W9-BAH-305

Weather America

LEWIS & CLARK LIBRARY
120 S. LAST CHANCE GULCH
HELENA, MONTANA 59601

2011

Third Edition

Weather America

A Thirty-Year Summary of Statistical Weather Data and Rankings

Grey House Publishing
AMENIA, NY 12501

LEWIS & CLARK LIBRARY
120 S. LAST CHANCE GULCH
HELENA, MONTANA 59601

PUBLISHER: Leslie Mackenzie
EDITOR: David Garoogian
EDITORIAL DIRECTOR: Laura Mars

PRODUCTION MANAGER: Kristen Thatcher
MARKETING DIRECTOR: Jessica Moody

EDITORIAL ADVISOR: Michael Rawlins, Phd
Manager, Climate System Research Center
Department of Geosciences, University of Massachusetts
WEATHER STATION MAPS: Michael Marturana

Grey House Publishing, Inc.
4919 Route 22
Amenia, NY 12501
518.789.8700
FAX 845.373.6390
www.greyhouse.com
e-mail: books @greyhouse.com

While every effort has been made to ensure the reliability of the information presented in this publication, Grey House Publishing neither guarantees the accuracy of the data contained herein nor assumes any responsibility for errors, omissions or discrepancies. Grey House accepts no payment for listing; inclusion in the publication of any organization, agency, institution, publication, service or individual does not imply endorsement of the editors or publisher.

Errors brought to the attention of the publisher and verified to the satisfaction of the publisher will be corrected in future editions.

Except by express prior written permission of the Copyright Proprietor no part of this work may be copied by any means of publication or communication now known or developed hereafter including, but not limited to, use in any directory or compilation or other print publication, in any information storage and retrieval system, in any other electronic device, or in any visual or audio-visual device or product.

This publication is an original and creative work, copyrighted by Grey House Publishing, Inc. and is fully protected by all applicable copyright laws, as well as by laws covering misappropriation, trade secrets and unfair competition.

Grey House has added value to the underlying factual material through one or more of the following efforts: unique and original selection; expression; arrangement; coordination; and classification.

Grey House Publishing, Inc. will defend its rights in this publication.

Copyright © 2011 Grey House Publishing, Inc.
All rights reserved

First edition published 1996
Third edition published 2011
Printed in Canada

ISBN: 978-1-59237-598-1 Softcover

Table of Contents

Introduction

This is the third edition of *Weather America*, the premier reference source organizing, analyzing, and ranking U.S. weather data for the last 30 years. Unique among dozens of weather data publications, *Weather America* provides the most comprehensive and useful compilation of weather data and statistics available.

More than 95% of the content from the last edition has been updated. This new edition includes valuable new data and features, including a detailed section on Billion Dollar Weather Disasters, as well as over 100 Full-Color State and National maps.

- **Coverage**: *Weather America* includes data for 2,021 weather stations. The 243 National and 1,778 Cooperative Stations were chosen based on not only state coverage, but also on geography, allowing users to see, for example, the variance in weather between oceanfront communities and mountainous regions.
- **Detail**: *Weather America* computes 32 data points for National and 19 for Cooperative Stations—five more data points than last edition. In addition, users will find **NEW Five-Year Average Charts, NEW Full-Color Maps, MORE detailed Storm Data,** and **MORE Rankings and Comparisons**.
- **Currency**: *Weather America* uses the most recent data available. Almost all weather data originates from the National Oceanic and Atmospheric Administration (NOAA), and more specifically within NOAA, the National Climatic Data Center (NCDC), in Asheville, North Carolina. NCDC organizes over 10,000 weather stations across the country, and, on a regular basis, collects, compiles, edits, and adjusts climatological data. Traditionally, 30 years of weather data is collected and presented every 10 years (e.g. 1961-1990, 1971-2000, etc.). Because more recent data exists, this edition is based on data from 1980-2009, the most recent thirty-year period for which complete year data is available.

Section One: State Chapters
More comprehensive than the previous edition, these chapters offer more data for complete, easy state research. Each state chapter opens with a narrative of the state's climatological conditions, covering Physical Features, General Climate, Precipitation, Relative Humidity, Storms, Drought, and Other Climatic Elements. Following the narrative are three state maps: A Full-Color General Reference Map with cities by population, roads, rivers, and lakes; a Full-Color Relief Map with capital cities and topography; and a Weather Station Map with major cities and larger type for easier reading.

Researchers will find state charts that list weather stations by county, by city, and by elevation. These charts are followed by National Weather Stations (operated by professional meteorologists) with a detailed climatological description and 32 data points, and then Cooperative Stations (manned primarily by volunteers) with 19 data points. The new data points charted in this edition include: Extreme Maximum Daily Precipitation; Days with ≥ 0.5 inches of Precipitation; and Maximum Snow Depth.

Following these station profiles are weather station rankings of 19 data points. These charts list the top 25 and the bottom 25 stations in the state for each data point. If states have fewer than 25 stations, all stations are listed.

Storm data is the final element of each state chapter. This chart includes specific location, exact date, storm type and severity, deaths, injuries, property and crop damage. Years covered are 2000- 2009.

Section Two: National Statistics

- **National Weather Rankings**: These National tables include detailed temperature, precipitation and snowfall data.
- **Five-Year Averages**: **NEW** to this section are Five-Year Averages, 1950–2009 for 19 data points.
- **All-Time Weather Records**: **NEW** This section includes state charts for six of the most basic weather criteria, such as Minimum and Maximum Temperature, Precipitation, Snowfall, and Snow Depth.
- **Storm Events**: Includes 20 charts with information on storms of any type with the greatest number of fatalities, injuries, property damage, and specific charts on hurricanes, tornadoes, floods, and hail.

Section Three: Appendices

- **Appendix A**: National, Regional and State Climate Centers with complete contact information, including web sites and contact names.
- **Appendix B**: **NEW** Glossary of Terms includes nearly 700 weather terms from Ablation and Absolute Humidity to Zone of Maximum Precipitation and Zulu Time.
- **Appendix C**: Map of U.S. NEXRAD (Doppler Radar) Network
- **Appendix D**: **NEW** Billion Dollar Climate and Weather Disasters that includes maps, charts, and timeline
- **Appendix E**: **NEW** Hurricane Strike Maps in full color
- **Appendix F**: **NEW** National Climate Maps in full color

This third edition of *Weather America* is also available online as an ebook through a number of our ebook vendors, including GVRL, ebrary, MyiLibrary, and NetLibrary.

Sources of the Data

The National Climactic Data Center (NCDC) has two main classes or types of weather stations; first-order stations which are staffed by professional meteorologists and cooperative stations which are staffed by volunteers. All 243 National Weather Service (NWS) stations included in this book are first-order stations.

The data in *Weather America* is compiled from several sources. The majority comes from the original NCDC computer tapes (DSI-3220 Summary of Month Cooperative). This data was used to create the entire table for each cooperative station and part of each National Weather Service station. The remainder of the data for each NWS station comes from the International Station Meteorological Climate Summary, Version 4.0, September 1996, which is also available from the NCDC.

Storm events come from the NCDC Storm Events Database which is accessible over the Internet at http://www4.ncdc.noaa.gov/cgi-win/wwcgi.dll?wwevent~storms.

Weather Station Tables

The weather station tables are grouped by type (National Weather Service and Cooperative) and then arranged alphabetically within each state section. The station name is almost always a place name, and is shown here just as it appears in NCDC data. The station name is followed by the county in which the station is located (or by county equivalent name), the elevation of the station (at the time beginning of the thirty year period) and the latitude and longitude.

The National Weather Service Station tables contain 32 data elements which were compiled from two different sources, the International Station Meteorological Climate Summary (ISMCS) and NCDC DSI-3220 data tapes. The following 13 elements are from the ISMCS: maximum precipitation, minimum precipitation, maximum snowfall, maximum 24-hour snowfall, thunderstorm days, foggy days, predominant sky cover, relative humidity (morning and afternoon), dewpoint, wind speed and direction, and maximum wind gust. The remaining 19 elements come from the DSI-3220 data tapes. The period of record (POR) for data from the DSI-3220 data tapes is 1980-2009. The POR for ISMCS data varies from station to station and appears in a note below each station.

The Cooperative Station tables contain 19 data elements which were all compiled from the DSI-3220 data tapes with a POR of 1980-2009.

Weather Elements (NWS and Cooperative Stations)

The following elements were compiled by the editor from the NCDC DSI-3220 data tapes using a period of record of 1980-2009.

The average temperatures (maximum, minimum, and mean) are the average (see Methodology below) of those temperatures for all available values for a given month. For example, for a given station the average maximum temperature for July is the arithmetic average of all available maximum July temperatures for that station. (Maximum means the highest recorded temperature, minimum means the lowest recorded temperature, and mean means an arithmetic average temperature.)

The extreme maximum temperature is the highest temperature recorded in each month over the period 1980-2009. The extreme minimum temperature is the lowest temperature recorded in each month over the same time period. The extreme maximum daily precipitation is the largest amount of precipitation recorded over a 24-hour period in each month from 1980-2009. The maximum snow depth is the maximum snow depth recorded in each month over the period 1980-2009.

The days for maximum temperature and minimum temperature are the average number of days those criteria were met for all available instances. The symbol ≥ means greater than or equal to, the symbol ≤ means less than or equal to. For example, for a given station, the number of days the maximum temperature was greater than or equal to 90°F in July, is just an arithmetic average of the number of days in all the available Julys for that station.

Heating and cooling degree days are based on the median temperature for a given day and its variance from 65°F. For example, for a given station if the day's high temperature was 50°F and the day's low temperature was 30°F, the median (midpoint) temperature was 40°F. 40°F is 25 degrees below 65°F, hence on this day there would be 25 heating degree days. The also applies for cooling degree days. For example, for a given station if the day's high temperature was 80°F and the day's low temperature was 70°F, the median (midpoint) temperature was 75°F. 75°F is 10 degrees above 65°F, hence on this day there would be 10 cooling degree days. All heating and/or cooling degree days in a month are summed for the month giving respective totals for each element for that month. These sums for a given month for a given station over the past thirty years are again summed and then arithmetically averaged. It should be noted that the heating and cooling degree days do not cancel each other out. It is possible to have both for a given station in the same month.

Precipitation data is computed the same as heating and cooling degree days. Mean precipitation and mean snowfall are arithmetic averages of cumulative totals for the month. All available values for the thirty year period for a given month for a given station are summed and then divided by the number of values. The same is true for days of greater than or equal to 0.1", 0.5",and 1.0" of precipitation, and days of greater than or equal to 1.0" of snow depth on the ground. The word trace appears for precipitation and snowfall amounts that are too small to measure.

Finally, remember that all values presented in the tables and the rankings are averages, maximums, or minimums of available data (see Methodology below) for that specific data element for the last thirty years (1980-2009).

Weather Elements (NWS Stations Only)

The following elements were taken directly from the International Station Meteorological Climate Summary. The periods of records vary per station and are noted at the bottom of each table.

Maximum precipitation, minimum precipitation, maximum snowfall, maximum snow depth, maximum 24-hour snowfall, thunderstorm days, foggy days, relative humidity (morning and afternoon), dewpoint, prevailing wind speed and direction, and maximum wind gust are all self-explanatory.

The word trace appears for precipitation and snowfall amounts that are too small to measure.

Predominant sky cover contains four possible entries: CLR (clear); SCT (scattered); BRK (broken); and OVR (overcast).

Inclusion Criteria—How Stations Were Selected

The basic criteria is that a station must have data for temperature, precipitation, heating and cooling degree days of sufficient quantity in order to create a meaningful average. More specifically, the definition of sufficiency here has two parts. First, there must be 22 values for a given data element, and second, ten of the nineteen elements included in the table must pass this sufficiency test. For example, in regard to mean maximum temperature (the first element on every data table), a given station needs to have a value for every month of at least 22 of the last thirty years in order to meet the criteria, and, in addition, every station included must have at least ten of the nineteen elements at least this minimal level of completeness in order to fulfill the criteria. We then removed stations that were geographicaly close together, giving preference to stations with better data quality. By using this procedure, 1,778 cooperative stations met these requirements and are included here. The 243 National Weather Service stations did not have to meet any minimum requirements.

Methodology

The following discussion applies only to data compiled from the NCDC DSI-3220 data tapes and excludes weather elements that are extreme maximums or minimums.

Weather America is based on an arithmetic average of all available data for a specific data element at a given station. For example, the average maximum daily high temperature during July for Alma, Michigan, was abstracted from NCDC source tapes for the thirty Julys, starting in July, 1980 and ending in July, 2009. These thirty figures were then summed and divided by thirty to produce an arithmetic average. As might be expected, there were not thirty values for every data element on every table. For a variety of reasons, NCDC data is sometimes incomplete. Thus the following standards were established.

For those data elements where there were 26-30 values, the data was taken to be essentially complete and an average was computed. For data elements where there were 22-25 values, the data was taken as being partly complete but still valid enough to use to compute an average. Such averages are shown in ***bold italic*** type to indicate that there was less than 26 values. For the few data elements where there were not even 22 values, no average was computed and 'na' appears in the space. If any of the twelve months for a given data element reported a value of 'na', no annual average was computed and the annual average was reported as 'na' as well.

Thus the basic computational methodology of *Weather America* is to provide an arithmetic average. Because of this, such a pure arithmetic average is somewhat different from the special type of average (called a "normal") which NCDC procedures produces and appears in federal publications.

Perhaps the best outline of the contrasting normalization methodology is found in the following paragraph (which appears as part of an NCDC technical document titled, CLIM81 1961-1990 NORMALS TD-9641 prepared by Lewis France of NCDC in May, 1992):

> Normals have been defined as the arithmetic mean of a climatological element computed over a long time period. International agreements eventually led to the decision that the appropriate time period would be three consecutive decades (Guttman, 1989). The data record should be consistent (have no changes in location, instruments, observation practices, etc.; these are identified here as "exposure changes") and have no missing values so a normal will reflect the actual average climatic conditions. If any significant exposure changes have occurred, the data record is said to be "inhomogeneous," and the normal may not reflect a true climatic average. Such data need to be adjusted to remove the nonclimatic inhomogeneities. The resulting (adjusted) record is then said to be "homogeneous." If no exposure changes have occurred at a station, the normal is calculated simply by averaging the appropriate 30 values from the 1961-1990 record.
>
> In the main, there are two "inhomogeneities" that NCDC is correcting for with normalization: adjusting for variances in time of day of observation (at the so-called First Order stations data is based on midnight to midnight observation times and this practice is not necessarily followed at cooperative stations which are staffed by volunteers), and second, estimating data that is either missing or incongruent.

A long discussion of the normalization process is not required here but a short note concerning comparative results of the two methodologies is appropriate.

When the editors first started compiling *Weather America* a concern arose because the normalization process would not be replicated: would our methodology produce strikingly different results than NCDC's? To allay concerns, results of the two processes were compared for the time period normalized results are available (1971-2000). In short, what was found was that the answer to this question is no. Never-the-less, users should be aware that because of both the time period covered (1980-2009) and the methodology used, data in *Weather America* is not compatible with data from other sources.

Potential cautions in using *Weather America*

First, as with any statistical reference work of this type, users need to be aware of the source of the data. The information here comes from NOAA, and it is the most comprehensive and reliable core data available. Although it is the best, it is not perfect. Most weather stations are staffed by volunteers, times of observation sometimes vary, stations occasionally are moved (especially over a thirty year period), equipment is changed or upgraded, and all of these factors affect the uniformity of the data. *Weather America* does not attempt to correct for these factors, and is not intended for either climatologists or atmospheric scientists. Users with concerns about data collection and reporting protocols are both referred to NCDC technical documentation, and also, they are perhaps better served by using the original computer tapes themselves as well.

Second, users need to be aware of the methodology here which is described above. Although this methodology has produced fully satisfactory results, it is not directly compatible with other methodologies, hence variances in the results published here and those which appear in other publications will doubtlessly arise.

Third, is the trap of that informal logical fallacy known as "hasty generalization," and its corollaries. This may involve presuming the future will be like the past (specifically, next year will be an average year), or it may involve misunderstanding the limitations of an arithmetic average, but more interestingly, it may involve those mistakes made most innocently by generalizing informally on too broad a basis. As weather is highly localized, the data should be taken in that context. A weather station collects data about climatic conditions at that spot, and that spot may or may not be an effective paradigm for an entire town or area. For example, the weather station in Burlington, Vermont is located at the airport about 3 miles east of the center of town. Most of Burlington is a lot closer to Lake Champlain, and that should mean to a careful user that there could be a significant difference between the temperature readings gathered at the weather station and readings that might be gathered at City Hall downtown. How much would this difference be? How could it be estimated? There are no answers here for these sorts of questions, but it is important for users of this book to raise them for themselves. (It is interesting to note that similar situations abound across the country. For example, compare different readings for the multiple stations in San Francisco, CA or for those around New York City.)

Our source of data has been consistent, so has our methodology. The data has been computed and reported consistently as well. As a result, the *Weather America* should prove valuable to the careful and informed reader.

Adapted from Introduction to the first edition, by Alfred N. Garwood

Al Gore on the Politicization of Global Warming

Since losing a highly contested election for president against George W. Bush in 2000, former vice president Al Gore has galvanized public interest in the issue of global warming by means of his slide shows and his heavily illustrated book and documentary film titled *An Inconvenient Truth*. Gore, who has long been interested in environmental issues, published his first book on the subject, *Earth in the Balance,* in 1992 when he was a senator.

As I've traveled around the world giving my slide show, there are two questions I most often get—particularly in the United States—from people who already know how serious the crisis has become...:

(1) "Why do so many people still believe this crisis isn't real?" and
(2) "Why is this a political issue at all?"

My response to the first question has been to try to make my slide show—and now this book—as clear and compelling as I can. As for why so many people still resist what the facts clearly show, I think, in part, the reason is that the truth about the climate crisis is an inconvenient one that means we are going to have to change the way we live our lives. Most of these changes will turn out to be for the better—things we really should do for other reasons anyway—but they are inconvenient nonetheless. Whether these changes involve something as minor as adjusting the thermostat and using different light bulbs, or as major as switching from oil and coal to renewable fuels, they will require effort.

But the answer to the first question is also linked to the second question. The truth about global warming is especially inconvenient and unwelcome to some powerful people and companies making enormous sums of money from activities they know full well have to change dramatically in order to ensure the planet's livability.

These people—especially those at a few multinational companies with the most at stake—have been spending many millions of dollars every year in figuring out ways of sowing public confusion about global warming. They've been particularly effective in building a coalition with other groups who agree to support each other's interests, and that coalition has thus far managed to paralyze America's ability to respond to global warming. The Bush/Cheney administration has received strong support from this coalition and seems to be doing everything it can to satisfy their concerns.

For example, many *scientists* working on global-warming research throughout the government have been ordered to watch what they say about the climate crisis and instructed not to talk to the news media. More important, all of America's policies related to global warming have been changed to reflect the unscientific view—the administration's view—that global warming is not a problem. Our negotiators in international forums dealing with global warming have been advised to try and stop any movement toward action that would inconvenience oil or coal companies, even if this means disrupting the diplomatic machinery in order to do it.

In addition, President Bush appointed the person in charge of the oil company disinformation campaign on global warming to head up all environmental policy in the White House. Even though this lawyer/lobbyist had no scientific training whatsoever, he was empowered by the president to edit and censor all warnings from the EPA and other government agencies about global warming.

Political leaders—especially the president—can have a major effect not only on public policy (especially when Congress is controlled by the president's party, is compliant, and does whatever the president wants it to) but also on public opinion, especially among those who count themselves followers of the president.

Consider this fact: Even as Americans in general have become increasingly concerned about global warming, opinion polls show members of the president's own party becoming less concerned, probably because they're naturally more inclined to give the president the benefit of the doubt.

The rationale offered by the so-called skeptics for opposing any action to solve the climate crisis has changed several times over the years. At first, opponents argued that global warming was not occurring at all; they said it was a myth. A few of them still say that today, but now there is so much undeniable evidence demolishing that assertion that, most naysayers have decided they need to change tactics. They now acknowledge that the globe is indeed warming, but in the very next breath, they claim it is just due to "natural causes."

***

Another related argument used by the deniers is that yes, global warming does seem to be happening, but it will probably be good for us. Certainly any effort to stop it, they continue, would no doubt be bad for the economy. But the latest—and in my opinion, most disgraceful argument put forth by opponents of change is: Yes it's happening, but there's nothing we can really do about it, so we might as well not even try. This faction favors the continued dumping of global-warming pollution into the atmosphere, even though they acknowledge that the crisis it's causing is real and harmful.

***

Part of the problem has to do with a long-term structural change in the way America's marketplace of ideas now operates. The one-way nature of our dominant communications medium, television, has combined with the increasing concentration of ownership over the vast majority of media outlets by a smaller and smaller number of large conglomerates that mix entertainment values with journalism to seriously damage the role of objectivity in America's public forum.

***

We have lost a lot of time that could have been spent solving the crisis, because the opponents of action have thus far successfully politicized the issue in the minds of many Americans. We can't afford inaction any longer, and, frankly, there's no excuse for it. We all want the same thing: for our children and the generations after them to inherit a clean and beautiful planet capable of supporting a healthy human civilization. That goal should transcend politics. Yes, the science is ongoing and always evolving, but there's already enough data, enough damage, to know without question that we're in trouble. This isn't an ideological debate with two sides, pro and con. There is only one Earth, and all of us who live on it share a common future. Right now we are facing a planetary emergency, and it is time for action, not for more phony controversies designed to insure political paralysis.

Source: Al Gore, *An Inconvenient Truth* (Emmaus, PA: Rodale, 2006), pp. 285-287. Reprinted with permission of Rodale Books

As has been the case with many controversial socio-political issues, college campuses were among the first places where concern about climate change found a large vocal and action-minded constituency. College administrators were confronted with student demands and student plans to green their campuses. With help from a variety of NGOs, a group of college and university presidents and chancellors signed a compact requiring the signatories on the following commitments to develop greening goals for their campuses, to publish their plans, and to provide continuously updated progress reports. By the summer of 2010, there were signatories from more than 650 schools.

Because having a green ethos can be a selling point for many schools, a growing number of college and university administrators have decided that obtaining LEED (Leadership in Energy and Environmental Design) certification for both new construction and the remodeling of old buildings is worth the additional expense.

We, the undersigned presidents and chancellors of colleges and universities, are deeply concerned about the unprecedented scale and speed of global warming and its potential for large-scale, adverse health, social, economic and ecological effects. We recognize the scientific consensus that global warming is real and is largely being caused by humans. We further recognize the need to reduce the global emission of greenhouse gases by 80% by mid-century at the latest, in order to avert the worst impacts of global warming and to reestablish the more stable climatic conditions that have made human progress over the last 10,000 years possible.

While we understand that there might be short-term challenges associated with this effort, we believe that there will be great short-, medium-, and long-term economic, health, social and environmental benefits, including achieving energy independence for the U.S. as quickly as possible.

We believe colleges and universities must exercise leadership in their communities and throughout society by modeling ways to minimize global warming emissions, and by providing the knowledge and the educated graduates to achieve climate neutrality. Campuses that address the climate challenge by reducing global warming emissions and by integrating sustainability into their curriculum will better serve their students and meet their social mandate to help create a thriving, ethical and civil society. These colleges and universities will be providing students with the knowledge and skills needed to address the critical, systemic challenges faced by the world in this new century and enable them to benefit from the economic opportunities that will arise as a result of solutions they develop.

We further believe that colleges and universities that exert leadership in addressing climate change will stabilize and reduce their long-term energy costs, attract excellent students and faculty, attract new sources of funding, and increase the support of alumni and local communities. Accordingly, we commit our institutions to taking the following steps in pursuit of climate neutrality.

1. Initiate the development of a comprehensive plan to achieve climate neutrality as soon as possible.
    a. Within two months of signing this document, create institutional structures to guide the development and implementation of the plan.
    b. Within one year of signing this document, complete a comprehensive inventory of all greenhouse gas emissions (including emissions from electricity, heating, commuting, and air travel) and update the inventory every other year thereafter.
    c. Within two years of signing this document, develop an institutional action plan for becoming climate neutral, which will include:
        i. A target date for achieving climate neutrality as soon as possible.
        ii. Interim targets for goals and actions that will lead to climate neutrality.
        iii. Actions to make climate neutrality and sustainability a part of the curriculum and other educational experience for all students.
        iv. Actions to expand research or other efforts necessary to achieve climate neutrality.
        v. Mechanisms for tracking progress on goals and actions.
2. Initiate two or more of the following tangible actions to reduce greenhouse gases while the more comprehensive plan is being developed.
    a. Establish a policy that all new campus construction will be built to at least the U.S. Green Building Council's LEED Silver standard or equivalent.
    b. Adopt an energy-efficient appliance purchasing policy requiring purchase of ENERGY STAR certified products in all areas for which such ratings exist.
    c. Establish a policy of offsetting all greenhouse gas emissions generated by air travel paid for by our institution.
3. Make the action plan, inventory, and periodic progress reports publicly available by providing them to the Association for the Advancement of Sustainability in Higher Education (AASHE) for posting and dissemination.

In recognition of the need to build support for this effort among college and university administrations across America, we will encourage other presidents to join this effort and become signatories to this commitment.

Source: Second Nature, Inc., American College and University President's Climate Commitment (2006), www.presidentsclimatecommitment.org/about/commitment text. Reprinted with permission of Second Nature, Inc.

ALABAMA

PHYSICAL FEATURES. The surface of Alabama rises as a rolling plain from the Gulf of Mexico in the southwest to foothills in the central part of the State. Thence there is a rise to the Appalachian Mountains which extend into the northeastern counties. Ridges from the Appalachians extend southward through the eastern counties, with elevations along these ridges as much as 600 to 800 feet above sea level in the southeast. The general elevation of the high northeastern area is about 800 feet above sea level, but some mountain summits rise to over 2,000 feet, the highest (Mount Cheaha in southwestern Cleburne County) being 2,407 feet.

GENERAL CLIMATE. The climate is temperate, becoming largely subtropical near the coast. The summers are long, hot, and humid, with little day-to-day temperature change. In the northeastern counties, higher altitudes help make the summer nights more comfortable. From late June through middle August, approximately a third of the evenings are made comfortable by local afternoon thundershowers which bring cool breezes over the areas where they occur.

In the coldest months of December, January, and February, there are frequent shifts between mild air, which has been moistened and warmed by the Gulf, and dry, cool continental air. Severely cold weather seldom occurs. Even in the northern third of the State, temperatures of zero or lower are rare and occur only when there is snow on the ground. Since cold air on clear nights collects in low places, there is considerable irregularity in the distribution of the last spring or first fall freezes in all sections.

PRECIPITATION. Precipitation is nearly all in the form of rain. Snow falls in the northern counties on an average of about twice each winter. The average fall in that area is only about three inches per year, and since this includes unusually heavy snows in a few individual winters, some winters have little or none. From late June through the first half of August, nearly all precipitation is from local thundershowers which occur mostly in the afternoons. During late August and in September, summer conditions of atmospheric temperature and moisture persist, but thundershowers become less frequent. However, late night and early morning thundershowers, characteristic of late summer on the coast, continue in the coastal counties until mid-September. Rains during October are nearly always from showers or thundershowers occurring ahead of temperature drops. Such changes become more frequent and more pronounced as winter approaches. Dry, sunny weather prevails most of the time in September and October, but from August through early October, heavy general rain may occur with a tropical disturbance or hurricane moving inland from the Gulf of Mexico. Since summer rain is heavier near the coast than elsewhere and winter rain is heavier in the north, the middle areas of the State get somewhat less precipitation for the year as a whole than the other areas.

Droughts may occur any time during the growing season from late April through October. Relatively long periods with little or no rain are more likely to occur in late summer and autumn than at any other time, while a secondary maximum of such periods occurs in May and June. Severe local droughts occur nearly every year, but severe statewide droughts are practically unknown.

Rivers in Alabama overflow about once a year on an average. Most floods occur from rains in late winter and early spring, with March the month of greatest flood frequency. The lower Tombigbee overflows most often, and in some stretches may stay over the banks most of the time in wet winter and spring seasons.

STORMS. Nearly all tornadoes occur during the season from November through early May. The greatest frequency is in March and April. The area covered by the average tornado is small. Destructive tropical hurricanes visit the coastal area on an average of about once in seven years between July and November. Windstorm damage may occur in local thundersqualls any time of the year.

Thunderstorms in the north and central sections occur on an average of one day each month in winter, on about 13 days in July, and on about 60 days during the year. Almost all the hail that falls in Alabama occurs in the period from February through May, although in the northern counties there are rare occurrences of damaging hail in June.

Heavy fog occurs mostly in winter. It occurs on an average of five days per year in Birmingham, eight days per year in Montgomery, and 31 days per year in Mobile, near the coast.

WINDS. In winter, winds from a northerly direction are most frequent. In summer, the wind is quite variable, but most often comes from southerly directions.

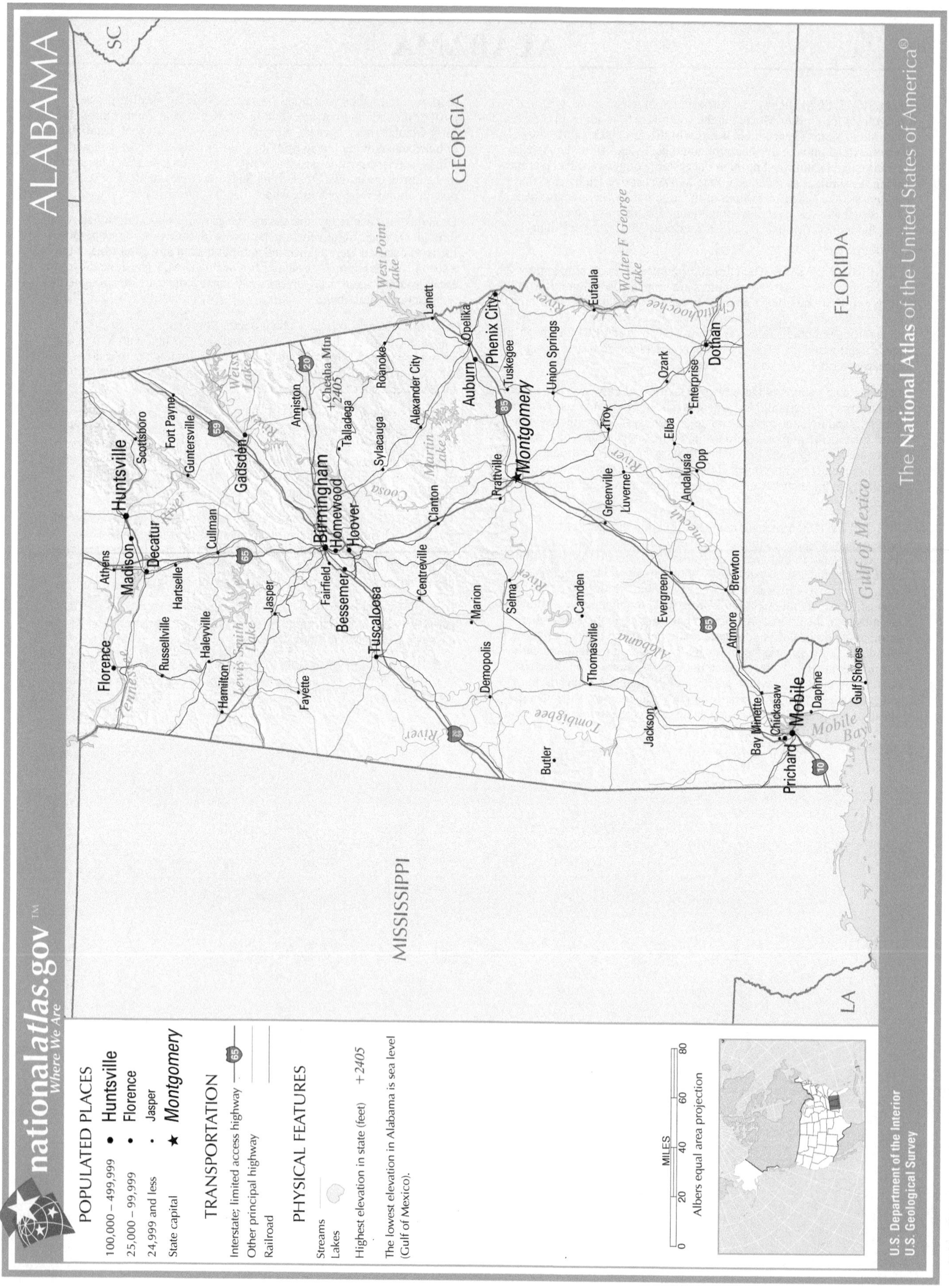
ALABAMA
nationalatlas.gov™
Where We Are
POPULATED PLACES
100,000 – 499,999 Huntsville
25,000 – 99,999 Florence
24,999 and less Jasper
State capital Montgomery
TRANSPORTATION
Interstate; limited access highway
Other principal highway
Railroad
PHYSICAL FEATURES
Streams
Lakes
Highest elevation in state (feet) +2405
The lowest elevation in Alabama is sea level (Gulf of Mexico).
MILES
0 20 40 60 80
Albers equal area projection
U.S. Department of the Interior
U.S. Geological Survey
The National Atlas of the United States of America®
SC
GEORGIA
FLORIDA
MISSISSIPPI
LA
Gulf of Mexico
Mobile Bay
Huntsville
Florence
Athens
Madison
Decatur
Scottsboro
Fort Payne
Guntersville
Hartselle
Cullman
Russellville
Haleyville
Hamilton
Jasper
Gadsden
Anniston
Cheaha Mtn +2405
Talladega
Birmingham
Homewood
Hoover
Fairfield
Bessemer
Tuscaloosa
Fayette
Sylacauga
Roanoke
Lanett
Alexander City
Opelika
Auburn
Phenix City
Tuskegee
Montgomery
Prattville
Clanton
Centreville
Marion
Selma
Demopolis
Camden
Thomasville
Union Springs
Eufaula
Troy
Ozark
Enterprise
Dothan
Elba
Opp
Andalusia
Greenville
Luverne
Evergreen
Brewton
Atmore
Jackson
Butler
Bay Minette
Chickasaw
Mobile
Prichard
Daphne
Gulf Shores
West Point Lake
Weiss Lake
Martin Lake
Lewis Smith Lake
Walter F George Lake
Tennessee River
Coosa River
Alabama River
Tombigbee River
Chattahoochee River
Conecuh River
Black Warrior River

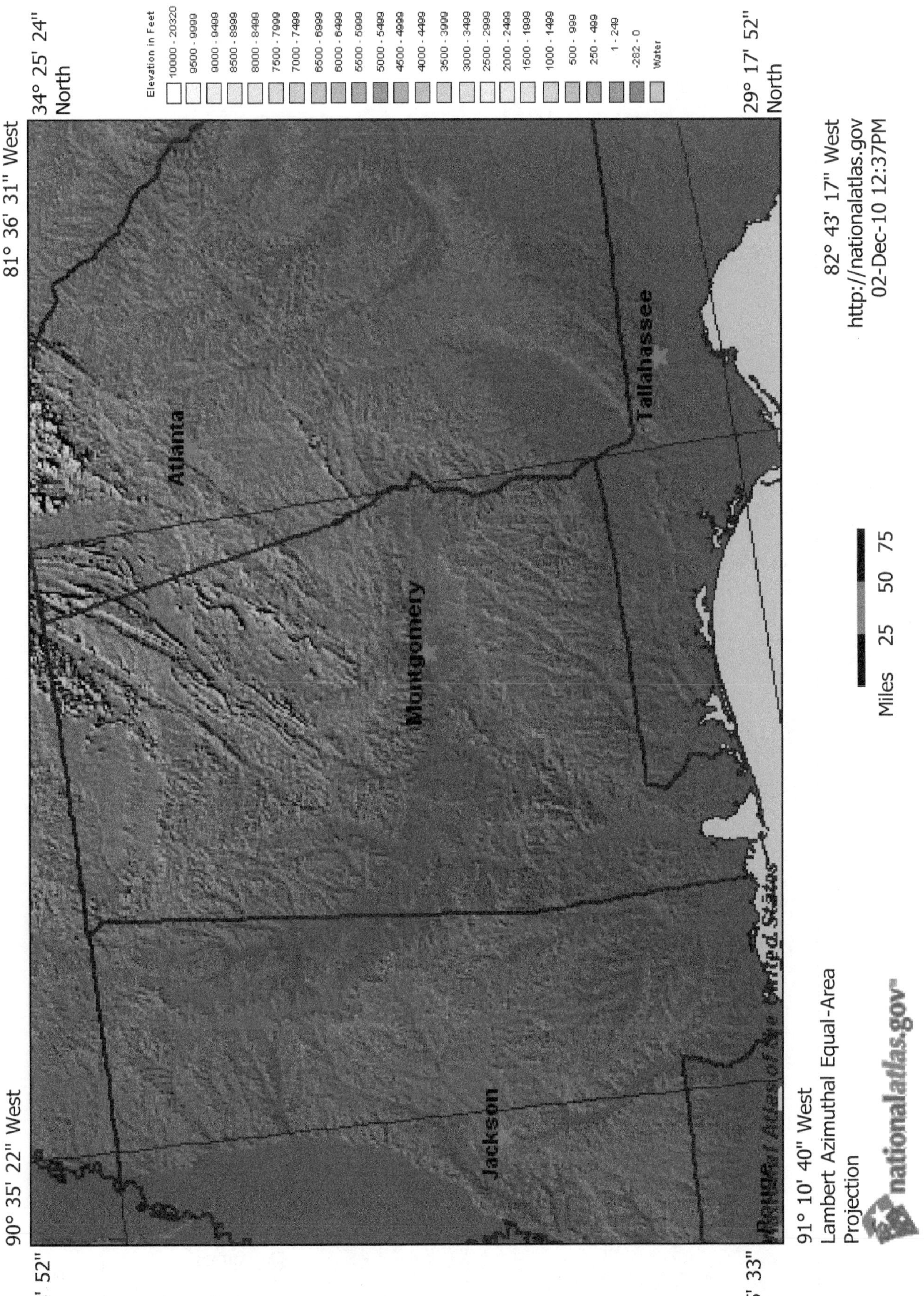
81° 36' 31" West
34° 25' 24" North
Elevation in Feet
10000 - 20320
9500 - 9999
9000 - 9499
8500 - 8999
8000 - 8499
7500 - 7999
7000 - 7499
6500 - 6999
6000 - 6499
5500 - 5999
5000 - 5499
4500 - 4999
4000 - 4499
3500 - 3999
3000 - 3499
2500 - 2999
2000 - 2499
1500 - 1999
1000 - 1499
500 - 999
250 - 499
1 - 249
-282 - 0
Water
29° 17' 52" North
Atlanta
Tallahassee
Montgomery
Jackson
Rouge
82° 43' 17" West
http://nationalatlas.gov
02-Dec-10 12:37PM
Miles 25 50 75
90° 35' 22" West
35° 38' 52" North
30° 25' 33" North
91° 10' 40" West
Lambert Azimuthal Equal-Area Projection
nationalatlas.gov

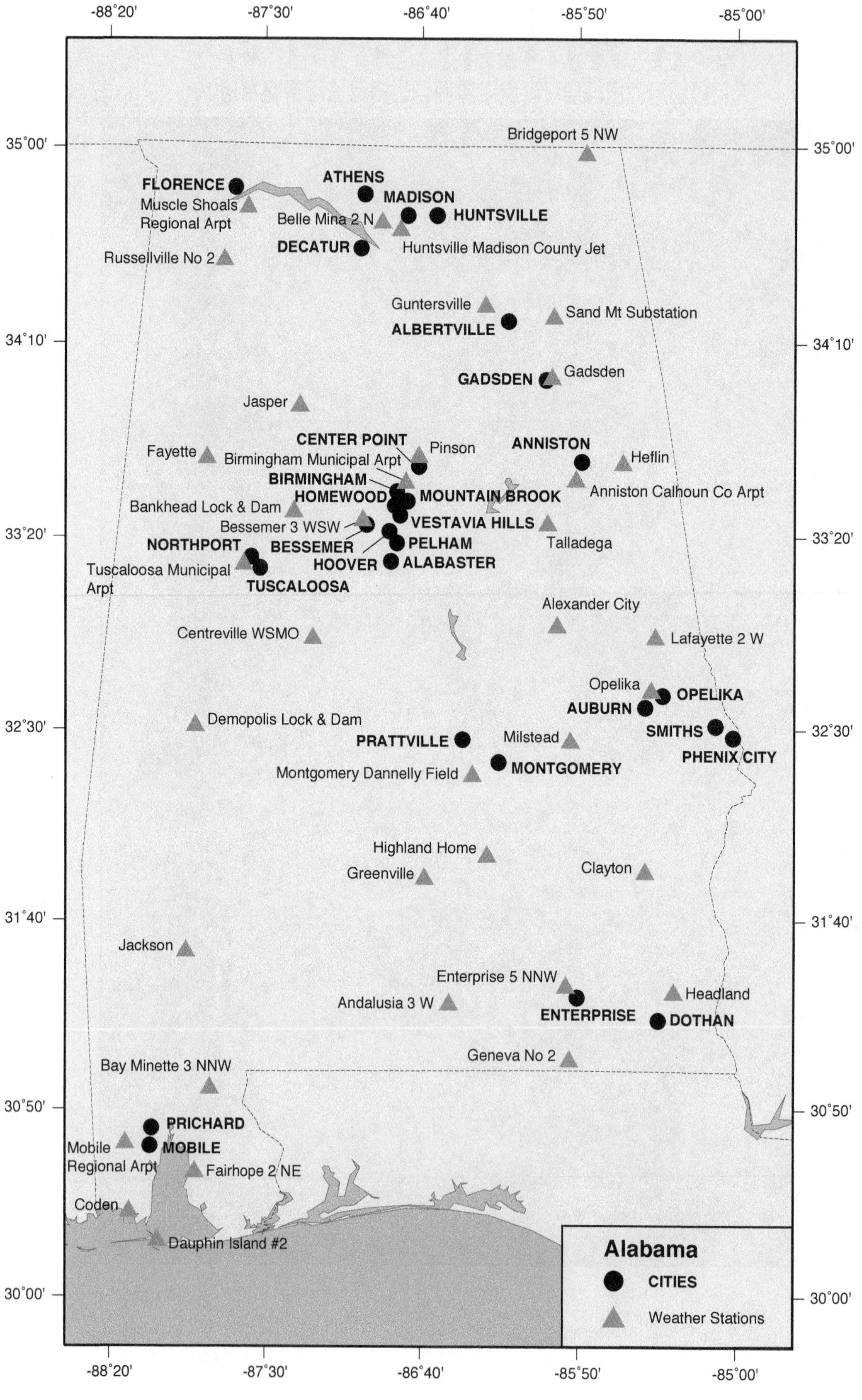
-88°20'
-87°30'
-86°40'
-85°50'
-85°00'
35°00'
34°10'
33°20'
32°30'
31°40'
30°50'
30°00'
Bridgeport 5 NW
FLORENCE
ATHENS
MADISON
HUNTSVILLE
Muscle Shoals Regional Arpt
Belle Mina 2 N
DECATUR
Huntsville Madison County Jet
Russellville No 2
Guntersville
Sand Mt Substation
ALBERTVILLE
GADSDEN
Gadsden
Jasper
CENTER POINT
Pinson
ANNISTON
Fayette
Birmingham Municipal Arpt
Heflin
BIRMINGHAM
HOMEWOOD
MOUNTAIN BROOK
Anniston Calhoun Co Arpt
Bankhead Lock & Dam
Bessemer 3 WSW
VESTAVIA HILLS
NORTHPORT
BESSEMER
PELHAM
Talladega
Tuscaloosa Municipal Arpt
HOOVER
ALABASTER
TUSCALOOSA
Alexander City
Centreville WSMO
Lafayette 2 W
Opelika
OPELIKA
AUBURN
Demopolis Lock & Dam
SMITHS
PRATTVILLE
Milstead
PHENIX CITY
Montgomery Dannelly Field
MONTGOMERY
Highland Home
Greenville
Clayton
Jackson
Enterprise 5 NNW
Headland
Andalusia 3 W
ENTERPRISE
DOTHAN
Geneva No 2
Bay Minette 3 NNW
PRICHARD
Mobile Regional Arpt
MOBILE
Fairhope 2 NE
Coden
Dauphin Island #2
Alabama
CITIES
Weather Stations

Alabama Weather Stations by County

County	Station Name
Baldwin	Bay Minette 3 NNW Fairhope 2 NE
Barbour	Clayton
Bibb	Centreville WSMO
Butler	Greenville
Calhoun	Anniston Calhoun Co Arpt
Chambers	Lafayette 2 W
Clarke	Jackson
Cleburne	Heflin
Coffee	Enterprise 5 NNW
Colbert	Muscle Shoals Regional Arpt
Covington	Andalusia 3 W
Crenshaw	Highland Home
Dekalb	Sand Mt Substation
Etowah	Gadsden
Fayette	Fayette
Franklin	Russellville No 2
Geneva	Geneva No 2
Henry	Headland
Jackson	Bridgeport 5 NW
Jefferson	Bessemer 3 WSW Birmingham Municipal Arpt Pinson
Lee	Opelika
Limestone	Belle Mina 2 N
Macon	Milstead
Madison	Huntsville Madison County Jetport
Marengo	Demopolis Lock and Dam
Marshall	Guntersville
Mobile	Coden Dauphin Island #2 Mobile Regional Arpt
Montgomery	Montgomery Dannelly Field
Talladega	Talladega
Tallapoosa	Alexander City

County	Station Name
Tuscaloosa	Bankhead Lock and Dam Tuscaloosa Municipal Arpt
Walker	Jasper

See User Guide for station inclusion criteria.

Alabama Weather Stations by City

City	Station Name	Miles
Alabaster	Bessemer 3 WSW	15.2
	Birmingham Municipal Arpt	23.4
Albertville	Gadsden	21.3
	Guntersville	8.6
	Sand Mt Substation	13.8
Anniston	Anniston Calhoun Co Arpt	5.7
	Heflin	12.6
	Talladega	24.8
Athens	Belle Mina 2 N	9.1
	Huntsville Madison County Jetport	14.5
Auburn	Lafayette 2 W	20.8
	Opelika	4.8
Bessemer	Bankhead Lock and Dam	23.0
	Bessemer 3 WSW	2.5
	Birmingham Municipal Arpt	17.1
Birmingham	Bessemer 3 WSW	14.3
	Birmingham Municipal Arpt	4.2
	Pinson	12.9
Center Point	Bessemer 3 WSW	25.0
	Birmingham Municipal Arpt	6.7
	Pinson	2.9
Decatur	Belle Mina 2 N	9.7
	Huntsville Madison County Jetport	13.0
Dothan	Headland	9.8
Enterprise	Enterprise 5 NNW	5.2
	Geneva No 2	19.3
Florence	Muscle Shoals Regional Arpt	6.5
	Russellville No 2	21.7
Gadsden	Gadsden	1.5
	Sand Mt Substation	19.0
Homewood	Bessemer 3 WSW	12.0
	Birmingham Municipal Arpt	7.7
	Pinson	16.6
Hoover	Bessemer 3 WSW	9.4
	Birmingham Municipal Arpt	15.2
	Pinson	24.1
Huntsville	Belle Mina 2 N	16.7
	Huntsville Madison County Jetport	11.7
Madison	Belle Mina 2 N	8.3
	Huntsville Madison County Jetport	5.1
Mobile	Coden	21.0
	Fairhope 2 NE	16.7
	Mobile Regional Arpt	7.5
Montgomery	Milstead	23.1
	Montgomery Dannelly Field	8.9

City	Station Name	Miles
Mountain Brook	Bessemer 3 WSW	16.2
	Birmingham Municipal Arpt	5.2
	Pinson	13.7
Northport	Bankhead Lock and Dam	19.5
	Tuscaloosa Municipal Arpt	2.8
Opelika	Lafayette 2 W	17.8
	Opelika	4.0
	West Point, GA	19.3
Pelham	Bessemer 3 WSW	13.0
	Birmingham Municipal Arpt	18.0
Phenix City	Columbus Metropolitan Arpt, GA	5.0
Prattville	Montgomery Dannelly Field	11.5
Prichard	Bay Minette 3 NNW	22.1
	Fairhope 2 NE	19.1
	Mobile Regional Arpt	9.7
Smiths	Opelika	22.6
	Columbus Metropolitan Arpt, GA	9.0
	West Point, GA	24.5
Tuscaloosa	Bankhead Lock and Dam	20.4
	Tuscaloosa Municipal Arpt	4.9
Vestavia Hills	Bessemer 3 WSW	12.8
	Birmingham Municipal Arpt	9.4
	Pinson	18.2

Note: Miles is the distance between the geographic center of the city and the weather station.

See User Guide for station inclusion criteria.

Alabama Weather Stations by Elevation

Feet	Station Name
1,194	Sand Mt Substation
850	Heflin
830	Russellville No 2
740	Lafayette 2 W
669	Bridgeport 5 NW
640	Alexander City
640	Opelika
624	Huntsville Madison County Jetport
620	Birmingham Municipal Arpt
610	Anniston Calhoun Co Arpt
607	Pinson
600	Belle Mina 2 N
594	Highland Home
578	Guntersville
564	Gadsden
540	Muscle Shoals Regional Arpt
500	Clayton
485	Jasper
470	Greenville
469	Enterprise 5 NNW
456	Centreville WSMO
448	Talladega
444	Bessemer 3 WSW
370	Headland
365	Fayette
279	Bankhead Lock and Dam
277	Bay Minette 3 NNW
250	Andalusia 3 W
220	Jackson
214	Milstead
214	Mobile Regional Arpt
202	Montgomery Dannelly Field
167	Tuscaloosa Municipal Arpt
145	Geneva No 2
100	Demopolis Lock and Dam
22	Fairhope 2 NE
12	Coden
7	Dauphin Island #2

See User Guide for station inclusion criteria.

Birmingham Municipal Airport

Birmingham is located in a hilly area of north-central Alabama in the foothills of the Appalachians about 300 miles inland from the Gulf of Mexico. There is a series of southwest to northeast valleys and ridges in the area.

The city is far enough inland to be protected from destructive tropical hurricanes, yet close enough that the Gulf has a pronounced modifying effect on the climate.

Although summers are long and hot, they are not generally excessively hot. On a typical mid-summer day, the temperature will be nearly 70 degrees at daybreak, approach 90 degrees at mid-day, and level off in the low 90s during the afternoon. It is not unusual for the temperature to remain below 100 degrees for several years in a row. However, every few years an extended heat wave will bring temperatures over 100 degrees. July is normally the hottest month but there is little difference from mid-June to mid-August. Rather persistent high humidity adds to the summer discomfort.

January is normally the coldest month but there is not much difference from mid-December to mid-February. Overall, winters are relatively mild. Even in cold spells, it is unusual for the temperature to remain below freezing all day. Sub-zero cold is extremely rare. Extremely low temperatures almost always occur under clear skies after a snowfall.

Snowfall is erratic. Sometimes there is a two- or three-year span with no measurable snow. On rare occasions, there may be a two to four inch snowstorm. The snow usually melts quickly. Even one or two inches of snow can effectively shut down this sunbelt city because of the hilly terrain, the wetness of the snow, and the unfamiliarity of motorists driving on snow and ice.

Birmingham is blessed with abundant rainfall. It is fairly well distributed throughout the year. However, some of the wetter winter months, plus March and July, have twice the rainfall of October, the driest month. Summer rainfall is almost entirely from scattered afternoon and early evening thunderstorms. Serious droughts are rare and most dry spells are not severe.

The stormiest time of the year with the greatest risk of severe thunderstorms and tornadoes is in spring, especially in March and April.

In a normal year, the last 32 degree minimum temperature in the spring is in mid to late March and the first in autumn is in early November.

Birmingham Municipal Airport *Jefferson County* Elevation: 620 ft. Latitude: 33° 34' N Longitude: 86° 45' W

	JAN	FEB	MAR	APR	MAY	JUN	JUL	AUG	SEP	OCT	NOV	DEC	YEAR
Mean Maximum Temp. (°F)	54.0	58.4	66.7	74.3	81.5	87.7	90.8	90.7	85.1	75.1	65.3	56.1	73.8
Mean Temp. (°F)	43.7	47.5	55.0	62.0	70.3	77.2	80.8	80.4	74.4	63.6	54.0	45.9	62.9
Mean Minimum Temp. (°F)	33.4	36.5	43.2	49.7	59.0	66.7	70.6	70.0	63.6	52.1	42.7	35.7	51.9
Extreme Maximum Temp. (°F)	78	83	89	92	96	100	106	105	100	91	85	79	106
Extreme Minimum Temp. (°F)	-6	4	2	27	39	45	58	52	39	28	20	1	-6
Days Maximum Temp. ≥ 90°F	0	0	0	0	2	12	20	19	7	0	0	0	60
Days Maximum Temp. ≤ 32°F	1	0	0	0	0	0	0	0	0	0	0	1	2
Days Minimum Temp. ≤ 32°F	16	10	5	1	0	0	0	0	0	0	6	14	52
Days Minimum Temp. ≤ 0°F	0	0	0	0	0	0	0	0	0	0	0	0	0
Heating Degree Days (base 65°F)	655	490	323	142	24	0	0	0	9	122	335	587	2,687
Cooling Degree Days (base 65°F)	1	3	19	61	194	374	496	483	298	86	12	3	2,030
Mean Precipitation (in.)	4.93	4.50	5.53	4.51	4.93	4.37	4.82	3.86	4.06	3.42	4.79	4.43	54.15
Maximum Precipitation (in.)*	11.0	17.7	15.8	13.8	11.1	8.4	13.7	10.8	10.4	11.9	15.3	14.0	76.5
Minimum Precipitation (in.)*	1.1	1.1	1.7	0.4	1.1	0.7	0.3	0.4	trace	0.1	0.4	0.8	39.2
Extreme Maximum Daily Precip. (in.)	4.71	3.42	4.69	4.13	5.71	3.51	5.47	3.40	9.75	6.94	4.41	4.03	9.75
Days With ≥ 0.1" Precipitation	8	7	7	6	7	8	8	6	5	5	7	7	81
Days With ≥ 0.5" Precipitation	4	4	4	3	3	3	3	3	3	2	3	3	38
Days With ≥ 1.0" Precipitation	1	1	2	1	2	1	1	1	1	1	2	1	15
Mean Snowfall (in.)	0.7	0.1	0.6	0.2	trace	trace	trace	0.0	trace	trace	trace	0.1	1.7
Maximum Snowfall (in.)*	7	2	13	5	0	0	0	0	0	trace	1	8	13
Maximum 24-hr. Snowfall (in.)*	5	2	10	5	0	0	0	0	0	trace	1	8	10
Maximum Snow Depth (in.)	4	1	13	5	trace	trace	trace	0	trace	trace	trace	trace	13
Days With ≥ 1.0" Snow Depth	0	0	0	0	0	0	0	0	0	0	0	0	0
Thunderstorm Days*	2	2	4	5	7	8	12	9	4	1	2	1	57
Foggy Days*	15	13	13	11	14	13	15	15	14	14	13	14	164
Predominant Sky Cover*	OVR	OVR	OVR	OVR	SCT	SCT	SCT	SCT	CLR	CLR	OVR	OVR	OVR
Mean Relative Humidity 7am (%)*	82	81	78	76	76	78	81	82	81	82	82	82	80
Mean Relative Humidity 4pm (%)*	57	53	48	46	51	54	58	55	54	50	52	58	53
Mean Dewpoint (°F)*	33	36	41	49	58	66	69	68	62	51	42	36	51
Prevailing Wind Direction*	N	N	S	S	S	NE	S	NE	NE	NE	N	N	NE
Prevailing Wind Speed (mph)*	9	9	10	10	9	6	7	6	6	6	9	9	8
Maximum Wind Gust (mph)*	66	61	69	71	89	59	61	66	52	43	66	53	89

Note: (*) Period of record is 1948-1995

The period of record for National Weather Service station data is 1980 – 2009 except where noted. See User Guide for detailed explanation of data.

Huntsville Airport

Huntsville has a temperate climate. Summers are characterized by warm and humid weather, with rather frequent thunderstorms. Winters are usually rather cool, but vary considerably from one year to the next.

The city of Huntsville is almost surrounded by the foothills of the Appalachian Mountains. The Tennessee River winds its way westward about seven miles to the south of the city, and the broad, fertile Tennessee River Valley, with flat to gently rolling terrain, extends to the west. The weather station is located at the Huntsville-Madison County Airport, which is 11 miles southwest of the center of Huntsville. Mountain ridges, with elevations from 1,200 to 1,600 feet above sea level, are located some 14 miles to the northeast, east, and southeast of the airport.

Cold air masses from the continent are predominant over the area during the winter season, but, at times, mild air from the Gulf of Mexico spreads northward to Huntsville or beyond, and may persist for several days. December through March account for about 43 percent of the normal annual precipitation. Severely cold weather seldom occurs.

In the transition from winter to spring, appearances of warm, moist air in place of the cold air become more frequent, and the greatest variety of weather usually occurs during this season. Spring season thunderstorms in the vicinity of the boundary between warm and cold air masses are likely to be accompanied by locally severe weather conditions.

Day to day weather changes in the summer season are rather small, other than the occurrence of thunderstorms that provide relief from the heat on about one-third of the days. Temperatures frequently rise to 90 degrees or higher, but reach 100 degrees only on rare occasions.

During the fall the weather is usually dry and pleasant. The air masses are cooler in the lower levels and the thunderstorm activity of summer decreases sharply. A major departure from the relatively dry weather of fall is an occasional rainy spell of one or more days.

Precipitation amounts for the drier months of the fall are appreciably less than for the relatively wet season in winter. However, with the exception of an infrequent long dry spell, precipitation provides adequate moisture for plant growth throughout the year. Precipitation is mostly in the form of rain, but snow can be expected each winter. The growing season is 214 days. The average date for the last occurrence of freezing temperatures in the spring is late March and the average date of the first freeze is late October.

Huntsville Airport *Madison County* Elevation: 624 ft. Latitude: 34° 39' N Longitude: 86° 47' W

	JAN	FEB	MAR	APR	MAY	JUN	JUL	AUG	SEP	OCT	NOV	DEC	YEAR
Mean Maximum Temp. (°F)	50.2	54.9	63.8	72.4	80.1	87.0	89.7	89.8	83.9	73.4	62.5	52.7	71.7
Mean Temp. (°F)	40.7	44.8	52.6	60.8	69.3	76.6	79.7	79.2	72.9	61.8	51.8	43.2	61.1
Mean Minimum Temp. (°F)	31.2	34.7	41.4	49.1	58.4	66.1	69.6	68.5	61.8	50.1	41.0	33.6	50.5
Extreme Maximum Temp. (°F)	77	83	88	91	96	101	104	105	101	91	84	79	105
Extreme Minimum Temp. (°F)	-11	1	6	25	39	47	56	51	38	29	19	-3	-11
Days Maximum Temp. ≥ 90°F	0	0	0	0	2	11	17	17	6	0	0	0	53
Days Maximum Temp. ≤ 32°F	2	1	0	0	0	0	0	0	0	0	0	1	4
Days Minimum Temp. ≤ 32°F	18	12	6	1	0	0	0	0	0	1	7	16	61
Days Minimum Temp. ≤ 0°F	0	0	0	0	0	0	0	0	0	0	0	0	0
Heating Degree Days (base 65°F)	746	565	388	169	31	0	0	0	15	153	395	670	3,132
Cooling Degree Days (base 65°F)	0	1	11	49	171	356	462	447	258	60	6	2	1,823
Mean Precipitation (in.)	4.89	4.78	5.61	4.39	5.24	4.27	4.04	3.61	3.96	3.51	4.88	5.72	54.90
Maximum Precipitation (in.)*	10.9	10.1	17.0	12.5	11.9	15.0	14.8	9.8	9.8	12.1	11.5	18.7	73.6
Minimum Precipitation (in.)*	1.3	0.6	1.6	0.4	1.5	0.2	0.8	0.7	0.5	trace	0.6	0.8	41.8
Extreme Maximum Daily Precip. (in.)	4.83	4.04	5.09	3.85	4.64	4.00	4.81	4.29	3.93	3.31	3.02	9.07	9.07
Days With ≥ 0.1" Precipitation	7	7	8	7	7	6	7	6	5	5	7	7	79
Days With ≥ 0.5" Precipitation	3	3	4	3	4	3	3	2	3	3	3	4	38
Days With ≥ 1.0" Precipitation	1	1	2	1	2	1	1	1	1	1	2	2	16
Mean Snowfall (in.)	***1.1***	***0.6***	na	na	na	na	na	na	na	na	na	***0.1***	na
Maximum Snowfall (in.)*	10	7	7	trace	0	0	0	0	0	trace	4	21	24
Maximum 24-hr. Snowfall (in.)*	7	4	5	trace	0	0	0	0	0	trace	4	16	16
Maximum Snow Depth (in.)	***9***	***3***	na	na	***trace***	na	na	na	na	na	na	***1***	na
Days With ≥ 1.0" Snow Depth	***1***	***1***	na	na	***0***	na	na	na	na	na	na	***0***	na
Thunderstorm Days*	1	2	4	5	7	8	10	8	4	2	2	1	54
Foggy Days*	13	11	11	8	12	13	16	17	15	13	12	13	154
Predominant Sky Cover*	OVR	OVR	OVR	OVR	OVR	OVR	OVR	OVR	OVR	OVR	OVR	OVR	OVR
Mean Relative Humidity 7am (%)*	82	81	79	78	79	81	84	86	85	86	84	81	82
Mean Relative Humidity 4pm (%)*	60	56	51	46	51	53	56	55	54	51	55	60	54
Mean Dewpoint (°F)*	30	33	39	47	57	65	69	68	62	50	41	33	50
Prevailing Wind Direction*	ESE	ESE	SE	SE	ESE	ESE	SE	ESE	ESE	ESE	ESE	SE	ESE
Prevailing Wind Speed (mph)*	9	9	10	10	8	7	7	7	8	8	9	10	9
Maximum Wind Gust (mph)*	62	58	70	59	69	67	63	58	52	54	94	54	94

Note: (*) Period of record is 1958-1995

Mobile Regional Airport

Mobile is located at the head of Mobile Bay and approximately 30 miles from the Gulf of Mexico. Its weather is influenced to a considerable extent by the Gulf.

The summers are consistently warm, but temperatures are seldom as high as they are at inland stations. Normally, in summer, the day begins in the low 70s and the temperature rises rapidly before noon to the high 80s or low 90s, when it is checked by the onset of the sea breeze. On the rare occasions when northerly winds prevail throughout the day, temperatures may reach the high 90s or rise slightly above 100 degrees.

Winter weather is usually mild except for occasional invasions of cold air that last about three days. January is the coldest month in the year. Unusual winters may produce readings that require extensive protective measures as some citrus fruit is grown in the area and outdoor nurseries are numerous.

Based on the 1951-1980 period, the average first occurrence of 32 degrees Fahrenheit in the fall is November 26 and the average last occurrence in the spring is February 27.

The yearly rainfall is among the highest in the United States. It is fairly evenly distributed throughout the year with a slight maximum at the height of the summer thunderstorm season and a slight minimum during the late fall. Rainfall is usually of the shower type and long periods of continuous rain are rare.

Frontal thunderstorms may occur in any month of the year. There may be a thunderstorm every other day in July and August. The summer storms are usually not too violent and seldom produce hail.

The area is subject to hurricanes from the West Indies, the western Caribbean, and the Gulf of Mexico.

Mobile Regional Airport *Mobile County* Elevation: 214 ft. Latitude: 30° 41' N Longitude: 88° 15' W

	JAN	FEB	MAR	APR	MAY	JUN	JUL	AUG	SEP	OCT	NOV	DEC	YEAR
Mean Maximum Temp. (°F)	61.1	64.6	71.4	77.4	84.5	89.2	91.1	90.7	87.0	79.0	70.5	62.9	77.5
Mean Temp. (°F)	50.8	54.0	60.5	66.5	74.1	79.8	81.9	81.7	77.6	68.4	59.6	52.6	67.3
Mean Minimum Temp. (°F)	40.4	43.5	49.5	55.4	63.7	70.3	72.7	72.6	68.2	57.6	48.5	42.3	57.1
Extreme Maximum Temp. (°F)	80	82	87	94	97	101	103	105	99	92	87	81	105
Extreme Minimum Temp. (°F)	3	11	21	32	44	49	63	60	47	30	26	8	3
Days Maximum Temp. ≥ 90°F	0	0	0	0	4	15	22	21	10	1	0	0	73
Days Maximum Temp. ≤ 32°F	0	0	0	0	0	0	0	0	0	0	0	0	0
Days Minimum Temp. ≤ 32°F	8	5	2	0	0	0	0	0	0	0	2	6	23
Days Minimum Temp. ≤ 0°F	0	0	0	0	0	0	0	0	0	0	0	0	0
Heating Degree Days (base 65°F)	441	315	178	59	3	0	0	0	1	51	199	393	1,640
Cooling Degree Days (base 65°F)	7	11	44	109	292	451	532	524	388	162	42	16	2,578
Mean Precipitation (in.)	5.44	4.98	6.45	5.25	5.34	6.07	6.99	6.93	5.24	3.65	5.00	5.05	66.39
Maximum Precipitation (in.)*	16.1	11.9	13.5	17.7	15.1	13.1	19.3	15.2	14.0	13.2	13.6	11.4	86.6
Minimum Precipitation (in.)*	1.0	1.3	0.6	0.5	0.4	1.2	1.7	1.5	0.6	trace	0.3	1.3	42.3
Extreme Maximum Daily Precip. (in.)	6.16	5.37	7.15	6.79	7.96	6.05	6.34	5.65	8.60	4.99	5.70	4.68	8.60
Days With ≥ 0.1" Precipitation	7	6	6	5	6	8	10	9	6	4	5	6	78
Days With ≥ 0.5" Precipitation	3	4	3	3	3	4	5	4	3	2	3	4	41
Days With ≥ 1.0" Precipitation	2	1	2	2	2	2	2	2	2	1	2	2	22
Mean Snowfall (in.)	trace	0.1	0.1	trace	trace	trace	trace	0.0	0.0	0.0	0.0	trace	0.2
Maximum Snowfall (in.)*	4	4	3	trace	0	0	0	0	0	0	trace	3	4
Maximum 24-hr. Snowfall (in.)*	4	4	2	trace	0	0	0	0	0	0	trace	3	4
Maximum Snow Depth (in.)	trace	1	2	trace	trace	trace	trace	0	0	0	0	trace	2
Days With ≥ 1.0" Snow Depth	0	0	0	0	0	0	0	0	0	0	0	0	0
Thunderstorm Days*	2	2	5	5	7	12	18	14	7	2	2	2	78
Foggy Days*	15	13	16	15	14	9	10	13	13	12	13	14	157
Predominant Sky Cover*	OVR	OVR	OVR	OVR	SCT	SCT	BRK	SCT	SCT	CLR	CLR	OVR	OVR
Mean Relative Humidity 7am (%)*	84	85	83	82	81	82	85	86	86	84	84	84	84
Mean Relative Humidity 4pm (%)*	60	58	55	54	57	62	67	65	61	55	58	62	60
Mean Dewpoint (°F)*	41	44	49	55	63	70	72	72	67	57	48	43	57
Prevailing Wind Direction*	N	N	S	S	S	S	S	NE	NE	NE	N	N	N
Prevailing Wind Speed (mph)*	13	13	12	12	10	9	8	8	9	8	12	12	10
Maximum Wind Gust (mph)*	48	61	55	61	62	67	64	74	97	59	58	56	97

Note: (*) Period of record is 1948-1995

Montgomery Dannelly Field

Montgomery is located in a gently rolling area of Alabama with no local topographic features which appreciably influence weather and climate. The National Weather Service Office is on the north side of Dannelly Field which is located about 6 airline miles south-southwest of the downtown bend in the Alabama River. Surrounding terrain is rather level with long gentle slopes toward the northeast and east.

During the months of June through September, inclusive, temperature and humidity conditions generally show little change from day to day. During the coldest months, December, January, and February, there are frequent shifts between mild and moist air from the Gulf of Mexico and dry, cool continental air.

From late June through the first half of August, nearly all precipitation is from local, mostly afternoon, thunderstorms, and there are apt to be considerable differences in day-to-day amounts of rainfall in different parts of the Montgomery area. In late August and in September, summer conditions of temperature and humidity persist as air continues to drift in from the Gulf, but local thunderstorms become less frequent because of the shortening of the days and the decrease in heat received from the sun. As this late summer season progresses, the local thunderstorms give way to thunderstorms which occur with cold fronts and occasional general rains associated with storms on the Gulf.

All types and intensities of rain, except the local thunderstorms of summer, may occur at any time from December through March or early April. Floods in the rivers are correspondingly most frequent during this period.

Most rain from late April through early June is in the form of showers or thunderstorms occurring in advance of approaching cool fronts, which become weaker and less frequent as summer approaches. It is during this spring season, and during the late summer and early autumn, that droughts sometimes occur.

Snow in Montgomery is important only as a curiosity.

Montgomery Dannelly Field *Montgomery County* Elevation: 202 ft. Latitude: 32° 18' N Longitude: 86° 24' W

	JAN	FEB	MAR	APR	MAY	JUN	JUL	AUG	SEP	OCT	NOV	DEC	YEAR
Mean Maximum Temp. (°F)	58.1	62.4	70.1	76.9	84.2	90.1	92.4	92.3	87.6	78.4	69.2	60.1	76.8
Mean Temp. (°F)	47.1	51.0	58.0	64.4	72.6	79.2	82.0	81.7	76.6	66.1	56.7	49.0	65.4
Mean Minimum Temp. (°F)	36.0	39.5	45.7	51.9	60.9	68.3	71.6	71.1	65.5	53.7	44.1	37.8	53.8
Extreme Maximum Temp. (°F)	83	84	89	94	96	103	104	106	101	95	87	85	106
Extreme Minimum Temp. (°F)	0	10	17	28	42	49	59	56	42	29	21	5	0
Days Maximum Temp. ≥ 90°F	0	0	0	0	5	18	24	24	13	2	0	0	86
Days Maximum Temp. ≤ 32°F	0	0	0	0	0	0	0	0	0	0	0	0	0
Days Minimum Temp. ≤ 32°F	13	7	2	0	0	0	0	0	0	0	4	11	37
Days Minimum Temp. ≤ 0°F	0	0	0	0	0	0	0	0	0	0	0	0	0
Heating Degree Days (base 65°F)	551	396	238	92	7	0	0	0	3	83	267	496	2,133
Cooling Degree Days (base 65°F)	3	6	27	80	249	433	535	526	358	122	24	7	2,370
Mean Precipitation (in.)	4.54	5.26	6.15	4.16	3.65	4.11	5.22	3.75	4.00	2.94	4.57	4.87	53.22
Maximum Precipitation (in.)*	16.5	13.4	16.8	15.6	23.1	14.4	11.9	10.4	10.6	9.1	21.3	11.3	135.
Minimum Precipitation (in.)*	0.7	1.8	1.9	0.5	0.7	0.3	1.6	0.8	0.4	trace	0.3	1.4	26.8
Extreme Maximum Daily Precip. (in.)	3.25	5.27	7.89	4.55	4.06	3.52	3.41	5.38	5.94	3.09	3.79	3.92	7.89
Days With ≥ 0.1" Precipitation	7	6	7	5	5	6	8	6	5	4	6	7	72
Days With ≥ 0.5" Precipitation	3	3	4	3	3	3	3	2	2	2	3	4	35
Days With ≥ 1.0" Precipitation	1	2	2	1	1	1	2	1	1	1	2	2	17
Mean Snowfall (in.)	na	na	na	na	na	na	na	na	na	na	na	na	na
Maximum Snowfall (in.)*	6	3	4	1	0	0	0	0	0	trace	trace	1	6
Maximum 24-hr. Snowfall (in.)*	3	3	4	1	0	0	0	0	0	trace	trace	1	4
Maximum Snow Depth (in.)	na	na	na	na	na	na	na	na	na	na	na	na	na
Days With ≥ 1.0" Snow Depth	na	na	na	na	na	na	na	na	na	na	na	na	na
Thunderstorm Days*	2	2	5	5	6	9	12	9	4	1	2	2	59
Foggy Days*	14	11	12	11	15	13	15	17	16	16	14	14	168
Predominant Sky Cover*	OVR	OVR	OVR	CLR	OVR	SCT	SCT	SCT	CLR	CLR	CLR	OVR	OVR
Mean Relative Humidity 7am (%)*	83	82	81	80	80	81	84	86	85	86	86	84	83
Mean Relative Humidity 4pm (%)*	56	51	48	46	51	54	59	56	55	50	52	56	53
Mean Dewpoint (°F)*	37	39	45	52	61	67	71	70	65	54	45	39	54
Prevailing Wind Direction*	NW	NW	S	S	S	SW	SW	E	E	E	NW	NW	E
Prevailing Wind Speed (mph)*	10	10	10	9	7	7	7	6	7	7	9	10	8
Maximum Wind Gust (mph)*	48	66	64	67	60	60	55	53	64	62	56	48	67

Note: (*) Period of record is 1948-1995

The period of record for National Weather Service station data is 1980 – 2009 except where noted. See User Guide for detailed explanation of data.

Alexander City *Tallapoosa County* Elevation: 640 ft. Latitude: 32° 57' N Longitude: 85° 57' W

	JAN	FEB	MAR	APR	MAY	JUN	JUL	AUG	SEP	OCT	NOV	DEC	YEAR
Mean Maximum Temp. (°F)	55.4	59.6	67.8	74.7	81.8	87.8	91.0	90.1	85.0	75.9	66.8	57.6	74.5
Mean Temp. (°F)	43.6	47.1	54.5	61.3	69.5	76.6	80.1	79.2	73.6	63.1	53.9	45.8	62.4
Mean Minimum Temp. (°F)	31.8	34.6	41.1	47.9	57.2	65.3	69.2	68.3	62.2	50.2	41.0	34.0	50.2
Extreme Maximum Temp. (°F)	78	81	89	92	96	102	104	105	99	93	86	80	105
Extreme Minimum Temp. (°F)	-6	5	12	25	39	42	56	53	38	29	18	-1	-6
Days Maximum Temp. ≥ 90°F	0	0	0	0	2	13	20	17	7	0	0	0	59
Days Maximum Temp. ≤ 32°F	0	0	0	0	0	0	0	0	0	0	0	0	0
Days Minimum Temp. ≤ 32°F	18	14	6	1	0	0	0	0	0	1	7	16	63
Days Minimum Temp. ≤ 0°F	0	0	0	0	0	0	0	0	0	0	0	0	0
Heating Degree Days (base 65°F)	657	501	331	150	26	0	0	0	9	125	335	591	2,725
Cooling Degree Days (base 65°F)	0	1	12	46	173	354	474	448	273	71	10	2	1,864
Mean Precipitation (in.)	5.24	5.18	5.82	4.24	4.29	4.41	5.39	4.38	4.21	3.16	4.56	4.72	55.60
Extreme Maximum Daily Precip. (in.)	3.45	3.50	3.39	3.50	2.90	3.55	5.02	3.40	4.73	3.00	3.02	4.17	5.02
Days With ≥ 0.1" Precipitation	8	7	7	6	6	7	8	7	5	4	6	7	78
Days With ≥ 0.5" Precipitation	4	4	4	3	3	3	4	3	3	2	3	3	39
Days With ≥ 1.0" Precipitation	2	2	2	1	1	1	2	1	2	1	2	2	19
Mean Snowfall (in.)	0.3	trace	0.2	trace	0.0	0.0	0.0	0.0	0.0	0.0	0.0	0.1	0.6
Maximum Snow Depth (in.)	0	0	7	0	0	0	0	0	0	0	0	trace	7
Days With ≥ 1.0" Snow Depth	0	0	0	0	0	0	0	0	0	0	0	0	0

Andalusia 3 W *Covington County* Elevation: 250 ft. Latitude: 31° 18' N Longitude: 86° 31' W

	JAN	FEB	MAR	APR	MAY	JUN	JUL	AUG	SEP	OCT	NOV	DEC	YEAR
Mean Maximum Temp. (°F)	60.8	64.8	72.3	78.2	85.1	90.0	91.7	91.2	87.6	79.6	71.0	63.2	78.0
Mean Temp. (°F)	47.6	50.7	57.4	63.1	71.2	77.9	80.3	79.9	75.3	65.2	56.3	50.0	64.6
Mean Minimum Temp. (°F)	34.1	36.8	42.4	48.0	57.3	65.7	68.8	68.4	62.9	51.1	42.0	36.6	51.2
Extreme Maximum Temp. (°F)	80	83	89	94	98	104	103	103	100	92	88	84	104
Extreme Minimum Temp. (°F)	0	10	16	27	38	44	58	55	39	28	16	2	0
Days Maximum Temp. ≥ 90°F	0	0	0	0	6	18	23	22	12	1	0	0	82
Days Maximum Temp. ≤ 32°F	0	0	0	0	0	0	0	0	0	0	0	0	0
Days Minimum Temp. ≤ 32°F	16	11	6	1	0	0	0	0	0	1	7	13	55
Days Minimum Temp. ≤ 0°F	0	0	0	0	0	0	0	0	0	0	0	0	0
Heating Degree Days (base 65°F)	536	404	254	116	13	0	0	0	5	92	274	466	2,160
Cooling Degree Days (base 65°F)	2	7	25	66	212	394	480	468	322	108	20	8	2,112
Mean Precipitation (in.)	5.18	5.11	6.69	4.38	4.00	5.56	6.03	5.59	4.52	3.71	4.77	4.65	60.19
Extreme Maximum Daily Precip. (in.)	3.95	7.76	12.34	4.00	3.14	7.30	5.25	4.20	17.88	12.80	4.18	7.10	17.88
Days With ≥ 0.1" Precipitation	7	6	6	5	5	8	8	7	5	3	5	5	70
Days With ≥ 0.5" Precipitation	4	3	4	3	3	3	4	3	2	2	3	3	37
Days With ≥ 1.0" Precipitation	2	2	2	1	1	1	2	2	1	1	2	1	18
Mean Snowfall (in.)	0.0	0.0	0.2	0.0	0.0	0.0	0.0	0.0	0.0	0.0	0.0	0.0	0.2
Maximum Snow Depth (in.)	0	1	0	0	0	0	0	0	0	0	0	0	1
Days With ≥ 1.0" Snow Depth	0	0	0	0	0	0	0	0	0	0	0	0	0

Anniston Calhoun Co Arpt *Calhoun County* Elevation: 610 ft. Latitude: 33° 35' N Longitude: 85° 51' W

	JAN	FEB	MAR	APR	MAY	JUN	JUL	AUG	SEP	OCT	NOV	DEC	YEAR
Mean Maximum Temp. (°F)	53.9	58.4	66.6	74.1	81.1	87.3	90.3	89.9	84.1	74.6	65.2	56.2	73.5
Mean Temp. (°F)	43.6	47.4	54.8	61.8	69.9	76.9	80.1	79.7	73.5	63.0	53.5	45.7	62.5
Mean Minimum Temp. (°F)	33.2	36.3	42.9	49.5	58.7	66.4	69.9	69.6	62.9	51.3	41.8	35.2	51.5
Extreme Maximum Temp. (°F)	79	84	88	92	96	102	105	106	99	91	85	79	106
Extreme Minimum Temp. (°F)	-5	8	12	26	39	46	55	52	40	28	20	3	-5
Days Maximum Temp. ≥ 90°F	0	0	0	0	2	11	18	17	6	0	0	0	54
Days Maximum Temp. ≤ 32°F	1	0	0	0	0	0	0	0	0	0	0	0	1
Days Minimum Temp. ≤ 32°F	16	11	5	1	0	0	0	0	0	1	7	14	55
Days Minimum Temp. ≤ 0°F	0	0	0	0	0	0	0	0	0	0	0	0	0
Heating Degree Days (base 65°F)	657	493	326	141	22	0	0	0	10	129	348	592	2,718
Cooling Degree Days (base 65°F)	1	1	15	52	182	362	477	464	274	74	11	2	1,915
Mean Precipitation (in.)	4.52	4.99	5.13	4.23	4.18	4.18	4.53	3.29	3.18	3.18	4.56	4.01	49.98
Extreme Maximum Daily Precip. (in.)	3.31	3.40	4.51	4.51	3.45	3.55	3.33	3.52	4.48	3.06	3.51	2.57	4.51
Days With ≥ 0.1" Precipitation	7	7	7	7	7	7	8	5	5	5	6	7	78
Days With ≥ 0.5" Precipitation	3	4	4	3	3	3	3	2	2	2	3	3	35
Days With ≥ 1.0" Precipitation	1	2	2	1	1	1	1	1	1	1	2	1	15
Mean Snowfall (in.)	na	na	na	na	na	na	na	na	na	na	na	na	na
Maximum Snow Depth (in.)	na	na	na	na	na	na	na	na	na	na	na	na	na
Days With ≥ 1.0" Snow Depth	na	na	na	na	na	na	na	na	na	na	na	na	na

Bankhead Lock and Dam *Tuscaloosa County* Elevation: 279 ft. Latitude: 33° 27' N Longitude: 87° 21' W

	JAN	FEB	MAR	APR	MAY	JUN	JUL	AUG	SEP	OCT	NOV	DEC	YEAR
Mean Maximum Temp. (°F)	53.9	58.5	66.7	74.6	81.9	88.9	91.8	91.5	86.1	75.8	66.0	56.3	74.3
Mean Temp. (°F)	42.5	46.2	53.8	61.1	69.5	76.9	80.3	80.0	73.9	62.9	53.4	45.1	62.1
Mean Minimum Temp. (°F)	31.1	33.9	40.9	47.5	57.1	64.9	68.7	68.3	61.7	50.0	40.7	33.8	49.9
Extreme Maximum Temp. (°F)	78	82	87	94	98	101	106	106	101	95	87	80	106
Extreme Minimum Temp. (°F)	-5	4	14	22	37	45	54	52	34	25	18	0	-5
Days Maximum Temp. ≥ 90°F	0	0	0	0	3	15	22	21	10	1	0	0	72
Days Maximum Temp. ≤ 32°F	1	0	0	0	0	0	0	0	0	0	0	1	2
Days Minimum Temp. ≤ 32°F	18	13	7	1	0	0	0	0	0	1	7	16	63
Days Minimum Temp. ≤ 0°F	0	0	0	0	0	0	0	0	0	0	0	0	0
Heating Degree Days (base 65°F)	691	527	351	159	27	1	0	0	11	127	351	612	2,857
Cooling Degree Days (base 65°F)	0	1	11	48	172	365	480	470	286	70	9	1	1,913
Mean Precipitation (in.)	5.95	5.64	5.87	4.80	4.63	4.94	5.59	3.97	4.14	4.13	5.12	5.23	60.01
Extreme Maximum Daily Precip. (in.)	4.92	5.55	4.39	5.94	4.50	3.53	4.25	4.60	6.30	7.80	4.10	10.03	10.03
Days With ≥ 0.1" Precipitation	8	7	8	7	6	8	8	7	5	5	7	7	83
Days With ≥ 0.5" Precipitation	4	4	4	3	3	4	4	3	3	3	4	4	43
Days With ≥ 1.0" Precipitation	2	2	2	2	2	2	2	1	1	2	2	2	22
Mean Snowfall (in.)	0.2	trace	0.0	0.0	0.0	0.0	0.0	0.0	0.0	0.0	0.0	trace	0.2
Maximum Snow Depth (in.)	0	1	0	0	0	0	0	0	0	0	0	trace	1
Days With ≥ 1.0" Snow Depth	0	0	0	0	0	0	0	0	0	0	0	0	0

The period of record for all cooperative weather station data is 1980 – 2009. See User Guide for detailed explanation of data.

Bay Minette 3 NNW *Baldwin County* Elevation: 277 ft. Latitude: 30° 56' N Longitude: 87° 48' W

	JAN	FEB	MAR	APR	MAY	JUN	JUL	AUG	SEP	OCT	NOV	DEC	YEAR
Mean Maximum Temp. (°F)	61.0	64.9	71.8	77.7	84.4	89.0	90.5	90.1	86.8	78.6	70.1	62.6	77.3
Mean Temp. (°F)	50.6	54.1	60.5	66.3	73.8	79.1	81.1	80.7	77.0	67.9	59.5	52.4	66.9
Mean Minimum Temp. (°F)	40.2	43.3	49.0	54.9	63.1	69.3	71.6	71.3	67.1	57.1	48.9	42.2	56.5
Extreme Maximum Temp. (°F)	81	83	87	93	96	101	103	104	100	91	85	82	104
Extreme Minimum Temp. (°F)	2	13	16	28	42	51	62	56	42	31	24	7	2
Days Maximum Temp. ≥ 90°F	0	0	0	0	3	14	20	19	9	0	0	0	65
Days Maximum Temp. ≤ 32°F	0	0	0	0	0	0	0	0	0	0	0	0	0
Days Minimum Temp. ≤ 32°F	8	5	1	0	0	0	0	0	0	0	2	7	23
Days Minimum Temp. ≤ 0°F	0	0	0	0	0	0	0	0	0	0	0	0	0
Heating Degree Days (base 65°F)	446	313	175	61	3	0	0	0	2	56	199	398	1,653
Cooling Degree Days (base 65°F)	7	11	42	107	282	431	505	494	368	151	41	15	2,454
Mean Precipitation (in.)	5.84	4.99	6.04	5.10	5.91	6.78	8.09	6.48	5.89	3.76	5.08	5.47	69.43
Extreme Maximum Daily Precip. (in.)	4.25	3.82	6.43	12.24	7.66	9.53	15.58	4.85	15.11	6.04	5.78	6.41	15.58
Days With ≥ 0.1" Precipitation	8	6	7	5	6	8	11	9	7	4	6	7	84
Days With ≥ 0.5" Precipitation	4	3	4	3	3	4	5	4	3	2	3	3	41
Days With ≥ 1.0" Precipitation	2	2	2	1	2	2	2	2	2	1	2	2	22
Mean Snowfall (in.)	trace	trace	0.1	0.0	0.0	0.0	0.0	0.0	0.0	0.0	0.0	0.1	0.2
Maximum Snow Depth (in.)	trace	1	trace	0	0	0	0	0	0	0	0	2	2
Days With ≥ 1.0" Snow Depth	0	0	0	0	0	0	0	0	0	0	0	0	0

Belle Mina 2 N *Limestone County* Elevation: 600 ft. Latitude: 34° 41' N Longitude: 86° 53' W

	JAN	FEB	MAR	APR	MAY	JUN	JUL	AUG	SEP	OCT	NOV	DEC	YEAR
Mean Maximum Temp. (°F)	50.2	54.4	63.4	72.1	80.2	87.4	90.7	90.6	84.8	74.0	63.1	52.5	72.0
Mean Temp. (°F)	39.8	43.2	51.1	59.5	68.3	75.8	79.2	78.3	72.0	60.6	50.8	41.8	60.0
Mean Minimum Temp. (°F)	29.3	32.0	38.9	46.8	56.3	64.1	67.7	66.0	59.1	47.2	38.5	31.0	48.1
Extreme Maximum Temp. (°F)	77	81	87	94	97	100	104	107	101	92	86	80	107
Extreme Minimum Temp. (°F)	-14	0	7	20	37	42	53	50	37	25	14	-5	-14
Days Maximum Temp. ≥ 90°F	0	0	0	0	2	12	20	19	7	0	0	0	60
Days Maximum Temp. ≤ 32°F	2	1	0	0	0	0	0	0	0	0	0	1	4
Days Minimum Temp. ≤ 32°F	20	16	9	2	0	0	0	0	0	2	10	19	78
Days Minimum Temp. ≤ 0°F	0	0	0	0	0	0	0	0	0	0	0	0	0
Heating Degree Days (base 65°F)	775	609	430	197	44	1	0	0	20	177	424	714	3,391
Cooling Degree Days (base 65°F)	0	0	8	38	153	331	447	421	235	49	6	1	1,689
Mean Precipitation (in.)	4.85	4.65	5.19	4.49	4.88	4.25	3.99	3.34	3.99	3.33	4.78	5.82	53.56
Extreme Maximum Daily Precip. (in.)	3.72	4.45	3.38	2.97	6.46	5.14	3.38	2.37	3.91	3.52	3.57	7.38	7.38
Days With ≥ 0.1" Precipitation	7	7	7	7	7	7	7	5	5	5	7	8	79
Days With ≥ 0.5" Precipitation	3	3	4	3	3	3	3	2	3	2	3	4	36
Days With ≥ 1.0" Precipitation	1	1	1	1	1	1	1	1	1	1	2	2	14
Mean Snowfall (in.)	0.6	0.4	0.4	trace	0.0	0.0	0.0	0.0	0.0	0.0	trace	0.1	1.5
Maximum Snow Depth (in.)	1	1	trace	0	0	0	0	0	0	0	trace	2	2
Days With ≥ 1.0" Snow Depth	0	0	0	0	0	0	0	0	0	0	0	0	0

Bessemer 3 WSW *Jefferson County* Elevation: 444 ft. Latitude: 33° 24' N Longitude: 87° 00' W

	JAN	FEB	MAR	APR	MAY	JUN	JUL	AUG	SEP	OCT	NOV	DEC	YEAR
Mean Maximum Temp. (°F)	55.6	60.4	68.5	76.2	83.4	89.8	92.9	92.5	87.3	76.9	66.9	57.8	75.7
Mean Temp. (°F)	43.9	47.8	54.9	62.3	70.6	77.4	80.9	80.3	74.6	63.6	53.9	46.0	63.0
Mean Minimum Temp. (°F)	32.1	35.2	41.3	48.3	57.8	65.0	68.9	67.9	61.9	50.2	41.0	34.1	50.3
Extreme Maximum Temp. (°F)	79	83	90	96	99	103	108	105	103	95	90	80	108
Extreme Minimum Temp. (°F)	-6	3	6	24	37	43	52	47	38	28	16	-1	-6
Days Maximum Temp. ≥ 90°F	0	0	0	1	5	17	24	23	12	1	0	0	83
Days Maximum Temp. ≤ 32°F	0	0	0	0	0	0	0	0	0	0	0	0	0
Days Minimum Temp. ≤ 32°F	17	12	6	2	0	0	0	0	0	1	7	16	61
Days Minimum Temp. ≤ 0°F	0	0	0	0	0	0	0	0	0	0	0	0	0
Heating Degree Days (base 65°F)	650	483	322	134	18	0	0	0	8	119	337	586	2,657
Cooling Degree Days (base 65°F)	1	2	15	59	200	380	501	482	304	83	11	2	2,040
Mean Precipitation (in.)	5.54	5.14	5.93	4.68	5.05	4.58	5.01	3.64	3.93	3.77	5.04	5.15	57.46
Extreme Maximum Daily Precip. (in.)	5.25	3.81	4.87	2.75	3.70	4.44	4.00	4.10	6.60	6.30	3.15	8.80	8.80
Days With ≥ 0.1" Precipitation	8	7	8	7	7	8	8	6	5	5	7	7	83
Days With ≥ 0.5" Precipitation	4	4	4	3	3	3	3	3	3	3	3	4	40
Days With ≥ 1.0" Precipitation	2	2	2	2	2	1	2	1	1	1	2	1	19
Mean Snowfall (in.)	0.3	0.0	0.6	0.0	0.0	0.0	0.0	0.0	0.0	0.0	0.0	0.0	0.9
Maximum Snow Depth (in.)	0	1	0	0	0	0	0	0	0	0	0	0	1
Days With ≥ 1.0" Snow Depth	0	0	0	0	0	0	0	0	0	0	0	0	0

Bridgeport 5 NW *Jackson County* Elevation: 669 ft. Latitude: 34° 59' N Longitude: 85° 48' W

	JAN	FEB	MAR	APR	MAY	JUN	JUL	AUG	SEP	OCT	NOV	DEC	YEAR
Mean Maximum Temp. (°F)	48.8	53.7	62.7	71.6	78.7	85.7	88.9	88.7	82.3	72.2	61.6	51.4	70.5
Mean Temp. (°F)	38.6	42.4	50.3	58.2	66.6	74.1	***77.6***	***77.2***	70.6	59.2	49.6	40.8	***58.8***
Mean Minimum Temp. (°F)	28.3	31.0	37.8	44.8	54.4	62.4	***66.4***	65.6	58.8	46.2	37.6	30.3	***47.0***
Extreme Maximum Temp. (°F)	75	76	86	89	95	97	100	103	98	90	84	76	103
Extreme Minimum Temp. (°F)	-13	-4	10	23	34	38	52	50	32	23	16	-5	-13
Days Maximum Temp. ≥ 90°F	0	0	0	0	1	8	14	14	4	0	0	0	41
Days Maximum Temp. ≤ 32°F	2	1	0	0	0	0	0	0	0	0	0	1	4
Days Minimum Temp. ≤ 32°F	21	16	10	3	0	0	0	0	0	3	10	19	82
Days Minimum Temp. ≤ 0°F	0	0	0	0	0	0	0	0	0	0	0	0	0
Heating Degree Days (base 65°F)	813	632	454	224	59	4	***0***	***0***	24	203	459	743	***3,615***
Cooling Degree Days (base 65°F)	0	0	4	26	116	284	***398***	***387***	198	29	3	0	***1,445***
Mean Precipitation (in.)	5.73	5.64	5.66	4.95	4.82	4.50	5.54	3.92	4.49	3.48	5.34	6.39	60.46
Extreme Maximum Daily Precip. (in.)	2.74	4.00	4.00	3.48	4.03	3.18	2.91	4.60	***3.94***	3.96	4.66	***6.90***	***6.90***
Days With ≥ 0.1" Precipitation	8	8	7	7	7	7	8	6	5	5	6	7	81
Days With ≥ 0.5" Precipitation	4	4	4	4	4	3	4	3	3	2	3	4	42
Days With ≥ 1.0" Precipitation	2	2	2	2	2	1	2	1	1	1	2	2	20
Mean Snowfall (in.)	0.7	0.2	trace	0.1	0.0	0.0	0.0	0.0	0.0	0.0	trace	trace	1.0
Maximum Snow Depth (in.)	3	***trace***	trace	***0***	0	0	0	0	0	0	trace	trace	***3***
Days With ≥ 1.0" Snow Depth	0	0	0	0	0	0	0	0	0	0	0	0	0

The period of record for all cooperative weather station data is 1980 – 2009. See User Guide for detailed explanation of data.

Centreville WSMO *Bibb County* Elevation: 456 ft. Latitude: 32° 54' N Longitude: 87° 15' W

	JAN	FEB	MAR	APR	MAY	JUN	JUL	AUG	SEP	OCT	NOV	DEC	YEAR
Mean Maximum Temp. (°F)	55.2	59.6	68.0	75.0	82.0	88.2	91.0	90.1	85.5	75.5	66.1	57.2	74.5
Mean Temp. (°F)	44.1	47.7	55.1	61.8	69.9	76.8	80.0	79.3	74.0	63.1	53.8	46.1	62.6
Mean Minimum Temp. (°F)	32.9	35.8	42.0	48.5	57.7	65.4	68.9	68.4	62.5	50.7	41.5	34.9	50.8
Extreme Maximum Temp. (°F)	80	86	89	92	96	100	105	102	102	92	87	82	105
Extreme Minimum Temp. (°F)	-6	5	14	27	38	48	54	54	38	26	16	1	-6
Days Maximum Temp. ≥ 90°F	0	0	0	0	2	13	20	18	8	1	0	0	62
Days Maximum Temp. ≤ 32°F	0	0	0	0	0	0	0	0	0	0	0	0	0
Days Minimum Temp. ≤ 32°F	16	12	6	1	0	0	0	0	0	1	7	15	58
Days Minimum Temp. ≤ 0°F	0	0	0	0	0	0	0	0	0	0	0	0	0
Heating Degree Days (base 65°F)	643	484	319	142	24	0	0	0	9	128	341	582	2,672
Cooling Degree Days (base 65°F)	1	3	16	52	181	361	472	450	286	77	13	3	1,915
Mean Precipitation (in.)	5.35	5.70	5.72	4.87	4.12	4.44	4.73	4.46	4.67	3.29	5.36	4.91	57.62
Extreme Maximum Daily Precip. (in.)	5.79	5.11	3.84	4.62	3.61	4.00	4.14	4.76	4.50	3.92	3.58	2.37	5.79
Days With ≥ 0.1" Precipitation	7	7	7	6	6	7	7	6	5	4	6	7	75
Days With ≥ 0.5" Precipitation	4	4	4	3	3	3	3	3	3	2	4	4	40
Days With ≥ 1.0" Precipitation	2	2	2	2	1	1	1	1	2	1	2	1	18
Mean Snowfall (in.)	0.3	trace	0.4	0.1	0.0	0.0	0.0	0.0	0.0	trace	trace	trace	0.8
Maximum Snow Depth (in.)	3	trace	8	trace	0	0	0	0	0	trace	trace	trace	8
Days With ≥ 1.0" Snow Depth	0	0	0	0	0	0	0	0	0	0	0	0	0

Clayton *Barbour County* Elevation: 500 ft. Latitude: 31° 53' N Longitude: 85° 29' W

	JAN	FEB	MAR	APR	MAY	JUN	JUL	AUG	SEP	OCT	NOV	DEC	YEAR
Mean Maximum Temp. (°F)	***57.9***	***62.1***	69.3	***76.2***	***83.4***	***88.3***	***90.9***	***90.2***	86.0	77.5	***69.2***	***59.9***	***75.9***
Mean Temp. (°F)	***46.3***	***50.0***	56.6	***62.9***	***71.1***	***77.3***	***80.0***	***79.3***	74.6	***64.8***	***56.8***	***48.1***	***64.0***
Mean Minimum Temp. (°F)	***34.7***	***37.8***	43.8	***49.6***	***58.8***	***66.3***	***69.1***	***68.2***	63.1	***52.2***	***44.2***	***36.2***	***52.0***
Extreme Maximum Temp. (°F)	***81***	***83***	87	94	97	101	104	105	98	93	***85***	***84***	***105***
Extreme Minimum Temp. (°F)	***-6***	***12***	13	27	36	49	57	***56***	42	28	***19***	***5***	-6
Days Maximum Temp. ≥ 90°F	***0***	***0***	0	0	4	12	20	18	9	1	***0***	***0***	***64***
Days Maximum Temp. ≤ 32°F	***0***	***0***	0	0	0	0	0	0	0	0	***0***	***0***	***0***
Days Minimum Temp. ≤ 32°F	***14***	***9***	5	1	0	0	0	***0***	0	1	***5***	***12***	***47***
Days Minimum Temp. ≤ 0°F	***0***	***0***	0	0	0	0	0	***0***	0	0	***0***	***0***	***0***
Heating Degree Days (base 65°F)	***574***	***424***	278	***123***	***16***	***0***	***0***	***0***	5	***94***	***264***	***521***	***2,299***
Cooling Degree Days (base 65°F)	***1***	***6***	23	***67***	***213***	***375***	***471***	***449***	299	***95***	***24***	***3***	***2,026***
Mean Precipitation (in.)	***4.28***	***4.67***	6.40	***3.56***	3.48	5.36	5.64	3.93	3.70	2.62	***4.20***	***3.79***	***51.63***
Extreme Maximum Daily Precip. (in.)	***3.12***	***4.50***	11.20	***3.00***	***3.20***	3.00	***8.00***	3.07	***5.20***	6.02	***5.30***	***3.54***	***11.20***
Days With ≥ 0.1" Precipitation	***6***	***6***	6	***5***	4	7	7	6	5	3	***5***	***5***	***65***
Days With ≥ 0.5" Precipitation	***3***	***3***	4	***2***	2	4	4	3	2	1	***3***	***3***	***34***
Days With ≥ 1.0" Precipitation	***1***	***2***	2	***1***	1	2	2	1	1	1	***1***	***1***	***16***
Mean Snowfall (in.)	***trace***	***0.0***	***0.0***	***0.0***	0.0	0.0	0.0	0.0	0.0	0.0	***0.0***	***0.2***	***0.2***
Maximum Snow Depth (in.)	***0***	***0***	***0***	***0***	0	0	0	0	0	***0***	***0***	***1***	***1***
Days With ≥ 1.0" Snow Depth	***0***	***0***	***0***	***0***	0	0	0	0	0	***0***	***0***	***0***	***0***

Coden *Mobile County* Elevation: 12 ft. Latitude: 30° 23' N Longitude: 88° 14' W

	JAN	FEB	MAR	APR	MAY	JUN	JUL	AUG	SEP	OCT	NOV	DEC	YEAR
Mean Maximum Temp. (°F)	60.4	63.6	***69.3***	***75.3***	***81.9***	***86.7***	***88.9***	***88.8***	***85.8***	78.4	69.5	62.6	***75.9***
Mean Temp. (°F)	49.9	52.8	***58.4***	***64.9***	***72.4***	***78.1***	***80.4***	***80.2***	***76.4***	67.7	58.0	52.0	***65.9***
Mean Minimum Temp. (°F)	39.3	41.9	***47.5***	***54.4***	***62.9***	***69.5***	***71.9***	***71.6***	***67.0***	57.0	46.4	41.5	***55.9***
Extreme Maximum Temp. (°F)	76	79	***84***	***87***	***93***	***98***	***100***	***101***	***96***	***90***	***83***	***80***	***101***
Extreme Minimum Temp. (°F)	1	12	***17***	***32***	***42***	***45***	***63***	***58***	***43***	***31***	***24***	7	***1***
Days Maximum Temp. ≥ 90°F	0	0	***0***	***0***	***0***	***6***	***13***	***13***	***5***	0	0	0	***37***
Days Maximum Temp. ≤ 32°F	0	0	***0***	***0***	***0***	***0***	***0***	***0***	***0***	0	0	0	***0***
Days Minimum Temp. ≤ 32°F	10	6	***2***	***0***	***0***	***0***	***0***	***0***	***0***	0	3	8	***29***
Days Minimum Temp. ≤ 0°F	0	0	***0***	***0***	***0***	***0***	***0***	***0***	***0***	0	0	0	***0***
Heating Degree Days (base 65°F)	465	345	***220***	***78***	***7***	***0***	***0***	***0***	***3***	58	232	407	***1,815***
Cooling Degree Days (base 65°F)	3	5	***24***	***81***	***244***	***401***	***486***	***477***	***352***	149	28	13	***2,263***
Mean Precipitation (in.)	5.89	5.78	***5.97***	***4.99***	***5.24***	***5.39***	***8.33***	***6.45***	***5.80***	4.30	4.57	5.10	***67.81***
Extreme Maximum Daily Precip. (in.)	7.06	8.40	***7.41***	***10.50***	***5.18***	***4.60***	***12.15***	***7.01***	***7.10***	***8.75***	***4.42***	***4.15***	***12.15***
Days With ≥ 0.1" Precipitation	7	6	***6***	***5***	***5***	***8***	***9***	***8***	***7***	5	5	6	***77***
Days With ≥ 0.5" Precipitation	4	3	***3***	***2***	***3***	***4***	***4***	***4***	***4***	3	3	3	***40***
Days With ≥ 1.0" Precipitation	2	2	***2***	***2***	***2***	***2***	***2***	***2***	***2***	1	2	2	***23***
Mean Snowfall (in.)	***0.0***	trace	***trace***	***0.0***	***0.0***	***0.0***	***0.0***	***0.0***	***0.0***	0.0	0.0	trace	***trace***
Maximum Snow Depth (in.)	***0***	trace	***trace***	***0***	***0***	***0***	***0***	***0***	***0***	***0***	***0***	***trace***	trace
Days With ≥ 1.0" Snow Depth	***0***	0	***0***	***0***	***0***	***0***	***0***	***0***	***0***	***0***	0	0	***0***

Dauphin Island #2 *Mobile County* Elevation: 7 ft. Latitude: 30° 15' N Longitude: 88° 05' W

	JAN	FEB	MAR	APR	MAY	JUN	JUL	AUG	SEP	OCT	NOV	DEC	YEAR
Mean Maximum Temp. (°F)	58.6	61.2	67.3	73.7	81.2	86.6	88.9	88.7	85.5	77.4	68.9	61.0	74.9
Mean Temp. (°F)	52.2	54.9	61.3	67.9	76.1	81.3	83.4	83.4	80.2	71.5	62.7	54.7	69.1
Mean Minimum Temp. (°F)	45.7	48.4	55.3	62.2	71.0	76.0	77.9	77.9	74.9	65.7	56.4	48.3	63.3
Extreme Maximum Temp. (°F)	75	76	80	88	95	96	101	99	95	91	84	79	101
Extreme Minimum Temp. (°F)	9	19	23	35	53	60	65	67	57	37	35	11	9
Days Maximum Temp. ≥ 90°F	0	0	0	0	0	5	13	13	4	0	0	0	35
Days Maximum Temp. ≤ 32°F	0	0	0	0	0	0	0	0	0	0	0	0	0
Days Minimum Temp. ≤ 32°F	2	1	0	0	0	0	0	0	0	0	0	1	4
Days Minimum Temp. ≤ 0°F	0	0	0	0	0	0	0	0	0	0	0	0	0
Heating Degree Days (base 65°F)	393	283	140	34	1	0	0	0	0	18	122	323	1,314
Cooling Degree Days (base 65°F)	2	3	34	128	353	497	579	576	464	227	60	9	2,932
Mean Precipitation (in.)	5.39	5.13	5.45	4.58	4.55	5.04	7.19	6.89	4.97	3.99	4.14	4.33	61.65
Extreme Maximum Daily Precip. (in.)	5.95	5.48	5.46	9.63	7.60	3.60	23.99	11.83	5.48	7.30	3.78	3.52	23.99
Days With ≥ 0.1" Precipitation	7	6	6	4	5	7	8	8	6	4	5	6	72
Days With ≥ 0.5" Precipitation	4	3	3	2	2	3	4	4	3	2	3	3	36
Days With ≥ 1.0" Precipitation	2	2	2	1	2	2	2	2	1	1	1	1	19
Mean Snowfall (in.)	0.0	0.0	0.0	0.0	0.0	0.0	0.0	0.0	0.0	0.0	0.0	0.0	0.0
Maximum Snow Depth (in.)	0	0	0	0	0	0	0	0	0	0	0	0	0
Days With ≥ 1.0" Snow Depth	0	0	0	0	0	0	0	0	0	0	0	0	0

The period of record for all cooperative weather station data is 1980 – 2009. See User Guide for detailed explanation of data.

Demopolis Lock and Dam *Marengo County* Elevation: 100 ft. Latitude: 32° 31' N Longitude: 87° 53' W

	JAN	FEB	MAR	APR	MAY	JUN	JUL	AUG	SEP	OCT	NOV	DEC	YEAR
Mean Maximum Temp. (°F)	55.9	60.1	68.4	75.8	83.4	89.1	91.7	91.3	86.3	76.6	67.2	58.1	75.3
Mean Temp. (°F)	44.8	48.4	55.9	63.0	71.4	77.9	80.8	80.3	75.0	64.2	54.7	46.8	63.6
Mean Minimum Temp. (°F)	33.7	36.7	43.4	50.2	59.3	66.6	69.9	69.2	63.7	51.7	42.1	35.4	51.8
Extreme Maximum Temp. (°F)	80	85	89	96	98	103	105	104	101	93	87	82	105
Extreme Minimum Temp. (°F)	-2	6	16	25	40	42	57	53	41	29	22	4	-2
Days Maximum Temp. ≥ 90°F	0	0	0	0	4	16	22	21	10	1	0	0	74
Days Maximum Temp. ≤ 32°F	1	0	0	0	0	0	0	0	0	0	0	1	2
Days Minimum Temp. ≤ 32°F	15	10	5	1	0	0	0	0	0	0	6	14	51
Days Minimum Temp. ≤ 0°F	0	0	0	0	0	0	0	0	0	0	0	0	0
Heating Degree Days (base 65°F)	621	467	296	122	16	0	0	0	7	111	318	563	2,521
Cooling Degree Days (base 65°F)	2	4	22	69	220	393	496	481	315	94	15	5	2,116
Mean Precipitation (in.)	5.44	5.26	5.34	4.63	4.18	4.11	4.62	4.35	3.65	3.68	4.60	4.71	54.57
Extreme Maximum Daily Precip. (in.)	3.82	4.05	3.74	5.05	3.70	4.58	4.70	4.00	4.24	5.22	3.62	3.62	5.22
Days With ≥ 0.1" Precipitation	8	7	7	6	6	7	7	6	5	5	6	7	77
Days With ≥ 0.5" Precipitation	4	4	4	3	3	3	3	3	3	2	3	4	39
Days With ≥ 1.0" Precipitation	2	2	2	1	1	1	1	1	1	1	2	1	16
Mean Snowfall (in.)	0.0	0.0	0.1	0.0	0.0	0.0	0.0	0.0	0.0	0.0	0.0	0.0	0.1
Maximum Snow Depth (in.)	0	0	0	0	0	0	0	0	0	0	0	0	0
Days With ≥ 1.0" Snow Depth	0	0	0	0	0	0	0	0	0	0	0	0	0

Enterprise 5 NNW *Coffee County* Elevation: 469 ft. Latitude: 31° 23' N Longitude: 85° 54' W

	JAN	FEB	MAR	APR	MAY	JUN	JUL	AUG	SEP	OCT	NOV	DEC	YEAR
Mean Maximum Temp. (°F)	58.3	62.9	70.0	76.4	83.7	88.3	90.2	89.6	86.0	77.7	69.5	60.4	76.1
Mean Temp. (°F)	48.4	52.5	58.8	65.0	72.9	78.6	80.8	80.3	76.2	67.2	59.0	50.5	65.9
Mean Minimum Temp. (°F)	38.5	42.1	47.6	53.6	62.1	68.8	71.4	71.0	66.4	56.5	48.4	40.6	55.6
Extreme Maximum Temp. (°F)	81	82	88	93	97	101	104	103	100	92	86	81	104
Extreme Minimum Temp. (°F)	-1	10	17	30	42	50	62	59	45	32	25	6	-1
Days Maximum Temp. ≥ 90°F	0	0	0	0	4	12	18	16	8	1	0	0	59
Days Maximum Temp. ≤ 32°F	0	0	0	0	0	0	0	0	0	0	0	0	0
Days Minimum Temp. ≤ 32°F	9	5	1	0	0	0	0	0	0	0	2	7	24
Days Minimum Temp. ≤ 0°F	0	0	0	0	0	0	0	0	0	0	0	0	0
Heating Degree Days (base 65°F)	509	356	216	85	7	0	0	0	2	63	211	448	1,897
Cooling Degree Days (base 65°F)	2	9	33	92	259	414	498	481	345	137	37	7	2,314
Mean Precipitation (in.)	5.13	4.72	5.84	3.95	3.42	5.07	6.35	4.32	3.98	3.08	4.08	3.83	53.77
Extreme Maximum Daily Precip. (in.)	3.62	4.97	8.55	4.36	3.87	4.70	9.27	3.48	6.55	8.34	3.36	3.88	9.27
Days With ≥ 0.1" Precipitation	6	6	6	5	5	7	9	7	5	4	5	5	70
Days With ≥ 0.5" Precipitation	3	3	3	2	2	3	4	3	2	2	3	3	33
Days With ≥ 1.0" Precipitation	1	1	2	1	1	1	2	1	1	1	1	1	14
Mean Snowfall (in.)	0.0	0.0	0.0	0.0	0.0	0.0	0.0	0.0	0.0	0.0	0.0	trace	trace
Maximum Snow Depth (in.)	0	0	0	0	0	0	0	0	0	0	0	0	0
Days With ≥ 1.0" Snow Depth	0	0	0	0	0	0	0	0	0	0	0	0	0

Fairhope 2 NE *Baldwin County* Elevation: 22 ft. Latitude: 30° 33' N Longitude: 87° 53' W

	JAN	FEB	MAR	APR	MAY	JUN	JUL	AUG	SEP	OCT	NOV	DEC	YEAR
Mean Maximum Temp. (°F)	61.0	64.3	70.7	76.9	84.0	88.7	90.6	90.5	87.4	79.5	71.0	63.3	77.3
Mean Temp. (°F)	50.5	53.6	59.9	66.1	73.8	79.6	81.8	81.4	77.6	68.4	59.9	52.7	67.1
Mean Minimum Temp. (°F)	39.9	42.8	49.1	55.2	63.6	70.5	72.9	72.3	67.7	57.4	48.7	42.1	56.8
Extreme Maximum Temp. (°F)	79	87	85	91	96	100	101	102	97	92	86	82	102
Extreme Minimum Temp. (°F)	5	14	21	35	45	52	62	60	47	33	26	9	5
Days Maximum Temp. ≥ 90°F	0	0	0	0	3	13	21	21	12	1	0	0	71
Days Maximum Temp. ≤ 32°F	0	0	0	0	0	0	0	0	0	0	0	0	0
Days Minimum Temp. ≤ 32°F	9	4	1	0	0	0	0	0	0	0	1	6	21
Days Minimum Temp. ≤ 0°F	0	0	0	0	0	0	0	0	0	0	0	0	0
Heating Degree Days (base 65°F)	449	327	187	61	3	0	0	0	1	50	191	392	1,661
Cooling Degree Days (base 65°F)	7	11	36	100	284	445	526	517	385	163	44	16	2,534
Mean Precipitation (in.)	5.62	5.41	5.94	4.80	4.95	6.65	8.01	6.95	5.91	4.23	5.03	4.57	68.07
Extreme Maximum Daily Precip. (in.)	8.00	8.61	6.20	13.75	6.54	7.80	14.52	5.74	9.18	7.37	4.88	3.30	14.52
Days With ≥ 0.1" Precipitation	7	6	6	5	5	9	10	9	7	5	6	6	81
Days With ≥ 0.5" Precipitation	4	3	3	2	2	4	5	4	3	3	3	3	39
Days With ≥ 1.0" Precipitation	2	2	2	1	2	2	3	2	2	1	2	2	23
Mean Snowfall (in.)	trace	trace	trace	trace	0.0	0.0	0.0	0.0	0.0	0.0	0.0	trace	trace
Maximum Snow Depth (in.)	trace	trace	trace	trace	0	0	0	0	0	0	0	trace	trace
Days With ≥ 1.0" Snow Depth	0	0	0	0	0	0	0	0	0	0	0	0	0

Fayette *Fayette County* Elevation: 365 ft. Latitude: 33° 41' N Longitude: 87° 49' W

	JAN	FEB	MAR	APR	MAY	JUN	JUL	AUG	SEP	OCT	NOV	DEC	YEAR
Mean Maximum Temp. (°F)	54.2	58.3	67.0	75.5	82.2	88.8	91.8	91.7	86.1	75.7	65.7	55.9	74.4
Mean Temp. (°F)	43.0	45.9	53.6	61.7	69.2	76.8	80.4	79.7	73.6	61.7	52.4	44.3	61.8
Mean Minimum Temp. (°F)	31.8	33.5	40.3	47.8	56.2	64.7	68.8	67.6	61.0	47.6	38.9	32.6	49.2
Extreme Maximum Temp. (°F)	78	85	89	94	97	102	105	106	100	93	87	81	106
Extreme Minimum Temp. (°F)	0	4	12	29	38	47	56	52	38	26	19	-1	-1
Days Maximum Temp. ≥ 90°F	0	0	0	0	3	15	21	21	9	1	0	0	70
Days Maximum Temp. ≤ 32°F	1	0	0	0	0	0	0	0	0	0	0	0	1
Days Minimum Temp. ≤ 32°F	17	15	8	1	0	0	0	0	0	2	10	17	70
Days Minimum Temp. ≤ 0°F	0	0	0	0	0	0	0	0	0	0	0	0	0
Heating Degree Days (base 65°F)	678	535	361	147	30	0	0	0	12	156	381	639	2,939
Cooling Degree Days (base 65°F)	1	1	15	55	167	360	483	463	276	61	8	2	1,892
Mean Precipitation (in.)	5.48	5.29	5.86	4.80	4.27	4.84	4.56	3.91	3.54	3.56	4.71	4.98	55.80
Extreme Maximum Daily Precip. (in.)	4.53	4.50	4.38	3.71	3.06	4.53	3.05	5.15	2.80	3.50	2.50	7.36	7.36
Days With ≥ 0.1" Precipitation	8	7	7	6	6	7	7	6	5	5	7	7	78
Days With ≥ 0.5" Precipitation	4	4	4	3	3	4	4	2	2	2	4	3	39
Days With ≥ 1.0" Precipitation	2	2	2	2	1	1	1	1	1	1	2	1	17
Mean Snowfall (in.)	0.3	trace	0.0	0.0	0.0	0.0	0.0	0.0	0.0	0.0	0.0	0.0	0.3
Maximum Snow Depth (in.)	4	0	0	0	0	0	0	0	0	0	0	0	4
Days With ≥ 1.0" Snow Depth	0	0	0	0	0	0	0	0	0	0	0	0	0

The period of record for all cooperative weather station data is 1980 – 2009. See User Guide for detailed explanation of data.

Gadsden *Etowah County* Elevation: 564 ft. Latitude: 34° 01' N Longitude: 85° 59' W

	JAN	FEB	MAR	APR	MAY	JUN	JUL	AUG	SEP	OCT	NOV	DEC	YEAR
Mean Maximum Temp. (°F)	51.9	56.6	65.9	74.1	81.3	87.5	90.7	90.5	84.6	74.8	64.2	55.0	73.1
Mean Temp. (°F)	41.4	45.4	53.6	61.5	69.6	76.9	80.6	80.0	73.8	62.9	52.6	44.4	61.9
Mean Minimum Temp. (°F)	30.9	34.2	41.3	48.7	58.0	66.3	70.4	69.5	63.0	51.1	40.9	33.6	50.7
Extreme Maximum Temp. (°F)	76	81	87	91	96	101	106	104	101	92	87	78	106
Extreme Minimum Temp. (°F)	-6	4	12	22	38	46	60	55	43	31	20	3	-6
Days Maximum Temp. ≥ 90°F	0	0	0	0	3	12	20	18	7	0	0	0	60
Days Maximum Temp. ≤ 32°F	1	0	0	0	0	0	0	0	0	0	0	0	1
Days Minimum Temp. ≤ 32°F	18	13	5	1	0	0	0	0	0	0	6	16	59
Days Minimum Temp. ≤ 0°F	0	0	0	0	0	0	0	0	0	0	0	0	0
Heating Degree Days (base 65°F)	725	549	358	151	27	0	0	0	10	129	372	634	2,955
Cooling Degree Days (base 65°F)	0	1	11	52	179	365	491	472	281	72	6	1	1,931
Mean Precipitation (in.)	5.13	4.98	5.50	4.73	4.79	4.52	4.98	3.73	4.02	3.56	4.99	4.30	55.23
Extreme Maximum Daily Precip. (in.)	***5.20***	4.50	4.02	3.90	3.50	***3.10***	***3.00***	***3.63***	5.10	***4.98***	***5.60***	***2.40***	***5.60***
Days With ≥ 0.1" Precipitation	8	7	7	7	7	7	7	6	5	5	6	7	79
Days With ≥ 0.5" Precipitation	4	4	4	3	3	3	3	2	2	2	3	3	36
Days With ≥ 1.0" Precipitation	1	2	2	2	2	1	2	1	1	1	2	1	18
Mean Snowfall (in.)	***trace***	0.1	trace	0.0	0.0	0.0	0.0	0.0	0.0	0.0	trace	trace	***0.1***
Maximum Snow Depth (in.)	***trace***	1	trace	0	0	0	0	0	0	***0***	trace	trace	***1***
Days With ≥ 1.0" Snow Depth	***0***	0	0	0	0	0	0	0	0	0	0	0	***0***

Geneva No 2 *Geneva County* Elevation: 145 ft. Latitude: 31° 03' N Longitude: 85° 53' W

	JAN	FEB	MAR	APR	MAY	JUN	JUL	AUG	SEP	OCT	NOV	DEC	YEAR
Mean Maximum Temp. (°F)	60.4	64.5	71.4	77.2	84.6	89.2	91.1	90.4	86.9	78.9	70.4	62.3	77.3
Mean Temp. (°F)	48.4	51.9	58.5	64.3	72.4	78.4	80.7	80.1	75.9	66.3	57.5	50.4	65.4
Mean Minimum Temp. (°F)	36.3	39.3	45.6	51.3	60.1	67.6	70.3	69.9	65.0	53.7	44.5	38.3	53.5
Extreme Maximum Temp. (°F)	81	84	89	94	96	102	103	101	99	93	86	83	103
Extreme Minimum Temp. (°F)	2	11	18	30	41	44	61	57	43	29	21	7	2
Days Maximum Temp. ≥ 90°F	0	0	0	1	6	16	22	20	10	1	0	0	76
Days Maximum Temp. ≤ 32°F	0	0	0	0	0	0	0	0	0	0	0	0	0
Days Minimum Temp. ≤ 32°F	13	8	3	0	0	0	0	0	0	0	5	12	41
Days Minimum Temp. ≤ 0°F	0	0	0	0	0	0	0	0	0	0	0	0	0
Heating Degree Days (base 65°F)	512	373	225	97	9	0	0	0	3	78	248	455	2,000
Cooling Degree Days (base 65°F)	4	9	30	81	245	409	494	476	338	125	31	9	2,251
Mean Precipitation (in.)	5.34	5.18	6.44	4.27	3.66	5.96	5.74	4.94	4.31	3.68	5.21	4.67	59.40
Extreme Maximum Daily Precip. (in.)	4.56	7.15	7.14	4.58	5.86	7.19	7.73	2.67	7.09	5.90	6.95	5.60	7.73
Days With ≥ 0.1" Precipitation	7	6	7	5	5	8	9	8	5	4	5	6	75
Days With ≥ 0.5" Precipitation	4	3	4	3	2	4	4	4	3	2	3	3	39
Days With ≥ 1.0" Precipitation	2	2	2	1	1	2	2	1	1	1	2	2	19
Mean Snowfall (in.)	0.0	trace	0.0	0.0	0.0	0.0	0.0	0.0	0.0	0.0	0.0	0.0	trace
Maximum Snow Depth (in.)	0	trace	0	0	0	0	0	0	0	0	0	0	trace
Days With ≥ 1.0" Snow Depth	0	0	0	0	0	0	0	0	0	0	0	0	0

Greenville *Butler County* Elevation: 470 ft. Latitude: 31° 51' N Longitude: 86° 39' W

	JAN	FEB	MAR	APR	MAY	JUN	JUL	AUG	SEP	OCT	NOV	DEC	YEAR
Mean Maximum Temp. (°F)	59.6	63.7	71.2	77.6	84.6	89.7	91.8	91.3	87.0	78.4	69.7	61.3	77.2
Mean Temp. (°F)	48.2	51.6	58.2	64.3	72.2	78.2	80.7	80.3	75.8	66.3	57.4	49.9	65.3
Mean Minimum Temp. (°F)	36.6	39.5	45.1	51.0	59.7	66.7	69.6	69.3	64.6	54.2	45.0	38.5	53.3
Extreme Maximum Temp. (°F)	80	85	89	96	98	105	105	105	101	96	91	84	105
Extreme Minimum Temp. (°F)	-1	9	15	28	38	50	56	50	39	28	18	5	-1
Days Maximum Temp. ≥ 90°F	0	0	0	0	5	16	22	21	11	1	0	0	76
Days Maximum Temp. ≤ 32°F	0	0	0	0	0	0	0	0	0	0	0	0	0
Days Minimum Temp. ≤ 32°F	11	9	4	1	0	0	0	0	0	1	4	11	41
Days Minimum Temp. ≤ 0°F	0	0	0	0	0	0	0	0	0	0	0	0	0
Heating Degree Days (base 65°F)	517	379	232	95	11	0	0	0	4	77	250	468	2,033
Cooling Degree Days (base 65°F)	2	8	29	81	241	404	494	481	335	125	28	8	2,236
Mean Precipitation (in.)	5.11	4.82	6.21	4.22	3.96	4.76	5.78	4.64	4.27	3.68	4.95	4.74	57.14
Extreme Maximum Daily Precip. (in.)	2.93	3.88	5.15	4.93	3.12	3.80	8.75	4.89	15.36	7.20	6.27	4.76	15.36
Days With ≥ 0.1" Precipitation	7	7	6	5	6	7	8	7	5	4	6	6	74
Days With ≥ 0.5" Precipitation	4	3	4	3	3	3	4	3	2	2	3	3	37
Days With ≥ 1.0" Precipitation	2	2	2	1	1	2	2	1	1	1	2	2	19
Mean Snowfall (in.)	0.1	trace	0.1	0.0	0.0	0.0	0.0	0.0	0.0	0.0	0.0	0.1	0.3
Maximum Snow Depth (in.)	0	trace	0	0	0	0	0	0	0	0	0	0	trace
Days With ≥ 1.0" Snow Depth	0	0	0	0	0	0	0	0	0	0	0	0	0

Guntersville *Marshall County* Elevation: 578 ft. Latitude: 34° 20' N Longitude: 86° 20' W

	JAN	FEB	MAR	APR	MAY	JUN	JUL	AUG	SEP	OCT	NOV	DEC	YEAR
Mean Maximum Temp. (°F)	51.6	56.5	64.7	72.5	80.5	87.3	90.3	90.2	84.6	74.1	63.6	53.5	72.5
Mean Temp. (°F)	41.9	45.6	53.0	60.6	69.4	76.8	80.0	79.5	73.8	62.7	52.8	43.8	61.7
Mean Minimum Temp. (°F)	32.1	34.7	41.3	48.6	58.3	66.2	69.7	68.8	63.0	51.3	42.0	34.1	50.8
Extreme Maximum Temp. (°F)	76	81	87	***94***	***96***	103	***106***	105	101	90	84	78	***106***
Extreme Minimum Temp. (°F)	-11	2	11	***25***	***40***	46	***54***	48	41	29	22	0	***-11***
Days Maximum Temp. ≥ 90°F	0	0	0	0	2	11	17	17	6	0	0	0	53
Days Maximum Temp. ≤ 32°F	1	1	0	0	0	0	0	0	0	0	0	1	3
Days Minimum Temp. ≤ 32°F	17	13	6	1	0	0	0	0	0	0	5	15	57
Days Minimum Temp. ≤ 0°F	0	0	0	0	0	0	0	0	0	0	0	0	0
Heating Degree Days (base 65°F)	710	543	375	167	26	0	0	0	8	127	366	649	2,971
Cooling Degree Days (base 65°F)	0	1	9	41	***169***	361	472	457	279	63	8	1	***1,861***
Mean Precipitation (in.)	4.66	5.03	5.27	4.45	4.55	4.02	4.49	3.76	3.91	2.96	4.46	5.21	52.77
Extreme Maximum Daily Precip. (in.)	4.45	***3.80***	4.06	***3.22***	***4.73***	3.31	***3.84***	5.76	4.76	***3.23***	***2.43***	***4.56***	***5.76***
Days With ≥ 0.1" Precipitation	7	7	7	7	6	7	7	5	5	5	6	8	***77***
Days With ≥ 0.5" Precipitation	3	4	4	4	3	3	3	2	2	2	3	4	37
Days With ≥ 1.0" Precipitation	1	1	2	1	1	1	1	1	1	1	2	2	15
Mean Snowfall (in.)	0.4	0.1	0.3	trace	0.0	0.0	0.0	0.0	0.0	trace	0.0	trace	0.8
Maximum Snow Depth (in.)	9	trace	trace	***trace***	***0***	0	***0***	0	0	***trace***	***0***	trace	***9***
Days With ≥ 1.0" Snow Depth	0	0	0	0	0	0	0	0	0	0	0	0	0

The period of record for all cooperative weather station data is 1980 – 2009. See User Guide for detailed explanation of data.

Headland *Henry County* Elevation: 370 ft. Latitude: 31° 21' N Longitude: 85° 20' W

	JAN	FEB	MAR	APR	MAY	JUN	JUL	AUG	SEP	OCT	NOV	DEC	YEAR
Mean Maximum Temp. (°F)	59.2	63.3	71.0	77.7	85.7	90.5	92.2	91.5	87.5	79.0	69.9	61.8	77.4
Mean Temp. (°F)	47.5	51.3	58.5	64.7	73.2	78.9	80.9	79.9	75.7	65.8	57.5	50.0	65.3
Mean Minimum Temp. (°F)	36.0	39.2	46.0	51.7	60.6	67.3	69.4	68.3	63.8	53.0	45.1	38.3	53.2
Extreme Maximum Temp. (°F)	80	83	88	94	100	104	108	106	101	93	86	82	108
Extreme Minimum Temp. (°F)	0	10	12	27	42	45	57	55	40	26	20	5	0
Days Maximum Temp. ≥ 90°F	0	0	0	1	8	19	24	23	12	1	0	0	88
Days Maximum Temp. ≤ 32°F	0	0	0	0	0	0	0	0	0	0	0	0	0
Days Minimum Temp. ≤ 32°F	12	7	2	0	0	0	0	0	0	1	3	9	34
Days Minimum Temp. ≤ 0°F	0	0	0	0	0	0	0	0	0	0	0	0	0
Heating Degree Days (base 65°F)	536	387	224	89	7	0	0	0	3	80	245	464	2,035
Cooling Degree Days (base 65°F)	2	7	30	88	267	425	500	470	331	113	26	6	2,265
Mean Precipitation (in.)	5.20	4.98	5.88	3.88	3.24	5.34	5.43	4.29	4.03	3.39	4.11	4.29	54.06
Extreme Maximum Daily Precip. (in.)	4.39	5.95	6.70	3.55	4.72	4.30	9.08	5.20	5.97	6.81	6.65	6.17	9.08
Days With ≥ 0.1" Precipitation	8	6	7	5	5	8	9	7	5	4	5	6	75
Days With ≥ 0.5" Precipitation	3	3	4	2	2	4	3	3	3	2	3	3	35
Days With ≥ 1.0" Precipitation	1	2	2	1	1	2	1	1	1	1	1	1	15
Mean Snowfall (in.)	0.0	trace	trace	0.0	0.0	0.0	0.0	0.0	0.0	0.0	0.0	trace	trace
Maximum Snow Depth (in.)	0	trace	0	0	0	0	0	0	0	0	0	trace	trace
Days With ≥ 1.0" Snow Depth	0	0	0	0	0	0	0	0	0	0	0	0	0

Heflin *Cleburne County* Elevation: 850 ft. Latitude: 33° 39' N Longitude: 85° 36' W

	JAN	FEB	MAR	APR	MAY	JUN	JUL	AUG	SEP	OCT	NOV	DEC	YEAR
Mean Maximum Temp. (°F)	52.7	56.6	65.1	72.5	79.4	85.8	89.0	88.5	83.0	73.5	64.1	54.5	72.1
Mean Temp. (°F)	41.4	44.5	52.0	58.9	67.0	74.4	78.1	77.5	71.4	60.3	51.2	43.2	60.0
Mean Minimum Temp. (°F)	30.1	32.4	38.9	45.3	54.6	63.0	67.1	66.4	59.8	47.0	38.2	31.9	47.9
Extreme Maximum Temp. (°F)	78	80	87	90	95	98	107	105	97	88	84	77	107
Extreme Minimum Temp. (°F)	-3	1	8	23	35	41	53	51	37	25	15	-10	-10
Days Maximum Temp. ≥ 90°F	0	0	0	0	0	7	14	13	4	0	0	0	38
Days Maximum Temp. ≤ 32°F	1	0	0	0	0	0	0	0	0	0	0	1	2
Days Minimum Temp. ≤ 32°F	19	15	9	3	0	0	0	0	0	2	10	18	76
Days Minimum Temp. ≤ 0°F	0	0	0	0	0	0	0	0	0	0	0	0	0
Heating Degree Days (base 65°F)	725	573	401	204	52	2	0	0	19	180	414	669	3,239
Cooling Degree Days (base 65°F)	0	0	6	28	121	291	413	394	219	41	5	1	1,519
Mean Precipitation (in.)	5.33	5.67	5.73	4.74	4.75	4.30	5.32	3.43	3.59	3.34	4.85	4.79	55.84
Extreme Maximum Daily Precip. (in.)	3.33	5.40	4.53	3.88	3.50	4.94	4.12	4.19	3.84	5.30	4.37	4.30	5.40
Days With ≥ 0.1" Precipitation	8	7	7	7	7	7	8	5	5	5	6	7	79
Days With ≥ 0.5" Precipitation	4	4	4	3	3	3	3	2	2	2	3	3	36
Days With ≥ 1.0" Precipitation	2	2	2	1	1	1	1	1	1	1	2	1	16
Mean Snowfall (in.)	0.7	0.2	0.6	0.2	0.0	0.0	0.0	0.0	0.0	trace	0.0	0.2	1.9
Maximum Snow Depth (in.)	2	trace	3	0	0	0	0	0	0	***trace***	0	trace	***3***
Days With ≥ 1.0" Snow Depth	0	0	0	0	0	0	0	0	0	0	0	0	0

Highland Home *Crenshaw County* Elevation: 594 ft. Latitude: 31° 57' N Longitude: 86° 19' W

	JAN	FEB	MAR	APR	MAY	JUN	JUL	AUG	SEP	OCT	NOV	DEC	YEAR
Mean Maximum Temp. (°F)	57.1	61.5	69.1	75.6	83.1	88.3	90.2	89.9	85.9	77.1	68.4	59.5	75.5
Mean Temp. (°F)	45.7	49.4	56.3	62.5	70.9	77.0	79.5	79.1	74.4	64.8	55.8	48.1	63.6
Mean Minimum Temp. (°F)	34.4	37.2	43.4	49.4	58.7	65.7	68.7	68.3	62.9	52.5	43.2	36.6	51.7
Extreme Maximum Temp. (°F)	79	83	87	94	95	104	105	104	102	93	88	81	105
Extreme Minimum Temp. (°F)	-3	7	13	24	37	45	55	53	41	29	20	4	-3
Days Maximum Temp. ≥ 90°F	0	0	0	0	3	14	18	17	8	1	0	0	61
Days Maximum Temp. ≤ 32°F	0	0	0	0	0	0	0	0	0	0	0	0	0
Days Minimum Temp. ≤ 32°F	14	10	5	1	0	0	0	0	0	1	6	12	49
Days Minimum Temp. ≤ 0°F	0	0	0	0	0	0	0	0	0	0	0	0	0
Heating Degree Days (base 65°F)	591	439	283	129	17	0	0	0	6	97	288	522	2,372
Cooling Degree Days (base 65°F)	1	5	20	62	207	366	456	445	296	99	20	5	1,982
Mean Precipitation (in.)	4.78	5.03	6.20	4.15	3.51	5.07	4.96	5.00	3.95	3.29	4.90	4.44	55.28
Extreme Maximum Daily Precip. (in.)	3.53	5.28	7.67	3.08	3.75	3.41	3.00	7.82	***6.91***	***5.35***	3.30	4.00	***7.82***
Days With ≥ 0.1" Precipitation	7	6	6	6	5	7	8	7	5	4	6	6	73
Days With ≥ 0.5" Precipitation	3	4	4	3	2	4	3	3	2	2	3	3	36
Days With ≥ 1.0" Precipitation	1	2	2	1	1	2	1	2	1	1	2	1	17
Mean Snowfall (in.)	trace	trace	0.2	trace	0.0	0.0	0.0	0.0	0.0	0.0	0.0	trace	0.2
Maximum Snow Depth (in.)	2	trace	6	trace	0	0	0	0	0	0	0	5	6
Days With ≥ 1.0" Snow Depth	0	0	0	0	0	0	0	0	0	0	0	0	0

Jackson *Clarke County* Elevation: 220 ft. Latitude: 31° 32' N Longitude: 87° 56' W

	JAN	FEB	MAR	APR	MAY	JUN	JUL	AUG	SEP	OCT	NOV	DEC	YEAR
Mean Maximum Temp. (°F)	60.0	***64.1***	***71.4***	77.8	84.8	***89.9***	91.7	***91.6***	87.3	78.8	69.9	***61.6***	***77.4***
Mean Temp. (°F)	48.4	***51.8***	***58.5***	64.6	72.7	***78.8***	81.2	***80.9***	76.3	66.3	56.9	***50.0***	***65.5***
Mean Minimum Temp. (°F)	36.8	***39.5***	***45.7***	51.4	60.5	***67.7***	70.7	70.2	65.2	53.7	43.9	***38.4***	***53.6***
Extreme Maximum Temp. (°F)	83	***83***	87	95	96	102	104	104	99	93	87	83	***104***
Extreme Minimum Temp. (°F)	3	***11***	18	29	39	48	58	55	40	28	21	6	***3***
Days Maximum Temp. ≥ 90°F	0	***0***	0	1	6	16	23	22	11	1	0	0	***80***
Days Maximum Temp. ≤ 32°F	0	***0***	0	0	0	0	0	0	0	0	0	0	***0***
Days Minimum Temp. ≤ 32°F	12	***9***	3	0	0	0	0	0	0	0	5	11	***40***
Days Minimum Temp. ≤ 0°F	0	***0***	0	0	0	0	0	0	0	0	0	0	***0***
Heating Degree Days (base 65°F)	512	***375***	***227***	94	9	***0***	0	***0***	3	83	263	***468***	***2,034***
Cooling Degree Days (base 65°F)	5	***9***	***33***	91	254	***422***	509	***499***	348	129	27	***10***	***2,336***
Mean Precipitation (in.)	5.50	5.00	6.06	4.40	4.86	5.41	6.01	4.82	4.37	3.26	5.06	5.29	60.04
Extreme Maximum Daily Precip. (in.)	3.93	3.79	6.38	3.75	8.00	5.70	4.21	5.00	8.76	4.40	4.05	6.45	8.76
Days With ≥ 0.1" Precipitation	7	6	6	5	6	7	9	7	5	4	6	6	74
Days With ≥ 0.5" Precipitation	4	3	3	2	3	4	4	3	2	2	3	3	36
Days With ≥ 1.0" Precipitation	2	2	2	2	2	2	2	1	1	1	2	2	21
Mean Snowfall (in.)	0.0	0.0	0.0	0.0	0.0	0.0	0.0	0.0	0.0	0.0	0.0	0.0	0.0
Maximum Snow Depth (in.)	0	0	0	0	0	0	0	0	0	0	0	0	0
Days With ≥ 1.0" Snow Depth	0	0	0	0	0	0	0	0	0	0	0	0	0

The period of record for all cooperative weather station data is 1980 – 2009. See User Guide for detailed explanation of data.

Jasper *Walker County* Elevation: 485 ft. Latitude: 33° 54' N Longitude: 87° 19' W

	JAN	FEB	MAR	APR	MAY	JUN	JUL	AUG	SEP	OCT	NOV	DEC	YEAR
Mean Maximum Temp. (°F)	52.4	56.9	65.8	73.6	80.6	87.3	90.4	90.5	85.0	74.6	64.2	55.1	73.0
Mean Temp. (°F)	41.0	44.5	52.4	59.7	68.3	75.6	79.3	78.9	72.6	61.4	51.3	43.7	60.7
Mean Minimum Temp. (°F)	29.6	32.1	39.0	45.8	55.8	63.8	68.1	67.2	60.2	48.1	38.3	32.3	48.4
Extreme Maximum Temp. (°F)	77	84	88	91	94	100	108	105	100	92	85	78	108
Extreme Minimum Temp. (°F)	-10	2	6	26	36	41	53	52	36	26	16	5	-10
Days Maximum Temp. ≥ 90°F	0	0	0	0	2	12	19	18	7	0	0	0	58
Days Maximum Temp. ≤ 32°F	1	1	0	0	0	0	0	0	0	0	0	0	2
Days Minimum Temp. ≤ 32°F	20	15	9	3	0	0	0	0	0	2	10	17	76
Days Minimum Temp. ≤ 0°F	0	0	0	0	0	0	0	0	0	0	0	0	0
Heating Degree Days (base 65°F)	739	574	393	187	42	1	0	0	16	161	411	654	3,178
Cooling Degree Days (base 65°F)	1	1	9	36	150	326	451	437	252	55	6	2	1,726
Mean Precipitation (in.)	5.58	5.37	5.88	5.50	5.63	4.63	5.02	3.32	4.57	4.27	5.24	5.87	60.88
Extreme Maximum Daily Precip. (in.)	3.74	4.70	5.27	5.10	6.09	2.77	3.60	3.05	4.55	4.70	3.90	3.80	6.09
Days With ≥ 0.1" Precipitation	8	7	8	7	8	8	8	6	5	6	7	7	85
Days With ≥ 0.5" Precipitation	4	4	4	3	4	4	4	3	3	3	4	4	44
Days With ≥ 1.0" Precipitation	2	2	2	2	2	1	2	1	1	1	2	2	20
Mean Snowfall (in.)	0.3	0.2	0.3	0.0	0.0	0.0	0.0	0.0	0.0	0.0	0.0	trace	0.8
Maximum Snow Depth (in.)	3	3	1	0	0	0	0	0	0	0	0	trace	3
Days With ≥ 1.0" Snow Depth	0	0	0	0	0	0	0	0	0	0	0	0	0

Lafayette 2 W *Chambers County* Elevation: 740 ft. Latitude: 32° 54' N Longitude: 85° 26' W

	JAN	FEB	MAR	APR	MAY	JUN	JUL	AUG	SEP	OCT	NOV	DEC	YEAR
Mean Maximum Temp. (°F)	55.9	60.3	68.8	75.7	82.6	88.2	90.5	89.9	84.7	75.6	66.9	57.7	74.7
Mean Temp. (°F)	43.7	47.4	54.8	61.4	69.5	76.1	79.0	78.5	72.8	62.5	53.8	45.4	62.1
Mean Minimum Temp. (°F)	31.5	34.6	40.7	47.1	56.3	63.9	67.4	67.0	60.7	49.4	40.6	33.1	49.3
Extreme Maximum Temp. (°F)	78	82	88	93	97	103	104	105	99	94	84	79	105
Extreme Minimum Temp. (°F)	-7	3	8	25	34	43	53	51	37	23	16	0	-7
Days Maximum Temp. ≥ 90°F	0	0	0	0	3	12	18	17	7	0	0	0	57
Days Maximum Temp. ≤ 32°F	0	0	0	0	0	0	0	0	0	0	0	0	0
Days Minimum Temp. ≤ 32°F	18	12	7	2	0	0	0	0	0	2	8	16	65
Days Minimum Temp. ≤ 0°F	0	0	0	0	0	0	0	0	0	0	0	0	0
Heating Degree Days (base 65°F)	652	492	320	146	28	1	0	0	9	140	339	602	2,729
Cooling Degree Days (base 65°F)	0	2	11	45	173	340	440	425	251	69	9	1	1,766
Mean Precipitation (in.)	5.04	5.01	6.05	4.61	4.44	4.22	5.28	3.80	3.81	3.14	4.08	4.77	54.25
Extreme Maximum Daily Precip. (in.)	3.01	4.29	5.70	4.10	4.02	4.69	4.00	6.38	6.30	2.50	5.00	2.95	6.38
Days With ≥ 0.1" Precipitation	7	7	7	6	6	7	8	6	5	5	6	7	77
Days With ≥ 0.5" Precipitation	4	3	4	3	3	3	4	3	3	2	3	3	38
Days With ≥ 1.0" Precipitation	2	2	2	1	1	1	2	1	1	1	1	1	16
Mean Snowfall (in.)	0.2	trace	0.1	trace	0.0	0.0	0.0	0.0	0.0	0.0	0.0	trace	0.3
Maximum Snow Depth (in.)	2	trace	5	0	0	0	0	0	0	0	0	0	5
Days With ≥ 1.0" Snow Depth	1	0	0	0	0	0	0	0	0	0	0	0	0

Milstead *Macon County* Elevation: 214 ft. Latitude: 32° 27' N Longitude: 85° 53' W

	JAN	FEB	MAR	APR	MAY	JUN	JUL	AUG	SEP	OCT	NOV	DEC	YEAR
Mean Maximum Temp. (°F)	57.2	61.3	69.1	75.7	83.2	89.0	91.7	91.1	86.4	77.1	68.5	59.2	75.8
Mean Temp. (°F)	45.6	49.1	56.0	62.5	70.9	77.8	81.0	80.3	75.0	64.3	55.5	47.7	63.8
Mean Minimum Temp. (°F)	34.0	36.7	42.8	49.1	58.5	66.6	70.3	69.4	63.6	51.5	42.5	36.2	51.8
Extreme Maximum Temp. (°F)	80	83	87	90	97	102	106	107	101	93	88	81	107
Extreme Minimum Temp. (°F)	-3	9	15	30	41	45	57	56	38	28	21	7	-3
Days Maximum Temp. ≥ 90°F	0	0	0	0	4	15	21	19	10	1	0	0	70
Days Maximum Temp. ≤ 32°F	0	0	0	0	0	0	0	0	0	0	0	0	0
Days Minimum Temp. ≤ 32°F	16	11	5	1	0	0	0	0	0	1	6	13	53
Days Minimum Temp. ≤ 0°F	0	0	0	0	0	0	0	0	0	0	0	0	0
Heating Degree Days (base 65°F)	595	449	291	128	18	0	0	0	6	105	295	535	2,422
Cooling Degree Days (base 65°F)	1	4	19	58	208	392	503	481	313	91	18	5	2,093
Mean Precipitation (in.)	4.54	4.99	6.24	4.22	3.73	4.18	4.72	3.89	3.94	2.86	4.82	4.26	52.39
Extreme Maximum Daily Precip. (in.)	2.83	5.03	5.78	4.95	4.58	3.71	4.75	4.57	4.32	6.60	4.37	3.14	6.60
Days With ≥ 0.1" Precipitation	7	7	7	5	6	7	7	6	5	4	5	6	72
Days With ≥ 0.5" Precipitation	3	3	4	3	2	3	3	2	3	2	3	3	34
Days With ≥ 1.0" Precipitation	1	2	2	1	1	1	1	1	1	1	2	1	15
Mean Snowfall (in.)	0.1	0.0	0.0	0.0	0.0	0.0	0.0	0.0	0.0	0.0	0.0	0.1	0.2
Maximum Snow Depth (in.)	0	trace	0	0	0	0	0	0	0	0	0	0	trace
Days With ≥ 1.0" Snow Depth	0	0	0	0	0	0	0	0	0	0	0	0	0

Muscle Shoals Regional Arpt *Colbert County* Elevation: 540 ft. Latitude: 34° 45' N Longitude: 87° 36' W

	JAN	FEB	MAR	APR	MAY	JUN	JUL	AUG	SEP	OCT	NOV	DEC	YEAR
Mean Maximum Temp. (°F)	50.3	54.9	64.1	73.0	80.3	87.8	90.8	90.9	84.3	73.6	63.4	52.8	72.2
Mean Temp. (°F)	40.8	44.8	53.0	61.3	69.4	77.0	80.4	79.8	73.0	61.7	52.3	43.2	61.4
Mean Minimum Temp. (°F)	31.2	34.5	41.9	49.7	58.4	66.1	70.0	68.7	61.7	49.8	41.2	33.6	50.6
Extreme Maximum Temp. (°F)	76	80	87	93	96	101	105	107	101	92	85	77	107
Extreme Minimum Temp. (°F)	-11	9	12	26	38	47	55	52	39	27	17	-5	-11
Days Maximum Temp. ≥ 90°F	0	0	0	0	2	13	19	19	7	0	0	0	60
Days Maximum Temp. ≤ 32°F	1	1	0	0	0	0	0	0	0	0	0	1	3
Days Minimum Temp. ≤ 32°F	18	13	5	1	0	0	0	0	0	1	7	15	60
Days Minimum Temp. ≤ 0°F	0	0	0	0	0	0	0	0	0	0	0	0	0
Heating Degree Days (base 65°F)	745	567	375	159	28	0	0	0	15	154	382	669	3,094
Cooling Degree Days (base 65°F)	1	1	12	56	172	366	485	467	263	60	7	1	1,891
Mean Precipitation (in.)	4.13	4.68	5.20	4.39	5.19	4.69	4.16	3.06	3.98	3.37	4.73	5.70	53.28
Extreme Maximum Daily Precip. (in.)	2.46	4.68	4.80	5.34	3.32	5.60	3.01	3.51	3.63	3.24	3.65	5.20	5.60
Days With ≥ 0.1" Precipitation	7	7	7	7	7	7	7	5	5	5	6	7	77
Days With ≥ 0.5" Precipitation	3	3	4	3	3	3	3	2	3	2	3	4	36
Days With ≥ 1.0" Precipitation	1	1	1	1	2	1	1	1	1	1	2	2	15
Mean Snowfall (in.)	na	na	na	na	na	na	na	na	na	na	na	na	na
Maximum Snow Depth (in.)	na	na	na	na	na	na	na	na	na	na	na	na	na
Days With ≥ 1.0" Snow Depth	na	na	na	na	na	na	na	na	na	na	na	na	na

The period of record for all cooperative weather station data is 1980 – 2009. See User Guide for detailed explanation of data.

Opelika *Lee County* Elevation: 640 ft. Latitude: 32° 40' N Longitude: 85° 27' W

	JAN	FEB	MAR	APR	MAY	JUN	JUL	AUG	SEP	OCT	NOV	DEC	YEAR
Mean Maximum Temp. (°F)	55.7	59.6	67.6	74.3	81.7	87.7	90.4	89.7	84.4	75.4	66.8	57.6	74.2
Mean Temp. (°F)	44.2	47.4	54.4	60.7	69.2	76.1	79.3	78.8	73.5	62.8	53.9	46.0	62.2
Mean Minimum Temp. (°F)	32.6	35.4	41.0	47.0	56.6	64.4	68.2	67.8	62.6	50.2	41.0	34.4	50.1
Extreme Maximum Temp. (°F)	78	84	88	91	95	101	103	103	99	91	86	80	103
Extreme Minimum Temp. (°F)	-7	5	12	25	36	37	53	55	39	26	6	5	-7
Days Maximum Temp. ≥ 90°F	0	0	0	0	2	12	18	16	6	0	0	0	54
Days Maximum Temp. ≤ 32°F	0	0	0	0	0	0	0	0	0	0	0	0	0
Days Minimum Temp. ≤ 32°F	17	12	7	2	0	0	0	0	0	1	7	15	61
Days Minimum Temp. ≤ 0°F	0	0	0	0	0	0	0	0	0	0	0	0	0
Heating Degree Days (base 65°F)	638	492	335	160	27	1	0	0	7	133	336	584	2,713
Cooling Degree Days (base 65°F)	1	1	11	38	165	339	450	434	269	72	10	2	1,792
Mean Precipitation (in.)	4.82	5.17	6.74	4.40	3.50	4.49	4.95	3.69	3.77	3.65	4.68	5.02	54.88
Extreme Maximum Daily Precip. (in.)	3.40	5.75	6.33	5.90	2.75	4.00	5.50	4.32	3.87	6.75	3.84	3.50	6.75
Days With ≥ 0.1" Precipitation	8	7	7	6	6	7	8	6	6	4	6	7	78
Days With ≥ 0.5" Precipitation	3	4	4	3	3	3	4	2	3	2	3	3	37
Days With ≥ 1.0" Precipitation	1	2	2	1	1	1	1	1	1	1	2	2	16
Mean Snowfall (in.)	trace	trace	0.1	0.0	0.0	0.0	0.0	0.0	0.0	0.0	0.0	trace	0.1
Maximum Snow Depth (in.)	trace	trace	0	0	0	0	0	0	0	0	0	trace	trace
Days With ≥ 1.0" Snow Depth	0	0	0	0	0	0	0	0	0	0	0	0	0

Pinson *Jefferson County* Elevation: 607 ft. Latitude: 33° 41' N Longitude: 86° 41' W

	JAN	FEB	MAR	APR	MAY	JUN	JUL	AUG	SEP	OCT	NOV	DEC	YEAR
Mean Maximum Temp. (°F)	53.7	58.5	67.5	75.0	81.7	87.7	90.7	90.7	84.9	74.7	64.9	55.7	73.8
Mean Temp. (°F)	42.0	46.0	53.5	60.6	68.7	75.6	79.3	78.9	72.8	61.6	52.0	44.1	61.3
Mean Minimum Temp. (°F)	30.2	33.5	39.5	46.3	55.6	63.5	67.8	67.1	60.5	48.5	39.0	32.5	48.7
Extreme Maximum Temp. (°F)	80	84	91	94	97	101	104	107	101	94	89	81	107
Extreme Minimum Temp. (°F)	-8	1	2	23	35	43	55	49	37	23	17	-2	-8
Days Maximum Temp. ≥ 90°F	0	0	0	1	3	13	20	19	8	0	0	0	64
Days Maximum Temp. ≤ 32°F	1	0	0	0	0	0	0	0	0	0	0	1	2
Days Minimum Temp. ≤ 32°F	20	14	9	3	0	0	0	0	0	2	10	18	76
Days Minimum Temp. ≤ 0°F	0	0	0	0	0	0	0	0	0	0	0	0	0
Heating Degree Days (base 65°F)	707	531	361	171	37	1	0	0	16	159	392	642	3,017
Cooling Degree Days (base 65°F)	1	1	12	47	157	327	450	439	255	61	8	2	1,760
Mean Precipitation (in.)	4.99	5.01	5.39	4.49	4.86	4.42	4.55	3.50	3.81	3.43	5.02	4.61	54.08
Extreme Maximum Daily Precip. (in.)	4.81	4.50	4.60	5.13	4.53	4.16	6.02	3.73	4.92	6.49	4.74	2.84	6.49
Days With ≥ 0.1" Precipitation	7	7	7	7	7	7	8	5	5	5	7	7	79
Days With ≥ 0.5" Precipitation	4	4	4	3	4	3	3	2	3	3	3	3	39
Days With ≥ 1.0" Precipitation	2	2	2	1	2	1	1	1	1	1	2	1	17
Mean Snowfall (in.)	0.6	0.3	0.7	0.2	0.0	0.0	0.0	0.0	0.0	trace	trace	0.1	1.9
Maximum Snow Depth (in.)	2	2	13	1	0	0	0	0	0	trace	trace	1	13
Days With ≥ 1.0" Snow Depth	0	0	0	0	0	0	0	0	0	0	0	0	0

Russellville No 2 *Franklin County* Elevation: 830 ft. Latitude: 34° 31' N Longitude: 87° 44' W

	JAN	FEB	MAR	APR	MAY	JUN	JUL	AUG	SEP	OCT	NOV	DEC	YEAR
Mean Maximum Temp. (°F)	50.2	54.3	63.1	71.5	79.2	86.2	89.5	89.7	83.9	72.8	62.5	52.3	71.3
Mean Temp. (°F)	39.5	42.9	50.8	58.5	66.9	74.5	78.3	77.9	71.6	59.9	50.5	41.8	59.4
Mean Minimum Temp. (°F)	28.8	31.5	38.4	45.5	54.6	62.7	67.1	66.2	59.3	46.9	38.5	31.3	47.6
Extreme Maximum Temp. (°F)	76	84	87	92	95	99	103	106	100	91	85	77	106
Extreme Minimum Temp. (°F)	-14	-1	5	23	34	39	54	50	35	24	15	-7	-14
Days Maximum Temp. ≥ 90°F	0	0	0	0	1	9	16	17	6	0	0	0	49
Days Maximum Temp. ≤ 32°F	2	1	0	0	0	0	0	0	0	0	0	1	4
Days Minimum Temp. ≤ 32°F	20	16	10	3	0	0	0	0	0	3	10	18	80
Days Minimum Temp. ≤ 0°F	0	0	0	0	0	0	0	0	0	0	0	0	0
Heating Degree Days (base 65°F)	783	619	443	223	59	4	0	0	23	197	433	712	3,496
Cooling Degree Days (base 65°F)	0	1	9	35	126	295	420	408	228	46	5	1	1,574
Mean Precipitation (in.)	4.82	4.92	5.19	4.96	5.97	4.26	4.64	3.59	3.99	3.72	4.93	5.63	56.62
Extreme Maximum Daily Precip. (in.)	3.20	6.75	4.00	3.85	6.10	3.30	2.98	6.85	4.55	3.30	3.80	4.74	6.85
Days With ≥ 0.1" Precipitation	6	7	7	7	7	6	7	5	5	5	7	7	76
Days With ≥ 0.5" Precipitation	4	4	4	4	3	3	3	2	3	3	3	4	40
Days With ≥ 1.0" Precipitation	1	1	2	2	2	1	1	1	1	1	2	2	17
Mean Snowfall (in.)	0.5	0.1	0.1	0.0	0.0	0.0	0.0	0.0	0.0	0.0	trace	0.1	0.8
Maximum Snow Depth (in.)	4	3	3	0	0	0	0	0	0	0	trace	1	4
Days With ≥ 1.0" Snow Depth	0	0	0	0	0	0	0	0	0	0	0	0	0

Sand Mt Substation *Dekalb County* Elevation: 1,194 ft. Latitude: 34° 17' N Longitude: 85° 58' W

	JAN	FEB	MAR	APR	MAY	JUN	JUL	AUG	SEP	OCT	NOV	DEC	YEAR
Mean Maximum Temp. (°F)	48.8	53.2	61.7	69.8	77.4	84.4	87.8	87.8	81.8	71.7	61.3	51.3	69.8
Mean Temp. (°F)	39.2	42.8	50.8	58.4	66.8	74.1	77.5	77.0	70.7	59.9	50.4	41.6	59.1
Mean Minimum Temp. (°F)	29.4	32.4	39.8	47.1	56.1	63.7	67.1	66.1	59.6	48.1	39.6	31.9	48.4
Extreme Maximum Temp. (°F)	74	79	85	88	92	97	103	103	97	89	82	76	103
Extreme Minimum Temp. (°F)	-13	0	11	24	35	45	54	50	35	23	17	-4	-13
Days Maximum Temp. ≥ 90°F	0	0	0	0	0	5	12	12	3	0	0	0	32
Days Maximum Temp. ≤ 32°F	2	1	0	0	0	0	0	0	0	0	0	1	4
Days Minimum Temp. ≤ 32°F	19	15	8	2	0	0	0	0	0	2	8	18	72
Days Minimum Temp. ≤ 0°F	0	0	0	0	0	0	0	0	0	0	0	0	0
Heating Degree Days (base 65°F)	794	621	438	221	56	3	0	1	24	190	434	719	3,501
Cooling Degree Days (base 65°F)	0	0	6	31	117	283	394	379	202	40	4	1	1,457
Mean Precipitation (in.)	5.00	5.09	5.45	4.49	4.39	4.01	4.44	3.62	4.41	3.26	4.87	4.98	54.01
Extreme Maximum Daily Precip. (in.)	4.00	4.54	3.50	3.26	4.78	2.84	5.75	5.10	6.41	4.09	4.36	4.89	6.41
Days With ≥ 0.1" Precipitation	8	7	8	8	7	7	7	6	5	5	7	7	82
Days With ≥ 0.5" Precipitation	4	3	4	3	3	3	3	2	3	2	3	3	36
Days With ≥ 1.0" Precipitation	1	2	2	1	1	1	1	1	1	1	2	2	16
Mean Snowfall (in.)	0.7	0.4	0.1	0.0	0.0	0.0	0.0	0.0	0.0	0.0	trace	0.1	1.3
Maximum Snow Depth (in.)	1	1	1	0	0	0	0	0	0	0	trace	3	3
Days With ≥ 1.0" Snow Depth	0	0	0	0	0	0	0	0	0	0	0	0	0

The period of record for all cooperative weather station data is 1980 – 2009. See User Guide for detailed explanation of data.

Talladega *Talladega County* Elevation: 448 ft. Latitude: 33° 25' N Longitude: 86° 08' W

	JAN	FEB	MAR	APR	MAY	JUN	JUL	AUG	SEP	OCT	NOV	DEC	YEAR
Mean Maximum Temp. (°F)	54.6	58.9	67.6	74.9	82.0	88.1	91.0	90.5	85.2	75.7	66.0	56.9	74.3
Mean Temp. (°F)	43.0	46.6	54.0	60.7	69.0	75.6	79.6	78.7	72.9	62.3	53.1	45.4	61.7
Mean Minimum Temp. (°F)	31.5	34.2	40.3	46.4	55.9	63.3	68.0	67.0	60.5	48.6	40.1	33.8	49.1
Extreme Maximum Temp. (°F)	78	82	88	91	96	100	107	104	98	90	85	79	107
Extreme Minimum Temp. (°F)	-5	3	6	24	36	41	54	49	38	24	14	1	-5
Days Maximum Temp. ≥ 90°F	0	0	0	0	2	13	19	19	7	0	0	0	60
Days Maximum Temp. ≤ 32°F	0	0	0	0	0	0	0	0	0	0	0	0	0
Days Minimum Temp. ≤ 32°F	17	13	8	2	0	0	0	0	0	2	8	15	65
Days Minimum Temp. ≤ 0°F	0	0	0	0	0	0	0	0	0	0	0	0	0
Heating Degree Days (base 65°F)	671	518	346	162	30	1	0	0	11	144	361	604	2,848
Cooling Degree Days (base 65°F)	0	2	12	40	162	327	458	434	253	65	9	2	1,764
Mean Precipitation (in.)	5.22	5.41	5.62	4.22	4.73	4.80	4.90	3.86	3.70	3.51	4.82	4.21	55.00
Extreme Maximum Daily Precip. (in.)	3.61	3.50	6.06	4.83	6.67	4.60	4.00	4.30	5.60	5.51	3.31	2.50	6.67
Days With ≥ 0.1" Precipitation	8	7	7	6	6	8	8	6	4	5	6	7	78
Days With ≥ 0.5" Precipitation	4	4	4	3	3	3	4	3	2	3	3	3	39
Days With ≥ 1.0" Precipitation	2	2	2	1	1	1	1	1	1	1	2	1	16
Mean Snowfall (in.)	0.4	0.0	0.6	0.1	0.0	0.0	0.0	0.0	0.0	0.0	0.0	trace	1.1
Maximum Snow Depth (in.)	trace	0	trace	0	0	0	0	0	0	0	0	trace	trace
Days With ≥ 1.0" Snow Depth	0	0	0	0	0	0	0	0	0	0	0	0	0

Tuscaloosa Municipal Arpt *Tuscaloosa County* Elevation: 167 ft. Latitude: 33° 13' N Longitude: 87° 37' W

	JAN	FEB	MAR	APR	MAY	JUN	JUL	AUG	SEP	OCT	NOV	DEC	YEAR
Mean Maximum Temp. (°F)	56.0	60.6	69.1	76.4	83.7	89.8	92.7	92.3	87.2	77.3	67.2	58.1	75.9
Mean Temp. (°F)	45.5	49.3	56.8	63.8	72.3	78.9	82.3	81.9	76.2	65.2	55.4	47.6	64.6
Mean Minimum Temp. (°F)	34.9	37.9	44.6	51.1	60.8	68.1	71.9	71.4	65.1	53.1	43.6	37.0	53.3
Extreme Maximum Temp. (°F)	79	84	90	94	96	101	105	107	102	94	87	82	107
Extreme Minimum Temp. (°F)	-1	7	12	29	41	45	60	56	42	29	21	2	-1
Days Maximum Temp. ≥ 90°F	0	0	0	0	5	17	24	23	12	1	0	0	82
Days Maximum Temp. ≤ 32°F	0	0	0	0	0	0	0	0	0	0	0	0	0
Days Minimum Temp. ≤ 32°F	15	9	4	0	0	0	0	0	0	0	5	13	46
Days Minimum Temp. ≤ 0°F	0	0	0	0	0	0	0	0	0	0	0	0	0
Heating Degree Days (base 65°F)	600	442	271	106	12	0	0	0	4	95	298	539	2,367
Cooling Degree Days (base 65°F)	2	5	25	76	244	426	544	531	347	108	18	5	2,331
Mean Precipitation (in.)	5.26	5.54	5.19	4.71	4.26	4.50	5.15	3.88	3.66	3.75	5.10	4.73	55.73
Extreme Maximum Daily Precip. (in.)	4.26	4.57	4.12	4.55	4.00	3.07	4.57	2.38	6.28	3.84	3.67	3.00	6.28
Days With ≥ 0.1" Precipitation	8	7	7	6	6	7	8	6	5	5	6	7	78
Days With ≥ 0.5" Precipitation	4	4	4	3	3	3	4	3	2	2	4	4	40
Days With ≥ 1.0" Precipitation	2	2	2	2	1	1	2	1	1	1	2	2	19
Mean Snowfall (in.)	0.1	0.0	0.2	trace	trace	0.0	0.0	0.0	0.0	0.0	0.0	trace	0.3
Maximum Snow Depth (in.)	3	trace	1	3	trace	0	0	0	0	0	0	trace	3
Days With ≥ 1.0" Snow Depth	0	0	0	0	0	0	0	0	0	0	0	0	0

The period of record for all cooperative weather station data is 1980 – 2009. See User Guide for detailed explanation of data.

Alabama Weather Station Rankings

Annual Extreme Maximum Temperature

Highest Rank	Highest Station Name	Highest °F	Lowest Rank	Lowest Station Name	Lowest °F
1	Bessemer 3 WSW	108	1	Coden	***101***
1	Headland	108	1	Dauphin Island #2	101
1	Jasper	***108***	3	Fairhope 2 NE	102
4	Belle Mina 2 N	107	4	Bridgeport 5 NW	103
4	Heflin	107	4	Geneva No 2	103
4	Milstead	***107***	4	Opelika	***103***
4	Muscle Shoals Regional Arpt	107	4	Sand Mt Substation	103
4	Pinson	107	8	Andalusia 3 W	104
4	Talladega	107	8	Bay Minette 3 NNW	104
4	Tuscaloosa Municipal Arpt	107	8	Enterprise 5 NNW	***104***
11	Anniston Calhoun Co Arpt	106	8	Jackson	***104***
11	Bankhead Lock and Dam	106	12	Alexander City	105
11	Birmingham Municipal Arpt	106	12	Centreville WSMO	105
11	Fayette	***106***	12	Clayton	***105***
11	Gadsden	106	12	Demopolis Lock and Dam	105
11	Guntersville	***106***	12	Greenville	105
11	Montgomery Dannelly Field	106	12	Highland Home	105
11	Russellville No 2	106	12	Huntsville Madison County Jetport	105
19	Alexander City	105	12	Lafayette 2 W	***105***
19	Centreville WSMO	105	12	Mobile Regional Arpt	105
19	Clayton	***105***	21	Anniston Calhoun Co Arpt	106
19	Demopolis Lock and Dam	105	21	Bankhead Lock and Dam	106
19	Greenville	105	21	Birmingham Municipal Arpt	106
19	Highland Home	105	21	Fayette	***106***
19	Huntsville Madison County Jetport	105	21	Gadsden	106

Annual Mean Maximum Temperature

Highest Rank	Highest Station Name	Highest °F	Lowest Rank	Lowest Station Name	Lowest °F
1	Andalusia 3 W	78.0	1	Sand Mt Substation	69.8
2	Mobile Regional Arpt	77.5	2	Bridgeport 5 NW	70.5
3	Headland	77.4	3	Russellville No 2	71.3
3	Jackson	***77.4***	4	Huntsville Madison County Jetport	71.7
5	Bay Minette 3 NNW	77.3	5	Belle Mina 2 N	72.0
5	Fairhope 2 NE	77.3	6	Heflin	72.1
5	Geneva No 2	77.3	7	Muscle Shoals Regional Arpt	72.2
8	Greenville	77.2	8	Guntersville	72.5
9	Montgomery Dannelly Field	76.8	9	Jasper	***73.0***
10	Enterprise 5 NNW	***76.1***	10	Gadsden	73.1
11	Clayton	***75.9***	11	Anniston Calhoun Co Arpt	73.5
11	Coden	***75.9***	12	Birmingham Municipal Arpt	73.8
11	Tuscaloosa Municipal Arpt	75.9	12	Pinson	73.8
14	Milstead	***75.8***	14	Bankhead Lock and Dam	74.3
15	Bessemer 3 WSW	75.7	14	Opelika	***74.3***
16	Highland Home	75.5	14	Talladega	74.3
17	Demopolis Lock and Dam	75.3	17	Fayette	***74.4***
18	Dauphin Island #2	74.9	18	Alexander City	74.5
19	Lafayette 2 W	***74.7***	18	Centreville WSMO	74.5
20	Alexander City	74.5	20	Lafayette 2 W	***74.7***
20	Centreville WSMO	74.5	21	Dauphin Island #2	74.9
22	Fayette	***74.4***	22	Demopolis Lock and Dam	75.3
23	Bankhead Lock and Dam	74.3	23	Highland Home	75.5
23	Opelika	***74.3***	24	Bessemer 3 WSW	75.7
23	Talladega	74.3	25	Milstead	***75.8***

Rankings include 25 highest/lowest stations. If state has less than 25 stations, all stations are included. The period of record is 1980–2009. See User Guide for detailed explanation of data.

Annual Mean Temperature

Highest

Rank	Station Name	°F
1	Dauphin Island #2	69.1
2	Mobile Regional Arpt	67.3
3	Fairhope 2 NE	67.1
4	Bay Minette 3 NNW	66.9
5	Coden	***65.9***
5	Enterprise 5 NNW	***65.9***
7	Jackson	***65.6***
8	Geneva No 2	65.4
8	Montgomery Dannelly Field	65.4
10	Greenville	65.3
10	Headland	65.3
12	Andalusia 3 W	64.6
12	Tuscaloosa Municipal Arpt	64.6
14	Clayton	***64.0***
15	Milstead	***63.8***
16	Demopolis Lock and Dam	63.6
16	Highland Home	63.6
18	Bessemer 3 WSW	63.0
19	Birmingham Municipal Arpt	62.9
20	Centreville WSMO	62.6
21	Anniston Calhoun Co Arpt	62.5
22	Alexander City	62.4
23	Opelika	***62.2***
24	Bankhead Lock and Dam	62.1
24	Lafayette 2 W	***62.1***

Lowest

Rank	Station Name	°F
1	Bridgeport 5 NW	***58.8***
2	Sand Mt Substation	59.1
3	Russellville No 2	59.4
4	Belle Mina 2 N	60.0
4	Heflin	60.0
6	Jasper	***60.7***
7	Huntsville Madison County Jetport	61.1
8	Pinson	61.3
9	Muscle Shoals Regional Arpt	61.4
10	Guntersville	61.7
10	Talladega	61.7
12	Fayette	***61.8***
13	Gadsden	61.9
14	Bankhead Lock and Dam	62.1
14	Lafayette 2 W	***62.1***
16	Opelika	***62.2***
17	Alexander City	62.4
18	Anniston Calhoun Co Arpt	62.5
19	Centreville WSMO	62.6
20	Birmingham Municipal Arpt	62.9
21	Bessemer 3 WSW	63.0
22	Demopolis Lock and Dam	63.6
22	Highland Home	63.6
24	Milstead	***63.8***
25	Clayton	***64.0***

Annual Mean Minimum Temperature

Highest

Rank	Station Name	°F
1	Dauphin Island #2	63.3
2	Mobile Regional Arpt	57.1
3	Fairhope 2 NE	56.8
4	Bay Minette 3 NNW	56.5
5	Coden	***55.9***
6	Enterprise 5 NNW	***55.6***
7	Montgomery Dannelly Field	53.9
8	Jackson	***53.6***
9	Geneva No 2	53.5
10	Greenville	53.3
10	Tuscaloosa Municipal Arpt	53.3
12	Headland	53.2
13	Birmingham Municipal Arpt	52.0
13	Clayton	***52.0***
15	Demopolis Lock and Dam	51.8
15	Highland Home	51.8
15	Milstead	***51.8***
18	Anniston Calhoun Co Arpt	51.5
19	Andalusia 3 W	51.2
20	Centreville WSMO	50.8
20	Guntersville	50.8
22	Gadsden	50.7
23	Muscle Shoals Regional Arpt	50.6
24	Huntsville Madison County Jetport	50.5
25	Bessemer 3 WSW	50.3

Lowest

Rank	Station Name	°F
1	Bridgeport 5 NW	***47.0***
2	Russellville No 2	47.6
3	Heflin	47.9
4	Belle Mina 2 N	48.1
5	Jasper	***48.4***
5	Sand Mt Substation	48.4
7	Pinson	48.7
8	Talladega	49.1
9	Fayette	***49.2***
10	Lafayette 2 W	***49.4***
11	Bankhead Lock and Dam	49.9
12	Opelika	***50.1***
13	Alexander City	50.2
14	Bessemer 3 WSW	50.3
15	Huntsville Madison County Jetport	50.5
16	Muscle Shoals Regional Arpt	50.6
17	Gadsden	50.7
18	Centreville WSMO	50.8
18	Guntersville	50.8
20	Andalusia 3 W	51.2
21	Anniston Calhoun Co Arpt	51.5
22	Demopolis Lock and Dam	51.8
22	Highland Home	51.8
22	Milstead	***51.8***
25	Birmingham Municipal Arpt	52.0

Rankings include 25 highest/lowest stations. If state has less than 25 stations, all stations are included. The period of record is 1980–2009. See User Guide for detailed explanation of data.

Annual Extreme Minimum Temperature

Highest			Lowest		
Rank	Station Name	°F	Rank	Station Name	°F
1	Dauphin Island #2	9	1	Belle Mina 2 N	-14
2	Fairhope 2 NE	5	1	Russellville No 2	-14
3	Jackson	***3***	3	Bridgeport 5 NW	-13
3	Mobile Regional Arpt	3	3	Sand Mt Substation	-13
5	Bay Minette 3 NNW	2	5	Guntersville	***-11***
5	Geneva No 2	2	5	Huntsville Madison County Jetport	-11
7	Coden	***1***	5	Muscle Shoals Regional Arpt	-11
8	Andalusia 3 W	0	8	Heflin	-10
8	Headland	0	8	Jasper	***-10***
8	Montgomery Dannelly Field	0	10	Pinson	-8
11	Enterprise 5 NNW	-1	11	Lafayette 2 W	***-7***
11	Fayette	***-1***	11	Opelika	***-7***
11	Greenville	-1	13	Alexander City	-6
11	Tuscaloosa Municipal Arpt	-1	13	Bessemer 3 WSW	-6
15	Demopolis Lock and Dam	-2	13	Birmingham Municipal Arpt	-6
16	Highland Home	-3	13	Centreville WSMO	-6
16	Milstead	***-3***	13	Clayton	***-6***
18	Anniston Calhoun Co Arpt	-5	13	Gadsden	-6
18	Bankhead Lock and Dam	-5	19	Anniston Calhoun Co Arpt	-5
18	Talladega	-5	19	Bankhead Lock and Dam	-5
21	Alexander City	-6	19	Talladega	-5
21	Bessemer 3 WSW	-6	22	Highland Home	-3
21	Birmingham Municipal Arpt	-6	22	Milstead	***-3***
21	Centreville WSMO	-6	24	Demopolis Lock and Dam	-2
21	Clayton	***-6***	25	Enterprise 5 NNW	-1

July Mean Maximum Temperature

Highest			Lowest		
Rank	Station Name	°F	Rank	Station Name	°F
1	Bessemer 3 WSW	92.9	1	Sand Mt Substation	87.8
2	Tuscaloosa Municipal Arpt	92.7	2	Bridgeport 5 NW	88.9
3	Montgomery Dannelly Field	92.4	2	Coden	***88.9***
4	Headland	92.2	2	Dauphin Island #2	88.9
5	Bankhead Lock and Dam	91.8	5	Heflin	89.0
5	Fayette	***91.8***	6	Russellville No 2	89.5
5	Greenville	91.8	7	Huntsville Madison County Jetport	89.7
8	Andalusia 3 W	91.7	8	Enterprise 5 NNW	90.2
8	Demopolis Lock and Dam	91.7	8	Highland Home	90.2
8	Jackson	91.7	10	Anniston Calhoun Co Arpt	90.3
8	Milstead	***91.7***	10	Guntersville	90.3
12	Geneva No 2	91.1	12	Jasper	90.4
12	Mobile Regional Arpt	91.1	12	Opelika	***90.4***
14	Alexander City	91.0	14	Bay Minette 3 NNW	90.5
14	Centreville WSMO	91.0	15	Fairhope 2 NE	90.6
14	Talladega	91.0	15	Lafayette 2 W	90.6
17	Clayton	***90.9***	17	Belle Mina 2 N	90.7
18	Birmingham Municipal Arpt	90.8	17	Gadsden	90.7
18	Muscle Shoals Regional Arpt	90.8	17	Pinson	90.7
20	Belle Mina 2 N	90.7	20	Birmingham Municipal Arpt	90.8
20	Gadsden	90.7	20	Muscle Shoals Regional Arpt	90.8
20	Pinson	90.7	22	Clayton	***90.9***
23	Fairhope 2 NE	90.6	23	Alexander City	91.0
23	Lafayette 2 W	90.6	23	Centreville WSMO	91.0
25	Bay Minette 3 NNW	90.5	23	Talladega	91.0

Rankings include 25 highest/lowest stations. If state has less than 25 stations, all stations are included. The period of record is 1980–2009. See User Guide for detailed explanation of data.

January Mean Minimum Temperature

Highest

Rank	Station Name	°F
1	Dauphin Island #2	45.7
2	Mobile Regional Arpt	40.5
3	Bay Minette 3 NNW	40.2
4	Fairhope 2 NE	39.9
5	Coden	39.3
6	Enterprise 5 NNW	38.5
7	Jackson	36.8
8	Greenville	36.6
9	Geneva No 2	36.3
10	Headland	36.1
11	Montgomery Dannelly Field	36.0
12	Tuscaloosa Municipal Arpt	34.9
13	Clayton	***34.7***
14	Highland Home	34.4
15	Andalusia 3 W	34.1
16	Milstead	34.0
17	Demopolis Lock and Dam	33.7
18	Birmingham Municipal Arpt	33.4
19	Anniston Calhoun Co Arpt	33.2
20	Centreville WSMO	32.9
21	Opelika	32.6
22	Bessemer 3 WSW	32.1
22	Guntersville	32.1
24	Alexander City	31.8
24	Fayette	***31.8***

Lowest

Rank	Station Name	°F
1	Bridgeport 5 NW	28.3
2	Russellville No 2	28.8
3	Belle Mina 2 N	29.3
4	Sand Mt Substation	29.4
5	Jasper	29.6
6	Heflin	30.1
7	Pinson	30.2
8	Gadsden	30.9
9	Bankhead Lock and Dam	31.1
10	Huntsville Madison County Jetport	31.2
10	Muscle Shoals Regional Arpt	31.2
12	Lafayette 2 W	31.5
12	Talladega	31.5
14	Alexander City	31.8
14	Fayette	***31.8***
16	Bessemer 3 WSW	32.1
16	Guntersville	32.1
18	Opelika	32.6
19	Centreville WSMO	32.9
20	Anniston Calhoun Co Arpt	33.2
21	Birmingham Municipal Arpt	33.4
22	Demopolis Lock and Dam	33.7
23	Milstead	34.0
24	Andalusia 3 W	34.1
25	Highland Home	34.4

Number of Days Annually Maximum Temperature ≥ 90°F

Highest

Rank	Station Name	Days
1	Headland	88
2	Montgomery Dannelly Field	86
3	Bessemer 3 WSW	83
4	Andalusia 3 W	82
4	Tuscaloosa Municipal Arpt	82
6	Jackson	***80***
7	Geneva No 2	76
7	Greenville	76
9	Demopolis Lock and Dam	74
10	Mobile Regional Arpt	73
11	Bankhead Lock and Dam	72
12	Fairhope 2 NE	71
13	Fayette	***70***
13	Milstead	***70***
15	Bay Minette 3 NNW	65
16	Clayton	***64***
16	Pinson	64
18	Centreville WSMO	62
19	Highland Home	61
20	Belle Mina 2 N	60
20	Birmingham Municipal Arpt	60
20	Gadsden	60
20	Muscle Shoals Regional Arpt	60
20	Talladega	60
25	Alexander City	59

Lowest

Rank	Station Name	Days
1	Sand Mt Substation	32
2	Dauphin Island #2	35
3	Coden	***37***
4	Heflin	38
5	Bridgeport 5 NW	41
6	Russellville No 2	49
7	Guntersville	53
7	Huntsville Madison County Jetport	53
9	Anniston Calhoun Co Arpt	54
9	Opelika	***54***
11	Lafayette 2 W	***57***
12	Jasper	***58***
13	Alexander City	59
13	Enterprise 5 NNW	59
15	Belle Mina 2 N	60
15	Birmingham Municipal Arpt	60
15	Gadsden	60
15	Muscle Shoals Regional Arpt	60
15	Talladega	60
20	Highland Home	61
21	Centreville WSMO	62
22	Clayton	***64***
22	Pinson	64
24	Bay Minette 3 NNW	65
25	Fayette	***70***

Rankings include 25 highest/lowest stations. If state has less than 25 stations, all stations are included. The period of record is 1980–2009. See User Guide for detailed explanation of data.

Number of Days Annually Maximum Temperature ≤ 32°F

Highest			Lowest		
Rank	Station Name	Days	Rank	Station Name	Days
1	Belle Mina 2 N	4	1	Alexander City	0
1	Bridgeport 5 NW	4	1	Andalusia 3 W	0
1	Huntsville Madison County Jetport	4	1	Bay Minette 3 NNW	0
1	Russellville No 2	4	1	Bessemer 3 WSW	0
1	Sand Mt Substation	4	1	Centreville WSMO	0
6	Guntersville	3	1	Clayton	***0***
6	Muscle Shoals Regional Arpt	3	1	Coden	***0***
8	Bankhead Lock and Dam	2	1	Dauphin Island #2	0
8	Birmingham Municipal Arpt	2	1	Enterprise 5 NNW	0
8	Demopolis Lock and Dam	2	1	Fairhope 2 NE	0
8	Heflin	2	1	Geneva No 2	0
8	Jasper	***2***	1	Greenville	0
8	Pinson	2	1	Headland	0
14	Anniston Calhoun Co Arpt	1	1	Highland Home	0
14	Fayette	***1***	1	Jackson	***0***
14	Gadsden	1	1	Lafayette 2 W	***0***
17	Alexander City	0	1	Milstead	***0***
17	Andalusia 3 W	0	1	Mobile Regional Arpt	0
17	Bay Minette 3 NNW	0	1	Montgomery Dannelly Field	0
17	Bessemer 3 WSW	0	1	Opelika	***0***
17	Centreville WSMO	0	1	Talladega	0
17	Clayton	***0***	1	Tuscaloosa Municipal Arpt	0
17	Coden	***0***	23	Anniston Calhoun Co Arpt	1
17	Dauphin Island #2	0	23	Fayette	***1***
17	Enterprise 5 NNW	0	23	Gadsden	1

Number of Days Annually Minimum Temperature ≤ 32°F

Highest			Lowest		
Rank	Station Name	Days	Rank	Station Name	Days
1	Bridgeport 5 NW	82	1	Dauphin Island #2	4
2	Russellville No 2	80	2	Fairhope 2 NE	21
3	Belle Mina 2 N	78	3	Bay Minette 3 NNW	23
4	Heflin	76	3	Mobile Regional Arpt	23
4	Jasper	***76***	5	Enterprise 5 NNW	***24***
4	Pinson	76	6	Coden	***29***
7	Sand Mt Substation	72	7	Headland	34
8	Fayette	***70***	8	Montgomery Dannelly Field	37
9	Lafayette 2 W	***65***	9	Jackson	***40***
9	Talladega	65	10	Geneva No 2	41
11	Alexander City	63	10	Greenville	41
11	Bankhead Lock and Dam	63	12	Tuscaloosa Municipal Arpt	46
13	Bessemer 3 WSW	61	13	Clayton	***47***
13	Huntsville Madison County Jetport	61	14	Highland Home	49
13	Opelika	***61***	15	Demopolis Lock and Dam	51
16	Muscle Shoals Regional Arpt	60	16	Birmingham Municipal Arpt	52
17	Gadsden	59	17	Milstead	***53***
18	Centreville WSMO	58	18	Andalusia 3 W	55
19	Guntersville	57	18	Anniston Calhoun Co Arpt	55
20	Andalusia 3 W	55	20	Guntersville	57
20	Anniston Calhoun Co Arpt	55	21	Centreville WSMO	58
22	Milstead	***53***	22	Gadsden	59
23	Birmingham Municipal Arpt	52	23	Muscle Shoals Regional Arpt	60
24	Demopolis Lock and Dam	51	24	Bessemer 3 WSW	61
25	Highland Home	49	24	Huntsville Madison County Jetport	61

Rankings include 25 highest/lowest stations. If state has less than 25 stations, all stations are included. The period of record is 1980–2009. See User Guide for detailed explanation of data.

Number of Days Annually Minimum Temperature ≤ 0°F

Highest			Lowest		
Rank	Station Name	Days	Rank	Station Name	Days
1	Alexander City	0	1	Alexander City	0
1	Andalusia 3 W	0	1	Andalusia 3 W	0
1	Anniston Calhoun Co Arpt	0	1	Anniston Calhoun Co Arpt	0
1	Bankhead Lock and Dam	0	1	Bankhead Lock and Dam	0
1	Bay Minette 3 NNW	0	1	Bay Minette 3 NNW	0
1	Belle Mina 2 N	0	1	Belle Mina 2 N	0
1	Bessemer 3 WSW	0	1	Bessemer 3 WSW	0
1	Birmingham Municipal Arpt	0	1	Birmingham Municipal Arpt	0
1	Bridgeport 5 NW	0	1	Bridgeport 5 NW	0
1	Centreville WSMO	0	1	Centreville WSMO	0
1	Clayton	***0***	1	Clayton	***0***
1	Coden	***0***	1	Coden	***0***
1	Dauphin Island #2	0	1	Dauphin Island #2	0
1	Demopolis Lock and Dam	0	1	Demopolis Lock and Dam	0
1	Enterprise 5 NNW	0	1	Enterprise 5 NNW	0
1	Fairhope 2 NE	0	1	Fairhope 2 NE	0
1	Fayette	***0***	1	Fayette	***0***
1	Gadsden	0	1	Gadsden	0
1	Geneva No 2	0	1	Geneva No 2	0
1	Greenville	0	1	Greenville	0
1	Guntersville	0	1	Guntersville	0
1	Headland	0	1	Headland	0
1	Heflin	0	1	Heflin	0
1	Highland Home	0	1	Highland Home	0
1	Huntsville Madison County Jetport	0	1	Huntsville Madison County Jetport	0

Number of Annual Heating Degree Days

Highest			Lowest		
Rank	Station Name	Num.	Rank	Station Name	Num.
1	Bridgeport 5 NW	***3,615***	1	Dauphin Island #2	1,314
2	Sand Mt Substation	3,501	2	Mobile Regional Arpt	1,640
3	Russellville No 2	3,496	3	Bay Minette 3 NNW	1,653
4	Belle Mina 2 N	3,391	4	Fairhope 2 NE	1,661
5	Heflin	3,239	5	Coden	***1,815***
6	Jasper	***3,178***	6	Enterprise 5 NNW	***1,897***
7	Huntsville Madison County Jetport	3,132	7	Geneva No 2	2,000
8	Muscle Shoals Regional Arpt	3,094	8	Greenville	2,033
9	Pinson	3,017	9	Jackson	***2,034***
10	Guntersville	2,971	10	Headland	2,035
11	Gadsden	2,955	11	Montgomery Dannelly Field	2,133
12	Fayette	***2,939***	12	Andalusia 3 W	2,160
13	Bankhead Lock and Dam	2,857	13	Clayton	***2,299***
14	Talladega	2,848	14	Tuscaloosa Municipal Arpt	2,367
15	Lafayette 2 W	***2,729***	15	Highland Home	2,372
16	Alexander City	2,725	16	Milstead	***2,422***
17	Anniston Calhoun Co Arpt	2,718	17	Demopolis Lock and Dam	2,521
18	Opelika	***2,713***	18	Bessemer 3 WSW	2,657
19	Birmingham Municipal Arpt	2,687	19	Centreville WSMO	2,672
20	Centreville WSMO	2,672	20	Birmingham Municipal Arpt	2,687
21	Bessemer 3 WSW	2,657	21	Opelika	***2,713***
22	Demopolis Lock and Dam	2,521	22	Anniston Calhoun Co Arpt	2,718
23	Milstead	***2,422***	23	Alexander City	2,725
24	Highland Home	2,372	24	Lafayette 2 W	***2,729***
25	Tuscaloosa Municipal Arpt	2,367	25	Talladega	2,848

Rankings include 25 highest/lowest stations. If state has less than 25 stations, all stations are included. The period of record is 1980–2009. See User Guide for detailed explanation of data.

Number of Annual Cooling Degree Days

Highest Rank	Station Name	Num.	Lowest Rank	Station Name	Num.
1	Dauphin Island #2	2,932	1	Bridgeport 5 NW	***1,445***
2	Mobile Regional Arpt	2,578	2	Sand Mt Substation	1,457
3	Fairhope 2 NE	2,534	3	Heflin	1,519
4	Bay Minette 3 NNW	2,454	4	Russellville No 2	1,574
5	Montgomery Dannelly Field	2,370	5	Belle Mina 2 N	1,689
6	Jackson	***2,336***	6	Jasper	***1,726***
7	Tuscaloosa Municipal Arpt	2,331	7	Pinson	1,760
8	Enterprise 5 NNW	***2,314***	8	Talladega	1,764
9	Headland	2,265	9	Lafayette 2 W	***1,766***
10	Coden	***2,263***	10	Opelika	***1,792***
11	Geneva No 2	2,251	11	Huntsville Madison County Jetport	1,823
12	Greenville	2,236	12	Guntersville	***1,861***
13	Demopolis Lock and Dam	2,116	13	Alexander City	1,864
14	Andalusia 3 W	2,112	14	Muscle Shoals Regional Arpt	1,891
15	Milstead	***2,093***	15	Fayette	***1,892***
16	Bessemer 3 WSW	2,040	16	Bankhead Lock and Dam	1,913
17	Birmingham Municipal Arpt	2,030	17	Anniston Calhoun Co Arpt	1,915
18	Clayton	***2,026***	17	Centreville WSMO	1,915
19	Highland Home	1,982	19	Gadsden	1,931
20	Gadsden	1,931	20	Highland Home	1,982
21	Anniston Calhoun Co Arpt	1,915	21	Clayton	***2,026***
21	Centreville WSMO	1,915	22	Birmingham Municipal Arpt	2,030
23	Bankhead Lock and Dam	1,913	23	Bessemer 3 WSW	2,040
24	Fayette	***1,892***	24	Milstead	***2,093***
25	Muscle Shoals Regional Arpt	1,891	25	Andalusia 3 W	2,112

Annual Precipitation

Highest Rank	Station Name	Inches	Lowest Rank	Station Name	Inches
1	Bay Minette 3 NNW	69.43	1	Anniston Calhoun Co Arpt	49.98
2	Fairhope 2 NE	68.07	2	Clayton	***51.63***
3	Coden	***67.81***	3	Milstead	***52.39***
4	Mobile Regional Arpt	66.39	4	Guntersville	52.77
5	Dauphin Island #2	61.65	5	Montgomery Dannelly Field	53.22
6	Jasper	60.88	6	Muscle Shoals Regional Arpt	53.28
7	Bridgeport 5 NW	60.46	7	Belle Mina 2 N	53.56
8	Andalusia 3 W	60.19	8	Enterprise 5 NNW	53.77
9	Jackson	60.04	9	Sand Mt Substation	54.01
10	Bankhead Lock and Dam	60.01	10	Headland	54.06
11	Geneva No 2	59.40	11	Pinson	54.08
12	Centreville WSMO	57.62	12	Birmingham Municipal Arpt	54.15
13	Bessemer 3 WSW	57.46	13	Lafayette 2 W	***54.25***
14	Greenville	57.14	14	Demopolis Lock and Dam	54.57
15	Russellville No 2	56.62	15	Opelika	***54.88***
16	Heflin	55.84	16	Huntsville Madison County Jetport	54.90
17	Fayette	***55.80***	17	Talladega	55.00
18	Tuscaloosa Municipal Arpt	55.73	18	Gadsden	55.23
19	Alexander City	55.60	19	Highland Home	55.28
20	Highland Home	55.28	20	Alexander City	55.60
21	Gadsden	55.23	21	Tuscaloosa Municipal Arpt	55.73
22	Talladega	55.00	22	Fayette	***55.80***
23	Huntsville Madison County Jetport	54.90	23	Heflin	55.84
24	Opelika	***54.88***	24	Russellville No 2	56.62
25	Demopolis Lock and Dam	54.57	25	Greenville	57.14

Rankings include 25 highest/lowest stations. If state has less than 25 stations, all stations are included. The period of record is 1980–2009. See User Guide for detailed explanation of data.

Annual Extreme Maximum Daily Precipitation

Highest

Rank	Station Name	Inches
1	Dauphin Island #2	23.99
2	Andalusia 3 W	17.88
3	Bay Minette 3 NNW	15.58
4	Greenville	15.36
5	Fairhope 2 NE	14.52
6	Coden	***12.15***
7	Clayton	***11.20***
8	Bankhead Lock and Dam	10.03
9	Birmingham Municipal Arpt	9.75
10	Enterprise 5 NNW	***9.27***
11	Headland	9.08
12	Huntsville Madison County Jetport	9.07
13	Bessemer 3 WSW	8.80
14	Jackson	8.76
15	Mobile Regional Arpt	8.60
16	Montgomery Dannelly Field	7.89
17	Highland Home	***7.82***
18	Geneva No 2	7.73
19	Belle Mina 2 N	7.38
20	Fayette	***7.36***
21	Bridgeport 5 NW	***6.90***
22	Russellville No 2	6.85
23	Opelika	***6.75***
24	Talladega	6.67
25	Milstead	***6.60***

Lowest

Rank	Station Name	Inches
1	Anniston Calhoun Co Arpt	4.51
2	Alexander City	5.02
3	Demopolis Lock and Dam	5.22
4	Heflin	5.40
5	Gadsden	***5.60***
5	Muscle Shoals Regional Arpt	5.60
7	Guntersville	***5.76***
8	Centreville WSMO	5.79
9	Jasper	***6.09***
10	Tuscaloosa Municipal Arpt	6.28
11	Lafayette 2 W	***6.38***
12	Sand Mt Substation	6.41
13	Pinson	6.49
14	Milstead	***6.60***
15	Talladega	6.67
16	Opelika	***6.75***
17	Russellville No 2	6.85
18	Bridgeport 5 NW	***6.90***
19	Fayette	***7.36***
20	Belle Mina 2 N	7.38
21	Geneva No 2	7.73
22	Highland Home	***7.82***
23	Montgomery Dannelly Field	7.89
24	Mobile Regional Arpt	8.60
25	Jackson	8.76

Number of Days Annually With ≥ 0.1 Inches of Precipitation

Highest

Rank	Station Name	Days
1	Jasper	85
2	Bay Minette 3 NNW	84
3	Bankhead Lock and Dam	83
3	Bessemer 3 WSW	83
5	Sand Mt Substation	82
6	Birmingham Municipal Arpt	81
6	Bridgeport 5 NW	81
6	Fairhope 2 NE	81
9	Belle Mina 2 N	79
9	Gadsden	79
9	Heflin	79
9	Huntsville Madison County Jetport	79
9	Pinson	79
14	Alexander City	78
14	Anniston Calhoun Co Arpt	78
14	Fayette	***78***
14	Mobile Regional Arpt	78
14	Opelika	***78***
14	Talladega	78
14	Tuscaloosa Municipal Arpt	78
21	Coden	***77***
21	Demopolis Lock and Dam	77
21	Guntersville	***77***
21	Lafayette 2 W	***77***
21	Muscle Shoals Regional Arpt	77

Lowest

Rank	Station Name	Days
1	Clayton	***65***
2	Andalusia 3 W	70
2	Enterprise 5 NNW	70
4	Dauphin Island #2	72
4	Milstead	***72***
4	Montgomery Dannelly Field	72
7	Highland Home	73
8	Greenville	74
8	Jackson	74
10	Centreville WSMO	75
10	Geneva No 2	75
10	Headland	75
13	Russellville No 2	76
14	Coden	***77***
14	Demopolis Lock and Dam	77
14	Guntersville	***77***
14	Lafayette 2 W	***77***
14	Muscle Shoals Regional Arpt	77
19	Alexander City	78
19	Anniston Calhoun Co Arpt	78
19	Fayette	***78***
19	Mobile Regional Arpt	78
19	Opelika	***78***
19	Talladega	78
19	Tuscaloosa Municipal Arpt	78

 Rankings include 25 highest/lowest stations. If state has less than 25 stations, all stations are included. The period of record is 1980–2009. See User Guide for detailed explanation of data.

Number of Days Annually With ≥ 0.5 Inches of Precipitation

Highest			Lowest		
Rank	Station Name	Days	Rank	Station Name	Days
1	Jasper	44	1	Enterprise 5 NNW	33
2	Bankhead Lock and Dam	43	2	Clayton	***34***
3	Bridgeport 5 NW	42	2	Milstead	***34***
4	Bay Minette 3 NNW	41	4	Anniston Calhoun Co Arpt	35
4	Mobile Regional Arpt	41	4	Headland	35
6	Bessemer 3 WSW	40	4	Montgomery Dannelly Field	35
6	Centreville WSMO	40	7	Belle Mina 2 N	36
6	Coden	***40***	7	Dauphin Island #2	36
6	Russellville No 2	40	7	Gadsden	36
6	Tuscaloosa Municipal Arpt	40	7	Heflin	36
11	Alexander City	39	7	Highland Home	36
11	Demopolis Lock and Dam	39	7	Jackson	36
11	Fairhope 2 NE	39	7	Muscle Shoals Regional Arpt	36
11	Fayette	***39***	7	Sand Mt Substation	36
11	Geneva No 2	39	15	Andalusia 3 W	37
11	Pinson	39	15	Greenville	37
11	Talladega	39	15	Guntersville	37
18	Birmingham Municipal Arpt	38	15	Opelika	***37***
18	Huntsville Madison County Jetport	38	19	Birmingham Municipal Arpt	38
18	Lafayette 2 W	***38***	19	Huntsville Madison County Jetport	38
21	Andalusia 3 W	37	19	Lafayette 2 W	***38***
21	Greenville	37	22	Alexander City	39
21	Guntersville	37	22	Demopolis Lock and Dam	39
21	Opelika	***37***	22	Fairhope 2 NE	39
25	Belle Mina 2 N	36	22	Fayette	***39***

Number of Days Annually With ≥ 1.0 Inches of Precipitation

Highest			Lowest		
Rank	Station Name	Days	Rank	Station Name	Days
1	Coden	***23***	1	Belle Mina 2 N	14
1	Fairhope 2 NE	23	1	Enterprise 5 NNW	14
3	Bankhead Lock and Dam	22	3	Anniston Calhoun Co Arpt	15
3	Bay Minette 3 NNW	22	3	Birmingham Municipal Arpt	15
3	Mobile Regional Arpt	22	3	Guntersville	15
6	Jackson	21	3	Headland	15
7	Bridgeport 5 NW	20	3	Milstead	***15***
7	Jasper	20	3	Muscle Shoals Regional Arpt	15
9	Alexander City	19	9	Clayton	***16***
9	Bessemer 3 WSW	19	9	Demopolis Lock and Dam	16
9	Dauphin Island #2	19	9	Heflin	16
9	Geneva No 2	19	9	Huntsville Madison County Jetport	16
9	Greenville	19	9	Lafayette 2 W	***16***
9	Tuscaloosa Municipal Arpt	19	9	Opelika	***16***
15	Andalusia 3 W	18	9	Sand Mt Substation	16
15	Centreville WSMO	18	9	Talladega	16
15	Gadsden	18	17	Fayette	***17***
18	Fayette	***17***	17	Highland Home	17
18	Highland Home	17	17	Montgomery Dannelly Field	17
18	Montgomery Dannelly Field	17	17	Pinson	17
18	Pinson	17	17	Russellville No 2	17
18	Russellville No 2	17	22	Andalusia 3 W	18
23	Clayton	***16***	22	Centreville WSMO	18
23	Demopolis Lock and Dam	16	22	Gadsden	18
23	Heflin	16	25	Alexander City	19

Annual Snowfall

Highest

Rank	Station Name	Inches
1	Heflin	1.9
1	Pinson	1.9
3	Birmingham Municipal Arpt	1.7
4	Belle Mina 2 N	1.5
5	Sand Mt Substation	1.3
6	Talladega	1.1
7	Bridgeport 5 NW	1.0
8	Bessemer 3 WSW	0.9
9	Centreville WSMO	0.8
9	Guntersville	0.8
9	Jasper	0.8
9	Russellville No 2	0.8
13	Alexander City	0.6
14	Fayette	***0.3***
14	Greenville	0.3
14	Lafayette 2 W	***0.3***
14	Tuscaloosa Municipal Arpt	0.3
18	Andalusia 3 W	0.2
18	Bankhead Lock and Dam	0.2
18	Bay Minette 3 NNW	0.2
18	Clayton	***0.2***
18	Highland Home	0.2
18	Milstead	***0.2***
18	Mobile Regional Arpt	0.2
25	Demopolis Lock and Dam	0.1

Lowest

Rank	Station Name	Inches
1	Dauphin Island #2	0.0
1	Jackson	0.0
3	Coden	***Trace***
3	Enterprise 5 NNW	Trace
3	Fairhope 2 NE	Trace
3	Geneva No 2	Trace
3	Headland	Trace
8	Demopolis Lock and Dam	0.1
8	Gadsden	***0.1***
8	Opelika	***0.1***
11	Andalusia 3 W	0.2
11	Bankhead Lock and Dam	0.2
11	Bay Minette 3 NNW	0.2
11	Clayton	***0.2***
11	Highland Home	0.2
11	Milstead	***0.2***
11	Mobile Regional Arpt	0.2
18	Fayette	***0.3***
18	Greenville	0.3
18	Lafayette 2 W	***0.3***
18	Tuscaloosa Municipal Arpt	0.3
22	Alexander City	0.6
23	Centreville WSMO	0.8
23	Guntersville	0.8
23	Jasper	0.8

Annual Maximum Snow Depth

Highest

Rank	Station Name	Inches
1	Birmingham Municipal Arpt	13
1	Pinson	13
3	Guntersville	***9***
4	Centreville WSMO	8
5	Alexander City	7
6	Highland Home	6
7	Lafayette 2 W	***5***
8	Fayette	***4***
8	Russellville No 2	4
10	Bridgeport 5 NW	***3***
10	Heflin	***3***
10	Jasper	***3***
10	Sand Mt Substation	3
10	Tuscaloosa Municipal Arpt	3
15	Bay Minette 3 NNW	2
15	Belle Mina 2 N	2
15	Mobile Regional Arpt	2
18	Andalusia 3 W	1
18	Bankhead Lock and Dam	1
18	Bessemer 3 WSW	1
18	Clayton	***1***
18	Gadsden	***1***
23	Coden	Trace
23	Fairhope 2 NE	Trace
23	Geneva No 2	Trace

Lowest

Rank	Station Name	Inches
1	Dauphin Island #2	0
1	Demopolis Lock and Dam	0
1	Enterprise 5 NNW	***0***
1	Jackson	0
5	Coden	Trace
5	Fairhope 2 NE	Trace
5	Geneva No 2	Trace
5	Greenville	Trace
5	Headland	Trace
5	Milstead	Trace
5	Opelika	Trace
5	Talladega	Trace
13	Andalusia 3 W	1
13	Bankhead Lock and Dam	1
13	Bessemer 3 WSW	1
13	Clayton	***1***
13	Gadsden	***1***
18	Bay Minette 3 NNW	2
18	Belle Mina 2 N	2
18	Mobile Regional Arpt	2
21	Bridgeport 5 NW	***3***
21	Heflin	***3***
21	Jasper	***3***
21	Sand Mt Substation	3
21	Tuscaloosa Municipal Arpt	3

Rankings include 25 highest/lowest stations. If state has less than 25 stations, all stations are included. The period of record is 1980–2009. See User Guide for detailed explanation of data.

Number of Days Annually With ≥ 1.0 Inch Snow Depth

Highest Rank	Station Name	Days	Lowest Rank	Station Name	Days
1	Alexander City	0	1	Alexander City	0
1	Andalusia 3 W	0	1	Andalusia 3 W	0
1	Bankhead Lock and Dam	0	1	Bankhead Lock and Dam	0
1	Bay Minette 3 NNW	0	1	Bay Minette 3 NNW	0
1	Belle Mina 2 N	0	1	Belle Mina 2 N	0
1	Bessemer 3 WSW	0	1	Bessemer 3 WSW	0
1	Birmingham Municipal Arpt	0	1	Birmingham Municipal Arpt	0
1	Bridgeport 5 NW	0	1	Bridgeport 5 NW	0
1	Centreville WSMO	0	1	Centreville WSMO	0
1	Clayton	***0***	1	Clayton	***0***
1	Coden	***0***	1	Coden	***0***
1	Dauphin Island #2	0	1	Dauphin Island #2	0
1	Demopolis Lock and Dam	0	1	Demopolis Lock and Dam	0
1	Enterprise 5 NNW	0	1	Enterprise 5 NNW	0
1	Fairhope 2 NE	0	1	Fairhope 2 NE	0
1	Fayette	***0***	1	Fayette	***0***
1	Gadsden	***0***	1	Gadsden	***0***
1	Geneva No 2	0	1	Geneva No 2	0
1	Greenville	0	1	Greenville	0
1	Guntersville	0	1	Guntersville	0
1	Headland	0	1	Headland	0
1	Heflin	0	1	Heflin	0
1	Highland Home	0	1	Highland Home	0
1	Jackson	0	1	Jackson	0
1	Jasper	0	1	Jasper	0

Rankings include 25 highest/lowest stations. If state has less than 25 stations, all stations are included. The period of record is 1980–2009. See User Guide for detailed explanation of data.

Significant Storm Events in Alabama: 2000 – 2009

Location or County	Date	Type	Mag.	Deaths	Injuries	Property Damage ($mil.)	Crop Damage ($mil.)
Tuscaloosa	12/16/00	Tornado	F4	11	144	12.5	0.0
Etowah	12/16/00	Tornado	F3	0	14	10.0	0.0
Dale	11/25/01	Tornado	F1	0	25	3.0	0.0
Jefferson	09/22/02	Flash Flood	na	0	0	5.8	0.0
Baldwin and Mobile Counties	09/24/02	Tropical Storm	na	0	0	6.5	0.0
Henry	11/05/02	Tornado	F2	1	20	3.0	0.0
Walker	11/10/02	Tornado	F3	7	40	2.5	0.0
Walker	11/10/02	Tornado	F3	3	20	2.5	0.0
Winston	11/10/02	Tornado	F3	1	15	0.2	0.0
Jefferson	05/07/03	Flash Flood	na	0	0	1,000.0	0.0
Chambers, Lee, and Russell Counties	05/07/03	Flood	na	0	0	4.4	0.2
Southwest Alabama	09/13/04	Hurricane Ivan	na	0	0	2,500.0	25.0
Jefferson County	09/16/04	High Wind	69 mph	0	0	10.0	0.0
Dallas County	09/16/04	High Wind	92 mph	0	0	10.0	0.2
Marengo County	09/16/04	High Wind	92 mph	0	0	10.0	0.2
Montgomery County	09/16/04	High Wind	75 mph	0	0	9.0	0.0
Greene County	09/16/04	High Wind	89 mph	0	0	5.0	0.0
Southwest Alabama	07/09/05	Hurricane Dennis	na	0	0	120.0	0.1
Southwest ALabama	08/27/05	Hurricane Katrina	na	0	0	1,000.0	0.0
Central Alabama	08/29/05	Tropical Storm	na	0	8	34.8	0.0
Coffee	03/01/07	Tornado	F4	9	50	250.0	0.0
Henry	03/01/07	Tornado	F1	0	2	11.0	0.0
Blount, Fayette, Lamar, Marion, Walker, and Winston Counties	08/08/07	Heat	na	1	17	0.0	0.0
Jackson	02/06/08	Tornado	F4	1	12	0.0	0.0
Lawrence	02/06/08	Tornado	F4	4	23	0.0	0.0
Autauga	02/17/08	Tornado	F3	0	50	10.0	0.0
Madison	06/29/08	Thunderstorm Wind	47 mph	1	12	1.0	0.0
Elmore	05/07/09	Flash Flood	na	0	0	4.9	0.0
Lower Baldwin County	11/09/09	High Surf	na	0	0	8.0	0.0

Note: Deaths, injuries, and damages are date and location specific.

ALASKA

PHYSICAL FEATURES. Alaska is the westernmost extension of the North American continent. Its east-west span covers a distance of 2,000 miles, and from north to south a distance of 1,100 miles. The state's coastline, 33,000 miles in length, is 50 percent longer than that of the conterminous U.S. In addition to the Aleutian Islands, hundreds of other islands are found along the northern coast of the Gulf of Alaska, the Alaska Peninsula, and the Bering Sea Coast. Alaska contains 375 million acres of land, and over 3 million lakes.

The two longest mountain ranges are the Brooks Range which separates the Arctic region from the interior, and the Alaska-Aleutian Range, which extends westward along the Alaska Peninsula and the Aleutian Islands, and northward about 200 miles from the Peninsula, then eastward to Canada. Other shorter but important ranges are the Chugach Mountains which form a rim to the central north Gulf of Alaska, and the Wrangell Mountains lying to the northeast of the Chugach Range and south of the Alaska Range. Both of these shorter ranges merge with the St. Elias Mountains, extending southeastward through Canada and across southeastern Alaska as the Coast Range. Numerous peaks in excess of 10,000 feet are found in all but the Brooks Range. The highest peak (20,320 feet above sea level) in the North American continent, Mt. McKinley, is found in Alaska, and several others tower above 16,000 feet.

Permafrost is a major factor in the geography of Alaska. It is defined as a layer of soil at variable depths beneath the surface of the earth in which the temperature has been below freezing continuously from a few to several thousands of years. It exists where summer heating fails to penetrate to the base of the layer of frozen ground. Permafrost covers most of the northern third of the State. Discontinuous or isolated patches also exist over the central portion in an overall area covering nearly a third of the State. No permafrost exists in the south-central and southern coastal portions, including southeastern Alaska, the Alaska Peninsula, and the Aleutian chain.

GENERAL CLIMATE. The geographical features already mentioned have a significant effect on Alaska's climate, which falls into four major zones. The climate zones are: (1) a Maritime Zone which includes southeastern Alaska, the South Coast, and southwestern islands, (2) a transition zone between marine and continental influences (this zone is difficult to define but generally comprises a very narrow band along the southern portion of the Copper River and the northern extreme of the South Coast—specifically the Chugach Mountains, Cook Inlet, Bristol Bay, and the coastal regions of the West-Central Division), (3) a continental zone made up of the remainders of the Copper River and West-Central Divisions, and the Interior Basin, and (4) an Arctic zone.

PRECIPITATION. In the maritime zone a coastal mountain range coupled with plentiful moisture produces annual precipitation amounts up to 200 inches in the southeastern panhandle, and up to 150 inches along the northern coast of the Gulf of Alaska. Amounts taper to near 60 inches on the southern side of the Alaska Range in the Peninsula and Aleutian Island sections. Precipitation amounts decrease rapidly to the north, with an average of 12 inches in the continental zone and less than 6 inches in the Arctic Region.

Snowfall makes up a large portion of the total annual precipitation.. Total snow depths on the ground are controlled by the temperature of an area. Fortunately, most of the areas of heavy snow have relatively mild temperatures which prevent total depths from becoming excessive.

TEMPERATURE. Mean annual temperatures in Alaska range from the low 40s under the maritime influence in the south to a chilly 10 degrees along the Arctic Slope north of the Brooks Mountain Range. The greatest seasonal temperature contrast between seasons is found in the central and eastern portion of the Continental Interior. In this area summer heating produces average maximum temperatures in the upper 70s with extreme readings in the 90s. In winter the lack of sunshine permits radiation to lower temperatures to the minus 50s and occasionally colder for two or three weeks at a time. Average winter minimums in this area are 20 to 30 degrees below zero. Elsewhere in the State, temperature contrasts are much more moderate. In the maritime zone the summer to winter range of average temperatures is from near 60 to the 20s. In the transition zone, temperatures range from the low 60s to near zero, except for the colder northern coastal region of the West-Central Division, where the range is from the mid 50s to near 10 below zero. The Arctic slope has a range extending from the upper 40s to 20 below zero.

Winter temperatures play a principal role in the flow of most of Alaska's rivers. Usually beginning in late October and extending into May (and sometimes early June for the northernmost streams), thick layers of ice form, permitting passage with all types of heavy equipment. Several rivers cease to flow completely during the coldest months.

WIND. A normal storm track along the Aleutian Island chain, the Alaska Peninsula and all of the coastal area of the Gulf of Alaska exposes these parts of the State to a large majority of the storms crossing the north Pacific, resulting in a variety of wind problems. Direct exposure to the wind of the storms themselves results in the frequent occurrence of winds in excess of 50 m.p.h. during all but the summer months, and on occasion even then for the land areas along the storm track. Wind velocities approaching 100 m.p.h. are not common but do occur, usually associated with mountainous terrain and narrow passes.

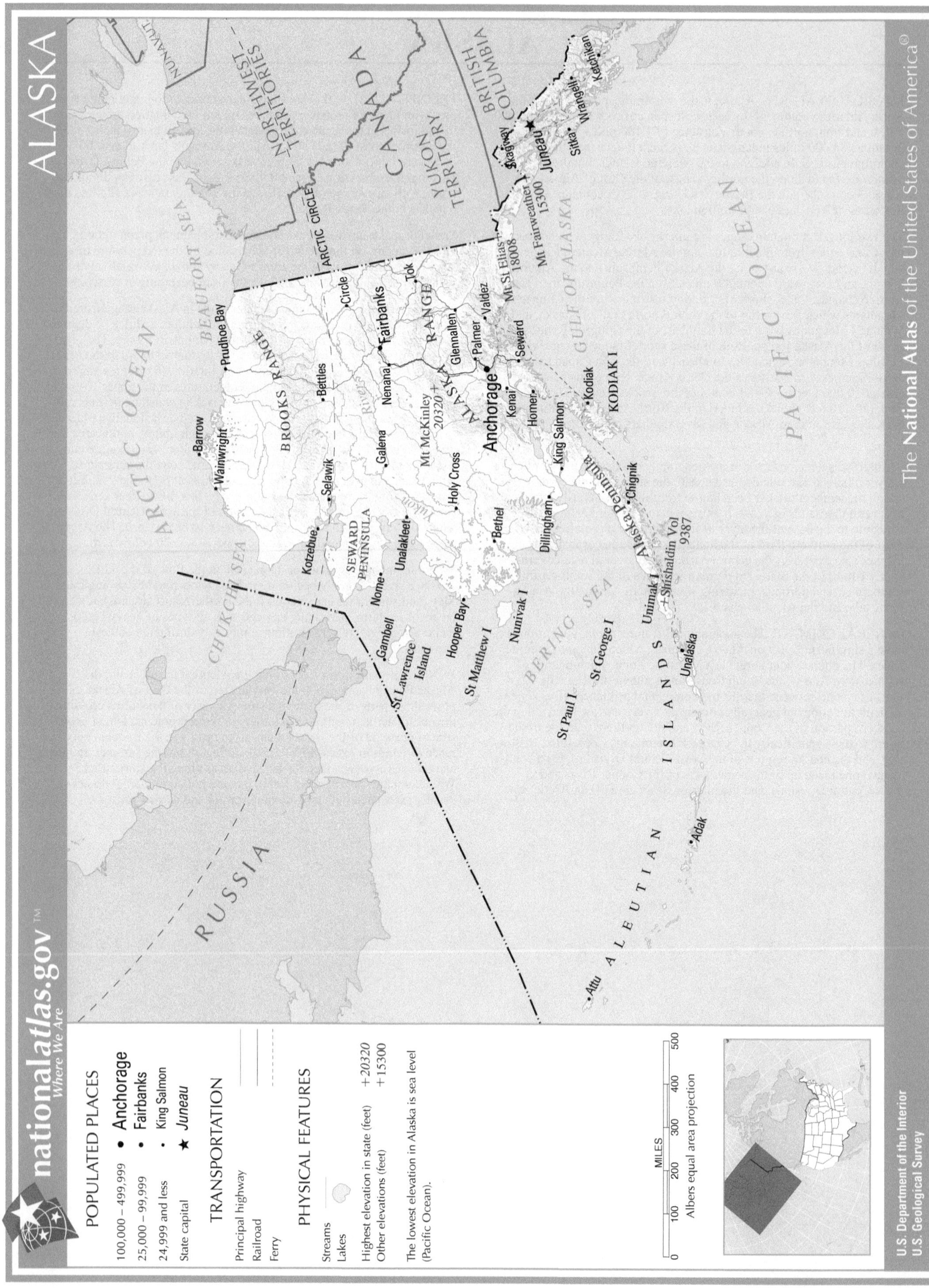
ALASKA
nationalatlas.gov™
Where We Are
POPULATED PLACES
100,000 – 499,999 Anchorage
25,000 – 99,999 Fairbanks
24,999 and less King Salmon
State capital Juneau
TRANSPORTATION
Principal highway
Railroad
Ferry
PHYSICAL FEATURES
Streams
Lakes
Highest elevation in state (feet) +20320
Other elevations (feet) +15300
The lowest elevation in Alaska is sea level (Pacific Ocean).
MILES
0 100 200 300 400 500
Albers equal area projection
U.S. Department of the Interior
U.S. Geological Survey
The National Atlas of the United States of America®
ARCTIC OCEAN
BEAUFORT SEA
CHUKCHI SEA
BERING SEA
GULF OF ALASKA
PACIFIC OCEAN
RUSSIA
CANADA
NORTHWEST TERRITORIES
NUNAVUT
YUKON TERRITORY
BRITISH COLUMBIA
ARCTIC CIRCLE
BROOKS RANGE
ALASKA RANGE
SEWARD PENINSULA
Alaska Peninsula
ALEUTIAN ISLANDS
KODIAK I
Yukon
Rivers
Mt McKinley 20320
Mt St Elias 18008
Mt Fairweather 15300
Shishaldin Vol 9387
Barrow
Wainwright
Prudhoe Bay
Bettles
Selawik
Kotzebue
Circle
Fairbanks
Tok
Nenana
Galena
Unalakleet
Nome
Holy Cross
Bethel
Hooper Bay
Dillingham
King Salmon
Anchorage
Palmer
Glennallen
Valdez
Kenai
Seward
Homer
Kodiak
Chignik
Skagway
Juneau
Sitka
Wrangell
Ketchikan
Gambell
St Lawrence Island
St Matthew I
Nunivak I
St Paul I
St George I
Unimak I
Unalaska
Adak
Attu

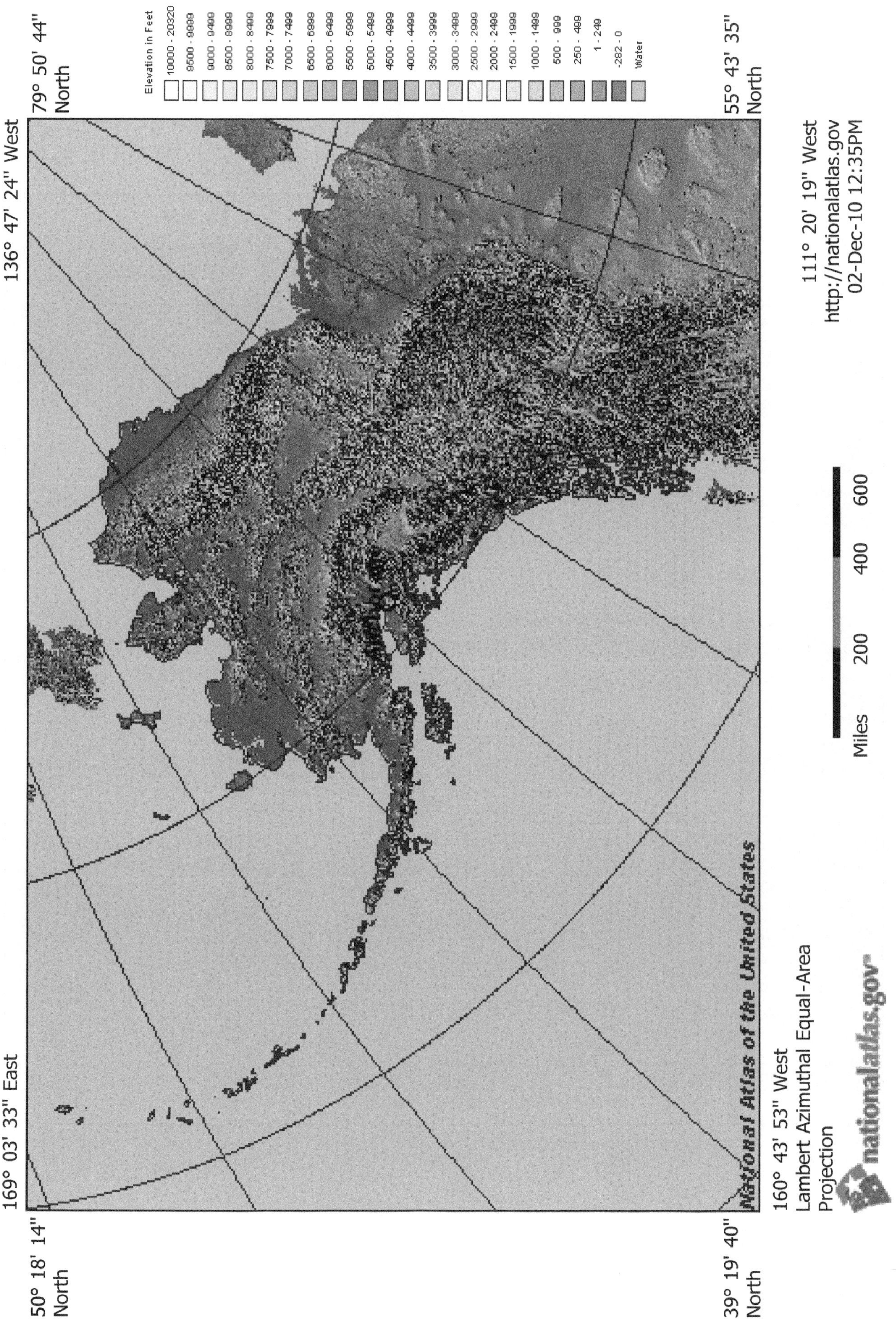
79° 50' 44" North
136° 47' 24" West
169° 03' 33" East
50° 18' 14" North
55° 43' 35" North
39° 19' 40" North
Elevation in Feet
10000 - 20320
9500 - 9999
9000 - 9499
8500 - 8999
8000 - 8499
7500 - 7999
7000 - 7499
6500 - 6999
6000 - 6499
5500 - 5999
5000 - 5499
4500 - 4999
4000 - 4499
3500 - 3999
3000 - 3499
2500 - 2999
2000 - 2499
1500 - 1999
1000 - 1499
500 - 999
250 - 499
1 - 249
-282 - 0
Water
National Atlas of the United States
160° 43' 53" West
Lambert Azimuthal Equal-Area
Projection
nationalatlas.gov
Miles
200
400
600
111° 20' 19" West
http://nationalatlas.gov
02-Dec-10 12:35PM

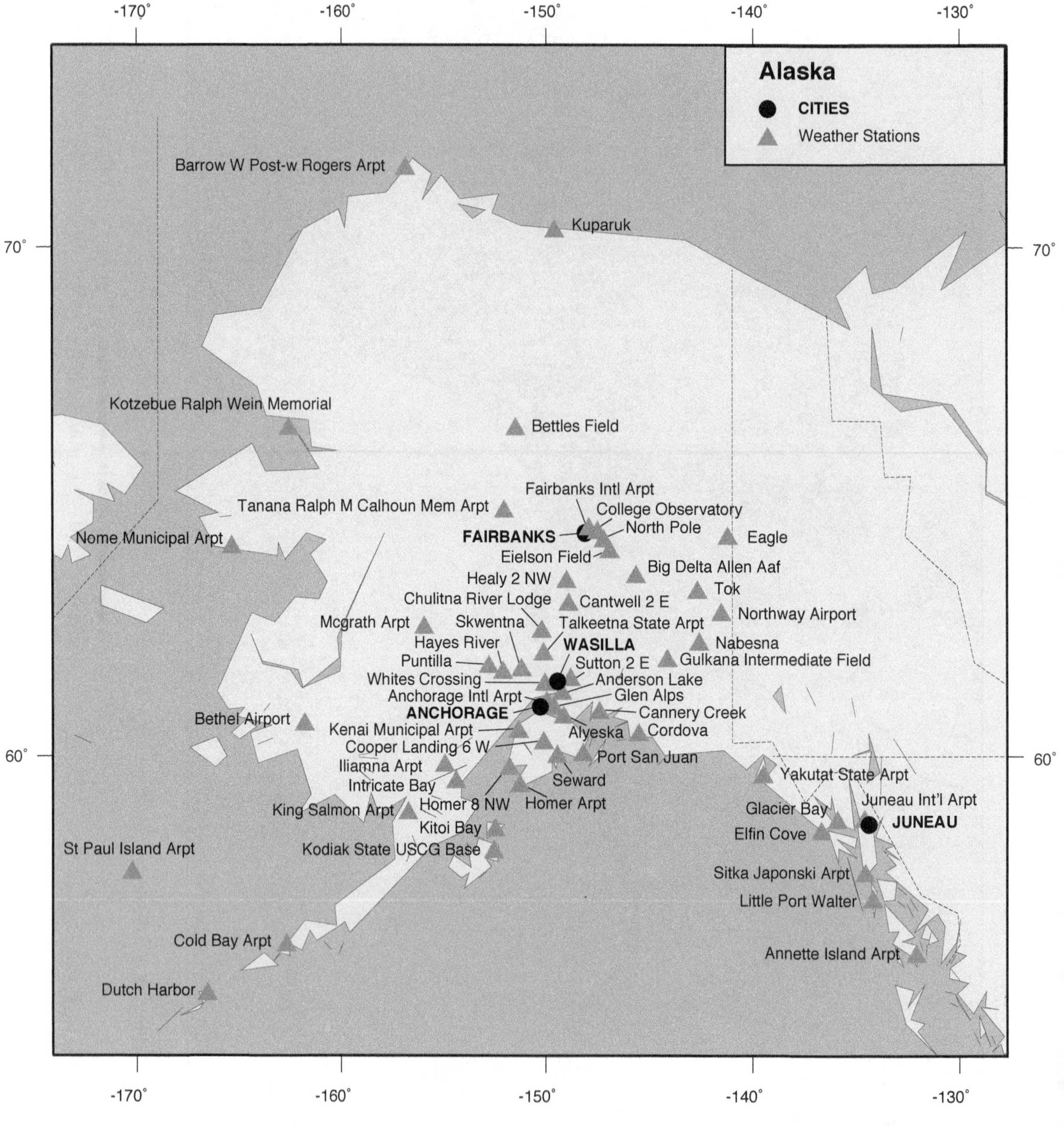
-170°
-160°
-150°
-140°
-130°
70°
60°
Alaska
CITIES
Weather Stations
Barrow W Post-w Rogers Arpt
Kuparuk
Kotzebue Ralph Wein Memorial
Bettles Field
Fairbanks Intl Arpt
Tanana Ralph M Calhoun Mem Arpt
College Observatory
FAIRBANKS
North Pole
Nome Municipal Arpt
Eagle
Eielson Field
Big Delta Allen Aaf
Healy 2 NW
Tok
Chulitna River Lodge
Cantwell 2 E
Northway Airport
Mcgrath Arpt
Skwentna
Talkeetna State Arpt
Hayes River
WASILLA
Nabesna
Puntilla
Sutton 2 E
Gulkana Intermediate Field
Whites Crossing
Anderson Lake
Anchorage Intl Arpt
Glen Alps
ANCHORAGE
Cannery Creek
Bethel Airport
Kenai Municipal Arpt
Alyeska
Cordova
Cooper Landing 6 W
Port San Juan
Iliamna Arpt
Seward
Yakutat State Arpt
Intricate Bay
Homer 8 NW
Homer Arpt
Juneau Int'l Arpt
King Salmon Arpt
Glacier Bay
JUNEAU
Kitoi Bay
Elfin Cove
St Paul Island Arpt
Kodiak State USCG Base
Sitka Japonski Arpt
Little Port Walter
Cold Bay Arpt
Annette Island Arpt
Dutch Harbor

Alaska Weather Stations by Borough

Borough	Station Name
Aleutians East	Cold Bay Arpt
Aleutians West	Dutch Harbor St Paul Island Arpt
Anchorage	Alyeska Anchorage Intl Arpt Glen Alps
Bethel	Bethel Airport
Bristol Bay	King Salmon Arpt
Denali	Cantwell 2 E Healy 2 NW
Fairbanks North Star	College Observatory Eielson Field Fairbanks Intl Arpt North Pole
Juneau	Juneau Int'l Arpt
Kenai Peninsula	Cooper Landing 6 W Homer 8 NW Homer Arpt Kenai Municipal Arpt Seward
Kodiak Island	Kitoi Bay Kodiak State USCG Base
Lake and Peninsula	Iliamna Arpt Intricate Bay
Matanuska-Susitna	Anderson Lake Chulitna River Lodge Hayes River Puntilla Skwentna Sutton 2 E Talkeetna State Arpt Whites Crossing
Nome	Nome Municipal Arpt
North Slope	Barrow W Post-W Rogers Arpt Kuparuk
Northwest Arctic	Kotzebue Ralph Wein Memorial
Prince of Wales-Outer Ketchikan	Annette Island Arpt
Sitka	Little Port Walter Sitka Japonski Arpt
Skagway-Hoonah-Angoon	Elfin Cove Glacier Bay
Southeast Fairbanks	Big Delta Allen AAF Eagle Northway Airport Tok

Borough	Station Name
Valdez-cordova	Cannery Creek Cordova Gulkana Intermediate Field Nabesna Port San Juan
Yakutat	Yakutat State Arpt
Yukon-Koyukuk	Bettles Field McGrath Arpt Tanana Ralph M Calhoun Mem Arpt

See User Guide for station inclusion criteria.

Alaska Weather Stations by City

City	Station Name	Miles
Anchorage	Anchorage Intl Arpt	6.8
	Glen Alps	7.4
College	College Observatory	0.8
	Fairbanks Intl Arpt	2.8
	North Pole	16.3
Fairbanks	College Observatory	4.2
	Eielson Field	21.5
	Fairbanks Intl Arpt	4.5
	North Pole	12.6
Juneau	Juneau Int'l Arpt	2.1
Kenai	Kenai Municipal Arpt	0.8
Knik-Fairview	Anderson Lake	9.9
	Whites Crossing	18.4
Lakes	Anderson Lake	1.2
	Sutton 2 E	16.1
	Whites Crossing	23.6
Palmer	Anderson Lake	7.2
	Sutton 2 E	10.9
Sitka	Sitka Japonski Arpt	0.8
Tanaina	Anderson Lake	3.2
	Sutton 2 E	19.3
	Whites Crossing	19.5
Wasilla	Anderson Lake	4.6
	Sutton 2 E	20.9
	Whites Crossing	19.6

Note: Miles is the distance between the geographic center of the city and the weather station.

See User Guide for station inclusion criteria.

Alaska Weather Stations by Elevation

Feet	Station Name
2,900	Nabesna
2,259	Glen Alps
2,149	Cantwell 2 E
1,832	Puntilla
1,712	Northway Airport
1,620	Tok
1,569	Gulkana Intermediate Field
1,490	Healy 2 NW
1,399	Chulitna River Lodge
1,268	Big Delta Allen AAF
1,000	Hayes River
1,000	Homer 8 NW
850	Eagle
644	Bettles Field
621	College Observatory
549	Sutton 2 E
546	Eielson Field
495	Anderson Lake
475	North Pole
436	Fairbanks Intl Arpt
375	Cooper Landing 6 W
345	Talkeetna State Arpt
344	McGrath Arpt
270	Whites Crossing
250	Alyeska
231	Tanana Ralph M Calhoun Mem Arpt
186	Iliamna Arpt
169	Intricate Bay
149	Skwentna
125	Bethel Airport
113	Anchorage Intl Arpt
108	Annette Island Arpt
96	Cold Bay Arpt
88	Homer Arpt
85	Kenai Municipal Arpt
75	Seward
63	Kuparuk
49	Glacier Bay
48	King Salmon Arpt
41	Cordova
36	Sitka Japonski Arpt
30	Barrow W Post-W Rogers Arpt
27	Yakutat State Arpt
21	St Paul Island Arpt
20	Elfin Cove
15	Kitoi Bay
15	Kodiak State USCG Base
14	Little Port Walter
13	Nome Municipal Arpt
12	Dutch Harbor
12	Juneau Int'l Arpt
9	Kotzebue Ralph Wein Memorial
5	Cannery Creek
0	Port San Juan

See User Guide for station inclusion criteria.

Anchorage Int'l Airport

Anchorage is in a broad valley with adjacent narrow bodies of water. Cook Inlet, including Knik Arm and Turnagain Arm, lies approximately 2 miles to the west, north, and south. The terrain rises gradually to the east for about 10 miles, Beyond this area, the Chugach Mountains acts as a barrier to the influx of warm, moist air from the Gulf of Alaska, so the average annual precipitation is only 10 to 15 percent of that at stations located on the Gulf of Alaska side of the Chugach Range. The Alaska Mountain Range lies in a long arc from southwest, through northwest, to northeast, approximately 100 miles distant from Anchorage. During the winter, this range is an effective barrier to the influx of very cold air from the north side of the range.

The four seasons are well marked in Anchorage. In the summer, high temperatures average about 60 degrees and low temperatures nearly 50 degrees. On summer days, temperatures on the east side of Anchorage may be about 10 degrees warmer than the official airport readings. Rain increases after mid-June. About two-thirds of the days in July and August are cloudy and one-third have rain.

Autumn is brief, beginning in early September and ending in mid-October. Temperatures begin to fall in September with snow becoming more frequent in October.

Winter can be considered as mid-October to early April when streams and lakes are frozen. Temperatures steadily decrease into January when the highs are near 20 degrees and lows near five degrees. On cold winter nights, temperatures on the east side of Anchorage may be 10-20 degrees lower than airport readings on the west side. Most winter precipitation is snow, but rain may occur on a few days.

Annual snowfall varies from about 70 inches on the west side to about 90 inches on the east side of Anchorage at low elevations. Along the Chugach Mountains, snow totals increase steadily with increasing elevations and winter arrives a month earlier and stays a month longer at the 1,000 to 2,000 foot level.

Spring begins in late April and May when days are warm and sunny, nights are cool, and precipitation is exceedingly small. Foliage turns green by late May.

The wind in Anchorage is generally light. However, on several days each winter, strong northerly winds, up to 90 mph, affect the entire Anchorage area.

The average occurrence of the first snow is mid-October, but has occurred as early as mid-September. The average date of the last snow is mid-April, but has occurred as late as early May. The growing season is about 125 days. Average occurrence of the last temperature of 32 degrees in spring is mid-May and the first in fall is mid-September. Daylight varies from about 19 hours in late June to 6 hours in late December with 12 hours of daylight occurring in late September and late March.

Anchorage Int'l Airport *Anchorage Borough* Elevation: 113 ft. Latitude: 61° 11' N Longitude: 150° 00' W

	JAN	FEB	MAR	APR	MAY	JUN	JUL	AUG	SEP	OCT	NOV	DEC	YEAR
Mean Maximum Temp. (°F)	23.0	26.7	33.9	44.7	55.8	62.8	65.4	63.4	55.1	40.4	27.8	24.5	43.6
Mean Temp. (°F)	17.0	20.3	26.6	36.9	47.7	55.2	58.8	56.7	48.5	34.8	22.3	18.7	37.0
Mean Minimum Temp. (°F)	11.0	13.8	19.3	29.1	39.6	47.6	52.2	49.9	41.9	29.0	16.7	12.9	30.2
Extreme Maximum Temp. (°F)	49	48	51	69	77	80	84	81	71	64	54	48	84
Extreme Minimum Temp. (°F)	-30	-28	-16	-4	24	34	39	31	19	-3	-15	-24	-30
Days Maximum Temp. ≥ 70°F	0	0	0	0	1	4	6	3	0	0	0	0	14
Days Maximum Temp. ≤ 32°F	24	19	12	2	0	0	0	0	0	5	21	24	107
Days Minimum Temp. ≤ 32°F	30	27	29	20	3	0	0	0	3	20	28	30	190
Days Minimum Temp. ≤ 0°F	7	5	1	0	0	0	0	0	0	0	3	5	21
Heating Degree Days (base 65°F)	1,483	1,259	1,184	836	529	288	187	252	489	930	1,276	1,429	10,142
Cooling Degree Days (base 65°F)	0	0	0	0	0	0	3	1	0	0	0	0	4
Mean Precipitation (in.)	0.75	0.72	0.59	0.43	0.76	1.02	1.80	3.24	3.04	2.12	1.08	1.09	16.64
Maximum Precipitation (in.)*	2.7	3.1	2.8	1.9	1.9	3.4	4.4	9.8	6.6	4.1	2.8	2.7	27.5
Minimum Precipitation (in.)*	trace	0.1	trace	trace	trace	0.2	0.4	0.3	0.8	0.3	0.1	0.1	8.1
Extreme Maximum Daily Precip. (in.)	1.10	0.70	1.25	1.32	0.97	0.90	1.52	2.76	1.32	1.60	0.77	0.78	2.76
Days With ≥ 0.1" Precipitation	2	3	2	1	2	3	5	9	9	6	4	4	50
Days With ≥ 0.5" Precipitation	0	0	0	0	0	0	1	2	1	1	0	0	5
Days With ≥ 1.0" Precipitation	0	0	0	0	0	0	0	0	0	0	0	0	0
Mean Snowfall (in.)	11.2	11.0	9.6	3.6	0.3	0.0	0.0	trace	0.4	8.1	12.8	16.4	73.4
Maximum Snowfall (in.)*	28	49	31	28	4	0	0	0	5	27	39	42	172
Maximum 24-hr. Snowfall (in.)*	8	12	14	8	4	0	0	0	3	9	11	16	16
Maximum Snow Depth (in.)	34	34	39	30	4	0	0	trace	2	15	28	34	39
Days With ≥ 1.0" Snow Depth	29	26	28	11	0	0	0	0	0	7	20	27	148
Thunderstorm Days*	0	0	0	0	< 1	< 1	< 1	< 1	< 1	0	0	0	2
Foggy Days*	11	9	5	4	1	2	4	5	6	7	10	12	76
Predominant Sky Cover*	OVR	OVR	OVR	OVR	OVR	OVR	OVR	OVR	OVR	OVR	OVR	OVR	OVR
Mean Relative Humidity 6am (%)*	74	74	72	75	73	74	80	84	84	78	78	78	77
Mean Relative Humidity 3pm (%)*	73	67	57	54	50	55	62	64	64	67	74	76	64
Mean Dewpoint (°F)*	8	11	15	25	34	43	49	48	41	27	15	10	27
Prevailing Wind Direction*	N	N	N	N	SSE	SSE	SSE	SSE	SSE	N	N	N	N
Prevailing Wind Speed (mph)*	9	9	8	7	13	13	12	10	10	8	8	8	9
Maximum Wind Gust (mph)*	73	74	75	51	48	46	40	54	53	60	63	62	75

Note: (*) Period of record is 1953-1995

The period of record for National Weather Service station data is 1980 – 2009 except where noted. See User Guide for detailed explanation of data.

Barrow W. Post-W. Rogers Airport

Barrow is the most northerly First-Order station operated by the National Weather Service. Although this station generally records one of the lowest mean temperatures for the winter months, the surrounding topography prevents the establishment of the lowest minima for the state. With the Arctic Ocean to the north, east, and west, and level tundra stretching 200 miles to the south, there are no natural wind barriers to assist in stilling the wind, permitting the lowering of temperatures by radiation, and no downslope drainage area to aid the flow of cold air to lower levels. Consequently, temperature inversions in the lower levels of the atmosphere are not as marked as those observed at stations in the central interior.

Temperatures at this northern station remain below the freezing point through most of the year, with the daily maxima reaching higher than 32 degrees on an average of only 109 days a year. Freezing temperatures have been observed every month of the year. February is generally the coldest month and March temperatures are but little higher than those observed in the winter months. In April, temperatures begin a general upward trend, with May becoming the definite transitional period from winter to the summer season. July is the warmest month of the year and the frequency of minimum temperatures of 32 degrees or less are about one day out of two for July and August. During late July or early August, the Arctic Ocean is usually ice-free for the first time in summer. September marks the end of the short summer is and by November about half of the daily mean temperatures are zero or below.

At 12:50 p.m. on November 18, the sun dips below the horizon and is not seen again until 11:51 a.m. on January 24. Then the amount of possible sunshine each day increases by never less than 9 minutes per day. By 1:06 a.m. on May 10th the possible sunshine has increased to 24 hours per day. The sun remains visible from that time to August 2, when it again sets for 1 hour and 25 minutes. The decrease in hours of sunshine is as rapid as the increase. The occurrence of cloudiness, precipitation, and heavy fog build up to a maximum along with the hours of sunshine. Maximum cloudiness does continue into the fall months, although the amount of sunshine, precipitation, and fog are on the decrease. Since an accurate estimate of cloudiness cannot be made under conditions of darkness, of cloudiness for that time is not recorded. However, it probably approximates that observed during late winter and spring months.

Variation of wind speed during the year is small, with the fall months being windiest. Extreme winds in the upper 40s and low 50s have been recorded for all months.

Barrow W. Post-W. Rogers Airport *North Slope Borough* Elevation: 30 ft. Latitude: 71° 17' N Longitude: 156° 46' W

	JAN	FEB	MAR	APR	MAY	JUN	JUL	AUG	SEP	OCT	NOV	DEC	YEAR
Mean Maximum Temp. (°F)	-7.3	-8.0	-6.4	8.1	25.7	40.6	46.7	43.6	35.3	21.5	5.7	-2.0	17.0
Mean Temp. (°F)	-13.4	-14.2	-12.8	1.4	21.1	35.8	40.7	38.7	31.8	16.9	0.2	-8.0	11.5
Mean Minimum Temp. (°F)	-19.4	-20.4	-19.2	-5.3	16.4	30.8	34.6	33.8	28.1	12.3	-5.4	-14.0	6.0
Extreme Maximum Temp. (°F)	33	36	34	39	47	72	79	74	62	40	35	32	79
Extreme Minimum Temp. (°F)	-52	-55	-46	-38	-19	12	25	21	2	-27	-38	-49	-55
Days Maximum Temp. ≥ 70°F	0	0	0	0	0	0	0	0	0	0	0	0	0
Days Maximum Temp. ≤ 32°F	31	28	31	29	24	3	0	1	11	28	30	31	247
Days Minimum Temp. ≤ 32°F	31	28	31	30	31	21	11	14	23	31	30	31	312
Days Minimum Temp. ≤ 0°F	30	26	29	21	2	0	0	0	0	6	20	28	162
Heating Degree Days (base 65°F)	2,435	2,244	2,418	1,907	1,355	871	748	808	990	1,484	1,945	2,267	19,472
Cooling Degree Days (base 65°F)	0	0	0	0	0	0	0	0	0	0	0	0	0
Mean Precipitation (in.)	0.13	0.13	0.08	0.14	0.16	0.33	0.95	1.09	0.72	0.41	0.18	0.13	4.45
Maximum Precipitation (in.)*	1.0	0.8	1.5	1.4	0.5	1.1	3.2	2.8	1.6	1.4	1.1	0.8	9.8
Minimum Precipitation (in.)*	trace	trace	trace	trace	trace	trace	0.1	0.1	trace	0.1	trace	trace	1.8
Extreme Maximum Daily Precip. (in.)	0.62	0.13	0.13	0.36	0.25	0.48	1.28	0.71	0.62	0.33	0.13	0.16	1.28
Days With ≥ 0.1" Precipitation	0	0	0	0	0	1	3	4	2	1	0	0	11
Days With ≥ 0.5" Precipitation	0	0	0	0	0	0	0	0	0	0	0	0	0
Days With ≥ 1.0" Precipitation	0	0	0	0	0	0	0	0	0	0	0	0	0
Mean Snowfall (in.)	2.8	2.6	1.9	2.9	2.5	0.7	0.2	0.9	4.5	8.8	5.4	3.3	36.5
Maximum Snowfall (in.)*	12	9	16	15	7	4	4	4	16	15	13	9	62
Maximum 24-hr. Snowfall (in.)*	5	3	7	4	4	3	3	2	5	5	4	3	7
Maximum Snow Depth (in.)	18	23	20	22	23	5	trace	3	7	12	18	140	140
Days With ≥ 1.0" Snow Depth	31	28	31	30	25	1	0	0	7	28	30	31	242
Thunderstorm Days*	< 1	< 1	< 1	0	0	< 1	< 1	< 1	0	0	< 1	< 1	1
Foggy Days*	14	14	13	14	20	22	23	24	20	17	15	14	210
Predominant Sky Cover*	CLR	CLR	CLR	OVR	OVR	OVR	OVR	OVR	OVR	OVR	OVR	OVR	OVR
Mean Relative Humidity 6am (%)*	68	67	66	74	87	91	92	94	92	85	77	70	81
Mean Relative Humidity 3pm (%)*	68	67	67	73	83	86	85	87	87	84	77	70	78
Mean Dewpoint (°F)*	-20	-23	-21	-6	17	31	36	35	28	12	-7	-18	6
Prevailing Wind Direction*	ENE	ENE	ENE	ENE	ENE	E	E	E	ENE	ENE	ENE	ENE	ENE
Prevailing Wind Speed (mph)*	14	13	14	14	15	14	14	15	15	16	15	14	14
Maximum Wind Gust (mph)*	58	74	56	48	41	43	55	48	66	55	53	67	74

Note: (*) Period of record is 1949-1995

Fairbanks Int'l Airport

Fairbanks is located in the Tanana Valley, in the interior of Alaska. It has a distinctly continental climate, with large variation of temperature from winter to summer.

The sun is above the horizon from 18 to 21 hours during June and July. During this period, daily average maximum temperatures reach the lower 70s. Temperatures of 80 degrees or higher occur on about 10 days each summer. In contrast, from November to early March, when the period of daylight ranges from 10 to less than 4 hours per day, the lowest temperature readings normally fall below zero quite regularly. Low temperatures of -40 degrees or colder occur each winter. The range of temperatures in summer is comparatively low, from the lower 30s to the mid 90s. In winter, this range is larger, from about 65 below to 45 degrees above. This large winter range of temperature reflects the great difference between frigid weather associated with dry northerly airflow from the Arctic to mild temperatures associated with southerly airflow from the Gulf of Alaska, accompanied by chinook winds off the Alaska Range, 80 miles to the south of Fairbanks.

Snow cover is persistent in Fairbanks, without interruption, from October through April. Snowfalls of four inches or more in a day occur only three times during winter. Blizzard conditions are almost never seen. Precipitation normally reaches a minimum in spring, and a maximum in August, when rainfall is common. During summer, thunderstorms occur in Fairbanks on an average of about eight days.

There are rolling hills reaching elevations up to 2,000 feet above Fairbanks to the north and east of the city. During winter, the uplands are often warmer than Fairbanks. During summer, the uplands are a few degrees cooler than the city. Precipitation in the uplands around Fairbanks is heavier than it is in the city by roughly 20 to 50 percent. Fairbanks exhibits an urban heat island, especially during winter. Low lying areas nearby, such as the community of North Pole, are often colder than the city.

During winter, with temperatures of -20 degrees or colder, ice fog frequently forms in the city. Cold snaps accompanied by ice fog generally last about a week, but can last three weeks in unusual situations. The fog is almost always less than 300 feet deep, so that the surrounding uplands are usually in the clear, with warmer temperatures. Visibility in the ice fog is sometimes quite low.

Hardy vegetables and grains grow luxuriantly. Freezing of local rivers normally begins in the first week of October, with ice normally supporting a persons weight by October 27. Rivers remain frozen and safe for travel until early April. Breakup usually occurs in the first week of May.

Fairbanks Int'l Airport *Fairbanks North Star Borough* Elevation: 436 ft. Latitude: 64° 49' N Longitude: 147° 51' W

	JAN	FEB	MAR	APR	MAY	JUN	JUL	AUG	SEP	OCT	NOV	DEC	YEAR
Mean Maximum Temp. (°F)	1.3	10.5	25.5	44.3	60.8	71.5	72.7	65.7	54.4	31.9	10.9	4.5	37.8
Mean Temp. (°F)	-7.4	-0.5	12.1	32.8	49.7	60.7	62.8	56.3	45.1	24.6	2.9	-3.9	27.9
Mean Minimum Temp. (°F)	-16.0	-11.5	-1.4	21.3	38.5	50.0	52.9	46.9	35.8	17.3	-5.1	-12.4	18.0
Extreme Maximum Temp. (°F)	52	47	56	76	88	94	93	93	78	72	49	45	94
Extreme Minimum Temp. (°F)	-51	-58	-43	-24	11	29	39	27	3	-27	-46	-53	-58
Days Maximum Temp. ≥ 70°F	0	0	0	0	5	18	21	10	1	0	0	0	55
Days Maximum Temp. ≤ 32°F	30	26	21	5	0	0	0	0	0	16	28	30	156
Days Minimum Temp. ≤ 32°F	31	28	31	26	6	0	0	0	10	29	30	31	222
Days Minimum Temp. ≤ 0°F	25	21	17	2	0	0	0	0	0	4	19	25	113
Heating Degree Days (base 65°F)	2,245	1,850	1,636	959	468	148	97	270	590	1,246	1,861	2,138	13,508
Cooling Degree Days (base 65°F)	0	0	0	0	1	27	37	8	0	0	0	0	73
Mean Precipitation (in.)	0.60	0.42	0.28	0.30	0.60	1.37	2.10	1.88	1.09	0.83	0.64	0.64	10.75
Maximum Precipitation (in.)*	2.4	1.8	2.2	0.9	1.7	3.5	4.9	6.2	3.0	2.2	3.3	3.2	18.5
Minimum Precipitation (in.)*	trace	trace	trace	trace	0.1	0.2	0.3	0.4	0.1	0.1	trace	trace	5.5
Extreme Maximum Daily Precip. (in.)	0.75	0.56	0.97	0.92	0.78	1.27	2.27	1.38	0.78	0.80	0.44	0.94	2.27
Days With ≥ 0.1" Precipitation	2	1	0	1	2	4	5	6	4	3	2	2	32
Days With ≥ 0.5" Precipitation	0	0	0	0	0	0	1	1	0	0	0	0	2
Days With ≥ 1.0" Precipitation	0	0	0	0	0	0	0	0	0	0	0	0	0
Mean Snowfall (in.)	10.6	7.8	4.9	2.9	0.9	trace	trace	trace	1.9	10.9	12.8	12.2	64.9
Maximum Snowfall (in.)*	40	43	30	12	14	0	0	trace	24	26	54	51	146
Maximum 24-hr. Snowfall (in.)*	10	16	13	6	9	0	0	trace	8	10	15	13	16
Maximum Snow Depth (in.)	46	42	54	49	14	trace	trace	trace	12	16	24	46	54
Days With ≥ 1.0" Snow Depth	31	28	31	22	1	0	0	0	1	17	30	31	192
Thunderstorm Days*	1	< 1	0	< 1	< 1	3	3	1	< 1	< 1	< 1	< 1	8
Foggy Days*	13	9	4	2	2	2	5	7	6	8	9	12	79
Predominant Sky Cover*	OVR	OVR	OVR	OVR	OVR	OVR	OVR	OVR	OVR	OVR	OVR	OVR	OVR
Mean Relative Humidity 6am (%)*	70	68	69	70	64	71	80	87	85	81	74	72	74
Mean Relative Humidity 3pm (%)*	70	64	54	46	38	44	51	55	56	69	74	72	58
Mean Dewpoint (°F)*	-13	-11	1	17	31	44	50	47	35	19	-1	-13	17
Prevailing Wind Direction*	N	N	N	N	N	SW	SW	SW	N	N	N	N	N
Prevailing Wind Speed (mph)*	6	6	7	8	8	10	9	9	7	7	6	6	7
Maximum Wind Gust (mph)*	47	40	46	40	44	48	63	54	51	40	46	38	63

Note: (*) Period of record is 1948-1995

Juneau Int'l Airport

Juneau lies well within the area of maritime influences which prevail over the coastal areas of southeastern Alaska, and is in the path of most storms that cross the Gulf of Alaska. Consequently, the area has little sunshine, generally moderate temperatures, and abundant precipitation. There are intervals, however, sometimes lasting for several days at a stretch, during which clear skies prevail. The rugged terrain creates considerable variations in both temperature and precipitation within relatively short distances.

Temperature variations, both daily and seasonal, are usually limited. There are, however, periods of comparatively severe cold, which usually start with strong northerly winds, and are most often caused by the flow of cold air from northwestern Canada through nearby mountain passes and over the Juneau ice field. During such periods strong, gusty winds, known locally as Taku Winds, often occur especially in downtown Juneau, Douglas, and other local areas.During periods of calm or light winds, temperature differences within short distances are frequently very pronounced. Variations in local sunlight and air drainage patterns produce wide differences in temperatures particularly between upland or sloping areas and areas of low, flat terrain. Juneau International Airport, located on low, flat terrain formed by the Mendenhall River delta, and in the path of drainage air from the Mendenhall Glacier, averages about 10 days a year with minimum readings below zero. Downtown Juneau, located on a sloping portion of a rugged mountain area, experiences on the average only about one day each year with minimum readings below zero. At the airport the growing season averages 146 days, from May 4 to September 28, while the downtown average is 181 days, from April 22 to October 21.

The months of February to June mark the period of lightest precipitation, with monthly averages of about three inches. After June the monthly amounts increase gradually, reaching an average of 7.71 inches in October. Due to the rugged topography, precipitation throughout the year tends to vary greatly within short distances. At the Juneau Airport, yearly precipitation is 53 inches while downtown, only eight miles away, it is 93 inches.

Although a trace of snow has fallen as early as September 9, first falls usually occur in the latter part of October, and sometimes not until the first part of December. On the average there is very little accumulation on the ground at low levels until the last of November, although at higher elevations, and particularly on mountain tops, a cover is usually established in early October. Ice accumulations are frequent problems in the Juneau area during the winter months.

Juneau Int'l Airport *Juneau Borough* Elevation: 12 ft. Latitude: 58° 21' N Longitude: 134° 35' W

	JAN	FEB	MAR	APR	MAY	JUN	JUL	AUG	SEP	OCT	NOV	DEC	YEAR
Mean Maximum Temp. (°F)	32.5	35.2	39.6	48.6	56.6	62.4	64.0	62.7	55.5	47.1	38.2	34.0	48.0
Mean Temp. (°F)	27.9	30.0	33.7	40.9	48.6	54.6	57.0	55.8	50.0	42.5	34.0	29.8	42.1
Mean Minimum Temp. (°F)	23.3	24.8	27.8	33.3	40.5	46.8	49.9	48.8	44.3	37.8	29.6	25.5	36.0
Extreme Maximum Temp. (°F)	55	57	61	74	76	85	85	84	73	61	55	54	85
Extreme Minimum Temp. (°F)	-9	-8	-3	13	26	33	39	37	27	11	-5	-10	-10
Days Maximum Temp. ≥ 70°F	0	0	0	0	2	6	7	5	0	0	0	0	20
Days Maximum Temp. ≤ 32°F	13	8	4	0	0	0	0	0	0	0	5	11	41
Days Minimum Temp. ≤ 32°F	23	21	21	12	2	0	0	0	1	7	17	21	125
Days Minimum Temp. ≤ 0°F	2	0	0	0	0	0	0	0	0	0	0	1	3
Heating Degree Days (base 65°F)	1,142	982	963	715	502	307	244	279	444	691	924	1,085	8,278
Cooling Degree Days (base 65°F)	0	0	0	0	0	1	2	1	0	0	0	0	4
Mean Precipitation (in.)	5.31	4.18	3.66	3.02	3.48	3.25	4.69	5.77	8.80	8.70	6.12	5.84	62.82
Maximum Precipitation (in.)*	9.1	8.2	6.5	5.3	9.2	6.0	7.9	12.3	15.1	15.3	11.2	9.9	85.1
Minimum Precipitation (in.)*	0.9	0.1	0.6	0.9	1.4	1.1	1.1	0.6	2.3	2.7	1.1	0.5	37.7
Extreme Maximum Daily Precip. (in.)	2.09	2.71	1.74	1.95	2.15	2.26	2.39	1.82	3.35	3.47	3.45	2.67	3.47
Days With ≥ 0.1" Precipitation	13	10	11	9	9	8	11	13	17	18	14	13	146
Days With ≥ 0.5" Precipitation	3	2	1	1	2	2	3	4	6	6	4	4	38
Days With ≥ 1.0" Precipitation	1	1	0	0	0	0	1	1	2	2	1	1	10
Mean Snowfall (in.)	28.1	17.1	11.1	0.9	trace	0.0	0.0	0.0	trace	0.8	12.9	16.8	87.7
Maximum Snowfall (in.)*	69	86	51	46	1	0	0	0	trace	16	70	55	212
Maximum 24-hr. Snowfall (in.)*	20	24	18	21	1	0	0	0	trace	9	17	20	24
Maximum Snow Depth (in.)	33	35	24	8	trace	0	0	0	trace	5	28	34	35
Days With ≥ 1.0" Snow Depth	20	15	12	1	0	0	0	0	0	0	6	13	67
Thunderstorm Days*	< 1	0	0	0	0	< 1	< 1	< 1	< 1	0	< 1	0	1
Foggy Days*	9	8	7	5	5	5	9	11	13	11	10	10	103
Predominant Sky Cover*	OVR	OVR	OVR	OVR	OVR	OVR	OVR	OVR	OVR	OVR	OVR	OVR	OVR
Mean Relative Humidity 6am (%)*	82	83	85	88	88	87	88	91	93	90	86	85	87
Mean Relative Humidity 3pm (%)*	79	74	69	63	62	64	70	73	78	80	81	83	73
Mean Dewpoint (°F)*	20	23	26	32	39	45	49	49	45	38	29	24	35
Prevailing Wind Direction*	ESE	ESE	ESE	ESE	ESE	ESE	N	N	ESE	ESE	ESE	ESE	ESE
Prevailing Wind Speed (mph)*	15	15	15	14	14	13	6	6	15	15	15	15	13
Maximum Wind Gust (mph)*	54	69	54	61	54	46	47	48	69	71	92	64	92

Note: (*) Period of record is 1948-1995

Nome Municipal Airport

The weather station at Nome is located at Nome Field, approximately 1 mile northwest of the city. Low, marshy flats lie between the station and Norton Sound to the south, exposing the station to winds from the southeast through the west. A series of foothills, with heights of 500 to 1,200 feet, extend from northwest through north to east at a distance of from four to eight miles. The terrain increases in ruggedness and height farther north, with the Kigluaik Mountains reaching a height of 5,000 feet at a distance of 30 miles. The ground along the coastal flats is swampy during the summer months, but is permanently frozen below a depth of two to three feet. Vegetation in the Nome area consists mostly of grass and numerous small flowering plants.

The moderating influence of the open water of Norton Sound is effective only from early June to about the middle of November. Storms moving through this area during these months result in extended periods of cloudiness and rain. There is a nearly continuous cloud cover during July and August. During the summer months the daily temperature range is very slight. The freezing of Norton Sound in November causes a rather abrupt change from a maritime to a continental climate. The majority of low pressure systems during this period take a path south of Nome, resulting in strong easterly winds, accompanied by frequent blizzards, with the winds later becoming northerly and reaching Nome across the colder frozen areas of northern Alaska.

Temperatures generally remain well below freezing from the middle of November to the latter part of April, with January usually the coldest month of the year. Temperatures usually begin to rise near the end of February and continue to rise until they reach a maximum in July.

Precipitation reaches its maximum during the late summer months and drops to a minimum in April and May. Snow begins to fall in September, but usually does not accumulate on the ground until the first part of November. The snow cover decreases rapidly in April and May, and normally disappears by the middle of June. Snow depths in Nome have exceeded 70 inches.

Severe windstorms do occur with winds over 70 mph recorded several times. Strong winds during the winter months when there is snow cover produce blowing snow conditions that severely hinder transportation in the area.

Nome Municipal Airport *Nome Borough* Elevation: 13 ft. Latitude: 64° 31' N Longitude: 165° 27' W

	JAN	FEB	MAR	APR	MAY	JUN	JUL	AUG	SEP	OCT	NOV	DEC	YEAR
Mean Maximum Temp. (°F)	13.1	15.5	18.9	27.7	43.2	54.9	58.2	55.9	48.6	34.6	23.2	16.8	34.2
Mean Temp. (°F)	5.2	7.7	10.9	20.7	36.9	47.8	52.3	50.1	42.7	28.7	16.9	9.4	27.4
Mean Minimum Temp. (°F)	-2.8	-0.2	2.7	13.6	30.6	40.7	46.3	44.1	36.7	22.9	10.7	2.0	20.6
Extreme Maximum Temp. (°F)	42	48	43	51	78	83	85	81	70	53	47	42	85
Extreme Minimum Temp. (°F)	-54	-41	-34	-22	-6	24	30	26	9	-6	-27	-32	-54
Days Maximum Temp. ≥ 70°F	0	0	0	0	0	2	3	1	0	0	0	0	6
Days Maximum Temp. ≤ 32°F	28	25	27	19	4	0	0	0	0	12	24	27	166
Days Minimum Temp. ≤ 32°F	31	28	31	28	18	2	0	1	9	25	29	31	233
Days Minimum Temp. ≤ 0°F	17	14	14	6	0	0	0	0	0	0	7	14	72
Heating Degree Days (base 65°F)	1,853	1,620	1,675	1,325	863	510	389	457	663	1,117	1,436	1,721	13,629
Cooling Degree Days (base 65°F)	0	0	0	0	0	1	2	0	0	0	0	0	3
Mean Precipitation (in.)	0.97	0.95	0.66	0.74	0.89	1.02	2.12	3.19	2.38	1.60	1.20	1.05	16.77
Maximum Precipitation (in.)*	2.1	2.1	1.9	2.1	2.0	4.1	4.7	7.8	7.5	3.8	4.4	2.2	24.3
Minimum Precipitation (in.)*	trace	trace	trace	trace	trace	trace	0.3	0.4	0.4	trace	trace	trace	7.4
Extreme Maximum Daily Precip. (in.)	0.68	0.56	0.65	0.49	0.76	0.95	1.59	1.72	1.27	1.50	0.84	0.67	1.72
Days With ≥ 0.1" Precipitation	3	4	2	3	3	3	6	8	7	5	4	4	52
Days With ≥ 0.5" Precipitation	0	0	0	0	0	0	1	2	1	0	0	0	4
Days With ≥ 1.0" Precipitation	0	0	0	0	0	0	0	0	0	0	0	0	0
Mean Snowfall (in.)	13.9	12.7	8.7	7.6	2.3	0.3	0.0	trace	0.5	4.6	12.5	13.8	76.9
Maximum Snowfall (in.)*	24	23	20	23	10	3	0	trace	4	14	31	30	102
Maximum 24-hr. Snowfall (in.)*	7	8	5	6	5	2	0	trace	2	6	9	8	9
Maximum Snow Depth (in.)	60	60	78	89	31	1	0	trace	2	10	24	46	89
Days With ≥ 1.0" Snow Depth	31	28	31	28	10	0	0	0	0	7	22	29	186
Thunderstorm Days*	< 1	< 1	0	0	< 1	< 1	< 1	< 1	0	0	0	< 1	2
Foggy Days*	10	7	9	9	10	12	16	15	8	7	8	9	120
Predominant Sky Cover*	OVR	OVR	OVR	OVR	OVR	OVR	OVR	OVR	OVR	OVR	OVR	OVR	OVR
Mean Relative Humidity 6am (%)*	75	73	74	79	80	81	86	88	84	80	77	75	79
Mean Relative Humidity 3pm (%)*	75	71	70	74	73	74	79	79	73	73	76	74	74
Mean Dewpoint (°F)*	0	-1	1	13	29	39	46	45	36	23	10	1	20
Prevailing Wind Direction*	E	E	NE	E	E	WSW	WSW	SW	N	N	ENE	E	N
Prevailing Wind Speed (mph)*	16	15	14	14	13	12	12	13	9	9	15	16	13
Maximum Wind Gust (mph)*	67	66	60	58	53	45	49	56	59	69	69	71	71

Note: (*) Period of record is 1948-1995

Alyeska *Anchorage Borough* Elevation: 250 ft. Latitude: 60° 58' N Longitude: 149° 08' W

	JAN	FEB	MAR	APR	MAY	JUN	JUL	AUG	SEP	OCT	NOV	DEC	YEAR
Mean Maximum Temp. (°F)	27.1	30.0	35.8	44.2	53.9	62.2	65.1	63.2	55.0	42.4	31.2	29.2	44.9
Mean Temp. (°F)	21.7	23.8	27.9	36.1	45.1	53.0	56.9	55.0	47.4	36.2	25.9	23.9	37.7
Mean Minimum Temp. (°F)	16.2	17.6	20.0	27.8	36.1	43.8	48.7	46.6	39.8	30.0	20.5	18.5	30.5
Extreme Maximum Temp. (°F)	50	52	51	67	78	82	82	88	75	62	51	50	88
Extreme Minimum Temp. (°F)	-30	-24	-12	-2	24	32	39	30	17	2	-12	-18	-30
Days Maximum Temp. ≥ 70°F	0	0	0	0	1	5	8	6	0	0	0	0	20
Days Maximum Temp. ≤ 32°F	17	13	8	1	0	0	0	0	0	3	14	16	72
Days Minimum Temp. ≤ 32°F	28	25	29	22	6	0	0	0	4	19	26	27	186
Days Minimum Temp. ≤ 0°F	5	4	1	0	0	0	0	0	0	0	1	3	14
Heating Degree Days (base 65°F)	1,337	1,157	1,143	861	612	354	244	306	522	885	1,168	1,268	9,857
Cooling Degree Days (base 65°F)	0	0	0	0	0	0	1	1	0	0	0	0	2
Mean Precipitation (in.)	8.55	6.20	5.24	5.43	3.12	2.35	2.61	4.81	7.95	7.98	7.10	9.34	70.68
Extreme Maximum Daily Precip. (in.)	4.24	5.29	4.90	3.18	2.15	1.70	1.99	3.04	4.20	4.52	5.34	5.30	5.34
Days With ≥ 0.1" Precipitation	13	11	10	10	7	6	7	10	13	13	12	15	127
Days With ≥ 0.5" Precipitation	5	4	3	4	2	1	1	3	5	5	5	6	44
Days With ≥ 1.0" Precipitation	3	2	1	2	1	0	0	1	2	2	2	3	19
Mean Snowfall (in.)	37.4	31.6	34.9	10.3	1.1	0.0	0.0	0.0	trace	11.5	32.4	53.4	212.6
Maximum Snow Depth (in.)	75	89	79	70	42	0	0	0	trace	32	35	62	89
Days With ≥ 1.0" Snow Depth	29	28	31	27	5	0	0	0	0	7	22	28	177

Anderson Lake *Matanuska-Susitna Borough* Elevation: 495 ft. Latitude: 61° 37' N Longitude: 149° 20' W

	JAN	FEB	MAR	APR	MAY	JUN	JUL	AUG	SEP	OCT	NOV	DEC	YEAR
Mean Maximum Temp. (°F)	24.4	***28.1***	34.9	46.2	57.6	64.3	66.1	63.2	54.8	41.8	28.4	***25.8***	***44.6***
Mean Temp. (°F)	17.9	***20.9***	27.2	37.4	47.2	54.3	57.6	54.9	47.0	35.0	21.9	***19.5***	***36.7***
Mean Minimum Temp. (°F)	11.4	***13.8***	19.4	28.5	36.8	44.3	49.0	46.5	39.0	28.2	15.3	***13.1***	***28.8***
Extreme Maximum Temp. (°F)	***48***	51	53	72	80	83	86	83	67	65	53	49	***86***
Extreme Minimum Temp. (°F)	-40	-35	-18	-7	11	21	37	29	17	-7	-23	***-21***	***-40***
Days Maximum Temp. ≥ 70°F	0	0	0	0	2	7	9	5	0	0	0	0	23
Days Maximum Temp. ≤ 32°F	***21***	15	11	2	0	0	0	0	0	5	18	20	***92***
Days Minimum Temp. ≤ 32°F	29	24	29	20	7	0	0	0	4	20	27	28	188
Days Minimum Temp. ≤ 0°F	8	5	2	0	0	0	0	0	0	0	5	***6***	***26***
Heating Degree Days (base 65°F)	1,452	***1,237***	1,166	822	544	314	226	308	534	921	1,288	***1,404***	***10,216***
Cooling Degree Days (base 65°F)	0	***0***	0	0	0	1	3	0	0	0	0	***0***	***4***
Mean Precipitation (in.)	***0.98***	0.93	0.78	0.41	1.21	1.60	2.55	3.40	3.13	1.80	1.24	***1.37***	***19.40***
Extreme Maximum Daily Precip. (in.)	***2.00***	***1.24***	0.71	1.11	6.03	1.70	***1.96***	1.94	***1.23***	3.40	1.20	***1.12***	***6.03***
Days With ≥ 0.1" Precipitation	***3***	3	2	1	3	4	7	9	7	4	4	***4***	***51***
Days With ≥ 0.5" Precipitation	***0***	0	0	0	0	1	1	2	2	1	1	***1***	***9***
Days With ≥ 1.0" Precipitation	***0***	0	0	0	0	0	0	0	0	0	0	0	***0***
Mean Snowfall (in.)	***10.7***	***9.9***	7.8	2.1	0.2	0.0	0.0	0.0	0.1	4.1	11.5	***14.4***	***60.8***
Maximum Snow Depth (in.)	***39***	39	38	22	4	0	0	0	2	9	24	31	***39***
Days With ≥ 1.0" Snow Depth	***25***	25	26	11	0	0	0	0	0	6	18	24	***135***

Annette Island Arpt *Prince of Wales-Outer Ketchikan Borough* Elevation: 108 ft. Latitude: 55° 03' N Longitude: 131° 34' W

	JAN	FEB	MAR	APR	MAY	JUN	JUL	AUG	SEP	OCT	NOV	DEC	YEAR
Mean Maximum Temp. (°F)	41.3	42.6	44.9	50.1	56.3	61.2	64.1	64.6	59.2	51.6	44.8	41.4	51.8
Mean Temp. (°F)	36.7	37.7	39.6	44.2	50.1	55.2	58.5	58.9	53.8	46.8	40.2	37.0	46.6
Mean Minimum Temp. (°F)	32.0	32.7	34.4	38.3	44.0	49.2	52.9	53.1	48.4	42.0	35.6	32.7	41.3
Extreme Maximum Temp. (°F)	61	65	64	77	84	93	88	87	82	68	61	57	93
Extreme Minimum Temp. (°F)	1	5	11	28	32	40	43	41	33	18	-3	7	-3
Days Maximum Temp. ≥ 70°F	0	0	0	0	2	4	6	6	1	0	0	0	19
Days Maximum Temp. ≤ 32°F	4	1	1	0	0	0	0	0	0	0	1	3	10
Days Minimum Temp. ≤ 32°F	15	13	11	3	0	0	0	0	0	2	9	14	67
Days Minimum Temp. ≤ 0°F	0	0	0	0	0	0	0	0	0	0	0	0	0
Heating Degree Days (base 65°F)	871	766	780	616	455	291	200	192	329	555	738	859	6,652
Cooling Degree Days (base 65°F)	0	0	0	0	0	5	7	7	0	0	0	0	19
Mean Precipitation (in.)	10.56	7.34	7.90	7.18	5.63	4.64	4.75	6.97	9.63	13.80	12.51	10.99	101.90
Extreme Maximum Daily Precip. (in.)	3.47	3.80	2.56	3.06	2.59	2.35	2.11	3.28	3.25	5.48	2.95	4.01	5.48
Days With ≥ 0.1" Precipitation	17	13	16	13	11	10	9	11	14	19	19	17	169
Days With ≥ 0.5" Precipitation	8	5	5	5	4	3	4	5	7	10	9	8	73
Days With ≥ 1.0" Precipitation	3	2	2	2	1	1	1	2	3	5	4	3	29
Mean Snowfall (in.)	8.5	7.1	6.4	1.4	0.1	trace	0.0	0.0	0.0	0.1	3.4	7.8	34.8
Maximum Snow Depth (in.)	21	8	11	4	trace	trace	0	0	0	2	3	19	21
Days With ≥ 1.0" Snow Depth	6	4	2	0	0	0	0	0	0	0	1	4	17

Bethel Airport *Bethel Borough* Elevation: 125 ft. Latitude: 60° 47' N Longitude: 161° 50' W

	JAN	FEB	MAR	APR	MAY	JUN	JUL	AUG	SEP	OCT	NOV	DEC	YEAR
Mean Maximum Temp. (°F)	12.5	17.7	23.1	34.7	50.5	60.9	63.6	59.9	52.1	35.9	23.1	16.6	37.5
Mean Temp. (°F)	6.6	11.1	15.8	27.1	41.9	52.3	56.2	53.4	45.5	30.3	17.4	10.3	30.7
Mean Minimum Temp. (°F)	0.6	4.5	8.4	19.5	33.4	43.8	48.8	46.9	39.0	24.7	11.6	3.9	23.7
Extreme Maximum Temp. (°F)	47	46	46	63	80	84	85	87	69	60	51	49	87
Extreme Minimum Temp. (°F)	-48	-39	-29	-14	7	30	35	28	19	-6	-26	-37	-48
Days Maximum Temp. ≥ 70°F	0	0	0	0	1	4	7	3	0	0	0	0	15
Days Maximum Temp. ≤ 32°F	25	21	21	11	1	0	0	0	0	10	21	24	134
Days Minimum Temp. ≤ 32°F	31	27	30	27	14	0	0	0	6	25	28	30	218
Days Minimum Temp. ≤ 0°F	15	12	11	3	0	0	0	0	0	1	7	13	62
Heating Degree Days (base 65°F)	1,810	1,522	1,521	1,130	708	374	267	353	577	1,069	1,424	1,694	12,449
Cooling Degree Days (base 65°F)	0	0	0	0	0	1	2	1	0	0	0	0	4
Mean Precipitation (in.)	0.78	0.73	0.74	0.73	1.15	1.77	2.38	3.21	2.69	1.64	1.52	1.09	18.43
Extreme Maximum Daily Precip. (in.)	1.08	1.03	0.73	0.92	1.35	1.36	1.00	1.73	1.28	1.32	1.45	0.66	1.73
Days With ≥ 0.1" Precipitation	2	2	3	3	4	6	7	9	8	5	5	3	57
Days With ≥ 0.5" Precipitation	0	0	0	0	0	1	1	2	1	1	1	0	7
Days With ≥ 1.0" Precipitation	0	0	0	0	0	0	0	0	0	0	0	0	0
Mean Snowfall (in.)	8.9	7.9	8.9	5.5	2.0	0.0	trace	0.0	0.6	4.2	12.4	11.3	61.7
Maximum Snow Depth (in.)	25	28	29	31	5	trace	trace	0	3	7	19	24	31
Days With ≥ 1.0" Snow Depth	31	26	28	15	1	0	0	0	0	6	22	26	155

The period of record for all cooperative weather station data is 1980 – 2009. See User Guide for detailed explanation of data.

Bettles Field *Yukon-Koyukuk Borough* Elevation: 644 ft. Latitude: 66° 55' N Longitude: 151° 31' W

	JAN	FEB	MAR	APR	MAY	JUN	JUL	AUG	SEP	OCT	NOV	DEC	YEAR
Mean Maximum Temp. (°F)	-1.9	4.6	16.7	33.8	54.5	69.0	70.0	62.1	48.5	25.5	6.0	1.7	32.5
Mean Temp. (°F)	-9.8	-5.0	4.5	22.8	44.3	58.3	59.9	52.5	40.5	18.9	-1.1	-5.9	23.3
Mean Minimum Temp. (°F)	-17.7	-14.5	-7.6	11.6	34.2	47.5	49.7	42.9	32.3	12.2	-8.1	-13.5	14.1
Extreme Maximum Temp. (°F)	48	38	49	63	86	92	93	88	73	57	42	35	93
Extreme Minimum Temp. (°F)	-69	-64	-49	-37	-7	28	30	23	0	-35	-54	-55	-69
Days Maximum Temp. ≥ 70°F	0	0	0	0	3	14	17	5	0	0	0	0	39
Days Maximum Temp. ≤ 32°F	30	27	27	12	1	0	0	0	1	22	29	31	180
Days Minimum Temp. ≤ 32°F	31	27	31	28	13	0	0	3	15	30	30	31	239
Days Minimum Temp. ≤ 0°F	24	21	21	7	0	0	0	0	0	7	20	25	125
Heating Degree Days (base 65°F)	2,320	1,979	1,872	1,261	635	211	173	382	730	1,423	1,983	2,201	15,170
Cooling Degree Days (base 65°F)	0	0	0	0	1	16	20	3	0	0	0	0	40
Mean Precipitation (in.)	0.84	0.88	0.56	0.59	0.89	1.47	2.32	2.66	1.89	1.07	0.84	0.91	14.92
Extreme Maximum Daily Precip. (in.)	0.91	0.99	0.74	0.98	1.02	1.00	1.63	2.96	1.08	1.00	1.35	0.78	2.96
Days With ≥ 0.1" Precipitation	3	3	2	2	3	5	7	7	6	3	3	3	47
Days With ≥ 0.5" Precipitation	0	0	0	0	0	1	1	1	1	0	0	0	4
Days With ≥ 1.0" Precipitation	0	0	0	0	0	0	0	0	0	0	0	0	0
Mean Snowfall (in.)	13.6	14.0	9.6	6.3	1.3	trace	trace	trace	2.8	12.7	14.9	16.5	91.7
Maximum Snow Depth (in.)	59	48	57	47	34	trace	trace	trace	8	22	42	59	59
Days With ≥ 1.0" Snow Depth	31	27	31	30	10	0	0	0	2	24	30	31	216

Big Delta Allen AAF *Southeast Fairbanks Borough* Elevation: 1,268 ft. Latitude: 64° 00' N Longitude: 145° 43' W

	JAN	FEB	MAR	APR	MAY	JUN	JUL	AUG	SEP	OCT	NOV	DEC	YEAR
Mean Maximum Temp. (°F)	6.3	13.9	25.0	43.0	58.0	67.7	69.9	64.2	52.8	31.4	13.5	9.5	37.9
Mean Temp. (°F)	-0.8	5.4	14.5	32.7	48.0	57.9	60.6	55.0	44.1	24.5	6.6	2.5	29.2
Mean Minimum Temp. (°F)	-7.9	-3.0	4.1	22.3	37.9	48.0	51.2	45.8	35.4	17.6	-0.3	-4.5	20.5
Extreme Maximum Temp. (°F)	54	51	58	71	85	90	87	90	74	74	50	55	90
Extreme Minimum Temp. (°F)	-59	-51	-40	-27	11	26	35	23	-2	-31	-47	-50	-59
Days Maximum Temp. ≥ 70°F	0	0	0	0	3	12	16	8	0	0	0	0	39
Days Maximum Temp. ≤ 32°F	27	23	20	5	0	0	0	0	1	16	27	28	147
Days Minimum Temp. ≤ 32°F	30	27	29	24	7	0	0	1	10	27	29	30	214
Days Minimum Temp. ≤ 0°F	19	13	12	2	0	0	0	0	0	4	15	18	83
Heating Degree Days (base 65°F)	2,042	1,683	1,559	964	521	216	146	309	619	1,248	1,751	1,937	12,995
Cooling Degree Days (base 65°F)	0	0	0	0	1	10	15	7	0	0	0	0	33
Mean Precipitation (in.)	0.29	0.39	0.18	0.20	0.91	2.24	2.72	1.95	1.05	0.73	0.56	0.36	11.58
Extreme Maximum Daily Precip. (in.)	0.49	0.59	0.53	0.55	1.11	2.02	2.27	1.34	1.44	0.49	0.44	0.30	2.27
Days With ≥ 0.1" Precipitation	1	1	0	1	3	6	7	6	3	3	2	2	35
Days With ≥ 0.5" Precipitation	0	0	0	0	0	1	2	1	0	0	0	0	4
Days With ≥ 1.0" Precipitation	0	0	0	0	0	0	0	0	0	0	0	0	0
Mean Snowfall (in.)	na	na	na	na	na	na	na	na	na	na	na	na	na
Maximum Snow Depth (in.)	na	na	na	na	na	na	na	na	na	na	na	na	na
Days With ≥ 1.0" Snow Depth	na	na	na	na	na	na	na	na	na	na	na	na	na

Cannery Creek *Valdez-Cordova Borough* Elevation: 5 ft. Latitude: 61° 01' N Longitude: 147° 31' W

	JAN	FEB	MAR	APR	MAY	JUN	JUL	AUG	SEP	OCT	NOV	DEC	YEAR
Mean Maximum Temp. (°F)	28.9	31.6	37.2	44.3	53.1	60.2	62.1	60.8	53.6	43.3	32.8	30.0	44.8
Mean Temp. (°F)	24.3	26.1	29.9	36.3	43.8	51.6	55.0	53.8	47.4	38.2	28.6	26.1	38.4
Mean Minimum Temp. (°F)	19.6	20.5	22.5	28.3	34.5	43.0	47.8	46.7	41.1	33.0	24.4	22.1	32.0
Extreme Maximum Temp. (°F)	59	43	52	64	74	78	80	78	67	58	48	44	80
Extreme Minimum Temp. (°F)	-18	-11	-4	1	22	29	35	30	23	8	-8	-12	-18
Days Maximum Temp. ≥ 70°F	0	0	0	0	1	2	4	2	0	0	0	0	9
Days Maximum Temp. ≤ 32°F	16	11	4	0	0	0	0	0	0	1	10	14	56
Days Minimum Temp. ≤ 32°F	30	27	30	24	11	0	0	0	3	15	26	29	195
Days Minimum Temp. ≤ 0°F	2	2	0	0	0	0	0	0	0	0	0	1	5
Heating Degree Days (base 65°F)	1,256	1,093	1,081	854	650	395	305	341	523	825	1,085	1,200	9,608
Cooling Degree Days (base 65°F)	0	0	0	0	0	0	1	0	0	0	0	0	1
Mean Precipitation (in.)	10.71	9.23	7.04	6.26	6.69	5.61	7.78	14.47	16.17	14.65	9.11	13.16	120.88
Extreme Maximum Daily Precip. (in.)	4.04	5.03	3.50	2.61	3.00	4.20	3.35	5.62	4.32	5.30	5.00	5.57	5.62
Days With ≥ 0.1" Precipitation	15	12	12	11	13	11	13	14	18	17	13	16	165
Days With ≥ 0.5" Precipitation	7	6	4	4	5	4	5	9	10	10	6	9	79
Days With ≥ 1.0" Precipitation	3	3	2	2	1	1	2	5	6	5	3	4	37
Mean Snowfall (in.)	28.4	26.5	24.5	6.8	0.7	0.0	0.0	0.0	0.0	3.3	17.9	34.2	142.3
Maximum Snow Depth (in.)	78	79	92	83	62	8	0	0	0	29	40	58	92
Days With ≥ 1.0" Snow Depth	31	28	30	30	18	0	0	0	0	2	21	30	190

Cantwell 2 E *Denali Borough* Elevation: 2,149 ft. Latitude: 63° 24' N Longitude: 148° 54' W

	JAN	FEB	MAR	APR	MAY	JUN	JUL	AUG	SEP	OCT	NOV	DEC	YEAR
Mean Maximum Temp. (°F)	10.8	17.4	25.4	38.4	52.6	64.7	66.0	60.5	49.7	32.2	16.8	14.3	37.4
Mean Temp. (°F)	1.0	6.0	12.1	26.6	40.7	51.5	55.1	50.4	40.4	23.4	8.0	4.7	26.6
Mean Minimum Temp. (°F)	-8.8	-5.5	-1.3	14.6	28.7	38.2	44.2	40.3	30.9	14.5	-0.8	-5.0	15.8
Extreme Maximum Temp. (°F)	44	52	58	64	78	87	85	87	71	66	51	45	87
Extreme Minimum Temp. (°F)	-49	-47	-45	-32	6	0	28	13	-11	-29	-36	-47	-49
Days Maximum Temp. ≥ 70°F	0	0	0	0	1	9	10	4	0	0	0	0	24
Days Maximum Temp. ≤ 32°F	28	24	22	6	0	0	0	0	1	14	26	27	148
Days Minimum Temp. ≤ 32°F	31	28	31	29	22	7	2	5	17	29	30	31	262
Days Minimum Temp. ≤ 0°F	21	17	17	4	0	0	0	0	0	6	16	19	100
Heating Degree Days (base 65°F)	1,986	1,668	1,638	1,147	747	400	301	446	733	1,285	1,707	1,868	13,926
Cooling Degree Days (base 65°F)	0	0	0	0	0	0	1	1	0	0	0	0	2
Mean Precipitation (in.)	0.94	0.70	0.46	0.42	0.75	1.72	2.72	3.20	2.60	1.21	0.78	0.95	16.45
Extreme Maximum Daily Precip. (in.)	0.70	0.52	0.60	0.39	0.60	1.24	4.16	1.71	1.18	1.55	1.58	1.25	4.16
Days With ≥ 0.1" Precipitation	3	2	2	2	2	5	7	9	7	3	3	3	48
Days With ≥ 0.5" Precipitation	0	0	0	0	0	1	1	2	1	0	0	0	5
Days With ≥ 1.0" Precipitation	0	0	0	0	0	0	0	0	0	0	0	0	0
Mean Snowfall (in.)	21.6	15.6	12.5	10.5	5.3	0.2	0.3	trace	3.8	16.1	17.9	20.5	124.3
Maximum Snow Depth (in.)	79	80	64	51	26	trace	0	trace	5	18	35	72	80
Days With ≥ 1.0" Snow Depth	31	28	31	30	10	0	0	0	1	18	29	31	209

The period of record for all cooperative weather station data is 1980 – 2009. See User Guide for detailed explanation of data.

Chulitna River Lodge *Matanuska-Susitna Borough* Elevation: 1,399 ft. Latitude: 62° 49' N Longitude: 149° 54' W

	JAN	FEB	MAR	APR	MAY	JUN	JUL	AUG	SEP	OCT	NOV	DEC	YEAR
Mean Maximum Temp. (°F)	18.6	23.1	30.3	***41.4***	53.8	64.9	***66.1***	61.4	51.2	35.2	23.1	20.3	***40.8***
Mean Temp. (°F)	12.7	16.4	21.3	***31.7***	43.6	54.1	***56.8***	52.9	42.9	29.0	17.4	14.5	***32.8***
Mean Minimum Temp. (°F)	6.7	9.6	12.2	***22.0***	33.5	43.4	***47.6***	44.5	34.6	22.7	11.7	8.6	***24.8***
Extreme Maximum Temp. (°F)	43	45	52	64	78	86	***86***	86	72	72	49	44	***86***
Extreme Minimum Temp. (°F)	-34	-29	-24	-6	6	12	***35***	27	3	-9	-19	-36	***-36***
Days Maximum Temp. ≥ 70°F	0	0	0	0	1	9	***10***	5	0	0	0	0	***25***
Days Maximum Temp. ≤ 32°F	25	22	16	3	0	0	***0***	0	0	10	23	25	***124***
Days Minimum Temp. ≤ 32°F	29	27	29	25	13	1	***0***	0	9	24	27	28	***212***
Days Minimum Temp. ≤ 0°F	9	7	5	1	0	0	***0***	0	0	0	4	7	***33***
Heating Degree Days (base 65°F)	1,619	1,370	1,350	***992***	656	325	***249***	***368***	656	1,110	1,420	1,561	***11,676***
Cooling Degree Days (base 65°F)	0	0	0	***0***	0	3	***4***	***1***	0	0	0	0	***8***
Mean Precipitation (in.)	2.35	2.06	1.62	1.29	1.13	1.81	***3.93***	5.98	5.66	3.25	2.45	2.77	***34.30***
Extreme Maximum Daily Precip. (in.)	2.05	2.00	1.70	1.31	0.92	1.48	na	3.65	2.46	***4.03***	***2.27***	2.16	na
Days With ≥ 0.1" Precipitation	6	6	4	3	4	5	***8***	11	10	7	6	7	***77***
Days With ≥ 0.5" Precipitation	1	1	1	1	0	1	***2***	4	4	2	1	1	***19***
Days With ≥ 1.0" Precipitation	0	0	0	0	0	0	***1***	1	1	0	0	0	***3***
Mean Snowfall (in.)	33.7	29.8	23.9	14.3	2.1	trace	0.0	trace	2.3	19.3	34.4	36.2	196.0
Maximum Snow Depth (in.)	99	97	112	95	66	20	0	0	28	35	70	72	112
Days With ≥ 1.0" Snow Depth	29	27	30	28	17	0	0	0	1	17	27	30	206

Cold Bay Arpt *Aleutians East Borough* Elevation: 96 ft. Latitude: 55° 12' N Longitude: 162° 43' W

	JAN	FEB	MAR	APR	MAY	JUN	JUL	AUG	SEP	OCT	NOV	DEC	YEAR
Mean Maximum Temp. (°F)	32.8	33.7	35.5	39.1	45.6	51.3	55.5	56.5	52.8	45.5	39.1	35.7	43.6
Mean Temp. (°F)	28.1	29.0	30.6	34.2	40.4	46.4	51.0	52.1	48.0	40.5	34.6	31.3	38.8
Mean Minimum Temp. (°F)	23.4	24.3	25.6	29.3	35.1	41.4	46.5	47.7	43.2	35.4	30.0	26.7	34.1
Extreme Maximum Temp. (°F)	51	50	54	54	68	72	70	74	76	59	59	54	76
Extreme Minimum Temp. (°F)	-13	-5	-2	5	22	27	33	32	26	6	10	-1	-13
Days Maximum Temp. ≥ 70°F	0	0	0	0	0	0	0	0	0	0	0	0	0
Days Maximum Temp. ≤ 32°F	12	9	8	4	0	0	0	0	0	0	4	8	45
Days Minimum Temp. ≤ 32°F	24	22	24	20	8	0	0	0	1	9	19	21	148
Days Minimum Temp. ≤ 0°F	0	0	0	0	0	0	0	0	0	0	0	0	0
Heating Degree Days (base 65°F)	1,137	1,012	1,061	917	755	552	427	392	502	753	904	1,039	9,451
Cooling Degree Days (base 65°F)	0	0	0	0	0	0	0	0	0	0	0	0	0
Mean Precipitation (in.)	3.25	3.00	2.74	2.36	2.70	2.79	2.48	3.70	4.82	4.78	4.91	4.44	41.97
Extreme Maximum Daily Precip. (in.)	2.85	2.75	2.29	2.16	1.90	2.92	1.77	1.97	2.12	2.74	3.78	3.63	3.78
Days With ≥ 0.1" Precipitation	9	8	8	6	7	8	7	10	12	13	13	12	113
Days With ≥ 0.5" Precipitation	1	1	1	1	1	1	1	2	3	2	3	2	19
Days With ≥ 1.0" Precipitation	0	0	0	0	0	0	0	1	1	1	1	1	5
Mean Snowfall (in.)	14.9	12.8	12.9	6.4	1.3	trace	0.0	trace	trace	2.7	10.1	13.1	74.2
Maximum Snow Depth (in.)	46	35	32	28	2	trace	0	trace	trace	11	11	23	46
Days With ≥ 1.0" Snow Depth	17	14	12	5	0	0	0	0	0	1	9	13	71

College Observatory *Fairbanks North Star Borough* Elevation: 621 ft. Latitude: 64° 52' N Longitude: 147° 50' W

	JAN	FEB	MAR	APR	MAY	JUN	JUL	AUG	SEP	OCT	NOV	DEC	YEAR
Mean Maximum Temp. (°F)	3.3	11.6	26.2	43.5	60.5	71.0	72.5	65.5	53.6	31.7	12.0	6.4	38.1
Mean Temp. (°F)	-4.0	2.4	14.3	31.9	48.4	59.3	61.7	55.1	43.6	24.0	5.0	-0.8	28.4
Mean Minimum Temp. (°F)	-11.2	-6.7	2.5	20.2	36.3	47.6	50.7	44.7	33.5	16.3	-1.9	-8.0	18.7
Extreme Maximum Temp. (°F)	52	49	57	71	86	94	92	93	77	71	47	44	94
Extreme Minimum Temp. (°F)	-55	-52	-35	-24	9	27	35	24	5	-23	-45	-47	-55
Days Maximum Temp. ≥ 70°F	0	0	0	0	5	17	21	9	1	0	0	0	53
Days Maximum Temp. ≤ 32°F	29	25	20	5	0	0	0	0	1	16	28	28	152
Days Minimum Temp. ≤ 32°F	30	28	31	27	10	0	0	1	13	29	30	30	229
Days Minimum Temp. ≤ 0°F	21	18	13	2	0	0	0	0	0	4	17	22	97
Heating Degree Days (base 65°F)	2,138	1,767	1,566	987	508	185	125	306	636	1,263	1,797	2,040	13,318
Cooling Degree Days (base 65°F)	0	0	0	0	1	21	29	7	0	0	0	0	58
Mean Precipitation (in.)	0.64	0.50	0.33	0.30	0.63	1.75	2.30	2.00	1.33	0.92	0.73	0.74	12.17
Extreme Maximum Daily Precip. (in.)	0.84	0.71	1.21	0.75	0.70	1.18	1.77	1.23	0.99	1.20	0.54	0.84	1.77
Days With ≥ 0.1" Precipitation	2	2	1	1	2	5	6	6	4	3	2	2	36
Days With ≥ 0.5" Precipitation	0	0	0	0	0	1	1	1	0	0	0	0	3
Days With ≥ 1.0" Precipitation	0	0	0	0	0	0	0	0	0	0	0	0	0
Mean Snowfall (in.)	10.3	7.6	5.2	3.0	0.7	trace	trace	0.0	1.7	11.3	13.0	12.2	65.0
Maximum Snow Depth (in.)	48	39	52	49	18	trace	trace	0	10	18	24	42	52
Days With ≥ 1.0" Snow Depth	31	28	31	23	2	0	0	0	1	19	30	30	195

Cooper Landing 6 W *Kenai Peninsula Borough* Elevation: 375 ft. Latitude: 60° 29' N Longitude: 149° 58' W

	JAN	FEB	MAR	APR	MAY	JUN	JUL	AUG	SEP	OCT	NOV	DEC	YEAR
Mean Maximum Temp. (°F)	24.2	***29.9***	37.2	47.1	57.8	65.8	68.3	66.0	56.6	42.7	30.3	26.9	***46.1***
Mean Temp. (°F)	16.0	***20.7***	26.2	36.2	45.4	53.1	57.1	54.6	46.4	34.0	22.3	19.3	***35.9***
Mean Minimum Temp. (°F)	7.8	***11.5***	15.2	25.2	32.9	40.3	45.9	43.1	36.2	25.4	14.2	11.8	***25.8***
Extreme Maximum Temp. (°F)	58	51	52	74	83	89	90	89	74	67	55	55	90
Extreme Minimum Temp. (°F)	-40	-34	-27	-11	18	26	29	23	6	-10	-19	-26	-40
Days Maximum Temp. ≥ 70°F	0	0	0	0	2	9	12	9	0	0	0	0	32
Days Maximum Temp. ≤ 32°F	18	12	7	1	0	0	0	0	0	3	14	16	71
Days Minimum Temp. ≤ 32°F	27	24	27	23	16	4	0	2	10	22	25	26	206
Days Minimum Temp. ≤ 0°F	10	7	6	0	0	0	0	0	0	1	5	7	36
Heating Degree Days (base 65°F)	1,513	***1,247***	1,194	858	601	352	241	318	551	953	1,277	1,411	***10,516***
Cooling Degree Days (base 65°F)	0	0	0	0	0	0	3	1	0	0	0	0	4
Mean Precipitation (in.)	na	na	***0.57***	0.82	0.61	0.76	1.74	2.40	3.02	3.03	***2.18***	na	na
Extreme Maximum Daily Precip. (in.)	na	na	na	na	na	na	na	na	na	na	na	na	na
Days With ≥ 0.1" Precipitation	***1***	***2***	***1***	1	1	2	3	4	4	3	***1***	1	***24***
Days With ≥ 0.5" Precipitation	***0***	***1***	***0***	0	0	0	1	1	1	1	***1***	0	***6***
Days With ≥ 1.0" Precipitation	***0***	***0***	***0***	0	0	0	0	0	1	0	***0***	0	***1***
Mean Snowfall (in.)	***8.1***	***8.0***	8.0	3.2	0.1	0.0	0.0	0.0	0.1	4.4	***6.4***	***9.9***	***48.2***
Maximum Snow Depth (in.)	46	***44***	***60***	32	2	0	0	0	2	12	18	42	***60***
Days With ≥ 1.0" Snow Depth	19	***21***	***20***	6	0	0	0	0	0	4	15	19	***104***

The period of record for all cooperative weather station data is 1980 – 2009. See User Guide for detailed explanation of data.

Cordova *Valdez-Cordova Borough* Elevation: 41 ft. Latitude: 60° 30' N Longitude: 145° 30' W

	JAN	FEB	MAR	APR	MAY	JUN	JUL	AUG	SEP	OCT	NOV	DEC	YEAR
Mean Maximum Temp. (°F)	33.4	35.9	39.4	46.4	53.9	59.2	61.6	61.8	56.2	47.0	37.4	34.5	47.2
Mean Temp. (°F)	26.4	28.3	31.2	38.1	45.4	51.4	54.6	53.9	48.2	39.8	30.5	28.1	39.7
Mean Minimum Temp. (°F)	19.3	20.6	23.0	29.6	36.9	43.5	47.6	46.0	40.2	32.6	23.6	21.6	32.0
Extreme Maximum Temp. (°F)	55	58	57	74	78	84	89	85	74	63	54	53	89
Extreme Minimum Temp. (°F)	-22	-23	-8	-2	22	31	34	29	21	5	-10	-16	-23
Days Maximum Temp. ≥ 70°F	0	0	0	0	1	3	3	3	0	0	0	0	10
Days Maximum Temp. ≤ 32°F	12	8	3	0	0	0	0	0	0	0	7	10	40
Days Minimum Temp. ≤ 32°F	24	22	24	19	7	0	0	0	5	15	22	24	162
Days Minimum Temp. ≤ 0°F	4	3	1	0	0	0	0	0	0	0	1	2	11
Heating Degree Days (base 65°F)	1,190	1,031	1,040	802	599	402	316	337	498	774	1,027	1,138	9,154
Cooling Degree Days (base 65°F)	0	0	0	0	0	0	1	0	0	0	0	0	1
Mean Precipitation (in.)	7.50	6.27	5.24	4.59	5.62	4.94	5.69	10.04	13.78	11.39	7.04	9.27	91.37
Extreme Maximum Daily Precip. (in.)	2.93	3.05	3.60	2.77	2.61	2.85	3.41	7.61	6.20	6.56	3.59	4.80	7.61
Days With ≥ 0.1" Precipitation	12	11	10	10	12	11	12	14	17	16	12	14	151
Days With ≥ 0.5" Precipitation	5	4	3	3	4	3	4	6	9	8	5	6	60
Days With ≥ 1.0" Precipitation	2	2	1	1	1	1	1	3	5	3	2	3	25
Mean Snowfall (in.)	na	***17.6***	***20.2***	***4.7***	***0.8***	***trace***	na	***trace***	***trace***	na	na	***23.5***	na
Maximum Snow Depth (in.)	***41***	***36***	***36***	***28***	na	***trace***	na	na	***4***	***10***	na	***27***	na
Days With ≥ 1.0" Snow Depth	***21***	***22***	***23***	***9***	***0***	***0***	***0***	***0***	***0***	***1***	na	20	na

Dutch Harbor *Aleutians West Borough* Elevation: 12 ft. Latitude: 53° 54' N Longitude: 166° 32' W

	JAN	FEB	MAR	APR	MAY	JUN	JUL	AUG	SEP	OCT	NOV	DEC	YEAR
Mean Maximum Temp. (°F)	37.0	37.8	***39.1***	***41.2***	46.3	51.8	56.9	58.9	54.2	47.6	***42.9***	***39.5***	***46.1***
Mean Temp. (°F)	32.2	***32.8***	***33.8***	***36.4***	41.5	46.8	51.4	53.1	48.7	42.3	***37.4***	***35.0***	***41.0***
Mean Minimum Temp. (°F)	27.4	***27.7***	***28.5***	***31.4***	36.6	41.8	45.9	47.3	43.2	37.0	***31.9***	***30.4***	***35.8***
Extreme Maximum Temp. (°F)	53	54	***61***	58	60	73	75	81	74	65	57	***59***	***81***
Extreme Minimum Temp. (°F)	-8	0	***2***	-5	15	30	21	30	19	11	8	***5***	***-8***
Days Maximum Temp. ≥ 70°F	0	0	***0***	0	0	0	1	1	0	0	0	***0***	***2***
Days Maximum Temp. ≤ 32°F	7	5	***4***	1	0	0	0	0	0	0	1	***3***	***21***
Days Minimum Temp. ≤ 32°F	22	20	***22***	16	5	0	0	0	1	5	14	***18***	***123***
Days Minimum Temp. ≤ 0°F	0	0	***0***	0	0	0	0	0	0	0	0	***0***	***0***
Heating Degree Days (base 65°F)	1,010	***903***	***962***	***851***	722	539	414	362	483	696	***821***	***924***	***8,687***
Cooling Degree Days (base 65°F)	0	***0***	***0***	***0***	0	0	0	1	0	0	***0***	***0***	***1***
Mean Precipitation (in.)	***7.78***	***6.71***	***5.50***	3.40	3.73	2.35	2.28	2.78	5.46	6.83	***7.23***	***8.26***	***62.31***
Extreme Maximum Daily Precip. (in.)	***4.00***	***3.40***	***2.30***	***1.94***	***3.62***	***2.03***	***4.80***	***2.22***	***2.00***	***3.26***	***4.10***	***3.00***	***4.80***
Days With ≥ 0.1" Precipitation	14	***13***	***11***	8	8	6	6	7	11	13	13	***15***	***125***
Days With ≥ 0.5" Precipitation	5	***4***	***3***	2	2	1	1	1	3	4	4	***5***	***35***
Days With ≥ 1.0" Precipitation	2	***2***	***1***	0	1	0	0	0	1	2	2	***3***	***14***
Mean Snowfall (in.)	24.9	***22.5***	***15.0***	6.0	0.2	0.0	0.0	0.0	0.0	0.6	***5.9***	***17.3***	***92.4***
Maximum Snow Depth (in.)	***55***	***58***	***54***	32	2	0	0	0	0	2	***9***	na	na
Days With ≥ 1.0" Snow Depth	***17***	***16***	***14***	7	0	0	0	0	0	1	***5***	***12***	***72***

Eagle *Southeast Fairbanks Borough* Elevation: 850 ft. Latitude: 64° 47' N Longitude: 141° 12' W

	JAN	FEB	MAR	APR	MAY	JUN	JUL	AUG	SEP	OCT	NOV	DEC	YEAR
Mean Maximum Temp. (°F)	-1.4	6.9	22.0	42.9	59.7	71.4	72.9	66.0	53.2	31.7	10.3	4.0	36.6
Mean Temp. (°F)	-9.8	-4.0	7.2	28.9	46.3	58.0	60.4	53.6	41.7	23.2	2.5	-4.2	25.3
Mean Minimum Temp. (°F)	-18.0	-14.8	-7.4	14.8	32.8	44.6	47.9	41.2	30.1	14.7	-5.2	-12.3	14.0
Extreme Maximum Temp. (°F)	50	49	53	74	87	95	92	92	77	69	47	47	95
Extreme Minimum Temp. (°F)	-68	-62	-52	-29	5	25	29	19	-7	-37	-48	-59	-68
Days Maximum Temp. ≥ 70°F	0	0	0	0	5	18	21	10	1	0	0	0	55
Days Maximum Temp. ≤ 32°F	29	26	22	6	0	0	0	0	1	15	28	29	156
Days Minimum Temp. ≤ 32°F	31	28	31	28	16	1	0	4	19	30	30	31	249
Days Minimum Temp. ≤ 0°F	24	21	20	5	0	0	0	0	0	5	18	23	116
Heating Degree Days (base 65°F)	2,322	1,949	1,789	1,076	574	216	153	349	693	1,289	1,874	2,150	14,434
Cooling Degree Days (base 65°F)	0	0	0	0	1	13	17	4	0	0	0	0	35
Mean Precipitation (in.)	0.52	0.48	0.38	0.25	1.14	1.65	2.38	1.92	1.29	0.96	0.72	0.69	12.38
Extreme Maximum Daily Precip. (in.)	0.42	0.50	0.57	0.37	1.38	1.36	1.67	1.86	1.45	0.77	0.66	0.44	1.86
Days With ≥ 0.1" Precipitation	2	2	2	1	4	6	8	6	5	4	3	3	46
Days With ≥ 0.5" Precipitation	0	0	0	0	0	0	1	1	0	0	0	0	2
Days With ≥ 1.0" Precipitation	0	0	0	0	0	0	0	0	0	0	0	0	0
Mean Snowfall (in.)	8.2	8.0	6.2	3.0	1.1	trace	0.0	trace	1.4	10.6	12.1	11.8	62.4
Maximum Snow Depth (in.)	28	28	36	32	17	trace	0	trace	6	16	19	25	36
Days With ≥ 1.0" Snow Depth	30	28	31	25	2	0	0	0	2	19	30	31	198

Eielson Field *Fairbanks North Star Borough* Elevation: 546 ft. Latitude: 64° 40' N Longitude: 147° 06' W

	JAN	FEB	MAR	APR	MAY	JUN	JUL	AUG	SEP	OCT	NOV	DEC	YEAR
Mean Maximum Temp. (°F)	0.7	9.9	26.1	44.0	60.1	70.1	71.6	65.0	54.0	31.5	8.2	3.1	37.0
Mean Temp. (°F)	-7.3	0.0	13.6	32.9	49.3	59.6	62.0	55.8	44.7	24.4	1.2	-4.6	27.6
Mean Minimum Temp. (°F)	-15.3	-9.9	0.8	21.7	38.4	49.0	52.3	46.5	35.4	17.2	-5.8	-12.2	18.2
Extreme Maximum Temp. (°F)	52	50	56	75	84	92	92	91	79	75	49	48	92
Extreme Minimum Temp. (°F)	-60	-54	-44	-23	9	27	34	22	5	-28	-45	-50	-60
Days Maximum Temp. ≥ 70°F	0	0	0	0	5	16	20	9	1	0	0	0	51
Days Maximum Temp. ≤ 32°F	28	25	21	5	0	0	0	0	0	16	27	28	150
Days Minimum Temp. ≤ 32°F	30	28	30	26	6	0	0	1	10	28	29	29	217
Days Minimum Temp. ≤ 0°F	24	20	15	2	0	0	0	0	0	4	20	23	108
Heating Degree Days (base 65°F)	2,248	1,836	1,590	957	481	175	111	286	602	1,252	1,911	2,170	13,619
Cooling Degree Days (base 65°F)	0	0	0	0	1	19	24	6	0	0	0	0	50
Mean Precipitation (in.)	0.37	0.32	0.28	0.23	0.73	1.87	2.52	2.50	1.29	0.82	0.54	0.49	11.96
Extreme Maximum Daily Precip. (in.)	0.37	0.73	7.00	0.58	0.98	1.48	***1.67***	1.79	1.12	1.04	1.40	***0.90***	***7.00***
Days With ≥ 0.1" Precipitation	1	1	1	1	2	5	6	7	4	2	2	1	33
Days With ≥ 0.5" Precipitation	0	0	0	0	0	1	1	1	0	0	0	0	3
Days With ≥ 1.0" Precipitation	0	0	0	0	0	0	0	0	0	0	0	0	0
Mean Snowfall (in.)	10.5	7.3	6.0	3.2	1.2	trace	trace	trace	2.0	***11.8***	14.1	12.2	***68.3***
Maximum Snow Depth (in.)	42	35	41	35	6	trace	***0***	trace	10	12	24	42	***42***
Days With ≥ 1.0" Snow Depth	30	28	30	14	0	0	***0***	0	1	16	29	30	***178***

The period of record for all cooperative weather station data is 1980 – 2009. See User Guide for detailed explanation of data.

Elfin Cove *Skagway-Hoonah-Angoon Borough* Elevation: 20 ft. Latitude: 58° 12' N Longitude: 136° 40' W

	JAN	FEB	MAR	APR	MAY	JUN	JUL	AUG	SEP	OCT	NOV	DEC	YEAR
Mean Maximum Temp. (°F)	35.8	37.3	40.0	45.9	51.6	55.8	58.1	59.2	55.4	***47.7***	39.8	37.1	***47.0***
Mean Temp. (°F)	32.7	33.9	35.8	40.7	46.3	51.0	54.1	54.7	51.1	***44.0***	36.7	34.2	***42.9***
Mean Minimum Temp. (°F)	29.6	30.4	31.6	35.5	41.0	46.3	50.0	50.2	46.7	***40.3***	33.6	31.2	***38.9***
Extreme Maximum Temp. (°F)	50	57	56	69	74	80	81	86	74	64	54	50	86
Extreme Minimum Temp. (°F)	1	7	9	20	31	35	40	39	30	20	5	8	1
Days Maximum Temp. ≥ 70°F	0	0	0	0	0	1	1	1	0	0	0	0	3
Days Maximum Temp. ≤ 32°F	8	5	2	0	0	0	0	0	0	0	3	6	24
Days Minimum Temp. ≤ 32°F	18	16	16	7	0	0	0	0	0	2	11	16	86
Days Minimum Temp. ≤ 0°F	0	0	0	0	0	0	0	0	0	0	0	0	0
Heating Degree Days (base 65°F)	994	873	897	721	572	412	333	313	411	***642***	841	949	***7,958***
Cooling Degree Days (base 65°F)	0	0	0	0	0	0	0	1	0	***0***	0	0	***1***
Mean Precipitation (in.)	10.56	7.89	7.69	5.88	4.58	3.25	4.50	7.24	12.68	15.47	12.00	11.40	103.14
Extreme Maximum Daily Precip. (in.)	3.30	4.56	2.51	2.98	2.32	1.85	1.75	3.26	8.61	***7.20***	6.36	3.60	***8.61***
Days With ≥ 0.1" Precipitation	18	14	15	13	11	10	12	14	18	19	18	18	180
Days With ≥ 0.5" Precipitation	7	6	5	3	3	1	2	5	10	10	9	8	69
Days With ≥ 1.0" Precipitation	3	2	2	1	1	0	0	2	4	4	3	3	25
Mean Snowfall (in.)	31.5	21.8	17.4	2.0	trace	0.0	0.0	0.0	trace	1.4	15.5	20.5	110.1
Maximum Snow Depth (in.)	56	60	62	53	trace	0	0	0	trace	10	56	40	62
Days With ≥ 1.0" Snow Depth	21	19	15	3	0	0	0	0	0	0	7	15	80

Glacier Bay *Skagway-Hoonah-Angoon Borough* Elevation: 49 ft. Latitude: 58° 27' N Longitude: 135° 53' W

	JAN	FEB	MAR	APR	MAY	JUN	JUL	AUG	SEP	OCT	NOV	DEC	YEAR
Mean Maximum Temp. (°F)	32.9	***34.8***	***38.8***	47.6	56.1	***61.4***	***63.6***	***62.2***	55.0	***46.6***	***37.8***	34.6	***47.6***
Mean Temp. (°F)	28.6	***29.9***	***33.1***	39.8	47.1	***52.6***	***55.3***	***54.4***	48.6	***41.2***	***33.3***	30.4	***41.2***
Mean Minimum Temp. (°F)	24.2	***24.9***	***27.3***	32.0	38.2	***43.8***	***47.0***	***46.5***	42.2	35.9	***28.7***	26.2	***34.7***
Extreme Maximum Temp. (°F)	56	49	54	73	77	***82***	81	81	71	64	***52***	53	***82***
Extreme Minimum Temp. (°F)	-8	-4	-5	3	8	***30***	37	38	25	5	***0***	-3	***-8***
Days Maximum Temp. ≥ 70°F	0	0	0	0	0	***3***	4	3	0	0	***0***	0	***10***
Days Maximum Temp. ≤ 32°F	11	7	3	0	0	***0***	0	0	0	0	***4***	9	***34***
Days Minimum Temp. ≤ 32°F	25	23	24	14	2	***0***	0	0	1	7	***18***	25	***139***
Days Minimum Temp. ≤ 0°F	0	0	0	0	0	***0***	0	0	0	0	***0***	0	***0***
Heating Degree Days (base 65°F)	1,120	***985***	***981***	750	548	***365***	***292***	***324***	484	***730***	***946***	1,065	***8,590***
Cooling Degree Days (base 65°F)	0	***0***	***0***	0	0	***0***	***0***	***0***	0	***0***	***0***	0	***0***
Mean Precipitation (in.)	6.59	***4.54***	3.75	2.76	3.45	***2.62***	3.78	5.86	10.06	11.29	***7.77***	7.59	***70.06***
Extreme Maximum Daily Precip. (in.)	2.30	***3.16***	na	***1.73***	na	***1.25***	***1.95***	na	***3.00***	na	na	***2.77***	na
Days With ≥ 0.1" Precipitation	13	9	10	8	9	***8***	9	11	15	17	***14***	13	***136***
Days With ≥ 0.5" Precipitation	4	2	2	1	1	***1***	2	3	6	7	***4***	5	***38***
Days With ≥ 1.0" Precipitation	1	1	0	0	0	***0***	1	1	3	3	***1***	1	***12***
Mean Snowfall (in.)	***33.2***	***23.1***	***15.1***	1.0	trace	***0.0***	0.0	0.0	0.0	1.0	na	22.0	na
Maximum Snow Depth (in.)	50	***62***	***80***	60	24	***0***	0	0	0	***13***	***40***	45	***80***
Days With ≥ 1.0" Snow Depth	26	***25***	26	13	1	***0***	0	0	0	1	***8***	22	***122***

Glen Alps *Anchorage Borough* Elevation: 2,259 ft. Latitude: 61° 06' N Longitude: 149° 41' W

	JAN	FEB	MAR	APR	MAY	JUN	JUL	AUG	SEP	OCT	NOV	DEC	YEAR
Mean Maximum Temp. (°F)	25.4	27.1	30.2	37.6	48.1	56.4	58.8	57.1	49.0	37.1	28.7	27.0	40.2
Mean Temp. (°F)	19.1	20.5	23.1	31.1	41.2	48.9	52.5	50.8	43.1	31.2	22.5	20.9	33.7
Mean Minimum Temp. (°F)	12.8	13.9	16.0	24.5	34.2	41.4	46.1	44.4	37.0	25.4	16.3	14.8	27.2
Extreme Maximum Temp. (°F)	52	55	55	63	71	76	76	84	65	56	51	46	84
Extreme Minimum Temp. (°F)	-37	-34	-15	-7	16	31	37	28	9	-4	-19	-22	-37
Days Maximum Temp. ≥ 70°F	0	0	0	0	0	1	2	1	0	0	0	0	4
Days Maximum Temp. ≤ 32°F	19	17	17	5	0	0	0	0	0	8	17	20	103
Days Minimum Temp. ≤ 32°F	31	28	31	27	12	0	0	0	6	24	29	30	218
Days Minimum Temp. ≤ 0°F	7	5	3	1	0	0	0	0	0	0	3	4	23
Heating Degree Days (base 65°F)	1,417	1,252	1,292	1,011	732	475	382	434	651	1,039	1,268	1,360	11,313
Cooling Degree Days (base 65°F)	0	0	0	0	0	0	1	0	0	0	0	0	1
Mean Precipitation (in.)	2.03	1.82	1.65	1.23	1.09	1.29	2.29	3.58	3.92	3.03	2.16	2.61	26.70
Extreme Maximum Daily Precip. (in.)	1.07	1.43	0.97	1.48	0.62	1.63	1.96	3.45	2.14	1.58	1.19	1.30	3.45
Days With ≥ 0.1" Precipitation	6	5	5	3	3	4	6	8	9	8	6	8	71
Days With ≥ 0.5" Precipitation	1	1	0	0	0	0	1	2	2	1	1	1	10
Days With ≥ 1.0" Precipitation	0	0	0	0	0	0	0	0	1	0	0	0	1
Mean Snowfall (in.)	24.7	24.1	23.7	13.5	3.1	trace	0.0	0.0	1.4	17.3	25.7	34.4	167.9
Maximum Snow Depth (in.)	88	***93***	***106***	***96***	57	trace	0	0	3	***26***	na	***85***	na
Days With ≥ 1.0" Snow Depth	31	***27***	***31***	***29***	10	0	0	0	1	***14***	na	***29***	na

Gulkana Intermediate Field *Valdez-Cordova Borough* Elevation: 1,569 ft. Latitude: 62° 09' N Longitude: 145° 27' W

	JAN	FEB	MAR	APR	MAY	JUN	JUL	AUG	SEP	OCT	NOV	DEC	YEAR
Mean Maximum Temp. (°F)	5.1	15.6	28.2	43.2	56.9	66.5	68.7	64.6	53.5	34.8	13.7	7.9	38.2
Mean Temp. (°F)	-2.8	5.7	15.7	31.8	45.2	54.5	57.7	53.5	43.3	26.7	5.9	0.2	28.1
Mean Minimum Temp. (°F)	-10.6	-4.3	3.1	20.4	33.4	42.4	46.6	42.3	33.1	18.6	-1.8	-7.6	18.0
Extreme Maximum Temp. (°F)	48	43	50	70	79	89	86	86	74	69	43	49	89
Extreme Minimum Temp. (°F)	-53	-50	-35	-27	17	26	29	20	2	-23	-44	-51	-53
Days Maximum Temp. ≥ 70°F	0	0	0	0	2	10	13	7	0	0	0	0	32
Days Maximum Temp. ≤ 32°F	28	24	18	3	0	0	0	0	1	12	27	28	141
Days Minimum Temp. ≤ 32°F	31	28	31	27	15	1	0	4	14	27	30	31	239
Days Minimum Temp. ≤ 0°F	22	18	14	2	0	0	0	0	0	3	17	22	98
Heating Degree Days (base 65°F)	2,102	1,675	1,525	989	608	311	224	352	644	1,181	1,769	2,009	13,389
Cooling Degree Days (base 65°F)	0	0	0	0	0	2	3	1	0	0	0	0	6
Mean Precipitation (in.)	0.49	0.49	0.31	0.24	0.65	1.38	1.82	1.83	1.55	1.02	0.69	0.78	11.25
Extreme Maximum Daily Precip. (in.)	0.54	0.61	0.56	0.61	1.51	1.07	1.10	1.22	1.40	0.76	0.96	0.86	1.51
Days With ≥ 0.1" Precipitation	2	2	1	1	2	4	5	6	5	4	2	2	36
Days With ≥ 0.5" Precipitation	0	0	0	0	0	0	1	1	0	0	0	0	2
Days With ≥ 1.0" Precipitation	0	0	0	0	0	0	0	0	0	0	0	0	0
Mean Snowfall (in.)	na	na	na	na	na	na	na	na	na	na	na	na	na
Maximum Snow Depth (in.)	na	na	na	na	na	na	na	na	na	na	na	na	na
Days With ≥ 1.0" Snow Depth	na	na	na	na	na	na	na	na	na	na	na	na	na

The period of record for all cooperative weather station data is 1980 – 2009. See User Guide for detailed explanation of data.

Hayes River *Matanuska-Susitna Borough* Elevation: 1,000 ft. Latitude: 61° 59' N Longitude: 152° 05' W

	JAN	FEB	MAR	APR	MAY	JUN	JUL	AUG	SEP	OCT	NOV	DEC	YEAR
Mean Maximum Temp. (°F)	21.7	26.3	31.6	41.6	52.2	65.3	67.8	64.1	54.0	38.5	26.4	21.8	42.6
Mean Temp. (°F)	14.2	17.1	21.0	31.7	41.8	53.7	57.8	54.6	45.1	30.5	18.7	14.5	33.4
Mean Minimum Temp. (°F)	6.6	7.9	10.3	21.7	31.4	41.9	47.7	44.9	36.1	22.5	10.8	7.1	24.1
Extreme Maximum Temp. (°F)	49	53	52	70	81	89	87	85	76	58	44	40	89
Extreme Minimum Temp. (°F)	-34	-32	-26	-20	-5	0	35	26	7	-9	-23	-29	-34
Days Maximum Temp. ≥ 70°F	0	0	0	0	1	9	13	7	0	0	0	0	30
Days Maximum Temp. ≤ 32°F	25	20	13	3	1	0	0	0	0	6	22	26	116
Days Minimum Temp. ≤ 32°F	30	28	30	27	16	1	0	1	8	28	29	30	228
Days Minimum Temp. ≤ 0°F	10	8	7	1	1	0	0	0	0	1	6	10	44
Heating Degree Days (base 65°F)	1,570	1,349	1,359	992	713	335	221	318	589	1,061	1,384	1,561	11,452
Cooling Degree Days (base 65°F)	0	0	0	0	0	3	5	1	0	0	0	0	9
Mean Precipitation (in.)	3.99	3.04	1.58	1.86	2.58	1.59	2.36	3.63	4.59	3.23	2.96	4.62	36.03
Extreme Maximum Daily Precip. (in.)	3.07	3.20	2.83	3.50	9.30	1.10	1.13	1.50	2.83	2.60	2.50	4.09	9.30
Days With ≥ 0.1" Precipitation	8	6	4	4	4	4	7	9	10	8	7	9	80
Days With ≥ 0.5" Precipitation	2	2	1	1	1	1	1	2	3	2	2	3	21
Days With ≥ 1.0" Precipitation	1	1	0	0	0	0	0	0	1	1	1	1	6
Mean Snowfall (in.)	46.5	31.6	21.5	12.1	1.5	0.0	0.0	0.0	0.6	10.6	34.5	48.7	207.6
Maximum Snow Depth (in.)	117	115	109	106	76	14	0	0	16	24	56	70	117
Days With ≥ 1.0" Snow Depth	30	28	30	29	18	0	0	0	1	12	26	30	204

Healy 2 NW *Denali Borough* Elevation: 1,490 ft. Latitude: 63° 53' N Longitude: 149° 01' W

	JAN	FEB	MAR	APR	MAY	JUN	JUL	AUG	SEP	OCT	NOV	DEC	YEAR
Mean Maximum Temp. (°F)	12.7	18.4	27.4	41.7	57.1	68.3	69.5	63.4	52.2	33.1	17.5	15.0	39.7
Mean Temp. (°F)	3.6	8.1	16.2	31.3	46.4	56.7	59.7	54.4	43.5	25.4	9.2	5.5	30.0
Mean Minimum Temp. (°F)	-5.5	-2.2	5.0	20.9	35.7	45.1	49.8	45.3	34.9	17.2	0.8	-4.0	20.3
Extreme Maximum Temp. (°F)	52	53	55	69	85	93	90	90	74	71	54	51	93
Extreme Minimum Temp. (°F)	-52	-51	-40	-25	4	27	32	20	-2	-20	-41	-44	-52
Days Maximum Temp. ≥ 70°F	0	0	0	0	2	12	16	6	0	0	0	0	36
Days Maximum Temp. ≤ 32°F	20	18	18	5	0	0	0	0	1	14	21	21	118
Days Minimum Temp. ≤ 32°F	28	26	29	23	10	0	0	1	12	25	28	28	210
Days Minimum Temp. ≤ 0°F	18	15	13	3	0	0	0	0	0	4	16	18	87
Heating Degree Days (base 65°F)	1,907	1,615	1,506	1,004	568	248	170	328	637	1,221	1,672	1,848	12,724
Cooling Degree Days (base 65°F)	0	0	0	0	0	7	13	7	0	0	0	0	27
Mean Precipitation (in.)	0.57	0.54	0.34	0.58	0.90	2.16	2.85	2.58	1.60	1.19	0.73	0.83	14.87
Extreme Maximum Daily Precip. (in.)	0.63	na	0.47	na	na	na	1.41	na	1.32	na	1.12	0.98	na
Days With ≥ 0.1" Precipitation	2	1	1	1	3	6	7	7	5	3	3	3	42
Days With ≥ 0.5" Precipitation	0	0	0	0	0	1	2	1	1	0	0	0	5
Days With ≥ 1.0" Precipitation	0	0	0	0	0	0	0	0	0	0	0	0	0
Mean Snowfall (in.)	10.4	7.8	7.1	4.0	1.0	trace	0.0	0.0	3.3	15.4	14.9	14.5	78.4
Maximum Snow Depth (in.)	31	40	34	35	14	trace	0	0	14	22	25	33	40
Days With ≥ 1.0" Snow Depth	28	25	28	22	3	0	0	0	2	18	27	28	181

Homer 8 NW *Kenai Peninsula Borough* Elevation: 1,000 ft. Latitude: 59° 45' N Longitude: 151° 39' W

	JAN	FEB	MAR	APR	MAY	JUN	JUL	AUG	SEP	OCT	NOV	DEC	YEAR
Mean Maximum Temp. (°F)	28.1	30.2	33.7	41.1	50.5	57.1	60.3	59.8	52.2	40.8	31.9	29.2	42.9
Mean Temp. (°F)	22.8	24.5	27.5	34.5	42.9	49.3	53.2	52.9	46.0	35.3	26.7	24.2	36.7
Mean Minimum Temp. (°F)	17.4	18.8	21.2	27.9	35.4	41.5	46.1	45.8	39.7	29.8	21.6	19.2	30.4
Extreme Maximum Temp. (°F)	47	52	50	67	76	78	78	82	66	57	51	46	82
Extreme Minimum Temp. (°F)	-30	-19	-6	-2	19	29	34	31	19	2	-12	-12	-30
Days Maximum Temp. ≥ 70°F	0	0	0	0	0	1	2	2	0	0	0	0	5
Days Maximum Temp. ≤ 32°F	17	13	11	2	0	0	0	0	0	4	14	18	79
Days Minimum Temp. ≤ 32°F	29	26	29	24	8	0	0	0	3	20	27	29	195
Days Minimum Temp. ≤ 0°F	4	2	1	0	0	0	0	0	0	0	1	1	9
Heating Degree Days (base 65°F)	1,304	1,137	1,156	908	677	463	358	369	565	914	1,141	1,257	10,249
Cooling Degree Days (base 65°F)	0	0	0	0	0	0	0	0	0	0	0	0	0
Mean Precipitation (in.)	2.39	1.74	1.35	1.32	1.48	1.51	2.38	3.26	4.50	3.77	2.98	2.86	29.54
Extreme Maximum Daily Precip. (in.)	1.29	1.27	1.10	1.38	0.89	1.17	1.68	1.52	2.38	3.10	2.84	2.00	3.10
Days With ≥ 0.1" Precipitation	7	6	5	4	5	5	7	9	10	9	7	8	82
Days With ≥ 0.5" Precipitation	1	1	0	0	0	1	1	2	3	2	2	1	14
Days With ≥ 1.0" Precipitation	0	0	0	0	0	0	0	0	1	1	0	0	2
Mean Snowfall (in.)	21.9	18.3	16.6	8.0	1.1	trace	0.0	0.0	0.2	5.6	14.5	22.1	108.3
Maximum Snow Depth (in.)	48	49	77	68	53	trace	0	0	1	10	28	40	77
Days With ≥ 1.0" Snow Depth	30	28	29	24	5	0	0	0	0	5	21	29	171

Homer Arpt *Kenai Peninsula Borough* Elevation: 88 ft. Latitude: 59° 39' N Longitude: 151° 29' W

	JAN	FEB	MAR	APR	MAY	JUN	JUL	AUG	SEP	OCT	NOV	DEC	YEAR
Mean Maximum Temp. (°F)	30.6	32.7	36.6	44.2	51.8	57.7	61.2	60.9	55.0	44.6	35.5	32.7	45.3
Mean Temp. (°F)	24.6	26.4	30.1	37.1	44.6	50.8	54.8	54.0	48.2	38.3	29.6	26.9	38.8
Mean Minimum Temp. (°F)	18.6	20.0	23.6	30.1	37.4	43.7	48.3	47.1	41.4	31.9	23.7	21.0	32.2
Extreme Maximum Temp. (°F)	51	56	51	65	71	75	81	78	69	60	55	51	81
Extreme Minimum Temp. (°F)	-24	-19	-6	3	23	33	37	33	23	8	-7	-9	-24
Days Maximum Temp. ≥ 70°F	0	0	0	0	0	0	1	1	0	0	0	0	2
Days Maximum Temp. ≤ 32°F	16	11	7	1	0	0	0	0	0	2	10	13	60
Days Minimum Temp. ≤ 32°F	27	25	26	20	5	0	0	0	3	17	24	26	173
Days Minimum Temp. ≤ 0°F	3	2	1	0	0	0	0	0	0	0	0	1	7
Heating Degree Days (base 65°F)	1,246	1,086	1,075	829	626	421	310	333	497	820	1,054	1,174	9,471
Cooling Degree Days (base 65°F)	0	0	0	0	0	0	0	0	0	0	0	0	0
Mean Precipitation (in.)	2.76	1.81	1.65	1.05	0.88	0.84	1.53	2.36	3.35	2.58	2.79	3.06	24.66
Extreme Maximum Daily Precip. (in.)	2.32	1.01	1.83	1.44	0.79	0.60	1.20	1.41	1.50	2.88	2.85	2.12	2.88
Days With ≥ 0.1" Precipitation	7	6	4	3	3	3	5	7	9	8	7	8	70
Days With ≥ 0.5" Precipitation	2	1	1	0	0	0	1	1	2	1	1	1	11
Days With ≥ 1.0" Precipitation	0	0	0	0	0	0	0	0	0	0	0	0	0
Mean Snowfall (in.)	na	na	na	na	na	na	na	na	na	na	na	na	na
Maximum Snow Depth (in.)	na	27	na	na	na	na	na	na	na	na	na	na	na
Days With ≥ 1.0" Snow Depth	na	18	na	na	na	na	na	na	na	na	na	na	na

The period of record for all cooperative weather station data is 1980 – 2009. See User Guide for detailed explanation of data.

Iliamna Arpt *Lake and Peninsula Borough* Elevation: 186 ft. Latitude: 59° 45' N Longitude: 154° 55' W

	JAN	FEB	MAR	APR	MAY	JUN	JUL	AUG	SEP	OCT	NOV	DEC	YEAR
Mean Maximum Temp. (°F)	23.5	26.5	30.6	40.1	51.7	59.4	63.0	61.4	53.8	40.5	30.3	27.3	42.3
Mean Temp. (°F)	17.4	20.0	23.6	33.2	44.1	51.8	56.3	55.0	47.9	34.9	24.7	21.4	35.9
Mean Minimum Temp. (°F)	11.3	13.6	16.5	26.3	36.6	44.2	49.5	48.5	42.1	29.3	18.9	15.4	29.4
Extreme Maximum Temp. (°F)	49	49	50	67	80	82	84	80	69	59	52	48	84
Extreme Minimum Temp. (°F)	-41	-31	-18	-12	13	31	39	31	18	-4	-15	-25	-41
Days Maximum Temp. ≥ 70°F	0	0	0	0	0	2	5	3	0	0	0	0	10
Days Maximum Temp. ≤ 32°F	17	14	14	4	0	0	0	0	0	6	14	15	84
Days Minimum Temp. ≤ 32°F	27	23	27	21	6	0	0	0	3	18	24	25	174
Days Minimum Temp. ≤ 0°F	9	7	5	1	0	0	0	0	0	0	2	7	31
Heating Degree Days (base 65°F)	1,470	1,268	1,279	947	639	389	265	305	505	926	1,204	1,346	10,543
Cooling Degree Days (base 65°F)	0	0	0	0	0	0	1	1	0	0	0	0	2
Mean Precipitation (in.)	1.36	1.13	0.88	0.87	1.07	1.37	2.47	4.18	4.53	3.20	2.26	1.43	24.75
Extreme Maximum Daily Precip. (in.)	1.46	0.97	0.99	0.73	2.00	2.08	1.61	3.50	2.39	2.32	1.79	1.21	3.50
Days With ≥ 0.1" Precipitation	4	4	3	3	3	3	6	9	9	7	6	5	62
Days With ≥ 0.5" Precipitation	0	0	0	0	0	1	1	3	3	2	1	0	11
Days With ≥ 1.0" Precipitation	0	0	0	0	0	0	0	1	1	1	0	0	3
Mean Snowfall (in.)	na	na	na	na	na	na	na	na	na	na	na	na	na
Maximum Snow Depth (in.)	na	na	na	na	na	na	na	na	na	na	na	na	na
Days With ≥ 1.0" Snow Depth	na	na	na	na	na	na	na	na	na	na	na	na	na

Intricate Bay *Lake and Peninsula Borough* Elevation: 169 ft. Latitude: 59° 34' N Longitude: 154° 28' W

	JAN	FEB	MAR	APR	MAY	JUN	JUL	AUG	SEP	OCT	NOV	DEC	YEAR
Mean Maximum Temp. (°F)	26.1	28.8	35.3	43.6	54.8	63.3	66.2	***63.8***	55.5	***42.7***	***33.5***	28.8	***45.2***
Mean Temp. (°F)	17.9	20.7	26.0	34.3	44.5	52.7	56.8	***54.8***	47.5	***35.4***	***26.6***	21.5	***36.6***
Mean Minimum Temp. (°F)	9.7	12.6	16.7	24.9	34.1	42.1	47.2	***45.8***	39.4	***28.0***	***19.7***	14.1	***27.9***
Extreme Maximum Temp. (°F)	60	53	52	64	79	82	84	***82***	70	***62***	***53***	49	***84***
Extreme Minimum Temp. (°F)	-43	-50	-33	-20	11	26	29	***22***	10	***-3***	***-16***	-32	***-50***
Days Maximum Temp. ≥ 70°F	0	0	0	0	1	6	8	***5***	0	***0***	***0***	0	***20***
Days Maximum Temp. ≤ 32°F	16	12	8	2	0	0	0	***0***	0	***3***	***12***	15	***68***
Days Minimum Temp. ≤ 32°F	27	24	26	22	12	2	0	***1***	6	***20***	***25***	27	***192***
Days Minimum Temp. ≤ 0°F	10	8	6	1	0	0	0	***0***	0	***0***	***2***	8	***35***
Heating Degree Days (base 65°F)	1,456	1,247	1,203	915	629	362	248	***309***	519	***912***	***1,146***	1,343	***10,289***
Cooling Degree Days (base 65°F)	0	0	0	0	0	0	1	***0***	0	***0***	***0***	0	***1***
Mean Precipitation (in.)	3.31	2.78	2.24	2.28	2.12	***1.57***	2.28	***4.12***	4.51	***3.96***	***3.66***	3.55	***36.38***
Extreme Maximum Daily Precip. (in.)	2.05	2.25	2.80	2.03	1.35	***1.06***	1.13	***1.63***	1.88	***2.50***	***3.10***	3.76	***3.76***
Days With ≥ 0.1" Precipitation	8	7	5	6	6	***5***	7	***10***	10	***9***	***7***	8	***88***
Days With ≥ 0.5" Precipitation	2	2	1	1	1	***1***	1	***3***	3	***2***	***2***	2	***21***
Days With ≥ 1.0" Precipitation	1	0	0	0	0	***0***	0	***1***	1	***1***	***1***	1	***6***
Mean Snowfall (in.)	14.2	10.8	7.4	***3.5***	0.2	0.0	0.0	***0.0***	trace	***3.4***	***10.3***	***17.1***	***66.9***
Maximum Snow Depth (in.)	***45***	***54***	***26***	***19***	7	***0***	0	***0***	***trace***	na	***24***	***40***	na
Days With ≥ 1.0" Snow Depth	***25***	18	***19***	8	0	0	0	***0***	0	***3***	***15***	24	***112***

Kenai Municipal Arpt *Kenai Peninsula Borough* Elevation: 85 ft. Latitude: 60° 34' N Longitude: 151° 15' W

	JAN	FEB	MAR	APR	MAY	JUN	JUL	AUG	SEP	OCT	NOV	DEC	YEAR
Mean Maximum Temp. (°F)	23.0	27.5	33.7	43.7	54.1	59.8	62.6	62.2	55.2	41.8	29.7	25.1	43.2
Mean Temp. (°F)	15.4	19.0	25.0	35.6	45.1	51.7	55.6	54.1	47.2	34.7	22.5	18.1	35.3
Mean Minimum Temp. (°F)	7.9	10.4	16.2	27.3	36.1	43.5	48.6	46.0	39.2	27.6	15.2	11.0	27.4
Extreme Maximum Temp. (°F)	47	52	51	69	79	84	82	83	70	63	55	48	84
Extreme Minimum Temp. (°F)	-45	-37	-28	-17	20	29	34	24	16	-12	-27	-31	-45
Days Maximum Temp. ≥ 70°F	0	0	0	0	1	2	3	3	0	0	0	0	9
Days Maximum Temp. ≤ 32°F	22	18	12	2	0	0	0	0	0	4	17	22	97
Days Minimum Temp. ≤ 32°F	29	27	29	22	9	1	0	0	6	20	27	30	200
Days Minimum Temp. ≤ 0°F	10	8	5	0	0	0	0	0	0	1	5	8	37
Heating Degree Days (base 65°F)	1,534	1,297	1,234	876	608	392	285	330	527	931	1,269	1,449	10,732
Cooling Degree Days (base 65°F)	0	0	0	0	0	0	0	0	0	0	0	0	0
Mean Precipitation (in.)	1.05	0.88	0.65	0.57	0.94	1.08	1.79	2.70	3.30	2.66	1.40	1.36	18.38
Extreme Maximum Daily Precip. (in.)	1.32	1.18	1.65	0.73	0.88	0.97	0.95	1.55	1.71	4.28	3.01	1.86	4.28
Days With ≥ 0.1" Precipitation	3	3	2	2	3	3	6	8	9	7	4	4	54
Days With ≥ 0.5" Precipitation	0	0	0	0	0	0	1	1	2	1	0	0	5
Days With ≥ 1.0" Precipitation	0	0	0	0	0	0	0	0	0	0	0	0	0
Mean Snowfall (in.)	na	na	na	na	na	na	na	na	na	na	na	na	na
Maximum Snow Depth (in.)	na	na	na	na	na	na	na	na	na	na	na	na	na
Days With ≥ 1.0" Snow Depth	na	na	na	na	na	na	na	na	na	na	na	na	na

King Salmon Arpt *Bristol Bay Borough* Elevation: 48 ft. Latitude: 58° 41' N Longitude: 156° 39' W

	JAN	FEB	MAR	APR	MAY	JUN	JUL	AUG	SEP	OCT	NOV	DEC	YEAR
Mean Maximum Temp. (°F)	23.5	26.8	33.0	42.6	53.7	60.9	64.0	62.6	55.4	41.3	30.5	26.2	43.4
Mean Temp. (°F)	16.0	18.8	24.6	33.9	44.2	51.5	55.7	54.6	47.5	33.6	23.0	18.4	35.1
Mean Minimum Temp. (°F)	8.5	10.8	16.1	25.1	34.6	42.0	47.3	46.5	39.6	25.8	15.5	10.5	26.9
Extreme Maximum Temp. (°F)	53	57	55	69	85	83	84	83	71	59	56	50	85
Extreme Minimum Temp. (°F)	-48	-43	-34	-15	14	27	33	25	15	-12	-28	-38	-48
Days Maximum Temp. ≥ 70°F	0	0	0	0	1	3	7	5	0	0	0	0	16
Days Maximum Temp. ≤ 32°F	18	14	12	4	0	0	0	0	0	6	14	16	84
Days Minimum Temp. ≤ 32°F	28	25	27	24	11	1	0	0	6	21	26	27	196
Days Minimum Temp. ≤ 0°F	10	9	5	1	0	0	0	0	0	1	6	10	42
Heating Degree Days (base 65°F)	1,514	1,302	1,247	926	640	400	283	318	518	968	1,254	1,441	10,811
Cooling Degree Days (base 65°F)	0	0	0	0	0	0	1	1	0	0	0	0	2
Mean Precipitation (in.)	1.03	0.77	0.72	0.92	1.36	1.70	2.33	2.96	3.27	2.18	1.53	1.24	20.01
Extreme Maximum Daily Precip. (in.)	1.05	0.69	0.72	0.62	0.81	1.30	1.11	1.59	1.24	1.31	1.37	1.15	1.59
Days With ≥ 0.1" Precipitation	4	2	3	3	5	6	7	9	10	7	5	4	65
Days With ≥ 0.5" Precipitation	0	0	0	0	0	0	1	1	1	1	0	0	4
Days With ≥ 1.0" Precipitation	0	0	0	0	0	0	0	0	0	0	0	0	0
Mean Snowfall (in.)	10.0	6.5	7.4	4.4	0.8	trace	0.0	trace	0.1	3.0	7.3	9.7	49.2
Maximum Snow Depth (in.)	20	16	15	9	3	trace	0	trace	1	10	8	17	20
Days With ≥ 1.0" Snow Depth	20	17	12	4	0	0	0	0	0	3	12	19	87

The period of record for all cooperative weather station data is 1980 – 2009. See User Guide for detailed explanation of data.

Kitoi Bay *Kodiak Island Borough* Elevation: 15 ft. Latitude: 58° 11' N Longitude: 152° 21' W

	JAN	FEB	MAR	APR	MAY	JUN	JUL	AUG	SEP	OCT	NOV	DEC	YEAR
Mean Maximum Temp. (°F)	33.9	35.4	39.1	44.1	51.5	57.1	61.2	62.5	56.2	46.3	38.0	35.3	46.7
Mean Temp. (°F)	29.1	30.3	32.8	37.5	44.2	50.3	54.6	55.2	49.3	40.0	33.0	30.4	40.6
Mean Minimum Temp. (°F)	24.3	25.0	26.5	30.8	36.9	43.5	47.9	47.9	42.4	33.7	28.0	25.4	34.4
Extreme Maximum Temp. (°F)	47	54	56	65	78	87	82	83	71	59	54	56	87
Extreme Minimum Temp. (°F)	-20	-6	-3	2	22	31	38	32	25	10	8	-2	-20
Days Maximum Temp. ≥ 70°F	0	0	0	0	1	2	4	4	0	0	0	0	11
Days Maximum Temp. ≤ 32°F	10	7	3	0	0	0	0	0	0	0	5	9	34
Days Minimum Temp. ≤ 32°F	25	21	24	17	6	0	0	0	2	14	22	24	155
Days Minimum Temp. ≤ 0°F	0	1	0	0	0	0	0	0	0	0	0	0	1
Heating Degree Days (base 65°F)	1,106	976	991	819	638	435	318	298	463	769	952	1,066	8,831
Cooling Degree Days (base 65°F)	0	0	0	0	0	0	1	0	0	0	0	0	1
Mean Precipitation (in.)	7.30	5.49	5.06	5.86	4.62	4.61	3.91	4.73	6.44	7.02	6.07	7.54	68.65
Extreme Maximum Daily Precip. (in.)	2.57	1.98	1.63	1.74	2.02	2.03	2.14	2.70	2.75	2.60	2.44	2.84	2.84
Days With ≥ 0.1" Precipitation	14	12	11	14	13	10	9	10	12	12	12	15	144
Days With ≥ 0.5" Precipitation	5	4	4	4	3	3	2	3	5	5	4	6	48
Days With ≥ 1.0" Precipitation	2	1	1	1	0	1	1	1	2	2	1	2	15
Mean Snowfall (in.)	10.1	8.6	5.8	2.7	0.2	0.0	0.0	0.0	0.0	0.9	5.4	12.3	46.0
Maximum Snow Depth (in.)	18	18	23	15	1	0	0	0	0	10	13	25	25
Days With ≥ 1.0" Snow Depth	13	11	7	3	0	0	0	0	0	1	4	12	51

Kodiak State USCG Base *Kodiak Island Borough* Elevation: 15 ft. Latitude: 57° 45' N Longitude: 152° 30' W

	JAN	FEB	MAR	APR	MAY	JUN	JUL	AUG	SEP	OCT	NOV	DEC	YEAR
Mean Maximum Temp. (°F)	35.5	36.3	38.8	43.7	50.6	55.7	60.6	62.1	56.3	47.2	39.7	36.8	46.9
Mean Temp. (°F)	30.7	31.2	33.5	38.1	44.8	50.2	55.0	55.6	49.9	41.0	34.4	31.6	41.3
Mean Minimum Temp. (°F)	25.9	26.0	28.1	32.5	38.9	44.6	49.3	49.1	43.4	34.7	28.9	26.4	35.7
Extreme Maximum Temp. (°F)	53	55	53	69	76	82	82	79	73	62	54	56	82
Extreme Minimum Temp. (°F)	-16	-8	1	9	24	33	37	34	26	13	5	-2	-16
Days Maximum Temp. ≥ 70°F	0	0	0	0	0	1	2	3	0	0	0	0	6
Days Maximum Temp. ≤ 32°F	8	6	4	1	0	0	0	0	0	0	4	7	30
Days Minimum Temp. ≤ 32°F	21	20	22	13	3	0	0	0	1	12	20	21	133
Days Minimum Temp. ≤ 0°F	0	1	0	0	0	0	0	0	0	0	0	0	1
Heating Degree Days (base 65°F)	1,056	950	971	799	620	438	306	284	447	738	913	1,027	8,549
Cooling Degree Days (base 65°F)	0	0	0	0	0	0	2	1	0	0	0	0	3
Mean Precipitation (in.)	8.62	6.07	5.59	5.73	5.62	6.04	4.75	4.49	7.54	8.27	6.91	8.82	78.45
Extreme Maximum Daily Precip. (in.)	4.79	3.00	2.57	2.99	2.70	3.75	3.54	3.92	5.16	7.44	2.87	4.16	7.44
Days With ≥ 0.1" Precipitation	13	11	11	12	10	11	9	8	11	11	11	13	131
Days With ≥ 0.5" Precipitation	7	5	4	4	4	4	3	3	5	5	5	7	56
Days With ≥ 1.0" Precipitation	2	1	1	1	1	2	1	1	2	2	2	3	19
Mean Snowfall (in.)	14.6	15.0	12.9	8.6	0.4	0.0	0.0	trace	trace	1.3	6.5	15.7	75.0
Maximum Snow Depth (in.)	24	21	22	18	trace	0	0	trace	trace	4	8	17	24
Days With ≥ 1.0" Snow Depth	10	10	7	3	0	0	0	0	0	1	4	10	45

Kotzebue Ralph Wein Memorial *Northwest Arctic Borough* Elevation: 9 ft. Latitude: 66° 53' N Longitude: 162° 36' W

	JAN	FEB	MAR	APR	MAY	JUN	JUL	AUG	SEP	OCT	NOV	DEC	YEAR
Mean Maximum Temp. (°F)	4.0	6.6	9.3	21.3	38.2	51.5	59.7	56.0	46.5	28.6	14.1	8.5	28.7
Mean Temp. (°F)	-2.8	-0.6	1.6	13.3	32.2	45.8	54.8	51.5	42.1	24.4	9.0	2.0	22.8
Mean Minimum Temp. (°F)	-9.5	-7.7	-6.2	5.3	26.1	40.0	49.9	47.1	37.6	20.2	3.8	-4.4	16.9
Extreme Maximum Temp. (°F)	37	40	38	48	71	85	82	76	68	54	40	37	85
Extreme Minimum Temp. (°F)	-49	-49	-45	-28	-11	24	32	29	13	-13	-28	-37	-49
Days Maximum Temp. ≥ 70°F	0	0	0	0	0	1	3	1	0	0	0	0	5
Days Maximum Temp. ≤ 32°F	30	27	30	23	8	0	0	0	1	19	28	30	196
Days Minimum Temp. ≤ 32°F	31	28	31	29	23	4	0	0	7	27	30	31	241
Days Minimum Temp. ≤ 0°F	21	19	21	12	1	0	0	0	0	1	13	20	108
Heating Degree Days (base 65°F)	2,101	1,854	1,967	1,546	1,011	571	312	411	681	1,252	1,677	1,951	15,334
Cooling Degree Days (base 65°F)	0	0	0	0	0	2	4	1	0	0	0	0	7
Mean Precipitation (in.)	0.63	0.67	0.45	0.52	0.40	0.60	1.43	2.13	1.56	1.01	0.73	0.72	10.85
Extreme Maximum Daily Precip. (in.)	0.43	0.64	0.64	0.55	0.44	0.70	0.83	1.08	0.95	1.32	1.00	0.83	1.32
Days With ≥ 0.1" Precipitation	2	2	1	2	1	2	4	6	5	3	3	3	34
Days With ≥ 0.5" Precipitation	0	0	0	0	0	0	0	1	0	0	0	0	1
Days With ≥ 1.0" Precipitation	0	0	0	0	0	0	0	0	0	0	0	0	0
Mean Snowfall (in.)	10.3	9.7	6.5	5.1	1.2	0.1	trace	trace	0.9	6.0	10.2	11.0	61.0
Maximum Snow Depth (in.)	41	58	62	53	42	5	trace	trace	2	10	22	35	62
Days With ≥ 1.0" Snow Depth	31	28	31	30	19	1	0	0	0	15	28	31	214

Kuparuk *North Slope Borough* Elevation: 63 ft. Latitude: 70° 19' N Longitude: 149° 35' W

	JAN	FEB	MAR	APR	MAY	JUN	JUL	AUG	SEP	OCT	NOV	DEC	YEAR
Mean Maximum Temp. (°F)	***-11.1***	-11.6	-8.2	8.5	28.3	47.4	55.8	***50.6***	***39.0***	***21.4***	***3.5***	***-4.5***	***18.3***
Mean Temp. (°F)	***-17.4***	-18.0	-15.4	1.0	22.6	40.2	47.4	***43.7***	***33.9***	***16.0***	***-3.0***	***-11.0***	***11.7***
Mean Minimum Temp. (°F)	***-23.6***	-24.4	-22.5	-6.5	16.9	32.9	38.8	***36.7***	***28.8***	***10.6***	***-9.6***	***-17.5***	***5.0***
Extreme Maximum Temp. (°F)	***37***	39	38	46	***67***	83	***82***	***82***	***66***	***49***	***37***	***35***	***83***
Extreme Minimum Temp. (°F)	***-55***	-58	-53	-37	***-21***	14	***18***	***18***	***2***	***-29***	***-44***	***-47***	***-58***
Days Maximum Temp. ≥ 70°F	***0***	0	0	0	0	1	3	***1***	***0***	***0***	***0***	***0***	***5***
Days Maximum Temp. ≤ 32°F	***31***	28	31	28	20	1	0	***0***	***8***	***28***	***30***	***31***	***236***
Days Minimum Temp. ≤ 32°F	***31***	28	31	30	30	15	4	***8***	***21***	***31***	***30***	***31***	***290***
Days Minimum Temp. ≤ 0°F	***30***	26	30	20	3	0	0	***0***	***0***	***7***	***23***	***28***	***167***
Heating Degree Days (base 65°F)	***2,559***	2,352	2,496	1,921	1,307	738	541	***654***	***927***	***1,515***	***2,042***	***2,361***	***19,413***
Cooling Degree Days (base 65°F)	***0***	0	0	0	0	0	0	***0***	***0***	***0***	***0***	***0***	***0***
Mean Precipitation (in.)	***0.12***	0.17	0.07	0.15	0.07	0.34	0.88	***1.05***	***0.50***	***0.35***	***0.15***	***0.13***	***3.98***
Extreme Maximum Daily Precip. (in.)	***0.25***	1.02	0.15	1.00	***0.50***	0.55	***0.70***	***0.80***	***0.71***	***0.80***	***0.21***	***0.25***	***1.02***
Days With ≥ 0.1" Precipitation	***0***	0	0	0	0	1	3	***4***	***2***	***1***	***0***	***0***	***11***
Days With ≥ 0.5" Precipitation	***0***	0	0	0	0	0	0	***0***	***0***	***0***	***0***	***0***	***0***
Days With ≥ 1.0" Precipitation	***0***	0	0	0	0	0	0	***0***	***0***	***0***	***0***	***0***	***0***
Mean Snowfall (in.)	***2.5***	2.6	2.2	2.8	1.8	0.5	trace	***0.3***	***3.1***	***8.3***	***4.2***	***3.5***	***31.8***
Maximum Snow Depth (in.)	***16***	15	14	16	***19***	5	***trace***	***trace***	7	***14***	***14***	***16***	***19***
Days With ≥ 1.0" Snow Depth	***31***	28	31	30	27	3	0	***0***	***5***	***27***	***30***	***31***	***243***

The period of record for all cooperative weather station data is 1980 – 2009. See User Guide for detailed explanation of data.

Little Port Walter *Sitka Borough* Elevation: 14 ft. Latitude: 56° 23' N Longitude: 134° 39' W

	JAN	FEB	MAR	APR	MAY	JUN	JUL	AUG	SEP	OCT	NOV	DEC	YEAR
Mean Maximum Temp. (°F)	38.3	39.6	42.1	47.6	54.2	59.6	62.7	62.4	57.0	49.7	42.8	39.4	49.6
Mean Temp. (°F)	33.9	34.7	36.6	41.1	46.7	52.3	55.9	55.7	51.0	44.6	38.1	35.1	43.8
Mean Minimum Temp. (°F)	29.5	29.9	31.1	34.4	39.2	44.9	49.1	49.0	45.0	39.4	33.4	30.8	38.0
Extreme Maximum Temp. (°F)	54	58	57	67	72	80	79	88	73	60	57	53	88
Extreme Minimum Temp. (°F)	8	10	8	24	28	34	37	40	31	23	4	9	4
Days Maximum Temp. ≥ 70°F	0	0	0	0	0	1	3	2	0	0	0	0	6
Days Maximum Temp. ≤ 32°F	5	3	1	0	0	0	0	0	0	0	2	4	15
Days Minimum Temp. ≤ 32°F	21	19	20	10	2	0	0	0	0	3	13	19	107
Days Minimum Temp. ≤ 0°F	0	0	0	0	0	0	0	0	0	0	0	0	0
Heating Degree Days (base 65°F)	956	849	872	712	560	375	274	281	412	627	798	919	7,635
Cooling Degree Days (base 65°F)	0	0	0	0	0	0	0	0	0	0	0	0	0
Mean Precipitation (in.)	26.65	18.94	19.04	15.55	12.04	8.19	7.66	14.42	23.64	33.24	28.97	27.92	236.26
Extreme Maximum Daily Precip. (in.)	13.52	6.20	8.53	8.41	7.35	6.00	5.34	8.42	10.12	13.55	12.51	9.12	13.55
Days With ≥ 0.1" Precipitation	22	17	19	17	14	11	10	13	18	23	23	21	208
Days With ≥ 0.5" Precipitation	14	11	12	9	7	5	5	7	12	16	16	15	129
Days With ≥ 1.0" Precipitation	9	8	6	5	4	3	2	4	8	12	11	10	82
Mean Snowfall (in.)	29.0	21.7	17.0	1.5	trace	0.0	0.0	0.0	0.0	0.4	11.3	21.9	102.8
Maximum Snow Depth (in.)	53	53	78	73	12	0	0	0	0	4	38	49	78
Days With ≥ 1.0" Snow Depth	20	18	15	4	0	0	0	0	0	0	7	15	79

McGrath Arpt *Yukon-Koyukuk Borough* Elevation: 344 ft. Latitude: 62° 57' N Longitude: 155° 36' W

	JAN	FEB	MAR	APR	MAY	JUN	JUL	AUG	SEP	OCT	NOV	DEC	YEAR
Mean Maximum Temp. (°F)	2.2	12.6	25.0	40.8	57.1	67.9	69.3	63.3	52.8	32.0	13.1	5.0	36.8
Mean Temp. (°F)	-6.7	1.7	12.0	29.7	46.6	57.3	60.0	54.5	44.4	25.3	5.4	-3.5	27.2
Mean Minimum Temp. (°F)	-15.5	-9.3	-1.1	18.6	36.1	46.6	50.7	45.6	36.1	18.6	-2.3	-12.1	17.7
Extreme Maximum Temp. (°F)	50	50	55	68	82	88	89	87	74	67	49	45	89
Extreme Minimum Temp. (°F)	-75	-61	-44	-40	-2	27	31	25	2	-28	-53	-59	-75
Days Maximum Temp. ≥ 70°F	0	0	0	0	3	12	15	6	1	0	0	0	37
Days Maximum Temp. ≤ 32°F	29	25	21	6	0	0	0	0	0	16	27	29	153
Days Minimum Temp. ≤ 32°F	31	28	31	27	10	0	0	1	10	28	30	31	227
Days Minimum Temp. ≤ 0°F	23	18	17	4	0	0	0	0	0	3	18	23	106
Heating Degree Days (base 65°F)	2,222	1,791	1,641	1,051	563	232	162	322	609	1,224	1,786	2,125	13,728
Cooling Degree Days (base 65°F)	0	0	0	0	0	6	14	3	0	0	0	0	23
Mean Precipitation (in.)	1.13	0.94	0.81	0.69	1.13	1.53	2.41	2.79	2.47	1.44	1.34	1.25	17.93
Extreme Maximum Daily Precip. (in.)	1.16	0.97	0.97	0.53	1.00	1.59	1.45	1.33	1.73	0.92	1.06	1.23	1.73
Days With ≥ 0.1" Precipitation	3	3	3	2	4	5	7	8	7	4	4	4	54
Days With ≥ 0.5" Precipitation	0	0	0	0	0	1	1	1	1	0	0	0	4
Days With ≥ 1.0" Precipitation	0	0	0	0	0	0	0	0	0	0	0	0	0
Mean Snowfall (in.)	16.9	13.4	11.4	4.9	1.0	trace	trace	trace	1.5	9.9	18.7	19.6	97.3
Maximum Snow Depth (in.)	51	51	68	43	30	trace	trace	trace	7	12	29	54	68
Days With ≥ 1.0" Snow Depth	31	28	31	27	4	0	0	0	1	16	29	31	198

Nabesna *Valdez-Cordova Borough* Elevation: 2,900 ft. Latitude: 62° 24' N Longitude: 143° 00' W

	JAN	FEB	MAR	APR	MAY	JUN	JUL	AUG	SEP	OCT	NOV	DEC	YEAR
Mean Maximum Temp. (°F)	1.2	10.0	22.6	39.3	53.4	63.3	65.3	61.5	49.7	29.7	9.9	4.8	34.2
Mean Temp. (°F)	-5.4	1.8	11.7	27.8	42.1	51.4	54.0	50.2	39.3	21.9	3.0	-1.7	24.7
Mean Minimum Temp. (°F)	-12.1	-6.5	0.7	16.1	30.8	39.5	42.6	38.9	28.8	14.1	-3.9	-8.1	15.1
Extreme Maximum Temp. (°F)	42	44	53	69	82	87	85	84	78	61	46	45	87
Extreme Minimum Temp. (°F)	-48	-47	-34	-22	10	26	22	17	0	-24	-40	-43	-48
Days Maximum Temp. ≥ 70°F	0	0	0	0	1	7	8	5	0	0	0	0	21
Days Maximum Temp. ≤ 32°F	30	26	25	5	0	0	0	0	1	18	28	30	163
Days Minimum Temp. ≤ 32°F	30	28	31	29	19	2	0	4	20	30	29	30	252
Days Minimum Temp. ≤ 0°F	24	18	15	2	0	0	0	0	0	3	18	23	103
Heating Degree Days (base 65°F)	2,184	1,786	1,648	1,111	704	403	334	452	764	1,328	1,858	2,067	14,639
Cooling Degree Days (base 65°F)	0	0	0	0	0	2	0	0	0	0	0	0	2
Mean Precipitation (in.)	0.26	0.36	0.16	0.30	0.98	2.14	3.00	1.66	1.07	0.75	0.43	0.35	11.46
Extreme Maximum Daily Precip. (in.)	0.52	1.00	0.30	1.33	1.06	1.56	2.05	1.15	1.10	4.00	0.65	0.51	4.00
Days With ≥ 0.1" Precipitation	1	1	1	1	3	5	7	5	3	2	1	1	31
Days With ≥ 0.5" Precipitation	0	0	0	0	0	1	2	1	1	0	0	0	5
Days With ≥ 1.0" Precipitation	0	0	0	0	0	0	0	0	0	0	0	0	0
Mean Snowfall (in.)	5.5	*6.6*	3.9	4.3	6.1	0.9	trace	0.2	2.7	8.3	8.6	7.1	*54.2*
Maximum Snow Depth (in.)	38	44	43	38	18	4	trace	trace	12	17	20	28	44
Days With ≥ 1.0" Snow Depth	31	28	29	25	3	0	0	0	2	16	28	31	193

North Pole *Fairbanks North Star Borough* Elevation: 475 ft. Latitude: 64° 45' N Longitude: 147° 20' W

	JAN	FEB	MAR	APR	MAY	JUN	JUL	AUG	SEP	OCT	NOV	DEC	YEAR
Mean Maximum Temp. (°F)	-0.8	10.5	27.1	45.2	60.9	71.4	72.8	65.6	54.1	31.2	8.9	1.8	37.4
Mean Temp. (°F)	-9.7	-1.0	12.4	31.6	47.5	58.4	61.0	54.4	43.1	22.9	0.5	-6.8	26.2
Mean Minimum Temp. (°F)	-18.5	-12.4	-2.3	18.0	34.1	45.3	49.1	43.1	32.1	14.6	-7.8	-15.3	15.0
Extreme Maximum Temp. (°F)	55	49	60	74	86	95	90	90	77	74	48	47	95
Extreme Minimum Temp. (°F)	-63	-59	-46	-32	6	22	34	21	-1	-29	-51	-56	-63
Days Maximum Temp. ≥ 70°F	0	0	0	0	5	18	21	10	1	0	0	0	55
Days Maximum Temp. ≤ 32°F	30	25	19	4	0	0	0	0	1	16	28	30	153
Days Minimum Temp. ≤ 32°F	31	28	31	28	14	1	0	3	16	30	30	31	243
Days Minimum Temp. ≤ 0°F	26	21	17	3	0	0	0	0	0	5	21	26	119
Heating Degree Days (base 65°F)	2,315	1,864	1,625	995	536	203	134	327	651	1,299	1,934	2,225	14,108
Cooling Degree Days (base 65°F)	0	0	0	0	1	11	17	4	0	0	0	0	33
Mean Precipitation (in.)	0.71	0.47	0.57	0.35	0.63	1.53	1.94	1.96	1.12	0.91	0.71	0.70	11.60
Extreme Maximum Daily Precip. (in.)	1.60	0.84	8.09	0.90	0.89	2.30	2.17	1.07	1.03	0.90	0.90	0.95	8.09
Days With ≥ 0.1" Precipitation	2	2	1	1	2	4	5	6	4	3	2	2	34
Days With ≥ 0.5" Precipitation	0	0	0	0	0	1	1	1	0	0	0	0	3
Days With ≥ 1.0" Precipitation	0	0	0	0	0	0	0	0	0	0	0	0	0
Mean Snowfall (in.)	8.6	5.7	3.7	1.8	0.4	0.0	0.0	0.0	1.1	8.9	10.8	9.8	50.8
Maximum Snow Depth (in.)	40	37	41	39	17	0	0	0	12	13	24	39	41
Days With ≥ 1.0" Snow Depth	31	28	30	22	1	0	0	0	1	19	30	31	193

The period of record for all cooperative weather station data is 1980 – 2009. See User Guide for detailed explanation of data.

Northway Airport *Southeast Fairbanks Borough* Elevation: 1,712 ft. Latitude: 62° 58' N Longitude: 141° 56' W

	JAN	FEB	MAR	APR	MAY	JUN	JUL	AUG	SEP	OCT	NOV	DEC	YEAR
Mean Maximum Temp. (°F)	-6.8	5.6	23.7	43.4	58.1	67.7	70.0	64.7	52.0	29.6	5.4	-4.1	34.1
Mean Temp. (°F)	-15.2	-5.8	7.7	29.6	46.0	56.0	59.1	53.7	41.5	21.6	-2.5	-12.1	23.3
Mean Minimum Temp. (°F)	-23.7	-17.2	-8.4	15.8	33.8	44.3	48.1	42.7	31.0	13.5	-10.5	-20.2	12.4
Extreme Maximum Temp. (°F)	43	41	53	74	85	89	86	88	79	68	33	51	89
Extreme Minimum Temp. (°F)	-65	-60	-50	-34	10	25	32	12	-6	-36	-55	-60	-65
Days Maximum Temp. ≥ 70°F	0	0	0	0	3	12	17	8	0	0	0	0	40
Days Maximum Temp. ≤ 32°F	31	28	23	4	0	0	0	0	1	19	30	31	167
Days Minimum Temp. ≤ 32°F	31	28	31	29	14	0	0	2	17	31	30	31	244
Days Minimum Temp. ≤ 0°F	29	24	21	3	0	0	0	0	0	4	23	29	133
Heating Degree Days (base 65°F)	2,492	2,001	1,773	1,056	583	267	183	345	698	1,339	2,027	2,396	15,160
Cooling Degree Days (base 65°F)	0	0	0	0	0	6	5	3	0	0	0	0	14
Mean Precipitation (in.)	0.26	0.20	0.18	0.24	1.01	2.02	2.65	1.43	1.06	0.51	0.36	0.24	10.16
Extreme Maximum Daily Precip. (in.)	0.79	0.32	0.37	0.53	1.00	1.27	2.79	1.56	1.08	0.69	0.53	0.26	2.79
Days With ≥ 0.1" Precipitation	1	1	0	1	3	5	7	5	4	1	1	1	30
Days With ≥ 0.5" Precipitation	0	0	0	0	0	1	1	0	0	0	0	0	2
Days With ≥ 1.0" Precipitation	0	0	0	0	0	0	0	0	0	0	0	0	0
Mean Snowfall (in.)	na	***5.2***	***4.1***	na	na	na	na	***trace***	***2.2***	***7.6***	***9.5***	***5.7***	na
Maximum Snow Depth (in.)	29	29	29	23	na	na	na	***trace***	***11***	17	20	24	na
Days With ≥ 1.0" Snow Depth	31	28	31	23	na	na	na	***0***	***2***	18	29	31	na

Port San Juan *Valdez-Cordova Borough* Elevation: 0 ft. Latitude: 60° 03' N Longitude: 148° 04' W

	JAN	FEB	MAR	APR	MAY	JUN	JUL	AUG	SEP	OCT	NOV	DEC	YEAR
Mean Maximum Temp. (°F)	34.8	34.9	37.7	43.1	51.6	58.8	62.2	***61.5***	54.5	45.5	38.1	36.4	***46.6***
Mean Temp. (°F)	30.4	30.2	32.6	37.2	44.3	***51.2***	55.8	***55.2***	48.8	40.3	33.5	31.9	***41.0***
Mean Minimum Temp. (°F)	25.9	25.6	27.4	31.3	37.0	***43.8***	49.4	***49.0***	43.0	34.9	28.8	27.4	***35.3***
Extreme Maximum Temp. (°F)	49	50	48	62	73	82	83	78	66	58	52	52	83
Extreme Minimum Temp. (°F)	-5	-1	6	9	23	27	33	30	27	9	2	6	-5
Days Maximum Temp. ≥ 70°F	0	0	0	0	0	2	3	2	0	0	0	0	7
Days Maximum Temp. ≤ 32°F	9	7	3	0	0	0	0	0	0	0	4	6	29
Days Minimum Temp. ≤ 32°F	23	21	23	15	4	0	0	0	1	11	20	22	140
Days Minimum Temp. ≤ 0°F	0	0	0	0	0	0	0	0	0	0	0	0	0
Heating Degree Days (base 65°F)	1,066	976	999	826	634	***407***	279	***296***	481	760	940	1,019	***8,683***
Cooling Degree Days (base 65°F)	0	0	0	0	0	***0***	***1***	***0***	0	0	0	0	***1***
Mean Precipitation (in.)	13.27	10.63	8.77	9.42	6.74	4.81	4.83	8.98	15.43	17.61	13.57	16.82	130.88
Extreme Maximum Daily Precip. (in.)	4.86	***3.91***	2.42	***3.20***	2.95	***3.36***	2.51	5.48	4.32	7.11	4.13	***3.82***	***7.11***
Days With ≥ 0.1" Precipitation	17	14	14	14	11	9	9	11	16	18	16	17	166
Days With ≥ 0.5" Precipitation	9	7	6	6	5	3	3	6	9	11	10	10	85
Days With ≥ 1.0" Precipitation	5	3	2	3	2	1	1	3	6	6	5	6	43
Mean Snowfall (in.)	21.7	22.1	19.3	6.0	0.5	0.0	0.0	0.0	0.0	1.5	12.6	23.9	107.6
Maximum Snow Depth (in.)	68	58	62	69	35	0	0	0	0	16	53	43	69
Days With ≥ 1.0" Snow Depth	22	21	23	13	1	0	0	0	0	2	10	21	113

Puntilla *Matanuska-Susitna Borough* Elevation: 1,832 ft. Latitude: 62° 06' N Longitude: 152° 45' W

	JAN	FEB	MAR	APR	MAY	JUN	JUL	AUG	SEP	OCT	NOV	DEC	YEAR
Mean Maximum Temp. (°F)	14.2	20.5	26.9	37.8	51.1	62.1	64.7	60.2	50.0	35.0	20.0	15.4	38.2
Mean Temp. (°F)	5.6	10.7	15.1	26.4	40.0	49.6	53.9	50.2	41.3	26.5	11.6	7.3	28.2
Mean Minimum Temp. (°F)	-3.0	0.9	3.3	14.9	28.8	37.2	43.1	40.1	32.6	17.9	3.2	-0.8	18.2
Extreme Maximum Temp. (°F)	41	42	52	62	80	85	83	83	72	61	52	40	85
Extreme Minimum Temp. (°F)	-50	-41	-38	-24	-2	8	25	19	9	-20	-35	-35	-50
Days Maximum Temp. ≥ 70°F	0	0	0	0	1	5	9	3	0	0	0	0	18
Days Maximum Temp. ≤ 32°F	28	23	20	6	0	0	0	0	0	***11***	27	28	***143***
Days Minimum Temp. ≤ 32°F	31	28	31	29	21	7	1	4	14	28	***30***	30	***254***
Days Minimum Temp. ≤ 0°F	18	13	14	5	0	0	0	0	0	3	13	16	82
Heating Degree Days (base 65°F)	1,841	1,531	1,542	1,153	767	455	338	452	703	1,186	1,596	***1,791***	***13,355***
Cooling Degree Days (base 65°F)	0	0	0	0	0	0	0	0	0	0	0	***0***	***0***
Mean Precipitation (in.)	1.24	***0.93***	***0.66***	0.41	0.44	1.06	2.83	2.60	1.67	***1.37***	***1.09***	***2.01***	***16.31***
Extreme Maximum Daily Precip. (in.)	1.03	1.00	1.00	1.00	1.50	3.50	6.03	6.01	1.54	***1.50***	2.00	***8.75***	***8.75***
Days With ≥ 0.1" Precipitation	4	3	2	1	2	3	6	6	6	***4***	4	***5***	***46***
Days With ≥ 0.5" Precipitation	0	0	0	0	0	0	1	1	1	***0***	0	***0***	***3***
Days With ≥ 1.0" Precipitation	0	0	0	0	0	0	0	0	0	***0***	0	***0***	***0***
Mean Snowfall (in.)	19.8	14.3	10.9	5.2	0.8	trace	trace	trace	1.0	8.2	14.9	***20.6***	***95.7***
Maximum Snow Depth (in.)	91	92	98	99	103	trace	0	trace	5	***15***	***35***	***75***	***103***
Days With ≥ 1.0" Snow Depth	30	27	29	27	10	0	0	0	1	***16***	***28***	28	***196***

Seward *Kenai Peninsula Borough* Elevation: 75 ft. Latitude: 60° 06' N Longitude: 149° 26' W

	JAN	FEB	MAR	APR	MAY	JUN	JUL	AUG	SEP	OCT	NOV	DEC	YEAR
Mean Maximum Temp. (°F)	31.7	33.4	37.8	44.6	52.7	58.4	61.6	61.5	55.0	***44.5***	***35.7***	33.3	***45.9***
Mean Temp. (°F)	26.9	28.3	32.2	38.6	46.3	52.3	56.2	55.8	49.4	***39.7***	***31.2***	28.7	***40.5***
Mean Minimum Temp. (°F)	22.1	23.2	26.5	32.5	39.9	46.1	50.8	49.9	43.7	34.9	***26.6***	24.0	***35.0***
Extreme Maximum Temp. (°F)	55	51	53	***68***	83	84	87	***86***	73	***59***	***51***	49	***87***
Extreme Minimum Temp. (°F)	-15	-15	0	1	29	30	40	***35***	30	***11***	***-2***	-8	***-15***
Days Maximum Temp. ≥ 70°F	0	0	0	0	1	2	3	4	0	0	0	0	10
Days Maximum Temp. ≤ 32°F	12	10	5	1	0	0	0	0	0	1	8	10	47
Days Minimum Temp. ≤ 32°F	24	22	23	12	1	0	0	0	0	9	21	23	135
Days Minimum Temp. ≤ 0°F	1	1	0	0	0	0	0	0	0	0	0	0	2
Heating Degree Days (base 65°F)	1,173	1,032	1,010	785	573	376	270	283	462	***776***	***1,007***	1,119	***8,866***
Cooling Degree Days (base 65°F)	0	0	0	0	0	1	4	3	0	***0***	***0***	0	***8***
Mean Precipitation (in.)	8.29	6.44	4.53	4.67	3.92	2.40	2.52	5.51	9.92	10.51	7.60	9.17	75.48
Extreme Maximum Daily Precip. (in.)	4.10	4.09	2.88	5.45	***6.64***	2.23	1.90	***4.17***	***9.81***	***15.05***	***4.03***	5.02	***15.05***
Days With ≥ 0.1" Precipitation	11	10	8	9	8	6	6	10	13	12	10	12	115
Days With ≥ 0.5" Precipitation	5	4	3	3	2	1	1	3	7	7	5	6	47
Days With ≥ 1.0" Precipitation	3	2	1	1	1	0	0	1	3	3	2	3	20
Mean Snowfall (in.)	17.7	15.5	11.8	5.1	0.3	0.0	0.0	0.0	trace	1.2	8.8	19.0	79.4
Maximum Snow Depth (in.)	40	34	***35***	***29***	2	0	0	***0***	***trace***	7	***16***	***38***	***40***
Days With ≥ 1.0" Snow Depth	19	18	18	7	0	0	0	0	0	1	8	17	88

The period of record for all cooperative weather station data is 1980 – 2009. See User Guide for detailed explanation of data.

Sitka Japonski Arpt *Sitka Borough* Elevation: 36 ft. Latitude: 57° 04' N Longitude: 135° 21' W

	JAN	FEB	MAR	APR	MAY	JUN	JUL	AUG	SEP	OCT	NOV	DEC	YEAR
Mean Maximum Temp. (°F)	40.4	41.1	43.1	48.2	53.1	57.8	60.4	61.9	57.6	50.6	43.6	41.0	49.9
Mean Temp. (°F)	36.3	36.4	38.0	42.5	47.7	52.8	56.2	57.2	52.9	46.2	39.4	37.0	45.2
Mean Minimum Temp. (°F)	32.2	31.7	32.9	36.8	42.3	47.8	52.0	52.4	48.1	41.7	35.2	32.9	40.5
Extreme Maximum Temp. (°F)	58	60	58	75	75	81	84	83	77	63	62	57	84
Extreme Minimum Temp. (°F)	4	7	5	15	29	37	42	41	33	20	2	6	2
Days Maximum Temp. ≥ 70°F	0	0	0	0	0	1	1	2	0	0	0	0	4
Days Maximum Temp. ≤ 32°F	3	2	1	0	0	0	0	0	0	0	1	3	10
Days Minimum Temp. ≤ 32°F	14	14	13	5	0	0	0	0	0	2	9	13	70
Days Minimum Temp. ≤ 0°F	0	0	0	0	0	0	0	0	0	0	0	0	0
Heating Degree Days (base 65°F)	882	803	830	668	528	360	265	237	357	576	760	862	7,128
Cooling Degree Days (base 65°F)	0	0	0	0	0	0	0	1	0	0	0	0	1
Mean Precipitation (in.)	8.48	6.39	6.03	4.42	4.26	2.96	3.99	6.99	12.12	13.29	10.24	8.84	88.01
Extreme Maximum Daily Precip. (in.)	3.51	4.09	2.19	3.13	2.55	2.36	2.22	3.33	3.74	3.32	4.74	3.28	4.74
Days With ≥ 0.1" Precipitation	16	12	14	11	11	8	11	13	18	21	17	16	168
Days With ≥ 0.5" Precipitation	6	4	4	3	3	1	2	5	9	11	8	6	62
Days With ≥ 1.0" Precipitation	2	1	1	0	1	0	0	2	4	4	3	2	20
Mean Snowfall (in.)	na	na	na	na	na	na	na	na	na	na	na	na	na
Maximum Snow Depth (in.)	na	na	na	na	na	na	na	na	na	na	na	na	na
Days With ≥ 1.0" Snow Depth	na	na	na	na	na	na	na	na	na	na	na	na	na

Skwentna *Matanuska-Susitna Borough* Elevation: 149 ft. Latitude: 61° 58' N Longitude: 151° 11' W

	JAN	FEB	MAR	APR	MAY	JUN	JUL	AUG	SEP	OCT	NOV	DEC	YEAR
Mean Maximum Temp. (°F)	17.7	25.3	35.4	45.5	58.4	67.8	70.2	***66.2***	55.9	40.2	24.3	19.3	***43.9***
Mean Temp. (°F)	9.5	14.3	23.0	34.6	46.2	55.7	***59.0***	***55.6***	46.0	32.1	16.5	11.6	***33.7***
Mean Minimum Temp. (°F)	1.0	3.6	10.5	23.7	33.9	43.6	***47.8***	44.9	36.0	23.8	8.6	3.9	***23.4***
Extreme Maximum Temp. (°F)	40	48	55	68	82	87	89	88	77	55	47	42	89
Extreme Minimum Temp. (°F)	-52	-53	-39	-18	0	28	33	25	6	-19	-30	-50	-53
Days Maximum Temp. ≥ 70°F	0	0	0	0	2	11	15	***9***	0	0	0	0	***37***
Days Maximum Temp. ≤ 32°F	24	19	9	1	0	0	0	0	0	5	23	25	106
Days Minimum Temp. ≤ 32°F	28	27	28	25	11	1	0	1	10	24	28	29	212
Days Minimum Temp. ≤ 0°F	13	11	7	1	0	0	0	0	0	1	8	12	53
Heating Degree Days (base 65°F)	1,714	1,426	1,296	904	576	275	***185***	***287***	565	1,015	1,449	1,649	***11,341***
Cooling Degree Days (base 65°F)	0	0	0	0	0	3	***6***	***1***	0	0	0	0	***10***
Mean Precipitation (in.)	2.33	1.99	1.09	1.09	1.12	1.31	2.05	3.63	3.87	3.48	2.15	3.29	27.40
Extreme Maximum Daily Precip. (in.)	1.67	1.66	0.88	1.26	1.52	1.08	***1.45***	***1.90***	***2.23***	4.87	***1.74***	6.71	***6.71***
Days With ≥ 0.1" Precipitation	6	5	3	3	4	4	6	8	9	7	5	6	66
Days With ≥ 0.5" Precipitation	1	1	0	0	0	1	1	2	2	2	1	2	13
Days With ≥ 1.0" Precipitation	0	0	0	0	0	0	0	1	1	1	0	1	4
Mean Snowfall (in.)	22.5	19.5	10.8	6.2	0.1	0.0	trace	trace	0.3	11.7	20.3	30.3	121.7
Maximum Snow Depth (in.)	80	88	64	59	31	0	trace	trace	3	22	37	56	88
Days With ≥ 1.0" Snow Depth	30	27	30	28	5	0	0	0	0	10	27	30	187

St Paul Island Arpt *Aleutians West Borough* Elevation: 21 ft. Latitude: 57° 10' N Longitude: 170° 13' W

	JAN	FEB	MAR	APR	MAY	JUN	JUL	AUG	SEP	OCT	NOV	DEC	YEAR
Mean Maximum Temp. (°F)	29.2	28.6	30.0	33.6	40.6	47.0	50.9	52.1	49.5	42.8	37.0	33.0	39.5
Mean Temp. (°F)	25.2	24.5	25.6	29.5	36.3	42.6	47.3	48.8	45.3	38.6	33.1	28.9	35.5
Mean Minimum Temp. (°F)	21.2	20.4	21.2	25.3	32.1	38.2	43.7	45.5	41.0	34.4	29.1	24.8	31.4
Extreme Maximum Temp. (°F)	44	42	50	49	59	62	65	66	58	52	46	43	66
Extreme Minimum Temp. (°F)	-9	-16	-13	-3	16	16	30	29	22	12	4	-2	-16
Days Maximum Temp. ≥ 70°F	0	0	0	0	0	0	0	0	0	0	0	0	0
Days Maximum Temp. ≤ 32°F	17	14	16	11	1	0	0	0	0	0	5	12	76
Days Minimum Temp. ≤ 32°F	27	25	28	26	16	2	0	0	2	11	20	23	180
Days Minimum Temp. ≤ 0°F	1	2	1	0	0	0	0	0	0	0	0	0	4
Heating Degree Days (base 65°F)	1,226	1,140	1,215	1,059	881	665	542	496	584	811	951	1,111	10,681
Cooling Degree Days (base 65°F)	0	0	0	0	0	0	0	0	0	0	0	0	0
Mean Precipitation (in.)	1.83	1.29	1.08	1.06	1.13	1.36	1.86	3.09	2.98	3.02	2.89	2.23	23.82
Extreme Maximum Daily Precip. (in.)	4.29	0.74	0.97	1.12	0.77	1.28	1.54	1.24	1.42	1.43	1.46	0.79	4.29
Days With ≥ 0.1" Precipitation	5	5	4	3	4	4	5	8	8	9	9	8	72
Days With ≥ 0.5" Precipitation	0	0	0	0	0	0	1	2	1	1	1	0	6
Days With ≥ 1.0" Precipitation	0	0	0	0	0	0	0	0	0	0	0	0	0
Mean Snowfall (in.)	13.7	11.1	9.2	6.2	1.1	trace	0.0	0.0	trace	2.0	8.2	11.4	62.9
Maximum Snow Depth (in.)	24	37	29	32	17	trace	trace	0	trace	4	16	26	37
Days With ≥ 1.0" Snow Depth	19	19	22	17	3	0	0	0	0	1	9	16	106

Sutton 2 E *Matanuska-Susitna Borough* Elevation: 549 ft. Latitude: 61° 43' N Longitude: 148° 53' W

	JAN	FEB	MAR	APR	MAY	JUN	JUL	AUG	SEP	OCT	NOV	DEC	YEAR
Mean Maximum Temp. (°F)	22.4	28.4	37.2	49.1	60.8	66.8	68.2	65.7	56.8	42.1	27.7	23.9	45.8
Mean Temp. (°F)	15.5	20.0	27.2	37.0	46.7	53.7	57.3	54.9	46.5	33.9	21.1	17.3	35.9
Mean Minimum Temp. (°F)	8.6	11.7	17.3	24.8	32.4	40.6	46.3	44.0	36.0	25.6	14.4	10.7	26.0
Extreme Maximum Temp. (°F)	49	54	55	78	82	85	85	85	73	67	49	52	85
Extreme Minimum Temp. (°F)	-40	-43	-31	-19	11	17	29	25	12	-21	-27	-36	-43
Days Maximum Temp. ≥ 70°F	0	0	0	0	3	10	12	7	0	0	0	0	32
Days Maximum Temp. ≤ 32°F	25	16	8	1	0	0	0	0	0	4	20	24	98
Days Minimum Temp. ≤ 32°F	31	27	30	26	17	3	0	1	10	23	29	30	227
Days Minimum Temp. ≤ 0°F	9	6	2	0	0	0	0	0	0	1	5	7	30
Heating Degree Days (base 65°F)	1,527	1,265	1,163	833	562	332	234	308	550	958	1,312	1,471	10,515
Cooling Degree Days (base 65°F)	0	0	0	0	0	0	1	0	0	0	0	0	1
Mean Precipitation (in.)	1.14	0.98	0.82	0.45	0.92	1.44	2.43	3.02	3.30	1.73	1.28	1.50	19.01
Extreme Maximum Daily Precip. (in.)	1.13	1.02	0.94	0.93	1.06	0.88	1.60	1.65	2.12	1.69	1.65	1.20	2.12
Days With ≥ 0.1" Precipitation	3	3	3	2	3	4	7	8	8	4	4	5	54
Days With ≥ 0.5" Precipitation	0	0	0	0	0	0	1	2	2	1	1	1	8
Days With ≥ 1.0" Precipitation	0	0	0	0	0	0	0	0	1	0	0	0	1
Mean Snowfall (in.)	12.4	9.2	8.7	2.7	1.1	0.0	0.0	0.0	0.3	6.2	***13.3***	15.5	***69.4***
Maximum Snow Depth (in.)	57	67	86	41	7	0	0	0	5	26	31	63	86
Days With ≥ 1.0" Snow Depth	29	27	29	16	0	0	0	0	0	9	22	28	160

The period of record for all cooperative weather station data is 1980 – 2009. See User Guide for detailed explanation of data.

Talkeetna State Arpt *Matanuska-Susitna Borough* Elevation: 345 ft. Latitude: 62° 19' N Longitude: 150° 06' W

	JAN	FEB	MAR	APR	MAY	JUN	JUL	AUG	SEP	OCT	NOV	DEC	YEAR
Mean Maximum Temp. (°F)	21.4	27.2	35.0	45.7	57.8	66.5	68.1	64.6	55.3	40.0	26.6	22.9	44.2
Mean Temp. (°F)	13.2	17.5	24.2	35.3	47.0	56.4	59.6	56.0	46.8	32.5	19.0	15.1	35.2
Mean Minimum Temp. (°F)	5.1	7.8	13.4	24.9	36.2	46.3	51.0	47.3	38.3	24.9	11.5	7.2	26.1
Extreme Maximum Temp. (°F)	46	52	54	77	87	88	89	89	77	63	51	54	89
Extreme Minimum Temp. (°F)	-46	-45	-33	-16	19	30	36	29	11	-16	-25	-37	-46
Days Maximum Temp. ≥ 70°F	0	0	0	0	2	11	13	7	0	0	0	0	33
Days Maximum Temp. ≤ 32°F	24	17	10	2	0	0	0	0	0	6	21	24	104
Days Minimum Temp. ≤ 32°F	31	27	30	26	9	0	0	0	7	24	29	30	213
Days Minimum Temp. ≤ 0°F	12	9	5	1	0	0	0	0	0	1	7	11	46
Heating Degree Days (base 65°F)	1,601	1,337	1,258	885	550	254	168	276	538	1,001	1,373	1,544	10,785
Cooling Degree Days (base 65°F)	0	0	0	0	0	4	8	3	0	0	0	0	15
Mean Precipitation (in.)	1.43	1.46	1.07	1.26	1.70	2.03	3.36	5.06	4.41	3.01	1.53	1.90	28.22
Extreme Maximum Daily Precip. (in.)	1.58	1.38	1.26	1.38	0.94	1.54	2.13	3.71	2.33	3.79	1.10	1.25	3.79
Days With ≥ 0.1" Precipitation	4	4	3	4	5	6	9	11	10	8	4	5	73
Days With ≥ 0.5" Precipitation	1	1	0	1	1	1	2	3	3	1	1	1	16
Days With ≥ 1.0" Precipitation	0	0	0	0	0	0	0	1	1	0	0	0	2
Mean Snowfall (in.)	na	na	na	na	na	na	na	na	na	na	na	na	na
Maximum Snow Depth (in.)	na	na	na	na	na	na	na	na	na	na	na	na	na
Days With ≥ 1.0" Snow Depth	na	na	na	na	na	na	na	na	na	na	na	na	na

Tanana Ralph M Calhoun Mem Arpt *Yukon-Koyukuk Borough* Elevation: 231 ft. Latitude: 65° 10' N Longitude: 152° 06' W

	JAN	FEB	MAR	APR	MAY	JUN	JUL	AUG	SEP	OCT	NOV	DEC	YEAR
Mean Maximum Temp. (°F)	-0.9	7.1	20.1	39.2	58.9	70.6	71.7	64.3	51.7	29.6	9.2	2.9	35.4
Mean Temp. (°F)	-8.8	-2.3	8.0	27.3	46.4	58.5	60.7	54.1	42.9	22.8	2.2	-4.7	25.6
Mean Minimum Temp. (°F)	-16.6	-11.6	-4.2	15.4	34.0	46.3	49.7	43.9	34.1	16.0	-4.9	-12.2	15.8
Extreme Maximum Temp. (°F)	41	38	50	70	85	91	89	86	73	66	45	35	91
Extreme Minimum Temp. (°F)	-76	-64	-48	-37	2	30	30	22	4	-23	-53	-59	-76
Days Maximum Temp. ≥ 70°F	0	0	0	0	4	17	19	7	0	0	0	0	47
Days Maximum Temp. ≤ 32°F	30	27	26	8	0	0	0	0	0	18	29	31	169
Days Minimum Temp. ≤ 32°F	31	28	31	27	13	0	0	2	13	29	30	31	235
Days Minimum Temp. ≤ 0°F	24	19	18	5	0	0	0	0	0	4	19	23	112
Heating Degree Days (base 65°F)	2,290	1,905	1,765	1,123	571	202	144	334	657	1,300	1,883	2,161	14,335
Cooling Degree Days (base 65°F)	0	0	0	0	0	13	19	3	0	0	0	0	35
Mean Precipitation (in.)	0.45	0.44	0.36	0.32	0.58	1.55	2.16	2.53	1.53	0.70	0.46	0.52	11.60
Extreme Maximum Daily Precip. (in.)	1.10	0.50	0.75	0.77	0.47	1.90	1.66	1.49	0.95	0.83	0.79	0.59	1.90
Days With ≥ 0.1" Precipitation	1	1	1	1	2	4	6	8	5	2	1	2	34
Days With ≥ 0.5" Precipitation	0	0	0	0	0	1	1	1	0	0	0	0	3
Days With ≥ 1.0" Precipitation	0	0	0	0	0	0	0	0	0	0	0	0	0
Mean Snowfall (in.)	na	***6.7***	na	***2.3***	na	na	na	***0.0***	***0.8***	***6.4***	na	***9.7***	na
Maximum Snow Depth (in.)	na	***55***	na	***46***	na	na	na	***0***	***4***	***9***	na	***34***	na
Days With ≥ 1.0" Snow Depth	na	***28***	na	***26***	na	na	na	***0***	***1***	***21***	na	***31***	na

Tok *Southeast Fairbanks Borough* Elevation: 1,620 ft. Latitude: 63° 21' N Longitude: 143° 03' W

	JAN	FEB	MAR	APR	MAY	JUN	JUL	AUG	SEP	OCT	NOV	DEC	YEAR
Mean Maximum Temp. (°F)	-3.1	8.1	25.6	44.9	60.8	***71.3***	73.4	68.1	54.1	31.2	8.1	-1.3	***36.8***
Mean Temp. (°F)	-11.9	-3.0	10.7	31.2	45.7	***56.0***	59.4	53.5	41.9	22.0	-0.6	-9.8	***24.6***
Mean Minimum Temp. (°F)	-20.7	-14.1	-4.2	17.4	30.5	***40.7***	45.5	38.9	29.6	12.7	-9.4	-18.3	***12.4***
Extreme Maximum Temp. (°F)	37	40	50	74	88	***93***	95	93	74	67	39	38	***95***
Extreme Minimum Temp. (°F)	-68	-61	-52	-33	10	***18***	27	13	6	-41	-53	-65	***-68***
Days Maximum Temp. ≥ 70°F	0	0	0	0	5	***18***	23	12	1	0	0	0	***59***
Days Maximum Temp. ≤ 32°F	31	28	22	3	0	***0***	0	0	0	16	30	31	***161***
Days Minimum Temp. ≤ 32°F	31	28	31	29	20	***4***	1	6	19	30	30	30	***259***
Days Minimum Temp. ≤ 0°F	28	22	18	3	0	***0***	0	0	0	5	23	28	***127***
Heating Degree Days (base 65°F)	2,388	1,922	1,680	1,010	592	***266***	177	356	687	1,327	1,968	2,323	***14,696***
Cooling Degree Days (base 65°F)	0	0	0	0	0	***4***	12	5	0	0	0	0	***21***
Mean Precipitation (in.)	0.37	0.19	0.16	0.12	0.69	***2.02***	2.20	1.03	0.81	0.61	0.55	0.44	***9.19***
Extreme Maximum Daily Precip. (in.)	1.05	0.61	0.50	0.51	***1.05***	***2.11***	2.25	0.94	***1.33***	1.03	2.00	1.30	***2.25***
Days With ≥ 0.1" Precipitation	1	0	1	0	2	***5***	5	3	2	2	2	1	***24***
Days With ≥ 0.5" Precipitation	0	0	0	0	0	***1***	1	0	0	0	0	0	***2***
Days With ≥ 1.0" Precipitation	0	0	0	0	0	***0***	0	0	0	0	0	0	***0***
Mean Snowfall (in.)	4.7	3.0	3.0	2.0	0.8	***0.0***	0.0	0.1	2.2	6.9	7.8	6.3	***36.8***
Maximum Snow Depth (in.)	30	27	26	22	15	***0***	0	3	***10***	16	27	31	***31***
Days With ≥ 1.0" Snow Depth	31	28	31	24	3	0	0	0	2	18	28	31	196

Whites Crossing *Matanuska-Susitna Borough* Elevation: 270 ft. Latitude: 61° 42' N Longitude: 150° 00' W

	JAN	FEB	MAR	APR	MAY	JUN	JUL	AUG	SEP	OCT	NOV	DEC	YEAR
Mean Maximum Temp. (°F)	15.5	23.9	34.5	46.6	59.5	67.2	68.9	65.6	55.3	38.6	21.8	17.1	42.9
Mean Temp. (°F)	7.1	12.8	21.2	34.5	46.7	55.6	59.0	55.6	45.8	30.1	13.3	8.9	32.5
Mean Minimum Temp. (°F)	-1.5	1.7	7.8	22.3	33.8	44.0	49.0	45.7	36.2	21.6	4.7	0.6	22.1
Extreme Maximum Temp. (°F)	47	49	52	69	83	88	89	86	72	69	54	49	89
Extreme Minimum Temp. (°F)	-50	-48	-36	-21	16	28	33	22	5	-20	-40	-42	-50
Days Maximum Temp. ≥ 70°F	0	0	0	0	3	11	13	8	0	0	0	0	35
Days Maximum Temp. ≤ 32°F	26	21	11	2	0	0	0	0	0	8	25	26	119
Days Minimum Temp. ≤ 32°F	29	28	29	27	13	1	0	1	10	25	29	29	221
Days Minimum Temp. ≤ 0°F	15	12	10	1	0	0	0	0	0	2	12	14	66
Heating Degree Days (base 65°F)	1,792	1,472	1,351	909	562	280	185	286	569	1,075	1,546	1,740	11,767
Cooling Degree Days (base 65°F)	0	0	0	0	0	3	6	2	0	0	0	0	11
Mean Precipitation (in.)	1.33	1.03	0.76	0.77	1.07	1.40	2.21	3.58	3.73	2.98	1.57	1.85	22.28
Extreme Maximum Daily Precip. (in.)	2.50	1.01	0.62	2.00	1.00	1.25	1.35	2.90	1.78	3.00	1.10	3.25	3.25
Days With ≥ 0.1" Precipitation	4	3	3	3	3	4	7	8	9	7	5	5	61
Days With ≥ 0.5" Precipitation	0	1	0	0	0	1	1	2	2	2	1	1	11
Days With ≥ 1.0" Precipitation	0	0	0	0	0	0	0	1	1	0	0	0	2
Mean Snowfall (in.)	11.9	9.5	7.2	2.8	trace	0.0	0.0	0.0	0.8	8.2	14.8	18.3	73.5
Maximum Snow Depth (in.)	69	69	64	48	16	0	0	0	8	34	56	76	76
Days With ≥ 1.0" Snow Depth	24	24	23	21	1	0	0	0	0	9	23	28	153

The period of record for all cooperative weather station data is 1980 – 2009. See User Guide for detailed explanation of data.

Yakutat State Arpt *Yakutat Borough* Elevation: 27 ft. Latitude: 59° 31' N Longitude: 139° 38' W

	JAN	FEB	MAR	APR	MAY	JUN	JUL	AUG	SEP	OCT	NOV	DEC	YEAR
Mean Maximum Temp. (°F)	33.7	36.4	39.6	45.8	52.3	57.3	60.2	60.6	55.6	47.5	38.6	35.1	46.9
Mean Temp. (°F)	28.0	29.8	32.2	38.0	44.8	50.9	54.5	53.9	48.5	41.2	32.5	29.6	40.3
Mean Minimum Temp. (°F)	22.2	23.2	24.7	30.1	37.3	44.3	48.7	47.1	41.4	34.9	26.4	24.1	33.7
Extreme Maximum Temp. (°F)	55	54	59	71	78	87	85	88	73	60	54	50	88
Extreme Minimum Temp. (°F)	-21	-20	-13	6	23	30	36	32	21	7	-4	-11	-21
Days Maximum Temp. ≥ 70°F	0	0	0	0	1	1	1	2	0	0	0	0	5
Days Maximum Temp. ≤ 32°F	12	6	3	0	0	0	0	0	0	0	5	10	36
Days Minimum Temp. ≤ 32°F	24	22	24	19	7	0	0	0	4	11	21	23	155
Days Minimum Temp. ≤ 0°F	2	1	0	0	0	0	0	0	0	0	0	1	4
Heating Degree Days (base 65°F)	1,141	988	1,011	804	619	418	320	338	488	731	968	1,090	8,916
Cooling Degree Days (base 65°F)	0	0	0	0	0	0	0	0	0	0	0	0	0
Mean Precipitation (in.)	13.73	11.14	10.93	9.47	8.33	6.46	8.06	14.42	21.07	22.21	14.61	15.67	156.10
Extreme Maximum Daily Precip. (in.)	7.44	7.00	6.81	3.66	4.65	4.81	7.12	6.85	6.57	6.05	5.83	10.22	10.22
Days With ≥ 0.1" Precipitation	18	14	16	14	13	11	12	14	19	21	18	18	188
Days With ≥ 0.5" Precipitation	9	7	7	6	5	4	5	8	12	14	10	10	97
Days With ≥ 1.0" Precipitation	5	4	3	3	3	2	2	5	7	8	5	5	52
Mean Snowfall (in.)	31.7	28.9	28.6	10.1	0.4	trace	0.0	trace	trace	3.5	19.4	27.6	150.2
Maximum Snow Depth (in.)	58	51	75	53	26	trace	0	trace	trace	20	34	37	75
Days With ≥ 1.0" Snow Depth	24	22	22	12	1	0	0	0	0	2	12	22	117

Alaska Weather Station Rankings

Annual Extreme Maximum Temperature

Highest			Lowest		
Rank	Station Name	°F	Rank	Station Name	°F
1	Eagle	95	1	St Paul Island Arpt	66
1	North Pole	95	2	Cold Bay Arpt	76
1	Tok	***95***	3	Barrow W Post-W Rogers Arpt	79
4	College Observatory	94	4	Cannery Creek	80
4	Fairbanks Intl Arpt	94	5	Dutch Harbor	***81***
6	Annette Island Arpt	93	5	Homer Arpt	81
6	Bettles Field	93	7	Glacier Bay	***82***
6	Healy 2 NW	***93***	7	Homer 8 NW	82
9	Eielson Field	92	7	Kodiak State USCG Base	82
10	Tanana Ralph M Calhoun Mem Arpt	91	10	Kuparuk	***83***
11	Big Delta Allen AAF	90	10	Port San Juan	83
11	Cooper Landing 6 W	90	12	Anchorage Intl Arpt	84
13	Cordova	89	12	Glen Alps	84
13	Gulkana Intermediate Field	89	12	Iliamna Arpt	84
13	Hayes River	***89***	12	Intricate Bay	***84***
13	McGrath Arpt	89	12	Kenai Municipal Arpt	84
13	Northway Airport	89	12	Sitka Japonski Arpt	84
13	Skwentna	89	18	Juneau Int'l Arpt	85
13	Talkeetna State Arpt	89	18	King Salmon Arpt	85
13	Whites Crossing	89	18	Kotzebue Ralph Wein Memorial	85
21	Alyeska	88	18	Nome Municipal Arpt	85
21	Little Port Walter	88	18	Puntilla	85
21	Yakutat State Arpt	88	18	Sutton 2 E	85
24	Bethel Airport	87	24	Anderson Lake	***86***
24	Cantwell 2 E	***87***	24	Chulitna River Lodge	***86***

Annual Mean Maximum Temperature

Highest			Lowest		
Rank	Station Name	°F	Rank	Station Name	°F
1	Annette Island Arpt	51.8	1	Barrow W Post-W Rogers Arpt	17.0
2	Sitka Japonski Arpt	49.9	2	Kuparuk	***18.3***
3	Little Port Walter	49.6	3	Kotzebue Ralph Wein Memorial	28.7
4	Juneau Int'l Arpt	48.0	4	Bettles Field	32.6
5	Glacier Bay	***47.6***	5	Northway Airport	34.1
6	Cordova	47.2	6	Nabesna	34.2
7	Elfin Cove	***47.0***	6	Nome Municipal Arpt	34.2
8	Kodiak State USCG Base	46.9	8	Tanana Ralph M Calhoun Mem Arpt	35.4
8	Yakutat State Arpt	46.9	9	Eagle	36.6
10	Kitoi Bay	46.7	10	McGrath Arpt	36.8
11	Port San Juan	***46.6***	10	Tok	***36.8***
12	Cooper Landing 6 W	***46.1***	12	Eielson Field	37.0
12	Dutch Harbor	***46.1***	13	Cantwell 2 E	***37.4***
14	Seward	***45.9***	13	North Pole	37.4
15	Sutton 2 E	45.8	15	Bethel Airport	37.6
16	Homer Arpt	45.3	16	Fairbanks Intl Arpt	37.8
17	Intricate Bay	***45.2***	17	Big Delta Allen AAF	37.9
18	Alyeska	44.9	18	College Observatory	38.2
19	Cannery Creek	44.8	18	Gulkana Intermediate Field	38.2
20	Anderson Lake	***44.6***	18	Puntilla	38.2
21	Talkeetna State Arpt	44.3	21	St Paul Island Arpt	39.5
22	Skwentna	***43.9***	22	Healy 2 NW	***39.7***
23	Anchorage Intl Arpt	43.6	23	Glen Alps	40.2
23	Cold Bay Arpt	43.6	24	Chulitna River Lodge	***40.8***
25	King Salmon Arpt	43.4	25	Iliamna Arpt	42.3

Rankings include 25 highest/lowest stations. If state has less than 25 stations, all stations are included. The period of record is 1980–2009. See User Guide for detailed explanation of data.

Annual Mean Temperature

Highest Rank	Station Name	°F	Lowest Rank	Station Name	°F
1	Annette Island Arpt	46.6	1	Barrow W Post-W Rogers Arpt	11.5
2	Sitka Japonski Arpt	45.2	2	Kuparuk	***11.7***
3	Little Port Walter	43.8	3	Kotzebue Ralph Wein Memorial	22.8
4	Elfin Cove	***43.0***	4	Bettles Field	23.3
5	Juneau Int'l Arpt	42.1	4	Northway Airport	23.3
6	Kodiak State USCG Base	41.3	6	Tok	***24.6***
7	Glacier Bay	***41.2***	7	Nabesna	24.7
8	Dutch Harbor	***41.0***	8	Eagle	25.3
8	Port San Juan	***41.0***	9	Tanana Ralph M Calhoun Mem Arpt	25.6
10	Kitoi Bay	40.6	10	North Pole	26.2
11	Seward	***40.5***	11	Cantwell 2 E	***26.7***
12	Yakutat State Arpt	40.3	12	McGrath Arpt	27.2
13	Cordova	39.7	13	Nome Municipal Arpt	27.4
14	Cold Bay Arpt	38.9	14	Eielson Field	27.6
15	Homer Arpt	38.8	15	Fairbanks Intl Arpt	27.9
16	Cannery Creek	38.4	16	Gulkana Intermediate Field	28.1
17	Alyeska	37.7	17	Puntilla	28.2
18	Anchorage Intl Arpt	37.0	18	College Observatory	28.4
19	Anderson Lake	***36.7***	19	Big Delta Allen AAF	29.3
19	Homer 8 NW	36.7	20	Healy 2 NW	***30.0***
21	Intricate Bay	***36.6***	21	Bethel Airport	30.7
22	Cooper Landing 6 W	***36.0***	22	Whites Crossing	32.5
23	Iliamna Arpt	35.9	23	Chulitna River Lodge	***32.8***
23	Sutton 2 E	35.9	24	Hayes River	***33.4***
25	St Paul Island Arpt	35.5	25	Skwentna	***33.7***

Annual Mean Minimum Temperature

Highest Rank	Station Name	°F	Lowest Rank	Station Name	°F
1	Annette Island Arpt	41.3	1	Kuparuk	***5.0***
2	Sitka Japonski Arpt	40.5	2	Barrow W Post-W Rogers Arpt	6.0
3	Elfin Cove	***38.9***	3	Northway Airport	12.4
4	Little Port Walter	38.0	3	Tok	***12.4***
5	Juneau Int'l Arpt	36.0	5	Eagle	14.0
6	Dutch Harbor	***35.8***	6	Bettles Field	14.1
7	Kodiak State USCG Base	35.7	7	North Pole	15.0
8	Port San Juan	***35.3***	8	Nabesna	15.1
9	Seward	***35.0***	9	Cantwell 2 E	***15.8***
10	Glacier Bay	***34.7***	9	Tanana Ralph M Calhoun Mem Arpt	15.8
11	Kitoi Bay	34.4	11	Kotzebue Ralph Wein Memorial	16.9
12	Cold Bay Arpt	34.1	12	McGrath Arpt	17.7
13	Yakutat State Arpt	33.7	13	Fairbanks Intl Arpt	18.0
14	Homer Arpt	32.2	13	Gulkana Intermediate Field	18.0
15	Cannery Creek	32.0	15	Eielson Field	18.2
15	Cordova	32.0	15	Puntilla	18.2
17	St Paul Island Arpt	31.4	17	College Observatory	18.7
18	Alyeska	30.5	18	Healy 2 NW	***20.3***
19	Homer 8 NW	30.4	19	Big Delta Allen AAF	20.5
20	Anchorage Intl Arpt	30.2	20	Nome Municipal Arpt	20.6
21	Iliamna Arpt	29.4	21	Whites Crossing	22.2
22	Anderson Lake	***28.8***	22	Skwentna	***23.4***
23	Intricate Bay	***27.9***	23	Bethel Airport	23.8
24	Kenai Municipal Arpt	27.4	24	Hayes River	***24.1***
25	Glen Alps	27.2	25	Chulitna River Lodge	***24.8***

Rankings include 25 highest/lowest stations. If state has less than 25 stations, all stations are included. The period of record is 1980–2009. See User Guide for detailed explanation of data.

Annual Extreme Minimum Temperature

Highest Rank	Station Name	°F	Lowest Rank	Station Name	°F
1	Little Port Walter	4	1	Tanana Ralph M Calhoun Mem Arpt	-76
2	Sitka Japonski Arpt	2	2	McGrath Arpt	-75
3	Elfin Cove	1	3	Bettles Field	-69
4	Annette Island Arpt	-3	4	Eagle	-68
5	Port San Juan	-5	4	Tok	*-68*
6	Dutch Harbor	*-8*	6	Northway Airport	-65
6	Glacier Bay	*-8*	7	North Pole	-63
8	Juneau Int'l Arpt	-10	8	Eielson Field	-60
9	Cold Bay Arpt	-13	9	Big Delta Allen AAF	-59
10	Seward	*-15*	10	Fairbanks Intl Arpt	-58
11	Kodiak State USCG Base	-16	10	Kuparuk	*-58*
11	St Paul Island Arpt	-16	12	Barrow W Post-W Rogers Arpt	-55
13	Cannery Creek	-18	12	College Observatory	-55
14	Kitoi Bay	-20	14	Nome Municipal Arpt	-54
15	Yakutat State Arpt	-21	15	Gulkana Intermediate Field	-53
16	Cordova	-23	15	Skwentna	-53
17	Homer Arpt	-24	17	Healy 2 NW	*-52*
18	Alyeska	-30	18	Intricate Bay	*-50*
18	Anchorage Intl Arpt	-30	18	Puntilla	-50
18	Homer 8 NW	-30	18	Whites Crossing	-50
21	Hayes River	*-34*	21	Cantwell 2 E	*-49*
22	Chulitna River Lodge	*-36*	21	Kotzebue Ralph Wein Memorial	-49
23	Glen Alps	-37	23	Bethel Airport	-48
24	Anderson Lake	*-40*	23	King Salmon Arpt	-48
24	Cooper Landing 6 W	-40	23	Nabesna	-48

July Mean Maximum Temperature

Highest Rank	Station Name	°F	Lowest Rank	Station Name	°F
1	Tok	73.4	1	Barrow W Post-W Rogers Arpt	46.7
2	Eagle	72.9	2	St Paul Island Arpt	50.9
3	North Pole	72.8	3	Cold Bay Arpt	55.5
4	Fairbanks Intl Arpt	72.7	4	Kuparuk	55.8
5	College Observatory	72.5	5	Dutch Harbor	56.9
6	Tanana Ralph M Calhoun Mem Arpt	71.7	6	Elfin Cove	58.1
7	Eielson Field	71.6	7	Nome Municipal Arpt	58.2
8	Skwentna	70.2	8	Glen Alps	58.8
9	Bettles Field	70.0	9	Kotzebue Ralph Wein Memorial	59.7
9	Northway Airport	70.0	10	Yakutat State Arpt	60.2
11	Big Delta Allen AAF	69.9	11	Homer 8 NW	60.3
12	Healy 2 NW	*69.5*	12	Sitka Japonski Arpt	60.4
13	McGrath Arpt	69.3	13	Kodiak State USCG Base	60.6
14	Whites Crossing	68.9	14	Homer Arpt	61.2
15	Gulkana Intermediate Field	68.7	14	Kitoi Bay	61.2
16	Cooper Landing 6 W	68.3	16	Cordova	61.6
17	Sutton 2 E	68.2	16	Seward	61.6
18	Talkeetna State Arpt	68.1	18	Cannery Creek	62.1
19	Hayes River	67.8	19	Port San Juan	62.2
20	Intricate Bay	66.2	20	Kenai Municipal Arpt	62.6
21	Anderson Lake	66.1	21	Little Port Walter	62.7
21	Chulitna River Lodge	*66.1*	22	Iliamna Arpt	63.0
23	Cantwell 2 E	*66.0*	23	Bethel Airport	63.6
24	Anchorage Intl Arpt	65.4	23	Glacier Bay	*63.6*
25	Nabesna	65.3	25	Juneau Int'l Arpt	64.0

Rankings include 25 highest/lowest stations. If state has less than 25 stations, all stations are included. The period of record is 1980–2009. See User Guide for detailed explanation of data.

January Mean Minimum Temperature

Highest			Lowest		
Rank	**Station Name**	**°F**	**Rank**	**Station Name**	**°F**
1	Sitka Japonski Arpt	32.2	1	Northway Airport	-23.7
2	Annette Island Arpt	32.0	2	Kuparuk	***-23.6***
3	Elfin Cove	29.6	3	Tok	-20.7
4	Little Port Walter	29.5	4	Barrow W Post-W Rogers Arpt	-19.4
5	Dutch Harbor	27.4	5	North Pole	-18.5
6	Kodiak State USCG Base	25.9	6	Eagle	-18.0
6	Port San Juan	25.9	7	Bettles Field	-17.7
8	Glacier Bay	24.3	8	Tanana Ralph M Calhoun Mem Arpt	-16.6
8	Kitoi Bay	24.3	9	Fairbanks Intl Arpt	-16.0
10	Cold Bay Arpt	23.4	10	McGrath Arpt	-15.5
11	Juneau Int'l Arpt	23.3	11	Eielson Field	-15.3
12	Yakutat State Arpt	22.2	12	Nabesna	-12.1
13	Seward	22.1	13	College Observatory	-11.3
14	St Paul Island Arpt	21.2	14	Gulkana Intermediate Field	-10.6
15	Cannery Creek	19.6	15	Kotzebue Ralph Wein Memorial	-9.5
16	Cordova	19.3	16	Cantwell 2 E	***-8.8***
17	Homer Arpt	18.6	17	Big Delta Allen AAF	-7.9
18	Homer 8 NW	17.4	18	Healy 2 NW	***-5.5***
19	Alyeska	16.2	19	Puntilla	-3.0
20	Glen Alps	12.8	20	Nome Municipal Arpt	-2.8
21	Anderson Lake	11.4	21	Whites Crossing	-1.5
22	Iliamna Arpt	11.3	22	Bethel Airport	0.6
23	Anchorage Intl Arpt	11.0	23	Skwentna	1.0
24	Intricate Bay	9.7	24	Talkeetna State Arpt	5.1
25	Sutton 2 E	8.6	25	Hayes River	***6.6***

Number of Days Annually Maximum Temperature ≥ 70°F

Highest			Lowest		
Rank	**Station Name**	**Days**	**Rank**	**Station Name**	**Days**
1	Tok	***59***	1	Barrow W Post-W Rogers Arpt	0
2	Eagle	55	1	Cold Bay Arpt	0
2	Fairbanks Intl Arpt	55	1	St Paul Island Arpt	0
2	North Pole	55	4	Dutch Harbor	***2***
5	College Observatory	53	4	Homer Arpt	2
6	Eielson Field	51	6	Elfin Cove	3
7	Tanana Ralph M Calhoun Mem Arpt	47	7	Glen Alps	4
8	Northway Airport	40	7	Sitka Japonski Arpt	4
9	Bettles Field	39	9	Homer 8 NW	5
9	Big Delta Allen AAF	39	9	Kotzebue Ralph Wein Memorial	5
11	McGrath Arpt	37	9	Kuparuk	***5***
11	Skwentna	***37***	9	Yakutat State Arpt	5
13	Healy 2 NW	***36***	13	Kodiak State USCG Base	6
14	Whites Crossing	35	13	Little Port Walter	6
15	Talkeetna State Arpt	33	13	Nome Municipal Arpt	6
16	Cooper Landing 6 W	32	16	Port San Juan	7
16	Gulkana Intermediate Field	32	17	Cannery Creek	9
16	Sutton 2 E	32	17	Kenai Municipal Arpt	9
19	Hayes River	***30***	19	Cordova	10
20	Chulitna River Lodge	***25***	19	Glacier Bay	***10***
21	Cantwell 2 E	***24***	19	Iliamna Arpt	10
22	Anderson Lake	23	19	Seward	10
23	Nabesna	21	23	Kitoi Bay	11
24	Alyeska	20	24	Anchorage Intl Arpt	14
24	Intricate Bay	***20***	25	Bethel Airport	15

Rankings include 25 highest/lowest stations. If state has less than 25 stations, all stations are included. The period of record is 1980–2009. See User Guide for detailed explanation of data.

Number of Days Annually Maximum Temperature ≤ 32°F

Highest			Lowest		
Rank	Station Name	Days	Rank	Station Name	Days
1	Barrow W Post-W Rogers Arpt	247	1	Annette Island Arpt	10
2	Kuparuk	***236***	1	Sitka Japonski Arpt	10
3	Kotzebue Ralph Wein Memorial	196	3	Little Port Walter	15
4	Bettles Field	180	4	Dutch Harbor	***21***
5	Tanana Ralph M Calhoun Mem Arpt	169	5	Elfin Cove	24
6	Northway Airport	167	6	Port San Juan	29
7	Nome Municipal Arpt	166	7	Kodiak State USCG Base	30
8	Nabesna	163	8	Glacier Bay	***34***
9	Tok	***161***	8	Kitoi Bay	34
10	Eagle	156	10	Yakutat State Arpt	36
10	Fairbanks Intl Arpt	156	11	Cordova	40
12	McGrath Arpt	153	12	Juneau Int'l Arpt	41
12	North Pole	153	13	Cold Bay Arpt	45
14	College Observatory	152	14	Seward	47
15	Eielson Field	150	15	Cannery Creek	56
16	Cantwell 2 E	***148***	16	Homer Arpt	60
17	Big Delta Allen AAF	147	17	Intricate Bay	***68***
18	Puntilla	***143***	18	Cooper Landing 6 W	71
19	Gulkana Intermediate Field	141	19	Alyeska	72
20	Bethel Airport	134	20	St Paul Island Arpt	76
21	Chulitna River Lodge	***124***	21	Homer 8 NW	79
22	Whites Crossing	119	22	Iliamna Arpt	84
23	Healy 2 NW	***118***	22	King Salmon Arpt	84
24	Hayes River	***116***	24	Anderson Lake	***92***
25	Anchorage Intl Arpt	107	25	Kenai Municipal Arpt	97

Number of Days Annually Minimum Temperature ≤ 32°F

Highest			Lowest		
Rank	Station Name	Days	Rank	Station Name	Days
1	Barrow W Post-W Rogers Arpt	312	1	Annette Island Arpt	67
2	Kuparuk	***290***	2	Sitka Japonski Arpt	70
3	Cantwell 2 E	***262***	3	Elfin Cove	86
4	Tok	***259***	4	Little Port Walter	107
5	Puntilla	***254***	5	Dutch Harbor	***123***
6	Nabesna	252	6	Juneau Int'l Arpt	125
7	Eagle	249	7	Kodiak State USCG Base	133
8	Northway Airport	244	8	Seward	135
9	North Pole	243	9	Glacier Bay	***139***
10	Kotzebue Ralph Wein Memorial	241	10	Port San Juan	140
11	Bettles Field	239	11	Cold Bay Arpt	148
11	Gulkana Intermediate Field	239	12	Kitoi Bay	155
13	Tanana Ralph M Calhoun Mem Arpt	235	12	Yakutat State Arpt	155
14	Nome Municipal Arpt	233	14	Cordova	162
15	College Observatory	229	15	Homer Arpt	173
16	Hayes River	***228***	16	Iliamna Arpt	174
17	McGrath Arpt	227	17	St Paul Island Arpt	180
17	Sutton 2 E	227	18	Alyeska	186
19	Fairbanks Intl Arpt	222	19	Anderson Lake	188
20	Whites Crossing	221	20	Anchorage Intl Arpt	190
21	Bethel Airport	218	21	Intricate Bay	***192***
21	Glen Alps	218	22	Cannery Creek	195
23	Eielson Field	217	22	Homer 8 NW	195
24	Big Delta Allen AAF	214	24	King Salmon Arpt	196
25	Talkeetna State Arpt	213	25	Kenai Municipal Arpt	200

Rankings include 25 highest/lowest stations. If state has less than 25 stations, all stations are included. The period of record is 1980–2009. See User Guide for detailed explanation of data.

Number of Days Annually Minimum Temperature ≤ 0°F

Highest			Lowest		
Rank	Station Name	Days	Rank	Station Name	Days
1	Kuparuk	***167***	1	Annette Island Arpt	0
2	Barrow W Post-W Rogers Arpt	162	1	Cold Bay Arpt	0
3	Northway Airport	133	1	Dutch Harbor	***0***
4	Tok	***127***	1	Elfin Cove	0
5	Bettles Field	125	1	Glacier Bay	***0***
6	North Pole	119	1	Little Port Walter	0
7	Eagle	116	1	Port San Juan	0
8	Fairbanks Intl Arpt	113	1	Sitka Japonski Arpt	0
9	Tanana Ralph M Calhoun Mem Arpt	112	9	Kitoi Bay	1
10	Eielson Field	108	9	Kodiak State USCG Base	1
10	Kotzebue Ralph Wein Memorial	108	11	Seward	2
12	McGrath Arpt	106	12	Juneau Int'l Arpt	3
13	Nabesna	103	13	St Paul Island Arpt	4
14	Cantwell 2 E	***100***	13	Yakutat State Arpt	4
15	Gulkana Intermediate Field	98	15	Cannery Creek	5
16	College Observatory	97	16	Homer Arpt	7
17	Healy 2 NW	***87***	17	Homer 8 NW	9
18	Big Delta Allen AAF	83	18	Cordova	11
19	Puntilla	82	19	Alyeska	14
20	Nome Municipal Arpt	72	20	Anchorage Intl Arpt	21
21	Whites Crossing	66	21	Glen Alps	23
22	Bethel Airport	62	22	Anderson Lake	***26***
23	Skwentna	53	23	Sutton 2 E	30
24	Talkeetna State Arpt	46	24	Iliamna Arpt	31
25	Hayes River	***44***	25	Chulitna River Lodge	***33***

Number of Annual Heating Degree Days

Highest			Lowest		
Rank	Station Name	Num.	Rank	Station Name	Num.
1	Barrow W Post-W Rogers Arpt	19,472	1	Annette Island Arpt	6,652
2	Kuparuk	***19,413***	2	Sitka Japonski Arpt	7,128
3	Kotzebue Ralph Wein Memorial	15,334	3	Little Port Walter	7,635
4	Bettles Field	15,170	4	Elfin Cove	***7,958***
5	Northway Airport	15,160	5	Juneau Int'l Arpt	8,278
6	Tok	***14,696***	6	Kodiak State USCG Base	8,549
7	Nabesna	14,639	7	Glacier Bay	***8,590***
8	Eagle	14,434	8	Port San Juan	***8,683***
9	Tanana Ralph M Calhoun Mem Arpt	14,335	9	Dutch Harbor	***8,687***
10	North Pole	14,108	10	Kitoi Bay	8,831
11	Cantwell 2 E	***13,926***	11	Seward	***8,866***
12	McGrath Arpt	13,728	12	Yakutat State Arpt	8,916
13	Nome Municipal Arpt	13,629	13	Cordova	9,154
14	Eielson Field	13,619	14	Cold Bay Arpt	9,451
15	Fairbanks Intl Arpt	13,508	15	Homer Arpt	9,471
16	Gulkana Intermediate Field	13,389	16	Cannery Creek	9,608
17	Puntilla	***13,355***	17	Alyeska	9,857
18	College Observatory	13,318	18	Anchorage Intl Arpt	10,142
19	Big Delta Allen AAF	12,995	19	Anderson Lake	***10,216***
20	Healy 2 NW	***12,724***	20	Homer 8 NW	10,249
21	Bethel Airport	12,449	21	Intricate Bay	***10,289***
22	Whites Crossing	11,767	22	Sutton 2 E	10,515
23	Chulitna River Lodge	***11,676***	23	Cooper Landing 6 W	***10,516***
24	Hayes River	***11,452***	24	Iliamna Arpt	10,543
25	Skwentna	***11,341***	25	St Paul Island Arpt	10,681

Rankings include 25 highest/lowest stations. If state has less than 25 stations, all stations are included. The period of record is 1980–2009. See User Guide for detailed explanation of data.

Number of Annual Cooling Degree Days

Highest

Rank	Station Name	Num.
1	Fairbanks Intl Arpt	73
2	College Observatory	58
3	Eielson Field	50
4	Bettles Field	40
5	Eagle	35
5	Tanana Ralph M Calhoun Mem Arpt	35
7	Big Delta Allen AAF	33
7	North Pole	33
9	Healy 2 NW	***27***
10	McGrath Arpt	23
11	Tok	***21***
12	Annette Island Arpt	19
13	Talkeetna State Arpt	15
14	Northway Airport	14
15	Whites Crossing	11
16	Skwentna	***10***
17	Hayes River	***9***
18	Chulitna River Lodge	***8***
18	Seward	***8***
20	Kotzebue Ralph Wein Memorial	7
21	Gulkana Intermediate Field	6
22	Anchorage Intl Arpt	4
22	Anderson Lake	***4***
22	Bethel Airport	4
22	Cooper Landing 6 W	4

Lowest

Rank	Station Name	Num.
1	Barrow W Post-W Rogers Arpt	0
1	Cold Bay Arpt	0
1	Glacier Bay	***0***
1	Homer 8 NW	0
1	Homer Arpt	0
1	Kenai Municipal Arpt	0
1	Kuparuk	***0***
1	Little Port Walter	0
1	Puntilla	***0***
1	St Paul Island Arpt	0
1	Yakutat State Arpt	0
12	Cannery Creek	1
12	Cordova	1
12	Dutch Harbor	***1***
12	Elfin Cove	***1***
12	Glen Alps	1
12	Intricate Bay	***1***
12	Kitoi Bay	1
12	Port San Juan	***1***
12	Sitka Japonski Arpt	1
12	Sutton 2 E	1
22	Alyeska	2
22	Cantwell 2 E	***2***
22	Iliamna Arpt	2
22	King Salmon Arpt	2

Annual Precipitation

Highest

Rank	Station Name	Inches
1	Little Port Walter	236.26
2	Yakutat State Arpt	156.10
3	Port San Juan	130.88
4	Cannery Creek	120.88
5	Elfin Cove	103.14
6	Annette Island Arpt	101.90
7	Cordova	91.37
8	Sitka Japonski Arpt	88.01
9	Kodiak State USCG Base	78.45
10	Seward	75.48
11	Alyeska	70.68
12	Glacier Bay	***70.06***
13	Kitoi Bay	68.65
14	Juneau Int'l Arpt	62.82
15	Dutch Harbor	***62.31***
16	Cold Bay Arpt	41.97
17	Intricate Bay	***36.38***
18	Hayes River	***36.03***
19	Chulitna River Lodge	***34.30***
20	Homer 8 NW	29.54
21	Talkeetna State Arpt	28.22
22	Skwentna	27.40
23	Glen Alps	26.70
24	Iliamna Arpt	24.75
25	Homer Arpt	24.66

Lowest

Rank	Station Name	Inches
1	Kuparuk	***3.98***
2	Barrow W Post-W Rogers Arpt	4.45
3	Tok	***9.19***
4	Northway Airport	10.16
5	Fairbanks Intl Arpt	10.75
6	Kotzebue Ralph Wein Memorial	10.85
7	Gulkana Intermediate Field	11.25
8	Nabesna	11.46
9	Big Delta Allen AAF	11.58
10	North Pole	11.60
10	Tanana Ralph M Calhoun Mem Arpt	11.60
12	Eielson Field	11.96
13	College Observatory	12.17
14	Eagle	12.38
15	Healy 2 NW	***14.87***
16	Bettles Field	14.92
17	Puntilla	***16.31***
18	Cantwell 2 E	***16.45***
19	Anchorage Intl Arpt	16.64
20	Nome Municipal Arpt	16.77
21	McGrath Arpt	17.93
22	Kenai Municipal Arpt	18.38
23	Bethel Airport	18.43
24	Sutton 2 E	19.01
25	Anderson Lake	***19.40***

Rankings include 25 highest/lowest stations. If state has less than 25 stations, all stations are included. The period of record is 1980–2009. See User Guide for detailed explanation of data.

Annual Extreme Maximum Daily Precipitation

Highest Rank	Station Name	Inches	Lowest Rank	Station Name	Inches
1	Seward	*15.05*	1	Kuparuk	*1.02*
2	Little Port Walter	13.55	2	Barrow W Post-W Rogers Arpt	1.28
3	Yakutat State Arpt	10.22	3	Kotzebue Ralph Wein Memorial	1.32
4	Hayes River	*9.30*	4	Gulkana Intermediate Field	1.51
5	Puntilla	*8.75*	5	King Salmon Arpt	1.59
6	Elfin Cove	*8.61*	6	Nome Municipal Arpt	1.72
7	North Pole	8.09	7	Bethel Airport	1.73
8	Cordova	7.61	7	McGrath Arpt	1.73
9	Kodiak State USCG Base	7.44	9	College Observatory	1.77
10	Port San Juan	*7.11*	10	Eagle	1.86
11	Eielson Field	*7.00*	11	Tanana Ralph M Calhoun Mem Arpt	1.90
12	Skwentna	*6.71*	12	Sutton 2 E	2.12
13	Anderson Lake	*6.03*	13	Tok	*2.25*
14	Cannery Creek	5.62	14	Big Delta Allen AAF	2.27
15	Annette Island Arpt	5.48	14	Fairbanks Intl Arpt	2.27
16	Alyeska	5.34	16	Anchorage Intl Arpt	2.76
17	Dutch Harbor	*4.80*	17	Northway Airport	2.79
18	Sitka Japonski Arpt	4.74	18	Kitoi Bay	2.84
19	St Paul Island Arpt	4.29	19	Homer Arpt	2.88
20	Kenai Municipal Arpt	4.28	20	Bettles Field	2.96
21	Cantwell 2 E	*4.16*	21	Homer 8 NW	3.10
22	Nabesna	4.00	22	Whites Crossing	3.25
23	Talkeetna State Arpt	3.79	23	Glen Alps	3.45
24	Cold Bay Arpt	3.78	24	Juneau Int'l Arpt	3.47
25	Intricate Bay	*3.76*	25	Iliamna Arpt	3.50

Number of Days Annually With ≥ 0.1 Inches of Precipitation

Highest Rank	Station Name	Days	Lowest Rank	Station Name	Days
1	Little Port Walter	208	1	Barrow W Post-W Rogers Arpt	11
2	Yakutat State Arpt	188	1	Kuparuk	*11*
3	Elfin Cove	180	3	Cooper Landing 6 W	*24*
4	Annette Island Arpt	169	3	Tok	*24*
5	Sitka Japonski Arpt	168	5	Northway Airport	30
6	Port San Juan	166	6	Nabesna	31
7	Cannery Creek	165	7	Fairbanks Intl Arpt	32
8	Cordova	151	8	Eielson Field	33
9	Juneau Int'l Arpt	146	9	Kotzebue Ralph Wein Memorial	34
10	Kitoi Bay	144	9	North Pole	34
11	Glacier Bay	*136*	9	Tanana Ralph M Calhoun Mem Arpt	34
12	Kodiak State USCG Base	131	12	Big Delta Allen AAF	35
13	Alyeska	127	13	College Observatory	36
14	Dutch Harbor	*125*	13	Gulkana Intermediate Field	36
15	Seward	115	15	Healy 2 NW	*42*
16	Cold Bay Arpt	113	16	Eagle	46
17	Intricate Bay	*88*	16	Puntilla	*46*
18	Homer 8 NW	82	18	Bettles Field	47
19	Hayes River	*80*	19	Cantwell 2 E	*48*
20	Chulitna River Lodge	*77*	20	Anchorage Intl Arpt	50
21	Talkeetna State Arpt	73	21	Anderson Lake	*51*
22	St Paul Island Arpt	72	22	Nome Municipal Arpt	52
23	Glen Alps	71	23	Kenai Municipal Arpt	54
24	Homer Arpt	70	23	McGrath Arpt	54
25	Skwentna	66	23	Sutton 2 E	54

Rankings include 25 highest/lowest stations. If state has less than 25 stations, all stations are included. The period of record is 1980–2009. See User Guide for detailed explanation of data.

Number of Days Annually With ≥ 0.5 Inches of Precipitation

Highest

Rank	Station Name	Days
1	Little Port Walter	129
2	Yakutat State Arpt	97
3	Port San Juan	85
4	Cannery Creek	79
5	Annette Island Arpt	73
6	Elfin Cove	69
7	Sitka Japonski Arpt	62
8	Cordova	60
9	Kodiak State USCG Base	56
10	Kitoi Bay	48
11	Seward	47
12	Alyeska	44
13	Glacier Bay	*38*
13	Juneau Int'l Arpt	38
15	Dutch Harbor	*35*
16	Hayes River	*21*
16	Intricate Bay	*21*
18	Chulitna River Lodge	*19*
18	Cold Bay Arpt	19
20	Talkeetna State Arpt	16
21	Homer 8 NW	14
22	Skwentna	13
23	Homer Arpt	11
23	Iliamna Arpt	11
23	Whites Crossing	11

Lowest

Rank	Station Name	Days
1	Barrow W Post-W Rogers Arpt	0
1	Kuparuk	*0*
3	Kotzebue Ralph Wein Memorial	1
4	Eagle	2
4	Fairbanks Intl Arpt	2
4	Gulkana Intermediate Field	2
4	Northway Airport	2
4	Tok	*2*
9	College Observatory	3
9	Eielson Field	3
9	North Pole	3
9	Puntilla	*3*
9	Tanana Ralph M Calhoun Mem Arpt	3
14	Bettles Field	4
14	Big Delta Allen AAF	4
14	King Salmon Arpt	4
14	McGrath Arpt	4
14	Nome Municipal Arpt	4
19	Anchorage Intl Arpt	5
19	Cantwell 2 E	*5*
19	Healy 2 NW	*5*
19	Kenai Municipal Arpt	5
19	Nabesna	5
24	Cooper Landing 6 W	*6*
24	St Paul Island Arpt	6

Number of Days Annually With ≥ 1.0 Inches of Precipitation

Highest

Rank	Station Name	Days
1	Little Port Walter	82
2	Yakutat State Arpt	52
3	Port San Juan	43
4	Cannery Creek	37
5	Annette Island Arpt	29
6	Cordova	25
6	Elfin Cove	25
8	Seward	20
8	Sitka Japonski Arpt	20
10	Alyeska	19
10	Kodiak State USCG Base	19
12	Kitoi Bay	15
13	Dutch Harbor	*14*
14	Glacier Bay	*12*
15	Juneau Int'l Arpt	10
16	Hayes River	*6*
16	Intricate Bay	*6*
18	Cold Bay Arpt	5
19	Skwentna	4
20	Chulitna River Lodge	*3*
20	Iliamna Arpt	3
22	Homer 8 NW	2
22	Talkeetna State Arpt	2
22	Whites Crossing	2
25	Cooper Landing 6 W	*1*

Lowest

Rank	Station Name	Days
1	Anchorage Intl Arpt	0
1	Anderson Lake	*0*
1	Barrow W Post-W Rogers Arpt	0
1	Bethel Airport	0
1	Bettles Field	0
1	Big Delta Allen AAF	0
1	Cantwell 2 E	*0*
1	College Observatory	0
1	Eagle	0
1	Eielson Field	0
1	Fairbanks Intl Arpt	0
1	Gulkana Intermediate Field	0
1	Healy 2 NW	*0*
1	Homer Arpt	0
1	Kenai Municipal Arpt	0
1	King Salmon Arpt	0
1	Kotzebue Ralph Wein Memorial	0
1	Kuparuk	*0*
1	McGrath Arpt	0
1	Nabesna	0
1	Nome Municipal Arpt	0
1	North Pole	0
1	Northway Airport	0
1	Puntilla	*0*
1	St Paul Island Arpt	0

Rankings include 25 highest/lowest stations. If state has less than 25 stations, all stations are included. The period of record is 1980–2009. See User Guide for detailed explanation of data.

Annual Snowfall

Rank	Station Name (Highest)	Inches	Rank	Station Name (Lowest)	Inches
1	Alyeska	212.6	1	Kuparuk	***31.8***
2	Hayes River	***207.6***	2	Annette Island Arpt	34.8
3	Chulitna River Lodge	196.0	3	Barrow W Post-W Rogers Arpt	36.5
4	Glen Alps	167.9	4	Tok	***36.8***
5	Yakutat State Arpt	150.2	5	Kitoi Bay	46.0
6	Cannery Creek	142.3	6	Cooper Landing 6 W	***48.2***
7	Cantwell 2 E	***124.3***	7	King Salmon Arpt	49.2
8	Skwentna	121.7	8	North Pole	50.8
9	Elfin Cove	110.1	9	Nabesna	***54.2***
10	Homer 8 NW	108.3	10	Anderson Lake	***60.8***
11	Port San Juan	107.6	11	Kotzebue Ralph Wein Memorial	61.0
12	Little Port Walter	102.8	12	Bethel Airport	61.7
13	McGrath Arpt	97.3	13	Eagle	62.4
14	Puntilla	***95.7***	14	St Paul Island Arpt	62.9
15	Dutch Harbor	***92.4***	15	Fairbanks Intl Arpt	64.9
16	Bettles Field	91.7	16	College Observatory	65.0
17	Juneau Int'l Arpt	87.7	17	Intricate Bay	***66.9***
18	Seward	79.4	18	Eielson Field	***68.3***
19	Healy 2 NW	***78.4***	19	Sutton 2 E	***69.4***
20	Nome Municipal Arpt	76.9	20	Anchorage Intl Arpt	73.4
21	Kodiak State USCG Base	75.0	21	Whites Crossing	73.5
22	Cold Bay Arpt	74.2	22	Cold Bay Arpt	74.2
23	Whites Crossing	73.5	23	Kodiak State USCG Base	75.0
24	Anchorage Intl Arpt	73.4	24	Nome Municipal Arpt	76.9
25	Sutton 2 E	***69.4***	25	Healy 2 NW	***78.4***

Annual Maximum Snow Depth

Rank	Station Name (Highest)	Inches	Rank	Station Name (Lowest)	Inches
1	Barrow W Post-W Rogers Arpt	140	1	Kuparuk	***19***
2	Hayes River	***117***	2	King Salmon Arpt	20
3	Chulitna River Lodge	112	3	Annette Island Arpt	21
4	Puntilla	***103***	4	Kodiak State USCG Base	24
5	Cannery Creek	92	5	Kitoi Bay	25
6	Alyeska	89	6	Bethel Airport	31
6	Nome Municipal Arpt	89	6	Tok	***31***
8	Skwentna	88	8	Juneau Int'l Arpt	35
9	Sutton 2 E	86	9	Eagle	36
10	Cantwell 2 E	***80***	10	St Paul Island Arpt	37
10	Glacier Bay	***80***	11	Anchorage Intl Arpt	39
12	Little Port Walter	78	11	Anderson Lake	***39***
13	Homer 8 NW	77	13	Healy 2 NW	***40***
14	Whites Crossing	76	13	Seward	***40***
15	Yakutat State Arpt	75	15	North Pole	41
16	Port San Juan	69	16	Eielson Field	***42***
17	McGrath Arpt	68	17	Nabesna	44
18	Elfin Cove	62	18	Cold Bay Arpt	46
18	Kotzebue Ralph Wein Memorial	62	19	College Observatory	52
20	Cooper Landing 6 W	***60***	20	Fairbanks Intl Arpt	54
21	Bettles Field	59	21	Bettles Field	59
22	Fairbanks Intl Arpt	54	22	Cooper Landing 6 W	***60***
23	College Observatory	52	23	Elfin Cove	62
24	Cold Bay Arpt	46	23	Kotzebue Ralph Wein Memorial	62
25	Nabesna	44	25	McGrath Arpt	68

Rankings include 25 highest/lowest stations. If state has less than 25 stations, all stations are included. The period of record is 1980–2009. See User Guide for detailed explanation of data.

Number of Days Annually With ≥ 1.0 Inch Snow Depth

Highest			Lowest		
Rank	Station Name	Days	Rank	Station Name	Days
1	Kuparuk	***243***	1	Annette Island Arpt	17
2	Barrow W Post-W Rogers Arpt	242	2	Kodiak State USCG Base	45
3	Bettles Field	216	3	Kitoi Bay	51
4	Kotzebue Ralph Wein Memorial	214	4	Juneau Int'l Arpt	67
5	Cantwell 2 E	***209***	5	Cold Bay Arpt	71
6	Chulitna River Lodge	206	6	Dutch Harbor	***72***
7	Hayes River	***204***	7	Little Port Walter	79
8	Eagle	198	8	Elfin Cove	80
8	McGrath Arpt	198	9	King Salmon Arpt	87
10	Puntilla	***196***	10	Seward	88
10	Tok	196	11	Cooper Landing 6 W	***104***
12	College Observatory	195	12	St Paul Island Arpt	106
13	Nabesna	193	13	Intricate Bay	***112***
13	North Pole	193	14	Port San Juan	113
15	Fairbanks Intl Arpt	192	15	Yakutat State Arpt	117
16	Cannery Creek	190	16	Glacier Bay	***122***
17	Skwentna	187	17	Anderson Lake	***135***
18	Nome Municipal Arpt	186	18	Anchorage Intl Arpt	148
19	Healy 2 NW	***181***	19	Whites Crossing	153
20	Eielson Field	***178***	20	Bethel Airport	155
21	Alyeska	177	21	Sutton 2 E	160
22	Homer 8 NW	171	22	Homer 8 NW	171
23	Sutton 2 E	160	23	Alyeska	177
24	Bethel Airport	155	24	Eielson Field	***178***
25	Whites Crossing	153	25	Healy 2 NW	***181***

Rankings include 25 highest/lowest stations. If state has less than 25 stations, all stations are included. The period of record is 1980–2009. See User Guide for detailed explanation of data.

Significant Storm Events in Alaska: 2000 – 2009

Location or County	Date	Type	Mag.	Deaths	Injuries	Property Damage ($mil.)	Crop Damage ($mil.)
North Slope Borough	08/10/00	High Wind	81 mph	0	0	7.7	0.0
Kuskokwim Delta	05/13/02	Flood	na	0	0	2.1	0.0
Kenai Peninsula	10/23/02	Flood	na	0	0	20.0	0.0
Anchorage Matanuska Valley and Kenai Peninsula	03/12/03	High Wind	110 mph	0	2	11.1	0.0
South Central Alaska	10/01/03	Flood	na	0	0	3.2	0.0
Western Alaska	10/18/04	Storm Surge	na	0	0	19.9	0.0
Pribilof Islands	10/22/04	Flood	na	0	0	5.0	0.0
Central and Eastern Beaufort Sea Coast	01/08/05	High Wind	75 mph	0	0	7.7	0.0
Southern Chukchi Sea Coast and Northwest Arctic Borough	09/22/05	Storm Surge	na	0	0	2.6	0.0
Haines Borough	11/20/05	Heavy Rain	na	0	0	2.0	0.0
Susitna Valley	08/18/06	Flood	na	0	0	20.0	0.0
Nern P.W. Snd	10/09/06	Flood	na	0	0	26.5	0.0
Copper River Basin	10/10/06	Flood	na	0	0	10.0	0.0
Susitna Valley	10/10/06	Flood	na	0	0	2.9	0.0
Western Arctic Coast-Villages of Wainwright and Kaktovik	07/29/08	High Surf	na	0	0	7.0	0.0
Tanana	07/30/08	Flood	na	0	0	2.6	0.0
Upr Tanana Vly Fortymile	05/04/09	Flood	na	0	0	6.3	0.0
Kuskokwim Delta	05/07/09	Flood	na	0	0	2.6	0.0
Yukon Flats Nearby Uplands	05/09/09	Flood	na	0	0	7.2	0.0
Tanana	05/12/09	Flood	na	0	0	5.9	0.0

Note: Deaths, injuries, and damages are date and location specific.

ARIZONA

PHYSICAL FEATURES. Arizona covers 113,909 square miles, with about 350 square miles of water surface. The State can be divided into three main topographical areas: (1) the northeastern portion is a high plateau averaging between 5,000 and 7,000 feet in elevation; (2) running diagonally from the southeastern to the northwestern corners of the State is a mountainous region with maximum elevations between about 9,000 and 12,000 feet above mean sea level; (3) the southwestern third of the State is made up of low mountain ranges and desert valleys. From the White Mountain area across the Mogollon Rim to the San Francisco Peaks is an unbroken stand of Ponderosa pine. The Kaibab plateau north of the Grand Canyon continues this timbered strip into southern Utah. The highest point in the State is Humphreys Peak with an elevation of 12,611 feet, located just northwest of Flagstaff. Baldy Peak, in the White Mountains of eastern Arizona, is the second highest in the State with an elevation of 11,490 feet.

The higher elevations of the State, running diagonally from the southeast to the northwest, average between 25 and 30 inches of precipitation (rain plus melted snow) annually, while the desert southwest has averages as low as three or four inches per year. The desert valleys of southwestern Arizona are an extension of the Sonora Desert of Mexico, with elevations as low as about 100 feet above sea level in the Lower Colorado River Valley. The plateau country in the northeastern corner of the State receives approximately 10 inches of precipitation annually. Higher ridges here are covered with junipers and pinon trees.

Nearly the entire State is in the Colorado River drainage basin emptying into the Gulf of California. The world-famed Grand Canyon lies within the State, extending from the junction of the Little Colorado with the main stream southwestward for approximately 217 miles. The Grand Canyon varies in width from four to 18 miles, and depths from the rim to the river bed range from 2,700 to as much as 5,700 feet. This is an outstanding example of arid or semiarid land erosion by a major river whose source is in a more rainy area.

GENERAL CLIMATE. Cold air masses from Canada sometimes penetrate into the State bringing temperatures well below zero in the high plateau and mountainous regions of central and northern Arizona. Great extremes occur between day and night temperatures throughout Arizona. The daily range between maximum and minimum temperatures sometimes runs as high as 50 to 60°F. during drier portions of the year. During winter months, daytime temperatures may average 70°F., with night temperatures often falling to freezing or slightly below in lower desert valleys. In the summer the pine-clad forests in the central part of the State may have afternoon temperatures of 80°F., while night temperatures drop to 35 to 40°F.

PRECIPITATION. Precipitation throughout Arizona is governed to a great extent by elevation and the season of the year. From November through March, storm systems from the Pacific Ocean cross the State. These winter storms occur frequently in the higher mountains of the central and northern parts of the State and sometimes bring with them heavy snows. Snow accumulation may reach depths of 100 inches or more during the winter. The gradual melting of this snow during the spring serves to maintain a supply of water in the main rivers of the State. Reservoirs on these streams supply water to the desert areas in the lower Salt River Valley and the lower Gila River Valley areas.

Summer rainfall begins early in July and usually extends to mid-September. Moisture-bearing winds sweep into Arizona from the southeast, with their source region in the Gulf of Mexico. Summer rains occur in the form of thundershowers which are caused, to a great extent, by excessive heating of the ground and the lifting of moisture-laden air along main mountain ranges. Thus, the heaviest thundershowers are usually found in mountainous regions of the central and southeastern portions of Arizona. These thunderstorms are often accompanied by strong winds and brief periods of blowing dust prior to the onset of rain. Hail occurs rather infrequently.

The average number of days with measurable precipitation per year varies from 72 in the Flagstaff region to 34 in Phoenix, 50 in Tucson, 53 in Winslow, and 15 in Yuma. A large portion of Arizona is included in the semiarid region of the United States. Long periods often occur with little or no precipitation. The air is generally dry and clear, with relatively low humidity and a high percentage of sunshine. April, May, and June are the months with the greatest number of clear days, while July and August, as well as December, January, and February have the cloudiest weather and lowest percent of sunshine. Humidities, while low when compared to most other states, are higher throughout much of Arizona during July and August, which is the thunderstorm season. Annual average humidity values, based on four readings per day, show Flagstaff with 55 percent, Phoenix 38 percent, Tucson 38 percent, Winslow 46 percent, and Yuma 33 percent. Yearly averages of percent of possible sunshine show Phoenix with 86 percent, Tucson 86 percent, and Yuma 92 percent. Due to high temperatures, the dryness of the air, and the high percentage of sunshine, evaporation rates in Arizona are high. Mean annual lake evaporation varies from about 80 inches in the southwestern corner of the State to about 50 inches in the northeastern corner. Phoenix averages about 72 inches and Tucson 70 inches per year.

The length of the growing season (period between freezes) varies tremendously over Arizona, averaging less than 3 months in some of the elevated areas of northern and eastern portions of the State. On the other hand, lower desert valleys sometimes have two or three years in succession without freezes.

Flood conditions occur infrequently, although heavy thundershowers during July and August at times cause flash floods that do considerable local damage. Floods on main rivers are mostly limited to the upper basins. Heaviest runoff usually occurs in connection with the arrival of tropical air over Arizona, which had its origin in hurricanes that dissipated in or off the west coast of Mexico. Heavy rains associated with these systems usually occur during August or September. High winds accompanying heavy thunderstorms during July and August sometimes reach peak gusts of about 100 miles per hour in local areas. Tornado funnels have been reported in Arizona.

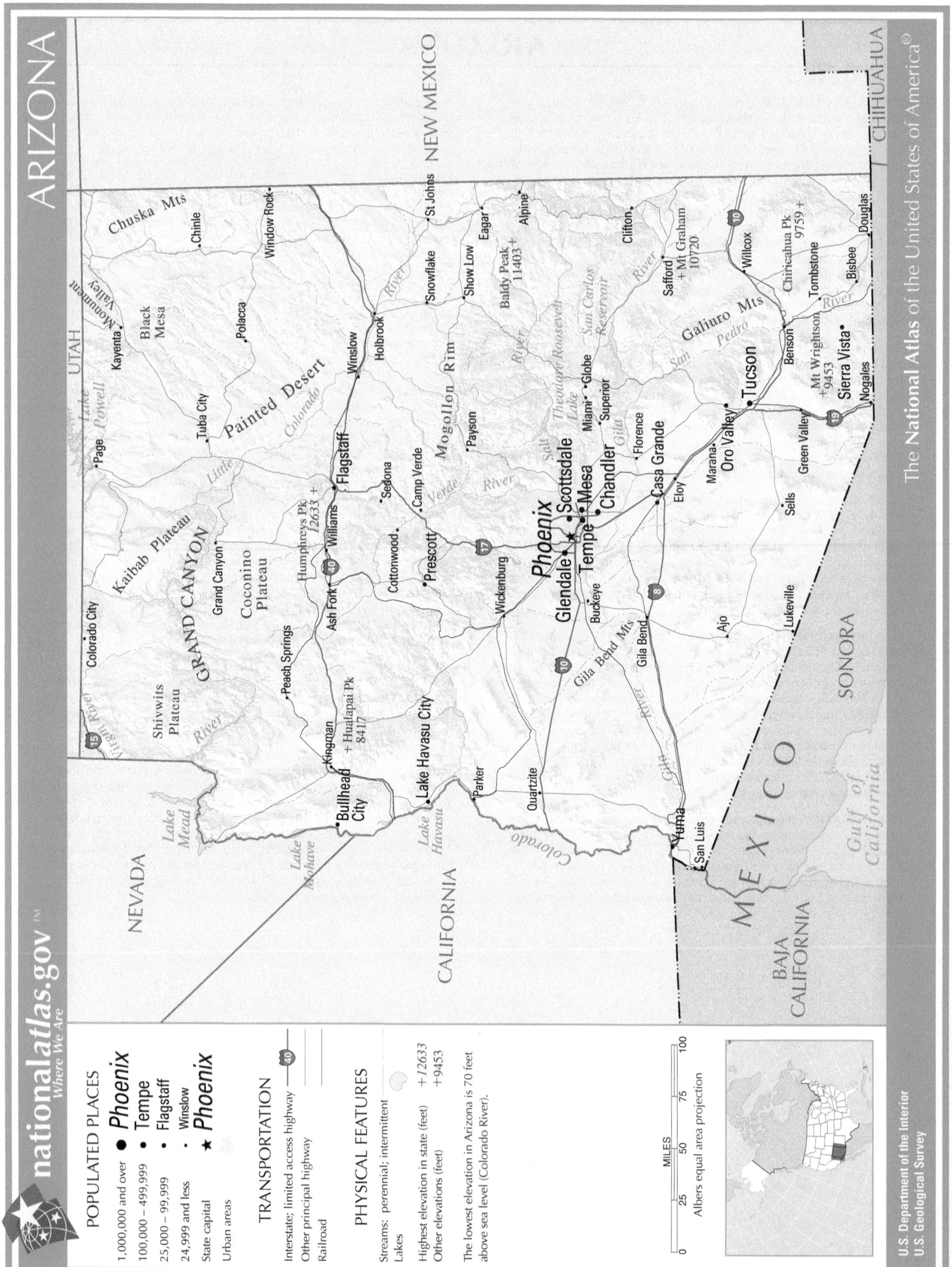
ARIZONA
nationalatlas.gov™
Where We Are
POPULATED PLACES
1,000,000 and over ● Phoenix
100,000 – 499,999 • Tempe
25,000 – 99,999 • Flagstaff
24,999 and less · Winslow
State capital ★ Phoenix
Urban areas
TRANSPORTATION
Interstate; limited access highway 40
Other principal highway
Railroad
PHYSICAL FEATURES
Streams: perennial; intermittent
Lakes
Highest elevation in state (feet) +12633
Other elevations (feet) +9453
The lowest elevation in Arizona is 70 feet above sea level (Colorado River).
MILES
0 25 50 75 100
Albers equal area projection
U.S. Department of the Interior
U.S. Geological Survey
The National Atlas of the United States of America®
NEVADA
UTAH
NEW MEXICO
CALIFORNIA
MEXICO
SONORA
CHIHUAHUA
BAJA CALIFORNIA
Gulf of California
Phoenix
Tucson
Mesa
Glendale
Scottsdale
Chandler
Tempe
Flagstaff
Yuma
Lake Havasu City
Bullhead City
Kingman
Prescott
Sierra Vista
Casa Grande
Oro Valley
Marana
Eloy
Florence
Superior
Globe
Miami
Payson
Show Low
Snowflake
Holbrook
Winslow
St Johns
Eagar
Alpine
Clifton
Safford
Willcox
Benson
Tombstone
Bisbee
Douglas
Nogales
Green Valley
Sells
Ajo
Lukeville
Gila Bend
Buckeye
Wickenburg
Quartzite
Parker
San Luis
Sedona
Camp Verde
Cottonwood
Williams
Ash Fork
Peach Springs
Grand Canyon
Colorado City
Page
Tuba City
Kayenta
Polacca
Chinle
Window Rock
Humphreys Pk 12633
Hualapai Pk 8417
Baldy Peak 11403
Mt Graham 10720
Chiricahua Pk 9759
Mt Wrightson 9453
GRAND CANYON
Kaibab Plateau
Coconino Plateau
Shivwits Plateau
Painted Desert
Mogollon Rim
Chuska Mts
Black Mesa
Monument Valley
Galiuro Mts
Gila Bend Mts
Lake Mead
Lake Mohave
Lake Havasu
Lake Powell
Theodore Roosevelt Lake
San Carlos Reservoir
Colorado
Little Colorado River
Verde River
Salt River
Gila River
San Pedro River
Virgin River
15
40
17
10
8
19

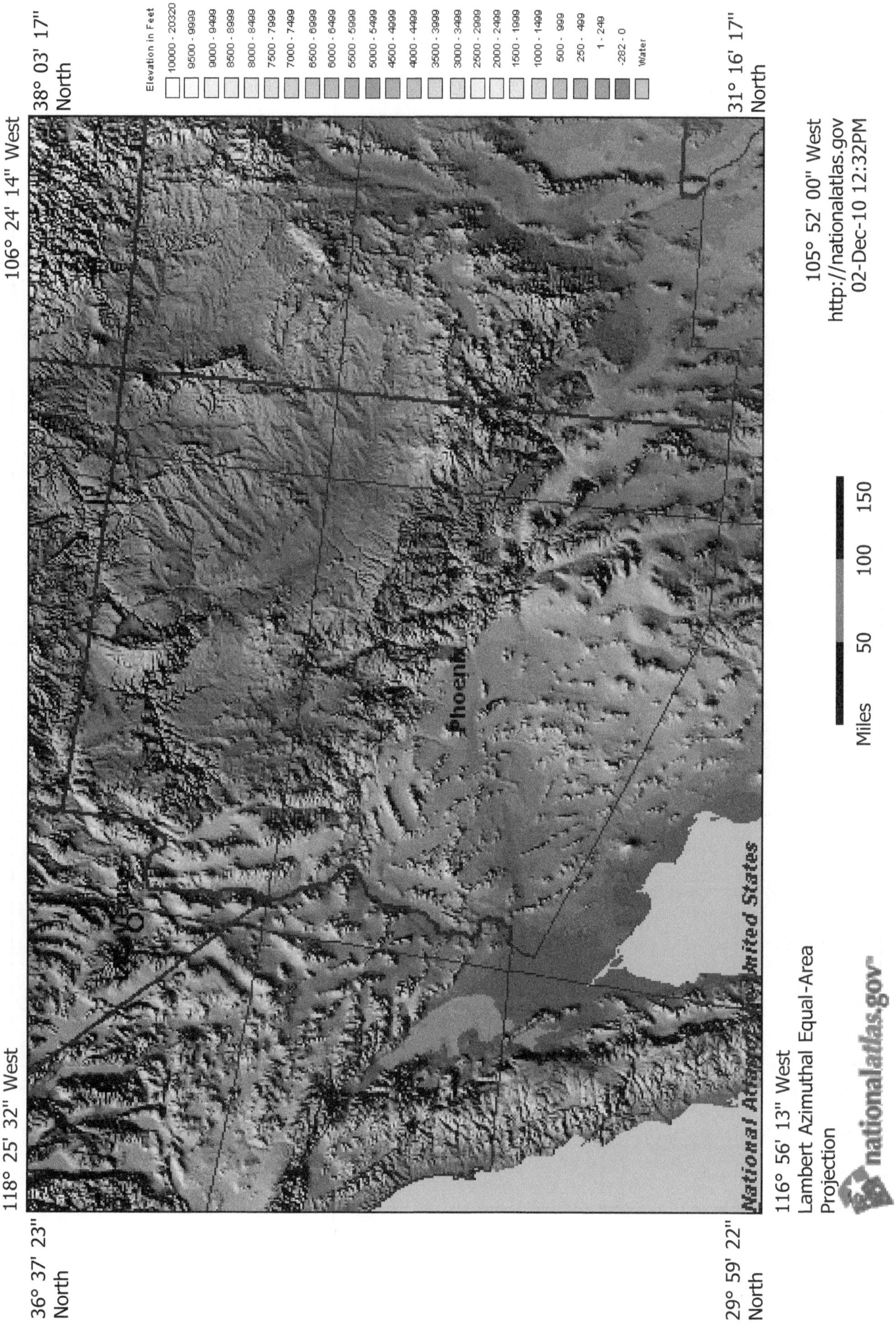
118° 25' 32" West
106° 24' 14" West
36° 37' 23" North
38° 03' 17" North
29° 59' 22" North
31° 16' 17" North
116° 56' 13" West
105° 52' 00" West
Elevation in Feet
10000 - 20320
9500 - 9999
9000 - 9499
8500 - 8999
8000 - 8499
7500 - 7999
7000 - 7499
6500 - 6999
6000 - 6499
5500 - 5999
5000 - 5499
4500 - 4999
4000 - 4499
3500 - 3999
3000 - 3499
2500 - 2999
2000 - 2499
1500 - 1999
1000 - 1499
500 - 999
250 - 499
1 - 249
-282 - 0
Water
Phoenix
Miles 50 100 150
Lambert Azimuthal Equal-Area Projection
http://nationalatlas.gov
02-Dec-10 12:32PM
nationalatlas.gov

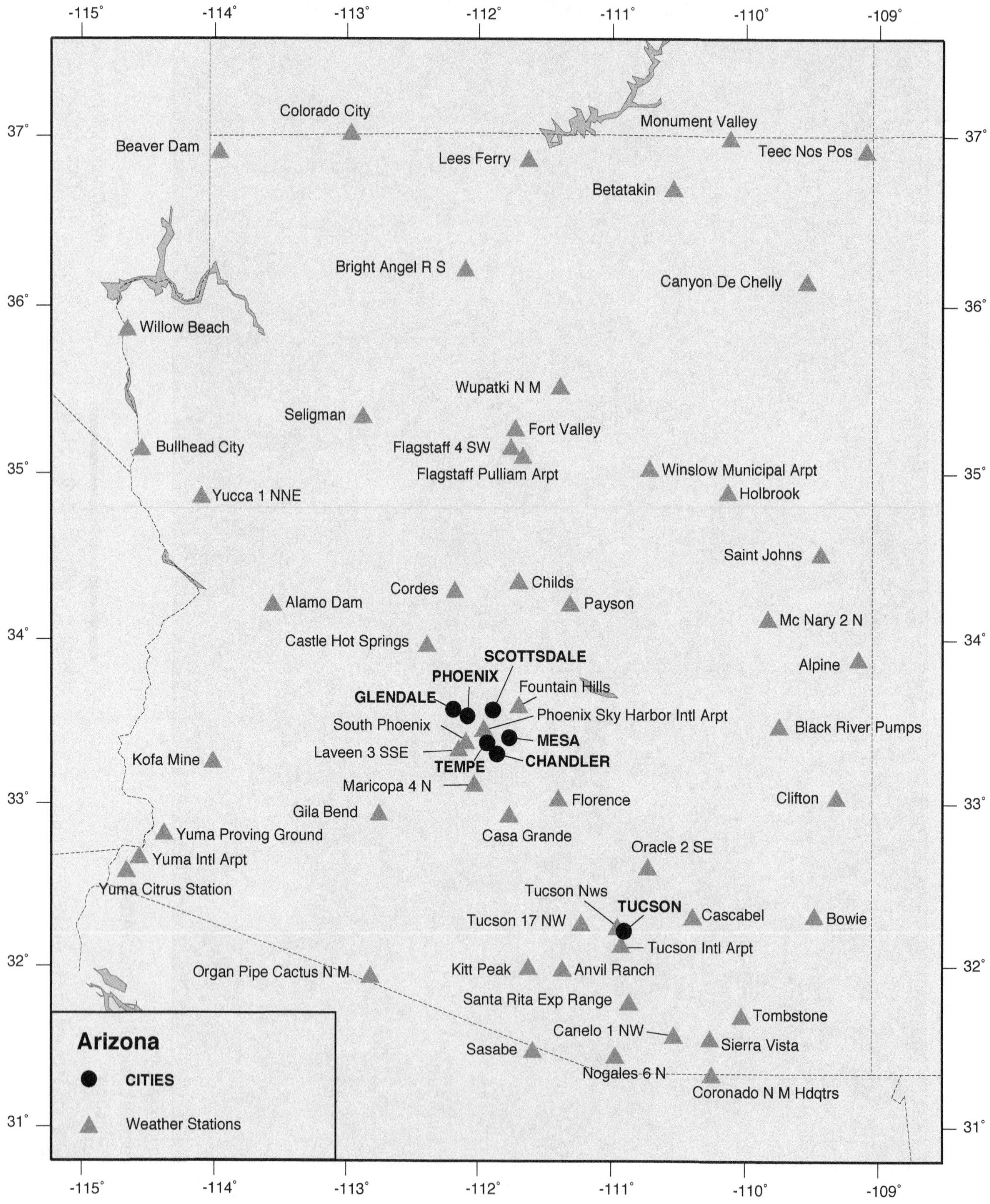
-115°
-114°
-113°
-112°
-111°
-110°
-109°
37°
36°
35°
34°
33°
32°
31°
Colorado City
Beaver Dam
Monument Valley
Teec Nos Pos
Lees Ferry
Betatakin
Bright Angel R S
Canyon De Chelly
Willow Beach
Wupatki N M
Seligman
Fort Valley
Bullhead City
Flagstaff 4 SW
Flagstaff Pulliam Arpt
Winslow Municipal Arpt
Holbrook
Yucca 1 NNE
Saint Johns
Cordes
Childs
Alamo Dam
Payson
Mc Nary 2 N
Castle Hot Springs
SCOTTSDALE
Alpine
PHOENIX
Fountain Hills
GLENDALE
Phoenix Sky Harbor Intl Arpt
South Phoenix
Black River Pumps
MESA
Laveen 3 SSE
CHANDLER
TEMPE
Kofa Mine
Maricopa 4 N
Clifton
Florence
Gila Bend
Casa Grande
Yuma Proving Ground
Yuma Intl Arpt
Oracle 2 SE
Yuma Citrus Station
Tucson Nws
TUCSON
Cascabel
Bowie
Tucson 17 NW
Tucson Intl Arpt
Kitt Peak
Anvil Ranch
Organ Pipe Cactus N M
Santa Rita Exp Range
Tombstone
Canelo 1 NW
Sierra Vista
Sasabe
Nogales 6 N
Coronado N M Hdqtrs
Arizona
CITIES
Weather Stations

Arizona Weather Stations by County

County	Station Name
Apache	Alpine
	Canyon De Chelly
	McNary 2 N
	Saint Johns
	Teec Nos Pos
Cochise	Bowie
	Cascabel
	Coronado N M Hdqtrs
	Sierra Vista
	Tombstone
Coconino	Bright Angel R S
	Flagstaff 4 SW
	Flagstaff Pulliam Arpt
	Fort Valley
	Lees Ferry
	Wupatki N M
Gila	Payson
Graham	Black River Pumps
Greenlee	Clifton
La Paz	Alamo Dam
Maricopa	Fountain Hills
	Gila Bend
	Laveen 3 SSE
	Phoenix Sky Harbor Intl Arpt
	South Phoenix
Mohave	Beaver Dam
	Bullhead City
	Colorado City
	Willow Beach
	Yucca 1 NNE
Navajo	Betatakin
	Holbrook
	Monument Valley
	Winslow Municipal Arpt
Pima	Anvil Ranch
	Kitt Peak
	Organ Pipe Cactus N M
	Santa Rita Exp Range
	Sasabe
	Tucson 17 NW
	Tucson Intl Arpt
	Tucson NWSO
Pinal	Casa Grande
	Florence
	Maricopa 4 N
	Oracle 2 SE
Santa Cruz	Canelo 1 NW
	Nogales 6 N
Yavapai	Castle Hot Springs
	Childs
	Cordes

County	Station Name
Yavapai *(cont.)*	Seligman
Yuma	Kofa Mine
	Yuma Citrus Station
	Yuma Intl Arpt
	Yuma Proving Ground

See User Guide for station inclusion criteria.

Arizona Weather Stations by City

City	Station Name	Miles
Apache Junction	Fountain Hills	16.3
	Phoenix Sky Harbor Intl Arpt	25.0
Avondale	Laveen 3 SSE	13.0
	Phoenix Sky Harbor Intl Arpt	19.5
	South Phoenix	15.6
Bullhead City	Bullhead City	2.3
	Needles Airport, CA	23.8
Casa Grande	Casa Grande	4.2
	Florence	22.3
	Maricopa 4 N	22.8
Casas Adobes	Oracle 2 SE	24.1
	Tucson 17 NW	12.7
	Tucson NWSO	8.6
	Tucson Intl Arpt	15.1
Catalina Foothills	Oracle 2 SE	22.3
	Tucson 17 NW	18.9
	Tucson NWSO	6.2
	Tucson Intl Arpt	12.3
Chandler	Fountain Hills	21.9
	Laveen 3 SSE	16.5
	Maricopa 4 N	16.4
	Phoenix Sky Harbor Intl Arpt	11.9
	South Phoenix	12.7
Drexel Heights	Anvil Ranch	22.8
	Tucson 17 NW	12.3
	Tucson NWSO	8.5
	Tucson Intl Arpt	5.2
El Mirage	Laveen 3 SSE	21.3
	Phoenix Sky Harbor Intl Arpt	22.3
	South Phoenix	21.3
Flagstaff	Flagstaff 4 SW	5.4
	Flagstaff Pulliam Arpt	5.1
	Fort Valley	7.3
Florence	Casa Grande	23.7
	Florence	1.6
Fortuna Foothills	Yuma Citrus Station	13.9
	Yuma Proving Ground	12.1
	Yuma Intl Arpt	10.7
Fountain Hills	Fountain Hills	0.9
	Phoenix Sky Harbor Intl Arpt	18.3
	South Phoenix	24.9
Gilbert	Fountain Hills	17.6
	Laveen 3 SSE	21.9
	Maricopa 4 N	22.1
	Phoenix Sky Harbor Intl Arpt	14.0
	South Phoenix	17.2
Glendale	Laveen 3 SSE	17.2
	Phoenix Sky Harbor Intl Arpt	15.1
	South Phoenix	15.4

City	Station Name	Miles
Goodyear	Laveen 3 SSE	15.8
	Phoenix Sky Harbor Intl Arpt	23.6
	South Phoenix	19.2
Green Valley	Anvil Ranch	24.1
	Santa Rita Exp Range	10.8
	Tucson Intl Arpt	19.3
Kingman	Yucca 1 NNE	23.4
Lake Havasu City	Parker Reservoir, CA	16.2
Marana	Tucson 17 NW	10.3
	Tucson NWSO	14.7
	Tucson Intl Arpt	20.2
Mesa	Fountain Hills	13.4
	Laveen 3 SSE	22.3
	Phoenix Sky Harbor Intl Arpt	12.2
	South Phoenix	16.9
New River	Castle Hot Springs	18.4
Oro Valley	Oracle 2 SE	19.0
	Tucson 17 NW	17.4
	Tucson NWSO	12.5
	Tucson Intl Arpt	19.4
Peoria	Laveen 3 SSE	20.0
	Phoenix Sky Harbor Intl Arpt	18.7
	South Phoenix	18.8
Phoenix	Fountain Hills	21.7
	Laveen 3 SSE	13.9
	Phoenix Sky Harbor Intl Arpt	7.7
	South Phoenix	9.9
Prescott	Cordes	24.8
Prescott Valley	Cordes	23.0
San Luis	Yuma Citrus Station	10.7
	Yuma Intl Arpt	15.2
Scottsdale	Fountain Hills	10.4
	Laveen 3 SSE	22.0
	Phoenix Sky Harbor Intl Arpt	9.7
	South Phoenix	16.3
Sierra Vista	Canelo 1 NW	14.4
	Coronado N M Hdqtrs	13.7
	Sierra Vista	0.5
	Tombstone	17.7
Sun City	Laveen 3 SSE	20.9
	Phoenix Sky Harbor Intl Arpt	20.6
	South Phoenix	20.2
Sun City West	Castle Hot Springs	21.7
Surprise	Castle Hot Springs	23.5
Tempe	Fountain Hills	18.9
	Laveen 3 SSE	13.4

See User Guide for station inclusion criteria.

City	Station Name	Miles
Tempe *(cont.)*	Maricopa 4 N	19.8
	Phoenix Sky Harbor Intl Arpt	5.3
	South Phoenix	8.1
Tucson	Tucson 17 NW	17.3
	Tucson NWSO	2.9
	Tucson Intl Arpt	5.8
Yuma	Yuma Citrus Station	5.4
	Yuma Proving Ground	16.3
	Yuma Intl Arpt	2.3

Note: Miles is the distance between the geographic center of the city and the weather station.

Arizona Weather Stations by Elevation

Feet	Station Name
8,399	Bright Angel R S
8,049	Alpine
7,347	Fort Valley
7,339	McNary 2 N
7,286	Betatakin
7,123	Flagstaff 4 SW
6,993	Flagstaff Pulliam Arpt
6,790	Kitt Peak
6,040	Black River Pumps
5,790	Saint Johns
5,609	Canyon De Chelly
5,563	Monument Valley
5,290	Teec Nos Pos
5,250	Seligman
5,242	Coronado N M Hdqtrs
5,069	Holbrook
5,009	Canelo 1 NW
5,009	Colorado City
4,913	Payson
4,908	Wupatki N M
4,890	Winslow Municipal Arpt
4,609	Tombstone
4,600	Sierra Vista
4,509	Oracle 2 SE
4,299	Santa Rita Exp Range
3,771	Cordes
3,770	Bowie
3,589	Sasabe
3,560	Nogales 6 N
3,520	Clifton
3,209	Lees Ferry
3,145	Cascabel
2,750	Anvil Ranch
2,648	Childs
2,561	Tucson 17 NW
2,548	Tucson Intl Arpt
2,478	Tucson NWSO
1,990	Castle Hot Springs
1,950	Yucca 1 NNE
1,875	Beaver Dam
1,774	Kofa Mine
1,678	Organ Pipe Cactus N M
1,575	Fountain Hills
1,504	Florence
1,461	Casa Grande
1,290	Alamo Dam
1,160	Maricopa 4 N
1,154	South Phoenix
1,115	Laveen 3 SSE
1,106	Phoenix Sky Harbor Intl Arpt
740	Willow Beach
734	Gila Bend
540	Bullhead City
324	Yuma Proving Ground
206	Yuma Intl Arpt
190	Yuma Citrus Station

See User Guide for station inclusion criteria.

Flagstaff Pulliam Airport

Flagstaff, elevation 7,000 feet, is situated on a volcanic plateau at the base of the highest mountains in Arizona. The climate may be classified as vigorous with cold winters, mild, pleasantly cool summers, moderate humidity, and considerable diurnal temperature change. Only limited farming exists due to the short growing season. The stormy months are January, February, March, July, and August.

The average first occurrence of 32 degrees Fahrenheit in the fall is September 21 and the average last occurrence in the spring is June 13.

Temperatures in Flagstaff are characteristic of high altitude climates. The average daily range of temperature is relatively high, especially in the winter months, October to March, as a result of extensive snow cover and clear skies. Winter minimum temperatures frequently reach zero or below and temperatures of -25 degrees or less have occurred. Summer maximum temperatures are often above 80 degrees and occasionally, temperatures have exceeded 95 degrees.

The Flagstaff area is semi-arid. Several months have recorded little or no precipitation. Over 90 consecutive days without measurable precipitation have occurred. Annual precipitation ranges from less than 10 inches to more than 35 inches. Winter snowfalls can be heavy, exceeding 100 inches during one month and over 200 inches during the winter season. However, accumulations are quite variable from year to year. Some winter months may experience little or no snow and the winter season has produced total snow accumulations of less than 12 inches.

Flagstaff Pulliam Airport *Coconino County* Elevation: 6,993 ft. Latitude: 35° 08' N Longitude: 111° 40' W

	JAN	FEB	MAR	APR	MAY	JUN	JUL	AUG	SEP	OCT	NOV	DEC	YEAR
Mean Maximum Temp. (°F)	43.3	45.7	51.2	59.0	68.8	78.7	82.2	79.4	73.7	63.0	51.5	43.6	61.7
Mean Temp. (°F)	30.4	32.6	37.4	43.7	51.9	60.3	66.5	64.7	57.8	47.2	37.3	30.3	46.7
Mean Minimum Temp. (°F)	17.4	19.4	23.5	28.3	35.0	41.8	50.7	50.0	42.0	31.3	23.1	16.9	31.6
Extreme Maximum Temp. (°F)	65	71	73	80	89	94	96	91	89	85	73	67	96
Extreme Minimum Temp. (°F)	-16	-23	-10	8	18	24	33	35	25	11	-6	-23	-23
Days Maximum Temp. ≥ 90°F	0	0	0	0	0	1	2	1	0	0	0	0	4
Days Maximum Temp. ≤ 32°F	3	2	1	0	0	0	0	0	0	0	1	4	11
Days Minimum Temp. ≤ 32°F	30	28	29	24	11	2	0	0	2	19	27	30	202
Days Minimum Temp. ≤ 0°F	2	1	0	0	0	0	0	0	0	0	0	1	4
Heating Degree Days (base 65°F)	1,067	910	850	632	399	156	25	45	211	547	823	1,070	6,735
Cooling Degree Days (base 65°F)	0	0	0	0	1	21	77	43	3	0	0	0	145
Mean Precipitation (in.)	2.09	2.36	2.21	1.17	0.67	0.38	2.49	3.06	2.33	1.59	1.68	1.79	21.82
Maximum Precipitation (in.)*	9.5	10.0	6.8	5.6	4.1	2.9	6.6	8.1	6.8	9.9	6.6	7.3	36.6
Minimum Precipitation (in.)*	0	trace	trace	trace	trace	0	trace	0.3	trace	trace	trace	trace	10.4
Extreme Maximum Daily Precip. (in.)	1.65	3.93	2.05	1.70	0.92	0.91	2.14	3.04	2.71	2.42	2.13	3.33	3.93
Days With ≥ 0.1" Precipitation	5	5	6	3	2	1	6	7	5	3	3	4	50
Days With ≥ 0.5" Precipitation	1	1	1	1	0	0	1	2	1	1	1	1	11
Days With ≥ 1.0" Precipitation	0	0	0	0	0	0	0	0	1	0	0	0	1
Mean Snowfall (in.)	***24.4***	***21.4***	***22.8***	***6.7***	***0.6***	***trace***	***trace***	***trace***	***0.1***	na	***10.2***	***15.6***	na
Maximum Snowfall (in.)*	63	46	79	58	8	trace	0	0	2	25	41	86	184
Maximum 24-hr. Snowfall (in.)*	16	21	26	11	7	trace	0	0	2	10	18	27	27
Maximum Snow Depth (in.)	na	***26***	na	na	na	na	na	na	na	na	na	***20***	na
Days With ≥ 1.0" Snow Depth	na	***14***	***8***	na	na	na	na	na	na	na	na	***12***	na
Thunderstorm Days*	< 1	1	1	2	5	5	18	18	9	3	1	< 1	63
Foggy Days*	10	8	8	4	2	< 1	1	2	3	4	6	8	56
Predominant Sky Cover*	CLR	CLR	CLR	CLR	CLR	CLR	BRK	BRK	CLR	CLR	CLR	CLR	CLR
Mean Relative Humidity 5am (%)*	75	75	73	67	64	55	70	79	75	71	72	73	71
Mean Relative Humidity 5pm (%)*	52	46	43	32	28	21	38	44	37	35	44	51	39
Mean Dewpoint (°F)*	16	18	19	21	25	28	44	46	38	27	20	16	27
Prevailing Wind Direction*	NE	SW	SW	SW	SW	SW	SW	SW	SW	NE	NE	NE	SW
Prevailing Wind Speed (mph)*	8	9	10	10	10	10	8	8	8	7	8	7	9
Maximum Wind Gust (mph)*	53	47	49	55	66	51	44	62	46	52	69	49	69

Note: (*) Period of record is 1950-1995

Phoenix Sky Harbor Int'l Arpt.

Phoenix is located in the Salt River Valley at an elevation of about 1,100 feet. The valley is oval shaped and flat except for scattered precipitous mountains rising a few hundred to as much as 1,500 feet above the valley floor. Sky Harbor Airport, where the weather observations are taken, is in the southern part of the city. Six miles to the south of the airport are the South Mountains rising to 2,500 feet. Eighteen miles southwest, the Estrella Mountains rise to 4,500 feet, and 30 miles to the west are the White Tank Mountains rising to 4,100 feet. The Superstition Mountains, over 30 miles to the east, rise to as much as 5,000 feet. The valley, though located in the Sonora Desert, supports large acreages of cotton, citrus, and other agriculture along with one of the largest urban populations in the United States. The water supply for this complex desert community is partly from reservoirs on the impounded Salt and Verde Rivers, and partly from a large underground water table.

Temperatures range from very hot in summer to mild in winter. Many winter days reach over 70 degrees and typical high temperatures in the middle of the winter are in the 60s. The climate becomes less attractive in the summer. The normal high temperature is over 90 degrees from early May through early October, and over 100 degrees from early June through early September. Many days each summer will exceed 110 degrees in the afternoon and remain above 85 degrees all night.

Indeed, the climate is very dry. Annual precipitation is only about seven inches, and afternoon humidities range from about 30 percent in winter to only about 10 percent in June. Rain comes mostly in two seasons. From about Thanksgiving to early April there are periodic rains from Pacific storms. Moisture from the south and southeast results in a summer thunderstorm peak in July and August. Usually the break from extreme dryness in June to the onset of thunderstorms in early July is very abrupt. Afternoon humidities suddenly double to about 20 percent, which with the great heat, gives a feeling of mugginess. Fog is rare, occurring about once per winter, and is unknown in the other seasons.

The valley is characterized by light winds. High winds associated with thunderstorms occur periodically in the summer. These occasionally create duststorms which move large distances across the deserts. Strong thunderstorm winds occur any month of the year, but are rare outside the summer months. Persistent strong winds of 30 mph or more are rare except for two or three events in an average spring due to Pacific storms.

The average first occurrence of 32 degrees Fahrenheit in the fall is December 13 and the average last occurrence in the spring is February 7.

Phoenix Sky Harbor Int'l Arpt. *Maricopa County* Elevation: 1,106 ft. Latitude: 33° 27' N Longitude: 111° 59' W

	JAN	FEB	MAR	APR	MAY	JUN	JUL	AUG	SEP	OCT	NOV	DEC	YEAR
Mean Maximum Temp. (°F)	67.4	71.0	77.0	85.4	94.9	104.0	106.2	104.5	99.9	88.6	75.9	66.4	86.8
Mean Temp. (°F)	56.5	59.9	65.2	72.8	82.1	90.8	94.8	93.6	88.3	76.6	64.2	55.6	75.0
Mean Minimum Temp. (°F)	45.6	48.7	53.4	60.1	69.2	77.5	83.3	82.6	76.7	64.6	52.5	44.8	63.2
Extreme Maximum Temp. (°F)	86	92	100	105	113	122	121	116	112	107	96	86	122
Extreme Minimum Temp. (°F)	29	28	38	40	50	60	68	64	57	44	35	26	26
Days Maximum Temp. ≥ 90°F	0	0	2	11	24	29	31	31	28	15	1	0	172
Days Maximum Temp. ≤ 32°F	0	0	0	0	0	0	0	0	0	0	0	0	0
Days Minimum Temp. ≤ 32°F	0	0	0	0	0	0	0	0	0	0	0	0	0
Days Minimum Temp. ≤ 0°F	0	0	0	0	0	0	0	0	0	0	0	0	0
Heating Degree Days (base 65°F)	259	156	77	19	1	0	0	0	0	7	90	286	895
Cooling Degree Days (base 65°F)	2	18	91	259	537	781	931	892	705	374	74	1	4,665
Mean Precipitation (in.)	0.88	0.94	0.98	0.29	0.12	0.03	1.00	0.99	0.64	0.56	0.64	0.85	7.92
Maximum Precipitation (in.)*	5.2	2.2	3.2	1.9	1.1	1.7	5.1	5.6	3.4	4.4	3.0	4.0	15.2
Minimum Precipitation (in.)*	0	0	0	0	0	0	trace	trace	0	0	0	0	2.8
Extreme Maximum Daily Precip. (in.)	1.22	1.46	1.98	0.74	0.46	0.18	1.90	1.59	1.66	2.32	1.58	1.35	2.32
Days With ≥ 0.1" Precipitation	2	2	2	1	0	0	2	2	1	1	1	2	16
Days With ≥ 0.5" Precipitation	1	0	1	0	0	0	1	1	0	0	0	1	5
Days With ≥ 1.0" Precipitation	0	0	0	0	0	0	0	0	0	0	0	0	0
Mean Snowfall (in.)	na	na	na	na	na	na	na	na	na	na	na	na	na
Maximum Snowfall (in.)*	trace	trace	0	0	0	0	0	0	0	0	0	trace	trace
Maximum 24-hr. Snowfall (in.)*	trace	trace	0	0	0	0	0	0	0	0	0	trace	trace
Maximum Snow Depth (in.)	na	na	na	na	na	na	na	na	na	na	na	na	na
Days With ≥ 1.0" Snow Depth	na	na	na	na	na	na	na	na	na	na	na	na	na
Thunderstorm Days*	< 1	1	1	1	1	1	6	7	4	1	1	< 1	24
Foggy Days*	2	1	1	< 1	< 1	0	< 1	< 1	< 1	< 1	1	2	7
Predominant Sky Cover*	CLR	CLR	CLR	CLR	CLR	CLR	CLR	CLR	CLR	CLR	CLR	CLR	CLR
Mean Relative Humidity 5am (%)*	68	63	57	45	37	33	46	53	50	52	59	66	52
Mean Relative Humidity 5pm (%)*	34	28	25	17	14	12	21	24	23	23	28	35	24
Mean Dewpoint (°F)*	33	33	34	33	36	40	56	59	52	43	36	33	41
Prevailing Wind Direction*	E	E	E	E	E	W	W	E	E	E	E	E	E
Prevailing Wind Speed (mph)*	6	7	7	7	7	9	8	7	7	7	6	6	7
Maximum Wind Gust (mph)*	60	54	52	49	59	73	86	78	61	61	60	68	86

Note: (*) Period of record is 1948-1995

The period of record for National Weather Service station data is 1980 – 2009 except where noted. See User Guide for detailed explanation of data.

Tucson Int'l Airport

Tucson lies at the foot of the Catalina Mountains, north of the airport. The area within about 15 miles of the airport station is flat or gently rolling, with many dry washes. The soil is sandy, and vegetation is mostly brush, cacti, and small trees. Rugged mountains encircle the valley. The mountains to the north, east, and south rise to over 5,000 feet above the airport. The western hills and mountains range from 500 to 4,000 feet.

The climate of Tucson is characterized by a long hot season, from April to October. Temperatures above 90 degrees prevail from May through September. Temperatures of 100 degrees or higher average 41 days annually, including 14 days each for June and July, but these extreme temperatures are moderated by low relative humidities. The temperature range is large, averaging 30 degrees or more a day.

More than 50 percent of the annual precipitation falls between July 1 and September 15, and over 20 percent falls from December through March. During the summer, scattered convective or orographic showers and thunderstorms often fill dry washes to overflowing. On occasion, brief, torrential downpours cause destructive flash floods in the Tucson area. Hail rarely occurs in thunderstorms. The December through March precipitation occurs as prolonged rainstorms that replenish the ground water. During these storms, snow often falls on the higher mountains, but snow in Tucson is infrequent. From the first of the year, the humidity decreases steadily until the summer thunderstorm season, when it shows a marked increase. From mid-September, the end of the thunderstorm season, the humidity decreases again until late November. Occasionally during the summer, humidities are high enough to produce discomfort, but only for short periods. During the hot season, humidity values sometimes fall below five percent.

Tucson lies in the zone receiving more sunshine than any other section of the United States. Cloudless days are commonplace, and average cloudiness is low.

Surface winds are generally light, with no major seasonal changes in velocity or direction. Occasional duststorms occur in areas where the ground has been disturbed. During the spring, winds may briefly be strong enough to cause some damage to trees and buildings. Usually local winds tend to be in the southeast quadrant during the night and early morning hours. Highest velocities usually occur with winds from the southwest and east to south.

Based on the 1951-1980 period, the average first occurrence of 32 degrees Fahrenheit in the fall is November 29 and the average last occurrence in the spring is February 28.

Tucson Int'l Airport *Pima County* Elevation: 2,548 ft. Latitude: 32° 08' N Longitude: 110° 57' W

	JAN	FEB	MAR	APR	MAY	JUN	JUL	AUG	SEP	OCT	NOV	DEC	YEAR
Mean Maximum Temp. (°F)	66.1	69.4	74.7	82.8	92.1	101.0	100.4	98.1	95.1	85.3	74.2	65.5	83.7
Mean Temp. (°F)	53.0	55.9	60.5	67.4	76.3	85.1	87.4	85.7	81.8	71.3	60.2	52.4	69.7
Mean Minimum Temp. (°F)	39.8	42.3	46.2	52.0	60.4	69.2	74.3	73.2	68.4	57.2	46.1	39.2	55.7
Extreme Maximum Temp. (°F)	87	91	99	104	109	117	114	112	107	102	93	83	117
Extreme Minimum Temp. (°F)	19	23	24	34	40	51	59	63	53	34	26	19	19
Days Maximum Temp. ≥ 90°F	0	0	1	7	21	29	30	29	25	10	0	0	152
Days Maximum Temp. ≤ 32°F	0	0	0	0	0	0	0	0	0	0	0	0	0
Days Minimum Temp. ≤ 32°F	4	2	1	0	0	0	0	0	0	0	1	5	13
Days Minimum Temp. ≤ 0°F	0	0	0	0	0	0	0	0	0	0	0	0	0
Heating Degree Days (base 65°F)	366	256	167	55	3	0	0	0	0	23	167	385	1,422
Cooling Degree Days (base 65°F)	1	4	33	133	360	611	701	647	510	226	30	1	3,257
Mean Precipitation (in.)	0.89	0.89	0.75	0.31	0.23	0.21	2.22	2.39	1.36	0.88	0.57	0.92	11.62
Maximum Precipitation (in.)*	4.8	2.9	2.3	1.7	1.1	1.5	6.2	7.9	5.1	5.0	1.9	5.0	21.9
Minimum Precipitation (in.)*	0	0	0	0	0	0	trace	0.2	0	0	0	0	5.3
Extreme Maximum Daily Precip. (in.)	1.32	1.04	0.97	1.17	0.53	0.66	1.90	2.29	2.15	2.96	1.40	2.10	2.96
Days With ≥ 0.1" Precipitation	2	2	2	1	1	1	5	5	3	2	2	2	28
Days With ≥ 0.5" Precipitation	0	0	1	0	0	0	1	2	1	1	0	1	7
Days With ≥ 1.0" Precipitation	0	0	0	0	0	0	1	0	0	0	0	0	1
Mean Snowfall (in.)	0.3	0.2	trace	trace	trace	0.0	trace	trace	trace	trace	trace	0.2	0.7
Maximum Snowfall (in.)*	5	4	6	2	0	0	0	0	0	0	6	7	8
Maximum 24-hr. Snowfall (in.)*	4	2	4	2	0	0	0	0	0	0	6	7	7
Maximum Snow Depth (in.)	1	trace	trace	trace	trace	0	trace	trace	trace	trace	trace	2	2
Days With ≥ 1.0" Snow Depth	0	0	0	0	0	0	0	0	0	0	0	0	0
Thunderstorm Days*	< 1	< 1	1	1	2	3	14	14	6	2	< 1	< 1	43
Foggy Days*	1	1	< 1	< 1	< 1	0	< 1	< 1	< 1	< 1	< 1	1	3
Predominant Sky Cover*	CLR	CLR	CLR	CLR	CLR	CLR	OVR	CLR	CLR	CLR	CLR	CLR	CLR
Mean Relative Humidity 5am (%)*	63	59	53	42	35	32	57	65	55	52	55	62	52
Mean Relative Humidity 5pm (%)*	32	26	22	15	13	13	28	32	26	24	27	34	25
Mean Dewpoint (°F)*	29	28	28	27	30	36	56	58	50	39	31	29	37
Prevailing Wind Direction*	SE	SE	SE	SE	SE	SE	SE	SE	SE	SE	SE	SE	SE
Prevailing Wind Speed (mph)*	8	8	8	8	8	8	9	8	9	9	8	8	8
Maximum Wind Gust (mph)*	55	48	53	55	55	58	81	76	71	49	51	47	81

Note: (*) Period of record is 1946-1995

Winslow Municipal Airport

Winslow is located in the Little Colorado River Valley. The adjacent terrain rises gradually in all directions except to the north-northwest along the river. The White Mountain area, 100 miles to the southeast, rises to over 11,000 feet. To the south and west the Mogollon Rim averages very close to 8,000 feet above sea level, while 60 miles to the northwest the San Francisco Peaks rise to 12,655 feet.

The surrounding high terrain has a considerable effect upon the climate and weather of the Winslow area. It acts as a barrier to the movement of low-level moist air currents, as well as to cold wintertime air masses from the plains states. As a consequence, the climate is very dry and relatively mild for the latitude and elevation.

The elevation of Winslow and the generally clear skies tend to create a large diurnal temperature variation during all seasons. Below-zero readings occur during the winter months about one year in three. Daytime temperatures over 70 degrees have been recorded during all winter months. Summer days are warm with temperatures of 90 degrees or higher occurring frequently from late May to mid-September. Because of the extremely low humidity, however, the high daytime temperatures are quite comfortable. The air cools rapidly after sunset so that nights are generally cool during the summer months.

Monthly and annual precipitation is extremely variable in amount. Moist air carried aloft over the surrounding mountains from the Gulf of Mexico and the Pacific Ocean during the summer and early fall helps produce the major portion of the annual precipitation. The lifting of the moist air over the mountains and the intense surface heating of the sparsely covered lower elevations causes considerable thunderstorm activity during this summer period. Snowfall during the winter is generally light, and because of warm daytime temperatures, it soon melts. The annual snowfall is about 10 inches, but occasionally a winter season will pass with only a trace being recorded. With the annual precipitation averaging about seven inches, agricultural activity in the vicinity of Winslow is restricted to small irrigated tracts.

More than 270 days during the year are clear or only partly cloudy. The average growing period is 186 days.

During the spring months, occasional high winds pick up considerable dust. During the late fall and winter months the prevailing wind direction is from the southeast, while in the spring and summer months the winds blow primarily from the southwest. Destructive weather such as tornadoes and ice storms rarely occur.

Winslow Municipal Airport *Navajo County* Elevation: 4,890 ft. Latitude: 35° 02' N Longitude: 110° 43' W

	JAN	FEB	MAR	APR	MAY	JUN	JUL	AUG	SEP	OCT	NOV	DEC	YEAR
Mean Maximum Temp. (°F)	48.4	54.7	62.2	70.5	80.3	90.4	93.3	89.9	83.8	72.1	58.9	47.5	71.0
Mean Temp. (°F)	35.2	40.2	46.7	54.0	63.3	72.4	77.9	75.7	68.4	56.0	43.8	34.3	55.7
Mean Minimum Temp. (°F)	22.0	25.7	31.1	37.5	46.2	54.4	62.4	61.5	52.9	39.8	28.6	21.1	40.3
Extreme Maximum Temp. (°F)	72	76	85	91	101	104	106	103	98	91	82	70	106
Extreme Minimum Temp. (°F)	-5	-3	-2	18	25	37	44	46	36	16	4	-11	-11
Days Maximum Temp. ≥ 90°F	0	0	0	0	4	18	24	17	6	0	0	0	69
Days Maximum Temp. ≤ 32°F	2	0	0	0	0	0	0	0	0	0	0	2	4
Days Minimum Temp. ≤ 32°F	28	22	18	7	1	0	0	0	0	6	21	28	131
Days Minimum Temp. ≤ 0°F	0	0	0	0	0	0	0	0	0	0	0	0	0
Heating Degree Days (base 65°F)	916	694	561	326	108	9	0	1	27	280	628	944	4,494
Cooling Degree Days (base 65°F)	0	0	0	3	61	238	406	339	135	7	0	0	1,189
Mean Precipitation (in.)	0.49	0.49	0.55	0.28	0.32	0.19	1.06	1.21	0.89	0.52	0.51	0.54	7.05
Maximum Precipitation (in.)*	1.4	2.0	2.1	1.2	1.4	3.2	2.7	4.8	2.5	5.6	1.7	3.7	12.3
Minimum Precipitation (in.)*	0	trace	0	trace	0	0	0	0.1	0	0	trace	trace	4.5
Extreme Maximum Daily Precip. (in.)	0.67	0.57	0.89	0.64	0.48	0.52	1.61	1.23	1.17	0.98	1.33	1.30	1.61
Days With ≥ 0.1" Precipitation	2	2	2	1	1	1	3	3	2	1	2	2	22
Days With ≥ 0.5" Precipitation	0	0	0	0	0	0	1	1	0	0	0	0	2
Days With ≥ 1.0" Precipitation	0	0	0	0	0	0	0	0	0	0	0	0	0
Mean Snowfall (in.)	na	na	na	na	na	na	na	na	na	na	na	na	na
Maximum Snowfall (in.)*	11	11	11	5	1	0	0	0	0	8	7	40	40
Maximum 24-hr. Snowfall (in.)*	5	8	5	3	1	0	0	0	0	7	3	15	15
Maximum Snow Depth (in.)	na	na	na	na	na	na	na	na	na	na	na	na	na
Days With ≥ 1.0" Snow Depth	na	na	na	na	na	na	na	na	na	na	na	na	na
Thunderstorm Days*	< 1	< 1	< 1	1	2	3	11	11	5	1	< 1	< 1	34
Foggy Days*	2	1	1	< 1	< 1	< 1	< 1	< 1	< 1	1	1	3	9
Predominant Sky Cover*	CLR	CLR	CLR	CLR	CLR	CLR	SCT	CLR	CLR	CLR	CLR	CLR	CLR
Mean Relative Humidity 5am (%)*	76	69	60	51	44	38	57	64	59	59	66	73	60
Mean Relative Humidity 5pm (%)*	47	34	25	19	16	14	26	29	25	26	33	47	29
Mean Dewpoint (°F)*	18	19	19	20	24	29	46	48	40	30	22	18	28
Prevailing Wind Direction*	SW	SW	SW	SW	SW	SW	SW	SW	SW	SW	SW	SE	SW
Prevailing Wind Speed (mph)*	10	12	14	15	14	14	12	10	12	10	10	7	12
Maximum Wind Gust (mph)*	53	58	73	73	74	68	56	66	52	54	55	59	74

Note: (*) Period of record is 1948-1979

The period of record for National Weather Service station data is 1980 – 2009 except where noted. See User Guide for detailed explanation of data.

Yuma Int'l Airport

Yuma has a desert climate. Winter is a period of mostly clear skies and abundant sunshine. Yuma records a higher percentage of sunshine than any other place in the United States. Even in December and January, Yuma averages more than eight hours of sunshine a day. Summers in the lower Colorado River Valley are long and hot. Afternoon temperatures reach at least 100 degrees on the average, from June 4 to September 24, and at least 105 degrees from June 22 to August 26. Extremes over 120 degrees have occurred. From mid July to mid September, moisture-laden air from the Gulf of California frequently invades the area. The water content of the air is higher than might be expected over a desert area.

Precipitation in the Yuma area is sparce. Normal annual precipitation is under three inches. The wettest years have produced less than 12 inches and the driest years less than one inch. Snow is rare in the Yuma area but amounts under two inches in a winter season have been recorded.

Yuma Int'l Airport *Yuma County* Elevation: 206 ft. Latitude: 32° 40' N Longitude: 114° 36' W

	JAN	FEB	MAR	APR	MAY	JUN	JUL	AUG	SEP	OCT	NOV	DEC	YEAR
Mean Maximum Temp. (°F)	na	na	na	na	na	na	na	na	na	na	na	na	na
Mean Temp. (°F)	na	na	na	na	na	na	na	na	na	na	na	na	na
Mean Minimum Temp. (°F)	na	na	na	na	na	na	na	na	na	na	na	na	na
Extreme Maximum Temp. (°F)	na	na	na	na	na	na	na	na	na	na	na	na	na
Extreme Minimum Temp. (°F)	na	na	na	na	na	na	na	na	na	na	na	na	na
Days Maximum Temp. ≥ 90°F	na	na	na	na	na	na	na	na	na	na	na	na	na
Days Maximum Temp. ≤ 32°F	na	na	na	na	na	na	na	na	na	na	na	na	na
Days Minimum Temp. ≤ 32°F	na	na	na	na	na	na	na	na	na	na	na	na	na
Days Minimum Temp. ≤ 0°F	na	na	na	na	na	na	na	na	na	na	na	na	na
Heating Degree Days (base 65°F)	na	na	na	na	na	na	na	na	na	na	na	na	na
Cooling Degree Days (base 65°F)	na	na	na	na	na	na	na	na	na	na	na	na	na
Mean Precipitation (in.)	na	na	na	na	na	na	na	na	na	na	na	na	na
Maximum Precipitation (in.)*	2.8	1.8	1.6	1.2	0.4	0.3	2.5	3.4	2.5	2.7	1.7	2.1	6.8
Minimum Precipitation (in.)*	0	0	0	0	0	0	0	0	0	0	0	0	0.3
Extreme Maximum Daily Precip. (in.)	na	na	na	na	na	na	na	na	na	na	na	na	na
Days With ≥ 0.1" Precipitation	na	na	na	na	na	na	na	na	na	na	na	na	na
Days With ≥ 0.5" Precipitation	na	na	na	na	na	na	na	na	na	na	na	na	na
Days With ≥ 1.0" Precipitation	na	na	na	na	na	na	na	na	na	na	na	na	na
Mean Snowfall (in.)	na	na	na	na	na	na	na	na	na	na	na	na	na
Maximum Snowfall (in.)*	0	0	0	0	0	0	0	0	0	0	0	trace	trace
Maximum 24-hr. Snowfall (in.)*	0	0	0	0	0	0	0	0	0	0	0	trace	trace
Maximum Snow Depth (in.)	na	na	na	na	na	na	na	na	na	na	na	na	na
Days With ≥ 1.0" Snow Depth	na	na	na	na	na	na	na	na	na	na	na	na	na
Thunderstorm Days*	< 1	< 1	< 1	< 1	< 1	< 1	2	2	1	1	< 1	< 1	6
Foggy Days*	1	< 1	0	< 1	0	0	< 1	< 1	< 1	< 1	< 1	1	2
Predominant Sky Cover*	CLR	CLR	CLR	CLR	CLR	CLR	CLR	CLR	CLR	CLR	CLR	CLR	CLR
Mean Relative Humidity 5am (%)*	55	52	49	45	42	39	48	55	55	52	51	53	50
Mean Relative Humidity 5pm (%)*	28	22	18	15	14	13	21	24	22	21	24	29	21
Mean Dewpoint (°F)*	29	30	31	33	38	44	58	61	55	44	34	29	40
Prevailing Wind Direction*	N	N	W	W	S	SSE	SSE	SSE	SSE	N	N	N	N
Prevailing Wind Speed (mph)*	10	10	10	10	9	12	13	12	10	8	9	9	10
Maximum Wind Gust (mph)*	43	40	43	40	40	44	58	67	76	43	43	46	76

Note: (*) Period of record is 1948-1979

Alamo Dam *La Paz County* Elevation: 1,290 ft. Latitude: 34° 14' N Longitude: 113° 35' W

	JAN	FEB	MAR	APR	MAY	JUN	JUL	AUG	SEP	OCT	NOV	DEC	YEAR
Mean Maximum Temp. (°F)	66.2	70.2	76.9	85.3	95.3	104.8	108.3	106.5	100.9	89.3	75.8	65.3	87.1
Mean Temp. (°F)	51.2	55.0	61.0	68.5	78.1	86.9	92.7	91.5	84.5	72.4	59.6	50.5	71.0
Mean Minimum Temp. (°F)	36.2	39.8	45.1	51.7	60.9	69.0	77.1	76.4	68.1	55.4	43.5	35.7	54.9
Extreme Maximum Temp. (°F)	81	88	102	106	114	123	124	119	115	110	96	84	124
Extreme Minimum Temp. (°F)	19	21	26	33	38	46	58	61	50	36	26	19	19
Days Maximum Temp. ≥ 90°F	0	0	3	11	24	29	31	30	28	16	1	0	173
Days Maximum Temp. ≤ 32°F	0	0	0	0	0	0	0	0	0	0	0	0	0
Days Minimum Temp. ≤ 32°F	8	3	0	0	0	0	0	0	0	0	1	9	21
Days Minimum Temp. ≤ 0°F	0	0	0	0	0	0	0	0	0	0	0	0	0
Heating Degree Days (base 65°F)	420	278	152	43	4	0	0	0	0	16	176	443	1,532
Cooling Degree Days (base 65°F)	0	1	36	155	417	664	868	828	593	251	22	0	3,835
Mean Precipitation (in.)	1.03	1.22	0.83	0.26	0.12	0.06	0.71	1.48	0.87	0.66	0.72	0.62	8.58
Extreme Maximum Daily Precip. (in.)	1.55	1.66	1.29	0.88	0.49	0.65	1.12	2.50	2.33	2.30	1.80	1.15	2.50
Days With ≥ 0.1" Precipitation	2	3	2	1	0	0	2	3	1	1	1	2	18
Days With ≥ 0.5" Precipitation	1	1	1	0	0	0	0	1	0	0	1	0	5
Days With ≥ 1.0" Precipitation	0	0	0	0	0	0	0	0	0	0	0	0	0
Mean Snowfall (in.)	0.0	0.1	0.0	0.0	0.0	0.0	0.0	0.0	0.0	0.0	trace	0.0	0.1
Maximum Snow Depth (in.)	0	2	0	0	0	0	0	0	0	0	trace	0	2
Days With ≥ 1.0" Snow Depth	0	0	0	0	0	0	0	0	0	0	0	0	0

Alpine *Apache County* Elevation: 8,049 ft. Latitude: 33° 51' N Longitude: 109° 09' W

	JAN	FEB	MAR	APR	MAY	JUN	JUL	AUG	SEP	OCT	NOV	DEC	YEAR
Mean Maximum Temp. (°F)	45.3	47.6	52.2	59.5	68.0	76.8	77.8	74.9	70.9	62.3	53.2	45.8	61.2
Mean Temp. (°F)	29.8	32.9	36.9	42.5	49.5	56.9	61.7	60.1	54.6	45.5	36.9	30.2	44.8
Mean Minimum Temp. (°F)	14.4	18.1	21.5	25.4	30.9	37.0	45.4	45.2	38.1	28.6	20.5	14.3	28.3
Extreme Maximum Temp. (°F)	65	66	71	79	92	93	91	87	83	81	75	68	93
Extreme Minimum Temp. (°F)	-15	-13	-11	5	15	19	27	29	20	7	-6	-22	-22
Days Maximum Temp. ≥ 90°F	0	0	0	0	0	0	0	0	0	0	0	0	0
Days Maximum Temp. ≤ 32°F	2	1	0	0	0	0	0	0	0	0	1	2	6
Days Minimum Temp. ≤ 32°F	30	27	29	25	18	7	1	0	5	22	27	30	221
Days Minimum Temp. ≤ 0°F	2	1	0	0	0	0	0	0	0	0	0	2	5
Heating Degree Days (base 65°F)	1,083	902	864	668	473	237	106	147	306	598	837	1,073	7,294
Cooling Degree Days (base 65°F)	0	0	0	0	0	2	9	2	0	0	0	0	13
Mean Precipitation (in.)	1.35	1.27	1.18	0.74	0.72	0.90	3.46	4.66	2.34	2.01	1.29	1.44	21.36
Extreme Maximum Daily Precip. (in.)	2.10	1.62	1.24	1.45	1.27	1.48	2.50	***2.77***	2.77	1.90	***2.02***	1.80	***2.77***
Days With ≥ 0.1" Precipitation	3	3	3	2	2	3	9	11	5	4	3	3	51
Days With ≥ 0.5" Precipitation	0	1	1	0	0	0	2	3	1	1	1	1	11
Days With ≥ 1.0" Precipitation	0	0	0	0	0	0	0	1	0	0	0	0	1
Mean Snowfall (in.)	9.8	7.9	6.8	2.5	0.5	trace	0.0	0.0	trace	1.4	4.1	8.2	41.2
Maximum Snow Depth (in.)	24	17	***16***	8	7	trace	0	0	trace	15	9	22	***24***
Days With ≥ 1.0" Snow Depth	7	6	***4***	0	0	0	0	0	0	0	2	4	***23***

Anvil Ranch *Pima County* Elevation: 2,750 ft. Latitude: 31° 59' N Longitude: 111° 23' W

	JAN	FEB	MAR	APR	MAY	JUN	JUL	AUG	SEP	OCT	NOV	DEC	YEAR
Mean Maximum Temp. (°F)	66.2	69.1	74.7	82.2	90.8	99.3	98.8	96.3	93.9	84.8	74.2	65.6	83.0
Mean Temp. (°F)	49.6	52.5	57.2	63.5	72.0	80.9	84.2	82.2	77.7	67.2	56.4	49.3	66.1
Mean Minimum Temp. (°F)	33.0	35.8	39.6	44.8	53.2	62.5	69.6	68.3	61.4	49.5	38.6	32.9	49.1
Extreme Maximum Temp. (°F)	87	97	97	102	106	114	111	109	106	102	94	86	114
Extreme Minimum Temp. (°F)	8	16	19	24	33	38	41	53	37	26	15	12	8
Days Maximum Temp. ≥ 90°F	0	0	1	5	18	28	29	28	24	8	1	0	142
Days Maximum Temp. ≤ 32°F	0	0	0	0	0	0	0	0	0	0	0	0	0
Days Minimum Temp. ≤ 32°F	15	9	4	1	0	0	0	0	0	1	6	15	51
Days Minimum Temp. ≤ 0°F	0	0	0	0	0	0	0	0	0	0	0	0	0
Heating Degree Days (base 65°F)	470	348	244	100	11	0	0	0	0	50	260	479	1,962
Cooling Degree Days (base 65°F)	0	1	9	61	236	485	602	541	388	125	8	0	2,456
Mean Precipitation (in.)	0.77	0.80	0.65	0.26	0.24	0.29	2.55	2.74	1.33	0.79	0.52	1.03	11.97
Extreme Maximum Daily Precip. (in.)	1.55	0.95	0.94	0.92	0.86	1.68	2.47	***2.20***	2.00	2.50	2.30	2.40	***2.50***
Days With ≥ 0.1" Precipitation	2	2	2	1	1	1	5	6	3	2	1	2	28
Days With ≥ 0.5" Precipitation	0	0	0	0	0	0	2	1	1	0	0	0	4
Days With ≥ 1.0" Precipitation	0	0	0	0	0	0	0	0	0	0	0	0	0
Mean Snowfall (in.)	trace	trace	0.0	0.0	0.0	0.0	0.0	0.0	0.0	0.0	0.0	trace	trace
Maximum Snow Depth (in.)	trace	0	0	0	0	0	0	0	0	0	0	0	trace
Days With ≥ 1.0" Snow Depth	0	0	0	0	0	0	0	0	0	0	0	0	0

Beaver Dam *Mohave County* Elevation: 1,875 ft. Latitude: 36° 54' N Longitude: 113° 57' W

	JAN	FEB	MAR	APR	MAY	JUN	JUL	AUG	SEP	OCT	NOV	DEC	YEAR
Mean Maximum Temp. (°F)	59.4	64.0	71.8	80.5	91.1	100.7	***106.3***	103.7	96.3	83.3	69.0	58.3	***82.0***
Mean Temp. (°F)	46.7	50.5	57.0	64.4	74.4	83.3	***89.7***	88.1	80.3	67.8	54.8	45.4	***66.9***
Mean Minimum Temp. (°F)	33.9	36.9	42.1	48.2	57.7	65.9	***73.1***	72.4	64.3	52.2	40.5	32.6	***51.7***
Extreme Maximum Temp. (°F)	80	87	96	101	113	116	120	116	114	106	89	77	120
Extreme Minimum Temp. (°F)	12	14	22	27	37	47	51	51	44	30	18	4	4
Days Maximum Temp. ≥ 90°F	0	0	1	6	18	27	30	30	25	8	0	0	145
Days Maximum Temp. ≤ 32°F	0	0	0	0	0	0	0	0	0	0	0	0	0
Days Minimum Temp. ≤ 32°F	13	7	3	1	0	0	0	0	0	0	5	15	44
Days Minimum Temp. ≤ 0°F	0	0	0	0	0	0	0	0	0	0	0	0	0
Heating Degree Days (base 65°F)	561	405	259	99	15	1	***0***	0	1	58	307	599	***2,305***
Cooling Degree Days (base 65°F)	0	1	17	88	313	557	***774***	723	468	151	7	0	***3,099***
Mean Precipitation (in.)	0.90	1.11	0.92	0.44	0.19	0.20	0.59	0.65	0.48	0.73	0.59	0.65	7.45
Extreme Maximum Daily Precip. (in.)	1.11	0.97	0.89	0.54	0.40	0.67	***1.25***	1.11	***1.38***	1.45	0.90	***1.75***	***1.75***
Days With ≥ 0.1" Precipitation	3	3	3	2	1	1	1	2	***1***	2	2	2	***23***
Days With ≥ 0.5" Precipitation	0	1	0	0	0	0	0	0	0	0	0	0	1
Days With ≥ 1.0" Precipitation	0	0	0	0	0	0	0	0	0	0	0	0	0
Mean Snowfall (in.)	trace	***0.0***	0.0	0.0	0.0	0.0	0.0	0.0	0.0	0.0	0.0	trace	***trace***
Maximum Snow Depth (in.)	0	***0***	0	0	0	0	0	0	0	***0***	0	1	***1***
Days With ≥ 1.0" Snow Depth	0	***0***	0	0	0	0	0	0	0	***0***	0	0	***0***

The period of record for all cooperative weather station data is 1980 – 2009. See User Guide for detailed explanation of data.

Betatakin *Navajo County* Elevation: 7,286 ft. Latitude: 36° 41' N Longitude: 110° 32' W

	JAN	FEB	MAR	APR	MAY	JUN	JUL	AUG	SEP	OCT	NOV	DEC	YEAR
Mean Maximum Temp. (°F)	40.5	44.0	51.6	60.7	71.1	81.8	85.5	82.8	75.4	63.0	49.5	40.1	62.2
Mean Temp. (°F)	31.1	34.0	40.2	47.5	57.5	67.5	72.0	70.0	63.1	51.5	39.5	30.9	50.4
Mean Minimum Temp. (°F)	21.6	24.0	28.7	34.4	43.8	53.2	58.5	57.1	50.8	39.9	29.4	21.6	38.6
Extreme Maximum Temp. (°F)	61	69	75	82	94	96	98	96	91	82	70	60	98
Extreme Minimum Temp. (°F)	-11	-14	4	14	23	32	39	41	32	14	-2	-14	-14
Days Maximum Temp. ≥ 90°F	0	0	0	0	0	3	8	3	0	0	0	0	14
Days Maximum Temp. ≤ 32°F	5	2	0	0	0	0	0	0	0	0	1	5	13
Days Minimum Temp. ≤ 32°F	29	25	22	12	3	0	0	0	0	6	18	28	143
Days Minimum Temp. ≤ 0°F	0	0	0	0	0	0	0	0	0	0	0	0	0
Heating Degree Days (base 65°F)	1,044	869	763	518	243	46	7	8	96	412	759	1,050	5,815
Cooling Degree Days (base 65°F)	0	0	0	0	17	127	232	170	46	1	0	0	593
Mean Precipitation (in.)	1.15	1.08	1.04	0.85	0.53	0.25	1.15	1.66	1.44	1.18	0.99	1.10	12.42
Extreme Maximum Daily Precip. (in.)	1.30	1.03	1.10	1.01	2.00	0.55	1.10	1.93	1.60	2.00	1.18	1.40	2.00
Days With ≥ 0.1" Precipitation	3	4	3	2	1	1	3	4	3	3	3	3	33
Days With ≥ 0.5" Precipitation	1	0	0	0	0	0	1	1	1	1	0	1	6
Days With ≥ 1.0" Precipitation	0	0	0	0	0	0	0	0	0	0	0	0	0
Mean Snowfall (in.)	9.6	8.3	5.6	3.7	0.7	trace	0.0	0.0	trace	0.4	4.7	9.3	42.3
Maximum Snow Depth (in.)	20	20	12	6	6	trace	0	0	trace	4	10	19	20
Days With ≥ 1.0" Snow Depth	15	11	5	1	0	0	0	0	0	0	3	8	43

Black River Pumps *Graham County* Elevation: 6,040 ft. Latitude: 33° 29' N Longitude: 109° 45' W

	JAN	FEB	MAR	APR	MAY	JUN	JUL	AUG	SEP	OCT	NOV	DEC	YEAR
Mean Maximum Temp. (°F)	50.3	53.3	58.4	66.8	76.3	86.4	87.7	84.4	79.9	70.3	58.4	50.7	68.6
Mean Temp. (°F)	35.8	38.6	42.9	49.7	58.4	68.0	71.9	70.1	64.6	54.2	42.9	35.7	52.7
Mean Minimum Temp. (°F)	21.2	23.9	27.3	32.5	40.6	49.4	56.1	55.6	49.3	38.1	27.4	20.7	36.8
Extreme Maximum Temp. (°F)	70	75	79	86	95	103	102	101	94	94	80	72	103
Extreme Minimum Temp. (°F)	-4	-3	1	12	24	26	44	42	34	14	6	-19	-19
Days Maximum Temp. ≥ 90°F	0	0	0	0	1	10	12	5	1	0	0	0	29
Days Maximum Temp. ≤ 32°F	0	0	0	0	0	0	0	0	0	0	0	1	1
Days Minimum Temp. ≤ 32°F	29	26	25	16	3	0	0	0	0	7	23	30	159
Days Minimum Temp. ≤ 0°F	0	0	0	0	0	0	0	0	0	0	0	1	1
Heating Degree Days (base 65°F)	900	739	678	452	208	28	1	4	60	333	657	902	4,962
Cooling Degree Days (base 65°F)	0	0	0	0	12	125	222	169	55	6	0	0	589
Mean Precipitation (in.)	1.88	1.76	1.52	0.72	0.61	0.53	3.68	3.46	2.01	1.42	1.28	1.61	20.48
Extreme Maximum Daily Precip. (in.)	4.01	1.25	1.75	1.17	1.16	1.61	2.38	1.77	2.00	2.02	2.00	1.87	4.01
Days With ≥ 0.1" Precipitation	4	5	4	2	2	1	8	8	4	3	3	4	48
Days With ≥ 0.5" Precipitation	1	1	1	0	0	0	2	2	1	1	1	1	11
Days With ≥ 1.0" Precipitation	0	0	0	0	0	0	1	0	0	0	0	0	1
Mean Snowfall (in.)	3.4	2.9	1.1	1.2	0.0	0.0	0.0	0.0	0.0	trace	0.4	1.4	10.4
Maximum Snow Depth (in.)	***15***	***12***	***10***	***2***	***0***	***0***	***0***	***0***	***0***	***0***	***0***	***6***	***15***
Days With ≥ 1.0" Snow Depth	***1***	1	***0***	0	0	0	0	0	0	0	0	0	***2***

Bowie *Cochise County* Elevation: 3,770 ft. Latitude: 32° 19' N Longitude: 109° 29' W

	JAN	FEB	MAR	APR	MAY	JUN	JUL	AUG	SEP	OCT	NOV	DEC	YEAR
Mean Maximum Temp. (°F)	60.7	65.4	71.7	80.0	88.9	97.7	97.1	93.9	90.3	80.7	69.1	60.1	79.6
Mean Temp. (°F)	46.4	50.5	55.7	62.8	71.3	80.1	82.4	80.1	75.2	64.7	53.3	45.9	64.0
Mean Minimum Temp. (°F)	32.0	35.5	39.7	45.6	53.8	62.4	67.6	66.3	60.0	48.6	37.6	31.7	48.4
Extreme Maximum Temp. (°F)	79	84	92	99	105	111	109	108	104	96	86	77	111
Extreme Minimum Temp. (°F)	13	16	17	27	36	38	55	52	45	27	17	13	13
Days Maximum Temp. ≥ 90°F	0	0	0	2	15	27	28	25	18	3	0	0	118
Days Maximum Temp. ≤ 32°F	0	0	0	0	0	0	0	0	0	0	0	0	0
Days Minimum Temp. ≤ 32°F	17	9	4	1	0	0	0	0	0	1	8	18	58
Days Minimum Temp. ≤ 0°F	0	0	0	0	0	0	0	0	0	0	0	0	0
Heating Degree Days (base 65°F)	571	404	284	107	11	0	0	0	1	76	344	584	2,382
Cooling Degree Days (base 65°F)	0	0	4	47	215	458	546	476	312	74	1	0	2,133
Mean Precipitation (in.)	1.01	0.92	0.61	0.31	0.39	0.44	2.17	2.37	1.09	0.94	0.81	1.20	12.26
Extreme Maximum Daily Precip. (in.)	0.96	1.30	0.85	0.51	1.16	2.15	1.91	2.69	1.72	2.35	1.20	1.70	2.69
Days With ≥ 0.1" Precipitation	3	3	2	1	1	1	5	5	3	2	2	3	31
Days With ≥ 0.5" Precipitation	0	1	0	0	0	0	1	1	1	1	0	1	6
Days With ≥ 1.0" Precipitation	0	0	0	0	0	0	0	0	0	0	0	0	0
Mean Snowfall (in.)	0.1	0.2	0.1	trace	0.0	0.0	0.0	0.0	0.0	0.0	0.0	0.5	0.9
Maximum Snow Depth (in.)	0	***trace***	0	0	0	0	0	0	0	0	0	0	trace
Days With ≥ 1.0" Snow Depth	0	***0***	0	0	0	0	0	0	0	0	0	0	***0***

Bright Angel R S *Coconino County* Elevation: 8,399 ft. Latitude: 36° 13' N Longitude: 112° 04' W

	JAN	FEB	MAR	APR	MAY	JUN	JUL	AUG	SEP	OCT	NOV	DEC	YEAR
Mean Maximum Temp. (°F)	38.7	39.6	45.4	***53.2***	***63.5***	74.6	78.3	75.0	68.6	57.0	46.2	***39.3***	***56.6***
Mean Temp. (°F)	27.8	28.8	33.5	***40.4***	***48.9***	58.0	63.1	60.8	54.5	44.0	34.6	***28.2***	***43.5***
Mean Minimum Temp. (°F)	16.9	18.0	21.5	***27.5***	***34.2***	41.3	47.8	46.5	40.5	31.0	23.0	***16.9***	***30.4***
Extreme Maximum Temp. (°F)	64	62	66	74	85	88	92	90	84	80	65	68	92
Extreme Minimum Temp. (°F)	-16	-23	-3	6	14	22	33	32	21	7	-1	-18	-23
Days Maximum Temp. ≥ 90°F	0	0	0	0	0	0	1	0	0	0	0	0	1
Days Maximum Temp. ≤ 32°F	8	6	2	0	0	0	0	0	0	0	2	6	24
Days Minimum Temp. ≤ 32°F	30	27	28	22	12	2	0	0	3	18	26	29	197
Days Minimum Temp. ≤ 0°F	1	1	0	0	0	0	0	0	0	0	0	1	3
Heating Degree Days (base 65°F)	1,146	1,016	972	***732***	***493***	209	83	133	308	644	906	***1,136***	***7,778***
Cooling Degree Days (base 65°F)	0	0	0	***0***	***0***	6	30	9	0	0	0	***0***	***45***
Mean Precipitation (in.)	3.58	3.52	3.21	1.55	0.68	0.42	1.99	2.64	1.92	1.81	1.64	2.44	25.40
Extreme Maximum Daily Precip. (in.)	3.18	3.50	***3.99***	***1.44***	***1.14***	0.99	2.02	2.20	3.16	***3.13***	2.48	2.66	***3.99***
Days With ≥ 0.1" Precipitation	6	6	5	***3***	2	1	5	6	3	3	3	5	***48***
Days With ≥ 0.5" Precipitation	3	3	2	1	0	0	1	2	1	1	1	2	17
Days With ≥ 1.0" Precipitation	1	1	1	0	0	0	0	1	0	0	0	0	4
Mean Snowfall (in.)	30.5	28.0	26.0	11.2	1.4	0.2	0.0	0.0	trace	3.8	11.9	20.2	133.2
Maximum Snow Depth (in.)	72	89	86	61	50	trace	0	0	trace	18	26	49	89
Days With ≥ 1.0" Snow Depth	29	27	28	13	2	0	0	0	0	2	10	24	135

The period of record for all cooperative weather station data is 1980 – 2009. See User Guide for detailed explanation of data.

Bullhead City *Mohave County* Elevation: 540 ft. Latitude: 35° 08' N Longitude: 114° 34' W

	JAN	FEB	MAR	APR	MAY	JUN	JUL	AUG	SEP	OCT	NOV	DEC	YEAR
Mean Maximum Temp. (°F)	66.2	71.3	79.6	88.4	98.3	107.8	112.2	110.3	103.5	90.5	75.6	65.4	89.1
Mean Temp. (°F)	55.1	58.8	64.9	72.6	82.0	90.5	96.1	95.0	87.7	75.3	62.8	54.2	74.6
Mean Minimum Temp. (°F)	43.9	46.3	50.1	56.7	65.7	73.1	80.0	79.7	71.8	60.0	49.9	43.0	60.0
Extreme Maximum Temp. (°F)	83	93	102	107	118	126	126	122	117	111	95	88	126
Extreme Minimum Temp. (°F)	28	28	33	40	47	50	64	60	54	39	31	23	23
Days Maximum Temp. ≥ 90°F	0	0	3	13	26	29	30	31	29	18	1	0	180
Days Maximum Temp. ≤ 32°F	0	0	0	0	0	0	0	0	0	0	0	0	0
Days Minimum Temp. ≤ 32°F	1	0	0	0	0	0	0	0	0	0	0	1	2
Days Minimum Temp. ≤ 0°F	0	0	0	0	0	0	0	0	0	0	0	0	0
Heating Degree Days (base 65°F)	302	181	79	14	0	0	0	0	0	6	112	329	1,023
Cooling Degree Days (base 65°F)	2	12	81	247	534	772	973	938	686	331	52	1	4,629
Mean Precipitation (in.)	0.94	1.03	0.73	0.14	0.07	0.01	0.28	0.71	0.35	0.43	0.42	0.51	5.62
Extreme Maximum Daily Precip. (in.)	1.04	1.70	1.15	0.75	0.55	0.15	2.29	3.05	1.69	1.45	1.23	1.07	3.05
Days With ≥ 0.1" Precipitation	2	2	2	1	0	0	1	1	1	1	1	1	13
Days With ≥ 0.5" Precipitation	1	1	1	0	0	0	0	1	0	0	0	0	4
Days With ≥ 1.0" Precipitation	0	0	0	0	0	0	0	0	0	0	0	0	0
Mean Snowfall (in.)	0.0	0.0	0.0	0.0	0.0	0.0	0.0	0.0	0.0	0.0	0.0	0.0	0.0
Maximum Snow Depth (in.)	0	0	0	0	0	0	0	0	0	0	0	0	0
Days With ≥ 1.0" Snow Depth	0	0	0	0	0	0	0	0	0	0	0	0	0

Canelo 1 NW *Santa Cruz County* Elevation: 5,009 ft. Latitude: 31° 34' N Longitude: 110° 32' W

	JAN	FEB	MAR	APR	MAY	JUN	JUL	AUG	SEP	OCT	NOV	DEC	YEAR
Mean Maximum Temp. (°F)	***58.4***	62.1	66.7	74.5	82.6	90.8	***88.8***	***85.7***	84.0	***75.9***	***66.1***	58.5	***74.5***
Mean Temp. (°F)	***43.3***	46.3	49.9	56.6	64.2	72.6	***74.8***	***72.7***	68.9	***59.8***	***50.1***	43.5	***58.6***
Mean Minimum Temp. (°F)	***28.1***	30.4	33.1	38.6	45.8	54.3	***60.8***	***59.6***	53.8	***43.6***	***34.0***	28.5	***42.6***
Extreme Maximum Temp. (°F)	***78***	81	88	94	101	106	***103***	99	97	92	***83***	77	***106***
Extreme Minimum Temp. (°F)	***7***	8	13	19	25	35	***49***	44	38	20	***14***	3	***3***
Days Maximum Temp. ≥ 90°F	***0***	0	0	0	5	18	***14***	6	3	0	***0***	0	***46***
Days Maximum Temp. ≤ 32°F	***0***	0	0	0	0	0	***0***	0	0	0	***0***	0	***0***
Days Minimum Temp. ≤ 32°F	***23***	17	15	6	1	0	***0***	0	0	2	***13***	22	***99***
Days Minimum Temp. ≤ 0°F	***0***	0	0	0	0	0	***0***	0	0	0	***0***	0	***0***
Heating Degree Days (base 65°F)	***666***	521	460	252	75	4	***0***	***0***	9	***171***	***442***	659	***3,259***
Cooling Degree Days (base 65°F)	***0***	0	0	5	58	238	***312***	***244***	133	***16***	***0***	0	***1,006***
Mean Precipitation (in.)	***1.40***	1.14	1.12	0.53	0.24	0.65	***4.01***	4.11	1.79	1.22	***0.95***	1.52	***18.68***
Extreme Maximum Daily Precip. (in.)	***2.52***	1.35	1.39	1.62	0.62	1.58	***2.77***	2.12	1.88	1.95	***1.55***	1.75	***2.77***
Days With ≥ 0.1" Precipitation	***3***	3	3	1	1	2	***8***	9	4	2	***2***	3	***41***
Days With ≥ 0.5" Precipitation	***1***	1	1	0	0	0	***3***	3	1	1	***1***	1	***13***
Days With ≥ 1.0" Precipitation	***0***	0	0	0	0	0	***1***	1	0	0	***0***	0	***2***
Mean Snowfall (in.)	***0.1***	0.1	0.2	0.0	0.0	0.0	***0.0***	0.0	0.0	0.0	***0.0***	***trace***	***0.4***
Maximum Snow Depth (in.)	***2***	***trace***	***3***	0	0	***0***	***0***	0	0	***0***	***0***	***4***	***4***
Days With ≥ 1.0" Snow Depth	***0***	***0***	0	0	0	0	***0***	0	0	0	***0***	***0***	***0***

Canyon De Chelly *Apache County* Elevation: 5,609 ft. Latitude: 36° 09' N Longitude: 109° 32' W

	JAN	FEB	MAR	APR	MAY	JUN	JUL	AUG	SEP	OCT	NOV	DEC	YEAR
Mean Maximum Temp. (°F)	45.1	51.6	60.6	69.4	79.4	89.5	93.0	89.6	82.7	70.2	56.2	44.8	69.3
Mean Temp. (°F)	32.7	38.1	45.4	53.0	62.1	71.1	76.7	74.5	66.5	54.2	42.0	32.4	54.1
Mean Minimum Temp. (°F)	20.2	24.6	30.2	36.6	44.8	52.7	60.4	59.4	50.2	38.1	27.8	20.0	38.7
Extreme Maximum Temp. (°F)	70	72	85	90	101	104	105	101	99	90	79	67	105
Extreme Minimum Temp. (°F)	-7	-11	2	18	22	33	40	40	23	15	-1	-14	-14
Days Maximum Temp. ≥ 90°F	0	0	0	0	3	17	24	16	3	0	0	0	63
Days Maximum Temp. ≤ 32°F	3	1	0	0	0	0	0	0	0	0	0	3	7
Days Minimum Temp. ≤ 32°F	28	24	19	9	1	0	0	0	0	8	22	28	139
Days Minimum Temp. ≤ 0°F	1	0	0	0	0	0	0	0	0	0	0	0	1
Heating Degree Days (base 65°F)	996	754	600	355	129	16	0	0	47	332	682	1,003	4,914
Cooling Degree Days (base 65°F)	0	0	0	2	48	206	371	302	99	3	0	0	1,031
Mean Precipitation (in.)	0.78	0.78	0.66	0.66	0.42	0.33	1.19	1.37	0.93	0.85	0.77	0.78	9.52
Extreme Maximum Daily Precip. (in.)	5.00	1.40	0.80	1.31	0.89	1.25	1.92	1.64	1.54	0.89	1.22	1.00	5.00
Days With ≥ 0.1" Precipitation	2	3	3	2	2	1	3	4	3	3	2	2	30
Days With ≥ 0.5" Precipitation	0	0	0	0	0	0	0	1	0	0	0	0	1
Days With ≥ 1.0" Precipitation	0	0	0	0	0	0	0	0	0	0	0	0	0
Mean Snowfall (in.)	1.6	1.0	0.8	0.1	0.0	0.0	0.0	0.0	0.0	0.1	0.6	1.4	5.6
Maximum Snow Depth (in.)	3	***8***	***2***	trace	0	0	0	0	0	trace	***3***	***3***	***8***
Days With ≥ 1.0" Snow Depth	0	0	0	0	0	0	0	0	0	0	0	0	0

Casa Grande *Pinal County* Elevation: 1,461 ft. Latitude: 32° 57' N Longitude: 111° 46' W

	JAN	FEB	MAR	APR	MAY	JUN	JUL	AUG	SEP	OCT	NOV	DEC	YEAR
Mean Maximum Temp. (°F)	68.2	71.8	78.3	86.9	96.1	104.9	106.2	104.0	99.7	***89.2***	76.8	66.6	***87.4***
Mean Temp. (°F)	53.3	56.5	62.0	69.2	78.1	86.5	91.2	89.7	84.1	***72.5***	***60.6***	52.1	***71.3***
Mean Minimum Temp. (°F)	38.4	41.0	45.7	51.5	60.1	68.1	76.2	75.4	68.4	***55.7***	***44.1***	37.4	***55.2***
Extreme Maximum Temp. (°F)	86	97	100	105	113	118	120	***115***	112	108	96	***87***	***120***
Extreme Minimum Temp. (°F)	17	23	26	30	42	46	57	***61***	48	29	***25***	***21***	***17***
Days Maximum Temp. ≥ 90°F	0	0	3	12	26	30	30	31	28	15	1	0	176
Days Maximum Temp. ≤ 32°F	0	0	0	0	0	0	0	0	0	0	0	0	0
Days Minimum Temp. ≤ 32°F	6	3	1	0	0	0	0	0	0	0	2	7	19
Days Minimum Temp. ≤ 0°F	0	0	0	0	0	0	0	0	0	0	0	0	0
Heating Degree Days (base 65°F)	357	240	130	35	1	0	0	0	0	***16***	***157***	395	***1,331***
Cooling Degree Days (base 65°F)	1	5	44	166	411	652	820	774	579	***254***	***30***	0	***3,736***
Mean Precipitation (in.)	0.81	0.95	0.88	0.29	0.21	0.08	0.90	1.81	0.77	***0.57***	0.62	1.00	***8.89***
Extreme Maximum Daily Precip. (in.)	1.40	1.50	1.20	0.79	0.75	***0.48***	1.08	***2.39***	***2.00***	***1.61***	***1.29***	1.41	***2.39***
Days With ≥ 0.1" Precipitation	2	2	2	1	1	0	2	3	2	1	1	2	19
Days With ≥ 0.5" Precipitation	1	1	1	0	0	0	1	1	1	0	0	1	7
Days With ≥ 1.0" Precipitation	0	0	0	0	0	0	0	1	0	0	0	0	1
Mean Snowfall (in.)	0.0	0.0	0.0	0.0	0.0	0.0	0.0	0.0	0.0	0.0	0.0	trace	trace
Maximum Snow Depth (in.)	0	0	0	0	0	0	0	***0***	0	0	0	trace	trace
Days With ≥ 1.0" Snow Depth	0	0	0	0	0	0	0	0	0	0	0	0	0

The period of record for all cooperative weather station data is 1980 – 2009. See User Guide for detailed explanation of data.

Cascabel *Cochise County* Elevation: 3,145 ft. Latitude: 32° 19' N Longitude: 110° 25' W

	JAN	FEB	MAR	APR	MAY	JUN	JUL	AUG	SEP	OCT	NOV	DEC	YEAR
Mean Maximum Temp. (°F)	65.3	68.5	74.1	82.4	91.4	100.4	99.4	96.4	93.4	84.0	73.2	64.5	82.7
Mean Temp. (°F)	47.9	50.6	54.8	61.2	69.3	78.2	82.2	80.7	75.7	65.2	54.3	47.1	63.9
Mean Minimum Temp. (°F)	30.5	32.7	35.5	40.0	47.2	55.9	65.0	65.0	57.9	46.3	35.4	29.8	45.1
Extreme Maximum Temp. (°F)	84	88	96	103	109	116	115	109	108	102	92	84	116
Extreme Minimum Temp. (°F)	7	9	15	20	25	38	44	51	41	19	11	10	7
Days Maximum Temp. ≥ 90°F	0	0	1	6	20	29	29	27	24	8	0	0	144
Days Maximum Temp. ≤ 32°F	0	0	0	0	0	0	0	0	0	0	0	0	0
Days Minimum Temp. ≤ 32°F	19	14	10	4	0	0	0	0	0	1	10	21	79
Days Minimum Temp. ≤ 0°F	0	0	0	0	0	0	0	0	0	0	0	0	0
Heating Degree Days (base 65°F)	524	401	312	140	23	0	0	0	1	73	315	547	2,336
Cooling Degree Days (base 65°F)	0	0	3	33	164	402	541	494	328	86	2	0	2,053
Mean Precipitation (in.)	1.13	1.20	0.94	0.36	0.31	0.37	2.65	2.86	1.33	1.02	0.76	1.23	14.16
Extreme Maximum Daily Precip. (in.)	1.88	1.86	0.82	0.84	0.65	1.28	4.12	5.03	1.70	1.80	1.39	1.63	5.03
Days With ≥ 0.1" Precipitation	3	3	2	1	1	1	6	6	3	2	2	3	33
Days With ≥ 0.5" Precipitation	1	1	1	0	0	0	1	2	1	1	0	1	9
Days With ≥ 1.0" Precipitation	0	0	0	0	0	0	0	1	0	0	0	0	1
Mean Snowfall (in.)	1.0	0.8	0.2	trace	0.0	0.0	0.0	0.0	0.0	0.0	trace	0.5	2.5
Maximum Snow Depth (in.)	2	trace	trace	trace	0	0	0	0	0	0	trace	4	4
Days With ≥ 1.0" Snow Depth	0	0	0	0	0	0	0	0	0	0	0	0	0

Castle Hot Springs *Yavapai County* Elevation: 1,990 ft. Latitude: 33° 59' N Longitude: 112° 22' W

	JAN	FEB	MAR	APR	MAY	JUN	JUL	AUG	SEP	OCT	NOV	DEC	YEAR
Mean Maximum Temp. (°F)	66.5	68.9	73.6	81.4	90.3	99.2	102.3	100.4	95.6	85.6	74.4	65.7	83.7
Mean Temp. (°F)	54.0	56.3	60.4	66.9	75.3	83.8	88.8	87.4	82.3	72.1	61.4	53.5	70.2
Mean Minimum Temp. (°F)	41.5	43.7	47.2	52.2	60.1	68.3	75.1	74.3	69.0	58.5	48.2	41.2	56.6
Extreme Maximum Temp. (°F)	87	91	94	99	110	116	120	113	109	104	93	84	120
Extreme Minimum Temp. (°F)	23	24	28	35	43	47	60	58	48	38	28	23	23
Days Maximum Temp. ≥ 90°F	0	0	1	6	17	28	31	29	26	10	1	0	149
Days Maximum Temp. ≤ 32°F	0	0	0	0	0	0	0	0	0	0	0	0	0
Days Minimum Temp. ≤ 32°F	2	1	0	0	0	0	0	0	0	0	0	2	5
Days Minimum Temp. ≤ 0°F	0	0	0	0	0	0	0	0	0	0	0	0	0
Heating Degree Days (base 65°F)	334	244	167	56	6	0	0	0	0	16	144	350	1,317
Cooling Degree Days (base 65°F)	1	6	33	120	332	570	743	702	527	243	41	0	3,318
Mean Precipitation (in.)	1.94	2.33	1.68	0.57	0.21	0.11	1.48	2.15	1.10	0.91	1.19	1.41	15.08
Extreme Maximum Daily Precip. (in.)	2.85	2.50	3.35	1.90	0.70	0.60	2.00	3.50	1.21	2.60	2.25	2.70	3.50
Days With ≥ 0.1" Precipitation	3	3	3	1	1	0	3	4	2	2	2	2	26
Days With ≥ 0.5" Precipitation	1	2	1	0	0	0	1	1	1	1	1	1	10
Days With ≥ 1.0" Precipitation	1	1	0	0	0	0	0	0	0	0	0	1	3
Mean Snowfall (in.)	trace	0.2	0.0	0.0	0.0	0.0	0.0	0.0	0.0	0.0	trace	trace	0.2
Maximum Snow Depth (in.)	trace	0	0	0	0	0	0	0	0	0	trace	trace	trace
Days With ≥ 1.0" Snow Depth	0	0	0	0	0	0	0	0	0	0	0	0	0

Childs *Yavapai County* Elevation: 2,648 ft. Latitude: 34° 21' N Longitude: 111° 42' W

	JAN	FEB	MAR	APR	MAY	JUN	JUL	AUG	SEP	OCT	NOV	DEC	YEAR
Mean Maximum Temp. (°F)	61.8	66.1	71.1	79.5	89.3	99.5	102.2	99.7	94.1	83.7	70.6	60.7	81.5
Mean Temp. (°F)	47.4	50.8	55.1	61.4	69.9	78.8	84.7	83.3	76.8	66.1	54.3	46.5	64.6
Mean Minimum Temp. (°F)	32.9	35.4	38.9	43.4	50.5	58.0	67.2	67.0	59.5	48.3	37.9	32.2	47.6
Extreme Maximum Temp. (°F)	81	88	94	100	110	116	117	112	109	106	96	83	117
Extreme Minimum Temp. (°F)	18	19	14	29	35	32	47	51	44	29	22	16	14
Days Maximum Temp. ≥ 90°F	0	0	0	5	16	27	30	29	24	9	0	0	140
Days Maximum Temp. ≤ 32°F	0	0	0	0	0	0	0	0	0	0	0	0	0
Days Minimum Temp. ≤ 32°F	15	8	3	1	0	0	0	0	0	0	6	17	50
Days Minimum Temp. ≤ 0°F	0	0	0	0	0	0	0	0	0	0	0	0	0
Heating Degree Days (base 65°F)	540	396	306	140	28	1	0	0	2	67	319	568	2,367
Cooling Degree Days (base 65°F)	0	0	4	41	187	422	618	575	363	106	4	0	2,320
Mean Precipitation (in.)	2.16	2.57	2.08	0.95	0.39	0.17	1.93	2.74	2.09	1.33	1.46	1.78	19.65
Extreme Maximum Daily Precip. (in.)	2.63	2.82	2.60	1.68	0.87	0.71	2.19	2.47	3.80	1.78	2.48	2.60	3.80
Days With ≥ 0.1" Precipitation	4	4	4	2	1	0	4	6	4	2	3	3	37
Days With ≥ 0.5" Precipitation	1	2	1	1	0	0	2	2	1	1	1	1	13
Days With ≥ 1.0" Precipitation	1	1	0	0	0	0	0	1	1	0	0	0	4
Mean Snowfall (in.)	0.1	0.6	0.0	0.0	0.0	0.0	0.0	0.0	0.0	0.0	0.2	0.2	1.1
Maximum Snow Depth (in.)	0	trace	0	0	0	0	0	0	0	0	trace	0	trace
Days With ≥ 1.0" Snow Depth	0	0	0	0	0	0	0	0	0	0	0	0	0

Clifton *Greenlee County* Elevation: 3,520 ft. Latitude: 33° 03' N Longitude: 109° 18' W

	JAN	FEB	MAR	APR	MAY	JUN	JUL	AUG	SEP	OCT	NOV	DEC	YEAR
Mean Maximum Temp. (°F)	60.6	65.2	71.7	80.5	89.5	99.0	99.5	96.4	91.8	81.2	68.3	59.5	80.3
Mean Temp. (°F)	47.3	51.6	57.5	65.5	74.3	83.5	85.9	83.7	78.6	67.3	54.6	46.5	66.4
Mean Minimum Temp. (°F)	34.0	37.9	43.2	50.3	59.1	68.1	72.3	71.1	65.2	53.3	40.8	33.5	52.4
Extreme Maximum Temp. (°F)	79	86	92	99	108	116	115	110	105	99	86	75	116
Extreme Minimum Temp. (°F)	20	18	19	33	34	30	56	51	42	32	23	16	16
Days Maximum Temp. ≥ 90°F	0	0	0	3	16	29	28	28	22	4	0	0	130
Days Maximum Temp. ≤ 32°F	0	0	0	0	0	0	0	0	0	0	0	0	0
Days Minimum Temp. ≤ 32°F	13	6	1	0	0	0	0	0	0	0	3	14	37
Days Minimum Temp. ≤ 0°F	0	0	0	0	0	0	0	0	0	0	0	0	0
Heating Degree Days (base 65°F)	541	372	239	68	8	0	0	0	0	52	311	565	2,156
Cooling Degree Days (base 65°F)	0	0	12	89	305	563	656	588	414	129	5	0	2,761
Mean Precipitation (in.)	1.29	1.35	1.01	0.50	0.53	0.47	2.36	3.00	1.66	1.31	1.27	1.37	16.12
Extreme Maximum Daily Precip. (in.)	1.41	1.97	1.16	0.91	1.34	1.00	1.98	1.93	2.45	1.34	1.97	1.76	2.45
Days With ≥ 0.1" Precipitation	3	3	3	1	2	1	6	7	4	3	3	3	39
Days With ≥ 0.5" Precipitation	1	1	1	0	0	0	1	2	1	1	1	1	10
Days With ≥ 1.0" Precipitation	0	0	0	0	0	0	0	0	0	0	0	0	0
Mean Snowfall (in.)	0.0	trace	0.0	0.0	0.0	0.0	0.0	0.0	0.0	0.0	0.0	0.1	0.1
Maximum Snow Depth (in.)	0	trace	0	0	0	0	0	0	0	0	0	0	trace
Days With ≥ 1.0" Snow Depth	0	0	0	0	0	0	0	0	0	0	0	0	0

The period of record for all cooperative weather station data is 1980 – 2009. See User Guide for detailed explanation of data.

Colorado City *Mohave County* Elevation: 5,009 ft. Latitude: 37° 00' N Longitude: 112° 58' W

	JAN	FEB	MAR	APR	MAY	JUN	JUL	AUG	SEP	OCT	NOV	DEC	YEAR
Mean Maximum Temp. (°F)	48.4	52.6	59.3	67.4	77.9	88.2	93.4	90.9	83.3	71.5	58.2	48.5	70.0
Mean Temp. (°F)	36.4	40.5	46.0	52.9	62.2	71.4	77.3	75.7	68.3	56.7	44.8	36.1	55.7
Mean Minimum Temp. (°F)	24.3	28.3	32.6	38.3	46.4	54.5	61.2	60.5	53.3	41.8	31.3	23.7	41.4
Extreme Maximum Temp. (°F)	70	78	88	90	98	105	110	105	98	92	80	69	110
Extreme Minimum Temp. (°F)	-4	-3	9	16	27	28	43	46	34	16	6	-9	-9
Days Maximum Temp. ≥ 90°F	0	0	0	0	3	15	23	20	5	0	0	0	66
Days Maximum Temp. ≤ 32°F	1	0	0	0	0	0	0	0	0	0	0	1	2
Days Minimum Temp. ≤ 32°F	27	20	16	6	1	0	0	0	0	4	16	26	116
Days Minimum Temp. ≤ 0°F	0	0	0	0	0	0	0	0	0	0	0	0	0
Heating Degree Days (base 65°F)	882	688	584	360	134	22	0	1	31	265	600	888	4,455
Cooling Degree Days (base 65°F)	0	0	0	4	53	220	389	339	138	14	0	0	1,157
Mean Precipitation (in.)	1.43	1.68	1.65	1.06	0.55	0.38	1.34	1.70	1.24	1.14	1.06	1.06	14.29
Extreme Maximum Daily Precip. (in.)	1.30	1.25	1.40	1.47	1.00	0.72	1.95	3.20	2.35	2.58	3.07	1.75	3.20
Days With ≥ 0.1" Precipitation	4	5	4	3	2	1	3	4	3	3	3	3	38
Days With ≥ 0.5" Precipitation	1	1	1	1	0	0	1	1	1	1	1	1	10
Days With ≥ 1.0" Precipitation	0	0	0	0	0	0	0	0	0	0	0	0	0
Mean Snowfall (in.)	4.2	3.7	2.8	0.7	trace	0.0	0.0	0.0	0.0	0.3	1.8	3.5	17.0
Maximum Snow Depth (in.)	12	7	5	trace	trace	0	0	0	0	3	6	9	12
Days With ≥ 1.0" Snow Depth	5	2	1	0	0	0	0	0	0	0	1	3	12

Cordes *Yavapai County* Elevation: 3,771 ft. Latitude: 34° 18' N Longitude: 112° 10' W

	JAN	FEB	MAR	APR	MAY	JUN	JUL	AUG	SEP	OCT	NOV	DEC	YEAR
Mean Maximum Temp. (°F)	58.7	60.9	65.9	73.6	83.0	92.8	96.2	93.9	88.4	78.1	66.6	58.3	76.4
Mean Temp. (°F)	46.3	48.2	52.0	58.1	66.5	75.4	81.0	79.6	73.8	63.6	53.0	45.8	61.9
Mean Minimum Temp. (°F)	33.8	35.4	38.1	42.6	49.9	57.9	65.8	65.2	59.1	49.0	39.4	33.3	47.4
Extreme Maximum Temp. (°F)	79	85	88	93	102	111	115	107	103	100	88	80	115
Extreme Minimum Temp. (°F)	15	12	20	24	31	37	50	48	40	28	19	8	8
Days Maximum Temp. ≥ 90°F	0	0	0	0	6	21	27	25	14	3	0	0	96
Days Maximum Temp. ≤ 32°F	0	0	0	0	0	0	0	0	0	0	0	0	0
Days Minimum Temp. ≤ 32°F	13	9	6	2	0	0	0	0	0	0	5	14	49
Days Minimum Temp. ≤ 0°F	0	0	0	0	0	0	0	0	0	0	0	0	0
Heating Degree Days (base 65°F)	574	469	397	218	62	4	0	0	6	105	356	588	2,779
Cooling Degree Days (base 65°F)	0	0	1	18	115	322	502	459	276	68	3	0	1,764
Mean Precipitation (in.)	1.71	2.06	1.46	0.63	0.43	0.19	1.80	2.24	1.94	0.99	1.19	1.48	16.12
Extreme Maximum Daily Precip. (in.)	1.72	2.74	2.31	1.20	0.98	0.63	1.62	3.32	2.55	2.19	2.00	3.15	3.32
Days With ≥ 0.1" Precipitation	3	4	3	1	1	1	4	4	3	2	2	3	31
Days With ≥ 0.5" Precipitation	1	1	1	0	0	0	1	1	1	1	1	1	9
Days With ≥ 1.0" Precipitation	0	1	0	0	0	0	0	1	1	0	0	0	3
Mean Snowfall (in.)	0.1	0.3	0.2	0.2	0.0	0.0	0.0	0.0	0.0	0.0	0.3	0.3	1.4
Maximum Snow Depth (in.)	trace	0	trace	0	0	0	0	0	0	0	0	0	trace
Days With ≥ 1.0" Snow Depth	0	0	0	0	0	0	0	0	0	0	0	0	0

Coronado N M Hdqtrs *Cochise County* Elevation: 5,242 ft. Latitude: 31° 21' N Longitude: 110° 15' W

	JAN	FEB	MAR	APR	MAY	JUN	JUL	AUG	SEP	OCT	NOV	DEC	YEAR
Mean Maximum Temp. (°F)	58.1	61.8	67.3	74.8	82.9	91.3	89.6	86.3	84.2	75.8	65.8	58.2	74.7
Mean Temp. (°F)	45.6	48.4	52.7	59.4	67.4	75.4	75.9	73.6	70.8	62.2	52.5	45.6	60.8
Mean Minimum Temp. (°F)	33.0	34.9	38.1	44.0	51.8	59.4	62.2	60.8	57.3	48.7	39.2	33.0	46.9
Extreme Maximum Temp. (°F)	77	82	86	93	101	105	103	99	97	94	82	78	105
Extreme Minimum Temp. (°F)	9	12	18	22	29	37	48	48	38	23	17	9	9
Days Maximum Temp. ≥ 90°F	0	0	0	0	5	19	16	8	4	0	0	0	52
Days Maximum Temp. ≤ 32°F	0	0	0	0	0	0	0	0	0	0	0	0	0
Days Minimum Temp. ≤ 32°F	15	11	7	3	0	0	0	0	0	0	6	15	57
Days Minimum Temp. ≤ 0°F	0	0	0	0	0	0	0	0	0	0	0	0	0
Heating Degree Days (base 65°F)	595	464	374	178	36	2	0	0	4	116	369	593	2,731
Cooling Degree Days (base 65°F)	0	0	1	18	117	319	346	273	184	37	0	0	1,295
Mean Precipitation (in.)	1.73	1.55	1.14	0.50	0.36	0.76	4.33	4.47	1.89	1.55	1.08	2.02	21.38
Extreme Maximum Daily Precip. (in.)	2.50	1.91	1.80	1.68	0.85	1.34	2.78	2.67	2.34	4.69	2.72	2.00	4.69
Days With ≥ 0.1" Precipitation	4	3	3	1	1	2	9	8	4	3	2	3	43
Days With ≥ 0.5" Precipitation	1	1	1	0	0	0	3	3	1	1	1	1	13
Days With ≥ 1.0" Precipitation	0	0	0	0	0	0	1	1	0	0	0	0	2
Mean Snowfall (in.)	0.9	1.2	0.7	trace	0.0	0.0	0.0	0.0	0.0	0.0	0.1	2.0	4.9
Maximum Snow Depth (in.)	16	3	*2*	1	0	0	0	0	0	0	1	4	*16*
Days With ≥ 1.0" Snow Depth	0	0	0	0	0	0	0	0	0	0	0	0	0

Flagstaff 4 SW *Coconino County* Elevation: 7,123 ft. Latitude: 35° 10' N Longitude: 111° 43' W

	JAN	FEB	MAR	APR	MAY	JUN	JUL	AUG	SEP	OCT	NOV	DEC	YEAR
Mean Maximum Temp. (°F)	*43.0*	*45.1*	*50.7*	*58.1*	*67.8*	77.0	81.4	78.4	72.7	*62.9*	51.6	43.0	*61.0*
Mean Temp. (°F)	*26.7*	*29.4*	*34.9*	*41.1*	*48.5*	56.0	63.2	61.6	54.6	*44.3*	34.3	26.6	*43.4*
Mean Minimum Temp. (°F)	*10.3*	*13.6*	*19.0*	*24.1*	*29.2*	34.9	45.0	44.7	36.4	*25.6*	16.9	10.0	*25.8*
Extreme Maximum Temp. (°F)	*63*	*70*	*73*	*80*	*87*	*91*	*96*	*92*	*88*	*84*	*73*	*66*	*96*
Extreme Minimum Temp. (°F)	*-28*	*-37*	*-18*	*3*	*8*	*17*	*25*	*26*	*19*	*4*	*-19*	*-36*	*-37*
Days Maximum Temp. ≥ 90°F	*0*	*0*	*0*	*0*	*0*	0	2	0	0	*0*	0	0	*2*
Days Maximum Temp. ≤ 32°F	*4*	*2*	*1*	*0*	*0*	0	0	0	0	*0*	1	4	*12*
Days Minimum Temp. ≤ 32°F	*30*	*28*	*30*	*26*	*22*	12	1	1	10	*26*	29	30	*245*
Days Minimum Temp. ≤ 0°F	*6*	*3*	*1*	*0*	*0*	0	0	0	0	*0*	1	5	*16*
Heating Degree Days (base 65°F)	*1,180*	*1,000*	*926*	*708*	*505*	269	85	114	306	*635*	914	1,185	*7,827*
Cooling Degree Days (base 65°F)	*0*	*0*	*0*	*0*	*0*	5	35	15	1	*0*	0	0	*56*
Mean Precipitation (in.)	*2.12*	*2.43*	*2.21*	*1.40*	*0.59*	0.43	2.29	3.47	2.27	*1.73*	1.67	2.00	*22.61*
Extreme Maximum Daily Precip. (in.)	*2.43*	*2.91*	*2.25*	*1.30*	*0.95*	*1.10*	*1.37*	*2.09*	*1.75*	*2.37*	*3.05*	*2.57*	*3.05*
Days With ≥ 0.1" Precipitation	*5*	*5*	*5*	*3*	*2*	1	6	8	4	*3*	3	4	*49*
Days With ≥ 0.5" Precipitation	*1*	*1*	*1*	*1*	*0*	0	2	2	2	*1*	1	1	*13*
Days With ≥ 1.0" Precipitation	*0*	*1*	*0*	*0*	*0*	0	0	1	1	*0*	0	0	*3*
Mean Snowfall (in.)	*18.4*	*17.5*	*15.6*	*8.0*	*0.4*	trace	0.0	0.0	trace	*1.5*	6.8	*13.1*	*81.3*
Maximum Snow Depth (in.)	*38*	*35*	*25*	*28*	*6*	*trace*	*0*	*0*	*0*	*10*	*16*	*27*	*38*
Days With ≥ 1.0" Snow Depth	*16*	*18*	*13*	*3*	*0*	0	0	0	0	*1*	5	14	*70*

The period of record for all cooperative weather station data is 1980 – 2009. See User Guide for detailed explanation of data.

Florence *Pinal County* Elevation: 1,504 ft. Latitude: 33° 02' N Longitude: 111° 24' W

	JAN	FEB	MAR	APR	MAY	JUN	JUL	AUG	SEP	OCT	NOV	DEC	YEAR
Mean Maximum Temp. (°F)	67.1	70.7	76.3	85.1	93.9	102.8	104.1	102.1	98.2	88.2	75.5	66.5	85.9
Mean Temp. (°F)	53.8	56.5	61.3	68.5	77.2	85.6	90.2	89.0	83.9	72.9	60.7	***53.1***	***71.1***
Mean Minimum Temp. (°F)	40.4	42.3	46.4	51.9	60.4	68.4	76.3	75.9	69.5	57.7	45.9	***39.6***	***56.2***
Extreme Maximum Temp. (°F)	86	91	98	104	114	116	119	116	114	112	95	86	119
Extreme Minimum Temp. (°F)	18	20	29	33	40	51	61	61	48	36	25	22	18
Days Maximum Temp. ≥ 90°F	0	0	1	10	23	29	31	30	28	15	1	0	168
Days Maximum Temp. ≤ 32°F	0	0	0	0	0	0	0	0	0	0	0	0	0
Days Minimum Temp. ≤ 32°F	3	2	1	0	0	0	0	0	0	0	1	5	12
Days Minimum Temp. ≤ 0°F	0	0	0	0	0	0	0	0	0	0	0	0	0
Heating Degree Days (base 65°F)	343	239	148	***42***	3	0	0	***0***	0	18	158	***364***	***1,315***
Cooling Degree Days (base 65°F)	2	6	41	***153***	389	624	789	***751***	572	270	35	***1***	***3,633***
Mean Precipitation (in.)	1.08	1.17	1.05	0.37	0.26	0.06	1.25	1.30	0.78	0.57	0.83	1.19	9.91
Extreme Maximum Daily Precip. (in.)	1.67	2.04	1.36	1.41	1.07	0.30	***3.25***	***2.30***	1.96	2.00	***2.50***	***1.52***	***3.25***
Days With ≥ 0.1" Precipitation	3	3	3	1	1	0	2	3	2	1	1	2	22
Days With ≥ 0.5" Precipitation	1	1	1	0	0	0	1	1	0	0	1	1	7
Days With ≥ 1.0" Precipitation	0	0	0	0	0	0	0	0	0	0	0	0	0
Mean Snowfall (in.)	0.0	0.0	0.0	0.0	0.0	0.0	0.0	0.0	0.0	0.0	0.0	trace	trace
Maximum Snow Depth (in.)	0	0	0	0	0	0	0	0	0	0	0	trace	trace
Days With ≥ 1.0" Snow Depth	0	0	0	0	0	0	0	0	0	0	0	0	0

Fort Valley *Coconino County* Elevation: 7,347 ft. Latitude: 35° 16' N Longitude: 111° 44' W

	JAN	FEB	MAR	APR	MAY	JUN	JUL	AUG	SEP	OCT	NOV	DEC	YEAR
Mean Maximum Temp. (°F)	43.4	45.7	51.1	58.7	69.0	79.4	81.7	78.8	73.5	63.7	52.3	44.2	61.8
Mean Temp. (°F)	28.0	30.4	35.3	41.1	49.0	57.2	63.1	61.8	55.1	45.1	35.5	28.3	44.2
Mean Minimum Temp. (°F)	12.4	15.2	19.5	23.4	29.1	35.0	44.4	44.7	36.8	26.4	18.6	12.4	26.5
Extreme Maximum Temp. (°F)	65	69	75	80	90	96	98	93	88	85	75	67	98
Extreme Minimum Temp. (°F)	-20	-32	-10	1	12	20	26	27	19	2	-11	-30	-32
Days Maximum Temp. ≥ 90°F	0	0	0	0	0	2	4	1	0	0	0	0	7
Days Maximum Temp. ≤ 32°F	3	2	1	0	0	0	0	0	0	0	1	3	10
Days Minimum Temp. ≤ 32°F	31	28	31	29	23	11	1	1	9	26	29	31	250
Days Minimum Temp. ≤ 0°F	5	2	0	0	0	0	0	0	0	0	1	4	12
Heating Degree Days (base 65°F)	1,142	970	913	710	487	233	82	104	290	610	878	1,131	7,550
Cooling Degree Days (base 65°F)	0	0	0	0	0	6	29	12	1	0	0	0	48
Mean Precipitation (in.)	2.40	2.57	2.15	1.12	0.75	0.29	2.48	3.09	2.32	1.20	1.64	1.62	21.63
Extreme Maximum Daily Precip. (in.)	2.03	***2.47***	***2.93***	***1.64***	0.89	0.61	***3.50***	4.00	***3.10***	***1.62***	***2.62***	***1.99***	***4.00***
Days With ≥ 0.1" Precipitation	4	5	4	2	2	1	5	6	5	2	3	3	42
Days With ≥ 0.5" Precipitation	2	2	1	1	0	0	1	2	1	1	1	1	13
Days With ≥ 1.0" Precipitation	1	0	0	0	0	0	0	1	1	0	0	0	3
Mean Snowfall (in.)	***14.8***	***10.7***	10.2	2.9	trace	trace	0.0	0.0	0.0	***0.5***	***5.4***	7.2	***51.7***
Maximum Snow Depth (in.)	na	na	na	na	***trace***	***0***	***0***	***0***	***0***	na	na	na	na
Days With ≥ 1.0" Snow Depth	na	na	***9***	***1***	0	0	0	0	0	***0***	***2***	***8***	na

Fountain Hills *Maricopa County* Elevation: 1,575 ft. Latitude: 33° 36' N Longitude: 111° 43' W

	JAN	FEB	MAR	APR	MAY	JUN	JUL	AUG	SEP	OCT	NOV	DEC	YEAR
Mean Maximum Temp. (°F)	66.5	70.3	76.6	85.0	94.6	103.9	106.1	104.7	99.9	89.1	75.7	65.7	86.5
Mean Temp. (°F)	54.0	57.0	62.1	69.4	78.5	86.9	91.5	90.8	85.5	74.5	62.0	53.4	72.1
Mean Minimum Temp. (°F)	41.4	43.6	47.6	53.8	62.2	69.9	76.7	76.8	71.1	59.9	48.3	41.0	57.7
Extreme Maximum Temp. (°F)	82	91	101	107	114	121	125	118	115	108	95	84	125
Extreme Minimum Temp. (°F)	23	25	29	36	44	49	57	62	51	37	29	24	23
Days Maximum Temp. ≥ 90°F	0	0	2	10	24	29	31	31	28	16	1	0	172
Days Maximum Temp. ≤ 32°F	0	0	0	0	0	0	0	0	0	0	0	0	0
Days Minimum Temp. ≤ 32°F	2	1	0	0	0	0	0	0	0	0	1	3	7
Days Minimum Temp. ≤ 0°F	0	0	0	0	0	0	0	0	0	0	0	0	0
Heating Degree Days (base 65°F)	336	228	134	39	3	0	0	0	0	12	132	354	1,238
Cooling Degree Days (base 65°F)	1	8	52	178	427	664	827	806	622	314	49	1	3,949
Mean Precipitation (in.)	1.50	1.53	1.58	0.46	0.22	0.06	0.99	1.30	0.98	0.71	0.93	1.33	11.59
Extreme Maximum Daily Precip. (in.)	2.00	2.01	2.05	1.00	0.56	0.70	1.26	1.52	1.95	1.65	2.24	2.30	2.30
Days With ≥ 0.1" Precipitation	3	3	3	1	1	0	2	3	2	2	2	3	25
Days With ≥ 0.5" Precipitation	1	1	1	0	0	0	1	1	1	0	1	1	8
Days With ≥ 1.0" Precipitation	0	0	0	0	0	0	0	0	0	0	0	0	0
Mean Snowfall (in.)	0.0	0.0	trace	0.0	0.0	0.0	0.0	0.0	0.0	0.0	0.0	0.0	trace
Maximum Snow Depth (in.)	0	0	0	0	0	0	0	0	0	0	0	0	0
Days With ≥ 1.0" Snow Depth	0	0	0	0	0	0	0	0	0	0	0	0	0

Gila Bend *Maricopa County* Elevation: 734 ft. Latitude: 32° 57' N Longitude: 112° 43' W

	JAN	FEB	MAR	APR	MAY	JUN	JUL	AUG	SEP	OCT	NOV	DEC	YEAR
Mean Maximum Temp. (°F)	70.2	74.1	80.5	88.8	97.8	106.4	109.0	107.5	102.9	91.8	79.0	69.1	89.8
Mean Temp. (°F)	55.8	59.2	64.7	71.8	80.5	88.9	94.5	93.6	87.9	75.7	63.4	54.8	74.2
Mean Minimum Temp. (°F)	41.3	44.4	48.9	54.7	63.1	71.3	79.9	79.8	72.9	59.5	47.8	40.5	58.7
Extreme Maximum Temp. (°F)	85	92	101	110	116	122	122	118	116	114	98	86	122
Extreme Minimum Temp. (°F)	16	24	32	39	45	54	63	63	53	38	27	19	16
Days Maximum Temp. ≥ 90°F	0	0	4	15	27	30	31	31	29	20	3	0	190
Days Maximum Temp. ≤ 32°F	0	0	0	0	0	0	0	0	0	0	0	0	0
Days Minimum Temp. ≤ 32°F	3	1	0	0	0	0	0	0	0	0	1	4	9
Days Minimum Temp. ≤ 0°F	0	0	0	0	0	0	0	0	0	0	0	0	0
Heating Degree Days (base 65°F)	282	170	78	17	1	0	0	0	0	8	103	309	968
Cooling Degree Days (base 65°F)	3	14	76	227	486	723	921	895	694	346	62	1	4,448
Mean Precipitation (in.)	0.65	0.97	0.67	0.22	0.20	0.01	0.78	1.16	0.48	0.37	0.61	0.77	6.89
Extreme Maximum Daily Precip. (in.)	1.05	1.62	1.35	1.10	1.85	0.20	1.61	1.90	1.50	1.30	2.01	1.29	2.01
Days With ≥ 0.1" Precipitation	2	2	2	1	0	0	2	3	1	1	1	2	17
Days With ≥ 0.5" Precipitation	0	1	0	0	0	0	0	1	0	0	0	1	3
Days With ≥ 1.0" Precipitation	0	0	0	0	0	0	0	0	0	0	0	0	0
Mean Snowfall (in.)	0.0	0.0	0.0	0.0	0.0	0.0	0.0	0.0	0.0	0.0	0.0	0.0	0.0
Maximum Snow Depth (in.)	0	0	0	0	0	0	0	0	0	0	0	0	0
Days With ≥ 1.0" Snow Depth	0	0	0	0	0	0	0	0	0	0	0	0	0

Holbrook *Navajo County* Elevation: 5,069 ft. Latitude: 34° 54' N Longitude: 110° 09' W

	JAN	FEB	MAR	APR	MAY	JUN	JUL	AUG	SEP	OCT	NOV	DEC	YEAR
Mean Maximum Temp. (°F)	50.4	56.9	64.0	71.9	81.4	91.0	94.3	91.3	85.3	74.1	61.2	49.8	72.6
Mean Temp. (°F)	35.6	40.7	46.9	54.1	63.0	71.7	77.5	75.6	68.5	56.4	44.4	35.4	55.8
Mean Minimum Temp. (°F)	20.9	24.5	29.7	36.2	44.5	52.3	60.5	59.9	51.6	38.8	27.6	20.9	38.9
Extreme Maximum Temp. (°F)	74	80	86	93	101	106	110	105	103	95	82	78	110
Extreme Minimum Temp. (°F)	-16	-2	4	18	19	32	41	44	28	17	6	-10	-16
Days Maximum Temp. ≥ 90°F	0	0	0	0	4	18	23	19	7	0	0	0	71
Days Maximum Temp. ≤ 32°F	1	0	0	0	0	0	0	0	0	0	0	1	2
Days Minimum Temp. ≤ 32°F	28	23	20	9	1	0	0	0	0	6	21	28	136
Days Minimum Temp. ≤ 0°F	0	0	0	0	0	0	0	0	0	0	0	0	0
Heating Degree Days (base 65°F)	904	681	555	325	107	10	0	0	25	267	610	912	4,396
Cooling Degree Days (base 65°F)	0	0	0	4	51	219	393	336	136	9	0	0	1,148
Mean Precipitation (in.)	0.59	0.63	0.74	0.32	0.28	0.18	1.17	1.59	1.07	0.79	0.57	0.71	8.64
Extreme Maximum Daily Precip. (in.)	0.87	2.50	1.20	0.53	0.74	0.62	1.23	1.32	1.08	***1.12***	1.02	1.60	***2.50***
Days With ≥ 0.1" Precipitation	2	1	2	1	1	1	3	4	3	2	1	2	23
Days With ≥ 0.5" Precipitation	0	0	0	0	0	0	1	1	1	0	0	0	3
Days With ≥ 1.0" Precipitation	0	0	0	0	0	0	0	0	0	0	0	0	0
Mean Snowfall (in.)	1.4	1.0	0.6	0.3	trace	0.0	0.0	0.0	0.0	trace	0.7	1.5	5.5
Maximum Snow Depth (in.)	3	***4***	4	trace	0	0	0	0	0	***trace***	***4***	***3***	***4***
Days With ≥ 1.0" Snow Depth	1	0	0	0	0	0	0	0	0	0	0	0	1

Kitt Peak *Pima County* Elevation: 6,790 ft. Latitude: 31° 58' N Longitude: 111° 36' W

	JAN	FEB	MAR	APR	MAY	JUN	JUL	AUG	SEP	OCT	NOV	DEC	YEAR
Mean Maximum Temp. (°F)	50.4	51.6	55.5	63.2	71.6	80.7	81.0	78.1	75.0	67.0	57.7	50.6	65.2
Mean Temp. (°F)	42.1	43.0	46.1	52.7	60.8	70.0	71.1	69.0	66.2	57.9	48.6	42.1	55.8
Mean Minimum Temp. (°F)	33.7	34.3	36.7	42.1	50.0	59.3	61.1	59.8	57.3	48.6	39.6	33.7	46.3
Extreme Maximum Temp. (°F)	71	77	78	88	90	98	98	91	88	88	76	72	98
Extreme Minimum Temp. (°F)	6	5	16	15	26	22	40	38	35	25	12	-1	-1
Days Maximum Temp. ≥ 90°F	0	0	0	0	0	2	2	0	0	0	0	0	4
Days Maximum Temp. ≤ 32°F	1	1	0	0	0	0	0	0	0	0	0	1	3
Days Minimum Temp. ≤ 32°F	13	11	11	5	1	0	0	0	0	1	6	12	60
Days Minimum Temp. ≤ 0°F	0	0	0	0	0	0	0	0	0	0	0	0	0
Heating Degree Days (base 65°F)	705	614	579	368	162	22	5	12	43	232	486	702	3,930
Cooling Degree Days (base 65°F)	0	0	0	4	39	179	201	142	85	18	0	0	668
Mean Precipitation (in.)	1.52	1.63	1.76	0.38	0.55	0.48	4.83	4.85	2.30	1.25	0.90	2.05	22.50
Extreme Maximum Daily Precip. (in.)	2.00	2.45	2.52	1.15	1.45	1.93	2.22	3.71	2.40	4.70	1.70	***3.20***	***4.70***
Days With ≥ 0.1" Precipitation	3	3	3	1	1	1	8	8	4	2	2	3	39
Days With ≥ 0.5" Precipitation	1	1	1	0	0	0	3	3	2	1	1	1	14
Days With ≥ 1.0" Precipitation	0	0	0	0	0	0	1	1	1	0	0	1	4
Mean Snowfall (in.)	2.2	3.6	2.5	1.0	trace	0.0	0.0	0.0	0.0	0.3	0.3	1.7	11.6
Maximum Snow Depth (in.)	10	19	13	7	trace	0	0	0	0	6	9	10	19
Days With ≥ 1.0" Snow Depth	2	2	2	0	0	0	0	0	0	0	0	1	7

Kofa Mine *Yuma County* Elevation: 1,774 ft. Latitude: 33° 16' N Longitude: 113° 58' W

	JAN	FEB	MAR	APR	MAY	JUN	JUL	AUG	SEP	OCT	NOV	DEC	YEAR
Mean Maximum Temp. (°F)	66.4	69.4	75.1	82.7	91.5	100.4	103.8	102.4	97.3	86.4	74.4	65.4	84.6
Mean Temp. (°F)	57.0	59.4	64.1	70.6	78.8	87.4	92.0	90.9	86.0	75.7	64.6	56.1	73.5
Mean Minimum Temp. (°F)	47.6	49.3	53.1	58.4	66.1	74.3	80.0	79.4	74.7	64.9	54.7	46.8	62.4
Extreme Maximum Temp. (°F)	85	93	97	104	112	117	119	116	111	109	94	82	119
Extreme Minimum Temp. (°F)	26	28	34	39	46	49	66	65	50	44	34	28	26
Days Maximum Temp. ≥ 90°F	0	0	1	7	19	28	31	30	27	12	1	0	156
Days Maximum Temp. ≤ 32°F	0	0	0	0	0	0	0	0	0	0	0	0	0
Days Minimum Temp. ≤ 32°F	0	0	0	0	0	0	0	0	0	0	0	0	0
Days Minimum Temp. ≤ 0°F	0	0	0	0	0	0	0	0	0	0	0	0	0
Heating Degree Days (base 65°F)	251	176	106	36	4	0	0	0	0	9	92	273	947
Cooling Degree Days (base 65°F)	8	24	86	210	439	678	842	810	637	347	87	4	4,172
Mean Precipitation (in.)	0.78	0.82	0.60	0.23	0.13	0.05	0.68	1.01	0.81	0.39	0.51	0.68	6.69
Extreme Maximum Daily Precip. (in.)	0.97	1.43	1.19	1.12	1.44	0.25	1.17	2.18	2.58	2.25	1.61	1.20	2.58
Days With ≥ 0.1" Precipitation	2	2	1	1	0	0	2	2	1	1	1	1	14
Days With ≥ 0.5" Precipitation	1	0	0	0	0	0	1	1	0	0	0	1	4
Days With ≥ 1.0" Precipitation	0	0	0	0	0	0	0	0	0	0	0	0	0
Mean Snowfall (in.)	0.0	trace	0.0	0.0	0.0	0.0	0.0	0.0	0.0	0.0	0.0	0.0	trace
Maximum Snow Depth (in.)	0	trace	0	0	0	0	0	0	0	0	0	0	trace
Days With ≥ 1.0" Snow Depth	0	0	0	0	0	0	0	0	0	0	0	0	0

Laveen 3 SSE *Maricopa County* Elevation: 1,115 ft. Latitude: 33° 20' N Longitude: 112° 09' W

	JAN	FEB	MAR	APR	MAY	JUN	JUL	AUG	SEP	OCT	NOV	DEC	YEAR
Mean Maximum Temp. (°F)	67.3	71.4	77.7	86.6	96.0	104.9	106.5	104.7	99.9	88.9	75.8	66.3	87.1
Mean Temp. (°F)	54.3	57.6	63.1	70.4	79.7	88.4	92.6	91.2	85.3	73.8	61.7	53.3	72.6
Mean Minimum Temp. (°F)	41.3	43.8	48.1	54.1	63.4	71.8	78.7	77.8	70.7	58.6	47.5	40.2	58.0
Extreme Maximum Temp. (°F)	86	90	102	108	115	122	125	118	118	107	97	85	125
Extreme Minimum Temp. (°F)	24	23	30	34	44	51	59	62	51	37	28	20	20
Days Maximum Temp. ≥ 90°F	0	0	3	12	25	30	31	31	28	15	1	0	176
Days Maximum Temp. ≤ 32°F	0	0	0	0	0	0	0	0	0	0	0	0	0
Days Minimum Temp. ≤ 32°F	3	1	0	0	0	0	0	0	0	0	1	3	8
Days Minimum Temp. ≤ 0°F	0	0	0	0	0	0	0	0	0	0	0	0	0
Heating Degree Days (base 65°F)	325	212	114	29	1	0	0	0	0	13	135	357	1,186
Cooling Degree Days (base 65°F)	1	8	60	197	466	707	864	818	615	293	41	1	4,071
Mean Precipitation (in.)	0.79	1.04	0.95	0.27	0.15	0.06	1.30	0.99	0.70	0.67	0.67	0.89	8.48
Extreme Maximum Daily Precip. (in.)	1.10	1.30	2.10	1.02	0.65	0.51	2.27	1.46	1.76	2.77	2.05	1.27	2.77
Days With ≥ 0.1" Precipitation	2	3	2	1	0	0	2	2	2	1	2	2	19
Days With ≥ 0.5" Precipitation	0	1	1	0	0	0	1	1	0	0	1	1	6
Days With ≥ 1.0" Precipitation	0	0	0	0	0	0	0	0	0	0	0	0	0
Mean Snowfall (in.)	0.0	0.0	0.0	0.0	0.0	0.0	0.0	0.0	0.0	0.0	0.0	0.0	0.0
Maximum Snow Depth (in.)	0	0	0	0	0	0	0	0	0	0	0	0	0
Days With ≥ 1.0" Snow Depth	0	0	0	0	0	0	0	0	0	0	0	0	0

The period of record for all cooperative weather station data is 1980 – 2009. See User Guide for detailed explanation of data.

Lees Ferry *Coconino County* Elevation: 3,209 ft. Latitude: 36° 52' N Longitude: 111° 36' W

	JAN	FEB	MAR	APR	MAY	JUN	JUL	AUG	SEP	OCT	NOV	DEC	YEAR
Mean Maximum Temp. (°F)	*50.6*	*57.6*	*67.7*	*77.8*	*88.6*	*100.7*	*103.8*	*100.2*	*91.4*	77.2	*60.9*	*49.4*	*77.2*
Mean Temp. (°F)	*39.9*	*45.5*	*54.0*	*62.9*	*73.2*	*83.8*	*88.4*	*85.2*	*76.4*	63.1	*49.0*	*39.4*	*63.4*
Mean Minimum Temp. (°F)	*29.1*	*33.3*	*40.3*	*47.9*	*57.7*	*66.8*	*72.9*	*70.1*	*61.4*	48.9	*37.1*	*29.1*	*49.5*
Extreme Maximum Temp. (°F)	70	*82*	89	99	*111*	*116*	119	114	*110*	99	82	*66*	*119*
Extreme Minimum Temp. (°F)	9	*11*	21	28	*35*	*39*	59	52	*44*	28	21	*9*	*9*
Days Maximum Temp. ≥ 90°F	0	*0*	0	3	*15*	*26*	29	28	*19*	3	0	*0*	*123*
Days Maximum Temp. ≤ 32°F	0	*0*	0	0	*0*	*0*	0	0	*0*	0	0	*0*	*0*
Days Minimum Temp. ≤ 32°F	21	*12*	*3*	0	*0*	*0*	0	0	*0*	0	8	*21*	*65*
Days Minimum Temp. ≤ 0°F	0	*0*	0	0	*0*	*0*	0	0	*0*	0	0	0	*0*
Heating Degree Days (base 65°F)	*772*	*546*	*338*	*118*	*16*	*0*	*0*	*0*	*4*	116	*474*	*786*	*3,170*
Cooling Degree Days (base 65°F)	*0*	*0*	*4*	*62*	*277*	*569*	*731*	*632*	*354*	62	*0*	*0*	*2,691*
Mean Precipitation (in.)	*0.50*	0.59	*0.56*	0.46	*0.38*	0.11	0.83	*1.18*	*0.68*	0.77	0.40	*0.35*	*6.81*
Extreme Maximum Daily Precip. (in.)	*0.60*	na	*1.50*	*1.49*	na	*0.42*	*1.32*	*1.75*	na	*1.18*	*0.83*	*0.70*	na
Days With ≥ 0.1" Precipitation	*1*	*2*	*2*	1	*1*	0	2	3	*2*	2	1	1	*18*
Days With ≥ 0.5" Precipitation	0	0	*0*	0	*0*	0	1	1	*0*	1	0	0	*3*
Days With ≥ 1.0" Precipitation	0	0	*0*	0	*0*	0	0	0	*0*	0	0	0	*0*
Mean Snowfall (in.)	*0.2*	*0.2*	*0.0*	0.0	*0.0*	0.0	0.0	0.0	*0.0*	0.0	0.1	*0.3*	*0.8*
Maximum Snow Depth (in.)	*trace*	*2*	*0*	*0*	*0*	*0*	*0*	*0*	*0*	*0*	*2*	*1*	*2*
Days With ≥ 1.0" Snow Depth	*0*	*0*	*0*	0	*0*	0	0	0	*0*	0	0	0	*0*

Maricopa 4 N *Pinal County* Elevation: 1,160 ft. Latitude: 33° 07' N Longitude: 112° 02' W

	JAN	FEB	MAR	APR	MAY	JUN	JUL	AUG	SEP	OCT	NOV	DEC	YEAR
Mean Maximum Temp. (°F)	67.5	71.6	78.2	87.0	96.6	105.7	107.6	105.5	100.7	89.3	76.2	66.4	87.7
Mean Temp. (°F)	51.8	55.4	61.1	68.5	77.9	86.8	92.1	90.8	84.3	71.5	58.9	50.6	70.8
Mean Minimum Temp. (°F)	36.0	39.2	43.9	50.0	59.2	67.9	76.7	76.1	67.8	53.7	41.6	34.7	53.9
Extreme Maximum Temp. (°F)	84	90	100	106	113	122	124	117	113	107	95	84	124
Extreme Minimum Temp. (°F)	15	17	25	31	39	48	60	56	46	30	23	17	15
Days Maximum Temp. ≥ 90°F	0	0	3	12	26	30	31	31	29	16	1	0	179
Days Maximum Temp. ≤ 32°F	0	0	0	0	0	0	0	0	0	0	0	0	0
Days Minimum Temp. ≤ 32°F	10	5	1	0	0	0	0	0	0	0	3	12	31
Days Minimum Temp. ≤ 0°F	0	0	0	0	0	0	0	0	0	0	0	0	0
Heating Degree Days (base 65°F)	402	266	147	37	2	0	0	0	0	22	193	440	1,509
Cooling Degree Days (base 65°F)	0	2	32	149	410	661	848	806	584	232	17	0	3,741
Mean Precipitation (in.)	0.79	0.88	1.01	0.29	0.17	0.08	0.95	0.95	0.72	0.45	0.57	0.97	7.83
Extreme Maximum Daily Precip. (in.)	1.13	1.18	1.96	0.94	1.29	0.53	1.43	1.27	1.21	1.75	1.44	1.20	1.96
Days With ≥ 0.1" Precipitation	2	2	2	1	0	0	2	2	2	1	1	2	17
Days With ≥ 0.5" Precipitation	0	1	1	0	0	0	1	1	0	0	0	1	5
Days With ≥ 1.0" Precipitation	0	0	0	0	0	0	0	0	0	0	0	0	0
Mean Snowfall (in.)	0.0	0.0	0.0	0.0	0.0	0.0	0.0	0.0	0.0	0.0	0.0	0.0	0.0
Maximum Snow Depth (in.)	0	0	0	0	0	0	0	0	0	0	0	0	0
Days With ≥ 1.0" Snow Depth	0	0	0	0	0	0	0	0	0	0	0	0	0

McNary 2 N *Apache County* Elevation: 7,339 ft. Latitude: 34° 07' N Longitude: 109° 51' W

	JAN	FEB	MAR	APR	MAY	JUN	JUL	AUG	SEP	OCT	NOV	DEC	YEAR
Mean Maximum Temp. (°F)	44.7	46.6	51.6	59.8	69.7	79.3	80.7	77.1	73.1	64.3	53.4	44.6	62.1
Mean Temp. (°F)	32.1	34.0	38.2	44.9	53.7	62.3	66.1	63.8	58.9	49.6	39.8	32.1	48.0
Mean Minimum Temp. (°F)	19.5	21.4	24.9	30.1	37.6	45.2	51.4	50.4	44.5	34.8	26.1	19.6	33.8
Extreme Maximum Temp. (°F)	68	72	74	80	89	93	98	89	88	83	79	73	98
Extreme Minimum Temp. (°F)	-8	-8	0	5	18	27	36	37	27	10	2	-13	-13
Days Maximum Temp. ≥ 90°F	0	0	0	0	0	1	2	0	0	0	0	0	3
Days Maximum Temp. ≤ 32°F	3	2	1	0	0	0	0	0	0	0	1	3	10
Days Minimum Temp. ≤ 32°F	30	27	28	19	6	1	0	0	1	10	24	29	175
Days Minimum Temp. ≤ 0°F	0	0	0	0	0	0	0	0	0	0	0	1	1
Heating Degree Days (base 65°F)	1,012	869	823	595	347	106	29	59	181	472	749	1,012	6,254
Cooling Degree Days (base 65°F)	0	0	0	0	2	31	69	28	3	0	0	0	133
Mean Precipitation (in.)	2.56	2.46	2.42	1.12	0.66	0.63	3.26	4.31	2.59	2.02	1.82	2.55	26.40
Extreme Maximum Daily Precip. (in.)	2.91	1.84	2.49	1.73	1.51	1.33	1.84	4.19	3.00	3.07	2.28	2.65	4.19
Days With ≥ 0.1" Precipitation	5	5	6	3	2	2	8	10	5	4	4	5	59
Days With ≥ 0.5" Precipitation	2	2	1	0	0	0	2	3	2	1	1	2	16
Days With ≥ 1.0" Precipitation	1	0	0	0	0	0	0	1	0	1	0	1	4
Mean Snowfall (in.)	15.8	16.3	13.8	4.4	0.5	trace	trace	0.0	0.0	2.1	6.2	13.8	72.9
Maximum Snow Depth (in.)	37	41	41	22	6	trace	trace	0	0	15	14	23	41
Days With ≥ 1.0" Snow Depth	21	19	12	3	0	0	0	0	0	1	5	15	76

Monument Valley *Navajo County* Elevation: 5,563 ft. Latitude: 36° 59' N Longitude: 110° 07' W

	JAN	FEB	MAR	APR	MAY	JUN	JUL	AUG	SEP	OCT	NOV	DEC	YEAR
Mean Maximum Temp. (°F)	40.7	47.3	58.1	67.3	77.6	88.1	92.2	*88.8*	*80.6*	67.9	51.5	40.9	*66.7*
Mean Temp. (°F)	32.5	37.8	*46.8*	54.8	65.0	75.6	79.5	*76.4*	*68.8*	56.6	42.2	32.7	*55.7*
Mean Minimum Temp. (°F)	24.3	28.2	*35.5*	42.4	52.3	63.1	67.0	*63.9*	57.1	45.2	32.9	24.6	*44.7*
Extreme Maximum Temp. (°F)	60	69	*77*	90	99	101	104	100	96	86	73	62	104
Extreme Minimum Temp. (°F)	-2	-4	*15*	10	32	36	49	37	21	22	7	-9	*-9*
Days Maximum Temp. ≥ 90°F	0	0	0	0	2	13	22	14	2	0	0	0	53
Days Maximum Temp. ≤ 32°F	5	1	0	0	0	0	0	0	0	0	0	4	10
Days Minimum Temp. ≤ 32°F	27	20	*11*	4	0	0	0	0	0	2	14	27	*105*
Days Minimum Temp. ≤ 0°F	0	0	*0*	0	0	0	0	0	0	0	0	0	*0*
Heating Degree Days (base 65°F)	1,000	762	*557*	309	91	7	0	*1*	*31*	269	677	993	*4,697*
Cooling Degree Days (base 65°F)	0	0	*0*	9	98	332	457	*359*	*152*	15	0	0	*1,422*
Mean Precipitation (in.)	0.26	0.20	*0.27*	0.25	0.33	*0.10*	0.54	0.79	0.70	0.68	0.32	*0.19*	*4.63*
Extreme Maximum Daily Precip. (in.)	1.10	1.15	na	0.97	*1.04*	*0.40*	*1.50*	*1.45*	1.06	1.77	*1.06*	*0.84*	na
Days With ≥ 0.1" Precipitation	1	1	*1*	1	*1*	*0*	1	2	2	1	0	*1*	*12*
Days With ≥ 0.5" Precipitation	0	0	*0*	0	*0*	*0*	0	0	0	0	0	*0*	*0*
Days With ≥ 1.0" Precipitation	0	0	*0*	0	*0*	*0*	0	0	0	0	0	*0*	*0*
Mean Snowfall (in.)	1.0	0.2	*0.4*	0.2	trace	0.0	0.0	0.0	0.0	trace	*0.7*	*2.6*	*5.1*
Maximum Snow Depth (in.)	*2*	*8*	*trace*	*4*	*0*	*0*	*0*	*0*	*0*	*trace*	*trace*	*1*	*8*
Days With ≥ 1.0" Snow Depth	*0*	0	*0*	0	0	0	0	0	0	0	*0*	*0*	*0*

Nogales 6 N *Santa Cruz County* Elevation: 3,560 ft. Latitude: 31° 27' N Longitude: 110° 58' W

	JAN	FEB	MAR	APR	MAY	JUN	JUL	AUG	SEP	OCT	NOV	DEC	YEAR
Mean Maximum Temp. (°F)	64.9	67.4	71.9	79.2	87.5	96.0	94.6	92.2	90.5	82.6	72.6	64.6	80.3
Mean Temp. (°F)	46.4	49.0	53.2	59.2	66.9	75.4	79.6	78.0	73.5	63.4	53.1	46.4	62.0
Mean Minimum Temp. (°F)	27.9	30.5	34.4	39.2	46.0	54.8	64.5	63.9	56.3	44.1	33.5	28.0	43.6
Extreme Maximum Temp. (°F)	85	85	93	99	107	112	109	107	102	99	90	84	112
Extreme Minimum Temp. (°F)	9	14	14	21	26	35	47	48	38	22	14	10	9
Days Maximum Temp. ≥ 90°F	0	0	0	2	12	26	25	22	19	6	0	0	112
Days Maximum Temp. ≤ 32°F	0	0	0	0	0	0	0	0	0	0	0	0	0
Days Minimum Temp. ≤ 32°F	24	18	12	5	0	0	0	0	0	2	14	24	99
Days Minimum Temp. ≤ 0°F	0	0	0	0	0	0	0	0	0	0	0	0	0
Heating Degree Days (base 65°F)	570	445	360	183	43	2	0	0	2	95	351	571	2,622
Cooling Degree Days (base 65°F)	0	0	1	16	108	321	458	412	263	53	1	0	1,633
Mean Precipitation (in.)	1.16	0.96	0.90	0.53	0.25	0.55	4.05	4.43	1.53	1.36	0.64	1.51	17.87
Extreme Maximum Daily Precip. (in.)	1.45	1.02	1.75	1.47	0.83	1.50	1.95	3.67	2.10	3.60	2.75	2.55	3.67
Days With ≥ 0.1" Precipitation	3	3	2	1	1	1	8	9	3	2	2	3	38
Days With ≥ 0.5" Precipitation	1	1	0	0	0	0	3	3	1	1	0	1	11
Days With ≥ 1.0" Precipitation	0	0	0	0	0	0	1	1	0	0	0	0	2
Mean Snowfall (in.)	0.2	trace	trace	0.0	0.0	0.0	0.0	0.0	0.0	0.0	0.0	0.3	0.5
Maximum Snow Depth (in.)	trace	trace	trace	0	0	0	0	0	0	0	0	4	4
Days With ≥ 1.0" Snow Depth	0	0	0	0	0	0	0	0	0	0	0	0	0

Oracle 2 SE *Pinal County* Elevation: 4,509 ft. Latitude: 32° 36' N Longitude: 110° 44' W

	JAN	FEB	MAR	APR	MAY	JUN	JUL	AUG	SEP	OCT	NOV	DEC	YEAR
Mean Maximum Temp. (°F)	55.4	58.7	63.9	71.8	82.6	91.8	91.8	88.7	85.6	76.0	63.5	55.1	73.7
Mean Temp. (°F)	45.2	47.7	52.0	58.9	69.0	78.2	79.8	77.4	73.7	63.8	52.4	44.9	61.9
Mean Minimum Temp. (°F)	35.0	36.6	40.1	46.0	55.4	64.5	67.7	66.0	61.8	51.6	41.2	34.7	50.0
Extreme Maximum Temp. (°F)	73	78	86	90	99	106	109	101	98	94	85	75	109
Extreme Minimum Temp. (°F)	10	12	15	24	32	45	46	52	44	28	18	12	10
Days Maximum Temp. ≥ 90°F	0	0	0	0	4	21	21	14	7	1	0	0	68
Days Maximum Temp. ≤ 32°F	0	0	0	0	0	0	0	0	0	0	0	0	0
Days Minimum Temp. ≤ 32°F	12	8	5	1	0	0	0	0	0	0	4	12	42
Days Minimum Temp. ≤ 0°F	0	0	0	0	0	0	0	0	0	0	0	0	0
Heating Degree Days (base 65°F)	607	484	397	199	34	1	0	0	3	101	373	616	2,815
Cooling Degree Days (base 65°F)	0	0	2	22	165	404	466	390	271	71	1	0	1,792
Mean Precipitation (in.)	2.31	2.57	2.26	0.91	0.49	0.33	3.27	4.24	1.93	1.47	1.60	2.19	23.57
Extreme Maximum Daily Precip. (in.)	2.00	3.03	2.45	1.68	1.74	0.85	2.45	2.73	2.28	2.56	2.55	1.88	3.03
Days With ≥ 0.1" Precipitation	4	4	4	2	1	1	6	7	4	3	2	4	42
Days With ≥ 0.5" Precipitation	2	2	2	1	0	0	2	2	1	1	1	2	16
Days With ≥ 1.0" Precipitation	1	1	1	0	0	0	1	1	0	0	0	1	6
Mean Snowfall (in.)	3.1	3.4	2.1	0.9	0.0	0.0	0.0	0.0	0.0	0.0	0.5	2.6	12.6
Maximum Snow Depth (in.)	2	***trace***	***3***	trace	0	***0***	0	0	0	***0***	***trace***	3	***3***
Days With ≥ 1.0" Snow Depth	0	0	0	0	0	0	0	0	0	0	0	0	0

Organ Pipe Cactus N M *Pima County* Elevation: 1,678 ft. Latitude: 31° 57' N Longitude: 112° 48' W

	JAN	FEB	MAR	APR	MAY	JUN	JUL	AUG	SEP	OCT	NOV	DEC	YEAR
Mean Maximum Temp. (°F)	69.8	72.9	78.0	85.4	93.2	101.3	103.5	102.2	98.5	88.8	77.5	68.7	86.7
Mean Temp. (°F)	54.9	57.7	61.9	68.1	75.7	83.8	89.0	88.0	83.4	72.8	61.7	54.2	70.9
Mean Minimum Temp. (°F)	40.0	42.5	45.8	50.8	58.2	66.3	74.4	73.7	68.1	56.8	45.9	39.7	55.2
Extreme Maximum Temp. (°F)	90	94	99	104	111	118	118	116	111	107	97	85	118
Extreme Minimum Temp. (°F)	21	19	28	31	42	48	52	59	48	34	26	21	19
Days Maximum Temp. ≥ 90°F	0	0	3	10	22	29	31	30	28	15	2	0	170
Days Maximum Temp. ≤ 32°F	0	0	0	0	0	0	0	0	0	0	0	0	0
Days Minimum Temp. ≤ 32°F	3	1	0	0	0	0	0	0	0	0	1	3	8
Days Minimum Temp. ≤ 0°F	0	0	0	0	0	0	0	0	0	0	0	0	0
Heating Degree Days (base 65°F)	307	209	133	43	4	0	0	0	0	13	127	327	1,163
Cooling Degree Days (base 65°F)	2	9	45	142	343	570	751	719	557	264	36	0	3,438
Mean Precipitation (in.)	0.91	0.94	0.96	0.28	0.07	0.11	1.41	2.37	0.81	0.54	0.48	1.22	10.10
Extreme Maximum Daily Precip. (in.)	1.37	1.49	1.64	1.64	0.41	1.00	2.03	2.19	2.25	2.01	1.10	1.89	2.25
Days With ≥ 0.1" Precipitation	2	2	2	1	0	0	3	4	2	1	1	2	20
Days With ≥ 0.5" Precipitation	1	1	1	0	0	0	1	2	1	0	0	1	8
Days With ≥ 1.0" Precipitation	0	0	0	0	0	0	0	1	0	0	0	0	1
Mean Snowfall (in.)	0.0	trace	0.0	0.0	0.0	0.0	0.0	0.0	0.0	0.0	0.0	trace	trace
Maximum Snow Depth (in.)	0	trace	0	0	0	0	0	0	0	0	0	trace	trace
Days With ≥ 1.0" Snow Depth	0	0	0	0	0	0	0	0	0	0	0	0	0

Payson *Gila County* Elevation: 4,913 ft. Latitude: 34° 14' N Longitude: 111° 20' W

	JAN	FEB	MAR	APR	MAY	JUN	JUL	AUG	SEP	OCT	NOV	DEC	YEAR
Mean Maximum Temp. (°F)	54.5	57.5	62.5	70.5	79.7	89.6	92.1	89.7	84.7	74.6	62.4	54.1	72.7
Mean Temp. (°F)	40.1	42.6	46.8	53.4	61.4	70.2	75.5	74.2	68.1	57.7	46.6	39.7	56.4
Mean Minimum Temp. (°F)	25.7	27.7	31.1	36.2	43.1	50.6	58.8	58.6	51.4	40.7	30.8	25.3	40.0
Extreme Maximum Temp. (°F)	74	80	84	91	99	106	107	104	99	94	83	75	107
Extreme Minimum Temp. (°F)	5	2	10	21	24	31	40	40	33	22	10	-2	-2
Days Maximum Temp. ≥ 90°F	0	0	0	0	3	15	22	17	6	1	0	0	64
Days Maximum Temp. ≤ 32°F	0	0	0	0	0	0	0	0	0	0	0	0	0
Days Minimum Temp. ≤ 32°F	27	21	19	9	1	0	0	0	0	3	19	27	126
Days Minimum Temp. ≤ 0°F	0	0	0	0	0	0	0	0	0	0	0	0	0
Heating Degree Days (base 65°F)	764	625	555	342	136	16	0	0	25	229	545	776	4,013
Cooling Degree Days (base 65°F)	0	0	0	1	31	177	333	291	124	9	0	0	966
Mean Precipitation (in.)	2.27	2.53	2.19	1.07	0.59	0.28	2.59	3.22	1.99	1.49	1.67	1.81	21.70
Extreme Maximum Daily Precip. (in.)	2.57	2.44	2.87	2.11	1.13	0.97	2.28	2.40	2.36	2.03	2.53	3.86	3.86
Days With ≥ 0.1" Precipitation	4	4	4	2	2	1	6	7	4	3	3	4	44
Days With ≥ 0.5" Precipitation	2	2	1	1	0	0	2	2	1	1	1	1	14
Days With ≥ 1.0" Precipitation	1	1	0	0	0	0	0	1	0	0	0	0	3
Mean Snowfall (in.)	5.4	5.0	3.5	1.9	trace	0.0	0.0	0.0	0.0	trace	1.6	3.3	20.7
Maximum Snow Depth (in.)	10	26	12	20	trace	0	0	0	0	trace	11	13	26
Days With ≥ 1.0" Snow Depth	2	1	1	0	0	0	0	0	0	0	0	2	6

The period of record for all cooperative weather station data is 1980 – 2009. See User Guide for detailed explanation of data.

Saint Johns *Apache County* Elevation: 5,790 ft. Latitude: 34° 31' N Longitude: 109° 24' W

	JAN	FEB	MAR	APR	MAY	JUN	JUL	AUG	SEP	OCT	NOV	DEC	YEAR
Mean Maximum Temp. (°F)	49.2	54.6	61.4	69.7	79.0	88.4	90.2	86.8	81.6	71.1	58.6	48.6	69.9
Mean Temp. (°F)	34.9	39.2	45.2	52.4	61.5	70.1	74.4	72.0	65.7	54.5	42.8	34.0	53.9
Mean Minimum Temp. (°F)	20.5	23.8	29.1	35.2	44.0	51.8	58.7	57.1	49.7	37.8	27.0	19.3	37.8
Extreme Maximum Temp. (°F)	73	75	83	88	99	101	102	101	93	89	80	70	102
Extreme Minimum Temp. (°F)	-4	-10	0	17	22	35	42	45	32	16	8	-25	-25
Days Maximum Temp. ≥ 90°F	0	0	0	0	2	14	18	10	1	0	0	0	45
Days Maximum Temp. ≤ 32°F	1	0	0	0	0	0	0	0	0	0	0	2	3
Days Minimum Temp. ≤ 32°F	27	24	21	11	1	0	0	0	0	7	23	29	143
Days Minimum Temp. ≤ 0°F	0	0	0	0	0	0	0	0	0	0	0	1	1
Heating Degree Days (base 65°F)	928	722	606	371	134	12	0	1	44	322	659	955	4,754
Cooling Degree Days (base 65°F)	0	0	0	1	33	173	300	224	71	2	0	0	804
Mean Precipitation (in.)	0.63	0.49	0.61	0.42	0.39	0.32	1.72	2.54	1.29	0.98	0.56	0.74	10.69
Extreme Maximum Daily Precip. (in.)	1.64	0.92	1.56	0.83	1.02	0.81	1.60	3.02	1.90	1.11	1.02	0.90	3.02
Days With ≥ 0.1" Precipitation	2	2	2	1	1	1	5	6	3	2	2	2	29
Days With ≥ 0.5" Precipitation	0	0	0	0	0	0	1	1	1	1	0	0	4
Days With ≥ 1.0" Precipitation	0	0	0	0	0	0	0	0	0	0	0	0	0
Mean Snowfall (in.)	1.5	0.8	0.9	0.2	trace	0.0	0.0	0.0	0.0	0.4	0.5	2.3	6.6
Maximum Snow Depth (in.)	5	8	14	3	trace	0	0	0	0	4	3	5	14
Days With ≥ 1.0" Snow Depth	0	0	0	0	0	0	0	0	0	0	0	0	0

Santa Rita Exp Range *Pima County* Elevation: 4,299 ft. Latitude: 31° 46' N Longitude: 110° 51' W

	JAN	FEB	MAR	APR	MAY	JUN	JUL	AUG	SEP	OCT	NOV	DEC	YEAR
Mean Maximum Temp. (°F)	***60.3***	***63.2***	68.2	***75.8***	84.5	***93.1***	***91.6***	***88.4***	86.5	***78.2***	***67.5***	***59.8***	***76.4***
Mean Temp. (°F)	***49.5***	***51.8***	56.0	***62.6***	71.1	***79.4***	***79.7***	***77.3***	75.1	***67.0***	***56.1***	***49.0***	***64.5***
Mean Minimum Temp. (°F)	***38.6***	***40.2***	43.8	***49.4***	57.6	***65.3***	***67.7***	***66.0***	63.6	***55.7***	***44.7***	***38.2***	***52.6***
Extreme Maximum Temp. (°F)	80	***82***	89	***95***	101	107	106	***102***	98	***93***	87	***76***	***107***
Extreme Minimum Temp. (°F)	14	***17***	26	***29***	36	46	50	***44***	48	32	23	***15***	***14***
Days Maximum Temp. ≥ 90°F	0	***0***	0	***0***	7	21	19	***14***	8	1	0	***0***	***70***
Days Maximum Temp. ≤ 32°F	0	***0***	0	***0***	0	0	0	0	0	0	0	***0***	***0***
Days Minimum Temp. ≤ 32°F	6	***4***	2	***1***	0	0	0	0	0	0	3	***6***	***22***
Days Minimum Temp. ≤ 0°F	0	***0***	0	***0***	0	0	0	0	0	0	0	***0***	***0***
Heating Degree Days (base 65°F)	***475***	***367***	284	***124***	19	***1***	***0***	***0***	1	***56***	***270***	***488***	***2,085***
Cooling Degree Days (base 65°F)	***0***	***1***	11	***59***	215	***439***	***463***	***387***	310	***125***	***10***	***0***	***2,020***
Mean Precipitation (in.)	1.65	***1.77***	1.50	***0.82***	0.35	0.48	4.81	4.63	2.34	1.62	1.19	***2.06***	***23.22***
Extreme Maximum Daily Precip. (in.)	1.43	***2.03***	***1.67***	***2.65***	0.97	***2.93***	***3.54***	***4.65***	2.06	na	***1.75***	***2.56***	na
Days With ≥ 0.1" Precipitation	4	***3***	3	***2***	1	1	8	9	5	***2***	2	***4***	***44***
Days With ≥ 0.5" Precipitation	1	***1***	1	***1***	0	0	3	3	2	1	1	***1***	***15***
Days With ≥ 1.0" Precipitation	0	***0***	0	***0***	0	0	1	1	1	0	0	***0***	***3***
Mean Snowfall (in.)	***0.9***	***0.8***	0.6	***0.0***	0.0	0.0	0.0	0.0	0.0	0.0	0.1	***0.5***	***2.9***
Maximum Snow Depth (in.)	***2***	***trace***	***3***	***2***	0	***0***	0	***0***	0	***0***	1	***2***	***3***
Days With ≥ 1.0" Snow Depth	***0***	***0***	0	***0***	0	0	0	0	0	0	0	***0***	***0***

Sasabe *Pima County* Elevation: 3,589 ft. Latitude: 31° 29' N Longitude: 111° 33' W

	JAN	FEB	MAR	APR	MAY	JUN	JUL	AUG	SEP	OCT	NOV	DEC	YEAR
Mean Maximum Temp. (°F)	63.7	65.9	70.1	77.8	86.3	95.0	94.8	91.8	89.9	81.4	***71.3***	63.7	***79.3***
Mean Temp. (°F)	49.8	51.9	55.6	61.6	69.1	78.0	81.0	78.8	75.4	66.2	***56.4***	49.7	***64.5***
Mean Minimum Temp. (°F)	36.0	37.9	41.1	45.4	51.8	60.9	67.1	65.6	61.0	51.0	***41.5***	35.6	***49.6***
Extreme Maximum Temp. (°F)	82	85	91	97	104	111	109	105	103	100	***90***	84	***111***
Extreme Minimum Temp. (°F)	16	***16***	24	28	34	43	51	51	45	27	***22***	18	***16***
Days Maximum Temp. ≥ 90°F	0	0	0	1	10	24	24	21	17	5	***0***	0	***102***
Days Maximum Temp. ≤ 32°F	0	0	0	0	0	0	0	0	0	0	***0***	0	***0***
Days Minimum Temp. ≤ 32°F	9	6	2	0	0	0	0	0	0	0	***3***	8	***28***
Days Minimum Temp. ≤ 0°F	0	0	0	0	0	0	0	0	0	0	***0***	0	***0***
Heating Degree Days (base 65°F)	464	364	291	133	28	1	0	0	1	59	***258***	468	***2,067***
Cooling Degree Days (base 65°F)	0	0	7	41	164	396	502	433	320	105	***7***	0	***1,975***
Mean Precipitation (in.)	1.10	1.43	1.10	0.52	0.19	0.34	3.57	3.61	1.82	1.10	***0.74***	1.73	***17.25***
Extreme Maximum Daily Precip. (in.)	1.76	2.22	1.46	1.90	1.44	0.72	2.65	4.10	2.11	3.41	***1.12***	3.20	***4.10***
Days With ≥ 0.1" Precipitation	2	3	2	1	0	1	6	7	3	2	***1***	3	***31***
Days With ≥ 0.5" Precipitation	1	1	1	0	0	0	2	2	1	1	***0***	1	***10***
Days With ≥ 1.0" Precipitation	0	0	0	0	0	0	1	1	0	0	***0***	1	***3***
Mean Snowfall (in.)	0.1	0.3	0.3	0.0	0.0	0.0	0.0	0.0	0.0	0.0	***0.0***	0.3	***1.0***
Maximum Snow Depth (in.)	0	***0***	2	0	0	0	0	0	0	0	***0***	0	***2***
Days With ≥ 1.0" Snow Depth	0	0	0	0	0	0	0	0	0	0	***0***	0	***0***

Seligman *Yavapai County* Elevation: 5,250 ft. Latitude: 35° 20' N Longitude: 112° 53' W

	JAN	FEB	MAR	APR	MAY	JUN	JUL	AUG	SEP	OCT	NOV	DEC	YEAR
Mean Maximum Temp. (°F)	52.3	55.9	61.9	69.2	78.8	88.3	92.1	89.4	83.8	73.3	61.4	52.4	71.6
Mean Temp. (°F)	37.8	40.6	45.2	51.3	59.6	68.1	74.1	72.5	65.9	55.3	44.8	37.4	54.4
Mean Minimum Temp. (°F)	23.3	25.2	28.5	33.3	40.5	47.8	56.1	55.6	48.0	37.2	28.2	22.4	37.2
Extreme Maximum Temp. (°F)	73	77	84	89	99	105	107	106	97	93	83	73	107
Extreme Minimum Temp. (°F)	-3	-3	9	14	23	31	39	40	30	15	4	-12	-12
Days Maximum Temp. ≥ 90°F	0	0	0	0	3	14	21	16	5	0	0	0	59
Days Maximum Temp. ≤ 32°F	0	0	0	0	0	0	0	0	0	0	0	0	0
Days Minimum Temp. ≤ 32°F	28	24	23	13	4	0	0	0	0	8	23	28	151
Days Minimum Temp. ≤ 0°F	0	0	0	0	0	0	0	0	0	0	0	0	0
Heating Degree Days (base 65°F)	836	685	607	405	181	31	0	1	45	297	599	848	4,535
Cooling Degree Days (base 65°F)	0	0	0	1	22	130	291	241	79	3	0	0	767
Mean Precipitation (in.)	1.18	1.19	1.12	0.58	0.40	0.31	1.85	2.11	1.41	0.96	0.87	0.87	12.85
Extreme Maximum Daily Precip. (in.)	1.50	1.09	1.08	0.76	0.74	1.01	2.25	2.19	2.60	3.08	1.15	1.57	3.08
Days With ≥ 0.1" Precipitation	3	3	3	2	1	1	4	5	3	2	2	3	32
Days With ≥ 0.5" Precipitation	1	1	0	0	0	0	1	1	1	1	1	0	7
Days With ≥ 1.0" Precipitation	0	0	0	0	0	0	0	0	0	0	0	0	0
Mean Snowfall (in.)	3.4	2.2	1.2	0.4	0.0	0.0	0.0	0.0	0.0	0.1	0.8	1.8	9.9
Maximum Snow Depth (in.)	10	8	4	trace	0	0	0	0	0	0	4	6	10
Days With ≥ 1.0" Snow Depth	2	1	0	0	0	0	0	0	0	0	0	1	4

The period of record for all cooperative weather station data is 1980 – 2009. See User Guide for detailed explanation of data.

Sierra Vista *Cochise County* Elevation: 4,600 ft. Latitude: 31° 33' N Longitude: 110° 17' W

	JAN	FEB	MAR	APR	MAY	JUN	JUL	AUG	SEP	OCT	NOV	DEC	YEAR
Mean Maximum Temp. (°F)	61.1	***64.6***	69.6	77.0	85.2	92.9	91.7	88.9	86.8	79.1	***68.4***	***61.1***	***77.2***
Mean Temp. (°F)	47.3	***50.6***	55.3	61.9	70.0	78.0	78.9	76.8	73.4	64.9	***54.2***	***47.1***	***63.2***
Mean Minimum Temp. (°F)	33.5	***36.5***	41.0	46.9	54.7	63.0	66.0	64.6	60.1	50.7	***40.1***	***33.1***	***49.2***
Extreme Maximum Temp. (°F)	81	***84***	91	97	102	107	108	102	98	96	***85***	79	***108***
Extreme Minimum Temp. (°F)	12	***11***	23	28	38	46	51	53	45	30	***19***	15	***11***
Days Maximum Temp. ≥ 90°F	0	***0***	0	1	8	23	20	15	9	1	***0***	0	***77***
Days Maximum Temp. ≤ 32°F	0	***0***	0	0	0	0	0	0	0	0	***0***	0	***0***
Days Minimum Temp. ≤ 32°F	14	***8***	3	0	0	0	0	0	0	0	***4***	15	***44***
Days Minimum Temp. ≤ 0°F	0	***0***	0	0	0	0	0	0	0	0	***0***	0	***0***
Heating Degree Days (base 65°F)	540	***401***	297	120	18	1	0	0	2	69	***319***	***547***	***2,314***
Cooling Degree Days (base 65°F)	0	***0***	4	35	180	396	437	373	262	72	***1***	***0***	***1,760***
Mean Precipitation (in.)	0.95	***0.64***	0.48	0.43	0.28	0.57	3.22	3.88	1.43	0.98	***0.51***	***1.02***	***14.39***
Extreme Maximum Daily Precip. (in.)	1.08	***0.80***	0.78	1.45	1.25	1.15	1.80	2.84	1.54	2.12	***1.69***	***1.77***	***2.84***
Days With ≥ 0.1" Precipitation	3	***2***	2	1	1	2	7	8	4	2	***1***	***2***	***35***
Days With ≥ 0.5" Precipitation	1	***0***	0	0	0	0	2	2	1	1	***0***	***1***	***8***
Days With ≥ 1.0" Precipitation	0	***0***	0	0	0	0	1	1	0	0	***0***	***0***	***2***
Mean Snowfall (in.)	***0.3***	***0.1***	0.2	trace	0.0	0.0	0.0	0.0	0.0	0.0	***0.0***	0.0	***0.6***
Maximum Snow Depth (in.)	***trace***	***0***	***0***	trace	0	***0***	0	0	0	***0***	***0***	***0***	trace
Days With ≥ 1.0" Snow Depth	***0***	***0***	0	0	0	0	0	0	0	0	***0***	0	***0***

South Phoenix *Maricopa County* Elevation: 1,154 ft. Latitude: 33° 23' N Longitude: 112° 04' W

	JAN	FEB	MAR	APR	MAY	JUN	JUL	AUG	SEP	OCT	NOV	DEC	YEAR
Mean Maximum Temp. (°F)	67.1	71.2	77.2	84.9	93.0	100.5	102.4	101.0	96.7	86.5	73.8	65.9	85.0
Mean Temp. (°F)	53.7	57.1	62.0	68.5	76.5	83.9	88.8	88.1	82.6	71.8	59.6	52.5	70.4
Mean Minimum Temp. (°F)	40.1	42.8	46.7	52.1	59.9	67.2	75.0	75.2	68.4	56.9	45.3	39.1	55.7
Extreme Maximum Temp. (°F)	83	90	98	101	110	114	113	112	109	105	91	83	114
Extreme Minimum Temp. (°F)	22	24	29	36	42	52	59	60	49	37	29	21	21
Days Maximum Temp. ≥ 90°F	0	0	2	9	23	29	31	31	28	11	0	0	164
Days Maximum Temp. ≤ 32°F	0	0	0	0	0	0	0	0	0	0	0	0	0
Days Minimum Temp. ≤ 32°F	4	1	0	0	0	0	0	0	0	0	1	4	10
Days Minimum Temp. ≤ 0°F	0	0	0	0	0	0	0	0	0	0	0	0	0
Heating Degree Days (base 65°F)	345	223	126	35	2	0	0	0	0	18	173	382	1,304
Cooling Degree Days (base 65°F)	0	5	39	147	365	573	743	722	534	234	18	0	3,380
Mean Precipitation (in.)	0.89	1.11	1.19	0.33	0.11	0.04	0.88	0.89	0.80	0.68	0.69	0.89	8.50
Extreme Maximum Daily Precip. (in.)	1.53	1.18	1.66	1.15	0.31	0.21	1.77	2.05	1.58	1.93	2.05	1.15	2.05
Days With ≥ 0.1" Precipitation	2	3	3	1	0	0	2	2	2	2	1	2	20
Days With ≥ 0.5" Precipitation	1	1	1	0	0	0	1	0	0	0	0	1	5
Days With ≥ 1.0" Precipitation	0	0	0	0	0	0	0	0	0	0	0	0	0
Mean Snowfall (in.)	0.0	0.0	0.0	0.0	0.0	0.0	0.0	0.0	0.0	0.0	0.0	0.0	0.0
Maximum Snow Depth (in.)	0	0	0	0	0	0	0	0	0	0	0	0	0
Days With ≥ 1.0" Snow Depth	0	0	0	0	0	0	0	0	0	0	0	0	0

Teec Nos Pos *Apache County* Elevation: 5,290 ft. Latitude: 36° 55' N Longitude: 109° 05' W

	JAN	FEB	MAR	APR	MAY	JUN	JUL	AUG	SEP	OCT	NOV	DEC	YEAR
Mean Maximum Temp. (°F)	43.8	50.4	59.8	68.9	78.3	89.6	93.3	90.3	82.7	69.7	***54.9***	44.5	***68.9***
Mean Temp. (°F)	33.3	38.8	46.5	54.8	63.8	74.2	79.0	76.8	68.5	55.8	***43.0***	***33.4***	***55.6***
Mean Minimum Temp. (°F)	22.9	27.2	33.1	40.6	49.2	58.7	64.8	63.3	54.3	41.8	***31.0***	***22.5***	***42.5***
Extreme Maximum Temp. (°F)	66	73	82	102	99	104	105	101	97	96	77	65	105
Extreme Minimum Temp. (°F)	-6	-11	10	20	30	39	44	49	23	21	11	-12	-12
Days Maximum Temp. ≥ 90°F	0	0	0	0	2	17	23	17	3	0	0	0	62
Days Maximum Temp. ≤ 32°F	3	1	0	0	0	0	0	0	0	0	0	2	6
Days Minimum Temp. ≤ 32°F	26	20	14	4	0	0	0	0	0	3	17	25	109
Days Minimum Temp. ≤ 0°F	0	0	0	0	0	0	0	0	0	0	0	0	0
Heating Degree Days (base 65°F)	976	733	567	307	105	8	0	0	33	284	***654***	***973***	***4,640***
Cooling Degree Days (base 65°F)	0	0	0	6	73	288	442	373	145	7	***0***	***0***	***1,334***
Mean Precipitation (in.)	0.68	0.52	0.64	0.61	0.57	0.20	0.88	1.15	0.79	0.90	0.45	0.64	8.03
Extreme Maximum Daily Precip. (in.)	1.80	1.50	0.83	1.30	1.05	0.65	2.00	2.07	1.75	2.00	0.84	3.50	3.50
Days With ≥ 0.1" Precipitation	2	2	2	2	1	1	2	3	2	2	2	2	23
Days With ≥ 0.5" Precipitation	0	0	0	0	0	0	1	1	0	0	0	0	2
Days With ≥ 1.0" Precipitation	0	0	0	0	0	0	0	0	0	0	0	0	0
Mean Snowfall (in.)	1.1	1.0	0.3	0.1	0.1	0.0	0.0	0.0	0.0	trace	0.3	0.4	3.3
Maximum Snow Depth (in.)	6	8	1	trace	trace	0	0	0	0	4	trace	3	8
Days With ≥ 1.0" Snow Depth	0	0	0	0	0	0	0	0	0	0	0	0	0

Tombstone *Cochise County* Elevation: 4,609 ft. Latitude: 31° 42' N Longitude: 110° 03' W

	JAN	FEB	MAR	APR	MAY	JUN	JUL	AUG	SEP	OCT	NOV	DEC	YEAR
Mean Maximum Temp. (°F)	60.2	63.7	69.4	77.4	86.0	94.8	93.4	90.1	87.8	79.1	68.1	60.1	77.5
Mean Temp. (°F)	48.2	51.1	55.5	62.5	70.8	79.1	79.9	77.7	74.7	65.7	55.5	48.3	64.1
Mean Minimum Temp. (°F)	36.0	38.3	41.7	47.6	55.5	63.3	66.4	65.2	61.5	52.3	42.7	36.4	50.6
Extreme Maximum Temp. (°F)	80	85	92	99	104	110	112	106	101	98	87	79	112
Extreme Minimum Temp. (°F)	16	18	22	28	35	46	57	54	47	29	20	16	16
Days Maximum Temp. ≥ 90°F	0	0	0	1	10	25	23	18	12	3	0	0	92
Days Maximum Temp. ≤ 32°F	0	0	0	0	0	0	0	0	0	0	0	0	0
Days Minimum Temp. ≤ 32°F	9	6	3	0	0	0	0	0	0	0	3	9	30
Days Minimum Temp. ≤ 0°F	0	0	0	0	0	0	0	0	0	0	0	0	0
Heating Degree Days (base 65°F)	516	388	292	118	17	0	0	0	1	66	285	511	2,194
Cooling Degree Days (base 65°F)	0	1	7	50	203	430	470	399	298	94	5	0	1,957
Mean Precipitation (in.)	0.94	0.75	0.69	0.30	0.26	0.63	2.82	3.08	1.60	0.97	0.71	1.08	13.83
Extreme Maximum Daily Precip. (in.)	1.35	1.05	1.00	1.54	0.97	2.30	***2.38***	1.97	2.20	2.10	2.15	1.80	***2.38***
Days With ≥ 0.1" Precipitation	2	2	2	1	1	1	6	7	3	2	2	3	32
Days With ≥ 0.5" Precipitation	1	0	0	0	0	0	2	2	1	1	0	1	8
Days With ≥ 1.0" Precipitation	0	0	0	0	0	0	0	1	0	0	0	0	1
Mean Snowfall (in.)	0.4	0.1	0.0	0.0	0.0	0.0	0.0	0.0	0.0	0.0	0.1	0.1	0.7
Maximum Snow Depth (in.)	10	6	trace	0	0	0	0	0	0	0	3	1	10
Days With ≥ 1.0" Snow Depth	0	0	0	0	0	0	0	0	0	0	0	0	0

The period of record for all cooperative weather station data is 1980 – 2009. See User Guide for detailed explanation of data.

Tucson 17 NW *Pima County* Elevation: 2,561 ft. Latitude: 32° 15' N Longitude: 111° 12' W

	JAN	FEB	MAR	APR	MAY	JUN	JUL	AUG	SEP	OCT	NOV	DEC	YEAR
Mean Maximum Temp. (°F)	66.5	69.2	75.3	83.0	92.6	101.0	101.3	98.8	96.0	***86.6***	***74.7***	***65.4***	***84.2***
Mean Temp. (°F)	53.6	56.0	61.3	68.0	77.0	85.6	88.0	86.1	82.5	***72.3***	***60.9***	***52.6***	***70.3***
Mean Minimum Temp. (°F)	40.6	42.8	47.3	53.1	61.4	70.2	74.8	73.4	68.9	***57.9***	***46.8***	***39.7***	***56.4***
Extreme Maximum Temp. (°F)	87	90	97	104	108	115	114	111	107	104	***95***	88	***115***
Extreme Minimum Temp. (°F)	20	19	26	27	44	51	55	58	46	35	***26***	23	***19***
Days Maximum Temp. ≥ 90°F	0	0	1	8	22	29	29	29	26	12	***1***	0	***157***
Days Maximum Temp. ≤ 32°F	0	0	0	0	0	0	0	0	0	0	***0***	0	***0***
Days Minimum Temp. ≤ 32°F	3	1	0	0	0	0	0	0	0	0	***1***	5	***10***
Days Minimum Temp. ≤ 0°F	0	0	0	0	0	0	0	0	0	0	***0***	0	***0***
Heating Degree Days (base 65°F)	351	255	154	57	4	0	0	0	0	***19***	***158***	***379***	***1,377***
Cooling Degree Days (base 65°F)	3	7	48	154	383	625	721	661	532	***251***	***42***	***1***	***3,428***
Mean Precipitation (in.)	0.96	0.97	0.93	0.36	0.22	0.36	2.20	2.86	1.35	0.89	***0.70***	***1.17***	***12.97***
Extreme Maximum Daily Precip. (in.)	***1.50***	***1.05***	***1.80***	***1.51***	***0.45***	***1.72***	1.90	***2.43***	3.42	***2.16***	***1.10***	na	na
Days With ≥ 0.1" Precipitation	3	3	2	1	1	1	5	5	3	2	***2***	***2***	***30***
Days With ≥ 0.5" Precipitation	0	1	1	0	0	0	1	2	1	1	***0***	***1***	***8***
Days With ≥ 1.0" Precipitation	0	0	0	0	0	0	1	1	0	0	***0***	***0***	***2***
Mean Snowfall (in.)	0.0	trace	0.0	0.0	0.0	0.0	0.0	0.0	0.0	0.0	***trace***	***trace***	***trace***
Maximum Snow Depth (in.)	0	trace	0	0	0	0	0	0	0	0	***trace***	0	trace
Days With ≥ 1.0" Snow Depth	0	0	0	0	0	0	0	0	0	0	***0***	0	***0***

Tucson NWSO *Pima County* Elevation: 2,478 ft. Latitude: 32° 14' N Longitude: 110° 57' W

	JAN	FEB	MAR	APR	MAY	JUN	JUL	AUG	SEP	OCT	NOV	DEC	YEAR
Mean Maximum Temp. (°F)	66.1	69.4	74.8	82.7	91.8	100.5	100.2	98.0	95.0	85.3	73.8	65.8	83.6
Mean Temp. (°F)	54.5	57.5	62.2	69.3	78.1	86.7	88.5	86.9	83.3	72.8	61.4	54.0	71.3
Mean Minimum Temp. (°F)	42.8	45.5	49.6	55.8	64.4	72.9	76.9	75.8	71.4	60.3	48.9	42.2	58.9
Extreme Maximum Temp. (°F)	86	90	98	104	110	115	115	112	106	103	92	84	115
Extreme Minimum Temp. (°F)	26	27	31	33	46	55	65	65	50	39	30	25	25
Days Maximum Temp. ≥ 90°F	0	0	1	7	21	29	30	29	26	10	0	0	153
Days Maximum Temp. ≤ 32°F	0	0	0	0	0	0	0	0	0	0	0	0	0
Days Minimum Temp. ≤ 32°F	2	1	0	0	0	0	0	0	0	0	0	2	5
Days Minimum Temp. ≤ 0°F	0	0	0	0	0	0	0	0	0	0	0	0	0
Heating Degree Days (base 65°F)	320	212	130	39	1	0	0	0	0	14	141	335	1,192
Cooling Degree Days (base 65°F)	1	7	51	174	415	658	737	686	554	263	39	1	3,586
Mean Precipitation (in.)	0.94	0.96	0.82	0.36	0.16	0.21	2.24	2.32	1.26	0.90	0.66	0.89	11.72
Extreme Maximum Daily Precip. (in.)	1.51	1.25	0.98	1.27	0.50	0.86	2.01	2.25	1.60	4.16	1.45	1.83	4.16
Days With ≥ 0.1" Precipitation	2	3	2	1	1	1	5	5	3	2	2	2	29
Days With ≥ 0.5" Precipitation	1	1	1	0	0	0	1	1	1	1	0	1	8
Days With ≥ 1.0" Precipitation	0	0	0	0	0	0	1	0	0	0	0	0	1
Mean Snowfall (in.)	0.2	trace	trace	trace	0.0	0.0	0.0	0.0	0.0	0.0	0.0	0.1	0.3
Maximum Snow Depth (in.)	trace	trace	0	trace	0	0	0	0	0	0	0	trace	trace
Days With ≥ 1.0" Snow Depth	0	0	0	0	0	0	0	0	0	0	0	0	0

Willow Beach *Mohave County* Elevation: 740 ft. Latitude: 35° 52' N Longitude: 114° 40' W

	JAN	FEB	MAR	APR	MAY	JUN	JUL	AUG	SEP	OCT	NOV	DEC	YEAR
Mean Maximum Temp. (°F)	***64.6***	69.3	***76.7***	85.6	95.5	105.6	110.5	108.5	101.6	88.8	73.5	***64.1***	***87.0***
Mean Temp. (°F)	***52.5***	56.9	***63.3***	***71.4***	80.7	89.5	95.0	93.5	***86.4***	74.2	60.9	***52.4***	***73.1***
Mean Minimum Temp. (°F)	***40.5***	44.5	***49.8***	***57.2***	65.9	73.3	79.4	78.5	***71.0***	59.7	48.1	***40.6***	***59.0***
Extreme Maximum Temp. (°F)	82	91	101	106	117	121	124	121	115	109	93	81	124
Extreme Minimum Temp. (°F)	26	25	35	42	48	51	65	65	55	41	31	21	21
Days Maximum Temp. ≥ 90°F	0	0	2	10	23	29	30	30	28	15	0	0	167
Days Maximum Temp. ≤ 32°F	0	0	0	0	0	0	0	0	0	0	0	0	0
Days Minimum Temp. ≤ 32°F	1	1	0	0	0	0	0	0	0	0	0	2	4
Days Minimum Temp. ≤ 0°F	0	0	0	0	0	0	0	0	0	0	0	0	0
Heating Degree Days (base 65°F)	***379***	227	***105***	***22***	1	0	0	0	***0***	11	149	***383***	***1,277***
Cooling Degree Days (base 65°F)	***0***	5	***59***	***221***	495	741	937	891	***647***	304	32	***0***	***4,332***
Mean Precipitation (in.)	0.78	1.04	0.74	0.24	0.16	0.08	0.37	0.47	0.41	0.52	0.34	0.54	5.69
Extreme Maximum Daily Precip. (in.)	***1.00***	1.46	1.99	0.94	0.61	0.52	1.37	1.64	1.68	***2.05***	***0.89***	***3.00***	***3.00***
Days With ≥ 0.1" Precipitation	2	3	2	1	1	0	1	1	1	1	1	1	15
Days With ≥ 0.5" Precipitation	0	1	0	0	0	0	0	0	0	0	0	0	1
Days With ≥ 1.0" Precipitation	0	0	0	0	0	0	0	0	0	0	0	0	0
Mean Snowfall (in.)	0.0	0.0	0.0	0.0	0.0	0.0	0.0	0.0	0.0	0.0	0.0	0.0	0.0
Maximum Snow Depth (in.)	0	0	0	0	0	0	0	0	0	***0***	0	0	***0***
Days With ≥ 1.0" Snow Depth	0	0	0	0	0	0	0	0	0	***0***	0	0	***0***

Wupatki N M *Coconino County* Elevation: 4,908 ft. Latitude: 35° 31' N Longitude: 111° 22' W

	JAN	FEB	MAR	APR	MAY	JUN	JUL	AUG	SEP	OCT	NOV	DEC	YEAR
Mean Maximum Temp. (°F)	48.1	55.1	63.1	71.3	81.3	91.7	95.1	91.5	84.7	72.4	58.3	46.5	71.6
Mean Temp. (°F)	37.1	42.6	49.6	57.1	66.6	76.4	80.8	78.0	70.9	58.9	46.1	35.9	58.3
Mean Minimum Temp. (°F)	26.1	30.0	36.1	42.9	52.0	61.1	66.6	64.5	57.0	45.3	33.9	25.2	45.1
Extreme Maximum Temp. (°F)	70	77	83	92	101	106	109	105	100	91	80	71	109
Extreme Minimum Temp. (°F)	4	-2	13	20	32	41	53	48	38	24	13	-5	-5
Days Maximum Temp. ≥ 90°F	0	0	0	0	5	20	26	21	7	0	0	0	79
Days Maximum Temp. ≤ 32°F	1	0	0	0	0	0	0	0	0	0	0	2	3
Days Minimum Temp. ≤ 32°F	26	17	9	2	0	0	0	0	0	2	12	26	94
Days Minimum Temp. ≤ 0°F	0	0	0	0	0	0	0	0	0	0	0	0	0
Heating Degree Days (base 65°F)	858	627	471	246	66	4	0	0	15	207	559	897	3,950
Cooling Degree Days (base 65°F)	0	0	0	16	123	353	497	412	199	25	0	0	1,625
Mean Precipitation (in.)	0.55	0.44	0.63	0.50	0.39	0.21	1.25	1.49	1.02	0.54	0.60	0.57	8.19
Extreme Maximum Daily Precip. (in.)	0.85	0.87	1.50	0.70	0.74	0.50	1.68	1.42	1.66	0.66	1.37	1.19	1.68
Days With ≥ 0.1" Precipitation	2	1	2	2	1	1	3	4	3	2	1	2	24
Days With ≥ 0.5" Precipitation	0	0	0	0	0	0	1	1	1	0	0	0	3
Days With ≥ 1.0" Precipitation	0	0	0	0	0	0	0	0	0	0	0	0	0
Mean Snowfall (in.)	1.3	0.8	0.5	0.4	trace	0.0	0.0	0.0	0.0	trace	0.5	1.6	5.1
Maximum Snow Depth (in.)	***5***	***4***	5	5	trace	0	0	0	0	***0***	***4***	12	***12***
Days With ≥ 1.0" Snow Depth	***1***	0	0	0	0	0	0	0	0	0	0	1	***2***

The period of record for all cooperative weather station data is 1980 – 2009. See User Guide for detailed explanation of data.

Yucca 1 NNE *Mohave County* Elevation: 1,950 ft. Latitude: 34° 53' N Longitude: 114° 08' W

	JAN	FEB	MAR	APR	MAY	JUN	JUL	AUG	SEP	OCT	NOV	DEC	YEAR
Mean Maximum Temp. (°F)	61.4	65.4	71.2	79.7	89.8	99.2	103.9	102.1	95.9	83.5	69.8	60.4	81.9
Mean Temp. (°F)	49.9	53.2	57.9	65.2	74.8	83.9	90.4	88.8	81.6	69.3	57.0	49.1	68.4
Mean Minimum Temp. (°F)	38.3	41.0	44.6	50.6	59.6	68.6	76.8	75.5	67.2	55.0	44.1	37.7	54.9
Extreme Maximum Temp. (°F)	84	87	97	103	112	117	120	119	111	105	89	79	120
Extreme Minimum Temp. (°F)	21	18	26	31	41	48	59	57	47	33	26	19	18
Days Maximum Temp. ≥ 90°F	0	0	1	5	17	26	30	30	25	9	0	0	143
Days Maximum Temp. ≤ 32°F	0	0	0	0	0	0	0	0	0	0	0	0	0
Days Minimum Temp. ≤ 32°F	6	3	1	0	0	0	0	0	0	0	1	6	17
Days Minimum Temp. ≤ 0°F	0	0	0	0	0	0	0	0	0	0	0	0	0
Heating Degree Days (base 65°F)	462	329	233	84	10	0	0	0	1	41	245	487	1,892
Cooling Degree Days (base 65°F)	0	2	21	96	320	574	792	744	506	181	12	0	3,248
Mean Precipitation (in.)	1.08	1.27	1.07	0.34	0.14	0.05	0.62	0.86	0.70	0.54	0.52	0.59	7.78
Extreme Maximum Daily Precip. (in.)	1.54	1.55	1.64	0.81	0.83	0.36	1.44	1.67	3.61	2.14	1.25	1.28	3.61
Days With ≥ 0.1" Precipitation	3	3	3	1	0	0	1	2	1	1	1	2	18
Days With ≥ 0.5" Precipitation	1	1	1	0	0	0	0	1	1	0	0	0	5
Days With ≥ 1.0" Precipitation	0	0	0	0	0	0	0	0	0	0	0	0	0
Mean Snowfall (in.)	0.0	0.1	0.0	0.0	0.0	0.0	0.0	0.0	0.0	0.0	0.0	0.0	0.1
Maximum Snow Depth (in.)	0	0	0	0	0	0	0	0	0	0	0	0	0
Days With ≥ 1.0" Snow Depth	0	0	0	0	0	0	0	0	0	0	0	0	0

Yuma Citrus Station *Yuma County* Elevation: 190 ft. Latitude: 32° 37' N Longitude: 114° 39' W

	JAN	FEB	MAR	APR	MAY	JUN	JUL	AUG	SEP	OCT	NOV	DEC	YEAR
Mean Maximum Temp. (°F)	na	na	na	na	na	na	na	na	na	na	na	na	na
Mean Temp. (°F)	na	na	na	na	na	na	na	na	na	na	na	na	na
Mean Minimum Temp. (°F)	na	na	na	na	na	na	na	na	na	na	na	na	na
Extreme Maximum Temp. (°F)	***83***	***93***	***101***	***106***	***115***	***122***	***124***	***119***	***115***	***110***	***95***	***81***	***124***
Extreme Minimum Temp. (°F)	***26***	***25***	***29***	***38***	***45***	***51***	***61***	***61***	***51***	***37***	***29***	***25***	***25***
Days Maximum Temp. ≥ 90°F	***0***	***0***	***3***	***10***	***21***	***26***	***27***	***27***	***25***	***15***	***1***	***0***	***155***
Days Maximum Temp. ≤ 32°F	***0***	***0***	***0***	***0***	***0***	***0***	***0***	***0***	***0***	***0***	***0***	***0***	***0***
Days Minimum Temp. ≤ 32°F	***1***	***1***	***0***	***0***	***0***	***0***	***0***	***0***	***0***	***0***	***0***	***2***	***4***
Days Minimum Temp. ≤ 0°F	***0***	***0***	***0***	***0***	***0***	***0***	***0***	***0***	***0***	***0***	***0***	***0***	***0***
Heating Degree Days (base 65°F)	na	na	na	na	na	na	na	na	na	na	na	na	na
Cooling Degree Days (base 65°F)	na	na	na	na	na	na	na	na	na	na	na	na	na
Mean Precipitation (in.)	***0.38***	***0.41***	***0.36***	***0.20***	***0.04***	***0.03***	***0.37***	***0.54***	***0.51***	***0.21***	***0.18***	***0.57***	***3.80***
Extreme Maximum Daily Precip. (in.)	***0.77***	***0.62***	***0.50***	***0.39***	***0.33***	***0.32***	***3.51***	***1.96***	***2.10***	***1.29***	***1.08***	***1.34***	***3.51***
Days With ≥ 0.1" Precipitation	***1***	***1***	***1***	***0***	***0***	***0***	***1***	***1***	***1***	***1***	***0***	***1***	***8***
Days With ≥ 0.5" Precipitation	***0***	***0***	***0***	***0***	***0***	***0***	***0***	***0***	***0***	***0***	***0***	***0***	***0***
Days With ≥ 1.0" Precipitation	***0***	***0***	***0***	***0***	***0***	***0***	***0***	***0***	***0***	***0***	***0***	***0***	***0***
Mean Snowfall (in.)	***0.0***	***0.0***	***0.0***	***0.0***	***0.0***	***0.0***	***0.0***	***0.0***	***0.0***	***0.0***	***0.0***	***0.0***	***0.0***
Maximum Snow Depth (in.)	***0***	***0***	***0***	***0***	***0***	***0***	***0***	***0***	***0***	***0***	***0***	***0***	***0***
Days With ≥ 1.0" Snow Depth	***0***	***0***	***0***	***0***	***0***	***0***	***0***	***0***	***0***	***0***	***0***	***0***	***0***

Yuma Proving Ground *Yuma County* Elevation: 324 ft. Latitude: 32° 50' N Longitude: 114° 24' W

	JAN	FEB	MAR	APR	MAY	JUN	JUL	AUG	SEP	OCT	NOV	DEC	YEAR
Mean Maximum Temp. (°F)	69.4	73.4	79.3	86.4	94.8	103.6	106.9	105.9	101.2	90.0	77.3	67.9	88.0
Mean Temp. (°F)	57.0	60.5	65.9	72.3	80.2	88.5	93.8	93.6	87.9	76.2	63.8	55.5	74.6
Mean Minimum Temp. (°F)	44.5	47.7	52.4	58.1	65.6	73.3	80.8	81.3	74.6	62.3	50.3	43.0	61.2
Extreme Maximum Temp. (°F)	88	94	103	106	117	121	124	118	116	112	95	85	124
Extreme Minimum Temp. (°F)	24	26	36	42	48	55	65	67	54	41	29	25	24
Days Maximum Temp. ≥ 90°F	0	0	4	11	24	29	31	31	28	17	2	0	177
Days Maximum Temp. ≤ 32°F	0	0	0	0	0	0	0	0	0	0	0	0	0
Days Minimum Temp. ≤ 32°F	1	0	0	0	0	0	0	0	0	0	0	1	2
Days Minimum Temp. ≤ 0°F	0	0	0	0	0	0	0	0	0	0	0	0	0
Heating Degree Days (base 65°F)	244	139	61	16	0	0	0	0	0	4	92	288	844
Cooling Degree Days (base 65°F)	2	20	94	240	479	711	901	894	696	359	63	1	4,460
Mean Precipitation (in.)	0.43	0.49	0.38	0.13	0.02	0.01	0.27	0.67	0.31	0.21	0.23	0.47	3.62
Extreme Maximum Daily Precip. (in.)	0.97	1.00	1.17	0.64	0.19	0.12	1.03	2.40	1.38	1.04	1.22	1.37	2.40
Days With ≥ 0.1" Precipitation	1	1	1	0	0	0	1	1	1	0	1	1	8
Days With ≥ 0.5" Precipitation	0	0	0	0	0	0	0	0	0	0	0	0	0
Days With ≥ 1.0" Precipitation	0	0	0	0	0	0	0	0	0	0	0	0	0
Mean Snowfall (in.)	0.0	0.0	0.0	0.0	0.0	0.0	0.0	0.0	0.0	0.0	0.0	0.0	0.0
Maximum Snow Depth (in.)	0	0	0	0	0	0	0	0	0	0	0	0	0
Days With ≥ 1.0" Snow Depth	0	0	0	0	0	0	0	0	0	0	0	0	0

The period of record for all cooperative weather station data is 1980 – 2009. See User Guide for detailed explanation of data.

Arizona Weather Station Rankings

Annual Extreme Maximum Temperature

Highest			Lowest		
Rank	Station Name	°F	Rank	Station Name	°F
1	Bullhead City	126	1	Bright Angel R S	92
2	Fountain Hills	125	2	Alpine	93
2	Laveen 3 SSE	125	3	Flagstaff 4 SW	***96***
4	Alamo Dam	124	3	Flagstaff Pulliam Arpt	96
4	Maricopa 4 N	124	5	Betatakin	98
4	Willow Beach	124	5	Fort Valley	98
4	Yuma Citrus Station	***124***	5	Kitt Peak	98
4	Yuma Proving Ground	124	5	McNary 2 N	98
9	Gila Bend	122	9	Saint Johns	102
9	Phoenix Sky Harbor Intl Arpt	122	10	Black River Pumps	103
11	Beaver Dam	120	11	Monument Valley	104
11	Casa Grande	***120***	12	Canyon De Chelly	105
11	Castle Hot Springs	120	12	Coronado N M Hdqtrs	105
11	Yucca 1 NNE	120	12	Teec Nos Pos	105
15	Florence	119	15	Canelo 1 NW	***106***
15	Kofa Mine	119	15	Winslow Municipal Arpt	106
15	Lees Ferry	***119***	17	Payson	107
18	Organ Pipe Cactus N M	118	17	Santa Rita Exp Range	***107***
19	Childs	***117***	17	Seligman	107
19	Tucson Intl Arpt	117	20	Sierra Vista	***108***
21	Cascabel	116	21	Oracle 2 SE	109
21	Clifton	***116***	21	Wupatki N M	109
23	Cordes	115	23	Colorado City	110
23	Tucson 17 NW	***115***	23	Holbrook	110
23	Tucson NWSO	115	25	Bowie	111

Annual Mean Maximum Temperature

Highest			Lowest		
Rank	Station Name	°F	Rank	Station Name	°F
1	Gila Bend	89.8	1	Bright Angel R S	***56.6***
2	Bullhead City	89.1	2	Flagstaff 4 SW	***61.0***
3	Yuma Proving Ground	88.0	3	Alpine	61.2
4	Maricopa 4 N	87.7	4	Flagstaff Pulliam Arpt	61.7
5	Casa Grande	***87.4***	5	Fort Valley	61.8
6	Laveen 3 SSE	87.2	6	McNary 2 N	62.1
7	Alamo Dam	87.1	7	Betatakin	62.2
8	Willow Beach	***87.0***	8	Kitt Peak	65.2
9	Phoenix Sky Harbor Intl Arpt	86.8	9	Monument Valley	***66.7***
10	Organ Pipe Cactus N M	86.7	10	Black River Pumps	68.6
11	Fountain Hills	86.5	11	Teec Nos Pos	***68.9***
12	Florence	85.9	12	Canyon De Chelly	69.4
13	South Phoenix	85.0	13	Saint Johns	69.9
14	Kofa Mine	84.6	14	Colorado City	70.0
15	Tucson 17 NW	***84.2***	15	Winslow Municipal Arpt	71.0
16	Castle Hot Springs	83.7	16	Seligman	71.6
16	Tucson Intl Arpt	83.7	16	Wupatki N M	71.6
18	Tucson NWSO	83.6	18	Holbrook	72.6
19	Anvil Ranch	83.0	19	Payson	72.7
20	Cascabel	82.7	20	Oracle 2 SE	73.7
21	Beaver Dam	***82.0***	21	Canelo 1 NW	***74.5***
22	Yucca 1 NNE	81.9	22	Coronado N M Hdqtrs	74.7
23	Childs	***81.5***	23	Cordes	76.4
24	Clifton	***80.3***	23	Santa Rita Exp Range	***76.4***
24	Nogales 6 N	80.3	25	Lees Ferry	***77.2***

Rankings include 25 highest/lowest stations. If state has less than 25 stations, all stations are included. The period of record is 1980–2009. See User Guide for detailed explanation of data.

Annual Mean Temperature

Highest Rank	Station Name	°F	Lowest Rank	Station Name	°F
1	Phoenix Sky Harbor Intl Arpt	75.0	1	Flagstaff 4 SW	***43.4***
2	Bullhead City	74.6	2	Bright Angel R S	***43.5***
2	Yuma Proving Ground	74.6	3	Fort Valley	44.2
4	Gila Bend	74.2	4	Alpine	44.8
5	Kofa Mine	73.5	5	Flagstaff Pulliam Arpt	46.7
6	Willow Beach	***73.1***	6	McNary 2 N	48.0
7	Laveen 3 SSE	72.6	7	Betatakin	50.4
8	Fountain Hills	72.1	8	Black River Pumps	52.7
9	Casa Grande	***71.3***	9	Saint Johns	53.9
9	Tucson NWSO	71.3	10	Canyon De Chelly	54.1
11	Florence	***71.1***	11	Seligman	54.4
12	Alamo Dam	71.0	12	Colorado City	55.7
12	Organ Pipe Cactus N M	71.0	12	Monument Valley	***55.7***
14	Maricopa 4 N	70.8	12	Teec Nos Pos	***55.7***
15	South Phoenix	70.4	12	Winslow Municipal Arpt	55.7
16	Tucson 17 NW	***70.3***	16	Holbrook	55.8
17	Castle Hot Springs	70.2	16	Kitt Peak	55.8
18	Tucson Intl Arpt	69.7	18	Payson	56.4
19	Yucca 1 NNE	68.4	19	Wupatki N M	58.3
20	Beaver Dam	***66.9***	20	Canelo 1 NW	***58.6***
21	Clifton	***66.4***	21	Coronado N M Hdqtrs	60.8
22	Anvil Ranch	66.1	22	Cordes	61.9
23	Childs	***64.6***	22	Oracle 2 SE	61.9
24	Santa Rita Exp Range	***64.5***	24	Nogales 6 N	62.0
24	Sasabe	***64.5***	25	Sierra Vista	***63.2***

Annual Mean Minimum Temperature

Highest Rank	Station Name	°F	Lowest Rank	Station Name	°F
1	Phoenix Sky Harbor Intl Arpt	63.3	1	Flagstaff 4 SW	***25.8***
2	Kofa Mine	62.4	2	Fort Valley	26.5
3	Yuma Proving Ground	61.2	3	Alpine	28.3
4	Bullhead City	60.0	4	Bright Angel R S	***30.4***
5	Willow Beach	***59.0***	5	Flagstaff Pulliam Arpt	31.6
6	Tucson NWSO	58.9	6	McNary 2 N	33.8
7	Gila Bend	58.7	7	Black River Pumps	36.9
8	Laveen 3 SSE	58.0	8	Seligman	37.2
9	Fountain Hills	57.7	9	Saint Johns	37.8
10	Castle Hot Springs	56.6	10	Betatakin	38.6
11	Tucson 17 NW	***56.4***	11	Canyon De Chelly	38.7
12	Florence	***56.2***	12	Holbrook	39.0
13	South Phoenix	55.7	13	Payson	40.0
13	Tucson Intl Arpt	55.7	14	Winslow Municipal Arpt	40.3
15	Casa Grande	***55.2***	15	Colorado City	41.4
15	Organ Pipe Cactus N M	55.2	16	Teec Nos Pos	***42.5***
17	Alamo Dam	54.9	17	Canelo 1 NW	***42.6***
17	Yucca 1 NNE	54.9	18	Nogales 6 N	43.6
19	Maricopa 4 N	53.9	19	Monument Valley	***44.7***
20	Santa Rita Exp Range	***52.6***	20	Cascabel	45.1
21	Clifton	***52.4***	20	Wupatki N M	45.1
22	Beaver Dam	***51.7***	22	Kitt Peak	46.4
23	Tombstone	50.6	23	Coronado N M Hdqtrs	46.9
24	Oracle 2 SE	50.0	24	Cordes	47.4
25	Sasabe	***49.6***	25	Childs	***47.6***

Rankings include 25 highest/lowest stations. If state has less than 25 stations, all stations are included. The period of record is 1980–2009. See User Guide for detailed explanation of data.

Annual Extreme Minimum Temperature

Highest Rank	Station Name	°F	Lowest Rank	Station Name	°F
1	Kofa Mine	26	1	Flagstaff 4 SW	***-37***
1	Phoenix Sky Harbor Intl Arpt	26	2	Fort Valley	-32
3	Tucson NWSO	25	3	Saint Johns	-25
3	Yuma Citrus Station	***25***	4	Bright Angel R S	-23
5	Yuma Proving Ground	24	4	Flagstaff Pulliam Arpt	-23
6	Bullhead City	23	6	Alpine	-22
6	Castle Hot Springs	23	7	Black River Pumps	-19
6	Fountain Hills	23	8	Holbrook	-16
9	South Phoenix	21	9	Betatakin	-14
9	Willow Beach	21	9	Canyon De Chelly	-14
11	Laveen 3 SSE	20	11	McNary 2 N	-13
12	Alamo Dam	19	12	Seligman	-12
12	Organ Pipe Cactus N M	19	12	Teec Nos Pos	-12
12	Tucson 17 NW	***19***	14	Winslow Municipal Arpt	-11
12	Tucson Intl Arpt	19	15	Colorado City	-9
16	Florence	18	15	Monument Valley	***-9***
16	Yucca 1 NNE	18	17	Wupatki N M	-5
18	Casa Grande	***17***	18	Payson	-2
19	Clifton	***16***	19	Kitt Peak	-1
19	Gila Bend	16	20	Canelo 1 NW	***3***
19	Sasabe	***16***	21	Beaver Dam	4
19	Tombstone	16	22	Cascabel	7
23	Maricopa 4 N	15	23	Anvil Ranch	8
24	Childs	***14***	23	Cordes	8
24	Santa Rita Exp Range	***14***	25	Coronado N M Hdqtrs	9

July Mean Maximum Temperature

Highest Rank	Station Name	°F	Lowest Rank	Station Name	°F
1	Bullhead City	112.2	1	Alpine	77.8
2	Willow Beach	110.5	2	Bright Angel R S	78.3
3	Gila Bend	109.0	3	McNary 2 N	80.7
4	Alamo Dam	108.3	4	Kitt Peak	81.0
5	Maricopa 4 N	107.6	5	Flagstaff 4 SW	81.4
6	Yuma Proving Ground	106.9	6	Fort Valley	81.7
7	Laveen 3 SSE	106.5	7	Flagstaff Pulliam Arpt	82.2
8	Beaver Dam	***106.3***	8	Betatakin	85.5
9	Casa Grande	106.2	9	Black River Pumps	87.7
9	Phoenix Sky Harbor Intl Arpt	106.2	10	Canelo 1 NW	***88.8***
11	Fountain Hills	106.1	11	Coronado N M Hdqtrs	89.6
12	Florence	104.1	12	Saint Johns	90.2
13	Kofa Mine	103.9	13	Santa Rita Exp Range	***91.6***
13	Yucca 1 NNE	103.9	14	Sierra Vista	91.7
15	Lees Ferry	***103.8***	15	Oracle 2 SE	91.8
16	Organ Pipe Cactus N M	103.5	16	Seligman	92.1
17	South Phoenix	102.4	17	Monument Valley	92.2
18	Castle Hot Springs	102.3	17	Payson	92.2
19	Childs	***102.2***	19	Canyon De Chelly	93.0
20	Tucson 17 NW	101.3	20	Teec Nos Pos	93.3
21	Tucson Intl Arpt	100.4	20	Winslow Municipal Arpt	93.3
22	Tucson NWSO	100.2	22	Colorado City	93.4
23	Clifton	99.5	22	Tombstone	93.4
24	Cascabel	99.4	24	Holbrook	94.3
25	Anvil Ranch	98.8	25	Nogales 6 N	94.6

Rankings include 25 highest/lowest stations. If state has less than 25 stations, all stations are included. The period of record is 1980–2009. See User Guide for detailed explanation of data.

January Mean Minimum Temperature

Highest Rank	Station Name	°F	Lowest Rank	Station Name	°F
1	Kofa Mine	47.6	1	Flagstaff 4 SW	***10.3***
2	Phoenix Sky Harbor Intl Arpt	45.6	2	Fort Valley	12.4
3	Yuma Proving Ground	44.5	3	Alpine	14.4
4	Bullhead City	43.9	4	Bright Angel R S	16.9
5	Tucson NWSO	42.9	5	Flagstaff Pulliam Arpt	17.4
6	Castle Hot Springs	41.5	6	McNary 2 N	19.5
7	Fountain Hills	41.4	7	Canyon De Chelly	20.2
8	Gila Bend	41.3	8	Saint Johns	20.5
8	Laveen 3 SSE	41.3	9	Holbrook	20.9
10	Tucson 17 NW	40.6	10	Black River Pumps	21.2
11	Willow Beach	***40.5***	11	Betatakin	21.6
12	Florence	40.4	12	Winslow Municipal Arpt	22.0
13	South Phoenix	40.2	13	Teec Nos Pos	22.9
14	Organ Pipe Cactus N M	40.0	14	Seligman	23.4
15	Tucson Intl Arpt	39.8	15	Colorado City	24.3
16	Santa Rita Exp Range	***38.6***	15	Monument Valley	24.3
17	Casa Grande	38.4	17	Payson	25.7
17	Yucca 1 NNE	38.4	18	Wupatki N M	26.1
19	Alamo Dam	36.2	19	Nogales 6 N	27.9
20	Tombstone	36.1	20	Canelo 1 NW	***28.1***
21	Maricopa 4 N	36.0	21	Lees Ferry	***29.1***
21	Sasabe	36.0	22	Cascabel	30.5
23	Oracle 2 SE	35.0	23	Bowie	32.0
24	Clifton	***34.0***	24	Childs	32.9
25	Beaver Dam	33.9	25	Coronado N M Hdqtrs	33.0

Number of Days Annually Maximum Temperature ≥ 90°F

Highest Rank	Station Name	Days	Lowest Rank	Station Name	Days
1	Gila Bend	190	1	Alpine	0
2	Bullhead City	180	2	Bright Angel R S	1
3	Maricopa 4 N	179	3	Flagstaff 4 SW	***2***
4	Yuma Proving Ground	177	4	McNary 2 N	3
5	Casa Grande	176	5	Flagstaff Pulliam Arpt	4
5	Laveen 3 SSE	176	5	Kitt Peak	4
7	Alamo Dam	173	7	Fort Valley	7
8	Fountain Hills	172	8	Betatakin	14
8	Phoenix Sky Harbor Intl Arpt	172	9	Black River Pumps	29
10	Organ Pipe Cactus N M	170	10	Saint Johns	45
11	Florence	168	11	Canelo 1 NW	***46***
12	Willow Beach	167	12	Coronado N M Hdqtrs	52
13	South Phoenix	164	13	Monument Valley	53
14	Tucson 17 NW	***157***	14	Seligman	59
15	Kofa Mine	156	15	Teec Nos Pos	62
16	Yuma Citrus Station	***155***	16	Canyon De Chelly	63
17	Tucson NWSO	153	17	Payson	64
18	Tucson Intl Arpt	152	18	Colorado City	66
19	Castle Hot Springs	149	19	Oracle 2 SE	68
20	Beaver Dam	145	20	Winslow Municipal Arpt	69
21	Cascabel	144	21	Santa Rita Exp Range	***70***
22	Yucca 1 NNE	143	22	Holbrook	71
23	Anvil Ranch	142	23	Sierra Vista	***77***
24	Childs	***140***	24	Wupatki N M	79
25	Clifton	***130***	25	Tombstone	92

Rankings include 25 highest/lowest stations. If state has less than 25 stations, all stations are included. The period of record is 1980–2009. See User Guide for detailed explanation of data.

Number of Days Annually Maximum Temperature ≤ 32°F					
Highest			Lowest		
Rank	Station Name	Days	Rank	Station Name	Days
1	Bright Angel R S	24	1	Alamo Dam	0
2	Betatakin	13	1	Anvil Ranch	0
3	Flagstaff 4 SW	***12***	1	Beaver Dam	0
4	Flagstaff Pulliam Arpt	11	1	Bowie	0
5	Fort Valley	10	1	Bullhead City	0
5	McNary 2 N	10	1	Canelo 1 NW	***0***
5	Monument Valley	10	1	Casa Grande	0
8	Canyon De Chelly	7	1	Cascabel	0
9	Alpine	6	1	Castle Hot Springs	0
9	Teec Nos Pos	6	1	Childs	***0***
11	Winslow Municipal Arpt	4	1	Clifton	***0***
12	Kitt Peak	3	1	Cordes	0
12	Saint Johns	3	1	Coronado N M Hdqtrs	0
12	Wupatki N M	3	1	Florence	0
15	Colorado City	2	1	Fountain Hills	0
15	Holbrook	2	1	Gila Bend	0
17	Black River Pumps	1	1	Kofa Mine	0
18	Alamo Dam	0	1	Laveen 3 SSE	0
18	Anvil Ranch	0	1	Lees Ferry	***0***
18	Beaver Dam	0	1	Maricopa 4 N	0
18	Bowie	0	1	Nogales 6 N	0
18	Bullhead City	0	1	Oracle 2 SE	0
18	Canelo 1 NW	***0***	1	Organ Pipe Cactus N M	0
18	Casa Grande	0	1	Payson	0
18	Cascabel	0	1	Phoenix Sky Harbor Intl Arpt	0

Number of Days Annually Minimum Temperature ≤ 32°F					
Highest			Lowest		
Rank	Station Name	Days	Rank	Station Name	Days
1	Fort Valley	250	1	Kofa Mine	0
2	Flagstaff 4 SW	***245***	1	Phoenix Sky Harbor Intl Arpt	0
3	Alpine	221	3	Bullhead City	2
4	Flagstaff Pulliam Arpt	202	3	Yuma Proving Ground	2
5	Bright Angel R S	197	5	Willow Beach	4
6	McNary 2 N	175	5	Yuma Citrus Station	***4***
7	Black River Pumps	159	7	Castle Hot Springs	5
8	Seligman	151	7	Tucson NWSO	5
9	Betatakin	143	9	Fountain Hills	7
9	Saint Johns	143	10	Laveen 3 SSE	8
11	Canyon De Chelly	139	10	Organ Pipe Cactus N M	8
12	Holbrook	136	12	Gila Bend	9
13	Winslow Municipal Arpt	131	13	South Phoenix	10
14	Payson	126	13	Tucson 17 NW	***10***
15	Colorado City	116	15	Florence	12
16	Teec Nos Pos	109	16	Tucson Intl Arpt	13
17	Monument Valley	***105***	17	Yucca 1 NNE	17
18	Canelo 1 NW	***99***	18	Casa Grande	19
18	Nogales 6 N	99	19	Alamo Dam	21
20	Wupatki N M	94	20	Santa Rita Exp Range	***22***
21	Cascabel	79	21	Sasabe	***28***
22	Lees Ferry	***65***	22	Tombstone	30
23	Kitt Peak	60	23	Maricopa 4 N	31
24	Bowie	58	24	Clifton	***37***
25	Coronado N M Hdqtrs	57	25	Oracle 2 SE	42

Rankings include 25 highest/lowest stations. If state has less than 25 stations, all stations are included. The period of record is 1980–2009. See User Guide for detailed explanation of data.

Number of Days Annually Minimum Temperature ≤ 0°F

Highest			Lowest		
Rank	Station Name	Days	Rank	Station Name	Days
1	Flagstaff 4 SW	***16***	1	Alamo Dam	0
2	Fort Valley	12	1	Anvil Ranch	0
3	Alpine	5	1	Beaver Dam	0
4	Flagstaff Pulliam Arpt	4	1	Betatakin	0
5	Bright Angel R S	3	1	Bowie	0
6	Black River Pumps	1	1	Bullhead City	0
6	Canyon De Chelly	1	1	Canelo 1 NW	***0***
6	McNary 2 N	1	1	Casa Grande	0
6	Saint Johns	1	1	Cascabel	0
10	Alamo Dam	0	1	Castle Hot Springs	0
10	Anvil Ranch	0	1	Childs	***0***
10	Beaver Dam	0	1	Clifton	***0***
10	Betatakin	0	1	Colorado City	0
10	Bowie	0	1	Cordes	0
10	Bullhead City	0	1	Coronado N M Hdqtrs	0
10	Canelo 1 NW	***0***	1	Florence	0
10	Casa Grande	0	1	Fountain Hills	0
10	Cascabel	0	1	Gila Bend	0
10	Castle Hot Springs	0	1	Holbrook	0
10	Childs	***0***	1	Kitt Peak	0
10	Clifton	***0***	1	Kofa Mine	0
10	Colorado City	0	1	Laveen 3 SSE	0
10	Cordes	0	1	Lees Ferry	***0***
10	Coronado N M Hdqtrs	0	1	Maricopa 4 N	0
10	Florence	0	1	Monument Valley	***0***

Number of Annual Heating Degree Days

Highest			Lowest		
Rank	Station Name	Num.	Rank	Station Name	Num.
1	Flagstaff 4 SW	***7,827***	1	Yuma Proving Ground	844
2	Bright Angel R S	***7,778***	2	Phoenix Sky Harbor Intl Arpt	895
3	Fort Valley	7,550	3	Kofa Mine	947
4	Alpine	7,294	4	Gila Bend	968
5	Flagstaff Pulliam Arpt	6,735	5	Bullhead City	1,023
6	McNary 2 N	6,254	6	Organ Pipe Cactus N M	1,163
7	Betatakin	5,815	7	Laveen 3 SSE	1,186
8	Black River Pumps	4,962	8	Tucson NWSO	1,192
9	Canyon De Chelly	4,914	9	Fountain Hills	1,238
10	Saint Johns	4,754	10	Willow Beach	***1,277***
11	Monument Valley	***4,697***	11	South Phoenix	1,304
12	Teec Nos Pos	***4,640***	12	Florence	***1,315***
13	Seligman	4,535	13	Castle Hot Springs	1,317
14	Winslow Municipal Arpt	4,494	14	Casa Grande	***1,331***
15	Colorado City	4,455	15	Tucson 17 NW	***1,377***
16	Holbrook	4,396	16	Tucson Intl Arpt	1,422
17	Payson	4,013	17	Maricopa 4 N	1,509
18	Wupatki N M	3,950	18	Alamo Dam	1,532
19	Kitt Peak	3,930	19	Yucca 1 NNE	1,892
20	Canelo 1 NW	***3,259***	20	Anvil Ranch	1,962
21	Lees Ferry	***3,170***	21	Sasabe	***2,067***
22	Oracle 2 SE	2,815	22	Santa Rita Exp Range	***2,085***
23	Cordes	2,779	23	Clifton	***2,156***
24	Coronado N M Hdqtrs	2,731	24	Tombstone	2,194
25	Nogales 6 N	2,622	25	Beaver Dam	***2,305***

 Rankings include 25 highest/lowest stations. If state has less than 25 stations, all stations are included. The period of record is 1980–2009. See User Guide for detailed explanation of data.

Number of Annual Cooling Degree Days

Highest Rank	Station Name	Num.	Lowest Rank	Station Name	Num.
1	Phoenix Sky Harbor Intl Arpt	4,665	1	Alpine	13
2	Bullhead City	4,629	2	Bright Angel R S	***45***
3	Yuma Proving Ground	4,460	3	Fort Valley	48
4	Gila Bend	4,448	4	Flagstaff 4 SW	***56***
5	Willow Beach	***4,332***	5	McNary 2 N	133
6	Kofa Mine	4,172	6	Flagstaff Pulliam Arpt	145
7	Laveen 3 SSE	4,071	7	Black River Pumps	589
8	Fountain Hills	3,949	8	Betatakin	593
9	Alamo Dam	3,835	9	Kitt Peak	668
10	Maricopa 4 N	3,741	10	Seligman	767
11	Casa Grande	***3,736***	11	Saint Johns	804
12	Florence	***3,633***	12	Payson	966
13	Tucson NWSO	3,586	13	Canelo 1 NW	***1,006***
14	Organ Pipe Cactus N M	3,438	14	Canyon De Chelly	1,031
15	Tucson 17 NW	***3,428***	15	Holbrook	1,148
16	South Phoenix	3,380	16	Colorado City	1,157
17	Castle Hot Springs	3,318	17	Winslow Municipal Arpt	1,189
18	Tucson Intl Arpt	3,257	18	Coronado N M Hdqtrs	1,295
19	Yucca 1 NNE	3,248	19	Teec Nos Pos	***1,334***
20	Beaver Dam	***3,099***	20	Monument Valley	***1,422***
21	Clifton	***2,761***	21	Wupatki N M	1,625
22	Lees Ferry	***2,691***	22	Nogales 6 N	1,633
23	Anvil Ranch	2,456	23	Sierra Vista	***1,760***
24	Childs	***2,320***	24	Cordes	1,764
25	Bowie	2,133	25	Oracle 2 SE	1,792

Annual Precipitation

Highest Rank	Station Name	Inches	Lowest Rank	Station Name	Inches
1	McNary 2 N	26.40	1	Yuma Proving Ground	3.62
2	Bright Angel R S	25.40	2	Yuma Citrus Station	***3.80***
3	Oracle 2 SE	23.57	3	Monument Valley	***4.63***
4	Santa Rita Exp Range	***23.22***	4	Bullhead City	5.62
5	Flagstaff 4 SW	***22.61***	5	Willow Beach	5.69
6	Kitt Peak	22.50	6	Kofa Mine	6.69
7	Flagstaff Pulliam Arpt	21.82	7	Lees Ferry	***6.81***
8	Payson	21.70	8	Gila Bend	6.89
9	Fort Valley	21.63	9	Winslow Municipal Arpt	7.05
10	Coronado N M Hdqtrs	21.38	10	Beaver Dam	7.45
11	Alpine	21.36	11	Yucca 1 NNE	7.78
12	Black River Pumps	20.48	12	Maricopa 4 N	7.83
13	Childs	***19.65***	13	Phoenix Sky Harbor Intl Arpt	7.92
14	Canelo 1 NW	***18.68***	14	Teec Nos Pos	8.03
15	Nogales 6 N	17.87	15	Wupatki N M	8.19
16	Sasabe	***17.25***	16	Laveen 3 SSE	8.48
17	Clifton	***16.12***	17	South Phoenix	8.50
17	Cordes	16.12	18	Alamo Dam	8.58
19	Castle Hot Springs	15.08	19	Holbrook	8.64
20	Sierra Vista	***14.39***	20	Casa Grande	***8.89***
21	Colorado City	14.29	21	Canyon De Chelly	9.52
22	Cascabel	14.16	22	Florence	9.91
23	Tombstone	13.83	23	Organ Pipe Cactus N M	10.10
24	Tucson 17 NW	***12.97***	24	Saint Johns	10.69
25	Seligman	12.85	25	Fountain Hills	11.59

Rankings include 25 highest/lowest stations. If state has less than 25 stations, all stations are included. The period of record is 1980–2009. See User Guide for detailed explanation of data.

Annual Extreme Maximum Daily Precipitation

Highest			Lowest		
Rank	Station Name	Inches	Rank	Station Name	Inches
1	Cascabel	5.03	1	Winslow Municipal Arpt	1.61
2	Canyon De Chelly	5.00	2	Wupatki N M	1.68
3	Kitt Peak	***4.70***	3	Beaver Dam	***1.75***
4	Coronado N M Hdqtrs	4.69	4	Maricopa 4 N	1.96
5	McNary 2 N	4.19	5	Betatakin	2.00
6	Tucson NWSO	4.16	6	Gila Bend	2.01
7	Sasabe	***4.10***	7	South Phoenix	2.05
8	Black River Pumps	4.01	8	Organ Pipe Cactus N M	2.25
9	Fort Valley	***4.00***	9	Fountain Hills	2.30
10	Bright Angel R S	***3.99***	10	Phoenix Sky Harbor Intl Arpt	2.32
11	Flagstaff Pulliam Arpt	3.93	11	Tombstone	***2.38***
12	Payson	3.86	12	Casa Grande	***2.39***
13	Childs	***3.80***	13	Yuma Proving Ground	2.40
14	Nogales 6 N	3.67	14	Clifton	***2.45***
15	Yucca 1 NNE	3.61	15	Alamo Dam	2.50
16	Yuma Citrus Station	***3.51***	15	Anvil Ranch	***2.50***
17	Castle Hot Springs	***3.50***	15	Holbrook	***2.50***
17	Teec Nos Pos	3.50	18	Kofa Mine	2.58
19	Cordes	3.32	19	Bowie	2.69
20	Florence	***3.25***	20	Alpine	***2.77***
21	Colorado City	3.20	20	Canelo 1 NW	***2.77***
22	Seligman	3.08	20	Laveen 3 SSE	2.77
23	Bullhead City	3.05	23	Sierra Vista	***2.84***
23	Flagstaff 4 SW	***3.05***	24	Tucson Intl Arpt	2.96
25	Oracle 2 SE	3.03	25	Willow Beach	***3.00***

Number of Days Annually With ≥ 0.1 Inches of Precipitation

Highest			Lowest		
Rank	Station Name	Days	Rank	Station Name	Days
1	McNary 2 N	59	1	Yuma Citrus Station	***8***
2	Alpine	51	1	Yuma Proving Ground	8
3	Flagstaff Pulliam Arpt	50	3	Monument Valley	***12***
4	Flagstaff 4 SW	***49***	4	Bullhead City	13
5	Black River Pumps	48	5	Kofa Mine	14
5	Bright Angel R S	***48***	6	Willow Beach	15
7	Payson	44	7	Phoenix Sky Harbor Intl Arpt	16
7	Santa Rita Exp Range	***44***	8	Gila Bend	17
9	Coronado N M Hdqtrs	43	8	Maricopa 4 N	17
10	Fort Valley	42	10	Alamo Dam	18
10	Oracle 2 SE	42	10	Lees Ferry	***18***
12	Canelo 1 NW	***41***	10	Yucca 1 NNE	18
13	Clifton	***39***	13	Casa Grande	19
13	Kitt Peak	39	13	Laveen 3 SSE	19
15	Colorado City	38	15	Organ Pipe Cactus N M	20
15	Nogales 6 N	38	15	South Phoenix	20
17	Childs	***37***	17	Florence	22
18	Sierra Vista	***35***	17	Winslow Municipal Arpt	22
19	Betatakin	33	19	Beaver Dam	***23***
19	Cascabel	33	19	Holbrook	23
21	Seligman	32	19	Teec Nos Pos	23
21	Tombstone	32	22	Wupatki N M	24
23	Bowie	31	23	Fountain Hills	25
23	Cordes	31	24	Castle Hot Springs	26
23	Sasabe	***31***	25	Anvil Ranch	28

Rankings include 25 highest/lowest stations. If state has less than 25 stations, all stations are included. The period of record is 1980–2009. See User Guide for detailed explanation of data.

Number of Days Annually With ≥ 0.5 Inches of Precipitation

Highest Rank	Station Name	Days	Lowest Rank	Station Name	Days
1	Bright Angel R S	17	1	Monument Valley	***0***
2	McNary 2 N	16	1	Yuma Citrus Station	***0***
2	Oracle 2 SE	16	1	Yuma Proving Ground	0
4	Santa Rita Exp Range	***15***	4	Beaver Dam	1
5	Kitt Peak	14	4	Canyon De Chelly	1
5	Payson	14	4	Willow Beach	1
7	Canelo 1 NW	***13***	7	Teec Nos Pos	2
7	Childs	***13***	7	Winslow Municipal Arpt	2
7	Coronado N M Hdqtrs	13	9	Gila Bend	3
7	Flagstaff 4 SW	***13***	9	Holbrook	3
7	Fort Valley	13	9	Lees Ferry	***3***
12	Alpine	11	9	Wupatki N M	3
12	Black River Pumps	11	13	Anvil Ranch	4
12	Flagstaff Pulliam Arpt	11	13	Bullhead City	4
12	Nogales 6 N	11	13	Kofa Mine	4
16	Castle Hot Springs	10	13	Saint Johns	4
16	Clifton	***10***	17	Alamo Dam	5
16	Colorado City	10	17	Maricopa 4 N	5
16	Sasabe	***10***	17	Phoenix Sky Harbor Intl Arpt	5
20	Cascabel	9	17	South Phoenix	5
20	Cordes	9	17	Yucca 1 NNE	5
22	Fountain Hills	8	22	Betatakin	6
22	Organ Pipe Cactus N M	8	22	Bowie	6
22	Sierra Vista	***8***	22	Laveen 3 SSE	6
22	Tombstone	8	25	Casa Grande	7

Number of Days Annually With ≥ 1.0 Inches of Precipitation

Highest Rank	Station Name	Days	Lowest Rank	Station Name	Days
1	Oracle 2 SE	6	1	Alamo Dam	0
2	Bright Angel R S	4	1	Anvil Ranch	0
2	Childs	***4***	1	Beaver Dam	0
2	Kitt Peak	4	1	Betatakin	0
2	McNary 2 N	4	1	Bowie	0
6	Castle Hot Springs	3	1	Bullhead City	0
6	Cordes	3	1	Canyon De Chelly	0
6	Flagstaff 4 SW	***3***	1	Clifton	***0***
6	Fort Valley	3	1	Colorado City	0
6	Payson	3	1	Florence	0
6	Santa Rita Exp Range	***3***	1	Fountain Hills	0
6	Sasabe	***3***	1	Gila Bend	0
13	Canelo 1 NW	***2***	1	Holbrook	0
13	Coronado N M Hdqtrs	2	1	Kofa Mine	0
13	Nogales 6 N	2	1	Laveen 3 SSE	0
13	Sierra Vista	***2***	1	Lees Ferry	***0***
13	Tucson 17 NW	***2***	1	Maricopa 4 N	0
18	Alpine	1	1	Monument Valley	***0***
18	Black River Pumps	1	1	Phoenix Sky Harbor Intl Arpt	0
18	Casa Grande	1	1	Saint Johns	0
18	Cascabel	1	1	Seligman	0
18	Flagstaff Pulliam Arpt	1	1	South Phoenix	0
18	Organ Pipe Cactus N M	1	1	Teec Nos Pos	0
18	Tombstone	1	1	Willow Beach	0
18	Tucson Intl Arpt	1	1	Winslow Municipal Arpt	0

Rankings include 25 highest/lowest stations. If state has less than 25 stations, all stations are included. The period of record is 1980–2009. See User Guide for detailed explanation of data.

Annual Snowfall

Highest			Lowest		
Rank	Station Name	Inches	Rank	Station Name	Inches
1	Bright Angel R S	133.2	1	Bullhead City	0.0
2	Flagstaff 4 SW	***81.3***	1	Gila Bend	0.0
3	McNary 2 N	72.9	1	Laveen 3 SSE	0.0
4	Fort Valley	***51.7***	1	Maricopa 4 N	0.0
5	Betatakin	42.3	1	South Phoenix	0.0
6	Alpine	41.2	1	Willow Beach	0.0
7	Payson	20.7	1	Yuma Citrus Station	***0.0***
8	Colorado City	17.0	1	Yuma Proving Ground	0.0
9	Oracle 2 SE	12.6	9	Anvil Ranch	Trace
10	Kitt Peak	11.6	9	Beaver Dam	***Trace***
11	Black River Pumps	10.4	9	Casa Grande	Trace
12	Seligman	9.9	9	Florence	Trace
13	Saint Johns	6.6	9	Fountain Hills	Trace
14	Canyon De Chelly	5.6	9	Kofa Mine	Trace
15	Holbrook	5.5	9	Organ Pipe Cactus N M	Trace
16	Monument Valley	***5.1***	9	Tucson 17 NW	***Trace***
16	Wupatki N M	5.1	17	Alamo Dam	0.1
18	Coronado N M Hdqtrs	4.9	17	Clifton	***0.1***
19	Teec Nos Pos	3.3	17	Yucca 1 NNE	0.1
20	Santa Rita Exp Range	***2.9***	20	Castle Hot Springs	0.2
21	Cascabel	2.5	21	Tucson NWSO	0.3
22	Cordes	1.4	22	Canelo 1 NW	***0.4***
23	Childs	***1.1***	23	Nogales 6 N	0.5
24	Sasabe	***1.0***	24	Sierra Vista	***0.6***
25	Bowie	0.9	25	Tombstone	0.7

Annual Maximum Snow Depth

Highest			Lowest		
Rank	Station Name	Inches	Rank	Station Name	Inches
1	Bright Angel R S	89	1	Bullhead City	0
2	McNary 2 N	41	1	Fountain Hills	0
3	Flagstaff 4 SW	***38***	1	Gila Bend	0
4	Payson	26	1	Laveen 3 SSE	0
5	Alpine	***24***	1	Maricopa 4 N	0
6	Betatakin	20	1	South Phoenix	0
7	Kitt Peak	19	1	Willow Beach	***0***
8	Coronado N M Hdqtrs	***16***	1	Yucca 1 NNE	0
9	Black River Pumps	***15***	1	Yuma Citrus Station	***0***
10	Saint Johns	14	1	Yuma Proving Ground	0
11	Colorado City	12	11	Anvil Ranch	Trace
11	Wupatki N M	***12***	11	Bowie	Trace
13	Seligman	10	11	Casa Grande	Trace
13	Tombstone	10	11	Castle Hot Springs	Trace
15	Canyon De Chelly	***8***	11	Childs	Trace
15	Monument Valley	***8***	11	Clifton	Trace
15	Teec Nos Pos	8	11	Cordes	Trace
18	Canelo 1 NW	***4***	11	Florence	Trace
18	Cascabel	4	11	Kofa Mine	Trace
18	Holbrook	***4***	11	Organ Pipe Cactus N M	Trace
18	Nogales 6 N	4	11	Sierra Vista	Trace
22	Oracle 2 SE	***3***	11	Tucson 17 NW	Trace
22	Santa Rita Exp Range	***3***	11	Tucson NWSO	Trace
24	Alamo Dam	2	24	Beaver Dam	***1***
24	Lees Ferry	***2***	25	Alamo Dam	2

Rankings include 25 highest/lowest stations. If state has less than 25 stations, all stations are included. The period of record is 1980–2009. See User Guide for detailed explanation of data.

Number of Days Annually With ≥ 1.0 Inch Snow Depth

Highest			Lowest		
Rank	Station Name	Days	Rank	Station Name	Days
1	Bright Angel R S	135	1	Alamo Dam	0
2	McNary 2 N	76	1	Anvil Ranch	0
3	Flagstaff 4 SW	*70*	1	Beaver Dam	*0*
4	Betatakin	43	1	Bowie	*0*
5	Alpine	*23*	1	Bullhead City	0
6	Colorado City	12	1	Canelo 1 NW	*0*
7	Kitt Peak	7	1	Canyon De Chelly	0
8	Payson	6	1	Casa Grande	0
9	Seligman	4	1	Cascabel	0
10	Black River Pumps	*2*	1	Castle Hot Springs	0
10	Wupatki N M	*2*	1	Childs	*0*
12	Holbrook	1	1	Clifton	*0*
13	Alamo Dam	0	1	Cordes	0
13	Anvil Ranch	0	1	Coronado N M Hdqtrs	0
13	Beaver Dam	*0*	1	Florence	0
13	Bowie	*0*	1	Fountain Hills	0
13	Bullhead City	0	1	Gila Bend	0
13	Canelo 1 NW	*0*	1	Kofa Mine	0
13	Canyon De Chelly	0	1	Laveen 3 SSE	0
13	Casa Grande	0	1	Lees Ferry	*0*
13	Cascabel	0	1	Maricopa 4 N	0
13	Castle Hot Springs	0	1	Monument Valley	*0*
13	Childs	*0*	1	Nogales 6 N	0
13	Clifton	*0*	1	Oracle 2 SE	0
13	Cordes	0	1	Organ Pipe Cactus N M	0

Significant Storm Events in Arizona: 2000 – 2009

Location or County	Date	Type	Mag.	Deaths	Injuries	Property Damage ($mil.)	Crop Damage ($mil.)
Tucson Metro Area	03/05/00	Winter Storm	na	2	10	0.0	0.0
Northern Arizona	03/20/00	Winter Storm	na	5	0	0.0	0.0
La Paz	10/22/00	Flash Flood	na	1	0	6.2	1.0
Maricopa	07/14/01	Thunderstorm Wind	92 mph	1	0	5.0	0.0
Maricopa	07/14/02	Thunderstorm Wind	105 mph	0	0	30.0	0.0
Maricopa	07/14/02	Thunderstorm Wind	69 mph	0	0	20.0	0.0
Maricopa	07/14/02	Thunderstorm Wind	100 mph	0	0	20.0	0.0
Cochise County	01/06/03	Dust Storm	na	1	25	0.0	0.0
Pima	06/17/03	Wildfire	na	0	0	66.0	0.0
Pima	07/01/03	Wildfire	na	0	0	66.0	0.0
Southern Arizona	05/20/05	Excessive Heat	na	12	0	0.0	0.0
Tohono Oodham Nation, Cochise and Santa Cruz Counties	07/02/05	Excessive Heat	na	9	0	0.0	0.0
Greater Phoenix Area	07/12/05	Excessive Heat	na	30	0	0.0	0.0
Maricopa	07/30/05	Flash Flood	na	0	0	3.0	0.0
Little Colorado River Valley, White Mountains, and Mogollon Rim	01/25/06	Ice Storm	na	5	0	0.0	0.0
Pinal County-Central Deserts	02/15/06	Dust Storm	na	2	13	0.0	0.0
Maricopa	07/25/06	Thunderstorm Wind	92 mph	0	1	150.0	0.0
Pima	07/31/06	Flood	na	0	0	3.0	0.0
Pinal	08/13/07	Thunderstorm Wind	86 mph	0	0	5.0	0.0
Santa Cruz	08/24/07	Flash Flood	na	0	0	10.0	0.0
Pima	08/13/08	Thunderstorm Wind	75 mph	0	0	2.5	0.0
Coconino	08/16/08	Flash Flood	na	0	0	10.0	0.0
Maricopa	08/28/08	Thunderstorm Wind	85 mph	0	0	20.0	0.0
Maricopa	08/28/08	Thunderstorm Wind	69 mph	0	1	4.0	0.0
Maricopa	08/28/08	Thunderstorm Wind	75 mph	0	0	2.0	0.0
Northern Gila County	05/30/09	Wildfire	na	0	0	3.0	0.0
Yavapai	09/10/09	Flash Flood	na	0	0	2.6	0.0
Western Mogollon Rim	10/02/09	Wildfire	na	0	0	2.5	0.0

Note: Deaths, injuries, and damages are date and location specific.

ARKANSAS

PHYSICAL FEATURES. Arkansas is divided geographically into two principal divisions on the basis of topography, and to a lesser extent, climate. The dividing line between these two sections cuts diagonally across the State from the northeast to the southwest. West and north of this line are the interior highlands; to the east and south are the lowlands.

Much of western and northern Arkansas is hilly and mountainous. In the southern part, or that portion south of the Arkansas River, are the Ouachita Mountains made up of a number of narrow east-west ridges separated by rather narrow valleys. Some of these ridges reach elevations of 2,500 feet or more. The Arkansas valley, between the Ozark and Ouachita highlands, is an area of fairly low relief with a few isolated ridges and mountains. One of these mountains in the Arkansas valley, Mt. Magazine, with an elevation of 2,823 feet above sea level, is the highest point in the State.

The Ozark Mountains and particularly that portion known as the Boston Mountains are the largest and most massive in Arkansas. It is this topographical feature of the State that has the most noticeable effect upon Arkansas weather.

GENERAL CLIMATE. Climatic differences between the two areas are not as great as the local differences between mountain and valley weather stations in the highlands. Generally, the climate of western and northern Arkansas is a little cooler and there are greater temperature extremes; humidities are lower and there is less cloudiness.

Average maximum or minimum temperatures show little variation over the State. Winter temperatures vary more noticeably from northwest to southeast than is the case in the summer. Maximum temperatures exceed 100°F. at times during July and August, particularly in the valley weather stations in the highlands. The winters are short, but cold periods of brief duration do occur. In the northern part of the State, zero temperatures are of occasional occurrence in January and February and zero has been recorded to the southern border.

PRECIPITATION. Precipitation in Arkansas is predominantly of the shower type except for occasional periods of general rain during the late fall, winter, and early spring. The average number of days with measurable precipitation averages around 100 per year.

Rainfall is normally abundant and well distributed throughout the year. However, extended rain-free periods, as well as flooding local storms, are by no means unusual.

Annual precipitation amounts display both local orographic influence and geographic location with the State. Just by virtue of being closer to the Gulf of Mexico moisture source, the southeast counties receive, on the average, five to six inches more rainfall per year than the northwest counties. However, noticeable exceptions to this are a number of Ozark and Ouachita Mountain weather stations where the year's totals average 55 to nearly 56 inches.

Winter and spring are the wettest times of the year. December and January are the wet months on the average in the southern counties and March through May is the wet period in the north. The fall of the year is uniformly the dry time of the year when monthly precipitation totals average two to three inches.

The State is subject to heavy local rains which frequently give storm totals of from five to 10 inches. Floods are frequent along the White, Black, and Ouachita Rivers. Disastrous floods are of rare occurrence.

Most of the State's precipitation falls as rain. Snow does occur, principally in the northwest. The average annual totals range from a little over a foot on the ground in the higher Ozark elevations in the northwest to one to two inches in the delta flat lands of the extreme southeast counties. Snowfall in these southern and eastern lowlands is generally light and remains on the ground only briefly.

Despite the generally abundant rainfall, short periods of dry weather are frequent over small areas of the State. Occasionally severe droughts of longer duration and involving large areas do occur. Severe droughts covering the greater part of the State occur infrequently.

OTHER CLIMATIC ELEMENTS. The long growing season, averaging from 180 days in the northwest up to more than 230 days in the principal cotton producing areas, favors agricultural activity. In addition to adequate moisture conditions, the eastern and southern Arkansas areas have dry, sunny weather during the early fall. Extended warm and humid summer periods are common.

An average of 17 tornadoes per year have been observed in Arkansas. The severe thunderstorms and tornadoes occur most frequently in the period March through May. With the advent of summer heat in June, the tornado occurrence falls off sharply.

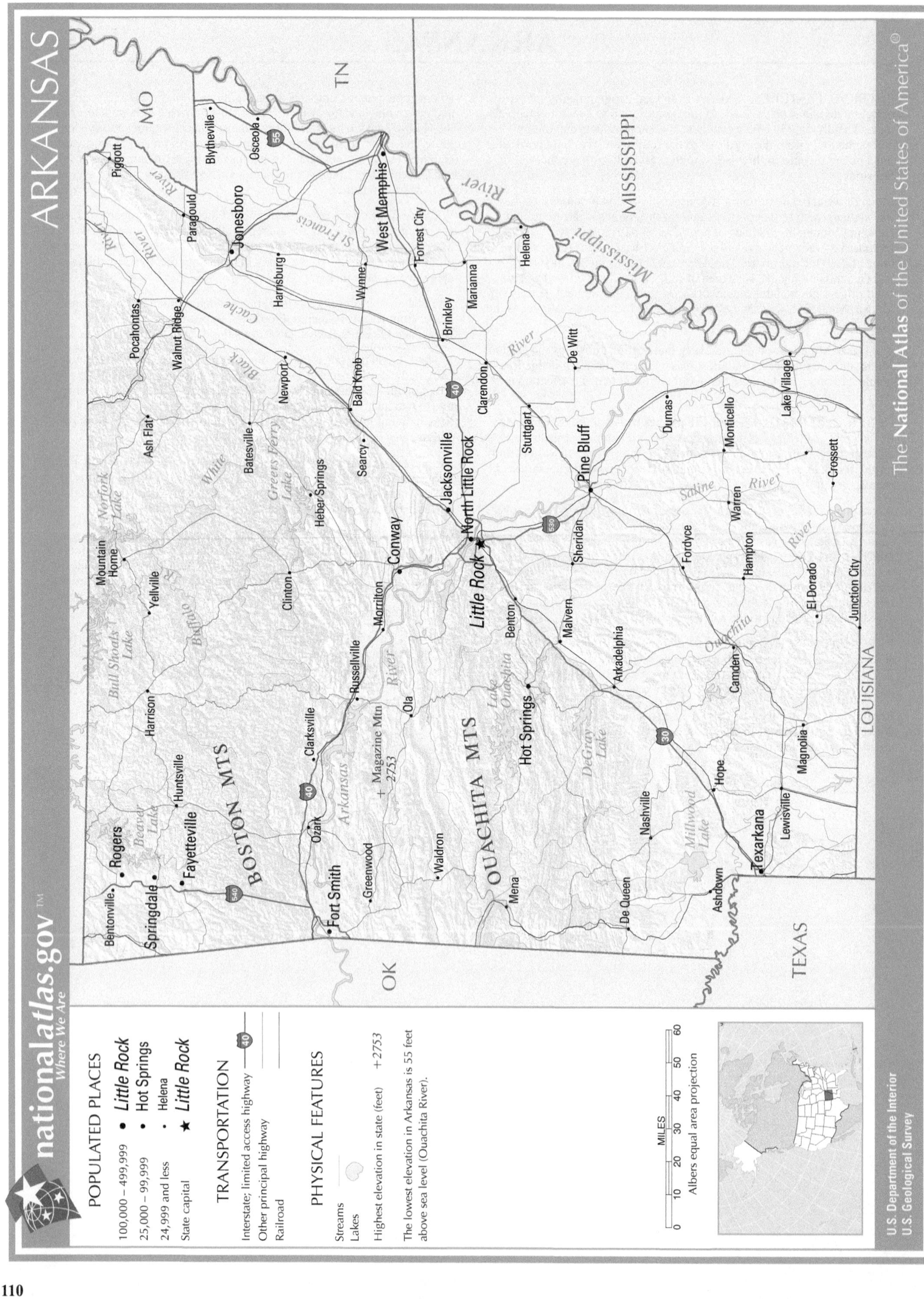
ARKANSAS
nationalatlas.gov™
Where We Are
POPULATED PLACES
100,000 – 499,999 • Little Rock
25,000 – 99,999 • Hot Springs
24,999 and less · Helena
State capital ★ Little Rock
TRANSPORTATION
Interstate; limited access highway 40
Other principal highway
Railroad
PHYSICAL FEATURES
Streams
Lakes
Highest elevation in state (feet) +2753
The lowest elevation in Arkansas is 55 feet above sea level (Ouachita River).
MILES
0 10 20 30 40 50 60
Albers equal area projection
U.S. Department of the Interior
U.S. Geological Survey
The National Atlas of the United States of America®
MO
TN
MISSISSIPPI
LOUISIANA
TEXAS
OK
BOSTON MTS
OUACHITA MTS
Magazine Mtn
2753
Mississippi River
St Francis
Cache River
Black River
White
Buffalo R
Arkansas River
Ouachita
Saline River
Norfork Lake
Bull Shoals Lake
Beaver Lake
Greers Ferry Lake
Lake Ouachita
DeGray Lake
Millwood Lake
Bentonville
Rogers
Springdale
Fayetteville
Fort Smith
Piggott
Paragould
Jonesboro
Blytheville
Osceola
West Memphis
Forrest City
Helena
Marianna
Harrisburg
Wynne
Brinkley
Pocahontas
Walnut Ridge
Newport
Bald Knob
Clarendon
De Witt
Stuttgart
Ash Flat
Batesville
Searcy
Jacksonville
North Little Rock
Little Rock
Pine Bluff
Heber Springs
Mountain Home
Yellville
Clinton
Conway
Morrilton
Russellville
Harrison
Huntsville
Clarksville
Ozark
Greenwood
Waldron
Mena
Ola
Benton
Malvern
Sheridan
Hot Springs
Arkadelphia
Fordyce
Hampton
Warren
Monticello
Dumas
Lake Village
Crossett
El Dorado
Junction City
Camden
Magnolia
Lewisville
Hope
Nashville
Texarkana
Ashdown
De Queen

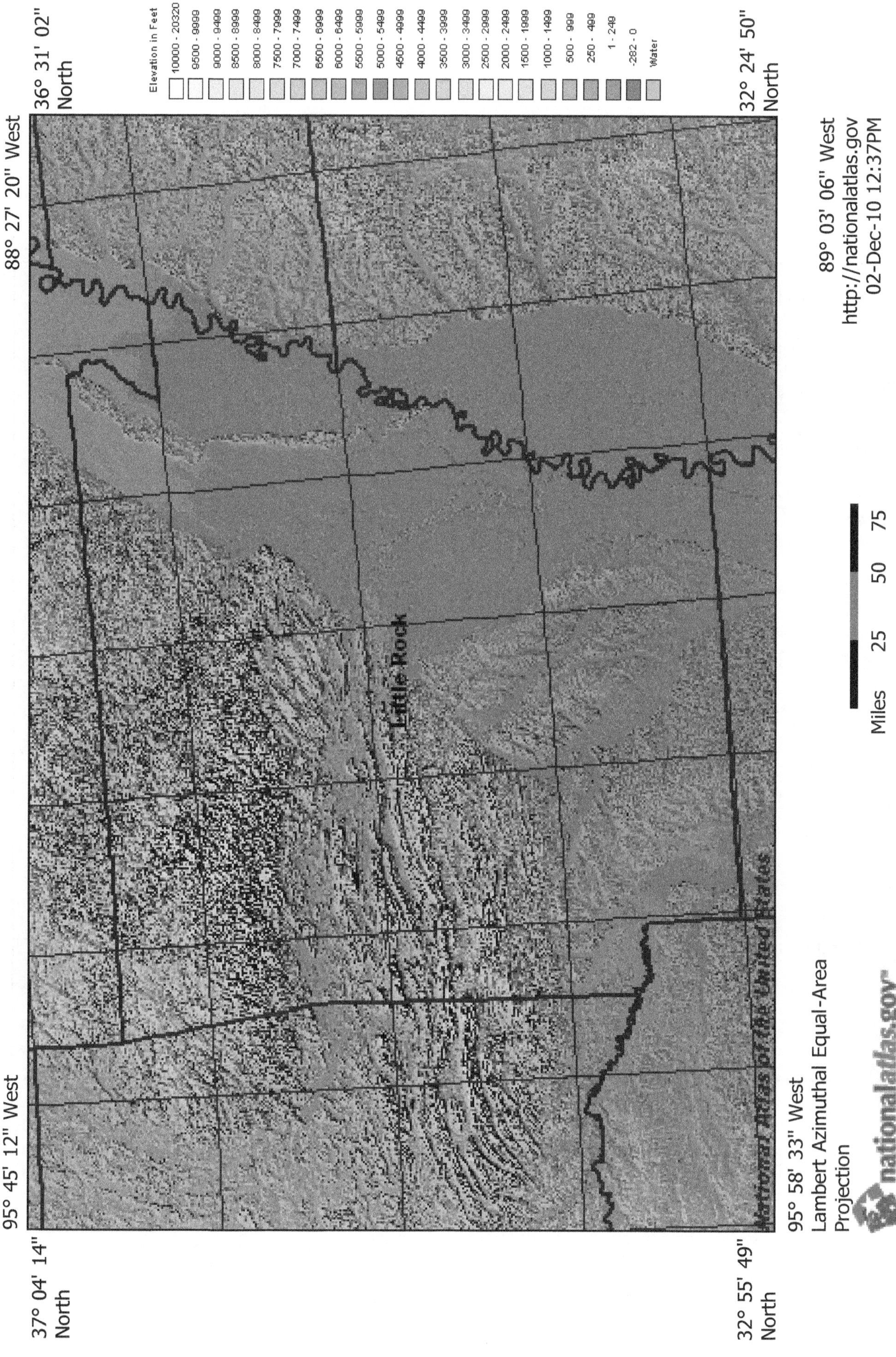
36° 31' 02" North
88° 27' 20" West
37° 04' 14" North
95° 45' 12" West
32° 24' 50" North
89° 03' 06" West
32° 55' 49" North
95° 58' 33" West
Elevation in Feet
10000 - 20320
9500 - 9999
9000 - 9499
8500 - 8999
8000 - 8499
7500 - 7999
7000 - 7499
6500 - 6999
6000 - 6499
5500 - 5999
5000 - 5499
4500 - 4999
4000 - 4499
3500 - 3999
3000 - 3499
2500 - 2999
2000 - 2499
1500 - 1999
1000 - 1499
500 - 999
250 - 499
1 - 249
-282 - 0
Water
Little Rock
National Atlas of the United States
Miles 25 50 75
Lambert Azimuthal Equal-Area Projection
http://nationalatlas.gov
02-Dec-10 12:37PM
nationalatlas.gov

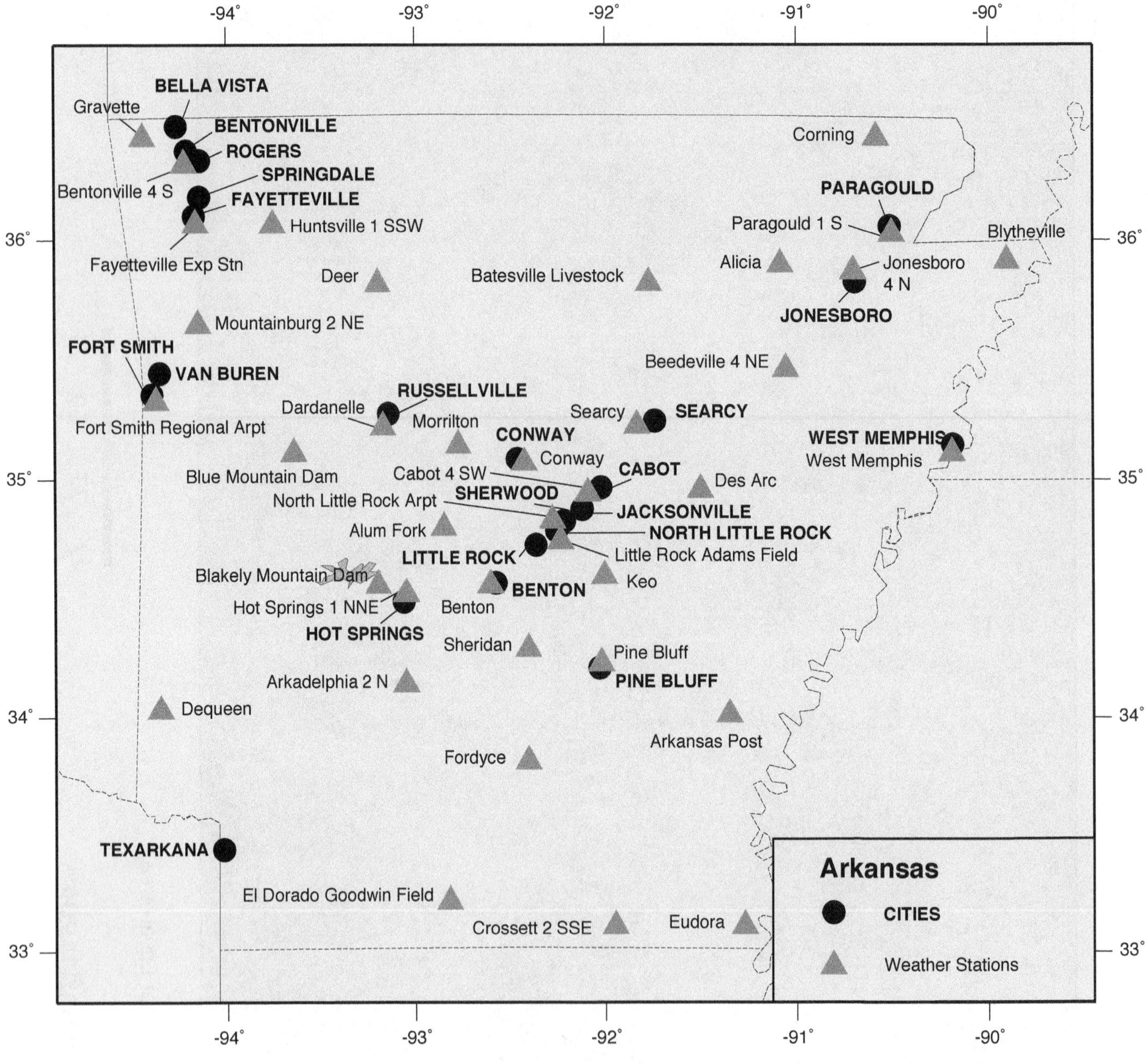
-94°
-93°
-92°
-91°
-90°
BELLA VISTA
Gravette
BENTONVILLE
ROGERS
Corning
SPRINGDALE
Bentonville 4 S
FAYETTEVILLE
PARAGOULD
Paragould 1 S
Huntsville 1 SSW
Blytheville
36°
Fayetteville Exp Stn
Alicia
Jonesboro 4 N
Deer
Batesville Livestock
JONESBORO
Mountainburg 2 NE
FORT SMITH
Beedeville 4 NE
VAN BUREN
RUSSELLVILLE
Dardanelle
Searcy
SEARCY
Fort Smith Regional Arpt
Morrilton
CONWAY
WEST MEMPHIS
West Memphis
Conway
Blue Mountain Dam
Cabot 4 SW
CABOT
Des Arc
35°
SHERWOOD
North Little Rock Arpt
JACKSONVILLE
Alum Fork
NORTH LITTLE ROCK
LITTLE ROCK
Little Rock Adams Field
Blakely Mountain Dam
Keo
BENTON
Hot Springs 1 NNE
Benton
HOT SPRINGS
Sheridan
Pine Bluff
PINE BLUFF
Arkadelphia 2 N
34°
Dequeen
Arkansas Post
Fordyce
TEXARKANA
Arkansas
El Dorado Goodwin Field
CITIES
Crossett 2 SSE
Eudora
33°
Weather Stations

Arkansas Weather Stations by County

County	Station Name
Arkansas	Arkansas Post
Ashley	Crossett 2 SSE
Benton	Bentonville 4 S Gravette
Chicot	Eudora
Clark	Arkadelphia 2 N
Clay	Corning
Conway	Morrilton
Craighead	Jonesboro 4 N
Crawford	Mountainburg 2 NE
Crittenden	West Memphis
Dallas	Fordyce
Faulkner	Conway
Garland	Blakely Mountain Dam Hot Springs 1 NNE
Grant	Sheridan
Greene	Paragould 1 S
Independence	Batesville Livestock
Jackson	Beedeville 4 NE
Jefferson	Pine Bluff
Lawrence	Alicia
Lonoke	Keo
Madison	Huntsville 1 SSW
Mississippi	Blytheville
Newton	Deer
Prairie	Des Arc
Pulaski	Cabot 4 SW Little Rock Adams Field North Little Rock Arpt
Saline	Alum Fork Benton
Sebastian	Fort Smith Regional Arpt
Sevier	Dequeen
Union	El Dorado Goodwin Field
Washington	Fayetteville Exp Stn

County	Station Name
White	Searcy
Yell	Blue Mountain Dam Dardanelle

See User Guide for station inclusion criteria.

Arkansas Weather Stations by City

City	Station Name	Miles
Bella Vista	Bentonville 4 S	10.6
	Gravette	10.6
	Anderson, MO	15.8
Benton	Alum Fork	22.2
	Benton	1.5
	Little Rock Adams Field	22.9
	Sheridan	21.3
Bentonville	Bentonville 4 S	3.9
	Fayetteville Exp Stn	18.9
	Gravette	14.2
	Anderson, MO	23.0
Cabot	Cabot 4 SW	3.8
	Conway	24.6
	Little Rock Adams Field	19.4
	North Little Rock Arpt	16.8
	Searcy	21.0
Conway	Cabot 4 SW	23.2
	Conway	1.4
	Morrilton	18.0
	North Little Rock Arpt	20.6
Fayetteville	Bentonville 4 S	16.7
	Fayetteville Exp Stn	1.5
	Huntsville 1 SSW	23.0
Fort Smith	Fort Smith Regional Arpt	2.5
	Mountainburg 2 NE	24.0
	Sallisaw 2 NW, OK	23.9
Hot Springs	Alum Fork	24.3
	Arkadelphia 2 N	23.6
	Blakely Mountain Dam	9.7
	Hot Springs 1 NNE	1.8
Jacksonville	Cabot 4 SW	5.5
	Conway	22.8
	Keo	20.3
	Little Rock Adams Field	10.8
	North Little Rock Arpt	8.8
Jonesboro	Alicia	22.3
	Jonesboro 4 N	3.9
	Paragould 1 S	17.9
Little Rock	Benton	17.9
	Cabot 4 SW	21.6
	Conway	24.6
	Keo	22.3
	Little Rock Adams Field	7.2
	North Little Rock Arpt	8.7
North Little Rock	Benton	24.9
	Cabot 4 SW	14.8
	Conway	22.7
	Keo	19.5
	Little Rock Adams Field	2.9
	North Little Rock Arpt	3.2
Paragould	Jonesboro 4 N	16.2
	Paragould 1 S	1.7

City	Station Name	Miles
Pine Bluff	Pine Bluff	1.6
	Sheridan	22.2
Rogers	Bentonville 4 S	4.4
	Fayetteville Exp Stn	15.9
	Gravette	18.7
Russellville	Dardanelle	3.5
	Morrilton	22.9
Searcy	Des Arc	23.7
	Searcy	5.4
Sherwood	Cabot 4 SW	10.9
	Conway	21.5
	Keo	20.0
	Little Rock Adams Field	5.8
	North Little Rock Arpt	3.2
Springdale	Bentonville 4 S	10.4
	Fayetteville Exp Stn	5.6
	Gravette	24.5
	Huntsville 1 SSW	23.3
Texarkana	Texarkana, TX	3.9
	Wright Patman Dam & Lock, TX	12.7
Van Buren	Fort Smith Regional Arpt	8.1
	Mountainburg 2 NE	17.7
West Memphis	West Memphis	2.3
	Memphis Intl Arpt, TN	12.2

Note: Miles is the distance between the geographic center of the city and the weather station.

See User Guide for station inclusion criteria.

Arkansas Weather Stations by Elevation

Feet	Station Name
2,375	Deer
1,783	Huntsville 1 SSW
1,270	Fayetteville Exp Stn
1,259	Gravette
1,220	Bentonville 4 S
792	Mountainburg 2 NE
698	Alum Fork
680	Hot Springs 1 NNE
570	Batesville Livestock
562	North Little Rock Arpt
449	Fort Smith Regional Arpt
425	Blakely Mountain Dam
425	Blue Mountain Dam
419	Dequeen
390	Jonesboro 4 N
370	Dardanelle
339	Morrilton
314	Conway
310	Benton
299	Corning
278	Cabot 4 SW
270	Paragould 1 S
256	Little Rock Adams Field
255	Alicia
251	Blytheville
251	El Dorado Goodwin Field
250	Sheridan
245	Searcy
240	Beedeville 4 NE
229	Fordyce
229	Keo
214	Pine Bluff
214	West Memphis
200	Des Arc
195	Arkadelphia 2 N
193	Arkansas Post
180	Crossett 2 SSE
134	Eudora

See User Guide for station inclusion criteria.

Fort Smith Regional Airport

The weather station at Fort Smith, Arkansas, was established on June 1, 1882 by the U. S. Army Signal Service. For the first 63 years, offices were located at several places within a few blocks of each other in downtown Fort Smith. Since 1945 the station has been at the Fort Smith Municipal Airport, about five miles southeast of its original location.

Fort Smith is located on the Arkansas River at its confluence with the Poteau River and at the point where it enters the state from Oklahoma. The river valley is broad and fairly flat, although elevations in the city of Fort Smith range from 390 feet at the river to about 700 feet. Within 20 miles to the north are the Boston Mountains with elevations to about 2,100 feet and about the same distance south are the Ouachita Mountains with a maximum elevation of about 2,600 feet. The general terrain in the area consists of low broken hills separated by creek and river bottom land.

The surrounding terrain has a definite influence on the weather of Fort Smith. Under conditions of light wind, the direction is prevailing northeast throughout the year. When there is a fairly strong inversion these winds may remain northeasterly even though a strong gradient is present. Although infrequent, dense fog will move in from the river to the east and persist longer than would be expected. In the summer this will result in uncomfortably high humidities and in the winter in cooler temperatures than reported at surrounding stations. Summertime temperatures in the mountains to the north are generally several degrees cooler than in the river valley.

Temperature extremes do occur. In summer there is an average of 10 days when the temperature rises to 100 degrees or higher. On the other hand, in about one year in five, the temperature does not reach 100 degrees. Wintertime temperatures rarely fall to zero or below.

Rainfall is well distributed throughout the growing season. January is the driest month, May the wettest. The difference is almost three inches, but rainfall is generally adequate for agricultural pursuits. Summer precipitation comes in the form of convective showers. Dry spells occur, but true droughts are infrequent.

Snowfall varies widely from season to season. Although snowfall averages a little over six inches, some years go by with no measurable amount being recorded. Ice storms are much more frequent, causing many problems with traffic movement.

Based on the 1951-1980 period, the average first occurrence of 32 degrees Fahrenheit in the fall is October 30 and the average last occurrence in the spring is April 3.

Fort Smith Regional Airport *Sebastian County* Elevation: 449 ft. Latitude: 35° 20' N Longitude: 94° 22' W

	JAN	FEB	MAR	APR	MAY	JUN	JUL	AUG	SEP	OCT	NOV	DEC	YEAR
Mean Maximum Temp. (°F)	50.0	55.5	64.5	73.5	80.4	87.9	93.3	93.3	85.5	74.7	62.7	51.5	72.7
Mean Temp. (°F)	39.5	44.2	52.7	61.3	69.7	77.6	82.3	81.9	73.9	62.6	51.4	41.3	61.5
Mean Minimum Temp. (°F)	28.9	32.8	40.8	49.0	59.0	67.3	71.3	70.5	62.2	50.5	40.0	31.1	50.3
Extreme Maximum Temp. (°F)	79	82	91	96	97	103	109	108	109	94	86	80	109
Extreme Minimum Temp. (°F)	-1	1	8	24	37	48	53	51	36	24	17	-5	-5
Days Maximum Temp. ≥ 90°F	0	0	0	1	3	13	24	23	10	1	0	0	75
Days Maximum Temp. ≤ 32°F	2	1	0	0	0	0	0	0	0	0	0	2	5
Days Minimum Temp. ≤ 32°F	22	14	6	1	0	0	0	0	0	1	7	18	69
Days Minimum Temp. ≤ 0°F	0	0	0	0	0	0	0	0	0	0	0	0	0
Heating Degree Days (base 65°F)	786	583	386	157	27	0	0	0	17	137	409	728	3,230
Cooling Degree Days (base 65°F)	1	1	11	53	180	386	543	532	289	70	7	1	2,074
Mean Precipitation (in.)	2.74	2.73	3.86	4.30	5.51	4.21	3.23	2.54	3.95	4.37	4.42	3.26	45.12
Maximum Precipitation (in.)*	11.3	7.9	8.5	10.3	13.4	10.4	10.4	6.6	9.0	12.0	13.9	10.1	61.2
Minimum Precipitation (in.)*	0.2	0.5	0.8	0.6	0.8	0.4	0.2	0.4	0.1	trace	0.6	0.3	26.4
Extreme Maximum Daily Precip. (in.)	3.68	2.80	4.66	4.56	3.84	2.73	3.28	3.92	3.52	5.72	3.71	3.54	5.72
Days With ≥ 0.1" Precipitation	5	4	6	6	8	6	5	4	5	6	6	5	66
Days With ≥ 0.5" Precipitation	2	2	3	3	4	3	2	2	3	3	3	3	33
Days With ≥ 1.0" Precipitation	1	1	1	1	2	1	1	1	1	1	2	1	14
Mean Snowfall (in.)	na	na	na	na	na	na	na	na	na	na	na	na	na
Maximum Snowfall (in.)*	13	12	5	trace	0	0	0	0	0	trace	5	7	22
Maximum 24-hr. Snowfall (in.)*	11	6	4	trace	0	0	0	0	0	trace	4	7	11
Maximum Snow Depth (in.)	na	na	na	na	na	na	na	na	na	na	na	na	na
Days With ≥ 1.0" Snow Depth	na	na	na	na	na	na	na	na	na	na	na	na	na
Thunderstorm Days*	1	2	5	7	8	8	8	7	5	3	3	2	59
Foggy Days*	11	9	8	6	8	7	6	9	9	9	9	10	101
Predominant Sky Cover*	OVR	OVR	OVR	OVR	OVR	CLR	CLR	CLR	CLR	CLR	OVR	OVR	OVR
Mean Relative Humidity 6am (%)*	81	81	79	82	88	89	89	89	89	87	83	82	85
Mean Relative Humidity 3pm (%)*	55	50	46	46	52	52	49	47	48	45	48	53	49
Mean Dewpoint (°F)*	28	31	37	47	58	66	69	67	61	50	38	31	49
Prevailing Wind Direction*	ENE	ENE	ENE	E	ENE	ENE	ENE	ENE	ENE	ENE	ENE	ENE	ENE
Prevailing Wind Speed (mph)*	8	8	8	9	7	6	7	7	7	7	7	8	7
Maximum Wind Gust (mph)*	54	58	56	76	71	71	85	63	55	60	60	59	85

Note: (*) Period of record is 1948-1995

 The period of record for National Weather Service station data is 1980 – 2009 except where noted. See User Guide for detailed explanation of data.

Little Rock Adams Field

Little Rock is located on the Arkansas River near the geographical center of the state. It is situated on the dividing line between the Ouachita Mountains to the west and the flat lowlands comprising the Mississippi River Valley to the east. Elevations range from 222 feet at the river level to 257 feet over much of the flat land, including the airport in the southeast, to near 600 feet in the hilly residential area of the western portions of the city. Two minor temperature variations are observed due to the terrain; somewhat lower minimum temperatures are observed in the airport vicinity and a slight downslope adiabatic heating effect accompanies airflow from the ridges and hills in the west and northwest.

The modified continental climate of Little Rock includes exposure to all of the North American air mass types. However, with its proximity to the Gulf of Mexico, the summer season is marked by prolonged periods of warm and humid weather. The growing season averages 233 days in which 62 percent of the normal precipitation occurs. Winters are mild, but polar and Arctic outbreaks are not uncommon.

Precipitation is fairly well distributed throughout the year. Summer rainfall is almost completely of the convective type. The driest period usually occurs in the late summer and early fall. Snow is almost negligible. Glaze and ice storms, although infrequent, are at times severe. Warm front weather in the winter and early spring, characterized by shallow surface cold air flow from the north under warm moist Gulf air, results in excellent conditions for the production of freezing precipitation.

Little Rock Adams Field *Pulaski County* Elevation: 256 ft. Latitude: 34° 45' N Longitude: 92° 14' W

	JAN	FEB	MAR	APR	MAY	JUN	JUL	AUG	SEP	OCT	NOV	DEC	YEAR
Mean Maximum Temp. (°F)	50.9	55.6	64.3	73.3	81.2	88.9	92.7	92.7	85.5	74.5	62.9	52.5	72.9
Mean Temp. (°F)	41.4	45.5	53.7	62.2	70.8	78.8	82.6	82.1	74.8	63.3	52.6	43.3	62.6
Mean Minimum Temp. (°F)	31.9	35.4	43.0	51.1	60.3	68.5	72.4	71.4	63.9	52.1	42.4	33.9	52.2
Extreme Maximum Temp. (°F)	80	85	86	95	98	105	112	109	104	93	85	80	112
Extreme Minimum Temp. (°F)	-2	5	15	28	41	49	59	52	42	29	20	-1	-2
Days Maximum Temp. ≥ 90°F	0	0	0	0	3	16	23	22	10	1	0	0	75
Days Maximum Temp. ≤ 32°F	2	1	0	0	0	0	0	0	0	0	0	2	5
Days Minimum Temp. ≤ 32°F	17	11	4	0	0	0	0	0	0	0	5	15	52
Days Minimum Temp. ≤ 0°F	0	0	0	0	0	0	0	0	0	0	0	0	0
Heating Degree Days (base 65°F)	725	546	361	137	19	0	0	0	11	124	374	669	2,966
Cooling Degree Days (base 65°F)	2	1	16	60	206	420	553	536	310	79	9	2	2,194
Mean Precipitation (in.)	3.53	3.55	4.83	5.18	4.86	3.58	3.27	2.54	3.31	4.93	5.27	4.96	49.81
Maximum Precipitation (in.)*	12.5	11.0	10.4	14.2	12.7	7.8	7.9	14.5	10.2	15.3	13.1	16.5	74.4
Minimum Precipitation (in.)*	0.5	0.9	0.7	0.5	0.7	trace	0.1	trace	0.3	0.1	0.3	1.3	28.3
Extreme Maximum Daily Precip. (in.)	4.21	2.79	2.83	4.44	4.12	2.64	3.58	2.56	4.38	5.11	6.23	5.76	6.23
Days With ≥ 0.1" Precipitation	6	6	7	7	8	6	5	4	5	6	6	6	72
Days With ≥ 0.5" Precipitation	2	3	4	4	3	3	2	2	2	3	3	3	34
Days With ≥ 1.0" Precipitation	1	1	2	2	1	1	1	1	1	2	2	1	16
Mean Snowfall (in.)	na	na	na	na	na	na	na	na	na	na	na	na	na
Maximum Snowfall (in.)*	14	10	7	trace	0	0	0	0	0	trace	5	10	33
Maximum 24-hr. Snowfall (in.)*	11	9	5	trace	0	0	0	0	0	trace	4	10	11
Maximum Snow Depth (in.)	*13*	na	na	na	na	na	na	na	na	na	na	na	na
Days With ≥ 1.0" Snow Depth	*1*	na	na	na	na	na	na	na	na	na	na	na	na
Thunderstorm Days*	2	2	5	6	7	8	9	7	4	3	3	2	58
Foggy Days*	14	12	11	10	13	11	12	14	15	13	12	13	150
Predominant Sky Cover*	OVR	OVR	OVR	OVR	OVR	SCT	SCT	SCT	CLR	CLR	OVR	OVR	OVR
Mean Relative Humidity 6am (%)*	80	80	78	82	87	87	88	88	88	86	82	81	84
Mean Relative Humidity 3pm (%)*	58	53	50	51	54	53	54	52	52	48	52	57	53
Mean Dewpoint (°F)*	30	33	40	49	59	67	70	69	62	51	41	33	51
Prevailing Wind Direction*	WSW	N	S	S	S	SW	SW	SW	NE	WSW	S	WSW	SW
Prevailing Wind Speed (mph)*	8	10	9	9	9	8	8	8	8	7	9	8	8
Maximum Wind Gust (mph)*	62	63	46	52	58	60	56	47	47	45	59	60	63

Note: (*) Period of record is 1948-1995

Alicia *Lawrence County* Elevation: 255 ft. Latitude: 35° 54' N Longitude: 91° 05' W

	JAN	FEB	MAR	APR	MAY	JUN	JUL	AUG	SEP	OCT	NOV	DEC	YEAR
Mean Maximum Temp. (°F)	47.3	52.5	61.9	72.1	80.9	89.0	92.3	91.7	84.7	74.1	61.0	49.4	71.4
Mean Temp. (°F)	38.1	42.5	51.1	60.6	69.8	78.2	81.7	80.4	72.6	61.6	50.6	40.4	60.6
Mean Minimum Temp. (°F)	28.8	32.5	40.3	49.1	58.7	67.3	71.0	69.1	60.5	49.1	40.1	31.3	49.8
Extreme Maximum Temp. (°F)	75	80	86	96	97	103	113	107	104	95	84	77	113
Extreme Minimum Temp. (°F)	-10	-1	13	26	38	44	54	48	38	25	15	-6	-10
Days Maximum Temp. ≥ 90°F	0	0	0	0	3	15	20	20	7	1	0	0	66
Days Maximum Temp. ≤ 32°F	3	1	0	0	0	0	0	0	0	0	0	2	6
Days Minimum Temp. ≤ 32°F	21	14	6	1	0	0	0	0	0	1	7	17	67
Days Minimum Temp. ≤ 0°F	0	0	0	0	0	0	0	0	0	0	0	0	0
Heating Degree Days (base 65°F)	829	630	431	171	27	0	0	0	17	158	430	756	3,449
Cooling Degree Days (base 65°F)	0	0	8	46	184	402	524	485	253	60	5	0	1,967
Mean Precipitation (in.)	3.27	3.23	3.96	4.64	4.60	2.95	3.20	2.62	3.22	4.06	4.57	4.45	44.77
Extreme Maximum Daily Precip. (in.)	2.74	3.64	4.00	3.19	6.00	2.08	4.33	2.60	4.65	4.35	3.12	4.44	6.00
Days With ≥ 0.1" Precipitation	5	5	6	6	7	5	5	4	4	5	6	6	64
Days With ≥ 0.5" Precipitation	2	2	3	3	3	2	2	2	2	3	3	3	30
Days With ≥ 1.0" Precipitation	1	1	1	2	1	1	1	1	1	1	2	1	14
Mean Snowfall (in.)	1.9	1.7	0.8	trace	0.0	0.0	0.0	0.0	0.0	0.0	0.0	0.8	5.2
Maximum Snow Depth (in.)	***6***	7	***5***	trace	0	0	0	0	0	***0***	0	3	***7***
Days With ≥ 1.0" Snow Depth	***0***	0	0	0	0	0	0	0	0	0	0	0	***0***

Alum Fork *Saline County* Elevation: 698 ft. Latitude: 34° 48' N Longitude: 92° 51' W

	JAN	FEB	MAR	APR	MAY	JUN	JUL	AUG	SEP	OCT	NOV	DEC	YEAR
Mean Maximum Temp. (°F)	51.3	56.0	64.6	73.3	79.5	86.7	91.3	91.4	84.4	73.9	62.5	52.3	72.3
Mean Temp. (°F)	40.9	44.7	52.8	61.2	68.9	76.3	80.4	80.1	73.1	62.3	51.9	42.3	61.2
Mean Minimum Temp. (°F)	30.5	33.3	40.9	49.1	58.2	65.9	69.6	68.7	61.7	50.7	41.2	32.3	50.2
Extreme Maximum Temp. (°F)	77	85	86	95	94	99	110	106	107	93	84	78	110
Extreme Minimum Temp. (°F)	-3	0	10	26	37	48	54	50	37	28	18	-3	-3
Days Maximum Temp. ≥ 90°F	0	0	0	0	1	9	19	20	8	0	0	0	57
Days Maximum Temp. ≤ 32°F	2	1	0	0	0	0	0	0	0	0	0	1	4
Days Minimum Temp. ≤ 32°F	19	14	6	1	0	0	0	0	0	0	7	17	64
Days Minimum Temp. ≤ 0°F	0	0	0	0	0	0	0	0	0	0	0	0	0
Heating Degree Days (base 65°F)	740	569	382	155	30	0	0	0	15	138	392	696	3,117
Cooling Degree Days (base 65°F)	1	1	10	49	157	346	485	475	263	62	5	1	1,855
Mean Precipitation (in.)	3.68	4.35	5.18	5.26	5.53	4.20	4.15	2.98	4.39	5.55	5.70	5.51	56.48
Extreme Maximum Daily Precip. (in.)	2.70	3.05	3.85	5.00	3.32	4.83	4.10	3.00	8.13	5.94	5.30	4.90	8.13
Days With ≥ 0.1" Precipitation	6	6	7	7	8	6	6	5	5	6	6	7	75
Days With ≥ 0.5" Precipitation	3	3	4	4	4	3	3	2	3	4	4	3	40
Days With ≥ 1.0" Precipitation	1	1	2	2	2	1	1	1	2	2	2	2	19
Mean Snowfall (in.)	0.6	1.3	0.1	trace	0.0	0.0	0.0	0.0	0.0	0.0	trace	0.4	2.4
Maximum Snow Depth (in.)	4	11	3	0	0	0	0	0	0	0	0	1	11
Days With ≥ 1.0" Snow Depth	0	1	0	0	0	0	0	0	0	0	0	0	1

Arkadelphia 2 N *Clark County* Elevation: 195 ft. Latitude: 34° 09' N Longitude: 93° 03' W

	JAN	FEB	MAR	APR	MAY	JUN	JUL	AUG	SEP	OCT	NOV	DEC	YEAR
Mean Maximum Temp. (°F)	54.0	58.5	67.6	75.7	82.0	88.7	92.5	92.5	86.0	75.4	64.6	54.8	74.4
Mean Temp. (°F)	42.5	46.4	54.7	62.1	70.3	77.6	81.2	***80.8***	73.6	62.5	53.0	43.7	***62.4***
Mean Minimum Temp. (°F)	31.0	34.2	41.8	48.8	58.5	66.4	69.7	***68.7***	61.3	49.4	41.3	32.7	***50.3***
Extreme Maximum Temp. (°F)	79	87	88	95	97	100	106	109	108	94	84	79	109
Extreme Minimum Temp. (°F)	1	5	14	25	37	46	55	48	34	26	20	0	0
Days Maximum Temp. ≥ 90°F	0	0	0	0	2	15	23	22	9	1	0	0	72
Days Maximum Temp. ≤ 32°F	1	1	0	0	0	0	0	0	0	0	0	1	3
Days Minimum Temp. ≤ 32°F	18	13	5	1	0	0	0	0	0	1	7	16	61
Days Minimum Temp. ≤ 0°F	0	0	0	0	0	0	0	0	0	0	0	0	0
Heating Degree Days (base 65°F)	690	522	328	135	19	0	0	***0***	14	137	362	653	***2,860***
Cooling Degree Days (base 65°F)	1	1	15	54	189	386	508	***496***	280	66	9	2	***2,007***
Mean Precipitation (in.)	3.93	4.20	4.90	4.75	6.51	4.08	4.36	2.75	3.89	5.44	5.23	5.32	55.36
Extreme Maximum Daily Precip. (in.)	4.02	3.12	7.02	4.28	4.94	4.63	5.49	4.02	6.90	5.83	6.11	7.14	7.14
Days With ≥ 0.1" Precipitation	6	6	6	6	7	6	5	4	4	6	6	6	68
Days With ≥ 0.5" Precipitation	3	3	3	3	4	3	3	2	2	3	3	3	35
Days With ≥ 1.0" Precipitation	1	1	2	2	2	2	2	1	1	2	2	2	20
Mean Snowfall (in.)	1.2	0.7	trace	0.0	0.0	0.0	0.0	0.0	0.0	0.0	trace	0.4	2.3
Maximum Snow Depth (in.)	10	5	trace	0	0	0	0	0	0	0	trace	6	10
Days With ≥ 1.0" Snow Depth	0	0	0	0	0	0	0	0	0	0	0	0	0

Arkansas Post *Arkansas County* Elevation: 193 ft. Latitude: 34° 01' N Longitude: 91° 21' W

	JAN	FEB	MAR	APR	MAY	JUN	JUL	AUG	SEP	OCT	NOV	DEC	YEAR
Mean Maximum Temp. (°F)	51.3	56.4	65.7	73.6	81.1	87.9	91.0	90.6	84.9	74.6	62.7	53.1	72.7
Mean Temp. (°F)	42.6	47.0	55.3	63.4	71.6	78.7	81.8	81.0	74.8	64.2	53.8	44.8	63.3
Mean Minimum Temp. (°F)	33.9	37.6	45.0	53.3	62.0	69.4	72.6	71.4	64.6	53.8	44.8	36.4	53.7
Extreme Maximum Temp. (°F)	77	82	87	93	95	101	106	103	103	94	82	81	106
Extreme Minimum Temp. (°F)	2	9	17	30	43	53	60	51	42	30	22	1	1
Days Maximum Temp. ≥ 90°F	0	0	0	0	2	11	20	19	7	0	0	0	59
Days Maximum Temp. ≤ 32°F	1	1	0	0	0	0	0	0	0	0	0	1	3
Days Minimum Temp. ≤ 32°F	15	9	3	0	0	0	0	0	0	0	3	11	41
Days Minimum Temp. ≤ 0°F	0	0	0	0	0	0	0	0	0	0	0	0	0
Heating Degree Days (base 65°F)	688	502	311	116	13	0	0	0	9	106	342	623	2,710
Cooling Degree Days (base 65°F)	1	2	17	75	224	417	529	504	310	90	11	2	2,182
Mean Precipitation (in.)	4.39	4.69	5.31	4.54	5.23	3.41	3.46	2.11	3.06	4.79	4.90	5.74	51.63
Extreme Maximum Daily Precip. (in.)	4.30	4.10	4.00	4.33	5.10	5.25	3.62	2.47	5.05	6.80	7.94	***4.60***	***7.94***
Days With ≥ 0.1" Precipitation	6	6	7	6	6	5	5	4	4	5	6	6	66
Days With ≥ 0.5" Precipitation	3	3	3	3	3	2	3	2	2	3	3	3	33
Days With ≥ 1.0" Precipitation	1	2	2	1	2	1	1	1	1	2	2	2	18
Mean Snowfall (in.)	1.2	0.4	0.1	trace	0.0	0.0	0.0	0.0	0.0	0.0	trace	0.3	2.0
Maximum Snow Depth (in.)	7	3	trace	trace	0	0	0	0	0	0	0	5	7
Days With ≥ 1.0" Snow Depth	1	0	0	0	0	0	0	0	0	0	0	0	1

The period of record for all cooperative weather station data is 1980 – 2009. See User Guide for detailed explanation of data.

Batesville Livestock *Independence County* Elevation: 570 ft. Latitude: 35° 50' N Longitude: 91° 46' W

	JAN	FEB	MAR	APR	MAY	JUN	JUL	AUG	SEP	OCT	NOV	DEC	YEAR
Mean Maximum Temp. (°F)	49.4	54.4	63.3	73.3	80.0	87.8	92.4	92.5	85.0	74.1	61.7	50.4	72.0
Mean Temp. (°F)	39.0	43.3	51.5	60.8	68.4	76.3	80.7	80.0	72.4	61.5	50.9	40.5	60.4
Mean Minimum Temp. (°F)	28.6	32.1	39.6	48.2	56.7	64.7	68.9	67.5	59.7	48.8	40.1	30.6	48.8
Extreme Maximum Temp. (°F)	78	83	87	94	96	105	111	110	108	94	86	78	111
Extreme Minimum Temp. (°F)	-11	-3	10	22	32	46	51	44	34	22	13	-9	-11
Days Maximum Temp. ≥ 90°F	0	0	0	0	2	12	22	21	10	1	0	0	68
Days Maximum Temp. ≤ 32°F	2	1	0	0	0	0	0	0	0	0	0	2	5
Days Minimum Temp. ≤ 32°F	21	15	8	1	0	0	0	0	0	2	8	18	73
Days Minimum Temp. ≤ 0°F	0	0	0	0	0	0	0	0	0	0	0	0	0
Heating Degree Days (base 65°F)	799	609	421	173	40	1	0	1	21	163	423	752	3,403
Cooling Degree Days (base 65°F)	0	1	9	52	152	345	493	474	249	61	7	1	1,844
Mean Precipitation (in.)	3.18	3.37	4.32	4.53	4.69	3.33	3.39	2.95	3.76	4.39	5.04	4.46	47.41
Extreme Maximum Daily Precip. (in.)	4.45	2.79	5.21	3.40	3.21	3.42	4.74	3.09	4.10	4.15	5.38	7.00	7.00
Days With ≥ 0.1" Precipitation	5	5	7	6	8	5	5	5	5	6	6	6	69
Days With ≥ 0.5" Precipitation	2	2	3	3	3	2	2	2	2	3	3	3	30
Days With ≥ 1.0" Precipitation	1	1	1	1	1	1	1	1	1	2	2	1	14
Mean Snowfall (in.)	2.1	2.1	0.4	0.0	0.0	0.0	0.0	0.0	0.0	0.1	0.3	0.8	5.8
Maximum Snow Depth (in.)	10	7	6	0	0	0	0	0	0	2	4	3	10
Days With ≥ 1.0" Snow Depth	2	2	0	0	0	0	0	0	0	0	0	1	5

Beedeville 4 NE *Jackson County* Elevation: 240 ft. Latitude: 35° 28' N Longitude: 91° 03' W

	JAN	FEB	MAR	APR	MAY	JUN	JUL	AUG	SEP	OCT	NOV	DEC	YEAR
Mean Maximum Temp. (°F)	47.1	52.5	61.8	72.1	80.3	87.9	91.5	90.5	83.9	73.6	60.9	49.7	71.0
Mean Temp. (°F)	38.9	43.4	51.7	61.3	70.2	78.1	81.6	79.7	72.4	61.8	51.3	41.4	61.0
Mean Minimum Temp. (°F)	30.7	34.2	41.5	50.5	60.1	68.2	71.6	68.9	60.8	50.0	41.6	33.0	50.9
Extreme Maximum Temp. (°F)	74	78	86	97	96	101	112	106	104	92	85	78	112
Extreme Minimum Temp. (°F)	-6	2	13	26	34	49	57	52	36	25	18	-5	-6
Days Maximum Temp. ≥ 90°F	0	0	0	0	2	13	20	19	7	1	0	0	62
Days Maximum Temp. ≤ 32°F	3	1	0	0	0	0	0	0	0	0	0	2	6
Days Minimum Temp. ≤ 32°F	18	12	6	1	0	0	0	0	0	1	6	15	59
Days Minimum Temp. ≤ 0°F	0	0	0	0	0	0	0	0	0	0	0	0	0
Heating Degree Days (base 65°F)	802	605	416	159	26	0	0	0	20	152	413	727	3,320
Cooling Degree Days (base 65°F)	0	0	10	54	195	399	521	464	248	61	7	1	1,960
Mean Precipitation (in.)	3.57	3.43	4.58	5.00	5.04	3.27	3.27	1.93	3.09	4.34	5.12	4.96	47.60
Extreme Maximum Daily Precip. (in.)	3.02	***3.42***	4.37	5.30	4.20	2.74	4.35	2.11	3.82	4.42	5.96	***6.72***	***6.72***
Days With ≥ 0.1" Precipitation	5	4	6	6	6	5	4	3	4	5	6	5	59
Days With ≥ 0.5" Precipitation	2	2	3	3	3	3	2	2	2	3	3	3	31
Days With ≥ 1.0" Precipitation	1	1	1	2	2	1	1	1	1	2	2	2	17
Mean Snowfall (in.)	0.8	0.9	0.3	0.0	0.0	0.0	0.0	0.0	0.0	trace	0.1	0.1	2.2
Maximum Snow Depth (in.)	11	4	***2***	0	0	0	0	0	0	trace	trace	2	***11***
Days With ≥ 1.0" Snow Depth	***0***	0	0	0	0	0	0	0	0	0	0	0	***0***

Benton *Saline County* Elevation: 310 ft. Latitude: 34° 34' N Longitude: 92° 36' W

	JAN	FEB	MAR	APR	MAY	JUN	JUL	AUG	SEP	OCT	NOV	DEC	YEAR
Mean Maximum Temp. (°F)	53.3	58.2	66.2	74.7	81.5	88.2	92.7	92.8	85.9	75.2	64.2	54.3	73.9
Mean Temp. (°F)	41.8	46.2	53.8	62.0	70.0	77.3	81.4	80.7	73.5	62.4	52.6	43.4	62.1
Mean Minimum Temp. (°F)	30.3	34.2	41.3	49.2	58.5	66.4	69.9	68.6	60.9	49.4	40.9	32.5	50.2
Extreme Maximum Temp. (°F)	79	87	86	95	97	101	112	108	106	94	84	79	112
Extreme Minimum Temp. (°F)	-3	1	14	23	38	49	56	46	36	20	12	-2	-3
Days Maximum Temp. ≥ 90°F	0	0	0	0	2	13	23	23	9	1	0	0	71
Days Maximum Temp. ≤ 32°F	1	1	0	0	0	0	0	0	0	0	0	1	3
Days Minimum Temp. ≤ 32°F	19	12	6	1	0	0	0	0	0	1	6	16	61
Days Minimum Temp. ≤ 0°F	0	0	0	0	0	0	0	0	0	0	0	0	0
Heating Degree Days (base 65°F)	714	526	353	141	23	0	0	0	16	140	374	664	2,951
Cooling Degree Days (base 65°F)	1	2	13	57	185	377	515	493	275	65	8	2	1,993
Mean Precipitation (in.)	3.76	3.53	4.63	5.41	4.88	4.09	4.07	2.85	4.44	5.11	5.28	5.02	53.07
Extreme Maximum Daily Precip. (in.)	4.12	3.40	3.35	***5.05***	4.10	4.65	5.60	3.17	8.00	5.53	6.03	***6.85***	***8.00***
Days With ≥ 0.1" Precipitation	5	5	6	6	7	5	5	4	5	6	6	6	66
Days With ≥ 0.5" Precipitation	3	2	3	4	4	3	2	2	2	3	3	3	34
Days With ≥ 1.0" Precipitation	1	1	1	2	1	1	1	1	1	2	2	2	16
Mean Snowfall (in.)	1.3	1.1	trace	0.0	0.0	0.0	0.0	0.0	0.0	0.0	0.1	0.1	2.6
Maximum Snow Depth (in.)	***6***	***4***	***1***	***0***	***0***	***0***	***0***	***0***	***0***	***0***	***2***	***2***	***6***
Days With ≥ 1.0" Snow Depth	***0***	0	0	0	0	0	0	0	0	0	0	0	***0***

Bentonville 4 S *Benton County* Elevation: 1,220 ft. Latitude: 36° 19' N Longitude: 94° 13' W

	JAN	FEB	MAR	APR	MAY	JUN	JUL	AUG	SEP	OCT	NOV	DEC	YEAR
Mean Maximum Temp. (°F)	45.7	50.7	58.7	69.0	76.2	83.7	89.3	89.6	81.8	71.1	58.5	47.7	68.5
Mean Temp. (°F)	34.8	38.7	46.6	56.3	64.7	72.8	77.9	77.2	69.2	58.1	47.0	36.9	56.7
Mean Minimum Temp. (°F)	23.8	26.6	34.5	43.5	53.3	61.8	66.5	64.8	56.5	45.0	35.5	26.0	44.8
Extreme Maximum Temp. (°F)	74	86	87	96	93	98	105	103	106	91	85	76	106
Extreme Minimum Temp. (°F)	-12	-16	-4	20	32	40	51	47	30	18	8	-15	-16
Days Maximum Temp. ≥ 90°F	0	0	0	0	1	4	16	17	6	0	0	0	44
Days Maximum Temp. ≤ 32°F	5	3	1	0	0	0	0	0	0	0	0	4	13
Days Minimum Temp. ≤ 32°F	25	21	13	4	0	0	0	0	0	3	13	23	102
Days Minimum Temp. ≤ 0°F	1	0	0	0	0	0	0	0	0	0	0	1	2
Heating Degree Days (base 65°F)	930	737	564	277	90	9	1	2	51	236	536	864	4,297
Cooling Degree Days (base 65°F)	0	0	3	23	89	248	409	388	184	29	3	0	1,376
Mean Precipitation (in.)	2.56	2.59	4.19	4.13	5.43	4.82	3.32	3.04	4.39	3.48	4.61	3.53	46.09
Extreme Maximum Daily Precip. (in.)	2.37	2.59	3.15	3.30	3.27	3.75	4.90	***2.14***	5.65	3.00	4.00	3.85	***5.65***
Days With ≥ 0.1" Precipitation	4	5	7	7	8	7	5	5	6	6	6	5	71
Days With ≥ 0.5" Precipitation	2	2	3	3	4	3	2	2	3	2	3	2	31
Days With ≥ 1.0" Precipitation	1	1	1	1	2	2	1	1	2	1	2	1	16
Mean Snowfall (in.)	***2.5***	2.4	2.0	trace	0.0	0.0	0.0	0.0	0.0	trace	0.2	1.8	***8.9***
Maximum Snow Depth (in.)	11	8	14	trace	0	0	0	0	0	trace	2	8	14
Days With ≥ 1.0" Snow Depth	2	2	1	0	0	0	0	0	0	0	0	2	7

Blakely Mountain Dam *Garland County* Elevation: 425 ft. Latitude: 34° 34' N Longitude: 93° 12' W

	JAN	FEB	MAR	APR	MAY	JUN	JUL	AUG	SEP	OCT	NOV	DEC	YEAR
Mean Maximum Temp. (°F)	***50.6***	55.0	63.4	72.6	***78.9***	86.9	91.7	91.8	84.5	73.4	62.2	52.6	***72.0***
Mean Temp. (°F)	***39.4***	42.8	50.7	59.0	***66.8***	74.6	***78.9***	78.5	71.4	60.4	***50.3***	41.6	***59.5***
Mean Minimum Temp. (°F)	28.2	30.7	37.9	45.3	***54.7***	62.6	***66.1***	65.1	58.3	47.3	***38.6***	30.5	***47.1***
Extreme Maximum Temp. (°F)	78	84	87	95	94	102	109	111	105	93	85	78	111
Extreme Minimum Temp. (°F)	2	1	12	24	34	45	54	45	35	25	15	0	0
Days Maximum Temp. ≥ 90°F	0	0	0	0	1	10	19	20	7	0	0	0	57
Days Maximum Temp. ≤ 32°F	1	1	0	0	0	0	0	0	0	0	0	1	3
Days Minimum Temp. ≤ 32°F	21	17	9	2	0	0	0	0	0	1	9	19	78
Days Minimum Temp. ≤ 0°F	0	0	0	0	0	0	0	0	0	0	0	0	0
Heating Degree Days (base 65°F)	***786***	621	442	202	***51***	2	***0***	0	23	180	***437***	718	***3,462***
Cooling Degree Days (base 65°F)	***0***	0	5	28	***114***	298	***439***	426	223	43	***3***	1	***1,580***
Mean Precipitation (in.)	3.62	4.21	5.14	5.21	5.81	4.31	4.38	2.68	4.03	5.49	5.78	5.29	55.95
Extreme Maximum Daily Precip. (in.)	3.56	4.50	4.24	3.89	4.10	6.00	4.24	4.99	6.36	***4.45***	***4.80***	***8.20***	***8.20***
Days With ≥ 0.1" Precipitation	6	6	6	6	7	6	5	4	5	6	6	6	69
Days With ≥ 0.5" Precipitation	2	3	3	3	3	3	3	1	3	3	3	3	33
Days With ≥ 1.0" Precipitation	1	1	2	2	2	1	1	1	1	2	2	1	17
Mean Snowfall (in.)	0.4	0.4	trace	0.0	0.0	0.0	0.0	0.0	0.0	0.0	0.0	0.1	0.9
Maximum Snow Depth (in.)	4	*7*	0	0	0	0	0	0	0	0	0	0	*7*
Days With ≥ 1.0" Snow Depth	0	0	0	0	0	0	0	0	0	0	0	0	0

Blue Mountain Dam *Yell County* Elevation: 425 ft. Latitude: 35° 07' N Longitude: 93° 39' W

	JAN	FEB	MAR	APR	MAY	JUN	JUL	AUG	SEP	OCT	NOV	DEC	YEAR
Mean Maximum Temp. (°F)	49.7	55.0	63.5	73.0	79.8	87.6	93.2	93.5	85.3	73.6	61.9	51.0	72.3
Mean Temp. (°F)	39.5	43.7	51.9	60.7	68.9	76.7	81.3	81.1	73.1	61.6	50.9	41.0	60.8
Mean Minimum Temp. (°F)	29.1	32.3	40.3	48.4	57.8	65.6	69.4	68.5	60.8	49.6	39.9	30.9	49.4
Extreme Maximum Temp. (°F)	79	82	90	99	100	104	111	112	109	96	85	80	112
Extreme Minimum Temp. (°F)	-2	3	11	26	37	46	51	49	36	22	16	-3	-3
Days Maximum Temp. ≥ 90°F	0	0	0	1	2	13	23	23	10	1	0	0	73
Days Maximum Temp. ≤ 32°F	2	1	0	0	0	0	0	0	0	0	0	2	5
Days Minimum Temp. ≤ 32°F	21	15	7	1	0	0	0	0	0	1	7	19	71
Days Minimum Temp. ≤ 0°F	0	0	0	0	0	0	0	0	0	0	0	0	0
Heating Degree Days (base 65°F)	786	598	410	173	36	1	0	0	21	161	425	739	3,350
Cooling Degree Days (base 65°F)	1	1	12	51	162	358	513	504	270	63	8	1	1,944
Mean Precipitation (in.)	3.20	3.32	4.58	4.40	5.42	3.69	3.30	2.90	3.85	4.32	4.87	4.46	48.31
Extreme Maximum Daily Precip. (in.)	4.48	3.36	6.53	3.14	6.15	3.45	2.36	3.04	6.48	4.57	5.09	8.25	8.25
Days With ≥ 0.1" Precipitation	5	5	7	6	8	6	5	5	5	6	6	6	70
Days With ≥ 0.5" Precipitation	2	2	3	3	4	3	2	2	2	3	3	3	32
Days With ≥ 1.0" Precipitation	1	1	1	1	2	1	1	1	1	1	2	1	14
Mean Snowfall (in.)	1.4	1.0	0.1	0.0	0.0	0.0	0.0	0.0	0.0	0.0	trace	0.5	3.0
Maximum Snow Depth (in.)	12	7	1	0	0	0	0	0	0	0	trace	5	12
Days With ≥ 1.0" Snow Depth	1	1	0	0	0	0	0	0	0	0	0	1	3

Blytheville *Mississippi County* Elevation: 251 ft. Latitude: 35° 55' N Longitude: 89° 54' W

	JAN	FEB	MAR	APR	MAY	JUN	JUL	AUG	SEP	OCT	NOV	DEC	YEAR
Mean Maximum Temp. (°F)	45.5	50.4	59.9	70.7	80.1	88.4	91.2	90.1	83.7	72.5	59.9	48.4	70.1
Mean Temp. (°F)	37.5	41.8	50.7	60.9	70.4	78.7	81.8	80.4	73.2	62.0	50.9	40.4	60.7
Mean Minimum Temp. (°F)	29.5	33.1	41.3	51.0	60.6	68.9	72.4	70.6	62.7	51.4	41.9	32.3	51.3
Extreme Maximum Temp. (°F)	79	78	85	94	96	103	108	105	100	92	85	79	108
Extreme Minimum Temp. (°F)	-14	-1	11	28	42	51	56	51	41	28	17	-7	-14
Days Maximum Temp. ≥ 90°F	0	0	0	0	3	14	20	18	7	0	0	0	62
Days Maximum Temp. ≤ 32°F	4	2	0	0	0	0	0	0	0	0	0	3	9
Days Minimum Temp. ≤ 32°F	20	13	5	0	0	0	0	0	0	0	5	16	59
Days Minimum Temp. ≤ 0°F	0	0	0	0	0	0	0	0	0	0	0	0	0
Heating Degree Days (base 65°F)	845	652	448	177	28	1	0	0	17	156	424	757	3,505
Cooling Degree Days (base 65°F)	0	1	10	60	202	417	529	484	270	70	7	1	2,051
Mean Precipitation (in.)	3.43	4.21	4.61	4.95	5.20	3.92	3.92	2.65	3.02	4.22	4.63	4.96	49.72
Extreme Maximum Daily Precip. (in.)	2.94	2.88	3.68	4.96	3.94	3.90	4.88	2.82	3.26	5.73	5.00	4.71	5.73
Days With ≥ 0.1" Precipitation	6	6	8	7	7	6	6	4	4	6	6	7	73
Days With ≥ 0.5" Precipitation	3	3	3	4	3	3	3	2	2	3	3	4	36
Days With ≥ 1.0" Precipitation	1	1	1	2	2	1	1	1	1	1	1	2	15
Mean Snowfall (in.)	0.4	***1.1***	0.1	0.0	0.0	0.0	0.0	0.0	0.0	0.0	trace	0.3	***1.9***
Maximum Snow Depth (in.)	2	5	24	0	0	0	0	0	0	0	trace	2	***24***
Days With ≥ 1.0" Snow Depth	***0***	1	0	0	0	0	0	0	0	0	0	0	***1***

Cabot 4 SW *Pulaski County* Elevation: 278 ft. Latitude: 34° 57' N Longitude: 92° 05' W

	JAN	FEB	MAR	APR	MAY	JUN	JUL	AUG	SEP	OCT	NOV	DEC	YEAR
Mean Maximum Temp. (°F)	50.6	55.4	64.0	72.6	79.7	87.2	91.2	91.0	84.9	74.1	62.3	51.7	72.1
Mean Temp. (°F)	40.3	44.3	52.4	60.7	68.8	76.6	80.2	79.4	72.6	61.4	51.1	41.7	60.8
Mean Minimum Temp. (°F)	30.0	33.1	40.8	48.7	57.9	65.8	69.0	67.8	60.4	48.6	39.9	31.5	49.5
Extreme Maximum Temp. (°F)	78	83	86	94	95	103	112	108	106	91	87	78	112
Extreme Minimum Temp. (°F)	-5	-1	11	24	37	46	51	49	36	24	14	-7	-7
Days Maximum Temp. ≥ 90°F	0	0	0	0	1	11	19	18	8	1	0	0	58
Days Maximum Temp. ≤ 32°F	2	1	0	0	0	0	0	0	0	0	0	2	5
Days Minimum Temp. ≤ 32°F	19	14	7	1	0	0	0	0	0	2	8	17	68
Days Minimum Temp. ≤ 0°F	0	0	0	0	0	0	0	0	0	0	0	0	0
Heating Degree Days (base 65°F)	758	582	394	171	34	1	0	0	19	162	416	718	3,255
Cooling Degree Days (base 65°F)	1	1	11	48	160	354	476	455	256	56	6	1	1,825
Mean Precipitation (in.)	3.55	3.50	4.95	5.00	5.50	3.53	3.30	2.90	3.48	4.74	5.80	4.81	51.06
Extreme Maximum Daily Precip. (in.)	4.00	3.24	3.50	4.27	3.63	2.95	4.00	3.26	7.55	4.22	7.76	4.53	7.76
Days With ≥ 0.1" Precipitation	5	6	7	7	7	5	5	4	4	5	7	6	68
Days With ≥ 0.5" Precipitation	3	3	3	3	4	3	2	2	2	3	4	3	35
Days With ≥ 1.0" Precipitation	1	1	1	2	2	1	1	1	1	2	2	1	16
Mean Snowfall (in.)	1.6	0.9	0.2	trace	0.0	0.0	0.0	0.0	0.0	trace	0.1	0.3	3.1
Maximum Snow Depth (in.)	10	6	1	trace	0	0	0	0	0	trace	2	4	10
Days With ≥ 1.0" Snow Depth	1	1	0	0	0	0	0	0	0	0	0	0	2

The period of record for all cooperative weather station data is 1980 – 2009. See User Guide for detailed explanation of data.

Conway *Faulkner County* Elevation: 314 ft. Latitude: 35° 05' N Longitude: 92° 26' W

	JAN	FEB	MAR	APR	MAY	JUN	JUL	AUG	SEP	OCT	NOV	DEC	YEAR
Mean Maximum Temp. (°F)	50.3	55.9	64.8	73.7	80.5	88.3	92.9	92.8	85.6	74.4	62.9	52.0	72.8
Mean Temp. (°F)	40.3	44.6	53.3	61.9	69.9	77.7	81.9	81.4	73.9	62.3	51.9	42.2	61.8
Mean Minimum Temp. (°F)	30.2	33.4	41.7	50.1	59.2	67.1	70.9	69.9	62.2	50.0	40.9	32.3	50.7
Extreme Maximum Temp. (°F)	79	84	89	92	95	101	111	108	107	95	84	78	111
Extreme Minimum Temp. (°F)	-5	3	14	27	37	48	55	50	37	27	14	-2	-5
Days Maximum Temp. ≥ 90°F	0	0	0	0	2	13	22	22	10	1	0	0	70
Days Maximum Temp. ≤ 32°F	2	1	0	0	0	0	0	0	0	0	0	2	5
Days Minimum Temp. ≤ 32°F	19	14	6	0	0	0	0	0	0	1	7	17	64
Days Minimum Temp. ≤ 0°F	0	0	0	0	0	0	0	0	0	0	0	0	0
Heating Degree Days (base 65°F)	760	570	376	144	25	0	0	0	15	144	392	701	3,127
Cooling Degree Days (base 65°F)	1	1	15	59	182	388	531	515	289	66	7	1	2,055
Mean Precipitation (in.)	3.44	3.45	4.71	5.00	4.73	3.77	2.82	2.74	3.11	4.58	4.72	4.96	48.03
Extreme Maximum Daily Precip. (in.)	2.34	2.48	2.50	4.50	3.57	3.67	2.37	2.20	2.35	4.22	3.91	4.95	4.95
Days With ≥ 0.1" Precipitation	6	6	6	6	7	6	5	4	5	6	6	6	69
Days With ≥ 0.5" Precipitation	2	2	3	3	3	3	2	2	2	3	3	3	31
Days With ≥ 1.0" Precipitation	1	1	1	2	1	1	1	1	1	2	2	2	16
Mean Snowfall (in.)	1.4	1.4	0.2	trace	0.0	0.0	0.0	0.0	0.0	trace	0.1	0.5	3.6
Maximum Snow Depth (in.)	13	9	4	0	0	0	0	0	0	0	2	2	13
Days With ≥ 1.0" Snow Depth	1	1	0	0	0	0	0	0	0	0	0	0	2

Corning *Clay County* Elevation: 299 ft. Latitude: 36° 26' N Longitude: 90° 35' W

	JAN	FEB	MAR	APR	MAY	JUN	JUL	AUG	SEP	OCT	NOV	DEC	YEAR
Mean Maximum Temp. (°F)	45.3	50.7	60.5	71.0	79.7	87.6	91.1	90.2	83.6	72.3	59.5	47.5	69.9
Mean Temp. (°F)	36.6	41.3	50.3	60.2	69.3	77.4	81.0	79.4	71.9	60.6	49.9	39.1	59.7
Mean Minimum Temp. (°F)	28.0	31.8	40.0	49.3	58.9	67.2	70.8	68.6	60.1	48.8	40.3	30.6	49.5
Extreme Maximum Temp. (°F)	74	78	85	95	95	102	109	106	103	92	84	76	109
Extreme Minimum Temp. (°F)	-13	-1	9	26	36	48	53	48	35	24	14	-8	-13
Days Maximum Temp. ≥ 90°F	0	0	0	0	2	12	20	17	7	0	0	0	58
Days Maximum Temp. ≤ 32°F	4	2	0	0	0	0	0	0	0	0	0	3	9
Days Minimum Temp. ≤ 32°F	22	15	7	1	0	0	0	0	0	1	7	18	71
Days Minimum Temp. ≤ 0°F	0	0	0	0	0	0	0	0	0	0	0	0	0
Heating Degree Days (base 65°F)	873	665	459	188	35	1	0	0	24	181	449	797	3,672
Cooling Degree Days (base 65°F)	0	0	9	50	176	382	503	455	237	51	4	1	1,868
Mean Precipitation (in.)	3.21	3.80	4.34	4.49	4.65	3.28	3.57	2.74	3.37	4.34	4.73	4.50	47.02
Extreme Maximum Daily Precip. (in.)	4.47	3.22	4.13	3.79	4.30	3.01	4.93	3.26	7.52	6.18	3.76	4.03	7.52
Days With ≥ 0.1" Precipitation	5	6	7	7	7	5	6	4	4	6	7	6	70
Days With ≥ 0.5" Precipitation	2	3	3	3	3	2	3	2	2	3	3	3	32
Days With ≥ 1.0" Precipitation	1	1	1	1	1	1	1	1	1	1	1	1	12
Mean Snowfall (in.)	2.3	2.7	0.9	trace	0.0	0.0	0.0	0.0	0.0	trace	0.1	1.5	7.5
Maximum Snow Depth (in.)	7	8	5	trace	0	0	0	0	0	trace	3	7	8
Days With ≥ 1.0" Snow Depth	1	2	0	0	0	0	0	0	0	0	0	2	5

Crossett 2 SSE *Ashley County* Elevation: 180 ft. Latitude: 33° 07' N Longitude: 91° 57' W

	JAN	FEB	MAR	APR	MAY	JUN	JUL	AUG	SEP	OCT	NOV	DEC	YEAR
Mean Maximum Temp. (°F)	54.1	58.4	66.7	75.1	81.9	88.5	91.9	92.1	86.5	76.3	65.5	55.9	74.4
Mean Temp. (°F)	42.3	46.0	53.6	61.7	69.5	76.8	80.2	79.7	73.3	62.2	52.7	44.3	61.9
Mean Minimum Temp. (°F)	30.4	33.5	40.5	48.4	57.1	65.0	68.5	67.2	60.1	48.0	39.9	32.6	49.3
Extreme Maximum Temp. (°F)	80	84	88	95	93	102	105	107	105	94	85	85	107
Extreme Minimum Temp. (°F)	1	5	11	26	35	43	52	50	34	22	18	0	0
Days Maximum Temp. ≥ 90°F	0	0	0	0	2	14	23	22	11	1	0	0	73
Days Maximum Temp. ≤ 32°F	1	1	0	0	0	0	0	0	0	0	0	1	3
Days Minimum Temp. ≤ 32°F	19	15	8	1	0	0	0	0	0	2	8	18	71
Days Minimum Temp. ≤ 0°F	0	0	0	0	0	0	0	0	0	0	0	0	0
Heating Degree Days (base 65°F)	699	533	358	150	28	1	0	0	17	151	372	639	2,948
Cooling Degree Days (base 65°F)	2	2	13	58	173	361	478	462	271	71	11	3	1,905
Mean Precipitation (in.)	5.21	5.64	5.31	4.76	5.75	4.09	3.84	3.49	3.48	4.95	4.88	5.89	57.29
Extreme Maximum Daily Precip. (in.)	3.80	9.30	3.30	5.50	4.50	2.80	6.02	4.50	8.10	6.40	4.00	4.23	9.30
Days With ≥ 0.1" Precipitation	7	7	7	5	7	6	6	5	5	6	6	7	74
Days With ≥ 0.5" Precipitation	3	4	4	3	4	3	3	2	2	3	3	4	38
Days With ≥ 1.0" Precipitation	2	2	2	2	2	1	1	1	1	2	2	2	20
Mean Snowfall (in.)	0.2	0.0	0.0	0.0	0.0	0.0	0.0	0.0	0.0	0.0	0.0	0.1	0.3
Maximum Snow Depth (in.)	trace	trace	0	0	0	0	0	0	0	0	0	trace	trace
Days With ≥ 1.0" Snow Depth	0	0	0	0	0	0	0	0	0	0	0	0	0

Dardanelle *Yell County* Elevation: 370 ft. Latitude: 35° 14' N Longitude: 93° 10' W

	JAN	FEB	MAR	APR	MAY	JUN	JUL	AUG	SEP	OCT	NOV	DEC	YEAR
Mean Maximum Temp. (°F)	51.3	57.2	65.7	74.9	81.4	88.6	92.9	93.4	85.9	75.2	62.5	51.6	73.4
Mean Temp. (°F)	40.7	45.5	53.5	62.0	69.9	77.3	81.4	81.2	73.6	62.8	51.6	41.8	61.8
Mean Minimum Temp. (°F)	30.1	33.7	41.1	49.0	58.3	65.9	69.8	68.9	61.3	50.3	40.6	31.9	50.1
Extreme Maximum Temp. (°F)	78	82	87	94	96	101	110	109	106	92	85	78	110
Extreme Minimum Temp. (°F)	-5	-1	12	24	36	47	53	47	36	26	15	-3	-5
Days Maximum Temp. ≥ 90°F	0	0	0	1	2	13	24	23	10	0	0	0	73
Days Maximum Temp. ≤ 32°F	1	1	0	0	0	0	0	0	0	0	0	1	3
Days Minimum Temp. ≤ 32°F	19	13	7	1	0	0	0	0	0	1	7	17	65
Days Minimum Temp. ≤ 0°F	0	0	0	0	0	0	0	0	0	0	0	0	0
Heating Degree Days (base 65°F)	747	546	363	140	24	0	0	0	14	130	403	713	3,080
Cooling Degree Days (base 65°F)	1	1	12	56	182	376	515	508	280	68	7	1	2,007
Mean Precipitation (in.)	3.37	3.46	4.50	4.78	5.27	3.75	3.61	2.47	3.66	4.63	4.93	4.44	48.87
Extreme Maximum Daily Precip. (in.)	4.73	3.02	4.88	3.66	4.55	4.09	3.93	3.18	3.89	7.15	5.04	3.62	7.15
Days With ≥ 0.1" Precipitation	5	5	6	6	7	6	5	4	5	6	6	6	67
Days With ≥ 0.5" Precipitation	2	3	3	3	4	2	3	2	3	3	3	3	34
Days With ≥ 1.0" Precipitation	1	1	1	2	2	1	1	1	1	2	2	1	16
Mean Snowfall (in.)	1.3	1.1	0.8	trace	0.0	0.0	0.0	0.0	0.0	trace	trace	0.6	3.8
Maximum Snow Depth (in.)	14	5	12	trace	0	0	0	0	0	trace	trace	4	14
Days With ≥ 1.0" Snow Depth	1	1	0	0	0	0	0	0	0	0	0	1	3

The period of record for all cooperative weather station data is 1980 – 2009. See User Guide for detailed explanation of data.

Deer *Newton County* Elevation: 2,375 ft. Latitude: 35° 50' N Longitude: 93° 12' W

	JAN	FEB	MAR	APR	MAY	JUN	JUL	AUG	SEP	OCT	NOV	DEC	YEAR
Mean Maximum Temp. (°F)	42.4	47.2	55.3	64.1	70.8	78.1	83.0	83.5	75.8	65.1	54.7	44.0	63.7
Mean Temp. (°F)	33.3	37.3	45.0	54.0	62.2	70.1	74.9	74.9	67.0	56.2	45.7	35.3	54.7
Mean Minimum Temp. (°F)	24.2	27.3	34.7	43.8	53.6	62.0	66.7	66.2	58.2	47.3	36.8	26.6	45.6
Extreme Maximum Temp. (°F)	69	78	83	88	85	92	102	102	97	86	79	70	102
Extreme Minimum Temp. (°F)	-20	-10	1	16	33	44	52	45	32	15	4	-13	-20
Days Maximum Temp. ≥ 90°F	0	0	0	0	0	0	4	6	1	0	0	0	11
Days Maximum Temp. ≤ 32°F	7	4	1	0	0	0	0	0	0	0	1	5	18
Days Minimum Temp. ≤ 32°F	24	18	13	3	0	0	0	0	0	1	11	22	92
Days Minimum Temp. ≤ 0°F	1	1	0	0	0	0	0	0	0	0	0	1	3
Heating Degree Days (base 65°F)	976	778	613	335	124	16	1	4	62	283	571	913	4,676
Cooling Degree Days (base 65°F)	0	0	1	11	44	176	315	317	128	18	1	0	1,011
Mean Precipitation (in.)	3.48	3.72	5.31	5.20	6.49	4.48	3.33	3.17	4.59	4.96	6.01	4.43	55.17
Extreme Maximum Daily Precip. (in.)	5.20	4.00	7.29	5.50	4.62	3.20	2.75	3.49	7.06	5.10	9.56	8.62	9.56
Days With ≥ 0.1" Precipitation	5	5	7	7	9	7	6	5	6	6	6	6	75
Days With ≥ 0.5" Precipitation	2	2	4	3	4	3	2	2	3	3	3	3	34
Days With ≥ 1.0" Precipitation	1	1	2	2	2	1	1	1	2	2	2	1	18
Mean Snowfall (in.)	3.4	3.8	1.8	0.3	0.0	0.0	0.0	0.0	0.0	trace	0.3	1.8	11.4
Maximum Snow Depth (in.)	15	14	14	4	0	0	0	0	0	1	4	8	15
Days With ≥ 1.0" Snow Depth	5	5	1	0	0	0	0	0	0	0	0	3	14

Dequeen *Sevier County* Elevation: 419 ft. Latitude: 34° 02' N Longitude: 94° 21' W

	JAN	FEB	MAR	APR	MAY	JUN	JUL	AUG	SEP	OCT	NOV	DEC	YEAR
Mean Maximum Temp. (°F)	53.6	58.2	66.1	74.1	80.9	88.1	92.5	93.7	86.7	76.0	64.7	54.9	74.1
Mean Temp. (°F)	41.6	45.6	53.2	60.9	69.5	77.2	81.2	81.6	74.3	63.0	52.4	43.4	62.0
Mean Minimum Temp. (°F)	29.6	32.9	40.2	47.6	58.1	66.2	69.9	69.3	61.8	50.0	40.1	31.9	49.8
Extreme Maximum Temp. (°F)	79	88	88	96	96	102	107	108	108	94	88	82	108
Extreme Minimum Temp. (°F)	0	4	11	25	37	47	56	52	37	21	18	-3	-3
Days Maximum Temp. ≥ 90°F	0	0	0	0	2	13	24	24	11	1	0	0	75
Days Maximum Temp. ≤ 32°F	1	1	0	0	0	0	0	0	0	0	0	1	3
Days Minimum Temp. ≤ 32°F	21	15	8	1	0	0	0	0	0	1	8	19	73
Days Minimum Temp. ≤ 0°F	0	0	0	0	0	0	0	0	0	0	0	0	0
Heating Degree Days (base 65°F)	717	543	371	161	28	0	0	0	15	132	380	664	3,011
Cooling Degree Days (base 65°F)	1	1	11	45	175	372	510	520	299	76	10	2	2,022
Mean Precipitation (in.)	3.64	3.73	5.14	4.77	6.34	4.69	3.40	2.37	4.23	5.68	4.92	5.13	54.04
Extreme Maximum Daily Precip. (in.)	4.91	2.73	5.98	6.55	3.72	2.86	4.96	3.35	7.92	4.90	4.65	6.24	7.92
Days With ≥ 0.1" Precipitation	5	6	6	6	8	6	5	4	5	6	6	6	69
Days With ≥ 0.5" Precipitation	3	3	4	3	4	3	2	2	3	3	3	3	36
Days With ≥ 1.0" Precipitation	1	1	2	2	2	2	1	1	2	2	2	1	19
Mean Snowfall (in.)	1.3	0.8	0.1	0.0	0.0	0.0	0.0	0.0	0.0	0.0	trace	0.3	2.5
Maximum Snow Depth (in.)	10	6	3	0	0	0	0	0	0	0	1	6	10
Days With ≥ 1.0" Snow Depth	0	0	0	0	0	0	0	0	0	0	0	0	0

Des Arc *Prairie County* Elevation: 200 ft. Latitude: 34° 58' N Longitude: 91° 30' W

	JAN	FEB	MAR	APR	MAY	JUN	JUL	AUG	SEP	OCT	NOV	DEC	YEAR
Mean Maximum Temp. (°F)	48.7	53.6	62.5	72.6	80.5	88.4	92.2	91.8	84.4	74.0	61.8	50.9	71.8
Mean Temp. (°F)	40.2	44.3	52.8	62.3	71.0	78.8	82.3	81.2	73.4	62.6	52.3	42.4	62.0
Mean Minimum Temp. (°F)	31.6	35.0	43.0	51.9	61.2	69.2	72.4	70.7	62.3	51.2	42.6	33.8	52.1
Extreme Maximum Temp. (°F)	78	80	83	93	97	105	108	109	103	95	87	77	109
Extreme Minimum Temp. (°F)	-5	4	15	28	40	53	60	52	40	28	19	-2	-5
Days Maximum Temp. ≥ 90°F	0	0	0	0	3	15	22	21	8	1	0	0	70
Days Maximum Temp. ≤ 32°F	2	1	0	0	0	0	0	0	0	0	0	2	5
Days Minimum Temp. ≤ 32°F	18	11	4	0	0	0	0	0	0	0	4	14	51
Days Minimum Temp. ≤ 0°F	0	0	0	0	0	0	0	0	0	0	0	0	0
Heating Degree Days (base 65°F)	764	579	386	142	22	0	0	0	15	140	386	694	3,128
Cooling Degree Days (base 65°F)	1	1	13	66	214	421	542	510	274	72	10	1	2,125
Mean Precipitation (in.)	3.59	4.02	5.14	5.00	4.68	3.20	3.02	2.32	3.22	4.74	4.82	4.87	48.62
Extreme Maximum Daily Precip. (in.)	***2.65***	***3.44***	***3.10***	***4.18***	4.00	***2.97***	3.45	***3.26***	3.30	***4.60***	***6.50***	***6.02***	***6.50***
Days With ≥ 0.1" Precipitation	6	6	8	7	7	5	5	4	5	6	6	6	71
Days With ≥ 0.5" Precipitation	2	3	4	3	3	2	2	2	2	3	3	3	32
Days With ≥ 1.0" Precipitation	1	1	2	2	1	1	1	1	1	1	2	1	15
Mean Snowfall (in.)	***0.8***	0.8	0.2	0.0	0.0	0.0	0.0	0.0	0.0	0.0	trace	0.1	***1.9***
Maximum Snow Depth (in.)	***trace***	***trace***	***trace***	0	0	0	0	0	0	***0***	***trace***	1	***1***
Days With ≥ 1.0" Snow Depth	***0***	***0***	0	0	0	0	0	0	0	0	0	0	***0***

El Dorado Goodwin Field *Union County* Elevation: 251 ft. Latitude: 33° 13' N Longitude: 92° 49' W

	JAN	FEB	MAR	APR	MAY	JUN	JUL	AUG	SEP	OCT	NOV	DEC	YEAR
Mean Maximum Temp. (°F)	55.6	60.0	68.8	76.3	82.9	89.4	93.2	93.4	87.3	76.9	66.1	57.4	75.6
Mean Temp. (°F)	44.7	48.4	56.4	63.7	71.7	78.5	82.2	81.8	75.2	64.4	54.4	46.6	64.0
Mean Minimum Temp. (°F)	33.7	36.7	44.0	51.1	60.4	67.6	71.2	70.2	63.1	51.9	42.6	35.7	52.3
Extreme Maximum Temp. (°F)	82	88	91	96	97	102	106	112	110	94	85	82	112
Extreme Minimum Temp. (°F)	1	7	14	26	39	48	55	51	39	26	1	3	1
Days Maximum Temp. ≥ 90°F	0	0	0	1	4	17	25	25	13	2	0	0	87
Days Maximum Temp. ≤ 32°F	1	0	0	0	0	0	0	0	0	0	0	1	2
Days Minimum Temp. ≤ 32°F	16	11	5	1	0	0	0	0	0	1	6	14	54
Days Minimum Temp. ≤ 0°F	0	0	0	0	0	0	0	0	0	0	0	0	0
Heating Degree Days (base 65°F)	627	469	286	111	16	0	0	0	10	109	329	568	2,525
Cooling Degree Days (base 65°F)	3	5	26	79	229	413	540	529	323	97	17	5	2,266
Mean Precipitation (in.)	4.24	4.56	4.87	4.34	5.00	4.98	3.55	3.22	2.99	4.59	4.68	5.15	52.17
Extreme Maximum Daily Precip. (in.)	2.90	3.95	3.55	6.09	4.50	8.77	3.07	3.70	4.81	6.60	4.80	3.65	8.77
Days With ≥ 0.1" Precipitation	6	6	7	6	8	6	5	5	4	5	6	6	70
Days With ≥ 0.5" Precipitation	3	3	4	3	3	3	2	2	2	3	3	3	34
Days With ≥ 1.0" Precipitation	1	2	2	2	1	2	1	1	1	1	1	2	17
Mean Snowfall (in.)	na	na	na	na	na	na	na	na	na	na	na	na	na
Maximum Snow Depth (in.)	na	na	na	na	na	na	na	***0***	na	na	na	na	na
Days With ≥ 1.0" Snow Depth	na	na	na	na	na	na	na	***0***	na	na	na	na	na

The period of record for all cooperative weather station data is 1980 – 2009. See User Guide for detailed explanation of data.

Eudora *Chicot County* Elevation: 134 ft. Latitude: 33° 07' N Longitude: 91° 16' W

	JAN	FEB	MAR	APR	MAY	JUN	JUL	AUG	SEP	OCT	NOV	DEC	YEAR
Mean Maximum Temp. (°F)	54.1	58.4	66.9	75.2	83.6	90.3	93.3	93.3	87.9	78.1	66.8	56.9	75.4
Mean Temp. (°F)	44.0	47.9	55.9	63.7	72.7	79.9	82.6	82.0	75.9	65.4	55.2	46.6	64.3
Mean Minimum Temp. (°F)	33.9	37.5	44.8	52.1	61.9	69.4	71.8	70.6	63.9	52.6	43.5	36.2	53.2
Extreme Maximum Temp. (°F)	80	83	89	96	96	103	105	107	108	98	89	83	108
Extreme Minimum Temp. (°F)	3	10	16	29	37	52	59	54	42	27	21	3	3
Days Maximum Temp. ≥ 90°F	0	0	0	0	6	19	25	25	15	3	0	0	93
Days Maximum Temp. ≤ 32°F	1	1	0	0	0	0	0	0	0	0	0	1	3
Days Minimum Temp. ≤ 32°F	15	9	3	0	0	0	0	0	0	0	4	13	44
Days Minimum Temp. ≤ 0°F	0	0	0	0	0	0	0	0	0	0	0	0	0
Heating Degree Days (base 65°F)	646	479	299	118	12	0	0	0	9	96	308	569	2,536
Cooling Degree Days (base 65°F)	2	3	24	85	259	454	553	534	343	114	20	5	2,396
Mean Precipitation (in.)	5.30	5.35	5.20	5.75	5.17	3.65	3.74	3.42	3.65	4.83	5.28	5.92	57.26
Extreme Maximum Daily Precip. (in.)	4.18	4.45	3.27	4.84	5.04	3.73	4.60	6.00	5.70	5.80	5.50	7.48	7.48
Days With ≥ 0.1" Precipitation	7	7	7	6	7	6	5	5	5	5	6	7	73
Days With ≥ 0.5" Precipitation	3	4	3	4	3	3	2	2	2	3	3	4	36
Days With ≥ 1.0" Precipitation	2	2	2	2	2	1	1	1	1	2	2	2	20
Mean Snowfall (in.)	trace	0.0	0.0	0.0	0.0	0.0	0.0	0.0	0.0	0.0	0.0	trace	trace
Maximum Snow Depth (in.)	trace	trace	0	0	0	0	0	0	0	0	0	trace	trace
Days With ≥ 1.0" Snow Depth	0	0	0	0	0	0	0	0	0	0	0	0	0

Fayetteville Exp Stn *Washington County* Elevation: 1,270 ft. Latitude: 36° 06' N Longitude: 94° 10' W

	JAN	FEB	MAR	APR	MAY	JUN	JUL	AUG	SEP	OCT	NOV	DEC	YEAR
Mean Maximum Temp. (°F)	45.8	50.8	58.5	68.6	75.7	83.5	89.4	89.7	81.3	70.3	58.2	48.6	68.4
Mean Temp. (°F)	35.6	39.9	47.8	57.4	65.6	73.7	79.3	78.6	70.2	58.7	47.9	38.7	57.8
Mean Minimum Temp. (°F)	25.3	28.9	37.0	46.2	55.3	63.9	69.1	67.4	59.0	47.1	37.6	28.7	47.1
Extreme Maximum Temp. (°F)	75	86	87	93	91	100	107	102	103	89	82	75	107
Extreme Minimum Temp. (°F)	-13	-8	-4	21	33	44	50	47	29	19	8	-12	-13
Days Maximum Temp. ≥ 90°F	0	0	0	0	0	3	15	15	5	0	0	0	38
Days Maximum Temp. ≤ 32°F	4	3	1	0	0	0	0	0	0	0	0	3	11
Days Minimum Temp. ≤ 32°F	22	17	10	2	0	0	0	0	0	2	9	18	80
Days Minimum Temp. ≤ 0°F	1	0	0	0	0	0	0	0	0	0	0	1	2
Heating Degree Days (base 65°F)	902	704	533	253	76	8	0	1	47	220	509	809	4,062
Cooling Degree Days (base 65°F)	0	0	5	33	101	276	449	431	209	35	3	0	1,542
Mean Precipitation (in.)	2.12	2.56	3.98	3.89	5.12	4.96	2.95	3.02	4.43	4.06	4.26	3.00	44.35
Extreme Maximum Daily Precip. (in.)	3.35	2.62	4.28	3.85	3.07	7.80	4.05	5.50	4.49	5.01	3.87	4.82	7.80
Days With ≥ 0.1" Precipitation	3	4	6	6	8	7	5	4	6	5	5	4	63
Days With ≥ 0.5" Precipitation	1	2	3	3	4	3	2	2	3	2	3	2	30
Days With ≥ 1.0" Precipitation	1	1	1	1	1	2	1	1	1	1	1	1	13
Mean Snowfall (in.)	1.7	1.8	0.1	trace	0.0	0.0	0.0	0.0	0.0	trace	trace	0.7	4.3
Maximum Snow Depth (in.)	10	6	9	trace	0	0	0	0	0	0	2	6	10
Days With ≥ 1.0" Snow Depth	1	1	0	0	0	0	0	0	0	0	0	1	3

Fordyce *Dallas County* Elevation: 229 ft. Latitude: 33° 49' N Longitude: 92° 24' W

	JAN	FEB	MAR	APR	MAY	JUN	JUL	AUG	SEP	OCT	NOV	DEC	YEAR
Mean Maximum Temp. (°F)	52.7	57.2	65.8	74.0	81.0	87.2	91.3	92.1	85.3	74.8	64.2	54.2	73.3
Mean Temp. (°F)	41.3	45.0	53.2	61.2	69.4	76.1	80.2	80.0	72.9	62.1	52.1	42.9	61.4
Mean Minimum Temp. (°F)	29.8	32.8	40.6	48.4	57.6	65.1	69.0	67.9	60.5	49.2	40.0	31.7	49.4
Extreme Maximum Temp. (°F)	80	84	88	95	94	99	106	106	105	94	88	80	106
Extreme Minimum Temp. (°F)	-1	3	12	27	37	44	51	48	39	26	19	-2	-2
Days Maximum Temp. ≥ 90°F	0	0	0	0	2	12	22	22	9	1	0	0	68
Days Maximum Temp. ≤ 32°F	1	1	0	0	0	0	0	0	0	0	0	1	3
Days Minimum Temp. ≤ 32°F	21	15	7	1	0	0	0	0	0	1	7	19	71
Days Minimum Temp. ≤ 0°F	0	0	0	0	0	0	0	0	0	0	0	0	0
Heating Degree Days (base 65°F)	730	558	371	157	30	1	0	0	17	149	388	679	3,080
Cooling Degree Days (base 65°F)	1	1	12	51	173	342	478	473	261	65	8	1	1,866
Mean Precipitation (in.)	4.31	4.88	5.43	4.67	5.62	4.62	4.12	2.60	3.37	5.80	4.98	5.93	56.33
Extreme Maximum Daily Precip. (in.)	3.02	3.35	4.77	5.10	3.32	5.25	4.80	4.38	6.80	5.18	5.00	5.45	6.80
Days With ≥ 0.1" Precipitation	6	7	7	7	7	6	6	4	4	6	6	7	73
Days With ≥ 0.5" Precipitation	3	4	4	3	4	3	3	2	2	3	3	4	38
Days With ≥ 1.0" Precipitation	1	2	1	2	2	1	1	1	1	2	2	2	18
Mean Snowfall (in.)	0.6	trace	trace	0.0	0.0	0.0	0.0	0.0	0.0	0.0	0.0	0.1	0.7
Maximum Snow Depth (in.)	trace	1	trace	0	0	0	0	0	0	0	0	trace	1
Days With ≥ 1.0" Snow Depth	0	0	0	0	0	0	0	0	0	0	0	0	0

Gravette *Benton County* Elevation: 1,259 ft. Latitude: 36° 26' N Longitude: 94° 27' W

	JAN	FEB	MAR	APR	MAY	JUN	JUL	AUG	SEP	OCT	NOV	DEC	YEAR
Mean Maximum Temp. (°F)	47.9	53.3	62.5	71.5	78.5	85.8	91.6	91.7	83.2	71.8	60.0	49.2	70.6
Mean Temp. (°F)	37.2	41.8	50.4	59.1	66.8	74.3	79.1	78.6	70.4	59.7	49.1	39.0	58.8
Mean Minimum Temp. (°F)	26.4	30.3	38.2	46.6	55.0	62.8	66.5	65.5	57.6	47.6	38.1	28.6	46.9
Extreme Maximum Temp. (°F)	76	88	90	95	94	100	108	106	108	91	86	77	108
Extreme Minimum Temp. (°F)	-15	-14	-1	17	29	42	48	44	28	15	6	-16	-16
Days Maximum Temp. ≥ 90°F	0	0	0	0	1	7	21	20	7	0	0	0	56
Days Maximum Temp. ≤ 32°F	3	2	0	0	0	0	0	0	0	0	0	3	8
Days Minimum Temp. ≤ 32°F	22	17	10	3	0	0	0	0	0	2	10	20	84
Days Minimum Temp. ≤ 0°F	1	0	0	0	0	0	0	0	0	0	0	1	2
Heating Degree Days (base 65°F)	856	649	455	212	59	4	0	1	39	199	475	801	3,750
Cooling Degree Days (base 65°F)	0	0	8	41	122	291	443	429	207	42	4	0	1,587
Mean Precipitation (in.)	2.65	2.74	4.07	4.34	5.53	4.80	3.03	3.42	4.61	4.09	4.19	3.38	46.85
Extreme Maximum Daily Precip. (in.)	5.07	2.70	6.27	3.26	3.13	3.44	3.96	2.12	5.90	4.97	4.04	3.63	6.27
Days With ≥ 0.1" Precipitation	4	5	6	7	8	7	5	5	5	6	6	4	68
Days With ≥ 0.5" Precipitation	2	2	3	3	4	3	2	3	3	3	3	2	33
Days With ≥ 1.0" Precipitation	1	1	1	1	2	1	1	1	2	1	1	1	14
Mean Snowfall (in.)	4.6	3.3	2.7	trace	0.0	0.0	0.0	0.0	0.0	0.1	0.5	3.8	15.0
Maximum Snow Depth (in.)	10	9	15	trace	0	0	0	0	0	1	3	10	15
Days With ≥ 1.0" Snow Depth	4	3	1	0	0	0	0	0	0	0	0	3	11

The period of record for all cooperative weather station data is 1980 – 2009. See User Guide for detailed explanation of data.

Hot Springs 1 NNE *Garland County* Elevation: 680 ft. Latitude: 34° 31' N Longitude: 93° 03' W

	JAN	FEB	MAR	APR	MAY	JUN	JUL	AUG	SEP	OCT	NOV	DEC	YEAR
Mean Maximum Temp. (°F)	52.0	57.1	65.8	74.6	81.5	89.3	94.6	94.9	87.0	75.1	63.3	52.8	74.0
Mean Temp. (°F)	41.1	45.2	53.1	61.6	69.8	77.6	82.1	81.8	73.9	62.4	51.8	42.3	61.9
Mean Minimum Temp. (°F)	30.1	33.1	40.3	48.6	58.0	65.8	69.7	68.6	60.7	49.6	40.3	31.8	49.7
Extreme Maximum Temp. (°F)	80	87	89	97	98	106	114	115	112	96	86	78	115
Extreme Minimum Temp. (°F)	0	4	10	24	36	49	52	50	37	25	18	-5	-5
Days Maximum Temp. ≥ 90°F	0	0	0	1	4	16	25	24	13	2	0	0	85
Days Maximum Temp. ≤ 32°F	1	1	0	0	0	0	0	0	0	0	0	1	3
Days Minimum Temp. ≤ 32°F	20	14	7	1	0	0	0	0	0	1	7	17	67
Days Minimum Temp. ≤ 0°F	0	0	0	0	0	0	0	0	0	0	0	0	0
Heating Degree Days (base 65°F)	734	555	376	152	28	1	0	0	16	145	395	697	3,099
Cooling Degree Days (base 65°F)	1	2	13	57	183	385	538	527	290	71	6	1	2,074
Mean Precipitation (in.)	3.69	4.15	5.19	5.23	6.11	4.24	4.40	2.87	4.11	5.82	5.59	5.40	56.80
Extreme Maximum Daily Precip. (in.)	3.50	3.72	3.20	5.82	12.97	5.40	3.21	4.73	6.65	5.65	4.20	6.65	12.97
Days With ≥ 0.1" Precipitation	6	6	7	7	8	6	6	5	5	6	6	7	75
Days With ≥ 0.5" Precipitation	3	3	4	3	4	3	3	2	2	3	4	3	37
Days With ≥ 1.0" Precipitation	1	1	2	2	2	1	1	1	1	2	2	2	18
Mean Snowfall (in.)	1.0	0.2	0.1	trace	0.0	0.0	0.0	0.0	0.0	trace	trace	0.1	1.4
Maximum Snow Depth (in.)	9	9	1	trace	0	0	0	0	0	trace	0	trace	9
Days With ≥ 1.0" Snow Depth	0	0	0	0	0	0	0	0	0	0	0	0	0

Huntsville 1 SSW *Madison County* Elevation: 1,783 ft. Latitude: 36° 04' N Longitude: 93° 45' W

	JAN	FEB	MAR	APR	MAY	JUN	JUL	AUG	SEP	OCT	NOV	DEC	YEAR
Mean Maximum Temp. (°F)	46.9	51.4	59.9	69.2	75.5	82.8	***88.0***	87.9	79.9	69.6	58.3	47.9	***68.1***
Mean Temp. (°F)	37.6	41.8	49.6	58.7	66.1	73.5	***78.1***	77.5	69.9	59.9	49.2	39.0	***58.4***
Mean Minimum Temp. (°F)	28.4	32.1	39.3	48.1	56.6	64.0	***68.2***	67.2	59.8	50.2	40.0	30.1	***48.7***
Extreme Maximum Temp. (°F)	76	86	86	92	91	97	106	106	103	89	83	74	106
Extreme Minimum Temp. (°F)	-18	-5	0	22	36	46	53	45	34	17	3	-13	-18
Days Maximum Temp. ≥ 90°F	0	0	0	0	0	3	12	13	3	0	0	0	31
Days Maximum Temp. ≤ 32°F	4	2	0	0	0	0	0	0	0	0	0	3	9
Days Minimum Temp. ≤ 32°F	20	15	9	1	0	0	0	0	0	1	7	18	71
Days Minimum Temp. ≤ 0°F	0	0	0	0	0	0	0	0	0	0	0	0	0
Heating Degree Days (base 65°F)	840	651	476	218	64	4	***0***	1	35	191	472	799	***3,751***
Cooling Degree Days (base 65°F)	0	0	6	36	104	265	***413***	397	189	40	4	0	***1,454***
Mean Precipitation (in.)	2.66	2.89	4.38	5.06	4.86	4.47	3.18	3.31	4.08	4.08	4.89	3.25	47.11
Extreme Maximum Daily Precip. (in.)	3.25	2.72	6.05	4.75	3.10	2.60	***2.55***	5.15	6.05	4.85	6.95	3.30	***6.95***
Days With ≥ 0.1" Precipitation	5	5	8	7	9	7	6	5	6	6	6	6	76
Days With ≥ 0.5" Precipitation	2	2	3	3	4	3	2	2	2	3	3	3	32
Days With ≥ 1.0" Precipitation	1	1	1	2	1	2	1	1	1	1	2	1	15
Mean Snowfall (in.)	3.5	4.0	2.5	0.1	0.0	0.0	0.0	0.0	0.0	trace	0.2	2.1	12.4
Maximum Snow Depth (in.)	17	14	14	trace	0	0	0	0	0	trace	3	7	17
Days With ≥ 1.0" Snow Depth	2	2	1	0	0	0	0	0	0	0	0	2	7

Jonesboro 4 N *Craighead County* Elevation: 390 ft. Latitude: 35° 53' N Longitude: 90° 42' W

	JAN	FEB	MAR	APR	MAY	JUN	JUL	AUG	SEP	OCT	NOV	DEC	YEAR
Mean Maximum Temp. (°F)	46.4	51.6	61.3	71.5	80.1	88.1	91.4	90.6	83.9	73.3	60.0	48.7	70.6
Mean Temp. (°F)	37.4	41.9	50.7	60.3	69.1	77.4	81.1	79.9	72.5	61.4	50.0	39.8	60.1
Mean Minimum Temp. (°F)	28.4	32.3	40.0	49.0	58.0	66.7	70.8	69.3	61.1	49.5	40.0	30.9	49.7
Extreme Maximum Temp. (°F)	74	78	85	95	95	105	107	106	101	93	85	77	107
Extreme Minimum Temp. (°F)	-11	-1	9	22	37	48	54	50	40	23	15	-7	-11
Days Maximum Temp. ≥ 90°F	0	0	0	0	2	13	20	18	7	1	0	0	61
Days Maximum Temp. ≤ 32°F	4	2	0	0	0	0	0	0	0	0	0	2	8
Days Minimum Temp. ≤ 32°F	21	14	8	1	0	0	0	0	0	1	7	18	70
Days Minimum Temp. ≤ 0°F	0	0	0	0	0	0	0	0	0	0	0	0	0
Heating Degree Days (base 65°F)	849	646	445	182	37	0	0	0	18	163	447	775	3,562
Cooling Degree Days (base 65°F)	0	0	8	47	170	380	506	471	250	57	5	1	1,895
Mean Precipitation (in.)	3.31	3.70	4.25	4.96	4.72	3.06	3.48	2.80	3.12	4.66	4.74	4.55	47.35
Extreme Maximum Daily Precip. (in.)	2.63	3.85	3.89	3.15	4.17	2.93	3.45	3.09	3.30	4.02	4.06	4.78	4.78
Days With ≥ 0.1" Precipitation	6	6	7	7	7	5	5	4	4	6	6	6	69
Days With ≥ 0.5" Precipitation	2	2	3	4	3	2	2	2	2	3	3	3	31
Days With ≥ 1.0" Precipitation	1	1	1	2	1	1	1	1	1	2	2	1	15
Mean Snowfall (in.)	2.2	1.5	0.6	trace	0.0	0.0	0.0	0.0	0.0	trace	trace	0.5	4.8
Maximum Snow Depth (in.)	4	***5***	5	trace	0	0	0	0	0	trace	trace	3	***5***
Days With ≥ 1.0" Snow Depth	0	1	0	0	0	0	0	0	0	0	0	0	1

Keo *Lonoke County* Elevation: 229 ft. Latitude: 34° 36' N Longitude: 92° 00' W

	JAN	FEB	MAR	APR	MAY	JUN	JUL	AUG	SEP	OCT	NOV	DEC	YEAR
Mean Maximum Temp. (°F)	50.1	54.9	63.9	73.4	80.6	87.4	90.5	89.8	83.7	73.7	61.9	51.8	71.8
Mean Temp. (°F)	41.5	45.8	53.9	62.9	71.1	78.3	81.4	80.3	73.4	63.2	52.8	43.5	62.3
Mean Minimum Temp. (°F)	32.8	36.5	43.9	52.4	61.6	69.1	72.2	70.7	63.2	52.6	43.6	35.1	52.8
Extreme Maximum Temp. (°F)	80	83	87	93	96	100	105	104	101	90	83	78	105
Extreme Minimum Temp. (°F)	-2	2	15	29	42	54	60	51	41	30	20	0	-2
Days Maximum Temp. ≥ 90°F	0	0	0	0	1	10	19	17	6	0	0	0	53
Days Maximum Temp. ≤ 32°F	2	1	0	0	0	0	0	0	0	0	0	2	5
Days Minimum Temp. ≤ 32°F	16	10	4	0	0	0	0	0	0	0	4	13	47
Days Minimum Temp. ≤ 0°F	0	0	0	0	0	0	0	0	0	0	0	0	0
Heating Degree Days (base 65°F)	723	539	352	128	17	0	0	0	13	125	369	661	2,927
Cooling Degree Days (base 65°F)	1	2	16	71	213	406	514	480	274	75	9	2	2,063
Mean Precipitation (in.)	3.39	3.75	4.73	5.15	4.61	3.56	3.50	1.95	3.26	4.68	4.77	5.17	48.52
Extreme Maximum Daily Precip. (in.)	3.66	2.81	3.75	6.00	4.63	7.77	3.58	3.16	3.68	5.61	4.31	7.54	7.77
Days With ≥ 0.1" Precipitation	6	6	7	6	7	5	5	4	4	5	6	6	67
Days With ≥ 0.5" Precipitation	2	3	3	3	3	2	2	1	2	3	3	3	30
Days With ≥ 1.0" Precipitation	1	1	1	1	1	1	1	0	1	1	2	2	13
Mean Snowfall (in.)	1.8	1.5	0.3	0.0	0.0	0.0	0.0	0.0	0.0	0.0	0.1	0.2	3.9
Maximum Snow Depth (in.)	10	7	3	0	0	0	0	0	0	0	trace	1	10
Days With ≥ 1.0" Snow Depth	1	1	0	0	0	0	0	0	0	0	0	1	3

The period of record for all cooperative weather station data is 1980 – 2009. See User Guide for detailed explanation of data.

Morrilton *Conway County* Elevation: 339 ft. Latitude: 35° 09' N Longitude: 92° 46' W

	JAN	FEB	MAR	APR	MAY	JUN	JUL	AUG	SEP	OCT	NOV	DEC	YEAR
Mean Maximum Temp. (°F)	50.2	55.7	64.0	73.4	80.6	88.0	93.1	93.3	85.9	74.5	62.0	51.5	72.7
Mean Temp. (°F)	39.3	43.5	51.6	60.5	69.0	76.7	81.1	80.3	72.6	61.2	50.2	40.7	60.6
Mean Minimum Temp. (°F)	28.3	31.3	39.1	47.5	57.3	65.4	69.1	67.3	59.3	47.8	38.3	29.9	48.4
Extreme Maximum Temp. (°F)	79	85	90	96	95	104	115	110	109	94	86	78	115
Extreme Minimum Temp. (°F)	-6	-2	12	24	36	47	54	43	34	26	15	-6	-6
Days Maximum Temp. ≥ 90°F	0	0	0	1	2	12	23	23	10	1	0	0	72
Days Maximum Temp. ≤ 32°F	2	1	0	0	0	0	0	0	0	0	0	1	4
Days Minimum Temp. ≤ 32°F	22	16	8	1	0	0	0	0	0	2	9	20	78
Days Minimum Temp. ≤ 0°F	0	0	0	0	0	0	0	0	0	0	0	0	0
Heating Degree Days (base 65°F)	790	601	417	173	35	1	0	0	19	165	444	745	3,390
Cooling Degree Days (base 65°F)	0	1	8	44	165	359	506	482	254	53	6	1	1,879
Mean Precipitation (in.)	3.37	3.71	4.69	4.71	4.83	3.72	3.19	2.83	3.46	4.92	5.49	4.80	49.72
Extreme Maximum Daily Precip. (in.)	2.72	3.60	4.55	5.11	7.10	3.22	3.55	3.81	4.13	3.95	6.27	4.60	7.10
Days With ≥ 0.1" Precipitation	6	5	7	6	7	5	5	5	5	6	6	7	70
Days With ≥ 0.5" Precipitation	2	3	3	3	3	3	2	2	2	3	3	3	32
Days With ≥ 1.0" Precipitation	1	1	1	2	1	1	1	1	1	2	2	1	15
Mean Snowfall (in.)	0.8	1.0	0.5	trace	0.0	0.0	0.0	0.0	0.0	trace	trace	0.5	2.8
Maximum Snow Depth (in.)	12	7	1	trace	0	0	0	0	0	na	trace	1	na
Days With ≥ 1.0" Snow Depth	1	1	0	0	0	0	0	0	0	0	0	0	2

Mountainburg 2 NE *Crawford County* Elevation: 792 ft. Latitude: 35° 39' N Longitude: 94° 09' W

	JAN	FEB	MAR	APR	MAY	JUN	JUL	AUG	SEP	OCT	NOV	DEC	YEAR
Mean Maximum Temp. (°F)	51.0	56.2	64.3	73.4	80.3	86.8	91.9	92.6	84.4	73.8	62.1	51.9	72.4
Mean Temp. (°F)	39.5	43.6	51.2	59.9	67.9	74.9	79.1	78.8	71.2	60.4	50.2	40.5	59.8
Mean Minimum Temp. (°F)	27.9	30.9	38.0	46.3	55.4	62.9	66.3	65.0	57.9	47.0	37.9	28.8	47.0
Extreme Maximum Temp. (°F)	76	86	89	93	96	100	107	107	108	92	85	78	108
Extreme Minimum Temp. (°F)	-6	-4	6	20	33	41	53	44	33	18	13	-9	-9
Days Maximum Temp. ≥ 90°F	0	0	0	0	2	10	22	22	7	0	0	0	63
Days Maximum Temp. ≤ 32°F	1	1	0	0	0	0	0	0	0	0	0	1	3
Days Minimum Temp. ≤ 32°F	22	17	10	2	0	0	0	0	0	2	10	21	84
Days Minimum Temp. ≤ 0°F	0	0	0	0	0	0	0	0	0	0	0	0	0
Heating Degree Days (base 65°F)	784	600	428	185	45	1	0	1	22	178	438	752	3,434
Cooling Degree Days (base 65°F)	0	1	7	38	141	304	445	437	216	43	2	1	1,635
Mean Precipitation (in.)	3.49	3.47	4.81	5.38	5.79	4.80	3.64	3.21	4.83	4.57	4.93	3.63	52.55
Extreme Maximum Daily Precip. (in.)	4.34	3.11	4.41	6.41	4.72	3.95	3.18	4.53	3.90	3.90	5.11	2.66	6.41
Days With ≥ 0.1" Precipitation	5	5	7	7	8	7	5	4	6	6	6	6	72
Days With ≥ 0.5" Precipitation	2	2	3	4	4	3	2	2	3	3	3	3	34
Days With ≥ 1.0" Precipitation	1	1	2	2	2	2	1	1	2	1	2	1	18
Mean Snowfall (in.)	1.3	0.9	0.6	trace	0.0	0.0	0.0	0.0	0.0	0.0	trace	0.4	3.2
Maximum Snow Depth (in.)	9	4	5	trace	0	0	0	0	0	0	trace	4	9
Days With ≥ 1.0" Snow Depth	1	1	0	0	0	0	0	0	0	0	0	1	3

North Little Rock Arpt *Pulaski County* Elevation: 562 ft. Latitude: 34° 50' N Longitude: 92° 16' W

	JAN	FEB	MAR	APR	MAY	JUN	JUL	AUG	SEP	OCT	NOV	DEC	YEAR
Mean Maximum Temp. (°F)	49.6	54.4	63.4	72.7	80.2	88.1	92.4	92.1	84.4	73.2	61.6	51.3	71.9
Mean Temp. (°F)	41.2	45.4	53.8	62.7	70.8	78.6	82.7	82.1	74.5	63.6	52.8	43.1	62.6
Mean Minimum Temp. (°F)	32.7	36.4	44.1	52.6	61.4	69.1	72.9	72.0	64.5	53.9	43.9	35.0	53.2
Extreme Maximum Temp. (°F)	81	83	87	94	97	102	110	111	105	92	84	78	111
Extreme Minimum Temp. (°F)	-6	4	14	30	40	52	60	53	41	27	19	-2	-6
Days Maximum Temp. ≥ 90°F	0	0	0	0	2	14	22	21	8	0	0	0	67
Days Maximum Temp. ≤ 32°F	2	1	0	0	0	0	0	0	0	0	0	2	5
Days Minimum Temp. ≤ 32°F	16	10	3	0	0	0	0	0	0	0	3	12	44
Days Minimum Temp. ≤ 0°F	0	0	0	0	0	0	0	0	0	0	0	0	0
Heating Degree Days (base 65°F)	733	548	360	134	22	0	0	0	13	121	370	672	2,973
Cooling Degree Days (base 65°F)	1	1	18	72	209	415	554	536	305	85	10	1	2,207
Mean Precipitation (in.)	3.41	3.55	4.84	4.84	5.01	3.28	3.65	2.64	3.39	4.88	5.40	5.02	49.91
Extreme Maximum Daily Precip. (in.)	2.83	3.06	3.48	4.43	3.86	2.29	3.58	4.20	4.83	5.23	7.01	5.01	7.01
Days With ≥ 0.1" Precipitation	6	6	7	7	8	6	5	4	5	6	6	7	73
Days With ≥ 0.5" Precipitation	2	3	4	3	3	2	2	2	2	3	4	3	33
Days With ≥ 1.0" Precipitation	1	1	1	2	1	1	1	1	1	2	2	2	16
Mean Snowfall (in.)	1.6	1.6	0.4	trace	trace	trace	trace	0.0	0.0	trace	0.2	0.5	4.3
Maximum Snow Depth (in.)	12	8	5	trace	trace	trace	trace	0	0	trace	4	3	12
Days With ≥ 1.0" Snow Depth	1	1	0	0	0	0	0	0	0	0	0	1	3

Paragould 1 S *Greene County* Elevation: 270 ft. Latitude: 36° 02' N Longitude: 90° 30' W

	JAN	FEB	MAR	APR	MAY	JUN	JUL	AUG	SEP	OCT	NOV	DEC	YEAR
Mean Maximum Temp. (°F)	46.5	51.7	61.1	71.3	79.7	87.7	90.7	90.1	83.6	73.1	60.3	48.8	70.4
Mean Temp. (°F)	37.9	42.4	51.0	60.8	69.7	77.8	81.1	79.9	72.9	61.7	50.7	40.5	60.5
Mean Minimum Temp. (°F)	29.3	33.0	40.9	50.1	59.7	67.8	71.5	69.7	61.9	50.3	41.1	32.1	50.6
Extreme Maximum Temp. (°F)	73	78	89	93	94	101	106	105	100	92	82	77	106
Extreme Minimum Temp. (°F)	-14	1	5	19	40	50	54	50	36	28	16	-6	-14
Days Maximum Temp. ≥ 90°F	0	0	0	0	1	12	19	17	6	0	0	0	55
Days Maximum Temp. ≤ 32°F	4	1	0	0	0	0	0	0	0	0	0	2	7
Days Minimum Temp. ≤ 32°F	20	14	6	1	0	0	0	0	0	0	6	16	63
Days Minimum Temp. ≤ 0°F	0	0	0	0	0	0	0	0	0	0	0	0	0
Heating Degree Days (base 65°F)	832	632	434	170	28	1	0	0	17	154	426	753	3,447
Cooling Degree Days (base 65°F)	0	0	8	49	181	392	506	471	260	59	5	0	1,931
Mean Precipitation (in.)	3.57	3.76	4.45	5.01	4.84	3.66	3.48	3.17	3.21	4.77	5.00	5.08	50.00
Extreme Maximum Daily Precip. (in.)	2.60	3.46	4.04	3.41	4.39	2.53	3.80	4.22	2.71	4.27	3.60	5.48	5.48
Days With ≥ 0.1" Precipitation	6	6	7	7	8	6	5	5	5	6	7	7	75
Days With ≥ 0.5" Precipitation	3	2	3	4	3	3	2	2	2	3	4	4	35
Days With ≥ 1.0" Precipitation	1	1	1	2	1	1	1	1	1	2	1	1	14
Mean Snowfall (in.)	0.6	0.5	0.2	0.0	0.0	0.0	0.0	0.0	0.0	0.0	trace	0.3	1.6
Maximum Snow Depth (in.)	4	5	3	0	0	0	0	0	0	0	trace	5	5
Days With ≥ 1.0" Snow Depth	1	1	0	0	0	0	0	0	0	0	0	0	2

The period of record for all cooperative weather station data is 1980 – 2009. See User Guide for detailed explanation of data.

Pine Bluff *Jefferson County* Elevation: 214 ft. Latitude: 34° 14' N Longitude: 92° 01' W

	JAN	FEB	MAR	APR	MAY	JUN	JUL	AUG	SEP	OCT	NOV	DEC	YEAR
Mean Maximum Temp. (°F)	50.9	55.6	64.3	73.6	81.4	88.2	92.0	91.7	85.4	74.9	64.0	53.4	73.0
Mean Temp. (°F)	41.5	45.4	53.6	62.4	71.1	78.5	82.1	81.5	74.5	63.5	53.3	43.8	62.6
Mean Minimum Temp. (°F)	32.0	35.2	42.9	51.2	60.8	68.7	72.2	71.2	63.4	52.1	42.5	34.1	52.2
Extreme Maximum Temp. (°F)	79	82	87	94	95	101	108	105	103	94	85	80	108
Extreme Minimum Temp. (°F)	1	8	16	29	40	49	59	55	39	28	20	1	1
Days Maximum Temp. ≥ 90°F	0	0	0	0	3	14	22	21	10	1	0	0	71
Days Maximum Temp. ≤ 32°F	2	1	0	0	0	0	0	0	0	0	0	2	5
Days Minimum Temp. ≤ 32°F	17	12	4	0	0	0	0	0	0	0	5	15	53
Days Minimum Temp. ≤ 0°F	0	0	0	0	0	0	0	0	0	0	0	0	0
Heating Degree Days (base 65°F)	725	548	364	142	20	0	0	0	13	124	359	652	2,947
Cooling Degree Days (base 65°F)	2	2	17	71	217	412	538	517	304	87	13	2	2,182
Mean Precipitation (in.)	4.09	4.47	5.18	5.10	5.20	3.69	4.07	3.10	3.84	5.46	4.45	5.60	54.25
Extreme Maximum Daily Precip. (in.)	4.57	2.82	3.32	4.35	4.15	3.03	4.33	3.82	5.40	3.95	3.50	4.38	5.40
Days With ≥ 0.1" Precipitation	7	7	7	7	7	6	6	4	4	6	6	7	74
Days With ≥ 0.5" Precipitation	3	4	3	3	3	2	3	2	2	3	3	4	35
Days With ≥ 1.0" Precipitation	1	1	2	2	1	1	1	1	1	2	1	2	16
Mean Snowfall (in.)	0.7	***trace***	trace	trace	0.0	0.0	0.0	0.0	0.0	0.0	trace	0.2	***0.9***
Maximum Snow Depth (in.)	5	trace	trace	trace	0	0	0	0	0	0	0	trace	5
Days With ≥ 1.0" Snow Depth	0	0	0	0	0	0	0	0	0	0	0	0	0

Searcy *White County* Elevation: 245 ft. Latitude: 35° 14' N Longitude: 91° 50' W

	JAN	FEB	MAR	APR	MAY	JUN	JUL	AUG	SEP	OCT	NOV	DEC	YEAR
Mean Maximum Temp. (°F)	50.2	55.5	64.4	74.0	81.8	89.5	93.4	93.0	85.9	74.3	62.4	51.6	73.0
Mean Temp. (°F)	39.8	44.1	52.5	61.6	70.3	78.2	82.0	81.0	73.5	61.6	51.3	41.4	61.4
Mean Minimum Temp. (°F)	29.3	32.6	40.5	49.0	58.6	66.9	70.6	69.0	61.1	48.9	40.1	31.3	49.8
Extreme Maximum Temp. (°F)	79	83	88	97	97	104	110	109	104	98	85	79	110
Extreme Minimum Temp. (°F)	-7	0	11	24	39	48	55	48	36	24	17	-4	-7
Days Maximum Temp. ≥ 90°F	0	0	0	0	4	16	24	23	10	1	0	0	78
Days Maximum Temp. ≤ 32°F	2	1	0	0	0	0	0	0	0	0	0	2	5
Days Minimum Temp. ≤ 32°F	21	15	7	1	0	0	0	0	0	1	8	18	71
Days Minimum Temp. ≤ 0°F	0	0	0	0	0	0	0	0	0	0	0	0	0
Heating Degree Days (base 65°F)	776	587	394	155	25	0	0	0	16	159	412	725	3,249
Cooling Degree Days (base 65°F)	1	1	13	58	195	404	533	503	278	61	7	1	2,055
Mean Precipitation (in.)	3.66	3.49	4.92	5.13	5.54	2.91	3.69	2.62	3.52	4.71	5.18	5.02	50.39
Extreme Maximum Daily Precip. (in.)	3.31	2.02	3.81	4.55	6.26	3.69	2.93	2.85	4.75	4.89	6.74	3.81	6.74
Days With ≥ 0.1" Precipitation	6	6	7	7	8	6	6	4	5	6	6	7	74
Days With ≥ 0.5" Precipitation	2	2	4	3	4	2	3	2	2	3	3	3	33
Days With ≥ 1.0" Precipitation	1	1	1	2	2	1	1	1	1	2	2	2	17
Mean Snowfall (in.)	0.7	0.7	trace	0.0	0.0	0.0	0.0	0.0	0.0	trace	0.1	0.2	1.7
Maximum Snow Depth (in.)	14	7	2	0	0	0	0	0	0	trace	trace	1	14
Days With ≥ 1.0" Snow Depth	0	0	0	0	0	0	0	0	0	0	0	0	0

Sheridan *Grant County* Elevation: 250 ft. Latitude: 34° 18' N Longitude: 92° 24' W

	JAN	FEB	MAR	APR	MAY	JUN	JUL	AUG	SEP	OCT	NOV	DEC	YEAR
Mean Maximum Temp. (°F)	51.7	57.1	65.7	74.6	81.6	88.5	92.5	92.3	85.7	75.2	63.7	53.4	73.5
Mean Temp. (°F)	40.4	44.8	53.1	61.4	69.7	77.2	81.2	80.5	73.4	61.9	51.5	42.4	61.5
Mean Minimum Temp. (°F)	29.1	32.5	40.4	48.1	57.9	66.0	69.8	68.6	61.1	48.5	39.3	31.4	49.4
Extreme Maximum Temp. (°F)	80	86	88	96	97	101	108	107	108	94	85	79	108
Extreme Minimum Temp. (°F)	-3	2	14	26	36	45	55	48	37	25	18	-8	-8
Days Maximum Temp. ≥ 90°F	0	0	0	0	3	14	23	21	9	1	0	0	71
Days Maximum Temp. ≤ 32°F	1	1	0	0	0	0	0	0	0	0	0	1	3
Days Minimum Temp. ≤ 32°F	21	16	7	1	0	0	0	0	0	1	9	18	73
Days Minimum Temp. ≤ 0°F	0	0	0	0	0	0	0	0	0	0	0	0	0
Heating Degree Days (base 65°F)	757	566	379	160	26	0	0	0	16	154	404	696	3,158
Cooling Degree Days (base 65°F)	2	1	15	57	180	374	508	488	276	64	8	2	1,975
Mean Precipitation (in.)	3.95	4.27	5.18	5.28	5.16	3.77	4.44	2.40	3.81	4.94	4.97	5.39	53.56
Extreme Maximum Daily Precip. (in.)	4.80	3.73	5.08	8.08	4.85	6.00	4.29	2.70	7.50	7.16	3.55	4.10	8.08
Days With ≥ 0.1" Precipitation	6	6	7	6	7	6	6	4	5	6	6	7	72
Days With ≥ 0.5" Precipitation	3	3	3	4	3	3	3	2	2	3	3	3	35
Days With ≥ 1.0" Precipitation	1	2	2	2	2	1	2	1	1	2	2	2	20
Mean Snowfall (in.)	1.6	0.6	0.2	trace	0.0	0.0	0.0	0.0	0.0	trace	trace	0.4	2.8
Maximum Snow Depth (in.)	6	4	1	trace	0	0	0	0	0	trace	trace	4	6
Days With ≥ 1.0" Snow Depth	0	0	0	0	0	0	0	0	0	0	0	1	1

West Memphis *Crittenden County* Elevation: 214 ft. Latitude: 35° 07' N Longitude: 90° 11' W

	JAN	FEB	MAR	APR	MAY	JUN	JUL	AUG	SEP	OCT	NOV	DEC	YEAR
Mean Maximum Temp. (°F)	48.1	53.4	62.1	71.4	80.3	88.0	90.9	90.4	84.7	74.2	61.9	51.1	71.4
Mean Temp. (°F)	39.2	43.6	52.0	60.9	70.3	78.2	81.4	80.3	73.9	62.6	52.1	42.3	61.4
Mean Minimum Temp. (°F)	30.2	33.8	41.8	50.3	60.2	68.4	71.9	70.2	63.0	51.0	42.3	33.5	51.4
Extreme Maximum Temp. (°F)	74	78	85	94	93	101	105	104	100	95	85	79	105
Extreme Minimum Temp. (°F)	-9	-8	10	25	37	51	59	48	36	29	16	-5	-9
Days Maximum Temp. ≥ 90°F	0	0	0	0	2	13	20	19	8	1	0	0	63
Days Maximum Temp. ≤ 32°F	3	1	0	0	0	0	0	0	0	0	0	2	6
Days Minimum Temp. ≤ 32°F	19	13	5	1	0	0	0	0	0	0	6	15	59
Days Minimum Temp. ≤ 0°F	0	0	0	0	0	0	0	0	0	0	0	0	0
Heating Degree Days (base 65°F)	793	598	407	171	27	0	0	0	17	143	388	696	3,240
Cooling Degree Days (base 65°F)	0	0	10	56	197	402	516	482	289	75	10	1	2,038
Mean Precipitation (in.)	3.83	3.97	5.13	5.41	5.13	3.91	3.52	2.81	3.28	4.44	5.34	6.09	52.86
Extreme Maximum Daily Precip. (in.)	3.20	3.20	3.88	3.15	4.34	2.61	2.23	2.65	3.52	5.72	6.44	7.25	7.25
Days With ≥ 0.1" Precipitation	7	6	7	7	7	6	5	4	5	5	7	7	73
Days With ≥ 0.5" Precipitation	3	3	3	4	4	3	2	2	2	3	3	4	36
Days With ≥ 1.0" Precipitation	1	1	2	2	2	1	1	1	1	1	2	2	17
Mean Snowfall (in.)	1.2	0.7	0.0	0.0	0.0	0.0	0.0	0.0	0.0	0.0	0.0	0.1	2.0
Maximum Snow Depth (in.)	3	***5***	4	0	0	0	0	0	0	0	0	1	***5***
Days With ≥ 1.0" Snow Depth	0	0	0	0	0	0	0	0	0	0	0	0	0

The period of record for all cooperative weather station data is 1980 – 2009. See User Guide for detailed explanation of data.

Arkansas Weather Station Rankings

Annual Extreme Maximum Temperature

Highest			Lowest		
Rank	**Station Name**	**°F**	**Rank**	**Station Name**	**°F**
1	Hot Springs 1 NNE	115	1	Deer	102
1	Morrilton	***115***	2	Keo	105
3	Alicia	113	2	West Memphis	105
4	Beedeville 4 NE	112	4	Arkansas Post	106
4	Benton	112	4	Bentonville 4 S	106
4	Blue Mountain Dam	112	4	Fordyce	106
4	Cabot 4 SW	112	4	Huntsville 1 SSW	106
4	El Dorado Goodwin Field	112	4	Paragould 1 S	106
4	Little Rock Adams Field	112	9	Crossett 2 SSE	107
10	Batesville Livestock	111	9	Fayetteville Exp Stn	***107***
10	Blakely Mountain Dam	111	9	Jonesboro 4 N	107
10	Conway	111	12	Blytheville	108
10	North Little Rock Arpt	111	12	Dequeen	108
14	Alum Fork	110	12	Eudora	108
14	Dardanelle	110	12	Gravette	108
14	Searcy	110	12	Mountainburg 2 NE	***108***
17	Arkadelphia 2 N	109	12	Pine Bluff	108
17	Corning	109	12	Sheridan	108
17	Des Arc	109	19	Arkadelphia 2 N	109
17	Fort Smith Regional Arpt	109	19	Corning	109
21	Blytheville	108	19	Des Arc	109
21	Dequeen	108	19	Fort Smith Regional Arpt	109
21	Eudora	108	23	Alum Fork	110
21	Gravette	108	23	Dardanelle	110
21	Mountainburg 2 NE	***108***	23	Searcy	110

Annual Mean Maximum Temperature

Highest			Lowest		
Rank	**Station Name**	**°F**	**Rank**	**Station Name**	**°F**
1	El Dorado Goodwin Field	75.6	1	Deer	63.7
2	Eudora	75.4	2	Huntsville 1 SSW	***68.1***
3	Arkadelphia 2 N	74.4	3	Fayetteville Exp Stn	***68.4***
3	Crossett 2 SSE	74.4	4	Bentonville 4 S	68.5
5	Dequeen	74.1	5	Corning	69.9
6	Hot Springs 1 NNE	74.0	6	Blytheville	70.1
7	Benton	73.9	7	Paragould 1 S	70.4
8	Sheridan	73.5	8	Gravette	70.6
9	Dardanelle	73.4	8	Jonesboro 4 N	70.6
10	Fordyce	73.3	10	Beedeville 4 NE	71.0
11	Pine Bluff	73.0	11	Alicia	71.4
11	Searcy	73.0	11	West Memphis	71.4
13	Little Rock Adams Field	72.9	13	Des Arc	71.8
14	Arkansas Post	72.8	13	Keo	71.8
14	Conway	72.8	15	Batesville Livestock	72.0
16	Fort Smith Regional Arpt	72.7	15	Blakely Mountain Dam	***72.0***
16	Morrilton	***72.7***	15	North Little Rock Arpt	72.0
18	Mountainburg 2 NE	***72.4***	18	Cabot 4 SW	72.1
19	Alum Fork	72.3	19	Alum Fork	72.3
19	Blue Mountain Dam	72.3	19	Blue Mountain Dam	72.3
21	Cabot 4 SW	72.1	21	Mountainburg 2 NE	***72.4***
22	Batesville Livestock	72.0	22	Fort Smith Regional Arpt	72.7
22	Blakely Mountain Dam	***72.0***	22	Morrilton	***72.7***
22	North Little Rock Arpt	72.0	24	Arkansas Post	72.8
25	Des Arc	71.8	24	Conway	72.8

Rankings include 25 highest/lowest stations. If state has less than 25 stations, all stations are included. The period of record is 1980–2009. See User Guide for detailed explanation of data.

Annual Mean Temperature

Highest			Lowest		
Rank	Station Name	°F	Rank	Station Name	°F
1	Eudora	64.3	1	Deer	54.7
2	El Dorado Goodwin Field	64.0	2	Bentonville 4 S	56.7
3	Arkansas Post	63.3	3	Fayetteville Exp Stn	***57.8***
4	Little Rock Adams Field	62.6	4	Huntsville 1 SSW	***58.4***
4	North Little Rock Arpt	62.6	5	Gravette	58.8
4	Pine Bluff	62.6	6	Blakely Mountain Dam	***59.6***
7	Arkadelphia 2 N	***62.4***	7	Corning	59.8
8	Keo	62.3	7	Mountainburg 2 NE	***59.8***
9	Benton	62.1	9	Jonesboro 4 N	60.1
10	Dequeen	62.0	10	Batesville Livestock	60.4
10	Des Arc	62.0	11	Paragould 1 S	60.5
12	Crossett 2 SSE	61.9	12	Alicia	60.6
12	Hot Springs 1 NNE	61.9	12	Morrilton	***60.6***
14	Conway	61.8	14	Blytheville	60.7
14	Dardanelle	61.8	15	Cabot 4 SW	60.8
16	Fort Smith Regional Arpt	61.5	16	Blue Mountain Dam	60.9
16	Sheridan	61.5	17	Beedeville 4 NE	61.0
18	Fordyce	61.4	18	Alum Fork	61.3
18	Searcy	61.4	19	Fordyce	61.4
18	West Memphis	61.4	19	Searcy	61.4
21	Alum Fork	61.3	19	West Memphis	61.4
22	Beedeville 4 NE	61.0	22	Fort Smith Regional Arpt	61.5
23	Blue Mountain Dam	60.9	22	Sheridan	61.5
24	Cabot 4 SW	60.8	24	Conway	61.8
25	Blytheville	60.7	24	Dardanelle	61.8

Annual Mean Minimum Temperature

Highest			Lowest		
Rank	Station Name	°F	Rank	Station Name	°F
1	Arkansas Post	53.7	1	Bentonville 4 S	44.8
2	Eudora	53.2	2	Deer	45.6
2	North Little Rock Arpt	53.2	3	Gravette	46.9
4	Keo	52.8	4	Mountainburg 2 NE	***47.0***
5	El Dorado Goodwin Field	52.3	5	Blakely Mountain Dam	***47.1***
6	Little Rock Adams Field	52.2	5	Fayetteville Exp Stn	***47.1***
6	Pine Bluff	52.2	7	Morrilton	***48.4***
8	Des Arc	52.1	8	Huntsville 1 SSW	***48.7***
9	West Memphis	51.4	9	Batesville Livestock	48.8
10	Blytheville	51.3	10	Crossett 2 SSE	49.3
11	Beedeville 4 NE	50.9	11	Blue Mountain Dam	49.4
12	Conway	50.7	11	Fordyce	49.4
13	Paragould 1 S	50.6	11	Sheridan	49.4
14	Arkadelphia 2 N	***50.3***	14	Cabot 4 SW	49.5
14	Fort Smith Regional Arpt	50.3	14	Corning	49.5
16	Alum Fork	50.2	16	Hot Springs 1 NNE	49.7
16	Benton	50.2	16	Jonesboro 4 N	49.7
18	Dardanelle	50.1	18	Alicia	49.8
19	Alicia	49.8	18	Dequeen	49.8
19	Dequeen	49.8	18	Searcy	49.8
19	Searcy	49.8	21	Dardanelle	50.1
22	Hot Springs 1 NNE	49.7	22	Alum Fork	50.2
22	Jonesboro 4 N	49.7	22	Benton	50.2
24	Cabot 4 SW	49.5	24	Arkadelphia 2 N	***50.3***
24	Corning	49.5	24	Fort Smith Regional Arpt	50.3

Rankings include 25 highest/lowest stations. If state has less than 25 stations, all stations are included. The period of record is 1980–2009. See User Guide for detailed explanation of data.

Annual Extreme Minimum Temperature

Highest			Lowest		
Rank	Station Name	°F	Rank	Station Name	°F
1	Eudora	3	1	Deer	-20
2	Arkansas Post	1	2	Huntsville 1 SSW	-18
2	El Dorado Goodwin Field	1	3	Bentonville 4 S	-16
2	Pine Bluff	1	3	Gravette	-16
5	Arkadelphia 2 N	0	5	Blytheville	-14
5	Blakely Mountain Dam	0	5	Paragould 1 S	-14
5	Crossett 2 SSE	0	7	Corning	-13
8	Fordyce	-2	7	Fayetteville Exp Stn	***-13***
8	Keo	-2	9	Batesville Livestock	-11
8	Little Rock Adams Field	-2	9	Jonesboro 4 N	-11
11	Alum Fork	-3	11	Alicia	-10
11	Benton	-3	12	Mountainburg 2 NE	***-9***
11	Blue Mountain Dam	-3	12	West Memphis	-9
11	Dequeen	-3	14	Sheridan	-8
15	Conway	-5	15	Cabot 4 SW	-7
15	Dardanelle	-5	15	Searcy	-7
15	Des Arc	-5	17	Beedeville 4 NE	-6
15	Fort Smith Regional Arpt	-5	17	Morrilton	***-6***
15	Hot Springs 1 NNE	-5	17	North Little Rock Arpt	-6
20	Beedeville 4 NE	-6	20	Conway	-5
20	Morrilton	***-6***	20	Dardanelle	-5
20	North Little Rock Arpt	-6	20	Des Arc	-5
23	Cabot 4 SW	-7	20	Fort Smith Regional Arpt	-5
23	Searcy	-7	20	Hot Springs 1 NNE	-5
25	Sheridan	-8	25	Alum Fork	-3

July Mean Maximum Temperature

Highest			Lowest		
Rank	Station Name	°F	Rank	Station Name	°F
1	Hot Springs 1 NNE	94.6	1	Deer	83.0
2	Searcy	93.4	2	Huntsville 1 SSW	***88.0***
3	Eudora	93.3	3	Bentonville 4 S	89.4
3	Fort Smith Regional Arpt	93.3	3	Fayetteville Exp Stn	***89.4***
5	Blue Mountain Dam	93.2	5	Keo	90.5
5	El Dorado Goodwin Field	93.2	6	Paragould 1 S	90.7
7	Morrilton	93.1	7	West Memphis	90.9
8	Conway	92.9	8	Arkansas Post	91.0
8	Dardanelle	92.9	9	Corning	91.1
10	Benton	92.7	10	Blytheville	91.2
10	Little Rock Adams Field	92.7	10	Cabot 4 SW	91.2
12	Arkadelphia 2 N	92.5	12	Alum Fork	91.3
12	Dequeen	92.5	12	Fordyce	91.3
12	Sheridan	92.5	14	Jonesboro 4 N	91.4
15	Batesville Livestock	92.4	15	Beedeville 4 NE	91.5
15	North Little Rock Arpt	92.4	16	Gravette	91.6
17	Alicia	92.3	17	Blakely Mountain Dam	91.7
18	Des Arc	92.2	18	Crossett 2 SSE	91.9
19	Pine Bluff	92.0	18	Mountainburg 2 NE	***91.9***
20	Crossett 2 SSE	91.9	20	Pine Bluff	92.0
20	Mountainburg 2 NE	***91.9***	21	Des Arc	92.2
22	Blakely Mountain Dam	91.7	22	Alicia	92.3
23	Gravette	91.6	23	Batesville Livestock	92.4
24	Beedeville 4 NE	91.5	23	North Little Rock Arpt	92.4
25	Jonesboro 4 N	91.4	25	Arkadelphia 2 N	92.5

January Mean Minimum Temperature

Highest			Lowest		
Rank	Station Name	°F	Rank	Station Name	°F
1	Arkansas Post	33.9	1	Bentonville 4 S	23.8
1	Eudora	33.9	2	Deer	24.2
3	El Dorado Goodwin Field	33.7	3	Fayetteville Exp Stn	***25.4***
4	Keo	32.8	4	Gravette	26.4
5	North Little Rock Arpt	32.7	5	Mountainburg 2 NE	***27.9***
6	Pine Bluff	32.0	6	Corning	28.0
7	Little Rock Adams Field	31.9	7	Blakely Mountain Dam	28.2
8	Des Arc	31.6	8	Morrilton	28.3
9	Arkadelphia 2 N	31.0	9	Huntsville 1 SSW	28.4
10	Beedeville 4 NE	30.7	9	Jonesboro 4 N	28.4
11	Alum Fork	30.5	11	Batesville Livestock	28.6
12	Crossett 2 SSE	30.4	12	Alicia	28.9
13	Benton	30.3	12	Fort Smith Regional Arpt	28.9
14	Conway	30.2	14	Blue Mountain Dam	29.1
14	West Memphis	30.2	14	Sheridan	29.1
16	Dardanelle	30.1	16	Paragould 1 S	29.3
16	Hot Springs 1 NNE	30.1	16	Searcy	29.3
18	Cabot 4 SW	30.0	18	Blytheville	29.5
19	Fordyce	29.8	19	Dequeen	29.6
20	Dequeen	29.6	20	Fordyce	29.8
21	Blytheville	29.5	21	Cabot 4 SW	30.0
22	Paragould 1 S	29.3	22	Dardanelle	30.1
22	Searcy	29.3	22	Hot Springs 1 NNE	30.1
24	Blue Mountain Dam	29.1	24	Conway	30.2
24	Sheridan	29.1	24	West Memphis	30.2

Number of Days Annually Maximum Temperature ≥ 90°F

Highest			Lowest		
Rank	Station Name	Days	Rank	Station Name	Days
1	Eudora	93	1	Deer	11
2	El Dorado Goodwin Field	87	2	Huntsville 1 SSW	31
3	Hot Springs 1 NNE	85	3	Fayetteville Exp Stn	***38***
4	Searcy	78	4	Bentonville 4 S	44
5	Dequeen	75	5	Keo	53
5	Fort Smith Regional Arpt	75	6	Paragould 1 S	55
5	Little Rock Adams Field	75	7	Gravette	56
8	Blue Mountain Dam	73	8	Alum Fork	57
8	Crossett 2 SSE	73	8	Blakely Mountain Dam	57
8	Dardanelle	73	10	Cabot 4 SW	58
11	Arkadelphia 2 N	72	10	Corning	58
11	Morrilton	***72***	12	Arkansas Post	59
13	Benton	71	13	Jonesboro 4 N	61
13	Pine Bluff	71	14	Beedeville 4 NE	62
13	Sheridan	71	14	Blytheville	62
16	Conway	70	16	Mountainburg 2 NE	***63***
16	Des Arc	70	16	West Memphis	63
18	Batesville Livestock	68	18	Alicia	66
18	Fordyce	68	19	North Little Rock Arpt	67
20	North Little Rock Arpt	67	20	Batesville Livestock	68
21	Alicia	66	20	Fordyce	68
22	Mountainburg 2 NE	***63***	22	Conway	70
22	West Memphis	63	22	Des Arc	70
24	Beedeville 4 NE	62	24	Benton	71
24	Blytheville	62	24	Pine Bluff	71

Rankings include 25 highest/lowest stations. If state has less than 25 stations, all stations are included. The period of record is 1980–2009. See User Guide for detailed explanation of data.

Number of Days Annually Maximum Temperature ≤ 32°F

Highest

Rank	Station Name	Days
1	Deer	18
2	Bentonville 4 S	13
3	Fayetteville Exp Stn	*11*
4	Blytheville	9
4	Corning	9
4	Huntsville 1 SSW	9
7	Gravette	8
7	Jonesboro 4 N	8
9	Paragould 1 S	7
10	Alicia	6
10	Beedeville 4 NE	6
10	West Memphis	6
13	Batesville Livestock	5
13	Blue Mountain Dam	5
13	Cabot 4 SW	5
13	Conway	5
13	Des Arc	5
13	Fort Smith Regional Arpt	5
13	Keo	5
13	Little Rock Adams Field	5
13	North Little Rock Arpt	5
13	Pine Bluff	5
13	Searcy	5
24	Alum Fork	4
24	Morrilton	*4*

Lowest

Rank	Station Name	Days
1	El Dorado Goodwin Field	2
2	Arkadelphia 2 N	3
2	Arkansas Post	3
2	Benton	3
2	Blakely Mountain Dam	3
2	Crossett 2 SSE	3
2	Dardanelle	3
2	Dequeen	3
2	Eudora	3
2	Fordyce	3
2	Hot Springs 1 NNE	3
2	Mountainburg 2 NE	*3*
2	Sheridan	3
14	Alum Fork	4
14	Morrilton	*4*
16	Batesville Livestock	5
16	Blue Mountain Dam	5
16	Cabot 4 SW	5
16	Conway	5
16	Des Arc	5
16	Fort Smith Regional Arpt	5
16	Keo	5
16	Little Rock Adams Field	5
16	North Little Rock Arpt	5
16	Pine Bluff	5

Number of Days Annually Minimum Temperature ≤ 32°F

Highest

Rank	Station Name	Days
1	Bentonville 4 S	102
2	Deer	92
3	Gravette	84
3	Mountainburg 2 NE	*84*
5	Fayetteville Exp Stn	*80*
6	Blakely Mountain Dam	78
6	Morrilton	*78*
8	Batesville Livestock	73
8	Dequeen	73
8	Sheridan	73
11	Blue Mountain Dam	71
11	Corning	71
11	Crossett 2 SSE	71
11	Fordyce	71
11	Huntsville 1 SSW	71
11	Searcy	71
17	Jonesboro 4 N	70
18	Fort Smith Regional Arpt	69
19	Cabot 4 SW	68
20	Alicia	67
20	Hot Springs 1 NNE	67
22	Dardanelle	65
23	Alum Fork	64
23	Conway	64
25	Paragould 1 S	63

Lowest

Rank	Station Name	Days
1	Arkansas Post	41
2	Eudora	44
2	North Little Rock Arpt	44
4	Keo	47
5	Des Arc	51
6	Little Rock Adams Field	52
7	Pine Bluff	53
8	El Dorado Goodwin Field	54
9	Beedeville 4 NE	59
9	Blytheville	59
9	West Memphis	59
12	Arkadelphia 2 N	61
12	Benton	61
14	Paragould 1 S	63
15	Alum Fork	64
15	Conway	64
17	Dardanelle	65
18	Alicia	67
18	Hot Springs 1 NNE	67
20	Cabot 4 SW	68
21	Fort Smith Regional Arpt	69
22	Jonesboro 4 N	70
23	Blue Mountain Dam	71
23	Corning	71
23	Crossett 2 SSE	71

Rankings include 25 highest/lowest stations. If state has less than 25 stations, all stations are included. The period of record is 1980–2009. See User Guide for detailed explanation of data.

Number of Days Annually Minimum Temperature ≤ 0°F

Highest			Lowest		
Rank	Station Name	Days	Rank	Station Name	Days
1	Deer	3	1	Alicia	0
2	Bentonville 4 S	2	1	Alum Fork	0
2	Fayetteville Exp Stn	***2***	1	Arkadelphia 2 N	0
2	Gravette	2	1	Arkansas Post	0
5	Alicia	0	1	Batesville Livestock	0
5	Alum Fork	0	1	Beedeville 4 NE	0
5	Arkadelphia 2 N	0	1	Benton	0
5	Arkansas Post	0	1	Blakely Mountain Dam	0
5	Batesville Livestock	0	1	Blue Mountain Dam	0
5	Beedeville 4 NE	0	1	Blytheville	0
5	Benton	0	1	Cabot 4 SW	0
5	Blakely Mountain Dam	0	1	Conway	0
5	Blue Mountain Dam	0	1	Corning	0
5	Blytheville	0	1	Crossett 2 SSE	0
5	Cabot 4 SW	0	1	Dardanelle	0
5	Conway	0	1	Dequeen	0
5	Corning	0	1	Des Arc	0
5	Crossett 2 SSE	0	1	El Dorado Goodwin Field	0
5	Dardanelle	0	1	Eudora	0
5	Dequeen	0	1	Fordyce	0
5	Des Arc	0	1	Fort Smith Regional Arpt	0
5	El Dorado Goodwin Field	0	1	Hot Springs 1 NNE	0
5	Eudora	0	1	Huntsville 1 SSW	0
5	Fordyce	0	1	Jonesboro 4 N	0
5	Fort Smith Regional Arpt	0	1	Keo	0

Number of Annual Heating Degree Days

Highest			Lowest		
Rank	Station Name	Num.	Rank	Station Name	Num.
1	Deer	4,676	1	El Dorado Goodwin Field	2,525
2	Bentonville 4 S	4,297	2	Eudora	2,536
3	Fayetteville Exp Stn	***4,062***	3	Arkansas Post	2,710
4	Huntsville 1 SSW	***3,751***	4	Arkadelphia 2 N	***2,860***
5	Gravette	3,750	5	Keo	2,927
6	Corning	3,672	6	Pine Bluff	2,947
7	Jonesboro 4 N	3,562	7	Crossett 2 SSE	2,948
8	Blytheville	3,505	8	Benton	2,951
9	Blakely Mountain Dam	***3,462***	9	Little Rock Adams Field	2,966
10	Alicia	3,449	10	North Little Rock Arpt	2,973
11	Paragould 1 S	3,447	11	Dequeen	3,011
12	Mountainburg 2 NE	***3,434***	12	Dardanelle	3,080
13	Batesville Livestock	3,403	12	Fordyce	3,080
14	Morrilton	***3,390***	14	Hot Springs 1 NNE	3,099
15	Blue Mountain Dam	3,350	15	Alum Fork	3,117
16	Beedeville 4 NE	3,320	16	Conway	3,127
17	Cabot 4 SW	3,255	17	Des Arc	3,128
18	Searcy	3,249	18	Sheridan	3,158
19	West Memphis	3,240	19	Fort Smith Regional Arpt	3,230
20	Fort Smith Regional Arpt	3,230	20	West Memphis	3,240
21	Sheridan	3,158	21	Searcy	3,249
22	Des Arc	3,128	22	Cabot 4 SW	3,255
23	Conway	3,127	23	Beedeville 4 NE	3,320
24	Alum Fork	3,117	24	Blue Mountain Dam	3,350
25	Hot Springs 1 NNE	3,099	25	Morrilton	***3,390***

Rankings include 25 highest/lowest stations. If state has less than 25 stations, all stations are included. The period of record is 1980–2009. See User Guide for detailed explanation of data.

Number of Annual Cooling Degree Days

Highest Rank	Station Name	Num.	Lowest Rank	Station Name	Num.
1	Eudora	2,396	1	Deer	1,011
2	El Dorado Goodwin Field	2,266	2	Bentonville 4 S	1,376
3	North Little Rock Arpt	2,207	3	Huntsville 1 SSW	***1,454***
4	Little Rock Adams Field	2,194	4	Fayetteville Exp Stn	***1,542***
5	Arkansas Post	2,182	5	Blakely Mountain Dam	***1,580***
5	Pine Bluff	2,182	6	Gravette	1,587
7	Des Arc	2,125	7	Mountainburg 2 NE	***1,635***
8	Fort Smith Regional Arpt	2,074	8	Cabot 4 SW	1,825
8	Hot Springs 1 NNE	2,074	9	Batesville Livestock	1,844
10	Keo	2,063	10	Alum Fork	1,855
11	Conway	2,055	11	Fordyce	1,866
11	Searcy	2,055	12	Corning	1,868
13	Blytheville	2,051	13	Morrilton	***1,879***
14	West Memphis	2,038	14	Jonesboro 4 N	1,895
15	Dequeen	2,022	15	Crossett 2 SSE	1,905
16	Arkadelphia 2 N	***2,007***	16	Paragould 1 S	1,931
16	Dardanelle	2,007	17	Blue Mountain Dam	1,944
18	Benton	1,993	18	Beedeville 4 NE	1,960
19	Sheridan	1,975	19	Alicia	1,967
20	Alicia	1,967	20	Sheridan	1,975
21	Beedeville 4 NE	1,960	21	Benton	1,993
22	Blue Mountain Dam	1,944	22	Arkadelphia 2 N	***2,007***
23	Paragould 1 S	1,931	22	Dardanelle	2,007
24	Crossett 2 SSE	1,905	24	Dequeen	2,022
25	Jonesboro 4 N	1,895	25	West Memphis	2,038

Annual Precipitation

Highest Rank	Station Name	Inches	Lowest Rank	Station Name	Inches
1	Crossett 2 SSE	57.29	1	Fayetteville Exp Stn	***44.35***
2	Eudora	57.26	2	Alicia	44.77
3	Hot Springs 1 NNE	56.80	3	Fort Smith Regional Arpt	45.12
4	Alum Fork	56.48	4	Bentonville 4 S	46.09
5	Fordyce	56.33	5	Gravette	46.85
6	Blakely Mountain Dam	55.95	6	Corning	47.02
7	Arkadelphia 2 N	55.36	7	Huntsville 1 SSW	47.11
8	Deer	55.17	8	Jonesboro 4 N	47.35
9	Pine Bluff	54.25	9	Batesville Livestock	47.41
10	Dequeen	54.04	10	Beedeville 4 NE	47.60
11	Sheridan	53.56	11	Conway	48.03
12	Benton	53.07	12	Blue Mountain Dam	48.31
13	West Memphis	52.86	13	Keo	48.52
14	Mountainburg 2 NE	***52.55***	14	Des Arc	48.62
15	El Dorado Goodwin Field	52.17	15	Dardanelle	48.87
16	Arkansas Post	51.63	16	Blytheville	49.72
17	Cabot 4 SW	51.06	16	Morrilton	***49.72***
18	Searcy	50.39	18	Little Rock Adams Field	49.81
19	Paragould 1 S	50.00	19	North Little Rock Arpt	49.91
20	North Little Rock Arpt	49.91	20	Paragould 1 S	50.00
21	Little Rock Adams Field	49.81	21	Searcy	50.39
22	Blytheville	49.72	22	Cabot 4 SW	51.06
22	Morrilton	***49.72***	23	Arkansas Post	51.63
24	Dardanelle	48.87	24	El Dorado Goodwin Field	52.17
25	Des Arc	48.62	25	Mountainburg 2 NE	***52.55***

Rankings include 25 highest/lowest stations. If state has less than 25 stations, all stations are included. The period of record is 1980–2009. See User Guide for detailed explanation of data.

Annual Extreme Maximum Daily Precipitation

Highest Rank	Station Name	Inches	Lowest Rank	Station Name	Inches
1	Hot Springs 1 NNE	12.97	1	Jonesboro 4 N	4.78
2	Deer	9.56	2	Conway	4.95
3	Crossett 2 SSE	9.30	3	Pine Bluff	5.40
4	El Dorado Goodwin Field	8.77	4	Paragould 1 S	5.48
5	Blue Mountain Dam	8.25	5	Bentonville 4 S	*5.65*
6	Blakely Mountain Dam	*8.20*	6	Fort Smith Regional Arpt	5.72
7	Alum Fork	8.13	7	Blytheville	5.73
8	Sheridan	8.08	8	Alicia	6.00
9	Benton	*8.00*	9	Little Rock Adams Field	6.23
10	Arkansas Post	*7.94*	10	Gravette	6.27
11	Dequeen	7.92	11	Mountainburg 2 NE	*6.41*
12	Fayetteville Exp Stn	*7.80*	12	Des Arc	*6.50*
13	Keo	7.77	13	Beedeville 4 NE	*6.72*
14	Cabot 4 SW	7.76	14	Searcy	6.74
15	Corning	7.52	15	Fordyce	6.80
16	Eudora	7.48	16	Huntsville 1 SSW	*6.95*
17	West Memphis	7.25	17	Batesville Livestock	7.00
18	Dardanelle	7.15	18	North Little Rock Arpt	7.01
19	Arkadelphia 2 N	7.14	19	Morrilton	*7.10*
20	Morrilton	*7.10*	20	Arkadelphia 2 N	7.14
21	North Little Rock Arpt	7.01	21	Dardanelle	7.15
22	Batesville Livestock	7.00	22	West Memphis	7.25
23	Huntsville 1 SSW	*6.95*	23	Eudora	7.48
24	Fordyce	6.80	24	Corning	7.52
25	Searcy	6.74	25	Cabot 4 SW	7.76

Number of Days Annually With ≥ 0.1 Inches of Precipitation

Highest Rank	Station Name	Days	Lowest Rank	Station Name	Days
1	Huntsville 1 SSW	76	1	Beedeville 4 NE	59
2	Alum Fork	75	2	Fayetteville Exp Stn	*63*
2	Deer	75	3	Alicia	64
2	Hot Springs 1 NNE	75	4	Arkansas Post	66
2	Paragould 1 S	75	4	Benton	66
6	Crossett 2 SSE	74	4	Fort Smith Regional Arpt	66
6	Pine Bluff	74	7	Dardanelle	67
6	Searcy	74	7	Keo	67
9	Blytheville	73	9	Arkadelphia 2 N	68
9	Eudora	73	9	Cabot 4 SW	68
9	Fordyce	73	9	Gravette	68
9	North Little Rock Arpt	73	12	Batesville Livestock	69
9	West Memphis	73	12	Blakely Mountain Dam	69
14	Little Rock Adams Field	72	12	Conway	69
14	Mountainburg 2 NE	*72*	12	Dequeen	69
14	Sheridan	72	12	Jonesboro 4 N	69
17	Bentonville 4 S	71	17	Blue Mountain Dam	70
17	Des Arc	71	17	Corning	70
19	Blue Mountain Dam	70	17	El Dorado Goodwin Field	70
19	Corning	70	17	Morrilton	*70*
19	El Dorado Goodwin Field	70	21	Bentonville 4 S	71
19	Morrilton	*70*	21	Des Arc	71
23	Batesville Livestock	69	23	Little Rock Adams Field	72
23	Blakely Mountain Dam	69	23	Mountainburg 2 NE	*72*
23	Conway	69	23	Sheridan	72

Rankings include 25 highest/lowest stations. If state has less than 25 stations, all stations are included. The period of record is 1980–2009. See User Guide for detailed explanation of data.

Number of Days Annually With ≥ 0.5 Inches of Precipitation

Highest

Rank	Station Name	Days
1	Alum Fork	40
2	Crossett 2 SSE	38
2	Fordyce	38
4	Hot Springs 1 NNE	37
5	Blytheville	36
5	Dequeen	36
5	Eudora	36
5	West Memphis	36
9	Arkadelphia 2 N	35
9	Cabot 4 SW	35
9	Paragould 1 S	35
9	Pine Bluff	35
9	Sheridan	35
14	Benton	34
14	Dardanelle	34
14	Deer	34
14	El Dorado Goodwin Field	34
14	Little Rock Adams Field	34
14	Mountainburg 2 NE	***34***
20	Arkansas Post	33
20	Blakely Mountain Dam	33
20	Fort Smith Regional Arpt	33
20	Gravette	33
20	North Little Rock Arpt	33
20	Searcy	33

Lowest

Rank	Station Name	Days
1	Alicia	30
1	Batesville Livestock	30
1	Fayetteville Exp Stn	***30***
1	Keo	30
5	Beedeville 4 NE	31
5	Bentonville 4 S	31
5	Conway	31
5	Jonesboro 4 N	31
9	Blue Mountain Dam	32
9	Corning	32
9	Des Arc	32
9	Huntsville 1 SSW	32
9	Morrilton	***32***
14	Arkansas Post	33
14	Blakely Mountain Dam	33
14	Fort Smith Regional Arpt	33
14	Gravette	33
14	North Little Rock Arpt	33
14	Searcy	33
20	Benton	34
20	Dardanelle	34
20	Deer	34
20	El Dorado Goodwin Field	34
20	Little Rock Adams Field	34
20	Mountainburg 2 NE	***34***

Number of Days Annually With ≥ 1.0 Inches of Precipitation

Highest

Rank	Station Name	Days
1	Arkadelphia 2 N	20
1	Crossett 2 SSE	20
1	Eudora	20
1	Sheridan	20
5	Alum Fork	19
5	Dequeen	19
7	Arkansas Post	18
7	Deer	18
7	Fordyce	18
7	Hot Springs 1 NNE	18
7	Mountainburg 2 NE	***18***
12	Beedeville 4 NE	17
12	Blakely Mountain Dam	17
12	El Dorado Goodwin Field	17
12	Searcy	17
12	West Memphis	17
17	Benton	16
17	Bentonville 4 S	16
17	Cabot 4 SW	16
17	Conway	16
17	Dardanelle	16
17	Little Rock Adams Field	16
17	North Little Rock Arpt	16
17	Pine Bluff	16
25	Blytheville	15

Lowest

Rank	Station Name	Days
1	Corning	12
2	Fayetteville Exp Stn	***13***
2	Keo	13
4	Alicia	14
4	Batesville Livestock	14
4	Blue Mountain Dam	14
4	Fort Smith Regional Arpt	14
4	Gravette	14
4	Paragould 1 S	14
10	Blytheville	15
10	Des Arc	15
10	Huntsville 1 SSW	15
10	Jonesboro 4 N	15
10	Morrilton	***15***
15	Benton	16
15	Bentonville 4 S	16
15	Cabot 4 SW	16
15	Conway	16
15	Dardanelle	16
15	Little Rock Adams Field	16
15	North Little Rock Arpt	16
15	Pine Bluff	16
23	Beedeville 4 NE	17
23	Blakely Mountain Dam	17
23	El Dorado Goodwin Field	17

Annual Snowfall

Highest Rank	Highest Station Name	Highest Inches	Lowest Rank	Lowest Station Name	Lowest Inches
1	Gravette	15.0	1	Eudora	Trace
2	Huntsville 1 SSW	12.4	2	Crossett 2 SSE	0.3
3	Deer	11.4	3	Fordyce	0.7
4	Bentonville 4 S	***8.9***	4	Blakely Mountain Dam	0.9
5	Corning	7.5	4	Pine Bluff	***0.9***
6	Batesville Livestock	5.8	6	Hot Springs 1 NNE	1.4
7	Alicia	5.2	7	Paragould 1 S	1.6
8	Jonesboro 4 N	4.8	8	Searcy	1.7
9	Fayetteville Exp Stn	***4.3***	9	Blytheville	***1.9***
9	North Little Rock Arpt	4.3	9	Des Arc	***1.9***
11	Keo	3.9	11	Arkansas Post	2.0
12	Dardanelle	3.8	11	West Memphis	2.0
13	Conway	3.6	13	Beedeville 4 NE	2.2
14	Mountainburg 2 NE	***3.2***	14	Arkadelphia 2 N	2.3
15	Cabot 4 SW	3.1	15	Alum Fork	2.4
16	Blue Mountain Dam	3.0	16	Dequeen	2.5
17	Morrilton	***2.8***	17	Benton	2.6
17	Sheridan	2.8	18	Morrilton	***2.8***
19	Benton	2.6	18	Sheridan	2.8
20	Dequeen	2.5	20	Blue Mountain Dam	3.0
21	Alum Fork	2.4	21	Cabot 4 SW	3.1
22	Arkadelphia 2 N	2.3	22	Mountainburg 2 NE	***3.2***
23	Beedeville 4 NE	2.2	23	Conway	3.6
24	Arkansas Post	2.0	24	Dardanelle	3.8
24	West Memphis	2.0	25	Keo	3.9

Annual Maximum Snow Depth

Highest Rank	Highest Station Name	Highest Inches	Lowest Rank	Lowest Station Name	Lowest Inches
1	Blytheville	***24***	1	Crossett 2 SSE	Trace
2	Huntsville 1 SSW	17	1	Eudora	Trace
3	Deer	15	3	Des Arc	***1***
3	Gravette	15	3	Fordyce	***1***
5	Bentonville 4 S	14	5	Jonesboro 4 N	***5***
5	Dardanelle	14	5	Paragould 1 S	***5***
5	Searcy	14	5	Pine Bluff	5
8	Conway	13	5	West Memphis	***5***
9	Blue Mountain Dam	12	9	Benton	***6***
9	North Little Rock Arpt	12	9	Sheridan	6
11	Alum Fork	11	11	Alicia	***7***
11	Beedeville 4 NE	***11***	11	Arkansas Post	7
13	Arkadelphia 2 N	10	11	Blakely Mountain Dam	***7***
13	Batesville Livestock	10	14	Corning	8
13	Cabot 4 SW	10	15	Hot Springs 1 NNE	9
13	Dequeen	10	15	Mountainburg 2 NE	***9***
13	Fayetteville Exp Stn	***10***	17	Arkadelphia 2 N	10
13	Keo	10	17	Batesville Livestock	10
19	Hot Springs 1 NNE	9	17	Cabot 4 SW	10
19	Mountainburg 2 NE	***9***	17	Dequeen	10
21	Corning	8	17	Fayetteville Exp Stn	***10***
22	Alicia	***7***	17	Keo	10
22	Arkansas Post	7	23	Alum Fork	11
22	Blakely Mountain Dam	***7***	23	Beedeville 4 NE	***11***
25	Benton	***6***	25	Blue Mountain Dam	12

Rankings include 25 highest/lowest stations. If state has less than 25 stations, all stations are included. The period of record is 1980–2009. See User Guide for detailed explanation of data.

Number of Days Annually With ≥ 1.0 Inch Snow Depth

Highest			Lowest		
Rank	Station Name	Days	Rank	Station Name	Days
1	Deer	14	1	Alicia	*0*
2	Gravette	11	1	Arkadelphia 2 N	0
3	Bentonville 4 S	7	1	Beedeville 4 NE	*0*
3	Huntsville 1 SSW	7	1	Benton	*0*
5	Batesville Livestock	5	1	Blakely Mountain Dam	0
5	Corning	5	1	Crossett 2 SSE	0
7	Blue Mountain Dam	3	1	Dequeen	0
7	Dardanelle	3	1	Des Arc	*0*
7	Fayetteville Exp Stn	*3*	1	Eudora	0
7	Keo	3	1	Fordyce	*0*
7	Mountainburg 2 NE	*3*	1	Hot Springs 1 NNE	0
7	North Little Rock Arpt	3	1	Pine Bluff	0
13	Cabot 4 SW	2	1	Searcy	0
13	Conway	2	1	West Memphis	0
13	Morrilton	*2*	15	Alum Fork	1
13	Paragould 1 S	*2*	15	Arkansas Post	1
17	Alum Fork	1	15	Blytheville	*1*
17	Arkansas Post	1	15	Jonesboro 4 N	1
17	Blytheville	*1*	15	Sheridan	1
17	Jonesboro 4 N	1	20	Cabot 4 SW	2
17	Sheridan	1	20	Conway	2
22	Alicia	*0*	20	Morrilton	*2*
22	Arkadelphia 2 N	0	20	Paragould 1 S	*2*
22	Beedeville 4 NE	*0*	24	Blue Mountain Dam	3
22	Benton	*0*	24	Dardanelle	3

Rankings include 25 highest/lowest stations. If state has less than 25 stations, all stations are included. The period of record is 1980–2009. See User Guide for detailed explanation of data.

Significant Storm Events in Arkansas: 2000 – 2009

Location or County	Date	Type	Mag.	Deaths	Injuries	Property Damage ($mil.)	Crop Damage ($mil.)
Southwest Arkansas	12/12/00	Ice Storm	na	0	0	360.0	0.0
Southwest Arkansas	12/24/00	Ice Storm	na	0	0	165.0	0.0
Columbia	10/11/01	Flash Flood	na	0	0	120.0	0.0
Ashley	11/24/01	Tornado	F3	3	11	2.0	0.0
Faulkner	12/18/02	Tornado	F3	1	13	0.0	0.0
Washington	07/13/03	Hail	2.75 in.	0	0	50.0	0.0
Union	01/12/05	Tornado	F3	2	13	3.0	0.0
Benton	03/12/06	Tornado	F3	0	12	5.0	0.0
Greene	04/02/06	Tornado	F3	0	47	25.0	0.0
Desha	02/24/07	Tornado	F3	0	28	45.0	0.0
Sharp	02/05/08	Tornado	F3	0	15	30.0	0.0
Stone	02/05/08	Tornado	F4	1	7	29.0	0.0
Van Buren	02/05/08	Tornado	F4	3	77	22.7	0.0
Baxter	02/05/08	Tornado	F2	1	35	15.7	0.0
Izard	02/05/08	Tornado	F3	2	20	11.5	0.0
Pope	02/05/08	Tornado	F3	5	15	11.5	0.0
Independence	03/18/08	Flood	na	0	0	20.0	0.5
Miller	03/31/08	Hail	4.00 in.	0	0	85.0	0.0
Pulaski	04/03/08	Tornado	F1	0	1	50.0	0.0
Cleburne	05/02/08	Tornado	F2	0	12	32.0	0.0
Arkansas	05/10/08	Tornado	F3	0	9	75.0	0.0
Northern Arkansas	01/26/09	Ice Storm	na	0	0	50.0	0.0
Baxter, Boone, Garland, and Marion Counties	01/26/09	Ice Storm	na	0	0	50.0	0.0
Johnson, Perry, Saline, and Van Buren Counties	01/26/09	Ice Storm	na	0	0	25.0	0.0
Polk	04/09/09	Tornado	F3	3	30	130.0	0.0
Pulaski	06/30/09	Hail	2.75 in.	0	0	60.0	1.0

Note: Deaths, injuries, and damages are date and location specific.

CALIFORNIA

PHYSICAL FEATURES. The State of California extends along the shore of the Pacific Ocean between latitudes 32.5° N. and 42° N. Its more than 1,340 miles of coastline constitute nearly three-fourths of the Pacific coastline of the conterminous United States. The total land area amounts to 158,693 square miles. With its major axis oriented in a northwest-southeast direction, the State is 800 miles in length. Its greatest east-west dimension at a given latitude is about 360 miles though its average width is only 250 miles. However, it spreads over more than 10° of longitude, a distance of 550 miles.

The topography of the State is varied. Included are Death Valley, the lowest point in the U.S., with an elevation of 276 feet below sea level, and less than 85 miles away, Mt. Whitney, the highest peak in the conterminous states, reaching to 14,495 feet above sea level. These wide ranges of altitude and latitude are responsible in part for the variety of climates and vegetation found in various areas of the State. Another significant factor is the continuous interaction of maritime air masses with those of continental origin. The combination of these influences results in pronounced climatic changes with short distances.

The Coast Range parallels the coastline from the Oregon border to just north of the Los Angeles Basin. It is generally no more than 50 miles from the coast to the crest of the range. The principal break in the Coast Range is at San Francisco Bay where a sea level opening permits an abundant inflow of marine air to the interior of the State under certain circulation patterns. In the northern end of the State, the Coast Range merges with the Cascade Range, farther inland, to create an extensive area of rugged terrain more than 200 miles in width. The Cascades, in turn, extend southeastward until they merge into the Sierra Nevada. The Sierra Nevada, like the Coast Range, lies parallel to the coast, but the crest over most of its length is about 150 miles inland. Thus, between the two ranges there is a broad, flat valley averaging 45 miles or more in width. In length the valley extends nearly 500 miles.

Both the extreme northeastern portion of California and the desert area of southern California east of the mountains lie within the Great Basin. The Great Basin extends from Utah to the Sierra Nevada and has no surface drainage to the ocean. It is an area of climatological extremes.

GENERAL CLIMATE. Along the western side of the Coast Range the climate is dominated by the Pacific Ocean. Warm winters, cool summers, small daily and seasonal temperature ranges, and high relative humidities are characteristic of this area. With increasing distance from the ocean the maritime influence decreases. Areas that are well protected from the ocean experience a more continental type of climate with warmer summers, colder winters, greater daily and seasonal temperature ranges, and generally lower relative humidities. Many parts of the State lie within a transitional zone, where conditions range between these two climatic extremes. Summer is a dry period over most of the State. With the northward migration of the semi-permanent Pacific high during summer, most storm tracks are deflected far to the north. In winter, the Pacific high decreases in intensity and drops further south, permitting storms to move into and across the State, producing widespread rain at low elevations and snow at high elevations.

The easternmost mountain chains form a barrier that protects much of California from the extremely cold air of the Great Basin in winter. The ranges of mountains to the west offer some protection to the interior from the strong flow of air off the Pacific Ocean. As a result, precipitation is heavy on the coastward or western side of both the Coast Range and the Sierra Nevada, and lighter on the eastern slopes. Temperature tends toward uniformity from day to day and from season to season on the ocean side of the Coast Range and in coastal valleys. East of the Sierra Nevada temperature patterns are continental in character with wide excursions from high readings to low. Between the two mountain chains and over much of the desert area the temperature regime is intermediate between the maritime and the continental models. Hot summers are the rule while winters are moderate to cold. In the basins and valleys adjoining the coast, climate is subject to wide variations within short distances as a result of the influence of topography on the circulation of marine air. The Los Angeles Basin and the San Francisco Bay area offer many varieties of climate within a few miles.

A dominating factor in the weather of California is the semi-permanent high pressure area of the north Pacific Ocean. This pressure center moves northward in summer, holding storm tracks well to the north, and as a result California receives little or no precipitation from this source during that period. In winter, the Pacific high retreats southward permitting storm centers to swing into and across California. These are the storms that bring widespread, moderate precipitation to the State. When changes in the circulation pattern permit storm centers to approach the California coast from a southwesterly direction, copious amounts of moisture are carried by the northeastward streaming air. This results in heavy rains and often produces widespread flooding.

There is another California weather characteristic that results from the location of the Pacific high. The steady flow of air from the northwest during the summer helps to drive the California Current of the Pacific Ocean as it sweeps southward almost parallel to the California coastline. However, since the mean drift is slightly offshore there is a band of upwelling immediately off the coast as water from deeper layers is drawn into the surface circulation. The water from below the surface is colder than the surface water, and as a result there is a semi-permanent band of cold water just offshore. The temperature of water reaching the surface from deeper levels ranges from about 49°F. in winter to 55°F. in late summer along the northern California coast, and from 57°F. to 65°F. on the southern California coast. Comparatively warm, moist Pacific air masses drifting over this band of cold water form a bank of fog which is swept inland by the prevailing northwest winds out of the high pressure center. In general, heat is added to the air as it moves inland during these summer months, and the fog quickly lifts to form a deck of low clouds that extend inland only a short distance before evaporating completely. Characteristically this deck of clouds extends inland further during the night and then recedes to the vicinity of the coast during the day.

PRECIPITATION. In the northern part of the State the months of heaviest precipitation are October through April. The rainy season becomes shorter in the southern part of the State, November through March marking the wet period here. During the rest of the year precipitation is infrequent and usually light. In the north and over the central and northern mountains there are usually from 60 to 100 days of precipitation per year, while in the southern desert there may be as few as 10 days. It is apparent, therefore, that the rainy season is made up of periods of stormy weather alternating with longer periods of pleasant weather. A typical winter storm situation brings intermittent rain over a period of from two to five days, followed by seven to 14 days of dry weather.

SNOWFALL. Snow has been reported at one time or another in nearly every part of California but it is very infrequent west of the Sierra Nevada except at high elevations of the Coast Range and the Cascades. In the Sierra Nevada, snow in moderate amounts is reported nearly every winter at elevations as low as 2,000 feet. Amounts and intensities increase with elevation to around 7,000 or 8,000 feet. Above 4,000 feet elevation snow remains on the ground for appreciable lengths of time each winter.

RELATIVE HUMIDITY. In general, relative humidities are moderate to high along the coast throughout the year. Inland humidities are high during the winter and low during the summer. Since the ocean is the source of the cool, humid, maritime air of summer, it follows that with increasing distance from the ocean, relative humidity tends to decrease. Where mountain barriers prevent the free flow of marine air inland, humidities decrease rapidly. Where openings in these barriers permit a significant influx of cool, moist air it mixes with the drier inland air, resulting in a more gradual decrease of moisture. This pattern is characteristic of most coastal valleys.

STORMS. Thunderstorms may occur in California at any time of the year. Near the coast and over the Central Valley there appears to be no prevailing season. The storms are usually light and infrequent. Over the interior mountain areas storms are more intense, and they may become unusually strong on occasion at intermediate and high elevations of the Sierra Nevada. Many California thunderstorms produce so little precipitation that range and forest fires often result from the lightning strikes. Heavy precipitation occasionally results. Some flash flooding has been reported as a result of thundershowers. Hail diameters from one quarter of an inch to one half inch are sometimes reported. Serious hail damage is infrequent. Tornadoes have been reported in California but with a frequency of only one or two per year. They are generally not severe, in many cases amounting to little more than a local whirlwind.

DROUGHT. Drought must be evaluated on a different basis than in other parts of the country. Typically there are extended periods every summer with little or no precipitation. This is the normal and expected condition. A deficiency of precipitation becomes significant in the State when the normal winter water supply fails to materialize.

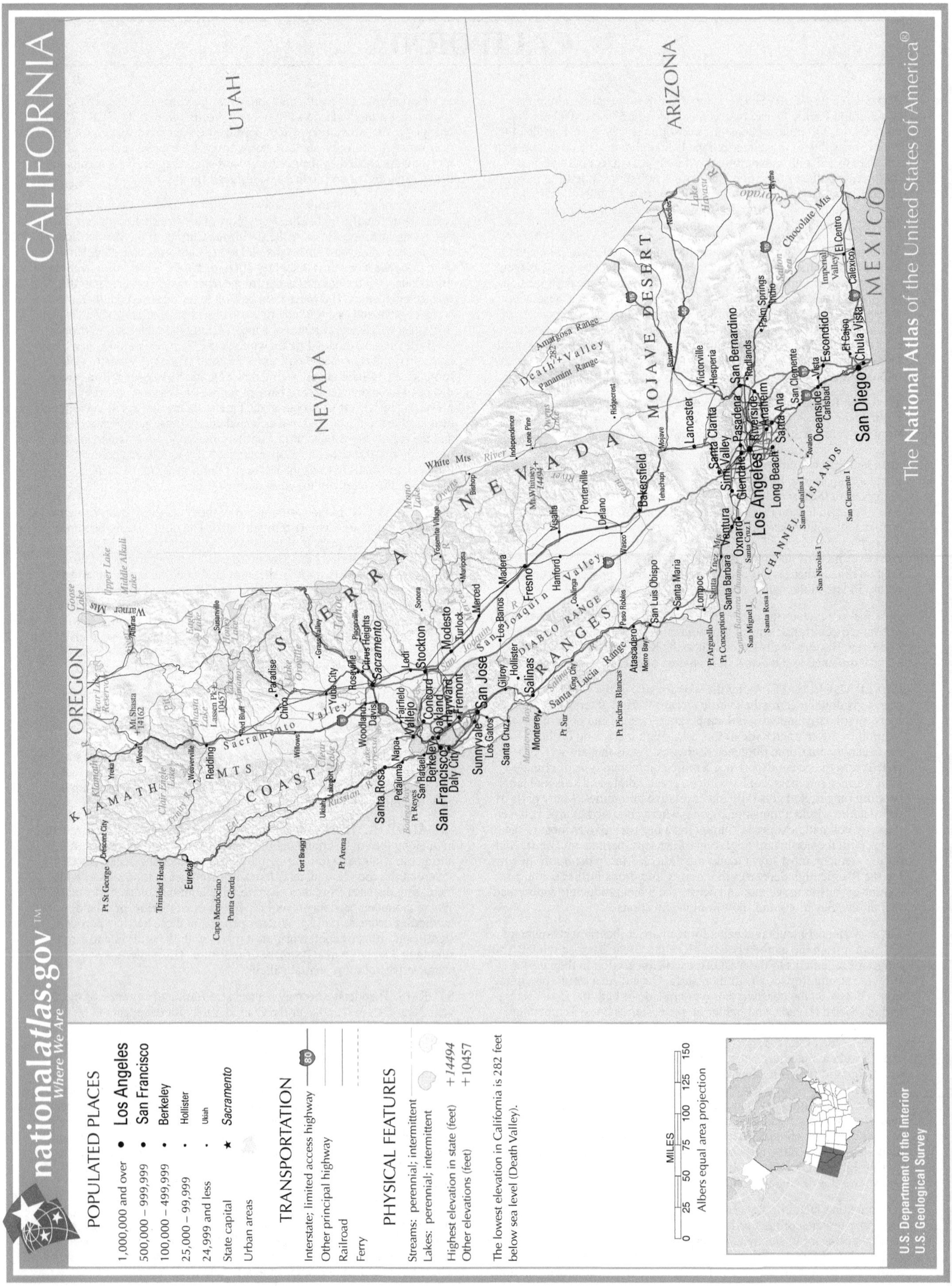
CALIFORNIA
nationalatlas.gov™
Where We Are
POPULATED PLACES
1,000,000 and over • Los Angeles
500,000 – 999,999 • San Francisco
100,000 – 499,999 • Berkeley
25,000 – 99,999 • Hollister
24,999 and less • Ukiah
State capital ★ Sacramento
Urban areas
TRANSPORTATION
Interstate; limited access highway
Other principal highway
Railroad
Ferry
PHYSICAL FEATURES
Streams: perennial; intermittent
Lakes: perennial; intermittent
Highest elevation in state (feet) +14494
Other elevations (feet) +10457
The lowest elevation in California is 282 feet below sea level (Death Valley).
MILES
0 25 50 75 100 125 150
Albers equal area projection
U.S. Department of the Interior
U.S. Geological Survey
The National Atlas of the United States of America®
OREGON
NEVADA
UTAH
ARIZONA
MEXICO
SIERRA NEVADA
MOJAVE DESERT
KLAMATH MTS
COAST RANGES
DIABLO RANGE
CHANNEL ISLANDS
Sacramento Valley
San Joaquin Valley
Death Valley
Los Angeles
San Diego
San Francisco
San Jose
Sacramento
Fresno
Bakersfield
Oakland
Stockton
Modesto
Santa Rosa
Salinas
Eureka
Redding
Mt. Shasta +14162
Lassen Pk +10457
Mt. Whitney +14494

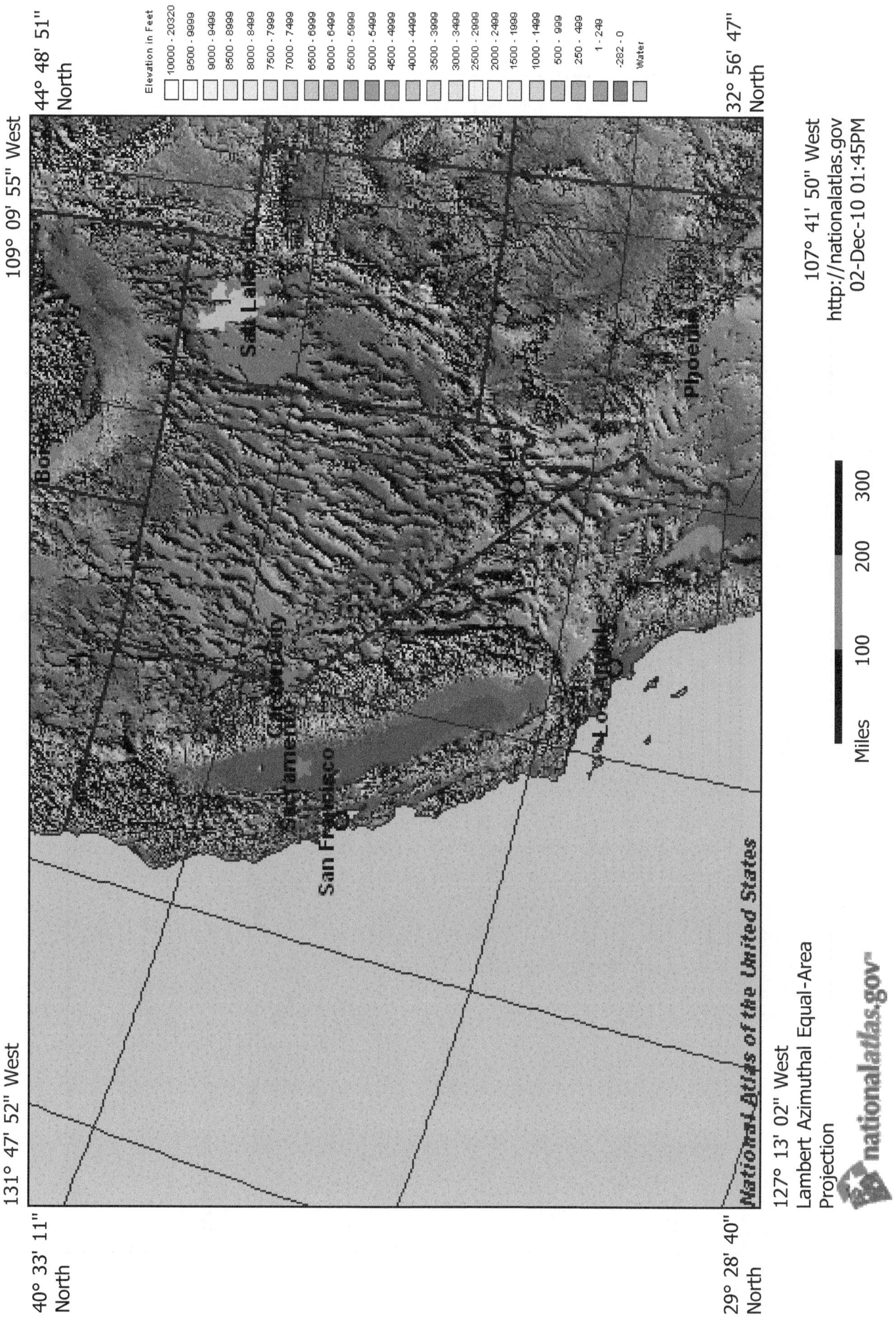
44° 48' 51" North
109° 09' 55" West
131° 47' 52" West
40° 33' 11" North
32° 56' 47" North
29° 28' 40" North
127° 13' 02" West
107° 41' 50" West
Elevation in Feet
10000 - 20320
9500 - 9999
9000 - 9499
8500 - 8999
8000 - 8499
7500 - 7999
7000 - 7499
6500 - 6999
6000 - 6499
5500 - 5999
5000 - 5499
4500 - 4999
4000 - 4499
3500 - 3999
3000 - 3499
2500 - 2999
2000 - 2499
1500 - 1999
1000 - 1499
500 - 999
250 - 499
1 - 249
-282 - 0
Water
Salt Lake City
Phoenix
San Francisco
Sacramento
Carson City
Miles
100
200
300
National Atlas of the United States
Lambert Azimuthal Equal-Area Projection
http://nationalatlas.gov
02-Dec-10 01:45PM
nationalatlas.gov

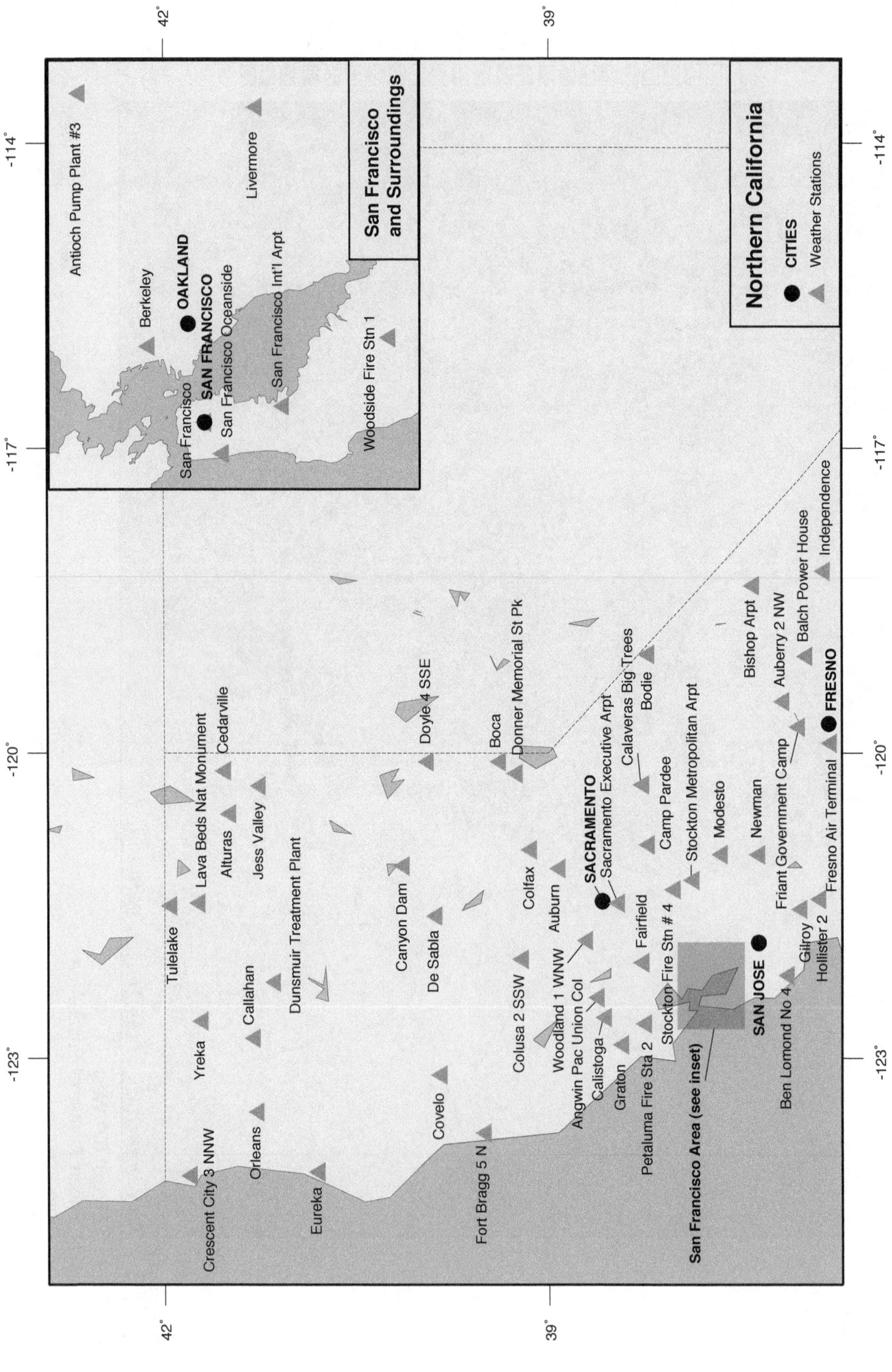
Northern California
CITIES
Weather Stations
San Francisco and Surroundings
Antioch Pump Plant #3
Berkeley
OAKLAND
SAN FRANCISCO
San Francisco
San Francisco Oceanside
San Francisco Int'l Arpt
Livermore
Woodside Fire Stn 1
Crescent City 3 NNW
Eureka
Orleans
Yreka
Callahan
Tulelake
Lava Beds Nat Monument
Alturas
Cedarville
Jess Valley
Dunsmuir Treatment Plant
Fort Bragg 5 N
Covelo
De Sabla
Canyon Dam
Doyle 4 SSE
Colusa 2 SSW
Colfax
Auburn
Woodland 1 WNW
Boca
Donner Memorial St Pk
Angwin Pac Union Col
Calistoga
Graton
Petaluma Fire Sta 2
SACRAMENTO
Sacramento Executive Arpt
Fairfield
Stockton Fire Stn # 4
Stockton Metropolitan Arpt
Camp Pardee
Calaveras Big Trees
Bodie
Modesto
San Francisco Area (see inset)
SAN JOSE
Ben Lomond No 4
Gilroy
Hollister 2
Newman
Friant Government Camp
Fresno Air Terminal
FRESNO
Auberry 2 NW
Balch Power House
Bishop Arpt
Independence
42°
39°
-114°
-117°
-120°
-123°

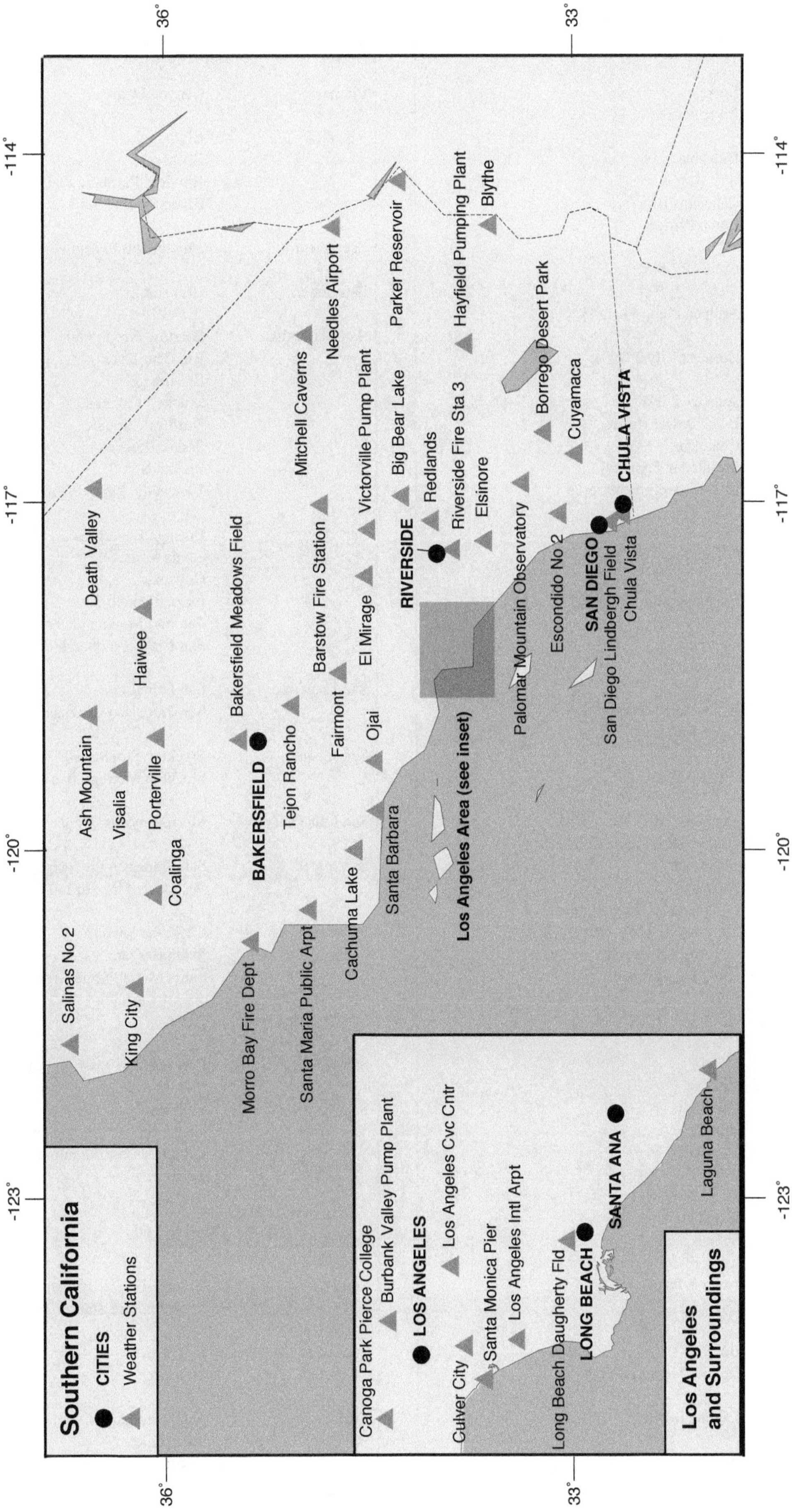
Southern California
CITIES
Weather Stations
Los Angeles and Surroundings
36°
33°
-114°
-117°
-120°
-123°
Salinas No 2
King City
Morro Bay Fire Dept
Santa Maria Public Arpt
Cachuma Lake
Santa Barbara
Coalinga
Porterville
Visalia
Ash Mountain
Haiwee
Death Valley
BAKERSFIELD
Bakersfield Meadows Field
Tejon Rancho
Fairmont
Ojai
Barstow Fire Station
El Mirage
Victorville Pump Plant
Mitchell Caverns
Needles Airport
Big Bear Lake
Parker Reservoir
RIVERSIDE
Redlands
Riverside Fire Sta 3
Elsinore
Hayfield Pumping Plant
Blythe
Borrego Desert Park
Cuyamaca
Palomar Mountain Observatory
Escondido No 2
SAN DIEGO
San Diego Lindbergh Field
Chula Vista
CHULA VISTA
Los Angeles Area (see inset)
Canoga Park Pierce College
Burbank Valley Pump Plant
LOS ANGELES
Los Angeles Cvc Cntr
Culver City
Santa Monica Pier
Los Angeles Intl Arpt
Long Beach Daugherty Fld
LONG BEACH
SANTA ANA
Laguna Beach

California Weather Stations by County

County	Station Name
Alameda	Berkeley
	Livermore
Butte	De Sabla
Calaveras	Calaveras Big Trees
	Camp Pardee
Colusa	Colusa 2 SSW
Contra Costa	Antioch Pump Plant #3
Del Norte	Crescent City 3 NNW
Fresno	Auberry 2 NW
	Balch Power House
	Coalinga
	Fresno Air Terminal
	Friant Government Camp
Humboldt	Eureka
	Orleans
Inyo	Bishop Arpt
	Death Valley
	Haiwee
	Independence
Kern	Bakersfield Meadows Field
	Tejon Rancho
Lassen	Doyle 4 SSE
Los Angeles	Burbank Valley Pump Plant
	Canoga Park Pierce College
	Culver City
	Fairmont
	Long Beach Daugherty Fld
	Los Angeles Civic Center
	Los Angeles Intl Arpt
	Santa Monica Pier
Mendocino	Covelo
	Fort Bragg 5 N
Modoc	Alturas
	Cedarville
	Jess Valley
Mono	Bodie
Monterey	King City
	Salinas No 2
Napa	Angwin Pac Union Col
	Calistoga
Nevada	Boca
	Donner Memorial St Pk
Orange	Laguna Beach
Placer	Auburn
	Colfax
Plumas	Canyon Dam
Riverside	Blythe
	Elsinore
	Hayfield Pumping Plant
	Riverside Fire Sta 3
Sacramento	Sacramento Executive Arpt
San Benito	Hollister 2
San Bernardino	Barstow Fire Station
	Big Bear Lake
	El Mirage
	Mitchell Caverns
	Needles Airport
	Parker Reservoir
	Redlands
	Victorville Pump Plant
San Diego	Borrego Desert Park
	Chula Vista
	Cuyamaca
	Escondido No 2
	Palomar Mountain Observatory
	San Diego Lindbergh Field
San Francisco	San Francisco
	San Francisco Oceanside
San Joaquin	Stockton Fire Stn #4
	Stockton Metropolitan Arpt
San Luis Obispo	Morro Bay Fire Dept
San Mateo	San Francisco Int'l Arpt
	Woodside Fire Stn 1
Santa Barbara	Cachuma Lake
	Santa Barbara
	Santa Maria Public Arpt
Santa Clara	Gilroy
Santa Cruz	Ben Lomond No 4
Siskiyou	Callahan
	Dunsmuir Treatment Plant
	Lava Beds Nat Monument
	Tulelake
	Yreka
Solano	Fairfield
Sonoma	Graton
	Petaluma Fire Station 2
Stanislaus	Modesto
	Newman
Tulare	Ash Mountain
	Porterville
	Visalia

See User Guide for station inclusion criteria.

County	Station Name
Ventura	Ojai
Yolo	Woodland 1 WNW

See User Guide for station inclusion criteria.

California Weather Stations by City

City	Station Name	Miles
Anaheim	Laguna Beach	20.8
	Long Beach Daugherty Fld	14.9
	Los Angeles Civic Center	24.0
Antioch	Antioch Pump Plant #3	3.7
	Fairfield	24.1
	Livermore	22.3
Bakersfield	Bakersfield Meadows Field	5.7
Berkeley	Berkeley	0.4
	San Francisco Oceanside	15.7
	San Francisco Int'l Arpt	18.9
	San Francisco	11.4
Burbank	Burbank Valley Pump Plant	1.5
	Canoga Park Pierce College	13.8
	Culver City	12.1
	Los Angeles Intl Arpt	17.6
	Los Angeles Civic Center	10.4
	Santa Monica Pier	16.0
Carlsbad	Escondido No 2	11.2
Chula Vista	Chula Vista	2.2
	San Diego Lindbergh Field	10.2
Concord	Antioch Pump Plant #3	15.2
	Berkeley	15.5
	Fairfield	21.0
	Livermore	24.6
Corona	Elsinore	19.6
	Riverside Fire Sta 3	12.0
Costa Mesa	Laguna Beach	10.8
	Long Beach Daugherty Fld	18.7
Daly City	Berkeley	16.6
	San Francisco Oceanside	3.6
	San Francisco Int'l Arpt	6.1
	San Francisco	5.8
	Woodside Fire Stn 1	21.2
Downey	Burbank Valley Pump Plant	21.1
	Culver City	16.3
	Long Beach Daugherty Fld	7.4
	Los Angeles Intl Arpt	15.3
	Los Angeles Civic Center	9.7
	Santa Monica Pier	21.5
East Los Angeles	Burbank Valley Pump Plant	14.8
	Culver City	13.3
	Long Beach Daugherty Fld	13.6
	Los Angeles Intl Arpt	14.8
	Los Angeles Civic Center	3.9
	Santa Monica Pier	19.1
El Monte	Burbank Valley Pump Plant	20.0
	Culver City	21.7
	Long Beach Daugherty Fld	18.3
	Los Angeles Intl Arpt	23.4
	Los Angeles Civic Center	11.9

City	Station Name	Miles
Escondido	Escondido No 2	1.6
	Palomar Mountain Observatory	22.5
Fairfield	Fairfield	1.6
Fontana	Redlands	15.8
	Riverside Fire Sta 3	10.6
Fremont	Livermore	14.6
	San Francisco Int'l Arpt	23.3
	Woodside Fire Stn 1	16.5
Fresno	Fresno Air Terminal	3.9
	Friant Government Camp	15.4
Fullerton	Laguna Beach	24.2
	Long Beach Daugherty Fld	14.1
	Los Angeles Civic Center	21.1
Garden Grove	Laguna Beach	18.5
	Long Beach Daugherty Fld	12.9
	Los Angeles Civic Center	24.8
Glendale	Burbank Valley Pump Plant	5.7
	Canoga Park Pierce College	18.0
	Culver City	13.1
	Long Beach Daugherty Fld	23.3
	Los Angeles Intl Arpt	18.0
	Los Angeles Civic Center	7.9
	Santa Monica Pier	18.1
Hayward	Berkeley	18.4
	Livermore	17.1
	San Francisco Oceanside	23.9
	San Francisco Int'l Arpt	17.8
	San Francisco	21.2
	Woodside Fire Stn 1	17.5
Huntington Beach	Laguna Beach	16.0
	Long Beach Daugherty Fld	13.5
Inglewood	Burbank Valley Pump Plant	15.7
	Canoga Park Pierce College	20.1
	Culver City	5.2
	Long Beach Daugherty Fld	13.4
	Los Angeles Intl Arpt	3.4
	Los Angeles Civic Center	9.2
	Santa Monica Pier	9.3
Irvine	Laguna Beach	9.1
	Long Beach Daugherty Fld	23.5
Lancaster	Fairmont	16.4
Long Beach	Culver City	20.1
	Long Beach Daugherty Fld	1.9
	Los Angeles Intl Arpt	16.4
	Los Angeles Civic Center	17.4
	Santa Monica Pier	23.7
Los Angeles	Burbank Valley Pump Plant	5.5
	Canoga Park Pierce College	10.0
	Culver City	7.2
	Long Beach Daugherty Fld	24.3

See User Guide for station inclusion criteria.

City	Station Name	Miles
Los Angeles *(cont.)*	Los Angeles Intl Arpt	13.0
	Los Angeles Civic Center	11.2
	Santa Monica Pier	9.8
Modesto	Modesto	0.9
	Newman	23.9
	Stockton Metropolitan Arpt	21.1
Moreno Valley	Elsinore	19.0
	Redlands	8.9
	Riverside Fire Sta 3	8.6
Norwalk	Burbank Valley Pump Plant	24.5
	Culver City	19.7
	Long Beach Daugherty Fld	6.9
	Los Angeles Intl Arpt	18.3
	Los Angeles Civic Center	13.2
	Santa Monica Pier	24.8
Oakland	Berkeley	5.7
	San Francisco Oceanside	15.8
	San Francisco Int'l Arpt	15.7
	San Francisco	11.8
	Woodside Fire Stn 1	24.9
Oceanside	Escondido No 2	14.2
Ontario	Riverside Fire Sta 3	16.1
Orange	Laguna Beach	17.6
	Long Beach Daugherty Fld	19.2
Oxnard	Ojai	18.3
Palmdale	Fairmont	20.7
Pasadena	Burbank Valley Pump Plant	12.6
	Canoga Park Pierce College	24.9
	Culver City	18.1
	Long Beach Daugherty Fld	22.3
	Los Angeles Intl Arpt	21.7
	Los Angeles Civic Center	9.3
	Santa Monica Pier	23.6
Pomona	Riverside Fire Sta 3	22.6
Rancho Cucamonga	Redlands	23.3
	Riverside Fire Sta 3	16.5
Rialto	Redlands	12.2
	Riverside Fire Sta 3	11.3
Richmond	Berkeley	6.4
	San Francisco Oceanside	17.0
	San Francisco Int'l Arpt	22.8
	San Francisco	13.3
Riverside	Elsinore	19.5
	Redlands	14.9
	Riverside Fire Sta 3	1.6
Roseville	Auburn	15.2
	Sacramento Executive Arpt	20.7
Sacramento	Sacramento Executive Arpt	3.7

City	Station Name	Miles
Sacramento *(cont.)*	Woodland 1 WNW	20.3
Salinas	Gilroy	21.9
	Hollister 2	16.6
	Salinas No 2	2.2
San Bernardino	Big Bear Lake	24.9
	Redlands	8.6
	Riverside Fire Sta 3	13.5
San Buenaventura (Ventura)	Ojai	12.0
San Diego	Chula Vista	11.0
	Escondido No 2	22.9
	San Diego Lindbergh Field	4.2
San Francisco	Berkeley	12.0
	San Francisco Oceanside	3.8
	San Francisco Int'l Arpt	10.1
	San Francisco	0.6
	Woodside Fire Stn 1	24.8
San Jose	Ben Lomond No 4	19.6
	Woodside Fire Stn 1	22.7
Santa Ana	Laguna Beach	14.3
	Long Beach Daugherty Fld	17.5
Santa Clara	Ben Lomond No 4	19.7
	Livermore	24.3
	Woodside Fire Stn 1	16.3
Santa Clarita	Burbank Valley Pump Plant	18.5
	Canoga Park Pierce College	16.5
	Fairmont	20.0
Santa Rosa	Angwin Pac Union Col	17.0
	Calistoga	12.1
	Graton	8.6
	Petaluma Fire Station 2	13.0
Simi Valley	Burbank Valley Pump Plant	23.1
	Canoga Park Pierce College	11.6
	Santa Monica Pier	23.2
South Gate	Burbank Valley Pump Plant	18.4
	Culver City	12.3
	Long Beach Daugherty Fld	8.1
	Los Angeles Intl Arpt	11.4
	Los Angeles Civic Center	7.4
	Santa Monica Pier	17.5
Stockton	Antioch Pump Plant #3	23.2
	Stockton Metropolitan Arpt	7.2
	Stockton Fire Stn #4	1.1
Sunnyvale	Ben Lomond No 4	20.0
	Livermore	25.0
	Woodside Fire Stn 1	13.1
Thousand Oaks	Canoga Park Pierce College	17.7
Torrance	Burbank Valley Pump Plant	24.0
	Culver City	12.9
	Long Beach Daugherty Fld	10.2

See User Guide for station inclusion criteria.

City	Station Name	Miles
Torrance *(cont.)*	Los Angeles Intl Arpt	7.4
	Los Angeles Civic Center	16.1
	Santa Monica Pier	14.4
Vallejo	Berkeley	17.2
	Fairfield	13.9
	Petaluma Fire Station 2	25.0
Victorville	El Mirage	16.4
	Victorville Pump Plant	3.1
Visalia	Porterville	24.1
	Visalia	0.8
West Covina	Long Beach Daugherty Fld	20.9
	Los Angeles Civic Center	18.2

Note: Miles is the distance between the geographic center of the city and the weather station.

See User Guide for station inclusion criteria.

California Weather Stations by Elevation

Feet	Station Name
8,370	Bodie
6,790	Big Bear Lake
5,937	Donner Memorial St Pk
5,575	Boca
5,549	Palomar Mountain Observatory
5,399	Jess Valley
4,770	Lava Beds Nat Monument
4,693	Calaveras Big Trees
4,669	Cedarville
4,640	Cuyamaca
4,560	Canyon Dam
4,399	Alturas
4,390	Doyle 4 SSE
4,350	Mitchell Caverns
4,102	Bishop Arpt
4,035	Tulelake
3,950	Independence
3,825	Haiwee
3,185	Callahan
3,060	Fairmont
2,950	El Mirage
2,857	Victorville Pump Plant
2,709	De Sabla
2,625	Yreka
2,399	Colfax
2,319	Barstow Fire Station
2,169	Dunsmuir Treatment Plant
2,089	Auberry 2 NW
1,720	Balch Power House
1,714	Angwin Pac Union Col
1,708	Ash Mountain
1,424	Tejon Rancho
1,410	Covelo
1,370	Hayfield Pumping Plant
1,317	Redlands
1,292	Auburn
1,285	Elsinore
914	Needles Airport
839	Riverside Fire Sta 3
805	Borrego Desert Park
790	Canoga Park Pierce College
780	Cachuma Lake
750	Ojai
737	Parker Reservoir
669	Coalinga
658	Camp Pardee
654	Burbank Valley Pump Plant
600	Escondido No 2
488	Bakersfield Meadows Field
479	Livermore
419	Ben Lomond No 4
410	Friant Government Camp
399	Orleans
393	Porterville
379	Woodside Fire Stn 1

Feet	Station Name
370	Calistoga
333	Fresno Air Terminal
325	Visalia
319	King City
310	Berkeley
274	Hollister 2
270	Los Angeles Civic Center
268	Blythe
253	Santa Maria Public Arpt
200	Graton
193	Gilroy
174	San Francisco
120	Fort Bragg 5 N
115	Morro Bay Fire Dept
100	Los Angeles Intl Arpt
90	Modesto
89	Newman
68	Woodland 1 WNW
60	Antioch Pump Plant #3
56	Chula Vista
55	Culver City
49	Colusa 2 SSW
44	Salinas No 2
40	Crescent City 3 NNW
40	Fairfield
35	Laguna Beach
35	San Francisco Oceanside
30	Petaluma Fire Station 2
24	Long Beach Daugherty Fld
21	Stockton Metropolitan Arpt
20	Eureka
15	Sacramento Executive Arpt
14	Santa Monica Pier
13	San Diego Lindbergh Field
12	Stockton Fire Stn #4
7	San Francisco Int'l Arpt
4	Santa Barbara
-193	Death Valley

See User Guide for station inclusion criteria.

Bakersfield Meadows Field

Bakersfield, situated in the extreme south end of the great San Joaquin Valley, is partially surrounded by a horseshoe-shaped rim of mountains with an open side to the northwest and the crest at an average distance of 40 miles.

The Sierra Nevada mountains to the northeast shut out most of the cold air that flows southward over the continent during winter. They also catch and store snow, which provides irrigation water for use during the dry months. The Tehachapi Mountains, forming the southern boundary, act as an obstruction to northwest wind, causing heavier precipitation on the windward slopes, high wind velocity over the ridges and, at times, continuing cloudiness in the south end of the valley after skies have cleared elsewhere.

Because of the nature of the surrounding topography, there are large climatic variations within relatively short distances. These zones of variation may be classified as valley, mountain, and desert areas. The overall climate, however, is warm and semi-arid. There is only one wet season during the year, as 90 percent of all precipitation falls from October through April, inclusive. Snow in the valley is infrequent, with only a trace occurring in about one year out of seven. Thunderstorms seldom occur in the valley.

Summers are cloudless, hot and dry. Cotton, potatoes, grapes, and cattle are the principal agricultural products. Severe freezes seldom occur and there are occasional years with no frost at all in certain warm areas.

Winters are mild and semi-arid, yet fairly humid. December and January are characterized by frequent fog, mostly nocturnal, which prevails when marine air is trapped in the valley by a high pressure system. In extreme cases this fog may last continuously for two or three weeks. Another local characteristic is the occasionally warm, dry, southeast chinook wind that spills through the Tehachapi Pass during winter. This wind usually attains velocities of 30 to 40 miles an hour, sometimes reaching as high as 60 miles an hour.

During summer months northwest sea breezes frequent the Bakersfield area about twice weekly. When above normal temperatures prevail for several days, the gradient builds up sufficiently to draw in cooler air from the coastal section. During prolonged periods of drought this late afternoon breeze may carry varying amounts of dust, and thermal instability sometimes causes the dust to rise as high as 7,000 feet.

Based on the 1951-1980 period, the average first occurrence of 32 degrees Fahrenheit in the fall is December 11 and the average last occurrence in the spring is January 31.

Bakersfield Meadows Field *Kern County* Elevation: 488 ft. Latitude: 35° 26' N Longitude: 119° 03' W

	JAN	FEB	MAR	APR	MAY	JUN	JUL	AUG	SEP	OCT	NOV	DEC	YEAR
Mean Maximum Temp. (°F)	57.2	63.8	69.5	76.0	84.4	91.6	97.8	96.4	90.6	80.2	66.3	57.2	77.6
Mean Temp. (°F)	48.2	53.1	57.7	62.7	70.5	77.3	83.6	82.3	76.9	67.1	55.2	47.7	65.2
Mean Minimum Temp. (°F)	39.0	42.3	45.9	49.3	56.6	63.0	69.3	68.1	63.2	54.0	44.1	38.1	52.7
Extreme Maximum Temp. (°F)	82	87	94	101	107	110	112	112	109	103	88	81	112
Extreme Minimum Temp. (°F)	23	25	32	33	37	45	52	55	47	38	28	19	19
Days Maximum Temp. ≥ 90°F	0	0	0	3	9	19	28	26	18	4	0	0	107
Days Maximum Temp. ≤ 32°F	0	0	0	0	0	0	0	0	0	0	0	0	0
Days Minimum Temp. ≤ 32°F	5	1	0	0	0	0	0	0	0	0	1	6	13
Days Minimum Temp. ≤ 0°F	0	0	0	0	0	0	0	0	0	0	0	0	0
Heating Degree Days (base 65°F)	515	330	230	122	28	3	0	0	2	52	290	529	2,101
Cooling Degree Days (base 65°F)	0	0	11	60	206	379	583	542	366	125	3	0	2,275
Mean Precipitation (in.)	1.18	1.21	1.24	0.51	0.18	0.08	trace	0.05	0.08	0.28	0.63	0.83	6.27
Maximum Precipitation (in.)*	2.6	4.7	4.3	2.6	2.4	1.1	0.3	1.2	1.1	1.8	3.0	2.0	10.9
Minimum Precipitation (in.)*	trace	trace	trace	0	0	0	0	0	0	0	0	0	1.9
Extreme Maximum Daily Precip. (in.)	1.42	0.97	0.99	0.74	0.64	0.44	0.05	1.00	0.34	0.96	0.99	0.98	1.42
Days With ≥ 0.1" Precipitation	3	4	4	2	1	0	0	0	0	1	2	2	19
Days With ≥ 0.5" Precipitation	0	1	0	0	0	0	0	0	0	0	0	0	1
Days With ≥ 1.0" Precipitation	0	0	0	0	0	0	0	0	0	0	0	0	0
Mean Snowfall (in.)	***0.1***	na	na	na	na	na	na	na	na	na	na	na	na
Maximum Snowfall (in.)*	trace	trace	2	0	0	0	0	0	0	0	0	trace	2
Maximum 24-hr. Snowfall (in.)*	trace	trace	2	0	0	0	0	0	0	0	0	trace	2
Maximum Snow Depth (in.)	na	na	na	na	na	na	na	na	na	na	na	na	na
Days With ≥ 1.0" Snow Depth	na	na	na	na	na	na	na	na	na	na	na	na	na
Thunderstorm Days*	< 1	< 1	1	< 1	< 1	< 1	< 1	< 1	1	< 1	< 1	< 1	2
Foggy Days*	18	10	4	1	< 1	< 1	< 1	< 1	1	2	10	18	64
Predominant Sky Cover*	OVR	OVR	CLR	CLR	CLR	CLR	CLR	CLR	CLR	CLR	CLR	OVR	CLR
Mean Relative Humidity 7am (%)*	86	82	75	63	53	46	44	50	56	63	77	86	65
Mean Relative Humidity 4pm (%)*	61	50	42	33	27	23	21	24	28	33	48	61	38
Mean Dewpoint (°F)*	39	41	41	42	44	48	51	53	51	46	42	39	45
Prevailing Wind Direction*	E	E	NNW	NW	NW	NW	NW	NW	NW	NW	E	E	NW
Prevailing Wind Speed (mph)*	6	6	9	10	10	10	10	9	9	8	6	6	8
Maximum Wind Gust (mph)*	48	58	51	48	45	58	36	49	48	48	49	63	63

Note: (*) Period of record is 1948-1995

The period of record for National Weather Service station data is 1980 – 2009 except where noted. See User Guide for detailed explanation of data.

Bishop Airport

The station at Bishop is located at the Municipal Airport two and a half miles east of the town, one mile west of the Owens River, on the floor of the Owens Valley, which is orientated northwest to southeast and at this point is 12 miles wide, level, and semi-arid. Peaks of the 12,000 to 14,000 feet Sierra Nevadas are 25 miles west, and the 12,000 to 14,000 feet White Mountains are 10 miles east. The northern end of the valley is partly cut off by 6,000 to 8,000 feet mountains about 45 miles distant. The southern end of the valley makes a gradual descent to the Mojave Desert about 150 miles distant.

During the summer and autumn, the Mojave Desert causes an early morning and late evening northerly wind. Conversely, in the heat of the afternoon, it causes a southerly wind that is occasionally strong. Summer skies are mostly clear with thunderstorms from May through August. The days are hot and dry, the nights cool.

Winter and spring, although seasons of adverse weather, are quite mild. The skies are partly cloudy with the years greatest amounts of precipitation falling during the months of November through April. At times, strong northerly winds blow, especially in the spring during the months of February, March, and April. East and west winds frequently give pronounced warm mountain wind effects and turbulence.

During the winter and spring, strong westerly winds aloft, flowing over the Sierra Nevadas, create the Sierra Wave, known to sailplane pilots the world over.

Based on the 1951-1980 period, the average first occurrence of 32 degrees Fahrenheit in the fall is October 13 and the average last occurrence in the spring is May 7.

Bishop Airport *Inyo County* Elevation: 4,102 ft. Latitude: 37° 22' N Longitude: 118° 21' W

	JAN	FEB	MAR	APR	MAY	JUN	JUL	AUG	SEP	OCT	NOV	DEC	YEAR
Mean Maximum Temp. (°F)	53.8	57.6	64.8	72.2	81.7	91.3	97.9	95.8	87.4	75.7	62.3	53.3	74.5
Mean Temp. (°F)	38.3	42.0	47.9	54.1	62.9	71.0	77.0	74.7	67.0	56.4	44.8	37.4	56.1
Mean Minimum Temp. (°F)	22.8	26.3	30.9	36.0	44.1	50.7	56.0	53.6	46.6	36.9	27.3	21.5	37.7
Extreme Maximum Temp. (°F)	76	81	85	93	102	107	110	107	112	97	84	77	112
Extreme Minimum Temp. (°F)	1	3	9	17	26	29	34	40	26	18	8	-8	-8
Days Maximum Temp. ≥ 90°F	0	0	0	0	6	20	29	28	14	1	0	0	98
Days Maximum Temp. ≤ 32°F	0	0	0	0	0	0	0	0	0	0	0	0	0
Days Minimum Temp. ≤ 32°F	29	23	18	9	1	0	0	0	0	7	24	30	141
Days Minimum Temp. ≤ 0°F	0	0	0	0	0	0	0	0	0	0	0	0	0
Heating Degree Days (base 65°F)	821	644	524	323	117	19	1	0	43	268	598	847	4,205
Cooling Degree Days (base 65°F)	0	0	0	4	60	206	379	309	111	8	0	0	1,077
Mean Precipitation (in.)	1.03	0.94	0.53	0.26	0.19	0.19	0.17	0.13	0.19	0.26	0.51	0.65	5.05
Maximum Precipitation (in.)*	8.9	6.0	2.9	2.3	1.3	1.3	1.5	0.6	1.3	1.6	2.6	5.8	17.1
Minimum Precipitation (in.)*	0	0	0	0	0	0	0	0	0	0	0	0	1.8
Extreme Maximum Daily Precip. (in.)	4.00	1.24	1.75	1.58	0.58	0.68	0.38	0.42	1.25	1.58	1.30	2.67	4.00
Days With ≥ 0.1" Precipitation	2	2	1	1	1	0	1	0	1	1	1	1	12
Days With ≥ 0.5" Precipitation	1	1	0	0	0	0	0	0	0	0	0	0	2
Days With ≥ 1.0" Precipitation	0	0	0	0	0	0	0	0	0	0	0	0	0
Mean Snowfall (in.)	na	na	na	na	na	na	na	na	na	na	na	na	na
Maximum Snowfall (in.)*	23	32	15	9	2	0	0	0	0	2	4	13	57
Maximum 24-hr. Snowfall (in.)*	13	12	8	7	2	0	0	0	0	2	2	6	13
Maximum Snow Depth (in.)	na	na	na	na	na	na	na	na	na	na	na	na	na
Days With ≥ 1.0" Snow Depth	na	na	na	na	na	na	na	na	na	na	na	na	na
Thunderstorm Days*	0	0	< 1	< 1	1	2	5	2	1	1	0	0	12
Foggy Days*	1	1	1	0	1	0	0	0	0	0	< 1	2	6
Predominant Sky Cover*	CLR	CLR	CLR	CLR	CLR	CLR	CLR	CLR	CLR	CLR	CLR	CLR	CLR
Mean Relative Humidity 7am (%)*	71	68	58	44	39	34	35	39	43	52	63	68	51
Mean Relative Humidity 4pm (%)*	35	27	21	17	16	13	14	14	15	18	27	35	21
Mean Dewpoint (°F)*	19	20	19	20	27	31	36	35	31	25	21	19	25
Prevailing Wind Direction*	NW	N	N	N	N	S	S	S	S	S	N	N	N
Prevailing Wind Speed (mph)*	7	13	14	13	13	13	13	13	12	12	12	12	12
Maximum Wind Gust (mph)*	60	63	59	62	66	60	60	75	53	56	93	68	93

Note: (*) Period of record is 1948-1995

Eureka

Humboldt Bay is one-quarter mile north and one mile west of the station. There are no hills in Eureka of any consequence. The land slopes upward gently from the Bay toward the Coast Range, which begins about 3 miles east of the station and reaches the top of its first ridge approximately 10 miles to the east. The elevation of the ridge is 2,000 feet and extends in a semicircle from a point 20 miles north of Eureka to a point 25 miles south.

The climate of Eureka is completely maritime with high humidity prevailing the entire year. The rainy season begins in October and continues through April, accounting for about 90 percent of the annual precipitation. The dry season from May through September is marked by considerable fog or low cloudiness that usually clears in the late morning.

Temperatures are moderate the entire year. Although record highs have reached the mid 80s and record lows near 20 degrees, the usual yearly range is from lows in the mid 30s to highs in the mid 70s.

The principal industries are lumbering, fishing, tourism, and dairy farming. There is very little truck farming due to the low temperatures and lack of sunshine, however, the climate is nearly ideal for berries and flowers.

Based on the 1951-1980 period, the average first occurrence of 32 degrees Fahrenheit in the fall is December 10 and the average last occurrence in the spring is February 6.

Eureka *Humboldt County* Elevation: 20 ft. Latitude: 40° 49' N Longitude: 124° 10' W

	JAN	FEB	MAR	APR	MAY	JUN	JUL	AUG	SEP	OCT	NOV	DEC	YEAR
Mean Maximum Temp. (°F)	55.8	56.6	57.0	58.1	60.5	62.6	63.9	64.6	64.1	62.0	58.5	55.4	59.9
Mean Temp. (°F)	48.8	49.7	50.2	51.6	54.5	56.8	58.4	59.1	57.6	55.0	51.4	48.4	53.5
Mean Minimum Temp. (°F)	41.7	42.7	43.5	45.1	48.4	50.9	53.0	53.5	51.1	48.0	44.3	41.3	47.0
Extreme Maximum Temp. (°F)	78	80	76	80	83	81	76	82	86	87	78	75	87
Extreme Minimum Temp. (°F)	4	27	30	32	35	40	46	45	41	34	29	22	4
Days Maximum Temp. ≥ 90°F	0	0	0	0	0	0	0	0	0	0	0	0	0
Days Maximum Temp. ≤ 32°F	0	0	0	0	0	0	0	0	0	0	0	0	0
Days Minimum Temp. ≤ 32°F	2	1	0	0	0	0	0	0	0	0	1	2	6
Days Minimum Temp. ≤ 0°F	0	0	0	0	0	0	0	0	0	0	0	0	0
Heating Degree Days (base 65°F)	496	427	450	395	319	240	198	177	215	305	400	508	4,130
Cooling Degree Days (base 65°F)	0	0	0	0	0	0	0	1	1	1	0	0	3
Mean Precipitation (in.)	6.30	5.57	5.30	3.20	1.71	0.69	0.18	0.30	0.55	2.14	5.53	7.98	39.45
Maximum Precipitation (in.)*	13.9	10.8	11.2	10.7	6.0	2.6	1.2	3.4	3.3	13.0	16.6	14.1	67.2
Minimum Precipitation (in.)*	0.7	0.1	1.2	0.3	trace	trace	0	trace	trace	trace	0.3	0.5	21.1
Extreme Maximum Daily Precip. (in.)	3.21	2.47	2.41	1.74	1.74	1.07	0.89	1.57	0.99	2.18	4.37	6.79	6.79
Days With ≥ 0.1" Precipitation	11	10	11	7	4	2	0	1	1	5	10	12	74
Days With ≥ 0.5" Precipitation	5	4	4	2	1	0	0	0	0	1	4	5	26
Days With ≥ 1.0" Precipitation	2	1	1	0	0	0	0	0	0	0	2	2	8
Mean Snowfall (in.)	trace	0.2	trace	trace	0.0	trace	0.0	0.0	0.0	0.0	trace	0.1	0.3
Maximum Snowfall (in.)*	3	4	1	trace	0	0	0	0	0	0	trace	2	4
Maximum 24-hr. Snowfall (in.)*	2	2	1	trace	0	0	0	0	0	0	trace	2	2
Maximum Snow Depth (in.)	8	8	6	trace	0	trace	0	0	0	0	trace	3	8
Days With ≥ 1.0" Snow Depth	0	0	0	0	0	0	0	0	0	0	0	0	0
Thunderstorm Days*	1	1	< 1	< 1	< 1	< 1	< 1	< 1	< 1	< 1	1	1	4
Foggy Days*	13	11	10	12	13	16	22	22	21	21	15	15	191
Predominant Sky Cover*	na	na	na	na	na	na	na	na	na	na	na	na	na
Mean Relative Humidity 7am (%)*	na	na	na	na	na	na	na	na	na	na	na	na	na
Mean Relative Humidity 4pm (%)*	na	na	na	na	na	na	na	na	na	na	na	na	na
Mean Dewpoint (°F)*	na	na	na	na	na	na	na	na	na	na	na	na	na
Prevailing Wind Direction*	na	na	na	na	na	na	na	na	na	na	na	na	na
Prevailing Wind Speed (mph)*	na	na	na	na	na	na	na	na	na	na	na	na	na
Maximum Wind Gust (mph)*	69	60	58	53	60	51	47	38	49	49	69	62	69

Note: (*) Period of record is 1941-1995

The period of record for National Weather Service station data is 1980 – 2009 except where noted. See User Guide for detailed explanation of data.

Fresno Air Terminal

Fresno is located about midway and toward the eastern edge of the San Joaquin Valley, which is oriented northwest to southeast and has a length of about 225 miles and an average width of 50 miles. The San Joaquin Valley is generally flat. About 15 miles east of Fresno the terrain slopes upward with the foothills of the Sierra Nevada. The Sierra Nevada attain an elevation of more than 14,000 feet 50 miles east of Fresno. West of the city 45 miles lie the foothills of the Coastal Range.

The climate of Fresno is dry and mild in winter and hot in summer. Nearly nine-tenths of the annual precipitation falls in the six months from November to April.

Due to clear skies during the summer and the protection of the San Joaquin Valley from marine effects, the normal daily maximum temperature reaches the high 90s during the latter part of July. The daily maximum temperature during the warmest month has ranged from 76 to 115 degrees. Low relative humidities and some wind movement substantially lower the sensible temperature during periods of high readings. Humidity readings of 15 percent are common on summer afternoons, and readings as low as eight percent have been recorded. In contrast to this, humidity readings average 90 percent during the morning hours of December and January.

Winds flow with the major axis of the San Joaquin Valley, generally from the northwest. This feature is especially beneficial since, during the warmest months, the northwest winds increase during the evenings. These refreshing breezes and the normally large temperature variation of about 35 degrees between the highest and lowest readings of the day, generally result in comfortable evening and night temperatures.

Winter temperatures are usually mild with infrequent cold spells dropping the readings below freezing. Heavy frost occurs almost every year, and the first frost usually occurs during the last week of November. The last frost in spring is usually in early March. The growing season is 291 days.

Although the heaviest rains recorded at Fresno for short periods have occurred in June, usually any rainfall during the summer is very light. Snow is a rare occurrence in Fresno.

Fresno enjoys a very high percentage of sunshine, receiving more than 80 percent of the possible amounts during all but the four months of November, December, January, and February.

During foggy periods, sunshine is reduced to a minimum and fog frequently lifts to a few hundred feet above the surface of the valley, appearing as a heavy, solid cloud layer.

Fresno Air Terminal *Fresno County* Elevation: 333 ft. Latitude: 36° 47' N Longitude: 119° 43' W

	JAN	FEB	MAR	APR	MAY	JUN	JUL	AUG	SEP	OCT	NOV	DEC	YEAR
Mean Maximum Temp. (°F)	55.0	61.9	67.6	75.0	84.4	92.1	98.6	97.1	90.9	79.5	65.2	54.9	76.9
Mean Temp. (°F)	46.9	51.9	56.7	62.2	70.3	77.1	83.1	81.6	76.1	66.1	54.4	46.5	64.4
Mean Minimum Temp. (°F)	38.8	41.9	45.6	49.3	56.1	62.0	67.6	66.0	61.3	52.7	43.5	38.1	51.9
Extreme Maximum Temp. (°F)	78	80	87	100	107	110	113	112	107	102	85	77	113
Extreme Minimum Temp. (°F)	23	24	32	32	41	46	54	55	46	39	29	18	18
Days Maximum Temp. ≥ 90°F	0	0	0	2	10	20	29	28	18	4	0	0	111
Days Maximum Temp. ≤ 32°F	0	0	0	0	0	0	0	0	0	0	0	0	0
Days Minimum Temp. ≤ 32°F	6	2	0	0	0	0	0	0	0	0	1	6	15
Days Minimum Temp. ≤ 0°F	0	0	0	0	0	0	0	0	0	0	0	0	0
Heating Degree Days (base 65°F)	553	363	257	127	27	2	0	0	2	58	313	565	2,267
Cooling Degree Days (base 65°F)	0	0	6	49	197	372	568	521	343	100	1	0	2,157
Mean Precipitation (in.)	2.25	2.04	2.07	0.88	0.43	0.21	0.01	0.01	0.17	0.61	1.01	1.59	11.28
Maximum Precipitation (in.)*	8.6	6.0	7.2	4.4	1.6	1.6	0.2	0.3	1.2	2.2	3.5	6.7	21.6
Minimum Precipitation (in.)*	trace	trace	0	trace	0	0	0	0	0	0	0	0	6.1
Extreme Maximum Daily Precip. (in.)	1.88	1.87	2.38	1.39	1.11	1.80	0.22	0.06	0.85	1.50	1.05	1.64	2.38
Days With ≥ 0.1" Precipitation	5	5	5	2	1	0	0	0	1	1	3	4	27
Days With ≥ 0.5" Precipitation	1	1	1	1	0	0	0	0	0	0	1	1	6
Days With ≥ 1.0" Precipitation	0	0	0	0	0	0	0	0	0	0	0	0	0
Mean Snowfall (in.)	na	na	na	na	na	na	na	na	na	na	na	na	na
Maximum Snowfall (in.)*	2	trace	trace	0	0	0	0	0	0	0	trace	1	2
Maximum 24-hr. Snowfall (in.)*	2	trace	trace	0	0	0	0	0	0	0	trace	1	2
Maximum Snow Depth (in.)	na	na	na	na	na	na	na	na	na	na	na	na	na
Days With ≥ 1.0" Snow Depth	na	na	na	na	na	na	na	na	na	na	na	na	na
Thunderstorm Days*	< 1	< 1	1	1	1	< 1	< 1	< 1	1	1	< 1	< 1	5
Foggy Days*	23	15	8	3	1	< 1	< 1	< 1	1	5	17	23	96
Predominant Sky Cover*	OVR	OVR	CLR	CLR	CLR	CLR	CLR	CLR	CLR	CLR	CLR	OVR	CLR
Mean Relative Humidity 7am (%)*	92	91	86	75	63	56	54	61	69	77	88	92	75
Mean Relative Humidity 4pm (%)*	67	56	46	35	27	23	21	24	27	34	53	68	40
Mean Dewpoint (°F)*	40	42	43	44	46	49	53	54	52	47	43	40	46
Prevailing Wind Direction*	SE	NW	NW	NW	NW	NW	WNW	WNW	WNW	NW	NW	ESE	NW
Prevailing Wind Speed (mph)*	7	8	9	9	10	9	9	8	8	8	8	7	8
Maximum Wind Gust (mph)*	55	49	48	48	44	39	30	36	39	51	46	48	55

Note: (*) Period of record is 1949-1995

Long Beach Daugherty Field

The climate of the Long Beach Airport is considerably influenced by local topography, which plays a greater role in the climatic conditions at this station than the more general movements of pressure systems which dominate other sections of the country.

The Pacific Ocean, four miles south and 12 miles west, has a moderating effect on temperatures. The annual range of temperatures at the airport is much less than is experienced at stations further inland in the Los Angeles basin. Low coastal hills lie immediately between the station and the sea, the highest being Signal Hill, one and five eithths miles southwest and 498 feet above sea level. The Palos Verdes Hills, 11 miles west-southwest of the station, slope upward to 1,480 feet above sea level. These natural barriers between the ocean and the station cause slightly greater ranges of high and low temperatures locally than at stations on the coast. During the winter months high temperatures are usually in the upper 60s, and lows in the 40s. In the summer highs are in the 70s and low 80s, and lows in the high 50s.

Precipitation is sparse during the summer months, with an average of only about 0.60 inch for the months of May through October. The greatest rainfall occurs during the winter months. The coastal hills influence the local precipitation with greater amounts of rainfall occurring just one or two miles south and southwest of the station. Snow is an extremely rare phenomenon locally, although the San Gabriel Mountains are blanketed in the higher elevations much of the winter, and occasionally have snow down to the 2,500-foot level. Thunderstorms occur only sporadically at Long Beach.

The coastal hills to the southwest combine with the lowest mountain passes leading to the interior desert valleys east of the Los Angeles basin to produce a sea breeze from a westerly component in the afternoon and early evening hours. Occasionally, strong dry northeasterly winds descend the mountain slopes in the fall, winter, and early spring months, but ordinarily by-pass the station. Actually, the highest winds at Long Beach are recorded in association with the winter and spring storms which invade southern California from the Pacific.

During the summer months low clouds are quite common in the late night and morning hours at this station due to its proximity to the ocean. By late morning or early afternoon the clouds have disappeared and the balance of the day is sunny and comfortable. Here again is a moderating influence on summertime temperatures locally which is not so prominent at stations further inland where the coastal cloudiness arrives later, burns off earlier, and penetrates less frequently.

Long Beach Daugherty Field *Los Angeles County* Elevation: 24 ft. Latitude: 33° 50' N Longitude: 118° 10' W

	JAN	FEB	MAR	APR	MAY	JUN	JUL	AUG	SEP	OCT	NOV	DEC	YEAR
Mean Maximum Temp. (°F)	67.4	67.3	68.6	72.0	73.7	77.1	82.2	83.9	82.2	77.4	72.1	67.1	74.2
Mean Temp. (°F)	56.9	57.8	59.6	62.7	65.8	69.1	73.4	74.5	72.8	67.9	61.5	56.4	64.9
Mean Minimum Temp. (°F)	46.4	48.1	50.6	53.4	57.8	61.0	64.5	65.1	63.3	58.3	50.9	45.7	55.4
Extreme Maximum Temp. (°F)	93	91	98	105	104	109	107	103	108	109	98	89	109
Extreme Minimum Temp. (°F)	30	34	37	40	47	51	57	58	54	45	35	28	28
Days Maximum Temp. ≥ 90°F	0	0	0	1	1	1	4	6	5	3	1	0	22
Days Maximum Temp. ≤ 32°F	0	0	0	0	0	0	0	0	0	0	0	0	0
Days Minimum Temp. ≤ 32°F	0	0	0	0	0	0	0	0	0	0	0	0	0
Days Minimum Temp. ≤ 0°F	0	0	0	0	0	0	0	0	0	0	0	0	0
Heating Degree Days (base 65°F)	249	204	170	97	32	5	0	0	1	16	118	260	1,152
Cooling Degree Days (base 65°F)	4	6	10	34	61	134	267	302	240	112	20	2	1,192
Mean Precipitation (in.)	2.61	3.25	1.95	0.58	0.22	0.07	0.03	0.03	0.18	0.58	0.98	1.66	12.14
Maximum Precipitation (in.)*	12.8	9.4	8.8	4.4	2.3	0.9	0.2	2.0	1.4	1.6	6.0	5.3	27.7
Minimum Precipitation (in.)*	0	0	0	0	0	0	0	0	0	0	0	trace	2.8
Extreme Maximum Daily Precip. (in.)	3.75	2.78	3.46	1.61	1.17	0.86	0.27	0.33	1.39	1.97	1.77	3.05	3.75
Days With ≥ 0.1" Precipitation	4	5	4	1	0	0	0	0	0	1	2	3	20
Days With ≥ 0.5" Precipitation	2	2	1	0	0	0	0	0	0	0	1	1	7
Days With ≥ 1.0" Precipitation	1	1	0	0	0	0	0	0	0	0	0	0	2
Mean Snowfall (in.)	na	na	na	na	na	na	na	na	na	na	na	na	na
Maximum Snowfall (in.)*	trace	0	0	0	0	0	0	0	0	0	0	0	trace
Maximum 24-hr. Snowfall (in.)*	trace	0	0	0	0	0	0	0	0	0	0	0	trace
Maximum Snow Depth (in.)	na	na	na	na	na	na	na	na	na	na	na	na	na
Days With ≥ 1.0" Snow Depth	na	na	na	na	na	na	na	na	na	na	na	na	na
Thunderstorm Days*	< 1	1	1	< 1	< 1	< 1	< 1	< 1	< 1	< 1	< 1	< 1	2
Foggy Days*	14	12	11	8	7	8	8	9	12	14	15	15	133
Predominant Sky Cover*	CLR	OVR	CLR	CLR	OVR	CLR	CLR	CLR	CLR	CLR	CLR	CLR	CLR
Mean Relative Humidity 7am (%)*	77	79	80	77	76	78	79	80	81	80	76	75	78
Mean Relative Humidity 4pm (%)*	54	54	55	52	55	56	54	54	55	55	52	53	54
Mean Dewpoint (°F)*	42	44	46	48	52	56	60	61	59	54	46	42	51
Prevailing Wind Direction*	WNW	WNW	W	S	S	S	S	WNW	WNW	WNW	NW	WNW	WNW
Prevailing Wind Speed (mph)*	7	8	10	9	9	8	8	8	8	8	7	7	8
Maximum Wind Gust (mph)*	49	49	49	47	43	40	28	29	51	49	78	45	78

Note: (*) Period of record is 1949-1995

Los Angeles Civic Center

The climate of Los Angeles is normally pleasant and mild through the year. The Pacific Ocean is the primary moderating influence. The coastal mountain ranges lying along the north and east sides of the Los Angeles coastal basin act as a buffer against extremes of summer heat and winter cold occurring in desert and plateau regions in the interior. A variable balance between mild sea breezes, and either hot or cold winds from the interior, results in some variety in weather conditions, but temperature and humidity are usually well within the comfort level. The climate of the Los Angeles metropolitan area is marked by a difference in temperature, humidity, cloudiness, fog, rain, and sunshine over fairly short distances.

These differences are closely related to the distance from, and elevation above, the Pacific Ocean. Both high and low temperatures become more extreme and the average relative humidity becomes lower inland and up slopes. Relative humidity is frequently high near the coast, but may be quite low along the foothills. During periods of high temperatures, the relative humidity is usually below normal. Like other Pacific Coast areas, most rainfall comes during the winter with nearly 85 percent of the annual total occurring from November through March, while summers are practically rainless. Precipitation generally increases with distance from the ocean, from a yearly total of around 12 inches in coastal sections to the south of the city to over 20 inches in foothill areas. Destructive flash floods occasionally develop in and below some mountain canyons. Snow is often visible on nearby mountains in the winter, but is extremely rare in the coastal basin.

Prevailing winds are from the west during the spring, summer, and early autumn, with northeasterly wind predominating the remainder of the year. At times, the lack of air movement, combined with a frequent and persistent temperature inversion, is associated with concentrations of air pollution in the Los Angeles coastal basin and some adjacent areas. In fall, winter, and early spring months, occasional foehn-like descending Santa Ana winds come from the northeast over ridges and through passes in the coastal mountains. Sunshine, fog, and clouds depend a great deal on topography and distance from the ocean. Low clouds are common at night and in the morning along the coast during spring and summer, but form later and clear earlier near the foothills so that annual cloudiness and fog frequencies are greatest near the ocean, and sunshine totals are highest on the inland side of the city. The sun shines about 75 percent of daytime hours at the Civic Center. Light fog may accompany the usual night and morning low clouds, but dense fog is more likely to occur during the night and early morning hours of the winter months.

Los Angeles Civic Center *Los Angeles County* Elevation: 270 ft. Latitude: 34° 03' N Longitude: 118° 14' W

	JAN	FEB	MAR	APR	MAY	JUN	JUL	AUG	SEP	OCT	NOV	DEC	YEAR
Mean Maximum Temp. (°F)	68.6	69.2	70.4	73.3	75.1	78.9	83.8	84.8	83.4	79.0	73.3	68.3	75.7
Mean Temp. (°F)	59.2	60.2	61.7	64.4	67.1	70.5	74.6	75.4	74.1	69.7	63.5	58.8	66.6
Mean Minimum Temp. (°F)	49.8	51.2	52.9	55.5	59.1	62.1	65.4	65.9	64.8	60.4	53.8	49.3	57.5
Extreme Maximum Temp. (°F)	91	95	98	106	101	112	107	105	110	108	99	89	112
Extreme Minimum Temp. (°F)	35	34	39	40	50	52	57	58	54	48	39	33	33
Days Maximum Temp. ≥ 90°F	0	0	0	2	1	2	4	6	6	4	1	0	26
Days Maximum Temp. ≤ 32°F	0	0	0	0	0	0	0	0	0	0	0	0	0
Days Minimum Temp. ≤ 32°F	0	0	0	0	0	0	0	0	0	0	0	0	0
Days Minimum Temp. ≤ 0°F	0	0	0	0	0	0	0	0	0	0	0	0	0
Heating Degree Days (base 65°F)	188	152	124	74	23	3	0	0	0	9	81	196	850
Cooling Degree Days (base 65°F)	15	23	28	63	95	175	304	329	281	163	44	11	1,531
Mean Precipitation (in.)	3.21	4.08	2.57	0.87	0.27	0.06	0.01	0.04	0.24	0.62	1.02	2.02	15.01
Maximum Precipitation (in.)*	10.0	12.4	8.1	9.9	3.6	1.1	trace	0.4	5.7	2.3	6.0	8.5	31.3
Minimum Precipitation (in.)*	trace	0	0	trace	0	0	0	0	0	0	0	0	4.1
Extreme Maximum Daily Precip. (in.)	3.30	3.03	4.10	1.44	1.18	0.76	0.13	0.44	1.95	1.41	1.96	5.55	5.55
Days With ≥ 0.1" Precipitation	4	5	4	2	1	0	0	0	1	1	2	3	23
Days With ≥ 0.5" Precipitation	2	3	2	1	0	0	0	0	0	1	1	1	11
Days With ≥ 1.0" Precipitation	1	1	1	0	0	0	0	0	0	0	0	0	3
Mean Snowfall (in.)	na	na	na	na	na	na	na	na	na	na	na	na	na
Maximum Snowfall (in.)*	trace	0	0	0	0	0	0	0	0	0	0	0	trace
Maximum 24-hr. Snowfall (in.)*	trace	0	0	0	0	0	0	0	0	0	0	0	trace
Maximum Snow Depth (in.)	na	na	na	na	na	na	na	na	na	na	na	na	na
Days With ≥ 1.0" Snow Depth	na	na	na	na	na	na	na	na	na	na	na	na	na
Thunderstorm Days*	< 1	1	< 1	1	< 1	< 1	< 1	< 1	< 1	< 1	< 1	< 1	2
Foggy Days*	3	4	3	4	4	6	5	5	8	6	5	3	56
Predominant Sky Cover*	na	na	na	na	na	na	na	na	na	na	na	na	na
Mean Relative Humidity 7am (%)*	na	na	na	na	na	na	na	na	na	na	na	na	na
Mean Relative Humidity 4pm (%)*	na	na	na	na	na	na	na	na	na	na	na	na	na
Mean Dewpoint (°F)*	na	na	na	na	na	na	na	na	na	na	na	na	na
Prevailing Wind Direction*	na	na	na	na	na	na	na	na	na	na	na	na	na
Prevailing Wind Speed (mph)*	na	na	na	na	na	na	na	na	na	na	na	na	na
Maximum Wind Gust (mph)*	na	na	na	na	na	na	na	na	na	na	na	na	na

Note: (*) Period of record is 1921-1963

Los Angeles Int'l Airport

Predominating influences on the climate of the Los Angeles International Airport are the Pacific Ocean, three miles to the west, the southern California coastal mountain ranges which line the inland side of the coastal plain surrounding the airport, and the large scale weather patterns associated with Pacific storm paths. Marine air covers the coastal plain most of the year but air from the interior reaches the coast at times, especially during the fall and winter months. The coast ranges act as a buffer to the more extreme conditions of the interior. Pronounced differences in temperature, humidity, cloudiness, fog, sunshine, and rain occur over fairly short distances on the coastal plains and the adjoining foothills due to the local topography and the decreased marine effect further inland. In general, temperature ranges are least and humidity highest close to the coast, while precipitation increases with elevation.

The most characteristic feature of the climate of the coastal plain around the station is the night and morning low cloudiness and sunny afternoons which prevail during the spring and summer months and occur often during the remainder of the year. The coastal low cloudiness, combined with the westerly sea breeze, produces mild temperatures throughout the year. Daily temperature range is usually less than 15 degrees in spring and summer and about 20 degrees in fall and winter. Hot weather is not frequent at any season along the coast. When high temperatures do occur, the humidity is almost always low. Nighttime temperatures are generally cool but minimum temperatures below 40 degrees are rare and periods of over 10 years have passed with no readings below freezing at the airport. Prevailing daytime winds are from the west, but night and early morning breezes are usually light and from the east and northeast. Strongest winds observed at the station have been from the west and north following winter storms. During the fall, winter, and spring, gusty dry northeasterly Santa Ana winds blow over southern California mountains and through passes to the coast, but rarely reach L.A. International Airport.

Precipitation occurs mainly in the winter. Measurable rain may fall on about one day in four from late October into early April, but in three years out of four, traces or less are reported for the entire months of July and August. Thunderstorms do not occur often near the coast, but showers and thunderstorms are observed over the coastal ranges during the summer. Traces of snow have fallen at Los Angeles International Airport only a few times, melting as they fell.

Visibility at Los Angeles International Airport is frequently restricted by haze, fog, or smoke. Low visibilities are favored by a layer of moist marine air with warm dry air above and light winds. Light fog occurs at some time nearly every month, but heavy fog is observed least during the summer.

Los Angeles Int'l Airport *Los Angeles County* Elevation: 100 ft. Latitude: 33° 56' N Longitude: 118° 24' W

	JAN	FEB	MAR	APR	MAY	JUN	JUL	AUG	SEP	OCT	NOV	DEC	YEAR
Mean Maximum Temp. (°F)	65.9	65.7	65.6	68.0	69.4	72.1	75.4	76.4	75.9	73.9	70.3	66.0	70.4
Mean Temp. (°F)	57.4	57.9	58.7	60.9	63.4	66.3	69.6	70.4	69.6	66.6	61.8	57.3	63.3
Mean Minimum Temp. (°F)	48.9	50.1	51.7	53.8	57.3	60.4	63.7	64.4	63.2	59.2	53.2	48.6	56.2
Extreme Maximum Temp. (°F)	91	90	95	102	94	104	97	97	106	103	96	90	106
Extreme Minimum Temp. (°F)	33	35	39	42	49	51	53	56	54	45	39	34	33
Days Maximum Temp. ≥ 90°F	0	0	0	1	0	0	0	0	1	1	0	0	3
Days Maximum Temp. ≤ 32°F	0	0	0	0	0	0	0	0	0	0	0	0	0
Days Minimum Temp. ≤ 32°F	0	0	0	0	0	0	0	0	0	0	0	0	0
Days Minimum Temp. ≤ 0°F	0	0	0	0	0	0	0	0	0	0	0	0	0
Heating Degree Days (base 65°F)	234	201	197	135	65	15	0	0	2	24	113	233	1,219
Cooling Degree Days (base 65°F)	7	8	8	20	22	60	148	175	146	79	23	3	699
Mean Precipitation (in.)	2.79	3.45	1.97	0.66	0.22	0.08	0.03	0.06	0.21	0.51	1.09	1.80	12.87
Maximum Precipitation (in.)*	12.7	11.1	6.4	4.5	2.5	0.7	0.3	2.5	1.9	1.8	7.5	5.7	29.5
Minimum Precipitation (in.)*	0	0	0	0	0	0	0	0	0	0	0	0	3.1
Extreme Maximum Daily Precip. (in.)	3.50	3.10	2.55	1.35	0.77	0.74	0.28	1.00	1.66	1.45	1.69	4.53	4.53
Days With ≥ 0.1" Precipitation	4	5	4	2	1	0	0	0	0	1	2	3	22
Days With ≥ 0.5" Precipitation	2	2	1	0	0	0	0	0	0	0	1	1	7
Days With ≥ 1.0" Precipitation	1	1	0	0	0	0	0	0	0	0	0	0	2
Mean Snowfall (in.)	na	na	na	na	na	na	na	na	na	na	na	na	na
Maximum Snowfall (in.)*	trace	0	0	0	0	0	0	0	0	0	0	0	trace
Maximum 24-hr. Snowfall (in.)*	trace	0	0	0	0	0	0	0	0	0	0	0	trace
Maximum Snow Depth (in.)	na	na	na	na	na	na	na	na	na	na	na	na	na
Days With ≥ 1.0" Snow Depth	na	na	na	na	na	na	na	na	na	na	na	na	na
Thunderstorm Days*	< 1	1	1	< 1	< 1	< 1	< 1	< 1	< 1	< 1	< 1	< 1	2
Foggy Days*	11	10	8	7	6	6	7	8	9	11	11	11	105
Predominant Sky Cover*	CLR	CLR	CLR	CLR	OVR	OVR	CLR	CLR	CLR	CLR	CLR	CLR	CLR
Mean Relative Humidity 7am (%)*	70	72	76	76	77	80	80	82	81	76	69	68	76
Mean Relative Humidity 4pm (%)*	61	62	64	64	66	67	67	68	67	66	61	61	64
Mean Dewpoint (°F)*	42	44	46	49	53	56	60	61	59	54	46	42	51
Prevailing Wind Direction*	WSW	WSW	WSW	WSW	WSW	WSW	WSW	WSW	WSW	WSW	WSW	WSW	WSW
Prevailing Wind Speed (mph)*	9	9	10	10	10	10	9	9	9	9	9	8	9
Maximum Wind Gust (mph)*	51	56	62	59	49	40	31	33	39	46	60	49	62

Note: (*) Period of record is 1948-1995

The period of record for National Weather Service station data is 1980 – 2009 except where noted. See User Guide for detailed explanation of data.

Sacramento Executive Airport

Sacramento, and the lower Sacramento Valley, has a mild climate with abundant sunshine most of the year. A nearly cloud-free sky prevails throughout the summer months, and in much of the spring and fall. The summers are usually dry with warm to hot afternoons and mostly mild nights. The rainy season generally is November through March. About 75 percent of the annual precipitation occurs then, but measurable rain falls only on an average of nine days per month during that period. The shielding effect of mountains to the north, east, and west usually modifies winter storms. The Sierra Nevada snow fields, only 70 miles east of Sacramento, usually provide an adequate water supply during the dry season, and an important recreational area in winter. Heavy snowfall and torrential rains frequently fall on the western Sierra slopes, and may produce flood conditions along the Sacramento River and its tributaries. In the valley, however, excessive rainfall as well as damaging winds are rare.

The prevailing wind at Sacramento is southerly every month but November, when it is northerly. Topographic effects, the north-south alignment of the valley, the coast range, and the Sierra Nevada strongly influence the wind flow in the valley. A sea level gap in the coast range permits cool, oceanic air to flow, occasionally, into the valley during the summer season with a marked lowering of temperature through the Sacramento-San Joaquin River Delta to the capital. In the spring and fall, a large north-to-south pressure gradient develops over the northern part of the state.

Extreme hot spells, with temperatures exceeding 100 degrees, are usually caused by air flow from a sub-tropical high pressure area that brings light to nearly calm winds and humidities below 20 percent.

Thunderstorms are few in number, usually mild in character, and occur mainly in the spring. An occasional thunderstorm may drift over the valley from the Sierra Nevada in the summer. Snow falls so rarely, and in such small amounts, that its occurrence may be disregarded as a climatic feature. Heavy fog occurs mostly in midwinter, never in summer, and seldom in spring or autumn. An occasional winter fog, under stagnant atmospheric conditions, may continue for several days. Light and moderate fogs are more frequent, and may come anytime during the wet, cold season. The fog is the radiational cooling type, and is usually confined to the early morning hours.

Based on the 1951-1980 period, the average first occurrence of 32 degrees Fahrenheit in the fall is December 1 and the average last occurrence in the spring is February 14.

Sacramento Executive Airport *Sacramento County* Elevation: 15 ft. Latitude: 38° 30' N Longitude: 121° 30' W

	JAN	FEB	MAR	APR	MAY	JUN	JUL	AUG	SEP	OCT	NOV	DEC	YEAR
Mean Maximum Temp. (°F)	54.3	60.5	65.4	71.7	80.2	87.1	92.4	91.5	87.4	78.1	64.2	54.2	73.9
Mean Temp. (°F)	46.6	51.1	54.9	59.2	65.8	71.5	75.6	74.9	71.7	64.2	53.6	46.3	61.3
Mean Minimum Temp. (°F)	38.9	41.7	44.3	46.6	51.4	55.8	58.7	58.2	55.9	50.3	43.0	38.3	48.6
Extreme Maximum Temp. (°F)	74	76	88	95	105	108	112	110	108	104	85	72	112
Extreme Minimum Temp. (°F)	21	23	31	31	37	41	48	51	42	36	26	18	18
Days Maximum Temp. ≥ 90°F	0	0	0	1	6	12	21	19	13	3	0	0	75
Days Maximum Temp. ≤ 32°F	0	0	0	0	0	0	0	0	0	0	0	0	0
Days Minimum Temp. ≤ 32°F	5	2	0	0	0	0	0	0	0	0	1	6	14
Days Minimum Temp. ≤ 0°F	0	0	0	0	0	0	0	0	0	0	0	0	0
Heating Degree Days (base 65°F)	562	386	308	186	62	9	0	0	7	76	336	573	2,505
Cooling Degree Days (base 65°F)	0	0	1	18	95	211	335	313	214	58	1	0	1,246
Mean Precipitation (in.)	3.66	3.63	2.74	1.13	0.68	0.21	0.01	0.05	0.30	0.89	1.99	3.12	18.41
Maximum Precipitation (in.)*	9.7	8.8	8.1	4.2	3.1	1.3	0.8	0.6	2.8	7.5	7.4	12.6	33.4
Minimum Precipitation (in.)*	0.2	0.1	0	0	0	0	0	0	0	0	trace	0	5.6
Extreme Maximum Daily Precip. (in.)	2.99	2.63	1.85	1.49	1.67	1.14	0.37	0.32	1.79	2.94	2.08	2.12	2.99
Days With ≥ 0.1" Precipitation	7	7	6	3	2	1	0	0	1	2	4	6	39
Days With ≥ 0.5" Precipitation	2	3	2	1	0	0	0	0	0	1	1	2	12
Days With ≥ 1.0" Precipitation	1	1	0	0	0	0	0	0	0	0	0	1	3
Mean Snowfall (in.)	na	na	na	na	na	na	na	na	na	na	na	na	na
Maximum Snowfall (in.)*	trace	2	trace	trace	0	0	0	0	0	0	0	trace	2
Maximum 24-hr. Snowfall (in.)*	trace	2	trace	trace	0	0	0	0	0	0	0	trace	2
Maximum Snow Depth (in.)	na	na	na	na	na	na	na	na	na	na	na	na	na
Days With ≥ 1.0" Snow Depth	na	na	na	na	na	na	na	na	na	na	na	na	na
Thunderstorm Days*	< 1	1	1	1	< 1	< 1	< 1	< 1	< 1	< 1	< 1	< 1	3
Foggy Days*	22	14	8	3	1	< 1	< 1	1	2	7	16	22	96
Predominant Sky Cover*	OVR	OVR	CLR	CLR	CLR	CLR	CLR	CLR	CLR	CLR	CLR	OVR	CLR
Mean Relative Humidity 7am (%)*	91	89	85	78	72	67	69	74	75	81	87	91	80
Mean Relative Humidity 4pm (%)*	70	59	52	43	36	31	29	29	31	38	56	70	45
Mean Dewpoint (°F)*	39	42	43	44	47	50	53	53	51	47	43	39	46
Prevailing Wind Direction*	SE	SE	SW	SW	SW	SW	SSW	SSW	SSW	NNW	NNW	SE	SW
Prevailing Wind Speed (mph)*	9	9	10	10	12	13	10	10	10	10	9	9	10
Maximum Wind Gust (mph)*	53	46	47	45	51	45	37	33	38	40	56	51	56

Note: (*) Period of record is 1947-1995

San Diego Lindbergh Field

The city of San Diego is located on San Diego Bay in the southwest corner of southern California. The prevailing winds and weather are tempered by the Pacific Ocean. Temperatures of freezing or below have rarely occurred at the station since the record began in 1871, but hot weather, 90 degrees or above, is more frequent.

Dry easterly winds sometimes blow in the vicinity for several days at a time, bringing temperatures in the 90s and at times even in the 100s in the eastern sections of the city and outlying suburbs. As these hot winds are predominant in the fall, highest temperatures occur in the months of September and October. Records show that over 60 percent of the days with 90 degrees or higher have occurred in these two months. High temperatures are almost invariably accompanied by very low relative humidities, which often drop below 20 percent and occasionally below 10 percent.

A marked feature of the climate is the wide variation in temperature within short distances. In nearby valleys daytimes are much warmer in summer and nights noticeably cooler in winter, and freezing occurs much more frequently than in the city. Although records show unusually small daily temperature ranges, only about 15 degrees between the highest and lowest readings, a few miles inland these ranges increase to 30 degrees or more.

Strong winds and gales associated with Pacific, or tropical storms, are infrequent due to the latitude.

The seasonal rainfall is about 10 inches in the city, but increases with elevation and distance from the coast. In the mountains to the north and east the average is between 20 and 40 inches, depending on slope and elevation. Most of the precipitation falls in winter, except in the mountains where there is an occasional thunderstorm. Eighty-five percent of the rainfall occurs from November through March, but wide variations take place in monthly and seasonal totals. In each occurrence of snowfall only a trace was recorded officially.

As on the rest of the Pacific Coast, a dominant characteristic of spring and summer is the nighttime and early morning cloudiness. Low clouds form regularly and frequently extend inland over the coastal valleys and foothills, but they usually dissipate during the morning and the afternoons are generally clear.

Considerable fog occurs along the coast, but the amount decreases with distance inland. The fall and winter months are usually the foggiest. Thunderstorms are rare, averaging about three a year in the city.

San Diego Lindbergh Field *San Diego County* Elevation: 13 ft. Latitude: 32° 44' N Longitude: 117° 10' W

	JAN	FEB	MAR	APR	MAY	JUN	JUL	AUG	SEP	OCT	NOV	DEC	YEAR
Mean Maximum Temp. (°F)	65.7	65.8	66.2	68.3	69.2	71.6	75.5	77.1	76.4	73.4	69.6	65.4	70.3
Mean Temp. (°F)	57.7	58.6	60.0	62.4	64.6	67.1	70.8	72.3	71.1	67.2	61.8	57.2	64.2
Mean Minimum Temp. (°F)	49.7	51.4	53.8	56.5	60.0	62.6	66.0	67.4	65.7	61.0	54.0	48.9	58.1
Extreme Maximum Temp. (°F)	87	90	93	98	93	100	99	94	107	104	90	87	107
Extreme Minimum Temp. (°F)	35	38	42	45	50	54	59	60	53	48	39	34	34
Days Maximum Temp. ≥ 90°F	0	0	0	0	0	0	0	0	1	1	0	0	2
Days Maximum Temp. ≤ 32°F	0	0	0	0	0	0	0	0	0	0	0	0	0
Days Minimum Temp. ≤ 32°F	0	0	0	0	0	0	0	0	0	0	0	0	0
Days Minimum Temp. ≤ 0°F	0	0	0	0	0	0	0	0	0	0	0	0	0
Heating Degree Days (base 65°F)	222	179	154	91	41	9	0	0	0	12	103	236	1,047
Cooling Degree Days (base 65°F)	3	5	6	21	35	80	186	232	189	87	14	1	859
Mean Precipitation (in.)	2.05	2.34	1.87	0.76	0.14	0.07	0.03	0.02	0.15	0.50	0.98	1.37	10.28
Maximum Precipitation (in.)*	9.1	5.4	7.0	3.7	1.8	0.9	0.2	2.1	1.9	1.8	5.8	6.6	19.4
Minimum Precipitation (in.)*	trace	0	trace	0	0	0	0	0	0	0	0	trace	3.4
Extreme Maximum Daily Precip. (in.)	2.24	2.18	2.03	1.42	0.77	0.49	0.23	0.17	0.90	2.70	2.04	1.60	2.70
Days With ≥ 0.1" Precipitation	4	4	4	2	0	0	0	0	0	1	2	3	20
Days With ≥ 0.5" Precipitation	1	2	1	0	0	0	0	0	0	0	1	1	6
Days With ≥ 1.0" Precipitation	0	1	0	0	0	0	0	0	0	0	0	0	1
Mean Snowfall (in.)	na	na	na	na	na	na	na	na	na	na	na	na	na
Maximum Snowfall (in.)*	trace	0	0	0	0	0	0	0	0	0	0	trace	trace
Maximum 24-hr. Snowfall (in.)*	trace	0	0	0	0	0	0	0	0	0	0	trace	trace
Maximum Snow Depth (in.)	na	na	na	na	na	na	na	na	na	na	na	na	na
Days With ≥ 1.0" Snow Depth	na	na	na	na	na	na	na	na	na	na	na	na	na
Thunderstorm Days*	< 1	< 1	< 1	< 1	< 1	< 1	< 1	< 1	< 1	< 1	< 1	< 1	6
Foggy Days*	11	9	8	6	6	7	6	7	9	11	11	11	102
Predominant Sky Cover*	CLR	CLR	OVR	OVR	OVR	OVR	OVR	OVR	CLR	CLR	CLR	CLR	OVR
Mean Relative Humidity 7am (%)*	70	72	73	72	74	78	80	79	78	75	69	68	74
Mean Relative Humidity 4pm (%)*	58	58	59	60	64	66	66	66	65	64	60	58	62
Mean Dewpoint (°F)*	43	45	47	50	53	57	61	62	61	56	48	43	52
Prevailing Wind Direction*	NW	WNW	WNW	WNW	WNW	WNW	WNW	WNW	WNW	WNW	WNW	NW	WNW
Prevailing Wind Speed (mph)*	8	9	10	10	9	9	9	9	9	9	9	8	9
Maximum Wind Gust (mph)*	64	52	53	43	40	37	30	33	44	35	48	44	64

Note: (*) Period of record is 1948-1995

The period of record for National Weather Service station data is 1980 – 2009 except where noted. See User Guide for detailed explanation of data.

San Francisco Mission

San Francisco is located at the northern end of a narrow peninsula which separates San Francisco Bay from the Pacific Ocean. It is known as the air conditioned city with cool pleasant summers and mild winters.

Precipitation averages about 20 inches a year with pronounced wet and dry seasons, characteristic of its Mediterranean climate. Little or no rain falls from June through September while about 80 percent of the annual total falls from November through March. Snow and freezing temperatures are extremely rare. On average, thunderstorms occur on only two days each year. The average annual wind speed is about nine mph.

Sea fogs, and the low stratus clouds associated with them are most common in the summertime, but may occur at any time of the year. In the summer the temperature of the Pacific Ocean is much lower than the temperature inland, particularly in the Central Valley of California. This condition tends to enhance the sea breeze effect common to coastal areas. Brisk westerly winds blow throughout the afternoon and evening hours. The fog is carried inland by these westerly winds in the late afternoon and evening and then evaporates during the subsequent forenoon.

The complex topography of San Francisco causes complex patterns of fog and sun as well as temperature. A range of hills with elevations of nearly 1000 feet above sea level, bisects the city from north to south. This range partially blocks the inland movement of the fog, but gaps in the hills permit small masses of fog to pass through, further complicating the pattern.

Sunshine varies greatly from one part of the city to another, especially in the summer. Spring and fall are the sunniest seasons. The percent of possible summer sunshine varies from an estimated 25 to 35 percent at the ocean to 70 to 80 percent in the sunniest area.

The extent and behavior of the summertime fog on a particular day depends on several factors. A typical day would find the fog covering the entire city at sunrise and little wind. During the forenoon the skies become sunny in the eastern part of the city with some partial clearing reaching the ocean for a couple of hours in the early afternoon. By early afternoon the winds pick up and by late afternoon the fog is rolling inland again.

Temperature patterns in the city are the same as those of sunshine. In the winter there is little variation, with average maximums from 55 to 60 degrees and average minimums in the mid to upper 40s. Average temperatures rise until June and remain nearly constant through August with average maximums in the lower 60s near the ocean and upper 60s in the sunny eastern half of the city. Summer minimums range from 50 to 55. The warmest time of the year is September and October when the fog diminishes greatly.

San Francisco Mission *San Francisco County* Elevation: 174 ft. Latitude: 37° 46' N Longitude: 122° 26' W

	JAN	FEB	MAR	APR	MAY	JUN	JUL	AUG	SEP	OCT	NOV	DEC	YEAR
Mean Maximum Temp. (°F)	58.0	61.3	62.9	64.3	65.5	67.9	68.2	69.3	71.2	70.5	64.3	58.4	65.2
Mean Temp. (°F)	52.2	54.8	56.1	57.1	58.6	60.6	61.4	62.5	63.5	62.4	57.5	52.6	58.3
Mean Minimum Temp. (°F)	46.3	48.2	49.1	49.9	51.6	53.3	54.6	55.6	55.7	54.3	50.7	46.7	51.3
Extreme Maximum Temp. (°F)	74	81	87	94	101	103	103	98	100	102	83	73	103
Extreme Minimum Temp. (°F)	36	31	39	23	43	47	48	50	49	47	40	28	23
Days Maximum Temp. ≥ 90°F	0	0	0	0	0	1	0	0	1	1	0	0	3
Days Maximum Temp. ≤ 32°F	0	0	0	0	0	0	0	0	0	0	0	0	0
Days Minimum Temp. ≤ 32°F	0	0	0	0	0	0	0	0	0	0	0	0	0
Days Minimum Temp. ≤ 0°F	0	0	0	0	0	0	0	0	0	0	0	0	0
Heating Degree Days (base 65°F)	391	284	274	239	205	145	121	91	78	110	221	379	2,538
Cooling Degree Days (base 65°F)	0	1	3	10	13	19	18	21	40	36	4	0	165
Mean Precipitation (in.)	4.40	4.50	3.20	1.37	0.68	0.16	0.01	0.06	0.21	1.06	3.06	4.43	23.14
Maximum Precipitation (in.)*	10.7	10.1	9.0	5.5	4.0	1.4	0.2	0.5	2.1	5.5	8.2	11.5	43.8
Minimum Precipitation (in.)*	0.5	trace	trace	trace	0	0	0	0	0	trace	0	0	10.0
Extreme Maximum Daily Precip. (in.)	4.22	2.93	2.57	1.27	1.42	0.70	0.04	0.54	0.63	2.48	5.54	3.61	5.54
Days With ≥ 0.1" Precipitation	8	8	7	4	2	0	0	0	1	2	5	8	45
Days With ≥ 0.5" Precipitation	3	3	2	1	0	0	0	0	0	1	2	3	15
Days With ≥ 1.0" Precipitation	1	1	0	0	0	0	0	0	0	0	1	1	4
Mean Snowfall (in.)	na	na	na	na	na	na	na	na	na	na	na	na	na
Maximum Snowfall (in.)*	trace	trace	trace	0	0	0	0	0	0	0	0	1	1
Maximum 24-hr. Snowfall (in.)*	trace	trace	trace	0	0	0	0	0	0	0	0	1	1
Maximum Snow Depth (in.)	na	na	na	na	na	na	na	na	na	na	na	na	na
Days With ≥ 1.0" Snow Depth	na	na	na	na	na	na	na	na	na	na	na	na	na
Thunderstorm Days*	< 1	1	< 1	1	0	< 1	1	1	< 1	1	< 1	0	5
Foggy Days*	< 1	1	0	0	0	0	0	0	0	0	0	0	1
Predominant Sky Cover*	na	na	na	na	na	na	na	na	na	na	na	na	na
Mean Relative Humidity 7am (%)*	na	na	na	na	na	na	na	na	na	na	na	na	na
Mean Relative Humidity 4pm (%)*	na	na	na	na	na	na	na	na	na	na	na	na	na
Mean Dewpoint (°F)*	na	na	na	na	na	na	na	na	na	na	na	na	na
Prevailing Wind Direction*	na	na	na	na	na	na	na	na	na	na	na	na	na
Prevailing Wind Speed (mph)*	na	na	na	na	na	na	na	na	na	na	na	na	na
Maximum Wind Gust (mph)*	na	na	na	na	na	na	na	na	na	na	na	na	na

Note: (*) Period of record is 1921-1992

San Francisco Int'l Airport

The station is located in the central Terminal Building of the San Francisco International Airport, which is on flat filled tideland on the west shore of San Francisco Bay. The bay borders the airport from the north to the south-southeast. San Bruno Mountain, five miles to the north-northwest, rises to 1,300 feet. A north-south trending ridge of coastal mountains, four miles to the west, varies in elevation from 700 to 1,900 feet, being highest southward along the peninsula. The Pacific Ocean west of the ridge is six miles from the airport. A broad gap to the northwest of the station, between San Bruno Mountain and the coastal mountains, allows a strong flow of marine air over the station and dominate the local climate.

San Francisco Airport enjoys a marine-type climate characterized by mild and moderately wet winters and by dry, cool summers. Winter rains, occurring from November through March, account for over 80 percent of the annual rainfall, and measurable precipitation occurs on an average of 10 days per month during this period. However, there are frequent dry periods lasting well over a week. Severe winter storms with gale winds and heavy rains occur only occasionally. Thunderstorms average two a year and may occur in any month.

The daily and annual range in temperature is small. A few frosty mornings occur during the winter but the temperature seldom drops below freezing. Winter temperatures generally rise to the high 50s in the early afternoon.

The summer weather is dominated by a cool sea breeze resulting in an average summer wind speed of nearly 15 mph. Winds are light in the early morning but normally reach 20 to 25 mph in the afternoon.

A sea fog, arriving over the station during the late evening or night as a low cloud, is another persistent feature of the summer weather. This high fog, occasionally producing drizzle or mist, usually disappears during the late forenoon. Despite the morning overcast, summer days are sunny. On the average a total of only 14 days during the four months from June through September are classified as cloudy.

Daytime temperatures are held down both by the morning low overcast and the afternoon strengthening sea breeze, resulting in daily maximum readings averaging about 70 degrees from May through August. However, during these months occasional hot spells, lasting a few days, are experienced without the usual high fog and sea breeze. September, when the sea breeze becomes less pronounced, is the warmest month with highs in the 70s. Low temperatures during the summer are in the mid-50s.

San Francisco Int'l Airport *San Mateo County* Elevation: 7 ft. Latitude: 37° 37' N Longitude: 122° 24' W

	JAN	FEB	MAR	APR	MAY	JUN	JUL	AUG	SEP	OCT	NOV	DEC	YEAR
Mean Maximum Temp. (°F)	56.3	59.6	62.1	64.8	67.5	70.6	72.1	72.7	73.5	70.5	63.0	56.6	65.8
Mean Temp. (°F)	50.1	52.9	54.8	56.9	59.5	62.1	63.6	64.4	64.5	61.7	55.7	50.5	58.0
Mean Minimum Temp. (°F)	43.9	46.1	47.4	48.9	51.3	53.5	55.1	56.0	55.4	52.8	48.4	44.3	50.3
Extreme Maximum Temp. (°F)	72	77	83	92	97	105	105	100	100	99	80	71	105
Extreme Minimum Temp. (°F)	31	31	37	39	42	46	48	49	48	43	35	27	27
Days Maximum Temp. ≥ 90°F	0	0	0	0	0	1	1	0	1	0	0	0	3
Days Maximum Temp. ≤ 32°F	0	0	0	0	0	0	0	0	0	0	0	0	0
Days Minimum Temp. ≤ 32°F	0	0	0	0	0	0	0	0	0	0	0	0	0
Days Minimum Temp. ≤ 0°F	0	0	0	0	0	0	0	0	0	0	0	0	0
Heating Degree Days (base 65°F)	453	337	312	244	178	102	62	46	53	118	272	443	2,620
Cooling Degree Days (base 65°F)	0	0	1	6	13	22	26	33	44	22	1	0	168
Mean Precipitation (in.)	4.15	4.23	2.96	1.22	0.45	0.11	0.01	0.04	0.17	0.92	2.30	3.88	20.44
Maximum Precipitation (in.)*	11.3	9.5	9.0	6.4	3.8	0.9	0.3	0.7	2.3	7.3	7.9	12.3	38.3
Minimum Precipitation (in.)*	0.2	trace	0	trace	trace	trace	0	trace	trace	trace	trace	trace	8.7
Extreme Maximum Daily Precip. (in.)	5.59	2.92	1.83	1.54	1.03	0.60	0.09	0.56	0.88	2.64	2.26	3.16	5.59
Days With ≥ 0.1" Precipitation	7	8	7	3	2	0	0	0	1	2	4	7	41
Days With ≥ 0.5" Precipitation	3	3	2	1	0	0	0	0	0	1	2	3	15
Days With ≥ 1.0" Precipitation	1	1	0	0	0	0	0	0	0	0	1	1	4
Mean Snowfall (in.)	na	na	na	na	na	na	na	na	na	na	na	na	na
Maximum Snowfall (in.)*	2	trace	trace	0	0	0	0	0	0	0	0	trace	2
Maximum 24-hr. Snowfall (in.)*	2	trace	trace	0	0	0	0	0	0	0	0	trace	2
Maximum Snow Depth (in.)	na	na	na	na	na	na	na	na	na	na	na	na	na
Days With ≥ 1.0" Snow Depth	na	na	na	na	na	na	na	na	na	na	na	na	na
Thunderstorm Days*	< 1	< 1	< 1	< 1	< 1	< 1	< 1	< 1	< 1	< 1	< 1	< 1	5
Foggy Days*	17	12	7	4	4	3	4	4	6	9	12	17	99
Predominant Sky Cover*	OVR	OVR	OVR	CLR	CLR	CLR	CLR	CLR	CLR	CLR	CLR	OVR	CLR
Mean Relative Humidity 7am (%)*	87	86	82	79	78	77	81	83	82	83	85	86	82
Mean Relative Humidity 4pm (%)*	68	66	64	62	61	60	61	62	60	60	63	68	63
Mean Dewpoint (°F)*	42	44	44	45	47	50	52	53	52	50	46	42	47
Prevailing Wind Direction*	SE	WNW	WNW	WNW	WNW	WNW	WNW	WNW	WNW	WNW	WNW	WNW	WNW
Prevailing Wind Speed (mph)*	9	13	14	15	16	16	15	14	13	13	12	10	14
Maximum Wind Gust (mph)*	78	69	64	61	62	58	52	49	56	64	68	74	78

Note: (*) Period of record is 1945-1995

Santa Maria Public Airport

Santa Maria Valley is a flat, fertile valley opening on the Pacific Ocean where it is widest and tapering inland for a distance approximately 30 miles. The valley is 10 miles wide at the site of the station, which is located 13 miles inland at an elevation of 236 feet. It is bounded by the foothills of the San Rafael Mountains, the Solomon Hills, and the Casmalia Hills ranging from 1,300 to 4,000 feet.

Located 150 miles west-northwest of Los Angeles and 250 miles south of San Francisco, Santa Maria has a maritime climate, displaying characteristics of those of both neighbors. Year-round mild temperatures moving through gradual transitions characterize the climate more than do clearly defined seasons. The annual range of temperatures is about 13 degrees, while the daily temperature range is about 20 degrees for May through September and a few degrees higher from October through April.

Based on the 1951-1980 period, the average first occurrence of 32 degrees Fahrenheit in the fall is December 5 and the average last occurrence in the spring is March 15.

The rainfall season, typical of the mid-California coast, is in the winter. About three-fourths of the total annual rainfall occurs from December through March in connection with Pacific cold fronts and storm centers passing inland. During the remainder of the year, and particularly from June to October, the northward displacement and intensification of the semipermanent Pacific anticyclone produces a circulation resulting in little or no precipitation here. Thunderstorms are rare.

During most days, clear, sunny afternoons prevail. But under the influence of the Pacific high, considerable advective and radiative cooling frequently produces nightly low stratus clouds, known as California stratus, and early-morning fog. Both clouds and fog, however, are generally dissipated before noon.

The unequal daytime solar heating over land and ocean, in conjunction with the Pacific high, gives rise to a consistent and prevailing westerly sea breeze during most afternoons. The winds generally decrease to a calm by sundown. Thus the two factors of nighttime stratus and daytime sea breezes effectively combine to maintain relatively cool days and warm nights with little diurnal change.

Santa Maria Public Airport *Santa Barbara County* Elevation: 253 ft. Latitude: 34° 55' N Longitude: 120° 28' W

	JAN	FEB	MAR	APR	MAY	JUN	JUL	AUG	SEP	OCT	NOV	DEC	YEAR
Mean Maximum Temp. (°F)	64.3	64.9	65.7	68.1	69.3	71.4	73.7	74.0	74.6	73.8	69.5	64.5	69.5
Mean Temp. (°F)	52.0	53.3	54.4	56.1	58.4	61.0	63.8	64.2	63.8	61.2	56.2	51.7	58.0
Mean Minimum Temp. (°F)	39.6	41.7	43.1	44.1	47.5	50.6	53.9	54.3	52.9	48.5	42.9	38.9	46.5
Extreme Maximum Temp. (°F)	87	89	95	103	95	110	104	104	101	108	96	85	110
Extreme Minimum Temp. (°F)	21	23	28	31	36	39	44	45	41	34	27	21	21
Days Maximum Temp. ≥ 90°F	0	0	0	1	0	0	0	0	1	2	0	0	4
Days Maximum Temp. ≤ 32°F	0	0	0	0	0	0	0	0	0	0	0	0	0
Days Minimum Temp. ≤ 32°F	4	2	1	0	0	0	0	0	0	0	1	5	13
Days Minimum Temp. ≤ 0°F	0	0	0	0	0	0	0	0	0	0	0	0	0
Heating Degree Days (base 65°F)	398	325	322	265	203	122	56	45	64	133	262	404	2,599
Cooling Degree Days (base 65°F)	0	1	1	6	5	10	28	26	33	22	5	0	137
Mean Precipitation (in.)	2.68	3.08	2.67	0.93	0.32	0.05	0.03	0.02	0.14	0.54	1.27	1.84	13.57
Maximum Precipitation (in.)*	11.8	9.7	9.4	4.2	2.4	0.9	0.4	0.9	3.0	2.1	4.7	4.8	26.8
Minimum Precipitation (in.)*	trace	0	trace	trace	0	trace	0	0	0	0	0	trace	3.3
Extreme Maximum Daily Precip. (in.)	2.27	1.92	3.14	2.14	1.74	0.72	0.35	0.23	0.76	1.40	1.52	1.74	3.14
Days With ≥ 0.1" Precipitation	5	6	5	2	1	0	0	0	0	1	3	4	27
Days With ≥ 0.5" Precipitation	2	2	2	1	0	0	0	0	0	0	1	1	9
Days With ≥ 1.0" Precipitation	1	1	1	0	0	0	0	0	0	0	0	0	3
Mean Snowfall (in.)	na	na	na	na	na	na	na	na	na	na	na	na	na
Maximum Snowfall (in.)*	trace	trace	0	0	0	0	0	0	0	0	trace	trace	trace
Maximum 24-hr. Snowfall (in.)*	trace	trace	0	0	0	0	0	0	0	0	trace	trace	trace
Maximum Snow Depth (in.)	na	na	na	na	na	na	na	na	na	na	na	na	na
Days With ≥ 1.0" Snow Depth	na	na	na	na	na	na	na	na	na	na	na	na	na
Thunderstorm Days*	< 1	< 1	1	< 1	< 1	< 1	< 1	< 1	1	< 1	< 1	< 1	2
Foggy Days*	14	14	15	18	21	25	28	28	26	22	15	14	240
Predominant Sky Cover*	CLR	OVR	CLR	CLR	CLR	CLR	CLR	CLR	CLR	CLR	CLR	CLR	CLR
Mean Relative Humidity 7am (%)*	81	84	86	83	84	84	88	90	88	84	80	79	84
Mean Relative Humidity 4pm (%)*	59	62	63	61	61	60	61	62	63	61	60	58	61
Mean Dewpoint (°F)*	40	43	44	46	48	51	53	54	54	49	43	40	47
Prevailing Wind Direction*	WNW	WNW	WNW	WNW	WNW	WNW	WNW	WNW	WNW	WNW	WNW	WNW	WNW
Prevailing Wind Speed (mph)*	9	12	13	14	14	13	12	10	10	12	10	9	12
Maximum Wind Gust (mph)*	54	58	53	47	47	45	41	35	38	37	40	52	58

Note: (*) Period of record is 1954-1995

The period of record for National Weather Service station data is 1980 – 2009 except where noted. See User Guide for detailed explanation of data.

Stockton Metropolitan Airport

Stockton, the county seat of San Joaquin County, is located near the center of the Great Central Valley of California. It is on the southeast corner of the broad delta formed by the confluence of the San Joaquin and Sacramento Rivers. The surrounding terrain is flat, irrigated farm and orchard land, near sea level, with the rivers and canals of the delta controlled by a system of levees.

Approximately 25 miles east and northeast of Stockton lie the foothills of the Sierra Nevada, rising gradually to an elevation of about 1,000 feet. Beyond the foothills, the mountains rise abruptly to the crest of the Sierra, at a distance of about 75 miles, with some peaks here exceeding 9,000 feet in elevation. On a few days during the year, when atmospheric conditions are favorable, the downslope effect of a north or northeast wind can bring unseasonably dry weather to the delta area, but on the whole the Sierra Nevada has little or no effect on the weather of San Joaquin County. The Sierra Nevada does affect the area, however, to the extent that the entire economy of the Great Valley depends upon the water supplied by the melting snows in the mountains.

To the west and southwest, the Coast Range, with peaks above 2,000 feet, form a barrier separating the Great Valley from the marine air which dominates the climate of the coastal communities. Several gaps in the Coast Range in the San Francisco Bay Area, however, permit the passage inland of a sea breeze which fans out into the delta and has a moderating effect on summer heat, with the result that Stockton enjoys slightly cooler summer days than communities in the upper San Joaquin and Sacramento Valleys.

The summer climate in Stockton is characterized by warm, dry days and relatively cool nights with clear skies and no rainfall. Winter brings mild temperatures and relatively light rains with frequent heavy fogs.

The annual rainfall averages about 14 inches, with 90 percent of the precipitation falling from November through April. Thunderstorms are infrequent, occurring on three or four days a year. Snow is practically unknown in the Stockton area.

In summer, temperatures exceeding 100 degrees can be expected on about 15 days. During these hot afternoons the air is extremely dry, with relative humidities running generally less than 20 percent. Even on these hot days, however, temperatures will fall into the low 60s at night. In winter the nighttime temperature on clear nights will fall to or slightly below freezing, and will rise in the afternoon into the low 50s.

In late autumn and early winter, clear still nights give rise to the formation of dense fogs, which normally settle in during the night and burn off sometime during the day. In December and January, the so-called fog season, under stagnant atmospheric conditions the fog may last for as long as four or five weeks, with only brief and temporary periods of clearing.

Stockton Metropolitan Airport *San Joaquin County* Elevation: 21 ft. Latitude: 37° 54' N Longitude: 121° 14' W

	JAN	FEB	MAR	APR	MAY	JUN	JUL	AUG	SEP	OCT	NOV	DEC	YEAR
Mean Maximum Temp. (°F)	54.5	61.4	66.8	73.4	81.8	88.7	94.2	92.9	88.4	78.6	64.8	54.3	75.0
Mean Temp. (°F)	46.5	51.2	55.2	60.1	67.1	73.1	77.5	76.5	72.8	64.5	53.7	46.0	62.0
Mean Minimum Temp. (°F)	38.4	40.9	43.5	46.8	52.4	57.4	60.9	60.1	57.2	50.3	42.5	37.6	49.0
Extreme Maximum Temp. (°F)	71	77	87	100	107	110	115	109	106	101	84	72	115
Extreme Minimum Temp. (°F)	20	22	28	32	39	45	49	50	43	36	25	17	17
Days Maximum Temp. ≥ 90°F	0	0	0	1	7	14	23	21	14	3	0	0	83
Days Maximum Temp. ≤ 32°F	0	0	0	0	0	0	0	0	0	0	0	0	0
Days Minimum Temp. ≤ 32°F	7	3	0	0	0	0	0	0	0	0	2	8	20
Days Minimum Temp. ≤ 0°F	0	0	0	0	0	0	0	0	0	0	0	0	0
Heating Degree Days (base 65°F)	567	384	297	163	46	5	0	0	5	72	334	581	2,454
Cooling Degree Days (base 65°F)	0	0	1	22	119	253	396	363	246	63	1	0	1,464
Mean Precipitation (in.)	2.73	2.51	2.10	0.93	0.53	0.08	0.02	0.01	0.29	0.77	1.61	2.12	13.70
Maximum Precipitation (in.)*	7.1	6.0	6.5	3.5	2.3	0.7	0.6	0.8	3.0	2.2	6.2	8.0	26.6
Minimum Precipitation (in.)*	0.1	0	trace	0	0	0	0	0	0	0	0	trace	5.4
Extreme Maximum Daily Precip. (in.)	2.01	1.62	1.39	1.03	1.66	0.23	0.50	0.06	1.38	1.46	1.50	1.92	2.01
Days With ≥ 0.1" Precipitation	6	6	6	3	1	0	0	0	1	2	4	5	34
Days With ≥ 0.5" Precipitation	2	2	1	0	0	0	0	0	0	1	1	1	8
Days With ≥ 1.0" Precipitation	0	0	0	0	0	0	0	0	0	0	0	0	0
Mean Snowfall (in.)	na	na	na	na	na	na	na	na	na	na	na	na	na
Maximum Snowfall (in.)*	trace	trace	trace	trace	0	0	0	0	0	0	0	trace	trace
Maximum 24-hr. Snowfall (in.)*	trace	trace	trace	trace	0	0	0	0	0	0	0	trace	trace
Maximum Snow Depth (in.)	na	na	na	na	na	na	na	na	na	na	na	na	na
Days With ≥ 1.0" Snow Depth	na	na	na	na	na	na	na	na	na	na	na	na	na
Thunderstorm Days*	< 1	< 1	1	1	< 1	< 1	< 1	< 1	< 1	< 1	< 1	< 1	2
Foggy Days*	24	17	11	5	2	< 1	< 1	< 1	2	8	18	24	111
Predominant Sky Cover*	OVR	OVR	OVR	CLR	CLR	CLR	CLR	CLR	CLR	CLR	OVR	OVR	CLR
Mean Relative Humidity 7am (%)*	90	90	85	76	65	60	61	65	70	77	87	91	76
Mean Relative Humidity 4pm (%)*	70	60	51	41	33	29	26	28	31	37	59	71	45
Mean Dewpoint (°F)*	39	42	42	43	46	49	52	52	51	47	44	40	46
Prevailing Wind Direction*	SE	SE	WNW	WNW	W	W	WNW	WNW	WNW	NW	SE	SE	WNW
Prevailing Wind Speed (mph)*	9	9	9	9	10	12	10	9	9	9	9	9	9
Maximum Wind Gust (mph)*	60	53	52	45	49	43	32	37	39	54	49	54	60

Note: (*) Period of record is 1948-1995

Alturas *Modoc County* Elevation: 4,399 ft. Latitude: 41° 30' N Longitude: 120° 33' W

	JAN	FEB	MAR	APR	MAY	JUN	JUL	AUG	SEP	OCT	NOV	DEC	YEAR
Mean Maximum Temp. (°F)	43.5	47.0	53.4	59.9	68.8	78.4	88.6	87.7	79.4	66.8	50.5	42.1	63.9
Mean Temp. (°F)	30.7	33.6	39.2	44.0	51.7	59.1	66.3	64.7	57.4	47.2	36.4	29.9	46.7
Mean Minimum Temp. (°F)	17.9	20.1	25.0	28.0	34.4	39.9	44.0	41.6	35.3	27.5	22.2	17.6	29.5
Extreme Maximum Temp. (°F)	62	72	78	85	95	102	108	104	100	90	83	72	108
Extreme Minimum Temp. (°F)	-13	-33	-3	7	17	21	28	26	17	1	-17	-25	-33
Days Maximum Temp. ≥ 90°F	0	0	0	0	1	4	15	13	4	0	0	0	37
Days Maximum Temp. ≤ 32°F	2	1	0	0	0	0	0	0	0	0	1	3	7
Days Minimum Temp. ≤ 32°F	27	25	26	22	12	4	1	1	10	23	24	27	202
Days Minimum Temp. ≤ 0°F	2	1	0	0	0	0	0	0	0	0	0	2	5
Heating Degree Days (base 65°F)	1,055	882	792	624	409	192	52	64	230	546	854	1,082	6,782
Cooling Degree Days (base 65°F)	0	0	0	0	3	25	100	61	9	0	0	0	198
Mean Precipitation (in.)	1.30	1.26	1.47	1.21	1.42	0.75	0.26	0.33	0.54	0.85	1.62	1.35	12.36
Extreme Maximum Daily Precip. (in.)	1.20	1.28	1.99	1.60	1.20	1.12	1.03	0.87	1.00	1.22	1.08	1.00	1.99
Days With ≥ 0.1" Precipitation	4	4	5	4	4	2	1	1	1	3	5	4	38
Days With ≥ 0.5" Precipitation	0	0	0	0	1	0	0	0	0	1	1	0	3
Days With ≥ 1.0" Precipitation	0	0	0	0	0	0	0	0	0	0	0	0	0
Mean Snowfall (in.)	4.5	2.8	2.4	0.6	0.5	trace	trace	0.0	0.0	0.1	3.2	3.3	17.4
Maximum Snow Depth (in.)	21	10	9	4	4	0	trace	0	0	1	12	14	21
Days With ≥ 1.0" Snow Depth	4	3	1	0	0	0	0	0	0	0	3	4	15

Angwin Pac Union Col *Napa County* Elevation: 1,714 ft. Latitude: 38° 34' N Longitude: 122° 26' W

	JAN	FEB	MAR	APR	MAY	JUN	JUL	AUG	SEP	OCT	NOV	DEC	YEAR
Mean Maximum Temp. (°F)	53.2	55.9	60.4	66.1	73.6	80.4	86.0	85.3	81.6	72.3	59.5	52.8	68.9
Mean Temp. (°F)	45.9	47.7	50.6	54.4	60.3	65.7	70.4	69.7	67.6	60.9	51.0	45.6	57.5
Mean Minimum Temp. (°F)	38.5	39.5	40.7	42.5	47.0	50.9	54.8	54.2	53.5	49.5	42.5	38.4	46.0
Extreme Maximum Temp. (°F)	77	75	84	91	101	104	105	104	101	99	82	74	105
Extreme Minimum Temp. (°F)	25	20	24	27	29	36	40	42	39	30	25	16	16
Days Maximum Temp. ≥ 90°F	0	0	0	0	1	5	10	9	5	1	0	0	31
Days Maximum Temp. ≤ 32°F	0	0	0	0	0	0	0	0	0	0	0	0	0
Days Minimum Temp. ≤ 32°F	5	4	3	2	0	0	0	0	0	0	2	5	21
Days Minimum Temp. ≤ 0°F	0	0	0	0	0	0	0	0	0	0	0	0	0
Heating Degree Days (base 65°F)	587	482	443	322	181	71	15	17	44	164	414	596	3,336
Cooling Degree Days (base 65°F)	0	0	2	10	43	99	190	171	129	44	1	0	689
Mean Precipitation (in.)	7.43	8.32	5.63	2.32	1.46	0.30	0.01	0.06	0.38	2.03	5.06	7.95	40.95
Extreme Maximum Daily Precip. (in.)	5.67	7.40	6.14	3.08	2.29	1.36	0.16	0.44	1.56	4.04	4.50	5.57	7.40
Days With ≥ 0.1" Precipitation	9	9	8	5	3	1	0	0	1	3	7	9	55
Days With ≥ 0.5" Precipitation	5	5	4	1	1	0	0	0	0	1	3	5	25
Days With ≥ 1.0" Precipitation	2	3	2	1	0	0	0	0	0	1	2	3	14
Mean Snowfall (in.)	trace	trace	trace	trace	trace	0.0	0.0	0.0	0.0	0.0	0.0	0.1	0.1
Maximum Snow Depth (in.)	2	1	4	0	0	0	0	0	0	0	0	trace	4
Days With ≥ 1.0" Snow Depth	0	0	0	0	0	0	0	0	0	0	0	0	0

Antioch Pump Plant #3 *Contra Costa County* Elevation: 60 ft. Latitude: 37° 59' N Longitude: 121° 44' W

	JAN	FEB	MAR	APR	MAY	JUN	JUL	AUG	SEP	OCT	NOV	DEC	YEAR
Mean Maximum Temp. (°F)	53.9	60.2	***65.4***	71.9	79.1	***86.1***	91.7	90.2	86.2	77.4	64.0	54.5	***73.4***
Mean Temp. (°F)	46.3	51.3	***55.3***	60.0	66.2	***71.8***	75.5	74.3	71.6	64.8	54.5	46.6	***61.5***
Mean Minimum Temp. (°F)	38.7	42.4	***45.2***	48.0	53.1	57.6	59.2	58.3	57.0	52.2	44.9	38.5	***49.6***
Extreme Maximum Temp. (°F)	70	76	88	94	103	109	110	109	107	101	82	73	110
Extreme Minimum Temp. (°F)	23	25	32	29	40	35	44	47	41	39	28	20	20
Days Maximum Temp. ≥ 90°F	0	0	0	0	4	10	20	15	10	2	0	0	61
Days Maximum Temp. ≤ 32°F	0	0	0	0	0	0	0	0	0	0	0	0	0
Days Minimum Temp. ≤ 32°F	5	1	0	0	0	0	0	0	0	0	1	5	12
Days Minimum Temp. ≤ 0°F	0	0	0	0	0	0	0	0	0	0	0	0	0
Heating Degree Days (base 65°F)	572	381	***294***	165	56	***9***	0	0	6	68	311	565	***2,427***
Cooling Degree Days (base 65°F)	0	0	***1***	22	101	***221***	332	294	210	69	2	0	***1,252***
Mean Precipitation (in.)	2.90	2.70	***2.37***	0.77	0.45	0.09	0.02	0.02	0.18	0.54	1.60	2.39	***14.03***
Extreme Maximum Daily Precip. (in.)	2.80	2.33	***1.40***	***1.44***	***1.10***	0.58	0.40	0.35	0.66	1.75	2.34	2.20	***2.80***
Days With ≥ 0.1" Precipitation	6	6	***6***	2	***1***	0	0	0	1	1	4	5	***32***
Days With ≥ 0.5" Precipitation	2	2	***1***	0	0	0	0	0	0	0	1	2	***8***
Days With ≥ 1.0" Precipitation	1	0	***0***	0	0	0	0	0	0	0	0	0	***1***
Mean Snowfall (in.)	0.0	trace	0.0	0.0	0.0	0.0	0.0	0.0	0.0	0.0	0.0	0.0	trace
Maximum Snow Depth (in.)	0	trace	0	0	0	0	0	0	0	0	0	0	trace
Days With ≥ 1.0" Snow Depth	0	0	0	0	0	0	0	0	0	0	0	0	0

Ash Mountain *Tulare County* Elevation: 1,708 ft. Latitude: 36° 29' N Longitude: 118° 50' W

	JAN	FEB	MAR	APR	MAY	JUN	JUL	AUG	SEP	OCT	NOV	DEC	YEAR
Mean Maximum Temp. (°F)	58.7	62.1	65.4	71.1	81.1	90.5	98.7	98.0	92.0	81.0	67.1	58.8	77.0
Mean Temp. (°F)	48.0	50.9	53.9	58.5	67.2	75.6	83.1	82.3	76.4	66.5	54.8	47.9	63.8
Mean Minimum Temp. (°F)	37.2	39.7	42.3	45.7	53.3	60.7	67.5	66.6	60.8	52.0	42.5	36.9	50.4
Extreme Maximum Temp. (°F)	80	83	89	97	106	109	118	114	109	103	89	80	118
Extreme Minimum Temp. (°F)	22	22	28	28	34	42	50	51	45	31	25	17	17
Days Maximum Temp. ≥ 90°F	0	0	0	1	7	17	29	28	19	6	0	0	107
Days Maximum Temp. ≤ 32°F	0	0	0	0	0	0	0	0	0	0	0	0	0
Days Minimum Temp. ≤ 32°F	7	3	1	1	0	0	0	0	0	0	2	7	21
Days Minimum Temp. ≤ 0°F	0	0	0	0	0	0	0	0	0	0	0	0	0
Heating Degree Days (base 65°F)	521	391	340	218	73	11	0	0	7	74	307	522	2,464
Cooling Degree Days (base 65°F)	0	0	3	28	148	336	568	545	354	128	6	0	2,116
Mean Precipitation (in.)	5.13	4.78	4.65	2.21	1.13	0.41	0.11	0.06	0.46	1.38	2.76	3.62	26.70
Extreme Maximum Daily Precip. (in.)	3.50	4.02	2.73	3.15	1.96	2.15	0.80	1.03	2.70	3.74	3.85	2.91	4.02
Days With ≥ 0.1" Precipitation	7	7	7	4	2	1	0	0	1	2	4	5	40
Days With ≥ 0.5" Precipitation	4	3	3	1	1	0	0	0	0	1	2	3	18
Days With ≥ 1.0" Precipitation	2	2	1	0	0	0	0	0	0	0	1	1	7
Mean Snowfall (in.)	0.3	0.1	0.1	trace	0.0	0.0	0.0	0.0	0.0	0.0	0.2	0.1	0.8
Maximum Snow Depth (in.)	2	2	1	trace	0	0	0	0	0	0	6	trace	6
Days With ≥ 1.0" Snow Depth	0	0	0	0	0	0	0	0	0	0	0	0	0

The period of record for all cooperative weather station data is 1980 – 2009. See User Guide for detailed explanation of data.

Auberry 2 NW *Fresno County* Elevation: 2,089 ft. Latitude: 37° 05' N Longitude: 119° 30' W

	JAN	FEB	MAR	APR	MAY	JUN	JUL	AUG	SEP	OCT	NOV	DEC	YEAR
Mean Maximum Temp. (°F)	55.4	58.3	62.1	68.6	78.7	87.7	94.7	93.7	87.4	76.1	62.9	55.1	73.4
Mean Temp. (°F)	46.0	48.8	52.0	57.1	65.7	73.8	81.1	80.2	74.5	64.3	52.6	45.8	61.8
Mean Minimum Temp. (°F)	36.6	39.3	41.9	45.5	52.7	59.9	67.6	66.7	61.6	52.5	42.2	36.5	50.2
Extreme Maximum Temp. (°F)	79	76	85	94	103	104	109	109	105	100	85	76	109
Extreme Minimum Temp. (°F)	21	17	25	27	28	36	44	46	41	33	25	10	10
Days Maximum Temp. ≥ 90°F	0	0	0	0	4	14	26	24	14	2	0	0	84
Days Maximum Temp. ≤ 32°F	0	0	0	0	0	0	0	0	0	0	0	0	0
Days Minimum Temp. ≤ 32°F	8	4	2	1	0	0	0	0	0	0	2	8	25
Days Minimum Temp. ≤ 0°F	0	0	0	0	0	0	0	0	0	0	0	0	0
Heating Degree Days (base 65°F)	582	450	398	252	90	16	0	0	12	104	368	587	2,859
Cooling Degree Days (base 65°F)	0	0	2	21	119	287	508	479	305	90	2	0	1,813
Mean Precipitation (in.)	5.29	4.67	4.29	1.97	1.00	0.31	0.07	0.05	0.37	1.38	2.51	3.89	25.80
Extreme Maximum Daily Precip. (in.)	3.95	2.70	3.43	2.85	2.22	2.01	1.17	0.38	1.41	2.98	3.90	4.08	4.08
Days With ≥ 0.1" Precipitation	7	7	6	3	2	1	0	0	1	2	4	6	39
Days With ≥ 0.5" Precipitation	4	4	3	1	1	0	0	0	0	1	2	3	19
Days With ≥ 1.0" Precipitation	2	2	1	1	0	0	0	0	0	0	1	1	8
Mean Snowfall (in.)	0.4	0.3	0.7	0.1	0.0	0.0	0.0	0.0	0.0	0.0	trace	0.4	1.9
Maximum Snow Depth (in.)	2	4	1	2	0	0	0	0	0	0	0	8	8
Days With ≥ 1.0" Snow Depth	0	0	0	0	0	0	0	0	0	0	0	0	0

Auburn *Placer County* Elevation: 1,292 ft. Latitude: 38° 54' N Longitude: 121° 05' W

	JAN	FEB	MAR	APR	MAY	JUN	JUL	AUG	SEP	OCT	NOV	DEC	YEAR
Mean Maximum Temp. (°F)	54.5	58.5	62.5	67.8	76.4	84.5	91.6	90.7	85.2	75.7	62.0	54.6	72.0
Mean Temp. (°F)	46.1	49.4	52.4	56.7	64.2	71.2	77.5	76.6	72.1	63.9	52.7	46.0	60.7
Mean Minimum Temp. (°F)	37.6	40.3	42.5	45.6	51.9	57.7	63.4	62.5	58.9	52.0	43.4	37.4	49.4
Extreme Maximum Temp. (°F)	73	76	86	89	101	103	107	107	103	98	82	74	107
Extreme Minimum Temp. (°F)	23	22	29	30	35	43	48	35	43	32	29	16	16
Days Maximum Temp. ≥ 90°F	0	0	0	0	3	9	19	18	10	2	0	0	61
Days Maximum Temp. ≤ 32°F	0	0	0	0	0	0	0	0	0	0	0	0	0
Days Minimum Temp. ≤ 32°F	6	2	1	0	0	0	0	0	0	0	1	7	17
Days Minimum Temp. ≤ 0°F	0	0	0	0	0	0	0	0	0	0	0	0	0
Heating Degree Days (base 65°F)	579	434	385	255	108	24	1	1	17	104	363	582	2,853
Cooling Degree Days (base 65°F)	0	0	1	14	89	216	397	369	235	75	1	0	1,397
Mean Precipitation (in.)	6.19	6.44	5.70	2.70	1.53	0.38	0.03	0.07	0.60	1.66	4.27	6.01	35.58
Extreme Maximum Daily Precip. (in.)	4.75	3.98	3.22	2.40	2.94	1.20	0.58	0.47	1.43	2.96	3.38	***4.02***	***4.75***
Days With ≥ 0.1" Precipitation	8	8	8	4	3	1	0	0	1	2	6	7	48
Days With ≥ 0.5" Precipitation	4	4	4	2	1	0	0	0	1	1	3	4	24
Days With ≥ 1.0" Precipitation	2	2	2	1	0	0	0	0	0	1	1	2	11
Mean Snowfall (in.)	0.1	0.2	0.3	0.2	0.0	0.0	0.0	0.0	0.0	0.0	0.2	0.1	1.1
Maximum Snow Depth (in.)	0	2	3	2	0	0	0	0	0	0	0	2	3
Days With ≥ 1.0" Snow Depth	0	0	0	0	0	0	0	0	0	0	0	0	0

Balch Power House *Fresno County* Elevation: 1,720 ft. Latitude: 36° 55' N Longitude: 119° 05' W

	JAN	FEB	MAR	APR	MAY	JUN	JUL	AUG	SEP	OCT	NOV	DEC	YEAR
Mean Maximum Temp. (°F)	52.5	57.5	63.8	69.8	78.3	86.4	94.7	94.7	89.2	77.9	60.5	52.0	73.1
Mean Temp. (°F)	45.1	48.6	53.1	57.8	65.6	73.1	81.1	81.1	75.8	65.7	52.2	44.9	62.0
Mean Minimum Temp. (°F)	37.7	39.5	42.3	45.8	52.9	59.7	67.5	67.5	62.5	53.4	43.7	37.9	50.9
Extreme Maximum Temp. (°F)	69	77	88	92	103	106	112	110	108	102	82	68	112
Extreme Minimum Temp. (°F)	20	22	28	23	22	41	49	50	43	37	23	20	20
Days Maximum Temp. ≥ 90°F	0	0	0	0	3	12	25	25	16	3	0	0	84
Days Maximum Temp. ≤ 32°F	0	0	0	0	0	0	0	0	0	0	0	0	0
Days Minimum Temp. ≤ 32°F	5	3	1	0	0	0	0	0	0	0	1	5	15
Days Minimum Temp. ≤ 0°F	0	0	0	0	0	0	0	0	0	0	0	0	0
Heating Degree Days (base 65°F)	610	458	366	228	80	16	0	0	8	80	379	615	2,840
Cooling Degree Days (base 65°F)	0	0	2	20	106	264	506	507	339	107	1	0	1,852
Mean Precipitation (in.)	6.14	5.66	4.95	2.60	1.27	0.45	0.16	0.03	0.66	1.61	2.96	4.41	30.90
Extreme Maximum Daily Precip. (in.)	3.49	4.31	4.67	4.21	2.40	2.02	2.51	0.32	3.16	4.80	5.06	***5.16***	***5.16***
Days With ≥ 0.1" Precipitation	6	7	7	4	2	1	0	0	1	2	4	5	39
Days With ≥ 0.5" Precipitation	4	4	3	2	1	0	0	0	0	1	2	3	20
Days With ≥ 1.0" Precipitation	2	2	1	0	0	0	0	0	0	0	1	1	7
Mean Snowfall (in.)	0.0	0.0	0.0	0.0	0.0	0.0	0.0	0.0	0.0	0.0	0.0	0.0	0.0
Maximum Snow Depth (in.)	0	22	0	0	0	0	0	0	0	0	0	2	22
Days With ≥ 1.0" Snow Depth	0	1	0	0	0	0	0	0	0	0	0	0	1

Barstow Fire Station *San Bernardino County* Elevation: 2,319 ft. Latitude: 34° 53' N Longitude: 117° 01' W

	JAN	FEB	MAR	APR	MAY	JUN	JUL	AUG	SEP	OCT	NOV	DEC	YEAR
Mean Maximum Temp. (°F)	60.7	64.6	70.7	78.3	86.8	96.4	102.1	100.8	93.7	82.0	68.7	59.2	80.3
Mean Temp. (°F)	47.7	51.4	56.7	63.3	71.1	79.7	85.6	84.4	77.5	66.6	54.8	46.3	65.4
Mean Minimum Temp. (°F)	34.7	38.1	42.6	48.3	55.4	63.0	69.1	68.0	61.2	51.0	40.9	33.4	50.5
Extreme Maximum Temp. (°F)	78	87	92	98	107	112	115	112	109	101	89	76	115
Extreme Minimum Temp. (°F)	12	18	26	30	32	36	48	40	34	32	20	16	12
Days Maximum Temp. ≥ 90°F	0	0	0	3	14	25	31	30	23	6	0	0	132
Days Maximum Temp. ≤ 32°F	0	0	0	0	0	0	0	0	0	0	0	0	0
Days Minimum Temp. ≤ 32°F	11	6	2	0	0	0	0	0	0	0	4	15	38
Days Minimum Temp. ≤ 0°F	0	0	0	0	0	0	0	0	0	0	0	0	0
Heating Degree Days (base 65°F)	529	380	261	112	28	2	0	0	3	61	303	574	2,253
Cooling Degree Days (base 65°F)	0	1	11	69	225	450	647	609	384	117	4	0	2,517
Mean Precipitation (in.)	0.85	0.99	0.67	0.21	0.09	0.06	0.33	0.24	0.29	0.28	0.45	0.56	5.02
Extreme Maximum Daily Precip. (in.)	1.25	1.57	1.52	0.98	0.32	0.60	1.31	0.80	1.36	1.35	1.20	1.25	1.57
Days With ≥ 0.1" Precipitation	3	3	2	1	0	0	1	1	1	1	1	2	16
Days With ≥ 0.5" Precipitation	1	1	0	0	0	0	0	0	0	0	0	0	2
Days With ≥ 1.0" Precipitation	0	0	0	0	0	0	0	0	0	0	0	0	0
Mean Snowfall (in.)	0.0	0.0	trace	0.0	0.0	0.0	0.0	0.0	0.0	0.0	0.0	0.3	0.3
Maximum Snow Depth (in.)	0	0	trace	0	0	0	0	0	0	0	0	7	7
Days With ≥ 1.0" Snow Depth	0	0	0	0	0	0	0	0	0	0	0	0	0

The period of record for all cooperative weather station data is 1980 – 2009. See User Guide for detailed explanation of data.

Ben Lomond No 4 *Santa Cruz County* Elevation: 419 ft. Latitude: 37° 05' N Longitude: 122° 05' W

	JAN	FEB	MAR	APR	MAY	JUN	JUL	AUG	SEP	OCT	NOV	DEC	YEAR
Mean Maximum Temp. (°F)	61.5	63.7	67.3	72.0	76.6	81.8	85.1	85.8	84.4	78.2	67.9	60.8	73.8
Mean Temp. (°F)	49.4	51.4	53.9	57.0	61.1	65.1	67.9	68.1	66.6	61.3	53.8	48.7	58.7
Mean Minimum Temp. (°F)	37.1	39.0	40.4	42.1	45.6	48.3	50.7	50.4	48.7	44.3	39.7	36.6	43.6
Extreme Maximum Temp. (°F)	82	87	92	100	105	110	112	110	107	112	95	79	112
Extreme Minimum Temp. (°F)	20	20	27	29	33	35	40	40	37	30	25	15	15
Days Maximum Temp. ≥ 90°F	0	0	0	1	3	6	8	9	9	4	0	0	40
Days Maximum Temp. ≤ 32°F	0	0	0	0	0	0	0	0	0	0	0	0	0
Days Minimum Temp. ≤ 32°F	10	5	3	1	0	0	0	0	0	0	5	11	35
Days Minimum Temp. ≤ 0°F	0	0	0	0	0	0	0	0	0	0	0	0	0
Heating Degree Days (base 65°F)	478	378	339	240	139	49	11	9	31	133	331	498	2,636
Cooling Degree Days (base 65°F)	0	0	1	8	26	58	108	113	85	26	1	0	426
Mean Precipitation (in.)	10.04	10.18	7.10	3.07	1.21	0.24	0.03	0.06	0.27	2.29	5.91	9.55	49.95
Extreme Maximum Daily Precip. (in.)	11.47	5.40	4.38	3.79	3.05	0.86	0.61	0.72	0.98	8.61	5.80	8.43	11.47
Days With ≥ 0.1" Precipitation	8	9	8	4	2	1	0	0	1	2	6	9	50
Days With ≥ 0.5" Precipitation	5	6	5	2	1	0	0	0	0	1	3	5	28
Days With ≥ 1.0" Precipitation	3	3	2	1	0	0	0	0	0	1	2	3	15
Mean Snowfall (in.)	trace	0.1	trace	0.0	0.0	0.0	0.0	0.0	0.0	0.0	trace	0.1	0.2
Maximum Snow Depth (in.)	0	trace	trace	0	0	0	0	0	0	0	trace	trace	trace
Days With ≥ 1.0" Snow Depth	0	0	0	0	0	0	0	0	0	0	0	0	0

Berkeley *Alameda County* Elevation: 310 ft. Latitude: 37° 52' N Longitude: 122° 16' W

	JAN	FEB	MAR	APR	MAY	JUN	JUL	AUG	SEP	OCT	NOV	DEC	YEAR
Mean Maximum Temp. (°F)	***56.8***	59.9	***62.6***	65.3	68.3	72.1	72.6	72.7	***73.4***	70.9	***63.3***	57.0	***66.2***
Mean Temp. (°F)	***50.3***	52.8	***54.6***	56.6	59.4	62.4	63.3	63.7	***64.1***	61.6	***55.6***	50.4	***57.9***
Mean Minimum Temp. (°F)	***43.7***	45.7	***46.6***	47.8	50.4	52.7	54.0	54.7	***54.5***	52.2	***47.9***	43.7	***49.5***
Extreme Maximum Temp. (°F)	***77***	77	87	95	101	107	99	***98***	***99***	***99***	***82***	***73***	***107***
Extreme Minimum Temp. (°F)	***29***	34	33	36	41	45	47	***47***	***44***	***42***	***35***	***24***	***24***
Days Maximum Temp. ≥ 90°F	***0***	0	0	0	0	1	0	0	2	1	***0***	0	***4***
Days Maximum Temp. ≤ 32°F	***0***	0	0	0	0	0	0	0	0	0	***0***	0	***0***
Days Minimum Temp. ≤ 32°F	***0***	0	0	0	0	0	0	0	0	0	***0***	0	***0***
Days Minimum Temp. ≤ 0°F	***0***	0	0	0	0	0	0	0	0	0	***0***	0	***0***
Heating Degree Days (base 65°F)	***450***	338	***316***	255	180	99	73	61	***67***	127	***276***	447	***2,689***
Cooling Degree Days (base 65°F)	***0***	0	***2***	9	14	29	27	28	***45***	27	***2***	0	***183***
Mean Precipitation (in.)	***4.98***	5.45	***3.70***	1.68	0.87	0.15	0.01	0.07	0.27	1.31	***3.29***	4.92	***26.70***
Extreme Maximum Daily Precip. (in.)	***6.98***	3.20	***2.60***	2.27	***1.92***	0.57	0.13	***0.69***	***0.57***	***3.93***	***3.89***	***4.73***	***6.98***
Days With ≥ 0.1" Precipitation	***8***	8	***6***	4	2	0	0	0	1	2	***6***	7	***44***
Days With ≥ 0.5" Precipitation	***3***	4	***3***	1	0	0	0	0	0	1	***3***	3	***18***
Days With ≥ 1.0" Precipitation	***1***	2	1	0	0	0	0	0	0	0	***1***	1	***6***
Mean Snowfall (in.)	***0.0***	0.0	0.0	0.0	0.0	0.0	0.0	0.0	0.0	0.0	***0.0***	0.0	***0.0***
Maximum Snow Depth (in.)	***0***	0	***0***	0	0	0	0	***0***	***0***	***0***	***0***	***0***	***0***
Days With ≥ 1.0" Snow Depth	***0***	0	***0***	0	0	0	0	0	0	***0***	***0***	0	***0***

Big Bear Lake *San Bernardino County* Elevation: 6,790 ft. Latitude: 34° 15' N Longitude: 116° 53' W

	JAN	FEB	MAR	APR	MAY	JUN	JUL	AUG	SEP	OCT	NOV	DEC	YEAR
Mean Maximum Temp. (°F)	47.5	48.0	52.3	59.0	68.1	76.4	81.4	80.1	74.0	64.6	54.7	47.6	62.8
Mean Temp. (°F)	34.6	35.4	38.7	44.1	51.9	59.0	64.8	63.8	57.8	48.8	40.5	34.4	47.8
Mean Minimum Temp. (°F)	21.6	22.6	25.1	29.1	35.6	41.5	48.1	47.4	41.5	33.0	26.2	21.2	32.8
Extreme Maximum Temp. (°F)	71	72	74	82	87	90	94	92	85	85	74	68	94
Extreme Minimum Temp. (°F)	-1	-3	2	7	22	26	32	31	22	16	3	-8	-8
Days Maximum Temp. ≥ 90°F	0	0	0	0	0	0	1	0	0	0	0	0	1
Days Maximum Temp. ≤ 32°F	2	1	0	0	0	0	0	0	0	0	0	2	5
Days Minimum Temp. ≤ 32°F	29	26	28	22	10	2	0	0	2	14	25	29	187
Days Minimum Temp. ≤ 0°F	0	0	0	0	0	0	0	0	0	0	0	0	0
Heating Degree Days (base 65°F)	937	832	808	621	401	181	50	62	212	494	728	941	6,267
Cooling Degree Days (base 65°F)	0	0	0	0	0	7	51	33	3	0	0	0	94
Mean Precipitation (in.)	4.37	4.33	2.82	0.98	0.37	0.15	0.67	1.03	0.41	0.89	1.42	2.55	19.99
Extreme Maximum Daily Precip. (in.)	5.00	4.10	3.06	1.70	1.41	0.85	1.80	2.60	1.30	3.25	3.78	3.12	5.00
Days With ≥ 0.1" Precipitation	5	5	5	2	1	0	1	2	1	1	2	3	28
Days With ≥ 0.5" Precipitation	2	2	2	1	0	0	0	1	0	0	1	2	11
Days With ≥ 1.0" Precipitation	1	1	1	0	0	0	0	0	0	0	0	1	4
Mean Snowfall (in.)	15.2	15.8	15.3	3.9	0.6	trace	0.0	0.0	0.1	1.2	4.5	10.3	66.9
Maximum Snow Depth (in.)	na	na	na	***12***	***2***	***0***	***0***	***0***	***0***	na	na	na	na
Days With ≥ 1.0" Snow Depth	na	na	na	0	0	0	0	0	0	0	0	***3***	na

Blythe *Riverside County* Elevation: 268 ft. Latitude: 33° 37' N Longitude: 114° 36' W

	JAN	FEB	MAR	APR	MAY	JUN	JUL	AUG	SEP	OCT	NOV	DEC	YEAR
Mean Maximum Temp. (°F)	67.8	72.8	79.8	88.0	96.9	105.2	***108.7***	107.5	101.5	90.3	***75.4***	66.2	***88.3***
Mean Temp. (°F)	54.0	58.4	64.3	71.5	79.8	87.5	***93.1***	92.4	85.3	73.5	***60.4***	52.6	***72.7***
Mean Minimum Temp. (°F)	40.2	43.9	48.7	55.0	62.7	69.7	***77.4***	77.3	69.2	56.7	***45.5***	39.0	***57.1***
Extreme Maximum Temp. (°F)	84	93	100	115	114	122	122	118	116	111	95	85	122
Extreme Minimum Temp. (°F)	0	26	31	39	44	53	59	58	50	36	27	24	0
Days Maximum Temp. ≥ 90°F	0	0	3	13	24	29	30	30	26	17	0	0	172
Days Maximum Temp. ≤ 32°F	0	0	0	0	0	0	0	0	0	0	0	0	0
Days Minimum Temp. ≤ 32°F	3	1	0	0	0	0	0	0	0	0	0	4	8
Days Minimum Temp. ≤ 0°F	0	0	0	0	0	0	0	0	0	0	0	0	0
Heating Degree Days (base 65°F)	335	187	78	16	0	0	***0***	0	0	9	***148***	378	***1,151***
Cooling Degree Days (base 65°F)	0	7	63	219	467	680	***877***	858	616	281	***23***	0	***4,091***
Mean Precipitation (in.)	0.52	0.60	0.32	0.10	0.06	trace	0.20	0.52	0.45	0.15	0.23	0.52	3.67
Extreme Maximum Daily Precip. (in.)	1.21	1.76	***1.48***	0.75	0.70	0.04	1.22	2.18	2.56	***0.92***	1.27	1.23	***2.56***
Days With ≥ 0.1" Precipitation	1	2	1	0	0	0	0	1	1	0	1	1	8
Days With ≥ 0.5" Precipitation	0	0	0	0	0	0	0	0	0	0	0	0	0
Days With ≥ 1.0" Precipitation	0	0	0	0	0	0	0	0	0	0	0	0	0
Mean Snowfall (in.)	0.0	0.0	0.0	0.0	0.0	0.0	0.0	0.0	0.0	0.0	0.0	0.0	0.0
Maximum Snow Depth (in.)	0	0	0	0	0	0	0	0	0	0	0	0	0
Days With ≥ 1.0" Snow Depth	0	0	0	0	0	0	0	0	0	***0***	0	0	***0***

The period of record for all cooperative weather station data is 1980 – 2009. See User Guide for detailed explanation of data.

Boca *Nevada County* Elevation: 5,575 ft. Latitude: 39° 23' N Longitude: 120° 06' W

	JAN	FEB	MAR	APR	MAY	JUN	JUL	AUG	SEP	OCT	NOV	DEC	YEAR
Mean Maximum Temp. (°F)	42.5	45.6	51.1	58.3	67.0	75.7	84.6	83.9	77.0	66.4	52.1	42.6	62.2
Mean Temp. (°F)	27.0	29.9	35.6	41.3	48.6	54.9	61.2	59.9	53.6	45.6	35.8	28.3	43.5
Mean Minimum Temp. (°F)	11.4	14.2	20.0	24.4	30.1	34.0	37.8	35.9	30.2	24.7	19.4	14.0	24.7
Extreme Maximum Temp. (°F)	64	68	75	81	90	96	103	99	95	89	78	68	103
Extreme Minimum Temp. (°F)	-30	-43	-7	6	13	17	22	22	15	10	-9	-28	-43
Days Maximum Temp. ≥ 90°F	0	0	0	0	0	1	7	5	1	0	0	0	14
Days Maximum Temp. ≤ 32°F	3	2	0	0	0	0	0	0	0	0	1	3	9
Days Minimum Temp. ≤ 32°F	30	28	30	28	21	13	6	8	20	28	28	30	270
Days Minimum Temp. ≤ 0°F	6	3	0	0	0	0	0	0	0	0	0	3	12
Heating Degree Days (base 65°F)	1,171	985	905	703	503	301	135	162	335	595	870	1,131	7,796
Cooling Degree Days (base 65°F)	0	0	0	0	0	3	25	10	0	0	0	0	38
Mean Precipitation (in.)	3.45	3.35	2.88	1.23	0.97	0.55	0.51	0.38	0.76	1.35	2.65	3.89	21.97
Extreme Maximum Daily Precip. (in.)	2.99	2.82	2.38	1.28	1.65	0.98	2.00	1.00	1.23	2.28	2.33	3.95	3.95
Days With ≥ 0.1" Precipitation	6	5	6	4	3	2	1	1	2	3	5	6	44
Days With ≥ 0.5" Precipitation	2	2	2	1	0	0	0	0	0	1	2	3	13
Days With ≥ 1.0" Precipitation	1	1	1	0	0	0	0	0	0	0	1	1	5
Mean Snowfall (in.)	19.5	19.8	15.9	5.6	1.1	0.1	0.0	0.0	0.2	1.0	8.9	20.8	92.9
Maximum Snow Depth (in.)	54	70	55	31	3	2	0	0	2	5	25	55	70
Days With ≥ 1.0" Snow Depth	23	21	13	2	0	0	0	0	0	1	6	20	86

Bodie *Mono County* Elevation: 8,370 ft. Latitude: 38° 13' N Longitude: 119° 01' W

	JAN	FEB	MAR	APR	MAY	JUN	JUL	AUG	SEP	OCT	NOV	DEC	YEAR
Mean Maximum Temp. (°F)	40.3	41.1	44.9	51.3	61.5	70.4	77.5	76.8	70.1	60.2	48.6	41.1	57.0
Mean Temp. (°F)	23.2	24.6	28.6	35.0	43.2	50.6	56.3	54.9	48.4	39.7	30.6	23.9	38.3
Mean Minimum Temp. (°F)	6.1	8.0	12.3	18.7	24.9	30.9	35.0	33.0	26.7	19.2	12.6	6.6	19.5
Extreme Maximum Temp. (°F)	60	61	68	75	82	90	91	88	88	83	70	64	91
Extreme Minimum Temp. (°F)	-27	-33	-15	-6	2	6	12	12	4	-6	-21	-31	-33
Days Maximum Temp. ≥ 90°F	0	0	0	0	0	0	0	0	0	0	0	0	0
Days Maximum Temp. ≤ 32°F	6	5	3	1	0	0	0	0	0	0	2	5	22
Days Minimum Temp. ≤ 32°F	31	28	31	29	26	18	11	15	24	29	30	31	303
Days Minimum Temp. ≤ 0°F	9	7	3	0	0	0	0	0	0	0	3	9	31
Heating Degree Days (base 65°F)	1,289	1,136	1,120	892	668	425	265	305	491	776	1,024	1,267	9,658
Cooling Degree Days (base 65°F)	0	0	0	0	0	0	1	0	0	0	0	0	1
Mean Precipitation (in.)	1.68	1.70	1.44	0.86	0.77	0.74	0.63	0.49	0.48	0.58	1.11	1.42	11.90
Extreme Maximum Daily Precip. (in.)	2.80	1.42	2.41	1.22	1.42	1.49	2.10	1.10	1.23	1.55	1.95	1.26	2.80
Days With ≥ 0.1" Precipitation	4	4	4	3	2	2	2	2	2	2	3	4	34
Days With ≥ 0.5" Precipitation	1	1	1	0	0	0	0	0	0	0	1	1	5
Days With ≥ 1.0" Precipitation	0	0	0	0	0	0	0	0	0	0	0	0	0
Mean Snowfall (in.)	13.0	13.8	14.8	5.7	3.0	0.5	trace	trace	0.4	2.2	9.3	***13.2***	***75.9***
Maximum Snow Depth (in.)	45	78	63	46	23	2	trace	1	8	18	19	42	78
Days With ≥ 1.0" Snow Depth	27	26	26	13	2	0	0	0	0	1	9	24	128

Borrego Desert Park *San Diego County* Elevation: 805 ft. Latitude: 33° 14' N Longitude: 116° 25' W

	JAN	FEB	MAR	APR	MAY	JUN	JUL	AUG	SEP	OCT	NOV	DEC	YEAR
Mean Maximum Temp. (°F)	69.7	72.2	78.4	85.2	93.9	102.8	107.5	106.4	101.0	90.1	78.3	68.9	87.9
Mean Temp. (°F)	57.1	59.5	64.3	69.9	77.5	85.6	91.7	91.2	85.7	75.5	64.5	56.3	73.2
Mean Minimum Temp. (°F)	44.5	46.6	50.1	54.4	61.1	68.3	75.8	75.9	70.4	60.9	50.7	43.6	58.5
Extreme Maximum Temp. (°F)	89	95	101	111	115	122	121	119	117	113	98	87	122
Extreme Minimum Temp. (°F)	24	24	23	35	42	48	56	57	49	41	32	23	23
Days Maximum Temp. ≥ 90°F	0	0	3	11	23	28	31	31	28	18	2	0	175
Days Maximum Temp. ≤ 32°F	0	0	0	0	0	0	0	0	0	0	0	0	0
Days Minimum Temp. ≤ 32°F	1	0	0	0	0	0	0	0	0	0	0	1	2
Days Minimum Temp. ≤ 0°F	0	0	0	0	0	0	0	0	0	0	0	0	0
Heating Degree Days (base 65°F)	242	171	96	39	6	0	0	0	0	7	86	266	913
Cooling Degree Days (base 65°F)	6	21	81	192	402	624	834	818	628	340	79	4	4,029
Mean Precipitation (in.)	1.16	1.53	0.81	0.18	0.07	0.02	0.30	0.50	0.31	0.26	0.35	0.82	6.31
Extreme Maximum Daily Precip. (in.)	2.02	2.42	2.46	0.56	1.04	0.23	1.15	2.05	1.36	1.51	1.40	2.10	2.46
Days With ≥ 0.1" Precipitation	2	3	2	1	0	0	1	1	1	1	1	2	15
Days With ≥ 0.5" Precipitation	1	1	0	0	0	0	0	0	0	0	0	1	3
Days With ≥ 1.0" Precipitation	0	0	0	0	0	0	0	0	0	0	0	0	0
Mean Snowfall (in.)	0.0	trace	0.0	0.0	0.0	0.0	0.0	0.0	0.0	0.0	0.0	0.0	trace
Maximum Snow Depth (in.)	0	trace	0	0	0	0	0	0	0	0	0	0	trace
Days With ≥ 1.0" Snow Depth	0	0	0	0	0	0	0	0	0	0	0	0	0

Burbank Valley Pump Plant *Los Angeles County* Elevation: 654 ft. Latitude: 34° 11' N Longitude: 118° 21' W

	JAN	FEB	MAR	APR	MAY	JUN	JUL	AUG	SEP	OCT	NOV	DEC	YEAR
Mean Maximum Temp. (°F)	69.0	69.5	71.5	75.0	77.4	82.1	88.1	89.5	87.4	81.6	74.3	68.5	77.8
Mean Temp. (°F)	55.7	56.9	59.0	62.5	66.1	70.3	75.3	76.1	73.8	67.9	60.3	55.0	64.9
Mean Minimum Temp. (°F)	42.4	44.3	46.4	50.1	54.8	58.5	62.5	62.5	60.2	54.1	46.2	41.5	52.0
Extreme Maximum Temp. (°F)	93	92	98	105	107	110	110	110	111	108	98	89	111
Extreme Minimum Temp. (°F)	26	29	22	33	42	46	52	52	46	41	30	25	22
Days Maximum Temp. ≥ 90°F	0	0	1	2	3	5	13	15	12	6	1	0	58
Days Maximum Temp. ≤ 32°F	0	0	0	0	0	0	0	0	0	0	0	0	0
Days Minimum Temp. ≤ 32°F	1	0	1	0	0	0	0	0	0	0	0	1	3
Days Minimum Temp. ≤ 0°F	0	0	0	0	0	0	0	0	0	0	0	0	0
Heating Degree Days (base 65°F)	284	229	194	115	45	9	0	0	3	29	153	303	1,364
Cooling Degree Days (base 65°F)	3	7	15	48	88	174	327	349	275	124	17	2	1,429
Mean Precipitation (in.)	3.48	4.83	3.22	1.08	0.32	0.11	0.02	0.07	0.23	0.85	1.03	2.15	17.39
Extreme Maximum Daily Precip. (in.)	4.52	4.50	5.45	2.30	1.80	1.01	0.18	0.67	1.10	3.00	2.00	3.49	5.45
Days With ≥ 0.1" Precipitation	5	5	4	2	1	0	0	0	1	1	2	3	24
Days With ≥ 0.5" Precipitation	2	3	2	1	0	0	0	0	0	1	1	2	12
Days With ≥ 1.0" Precipitation	1	2	1	0	0	0	0	0	0	0	0	1	5
Mean Snowfall (in.)	0.0	0.0	0.0	0.0	0.0	0.0	0.0	0.0	0.0	0.0	0.0	0.0	0.0
Maximum Snow Depth (in.)	0	0	0	0	0	0	0	0	0	0	0	0	0
Days With ≥ 1.0" Snow Depth	0	0	0	0	0	0	0	0	0	0	0	0	0

The period of record for all cooperative weather station data is 1980 – 2009. See User Guide for detailed explanation of data.

Cachuma Lake *Santa Barbara County* Elevation: 780 ft. Latitude: 34° 35' N Longitude: 119° 59' W

	JAN	FEB	MAR	APR	MAY	JUN	JUL	AUG	SEP	OCT	NOV	DEC	YEAR
Mean Maximum Temp. (°F)	66.4	67.3	70.1	74.8	79.4	85.1	91.2	92.0	88.8	82.8	73.8	66.4	78.2
Mean Temp. (°F)	52.9	54.3	56.5	59.6	63.6	67.7	72.2	72.7	70.5	65.5	58.5	52.6	62.2
Mean Minimum Temp. (°F)	39.4	41.3	42.9	44.4	47.8	50.3	53.3	53.4	52.1	48.2	43.2	38.8	46.2
Extreme Maximum Temp. (°F)	87	92	95	105	104	113	112	112	112	110	100	87	113
Extreme Minimum Temp. (°F)	20	22	27	30	35	37	42	43	40	27	28	16	16
Days Maximum Temp. ≥ 90°F	0	0	0	2	4	9	18	20	14	8	1	0	76
Days Maximum Temp. ≤ 32°F	0	0	0	0	0	0	0	0	0	0	0	0	0
Days Minimum Temp. ≤ 32°F	4	2	1	0	0	0	0	0	0	0	1	4	12
Days Minimum Temp. ≤ 0°F	0	0	0	0	0	0	0	0	0	0	0	0	0
Heating Degree Days (base 65°F)	368	299	261	178	89	22	2	1	8	61	204	377	1,870
Cooling Degree Days (base 65°F)	0	3	5	23	52	112	232	247	180	84	15	0	953
Mean Precipitation (in.)	4.79	5.35	3.90	1.27	0.45	0.05	0.01	0.03	0.14	0.91	1.59	3.17	21.66
Extreme Maximum Daily Precip. (in.)	6.25	6.63	6.10	2.47	2.04	0.41	0.07	0.59	0.54	4.09	2.26	7.23	7.23
Days With ≥ 0.1" Precipitation	6	6	5	2	1	0	0	0	0	1	3	4	28
Days With ≥ 0.5" Precipitation	3	3	2	1	0	0	0	0	0	0	1	2	12
Days With ≥ 1.0" Precipitation	1	2	1	0	0	0	0	0	0	0	1	1	6
Mean Snowfall (in.)	0.0	0.0	0.0	0.0	0.0	0.0	0.0	0.0	0.0	0.0	0.0	0.0	0.0
Maximum Snow Depth (in.)	0	0	0	0	0	0	0	0	0	0	0	0	0
Days With ≥ 1.0" Snow Depth	0	0	0	0	0	0	0	0	0	0	0	0	0

Calaveras Big Trees *Calaveras County* Elevation: 4,693 ft. Latitude: 38° 17' N Longitude: 120° 19' W

	JAN	FEB	MAR	APR	MAY	JUN	JUL	AUG	SEP	OCT	NOV	DEC	YEAR
Mean Maximum Temp. (°F)	43.9	45.1	48.6	54.5	63.8	73.0	80.6	80.1	73.0	63.0	50.9	43.6	60.0
Mean Temp. (°F)	36.4	37.0	39.9	44.4	52.4	60.2	67.2	66.6	60.7	52.0	42.0	36.2	49.6
Mean Minimum Temp. (°F)	28.8	28.9	31.0	34.2	40.9	47.4	53.7	53.2	48.3	41.0	33.1	28.7	39.1
Extreme Maximum Temp. (°F)	62	68	72	82	93	91	95	98	92	88	73	65	98
Extreme Minimum Temp. (°F)	5	5	14	18	10	30	32	41	31	25	14	3	3
Days Maximum Temp. ≥ 90°F	0	0	0	0	0	0	2	1	0	0	0	0	3
Days Maximum Temp. ≤ 32°F	2	2	1	0	0	0	0	0	0	0	1	3	9
Days Minimum Temp. ≤ 32°F	23	21	19	13	4	0	0	0	0	4	14	23	121
Days Minimum Temp. ≤ 0°F	0	0	0	0	0	0	0	0	0	0	0	0	0
Heating Degree Days (base 65°F)	881	783	772	612	390	167	37	38	155	400	682	886	5,803
Cooling Degree Days (base 65°F)	0	0	0	0	5	30	113	96	31	4	0	0	279
Mean Precipitation (in.)	10.39	10.33	8.33	4.38	2.53	0.73	0.14	0.09	0.90	3.06	6.11	9.01	56.00
Extreme Maximum Daily Precip. (in.)	7.85	6.25	5.18	4.52	2.85	1.51	2.14	0.80	2.26	5.50	5.79	4.72	7.85
Days With ≥ 0.1" Precipitation	9	9	9	6	4	1	0	0	1	3	7	9	58
Days With ≥ 0.5" Precipitation	6	5	5	3	2	0	0	0	1	2	3	5	32
Days With ≥ 1.0" Precipitation	4	4	3	2	1	0	0	0	0	1	2	3	20
Mean Snowfall (in.)	22.9	25.6	23.8	11.1	1.7	0.1	0.0	0.0	trace	0.6	6.3	20.6	112.7
Maximum Snow Depth (in.)	***58***	***54***	na	***84***	1	trace	0	0	***0***	***7***	***20***	***36***	na
Days With ≥ 1.0" Snow Depth	***3***	***4***	***5***	***1***	0	0	0	0	0	0	1	2	***16***

Calistoga *Napa County* Elevation: 370 ft. Latitude: 38° 35' N Longitude: 122° 34' W

	JAN	FEB	MAR	APR	MAY	JUN	JUL	AUG	SEP	OCT	NOV	DEC	YEAR
Mean Maximum Temp. (°F)	***59.7***	63.9	67.8	***72.6***	79.6	86.4	92.4	91.5	88.2	79.8	***66.9***	***58.7***	***75.6***
Mean Temp. (°F)	***48.3***	51.4	54.3	***57.5***	63.1	68.4	72.6	71.8	69.2	62.5	***53.6***	***47.6***	***60.0***
Mean Minimum Temp. (°F)	***36.9***	38.9	40.8	42.4	46.6	50.4	52.8	52.1	50.1	45.2	***40.3***	***36.6***	***44.4***
Extreme Maximum Temp. (°F)	80	88	89	102	104	106	111	109	110	106	91	83	111
Extreme Minimum Temp. (°F)	18	17	21	20	29	35	37	38	35	27	21	12	12
Days Maximum Temp. ≥ 90°F	0	0	0	1	4	11	19	18	14	5	0	0	72
Days Maximum Temp. ≤ 32°F	0	0	0	0	0	0	0	0	0	0	0	0	0
Days Minimum Temp. ≤ 32°F	9	6	3	1	0	0	0	0	0	0	4	10	33
Days Minimum Temp. ≤ 0°F	0	0	0	0	0	0	0	0	0	0	0	0	0
Heating Degree Days (base 65°F)	***510***	379	328	***230***	107	25	2	2	15	111	***335***	***532***	***2,576***
Cooling Degree Days (base 65°F)	***0***	1	3	***13***	55	133	244	219	149	41	***1***	***0***	***859***
Mean Precipitation (in.)	7.48	8.03	5.69	2.04	1.31	0.27	0.03	0.07	0.33	1.98	4.59	8.05	39.87
Extreme Maximum Daily Precip. (in.)	5.80	8.10	5.63	2.17	2.30	1.03	0.53	0.83	1.18	3.06	3.58	5.90	8.10
Days With ≥ 0.1" Precipitation	8	8	7	4	2	1	0	0	1	3	5	8	47
Days With ≥ 0.5" Precipitation	4	5	4	1	1	0	0	0	0	1	3	5	24
Days With ≥ 1.0" Precipitation	2	3	2	0	0	0	0	0	0	1	1	3	12
Mean Snowfall (in.)	trace	trace	0.0	0.0	0.0	0.0	0.0	0.0	0.0	0.0	0.0	0.0	trace
Maximum Snow Depth (in.)	trace	trace	0	0	0	0	0	0	0	0	0	0	trace
Days With ≥ 1.0" Snow Depth	0	0	0	0	0	0	0	0	0	0	0	0	0

Callahan *Siskiyou County* Elevation: 3,185 ft. Latitude: 41° 19' N Longitude: 122° 48' W

	JAN	FEB	MAR	APR	MAY	JUN	JUL	AUG	SEP	OCT	NOV	DEC	YEAR
Mean Maximum Temp. (°F)	45.4	50.8	56.8	63.1	70.9	78.6	86.9	86.3	79.5	67.6	51.5	44.1	65.1
Mean Temp. (°F)	35.9	39.6	43.7	48.5	55.0	61.2	68.2	67.1	60.8	51.6	40.8	35.2	50.6
Mean Minimum Temp. (°F)	26.4	28.4	30.5	33.8	39.0	43.8	49.4	47.8	42.0	35.5	30.1	26.3	36.1
Extreme Maximum Temp. (°F)	65	72	76	86	98	100	103	102	98	90	75	64	103
Extreme Minimum Temp. (°F)	6	-1	14	19	25	23	30	34	27	16	11	-6	-6
Days Maximum Temp. ≥ 90°F	0	0	0	0	1	3	11	10	3	0	0	0	28
Days Maximum Temp. ≤ 32°F	1	0	0	0	0	0	0	0	0	0	0	1	2
Days Minimum Temp. ≤ 32°F	25	21	20	14	6	1	0	0	1	11	21	25	145
Days Minimum Temp. ≤ 0°F	0	0	0	0	0	0	0	0	0	0	0	0	0
Heating Degree Days (base 65°F)	896	711	654	489	312	140	28	30	144	410	720	917	5,451
Cooling Degree Days (base 65°F)	0	0	0	0	8	34	133	101	23	1	0	0	300
Mean Precipitation (in.)	3.45	2.84	2.15	1.28	1.30	0.79	0.46	0.31	0.44	1.24	2.97	3.99	21.22
Extreme Maximum Daily Precip. (in.)	4.36	2.42	2.23	1.17	1.86	1.21	1.03	2.51	1.01	1.99	2.22	3.98	4.36
Days With ≥ 0.1" Precipitation	7	6	5	3	3	2	1	1	1	3	6	7	45
Days With ≥ 0.5" Precipitation	2	2	1	1	1	0	0	0	0	1	2	2	12
Days With ≥ 1.0" Precipitation	1	1	0	0	0	0	0	0	0	0	1	1	4
Mean Snowfall (in.)	0.9	0.3	1.2	0.3	0.1	0.0	0.0	0.0	0.0	0.1	1.0	1.6	5.5
Maximum Snow Depth (in.)	11	12	0	1	0	0	0	0	0	0	5	10	12
Days With ≥ 1.0" Snow Depth	0	0	0	0	0	0	0	0	0	0	0	0	0

The period of record for all cooperative weather station data is 1980 – 2009. See User Guide for detailed explanation of data.

Camp Pardee *Calaveras County* Elevation: 658 ft. Latitude: 38° 15' N Longitude: 120° 52' W

	JAN	FEB	MAR	APR	MAY	JUN	JUL	AUG	SEP	OCT	NOV	DEC	YEAR
Mean Maximum Temp. (°F)	53.9	59.9	64.7	70.7	80.2	88.8	95.3	94.1	88.7	78.2	63.9	54.5	74.4
Mean Temp. (°F)	46.7	51.1	54.8	59.0	66.2	73.2	78.9	77.9	74.0	65.7	54.8	47.1	62.4
Mean Minimum Temp. (°F)	39.4	42.4	44.8	47.1	52.2	57.5	62.4	61.7	59.2	53.1	45.7	39.6	50.4
Extreme Maximum Temp. (°F)	71	75	85	99	108	108	113	111	106	102	83	73	113
Extreme Minimum Temp. (°F)	25	23	30	33	38	43	49	50	42	38	29	18	18
Days Maximum Temp. ≥ 90°F	0	0	0	1	5	14	25	23	15	3	0	0	86
Days Maximum Temp. ≤ 32°F	0	0	0	0	0	0	0	0	0	0	0	0	0
Days Minimum Temp. ≤ 32°F	4	1	0	0	0	0	0	0	0	0	0	4	9
Days Minimum Temp. ≤ 0°F	0	0	0	0	0	0	0	0	0	0	0	0	0
Heating Degree Days (base 65°F)	563	387	314	200	71	10	0	0	7	72	303	549	2,476
Cooling Degree Days (base 65°F)	0	0	2	24	114	260	436	407	282	98	3	0	1,626
Mean Precipitation (in.)	4.27	3.92	3.85	1.89	1.14	0.29	0.04	0.04	0.44	1.24	2.51	3.59	23.22
Extreme Maximum Daily Precip. (in.)	2.52	2.14	2.05	2.84	5.33	1.37	0.70	0.22	2.41	2.24	1.95	2.05	5.33
Days With ≥ 0.1" Precipitation	8	7	7	4	2	1	0	0	1	2	5	7	44
Days With ≥ 0.5" Precipitation	3	3	3	1	1	0	0	0	0	1	2	3	17
Days With ≥ 1.0" Precipitation	1	1	1	0	0	0	0	0	0	0	1	1	5
Mean Snowfall (in.)	0.0	0.0	0.0	0.0	0.0	0.0	0.0	0.0	0.0	0.0	0.0	0.0	0.0
Maximum Snow Depth (in.)	0	0	0	0	0	0	0	0	0	0	0	0	0
Days With ≥ 1.0" Snow Depth	0	0	0	0	0	0	0	0	0	0	0	0	0

Canoga Park Pierce College *Los Angeles County* Elevation: 790 ft. Latitude: 34° 11' N Longitude: 118° 34' W

	JAN	FEB	MAR	APR	MAY	JUN	JUL	AUG	SEP	OCT	NOV	DEC	YEAR
Mean Maximum Temp. (°F)	69.2	70.1	73.1	78.2	82.3	88.7	95.3	97.0	92.5	***84.8***	74.9	69.2	***81.3***
Mean Temp. (°F)	54.6	55.8	57.9	61.7	66.0	71.2	76.2	77.3	73.8	***67.3***	58.7	54.0	***64.5***
Mean Minimum Temp. (°F)	40.0	41.5	42.7	45.2	49.7	53.5	57.1	57.6	55.0	***49.6***	42.5	38.7	***47.8***
Extreme Maximum Temp. (°F)	92	94	101	105	113	113	115	116	114	***110***	97	93	***116***
Extreme Minimum Temp. (°F)	24	18	28	30	38	40	46	45	42	***35***	24	20	***18***
Days Maximum Temp. ≥ 90°F	0	0	1	5	7	15	25	27	19	***10***	2	0	***111***
Days Maximum Temp. ≤ 32°F	0	0	0	0	0	0	0	0	0	***0***	0	0	***0***
Days Minimum Temp. ≤ 32°F	4	3	1	0	0	0	0	0	0	***0***	1	5	***14***
Days Minimum Temp. ≤ 0°F	0	0	0	0	0	0	0	0	0	***0***	0	0	***0***
Heating Degree Days (base 65°F)	317	258	224	134	61	12	0	0	5	***40***	194	337	***1,582***
Cooling Degree Days (base 65°F)	3	4	10	42	100	204	355	390	275	***116***	12	1	***1,512***
Mean Precipitation (in.)	3.68	5.19	3.25	1.03	0.35	0.07	0.02	0.06	0.15	***0.89***	1.39	2.59	***18.67***
Extreme Maximum Daily Precip. (in.)	4.62	5.78	***6.06***	2.49	1.97	0.52	***0.17***	***0.54***	***0.75***	***3.20***	***2.33***	***4.62***	***6.06***
Days With ≥ 0.1" Precipitation	5	5	4	2	1	0	0	0	0	***1***	2	3	***23***
Days With ≥ 0.5" Precipitation	2	3	2	1	0	0	0	0	0	***0***	1	2	***11***
Days With ≥ 1.0" Precipitation	1	2	1	0	0	0	0	0	0	***0***	0	1	***5***
Mean Snowfall (in.)	0.0	trace	0.0	0.0	0.0	0.0	0.0	0.0	0.0	***0.0***	0.0	trace	***trace***
Maximum Snow Depth (in.)	0	0	0	0	0	0	0	0	0	***0***	0	trace	trace
Days With ≥ 1.0" Snow Depth	0	0	0	0	0	0	0	0	0	***0***	0	0	***0***

Canyon Dam *Plumas County* Elevation: 4,560 ft. Latitude: 40° 10' N Longitude: 121° 05' W

	JAN	FEB	MAR	APR	MAY	JUN	JUL	AUG	SEP	OCT	NOV	DEC	YEAR
Mean Maximum Temp. (°F)	40.4	43.9	50.2	57.5	67.8	76.0	84.2	83.5	76.5	64.3	48.6	40.2	61.1
Mean Temp. (°F)	32.2	34.6	39.2	44.5	52.8	59.8	66.5	65.4	59.4	49.8	39.0	32.3	48.0
Mean Minimum Temp. (°F)	24.0	25.2	28.1	31.4	37.8	43.6	48.8	47.3	42.3	35.3	29.2	24.3	34.8
Extreme Maximum Temp. (°F)	57	63	71	81	92	96	102	102	97	85	69	60	102
Extreme Minimum Temp. (°F)	-5	-10	8	14	23	27	34	31	26	19	9	-11	-11
Days Maximum Temp. ≥ 90°F	0	0	0	0	0	1	7	5	1	0	0	0	14
Days Maximum Temp. ≤ 32°F	3	1	0	0	0	0	0	0	0	0	0	3	7
Days Minimum Temp. ≤ 32°F	29	26	26	18	6	1	0	0	1	10	22	28	167
Days Minimum Temp. ≤ 0°F	0	0	0	0	0	0	0	0	0	0	0	0	0
Heating Degree Days (base 65°F)	1,011	853	793	610	374	173	46	52	176	465	775	1,008	6,336
Cooling Degree Days (base 65°F)	0	0	0	0	3	23	101	71	16	0	0	0	214
Mean Precipitation (in.)	6.09	6.64	5.18	2.62	1.61	0.75	0.16	0.19	0.71	2.10	4.53	6.49	37.07
Extreme Maximum Daily Precip. (in.)	4.10	3.22	3.41	2.49	2.15	1.18	0.60	1.07	1.97	2.74	3.42	3.79	4.10
Days With ≥ 0.1" Precipitation	9	9	8	5	4	2	0	1	1	3	7	9	58
Days With ≥ 0.5" Precipitation	4	4	4	2	1	1	0	0	1	2	3	4	26
Days With ≥ 1.0" Precipitation	2	2	2	1	0	0	0	0	0	1	1	2	11
Mean Snowfall (in.)	25.8	24.5	16.7	7.0	0.3	0.0	0.0	0.0	0.1	0.9	8.0	22.7	106.0
Maximum Snow Depth (in.)	115	101	95	50	4	0	0	0	2	4	31	72	115
Days With ≥ 1.0" Snow Depth	26	25	19	5	0	0	0	0	0	0	5	21	101

Cedarville *Modoc County* Elevation: 4,669 ft. Latitude: 41° 32' N Longitude: 120° 10' W

	JAN	FEB	MAR	APR	MAY	JUN	JUL	AUG	SEP	OCT	NOV	DEC	YEAR
Mean Maximum Temp. (°F)	40.7	44.4	51.1	57.4	66.7	76.5	86.9	86.0	77.5	64.9	48.8	40.1	61.7
Mean Temp. (°F)	30.9	34.2	39.9	45.4	53.7	62.0	70.7	69.1	60.5	49.4	37.5	30.3	48.6
Mean Minimum Temp. (°F)	21.0	24.0	28.8	33.4	40.6	47.4	54.5	52.1	43.3	33.9	26.3	20.4	35.5
Extreme Maximum Temp. (°F)	60	69	78	82	93	99	107	102	98	90	75	63	107
Extreme Minimum Temp. (°F)	-6	-17	-1	14	23	29	36	33	24	11	-5	-28	-28
Days Maximum Temp. ≥ 90°F	0	0	0	0	0	3	13	10	3	0	0	0	29
Days Maximum Temp. ≤ 32°F	5	2	0	0	0	0	0	0	0	0	1	5	13
Days Minimum Temp. ≤ 32°F	28	24	22	13	4	0	0	0	2	13	23	28	157
Days Minimum Temp. ≤ 0°F	0	0	0	0	0	0	0	0	0	0	0	1	1
Heating Degree Days (base 65°F)	1,051	864	770	580	356	143	23	26	167	477	817	1,070	6,344
Cooling Degree Days (base 65°F)	0	0	0	0	12	59	207	159	37	1	0	0	475
Mean Precipitation (in.)	1.61	1.28	1.39	1.24	1.21	0.67	0.20	0.26	0.44	0.79	1.75	1.66	12.50
Extreme Maximum Daily Precip. (in.)	2.38	1.92	1.34	1.00	1.22	1.86	0.76	0.85	1.37	1.31	1.48	1.21	2.38
Days With ≥ 0.1" Precipitation	4	4	4	4	4	2	1	1	1	3	5	5	38
Days With ≥ 0.5" Precipitation	1	0	0	0	0	0	0	0	0	0	1	1	3
Days With ≥ 1.0" Precipitation	0	0	0	0	0	0	0	0	0	0	0	0	0
Mean Snowfall (in.)	3.4	2.4	1.1	0.7	trace	trace	0.0	0.0	trace	0.1	1.8	3.7	13.2
Maximum Snow Depth (in.)	14	10	5	3	1	1	0	0	trace	3	10	17	17
Days With ≥ 1.0" Snow Depth	7	2	1	1	0	0	0	0	0	0	1	3	15

The period of record for all cooperative weather station data is 1980 – 2009. See User Guide for detailed explanation of data.

Chula Vista *San Diego County* Elevation: 56 ft. Latitude: 32° 38' N Longitude: 117° 05' W

	JAN	FEB	MAR	APR	MAY	JUN	JUL	AUG	SEP	OCT	NOV	DEC	YEAR
Mean Maximum Temp. (°F)	68.3	67.9	67.9	69.5	70.0	71.9	75.6	77.8	78.0	75.6	71.1	67.6	71.8
Mean Temp. (°F)	57.2	57.8	59.0	61.2	63.9	66.3	69.9	71.7	70.9	66.6	60.5	56.4	63.4
Mean Minimum Temp. (°F)	46.0	47.7	50.2	52.9	57.6	60.6	64.2	65.5	63.6	58.0	49.8	45.3	55.1
Extreme Maximum Temp. (°F)	90	90	95	102	95	97	100	96	108	106	96	84	108
Extreme Minimum Temp. (°F)	30	29	32	15	44	49	54	42	43	44	35	28	15
Days Maximum Temp. ≥ 90°F	0	0	0	0	0	0	0	0	1	1	0	0	2
Days Maximum Temp. ≤ 32°F	0	0	0	0	0	0	0	0	0	0	0	0	0
Days Minimum Temp. ≤ 32°F	0	0	0	0	0	0	0	0	0	0	0	0	0
Days Minimum Temp. ≤ 0°F	0	0	0	0	0	0	0	0	0	0	0	0	0
Heating Degree Days (base 65°F)	240	201	184	122	55	14	0	0	1	21	138	259	1,235
Cooling Degree Days (base 65°F)	3	4	5	15	26	59	161	215	185	79	10	0	762
Mean Precipitation (in.)	1.90	2.29	1.78	0.66	0.09	0.06	0.03	0.01	0.14	0.44	0.99	1.22	9.61
Extreme Maximum Daily Precip. (in.)	2.14	2.42	1.79	0.77	1.45	0.40	0.43	0.15	1.20	1.10	2.15	1.74	2.42
Days With ≥ 0.1" Precipitation	4	4	3	2	0	0	0	0	0	1	2	3	19
Days With ≥ 0.5" Precipitation	1	2	1	0	0	0	0	0	0	0	1	1	6
Days With ≥ 1.0" Precipitation	0	0	0	0	0	0	0	0	0	0	0	0	0
Mean Snowfall (in.)	trace	0.0	0.0	0.0	0.0	0.0	0.0	0.0	trace	0.0	0.0	0.2	0.2
Maximum Snow Depth (in.)	trace	0	0	0	0	0	0	0	trace	0	0	0	trace
Days With ≥ 1.0" Snow Depth	0	0	0	0	0	0	0	0	0	0	0	0	0

Coalinga *Fresno County* Elevation: 669 ft. Latitude: 36° 08' N Longitude: 120° 22' W

	JAN	FEB	MAR	APR	MAY	JUN	JUL	AUG	SEP	OCT	NOV	DEC	YEAR
Mean Maximum Temp. (°F)	58.9	65.2	71.4	78.1	87.3	94.4	100.2	98.8	93.4	82.9	68.5	59.5	79.9
Mean Temp. (°F)	48.2	52.9	57.6	62.5	70.7	77.5	83.5	81.8	76.6	66.8	55.1	47.9	65.1
Mean Minimum Temp. (°F)	37.4	40.5	43.7	47.0	54.1	60.5	66.8	64.7	59.8	50.6	41.7	36.2	50.2
Extreme Maximum Temp. (°F)	77	87	92	101	110	111	115	113	110	103	90	79	115
Extreme Minimum Temp. (°F)	17	21	29	31	38	41	44	51	44	30	26	11	11
Days Maximum Temp. ≥ 90°F	0	0	0	4	13	22	30	29	21	7	0	0	126
Days Maximum Temp. ≤ 32°F	0	0	0	0	0	0	0	0	0	0	0	0	0
Days Minimum Temp. ≤ 32°F	9	3	0	0	0	0	0	0	0	0	3	10	25
Days Minimum Temp. ≤ 0°F	0	0	0	0	0	0	0	0	0	0	0	0	0
Heating Degree Days (base 65°F)	515	337	232	122	26	2	0	0	3	53	293	524	2,107
Cooling Degree Days (base 65°F)	0	0	8	55	208	382	581	528	357	115	2	0	2,236
Mean Precipitation (in.)	1.91	1.74	1.48	0.47	0.26	0.07	0.01	0.03	0.18	0.39	0.52	1.07	8.13
Extreme Maximum Daily Precip. (in.)	2.59	1.99	3.74	1.09	1.55	0.70	0.08	0.25	0.98	1.19	1.15	1.39	3.74
Days With ≥ 0.1" Precipitation	4	4	3	1	1	0	0	0	0	1	2	3	19
Days With ≥ 0.5" Precipitation	1	1	1	0	0	0	0	0	0	0	0	1	4
Days With ≥ 1.0" Precipitation	0	0	0	0	0	0	0	0	0	0	0	0	0
Mean Snowfall (in.)	0.0	trace	0.0	0.0	0.0	0.0	0.0	0.0	0.0	0.0	0.0	0.0	trace
Maximum Snow Depth (in.)	0	trace	0	0	0	0	0	0	0	0	0	0	trace
Days With ≥ 1.0" Snow Depth	0	0	0	0	0	0	0	0	0	0	0	0	0

Colfax *Placer County* Elevation: 2,399 ft. Latitude: 39° 07' N Longitude: 120° 57' W

	JAN	FEB	MAR	APR	MAY	JUN	JUL	AUG	SEP	OCT	NOV	DEC	YEAR
Mean Maximum Temp. (°F)	54.7	56.8	60.4	66.0	74.7	83.0	90.9	90.2	84.7	74.1	60.0	53.6	70.8
Mean Temp. (°F)	44.9	46.7	49.5	54.0	61.6	69.0	75.9	74.8	69.7	60.6	49.7	44.2	58.4
Mean Minimum Temp. (°F)	35.1	36.4	38.4	41.9	48.4	54.9	60.8	59.4	54.6	47.0	39.2	34.8	45.9
Extreme Maximum Temp. (°F)	77	80	83	89	100	102	107	105	103	100	84	79	107
Extreme Minimum Temp. (°F)	18	15	24	22	30	38	44	44	36	31	22	14	14
Days Maximum Temp. ≥ 90°F	0	0	0	0	2	7	19	17	10	2	0	0	57
Days Maximum Temp. ≤ 32°F	0	0	0	0	0	0	0	0	0	0	0	0	0
Days Minimum Temp. ≤ 32°F	11	8	6	2	0	0	0	0	0	0	4	11	42
Days Minimum Temp. ≤ 0°F	0	0	0	0	0	0	0	0	0	0	0	0	0
Heating Degree Days (base 65°F)	616	512	475	331	158	42	3	1	34	170	453	637	3,432
Cooling Degree Days (base 65°F)	0	0	1	6	59	168	346	312	181	41	0	0	1,114
Mean Precipitation (in.)	7.98	8.45	6.93	3.22	1.72	0.62	0.05	0.14	0.82	2.38	6.02	8.25	46.58
Extreme Maximum Daily Precip. (in.)	4.18	5.90	3.80	2.88	2.00	1.86	0.82	0.93	2.06	2.61	3.99	4.20	5.90
Days With ≥ 0.1" Precipitation	9	9	9	5	3	1	0	0	1	3	7	9	56
Days With ≥ 0.5" Precipitation	5	5	5	2	1	0	0	0	0	2	4	5	29
Days With ≥ 1.0" Precipitation	3	3	2	1	0	0	0	0	0	1	2	3	15
Mean Snowfall (in.)	1.7	3.2	1.9	0.5	0.0	0.0	0.0	0.0	0.0	0.0	0.3	1.9	9.5
Maximum Snow Depth (in.)	0	16	1	trace	0	0	0	0	0	1	trace	5	16
Days With ≥ 1.0" Snow Depth	0	0	0	0	0	0	0	0	0	0	0	0	0

Colusa 2 SSW *Colusa County* Elevation: 49 ft. Latitude: 39° 12' N Longitude: 122° 01' W

	JAN	FEB	MAR	APR	MAY	JUN	JUL	AUG	SEP	OCT	NOV	DEC	YEAR
Mean Maximum Temp. (°F)	54.4	60.4	66.5	73.6	81.8	88.8	93.7	92.5	89.0	79.4	64.0	54.4	74.9
Mean Temp. (°F)	46.4	50.9	55.3	59.9	67.6	73.3	76.7	75.0	71.5	63.8	52.9	46.1	61.6
Mean Minimum Temp. (°F)	38.3	41.5	44.1	46.1	53.5	57.8	59.6	57.5	53.9	48.1	41.8	37.6	48.3
Extreme Maximum Temp. (°F)	75	78	88	98	106	108	111	111	108	105	85	72	111
Extreme Minimum Temp. (°F)	21	21	27	30	36	38	40	43	35	34	24	18	18
Days Maximum Temp. ≥ 90°F	0	0	0	1	7	14	23	21	15	4	0	0	85
Days Maximum Temp. ≤ 32°F	0	0	0	0	0	0	0	0	0	0	0	0	0
Days Minimum Temp. ≤ 32°F	6	2	0	0	0	0	0	0	0	0	2	7	17
Days Minimum Temp. ≤ 0°F	0	0	0	0	0	0	0	0	0	0	0	0	0
Heating Degree Days (base 65°F)	570	391	297	171	47	6	0	0	10	89	357	580	2,518
Cooling Degree Days (base 65°F)	0	0	3	24	136	263	369	317	211	59	1	0	1,383
Mean Precipitation (in.)	3.54	3.20	2.53	0.90	0.73	0.23	0.01	0.06	0.29	0.90	2.14	2.90	17.43
Extreme Maximum Daily Precip. (in.)	3.03	3.56	2.80	1.05	1.38	0.66	0.16	0.56	2.17	1.40	1.92	2.05	3.56
Days With ≥ 0.1" Precipitation	7	6	6	3	2	1	0	0	1	2	5	6	39
Days With ≥ 0.5" Precipitation	3	2	2	0	1	0	0	0	0	1	1	2	12
Days With ≥ 1.0" Precipitation	1	1	0	0	0	0	0	0	0	0	0	1	3
Mean Snowfall (in.)	0.0	0.0	0.0	0.0	0.0	0.0	0.0	0.0	0.0	0.0	0.0	trace	trace
Maximum Snow Depth (in.)	0	0	0	0	0	0	0	0	0	0	0	4	4
Days With ≥ 1.0" Snow Depth	0	0	0	0	0	0	0	0	0	0	0	0	0

The period of record for all cooperative weather station data is 1980 – 2009. See User Guide for detailed explanation of data.

Covelo *Mendocino County* Elevation: 1,410 ft. Latitude: 39° 49' N Longitude: 123° 15' W

	JAN	FEB	MAR	APR	MAY	JUN	JUL	AUG	SEP	OCT	NOV	DEC	YEAR
Mean Maximum Temp. (°F)	53.5	58.0	63.1	68.5	76.6	84.7	93.3	92.8	88.0	76.2	59.5	52.0	72.2
Mean Temp. (°F)	42.8	45.9	49.6	53.4	59.7	66.2	72.8	71.5	66.7	57.7	47.4	41.8	56.3
Mean Minimum Temp. (°F)	31.9	33.8	35.9	38.3	42.8	47.7	52.2	50.1	45.4	39.1	35.2	31.5	40.3
Extreme Maximum Temp. (°F)	78	82	88	94	104	106	110	115	107	104	82	70	115
Extreme Minimum Temp. (°F)	13	13	22	23	28	31	37	38	32	22	15	9	9
Days Maximum Temp. ≥ 90°F	0	0	0	0	3	9	22	22	14	3	0	0	73
Days Maximum Temp. ≤ 32°F	0	0	0	0	0	0	0	0	0	0	0	0	0
Days Minimum Temp. ≤ 32°F	17	13	10	5	1	0	0	0	0	4	12	17	79
Days Minimum Temp. ≤ 0°F	0	0	0	0	0	0	0	0	0	0	0	0	0
Heating Degree Days (base 65°F)	683	533	472	342	183	52	6	3	43	231	522	713	3,783
Cooling Degree Days (base 65°F)	0	0	0	2	26	96	253	211	102	12	0	0	702
Mean Precipitation (in.)	7.70	7.18	5.47	2.78	1.66	0.48	0.04	0.17	0.44	2.10	5.57	8.45	42.04
Extreme Maximum Daily Precip. (in.)	4.04	3.75	2.76	1.93	2.09	0.87	0.45	0.92	1.02	1.95	2.95	***5.70***	***5.70***
Days With ≥ 0.1" Precipitation	10	10	8	5	4	1	0	0	1	4	8	10	61
Days With ≥ 0.5" Precipitation	6	5	4	2	1	0	0	0	0	2	4	5	29
Days With ≥ 1.0" Precipitation	2	3	2	1	0	0	0	0	0	1	2	3	14
Mean Snowfall (in.)	0.6	0.5	0.1	0.1	0.0	0.0	0.0	0.0	0.0	0.0	0.1	0.4	1.8
Maximum Snow Depth (in.)	trace	0	1	trace	0	0	0	0	0	0	0	***0***	***1***
Days With ≥ 1.0" Snow Depth	0	0	0	0	0	0	0	0	0	0	0	0	0

Crescent City 3 NNW *Del Norte County* Elevation: 40 ft. Latitude: 41° 48' N Longitude: 124° 13' W

	JAN	FEB	MAR	APR	MAY	JUN	JUL	AUG	SEP	OCT	NOV	DEC	YEAR
Mean Maximum Temp. (°F)	55.0	56.0	56.6	58.3	60.9	63.3	65.7	66.0	65.7	62.8	57.3	54.5	60.2
Mean Temp. (°F)	47.9	48.7	49.4	50.9	53.7	56.2	58.6	59.0	57.5	54.7	50.3	47.3	52.9
Mean Minimum Temp. (°F)	40.8	41.4	42.2	43.6	46.4	49.0	51.5	51.8	49.3	46.5	43.4	40.1	45.5
Extreme Maximum Temp. (°F)	75	78	76	84	90	87	88	84	92	93	76	80	93
Extreme Minimum Temp. (°F)	24	24	28	30	34	37	40	40	37	29	27	19	19
Days Maximum Temp. ≥ 90°F	0	0	0	0	0	0	0	0	0	0	0	0	0
Days Maximum Temp. ≤ 32°F	0	0	0	0	0	0	0	0	0	0	0	0	0
Days Minimum Temp. ≤ 32°F	3	2	1	0	0	0	0	0	0	0	1	4	11
Days Minimum Temp. ≤ 0°F	0	0	0	0	0	0	0	0	0	0	0	0	0
Heating Degree Days (base 65°F)	524	454	476	415	344	259	193	181	220	316	433	541	4,356
Cooling Degree Days (base 65°F)	0	0	0	0	1	0	1	1	2	3	0	0	8
Mean Precipitation (in.)	10.25	8.73	8.88	5.65	3.29	1.71	0.37	0.56	1.05	4.37	9.67	13.23	67.76
Extreme Maximum Daily Precip. (in.)	***7.73***	***5.40***	na	na	na	***1.47***	***2.11***	2.00	***1.89***	na	na	na	na
Days With ≥ 0.1" Precipitation	11	10	11	8	5	3	1	1	2	5	10	12	79
Days With ≥ 0.5" Precipitation	6	5	5	3	2	1	0	0	1	3	6	7	39
Days With ≥ 1.0" Precipitation	3	3	2	1	1	0	0	0	0	1	3	4	18
Mean Snowfall (in.)	0.0	0.0	0.0	trace	0.0	0.0	0.0	0.0	0.0	0.0	0.0	0.0	trace
Maximum Snow Depth (in.)	0	0	0	0	0	0	0	0	0	0	0	0	0
Days With ≥ 1.0" Snow Depth	0	0	0	0	0	0	0	0	0	0	0	0	0

Culver City *Los Angeles County* Elevation: 55 ft. Latitude: 34° 01' N Longitude: 118° 24' W

	JAN	FEB	MAR	APR	MAY	JUN	JUL	AUG	SEP	OCT	NOV	DEC	YEAR
Mean Maximum Temp. (°F)	66.4	67.3	***68.7***	72.1	73.3	76.2	79.6	80.4	***79.4***	***75.9***	70.1	65.9	***72.9***
Mean Temp. (°F)	57.1	57.9	***59.6***	62.6	64.9	68.0	71.2	71.8	***70.7***	***66.6***	60.8	56.6	***64.0***
Mean Minimum Temp. (°F)	47.7	48.4	***50.4***	53.1	56.5	59.9	62.7	63.1	***62.0***	***57.3***	51.5	47.3	***55.0***
Extreme Maximum Temp. (°F)	87	90	***91***	105	97	107	102	103	110	104	96	90	***110***
Extreme Minimum Temp. (°F)	34	33	34	32	46	46	50	46	51	42	40	33	32
Days Maximum Temp. ≥ 90°F	0	0	0	1	0	1	1	1	2	1	0	0	7
Days Maximum Temp. ≤ 32°F	0	0	0	0	0	0	0	0	0	0	0	0	0
Days Minimum Temp. ≤ 32°F	0	0	0	0	0	0	0	0	0	0	0	0	0
Days Minimum Temp. ≤ 0°F	0	0	0	0	0	0	0	0	0	0	0	0	0
Heating Degree Days (base 65°F)	245	201	***170***	100	38	6	0	0	***1***	***26***	133	255	***1,175***
Cooling Degree Days (base 65°F)	4	6	***8***	35	43	103	199	217	***179***	***82***	14	1	***891***
Mean Precipitation (in.)	3.09	3.70	2.43	0.64	0.19	0.03	0.02	0.01	0.09	0.58	0.97	1.91	13.66
Extreme Maximum Daily Precip. (in.)	***3.19***	***4.04***	***4.10***	***1.98***	***1.06***	***0.34***	0.10	0.22	***0.61***	na	1.90	***2.60***	na
Days With ≥ 0.1" Precipitation	***5***	4	3	1	0	0	0	0	0	1	1	3	***18***
Days With ≥ 0.5" Precipitation	***2***	2	2	0	0	0	0	0	0	0	1	1	***8***
Days With ≥ 1.0" Precipitation	***1***	1	1	0	0	0	0	0	0	0	0	1	***4***
Mean Snowfall (in.)	trace	0.0	0.0	0.0	0.0	0.0	0.0	0.0	0.0	0.0	0.0	0.0	trace
Maximum Snow Depth (in.)	0	0	***0***	0	0	0	0	0	0	0	0	0	***0***
Days With ≥ 1.0" Snow Depth	0	0	0	0	0	0	0	0	0	0	0	0	0

Cuyamaca *San Diego County* Elevation: 4,640 ft. Latitude: 32° 59' N Longitude: 116° 35' W

	JAN	FEB	MAR	APR	MAY	JUN	JUL	AUG	SEP	OCT	NOV	DEC	YEAR
Mean Maximum Temp. (°F)	51.8	52.7	56.4	61.1	68.6	77.1	84.5	85.0	79.9	69.6	59.5	52.2	66.6
Mean Temp. (°F)	41.3	42.0	45.2	49.0	55.4	62.8	70.1	70.0	64.3	54.7	46.7	40.7	53.5
Mean Minimum Temp. (°F)	30.7	31.3	33.9	36.9	42.1	48.4	55.6	55.0	48.6	39.6	33.8	29.2	40.4
Extreme Maximum Temp. (°F)	74	74	80	86	92	98	103	99	99	91	80	75	103
Extreme Minimum Temp. (°F)	9	4	10	20	22	29	36	37	25	21	14	5	4
Days Maximum Temp. ≥ 90°F	0	0	0	0	0	1	6	7	2	0	0	0	16
Days Maximum Temp. ≤ 32°F	0	0	0	0	0	0	0	0	0	0	0	0	0
Days Minimum Temp. ≤ 32°F	20	17	13	7	1	0	0	0	0	4	13	21	96
Days Minimum Temp. ≤ 0°F	0	0	0	0	0	0	0	0	0	0	0	0	0
Heating Degree Days (base 65°F)	728	643	608	474	301	115	16	16	85	318	542	745	4,591
Cooling Degree Days (base 65°F)	0	0	0	0	8	55	180	179	71	5	0	0	498
Mean Precipitation (in.)	5.99	6.64	5.78	2.46	0.82	0.21	0.41	0.85	0.74	1.10	3.06	4.58	32.64
Extreme Maximum Daily Precip. (in.)	6.32	5.35	7.37	2.62	1.98	1.56	1.10	2.20	2.69	1.54	4.84	5.63	7.37
Days With ≥ 0.1" Precipitation	6	6	6	4	2	0	1	2	1	2	4	5	39
Days With ≥ 0.5" Precipitation	3	4	4	2	1	0	0	1	0	1	2	3	21
Days With ≥ 1.0" Precipitation	2	2	2	1	0	0	0	0	0	0	1	1	9
Mean Snowfall (in.)	4.6	6.6	6.5	2.8	0.1	0.0	0.0	0.0	0.0	trace	0.9	2.3	23.8
Maximum Snow Depth (in.)	13	28	24	12	0	0	0	0	0	trace	1	16	28
Days With ≥ 1.0" Snow Depth	2	1	2	0	0	0	0	0	0	0	0	1	6

The period of record for all cooperative weather station data is 1980 – 2009. See User Guide for detailed explanation of data.

De Sabla *Butte County* Elevation: 2,709 ft. Latitude: 39° 52' N Longitude: 121° 37' W

	JAN	FEB	MAR	APR	MAY	JUN	JUL	AUG	SEP	OCT	NOV	DEC	YEAR
Mean Maximum Temp. (°F)	52.6	55.1	59.6	65.4	73.9	82.6	90.4	89.9	84.2	73.2	58.3	51.3	69.7
Mean Temp. (°F)	42.6	44.4	47.7	52.2	59.5	66.7	72.9	72.1	67.1	58.4	47.3	41.8	56.1
Mean Minimum Temp. (°F)	32.5	33.7	35.7	38.9	44.9	50.7	55.4	54.3	49.9	43.7	36.2	32.4	42.4
Extreme Maximum Temp. (°F)	73	77	83	90	97	103	107	108	105	99	80	74	108
Extreme Minimum Temp. (°F)	12	11	20	22	27	31	39	38	30	19	15	6	6
Days Maximum Temp. ≥ 90°F	0	0	0	0	2	7	19	18	10	2	0	0	58
Days Maximum Temp. ≤ 32°F	0	0	0	0	0	0	0	0	0	0	0	0	0
Days Minimum Temp. ≤ 32°F	16	12	10	5	1	0	0	0	0	2	9	16	71
Days Minimum Temp. ≤ 0°F	0	0	0	0	0	0	0	0	0	0	0	0	0
Heating Degree Days (base 65°F)	689	576	530	382	200	63	7	5	57	224	526	711	3,970
Cooling Degree Days (base 65°F)	0	0	0	4	34	119	260	234	128	27	0	0	806
Mean Precipitation (in.)	11.56	12.06	9.42	4.89	2.88	0.94	0.05	0.15	1.14	3.52	7.65	13.61	67.87
Extreme Maximum Daily Precip. (in.)	8.37	7.72	5.99	3.60	2.93	1.76	0.62	1.22	***2.61***	3.36	4.92	7.85	***8.37***
Days With ≥ 0.1" Precipitation	11	10	10	7	4	2	0	0	2	4	8	10	68
Days With ≥ 0.5" Precipitation	6	7	6	3	2	1	0	0	1	2	5	7	40
Days With ≥ 1.0" Precipitation	4	4	4	2	1	0	0	0	0	1	3	5	24
Mean Snowfall (in.)	1.9	0.1	2.2	0.3	0.0	0.0	0.0	0.0	0.0	0.0	0.0	0.2	4.7
Maximum Snow Depth (in.)	30	0	15	13	0	0	0	0	0	0	1	7	30
Days With ≥ 1.0" Snow Depth	1	0	0	0	0	0	0	0	0	0	0	0	1

Death Valley *Inyo County* Elevation: -193 ft. Latitude: 36° 28' N Longitude: 116° 52' W

	JAN	FEB	MAR	APR	MAY	JUN	JUL	AUG	SEP	OCT	NOV	DEC	YEAR
Mean Maximum Temp. (°F)	66.9	73.4	81.7	90.5	100.5	109.8	116.4	114.7	106.5	92.8	77.1	65.4	91.3
Mean Temp. (°F)	53.0	59.5	67.7	76.0	86.2	95.1	101.8	99.8	90.7	76.7	62.2	51.5	76.7
Mean Minimum Temp. (°F)	39.1	45.5	53.7	61.4	71.9	80.3	87.1	84.9	74.9	60.6	47.3	37.5	62.0
Extreme Maximum Temp. (°F)	84	97	102	112	122	128	129	127	123	113	98	88	129
Extreme Minimum Temp. (°F)	0	26	26	23	46	54	67	66	55	37	30	22	0
Days Maximum Temp. ≥ 90°F	0	1	6	17	27	30	31	31	29	21	1	0	194
Days Maximum Temp. ≤ 32°F	0	0	0	0	0	0	0	0	0	0	0	0	0
Days Minimum Temp. ≤ 32°F	3	1	0	0	0	0	0	0	0	0	0	6	10
Days Minimum Temp. ≤ 0°F	0	0	0	0	0	0	0	0	0	0	0	0	0
Heating Degree Days (base 65°F)	365	169	45	8	1	0	0	0	0	5	128	412	1,133
Cooling Degree Days (base 65°F)	1	19	136	344	665	909	1,146	1,086	778	375	51	2	5,512
Mean Precipitation (in.)	0.36	0.47	0.33	0.13	0.05	0.03	0.09	0.13	0.21	0.07	0.17	0.17	2.21
Extreme Maximum Daily Precip. (in.)	0.99	0.99	0.96	1.47	0.30	0.40	0.28	0.66	1.11	0.40	0.80	0.55	1.47
Days With ≥ 0.1" Precipitation	1	1	1	0	0	0	0	0	1	0	0	1	5
Days With ≥ 0.5" Precipitation	0	0	0	0	0	0	0	0	0	0	0	0	0
Days With ≥ 1.0" Precipitation	0	0	0	0	0	0	0	0	0	0	0	0	0
Mean Snowfall (in.)	0.0	0.0	0.0	0.0	0.0	0.0	0.0	0.0	0.0	0.0	0.0	0.0	0.0
Maximum Snow Depth (in.)	0	0	0	0	0	0	0	0	0	0	0	0	0
Days With ≥ 1.0" Snow Depth	0	0	0	0	0	0	0	0	0	0	0	0	0

Donner Memorial St Pk *Nevada County* Elevation: 5,937 ft. Latitude: 39° 19' N Longitude: 120° 14' W

	JAN	FEB	MAR	APR	MAY	JUN	JUL	AUG	SEP	OCT	NOV	DEC	YEAR
Mean Maximum Temp. (°F)	40.5	42.7	47.6	54.1	63.7	72.5	81.2	81.0	73.9	62.7	48.7	39.4	59.0
Mean Temp. (°F)	28.1	29.8	34.6	40.1	48.0	54.9	61.6	61.1	54.8	45.6	35.7	27.7	43.5
Mean Minimum Temp. (°F)	15.6	16.8	21.5	26.1	32.3	37.3	42.0	41.3	35.6	28.6	22.7	16.0	28.0
Extreme Maximum Temp. (°F)	60	65	72	79	88	95	99	99	92	90	74	61	99
Extreme Minimum Temp. (°F)	-13	-27	-2	5	14	22	27	28	24	12	-3	-16	-27
Days Maximum Temp. ≥ 90°F	0	0	0	0	0	0	3	2	0	0	0	0	5
Days Maximum Temp. ≤ 32°F	5	3	2	0	0	0	0	0	0	0	2	6	18
Days Minimum Temp. ≤ 32°F	31	27	30	26	17	6	1	1	9	25	28	30	231
Days Minimum Temp. ≤ 0°F	1	1	0	0	0	0	0	0	0	0	0	2	4
Heating Degree Days (base 65°F)	1,137	989	941	734	522	300	125	130	301	593	871	1,148	7,791
Cooling Degree Days (base 65°F)	0	0	0	0	0	4	26	17	1	0	0	0	48
Mean Precipitation (in.)	6.82	6.53	5.61	2.51	1.74	0.74	0.33	0.42	0.95	2.02	4.99	6.69	39.35
Extreme Maximum Daily Precip. (in.)	4.04	4.36	4.56	2.29	2.40	0.77	1.50	1.31	1.55	3.50	3.31	6.00	6.00
Days With ≥ 0.1" Precipitation	9	8	8	5	4	2	1	1	2	3	7	8	58
Days With ≥ 0.5" Precipitation	4	4	4	2	1	0	0	0	1	1	3	4	24
Days With ≥ 1.0" Precipitation	2	2	2	0	0	0	0	0	0	0	2	2	10
Mean Snowfall (in.)	39.6	40.9	33.5	15.5	2.9	0.5	0.0	0.0	0.2	2.6	14.3	35.4	185.4
Maximum Snow Depth (in.)	68	94	76	74	46	4	0	0	2	12	32	62	94
Days With ≥ 1.0" Snow Depth	30	27	28	13	3	0	0	0	0	1	8	24	134

Doyle 4 SSE *Lassen County* Elevation: 4,390 ft. Latitude: 39° 58' N Longitude: 120° 05' W

	JAN	FEB	MAR	APR	MAY	JUN	JUL	AUG	SEP	OCT	NOV	DEC	YEAR
Mean Maximum Temp. (°F)	42.9	48.2	55.7	62.2	71.1	79.6	88.2	87.3	79.2	67.4	52.0	42.1	64.7
Mean Temp. (°F)	33.4	37.5	43.3	48.1	55.3	62.3	69.1	67.8	60.9	51.1	40.0	32.7	50.1
Mean Minimum Temp. (°F)	23.8	26.8	30.8	34.0	39.5	44.9	49.8	48.3	42.5	34.8	27.9	23.1	35.5
Extreme Maximum Temp. (°F)	70	70	80	85	95	101	104	104	98	89	75	66	104
Extreme Minimum Temp. (°F)	-4	-17	7	14	22	27	30	28	25	12	-2	-25	-25
Days Maximum Temp. ≥ 90°F	0	0	0	0	1	3	15	12	3	0	0	0	34
Days Maximum Temp. ≤ 32°F	3	1	0	0	0	0	0	0	0	0	1	4	9
Days Minimum Temp. ≤ 32°F	26	21	19	13	5	1	0	0	2	12	21	26	146
Days Minimum Temp. ≤ 0°F	0	0	0	0	0	0	0	0	0	0	0	1	1
Heating Degree Days (base 65°F)	973	770	665	501	302	119	21	24	146	423	743	995	5,682
Cooling Degree Days (base 65°F)	0	0	0	0	9	44	154	119	29	0	0	0	355
Mean Precipitation (in.)	2.15	2.32	1.87	0.90	0.97	0.66	0.36	0.30	0.65	0.97	2.34	2.43	15.92
Extreme Maximum Daily Precip. (in.)	3.58	4.48	4.13	1.44	1.30	1.73	2.15	0.95	1.05	2.38	3.63	4.06	4.48
Days With ≥ 0.1" Precipitation	4	3	3	3	3	2	1	1	2	2	4	4	32
Days With ≥ 0.5" Precipitation	1	1	1	0	0	0	0	0	0	1	1	1	6
Days With ≥ 1.0" Precipitation	1	1	0	0	0	0	0	0	0	0	1	1	4
Mean Snowfall (in.)	7.3	4.0	3.9	1.5	0.1	trace	0.0	0.0	0.2	0.2	2.5	6.8	26.5
Maximum Snow Depth (in.)	20	12	6	6	trace	trace	0	0	4	trace	12	22	22
Days With ≥ 1.0" Snow Depth	9	4	1	0	0	0	0	0	0	0	2	6	22

The period of record for all cooperative weather station data is 1980 – 2009. See User Guide for detailed explanation of data.

Dunsmuir Treatment Plant *Siskiyou County* Elevation: 2,169 ft. Latitude: 41° 11' N Longitude: 122° 16' W

	JAN	FEB	MAR	APR	MAY	JUN	JUL	AUG	SEP	OCT	NOV	DEC	YEAR
Mean Maximum Temp. (°F)	49.8	53.7	58.8	65.6	74.2	81.9	90.0	89.6	83.9	72.5	56.8	49.5	68.9
Mean Temp. (°F)	40.0	42.4	46.2	51.5	59.2	66.1	71.9	70.4	65.0	56.0	45.3	39.9	54.5
Mean Minimum Temp. (°F)	30.1	31.1	33.5	37.4	44.1	50.2	53.7	51.2	46.2	39.5	33.7	30.2	40.1
Extreme Maximum Temp. (°F)	70	78	83	92	99	102	108	109	106	99	82	75	109
Extreme Minimum Temp. (°F)	12	8	19	22	29	34	39	41	31	25	18	4	4
Days Maximum Temp. ≥ 90°F	0	0	0	0	3	7	18	17	10	1	0	0	56
Days Maximum Temp. ≤ 32°F	0	0	0	0	0	0	0	0	0	0	0	0	0
Days Minimum Temp. ≤ 32°F	23	18	14	6	0	0	0	0	0	2	14	23	100
Days Minimum Temp. ≤ 0°F	0	0	0	0	0	0	0	0	0	0	0	0	0
Heating Degree Days (base 65°F)	768	631	576	400	203	63	8	7	68	280	585	772	4,361
Cooling Degree Days (base 65°F)	0	0	0	1	31	102	230	183	76	9	0	0	632
Mean Precipitation (in.)	11.05	10.64	9.02	4.37	3.02	1.19	0.24	0.26	0.87	3.24	7.92	11.89	63.71
Extreme Maximum Daily Precip. (in.)	6.44	4.85	4.95	2.90	4.20	3.06	0.88	1.20	2.06	4.50	4.53	5.80	6.44
Days With ≥ 0.1" Precipitation	11	10	10	7	5	3	1	1	2	4	9	11	74
Days With ≥ 0.5" Precipitation	7	7	6	3	2	1	0	0	1	2	5	7	41
Days With ≥ 1.0" Precipitation	4	4	3	1	1	0	0	0	0	1	3	4	21
Mean Snowfall (in.)	8.0	7.5	4.5	0.5	0.0	0.0	0.0	0.0	0.0	trace	1.7	8.1	30.3
Maximum Snow Depth (in.)	30	20	15	5	0	0	0	0	0	trace	4	24	30
Days With ≥ 1.0" Snow Depth	10	5	2	0	0	0	0	0	0	0	1	6	24

El Mirage *San Bernardino County* Elevation: 2,950 ft. Latitude: 34° 35' N Longitude: 117° 38' W

	JAN	FEB	MAR	APR	MAY	JUN	JUL	AUG	SEP	OCT	NOV	DEC	YEAR
Mean Maximum Temp. (°F)	57.3	60.3	65.8	72.8	81.8	91.3	98.1	97.0	89.5	77.8	65.3	56.5	76.1
Mean Temp. (°F)	43.7	46.7	51.4	56.9	65.3	73.4	79.5	78.4	71.7	61.2	50.2	42.6	60.1
Mean Minimum Temp. (°F)	30.0	33.0	37.0	40.8	48.7	55.4	60.9	59.8	53.9	44.5	35.1	28.6	44.0
Extreme Maximum Temp. (°F)	75	82	88	95	104	110	112	108	103	95	84	78	112
Extreme Minimum Temp. (°F)	5	13	18	23	30	32	41	44	33	26	14	1	1
Days Maximum Temp. ≥ 90°F	0	0	0	1	7	20	29	28	17	3	0	0	105
Days Maximum Temp. ≤ 32°F	0	0	0	0	0	0	0	0	0	0	0	0	0
Days Minimum Temp. ≤ 32°F	21	13	7	3	0	0	0	0	0	1	10	22	77
Days Minimum Temp. ≤ 0°F	0	0	0	0	0	0	0	0	0	0	0	0	0
Heating Degree Days (base 65°F)	654	511	416	255	92	16	0	0	20	152	438	688	3,242
Cooling Degree Days (base 65°F)	0	0	1	17	107	273	458	423	230	41	0	0	1,550
Mean Precipitation (in.)	0.97	1.21	0.92	0.28	0.18	0.06	0.16	0.32	0.22	0.30	0.34	0.76	5.72
Extreme Maximum Daily Precip. (in.)	1.07	2.45	2.01	0.89	1.33	0.37	0.65	1.29	0.76	1.35	1.13	1.51	2.45
Days With ≥ 0.1" Precipitation	3	2	3	1	0	0	1	1	1	1	1	2	16
Days With ≥ 0.5" Precipitation	1	1	0	0	0	0	0	0	0	0	0	0	2
Days With ≥ 1.0" Precipitation	0	0	0	0	0	0	0	0	0	0	0	0	0
Mean Snowfall (in.)	0.2	0.2	0.2	trace	0.0	0.0	0.0	0.0	0.0	0.0	trace	0.7	1.3
Maximum Snow Depth (in.)	1	3	1	0	0	0	0	0	0	0	1	13	13
Days With ≥ 1.0" Snow Depth	0	0	0	0	0	0	0	0	0	0	0	0	0

Elsinore *Riverside County* Elevation: 1,285 ft. Latitude: 33° 40' N Longitude: 117° 20' W

	JAN	FEB	MAR	APR	MAY	JUN	JUL	AUG	SEP	OCT	NOV	DEC	YEAR
Mean Maximum Temp. (°F)	***66.0***	67.9	72.1	77.5	***83.8***	***90.9***	***97.8***	***98.8***	***93.4***	***83.4***	***72.4***	65.7	***80.8***
Mean Temp. (°F)	***52.6***	54.5	57.8	62.1	***68.3***	***73.7***	***79.5***	***80.7***	***76.2***	***67.6***	***57.8***	51.9	***65.2***
Mean Minimum Temp. (°F)	***39.1***	41.0	43.6	46.7	***52.7***	***56.5***	***61.1***	***62.5***	***59.0***	***51.9***	***43.1***	38.0	***49.6***
Extreme Maximum Temp. (°F)	91	92	98	103	109	112	114	115	111	106	96	88	115
Extreme Minimum Temp. (°F)	21	20	29	31	39	44	42	***51***	43	33	26	19	***19***
Days Maximum Temp. ≥ 90°F	0	0	1	4	8	16	25	***27***	19	7	1	0	***108***
Days Maximum Temp. ≤ 32°F	0	0	0	0	0	0	0	0	0	0	0	0	0
Days Minimum Temp. ≤ 32°F	4	2	1	0	0	0	0	0	0	0	1	4	12
Days Minimum Temp. ≤ 0°F	0	0	0	0	0	0	0	0	0	0	0	0	0
Heating Degree Days (base 65°F)	***378***	292	223	122	***31***	***5***	***0***	***0***	***2***	***36***	***218***	400	***1,707***
Cooling Degree Days (base 65°F)	***0***	1	8	41	***140***	***273***	***457***	***493***	***345***	***122***	***9***	1	***1,890***
Mean Precipitation (in.)	2.51	3.17	1.79	0.63	0.18	0.01	0.19	0.01	0.18	0.58	0.79	1.57	11.61
Extreme Maximum Daily Precip. (in.)	3.20	5.06	2.80	0.88	0.63	0.16	1.50	0.12	1.45	2.28	***1.63***	2.65	***5.06***
Days With ≥ 0.1" Precipitation	4	4	3	2	0	0	0	0	0	1	2	3	19
Days With ≥ 0.5" Precipitation	1	2	1	0	0	0	0	0	0	0	1	1	6
Days With ≥ 1.0" Precipitation	1	1	0	0	0	0	0	0	0	0	0	0	2
Mean Snowfall (in.)	0.0	0.0	0.0	0.0	0.0	0.0	0.0	0.0	0.0	0.0	trace	0.0	trace
Maximum Snow Depth (in.)	0	0	0	0	0	0	0	0	0	0	trace	0	trace
Days With ≥ 1.0" Snow Depth	0	0	0	0	0	0	0	0	0	0	0	0	0

Escondido No 2 *San Diego County* Elevation: 600 ft. Latitude: 33° 07' N Longitude: 117° 06' W

	JAN	FEB	MAR	APR	MAY	JUN	JUL	AUG	SEP	OCT	NOV	DEC	YEAR
Mean Maximum Temp. (°F)	***68.7***	69.1	***70.4***	***74.6***	***76.8***	82.0	87.3	***88.6***	***86.3***	***80.2***	***73.5***	69.0	***77.2***
Mean Temp. (°F)	***55.9***	56.9	***58.7***	***62.5***	***65.8***	70.0	74.8	***76.0***	***73.9***	***67.7***	***60.1***	55.4	***64.8***
Mean Minimum Temp. (°F)	***43.0***	44.6	***47.1***	***50.3***	***54.7***	58.1	62.2	***63.4***	***61.3***	***55.1***	***46.7***	41.7	***52.3***
Extreme Maximum Temp. (°F)	92	94	97	103	***103***	105	112	***109***	***108***	***105***	98	90	***112***
Extreme Minimum Temp. (°F)	25	27	32	36	***31***	41	52	***54***	***49***	***39***	30	26	***25***
Days Maximum Temp. ≥ 90°F	0	0	0	1	2	4	10	***13***	10	4	1	0	***45***
Days Maximum Temp. ≤ 32°F	0	0	0	0	0	0	0	***0***	0	0	0	0	***0***
Days Minimum Temp. ≤ 32°F	1	1	0	0	0	0	0	***0***	0	0	0	1	***3***
Days Minimum Temp. ≤ 0°F	0	0	0	0	0	0	0	***0***	0	0	0	0	***0***
Heating Degree Days (base 65°F)	***278***	226	***194***	***102***	***43***	6	0	***0***	***2***	***23***	***153***	292	***1,319***
Cooling Degree Days (base 65°F)	***2***	4	***7***	***34***	***74***	162	310	***349***	***274***	***113***	***13***	1	***1,343***
Mean Precipitation (in.)	3.15	3.54	2.74	1.11	0.24	0.13	0.09	***0.08***	0.21	0.60	1.25	1.65	***14.79***
Extreme Maximum Daily Precip. (in.)	***3.24***	***2.00***	***2.62***	***1.80***	***0.80***	0.75	0.74	***1.45***	***1.72***	***1.95***	***2.00***	***1.82***	***3.24***
Days With ≥ 0.1" Precipitation	5	5	4	3	1	0	0	***0***	0	1	3	4	***26***
Days With ≥ 0.5" Precipitation	2	2	2	1	0	0	0	***0***	0	0	1	1	***9***
Days With ≥ 1.0" Precipitation	1	1	1	0	0	0	0	***0***	0	0	0	0	***3***
Mean Snowfall (in.)	0.0	0.0	0.0	0.0	0.0	0.0	0.0	***0.0***	0.0	0.0	0.0	0.0	***0.0***
Maximum Snow Depth (in.)	0	0	0	0	***0***	0	0	***0***	***0***	***0***	0	0	***0***
Days With ≥ 1.0" Snow Depth	0	0	0	0	0	0	0	***0***	0	0	0	0	***0***

The period of record for all cooperative weather station data is 1980 – 2009. See User Guide for detailed explanation of data.

Fairfield *Solano County* Elevation: 40 ft. Latitude: 38° 16' N Longitude: 122° 04' W

	JAN	FEB	MAR	APR	MAY	JUN	JUL	AUG	SEP	OCT	NOV	DEC	YEAR
Mean Maximum Temp. (°F)	55.4	61.7	66.7	72.1	79.0	85.6	90.4	89.8	87.2	78.5	65.5	55.7	74.0
Mean Temp. (°F)	46.8	51.6	55.5	59.4	65.1	70.2	73.7	73.1	71.0	64.5	54.6	46.9	61.0
Mean Minimum Temp. (°F)	38.3	41.4	44.2	46.6	51.1	54.7	56.7	56.5	54.7	50.5	43.6	38.1	48.0
Extreme Maximum Temp. (°F)	74	79	87	97	111	111	114	111	109	102	87	77	114
Extreme Minimum Temp. (°F)	22	24	30	30	36	42	42	40	39	33	21	17	17
Days Maximum Temp. ≥ 90°F	0	0	0	1	5	10	16	15	12	3	0	0	62
Days Maximum Temp. ≤ 32°F	0	0	0	0	0	0	0	0	0	0	0	0	0
Days Minimum Temp. ≤ 32°F	5	1	0	0	0	0	0	0	0	0	1	6	13
Days Minimum Temp. ≤ 0°F	0	0	0	0	0	0	0	0	0	0	0	0	0
Heating Degree Days (base 65°F)	557	373	290	182	73	14	1	2	9	74	308	554	2,437
Cooling Degree Days (base 65°F)	0	0	2	20	82	176	276	260	195	66	2	0	1,079
Mean Precipitation (in.)	4.71	5.08	3.44	1.28	0.76	0.16	0.00	0.03	0.21	1.15	2.86	4.91	24.59
Extreme Maximum Daily Precip. (in.)	3.64	3.81	2.83	2.38	2.17	1.63	0.13	0.41	0.77	5.10	2.48	5.58	5.58
Days With ≥ 0.1" Precipitation	8	7	7	3	2	0	0	0	1	2	5	7	42
Days With ≥ 0.5" Precipitation	3	4	2	1	1	0	0	0	0	1	2	3	17
Days With ≥ 1.0" Precipitation	1	1	1	0	0	0	0	0	0	0	1	1	5
Mean Snowfall (in.)	0.0	0.0	0.0	0.0	0.0	0.0	0.0	0.0	0.0	0.0	0.0	0.1	0.1
Maximum Snow Depth (in.)	0	0	0	0	0	0	0	0	0	0	0	0	0
Days With ≥ 1.0" Snow Depth	0	0	0	0	0	0	0	0	0	0	0	0	0

Fairmont *Los Angeles County* Elevation: 3,060 ft. Latitude: 34° 42' N Longitude: 118° 26' W

	JAN	FEB	MAR	APR	MAY	JUN	JUL	AUG	SEP	OCT	NOV	DEC	YEAR
Mean Maximum Temp. (°F)	54.7	56.7	62.0	67.7	75.5	84.3	91.1	91.6	85.9	75.4	62.9	54.4	71.9
Mean Temp. (°F)	45.8	47.6	52.0	56.4	63.8	72.2	78.7	79.0	73.4	63.7	52.9	45.5	60.9
Mean Minimum Temp. (°F)	36.7	38.4	41.9	45.2	52.1	60.1	66.3	66.3	60.8	51.9	42.8	36.6	49.9
Extreme Maximum Temp. (°F)	75	78	87	93	100	108	111	107	105	96	84	77	111
Extreme Minimum Temp. (°F)	12	12	22	19	17	32	48	22	34	31	22	11	11
Days Maximum Temp. ≥ 90°F	0	0	0	0	3	10	19	20	12	2	0	0	66
Days Maximum Temp. ≤ 32°F	0	0	0	0	0	0	0	0	0	0	0	0	0
Days Minimum Temp. ≤ 32°F	8	5	3	1	0	0	0	0	0	0	2	8	27
Days Minimum Temp. ≤ 0°F	0	0	0	0	0	0	0	0	0	0	0	0	0
Heating Degree Days (base 65°F)	590	486	400	275	135	31	1	2	24	120	360	596	3,020
Cooling Degree Days (base 65°F)	0	0	4	24	103	253	435	443	283	86	3	0	1,634
Mean Precipitation (in.)	3.55	4.43	2.27	0.96	0.38	0.07	0.09	0.07	0.20	0.72	1.20	2.20	16.14
Extreme Maximum Daily Precip. (in.)	3.85	3.94	2.27	1.97	1.72	0.81	0.41	0.51	0.73	2.56	2.42	3.50	3.94
Days With ≥ 0.1" Precipitation	5	5	4	2	1	0	0	0	1	1	2	3	24
Days With ≥ 0.5" Precipitation	2	3	2	1	0	0	0	0	0	0	1	1	10
Days With ≥ 1.0" Precipitation	1	2	1	0	0	0	0	0	0	0	0	1	5
Mean Snowfall (in.)	trace	0.9	0.2	0.0	0.0	0.0	0.0	0.0	0.0	0.0	trace	1.9	3.0
Maximum Snow Depth (in.)	5	5	1	0	0	0	0	0	0	0	1	26	26
Days With ≥ 1.0" Snow Depth	0	0	0	0	0	0	0	0	0	0	0	0	0

Fort Bragg 5 N *Mendocino County* Elevation: 120 ft. Latitude: 39° 31' N Longitude: 123° 46' W

	JAN	FEB	MAR	APR	MAY	JUN	JUL	AUG	SEP	OCT	NOV	DEC	YEAR
Mean Maximum Temp. (°F)	54.8	56.1	57.5	59.3	61.9	64.3	66.4	66.5	66.0	63.4	58.1	54.3	60.7
Mean Temp. (°F)	47.5	48.5	49.5	51.0	53.6	56.0	57.8	58.1	57.3	54.8	50.4	47.1	52.6
Mean Minimum Temp. (°F)	40.2	40.9	41.5	42.7	45.2	47.7	49.2	49.6	48.6	46.1	42.6	39.9	44.5
Extreme Maximum Temp. (°F)	76	79	76	80	89	86	83	83	85	94	77	70	94
Extreme Minimum Temp. (°F)	26	24	29	30	35	37	38	42	38	33	29	18	18
Days Maximum Temp. ≥ 90°F	0	0	0	0	0	0	0	0	0	0	0	0	0
Days Maximum Temp. ≤ 32°F	0	0	0	0	0	0	0	0	0	0	0	0	0
Days Minimum Temp. ≤ 32°F	3	2	1	0	0	0	0	0	0	0	1	4	11
Days Minimum Temp. ≤ 0°F	0	0	0	0	0	0	0	0	0	0	0	0	0
Heating Degree Days (base 65°F)	536	461	472	412	348	264	215	209	225	313	432	547	4,434
Cooling Degree Days (base 65°F)	0	0	0	0	1	1	1	1	1	2	0	0	7
Mean Precipitation (in.)	7.07	7.06	5.94	3.10	1.73	0.58	0.10	0.22	0.45	2.34	5.27	8.30	42.16
Extreme Maximum Daily Precip. (in.)	3.84	3.06	2.93	2.21	1.78	1.74	0.33	2.05	1.16	3.78	2.55	4.36	4.36
Days With ≥ 0.1" Precipitation	11	11	10	7	4	1	0	0	1	4	9	12	70
Days With ≥ 0.5" Precipitation	5	5	4	2	1	0	0	0	0	2	4	6	29
Days With ≥ 1.0" Precipitation	2	2	2	1	0	0	0	0	0	1	1	3	12
Mean Snowfall (in.)	0.0	trace	trace	0.0	0.0	0.0	0.0	0.0	0.0	0.0	0.0	0.0	trace
Maximum Snow Depth (in.)	0	trace	trace	0	0	0	0	0	0	0	0	0	trace
Days With ≥ 1.0" Snow Depth	0	0	0	0	0	0	0	0	0	0	0	0	0

Friant Government Camp *Fresno County* Elevation: 410 ft. Latitude: 37° 00' N Longitude: 119° 43' W

	JAN	FEB	MAR	APR	MAY	JUN	JUL	AUG	SEP	OCT	NOV	DEC	YEAR
Mean Maximum Temp. (°F)	56.0	62.0	67.1	74.5	84.9	93.0	99.7	98.6	92.4	81.5	66.9	56.4	77.7
Mean Temp. (°F)	47.0	51.4	54.7	59.1	67.3	74.4	80.5	79.3	74.5	65.7	54.5	46.6	62.9
Mean Minimum Temp. (°F)	38.0	40.7	42.4	43.7	49.7	55.7	61.2	60.0	56.5	49.8	42.1	36.8	48.1
Extreme Maximum Temp. (°F)	77	79	88	99	108	109	114	114	108	102	87	79	114
Extreme Minimum Temp. (°F)	22	21	28	28	34	37	45	38	41	33	26	16	16
Days Maximum Temp. ≥ 90°F	0	0	0	2	10	21	29	29	20	6	0	0	117
Days Maximum Temp. ≤ 32°F	0	0	0	0	0	0	0	0	0	0	0	0	0
Days Minimum Temp. ≤ 32°F	6	2	1	1	0	0	0	0	0	0	2	8	20
Days Minimum Temp. ≤ 0°F	0	0	0	0	0	0	0	0	0	0	0	0	0
Heating Degree Days (base 65°F)	550	379	315	196	57	8	0	0	6	73	310	563	2,457
Cooling Degree Days (base 65°F)	0	0	3	26	137	296	487	452	297	101	3	0	1,802
Mean Precipitation (in.)	3.07	2.71	2.65	1.12	0.49	0.20	0.01	0.01	0.18	0.84	1.41	2.14	14.83
Extreme Maximum Daily Precip. (in.)	3.05	1.93	2.45	1.36	1.59	1.38	0.10	0.08	1.33	1.58	1.29	1.35	3.05
Days With ≥ 0.1" Precipitation	6	6	6	3	1	0	0	0	0	2	3	5	32
Days With ≥ 0.5" Precipitation	2	2	2	1	0	0	0	0	0	1	1	2	11
Days With ≥ 1.0" Precipitation	1	0	0	0	0	0	0	0	0	0	0	0	1
Mean Snowfall (in.)	0.0	0.0	0.0	0.0	0.0	0.0	0.0	0.0	0.0	0.0	0.0	0.0	0.0
Maximum Snow Depth (in.)	0	0	0	0	0	0	0	0	0	0	0	0	0
Days With ≥ 1.0" Snow Depth	0	0	0	0	0	0	0	0	0	0	0	0	0

The period of record for all cooperative weather station data is 1980 – 2009. See User Guide for detailed explanation of data.

Gilroy *Santa Clara County* Elevation: 193 ft. Latitude: 37° 00' N Longitude: 121° 34' W

	JAN	FEB	MAR	APR	MAY	JUN	JUL	AUG	SEP	OCT	NOV	DEC	YEAR
Mean Maximum Temp. (°F)	60.2	64.0	68.1	73.0	78.4	83.7	88.0	87.7	85.3	78.7	67.9	60.3	74.6
Mean Temp. (°F)	49.5	52.7	56.1	59.4	64.1	68.3	71.6	71.4	69.4	63.8	55.3	49.2	60.9
Mean Minimum Temp. (°F)	38.7	41.4	44.0	45.7	49.7	52.9	55.2	55.1	53.4	48.9	42.7	38.0	47.2
Extreme Maximum Temp. (°F)	79	86	90	100	106	110	112	112	104	107	94	76	112
Extreme Minimum Temp. (°F)	19	23	30	27	38	40	41	30	30	35	28	17	17
Days Maximum Temp. ≥ 90°F	0	0	0	1	3	6	11	11	9	4	0	0	45
Days Maximum Temp. ≤ 32°F	0	0	0	0	0	0	0	0	0	0	0	0	0
Days Minimum Temp. ≤ 32°F	7	3	0	0	0	0	0	0	0	0	2	7	19
Days Minimum Temp. ≤ 0°F	0	0	0	0	0	0	0	0	0	0	0	0	0
Heating Degree Days (base 65°F)	473	341	273	180	81	21	2	1	13	85	286	483	2,239
Cooling Degree Days (base 65°F)	0	0	3	19	59	127	214	208	151	56	2	0	839
Mean Precipitation (in.)	4.41	4.10	3.32	1.16	0.48	0.10	0.03	0.03	0.25	1.00	2.22	3.59	20.69
Extreme Maximum Daily Precip. (in.)	3.55	2.88	2.82	1.58	1.87	0.43	0.56	0.50	0.95	5.95	2.80	2.81	5.95
Days With ≥ 0.1" Precipitation	7	7	6	3	1	0	0	0	1	2	4	6	37
Days With ≥ 0.5" Precipitation	3	3	2	1	0	0	0	0	0	1	2	2	14
Days With ≥ 1.0" Precipitation	1	1	1	0	0	0	0	0	0	0	0	1	4
Mean Snowfall (in.)	0.0	0.0	0.0	0.0	0.0	0.0	0.0	0.0	0.0	0.0	0.0	0.0	0.0
Maximum Snow Depth (in.)	0	0	0	0	0	0	0	0	0	0	0	0	0
Days With ≥ 1.0" Snow Depth	0	0	0	0	0	0	0	0	0	0	0	0	0

Graton *Sonoma County* Elevation: 200 ft. Latitude: 38° 26' N Longitude: 122° 52' W

	JAN	FEB	MAR	APR	MAY	JUN	JUL	AUG	SEP	OCT	NOV	DEC	YEAR
Mean Maximum Temp. (°F)	57.4	62.1	66.1	70.6	76.0	81.5	83.6	83.9	83.0	77.7	66.4	57.5	72.2
Mean Temp. (°F)	46.7	50.0	52.9	55.7	60.2	64.4	66.3	66.4	65.0	60.3	52.5	46.4	57.2
Mean Minimum Temp. (°F)	36.0	37.9	39.5	40.8	44.3	47.3	49.1	48.8	46.9	42.9	38.6	35.2	42.3
Extreme Maximum Temp. (°F)	84	82	90	98	101	108	110	107	107	106	88	77	110
Extreme Minimum Temp. (°F)	19	17	25	28	33	35	38	40	34	29	23	14	14
Days Maximum Temp. ≥ 90°F	0	0	0	0	2	5	6	7	7	3	0	0	30
Days Maximum Temp. ≤ 32°F	0	0	0	0	0	0	0	0	0	0	0	0	0
Days Minimum Temp. ≤ 32°F	12	7	3	1	0	0	0	0	0	1	6	14	44
Days Minimum Temp. ≤ 0°F	0	0	0	0	0	0	0	0	0	0	0	0	0
Heating Degree Days (base 65°F)	560	417	370	275	162	64	27	24	51	157	367	571	3,045
Cooling Degree Days (base 65°F)	0	0	1	4	19	53	75	75	57	19	0	0	303
Mean Precipitation (in.)	8.22	7.88	5.69	2.29	1.31	0.30	0.01	0.08	0.33	1.91	5.28	8.10	41.40
Extreme Maximum Daily Precip. (in.)	5.72	4.94	6.49	3.19	2.33	1.39	0.09	1.40	0.97	2.79	3.35	6.70	6.70
Days With ≥ 0.1" Precipitation	10	9	8	5	2	1	0	0	1	3	7	9	55
Days With ≥ 0.5" Precipitation	5	5	4	2	1	0	0	0	0	1	4	5	27
Days With ≥ 1.0" Precipitation	3	3	2	0	0	0	0	0	0	1	2	3	14
Mean Snowfall (in.)	0.0	0.0	0.0	trace	0.0	0.0	0.0	0.0	0.0	0.0	0.0	0.0	trace
Maximum Snow Depth (in.)	0	0	0	trace	0	0	0	0	0	0	0	0	trace
Days With ≥ 1.0" Snow Depth	0	0	0	0	0	0	0	0	0	0	0	0	0

Haiwee *Inyo County* Elevation: 3,825 ft. Latitude: 36° 08' N Longitude: 117° 57' W

	JAN	FEB	MAR	APR	MAY	JUN	JUL	AUG	SEP	OCT	NOV	DEC	YEAR
Mean Maximum Temp. (°F)	54.1	57.8	64.7	72.0	81.9	90.9	96.8	95.7	88.3	77.7	64.0	53.7	74.8
Mean Temp. (°F)	41.4	44.7	50.6	56.9	66.0	74.4	80.4	79.2	71.8	61.7	49.8	41.3	59.9
Mean Minimum Temp. (°F)	28.7	31.6	36.5	41.8	50.3	57.7	63.8	62.6	55.2	45.7	35.5	28.9	44.9
Extreme Maximum Temp. (°F)	74	79	88	96	106	109	117	113	108	97	87	76	117
Extreme Minimum Temp. (°F)	-8	2	19	22	32	38	44	49	28	26	16	1	-8
Days Maximum Temp. ≥ 90°F	0	0	0	1	7	18	27	27	15	3	0	0	98
Days Maximum Temp. ≤ 32°F	0	0	0	0	0	0	0	0	0	0	0	0	0
Days Minimum Temp. ≤ 32°F	23	14	8	2	0	0	0	0	0	1	9	22	79
Days Minimum Temp. ≤ 0°F	0	0	0	0	0	0	0	0	0	0	0	0	0
Heating Degree Days (base 65°F)	723	568	439	252	79	10	0	0	16	142	450	727	3,406
Cooling Degree Days (base 65°F)	0	0	0	16	117	298	484	446	227	47	0	0	1,635
Mean Precipitation (in.)	1.25	1.60	1.07	0.33	0.20	0.08	0.38	0.32	0.25	0.21	0.58	0.92	7.19
Extreme Maximum Daily Precip. (in.)	2.35	1.44	2.65	0.73	0.58	0.50	1.03	1.53	1.60	0.76	1.86	1.68	2.65
Days With ≥ 0.1" Precipitation	3	3	2	1	1	0	1	1	1	1	1	2	17
Days With ≥ 0.5" Precipitation	1	1	1	0	0	0	0	0	0	0	0	1	4
Days With ≥ 1.0" Precipitation	0	0	0	0	0	0	0	0	0	0	0	0	0
Mean Snowfall (in.)	0.4	*0.3*	0.0	0.1	0.0	0.0	0.0	0.0	0.0	*0.0*	0.1	*0.4*	*1.3*
Maximum Snow Depth (in.)	na	na	na	na	na	na	na	na	na	na	na	na	na
Days With ≥ 1.0" Snow Depth	na	na	na	na	na	na	na	na	na	na	na	na	na

Hayfield Pumping Plant *Riverside County* Elevation: 1,370 ft. Latitude: 33° 42' N Longitude: 115° 38' W

	JAN	FEB	MAR	APR	MAY	JUN	JUL	AUG	SEP	OCT	NOV	DEC	YEAR
Mean Maximum Temp. (°F)	66.5	69.7	75.6	82.8	91.4	100.1	104.8	103.7	98.5	87.3	75.0	66.0	85.1
Mean Temp. (°F)	53.1	55.9	61.1	67.3	75.7	83.4	89.8	89.0	82.7	71.3	60.2	52.2	70.1
Mean Minimum Temp. (°F)	39.5	42.1	46.5	51.7	60.0	66.7	74.7	74.2	66.7	55.2	45.3	38.4	55.1
Extreme Maximum Temp. (°F)	84	91	99	105	111	119	119	116	113	108	94	84	119
Extreme Minimum Temp. (°F)	18	21	25	34	41	49	56	58	46	36	23	18	18
Days Maximum Temp. ≥ 90°F	0	0	1	7	20	27	31	31	26	13	1	0	157
Days Maximum Temp. ≤ 32°F	0	0	0	0	0	0	0	0	0	0	0	0	0
Days Minimum Temp. ≤ 32°F	5	3	1	0	0	0	0	0	0	0	1	7	17
Days Minimum Temp. ≤ 0°F	0	0	0	0	0	0	0	0	0	0	0	0	0
Heating Degree Days (base 65°F)	364	254	154	55	7	0	0	0	0	21	163	391	1,409
Cooling Degree Days (base 65°F)	1	5	40	128	346	559	774	751	539	221	26	1	3,391
Mean Precipitation (in.)	0.76	0.82	0.58	0.10	0.10	trace	0.25	0.68	0.33	0.24	0.27	0.58	4.71
Extreme Maximum Daily Precip. (in.)	1.80	1.27	1.63	0.39	1.62	0.06	1.45	2.70	2.80	1.04	1.08	3.00	3.00
Days With ≥ 0.1" Precipitation	2	2	1	0	0	0	0	1	1	1	1	1	10
Days With ≥ 0.5" Precipitation	0	1	0	0	0	0	0	0	0	0	0	0	1
Days With ≥ 1.0" Precipitation	0	0	0	0	0	0	0	0	0	0	0	0	0
Mean Snowfall (in.)	trace	0.0	0.0	0.0	0.0	0.0	0.0	0.0	0.0	0.0	0.0	0.0	trace
Maximum Snow Depth (in.)	trace	0	0	0	0	0	0	0	0	0	0	0	trace
Days With ≥ 1.0" Snow Depth	0	0	0	0	0	0	0	0	0	0	0	0	0

 The period of record for all cooperative weather station data is 1980 – 2009. See User Guide for detailed explanation of data.

Hollister 2 *San Benito County* Elevation: 274 ft. Latitude: 36° 51' N Longitude: 121° 25' W

	JAN	FEB	MAR	APR	MAY	JUN	JUL	AUG	SEP	OCT	NOV	DEC	YEAR
Mean Maximum Temp. (°F)	59.9	62.6	65.9	70.3	74.1	78.3	80.8	81.5	81.1	76.6	67.1	59.6	71.5
Mean Temp. (°F)	49.1	51.8	54.3	57.3	61.0	64.7	67.0	67.5	66.7	62.2	54.5	48.6	58.7
Mean Minimum Temp. (°F)	38.1	40.9	42.5	44.3	48.0	50.9	53.1	53.6	52.3	47.7	41.8	37.4	45.9
Extreme Maximum Temp. (°F)	77	82	89	99	105	108	112	110	105	107	94	78	112
Extreme Minimum Temp. (°F)	20	20	25	27	37	38	44	45	40	34	24	14	14
Days Maximum Temp. ≥ 90°F	0	0	0	1	2	3	4	5	6	3	0	0	24
Days Maximum Temp. ≤ 32°F	0	0	0	0	0	0	0	0	0	0	0	0	0
Days Minimum Temp. ≤ 32°F	8	3	1	0	0	0	0	0	0	0	2	8	22
Days Minimum Temp. ≤ 0°F	0	0	0	0	0	0	0	0	0	0	0	0	0
Heating Degree Days (base 65°F)	488	367	327	235	147	63	26	18	32	117	310	503	2,633
Cooling Degree Days (base 65°F)	0	0	2	11	31	59	94	104	91	36	1	0	429
Mean Precipitation (in.)	2.89	2.85	2.24	0.88	0.39	0.06	0.04	0.01	0.21	0.69	1.60	2.11	13.97
Extreme Maximum Daily Precip. (in.)	2.82	2.33	2.05	1.43	0.88	0.50	0.61	0.18	1.30	2.31	1.86	2.00	2.82
Days With ≥ 0.1" Precipitation	6	6	6	3	1	0	0	0	0	2	4	5	33
Days With ≥ 0.5" Precipitation	2	2	1	0	0	0	0	0	0	0	1	1	7
Days With ≥ 1.0" Precipitation	0	1	0	0	0	0	0	0	0	0	0	0	1
Mean Snowfall (in.)	0.0	0.0	0.0	0.0	0.0	0.0	0.0	0.0	0.0	0.0	0.0	0.0	0.0
Maximum Snow Depth (in.)	0	0	0	0	0	0	0	0	0	0	0	0	0
Days With ≥ 1.0" Snow Depth	0	0	0	0	0	0	0	0	0	0	0	0	0

Independence *Inyo County* Elevation: 3,950 ft. Latitude: 36° 48' N Longitude: 118° 12' W

	JAN	FEB	MAR	APR	MAY	JUN	JUL	AUG	SEP	OCT	NOV	DEC	YEAR
Mean Maximum Temp. (°F)	55.8	59.5	66.5	74.0	83.9	93.2	99.6	97.9	90.3	78.2	64.8	54.8	76.5
Mean Temp. (°F)	42.4	46.1	52.0	58.7	68.2	76.8	82.6	80.7	73.6	62.1	50.1	41.5	61.2
Mean Minimum Temp. (°F)	29.0	32.7	37.6	43.4	52.4	60.3	65.7	63.4	56.8	46.0	35.4	28.2	45.9
Extreme Maximum Temp. (°F)	80	86	90	102	105	110	114	109	108	98	91	76	114
Extreme Minimum Temp. (°F)	9	12	16	21	30	38	43	49	40	27	16	-2	-2
Days Maximum Temp. ≥ 90°F	0	0	0	1	9	21	29	29	18	3	0	0	110
Days Maximum Temp. ≤ 32°F	0	0	0	0	0	0	0	0	0	0	0	0	0
Days Minimum Temp. ≤ 32°F	22	13	7	2	0	0	0	0	0	1	10	24	79
Days Minimum Temp. ≤ 0°F	0	0	0	0	0	0	0	0	0	0	0	0	0
Heating Degree Days (base 65°F)	693	529	397	211	59	8	0	0	9	138	441	721	3,206
Cooling Degree Days (base 65°F)	0	0	3	29	163	368	554	493	274	55	1	0	1,940
Mean Precipitation (in.)	1.09	1.15	0.64	0.21	0.11	0.17	0.10	0.12	0.16	0.21	0.68	0.75	5.39
Extreme Maximum Daily Precip. (in.)	2.18	2.06	2.57	0.50	0.40	0.93	0.40	0.71	0.56	1.05	3.05	1.58	3.05
Days With ≥ 0.1" Precipitation	2	3	1	1	0	0	0	0	0	1	1	2	11
Days With ≥ 0.5" Precipitation	1	1	0	0	0	0	0	0	0	0	0	0	2
Days With ≥ 1.0" Precipitation	0	0	0	0	0	0	0	0	0	0	0	0	0
Mean Snowfall (in.)	0.4	0.2	trace	trace	0.0	0.0	0.0	0.0	0.0	0.0	trace	***0.3***	***0.9***
Maximum Snow Depth (in.)	na	na	na	na	***0***	na	***0***	***0***	***0***	na	na	na	na
Days With ≥ 1.0" Snow Depth	na	na	na	na	***0***	na	***0***	***0***	***0***	na	na	na	na

Jess Valley *Modoc County* Elevation: 5,399 ft. Latitude: 41° 16' N Longitude: 120° 18' W

	JAN	FEB	MAR	APR	MAY	JUN	JUL	AUG	SEP	OCT	NOV	DEC	YEAR
Mean Maximum Temp. (°F)	42.1	44.3	49.1	55.1	64.4	73.2	83.4	82.7	76.1	63.7	49.2	41.3	60.4
Mean Temp. (°F)	31.2	32.9	37.2	41.9	49.8	57.1	65.4	64.3	58.0	47.9	37.2	30.5	46.1
Mean Minimum Temp. (°F)	20.5	21.7	25.4	28.5	34.9	41.0	47.3	45.8	39.7	32.0	25.1	19.6	31.8
Extreme Maximum Temp. (°F)	62	66	75	81	89	95	102	98	95	88	78	64	102
Extreme Minimum Temp. (°F)	-8	-28	1	6	18	21	29	30	19	8	-5	-26	-28
Days Maximum Temp. ≥ 90°F	0	0	0	0	0	1	5	5	1	0	0	0	12
Days Maximum Temp. ≤ 32°F	4	2	1	0	0	0	0	0	0	0	2	5	14
Days Minimum Temp. ≤ 32°F	28	25	26	22	11	3	0	0	5	16	24	27	187
Days Minimum Temp. ≤ 0°F	1	1	0	0	0	0	0	0	0	0	0	2	4
Heating Degree Days (base 65°F)	1,040	900	854	687	467	243	62	73	217	528	828	1,064	6,963
Cooling Degree Days (base 65°F)	0	0	0	0	2	12	80	57	14	0	0	0	165
Mean Precipitation (in.)	1.89	1.58	2.03	2.13	2.56	1.52	0.46	0.48	0.78	1.22	2.22	2.14	19.01
Extreme Maximum Daily Precip. (in.)	1.00	1.36	***1.68***	2.05	2.06	2.10	0.89	1.22	1.80	1.61	***1.21***	***1.30***	***2.10***
Days With ≥ 0.1" Precipitation	6	5	6	7	6	4	1	1	2	4	7	6	55
Days With ≥ 0.5" Precipitation	1	1	1	1	2	1	0	0	0	1	1	1	10
Days With ≥ 1.0" Precipitation	0	0	0	0	0	0	0	0	0	0	0	0	0
Mean Snowfall (in.)	12.0	10.0	11.9	10.1	4.2	0.4	0.1	0.0	0.2	2.5	10.8	13.1	75.3
Maximum Snow Depth (in.)	27	16	13	9	10	trace	trace	0	trace	5	12	18	27
Days With ≥ 1.0" Snow Depth	9	6	3	0	0	0	0	0	0	0	4	8	30

King City *Monterey County* Elevation: 319 ft. Latitude: 36° 12' N Longitude: 121° 08' W

	JAN	FEB	MAR	APR	MAY	JUN	JUL	AUG	SEP	OCT	NOV	DEC	YEAR
Mean Maximum Temp. (°F)	63.1	65.8	69.3	74.1	78.5	82.7	85.1	85.4	84.7	79.3	69.2	62.4	75.0
Mean Temp. (°F)	50.1	52.7	55.5	58.6	62.7	66.3	69.0	69.1	67.7	62.4	54.6	49.3	59.8
Mean Minimum Temp. (°F)	37.0	39.6	41.6	43.0	46.8	49.9	52.8	52.7	50.5	45.4	39.9	36.0	44.6
Extreme Maximum Temp. (°F)	83	86	93	104	106	112	111	109	111	109	93	84	112
Extreme Minimum Temp. (°F)	17	20	29	28	35	38	40	43	36	29	23	14	14
Days Maximum Temp. ≥ 90°F	0	0	0	2	3	6	7	7	8	4	0	0	37
Days Maximum Temp. ≤ 32°F	0	0	0	0	0	0	0	0	0	0	0	0	0
Days Minimum Temp. ≤ 32°F	9	5	2	0	0	0	0	0	0	0	5	12	33
Days Minimum Temp. ≤ 0°F	0	0	0	0	0	0	0	0	0	0	0	0	0
Heating Degree Days (base 65°F)	457	342	290	201	104	32	5	4	20	110	308	481	2,354
Cooling Degree Days (base 65°F)	0	0	2	15	39	79	135	137	106	36	2	0	551
Mean Precipitation (in.)	2.27	2.61	2.22	0.78	0.31	0.05	0.01	0.01	0.18	0.62	1.09	1.86	12.01
Extreme Maximum Daily Precip. (in.)	2.01	2.70	3.00	1.58	0.80	0.40	0.09	0.12	0.43	1.88	1.28	2.26	3.00
Days With ≥ 0.1" Precipitation	5	5	5	2	1	0	0	0	0	1	3	4	26
Days With ≥ 0.5" Precipitation	1	2	1	0	0	0	0	0	0	0	1	1	6
Days With ≥ 1.0" Precipitation	0	1	0	0	0	0	0	0	0	0	0	0	1
Mean Snowfall (in.)	0.0	0.0	0.0	0.0	0.0	0.0	0.0	0.0	0.0	0.0	0.0	trace	trace
Maximum Snow Depth (in.)	0	0	0	0	0	0	0	0	0	0	0	0	0
Days With ≥ 1.0" Snow Depth	0	0	0	0	0	0	0	0	0	0	0	0	0

The period of record for all cooperative weather station data is 1980 – 2009. See User Guide for detailed explanation of data.

Laguna Beach *Orange County* Elevation: 35 ft. Latitude: 33° 33' N Longitude: 117° 47' W

	JAN	FEB	MAR	APR	MAY	JUN	JUL	AUG	SEP	OCT	NOV	DEC	YEAR
Mean Maximum Temp. (°F)	67.3	67.9	68.8	71.4	72.7	74.8	78.7	79.7	79.4	76.1	71.2	67.1	72.9
Mean Temp. (°F)	55.4	56.3	57.7	60.2	63.3	65.8	69.3	69.8	68.9	65.1	59.2	54.9	62.2
Mean Minimum Temp. (°F)	43.5	44.7	46.6	49.0	53.8	56.7	59.8	59.9	58.4	54.1	47.1	42.8	51.4
Extreme Maximum Temp. (°F)	89	90	92	97	100	100	104	97	102	98	93	85	104
Extreme Minimum Temp. (°F)	27	30	32	35	39	39	43	49	45	40	28	30	27
Days Maximum Temp. ≥ 90°F	0	0	0	0	0	0	0	1	1	1	0	0	3
Days Maximum Temp. ≤ 32°F	0	0	0	0	0	0	0	0	0	0	0	0	0
Days Minimum Temp. ≤ 32°F	1	0	0	0	0	0	0	0	0	0	0	1	2
Days Minimum Temp. ≤ 0°F	0	0	0	0	0	0	0	0	0	0	0	0	0
Heating Degree Days (base 65°F)	293	242	222	146	71	26	3	2	9	43	174	306	1,537
Cooling Degree Days (base 65°F)	1	2	3	9	25	58	142	159	134	53	5	0	591
Mean Precipitation (in.)	2.63	3.53	2.13	0.92	0.22	0.11	0.05	0.03	0.26	0.62	1.21	1.96	13.67
Extreme Maximum Daily Precip. (in.)	2.45	3.00	2.97	1.31	0.54	0.88	0.32	0.16	1.01	2.20	2.00	5.50	5.50
Days With ≥ 0.1" Precipitation	4	5	4	2	1	0	0	0	1	1	2	3	23
Days With ≥ 0.5" Precipitation	2	2	2	1	0	0	0	0	0	0	1	1	9
Days With ≥ 1.0" Precipitation	1	1	1	0	0	0	0	0	0	0	0	0	3
Mean Snowfall (in.)	0.0	0.0	0.0	0.0	0.0	0.0	0.0	0.0	0.0	0.0	0.0	0.0	0.0
Maximum Snow Depth (in.)	0	0	0	0	0	0	0	0	0	0	0	0	0
Days With ≥ 1.0" Snow Depth	0	0	0	0	0	0	0	0	0	0	0	0	0

Lava Beds Nat Monument *Siskiyou County* Elevation: 4,770 ft. Latitude: 41° 44' N Longitude: 121° 30' W

	JAN	FEB	MAR	APR	MAY	JUN	JUL	AUG	SEP	OCT	NOV	DEC	YEAR
Mean Maximum Temp. (°F)	41.9	45.3	50.7	57.1	66.1	74.8	84.6	84.9	76.7	64.7	48.7	40.7	61.4
Mean Temp. (°F)	32.5	35.2	39.5	44.6	52.4	59.6	68.1	67.9	60.7	50.5	38.2	31.6	48.4
Mean Minimum Temp. (°F)	23.1	25.1	28.2	32.1	38.7	44.3	51.6	50.8	44.5	36.1	27.7	22.6	35.4
Extreme Maximum Temp. (°F)	60	68	75	88	94	98	103	102	99	89	74	64	103
Extreme Minimum Temp. (°F)	-1	-13	7	14	20	27	33	30	24	11	2	-18	-18
Days Maximum Temp. ≥ 90°F	0	0	0	0	0	2	9	8	2	0	0	0	21
Days Maximum Temp. ≤ 32°F	3	2	0	0	0	0	0	0	0	0	1	4	10
Days Minimum Temp. ≤ 32°F	28	24	23	16	7	2	0	0	2	10	22	28	162
Days Minimum Temp. ≤ 0°F	0	0	0	0	0	0	0	0	0	0	0	0	0
Heating Degree Days (base 65°F)	1,002	835	784	605	396	193	44	40	168	447	796	1,028	6,338
Cooling Degree Days (base 65°F)	0	0	0	0	12	36	148	137	44	3	0	0	380
Mean Precipitation (in.)	1.69	1.94	1.91	1.10	1.23	0.92	0.60	0.44	0.53	1.01	1.63	1.71	14.71
Extreme Maximum Daily Precip. (in.)	3.37	2.16	1.64	0.64	1.06	1.84	1.77	1.52	1.50	1.49	1.78	2.17	3.37
Days With ≥ 0.1" Precipitation	4	5	5	3	3	3	2	1	2	3	4	4	39
Days With ≥ 0.5" Precipitation	1	1	1	0	1	0	0	0	0	1	1	1	7
Days With ≥ 1.0" Precipitation	0	0	0	0	0	0	0	0	0	0	0	0	0
Mean Snowfall (in.)	10.1	7.7	7.5	3.3	1.1	0.1	trace	0.0	trace	0.3	4.5	8.6	43.2
Maximum Snow Depth (in.)	26	22	20	8	6	1	0	0	trace	2	17	20	26
Days With ≥ 1.0" Snow Depth	15	11	6	2	0	0	0	0	0	0	5	13	52

Livermore *Alameda County* Elevation: 479 ft. Latitude: 37° 40' N Longitude: 121° 46' W

	JAN	FEB	MAR	APR	MAY	JUN	JUL	AUG	SEP	OCT	NOV	DEC	YEAR
Mean Maximum Temp. (°F)	56.6	61.4	66.0	71.2	77.3	83.5	89.3	88.8	85.8	77.6	65.1	56.7	73.3
Mean Temp. (°F)	47.7	51.4	54.8	58.5	63.6	68.6	72.9	72.6	70.2	63.5	54.2	47.7	60.5
Mean Minimum Temp. (°F)	38.7	41.3	43.5	45.7	49.9	53.8	56.5	56.3	54.5	49.5	43.2	38.6	47.6
Extreme Maximum Temp. (°F)	73	77	88	96	104	109	112	110	110	106	86	71	112
Extreme Minimum Temp. (°F)	22	24	31	33	36	42	47	44	39	35	27	18	18
Days Maximum Temp. ≥ 90°F	0	0	0	1	3	8	16	15	11	3	0	0	57
Days Maximum Temp. ≤ 32°F	0	0	0	0	0	0	0	0	0	0	0	0	0
Days Minimum Temp. ≤ 32°F	6	3	0	0	0	0	0	0	0	0	1	6	16
Days Minimum Temp. ≤ 0°F	0	0	0	0	0	0	0	0	0	0	0	0	0
Heating Degree Days (base 65°F)	530	379	311	203	96	24	2	1	11	87	319	530	2,493
Cooling Degree Days (base 65°F)	0	0	1	14	59	140	255	243	172	49	1	0	934
Mean Precipitation (in.)	2.86	2.94	2.35	0.98	0.49	0.09	0.03	0.05	0.22	0.78	1.75	2.49	15.03
Extreme Maximum Daily Precip. (in.)	2.29	1.95	1.79	1.62	0.82	0.60	0.67	0.50	1.02	2.21	1.98	2.09	2.29
Days With ≥ 0.1" Precipitation	6	7	6	3	2	0	0	0	1	1	4	6	36
Days With ≥ 0.5" Precipitation	2	2	1	0	0	0	0	0	0	1	1	2	9
Days With ≥ 1.0" Precipitation	1	0	0	0	0	0	0	0	0	0	0	0	1
Mean Snowfall (in.)	0.0	0.0	trace	0.0	0.0	0.0	0.0	0.0	0.0	0.0	0.0	trace	trace
Maximum Snow Depth (in.)	0	0	trace	0	0	0	0	0	0	0	0	trace	trace
Days With ≥ 1.0" Snow Depth	0	0	0	0	0	0	0	0	0	0	0	0	0

Mitchell Caverns *San Bernardino County* Elevation: 4,350 ft. Latitude: 34° 57' N Longitude: 115° 33' W

	JAN	FEB	MAR	APR	MAY	JUN	JUL	AUG	SEP	OCT	NOV	DEC	YEAR
Mean Maximum Temp. (°F)	54.6	56.5	62.0	69.5	78.9	88.1	93.2	91.2	85.2	74.0	62.3	54.1	72.5
Mean Temp. (°F)	46.7	48.1	52.6	59.0	68.1	77.1	82.2	80.5	74.6	64.4	53.6	46.1	62.7
Mean Minimum Temp. (°F)	38.6	39.7	43.3	48.5	57.2	66.1	71.3	69.8	63.9	54.7	44.8	38.0	53.0
Extreme Maximum Temp. (°F)	73	81	83	89	98	105	110	106	100	97	82	75	110
Extreme Minimum Temp. (°F)	17	12	21	26	32	35	48	44	38	30	22	11	11
Days Maximum Temp. ≥ 90°F	0	0	0	0	3	14	24	20	8	1	0	0	70
Days Maximum Temp. ≤ 32°F	0	0	0	0	0	0	0	0	0	0	0	0	0
Days Minimum Temp. ≤ 32°F	5	4	2	1	0	0	0	0	0	0	2	6	20
Days Minimum Temp. ≤ 0°F	0	0	0	0	0	0	0	0	0	0	0	0	0
Heating Degree Days (base 65°F)	562	471	382	213	59	7	0	0	11	110	342	580	2,737
Cooling Degree Days (base 65°F)	0	0	5	39	162	377	540	489	305	97	5	0	2,019
Mean Precipitation (in.)	1.51	1.92	1.47	0.58	0.19	0.10	1.03	1.41	0.97	0.77	0.63	1.23	11.81
Extreme Maximum Daily Precip. (in.)	2.34	4.50	2.61	0.96	0.95	0.63	5.66	2.70	2.66	1.62	1.75	5.10	5.66
Days With ≥ 0.1" Precipitation	3	3	2	1	1	0	2	2	2	1	1	2	20
Days With ≥ 0.5" Precipitation	1	1	1	0	0	0	1	1	1	1	1	1	9
Days With ≥ 1.0" Precipitation	0	1	0	0	0	0	0	0	0	0	0	0	1
Mean Snowfall (in.)	0.3	0.3	0.6	0.1	trace	0.0	0.0	0.0	0.0	trace	0.1	0.8	2.2
Maximum Snow Depth (in.)	5	1	trace	trace	0	0	0	0	0	trace	6	8	8
Days With ≥ 1.0" Snow Depth	0	0	0	0	0	0	0	0	0	0	0	0	0

The period of record for all cooperative weather station data is 1980 – 2009. See User Guide for detailed explanation of data.

Modesto *Stanislaus County* Elevation: 90 ft. Latitude: 37° 39' N Longitude: 121° 00' W

	JAN	FEB	MAR	APR	MAY	JUN	JUL	AUG	SEP	OCT	NOV	DEC	YEAR
Mean Maximum Temp. (°F)	54.8	62.3	68.2	74.3	82.4	89.0	94.5	93.0	88.2	78.4	64.9	54.7	75.4
Mean Temp. (°F)	47.1	52.6	57.1	61.6	68.4	74.0	78.6	77.3	73.3	65.1	54.4	46.8	63.0
Mean Minimum Temp. (°F)	39.4	42.8	45.9	49.0	54.3	59.0	62.6	61.7	58.4	51.8	44.0	38.9	50.6
Extreme Maximum Temp. (°F)	75	80	87	100	107	111	113	108	105	101	88	75	113
Extreme Minimum Temp. (°F)	23	24	33	34	39	45	51	51	44	39	27	19	19
Days Maximum Temp. ≥ 90°F	0	0	0	2	7	15	24	22	14	2	0	0	86
Days Maximum Temp. ≤ 32°F	0	0	0	0	0	0	0	0	0	0	0	0	0
Days Minimum Temp. ≤ 32°F	4	1	0	0	0	0	0	0	0	0	1	5	11
Days Minimum Temp. ≤ 0°F	0	0	0	0	0	0	0	0	0	0	0	0	0
Heating Degree Days (base 65°F)	547	345	243	131	37	4	0	0	4	64	313	557	2,245
Cooling Degree Days (base 65°F)	0	0	4	37	148	282	427	389	260	76	2	0	1,625
Mean Precipitation (in.)	2.61	2.36	2.09	0.90	0.62	0.13	0.02	0.02	0.25	0.66	1.28	1.96	12.90
Extreme Maximum Daily Precip. (in.)	1.70	1.91	2.19	1.63	1.67	1.14	0.52	0.19	1.05	1.57	1.14	1.81	2.19
Days With ≥ 0.1" Precipitation	6	6	5	3	1	0	0	0	1	1	3	5	31
Days With ≥ 0.5" Precipitation	2	2	1	0	0	0	0	0	0	0	1	1	7
Days With ≥ 1.0" Precipitation	0	0	0	0	0	0	0	0	0	0	0	0	0
Mean Snowfall (in.)	na	na	na	na	na	na	na	na	na	na	na	na	na
Maximum Snow Depth (in.)	na	na	na	na	na	na	na	na	na	na	na	na	na
Days With ≥ 1.0" Snow Depth	na	na	na	na	na	na	na	na	na	na	na	na	na

Morro Bay Fire Dept *San Luis Obispo County* Elevation: 115 ft. Latitude: 35° 22' N Longitude: 120° 51' W

	JAN	FEB	MAR	APR	MAY	JUN	JUL	AUG	SEP	OCT	NOV	DEC	YEAR
Mean Maximum Temp. (°F)	62.5	62.9	63.5	64.4	63.5	64.2	65.8	66.5	67.5	68.4	66.7	62.4	64.9
Mean Temp. (°F)	52.5	53.5	54.3	55.0	55.9	57.3	59.3	60.0	59.9	59.3	56.6	52.3	56.3
Mean Minimum Temp. (°F)	42.4	44.0	45.0	45.6	48.2	50.3	52.7	53.4	52.4	50.1	46.4	42.2	47.7
Extreme Maximum Temp. (°F)	83	87	92	100	91	98	88	90	102	97	90	81	102
Extreme Minimum Temp. (°F)	23	25	32	34	34	39	35	40	41	37	31	22	22
Days Maximum Temp. ≥ 90°F	0	0	0	0	0	0	0	0	0	0	0	0	0
Days Maximum Temp. ≤ 32°F	0	0	0	0	0	0	0	0	0	0	0	0	0
Days Minimum Temp. ≤ 32°F	1	1	0	0	0	0	0	0	0	0	0	2	4
Days Minimum Temp. ≤ 0°F	0	0	0	0	0	0	0	0	0	0	0	0	0
Heating Degree Days (base 65°F)	382	320	326	298	278	228	173	154	158	185	253	386	3,141
Cooling Degree Days (base 65°F)	0	1	1	5	2	2	3	5	13	15	5	0	52
Mean Precipitation (in.)	3.42	3.85	3.27	1.07	0.42	0.08	0.03	0.05	0.24	0.77	1.40	2.50	17.10
Extreme Maximum Daily Precip. (in.)	3.70	2.63	8.82	2.55	2.23	0.63	0.22	0.67	1.05	1.98	1.49	2.51	8.82
Days With ≥ 0.1" Precipitation	6	7	5	3	1	0	0	0	1	2	3	5	33
Days With ≥ 0.5" Precipitation	2	3	2	1	0	0	0	0	0	0	1	2	11
Days With ≥ 1.0" Precipitation	1	1	1	0	0	0	0	0	0	0	0	1	4
Mean Snowfall (in.)	0.0	trace	0.0	0.0	0.0	0.0	0.0	0.0	0.0	0.0	0.0	0.0	trace
Maximum Snow Depth (in.)	0	trace	0	0	0	0	0	0	0	0	0	0	trace
Days With ≥ 1.0" Snow Depth	0	0	0	0	0	0	0	0	0	0	0	0	0

Needles Airport *San Bernardino County* Elevation: 914 ft. Latitude: 34° 46' N Longitude: 114° 37' W

	JAN	FEB	MAR	APR	MAY	JUN	JUL	AUG	SEP	OCT	NOV	DEC	YEAR
Mean Maximum Temp. (°F)	65.6	70.4	78.0	85.9	95.5	104.7	109.3	107.4	101.2	88.5	74.2	64.4	87.1
Mean Temp. (°F)	54.7	58.6	64.9	72.2	81.8	90.8	96.8	95.1	88.0	75.3	62.3	53.6	74.5
Mean Minimum Temp. (°F)	43.7	46.7	51.6	58.5	68.1	76.8	84.2	82.7	74.8	62.0	50.4	42.8	61.9
Extreme Maximum Temp. (°F)	85	92	99	106	114	121	125	121	115	109	92	80	125
Extreme Minimum Temp. (°F)	24	24	32	41	48	53	57	68	47	40	32	13	13
Days Maximum Temp. ≥ 90°F	0	0	2	11	24	29	31	30	28	15	0	0	170
Days Maximum Temp. ≤ 32°F	0	0	0	0	0	0	0	0	0	0	0	0	0
Days Minimum Temp. ≤ 32°F	1	0	0	0	0	0	0	0	0	0	0	1	2
Days Minimum Temp. ≤ 0°F	0	0	0	0	0	0	0	0	0	0	0	0	0
Heating Degree Days (base 65°F)	313	186	81	18	1	0	0	0	0	8	123	347	1,077
Cooling Degree Days (base 65°F)	1	12	84	243	529	780	992	940	698	333	50	1	4,663
Mean Precipitation (in.)	0.73	0.77	0.58	0.22	0.09	0.03	0.22	0.64	0.38	0.23	0.39	0.45	4.73
Extreme Maximum Daily Precip. (in.)	1.14	1.52	0.99	0.79	0.41	0.48	1.43	1.48	2.10	0.95	1.42	1.34	2.10
Days With ≥ 0.1" Precipitation	2	2	1	1	0	0	1	1	1	1	1	1	12
Days With ≥ 0.5" Precipitation	0	0	0	0	0	0	0	0	0	0	0	0	0
Days With ≥ 1.0" Precipitation	0	0	0	0	0	0	0	0	0	0	0	0	0
Mean Snowfall (in.)	***0.0***	na	na	na	na	na	na	na	na	na	na	na	na
Maximum Snow Depth (in.)	***0***	na	na	na	na	na	na	na	na	na	na	na	na
Days With ≥ 1.0" Snow Depth	***0***	na	na	na	na	na	na	na	na	na	na	na	na

Newman *Stanislaus County* Elevation: 89 ft. Latitude: 37° 19' N Longitude: 121° 01' W

	JAN	FEB	MAR	APR	MAY	JUN	JUL	AUG	SEP	OCT	NOV	DEC	YEAR
Mean Maximum Temp. (°F)	56.3	63.4	69.7	76.9	***85.1***	92.5	96.8	95.0	90.8	81.6	67.2	57.0	***77.7***
Mean Temp. (°F)	47.0	51.9	56.4	61.2	***68.6***	74.6	78.8	77.3	73.5	65.5	54.4	46.9	***63.0***
Mean Minimum Temp. (°F)	37.6	40.4	43.0	45.5	***52.0***	56.7	60.7	59.5	56.1	49.2	41.6	36.7	***48.3***
Extreme Maximum Temp. (°F)	76	80	96	101	***111***	112	116	111	108	104	86	74	***116***
Extreme Minimum Temp. (°F)	15	20	25	28	***35***	41	44	46	35	32	25	15	***15***
Days Maximum Temp. ≥ 90°F	0	0	0	2	***10***	20	27	26	18	5	0	0	***108***
Days Maximum Temp. ≤ 32°F	0	0	0	0	***0***	0	0	0	0	0	0	0	***0***
Days Minimum Temp. ≤ 32°F	8	3	0	1	***0***	0	0	0	0	0	3	9	***24***
Days Minimum Temp. ≤ 0°F	0	0	0	0	***0***	0	0	0	0	0	0	0	***0***
Heating Degree Days (base 65°F)	551	364	263	143	***35***	3	0	0	3	57	312	554	***2,285***
Cooling Degree Days (base 65°F)	0	0	3	36	***153***	300	434	388	264	79	1	0	***1,658***
Mean Precipitation (in.)	2.62	2.28	1.73	0.61	0.43	0.06	0.01	0.01	0.25	0.60	1.19	1.72	11.51
Extreme Maximum Daily Precip. (in.)	4.10	2.03	2.53	1.22	***1.70***	0.37	0.24	0.10	1.18	2.07	1.98	1.42	***4.10***
Days With ≥ 0.1" Precipitation	5	6	4	2	***1***	0	0	0	1	1	3	5	***28***
Days With ≥ 0.5" Precipitation	2	1	1	0	0	0	0	0	0	0	1	1	6
Days With ≥ 1.0" Precipitation	0	0	0	0	0	0	0	0	0	0	0	0	0
Mean Snowfall (in.)	0.0	0.0	0.0	0.0	0.0	0.0	0.0	0.0	0.0	0.0	0.0	0.0	0.0
Maximum Snow Depth (in.)	0	0	0	0	0	0	0	0	0	0	0	0	0
Days With ≥ 1.0" Snow Depth	0	0	0	0	0	0	0	0	0	0	0	0	0

The period of record for all cooperative weather station data is 1980 – 2009. See User Guide for detailed explanation of data.

Ojai *Ventura County* Elevation: 750 ft. Latitude: 34° 27' N Longitude: 119° 14' W

	JAN	FEB	MAR	APR	MAY	JUN	JUL	AUG	SEP	OCT	NOV	DEC	YEAR
Mean Maximum Temp. (°F)	67.9	68.6	70.6	75.4	78.1	82.7	89.1	90.6	88.1	81.4	73.2	67.4	77.8
Mean Temp. (°F)	52.5	53.8	55.9	59.6	63.2	67.3	72.6	73.1	70.7	64.5	57.0	51.7	61.8
Mean Minimum Temp. (°F)	37.0	39.1	41.2	43.9	48.3	51.8	56.0	55.5	53.3	47.5	40.8	36.0	45.9
Extreme Maximum Temp. (°F)	90	92	96	103	105	110	111	109	110	107	100	88	111
Extreme Minimum Temp. (°F)	19	22	28	29	36	39	44	42	39	31	24	16	16
Days Maximum Temp. ≥ 90°F	0	0	0	2	3	6	14	16	14	6	1	0	62
Days Maximum Temp. ≤ 32°F	0	0	0	0	0	0	0	0	0	0	0	0	0
Days Minimum Temp. ≤ 32°F	8	5	1	0	0	0	0	0	0	0	2	9	25
Days Minimum Temp. ≤ 0°F	0	0	0	0	0	0	0	0	0	0	0	0	0
Heating Degree Days (base 65°F)	382	311	278	174	96	31	1	1	14	73	238	404	2,003
Cooling Degree Days (base 65°F)	0	2	2	20	46	105	243	258	192	63	6	0	937
Mean Precipitation (in.)	4.74	5.64	3.65	1.18	0.44	0.08	0.04	0.05	0.20	0.93	1.64	2.74	21.33
Extreme Maximum Daily Precip. (in.)	7.10	5.60	4.82	2.67	1.45	0.80	0.43	0.97	0.80	3.14	4.89	4.65	7.10
Days With ≥ 0.1" Precipitation	5	5	5	2	1	0	0	0	0	1	2	3	24
Days With ≥ 0.5" Precipitation	3	3	2	1	0	0	0	0	0	0	1	2	12
Days With ≥ 1.0" Precipitation	1	2	1	0	0	0	0	0	0	0	0	1	5
Mean Snowfall (in.)	0.0	0.0	0.0	0.0	0.0	0.0	0.0	0.0	0.0	0.0	0.0	0.0	0.0
Maximum Snow Depth (in.)	0	0	0	0	0	0	0	0	0	0	0	0	0
Days With ≥ 1.0" Snow Depth	0	0	0	0	0	0	0	0	0	0	0	0	0

Orleans *Humboldt County* Elevation: 399 ft. Latitude: 41° 18' N Longitude: 123° 32' W

	JAN	FEB	MAR	APR	MAY	JUN	JUL	AUG	SEP	OCT	NOV	DEC	YEAR
Mean Maximum Temp. (°F)	51.3	56.8	63.4	70.1	77.2	83.9	92.1	91.9	86.5	73.1	56.9	49.9	71.1
Mean Temp. (°F)	43.7	47.4	51.8	56.2	61.9	67.4	73.6	73.0	68.3	58.9	49.0	43.0	57.8
Mean Minimum Temp. (°F)	36.0	37.8	40.2	42.2	46.6	50.9	55.1	54.1	49.9	44.6	41.0	36.0	44.5
Extreme Maximum Temp. (°F)	70	78	86	97	102	106	112	110	107	98	77	68	112
Extreme Minimum Temp. (°F)	12	16	27	29	31	38	43	39	35	27	21	5	5
Days Maximum Temp. ≥ 90°F	0	0	0	1	4	8	20	20	12	1	0	0	66
Days Maximum Temp. ≤ 32°F	0	0	0	0	0	0	0	0	0	0	0	0	0
Days Minimum Temp. ≤ 32°F	9	6	2	1	0	0	0	0	0	1	3	9	31
Days Minimum Temp. ≤ 0°F	0	0	0	0	0	0	0	0	0	0	0	0	0
Heating Degree Days (base 65°F)	654	492	402	262	133	36	3	1	26	196	474	677	3,356
Cooling Degree Days (base 65°F)	0	0	0	6	44	115	278	257	129	14	0	0	843
Mean Precipitation (in.)	8.81	7.47	6.38	3.58	2.30	0.89	0.19	0.35	0.74	3.28	7.71	10.83	52.53
Extreme Maximum Daily Precip. (in.)	4.50	3.07	2.64	1.88	***2.29***	1.85	1.18	3.15	1.65	3.63	5.46	4.69	***5.46***
Days With ≥ 0.1" Precipitation	11	10	10	7	5	2	0	1	2	5	11	13	77
Days With ≥ 0.5" Precipitation	6	5	5	2	1	1	0	0	0	2	5	7	34
Days With ≥ 1.0" Precipitation	3	3	2	1	1	0	0	0	0	1	2	4	17
Mean Snowfall (in.)	0.9	1.1	0.3	trace	trace	0.0	0.0	0.0	0.0	0.0	0.1	1.4	3.8
Maximum Snow Depth (in.)	2	4	trace	0	trace	0	0	0	0	0	trace	2	4
Days With ≥ 1.0" Snow Depth	0	0	0	0	0	0	0	0	0	0	0	0	0

Palomar Mountain Observatory *San Diego County* Elevation: 5,549 ft. Latitude: 33° 23' N Longitude: 116° 50' W

	JAN	FEB	MAR	APR	MAY	JUN	JUL	AUG	SEP	OCT	NOV	DEC	YEAR
Mean Maximum Temp. (°F)	50.7	51.0	55.8	61.7	69.4	78.1	84.0	83.8	78.5	67.9	57.5	50.5	65.7
Mean Temp. (°F)	43.0	43.1	46.7	51.4	58.6	67.0	73.4	73.6	68.4	58.6	49.2	42.9	56.3
Mean Minimum Temp. (°F)	35.3	35.2	37.6	41.1	47.7	55.9	62.4	63.2	58.0	49.3	40.9	35.3	46.8
Extreme Maximum Temp. (°F)	68	69	78	84	91	98	98	99	92	92	79	72	99
Extreme Minimum Temp. (°F)	14	12	18	19	20	30	39	41	34	30	19	17	12
Days Maximum Temp. ≥ 90°F	0	0	0	0	0	1	5	3	1	0	0	0	10
Days Maximum Temp. ≤ 32°F	1	1	0	0	0	0	0	0	0	0	0	1	3
Days Minimum Temp. ≤ 32°F	12	11	9	6	2	0	0	0	0	1	5	11	57
Days Minimum Temp. ≤ 0°F	0	0	0	0	0	0	0	0	0	0	0	0	0
Heating Degree Days (base 65°F)	674	611	559	406	229	66	5	3	48	221	468	678	3,968
Cooling Degree Days (base 65°F)	0	0	0	4	36	134	273	277	154	31	1	0	910
Mean Precipitation (in.)	5.67	6.74	4.79	1.73	0.58	0.13	0.37	0.84	0.54	1.11	2.40	3.31	28.21
Extreme Maximum Daily Precip. (in.)	***5.65***	***4.97***	9.58	2.42	2.19	1.42	1.50	1.65	2.26	6.20	4.86	na	na
Days With ≥ 0.1" Precipitation	5	6	4	3	1	0	1	1	1	2	3	3	30
Days With ≥ 0.5" Precipitation	3	4	3	1	0	0	0	1	0	1	2	2	17
Days With ≥ 1.0" Precipitation	2	2	2	1	0	0	0	0	0	0	1	1	9
Mean Snowfall (in.)	2.9	5.0	7.6	1.9	trace	trace	0.0	0.0	0.0	trace	0.8	3.9	22.1
Maximum Snow Depth (in.)	16	21	25	15	2	0	0	0	0	1	14	27	27
Days With ≥ 1.0" Snow Depth	3	3	2	1	0	0	0	0	0	0	1	2	12

Parker Reservoir *San Bernardino County* Elevation: 737 ft. Latitude: 34° 17' N Longitude: 114° 10' W

	JAN	FEB	MAR	APR	MAY	JUN	JUL	AUG	SEP	OCT	NOV	DEC	YEAR
Mean Maximum Temp. (°F)	65.8	70.4	77.4	85.2	94.6	103.5	107.7	106.3	100.4	88.6	74.9	64.8	86.6
Mean Temp. (°F)	54.8	58.9	65.3	72.5	81.8	90.4	95.5	94.2	88.0	76.0	63.0	53.9	74.5
Mean Minimum Temp. (°F)	43.8	47.3	53.1	59.8	69.0	77.2	83.3	82.1	75.5	63.3	51.1	42.9	62.4
Extreme Maximum Temp. (°F)	86	92	100	106	115	121	123	119	115	110	95	82	123
Extreme Minimum Temp. (°F)	30	27	35	41	50	56	64	67	53	38	36	25	25
Days Maximum Temp. ≥ 90°F	0	0	2	10	24	29	31	31	28	16	1	0	172
Days Maximum Temp. ≤ 32°F	0	0	0	0	0	0	0	0	0	0	0	0	0
Days Minimum Temp. ≤ 32°F	0	0	0	0	0	0	0	0	0	0	0	1	1
Days Minimum Temp. ≤ 0°F	0	0	0	0	0	0	0	0	0	0	0	0	0
Heating Degree Days (base 65°F)	310	181	80	18	1	0	0	0	0	8	113	338	1,049
Cooling Degree Days (base 65°F)	1	14	95	252	529	768	952	913	696	356	61	0	4,637
Mean Precipitation (in.)	1.09	1.10	0.80	0.19	0.08	0.01	0.47	0.64	0.61	0.43	0.39	0.64	6.45
Extreme Maximum Daily Precip. (in.)	2.35	1.75	1.02	1.01	0.51	0.12	1.80	1.47	2.02	1.49	1.77	0.98	2.35
Days With ≥ 0.1" Precipitation	2	2	2	1	0	0	1	1	1	1	1	1	13
Days With ≥ 0.5" Precipitation	1	1	1	0	0	0	0	0	0	0	0	0	3
Days With ≥ 1.0" Precipitation	0	0	0	0	0	0	0	0	0	0	0	0	0
Mean Snowfall (in.)	0.0	0.0	0.0	0.0	0.0	0.0	0.0	0.0	0.0	0.0	0.0	0.0	0.0
Maximum Snow Depth (in.)	0	0	0	0	0	0	0	0	0	0	0	0	0
Days With ≥ 1.0" Snow Depth	0	0	0	0	0	0	0	0	0	0	0	0	0

The period of record for all cooperative weather station data is 1980 – 2009. See User Guide for detailed explanation of data.

Petaluma Fire Station 2 *Sonoma County* Elevation: 30 ft. Latitude: 38° 16' N Longitude: 122° 39' W

	JAN	FEB	MAR	APR	MAY	JUN	JUL	AUG	SEP	OCT	NOV	DEC	YEAR
Mean Maximum Temp. (°F)	57.3	61.9	65.1	68.8	73.2	78.6	82.0	82.1	81.4	76.0	65.2	57.3	70.7
Mean Temp. (°F)	48.0	51.2	53.7	56.3	60.4	64.7	67.2	67.3	66.3	61.6	53.6	47.9	58.2
Mean Minimum Temp. (°F)	38.6	40.5	42.2	43.8	47.4	50.7	52.3	52.4	51.1	47.2	41.9	38.4	45.5
Extreme Maximum Temp. (°F)	80	81	87	97	100	107	107	104	103	106	87	79	107
Extreme Minimum Temp. (°F)	21	18	29	24	27	33	35	36	37	29	23	20	18
Days Maximum Temp. ≥ 90°F	0	0	0	0	1	3	4	5	6	2	0	0	21
Days Maximum Temp. ≤ 32°F	0	0	0	0	0	0	0	0	0	0	0	0	0
Days Minimum Temp. ≤ 32°F	6	3	1	0	0	0	0	0	0	0	3	7	20
Days Minimum Temp. ≤ 0°F	0	0	0	0	0	0	0	0	0	0	0	0	0
Heating Degree Days (base 65°F)	520	382	344	260	156	57	17	13	29	121	338	524	2,761
Cooling Degree Days (base 65°F)	0	0	0	5	21	53	91	91	74	23	1	0	359
Mean Precipitation (in.)	4.83	5.53	3.69	1.47	0.82	0.18	0.02	0.06	0.21	1.29	3.09	5.09	26.28
Extreme Maximum Daily Precip. (in.)	3.62	3.28	3.69	1.65	1.78	0.75	0.19	1.00	0.90	2.55	2.51	4.29	4.29
Days With ≥ 0.1" Precipitation	8	8	7	4	2	0	0	0	1	2	6	9	47
Days With ≥ 0.5" Precipitation	3	4	2	1	1	0	0	0	0	1	2	3	17
Days With ≥ 1.0" Precipitation	1	2	1	0	0	0	0	0	0	0	1	1	6
Mean Snowfall (in.)	0.0	trace	0.0	trace	0.0	0.0	0.0	0.0	0.0	0.0	0.0	0.0	trace
Maximum Snow Depth (in.)	0	trace	0	trace	0	0	0	0	0	0	0	0	trace
Days With ≥ 1.0" Snow Depth	0	0	0	0	0	0	0	0	0	0	0	0	0

Porterville *Tulare County* Elevation: 393 ft. Latitude: 36° 04' N Longitude: 119° 01' W

	JAN	FEB	MAR	APR	MAY	JUN	JUL	AUG	SEP	OCT	NOV	DEC	YEAR
Mean Maximum Temp. (°F)	58.3	65.0	70.8	77.4	85.5	92.9	98.0	97.3	92.3	82.9	68.4	58.5	78.9
Mean Temp. (°F)	48.4	53.5	58.2	63.3	70.3	77.0	82.3	81.2	76.4	67.4	55.6	47.9	65.1
Mean Minimum Temp. (°F)	38.4	41.9	45.6	49.0	55.0	61.0	66.4	65.1	60.4	52.0	42.7	37.3	51.2
Extreme Maximum Temp. (°F)	79	85	91	99	109	108	111	112	108	103	88	80	112
Extreme Minimum Temp. (°F)	24	23	32	32	38	45	51	52	45	33	27	16	16
Days Maximum Temp. ≥ 90°F	0	0	0	3	10	21	29	29	20	7	0	0	119
Days Maximum Temp. ≤ 32°F	0	0	0	0	0	0	0	0	0	0	0	0	0
Days Minimum Temp. ≤ 32°F	6	2	0	0	0	0	0	0	0	0	2	7	17
Days Minimum Temp. ≤ 0°F	0	0	0	0	0	0	0	0	0	0	0	0	0
Heating Degree Days (base 65°F)	508	320	215	109	27	2	0	0	2	44	280	523	2,030
Cooling Degree Days (base 65°F)	0	1	11	64	197	368	542	510	350	127	4	0	2,174
Mean Precipitation (in.)	2.20	1.97	2.16	0.92	0.42	0.11	0.02	0.01	0.20	0.49	1.24	1.46	11.20
Extreme Maximum Daily Precip. (in.)	1.50	1.15	1.49	1.09	1.59	0.80	0.22	0.08	0.92	0.78	1.32	1.13	1.59
Days With ≥ 0.1" Precipitation	5	5	5	3	1	0	0	0	0	1	3	4	27
Days With ≥ 0.5" Precipitation	2	1	1	1	0	0	0	0	0	0	1	1	7
Days With ≥ 1.0" Precipitation	0	0	0	0	0	0	0	0	0	0	0	0	0
Mean Snowfall (in.)	0.0	0.0	0.0	0.0	0.0	0.0	0.0	0.0	0.0	0.0	0.0	0.0	0.0
Maximum Snow Depth (in.)	3	0	0	0	0	0	0	0	0	0	0	0	3
Days With ≥ 1.0" Snow Depth	0	0	0	0	0	0	0	0	0	0	0	0	0

Redlands *San Bernardino County* Elevation: 1,317 ft. Latitude: 34° 03' N Longitude: 117° 11' W

	JAN	FEB	MAR	APR	MAY	JUN	JUL	AUG	SEP	OCT	NOV	DEC	YEAR
Mean Maximum Temp. (°F)	67.2	67.9	70.9	75.7	80.9	88.1	95.1	95.9	91.6	82.4	73.9	66.9	79.7
Mean Temp. (°F)	54.3	55.5	58.1	62.0	67.1	72.7	78.7	79.4	75.7	67.7	59.5	53.7	65.4
Mean Minimum Temp. (°F)	41.3	43.0	45.3	48.2	53.3	57.2	62.3	62.8	59.8	52.9	45.1	40.5	51.0
Extreme Maximum Temp. (°F)	93	92	97	106	109	109	118	113	112	110	98	86	118
Extreme Minimum Temp. (°F)	19	25	31	33	38	41	49	49	46	38	29	24	19
Days Maximum Temp. ≥ 90°F	0	0	1	3	6	14	26	27	19	7	1	0	104
Days Maximum Temp. ≤ 32°F	0	0	0	0	0	0	0	0	0	0	0	0	0
Days Minimum Temp. ≤ 32°F	1	1	0	0	0	0	0	0	0	0	0	2	4
Days Minimum Temp. ≤ 0°F	0	0	0	0	0	0	0	0	0	0	0	0	0
Heating Degree Days (base 65°F)	328	270	221	132	46	8	0	0	3	37	176	344	1,565
Cooling Degree Days (base 65°F)	2	4	14	49	118	245	433	454	330	128	19	1	1,797
Mean Precipitation (in.)	2.73	3.32	2.11	0.96	0.31	0.11	0.08	0.13	0.28	0.63	0.98	1.57	13.21
Extreme Maximum Daily Precip. (in.)	2.53	3.05	2.05	1.88	1.16	1.00	0.35	0.88	0.99	2.75	1.98	2.20	3.05
Days With ≥ 0.1" Precipitation	5	5	4	2	1	0	0	0	1	1	2	3	24
Days With ≥ 0.5" Precipitation	2	2	1	1	0	0	0	0	0	0	1	1	8
Days With ≥ 1.0" Precipitation	1	1	1	0	0	0	0	0	0	0	0	0	3
Mean Snowfall (in.)	0.0	0.0	0.0	0.0	0.0	0.0	0.0	0.0	0.0	0.0	0.0	0.0	0.0
Maximum Snow Depth (in.)	0	0	0	0	0	0	0	0	0	0	0	0	0
Days With ≥ 1.0" Snow Depth	0	0	0	0	0	0	0	0	0	0	0	0	0

Riverside Fire Sta 3 *Riverside County* Elevation: 839 ft. Latitude: 33° 57' N Longitude: 117° 23' W

	JAN	FEB	MAR	APR	MAY	JUN	JUL	AUG	SEP	OCT	NOV	DEC	YEAR
Mean Maximum Temp. (°F)	69.1	69.8	72.9	77.5	82.2	88.3	94.9	95.9	91.7	83.3	74.9	68.8	80.8
Mean Temp. (°F)	55.9	57.1	59.7	63.6	68.5	73.5	79.2	80.0	76.3	68.8	60.5	55.0	66.5
Mean Minimum Temp. (°F)	42.7	44.3	46.5	49.7	54.8	58.7	63.5	64.1	60.9	54.2	46.1	41.2	52.2
Extreme Maximum Temp. (°F)	92	91	99	105	110	111	116	113	112	109	98	89	116
Extreme Minimum Temp. (°F)	26	22	32	35	43	46	51	51	45	41	28	22	22
Days Maximum Temp. ≥ 90°F	0	0	1	4	6	14	25	26	18	8	1	0	103
Days Maximum Temp. ≤ 32°F	0	0	0	0	0	0	0	0	0	0	0	0	0
Days Minimum Temp. ≤ 32°F	1	1	0	0	0	0	0	0	0	0	0	2	4
Days Minimum Temp. ≤ 0°F	0	0	0	0	0	0	0	0	0	0	0	0	0
Heating Degree Days (base 65°F)	278	224	173	90	22	3	0	0	1	23	149	304	1,267
Cooling Degree Days (base 65°F)	3	5	17	57	139	265	448	471	348	146	20	2	1,921
Mean Precipitation (in.)	2.03	2.68	1.73	0.65	0.15	0.08	0.04	0.12	0.14	0.48	0.81	1.11	10.02
Extreme Maximum Daily Precip. (in.)	2.22	2.45	1.60	1.05	0.82	0.83	0.25	1.84	0.64	2.50	2.05	*2.16*	*2.50*
Days With ≥ 0.1" Precipitation	4	5	3	1	0	0	0	0	0	1	2	2	18
Days With ≥ 0.5" Precipitation	1	2	1	0	0	0	0	0	0	0	1	0	5
Days With ≥ 1.0" Precipitation	0	1	1	0	0	0	0	0	0	0	0	0	2
Mean Snowfall (in.)	0.0	0.0	0.0	0.0	0.0	0.0	0.0	0.0	0.0	0.0	0.0	0.0	0.0
Maximum Snow Depth (in.)	0	0	0	0	0	0	0	0	0	0	0	0	0
Days With ≥ 1.0" Snow Depth	0	0	0	0	0	0	0	0	0	0	0	0	0

The period of record for all cooperative weather station data is 1980 – 2009. See User Guide for detailed explanation of data.

Salinas No 2 *Monterey County* Elevation: 44 ft. Latitude: 36° 40' N Longitude: 121° 40' W

	JAN	FEB	MAR	APR	MAY	JUN	JUL	AUG	SEP	OCT	NOV	DEC	YEAR
Mean Maximum Temp. (°F)	62.8	64.4	65.8	67.7	68.8	70.6	71.6	73.1	74.7	73.6	68.0	62.7	68.7
Mean Temp. (°F)	52.2	54.0	55.3	57.0	59.2	61.4	63.1	64.3	64.2	61.7	56.5	52.0	58.4
Mean Minimum Temp. (°F)	41.5	43.4	44.8	46.2	49.5	52.1	54.6	55.3	53.7	49.7	44.8	41.3	48.1
Extreme Maximum Temp. (°F)	85	85	89	100	99	103	97	99	103	105	94	80	105
Extreme Minimum Temp. (°F)	22	26	31	32	37	42	43	45	42	36	27	24	22
Days Maximum Temp. ≥ 90°F	0	0	0	1	1	1	0	0	1	1	0	0	5
Days Maximum Temp. ≤ 32°F	0	0	0	0	0	0	0	0	0	0	0	0	0
Days Minimum Temp. ≤ 32°F	2	1	0	0	0	0	0	0	0	0	0	3	6
Days Minimum Temp. ≤ 0°F	0	0	0	0	0	0	0	0	0	0	0	0	0
Heating Degree Days (base 65°F)	391	307	294	242	181	113	68	44	53	121	254	396	2,464
Cooling Degree Days (base 65°F)	0	1	1	7	9	11	17	28	36	26	4	0	140
Mean Precipitation (in.)	2.98	3.01	2.61	0.97	0.40	0.09	0.03	0.04	0.14	0.67	1.67	2.27	14.88
Extreme Maximum Daily Precip. (in.)	2.96	2.38	1.87	1.06	0.85	0.47	0.67	0.35	1.03	1.50	2.05	1.59	2.96
Days With ≥ 0.1" Precipitation	5	6	5	3	1	0	0	0	0	1	3	5	29
Days With ≥ 0.5" Precipitation	2	2	2	0	0	0	0	0	0	1	1	1	9
Days With ≥ 1.0" Precipitation	1	0	0	0	0	0	0	0	0	0	0	0	1
Mean Snowfall (in.)	0.0	0.0	0.0	0.0	0.0	0.0	0.0	0.0	0.0	0.0	0.0	0.0	0.0
Maximum Snow Depth (in.)	0	0	0	0	0	0	0	0	0	0	0	0	0
Days With ≥ 1.0" Snow Depth	0	0	0	0	0	0	0	0	0	0	0	0	0

San Francisco Oceanside *San Francisco County* Elevation: 35 ft. Latitude: 37° 44' N Longitude: 122° 30' W

	JAN	FEB	MAR	APR	MAY	JUN	JUL	AUG	SEP	OCT	NOV	DEC	YEAR
Mean Maximum Temp. (°F)	57.8	59.8	60.1	60.5	60.6	62.0	62.9	63.9	65.1	65.1	62.4	58.0	61.5
Mean Temp. (°F)	51.4	53.2	53.6	54.4	55.5	57.1	58.5	59.5	59.8	58.9	55.6	51.6	55.8
Mean Minimum Temp. (°F)	45.0	46.5	47.1	48.3	50.3	52.2	54.0	55.1	54.4	52.7	48.8	45.0	49.9
Extreme Maximum Temp. (°F)	74	77	81	90	98	87	79	92	92	91	83	73	98
Extreme Minimum Temp. (°F)	29	31	29	35	40	41	46	41	31	40	36	26	26
Days Maximum Temp. ≥ 90°F	0	0	0	0	0	0	0	0	0	0	0	0	0
Days Maximum Temp. ≤ 32°F	0	0	0	0	0	0	0	0	0	0	0	0	0
Days Minimum Temp. ≤ 32°F	0	0	0	0	0	0	0	0	0	0	0	0	0
Days Minimum Temp. ≤ 0°F	0	0	0	0	0	0	0	0	0	0	0	0	0
Heating Degree Days (base 65°F)	415	327	346	314	290	232	197	167	155	195	277	410	3,325
Cooling Degree Days (base 65°F)	0	0	0	3	1	1	1	3	6	10	2	0	27
Mean Precipitation (in.)	3.94	4.17	2.75	1.05	0.71	0.13	0.01	0.06	0.13	0.86	2.48	4.01	20.30
Extreme Maximum Daily Precip. (in.)	2.40	3.90	2.52	1.15	1.44	0.69	0.07	0.64	0.40	na	1.87	3.43	na
Days With ≥ 0.1" Precipitation	7	8	6	3	2	0	0	0	0	1	4	7	38
Days With ≥ 0.5" Precipitation	3	3	2	1	0	0	0	0	0	1	2	2	14
Days With ≥ 1.0" Precipitation	1	1	0	0	0	0	0	0	0	0	1	1	4
Mean Snowfall (in.)	0.0	0.0	0.0	0.0	0.0	0.0	0.0	0.0	0.0	0.0	0.0	0.0	0.0
Maximum Snow Depth (in.)	0	0	0	0	0	0	0	0	0	0	0	0	0
Days With ≥ 1.0" Snow Depth	0	0	0	0	0	0	0	0	0	0	0	0	0

Santa Barbara *Santa Barbara County* Elevation: 4 ft. Latitude: 34° 25' N Longitude: 119° 41' W

	JAN	FEB	MAR	APR	MAY	JUN	JUL	AUG	SEP	OCT	NOV	DEC	YEAR
Mean Maximum Temp. (°F)	64.9	65.5	66.7	69.6	69.9	71.9	75.2	76.6	75.7	73.1	69.1	65.3	70.3
Mean Temp. (°F)	55.5	56.5	57.9	60.4	61.9	64.2	67.4	68.1	67.4	64.3	59.4	55.5	61.5
Mean Minimum Temp. (°F)	45.7	47.3	49.1	51.1	53.8	56.5	59.4	59.5	59.0	55.4	49.6	45.6	52.7
Extreme Maximum Temp. (°F)	89	89	96	101	97	103	105	96	98	102	95	84	105
Extreme Minimum Temp. (°F)	22	30	32	37	36	45	46	43	40	34	37	26	22
Days Maximum Temp. ≥ 90°F	0	0	0	1	0	0	0	0	1	1	0	0	3
Days Maximum Temp. ≤ 32°F	0	0	0	0	0	0	0	0	0	0	0	0	0
Days Minimum Temp. ≤ 32°F	0	0	0	0	0	0	0	0	0	0	0	0	0
Days Minimum Temp. ≤ 0°F	0	0	0	0	0	0	0	0	0	0	0	0	0
Heating Degree Days (base 65°F)	291	236	218	150	106	48	9	6	15	56	169	289	1,593
Cooling Degree Days (base 65°F)	2	2	5	17	18	32	90	109	92	41	8	1	417
Mean Precipitation (in.)	4.33	4.83	3.16	0.98	0.33	0.09	0.01	0.02	0.12	0.84	1.51	2.61	18.83
Extreme Maximum Daily Precip. (in.)	8.00	3.50	4.75	3.30	1.09	0.62	0.10	0.12	1.45	3.12	5.90	3.75	8.00
Days With ≥ 0.1" Precipitation	5	5	4	2	1	0	0	0	0	1	2	3	23
Days With ≥ 0.5" Precipitation	3	3	2	1	0	0	0	0	0	1	1	2	13
Days With ≥ 1.0" Precipitation	1	2	1	0	0	0	0	0	0	0	0	1	5
Mean Snowfall (in.)	0.0	0.0	0.0	0.0	0.0	0.0	0.0	0.0	0.0	0.0	0.0	0.0	0.0
Maximum Snow Depth (in.)	0	0	0	0	0	0	0	0	0	0	0	0	0
Days With ≥ 1.0" Snow Depth	0	0	0	0	0	0	0	0	0	0	0	0	0

Santa Monica Pier *Los Angeles County* Elevation: 14 ft. Latitude: 34° 00' N Longitude: 118° 30' W

	JAN	FEB	MAR	APR	MAY	JUN	JUL	AUG	SEP	OCT	NOV	DEC	YEAR
Mean Maximum Temp. (°F)	63.7	63.4	63.0	64.2	64.6	66.8	69.8	70.4	70.6	69.6	67.1	63.8	66.4
Mean Temp. (°F)	57.2	57.5	57.8	59.4	60.8	63.4	66.2	66.8	66.6	64.7	61.0	57.2	61.6
Mean Minimum Temp. (°F)	50.7	51.5	52.7	54.5	57.0	60.0	62.6	63.2	62.6	59.8	54.9	50.6	56.7
Extreme Maximum Temp. (°F)	84	89	85	99	86	90	84	95	89	99	91	85	99
Extreme Minimum Temp. (°F)	39	35	41	43	43	51	53	55	55	48	37	37	35
Days Maximum Temp. ≥ 90°F	0	0	0	0	0	0	0	0	0	0	0	0	0
Days Maximum Temp. ≤ 32°F	0	0	0	0	0	0	0	0	0	0	0	0	0
Days Minimum Temp. ≤ 32°F	0	0	0	0	0	0	0	0	0	0	0	0	0
Days Minimum Temp. ≤ 0°F	0	0	0	0	0	0	0	0	0	0	0	0	0
Heating Degree Days (base 65°F)	240	213	220	172	128	59	15	12	18	46	130	238	1,491
Cooling Degree Days (base 65°F)	7	7	4	11	6	17	60	75	73	44	18	4	326
Mean Precipitation (in.)	3.09	3.66	1.89	0.46	0.22	0.05	0.01	0.03	0.15	0.50	1.05	1.79	12.90
Extreme Maximum Daily Precip. (in.)	4.67	3.88	2.65	1.11	1.73	0.55	0.08	0.36	1.00	1.45	2.00	2.25	4.67
Days With ≥ 0.1" Precipitation	4	5	3	1	0	0	0	0	0	1	2	3	19
Days With ≥ 0.5" Precipitation	2	3	1	0	0	0	0	0	0	0	1	1	8
Days With ≥ 1.0" Precipitation	1	1	1	0	0	0	0	0	0	0	0	1	4
Mean Snowfall (in.)	0.0	0.0	0.0	0.0	0.0	0.0	0.0	0.0	0.0	0.0	0.0	0.0	0.0
Maximum Snow Depth (in.)	0	0	0	0	0	0	0	0	0	0	0	0	0
Days With ≥ 1.0" Snow Depth	0	0	0	0	0	0	0	0	0	0	0	0	0

The period of record for all cooperative weather station data is 1980 – 2009. See User Guide for detailed explanation of data.

Stockton Fire Stn #4 *San Joaquin County* Elevation: 12 ft. Latitude: 38° 00' N Longitude: 121° 19' W

	JAN	FEB	MAR	APR	MAY	JUN	JUL	AUG	SEP	OCT	NOV	DEC	YEAR
Mean Maximum Temp. (°F)	55.7	63.0	68.3	74.4	81.9	88.4	93.5	92.8	89.4	80.5	66.3	56.3	75.9
Mean Temp. (°F)	46.2	51.3	55.6	60.1	66.3	71.6	75.3	74.4	71.3	63.9	53.6	45.9	61.3
Mean Minimum Temp. (°F)	36.8	39.7	42.7	45.8	50.7	54.8	57.0	56.1	53.2	47.2	40.9	35.8	46.7
Extreme Maximum Temp. (°F)	72	78	87	99	106	110	112	110	105	102	85	73	112
Extreme Minimum Temp. (°F)	17	13	24	27	34	31	40	37	29	29	23	15	13
Days Maximum Temp. ≥ 90°F	0	0	0	1	6	13	22	21	15	4	0	0	82
Days Maximum Temp. ≤ 32°F	0	0	0	0	0	0	0	0	0	0	0	0	0
Days Minimum Temp. ≤ 32°F	9	4	2	0	0	0	0	0	0	0	3	9	27
Days Minimum Temp. ≤ 0°F	0	0	0	0	0	0	0	0	0	0	0	0	0
Heating Degree Days (base 65°F)	575	381	291	163	62	11	1	2	13	88	337	585	2,509
Cooling Degree Days (base 65°F)	0	0	3	23	109	216	326	302	211	62	1	0	1,253
Mean Precipitation (in.)	3.43	3.24	2.63	1.38	0.59	0.11	0.02	0.02	0.28	0.95	2.07	2.94	17.66
Extreme Maximum Daily Precip. (in.)	2.76	2.30	1.46	1.57	1.62	0.40	0.35	0.30	1.05	2.90	2.14	2.30	2.90
Days With ≥ 0.1" Precipitation	7	6	6	3	1	0	0	0	1	2	4	6	36
Days With ≥ 0.5" Precipitation	2	2	2	1	0	0	0	0	0	1	2	2	12
Days With ≥ 1.0" Precipitation	1	1	1	0	0	0	0	0	0	0	0	0	3
Mean Snowfall (in.)	0.0	0.0	0.0	0.0	0.0	0.0	0.0	0.0	0.0	0.0	0.0	0.0	0.0
Maximum Snow Depth (in.)	0	0	0	0	0	0	0	0	0	0	0	0	0
Days With ≥ 1.0" Snow Depth	0	0	0	0	0	0	0	0	0	0	0	0	0

Tejon Rancho *Kern County* Elevation: 1,424 ft. Latitude: 35° 02' N Longitude: 118° 45' W

	JAN	FEB	MAR	APR	MAY	JUN	JUL	AUG	SEP	OCT	NOV	DEC	YEAR
Mean Maximum Temp. (°F)	59.3	63.4	68.5	75.1	83.8	91.4	97.6	96.5	91.3	80.9	66.7	59.0	77.8
Mean Temp. (°F)	46.5	50.5	54.8	59.9	68.0	75.2	81.2	79.7	75.3	65.7	53.2	46.5	63.0
Mean Minimum Temp. (°F)	33.6	37.6	41.0	44.6	52.1	58.9	64.9	62.8	59.3	50.4	39.7	33.9	48.2
Extreme Maximum Temp. (°F)	82	84	89	100	109	108	113	109	108	101	90	81	113
Extreme Minimum Temp. (°F)	6	14	17	16	24	31	39	41	34	26	15	11	6
Days Maximum Temp. ≥ 90°F	0	0	0	2	8	18	27	27	19	5	0	0	106
Days Maximum Temp. ≤ 32°F	0	0	0	0	0	0	0	0	0	0	0	0	0
Days Minimum Temp. ≤ 32°F	13	6	3	2	0	0	0	0	0	1	4	12	41
Days Minimum Temp. ≤ 0°F	0	0	0	0	0	0	0	0	0	0	0	0	0
Heating Degree Days (base 65°F)	569	403	314	185	56	9	0	0	4	79	348	568	2,535
Cooling Degree Days (base 65°F)	0	0	3	38	155	320	511	462	319	108	2	0	1,918
Mean Precipitation (in.)	2.17	2.14	2.21	1.11	0.46	0.14	0.02	0.08	0.21	0.53	1.55	1.35	11.97
Extreme Maximum Daily Precip. (in.)	***2.19***	***1.68***	2.05	1.57	0.99	0.74	0.24	1.34	1.34	1.40	1.83	1.65	***2.19***
Days With ≥ 0.1" Precipitation	4	5	5	2	1	0	0	0	0	1	3	3	24
Days With ≥ 0.5" Precipitation	1	1	2	1	0	0	0	0	0	0	1	1	7
Days With ≥ 1.0" Precipitation	0	0	0	0	0	0	0	0	0	0	0	0	0
Mean Snowfall (in.)	0.0	0.0	0.0	0.0	0.0	0.0	0.0	0.0	0.0	0.0	0.0	trace	trace
Maximum Snow Depth (in.)	0	0	0	0	0	0	0	0	0	0	0	0	0
Days With ≥ 1.0" Snow Depth	0	0	0	0	0	0	0	0	0	0	0	0	0

Tulelake *Siskiyou County* Elevation: 4,035 ft. Latitude: 41° 57' N Longitude: 121° 28' W

	JAN	FEB	MAR	APR	MAY	JUN	JUL	AUG	SEP	OCT	NOV	DEC	YEAR
Mean Maximum Temp. (°F)	40.5	45.8	52.4	59.5	68.0	76.1	84.3	84.1	77.0	65.1	47.9	39.5	61.7
Mean Temp. (°F)	30.7	34.5	39.2	44.8	52.8	59.4	65.4	64.0	57.2	47.9	36.6	29.9	46.9
Mean Minimum Temp. (°F)	20.9	23.1	26.0	30.1	37.5	42.8	46.5	43.9	37.4	30.6	25.2	20.2	32.0
Extreme Maximum Temp. (°F)	60	69	76	84	95	96	101	102	99	89	71	59	102
Extreme Minimum Temp. (°F)	-14	-24	6	10	16	24	31	27	21	7	-9	-16	-24
Days Maximum Temp. ≥ 90°F	0	0	0	0	0	1	7	6	2	0	0	0	16
Days Maximum Temp. ≤ 32°F	4	2	0	0	0	0	0	0	0	0	1	5	12
Days Minimum Temp. ≤ 32°F	28	24	25	19	8	1	0	0	6	19	24	28	182
Days Minimum Temp. ≤ 0°F	1	1	0	0	0	0	0	0	0	0	0	1	3
Heating Degree Days (base 65°F)	1,055	857	792	599	378	183	60	74	234	524	846	1,083	6,685
Cooling Degree Days (base 65°F)	0	0	0	0	0	5	23	80	50	9	0	0	167
Mean Precipitation (in.)	1.37	1.18	1.14	0.98	1.10	0.82	0.34	0.33	0.49	0.79	1.35	1.41	11.30
Extreme Maximum Daily Precip. (in.)	1.20	1.32	1.32	1.03	0.82	1.28	1.05	1.37	1.22	0.84	1.21	1.65	1.65
Days With ≥ 0.1" Precipitation	5	4	4	3	4	2	1	1	1	2	4	4	35
Days With ≥ 0.5" Precipitation	0	0	0	0	0	0	0	0	0	0	0	1	1
Days With ≥ 1.0" Precipitation	0	0	0	0	0	0	0	0	0	0	0	0	0
Mean Snowfall (in.)	6.1	4.0	2.3	1.1	0.1	0.0	0.0	0.0	0.0	0.2	3.3	5.8	22.9
Maximum Snow Depth (in.)	21	11	4	2	0	0	0	0	0	1	5	10	21
Days With ≥ 1.0" Snow Depth	7	5	1	0	0	0	0	0	0	0	3	7	23

Victorville Pump Plant *San Bernardino County* Elevation: 2,857 ft. Latitude: 34° 32' N Longitude: 117° 18' W

	JAN	FEB	MAR	APR	MAY	JUN	JUL	AUG	SEP	OCT	NOV	DEC	YEAR
Mean Maximum Temp. (°F)	59.9	62.7	67.9	74.9	83.6	92.7	98.4	98.2	91.9	80.8	67.9	59.3	78.2
Mean Temp. (°F)	46.0	49.0	53.1	59.0	66.5	74.2	80.2	80.0	73.8	63.2	52.1	45.0	61.8
Mean Minimum Temp. (°F)	32.0	35.1	38.4	43.0	49.4	55.6	62.0	61.6	55.6	45.6	36.3	30.7	45.4
Extreme Maximum Temp. (°F)	79	84	93	100	108	111	116	112	113	101	88	79	116
Extreme Minimum Temp. (°F)	9	16	21	25	32	36	36	44	34	28	16	6	6
Days Maximum Temp. ≥ 90°F	0	0	0	2	9	20	27	28	20	6	0	0	112
Days Maximum Temp. ≤ 32°F	0	0	0	0	0	0	0	0	0	0	0	0	0
Days Minimum Temp. ≤ 32°F	18	10	5	1	0	0	0	0	0	1	9	20	64
Days Minimum Temp. ≤ 0°F	0	0	0	0	0	0	0	0	0	0	0	0	0
Heating Degree Days (base 65°F)	583	447	363	203	73	12	2	0	13	116	381	612	2,805
Cooling Degree Days (base 65°F)	0	0	3	29	127	294	479	471	283	67	1	0	1,754
Mean Precipitation (in.)	0.98	1.33	1.02	0.35	0.16	0.05	0.19	0.21	0.19	0.36	0.45	0.87	6.16
Extreme Maximum Daily Precip. (in.)	1.50	3.00	2.68	1.16	0.82	0.64	0.98	0.81	1.06	1.65	1.38	1.70	3.00
Days With ≥ 0.1" Precipitation	2	3	2	1	0	0	1	0	1	1	1	2	14
Days With ≥ 0.5" Precipitation	1	1	1	0	0	0	0	0	0	0	0	1	4
Days With ≥ 1.0" Precipitation	0	0	0	0	0	0	0	0	0	0	0	0	0
Mean Snowfall (in.)	trace	trace	0.0	0.0	0.0	0.0	0.0	0.0	0.0	0.0	0.0	0.0	trace
Maximum Snow Depth (in.)	0	0	0	0	0	0	0	0	0	0	0	0	0
Days With ≥ 1.0" Snow Depth	0	0	0	0	0	0	0	0	0	0	0	0	0

The period of record for all cooperative weather station data is 1980 – 2009. See User Guide for detailed explanation of data.

Visalia *Tulare County* Elevation: 325 ft. Latitude: 36° 20' N Longitude: 119° 18' W

	JAN	FEB	MAR	APR	MAY	JUN	JUL	AUG	SEP	OCT	NOV	DEC	YEAR
Mean Maximum Temp. (°F)	55.0	61.8	67.5	73.9	82.1	89.3	94.4	93.2	88.1	78.3	64.8	54.8	75.3
Mean Temp. (°F)	46.9	52.0	56.8	61.6	69.0	75.4	80.5	79.0	74.1	65.4	54.2	46.3	63.4
Mean Minimum Temp. (°F)	38.7	42.2	46.1	49.4	55.8	61.4	66.5	64.7	60.2	52.5	43.6	37.7	51.6
Extreme Maximum Temp. (°F)	79	81	87	97	105	107	108	105	104	98	86	78	108
Extreme Minimum Temp. (°F)	23	27	31	34	41	48	52	55	41	38	30	21	21
Days Maximum Temp. ≥ 90°F	0	0	0	1	6	15	25	23	13	2	0	0	85
Days Maximum Temp. ≤ 32°F	0	0	0	0	0	0	0	0	0	0	0	0	0
Days Minimum Temp. ≤ 32°F	4	1	0	0	0	0	0	0	0	0	0	6	11
Days Minimum Temp. ≤ 0°F	0	0	0	0	0	0	0	0	0	0	0	0	0
Heating Degree Days (base 65°F)	555	360	252	134	33	3	0	0	3	63	319	574	2,296
Cooling Degree Days (base 65°F)	0	0	5	41	164	320	486	440	284	82	1	0	1,823
Mean Precipitation (in.)	2.11	1.87	1.93	0.97	0.35	0.14	0.01	0.01	0.15	0.55	1.09	1.59	10.77
Extreme Maximum Daily Precip. (in.)	3.00	2.15	1.60	2.22	0.73	0.95	0.25	0.11	0.90	1.47	1.57	2.41	3.00
Days With ≥ 0.1" Precipitation	5	5	5	2	1	0	0	0	0	1	3	4	26
Days With ≥ 0.5" Precipitation	1	1	1	1	0	0	0	0	0	0	1	1	6
Days With ≥ 1.0" Precipitation	0	0	0	0	0	0	0	0	0	0	0	0	0
Mean Snowfall (in.)	0.1	0.0	0.0	0.0	0.0	0.0	0.0	0.0	0.0	0.0	0.0	0.0	0.1
Maximum Snow Depth (in.)	2	0	0	0	0	0	0	0	0	0	0	0	2
Days With ≥ 1.0" Snow Depth	0	0	0	0	0	0	0	0	0	0	0	0	0

Woodland 1 WNW *Yolo County* Elevation: 68 ft. Latitude: 38° 41' N Longitude: 121° 48' W

	JAN	FEB	MAR	APR	MAY	JUN	JUL	AUG	SEP	OCT	NOV	DEC	YEAR
Mean Maximum Temp. (°F)	54.5	60.4	66.7	73.6	82.2	90.0	95.2	94.1	89.9	79.0	64.5	54.6	75.4
Mean Temp. (°F)	47.0	51.5	56.2	61.0	68.0	74.1	77.6	76.6	73.8	65.4	54.5	46.7	62.7
Mean Minimum Temp. (°F)	39.4	42.5	45.6	48.3	53.8	58.2	59.9	59.0	57.7	51.9	44.4	38.8	49.9
Extreme Maximum Temp. (°F)	73	77	85	97	105	109	113	110	107	105	84	73	113
Extreme Minimum Temp. (°F)	23	25	32	33	39	46	49	50	47	38	28	19	19
Days Maximum Temp. ≥ 90°F	0	0	0	1	7	16	25	24	17	4	0	0	94
Days Maximum Temp. ≤ 32°F	0	0	0	0	0	0	0	0	0	0	0	0	0
Days Minimum Temp. ≤ 32°F	4	1	0	0	0	0	0	0	0	0	1	5	11
Days Minimum Temp. ≤ 0°F	0	0	0	0	0	0	0	0	0	0	0	0	0
Heating Degree Days (base 65°F)	551	376	272	149	40	4	0	0	3	62	310	559	2,326
Cooling Degree Days (base 65°F)	0	0	5	35	140	283	397	366	273	82	1	0	1,582
Mean Precipitation (in.)	4.27	4.51	3.00	1.29	0.64	0.16	0.01	0.07	0.37	1.05	2.37	3.55	21.29
Extreme Maximum Daily Precip. (in.)	3.18	3.39	2.15	2.70	2.03	0.47	0.11	0.97	2.74	2.74	2.13	3.60	3.60
Days With ≥ 0.1" Precipitation	7	7	6	3	2	1	0	0	1	2	4	6	39
Days With ≥ 0.5" Precipitation	3	3	2	1	0	0	0	0	0	1	2	2	14
Days With ≥ 1.0" Precipitation	1	1	1	0	0	0	0	0	0	0	0	1	4
Mean Snowfall (in.)	0.0	0.0	0.0	0.0	0.0	0.0	0.0	0.0	0.0	0.0	0.0	trace	trace
Maximum Snow Depth (in.)	trace	0	0	0	0	0	0	0	0	0	0	0	trace
Days With ≥ 1.0" Snow Depth	0	0	0	0	0	0	0	0	0	0	0	0	0

Woodside Fire Stn 1 *San Mateo County* Elevation: 379 ft. Latitude: 37° 26' N Longitude: 122° 15' W

	JAN	FEB	MAR	APR	MAY	JUN	JUL	AUG	SEP	OCT	NOV	DEC	YEAR
Mean Maximum Temp. (°F)	60.5	63.9	***68.2***	73.1	78.3	83.8	***88.5***	***88.7***	***86.2***	***79.3***	***67.1***	***60.2***	***74.8***
Mean Temp. (°F)	48.8	51.6	***54.7***	57.9	62.2	66.3	***70.1***	***69.8***	***68.0***	***62.5***	***53.8***	***48.5***	***59.5***
Mean Minimum Temp. (°F)	37.0	39.2	***41.2***	42.6	46.0	48.7	***51.6***	***50.9***	***49.8***	***45.6***	***40.4***	***36.9***	***44.2***
Extreme Maximum Temp. (°F)	84	84	91	99	105	***108***	114	114	108	***106***	***90***	***76***	***114***
Extreme Minimum Temp. (°F)	21	17	29	30	33	***36***	38	38	38	***30***	***23***	***20***	***17***
Days Maximum Temp. ≥ 90°F	0	0	0	1	3	7	12	12	9	***3***	0	0	***47***
Days Maximum Temp. ≤ 32°F	0	0	0	0	0	0	0	0	0	***0***	0	0	***0***
Days Minimum Temp. ≤ 32°F	10	4	1	0	0	0	0	0	0	***0***	3	10	***28***
Days Minimum Temp. ≤ 0°F	0	0	0	0	0	0	0	0	0	***0***	0	0	***0***
Heating Degree Days (base 65°F)	497	373	***313***	219	119	45	***8***	***6***	***22***	***107***	***331***	***503***	***2,543***
Cooling Degree Days (base 65°F)	0	0	***2***	11	39	90	***173***	***162***	***120***	***36***	***1***	***0***	***634***
Mean Precipitation (in.)	6.09	6.02	4.40	1.77	0.76	0.16	0.01	0.05	0.18	1.25	3.67	5.70	30.06
Extreme Maximum Daily Precip. (in.)	4.15	***3.21***	2.60	2.00	0.88	***0.86***	0.17	0.86	0.58	***2.70***	***3.53***	***4.64***	***4.64***
Days With ≥ 0.1" Precipitation	8	8	8	4	2	0	0	0	1	2	5	7	45
Days With ≥ 0.5" Precipitation	4	4	3	1	0	0	0	0	0	1	3	4	20
Days With ≥ 1.0" Precipitation	2	2	1	0	0	0	0	0	0	0	1	2	8
Mean Snowfall (in.)	0.0	0.0	0.0	0.0	0.0	0.0	0.0	0.0	0.0	0.0	0.0	0.0	0.0
Maximum Snow Depth (in.)	0	0	0	0	0	***0***	0	0	0	***0***	0	0	***0***
Days With ≥ 1.0" Snow Depth	0	0	0	0	0	0	0	0	0	***0***	0	0	***0***

Yreka *Siskiyou County* Elevation: 2,625 ft. Latitude: 41° 42' N Longitude: 122° 38' W

	JAN	FEB	MAR	APR	MAY	JUN	JUL	AUG	SEP	OCT	NOV	DEC	YEAR
Mean Maximum Temp. (°F)	45.9	51.4	57.9	64.1	73.4	81.6	91.7	91.2	83.1	70.3	53.0	44.8	67.4
Mean Temp. (°F)	35.3	39.1	43.9	49.1	56.8	63.7	71.7	70.8	63.5	52.8	40.9	34.6	51.9
Mean Minimum Temp. (°F)	24.7	26.6	29.9	34.1	40.2	45.8	51.8	50.4	43.8	35.2	28.8	24.3	36.3
Extreme Maximum Temp. (°F)	64	73	79	91	103	106	109	110	106	93	76	65	110
Extreme Minimum Temp. (°F)	6	-2	12	17	21	31	34	33	28	12	10	-5	-5
Days Maximum Temp. ≥ 90°F	0	0	0	0	3	7	20	20	9	1	0	0	60
Days Maximum Temp. ≤ 32°F	0	0	0	0	0	0	0	0	0	0	0	1	1
Days Minimum Temp. ≤ 32°F	27	23	22	12	4	0	0	0	1	10	22	27	148
Days Minimum Temp. ≤ 0°F	0	0	0	0	0	0	0	0	0	0	0	0	0
Heating Degree Days (base 65°F)	913	727	647	470	270	109	17	14	105	375	716	937	5,300
Cooling Degree Days (base 65°F)	0	0	0	1	24	78	232	201	66	3	0	0	605
Mean Precipitation (in.)	3.15	2.12	1.60	1.20	1.31	1.00	0.51	0.36	0.56	1.03	2.88	3.96	19.68
Extreme Maximum Daily Precip. (in.)	2.62	1.83	1.35	1.28	2.80	1.93	0.77	1.02	2.15	1.50	2.38	3.28	3.28
Days With ≥ 0.1" Precipitation	7	5	4	3	4	2	1	1	1	3	6	7	44
Days With ≥ 0.5" Precipitation	2	1	1	0	1	0	0	0	0	1	2	2	10
Days With ≥ 1.0" Precipitation	1	0	0	0	0	0	0	0	0	0	1	1	3
Mean Snowfall (in.)	3.7	2.5	0.8	0.2	trace	0.0	0.0	0.0	0.0	0.1	1.2	3.7	12.2
Maximum Snow Depth (in.)	14	10	1	***2***	0	***0***	0	0	0	***0***	5	12	***14***
Days With ≥ 1.0" Snow Depth	2	1	0	0	0	0	0	0	0	0	1	2	6

The period of record for all cooperative weather station data is 1980 – 2009. See User Guide for detailed explanation of data.

California Weather Station Rankings

Annual Extreme Maximum Temperature

Highest			Lowest		
Rank	**Station Name**	**°F**	**Rank**	**Station Name**	**°F**
1	Death Valley	129	1	Eureka	87
2	Needles Airport	125	2	Bodie	91
3	Parker Reservoir	123	3	Crescent City 3 NNW	93
4	Blythe	122	4	Big Bear Lake	94
4	Borrego Desert Park	122	4	Fort Bragg 5 N	94
6	Hayfield Pumping Plant	119	6	Calaveras Big Trees	98
7	Ash Mountain	118	6	San Francisco Oceanside	***98***
7	Redlands	118	8	Donner Memorial St Pk	99
9	Haiwee	117	8	Palomar Mountain Observatory	99
10	Canoga Park Pierce College	***116***	8	Santa Monica Pier	***99***
10	Newman	***116***	11	Canyon Dam	102
10	Riverside Fire Sta 3	116	11	Jess Valley	102
10	Victorville Pump Plant	116	11	Morro Bay Fire Dept	102
14	Barstow Fire Station	115	11	Tulelake	102
14	Coalinga	115	15	Boca	103
14	Covelo	115	15	Callahan	103
14	Elsinore	115	15	Cuyamaca	103
14	Stockton Metropolitan Arpt	115	15	Lava Beds Nat Monument	103
19	Fairfield	114	15	San Francisco	103
19	Friant Government Camp	114	20	Doyle 4 SSE	104
19	Independence	114	20	Laguna Beach	***104***
19	Woodside Fire Stn 1	***114***	22	Angwin Pac Union Col	105
23	Cachuma Lake	113	22	Salinas No 2	105
23	Camp Pardee	113	22	San Francisco Int'l Arpt	105
23	Fresno Air Terminal	113	22	Santa Barbara	***105***

Annual Mean Maximum Temperature

Highest			Lowest		
Rank	**Station Name**	**°F**	**Rank**	**Station Name**	**°F**
1	Death Valley	91.3	1	Bodie	57.0
2	Blythe	***88.3***	2	Donner Memorial St Pk	59.0
3	Borrego Desert Park	87.9	3	Eureka	59.9
4	Needles Airport	87.1	4	Calaveras Big Trees	60.0
5	Parker Reservoir	86.6	5	Crescent City 3 NNW	60.2
6	Hayfield Pumping Plant	85.1	6	Jess Valley	60.4
7	Canoga Park Pierce College	***81.3***	7	Fort Bragg 5 N	60.7
8	Elsinore	***80.8***	8	Canyon Dam	61.1
8	Riverside Fire Sta 3	80.8	9	Lava Beds Nat Monument	***61.4***
10	Barstow Fire Station	80.3	10	San Francisco Oceanside	***61.5***
11	Coalinga	79.9	11	Cedarville	61.7
12	Redlands	79.7	11	Tulelake	61.7
13	Porterville	***78.9***	13	Boca	62.2
14	Cachuma Lake	78.2	14	Big Bear Lake	62.8
14	Victorville Pump Plant	78.2	15	Alturas	63.9
16	Burbank Valley Pump Plant	77.8	16	Doyle 4 SSE	64.7
16	Ojai	77.8	17	Morro Bay Fire Dept	64.9
16	Tejon Rancho	77.8	18	Callahan	65.1
19	Friant Government Camp	77.7	19	San Francisco	65.2
19	Newman	***77.7***	20	Palomar Mountain Observatory	65.7
21	Bakersfield Meadows Field	77.6	21	San Francisco Int'l Arpt	65.8
22	Escondido No 2	***77.2***	22	Berkeley	***66.2***
23	Ash Mountain	77.1	23	Santa Monica Pier	***66.4***
24	Fresno Air Terminal	76.9	24	Cuyamaca	66.6
25	Independence	76.5	25	Yreka	67.4

Rankings include 25 highest/lowest stations. If state has less than 25 stations, all stations are included. The period of record is 1980–2009. See User Guide for detailed explanation of data.

Annual Mean Temperature

Highest			Lowest		
Rank	Station Name	°F	Rank	Station Name	°F
1	Death Valley	76.7	1	Bodie	38.3
2	Needles Airport	74.5	2	Boca	43.5
2	Parker Reservoir	74.5	2	Donner Memorial St Pk	43.5
4	Borrego Desert Park	73.2	4	Jess Valley	46.1
5	Blythe	***72.7***	5	Alturas	46.7
6	Hayfield Pumping Plant	70.1	6	Tulelake	46.9
7	Los Angeles Civic Center	66.6	7	Big Bear Lake	47.8
8	Riverside Fire Sta 3	66.5	8	Canyon Dam	48.0
9	Barstow Fire Station	65.4	9	Lava Beds Nat Monument	***48.4***
9	Redlands	65.4	10	Cedarville	48.6
11	Bakersfield Meadows Field	65.2	11	Calaveras Big Trees	49.6
11	Elsinore	***65.2***	12	Doyle 4 SSE	50.1
13	Coalinga	65.1	13	Callahan	50.6
13	Porterville	***65.1***	14	Yreka	51.9
15	Burbank Valley Pump Plant	64.9	15	Fort Bragg 5 N	52.6
15	Long Beach Daugherty Fld	64.9	16	Crescent City 3 NNW	52.9
17	Escondido No 2	***64.8***	17	Cuyamaca	53.5
18	Canoga Park Pierce College	***64.6***	17	Eureka	53.5
19	Fresno Air Terminal	64.4	19	Dunsmuir Treatment Plant	54.5
20	San Diego Lindbergh Field	64.2	20	San Francisco Oceanside	***55.8***
21	Culver City	***64.0***	21	Bishop Arpt	56.1
22	Ash Mountain	63.8	21	De Sabla	56.1
23	Chula Vista	***63.5***	23	Covelo	56.3
24	Visalia	63.4	23	Morro Bay Fire Dept	56.3
25	Los Angeles Intl Arpt	63.3	23	Palomar Mountain Observatory	56.3

Annual Mean Minimum Temperature

Highest			Lowest		
Rank	Station Name	°F	Rank	Station Name	°F
1	Parker Reservoir	62.4	1	Bodie	19.5
2	Death Valley	62.0	2	Boca	24.7
3	Needles Airport	61.9	3	Donner Memorial St Pk	28.0
4	Borrego Desert Park	58.5	4	Alturas	29.5
5	San Diego Lindbergh Field	58.1	5	Jess Valley	31.8
6	Los Angeles Civic Center	57.5	6	Tulelake	32.0
7	Blythe	***57.1***	7	Big Bear Lake	32.8
8	Santa Monica Pier	***56.7***	8	Canyon Dam	34.8
9	Los Angeles Intl Arpt	56.2	9	Lava Beds Nat Monument	***35.4***
10	Long Beach Daugherty Fld	55.4	10	Cedarville	35.5
11	Chula Vista	***55.1***	10	Doyle 4 SSE	35.5
11	Hayfield Pumping Plant	55.1	12	Callahan	36.1
13	Culver City	***55.0***	13	Yreka	36.3
14	Mitchell Caverns	53.0	14	Bishop Arpt	37.7
15	Bakersfield Meadows Field	52.8	15	Calaveras Big Trees	39.1
16	Santa Barbara	***52.7***	16	Dunsmuir Treatment Plant	40.1
17	Escondido No 2	***52.4***	17	Covelo	40.3
18	Riverside Fire Sta 3	52.2	18	Cuyamaca	40.4
19	Burbank Valley Pump Plant	52.0	19	Graton	42.3
20	Fresno Air Terminal	51.9	20	De Sabla	42.4
21	Visalia	51.6	21	Ben Lomond No 4	43.6
22	Laguna Beach	***51.4***	22	El Mirage	44.0
23	San Francisco	51.3	23	Woodside Fire Stn 1	***44.2***
24	Porterville	***51.2***	24	Calistoga	***44.4***
25	Redlands	51.0	25	Fort Bragg 5 N	44.5

Rankings include 25 highest/lowest stations. If state has less than 25 stations, all stations are included. The period of record is 1980–2009. See User Guide for detailed explanation of data.

Annual Extreme Minimum Temperature

Highest			Lowest		
Rank	Station Name	°F	Rank	Station Name	°F
1	Santa Monica Pier	***35***	1	Boca	-43
2	San Diego Lindbergh Field	34	2	Alturas	-33
3	Los Angeles Civic Center	33	2	Bodie	-33
3	Los Angeles Intl Arpt	33	4	Cedarville	-28
5	Culver City	32	4	Jess Valley	-28
6	Long Beach Daugherty Fld	28	6	Donner Memorial St Pk	-27
7	Laguna Beach	***27***	7	Doyle 4 SSE	-25
7	San Francisco Int'l Arpt	27	8	Tulelake	-24
9	San Francisco Oceanside	***26***	9	Lava Beds Nat Monument	-18
10	Escondido No 2	***25***	10	Canyon Dam	-11
10	Parker Reservoir	25	11	Big Bear Lake	-8
12	Berkeley	***24***	11	Bishop Arpt	-8
13	Borrego Desert Park	23	11	Haiwee	-8
13	San Francisco	23	14	Callahan	-6
15	Burbank Valley Pump Plant	22	15	Yreka	-5
15	Morro Bay Fire Dept	22	16	Independence	-2
15	Riverside Fire Sta 3	22	17	Blythe	0
15	Salinas No 2	22	17	Death Valley	0
15	Santa Barbara	***22***	19	El Mirage	1
20	Santa Maria Public Arpt	21	20	Calaveras Big Trees	3
20	Visalia	21	21	Cuyamaca	4
22	Antioch Pump Plant #3	20	21	Dunsmuir Treatment Plant	4
22	Balch Power House	20	21	Eureka	4
24	Bakersfield Meadows Field	19	24	Orleans	5
24	Crescent City 3 NNW	19	25	De Sabla	6

July Mean Maximum Temperature

Highest			Lowest		
Rank	Station Name	°F	Rank	Station Name	°F
1	Death Valley	116.4	1	San Francisco Oceanside	62.9
2	Needles Airport	109.3	2	Eureka	63.9
3	Blythe	***108.7***	3	Crescent City 3 NNW	65.7
4	Parker Reservoir	107.7	4	Morro Bay Fire Dept	65.8
5	Borrego Desert Park	107.5	5	Fort Bragg 5 N	66.4
6	Hayfield Pumping Plant	104.8	6	San Francisco	68.2
7	Barstow Fire Station	102.1	7	Santa Monica Pier	69.8
8	Coalinga	100.2	8	Salinas No 2	71.6
9	Friant Government Camp	99.7	9	San Francisco Int'l Arpt	72.1
10	Independence	99.6	10	Berkeley	72.6
11	Ash Mountain	98.7	11	Santa Maria Public Arpt	73.7
12	Fresno Air Terminal	98.6	12	Santa Barbara	75.2
13	Victorville Pump Plant	98.4	13	Los Angeles Intl Arpt	75.4
14	El Mirage	98.1	14	San Diego Lindbergh Field	75.5
15	Porterville	***98.0***	15	Chula Vista	***75.7***
16	Bishop Arpt	97.9	16	Bodie	77.5
17	Bakersfield Meadows Field	97.8	17	Laguna Beach	78.7
17	Elsinore	***97.8***	18	Culver City	79.6
19	Tejon Rancho	97.6	19	Calaveras Big Trees	80.6
20	Haiwee	96.8	20	Hollister 2	80.8
20	Newman	96.8	21	Donner Memorial St Pk	81.2
22	Camp Pardee	95.3	22	Big Bear Lake	81.4
22	Canoga Park Pierce College	95.3	23	Petaluma Fire Station 2	82.0
24	Woodland 1 WNW	95.2	24	Long Beach Daugherty Fld	82.2
25	Redlands	95.1	25	Jess Valley	83.4

Rankings include 25 highest/lowest stations. If state has less than 25 stations, all stations are included. The period of record is 1980–2009. See User Guide for detailed explanation of data.

January Mean Minimum Temperature

Highest Rank	Station Name	°F	Lowest Rank	Station Name	°F
1	Santa Monica Pier	50.8	1	Bodie	6.1
2	Los Angeles Civic Center	49.8	2	Boca	11.4
3	San Diego Lindbergh Field	49.7	3	Donner Memorial St Pk	15.6
4	Los Angeles Intl Arpt	48.9	4	Alturas	17.9
5	Culver City	47.7	5	Jess Valley	20.5
6	Long Beach Daugherty Fld	46.4	6	Tulelake	20.9
7	San Francisco	46.3	7	Cedarville	21.0
8	Chula Vista	46.0	8	Big Bear Lake	21.6
9	Santa Barbara	45.8	9	Bishop Arpt	22.8
10	San Francisco Oceanside	***45.0***	10	Lava Beds Nat Monument	23.1
11	Borrego Desert Park	44.5	11	Doyle 4 SSE	23.8
12	San Francisco Int'l Arpt	43.9	12	Canyon Dam	24.0
13	Parker Reservoir	43.8	13	Yreka	24.7
14	Berkeley	***43.7***	14	Callahan	26.4
14	Needles Airport	43.7	15	Haiwee	28.7
16	Laguna Beach	***43.5***	16	Calaveras Big Trees	28.8
17	Escondido No 2	***43.0***	17	Independence	29.0
18	Riverside Fire Sta 3	42.7	18	El Mirage	30.0
19	Burbank Valley Pump Plant	42.4	19	Dunsmuir Treatment Plant	30.1
19	Morro Bay Fire Dept	42.4	20	Cuyamaca	30.7
21	Eureka	41.7	21	Covelo	31.9
22	Salinas No 2	41.5	22	Victorville Pump Plant	32.0
23	Redlands	41.3	23	De Sabla	32.5
24	Crescent City 3 NNW	40.8	24	Tejon Rancho	33.6
25	Blythe	40.2	25	Barstow Fire Station	34.7

Number of Days Annually Maximum Temperature ≥ 90°F

Highest Rank	Station Name	Days	Lowest Rank	Station Name	Days
1	Death Valley	194	1	Bodie	0
2	Borrego Desert Park	175	1	Crescent City 3 NNW	0
3	Blythe	172	1	Eureka	0
3	Parker Reservoir	172	1	Fort Bragg 5 N	0
5	Needles Airport	170	1	Morro Bay Fire Dept	0
6	Hayfield Pumping Plant	157	1	San Francisco Oceanside	0
7	Barstow Fire Station	132	1	Santa Monica Pier	***0***
8	Coalinga	126	8	Big Bear Lake	1
9	Porterville	***119***	9	Chula Vista	2
10	Friant Government Camp	117	9	San Diego Lindbergh Field	2
11	Victorville Pump Plant	112	11	Calaveras Big Trees	3
12	Canoga Park Pierce College	***111***	11	Laguna Beach	3
12	Fresno Air Terminal	111	11	Los Angeles Intl Arpt	3
14	Independence	110	11	San Francisco	3
15	Elsinore	***108***	11	San Francisco Int'l Arpt	3
15	Newman	***108***	11	Santa Barbara	***3***
17	Ash Mountain	107	17	Berkeley	***4***
17	Bakersfield Meadows Field	107	17	Santa Maria Public Arpt	4
19	Tejon Rancho	106	19	Donner Memorial St Pk	5
20	El Mirage	105	19	Salinas No 2	5
21	Redlands	104	21	Culver City	7
22	Riverside Fire Sta 3	103	22	Palomar Mountain Observatory	10
23	Bishop Arpt	98	23	Jess Valley	12
23	Haiwee	98	24	Boca	14
25	Woodland 1 WNW	94	24	Canyon Dam	14

Rankings include 25 highest/lowest stations. If state has less than 25 stations, all stations are included. The period of record is 1980–2009. See User Guide for detailed explanation of data.

Number of Days Annually Maximum Temperature ≤ 32°F

Highest			Lowest		
Rank	Station Name	Days	Rank	Station Name	Days
1	Bodie	22	1	Angwin Pac Union Col	0
2	Donner Memorial St Pk	18	1	Antioch Pump Plant #3	0
3	Jess Valley	14	1	Ash Mountain	0
4	Cedarville	13	1	Auberry 2 NW	0
5	Tulelake	12	1	Auburn	0
6	Lava Beds Nat Monument	10	1	Bakersfield Meadows Field	0
7	Boca	9	1	Balch Power House	0
7	Calaveras Big Trees	9	1	Barstow Fire Station	0
7	Doyle 4 SSE	9	1	Ben Lomond No 4	0
10	Alturas	7	1	Berkeley	*0*
10	Canyon Dam	7	1	Bishop Arpt	0
12	Big Bear Lake	5	1	Blythe	0
13	Palomar Mountain Observatory	3	1	Borrego Desert Park	0
14	Callahan	2	1	Burbank Valley Pump Plant	0
15	Yreka	1	1	Cachuma Lake	0
16	Angwin Pac Union Col	0	1	Calistoga	0
16	Antioch Pump Plant #3	0	1	Camp Pardee	0
16	Ash Mountain	0	1	Canoga Park Pierce College	*0*
16	Auberry 2 NW	0	1	Chula Vista	0
16	Auburn	0	1	Coalinga	0
16	Bakersfield Meadows Field	0	1	Colfax	0
16	Balch Power House	0	1	Colusa 2 SSW	0
16	Barstow Fire Station	0	1	Covelo	0
16	Ben Lomond No 4	0	1	Crescent City 3 NNW	0
16	Berkeley	*0*	1	Culver City	0

Number of Days Annually Minimum Temperature ≤ 32°F

Highest			Lowest		
Rank	Station Name	Days	Rank	Station Name	Days
1	Bodie	303	1	Berkeley	*0*
2	Boca	270	1	Chula Vista	0
3	Donner Memorial St Pk	231	1	Culver City	0
4	Alturas	202	1	Long Beach Daugherty Fld	0
5	Big Bear Lake	187	1	Los Angeles Civic Center	0
5	Jess Valley	187	1	Los Angeles Intl Arpt	0
7	Tulelake	182	1	San Diego Lindbergh Field	0
8	Canyon Dam	167	1	San Francisco	0
9	Lava Beds Nat Monument	162	1	San Francisco Int'l Arpt	0
10	Cedarville	157	1	San Francisco Oceanside	0
11	Yreka	148	1	Santa Barbara	*0*
12	Doyle 4 SSE	146	1	Santa Monica Pier	*0*
13	Callahan	145	13	Parker Reservoir	1
14	Bishop Arpt	141	14	Borrego Desert Park	2
15	Calaveras Big Trees	121	14	Laguna Beach	2
16	Dunsmuir Treatment Plant	100	14	Needles Airport	2
17	Cuyamaca	96	17	Burbank Valley Pump Plant	3
18	Covelo	79	17	Escondido No 2	*3*
18	Haiwee	79	19	Morro Bay Fire Dept	4
18	Independence	79	19	Redlands	4
21	El Mirage	77	19	Riverside Fire Sta 3	4
22	De Sabla	71	22	Eureka	6
23	Victorville Pump Plant	64	22	Salinas No 2	6
24	Palomar Mountain Observatory	57	24	Blythe	8
25	Graton	44	25	Camp Pardee	9

Rankings include 25 highest/lowest stations. If state has less than 25 stations, all stations are included. The period of record is 1980–2009. See User Guide for detailed explanation of data.

Number of Days Annually Minimum Temperature ≤ 0°F

Highest Rank	Station Name	Days	Lowest Rank	Station Name	Days
1	Bodie	31	1	Angwin Pac Union Col	0
2	Boca	12	1	Antioch Pump Plant #3	0
3	Alturas	5	1	Ash Mountain	0
4	Donner Memorial St Pk	4	1	Auberry 2 NW	0
4	Jess Valley	4	1	Auburn	0
6	Tulelake	3	1	Bakersfield Meadows Field	0
7	Cedarville	1	1	Balch Power House	0
7	Doyle 4 SSE	1	1	Barstow Fire Station	0
9	Angwin Pac Union Col	0	1	Ben Lomond No 4	0
9	Antioch Pump Plant #3	0	1	Berkeley	*0*
9	Ash Mountain	0	1	Big Bear Lake	0
9	Auberry 2 NW	0	1	Bishop Arpt	0
9	Auburn	0	1	Blythe	0
9	Bakersfield Meadows Field	0	1	Borrego Desert Park	0
9	Balch Power House	0	1	Burbank Valley Pump Plant	0
9	Barstow Fire Station	0	1	Cachuma Lake	0
9	Ben Lomond No 4	0	1	Calaveras Big Trees	0
9	Berkeley	*0*	1	Calistoga	0
9	Big Bear Lake	0	1	Callahan	0
9	Bishop Arpt	0	1	Camp Pardee	0
9	Blythe	0	1	Canoga Park Pierce College	*0*
9	Borrego Desert Park	0	1	Canyon Dam	0
9	Burbank Valley Pump Plant	0	1	Chula Vista	0
9	Cachuma Lake	0	1	Coalinga	0
9	Calaveras Big Trees	0	1	Colfax	0

Number of Annual Heating Degree Days

Highest Rank	Station Name	Num.	Lowest Rank	Station Name	Num.
1	Bodie	9,658	1	Los Angeles Civic Center	850
2	Boca	7,796	2	Borrego Desert Park	913
3	Donner Memorial St Pk	7,791	3	San Diego Lindbergh Field	1,047
4	Jess Valley	6,963	4	Parker Reservoir	1,049
5	Alturas	6,782	5	Needles Airport	1,077
6	Tulelake	6,685	6	Death Valley	1,133
7	Cedarville	6,344	7	Blythe	*1,151*
8	Lava Beds Nat Monument	*6,338*	8	Long Beach Daugherty Fld	1,152
9	Canyon Dam	6,336	9	Culver City	*1,175*
10	Big Bear Lake	6,267	10	Los Angeles Intl Arpt	1,219
11	Calaveras Big Trees	5,803	11	Chula Vista	*1,235*
12	Doyle 4 SSE	5,682	12	Riverside Fire Sta 3	1,267
13	Callahan	5,451	13	Escondido No 2	*1,319*
14	Yreka	5,300	14	Burbank Valley Pump Plant	1,364
15	Cuyamaca	4,591	15	Hayfield Pumping Plant	1,409
16	Fort Bragg 5 N	4,434	16	Santa Monica Pier	*1,491*
17	Dunsmuir Treatment Plant	4,361	17	Laguna Beach	*1,537*
18	Crescent City 3 NNW	4,356	18	Redlands	1,565
19	Bishop Arpt	4,205	19	Canoga Park Pierce College	*1,582*
20	Eureka	4,130	20	Santa Barbara	*1,593*
21	De Sabla	3,970	21	Elsinore	*1,707*
22	Palomar Mountain Observatory	3,968	22	Cachuma Lake	1,870
23	Covelo	3,783	23	Ojai	2,003
24	Colfax	3,432	24	Porterville	*2,030*
25	Haiwee	3,406	25	Bakersfield Meadows Field	2,101

 Rankings include 25 highest/lowest stations. If state has less than 25 stations, all stations are included. The period of record is 1980–2009. See User Guide for detailed explanation of data.

Number of Annual Cooling Degree Days

Highest Rank	Station Name	Num.	Lowest Rank	Station Name	Num.
1	Death Valley	5,512	1	Bodie	1
2	Needles Airport	4,663	2	Eureka	3
3	Parker Reservoir	4,637	3	Fort Bragg 5 N	7
4	Blythe	***4,091***	4	Crescent City 3 NNW	8
5	Borrego Desert Park	4,029	5	San Francisco Oceanside	***27***
6	Hayfield Pumping Plant	3,391	6	Boca	38
7	Barstow Fire Station	2,517	7	Donner Memorial St Pk	48
8	Bakersfield Meadows Field	2,275	8	Morro Bay Fire Dept	52
9	Coalinga	2,236	9	Big Bear Lake	94
10	Porterville	***2,174***	10	Santa Maria Public Arpt	137
11	Fresno Air Terminal	2,157	11	Salinas No 2	140
12	Ash Mountain	2,116	12	Jess Valley	165
13	Mitchell Caverns	2,019	12	San Francisco	165
14	Independence	1,940	14	Tulelake	167
15	Riverside Fire Sta 3	1,921	15	San Francisco Int'l Arpt	168
16	Tejon Rancho	1,918	16	Berkeley	***183***
17	Elsinore	***1,890***	17	Alturas	198
18	Balch Power House	1,852	18	Canyon Dam	214
19	Visalia	1,823	19	Calaveras Big Trees	279
20	Auberry 2 NW	1,813	20	Callahan	300
21	Friant Government Camp	1,802	21	Graton	303
22	Redlands	1,797	22	Santa Monica Pier	***326***
23	Victorville Pump Plant	1,754	23	Doyle 4 SSE	355
24	Newman	***1,658***	24	Petaluma Fire Station 2	359
25	Haiwee	1,635	25	Lava Beds Nat Monument	***380***

Annual Precipitation

Highest Rank	Station Name	Inches	Lowest Rank	Station Name	Inches
1	De Sabla	67.87	1	Death Valley	2.21
2	Crescent City 3 NNW	67.76	2	Blythe	3.67
3	Dunsmuir Treatment Plant	63.71	3	Hayfield Pumping Plant	4.71
4	Calaveras Big Trees	56.00	4	Needles Airport	4.73
5	Orleans	52.53	5	Barstow Fire Station	5.02
6	Ben Lomond No 4	49.95	6	Bishop Arpt	5.05
7	Colfax	46.58	7	Independence	5.39
8	Fort Bragg 5 N	42.16	8	El Mirage	5.72
9	Covelo	42.04	9	Victorville Pump Plant	6.16
10	Graton	41.40	10	Bakersfield Meadows Field	6.27
11	Angwin Pac Union Col	40.95	11	Borrego Desert Park	6.31
12	Calistoga	39.87	12	Parker Reservoir	6.45
13	Eureka	39.45	13	Haiwee	7.19
14	Donner Memorial St Pk	39.35	14	Coalinga	8.13
15	Canyon Dam	37.07	15	Chula Vista	9.61
16	Auburn	35.58	16	Riverside Fire Sta 3	10.02
17	Cuyamaca	32.64	17	San Diego Lindbergh Field	10.28
18	Balch Power House	30.90	18	Visalia	10.77
19	Woodside Fire Stn 1	30.06	19	Porterville	***11.20***
20	Palomar Mountain Observatory	28.21	20	Fresno Air Terminal	11.28
21	Ash Mountain	26.70	21	Tulelake	11.30
21	Berkeley	***26.70***	22	Newman	11.51
23	Petaluma Fire Station 2	26.28	23	Elsinore	11.61
24	Auberry 2 NW	25.80	24	Mitchell Caverns	11.81
25	Fairfield	24.59	25	Bodie	11.90

Rankings include 25 highest/lowest stations. If state has less than 25 stations, all stations are included. The period of record is 1980–2009. See User Guide for detailed explanation of data.

Annual Extreme Maximum Daily Precipitation

Highest Rank	Highest Station Name	Highest Inches	Lowest Rank	Lowest Station Name	Lowest Inches
1	Ben Lomond No 4	11.47	1	Bakersfield Meadows Field	1.42
2	Morro Bay Fire Dept	8.82	2	Death Valley	1.47
3	De Sabla	*8.37*	3	Barstow Fire Station	1.57
4	Calistoga	8.10	4	Porterville	*1.59*
5	Santa Barbara	*8.00*	5	Tulelake	1.65
6	Calaveras Big Trees	7.85	6	Alturas	1.99
7	Angwin Pac Union Col	7.40	7	Stockton Metropolitan Arpt	2.01
8	Cuyamaca	7.37	8	Jess Valley	*2.10*
9	Cachuma Lake	7.23	8	Needles Airport	2.10
10	Ojai	7.10	10	Modesto	2.19
11	Berkeley	*6.98*	10	Tejon Rancho	*2.19*
12	Eureka	6.79	12	Livermore	2.29
13	Graton	6.70	13	Parker Reservoir	2.35
14	Dunsmuir Treatment Plant	6.44	14	Cedarville	2.38
15	Canoga Park Pierce College	*6.06*	14	Fresno Air Terminal	2.38
16	Donner Memorial St Pk	6.00	16	Chula Vista	*2.42*
17	Gilroy	5.95	17	El Mirage	2.45
18	Colfax	5.90	18	Borrego Desert Park	2.46
19	Covelo	*5.70*	19	Riverside Fire Sta 3	*2.50*
20	Mitchell Caverns	5.66	20	Blythe	*2.56*
21	San Francisco Int'l Arpt	5.59	21	Haiwee	2.65
22	Fairfield	5.58	22	San Diego Lindbergh Field	2.70
23	Los Angeles Civic Center	5.55	23	Antioch Pump Plant #3	*2.80*
24	San Francisco	5.54	23	Bodie	2.80
25	Laguna Beach	*5.50*	25	Hollister 2	2.82

Number of Days Annually With ≥ 0.1 Inches of Precipitation

Highest Rank	Highest Station Name	Highest Days	Lowest Rank	Lowest Station Name	Lowest Days
1	Crescent City 3 NNW	79	1	Death Valley	5
2	Orleans	77	2	Blythe	8
3	Dunsmuir Treatment Plant	74	3	Hayfield Pumping Plant	10
3	Eureka	74	4	Independence	11
5	Fort Bragg 5 N	70	5	Bishop Arpt	12
6	De Sabla	68	5	Needles Airport	12
7	Covelo	61	7	Parker Reservoir	13
8	Calaveras Big Trees	58	8	Victorville Pump Plant	14
8	Canyon Dam	58	9	Borrego Desert Park	15
8	Donner Memorial St Pk	58	10	Barstow Fire Station	16
11	Colfax	56	10	El Mirage	16
12	Angwin Pac Union Col	55	12	Haiwee	17
12	Graton	55	13	Culver City	*18*
12	Jess Valley	55	13	Riverside Fire Sta 3	18
15	Ben Lomond No 4	50	15	Bakersfield Meadows Field	19
16	Auburn	48	15	Chula Vista	19
17	Calistoga	47	15	Coalinga	19
17	Petaluma Fire Station 2	47	15	Elsinore	19
19	Callahan	45	15	Santa Monica Pier	*19*
19	San Francisco	45	20	Long Beach Daugherty Fld	20
19	Woodside Fire Stn 1	45	20	Mitchell Caverns	20
22	Berkeley	*44*	20	San Diego Lindbergh Field	20
22	Boca	44	23	Los Angeles Intl Arpt	22
22	Camp Pardee	44	24	Canoga Park Pierce College	*23*
22	Yreka	44	24	Laguna Beach	23

Rankings include 25 highest/lowest stations. If state has less than 25 stations, all stations are included. The period of record is 1980–2009. See User Guide for detailed explanation of data.

Number of Days Annually With ≥ 0.5 Inches of Precipitation

Highest Rank	Station Name	Days	Lowest Rank	Station Name	Days
1	Dunsmuir Treatment Plant	41	1	Blythe	0
2	De Sabla	40	1	Death Valley	0
3	Crescent City 3 NNW	39	1	Needles Airport	0
4	Orleans	34	4	Bakersfield Meadows Field	1
5	Calaveras Big Trees	32	4	Hayfield Pumping Plant	1
6	Colfax	29	4	Tulelake	1
6	Covelo	29	7	Barstow Fire Station	2
6	Fort Bragg 5 N	29	7	Bishop Arpt	2
9	Ben Lomond No 4	28	7	El Mirage	2
10	Graton	27	7	Independence	2
11	Canyon Dam	26	11	Alturas	3
11	Eureka	26	11	Borrego Desert Park	3
13	Angwin Pac Union Col	25	11	Cedarville	3
14	Auburn	24	11	Parker Reservoir	3
14	Calistoga	24	15	Coalinga	4
14	Donner Memorial St Pk	24	15	Haiwee	4
17	Cuyamaca	21	15	Victorville Pump Plant	4
18	Balch Power House	20	18	Bodie	5
18	Woodside Fire Stn 1	20	18	Riverside Fire Sta 3	5
20	Auberry 2 NW	19	20	Chula Vista	6
21	Ash Mountain	18	20	Doyle 4 SSE	6
21	Berkeley	*18*	20	Elsinore	6
23	Camp Pardee	17	20	Fresno Air Terminal	6
23	Fairfield	17	20	King City	6
23	Palomar Mountain Observatory	17	20	Newman	6

Number of Days Annually With ≥ 1.0 Inches of Precipitation

Highest Rank	Station Name	Days	Lowest Rank	Station Name	Days
1	De Sabla	24	1	Alturas	0
2	Dunsmuir Treatment Plant	21	1	Bakersfield Meadows Field	0
3	Calaveras Big Trees	20	1	Barstow Fire Station	0
4	Crescent City 3 NNW	18	1	Bishop Arpt	0
5	Orleans	17	1	Blythe	0
6	Ben Lomond No 4	15	1	Bodie	0
6	Colfax	15	1	Borrego Desert Park	0
8	Angwin Pac Union Col	14	1	Cedarville	0
8	Covelo	14	1	Chula Vista	0
8	Graton	14	1	Coalinga	0
11	Calistoga	12	1	Death Valley	0
11	Fort Bragg 5 N	12	1	El Mirage	0
13	Auburn	11	1	Fresno Air Terminal	0
13	Canyon Dam	11	1	Haiwee	0
15	Donner Memorial St Pk	10	1	Hayfield Pumping Plant	0
16	Cuyamaca	9	1	Independence	0
16	Palomar Mountain Observatory	9	1	Jess Valley	0
18	Auberry 2 NW	8	1	Lava Beds Nat Monument	0
18	Eureka	8	1	Modesto	0
18	Woodside Fire Stn 1	8	1	Needles Airport	0
21	Ash Mountain	7	1	Newman	0
21	Balch Power House	7	1	Parker Reservoir	0
23	Berkeley	*6*	1	Porterville	*0*
23	Cachuma Lake	6	1	Stockton Metropolitan Arpt	0
23	Petaluma Fire Station 2	6	1	Tejon Rancho	0

Rankings include 25 highest/lowest stations. If state has less than 25 stations, all stations are included. The period of record is 1980–2009. See User Guide for detailed explanation of data.

Annual Snowfall

Highest Rank	Station Name	Inches	Lowest Rank	Station Name	Inches
1	Donner Memorial St Pk	185.4	1	Balch Power House	0.0
2	Calaveras Big Trees	112.7	1	Berkeley	*0.0*
3	Canyon Dam	106.0	1	Blythe	0.0
4	Boca	92.9	1	Burbank Valley Pump Plant	0.0
5	Bodie	*75.9*	1	Cachuma Lake	0.0
6	Jess Valley	75.3	1	Camp Pardee	0.0
7	Big Bear Lake	66.9	1	Death Valley	0.0
8	Lava Beds Nat Monument	43.2	1	Escondido No 2	*0.0*
9	Dunsmuir Treatment Plant	30.3	1	Friant Government Camp	0.0
10	Doyle 4 SSE	26.5	1	Gilroy	0.0
11	Cuyamaca	23.8	1	Hollister 2	0.0
12	Tulelake	22.9	1	Laguna Beach	0.0
13	Palomar Mountain Observatory	22.1	1	Newman	0.0
14	Alturas	17.4	1	Ojai	0.0
15	Cedarville	13.2	1	Parker Reservoir	0.0
16	Yreka	12.2	1	Porterville	*0.0*
17	Colfax	9.5	1	Redlands	0.0
18	Callahan	5.5	1	Riverside Fire Sta 3	0.0
19	De Sabla	4.7	1	Salinas No 2	0.0
20	Orleans	3.8	1	San Francisco Oceanside	*0.0*
21	Fairmont	3.0	1	Santa Barbara	0.0
22	Mitchell Caverns	2.2	1	Santa Monica Pier	0.0
23	Auberry 2 NW	1.9	1	Stockton Fire Stn #4	0.0
24	Covelo	1.8	1	Woodside Fire Stn 1	0.0
25	El Mirage	1.3	25	Antioch Pump Plant #3	Trace

Annual Maximum Snow Depth

Highest Rank	Station Name	Inches	Lowest Rank	Station Name	Inches
1	Canyon Dam	115	1	Berkeley	*0*
2	Donner Memorial St Pk	94	1	Blythe	0
3	Bodie	78	1	Burbank Valley Pump Plant	0
4	Boca	70	1	Cachuma Lake	0
5	De Sabla	30	1	Camp Pardee	0
5	Dunsmuir Treatment Plant	30	1	Crescent City 3 NNW	0
7	Cuyamaca	28	1	Culver City	*0*
8	Jess Valley	27	1	Death Valley	0
8	Palomar Mountain Observatory	27	1	Escondido No 2	*0*
10	Fairmont	26	1	Fairfield	0
10	Lava Beds Nat Monument	26	1	Friant Government Camp	0
12	Balch Power House	22	1	Gilroy	0
12	Doyle 4 SSE	22	1	Hollister 2	0
14	Alturas	21	1	King City	0
14	Tulelake	21	1	Laguna Beach	*0*
16	Cedarville	17	1	Newman	0
17	Colfax	16	1	Ojai	0
18	Yreka	*14*	1	Parker Reservoir	0
19	El Mirage	13	1	Redlands	0
20	Callahan	12	1	Riverside Fire Sta 3	0
21	Auberry 2 NW	8	1	Salinas No 2	0
21	Eureka	8	1	San Francisco Oceanside	*0*
21	Mitchell Caverns	*8*	1	Santa Barbara	0
24	Barstow Fire Station	7	1	Santa Monica Pier	*0*
25	Ash Mountain	6	1	Stockton Fire Stn #4	0

 Rankings include 25 highest/lowest stations. If state has less than 25 stations, all stations are included. The period of record is 1980–2009. See User Guide for detailed explanation of data.

Number of Days Annually With ≥ 1.0 Inch Snow Depth

Highest			Lowest		
Rank	**Station Name**	**Days**	**Rank**	**Station Name**	**Days**
1	Donner Memorial St Pk	134	1	Angwin Pac Union Col	0
2	Bodie	128	1	Antioch Pump Plant #3	0
3	Canyon Dam	101	1	Ash Mountain	0
4	Boca	86	1	Auberry 2 NW	0
5	Lava Beds Nat Monument	52	1	Auburn	0
6	Jess Valley	30	1	Barstow Fire Station	0
7	Dunsmuir Treatment Plant	24	1	Ben Lomond No 4	0
8	Tulelake	23	1	Berkeley	***0***
9	Doyle 4 SSE	22	1	Blythe	***0***
10	Calaveras Big Trees	***16***	1	Borrego Desert Park	0
11	Alturas	15	1	Burbank Valley Pump Plant	0
11	Cedarville	15	1	Cachuma Lake	0
13	Palomar Mountain Observatory	12	1	Calistoga	0
14	Cuyamaca	6	1	Callahan	0
14	Yreka	6	1	Camp Pardee	0
16	Balch Power House	1	1	Canoga Park Pierce College	***0***
16	De Sabla	1	1	Chula Vista	0
18	Angwin Pac Union Col	0	1	Coalinga	0
18	Antioch Pump Plant #3	0	1	Colfax	0
18	Ash Mountain	0	1	Colusa 2 SSW	0
18	Auberry 2 NW	0	1	Covelo	0
18	Auburn	0	1	Crescent City 3 NNW	0
18	Barstow Fire Station	0	1	Culver City	0
18	Ben Lomond No 4	0	1	Death Valley	0
18	Berkeley	***0***	1	El Mirage	0

Significant Storm Events in California: 2000 – 2009

Location or County	Date	Type	Mag.	Deaths	Injuries	Property Damage ($mil.)	Crop Damage ($mil.)
Riverside, San Bernardino, and San Diego County Mountains	03/04/00	Winter Storm	na	3	13	0.0	0.0
Interior Northern California	06/13/00	Excessive Heat	na	1	15	0.0	0.0
Bay Area	06/14/00	Excessive Heat	na	9	102	0.0	0.0
Tehama	09/29/00	Wild/Forest Fire	na	0	0	547.0	0.0
San Diego Co. Deserts and Coachella Valley	05/07/01	Excessive Heat	na	1	19	0.0	0.0
Kern County Mountains	01/03/02	Fog	na	1	15	0.8	0.0
Central and Southern San Joaquin Co. Valley	02/05/02	Fog	na	3	40	0.4	0.0
San Diego	02/10/02	Wild/Forest Fire	na	0	19	16.0	2.0
Tulare	08/01/02	Wild/Forest Fire	na	0	0	45.7	0.0
San Diego	08/01/02	Wild/Forest Fire	na	0	38	10.0	0.0
Los Angeles	09/01/02	Wild/Forest Fire	na	0	14	12.7	0.0
Los Angeles	09/22/02	Wild/Forest Fire	na	0	14	15.3	0.0
Southern California	01/05/03	High Wind	100 mph	2	11	3.2	28.0
San Diego	07/16/03	Wildfire	na	0	14	1.0	0.0
San Bernardino	10/21/03	Wildfire	na	0	35	50.0	0.0
San Diego	10/25/03	Wildfire	na	14	90	1,040.0	6.5
San Bernardino	10/25/03	Wildfire	na	4	5	696.4	0.0
San Diego	10/26/03	Wildfire	na	2	18	55.2	22.0
San Bernardino	11/01/03	Wildfire	na	2	7	278.6	0.0
San Diego	11/01/03	Wildfire	na	0	23	16.9	0.0
San Bernardino County Mountain	12/25/03	Landslide	na	14	10	5.0	0.0
San Bernardino County Mountain-Cajon Pass	04/01/04	Dense Fog	na	0	24	1.4	0.0
Riverside and San Diego County Valleys	05/02/04	Wildfire	na	0	18	8.0	0.0
San Bernardino	01/07/05	Heavy Rain	na	0	0	70.0	2.0
Los Angeles, Southern Santa Barbara, and Ventura Counties	01/10/05	Landslide	na	10	0	0.0	0.0
San Bernardino	02/18/05	Heavy Rain	na	0	0	40.0	0.0
Del Norte, Humboldt, Mendocino, and Trinity Counties	12/28/05	Landslide	na	0	0	55.9	0.0
Klamath and Russian River Basins	12/29/05	Flood	na	0	0	60.8	8.0
Napa	12/31/05	Flood	na	0	0	115.0	32.5
Marin	12/31/05	Flood	na	0	0	108.0	0.0
Sonoma	12/31/05	Flood	na	0	0	104.0	3.0
Marin	01/01/06	Flood	na	0	0	108.0	0.0
Sonoma	01/01/06	Flood	na	0	0	104.0	3.0
Coastal North Bay Area	03/11/06	Winter Weather	na	2	15	0.0	0.0
San Bernardino County Mountain-Apple and Lucerne Valleys	07/09/06	Wildfire	na	1	18	11.7	0.0
Interior Central California	07/16/06	Excessive Heat	na	46	18	0.1	492.4
Southern California	07/21/06	Excessive Heat	na	16	27	0.0	0.0
Santa Monica Mountains Recreational Area	01/08/07	Wildfire	na	0	0	60.0	0.0
Greater Lake Tahoe Area	06/24/07	Wildfire	na	0	3	500.0	0.0
San Diego County Coast	10/03/07	Landslide	na	0	0	48.0	0.0
San Diego County Valleys	10/21/07	Wildfire	na	8	61	75.0	0.0
San Diego County	10/21/07	Wildfire	na	0	0	50.0	0.0
Orange County Coast, Santa Ana Mountains and Foothills	10/21/07	Wildfire	na	0	16	10.0	0.0
San Diego County Valleys	10/22/07	Wildfire	na	0	5	151.1	15.0
San Bernardino County Mountain	10/22/07	Wildfire	na	0	9	65.0	0.0
San Bernardino County Mountain	10/22/07	Wildfire	na	0	1	50.0	0.0
San Diego County	10/23/07	Wildfire	na	0	15	5.0	0.0
Orange County Coastal Areas, San Bernardino and Riverside Counties	11/15/08	Wildfire	na	0	0	150.0	0.0
Santa Barbara County	05/05/09	Wildfire	na	0	30	17.0	0.0

Note: Deaths, injuries, and damages are date and location specific.

COLORADO

PHYSICAL FEATURES. Colorado lies astride the highest mountains of the Continental Divide. Nearly rectangular, its north and south boundaries are the 41° and 37° N. parallels, and the east and west boundaries are the 102° and 109° W. meridians. It is eighth in size among the 50 states, with an area of 104,247 square miles. Although primarily a mountain state, nearly 40 percent of its area is taken up by the eastern high plains.

The principal features of Colorado geography are its inland continental location in the middle latitudes, and the mountains and ranges extending north and south approximately through the middle of the State. With an average altitude about 6,800 feet above sea level, Colorado is the highest state in the Union. Roughly three-quarters of the Nation's land above 10,000 feet altitude lies within its borders. The State has 54 mountains 14,000 feet or higher, and about 830 mountains between 11,000 and 14,000 feet in elevation.

Emerging gradually from the plains of Kansas and Nebraska, the high plains of Colorado slope gently upward for a distance of some 200 miles from the eastern border to the base of the foothills of the Rocky Mountains. The eastern portion of the State is generally level to rolling prairie broken by occasional hills and bluffs. The northern part of the plains area slopes to the northeast and the southern part to the southeast, divided by higher country and hills extending eastward from the mountains near the center of the State. Elevations along the eastern border range from about 3,350 feet at the lowest point in the State (where the Arkansas River crosses the border) to near 4,000 feet.

At elevations between 5,000 and 6,000 feet the plains give way abruptly to foothills with elevations of 7,000 to 9,000 feet. Backing the foothills are the mountain ranges above 9,000 feet with the higher peaks over 14,000 feet. West of these "front ranges" are additional ranges, generally extending north and south, but with many spurs and extensions in other directions. These ranges enclose numerous high mountain peaks and valleys. Farther westward the mountains give way to rugged plateau country in the form of high mesas (some more than 10,000 feet in elevation) which extends to the western border of the State. This land is often cut by rugged canyons, the work of the many streams fed by accumulations of winter snow.

All rivers in Colorado rise within its borders and flow outward, with the exception of the Green River which flows diagonally across the extreme northwestern corner of the State. Four of the Nation's major rivers have their source in Colorado: the Colorado, the Rio Grande, the Arkansas, and the Platte.

GENERAL CLIMATE. Most of Colorado has a cool and invigorating climate that could be termed a highland or mountain climate of a continental location. During summer there are hot days in the plains, but these are often relieved by afternoon thundershowers. Mountain regions are nearly always cool. Humidity is generally quite low; this favors rapid evaporation and a relatively comfortable feeling even on hot days. The thin atmosphere allows greater penetration of solar radiation and results in pleasant daytime conditions even during the winter. This is why skiers at high elevations are often pictured in very light clothing, although surrounded by heavy snow.

The climates of local areas are profoundly affected by differences in elevation, and to a lesser degree, by the orientation of mountain ranges and valleys with respect to general air movements. While temperature decreases, and precipitation generally increases with altitude, these patterns are modified by the orientation of mountain slopes with respect to the prevailing winds and by the effect of topographical features in creating local air movements.

As a result of the State's distance from major sources of moisture (the Pacific Ocean and the Gulf of Mexico), precipitation is generally light in the lower elevations. Prevailing air currents reach Colorado from westerly directions. Eastward-moving storms originating in the Pacific Ocean lose much of their moisture in passage over mountain ranges to the west; a large part of the remaining moisture falls as rain or snow on the mountaintops and westward-facing slopes. Eastern slope areas receive relatively small amounts of precipitation from these storms.

Storms moving from the north usually carry little moisture. The frequency of such storms increases during the fall and winter months, and decreases rapidly in the spring. The accompanying outbreaks of polar air are responsible for the sudden drops in temperature often experienced in the plains section. Occasionally these outbreaks are attended by strong northerly winds which come in contact with moist air from the south; the interaction of these air masses causes a heavy fall of snow and the most severe of all weather conditions of the high plains, the blizzard. This cold air is frequently too shallow to cross the mountains to the western portion of the State so while the plains are in the grip of a very severe storm, the weather in the mountains and western valleys may be mild.

Occasionally, when the plains are covered with a shallow layer of cold air, strong westerly winds aloft work their way to the surface. Warmed by rapid descent from higher levels, these winds bring large and sudden temperature rises. This phenomenon is called the "chinook" of the high plains and temperature rises of 25 to 35°F. within a short time are not uncommon. Chinook winds greatly moderate average winter temperatures in areas near enough to the mountains to experience them frequently.

Warm, moist air from the south moves into Colorado most frequently in the spring. As this air is carried northward and westward to higher elevations, the heaviest and most general rainfalls of the year occur over the eastern portions of the State. Frequent showers and thunderstorms continue well into the summer.

CLIMATE OF THE EASTERN PLAINS. The climate of the plains is comparatively uniform from place to place, with characteristic features of low relative humidity, abundant sunshine, light rainfall, moderate to high wind movement, and a large daily range in temperature. Because of the very low relative humidity, hot days cause less discomfort than in more humid areas. Summer precipitation in the plains is largely from thunderstorm activity and is sometimes extremely heavy. Strong winds occur frequently in winter and spring. These winds tend to dry out soils, which are not well supplied with moisture because of the low annual precipitation. During periods of drought such winds give rise to the duststorms which are especially characteristic of the southeastern plains.

At the western edge of the plains and near the foothills of the mountains, there are a number of significant changes in climate as compared to the plains proper. Average wind movement is less. Temperature changes from day to day are not as great; summer temperatures are lower, and winter temperatures are higher. Precipitation, which decreases gradually from the eastern border to a minimum near the mountains, increases rapidly with the increasing elevation of the foothills and proximity to higher ranges.

CLIMATE OF WESTERN COLORADO. The rugged topography of western Colorado causes large variations in climate within short distances, and few climatic generalizations apply to the whole area. Snow-covered mountain peaks and valleys often have very cold nighttime temperatures in winter, when skies are clear and the air is still — occasionally to 50°F below zero. Summer in the mountains is a cool and refreshing season. At typical mountain weather stations the average July temperature is in the neighborhood of 60°F. The highest temperatures are usually in the 70s and 80s, but may reach 95°F. Above 7,000 feet, the nights are quite cool throughout the summer, while bright sunshine makes the days comfortably warm.

Precipitation west of the Continental Divide is more evenly distributed throughout the year than in the eastern plains. For most of western Colorado, the greatest monthly precipitation occurs in the winter months, while June is the driest month. In contrast, June is one of the wetter months in most of the eastern portion of the State.

STORMS. Thunderstorms are quite prevalent in the eastern plains and along the eastern slopes of the mountains during the spring and summer. These often become quite severe, and the frequency of hail damage to crops in northeastern Colorado is quite high. Tornadoes almost never occur in the mountains, and are relatively infrequent over the eastern plains. A spring flood potential results from the melting of snow. In years when snow cover is heavy, or when there is a sudden warming in the spring at high elevations, there may be extensive flooding. Heavy thunderstorms in the eastern foothills and plains occasionally cause damaging flash floods. Similar flash floods occur on the western slopes but with somewhat lower frequency.

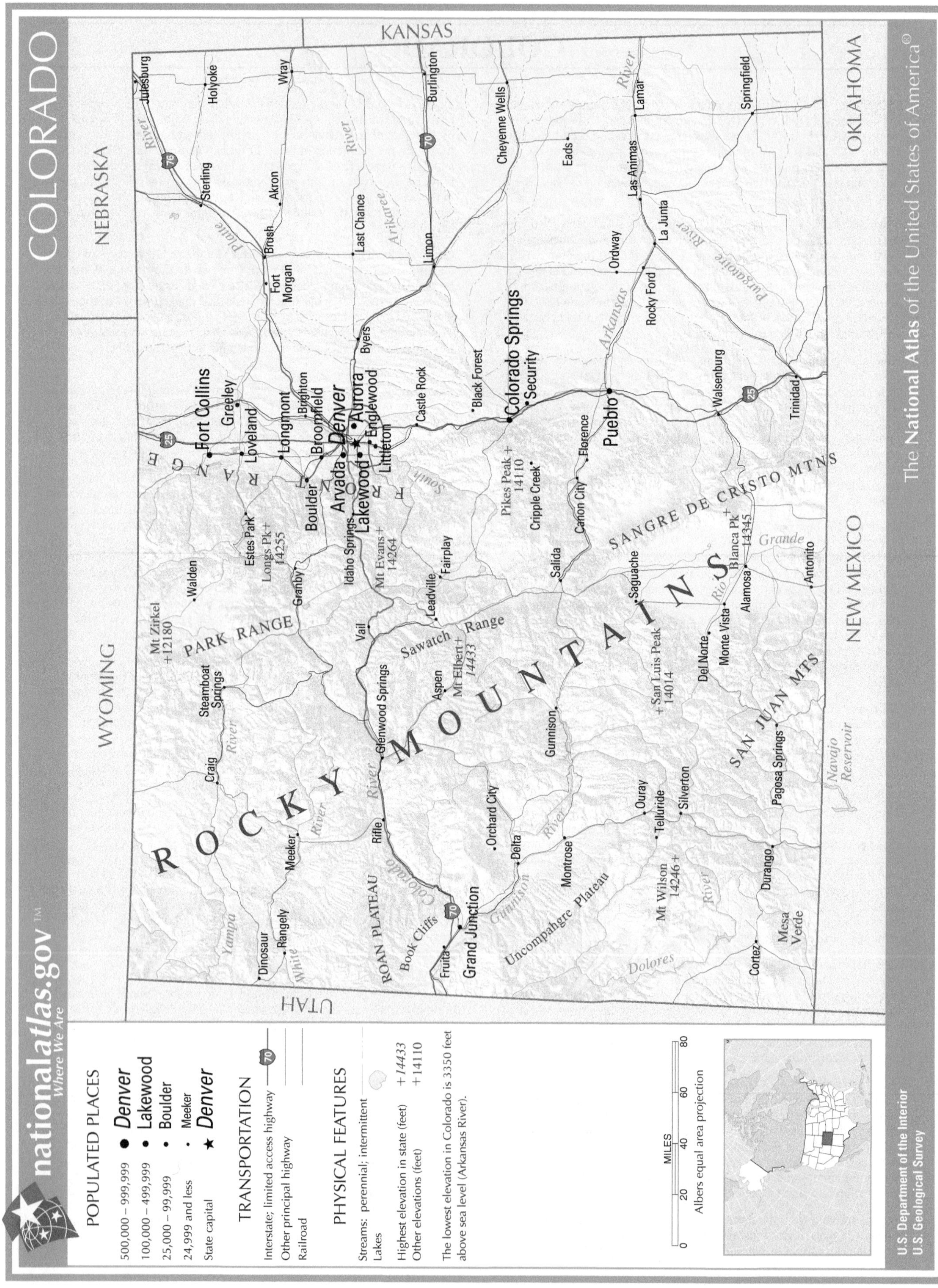
COLORADO
nationalatlas.gov™
Where We Are
POPULATED PLACES
500,000 – 999,999 Denver
100,000 – 499,999 Lakewood
25,000 – 99,999 Boulder
24,999 and less Meeker
State capital Denver
TRANSPORTATION
Interstate; limited access highway
Other principal highway
Railroad
PHYSICAL FEATURES
Streams: perennial; intermittent
Lakes
Highest elevation in state (feet) +14433
Other elevations (feet) +14110
The lowest elevation in Colorado is 3350 feet above sea level (Arkansas River).
MILES
0 20 40 60 80
Albers equal area projection
U.S. Department of the Interior
U.S. Geological Survey
The National Atlas of the United States of America®
WYOMING
NEBRASKA
KANSAS
OKLAHOMA
NEW MEXICO
UTAH
ROCKY MOUNTAINS
FRONT RANGE
PARK RANGE
Sawatch Range
SANGRE DE CRISTO MTNS
SAN JUAN MTS
ROAN PLATEAU
Book Cliffs
Uncompahgre Plateau
Mt Zirkel +12180
Longs Pk +14255
Mt Evans +14264
Mt Elbert +14433
Pikes Peak +14110
San Luis Peak +14014
Blanca Pk +14345
Mt Wilson 14246 +
Julesburg
Holyoke
Wray
Burlington
Sterling
Akron
Brush
Fort Morgan
Last Chance
Limon
Cheyenne Wells
Eads
Lamar
Springfield
Las Animas
La Junta
Ordway
Rocky Ford
Fort Collins
Greeley
Loveland
Longmont
Brighton
Broomfield
Boulder
Denver
Aurora
Arvada
Lakewood
Englewood
Littleton
Byers
Castle Rock
Black Forest
Colorado Springs
Security
Pueblo
Walsenburg
Trinidad
Florence
Canon City
Cripple Creek
Estes Park
Walden
Granby
Idaho Springs
Fairplay
Leadville
Vail
Salida
Saguache
Alamosa
Antonito
Monte Vista
Del Norte
Steamboat Springs
Craig
Meeker
Rangely
Dinosaur
Rifle
Glenwood Springs
Aspen
Gunnison
Orchard City
Delta
Montrose
Grand Junction
Fruita
Ouray
Telluride
Silverton
Pagosa Springs
Durango
Cortez
Mesa Verde
Navajo Reservoir
Platte River
Arikaree
Arkansas
Purgatoire River
Rio Grande
South Platte
Yampa River
White River
Colorado River
Gunnison
Dolores
76
70
25

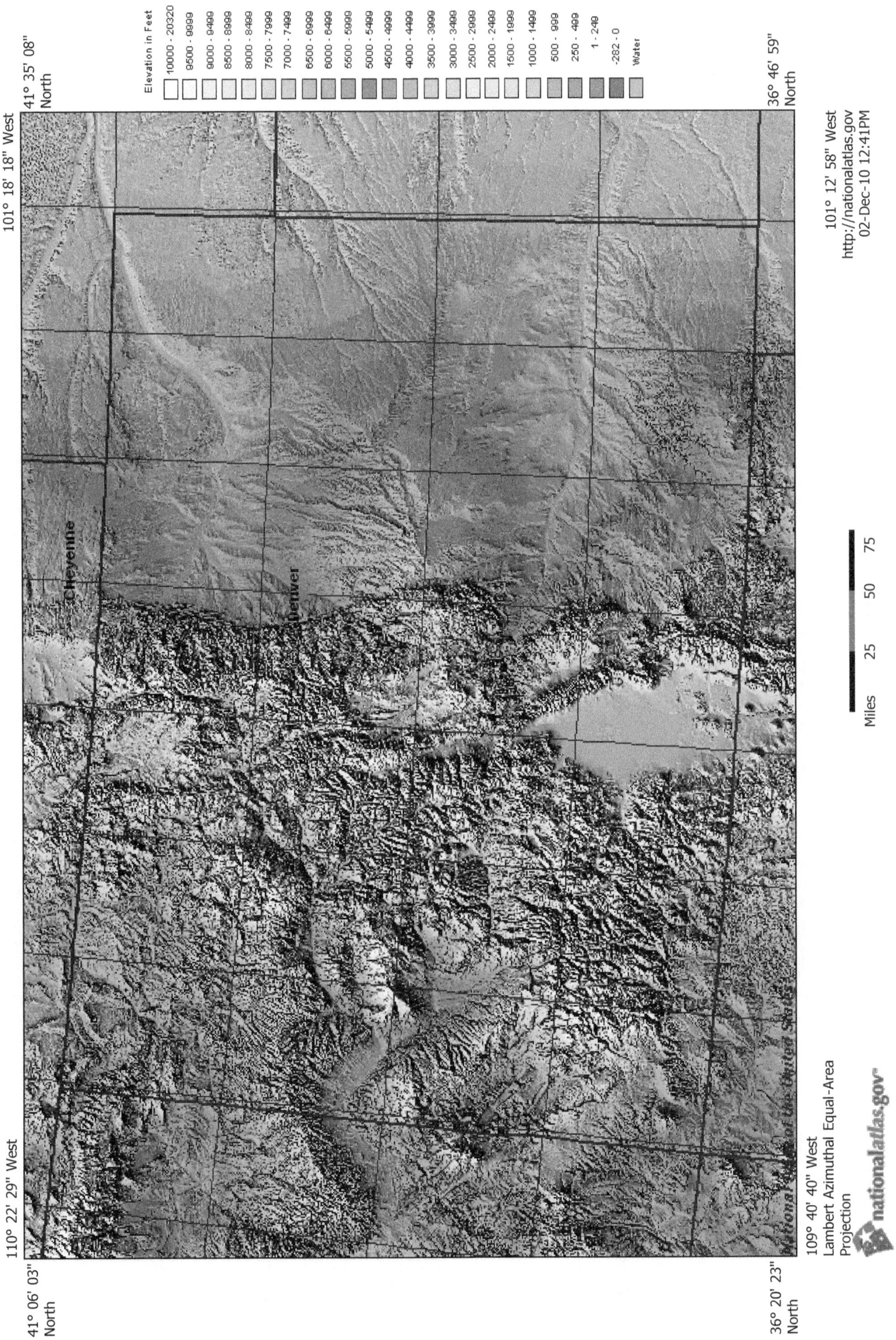
Elevation in Feet
10000 - 20320
9500 - 9999
9000 - 9499
8500 - 8999
8000 - 8499
7500 - 7999
7000 - 7499
6500 - 6999
6000 - 6499
5500 - 5999
5000 - 5499
4500 - 4999
4000 - 4499
3500 - 3999
3000 - 3499
2500 - 2999
2000 - 2499
1500 - 1999
1000 - 1499
500 - 999
250 - 499
1 - 249
-282 - 0
Water
41° 35' 08" North
101° 18' 18" West
36° 46' 59" North
101° 12' 58" West
http://nationalatlas.gov
02-Dec-10 12:41PM
Cheyenne
Denver
Miles
25
50
75
110° 22' 29" West
41° 06' 03" North
36° 20' 23" North
109° 40' 40" West
Lambert Azimuthal Equal-Area Projection
nationalatlas.gov

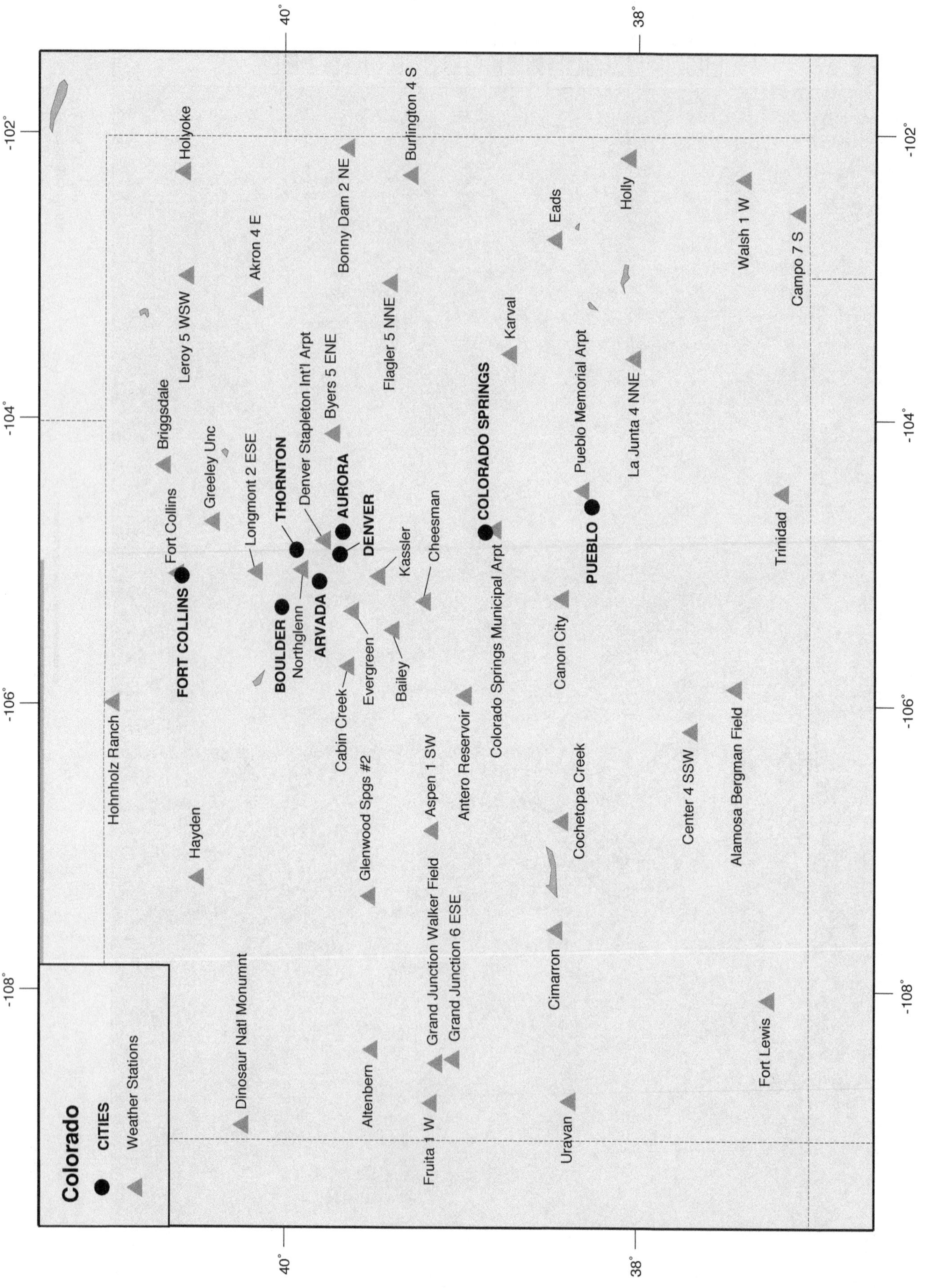
Colorado
CITIES
Weather Stations
-102°
-104°
-106°
-108°
40°
38°
Holyoke
Burlington 4 S
Bonny Dam 2 NE
Akron 4 E
Leroy 5 WSW
Briggsdale
Flagler 5 NNE
Byers 5 ENE
Denver Stapleton Int'l Arpt
THORNTON
AURORA
DENVER
Longmont 2 ESE
Greeley Unc
Fort Collins
FORT COLLINS
BOULDER
Northglenn
ARVADA
Evergreen
Kassler
Cheesman
Bailey
Cabin Creek
Karval
COLORADO SPRINGS
Colorado Springs Municipal Arpt
Eads
Holly
Walsh 1 W
Campo 7 S
Pueblo Memorial Arpt
PUEBLO
La Junta 4 NNE
Trinidad
Canon City
Hohnholz Ranch
Hayden
Glenwood Spgs #2
Aspen 1 SW
Antero Reservoir
Cochetopa Creek
Center 4 SSW
Alamosa Bergman Field
Dinosaur Natl Monumnt
Altenbern
Grand Junction Walker Field
Grand Junction 6 ESE
Fruita 1 W
Cimarron
Uravan
Fort Lewis

Colorado Weather Stations by County

County	Station Name
Adams	Byers 5 ENE Northglenn
Alamosa	Alamosa Bergman Field
Baca	Campo 7 S Walsh 1 W
Boulder	Boulder Longmont 2 ESE
Clear Creek	Cabin Creek
Denver	Denver Stapleton Int'l Arpt
El Paso	Colorado Springs Municipal Arpt
Fremont	Canon City
Garfield	Altenbern Glenwood Spgs #2
Gunnison	Cochetopa Creek
Jefferson	Cheesman Evergreen Kassler
Kiowa	Eads
Kit Carson	Burlington 4 S Flagler 5 NNE
La Plata	Fort Lewis
Larimer	Fort Collins Hohnholz Ranch
Las Animas	Trinidad
Lincoln	Karval
Logan	Leroy 5 WSW
Mesa	Fruita 1 W Grand Junction 6 ESE Grand Junction Walker Field
Moffat	Dinosaur Natl Monumnt
Montrose	Cimarron Uravan
Otero	La Junta 4 NNE
Park	Antero Reservoir Bailey
Phillips	Holyoke
Pitkin	Aspen 1 SW
Prowers	Holly

County	Station Name
Pueblo	Pueblo Memorial Arpt
Rio Grande	Center 4 SSW
Routt	Hayden
Washington	Akron 4 E
Weld	Briggsdale Greeley Unc
Yuma	Bonny Dam 2 NE

See User Guide for station inclusion criteria.

Colorado Weather Stations by City

City	Station Name	Miles
Arvada	Boulder	15.0
	Denver Stapleton Int'l Arpt	13.1
	Evergreen	17.3
	Kassler	23.4
	Longmont 2 ESE	23.9
	Northglenn	7.1
Aurora	Denver Stapleton Int'l Arpt	5.7
	Kassler	20.9
	Northglenn	17.7
Black Forest	Colorado Springs Municipal Arpt	15.0
Boulder	Boulder	1.0
	Longmont 2 ESE	14.7
	Northglenn	15.1
Brighton	Boulder	24.3
	Denver Stapleton Int'l Arpt	15.2
	Longmont 2 ESE	18.7
	Northglenn	12.5
Broomfield	Boulder	12.1
	Denver Stapleton Int'l Arpt	15.2
	Evergreen	24.6
	Longmont 2 ESE	16.4
	Northglenn	3.0
Castle Rock	Kassler	15.0
Castlewood	Denver Stapleton Int'l Arpt	12.7
	Evergreen	22.1
	Kassler	12.5
	Northglenn	22.6
Cimarron Hills	Colorado Springs Municipal Arpt	3.0
Clifton	Fruita 1 W	16.6
	Grand Junction Walker Field	5.5
	Grand Junction 6 ESE	1.8
Colorado Springs	Colorado Springs Municipal Arpt	5.1
Columbine	Denver Stapleton Int'l Arpt	16.5
	Evergreen	13.5
	Kassler	7.3
	Northglenn	21.9
Commerce City	Boulder	22.5
	Denver Stapleton Int'l Arpt	4.5
	Northglenn	7.8
Denver	Denver Stapleton Int'l Arpt	6.2
	Evergreen	19.6
	Kassler	17.8
	Northglenn	12.8
Englewood	Denver Stapleton Int'l Arpt	10.5
	Evergreen	17.5
	Kassler	12.8
	Northglenn	17.6
Fort Collins	Fort Collins	2.0
	Greeley Unc	22.8

City	Station Name	Miles
Fountain	Colorado Springs Municipal Arpt	8.4
Grand Junction	Fruita 1 W	11.9
	Grand Junction Walker Field	3.8
	Grand Junction 6 ESE	5.4
Greeley	Fort Collins	22.4
	Greeley Unc	1.4
	Longmont 2 ESE	25.0
Highlands Ranch	Denver Stapleton Int'l Arpt	16.3
	Evergreen	19.8
	Kassler	8.3
	Northglenn	24.8
Ken Caryl	Bailey	23.7
	Denver Stapleton Int'l Arpt	18.1
	Evergreen	11.8
	Kassler	6.7
	Northglenn	22.6
Lafayette	Boulder	8.8
	Denver Stapleton Int'l Arpt	20.0
	Longmont 2 ESE	12.1
	Northglenn	7.8
Lakewood	Boulder	22.2
	Denver Stapleton Int'l Arpt	13.3
	Evergreen	12.4
	Kassler	15.2
	Northglenn	14.3
Littleton	Denver Stapleton Int'l Arpt	13.8
	Evergreen	16.4
	Kassler	9.4
	Northglenn	20.7
Longmont	Boulder	14.7
	Longmont 2 ESE	2.4
	Northglenn	19.7
Loveland	Fort Collins	12.1
	Greeley Unc	20.4
	Longmont 2 ESE	16.7
Northglenn	Boulder	16.7
	Denver Stapleton Int'l Arpt	10.9
	Longmont 2 ESE	19.1
	Northglenn	1.8
Parker	Denver Stapleton Int'l Arpt	18.1
	Kassler	18.0
Pueblo	Pueblo Memorial Arpt	6.8
Pueblo West	Pueblo Memorial Arpt	13.8
Security-Widefield	Colorado Springs Municipal Arpt	4.9
Southglenn	Denver Stapleton Int'l Arpt	13.2
	Evergreen	19.6
	Kassler	10.6
	Northglenn	21.8

See User Guide for station inclusion criteria.

City	Station Name	Miles
Thornton	Boulder	17.7
	Denver Stapleton Int'l Arpt	11.0
	Longmont 2 ESE	18.6
	Northglenn	3.5
Westminster	Boulder	14.3
	Denver Stapleton Int'l Arpt	12.3
	Evergreen	21.7
	Longmont 2 ESE	20.3
	Northglenn	2.7
Wheat Ridge	Boulder	18.3
	Denver Stapleton Int'l Arpt	12.0
	Evergreen	15.3
	Kassler	19.9
	Northglenn	9.7

Note: Miles is the distance between the geographic center of the city and the weather station.

Colorado Weather Stations by Elevation

Feet	Station Name
10,020	Cabin Creek
8,919	Antero Reservoir
8,163	Aspen 1 SW
8,000	Cochetopa Creek
7,759	Hohnholz Ranch
7,729	Bailey
7,672	Center 4 SSW
7,600	Fort Lewis
7,533	Alamosa Bergman Field
7,000	Evergreen
6,896	Cimarron
6,879	Cheesman
6,439	Hayden
6,140	Colorado Springs Municipal Arpt
6,029	Trinidad
5,919	Dinosaur Natl Monumnt
5,750	Glenwood Spgs #2
5,678	Altenbern
5,500	Kassler
5,483	Boulder
5,366	Northglenn
5,330	Canon City
5,286	Denver Stapleton Int'l Arpt
5,100	Byers 5 ENE
5,075	Karval
5,009	Uravan
5,003	Fort Collins
4,950	Longmont 2 ESE
4,875	Flagler 5 NNE
4,839	Grand Junction Walker Field
4,833	Briggsdale
4,759	Grand Junction 6 ESE
4,714	Greeley Unc
4,684	Pueblo Memorial Arpt
4,540	Akron 4 E
4,479	Fruita 1 W
4,470	Leroy 5 WSW
4,210	Eads
4,209	Burlington 4 S
4,203	La Junta 4 NNE
4,118	Campo 7 S
3,977	Walsh 1 W
3,729	Holyoke
3,716	Bonny Dam 2 NE
3,390	Holly

See User Guide for station inclusion criteria.

Alamosa Bergman Field

Alamosa is located in the south-central part of Colorado, near the center of the San Luis Valley which lies in a broad depression between mountain ranges converging to the north. The valley is the first of a series of basins along the Rio Grande River. The mountain ranges to the east reach altitudes over 14,000 feet and those to the west are between 13,000 and 14,000 feet. The length of the valley from north to south is over 80 miles, and its greatest width is about 50 miles. The valley floor ranges in altitude from 7,500 to near 8,000 feet and has a remarkably flat surface, except for a range of low hills across the southern portion. From the lowest areas which lie along an axis near the eastern border, the valley floor rises to the foothills, steeply to the east and more gently to the west.

The climate of the San Luis Valley is marked by cold winters and moderate summers, light precipitation, and much sunshine. At Alamosa about 80 percent of the annual precipitation occurs from April to October, most of it in the form of scattered light showers and thunderstorms that develop over the mountains and move into the valley during the afternoon. More than half of these thunderstorms occur during July and August; hail frequently falls in some parts of the valley during these storms. Winter snows occur mainly in frequent light falls, with occasional falls as early as September or as late as May. A good snow cover will remain on the ground for several weeks during the coldest months.

All agriculture in the valley is dependent on irrigation, using water supplied by the more abundant precipitation in the surrounding mountains. Summer grazing of cattle and sheep on nearby mountain ranges and smaller valleys is extensive. A wide variety of vegetables, grains and feed crops are grown locally, with potatoes being the main commercial crop.

Summer is characterized by frequent days with maximum temperatures in the middle 80s and minimum temperatures in the low 40s. Relative humidity ranges from about 76 percent in the early mornings to around 40 percent during the afternoons. Winds are light during the coldest weather, but are strong with occasional blowing dust during the spring and early summer months.

Based on the 1951-1980 period, the average first occurrence of 32 degrees Fahrenheit in the fall is September 8 and the average last occurrence in the spring is June 8.

Alamosa Bergman Field *Alamosa County* Elevation: 7,533 ft. Latitude: 37° 26' N Longitude: 105° 52' W

	JAN	FEB	MAR	APR	MAY	JUN	JUL	AUG	SEP	OCT	NOV	DEC	YEAR
Mean Maximum Temp. (°F)	34.8	40.8	50.5	59.6	69.4	78.9	82.8	79.9	73.3	61.8	47.5	36.1	59.6
Mean Temp. (°F)	16.7	23.5	33.7	41.9	51.4	59.8	64.8	62.9	55.1	43.1	29.9	18.6	41.8
Mean Minimum Temp. (°F)	-1.5	6.1	16.9	24.1	33.5	40.6	46.8	45.8	36.8	24.3	12.2	1.0	23.9
Extreme Maximum Temp. (°F)	60	66	73	80	90	95	96	91	87	80	71	60	96
Extreme Minimum Temp. (°F)	-40	-30	-14	-4	13	24	30	30	15	-9	-26	-33	-40
Days Maximum Temp. ≥ 90°F	0	0	0	0	0	1	2	0	0	0	0	0	3
Days Maximum Temp. ≤ 32°F	13	6	1	0	0	0	0	0	0	0	3	11	34
Days Minimum Temp. ≤ 32°F	31	28	31	27	13	2	0	0	8	27	30	31	228
Days Minimum Temp. ≤ 0°F	17	9	1	0	0	0	0	0	0	0	4	15	46
Heating Degree Days (base 65°F)	1,493	1,168	962	687	415	158	37	74	292	673	1,047	1,434	8,440
Cooling Degree Days (base 65°F)	0	0	0	0	0	8	39	16	0	0	0	0	63
Mean Precipitation (in.)	0.25	0.27	0.51	0.62	0.60	0.48	0.95	1.26	0.89	0.70	0.42	0.32	7.27
Maximum Precipitation (in.)*	0.8	1.4	1.6	1.7	1.8	2.6	3.5	5.4	1.9	2.4	1.2	1.5	11.5
Minimum Precipitation (in.)*	trace	trace	trace	trace	trace	trace	trace	0.2	trace	0	trace	trace	3.4
Extreme Maximum Daily Precip. (in.)	0.38	0.36	1.15	1.04	0.71	0.57	1.49	1.08	1.17	0.85	0.71	0.62	1.49
Days With ≥ 0.1" Precipitation	1	1	2	2	2	2	3	4	3	2	1	1	24
Days With ≥ 0.5" Precipitation	0	0	0	0	0	0	0	1	0	0	0	0	1
Days With ≥ 1.0" Precipitation	0	0	0	0	0	0	0	0	0	0	0	0	0
Mean Snowfall (in.)	4.1	3.5	4.9	3.7	1.0	trace	trace	0.0	trace	2.2	3.4	4.6	27.4
Maximum Snowfall (in.)*	14	16	29	14	14	1	0	0	4	20	20	28	69
Maximum 24-hr. Snowfall (in.)*	7	10	14	9	8	1	0	0	4	13	8	16	16
Maximum Snow Depth (in.)	10	10	11	5	3	trace	0	0	trace	12	8	10	12
Days With ≥ 1.0" Snow Depth	15	10	3	1	0	0	0	0	0	1	4	10	44
Thunderstorm Days*	0	< 1	< 1	2	7	9	9	8	6	1	0	0	42
Foggy Days*	14	10	7	6	4	2	2	6	6	5	9	13	84
Predominant Sky Cover*	CLR	CLR	CLR	SCT	SCT	SCT	SCT	SCT	CLR	CLR	CLR	CLR	CLR
Mean Relative Humidity 5am (%)*	78	78	75	71	74	76	84	86	82	77	78	77	78
Mean Relative Humidity 5pm (%)*	58	49	38	29	29	26	36	39	34	34	49	59	40
Mean Dewpoint (°F)*	7	12	16	19	27	34	44	45	36	25	16	8	24
Prevailing Wind Direction*	SW	SW	SW	SW	SW	SW	S	S	S	S	S	SW	SW
Prevailing Wind Speed (mph)*	9	10	14	15	15	14	9	8	9	9	10	8	12
Maximum Wind Gust (mph)*	69	66	71	67	70	68	58	48	56	62	54	54	71

Note: (*) Period of record is 1948-1995

Colorado Springs Muni Airport

At an elevation near 6,200 feet above sea level, Colorado Springs is located in relatively flat semi-arid country on the eastern slope of the Rocky Mountains. Immediately to the west the mountains rise abruptly to heights ranging from 10,000 to 14,000 feet but generally averaging near 11,000 feet. To the east lie gently undulating prairie lands. The land slopes upward to the north, reaching an average height of about 8,000 feet in 20 miles at the top of Palmer Lake Divide.

Colorado Springs is in the Arkansas River drainage basin. The principal tributary feeding the Arkansas from this area is Fountain Creek which rises in the high mountains west of the city and is fed by Monument Creek originating to the north in the Palmer Lake Divide area.

Other topographical features of the area, and particularly its wide range of elevations, help to give Colorado Springs the various and altogether delightful plains and mountain mixture of climate that has established the locality as a highly desirable place to live. The higher elevations immediately to the west and north of the city produce significant differences in temperature and precipitation. Precipitation amounts at these higher elevations are approximately twice those at nearby lower elevations and the number of rainy days is almost triple.

In Colorado Springs itself, precipitation is relatively sparse. Over 80 percent of it falls between April 1 and September 30, mostly as heavy downpours accompanying summer thunderstorms. Temperatures, in view of the station latitude and elevation, are mild. Uncomfortable extremes, in either summer or winter, are comparatively rare and of short duration. Relative humidity is normally low and wind movement moderately high. This is notably true of the west-to-east movement of the chinook winds, that cause rapid rises in winter temperatures and remind us that the Indian meaning of chinook is snow eater.

Colorado Springs is best known as a resort city, but is also important to the high-tech industry and military community. Several military installations, including the United States Air Force Academy and the Space Command are located within or near the city. The surrounding prairie is also important for cattle raising and a considerable amount of grazing land is used for sheep in the summer months. The growing season varies considerably in length but averages from the first week in May to the first week of October.

Colorado Springs Muni Airport *El Paso County* Elevation: 6,140 ft. Latitude: 38° 49' N Longitude: 104° 43' W

	JAN	FEB	MAR	APR	MAY	JUN	JUL	AUG	SEP	OCT	NOV	DEC	YEAR
Mean Maximum Temp. (°F)	43.1	45.3	52.2	59.9	69.2	79.2	85.2	81.8	74.6	63.2	51.2	42.5	62.3
Mean Temp. (°F)	30.4	32.5	39.1	46.5	56.0	65.3	71.1	68.8	60.9	49.4	38.3	30.1	49.0
Mean Minimum Temp. (°F)	17.7	19.6	25.9	33.2	42.7	51.3	57.0	55.7	47.3	35.7	25.3	17.7	35.7
Extreme Maximum Temp. (°F)	73	74	78	87	94	99	100	99	94	85	78	75	100
Extreme Minimum Temp. (°F)	-20	-19	-3	7	22	36	46	39	22	7	-5	-24	-24
Days Maximum Temp. ≥ 90°F	0	0	0	0	0	4	10	3	1	0	0	0	18
Days Maximum Temp. ≤ 32°F	6	5	2	1	0	0	0	0	0	1	3	6	24
Days Minimum Temp. ≤ 32°F	30	27	25	14	2	0	0	0	1	10	24	30	163
Days Minimum Temp. ≤ 0°F	2	2	0	0	0	0	0	0	0	0	0	2	6
Heating Degree Days (base 65°F)	1,065	912	797	547	284	74	8	19	152	476	795	1,074	6,203
Cooling Degree Days (base 65°F)	0	0	0	1	11	89	204	142	37	1	0	0	485
Mean Precipitation (in.)	0.32	0.34	1.03	1.49	2.16	2.54	2.80	3.41	1.21	0.80	0.41	0.34	16.85
Maximum Precipitation (in.)*	1.2	2.4	2.4	3.6	5.0	7.8	5.1	6.1	3.0	5.0	2.0	1.0	21.9
Minimum Precipitation (in.)*	trace	trace	0.3	0.1	0.7	0.1	0.7	1.4	0	trace	trace	trace	12.6
Extreme Maximum Daily Precip. (in.)	0.77	1.49	1.63	2.63	1.85	2.51	3.63	3.98	4.29	1.13	0.67	0.66	4.29
Days With ≥ 0.1" Precipitation	1	1	3	4	5	5	6	7	3	2	1	1	39
Days With ≥ 0.5" Precipitation	0	0	0	1	1	2	1	2	0	0	0	0	7
Days With ≥ 1.0" Precipitation	0	0	0	0	0	0	1	1	0	0	0	0	2
Mean Snowfall (in.)	5.7	4.7	8.3	5.3	0.7	trace	trace	trace	0.3	3.1	4.8	5.9	38.8
Maximum Snowfall (in.)*	29	23	23	20	19	0	0	0	2	26	26	18	88
Maximum 24-hr. Snowfall (in.)*	22	15	12	7	15	0	0	0	1	9	9	9	22
Maximum Snow Depth (in.)	16	12	15	12	5	trace	trace	trace	2	20	9	8	20
Days With ≥ 1.0" Snow Depth	6	4	4	2	0	0	0	0	0	1	3	6	26
Thunderstorm Days*	0	< 1	1	2	8	10	12	13	4	1	0	0	51
Foggy Days*	6	7	7	6	5	4	3	4	4	4	6	7	63
Predominant Sky Cover*	CLR	CLR	OVR	OVR	OVR	CLR	SCT	CLR	CLR	CLR	CLR	CLR	CLR
Mean Relative Humidity 5am (%)*	57	59	62	63	67	66	68	70	65	58	59	56	63
Mean Relative Humidity 5pm (%)*	46	41	39	36	38	35	39	41	36	36	45	47	40
Mean Dewpoint (°F)*	10	13	16	23	33	41	47	47	38	26	17	11	27
Prevailing Wind Direction*	NNE	N	N	N	N	SSE	N	N	N	N	NNE	NNE	N
Prevailing Wind Speed (mph)*	9	12	14	14	13	12	10	10	10	12	9	9	12
Maximum Wind Gust (mph)*	63	61	71	64	70	64	58	56	54	58	62	68	71

Note: (*) Period of record is 1978-1995

Denver Stapleton Int'l Airport

Denver enjoys the invigorating climate that prevails over much of the central Rocky Mountain region, without the extremely cold mornings of the high elevations during winter, or the hot afternoons of summer at lower altitudes. Extremely warm or cold weather in Denver is usually of short duration.

Situated a long distance from any moisture source, and separated from the Pacific Ocean by several high mountain barriers, Denver enjoys low relative humidity, light precipitation, and abundant sunshine.

Air masses from four different sources influence Denver weather. These include arctic air from Canada and Alaska, warm, moist air from the Gulf of Mexico, warm, dry air from Mexico and the southwestern deserts, and Pacific air modified by its passage over mountains to the west.

In winter, the high altitude and mountains to the west combine to moderate temperatures in Denver. Invasions of cold air from the north, intensified by the high altitude, can be abrupt and severe. However, many of the cold air masses that spread southward out of Canada never reach the altitude of Denver, but move off over the lower plains to the east. Surges of air from the west are moderated in their descent down the east face of the Rockies, and reach Denver in the form of chinook winds that often raise temperatures into the 60s, even in midwinter.

In spring, polar air often collides with warm, moist air from the Gulf of Mexico and these collisions result in frequent, rapid and drastic weather changes. Spring is the cloudiest, windiest, and wettest season in the city. Much of the precipitation falls as snow, especially in March and early April. Stormy periods are interspersed with stretches of mild, sunny weather that quickly melt previous snow cover.

Summer precipitation falls mainly from scattered thunderstorms during the afternoon and evening. Mornings are usually clear and sunny, with clouds forming during early afternoon to cut off the sunshine at what would otherwise be the hottest part of the day. Severe thunderstorms, with large hail and heavy rain occasionally occur in the city, but these conditions are more common on the plains to the east.

Autumn is the most pleasant season. Few thunderstorms occur and invasions of cold air are infrequent. As a result, there is more sunshine and less severe weather than at any other time of the year.

Based on the 1951-1980 period, the average first occurrence of 32 degrees Fahrenheit in the fall is October 8 and the average last occurrence in the spring is May 3.

Denver Stapleton Int'l Airport *Denver County* Elevation: 5,286 ft. Latitude: 39° 46' N Longitude: 104° 52' W

	JAN	FEB	MAR	APR	MAY	JUN	JUL	AUG	SEP	OCT	NOV	DEC	YEAR
Mean Maximum Temp. (°F)	44.9	46.9	54.2	61.6	71.2	82.1	88.7	86.0	77.5	65.2	52.8	44.0	64.6
Mean Temp. (°F)	31.7	33.9	41.0	48.4	58.0	67.9	74.2	72.0	63.0	50.8	39.4	31.0	50.9
Mean Minimum Temp. (°F)	18.4	20.9	27.8	35.1	44.7	53.6	59.5	57.8	48.4	36.3	25.9	17.9	37.2
Extreme Maximum Temp. (°F)	74	74	82	90	96	104	104	102	97	89	81	75	104
Extreme Minimum Temp. (°F)	-19	-24	-5	7	25	36	44	43	17	7	-8	-25	-25
Days Maximum Temp. ≥ 90°F	0	0	0	0	1	7	16	11	3	0	0	0	38
Days Maximum Temp. ≤ 32°F	6	4	2	0	0	0	0	0	0	0	2	6	20
Days Minimum Temp. ≤ 32°F	29	26	23	11	1	0	0	0	1	9	24	29	153
Days Minimum Temp. ≤ 0°F	2	2	0	0	0	0	0	0	0	0	0	2	6
Heating Degree Days (base 65°F)	1,026	872	736	494	234	49	4	8	124	436	761	1,047	5,791
Cooling Degree Days (base 65°F)	0	0	0	2	24	142	296	231	69	2	0	0	766
Mean Precipitation (in.)	0.49	0.46	1.29	1.74	2.33	1.57	2.09	2.07	1.07	1.06	0.82	0.61	15.60
Maximum Precipitation (in.)*	1.4	1.6	4.6	4.1	7.3	4.7	6.4	5.8	4.7	4.2	2.7	2.8	23.3
Minimum Precipitation (in.)*	trace	trace	0.2	trace	0.1	0.1	0.5	0.1	trace	0	trace	trace	7.5
Extreme Maximum Daily Precip. (in.)	0.64	0.41	3.10	1.29	1.96	1.76	3.83	3.81	1.31	1.33	0.72	2.00	3.83
Days With ≥ 0.1" Precipitation	2	2	4	5	5	4	4	4	3	3	3	2	41
Days With ≥ 0.5" Precipitation	0	0	0	1	1	1	1	1	0	1	0	0	6
Days With ≥ 1.0" Precipitation	0	0	0	0	0	0	1	0	0	0	0	0	1
Mean Snowfall (in.)	7.3	5.8	10.9	7.5	1.0	trace	trace	trace	1.3	4.0	8.8	8.4	55.0
Maximum Snowfall (in.)*	24	18	31	26	14	trace	0	0	17	31	30	31	112
Maximum 24-hr. Snowfall (in.)*	14	10	18	17	9	trace	0	0	12	10	14	24	24
Maximum Snow Depth (in.)	14	11	22	11	7	trace	trace	trace	8	17	16	24	24
Days With ≥ 1.0" Snow Depth	13	8	5	2	0	0	0	0	0	1	6	12	47
Thunderstorm Days*	< 1	< 1	< 1	2	6	10	10	8	3	1	< 1	0	40
Foggy Days*	5	6	7	5	5	3	2	3	4	4	6	5	55
Predominant Sky Cover*	CLR	OVR	OVR	OVR	OVR	SCT	SCT	SCT	CLR	CLR	CLR	CLR	CLR
Mean Relative Humidity 5am (%)*	62	66	67	66	70	68	68	68	66	63	66	63	66
Mean Relative Humidity 5pm (%)*	49	44	39	35	38	34	33	34	32	35	47	50	39
Mean Dewpoint (°F)*	13	16	19	26	36	43	48	47	39	28	20	14	29
Prevailing Wind Direction*	S	S	S	S	S	S	S	S	S	SSW	S	S	S
Prevailing Wind Speed (mph)*	9	9	9	10	10	9	9	9	8	8	8	9	9
Maximum Wind Gust (mph)*	62	66	62	70	63	64	70	59	59	60	56	67	70

Note: (*) Period of record is 1948-1995

Grand Junction Walker Field

Grand Junction is located at the junction of the Colorado and Gunnison Rivers. It is on the west slope of the Rockies, in a large mountain valley. The area has a climate marked by the wide seasonal range usual to interior localities at this latitude. Thanks, however, to the protective topography of the vicinity, sudden and severe weather changes are very infrequent. The valley floor slopes from 4,800 feet near Palisade to 4,400 feet at the west end near Fruita. Mountains are on all sides at distances of from 10 to 60 miles and reach heights of 9,000 to over 12,000 feet.

This mountain valley location, with attendant valley breezes, provides protection from spring and fall frosts. This results in a growing season averaging 191 days in the city. This varies considerably in the outlying districts. It is about the same in the upper valley around Palisade, and three to four weeks shorter near the river west of Grand Junction. The growing season is sufficiently long to permit commercial growth of almost all fruits except citrus varieties. Summer grazing of cattle and sheep on nearby mountain ranges is extensive.

The interior, continental location, ringed by mountains on all sides, results in quite low precipitation in all seasons. Consequently, agriculture is dependent on irrigation. Adequate supplies of water are available from mountain snows and rains. Summer rains occur chiefly as scattered light showers and thunderstorms which develop over nearby mountains. Winter snows are fairly frequent, but are mostly light and quick to melt. Even the infrequent snows of from four to eight inches seldom remain on the ground for prolonged periods. Blizzard conditions in the valley are extremely rare.

Temperatures above 100 degrees are infrequent, and about one-third of the winters have no readings below zero. Summer days with maximum temperatures in the middle 90s and minimums in the low 60s are common. Relative humidity is very low during the summer, with values similar to other dry locations such as the southern parts of New Mexico and Arizona. Spells of cold winter weather are sometimes prolonged due to cold air becoming trapped in the valley. Winds are usually very light during the coldest weather. Changes in winter are normally gradual, and abrupt changes are much less frequent than in eastern Colorado. Cold waves are rare. Sunny days predominate in all seasons.

The prevailing wind is from the east-southeast due to the valley breeze effect. The strongest winds are associated with thunderstorms or with pre-frontal weather. They usually are from the south or southwest.

Grand Junction Walker Field *Mesa County* Elevation: 4,839 ft. Latitude: 39° 08' N Longitude: 108° 32' W

	JAN	FEB	MAR	APR	MAY	JUN	JUL	AUG	SEP	OCT	NOV	DEC	YEAR
Mean Maximum Temp. (°F)	38.6	46.4	57.0	65.8	76.6	88.1	93.7	90.3	80.6	66.6	51.0	39.2	66.1
Mean Temp. (°F)	28.5	35.6	44.6	52.4	62.3	72.6	78.8	76.2	66.7	53.6	39.8	29.3	53.4
Mean Minimum Temp. (°F)	18.3	24.8	32.2	38.9	47.9	57.1	63.9	62.1	52.8	40.5	28.6	19.4	40.5
Extreme Maximum Temp. (°F)	57	68	81	89	101	105	106	103	100	88	76	64	106
Extreme Minimum Temp. (°F)	-8	-18	6	16	26	35	44	45	31	18	-4	-17	-18
Days Maximum Temp. ≥ 90°F	0	0	0	0	2	15	25	19	4	0	0	0	65
Days Maximum Temp. ≤ 32°F	7	2	0	0	0	0	0	0	0	0	1	6	16
Days Minimum Temp. ≤ 32°F	30	24	16	6	0	0	0	0	0	4	22	30	132
Days Minimum Temp. ≤ 0°F	2	0	0	0	0	0	0	0	0	0	0	1	3
Heating Degree Days (base 65°F)	1,125	825	625	375	138	17	0	1	60	352	749	1,099	5,366
Cooling Degree Days (base 65°F)	0	0	0	3	59	252	436	356	118	5	0	0	1,229
Mean Precipitation (in.)	0.58	0.56	0.93	0.90	0.90	0.45	0.62	0.95	1.19	1.05	0.73	0.57	9.43
Maximum Precipitation (in.)*	2.5	1.5	2.0	1.9	2.0	2.1	1.9	3.5	2.8	3.4	2.0	1.9	15.7
Minimum Precipitation (in.)*	trace	trace	trace	0.1	trace	trace	trace	trace	trace	0	trace	trace	4.4
Extreme Maximum Daily Precip. (in.)	0.59	0.53	1.00	0.83	0.96	0.91	0.76	1.31	1.21	0.88	0.80	0.60	1.31
Days With ≥ 0.1" Precipitation	2	2	3	3	3	2	2	3	4	3	2	2	31
Days With ≥ 0.5" Precipitation	0	0	0	0	0	0	0	0	1	0	0	0	1
Days With ≥ 1.0" Precipitation	0	0	0	0	0	0	0	0	0	0	0	0	0
Mean Snowfall (in.)	4.8	3.2	2.8	0.9	trace	trace	trace	trace	trace	0.4	2.1	4.9	19.1
Maximum Snowfall (in.)*	34	18	15	14	5	0	0	0	3	6	12	19	56
Maximum 24-hr. Snowfall (in.)*	8	9	6	6	5	0	0	0	3	3	8	5	9
Maximum Snow Depth (in.)	9	11	3	4	trace	trace	trace	trace	trace	1	5	11	11
Days With ≥ 1.0" Snow Depth	11	5	1	0	0	0	0	0	0	0	1	6	24
Thunderstorm Days*	< 1	< 1	1	2	5	5	8	8	5	2	< 1	< 1	36
Foggy Days*	8	5	3	1	< 1	< 1	< 1	< 1	< 1	1	3	5	26
Predominant Sky Cover*	OVR	OVR	OVR	OVR	SCT	CLR	SCT	SCT	CLR	CLR	CLR	OVR	CLR
Mean Relative Humidity 5am (%)*	77	73	64	56	52	43	47	51	51	57	69	76	60
Mean Relative Humidity 5pm (%)*	62	50	36	27	24	18	21	24	25	32	47	60	35
Mean Dewpoint (°F)*	16	20	22	25	31	34	43	44	36	29	24	18	28
Prevailing Wind Direction*	ESE	ESE	ESE	ESE	ESE	SE	SE	SE	ESE	ESE	ESE	ESE	ESE
Prevailing Wind Speed (mph)*	7	8	9	9	10	10	10	9	10	9	8	8	9
Maximum Wind Gust (mph)*	59	59	59	78	62	69	64	74	64	54	53	45	78

Note: (*) Period of record is 1948-1995

Pueblo Memorial Airport

The city of Pueblo is located about 40 miles east-southeast of the Royal Gorge, at the junction of the Arkansas and Fountain Rivers. The mountains west of the city extend from within 25 miles to the southwest to about 35 miles to the northwest. Lake Pueblo, the largest body of water in southern Colorado, is located 7 miles west of the city and provides a variety of water sports, fishing, picnicing, and a wildlife preserve. The countryside surrounding Pueblo consists of rolling plains, broken by normally dry arroyos, and is generally treeless, covered mainly with sparse bunchgrass and occasional cacti. The business section of the city is 4,663 feet above sea level. The National Weather Service Office is located at Pueblo Memorial Airport, six miles east of the Pueblo Post Office, and about one and a half miles north of the Arkansas River. Terrain at the airport is relatively flat, and from 50 to 100 feet above the river. The air quality in Pueblo is rated the best of large Colorado cities along the front range.

The climate is semi-arid and marked by large daily temperature variations. The temperature reaches 90 degrees or more about half the time during the summer, but thanks to the low relative humidity, the heat is not oppressive. Summer nights are invariably cool since mountain breezes prevail from shortly after sunset to about noon the following day. The sun shines about 76 percent of the time. Winter is comparatively mild due to the abundant sunshine and the protection afforded by the nearby mountains. Temperatures reach 50 degrees or higher in the winter. The temperature drops to zero or below about eight times during the winter. Cold spells are generally broken after a few days by chinook winds, a very dry, warm, downslope westerly wind.

The probability of measurable precipitation in summer is one day out of four and in winter one out of eight. Summer rains usually occur in the form of afternoon thunderstorms. Blowing dust frequently develops during the spring months of abnormally dry years, especially in areas where dry farming has been attempted.

Agriculture consists chiefly of cattle grazing on the dry plains and irrigated farming near streams. Sugar beets, corn, chili peppers, and melons are the most important crops. In addition, a variety of vegetables, from asparagus to zucchini, are grown. Some dry farming is attempted, but the extent of such operations is limited by the annual precipitation of less than 12 inches.

Pueblo Memorial Airport *Pueblo County* Elevation: 4,684 ft. Latitude: 38° 17' N Longitude: 104° 30' W

	JAN	FEB	MAR	APR	MAY	JUN	JUL	AUG	SEP	OCT	NOV	DEC	YEAR
Mean Maximum Temp. (°F)	47.1	51.3	59.4	67.6	77.1	87.7	93.4	89.9	81.9	69.6	56.5	46.7	69.0
Mean Temp. (°F)	30.8	34.6	42.7	50.9	60.8	70.3	76.3	73.9	65.0	52.0	39.6	30.7	52.3
Mean Minimum Temp. (°F)	14.4	17.9	26.0	34.1	44.5	53.0	59.1	57.8	48.0	34.4	22.7	14.6	35.6
Extreme Maximum Temp. (°F)	81	81	86	93	102	108	109	105	101	94	85	82	109
Extreme Minimum Temp. (°F)	-19	-26	-6	2	24	35	44	42	21	4	-17	-25	-26
Days Maximum Temp. ≥ 90°F	0	0	0	0	3	14	23	19	7	0	0	0	66
Days Maximum Temp. ≤ 32°F	5	3	1	0	0	0	0	0	0	0	2	5	16
Days Minimum Temp. ≤ 32°F	30	27	25	12	1	0	0	0	1	13	26	30	165
Days Minimum Temp. ≤ 0°F	3	2	0	0	0	0	0	0	0	0	0	3	8
Heating Degree Days (base 65°F)	1,053	851	684	419	160	20	1	3	83	398	754	1,056	5,482
Cooling Degree Days (base 65°F)	0	0	0	2	37	187	358	286	90	3	0	0	963
Mean Precipitation (in.)	0.36	0.28	0.93	1.46	1.49	1.34	2.01	2.41	0.78	0.72	0.48	0.36	12.62
Maximum Precipitation (in.)*	0.9	1.4	2.3	4.0	5.4	4.3	5.1	5.8	2.7	4.9	2.5	1.0	23.1
Minimum Precipitation (in.)*	trace	trace	0	trace	0.3	trace	0.1	0.1	trace	trace	trace	trace	6.3
Extreme Maximum Daily Precip. (in.)	0.55	0.60	1.26	2.00	2.67	1.58	1.95	2.28	1.57	1.28	0.78	0.54	2.67
Days With ≥ 0.1" Precipitation	1	1	3	4	4	3	5	5	2	2	1	1	32
Days With ≥ 0.5" Precipitation	0	0	0	1	1	1	1	1	0	0	0	0	5
Days With ≥ 1.0" Precipitation	0	0	0	0	0	0	0	1	0	0	0	0	1
Mean Snowfall (in.)	6.5	3.6	5.7	4.2	0.5	trace	trace	trace	0.3	1.3	4.2	5.4	31.7
Maximum Snowfall (in.)*	18	14	16	21	11	0	0	0	14	16	26	15	72
Maximum 24-hr. Snowfall (in.)*	12	8	9	13	6	0	0	0	10	13	16	7	16
Maximum Snow Depth (in.)	10	7	10	9	3	trace	trace	trace	1	8	11	8	11
Days With ≥ 1.0" Snow Depth	7	3	1	1	0	0	0	0	0	0	2	5	19
Thunderstorm Days*	0	0	< 1	2	6	8	11	9	3	1	< 1	0	40
Foggy Days*	5	5	5	3	3	2	1	2	4	3	5	5	43
Predominant Sky Cover*	CLR	CLR	OVR	CLR	OVR	CLR	SCT	SCT	CLR	CLR	CLR	CLR	CLR
Mean Relative Humidity 5am (%)*	70	69	68	66	70	71	72	75	71	67	73	69	70
Mean Relative Humidity 5pm (%)*	49	40	35	30	32	29	32	34	32	32	45	49	37
Mean Dewpoint (°F)*	15	17	21	27	37	45	51	52	42	30	23	16	31
Prevailing Wind Direction*	W	W	W	SE	SE	SE	SE	SE	SE	W	W	W	SE
Prevailing Wind Speed (mph)*	9	9	12	10	12	12	10	10	9	8	8	9	10
Maximum Wind Gust (mph)*	68	71	86	73	76	69	70	63	59	67	68	63	86

Note: (*) Period of record is 1954-1995

Akron 4 E *Washington County* Elevation: 4,540 ft. Latitude: 40° 09' N Longitude: 103° 09' W

	JAN	FEB	MAR	APR	MAY	JUN	JUL	AUG	SEP	OCT	NOV	DEC	YEAR
Mean Maximum Temp. (°F)	40.4	44.0	52.4	60.9	70.7	81.6	89.3	86.8	78.1	64.8	50.9	40.4	63.4
Mean Temp. (°F)	27.6	31.0	38.6	46.6	56.8	66.8	73.8	71.6	62.6	49.6	37.5	27.6	49.2
Mean Minimum Temp. (°F)	14.7	17.9	24.8	32.3	42.8	51.9	58.1	56.4	47.0	34.4	23.9	14.7	34.9
Extreme Maximum Temp. (°F)	75	75	83	90	98	105	107	105	102	92	81	75	107
Extreme Minimum Temp. (°F)	-21	-26	-13	0	17	31	41	36	14	1	-10	-32	-32
Days Maximum Temp. ≥ 90°F	0	0	0	0	1	8	17	14	5	0	0	0	45
Days Maximum Temp. ≤ 32°F	9	6	3	1	0	0	0	0	0	1	4	8	32
Days Minimum Temp. ≤ 32°F	31	27	26	15	2	0	0	0	1	12	25	30	169
Days Minimum Temp. ≤ 0°F	3	2	0	0	0	0	0	0	0	0	0	3	8
Heating Degree Days (base 65°F)	1,153	955	811	546	270	66	7	14	141	473	820	1,154	6,410
Cooling Degree Days (base 65°F)	0	0	0	1	21	126	286	227	74	4	0	0	739
Mean Precipitation (in.)	0.37	0.39	0.95	1.39	2.65	2.44	2.62	2.59	1.15	1.05	0.59	0.44	16.63
Extreme Maximum Daily Precip. (in.)	1.00	1.03	2.06	1.43	2.04	1.81	3.75	2.39	2.18	1.88	1.40	1.10	3.75
Days With ≥ 0.1" Precipitation	1	1	2	4	6	5	6	5	3	3	2	1	39
Days With ≥ 0.5" Precipitation	0	0	0	1	2	2	2	2	1	0	0	0	10
Days With ≥ 1.0" Precipitation	0	0	0	0	0	0	0	1	0	0	0	0	1
Mean Snowfall (in.)	***4.4***	4.4	***5.1***	3.7	0.3	0.0	0.0	0.0	0.3	1.6	***5.0***	***5.6***	***30.4***
Maximum Snow Depth (in.)	***30***	11	***9***	9	2	0	0	4	5	8	***9***	na	na
Days With ≥ 1.0" Snow Depth	***12***	10	***5***	2	0	0	0	0	0	1	***5***	***13***	***48***

Altenbern *Garfield County* Elevation: 5,678 ft. Latitude: 39° 30' N Longitude: 108° 23' W

	JAN	FEB	MAR	APR	MAY	JUN	JUL	AUG	SEP	OCT	NOV	DEC	YEAR
Mean Maximum Temp. (°F)	38.0	43.7	54.0	62.8	72.6	83.5	89.3	86.2	77.5	64.7	49.3	38.1	63.3
Mean Temp. (°F)	24.9	30.7	39.3	46.5	55.2	63.7	69.7	67.8	59.5	48.1	35.3	25.4	47.2
Mean Minimum Temp. (°F)	11.8	17.7	24.5	30.0	37.8	43.9	50.1	49.4	41.5	31.4	21.2	12.6	31.0
Extreme Maximum Temp. (°F)	57	67	80	84	97	102	104	99	96	87	72	61	104
Extreme Minimum Temp. (°F)	-19	-28	-3	5	19	22	30	26	20	8	-11	-23	-28
Days Maximum Temp. ≥ 90°F	0	0	0	0	0	6	17	9	1	0	0	0	33
Days Maximum Temp. ≤ 32°F	7	2	0	0	0	0	0	0	0	0	1	7	17
Days Minimum Temp. ≤ 32°F	31	27	28	20	6	1	0	0	3	18	28	31	193
Days Minimum Temp. ≤ 0°F	5	1	0	0	0	0	0	0	0	0	0	4	10
Heating Degree Days (base 65°F)	1,235	964	790	550	299	80	8	15	171	516	886	1,223	6,737
Cooling Degree Days (base 65°F)	0	0	0	0	3	49	162	110	14	0	0	0	338
Mean Precipitation (in.)	1.20	1.30	1.47	1.63	1.78	0.96	1.39	1.50	1.93	2.00	1.44	1.11	17.71
Extreme Maximum Daily Precip. (in.)	1.03	1.47	1.74	0.82	1.19	1.82	1.32	1.70	1.49	1.87	1.26	1.64	1.87
Days With ≥ 0.1" Precipitation	4	4	5	5	5	3	4	4	5	6	4	4	53
Days With ≥ 0.5" Precipitation	0	1	0	1	1	0	1	1	1	1	1	0	8
Days With ≥ 1.0" Precipitation	0	0	0	0	0	0	0	0	0	0	0	0	0
Mean Snowfall (in.)	13.7	10.7	7.6	2.8	0.4	0.0	0.0	0.0	0.0	1.3	7.2	14.5	58.2
Maximum Snow Depth (in.)	34	37	25	7	trace	0	0	0	0	4	14	22	37
Days With ≥ 1.0" Snow Depth	22	13	3	0	0	0	0	0	0	0	4	16	58

Antero Reservoir *Park County* Elevation: 8,919 ft. Latitude: 39° 00' N Longitude: 105° 54' W

	JAN	FEB	MAR	APR	MAY	JUN	JUL	AUG	SEP	OCT	NOV	DEC	YEAR
Mean Maximum Temp. (°F)	33.5	35.9	42.2	49.3	59.9	70.5	76.5	73.6	67.0	55.8	43.0	33.5	53.4
Mean Temp. (°F)	14.7	17.5	26.4	34.1	44.0	52.6	58.5	56.6	48.9	37.6	26.2	15.4	36.0
Mean Minimum Temp. (°F)	-4.2	-0.8	10.5	18.8	28.0	34.7	40.3	39.6	30.8	19.3	9.3	-2.8	18.6
Extreme Maximum Temp. (°F)	60	58	64	72	81	85	88	87	82	78	68	58	88
Extreme Minimum Temp. (°F)	-46	-51	-31	-18	5	17	27	24	11	-13	-29	-44	-51
Days Maximum Temp. ≥ 90°F	0	0	0	0	0	0	0	0	0	0	0	0	0
Days Maximum Temp. ≤ 32°F	13	10	5	2	0	0	0	0	0	1	5	13	49
Days Minimum Temp. ≤ 32°F	31	28	31	29	24	10	1	2	18	30	30	31	265
Days Minimum Temp. ≤ 0°F	19	15	6	1	0	0	0	0	0	0	6	18	65
Heating Degree Days (base 65°F)	1,554	1,336	1,191	920	644	366	197	253	476	844	1,157	1,533	10,471
Cooling Degree Days (base 65°F)	0	0	0	0	0	0	1	0	0	0	0	0	1
Mean Precipitation (in.)	0.25	0.29	0.57	0.71	1.10	1.20	1.95	2.37	1.01	0.72	0.33	0.31	10.81
Extreme Maximum Daily Precip. (in.)	0.46	0.80	0.55	0.76	1.20	1.48	2.18	1.76	1.29	1.29	1.07	0.49	2.18
Days With ≥ 0.1" Precipitation	1	1	2	2	3	4	6	6	3	2	1	1	32
Days With ≥ 0.5" Precipitation	0	0	0	0	1	1	1	1	0	0	0	0	4
Days With ≥ 1.0" Precipitation	0	0	0	0	0	0	0	0	0	0	0	0	0
Mean Snowfall (in.)	4.5	5.3	9.1	8.7	3.0	0.1	0.0	0.0	0.4	4.1	5.6	5.6	46.4
Maximum Snow Depth (in.)	14	25	24	19	20	4	0	0	3	12	15	11	25
Days With ≥ 1.0" Snow Depth	17	16	13	6	1	0	0	0	0	3	9	17	82

Aspen 1 SW *Pitkin County* Elevation: 8,163 ft. Latitude: 39° 11' N Longitude: 106° 50' W

	JAN	FEB	MAR	APR	MAY	JUN	JUL	AUG	SEP	OCT	NOV	DEC	YEAR
Mean Maximum Temp. (°F)	35.2	39.2	45.4	52.5	62.8	72.5	78.2	75.8	68.8	57.5	44.0	34.6	55.5
Mean Temp. (°F)	22.0	25.5	32.4	39.4	48.8	57.0	62.7	61.1	53.9	43.5	31.6	22.1	41.7
Mean Minimum Temp. (°F)	8.9	11.8	19.4	26.2	34.7	41.4	47.1	46.4	39.0	29.4	19.1	9.6	27.8
Extreme Maximum Temp. (°F)	58	60	68	74	86	88	92	89	86	77	70	62	92
Extreme Minimum Temp. (°F)	-20	-25	-14	0	15	20	29	29	18	6	-11	-23	-25
Days Maximum Temp. ≥ 90°F	0	0	0	0	0	0	0	0	0	0	0	0	0
Days Maximum Temp. ≤ 32°F	12	6	2	0	0	0	0	0	0	1	5	12	38
Days Minimum Temp. ≤ 32°F	31	28	30	24	11	2	0	0	5	20	29	31	211
Days Minimum Temp. ≤ 0°F	6	3	1	0	0	0	0	0	0	0	1	6	17
Heating Degree Days (base 65°F)	1,325	1,110	1,003	763	497	239	91	123	326	661	998	1,325	8,461
Cooling Degree Days (base 65°F)	0	0	0	0	0	4	24	9	1	0	0	0	38
Mean Precipitation (in.)	1.86	2.11	2.65	2.44	2.11	1.34	1.87	1.54	2.04	2.03	2.37	2.02	24.38
Extreme Maximum Daily Precip. (in.)	1.15	1.92	1.56	1.05	1.30	2.35	1.20	1.00	1.07	0.96	1.80	1.16	2.35
Days With ≥ 0.1" Precipitation	6	6	8	8	6	4	6	6	7	6	7	7	77
Days With ≥ 0.5" Precipitation	1	1	1	1	1	0	1	0	1	1	1	1	10
Days With ≥ 1.0" Precipitation	0	0	0	0	0	0	0	0	0	0	0	0	0
Mean Snowfall (in.)	26.7	27.3	28.1	19.4	7.7	0.9	0.0	0.0	1.2	10.8	26.7	28.1	176.9
Maximum Snow Depth (in.)	44	54	60	48	26	9	0	0	6	17	***24***	40	***60***
Days With ≥ 1.0" Snow Depth	31	28	30	19	3	0	0	0	0	4	20	30	165

The period of record for all cooperative weather station data is 1980 – 2009. See User Guide for detailed explanation of data.

Bailey *Park County* Elevation: 7,729 ft. Latitude: 39° 24' N Longitude: 105° 29' W

	JAN	FEB	MAR	APR	MAY	JUN	JUL	AUG	SEP	OCT	NOV	DEC	YEAR
Mean Maximum Temp. (°F)	37.9	40.6	46.7	53.3	62.6	73.1	78.5	75.8	69.1	58.0	45.1	37.1	56.5
Mean Temp. (°F)	23.1	25.5	31.9	38.3	47.1	55.7	61.3	59.4	51.8	41.2	30.5	22.8	40.7
Mean Minimum Temp. (°F)	8.3	10.4	17.1	23.2	31.4	38.3	44.0	43.0	34.4	24.4	16.0	8.6	24.9
Extreme Maximum Temp. (°F)	61	62	70	75	86	90	93	89	86	81	68	65	93
Extreme Minimum Temp. (°F)	-28	-32	-20	-11	13	24	28	26	7	-9	-18	-32	-32
Days Maximum Temp. ≥ 90°F	0	0	0	0	0	0	1	0	0	0	0	0	1
Days Maximum Temp. ≤ 32°F	9	5	3	2	0	0	0	0	0	1	4	10	34
Days Minimum Temp. ≤ 32°F	31	28	30	28	18	4	0	1	11	28	29	31	239
Days Minimum Temp. ≤ 0°F	7	5	2	0	0	0	0	0	0	0	2	7	23
Heating Degree Days (base 65°F)	1,292	1,109	1,018	796	549	273	120	170	390	731	1,028	1,300	8,776
Cooling Degree Days (base 65°F)	0	0	0	0	0	2	11	4	0	0	0	0	17
Mean Precipitation (in.)	0.49	0.54	1.45	1.92	2.05	1.84	2.59	2.96	1.31	1.19	0.83	0.58	17.75
Extreme Maximum Daily Precip. (in.)	0.58	0.53	1.94	1.69	1.90	1.58	1.74	2.12	1.10	1.64	1.18	1.45	2.12
Days With ≥ 0.1" Precipitation	2	2	4	5	6	5	7	8	4	3	3	2	51
Days With ≥ 0.5" Precipitation	0	0	1	1	1	1	2	1	1	1	0	0	9
Days With ≥ 1.0" Precipitation	0	0	0	0	0	0	0	1	0	0	0	0	1
Mean Snowfall (in.)	8.4	9.2	17.9	16.8	3.6	0.1	0.0	0.0	1.7	7.1	11.3	10.0	86.1
Maximum Snow Depth (in.)	45	40	41	34	24	3	0	0	8	20	19	40	45
Days With ≥ 1.0" Snow Depth	30	28	26	13	2	0	0	0	1	5	21	28	154

Bonny Dam 2 NE *Yuma County* Elevation: 3,716 ft. Latitude: 39° 39' N Longitude: 102° 07' W

	JAN	FEB	MAR	APR	MAY	JUN	JUL	AUG	SEP	OCT	NOV	DEC	YEAR
Mean Maximum Temp. (°F)	***41.6***	45.9	***54.5***	62.9	73.0	***83.6***	***90.6***	***88.3***	***79.4***	***66.6***	***53.4***	***42.8***	***65.2***
Mean Temp. (°F)	***28.9***	32.5	***40.5***	48.4	59.0	***69.2***	***75.7***	***73.7***	***64.4***	***51.4***	***39.5***	***29.8***	***51.1***
Mean Minimum Temp. (°F)	***16.1***	18.7	***26.4***	33.9	45.0	***54.7***	***60.7***	***59.2***	***49.4***	36.3	***25.7***	***16.7***	***36.9***
Extreme Maximum Temp. (°F)	79	79	87	95	101	105	109	105	102	93	85	80	109
Extreme Minimum Temp. (°F)	-30	-25	-9	7	25	35	45	41	14	6	-4	-24	-30
Days Maximum Temp. ≥ 90°F	0	0	0	0	2	8	17	14	6	0	0	0	47
Days Maximum Temp. ≤ 32°F	7	5	2	1	0	0	0	0	0	0	2	6	23
Days Minimum Temp. ≤ 32°F	29	26	23	12	2	0	0	0	1	9	22	27	151
Days Minimum Temp. ≤ 0°F	2	2	0	0	0	0	0	0	0	0	0	2	6
Heating Degree Days (base 65°F)	***1,113***	912	***754***	493	213	***40***	***3***	***8***	***111***	***421***	***757***	***1,084***	***5,909***
Cooling Degree Days (base 65°F)	***0***	0	***0***	2	35	***172***	***341***	***286***	***99***	***7***	***0***	***0***	***942***
Mean Precipitation (in.)	0.45	0.45	1.11	1.80	2.91	2.66	2.96	2.29	1.61	1.27	0.62	0.44	18.57
Extreme Maximum Daily Precip. (in.)	0.96	***0.60***	***1.72***	***1.97***	***2.30***	***1.75***	***3.40***	***4.60***	***2.50***	***1.92***	***0.97***	***1.50***	***4.60***
Days With ≥ 0.1" Precipitation	1	2	3	4	5	5	5	4	3	2	2	1	37
Days With ≥ 0.5" Precipitation	0	0	1	1	1	2	2	1	1	1	0	0	10
Days With ≥ 1.0" Precipitation	0	0	0	0	1	1	1	1	0	0	0	0	4
Mean Snowfall (in.)	4.6	4.5	3.5	2.7	0.1	0.0	0.0	0.0	0.3	1.2	2.2	4.1	23.2
Maximum Snow Depth (in.)	16	11	14	16	1	0	0	0	2	12	12	16	16
Days With ≥ 1.0" Snow Depth	9	7	4	1	0	0	0	0	0	1	2	7	31

Boulder *Boulder County* Elevation: 5,483 ft. Latitude: 40° 00' N Longitude: 105° 16' W

	JAN	FEB	MAR	APR	MAY	JUN	JUL	AUG	SEP	OCT	NOV	DEC	YEAR
Mean Maximum Temp. (°F)	46.2	48.0	55.5	63.0	71.8	81.6	87.6	85.3	77.2	65.5	53.3	45.6	65.0
Mean Temp. (°F)	33.8	35.4	42.3	49.3	57.7	66.5	72.5	70.7	62.5	51.6	40.8	33.6	51.4
Mean Minimum Temp. (°F)	21.4	22.9	29.0	35.6	43.6	51.4	57.3	56.1	47.8	37.6	28.3	21.5	37.7
Extreme Maximum Temp. (°F)	73	77	80	88	95	101	101	100	100	89	78	76	101
Extreme Minimum Temp. (°F)	-19	-24	-6	2	24	33	44	40	15	5	-8	-15	-24
Days Maximum Temp. ≥ 90°F	0	0	0	0	1	6	14	9	2	0	0	0	32
Days Maximum Temp. ≤ 32°F	4	3	1	0	0	0	0	0	0	0	2	4	14
Days Minimum Temp. ≤ 32°F	27	23	21	12	1	0	0	0	1	8	19	27	139
Days Minimum Temp. ≤ 0°F	2	1	0	0	0	0	0	0	0	0	0	1	4
Heating Degree Days (base 65°F)	960	830	698	466	239	57	6	10	123	414	719	968	5,490
Cooling Degree Days (base 65°F)	0	0	0	0	2	19	110	244	195	56	4	0	630
Mean Precipitation (in.)	0.74	0.82	2.05	2.65	2.79	2.10	1.76	1.90	1.66	1.55	1.37	0.88	20.27
Extreme Maximum Daily Precip. (in.)	1.04	0.75	2.47	3.56	3.51	3.13	1.81	2.00	1.56	1.83	1.19	1.14	3.56
Days With ≥ 0.1" Precipitation	2	3	5	5	6	5	4	4	4	4	3	3	48
Days With ≥ 0.5" Precipitation	0	0	1	2	2	1	1	1	1	1	1	0	11
Days With ≥ 1.0" Precipitation	0	0	0	0	0	0	0	0	0	0	0	0	0
Mean Snowfall (in.)	11.5	11.3	17.4	11.7	0.6	trace	0.0	0.0	1.4	5.8	14.6	13.4	87.7
Maximum Snow Depth (in.)	17	***13***	16	16	4	trace	0	0	9	25	***22***	***19***	***25***
Days With ≥ 1.0" Snow Depth	13	***10***	6	3	0	0	0	0	0	2	***8***	14	***56***

Briggsdale *Weld County* Elevation: 4,833 ft. Latitude: 40° 39' N Longitude: 104° 20' W

	JAN	FEB	MAR	APR	MAY	JUN	JUL	AUG	SEP	OCT	NOV	DEC	YEAR
Mean Maximum Temp. (°F)	42.4	45.7	54.5	63.1	72.9	82.8	89.6	87.4	78.6	65.3	50.9	40.9	64.5
Mean Temp. (°F)	27.6	30.8	39.0	47.0	57.1	66.4	72.7	70.8	61.4	48.7	35.8	26.2	48.6
Mean Minimum Temp. (°F)	12.6	15.6	23.4	30.9	41.3	50.0	55.7	54.1	44.2	32.1	20.6	11.4	32.7
Extreme Maximum Temp. (°F)	71	74	80	89	96	102	106	103	98	88	78	75	106
Extreme Minimum Temp. (°F)	-30	-32	-14	4	18	30	35	35	17	1	-17	-38	-38
Days Maximum Temp. ≥ 90°F	0	0	0	0	1	8	17	12	3	0	0	0	41
Days Maximum Temp. ≤ 32°F	6	4	2	0	0	0	0	0	0	0	3	7	22
Days Minimum Temp. ≤ 32°F	30	27	28	17	3	0	0	0	2	15	27	30	179
Days Minimum Temp. ≤ 0°F	5	3	0	0	0	0	0	0	0	0	1	5	14
Heating Degree Days (base 65°F)	1,151	961	799	532	251	59	5	9	145	498	870	1,198	6,478
Cooling Degree Days (base 65°F)	0	0	0	0	14	108	249	195	43	0	0	0	609
Mean Precipitation (in.)	0.19	0.19	0.75	1.16	2.08	1.87	2.27	1.96	1.23	0.81	0.45	0.27	13.23
Extreme Maximum Daily Precip. (in.)	0.37	0.48	1.60	2.07	2.40	2.40	2.46	2.63	1.31	1.42	0.55	0.54	2.63
Days With ≥ 0.1" Precipitation	1	1	2	3	5	4	4	4	3	3	2	1	33
Days With ≥ 0.5" Precipitation	0	0	0	1	1	1	1	1	1	0	0	0	6
Days With ≥ 1.0" Precipitation	0	0	0	0	0	0	1	0	0	0	0	0	1
Mean Snowfall (in.)	2.4	1.6	2.6	1.1	0.1	0.0	0.0	0.0	0.2	0.8	1.9	3.0	13.7
Maximum Snow Depth (in.)	***5***	na	***8***	4	0	0	0	0	2	***10***	***12***	***19***	na
Days With ≥ 1.0" Snow Depth	***1***	***1***	1	0	0	0	0	0	0	0	1	2	***6***

The period of record for all cooperative weather station data is 1980 – 2009. See User Guide for detailed explanation of data.

Burlington 4 S *Kit Carson County* Elevation: 4,209 ft. Latitude: 39° 15' N Longitude: 102° 17' W

	JAN	FEB	MAR	APR	MAY	JUN	JUL	AUG	SEP	OCT	NOV	DEC	YEAR
Mean Maximum Temp. (°F)	42.8	46.1	54.6	64.0	73.3	***84.2***	90.4	88.0	79.6	66.6	52.6	43.1	***65.4***
Mean Temp. (°F)	30.3	33.2	40.5	49.3	59.3	***69.6***	75.4	73.6	64.7	51.9	39.5	30.7	***51.5***
Mean Minimum Temp. (°F)	17.7	20.2	26.4	34.6	45.2	***55.1***	60.4	59.1	49.8	37.2	26.3	18.2	***37.5***
Extreme Maximum Temp. (°F)	76	77	86	93	100	107	109	107	99	97	84	78	109
Extreme Minimum Temp. (°F)	-18	-23	-7	5	26	37	46	40	20	8	-3	-19	-23
Days Maximum Temp. ≥ 90°F	0	0	0	0	2	9	17	14	5	0	0	0	47
Days Maximum Temp. ≤ 32°F	7	5	2	1	0	0	0	0	0	0	3	6	24
Days Minimum Temp. ≤ 32°F	29	26	22	12	2	0	0	0	1	9	22	29	152
Days Minimum Temp. ≤ 0°F	2	2	0	0	0	0	0	0	0	0	0	2	6
Heating Degree Days (base 65°F)	1,071	894	752	467	208	***38***	4	7	103	405	759	1,057	***5,765***
Cooling Degree Days (base 65°F)	0	0	0	4	37	***183***	333	280	101	6	0	0	***944***
Mean Precipitation (in.)	0.35	0.42	0.98	1.43	2.59	2.71	2.93	2.36	1.07	1.44	0.48	0.43	17.19
Extreme Maximum Daily Precip. (in.)	0.70	0.60	2.42	1.76	2.10	2.55	3.51	2.56	1.61	2.83	1.15	0.95	3.51
Days With ≥ 0.1" Precipitation	1	1	2	3	6	5	6	4	2	3	1	1	35
Days With ≥ 0.5" Precipitation	0	0	1	1	1	2	2	2	1	1	0	0	11
Days With ≥ 1.0" Precipitation	0	0	0	0	1	0	1	1	0	0	0	0	3
Mean Snowfall (in.)	5.7	4.9	6.1	4.8	0.2	0.0	0.0	0.0	trace	2.1	3.2	4.8	31.8
Maximum Snow Depth (in.)	13	***9***	16	24	2	0	0	0	1	22	9	18	***24***
Days With ≥ 1.0" Snow Depth	5	***5***	2	1	0	0	0	0	0	1	2	5	***21***

Byers 5 ENE *Adams County* Elevation: 5,100 ft. Latitude: 39° 44' N Longitude: 104° 08' W

	JAN	FEB	MAR	APR	MAY	JUN	JUL	AUG	SEP	OCT	NOV	DEC	YEAR
Mean Maximum Temp. (°F)	42.6	45.8	54.4	62.8	72.4	83.3	90.4	87.4	79.1	66.3	52.4	42.5	64.9
Mean Temp. (°F)	28.2	31.4	39.5	47.5	57.2	67.1	73.7	71.5	62.7	50.0	37.5	28.1	49.5
Mean Minimum Temp. (°F)	13.7	16.9	24.7	32.1	42.1	50.9	56.9	55.5	46.2	33.6	22.5	13.6	34.0
Extreme Maximum Temp. (°F)	74	76	85	92	98	105	106	104	101	91	81	76	106
Extreme Minimum Temp. (°F)	-32	-27	-15	0	20	32	40	37	10	-3	-14	-33	-33
Days Maximum Temp. ≥ 90°F	0	0	0	0	1	9	18	13	5	0	0	0	46
Days Maximum Temp. ≤ 32°F	6	4	2	0	0	0	0	0	0	0	3	7	22
Days Minimum Temp. ≤ 32°F	31	27	27	16	3	0	0	0	1	14	26	30	175
Days Minimum Temp. ≤ 0°F	4	2	0	0	0	0	0	0	0	0	1	4	11
Heating Degree Days (base 65°F)	1,135	943	782	520	251	57	5	8	129	461	820	1,138	6,249
Cooling Degree Days (base 65°F)	0	0	0	1	18	126	281	217	66	2	0	0	711
Mean Precipitation (in.)	0.42	0.38	1.15	1.65	2.47	1.93	2.30	2.12	1.03	1.00	0.69	0.46	15.60
Extreme Maximum Daily Precip. (in.)	0.60	0.56	2.27	2.23	1.98	1.75	3.26	1.74	1.38	1.82	1.22	0.89	3.26
Days With ≥ 0.1" Precipitation	2	2	3	4	6	4	5	5	3	3	2	2	41
Days With ≥ 0.5" Precipitation	0	0	1	1	1	1	1	1	1	1	0	0	8
Days With ≥ 1.0" Precipitation	0	0	0	0	0	0	0	0	0	0	0	0	0
Mean Snowfall (in.)	6.2	4.9	8.5	6.2	0.6	0.0	0.0	0.0	1.0	3.6	6.4	6.8	44.2
Maximum Snow Depth (in.)	18	17	13	18	3	0	0	0	10	19	15	18	19
Days With ≥ 1.0" Snow Depth	15	11	5	2	0	0	0	0	0	2	6	14	55

Cabin Creek *Clear Creek County* Elevation: 10,020 ft. Latitude: 39° 39' N Longitude: 105° 42' W

	JAN	FEB	MAR	APR	MAY	JUN	JUL	AUG	SEP	OCT	NOV	DEC	YEAR
Mean Maximum Temp. (°F)	32.2	33.2	37.9	43.4	53.4	64.0	69.3	67.2	60.7	49.9	39.1	32.5	48.6
Mean Temp. (°F)	20.8	21.7	26.1	31.5	41.5	50.6	55.9	54.2	47.6	37.9	27.8	21.3	36.4
Mean Minimum Temp. (°F)	9.4	10.2	14.3	19.9	29.6	37.4	42.5	41.2	34.6	26.0	16.5	10.1	24.3
Extreme Maximum Temp. (°F)	56	54	62	64	75	80	83	78	78	72	62	57	83
Extreme Minimum Temp. (°F)	-25	-26	-18	-14	10	19	27	27	9	-5	-16	-23	-26
Days Maximum Temp. ≥ 90°F	0	0	0	0	0	0	0	0	0	0	0	0	0
Days Maximum Temp. ≤ 32°F	16	12	9	4	1	0	0	0	0	2	8	14	66
Days Minimum Temp. ≤ 32°F	31	28	31	28	20	7	1	1	10	25	29	31	242
Days Minimum Temp. ≤ 0°F	6	4	3	1	0	0	0	0	0	0	2	5	21
Heating Degree Days (base 65°F)	1,363	1,217	1,198	998	721	425	275	328	516	833	1,109	1,347	10,330
Cooling Degree Days (base 65°F)	0	0	0	0	0	0	0	0	0	0	0	0	0
Mean Precipitation (in.)	0.82	0.88	1.89	2.62	1.99	1.75	2.70	2.95	1.64	1.28	1.15	0.95	20.62
Extreme Maximum Daily Precip. (in.)	0.80	0.80	2.20	3.00	1.55	1.40	1.52	1.25	1.01	1.60	1.20	1.25	3.00
Days With ≥ 0.1" Precipitation	3	3	5	7	5	5	7	9	5	4	4	3	60
Days With ≥ 0.5" Precipitation	0	0	1	2	1	1	1	1	1	1	1	0	10
Days With ≥ 1.0" Precipitation	0	0	0	0	0	0	0	0	0	0	0	0	0
Mean Snowfall (in.)	13.2	14.2	27.5	26.4	7.5	0.4	0.0	0.1	2.4	9.8	14.9	15.7	132.1
Maximum Snow Depth (in.)	***34***	***30***	***65***	***42***	***20***	***3***	***0***	***0***	***3***	***16***	***20***	na	na
Days With ≥ 1.0" Snow Depth	***15***	16	17	10	2	0	0	0	0	3	10	***19***	***92***

Campo 7 S *Baca County* Elevation: 4,118 ft. Latitude: 37° 01' N Longitude: 102° 33' W

	JAN	FEB	MAR	APR	MAY	JUN	JUL	AUG	SEP	OCT	NOV	DEC	YEAR
Mean Maximum Temp. (°F)	48.6	52.1	60.1	69.2	78.3	87.4	92.3	89.9	82.8	71.1	58.1	48.2	69.8
Mean Temp. (°F)	33.9	37.0	44.3	53.1	63.0	71.9	77.0	75.1	67.1	54.9	42.7	33.7	54.5
Mean Minimum Temp. (°F)	19.1	21.7	28.6	36.9	47.6	56.4	61.6	60.4	51.4	38.7	27.4	19.2	39.1
Extreme Maximum Temp. (°F)	82	80	94	98	102	109	110	106	106	98	87	79	110
Extreme Minimum Temp. (°F)	-20	-26	2	10	27	38	47	44	27	9	-5	-26	-26
Days Maximum Temp. ≥ 90°F	0	0	0	1	5	14	21	17	8	1	0	0	67
Days Maximum Temp. ≤ 32°F	4	3	1	0	0	0	0	0	0	0	1	4	13
Days Minimum Temp. ≤ 32°F	30	***25***	21	9	1	0	0	0	1	7	21	30	***145***
Days Minimum Temp. ≤ 0°F	1	1	0	0	0	0	0	0	0	0	0	1	3
Heating Degree Days (base 65°F)	958	788	635	360	132	18	2	4	65	321	661	962	4,906
Cooling Degree Days (base 65°F)	0	0	1	9	76	231	380	326	135	12	0	0	1,170
Mean Precipitation (in.)	0.36	0.36	1.03	1.45	2.11	2.46	2.65	2.88	1.32	1.35	0.46	0.49	16.92
Extreme Maximum Daily Precip. (in.)	0.82	0.67	2.62	1.64	3.05	3.22	2.75	3.44	2.37	3.50	0.83	0.86	3.50
Days With ≥ 0.1" Precipitation	1	1	3	3	4	5	5	5	3	2	1	1	34
Days With ≥ 0.5" Precipitation	0	0	0	1	1	2	2	2	1	1	0	0	10
Days With ≥ 1.0" Precipitation	0	0	0	0	0	1	1	1	0	0	0	0	3
Mean Snowfall (in.)	5.3	2.8	4.4	1.0	0.1	0.0	0.0	0.0	0.1	1.3	1.7	6.2	22.9
Maximum Snow Depth (in.)	***13***	***8***	***8***	***6***	***1***	0	***0***	***0***	0	***16***	***7***	***8***	***16***
Days With ≥ 1.0" Snow Depth	***3***	***2***	***1***	0	0	0	0	0	0	0	1	2	***9***

The period of record for all cooperative weather station data is 1980 – 2009. See User Guide for detailed explanation of data.

Canon City *Fremont County* Elevation: 5,330 ft. Latitude: 38° 25' N Longitude: 105° 14' W

	JAN	FEB	MAR	APR	MAY	JUN	JUL	AUG	SEP	OCT	NOV	DEC	YEAR
Mean Maximum Temp. (°F)	49.1	51.0	57.7	64.7	73.8	83.4	89.3	86.1	79.1	68.6	57.0	48.1	67.3
Mean Temp. (°F)	34.9	36.6	43.2	50.1	59.4	68.4	74.7	72.2	64.3	53.3	42.7	34.3	52.8
Mean Minimum Temp. (°F)	20.7	22.3	28.6	35.6	44.9	53.3	60.0	58.3	49.5	37.9	28.3	20.5	38.3
Extreme Maximum Temp. (°F)	76	77	82	88	98	102	105	100	95	90	83	76	105
Extreme Minimum Temp. (°F)	-15	-16	-8	7	22	34	46	44	25	12	-7	-25	-25
Days Maximum Temp. ≥ 90°F	0	0	0	0	1	8	17	10	3	0	0	0	39
Days Maximum Temp. ≤ 32°F	3	3	1	0	0	0	0	0	0	0	2	4	13
Days Minimum Temp. ≤ 32°F	27	25	21	11	1	0	0	0	0	8	20	27	140
Days Minimum Temp. ≤ 0°F	1	2	0	0	0	0	0	0	0	0	0	1	4
Heating Degree Days (base 65°F)	927	795	670	442	196	38	3	8	94	363	662	944	5,142
Cooling Degree Days (base 65°F)	0	0	0	3	29	146	309	238	79	6	0	0	810
Mean Precipitation (in.)	0.59	0.46	1.11	1.65	1.52	1.08	1.98	2.21	1.09	0.76	0.72	0.51	13.68
Extreme Maximum Daily Precip. (in.)	3.00	1.03	1.16	3.21	2.25	1.10	1.65	2.15	1.25	1.18	0.85	0.97	3.21
Days With ≥ 0.1" Precipitation	1	2	3	3	4	3	5	5	3	2	2	2	35
Days With ≥ 0.5" Precipitation	0	0	1	1	1	0	1	1	0	0	0	0	5
Days With ≥ 1.0" Precipitation	0	0	0	0	0	0	0	0	0	0	0	0	0
Mean Snowfall (in.)	7.0	6.6	7.4	4.6	0.6	0.0	0.0	0.0	0.1	2.0	6.2	7.5	42.0
Maximum Snow Depth (in.)	9	19	13	8	14	0	0	0	2	9	9	13	19
Days With ≥ 1.0" Snow Depth	7	5	3	1	0	0	0	0	0	1	4	9	30

Center 4 SSW *Rio Grande County* Elevation: 7,672 ft. Latitude: 37° 42' N Longitude: 106° 09' W

	JAN	FEB	MAR	APR	MAY	JUN	JUL	AUG	SEP	OCT	NOV	DEC	YEAR
Mean Maximum Temp. (°F)	32.9	39.3	49.2	58.5	67.4	76.2	80.1	78.2	72.6	61.5	46.3	34.7	58.1
Mean Temp. (°F)	16.3	22.9	34.1	42.5	51.4	58.7	63.2	61.6	55.3	44.3	30.7	18.9	41.6
Mean Minimum Temp. (°F)	-0.3	6.4	18.9	26.3	35.3	41.1	46.2	45.0	37.9	27.0	14.9	3.0	25.1
Extreme Maximum Temp. (°F)	59	65	71	79	88	90	92	89	87	80	68	60	92
Extreme Minimum Temp. (°F)	-34	-32	-12	1	16	25	31	28	12	-1	-15	-29	-34
Days Maximum Temp. ≥ 90°F	0	0	0	0	0	0	1	0	0	0	0	0	1
Days Maximum Temp. ≤ 32°F	15	7	1	0	0	0	0	0	0	0	4	12	39
Days Minimum Temp. ≤ 32°F	31	28	30	25	10	1	0	0	5	24	30	31	215
Days Minimum Temp. ≤ 0°F	16	9	1	0	0	0	0	0	0	0	2	11	39
Heating Degree Days (base 65°F)	1,504	1,186	953	669	417	187	69	105	284	634	1,024	1,423	8,455
Cooling Degree Days (base 65°F)	0	0	0	0	0	4	20	7	0	0	0	0	31
Mean Precipitation (in.)	0.18	0.19	0.42	0.47	0.64	0.68	1.10	1.26	0.90	0.59	0.35	0.28	7.06
Extreme Maximum Daily Precip. (in.)	0.28	0.63	0.81	0.86	0.79	0.94	2.18	1.07	0.84	0.84	0.82	0.65	2.18
Days With ≥ 0.1" Precipitation	1	1	1	2	2	2	3	4	3	2	1	1	23
Days With ≥ 0.5" Precipitation	0	0	0	0	0	0	0	0	0	0	0	0	0
Days With ≥ 1.0" Precipitation	0	0	0	0	0	0	0	0	0	0	0	0	0
Mean Snowfall (in.)	4.8	3.9	5.1	1.9	0.6	0.0	0.0	0.0	0.0	1.2	3.5	5.1	26.1
Maximum Snow Depth (in.)	na	na	na	8	2	0	0	0	0	10	8	na	na
Days With ≥ 1.0" Snow Depth	na	na	2	0	0	0	0	0	0	0	2	4	na

Cheesman *Jefferson County* Elevation: 6,879 ft. Latitude: 39° 13' N Longitude: 105° 17' W

	JAN	FEB	MAR	APR	MAY	JUN	JUL	AUG	SEP	OCT	NOV	DEC	YEAR
Mean Maximum Temp. (°F)	44.8	46.4	51.0	57.3	67.0	77.6	83.8	81.3	74.2	63.6	51.9	44.1	61.9
Mean Temp. (°F)	26.6	28.5	34.6	41.0	50.3	59.6	65.4	63.1	55.6	45.1	34.9	26.8	44.3
Mean Minimum Temp. (°F)	8.3	10.5	18.1	24.6	33.6	41.6	46.8	44.8	36.9	26.6	17.8	9.5	26.6
Extreme Maximum Temp. (°F)	69	72	75	82	91	99	98	97	96	90	76	69	99
Extreme Minimum Temp. (°F)	-28	-31	-28	-6	13	18	25	26	11	-3	-15	-29	-31
Days Maximum Temp. ≥ 90°F	0	0	0	0	0	1	6	2	0	0	0	0	9
Days Maximum Temp. ≤ 32°F	4	3	2	1	0	0	0	0	0	1	2	5	18
Days Minimum Temp. ≤ 32°F	31	28	30	26	14	2	1	1	8	24	28	31	224
Days Minimum Temp. ≤ 0°F	8	5	2	0	0	0	0	0	0	0	2	7	24
Heating Degree Days (base 65°F)	1,183	1,027	936	713	450	172	52	88	279	609	897	1,177	7,583
Cooling Degree Days (base 65°F)	0	0	0	0	1	17	69	37	4	0	0	0	128
Mean Precipitation (in.)	0.46	0.55	1.40	1.65	1.84	2.01	2.32	3.06	1.25	1.06	0.72	0.60	16.92
Extreme Maximum Daily Precip. (in.)	0.66	0.58	1.98	1.30	1.45	1.22	2.17	2.02	1.15	2.04	0.83	1.44	2.17
Days With ≥ 0.1" Precipitation	2	2	4	5	5	5	6	8	4	3	2	2	48
Days With ≥ 0.5" Precipitation	0	0	1	1	1	1	1	2	1	1	0	0	9
Days With ≥ 1.0" Precipitation	0	0	0	0	0	0	0	0	0	0	0	0	0
Mean Snowfall (in.)	7.2	7.2	13.6	9.3	1.5	trace	0.0	0.0	0.7	5.5	8.2	8.9	62.1
Maximum Snow Depth (in.)	18	12	28	17	6	trace	0	0	8	22	15	28	28
Days With ≥ 1.0" Snow Depth	12	9	8	4	1	0	0	0	0	2	7	11	54

Cimarron *Montrose County* Elevation: 6,896 ft. Latitude: 38° 27' N Longitude: 107° 34' W

	JAN	FEB	MAR	APR	MAY	JUN	JUL	AUG	SEP	OCT	NOV	DEC	YEAR
Mean Maximum Temp. (°F)	34.1	38.3	48.8	58.4	69.3	79.7	84.7	82.3	74.3	62.9	47.1	35.0	59.6
Mean Temp. (°F)	18.2	23.4	33.9	42.1	50.8	58.5	64.6	63.3	55.0	44.0	31.6	20.0	42.1
Mean Minimum Temp. (°F)	2.3	8.4	18.9	25.6	32.2	37.2	44.4	44.3	35.6	25.1	16.0	4.9	24.6
Extreme Maximum Temp. (°F)	54	65	81	85	91	96	97	93	92	83	72	56	97
Extreme Minimum Temp. (°F)	-35	-35	-18	-3	15	20	29	27	14	0	-18	-33	-35
Days Maximum Temp. ≥ 90°F	0	0	0	0	0	1	5	2	0	0	0	0	8
Days Maximum Temp. ≤ 32°F	13	6	1	0	0	0	0	0	0	0	2	12	34
Days Minimum Temp. ≤ 32°F	30	28	30	25	17	6	1	1	11	25	28	31	233
Days Minimum Temp. ≤ 0°F	15	8	2	0	0	0	0	0	0	0	2	12	39
Heating Degree Days (base 65°F)	1,444	1,170	957	684	434	193	43	68	296	643	995	1,390	8,317
Cooling Degree Days (base 65°F)	0	0	0	0	0	4	38	23	2	0	0	0	67
Mean Precipitation (in.)	0.94	0.87	0.97	1.20	1.18	0.77	1.29	1.44	1.79	1.41	1.15	1.02	14.03
Extreme Maximum Daily Precip. (in.)	1.20	1.50	1.22	1.41	0.90	1.22	1.75	1.28	1.57	1.25	1.08	1.50	1.75
Days With ≥ 0.1" Precipitation	3	3	3	3	4	2	4	4	5	5	4	3	43
Days With ≥ 0.5" Precipitation	0	0	0	0	1	0	1	1	1	1	0	0	5
Days With ≥ 1.0" Precipitation	0	0	0	0	0	0	0	0	0	0	0	0	0
Mean Snowfall (in.)	13.0	11.5	11.6	5.6	0.6	trace	0.0	0.0	trace	1.4	9.4	15.6	68.7
Maximum Snow Depth (in.)	na	na	na	15	trace	trace	0	0	trace	4	na	na	na
Days With ≥ 1.0" Snow Depth	na	8	3	1	0	0	0	0	0	0	2	8	na

The period of record for all cooperative weather station data is 1980 – 2009. See User Guide for detailed explanation of data.

Cochetopa Creek *Gunnison County* Elevation: 8,000 ft. Latitude: 38° 27' N Longitude: 106° 46' W

	JAN	FEB	MAR	APR	MAY	JUN	JUL	AUG	SEP	OCT	NOV	DEC	YEAR
Mean Maximum Temp. (°F)	30.3	35.6	45.8	55.9	66.3	76.3	81.6	79.6	72.6	60.8	45.5	32.4	56.9
Mean Temp. (°F)	13.4	19.0	30.2	39.2	48.1	56.5	62.4	61.0	53.1	41.6	28.7	16.2	39.1
Mean Minimum Temp. (°F)	-3.4	2.4	14.5	22.4	29.8	36.5	43.2	42.3	33.6	22.5	11.8	-0.1	21.3
Extreme Maximum Temp. (°F)	50	58	70	78	88	93	94	93	90	80	67	56	94
Extreme Minimum Temp. (°F)	-36	-36	-21	-5	11	18	30	24	13	1	-16	-36	-36
Days Maximum Temp. ≥ 90°F	0	0	0	0	0	0	2	0	0	0	0	0	2
Days Maximum Temp. ≤ 32°F	18	10	2	0	0	0	0	0	0	0	4	15	49
Days Minimum Temp. ≤ 32°F	31	28	31	28	21	7	1	1	13	28	30	31	250
Days Minimum Temp. ≤ 0°F	20	12	3	0	0	0	0	0	0	0	4	17	56
Heating Degree Days (base 65°F)	1,593	1,294	1,073	769	518	251	92	126	350	717	1,082	1,508	9,373
Cooling Degree Days (base 65°F)	0	0	0	0	0	2	19	8	1	0	0	0	30
Mean Precipitation (in.)	0.65	0.69	0.77	0.93	1.02	0.76	1.45	1.73	1.25	0.78	0.70	0.75	11.48
Extreme Maximum Daily Precip. (in.)	0.78	0.60	0.48	0.73	0.77	1.05	0.94	1.36	0.90	0.66	0.86	1.04	1.36
Days With ≥ 0.1" Precipitation	2	3	3	3	4	2	5	5	4	3	3	3	40
Days With ≥ 0.5" Precipitation	0	0	0	0	0	0	1	1	1	0	0	0	3
Days With ≥ 1.0" Precipitation	0	0	0	0	0	0	0	0	0	0	0	0	0
Mean Snowfall (in.)	9.8	9.3	7.4	5.3	1.0	trace	0.0	0.0	trace	1.7	6.6	10.6	51.7
Maximum Snow Depth (in.)	28	31	32	21	7	trace	0	0	1	6	11	25	32
Days With ≥ 1.0" Snow Depth	14	14	12	4	1	0	0	0	0	1	7	13	66

Dinosaur Natl Monumnt *Moffat County* Elevation: 5,919 ft. Latitude: 40° 15' N Longitude: 108° 58' W

	JAN	FEB	MAR	APR	MAY	JUN	JUL	AUG	SEP	OCT	NOV	DEC	YEAR
Mean Maximum Temp. (°F)	33.4	39.5	51.4	61.5	72.5	84.3	91.2	88.3	78.0	63.4	46.5	34.3	62.0
Mean Temp. (°F)	22.6	27.9	38.8	47.1	57.0	67.2	74.1	71.8	62.2	49.5	35.3	24.0	48.1
Mean Minimum Temp. (°F)	11.8	16.3	26.1	32.7	41.4	50.1	57.1	55.2	46.4	35.6	24.0	13.6	34.2
Extreme Maximum Temp. (°F)	57	64	76	87	96	100	104	100	96	82	70	58	104
Extreme Minimum Temp. (°F)	-21	-24	-1	8	16	31	28	34	21	5	-6	-29	-29
Days Maximum Temp. ≥ 90°F	0	0	0	0	1	8	20	13	2	0	0	0	44
Days Maximum Temp. ≤ 32°F	13	6	1	0	0	0	0	0	0	0	2	12	34
Days Minimum Temp. ≤ 32°F	30	27	25	14	4	0	0	0	1	10	26	30	167
Days Minimum Temp. ≤ 0°F	4	2	0	0	0	0	0	0	0	0	0	3	9
Heating Degree Days (base 65°F)	1,308	1,042	806	529	257	52	2	5	123	475	884	1,264	6,747
Cooling Degree Days (base 65°F)	0	0	0	0	15	125	292	222	47	0	0	0	701
Mean Precipitation (in.)	0.61	0.63	0.82	1.15	1.29	0.81	0.92	0.92	1.39	1.54	0.85	0.56	11.49
Extreme Maximum Daily Precip. (in.)	0.81	1.00	1.33	1.20	1.03	1.35	1.07	0.98	1.54	1.61	0.83	0.72	1.61
Days With ≥ 0.1" Precipitation	2	2	3	3	4	3	3	3	4	4	3	2	36
Days With ≥ 0.5" Precipitation	0	0	0	1	1	0	0	0	1	1	0	0	4
Days With ≥ 1.0" Precipitation	0	0	0	0	0	0	0	0	0	0	0	0	0
Mean Snowfall (in.)	8.1	6.0	4.5	2.3	0.3	trace	0.0	0.0	trace	0.9	4.7	7.5	34.3
Maximum Snow Depth (in.)	22	23	22	5	1	trace	0	0	trace	2	14	17	23
Days With ≥ 1.0" Snow Depth	22	16	4	0	0	0	0	0	0	0	3	14	59

Eads *Kiowa County* Elevation: 4,210 ft. Latitude: 38° 29' N Longitude: 102° 47' W

	JAN	FEB	MAR	APR	MAY	JUN	JUL	AUG	SEP	OCT	NOV	DEC	YEAR
Mean Maximum Temp. (°F)	43.4	***47.5***	57.2	66.1	75.7	86.1	91.8	88.8	81.1	68.4	54.6	***44.3***	***67.1***
Mean Temp. (°F)	29.0	***33.2***	42.0	50.4	60.5	70.6	76.3	74.0	65.4	52.4	39.6	***30.0***	***52.0***
Mean Minimum Temp. (°F)	14.6	***18.8***	26.9	34.7	45.3	55.0	61.0	59.1	49.6	35.8	24.5	***15.7***	***36.7***
Extreme Maximum Temp. (°F)	77	***80***	90	94	102	105	108	***105***	106	92	83	***76***	***108***
Extreme Minimum Temp. (°F)	-27	***-19***	-1	10	26	33	48	***44***	20	10	-12	***-18***	***-27***
Days Maximum Temp. ≥ 90°F	0	***0***	0	0	3	12	21	16	7	0	0	***0***	***59***
Days Maximum Temp. ≤ 32°F	7	***5***	2	0	0	0	0	0	0	0	2	***6***	***22***
Days Minimum Temp. ≤ 32°F	30	***27***	23	11	1	0	0	0	1	11	24	***31***	***159***
Days Minimum Temp. ≤ 0°F	3	***1***	0	0	0	0	0	0	0	0	0	***2***	***6***
Heating Degree Days (base 65°F)	1,108	***895***	705	435	179	27	3	5	90	389	757	***1,076***	***5,669***
Cooling Degree Days (base 65°F)	0	***0***	0	3	47	201	361	290	107	6	0	***0***	***1,015***
Mean Precipitation (in.)	***0.30***	***0.41***	***0.97***	1.56	2.25	2.19	2.44	2.68	1.08	1.22	0.45	***0.41***	***15.96***
Extreme Maximum Daily Precip. (in.)	0.66	***0.80***	***1.30***	***2.19***	***3.18***	***2.55***	***2.75***	***2.49***	***1.40***	***3.10***	***0.72***	***1.05***	***3.18***
Days With ≥ 0.1" Precipitation	1	***1***	***2***	***3***	5	4	4	5	3	2	2	***1***	***33***
Days With ≥ 0.5" Precipitation	0	***0***	***0***	***1***	1	2	2	2	1	1	0	***0***	***10***
Days With ≥ 1.0" Precipitation	0	***0***	***0***	0	0	0	1	1	0	0	0	***0***	***2***
Mean Snowfall (in.)	***3.4***	***1.7***	3.3	***1.4***	0.0	0.0	0.0	0.0	0.2	trace	1.7	***2.4***	***14.1***
Maximum Snow Depth (in.)	***12***	na	na	***10***	***0***	***0***	***0***	***0***	***0***	***1***	na	na	na
Days With ≥ 1.0" Snow Depth	na	na	na	***0***	0	0	0	0	0	0	***0***	***2***	na

Evergreen *Jefferson County* Elevation: 7,000 ft. Latitude: 39° 38' N Longitude: 105° 19' W

	JAN	FEB	MAR	APR	MAY	JUN	JUL	AUG	SEP	OCT	NOV	DEC	YEAR
Mean Maximum Temp. (°F)	44.7	45.6	50.6	56.8	65.0	75.6	81.6	79.5	72.4	61.5	50.9	44.5	60.7
Mean Temp. (°F)	27.8	29.2	35.2	41.4	49.8	58.7	64.6	62.9	55.2	44.4	34.9	27.9	44.3
Mean Minimum Temp. (°F)	10.9	12.7	19.7	26.0	34.7	41.9	47.5	46.3	37.9	27.2	18.8	11.2	27.9
Extreme Maximum Temp. (°F)	72	69	78	82	92	96	96	96	92	85	77	69	96
Extreme Minimum Temp. (°F)	-22	-28	-18	-5	16	27	33	30	8	-3	-11	-29	-29
Days Maximum Temp. ≥ 90°F	0	0	0	0	0	1	3	1	0	0	0	0	5
Days Maximum Temp. ≤ 32°F	4	4	2	1	0	0	0	0	0	1	3	5	20
Days Minimum Temp. ≤ 32°F	31	28	30	26	11	1	0	0	6	26	29	31	219
Days Minimum Temp. ≤ 0°F	5	3	1	0	0	0	0	0	0	0	1	5	15
Heating Degree Days (base 65°F)	1,145	1,004	917	702	464	191	56	84	291	632	896	1,143	7,525
Cooling Degree Days (base 65°F)	0	0	0	0	1	10	49	28	3	0	0	0	91
Mean Precipitation (in.)	0.62	0.66	1.81	2.40	2.50	2.10	2.21	2.57	1.47	1.30	0.90	0.74	19.28
Extreme Maximum Daily Precip. (in.)	0.92	0.70	2.40	1.89	2.10	2.73	2.10	1.56	1.15	1.81	1.35	1.48	2.73
Days With ≥ 0.1" Precipitation	2	2	4	5	6	5	6	7	4	3	3	2	49
Days With ≥ 0.5" Precipitation	0	0	1	1	1	1	1	1	1	1	0	0	8
Days With ≥ 1.0" Precipitation	0	0	0	0	0	0	0	0	0	0	0	0	0
Mean Snowfall (in.)	9.2	8.9	18.2	14.5	2.6	0.0	0.0	0.0	1.4	6.5	11.5	9.8	82.6
Maximum Snow Depth (in.)	na	na	na	na	na	na	na	na	na	na	na	na	na
Days With ≥ 1.0" Snow Depth	na	na	na	na	1	0	0	0	0	1	***4***	***10***	na

The period of record for all cooperative weather station data is 1980 – 2009. See User Guide for detailed explanation of data.

Flagler 5 NNE *Kit Carson County* Elevation: 4,875 ft. Latitude: 39° 22' N Longitude: 103° 03' W

	JAN	FEB	MAR	APR	MAY	JUN	JUL	AUG	SEP	OCT	NOV	DEC	YEAR
Mean Maximum Temp. (°F)	43.0	45.6	***54.0***	***61.6***	71.6	81.8	88.3	85.8	***78.1***	66.3	***52.0***	***42.5***	***64.2***
Mean Temp. (°F)	28.7	31.8	***39.0***	***46.4***	56.7	66.4	72.7	70.9	***62.5***	***50.3***	***37.6***	***29.0***	***49.3***
Mean Minimum Temp. (°F)	14.6	17.8	***24.0***	***31.2***	41.9	51.0	57.1	56.0	***46.8***	***34.4***	***23.3***	***15.4***	***34.4***
Extreme Maximum Temp. (°F)	78	77	82	90	99	102	103	103	98	93	81	76	103
Extreme Minimum Temp. (°F)	-29	-25	-10	4	20	31	37	33	21	-6	-11	-29	-29
Days Maximum Temp. ≥ 90°F	0	0	0	0	1	7	14	11	3	0	0	0	36
Days Maximum Temp. ≤ 32°F	6	5	2	0	0	0	0	0	0	0	3	6	22
Days Minimum Temp. ≤ 32°F	29	26	24	15	3	0	0	0	1	11	23	27	159
Days Minimum Temp. ≤ 0°F	3	2	0	0	0	0	0	0	0	0	0	2	7
Heating Degree Days (base 65°F)	1,117	932	***800***	***553***	266	62	8	14	***133***	***452***	***813***	***1,109***	***6,259***
Cooling Degree Days (base 65°F)	0	0	***0***	***1***	19	111	255	204	***64***	***3***	***0***	***0***	***657***
Mean Precipitation (in.)	0.33	0.32	0.92	1.44	2.47	2.87	2.89	2.45	1.24	0.98	0.45	0.38	16.74
Extreme Maximum Daily Precip. (in.)	0.78	0.92	1.87	1.93	2.22	3.24	3.30	2.35	1.65	1.87	0.90	1.20	3.30
Days With ≥ 0.1" Precipitation	1	1	2	3	5	5	5	5	2	2	2	1	34
Days With ≥ 0.5" Precipitation	0	0	1	1	2	2	2	2	1	0	0	0	11
Days With ≥ 1.0" Precipitation	0	0	0	0	1	1	1	1	0	0	0	0	4
Mean Snowfall (in.)	4.0	3.7	6.1	4.5	0.8	0.0	0.0	0.0	0.4	2.1	4.4	4.9	30.9
Maximum Snow Depth (in.)	19	17	12	14	8	0	0	0	5	12	14	14	19
Days With ≥ 1.0" Snow Depth	5	4	3	2	0	0	0	0	0	1	3	3	21

Fort Collins *Larimer County* Elevation: 5,003 ft. Latitude: 40° 35' N Longitude: 105° 05' W

	JAN	FEB	MAR	APR	MAY	JUN	JUL	AUG	SEP	OCT	NOV	DEC	YEAR
Mean Maximum Temp. (°F)	43.9	46.6	54.4	62.2	71.0	80.5	86.6	83.9	75.8	63.8	51.5	43.0	63.6
Mean Temp. (°F)	30.6	33.5	41.0	48.6	57.6	66.3	72.3	70.1	61.5	49.7	38.6	30.1	50.0
Mean Minimum Temp. (°F)	17.3	20.4	27.6	34.9	44.2	52.1	58.0	56.2	47.0	35.7	25.6	17.3	36.3
Extreme Maximum Temp. (°F)	73	76	79	89	97	100	103	99	97	88	81	73	103
Extreme Minimum Temp. (°F)	-28	-19	-6	8	27	34	44	39	18	4	-7	-24	-28
Days Maximum Temp. ≥ 90°F	0	0	0	0	0	5	11	6	1	0	0	0	23
Days Maximum Temp. ≤ 32°F	5	3	2	0	0	0	0	0	0	0	2	5	17
Days Minimum Temp. ≤ 32°F	30	26	23	11	1	0	0	0	1	10	24	30	156
Days Minimum Temp. ≤ 0°F	2	1	0	0	0	0	0	0	0	0	0	2	5
Heating Degree Days (base 65°F)	1,058	884	738	486	236	55	5	10	138	467	786	1,073	5,936
Cooling Degree Days (base 65°F)	0	0	0	0	14	102	239	174	38	1	0	0	568
Mean Precipitation (in.)	0.43	0.41	1.62	2.05	2.48	2.11	1.71	1.57	1.35	1.14	0.76	0.50	16.13
Extreme Maximum Daily Precip. (in.)	0.51	0.62	3.48	2.41	3.17	2.49	4.63	2.49	1.29	1.20	0.87	1.30	4.63
Days With ≥ 0.1" Precipitation	2	1	3	4	5	4	3	3	3	3	3	1	35
Days With ≥ 0.5" Precipitation	0	0	1	1	1	1	1	1	1	1	0	0	8
Days With ≥ 1.0" Precipitation	0	0	0	0	0	0	0	0	0	0	0	0	0
Mean Snowfall (in.)	8.0	6.6	12.7	6.3	0.5	trace	trace	trace	0.9	3.6	8.6	8.3	55.5
Maximum Snow Depth (in.)	14	12	23	10	4	trace	trace	trace	4	15	10	17	23
Days With ≥ 1.0" Snow Depth	13	8	5	2	0	0	0	0	0	1	5	12	46

Fort Lewis *La Plata County* Elevation: 7,600 ft. Latitude: 37° 14' N Longitude: 108° 03' W

	JAN	FEB	MAR	APR	MAY	JUN	JUL	AUG	SEP	OCT	NOV	DEC	YEAR
Mean Maximum Temp. (°F)	37.6	41.2	48.0	57.2	66.9	77.5	81.9	78.7	71.9	60.5	46.9	38.0	58.9
Mean Temp. (°F)	24.3	27.9	34.6	42.2	50.4	59.4	65.6	63.7	56.4	45.4	33.8	25.0	44.1
Mean Minimum Temp. (°F)	10.8	14.6	21.2	27.0	33.9	41.2	49.3	48.7	40.8	30.2	20.5	11.9	29.2
Extreme Maximum Temp. (°F)	57	60	68	77	91	93	95	93	88	79	70	59	95
Extreme Minimum Temp. (°F)	-25	-20	-7	2	13	22	29	32	20	5	-6	-24	-25
Days Maximum Temp. ≥ 90°F	0	0	0	0	0	0	1	0	0	0	0	0	1
Days Maximum Temp. ≤ 32°F	8	3	1	0	0	0	0	0	0	0	2	8	22
Days Minimum Temp. ≤ 32°F	30	28	29	24	12	3	0	0	3	18	27	30	204
Days Minimum Temp. ≤ 0°F	5	2	0	0	0	0	0	0	0	0	1	4	12
Heating Degree Days (base 65°F)	1,256	1,042	935	678	444	174	35	64	255	601	931	1,234	7,649
Cooling Degree Days (base 65°F)	0	0	0	0	0	13	61	30	3	0	0	0	107
Mean Precipitation (in.)	1.63	1.46	1.55	1.15	1.02	0.59	2.08	2.41	2.16	1.62	1.57	1.21	18.45
Extreme Maximum Daily Precip. (in.)	1.67	1.12	1.32	2.24	***1.06***	0.85	1.65	***2.09***	2.30	1.66	1.68	1.35	***2.30***
Days With ≥ 0.1" Precipitation	4	4	4	3	3	2	5	6	4	4	3	3	45
Days With ≥ 0.5" Precipitation	1	1	1	1	0	0	1	1	1	1	1	1	10
Days With ≥ 1.0" Precipitation	0	0	0	0	0	0	0	0	1	0	0	0	1
Mean Snowfall (in.)	21.3	17.5	12.5	5.3	0.5	0.0	0.0	0.0	trace	1.6	10.3	16.8	85.8
Maximum Snow Depth (in.)	48	49	39	35	2	0	0	0	1	7	17	30	49
Days With ≥ 1.0" Snow Depth	27	24	18	3	0	0	0	0	0	1	7	21	101

Fruita 1 W *Mesa County* Elevation: 4,479 ft. Latitude: 39° 10' N Longitude: 108° 45' W

	JAN	FEB	MAR	APR	MAY	JUN	JUL	AUG	SEP	OCT	NOV	DEC	YEAR
Mean Maximum Temp. (°F)	39.7	46.8	57.8	66.8	***76.8***	***87.8***	93.6	90.4	82.1	68.2	53.4	40.8	***67.0***
Mean Temp. (°F)	26.7	33.3	42.6	50.5	***60.1***	***69.2***	75.5	73.2	***64.1***	51.0	38.7	28.2	***51.1***
Mean Minimum Temp. (°F)	13.8	19.9	27.3	34.1	43.2	***50.5***	57.4	56.0	45.9	33.8	24.1	15.5	***35.1***
Extreme Maximum Temp. (°F)	60	70	83	89	100	105	111	105	98	93	75	63	111
Extreme Minimum Temp. (°F)	-21	-36	4	14	27	29	41	37	24	14	-7	-18	-36
Days Maximum Temp. ≥ 90°F	0	0	0	0	2	13	22	19	5	0	0	0	61
Days Maximum Temp. ≤ 32°F	7	1	0	0	0	0	0	0	0	0	0	5	13
Days Minimum Temp. ≤ 32°F	29	25	23	12	2	0	0	0	1	14	26	29	161
Days Minimum Temp. ≤ 0°F	3	1	0	0	0	0	0	0	0	0	0	2	6
Heating Degree Days (base 65°F)	1,181	889	688	430	***177***	***30***	1	2	***86***	428	779	1,135	***5,826***
Cooling Degree Days (base 65°F)	0	0	0	1	***32***	***161***	335	264	***65***	1	0	0	***859***
Mean Precipitation (in.)	0.68	0.61	0.92	0.77	0.91	0.54	0.74	0.91	0.98	1.10	0.79	0.67	9.62
Extreme Maximum Daily Precip. (in.)	0.76	***0.85***	***0.84***	0.93	***1.45***	1.57	1.18	0.90	***1.00***	1.18	1.03	0.80	***1.57***
Days With ≥ 0.1" Precipitation	2	2	3	2	2	1	2	3	3	3	2	2	27
Days With ≥ 0.5" Precipitation	0	0	0	0	0	0	0	0	0	1	0	0	1
Days With ≥ 1.0" Precipitation	0	0	0	0	0	0	0	0	0	0	0	0	0
Mean Snowfall (in.)	3.0	1.1	0.5	0.2	trace	0.0	0.0	0.0	0.0	0.1	na	***2.8***	na
Maximum Snow Depth (in.)	8	***6***	***3***	***1***	***trace***	***0***	***0***	***0***	***0***	***trace***	na	***9***	na
Days With ≥ 1.0" Snow Depth	4	***1***	0	0	0	0	0	0	0	0	na	3	na

The period of record for all cooperative weather station data is 1980 – 2009. See User Guide for detailed explanation of data.

Glenwood Spgs #2 *Garfield County* Elevation: 5,750 ft. Latitude: 39° 32' N Longitude: 107° 19' W

	JAN	FEB	MAR	APR	MAY	JUN	JUL	AUG	SEP	OCT	NOV	DEC	YEAR
Mean Maximum Temp. (°F)	37.8	43.4	53.5	62.2	***72.1***	82.8	89.0	86.9	78.0	65.0	49.5	37.7	***63.2***
Mean Temp. (°F)	26.0	31.2	40.1	47.2	***55.8***	64.3	70.9	69.4	60.8	49.0	36.9	26.5	***48.2***
Mean Minimum Temp. (°F)	14.1	19.1	26.6	32.1	39.3	45.9	52.7	51.8	43.6	33.1	24.2	15.2	33.1
Extreme Maximum Temp. (°F)	56	67	75	84	95	100	102	100	96	86	75	65	102
Extreme Minimum Temp. (°F)	-15	-24	-5	10	23	29	37	35	26	12	-12	-20	-24
Days Maximum Temp. ≥ 90°F	0	0	0	0	0	6	16	11	2	0	0	0	35
Days Maximum Temp. ≤ 32°F	8	2	1	0	0	0	0	0	0	0	1	8	20
Days Minimum Temp. ≤ 32°F	30	26	24	15	3	0	0	0	2	15	25	30	170
Days Minimum Temp. ≤ 0°F	3	1	0	0	0	0	0	0	0	0	0	2	6
Heating Degree Days (base 65°F)	1,203	949	765	527	***287***	76	6	10	144	488	836	1,187	***6,478***
Cooling Degree Days (base 65°F)	0	0	0	0	***3***	63	195	153	26	0	0	0	***440***
Mean Precipitation (in.)	1.32	1.14	1.38	1.52	1.90	1.05	1.11	1.27	1.96	1.88	1.41	1.22	17.16
Extreme Maximum Daily Precip. (in.)	1.23	1.22	1.31	1.30	***2.09***	***1.32***	0.92	1.40	1.93	1.55	***1.13***	1.00	***2.09***
Days With ≥ 0.1" Precipitation	4	4	4	4	4	3	3	4	5	4	4	4	47
Days With ≥ 0.5" Precipitation	0	0	0	1	1	0	0	1	1	1	1	0	6
Days With ≥ 1.0" Precipitation	0	0	0	0	0	0	0	0	0	0	0	0	0
Mean Snowfall (in.)	14.8	8.0	***4.7***	***1.2***	0.2	0.0	0.0	0.0	0.0	1.0	***5.6***	12.3	***47.8***
Maximum Snow Depth (in.)	***30***	na	***16***	***4***	***2***	***0***	***0***	***0***	***0***	***3***	na	na	na
Days With ≥ 1.0" Snow Depth	***16***	***12***	***3***	1	0	0	0	0	0	0	***2***	***11***	***45***

Grand Junction 6 ESE *Mesa County* Elevation: 4,759 ft. Latitude: 39° 03' N Longitude: 108° 28' W

	JAN	FEB	MAR	APR	MAY	JUN	JUL	AUG	SEP	OCT	NOV	DEC	YEAR
Mean Maximum Temp. (°F)	40.1	47.1	57.3	65.9	76.2	87.3	93.2	90.2	80.9	67.4	52.2	40.8	66.5
Mean Temp. (°F)	29.5	36.0	45.2	52.9	62.6	72.5	78.7	76.1	67.0	54.1	40.8	30.4	53.8
Mean Minimum Temp. (°F)	18.8	24.9	33.0	39.8	49.0	57.7	64.1	62.0	53.0	40.8	29.4	20.0	41.0
Extreme Maximum Temp. (°F)	59	68	81	88	100	104	107	103	99	87	75	67	107
Extreme Minimum Temp. (°F)	-10	-21	8	17	28	35	47	44	29	15	5	-13	-21
Days Maximum Temp. ≥ 90°F	0	0	0	0	2	14	23	19	4	0	0	0	62
Days Maximum Temp. ≤ 32°F	6	2	0	0	0	0	0	0	0	0	0	5	13
Days Minimum Temp. ≤ 32°F	30	24	15	5	0	0	0	0	0	4	20	30	128
Days Minimum Temp. ≤ 0°F	1	0	0	0	0	0	0	0	0	0	0	0	1
Heating Degree Days (base 65°F)	1,093	814	608	363	136	20	0	1	59	337	719	1,065	5,215
Cooling Degree Days (base 65°F)	0	0	0	6	70	253	432	353	125	6	0	0	1,245
Mean Precipitation (in.)	0.46	0.49	0.86	0.94	0.97	0.52	0.76	0.81	1.12	1.01	0.81	0.51	9.26
Extreme Maximum Daily Precip. (in.)	0.58	0.70	1.19	0.88	0.88	1.10	1.20	0.97	1.10	1.05	0.89	0.83	1.20
Days With ≥ 0.1" Precipitation	2	2	3	3	3	2	2	3	4	3	2	2	31
Days With ≥ 0.5" Precipitation	0	0	0	0	0	0	0	0	0	0	0	0	0
Days With ≥ 1.0" Precipitation	0	0	0	0	0	0	0	0	0	0	0	0	0
Mean Snowfall (in.)	3.2	2.2	1.5	0.5	trace	0.0	0.0	0.0	0.0	0.1	1.6	3.6	12.7
Maximum Snow Depth (in.)	9	***8***	3	2	0	0	0	0	0	***1***	6	***14***	***14***
Days With ≥ 1.0" Snow Depth	***5***	2	1	0	0	0	0	0	0	0	1	5	***14***

Greeley Unc *Weld County* Elevation: 4,714 ft. Latitude: 40° 24' N Longitude: 104° 42' W

	JAN	FEB	MAR	APR	MAY	JUN	JUL	AUG	SEP	OCT	NOV	DEC	YEAR
Mean Maximum Temp. (°F)	42.1	46.6	56.5	64.8	74.2	84.2	90.4	88.0	79.8	66.4	51.8	41.6	65.5
Mean Temp. (°F)	29.3	33.2	42.0	50.0	59.5	68.7	74.6	72.4	63.7	51.1	38.6	29.2	51.0
Mean Minimum Temp. (°F)	16.5	19.9	27.4	35.1	44.6	53.0	58.6	56.8	47.6	35.8	25.2	16.7	36.4
Extreme Maximum Temp. (°F)	74	76	83	92	101	110	112	105	99	92	84	75	112
Extreme Minimum Temp. (°F)	-25	-20	-5	10	24	34	46	41	17	5	-7	-24	-25
Days Maximum Temp. ≥ 90°F	0	0	0	0	2	10	18	14	5	0	0	0	49
Days Maximum Temp. ≤ 32°F	7	4	1	0	0	0	0	0	0	0	2	7	21
Days Minimum Temp. ≤ 32°F	30	27	24	11	1	0	0	0	1	10	24	30	158
Days Minimum Temp. ≤ 0°F	3	2	0	0	0	0	0	0	0	0	0	2	7
Heating Degree Days (base 65°F)	1,099	892	706	446	196	38	3	5	102	426	787	1,105	5,805
Cooling Degree Days (base 65°F)	0	0	0	1	30	154	306	243	71	2	0	0	807
Mean Precipitation (in.)	0.51	0.40	1.14	1.71	2.32	1.87	1.67	1.43	1.08	1.04	0.73	0.52	14.42
Extreme Maximum Daily Precip. (in.)	0.88	0.79	1.91	2.56	2.77	2.74	3.48	3.08	1.40	1.96	1.10	1.10	3.48
Days With ≥ 0.1" Precipitation	2	1	3	4	5	5	3	3	3	3	2	2	36
Days With ≥ 0.5" Precipitation	0	0	1	1	1	1	1	1	1	0	0	0	7
Days With ≥ 1.0" Precipitation	0	0	0	0	0	0	0	0	0	0	0	0	0
Mean Snowfall (in.)	6.5	4.6	7.6	5.0	0.6	0.0	0.0	0.0	0.6	2.8	6.6	6.4	40.7
Maximum Snow Depth (in.)	15	13	13	9	5	0	0	0	5	20	16	20	20
Days With ≥ 1.0" Snow Depth	15	8	3	1	0	0	0	0	0	1	5	12	45

Hayden *Routt County* Elevation: 6,439 ft. Latitude: 40° 30' N Longitude: 107° 15' W

	JAN	FEB	MAR	APR	MAY	JUN	JUL	AUG	SEP	OCT	NOV	DEC	YEAR
Mean Maximum Temp. (°F)	30.7	35.0	46.4	58.6	68.8	79.1	85.6	83.4	74.5	61.5	44.9	32.0	58.4
Mean Temp. (°F)	19.6	23.5	34.0	43.9	53.0	61.4	67.8	66.2	57.6	46.0	32.7	21.1	43.9
Mean Minimum Temp. (°F)	8.5	12.0	21.6	29.2	37.1	43.6	50.0	49.0	40.7	30.4	20.5	10.2	29.4
Extreme Maximum Temp. (°F)	60	61	74	81	92	95	98	95	92	83	74	61	98
Extreme Minimum Temp. (°F)	-34	-44	-16	3	17	26	32	32	14	2	-14	-33	-44
Days Maximum Temp. ≥ 90°F	0	0	0	0	0	2	8	3	0	0	0	0	13
Days Maximum Temp. ≤ 32°F	18	10	2	0	0	0	0	0	0	0	5	16	51
Days Minimum Temp. ≤ 32°F	31	28	29	20	7	1	0	0	4	19	28	31	198
Days Minimum Temp. ≤ 0°F	7	5	1	0	0	0	0	0	0	0	1	6	20
Heating Degree Days (base 65°F)	1,402	1,167	954	626	367	129	17	29	223	582	961	1,353	7,810
Cooling Degree Days (base 65°F)	0	0	0	0	1	27	111	74	7	0	0	0	220
Mean Precipitation (in.)	1.69	1.35	1.37	1.75	1.70	1.18	1.37	1.38	1.80	1.69	1.55	1.53	18.36
Extreme Maximum Daily Precip. (in.)	0.85	1.06	0.78	1.59	1.33	1.47	1.14	1.10	1.84	1.46	1.08	1.34	1.84
Days With ≥ 0.1" Precipitation	6	5	5	6	5	4	4	4	5	5	5	5	59
Days With ≥ 0.5" Precipitation	1	0	0	1	1	0	1	0	1	1	1	0	7
Days With ≥ 1.0" Precipitation	0	0	0	0	0	0	0	0	0	0	0	0	0
Mean Snowfall (in.)	26.1	18.5	14.7	8.9	1.3	trace	0.0	0.0	0.3	5.5	16.9	22.6	114.8
Maximum Snow Depth (in.)	38	37	30	24	4	trace	0	0	trace	8	13	40	40
Days With ≥ 1.0" Snow Depth	30	28	18	2	0	0	0	0	0	2	13	27	120

The period of record for all cooperative weather station data is 1980 – 2009. See User Guide for detailed explanation of data.

Hohnholz Ranch *Larimer County* Elevation: 7,759 ft. Latitude: 40° 58' N Longitude: 106° 00' W

	JAN	FEB	MAR	APR	MAY	JUN	JUL	AUG	SEP	OCT	NOV	DEC	YEAR
Mean Maximum Temp. (°F)	34.5	36.8	43.5	52.1	62.2	72.7	79.7	77.3	69.3	57.3	42.6	33.7	55.1
Mean Temp. (°F)	21.1	22.7	29.6	36.7	45.7	54.5	60.5	58.1	49.9	39.7	28.7	20.3	38.9
Mean Minimum Temp. (°F)	7.6	8.4	15.6	21.2	29.1	36.3	41.3	38.8	30.4	22.0	14.7	6.9	22.7
Extreme Maximum Temp. (°F)	60	57	67	76	84	90	92	90	87	77	68	59	92
Extreme Minimum Temp. (°F)	-33	-38	-31	-13	5	20	27	22	10	-9	-21	-40	-40
Days Maximum Temp. ≥ 90°F	0	0	0	0	0	0	1	0	0	0	0	0	1
Days Maximum Temp. ≤ 32°F	13	8	5	1	0	0	0	0	0	1	6	13	47
Days Minimum Temp. ≤ 32°F	31	28	30	28	22	6	1	4	18	28	29	31	256
Days Minimum Temp. ≤ 0°F	9	7	3	1	0	0	0	0	0	0	3	9	32
Heating Degree Days (base 65°F)	1,355	1,191	1,092	843	592	310	142	211	448	779	1,083	1,378	9,424
Cooling Degree Days (base 65°F)	0	0	0	0	0	1	10	2	0	0	0	0	13
Mean Precipitation (in.)	0.77	0.83	1.22	1.57	1.73	1.68	1.32	1.45	1.38	1.02	0.90	0.81	14.68
Extreme Maximum Daily Precip. (in.)	0.70	0.78	1.29	2.05	1.00	1.81	0.83	0.98	1.46	1.30	0.60	0.84	2.05
Days With ≥ 0.1" Precipitation	3	3	4	5	5	5	4	5	4	3	3	3	47
Days With ≥ 0.5" Precipitation	0	0	0	0	1	1	1	1	1	0	0	0	5
Days With ≥ 1.0" Precipitation	0	0	0	0	0	0	0	0	0	0	0	0	0
Mean Snowfall (in.)	12.5	13.5	17.7	16.7	7.8	0.9	trace	trace	2.2	9.1	12.4	13.8	106.6
Maximum Snow Depth (in.)	16	26	24	18	12	6	trace	trace	6	24	10	21	26
Days With ≥ 1.0" Snow Depth	28	26	18	8	2	0	0	0	1	4	16	26	129

Holly *Prowers County* Elevation: 3,390 ft. Latitude: 38° 03' N Longitude: 102° 07' W

	JAN	FEB	MAR	APR	MAY	JUN	JUL	AUG	SEP	OCT	NOV	DEC	YEAR
Mean Maximum Temp. (°F)	44.9	49.5	59.2	69.2	78.2	88.7	94.1	91.3	83.1	71.4	56.5	45.7	69.3
Mean Temp. (°F)	29.7	33.9	42.8	52.2	62.3	72.5	78.1	75.9	66.7	54.0	40.3	30.7	53.3
Mean Minimum Temp. (°F)	14.4	18.3	26.3	35.1	46.4	56.2	62.0	60.4	50.2	36.6	24.2	15.7	37.2
Extreme Maximum Temp. (°F)	79	84	92	99	104	109	109	107	104	96	86	75	109
Extreme Minimum Temp. (°F)	-28	-22	-9	10	25	36	40	40	19	13	-9	-22	-28
Days Maximum Temp. ≥ 90°F	0	0	0	1	4	15	23	19	9	1	0	0	72
Days Maximum Temp. ≤ 32°F	6	4	1	0	0	0	0	0	0	0	1	5	17
Days Minimum Temp. ≤ 32°F	31	27	24	12	1	0	0	0	1	9	25	30	160
Days Minimum Temp. ≤ 0°F	2	2	0	0	0	0	0	0	0	0	0	2	6
Heating Degree Days (base 65°F)	1,089	873	683	387	140	15	2	2	75	344	734	1,057	5,401
Cooling Degree Days (base 65°F)	0	0	0	9	63	247	413	347	132	10	0	0	1,221
Mean Precipitation (in.)	0.34	0.39	1.06	1.42	2.35	2.72	2.67	3.24	1.27	1.28	0.57	0.44	17.75
Extreme Maximum Daily Precip. (in.)	1.31	0.78	1.14	1.96	2.46	3.39	2.38	3.55	1.91	3.32	1.37	0.66	3.55
Days With ≥ 0.1" Precipitation	1	1	3	3	5	5	5	4	3	3	2	1	36
Days With ≥ 0.5" Precipitation	0	0	1	1	1	2	2	2	1	1	0	0	11
Days With ≥ 1.0" Precipitation	0	0	0	0	1	1	1	1	0	0	0	0	4
Mean Snowfall (in.)	4.8	4.0	5.3	1.8	trace	0.0	0.0	0.0	0.1	0.6	2.5	4.5	23.6
Maximum Snow Depth (in.)	22	17	7	10	0	0	0	0	1	15	14	22	22
Days With ≥ 1.0" Snow Depth	8	6	2	0	0	0	0	0	0	0	1	4	21

Holyoke *Phillips County* Elevation: 3,729 ft. Latitude: 40° 35' N Longitude: 102° 18' W

	JAN	FEB	MAR	APR	MAY	JUN	JUL	AUG	SEP	OCT	NOV	DEC	YEAR
Mean Maximum Temp. (°F)	41.7	45.2	53.2	62.3	71.9	81.6	87.8	85.8	77.4	64.7	52.6	42.1	63.8
Mean Temp. (°F)	28.6	31.7	39.2	48.1	58.7	68.2	74.1	72.3	62.9	50.1	38.5	28.6	50.1
Mean Minimum Temp. (°F)	15.4	18.1	25.2	33.9	45.4	54.8	60.4	58.8	48.4	35.4	24.4	15.2	36.3
Extreme Maximum Temp. (°F)	75	77	84	92	98	103	107	107	98	93	83	73	107
Extreme Minimum Temp. (°F)	-19	-24	-11	8	22	34	46	42	18	3	-9	-33	-33
Days Maximum Temp. ≥ 90°F	0	0	0	0	1	7	14	11	4	0	0	0	37
Days Maximum Temp. ≤ 32°F	7	6	3	0	0	0	0	0	0	0	2	8	26
Days Minimum Temp. ≤ 32°F	31	27	25	13	1	0	0	0	1	11	25	30	164
Days Minimum Temp. ≤ 0°F	3	2	0	0	0	0	0	0	0	0	0	3	8
Heating Degree Days (base 65°F)	1,123	936	793	501	223	46	6	11	131	459	789	1,121	6,139
Cooling Degree Days (base 65°F)	0	0	0	2	33	149	295	245	74	4	0	0	802
Mean Precipitation (in.)	0.46	0.49	1.12	1.87	3.04	2.93	2.84	2.30	1.32	1.19	0.64	0.42	18.62
Extreme Maximum Daily Precip. (in.)	1.26	0.68	2.06	1.58	2.13	3.51	3.02	2.37	2.45	1.92	0.81	1.00	3.51
Days With ≥ 0.1" Precipitation	2	2	3	4	6	6	5	4	3	3	2	1	41
Days With ≥ 0.5" Precipitation	0	0	1	1	2	2	2	2	1	1	0	0	12
Days With ≥ 1.0" Precipitation	0	0	0	0	1	1	1	1	0	0	0	0	4
Mean Snowfall (in.)	5.2	4.5	6.0	3.4	trace	0.0	0.0	0.0	0.4	1.5	4.5	5.0	30.5
Maximum Snow Depth (in.)	12	11	12	8	1	0	0	0	6	8	12	17	17
Days With ≥ 1.0" Snow Depth	7	6	4	2	0	0	0	0	0	1	2	6	28

Karval *Lincoln County* Elevation: 5,075 ft. Latitude: 38° 44' N Longitude: 103° 33' W

	JAN	FEB	MAR	APR	MAY	JUN	JUL	AUG	SEP	OCT	NOV	DEC	YEAR
Mean Maximum Temp. (°F)	44.6	47.4	55.3	63.6	72.6	82.1	88.8	85.9	78.4	66.7	53.0	43.8	65.2
Mean Temp. (°F)	30.3	33.2	40.5	48.4	57.9	67.2	na	71.5	63.0	51.1	38.8	30.0	na
Mean Minimum Temp. (°F)	15.9	18.9	25.6	33.2	43.1	52.3	57.9	57.1	47.5	35.3	24.5	16.2	35.6
Extreme Maximum Temp. (°F)	77	79	84	90	98	102	103	103	99	90	83	78	103
Extreme Minimum Temp. (°F)	-29	-24	-5	6	20	34	43	41	25	5	-6	-28	-29
Days Maximum Temp. ≥ 90°F	0	0	0	0	1	7	15	11	3	0	0	0	37
Days Maximum Temp. ≤ 32°F	6	5	2	1	0	0	0	0	0	0	3	7	24
Days Minimum Temp. ≤ 32°F	30	27	25	14	2	0	0	0	1	10	23	30	162
Days Minimum Temp. ≤ 0°F	2	2	0	0	0	0	0	0	0	0	0	2	6
Heating Degree Days (base 65°F)	1,070	894	752	492	237	49	na	11	124	427	779	1,078	na
Cooling Degree Days (base 65°F)	0	0	0	2	22	122	na	218	69	4	0	0	na
Mean Precipitation (in.)	0.31	0.31	0.84	1.42	2.18	2.01	2.45	2.31	0.96	0.96	0.39	0.31	14.45
Extreme Maximum Daily Precip. (in.)	0.63	0.90	1.31	3.00	2.56	1.93	4.30	1.88	1.60	1.61	0.70	0.79	4.30
Days With ≥ 0.1" Precipitation	1	1	2	3	5	5	5	5	3	2	1	1	34
Days With ≥ 0.5" Precipitation	0	0	1	1	1	1	1	2	1	1	0	0	9
Days With ≥ 1.0" Precipitation	0	0	0	0	0	0	1	1	0	0	0	0	2
Mean Snowfall (in.)	4.4	3.0	5.4	2.7	0.3	0.0	0.0	0.0	0.1	1.4	3.2	4.4	24.9
Maximum Snow Depth (in.)	13	9	10	10	6	0	0	0	1	18	10	7	18
Days With ≥ 1.0" Snow Depth	9	6	3	1	0	0	0	0	0	1	4	9	33

The period of record for all cooperative weather station data is 1980 – 2009. See User Guide for detailed explanation of data.

Kassler *Jefferson County* Elevation: 5,500 ft. Latitude: 39° 29' N Longitude: 105° 06' W

	JAN	FEB	MAR	APR	MAY	JUN	JUL	AUG	SEP	OCT	NOV	DEC	YEAR
Mean Maximum Temp. (°F)	47.1	48.4	54.6	61.8	70.6	81.2	87.9	85.5	77.6	66.0	54.6	46.0	65.1
Mean Temp. (°F)	31.8	33.5	40.2	47.4	56.7	66.5	73.2	71.3	62.7	50.8	39.9	31.0	50.4
Mean Minimum Temp. (°F)	16.7	18.7	25.8	33.0	42.9	51.8	58.5	57.0	47.8	35.5	25.1	16.1	35.7
Extreme Maximum Temp. (°F)	76	76	83	88	97	105	105	101	98	90	82	75	105
Extreme Minimum Temp. (°F)	-23	-25	-10	0	22	32	37	40	18	-8	-10	-31	-31
Days Maximum Temp. ≥ 90°F	0	0	0	0	1	6	14	9	3	0	0	0	33
Days Maximum Temp. ≤ 32°F	4	4	2	0	0	0	0	0	0	0	2	5	17
Days Minimum Temp. ≤ 32°F	29	26	24	14	3	0	0	0	1	11	23	29	160
Days Minimum Temp. ≤ 0°F	3	2	0	0	0	0	0	0	0	0	0	3	8
Heating Degree Days (base 65°F)	1,021	885	761	521	268	67	7	12	134	439	748	1,045	5,908
Cooling Degree Days (base 65°F)	0	0	0	2	19	119	270	214	73	4	0	0	701
Mean Precipitation (in.)	0.57	0.58	1.78	2.31	2.52	1.78	1.49	2.02	1.44	1.51	1.18	0.83	18.01
Extreme Maximum Daily Precip. (in.)	0.55	0.60	1.83	1.77	2.40	2.36	1.11	2.49	1.38	2.04	1.27	1.52	2.49
Days With ≥ 0.1" Precipitation	2	2	5	5	6	5	4	5	4	3	3	2	46
Days With ≥ 0.5" Precipitation	0	0	1	1	2	1	1	1	1	1	1	0	10
Days With ≥ 1.0" Precipitation	0	0	0	0	0	0	0	0	0	0	0	0	0
Mean Snowfall (in.)	9.9	8.0	14.1	8.1	0.4	0.0	0.0	0.0	0.6	4.2	10.4	14.1	69.8
Maximum Snow Depth (in.)	26	10	38	18	3	0	0	0	8	29	20	26	38
Days With ≥ 1.0" Snow Depth	12	8	7	3	0	0	0	0	0	2	7	12	51

La Junta 4 NNE *Otero County* Elevation: 4,203 ft. Latitude: 38° 03' N Longitude: 103° 32' W

	JAN	FEB	MAR	APR	MAY	JUN	JUL	AUG	SEP	OCT	NOV	DEC	YEAR
Mean Maximum Temp. (°F)	45.1	48.9	59.9	68.8	78.0	89.2	94.8	91.9	83.2	70.3	56.6	45.5	69.3
Mean Temp. (°F)	31.2	34.8	44.7	53.3	63.0	73.4	78.9	76.8	67.6	54.4	41.4	31.6	54.3
Mean Minimum Temp. (°F)	17.3	20.6	29.4	37.7	47.9	57.5	63.1	61.7	51.9	38.5	26.3	17.7	39.1
Extreme Maximum Temp. (°F)	78	81	88	95	104	110	108	108	104	93	85	81	110
Extreme Minimum Temp. (°F)	-12	-20	0	17	25	38	50	43	22	9	-9	-21	-21
Days Maximum Temp. ≥ 90°F	0	0	0	1	4	16	25	21	9	1	0	0	77
Days Maximum Temp. ≤ 32°F	7	4	1	0	0	0	0	0	0	0	1	6	19
Days Minimum Temp. ≤ 32°F	30	26	21	7	0	0	0	0	1	6	23	30	144
Days Minimum Temp. ≤ 0°F	2	2	0	0	0	0	0	0	0	0	0	2	6
Heating Degree Days (base 65°F)	1,036	847	623	356	126	12	1	2	65	331	700	1,028	5,127
Cooling Degree Days (base 65°F)	0	0	1	10	71	269	440	376	149	11	0	0	1,327
Mean Precipitation (in.)	0.30	0.34	0.83	1.38	1.66	1.33	1.63	1.45	0.83	0.82	0.37	0.27	11.21
Extreme Maximum Daily Precip. (in.)	0.64	0.80	1.20	2.21	1.58	1.13	1.79	1.72	0.91	2.19	1.14	0.84	2.21
Days With ≥ 0.1" Precipitation	1	1	2	4	4	3	4	3	2	2	1	1	28
Days With ≥ 0.5" Precipitation	0	0	0	1	1	1	1	1	0	0	0	0	5
Days With ≥ 1.0" Precipitation	0	0	0	0	0	0	0	0	0	0	0	0	0
Mean Snowfall (in.)	na	na	na	na	na	na	na	na	na	na	na	na	na
Maximum Snow Depth (in.)	na	na	na	na	na	na	na	na	na	na	na	na	na
Days With ≥ 1.0" Snow Depth	na	na	na	na	na	na	na	na	na	na	na	na	na

Leroy 5 WSW *Logan County* Elevation: 4,470 ft. Latitude: 40° 31' N Longitude: 103° 00' W

	JAN	FEB	MAR	APR	MAY	JUN	JUL	AUG	SEP	OCT	NOV	DEC	YEAR
Mean Maximum Temp. (°F)	40.0	43.7	52.1	60.9	70.4	81.4	89.2	86.5	77.9	65.0	50.6	40.4	63.2
Mean Temp. (°F)	27.8	31.2	38.7	46.9	56.9	67.1	74.1	71.9	62.8	50.3	37.8	28.2	49.5
Mean Minimum Temp. (°F)	15.6	18.6	25.4	32.7	43.4	52.8	59.1	57.3	47.6	35.5	25.0	16.1	35.7
Extreme Maximum Temp. (°F)	75	74	84	91	98	107	108	105	102	92	80	72	108
Extreme Minimum Temp. (°F)	-23	-25	-9	4	20	35	35	41	14	3	-8	-25	-25
Days Maximum Temp. ≥ 90°F	0	0	0	0	1	6	16	12	5	0	0	0	40
Days Maximum Temp. ≤ 32°F	9	6	4	1	0	0	0	0	0	0	4	8	32
Days Minimum Temp. ≤ 32°F	30	27	25	15	2	0	0	0	1	10	23	30	163
Days Minimum Temp. ≤ 0°F	3	2	1	0	0	0	0	0	0	0	1	3	10
Heating Degree Days (base 65°F)	1,145	951	807	539	267	61	7	14	139	454	810	1,132	6,326
Cooling Degree Days (base 65°F)	0	0	0	1	22	131	298	234	79	5	0	0	770
Mean Precipitation (in.)	0.35	0.39	0.97	1.50	2.79	2.73	3.11	2.18	1.25	1.02	0.55	0.39	17.23
Extreme Maximum Daily Precip. (in.)	0.95	1.41	1.60	1.83	2.51	3.87	5.03	2.53	1.41	1.53	0.82	1.17	5.03
Days With ≥ 0.1" Precipitation	1	2	3	4	7	6	5	5	3	3	2	2	43
Days With ≥ 0.5" Precipitation	0	0	0	1	2	2	2	2	1	0	0	0	10
Days With ≥ 1.0" Precipitation	0	0	0	0	0	0	1	1	0	0	0	0	2
Mean Snowfall (in.)	5.9	5.6	8.0	6.5	0.4	trace	0.0	0.0	1.1	2.2	6.5	6.5	42.7
Maximum Snow Depth (in.)	15	14	10	13	5	trace	0	0	10	7	23	24	24
Days With ≥ 1.0" Snow Depth	13	10	6	3	0	0	0	0	0	1	5	11	49

Longmont 2 ESE *Boulder County* Elevation: 4,950 ft. Latitude: 40° 10' N Longitude: 105° 04' W

	JAN	FEB	MAR	APR	MAY	JUN	JUL	AUG	SEP	OCT	NOV	DEC	YEAR
Mean Maximum Temp. (°F)	44.0	46.3	54.7	63.0	72.4	82.8	89.5	87.5	79.0	66.6	52.0	44.4	65.2
Mean Temp. (°F)	28.4	31.3	39.4	47.4	57.2	66.6	72.4	70.5	61.4	49.3	36.9	29.0	49.2
Mean Minimum Temp. (°F)	12.9	16.2	24.1	31.8	41.9	50.3	55.3	53.3	44.0	32.1	21.8	13.5	33.1
Extreme Maximum Temp. (°F)	75	77	85	88	100	106	105	104	100	90	80	73	106
Extreme Minimum Temp. (°F)	-30	-28	-12	6	18	29	40	37	18	1	-16	-31	-31
Days Maximum Temp. ≥ 90°F	0	0	0	0	1	9	17	14	5	0	0	0	46
Days Maximum Temp. ≤ 32°F	6	4	2	0	0	0	0	0	0	0	3	5	20
Days Minimum Temp. ≤ 32°F	31	27	27	16	3	0	0	0	2	15	27	31	179
Days Minimum Temp. ≤ 0°F	4	3	0	0	0	0	0	0	0	0	1	4	12
Heating Degree Days (base 65°F)	1,127	946	786	521	253	59	6	12	150	478	836	1,111	6,285
Cooling Degree Days (base 65°F)	0	0	0	0	18	112	244	188	51	1	0	0	614
Mean Precipitation (in.)	0.43	0.41	1.41	1.79	2.33	1.68	1.16	1.42	1.30	0.78	0.88	0.51	14.10
Extreme Maximum Daily Precip. (in.)	0.61	0.45	2.04	2.07	1.81	2.29	1.52	1.65	1.22	1.05	0.84	0.68	2.29
Days With ≥ 0.1" Precipitation	2	2	3	5	5	4	4	3	4	2	3	1	38
Days With ≥ 0.5" Precipitation	0	0	1	1	1	1	1	1	1	0	0	0	7
Days With ≥ 1.0" Precipitation	0	0	0	0	1	0	0	0	0	0	0	0	1
Mean Snowfall (in.)	4.7	3.3	4.6	3.3	0.2	0.0	0.0	0.0	0.4	1.2	4.7	6.2	28.6
Maximum Snow Depth (in.)	na	na	na	na	na	na	na	na	na	na	na	na	na
Days With ≥ 1.0" Snow Depth	na	na	na	1	0	0	0	0	0	0	2	na	na

The period of record for all cooperative weather station data is 1980 – 2009. See User Guide for detailed explanation of data.

Northglenn *Adams County* Elevation: 5,366 ft. Latitude: 39° 54' N Longitude: 105° 01' W

	JAN	FEB	MAR	APR	MAY	JUN	JUL	AUG	SEP	OCT	NOV	DEC	YEAR
Mean Maximum Temp. (°F)	46.6	49.0	55.9	63.1	72.8	83.1	89.6	86.9	78.1	66.4	53.4	45.1	65.8
Mean Temp. (°F)	32.9	35.0	41.8	48.7	58.3	67.6	73.6	71.4	62.7	51.4	39.8	31.7	51.2
Mean Minimum Temp. (°F)	19.2	21.0	27.6	34.3	43.8	52.0	57.5	55.9	47.3	36.3	26.2	18.3	36.6
Extreme Maximum Temp. (°F)	77	77	83	90	101	103	108	110	101	92	83	77	110
Extreme Minimum Temp. (°F)	-15	-30	-5	6	12	30	33	41	18	5	-6	-24	-30
Days Maximum Temp. ≥ 90°F	0	0	0	0	1	8	17	13	4	0	0	0	43
Days Maximum Temp. ≤ 32°F	5	4	2	0	0	0	0	0	0	0	2	5	18
Days Minimum Temp. ≤ 32°F	28	26	22	12	2	0	0	0	1	9	23	29	152
Days Minimum Temp. ≤ 0°F	2	1	0	0	0	0	0	0	0	0	0	2	5
Heating Degree Days (base 65°F)	989	840	714	483	229	50	7	10	131	421	748	1,028	5,650
Cooling Degree Days (base 65°F)	0	0	0	2	27	134	280	217	70	4	0	0	734
Mean Precipitation (in.)	0.40	0.37	1.16	1.94	2.11	1.61	1.78	1.56	1.07	0.99	0.72	0.55	14.26
Extreme Maximum Daily Precip. (in.)	0.51	0.48	2.00	2.27	2.20	1.53	2.15	2.45	1.13	1.45	0.80	1.49	2.45
Days With ≥ 0.1" Precipitation	1	1	3	4	5	4	4	4	3	3	2	2	36
Days With ≥ 0.5" Precipitation	0	0	1	1	1	1	1	1	0	0	0	0	6
Days With ≥ 1.0" Precipitation	0	0	0	0	0	0	1	0	0	0	0	0	1
Mean Snowfall (in.)	6.5	5.1	6.8	5.9	0.5	0.0	0.0	0.0	0.5	2.4	7.2	7.8	42.7
Maximum Snow Depth (in.)	10	6	21	12	3	0	0	0	5	na	14	22	na
Days With ≥ 1.0" Snow Depth	8	6	5	2	0	0	0	0	0	1	6	10	38

Trinidad *Las Animas County* Elevation: 6,029 ft. Latitude: 37° 11' N Longitude: 104° 29' W

	JAN	FEB	MAR	APR	MAY	JUN	JUL	AUG	SEP	OCT	NOV	DEC	YEAR
Mean Maximum Temp. (°F)	49.4	51.9	58.5	66.4	75.1	83.9	87.6	85.0	79.5	69.3	57.2	48.2	67.7
Mean Temp. (°F)	34.8	37.1	43.6	50.7	59.8	68.4	72.6	70.6	64.3	53.5	42.4	34.1	52.7
Mean Minimum Temp. (°F)	20.1	22.2	28.6	34.9	44.4	52.8	57.6	56.2	49.0	37.6	27.6	20.0	37.6
Extreme Maximum Temp. (°F)	78	75	81	89	96	101	101	98	94	89	80	78	101
Extreme Minimum Temp. (°F)	-15	-20	-10	2	25	32	43	41	23	2	-7	-16	-20
Days Maximum Temp. ≥ 90°F	0	0	0	0	1	7	12	6	1	0	0	0	27
Days Maximum Temp. ≤ 32°F	3	2	1	0	0	0	0	0	0	0	1	4	11
Days Minimum Temp. ≤ 32°F	29	25	21	12	2	0	0	0	1	8	22	29	149
Days Minimum Temp. ≤ 0°F	1	1	0	0	0	0	0	0	0	0	0	1	3
Heating Degree Days (base 65°F)	931	782	658	424	183	31	2	6	81	353	672	950	5,073
Cooling Degree Days (base 65°F)	0	0	0	1	28	140	246	186	66	3	0	0	670
Mean Precipitation (in.)	0.51	0.52	1.13	1.34	1.81	1.76	2.61	2.65	1.36	1.14	0.85	0.58	16.26
Extreme Maximum Daily Precip. (in.)	0.90	0.90	0.93	2.15	1.55	1.98	2.50	4.20	1.87	1.90	1.14	1.47	4.20
Days With ≥ 0.1" Precipitation	2	2	3	3	4	5	5	6	3	3	2	2	40
Days With ≥ 0.5" Precipitation	0	0	1	1	1	1	2	2	1	1	1	0	11
Days With ≥ 1.0" Precipitation	0	0	0	0	0	0	0	0	0	0	0	0	0
Mean Snowfall (in.)	7.2	6.7	9.1	7.0	0.7	0.0	trace	0.0	0.2	3.5	6.2	9.0	49.6
Maximum Snow Depth (in.)	22	13	10	17	10	0	trace	0	2	11	15	31	31
Days With ≥ 1.0" Snow Depth	5	5	3	1	0	0	0	0	0	1	2	7	24

Uravan *Montrose County* Elevation: 5,009 ft. Latitude: 38° 23' N Longitude: 108° 45' W

	JAN	FEB	MAR	APR	MAY	JUN	JUL	AUG	SEP	OCT	NOV	DEC	YEAR
Mean Maximum Temp. (°F)	43.7	50.2	59.2	67.5	78.4	89.9	95.8	92.5	83.7	70.8	55.4	44.0	69.3
Mean Temp. (°F)	30.1	36.5	44.4	51.7	61.7	71.4	77.8	75.6	66.3	53.8	40.9	30.9	53.4
Mean Minimum Temp. (°F)	16.4	22.6	29.6	35.8	44.9	52.9	59.8	58.7	48.9	36.8	26.4	17.8	37.6
Extreme Maximum Temp. (°F)	66	73	85	90	101	107	110	106	103	90	80	65	110
Extreme Minimum Temp. (°F)	-10	-10	2	15	29	30	44	42	31	16	-11	-15	-15
Days Maximum Temp. ≥ 90°F	0	0	0	0	3	17	27	22	8	0	0	0	77
Days Maximum Temp. ≤ 32°F	2	1	0	0	0	0	0	0	0	0	0	2	5
Days Minimum Temp. ≤ 32°F	30	26	21	9	1	0	0	0	0	8	24	30	149
Days Minimum Temp. ≤ 0°F	2	0	0	0	0	0	0	0	0	0	0	1	3
Heating Degree Days (base 65°F)	1,075	799	630	393	145	19	0	1	56	342	715	1,049	5,224
Cooling Degree Days (base 65°F)	0	0	0	1	48	219	403	337	104	2	0	0	1,114
Mean Precipitation (in.)	0.77	0.92	1.05	0.95	0.92	0.53	1.11	1.43	1.76	1.53	0.99	0.92	12.88
Extreme Maximum Daily Precip. (in.)	1.00	0.80	0.95	0.80	0.85	1.18	1.25	1.15	1.85	1.43	0.94	0.93	1.85
Days With ≥ 0.1" Precipitation	3	3	4	4	3	1	3	4	4	4	3	3	39
Days With ≥ 0.5" Precipitation	0	0	0	0	0	0	0	1	1	1	0	0	3
Days With ≥ 1.0" Precipitation	0	0	0	0	0	0	0	0	0	0	0	0	0
Mean Snowfall (in.)	na	0.9	0.4	0.3	0.0	0.0	0.0	0.0	0.0	0.2	0.3	na	na
Maximum Snow Depth (in.)	na	na	na	na	na	na	na	na	na	na	na	na	na
Days With ≥ 1.0" Snow Depth	na	na	0	0	0	0	0	0	0	0	0	na	na

Walsh 1 W *Baca County* Elevation: 3,977 ft. Latitude: 37° 23' N Longitude: 102° 18' W

	JAN	FEB	MAR	APR	MAY	JUN	JUL	AUG	SEP	OCT	NOV	DEC	YEAR
Mean Maximum Temp. (°F)	45.6	49.6	58.0	67.4	76.8	87.0	92.4	89.2	81.7	69.4	56.5	46.2	68.3
Mean Temp. (°F)	32.0	35.5	43.3	52.1	62.1	72.0	77.2	75.0	66.9	54.2	42.1	32.4	53.7
Mean Minimum Temp. (°F)	18.4	21.3	28.4	36.7	47.4	56.9	62.0	60.9	52.0	39.0	27.8	19.0	39.2
Extreme Maximum Temp. (°F)	80	82	88	96	102	108	106	106	102	93	88	78	108
Extreme Minimum Temp. (°F)	-25	-19	-4	8	28	38	45	41	20	8	-7	-20	-25
Days Maximum Temp. ≥ 90°F	0	0	0	1	4	13	22	17	7	1	0	0	65
Days Maximum Temp. ≤ 32°F	6	4	2	0	0	0	0	0	0	0	2	6	20
Days Minimum Temp. ≤ 32°F	30	25	21	10	1	0	0	0	0	7	21	30	145
Days Minimum Temp. ≤ 0°F	1	1	0	0	0	0	0	0	0	0	0	2	4
Heating Degree Days (base 65°F)	1,015	827	668	391	146	20	2	5	73	341	679	1,003	5,170
Cooling Degree Days (base 65°F)	0	0	0	9	64	236	388	323	137	14	0	0	1,171
Mean Precipitation (in.)	0.50	0.45	1.11	1.69	2.24	2.63	3.54	2.99	1.38	1.55	0.59	0.55	19.22
Extreme Maximum Daily Precip. (in.)	1.04	0.87	2.02	1.93	2.95	2.54	4.30	3.20	1.82	3.33	1.32	1.61	4.30
Days With ≥ 0.1" Precipitation	2	1	3	4	5	5	5	5	3	3	2	2	40
Days With ≥ 0.5" Precipitation	0	0	1	1	1	2	2	2	1	1	0	0	11
Days With ≥ 1.0" Precipitation	0	0	0	0	0	1	1	1	0	0	0	0	3
Mean Snowfall (in.)	5.1	3.4	4.4	1.6	0.1	0.0	0.0	0.0	0.2	0.7	2.2	5.0	22.7
Maximum Snow Depth (in.)	28	10	9	13	3	0	0	0	2	9	11	28	28
Days With ≥ 1.0" Snow Depth	7	5	3	1	0	0	0	0	0	0	2	5	23

The period of record for all cooperative weather station data is 1980 – 2009. See User Guide for detailed explanation of data.

Colorado Weather Station Rankings

Annual Extreme Maximum Temperature

Highest			Lowest		
Rank	Station Name	°F	Rank	Station Name	°F
1	Greeley Unc	112	1	Cabin Creek	83
2	Fruita 1 W	111	2	Antero Reservoir	88
3	Campo 7 S	110	3	Aspen 1 SW	92
3	La Junta 4 NNE	***110***	3	Center 4 SSW	92
3	Northglenn	***110***	3	Hohnholz Ranch	***92***
3	Uravan	110	6	Bailey	93
7	Bonny Dam 2 NE	109	7	Cochetopa Creek	94
7	Burlington 4 S	109	8	Fort Lewis	95
7	Holly	109	9	Alamosa Bergman Field	96
7	Pueblo Memorial Arpt	109	9	Evergreen	96
11	Eads	***108***	11	Cimarron	97
11	Leroy 5 WSW	108	12	Hayden	98
11	Walsh 1 W	108	13	Cheesman	99
14	Akron 4 E	107	14	Colorado Springs Municipal Arpt	100
14	Grand Junction 6 ESE	107	15	Boulder	101
14	Holyoke	107	15	Trinidad	101
17	Briggsdale	106	17	Glenwood Spgs #2	102
17	Byers 5 ENE	106	18	Flagler 5 NNE	103
17	Grand Junction Walker Field	106	18	Fort Collins	103
17	Longmont 2 ESE	***106***	18	Karval	103
21	Canon City	***105***	21	Altenbern	104
21	Kassler	105	21	Denver Stapleton Int'l Arpt	104
23	Altenbern	104	21	Dinosaur Natl Monumnt	104
23	Denver Stapleton Int'l Arpt	104	24	Canon City	***105***
23	Dinosaur Natl Monumnt	104	24	Kassler	105

Annual Mean Maximum Temperature

Highest			Lowest		
Rank	Station Name	°F	Rank	Station Name	°F
1	Campo 7 S	69.8	1	Cabin Creek	48.6
2	La Junta 4 NNE	***69.4***	2	Antero Reservoir	53.4
3	Holly	69.3	3	Hohnholz Ranch	***55.1***
3	Uravan	69.3	4	Aspen 1 SW	55.5
5	Pueblo Memorial Arpt	69.0	5	Bailey	56.5
6	Walsh 1 W	68.3	6	Cochetopa Creek	56.9
7	Trinidad	67.7	7	Center 4 SSW	58.1
8	Canon City	***67.3***	8	Hayden	58.4
9	Eads	***67.1***	9	Fort Lewis	58.9
10	Fruita 1 W	***67.0***	10	Alamosa Bergman Field	59.6
11	Grand Junction 6 ESE	66.6	10	Cimarron	59.6
12	Grand Junction Walker Field	66.2	12	Evergreen	60.7
13	Northglenn	***65.8***	13	Cheesman	61.9
14	Burlington 4 S	***65.5***	14	Dinosaur Natl Monumnt	62.0
14	Greeley Unc	65.5	15	Colorado Springs Municipal Arpt	62.3
16	Bonny Dam 2 NE	***65.2***	16	Glenwood Spgs #2	***63.2***
16	Karval	65.2	16	Leroy 5 WSW	63.2
16	Longmont 2 ESE	***65.2***	18	Altenbern	63.3
19	Kassler	65.1	19	Akron 4 E	63.4
20	Boulder	65.0	20	Fort Collins	63.6
20	Byers 5 ENE	65.0	21	Holyoke	63.9
22	Denver Stapleton Int'l Arpt	64.6	22	Flagler 5 NNE	***64.2***
23	Briggsdale	64.5	23	Briggsdale	64.5
24	Flagler 5 NNE	***64.2***	24	Denver Stapleton Int'l Arpt	64.6
25	Holyoke	63.9	25	Boulder	65.0

Rankings include 25 highest/lowest stations. If state has less than 25 stations, all stations are included. The period of record is 1980–2009. See User Guide for detailed explanation of data.

Annual Mean Temperature

Highest Rank	Station Name	°F	Lowest Rank	Station Name	°F
1	Campo 7 S	54.5	1	Antero Reservoir	36.0
2	La Junta 4 NNE	*54.3*	2	Cabin Creek	36.4
3	Grand Junction 6 ESE	53.8	3	Hohnholz Ranch	*38.9*
3	Walsh 1 W	53.8	4	Cochetopa Creek	39.1
5	Grand Junction Walker Field	53.4	5	Bailey	40.7
5	Uravan	53.4	6	Center 4 SSW	41.6
7	Holly	53.3	7	Aspen 1 SW	41.7
8	Canon City	*52.8*	8	Alamosa Bergman Field	41.8
9	Trinidad	52.7	9	Cimarron	42.1
10	Pueblo Memorial Arpt	52.3	10	Hayden	43.9
11	Eads	*52.0*	11	Fort Lewis	44.1
12	Burlington 4 S	*51.5*	12	Cheesman	44.3
13	Boulder	51.4	12	Evergreen	44.3
14	Northglenn	*51.3*	14	Altenbern	47.2
15	Bonny Dam 2 NE	*51.1*	15	Dinosaur Natl Monumnt	48.1
15	Fruita 1 W	*51.1*	16	Glenwood Spgs #2	*48.2*
17	Greeley Unc	51.0	17	Briggsdale	48.6
18	Denver Stapleton Int'l Arpt	50.9	18	Colorado Springs Municipal Arpt	49.0
19	Kassler	50.4	19	Akron 4 E	49.2
20	Holyoke	50.1	19	Longmont 2 ESE	*49.2*
21	Fort Collins	50.0	21	Flagler 5 NNE	*49.4*
22	Byers 5 ENE	49.5	22	Byers 5 ENE	49.5
22	Leroy 5 WSW	49.5	22	Leroy 5 WSW	49.5
24	Flagler 5 NNE	*49.4*	24	Fort Collins	50.0
25	Akron 4 E	49.2	25	Holyoke	50.1

Annual Mean Minimum Temperature

Highest Rank	Station Name	°F	Lowest Rank	Station Name	°F
1	Grand Junction 6 ESE	41.0	1	Antero Reservoir	18.6
2	Grand Junction Walker Field	40.5	2	Cochetopa Creek	21.3
3	Walsh 1 W	39.2	3	Hohnholz Ranch	*22.7*
4	Campo 7 S	39.1	4	Alamosa Bergman Field	23.9
4	La Junta 4 NNE	*39.1*	5	Cabin Creek	24.3
6	Canon City	*38.3*	6	Cimarron	24.6
7	Boulder	37.7	7	Bailey	24.9
8	Trinidad	37.6	8	Center 4 SSW	25.1
8	Uravan	37.6	9	Cheesman	26.6
10	Burlington 4 S	*37.5*	10	Aspen 1 SW	27.8
11	Denver Stapleton Int'l Arpt	37.2	11	Evergreen	27.9
11	Holly	37.2	12	Fort Lewis	29.2
13	Bonny Dam 2 NE	*36.9*	13	Hayden	29.4
14	Eads	*36.7*	14	Altenbern	31.0
15	Northglenn	*36.6*	15	Briggsdale	32.7
16	Fort Collins	36.4	16	Glenwood Spgs #2	33.1
16	Greeley Unc	36.4	16	Longmont 2 ESE	*33.1*
18	Holyoke	36.3	18	Byers 5 ENE	34.1
19	Leroy 5 WSW	35.8	19	Dinosaur Natl Monumnt	34.2
20	Colorado Springs Municipal Arpt	35.7	20	Flagler 5 NNE	*34.5*
20	Kassler	35.7	21	Akron 4 E	34.9
22	Karval	*35.6*	22	Fruita 1 W	*35.1*
22	Pueblo Memorial Arpt	35.6	23	Karval	*35.6*
24	Fruita 1 W	*35.1*	23	Pueblo Memorial Arpt	35.6
25	Akron 4 E	34.9	25	Colorado Springs Municipal Arpt	35.7

Rankings include 25 highest/lowest stations. If state has less than 25 stations, all stations are included. The period of record is 1980–2009. See User Guide for detailed explanation of data.

Annual Extreme Minimum Temperature

Highest

Rank	Station Name	°F
1	Uravan	-15
2	Grand Junction Walker Field	-18
3	Trinidad	-20
4	Grand Junction 6 ESE	-21
4	La Junta 4 NNE	***-21***
6	Burlington 4 S	-23
7	Boulder	-24
7	Colorado Springs Municipal Arpt	-24
7	Glenwood Spgs #2	-24
10	Aspen 1 SW	-25
10	Canon City	***-25***
10	Denver Stapleton Int'l Arpt	-25
10	Fort Lewis	-25
10	Greeley Unc	-25
10	Leroy 5 WSW	-25
10	Walsh 1 W	-25
17	Cabin Creek	-26
17	Campo 7 S	-26
17	Pueblo Memorial Arpt	-26
20	Eads	***-27***
21	Altenbern	-28
21	Fort Collins	-28
21	Holly	-28
24	Dinosaur Natl Monumnt	-29
24	Evergreen	-29

Lowest

Rank	Station Name	°F
1	Antero Reservoir	-51
2	Hayden	-44
3	Alamosa Bergman Field	-40
3	Hohnholz Ranch	***-40***
5	Briggsdale	-38
6	Cochetopa Creek	-36
6	Fruita 1 W	-36
8	Cimarron	-35
9	Center 4 SSW	-34
10	Byers 5 ENE	-33
10	Holyoke	-33
12	Akron 4 E	-32
12	Bailey	-32
14	Cheesman	-31
14	Kassler	-31
14	Longmont 2 ESE	***-31***
17	Bonny Dam 2 NE	-30
17	Northglenn	***-30***
19	Dinosaur Natl Monumnt	-29
19	Evergreen	-29
19	Flagler 5 NNE	-29
19	Karval	-29
23	Altenbern	-28
23	Fort Collins	-28
23	Holly	-28

July Mean Maximum Temperature

Highest

Rank	Station Name	°F
1	Uravan	95.8
2	La Junta 4 NNE	94.8
3	Holly	94.1
4	Grand Junction Walker Field	93.7
5	Fruita 1 W	93.6
6	Pueblo Memorial Arpt	93.4
7	Grand Junction 6 ESE	93.2
8	Walsh 1 W	92.4
9	Campo 7 S	92.3
10	Eads	91.8
11	Dinosaur Natl Monumnt	91.2
12	Bonny Dam 2 NE	***90.6***
13	Burlington 4 S	90.4
13	Byers 5 ENE	90.4
13	Greeley Unc	90.4
16	Briggsdale	89.6
16	Northglenn	***89.6***
18	Longmont 2 ESE	***89.5***
19	Akron 4 E	89.3
19	Altenbern	89.3
19	Canon City	89.3
22	Leroy 5 WSW	89.2
23	Glenwood Spgs #2	89.0
24	Karval	88.8
25	Denver Stapleton Int'l Arpt	88.7

Lowest

Rank	Station Name	°F
1	Cabin Creek	69.3
2	Antero Reservoir	76.5
3	Aspen 1 SW	78.2
4	Bailey	78.5
5	Hohnholz Ranch	***79.7***
6	Center 4 SSW	80.1
7	Cochetopa Creek	81.6
7	Evergreen	81.6
9	Fort Lewis	81.9
10	Alamosa Bergman Field	82.8
11	Cheesman	83.9
12	Cimarron	84.7
13	Colorado Springs Municipal Arpt	85.2
14	Hayden	85.6
15	Fort Collins	86.6
16	Boulder	87.6
16	Trinidad	87.6
18	Holyoke	87.8
19	Kassler	87.9
20	Flagler 5 NNE	88.4
21	Denver Stapleton Int'l Arpt	88.7
22	Karval	88.8
23	Glenwood Spgs #2	89.0
24	Leroy 5 WSW	89.2
25	Akron 4 E	89.3

Rankings include 25 highest/lowest stations. If state has less than 25 stations, all stations are included. The period of record is 1980–2009. See User Guide for detailed explanation of data.

January Mean Minimum Temperature

Highest Rank	Highest Station Name	°F	Lowest Rank	Lowest Station Name	°F
1	Boulder	21.4	1	Antero Reservoir	-4.2
2	Canon City	20.7	2	Cochetopa Creek	-3.4
3	Trinidad	20.1	3	Alamosa Bergman Field	-1.5
4	Northglenn	***19.2***	4	Center 4 SSW	-0.3
5	Campo 7 S	19.1	5	Cimarron	2.3
6	Grand Junction 6 ESE	18.8	6	Hohnholz Ranch	***7.6***
7	Denver Stapleton Int'l Arpt	18.4	7	Bailey	8.3
7	Walsh 1 W	18.4	7	Cheesman	8.3
9	Grand Junction Walker Field	18.3	9	Hayden	8.5
10	Burlington 4 S	17.7	10	Aspen 1 SW	8.9
10	Colorado Springs Municipal Arpt	17.7	11	Cabin Creek	9.4
12	Fort Collins	17.3	12	Evergreen	10.9
12	La Junta 4 NNE	17.3	12	Fort Lewis	10.9
14	Kassler	16.7	14	Altenbern	11.8
15	Greeley Unc	16.5	14	Dinosaur Natl Monumnt	11.8
16	Uravan	16.4	16	Briggsdale	12.6
17	Bonny Dam 2 NE	***16.1***	17	Longmont 2 ESE	***12.9***
18	Karval	15.9	18	Byers 5 ENE	13.7
19	Leroy 5 WSW	15.6	19	Fruita 1 W	13.8
20	Holyoke	15.4	20	Glenwood Spgs #2	14.1
21	Akron 4 E	14.7	21	Holly	14.4
22	Eads	14.6	21	Pueblo Memorial Arpt	14.4
22	Flagler 5 NNE	14.6	23	Eads	14.6
24	Holly	14.4	23	Flagler 5 NNE	14.6
24	Pueblo Memorial Arpt	14.4	25	Akron 4 E	14.7

Number of Days Annually Maximum Temperature ≥ 90°F

Highest Rank	Highest Station Name	Days	Lowest Rank	Lowest Station Name	Days
1	La Junta 4 NNE	***77***	1	Antero Reservoir	0
1	Uravan	77	1	Aspen 1 SW	0
3	Holly	72	1	Cabin Creek	0
4	Campo 7 S	67	4	Bailey	1
5	Pueblo Memorial Arpt	66	4	Center 4 SSW	1
6	Grand Junction Walker Field	65	4	Fort Lewis	1
6	Walsh 1 W	65	4	Hohnholz Ranch	***1***
8	Grand Junction 6 ESE	62	8	Cochetopa Creek	2
9	Fruita 1 W	61	9	Alamosa Bergman Field	3
10	Eads	***59***	10	Evergreen	5
11	Greeley Unc	49	11	Cimarron	8
12	Bonny Dam 2 NE	47	12	Cheesman	9
12	Burlington 4 S	47	13	Hayden	13
14	Byers 5 ENE	46	14	Colorado Springs Municipal Arpt	18
14	Longmont 2 ESE	***46***	15	Fort Collins	23
16	Akron 4 E	45	16	Trinidad	27
17	Dinosaur Natl Monumnt	44	17	Boulder	32
18	Northglenn	***43***	18	Altenbern	33
19	Briggsdale	41	18	Kassler	33
20	Leroy 5 WSW	40	20	Glenwood Spgs #2	35
21	Canon City	***39***	21	Flagler 5 NNE	36
22	Denver Stapleton Int'l Arpt	38	22	Holyoke	37
23	Holyoke	37	22	Karval	37
23	Karval	37	24	Denver Stapleton Int'l Arpt	38
25	Flagler 5 NNE	36	25	Canon City	***39***

Number of Days Annually Maximum Temperature ≤ 32°F					
Highest			Lowest		
Rank	Station Name	Days	Rank	Station Name	Days
1	Cabin Creek	66	1	Uravan	5
2	Hayden	51	2	Trinidad	11
3	Antero Reservoir	49	3	Campo 7 S	13
3	Cochetopa Creek	49	3	Canon City	*13*
5	Hohnholz Ranch	*47*	3	Fruita 1 W	13
6	Center 4 SSW	39	3	Grand Junction 6 ESE	13
7	Aspen 1 SW	38	7	Boulder	14
8	Alamosa Bergman Field	34	8	Grand Junction Walker Field	16
8	Bailey	34	8	Pueblo Memorial Arpt	16
8	Cimarron	34	10	Altenbern	17
8	Dinosaur Natl Monumnt	34	10	Fort Collins	17
12	Akron 4 E	32	10	Holly	17
12	Leroy 5 WSW	32	10	Kassler	17
14	Holyoke	26	14	Cheesman	18
15	Burlington 4 S	24	14	Northglenn	*18*
15	Colorado Springs Municipal Arpt	24	16	La Junta 4 NNE	*19*
15	Karval	24	17	Denver Stapleton Int'l Arpt	20
18	Bonny Dam 2 NE	23	17	Evergreen	20
19	Briggsdale	22	17	Glenwood Spgs #2	20
19	Byers 5 ENE	22	17	Longmont 2 ESE	*20*
19	Eads	*22*	17	Walsh 1 W	20
19	Flagler 5 NNE	22	22	Greeley Unc	21
19	Fort Lewis	22	23	Briggsdale	22
24	Greeley Unc	21	23	Byers 5 ENE	22
25	Denver Stapleton Int'l Arpt	20	23	Eads	*22*

Number of Days Annually Minimum Temperature ≤ 32°F					
Highest			Lowest		
Rank	Station Name	Days	Rank	Station Name	Days
1	Antero Reservoir	265	1	Grand Junction 6 ESE	128
2	Hohnholz Ranch	*256*	2	Grand Junction Walker Field	132
3	Cochetopa Creek	250	3	Boulder	139
4	Cabin Creek	242	4	Canon City	*140*
5	Bailey	239	5	La Junta 4 NNE	*144*
6	Cimarron	233	6	Campo 7 S	*145*
7	Alamosa Bergman Field	228	6	Walsh 1 W	145
8	Cheesman	224	8	Trinidad	149
9	Evergreen	219	8	Uravan	149
10	Center 4 SSW	215	10	Bonny Dam 2 NE	151
11	Aspen 1 SW	211	11	Burlington 4 S	152
12	Fort Lewis	204	11	Northglenn	*152*
13	Hayden	198	13	Denver Stapleton Int'l Arpt	153
14	Altenbern	193	14	Fort Collins	156
15	Briggsdale	179	15	Greeley Unc	158
15	Longmont 2 ESE	*179*	16	Eads	*159*
17	Byers 5 ENE	175	16	Flagler 5 NNE	159
18	Glenwood Spgs #2	170	18	Holly	160
19	Akron 4 E	169	18	Kassler	160
20	Dinosaur Natl Monumnt	167	20	Fruita 1 W	161
21	Pueblo Memorial Arpt	165	21	Karval	162
22	Holyoke	164	22	Colorado Springs Municipal Arpt	163
23	Colorado Springs Municipal Arpt	163	22	Leroy 5 WSW	163
23	Leroy 5 WSW	163	24	Holyoke	164
25	Karval	162	25	Pueblo Memorial Arpt	165

Rankings include 25 highest/lowest stations. If state has less than 25 stations, all stations are included. The period of record is 1980–2009. See User Guide for detailed explanation of data.

Number of Days Annually Minimum Temperature ≤ 0°F

Highest			Lowest		
Rank	Station Name	Days	Rank	Station Name	Days
1	Antero Reservoir	65	1	Grand Junction 6 ESE	1
2	Cochetopa Creek	56	2	Campo 7 S	3
3	Alamosa Bergman Field	46	2	Grand Junction Walker Field	3
4	Center 4 SSW	39	2	Trinidad	3
4	Cimarron	39	2	Uravan	3
6	Hohnholz Ranch	***32***	6	Boulder	4
7	Cheesman	24	6	Canon City	***4***
8	Bailey	23	6	Walsh 1 W	4
9	Cabin Creek	21	9	Fort Collins	5
10	Hayden	20	9	Northglenn	***5***
11	Aspen 1 SW	17	11	Bonny Dam 2 NE	6
12	Evergreen	15	11	Burlington 4 S	6
13	Briggsdale	14	11	Colorado Springs Municipal Arpt	6
14	Fort Lewis	12	11	Denver Stapleton Int'l Arpt	6
14	Longmont 2 ESE	***12***	11	Eads	***6***
16	Byers 5 ENE	11	11	Fruita 1 W	6
17	Altenbern	10	11	Glenwood Spgs #2	6
17	Leroy 5 WSW	10	11	Holly	6
19	Dinosaur Natl Monumnt	9	11	Karval	6
20	Akron 4 E	8	11	La Junta 4 NNE	***6***
20	Holyoke	8	21	Flagler 5 NNE	7
20	Kassler	8	21	Greeley Unc	7
20	Pueblo Memorial Arpt	8	23	Akron 4 E	8
24	Flagler 5 NNE	7	23	Holyoke	8
24	Greeley Unc	7	23	Kassler	8

Number of Annual Heating Degree Days

Highest			Lowest		
Rank	Station Name	Num.	Rank	Station Name	Num.
1	Antero Reservoir	10,471	1	Campo 7 S	4,906
2	Cabin Creek	10,330	2	Trinidad	5,073
3	Hohnholz Ranch	***9,424***	3	La Junta 4 NNE	***5,127***
4	Cochetopa Creek	9,373	4	Canon City	***5,142***
5	Bailey	8,776	5	Walsh 1 W	5,170
6	Aspen 1 SW	8,461	6	Grand Junction 6 ESE	5,215
7	Center 4 SSW	8,455	7	Uravan	5,224
8	Alamosa Bergman Field	8,440	8	Grand Junction Walker Field	5,366
9	Cimarron	8,317	9	Holly	5,401
10	Hayden	7,810	10	Pueblo Memorial Arpt	5,482
11	Fort Lewis	7,649	11	Boulder	5,490
12	Cheesman	7,583	12	Northglenn	***5,650***
13	Evergreen	7,525	13	Eads	***5,669***
14	Dinosaur Natl Monumnt	6,747	14	Burlington 4 S	***5,765***
15	Altenbern	6,737	15	Denver Stapleton Int'l Arpt	5,791
16	Briggsdale	6,478	16	Greeley Unc	5,805
16	Glenwood Spgs #2	***6,478***	17	Fruita 1 W	***5,826***
18	Akron 4 E	6,410	18	Kassler	5,908
19	Leroy 5 WSW	6,326	19	Bonny Dam 2 NE	***5,909***
20	Longmont 2 ESE	***6,285***	20	Fort Collins	5,936
21	Flagler 5 NNE	***6,259***	21	Holyoke	6,139
22	Byers 5 ENE	6,249	22	Colorado Springs Municipal Arpt	6,203
23	Colorado Springs Municipal Arpt	6,203	23	Byers 5 ENE	6,249
24	Holyoke	6,139	24	Flagler 5 NNE	***6,259***
25	Fort Collins	5,936	25	Longmont 2 ESE	***6,285***

Rankings include 25 highest/lowest stations. If state has less than 25 stations, all stations are included. The period of record is 1980–2009. See User Guide for detailed explanation of data.

Number of Annual Cooling Degree Days

Highest			Lowest		
Rank	Station Name	Num.	Rank	Station Name	Num.
1	La Junta 4 NNE	***1,327***	1	Cabin Creek	0
2	Grand Junction 6 ESE	1,245	2	Antero Reservoir	1
3	Grand Junction Walker Field	1,229	3	Hohnholz Ranch	***13***
4	Holly	1,221	4	Bailey	17
5	Walsh 1 W	1,171	5	Cochetopa Creek	30
6	Campo 7 S	1,170	6	Center 4 SSW	31
7	Uravan	1,114	7	Aspen 1 SW	38
8	Eads	***1,015***	8	Alamosa Bergman Field	63
9	Pueblo Memorial Arpt	963	9	Cimarron	67
10	Burlington 4 S	***944***	10	Evergreen	91
11	Bonny Dam 2 NE	***942***	11	Fort Lewis	107
12	Fruita 1 W	***859***	12	Cheesman	128
13	Canon City	***810***	13	Hayden	220
14	Greeley Unc	807	14	Altenbern	338
15	Holyoke	802	15	Glenwood Spgs #2	***440***
16	Leroy 5 WSW	770	16	Colorado Springs Municipal Arpt	485
17	Denver Stapleton Int'l Arpt	766	17	Fort Collins	568
18	Akron 4 E	739	18	Briggsdale	609
19	Northglenn	***734***	19	Longmont 2 ESE	***614***
20	Byers 5 ENE	711	20	Boulder	630
21	Dinosaur Natl Monumnt	701	21	Flagler 5 NNE	***657***
21	Kassler	701	22	Trinidad	670
23	Trinidad	670	23	Dinosaur Natl Monumnt	701
24	Flagler 5 NNE	***657***	23	Kassler	701
25	Boulder	630	25	Byers 5 ENE	711

Annual Precipitation

Highest			Lowest		
Rank	Station Name	Inches	Rank	Station Name	Inches
1	Aspen 1 SW	24.38	1	Center 4 SSW	7.06
2	Cabin Creek	20.62	2	Alamosa Bergman Field	7.27
3	Boulder	20.27	3	Grand Junction 6 ESE	9.26
4	Evergreen	19.28	4	Grand Junction Walker Field	9.43
5	Walsh 1 W	19.22	5	Fruita 1 W	9.62
6	Holyoke	18.62	6	Antero Reservoir	10.81
7	Bonny Dam 2 NE	18.57	7	La Junta 4 NNE	***11.21***
8	Fort Lewis	18.45	8	Cochetopa Creek	11.48
9	Hayden	18.36	9	Dinosaur Natl Monumnt	11.49
10	Kassler	18.01	10	Pueblo Memorial Arpt	12.62
11	Bailey	17.75	11	Uravan	12.88
11	Holly	17.75	12	Briggsdale	13.23
13	Altenbern	17.71	13	Canon City	***13.68***
14	Leroy 5 WSW	17.23	14	Cimarron	14.03
15	Burlington 4 S	17.19	15	Longmont 2 ESE	***14.10***
16	Glenwood Spgs #2	17.16	16	Northglenn	***14.26***
17	Campo 7 S	16.92	17	Greeley Unc	14.42
17	Cheesman	16.92	18	Karval	14.45
19	Colorado Springs Municipal Arpt	16.85	19	Hohnholz Ranch	***14.68***
20	Flagler 5 NNE	16.74	20	Byers 5 ENE	15.60
21	Akron 4 E	16.63	20	Denver Stapleton Int'l Arpt	15.60
22	Trinidad	16.26	22	Eads	***15.96***
23	Fort Collins	16.13	23	Fort Collins	16.13
24	Eads	***15.96***	24	Trinidad	16.26
25	Byers 5 ENE	15.60	25	Akron 4 E	16.63

Rankings include 25 highest/lowest stations. If state has less than 25 stations, all stations are included. The period of record is 1980–2009. See User Guide for detailed explanation of data.

Annual Extreme Maximum Daily Precipitation

Rank	Station Name (Highest)	Inches	Rank	Station Name (Lowest)	Inches
1	Leroy 5 WSW	5.03	1	Grand Junction 6 ESE	1.20
2	Fort Collins	4.63	2	Grand Junction Walker Field	1.31
3	Bonny Dam 2 NE	***4.60***	3	Cochetopa Creek	1.36
4	Karval	4.30	4	Alamosa Bergman Field	1.49
4	Walsh 1 W	4.30	5	Fruita 1 W	***1.57***
6	Colorado Springs Municipal Arpt	4.29	6	Dinosaur Natl Monumnt	1.61
7	Trinidad	4.20	7	Cimarron	1.75
8	Denver Stapleton Int'l Arpt	3.83	8	Hayden	1.84
9	Akron 4 E	3.75	9	Uravan	1.85
10	Boulder	3.56	10	Altenbern	1.87
11	Holly	3.55	11	Hohnholz Ranch	***2.05***
12	Burlington 4 S	3.51	12	Glenwood Spgs #2	***2.09***
12	Holyoke	3.51	13	Bailey	2.12
14	Campo 7 S	3.50	14	Cheesman	2.17
15	Greeley Unc	3.48	15	Antero Reservoir	2.18
16	Flagler 5 NNE	3.30	15	Center 4 SSW	2.18
17	Byers 5 ENE	3.26	17	La Junta 4 NNE	***2.21***
18	Canon City	***3.21***	18	Longmont 2 ESE	***2.29***
19	Eads	***3.18***	19	Fort Lewis	***2.30***
20	Cabin Creek	3.00	20	Aspen 1 SW	2.35
21	Evergreen	2.73	21	Northglenn	***2.45***
22	Pueblo Memorial Arpt	2.67	22	Kassler	2.49
23	Briggsdale	2.63	23	Briggsdale	2.63
24	Kassler	2.49	24	Pueblo Memorial Arpt	2.67
25	Northglenn	***2.45***	25	Evergreen	2.73

Number of Days Annually With ≥ 0.1 Inches of Precipitation

Rank	Station Name (Highest)	Days	Rank	Station Name (Lowest)	Days
1	Aspen 1 SW	77	1	Center 4 SSW	23
2	Cabin Creek	60	2	Alamosa Bergman Field	24
3	Hayden	59	3	Fruita 1 W	27
4	Altenbern	53	4	La Junta 4 NNE	***28***
5	Bailey	51	5	Grand Junction 6 ESE	31
6	Evergreen	49	5	Grand Junction Walker Field	31
7	Boulder	48	7	Antero Reservoir	32
7	Cheesman	48	7	Pueblo Memorial Arpt	32
9	Glenwood Spgs #2	47	9	Briggsdale	33
9	Hohnholz Ranch	***47***	9	Eads	***33***
11	Kassler	46	11	Campo 7 S	34
12	Fort Lewis	45	11	Flagler 5 NNE	34
13	Cimarron	43	11	Karval	34
13	Leroy 5 WSW	43	14	Burlington 4 S	35
15	Byers 5 ENE	41	14	Canon City	***35***
15	Denver Stapleton Int'l Arpt	41	14	Fort Collins	35
15	Holyoke	41	17	Dinosaur Natl Monumnt	36
18	Cochetopa Creek	40	17	Greeley Unc	36
18	Trinidad	40	17	Holly	36
18	Walsh 1 W	40	17	Northglenn	***36***
21	Akron 4 E	39	21	Bonny Dam 2 NE	37
21	Colorado Springs Municipal Arpt	39	22	Longmont 2 ESE	***38***
21	Uravan	39	23	Akron 4 E	39
24	Longmont 2 ESE	***38***	23	Colorado Springs Municipal Arpt	39
25	Bonny Dam 2 NE	37	23	Uravan	39

Rankings include 25 highest/lowest stations. If state has less than 25 stations, all stations are included. The period of record is 1980–2009. See User Guide for detailed explanation of data.

Number of Days Annually With ≥ 0.5 Inches of Precipitation

Highest			Lowest		
Rank	Station Name	Days	Rank	Station Name	Days
1	Holyoke	12	1	Center 4 SSW	0
2	Boulder	11	1	Grand Junction 6 ESE	0
2	Burlington 4 S	11	3	Alamosa Bergman Field	1
2	Flagler 5 NNE	11	3	Fruita 1 W	1
2	Holly	11	3	Grand Junction Walker Field	1
2	Trinidad	11	6	Cochetopa Creek	3
2	Walsh 1 W	11	6	Uravan	3
8	Akron 4 E	10	8	Antero Reservoir	4
8	Aspen 1 SW	10	8	Dinosaur Natl Monumnt	4
8	Bonny Dam 2 NE	10	10	Canon City	*5*
8	Cabin Creek	10	10	Cimarron	5
8	Campo 7 S	10	10	Hohnholz Ranch	*5*
8	Eads	*10*	10	La Junta 4 NNE	*5*
8	Fort Lewis	10	10	Pueblo Memorial Arpt	5
8	Kassler	10	15	Briggsdale	6
8	Leroy 5 WSW	10	15	Denver Stapleton Int'l Arpt	6
17	Bailey	9	15	Glenwood Spgs #2	6
17	Cheesman	9	15	Northglenn	*6*
17	Karval	9	19	Colorado Springs Municipal Arpt	7
20	Altenbern	8	19	Greeley Unc	7
20	Byers 5 ENE	8	19	Hayden	7
20	Evergreen	8	19	Longmont 2 ESE	*7*
20	Fort Collins	8	23	Altenbern	8
24	Colorado Springs Municipal Arpt	7	23	Byers 5 ENE	8
24	Greeley Unc	7	23	Evergreen	8

Number of Days Annually With ≥ 1.0 Inches of Precipitation

Highest			Lowest		
Rank	Station Name	Days	Rank	Station Name	Days
1	Bonny Dam 2 NE	4	1	Alamosa Bergman Field	0
1	Flagler 5 NNE	4	1	Altenbern	0
1	Holly	4	1	Antero Reservoir	0
1	Holyoke	4	1	Aspen 1 SW	0
5	Burlington 4 S	3	1	Boulder	0
5	Campo 7 S	3	1	Byers 5 ENE	0
5	Walsh 1 W	3	1	Cabin Creek	0
8	Colorado Springs Municipal Arpt	2	1	Canon City	*0*
8	Eads	*2*	1	Center 4 SSW	0
8	Karval	2	1	Cheesman	0
8	Leroy 5 WSW	2	1	Cimarron	0
12	Akron 4 E	1	1	Cochetopa Creek	0
12	Bailey	1	1	Dinosaur Natl Monumnt	0
12	Briggsdale	1	1	Evergreen	0
12	Denver Stapleton Int'l Arpt	1	1	Fruita 1 W	0
12	Fort Lewis	1	1	Fort Collins	0
12	Longmont 2 ESE	*1*	1	Glenwood Spgs #2	0
12	Northglenn	*1*	1	Grand Junction 6 ESE	0
12	Pueblo Memorial Arpt	1	1	Grand Junction Walker Field	0
20	Alamosa Bergman Field	0	1	Greeley Unc	0
20	Altenbern	0	1	Hayden	0
20	Antero Reservoir	0	1	Hohnholz Ranch	*0*
20	Aspen 1 SW	0	1	Kassler	0
20	Boulder	0	1	La Junta 4 NNE	*0*
20	Byers 5 ENE	0	1	Trinidad	0

Rankings include 25 highest/lowest stations. If state has less than 25 stations, all stations are included. The period of record is 1980–2009. See User Guide for detailed explanation of data.

Annual Snowfall

Highest			Lowest		
Rank	Station Name	Inches	Rank	Station Name	Inches
1	Aspen 1 SW	176.9	1	Grand Junction 6 ESE	12.7
2	Cabin Creek	132.1	2	Briggsdale	13.7
3	Hayden	114.8	3	Eads	***14.1***
4	Hohnholz Ranch	***106.6***	4	Grand Junction Walker Field	19.1
5	Boulder	87.7	5	Walsh 1 W	22.7
6	Bailey	86.1	6	Campo 7 S	22.9
7	Fort Lewis	85.8	7	Bonny Dam 2 NE	23.2
8	Evergreen	82.6	8	Holly	23.6
9	Kassler	69.8	9	Karval	24.9
10	Cimarron	68.7	10	Center 4 SSW	26.1
11	Cheesman	62.1	11	Alamosa Bergman Field	27.4
12	Altenbern	58.2	12	Longmont 2 ESE	***28.6***
13	Fort Collins	55.5	13	Akron 4 E	***30.4***
14	Denver Stapleton Int'l Arpt	55.0	14	Holyoke	***30.5***
15	Cochetopa Creek	51.7	15	Flagler 5 NNE	30.9
16	Trinidad	49.6	16	Pueblo Memorial Arpt	31.7
17	Glenwood Spgs #2	***47.8***	17	Burlington 4 S	31.8
18	Antero Reservoir	46.4	18	Dinosaur Natl Monumnt	34.3
19	Byers 5 ENE	44.2	19	Colorado Springs Municipal Arpt	38.8
20	Leroy 5 WSW	42.7	20	Greeley Unc	40.7
20	Northglenn	***42.7***	21	Canon City	***42.0***
22	Canon City	***42.0***	22	Leroy 5 WSW	42.7
23	Greeley Unc	40.7	22	Northglenn	***42.7***
24	Colorado Springs Municipal Arpt	38.8	24	Byers 5 ENE	44.2
25	Dinosaur Natl Monumnt	34.3	25	Antero Reservoir	46.4

Annual Maximum Snow Depth

Highest			Lowest		
Rank	Station Name	Inches	Rank	Station Name	Inches
1	Aspen 1 SW	***60***	1	Grand Junction Walker Field	11
2	Fort Lewis	49	1	Pueblo Memorial Arpt	11
3	Bailey	45	3	Alamosa Bergman Field	12
4	Hayden	40	4	Grand Junction 6 ESE	***14***
5	Kassler	38	5	Bonny Dam 2 NE	16
6	Altenbern	37	5	Campo 7 S	***16***
7	Cochetopa Creek	32	7	Holyoke	***17***
8	Trinidad	31	8	Karval	18
9	Cheesman	28	9	Byers 5 ENE	19
9	Walsh 1 W	28	9	Canon City	***19***
11	Hohnholz Ranch	***26***	9	Flagler 5 NNE	19
12	Antero Reservoir	25	12	Colorado Springs Municipal Arpt	20
12	Boulder	***25***	12	Greeley Unc	20
14	Burlington 4 S	***24***	14	Holly	22
14	Denver Stapleton Int'l Arpt	24	15	Dinosaur Natl Monumnt	23
14	Leroy 5 WSW	24	15	Fort Collins	23
17	Dinosaur Natl Monumnt	23	17	Burlington 4 S	***24***
17	Fort Collins	23	17	Denver Stapleton Int'l Arpt	24
19	Holly	22	17	Leroy 5 WSW	24
20	Colorado Springs Municipal Arpt	20	20	Antero Reservoir	25
20	Greeley Unc	20	20	Boulder	***25***
22	Byers 5 ENE	19	22	Hohnholz Ranch	***26***
22	Canon City	***19***	23	Cheesman	28
22	Flagler 5 NNE	19	23	Walsh 1 W	28
25	Karval	18	25	Trinidad	31

Rankings include 25 highest/lowest stations. If state has less than 25 stations, all stations are included. The period of record is 1980–2009. See User Guide for detailed explanation of data.

Number of Days Annually With ≥ 1.0 Inch Snow Depth					
Highest			Lowest		
Rank	Station Name	Days	Rank	Station Name	Days
1	Aspen 1 SW	165	1	Briggsdale	***6***
2	Bailey	154	2	Campo 7 S	***9***
3	Hohnholz Ranch	***129***	3	Grand Junction 6 ESE	***14***
4	Hayden	120	4	Pueblo Memorial Arpt	19
5	Fort Lewis	101	5	Burlington 4 S	***21***
6	Cabin Creek	***92***	5	Flagler 5 NNE	21
7	Antero Reservoir	82	5	Holly	21
8	Cochetopa Creek	66	8	Walsh 1 W	23
9	Dinosaur Natl Monumnt	59	9	Grand Junction Walker Field	24
10	Altenbern	58	9	Trinidad	24
11	Boulder	***56***	11	Colorado Springs Municipal Arpt	26
12	Byers 5 ENE	55	12	Holyoke	28
13	Cheesman	54	13	Canon City	***30***
14	Kassler	51	14	Bonny Dam 2 NE	31
15	Leroy 5 WSW	49	15	Karval	33
16	Akron 4 E	***48***	16	Northglenn	***38***
17	Denver Stapleton Int'l Arpt	47	17	Alamosa Bergman Field	44
18	Fort Collins	46	18	Glenwood Spgs #2	***45***
19	Glenwood Spgs #2	***45***	18	Greeley Unc	45
19	Greeley Unc	45	20	Fort Collins	46
21	Alamosa Bergman Field	44	21	Denver Stapleton Int'l Arpt	47
22	Northglenn	***38***	22	Akron 4 E	***48***
23	Karval	33	23	Leroy 5 WSW	49
24	Bonny Dam 2 NE	31	24	Kassler	51
25	Canon City	***30***	25	Cheesman	54

Rankings include 25 highest/lowest stations. If state has less than 25 stations, all stations are included. The period of record is 1980–2009. See User Guide for detailed explanation of data.

Significant Storm Events in Colorado: 2000 – 2009

Location or County	Date	Type	Mag.	Deaths	Injuries	Property Damage ($mil.)	Crop Damage ($mil.)
Jefferson	06/12/00	Wild/Forest Fire	na	0	0	12.0	0.0
Southeast Colorado	04/11/01	High Wind	79 mph	0	0	6.1	0.0
El Paso	05/28/01	Tornado	F2	0	4	8.0	0.0
Bent	06/07/01	Hail	3.00 in.	0	0	6.0	3.0
Adams	06/20/01	Hail	2.50 in.	0	5	49.0	0.0
Denver	06/20/01	Hail	2.00 in.	0	0	10.0	0.0
Teller	06/09/02	Wild/Forest Fire	na	0	2	6.0	0.0
El Paso	06/14/02	Hail	1.00 in.	0	0	24.0	0.0
Rio Grande	06/19/02	Wild/Forest Fire	na	0	0	11.0	0.0
Rio Grande	07/01/02	Wild/Forest Fire	na	0	0	11.0	0.0
La Plata	07/01/02	Wild/Forest Fire	na	0	0	8.0	0.0
Teller	07/01/02	Wild/Forest Fire	na	0	2	6.0	0.0
North Central Colorado	03/17/03	Blizzard	na	0	2	62.0	0.0
North Central Colorado	03/17/03	Winter Storm	na	0	0	31.0	0.0
Denver	06/09/04	Hail	0.75 in.	0	0	146.5	0.0
Douglas	07/07/06	Flash Flood	na	0	0	13.3	0.0
Weld	05/22/08	Tornado	F3	1	78	147.0	0.0
Arapahoe	06/07/09	Hail	3.00 in.	0	0	161.0	0.0
Jefferson	07/20/09	Hail	1.25 in.	0	0	350.0	0.0
Pueblo	07/29/09	Hail	1.75 in.	0	7	90.0	20.0

Note: Deaths, injuries, and damages are date and location specific.

CONNECTICUT

PHYSICAL FEATURES. Connecticut occupies the southwestern portion of the region known as New England. The State extends for 90 miles in an east-west direction and 75 miles from north to south. The total area of 5,009 square miles makes Connecticut the third smallest state in the Nation.

The topography of Connecticut is predominantly hilly. The highest terrain is found in the northwest portion of the State, with elevations of 1,000 to 2,000 feet. The southwestern quarter and most of the eastern half have elevations of 300 to 1,000 feet. The State of Connecticut is bisected by the Connecticut River which rises in Canada. Smaller river basins in the State with their headwaters in the southern half of Massachusetts include the Housatonic in the west and the Shetucket, Quinebaug, and Thames in the east. The narrow river valleys and steep hillsides in much of the western highlands make for destructive flash floods during periods of unusually heavy or intense rainfall.

The entire southern border of Connecticut is washed by the waters of Long Island Sound. The coastline of approximately 100 miles is indented by small coves and the mouths of numerous rivers and streams. Beaches are found along the greater length.

GENERAL CLIMATE. The chief characteristics of Connecticut's climate are: (1) equable distribution of precipitation among the four seasons, (2) large ranges of temperature both daily and annually, (3) great differences in the same season or month of different years, and (4) considerable diversity of the weather over short periods of time.

Connecticut lies in the "prevailing westerlies," the belt of generally eastward air movement which encircles the globe in middle latitudes. Embedded in this circulation are extensive masses of air originating in higher and lower latitudes and interacting to produce low-pressure storm systems. A large number of storm centers and air-mass fronts pass near or over Connecticut during a year. Three types of air affect this State: (1) cold, dry air pouring down from subarctic North America, (2) warm, moist air streaming up on a long overland journey from the Gulf of Mexico and subtropical waters of the Atlantic, and (3) cool, damp air moving in from the North Atlantic. Because the flow of air is usually from continental areas, Connecticut is more influenced by the first two types than it is by the third. The procession of contrasting air masses and the relatively frequent passage of storms bring about a roughly twice weekly alternation from fair to cloudy or storm conditions, usually attended by abrupt changes in temperature, moisture, sunshine, and wind direction and speed. There is no regular or persistent rhythm to this sequence; it is sometimes interrupted by periods during which the weather pattern continues much the same for several days, and infrequently for a few weeks.

TEMPERATURE. Despite the small size of Connecticut, there is a difference of about 6°F. in mean annual temperature from north to south. The greater contrast of temperature over the State occurs during the winter season. The number of days with minimum temperatures of zero or below average about 10 per year at the higher elevations, about five in the lower uplands and central valley, and two or less along the shore of Long Island Sound. Summer temperatures are comparatively uniform over the State. The central valley experiences the greatest number of hot days. Temperatures of 90°F. or higher occur on an average on about 10 days per year. At the higher elevations and near the coast, the average number is approximately three days per year. In much of the western and eastern highlands, the occurrence of 90°F. temperatures is a little less frequent than in the central valley.

During the warmest month of the summer the average minimum temperature ranges from about 56°F. in the cool northwestern corner of the State to about 63°F. in the warmer coastal sections. Over most of the State the average July minimum temperature is within a degree or two of 60°F.

The period free from temperatures of 32°F. or lower has an average length of 155 to 170 days over the greater portion of Connecticut. In the northwest as well as in local areas of the western and eastern highlands, the freeze-free season lasts about 125 to 135 days. Along the immediate coast approximately 190 days will elapse between the last spring and first fall freeze.

PRECIPITATION. Precipitation tends to become evenly distributed throughout the year in all parts of Connecticut. Low-pressure centers and their accompanying air mass fronts are the principal year-round producers of precipitation. Storms moving up the Atlantic coast generally yield the heaviest amounts of rain and snow. In the summer bands and patches of thunderstorms and convective showers add considerable precipitation and make up the difference resulting from decreased activity of low-pressure storm centers. Thunderstorms are of brief duration and often scattered in comparison with the general storms, but they yield the heaviest local rainfall.

Variations in precipitation from month to month are sometimes extreme. A month yielding five inches or more may be preceded or followed by one with less than two inches of precipitation, in any season. Months with less than one inch are known to occur, as well as those with precipitation in excess of 10 inches. Such large fluctuations, however, are not characteristic of the precipitation supply in Connecticut. Consequently, prolonged droughts and widespread floods are infrequent.

While there are no pronounced wet and dry months as in other climates, February and October are relatively dry. The average total precipitation for each of these months is three inches or slightly less in comparison with 3.5 to four inches in the other 10 months. Measurable precipitation falls on an average of one day in three, with the yearly total approximating 120 days. Periods of five days or more of successive daily precipitation occur a few times during most years.

The average annual snowfall increases from the coast to the northwestern corner of the State. Most of the snow falls in January and February, but in the majority of winters substantial amounts fall in December or March storms as well. Except for the northwestern highlands, snowfalls of more than one inch are quite rare before mid-November and after April 15. The average number of days per year with snow on the ground similarly shows an increase from the shore to the northwest. During an average winter a measurable snow cover is present most of the time from late December through the early half of March in the greater portion of the State. In the immediate coastal areas a snow cover does not last more than a few days unless a heavy snowstorm is followed by prolonged cold temperatures.

OTHER CLIMATIC ELEMENTS. During the colder months the prevailing wind is northwest to north over Connecticut, while from April through September southwest or south winds predominate. The mean hourly speed ranges from about seven m.p.h. in the summer and early fall to about 10 m.p.h. in the winter and spring seasons. An important feature of the climate is the sea breeze along the coast. During the summer and late spring this onshore wind blows from the cool ocean during the afternoon and penetrates inland from five to 10 miles. It occurs often enough to give lower mean summer maximum temperatures in a narrow coastal belt than prevail over interior lowlands.

Thunderstorms occur on an average of 20 to 30 days per year, with the greatest frequency during the summer months and in the afternoon or evening hours. Often these storms are accompanied by destructive hail and/or wind. Aside from infrequent tornadoes and hurricanes, coastal storms or "northeasters" are the most serious weather hazard in Connecticut. They generate very strong winds and heavy rain and produce the greatest snowstorms in the winter. If these storms occur at the time of high tide, heavy water damage results along the shore. In occasional years a tornado or storm with tornadic characteristics strikes some part of the State. The central valley appears to be the most likely to be struck, and the summer months the most likely season. Storms of tropical origin occasionally affect Connecticut during the summer or fall months, as they move on a path well out over the ocean.

The Connecticut River shows an annual rise in early spring as the result of the melting of high elevation snow in northern and central New England. A secondary period of flooding (occasionally of major proportions) is caused by heavy rains which may be associated with hurricanes or storms of tropical origin in late summer or fall, normally the low water season.

The percentage of possible sunshine averages 55 to 60 percent, ranging from 45 percent in the interior during the months of November through January to near 65 percent along the coast in the summer. The average number of clear days per year is between 100 and 125, with the greatest number per month usually occurring in September and October. An average of about 140 cloudy days occur per year. Heavy or dense fog is observed on an average of about 25 days per year in both coastal and inland sections. In the former section, heavy fog is most common during the late winter and spring seasons, while inland the late summer and fall is the period of maximum occurrence. The humidity tends to be lowest in the spring and highest in the late summer and early fall.

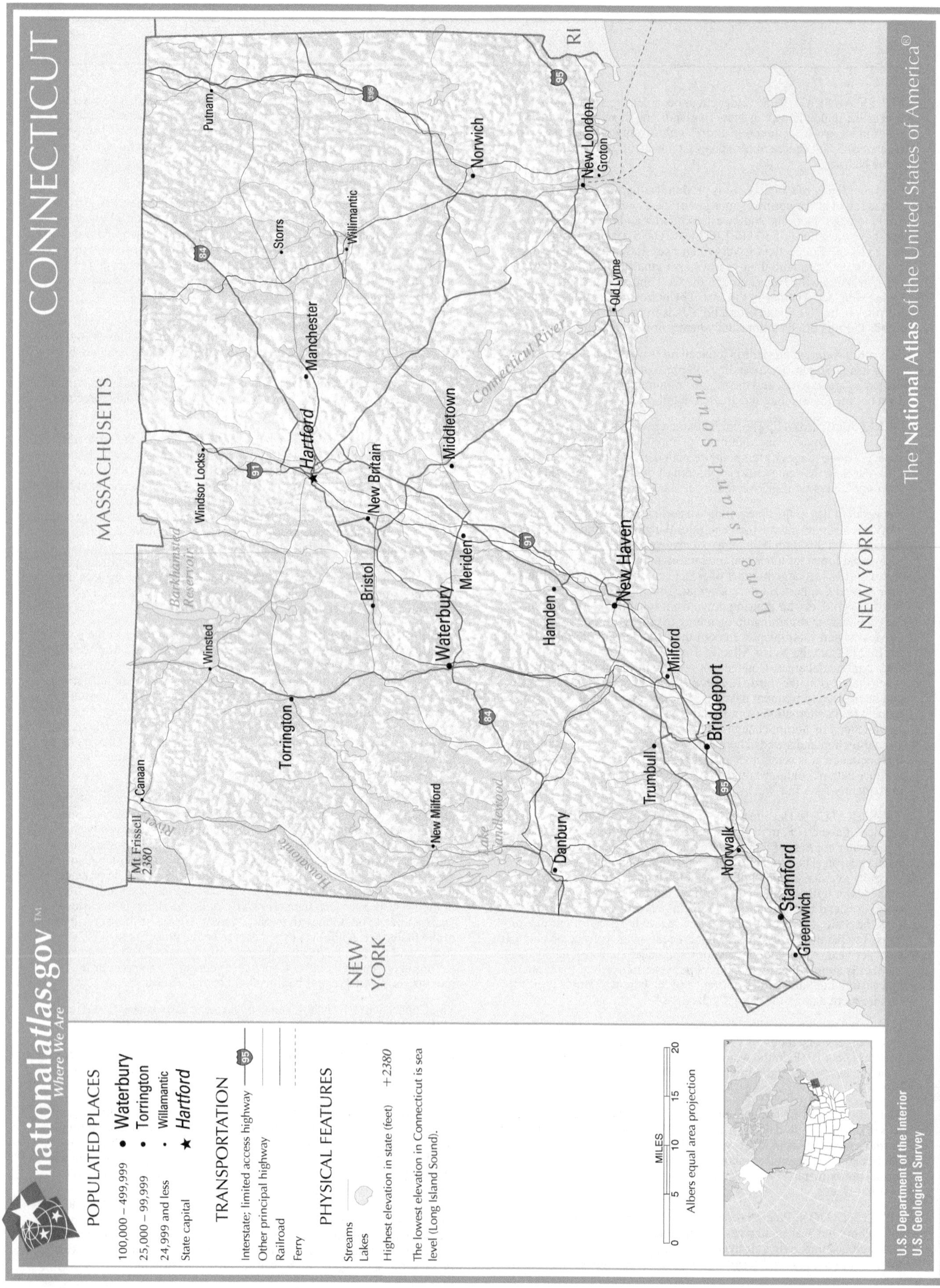
CONNECTICUT
nationalatlas.gov™
Where We Are
POPULATED PLACES
100,000 – 499,999 Waterbury
25,000 – 99,999 Torrington
24,999 and less Willamantic
State capital Hartford
TRANSPORTATION
Interstate; limited access highway
Other principal highway
Railroad
Ferry
PHYSICAL FEATURES
Streams
Lakes
Highest elevation in state (feet) +2380
The lowest elevation in Connecticut is sea level (Long Island Sound).
MILES
0 5 10 15 20
Albers equal area projection
MASSACHUSETTS
RI
NEW YORK
NEW YORK
Long Island Sound
Connecticut River
Housatonic River
Barkhamsted Reservoir
Lake Candlewood
Mt Frissell 2380
Canaan
Winsted
Torrington
New Milford
Danbury
Windsor Locks
Hartford
Manchester
Putnam
Storrs
Willimantic
Norwich
New London
Groton
Old Lyme
Middletown
New Britain
Bristol
Meriden
Waterbury
Hamden
New Haven
Milford
Bridgeport
Trumbull
Norwalk
Stamford
Greenwich
95
395
84
91
The National Atlas of the United States of America®
U.S. Department of the Interior
U.S. Geological Survey

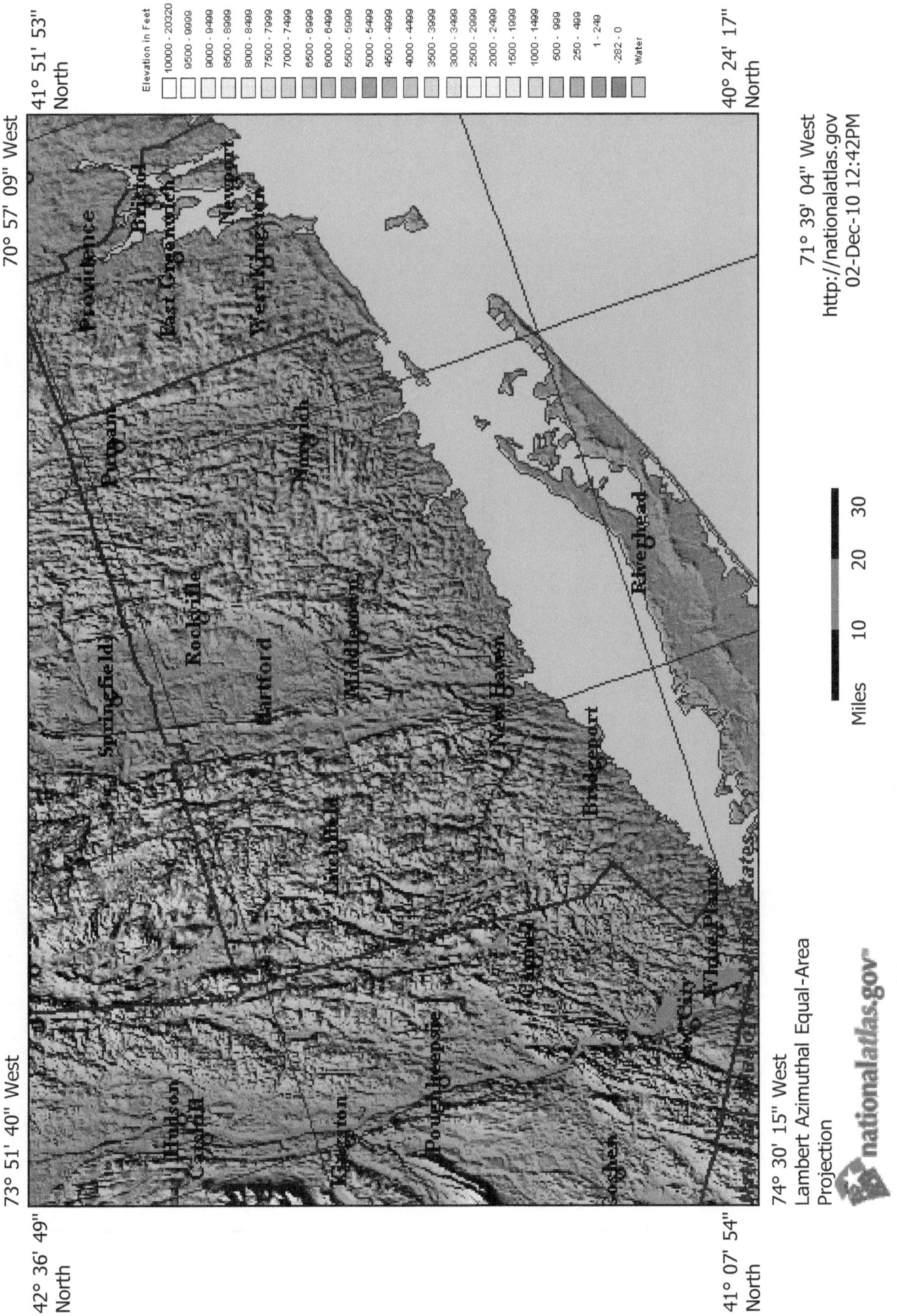

73° 51' 40" West
70° 57' 09" West
42° 36' 49" North
41° 51' 53" North
41° 07' 54" North
40° 24' 17" North
74° 30' 15" West
71° 39' 04" West
Lambert Azimuthal Equal-Area Projection
http://nationalatlas.gov
02-Dec-10 12:42PM
Elevation in Feet
10000 - 20320
9500 - 9999
9000 - 9499
8500 - 8999
8000 - 8499
7500 - 7999
7000 - 7499
6500 - 6999
6000 - 6499
5500 - 5999
5000 - 5499
4500 - 4999
4000 - 4499
3500 - 3999
3000 - 3499
2500 - 2999
2000 - 2499
1500 - 1999
1000 - 1499
500 - 999
250 - 499
1 - 249
-282 - 0
Water
Miles 10 20 30
Providence
East Greenwich
Bristol
Newport
West Kingston
Putnam
Norwich
Rockville
Hartford
Springfield
Middletown
New Haven
Riverhead
Bridgeport
Poughkeepsie
Kingston
Hudson
Catskill
nationalatlas.gov

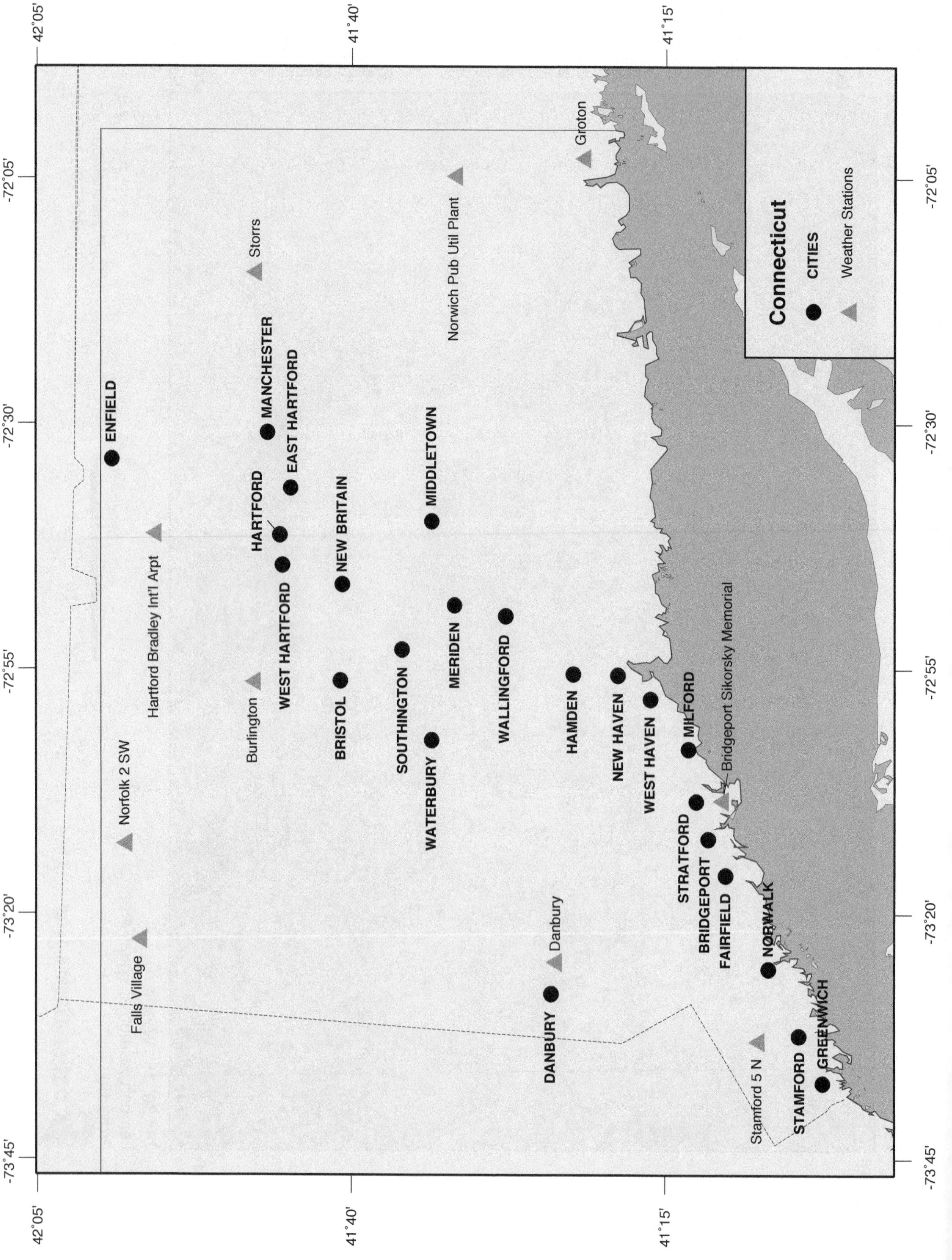
Connecticut
CITIES
Weather Stations
42°05'
41°40'
41°15'
-73°45'
-73°20'
-72°55'
-72°30'
-72°05'
ENFIELD
MANCHESTER
EAST HARTFORD
HARTFORD
WEST HARTFORD
NEW BRITAIN
MIDDLETOWN
BRISTOL
SOUTHINGTON
MERIDEN
WALLINGFORD
WATERBURY
HAMDEN
NEW HAVEN
WEST HAVEN
MILFORD
STRATFORD
BRIDGEPORT
FAIRFIELD
NORWALK
DANBURY
STAMFORD
GREENWICH
Storrs
Norwich Pub Util Plant
Groton
Hartford Bradley Int'l Arpt
Burlington
Norfolk 2 SW
Falls Village
Danbury
Bridgeport Sikorsky Memorial
Stamford 5 N

Connecticut Weather Stations by County

County	Station Name
Fairfield	Bridgeport Sikorsky Memorial Danbury Stamford 5 N
Hartford	Burlington Hartford Bradley Int'l Arpt
Litchfield	Falls Village Norfolk 2 SW
New London	Groton Norwich Public Util Plant
Tolland	Storrs

See User Guide for station inclusion criteria.

Connecticut Weather Stations by City

City	Station Name	Miles
Bridgeport	Bridgeport Sikorsky Memorial	2.5
	Danbury	18.4
	Stamford 5 N	19.1
Bristol	Burlington	8.1
	Hartford Bradley Int'l Arpt	21.5
	Norfolk 2 SW	24.6
Danbury	Bridgeport Sikorsky Memorial	22.1
	Danbury	2.2
	Stamford 5 N	20.4
	Yorktown Heights 1 W, NY	20.1
East Hartford	Burlington	16.7
	Hartford Bradley Int'l Arpt	12.3
	Storrs	18.9
Enfield	Burlington	23.2
	Hartford Bradley Int'l Arpt	7.4
	Storrs	20.8
	East Brimfield Lake, MA	23.7
Fairfield	Bridgeport Sikorsky Memorial	5.6
	Danbury	17.8
	Stamford 5 N	15.8
Greenwich	Stamford 5 N	6.3
	Dobbs Ferry Ardsley, NY	11.5
	Mineola, NY	21.3
	New York Laguardia Arpt, NY	22.5
	Yorktown Heights 1 W, NY	18.2
Hamden	Bridgeport Sikorsky Memorial	17.6
Hartford	Burlington	12.8
	Hartford Bradley Int'l Arpt	11.8
	Storrs	22.8
Manchester	Burlington	21.1
	Hartford Bradley Int'l Arpt	13.4
	Storrs	14.2
Meriden	Burlington	19.7
Middletown	Burlington	21.7
Milford	Bridgeport Sikorsky Memorial	5.4
	Danbury	22.5
	Riverhead Research Farm, NY	24.8
New Britain	Burlington	11.5
	Hartford Bradley Int'l Arpt	18.5
New Haven	Bridgeport Sikorsky Memorial	14.7
Norwalk	Bridgeport Sikorsky Memorial	14.9
	Danbury	19.9
	Stamford 5 N	6.8
	Dobbs Ferry Ardsley, NY	22.9
	Yorktown Heights 1 W, NY	22.4
Southington	Burlington	14.2
Stamford	Bridgeport Sikorsky Memorial	21.7
	Danbury	23.5
	Stamford 5 N	3.1
	Dobbs Ferry Ardsley, NY	16.1
	Mineola, NY	23.8
	Yorktown Heights 1 W, NY	19.0
Stratford	Bridgeport Sikorsky Memorial	1.7
	Danbury	19.9
	Stamford 5 N	22.4
Wallingford	Burlington	24.3
Waterbury	Burlington	17.6
	Danbury	22.6
West Hartford	Burlington	10.3
	Hartford Bradley Int'l Arpt	12.1
West Haven	Bridgeport Sikorsky Memorial	11.4
	Riverhead Research Farm, NY	24.6

Note: Miles is the distance between the geographic center of the city and the weather station.

See User Guide for station inclusion criteria.

Connecticut Weather Stations by Elevation

Feet	Station Name
1,339	Norfolk 2 SW
649	Storrs
549	Falls Village
509	Burlington
404	Danbury
189	Stamford 5 N
160	Hartford Bradley Int'l Arpt
40	Groton
20	Norwich Public Util Plant
9	Bridgeport Sikorsky Memorial

See User Guide for station inclusion criteria.

Bridgeport Sikorsky Memorial

The airport is located on Stratford Point, a peninsula jutting out into Long Island Sound. Station instrumentation is located approximately 1 mile from the sound. Land around the airport is flat, with marshes to the south. The terrain is of glacial origin, rising in a rolling, mostly wooded manner, to the foothills of the Berkshires, 30 miles to the north and northwest.

Cities in close proximity to the station are Bridgeport, Fairfield, and Milford, while Danbury, New Haven, Norwalk and Stamford are located within a 35-mile radius.

The most pronounced topographical effect is the land-sea breeze, an occurrence generally associated with the spring through early autumn months.

Mean monthly temperatures during the summer months average three to five degrees lower than nearby inland stations because of the sea-breeze effect. Temperatures during the fall and winter months are moderated because of the proximity of Long Island Sound.

Winter snowfall is generally around 10 inches less than areas a few miles inland, also due to the proximity of the station to Long Island Sound.

One of the hazards along the coastal areas is the flooding of low-lying areas (usually during periods of high tide) with the approach of slow-moving deepening low pressure systems, resulting in 3 to 5 feet higher tides than normal.

Bridgeport Sikorsky Memorial *Fairfield County* Elevation: 9 ft. Latitude: 41° 11' N Longitude: 73° 09' W

	JAN	FEB	MAR	APR	MAY	JUN	JUL	AUG	SEP	OCT	NOV	DEC	YEAR
Mean Maximum Temp. (°F)	37.1	39.6	46.9	57.3	67.4	76.8	82.0	80.8	74.0	63.2	53.0	42.4	60.0
Mean Temp. (°F)	30.2	32.3	39.0	49.1	59.0	68.5	74.2	73.3	66.0	54.8	45.4	35.4	52.3
Mean Minimum Temp. (°F)	23.1	25.0	31.1	40.9	50.5	60.1	66.2	65.6	57.9	46.4	37.8	28.3	44.4
Extreme Maximum Temp. (°F)	68	67	84	91	97	97	100	100	93	89	78	76	100
Extreme Minimum Temp. (°F)	-7	2	6	18	36	44	49	44	38	26	17	-4	-7
Days Maximum Temp. ≥ 90°F	0	0	0	0	0	1	3	2	0	0	0	0	6
Days Maximum Temp. ≤ 32°F	9	6	1	0	0	0	0	0	0	0	0	4	20
Days Minimum Temp. ≤ 32°F	26	23	17	2	0	0	0	0	0	1	8	21	98
Days Minimum Temp. ≤ 0°F	1	0	0	0	0	0	0	0	0	0	0	0	1
Heating Degree Days (base 65°F)	1,073	918	799	471	201	30	1	3	60	319	581	912	5,368
Cooling Degree Days (base 65°F)	0	0	0	2	23	141	292	266	96	9	0	0	829
Mean Precipitation (in.)	3.08	2.63	3.94	4.29	3.78	3.62	3.50	3.96	3.47	3.69	3.41	3.22	42.59
Maximum Precipitation (in.)*	11.2	6.6	9.4	10.7	9.5	17.7	12.8	13.3	7.4	10.7	10.2	7.9	73.9
Minimum Precipitation (in.)*	0.4	0.4	0.7	0.7	0.4	0.1	0.5	0.7	0.4	0.3	0.4	0.3	23.0
Extreme Maximum Daily Precip. (in.)	2.80	2.05	3.59	5.30	2.97	4.79	3.93	4.66	3.34	4.12	2.64	2.38	5.30
Days With ≥ 0.1" Precipitation	6	6	7	7	7	7	6	6	5	6	6	7	76
Days With ≥ 0.5" Precipitation	2	2	3	2	2	2	2	3	2	3	3	2	28
Days With ≥ 1.0" Precipitation	1	1	1	1	1	1	1	1	1	1	1	1	12
Mean Snowfall (in.)	***7.6***	***7.1***	***5.3***	***1.1***	***0.0***	na	na	***trace***	***0.0***	***trace***	***0.7***	***5.2***	na
Maximum Snowfall (in.)*	26	28	22	6	trace	0	0	0	0	1	7	21	60
Maximum 24-hr. Snowfall (in.)*	16	16	11	6	trace	0	0	0	0	1	6	15	16
Maximum Snow Depth (in.)	***20***	***20***	***9***	***6***	***0***	na	***trace***	***trace***	***0***	***trace***	***5***	***10***	na
Days With ≥ 1.0" Snow Depth	***10***	***7***	***4***	***0***	***0***	na	***0***	***0***	***0***	***0***	***0***	***5***	na
Thunderstorm Days*	< 1	< 1	1	2	3	4	5	4	2	1	< 1	< 1	22
Foggy Days*	12	12	14	14	16	16	16	17	15	14	13	13	172
Predominant Sky Cover*	OVR	OVR	OVR	OVR	OVR	OVR	OVR	OVR	OVR	OVR	OVR	OVR	OVR
Mean Relative Humidity 7am (%)*	73	72	72	72	75	77	79	80	81	79	77	74	76
Mean Relative Humidity 4pm (%)*	61	59	56	55	58	60	60	61	61	60	62	63	60
Mean Dewpoint (°F)*	20	20	26	36	47	57	63	63	56	46	35	25	41
Prevailing Wind Direction*	WNW	NW	NW	SW	SW	SW	SW	SW	SW	NE	WNW	WNW	WSW
Prevailing Wind Speed (mph)*	15	16	16	13	12	10	10	10	13	12	14	15	13
Maximum Wind Gust (mph)*	69	66	71	63	59	55	62	77	69	76	61	66	77

Note: (*) Period of record is 1948-1995

The period of record for National Weather Service station data is 1980 – 2009 except where noted. See User Guide for detailed explanation of data.

Hartford Bradley Int'l Airport

Bradley International Airport is located about 3 miles west of the Connecticut River on a slight rise of ground in a broad portion of the Connecticut River Valley between north-south mountain ranges whose heights do not exceed 1,200 feet.

The station is in the northern temperate climate zone. The prevailing west to east movement of air brings the majority of weather systems into Connecticut from the west. The average wintertime position of the Polar Front boundary between cold, dry polar air and warm, moist tropical air is just south of New England, which helps to explain the extensive winter storm activity and day to day variability of local weather. In summer, the Polar Front has an average position along the New England-Canada border with this station in a warm and pleasant atmosphere.

Relative to continent and ocean, is also significant. Rapid weather changes result when storms move northward along the mid-Atlantic coast, frequently producing strong and persistent northeast winds associated with storms known locally as coastals or northeasters. Seasonally, weather characteristics vary from the cold and dry continental-polar air of winter to the warm and humid maritime air of summer.

Summer thunderstorms develop in the Berkshire Mountains to the west and northwest, move over the Connecticut Valley, and when accompanied by wind and hail, sometimes cause considerable damage to crops, particularly tobacco. During the winter, rain often falls through cold air trapped in the valley, creating extremely hazardous ice conditions. On clear nights in the late summer or early autumn, cool air drainage into the valley, and moisture from the Connecticut River, produce steam and/or ground fog which becomes quite dense throughout the valley, hampering ground and air transportation.

The mean date of the last springtime temperature of 32 degrees or lower is April 22, and the mean date of the first autumn temperature of 32 degrees is October 15.

Hartford Bradley Int'l Airport *Hartford County* Elevation: 160 ft. Latitude: 41° 56' N Longitude: 72° 41' W

	JAN	FEB	MAR	APR	MAY	JUN	JUL	AUG	SEP	OCT	NOV	DEC	YEAR
Mean Maximum Temp. (°F)	34.5	38.3	47.4	60.2	71.1	79.6	84.5	82.7	74.9	63.0	51.4	39.6	60.6
Mean Temp. (°F)	26.1	29.5	37.5	49.3	59.4	68.4	73.5	72.0	63.8	52.0	42.3	31.4	50.4
Mean Minimum Temp. (°F)	17.7	20.5	27.7	38.3	47.7	57.1	62.5	61.2	52.6	41.0	33.0	23.2	40.2
Extreme Maximum Temp. (°F)	72	73	89	95	99	98	101	102	99	89	80	76	102
Extreme Minimum Temp. (°F)	-21	-13	-6	14	28	37	45	39	30	21	1	-14	-21
Days Maximum Temp. ≥ 90°F	0	0	0	0	1	3	6	5	1	0	0	0	16
Days Maximum Temp. ≤ 32°F	13	8	2	0	0	0	0	0	0	0	0	7	30
Days Minimum Temp. ≤ 32°F	28	25	22	7	1	0	0	0	0	6	16	26	131
Days Minimum Temp. ≤ 0°F	3	1	0	0	0	0	0	0	0	0	0	1	5
Heating Degree Days (base 65°F)	1,198	999	845	470	200	38	3	10	103	402	676	1,034	5,978
Cooling Degree Days (base 65°F)	0	0	0	5	34	145	274	233	73	7	0	0	771
Mean Precipitation (in.)	3.20	2.93	3.66	3.86	4.29	4.32	4.16	3.86	4.06	4.27	3.85	3.40	45.86
Maximum Precipitation (in.)*	9.6	7.3	9.5	9.9	12.0	13.6	8.4	21.9	9.0	11.6	8.5	8.4	64.5
Minimum Precipitation (in.)*	0.4	0.4	0.3	1.4	0.7	0.3	1.1	0.5	0.8	0.3	0.5	0.8	29.0
Extreme Maximum Daily Precip. (in.)	2.00	2.53	2.52	3.21	4.81	5.88	3.32	4.05	5.72	5.26	2.90	1.97	5.88
Days With ≥ 0.1" Precipitation	6	6	7	7	8	7	7	6	6	6	6	7	79
Days With ≥ 0.5" Precipitation	3	2	3	2	3	3	3	2	2	3	3	2	31
Days With ≥ 1.0" Precipitation	1	1	1	1	1	1	1	1	1	1	1	1	12
Mean Snowfall (in.)	***13.6***	***11.9***	8.5	***1.1***	***trace***	***trace***	***0.0***	***trace***	***0.0***	***trace***	***2.2***	9.4	***46.7***
Maximum Snowfall (in.)*	37	32	43	14	1	0	0	0	0	2	9	35	88
Maximum 24-hr. Snowfall (in.)*	14	14	14	14	1	0	0	0	0	2	8	14	14
Maximum Snow Depth (in.)	na	na	na	na	na	na	na	na	na	na	na	na	na
Days With ≥ 1.0" Snow Depth	na	na	na	na	na	na	na	na	na	na	na	na	na
Thunderstorm Days*	< 1	< 1	1	1	2	4	5	4	2	1	< 1	< 1	20
Foggy Days*	12	10	12	12	13	15	16	17	16	14	13	12	162
Predominant Sky Cover*	OVR	OVR	OVR	OVR	OVR	OVR	OVR	OVR	OVR	OVR	OVR	OVR	OVR
Mean Relative Humidity 7am (%)*	73	73	72	70	73	77	79	83	86	84	79	76	77
Mean Relative Humidity 4pm (%)*	58	54	51	46	48	51	52	54	55	53	58	61	53
Mean Dewpoint (°F)*	15	17	24	33	45	56	61	60	53	42	32	20	38
Prevailing Wind Direction*	NW	NW	NW	S	S	S	S	S	S	S	N	NW	S
Prevailing Wind Speed (mph)*	12	13	13	10	9	9	8	8	8	8	8	12	10
Maximum Wind Gust (mph)*	66	53	62	60	48	59	89	58	66	86	64	58	89

Note: (*) Period of record is 1949-1995

Burlington *Hartford County* Elevation: 509 ft. Latitude: 41° 48' N Longitude: 72° 56' W

	JAN	FEB	MAR	APR	MAY	JUN	JUL	AUG	SEP	OCT	NOV	DEC	YEAR
Mean Maximum Temp. (°F)	35.0	38.4	46.4	58.7	69.6	77.7	82.4	80.8	73.6	62.1	51.5	40.2	59.7
Mean Temp. (°F)	25.0	28.0	35.8	47.3	57.8	66.4	71.2	69.9	62.2	50.5	41.3	31.0	48.9
Mean Minimum Temp. (°F)	15.3	17.4	25.1	35.8	45.9	55.1	60.0	58.8	50.8	38.8	31.1	21.7	38.0
Extreme Maximum Temp. (°F)	72	70	83	94	95	95	100	97	95	89	80	75	100
Extreme Minimum Temp. (°F)	-18	-10	-3	14	27	35	40	37	24	19	1	-13	-18
Days Maximum Temp. ≥ 90°F	0	0	0	0	1	2	4	3	1	0	0	0	11
Days Maximum Temp. ≤ 32°F	12	8	3	0	0	0	0	0	0	0	0	7	30
Days Minimum Temp. ≤ 32°F	29	26	25	10	1	0	0	0	0	8	19	27	145
Days Minimum Temp. ≤ 0°F	3	1	0	0	0	0	0	0	0	0	0	1	5
Heating Degree Days (base 65°F)	1,232	1,041	899	529	242	60	9	19	130	447	704	1,047	6,359
Cooling Degree Days (base 65°F)	0	0	0	3	24	108	209	176	53	4	0	0	577
Mean Precipitation (in.)	3.62	3.40	4.36	4.65	4.70	4.69	4.73	4.76	4.77	5.05	4.47	3.92	53.12
Extreme Maximum Daily Precip. (in.)	2.78	2.84	4.79	5.27	6.31	6.13	3.85	3.76	7.77	7.21	2.81	3.15	7.77
Days With ≥ 0.1" Precipitation	6	6	7	7	8	7	7	7	6	6	6	6	79
Days With ≥ 0.5" Precipitation	3	2	3	3	3	3	3	3	3	3	3	3	35
Days With ≥ 1.0" Precipitation	1	1	1	1	1	2	1	1	1	2	1	1	14
Mean Snowfall (in.)	*7.0*	*5.2*	*4.5*	0.5	0.0	0.0	0.0	0.0	0.0	trace	0.6	*4.4*	*22.2*
Maximum Snow Depth (in.)	na	na	na	*trace*	*0*	*0*	*0*	*0*	*0*	*trace*	na	na	na
Days With ≥ 1.0" Snow Depth	na	na	*4*	0	0	0	0	0	0	0	*0*	na	na

Danbury *Fairfield County* Elevation: 404 ft. Latitude: 41° 24' N Longitude: 73° 25' W

	JAN	FEB	MAR	APR	MAY	JUN	JUL	AUG	SEP	OCT	NOV	DEC	YEAR
Mean Maximum Temp. (°F)	35.4	39.5	48.2	61.1	72.0	80.3	84.9	82.7	74.8	62.7	51.1	40.2	61.1
Mean Temp. (°F)	26.9	30.2	37.9	49.5	59.6	68.7	73.7	72.0	63.7	51.8	42.0	32.2	50.7
Mean Minimum Temp. (°F)	18.4	20.8	27.5	37.9	47.4	57.1	62.3	61.3	52.7	41.0	32.8	24.0	40.3
Extreme Maximum Temp. (°F)	69	73	92	95	97	98	106	103	98	87	80	76	106
Extreme Minimum Temp. (°F)	-18	-8	-3	14	26	36	44	38	31	19	10	-11	-18
Days Maximum Temp. ≥ 90°F	0	0	0	0	1	4	7	4	1	0	0	0	17
Days Maximum Temp. ≤ 32°F	12	7	2	0	0	0	0	0	0	0	0	6	27
Days Minimum Temp. ≤ 32°F	28	25	22	8	1	0	0	0	0	6	16	26	132
Days Minimum Temp. ≤ 0°F	2	1	0	0	0	0	0	0	0	0	0	0	3
Heating Degree Days (base 65°F)	1,174	979	836	463	196	37	2	8	105	407	684	1,011	5,902
Cooling Degree Days (base 65°F)	0	0	1	6	37	155	278	234	74	6	0	0	791
Mean Precipitation (in.)	3.67	3.13	4.58	4.51	4.10	4.95	4.74	4.37	4.87	4.69	4.31	4.20	52.12
Extreme Maximum Daily Precip. (in.)	3.75	2.98	3.29	3.46	3.62	4.44	5.81	4.00	9.55	5.53	4.00	4.12	9.55
Days With ≥ 0.1" Precipitation	7	6	8	8	8	8	6	7	6	6	7	7	84
Days With ≥ 0.5" Precipitation	2	2	3	3	3	3	3	3	3	3	3	3	34
Days With ≥ 1.0" Precipitation	1	1	1	1	1	1	1	1	1	1	2	1	13
Mean Snowfall (in.)	12.4	11.6	9.9	1.7	trace	0.0	0.0	0.0	0.0	trace	1.3	9.2	46.1
Maximum Snow Depth (in.)	36	28	19	10	trace	0	0	0	0	trace	4	18	36
Days With ≥ 1.0" Snow Depth	15	13	7	1	0	0	0	0	0	0	1	9	46

Falls Village *Litchfield County* Elevation: 549 ft. Latitude: 41° 57' N Longitude: 73° 22' W

	JAN	FEB	MAR	APR	MAY	JUN	JUL	AUG	SEP	OCT	NOV	DEC	YEAR
Mean Maximum Temp. (°F)	34.5	38.2	46.7	60.0	71.6	79.0	83.3	81.4	73.6	61.8	50.3	38.9	59.9
Mean Temp. (°F)	24.4	27.4	35.4	47.3	58.0	66.2	70.8	69.4	61.6	49.9	40.1	29.5	48.3
Mean Minimum Temp. (°F)	14.1	16.6	24.0	34.6	44.3	53.4	58.1	57.4	49.6	37.9	29.8	20.1	36.7
Extreme Maximum Temp. (°F)	67	70	88	93	94	95	100	99	94	84	81	72	100
Extreme Minimum Temp. (°F)	-27	-21	-10	10	23	31	40	34	27	17	5	-16	-27
Days Maximum Temp. ≥ 90°F	0	0	0	0	1	2	5	3	0	0	0	0	11
Days Maximum Temp. ≤ 32°F	13	8	2	0	0	0	0	0	0	0	1	7	31
Days Minimum Temp. ≤ 32°F	29	26	26	13	3	0	0	0	1	10	19	28	155
Days Minimum Temp. ≤ 0°F	5	3	0	0	0	0	0	0	0	0	0	1	9
Heating Degree Days (base 65°F)	1,253	1,057	911	527	233	58	9	22	141	465	741	1,093	6,510
Cooling Degree Days (base 65°F)	0	0	0	3	23	102	194	166	46	2	0	0	536
Mean Precipitation (in.)	2.92	2.59	3.43	3.71	4.07	4.77	4.60	4.04	4.06	4.17	3.74	3.29	45.39
Extreme Maximum Daily Precip. (in.)	1.61	3.22	2.60	3.09	3.89	4.15	6.02	3.49	4.76	8.23	2.35	2.32	8.23
Days With ≥ 0.1" Precipitation	6	6	7	7	8	8	7	7	6	7	7	6	82
Days With ≥ 0.5" Precipitation	2	1	2	3	3	3	3	3	2	3	3	2	30
Days With ≥ 1.0" Precipitation	1	0	1	1	1	1	1	1	1	1	1	1	11
Mean Snowfall (in.)	*6.7*	*4.9*	4.2	0.7	0.0	0.0	0.0	0.0	0.0	0.0	0.6	*4.5*	*21.6*
Maximum Snow Depth (in.)	*31*	na	*22*	18	0	0	0	0	0	0	8	*11*	na
Days With ≥ 1.0" Snow Depth	*3*	*3*	*3*	0	0	0	0	0	0	0	0	*2*	*11*

Groton *New London County* Elevation: 40 ft. Latitude: 41° 21' N Longitude: 72° 03' W

	JAN	FEB	MAR	APR	MAY	JUN	JUL	AUG	SEP	OCT	NOV	DEC	YEAR
Mean Maximum Temp. (°F)	37.7	40.2	47.2	56.4	*66.3*	75.0	80.4	79.4	73.0	62.3	53.0	42.8	*59.5*
Mean Temp. (°F)	29.3	31.8	38.5	47.8	*57.2*	66.2	72.0	71.2	64.3	53.2	44.6	34.7	*50.9*
Mean Minimum Temp. (°F)	21.0	23.3	29.8	39.2	*48.0*	57.4	63.6	63.1	55.7	44.1	36.1	26.6	*42.3*
Extreme Maximum Temp. (°F)	64	65	78	88	*91*	95	101	94	93	82	75	69	*101*
Extreme Minimum Temp. (°F)	-13	-9	5	14	*33*	40	47	44	32	25	8	-10	*-13*
Days Maximum Temp. ≥ 90°F	0	0	0	0	*0*	1	2	1	0	0	0	0	*4*
Days Maximum Temp. ≤ 32°F	9	5	1	0	*0*	0	0	0	0	0	0	4	*19*
Days Minimum Temp. ≤ 32°F	27	24	19	4	*0*	0	0	0	0	2	11	23	*110*
Days Minimum Temp. ≤ 0°F	1	0	0	0	*0*	0	0	0	0	0	0	0	*1*
Heating Degree Days (base 65°F)	1,099	932	815	510	*248*	48	3	7	84	362	606	931	*5,645*
Cooling Degree Days (base 65°F)	0	0	0	1	*12*	92	227	207	71	5	0	0	*615*
Mean Precipitation (in.)	3.64	3.34	4.94	4.61	*3.37*	3.94	3.69	4.42	4.13	3.79	4.45	4.11	*48.43*
Extreme Maximum Daily Precip. (in.)	2.41	2.86	3.15	3.29	*2.43*	6.30	4.38	4.70	3.83	2.58	3.39	3.68	*6.30*
Days With ≥ 0.1" Precipitation	7	6	8	7	*7*	6	6	6	6	6	7	8	*80*
Days With ≥ 0.5" Precipitation	3	2	3	3	*2*	2	3	3	3	3	3	3	*33*
Days With ≥ 1.0" Precipitation	1	1	1	1	*1*	1	1	1	1	1	1	1	*12*
Mean Snowfall (in.)	7.2	6.4	3.3	0.8	*0.0*	0.0	0.0	0.0	0.0	trace	0.8	4.5	*23.0*
Maximum Snow Depth (in.)	19	14	*7*	6	*0*	0	0	0	0	trace	6	9	*19*
Days With ≥ 1.0" Snow Depth	9	6	*2*	0	*0*	0	0	0	0	0	0	4	*21*

The period of record for all cooperative weather station data is 1980 – 2009. See User Guide for detailed explanation of data.

Norfolk 2 SW *Litchfield County* Elevation: 1,339 ft. Latitude: 41° 58' N Longitude: 73° 13' W

	JAN	FEB	MAR	APR	MAY	JUN	JUL	AUG	SEP	OCT	NOV	DEC	YEAR
Mean Maximum Temp. (°F)	29.4	32.3	40.5	54.1	65.3	73.3	77.8	75.9	68.1	56.2	44.9	33.6	54.3
Mean Temp. (°F)	21.2	23.5	31.3	44.0	54.9	63.5	68.2	66.6	58.8	47.2	37.4	26.4	45.3
Mean Minimum Temp. (°F)	13.0	14.7	22.1	33.8	44.5	53.7	58.5	57.3	49.5	38.2	29.8	19.1	36.2
Extreme Maximum Temp. (°F)	62	63	79	89	88	92	92	92	89	81	75	67	92
Extreme Minimum Temp. (°F)	-21	-12	-8	7	26	32	43	37	29	21	4	-20	-21
Days Maximum Temp. ≥ 90°F	0	0	0	0	0	0	1	0	0	0	0	0	1
Days Maximum Temp. ≤ 32°F	19	15	7	0	0	0	0	0	0	0	3	14	58
Days Minimum Temp. ≤ 32°F	29	27	27	14	2	0	0	0	0	9	20	28	156
Days Minimum Temp. ≤ 0°F	5	3	1	0	0	0	0	0	0	0	0	2	11
Heating Degree Days (base 65°F)	1,351	1,166	1,037	627	319	104	25	48	204	547	822	1,190	7,440
Cooling Degree Days (base 65°F)	0	0	0	2	13	65	130	105	25	2	0	0	342
Mean Precipitation (in.)	3.86	3.45	4.32	4.48	4.41	4.88	4.74	4.70	4.29	4.89	4.64	4.25	52.91
Extreme Maximum Daily Precip. (in.)	1.93	2.37	3.55	4.12	2.82	4.90	3.62	2.95	5.80	6.52	3.00	3.30	6.52
Days With ≥ 0.1" Precipitation	7	7	8	8	9	8	8	7	7	7	7	8	91
Days With ≥ 0.5" Precipitation	3	2	3	3	3	3	4	3	3	3	3	3	36
Days With ≥ 1.0" Precipitation	1	1	1	1	1	1	1	1	1	1	1	1	12
Mean Snowfall (in.)	19.6	16.4	15.1	5.4	trace	trace	0.0	0.0	0.0	0.7	4.5	16.6	78.3
Maximum Snow Depth (in.)	39	34	40	21	trace	trace	0	0	0	10	10	29	40
Days With ≥ 1.0" Snow Depth	25	25	22	4	0	0	0	0	0	0	4	20	100

Norwich Public Util Plant *New London County* Elevation: 20 ft. Latitude: 41° 32' N Longitude: 72° 04' W

	JAN	FEB	MAR	APR	MAY	JUN	JUL	AUG	SEP	OCT	NOV	DEC	YEAR
Mean Maximum Temp. (°F)	37.9	41.1	48.6	59.8	70.5	78.7	83.8	82.6	75.3	64.0	53.6	42.6	61.5
Mean Temp. (°F)	28.2	31.4	38.3	48.8	58.7	67.5	73.1	72.0	64.1	52.5	43.3	33.4	50.9
Mean Minimum Temp. (°F)	18.8	21.5	27.9	37.8	46.9	56.2	62.3	61.2	52.6	40.9	32.8	24.1	40.2
Extreme Maximum Temp. (°F)	68	72	85	94	98	98	101	102	97	87	79	77	102
Extreme Minimum Temp. (°F)	-13	-17	3	17	27	33	43	40	30	18	6	-13	-17
Days Maximum Temp. ≥ 90°F	0	0	0	0	1	2	5	4	1	0	0	0	13
Days Maximum Temp. ≤ 32°F	9	5	1	0	0	0	0	0	0	0	0	5	20
Days Minimum Temp. ≤ 32°F	28	24	21	8	0	0	0	0	0	6	16	26	129
Days Minimum Temp. ≤ 0°F	2	0	0	0	0	0	0	0	0	0	0	0	2
Heating Degree Days (base 65°F)	1,134	943	820	480	214	43	3	8	93	387	645	973	5,743
Cooling Degree Days (base 65°F)	0	0	0	2	25	124	261	233	71	6	0	0	722
Mean Precipitation (in.)	4.10	3.86	5.20	5.12	3.94	4.31	3.87	4.81	4.19	4.88	4.81	4.59	53.68
Extreme Maximum Daily Precip. (in.)	3.18	2.89	3.62	4.28	4.31	6.11	4.81	5.21	4.01	6.18	3.24	3.47	6.18
Days With ≥ 0.1" Precipitation	7	6	8	7	7	6	6	6	6	6	6	7	78
Days With ≥ 0.5" Precipitation	3	3	3	3	3	3	2	3	3	3	3	3	35
Days With ≥ 1.0" Precipitation	1	1	1	1	1	1	1	1	1	1	2	1	13
Mean Snowfall (in.)	***6.1***	na	3.3	0.8	0.0	0.0	0.0	trace	0.0	0.0	0.2	***5.0***	na
Maximum Snow Depth (in.)	25	na	***8***	***3***	***0***	***0***	***0***	***trace***	***0***	***0***	4	***17***	na
Days With ≥ 1.0" Snow Depth	***8***	***7***	3	0	0	0	0	0	0	0	0	***5***	***23***

Stamford 5 N *Fairfield County* Elevation: 189 ft. Latitude: 41° 07' N Longitude: 73° 33' W

	JAN	FEB	MAR	APR	MAY	JUN	JUL	AUG	SEP	OCT	NOV	DEC	YEAR
Mean Maximum Temp. (°F)	***38.4***	***42.0***	***50.5***	***62.5***	***73.3***	81.1	85.5	83.5	***76.2***	65.0	54.2	43.1	***62.9***
Mean Temp. (°F)	***28.9***	***32.0***	***39.8***	***50.5***	***60.6***	68.8	73.8	72.3	***65.0***	53.6	44.1	34.2	***52.0***
Mean Minimum Temp. (°F)	***19.5***	***21.9***	***29.0***	***38.5***	***48.0***	56.6	62.0	61.1	***53.8***	42.0	33.9	25.2	***40.9***
Extreme Maximum Temp. (°F)	***69***	***74***	***85***	***96***	***97***	***97***	***102***	***104***	***97***	***85***	***82***	***76***	***104***
Extreme Minimum Temp. (°F)	***-18***	***-6***	***1***	***16***	***29***	***35***	***44***	***39***	***33***	***21***	***13***	***-13***	***-18***
Days Maximum Temp. ≥ 90°F	***0***	***0***	***0***	***0***	***1***	3	7	5	***1***	0	0	0	***17***
Days Maximum Temp. ≤ 32°F	***8***	***4***	***1***	***0***	***0***	0	0	0	***0***	0	0	3	***16***
Days Minimum Temp. ≤ 32°F	***27***	***24***	***20***	***7***	***1***	0	0	0	***0***	5	14	24	***122***
Days Minimum Temp. ≤ 0°F	***2***	***0***	***0***	***0***	***0***	0	0	0	***0***	0	0	0	***2***
Heating Degree Days (base 65°F)	***1,110***	***929***	***776***	***433***	***166***	29	1	5	***78***	353	622	949	***5,451***
Cooling Degree Days (base 65°F)	***0***	***0***	***0***	***4***	***38***	150	281	240	***86***	5	0	0	***804***
Mean Precipitation (in.)	***4.14***	***3.19***	***4.86***	***5.04***	***4.87***	4.46	3.96	4.05	***4.93***	4.40	4.74	3.99	***52.63***
Extreme Maximum Daily Precip. (in.)	***2.94***	***2.82***	na	***4.10***	na	***3.08***	***4.04***	***2.52***	na	***3.76***	***2.64***	***3.02***	na
Days With ≥ 0.1" Precipitation	***7***	***6***	***7***	***8***	***8***	7	6	7	***6***	6	7	7	***82***
Days With ≥ 0.5" Precipitation	***3***	***2***	***3***	***3***	***3***	3	3	3	***3***	3	3	3	***35***
Days With ≥ 1.0" Precipitation	***1***	***1***	***1***	***1***	***1***	1	1	1	***2***	1	2	1	***14***
Mean Snowfall (in.)	***9.9***	***8.5***	***5.8***	***1.0***	***0.0***	0.0	0.0	0.0	***0.0***	trace	0.9	5.6	***31.7***
Maximum Snow Depth (in.)	***20***	na	***15***	***10***	***0***	***0***	***0***	***0***	***0***	***trace***	***2***	na	na
Days With ≥ 1.0" Snow Depth	na	na	***3***	***0***	***0***	0	0	0	***0***	***0***	***0***	***3***	na

Storrs *Tolland County* Elevation: 649 ft. Latitude: 41° 48' N Longitude: 72° 15' W

	JAN	FEB	MAR	APR	MAY	JUN	JUL	AUG	SEP	OCT	NOV	DEC	YEAR
Mean Maximum Temp. (°F)	33.2	***36.3***	44.2	***56.1***	66.7	75.0	79.5	78.3	71.3	60.3	50.2	38.8	***57.5***
Mean Temp. (°F)	25.4	***28.2***	35.8	***46.9***	56.8	65.7	70.7	69.4	62.2	51.1	42.1	31.5	***48.8***
Mean Minimum Temp. (°F)	17.6	***20.0***	27.4	***37.7***	46.9	56.3	61.8	60.5	53.0	41.8	34.0	24.1	***40.1***
Extreme Maximum Temp. (°F)	67	***69***	81	***91***	***92***	95	95	96	95	84	78	73	***96***
Extreme Minimum Temp. (°F)	-10	***-12***	0	***14***	***28***	36	45	39	31	22	9	-11	***-12***
Days Maximum Temp. ≥ 90°F	0	***0***	0	***0***	0	0	1	1	0	0	0	0	***2***
Days Maximum Temp. ≤ 32°F	14	***10***	4	***0***	0	0	0	0	0	0	1	8	***37***
Days Minimum Temp. ≤ 32°F	28	***25***	22	***7***	0	0	0	0	0	4	13	25	***124***
Days Minimum Temp. ≤ 0°F	3	***1***	0	***0***	0	0	0	0	0	0	0	1	***5***
Heating Degree Days (base 65°F)	1,219	***1,037***	900	***538***	264	67	9	20	124	429	680	1,032	***6,319***
Cooling Degree Days (base 65°F)	0	***0***	0	***3***	17	95	192	163	49	4	0	0	***523***
Mean Precipitation (in.)	3.58	***3.41***	4.25	***4.53***	3.84	4.25	4.21	3.88	4.12	4.81	4.59	4.10	***49.57***
Extreme Maximum Daily Precip. (in.)	2.50	***2.79***	4.17	***3.28***	***2.90***	4.07	4.01	4.25	4.35	5.48	2.61	4.20	***5.48***
Days With ≥ 0.1" Precipitation	6	***6***	7	***8***	8	7	7	6	6	6	7	7	***81***
Days With ≥ 0.5" Precipitation	3	***2***	3	***3***	3	2	3	3	3	3	3	3	***34***
Days With ≥ 1.0" Precipitation	1	***1***	1	***1***	1	1	1	1	1	2	2	1	***14***
Mean Snowfall (in.)	na	na	***5.1***	***1.2***	0.0	0.0	0.0	0.0	0.0	trace	1.1	***6.5***	na
Maximum Snow Depth (in.)	na	na	na	na	na	na	na	na	na	na	na	na	na
Days With ≥ 1.0" Snow Depth	na	na	***5***	***0***	0	0	0	0	0	0	***1***	na	na

The period of record for all cooperative weather station data is 1980 – 2009. See User Guide for detailed explanation of data.

Connecticut Weather Station Rankings

Annual Extreme Maximum Temperature

Rank	Station Name (Highest)	°F	Rank	Station Name (Lowest)	°F
1	Danbury	***106***	1	Norfolk 2 SW	92
2	Stamford 5 N	***104***	2	Storrs	***96***
3	Hartford Bradley Int'l Arpt	102	3	Bridgeport Sikorsky Memorial	100
3	Norwich Public Util Plant	102	3	Burlington	100
5	Groton	***101***	3	Falls Village	100
6	Bridgeport Sikorsky Memorial	100	6	Groton	***101***
6	Burlington	100	7	Hartford Bradley Int'l Arpt	102
6	Falls Village	100	7	Norwich Public Util Plant	102
9	Storrs	***96***	9	Stamford 5 N	***104***
10	Norfolk 2 SW	92	10	Danbury	***106***

Annual Mean Maximum Temperature

Rank	Station Name (Highest)	°F	Rank	Station Name (Lowest)	°F
1	Stamford 5 N	***62.9***	1	Norfolk 2 SW	54.3
2	Norwich Public Util Plant	61.5	2	Storrs	***57.5***
3	Danbury	***61.1***	3	Groton	***59.5***
4	Hartford Bradley Int'l Arpt	60.6	4	Burlington	59.7
5	Bridgeport Sikorsky Memorial	60.0	5	Falls Village	59.9
6	Falls Village	59.9	6	Bridgeport Sikorsky Memorial	60.0
7	Burlington	59.7	7	Hartford Bradley Int'l Arpt	60.6
8	Groton	***59.5***	8	Danbury	***61.1***
9	Storrs	***57.5***	9	Norwich Public Util Plant	61.5
10	Norfolk 2 SW	54.3	10	Stamford 5 N	***62.9***

 Rankings include 25 highest/lowest stations. If state has less than 25 stations, all stations are included. The period of record is 1980–2009. See User Guide for detailed explanation of data.

Annual Mean Temperature

Highest Rank	Station Name	°F	Lowest Rank	Station Name	°F
1	Bridgeport Sikorsky Memorial	52.3	1	Norfolk 2 SW	45.3
2	Stamford 5 N	***52.0***	2	Falls Village	48.3
3	Norwich Public Util Plant	51.0	3	Storrs	***48.8***
4	Groton	***50.9***	4	Burlington	48.9
5	Danbury	***50.7***	5	Hartford Bradley Int'l Arpt	50.4
6	Hartford Bradley Int'l Arpt	50.4	6	Danbury	***50.7***
7	Burlington	48.9	7	Groton	***50.9***
8	Storrs	***48.8***	8	Norwich Public Util Plant	51.0
9	Falls Village	48.3	9	Stamford 5 N	***52.0***
10	Norfolk 2 SW	45.3	10	Bridgeport Sikorsky Memorial	52.3

Annual Mean Minimum Temperature

Highest Rank	Station Name	°F	Lowest Rank	Station Name	°F
1	Bridgeport Sikorsky Memorial	44.4	1	Norfolk 2 SW	36.2
2	Groton	***42.3***	2	Falls Village	36.7
3	Stamford 5 N	***41.0***	3	Burlington	38.0
4	Danbury	***40.3***	4	Storrs	***40.1***
5	Hartford Bradley Int'l Arpt	40.2	5	Hartford Bradley Int'l Arpt	40.2
5	Norwich Public Util Plant	40.2	5	Norwich Public Util Plant	40.2
7	Storrs	***40.1***	7	Danbury	***40.3***
8	Burlington	38.0	8	Stamford 5 N	***41.0***
9	Falls Village	36.7	9	Groton	***42.3***
10	Norfolk 2 SW	36.2	10	Bridgeport Sikorsky Memorial	44.4

Rankings include 25 highest/lowest stations. If state has less than 25 stations, all stations are included. The period of record is 1980–2009. See User Guide for detailed explanation of data.

Annual Extreme Minimum Temperature

Highest

Rank	Station Name	°F
1	Bridgeport Sikorsky Memorial	-7
2	Storrs	***-12***
3	Groton	***-13***
4	Norwich Public Util Plant	-17
5	Burlington	-18
5	Danbury	***-18***
5	Stamford 5 N	***-18***
8	Hartford Bradley Int'l Arpt	-21
8	Norfolk 2 SW	-21
10	Falls Village	-27

Lowest

Rank	Station Name	°F
1	Falls Village	-27
2	Hartford Bradley Int'l Arpt	-21
2	Norfolk 2 SW	-21
4	Burlington	-18
4	Danbury	***-18***
4	Stamford 5 N	***-18***
7	Norwich Public Util Plant	-17
8	Groton	***-13***
9	Storrs	***-12***
10	Bridgeport Sikorsky Memorial	-7

July Mean Maximum Temperature

Highest

Rank	Station Name	°F
1	Stamford 5 N	85.5
2	Danbury	***84.9***
3	Hartford Bradley Int'l Arpt	84.5
4	Norwich Public Util Plant	83.8
5	Falls Village	83.3
6	Burlington	82.4
7	Bridgeport Sikorsky Memorial	82.0
8	Groton	80.4
9	Storrs	79.5
10	Norfolk 2 SW	77.8

Lowest

Rank	Station Name	°F
1	Norfolk 2 SW	77.8
2	Storrs	79.5
3	Groton	80.4
4	Bridgeport Sikorsky Memorial	82.0
5	Burlington	82.4
6	Falls Village	83.3
7	Norwich Public Util Plant	83.8
8	Hartford Bradley Int'l Arpt	84.5
9	Danbury	***84.9***
10	Stamford 5 N	85.5

Rankings include 25 highest/lowest stations. If state has less than 25 stations, all stations are included. The period of record is 1980–2009. See User Guide for detailed explanation of data.

January Mean Minimum Temperature

Highest Rank	Station Name	°F	Lowest Rank	Station Name	°F
1	Bridgeport Sikorsky Memorial	23.1	1	Norfolk 2 SW	13.0
2	Groton	21.0	2	Falls Village	14.1
3	Stamford 5 N	*19.5*	3	Burlington	15.3
4	Norwich Public Util Plant	18.8	4	Storrs	17.6
5	Danbury	*18.4*	5	Hartford Bradley Int'l Arpt	17.7
6	Hartford Bradley Int'l Arpt	17.7	6	Danbury	*18.4*
7	Storrs	17.6	7	Norwich Public Util Plant	18.8
8	Burlington	15.3	8	Stamford 5 N	*19.5*
9	Falls Village	14.1	9	Groton	21.0
10	Norfolk 2 SW	13.0	10	Bridgeport Sikorsky Memorial	23.1

Number of Days Annually Maximum Temperature ≥ 90°F

Highest Rank	Station Name	Days	Lowest Rank	Station Name	Days
1	Danbury	*17*	1	Norfolk 2 SW	1
1	Stamford 5 N	*17*	2	Storrs	*2*
3	Hartford Bradley Int'l Arpt	16	3	Groton	*4*
4	Norwich Public Util Plant	13	4	Bridgeport Sikorsky Memorial	6
5	Burlington	11	5	Burlington	11
5	Falls Village	11	5	Falls Village	11
7	Bridgeport Sikorsky Memorial	6	7	Norwich Public Util Plant	13
8	Groton	*4*	8	Hartford Bradley Int'l Arpt	16
9	Storrs	*2*	9	Danbury	*17*
10	Norfolk 2 SW	1	9	Stamford 5 N	*17*

Rankings include 25 highest/lowest stations. If state has less than 25 stations, all stations are included. The period of record is 1980–2009. See User Guide for detailed explanation of data.

Number of Days Annually Maximum Temperature ≤ 32°F

Highest

Rank	Station Name	Days
1	Norfolk 2 SW	58
2	Storrs	***37***
3	Falls Village	31
4	Burlington	30
4	Hartford Bradley Int'l Arpt	30
6	Danbury	***27***
7	Bridgeport Sikorsky Memorial	20
7	Norwich Public Util Plant	20
9	Groton	***19***
10	Stamford 5 N	***16***

Lowest

Rank	Station Name	Days
1	Stamford 5 N	***16***
2	Groton	***19***
3	Bridgeport Sikorsky Memorial	20
3	Norwich Public Util Plant	20
5	Danbury	***27***
6	Burlington	30
6	Hartford Bradley Int'l Arpt	30
8	Falls Village	31
9	Storrs	***37***
10	Norfolk 2 SW	58

Number of Days Annually Minimum Temperature ≤ 32°F

Highest

Rank	Station Name	Days
1	Norfolk 2 SW	156
2	Falls Village	155
3	Burlington	145
4	Danbury	***132***
5	Hartford Bradley Int'l Arpt	131
6	Norwich Public Util Plant	129
7	Storrs	***124***
8	Stamford 5 N	***122***
9	Groton	***110***
10	Bridgeport Sikorsky Memorial	98

Lowest

Rank	Station Name	Days
1	Bridgeport Sikorsky Memorial	98
2	Groton	***110***
3	Stamford 5 N	***122***
4	Storrs	***124***
5	Norwich Public Util Plant	129
6	Hartford Bradley Int'l Arpt	131
7	Danbury	***132***
8	Burlington	145
9	Falls Village	155
10	Norfolk 2 SW	156

Rankings include 25 highest/lowest stations. If state has less than 25 stations, all stations are included. The period of record is 1980–2009. See User Guide for detailed explanation of data.

Number of Days Annually Minimum Temperature ≤ 0°F

Highest			Lowest		
Rank	Station Name	Days	Rank	Station Name	Days
1	Norfolk 2 SW	11	1	Bridgeport Sikorsky Memorial	1
2	Falls Village	9	1	Groton	*1*
3	Burlington	5	3	Norwich Public Util Plant	2
3	Hartford Bradley Int'l Arpt	5	3	Stamford 5 N	*2*
3	Storrs	*5*	5	Danbury	*3*
6	Danbury	*3*	6	Burlington	5
7	Norwich Public Util Plant	2	6	Hartford Bradley Int'l Arpt	5
7	Stamford 5 N	*2*	6	Storrs	*5*
9	Bridgeport Sikorsky Memorial	1	9	Falls Village	9
9	Groton	*1*	10	Norfolk 2 SW	11

Number of Annual Heating Degree Days

Highest			Lowest		
Rank	Station Name	Num.	Rank	Station Name	Num.
1	Norfolk 2 SW	7,440	1	Bridgeport Sikorsky Memorial	5,368
2	Falls Village	6,510	2	Stamford 5 N	*5,451*
3	Burlington	6,359	3	Groton	*5,645*
4	Storrs	*6,319*	4	Norwich Public Util Plant	5,743
5	Hartford Bradley Int'l Arpt	5,978	5	Danbury	*5,902*
6	Danbury	*5,902*	6	Hartford Bradley Int'l Arpt	5,978
7	Norwich Public Util Plant	5,743	7	Storrs	*6,319*
8	Groton	*5,645*	8	Burlington	6,359
9	Stamford 5 N	*5,451*	9	Falls Village	6,510
10	Bridgeport Sikorsky Memorial	5,368	10	Norfolk 2 SW	7,440

Number of Annual Cooling Degree Days

Highest			Lowest		
Rank	Station Name	Num.	Rank	Station Name	Num.
1	Bridgeport Sikorsky Memorial	829	1	Norfolk 2 SW	342
2	Stamford 5 N	***804***	2	Storrs	***523***
3	Danbury	***791***	3	Falls Village	536
4	Hartford Bradley Int'l Arpt	771	4	Burlington	577
5	Norwich Public Util Plant	722	5	Groton	***615***
6	Groton	***615***	6	Norwich Public Util Plant	722
7	Burlington	577	7	Hartford Bradley Int'l Arpt	771
8	Falls Village	536	8	Danbury	***791***
9	Storrs	***523***	9	Stamford 5 N	***804***
10	Norfolk 2 SW	342	10	Bridgeport Sikorsky Memorial	829

Annual Precipitation

Highest			Lowest		
Rank	Station Name	Inches	Rank	Station Name	Inches
1	Norwich Public Util Plant	53.68	1	Bridgeport Sikorsky Memorial	42.59
2	Burlington	53.12	2	Falls Village	45.39
3	Norfolk 2 SW	52.91	3	Hartford Bradley Int'l Arpt	45.86
4	Stamford 5 N	***52.63***	4	Groton	***48.43***
5	Danbury	***52.12***	5	Storrs	***49.57***
6	Storrs	***49.57***	6	Danbury	***52.12***
7	Groton	***48.43***	7	Stamford 5 N	***52.63***
8	Hartford Bradley Int'l Arpt	45.86	8	Norfolk 2 SW	52.91
9	Falls Village	45.39	9	Burlington	53.12
10	Bridgeport Sikorsky Memorial	42.59	10	Norwich Public Util Plant	53.68

Rankings include 25 highest/lowest stations. If state has less than 25 stations, all stations are included. The period of record is 1980–2009. See User Guide for detailed explanation of data.

Annual Extreme Maximum Daily Precipitation

Highest			Lowest		
Rank	Station Name	Inches	Rank	Station Name	Inches
1	Danbury	***9.55***	1	Bridgeport Sikorsky Memorial	5.30
2	Falls Village	8.23	2	Storrs	***5.48***
3	Burlington	7.77	3	Hartford Bradley Int'l Arpt	5.88
4	Norfolk 2 SW	6.52	4	Norwich Public Util Plant	6.18
5	Groton	***6.30***	5	Groton	***6.30***
6	Norwich Public Util Plant	6.18	6	Norfolk 2 SW	6.52
7	Hartford Bradley Int'l Arpt	5.88	7	Burlington	7.77
8	Storrs	***5.48***	8	Falls Village	8.23
9	Bridgeport Sikorsky Memorial	5.30	9	Danbury	***9.55***

Number of Days Annually With ≥ 0.1 Inches of Precipitation

Highest			Lowest		
Rank	Station Name	Days	Rank	Station Name	Days
1	Norfolk 2 SW	91	1	Bridgeport Sikorsky Memorial	76
2	Danbury	***84***	2	Norwich Public Util Plant	78
3	Falls Village	82	3	Burlington	79
3	Stamford 5 N	***82***	3	Hartford Bradley Int'l Arpt	79
5	Storrs	***81***	5	Groton	***80***
6	Groton	***80***	6	Storrs	***81***
7	Burlington	79	7	Falls Village	82
7	Hartford Bradley Int'l Arpt	79	7	Stamford 5 N	***82***
9	Norwich Public Util Plant	78	9	Danbury	***84***
10	Bridgeport Sikorsky Memorial	76	10	Norfolk 2 SW	91

Number of Days Annually With ≥ 0.5 Inches of Precipitation

Highest Rank	Highest Station Name	Highest Days	Lowest Rank	Lowest Station Name	Lowest Days
1	Norfolk 2 SW	36	1	Bridgeport Sikorsky Memorial	28
2	Burlington	35	2	Falls Village	30
2	Norwich Public Util Plant	35	3	Hartford Bradley Int'l Arpt	31
2	Stamford 5 N	*35*	4	Groton	*33*
5	Danbury	*34*	5	Danbury	*34*
5	Storrs	*34*	5	Storrs	*34*
7	Groton	*33*	7	Burlington	35
8	Hartford Bradley Int'l Arpt	31	7	Norwich Public Util Plant	35
9	Falls Village	30	7	Stamford 5 N	*35*
10	Bridgeport Sikorsky Memorial	28	10	Norfolk 2 SW	36

Number of Days Annually With ≥ 1.0 Inches of Precipitation

Highest Rank	Highest Station Name	Highest Days	Lowest Rank	Lowest Station Name	Lowest Days
1	Burlington	14	1	Falls Village	11
1	Stamford 5 N	*14*	2	Bridgeport Sikorsky Memorial	12
1	Storrs	*14*	2	Groton	*12*
4	Danbury	*13*	2	Hartford Bradley Int'l Arpt	12
4	Norwich Public Util Plant	13	2	Norfolk 2 SW	12
6	Bridgeport Sikorsky Memorial	12	6	Danbury	*13*
6	Groton	*12*	6	Norwich Public Util Plant	13
6	Hartford Bradley Int'l Arpt	12	8	Burlington	14
6	Norfolk 2 SW	12	8	Stamford 5 N	*14*
10	Falls Village	11	8	Storrs	*14*

 Rankings include 25 highest/lowest stations. If state has less than 25 stations, all stations are included. The period of record is 1980–2009. See User Guide for detailed explanation of data.

Annual Snowfall

Highest

Rank	Station Name	Inches
1	Norfolk 2 SW	78.3
2	Hartford Bradley Int'l Arpt	*46.7*
3	Danbury	*46.1*
4	Stamford 5 N	*31.7*
5	Groton	*23.0*
6	Burlington	*22.2*
7	Falls Village	*21.6*

Lowest

Rank	Station Name	Inches
1	Falls Village	*21.6*
2	Burlington	*22.2*
3	Groton	*23.0*
4	Stamford 5 N	*31.7*
5	Danbury	*46.1*
6	Hartford Bradley Int'l Arpt	*46.7*
7	Norfolk 2 SW	78.3

Annual Maximum Snow Depth

Highest

Rank	Station Name	Inches
1	Norfolk 2 SW	40
2	Danbury	*36*
3	Groton	*19*

Lowest

Rank	Station Name	Inches
1	Groton	*19*
2	Danbury	*36*
3	Norfolk 2 SW	40

Rankings include 25 highest/lowest stations. If state has less than 25 stations, all stations are included. The period of record is 1980–2009. See User Guide for detailed explanation of data.

Number of Days Annually With ≥ 1.0 Inch Snow Depth

Highest			Lowest		
Rank	Station Name	Days	Rank	Station Name	Days
1	Norfolk 2 SW	100	1	Falls Village	*11*
2	Danbury	*46*	2	Groton	*21*
3	Norwich Public Util Plant	*23*	3	Norwich Public Util Plant	*23*
4	Groton	*21*	4	Danbury	*46*
5	Falls Village	*11*	5	Norfolk 2 SW	100

Rankings include 25 highest/lowest stations. If state has less than 25 stations, all stations are included. The period of record is 1980–2009. See User Guide for detailed explanation of data.

Significant Storm Events in Connecticut: 2000 – 2009

Location or County	Date	Type	Mag.	Deaths	Injuries	Property Damage ($mil.)	Crop Damage ($mil.)
Middlesex	05/10/00	Lightning	na	1	0	0.0	0.0
New Haven	06/02/00	Thunderstorm Wind	58 mph	1	0	0.0	0.0
Fairfield	08/11/00	Flash Flood	na	0	0	6.0	0.0
Hartford, Tolland, and Windham Counties	03/05/01	Heavy Snow	na	0	0	5.0	0.0
Hartford, Tolland, and Windham Counties	03/09/01	Heavy Snow	na	0	0	2.0	0.0
Fairfield	05/24/02	Wind	na	1	0	0.0	0.0
Fairfield, Middlesex, New Haven, and New London Counties	07/02/02	Excessive Heat	na	1	0	0.0	0.0
Fairfield, Middlesex, New Haven, and New London Counties	09/11/02	Wind	na	1	0	0.0	0.0
New Haven	10/19/02	Rip Currents	na	2	0	0.0	0.0
Hartford and Tolland Counties	11/16/02	Ice Storm	na	0	0	2.5	0.0
Northern Litchfield County	01/23/05	Winter Storm	na	1	0	0.0	0.0
North Central and Northeast Connecticut	10/15/05	Flood	na	2	0	6.0	0.0
New Haven	04/23/06	Flood	na	1	0	0.0	0.0
Fairfield	07/12/06	Tornado	F1	0	0	2.0	0.0
Fairfield	10/11/07	Flash Flood	na	0	0	2.0	0.0
New Haven	06/08/08	Lightning	na	1	4	0.0	0.0
Fairfield	09/06/08	Flash Flood	na	1	0	0.0	0.0
Southern Fairfield County	01/06/09	Winter Weather	na	1	1	0.0	0.0
Northern Fairfield, New Haven, and New London Counties	01/06/09	Ice Storm	na	1	3	0.0	0.0
Southern Litchfield County	12/29/09	High Wind	58 mph	1	0	0.0	0.0

Note: Deaths, injuries, and damages are date and location specific.

DELAWARE

PHYSICAL FEATURES. The State of Delaware is located on the east coast of the United States midway between the north and the south. Delaware lies in a north-south position, spanning a distance of 96 miles. The width increases from nine miles in the northern portion to 35 miles in the extreme southern portion. The State occupies the eastern and northern portion of the Delmarva Peninsula which is bounded by the Chesapeake Bay on the west and the Delaware Bay and Atlantic Ocean on the east. The total area of Delaware is 2,057 square miles.

Over 95 percent of the land area of the State is more or less flat and without topographic features; however, the extreme northern portion, about 120 square miles, which lies on the Piedmont, is undulating and hilly with elevations rising to 438 feet above mean sea level. This increase in elevation no doubt contributes to a slight decrease in local temperatures under certain circumstances.

GENERAL CLIMATE. Since the flow of the atmosphere in temperate latitudes is from west to east, the distribution of land and water masses, i.e., the expansive North American continent situated immediately to the west, predisposes the Delaware area to a continental type of climate. This type of climate in middle latitudes is marked by well-defined seasons. Winter is the dormant season for plant growth and is one of low temperature rather than drought. In spring and fall the changeability of the weather is a striking characteristic. It is occasioned by a rapid succession of warm and cold periods associated with storms, which generally move from a westerly direction over the eastern portion of the United States. Summers are warm to hot. The higher atmospheric humidity along the sea coast causes the summer heat to be more oppressive or sultry and the winter cold more raw and penetrating than in drier climates of the interior.

The topography of the eastern United States is characterized by the Appalachian Mountains, which extend along a northeast-southwest axis about 150 miles to the northwest of Delaware. To the west and northwest of Delaware, these mountains range in height from 2,000 to 3,000 feet above mean sea level and contribute to some slight tempering of the cold air masses which move rapidly out of the interior of the continent over the Delaware region in the winter.

A semipermanent high pressure area with a clockwise circulation virtually overspreads the entire Atlantic Ocean at middle latitudes and exerts a pronounced effect on the weather regimes of the east coast. During the winter season the Atlantic High (or Azores High) maintains an average position between latitude 30 N. and 33 N. and longitudes 25 W. and 35 W. and overspreads the eastern portion of the south Atlantic Ocean. As the summer season approaches, the Atlantic High moves westward and slightly northward to a mean position between latitudes 32 N. and 35 N. and longitudes 40 W. and 45 W. During this period it becomes more intense and widespread as the semipermanent low of the north Atlantic Ocean becomes smaller and weaker. In the summer location the Atlantic High dominates the flow of air over the eastern United States much of the time. A persistence of the Atlantic High in a westerly position in the vicinity of Bermuda results in a prolonged flow of moist, warm tropical air over the entire eastern United States. Weather in this type of air mass consists of scattered thunderstorms, considerable daytime cloudiness, and hot, sultry conditions. In the westerly position the High exerts blocking action on Lows which are forced to travel across more northerly latitudes. Persistence of this High over the eastern United States frequently results in drought conditions over the Delaware region, as the dry, subsiding air of the High prevents the formation of precipitation.

WINDS. Prevailing surface winds in northern Delaware blow from the northwesterly quadrant in all months except June, when southerly winds prevail. However, during the periods of May and July through September, winds come from the southwesterly quadrant a high proportion of the time. In southern Delaware surface winds prevail from the southwesterly quadrant from May through September and from the northwesterly quadrant from October through April.

Average wind speeds are higher during the period January through April, largely due to the rapid succession of well-developed storm systems which migrate from a westerly to easterly direction. During this period average wind speeds of about 10 miles per hour prevail. From July through October winds are somewhat lighter, averaging from seven to nine miles per hour.

During the fall, winter, and spring seasons, it is not unusual to experience brief windstorms associated with violent, fast-moving cold fronts with gusts from 50 to 60 m.p.h. In the summer, rare occurrences of violent windstorms are associated with severe thunderstorms. From June through October, it is estimated that wind speeds of more than 75 m.p.h. could occur anywhere in Delaware during the rare event of a hurricane traversing or passing very near the State.

Delaware lies in the mean zone of the westerlies in the winter and slightly south of the tracks followed by most of the migrating cyclones in their movement from some point in the United States to the region of semipermanent low pressure in the Iceland or North Atlantic area. Cyclones which have their origin in the south Pacific coastal region, Texas, or the Gulf or South Atlantic States have a greater tendency to follow a track through the Delaware region. Storms of the south Pacific coast, Texas, east Gulf, and sometimes of the south Atlantic bring the heaviest widespread rains to the Delaware area.

TEMPERATURE. The difference in latitude of northern Delaware and southern Delaware contributes in some part to the difference in mean temperature between these two regions of the State. The mean temperature difference of 3 to 4°F. between northern and southern portions in winter and 1 to 2°F. in summer is largely but not entirely due to the variation in solar radiational heating. In the extreme northern portion where elevations range from 300 to 400 feet on the higher hills, altitude is a controlling factor, although a small one, and reduces temperatures by approximately 1 on the average as compared to the nearby lower terrain.

In order for ocean currents to have a direct temperature control, the winds must be prevailing onshore. The relatively frequent occurrence of easterly winds associated with cyclonic storms to the southeast brings about advection of air off the mild waters and consequently tends to raise the normal winter temperatures and lower the summer temperatures. Therefore, mean winter temperatures of Delaware are roughly 5°F. higher than for regions of the continental interior at the same latitude.

The climate of Delaware is humid, temperate, with hot summers and mild winters. The winter climate is intermediate between the cold of the northeast and the mild weather of the south. The average frost penetration ranges from about five inches in southern Delaware to about 10 inches in northern Delaware. Summer weather is characterized by considerable warm weather, including at least several hot, humid periods. However, nights are usually quite comfortable. The average length of the growing (frost-free) season ranges from about 175 to 195 days.

PRECIPITATION. The average annual precipitation ranges from 44 inches in northern Delaware to 47 inches in southern Delaware. The monthly distribution is fairly uniform throughout the year, with July and August the months with heaviest amounts. Precipitation in the summer season is less dependable and more variable than in winter. The seasonal increase in evapotranspiration during the summer results in a rapid loss of soil moisture and contributes to the development of drought conditions. Flooding occurs infrequently, and results largely from tides pushed by strong easterly winds. The passage through the area of storms of tropical origin, usually during the late summer or fall, with their high winds and intense rains constitute the most serious flood threat.

The mean snowfall is 18 inches in northern Delaware and 14 inches in southern Delaware. The snow season runs from December through March, with a few light flurries in some years as early as November or late October and as late as early April. Heaviest snowfalls in Delaware generally occur in February and March.

STORMS. Thunderstorms occur at a given station on the average of 30 to 33 days per year. The Atlantic coastal region has fewer thunderstorms than interior portions, on the average. They have been observed in every month of the year; however, July is the month with the greatest frequency of thunderstorms, on the average. Hail is uncommon in Delaware. The frequency of occurrence of tornadoes in Delaware is estimated at about one in two or three years, on the average.

Average relative humidity in Delaware is lowest in winter and early spring, and highest in the late summer and early fall. February and March have average relative humidities of about 60 to 65 percent, whereas August, September, and October have average relative humidities of about 75 to 80 percent.

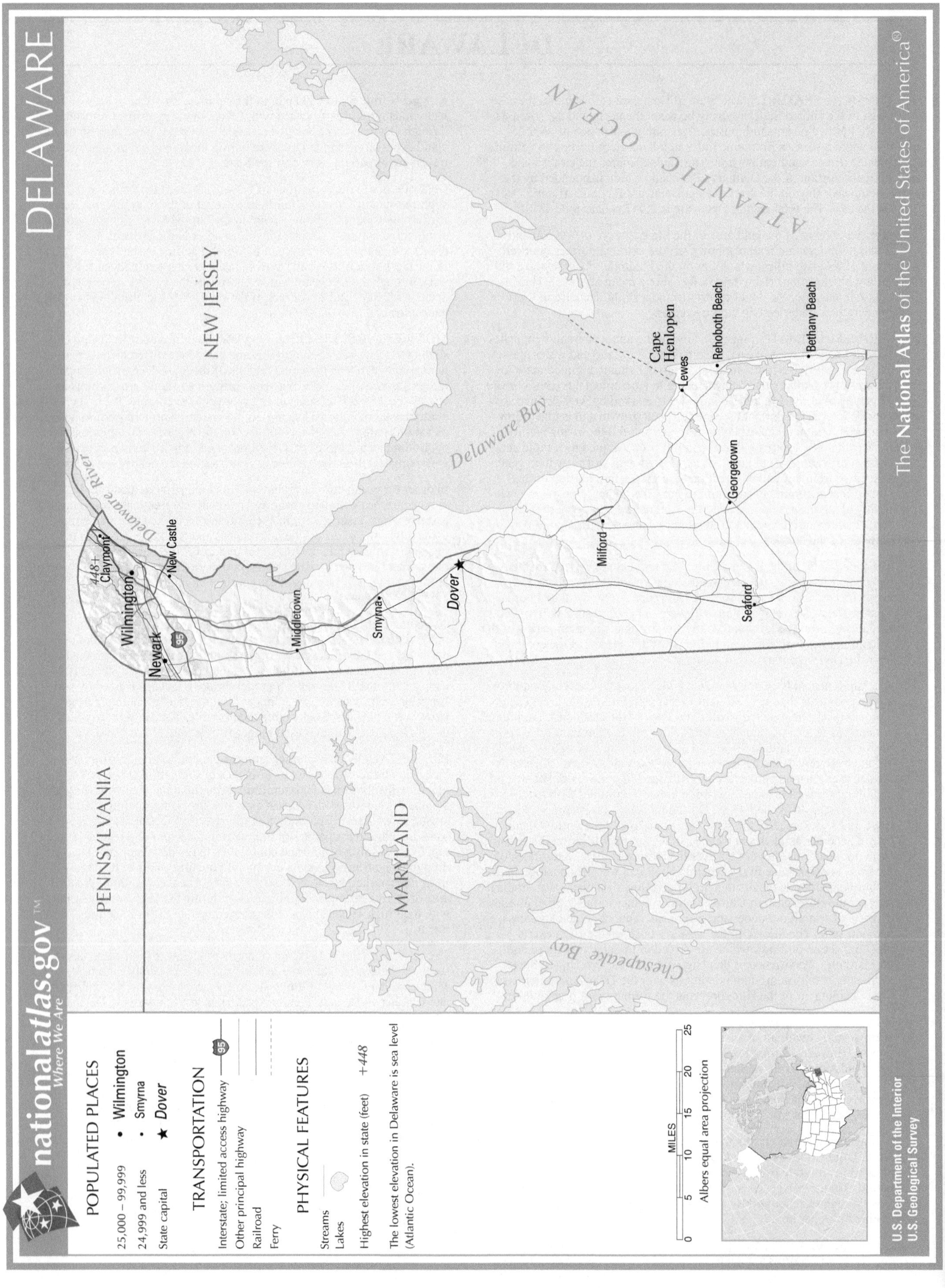
DELAWARE
nationalatlas.gov™
Where We Are
POPULATED PLACES
25,000 – 99,999 • Wilmington
24,999 and less • Smyrna
State capital ★ Dover
TRANSPORTATION
Interstate; limited access highway
Other principal highway
Railroad
Ferry
PHYSICAL FEATURES
Streams
Lakes
Highest elevation in state (feet) +448
The lowest elevation in Delaware is sea level (Atlantic Ocean).
MILES
0 5 10 15 20 25
Albers equal area projection
U.S. Department of the Interior
U.S. Geological Survey
The National Atlas of the United States of America®
PENNSYLVANIA
NEW JERSEY
MARYLAND
ATLANTIC OCEAN
Delaware Bay
Delaware River
Chesapeake Bay
Wilmington
Newark
Claymont
New Castle
Middletown
Smyrna
Dover
Milford
Georgetown
Seaford
Lewes
Cape Henlopen
Rehoboth Beach
Bethany Beach
448+
95

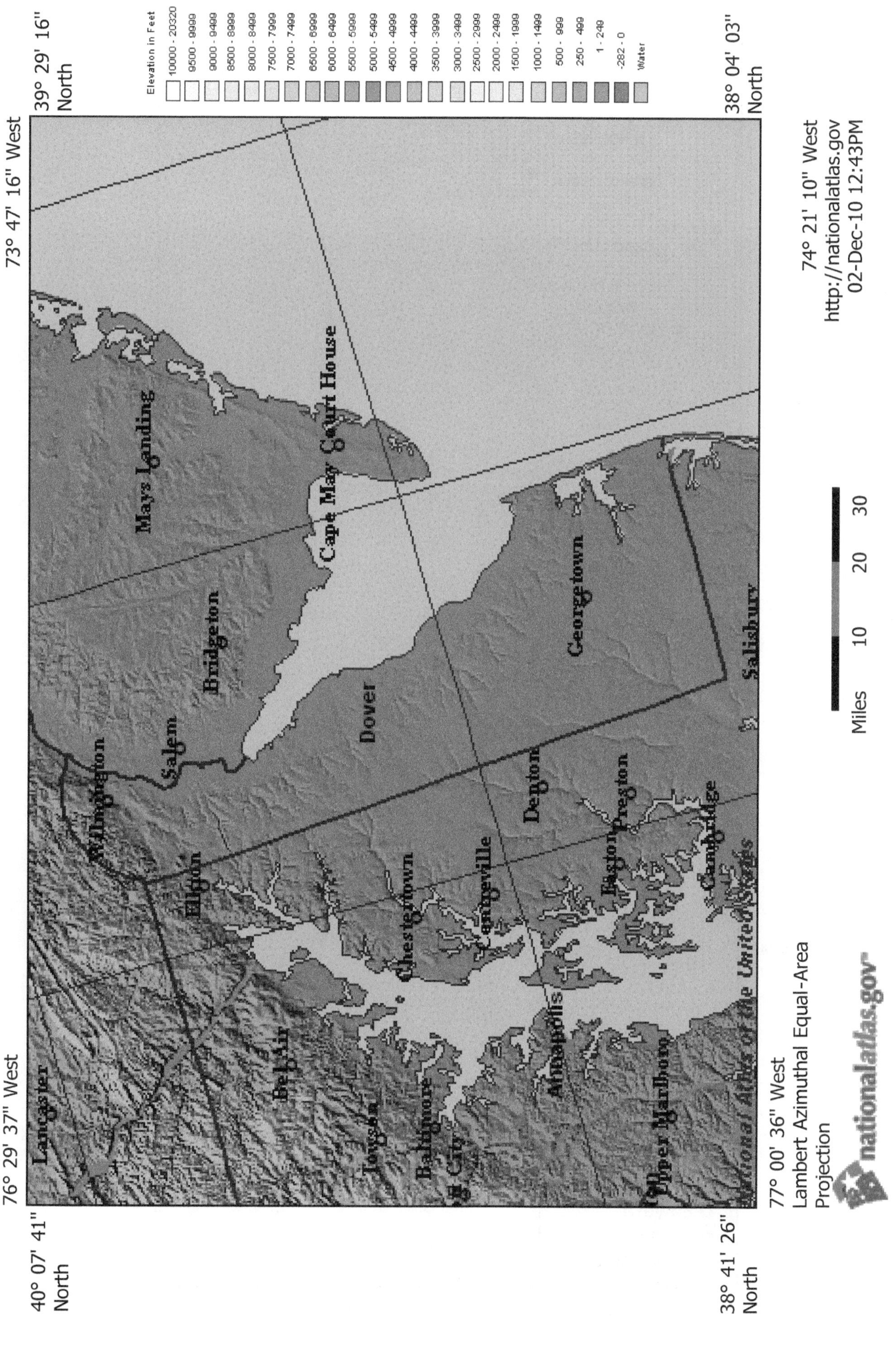
Elevation in Feet
10000 - 20320
9500 - 9999
9000 - 9499
8500 - 8999
8000 - 8499
7500 - 7999
7000 - 7499
6500 - 6999
6000 - 6499
5500 - 5999
5000 - 5499
4500 - 4999
4000 - 4499
3500 - 3999
3000 - 3499
2500 - 2999
2000 - 2499
1500 - 1999
1000 - 1499
500 - 999
250 - 499
1 - 249
-282 - 0
Water
39° 29' 16" North
73° 47' 16" West
38° 04' 03" North
74° 21' 10" West
http://nationalatlas.gov
02-Dec-10 12:43PM
40° 07' 41" North
76° 29' 37" West
38° 41' 26" North
77° 00' 36" West
Lambert Azimuthal Equal-Area Projection
Miles 10 20 30
Mays Landing
Cape May Court House
Bridgeton
Salem
Wilmington
Dover
Georgetown
Salisbury
Denton
Preston
Cambridge
Easton
Elkton
Centreville
Chestertown
Annapolis
Bel Air
Baltimore
Towson
Lancaster
Upper Marlboro
National Atlas of the United States
nationalatlas.gov

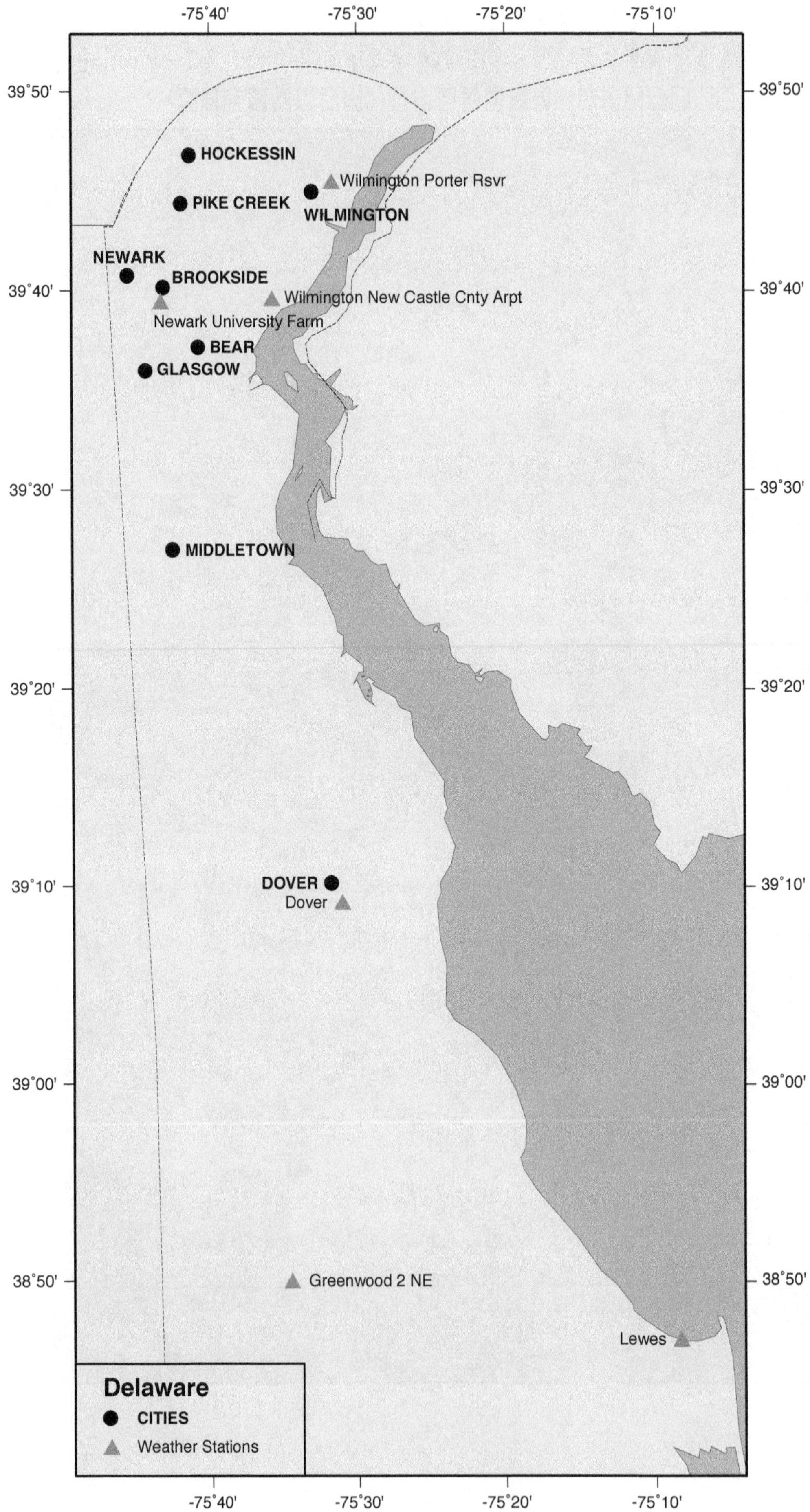
-75°40'
-75°30'
-75°20'
-75°10'
39°50'
39°40'
39°30'
39°20'
39°10'
39°00'
38°50'
HOCKESSIN
Wilmington Porter Rsvr
PIKE CREEK
WILMINGTON
NEWARK
BROOKSIDE
Wilmington New Castle Cnty Arpt
Newark University Farm
BEAR
GLASGOW
MIDDLETOWN
DOVER
Dover
Greenwood 2 NE
Lewes
Delaware
CITIES
Weather Stations

Delaware Weather Stations by County

County	Station Name
Kent	Dover
New Castle	Newark University Farm Wilmington New Castle Cnty Arpt Wilmington Porter Rsvr
Sussex	Greenwood 2 NE Lewes

See User Guide for station inclusion criteria.

Delaware Weather Stations by City

City	Station Name	Miles
Bear	Newark University Farm	4.0
	Wilmington New Castle Cnty Arpt	5.5
	Wilmington Porter Rsvr	12.9
	Marcus Hook, PA	19.6
	Octoraro Lake, PA	23.0
Brookside	Newark University Farm	0.9
	Wilmington New Castle Cnty Arpt	6.3
	Wilmington Porter Rsvr	11.9
	Conowingo Dam, MD	23.9
	Coatesville 2 W, PA	23.1
	Marcus Hook, PA	19.0
	Octoraro Lake, PA	19.8
Dover	Dover	1.3
	Greenwood 2 NE	24.3
Glasgow	Newark University Farm	4.5
	Wilmington New Castle Cnty Arpt	8.7
	Wilmington Porter Rsvr	15.8
	Aberdeen Phillips Field, MD	24.6
	Conowingo Dam, MD	23.0
	Marcus Hook, PA	22.7
	Octoraro Lake, PA	21.5
Hockessin	Newark University Farm	8.3
	Wilmington New Castle Cnty Arpt	9.2
	Wilmington Porter Rsvr	8.2
	Coatesville 2 W, PA	16.9
	Marcus Hook, PA	14.6
	Octoraro Lake, PA	19.3
	Philadelphia Int'l Arpt, PA	24.8
Middletown	Dover	23.5
	Newark University Farm	14.7
	Wilmington New Castle Cnty Arpt	15.9
	Wilmington Porter Rsvr	23.6
	Aberdeen Phillips Field, MD	24.3
Newark	Newark University Farm	1.6
	Wilmington New Castle Cnty Arpt	8.5
	Wilmington Porter Rsvr	13.4
	Conowingo Dam, MD	21.8
	Coatesville 2 W, PA	21.7
	Marcus Hook, PA	20.4
	Octoraro Lake, PA	17.6
Pike Creek	Newark University Farm	5.2
	Wilmington New Castle Cnty Arpt	7.1
	Wilmington Porter Rsvr	9.0
	Coatesville 2 W, PA	19.3
	Marcus Hook, PA	15.9
	Octoraro Lake, PA	19.2
Wilmington	Newark University Farm	11.2
	Wilmington New Castle Cnty Arpt	6.3
	Wilmington Porter Rsvr	1.6
	Seabrook Farms, NJ	24.2
	Coatesville 2 W, PA	23.2
	Marcus Hook, PA	8.6
	Philadelphia Int'l Arpt, PA	18.8

Note: Miles is the distance between the geographic center of the city and the weather station.

See User Guide for station inclusion criteria.

Delaware Weather Stations by Elevation

Feet	Station Name
270	Wilmington Porter Rsvr
89	Newark University Farm
74	Wilmington New Castle Cnty Arpt
44	Greenwood 2 NE
29	Dover
15	Lewes

See User Guide for station inclusion criteria.

Wilmington Arpt

Delaware is part of the Atlantic Coastal Plain consisting mainly of flat low land with many marshes. Small streams and tidal estuaries comprise the drainage of the State. Wilmington, at the northern end of the State, marks the beginning of low rolling hills extending northward and northwestward into Pennsylvania. The Delaware River, the Delaware Bay, and the Atlantic Ocean are along the eastern boundary of the State. The broad Chesapeake Bay lies 35 miles, or less, to the west of the western boundary of nearly the entire State. These large water areas considerably influence the climate of the Wilmington, Delaware region.

Summers are warm and humid, winters are usually mild. During the summer maximum temperatures are usually in the 80s. The temperature reaches 100 degrees on the average once in six years. During January, the coldest month of the year, the daily average temperature is 32 degrees. Temperatures of zero may be expected once in four years. Most of the winter precipitation falls as rain. Seasonal snowfall has been as little as one inch, and as much as 50 inches. Snow is frequently mixed with rain and sleet, and seldom remains on the ground more than a few days.

The proximity of large water areas and the inflow of southerly winds cause the relative humidity to be quite high all year. During the summer months the relative humidity is approximately 75 percent. Fog is relatively frequent and may occur in any month. Light southeast winds blowing up the Delaware Bay favor the formation of fog. Light north-northeast winds bring in smoke from Philadelphia and from the heavy industry area located along the Delaware River north of Wilmington.

Rainfall distribution throughout the year is fairly uniform, however, the greatest amounts normally come during the summer months. Mostly, the summer rainfall comes in the form of thunderstorms. Moisture deficiencies for crops occur occasionally, but severe droughts are rare. During the fall, winter, and spring seasons, much of the rainfall comes from storms forming over the southern states or the South Atlantic and moving northward along the coast. During the late summer and early fall, hurricanes occasionally cause heavy rainfall, but winds seldom reach hurricane force in Wilmington. Heavy rains occasionally cause minor flooding. Strong easterly and southeasterly winds sometimes cause high tides in the Delaware Bay and the Delaware River.

Based on the 1951-1980 period, the average first occurrence of 32 degrees Fahrenheit in the fall is October 29 and the average last occurrence in the spring is April 13.

Wilmington Arpt *New Castle County* Elevation: 74 ft. Latitude: 39° 40' N Longitude: 75° 36' W

	JAN	FEB	MAR	APR	MAY	JUN	JUL	AUG	SEP	OCT	NOV	DEC	YEAR
Mean Maximum Temp. (°F)	40.3	43.7	52.3	63.5	73.0	81.6	86.1	84.4	77.6	66.2	55.6	44.7	64.1
Mean Temp. (°F)	32.4	35.1	42.8	53.2	62.8	71.9	76.8	75.2	67.9	56.1	46.5	36.7	54.8
Mean Minimum Temp. (°F)	24.5	26.5	33.3	42.9	52.4	62.2	67.4	66.0	58.2	46.0	37.2	28.6	45.4
Extreme Maximum Temp. (°F)	71	78	86	94	96	100	100	100	100	90	80	75	100
Extreme Minimum Temp. (°F)	-14	0	2	18	33	44	48	43	37	26	17	-7	-14
Days Maximum Temp. ≥ 90°F	0	0	0	0	1	4	9	6	2	0	0	0	22
Days Maximum Temp. ≤ 32°F	7	4	1	0	0	0	0	0	0	0	0	4	16
Days Minimum Temp. ≤ 32°F	24	21	14	2	0	0	0	0	0	1	10	21	93
Days Minimum Temp. ≤ 0°F	0	0	0	0	0	0	0	0	0	0	0	0	0
Heating Degree Days (base 65°F)	1,003	838	683	357	130	13	0	2	45	289	550	870	4,780
Cooling Degree Days (base 65°F)	0	0	1	11	67	228	373	326	138	20	0	0	1,164
Mean Precipitation (in.)	3.00	2.51	3.97	3.56	3.88	3.95	4.48	3.24	4.17	3.36	3.10	3.43	42.65
Maximum Precipitation (in.)*	8.4	7.0	7.5	6.8	7.4	7.5	12.6	12.1	9.5	8.0	7.8	7.9	54.7
Minimum Precipitation (in.)*	0.5	0.8	0.8	0.3	0.2	0.2	0.2	0.3	0.8	0.2	0.5	0.2	24.9
Extreme Maximum Daily Precip. (in.)	2.51	2.15	3.21	4.36	2.72	3.58	6.63	2.66	8.29	2.56	2.02	2.28	8.29
Days With ≥ 0.1" Precipitation	6	5	7	6	7	7	7	5	5	5	6	6	72
Days With ≥ 0.5" Precipitation	2	2	3	3	3	3	3	2	3	2	2	3	31
Days With ≥ 1.0" Precipitation	1	0	1	1	1	1	1	1	1	1	1	1	11
Mean Snowfall (in.)	6.7	***6.4***	2.1	***0.3***	***trace***	***trace***	***trace***	***0.0***	***0.0***	***trace***	***0.4***	3.3	***19.2***
Maximum Snowfall (in.)*	21	28	20	3	trace	0	0	0	0	3	12	22	49
Maximum 24-hr. Snowfall (in.)*	12	15	13	2	trace	0	0	0	0	3	7	12	15
Maximum Snow Depth (in.)	***13***	***25***	***9***	***2***	***trace***	***trace***	***trace***	***0***	***0***	***0***	***6***	***13***	***25***
Days With ≥ 1.0" Snow Depth	***7***	***5***	***2***	***0***	***0***	***0***	***0***	***0***	***0***	***0***	***0***	***3***	***17***
Thunderstorm Days*	< 1	< 1	1	2	4	6	6	6	2	1	1	< 1	29
Foggy Days*	12	11	13	12	15	15	16	17	16	15	13	13	168
Predominant Sky Cover*	OVR	OVR	OVR	OVR	OVR	OVR	OVR	OVR	OVR	OVR	OVR	OVR	OVR
Mean Relative Humidity 7am (%)*	75	74	74	73	76	78	80	83	85	84	80	76	78
Mean Relative Humidity 4pm (%)*	60	56	52	50	53	54	55	57	56	55	58	61	55
Mean Dewpoint (°F)*	22	23	29	39	50	60	65	64	58	46	36	26	43
Prevailing Wind Direction*	WNW	NW	NW	WNW	S	S	S	S	NW	NW	NW	NW	NW
Prevailing Wind Speed (mph)*	13	13	14	12	10	9	9	9	8	9	12	12	10
Maximum Wind Gust (mph)*	67	58	71	62	71	61	66	60	64	58	59	69	71

Note: (*) Period of record is 1948-1995

Dover *Kent County* Elevation: 29 ft. Latitude: 39° 09' N Longitude: 75° 31' W

	JAN	FEB	MAR	APR	MAY	JUN	JUL	AUG	SEP	OCT	NOV	DEC	YEAR
Mean Maximum Temp. (°F)	44.0	47.2	54.8	65.5	74.5	83.0	87.2	85.5	79.3	68.9	58.8	48.2	66.4
Mean Temp. (°F)	35.6	38.1	45.1	54.9	64.1	73.1	77.7	76.3	69.7	58.8	49.3	39.7	56.9
Mean Minimum Temp. (°F)	27.2	28.9	35.4	44.3	53.6	63.2	68.2	67.0	60.0	48.5	39.7	31.2	47.3
Extreme Maximum Temp. (°F)	74	77	86	97	97	100	101	100	98	90	81	75	101
Extreme Minimum Temp. (°F)	-5	2	9	17	36	45	52	45	40	27	17	1	-5
Days Maximum Temp. ≥ 90°F	0	0	0	0	1	5	11	7	2	0	0	0	26
Days Maximum Temp. ≤ 32°F	5	2	0	0	0	0	0	0	0	0	0	2	9
Days Minimum Temp. ≤ 32°F	22	19	12	2	0	0	0	0	0	1	7	18	81
Days Minimum Temp. ≤ 0°F	0	0	0	0	0	0	0	0	0	0	0	0	0
Heating Degree Days (base 65°F)	905	755	614	314	107	9	0	1	28	221	469	777	4,200
Cooling Degree Days (base 65°F)	0	0	3	18	86	258	402	356	175	34	3	0	1,335
Mean Precipitation (in.)	3.43	2.98	4.38	3.94	4.27	4.13	4.00	4.32	4.19	3.34	3.42	3.59	45.99
Extreme Maximum Daily Precip. (in.)	2.41	2.30	3.33	3.87	4.01	3.81	5.00	5.20	5.30	2.95	2.65	2.90	5.30
Days With ≥ 0.1" Precipitation	6	6	7	8	8	7	7	6	6	5	6	7	79
Days With ≥ 0.5" Precipitation	2	2	3	3	3	3	2	3	3	2	3	2	31
Days With ≥ 1.0" Precipitation	1	1	1	1	1	1	1	1	1	1	1	1	12
Mean Snowfall (in.)	4.9	5.2	0.6	0.0	0.0	0.0	0.0	0.0	0.0	0.0	0.2	2.3	13.2
Maximum Snow Depth (in.)	16	25	4	0	0	0	0	0	0	0	5	18	25
Days With ≥ 1.0" Snow Depth	4	4	0	0	0	0	0	0	0	0	0	2	10

Greenwood 2 NE *Sussex County* Elevation: 44 ft. Latitude: 38° 49' N Longitude: 75° 35' W

	JAN	FEB	MAR	APR	MAY	JUN	JUL	AUG	SEP	OCT	NOV	DEC	YEAR
Mean Maximum Temp. (°F)	44.3	46.1	54.6	64.6	73.7	82.4	86.5	84.9	78.6	68.1	58.0	47.4	65.8
Mean Temp. (°F)	35.6	36.8	44.2	53.6	62.6	72.1	76.6	74.9	68.2	56.9	48.0	38.3	55.6
Mean Minimum Temp. (°F)	26.8	27.4	33.7	42.5	51.5	61.7	66.5	64.8	57.8	45.7	37.9	29.1	45.4
Extreme Maximum Temp. (°F)	76	76	87	93	94	101	100	100	95	91	81	77	101
Extreme Minimum Temp. (°F)	-8	-4	2	22	32	43	44	42	38	25	9	3	-8
Days Maximum Temp. ≥ 90°F	0	0	0	0	1	4	10	6	1	0	0	0	22
Days Maximum Temp. ≤ 32°F	5	3	1	0	0	0	0	0	0	0	0	3	12
Days Minimum Temp. ≤ 32°F	22	21	15	4	0	0	0	0	0	2	10	21	95
Days Minimum Temp. ≤ 0°F	0	0	0	0	0	0	0	0	0	0	0	0	0
Heating Degree Days (base 65°F)	904	790	642	349	136	15	0	2	38	268	506	820	4,470
Cooling Degree Days (base 65°F)	0	0	3	13	68	234	366	314	140	24	2	0	1,164
Mean Precipitation (in.)	3.61	2.81	4.19	3.59	3.78	3.85	4.27	3.98	4.32	3.55	3.57	3.71	45.23
Extreme Maximum Daily Precip. (in.)	3.83	2.08	3.38	3.10	2.58	4.08	3.37	3.00	6.41	2.75	2.60	2.66	6.41
Days With ≥ 0.1" Precipitation	7	6	7	7	7	7	6	6	6	6	6	7	78
Days With ≥ 0.5" Precipitation	3	2	3	3	2	3	2	3	2	3	3	3	32
Days With ≥ 1.0" Precipitation	1	1	1	1	1	1	1	1	1	1	1	1	12
Mean Snowfall (in.)	3.7	4.4	1.3	0.3	0.0	0.0	0.0	0.0	0.0	0.0	0.4	2.0	12.1
Maximum Snow Depth (in.)	16	12	12	3	0	0	0	0	0	0	5	8	16
Days With ≥ 1.0" Snow Depth	3	5	1	0	0	0	0	0	0	0	0	3	12

Lewes *Sussex County* Elevation: 15 ft. Latitude: 38° 46' N Longitude: 75° 08' W

	JAN	FEB	MAR	APR	MAY	JUN	JUL	AUG	SEP	OCT	NOV	DEC	YEAR
Mean Maximum Temp. (°F)	45.2	47.6	54.9	65.3	74.5	83.0	86.9	85.2	79.1	69.2	59.4	49.6	66.7
Mean Temp. (°F)	37.4	39.3	45.9	55.5	64.6	73.7	78.2	76.8	70.8	60.2	50.9	41.7	57.9
Mean Minimum Temp. (°F)	29.5	31.0	36.8	45.6	54.6	64.4	69.5	68.4	62.5	51.2	42.4	33.8	49.1
Extreme Maximum Temp. (°F)	73	86	89	92	97	102	101	101	98	89	83	77	102
Extreme Minimum Temp. (°F)	-11	3	11	18	35	41	53	47	41	30	20	3	-11
Days Maximum Temp. ≥ 90°F	0	0	0	0	1	7	11	7	1	0	0	0	27
Days Maximum Temp. ≤ 32°F	4	2	0	0	0	0	0	0	0	0	0	2	8
Days Minimum Temp. ≤ 32°F	19	16	9	1	0	0	0	0	0	0	4	14	63
Days Minimum Temp. ≤ 0°F	0	0	0	0	0	0	0	0	0	0	0	0	0
Heating Degree Days (base 65°F)	851	719	591	300	100	9	0	1	16	183	422	715	3,907
Cooling Degree Days (base 65°F)	0	0	5	21	93	278	418	374	197	42	5	1	1,434
Mean Precipitation (in.)	3.67	2.97	4.27	3.72	3.63	3.52	4.64	4.70	4.09	3.63	3.62	3.86	46.32
Extreme Maximum Daily Precip. (in.)	3.41	1.76	2.73	3.77	3.71	5.00	4.14	6.30	5.10	2.45	2.85	2.54	6.30
Days With ≥ 0.1" Precipitation	6	6	7	7	7	6	7	6	5	5	6	7	75
Days With ≥ 0.5" Precipitation	3	2	3	3	3	2	3	3	2	3	3	3	33
Days With ≥ 1.0" Precipitation	1	1	1	1	1	1	1	1	1	1	1	1	12
Mean Snowfall (in.)	3.0	4.0	0.9	0.0	0.0	0.0	0.0	0.0	0.0	0.0	0.2	1.2	9.3
Maximum Snow Depth (in.)	15	9	6	0	0	0	0	0	0	0	5	4	15
Days With ≥ 1.0" Snow Depth	0	0	0	0	0	0	0	0	0	0	0	0	0

Newark University Farm *New Castle County* Elevation: 89 ft. Latitude: 39° 40' N Longitude: 75° 44' W

	JAN	FEB	MAR	APR	MAY	JUN	JUL	AUG	SEP	OCT	NOV	DEC	YEAR
Mean Maximum Temp. (°F)	41.8	45.7	54.1	65.8	75.8	84.1	88.1	86.2	79.4	68.1	57.2	46.0	66.0
Mean Temp. (°F)	32.9	36.0	43.2	53.6	63.7	72.3	77.1	75.2	68.3	56.4	46.6	37.1	55.2
Mean Minimum Temp. (°F)	24.0	26.2	32.3	41.4	51.7	60.4	66.1	64.2	57.1	44.7	36.1	28.1	44.3
Extreme Maximum Temp. (°F)	72	76	89	94	96	99	105	103	100	89	80	75	105
Extreme Minimum Temp. (°F)	-10	-1	4	14	33	39	41	42	36	26	15	-6	-10
Days Maximum Temp. ≥ 90°F	0	0	0	0	2	6	13	8	2	0	0	0	31
Days Maximum Temp. ≤ 32°F	5	3	0	0	0	0	0	0	0	0	0	3	11
Days Minimum Temp. ≤ 32°F	25	21	17	4	0	0	0	0	0	2	11	21	101
Days Minimum Temp. ≤ 0°F	1	0	0	0	0	0	0	0	0	0	0	0	1
Heating Degree Days (base 65°F)	987	815	670	347	110	12	0	2	43	279	545	859	4,669
Cooling Degree Days (base 65°F)	0	0	1	12	77	237	381	326	148	20	1	0	1,203
Mean Precipitation (in.)	3.11	2.63	4.39	3.52	4.32	3.75	4.67	3.55	4.62	3.29	3.51	3.51	44.87
Extreme Maximum Daily Precip. (in.)	2.21	na	2.89	2.31	2.62	2.74	6.22	3.08	8.67	3.35	2.74	3.42	na
Days With ≥ 0.1" Precipitation	6	5	8	7	8	6	7	6	5	5	6	6	75
Days With ≥ 0.5" Precipitation	2	2	3	2	3	2	3	2	3	2	2	2	28
Days With ≥ 1.0" Precipitation	1	0	1	1	1	1	1	1	1	1	1	1	11
Mean Snowfall (in.)	4.3	1.5	1.4	trace	0.0	0.0	0.0	0.0	0.0	0.0	0.1	0.9	8.2
Maximum Snow Depth (in.)	16	16	14	trace	0	na	0	0	0	0	na	6	na
Days With ≥ 1.0" Snow Depth	4	3	1	0	0	0	0	0	0	0	0	2	10

The period of record for all cooperative weather station data is 1980 – 2009. See User Guide for detailed explanation of data.

Wilmington Porter Rsvr *New Castle County* Elevation: 270 ft. Latitude: 39° 46' N Longitude: 75° 32' W

	JAN	FEB	MAR	APR	MAY	JUN	JUL	AUG	SEP	OCT	NOV	DEC	YEAR
Mean Maximum Temp. (°F)	39.3	42.6	50.9	62.3	72.1	80.8	85.1	83.4	76.1	64.8	54.3	43.6	62.9
Mean Temp. (°F)	32.2	34.9	42.3	53.0	62.8	71.8	76.5	74.9	67.6	56.1	46.3	36.5	54.6
Mean Minimum Temp. (°F)	25.2	27.2	33.7	43.6	53.4	62.8	67.8	66.4	58.9	47.3	38.2	29.3	46.1
Extreme Maximum Temp. (°F)	70	74	87	94	94	97	100	100	97	86	80	73	100
Extreme Minimum Temp. (°F)	-9	2	5	19	38	45	52	43	41	28	18	-1	-9
Days Maximum Temp. ≥ 90°F	0	0	0	0	1	3	7	5	1	0	0	0	17
Days Maximum Temp. ≤ 32°F	8	5	1	0	0	0	0	0	0	0	0	4	18
Days Minimum Temp. ≤ 32°F	24	21	13	2	0	0	0	0	0	0	8	20	88
Days Minimum Temp. ≤ 0°F	0	0	0	0	0	0	0	0	0	0	0	0	0
Heating Degree Days (base 65°F)	1,009	845	698	364	129	13	0	2	47	288	556	878	4,829
Cooling Degree Days (base 65°F)	0	0	2	10	67	225	363	317	131	18	0	0	1,133
Mean Precipitation (in.)	3.71	2.82	4.57	4.23	4.40	4.27	5.11	3.69	4.79	3.88	3.48	4.00	48.95
Extreme Maximum Daily Precip. (in.)	2.77	1.91	3.77	2.66	3.62	4.25	6.22	3.96	9.30	3.12	2.32	2.80	9.30
Days With ≥ 0.1" Precipitation	7	6	7	7	7	7	7	6	6	6	6	6	78
Days With ≥ 0.5" Precipitation	3	2	3	3	3	3	3	2	3	3	3	3	34
Days With ≥ 1.0" Precipitation	1	1	1	1	1	1	2	1	1	1	1	1	13
Mean Snowfall (in.)	5.8	5.0	2.0	0.1	0.0	0.0	0.0	0.0	0.0	0.0	0.3	1.9	15.1
Maximum Snow Depth (in.)	22	19	9	1	0	0	0	0	0	0	1	11	22
Days With ≥ 1.0" Snow Depth	4	4	1	0	0	0	0	0	0	0	0	2	11

The period of record for all cooperative weather station data is 1980 – 2009. See User Guide for detailed explanation of data.

Delaware Weather Station Rankings

Annual Extreme Maximum Temperature

Highest			Lowest		
Rank	Station Name	°F	Rank	Station Name	°F
1	Newark University Farm	***105***	1	Wilmington New Castle Cnty Arpt	100
2	Lewes	102	1	Wilmington Porter Rsvr	100
3	Dover	101	3	Dover	101
3	Greenwood 2 NE	***101***	3	Greenwood 2 NE	***101***
5	Wilmington New Castle Cnty Arpt	100	5	Lewes	102
5	Wilmington Porter Rsvr	100	6	Newark University Farm	***105***

Annual Mean Maximum Temperature

Highest			Lowest		
Rank	Station Name	°F	Rank	Station Name	°F
1	Lewes	66.7	1	Wilmington Porter Rsvr	62.9
2	Dover	66.4	2	Wilmington New Castle Cnty Arpt	64.1
3	Newark University Farm	***66.0***	3	Greenwood 2 NE	***65.8***
4	Greenwood 2 NE	***65.8***	4	Newark University Farm	***66.0***
5	Wilmington New Castle Cnty Arpt	64.1	5	Dover	66.4
6	Wilmington Porter Rsvr	62.9	6	Lewes	66.7

Annual Mean Temperature

Highest Rank	Station Name	°F	Lowest Rank	Station Name	°F
1	Lewes	57.9	1	Wilmington Porter Rsvr	54.6
2	Dover	56.9	2	Wilmington New Castle Cnty Arpt	54.8
3	Greenwood 2 NE	***55.6***	3	Newark University Farm	***55.2***
4	Newark University Farm	***55.2***	4	Greenwood 2 NE	***55.6***
5	Wilmington New Castle Cnty Arpt	54.8	5	Dover	56.9
6	Wilmington Porter Rsvr	54.6	6	Lewes	57.9

Annual Mean Minimum Temperature

Highest Rank	Station Name	°F	Lowest Rank	Station Name	°F
1	Lewes	49.2	1	Newark University Farm	***44.4***
2	Dover	47.3	2	Wilmington New Castle Cnty Arpt	45.4
3	Wilmington Porter Rsvr	46.1	3	Greenwood 2 NE	***45.5***
4	Greenwood 2 NE	***45.5***	4	Wilmington Porter Rsvr	46.1
5	Wilmington New Castle Cnty Arpt	45.4	5	Dover	47.3
6	Newark University Farm	***44.4***	6	Lewes	49.2

 Rankings include 25 highest/lowest stations. If state has less than 25 stations, all stations are included. The period of record is 1980–2009. See User Guide for detailed explanation of data.

Annual Extreme Minimum Temperature

Highest Rank	Station Name	°F	Lowest Rank	Station Name	°F
1	Dover	-5	1	Wilmington New Castle Cnty Arpt	-14
2	Greenwood 2 NE	***-8***	2	Lewes	-11
3	Wilmington Porter Rsvr	-9	3	Newark University Farm	***-10***
4	Newark University Farm	***-10***	4	Wilmington Porter Rsvr	-9
5	Lewes	-11	5	Greenwood 2 NE	***-8***
6	Wilmington New Castle Cnty Arpt	-14	6	Dover	-5

July Mean Maximum Temperature

Highest Rank	Station Name	°F	Lowest Rank	Station Name	°F
1	Newark University Farm	***88.1***	1	Wilmington Porter Rsvr	85.2
2	Dover	87.2	2	Wilmington New Castle Cnty Arpt	86.1
3	Lewes	86.9	3	Greenwood 2 NE	***86.5***
4	Greenwood 2 NE	***86.5***	4	Lewes	86.9
5	Wilmington New Castle Cnty Arpt	86.1	5	Dover	87.2
6	Wilmington Porter Rsvr	85.2	6	Newark University Farm	***88.1***

Rankings include 25 highest/lowest stations. If state has less than 25 stations, all stations are included. The period of record is 1980–2009. See User Guide for detailed explanation of data.

January Mean Minimum Temperature

Highest			Lowest		
Rank	**Station Name**	**°F**	**Rank**	**Station Name**	**°F**
1	Lewes	29.5	1	Newark University Farm	***24.0***
2	Dover	27.2	2	Wilmington New Castle Cnty Arpt	24.5
3	Greenwood 2 NE	***26.8***	3	Wilmington Porter Rsvr	25.2
4	Wilmington Porter Rsvr	25.2	4	Greenwood 2 NE	***26.8***
5	Wilmington New Castle Cnty Arpt	24.5	5	Dover	27.2
6	Newark University Farm	***24.0***	6	Lewes	29.5

Number of Days Annually Maximum Temperature ≥ 90°F

Highest			Lowest		
Rank	**Station Name**	**Days**	**Rank**	**Station Name**	**Days**
1	Newark University Farm	***31***	1	Wilmington Porter Rsvr	17
2	Lewes	27	2	Greenwood 2 NE	***22***
3	Dover	26	2	Wilmington New Castle Cnty Arpt	22
4	Greenwood 2 NE	***22***	4	Dover	26
4	Wilmington New Castle Cnty Arpt	22	5	Lewes	27
6	Wilmington Porter Rsvr	17	6	Newark University Farm	***31***

Rankings include 25 highest/lowest stations. If state has less than 25 stations, all stations are included. The period of record is 1980–2009. See User Guide for detailed explanation of data.

Number of Days Annually Maximum Temperature ≤ 32°F

Highest Rank	Station Name	Days	Lowest Rank	Station Name	Days
1	Wilmington Porter Rsvr	18	1	Lewes	8
2	Wilmington New Castle Cnty Arpt	16	2	Dover	9
3	Greenwood 2 NE	*12*	3	Newark University Farm	*11*
4	Newark University Farm	*11*	4	Greenwood 2 NE	*12*
5	Dover	9	5	Wilmington New Castle Cnty Arpt	16
6	Lewes	8	6	Wilmington Porter Rsvr	18

Number of Days Annually Minimum Temperature ≤ 32°F

Highest Rank	Station Name	Days	Lowest Rank	Station Name	Days
1	Newark University Farm	*101*	1	Lewes	63
2	Greenwood 2 NE	*95*	2	Dover	81
3	Wilmington New Castle Cnty Arpt	93	3	Wilmington Porter Rsvr	88
4	Wilmington Porter Rsvr	88	4	Wilmington New Castle Cnty Arpt	93
5	Dover	81	5	Greenwood 2 NE	*95*
6	Lewes	63	6	Newark University Farm	*101*

Rankings include 25 highest/lowest stations. If state has less than 25 stations, all stations are included. The period of record is 1980–2009. See User Guide for detailed explanation of data.

Number of Days Annually Minimum Temperature ≤ 0°F

Highest			Lowest		
Rank	**Station Name**	**Days**	**Rank**	**Station Name**	**Days**
1	Newark University Farm	*1*	1	Dover	0
2	Dover	0	1	Greenwood 2 NE	*0*
2	Greenwood 2 NE	*0*	1	Lewes	0
2	Lewes	0	1	Wilmington New Castle Cnty Arpt	0
2	Wilmington New Castle Cnty Arpt	0	1	Wilmington Porter Rsvr	0
2	Wilmington Porter Rsvr	0	6	Newark University Farm	*1*

Number of Annual Heating Degree Days

Highest			Lowest		
Rank	**Station Name**	**Num.**	**Rank**	**Station Name**	**Num.**
1	Wilmington Porter Rsvr	4,829	1	Lewes	3,907
2	Wilmington New Castle Cnty Arpt	4,780	2	Dover	4,200
3	Newark University Farm	*4,669*	3	Greenwood 2 NE	*4,470*
4	Greenwood 2 NE	*4,470*	4	Newark University Farm	*4,669*
5	Dover	4,200	5	Wilmington New Castle Cnty Arpt	4,780
6	Lewes	3,907	6	Wilmington Porter Rsvr	4,829

Rankings include 25 highest/lowest stations. If state has less than 25 stations, all stations are included. The period of record is 1980–2009. See User Guide for detailed explanation of data.

Number of Annual Cooling Degree Days

Highest			Lowest		
Rank	**Station Name**	**Num.**	**Rank**	**Station Name**	**Num.**
1	Lewes	1,434	1	Wilmington Porter Rsvr	1,133
2	Dover	1,335	2	Greenwood 2 NE	***1,164***
3	Newark University Farm	***1,203***	2	Wilmington New Castle Cnty Arpt	1,164
4	Greenwood 2 NE	***1,164***	4	Newark University Farm	***1,203***
4	Wilmington New Castle Cnty Arpt	1,164	5	Dover	1,335
6	Wilmington Porter Rsvr	1,133	6	Lewes	1,434

Annual Precipitation

Highest			Lowest		
Rank	**Station Name**	**Inches**	**Rank**	**Station Name**	**Inches**
1	Wilmington Porter Rsvr	48.95	1	Wilmington New Castle Cnty Arpt	42.65
2	Lewes	46.32	2	Newark University Farm	***44.87***
3	Dover	45.99	3	Greenwood 2 NE	***45.23***
4	Greenwood 2 NE	***45.23***	4	Dover	45.99
5	Newark University Farm	***44.87***	5	Lewes	46.32
6	Wilmington New Castle Cnty Arpt	42.65	6	Wilmington Porter Rsvr	48.95

Annual Extreme Maximum Daily Precipitation

Highest			Lowest		
Rank	Station Name	Inches	Rank	Station Name	Inches
1	Wilmington Porter Rsvr	9.30	1	Dover	5.30
2	Wilmington New Castle Cnty Arpt	8.29	2	Lewes	6.30
3	Greenwood 2 NE	***6.41***	3	Greenwood 2 NE	***6.41***
4	Lewes	6.30	4	Wilmington New Castle Cnty Arpt	8.29
5	Dover	5.30	5	Wilmington Porter Rsvr	9.30

Number of Days Annually With ≥ 0.1 Inches of Precipitation

Highest			Lowest		
Rank	Station Name	Days	Rank	Station Name	Days
1	Dover	79	1	Wilmington New Castle Cnty Arpt	72
2	Greenwood 2 NE	***78***	2	Lewes	75
2	Wilmington Porter Rsvr	78	2	Newark University Farm	***75***
4	Lewes	75	4	Greenwood 2 NE	***78***
4	Newark University Farm	***75***	4	Wilmington Porter Rsvr	78
6	Wilmington New Castle Cnty Arpt	72	6	Dover	79

 Rankings include 25 highest/lowest stations. If state has less than 25 stations, all stations are included. The period of record is 1980–2009. See User Guide for detailed explanation of data.

Number of Days Annually With ≥ 0.5 Inches of Precipitation

Highest			Lowest		
Rank	Station Name	Days	Rank	Station Name	Days
1	Wilmington Porter Rsvr	34	1	Newark University Farm	*28*
2	Lewes	33	2	Dover	31
3	Greenwood 2 NE	*32*	2	Wilmington New Castle Cnty Arpt	31
4	Dover	31	4	Greenwood 2 NE	*32*
4	Wilmington New Castle Cnty Arpt	31	5	Lewes	33
6	Newark University Farm	*28*	6	Wilmington Porter Rsvr	34

Number of Days Annually With ≥ 1.0 Inches of Precipitation

Highest			Lowest		
Rank	Station Name	Days	Rank	Station Name	Days
1	Wilmington Porter Rsvr	13	1	Newark University Farm	*11*
2	Dover	12	1	Wilmington New Castle Cnty Arpt	11
2	Greenwood 2 NE	*12*	3	Dover	12
2	Lewes	12	3	Greenwood 2 NE	*12*
5	Newark University Farm	*11*	3	Lewes	12
5	Wilmington New Castle Cnty Arpt	11	6	Wilmington Porter Rsvr	13

Rankings include 25 highest/lowest stations. If state has less than 25 stations, all stations are included. The period of record is 1980–2009. See User Guide for detailed explanation of data.

Annual Snowfall

Highest			Lowest		
Rank	Station Name	Inches	Rank	Station Name	Inches
1	Wilmington New Castle Cnty Arpt	***19.2***	1	Newark University Farm	***8.2***
2	Wilmington Porter Rsvr	15.1	2	Lewes	9.3
3	Dover	13.2	3	Greenwood 2 NE	***12.1***
4	Greenwood 2 NE	***12.1***	4	Dover	13.2
5	Lewes	9.3	5	Wilmington Porter Rsvr	15.1
6	Newark University Farm	***8.2***	6	Wilmington New Castle Cnty Arpt	***19.2***

Annual Maximum Snow Depth

Highest			Lowest		
Rank	Station Name	Inches	Rank	Station Name	Inches
1	Dover	25	1	Lewes	15
1	Wilmington New Castle Cnty Arpt	***25***	2	Greenwood 2 NE	***16***
3	Wilmington Porter Rsvr	22	3	Wilmington Porter Rsvr	22
4	Greenwood 2 NE	***16***	4	Dover	25
5	Lewes	15	4	Wilmington New Castle Cnty Arpt	***25***

 Rankings include 25 highest/lowest stations. If state has less than 25 stations, all stations are included. The period of record is 1980–2009. See User Guide for detailed explanation of data.

Number of Days Annually With ≥ 1.0 Inch Snow Depth

Highest			Lowest		
Rank	**Station Name**	**Days**	**Rank**	**Station Name**	**Days**
1	Wilmington New Castle Cnty Arpt	*17*	1	Lewes	0
2	Greenwood 2 NE	*12*	2	Dover	10
3	Wilmington Porter Rsvr	11	2	Newark University Farm	*10*
4	Dover	10	4	Wilmington Porter Rsvr	11
4	Newark University Farm	*10*	5	Greenwood 2 NE	*12*
6	Lewes	0	6	Wilmington New Castle Cnty Arpt	*17*

Rankings include 25 highest/lowest stations. If state has less than 25 stations, all stations are included. The period of record is 1980–2009. See User Guide for detailed explanation of data.

Significant Storm Events in Delaware: 2000 – 2009

Location or County	Date	Type	Mag.	Deaths	Injuries	Property Damage ($mil.)	Crop Damage ($mil.)
Sussex	08/11/01	Flash Flood	na	0	0	1.1	0.0
Sussex	08/25/01	Rip Currents	na	1	0	0.0	0.0
Sussex	09/29/02	Rip Currents	na	1	0	0.0	0.0
Kent, Sussex and New Castle Counties	02/16/03	Winter Storm	na	0	0	4.4	0.0
Coastal Areas, Kent and Inland Sussex County	02/17/03	Astronomical High Tide	na	0	0	1.0	0.0
New Castle	09/15/03	Flash Flood	na	0	1	16.1	0.0
Coastal Areas, Kent and Inland Sussex County	09/18/03	Tropical Storm	na	0	0	17.7	0.0
New Castle County	09/18/03	High Wind	58 mph	0	0	9.5	0.0
New Castle	09/28/04	Tornado	F2	0	0	1.0	0.0
Kent, Sussex and New Castle Counties	12/01/04	Strong Wind	53 mph	1	1	0.1	0.0
Sussex	09/05/05	Rip Current	na	1	0	0.0	0.0
Sussex	06/25/06	Flash Flood	na	0	0	1.0	0.0
Kent, Sussex and New Castle Counties	08/01/06	Excessive Heat	na	2	5	0.0	0.0
Kent, Sussex and New Castle Counties	02/06/07	Extreme Cold/Wind Chill	na	1	1	0.0	0.0
Kent and New Castle Counties	02/13/07	Winter Storm	na	1	0	0.0	0.0
Kent and New Castle Counties	02/25/07	Winter Storm	na	2	0	0.0	0.0
Coastal Areas and Inland Sussex County	11/12/09	Coastal Flood	na	0	0	40.0	0.0

Note: Deaths, injuries, and damages are date and location specific.

FLORIDA

PHYSICAL FEATURES. Florida, situated between latitudes 24° 30' and 31° N., and longitudes 80° and 87° 30' W., is largely a lowland peninsula comprising about 54,100 square miles of land area and is surrounded on three sides by the waters of the Atlantic Ocean and the Gulf of Mexico. Countless shallow lakes, which exist particularly on the peninsula and range in size from small cypress ponds to that of Lake Okeechobee, account for approximately 4,400 square miles of additional water area.

No point in the State is more than 70 miles from salt water, and the highest natural land in the Northwest Division is only 345 feet above sea level. Coastal areas are low and flat and are indented by many small bays or inlets. Many small islands dot the shorelines. The elevation of most of the interior ranges from 50 to 100 feet above sea level, though gentle hills in the interior of the peninsula and across the northern and western portions of the State rise above 200 feet.

A large portion of the southern one-third of the peninsula is the swampland known as the Everglades. An ill-defined divide of low, rolling hills, extending north-to-south near the middle of the peninsula and terminating north of Lake Okeechobee, gives rise to most peninsula streams, chains of lakes, and many springs. Stream gradients are slight and often insufficient to handle the runoff following heavy rainfall. Consequently, there are sizable areas of swamp and marshland near these streams.

GENERAL CLIMATE. Climate is probably Florida's greatest natural resource. General climatic conditions range from a zone of transition between temperate and subtropical conditions in the extreme northern interior portion of the State to the tropical conditions found on the Florida Keys. The chief factors of climatic control are: latitude, proximity to the Atlantic Ocean and Gulf of Mexico, and numerous inland lakes.

Summers throughout the State are long, warm, and relatively humid; winters, although punctuated with periodic invasions of cool to occasionally cold air from the north, are mild because of the southern latitude and relatively warm adjacent ocean waters. The Gulf Stream, which flows around the western tip of Cuba, through the Straits of Florida, and northward along the lower east coast, exerts a warming influence to the southern east coast largely because the predominate wind direction is from the east. Coastal weather stations throughout the State average slightly warmer in winter and cooler in summer than do inland weather stations at the same latitude.

Florida enjoys abundant rainfall. Except for the northwestern portion of the State, the average year can be divided into two seasons—the so-called "rainy season" and the long, relatively dry season. On the peninsula, generally more than one-half of the precipitation for an average year can be expected to fall during the four-month period, June through September. In northwest Florida, there is a secondary rainfall maximum in late winter and in early spring.

The summer heat is tempered by sea breezes along the coast and by frequent afternoon or early evening thunderstorms in all areas. During the warm season, sea breezes are felt almost daily within several miles of the coast and occasionally 20 to 30 miles inland. Thundershowers, which on the average occur about one-half of the days in summer, frequently are accompanied by as much as a rapid 10 to 20°F. drop in temperature, resulting in comfortable weather for the remainder of the day. Gentle breezes occur almost daily in all areas and serve to mitigate further the oppressiveness that otherwise would accompany the prevailing summer temperature and humidity conditions. Because most of the large-scale wind patterns affecting Florida have passed over water surfaces, hot drying winds seldom occur.

Most of the summer rainfall is derived from "local" showers or thundershowers. Many weather stations average more than 80 thundershowers per year, and some average more than 100. Showers are often heavy, usually lasting only one or two hours, and generally occur near the hottest part of the day. The more severe thundershowers are occasionally attended by hail or locally strong winds which may inflict serious local damage to crops and property. Day-long summer rains are usually associated with tropical disturbances and are infrequent. Even in the wet season, the rainfall duration is generally less than 10 percent of the time.

DROUGHTS. Florida is not immune from drought, even though annual rainfall amounts are relatively large. Prolonged periods of deficient rainfall are occasionally experienced even during the time of the expected rainy season. Several such dry periods, in the course of one or two years, can lead to significantly lowered water tables and lake levels which, in turn, may cause serious water shortages for those communities that depend upon lakes and shallow wells for their water supply. Statewide droughts during summer are rare, but it is not unusual during a drought in one portion of the State for other portions to receive generous rainfall. In a few instances, individual weather stations have experienced periods of a month or more without rainfall.

SNOW. Snowfall in Florida is unusual, although measurable amounts have fallen in the northern portions at irregular intervals, and a trace of snow has been recorded as far south as Fort Myers.

WIND. Prevailing winds over the southern peninsula are southeast and east. Over the remainder of the State, wind directions are influenced locally by convectional forces inland and by the land-and-sea-breeze-effect near the coast. Consequently, prevailing directions are somewhat erratic, but, in general, follow a pattern from the north in winter and from the south in summer. The windiest months are March and April. High local winds of short duration occur occasionally in connection with thunderstorms in summer and with cold fronts moving across the State in other seasons. Tornadoes, funnel clouds, and waterspouts also occur, averaging 10 to 15 in a year. Tornadoes have occurred in all seasons, but are most frequent in spring; they also occur in connection with tropical storms. Generally, tornado paths in Florida are short. Occasionally, waterspouts come inland, but they usually dissipate soon after reaching land and affect only very small areas.

TROPICAL STORMS. Storms that produce high winds and are often destructive are usually tropical in origin. Florida, jutting out into the ocean between the subtropical Atlantic and the Gulf of Mexico, is the most exposed of all States to these storms. In particular, hurricanes can approach from the Atlantic Ocean to the east, from the Caribbean Sea to the south, and from the Gulf of Mexico to the west.

The vulnerability of the State to tropical storms varies with the progress of the hurricane season. In August and early September, tropical storms normally approach the State from the east or southeast, but as the season progresses into late September and October, the region of maximum hurricane activity (insofar as Florida is concerned) shifts to the western Caribbean. Most of those storms that move into Florida approach the State from the south or southwest, entering the Keys, the Miami area, or along the west coast. Some of the world's heaviest rainfalls have occurred within tropical cyclones. Rainfall over 20 inches in 24 hours is not uncommon. The intensity of the rainfall, however, does not seem to bear any relation to the intensity of the wind circulation.

OTHER CLIMATIC ELEMENTS. The climate of Florida is humid. Inland areas with greater temperature extremes enjoy slightly lower relative humidity, especially during times of hot weather. On the average, variations in relative humidity from one place to another are small; humidities range from about 50 to 65 percent during the afternoon hours to about 85 to 95 percent during the night and early morning hours.

Heavy fogs are usually confined to the night and early morning hours in the late fall, winter, and early spring months. On the average, they occur about 35 to 40 days in a year over the extreme northern portion; about 25 to 30 days in a year over the central portion; and less than 10 days in a year over the extreme southern portion of the State. These fogs usually dissipate or thin soon after sunrise; heavy daytime fog is seldom observed in Florida.

Florida has been nicknamed the Sunshine State. Sunshine measurements made at widely separated stations in the State indicate the sun shines about two-thirds of the possible sunlight hours during the year, ranging from slightly more than 60 percent of possible in December and January to more than 70 percent of possible in April and May. In general, southern Florida enjoys a higher percentage of possible sunshine hours than does northern Florida. The length of day operates to Florida's advantage. In winter, when sunshine is highly valued, the sun can shine longer in Florida than in the more northern latitudes. In summer, the situation reverses itself with longer days returning to the north.

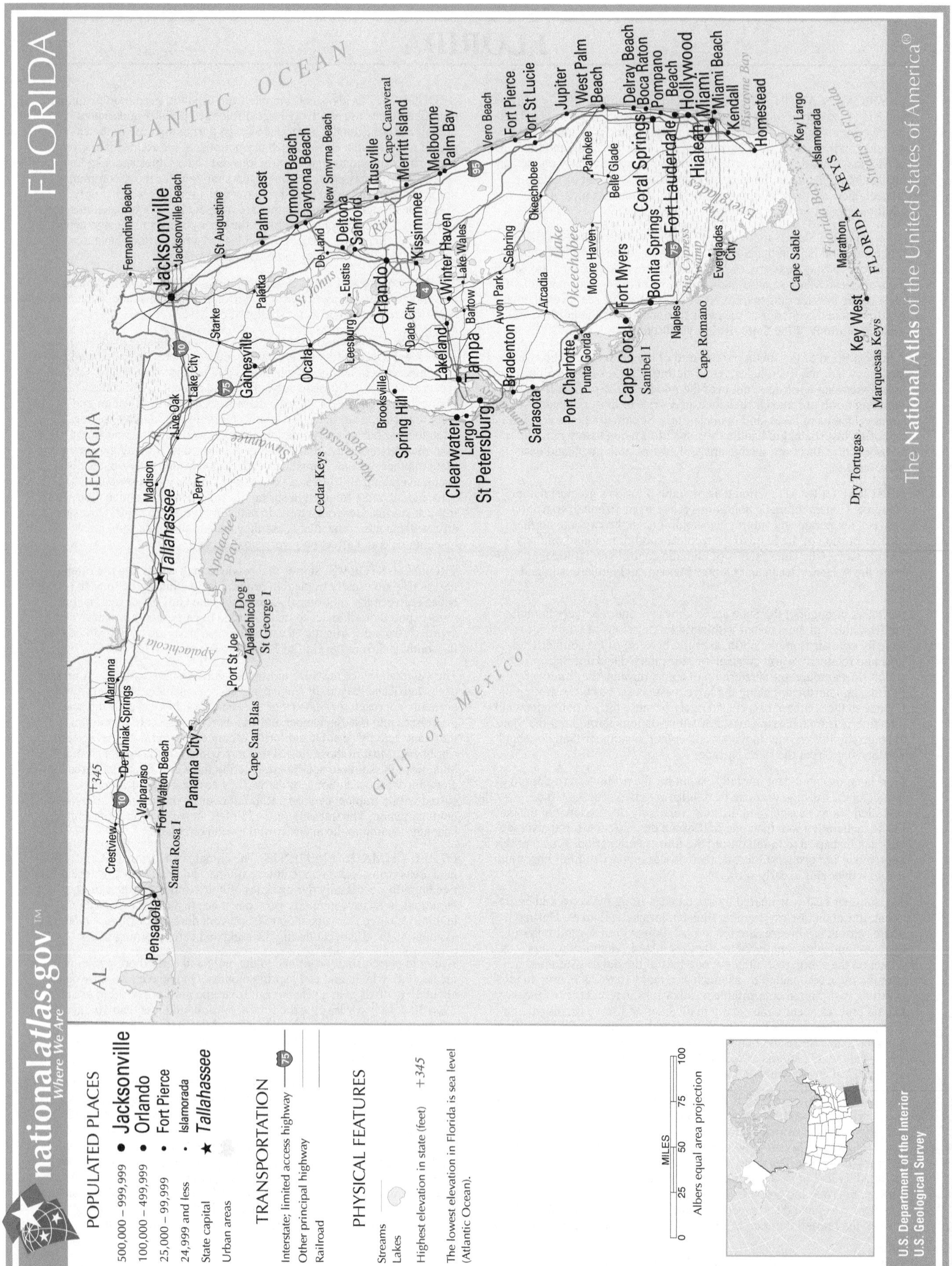
FLORIDA
nationalatlas.gov™
Where We Are
POPULATED PLACES
500,000 – 999,999 Jacksonville
100,000 – 499,999 Orlando
25,000 – 99,999 Fort Pierce
24,999 and less Islamorada
State capital Tallahassee
Urban areas
TRANSPORTATION
Interstate; limited access highway
Other principal highway
Railroad
PHYSICAL FEATURES
Streams
Lakes
Highest elevation in state (feet) +345
The lowest elevation in Florida is sea level (Atlantic Ocean).
MILES
0 25 50 75 100
Albers equal area projection
U.S. Department of the Interior
U.S. Geological Survey
The National Atlas of the United States of America®
ATLANTIC OCEAN
Gulf of Mexico
GEORGIA
AL
Pensacola
Crestview
Valparaiso
Fort Walton Beach
Santa Rosa I
De Funiak Springs
Panama City
Marianna
Cape San Blas
Port St Joe
Apalachicola
St George I
Dog I
Apalachicola R
Tallahassee
Apalachee Bay
Madison
Perry
Live Oak
Lake City
Suwannee
Cedar Keys
Waccasassa Bay
Gainesville
Starke
Jacksonville
Fernandina Beach
Jacksonville Beach
St Augustine
Palatka
Palm Coast
Ormond Beach
Daytona Beach
New Smyrna Beach
Ocala
Leesburg
Eustis
De Land
Deltona
Sanford
St Johns River
Orlando
Titusville
Cape Canaveral
Merritt Island
Kissimmee
Melbourne
Palm Bay
Brooksville
Spring Hill
Dade City
Lakeland
Tampa
Clearwater
Largo
St Petersburg
Tampa Bay
Bradenton
Sarasota
Bartow
Winter Haven
Lake Wales
Avon Park
Sebring
Vero Beach
Fort Pierce
Port St Lucie
Okeechobee
Lake Okeechobee
Arcadia
Port Charlotte
Punta Gorda
Cape Coral
Sanibel I
Fort Myers
Moore Haven
Pahokee
Belle Glade
Jupiter
West Palm Beach
Delray Beach
Boca Raton
Pompano Beach
Coral Springs
Fort Lauderdale
Hollywood
Hialeah
Miami
Miami Beach
Kendall
Homestead
Biscayne Bay
Bonita Springs
Naples
Big Cypress Swamp
The Everglades
Everglades City
Cape Romano
Cape Sable
Florida Bay
Key Largo
Islamorada
Marathon
FLORIDA KEYS
Straits of Florida
Key West
Marquesas Keys
Dry Tortugas
+345

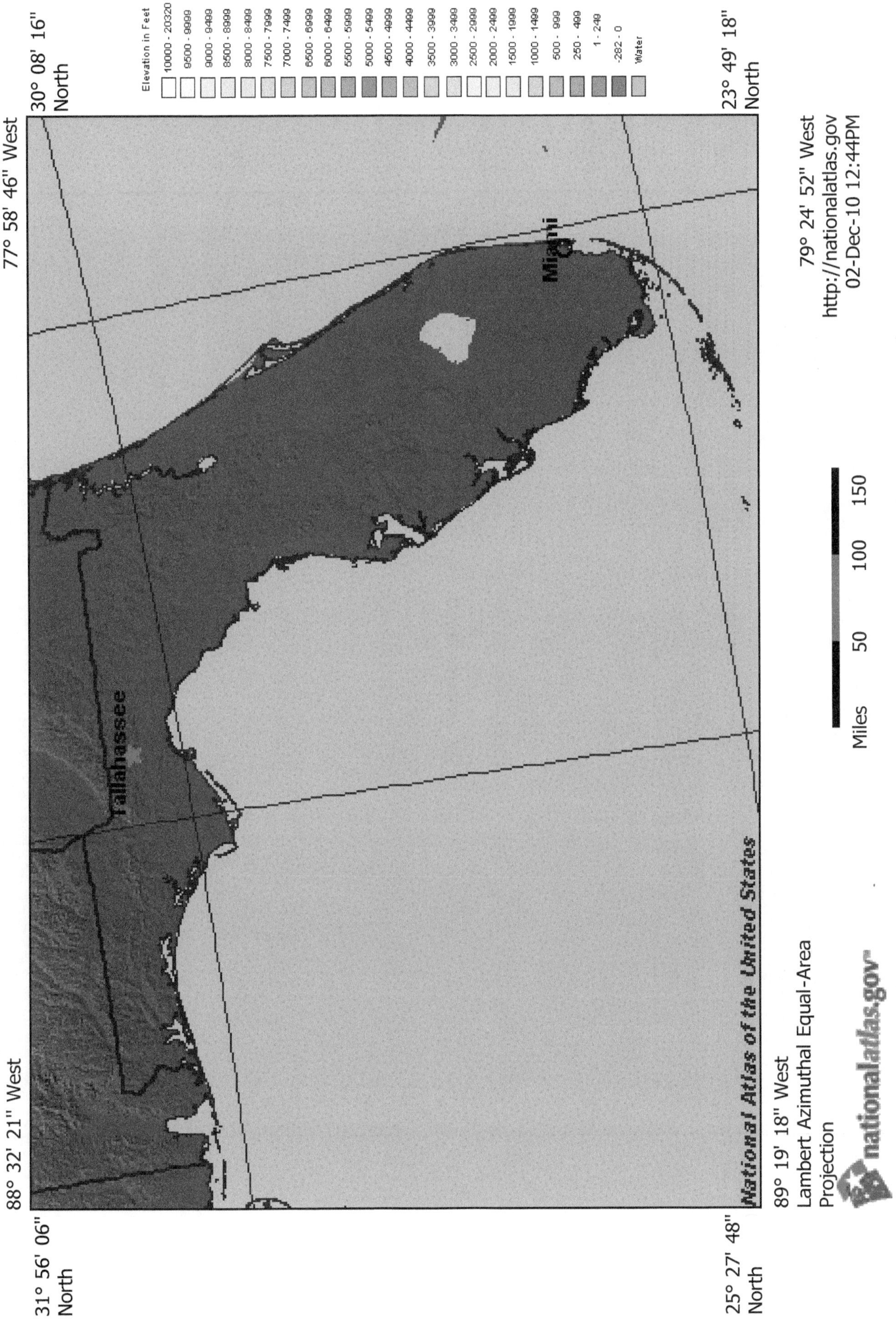
30° 08' 16" North
77° 58' 46" West
Elevation in Feet
10000 - 20320
9500 - 9999
9000 - 9499
8500 - 8999
8000 - 8499
7500 - 7999
7000 - 7499
6500 - 6999
6000 - 6499
5500 - 5999
5000 - 5499
4500 - 4999
4000 - 4499
3500 - 3999
3000 - 3499
2500 - 2999
2000 - 2499
1500 - 1999
1000 - 1499
500 - 999
250 - 499
1 - 249
-282 - 0
Water
23° 49' 18" North
79° 24' 52" West
http://nationalatlas.gov
02-Dec-10 12:44PM
Miami
Tallahassee
Miles 50 100 150
National Atlas of the United States
88° 32' 21" West
31° 56' 06" North
89° 19' 18" West
Lambert Azimuthal Equal-Area Projection
nationalatlas.gov
25° 27' 48" North

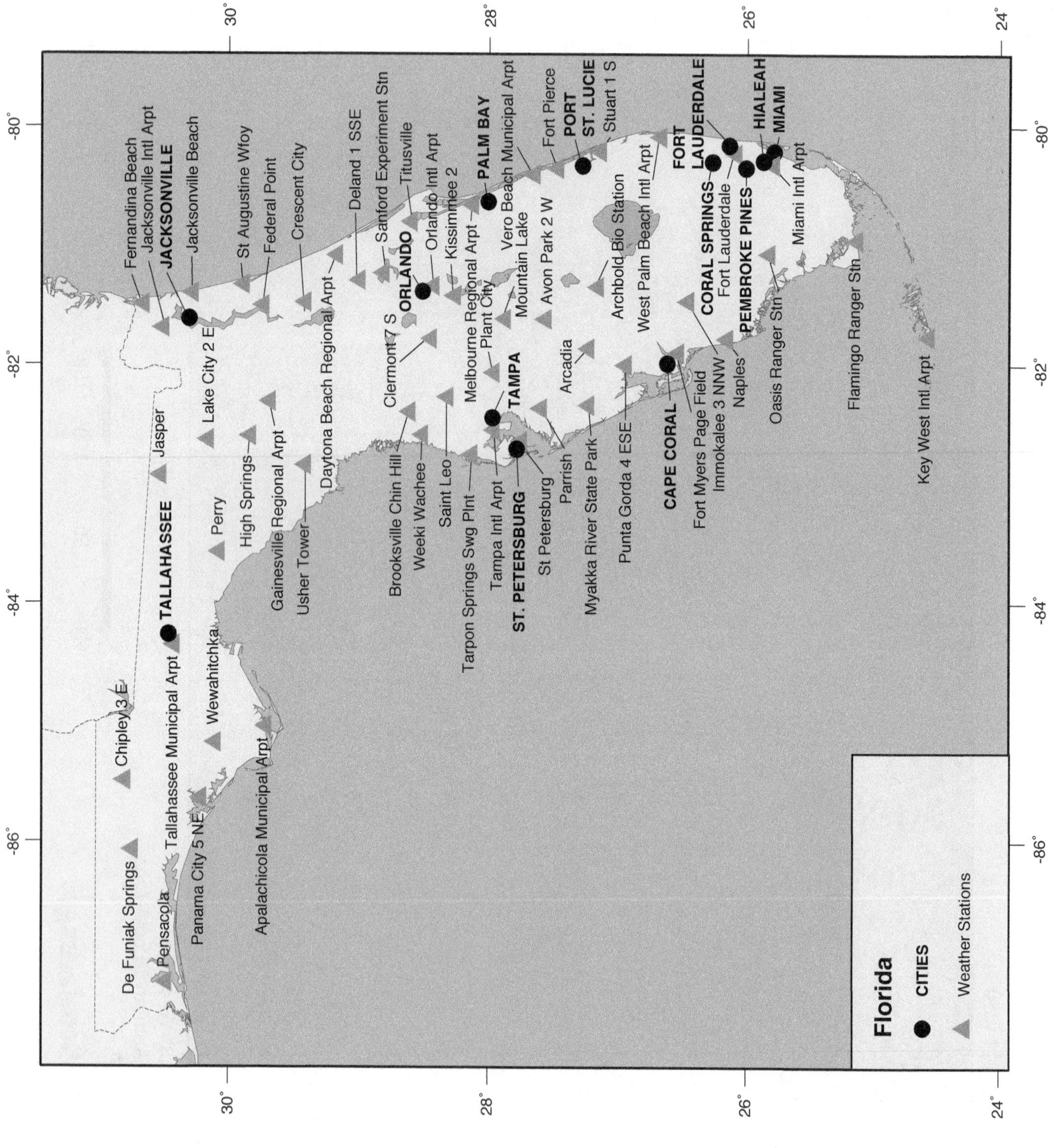
Florida
CITIES
Weather Stations
30°
28°
26°
24°
-80°
-82°
-84°
-86°
Fernandina Beach
Jacksonville Intl Arpt
JACKSONVILLE
Jacksonville Beach
St Augustine Wfoy
Federal Point
Crescent City
Deland 1 SSE
Sanford Experiment Stn
Titusville
Orlando Intl Arpt
ORLANDO
Kissimmee 2
Melbourne Regional Arpt
PALM BAY
Vero Beach Municipal Arpt
Mountain Lake
Plant City
Fort Pierce
PORT ST. LUCIE
Stuart 1 S
Avon Park 2 W
Archbold Bio Station
West Palm Beach Intl Arpt
FORT LAUDERDALE
CORAL SPRINGS
Fort Lauderdale
PEMBROKE PINES
HIALEAH
MIAMI
Miami Intl Arpt
Oasis Ranger Stn
Flamingo Ranger Stn
Key West Intl Arpt
Naples
Immokalee 3 NNW
Fort Myers Page Field
CAPE CORAL
Punta Gorda 4 ESE
Myakka River State Park
Arcadia
Parrish
St Petersburg
ST. PETERSBURG
Tampa Intl Arpt
TAMPA
Tarpon Springs Swg Plnt
Saint Leo
Weeki Wachee
Brooksville Chin Hill
Clermont 7 S
Daytona Beach Regional Arpt
Usher Tower
Gainesville Regional Arpt
High Springs
Perry
Lake City 2 E
Jasper
TALLAHASSEE
Tallahassee Municipal Arpt
Wewahitchka
Apalachicola Municipal Arpt
Chipley 3 E
De Funiak Springs
Pensacola
Panama City 5 NE

Florida Weather Stations by County

County	Station Name
Alachua	Gainesville Regional Arpt High Springs
Bay	Panama City 5 NE
Brevard	Melbourne Regional Arpt Titusville
Broward	Fort Lauderdale
Charlotte	Punta Gorda 4 ESE
Collier	Immokalee 3 NNW Naples Oasis Ranger Station
Columbia	Lake City 2 E
Dade	Miami Intl Arpt
Desoto	Arcadia
Duval	Jacksonville Beach Jacksonville Intl Arpt
Escambia	Pensacola Regional Arpt
Franklin	Apalachicola Municipal Arpt
Gulf	Wewahitchka
Hamilton	Jasper
Hernando	Brooksville Chin Hill Weeki Wachee
Highlands	Archbold Bio Station Avon Park 2 W
Hillsborough	Plant City Tampa Intl Arpt
Indian River	Vero Beach Municipal Arpt
Lake	Clermont 7 S
Lee	Fort Myers Page Field
Leon	Tallahassee Municipal Arpt
Levy	Usher Tower
Manatee	Parrish
Martin	Stuart 1 S
Monroe	Flamingo Ranger Stn Key West Intl Arpt
Nassau	Fernandina Beach
Orange	Orlando Intl Arpt
Osceola	Kissimmee 2

County	Station Name
Palm Beach	West Palm Beach Intl Arpt
Pasco	Saint Leo
Pinellas	St Petersburg Tarpon Springs Sewage Plant
Polk	Mountain Lake
Putnam	Crescent City Federal Point
Sarasota	Myakka River State Park
Seminole	Sanford Experiment Stn
St. Johns	St Augustine WFOY
St. Lucie	Fort Pierce
Taylor	Perry
Volusia	Daytona Beach Regional Arpt Deland 1 SSE
Walton	De Funiak Springs
Washington	Chipley 3 E

See User Guide for station inclusion criteria.

Florida Weather Stations by City

City	Station Name	Miles
Boca Raton	Fort Lauderdale	19.6
	West Palm Beach Intl Arpt	21.7
Boynton Beach	West Palm Beach Intl Arpt	10.6
Brandon	Parrish	22.1
	Plant City	11.2
	St Petersburg	23.9
	Tampa Intl Arpt	15.1
Cape Coral	Fort Myers Page Field	6.4
	Punta Gorda 4 ESE	21.7
Carol City	Fort Lauderdale	11.7
	Miami Intl Arpt	9.0
Clearwater	St Petersburg	16.4
	Tampa Intl Arpt	13.7
	Tarpon Springs Sewage Plant	11.9
Coral Springs	Fort Lauderdale	12.2
Davie	Fort Lauderdale	5.3
	Miami Intl Arpt	18.3
Daytona Beach	Daytona Beach Regional Arpt	2.4
	Deland 1 SSE	20.6
Deerfield Beach	Fort Lauderdale	15.1
Delray Beach	West Palm Beach Intl Arpt	15.8
Deltona	Daytona Beach Regional Arpt	21.2
	Deland 1 SSE	9.0
	Sanford Experiment Stn	7.4
Fort Lauderdale	Fort Lauderdale	4.6
	Miami Intl Arpt	24.4
Fort Myers	Fort Myers Page Field	3.0
	Punta Gorda 4 ESE	21.9
Fountainbleau	Fort Lauderdale	24.4
	Miami Intl Arpt	4.3
Gainesville	Gainesville Regional Arpt	4.4
	High Springs	19.1
Hialeah	Fort Lauderdale	17.5
	Miami Intl Arpt	3.3
Hollywood	Fort Lauderdale	5.7
	Miami Intl Arpt	15.9
Jacksonville	Jacksonville Intl Arpt	14.2
	Jacksonville Beach	14.1
Kendall	Miami Intl Arpt	10.4
Kissimmee	Clermont 7 S	22.8
	Kissimmee 2	1.9
	Orlando Intl Arpt	9.7
Lakeland	Mountain Lake	22.9

City	Station Name	Miles
Lakeland *(cont.)*	Plant City	11.0
Largo	St Petersburg	13.3
	Tampa Intl Arpt	15.6
	Tarpon Springs Sewage Plant	16.8
Lehigh Acres	Fort Myers Page Field	13.8
	Immokalee 3 NNW	16.4
Melbourne	Melbourne Regional Arpt	0.5
Miami	Fort Lauderdale	21.9
	Miami Intl Arpt	5.1
Miami Beach	Fort Lauderdale	20.0
	Miami Intl Arpt	10.4
Miramar	Fort Lauderdale	9.3
	Miami Intl Arpt	11.6
North Port	Myakka River State Park	13.6
	Punta Gorda 4 ESE	16.4
Orlando	Clermont 7 S	23.0
	Kissimmee 2	17.2
	Orlando Intl Arpt	7.4
	Sanford Experiment Stn	20.7
Palm Bay	Melbourne Regional Arpt	7.6
Palm Coast	Crescent City	18.3
	Federal Point	23.1
	St Augustine WFOY	24.8
Pembroke Pines	Fort Lauderdale	9.6
	Miami Intl Arpt	13.5
Plantation	Fort Lauderdale	4.3
	Miami Intl Arpt	21.7
Pompano Beach	Fort Lauderdale	10.2
Port St. Lucie	Fort Pierce	12.7
	Stuart 1 S	10.5
Spring Hill	Brooksville Chin Hill	14.7
	Saint Leo	19.9
	Weeki Wachee	3.4
St. Petersburg	Parrish	22.6
	St Petersburg	2.4
	Tampa Intl Arpt	15.0
Sunrise	Fort Lauderdale	6.5
	Miami Intl Arpt	23.7
Tallahassee	Tallahassee Municipal Arpt	5.9
Tampa	Plant City	20.3
	St Petersburg	17.9
	Tampa Intl Arpt	4.4
	Tarpon Springs Sewage Plant	21.2

See User Guide for station inclusion criteria.

City	Station Name	Miles
Town 'n' Country	St Petersburg	17.3
	Tampa Intl Arpt	4.1
	Tarpon Springs Sewage Plant	14.2
West Palm Beach	West Palm Beach Intl Arpt	2.8
Weston	Fort Lauderdale	11.7
	Miami Intl Arpt	20.7

Note: Miles is the distance between the geographic center of the city and the weather station.

Florida Weather Stations by Elevation

Feet	Station Name
240	Brooksville Chin Hill
229	De Funiak Springs
194	Lake City 2 E
189	Saint Leo
153	Avon Park 2 W
146	Jasper
140	Archbold Bio Station
133	Gainesville Regional Arpt
129	Chipley 3 E
125	Mountain Lake
120	Plant City
111	Pensacola Regional Arpt
109	Clermont 7 S
96	Orlando Intl Arpt
64	High Springs
62	Arcadia
60	Kissimmee 2
60	Parrish
55	Crescent City
55	Tallahassee Municipal Arpt
44	Perry
42	Wewahitchka
35	Immokalee 3 NNW
35	Melbourne Regional Arpt
35	Miami Intl Arpt
33	Usher Tower
32	Panama City 5 NE
28	Daytona Beach Regional Arpt
25	Jacksonville Intl Arpt
24	Deland 1 SSE
24	Fort Pierce
23	Vero Beach Municipal Arpt
20	Apalachicola Municipal Arpt
20	Myakka River State Park
20	Punta Gorda 4 ESE
20	Weeki Wachee
19	Tampa Intl Arpt
18	West Palm Beach Intl Arpt
16	Fort Lauderdale
15	Fort Myers Page Field
15	Sanford Experiment Stn
13	Fernandina Beach
9	Jacksonville Beach
9	Stuart 1 S
7	Oasis Ranger Station
7	St Augustine WFOY
7	St Petersburg
7	Tarpon Springs Sewage Plant
4	Federal Point
4	Naples
4	Titusville
3	Key West Intl Arpt
2	Flamingo Ranger Stn

See User Guide for station inclusion criteria.

Apalachicola Municipal Airport

Apalachicola is located in a coastal area that is low and flat and bordered by the Gulf of Mexico from the east-northeast through the south to the west-southwest. There are many rivers, creeks, lakes, and bays to the north. Apalachicola is situated at the mouth of the Apalachicola River and on the Apalachicola Bay. Several islands to the east and south offer very good protection from the occasionally rough seas of the Gulf. The land area is generally sandy, and is heavily covered with pine and cypress forests and scattered palmetto palms.

The climate of this locality is typical of that experienced on the northern Gulf of Mexico. Because of the moderating effect of the surrounding Gulf, temperatures are usually mild and subtropical in nature, but are subject to occasional wide winter variations.

Average annual rainfall is about 57 inches, but actual monthly and yearly totals vary widely. Sandy soil and generally adequate drainage allow rapid absorption and runoff during occasional tropical downpours. Thunderstorms occur in all months. About three-fourths of the average annual number occur during the summer months. Very few tropical storms affect Apalachicola.

Hail has fallen on occasions, but averages less than one occurrence a year. There is no record of sleet or glaze. Snow has fallen on rare occasions, but generally melted as it fell. A measurable amount of snow is rare.

Apalachicola Municipal Airport *Franklin County* Elevation: 20 ft. Latitude: 29° 44' N Longitude: 85° 02' W

	JAN	FEB	MAR	APR	MAY	JUN	JUL	AUG	SEP	OCT	NOV	DEC	YEAR
Mean Maximum Temp. (°F)	63.6	66.2	71.1	76.9	84.2	88.8	90.8	90.2	87.5	80.9	73.0	65.8	78.2
Mean Temp. (°F)	53.4	56.2	61.3	67.0	74.5	80.3	82.5	82.2	79.1	71.1	62.5	55.7	68.8
Mean Minimum Temp. (°F)	43.3	46.0	51.4	57.1	64.7	71.8	74.3	74.2	70.7	61.2	52.0	45.6	59.4
Extreme Maximum Temp. (°F)	80	80	85	90	98	100	101	103	97	94	90	83	103
Extreme Minimum Temp. (°F)	9	19	22	36	47	48	63	62	51	33	31	14	9
Days Maximum Temp. ≥ 90°F	0	0	0	0	3	13	20	18	9	1	0	0	64
Days Maximum Temp. ≤ 32°F	0	0	0	0	0	0	0	0	0	0	0	0	0
Days Minimum Temp. ≤ 32°F	5	2	1	0	0	0	0	0	0	0	0	3	11
Days Minimum Temp. ≤ 0°F	0	0	0	0	0	0	0	0	0	0	0	0	0
Heating Degree Days (base 65°F)	358	253	146	41	0	0	0	0	0	23	134	300	1,255
Cooling Degree Days (base 65°F)	7	9	37	107	302	466	551	540	431	218	66	20	2,754
Mean Precipitation (in.)	4.38	4.02	5.14	3.05	2.27	5.38	6.99	8.04	6.87	4.25	3.40	3.24	57.03
Maximum Precipitation (in.)*	20.8	8.9	13.5	12.1	12.1	18.3	18.1	21.1	18.3	11.2	6.7	9.7	88.2
Minimum Precipitation (in.)*	0.8	0.5	0.7	0.1	0.3	0.3	0.8	2.3	0.6	0.1	0.5	0.9	38.1
Extreme Maximum Daily Precip. (in.)	3.96	4.37	***3.73***	6.21	6.80	***4.74***	5.50	9.26	7.66	10.67	5.48	4.52	***10.67***
Days With ≥ 0.1" Precipitation	6	5	5	4	3	7	9	9	7	4	4	5	68
Days With ≥ 0.5" Precipitation	3	2	3	2	1	4	4	5	4	2	2	2	34
Days With ≥ 1.0" Precipitation	1	1	2	1	1	2	2	3	2	1	1	1	18
Mean Snowfall (in.)	trace	trace	trace	0.0	0.0	0.0	0.0	0.0	0.0	0.0	0.0	trace	trace
Maximum Snowfall (in.)*	trace	trace	trace	0	0	0	0	0	0	0	0	trace	trace
Maximum 24-hr. Snowfall (in.)*	trace	trace	trace	0	0	0	0	0	0	0	0	trace	trace
Maximum Snow Depth (in.)	trace	trace	0	0	0	0	0	0	0	0	0	trace	trace
Days With ≥ 1.0" Snow Depth	0	0	0	0	0	0	0	0	0	0	0	0	0
Thunderstorm Days*	2	3	4	3	5	11	17	17	10	2	2	2	78
Foggy Days*	17	15	17	14	12	8	7	8	9	11	13	16	147
Predominant Sky Cover*	OVR	OVR	OVR	CLR	SCT	SCT	SCT	SCT	SCT	CLR	CLR	OVR	OVR
Mean Relative Humidity 7am (%)*	83	86	88	87	87	87	89	91	89	86	86	85	87
Mean Relative Humidity 4pm (%)*	62	64	66	62	65	67	70	69	67	60	64	65	65
Mean Dewpoint (°F)*	42	47	53	58	66	71	74	74	70	60	54	47	60
Prevailing Wind Direction*	N	SE	SE	SE	S	SW	SW	SE	NE	NE	NE	N	SE
Prevailing Wind Speed (mph)*	10	9	10	10	8	8	7	9	8	8	8	10	9
Maximum Wind Gust (mph)*	41	49	41	43	61	38	41	68	68	44	85	47	85

Note: (*) Period of record is 1948-1992

Daytona Beach Regional Airport

Daytona Beach is located on the Atlantic Ocean. The Halifax River, part of the Florida Inland Waterway, runs through the city. The terrain in the area is flat and the soil is mostly sandy. Elevations in the area range from three to 15 feet above mean sea level near the ocean to about 31 feet at the airport and on a ridge running along the western city limits.

Nearness to the ocean results in a climate tempered by the effect of land and sea breezes. In the summer, while maximum temperatures reach 90 degrees or above during the late morning or early afternoon, the number of hours of 90 degrees or above is relatively small due to the beginning of the sea breeze near midday and the occurrence of local afternoon convective thunderstorms which lower the temperature to the comfortable 80s. Winters, although subject to invasions of cold air, are relatively mild due to the nearness of the ocean and latitudinal location.

The rainy season from June through mid-October produces 60 percent of the annual rainfall. The major portion of the summer rainfall occurs in the form of local convective thunderstorms which are occasionally heavy and produce as much as two or three inches of rain. The more severe thunderstorms may be attended by strong gusty winds. Almost all rainfall during the winter months is associated with frontal passages.

Long periods of cloudiness and rain are infrequent, usually not lasting over two or three days. These periods are usually associated with a stationary front, a so-called northeaster, or a tropical disturbance.

Tropical disturbances or hurricanes are not considered a great threat to this area of the state. Generally hurricanes in this latitude tend to pass well offshore or lose much of their intensity while crossing the state before reaching this area. Only in gusts have hurricane-force winds been recorded at this station.

Heavy fog occurs mostly during the winter and early spring. These fogs usually form by radiational cooling at night and dissipate soon after sunrise. On rare occasions sea fog moves in from the ocean and persists for two or three days. There is no significant source in the area for air pollution.

Daytona Beach Regional Airport *Volusia County* Elevation: 28 ft. Latitude: 29° 11' N Longitude: 81° 04' W

	JAN	FEB	MAR	APR	MAY	JUN	JUL	AUG	SEP	OCT	NOV	DEC	YEAR
Mean Maximum Temp. (°F)	68.8	71.1	75.1	79.5	84.9	88.6	90.5	89.9	87.2	82.3	76.2	70.8	80.4
Mean Temp. (°F)	58.1	60.6	64.7	68.9	75.1	79.9	81.7	81.6	79.7	74.1	66.8	60.8	71.0
Mean Minimum Temp. (°F)	47.3	50.0	54.2	58.4	65.1	71.1	72.9	73.3	72.2	65.9	57.3	50.8	61.5
Extreme Maximum Temp. (°F)	87	89	92	94	99	101	102	100	96	93	88	88	102
Extreme Minimum Temp. (°F)	15	26	26	36	45	52	60	65	53	41	33	19	15
Days Maximum Temp. ≥ 90°F	0	0	0	1	7	12	19	16	7	1	0	0	63
Days Maximum Temp. ≤ 32°F	0	0	0	0	0	0	0	0	0	0	0	0	0
Days Minimum Temp. ≤ 32°F	2	1	0	0	0	0	0	0	0	0	0	1	4
Days Minimum Temp. ≤ 0°F	0	0	0	0	0	0	0	0	0	0	0	0	0
Heating Degree Days (base 65°F)	239	161	91	28	1	0	0	0	0	7	61	179	767
Cooling Degree Days (base 65°F)	32	42	88	153	319	453	524	522	448	297	122	56	3,056
Mean Precipitation (in.)	2.67	2.67	4.11	2.23	3.09	5.92	5.89	6.35	6.91	4.58	2.76	2.66	49.84
Maximum Precipitation (in.)*	7.2	9.1	8.1	7.1	12.3	15.2	14.4	19.9	15.2	13.0	12.9	12.0	79.3
Minimum Precipitation (in.)*	0.1	0.6	0.3	trace	0.1	1.0	0.2	2.0	0.4	0.2	trace	0.1	31.4
Extreme Maximum Daily Precip. (in.)	5.67	2.91	4.28	3.68	6.37	4.54	3.43	7.00	9.02	6.84	8.99	3.65	9.02
Days With ≥ 0.1" Precipitation	4	4	5	4	4	9	9	9	9	6	4	4	71
Days With ≥ 0.5" Precipitation	1	2	3	1	2	4	4	4	4	3	2	2	32
Days With ≥ 1.0" Precipitation	1	1	1	1	1	1	2	2	2	1	1	1	15
Mean Snowfall (in.)	na	na	na	na	na	na	na	na	na	na	na	na	na
Maximum Snowfall (in.)*	trace	trace	0	0	0	0	0	0	0	0	0	trace	trace
Maximum 24-hr. Snowfall (in.)*	trace	trace	0	0	0	0	0	0	0	0	0	trace	trace
Maximum Snow Depth (in.)	na	na	na	na	na	na	na	na	na	na	na	na	na
Days With ≥ 1.0" Snow Depth	na	na	na	na	na	na	na	na	na	na	na	na	na
Thunderstorm Days*	1	2	3	4	8	14	17	15	9	3	1	1	78
Foggy Days*	15	12	12	10	10	10	8	9	8	9	12	14	129
Predominant Sky Cover*	OVR	OVR	CLR	CLR	SCT	SCT	SCT	SCT	SCT	SCT	CLR	OVR	SCT
Mean Relative Humidity 7am (%)*	87	86	86	85	85	87	89	91	90	87	87	87	87
Mean Relative Humidity 4pm (%)*	61	59	57	56	61	68	69	71	71	66	64	63	64
Mean Dewpoint (°F)*	49	50	54	58	65	70	72	73	71	65	57	52	61
Prevailing Wind Direction*	NW	N	WSW	ESE	ESE	E	SW	E	ENE	ENE	NW	NW	E
Prevailing Wind Speed (mph)*	9	12	12	12	12	10	7	10	12	12	8	8	10
Maximum Wind Gust (mph)*	62	58	77	58	69	74	67	68	55	56	55	60	77

Note: (*) Period of record is 1948-1995

Fort Myers Page Field

Located on the south bank of the Caloosahatchee River, about 15 miles from the Gulf of Mexico, Fort Myers has a climate characterized as subtropical, with temperature extremes of both summer and winter tempered by the marine influence of the Gulf.

Temperatures generally range from the low 60s in winter to the low 80s in summer. Winters are mild, with many bright, warm days and moderately cool nights. Occasional cold snaps bring temperatures in the 30s, but only rarely do temperatures drop into the 20s. Frost occurs in the farming areas on only a few occasions each year, and usually is light and scattered. In the summer, temperatures have reached 100 degrees, but these occurrences are very rare.

About two-thirds of annual precipitation occurs during June through September. There are frequent long periods during the winter when only very light, or no rain falls. Most rain during the summer occurs as late afternoon or early evening thunderstorms, which bring welcome cooling on hot summer days. These showers seldom last long, even though they yield large amounts of rain. Exceptions are during the late summer or fall when tropical storms or hurricanes may pass near the Fort Myers area. These may result in heavy downpours that may reach torrential proportions. 24 hour amounts of from six to over 10 inches may occur.

The prevailing wind direction is east and, except during the passage of tropical storms, high velocities are not experienced. During winter and spring there are usually a few days with 20 to 30 mph winds and thunderstorms are sometimes accompanied by strong gusts for brief periods. Winds approximating 100 mph have been experienced with the passage of hurricanes during the fall months.

Thunderstorms have occurred during every month, but are infrequent from November to April. From June through September they occur on 2 out of every 3 days on an average, and as a general rule, in the late afternoons or early evenings. Heavy fog is rather infrequent, occurring mostly in winter during the early mornings. There is seldom a day without sunshine at some time.

Relative humidity is high during the night, dropping off in the middle of the day.

Fort Myers Page Field *Lee County* Elevation: 15 ft. Latitude: 26° 35' N Longitude: 81° 52' W

	JAN	FEB	MAR	APR	MAY	JUN	JUL	AUG	SEP	OCT	NOV	DEC	YEAR
Mean Maximum Temp. (°F)	74.8	77.1	80.4	84.4	89.2	91.3	91.7	91.8	90.2	86.6	81.2	76.6	84.6
Mean Temp. (°F)	64.3	66.6	70.0	73.8	78.8	82.5	83.2	83.4	82.3	77.8	71.7	66.6	75.1
Mean Minimum Temp. (°F)	53.7	56.0	59.6	63.1	68.4	73.6	74.6	75.0	74.3	69.1	62.2	56.6	65.5
Extreme Maximum Temp. (°F)	90	89	93	96	99	103	100	98	96	95	95	88	103
Extreme Minimum Temp. (°F)	28	32	33	42	54	60	67	69	64	47	40	27	27
Days Maximum Temp. ≥ 90°F	0	0	0	3	15	23	26	26	20	7	0	0	120
Days Maximum Temp. ≤ 32°F	0	0	0	0	0	0	0	0	0	0	0	0	0
Days Minimum Temp. ≤ 32°F	0	0	0	0	0	0	0	0	0	0	0	0	0
Days Minimum Temp. ≤ 0°F	0	0	0	0	0	0	0	0	0	0	0	0	0
Heating Degree Days (base 65°F)	104	58	23	3	0	0	0	0	0	2	14	69	273
Cooling Degree Days (base 65°F)	89	109	186	273	436	531	571	577	526	407	223	126	4,054
Mean Precipitation (in.)	1.92	2.06	2.72	1.93	3.01	10.04	9.12	10.15	8.46	2.71	1.97	1.71	55.80
Maximum Precipitation (in.)*	7.9	10.8	18.6	5.7	10.3	20.1	16.7	16.7	16.6	11.9	8.1	5.2	74.8
Minimum Precipitation (in.)*	0	0.1	trace	trace	0.3	2.0	2.3	4.0	1.9	0	trace	trace	32.8
Extreme Maximum Daily Precip. (in.)	2.63	2.55	3.41	2.36	7.75	4.70	3.84	5.12	6.39	4.83	4.68	2.48	7.75
Days With ≥ 0.1" Precipitation	3	3	4	3	4	12	13	13	11	4	3	3	76
Days With ≥ 0.5" Precipitation	1	1	2	1	2	6	6	7	5	2	1	1	35
Days With ≥ 1.0" Precipitation	1	1	1	1	1	4	3	4	3	1	0	0	20
Mean Snowfall (in.)	na	na	na	na	na	na	na	na	na	na	na	na	na
Maximum Snowfall (in.)*	0	0	0	0	0	0	0	0	0	0	0	0	0
Maximum 24-hr. Snowfall (in.)*	0	0	0	0	0	0	0	0	0	0	0	0	0
Maximum Snow Depth (in.)	na	na	na	na	na	na	na	na	na	na	na	na	na
Days With ≥ 1.0" Snow Depth	na	na	na	na	na	na	na	na	na	na	na	na	na
Thunderstorm Days*	1	1	2	3	6	16	22	21	14	4	1	1	92
Foggy Days*	15	12	13	10	9	6	3	3	4	8	11	13	107
Predominant Sky Cover*	CLR	CLR	CLR	CLR	SCT	SCT	BRK	BRK	SCT	SCT	SCT	CLR	SCT
Mean Relative Humidity 7am (%)*	90	89	89	88	87	89	90	91	92	90	90	90	90
Mean Relative Humidity 4pm (%)*	56	54	52	50	53	64	68	67	66	59	58	57	59
Mean Dewpoint (°F)*	55	55	58	61	66	72	73	74	73	67	61	57	64
Prevailing Wind Direction*	NE	NE	ENE	E	E	E	E	E	ENE	NE	NE	NE	ENE
Prevailing Wind Speed (mph)*	8	9	9	9	8	7	7	7	7	9	8	8	8
Maximum Wind Gust (mph)*	45	46	39	38	45	71	45	48	41	40	37	47	71

Note: (*) Period of record is 1948-1995

Gainesville Regional Airport

Gainsville lies in the north central part of the Florida peninsula, almost midway between the coasts of the Atlantic Ocean and the Gulf of Mexico. The terrain is fairly level with several nearby lakes to the east and south. Due to its centralized location, maritime influences are somewhat less than they would be along coastlines at the same latitude.

Maximum temperatures in summer average slightly more than 90 degrees. From June to September, the number of days when temperatures exceed 89 degrees is 84 on average. Record high temperatures are in excess of 100 degrees. Minimum temperatures in winter average a little more than 44 degrees. The average number of days per year when temperatures are freezing or below is 18. Record lows occur in the teens. Low temperatures are a consequence of cold winds from the north or nighttime radiational cooling of the ground in contact with rather calm air.

Rainfall is appreciable in every month but is most abundant from showers and thunderstorms in summer. The average number of thunderstorm hours yearly is approximately 160. In winter, large-scale cyclone and frontal activity is responsible for some of the precipitation. Monthly average values range from about two inches in November to about eight inches in August. Snowfall is practically unknown.

Because of its inland location, Gainesville does not have serious problems with hurricanes. An occasional hurricane will cross the Gulf or Atlantic coast and head toward Gainesville, but before it arrives it is weakened by surface friction and a depletion of water vapor.

Gainesville Regional Airport *Alachua County* Elevation: 133 ft. Latitude: 29° 42' N Longitude: 82° 17' W

	JAN	FEB	MAR	APR	MAY	JUN	JUL	AUG	SEP	OCT	NOV	DEC	YEAR
Mean Maximum Temp. (°F)	66.9	70.0	75.2	80.3	86.9	89.9	90.8	90.1	87.4	81.3	74.5	68.2	80.1
Mean Temp. (°F)	55.0	57.8	62.7	67.6	74.7	79.6	81.1	80.9	78.3	71.0	63.0	56.6	69.0
Mean Minimum Temp. (°F)	43.1	45.6	50.3	54.9	62.5	69.2	71.4	71.6	69.2	60.7	51.5	44.9	57.9
Extreme Maximum Temp. (°F)	83	87	90	95	98	102	108	99	97	93	88	84	108
Extreme Minimum Temp. (°F)	10	18	26	33	42	58	61	61	52	32	25	16	10
Days Maximum Temp. ≥ 90°F	0	0	0	1	10	17	22	20	10	1	0	0	81
Days Maximum Temp. ≤ 32°F	0	0	0	0	0	0	0	0	0	0	0	0	0
Days Minimum Temp. ≤ 32°F	6	3	1	0	0	0	0	0	0	0	1	4	15
Days Minimum Temp. ≤ 0°F	0	0	0	0	0	0	0	0	0	0	0	0	0
Heating Degree Days (base 65°F)	319	220	127	45	2	0	0	0	0	25	126	279	1,143
Cooling Degree Days (base 65°F)	17	25	64	130	310	444	508	500	406	220	72	26	2,722
Mean Precipitation (in.)	3.41	3.14	4.18	2.41	2.48	6.65	6.17	6.54	4.78	3.03	2.03	2.40	47.22
Maximum Precipitation (in.)*	9.0	6.9	9.8	6.0	7.2	14.8	12.2	15.8	12.0	8.0	4.5	6.4	70.8
Minimum Precipitation (in.)*	0.5	0.3	0.7	0.4	0.2	2.2	1.5	2.5	1.9	trace	0.3	0.2	40.5
Extreme Maximum Daily Precip. (in.)	2.48	4.60	3.31	2.62	3.42	4.31	4.96	3.45	6.16	5.13	2.29	4.62	6.16
Days With ≥ 0.1" Precipitation	6	4	6	4	4	11	10	11	7	4	3	4	74
Days With ≥ 0.5" Precipitation	2	2	3	2	2	5	4	4	3	2	1	1	31
Days With ≥ 1.0" Precipitation	1	1	1	1	1	2	2	2	1	1	1	1	15
Mean Snowfall (in.)	na	na	na	na	na	na	na	na	na	na	na	na	na
Maximum Snowfall (in.)*	0	trace	0	0	0	0	0	0	0	0	0	trace	trace
Maximum 24-hr. Snowfall (in.)*	0	trace	0	0	0	0	0	0	0	0	0	trace	trace
Maximum Snow Depth (in.)	na	na	na	na	na	na	na	na	na	na	na	na	na
Days With ≥ 1.0" Snow Depth	na	na	na	na	na	na	na	na	na	na	na	na	na
Thunderstorm Days*	1	2	3	3	6	13	20	17	8	3	1	1	78
Foggy Days*	19	17	20	21	22	23	21	24	23	21	21	19	251
Predominant Sky Cover*	OVR	OVR	CLR	CLR	SCT	BRK	SCT	BRK	SCT	CLR	CLR	OVR	SCT
Mean Relative Humidity 7am (%)*	90	90	92	92	91	93	94	96	96	94	94	92	93
Mean Relative Humidity 4pm (%)*	60	55	52	50	51	61	67	67	67	63	63	61	60
Mean Dewpoint (°F)*	47	49	53	56	63	70	73	73	70	63	57	49	60
Prevailing Wind Direction*	WNW	W	W	W	ESE	WSW	WSW	E	E	NE	NE	NW	E
Prevailing Wind Speed (mph)*	9	10	10	9	9	9	9	7	8	9	9	8	9
Maximum Wind Gust (mph)*	na	na	na	na	na	na	na	na	na	na	na	na	na

Note: (*) Period of record is 1962-1995

The period of record for National Weather Service station data is 1980 – 2009 except where noted. See User Guide for detailed explanation of data.

Jacksonville Int'l Airport

Jacksonville, a very large metropolitan area covering 840 square miles, extends from the Atlantic Ocean to about 40 miles inland. Downtown Jacksonville is located some 16 miles inland on the St. Johns River. The surrounding terrain is level. Easterly winds blowing about 40 percent of the time produce a maritime influence that modifies to some extent the heat of summer and the cold of winter. Summers are long, warm and relatively humid. Winters, although punctuated with periodic invasions of cool to occasionally cold air from the north, are mild because of the southern latitude and the proximity to the warm Atlantic Ocean waters. Because of the nearness to the ocean, climatic features across the city vary. For example, during the summer months temperatures at Jacksonville International Airport, located 17 miles inland, usually reach into the low and mid-90s before being tempered by sea breezes. Temperatures along the beaches rarely exceed 90 degrees. Summer thunderstorms usually occur before the noon hour along the beaches, while afternoon thunderstorms are the rule inland.

The annual temperature for Jacksonville is between 68 and 69 degrees. June, July, and August are the hottest months, with temperatures averaging near 80 degrees. December, January, and February are the coolest months, with temperatures near the middle 50s. Temperatures exceed 95 degrees only about ten times a year. Night temperatures in summer are usually comfortable, rarely failing to drop below 80 degrees.

The greatest rainfall, mostly in the form of local thundershowers, occurs during the summer months when a measurable amount can be expected one day in two. Rainfall of one inch or more in 24 hours normally occurs about fourteen times a year, and very infrequently heavy rains, associated with tropical storms, reach amounts of several inches with durations of more than 24 hours.

The atmosphere is moist, with an average relative humidity of about 75 percent, ranging from about 90 percent in early morning hours to about 55 percent during the afternoon.

Prevailing winds are northeasterly in the fall and winter months, and southwesterly in spring and summer. Wind movement, which averages slightly less than nine mph, is two to three mph higher in the early afternoon than the early morning hours, and slightly higher in spring than in other seasons of the year. Although this area is in the Hurricane Belt, this section of the coast has been very fortunate in escaping hurricane-force winds. Most hurricanes reaching this latitude have tended to move parallel to the coastline, keeping well out to sea.

Jacksonville Int'l Airport *Duval County* Elevation: 25 ft. Latitude: 30° 30' N Longitude: 81° 42' W

	JAN	FEB	MAR	APR	MAY	JUN	JUL	AUG	SEP	OCT	NOV	DEC	YEAR
Mean Maximum Temp. (°F)	65.0	68.3	73.8	79.2	85.5	89.9	92.0	90.8	87.0	80.3	73.4	66.7	79.3
Mean Temp. (°F)	53.3	56.6	61.9	67.0	74.1	79.9	82.3	81.7	78.2	70.4	62.3	55.5	68.6
Mean Minimum Temp. (°F)	41.7	44.8	49.9	54.8	62.6	69.9	72.6	72.6	69.5	60.5	51.0	44.2	57.8
Extreme Maximum Temp. (°F)	84	86	89	94	98	103	103	102	98	94	88	84	103
Extreme Minimum Temp. (°F)	7	19	23	31	45	47	62	59	48	33	25	11	7
Days Maximum Temp. ≥ 90°F	0	0	0	1	8	16	24	20	9	1	0	0	79
Days Maximum Temp. ≤ 32°F	0	0	0	0	0	0	0	0	0	0	0	0	0
Days Minimum Temp. ≤ 32°F	7	3	1	0	0	0	0	0	0	0	1	4	16
Days Minimum Temp. ≤ 0°F	0	0	0	0	0	0	0	0	0	0	0	0	0
Heating Degree Days (base 65°F)	367	254	149	54	4	0	0	0	0	27	140	311	1,306
Cooling Degree Days (base 65°F)	13	21	59	121	292	454	544	525	404	203	64	23	2,723
Mean Precipitation (in.)	3.25	3.13	4.12	2.74	2.52	6.48	6.59	6.67	8.12	4.02	2.14	2.79	52.57
Maximum Precipitation (in.)*	10.2	8.8	10.2	11.6	10.4	14.0	16.2	16.2	19.4	13.4	5.0	7.1	79.6
Minimum Precipitation (in.)*	0.1	0.5	0.7	0.1	0.2	1.6	2.0	2.2	1.0	0.3	trace	trace	31.2
Extreme Maximum Daily Precip. (in.)	2.90	2.92	4.36	2.40	5.07	6.07	3.97	6.80	6.40	7.83	2.68	3.96	7.83
Days With ≥ 0.1" Precipitation	5	5	6	4	4	9	10	10	9	5	4	4	75
Days With ≥ 0.5" Precipitation	2	2	3	2	2	4	4	4	4	2	1	2	32
Days With ≥ 1.0" Precipitation	1	1	1	1	1	2	2	2	2	1	1	1	16
Mean Snowfall (in.)	***trace***	***trace***	***trace***	***trace***	***0.0***	***trace***	***trace***	***0.0***	***0.0***	na	na	na	na
Maximum Snowfall (in.)*	trace	2	1	0	0	0	0	0	0	0	0	1	2
Maximum 24-hr. Snowfall (in.)*	trace	2	1	0	0	0	0	0	0	0	0	1	2
Maximum Snow Depth (in.)	***trace***	***trace***	***trace***	***trace***	***0***	***trace***	***trace***	***0***	***0***	na	na	na	na
Days With ≥ 1.0" Snow Depth	***0***	***0***	***0***	***0***	***0***	***0***	***0***	***0***	***0***	na	na	na	na
Thunderstorm Days*	1	2	3	4	6	11	16	13	7	2	1	1	67
Foggy Days*	18	14	15	13	14	13	11	15	16	17	16	17	179
Predominant Sky Cover*	OVR	OVR	OVR	CLR	SCT	BRK	BRK	SCT	SCT	CLR	CLR	OVR	OVR
Mean Relative Humidity 7am (%)*	87	86	87	87	87	88	89	92	92	91	90	88	89
Mean Relative Humidity 4pm (%)*	57	53	50	49	54	61	64	66	67	62	59	59	58
Mean Dewpoint (°F)*	44	46	50	56	63	70	72	73	70	62	53	47	59
Prevailing Wind Direction*	NW	NW	WSW	SE	SE	SW	SW	SW	NE	NE	NW	NW	SW
Prevailing Wind Speed (mph)*	9	10	10	10	10	8	7	7	10	12	8	9	9
Maximum Wind Gust (mph)*	64	62	66	67	71	67	69	66	59	43	49	61	71

Note: (*) Period of record is 1948-1995

The period of record for National Weather Service station data is 1980 – 2009 except where noted. See User Guide for detailed explanation of data.

Key West Int'l Airport

Key West is located at the end of the Overseas Highway and near the western end of the Florida Keys, which are a chain of islands swinging in a southwesterly arc from the southeast coast of the Florida peninsula. The nearest point of the mainland is about 60 statute miles to the northeast, while Cuba at its closest point is 98 miles south. The city occupies the island of the same name which is three and a half miles long and one mile wide. Its mean elevation is around eight feet. The maximum elevation of 18 feet covers only about one acre in the western portion. Soil is a thin layer of sand, or marlfill, overlying a stratum of Oolitic limestone. Vegetation on the eastern end of the island is scanty, chiefly of low growth. The western end, where settlement and landscaping are older, has a little heavier growth. The airport and Weather Service Office are located on the southeast shore on partially filled mangrove swamp.

The waters surrounding the key are quite shallow up to the mainland on the northeast and for six miles to the reef on the south. There is little wave action because the reef disrupts any established wave pattern.

Because of the nearness of the Gulf Stream in the Straits of Florida, about 12 miles south and southeast, and the tempering effects of the Gulf of Mexico to the west and north, Key West has a notably mild, tropical-maritime climate in which the average temperatures during the winter are about 14 degrees lower than in summer. Cold fronts are strongly modified by the warm water as they move in from northerly quadrants in winter. There is no known record of frost, ice, sleet, or snow in Key West. Prevailing easterly tradewinds and sea breezes suppress the usual summertime heating. Diurnal variations throughout the year average only about 10 degrees.

Precipitation is characterized by dry and wet seasons. The period of December through April receives abundant sunshine and slightly less than 25 percent of the annual rainfall. This rainfall usually occurs in advance of cold fronts in a few heavy showers, or occasionally five to eight light showers per month. June through October is normally the wet season, receiving approximately 53 percent of the yearly total in numerous showers and thunderstorms. Early morning is the favored time for diurnal showers. Easterly waves during this season occasionally bring excessive rainfall, while infrequent hurricanes may be accompanied by unusually heavy amounts. Humidity remains relatively high during the entire year.

Key West Int'l Airport *Monroe County* Elevation: 3 ft. Latitude: 24° 33' N Longitude: 81° 45' W

	JAN	FEB	MAR	APR	MAY	JUN	JUL	AUG	SEP	OCT	NOV	DEC	YEAR
Mean Maximum Temp. (°F)	74.9	76.5	78.8	81.7	85.2	88.2	89.6	89.9	88.3	85.0	80.4	76.6	82.9
Mean Temp. (°F)	69.7	71.3	73.7	76.7	80.5	83.5	84.7	84.7	83.4	80.5	76.1	71.9	78.1
Mean Minimum Temp. (°F)	64.5	66.1	68.5	71.7	75.7	78.7	79.8	79.6	78.5	76.1	71.7	67.1	73.2
Extreme Maximum Temp. (°F)	86	85	88	90	91	93	94	98	95	91	89	86	98
Extreme Minimum Temp. (°F)	41	45	47	48	64	70	71	71	69	61	52	44	41
Days Maximum Temp. ≥ 90°F	0	0	0	0	1	8	17	20	9	1	0	0	56
Days Maximum Temp. ≤ 32°F	0	0	0	0	0	0	0	0	0	0	0	0	0
Days Minimum Temp. ≤ 32°F	0	0	0	0	0	0	0	0	0	0	0	0	0
Days Minimum Temp. ≤ 0°F	0	0	0	0	0	0	0	0	0	0	0	0	0
Heating Degree Days (base 65°F)	27	14	6	0	0	0	0	0	0	0	1	13	61
Cooling Degree Days (base 65°F)	180	198	282	358	487	561	619	619	559	489	340	233	4,925
Mean Precipitation (in.)	2.04	1.37	2.07	2.13	3.05	4.13	3.57	5.41	6.33	4.81	3.12	2.21	40.24
Maximum Precipitation (in.)*	17.6	4.5	9.7	10.6	12.9	14.4	11.7	10.4	18.4	21.6	27.7	11.2	62.9
Minimum Precipitation (in.)*	trace	trace	trace	0	0.3	0.3	0.4	2.2	1.7	0.7	trace	0.1	20.0
Extreme Maximum Daily Precip. (in.)	6.42	2.34	5.26	6.19	4.04	5.14	4.25	9.66	5.73	7.30	22.75	6.66	22.75
Days With ≥ 0.1" Precipitation	3	3	3	3	4	6	7	9	10	7	4	3	62
Days With ≥ 0.5" Precipitation	1	1	1	1	2	3	2	3	4	3	1	1	23
Days With ≥ 1.0" Precipitation	0	0	1	1	1	1	1	2	2	1	1	1	12
Mean Snowfall (in.)	na	na	na	na	na	na	na	na	na	na	na	na	na
Maximum Snowfall (in.)*	0	0	0	0	0	0	0	0	0	0	0	0	0
Maximum 24-hr. Snowfall (in.)*	0	0	0	0	0	0	0	0	0	0	0	0	0
Maximum Snow Depth (in.)	na	na	na	na	na	na	na	na	na	na	na	na	na
Days With ≥ 1.0" Snow Depth	na	na	na	na	na	na	na	na	na	na	na	na	na
Thunderstorm Days*	1	1	2	2	4	10	13	15	12	4	1	1	66
Foggy Days*	3	1	1	< 1	< 1	< 1	< 1	< 1	< 1	< 1	1	1	7
Predominant Sky Cover*	SCT	SCT	SCT	SCT	SCT	SCT	SCT	SCT	SCT	SCT	SCT	SCT	SCT
Mean Relative Humidity 7am (%)*	82	81	79	76	76	78	76	78	81	82	83	82	79
Mean Relative Humidity 4pm (%)*	69	67	66	63	65	68	66	67	69	69	70	70	68
Mean Dewpoint (°F)*	62	62	64	66	70	74	74	75	74	71	67	63	69
Prevailing Wind Direction*	NE	NE	SE	ESE	ESE	SE	ESE	ESE	ESE	ENE	NE	NE	ESE
Prevailing Wind Speed (mph)*	12	12	13	14	13	10	12	12	12	13	13	12	12
Maximum Wind Gust (mph)*	58	55	75	78	53	70	67	56	87	90	69	54	90

Note: (*) Period of record is 1948-1995

Miami Int'l Airport

Miami is located on the lower east coast of Florida. To the east of the city lies Biscayne Bay, an arm of the ocean, about 15 miles long and three miles wide. East of the bay is the island of Miami Beach, a mile or less wide and about 10 miles long, and beyond Miami Beach is the Atlantic Ocean. The surrounding countryside is level and sparsely wooded.

The climate of Miami is essentially subtropical marine, featured by a long and warm summer, with abundant rainfall, followed by a mild, dry winter. The marine influence is evidenced by the low daily range of temperature and the rapid warming of cold air masses which pass to the east of the state. The Miami area is subject to winds from the east or southeast about half the time, and in several specific respects has a climate whose features differ from those farther inland.

One of these features is the annual precipitation for the area. During the early morning hours more rainfall occurs at Miami Beach than at the airport, while during the afternoon the reverse is true. The airport office is about nine miles inland.

An even more striking difference appears in the annual number of days with temperatures reaching 90 degrees or higher, with inland stations having about four times more than the beach. Minimum temperature contrasts also are particularly marked under proper conditions, with the difference between inland locations and the Miami Beach station frequently reaching to 15 degrees or more, especially in winter.

Freezing temperatures occur occasionally in the suburbs and farming districts southwest, west, and northwest of the city, but rarely near the ocean.

Hurricanes occasionally affect the area. The months of greatest frequency are September and October. Destructive tornadoes are very rare. Funnel clouds are occasionally sighted and a few touch the ground briefly but significant damage is seldom reported. Waterspouts are often visible from the beaches during the summer months, however, significant damage is seldom reported. June, July, and August have the highest frequency of dangerous lightning events.

Miami Int'l Airport *Dade County* Elevation: 35 ft. Latitude: 25° 49' N Longitude: 80° 18' W

	JAN	FEB	MAR	APR	MAY	JUN	JUL	AUG	SEP	OCT	NOV	DEC	YEAR
Mean Maximum Temp. (°F)	76.2	77.9	80.2	83.1	86.6	89.0	90.5	90.6	89.0	85.9	81.4	77.8	84.0
Mean Temp. (°F)	68.1	70.0	72.6	75.6	79.6	82.4	83.8	83.9	82.7	79.7	74.7	70.5	77.0
Mean Minimum Temp. (°F)	59.9	62.1	64.9	68.0	72.5	75.7	77.0	77.1	76.3	73.3	67.9	63.1	69.8
Extreme Maximum Temp. (°F)	88	89	93	94	96	98	98	98	97	95	91	89	98
Extreme Minimum Temp. (°F)	30	37	32	48	56	60	69	69	68	53	45	30	30
Days Maximum Temp. ≥ 90°F	0	0	1	2	6	13	22	23	14	4	0	0	85
Days Maximum Temp. ≤ 32°F	0	0	0	0	0	0	0	0	0	0	0	0	0
Days Minimum Temp. ≤ 32°F	0	0	0	0	0	0	0	0	0	0	0	0	0
Days Minimum Temp. ≤ 0°F	0	0	0	0	0	0	0	0	0	0	0	0	0
Heating Degree Days (base 65°F)	51	27	13	1	0	0	0	0	0	0	3	32	127
Cooling Degree Days (base 65°F)	154	175	255	325	459	529	590	593	536	461	301	208	4,586
Mean Precipitation (in.)	1.65	2.12	3.01	3.18	5.29	9.53	6.57	8.97	9.51	6.48	3.30	2.00	61.61
Maximum Precipitation (in.)*	6.7	8.1	10.6	10.2	18.5	22.4	11.2	16.6	24.4	21.6	13.8	6.4	89.3
Minimum Precipitation (in.)*	trace	0.1	trace	0	0.4	2.0	1.8	1.6	2.6	1.3	0.1	0.1	37.0
Extreme Maximum Daily Precip. (in.)	2.26	4.42	3.17	7.25	4.39	5.89	4.67	6.57	4.63	12.56	7.56	5.06	12.56
Days With ≥ 0.1" Precipitation	3	4	4	4	7	12	11	13	13	8	5	3	87
Days With ≥ 0.5" Precipitation	1	1	2	2	3	6	4	6	6	4	2	1	38
Days With ≥ 1.0" Precipitation	0	1	1	1	2	3	2	3	3	2	1	0	19
Mean Snowfall (in.)	*0.0*	*0.0*	*0.0*	na	na	na	na	na	na	na	na	na	na
Maximum Snowfall (in.)*	0	0	0	0	0	0	0	0	0	0	0	0	0
Maximum 24-hr. Snowfall (in.)*	0	0	0	0	0	0	0	0	0	0	0	0	0
Maximum Snow Depth (in.)	*0*	*0*	*0*	na	na	na	na	na	na	na	na	na	na
Days With ≥ 1.0" Snow Depth	*0*	*0*	*0*	na	na	na	na	na	na	na	na	na	na
Thunderstorm Days*	1	1	2	3	6	12	15	16	12	5	1	1	75
Foggy Days*	7	5	4	3	3	1	1	1	1	3	5	6	40
Predominant Sky Cover*	SCT	SCT	SCT	SCT	SCT	SCT	SCT	SCT	SCT	SCT	SCT	SCT	SCT
Mean Relative Humidity 7am (%)*	85	84	82	80	81	84	84	86	88	87	85	84	84
Mean Relative Humidity 4pm (%)*	60	58	57	57	61	68	66	67	69	65	63	60	63
Mean Dewpoint (°F)*	58	58	60	63	68	72	73	74	73	69	64	59	66
Prevailing Wind Direction*	NNW	ESE	SE	ESE	ESE	ESE	ESE	ESE	E	ENE	ENE	NNW	ESE
Prevailing Wind Speed (mph)*	9	12	12	12	10	10	9	9	9	12	13	9	10
Maximum Wind Gust (mph)*	58	61	60	78	62	68	56	115	94	125	53	46	125

Note: (*) Period of record is 1948-1995

Orlando Int'l Airport

Orlando is located in the central section of the Florida peninsula, surrounded by many lakes. Relative humidities remain high the year-round, with values near 90 percent at night and 40 to 50 percent in the afternoon. On some winter days, the humidity may drop to 20 percent.

The rainy season extends from June through September, sometimes through October when tropical storms are near. During this period, scattered afternoon thunderstorms are an almost daily occurrence, and these bring a drop in temperature to make the climate bearable. Summer temperatures above 95 degrees are rather rare. There is usually a breeze which contributes to the general comfort.

During the winter months rainfall is light. While temperatures, on infrequent occasion, may drop at night to near freezing, they rise rapidly during the day and, in brilliant sunshine, afternoons are pleasant.

Frozen precipitation in the form of snowflakes, snow pellets, or sleet is rare. However, hail is occasionally reported during thunderstorms.

Hurricanes are usually not considered a great threat to Orlando, since, to reach this area, they must pass over a substantial stretch of land and, in so doing, lose much of their punch. Sustained hurricane winds of 75 mph or higher rarely occur. Orlando, being inland, is relatively safe from high water, although heavy rains sometimes briefly flood sections of the city.

Orlando Int'l Airport *Orange County* Elevation: 96 ft. Latitude: 28° 26' N Longitude: 81° 20' W

	JAN	FEB	MAR	APR	MAY	JUN	JUL	AUG	SEP	OCT	NOV	DEC	YEAR
Mean Maximum Temp. (°F)	71.4	74.1	78.3	82.5	88.1	90.7	91.8	91.7	89.5	84.6	78.3	73.0	82.8
Mean Temp. (°F)	60.4	63.1	67.2	71.2	77.2	81.3	82.7	82.8	81.1	75.5	68.5	62.8	72.8
Mean Minimum Temp. (°F)	49.4	52.0	56.0	59.9	66.3	71.8	73.5	74.0	72.7	66.4	58.6	52.6	62.8
Extreme Maximum Temp. (°F)	87	89	92	95	99	100	101	100	98	95	89	87	101
Extreme Minimum Temp. (°F)	19	26	25	38	48	53	64	65	57	43	35	20	19
Days Maximum Temp. ≥ 90°F	0	0	0	3	13	20	25	25	18	4	0	0	108
Days Maximum Temp. ≤ 32°F	0	0	0	0	0	0	0	0	0	0	0	0	0
Days Minimum Temp. ≤ 32°F	1	0	0	0	0	0	0	0	0	0	0	0	1
Days Minimum Temp. ≤ 0°F	0	0	0	0	0	0	0	0	0	0	0	0	0
Heating Degree Days (base 65°F)	184	111	56	12	0	0	0	0	0	5	40	135	543
Cooling Degree Days (base 65°F)	49	64	130	205	386	495	555	560	491	338	151	74	3,498
Mean Precipitation (in.)	2.31	2.29	3.52	2.66	3.58	7.64	7.30	7.04	5.99	3.32	2.34	2.57	50.56
Maximum Precipitation (in.)*	7.2	8.3	11.4	9.1	10.4	15.3	13.3	11.6	10.3	5.6	10.3	5.3	67.8
Minimum Precipitation (in.)*	0.2	0.1	1.1	0.1	0.5	3.5	2.6	2.9	2.5	0.4	0.2	0.2	31.7
Extreme Maximum Daily Precip. (in.)	4.17	2.47	4.06	5.13	3.85	4.40	5.28	4.73	5.08	4.70	3.83	3.29	5.28
Days With ≥ 0.1" Precipitation	4	4	5	4	5	11	11	11	9	5	4	4	77
Days With ≥ 0.5" Precipitation	1	1	2	2	3	6	5	4	4	2	1	2	33
Days With ≥ 1.0" Precipitation	1	1	1	1	1	2	2	2	2	1	1	1	16
Mean Snowfall (in.)	0.0	0.0	trace	trace	trace	trace	trace	trace	0.0	0.0	0.0	0.0	trace
Maximum Snowfall (in.)*	trace	0	0	0	0	0	0	0	0	0	0	0	trace
Maximum 24-hr. Snowfall (in.)*	trace	0	0	0	0	0	0	0	0	0	0	0	trace
Maximum Snow Depth (in.)	0	0	trace	trace	trace	trace	trace	trace	0	0	0	0	trace
Days With ≥ 1.0" Snow Depth	0	0	0	0	0	0	0	0	0	0	0	0	0
Thunderstorm Days*	1	2	3	3	8	16	19	19	11	3	1	1	87
Foggy Days*	16	14	15	13	13	12	10	9	11	14	16	17	160
Predominant Sky Cover*	OVR	OVR	OVR	CLR	SCT	BRK	BRK	BRK	BRK	SCT	OVR	OVR	BRK
Mean Relative Humidity 7am (%)*	88	89	90	88	89	91	91	93	93	91	91	90	90
Mean Relative Humidity 4pm (%)*	54	50	48	47	51	61	64	66	65	59	58	58	57
Mean Dewpoint (°F)*	50	51	55	58	65	71	72	73	72	65	59	53	62
Prevailing Wind Direction*	N	N	S	E	E	S	S	E	NE	N	N	N	N
Prevailing Wind Speed (mph)*	9	9	10	9	9	8	8	8	8	8	9	9	9
Maximum Wind Gust (mph)*	48	51	62	56	68	62	74	62	56	40	49	44	74

Note: (*) Period of record is 1974-1995

Pensacola Regional Airport

Pensacola is situated on a somewhat hilly, sandy slope which borders Pensacola Bay, an expanse of deep water several miles in width. The bay is separated from the Gulf of Mexico by a long, narrow island that forms a natural breakwater for the harbor. Elevations in the city range from a few feet above sea level to more than 100 feet in portions of the residential sections, and most of the city is well above storm tides.

The Gulf of Mexico, about six miles distant, moderates the climate of Pensacola by tempering the cold Northers of winter and causing cool and refreshing sea breezes during the daytime in summer.

The average temperature for the summer months is around 80 degrees with an average daily range of 12.5 degrees. Temperatures of 90 degrees or higher occur on the average of 39 times yearly. A temperature of 100 degrees or higher occurs occasionally. The average winter temperature is in the low to mid 50s with an average daily range of 15.7 degrees. On the average, the temperature falls to freezing or below on only nine days of the year. The average occurrence of the last temperature as low as 32 degrees in spring is mid-February, and the average earliest occurrence in autumn is early December, making the average growing season 292 days. Severe cold waves are rather infrequent.

Rainfall is usually well distributed through the year with the greatest frequency normally being in July and August. The greatest monthly rainfall occurs, on average, in July and least in October. Much of the rainfall in summer occurs during the daylight hours and comes in the form of thunderstorms, often producing excessive amounts. Winter rains are frequently lighter, but extend over longer periods. Snow has occurred in about 30 percent of the winters but measurable amounts are less frequent.

A moderate sea breeze usually blows off the Gulf of Mexico during most of the day in summer. Seriously destructive hurricanes are occasionally experienced in this vicinity but loss of life is rare. Hurricanes have occurred from early July to mid-October.

Pensacola Regional Airport *Escambia County* Elevation: 111 ft. Latitude: 30° 29' N Longitude: 87° 11' W

	JAN	FEB	MAR	APR	MAY	JUN	JUL	AUG	SEP	OCT	NOV	DEC	YEAR
Mean Maximum Temp. (°F)	61.4	64.4	70.3	76.1	83.6	89.0	90.6	90.1	87.0	79.2	70.7	63.2	77.1
Mean Temp. (°F)	52.0	55.0	60.9	66.8	74.8	80.7	82.6	82.2	78.7	69.8	60.9	53.9	68.2
Mean Minimum Temp. (°F)	42.6	45.5	51.4	57.5	65.9	72.4	74.5	74.2	70.3	60.2	51.1	44.5	59.2
Extreme Maximum Temp. (°F)	80	81	86	96	98	102	106	104	98	91	86	80	106
Extreme Minimum Temp. (°F)	5	15	22	33	48	56	66	60	49	32	27	11	5
Days Maximum Temp. ≥ 90°F	0	0	0	0	3	13	19	18	9	0	0	0	62
Days Maximum Temp. ≤ 32°F	0	0	0	0	0	0	0	0	0	0	0	0	0
Days Minimum Temp. ≤ 32°F	5	3	1	0	0	0	0	0	0	0	0	4	13
Days Minimum Temp. ≤ 0°F	0	0	0	0	0	0	0	0	0	0	0	0	0
Heating Degree Days (base 65°F)	402	287	162	48	1	0	0	0	1	34	166	353	1,454
Cooling Degree Days (base 65°F)	7	11	41	110	312	479	553	540	418	190	50	15	2,726
Mean Precipitation (in.)	4.64	5.02	5.95	4.47	4.08	6.45	7.35	6.62	6.12	4.92	4.57	4.52	64.71
Maximum Precipitation (in.)*	18.8	11.7	13.0	15.5	10.3	21.1	20.4	14.1	15.7	14.8	12.0	15.3	92.7
Minimum Precipitation (in.)*	0.6	0.5	0.8	0.4	0.1	0.3	1.7	0.9	0.4	0	0.3	0.6	28.5
Extreme Maximum Daily Precip. (in.)	3.70	4.70	7.48	6.87	4.94	6.04	5.00	5.68	9.10	8.94	4.90	3.50	9.10
Days With ≥ 0.1" Precipitation	7	6	6	5	5	8	10	9	6	4	5	6	77
Days With ≥ 0.5" Precipitation	3	3	4	3	2	4	5	4	3	3	3	3	40
Days With ≥ 1.0" Precipitation	1	2	2	1	1	2	2	2	2	2	2	1	20
Mean Snowfall (in.)	na	na	na	na	na	na	na	na	na	na	na	na	na
Maximum Snowfall (in.)*	3	2	2	0	0	0	0	0	0	0	0	trace	3
Maximum 24-hr. Snowfall (in.)*	2	2	2	0	0	0	0	0	0	0	0	trace	2
Maximum Snow Depth (in.)	na	na	na	na	na	na	na	na	na	na	na	na	na
Days With ≥ 1.0" Snow Depth	na	na	na	na	na	na	na	na	na	na	na	na	na
Thunderstorm Days*	2	3	4	4	5	10	15	14	7	2	2	1	69
Foggy Days*	18	15	18	16	15	13	12	15	14	14	14	17	181
Predominant Sky Cover*	OVR	OVR	OVR	CLR	SCT	SCT	SCT	SCT	SCT	CLR	CLR	OVR	SCT
Mean Relative Humidity 7am (%)*	84	84	82	80	78	79	81	83	83	81	83	85	82
Mean Relative Humidity 4pm (%)*	64	62	60	59	61	63	67	67	64	59	63	67	63
Mean Dewpoint (°F)*	44	47	50	56	65	71	73	73	68	59	51	46	58
Prevailing Wind Direction*	NNW	N	NNW	SE	SSE	SSW	SW	NE	N	N	NNW	N	N
Prevailing Wind Speed (mph)*	10	10	12	12	10	9	8	7	8	8	10	9	9
Maximum Wind Gust (mph)*	na	na	na	na	na	na	na	na	na	na	na	na	na

Note: (*) Period of record is 1948-1995

Tallahassee Municipal Airport

Located about 20 miles from the Gulf of Mexico, Tallahassee has a mild, moist climate of the Gulf States. In contrast to the southern part of the Florida Peninsula, there is a definite march of the four seasons with considerable winter rainfall and quite a bit less winter sunshine. The annual average temperature is about 68 degrees.

During the winter, topographic effects and cold air drainage into lower elevations produce a wide variation of low temperatures on cold, clear and calm nights. Freezing temperatures at the airport and surrounding suburban areas average about thirty-six occurrences each winter, but freezing temperatures in the city are about half that number. Temperatures of 25 degrees or lower in the suburban areas average about twelve times per winter, with temperatures dropping into the teens on occasions. Below zero temperatures are rarely recorded. Snow in Tallahassee is infrequent. The date for the last occurrence of 32 degrees is February 28, but has been as late as April 8. The date of the first occurrence of 32 degrees in the fall is November 25, but has been as early as October 18. This gives an average growing season of some 270 days.

Summer is the least pleasant time of the year. Thunderstorms occur every other day. Rather high temperatures and very high humidities cause considerable discomfort. Occurrences of temperatures of 90 degrees or higher average about 90 days per year, but only about 22 of these days have readings as high as 95 degrees. Temperatures reach 100 degrees once or twice in less than half the years. In general, summertime cloudiness holds the high temperatures about 90 degrees.

July is the wettest month followed by August, September, and June. The driest months are October, November, and April.

Extended droughts are infrequent, shorter droughts are rather common, but both are significant. Droughts, or rainfall deficiencies, when extended over months or years, cause the disappearance of large lakes and cypress ponds. Droughts of shorter duration create fire danger in the nearby forests.

High winds are infrequent and of short duration, usually associated with strong cold fronts in the late winter and early spring months. The likelihood of a hurricane occurrence in our coastal area is about once every 17 years with fringe effects felt about once every five years.

Tallahassee Municipal Airport *Leon County* Elevation: 55 ft. Latitude: 30° 24' N Longitude: 84° 21' W

	JAN	FEB	MAR	APR	MAY	JUN	JUL	AUG	SEP	OCT	NOV	DEC	YEAR
Mean Maximum Temp. (°F)	63.9	67.9	74.1	80.0	87.1	91.1	92.3	91.7	88.6	81.4	73.1	65.7	79.7
Mean Temp. (°F)	51.6	55.0	60.8	66.1	74.3	80.2	82.1	81.8	78.4	69.4	60.4	53.5	67.8
Mean Minimum Temp. (°F)	39.2	42.0	47.3	52.2	61.5	69.3	71.9	71.9	68.1	57.4	47.6	41.3	55.8
Extreme Maximum Temp. (°F)	82	86	91	95	100	103	103	103	99	94	87	83	103
Extreme Minimum Temp. (°F)	6	14	20	29	38	46	59	57	45	29	23	13	6
Days Maximum Temp. ≥ 90°F	0	0	0	2	10	20	25	23	15	2	0	0	97
Days Maximum Temp. ≤ 32°F	0	0	0	0	0	0	0	0	0	0	0	0	0
Days Minimum Temp. ≤ 32°F	11	6	3	0	0	0	0	0	0	0	3	9	32
Days Minimum Temp. ≤ 0°F	0	0	0	0	0	0	0	0	0	0	0	0	0
Heating Degree Days (base 65°F)	416	290	170	66	3	0	0	0	1	44	182	364	1,536
Cooling Degree Days (base 65°F)	6	12	46	106	299	463	537	530	409	189	50	15	2,662
Mean Precipitation (in.)	4.21	4.75	6.12	3.14	3.54	7.65	7.39	7.13	4.83	3.37	3.47	3.88	59.48
Maximum Precipitation (in.)*	18.9	11.5	16.5	13.1	11.7	17.4	20.1	15.7	20.3	12.3	10.4	12.6	104.
Minimum Precipitation (in.)*	0.2	0.8	1.0	0.3	trace	2.1	2.3	2.4	0.1	trace	0.4	0.9	31.0
Extreme Maximum Daily Precip. (in.)	4.93	4.99	6.40	3.71	5.09	8.17	4.43	6.30	7.86	7.79	4.35	5.34	8.17
Days With ≥ 0.1" Precipitation	6	6	6	4	5	9	11	9	6	4	4	5	75
Days With ≥ 0.5" Precipitation	3	3	3	2	2	5	5	5	3	2	2	3	38
Days With ≥ 1.0" Precipitation	1	1	2	1	1	2	2	2	1	1	1	1	16
Mean Snowfall (in.)	na	na	na	na	na	na	na	na	na	na	na	na	na
Maximum Snowfall (in.)*	trace	3	trace	0	0	0	0	0	0	0	0	1	3
Maximum 24-hr. Snowfall (in.)*	trace	2	trace	0	0	0	0	0	0	0	0	1	2
Maximum Snow Depth (in.)	na	na	na	na	na	na	na	na	na	na	na	na	na
Days With ≥ 1.0" Snow Depth	na	na	na	na	na	na	na	na	na	na	na	na	na
Thunderstorm Days*	2	2	4	4	8	14	19	16	8	2	2	2	83
Foggy Days*	17	16	18	17	19	18	17	19	18	16	16	17	208
Predominant Sky Cover*	OVR	OVR	OVR	CLR	SCT	SCT	BRK	SCT	SCT	CLR	CLR	OVR	OVR
Mean Relative Humidity 7am (%)*	87	87	88	89	89	91	93	94	92	90	89	87	90
Mean Relative Humidity 4pm (%)*	54	51	49	46	50	58	66	64	60	51	52	55	55
Mean Dewpoint (°F)*	42	44	49	55	62	69	72	72	69	58	49	44	57
Prevailing Wind Direction*	N	N	S	S	S	S	S	E	ENE	N	N	N	N
Prevailing Wind Speed (mph)*	8	9	10	10	9	8	7	6	8	7	8	8	8
Maximum Wind Gust (mph)*	53	51	53	54	81	76	67	64	83	58	68	43	83

Note: (*) Period of record is 1948-1995

Tampa Int'l Airport

Tampa is on west central coast of the Florida Peninsula. Very near the Gulf of Mexico at the upper end of Tampa Bay, land and sea breezes modify the subtropical climate. Major rivers flowing into the area are the Hillsborough, the Alafia, and the Little Manatee.

Winters are mild. Summers are long, rather warm, and humid. Low temperatures are about 50 degrees in the winter and 70 degrees during the summer. Afternoon highs range from the low 70s in the winter to around 90 degrees from June through September. Invasions of cold northern air produce an occasional cool winter morning. Freezing temperatures occur on one or two mornings per year during December, January, and February. In some years no freezing temperatures occur. Temperatures rarely fail to recover to the 60s on the cooler winter days. Temperatures above the low 90s are uncommon because of the afternoon sea breezes and thunderstorms. An outstanding feature of the Tampa climate is the summer thunderstorm season. Most of the thunderstorms occur in the late afternoon hours from June through September. The resulting sudden drop in temperature from about 90 degrees to around 70 degrees makes for a pleasant change. Between a dry spring and a dry fall, some 30 inches of rain, about 60 percent of the annual total, falls during the summer months. Snowfall is very rare.

A large part of the generally flat sandy land near the coast has an elevation of under 15 feet above sea level. This does make the area vulnerable to tidal surges. Tropical storms threaten the area on a few occasions most years. The greatest risk of hurricanes has been during the months of June and October. Many hurricanes, by replenishing the soil moisture and raising the water table, do far more good than harm. The heaviest rains in a 24-hour period, around 12 inches, have been associated with hurricanes.

Fittingly named the Suncoast, the sun shines more than 65 percent of the possible, with the sunniest months being April and May. Afternoon humidities are usually 60 percent or higher in the summer months, but range from 50 to 60 percent the remainder of the year.

Night ground fogs occur frequently during the cooler winter months. Prevailing winds are easterly, but westerly afternoon and early evening sea breezes occur most months of the year. Winds in excess of 25 mph are not common and usually occur only with thunderstorms or tropical disturbances.

Based on the 1951-1980 period, the average first occurrence of 32 degrees Fahrenheit in the fall is December 26 and the average last occurrence in the spring is February 3.

Tampa Int'l Airport *Hillsborough County* Elevation: 19 ft. Latitude: 27° 58' N Longitude: 82° 32' W

	JAN	FEB	MAR	APR	MAY	JUN	JUL	AUG	SEP	OCT	NOV	DEC	YEAR
Mean Maximum Temp. (°F)	70.5	72.9	76.9	81.2	87.4	89.9	90.4	90.5	89.2	84.5	78.2	72.6	82.0
Mean Temp. (°F)	60.8	63.3	67.3	71.7	78.1	82.0	82.8	83.0	81.5	75.9	68.9	63.2	73.2
Mean Minimum Temp. (°F)	51.1	53.6	57.7	62.1	68.8	74.0	75.3	75.4	73.7	67.3	59.6	53.7	64.3
Extreme Maximum Temp. (°F)	86	87	89	92	97	99	97	97	96	94	90	86	99
Extreme Minimum Temp. (°F)	21	25	29	40	49	53	65	68	57	42	36	19	19
Days Maximum Temp. ≥ 90°F	0	0	0	1	9	17	21	22	17	4	0	0	91
Days Maximum Temp. ≤ 32°F	0	0	0	0	0	0	0	0	0	0	0	0	0
Days Minimum Temp. ≤ 32°F	1	0	0	0	0	0	0	0	0	0	0	0	1
Days Minimum Temp. ≤ 0°F	0	0	0	0	0	0	0	0	0	0	0	0	0
Heating Degree Days (base 65°F)	177	108	56	12	0	0	0	0	0	4	39	133	529
Cooling Degree Days (base 65°F)	54	67	134	219	414	516	560	564	501	350	163	83	3,625
Mean Precipitation (in.)	2.17	2.80	2.94	2.06	2.17	6.65	7.05	7.71	6.39	2.30	1.57	2.46	46.27
Maximum Precipitation (in.)*	8.0	7.9	12.6	6.6	17.6	13.8	20.6	18.6	14.0	7.4	6.1	6.7	76.6
Minimum Precipitation (in.)*	trace	0.2	0.1	trace	0.1	1.9	1.6	2.3	1.3	0.1	trace	0.1	28.9
Extreme Maximum Daily Precip. (in.)	3.40	8.28	3.26	5.44	3.94	5.29	4.72	4.15	7.59	2.69	2.29	4.32	8.28
Days With ≥ 0.1" Precipitation	4	4	4	3	3	9	11	11	8	4	3	3	67
Days With ≥ 0.5" Precipitation	2	2	2	1	1	4	5	5	4	1	1	1	29
Days With ≥ 1.0" Precipitation	1	1	1	1	1	2	2	3	2	1	0	1	16
Mean Snowfall (in.)	trace	0.0	trace	trace	0.0	0.0	trace	0.0	0.0	0.0	0.0	trace	trace
Maximum Snowfall (in.)*	trace	trace	trace	0	0	0	0	0	0	0	0	trace	trace
Maximum 24-hr. Snowfall (in.)*	trace	trace	trace	0	0	0	0	0	0	0	0	trace	trace
Maximum Snow Depth (in.)	trace	0	0	trace	0	0	trace	0	0	0	0	trace	trace
Days With ≥ 1.0" Snow Depth	0	0	0	0	0	0	0	0	0	0	0	0	0
Thunderstorm Days*	1	2	3	3	5	14	21	20	12	3	1	1	86
Foggy Days*	15	13	13	10	10	8	6	8	9	9	12	14	127
Predominant Sky Cover*	OVR	OVR	SCT	CLR	SCT	SCT	BRK	BRK	SCT	SCT	CLR	CLR	SCT
Mean Relative Humidity 7am (%)*	87	87	87	86	85	86	88	90	91	89	88	87	88
Mean Relative Humidity 4pm (%)*	57	55	54	51	52	60	65	66	64	57	56	58	58
Mean Dewpoint (°F)*	51	52	56	60	65	71	73	73	72	65	58	53	62
Prevailing Wind Direction*	NE	E	E	E	E	W	E	E	ENE	NE	NE	NE	ENE
Prevailing Wind Speed (mph)*	8	8	8	9	9	10	7	7	8	9	8	8	8
Maximum Wind Gust (mph)*	55	73	58	56	99	78	67	59	75	53	54	60	99

Note: (*) Period of record is 1948-1995

Vero Beach

Vero Beach is located on the southeast coast of Florida, separated from the Atlantic Ocean by the Inland Waterway and a narrow island offshore. Its climate is strongly influenced by this maritime location. Temperatures in summer rarely reach 100 degrees. The average maximum temperature in July and August is about 90 degrees. In winter the average minimum temperature is slightly above 50 degrees with record lows near 20 degrees. On average, only one day a year experiences freezing temperatures, usually in January.

Rainfall occurs in all seasons but most abundantly in summer when showers are common. Thunderstorms are present approximately 70 to 80 days a year. Monthly precipitation amounts in winter are about half those in summer, and are due in part to cold frontal systems traversing the region. Throughout the year, relative humidity at 7 A.M. tends to range from 80 to 90 percent. The 1 P.M. humidity ranges from 60 to 70 percent with lower values occurring in midafternoon when temperatures are the highest.

Vero Beach lies at the northern boundary of a tropical rainy region. Within that region during summer and fall there may be hurricane activity. Of those hurricanes that pass close to Vero Beach, many move northward offshore, some cross the peninsula of Florida moving generally eastward but being weakened by their passage over land, and some enter the coastal area from the Atlantic Ocean. The frequency of the latter group has been small, about five in 114 years.

Vero Beach *Indian River County* Elevation: 23 ft. Latitude: 27° 39' N Longitude: 80° 25' W

	JAN	FEB	MAR	APR	MAY	JUN	JUL	AUG	SEP	OCT	NOV	DEC	YEAR
Mean Maximum Temp. (°F)	***73.3***	***75.3***	77.9	80.9	85.3	88.6	90.1	90.2	88.4	84.5	79.3	74.8	***82.4***
Mean Temp. (°F)	***62.9***	***64.9***	68.0	71.0	76.5	80.4	81.7	81.8	80.9	76.8	70.6	65.2	***73.4***
Mean Minimum Temp. (°F)	***52.4***	***54.3***	58.0	61.1	67.7	72.0	73.3	73.5	73.3	69.0	61.8	55.5	***64.3***
Extreme Maximum Temp. (°F)	***88***	***89***	***93***	***94***	***99***	***102***	***99***	***98***	***98***	***94***	***92***	***87***	***102***
Extreme Minimum Temp. (°F)	***21***	***28***	***32***	***36***	***47***	***62***	***67***	***67***	***61***	***46***	***37***	***23***	***21***
Days Maximum Temp. ≥ 90°F	***0***	***0***	0	1	4	11	18	19	9	3	0	0	***65***
Days Maximum Temp. ≤ 32°F	***0***	***0***	0	0	0	0	0	0	0	0	0	0	***0***
Days Minimum Temp. ≤ 32°F	***1***	***0***	0	0	0	0	0	0	0	0	0	0	***1***
Days Minimum Temp. ≤ 0°F	***0***	***0***	0	0	0	0	0	0	0	0	0	0	***0***
Heating Degree Days (base 65°F)	***134***	***88***	49	15	0	0	0	0	0	3	23	92	***404***
Cooling Degree Days (base 65°F)	***75***	***89***	148	202	363	468	524	529	483	376	197	104	***3,558***
Mean Precipitation (in.)	***2.63***	***2.27***	3.79	2.73	3.27	6.82	6.16	6.77	7.06	4.97	3.22	2.25	***51.94***
Maximum Precipitation (in.)*	8.9	6.8	12.8	8.8	5.8	10.8	11.1	11.7	15.4	12.4	11.8	5.9	66.7
Minimum Precipitation (in.)*	0.3	0.3	0.2	trace	0.3	1.5	2.9	2.0	1.7	0.8	0.3	0.2	35.2
Extreme Maximum Daily Precip. (in.)	***2.81***	***2.54***	***6.80***	***3.72***	***2.82***	***3.95***	***4.21***	***6.33***	***7.30***	***6.09***	***4.82***	***2.58***	***7.30***
Days With ≥ 0.1" Precipitation	***4***	***4***	5	4	5	9	9	9	10	8	5	4	***76***
Days With ≥ 0.5" Precipitation	***2***	***2***	3	2	2	4	4	4	5	3	2	2	***35***
Days With ≥ 1.0" Precipitation	***1***	***1***	1	1	1	2	2	2	2	1	1	1	***16***
Mean Snowfall (in.)	na	na	na	na	na	na	na	na	na	na	na	na	na
Maximum Snowfall (in.)*	0	0	0	0	0	0	0	0	0	0	0	0	0
Maximum 24-hr. Snowfall (in.)*	0	0	0	0	0	0	0	0	0	0	0	0	0
Maximum Snow Depth (in.)	na	na	na	na	na	na	na	na	na	na	na	na	na
Days With ≥ 1.0" Snow Depth	na	na	na	na	na	na	na	na	na	na	na	na	na
Thunderstorm Days*	1	1	3	4	6	12	16	15	10	4	1	< 1	73
Foggy Days*	12	12	12	10	10	8	7	9	7	9	11	12	119
Predominant Sky Cover*	SCT	SCT	SCT	SCT	SCT	SCT	SCT	SCT	SCT	SCT	SCT	SCT	SCT
Mean Relative Humidity 7am (%)*	89	88	86	84	83	86	88	90	90	87	87	88	87
Mean Relative Humidity 4pm (%)*	63	60	59	58	62	69	69	70	70	68	66	64	65
Mean Dewpoint (°F)*	56	56	58	61	67	72	73	74	73	68	62	56	65
Prevailing Wind Direction*	NW	ESE	SE	ESE	ESE	ESE	ESE	ESE	ENE	NE	NW	NW	ESE
Prevailing Wind Speed (mph)*	10	12	14	12	12	12	10	10	10	12	9	9	12
Maximum Wind Gust (mph)*	na	na	na	na	na	na	na	na	na	na	na	na	na

Note: (*) Period of record is 1949-1995

West Palm Beach Int'l Airport

West Palm Beach and Palm Beach, both located on the coastal sand ridge of southeastern Florida, are separated by Lake Worth, a portion of the Inland Waterway. The entire coastal ridge is only about five miles wide and in early times the Everglades reached to its western edge. Now most of the swampland has been drained and is devoted to agriculture, the peat-like muck soil being very fertile when fortified with certain lacking minerals. The Atlantic Ocean forms the eastern edge of Palm Beach, and the Gulf Stream flows northward about two miles offshore, its nearest approach to the Florida coast.

Because of its southerly location and marine influences, the Palm Beach area has a notably equable climate. Cold continental air must either travel over water or flow down the Florida Peninsula to reach the area, and in either case its cold is appreciably modified. Actually, the coldest weather, with infrequent frosts, is experienced the second or third night after the arrival of the cold air, due to the loss of heat through radiation cooling. The frequency of temperatures as low as the freezing mark is about one per three years at the National Weather Service Office, but in the farmlands farther from the coast the frequency of light freezes is much higher.

Summer temperatures are tempered by the ocean breeze, and by the frequent formation of cumulus clouds, which shade the land somewhat without completely obscuring the sun. Temperatures of 89 degrees or higher have occurred in all months of the year, but the 100 degree mark has rarely occurred. August is the warmest month and has an average maximum temperature of about 90 degrees. The occurrence of 90 degree temperatures in August is so common that such can be expected on more than two-thirds of the days. However, temperatures as high as 100 degrees rarely occur.

The moist, unstable air in this area results in frequent showers, usually of short duration. Thunderstorms are frequent during the summer, occurring every other day. Rainfall is heaviest during the summer and fall, the fall rainfall occurring from occasional heavy rains accompanying tropical disturbances. High winds, associated with hurricanes, have been estimated at about 140 mph in the city.

Flying weather is usually very good in this area, with instrument weather occurring only rarely. Heavy fog occurs on an average of only one morning a month in the winter and spring, and almost never in the summer and fall.

West Palm Beach Int'l Airport *Palm Beach County* Elevation: 18 ft. Latitude: 26° 41' N Longitude: 80° 06' W

	JAN	FEB	MAR	APR	MAY	JUN	JUL	AUG	SEP	OCT	NOV	DEC	YEAR
Mean Maximum Temp. (°F)	75.0	76.8	79.1	82.0	85.9	88.7	90.2	90.3	88.5	85.2	80.4	76.5	83.2
Mean Temp. (°F)	66.0	68.0	70.8	73.9	78.5	81.5	82.9	83.1	81.9	78.5	73.0	68.4	75.5
Mean Minimum Temp. (°F)	57.0	59.2	62.5	65.8	71.0	74.3	75.5	75.9	75.1	71.8	65.5	60.3	67.8
Extreme Maximum Temp. (°F)	87	88	93	95	97	98	99	99	95	95	91	90	99
Extreme Minimum Temp. (°F)	28	32	30	43	51	61	69	69	67	48	40	28	28
Days Maximum Temp. ≥ 90°F	0	0	0	1	4	11	19	21	11	2	0	0	69
Days Maximum Temp. ≤ 32°F	0	0	0	0	0	0	0	0	0	0	0	0	0
Days Minimum Temp. ≤ 32°F	0	0	0	0	0	0	0	0	0	0	0	0	0
Days Minimum Temp. ≤ 0°F	0	0	0	0	0	0	0	0	0	0	0	0	0
Heating Degree Days (base 65°F)	80	46	23	4	0	0	0	0	0	1	10	53	217
Cooling Degree Days (base 65°F)	118	138	212	278	424	502	561	569	512	427	257	166	4,164
Mean Precipitation (in.)	3.20	2.80	4.31	3.58	4.74	8.24	5.86	7.89	8.37	5.19	4.88	3.31	62.37
Maximum Precipitation (in.)*	11.0	8.7	16.8	12.6	15.2	17.9	13.3	20.1	24.9	18.7	14.6	11.7	85.9
Minimum Precipitation (in.)*	0.2	0.3	0.3	trace	0.4	1.1	1.2	1.7	1.8	1.2	0.2	0.1	37.3
Extreme Maximum Daily Precip. (in.)	6.78	4.97	5.58	5.10	5.49	3.95	3.57	8.01	8.79	7.10	7.41	8.21	8.79
Days With ≥ 0.1" Precipitation	4	5	5	5	6	11	10	11	12	7	5	5	86
Days With ≥ 0.5" Precipitation	2	2	3	2	3	6	4	5	5	3	2	2	39
Days With ≥ 1.0" Precipitation	1	1	1	1	2	3	2	2	2	1	1	1	18
Mean Snowfall (in.)	na	na	na	na	na	na	na	na	na	na	na	na	na
Maximum Snowfall (in.)*	trace	0	0	0	0	0	0	0	0	0	0	0	trace
Maximum 24-hr. Snowfall (in.)*	trace	0	0	0	0	0	0	0	0	0	0	0	trace
Maximum Snow Depth (in.)	na	na	na	na	na	na	na	na	na	na	na	na	na
Days With ≥ 1.0" Snow Depth	na	na	na	na	na	na	na	na	na	na	na	na	na
Thunderstorm Days*	1	1	3	4	7	13	16	16	11	4	2	1	79
Foggy Days*	7	6	6	4	3	3	2	2	2	4	5	6	50
Predominant Sky Cover*	SCT	SCT	SCT	SCT	SCT	SCT	SCT	SCT	SCT	SCT	SCT	SCT	SCT
Mean Relative Humidity 7am (%)*	84	84	83	79	80	84	85	86	87	85	84	84	84
Mean Relative Humidity 4pm (%)*	61	59	58	58	63	69	68	68	70	66	64	62	64
Mean Dewpoint (°F)*	56	57	59	62	67	72	73	73	73	68	63	58	65
Prevailing Wind Direction*	NW	NW	SE	SE	ESE	ESE	ESE	ESE	E	ENE	E	NW	E
Prevailing Wind Speed (mph)*	10	10	13	13	12	10	10	10	12	14	14	10	12
Maximum Wind Gust (mph)*	62	52	74	63	74	92	59	66	75	49	47	53	92

Note: (*) Period of record is 1948-1995

Arcadia *Desoto County* Elevation: 62 ft. Latitude: 27° 14' N Longitude: 81° 51' W

	JAN	FEB	MAR	APR	MAY	JUN	JUL	AUG	SEP	OCT	NOV	DEC	YEAR
Mean Maximum Temp. (°F)	73.4	75.8	79.7	83.6	89.0	90.9	91.5	91.3	89.6	85.6	79.7	74.9	83.8
Mean Temp. (°F)	60.6	63.0	67.1	70.5	76.6	80.2	81.4	81.5	80.1	75.1	68.3	63.2	72.3
Mean Minimum Temp. (°F)	47.7	50.1	54.4	57.4	63.8	69.3	71.3	71.6	70.6	64.6	56.8	51.5	60.8
Extreme Maximum Temp. (°F)	88	90	93	95	98	104	100	98	97	96	92	87	104
Extreme Minimum Temp. (°F)	18	25	26	36	50	52	61	62	59	38	33	22	18
Days Maximum Temp. ≥ 90°F	0	0	0	3	16	21	25	25	19	5	0	0	114
Days Maximum Temp. ≤ 32°F	0	0	0	0	0	0	0	0	0	0	0	0	0
Days Minimum Temp. ≤ 32°F	3	1	0	0	0	0	0	0	0	0	0	1	5
Days Minimum Temp. ≤ 0°F	0	0	0	0	0	0	0	0	0	0	0	0	0
Heating Degree Days (base 65°F)	177	113	56	17	0	0	0	0	0	6	40	127	536
Cooling Degree Days (base 65°F)	48	63	127	189	366	461	517	518	460	326	145	77	3,297
Mean Precipitation (in.)	1.86	2.52	3.06	2.20	3.69	9.12	7.71	7.70	7.00	2.64	2.09	1.82	51.41
Extreme Maximum Daily Precip. (in.)	2.70	3.05	4.00	2.35	***6.28***	5.70	***4.00***	***2.63***	6.00	4.50	4.00	2.87	***6.28***
Days With ≥ 0.1" Precipitation	3	3	4	3	4	10	10	11	8	4	3	3	66
Days With ≥ 0.5" Precipitation	1	2	2	1	2	6	6	5	4	2	1	1	33
Days With ≥ 1.0" Precipitation	1	1	1	1	1	3	2	2	2	1	1	1	17
Mean Snowfall (in.)	0.0	0.0	0.0	0.0	0.0	0.0	0.0	0.0	0.0	0.0	0.0	0.0	0.0
Maximum Snow Depth (in.)	0	0	0	0	0	0	0	0	0	0	0	0	0
Days With ≥ 1.0" Snow Depth	0	0	0	0	0	0	0	0	0	0	0	0	0

Archbold Bio Station *Highlands County* Elevation: 140 ft. Latitude: 27° 11' N Longitude: 81° 21' W

	JAN	FEB	MAR	APR	MAY	JUN	JUL	AUG	SEP	OCT	NOV	DEC	YEAR
Mean Maximum Temp. (°F)	74.3	77.2	80.9	84.9	89.9	91.9	93.0	92.9	90.8	86.7	80.7	75.8	84.9
Mean Temp. (°F)	60.5	63.1	66.8	70.1	75.6	79.7	80.8	81.2	79.9	75.0	68.5	63.2	72.0
Mean Minimum Temp. (°F)	46.7	48.9	52.7	55.2	61.2	67.5	68.7	69.5	69.0	63.2	56.2	50.5	59.1
Extreme Maximum Temp. (°F)	89	92	94	98	99	102	103	99	99	97	92	89	103
Extreme Minimum Temp. (°F)	13	18	24	27	36	52	58	60	55	35	27	18	13
Days Maximum Temp. ≥ 90°F	0	0	2	6	18	23	28	28	22	9	0	0	136
Days Maximum Temp. ≤ 32°F	0	0	0	0	0	0	0	0	0	0	0	0	0
Days Minimum Temp. ≤ 32°F	4	2	1	0	0	0	0	0	0	0	0	2	9
Days Minimum Temp. ≤ 0°F	0	0	0	0	0	0	0	0	0	0	0	0	0
Heating Degree Days (base 65°F)	185	119	66	26	1	0	0	0	0	5	41	130	573
Cooling Degree Days (base 65°F)	53	70	128	185	336	448	498	509	455	322	153	80	3,237
Mean Precipitation (in.)	2.00	2.53	3.48	2.31	3.39	8.18	8.09	8.00	6.42	3.07	2.00	1.92	51.39
Extreme Maximum Daily Precip. (in.)	3.98	4.29	4.68	3.20	2.69	4.88	3.99	5.97	4.41	6.07	4.04	2.44	6.07
Days With ≥ 0.1" Precipitation	3	4	4	4	5	11	11	11	10	5	3	3	74
Days With ≥ 0.5" Precipitation	1	1	2	2	2	5	5	5	4	2	1	1	31
Days With ≥ 1.0" Precipitation	1	1	1	1	1	3	3	2	2	1	1	1	18
Mean Snowfall (in.)	0.0	0.0	0.0	0.0	0.0	0.0	0.0	0.0	0.0	0.0	0.0	0.0	0.0
Maximum Snow Depth (in.)	0	0	0	0	0	0	0	0	0	0	0	0	0
Days With ≥ 1.0" Snow Depth	0	0	0	0	0	0	0	0	0	0	0	0	0

Avon Park 2 W *Highlands County* Elevation: 153 ft. Latitude: 27° 36' N Longitude: 81° 32' W

	JAN	FEB	MAR	APR	MAY	JUN	JUL	AUG	SEP	OCT	NOV	DEC	YEAR
Mean Maximum Temp. (°F)	72.2	75.4	79.0	83.3	88.5	90.6	91.6	91.5	89.5	85.2	79.0	74.1	83.3
Mean Temp. (°F)	60.1	63.3	67.1	71.0	76.8	80.5	81.7	81.9	80.3	75.2	68.2	62.7	72.4
Mean Minimum Temp. (°F)	47.8	51.2	55.0	58.7	65.0	70.3	71.9	72.2	71.0	65.1	57.4	51.3	61.4
Extreme Maximum Temp. (°F)	88	91	92	95	99	101	100	99	98	96	91	88	101
Extreme Minimum Temp. (°F)	18	26	23	36	44	50	64	59	58	38	33	23	18
Days Maximum Temp. ≥ 90°F	0	0	1	3	13	20	24	24	18	5	0	0	108
Days Maximum Temp. ≤ 32°F	0	0	0	0	0	0	0	0	0	0	0	0	0
Days Minimum Temp. ≤ 32°F	2	1	0	0	0	0	0	0	0	0	0	1	4
Days Minimum Temp. ≤ 0°F	0	0	0	0	0	0	0	0	0	0	0	0	0
Heating Degree Days (base 65°F)	198	112	61	18	1	0	0	0	0	6	43	141	580
Cooling Degree Days (base 65°F)	52	72	132	205	372	472	526	530	465	328	146	79	3,379
Mean Precipitation (in.)	2.17	2.44	3.06	2.24	3.23	8.52	7.05	7.32	6.93	2.97	2.14	2.04	50.11
Extreme Maximum Daily Precip. (in.)	3.65	4.13	4.85	2.51	3.26	6.90	3.11	4.05	4.40	4.00	9.03	4.25	9.03
Days With ≥ 0.1" Precipitation	4	4	4	3	5	10	11	11	9	5	3	3	72
Days With ≥ 0.5" Precipitation	1	1	2	2	2	6	5	5	4	2	1	1	32
Days With ≥ 1.0" Precipitation	1	1	1	1	1	3	2	2	2	1	1	1	17
Mean Snowfall (in.)	0.0	0.0	0.0	0.0	0.0	0.0	0.0	0.0	0.0	0.0	0.0	0.0	0.0
Maximum Snow Depth (in.)	0	0	0	0	0	0	0	0	0	0	0	0	0
Days With ≥ 1.0" Snow Depth	0	0	0	0	0	0	0	0	0	0	0	0	0

Brooksville Chin Hill *Hernando County* Elevation: 240 ft. Latitude: 28° 37' N Longitude: 82° 22' W

	JAN	FEB	MAR	APR	MAY	JUN	JUL	AUG	SEP	OCT	NOV	DEC	YEAR
Mean Maximum Temp. (°F)	70.7	73.2	78.0	81.9	***87.9***	89.6	90.3	90.2	88.7	83.8	77.6	72.1	***82.0***
Mean Temp. (°F)	59.4	61.7	66.3	70.3	***76.3***	79.8	81.0	81.1	79.5	74.0	66.9	61.4	***71.5***
Mean Minimum Temp. (°F)	48.0	50.2	54.6	58.6	***64.6***	70.0	71.7	71.9	70.2	64.1	56.3	50.5	***60.9***
Extreme Maximum Temp. (°F)	86	88	90	96	100	104	100	99	96	95	89	86	104
Extreme Minimum Temp. (°F)	13	21	20	35	48	55	61	62	54	34	31	15	13
Days Maximum Temp. ≥ 90°F	0	0	0	2	10	17	20	19	14	3	0	0	85
Days Maximum Temp. ≤ 32°F	0	0	0	0	0	0	0	0	0	0	0	0	0
Days Minimum Temp. ≤ 32°F	2	1	0	0	0	0	0	0	0	0	0	2	5
Days Minimum Temp. ≤ 0°F	0	0	0	0	0	0	0	0	0	0	0	0	0
Heating Degree Days (base 65°F)	210	137	64	20	***0***	0	0	0	0	7	56	165	***659***
Cooling Degree Days (base 65°F)	42	50	112	185	***357***	451	504	506	443	293	121	60	***3,124***
Mean Precipitation (in.)	3.10	3.21	4.01	2.65	2.66	7.90	8.34	8.02	6.15	2.56	2.19	2.47	53.26
Extreme Maximum Daily Precip. (in.)	3.18	4.48	5.40	4.00	3.51	5.39	3.88	3.45	6.22	4.05	5.77	4.00	6.22
Days With ≥ 0.1" Precipitation	4	4	5	3	4	10	11	12	8	4	3	4	72
Days With ≥ 0.5" Precipitation	2	2	3	2	2	5	5	5	3	1	1	2	33
Days With ≥ 1.0" Precipitation	1	1	1	1	1	3	3	2	2	1	1	1	18
Mean Snowfall (in.)	0.0	0.0	0.0	0.0	0.0	0.0	0.0	0.0	0.0	0.0	0.0	0.0	0.0
Maximum Snow Depth (in.)	0	0	0	0	0	0	0	0	0	0	0	0	0
Days With ≥ 1.0" Snow Depth	0	0	0	0	0	0	0	0	0	0	0	0	0

The period of record for all cooperative weather station data is 1980 – 2009. See User Guide for detailed explanation of data.

Chipley 3 E *Washington County* Elevation: 129 ft. Latitude: 30° 47' N Longitude: 85° 29' W

	JAN	FEB	MAR	APR	MAY	JUN	JUL	AUG	SEP	OCT	NOV	DEC	YEAR
Mean Maximum Temp. (°F)	61.6	65.4	72.5	78.6	86.1	90.2	91.9	91.3	87.7	80.2	71.6	63.5	78.4
Mean Temp. (°F)	49.5	52.9	59.6	65.4	73.4	79.2	81.4	80.9	76.4	67.4	58.8	51.7	66.4
Mean Minimum Temp. (°F)	37.3	40.4	46.6	52.1	60.7	68.2	70.9	70.4	65.0	54.4	45.9	39.8	54.3
Extreme Maximum Temp. (°F)	80	83	90	94	100	104	104	102	106	94	88	82	106
Extreme Minimum Temp. (°F)	2	13	20	31	42	47	61	55	43	29	26	10	2
Days Maximum Temp. ≥ 90°F	0	0	0	1	8	18	23	22	13	2	0	0	87
Days Maximum Temp. ≤ 32°F	0	0	0	0	0	0	0	0	0	0	0	0	0
Days Minimum Temp. ≤ 32°F	11	7	2	0	0	0	0	0	0	0	3	9	32
Days Minimum Temp. ≤ 0°F	0	0	0	0	0	0	0	0	0	0	0	0	0
Heating Degree Days (base 65°F)	476	345	198	78	5	0	0	0	2	63	215	419	1,801
Cooling Degree Days (base 65°F)	5	9	36	96	272	433	515	499	351	144	35	12	2,407
Mean Precipitation (in.)	5.22	4.97	5.98	4.27	3.62	6.27	7.11	6.00	4.70	3.51	3.99	4.28	59.92
Extreme Maximum Daily Precip. (in.)	5.40	3.65	5.20	3.82	3.43	6.83	4.70	4.51	8.10	4.95	6.73	8.00	8.10
Days With ≥ 0.1" Precipitation	7	6	7	5	5	9	11	8	6	4	5	6	79
Days With ≥ 0.5" Precipitation	4	3	4	3	3	5	5	4	3	2	3	3	42
Days With ≥ 1.0" Precipitation	2	2	2	2	1	2	2	2	1	1	1	1	19
Mean Snowfall (in.)	0.0	0.0	0.0	0.0	0.0	0.0	0.0	0.0	0.0	0.0	0.0	0.0	0.0
Maximum Snow Depth (in.)	0	0	0	0	0	0	0	0	0	0	0	0	0
Days With ≥ 1.0" Snow Depth	0	0	0	0	0	0	0	0	0	0	0	0	0

Clermont 7 S *Lake County* Elevation: 109 ft. Latitude: 28° 27' N Longitude: 81° 45' W

	JAN	FEB	MAR	APR	MAY	JUN	JUL	AUG	SEP	OCT	NOV	DEC	YEAR
Mean Maximum Temp. (°F)	70.8	73.4	78.2	82.8	88.0	90.4	91.8	91.2	88.9	83.8	77.7	72.3	82.4
Mean Temp. (°F)	59.6	62.1	66.6	70.7	76.4	80.4	82.0	81.8	80.1	74.6	67.7	61.8	72.0
Mean Minimum Temp. (°F)	48.4	50.7	55.1	58.5	64.8	70.4	72.1	72.5	71.3	65.3	57.7	51.2	61.5
Extreme Maximum Temp. (°F)	89	89	91	94	100	102	101	98	98	95	90	89	102
Extreme Minimum Temp. (°F)	18	17	25	37	51	51	62	64	55	38	34	19	17
Days Maximum Temp. ≥ 90°F	0	0	0	3	12	18	23	21	15	3	0	0	95
Days Maximum Temp. ≤ 32°F	0	0	0	0	0	0	0	0	0	0	0	0	0
Days Minimum Temp. ≤ 32°F	2	1	0	0	0	0	0	0	0	0	0	1	4
Days Minimum Temp. ≤ 0°F	0	0	0	0	0	0	0	0	0	0	0	0	0
Heating Degree Days (base 65°F)	202	132	63	16	0	0	0	0	0	7	46	154	620
Cooling Degree Days (base 65°F)	43	55	121	193	361	469	533	528	461	311	134	61	3,270
Mean Precipitation (in.)	2.92	2.53	3.85	2.28	3.21	8.31	6.83	7.86	5.33	2.61	2.16	2.72	50.61
Extreme Maximum Daily Precip. (in.)	4.90	3.80	3.30	3.35	3.06	4.36	4.48	4.95	4.07	3.60	6.90	4.28	6.90
Days With ≥ 0.1" Precipitation	4	4	5	4	4	11	10	11	8	4	3	4	72
Days With ≥ 0.5" Precipitation	2	2	3	2	2	5	5	5	3	2	1	2	34
Days With ≥ 1.0" Precipitation	1	1	1	1	1	3	2	2	1	1	1	1	16
Mean Snowfall (in.)	0.0	0.0	0.0	0.0	0.0	0.0	0.0	0.0	0.0	0.0	0.0	0.0	0.0
Maximum Snow Depth (in.)	0	0	0	0	0	0	0	0	0	0	0	trace	trace
Days With ≥ 1.0" Snow Depth	0	0	0	0	0	0	0	0	0	0	0	0	0

Crescent City *Putnam County* Elevation: 55 ft. Latitude: 29° 26' N Longitude: 81° 30' W

	JAN	FEB	MAR	APR	MAY	JUN	JUL	AUG	SEP	OCT	NOV	DEC	YEAR
Mean Maximum Temp. (°F)	67.9	70.9	75.4	80.4	86.0	89.8	***91.5***	91.5	88.4	***82.6***	75.8	70.2	***80.9***
Mean Temp. (°F)	56.9	59.9	64.5	***69.8***	76.1	80.9	***82.5***	82.7	80.3	***73.9***	66.1	***59.6***	***71.1***
Mean Minimum Temp. (°F)	45.9	48.8	53.6	***59.1***	66.2	72.0	***73.5***	73.9	72.2	***65.1***	56.4	***49.0***	***61.3***
Extreme Maximum Temp. (°F)	84	90	90	95	97	101	106	105	100	97	91	85	106
Extreme Minimum Temp. (°F)	15	25	30	30	46	60	63	65	56	40	32	14	14
Days Maximum Temp. ≥ 90°F	0	0	0	2	9	16	22	23	12	2	0	0	86
Days Maximum Temp. ≤ 32°F	0	0	0	0	0	0	0	0	0	0	0	0	0
Days Minimum Temp. ≤ 32°F	3	1	0	0	0	0	0	0	0	0	0	1	5
Days Minimum Temp. ≤ 0°F	0	0	0	0	0	0	0	0	0	0	0	0	0
Heating Degree Days (base 65°F)	266	174	93	***27***	1	0	***0***	0	0	***9***	67	***205***	***842***
Cooling Degree Days (base 65°F)	23	35	86	***176***	353	485	***551***	555	466	***292***	108	***45***	***3,175***
Mean Precipitation (in.)	2.82	2.77	3.91	2.33	3.23	6.60	6.61	6.37	6.04	3.15	2.31	2.02	48.16
Extreme Maximum Daily Precip. (in.)	3.00	2.80	3.10	5.03	4.41	3.48	2.55	3.32	3.32	***2.44***	2.77	2.33	***5.03***
Days With ≥ 0.1" Precipitation	5	5	5	4	5	10	10	11	9	6	4	4	78
Days With ≥ 0.5" Precipitation	2	2	3	2	2	5	4	4	4	2	2	1	33
Days With ≥ 1.0" Precipitation	1	1	2	1	1	2	2	2	2	1	1	1	17
Mean Snowfall (in.)	0.0	0.0	0.0	0.0	0.0	0.0	0.0	0.0	0.0	0.0	0.0	trace	trace
Maximum Snow Depth (in.)	0	0	0	0	0	0	0	0	0	0	0	trace	trace
Days With ≥ 1.0" Snow Depth	0	0	0	0	0	0	0	0	0	0	0	0	0

De Funiak Springs *Walton County* Elevation: 229 ft. Latitude: 30° 44' N Longitude: 86° 04' W

	JAN	FEB	MAR	APR	MAY	JUN	JUL	AUG	SEP	OCT	NOV	DEC	YEAR
Mean Maximum Temp. (°F)	62.2	65.9	72.6	78.8	85.9	***90.6***	***92.0***	91.3	***87.8***	***80.0***	***71.2***	63.6	***78.5***
Mean Temp. (°F)	50.1	53.7	59.8	65.6	73.6	***79.5***	***81.4***	80.9	***76.8***	***67.7***	***58.6***	52.1	***66.7***
Mean Minimum Temp. (°F)	37.9	41.5	47.0	52.3	61.4	***68.3***	***70.8***	70.4	***65.8***	***55.4***	***46.0***	40.5	***54.8***
Extreme Maximum Temp. (°F)	80	82	90	96	***99***	***104***	***105***	***101***	***99***	***94***	***88***	***82***	***105***
Extreme Minimum Temp. (°F)	3	12	19	28	***40***	***44***	***60***	***60***	***40***	***28***	***22***	7	***3***
Days Maximum Temp. ≥ 90°F	0	0	0	1	7	***18***	22	22	***13***	1	***0***	0	***84***
Days Maximum Temp. ≤ 32°F	0	0	0	0	0	***0***	0	0	***0***	0	***0***	0	***0***
Days Minimum Temp. ≤ 32°F	11	5	2	0	0	***0***	0	0	***0***	0	***3***	8	***29***
Days Minimum Temp. ≤ 0°F	0	0	0	0	0	***0***	0	0	***0***	0	***0***	0	***0***
Heating Degree Days (base 65°F)	460	322	191	72	5	***0***	***0***	0	***2***	***55***	***217***	407	***1,731***
Cooling Degree Days (base 65°F)	5	10	37	96	280	***441***	***515***	500	***364***	***148***	***32***	13	***2,441***
Mean Precipitation (in.)	4.35	5.31	5.87	4.14	4.64	***6.92***	7.41	6.73	***5.61***	3.80	***4.78***	4.65	***64.21***
Extreme Maximum Daily Precip. (in.)	3.60	6.25	3.96	4.25	***5.00***	***10.55***	***7.50***	***3.80***	***7.73***	***3.77***	***6.72***	***4.50***	***10.55***
Days With ≥ 0.1" Precipitation	6	6	7	5	5	***9***	11	10	***7***	4	***5***	6	***81***
Days With ≥ 0.5" Precipitation	3	3	4	3	3	***5***	5	5	***3***	2	***3***	3	***42***
Days With ≥ 1.0" Precipitation	1	2	2	1	1	***2***	2	2	***2***	1	***2***	2	***20***
Mean Snowfall (in.)	trace	0.0	trace	0.0	0.0	***0.0***	0.0	0.0	***0.0***	0.0	***0.0***	0.0	***trace***
Maximum Snow Depth (in.)	trace	0	0	0	***0***	***0***	***0***	***0***	***0***	***0***	***0***	***0***	trace
Days With ≥ 1.0" Snow Depth	0	0	0	0	0	***0***	0	0	***0***	***0***	***0***	0	***0***

The period of record for all cooperative weather station data is 1980 – 2009. See User Guide for detailed explanation of data.

Deland 1 SSE *Volusia County* Elevation: 24 ft. Latitude: 29° 01' N Longitude: 81° 18' W

	JAN	FEB	MAR	APR	MAY	JUN	JUL	AUG	SEP	OCT	NOV	DEC	YEAR
Mean Maximum Temp. (°F)	69.4	72.3	76.9	81.2	86.2	89.5	91.4	90.9	88.1	83.0	76.7	71.4	81.4
Mean Temp. (°F)	57.2	60.1	64.4	68.8	74.7	79.8	81.7	81.6	79.4	73.2	65.6	59.9	70.5
Mean Minimum Temp. (°F)	45.1	47.9	51.9	56.2	63.1	70.2	72.0	72.3	70.7	63.3	54.4	48.1	59.6
Extreme Maximum Temp. (°F)	85	87	93	93	98	101	101	102	96	94	91	87	102
Extreme Minimum Temp. (°F)	16	21	27	30	42	56	61	60	55	34	28	18	16
Days Maximum Temp. ≥ 90°F	0	0	0	2	8	15	22	21	11	3	0	0	82
Days Maximum Temp. ≤ 32°F	0	0	0	0	0	0	0	0	0	0	0	0	0
Days Minimum Temp. ≤ 32°F	4	2	1	0	0	0	0	0	0	0	0	2	9
Days Minimum Temp. ≤ 0°F	0	0	0	0	0	0	0	0	0	0	0	0	0
Heating Degree Days (base 65°F)	259	172	96	31	1	0	0	0	0	11	72	197	839
Cooling Degree Days (base 65°F)	25	39	84	150	307	451	526	522	440	272	97	44	2,957
Mean Precipitation (in.)	2.99	2.89	4.14	2.65	3.57	8.10	8.49	8.40	7.87	4.05	2.74	2.83	58.72
Extreme Maximum Daily Precip. (in.)	3.79	2.50	6.05	5.00	5.20	3.40	4.20	6.00	5.60	2.90	5.09	2.75	6.05
Days With ≥ 0.1" Precipitation	4	5	6	4	5	12	12	11	10	7	5	4	85
Days With ≥ 0.5" Precipitation	2	2	3	2	2	5	6	5	5	3	2	2	39
Days With ≥ 1.0" Precipitation	1	1	1	1	1	3	3	3	3	1	1	1	20
Mean Snowfall (in.)	0.0	0.0	0.0	0.0	0.0	0.0	0.0	0.0	0.0	0.0	0.0	0.0	0.0
Maximum Snow Depth (in.)	0	0	0	0	0	0	0	0	0	0	0	0	0
Days With ≥ 1.0" Snow Depth	0	0	0	0	0	0	0	0	0	0	0	0	0

Federal Point *Putnam County* Elevation: 4 ft. Latitude: 29° 45' N Longitude: 81° 32' W

	JAN	FEB	MAR	APR	MAY	JUN	JUL	AUG	SEP	OCT	NOV	DEC	YEAR
Mean Maximum Temp. (°F)	65.8	69.4	74.9	80.5	87.0	90.3	91.9	90.5	87.2	80.9	73.4	67.4	79.9
Mean Temp. (°F)	56.2	59.4	64.4	69.3	75.9	80.5	82.2	81.5	78.9	72.5	64.7	58.6	70.3
Mean Minimum Temp. (°F)	46.8	49.3	53.8	58.1	64.7	70.7	72.5	72.5	70.5	64.1	56.0	49.7	60.7
Extreme Maximum Temp. (°F)	95	84	89	95	100	103	104	102	100	93	88	83	104
Extreme Minimum Temp. (°F)	11	23	24	37	46	56	62	63	55	40	28	16	11
Days Maximum Temp. ≥ 90°F	0	0	0	1	9	17	24	20	9	1	0	0	81
Days Maximum Temp. ≤ 32°F	0	0	0	0	0	0	0	0	0	0	0	0	0
Days Minimum Temp. ≤ 32°F	2	1	0	0	0	0	0	0	0	0	0	1	4
Days Minimum Temp. ≤ 0°F	0	0	0	0	0	0	0	0	0	0	0	0	0
Heating Degree Days (base 65°F)	280	182	91	23	0	0	0	0	0	10	85	224	895
Cooling Degree Days (base 65°F)	15	27	79	160	345	473	541	519	425	251	84	30	2,949
Mean Precipitation (in.)	2.67	3.16	3.65	2.35	2.93	6.44	6.20	6.71	7.50	3.68	2.36	2.02	49.67
Extreme Maximum Daily Precip. (in.)	2.81	3.68	2.77	2.60	3.35	6.32	***6.05***	5.68	5.05	3.33	2.47	2.85	***6.32***
Days With ≥ 0.1" Precipitation	4	5	5	3	4	9	9	10	9	5	4	4	71
Days With ≥ 0.5" Precipitation	2	2	2	1	2	4	4	4	4	2	2	1	30
Days With ≥ 1.0" Precipitation	1	1	1	1	1	2	1	2	2	1	1	1	15
Mean Snowfall (in.)	0.0	0.0	0.0	0.0	0.0	0.0	0.0	0.0	0.0	0.0	0.0	0.0	0.0
Maximum Snow Depth (in.)	0	0	0	0	0	0	0	0	0	0	0	0	0
Days With ≥ 1.0" Snow Depth	0	0	0	0	0	0	0	0	0	0	0	0	0

Fernandina Beach *Nassau County* Elevation: 13 ft. Latitude: 30° 40' N Longitude: 81° 28' W

	JAN	FEB	MAR	APR	MAY	JUN	JUL	AUG	SEP	OCT	NOV	DEC	YEAR
Mean Maximum Temp. (°F)	62.6	65.2	70.6	76.0	82.6	87.2	89.9	88.6	85.0	78.4	71.3	64.4	76.8
Mean Temp. (°F)	53.4	56.1	61.4	66.8	74.1	79.6	82.0	81.4	78.5	71.4	63.2	55.9	68.7
Mean Minimum Temp. (°F)	44.2	46.9	52.2	57.6	65.6	72.0	74.0	74.2	72.0	64.4	55.0	47.3	60.4
Extreme Maximum Temp. (°F)	82	85	88	94	96	100	102	101	99	94	87	83	102
Extreme Minimum Temp. (°F)	4	20	22	37	40	52	63	61	52	39	31	12	4
Days Maximum Temp. ≥ 90°F	0	0	0	1	4	9	16	12	4	1	0	0	47
Days Maximum Temp. ≤ 32°F	0	0	0	0	0	0	0	0	0	0	0	0	0
Days Minimum Temp. ≤ 32°F	3	1	0	0	0	0	0	0	0	0	0	2	6
Days Minimum Temp. ≤ 0°F	0	0	0	0	0	0	0	0	0	0	0	0	0
Heating Degree Days (base 65°F)	362	261	149	50	2	0	0	0	0	17	115	296	1,252
Cooling Degree Days (base 65°F)	9	15	45	111	291	446	532	516	412	223	67	21	2,688
Mean Precipitation (in.)	3.36	3.16	4.04	2.92	2.28	5.34	5.47	5.68	6.85	4.82	2.13	2.93	48.98
Extreme Maximum Daily Precip. (in.)	2.82	3.21	6.46	3.24	2.76	5.64	3.07	4.70	5.19	6.72	3.10	3.96	6.72
Days With ≥ 0.1" Precipitation	6	5	6	4	4	8	9	9	8	5	4	4	72
Days With ≥ 0.5" Precipitation	2	2	3	2	2	4	4	3	5	3	1	2	33
Days With ≥ 1.0" Precipitation	1	1	1	1	1	1	2	2	2	1	1	1	15
Mean Snowfall (in.)	0.0	0.0	trace	0.0	0.0	0.0	0.0	0.0	0.0	0.0	0.0	0.0	trace
Maximum Snow Depth (in.)	0	0	trace	0	0	0	0	0	0	0	0	0	trace
Days With ≥ 1.0" Snow Depth	0	0	0	0	0	0	0	0	0	0	0	0	0

Flamingo Ranger Stn *Monroe County* Elevation: 2 ft. Latitude: 25° 09' N Longitude: 80° 55' W

	JAN	FEB	MAR	APR	MAY	JUN	JUL	AUG	SEP	OCT	NOV	DEC	YEAR
Mean Maximum Temp. (°F)	76.6	77.7	79.9	83.2	86.5	88.8	90.0	90.3	89.3	86.4	82.3	78.8	84.2
Mean Temp. (°F)	66.4	67.8	70.4	73.7	77.8	81.3	82.2	82.4	81.5	78.2	73.4	69.3	75.4
Mean Minimum Temp. (°F)	56.1	57.7	60.7	64.1	69.0	73.8	74.4	74.5	73.6	70.0	64.4	59.8	66.5
Extreme Maximum Temp. (°F)	88	92	89	93	96	104	100	97	102	99	91	92	104
Extreme Minimum Temp. (°F)	29	24	33	44	52	60	62	63	60	41	39	25	24
Days Maximum Temp. ≥ 90°F	0	0	0	0	4	11	19	22	15	3	0	0	74
Days Maximum Temp. ≤ 32°F	0	0	0	0	0	0	0	0	0	0	0	0	0
Days Minimum Temp. ≤ 32°F	0	0	0	0	0	0	0	0	0	0	0	0	0
Days Minimum Temp. ≤ 0°F	0	0	0	0	0	0	0	0	0	0	0	0	0
Heating Degree Days (base 65°F)	64	43	20	3	0	0	0	0	0	1	6	34	171
Cooling Degree Days (base 65°F)	114	128	193	270	404	496	540	547	502	417	264	176	4,051
Mean Precipitation (in.)	1.70	1.58	1.99	1.98	3.43	7.37	5.55	6.90	6.88	3.93	2.64	1.42	45.37
Extreme Maximum Daily Precip. (in.)	3.85	3.60	4.00	***3.10***	5.63	6.78	3.30	8.20	2.50	2.54	4.53	***2.53***	***8.20***
Days With ≥ 0.1" Precipitation	3	3	3	3	5	9	9	9	10	5	4	2	65
Days With ≥ 0.5" Precipitation	1	1	1	1	2	4	3	4	4	2	2	1	26
Days With ≥ 1.0" Precipitation	0	0	1	0	1	2	2	2	2	1	1	0	12
Mean Snowfall (in.)	0.0	0.0	0.0	0.0	0.0	0.0	0.0	0.0	0.0	0.0	0.0	0.0	0.0
Maximum Snow Depth (in.)	0	0	0	0	0	0	0	0	0	0	0	0	0
Days With ≥ 1.0" Snow Depth	0	0	0	0	0	0	0	0	0	0	0	0	0

The period of record for all cooperative weather station data is 1980 – 2009. See User Guide for detailed explanation of data.

Fort Lauderdale *Broward County* Elevation: 16 ft. Latitude: 26° 06' N Longitude: 80° 12' W

	JAN	FEB	MAR	APR	MAY	JUN	JUL	AUG	SEP	OCT	NOV	DEC	YEAR
Mean Maximum Temp. (°F)	76.1	77.6	79.6	82.4	85.8	88.4	89.8	90.2	88.8	85.9	81.1	77.4	83.6
Mean Temp. (°F)	67.5	69.0	71.5	74.5	78.5	81.4	82.8	83.2	82.1	79.1	73.9	69.6	76.1
Mean Minimum Temp. (°F)	58.7	60.4	63.3	66.5	71.2	74.5	75.7	76.2	75.4	72.3	66.6	61.8	68.5
Extreme Maximum Temp. (°F)	87	89	92	94	98	98	99	97	97	98	91	89	99
Extreme Minimum Temp. (°F)	29	34	32	44	54	63	68	66	68	52	42	30	29
Days Maximum Temp. ≥ 90°F	0	0	0	1	5	10	16	20	11	3	0	0	66
Days Maximum Temp. ≤ 32°F	0	0	0	0	0	0	0	0	0	0	0	0	0
Days Minimum Temp. ≤ 32°F	0	0	0	0	0	0	0	0	0	0	0	0	0
Days Minimum Temp. ≤ 0°F	0	0	0	0	0	0	0	0	0	0	0	0	0
Heating Degree Days (base 65°F)	57	32	15	2	0	0	0	0	0	0	6	37	149
Cooling Degree Days (base 65°F)	140	151	224	293	425	500	559	571	519	445	278	187	4,292
Mean Precipitation (in.)	2.66	2.98	3.50	3.36	6.15	9.92	7.36	7.43	9.15	6.80	4.06	2.43	65.80
Extreme Maximum Daily Precip. (in.)	5.82	4.66	4.78	7.60	5.73	8.28	4.62	4.57	5.35	7.09	6.77	5.38	8.28
Days With ≥ 0.1" Precipitation	5	4	5	4	7	12	11	11	12	9	6	4	90
Days With ≥ 0.5" Precipitation	2	2	2	2	4	6	5	5	5	4	2	1	40
Days With ≥ 1.0" Precipitation	1	1	1	1	2	3	2	2	3	2	1	1	20
Mean Snowfall (in.)	0.0	0.0	0.0	0.0	0.0	0.0	0.0	0.0	0.0	0.0	0.0	0.0	0.0
Maximum Snow Depth (in.)	0	0	0	0	0	0	0	0	0	0	0	0	0
Days With ≥ 1.0" Snow Depth	0	0	0	0	0	0	0	0	0	0	0	0	0

Fort Pierce *St. Lucie County* Elevation: 24 ft. Latitude: 27° 28' N Longitude: 80° 21' W

	JAN	FEB	MAR	APR	MAY	JUN	JUL	AUG	SEP	OCT	NOV	DEC	YEAR
Mean Maximum Temp. (°F)	73.8	75.6	78.5	81.7	86.1	89.3	91.1	90.9	89.2	85.4	80.1	75.6	83.1
Mean Temp. (°F)	62.7	64.7	68.0	71.5	76.8	80.4	81.9	81.9	80.8	76.7	70.3	65.2	73.4
Mean Minimum Temp. (°F)	51.5	53.8	57.5	61.2	67.5	71.5	72.6	72.9	72.3	68.0	60.5	54.7	63.7
Extreme Maximum Temp. (°F)	89	89	91	94	98	100	101	98	99	98	92	88	101
Extreme Minimum Temp. (°F)	19	25	26	33	45	56	64	61	63	42	34	19	19
Days Maximum Temp. ≥ 90°F	0	0	1	1	6	14	23	23	15	4	0	0	87
Days Maximum Temp. ≤ 32°F	0	0	0	0	0	0	0	0	0	0	0	0	0
Days Minimum Temp. ≤ 32°F	1	0	0	0	0	0	0	0	0	0	0	1	2
Days Minimum Temp. ≤ 0°F	0	0	0	0	0	0	0	0	0	0	0	0	0
Heating Degree Days (base 65°F)	135	87	48	12	0	0	0	0	0	3	25	96	406
Cooling Degree Days (base 65°F)	70	85	149	214	374	470	531	531	480	373	192	108	3,577
Mean Precipitation (in.)	2.40	3.00	3.58	2.97	3.87	5.65	5.82	7.42	7.77	5.75	3.67	2.18	54.08
Extreme Maximum Daily Precip. (in.)	2.66	3.34	5.01	3.25	3.10	4.02	3.84	12.11	7.00	8.53	4.26	2.84	12.11
Days With ≥ 0.1" Precipitation	4	4	5	4	6	9	8	10	10	8	5	4	77
Days With ≥ 0.5" Precipitation	2	2	2	2	3	4	3	5	4	4	2	1	34
Days With ≥ 1.0" Precipitation	1	1	1	1	1	2	2	2	2	2	1	1	17
Mean Snowfall (in.)	0.0	0.0	0.0	0.0	0.0	0.0	0.0	0.0	0.0	0.0	0.0	0.0	0.0
Maximum Snow Depth (in.)	0	0	0	0	0	0	0	0	0	0	0	0	0
Days With ≥ 1.0" Snow Depth	0	0	0	0	0	0	0	0	0	0	0	0	0

High Springs *Alachua County* Elevation: 64 ft. Latitude: 29° 50' N Longitude: 82° 36' W

	JAN	FEB	MAR	APR	MAY	JUN	JUL	AUG	SEP	OCT	NOV	DEC	YEAR
Mean Maximum Temp. (°F)	68.4	72.1	77.6	83.1	89.0	91.7	92.9	92.2	89.5	83.2	76.5	69.9	82.2
Mean Temp. (°F)	54.5	57.8	63.1	67.9	75.3	80.2	81.8	81.6	78.5	70.7	62.9	56.4	69.2
Mean Minimum Temp. (°F)	40.6	43.5	48.5	52.7	61.7	68.8	70.8	71.0	67.5	58.3	49.1	42.7	56.3
Extreme Maximum Temp. (°F)	87	88	92	96	101	104	107	104	99	99	90	89	107
Extreme Minimum Temp. (°F)	9	17	20	30	41	45	55	59	49	29	23	8	8
Days Maximum Temp. ≥ 90°F	0	0	0	3	15	21	24	24	17	4	0	0	108
Days Maximum Temp. ≤ 32°F	0	0	0	0	0	0	0	0	0	0	0	0	0
Days Minimum Temp. ≤ 32°F	9	5	2	0	0	0	0	0	0	0	2	7	25
Days Minimum Temp. ≤ 0°F	0	0	0	0	0	0	0	0	0	0	0	0	0
Heating Degree Days (base 65°F)	333	221	121	43	2	0	0	0	0	27	126	288	1,161
Cooling Degree Days (base 65°F)	14	24	69	136	330	462	528	522	415	211	71	26	2,808
Mean Precipitation (in.)	3.71	3.63	4.42	2.95	2.75	7.17	7.15	7.36	4.59	3.20	2.26	2.64	51.83
Extreme Maximum Daily Precip. (in.)	2.92	5.13	3.05	3.27	5.93	3.60	5.50	3.30	5.50	10.00	2.44	5.60	10.00
Days With ≥ 0.1" Precipitation	6	5	6	4	5	9	11	11	7	5	4	4	77
Days With ≥ 0.5" Precipitation	3	2	3	2	2	4	5	5	3	2	2	2	35
Days With ≥ 1.0" Precipitation	1	1	2	1	1	2	2	3	1	1	1	1	17
Mean Snowfall (in.)	0.0	0.0	0.0	0.0	0.0	0.0	0.0	0.0	0.0	0.0	0.0	0.0	0.0
Maximum Snow Depth (in.)	0	0	0	0	0	0	0	0	0	0	0	0	0
Days With ≥ 1.0" Snow Depth	0	0	0	0	0	0	0	0	0	0	0	0	0

Immokalee 3 NNW *Collier County* Elevation: 35 ft. Latitude: 26° 28' N Longitude: 81° 26' W

	JAN	FEB	MAR	APR	MAY	JUN	JUL	AUG	SEP	OCT	NOV	DEC	YEAR
Mean Maximum Temp. (°F)	***76.3***	78.1	***80.9***	***84.8***	89.1	91.1	***92.0***	91.8	***90.2***	86.8	***81.6***	***77.5***	***85.0***
Mean Temp. (°F)	***63.9***	65.5	***68.7***	***72.0***	77.0	80.8	***82.0***	82.4	***81.1***	76.8	***70.7***	***65.8***	73.9
Mean Minimum Temp. (°F)	***51.5***	52.9	***56.3***	***59.1***	64.7	70.5	***72.0***	72.9	***72.0***	66.6	***59.9***	***54.0***	***62.7***
Extreme Maximum Temp. (°F)	***89***	90	99	***96***	100	102	***98***	100	***98***	95	92	89	***102***
Extreme Minimum Temp. (°F)	***20***	25	30	***40***	50	54	***63***	67	***64***	41	35	24	***20***
Days Maximum Temp. ≥ 90°F	***0***	0	1	***5***	15	21	***27***	26	***20***	8	0	0	***123***
Days Maximum Temp. ≤ 32°F	***0***	0	0	***0***	0	0	***0***	0	***0***	0	0	0	***0***
Days Minimum Temp. ≤ 32°F	***1***	1	0	***0***	0	0	***0***	0	***0***	0	0	0	***2***
Days Minimum Temp. ≤ 0°F	***0***	0	0	***0***	0	0	***0***	0	***0***	0	0	0	***0***
Heating Degree Days (base 65°F)	***109***	78	***36***	***8***	0	0	***0***	0	***0***	2	***21***	***79***	***333***
Cooling Degree Days (base 65°F)	***82***	99	***156***	***225***	378	482	***535***	545	***490***	372	***200***	***110***	***3,674***
Mean Precipitation (in.)	***2.17***	2.58	2.81	***2.34***	3.69	7.60	***7.58***	7.85	***6.12***	3.15	***2.04***	1.71	***49.64***
Extreme Maximum Daily Precip. (in.)	***3.71***	***2.75***	***3.05***	***3.23***	***5.30***	***3.00***	***4.44***	***4.31***	***5.79***	***3.82***	***6.45***	***2.61***	***6.45***
Days With ≥ 0.1" Precipitation	***3***	4	4	***3***	5	10	***11***	12	***9***	5	3	3	***72***
Days With ≥ 0.5" Precipitation	***1***	2	2	***1***	2	5	***5***	5	***4***	2	1	1	***31***
Days With ≥ 1.0" Precipitation	***1***	1	1	***1***	1	2	***2***	2	***2***	1	1	1	***16***
Mean Snowfall (in.)	***0.0***	0.0	0.0	***0.0***	0.0	0.0	***0.0***	0.0	***0.0***	0.0	0.0	0.0	***0.0***
Maximum Snow Depth (in.)	***0***	0	0	***0***	0	0	***0***	0	***0***	***0***	0	0	***0***
Days With ≥ 1.0" Snow Depth	***0***	0	0	***0***	0	0	***0***	0	***0***	***0***	0	0	***0***

Jacksonville Beach *Duval County* Elevation: 9 ft. Latitude: 30° 17' N Longitude: 81° 24' W

	JAN	FEB	MAR	APR	MAY	JUN	JUL	AUG	SEP	OCT	NOV	DEC	YEAR
Mean Maximum Temp. (°F)	63.7	66.1	70.8	76.4	82.6	86.8	89.5	88.5	85.5	79.7	72.0	66.0	77.3
Mean Temp. (°F)	54.9	57.6	62.6	68.0	74.9	79.8	81.9	81.6	79.4	73.0	64.2	57.9	69.7
Mean Minimum Temp. (°F)	46.2	49.1	54.3	59.6	67.2	72.6	74.3	74.8	73.3	66.4	56.4	49.8	62.0
Extreme Maximum Temp. (°F)	85	85	89	94	98	99	103	102	96	94	88	83	103
Extreme Minimum Temp. (°F)	14	21	24	37	51	55	67	66	53	40	29	15	14
Days Maximum Temp. ≥ 90°F	0	0	0	1	3	7	13	10	3	1	0	0	38
Days Maximum Temp. ≤ 32°F	0	0	0	0	0	0	0	0	0	0	0	0	0
Days Minimum Temp. ≤ 32°F	2	1	0	0	0	0	0	0	0	0	0	1	4
Days Minimum Temp. ≤ 0°F	0	0	0	0	0	0	0	0	0	0	0	0	0
Heating Degree Days (base 65°F)	316	220	120	34	1	0	0	0	0	10	93	241	1,035
Cooling Degree Days (base 65°F)	11	18	52	132	315	449	530	523	441	266	76	28	2,841
Mean Precipitation (in.)	3.34	2.93	3.86	2.66	2.48	5.68	4.97	6.81	7.22	5.37	2.38	2.61	50.31
Extreme Maximum Daily Precip. (in.)	2.80	2.50	3.32	4.59	4.42	5.01	3.18	12.56	8.01	7.62	4.35	3.57	12.56
Days With ≥ 0.1" Precipitation	5	5	6	4	4	8	8	9	9	6	4	4	72
Days With ≥ 0.5" Precipitation	2	2	3	2	2	3	3	4	4	3	2	2	32
Days With ≥ 1.0" Precipitation	1	1	1	1	1	2	1	2	2	2	1	1	16
Mean Snowfall (in.)	0.0	0.0	0.0	0.0	0.0	0.0	0.0	0.0	0.0	0.0	0.0	0.1	0.1
Maximum Snow Depth (in.)	0	0	0	0	0	0	0	0	0	0	0	0	0
Days With ≥ 1.0" Snow Depth	0	0	0	0	0	0	0	0	0	0	0	0	0

Jasper *Hamilton County* Elevation: 146 ft. Latitude: 30° 31' N Longitude: 82° 57' W

	JAN	FEB	MAR	APR	MAY	JUN	JUL	AUG	SEP	OCT	NOV	DEC	YEAR
Mean Maximum Temp. (°F)	64.0	67.5	73.4	79.0	85.7	89.9	91.6	91.1	88.1	81.0	73.5	66.0	79.2
Mean Temp. (°F)	51.2	54.6	60.1	65.6	73.1	78.9	81.1	80.6	77.2	68.6	60.4	53.3	67.1
Mean Minimum Temp. (°F)	38.3	41.6	46.8	52.3	60.4	67.8	70.5	70.2	66.2	56.2	47.3	40.6	54.8
Extreme Maximum Temp. (°F)	82	84	88	93	99	103	102	103	102	97	89	86	103
Extreme Minimum Temp. (°F)	4	14	19	27	42	47	58	58	45	31	24	12	4
Days Maximum Temp. ≥ 90°F	0	0	0	1	7	17	23	21	14	2	0	0	85
Days Maximum Temp. ≤ 32°F	0	0	0	0	0	0	0	0	0	0	0	0	0
Days Minimum Temp. ≤ 32°F	11	5	2	0	0	0	0	0	0	0	3	9	30
Days Minimum Temp. ≤ 0°F	0	0	0	0	0	0	0	0	0	0	0	0	0
Heating Degree Days (base 65°F)	429	301	184	71	7	0	0	0	0	48	179	372	1,591
Cooling Degree Days (base 65°F)	8	12	41	98	264	424	504	492	373	166	48	16	2,446
Mean Precipitation (in.)	4.35	4.34	5.34	3.04	2.80	6.04	6.11	5.93	4.52	3.40	2.55	3.05	51.47
Extreme Maximum Daily Precip. (in.)	3.60	5.00	6.62	4.40	3.25	4.40	3.52	4.25	6.05	4.88	2.40	2.50	6.62
Days With ≥ 0.1" Precipitation	6	6	6	4	5	9	10	10	6	4	3	5	74
Days With ≥ 0.5" Precipitation	3	3	3	2	2	4	4	4	3	2	2	2	34
Days With ≥ 1.0" Precipitation	2	1	1	1	1	2	2	2	1	1	1	1	16
Mean Snowfall (in.)	0.0	0.0	trace	0.0	0.0	0.0	0.0	0.0	0.0	0.0	0.0	0.1	0.1
Maximum Snow Depth (in.)	0	0	trace	0	0	0	0	0	0	0	0	0	trace
Days With ≥ 1.0" Snow Depth	0	0	0	0	0	0	0	0	0	0	0	0	0

Kissimmee 2 *Osceola County* Elevation: 60 ft. Latitude: 28° 17' N Longitude: 81° 25' W

	JAN	FEB	MAR	APR	MAY	JUN	JUL	AUG	SEP	OCT	NOV	DEC	YEAR
Mean Maximum Temp. (°F)	72.9	75.3	78.7	82.8	87.6	90.4	91.7	91.6	89.5	84.9	79.3	73.9	83.2
Mean Temp. (°F)	60.9	63.3	67.0	70.9	76.5	80.8	82.3	82.4	80.7	75.3	68.5	62.6	72.6
Mean Minimum Temp. (°F)	48.9	51.3	55.3	58.9	65.3	71.2	72.9	73.2	71.9	65.6	57.8	51.2	61.9
Extreme Maximum Temp. (°F)	86	89	91	98	98	101	101	100	97	95	89	87	101
Extreme Minimum Temp. (°F)	19	27	25	39	46	53	66	66	56	40	35	20	19
Days Maximum Temp. ≥ 90°F	0	0	0	2	10	19	24	24	17	4	0	0	100
Days Maximum Temp. ≤ 32°F	0	0	0	0	0	0	0	0	0	0	0	0	0
Days Minimum Temp. ≤ 32°F	2	1	0	0	0	0	0	0	0	0	0	1	4
Days Minimum Temp. ≤ 0°F	0	0	0	0	0	0	0	0	0	0	0	0	0
Heating Degree Days (base 65°F)	173	107	56	13	0	0	0	0	0	5	39	138	531
Cooling Degree Days (base 65°F)	52	66	126	198	363	481	543	547	478	331	152	71	3,408
Mean Precipitation (in.)	2.37	2.66	3.49	2.11	3.60	7.42	7.07	7.75	6.34	3.23	2.30	2.33	50.67
Extreme Maximum Daily Precip. (in.)	4.31	2.90	3.50	4.29	4.70	5.86	7.65	4.25	4.95	4.19	5.50	2.49	7.65
Days With ≥ 0.1" Precipitation	4	4	5	3	5	10	11	11	9	5	3	3	73
Days With ≥ 0.5" Precipitation	2	2	2	1	2	5	4	5	4	2	1	1	31
Days With ≥ 1.0" Precipitation	1	1	1	0	1	2	2	2	2	1	1	1	15
Mean Snowfall (in.)	0.0	0.0	0.0	0.0	0.0	0.0	0.0	0.0	0.0	0.0	0.0	0.0	0.0
Maximum Snow Depth (in.)	0	0	0	0	0	0	0	0	0	0	0	0	0
Days With ≥ 1.0" Snow Depth	0	0	0	0	0	0	0	0	0	0	0	0	0

Lake City 2 E *Columbia County* Elevation: 194 ft. Latitude: 30° 11' N Longitude: 82° 36' W

	JAN	FEB	MAR	APR	MAY	JUN	JUL	AUG	SEP	OCT	NOV	DEC	YEAR
Mean Maximum Temp. (°F)	64.8	68.4	74.3	79.6	86.4	90.1	91.4	90.8	87.5	80.8	73.6	66.9	79.6
Mean Temp. (°F)	53.5	56.8	62.3	67.4	74.5	79.8	81.5	81.2	77.9	70.3	62.6	55.8	68.6
Mean Minimum Temp. (°F)	42.1	45.2	50.2	55.3	62.5	69.4	71.6	71.5	68.2	59.7	51.5	44.8	57.7
Extreme Maximum Temp. (°F)	84	85	89	96	99	104	102	104	97	94	89	91	104
Extreme Minimum Temp. (°F)	7	16	19	34	42	49	57	60	47	35	26	9	7
Days Maximum Temp. ≥ 90°F	0	0	0	1	9	18	23	21	11	1	0	0	84
Days Maximum Temp. ≤ 32°F	0	0	0	0	0	0	0	0	0	0	0	0	0
Days Minimum Temp. ≤ 32°F	7	3	1	0	0	0	0	0	0	0	1	4	16
Days Minimum Temp. ≤ 0°F	0	0	0	0	0	0	0	0	0	0	0	0	0
Heating Degree Days (base 65°F)	364	247	141	52	4	0	0	0	0	29	137	303	1,277
Cooling Degree Days (base 65°F)	14	22	64	130	305	450	519	508	393	199	70	26	2,700
Mean Precipitation (in.)	4.18	3.60	5.19	3.07	2.78	7.22	7.16	6.99	5.46	3.03	2.29	2.79	53.76
Extreme Maximum Daily Precip. (in.)	3.44	2.55	3.90	4.30	2.18	4.25	5.33	4.05	7.90	4.05	2.24	5.19	7.90
Days With ≥ 0.1" Precipitation	6	5	6	4	5	10	10	10	7	4	4	4	75
Days With ≥ 0.5" Precipitation	3	3	3	2	2	5	5	4	3	2	2	2	36
Days With ≥ 1.0" Precipitation	1	1	2	1	1	2	2	2	2	1	1	1	17
Mean Snowfall (in.)	0.0	0.0	0.0	0.0	0.0	0.0	0.0	0.0	0.0	0.0	0.0	0.0	0.0
Maximum Snow Depth (in.)	0	0	0	0	0	0	0	0	0	0	0	0	0
Days With ≥ 1.0" Snow Depth	0	0	0	0	0	0	0	0	0	0	0	0	0

The period of record for all cooperative weather station data is 1980 – 2009. See User Guide for detailed explanation of data.

Melbourne Regional Arpt *Brevard County* Elevation: 35 ft. Latitude: 28° 07' N Longitude: 80° 39' W

	JAN	FEB	MAR	APR	MAY	JUN	JUL	AUG	SEP	OCT	NOV	DEC	YEAR
Mean Maximum Temp. (°F)	71.6	73.7	77.1	80.6	85.2	88.9	90.3	90.0	87.9	83.7	78.3	73.3	81.7
Mean Temp. (°F)	61.0	63.3	66.8	70.5	76.2	80.3	81.5	81.6	80.4	76.0	69.2	63.6	72.5
Mean Minimum Temp. (°F)	50.4	52.8	56.5	60.4	67.2	71.6	72.7	73.2	72.7	68.2	60.2	53.7	63.3
Extreme Maximum Temp. (°F)	88	88	93	97	97	101	102	101	96	94	91	89	102
Extreme Minimum Temp. (°F)	22	28	25	25	47	55	62	60	58	45	37	21	21
Days Maximum Temp. ≥ 90°F	0	0	1	1	5	12	19	18	8	2	0	0	66
Days Maximum Temp. ≤ 32°F	0	0	0	0	0	0	0	0	0	0	0	0	0
Days Minimum Temp. ≤ 32°F	1	1	0	0	0	0	0	0	0	0	0	1	3
Days Minimum Temp. ≤ 0°F	0	0	0	0	0	0	0	0	0	0	0	0	0
Heating Degree Days (base 65°F)	170	109	59	17	0	0	0	0	0	4	34	123	516
Cooling Degree Days (base 65°F)	54	67	122	190	355	464	520	522	468	351	168	85	3,366
Mean Precipitation (in.)	2.37	2.51	3.02	2.11	3.42	6.64	6.05	7.54	7.53	5.11	2.91	2.54	51.75
Extreme Maximum Daily Precip. (in.)	4.13	3.76	5.24	2.60	5.21	6.57	3.59	11.85	7.98	4.80	4.70	6.77	11.85
Days With ≥ 0.1" Precipitation	4	4	4	4	5	9	9	10	9	7	4	4	73
Days With ≥ 0.5" Precipitation	2	2	2	2	2	4	5	5	5	3	1	2	35
Days With ≥ 1.0" Precipitation	1	1	1	0	1	2	2	2	2	1	1	1	15
Mean Snowfall (in.)	0.0	0.0	0.0	0.0	0.0	0.0	0.0	0.0	0.0	0.0	0.0	0.0	0.0
Maximum Snow Depth (in.)	0	0	0	0	0	0	0	0	0	0	0	0	0
Days With ≥ 1.0" Snow Depth	0	0	0	0	0	0	0	0	0	0	0	0	0

Mountain Lake *Polk County* Elevation: 125 ft. Latitude: 27° 56' N Longitude: 81° 36' W

	JAN	FEB	MAR	APR	MAY	JUN	JUL	AUG	SEP	OCT	NOV	DEC	YEAR
Mean Maximum Temp. (°F)	73.3	76.2	80.2	84.4	89.4	91.7	92.4	92.4	90.2	85.5	79.4	74.4	84.1
Mean Temp. (°F)	61.2	63.8	67.9	71.8	77.4	81.2	82.1	82.3	80.7	75.3	68.5	63.1	72.9
Mean Minimum Temp. (°F)	49.0	51.4	55.5	59.1	65.4	70.6	71.7	72.2	71.1	65.1	57.6	51.8	61.7
Extreme Maximum Temp. (°F)	89	91	93	96	99	101	105	100	98	96	91	88	105
Extreme Minimum Temp. (°F)	16	24	25	34	44	50	53	62	57	36	31	16	16
Days Maximum Temp. ≥ 90°F	0	0	1	5	16	21	26	26	19	6	0	0	120
Days Maximum Temp. ≤ 32°F	0	0	0	0	0	0	0	0	0	0	0	0	0
Days Minimum Temp. ≤ 32°F	2	1	0	0	0	0	0	0	0	0	0	1	4
Days Minimum Temp. ≤ 0°F	0	0	0	0	0	0	0	0	0	0	0	0	0
Heating Degree Days (base 65°F)	171	102	50	11	0	0	0	0	0	4	40	130	508
Cooling Degree Days (base 65°F)	59	74	145	221	392	492	536	543	477	332	151	77	3,499
Mean Precipitation (in.)	2.32	2.34	3.22	2.22	3.38	8.05	7.09	6.99	6.12	2.88	2.15	2.49	49.25
Extreme Maximum Daily Precip. (in.)	3.85	3.11	2.80	3.00	3.11	4.65	3.65	4.20	4.60	6.00	3.16	3.80	6.00
Days With ≥ 0.1" Precipitation	4	4	5	4	5	11	11	11	8	5	3	3	74
Days With ≥ 0.5" Precipitation	1	1	2	2	2	5	5	5	3	2	1	2	31
Days With ≥ 1.0" Precipitation	1	1	1	1	1	3	2	2	2	1	1	1	17
Mean Snowfall (in.)	0.0	0.0	0.0	0.0	0.0	0.0	0.0	0.0	0.0	0.0	0.0	0.0	0.0
Maximum Snow Depth (in.)	0	0	0	0	0	0	0	0	0	0	0	0	0
Days With ≥ 1.0" Snow Depth	0	0	0	0	0	0	0	0	0	0	0	0	0

Myakka River State Park *Sarasota County* Elevation: 20 ft. Latitude: 27° 14' N Longitude: 82° 19' W

	JAN	FEB	MAR	APR	MAY	JUN	JUL	AUG	SEP	OCT	NOV	DEC	YEAR
Mean Maximum Temp. (°F)	75.1	77.9	81.3	85.3	90.7	92.5	92.9	93.0	91.5	87.4	81.4	76.5	85.5
Mean Temp. (°F)	62.2	64.7	68.3	71.7	77.2	81.1	82.2	82.8	81.4	76.3	69.5	64.4	73.5
Mean Minimum Temp. (°F)	49.2	51.6	55.1	58.2	63.6	69.6	71.5	72.5	71.2	65.1	57.5	52.2	61.4
Extreme Maximum Temp. (°F)	89	91	93	98	104	105	101	104	103	97	95	89	105
Extreme Minimum Temp. (°F)	18	22	28	36	45	50	63	60	58	37	33	22	18
Days Maximum Temp. ≥ 90°F	0	0	2	6	20	25	27	28	23	12	1	0	144
Days Maximum Temp. ≤ 32°F	0	0	0	0	0	0	0	0	0	0	0	0	0
Days Minimum Temp. ≤ 32°F	2	1	0	0	0	0	0	0	0	0	0	1	4
Days Minimum Temp. ≤ 0°F	0	0	0	0	0	0	0	0	0	0	0	0	0
Heating Degree Days (base 65°F)	146	84	41	9	0	0	0	0	0	3	29	105	417
Cooling Degree Days (base 65°F)	64	84	150	218	385	488	542	559	499	359	170	93	3,611
Mean Precipitation (in.)	2.84	2.86	3.66	2.60	2.69	9.26	9.52	9.69	7.95	3.30	2.24	2.38	58.99
Extreme Maximum Daily Precip. (in.)	3.70	6.15	4.70	4.00	2.60	8.75	5.52	4.00	6.00	5.30	7.25	3.34	8.75
Days With ≥ 0.1" Precipitation	4	4	4	3	4	11	13	13	10	5	3	4	78
Days With ≥ 0.5" Precipitation	2	2	2	2	2	6	6	6	5	2	1	1	37
Days With ≥ 1.0" Precipitation	1	1	1	1	1	3	3	3	3	1	1	1	20
Mean Snowfall (in.)	0.0	0.0	0.0	0.0	0.0	0.0	0.0	0.0	0.0	0.0	0.0	trace	trace
Maximum Snow Depth (in.)	0	0	0	0	0	0	0	0	0	0	0	trace	trace
Days With ≥ 1.0" Snow Depth	0	0	0	0	0	0	0	0	0	0	0	0	0

Naples *Collier County* Elevation: 4 ft. Latitude: 26° 10' N Longitude: 81° 47' W

	JAN	FEB	MAR	APR	MAY	JUN	JUL	AUG	SEP	OCT	NOV	DEC	YEAR
Mean Maximum Temp. (°F)	75.9	77.8	80.8	83.9	88.2	90.6	92.0	92.2	90.9	87.5	82.2	77.9	85.0
Mean Temp. (°F)	64.9	66.8	70.1	73.2	78.0	81.5	82.7	83.0	82.1	78.1	72.2	67.3	75.0
Mean Minimum Temp. (°F)	53.8	55.8	59.3	62.5	67.7	72.4	73.3	73.8	73.2	68.6	62.1	56.7	64.9
Extreme Maximum Temp. (°F)	88	90	91	93	95	98	98	97	99	96	93	89	99
Extreme Minimum Temp. (°F)	26	28	33	40	52	59	63	69	59	46	37	27	26
Days Maximum Temp. ≥ 90°F	0	0	1	2	11	21	28	28	23	11	1	0	126
Days Maximum Temp. ≤ 32°F	0	0	0	0	0	0	0	0	0	0	0	0	0
Days Minimum Temp. ≤ 32°F	0	0	0	0	0	0	0	0	0	0	0	0	0
Days Minimum Temp. ≤ 0°F	0	0	0	0	0	0	0	0	0	0	0	0	0
Heating Degree Days (base 65°F)	94	55	25	5	0	0	0	0	0	1	12	59	251
Cooling Degree Days (base 65°F)	97	113	188	259	409	503	555	566	518	415	233	138	3,994
Mean Precipitation (in.)	2.02	2.13	2.17	2.22	3.46	8.46	9.07	8.73	8.85	3.87	2.06	1.71	54.75
Extreme Maximum Daily Precip. (in.)	6.10	2.65	2.52	4.60	4.53	3.75	7.66	3.85	6.51	5.20	4.82	2.20	7.66
Days With ≥ 0.1" Precipitation	3	3	3	3	5	11	13	13	12	6	3	3	78
Days With ≥ 0.5" Precipitation	1	1	2	1	2	5	6	6	6	2	1	1	34
Days With ≥ 1.0" Precipitation	1	1	1	1	1	3	3	3	3	1	1	0	19
Mean Snowfall (in.)	0.0	0.0	0.0	0.0	0.0	0.0	0.0	0.0	0.0	0.0	0.0	0.0	0.0
Maximum Snow Depth (in.)	0	0	0	0	0	0	0	0	0	0	0	0	0
Days With ≥ 1.0" Snow Depth	0	0	0	0	0	0	0	0	0	0	0	0	0

The period of record for all cooperative weather station data is 1980 – 2009. See User Guide for detailed explanation of data.

Oasis Ranger Station *Collier County* Elevation: 7 ft. Latitude: 25° 51' N Longitude: 81° 02' W

	JAN	FEB	MAR	APR	MAY	JUN	JUL	AUG	SEP	OCT	NOV	DEC	YEAR
Mean Maximum Temp. (°F)	78.6	80.7	83.2	86.7	90.8	92.5	93.7	93.9	92.4	88.9	84.0	80.2	87.1
Mean Temp. (°F)	66.7	68.6	70.9	73.7	78.0	82.2	84.2	84.7	83.8	79.8	74.0	69.2	76.3
Mean Minimum Temp. (°F)	54.7	56.5	58.6	60.7	65.1	71.8	74.6	75.4	75.1	70.7	63.9	58.2	65.4
Extreme Maximum Temp. (°F)	90	91	94	97	100	103	101	101	100	98	96	91	103
Extreme Minimum Temp. (°F)	26	26	32	41	50	58	62	62	63	48	39	26	26
Days Maximum Temp. ≥ 90°F	0	0	3	8	21	26	29	29	25	15	2	0	158
Days Maximum Temp. ≤ 32°F	0	0	0	0	0	0	0	0	0	0	0	0	0
Days Minimum Temp. ≤ 32°F	0	0	0	0	0	0	0	0	0	0	0	0	0
Days Minimum Temp. ≤ 0°F	0	0	0	0	0	0	0	0	0	0	0	0	0
Heating Degree Days (base 65°F)	65	38	20	3	0	0	0	0	0	0	6	38	170
Cooling Degree Days (base 65°F)	125	146	210	271	410	523	601	616	570	466	282	176	4,396
Mean Precipitation (in.)	1.84	1.79	2.86	2.78	5.10	10.59	7.88	9.34	8.03	4.20	2.14	1.60	58.15
Extreme Maximum Daily Precip. (in.)	3.20	3.59	3.65	3.05	4.71	6.85	5.72	8.05	5.72	4.60	5.05	2.18	8.05
Days With ≥ 0.1" Precipitation	3	3	4	4	6	13	12	13	11	6	3	2	80
Days With ≥ 0.5" Precipitation	1	1	2	2	3	6	5	6	5	2	1	1	35
Days With ≥ 1.0" Precipitation	0	0	1	1	2	4	3	3	2	1	1	1	19
Mean Snowfall (in.)	0.0	0.0	0.0	0.0	0.0	0.0	0.0	0.0	0.0	0.0	0.0	0.0	0.0
Maximum Snow Depth (in.)	0	0	0	0	0	0	0	0	0	0	0	0	0
Days With ≥ 1.0" Snow Depth	0	0	0	0	0	0	0	0	0	0	0	0	0

Panama City 5 NE *Bay County* Elevation: 32 ft. Latitude: 30° 13' N Longitude: 85° 36' W

	JAN	FEB	MAR	APR	MAY	JUN	JUL	AUG	SEP	OCT	NOV	DEC	YEAR
Mean Maximum Temp. (°F)	63.1	66.0	71.5	77.0	83.9	88.4	90.0	90.0	87.9	80.7	72.7	65.0	78.0
Mean Temp. (°F)	51.8	54.7	60.1	65.8	73.4	79.2	81.3	81.2	78.2	69.2	60.8	53.7	67.4
Mean Minimum Temp. (°F)	40.4	43.3	48.7	54.5	62.8	70.1	72.6	72.3	68.4	57.7	48.9	42.4	56.8
Extreme Maximum Temp. (°F)	79	82	86	93	100	101	101	102	98	92	86	82	102
Extreme Minimum Temp. (°F)	6	15	23	34	40	46	60	59	45	33	25	11	6
Days Maximum Temp. ≥ 90°F	0	0	0	0	2	12	17	19	12	1	0	0	63
Days Maximum Temp. ≤ 32°F	0	0	0	0	0	0	0	0	0	0	0	0	0
Days Minimum Temp. ≤ 32°F	9	4	1	0	0	0	0	0	0	0	1	6	21
Days Minimum Temp. ≤ 0°F	0	0	0	0	0	0	0	0	0	0	0	0	0
Heating Degree Days (base 65°F)	410	296	180	63	4	0	0	0	1	40	167	359	1,520
Cooling Degree Days (base 65°F)	7	10	36	93	271	434	511	509	402	177	48	16	2,514
Mean Precipitation (in.)	5.00	5.09	5.86	3.99	3.06	6.37	7.58	6.98	5.99	3.79	4.44	4.02	62.17
Extreme Maximum Daily Precip. (in.)	4.04	7.20	4.44	10.72	4.40	5.80	3.80	4.28	12.80	5.85	6.67	6.35	12.80
Days With ≥ 0.1" Precipitation	7	6	6	4	4	9	10	10	7	4	5	6	78
Days With ≥ 0.5" Precipitation	3	3	3	2	2	4	5	5	3	2	3	2	37
Days With ≥ 1.0" Precipitation	1	2	2	1	1	2	3	2	2	1	1	1	19
Mean Snowfall (in.)	0.0	0.0	0.0	0.0	0.0	0.0	0.0	0.0	0.0	0.0	0.0	0.0	0.0
Maximum Snow Depth (in.)	0	0	0	0	0	0	0	0	0	0	0	0	0
Days With ≥ 1.0" Snow Depth	0	0	0	0	0	0	0	0	0	0	0	0	0

Parrish *Manatee County* Elevation: 60 ft. Latitude: 27° 37' N Longitude: 82° 21' W

	JAN	FEB	MAR	APR	MAY	JUN	JUL	AUG	SEP	OCT	NOV	DEC	YEAR
Mean Maximum Temp. (°F)	71.8	74.3	77.8	81.8	86.9	89.8	90.6	90.6	89.2	84.8	78.9	73.8	82.5
Mean Temp. (°F)	60.7	62.9	66.7	70.4	75.9	80.4	81.6	81.9	80.5	75.1	68.4	62.8	72.3
Mean Minimum Temp. (°F)	49.5	51.5	55.5	59.1	64.9	71.0	72.6	73.0	71.7	65.3	57.8	51.7	62.0
Extreme Maximum Temp. (°F)	86	88	91	92	96	101	98	101	99	93	90	87	101
Extreme Minimum Temp. (°F)	18	24	29	36	41	51	65	64	57	42	31	23	18
Days Maximum Temp. ≥ 90°F	0	0	0	1	8	18	22	22	17	4	0	0	92
Days Maximum Temp. ≤ 32°F	0	0	0	0	0	0	0	0	0	0	0	0	0
Days Minimum Temp. ≤ 32°F	1	1	0	0	0	0	0	0	0	0	0	1	3
Days Minimum Temp. ≤ 0°F	0	0	0	0	0	0	0	0	0	0	0	0	0
Heating Degree Days (base 65°F)	180	118	61	18	1	0	0	0	0	6	41	138	563
Cooling Degree Days (base 65°F)	54	65	121	188	346	469	523	530	472	325	150	76	3,319
Mean Precipitation (in.)	2.78	2.75	3.42	2.41	2.66	8.07	8.08	8.75	8.16	2.89	2.32	2.28	54.57
Extreme Maximum Daily Precip. (in.)	4.50	3.62	6.00	3.50	3.81	6.90	3.76	4.50	8.27	3.70	4.96	3.97	8.27
Days With ≥ 0.1" Precipitation	4	4	4	3	4	9	12	12	9	4	3	3	71
Days With ≥ 0.5" Precipitation	2	2	2	2	2	5	6	6	5	2	1	1	36
Days With ≥ 1.0" Precipitation	1	1	1	1	1	3	3	3	2	1	1	1	19
Mean Snowfall (in.)	0.0	0.0	0.0	0.0	0.0	0.0	0.0	0.0	0.0	0.0	0.0	0.0	0.0
Maximum Snow Depth (in.)	0	0	0	0	0	0	0	0	0	0	0	0	0
Days With ≥ 1.0" Snow Depth	0	0	0	0	0	0	0	0	0	0	0	0	0

Perry *Taylor County* Elevation: 44 ft. Latitude: 30° 06' N Longitude: 83° 34' W

	JAN	FEB	MAR	APR	MAY	JUN	JUL	AUG	SEP	OCT	NOV	DEC	YEAR
Mean Maximum Temp. (°F)	67.4	70.8	76.1	81.2	87.7	90.9	92.4	91.9	89.6	83.2	76.0	69.2	81.4
Mean Temp. (°F)	54.3	57.3	62.4	67.3	74.6	79.7	81.7	81.5	78.6	70.7	62.6	56.1	68.9
Mean Minimum Temp. (°F)	41.2	43.9	48.5	53.3	61.3	68.4	71.0	71.0	67.5	58.1	49.2	43.0	56.4
Extreme Maximum Temp. (°F)	82	85	90	94	100	103	104	102	98	94	89	86	104
Extreme Minimum Temp. (°F)	7	14	19	29	40	46	59	58	45	28	20	12	7
Days Maximum Temp. ≥ 90°F	0	0	0	2	11	20	25	24	18	4	0	0	104
Days Maximum Temp. ≤ 32°F	0	0	0	0	0	0	0	0	0	0	0	0	0
Days Minimum Temp. ≤ 32°F	8	5	2	0	0	0	0	0	0	0	2	7	24
Days Minimum Temp. ≤ 0°F	0	0	0	0	0	0	0	0	0	0	0	0	0
Heating Degree Days (base 65°F)	338	231	134	50	3	0	0	0	0	31	136	294	1,217
Cooling Degree Days (base 65°F)	13	21	59	125	307	448	525	518	414	213	72	26	2,741
Mean Precipitation (in.)	4.45	3.87	5.31	2.98	2.70	6.69	8.16	8.01	4.88	3.24	2.42	3.04	55.75
Extreme Maximum Daily Precip. (in.)	3.20	5.20	5.80	4.59	3.19	5.45	10.26	12.10	4.73	5.07	3.79	3.48	12.10
Days With ≥ 0.1" Precipitation	6	5	6	4	4	9	11	11	7	4	4	5	76
Days With ≥ 0.5" Precipitation	3	3	3	2	2	4	5	5	3	2	1	2	35
Days With ≥ 1.0" Precipitation	1	1	2	1	1	2	2	2	2	1	1	1	17
Mean Snowfall (in.)	0.0	0.0	0.0	0.0	0.0	0.0	0.0	0.0	0.0	0.0	0.0	0.0	0.0
Maximum Snow Depth (in.)	0	0	0	0	0	0	0	0	0	0	0	0	0
Days With ≥ 1.0" Snow Depth	0	0	0	0	0	0	0	0	0	0	0	0	0

The period of record for all cooperative weather station data is 1980 – 2009. See User Guide for detailed explanation of data.

Plant City *Hillsborough County* Elevation: 120 ft. Latitude: 28° 01' N Longitude: 82° 08' W

	JAN	FEB	MAR	APR	MAY	JUN	JUL	AUG	SEP	OCT	NOV	DEC	YEAR
Mean Maximum Temp. (°F)	72.5	75.1	78.9	83.0	88.5	90.7	91.6	91.4	89.7	85.1	79.0	74.0	83.3
Mean Temp. (°F)	60.8	63.4	67.1	71.0	76.9	80.8	82.0	82.0	80.5	75.0	68.1	62.9	72.5
Mean Minimum Temp. (°F)	49.0	51.6	55.3	58.9	65.2	70.8	72.2	72.6	71.1	65.0	57.2	51.7	61.7
Extreme Maximum Temp. (°F)	87	89	90	93	99	102	102	99	98	94	89	89	102
Extreme Minimum Temp. (°F)	17	25	24	35	43	49	59	64	55	38	29	20	17
Days Maximum Temp. ≥ 90°F	0	0	0	2	12	20	25	24	18	5	0	0	106
Days Maximum Temp. ≤ 32°F	0	0	0	0	0	0	0	0	0	0	0	0	0
Days Minimum Temp. ≤ 32°F	2	1	0	0	0	0	0	0	0	0	0	1	4
Days Minimum Temp. ≤ 0°F	0	0	0	0	0	0	0	0	0	0	0	0	0
Heating Degree Days (base 65°F)	179	111	59	16	0	0	0	0	0	6	44	135	550
Cooling Degree Days (base 65°F)	55	72	131	203	375	480	533	534	470	323	144	76	3,396
Mean Precipitation (in.)	2.67	2.79	3.48	2.59	3.53	8.64	7.59	8.43	6.98	2.42	1.95	2.57	53.64
Extreme Maximum Daily Precip. (in.)	4.46	3.85	3.21	2.87	3.10	4.65	3.52	3.82	7.70	2.55	4.60	3.56	7.70
Days With ≥ 0.1" Precipitation	4	4	4	4	5	11	12	12	8	4	3	4	75
Days With ≥ 0.5" Precipitation	2	2	2	2	2	6	5	6	4	1	1	2	35
Days With ≥ 1.0" Precipitation	1	1	1	1	1	3	2	3	2	1	1	1	18
Mean Snowfall (in.)	0.0	0.0	0.0	0.0	0.0	0.0	0.0	0.0	0.0	0.0	0.0	0.0	0.0
Maximum Snow Depth (in.)	0	0	0	0	0	0	0	0	0	0	0	0	0
Days With ≥ 1.0" Snow Depth	0	0	0	0	0	0	0	0	0	0	0	0	0

Punta Gorda 4 ESE *Charlotte County* Elevation: 20 ft. Latitude: 26° 55' N Longitude: 82° 00' W

	JAN	FEB	MAR	APR	MAY	JUN	JUL	AUG	SEP	OCT	NOV	DEC	YEAR
Mean Maximum Temp. (°F)	74.8	77.1	80.5	84.4	89.3	91.5	92.1	92.3	90.6	86.7	81.0	76.5	84.7
Mean Temp. (°F)	63.4	65.5	69.0	72.7	77.8	81.8	82.9	83.2	81.9	77.0	70.4	65.6	74.3
Mean Minimum Temp. (°F)	51.8	54.0	57.5	60.9	66.2	72.0	73.7	74.1	73.1	67.2	59.7	54.7	63.7
Extreme Maximum Temp. (°F)	89	92	93	93	98	102	99	99	95	98	93	96	102
Extreme Minimum Temp. (°F)	23	27	29	41	49	57	63	66	61	43	37	25	23
Days Maximum Temp. ≥ 90°F	0	0	0	2	15	24	27	27	22	7	0	0	124
Days Maximum Temp. ≤ 32°F	0	0	0	0	0	0	0	0	0	0	0	0	0
Days Minimum Temp. ≤ 32°F	1	0	0	0	0	0	0	0	0	0	0	0	1
Days Minimum Temp. ≤ 0°F	0	0	0	0	0	0	0	0	0	0	0	0	0
Heating Degree Days (base 65°F)	119	69	31	5	0	0	0	0	0	2	21	80	327
Cooling Degree Days (base 65°F)	76	90	162	241	403	510	564	572	512	380	189	106	3,805
Mean Precipitation (in.)	1.85	2.37	3.12	1.94	2.52	8.62	8.27	8.56	6.58	3.01	1.94	1.83	50.61
Extreme Maximum Daily Precip. (in.)	2.65	3.00	5.02	2.98	3.50	10.65	4.00	10.35	6.30	4.90	4.50	2.90	10.65
Days With ≥ 0.1" Precipitation	3	4	4	3	4	10	12	11	10	5	3	3	72
Days With ≥ 0.5" Precipitation	1	2	2	1	2	5	6	6	4	2	1	1	33
Days With ≥ 1.0" Precipitation	0	1	1	1	1	3	3	2	2	1	0	1	16
Mean Snowfall (in.)	0.0	0.0	0.0	0.0	0.0	0.0	0.0	0.0	0.0	0.0	0.0	0.0	0.0
Maximum Snow Depth (in.)	0	0	0	0	0	0	0	0	0	0	0	0	0
Days With ≥ 1.0" Snow Depth	0	0	0	0	0	0	0	0	0	0	0	0	0

Saint Leo *Pasco County* Elevation: 189 ft. Latitude: 28° 20' N Longitude: 82° 16' W

	JAN	FEB	MAR	APR	MAY	JUN	JUL	AUG	SEP	OCT	NOV	DEC	YEAR
Mean Maximum Temp. (°F)	72.4	75.3	79.5	83.9	89.9	91.8	92.4	92.4	90.6	85.8	79.3	73.8	83.9
Mean Temp. (°F)	60.9	63.5	67.5	71.7	77.7	81.4	82.6	82.6	80.8	75.2	68.4	62.7	72.9
Mean Minimum Temp. (°F)	49.3	51.7	55.5	59.5	65.5	71.0	72.6	72.7	71.0	64.6	57.5	51.6	61.9
Extreme Maximum Temp. (°F)	87	89	92	95	99	103	100	100	98	96	92	88	103
Extreme Minimum Temp. (°F)	18	22	24	38	46	54	64	66	53	39	35	20	18
Days Maximum Temp. ≥ 90°F	0	0	1	4	18	23	27	26	22	7	0	0	128
Days Maximum Temp. ≤ 32°F	0	0	0	0	0	0	0	0	0	0	0	0	0
Days Minimum Temp. ≤ 32°F	1	1	0	0	0	0	0	0	0	0	0	1	3
Days Minimum Temp. ≤ 0°F	0	0	0	0	0	0	0	0	0	0	0	0	0
Heating Degree Days (base 65°F)	177	108	54	12	0	0	0	0	0	5	43	140	539
Cooling Degree Days (base 65°F)	55	72	139	221	402	500	551	551	482	329	152	76	3,530
Mean Precipitation (in.)	3.21	2.98	3.99	2.58	2.90	7.75	8.11	7.54	6.84	3.11	2.25	2.75	54.01
Extreme Maximum Daily Precip. (in.)	2.60	4.37	3.82	2.01	3.17	3.74	3.14	3.27	5.61	3.70	9.27	4.39	9.27
Days With ≥ 0.1" Precipitation	5	5	5	4	4	10	12	12	9	5	4	4	79
Days With ≥ 0.5" Precipitation	2	2	3	2	2	5	6	5	4	2	1	2	36
Days With ≥ 1.0" Precipitation	1	1	1	1	1	3	3	2	2	1	0	1	17
Mean Snowfall (in.)	0.0	0.0	0.0	0.0	0.0	0.0	0.0	0.0	0.0	0.0	0.0	0.0	0.0
Maximum Snow Depth (in.)	0	0	0	0	0	0	0	0	0	0	0	0	0
Days With ≥ 1.0" Snow Depth	0	0	0	0	0	0	0	0	0	0	0	0	0

Sanford Experiment Stn *Seminole County* Elevation: 15 ft. Latitude: 28° 48' N Longitude: 81° 14' W

	JAN	FEB	MAR	APR	MAY	JUN	JUL	AUG	SEP	OCT	NOV	DEC	YEAR
Mean Maximum Temp. (°F)	70.0	72.6	77.0	81.5	87.3	90.6	92.0	91.8	89.1	83.9	77.7	71.8	82.1
Mean Temp. (°F)	59.0	61.5	65.8	70.0	76.0	80.7	82.4	82.4	80.4	74.7	67.8	61.5	71.8
Mean Minimum Temp. (°F)	47.9	50.2	54.5	58.5	64.8	70.7	72.7	73.0	71.6	65.4	57.9	51.2	61.5
Extreme Maximum Temp. (°F)	89	89	92	96	100	102	103	100	98	96	92	87	103
Extreme Minimum Temp. (°F)	19	26	27	36	45	52	60	65	52	39	35	19	19
Days Maximum Temp. ≥ 90°F	0	0	0	2	11	19	25	24	16	4	0	0	101
Days Maximum Temp. ≤ 32°F	0	0	0	0	0	0	0	0	0	0	0	0	0
Days Minimum Temp. ≤ 32°F	2	1	0	0	0	0	0	0	0	0	0	1	4
Days Minimum Temp. ≤ 0°F	0	0	0	0	0	0	0	0	0	0	0	0	0
Heating Degree Days (base 65°F)	217	143	76	22	1	0	0	0	0	6	49	162	676
Cooling Degree Days (base 65°F)	38	48	108	179	350	476	546	547	469	314	140	61	3,276
Mean Precipitation (in.)	2.79	2.64	3.84	2.62	3.15	7.27	7.38	8.15	5.86	3.79	2.79	2.60	52.88
Extreme Maximum Daily Precip. (in.)	4.00	3.41	4.13	6.50	5.45	4.00	***6.15***	8.27	3.70	3.11	10.17	3.07	***10.17***
Days With ≥ 0.1" Precipitation	4	4	5	4	5	10	9	10	8	6	4	4	73
Days With ≥ 0.5" Precipitation	2	2	3	2	2	5	5	5	4	2	1	2	35
Days With ≥ 1.0" Precipitation	1	1	1	1	1	2	2	3	2	1	1	1	17
Mean Snowfall (in.)	0.0	0.0	0.0	0.0	0.0	0.0	0.0	0.0	0.0	0.0	0.0	0.0	0.0
Maximum Snow Depth (in.)	0	0	0	0	0	0	0	0	0	0	0	0	0
Days With ≥ 1.0" Snow Depth	0	0	0	0	0	0	0	0	0	0	0	0	0

The period of record for all cooperative weather station data is 1980 – 2009. See User Guide for detailed explanation of data.

St Augustine WFOY *St. Johns County* Elevation: 7 ft. Latitude: 29° 54' N Longitude: 81° 19' W

	JAN	FEB	MAR	APR	MAY	JUN	JUL	AUG	SEP	OCT	NOV	DEC	YEAR
Mean Maximum Temp. (°F)	66.7	69.3	73.5	78.8	84.2	88.2	90.6	89.7	86.6	81.2	74.5	68.4	79.3
Mean Temp. (°F)	56.6	59.0	63.5	68.7	74.9	79.6	81.7	81.3	79.2	73.2	65.5	59.0	70.2
Mean Minimum Temp. (°F)	46.3	48.7	53.5	58.5	65.5	70.9	72.7	72.9	71.7	65.2	56.5	49.6	61.0
Extreme Maximum Temp. (°F)	86	87	93	95	98	101	103	101	98	93	88	86	103
Extreme Minimum Temp. (°F)	10	21	23	34	45	52	59	61	51	36	34	16	10
Days Maximum Temp. ≥ 90°F	0	0	0	1	5	11	18	15	7	1	0	0	58
Days Maximum Temp. ≤ 32°F	0	0	0	0	0	0	0	0	0	0	0	0	0
Days Minimum Temp. ≤ 32°F	3	1	0	0	0	0	0	0	0	0	0	2	6
Days Minimum Temp. ≤ 0°F	0	0	0	0	0	0	0	0	0	0	0	0	0
Heating Degree Days (base 65°F)	272	187	104	28	1	0	0	0	0	10	77	215	894
Cooling Degree Days (base 65°F)	17	25	64	145	315	444	523	512	432	271	100	36	2,884
Mean Precipitation (in.)	2.79	3.02	4.06	2.68	3.00	5.71	4.72	6.41	7.54	4.70	2.36	2.45	49.44
Extreme Maximum Daily Precip. (in.)	2.23	4.40	3.77	3.83	2.50	8.07	4.50	5.25	4.00	11.28	4.65	3.90	11.28
Days With ≥ 0.1" Precipitation	5	5	5	4	4	8	8	9	9	6	4	4	71
Days With ≥ 0.5" Precipitation	2	2	3	2	2	4	3	4	4	3	1	1	31
Days With ≥ 1.0" Precipitation	1	1	1	1	1	2	1	2	2	1	0	1	14
Mean Snowfall (in.)	0.0	0.0	trace	0.0	0.0	0.0	0.0	0.0	0.0	0.0	trace	0.0	trace
Maximum Snow Depth (in.)	0	0	trace	0	0	0	0	0	0	0	trace	0	trace
Days With ≥ 1.0" Snow Depth	0	0	0	0	0	0	0	0	0	0	0	0	0

St Petersburg *Pinellas County* Elevation: 7 ft. Latitude: 27° 46' N Longitude: 82° 38' W

	JAN	FEB	MAR	APR	MAY	JUN	JUL	AUG	SEP	OCT	NOV	DEC	YEAR
Mean Maximum Temp. (°F)	69.4	71.8	75.6	80.1	86.0	89.2	90.4	90.2	88.4	83.4	76.7	71.5	81.1
Mean Temp. (°F)	61.8	64.1	68.1	72.7	78.7	82.4	83.6	83.6	82.0	76.9	69.8	64.2	74.0
Mean Minimum Temp. (°F)	54.1	56.3	60.5	65.2	71.3	75.5	76.8	77.0	75.6	70.4	62.9	56.8	66.9
Extreme Maximum Temp. (°F)	88	83	88	93	95	99	100	99	97	94	88	88	100
Extreme Minimum Temp. (°F)	27	28	34	46	55	64	67	67	52	49	43	24	24
Days Maximum Temp. ≥ 90°F	0	0	0	0	4	14	21	20	13	2	0	0	74
Days Maximum Temp. ≤ 32°F	0	0	0	0	0	0	0	0	0	0	0	0	0
Days Minimum Temp. ≤ 32°F	0	0	0	0	0	0	0	0	0	0	0	0	0
Days Minimum Temp. ≤ 0°F	0	0	0	0	0	0	0	0	0	0	0	0	0
Heating Degree Days (base 65°F)	143	84	39	5	0	0	0	0	0	2	26	102	401
Cooling Degree Days (base 65°F)	50	64	142	242	431	528	584	584	517	379	177	83	3,781
Mean Precipitation (in.)	2.60	2.75	3.50	2.32	2.20	6.48	7.26	8.31	7.99	2.81	1.96	2.75	50.93
Extreme Maximum Daily Precip. (in.)	4.07	3.81	3.94	5.08	4.50	7.45	5.05	4.64	8.31	2.12	3.22	4.24	8.31
Days With ≥ 0.1" Precipitation	4	4	5	3	3	8	11	11	9	4	3	4	69
Days With ≥ 0.5" Precipitation	2	2	2	2	1	4	5	6	4	2	1	2	33
Days With ≥ 1.0" Precipitation	1	1	1	1	1	2	2	3	2	1	1	1	17
Mean Snowfall (in.)	0.0	0.0	0.0	0.0	0.0	0.0	0.0	0.0	0.0	0.0	0.0	0.0	0.0
Maximum Snow Depth (in.)	0	0	0	0	0	0	0	0	0	0	0	0	0
Days With ≥ 1.0" Snow Depth	0	0	0	0	0	0	0	0	0	0	0	0	0

Stuart 1 S *Martin County* Elevation: 9 ft. Latitude: 27° 10' N Longitude: 80° 14' W

	JAN	FEB	MAR	APR	MAY	JUN	JUL	AUG	SEP	OCT	NOV	DEC	YEAR
Mean Maximum Temp. (°F)	***75.3***	75.9	78.2	***81.8***	85.6	***88.9***	***90.3***	***90.3***	***88.8***	85.3	***80.1***	***76.4***	***83.1***
Mean Temp. (°F)	***65.7***	66.6	69.4	***73.1***	77.7	***81.2***	***82.5***	***82.8***	***81.7***	78.1	***72.3***	***67.9***	***74.9***
Mean Minimum Temp. (°F)	***56.1***	57.3	60.5	***64.4***	69.7	***73.4***	***74.7***	***75.3***	***74.6***	70.8	***64.4***	***59.4***	***66.7***
Extreme Maximum Temp. (°F)	89	89	92	94	96	98	101	99	97	96	89	88	101
Extreme Minimum Temp. (°F)	23	28	26	39	51	55	64	63	65	44	39	27	23
Days Maximum Temp. ≥ 90°F	0	0	0	1	5	12	17	18	12	3	0	0	68
Days Maximum Temp. ≤ 32°F	0	0	0	0	0	0	0	0	0	0	0	0	0
Days Minimum Temp. ≤ 32°F	0	0	0	0	0	0	0	0	0	0	0	0	0
Days Minimum Temp. ≤ 0°F	0	0	0	0	0	0	0	0	0	0	0	0	0
Heating Degree Days (base 65°F)	***79***	57	29	***5***	0	***0***	***0***	***0***	***0***	2	***13***	***51***	***236***
Cooling Degree Days (base 65°F)	***108***	108	173	***254***	399	***493***	***551***	***560***	***509***	414	***238***	***149***	***3,956***
Mean Precipitation (in.)	2.55	3.37	4.70	2.91	5.12	6.92	6.53	8.23	7.93	6.62	4.20	2.68	61.76
Extreme Maximum Daily Precip. (in.)	3.55	3.55	6.20	***2.10***	4.43	***7.55***	***4.07***	***10.12***	5.51	16.05	6.77	***3.70***	***16.05***
Days With ≥ 0.1" Precipitation	4	5	6	5	7	10	10	11	10	9	6	4	87
Days With ≥ 0.5" Precipitation	2	2	3	2	3	4	4	5	4	3	2	1	35
Days With ≥ 1.0" Precipitation	1	1	1	1	2	2	2	2	2	1	1	1	17
Mean Snowfall (in.)	0.0	0.0	0.0	0.0	0.0	0.0	0.0	0.0	0.0	0.0	0.0	0.0	0.0
Maximum Snow Depth (in.)	0	0	0	0	0	0	0	0	0	0	0	0	0
Days With ≥ 1.0" Snow Depth	0	0	0	0	0	0	0	0	0	0	0	0	0

Tarpon Springs Sewage Plant *Pinellas County* Elevation: 7 ft. Latitude: 28° 09' N Longitude: 82° 45' W

	JAN	FEB	MAR	APR	MAY	JUN	JUL	AUG	SEP	OCT	NOV	DEC	YEAR
Mean Maximum Temp. (°F)	71.0	73.4	77.4	81.5	87.0	90.2	91.3	91.5	89.9	84.9	78.4	73.2	82.5
Mean Temp. (°F)	60.7	63.2	67.3	71.6	77.3	81.6	82.9	83.1	81.3	75.6	68.4	63.0	73.0
Mean Minimum Temp. (°F)	50.4	52.9	57.2	61.7	67.7	73.0	74.4	74.6	72.6	66.2	58.4	52.9	63.5
Extreme Maximum Temp. (°F)	89	88	91	92	97	100	102	99	97	93	90	88	102
Extreme Minimum Temp. (°F)	19	23	31	37	45	51	63	65	55	42	29	21	19
Days Maximum Temp. ≥ 90°F	0	0	0	1	8	18	23	24	19	5	0	0	98
Days Maximum Temp. ≤ 32°F	0	0	0	0	0	0	0	0	0	0	0	0	0
Days Minimum Temp. ≤ 32°F	1	0	0	0	0	0	0	0	0	0	0	1	2
Days Minimum Temp. ≤ 0°F	0	0	0	0	0	0	0	0	0	0	0	0	0
Heating Degree Days (base 65°F)	180	110	53	10	0	0	0	0	0	4	46	134	537
Cooling Degree Days (base 65°F)	53	64	132	215	390	505	561	567	496	340	155	79	3,557
Mean Precipitation (in.)	3.01	2.74	3.67	2.30	2.09	6.58	7.99	7.89	7.05	3.38	2.24	2.93	51.87
Extreme Maximum Daily Precip. (in.)	4.21	4.30	2.80	3.53	3.07	6.32	7.45	4.60	6.51	8.00	6.50	4.40	8.00
Days With ≥ 0.1" Precipitation	5	4	5	4	3	8	10	11	9	5	4	4	72
Days With ≥ 0.5" Precipitation	2	2	3	2	2	4	5	5	4	2	1	2	34
Days With ≥ 1.0" Precipitation	1	1	1	1	1	2	3	2	2	1	0	1	16
Mean Snowfall (in.)	0.0	0.0	0.0	0.0	0.0	0.0	0.0	0.0	0.0	0.0	0.0	0.0	0.0
Maximum Snow Depth (in.)	0	0	0	0	0	0	0	0	0	0	0	0	0
Days With ≥ 1.0" Snow Depth	0	0	0	0	0	0	0	0	0	0	0	0	0

The period of record for all cooperative weather station data is 1980 – 2009. See User Guide for detailed explanation of data.

Titusville *Brevard County* Elevation: 4 ft. Latitude: 28° 37' N Longitude: 80° 49' W

	JAN	FEB	MAR	APR	MAY	JUN	JUL	AUG	SEP	OCT	NOV	DEC	YEAR
Mean Maximum Temp. (°F)	69.6	72.0	76.2	80.2	85.4	89.0	91.1	90.8	88.3	83.5	77.4	72.0	81.3
Mean Temp. (°F)	59.3	61.8	66.4	70.2	76.1	80.3	82.0	82.0	80.3	75.1	68.3	62.2	72.0
Mean Minimum Temp. (°F)	48.8	51.5	56.5	60.1	66.8	71.4	72.9	73.1	72.2	66.7	59.1	52.3	62.6
Extreme Maximum Temp. (°F)	88	88	92	95	101	103	101	100	99	95	93	88	103
Extreme Minimum Temp. (°F)	19	23	26	38	48	56	63	62	57	43	36	19	19
Days Maximum Temp. ≥ 90°F	0	0	0	1	7	14	22	21	11	3	0	0	79
Days Maximum Temp. ≤ 32°F	0	0	0	0	0	0	0	0	0	0	0	0	0
Days Minimum Temp. ≤ 32°F	1	0	0	0	0	0	0	0	0	0	0	1	2
Days Minimum Temp. ≤ 0°F	0	0	0	0	0	0	0	0	0	0	0	0	0
Heating Degree Days (base 65°F)	210	135	67	19	0	0	0	0	0	5	45	149	630
Cooling Degree Days (base 65°F)	39	51	119	181	352	464	536	532	465	326	149	69	3,283
Mean Precipitation (in.)	2.74	2.73	3.67	2.87	3.16	6.63	6.74	7.40	7.11	4.72	3.00	2.56	53.33
Extreme Maximum Daily Precip. (in.)	4.90	2.90	6.50	5.25	4.83	3.55	4.60	8.60	3.50	6.75	3.00	2.10	8.60
Days With ≥ 0.1" Precipitation	4	4	5	4	5	10	9	11	10	7	5	5	79
Days With ≥ 0.5" Precipitation	2	2	3	2	2	5	4	5	5	3	2	2	37
Days With ≥ 1.0" Precipitation	1	1	1	1	1	2	2	2	2	2	1	1	17
Mean Snowfall (in.)	0.0	0.0	0.0	0.0	0.0	0.0	0.0	0.0	0.0	0.0	0.0	0.0	0.0
Maximum Snow Depth (in.)	0	0	0	0	0	0	0	0	0	0	0	0	0
Days With ≥ 1.0" Snow Depth	0	0	0	0	0	0	0	0	0	0	0	0	0

Usher Tower *Levy County* Elevation: 33 ft. Latitude: 29° 25' N Longitude: 82° 49' W

	JAN	FEB	MAR	APR	MAY	JUN	JUL	AUG	SEP	OCT	NOV	DEC	YEAR
Mean Maximum Temp. (°F)	67.8	71.2	76.6	81.6	87.7	90.4	91.3	90.5	88.6	83.0	75.6	69.4	81.1
Mean Temp. (°F)	55.5	58.7	63.5	68.3	74.6	79.4	81.1	80.9	78.6	71.7	63.5	57.4	69.4
Mean Minimum Temp. (°F)	43.1	46.2	50.4	54.9	61.4	68.5	70.8	71.3	68.7	60.3	51.4	45.3	57.7
Extreme Maximum Temp. (°F)	86	86	91	96	102	105	102	100	99	96	92	86	105
Extreme Minimum Temp. (°F)	9	17	22	30	42	44	59	59	48	28	24	12	9
Days Maximum Temp. ≥ 90°F	0	0	0	1	10	19	23	21	13	2	0	0	89
Days Maximum Temp. ≤ 32°F	0	0	0	0	0	0	0	0	0	0	0	0	0
Days Minimum Temp. ≤ 32°F	7	3	1	0	0	0	0	0	0	0	1	5	17
Days Minimum Temp. ≤ 0°F	0	0	0	0	0	0	0	0	0	0	0	0	0
Heating Degree Days (base 65°F)	305	197	109	35	1	0	0	0	0	18	117	259	1,041
Cooling Degree Days (base 65°F)	16	25	70	139	304	440	505	501	416	232	79	30	2,757
Mean Precipitation (in.)	3.97	3.43	4.39	3.31	2.33	8.01	8.38	9.55	6.89	3.22	2.69	2.79	58.96
Extreme Maximum Daily Precip. (in.)	4.26	6.32	3.70	8.41	3.31	6.36	5.30	4.82	7.68	5.84	3.52	4.70	8.41
Days With ≥ 0.1" Precipitation	6	5	6	4	4	10	12	13	8	4	4	4	80
Days With ≥ 0.5" Precipitation	3	2	3	2	2	5	6	6	4	2	2	2	39
Days With ≥ 1.0" Precipitation	1	1	1	1	1	2	3	3	2	1	1	1	18
Mean Snowfall (in.)	0.0	trace	0.0	0.0	0.0	0.0	0.0	0.0	0.0	0.0	0.0	0.0	trace
Maximum Snow Depth (in.)	0	trace	0	0	0	0	0	0	0	0	0	0	trace
Days With ≥ 1.0" Snow Depth	0	0	0	0	0	0	0	0	0	0	0	0	0

Weeki Wachee *Hernando County* Elevation: 20 ft. Latitude: 28° 31' N Longitude: 82° 35' W

	JAN	FEB	MAR	APR	MAY	JUN	JUL	AUG	SEP	OCT	NOV	DEC	YEAR
Mean Maximum Temp. (°F)	70.4	73.0	77.2	81.9	87.3	90.3	91.5	91.5	90.2	85.2	78.9	72.5	82.5
Mean Temp. (°F)	57.6	60.2	64.8	69.2	75.3	80.3	81.6	81.7	79.9	73.8	66.5	59.9	70.9
Mean Minimum Temp. (°F)	44.7	47.4	52.3	56.5	63.3	70.3	71.8	71.7	69.7	62.3	54.0	47.2	59.3
Extreme Maximum Temp. (°F)	88	89	92	96	100	100	100	98	98	97	91	90	100
Extreme Minimum Temp. (°F)	13	21	21	34	45	47	60	64	48	32	27	19	13
Days Maximum Temp. ≥ 90°F	0	0	0	2	9	18	23	24	18	6	0	0	100
Days Maximum Temp. ≤ 32°F	0	0	0	0	0	0	0	0	0	0	0	0	0
Days Minimum Temp. ≤ 32°F	5	2	1	0	0	0	0	0	0	0	0	3	11
Days Minimum Temp. ≤ 0°F	0	0	0	0	0	0	0	0	0	0	0	0	0
Heating Degree Days (base 65°F)	260	172	97	29	1	0	0	0	0	11	71	208	849
Cooling Degree Days (base 65°F)	36	43	97	164	328	466	522	523	455	289	121	56	3,100
Mean Precipitation (in.)	3.48	2.94	4.12	2.46	2.25	6.97	8.64	7.05	6.70	2.58	1.98	2.34	51.51
Extreme Maximum Daily Precip. (in.)	***5.70***	***4.00***	***3.40***	***2.70***	***2.41***	***4.75***	***3.73***	***3.55***	***5.07***	3.30	3.50	***3.25***	***5.70***
Days With ≥ 0.1" Precipitation	4	3	4	3	3	7	10	9	7	3	3	3	59
Days With ≥ 0.5" Precipitation	2	2	3	2	2	4	5	5	4	1	1	1	32
Days With ≥ 1.0" Precipitation	1	1	1	1	1	3	3	2	2	1	1	1	18
Mean Snowfall (in.)	0.0	0.0	0.0	0.0	0.0	0.0	0.0	0.0	0.0	0.0	0.0	0.0	0.0
Maximum Snow Depth (in.)	0	0	0	0	0	0	0	0	0	0	0	0	0
Days With ≥ 1.0" Snow Depth	0	0	0	0	0	0	0	0	0	0	0	0	0

Wewahitchka *Gulf County* Elevation: 42 ft. Latitude: 30° 07' N Longitude: 85° 12' W

	JAN	FEB	MAR	APR	MAY	JUN	JUL	AUG	SEP	OCT	NOV	DEC	YEAR
Mean Maximum Temp. (°F)	64.1	67.5	73.3	79.2	85.7	90.0	90.8	90.3	87.4	80.2	73.2	65.8	78.9
Mean Temp. (°F)	52.4	55.5	61.3	66.5	73.8	79.4	81.2	80.9	77.5	68.6	61.0	54.0	67.7
Mean Minimum Temp. (°F)	40.5	43.4	49.2	53.8	61.7	68.9	71.7	71.5	67.8	56.8	48.8	42.3	56.4
Extreme Maximum Temp. (°F)	83	86	93	93	98	104	103	100	99	94	93	87	104
Extreme Minimum Temp. (°F)	12	15	20	34	41	47	61	61	47	30	22	11	11
Days Maximum Temp. ≥ 90°F	0	0	0	1	6	17	20	19	11	1	0	0	75
Days Maximum Temp. ≤ 32°F	0	0	0	0	0	0	0	0	0	0	0	0	0
Days Minimum Temp. ≤ 32°F	9	5	1	0	0	0	0	0	0	0	1	6	22
Days Minimum Temp. ≤ 0°F	0	0	0	0	0	0	0	0	0	0	0	0	0
Heating Degree Days (base 65°F)	392	276	156	55	3	0	0	0	0	46	164	350	1,442
Cooling Degree Days (base 65°F)	8	14	46	109	281	440	509	500	384	164	55	17	2,527
Mean Precipitation (in.)	4.95	4.82	5.77	3.74	2.98	6.70	8.58	7.77	5.50	3.38	3.53	3.70	61.42
Extreme Maximum Daily Precip. (in.)	5.70	6.25	7.31	5.15	7.50	4.04	4.48	5.65	8.00	5.60	3.65	3.90	8.00
Days With ≥ 0.1" Precipitation	7	6	6	5	5	10	13	12	8	5	5	6	88
Days With ≥ 0.5" Precipitation	4	3	3	2	2	4	6	5	3	2	2	3	39
Days With ≥ 1.0" Precipitation	1	2	2	1	1	2	3	2	1	1	1	1	18
Mean Snowfall (in.)	0.0	0.0	0.0	0.0	0.0	0.0	0.0	0.0	0.0	0.0	0.0	0.0	0.0
Maximum Snow Depth (in.)	0	0	0	0	0	0	0	0	0	0	0	0	0
Days With ≥ 1.0" Snow Depth	0	0	0	0	0	0	0	0	0	0	0	0	0

The period of record for all cooperative weather station data is 1980 – 2009. See User Guide for detailed explanation of data.

Florida Weather Station Rankings

Annual Extreme Maximum Temperature

Highest			Lowest		
Rank	Station Name	°F	Rank	Station Name	°F
1	Gainesville Regional Arpt	***108***	1	Key West Intl Arpt	98
2	High Springs	107	1	Miami Intl Arpt	98
3	Chipley 3 E	106	3	Fort Lauderdale	99
3	Crescent City	106	3	Naples	99
3	Pensacola Regional Arpt	106	3	Tampa Intl Arpt	99
6	De Funiak Springs	***105***	3	West Palm Beach Intl Arpt	99
6	Mountain Lake	105	7	St Petersburg	100
6	Myakka River State Park	105	7	Weeki Wachee	100
6	Usher Tower	105	9	Avon Park 2 W	101
10	Arcadia	104	9	Fort Pierce	101
10	Brooksville Chin Hill	104	9	Kissimmee 2	101
10	Federal Point	104	9	Orlando Intl Arpt	101
10	Flamingo Ranger Stn	104	9	Parrish	101
10	Lake City 2 E	104	9	Stuart 1 S	101
10	Perry	104	15	Clermont 7 S	102
10	Wewahitchka	104	15	Daytona Beach Regional Arpt	102
17	Apalachicola Municipal Arpt	103	15	Deland 1 SSE	102
17	Archbold Bio Station	103	15	Fernandina Beach	102
17	Fort Myers Page Field	103	15	Immokalee 3 NNW	***102***
17	Jacksonville Beach	103	15	Melbourne Regional Arpt	102
17	Jacksonville Intl Arpt	103	15	Panama City 5 NE	102
17	Jasper	103	15	Plant City	102
17	Oasis Ranger Station	103	15	Punta Gorda 4 ESE	102
17	Saint Leo	103	15	Tarpon Springs Sewage Plant	102
17	Sanford Experiment Stn	103	15	Vero Beach Municipal Arpt	***102***

Annual Mean Maximum Temperature

Highest			Lowest		
Rank	Station Name	°F	Rank	Station Name	°F
1	Oasis Ranger Station	87.1	1	Fernandina Beach	76.8
2	Myakka River State Park	85.5	2	Pensacola Regional Arpt	77.1
3	Immokalee 3 NNW	***85.0***	3	Jacksonville Beach	77.3
3	Naples	85.0	4	Panama City 5 NE	78.0
5	Archbold Bio Station	84.9	5	Apalachicola Municipal Arpt	78.3
6	Punta Gorda 4 ESE	84.7	6	Chipley 3 E	78.4
7	Fort Myers Page Field	84.6	7	De Funiak Springs	***78.5***
8	Flamingo Ranger Stn	84.2	8	Wewahitchka	79.0
9	Mountain Lake	84.1	9	Jasper	79.2
10	Miami Intl Arpt	84.0	10	Jacksonville Intl Arpt	79.3
11	Saint Leo	83.9	10	St Augustine WFOY	79.3
12	Arcadia	83.8	12	Lake City 2 E	79.6
13	Fort Lauderdale	83.6	13	Tallahassee Municipal Arpt	79.7
14	Avon Park 2 W	83.3	14	Federal Point	79.9
14	Plant City	83.3	15	Gainesville Regional Arpt	***80.1***
16	Kissimmee 2	83.2	16	Daytona Beach Regional Arpt	80.4
16	West Palm Beach Intl Arpt	83.2	17	Crescent City	***80.9***
18	Fort Pierce	83.1	18	St Petersburg	81.1
18	Stuart 1 S	***83.1***	18	Usher Tower	81.1
20	Key West Intl Arpt	82.9	20	Titusville	81.3
21	Orlando Intl Arpt	82.8	21	Deland 1 SSE	81.4
22	Parrish	82.5	21	Perry	81.4
22	Tarpon Springs Sewage Plant	82.5	23	Melbourne Regional Arpt	81.7
22	Weeki Wachee	82.5	24	Brooksville Chin Hill	***82.0***
25	Clermont 7 S	82.4	24	Tampa Intl Arpt	82.0

Rankings include 25 highest/lowest stations. If state has less than 25 stations, all stations are included. The period of record is 1980–2009. See User Guide for detailed explanation of data.

Annual Mean Temperature

Highest Rank	Highest Station Name	Highest °F	Lowest Rank	Lowest Station Name	Lowest °F
1	Key West Intl Arpt	78.1	1	Chipley 3 E	66.4
2	Miami Intl Arpt	77.0	2	De Funiak Springs	***66.7***
3	Oasis Ranger Station	76.3	3	Jasper	67.1
4	Fort Lauderdale	76.1	4	Panama City 5 NE	67.5
5	West Palm Beach Intl Arpt	75.6	5	Wewahitchka	67.7
6	Flamingo Ranger Stn	75.4	6	Tallahassee Municipal Arpt	67.8
7	Fort Myers Page Field	75.1	7	Pensacola Regional Arpt	68.2
8	Naples	75.0	8	Jacksonville Intl Arpt	68.6
9	Stuart 1 S	***74.9***	8	Lake City 2 E	68.6
10	Punta Gorda 4 ESE	74.3	10	Fernandina Beach	68.7
11	St Petersburg	74.0	11	Apalachicola Municipal Arpt	68.8
12	Immokalee 3 NNW	***73.9***	12	Perry	68.9
13	Myakka River State Park	73.5	13	Gainesville Regional Arpt	***69.0***
14	Fort Pierce	73.4	14	High Springs	69.2
14	Vero Beach Municipal Arpt	***73.4***	15	Usher Tower	69.4
16	Tampa Intl Arpt	73.2	16	Jacksonville Beach	69.7
17	Tarpon Springs Sewage Plant	73.0	17	St Augustine WFOY	70.2
18	Mountain Lake	72.9	18	Federal Point	70.4
18	Saint Leo	72.9	19	Deland 1 SSE	70.5
20	Orlando Intl Arpt	72.8	20	Weeki Wachee	70.9
21	Kissimmee 2	72.6	21	Daytona Beach Regional Arpt	71.0
22	Melbourne Regional Arpt	72.5	22	Crescent City	***71.1***
22	Plant City	72.5	23	Brooksville Chin Hill	***71.5***
24	Avon Park 2 W	72.4	24	Sanford Experiment Stn	71.9
25	Arcadia	72.3	25	Archbold Bio Station	72.0

Annual Mean Minimum Temperature

Highest Rank	Highest Station Name	Highest °F	Lowest Rank	Lowest Station Name	Lowest °F
1	Key West Intl Arpt	73.2	1	Chipley 3 E	54.3
2	Miami Intl Arpt	69.8	2	De Funiak Springs	***54.8***
3	Fort Lauderdale	68.6	2	Jasper	54.8
4	West Palm Beach Intl Arpt	67.8	4	Tallahassee Municipal Arpt	55.8
5	St Petersburg	66.9	5	High Springs	56.3
6	Stuart 1 S	***66.7***	6	Perry	56.4
7	Flamingo Ranger Stn	66.5	6	Wewahitchka	56.4
8	Fort Myers Page Field	65.5	8	Panama City 5 NE	56.8
9	Oasis Ranger Station	65.4	9	Lake City 2 E	57.7
10	Naples	64.9	9	Usher Tower	57.7
11	Tampa Intl Arpt	64.4	11	Jacksonville Intl Arpt	57.8
12	Vero Beach Municipal Arpt	***64.3***	12	Gainesville Regional Arpt	***57.9***
13	Fort Pierce	63.7	13	Archbold Bio Station	59.1
13	Punta Gorda 4 ESE	63.7	14	Pensacola Regional Arpt	59.2
15	Tarpon Springs Sewage Plant	63.5	15	Weeki Wachee	59.3
16	Melbourne Regional Arpt	63.3	16	Apalachicola Municipal Arpt	59.4
17	Orlando Intl Arpt	62.8	17	Deland 1 SSE	59.6
18	Immokalee 3 NNW	***62.7***	18	Fernandina Beach	60.5
19	Titusville	62.6	19	Federal Point	60.7
20	Jacksonville Beach	62.0	20	Arcadia	60.8
20	Kissimmee 2	62.0	21	Brooksville Chin Hill	***60.9***
20	Parrish	62.0	22	St Augustine WFOY	61.0
23	Saint Leo	61.9	23	Crescent City	***61.3***
24	Mountain Lake	61.7	24	Avon Park 2 W	61.4
24	Plant City	61.7	24	Myakka River State Park	61.4

Rankings include 25 highest/lowest stations. If state has less than 25 stations, all stations are included. The period of record is 1980–2009. See User Guide for detailed explanation of data.

Annual Extreme Minimum Temperature

Highest Rank	Station Name	°F	Lowest Rank	Station Name	°F
1	Key West Intl Arpt	41	1	Chipley 3 E	2
2	Miami Intl Arpt	30	2	De Funiak Springs	*3*
3	Fort Lauderdale	29	3	Fernandina Beach	4
4	West Palm Beach Intl Arpt	28	3	Jasper	4
5	Fort Myers Page Field	27	5	Pensacola Regional Arpt	5
6	Naples	26	6	Panama City 5 NE	6
6	Oasis Ranger Station	26	6	Tallahassee Municipal Arpt	6
8	Flamingo Ranger Stn	24	8	Jacksonville Intl Arpt	7
8	St Petersburg	24	8	Lake City 2 E	7
10	Punta Gorda 4 ESE	23	8	Perry	7
10	Stuart 1 S	23	11	High Springs	8
12	Melbourne Regional Arpt	21	12	Apalachicola Municipal Arpt	9
12	Vero Beach Municipal Arpt	***21***	12	Usher Tower	9
14	Immokalee 3 NNW	***20***	14	Gainesville Regional Arpt	***10***
15	Fort Pierce	19	14	St Augustine WFOY	10
15	Kissimmee 2	19	16	Federal Point	11
15	Orlando Intl Arpt	19	16	Wewahitchka	11
15	Sanford Experiment Stn	19	18	Archbold Bio Station	13
15	Tampa Intl Arpt	19	18	Brooksville Chin Hill	13
15	Tarpon Springs Sewage Plant	19	18	Weeki Wachee	13
15	Titusville	19	21	Crescent City	14
22	Arcadia	18	21	Jacksonville Beach	14
22	Avon Park 2 W	18	23	Daytona Beach Regional Arpt	15
22	Myakka River State Park	18	24	Deland 1 SSE	16
22	Parrish	18	24	Mountain Lake	16

July Mean Maximum Temperature

Highest Rank	Station Name	°F	Lowest Rank	Station Name	°F
1	Oasis Ranger Station	93.7	1	Jacksonville Beach	89.5
2	Archbold Bio Station	93.0	2	Key West Intl Arpt	89.6
3	High Springs	92.9	3	Fort Lauderdale	89.8
3	Myakka River State Park	92.9	4	Fernandina Beach	89.9
5	Saint Leo	92.5	5	Flamingo Ranger Stn	90.0
6	Mountain Lake	92.4	5	Panama City 5 NE	90.0
6	Perry	92.4	7	Vero Beach Municipal Arpt	90.1
8	Tallahassee Municipal Arpt	92.3	8	West Palm Beach Intl Arpt	90.2
9	Punta Gorda 4 ESE	92.1	9	Brooksville Chin Hill	90.3
10	De Funiak Springs	***92.0***	9	Melbourne Regional Arpt	90.3
10	Immokalee 3 NNW	***92.0***	9	Stuart 1 S	***90.3***
10	Jacksonville Intl Arpt	92.0	12	St Petersburg	90.4
10	Naples	92.0	12	Tampa Intl Arpt	90.4
10	Sanford Experiment Stn	92.0	14	Daytona Beach Regional Arpt	90.5
15	Chipley 3 E	91.9	14	Miami Intl Arpt	90.5
15	Federal Point	91.9	16	Parrish	90.6
17	Clermont 7 S	91.8	16	Pensacola Regional Arpt	90.6
17	Orlando Intl Arpt	91.8	16	St Augustine WFOY	90.6
19	Fort Myers Page Field	91.7	19	Apalachicola Municipal Arpt	90.8
19	Kissimmee 2	91.7	19	Gainesville Regional Arpt	90.8
21	Avon Park 2 W	91.6	19	Wewahitchka	90.8
21	Jasper	91.6	22	Titusville	91.1
21	Plant City	91.6	23	Fort Pierce	91.2
24	Arcadia	91.5	24	Tarpon Springs Sewage Plant	91.3
24	Crescent City	***91.5***	25	Deland 1 SSE	91.4

Rankings include 25 highest/lowest stations. If state has less than 25 stations, all stations are included. The period of record is 1980–2009. See User Guide for detailed explanation of data.

January Mean Minimum Temperature

Highest Rank	Station Name	°F	Lowest Rank	Station Name	°F
1	Key West Intl Arpt	64.5	1	Chipley 3 E	37.3
2	Miami Intl Arpt	59.9	2	De Funiak Springs	37.9
3	Fort Lauderdale	58.7	3	Jasper	38.3
4	West Palm Beach Intl Arpt	57.0	4	Tallahassee Municipal Arpt	39.2
5	Flamingo Ranger Stn	56.1	5	Panama City 5 NE	40.4
5	Stuart 1 S	***56.1***	6	Wewahitchka	40.5
7	Oasis Ranger Station	54.7	7	High Springs	40.6
8	St Petersburg	54.1	8	Perry	41.2
9	Naples	53.8	9	Jacksonville Intl Arpt	41.7
10	Fort Myers Page Field	53.7	10	Lake City 2 E	42.1
11	Vero Beach Municipal Arpt	***52.4***	11	Pensacola Regional Arpt	42.6
12	Punta Gorda 4 ESE	51.8	12	Gainesville Regional Arpt	***43.1***
13	Fort Pierce	51.5	12	Usher Tower	43.1
13	Immokalee 3 NNW	***51.5***	14	Apalachicola Municipal Arpt	43.3
15	Tampa Intl Arpt	51.1	15	Fernandina Beach	44.2
16	Melbourne Regional Arpt	50.4	16	Weeki Wachee	44.7
16	Tarpon Springs Sewage Plant	50.4	17	Deland 1 SSE	45.1
18	Parrish	49.6	18	Crescent City	45.9
19	Orlando Intl Arpt	49.4	19	Jacksonville Beach	46.2
20	Saint Leo	49.3	20	St Augustine WFOY	46.3
21	Myakka River State Park	49.2	21	Archbold Bio Station	46.7
22	Mountain Lake	49.0	22	Federal Point	46.8
22	Plant City	49.0	23	Daytona Beach Regional Arpt	47.4
24	Kissimmee 2	48.9	24	Arcadia	47.7
25	Titusville	48.8	25	Avon Park 2 W	47.8

Number of Days Annually Maximum Temperature ≥ 90°F

Highest Rank	Station Name	Days	Lowest Rank	Station Name	Days
1	Oasis Ranger Station	158	1	Jacksonville Beach	38
2	Myakka River State Park	144	2	Fernandina Beach	47
3	Archbold Bio Station	136	3	Key West Intl Arpt	56
4	Saint Leo	128	4	St Augustine WFOY	58
5	Naples	126	5	Pensacola Regional Arpt	62
6	Punta Gorda 4 ESE	124	6	Daytona Beach Regional Arpt	63
7	Immokalee 3 NNW	***123***	6	Panama City 5 NE	63
8	Fort Myers Page Field	120	8	Apalachicola Municipal Arpt	64
8	Mountain Lake	120	9	Vero Beach Municipal Arpt	***65***
10	Arcadia	114	10	Fort Lauderdale	66
11	Avon Park 2 W	108	10	Melbourne Regional Arpt	66
11	High Springs	108	12	Stuart 1 S	68
11	Orlando Intl Arpt	108	13	West Palm Beach Intl Arpt	69
14	Plant City	106	14	Flamingo Ranger Stn	74
15	Perry	104	14	St Petersburg	74
16	Sanford Experiment Stn	101	16	Wewahitchka	75
17	Kissimmee 2	100	17	Jacksonville Intl Arpt	79
17	Weeki Wachee	100	17	Titusville	79
19	Tarpon Springs Sewage Plant	98	19	Federal Point	81
20	Tallahassee Municipal Arpt	97	19	Gainesville Regional Arpt	***81***
21	Clermont 7 S	95	21	Deland 1 SSE	82
22	Parrish	92	22	De Funiak Springs	***84***
23	Tampa Intl Arpt	91	22	Lake City 2 E	84
24	Usher Tower	89	24	Brooksville Chin Hill	85
25	Chipley 3 E	87	24	Jasper	85

Number of Days Annually Maximum Temperature ≤ 32°F

Highest

Rank	Station Name	Days
1	Apalachicola Municipal Arpt	0
1	Arcadia	0
1	Archbold Bio Station	0
1	Avon Park 2 W	0
1	Brooksville Chin Hill	0
1	Chipley 3 E	0
1	Clermont 7 S	0
1	Crescent City	0
1	Daytona Beach Regional Arpt	0
1	De Funiak Springs	*0*
1	Deland 1 SSE	0
1	Federal Point	0
1	Fernandina Beach	0
1	Flamingo Ranger Stn	0
1	Fort Lauderdale	0
1	Fort Myers Page Field	0
1	Fort Pierce	0
1	Gainesville Regional Arpt	*0*
1	High Springs	0
1	Immokalee 3 NNW	*0*
1	Jacksonville Beach	0
1	Jacksonville Intl Arpt	0
1	Jasper	0
1	Key West Intl Arpt	0
1	Kissimmee 2	0

Lowest

Rank	Station Name	Days
1	Apalachicola Municipal Arpt	0
1	Arcadia	0
1	Archbold Bio Station	0
1	Avon Park 2 W	0
1	Brooksville Chin Hill	0
1	Chipley 3 E	0
1	Clermont 7 S	0
1	Crescent City	0
1	Daytona Beach Regional Arpt	0
1	De Funiak Springs	*0*
1	Deland 1 SSE	0
1	Federal Point	0
1	Fernandina Beach	0
1	Flamingo Ranger Stn	0
1	Fort Lauderdale	0
1	Fort Myers Page Field	0
1	Fort Pierce	0
1	Gainesville Regional Arpt	*0*
1	High Springs	0
1	Immokalee 3 NNW	*0*
1	Jacksonville Beach	0
1	Jacksonville Intl Arpt	0
1	Jasper	0
1	Key West Intl Arpt	0
1	Kissimmee 2	0

Number of Days Annually Minimum Temperature ≤ 32°F

Highest

Rank	Station Name	Days
1	Chipley 3 E	32
1	Tallahassee Municipal Arpt	32
3	Jasper	30
4	De Funiak Springs	*29*
5	High Springs	25
6	Perry	24
7	Wewahitchka	22
8	Panama City 5 NE	21
9	Usher Tower	17
10	Jacksonville Intl Arpt	16
10	Lake City 2 E	16
12	Gainesville Regional Arpt	*15*
13	Pensacola Regional Arpt	13
14	Apalachicola Municipal Arpt	11
14	Weeki Wachee	11
16	Archbold Bio Station	9
16	Deland 1 SSE	9
18	Fernandina Beach	6
18	St Augustine WFOY	6
20	Arcadia	5
20	Brooksville Chin Hill	5
20	Crescent City	5
23	Avon Park 2 W	4
23	Clermont 7 S	4
23	Daytona Beach Regional Arpt	4

Lowest

Rank	Station Name	Days
1	Flamingo Ranger Stn	0
1	Fort Lauderdale	0
1	Fort Myers Page Field	0
1	Key West Intl Arpt	0
1	Miami Intl Arpt	0
1	Naples	0
1	Oasis Ranger Station	0
1	St Petersburg	0
1	Stuart 1 S	0
1	West Palm Beach Intl Arpt	0
11	Orlando Intl Arpt	1
11	Punta Gorda 4 ESE	1
11	Tampa Intl Arpt	1
11	Vero Beach Municipal Arpt	*1*
15	Fort Pierce	2
15	Immokalee 3 NNW	*2*
15	Tarpon Springs Sewage Plant	2
15	Titusville	2
19	Melbourne Regional Arpt	3
19	Parrish	3
19	Saint Leo	3
22	Avon Park 2 W	4
22	Clermont 7 S	4
22	Daytona Beach Regional Arpt	4
22	Federal Point	4

Rankings include 25 highest/lowest stations. If state has less than 25 stations, all stations are included. The period of record is 1980–2009. See User Guide for detailed explanation of data.

Number of Days Annually Minimum Temperature ≤ 0°F

Highest Rank	Station Name	Days	Lowest Rank	Station Name	Days
1	Apalachicola Municipal Arpt	0	1	Apalachicola Municipal Arpt	0
1	Arcadia	0	1	Arcadia	0
1	Archbold Bio Station	0	1	Archbold Bio Station	0
1	Avon Park 2 W	0	1	Avon Park 2 W	0
1	Brooksville Chin Hill	0	1	Brooksville Chin Hill	0
1	Chipley 3 E	0	1	Chipley 3 E	0
1	Clermont 7 S	0	1	Clermont 7 S	0
1	Crescent City	0	1	Crescent City	0
1	Daytona Beach Regional Arpt	0	1	Daytona Beach Regional Arpt	0
1	De Funiak Springs	***0***	1	De Funiak Springs	***0***
1	Deland 1 SSE	0	1	Deland 1 SSE	0
1	Federal Point	0	1	Federal Point	0
1	Fernandina Beach	0	1	Fernandina Beach	0
1	Flamingo Ranger Stn	0	1	Flamingo Ranger Stn	0
1	Fort Lauderdale	0	1	Fort Lauderdale	0
1	Fort Myers Page Field	0	1	Fort Myers Page Field	0
1	Fort Pierce	0	1	Fort Pierce	0
1	Gainesville Regional Arpt	***0***	1	Gainesville Regional Arpt	***0***
1	High Springs	0	1	High Springs	0
1	Immokalee 3 NNW	***0***	1	Immokalee 3 NNW	***0***
1	Jacksonville Beach	0	1	Jacksonville Beach	0
1	Jacksonville Intl Arpt	0	1	Jacksonville Intl Arpt	0
1	Jasper	0	1	Jasper	0
1	Key West Intl Arpt	0	1	Key West Intl Arpt	0
1	Kissimmee 2	0	1	Kissimmee 2	0

Number of Annual Heating Degree Days

Highest Rank	Station Name	Num.	Lowest Rank	Station Name	Num.
1	Chipley 3 E	1,801	1	Key West Intl Arpt	61
2	De Funiak Springs	***1,731***	2	Miami Intl Arpt	127
3	Jasper	1,591	3	Fort Lauderdale	149
4	Tallahassee Municipal Arpt	1,536	4	Oasis Ranger Station	170
5	Panama City 5 NE	1,520	5	Flamingo Ranger Stn	171
6	Pensacola Regional Arpt	1,454	6	West Palm Beach Intl Arpt	217
7	Wewahitchka	1,442	7	Stuart 1 S	***236***
8	Jacksonville Intl Arpt	1,306	8	Naples	251
9	Lake City 2 E	1,277	9	Fort Myers Page Field	273
10	Apalachicola Municipal Arpt	1,255	10	Punta Gorda 4 ESE	327
11	Fernandina Beach	1,252	11	Immokalee 3 NNW	***333***
12	Perry	1,217	12	St Petersburg	401
13	High Springs	1,161	13	Vero Beach Municipal Arpt	***404***
14	Gainesville Regional Arpt	***1,143***	14	Fort Pierce	406
15	Usher Tower	1,041	15	Myakka River State Park	417
16	Jacksonville Beach	1,035	16	Mountain Lake	508
17	Federal Point	895	17	Melbourne Regional Arpt	516
18	St Augustine WFOY	894	18	Tampa Intl Arpt	529
19	Weeki Wachee	849	19	Kissimmee 2	531
20	Crescent City	***842***	20	Arcadia	536
21	Deland 1 SSE	839	21	Tarpon Springs Sewage Plant	537
22	Daytona Beach Regional Arpt	767	22	Saint Leo	539
23	Sanford Experiment Stn	676	23	Orlando Intl Arpt	543
24	Brooksville Chin Hill	***659***	24	Plant City	550
25	Titusville	630	25	Parrish	563

Rankings include 25 highest/lowest stations. If state has less than 25 stations, all stations are included. The period of record is 1980–2009. See User Guide for detailed explanation of data.

Number of Annual Cooling Degree Days

Highest

Rank	Station Name	Num.
1	Key West Intl Arpt	4,925
2	Miami Intl Arpt	4,586
3	Oasis Ranger Station	4,396
4	Fort Lauderdale	4,292
5	West Palm Beach Intl Arpt	4,164
6	Fort Myers Page Field	4,054
7	Flamingo Ranger Stn	4,051
8	Naples	3,994
9	Stuart 1 S	***3,956***
10	Punta Gorda 4 ESE	3,805
11	St Petersburg	3,781
12	Immokalee 3 NNW	***3,674***
13	Tampa Intl Arpt	3,625
14	Myakka River State Park	3,611
15	Fort Pierce	3,577
16	Vero Beach Municipal Arpt	***3,558***
17	Tarpon Springs Sewage Plant	3,557
18	Saint Leo	3,530
19	Mountain Lake	3,499
20	Orlando Intl Arpt	3,498
21	Kissimmee 2	3,408
22	Plant City	3,396
23	Avon Park 2 W	3,379
24	Melbourne Regional Arpt	3,366
25	Parrish	3,319

Lowest

Rank	Station Name	Num.
1	Chipley 3 E	2,407
2	De Funiak Springs	***2,441***
3	Jasper	2,446
4	Panama City 5 NE	2,514
5	Wewahitchka	2,527
6	Tallahassee Municipal Arpt	2,662
7	Fernandina Beach	2,688
8	Lake City 2 E	2,700
9	Gainesville Regional Arpt	***2,722***
10	Jacksonville Intl Arpt	2,723
11	Pensacola Regional Arpt	2,726
12	Perry	2,741
13	Apalachicola Municipal Arpt	2,754
14	Usher Tower	2,757
15	High Springs	2,808
16	Jacksonville Beach	2,841
17	St Augustine WFOY	2,884
18	Federal Point	2,949
19	Deland 1 SSE	2,957
20	Daytona Beach Regional Arpt	3,056
21	Weeki Wachee	3,100
22	Brooksville Chin Hill	***3,124***
23	Crescent City	***3,175***
24	Archbold Bio Station	3,237
25	Clermont 7 S	3,270

Annual Precipitation

Highest

Rank	Station Name	Inches
1	Fort Lauderdale	65.80
2	Pensacola Regional Arpt	64.71
3	De Funiak Springs	***64.21***
4	West Palm Beach Intl Arpt	62.37
5	Panama City 5 NE	62.17
6	Stuart 1 S	61.76
7	Miami Intl Arpt	61.61
8	Wewahitchka	61.42
9	Chipley 3 E	59.92
10	Tallahassee Municipal Arpt	59.48
11	Myakka River State Park	58.99
12	Usher Tower	58.96
13	Deland 1 SSE	58.72
14	Oasis Ranger Station	58.15
15	Apalachicola Municipal Arpt	57.03
16	Fort Myers Page Field	55.80
17	Perry	55.75
18	Naples	54.75
19	Parrish	54.57
20	Fort Pierce	54.08
21	Saint Leo	54.01
22	Lake City 2 E	53.76
23	Plant City	53.64
24	Titusville	53.33
25	Brooksville Chin Hill	53.26

Lowest

Rank	Station Name	Inches
1	Key West Intl Arpt	40.24
2	Flamingo Ranger Stn	45.37
3	Tampa Intl Arpt	46.27
4	Gainesville Regional Arpt	***47.22***
5	Crescent City	48.16
6	Fernandina Beach	48.98
7	Mountain Lake	49.25
8	St Augustine WFOY	49.44
9	Immokalee 3 NNW	***49.64***
10	Federal Point	49.67
11	Daytona Beach Regional Arpt	49.84
12	Avon Park 2 W	50.11
13	Jacksonville Beach	50.31
14	Orlando Intl Arpt	50.56
15	Clermont 7 S	50.61
15	Punta Gorda 4 ESE	50.61
17	Kissimmee 2	50.67
18	St Petersburg	50.93
19	Archbold Bio Station	51.39
20	Arcadia	51.41
21	Jasper	51.47
22	Weeki Wachee	51.51
23	Melbourne Regional Arpt	51.75
24	High Springs	51.83
25	Tarpon Springs Sewage Plant	51.87

Rankings include 25 highest/lowest stations. If state has less than 25 stations, all stations are included. The period of record is 1980–2009. See User Guide for detailed explanation of data.

Annual Extreme Maximum Daily Precipitation

Highest Rank	Station Name	Inches	Lowest Rank	Station Name	Inches
1	Key West Intl Arpt	22.75	1	Crescent City	***5.03***
2	Stuart 1 S	***16.05***	2	Orlando Intl Arpt	5.28
3	Panama City 5 NE	12.80	3	Weeki Wachee	***5.70***
4	Jacksonville Beach	12.56	4	Mountain Lake	6.00
4	Miami Intl Arpt	12.56	5	Deland 1 SSE	6.05
6	Fort Pierce	12.11	6	Archbold Bio Station	6.07
7	Perry	12.10	7	Gainesville Regional Arpt	***6.16***
8	Melbourne Regional Arpt	11.85	8	Brooksville Chin Hill	6.22
9	St Augustine WFOY	11.28	9	Arcadia	***6.28***
10	Apalachicola Municipal Arpt	***10.67***	10	Federal Point	***6.32***
11	Punta Gorda 4 ESE	10.65	11	Immokalee 3 NNW	***6.45***
12	De Funiak Springs	***10.55***	12	Jasper	6.62
13	Sanford Experiment Stn	***10.17***	13	Fernandina Beach	6.72
14	High Springs	10.00	14	Clermont 7 S	6.90
15	Saint Leo	9.27	15	Vero Beach Municipal Arpt	***7.30***
16	Pensacola Regional Arpt	9.10	16	Kissimmee 2	7.65
17	Avon Park 2 W	9.03	17	Naples	7.66
18	Daytona Beach Regional Arpt	9.02	18	Plant City	7.70
19	West Palm Beach Intl Arpt	8.79	19	Fort Myers Page Field	7.75
20	Myakka River State Park	8.75	20	Jacksonville Intl Arpt	7.83
21	Titusville	8.60	21	Lake City 2 E	7.90
22	Usher Tower	8.41	22	Tarpon Springs Sewage Plant	8.00
23	St Petersburg	8.31	22	Wewahitchka	8.00
24	Fort Lauderdale	8.28	24	Oasis Ranger Station	8.05
24	Tampa Intl Arpt	8.28	25	Chipley 3 E	8.10

Number of Days Annually With ≥ 0.1 Inches of Precipitation

Highest Rank	Station Name	Days	Lowest Rank	Station Name	Days
1	Fort Lauderdale	90	1	Weeki Wachee	59
2	Wewahitchka	88	2	Key West Intl Arpt	62
3	Miami Intl Arpt	87	3	Flamingo Ranger Stn	65
3	Stuart 1 S	87	4	Arcadia	66
5	West Palm Beach Intl Arpt	86	5	Tampa Intl Arpt	67
6	Deland 1 SSE	85	6	Apalachicola Municipal Arpt	68
7	De Funiak Springs	***81***	7	St Petersburg	69
8	Oasis Ranger Station	80	8	Daytona Beach Regional Arpt	71
8	Usher Tower	80	8	Federal Point	71
10	Chipley 3 E	79	8	Parrish	71
10	Saint Leo	79	8	St Augustine WFOY	71
10	Titusville	79	12	Avon Park 2 W	72
13	Crescent City	78	12	Brooksville Chin Hill	72
13	Myakka River State Park	78	12	Clermont 7 S	72
13	Naples	78	12	Fernandina Beach	72
13	Panama City 5 NE	78	12	Immokalee 3 NNW	***72***
17	Fort Pierce	77	12	Jacksonville Beach	72
17	High Springs	77	12	Punta Gorda 4 ESE	72
17	Orlando Intl Arpt	77	12	Tarpon Springs Sewage Plant	72
17	Pensacola Regional Arpt	77	20	Kissimmee 2	73
21	Fort Myers Page Field	76	20	Melbourne Regional Arpt	73
21	Perry	76	20	Sanford Experiment Stn	73
21	Vero Beach Municipal Arpt	***76***	23	Archbold Bio Station	74
24	Jacksonville Intl Arpt	75	23	Gainesville Regional Arpt	***74***
24	Lake City 2 E	75	23	Jasper	74

Rankings include 25 highest/lowest stations. If state has less than 25 stations, all stations are included. The period of record is 1980–2009. See User Guide for detailed explanation of data.

Number of Days Annually With ≥ 0.5 Inches of Precipitation

Highest			Lowest		
Rank	Station Name	Days	Rank	Station Name	Days
1	Chipley 3 E	42	1	Key West Intl Arpt	23
1	De Funiak Springs	***42***	2	Flamingo Ranger Stn	26
3	Fort Lauderdale	40	3	Tampa Intl Arpt	29
3	Pensacola Regional Arpt	40	4	Federal Point	30
5	Deland 1 SSE	39	5	Archbold Bio Station	31
5	Usher Tower	39	5	Gainesville Regional Arpt	***31***
5	West Palm Beach Intl Arpt	39	5	Immokalee 3 NNW	***31***
5	Wewahitchka	39	5	Kissimmee 2	31
9	Miami Intl Arpt	38	5	Mountain Lake	31
9	Tallahassee Municipal Arpt	38	5	St Augustine WFOY	31
11	Myakka River State Park	37	11	Avon Park 2 W	32
11	Panama City 5 NE	37	11	Daytona Beach Regional Arpt	32
11	Titusville	37	11	Jacksonville Beach	32
14	Lake City 2 E	36	11	Jacksonville Intl Arpt	32
14	Parrish	36	11	Weeki Wachee	32
14	Saint Leo	36	16	Arcadia	33
17	Fort Myers Page Field	35	16	Brooksville Chin Hill	33
17	High Springs	35	16	Crescent City	33
17	Melbourne Regional Arpt	35	16	Fernandina Beach	33
17	Oasis Ranger Station	35	16	Orlando Intl Arpt	33
17	Perry	35	16	Punta Gorda 4 ESE	33
17	Plant City	35	16	St Petersburg	33
17	Sanford Experiment Stn	35	23	Apalachicola Municipal Arpt	34
17	Stuart 1 S	35	23	Clermont 7 S	34
17	Vero Beach Municipal Arpt	***35***	23	Fort Pierce	34

Number of Days Annually With ≥ 1.0 Inches of Precipitation

Highest			Lowest		
Rank	Station Name	Days	Rank	Station Name	Days
1	De Funiak Springs	***20***	1	Flamingo Ranger Stn	12
1	Deland 1 SSE	20	1	Key West Intl Arpt	12
1	Fort Lauderdale	20	3	St Augustine WFOY	14
1	Fort Myers Page Field	20	4	Daytona Beach Regional Arpt	15
1	Myakka River State Park	20	4	Federal Point	15
1	Pensacola Regional Arpt	20	4	Fernandina Beach	15
7	Chipley 3 E	19	4	Gainesville Regional Arpt	***15***
7	Miami Intl Arpt	19	4	Kissimmee 2	15
7	Naples	19	4	Melbourne Regional Arpt	15
7	Oasis Ranger Station	19	10	Clermont 7 S	16
7	Panama City 5 NE	19	10	Immokalee 3 NNW	***16***
7	Parrish	19	10	Jacksonville Beach	16
13	Apalachicola Municipal Arpt	18	10	Jacksonville Intl Arpt	16
13	Archbold Bio Station	18	10	Jasper	16
13	Brooksville Chin Hill	18	10	Orlando Intl Arpt	16
13	Plant City	18	10	Punta Gorda 4 ESE	16
13	Usher Tower	18	10	Tallahassee Municipal Arpt	16
13	Weeki Wachee	18	10	Tampa Intl Arpt	16
13	West Palm Beach Intl Arpt	18	10	Tarpon Springs Sewage Plant	16
13	Wewahitchka	18	10	Vero Beach Municipal Arpt	***16***
21	Arcadia	17	21	Arcadia	17
21	Avon Park 2 W	17	21	Avon Park 2 W	17
21	Crescent City	17	21	Crescent City	17
21	Fort Pierce	17	21	Fort Pierce	17
21	High Springs	17	21	High Springs	17

Rankings include 25 highest/lowest stations. If state has less than 25 stations, all stations are included. The period of record is 1980–2009. See User Guide for detailed explanation of data.

Annual Snowfall

Highest			Lowest		
Rank	Station Name	Inches	Rank	Station Name	Inches
1	Jacksonville Beach	0.1	1	Arcadia	0.0
1	Jasper	0.1	1	Archbold Bio Station	0.0
3	Apalachicola Municipal Arpt	Trace	1	Avon Park 2 W	0.0
3	Crescent City	Trace	1	Brooksville Chin Hill	0.0
3	De Funiak Springs	***Trace***	1	Chipley 3 E	0.0
3	Fernandina Beach	Trace	1	Clermont 7 S	0.0
3	Myakka River State Park	Trace	1	Deland 1 SSE	0.0
3	Orlando Intl Arpt	Trace	1	Federal Point	0.0
3	St Augustine WFOY	Trace	1	Flamingo Ranger Stn	0.0
3	Tampa Intl Arpt	Trace	1	Fort Lauderdale	0.0
3	Usher Tower	Trace	1	Fort Pierce	0.0
12	Arcadia	0.0	1	High Springs	0.0
12	Archbold Bio Station	0.0	1	Immokalee 3 NNW	***0.0***
12	Avon Park 2 W	0.0	1	Kissimmee 2	0.0
12	Brooksville Chin Hill	0.0	1	Lake City 2 E	0.0
12	Chipley 3 E	0.0	1	Melbourne Regional Arpt	0.0
12	Clermont 7 S	0.0	1	Mountain Lake	0.0
12	Deland 1 SSE	0.0	1	Naples	0.0
12	Federal Point	0.0	1	Oasis Ranger Station	0.0
12	Flamingo Ranger Stn	0.0	1	Panama City 5 NE	0.0
12	Fort Lauderdale	0.0	1	Parrish	0.0
12	Fort Pierce	0.0	1	Perry	0.0
12	High Springs	0.0	1	Plant City	0.0
12	Immokalee 3 NNW	***0.0***	1	Punta Gorda 4 ESE	0.0
12	Kissimmee 2	0.0	1	Saint Leo	0.0

Annual Maximum Snow Depth

Highest			Lowest		
Rank	Station Name	Inches	Rank	Station Name	Inches
1	Apalachicola Municipal Arpt	Trace	1	Arcadia	0
1	Clermont 7 S	Trace	1	Archbold Bio Station	0
1	Crescent City	Trace	1	Avon Park 2 W	0
1	De Funiak Springs	Trace	1	Brooksville Chin Hill	0
1	Fernandina Beach	Trace	1	Chipley 3 E	0
1	Jasper	Trace	1	Deland 1 SSE	0
1	Myakka River State Park	Trace	1	Federal Point	0
1	Orlando Intl Arpt	Trace	1	Flamingo Ranger Stn	0
1	St Augustine WFOY	Trace	1	Fort Lauderdale	0
1	Tampa Intl Arpt	Trace	1	Fort Pierce	0
1	Usher Tower	Trace	1	High Springs	0
12	Arcadia	0	1	Immokalee 3 NNW	***0***
12	Archbold Bio Station	0	1	Jacksonville Beach	0
12	Avon Park 2 W	0	1	Kissimmee 2	0
12	Brooksville Chin Hill	0	1	Lake City 2 E	0
12	Chipley 3 E	0	1	Melbourne Regional Arpt	0
12	Deland 1 SSE	0	1	Mountain Lake	0
12	Federal Point	0	1	Naples	0
12	Flamingo Ranger Stn	0	1	Oasis Ranger Station	0
12	Fort Lauderdale	0	1	Panama City 5 NE	0
12	Fort Pierce	0	1	Parrish	0
12	High Springs	0	1	Perry	0
12	Immokalee 3 NNW	***0***	1	Plant City	0
12	Jacksonville Beach	0	1	Punta Gorda 4 ESE	0
12	Kissimmee 2	0	1	Saint Leo	0

Rankings include 25 highest/lowest stations. If state has less than 25 stations, all stations are included. The period of record is 1980–2009. See User Guide for detailed explanation of data.

Number of Days Annually With ≥ 1.0 Inch Snow Depth					
Highest			Lowest		
Rank	Station Name	Days	Rank	Station Name	Days
1	Apalachicola Municipal Arpt	0	1	Apalachicola Municipal Arpt	0
1	Arcadia	0	1	Arcadia	0
1	Archbold Bio Station	0	1	Archbold Bio Station	0
1	Avon Park 2 W	0	1	Avon Park 2 W	0
1	Brooksville Chin Hill	0	1	Brooksville Chin Hill	0
1	Chipley 3 E	0	1	Chipley 3 E	0
1	Clermont 7 S	0	1	Clermont 7 S	0
1	Crescent City	0	1	Crescent City	0
1	De Funiak Springs	*0*	1	De Funiak Springs	*0*
1	Deland 1 SSE	0	1	Deland 1 SSE	0
1	Federal Point	0	1	Federal Point	0
1	Fernandina Beach	0	1	Fernandina Beach	0
1	Flamingo Ranger Stn	0	1	Flamingo Ranger Stn	0
1	Fort Lauderdale	0	1	Fort Lauderdale	0
1	Fort Pierce	0	1	Fort Pierce	0
1	High Springs	0	1	High Springs	0
1	Immokalee 3 NNW	*0*	1	Immokalee 3 NNW	*0*
1	Jacksonville Beach	0	1	Jacksonville Beach	0
1	Jasper	0	1	Jasper	0
1	Kissimmee 2	0	1	Kissimmee 2	0
1	Lake City 2 E	0	1	Lake City 2 E	0
1	Melbourne Regional Arpt	0	1	Melbourne Regional Arpt	0
1	Mountain Lake	0	1	Mountain Lake	0
1	Myakka River State Park	0	1	Myakka River State Park	0
1	Naples	0	1	Naples	0

 Rankings include 25 highest/lowest stations. If state has less than 25 stations, all stations are included. The period of record is 1980–2009. See User Guide for detailed explanation of data.

Significant Storm Events in Florida: 2000 – 2009

Location or County	Date	Type	Mag.	Deaths	Injuries	Property Damage ($mil.)	Crop Damage ($mil.)
Broward and Miami-Dade Co.	10/03/00	Flood	na	0	0	450.0	500.0
Washington	03/15/01	Tornado	F2	1	21	1.5	0.0
Miami-Dade	03/27/03	Tornado	F2	1	14	8.0	0.0
Okaloosa	06/08/03	Rip Current	na	1	10	0.0	0.0
Walton	06/08/03	Rip Current	na	6	0	0.0	0.0
Palm Beach	08/07/03	Tornado	F1	0	28	80.0	0.0
Southwest and West Central Florida	08/13/04	Hurricane Charley	na	7	780	5,420.0	285.0
Osceola, Orange, Seminole, and Volusia Co.	08/13/04	High Wind	105 mph	4	0	1,300.0	0.0
Hardee, Highlands, and Polk Counties	08/13/04	High Wind	108 mph	1	12	929.0	175.0
Hillsborough County	08/13/04	Tropical Storm	na	0	0	78.0	0.0
Volusia Co.	08/13/04	Hurricane Charley	na	2	0	52.0	0.0
Brevard, Indian River, Martin, St Lucie, and Volusia Co.	09/04/04	Hurricane Frances	na	0	0	4,830.0	93.2
Southeast Florida	09/04/04	Hurricane Frances	na	0	0	621.0	90.0
Central Florida	09/05/04	Tropical Storm	na	1	0	179.4	0.0
Hardee, Highlands, Polk, and Sumter Counties	09/05/04	High Wind	69 mph	0	0	127.2	0.0
Extreme Western Florida Panhandle	09/13/04	Hurricane Ivan	na	7	0	4,000.0	25.0
Northwestern Florida	09/15/04	Hurricane Ivan	na	6	16	90.4	0.0
Highlands and Polk Counties	09/25/04	High Wind	70 mph	0	0	702.0	0.0
Brevard, Indian River, Martin, St. Lucie, and Volusia Co.	09/25/04	Hurricane Jeanne	na	0	0	379.9	8.7
Glades, Hendry, Palm Beach, Broward, and Miami-Dade Co.	09/25/04	Hurricane Jeanne	na	0	0	323.0	30.0
West Central Florida	09/25/04	Tropical Storm	na	0	0	134.8	0.0
Lake, Okeechobee, Orange, Osceola, and Seminole Counties	09/25/04	Strong Wind	47 mph	1	0	70.0	48.4
Extreme Northwest Florida	07/09/05	Hurricane Dennis	na	0	0	1,500.0	0.3
Northwestern Florida	07/09/05	Hurricane Dennis	na	0	0	62.0	0.0
Southeast Florida	08/25/05	Hurricane Katrina	na	6	0	100.0	423.0
Northwest Florida	08/27/05	Tropical Storm	na	0	0	100.0	0.0
Monroe County and Florida Keys	10/23/05	Hurricane Wilma	na	0	6	99.0	0.0
South Florida	10/24/05	Hurricane Wilma	na	5	0	10,000.0	0.0
Lee Co.	10/24/05	Hurricane Wilma	na	0	0	101.0	0.0
Okaloosa	01/13/06	Tornado	F0	0	13	2.0	0.0
Volusia	12/25/06	Tornado	F0	0	6	50.0	0.0
Sumter	02/02/07	Tornado	F3	0	15	62.0	0.0
Volusia	02/02/07	Tornado	F3	0	42	52.0	0.0
Volusia	02/02/07	Tornado	F3	0	42	52.0	0.0
Lake	02/02/07	Tornado	F3	8	10	52.0	0.0
Lake	02/02/07	Tornado	F3	13	9	46.0	0.0
St Lucie	08/19/08	Flood	na	0	0	67.0	20.0
Brevard	08/20/08	Flash Flood	na	0	0	70.0	0.0
Volusia	05/19/09	Flood	na	0	0	68.6	0.0
Polk	07/04/09	Lightning	na	1	26	0.0	0.0

Note: Deaths, injuries, and damages are date and location specific.

GEORGIA

PHYSICAL FEATURES. Georgia is located roughly between latitudes 30° and 35° N. and longitudes 81° and 86° W. From north to south its length is 320 miles, and its maximum width is about 250 miles. With an area of almost 59,000 square miles, it is the largest State east of the Mississippi River. Its elevation ranges from near sea level along the southeast coast to almost 5,000 feet at its highest point in the northeast.

Georgia's land area is made up of four principal physiographic provinces: the Blue Ridge or Mountain Province, the Valley and Ridge Province, the Piedmont Province, and the Coastal Plain Province.

The Blue Ridge or Mountain Province is located in the northeastern part of the State. The terrain in this area is characterized by forest-covered mountains and narrow valleys with rapidly flowing streams. The average elevation of the area is less than 2,000 feet, but the higher mountains reach altitudes between 4,000 and 5,000 feet above sea level. The Valley and Ridge Province, located in northwest Georgia, is composed of wide, flat valleys separated by narrow, steep, wooded ridges than run more or less northeast-southwest. The elevation of the valleys ranges mostly between 500 and 800 feet above sea level, with the ridges rising to heights of 600 to 2,000 feet.

The Piedmont Plateau Province is a wide area extending from the foothills of the Appalachian Mountains to the Coastal Plain and comprising nearly one-third of the area of the State. The terrain is mostly hilly in the north to rolling in the south, where it merges with the Coastal Plain. Elevations range from near 1,200 feet in the north to less than 500 feet in the south. The boundary between the Piedmont Province and the Coastal Plain is called the Fall Line, because of the steep fall of rivers as they cross this boundary. The Fall Line extends across the State from west-southwest to east-northeast. The Coastal Plain Province includes all of Georgia south of the Fall Line and comprises about three-fifths of the total area of the State. The terrain is slightly rolling to level and ranges in altitude from near sea level along the coast to a maximum of 600 feet. The low-lying coastal sections are rather marshy and the large slow-moving streams are bordered by wide, swampy, densely wooded areas.

Georgia streams are divided into two main groups — those flowing southeastward into the Atlantic and those flowing southward directly into the Gulf of Mexico, or indirectly into the Gulf through the Alabama-Mobile and Tennessee River systems. The Chattahoochee Ridge marks the dividing line between the parts of the State that are drained into the Atlantic and into the Gulf. The main streams in the Atlantic drainage system are the Savannah and Altamaha Rivers. The Savannah and its headwater streams form the boundary between Georgia and South Carolina throughout its entire length. The Altamaha drains a large area of central Georgia. The Chattahoochee and Flint River systems constitute the major streams of west Georgia, which drain directly into the Gulf of Mexico.

GENERAL CLIMATE. Georgia's climate is determined primarily by its latitude, the proximity of the Gulf of Mexico and the Atlantic Ocean, and by the altitude.

Average annual rainfall in Georgia ranges from more than 75 inches in the extreme northeast corner to about 40 inches in a small area of the East Central Division. Total rainfall varies greatly from year to year in all parts of the State, and most stations with several years of record show more than twice as much rain in their wettest year as in their driest. The distribution of rainfall throughout the year is also highly variable in all parts of the State, but the extremes occur at different seasons in different areas.

Most of the State shows two maxima and two minima in the annual rainfall curve. One maximum occurs in winter and early spring and the other in midsummer. The driest season for all the State is autumn, with most areas showing a secondary minimum about May. In the northern third of the State, the cool season rainfall maximum predominates, with either January or March normally the wettest month. This is due to the greater influence in that area of the cyclonic storms that move across the country with regularity during winter and early spring. The mountains of north Georgia add enough lift to the moist air that is drawn into the forward side of these storms from the Gulf to add materially to the total annual rainfall of the area. Most sections of central and south Georgia have their greatest rainfall in midsummer, with a secondary maximum about March. The lower east coastal area has its highest normal rainfall in September, due to the occasional extremely heavy rains that occur with late summer and autumn tropical storms. October is normally the driest month in most of the State. Snowfall is light in Georgia and of no significance at all in most of the State.

Due to its latitude and proximity to the warm waters of the Gulf of Mexico and Atlantic Ocean, most of Georgia has warm, humid summers and short, mild winters. However, in the northern part of the State, altitude becomes the more predominant influence with resulting cool summers and colder, but not severe, winters. All four seasons are apparent, but spring is usually short and blustery with rather frequent periods of storminess of varying intensity. In autumn long periods of mild, sunny weather are the rule for all of Georgia.

TEMPERATURE. Average summer temperatures range from about 73°F. in the extreme north to nearly 82°F. in parts of south Georgia. There is little difference in summer averages over the southern two-thirds of the State, where they range between 80 and 82°F. Summer days are characteristically warm and humid in this area, with high temperatures exceeding 90°F. on most days and reaching 100°F. during most years. Temperatures usually drop to the middle or low 70s, or even below 70°F. by early morning, giving some relief from the daytime warmth. The flow of moist air from the Gulf over the warm land surface results in frequent afternoon thundershowers in south and central Georgia during summer. These showers not only provide most of the summer rainfall, but oftentimes bring welcome relief from the afternoon heat. All parts of the State have experienced 100°F. weather at one time or another during the period of official records, but such occurrences are highly unusual in the mountain section of the north.

Winter temperatures show more variation from north to south than do those of summer. There is also a much greater variation in winter from day to day in all sections of the State. The average temperature for the three winter months ranges from 41°F. in the north to about 56°F. on the lower east coast, with the increase being almost uniform from north to south. All of Georgia experiences freezing temperatures almost every year, but the frequency of such occurrences varies greatly from the mountains to the coast. The average annual number of days with a temperature of 32°F. or less ranges from 110 in the north to about 10 in the lower coastal region.

Georgia winters are characterized by frequent and sometimes large fluctuations in temperature. The cold snaps, which usually occur with regularity from mid-November to mid-March, alternate with longer periods of mild weather. Daytime temperatures almost always rise to above freezing in the southern three-fourths of the State, even during the coldest weather. There is approximately four months difference in the average length of the freeze-free growing season from north to south, ranging from about 170 days in the northernmost areas to near 300 days on the lower coast.

Relative humidity averages are moderately high in most of Georgia, as would be expected from its location in relation to the Gulf of Mexico and the Atlantic Ocean and from the high frequency of wind flow from the direction of these warm waters. Year-round averages at about 7:00 a.m. are approximately 85 percent, or slightly higher in the south. By 1:00 p.m. the average drops to about 55 percent. Monthly averages for both morning and afternoon are higher in summer than in other seasons in all sections of the State.

STORMS. Several tornadoes may be expected in Georgia each year. These storms have occurred during every month of the year, but have their highest frequency in spring. Approximately 50 percent of Georgia's tornadoes have occurred in March and April. Local windstorms, other than tornadoes, occur frequently in spring and early summer. These storms usually occur in connection with thunderstorms, the more severe of which may also produce hail. The southeast Georgia coast has been battered by hurricane winds on a few occasions but, since most of these storms do not reach the State or move into the State after having traveled over land areas, they usually produce only moderate winds and heavy to copious rains. Tropical storm rainfall contributes materially to the precipitation normals for the late summer and fall months in southeast Georgia and to a lesser extent in other areas of the State.

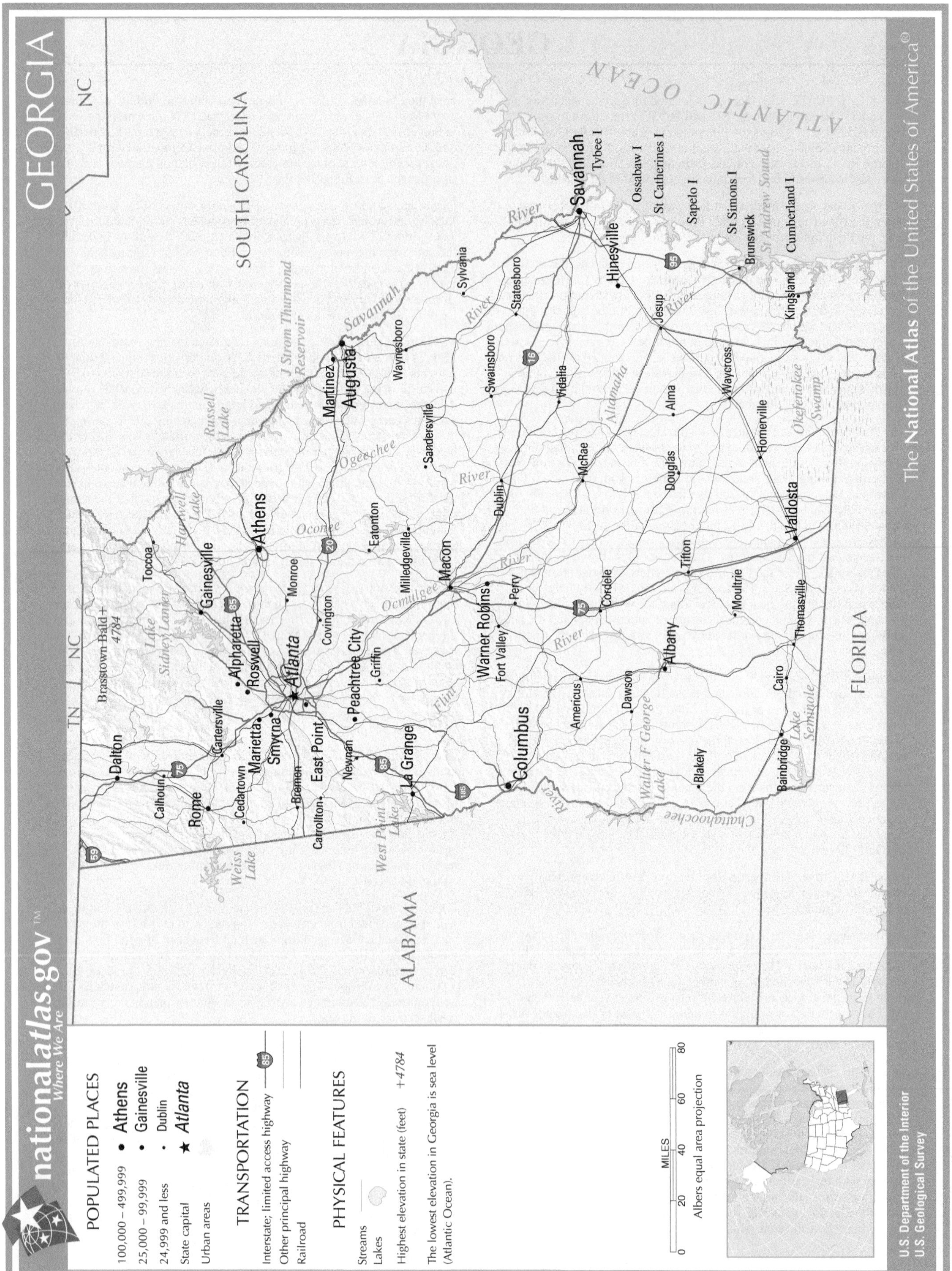
GEORGIA
nationalatlas.gov™
Where We Are
POPULATED PLACES
100,000 – 499,999 • Athens
25,000 – 99,999 • Gainesville
24,999 and less · Dublin
State capital ★ Atlanta
Urban areas
TRANSPORTATION
Interstate; limited access highway
Other principal highway
Railroad
PHYSICAL FEATURES
Streams
Lakes
Highest elevation in state (feet) +4784
The lowest elevation in Georgia is sea level (Atlantic Ocean).
MILES
0 20 40 60 80
Albers equal area projection
U.S. Department of the Interior
U.S. Geological Survey
The National Atlas of the United States of America®
SOUTH CAROLINA
NC
TN
ALABAMA
FLORIDA
ATLANTIC OCEAN
Brasstown Bald + 4784
Atlanta
Athens
Augusta
Savannah
Columbus
Macon
Albany
Valdosta
Warner Robins
Roswell
Alpharetta
Marietta
Smyrna
East Point
Peachtree City
Gainesville
Dalton
Rome
La Grange
Martinez
Hinesville
Toccoa
Calhoun
Cartersville
Cedartown
Bremen
Carrollton
Newnan
Griffin
Covington
Monroe
Eatonton
Milledgeville
Sandersville
Waynesboro
Sylvania
Statesboro
Swainsboro
Vidalia
Dublin
McRae
Perry
Fort Valley
Cordele
Americus
Dawson
Tifton
Moultrie
Thomasville
Cairo
Bainbridge
Blakely
Douglas
Alma
Jesup
Waycross
Homerville
Brunswick
Kingsland
Tybee I
Ossabaw I
St Catherines I
Sapelo I
St Simons I
Cumberland I
St Andrew Sound
Okefenokee Swamp
Savannah River
Ogeechee River
Oconee River
Ocmulgee River
Altamaha River
Flint River
Chattahoochee River
J Strom Thurmond Reservoir
Russell Lake
Hartwell Lake
Lake Sidney Lanier
Weiss Lake
West Point Lake
Walter F George Lake
Lake Seminole
59
75
85
185
20
16
95

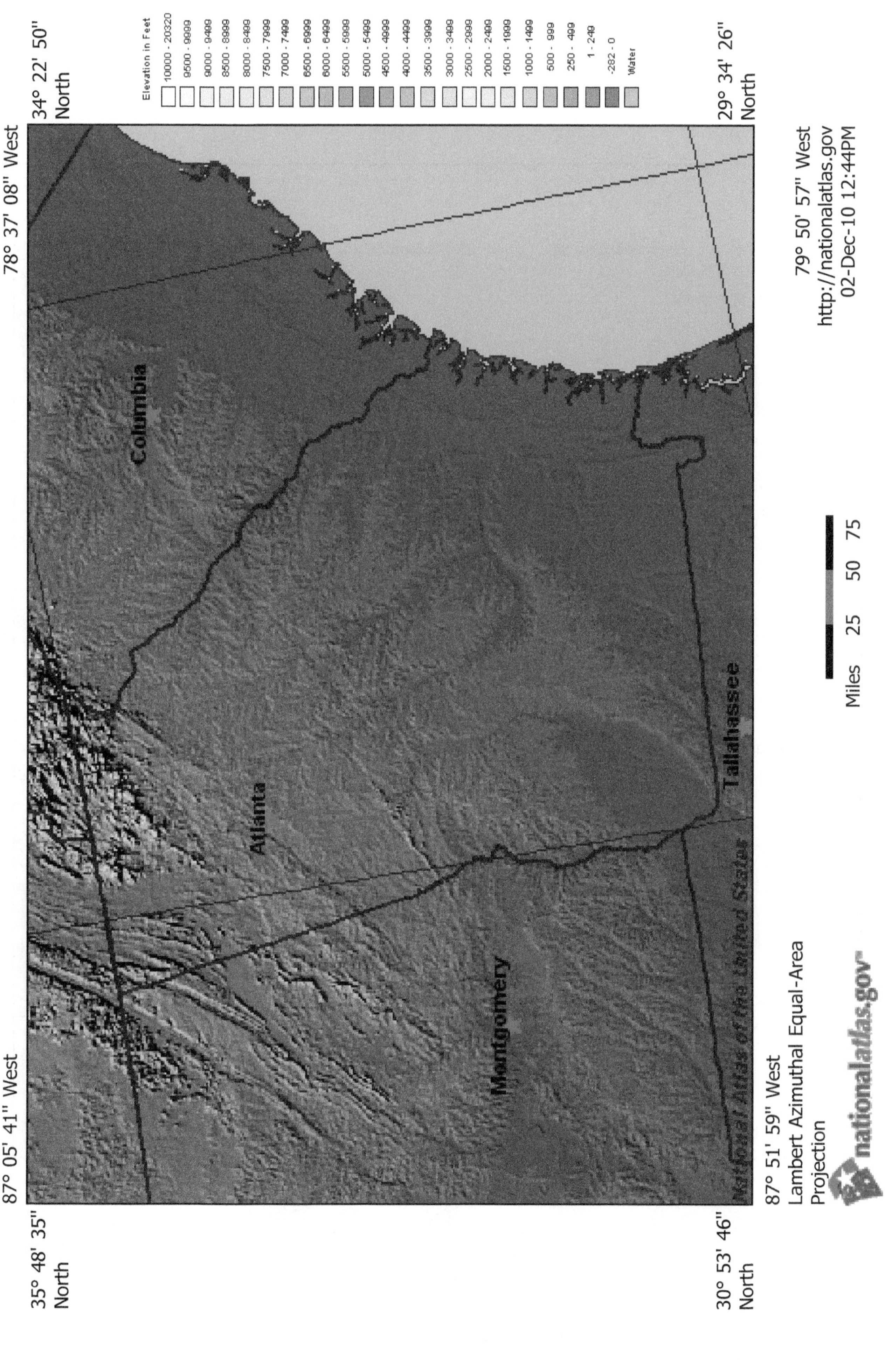
34° 22' 50" North
78° 37' 08" West
35° 48' 35" North
87° 05' 41" West
30° 53' 46" North
87° 51' 59" West
29° 34' 26" North
79° 50' 57" West
Elevation in Feet
10000 - 20320
9500 - 9999
9000 - 9499
8500 - 8999
8000 - 8499
7500 - 7999
7000 - 7499
6500 - 6999
6000 - 6499
5500 - 5999
5000 - 5499
4500 - 4999
4000 - 4499
3500 - 3999
3000 - 3499
2500 - 2999
2000 - 2499
1500 - 1999
1000 - 1499
500 - 999
250 - 499
1 - 249
-282 - 0
Water
Columbia
Atlanta
Montgomery
Tallahassee
National Atlas of the United States
Miles 25 50 75
Lambert Azimuthal Equal-Area Projection
http://nationalatlas.gov
02-Dec-10 12:44PM
nationalatlas.gov

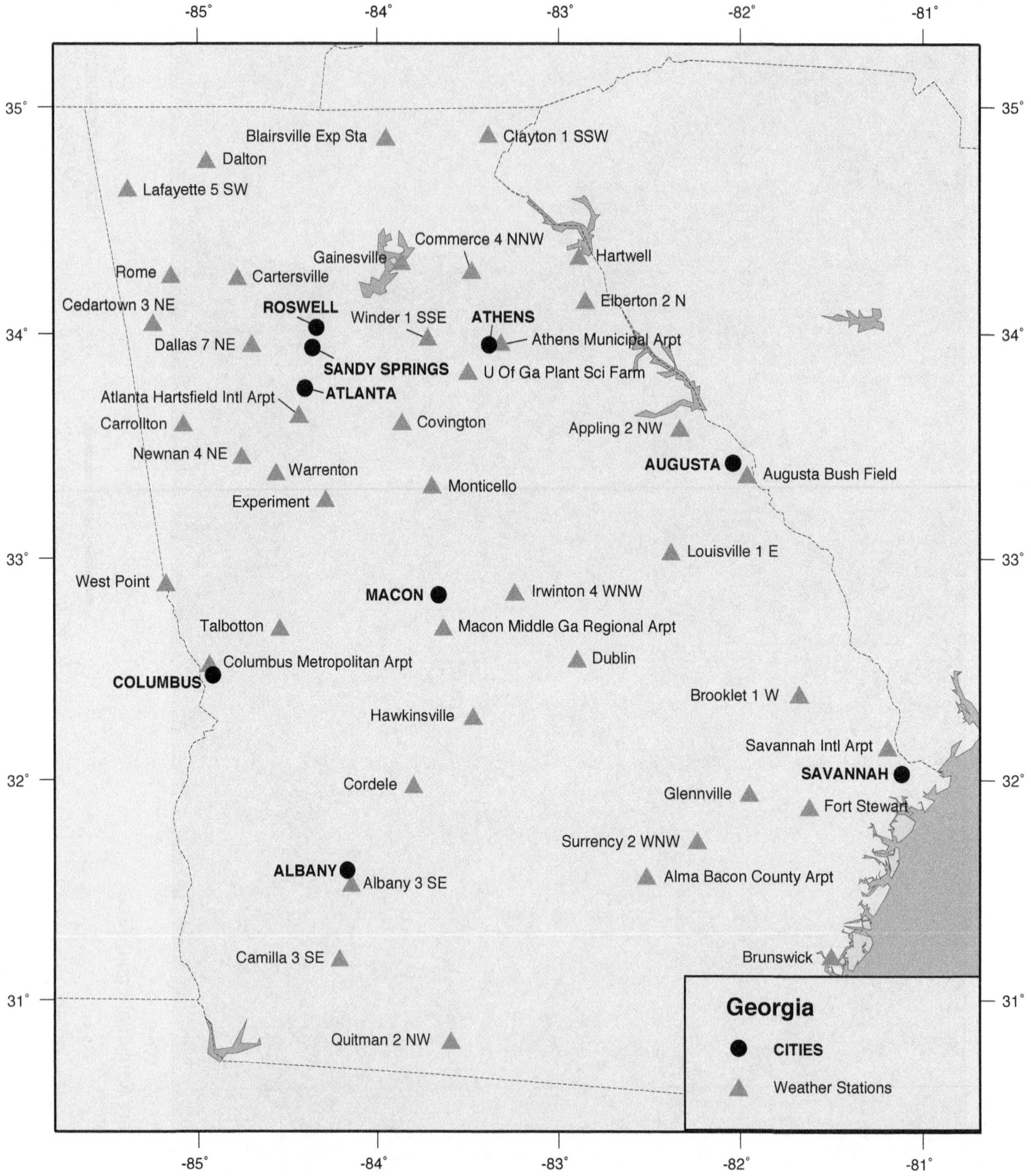
-85°
-84°
-83°
-82°
-81°
35°
34°
33°
32°
31°
Blairsville Exp Sta
Clayton 1 SSW
Dalton
Lafayette 5 SW
Commerce 4 NNW
Gainesville
Hartwell
Rome
Cartersville
Elberton 2 N
Cedartown 3 NE
ROSWELL
Winder 1 SSE
ATHENS
Dallas 7 NE
Athens Municipal Arpt
SANDY SPRINGS
U Of Ga Plant Sci Farm
Atlanta Hartsfield Intl Arpt
ATLANTA
Carrollton
Covington
Appling 2 NW
Newnan 4 NE
AUGUSTA
Warrenton
Augusta Bush Field
Monticello
Experiment
Louisville 1 E
West Point
MACON
Irwinton 4 WNW
Talbotton
Macon Middle Ga Regional Arpt
Columbus Metropolitan Arpt
Dublin
COLUMBUS
Brooklet 1 W
Hawkinsville
Savannah Intl Arpt
SAVANNAH
Cordele
Glennville
Fort Stewart
Surrency 2 WNW
ALBANY
Alma Bacon County Arpt
Albany 3 SE
Camilla 3 SE
Brunswick
Quitman 2 NW
Georgia
CITIES
Weather Stations

Georgia Weather Stations by County

County	Station Name
Appling	Surrency 2 WNW
Bacon	Alma Bacon County Arpt
Barrow	Winder 1 SSE
Bartow	Cartersville
Bibb	Macon Middle GA Regional Arpt
Brooks	Quitman 2 NW
Bulloch	Brooklet 1 W
Carroll	Carrollton
Chatham	Savannah Intl Arpt
Clarke	Athens Municipal Arpt
Columbia	Appling 2 NW
Coweta	Newnan 4 NE
Crisp	Cordele
Dougherty	Albany 3 SE
Elbert	Elberton 2 N
Floyd	Rome
Fulton	Atlanta Hartsfield Intl Arpt
Glynn	Brunswick
Hall	Gainesville
Hart	Hartwell
Jackson	Commerce 4 NNW
Jasper	Monticello
Jefferson	Louisville 1 E
Laurens	Dublin
Liberty	Fort Stewart
Mitchell	Camilla 3 SE
Muscogee	Columbus Metropolitan Arpt
Newton	Covington
Oconee	U of GA Plant Sci Farm
Paulding	Dallas 7 NE
Polk	Cedartown 3 NE
Pulaski	Hawkinsville

County	Station Name
Rabun	Clayton 1 SSW
Richmond	Augusta Bush Field
Spalding	Experiment
Talbot	Talbotton
Tattnall	Glennville
Troup	West Point
Union	Blairsville Exp Sta
Walker	Lafayette 5 SW
Warren	Warrenton
Whitfield	Dalton
Wilkinson	Irwinton 4 WNW

See User Guide for station inclusion criteria.

Georgia Weather Stations by City

City	Station Name	Miles
Albany	Albany 3 SE	3.9
Athens	Athens Municipal Arpt	2.7
	Commerce 4 NNW	22.7
	U of GA Plant Sci Farm	10.5
	Winder 1 SSE	19.4
Atlanta	Atlanta Hartsfield Intl Arpt	9.0
	Dallas 7 NE	24.9
Augusta	Appling 2 NW	19.2
	Augusta Bush Field	6.3
	Aiken 4 NE, SC	23.8
	Clark Hill 1 W, SC	18.2
Candler-McAfee	Atlanta Hartsfield Intl Arpt	11.4
	Covington	23.9
Columbus	Columbus Metropolitan Arpt	2.5
Dalton	Dalton	2.0
	Lafayette 5 SW	23.9
	Chattanooga Lovell Field, TN	22.1
Douglasville	Atlanta Hartsfield Intl Arpt	18.7
	Carrollton	22.6
	Dallas 7 NE	16.6
	Newnan 4 NE	20.5
Dunwoody	Atlanta Hartsfield Intl Arpt	22.4
East Point	Atlanta Hartsfield Intl Arpt	3.2
	Newnan 4 NE	24.3
	Warrenton	22.2
Gainesville	Commerce 4 NNW	20.2
	Gainesville	1.9
	Winder 1 SSE	23.2
Hinesville	Fort Stewart	3.0
	Glennville	20.3
Kennesaw	Cartersville	16.8
	Dallas 7 NE	8.1
LaGrange	West Point	15.0
Lawrenceville	Covington	24.9
	Winder 1 SSE	15.8
Mableton	Atlanta Hartsfield Intl Arpt	14.7
	Dallas 7 NE	15.6
Macon	Irwinton 4 WNW	24.9
	Macon Middle GA Regional Arpt	10.5
Marietta	Atlanta Hartsfield Intl Arpt	22.4
	Cartersville	24.4
	Dallas 7 NE	12.6
Martinez	Appling 2 NW	14.0
	Augusta Bush Field	13.0
	Aiken 4 NE, SC	24.5
	Clark Hill 1 W, SC	11.3

City	Station Name	Miles
Martinez *(cont.)*	Johnston 4 SW, SC	23.1
Newnan	Carrollton	22.8
	Newnan 4 NE	5.0
	Warrenton	13.0
North Atlanta	Atlanta Hartsfield Intl Arpt	16.5
Peachtree City	Atlanta Hartsfield Intl Arpt	18.2
	Experiment	18.7
	Newnan 4 NE	12.9
	Warrenton	2.0
Redan	Atlanta Hartsfield Intl Arpt	17.2
	Covington	18.7
Rome	Cartersville	23.3
	Cedartown 3 NE	14.9
	Rome	2.4
Roswell	Dallas 7 NE	23.7
Sandy Springs	Atlanta Hartsfield Intl Arpt	21.6
	Dallas 7 NE	22.3
Savannah	Savannah Intl Arpt	8.0
Smyrna	Atlanta Hartsfield Intl Arpt	16.8
	Dallas 7 NE	15.7
Statesboro	Brooklet 1 W	7.2
Tucker	Atlanta Hartsfield Intl Arpt	19.5
Valdosta	Quitman 2 NW	18.1
Warner Robins	Hawkinsville	24.9
	Macon Middle GA Regional Arpt	4.9

Note: Miles is the distance between the geographic center of the city and the weather station.

See User Guide for station inclusion criteria.

Georgia Weather Stations by Elevation

Feet	Station Name
1,917	Blairsville Exp Sta
1,879	Clayton 1 SSW
1,169	Gainesville
1,100	Dallas 7 NE
1,009	Atlanta Hartsfield Intl Arpt
995	Carrollton
959	Winder 1 SSE
924	Experiment
919	Newnan 4 NE
839	U of GA Plant Sci Farm
799	Athens Municipal Arpt
799	Lafayette 5 SW
785	Cedartown 3 NE
770	Covington
750	Commerce 4 NNW
729	Talbotton
720	Cartersville
700	Dalton
689	Hartwell
620	Rome
575	West Point
540	Elberton 2 N
529	Monticello
515	Irwinton 4 WNW
509	Warrenton
392	Columbus Metropolitan Arpt
370	Appling 2 NW
354	Macon Middle GA Regional Arpt
321	Louisville 1 E
308	Cordele
271	Hawkinsville
229	Dublin
200	Surrency 2 WNW
198	Alma Bacon County Arpt
189	Brooklet 1 W
185	Quitman 2 NW
180	Albany 3 SE
174	Camilla 3 SE
169	Glennville
131	Augusta Bush Field
91	Fort Stewart
45	Savannah Intl Arpt
13	Brunswick

See User Guide for station inclusion criteria.

Athens Municipal Airport

Athens is located in northeast Georgia, in the Piedmont Plateau section of the state. The terrain is rolling to hilly with the elevation within the city averaging about 700 feet above sea level, and that of the county ranging mostly between 600 and 850 feet. The Atlantic Ocean 200 miles to the southeast, the Gulf of Mexico 275 miles to the south, and the southern Appalachian Mountains to the north and northwest, all exert some influence on the climate of Athens, with the total effect being a moderation of both summer and winter weather.

Summers are warm and somewhat humid in Athens, but there is a noticeable absence of prolonged periods of extreme heat. The maximum temperature reaches 90 degrees or higher on about one-half the days during the three months, June through August, but a temperature of 100 degrees or higher occurs during fewer than one-half the years.

With the mountains to the north serving as a partial barrier to the flow of extremely cold air into the area, winters in Athens are not severe. Cold spells are usually short-lived, interspersed with periods of warm southerly air flow, making normal outside activities possible throughout most years.

Average annual precipitation in Athens is fairly evenly distributed throughout the year, with slight maxima in winter, early spring, and in midsummer. In spite of what appears to be an abundant supply of moisture, dry spells occur during most years. Fortunately, they are more frequent in autumn when long periods of clear, mild, weather but offer ideal conditions for harvesting operations.

Snowfall is not of much importance in the area. Measurable amounts occur rather infrequently, but occasionally there is sufficient fall to cause some accumulation on the ground.

The average length of the freeze-free growing season in Athens is 220 days, from early April, the average occurrence of the last spring freeze, to early November, the average occurrence of the first fall freeze.

Thunderstorms occur in all months of the year but are most frequent in June and July. Severe thunderstorms are infrequent, but may occur as isolated summer storms, or in squall lines of winter and spring. A few tornadoes have crossed the city and county since 1930, causing several deaths.

Athens Municipal Airport *Clarke County* Elevation: 799 ft. Latitude: 33° 57' N Longitude: 83° 20' W

	JAN	FEB	MAR	APR	MAY	JUN	JUL	AUG	SEP	OCT	NOV	DEC	YEAR
Mean Maximum Temp. (°F)	53.4	57.8	65.7	73.5	81.2	88.0	91.0	89.5	83.4	73.7	64.6	55.5	73.1
Mean Temp. (°F)	43.5	47.2	54.2	61.5	69.8	77.3	80.5	79.5	73.2	62.7	53.6	45.4	62.4
Mean Minimum Temp. (°F)	33.5	36.5	42.7	49.4	58.3	66.4	70.0	69.3	63.0	51.6	42.5	35.3	51.5
Extreme Maximum Temp. (°F)	78	81	89	93	95	103	103	107	98	92	84	79	107
Extreme Minimum Temp. (°F)	-4	7	11	26	37	49	57	56	44	27	16	3	-4
Days Maximum Temp. ≥ 90°F	0	0	0	0	3	13	20	16	5	0	0	0	57
Days Maximum Temp. ≤ 32°F	1	0	0	0	0	0	0	0	0	0	0	0	1
Days Minimum Temp. ≤ 32°F	15	10	4	0	0	0	0	0	0	1	5	13	48
Days Minimum Temp. ≤ 0°F	0	0	0	0	0	0	0	0	0	0	0	0	0
Heating Degree Days (base 65°F)	660	498	337	148	24	1	0	0	9	128	344	601	2,750
Cooling Degree Days (base 65°F)	0	1	9	48	180	375	488	455	263	63	8	1	1,891
Mean Precipitation (in.)	4.07	4.40	4.68	3.17	3.06	4.14	4.47	3.36	3.94	3.55	3.75	3.73	46.32
Maximum Precipitation (in.)*	9.5	9.2	10.9	9.5	11.3	13.3	10.5	7.4	10.3	7.7	9.2	8.4	71.4
Minimum Precipitation (in.)*	0.6	0.8	1.1	0.7	0.4	0.9	1.4	0.5	0.6	trace	1.0	0.8	32.4
Extreme Maximum Daily Precip. (in.)	2.49	2.71	3.73	3.51	3.67	7.34	6.22	4.32	3.69	5.43	3.07	3.60	7.34
Days With ≥ 0.1" Precipitation	7	7	7	6	6	7	7	5	5	4	5	6	72
Days With ≥ 0.5" Precipitation	3	3	3	2	2	3	3	2	3	2	3	2	31
Days With ≥ 1.0" Precipitation	1	1	2	1	1	1	1	1	1	1	1	1	13
Mean Snowfall (in.)	na	na	na	na	na	na	na	na	na	na	na	na	na
Maximum Snowfall (in.)*	7	5	9	0	0	0	0	0	0	0	2	3	11
Maximum 24-hr. Snowfall (in.)*	7	5	9	0	0	0	0	0	0	0	2	3	9
Maximum Snow Depth (in.)	na	na	na	na	na	na	na	na	na	na	na	na	na
Days With ≥ 1.0" Snow Depth	na	na	na	na	na	na	na	na	na	na	na	na	na
Thunderstorm Days*	1	1	3	4	6	9	12	8	3	1	1	1	50
Foggy Days*	15	12	13	11	16	16	19	22	20	16	13	14	187
Predominant Sky Cover*	OVR	OVR	OVR	CLR	OVR	OVR	OVR	SCT	OVR	CLR	CLR	OVR	OVR
Mean Relative Humidity 7am (%)*	80	79	80	82	86	87	90	92	92	89	85	81	85
Mean Relative Humidity 4pm (%)*	54	50	48	45	51	53	57	57	57	52	51	54	52
Mean Dewpoint (°F)*	31	32	39	47	57	65	69	69	63	51	41	34	50
Prevailing Wind Direction*	WNW	WNW	WNW	WNW	WNW	WSW	WSW	NE	NE	NE	WNW	WNW	WNW
Prevailing Wind Speed (mph)*	10	10	10	10	8	7	7	7	8	8	9	10	9
Maximum Wind Gust (mph)*	55	56	83	60	52	58	78	49	55	47	59	45	83

Note: (*) Period of record is 1948-1995

The period of record for National Weather Service station data is 1980 – 2009 except where noted. See User Guide for detailed explanation of data.

Atlanta Hartsfield Int'l Arpt.

Atlanta is located in the foothills of the southern Appalachians in north-central Georgia. The terrain is rolling to hilly and slopes downward toward the east, west, and south so that drainage of the major river systems is generally into the Gulf of Mexico from the western and southern sections of the city and to the Atlantic from the eastern portions of the city.

The Gulf of Mexico and the Atlantic Ocean are approximately 250 miles south and southeast of the city, respectively. Both the Appalachian chain of mountains and the two nearby maritime bodies exert an important influence on the Atlanta climate. Temperatures are moderated throughout the year while abundant precipitation fosters natural vegetation and growth of crops. Summer temperatures in Atlanta are moderated somewhat by elevation but are still rather warm. However, prolonged periods of hot weather are unusual and 100 degree heat is rarely experienced.

With the mountains to the north blocking the southward movement of Polar air masses, Atlanta winters are rather mild. Cold spells are not unusual but they are rather short-lived and seldom disrupt outdoor activities for an extended period of time. Late March is the average date of the last temperature of 32 degrees in the spring and mid-November is the average date of the first temperature of 32 degrees in the fall, which gives an average growing season of about 234 days.

Minimum dry precipitation periods occur mainly during the late summer and early autumn. Maximum thunderstorm activity occurs during July, but severe local thunderstorms occur most frequently in March, April, and May, some spawning highly damaging tornadoes.

The average annual snowfall varies widely from year to year. A fall of four inches or more occurs about once every five years. Most snows melt in a short period of time due to the rapid warming which often follows the storm. Ice storms, freezing rain or glaze, occur about two out of every three years, causing hazardous travel and disruption of utilities. Severe ice storms occur about once in ten years, causing major disruption of utilities and significant property damage.

The Bermuda High pressure area has a dominant effect on Atlanta weather, particularly in the summer months. East or northeast winds produce the most unpleasant weather although southerly winds are quite humid during the summer. The generally light wind conditions contribute to the formation of an occasional early morning fog.

Atlanta Hartsfield Int'l Arpt. *Fulton County* Elevation: 1,009 ft. Latitude: 33° 38' N Longitude: 84° 26' W

	JAN	FEB	MAR	APR	MAY	JUN	JUL	AUG	SEP	OCT	NOV	DEC	YEAR
Mean Maximum Temp. (°F)	52.9	57.2	65.1	72.7	80.3	86.8	89.6	88.5	82.4	72.8	63.9	54.7	72.2
Mean Temp. (°F)	43.7	47.5	54.6	62.0	70.3	77.4	80.5	79.6	73.6	63.3	54.1	45.7	62.7
Mean Minimum Temp. (°F)	34.5	37.7	44.2	51.3	60.3	67.9	71.3	70.6	64.7	53.8	44.2	36.7	53.1
Extreme Maximum Temp. (°F)	78	80	89	93	95	99	105	104	97	89	83	79	105
Extreme Minimum Temp. (°F)	-8	6	11	27	41	50	60	55	43	32	22	0	-8
Days Maximum Temp. ≥ 90°F	0	0	0	0	1	10	16	13	3	0	0	0	43
Days Maximum Temp. ≤ 32°F	1	0	0	0	0	0	0	0	0	0	0	0	1
Days Minimum Temp. ≤ 32°F	13	9	3	0	0	0	0	0	0	0	3	11	39
Days Minimum Temp. ≤ 0°F	0	0	0	0	0	0	0	0	0	0	0	0	0
Heating Degree Days (base 65°F)	653	490	327	139	21	1	0	0	10	116	331	592	2,680
Cooling Degree Days (base 65°F)	0	1	13	57	192	379	487	459	274	70	9	1	1,942
Mean Precipitation (in.)	4.21	4.62	5.05	3.34	3.71	3.93	5.14	3.84	4.57	3.35	3.99	3.88	49.63
Maximum Precipitation (in.)*	10.2	12.8	11.7	11.9	8.4	10.0	17.7	8.7	11.6	11.0	15.7	9.9	71.2
Minimum Precipitation (in.)*	0.8	0.8	1.9	0.5	0.4	0.2	0.6	0.5	trace	trace	0.8	0.7	31.8
Extreme Maximum Daily Precip. (in.)	2.59	3.65	4.32	2.78	3.03	3.78	5.14	3.72	4.93	6.68	4.05	3.10	6.68
Days With ≥ 0.1" Precipitation	7	7	7	6	6	7	8	6	5	4	6	6	75
Days With ≥ 0.5" Precipitation	3	3	3	2	3	3	3	3	3	2	3	3	34
Days With ≥ 1.0" Precipitation	1	1	2	1	1	1	2	1	1	1	1	1	14
Mean Snowfall (in.)	***1.3***	na	***0.9***	na	na	***0.0***	***trace***	***0.0***	***0.0***	***trace***	***trace***	***0.3***	na
Maximum Snowfall (in.)*	7	4	8	trace	0	0	0	0	0	trace	1	3	10
Maximum 24-hr. Snowfall (in.)*	5	4	8	trace	0	0	0	0	0	trace	1	2	8
Maximum Snow Depth (in.)	5	1	4	trace	0	0	trace	0	0	trace	trace	2	5
Days With ≥ 1.0" Snow Depth	1	0	0	0	0	0	0	0	0	0	0	0	1
Thunderstorm Days*	1	2	3	4	6	8	10	7	3	1	1	1	47
Foggy Days*	14	11	11	9	11	11	14	16	14	12	12	13	148
Predominant Sky Cover*	OVR	OVR	OVR	OVR	OVR	SCT	SCT	SCT	OVR	CLR	OVR	OVR	OVR
Mean Relative Humidity 7am (%)*	79	77	78	78	82	84	88	89	88	84	81	80	82
Mean Relative Humidity 4pm (%)*	56	50	48	45	49	53	57	56	56	51	52	56	52
Mean Dewpoint (°F)*	32	33	39	47	56	64	68	68	62	51	41	34	49
Prevailing Wind Direction*	NW	NW	NW	NW	NW	NW	W	E	ENE	ENE	NW	NW	NW
Prevailing Wind Speed (mph)*	13	13	13	12	10	9	8	8	10	9	12	12	10
Maximum Wind Gust (mph)*	62	71	70	61	73	60	77	61	58	48	56	67	77

Note: (*) Period of record is 1945-1995

Augusta Bush Field

The boundary between the Piedmont Plateau and the Coastal Plain, known as the Fall Line, crosses the Savannah River basin in a general north-east-southwest direction near Augusta, Georgia. The Weather Service Office at Bush Field is located in the Savannah River Valley approximately two miles west of the river and 203 miles above the mouth of the Savannah. Hills some 200 feet higher than the station are found slightly more than one mile to the west and approximately four miles to the southwest, and some five miles to the south and southeast. Swampland is found immediately to the north, east, and south of the station.

The length of the growing season averages 241 days. The average last occurrence in the spring of temperatures of 32 degrees is mid-March, and the first in the fall is mid-November.

Measurable snow is a rarity and then remains on the ground only a short time. Ice storms, damaging winds, and very low temperatures are also of rare occurrence.

Augusta has been protected, to a great extent, from flooding of the Savannah River by the construction of two multipurpose dams. The Clark Hill Dam is located 21.7 miles above the city and Hartwell Dam has been constructed 89 miles above Augusta.

Augusta Bush Field *Richmond County* Elevation: 131 ft. Latitude: 33° 22' N Longitude: 81° 58' W

	JAN	FEB	MAR	APR	MAY	JUN	JUL	AUG	SEP	OCT	NOV	DEC	YEAR
Mean Maximum Temp. (°F)	57.6	62.0	69.5	76.8	84.5	90.3	92.9	91.5	86.2	77.0	68.5	59.8	76.4
Mean Temp. (°F)	45.5	49.1	55.9	62.7	71.0	78.4	81.6	80.6	74.7	64.3	55.2	47.4	63.9
Mean Minimum Temp. (°F)	33.4	36.2	42.4	48.5	57.5	66.5	70.3	69.6	63.2	51.5	41.8	35.0	51.3
Extreme Maximum Temp. (°F)	82	85	91	96	99	104	107	108	101	95	87	82	108
Extreme Minimum Temp. (°F)	-1	11	12	26	36	47	54	52	42	27	18	5	-1
Days Maximum Temp. ≥ 90°F	0	0	0	1	7	18	25	20	10	1	0	0	82
Days Maximum Temp. ≤ 32°F	0	0	0	0	0	0	0	0	0	0	0	0	0
Days Minimum Temp. ≤ 32°F	15	11	5	1	0	0	0	0	0	1	6	14	53
Days Minimum Temp. ≤ 0°F	0	0	0	0	0	0	0	0	0	0	0	0	0
Heating Degree Days (base 65°F)	600	446	290	121	17	0	0	0	6	105	304	541	2,430
Cooling Degree Days (base 65°F)	2	2	16	58	209	410	522	489	303	90	15	3	2,119
Mean Precipitation (in.)	3.87	3.94	4.47	2.84	2.67	4.79	4.21	4.27	3.33	3.30	2.85	3.38	43.92
Maximum Precipitation (in.)*	8.9	7.7	11.9	8.4	9.6	8.8	12.2	11.3	9.5	14.8	7.8	8.6	66.0
Minimum Precipitation (in.)*	0.8	0.3	0.9	0.6	0.5	0.7	1.0	0.6	0.3	trace	0.1	0.3	31.5
Extreme Maximum Daily Precip. (in.)	2.66	3.50	3.73	2.73	4.44	3.42	3.64	4.21	7.30	5.32	3.43	2.65	7.30
Days With ≥ 0.1" Precipitation	7	6	6	5	5	7	7	7	4	4	4	6	68
Days With ≥ 0.5" Precipitation	3	3	3	2	2	3	3	3	2	2	2	2	30
Days With ≥ 1.0" Precipitation	1	1	1	1	1	2	1	1	1	1	1	1	13
Mean Snowfall (in.)	0.3	0.4	0.0	***trace***	***0.0***	***trace***	***0.0***	***0.0***	***0.0***	***0.0***	0.0	0.1	***0.8***
Maximum Snowfall (in.)*	3	14	1	0	0	0	0	0	0	0	trace	1	14
Maximum 24-hr. Snowfall (in.)*	3	8	1	0	0	0	0	0	0	0	trace	1	8
Maximum Snow Depth (in.)	3	4	1	***trace***	***0***	***trace***	***0***	***0***	***0***	***0***	0	1	***4***
Days With ≥ 1.0" Snow Depth	0	0	0	***0***	***0***	***0***	***0***	***0***	***0***	***0***	0	0	***0***
Thunderstorm Days*	1	2	3	4	6	10	13	10	4	1	1	1	56
Foggy Days*	15	12	13	13	16	17	18	22	20	17	16	15	194
Predominant Sky Cover*	OVR	OVR	OVR	CLR	OVR	SCT	SCT	SCT	OVR	CLR	CLR	OVR	OVR
Mean Relative Humidity 7am (%)*	84	82	84	85	86	86	88	91	92	91	88	85	87
Mean Relative Humidity 4pm (%)*	51	47	45	43	47	51	56	56	55	49	47	51	50
Mean Dewpoint (°F)*	34	36	41	49	59	66	70	70	64	53	43	36	52
Prevailing Wind Direction*	W	WNW	WNW	SE	SE	SE	SE	SE	NE	NE	WNW	W	SE
Prevailing Wind Speed (mph)*	10	12	12	8	7	7	7	6	8	8	9	9	8
Maximum Wind Gust (mph)*	55	55	66	54	58	60	69	62	47	63	48	49	69

Note: (*) Period of record is 1949-1995

The period of record for National Weather Service station data is 1980 – 2009 except where noted. See User Guide for detailed explanation of data.

Columbus Metropolitan Airport

Columbus is located on the Chattahoochee River at the western boundary of Georgia, about 225 miles west of the Atlantic Ocean and 170 miles north of the Gulf of Mexico. Elevation of the ground above sea level ranges from 200 to 500 feet and effects of terrain on the weather are negligible. The climate is that of the humid southeast, with pronounced maritime effects at some periods, and equally pronounced continental effects at others.

Annual rainfall is variable, the months of highest rainfall are generally March and July, and the driest are usually October and November. Heavy mid-summer rainfall is commonly the result of frequent local thunderstorms. Heavy rains which occasionally come in autumn are likely to be due to Gulf or Caribbean hurricanes moving inland near the Columbus area.

Snow is rare, but almost every winter sees a few snowflakes falling in the area and occasionally a moderate to heavy snowfall is experienced.

The coldest month is usually January and the warmest is usually July.

Most days in summer will have a high temperature of 90 degrees or more, but few will reach 100 degrees. During many winters the minimum temperature does not drop below 20 degrees, but about one year in ten it will drop to 10 degrees or lower.

Based on the 1951-1980 period, the average first occurrence of 32 degrees Fahrenheit in the fall is November 9 and the average last occurrence in the spring is March 21.

Columbus Metropolitan Airport *Muscogee County* Elevation: 392 ft. Latitude: 32° 31' N Longitude: 84° 57' W

	JAN	FEB	MAR	APR	MAY	JUN	JUL	AUG	SEP	OCT	NOV	DEC	YEAR
Mean Maximum Temp. (°F)	57.7	62.2	69.6	76.6	83.9	89.9	92.2	91.4	86.2	77.1	68.3	59.5	76.2
Mean Temp. (°F)	47.5	51.2	58.0	64.6	72.9	79.8	82.5	81.9	76.6	66.3	57.2	49.3	65.6
Mean Minimum Temp. (°F)	37.2	40.2	46.2	52.5	61.9	69.6	72.8	72.3	66.8	55.6	46.1	39.0	55.0
Extreme Maximum Temp. (°F)	82	83	89	93	97	103	104	104	100	93	86	80	104
Extreme Minimum Temp. (°F)	-2	10	16	30	44	49	60	58	45	32	24	8	-2
Days Maximum Temp. ≥ 90°F	0	0	0	0	5	17	23	21	10	1	0	0	77
Days Maximum Temp. ≤ 32°F	0	0	0	0	0	0	0	0	0	0	0	0	0
Days Minimum Temp. ≤ 32°F	11	6	2	0	0	0	0	0	0	0	2	9	30
Days Minimum Temp. ≤ 0°F	0	0	0	0	0	0	0	0	0	0	0	0	0
Heating Degree Days (base 65°F)	537	388	237	88	6	0	0	0	2	72	251	485	2,066
Cooling Degree Days (base 65°F)	1	4	26	81	258	449	551	530	356	121	24	4	2,405
Mean Precipitation (in.)	3.80	4.44	5.70	3.66	3.23	3.73	4.80	3.84	3.03	2.60	4.03	4.27	47.13
Maximum Precipitation (in.)*	8.3	9.4	12.5	11.7	8.4	10.8	13.2	10.1	6.9	8.4	12.4	9.4	73.2
Minimum Precipitation (in.)*	0.7	1.0	1.4	0.1	0.2	0.7	1.7	0.8	0.2	0	0.3	0.4	30.2
Extreme Maximum Daily Precip. (in.)	3.21	5.54	5.38	5.74	4.54	3.40	5.45	4.10	3.61	4.13	5.44	3.63	5.74
Days With ≥ 0.1" Precipitation	7	6	7	5	5	7	8	6	5	4	5	6	71
Days With ≥ 0.5" Precipitation	3	3	4	3	2	3	3	2	2	2	2	3	32
Days With ≥ 1.0" Precipitation	1	1	2	1	1	1	1	1	1	1	1	1	13
Mean Snowfall (in.)	***0.2***	***trace***	***0.2***	***trace***	***trace***	***0.0***	na	na	na	na	na	na	na
Maximum Snowfall (in.)*	2	14	3	trace	0	0	0	0	0	0	trace	2	14
Maximum 24-hr. Snowfall (in.)*	1	11	3	trace	0	0	0	0	0	0	trace	1	11
Maximum Snow Depth (in.)	***1***	***trace***	***1***	***trace***	***trace***	***0***	***0***	na	na	na	na	na	na
Days With ≥ 1.0" Snow Depth	***0***	***0***	***0***	***0***	***0***	***0***	***0***	na	na	na	na	na	na
Thunderstorm Days*	1	2	4	4	6	8	13	9	4	1	1	1	54
Foggy Days*	15	13	14	12	15	15	19	19	16	14	14	15	181
Predominant Sky Cover*	OVR	OVR	OVR	CLR	OVR	SCT	SCT	SCT	OVR	CLR	CLR	OVR	OVR
Mean Relative Humidity 7am (%)*	84	83	85	86	86	86	90	91	90	89	87	85	87
Mean Relative Humidity 4pm (%)*	54	50	46	43	48	51	57	55	54	49	50	54	51
Mean Dewpoint (°F)*	36	38	43	51	60	66	71	70	65	54	45	39	53
Prevailing Wind Direction*	NW	NW	NW	NW	ENE	ENE	SW	ENE	ENE	ENE	ENE	ENE	ENE
Prevailing Wind Speed (mph)*	10	10	10	10	8	8	8	7	9	9	8	9	9
Maximum Wind Gust (mph)*	58	61	99	67	82	54	64	71	61	52	52	56	99

Note: (*) Period of record is 1948-1995

Macon Regional Airport

Located very near the geographical center of Georgia, Macon is well situated to escape rigorous climatic extremes. The climate is a blend of the maritime and continental types. Rarely does either dominate for long unbroken periods. The prevailing northwesterly winds of winter and early spring are frequently superseded by southerly flows of warm, moist tropical air. The southern extremity of the Appalachians presents an effective barrier to the rapid flow of cold air in winter. In summertime the prevailing southerlies frequently give way to the drier westerly and northerly winds. In short, the climate is truly equable.

Severe storms occur occasionally in this locality. Tornadoes occur, about twice each year within the area covered by Bibb and adjacent counties. Thunderstorms occur on approximately two days out of five from June through August. Occasionally, thunderstorms are accompanied by severe squalls, but property damage from this cause has been heavy in only a few instances. As Macon is some 200 miles from both the Atlantic and the Gulf of Mexico, hurricanes offer no direct threat, and secondary effects are generally milder than those produced by the heavier thunderstorms. Property damage of a minor nature occurs occasionally due to gale force winds and heavy rainfall.

Snow occurs at some time during most winters, but amounts of snow are usually quite small. However, on rare occasions heavy snow does occur in this area.

Based on the 1951-1980 period, the average first occurrence of 32 degrees Fahrenheit in the fall is November 8 and the average last occurrence in the spring is March 17.

The National Weather Service Office is surrounded by predominantly flat terrain. Flanking the station on the west, a range of wooded hills about 300 feet in height runs in a general northwest-southeast direction. The nearest point of these hills is about two and a half miles to the southwest. Most of the countryside is well wooded, except for a few farms. Much of the outlying area is swampy, especially in the river and creek bottoms. Besides the swamps, the only bodies of water in the vicinity are the Ocmulgee River, Echeconnee Creek, and Tobesofkee Creek. These have little influence on the climate, except that when other conditions are favorable, they contribute to the formation of fog.

Macon Regional Airport *Bibb County* Elevation: 354 ft. Latitude: 32° 41' N Longitude: 83° 39' W

	JAN	FEB	MAR	APR	MAY	JUN	JUL	AUG	SEP	OCT	NOV	DEC	YEAR
Mean Maximum Temp. (°F)	58.1	62.4	69.7	76.8	84.7	90.3	92.8	91.6	86.2	77.4	68.8	60.0	76.6
Mean Temp. (°F)	46.9	50.5	57.2	63.7	72.2	79.2	82.1	81.2	75.4	65.2	56.2	48.5	64.9
Mean Minimum Temp. (°F)	35.6	38.5	44.7	50.5	59.6	68.0	71.4	70.7	64.5	52.9	43.5	37.1	53.1
Extreme Maximum Temp. (°F)	81	85	90	96	98	105	108	105	102	94	86	81	108
Extreme Minimum Temp. (°F)	-6	10	14	28	40	50	56	56	44	27	20	7	-6
Days Maximum Temp. ≥ 90°F	0	0	0	1	7	18	24	22	10	1	0	0	83
Days Maximum Temp. ≤ 32°F	0	0	0	0	0	0	0	0	0	0	0	0	0
Days Minimum Temp. ≤ 32°F	13	8	3	1	0	0	0	0	0	1	5	12	43
Days Minimum Temp. ≤ 0°F	0	0	0	0	0	0	0	0	0	0	0	0	0
Heating Degree Days (base 65°F)	556	407	256	103	11	0	0	0	4	91	277	508	2,213
Cooling Degree Days (base 65°F)	1	3	21	71	240	432	538	509	323	103	20	4	2,265
Mean Precipitation (in.)	4.17	4.33	4.83	3.00	2.67	3.93	4.51	4.02	3.57	2.80	3.27	4.02	45.12
Maximum Precipitation (in.)*	10.9	9.3	11.9	8.4	11.8	9.1	18.2	8.6	8.8	9.4	10.3	10.4	60.7
Minimum Precipitation (in.)*	0.7	0.6	1.2	0.1	0.3	0.9	0.4	1.1	0.3	0	0.4	0.6	26.0
Extreme Maximum Daily Precip. (in.)	4.73	3.98	4.28	2.78	3.43	4.07	3.19	3.06	5.30	4.01	3.06	2.72	5.30
Days With ≥ 0.1" Precipitation	7	6	7	5	5	7	8	6	5	4	5	6	71
Days With ≥ 0.5" Precipitation	3	3	3	2	2	2	3	3	2	2	2	3	30
Days With ≥ 1.0" Precipitation	1	2	1	1	1	1	1	1	1	1	1	1	13
Mean Snowfall (in.)	na	na	na	na	na	na	na	na	na	na	na	na	na
Maximum Snowfall (in.)*	4	17	3	0	0	0	0	0	0	0	trace	2	17
Maximum 24-hr. Snowfall (in.)*	4	11	3	0	0	0	0	0	0	0	trace	1	11
Maximum Snow Depth (in.)	na	na	na	na	na	na	na	na	na	na	na	na	na
Days With ≥ 1.0" Snow Depth	na	na	na	na	na	na	na	na	na	na	na	na	na
Thunderstorm Days*	1	2	3	4	6	9	13	9	3	1	1	1	53
Foggy Days*	14	12	14	11	15	15	17	21	21	16	14	15	185
Predominant Sky Cover*	OVR	OVR	OVR	CLR	OVR	SCT	BRK	SCT	OVR	CLR	CLR	OVR	OVR
Mean Relative Humidity 7am (%)*	83	83	84	85	86	86	89	91	92	89	87	84	87
Mean Relative Humidity 4pm (%)*	52	48	46	42	46	51	55	54	54	48	47	52	50
Mean Dewpoint (°F)*	36	37	43	50	59	66	70	70	65	53	44	38	53
Prevailing Wind Direction*	NW	NW	WNW	WNW	WNW	WNW	WSW	NE	NE	NE	NW	NW	WNW
Prevailing Wind Speed (mph)*	10	10	10	9	8	8	7	8	9	9	9	10	9
Maximum Wind Gust (mph)*	59	87	74	64	71	59	63	54	44	45	58	59	87

Note: (*) Period of record is 1948-1995

The period of record for National Weather Service station data is 1980 – 2009 except where noted. See User Guide for detailed explanation of data.

Savannah Int'l Airport

Savannah is surrounded by flat terrain, low and marshy to the north and east, and rising to several feet above sea level to the west and south. About half the land to the west and south is cleared and the other half is wooded and swampy.

The area has a temperate climate, with a seasonal low temperature of 51 degrees in winter, 66 degrees in spring, 80 degrees in summer, and 66 degrees in autumn. The lowest temperatures are below 10 degrees and the highest temperatures are about 100 degrees.

The normal annual rainfall is about 49 inches. About half falls in the thunderstorm season of June 15 through September 15. The remainder, produced principally by squall-line and frontal showers, is spread over the other nine months with a minor peak in March. Considerable periods of fair, mild weather are experienced in October, November, April, and to a less extent, in May. Snow is a rarity and even a trace does not occur on an average of once a year. The heaviest snowfalls are under five inches. Severe tropical storms affect this area about once in ten years. Rainfall from these storms constitute the heaviest sustained precipitation. Accumulations exceeding 22 inches have occurred.

The present exposure of the thermometers gives readings more nearly commensurate with those of suburban street levels of Savannah than was the case of previous locations atop various buildings. During that time, especially on still, clear nights, temperatures near the ground and in lower inland areas were as much as 15 degrees lower than the official low temperature. Present differences on comparable nights range from three to eight degrees.

Sunshine is adequate at all seasons and seldom are there two or more days in succession without it. Sea and land-breeze effect is usually not felt in Savannah, though it is a daily feature on the nearby islands. Dry, continental air masses reach this area in summer mostly by sliding down the Atlantic coast and giving cooler northeast winds. Such masses reaching this area from the northwest or west in summer bring mostly clear skies and high temperatures.

Based on the 1951-1980 period, the average first occurrence of 32 degrees Fahrenheit in the fall is November 15 and the average last occurrence in the spring is March 10.

Savannah Int'l Airport *Chatham County* Elevation: 45 ft. Latitude: 32° 07' N Longitude: 81° 12' W

	JAN	FEB	MAR	APR	MAY	JUN	JUL	AUG	SEP	OCT	NOV	DEC	YEAR
Mean Maximum Temp. (°F)	60.5	64.4	70.9	77.6	84.5	89.7	92.5	90.6	86.0	78.1	70.5	62.6	77.3
Mean Temp. (°F)	49.9	53.3	59.5	65.8	73.4	79.9	82.8	81.7	77.1	68.0	59.4	52.0	66.9
Mean Minimum Temp. (°F)	39.2	42.1	48.1	53.9	62.3	70.0	73.1	72.7	68.1	57.8	48.3	41.3	56.4
Extreme Maximum Temp. (°F)	82	86	89	95	98	104	105	102	98	97	86	82	105
Extreme Minimum Temp. (°F)	3	18	20	28	43	51	62	57	48	33	23	9	3
Days Maximum Temp. ≥ 90°F	0	0	0	1	6	16	24	20	8	1	0	0	76
Days Maximum Temp. ≤ 32°F	0	0	0	0	0	0	0	0	0	0	0	0	0
Days Minimum Temp. ≤ 32°F	9	5	1	0	0	0	0	0	0	0	1	7	23
Days Minimum Temp. ≤ 0°F	0	0	0	0	0	0	0	0	0	0	0	0	0
Heating Degree Days (base 65°F)	466	336	199	72	7	0	0	0	1	52	201	407	1,741
Cooling Degree Days (base 65°F)	5	11	35	102	274	453	559	523	371	152	39	11	2,535
Mean Precipitation (in.)	3.58	2.72	3.90	3.15	3.00	5.87	5.60	6.41	4.67	3.72	2.34	2.94	47.90
Maximum Precipitation (in.)*	9.0	7.9	9.6	10.6	10.1	14.4	20.1	17.0	13.5	19.8	5.3	5.8	73.2
Minimum Precipitation (in.)*	0.4	0.3	0.2	0.4	0.5	0.8	1.3	1.0	0.3	trace	0.1	0.1	32.8
Extreme Maximum Daily Precip. (in.)	3.27	2.44	2.94	3.66	3.35	6.60	3.15	5.75	5.66	7.11	2.23	7.12	7.12
Days With ≥ 0.1" Precipitation	6	5	6	4	5	8	8	9	6	4	4	5	70
Days With ≥ 0.5" Precipitation	2	2	3	2	2	3	4	4	3	2	2	2	31
Days With ≥ 1.0" Precipitation	1	1	1	1	1	2	2	2	1	1	1	1	15
Mean Snowfall (in.)	trace	0.1	0.1	***trace***	***0.0***	trace	***trace***	***0.0***	0.0	0.0	***trace***	***0.2***	***0.4***
Maximum Snowfall (in.)*	2	4	1	0	0	0	0	0	0	0	trace	4	5
Maximum 24-hr. Snowfall (in.)*	1	4	1	0	0	0	0	0	0	0	trace	3	4
Maximum Snow Depth (in.)	trace	1	trace	***trace***	***0***	trace	***trace***	***0***	0	***0***	***trace***	***4***	***4***
Days With ≥ 1.0" Snow Depth	0	0	0	***0***	***0***	0	***0***	***0***	0	***0***	***0***	***0***	***0***
Thunderstorm Days*	1	1	3	4	7	10	15	12	6	2	1	1	63
Foggy Days*	14	12	14	12	15	15	13	18	18	15	14	13	173
Predominant Sky Cover*	OVR	OVR	OVR	CLR	OVR	SCT	SCT	SCT	OVR	CLR	CLR	OVR	OVR
Mean Relative Humidity 7am (%)*	83	82	83	84	85	87	88	91	91	88	86	83	86
Mean Relative Humidity 4pm (%)*	53	50	49	48	52	58	61	63	62	55	53	54	55
Mean Dewpoint (°F)*	38	40	46	53	61	68	72	72	68	57	48	41	55
Prevailing Wind Direction*	WNW	WNW	WNW	WSW	SSE	SW	SW	SW	NE	NE	NE	WNW	NE
Prevailing Wind Speed (mph)*	12	12	12	9	9	8	7	7	9	9	9	10	9
Maximum Wind Gust (mph)*	60	59	68	74	68	81	64	58	68	61	62	54	81

Note: (*) Period of record is 1950-1995

Albany 3 SE *Dougherty County* Elevation: 180 ft. Latitude: 31° 32' N Longitude: 84° 08' W

	JAN	FEB	MAR	APR	MAY	JUN	JUL	AUG	SEP	OCT	NOV	DEC	YEAR
Mean Maximum Temp. (°F)	60.3	64.7	71.7	78.3	85.7	90.5	93.1	92.1	88.1	79.9	71.1	62.7	78.2
Mean Temp. (°F)	47.8	51.8	58.2	64.4	72.6	79.0	82.0	81.4	76.8	67.0	57.8	50.3	65.8
Mean Minimum Temp. (°F)	35.3	38.8	44.6	50.4	59.4	67.6	70.8	70.7	65.5	54.0	44.4	37.8	53.3
Extreme Maximum Temp. (°F)	82	86	91	94	98	104	107	104	102	98	90	83	107
Extreme Minimum Temp. (°F)	1	16	10	27	41	46	58	56	44	28	23	8	1
Days Maximum Temp. ≥ 90°F	0	0	0	1	8	19	24	23	14	2	0	0	91
Days Maximum Temp. ≤ 32°F	0	0	0	0	0	0	0	0	0	0	0	0	0
Days Minimum Temp. ≤ 32°F	14	9	4	1	0	0	0	0	0	0	4	11	43
Days Minimum Temp. ≤ 0°F	0	0	0	0	0	0	0	0	0	0	0	0	0
Heating Degree Days (base 65°F)	529	376	234	96	8	0	0	0	2	69	240	457	2,011
Cooling Degree Days (base 65°F)	2	9	29	84	251	428	535	515	364	137	30	8	2,392
Mean Precipitation (in.)	5.08	4.49	5.58	3.45	3.16	5.01	5.78	5.13	3.66	2.74	3.50	4.02	51.60
Extreme Maximum Daily Precip. (in.)	3.05	3.55	6.00	3.53	4.48	4.60	4.25	4.49	5.52	5.56	5.65	2.75	6.00
Days With ≥ 0.1" Precipitation	7	6	7	5	4	8	9	8	5	4	5	6	74
Days With ≥ 0.5" Precipitation	3	3	4	2	2	3	4	4	2	2	2	3	34
Days With ≥ 1.0" Precipitation	2	2	2	1	1	2	2	1	1	1	1	1	17
Mean Snowfall (in.)	trace	0.0	0.0	0.0	0.0	0.0	0.0	0.0	0.0	0.0	0.0	0.0	trace
Maximum Snow Depth (in.)	trace	0	0	0	0	0	0	0	0	0	0	0	trace
Days With ≥ 1.0" Snow Depth	0	0	0	0	0	0	0	0	0	0	0	0	0

Alma Bacon County Arpt *Bacon County* Elevation: 198 ft. Latitude: 31° 32' N Longitude: 82° 31' W

	JAN	FEB	MAR	APR	MAY	JUN	JUL	AUG	SEP	OCT	NOV	DEC	YEAR
Mean Maximum Temp. (°F)	61.8	65.7	72.1	78.6	85.6	90.2	92.4	91.3	86.9	79.3	71.4	63.7	78.2
Mean Temp. (°F)	51.0	54.4	60.1	66.1	73.5	79.5	82.0	81.3	77.0	68.4	59.9	52.8	67.2
Mean Minimum Temp. (°F)	40.1	43.0	48.1	53.5	61.4	68.7	71.5	71.2	67.1	57.4	48.5	41.9	56.0
Extreme Maximum Temp. (°F)	82	86	88	96	97	104	104	105	101	95	87	82	105
Extreme Minimum Temp. (°F)	-1	13	18	30	44	47	59	58	42	30	26	9	-1
Days Maximum Temp. ≥ 90°F	0	0	0	1	8	18	25	22	11	1	0	0	86
Days Maximum Temp. ≤ 32°F	0	0	0	0	0	0	0	0	0	0	0	0	0
Days Minimum Temp. ≤ 32°F	9	4	2	0	0	0	0	0	0	0	2	7	24
Days Minimum Temp. ≤ 0°F	0	0	0	0	0	0	0	0	0	0	0	0	0
Heating Degree Days (base 65°F)	435	309	183	65	4	0	0	0	1	47	187	383	1,614
Cooling Degree Days (base 65°F)	7	13	39	105	275	442	533	512	368	159	41	12	2,506
Mean Precipitation (in.)	4.24	3.78	5.10	2.91	2.51	5.29	5.36	5.46	3.62	3.21	2.48	3.28	47.24
Extreme Maximum Daily Precip. (in.)	5.84	4.70	5.25	3.86	3.86	4.01	5.04	4.56	4.18	5.69	3.08	3.78	5.84
Days With ≥ 0.1" Precipitation	7	5	6	4	4	9	9	8	6	4	4	5	71
Days With ≥ 0.5" Precipitation	3	3	3	2	2	4	3	4	2	2	2	2	32
Days With ≥ 1.0" Precipitation	1	1	2	1	1	1	1	1	1	1	1	1	13
Mean Snowfall (in.)	na	na	na	na	na	na	***0.0***	na	na	na	na	na	na
Maximum Snow Depth (in.)	na	na	na	na	na	na	***0***	na	na	na	na	na	na
Days With ≥ 1.0" Snow Depth	na	na	na	na	na	na	***0***	na	na	na	na	na	na

Appling 2 NW *Columbia County* Elevation: 370 ft. Latitude: 33° 34' N Longitude: 82° 20' W

	JAN	FEB	MAR	APR	MAY	JUN	JUL	AUG	SEP	OCT	NOV	DEC	YEAR
Mean Maximum Temp. (°F)	55.1	59.6	67.3	74.7	82.0	87.8	91.0	89.6	84.3	75.1	66.5	57.3	74.2
Mean Temp. (°F)	43.0	46.6	53.5	60.7	68.7	76.2	79.6	78.5	72.6	61.8	52.9	45.0	61.6
Mean Minimum Temp. (°F)	30.8	33.5	39.7	46.6	55.4	64.6	68.2	67.4	60.7	48.3	39.2	32.6	48.9
Extreme Maximum Temp. (°F)	81	83	88	93	96	102	106	105	102	93	88	80	106
Extreme Minimum Temp. (°F)	-4	6	6	22	33	40	52	53	38	25	18	1	-4
Days Maximum Temp. ≥ 90°F	0	0	0	1	3	12	20	16	7	0	0	0	59
Days Maximum Temp. ≤ 32°F	0	0	0	0	0	0	0	0	0	0	0	0	0
Days Minimum Temp. ≤ 32°F	19	14	8	2	0	0	0	0	0	1	9	18	71
Days Minimum Temp. ≤ 0°F	0	0	0	0	0	0	0	0	0	0	0	0	0
Heating Degree Days (base 65°F)	676	516	359	165	34	1	0	0	12	142	364	615	2,884
Cooling Degree Days (base 65°F)	0	1	9	41	155	344	461	427	246	49	7	1	1,741
Mean Precipitation (in.)	4.31	4.11	4.95	3.02	3.05	4.52	3.93	3.80	3.61	3.67	3.34	3.63	45.94
Extreme Maximum Daily Precip. (in.)	2.85	3.30	4.50	3.50	3.60	7.00	2.90	3.20	9.30	9.50	4.20	3.30	9.50
Days With ≥ 0.1" Precipitation	7	6	6	5	5	7	7	6	5	4	4	6	68
Days With ≥ 0.5" Precipitation	4	3	4	2	2	3	3	3	2	2	2	3	33
Days With ≥ 1.0" Precipitation	2	2	2	1	1	2	1	1	1	1	1	1	16
Mean Snowfall (in.)	trace	trace	0.2	0.0	0.0	0.0	0.0	0.0	0.0	0.0	0.0	0.0	0.2
Maximum Snow Depth (in.)	4	trace	trace	0	0	0	0	0	0	0	0	0	4
Days With ≥ 1.0" Snow Depth	0	0	0	0	0	0	0	0	0	0	0	0	0

Blairsville Exp Sta *Union County* Elevation: 1,917 ft. Latitude: 34° 51' N Longitude: 83° 57' W

	JAN	FEB	MAR	APR	MAY	JUN	JUL	AUG	SEP	OCT	NOV	DEC	YEAR
Mean Maximum Temp. (°F)	48.4	52.3	59.7	67.8	75.2	81.6	84.5	83.9	78.2	69.6	60.5	51.4	67.8
Mean Temp. (°F)	36.6	40.0	46.9	54.2	62.4	69.8	73.3	72.6	66.4	56.2	47.5	39.6	55.5
Mean Minimum Temp. (°F)	24.8	27.6	34.1	40.6	49.6	58.0	62.1	61.1	54.6	42.8	34.5	27.8	43.1
Extreme Maximum Temp. (°F)	74	76	83	88	88	95	97	97	93	85	83	74	97
Extreme Minimum Temp. (°F)	-16	-8	-5	16	28	35	48	45	32	20	9	-8	-16
Days Maximum Temp. ≥ 90°F	0	0	0	0	0	1	5	3	0	0	0	0	9
Days Maximum Temp. ≤ 32°F	2	1	0	0	0	0	0	0	0	0	0	1	4
Days Minimum Temp. ≤ 32°F	23	20	15	6	1	0	0	0	0	6	15	22	108
Days Minimum Temp. ≤ 0°F	0	0	0	0	0	0	0	0	0	0	0	0	0
Heating Degree Days (base 65°F)	873	701	555	322	117	14	1	1	51	276	518	780	4,209
Cooling Degree Days (base 65°F)	0	0	1	5	44	164	266	242	101	11	1	0	835
Mean Precipitation (in.)	5.19	4.78	5.42	4.46	4.31	4.84	4.69	4.39	4.77	3.55	4.99	4.72	56.11
Extreme Maximum Daily Precip. (in.)	4.50	3.70	4.86	2.70	2.72	4.75	3.29	2.85	5.30	3.56	4.70	2.10	5.30
Days With ≥ 0.1" Precipitation	8	7	8	8	8	8	8	7	7	5	7	8	89
Days With ≥ 0.5" Precipitation	4	3	4	3	3	3	3	3	3	2	3	3	37
Days With ≥ 1.0" Precipitation	2	1	2	1	1	1	1	1	2	1	2	2	17
Mean Snowfall (in.)	1.0	0.6	1.0	0.3	0.0	0.0	0.0	0.0	0.0	trace	trace	0.1	3.0
Maximum Snow Depth (in.)	trace	trace	trace	2	0	0	0	0	0	trace	trace	trace	2
Days With ≥ 1.0" Snow Depth	0	0	0	0	0	0	0	0	0	0	0	0	0

The period of record for all cooperative weather station data is 1980 – 2009. See User Guide for detailed explanation of data.

Brooklet 1 W *Bulloch County* Elevation: 189 ft. Latitude: 32° 22' N Longitude: 81° 41' W

	JAN	FEB	MAR	APR	MAY	JUN	JUL	AUG	SEP	OCT	NOV	DEC	YEAR
Mean Maximum Temp. (°F)	59.6	63.6	70.3	77.7	84.9	90.1	92.7	90.8	85.8	78.0	70.0	61.8	77.1
Mean Temp. (°F)	48.8	52.3	58.6	65.3	73.1	79.5	82.1	80.7	75.9	66.9	58.4	50.9	66.0
Mean Minimum Temp. (°F)	38.0	40.8	46.7	52.9	61.2	68.8	71.5	70.7	66.0	55.8	46.8	40.0	54.9
Extreme Maximum Temp. (°F)	81	85	90	95	98	104	109	104	100	93	86	82	109
Extreme Minimum Temp. (°F)	1	15	15	30	40	49	59	56	46	30	24	7	1
Days Maximum Temp. ≥ 90°F	0	0	0	1	7	17	24	20	8	1	0	0	78
Days Maximum Temp. ≤ 32°F	0	0	0	0	0	0	0	0	0	0	0	0	0
Days Minimum Temp. ≤ 32°F	10	6	2	0	0	0	0	0	0	0	2	8	28
Days Minimum Temp. ≤ 0°F	0	0	0	0	0	0	0	0	0	0	0	0	0
Heating Degree Days (base 65°F)	498	362	221	80	7	0	0	0	2	63	221	439	1,893
Cooling Degree Days (base 65°F)	3	8	28	95	264	441	537	496	336	128	31	8	2,375
Mean Precipitation (in.)	3.98	3.37	3.94	2.92	2.89	5.28	4.62	5.96	3.72	3.04	2.74	3.19	45.65
Extreme Maximum Daily Precip. (in.)	3.80	2.60	2.86	3.03	2.71	4.64	3.61	6.57	3.48	3.47	4.10	2.97	6.57
Days With ≥ 0.1" Precipitation	7	5	6	5	5	8	8	8	6	4	4	5	71
Days With ≥ 0.5" Precipitation	3	2	3	2	2	3	3	4	3	2	2	2	31
Days With ≥ 1.0" Precipitation	1	1	1	1	1	2	1	2	1	1	1	1	14
Mean Snowfall (in.)	trace	trace	0.0	0.0	0.0	0.0	0.0	0.0	0.0	0.0	0.0	0.1	0.1
Maximum Snow Depth (in.)	trace	1	0	0	0	0	0	0	0	0	0	trace	1
Days With ≥ 1.0" Snow Depth	0	0	0	0	0	0	0	0	0	0	0	0	0

Brunswick *Glynn County* Elevation: 13 ft. Latitude: 31° 10' N Longitude: 81° 30' W

	JAN	FEB	MAR	APR	MAY	JUN	JUL	AUG	SEP	OCT	NOV	DEC	YEAR
Mean Maximum Temp. (°F)	62.3	66.0	71.6	77.9	84.5	89.5	92.5	90.8	86.2	79.3	71.7	64.3	78.0
Mean Temp. (°F)	52.0	55.7	61.3	67.4	74.8	80.6	83.2	82.3	78.3	70.4	61.8	54.4	68.5
Mean Minimum Temp. (°F)	41.5	45.3	51.0	56.8	65.0	71.6	73.9	73.7	70.3	61.5	51.9	44.4	58.9
Extreme Maximum Temp. (°F)	85	89	88	99	98	103	106	103	101	95	88	87	106
Extreme Minimum Temp. (°F)	5	18	21	33	38	51	59	62	40	39	30	11	5
Days Maximum Temp. ≥ 90°F	0	0	0	1	6	15	24	18	7	1	0	0	72
Days Maximum Temp. ≤ 32°F	0	0	0	0	0	0	0	0	0	0	0	0	0
Days Minimum Temp. ≤ 32°F	6	3	0	0	0	0	0	0	0	0	0	3	12
Days Minimum Temp. ≤ 0°F	0	0	0	0	0	0	0	0	0	0	0	0	0
Heating Degree Days (base 65°F)	404	273	156	52	5	0	0	0	0	29	146	339	1,404
Cooling Degree Days (base 65°F)	7	15	49	130	316	475	573	543	404	203	58	18	2,791
Mean Precipitation (in.)	3.62	3.76	4.21	2.80	2.49	5.82	5.00	6.70	6.26	4.56	2.25	2.64	50.11
Extreme Maximum Daily Precip. (in.)	3.10	4.43	3.50	3.24	2.93	4.39	2.77	3.49	4.95	6.53	2.70	2.54	6.53
Days With ≥ 0.1" Precipitation	6	5	6	4	4	9	8	9	8	5	4	5	73
Days With ≥ 0.5" Precipitation	2	2	3	2	2	3	3	5	4	2	2	2	32
Days With ≥ 1.0" Precipitation	1	1	1	1	1	2	2	2	2	1	1	1	16
Mean Snowfall (in.)	0.0	0.0	0.0	0.0	0.0	0.0	0.0	0.0	0.0	0.0	0.0	0.0	0.0
Maximum Snow Depth (in.)	0	0	0	0	0	0	0	0	0	0	0	0	0
Days With ≥ 1.0" Snow Depth	0	0	0	0	0	0	0	0	0	0	0	0	0

Camilla 3 SE *Mitchell County* Elevation: 174 ft. Latitude: 31° 11' N Longitude: 84° 12' W

	JAN	FEB	MAR	APR	MAY	JUN	JUL	AUG	SEP	OCT	NOV	DEC	YEAR
Mean Maximum Temp. (°F)	61.4	65.6	72.1	78.5	85.8	90.0	91.9	90.9	87.3	79.9	71.6	63.6	78.2
Mean Temp. (°F)	50.1	53.8	59.8	65.9	73.8	79.5	81.8	81.0	76.8	67.9	59.3	52.1	66.8
Mean Minimum Temp. (°F)	38.7	41.9	47.5	53.3	61.8	69.0	71.6	71.1	66.4	55.7	46.9	40.7	55.4
Extreme Maximum Temp. (°F)	83	87	90	95	100	103	107	103	100	98	90	85	107
Extreme Minimum Temp. (°F)	2	12	17	32	42	49	60	60	47	31	25	10	2
Days Maximum Temp. ≥ 90°F	0	0	0	1	7	16	22	20	10	2	0	0	78
Days Maximum Temp. ≤ 32°F	0	0	0	0	0	0	0	0	0	0	0	0	0
Days Minimum Temp. ≤ 32°F	10	6	2	0	0	0	0	0	0	0	3	9	30
Days Minimum Temp. ≤ 0°F	0	0	0	0	0	0	0	0	0	0	0	0	0
Heating Degree Days (base 65°F)	459	321	191	69	5	0	0	0	1	54	204	403	1,707
Cooling Degree Days (base 65°F)	4	11	37	103	284	443	526	503	363	149	39	10	2,472
Mean Precipitation (in.)	5.15	4.74	6.05	3.67	2.53	5.33	5.77	4.93	3.71	2.89	3.35	3.84	51.96
Extreme Maximum Daily Precip. (in.)	4.32	5.50	6.20	4.72	2.77	4.05	3.97	6.04	5.05	3.80	5.04	4.03	6.20
Days With ≥ 0.1" Precipitation	7	6	6	5	4	8	9	7	5	4	4	5	70
Days With ≥ 0.5" Precipitation	3	3	4	2	2	4	4	3	2	2	2	3	34
Days With ≥ 1.0" Precipitation	2	2	2	1	1	2	2	1	1	1	1	1	17
Mean Snowfall (in.)	0.0	0.0	0.0	0.0	0.0	0.0	0.0	0.0	0.0	0.0	0.0	0.0	0.0
Maximum Snow Depth (in.)	0	0	0	0	0	0	0	0	0	0	0	0	0
Days With ≥ 1.0" Snow Depth	0	0	0	0	0	0	0	0	0	0	0	0	0

Carrollton *Carroll County* Elevation: 995 ft. Latitude: 33° 36' N Longitude: 85° 05' W

	JAN	FEB	MAR	APR	MAY	JUN	JUL	AUG	SEP	OCT	NOV	DEC	YEAR
Mean Maximum Temp. (°F)	52.8	57.4	65.6	73.2	80.2	86.0	88.6	87.5	81.8	72.8	64.0	54.7	72.0
Mean Temp. (°F)	42.1	45.8	52.7	59.9	67.9	74.7	78.0	77.1	70.9	60.6	52.0	44.1	60.5
Mean Minimum Temp. (°F)	31.3	34.2	39.8	46.6	55.6	63.2	67.3	66.7	60.0	48.3	39.9	33.4	48.9
Extreme Maximum Temp. (°F)	74	79	86	90	94	100	103	102	95	88	82	77	103
Extreme Minimum Temp. (°F)	-9	4	9	24	30	41	49	53	38	25	17	3	-9
Days Maximum Temp. ≥ 90°F	0	0	0	0	1	7	13	10	2	0	0	0	33
Days Maximum Temp. ≤ 32°F	1	0	0	0	0	0	0	0	0	0	0	0	1
Days Minimum Temp. ≤ 32°F	17	13	7	2	0	0	0	0	0	2	8	16	65
Days Minimum Temp. ≤ 0°F	0	0	0	0	0	0	0	0	0	0	0	0	0
Heating Degree Days (base 65°F)	702	536	380	174	33	1	0	0	18	167	387	643	3,041
Cooling Degree Days (base 65°F)	0	0	5	28	131	298	409	383	202	37	3	1	1,497
Mean Precipitation (in.)	4.68	5.16	5.50	4.14	4.03	3.78	4.70	3.45	3.77	3.52	4.49	4.42	51.64
Extreme Maximum Daily Precip. (in.)	3.96	5.65	4.92	3.19	6.23	2.44	3.37	2.50	7.66	4.52	4.72	3.25	7.66
Days With ≥ 0.1" Precipitation	7	6	7	6	6	7	7	6	5	4	6	7	74
Days With ≥ 0.5" Precipitation	3	4	4	3	3	3	3	3	2	2	3	3	36
Days With ≥ 1.0" Precipitation	1	2	2	1	1	1	1	1	1	1	2	1	15
Mean Snowfall (in.)	0.3	trace	0.0	0.0	0.0	0.0	0.0	0.0	0.0	0.0	0.0	0.1	0.4
Maximum Snow Depth (in.)	3	trace	0	0	0	0	0	0	0	0	0	trace	3
Days With ≥ 1.0" Snow Depth	0	0	0	0	0	0	0	0	0	0	0	0	0

Cartersville *Bartow County* Elevation: 720 ft. Latitude: 34° 14' N Longitude: 84° 47' W

	JAN	FEB	MAR	APR	MAY	JUN	JUL	AUG	SEP	OCT	NOV	DEC	YEAR
Mean Maximum Temp. (°F)	52.1	57.2	66.1	***73.8***	80.3	86.3	89.6	88.5	82.7	73.5	63.7	54.1	***72.3***
Mean Temp. (°F)	41.9	46.0	53.5	***60.7***	68.3	75.2	78.7	77.9	72.0	61.6	52.2	44.0	***61.0***
Mean Minimum Temp. (°F)	31.7	34.7	40.8	***47.6***	56.3	64.1	67.7	67.2	61.3	49.6	40.8	33.9	***49.6***
Extreme Maximum Temp. (°F)	79	80	87	93	96	101	104	103	98	89	83	82	104
Extreme Minimum Temp. (°F)	-9	1	10	22	35	44	54	52	34	25	14	-3	-9
Days Maximum Temp. ≥ 90°F	0	0	0	0	1	8	16	13	4	0	0	0	42
Days Maximum Temp. ≤ 32°F	1	0	0	0	0	0	0	0	0	0	0	0	1
Days Minimum Temp. ≤ 32°F	16	12	7	2	0	0	0	0	0	1	8	15	61
Days Minimum Temp. ≤ 0°F	0	0	0	0	0	0	0	0	0	0	0	0	0
Heating Degree Days (base 65°F)	708	532	360	***163***	39	1	0	0	16	152	384	644	***2,999***
Cooling Degree Days (base 65°F)	0	1	10	***41***	149	315	431	406	233	51	7	1	***1,645***
Mean Precipitation (in.)	3.24	3.81	***4.39***	3.30	2.93	3.18	4.05	2.97	3.25	2.43	3.00	3.43	***39.98***
Extreme Maximum Daily Precip. (in.)	***2.50***	***3.20***	***6.00***	***2.03***	***3.00***	***2.25***	***3.20***	***2.90***	***4.05***	***2.20***	***3.62***	***3.00***	***6.00***
Days With ≥ 0.1" Precipitation	5	5	***5***	5	4	5	5	5	4	3	4	5	***55***
Days With ≥ 0.5" Precipitation	2	3	***3***	3	2	2	3	2	2	1	2	2	***27***
Days With ≥ 1.0" Precipitation	1	2	***1***	1	1	1	1	1	1	1	1	1	***13***
Mean Snowfall (in.)	0.3	0.2	0.1	trace	0.0	0.0	0.0	0.0	0.0	0.0	0.0	0.1	0.7
Maximum Snow Depth (in.)	0	1	2	trace	0	0	0	0	0	0	0	trace	2
Days With ≥ 1.0" Snow Depth	0	0	0	0	0	0	0	0	0	0	0	0	0

Cedartown 3 NE *Polk County* Elevation: 785 ft. Latitude: 34° 03' N Longitude: 85° 15' W

	JAN	FEB	MAR	APR	MAY	JUN	JUL	AUG	SEP	OCT	NOV	DEC	YEAR
Mean Maximum Temp. (°F)	52.9	56.9	66.1	74.0	80.5	87.2	90.1	89.5	83.6	74.0	64.1	54.4	72.8
Mean Temp. (°F)	41.9	45.1	52.9	60.3	68.0	75.5	79.0	78.2	71.7	61.0	51.6	43.6	60.7
Mean Minimum Temp. (°F)	30.9	33.2	39.5	46.6	55.3	63.7	67.8	66.9	59.8	48.0	39.0	32.8	48.6
Extreme Maximum Temp. (°F)	78	83	88	92	95	100	104	104	98	95	85	79	104
Extreme Minimum Temp. (°F)	-9	3	5	24	33	44	52	50	30	24	18	0	-9
Days Maximum Temp. ≥ 90°F	0	0	0	0	2	10	18	15	5	0	0	0	50
Days Maximum Temp. ≤ 32°F	1	0	0	0	0	0	0	0	0	0	0	0	1
Days Minimum Temp. ≤ 32°F	18	14	8	2	0	0	0	0	0	2	10	16	70
Days Minimum Temp. ≤ 0°F	0	0	0	0	0	0	0	0	0	0	0	0	0
Heating Degree Days (base 65°F)	708	558	378	173	40	1	0	0	16	162	401	657	3,094
Cooling Degree Days (base 65°F)	0	1	8	39	139	321	440	417	224	46	5	2	1,642
Mean Precipitation (in.)	4.63	4.87	5.29	4.00	4.33	4.17	4.85	3.81	3.73	3.57	4.30	4.21	51.76
Extreme Maximum Daily Precip. (in.)	4.35	4.10	4.00	3.50	2.76	3.50	3.76	3.06	3.77	5.08	4.90	2.44	5.08
Days With ≥ 0.1" Precipitation	7	7	7	6	7	7	7	5	5	5	6	7	76
Days With ≥ 0.5" Precipitation	3	3	3	3	3	3	3	3	2	2	3	3	34
Days With ≥ 1.0" Precipitation	1	1	2	1	1	1	1	1	1	1	1	1	13
Mean Snowfall (in.)	0.8	0.3	0.7	0.2	0.0	0.0	0.0	0.0	0.0	0.0	0.0	0.1	2.1
Maximum Snow Depth (in.)	3	2	15	5	0	0	0	0	0	0	0	trace	15
Days With ≥ 1.0" Snow Depth	1	0	0	0	0	0	0	0	0	0	0	0	1

Clayton 1 SSW *Rabun County* Elevation: 1,879 ft. Latitude: 34° 52' N Longitude: 83° 24' W

	JAN	FEB	MAR	APR	MAY	JUN	JUL	AUG	SEP	OCT	NOV	DEC	YEAR
Mean Maximum Temp. (°F)	50.6	54.4	62.0	69.9	76.6	82.6	85.4	84.6	79.0	70.6	61.8	52.8	69.2
Mean Temp. (°F)	39.2	42.2	48.6	55.9	63.4	70.5	73.9	73.4	67.5	57.8	49.1	41.3	56.9
Mean Minimum Temp. (°F)	27.8	29.9	35.2	41.9	50.1	58.4	62.4	62.1	55.9	45.0	36.2	29.7	44.6
Extreme Maximum Temp. (°F)	76	78	84	89	92	97	97	98	92	86	82	75	98
Extreme Minimum Temp. (°F)	-11	3	6	12	28	36	48	47	32	21	14	-4	-11
Days Maximum Temp. ≥ 90°F	0	0	0	0	0	2	5	4	1	0	0	0	12
Days Maximum Temp. ≤ 32°F	1	0	0	0	0	0	0	0	0	0	0	0	1
Days Minimum Temp. ≤ 32°F	21	18	12	4	0	0	0	0	0	3	12	21	91
Days Minimum Temp. ≤ 0°F	0	0	0	0	0	0	0	0	0	0	0	0	0
Heating Degree Days (base 65°F)	791	639	501	275	92	10	0	1	39	230	472	729	3,779
Cooling Degree Days (base 65°F)	0	0	1	9	50	181	283	269	121	14	1	0	929
Mean Precipitation (in.)	6.28	5.94	6.53	5.00	5.01	5.62	5.36	5.87	6.15	4.79	5.97	6.31	68.83
Extreme Maximum Daily Precip. (in.)	4.64	3.36	4.33	2.75	3.83	4.00	4.75	4.85	12.75	3.90	4.75	2.91	12.75
Days With ≥ 0.1" Precipitation	8	7	8	8	7	8	8	8	7	6	7	8	90
Days With ≥ 0.5" Precipitation	4	4	4	3	3	4	4	4	3	3	4	4	44
Days With ≥ 1.0" Precipitation	2	2	2	2	1	2	2	2	2	2	2	2	23
Mean Snowfall (in.)	1.2	1.0	0.3	0.0	0.0	0.0	0.0	0.0	0.0	0.0	0.0	0.2	2.7
Maximum Snow Depth (in.)	14	4	trace	trace	0	0	0	0	0	0	2	4	14
Days With ≥ 1.0" Snow Depth	0	0	0	0	0	0	0	0	0	0	0	0	0

Commerce 4 NNW *Jackson County* Elevation: 750 ft. Latitude: 34° 16' N Longitude: 83° 29' W

	JAN	FEB	MAR	APR	MAY	JUN	JUL	AUG	SEP	OCT	NOV	DEC	YEAR
Mean Maximum Temp. (°F)	52.5	56.5	65.0	72.9	79.9	86.9	89.9	88.6	82.5	72.9	63.5	54.9	72.2
Mean Temp. (°F)	41.8	45.2	52.6	59.8	67.7	75.6	79.0	77.9	71.4	61.0	51.6	44.0	60.6
Mean Minimum Temp. (°F)	31.1	33.8	40.1	46.6	55.4	64.2	68.0	67.1	60.3	49.0	39.7	32.9	49.0
Extreme Maximum Temp. (°F)	75	80	88	92	95	100	105	105	97	90	83	79	105
Extreme Minimum Temp. (°F)	-5	6	11	25	35	43	55	55	38	26	16	0	-5
Days Maximum Temp. ≥ 90°F	0	0	0	0	1	9	17	13	4	0	0	0	44
Days Maximum Temp. ≤ 32°F	1	0	0	0	0	0	0	0	0	0	0	0	1
Days Minimum Temp. ≤ 32°F	18	13	7	1	0	0	0	0	0	1	8	16	64
Days Minimum Temp. ≤ 0°F	0	0	0	0	0	0	0	0	0	0	0	0	0
Heating Degree Days (base 65°F)	712	554	383	181	40	1	0	0	16	160	399	646	3,092
Cooling Degree Days (base 65°F)	0	0	5	31	130	325	441	407	215	42	4	1	1,601
Mean Precipitation (in.)	4.73	4.91	5.08	3.49	3.28	4.58	3.86	3.97	3.97	4.17	4.04	4.46	50.54
Extreme Maximum Daily Precip. (in.)	3.07	3.21	4.05	2.60	2.00	4.85	2.82	4.37	5.68	6.32	3.86	2.75	6.32
Days With ≥ 0.1" Precipitation	8	7	7	6	6	7	7	6	5	5	6	7	77
Days With ≥ 0.5" Precipitation	3	3	3	3	2	3	3	2	3	3	3	3	34
Days With ≥ 1.0" Precipitation	2	1	2	1	1	1	1	1	1	2	1	1	15
Mean Snowfall (in.)	0.6	0.2	0.1	0.0	0.0	0.0	0.0	0.0	0.0	0.0	0.0	trace	0.9
Maximum Snow Depth (in.)	1	3	7	0	0	0	0	0	0	0	0	trace	7
Days With ≥ 1.0" Snow Depth	0	0	0	0	0	0	0	0	0	0	0	0	0

The period of record for all cooperative weather station data is 1980 – 2009. See User Guide for detailed explanation of data.

Cordele *Crisp County* Elevation: 308 ft. Latitude: 31° 59' N Longitude: 83° 47' W

	JAN	FEB	MAR	APR	MAY	JUN	JUL	AUG	SEP	OCT	NOV	DEC	YEAR
Mean Maximum Temp. (°F)	60.1	64.4	72.1	79.6	87.1	92.3	94.6	92.9	88.1	79.5	70.4	61.7	78.6
Mean Temp. (°F)	49.2	52.9	59.6	66.5	74.5	80.8	83.4	82.1	77.1	67.4	58.5	50.8	66.9
Mean Minimum Temp. (°F)	38.2	41.2	47.0	53.3	61.9	69.3	72.1	71.2	66.0	55.3	46.6	39.8	55.2
Extreme Maximum Temp. (°F)	79	84	90	96	100	106	104	104	101	96	87	81	106
Extreme Minimum Temp. (°F)	-3	13	15	30	44	47	59	56	46	30	23	8	-3
Days Maximum Temp. ≥ 90°F	0	0	0	2	11	22	27	25	14	2	0	0	103
Days Maximum Temp. ≤ 32°F	0	0	0	0	0	0	0	0	0	0	0	0	0
Days Minimum Temp. ≤ 32°F	10	6	2	0	0	0	0	0	0	0	3	8	29
Days Minimum Temp. ≤ 0°F	0	0	0	0	0	0	0	0	0	0	0	0	0
Heating Degree Days (base 65°F)	487	347	200	67	4	0	0	0	2	61	221	442	1,831
Cooling Degree Days (base 65°F)	4	9	39	117	306	481	577	537	371	144	33	8	2,626
Mean Precipitation (in.)	4.46	3.92	5.01	3.40	2.78	4.54	4.18	4.05	4.27	2.20	3.25	3.93	45.99
Extreme Maximum Daily Precip. (in.)	2.92	3.95	5.60	4.25	3.16	3.51	4.08	3.15	9.28	3.20	4.13	3.75	9.28
Days With ≥ 0.1" Precipitation	7	6	6	5	5	8	7	7	5	3	5	6	70
Days With ≥ 0.5" Precipitation	3	3	3	2	2	3	3	3	2	1	2	3	30
Days With ≥ 1.0" Precipitation	2	1	2	1	1	1	1	1	1	1	1	1	14
Mean Snowfall (in.)	0.0	0.0	0.0	0.0	0.0	0.0	0.0	0.0	0.0	0.0	0.0	0.0	0.0
Maximum Snow Depth (in.)	0	0	0	0	0	0	0	0	0	0	0	0	0
Days With ≥ 1.0" Snow Depth	0	0	0	0	0	0	0	0	0	0	0	0	0

Covington *Newton County* Elevation: 770 ft. Latitude: 33° 36' N Longitude: 83° 53' W

	JAN	FEB	MAR	APR	MAY	JUN	JUL	AUG	SEP	OCT	NOV	DEC	YEAR
Mean Maximum Temp. (°F)	52.9	***57.2***	66.4	74.0	81.5	87.7	90.6	89.0	83.2	73.4	64.2	54.7	***72.9***
Mean Temp. (°F)	42.3	***46.0***	53.8	60.8	69.1	76.5	79.6	78.6	72.5	61.8	52.4	44.1	***61.5***
Mean Minimum Temp. (°F)	31.7	***34.8***	41.0	47.6	56.6	65.1	68.6	68.1	61.8	50.2	40.6	33.4	***50.0***
Extreme Maximum Temp. (°F)	75	***81***	89	95	95	101	104	105	98	91	84	78	***105***
Extreme Minimum Temp. (°F)	-7	***9***	12	24	37	46	55	55	34	25	15	1	***-7***
Days Maximum Temp. ≥ 90°F	0	***0***	0	0	3	12	18	14	5	0	0	0	***52***
Days Maximum Temp. ≤ 32°F	1	***0***	0	0	0	0	0	0	0	0	0	0	***1***
Days Minimum Temp. ≤ 32°F	17	***12***	6	1	0	0	0	0	0	1	8	16	***61***
Days Minimum Temp. ≤ 0°F	0	***0***	0	0	0	0	0	0	0	0	0	0	***0***
Heating Degree Days (base 65°F)	695	***531***	351	161	30	1	0	0	12	145	378	642	***2,946***
Cooling Degree Days (base 65°F)	0	***1***	10	41	162	351	461	428	245	53	7	1	***1,760***
Mean Precipitation (in.)	4.19	***4.88***	5.14	3.33	3.35	4.20	4.48	4.16	4.00	3.37	3.99	3.95	***49.04***
Extreme Maximum Daily Precip. (in.)	2.03	***3.90***	6.07	3.30	3.46	3.91	4.25	4.79	4.19	4.12	4.30	2.67	***6.07***
Days With ≥ 0.1" Precipitation	7	***7***	7	6	6	7	6	7	6	5	6	6	***76***
Days With ≥ 0.5" Precipitation	3	***3***	4	2	2	3	3	3	3	2	3	3	***34***
Days With ≥ 1.0" Precipitation	1	***1***	2	1	1	1	1	1	1	1	1	1	***13***
Mean Snowfall (in.)	0.7	***0.2***	0.4	0.0	0.0	0.0	0.0	0.0	0.0	0.0	0.0	0.1	***1.4***
Maximum Snow Depth (in.)	6	***3***	3	0	0	0	0	0	0	0	0	3	***6***
Days With ≥ 1.0" Snow Depth	1	***0***	0	0	0	0	0	0	0	0	0	0	***1***

Dallas 7 NE *Paulding County* Elevation: 1,100 ft. Latitude: 33° 59' N Longitude: 84° 45' W

	JAN	FEB	MAR	APR	MAY	JUN	JUL	AUG	SEP	OCT	NOV	DEC	YEAR
Mean Maximum Temp. (°F)	51.5	55.8	64.2	72.4	79.7	86.5	89.6	88.8	82.9	73.1	63.6	53.8	71.8
Mean Temp. (°F)	40.4	43.9	51.3	59.1	67.1	74.7	78.3	77.5	71.1	60.3	51.1	42.7	59.8
Mean Minimum Temp. (°F)	29.2	31.9	38.4	45.7	54.4	62.9	66.9	66.1	59.3	47.5	38.6	31.6	47.7
Extreme Maximum Temp. (°F)	80	80	89	93	96	101	104	104	98	89	85	80	104
Extreme Minimum Temp. (°F)	-12	-2	8	21	34	40	54	50	38	25	15	-2	-12
Days Maximum Temp. ≥ 90°F	0	0	0	0	1	10	17	15	5	0	0	0	48
Days Maximum Temp. ≤ 32°F	1	1	0	0	0	0	0	0	0	0	0	1	3
Days Minimum Temp. ≤ 32°F	20	16	10	3	0	0	0	0	0	2	10	19	80
Days Minimum Temp. ≤ 0°F	0	0	0	0	0	0	0	0	0	0	0	0	0
Heating Degree Days (base 65°F)	757	591	425	208	54	3	0	0	21	180	415	685	3,339
Cooling Degree Days (base 65°F)	0	0	7	36	125	302	418	394	211	42	5	1	1,541
Mean Precipitation (in.)	4.96	5.12	5.30	3.99	4.06	4.11	5.04	4.39	4.29	3.49	4.30	4.40	53.45
Extreme Maximum Daily Precip. (in.)	3.95	6.20	4.96	3.25	5.95	3.28	5.68	5.50	8.43	3.65	4.25	4.60	8.43
Days With ≥ 0.1" Precipitation	8	7	8	7	7	7	7	6	5	5	6	7	80
Days With ≥ 0.5" Precipitation	4	4	3	3	2	3	3	3	3	2	3	3	36
Days With ≥ 1.0" Precipitation	2	2	2	1	1	1	2	1	1	1	2	1	17
Mean Snowfall (in.)	1.3	0.7	1.1	0.2	0.0	0.0	0.0	0.0	0.0	0.0	trace	0.3	3.6
Maximum Snow Depth (in.)	8	3	9	2	0	0	0	0	0	0	trace	1	9
Days With ≥ 1.0" Snow Depth	1	0	0	0	0	0	0	0	0	0	0	0	1

Dalton *Whitfield County* Elevation: 700 ft. Latitude: 34° 45' N Longitude: 84° 57' W

	JAN	FEB	MAR	APR	MAY	JUN	JUL	AUG	SEP	OCT	NOV	DEC	YEAR
Mean Maximum Temp. (°F)	*49.8*	*54.7*	*63.5*	*71.8*	*79.6*	*85.9*	*89.6*	*89.0*	*83.5*	*73.4*	*63.2*	*53.1*	*71.4*
Mean Temp. (°F)	*39.8*	*43.9*	*51.5*	*59.2*	*67.8*	*75.1*	*79.2*	*78.3*	*72.2*	*60.8*	*51.6*	*42.9*	*60.2*
Mean Minimum Temp. (°F)	*29.8*	*33.0*	*39.5*	*46.4*	*55.9*	*64.3*	*68.8*	*67.6*	*60.9*	*48.2*	*39.9*	*32.7*	*48.9*
Extreme Maximum Temp. (°F)	*76*	*79*	*87*	*91*	*93*	*103*	*102*	*103*	*99*	*90*	*85*	*76*	*103*
Extreme Minimum Temp. (°F)	*-10*	*3*	*7*	*25*	*38*	*42*	*55*	*53*	*38*	*28*	*21*	*-4*	*-10*
Days Maximum Temp. ≥ 90°F	*0*	*0*	*0*	*0*	*1*	*8*	*15*	*13*	*6*	*0*	*0*	*0*	*43*
Days Maximum Temp. ≤ 32°F	*2*	*1*	*0*	*0*	*0*	*0*	*0*	*0*	*0*	*0*	*0*	*1*	*4*
Days Minimum Temp. ≤ 32°F	*19*	*14*	*7*	*1*	*0*	*0*	*0*	*0*	*0*	*1*	*7*	*16*	*65*
Days Minimum Temp. ≤ 0°F	*0*	*0*	*0*	*0*	*0*	*0*	*0*	*0*	*0*	*0*	*0*	*0*	*0*
Heating Degree Days (base 65°F)	*773*	*592*	*416*	*200*	*44*	*2*	*0*	*0*	*18*	*165*	*399*	*678*	*3,287*
Cooling Degree Days (base 65°F)	*0*	*0*	*6*	*32*	*137*	*312*	*448*	*419*	*240*	*42*	*4*	*1*	*1,641*
Mean Precipitation (in.)	*5.17*	*5.02*	*5.72*	*4.18*	*4.35*	*4.94*	*4.70*	*3.61*	*4.89*	*3.16*	*5.01*	*4.58*	*55.33*
Extreme Maximum Daily Precip. (in.)	*3.81*	*3.48*	*3.56*	*3.50*	*3.78*	na	*2.91*	*3.01*	*4.35*	*3.90*	na	*2.87*	na
Days With ≥ 0.1" Precipitation	*7*	*7*	*8*	*6*	*6*	*7*	*8*	*6*	*6*	*5*	*7*	*7*	*80*
Days With ≥ 0.5" Precipitation	*4*	*4*	*4*	*3*	*3*	*3*	*3*	*2*	*3*	*2*	*3*	*4*	*38*
Days With ≥ 1.0" Precipitation	*2*	*2*	*2*	*1*	*1*	*2*	*1*	*1*	*2*	*1*	*2*	*2*	*19*
Mean Snowfall (in.)	*0.7*	*0.6*	*0.9*	*0.1*	*0.0*	*0.0*	*0.0*	*0.0*	*0.0*	*trace*	*0.0*	*trace*	*2.3*
Maximum Snow Depth (in.)	*2*	*4*	*0*	*trace*	*0*	*0*	*0*	*0*	*0*	*trace*	*0*	*trace*	*4*
Days With ≥ 1.0" Snow Depth	*0*	*0*	*0*	*0*	*0*	*0*	*0*	*0*	*0*	*0*	*0*	*0*	*0*

The period of record for all cooperative weather station data is 1980 – 2009. See User Guide for detailed explanation of data.

Dublin *Laurens County* Elevation: 229 ft. Latitude: 32° 33' N Longitude: 82° 54' W

	JAN	FEB	MAR	APR	MAY	JUN	JUL	AUG	SEP	OCT	NOV	DEC	YEAR
Mean Maximum Temp. (°F)	57.8	62.3	69.9	77.6	85.5	91.0	94.0	92.2	86.8	77.7	68.9	60.1	77.0
Mean Temp. (°F)	46.1	49.6	56.5	63.6	72.0	78.8	82.1	80.9	75.1	65.0	55.8	48.1	64.5
Mean Minimum Temp. (°F)	34.3	36.9	43.0	49.5	58.4	66.6	70.3	69.5	63.3	52.1	42.7	36.1	51.9
Extreme Maximum Temp. (°F)	81	85	89	98	99	105	109	109	103	95	90	82	109
Extreme Minimum Temp. (°F)	0	11	14	28	40	45	56	56	40	29	20	5	0
Days Maximum Temp. ≥ 90°F	0	0	0	1	9	19	26	22	11	1	0	0	89
Days Maximum Temp. ≤ 32°F	0	0	0	0	0	0	0	0	0	0	0	0	0
Days Minimum Temp. ≤ 32°F	15	10	4	1	0	0	0	0	0	0	6	13	49
Days Minimum Temp. ≤ 0°F	0	0	0	0	0	0	0	0	0	0	0	0	0
Heating Degree Days (base 65°F)	581	431	276	110	14	0	0	0	5	93	287	521	2,318
Cooling Degree Days (base 65°F)	2	4	19	73	237	421	539	499	315	98	18	4	2,229
Mean Precipitation (in.)	4.33	3.75	4.93	3.06	2.37	4.77	4.57	4.69	3.58	3.23	3.14	3.87	46.29
Extreme Maximum Daily Precip. (in.)	3.30	2.70	3.95	3.00	3.34	5.70	2.20	4.80	5.12	4.00	4.09	3.88	5.70
Days With ≥ 0.1" Precipitation	7	6	6	5	4	8	7	7	5	4	5	6	70
Days With ≥ 0.5" Precipitation	3	3	4	2	2	4	4	3	2	2	2	3	34
Days With ≥ 1.0" Precipitation	1	1	2	1	1	1	2	2	1	1	1	1	15
Mean Snowfall (in.)	0.1	trace	trace	0.0	0.0	0.0	0.0	0.0	0.0	0.0	0.0	0.0	0.1
Maximum Snow Depth (in.)	0	trace	trace	0	0	0	0	0	0	0	0	0	trace
Days With ≥ 1.0" Snow Depth	0	0	0	0	0	0	0	0	0	0	0	0	0

Elberton 2 N *Elbert County* Elevation: 540 ft. Latitude: 34° 09' N Longitude: 82° 51' W

	JAN	FEB	MAR	APR	MAY	JUN	JUL	AUG	SEP	OCT	NOV	DEC	YEAR
Mean Maximum Temp. (°F)	52.6	56.9	65.3	73.1	79.6	86.0	88.8	87.5	81.7	72.3	63.3	54.1	71.8
Mean Temp. (°F)	40.9	44.1	51.5	58.9	66.7	74.4	77.8	76.8	70.4	59.6	50.2	42.4	59.5
Mean Minimum Temp. (°F)	29.2	31.3	37.7	44.7	53.7	62.8	66.8	66.0	58.9	46.8	37.1	30.7	47.1
Extreme Maximum Temp. (°F)	76	79	86	92	93	100	104	106	95	92	81	76	106
Extreme Minimum Temp. (°F)	-5	6	10	21	32	40	50	51	35	22	13	2	-5
Days Maximum Temp. ≥ 90°F	0	0	0	0	1	8	14	11	3	0	0	0	37
Days Maximum Temp. ≤ 32°F	0	0	0	0	0	0	0	0	0	0	0	0	0
Days Minimum Temp. ≤ 32°F	20	17	10	3	0	0	0	0	0	3	12	19	84
Days Minimum Temp. ≤ 0°F	0	0	0	0	0	0	0	0	0	0	0	0	0
Heating Degree Days (base 65°F)	741	584	413	203	51	3	0	0	22	195	439	694	3,345
Cooling Degree Days (base 65°F)	0	0	4	27	110	293	404	372	189	33	3	1	1,436
Mean Precipitation (in.)	4.37	4.42	5.01	3.18	3.36	4.12	4.81	4.11	3.50	3.49	3.79	3.89	48.05
Extreme Maximum Daily Precip. (in.)	4.02	2.80	4.30	2.91	2.42	3.60	8.79	6.70	4.53	3.16	3.25	3.25	8.79
Days With ≥ 0.1" Precipitation	7	7	7	6	6	7	7	6	5	4	6	6	74
Days With ≥ 0.5" Precipitation	3	3	3	2	3	3	3	3	2	2	3	3	33
Days With ≥ 1.0" Precipitation	1	1	2	1	1	1	1	1	1	1	1	1	13
Mean Snowfall (in.)	0.1	0.0	trace	0.0	0.0	0.0	0.0	0.0	0.0	0.0	0.0	0.0	0.1
Maximum Snow Depth (in.)	trace	0	10	0	0	0	0	0	0	0	0	0	10
Days With ≥ 1.0" Snow Depth	0	0	0	0	0	0	0	0	0	0	0	0	0

Experiment *Spalding County* Elevation: 924 ft. Latitude: 33° 16' N Longitude: 84° 17' W

	JAN	FEB	MAR	APR	MAY	JUN	JUL	AUG	SEP	OCT	NOV	DEC	YEAR
Mean Maximum Temp. (°F)	*53.0*	*57.8*	*64.9*	*72.5*	*80.0*	*86.0*	*89.4*	*87.9*	*82.6*	*73.4*	*64.9*	*55.7*	*72.3*
Mean Temp. (°F)	*42.4*	*46.7*	*53.4*	*60.5*	*68.6*	*75.5*	*78.8*	*77.4*	*71.7*	*61.5*	*53.4*	*44.9*	*61.2*
Mean Minimum Temp. (°F)	*31.8*	*35.5*	*41.9*	*48.5*	*57.2*	*64.7*	*68.1*	*66.8*	*60.8*	*49.7*	*41.8*	*34.1*	*50.1*
Extreme Maximum Temp. (°F)	*78*	*80*	*85*	*91*	*95*	*99*	*102*	*101*	*97*	*90*	*83*	*77*	*102*
Extreme Minimum Temp. (°F)	*-8*	*7*	*11*	*25*	*35*	*44*	*57*	*51*	*40*	*27*	*22*	*0*	*-8*
Days Maximum Temp. ≥ 90°F	*0*	*0*	*0*	*0*	*1*	*8*	*16*	*12*	*4*	*0*	*0*	*0*	*41*
Days Maximum Temp. ≤ 32°F	*1*	*0*	*0*	*0*	*0*	*0*	*0*	*0*	*0*	*0*	*0*	*0*	*1*
Days Minimum Temp. ≤ 32°F	*17*	*11*	*5*	*1*	*0*	*0*	*0*	*0*	*0*	*1*	*6*	*15*	*56*
Days Minimum Temp. ≤ 0°F	*0*	*0*	*0*	*0*	*0*	*0*	*0*	*0*	*0*	*0*	*0*	*0*	*0*
Heating Degree Days (base 65°F)	*692*	*512*	*360*	*169*	*32*	*2*	*0*	*1*	*16*	*150*	*350*	*617*	*2,901*
Cooling Degree Days (base 65°F)	*0*	*1*	*9*	*41*	*152*	*322*	*435*	*391*	*225*	*48*	*8*	*1*	*1,633*
Mean Precipitation (in.)	*4.54*	*4.62*	*5.14*	*3.68*	*3.47*	*4.27*	*4.83*	*3.82*	*3.58*	*3.08*	*3.92*	*3.87*	*48.82*
Extreme Maximum Daily Precip. (in.)	*2.48*	*4.44*	*6.30*	*3.18*	*2.73*	*2.76*	*10.50*	*3.27*	*4.80*	*3.15*	*2.54*	*2.70*	*10.50*
Days With ≥ 0.1" Precipitation	*8*	*7*	*7*	*6*	*6*	*7*	*7*	*6*	*6*	*5*	*6*	*7*	*78*
Days With ≥ 0.5" Precipitation	*4*	*3*	*3*	*2*	*3*	*3*	*3*	*2*	*2*	*2*	*3*	*3*	*33*
Days With ≥ 1.0" Precipitation	*1*	*1*	*2*	*1*	*1*	*1*	*1*	*1*	*1*	*1*	*1*	*1*	*13*
Mean Snowfall (in.)	*0.3*	*trace*	*0.3*	*0.0*	*0.0*	*0.0*	*0.0*	*0.0*	*0.0*	*0.0*	*0.0*	*0.0*	*0.6*
Maximum Snow Depth (in.)	*trace*	*0*	*5*	*0*	*0*	*0*	*0*	*0*	*0*	*0*	*0*	*2*	*5*
Days With ≥ 1.0" Snow Depth	*0*	*0*	*0*	*0*	*0*	*0*	*0*	*0*	*0*	*0*	*0*	*0*	*0*

Fort Stewart *Liberty County* Elevation: 91 ft. Latitude: 31° 52' N Longitude: 81° 38' W

	JAN	FEB	MAR	APR	MAY	JUN	JUL	AUG	SEP	OCT	NOV	DEC	YEAR
Mean Maximum Temp. (°F)	62.9	66.7	73.2	79.5	86.4	91.0	93.4	91.5	87.6	79.7	72.3	64.6	79.1
Mean Temp. (°F)	51.8	55.1	61.0	67.0	74.5	80.4	83.0	81.9	77.8	69.1	60.9	53.6	68.0
Mean Minimum Temp. (°F)	40.6	43.1	48.7	54.5	62.6	69.7	72.6	72.2	68.0	58.3	49.5	42.6	56.9
Extreme Maximum Temp. (°F)	87	85	89	97	100	110	110	106	100	95	88	83	110
Extreme Minimum Temp. (°F)	0	16	19	29	44	55	62	56	48	27	25	10	0
Days Maximum Temp. ≥ 90°F	0	0	0	2	9	19	26	22	11	1	0	0	90
Days Maximum Temp. ≤ 32°F	0	0	0	0	0	0	0	0	0	0	0	0	0
Days Minimum Temp. ≤ 32°F	8	4	1	0	0	0	0	0	0	0	1	6	20
Days Minimum Temp. ≤ 0°F	0	0	0	0	0	0	0	0	0	0	0	0	0
Heating Degree Days (base 65°F)	409	289	164	55	3	0	0	0	0	41	165	359	1,485
Cooling Degree Days (base 65°F)	7	14	46	122	305	468	565	531	391	175	49	14	2,687
Mean Precipitation (in.)	4.01	3.44	3.93	2.91	2.90	5.50	5.91	6.31	4.22	3.94	2.65	2.99	48.71
Extreme Maximum Daily Precip. (in.)	3.45	3.80	4.07	3.35	3.02	4.45	3.00	4.53	3.21	6.00	2.70	2.30	6.00
Days With ≥ 0.1" Precipitation	7	5	6	4	5	8	9	9	6	5	4	5	73
Days With ≥ 0.5" Precipitation	3	2	3	2	2	4	4	4	3	2	2	2	33
Days With ≥ 1.0" Precipitation	1	1	1	1	1	2	2	2	2	1	1	1	16
Mean Snowfall (in.)	trace	0.0	trace	0.0	0.0	0.0	0.0	0.0	0.0	0.0	0.0	0.1	0.1
Maximum Snow Depth (in.)	trace	0	0	0	0	0	0	0	0	0	0	4	4
Days With ≥ 1.0" Snow Depth	0	0	0	0	0	0	0	0	0	0	0	0	0

The period of record for all cooperative weather station data is 1980 – 2009. See User Guide for detailed explanation of data.

Gainesville *Hall County* Elevation: 1,169 ft. Latitude: 34° 18' N Longitude: 83° 52' W

	JAN	FEB	MAR	APR	MAY	JUN	JUL	AUG	SEP	OCT	NOV	DEC	YEAR
Mean Maximum Temp. (°F)	50.9	55.3	63.5	71.5	78.1	84.8	88.1	87.1	80.7	71.5	62.7	53.3	70.6
Mean Temp. (°F)	41.4	44.8	52.0	59.6	67.2	74.7	78.4	77.4	71.0	61.0	52.2	43.9	60.3
Mean Minimum Temp. (°F)	31.8	34.3	40.4	47.7	56.1	64.5	68.5	67.8	61.3	50.4	41.6	34.5	49.9
Extreme Maximum Temp. (°F)	76	78	86	93	93	98	103	101	96	88	84	78	103
Extreme Minimum Temp. (°F)	-8	8	10	26	37	45	56	55	42	28	18	-1	-8
Days Maximum Temp. ≥ 90°F	0	0	0	0	0	6	13	10	2	0	0	0	31
Days Maximum Temp. ≤ 32°F	1	1	0	0	0	0	0	0	0	0	0	1	3
Days Minimum Temp. ≤ 32°F	17	12	6	1	0	0	0	0	0	0	5	14	55
Days Minimum Temp. ≤ 0°F	0	0	0	0	0	0	0	0	0	0	0	0	0
Heating Degree Days (base 65°F)	724	565	401	189	46	2	0	0	16	158	381	647	3,129
Cooling Degree Days (base 65°F)	0	0	5	34	120	299	421	393	203	40	4	1	1,520
Mean Precipitation (in.)	5.24	5.04	5.59	3.65	3.81	4.27	4.24	4.26	4.67	3.94	4.33	4.58	53.62
Extreme Maximum Daily Precip. (in.)	3.95	3.82	4.80	2.18	2.65	4.62	3.56	5.03	6.04	4.30	4.15	4.27	6.04
Days With ≥ 0.1" Precipitation	8	7	8	7	7	7	7	7	6	5	6	7	82
Days With ≥ 0.5" Precipitation	4	4	4	3	3	3	3	3	3	2	3	3	38
Days With ≥ 1.0" Precipitation	2	2	2	1	1	1	1	1	1	1	2	1	16
Mean Snowfall (in.)	1.2	0.5	0.2	0.0	0.0	0.0	0.0	0.0	0.0	0.0	0.0	0.2	2.1
Maximum Snow Depth (in.)	4	3	trace	0	0	0	0	0	0	0	0	1	4
Days With ≥ 1.0" Snow Depth	0	0	0	0	0	0	0	0	0	0	0	0	0

Glennville *Tattnall County* Elevation: 169 ft. Latitude: 31° 56' N Longitude: 81° 56' W

	JAN	FEB	MAR	APR	MAY	JUN	JUL	AUG	SEP	OCT	NOV	DEC	YEAR
Mean Maximum Temp. (°F)	60.9	65.0	71.9	78.4	85.7	90.9	***93.0***	91.2	86.7	78.7	71.0	62.9	***78.0***
Mean Temp. (°F)	49.7	53.1	59.4	65.5	73.6	79.9	***82.4***	81.3	76.7	67.6	59.3	51.7	***66.7***
Mean Minimum Temp. (°F)	38.4	41.2	46.8	52.7	61.3	69.0	***71.7***	71.5	66.6	56.4	47.5	40.4	***55.3***
Extreme Maximum Temp. (°F)	82	85	89	97	99	110	106	103	100	95	88	83	110
Extreme Minimum Temp. (°F)	1	14	17	31	44	52	59	52	40	33	24	9	1
Days Maximum Temp. ≥ 90°F	0	0	0	1	7	19	23	21	10	1	0	0	82
Days Maximum Temp. ≤ 32°F	0	0	0	0	0	0	0	0	0	0	0	0	0
Days Minimum Temp. ≤ 32°F	10	6	2	0	0	0	0	0	0	0	2	8	28
Days Minimum Temp. ≤ 0°F	0	0	0	0	0	0	0	0	0	0	0	0	0
Heating Degree Days (base 65°F)	473	340	201	76	5	0	***0***	0	1	56	202	416	***1,770***
Cooling Degree Days (base 65°F)	4	10	34	98	279	454	***546***	514	357	143	38	10	***2,487***
Mean Precipitation (in.)	3.99	3.68	4.28	2.99	2.71	4.86	4.98	6.22	3.70	3.32	2.62	3.05	46.40
Extreme Maximum Daily Precip. (in.)	3.32	4.02	3.10	4.12	2.85	5.43	4.00	***6.30***	4.00	7.90	3.50	2.16	***7.90***
Days With ≥ 0.1" Precipitation	7	5	6	4	4	7	8	9	5	4	4	4	67
Days With ≥ 0.5" Precipitation	3	2	3	2	2	3	3	4	3	2	2	2	31
Days With ≥ 1.0" Precipitation	1	1	1	1	1	1	1	2	1	1	1	1	13
Mean Snowfall (in.)	trace	trace	0.0	0.0	0.0	0.0	0.0	0.0	0.0	0.0	0.0	0.1	0.1
Maximum Snow Depth (in.)	trace	trace	0	0	0	0	0	0	0	0	0	trace	trace
Days With ≥ 1.0" Snow Depth	0	0	0	0	0	0	0	0	0	0	0	0	0

Hartwell *Hart County* Elevation: 689 ft. Latitude: 34° 21' N Longitude: 82° 56' W

	JAN	FEB	MAR	APR	MAY	JUN	JUL	AUG	SEP	OCT	NOV	DEC	YEAR
Mean Maximum Temp. (°F)	52.2	56.5	64.9	72.7	79.5	86.1	89.1	87.5	81.3	71.9	63.7	54.9	71.7
Mean Temp. (°F)	42.6	46.2	53.6	61.0	68.8	76.2	79.6	78.4	72.1	62.1	53.3	45.1	61.6
Mean Minimum Temp. (°F)	33.0	35.8	42.2	49.2	58.2	66.4	70.1	69.3	62.9	52.3	42.8	35.5	51.5
Extreme Maximum Temp. (°F)	78	79	88	94	98	100	105	108	96	91	81	79	108
Extreme Minimum Temp. (°F)	-5	7	11	27	40	46	60	55	44	31	21	3	-5
Days Maximum Temp. ≥ 90°F	0	0	0	0	1	9	15	11	3	0	0	0	39
Days Maximum Temp. ≤ 32°F	1	0	0	0	0	0	0	0	0	0	0	0	1
Days Minimum Temp. ≤ 32°F	15	10	4	0	0	0	0	0	0	0	4	12	45
Days Minimum Temp. ≤ 0°F	0	0	0	0	0	0	0	0	0	0	0	0	0
Heating Degree Days (base 65°F)	687	526	355	158	30	1	0	0	10	133	353	605	2,858
Cooling Degree Days (base 65°F)	0	0	7	43	153	343	459	423	231	50	6	1	1,716
Mean Precipitation (in.)	4.42	4.38	5.25	3.29	3.47	4.07	4.05	3.72	4.52	3.98	3.90	4.67	49.72
Extreme Maximum Daily Precip. (in.)	2.62	3.07	5.00	2.73	2.36	3.55	4.05	7.20	5.90	4.00	5.15	4.53	7.20
Days With ≥ 0.1" Precipitation	6	6	6	6	5	6	6	6	5	5	5	7	69
Days With ≥ 0.5" Precipitation	3	3	3	2	2	2	3	2	2	2	3	3	30
Days With ≥ 1.0" Precipitation	2	1	2	1	1	1	1	1	1	1	1	2	15
Mean Snowfall (in.)	0.7	0.3	0.1	0.0	0.0	0.0	0.0	0.0	0.0	0.0	0.0	0.1	1.2
Maximum Snow Depth (in.)	7	2	4	0	0	0	0	0	0	0	0	0	7
Days With ≥ 1.0" Snow Depth	0	0	0	0	0	0	0	0	0	0	0	0	0

Hawkinsville *Pulaski County* Elevation: 271 ft. Latitude: 32° 17' N Longitude: 83° 28' W

	JAN	FEB	MAR	APR	MAY	JUN	JUL	AUG	SEP	OCT	NOV	DEC	YEAR
Mean Maximum Temp. (°F)	58.3	62.8	70.2	77.1	84.9	90.5	***93.0***	91.7	87.0	78.0	69.5	60.9	***77.0***
Mean Temp. (°F)	46.6	50.4	57.3	63.7	72.4	79.1	***81.7***	80.9	75.5	65.5	56.6	49.1	***64.9***
Mean Minimum Temp. (°F)	34.8	37.9	44.3	50.2	59.7	67.7	***70.5***	70.0	64.0	53.1	43.7	37.2	***52.8***
Extreme Maximum Temp. (°F)	80	84	90	96	97	104	105	105	102	98	87	83	105
Extreme Minimum Temp. (°F)	-2	11	15	28	41	45	57	52	37	31	21	8	-2
Days Maximum Temp. ≥ 90°F	0	0	0	1	8	19	22	22	11	1	0	0	84
Days Maximum Temp. ≤ 32°F	0	0	0	0	0	0	0	0	0	0	0	0	0
Days Minimum Temp. ≤ 32°F	14	8	3	0	0	0	0	0	0	0	5	12	42
Days Minimum Temp. ≤ 0°F	0	0	0	0	0	0	0	0	0	0	0	0	0
Heating Degree Days (base 65°F)	565	412	255	107	11	0	***0***	0	5	85	267	491	***2,198***
Cooling Degree Days (base 65°F)	2	4	22	75	245	431	***525***	499	327	108	23	5	***2,266***
Mean Precipitation (in.)	4.56	3.88	4.80	3.33	2.85	4.33	4.34	3.86	3.84	3.05	3.31	3.93	46.08
Extreme Maximum Daily Precip. (in.)	2.81	3.16	4.00	3.20	2.78	4.08	3.70	3.04	5.12	7.28	3.37	4.92	7.28
Days With ≥ 0.1" Precipitation	7	6	6	5	5	7	7	6	5	4	5	6	69
Days With ≥ 0.5" Precipitation	3	3	3	2	2	2	3	3	2	2	2	3	30
Days With ≥ 1.0" Precipitation	1	1	2	1	1	1	1	1	1	1	1	1	13
Mean Snowfall (in.)	0.1	trace	0.1	0.0	0.0	0.0	0.0	0.0	0.0	0.0	0.0	trace	0.2
Maximum Snow Depth (in.)	0	trace	0	0	0	0	0	***0***	0	0	0	0	trace
Days With ≥ 1.0" Snow Depth	0	0	0	0	0	0	0	0	0	0	0	0	0

The period of record for all cooperative weather station data is 1980 – 2009. See User Guide for detailed explanation of data.

Irwinton 4 WNW *Wilkinson County* Elevation: 515 ft. Latitude: 32° 50' N Longitude: 83° 14' W

	JAN	FEB	MAR	APR	MAY	JUN	JUL	AUG	SEP	OCT	NOV	DEC	YEAR
Mean Maximum Temp. (°F)	58.7	62.9	70.8	77.8	84.4	90.0	93.0	91.5	86.5	77.9	69.5	60.3	76.9
Mean Temp. (°F)	***47.3***	50.9	57.9	64.4	72.1	78.7	81.8	80.8	75.6	66.2	57.0	49.2	***65.2***
Mean Minimum Temp. (°F)	35.9	38.9	44.9	50.9	59.8	67.3	70.6	70.0	64.6	54.4	44.5	38.1	53.3
Extreme Maximum Temp. (°F)	81	85	90	96	96	103	107	105	102	93	86	81	107
Extreme Minimum Temp. (°F)	-4	8	10	28	33	44	60	56	40	29	24	5	-4
Days Maximum Temp. ≥ 90°F	0	0	0	1	6	17	24	21	10	0	0	0	79
Days Maximum Temp. ≤ 32°F	0	0	0	0	0	0	0	0	0	0	0	0	0
Days Minimum Temp. ≤ 32°F	11	8	2	0	0	0	0	0	0	0	3	9	33
Days Minimum Temp. ≤ 0°F	0	0	0	0	0	0	0	0	0	0	0	0	0
Heating Degree Days (base 65°F)	***542***	396	237	92	9	0	0	0	3	71	252	487	***2,089***
Cooling Degree Days (base 65°F)	***2***	4	24	80	238	416	528	497	330	113	19	4	***2,255***
Mean Precipitation (in.)	4.13	4.01	4.74	3.06	2.74	3.91	4.24	4.16	3.69	2.81	3.11	3.94	44.54
Extreme Maximum Daily Precip. (in.)	3.57	3.90	4.05	2.36	3.23	3.59	***3.05***	3.76	5.29	***3.60***	4.00	***3.83***	***5.29***
Days With ≥ 0.1" Precipitation	6	5	6	5	5	6	7	7	5	4	5	5	66
Days With ≥ 0.5" Precipitation	3	3	3	2	2	2	3	3	2	2	2	2	29
Days With ≥ 1.0" Precipitation	1	1	2	1	1	1	1	1	1	1	1	1	13
Mean Snowfall (in.)	0.1	trace	0.1	0.0	0.0	0.0	0.0	0.0	0.0	0.0	0.0	trace	0.2
Maximum Snow Depth (in.)	trace	trace	trace	0	0	0	0	0	0	0	0	0	trace
Days With ≥ 1.0" Snow Depth	0	0	0	0	0	0	0	0	0	0	0	0	0

Lafayette 5 SW *Walker County* Elevation: 799 ft. Latitude: 34° 39' N Longitude: 85° 22' W

	JAN	FEB	MAR	APR	MAY	JUN	JUL	AUG	SEP	OCT	NOV	DEC	YEAR
Mean Maximum Temp. (°F)	49.6	54.3	63.2	71.3	78.4	85.1	88.7	88.3	82.1	72.0	61.6	51.8	70.5
Mean Temp. (°F)	39.1	42.8	50.3	57.9	65.8	73.4	77.2	76.7	70.4	59.5	49.6	41.4	58.7
Mean Minimum Temp. (°F)	28.6	31.3	37.4	44.4	53.1	61.7	65.7	65.0	58.6	46.9	37.6	31.0	46.8
Extreme Maximum Temp. (°F)	75	80	88	90	93	97	106	104	98	90	88	75	106
Extreme Minimum Temp. (°F)	-13	-3	7	22	34	41	49	49	36	26	16	-2	-13
Days Maximum Temp. ≥ 90°F	0	0	0	0	1	7	13	12	4	0	0	0	37
Days Maximum Temp. ≤ 32°F	2	1	0	0	0	0	0	0	0	0	0	1	4
Days Minimum Temp. ≤ 32°F	21	16	10	3	0	0	0	0	0	2	11	19	82
Days Minimum Temp. ≤ 0°F	0	0	0	0	0	0	0	0	0	0	0	0	0
Heating Degree Days (base 65°F)	795	622	452	226	66	4	0	0	22	193	458	725	3,563
Cooling Degree Days (base 65°F)	0	0	3	20	97	263	386	369	190	30	3	0	1,361
Mean Precipitation (in.)	5.51	5.56	5.78	4.51	4.84	4.22	4.80	3.83	4.51	3.65	5.52	5.63	58.36
Extreme Maximum Daily Precip. (in.)	4.01	6.99	4.09	2.95	4.60	3.30	4.69	2.95	7.25	4.41	5.53	3.91	7.25
Days With ≥ 0.1" Precipitation	8	7	7	7	7	7	8	6	6	5	7	8	83
Days With ≥ 0.5" Precipitation	4	4	4	3	3	3	3	3	3	2	3	4	39
Days With ≥ 1.0" Precipitation	2	2	2	1	1	1	2	1	1	1	2	2	18
Mean Snowfall (in.)	0.6	0.5	0.7	0.1	0.0	0.0	0.0	0.0	0.0	trace	trace	0.1	2.0
Maximum Snow Depth (in.)	2	***trace***	2	0	0	***0***	0	0	***0***	trace	trace	trace	***2***
Days With ≥ 1.0" Snow Depth	0	0	0	0	0	0	0	0	0	0	0	0	0

Louisville 1 E *Jefferson County* Elevation: 321 ft. Latitude: 33° 01' N Longitude: 82° 23' W

	JAN	FEB	MAR	APR	MAY	JUN	JUL	AUG	SEP	OCT	NOV	DEC	YEAR
Mean Maximum Temp. (°F)	58.7	63.1	70.4	77.6	84.9	90.3	92.9	91.5	86.5	77.7	69.4	60.5	77.0
Mean Temp. (°F)	47.0	50.6	57.1	63.9	71.9	78.8	81.8	80.7	75.3	65.3	56.8	48.7	64.8
Mean Minimum Temp. (°F)	35.2	38.1	43.8	50.1	59.0	67.3	70.7	69.8	63.9	52.8	44.1	36.9	52.6
Extreme Maximum Temp. (°F)	80	85	91	96	99	105	105	106	102	94	87	85	106
Extreme Minimum Temp. (°F)	-2	12	14	26	38	46	56	53	42	27	20	6	-2
Days Maximum Temp. ≥ 90°F	0	0	0	1	7	17	24	20	10	1	0	0	80
Days Maximum Temp. ≤ 32°F	0	0	0	0	0	0	0	0	0	0	0	0	0
Days Minimum Temp. ≤ 32°F	13	9	4	1	0	0	0	0	0	1	5	12	45
Days Minimum Temp. ≤ 0°F	0	0	0	0	0	0	0	0	0	0	0	0	0
Heating Degree Days (base 65°F)	553	406	259	103	13	0	0	0	4	87	262	501	2,188
Cooling Degree Days (base 65°F)	2	5	22	76	236	422	528	492	318	103	22	4	2,230
Mean Precipitation (in.)	4.31	3.85	4.85	2.98	2.81	4.24	3.93	4.31	3.74	3.25	2.86	3.74	44.87
Extreme Maximum Daily Precip. (in.)	2.93	3.55	3.21	2.86	1.92	5.57	4.36	5.28	6.96	16.42	3.27	3.31	16.42
Days With ≥ 0.1" Precipitation	7	6	6	5	5	6	7	7	4	4	5	6	68
Days With ≥ 0.5" Precipitation	3	3	4	2	2	3	3	3	2	1	2	3	31
Days With ≥ 1.0" Precipitation	1	1	2	1	1	1	1	1	1	1	1	1	13
Mean Snowfall (in.)	0.1	trace	trace	0.0	0.0	0.0	0.0	0.0	0.0	0.0	trace	0.1	0.2
Maximum Snow Depth (in.)	3	1	trace	0	0	0	0	0	0	0	trace	trace	3
Days With ≥ 1.0" Snow Depth	0	0	0	0	0	0	0	0	0	0	0	0	0

Monticello *Jasper County* Elevation: 529 ft. Latitude: 33° 19' N Longitude: 83° 42' W

	JAN	FEB	MAR	APR	MAY	JUN	JUL	AUG	SEP	OCT	NOV	DEC	YEAR
Mean Maximum Temp. (°F)	55.6	59.8	67.7	74.9	82.0	87.8	90.6	89.4	84.2	75.5	66.8	57.4	74.3
Mean Temp. (°F)	44.1	47.4	54.3	61.4	69.3	76.5	79.8	78.8	73.0	63.1	54.0	45.7	62.3
Mean Minimum Temp. (°F)	32.5	35.1	40.9	47.9	56.5	65.3	69.0	68.3	61.8	50.8	41.2	34.0	50.3
Extreme Maximum Temp. (°F)	79	82	88	93	95	100	103	103	99	91	83	78	103
Extreme Minimum Temp. (°F)	-7	7	12	25	37	48	55	52	42	24	15	2	-7
Days Maximum Temp. ≥ 90°F	0	0	0	0	3	12	19	15	6	0	0	0	55
Days Maximum Temp. ≤ 32°F	0	0	0	0	0	0	0	0	0	0	0	0	0
Days Minimum Temp. ≤ 32°F	16	12	6	1	0	0	0	0	0	1	7	15	58
Days Minimum Temp. ≤ 0°F	0	0	0	0	0	0	0	0	0	0	0	0	0
Heating Degree Days (base 65°F)	642	492	335	148	27	1	0	0	9	118	332	592	2,696
Cooling Degree Days (base 65°F)	0	1	11	48	166	354	467	436	257	69	8	1	1,818
Mean Precipitation (in.)	4.10	4.40	5.14	3.31	2.69	3.78	4.75	3.60	3.27	2.97	3.72	3.72	45.45
Extreme Maximum Daily Precip. (in.)	2.93	4.08	4.48	2.27	2.00	2.40	4.00	4.03	4.20	5.50	4.90	4.50	5.50
Days With ≥ 0.1" Precipitation	7	6	6	6	5	7	7	6	5	4	5	5	69
Days With ≥ 0.5" Precipitation	3	3	4	2	2	3	3	2	2	2	3	3	32
Days With ≥ 1.0" Precipitation	1	1	2	1	1	1	1	1	1	1	1	1	13
Mean Snowfall (in.)	0.4	0.0	0.1	0.0	0.0	0.0	0.0	0.0	0.0	trace	0.0	trace	0.5
Maximum Snow Depth (in.)	3	trace	0	0	0	0	0	0	0	trace	0	trace	3
Days With ≥ 1.0" Snow Depth	0	0	0	0	0	0	0	0	0	0	0	0	0

The period of record for all cooperative weather station data is 1980 – 2009. See User Guide for detailed explanation of data.

Newnan 4 NE *Coweta County* Elevation: 919 ft. Latitude: 33° 27' N Longitude: 84° 47' W

	JAN	FEB	MAR	APR	MAY	JUN	JUL	AUG	SEP	OCT	NOV	DEC	YEAR
Mean Maximum Temp. (°F)	54.3	58.4	66.7	74.0	80.6	86.4	89.0	88.2	82.7	73.5	65.3	55.8	72.9
Mean Temp. (°F)	43.4	46.8	54.0	60.9	68.6	75.4	78.6	77.7	71.9	61.6	53.5	45.0	61.5
Mean Minimum Temp. (°F)	32.5	35.2	41.2	47.7	56.6	64.4	68.1	67.2	60.9	49.6	41.7	34.2	49.9
Extreme Maximum Temp. (°F)	77	79	85	92	94	98	102	101	97	91	88	77	102
Extreme Minimum Temp. (°F)	-8	4	11	24	37	41	56	52	37	26	19	1	-8
Days Maximum Temp. ≥ 90°F	0	0	0	0	1	9	14	11	3	0	0	0	38
Days Maximum Temp. ≤ 32°F	1	0	0	0	0	0	0	0	0	0	0	0	1
Days Minimum Temp. ≤ 32°F	16	12	7	2	0	0	0	0	0	1	7	15	60
Days Minimum Temp. ≤ 0°F	0	0	0	0	0	0	0	0	0	0	0	0	0
Heating Degree Days (base 65°F)	662	508	346	158	32	1	0	0	15	150	344	613	2,829
Cooling Degree Days (base 65°F)	0	1	11	41	151	321	428	400	227	50	7	1	1,638
Mean Precipitation (in.)	4.55	4.90	5.32	3.70	3.72	3.82	4.81	3.85	4.01	3.07	4.24	3.97	49.96
Extreme Maximum Daily Precip. (in.)	3.52	5.68	5.60	2.83	3.10	3.76	6.98	3.90	4.73	3.53	3.30	3.35	6.98
Days With ≥ 0.1" Precipitation	7	7	7	6	6	7	7	6	5	5	6	6	75
Days With ≥ 0.5" Precipitation	3	3	3	3	3	3	3	3	3	2	3	3	35
Days With ≥ 1.0" Precipitation	1	2	2	1	1	1	1	1	1	1	1	1	14
Mean Snowfall (in.)	0.8	0.1	0.6	0.0	0.0	0.0	0.0	0.0	0.0	0.0	0.0	0.2	1.7
Maximum Snow Depth (in.)	7	1	7	trace	0	0	0	0	0	0	0	3	7
Days With ≥ 1.0" Snow Depth	1	0	0	0	0	0	0	0	0	0	0	0	1

Quitman 2 NW *Brooks County* Elevation: 185 ft. Latitude: 30° 48' N Longitude: 83° 35' W

	JAN	FEB	MAR	APR	MAY	JUN	JUL	AUG	SEP	OCT	NOV	DEC	YEAR
Mean Maximum Temp. (°F)	61.8	66.7	72.7	79.0	86.1	90.4	92.0	90.8	87.6	80.0	71.9	63.5	78.6
Mean Temp. (°F)	49.7	54.0	59.9	65.5	73.2	79.0	81.0	80.2	76.2	67.2	59.0	51.3	66.4
Mean Minimum Temp. (°F)	37.6	41.3	47.0	52.0	60.2	67.6	69.9	69.5	64.8	54.4	46.1	39.1	54.1
Extreme Maximum Temp. (°F)	82	85	88	92	98	105	103	102	98	97	87	85	105
Extreme Minimum Temp. (°F)	3	14	18	29	40	54	59	57	42	31	25	6	3
Days Maximum Temp. ≥ 90°F	0	0	0	1	7	18	24	21	12	2	0	0	85
Days Maximum Temp. ≤ 32°F	0	0	0	0	0	0	0	0	0	0	0	0	0
Days Minimum Temp. ≤ 32°F	11	5	2	0	0	0	0	0	0	0	3	9	30
Days Minimum Temp. ≤ 0°F	0	0	0	0	0	0	0	0	0	0	0	0	0
Heating Degree Days (base 65°F)	472	312	189	74	6	0	0	0	2	61	210	427	1,753
Cooling Degree Days (base 65°F)	4	9	37	96	267	427	501	479	346	136	37	9	2,348
Mean Precipitation (in.)	4.99	4.39	5.50	3.29	2.27	5.85	***6.02***	5.80	4.13	3.53	3.01	3.30	***52.08***
Extreme Maximum Daily Precip. (in.)	4.95	***5.55***	8.35	***6.95***	***3.85***	***9.51***	***3.10***	***6.90***	***8.77***	***5.95***	***4.10***	***3.05***	***9.51***
Days With ≥ 0.1" Precipitation	4	4	5	3	3	6	6	4	4	3	3	3	48
Days With ≥ 0.5" Precipitation	3	3	3	2	2	4	4	3	2	2	2	2	32
Days With ≥ 1.0" Precipitation	2	1	2	1	1	2	2	2	1	1	1	1	17
Mean Snowfall (in.)	0.0	trace	trace	0.0	0.0	0.0	0.0	0.0	0.0	0.0	0.0	0.1	0.1
Maximum Snow Depth (in.)	0	trace	trace	0	0	0	0	0	0	0	0	0	trace
Days With ≥ 1.0" Snow Depth	0	0	0	0	0	0	0	0	0	0	0	0	0

Rome *Floyd County* Elevation: 620 ft. Latitude: 34° 15' N Longitude: 85° 09' W

	JAN	FEB	MAR	APR	MAY	JUN	JUL	AUG	SEP	OCT	NOV	DEC	YEAR
Mean Maximum Temp. (°F)	51.2	55.9	64.6	72.6	79.4	85.5	88.6	87.9	82.1	72.3	63.0	53.4	71.4
Mean Temp. (°F)	40.6	44.4	52.0	59.5	67.4	74.8	78.5	77.6	71.3	60.1	51.0	42.9	60.0
Mean Minimum Temp. (°F)	30.0	32.7	39.3	46.4	55.4	64.0	68.3	67.3	60.4	47.9	39.1	32.3	48.6
Extreme Maximum Temp. (°F)	78	80	89	93	94	100	102	105	98	90	83	79	105
Extreme Minimum Temp. (°F)	-9	5	8	23	35	42	54	53	39	23	20	-2	-9
Days Maximum Temp. ≥ 90°F	0	0	0	0	1	8	14	12	4	0	0	0	39
Days Maximum Temp. ≤ 32°F	1	0	0	0	0	0	0	0	0	0	0	1	2
Days Minimum Temp. ≤ 32°F	19	15	8	2	0	0	0	0	0	2	9	17	72
Days Minimum Temp. ≤ 0°F	0	0	0	0	0	0	0	0	0	0	0	0	0
Heating Degree Days (base 65°F)	749	578	404	190	46	3	0	0	19	183	416	680	3,268
Cooling Degree Days (base 65°F)	0	0	6	32	128	303	424	398	215	39	4	1	1,550
Mean Precipitation (in.)	4.78	4.78	5.83	4.32	4.10	4.85	5.03	4.41	3.72	3.68	4.46	4.48	54.44
Extreme Maximum Daily Precip. (in.)	4.21	4.92	4.10	3.49	2.69	3.17	4.05	4.92	4.95	6.67	3.70	2.61	6.67
Days With ≥ 0.1" Precipitation	8	7	7	7	7	7	7	6	6	5	6	7	80
Days With ≥ 0.5" Precipitation	4	3	4	3	3	4	3	3	3	2	3	3	38
Days With ≥ 1.0" Precipitation	1	1	2	1	1	2	1	1	1	1	2	1	15
Mean Snowfall (in.)	0.5	trace	0.5	0.2	0.0	0.0	0.0	0.0	0.0	0.0	trace	trace	1.2
Maximum Snow Depth (in.)	trace	trace	14	0	0	0	0	0	0	0	trace	trace	14
Days With ≥ 1.0" Snow Depth	0	0	0	0	0	0	0	0	0	0	0	0	0

Surrency 2 WNW *Appling County* Elevation: 200 ft. Latitude: 31° 44' N Longitude: 82° 14' W

	JAN	FEB	MAR	APR	MAY	JUN	JUL	AUG	SEP	OCT	NOV	DEC	YEAR
Mean Maximum Temp. (°F)	61.5	66.2	72.7	79.3	86.0	90.2	92.7	90.8	86.8	79.4	71.2	63.2	78.3
Mean Temp. (°F)	49.8	53.6	59.4	65.2	72.5	78.4	81.3	79.8	75.7	67.0	58.9	51.6	66.1
Mean Minimum Temp. (°F)	38.0	40.9	46.2	51.1	58.8	66.4	70.0	68.8	64.6	54.5	46.5	39.9	53.8
Extreme Maximum Temp. (°F)	80	88	87	96	97	103	105	102	99	94	85	82	105
Extreme Minimum Temp. (°F)	1	12	17	29	39	48	57	56	41	26	19	9	1
Days Maximum Temp. ≥ 90°F	0	0	0	1	7	17	24	21	9	1	0	0	80
Days Maximum Temp. ≤ 32°F	0	0	0	0	0	0	0	0	0	0	0	0	0
Days Minimum Temp. ≤ 32°F	11	7	3	1	0	0	0	0	0	0	5	9	36
Days Minimum Temp. ≤ 0°F	0	0	0	0	0	0	0	0	0	0	0	0	0
Heating Degree Days (base 65°F)	470	329	198	79	8	0	0	0	2	62	212	418	1,778
Cooling Degree Days (base 65°F)	5	11	33	91	246	408	513	466	330	130	35	8	2,276
Mean Precipitation (in.)	4.24	3.56	4.66	2.61	2.43	4.95	5.26	5.97	3.50	3.02	2.28	3.21	45.69
Extreme Maximum Daily Precip. (in.)	3.26	3.00	4.00	3.20	2.29	4.22	3.02	8.03	4.43	3.42	3.55	2.57	8.03
Days With ≥ 0.1" Precipitation	7	5	7	5	5	8	8	8	6	4	4	5	72
Days With ≥ 0.5" Precipitation	3	3	3	2	2	3	4	4	2	2	2	2	32
Days With ≥ 1.0" Precipitation	1	1	2	1	1	1	2	2	1	1	1	1	15
Mean Snowfall (in.)	trace	trace	trace	0.0	0.0	0.0	0.0	0.0	0.0	0.0	0.0	0.1	0.1
Maximum Snow Depth (in.)	trace	trace	trace	0	0	0	0	0	0	0	0	0	trace
Days With ≥ 1.0" Snow Depth	0	0	0	0	0	0	0	0	0	0	0	0	0

The period of record for all cooperative weather station data is 1980 – 2009. See User Guide for detailed explanation of data.

Talbotton *Talbot County* Elevation: 729 ft. Latitude: 32° 41' N Longitude: 84° 33' W

	JAN	FEB	MAR	APR	MAY	JUN	JUL	AUG	SEP	OCT	NOV	DEC	YEAR
Mean Maximum Temp. (°F)	57.5	61.7	69.8	76.1	82.4	87.8	89.9	89.4	***84.4***	75.6	67.5	59.1	***75.1***
Mean Temp. (°F)	45.7	49.0	56.1	62.3	69.6	76.2	79.1	78.5	***73.1***	63.1	54.6	47.4	***62.9***
Mean Minimum Temp. (°F)	33.9	36.3	42.4	48.5	56.7	64.5	68.3	67.7	***61.8***	50.5	41.7	35.6	***50.7***
Extreme Maximum Temp. (°F)	80	83	89	93	96	102	104	104	100	94	85	79	104
Extreme Minimum Temp. (°F)	-5	6	12	25	33	42	48	52	40	27	18	4	-5
Days Maximum Temp. ≥ 90°F	0	0	0	0	3	12	17	16	6	0	0	0	54
Days Maximum Temp. ≤ 32°F	0	0	0	0	0	0	0	0	0	0	0	0	0
Days Minimum Temp. ≤ 32°F	15	11	6	1	0	0	0	0	0	1	7	13	54
Days Minimum Temp. ≤ 0°F	0	0	0	0	0	0	0	0	0	0	0	0	0
Heating Degree Days (base 65°F)	591	448	285	126	23	1	1	0	***7***	120	315	541	***2,458***
Cooling Degree Days (base 65°F)	0	2	17	53	171	343	446	427	***259***	67	11	2	***1,798***
Mean Precipitation (in.)	4.17	4.76	5.59	3.46	3.03	4.27	4.65	3.92	3.87	3.11	4.06	4.47	49.36
Extreme Maximum Daily Precip. (in.)	2.44	3.40	9.00	4.80	2.45	4.50	4.29	4.05	4.71	3.95	3.60	3.40	9.00
Days With ≥ 0.1" Precipitation	7	6	7	5	5	6	7	6	5	4	5	6	69
Days With ≥ 0.5" Precipitation	3	3	4	2	2	3	3	3	3	2	3	3	34
Days With ≥ 1.0" Precipitation	1	2	2	1	1	1	1	1	1	1	1	2	15
Mean Snowfall (in.)	0.2	trace	0.1	0.0	0.0	0.0	0.0	0.0	0.0	0.0	0.0	trace	0.3
Maximum Snow Depth (in.)	1	0	1	0	0	0	0	0	0	0	0	2	2
Days With ≥ 1.0" Snow Depth	0	0	0	0	0	0	0	0	0	0	0	0	0

U of GA Plant Sci Farm *Oconee County* Elevation: 839 ft. Latitude: 33° 52' N Longitude: 83° 32' W

	JAN	FEB	MAR	APR	MAY	JUN	JUL	AUG	SEP	OCT	NOV	DEC	YEAR
Mean Maximum Temp. (°F)	53.0	57.2	65.2	73.1	81.1	87.8	90.8	89.2	83.2	74.0	64.7	55.4	72.9
Mean Temp. (°F)	42.6	46.0	53.2	60.6	69.1	76.5	79.8	78.4	72.2	62.2	53.1	45.0	61.6
Mean Minimum Temp. (°F)	32.1	34.8	41.2	48.0	57.0	65.3	68.8	67.6	61.2	50.3	41.4	34.5	50.2
Extreme Maximum Temp. (°F)	78	79	87	94	96	100	104	104	98	90	85	78	104
Extreme Minimum Temp. (°F)	-1	6	9	26	37	47	56	54	42	25	17	0	-1
Days Maximum Temp. ≥ 90°F	0	0	0	0	3	13	19	15	5	0	0	0	55
Days Maximum Temp. ≤ 32°F	1	0	0	0	0	0	0	0	0	0	0	0	1
Days Minimum Temp. ≤ 32°F	16	12	6	1	0	0	0	0	0	1	6	14	56
Days Minimum Temp. ≤ 0°F	0	0	0	0	0	0	0	0	0	0	0	0	0
Heating Degree Days (base 65°F)	687	531	365	170	30	1	0	0	13	136	358	615	2,906
Cooling Degree Days (base 65°F)	0	0	7	44	164	354	466	424	237	56	6	1	1,759
Mean Precipitation (in.)	4.43	4.65	5.06	3.28	3.36	4.34	4.67	3.93	4.43	3.31	4.17	3.96	49.59
Extreme Maximum Daily Precip. (in.)	2.90	3.15	3.20	3.00	4.10	4.35	5.21	4.90	4.53	3.50	3.70	2.38	5.21
Days With ≥ 0.1" Precipitation	7	7	7	6	6	7	7	6	6	4	6	6	75
Days With ≥ 0.5" Precipitation	3	3	4	2	2	3	3	3	3	2	3	3	34
Days With ≥ 1.0" Precipitation	1	1	2	1	1	1	1	1	1	1	1	1	13
Mean Snowfall (in.)	0.3	0.1	0.3	0.0	0.0	0.0	0.0	0.0	0.0	0.0	0.0	0.0	0.7
Maximum Snow Depth (in.)	0	0	0	0	0	0	0	0	0	0	0	0	0
Days With ≥ 1.0" Snow Depth	0	0	0	0	0	0	0	0	0	0	0	0	0

Warrenton *Warren County* Elevation: 509 ft. Latitude: 33° 22' N Longitude: 84° 34' W

	JAN	FEB	MAR	APR	MAY	JUN	JUL	AUG	SEP	OCT	NOV	DEC	YEAR
Mean Maximum Temp. (°F)	54.5	59.2	66.7	74.3	81.9	88.5	91.1	89.6	84.1	74.6	66.3	57.1	74.0
Mean Temp. (°F)	43.3	47.0	53.7	61.0	69.2	76.7	79.9	78.8	73.0	62.5	53.7	45.6	62.0
Mean Minimum Temp. (°F)	32.1	34.7	40.6	47.6	56.6	64.8	68.6	68.0	61.9	50.4	41.1	34.1	50.0
Extreme Maximum Temp. (°F)	79	82	88	93	96	102	108	105	99	90	84	79	108
Extreme Minimum Temp. (°F)	-3	8	11	26	37	44	53	52	43	27	21	5	-3
Days Maximum Temp. ≥ 90°F	0	0	0	0	3	12	19	16	6	0	0	0	56
Days Maximum Temp. ≤ 32°F	0	0	0	0	0	0	0	0	0	0	0	0	0
Days Minimum Temp. ≤ 32°F	17	12	7	1	0	0	0	0	0	1	6	15	59
Days Minimum Temp. ≤ 0°F	0	0	0	0	0	0	0	0	0	0	0	0	0
Heating Degree Days (base 65°F)	666	504	353	155	28	1	0	0	9	135	342	596	2,789
Cooling Degree Days (base 65°F)	1	0	9	42	167	358	468	436	256	65	10	1	1,813
Mean Precipitation (in.)	4.46	4.35	5.25	3.14	3.14	4.14	4.07	4.55	3.88	3.66	3.50	3.83	47.97
Extreme Maximum Daily Precip. (in.)	2.40	3.60	5.15	3.95	3.00	4.16	4.65	3.50	7.19	3.87	3.80	3.02	7.19
Days With ≥ 0.1" Precipitation	7	6	6	5	5	6	6	7	5	4	4	6	67
Days With ≥ 0.5" Precipitation	3	3	4	3	2	3	3	3	2	2	2	3	33
Days With ≥ 1.0" Precipitation	2	1	2	1	1	1	1	1	1	1	1	1	14
Mean Snowfall (in.)	0.2	0.0	0.1	0.0	0.0	0.0	0.0	0.0	0.0	0.0	0.0	0.0	0.3
Maximum Snow Depth (in.)	0	0	0	0	0	0	0	0	0	0	0	0	0
Days With ≥ 1.0" Snow Depth	0	0	0	0	0	0	0	0	0	0	0	0	0

West Point *Troup County* Elevation: 575 ft. Latitude: 32° 52' N Longitude: 85° 11' W

	JAN	FEB	MAR	APR	MAY	JUN	JUL	AUG	SEP	OCT	NOV	DEC	YEAR
Mean Maximum Temp. (°F)	55.4	59.8	67.3	74.6	81.9	88.2	91.0	90.0	84.7	75.4	66.9	57.7	74.4
Mean Temp. (°F)	43.8	47.5	54.4	61.2	69.5	76.8	80.2	79.4	73.7	63.0	54.3	46.3	62.5
Mean Minimum Temp. (°F)	32.1	35.1	41.4	47.8	57.0	65.3	69.4	68.8	62.6	50.6	41.8	34.8	50.5
Extreme Maximum Temp. (°F)	80	81	88	91	96	102	106	104	99	91	86	80	106
Extreme Minimum Temp. (°F)	-8	7	13	27	39	44	55	51	41	29	21	2	-8
Days Maximum Temp. ≥ 90°F	0	0	0	0	3	13	20	17	7	0	0	0	60
Days Maximum Temp. ≤ 32°F	0	0	0	0	0	0	0	0	0	0	0	0	0
Days Minimum Temp. ≤ 32°F	18	13	5	1	0	0	0	0	0	0	6	14	57
Days Minimum Temp. ≤ 0°F	0	0	0	0	0	0	0	0	0	0	0	0	0
Heating Degree Days (base 65°F)	651	491	330	148	23	0	0	0	8	122	323	576	2,672
Cooling Degree Days (base 65°F)	0	1	9	42	169	361	479	454	275	68	10	1	1,869
Mean Precipitation (in.)	4.40	4.79	5.40	4.07	3.36	3.81	5.09	3.69	3.54	3.12	4.28	4.49	50.04
Extreme Maximum Daily Precip. (in.)	3.50	4.90	4.60	4.00	6.00	3.50	4.95	3.30	4.33	4.55	3.45	4.00	6.00
Days With ≥ 0.1" Precipitation	6	6	6	5	5	6	7	6	5	4	5	6	67
Days With ≥ 0.5" Precipitation	3	3	3	3	2	3	3	2	2	2	3	3	32
Days With ≥ 1.0" Precipitation	1	2	2	1	1	1	1	1	1	1	2	1	15
Mean Snowfall (in.)	trace	0.0	trace	0.0	0.0	0.0	0.0	0.0	0.0	0.0	0.0	0.1	0.1
Maximum Snow Depth (in.)	0	0	3	0	0	0	0	0	0	0	0	0	3
Days With ≥ 1.0" Snow Depth	0	0	0	0	0	0	0	0	0	0	0	0	0

The period of record for all cooperative weather station data is 1980 – 2009. See User Guide for detailed explanation of data.

Winder 1 SSE *Barrow County* Elevation: 959 ft. Latitude: 33° 59' N Longitude: 83° 43' W

	JAN	FEB	MAR	APR	MAY	JUN	JUL	AUG	SEP	OCT	NOV	DEC	YEAR
Mean Maximum Temp. (°F)	53.1	57.6	65.5	73.6	80.6	86.5	89.7	88.3	82.3	73.3	64.4	54.6	72.5
Mean Temp. (°F)	42.5	46.2	52.7	60.2	67.7	74.9	78.5	77.3	71.5	61.7	52.9	44.2	60.9
Mean Minimum Temp. (°F)	31.9	34.8	39.8	46.7	54.8	63.1	67.2	66.3	60.6	50.2	41.4	33.8	49.2
Extreme Maximum Temp. (°F)	80	79	85	94	93	100	104	103	96	89	84	76	104
Extreme Minimum Temp. (°F)	-8	2	5	24	34	46	51	53	37	27	22	0	-8
Days Maximum Temp. ≥ 90°F	0	0	0	0	2	8	17	12	3	0	0	0	42
Days Maximum Temp. ≤ 32°F	0	0	0	0	0	0	0	0	0	0	0	0	0
Days Minimum Temp. ≤ 32°F	17	12	7	1	0	0	0	0	0	1	6	15	59
Days Minimum Temp. ≤ 0°F	0	0	0	0	0	0	0	0	0	0	0	0	0
Heating Degree Days (base 65°F)	688	524	380	173	38	1	0	0	16	141	361	633	2,955
Cooling Degree Days (base 65°F)	0	0	5	35	130	303	425	390	217	47	5	1	1,558
Mean Precipitation (in.)	4.58	4.44	5.24	3.54	3.47	4.13	3.98	3.78	4.24	3.31	3.71	3.32	47.74
Extreme Maximum Daily Precip. (in.)	3.10	3.36	4.80	4.30	2.42	3.43	5.55	4.51	4.23	4.35	2.46	2.91	5.55
Days With ≥ 0.1" Precipitation	6	6	7	5	5	7	6	6	6	4	5	5	68
Days With ≥ 0.5" Precipitation	3	3	4	3	2	3	3	2	3	2	3	2	33
Days With ≥ 1.0" Precipitation	2	2	2	1	1	1	1	1	1	1	2	1	16
Mean Snowfall (in.)	0.5	0.1	0.0	0.0	0.0	0.0	0.0	0.0	0.0	0.0	0.0	0.2	0.8
Maximum Snow Depth (in.)	2	2	0	0	0	0	0	0	0	0	0	2	2
Days With ≥ 1.0" Snow Depth	0	0	0	0	0	0	0	0	0	0	0	0	0

The period of record for all cooperative weather station data is 1980 – 2009. See User Guide for detailed explanation of data.

Georgia Weather Station Rankings

Annual Extreme Maximum Temperature

Highest

Rank	Station Name	°F
1	Fort Stewart	110
1	Glennville	110
3	Brooklet 1 W	109
3	Dublin	109
5	Augusta Bush Field	108
5	Hartwell	108
5	Macon Middle GA Regional Arpt	108
5	Warrenton	108
9	Albany 3 SE	107
9	Athens Municipal Arpt	107
9	Camilla 3 SE	107
9	Irwinton 4 WNW	107
13	Appling 2 NW	106
13	Brunswick	106
13	Cordele	106
13	Elberton 2 N	106
13	Lafayette 5 SW	106
13	Louisville 1 E	106
13	West Point	106
20	Alma Bacon County Arpt	105
20	Atlanta Hartsfield Intl Arpt	105
20	Commerce 4 NNW	105
20	Covington	***105***
20	Hawkinsville	105
20	Quitman 2 NW	105

Lowest

Rank	Station Name	°F
1	Blairsville Exp Sta	97
2	Clayton 1 SSW	98
3	Experiment	***102***
3	Newnan 4 NE	102
5	Carrollton	103
5	Dalton	***103***
5	Gainesville	103
5	Monticello	103
9	Cartersville	104
9	Cedartown 3 NE	104
9	Columbus Metropolitan Arpt	104
9	Dallas 7 NE	104
9	Talbotton	104
9	U of GA Plant Sci Farm	104
9	Winder 1 SSE	***104***
16	Alma Bacon County Arpt	105
16	Atlanta Hartsfield Intl Arpt	105
16	Commerce 4 NNW	105
16	Covington	***105***
16	Hawkinsville	105
16	Quitman 2 NW	105
16	Rome	105
16	Savannah Intl Arpt	105
16	Surrency 2 WNW	***105***
25	Appling 2 NW	106

Annual Mean Maximum Temperature

Highest

Rank	Station Name	°F
1	Fort Stewart	79.1
2	Cordele	78.6
2	Quitman 2 NW	78.6
4	Surrency 2 WNW	***78.3***
5	Albany 3 SE	78.2
5	Alma Bacon County Arpt	78.2
5	Camilla 3 SE	78.2
8	Brunswick	78.0
8	Glennville	***78.0***
10	Savannah Intl Arpt	77.3
11	Brooklet 1 W	77.1
12	Dublin	77.0
12	Hawkinsville	***77.0***
12	Louisville 1 E	77.0
15	Irwinton 4 WNW	76.9
16	Macon Middle GA Regional Arpt	76.6
17	Augusta Bush Field	76.4
18	Columbus Metropolitan Arpt	76.2
19	Talbotton	***75.1***
20	West Point	74.4
21	Monticello	74.3
22	Appling 2 NW	74.2
23	Warrenton	74.0
24	Athens Municipal Arpt	73.1
25	Covington	***72.9***

Lowest

Rank	Station Name	°F
1	Blairsville Exp Sta	67.8
2	Clayton 1 SSW	69.2
3	Lafayette 5 SW	70.5
4	Gainesville	70.6
5	Dalton	***71.4***
5	Rome	71.4
7	Hartwell	71.7
8	Dallas 7 NE	71.8
8	Elberton 2 N	71.8
10	Carrollton	72.1
11	Atlanta Hartsfield Intl Arpt	72.2
11	Commerce 4 NNW	72.2
13	Cartersville	***72.3***
13	Experiment	***72.3***
15	Winder 1 SSE	***72.5***
16	Cedartown 3 NE	72.8
17	Covington	***72.9***
17	Newnan 4 NE	72.9
17	U of GA Plant Sci Farm	72.9
20	Athens Municipal Arpt	73.1
21	Warrenton	74.0
22	Appling 2 NW	74.2
23	Monticello	74.3
24	West Point	74.4
25	Talbotton	***75.1***

Rankings include 25 highest/lowest stations. If state has less than 25 stations, all stations are included. The period of record is 1980–2009. See User Guide for detailed explanation of data.

Annual Mean Temperature

Highest

Rank	Station Name	°F
1	Brunswick	68.5
2	Fort Stewart	68.0
3	Alma Bacon County Arpt	67.2
4	Cordele	66.9
4	Savannah Intl Arpt	66.9
6	Camilla 3 SE	66.8
7	Glennville	***66.7***
8	Quitman 2 NW	66.4
9	Surrency 2 WNW	***66.1***
10	Brooklet 1 W	66.0
11	Albany 3 SE	65.8
12	Columbus Metropolitan Arpt	65.6
13	Irwinton 4 WNW	***65.2***
14	Hawkinsville	***64.9***
14	Macon Middle GA Regional Arpt	64.9
16	Louisville 1 E	64.8
17	Dublin	64.5
18	Augusta Bush Field	63.9
19	Talbotton	***62.9***
20	Atlanta Hartsfield Intl Arpt	62.7
21	West Point	62.5
22	Athens Municipal Arpt	62.4
23	Monticello	62.3
24	Warrenton	62.0
25	Appling 2 NW	61.6

Lowest

Rank	Station Name	°F
1	Blairsville Exp Sta	55.5
2	Clayton 1 SSW	56.9
3	Lafayette 5 SW	58.7
4	Elberton 2 N	59.5
5	Dallas 7 NE	59.8
6	Rome	60.0
7	Dalton	***60.2***
8	Gainesville	60.3
9	Carrollton	60.5
10	Commerce 4 NNW	60.6
11	Cedartown 3 NE	60.7
12	Winder 1 SSE	***60.9***
13	Cartersville	***61.0***
14	Experiment	***61.2***
15	Covington	***61.5***
15	Newnan 4 NE	61.5
17	Appling 2 NW	61.6
17	Hartwell	61.6
17	U of GA Plant Sci Farm	61.6
20	Warrenton	62.0
21	Monticello	62.3
22	Athens Municipal Arpt	62.4
23	West Point	62.5
24	Atlanta Hartsfield Intl Arpt	62.7
25	Talbotton	***62.9***

Annual Mean Minimum Temperature

Highest

Rank	Station Name	°F
1	Brunswick	58.9
2	Fort Stewart	56.9
3	Savannah Intl Arpt	56.4
4	Alma Bacon County Arpt	56.0
5	Camilla 3 SE	55.4
6	Glennville	***55.3***
7	Cordele	55.2
8	Columbus Metropolitan Arpt	55.0
9	Brooklet 1 W	54.9
10	Quitman 2 NW	54.1
11	Surrency 2 WNW	***53.8***
12	Albany 3 SE	53.3
12	Irwinton 4 WNW	53.3
14	Atlanta Hartsfield Intl Arpt	53.1
14	Macon Middle GA Regional Arpt	53.1
16	Hawkinsville	***52.8***
17	Louisville 1 E	52.6
18	Dublin	51.9
19	Athens Municipal Arpt	51.6
20	Hartwell	51.5
21	Augusta Bush Field	51.3
22	Talbotton	***50.7***
23	West Point	50.6
24	Monticello	50.3
25	U of GA Plant Sci Farm	50.2

Lowest

Rank	Station Name	°F
1	Blairsville Exp Sta	43.1
2	Clayton 1 SSW	44.6
3	Lafayette 5 SW	46.8
4	Elberton 2 N	47.1
5	Dallas 7 NE	47.7
6	Cedartown 3 NE	48.6
6	Rome	48.6
8	Appling 2 NW	48.9
8	Carrollton	48.9
8	Dalton	***48.9***
11	Commerce 4 NNW	49.0
12	Winder 1 SSE	***49.2***
13	Cartersville	***49.6***
14	Gainesville	49.9
14	Newnan 4 NE	49.9
16	Covington	***50.0***
16	Warrenton	50.0
18	Experiment	***50.1***
19	U of GA Plant Sci Farm	50.2
20	Monticello	50.3
21	West Point	50.6
22	Talbotton	***50.7***
23	Augusta Bush Field	51.3
24	Hartwell	51.5
25	Athens Municipal Arpt	51.6

Rankings include 25 highest/lowest stations. If state has less than 25 stations, all stations are included. The period of record is 1980–2009. See User Guide for detailed explanation of data.

Annual Extreme Minimum Temperature

Highest

Rank	Station Name	°F
1	Brunswick	5
2	Quitman 2 NW	3
2	Savannah Intl Arpt	3
4	Camilla 3 SE	2
5	Albany 3 SE	1
5	Brooklet 1 W	1
5	Glennville	1
5	Surrency 2 WNW	*1*
9	Dublin	0
9	Fort Stewart	0
11	Alma Bacon County Arpt	-1
11	Augusta Bush Field	-1
11	U of GA Plant Sci Farm	-1
14	Columbus Metropolitan Arpt	-2
14	Hawkinsville	-2
14	Louisville 1 E	-2
17	Cordele	-3
17	Warrenton	-3
19	Appling 2 NW	-4
19	Athens Municipal Arpt	-4
19	Irwinton 4 WNW	-4
22	Commerce 4 NNW	-5
22	Elberton 2 N	-5
22	Hartwell	-5
22	Talbotton	-5

Lowest

Rank	Station Name	°F
1	Blairsville Exp Sta	-16
2	Lafayette 5 SW	-13
3	Dallas 7 NE	-12
4	Clayton 1 SSW	-11
5	Dalton	***-10***
6	Carrollton	-9
6	Cartersville	-9
6	Cedartown 3 NE	-9
6	Rome	-9
10	Atlanta Hartsfield Intl Arpt	-8
10	Experiment	***-8***
10	Gainesville	-8
10	Newnan 4 NE	-8
10	West Point	-8
10	Winder 1 SSE	***-8***
16	Covington	***-7***
16	Monticello	-7
18	Macon Middle GA Regional Arpt	-6
19	Commerce 4 NNW	-5
19	Elberton 2 N	-5
19	Hartwell	-5
19	Talbotton	-5
23	Appling 2 NW	-4
23	Athens Municipal Arpt	-4
23	Irwinton 4 WNW	-4

July Mean Maximum Temperature

Highest

Rank	Station Name	°F
1	Cordele	94.6
2	Dublin	94.0
3	Fort Stewart	93.4
4	Albany 3 SE	93.1
5	Glennville	***93.0***
5	Hawkinsville	***93.0***
5	Irwinton 4 WNW	93.0
8	Augusta Bush Field	92.9
8	Louisville 1 E	92.9
10	Macon Middle GA Regional Arpt	92.8
11	Brooklet 1 W	92.7
11	Surrency 2 WNW	***92.7***
13	Brunswick	92.5
13	Savannah Intl Arpt	92.5
15	Alma Bacon County Arpt	92.4
16	Columbus Metropolitan Arpt	92.2
17	Quitman 2 NW	92.0
18	Camilla 3 SE	91.9
19	Warrenton	91.1
20	Appling 2 NW	91.0
20	Athens Municipal Arpt	91.0
20	West Point	91.0
23	U of GA Plant Sci Farm	90.8
24	Covington	90.6
24	Monticello	90.6

Lowest

Rank	Station Name	°F
1	Blairsville Exp Sta	84.5
2	Clayton 1 SSW	85.4
3	Gainesville	88.1
4	Carrollton	88.6
4	Rome	88.6
6	Lafayette 5 SW	88.7
7	Elberton 2 N	88.8
8	Newnan 4 NE	89.0
9	Hartwell	89.1
10	Experiment	***89.4***
11	Cartersville	89.6
11	Dallas 7 NE	89.6
11	Dalton	***89.6***
14	Atlanta Hartsfield Intl Arpt	89.7
14	Winder 1 SSE	89.7
16	Commerce 4 NNW	89.9
16	Talbotton	89.9
18	Cedartown 3 NE	90.1
19	Covington	90.6
19	Monticello	90.6
21	U of GA Plant Sci Farm	90.8
22	Appling 2 NW	91.0
22	Athens Municipal Arpt	91.0
22	West Point	91.0
25	Warrenton	91.1

Rankings include 25 highest/lowest stations. If state has less than 25 stations, all stations are included. The period of record is 1980–2009. See User Guide for detailed explanation of data.

January Mean Minimum Temperature

Highest			Lowest		
Rank	Station Name	°F	Rank	Station Name	°F
1	Brunswick	41.5	1	Blairsville Exp Sta	24.8
2	Fort Stewart	40.6	2	Clayton 1 SSW	27.8
3	Alma Bacon County Arpt	40.1	3	Lafayette 5 SW	28.6
4	Savannah Intl Arpt	39.2	4	Dallas 7 NE	29.2
5	Camilla 3 SE	38.7	4	Elberton 2 N	29.2
6	Glennville	38.4	6	Dalton	***29.8***
7	Cordele	38.2	7	Rome	30.0
8	Brooklet 1 W	38.0	8	Appling 2 NW	30.8
8	Surrency 2 WNW	***38.0***	9	Cedartown 3 NE	30.9
10	Quitman 2 NW	37.6	10	Commerce 4 NNW	31.1
11	Columbus Metropolitan Arpt	37.2	11	Carrollton	31.3
12	Irwinton 4 WNW	35.9	12	Cartersville	31.7
13	Macon Middle GA Regional Arpt	35.6	12	Covington	31.7
14	Albany 3 SE	35.3	14	Experiment	***31.8***
15	Louisville 1 E	35.2	14	Gainesville	31.8
16	Hawkinsville	34.8	16	Winder 1 SSE	31.9
17	Atlanta Hartsfield Intl Arpt	34.5	17	Warrenton	32.1
18	Dublin	34.3	17	West Point	32.1
19	Talbotton	33.9	19	U of GA Plant Sci Farm	32.2
20	Athens Municipal Arpt	33.5	20	Monticello	32.5
21	Augusta Bush Field	33.4	20	Newnan 4 NE	32.5
22	Hartwell	33.0	22	Hartwell	33.0
23	Monticello	32.5	23	Augusta Bush Field	33.4
23	Newnan 4 NE	32.5	24	Athens Municipal Arpt	33.5
25	U of GA Plant Sci Farm	32.2	25	Talbotton	33.9

Number of Days Annually Maximum Temperature ≥ 90°F

Highest			Lowest		
Rank	Station Name	Days	Rank	Station Name	Days
1	Cordele	103	1	Blairsville Exp Sta	9
2	Albany 3 SE	91	2	Clayton 1 SSW	12
3	Fort Stewart	90	3	Gainesville	31
4	Dublin	89	4	Carrollton	33
5	Alma Bacon County Arpt	86	5	Elberton 2 N	37
6	Quitman 2 NW	85	5	Lafayette 5 SW	37
7	Hawkinsville	84	7	Newnan 4 NE	38
8	Macon Middle GA Regional Arpt	83	8	Hartwell	39
9	Augusta Bush Field	82	8	Rome	39
9	Glennville	82	10	Experiment	***41***
11	Louisville 1 E	80	11	Cartersville	42
11	Surrency 2 WNW	***80***	11	Winder 1 SSE	***42***
13	Irwinton 4 WNW	79	13	Atlanta Hartsfield Intl Arpt	43
14	Brooklet 1 W	78	13	Dalton	***43***
14	Camilla 3 SE	78	15	Commerce 4 NNW	44
16	Columbus Metropolitan Arpt	77	16	Dallas 7 NE	48
17	Savannah Intl Arpt	76	17	Cedartown 3 NE	50
18	Brunswick	72	18	Covington	***52***
19	West Point	60	19	Talbotton	54
20	Appling 2 NW	59	20	Monticello	55
21	Athens Municipal Arpt	57	20	U of GA Plant Sci Farm	55
22	Warrenton	56	22	Warrenton	56
23	Monticello	55	23	Athens Municipal Arpt	57
23	U of GA Plant Sci Farm	55	24	Appling 2 NW	59
25	Talbotton	54	25	West Point	60

Number of Days Annually Maximum Temperature ≤ 32°F

Highest			Lowest		
Rank	Station Name	Days	Rank	Station Name	Days
1	Blairsville Exp Sta	4	1	Albany 3 SE	0
1	Dalton	*4*	1	Alma Bacon County Arpt	0
1	Lafayette 5 SW	4	1	Appling 2 NW	0
4	Dallas 7 NE	3	1	Augusta Bush Field	0
4	Gainesville	3	1	Brooklet 1 W	0
6	Rome	2	1	Brunswick	0
7	Athens Municipal Arpt	1	1	Camilla 3 SE	0
7	Atlanta Hartsfield Intl Arpt	1	1	Columbus Metropolitan Arpt	0
7	Carrollton	1	1	Cordele	0
7	Cartersville	1	1	Dublin	0
7	Cedartown 3 NE	1	1	Elberton 2 N	0
7	Clayton 1 SSW	1	1	Fort Stewart	0
7	Commerce 4 NNW	1	1	Glennville	0
7	Covington	*1*	1	Hawkinsville	0
7	Experiment	*1*	1	Irwinton 4 WNW	0
7	Hartwell	1	1	Louisville 1 E	0
7	Newnan 4 NE	1	1	Macon Middle GA Regional Arpt	0
7	U of GA Plant Sci Farm	1	1	Monticello	0
19	Albany 3 SE	0	1	Quitman 2 NW	0
19	Alma Bacon County Arpt	0	1	Savannah Intl Arpt	0
19	Appling 2 NW	0	1	Surrency 2 WNW	*0*
19	Augusta Bush Field	0	1	Talbotton	0
19	Brooklet 1 W	0	1	Warrenton	0
19	Brunswick	0	1	West Point	0
19	Camilla 3 SE	0	1	Winder 1 SSE	*0*

Number of Days Annually Minimum Temperature ≤ 32°F

Highest			Lowest		
Rank	Station Name	Days	Rank	Station Name	Days
1	Blairsville Exp Sta	108	1	Brunswick	12
2	Clayton 1 SSW	91	2	Fort Stewart	20
3	Elberton 2 N	84	3	Savannah Intl Arpt	23
4	Lafayette 5 SW	82	4	Alma Bacon County Arpt	24
5	Dallas 7 NE	80	5	Brooklet 1 W	28
6	Rome	72	5	Glennville	28
7	Appling 2 NW	71	7	Cordele	29
8	Cedartown 3 NE	70	8	Camilla 3 SE	30
9	Carrollton	65	8	Columbus Metropolitan Arpt	30
9	Dalton	*65*	8	Quitman 2 NW	30
11	Commerce 4 NNW	64	11	Irwinton 4 WNW	33
12	Cartersville	61	12	Surrency 2 WNW	*36*
12	Covington	*61*	13	Atlanta Hartsfield Intl Arpt	39
14	Newnan 4 NE	60	14	Hawkinsville	42
15	Warrenton	59	15	Albany 3 SE	43
15	Winder 1 SSE	*59*	15	Macon Middle GA Regional Arpt	43
17	Monticello	58	17	Hartwell	45
18	West Point	57	17	Louisville 1 E	45
19	Experiment	*56*	19	Athens Municipal Arpt	48
19	U of GA Plant Sci Farm	56	20	Dublin	49
21	Gainesville	55	21	Augusta Bush Field	53
22	Talbotton	54	22	Talbotton	54
23	Augusta Bush Field	53	23	Gainesville	55
24	Dublin	49	24	Experiment	*56*
25	Athens Municipal Arpt	48	24	U of GA Plant Sci Farm	56

 Rankings include 25 highest/lowest stations. If state has less than 25 stations, all stations are included. The period of record is 1980–2009. See User Guide for detailed explanation of data.

Number of Days Annually Minimum Temperature ≤ 0°F

Highest			Lowest		
Rank	Station Name	Days	Rank	Station Name	Days
1	Albany 3 SE	0	1	Albany 3 SE	0
1	Alma Bacon County Arpt	0	1	Alma Bacon County Arpt	0
1	Appling 2 NW	0	1	Appling 2 NW	0
1	Athens Municipal Arpt	0	1	Athens Municipal Arpt	0
1	Atlanta Hartsfield Intl Arpt	0	1	Atlanta Hartsfield Intl Arpt	0
1	Augusta Bush Field	0	1	Augusta Bush Field	0
1	Blairsville Exp Sta	0	1	Blairsville Exp Sta	0
1	Brooklet 1 W	0	1	Brooklet 1 W	0
1	Brunswick	0	1	Brunswick	0
1	Camilla 3 SE	0	1	Camilla 3 SE	0
1	Carrollton	0	1	Carrollton	0
1	Cartersville	0	1	Cartersville	0
1	Cedartown 3 NE	0	1	Cedartown 3 NE	0
1	Clayton 1 SSW	0	1	Clayton 1 SSW	0
1	Columbus Metropolitan Arpt	0	1	Columbus Metropolitan Arpt	0
1	Commerce 4 NNW	0	1	Commerce 4 NNW	0
1	Cordele	0	1	Cordele	0
1	Covington	***0***	1	Covington	***0***
1	Dallas 7 NE	0	1	Dallas 7 NE	0
1	Dalton	***0***	1	Dalton	***0***
1	Dublin	0	1	Dublin	0
1	Elberton 2 N	0	1	Elberton 2 N	0
1	Experiment	***0***	1	Experiment	***0***
1	Fort Stewart	0	1	Fort Stewart	0
1	Gainesville	0	1	Gainesville	0

Number of Annual Heating Degree Days

Highest			Lowest		
Rank	Station Name	Num.	Rank	Station Name	Num.
1	Blairsville Exp Sta	4,209	1	Brunswick	1,404
2	Clayton 1 SSW	3,779	2	Fort Stewart	1,485
3	Lafayette 5 SW	3,563	3	Alma Bacon County Arpt	1,614
4	Elberton 2 N	3,345	4	Camilla 3 SE	1,707
5	Dallas 7 NE	3,339	5	Savannah Intl Arpt	1,741
6	Dalton	***3,287***	6	Quitman 2 NW	1,753
7	Rome	3,268	7	Glennville	***1,770***
8	Gainesville	3,129	8	Surrency 2 WNW	***1,778***
9	Cedartown 3 NE	3,094	9	Cordele	1,831
10	Commerce 4 NNW	3,092	10	Brooklet 1 W	1,893
11	Carrollton	3,041	11	Albany 3 SE	2,011
12	Cartersville	***2,999***	12	Columbus Metropolitan Arpt	2,066
13	Winder 1 SSE	***2,955***	13	Irwinton 4 WNW	***2,089***
14	Covington	***2,946***	14	Louisville 1 E	2,188
15	U of GA Plant Sci Farm	2,906	15	Hawkinsville	***2,198***
16	Experiment	***2,901***	16	Macon Middle GA Regional Arpt	2,213
17	Appling 2 NW	2,884	17	Dublin	2,318
18	Hartwell	2,858	18	Augusta Bush Field	2,430
19	Newnan 4 NE	2,829	19	Talbotton	***2,458***
20	Warrenton	2,789	20	West Point	2,672
21	Athens Municipal Arpt	2,750	21	Atlanta Hartsfield Intl Arpt	2,680
22	Monticello	2,696	22	Monticello	2,696
23	Atlanta Hartsfield Intl Arpt	2,680	23	Athens Municipal Arpt	2,750
24	West Point	2,672	24	Warrenton	2,789
25	Talbotton	***2,458***	25	Newnan 4 NE	2,829

Rankings include 25 highest/lowest stations. If state has less than 25 stations, all stations are included. The period of record is 1980–2009. See User Guide for detailed explanation of data.

Number of Annual Cooling Degree Days

Highest Rank	Station Name	Num.	Lowest Rank	Station Name	Num.
1	Brunswick	2,791	1	Blairsville Exp Sta	835
2	Fort Stewart	2,687	2	Clayton 1 SSW	929
3	Cordele	2,626	3	Lafayette 5 SW	1,361
4	Savannah Intl Arpt	2,535	4	Elberton 2 N	1,436
5	Alma Bacon County Arpt	2,506	5	Carrollton	1,497
6	Glennville	***2,487***	6	Gainesville	1,520
7	Camilla 3 SE	2,472	7	Dallas 7 NE	1,541
8	Columbus Metropolitan Arpt	2,405	8	Rome	1,550
9	Albany 3 SE	2,392	9	Winder 1 SSE	***1,558***
10	Brooklet 1 W	2,375	10	Commerce 4 NNW	1,601
11	Quitman 2 NW	2,348	11	Experiment	***1,633***
12	Surrency 2 WNW	***2,276***	12	Newnan 4 NE	1,638
13	Hawkinsville	***2,266***	13	Dalton	***1,641***
14	Macon Middle GA Regional Arpt	2,265	14	Cedartown 3 NE	1,642
15	Irwinton 4 WNW	***2,255***	15	Cartersville	***1,645***
16	Louisville 1 E	2,230	16	Hartwell	1,716
17	Dublin	2,229	17	Appling 2 NW	1,741
18	Augusta Bush Field	2,119	18	U of GA Plant Sci Farm	1,759
19	Atlanta Hartsfield Intl Arpt	1,942	19	Covington	***1,760***
20	Athens Municipal Arpt	1,891	20	Talbotton	***1,798***
21	West Point	1,869	21	Warrenton	1,813
22	Monticello	1,818	22	Monticello	1,818
23	Warrenton	1,813	23	West Point	1,869
24	Talbotton	***1,798***	24	Athens Municipal Arpt	1,891
25	Covington	***1,760***	25	Atlanta Hartsfield Intl Arpt	1,942

Annual Precipitation

Highest Rank	Station Name	Inches	Lowest Rank	Station Name	Inches
1	Clayton 1 SSW	68.83	1	Cartersville	***39.98***
2	Lafayette 5 SW	58.36	2	Augusta Bush Field	43.92
3	Blairsville Exp Sta	56.11	3	Irwinton 4 WNW	44.54
4	Dalton	***55.33***	4	Louisville 1 E	44.87
5	Rome	54.44	5	Macon Middle GA Regional Arpt	45.12
6	Gainesville	53.62	6	Monticello	45.45
7	Dallas 7 NE	53.45	7	Brooklet 1 W	45.65
8	Quitman 2 NW	***52.08***	8	Surrency 2 WNW	***45.69***
9	Camilla 3 SE	51.96	9	Appling 2 NW	45.94
10	Cedartown 3 NE	51.76	10	Cordele	45.99
11	Carrollton	51.64	11	Hawkinsville	46.08
12	Albany 3 SE	51.60	12	Dublin	46.29
13	Commerce 4 NNW	50.54	13	Athens Municipal Arpt	46.32
14	Brunswick	50.11	14	Glennville	46.40
15	West Point	50.04	15	Columbus Metropolitan Arpt	47.13
16	Newnan 4 NE	49.96	16	Alma Bacon County Arpt	47.24
17	Hartwell	49.72	17	Winder 1 SSE	***47.74***
18	Atlanta Hartsfield Intl Arpt	49.63	18	Savannah Intl Arpt	47.90
19	U of GA Plant Sci Farm	49.59	19	Warrenton	47.97
20	Talbotton	49.36	20	Elberton 2 N	48.05
21	Covington	***49.04***	21	Fort Stewart	48.71
22	Experiment	***48.82***	22	Experiment	***48.82***
23	Fort Stewart	48.71	23	Covington	***49.04***
24	Elberton 2 N	48.05	24	Talbotton	49.36
25	Warrenton	47.97	25	U of GA Plant Sci Farm	49.59

 Rankings include 25 highest/lowest stations. If state has less than 25 stations, all stations are included. The period of record is 1980–2009. See User Guide for detailed explanation of data.

Annual Extreme Maximum Daily Precipitation

Highest			Lowest		
Rank	Station Name	Inches	Rank	Station Name	Inches
1	Louisville 1 E	16.42	1	Cedartown 3 NE	5.08
2	Clayton 1 SSW	12.75	2	U of GA Plant Sci Farm	5.21
3	Experiment	***10.50***	3	Irwinton 4 WNW	***5.29***
4	Quitman 2 NW	***9.51***	4	Blairsville Exp Sta	5.30
5	Appling 2 NW	9.50	4	Macon Middle GA Regional Arpt	5.30
6	Cordele	9.28	6	Monticello	5.50
7	Talbotton	9.00	7	Winder 1 SSE	***5.55***
8	Elberton 2 N	8.79	8	Dublin	5.70
9	Dallas 7 NE	8.43	9	Columbus Metropolitan Arpt	5.74
10	Surrency 2 WNW	***8.03***	10	Alma Bacon County Arpt	5.84
11	Glennville	***7.90***	11	Albany 3 SE	6.00
12	Carrollton	7.66	11	Cartersville	***6.00***
13	Athens Municipal Arpt	7.34	11	Fort Stewart	6.00
14	Augusta Bush Field	7.30	11	West Point	6.00
15	Hawkinsville	7.28	15	Gainesville	6.04
16	Lafayette 5 SW	7.25	16	Covington	***6.07***
17	Hartwell	7.20	17	Camilla 3 SE	6.20
18	Warrenton	7.19	18	Commerce 4 NNW	6.32
19	Savannah Intl Arpt	7.12	19	Brunswick	6.53
20	Newnan 4 NE	6.98	20	Brooklet 1 W	6.57
21	Atlanta Hartsfield Intl Arpt	6.68	21	Rome	6.67
22	Rome	6.67	22	Atlanta Hartsfield Intl Arpt	6.68
23	Brooklet 1 W	6.57	23	Newnan 4 NE	6.98
24	Brunswick	6.53	24	Savannah Intl Arpt	7.12
25	Commerce 4 NNW	6.32	25	Warrenton	7.19

Number of Days Annually With ≥ 0.1 Inches of Precipitation

Highest			Lowest		
Rank	Station Name	Days	Rank	Station Name	Days
1	Clayton 1 SSW	90	1	Quitman 2 NW	48
2	Blairsville Exp Sta	89	2	Cartersville	***55***
3	Lafayette 5 SW	83	3	Irwinton 4 WNW	66
4	Gainesville	82	4	Glennville	67
5	Dallas 7 NE	80	4	Warrenton	67
5	Dalton	***80***	4	West Point	67
5	Rome	80	7	Appling 2 NW	68
8	Experiment	***78***	7	Augusta Bush Field	68
9	Commerce 4 NNW	77	7	Louisville 1 E	68
10	Cedartown 3 NE	76	7	Winder 1 SSE	***68***
10	Covington	***76***	11	Hartwell	69
12	Atlanta Hartsfield Intl Arpt	75	11	Hawkinsville	69
12	Newnan 4 NE	75	11	Monticello	69
12	U of GA Plant Sci Farm	75	11	Talbotton	69
15	Albany 3 SE	74	15	Camilla 3 SE	70
15	Carrollton	74	15	Cordele	70
15	Elberton 2 N	74	15	Dublin	70
18	Brunswick	73	15	Savannah Intl Arpt	70
18	Fort Stewart	73	19	Alma Bacon County Arpt	71
20	Athens Municipal Arpt	72	19	Brooklet 1 W	71
20	Surrency 2 WNW	***72***	19	Columbus Metropolitan Arpt	71
22	Alma Bacon County Arpt	71	19	Macon Middle GA Regional Arpt	71
22	Brooklet 1 W	71	23	Athens Municipal Arpt	72
22	Columbus Metropolitan Arpt	71	23	Surrency 2 WNW	***72***
22	Macon Middle GA Regional Arpt	71	25	Brunswick	73

Rankings include 25 highest/lowest stations. If state has less than 25 stations, all stations are included. The period of record is 1980–2009. See User Guide for detailed explanation of data.

Number of Days Annually With ≥ 0.5 Inches of Precipitation

Highest			Lowest		
Rank	Station Name	Days	Rank	Station Name	Days
1	Clayton 1 SSW	44	1	Cartersville	***27***
2	Lafayette 5 SW	39	2	Irwinton 4 WNW	29
3	Dalton	***38***	3	Augusta Bush Field	30
3	Gainesville	38	3	Cordele	30
3	Rome	38	3	Hartwell	30
6	Blairsville Exp Sta	37	3	Hawkinsville	30
7	Carrollton	36	3	Macon Middle GA Regional Arpt	30
7	Dallas 7 NE	36	8	Athens Municipal Arpt	31
9	Newnan 4 NE	35	8	Brooklet 1 W	31
10	Albany 3 SE	34	8	Glennville	31
10	Atlanta Hartsfield Intl Arpt	34	8	Louisville 1 E	31
10	Camilla 3 SE	34	8	Savannah Intl Arpt	31
10	Cedartown 3 NE	34	13	Alma Bacon County Arpt	32
10	Commerce 4 NNW	34	13	Brunswick	32
10	Covington	***34***	13	Columbus Metropolitan Arpt	32
10	Dublin	34	13	Monticello	32
10	Talbotton	34	13	Quitman 2 NW	32
10	U of GA Plant Sci Farm	34	13	Surrency 2 WNW	***32***
19	Appling 2 NW	33	13	West Point	32
19	Elberton 2 N	33	20	Appling 2 NW	33
19	Experiment	***33***	20	Elberton 2 N	33
19	Fort Stewart	33	20	Experiment	***33***
19	Warrenton	33	20	Fort Stewart	33
19	Winder 1 SSE	***33***	20	Warrenton	33
25	Alma Bacon County Arpt	32	20	Winder 1 SSE	***33***

Number of Days Annually With ≥ 1.0 Inches of Precipitation

Highest			Lowest		
Rank	Station Name	Days	Rank	Station Name	Days
1	Clayton 1 SSW	23	1	Alma Bacon County Arpt	13
2	Dalton	***19***	1	Athens Municipal Arpt	13
3	Lafayette 5 SW	18	1	Augusta Bush Field	13
4	Albany 3 SE	17	1	Cartersville	***13***
4	Blairsville Exp Sta	17	1	Cedartown 3 NE	13
4	Camilla 3 SE	17	1	Columbus Metropolitan Arpt	13
4	Dallas 7 NE	17	1	Covington	***13***
4	Quitman 2 NW	17	1	Elberton 2 N	13
9	Appling 2 NW	16	1	Experiment	***13***
9	Brunswick	16	1	Glennville	13
9	Fort Stewart	16	1	Hawkinsville	13
9	Gainesville	16	1	Irwinton 4 WNW	13
9	Winder 1 SSE	***16***	1	Louisville 1 E	13
14	Carrollton	15	1	Macon Middle GA Regional Arpt	13
14	Commerce 4 NNW	15	1	Monticello	13
14	Dublin	15	1	U of GA Plant Sci Farm	13
14	Hartwell	15	17	Atlanta Hartsfield Intl Arpt	14
14	Rome	15	17	Brooklet 1 W	14
14	Savannah Intl Arpt	15	17	Cordele	14
14	Surrency 2 WNW	***15***	17	Newnan 4 NE	14
14	Talbotton	15	17	Warrenton	14
14	West Point	15	22	Carrollton	15
23	Atlanta Hartsfield Intl Arpt	14	22	Commerce 4 NNW	15
23	Brooklet 1 W	14	22	Dublin	15
23	Cordele	14	22	Hartwell	15

Rankings include 25 highest/lowest stations. If state has less than 25 stations, all stations are included. The period of record is 1980–2009. See User Guide for detailed explanation of data.

Annual Snowfall

Highest Rank	Station Name	Inches	Lowest Rank	Station Name	Inches
1	Dallas 7 NE	3.6	1	Brunswick	0.0
2	Blairsville Exp Sta	3.0	1	Camilla 3 SE	0.0
3	Clayton 1 SSW	2.7	1	Cordele	0.0
4	Dalton	*2.3*	4	Albany 3 SE	Trace
5	Cedartown 3 NE	2.1	5	Brooklet 1 W	0.1
5	Gainesville	2.1	5	Dublin	0.1
7	Lafayette 5 SW	2.0	5	Elberton 2 N	0.1
8	Newnan 4 NE	1.7	5	Fort Stewart	0.1
9	Covington	*1.4*	5	Glennville	0.1
10	Hartwell	1.2	5	Quitman 2 NW	0.1
10	Rome	1.2	5	Surrency 2 WNW	*0.1*
12	Commerce 4 NNW	0.9	5	West Point	0.1
13	Augusta Bush Field	*0.8*	13	Appling 2 NW	0.2
13	Winder 1 SSE	*0.8*	13	Hawkinsville	0.2
15	Cartersville	0.7	13	Irwinton 4 WNW	0.2
15	U of GA Plant Sci Farm	0.7	13	Louisville 1 E	0.2
17	Experiment	*0.6*	17	Talbotton	0.3
18	Monticello	0.5	17	Warrenton	0.3
19	Carrollton	0.4	19	Carrollton	0.4
19	Savannah Intl Arpt	*0.4*	19	Savannah Intl Arpt	*0.4*
21	Talbotton	0.3	21	Monticello	0.5
21	Warrenton	0.3	22	Experiment	*0.6*
23	Appling 2 NW	0.2	23	Cartersville	0.7
23	Hawkinsville	0.2	23	U of GA Plant Sci Farm	0.7
23	Irwinton 4 WNW	0.2	25	Augusta Bush Field	*0.8*

Annual Maximum Snow Depth

Highest Rank	Station Name	Inches	Lowest Rank	Station Name	Inches
1	Cedartown 3 NE	15	1	Brunswick	0
2	Clayton 1 SSW	14	1	Camilla 3 SE	0
2	Rome	14	1	Cordele	0
4	Elberton 2 N	10	1	U of GA Plant Sci Farm	0
5	Dallas 7 NE	9	1	Warrenton	0
6	Commerce 4 NNW	7	6	Albany 3 SE	Trace
6	Hartwell	7	6	Dublin	Trace
6	Newnan 4 NE	*7*	6	Glennville	Trace
9	Covington	*6*	6	Hawkinsville	Trace
10	Atlanta Hartsfield Intl Arpt	5	6	Irwinton 4 WNW	Trace
10	Experiment	*5*	6	Quitman 2 NW	Trace
12	Appling 2 NW	4	6	Surrency 2 WNW	Trace
12	Augusta Bush Field	*4*	13	Brooklet 1 W	1
12	Dalton	*4*	14	Blairsville Exp Sta	2
12	Fort Stewart	4	14	Cartersville	2
12	Gainesville	4	14	Lafayette 5 SW	*2*
12	Savannah Intl Arpt	*4*	14	Talbotton	2
18	Carrollton	3	14	Winder 1 SSE	*2*
18	Louisville 1 E	3	19	Carrollton	3
18	Monticello	3	19	Louisville 1 E	3
18	West Point	3	19	Monticello	3
22	Blairsville Exp Sta	2	19	West Point	3
22	Cartersville	2	23	Appling 2 NW	4
22	Lafayette 5 SW	*2*	23	Augusta Bush Field	*4*
22	Talbotton	2	23	Dalton	*4*

Rankings include 25 highest/lowest stations. If state has less than 25 stations, all stations are included. The period of record is 1980–2009. See User Guide for detailed explanation of data.

Number of Days Annually With ≥ 1.0 Inch Snow Depth

Highest

Rank	Station Name	Days
1	Atlanta Hartsfield Intl Arpt	1
1	Cedartown 3 NE	1
1	Covington	*1*
1	Dallas 7 NE	1
1	Newnan 4 NE	*1*
6	Albany 3 SE	0
6	Appling 2 NW	0
6	Augusta Bush Field	*0*
6	Blairsville Exp Sta	0
6	Brooklet 1 W	0
6	Brunswick	0
6	Camilla 3 SE	0
6	Carrollton	0
6	Cartersville	0
6	Clayton 1 SSW	0
6	Commerce 4 NNW	0
6	Cordele	0
6	Dalton	*0*
6	Dublin	0
6	Elberton 2 N	0
6	Experiment	*0*
6	Fort Stewart	0
6	Gainesville	0
6	Glennville	0
6	Hartwell	0

Lowest

Rank	Station Name	Days
1	Albany 3 SE	0
1	Appling 2 NW	0
1	Augusta Bush Field	*0*
1	Blairsville Exp Sta	0
1	Brooklet 1 W	0
1	Brunswick	0
1	Camilla 3 SE	0
1	Carrollton	0
1	Cartersville	0
1	Clayton 1 SSW	0
1	Commerce 4 NNW	0
1	Cordele	0
1	Dalton	*0*
1	Dublin	0
1	Elberton 2 N	0
1	Experiment	*0*
1	Fort Stewart	0
1	Gainesville	0
1	Glennville	0
1	Hartwell	0
1	Hawkinsville	0
1	Irwinton 4 WNW	0
1	Lafayette 5 SW	0
1	Louisville 1 E	0
1	Monticello	0

Rankings include 25 highest/lowest stations. If state has less than 25 stations, all stations are included. The period of record is 1980–2009. See User Guide for detailed explanation of data.

Significant Storm Events in Georgia: 2000 – 2009

Location or County	Date	Type	Mag.	Deaths	Injuries	Property Damage ($mil.)	Crop Damage ($mil.)
Northern Georgia	01/22/00	Ice Storm	na	0	1	48.0	0.0
Mitchell	02/13/00	Tornado	F3	11	175	20.0	2.0
Grady	02/14/00	Tornado	F3	6	15	3.5	3.0
Tift	02/14/00	Tornado	F2	0	10	2.0	0.0
Fulton	07/23/00	Thunderstorm Wind	na	0	0	8.0	0.0
Gordon	05/01/02	Thunderstorm Wind	100 mph	0	0	11.6	0.0
Pickens	11/11/02	Tornado	F2	0	10	5.6	0.0
Mitchell	03/20/03	Tornado	F3	4	200	6.0	0.0
Troup	05/07/03	Flash Flood	na	1	0	10.0	0.0
North and Central Georgia	09/06/04	High Wind	41 mph	0	0	14.0	26.5
Fulton	09/16/04	Flash Flood	na	0	0	20.0	0.0
Northern Georgia	09/16/04	High Wind	75 mph	0	2	14.2	0.0
North and Central Georgia	01/28/05	Winter Storm	na	0	0	9.7	0.0
Miller	03/22/05	Tornado	F3	0	10	5.5	0.0
Henry	07/06/05	Tornado	F2	0	0	70.0	0.0
Sumter	03/01/07	Tornado	F3	2	8	110.0	0.0
Muscogee	03/01/07	Tornado	F2	0	1	28.0	0.0
Baker	03/01/07	Tornado	F2	6	3	1.2	0.0
Charlton and Ware Counties	05/01/07	Wildfire	na	0	0	21.7	0.0
Carroll	02/26/08	Tornado	F3	0	1	8.0	0.0
Fulton	03/14/08	Tornado	F2	1	30	25.0	0.0
Johnson	05/11/08	Tornado	F1	0	5	15.0	0.0
Mcintosh	05/11/08	Tornado	F4	0	9	12.5	0.0
Cherokee	05/20/08	Tornado	F1	0	4	46.0	0.0
Fayette	02/18/09	Hail	3.00 in.	0	0	8.0	0.0
Thomas	02/19/09	Tornado	F2	0	0	10.0	0.0
Richmond	04/10/09	Tornado	F3	0	12	5.0	0.0

Note: Deaths, injuries, and damages are date and location specific.

HAWAII

PHYSICAL FEATURES. West and south of California, 2,100 miles away, lies Hawaii. Among the 50 states it is the only one surrounded by the ocean. It is the only state within the tropics. Both of these facts contribute significantly to its climate, as do also its division into separate, widely-spaced islands and its topographic diversity.

The islands of the State are the easternmost members of the Hawaiian Island Chain. This Chain extends for a distance of 2,000 miles from the Kure and Midway Islands at the northwest to the Island of Hawaii at the extreme southeast end. In longitude, the Hawaiian Chain reaches from 178° to 154° W.; in latitude, from 28° to 19° N. The islands of the State of Hawaii cover a far lesser range: from 160° to 154° W. and from 22° to 19° N. They occupy a narrow zone 430 miles long. There are six major islands in the State. From west to east these are Kauai, Oahu, Molokai, Lanai, Maui, and Hawaii. Taken together with the much smaller islands of Niihau and Kahoolawe, their total area is 6,424 square miles. The islands are terrestrial, summit portions of the long range of volcanic mountains that comprise the Hawaiian Chain. The mountainous nature of Hawaii is indicated by the fact that 50 percent of the State lies above an elevation of 2,000 feet and 10 percent lies above 7,000 feet. Almost half of the area of Hawaii lies within five miles of the coast. Because of this extreme insularity the marine influence upon the climate is very great, yet the mountains, especially the massive ones on Hawaii and Maui, strongly modify the marine effect and result in conditions that are semi-continental in some localities.

GENERAL CLIMATE. The most prominent feature of the circulation of air across the tropical Pacific is the trade-wind flow in a general east-to-west direction. In the central North Pacific the trade winds blow from the northeast quadrant, and represent the outflow of air from the great region of high pressure, the Pacific Anticyclone, whose typical location is well north and east of the Hawaiian Island Chain. The Pacific High, and with it the trade-wind zone, moves north and south with the sun, so that it reaches its northernmost position in the summer half-year. This brings the heart of the trade winds across Hawaii during the period May through September, when the trades are prevalent 80 to 95 percent of the time. From October through April, Hawaii is located to the north of the heart of the trade winds. Nevertheless, the trades still blow across the islands much of the time.

The dominance of the trades and the influence of terrain give special character to the climate of the Islands. Completely cloudless skies are extremely rare, even though much of the time the dense cloud cover is confined to the mountain areas and windward slopes, while the leeward lowlands have only a few scattered clouds. Showers are very common; while some of these are very heavy, the vast majority are light and brief — a sudden sprinkle of rain. Even the heavy showers are of a special character, in that they are seldom accompanied by thunder and lightning. Finally, the trade winds provide a system of natural ventilation much of the time throughout most of the State and bring to the land, at least in the lower lying regions, the mildly warm temperatures that are characteristic of air that has moved great distances across the tropical seas.

The relatively slight variations in the length of the daylight period in Hawaii, together with the smaller annual variations in the altitude of the sun above the horizon, result in relatively small variations in the amount of incoming solar energy from one time of the year to another. This small variation partly explains why seasonal changes in temperature are so slight throughout much of Hawaii. The other principal reason for the slightness of the variation is the virtually constant flow of fresh ocean air across the islands. Just as the temperature of the ocean surface varies comparatively little from season to season, so does the temperature of air that has moved great distances across the ocean.

The rugged configuration of the islands produces marked variations in conditions from one locality to another. Air swept inland on the trade winds or as part of storm circulations is shunted one way and another by the mountains and valleys and great open slopes. This complex three-dimensional flow of air results in striking differences from place to place in windspeed, cloudiness, and rainfall. Together with variations in the elevation of the land, it results in differences in air temperature.

The native Hawaiians recognize only two seasons. KAU is the fruitful season, the season when the sun was directly or almost directly overhead, when the weather was warmer, and when the trade winds were most reliable. HOO-ILO is the season when the sun was in the south, when the weather was cooler, and when the trade winds were most often interrupted by other winds. Modern analysis of the climatic records shows the soundness of the Hawaiian seasons.

In terms of variations in climatic conditions from one part of the State to another, the most striking contrasts are those in rainfall. At one extreme the annual rainfall averages 20 inches and less in leeward coastal areas and near the summits of the very high mountains, Mauna Loa and Mauna Kea. At the other extreme the annual average exceeds 300 inches along the lower windward slopes of these high mountains and of Haleakala and at or near the summit of the lower mountains.

In general the Hawaiian climate is characterized by a two-season year, by mild and fairly uniform temperature conditions everywhere but at high elevations, by strikingly marked geographic differences in rainfall, by generally humid conditions and high cloudiness except on the driest coasts and at high elevations, and by a general dominance of trade-wind flow especially at elevations below a few thousand feet.

The surface waters of the open ocean around Hawaii have an average temperature that ranges from a minimum of 73 or 74°F. between late February and early April to a maximum of 79 or 80°F. in late September or early October. With temperatures as mild as these — and with temperatures almost as mild for hundreds of miles around, even to the north — the air that reaches Hawaii is neither very hot nor cold. The mild, equable temperatures of the ocean give rise to mild, equable temperatures in the air that moves across the oceans and onto the islands of Hawaii.

PRECIPITATION. If the islands of the State of Hawaii did not exist, the average annual rainfall upon the water where the islands actually lie would be about 25 inches. Instead, the actual average is about 70 inches. Thus the islands extract from the air that passes across them about 45 inches of rainfall that otherwise would not fall. The mountains are dominantly responsible for this added water bonus. The driest areas are on the upper slopes of the high mountains, on leeward coasts, or in leeward locations in the interior of the islands. In the driest of these areas the average annual rainfall is less than 10 inches. The contrast in rainfall between the rainier winter season and the drier summer season is generally most pronounced at low elevations in the areas with low annual rainfall. In the lowlands at all times of the year, rainfall is most likely to occur during the nighttime or in the morning hours, and least likely to occur during midafternoon.

In most parts of the tropics the rainfall is highly variable from one year to another. Hawaii is no exception. Even in areas where the rainfall is very high and the monthly averages are all above 10 inches, the rainfall of particular months may vary by 200 to 300% from one year to another and there may be very occasional months with only one or two inches of rain. With such wide swings in rainfall it is inevitable that there are occasional droughts.

STORMS. Intense local rainstorms other than those that occur under trade-wind conditions are small features that seldom cover more than a few square miles and sometimes less than a single square mile. They occur most typically in the late afternoon or early evening. In some areas in which there are well developed sea breezes, they are common occurrences, especially in summer. In most areas, however, they are apt to occur on only a few days per year when the overall winds are light and variable or when there is a gentle flow of air from a southerly direction.

Intense local storms are sometimes accompanied by lightning and thunder. Lightning and thunder also occasionally accompany very intense rainfall along a cold front moving across the islands. Thunderstorms are reported from somewhere in the State on 20 to 30 days a year, and more often in winter than in summer. Waterspouts and other funnel clouds are not uncommon in the Hawaiian area, about 20 of them being sighted in the average year. Often they are accompanied by towering cumulus clouds and rain, although they have also been observed under trade wind conditions. Hail falls somewhere in Hawaii between five and 10 times in the average year. Almost always it is quite small — 1/4 inch or less in diameter — but on several occasions hail the size of marbles, and discs about 5/8 of an inch in diameter, have been reported.

Kona storms, like cold front storms, are features of the winter season. They are so-called because they often bring winds from "kona" or leeward directions. Kona rains last from several hours to several days.

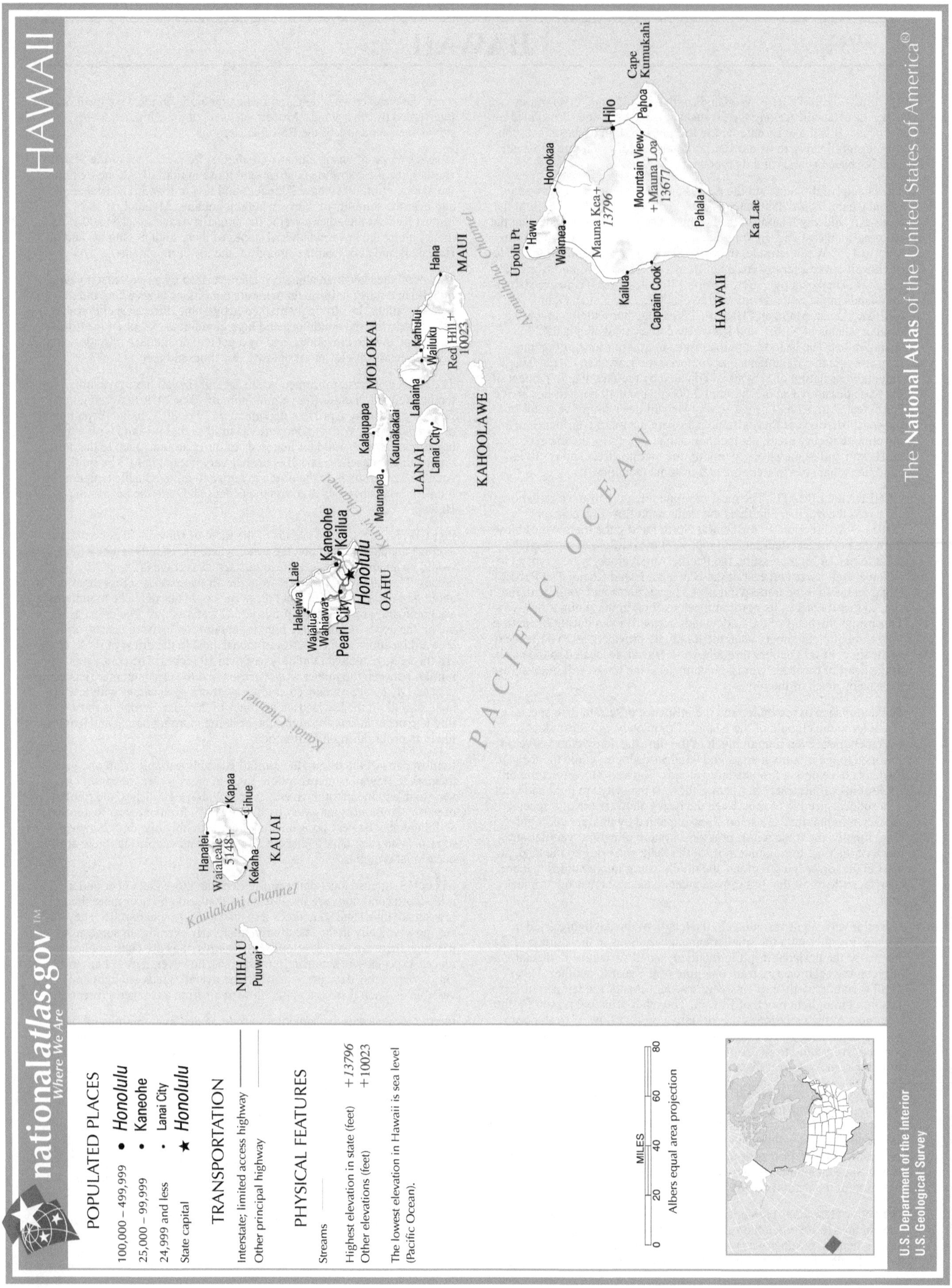
HAWAII
nationalatlas.gov
Where We Are
POPULATED PLACES
100,000 – 499,999 Honolulu
25,000 – 99,999 Kaneohe
24,999 and less Lanai City
State capital Honolulu
TRANSPORTATION
Interstate; limited access highway
Other principal highway
PHYSICAL FEATURES
Streams
Highest elevation in state (feet) +13796
Other elevations (feet) +10023
The lowest elevation in Hawaii is sea level (Pacific Ocean).
MILES
0 20 40 60 80
Albers equal area projection
U.S. Department of the Interior
U.S. Geological Survey
The National Atlas of the United States of America®
NIIHAU
Puuwai
Kaulakahi Channel
KAUAI
Hanalei
Waialeale 5148
Kekaha
Kapaa
Lihue
Kauai Channel
OAHU
Haleiwa
Waialua
Wahiawa
Laie
Pearl City
Honolulu
Kaneohe
Kailua
Kaiwi Channel
MOLOKAI
Kalaupapa
Kaunakakai
Maunaloa
LANAI
Lanai City
KAHOOLAWE
MAUI
Lahaina
Wailuku
Kahului
Red Hill 10023
Hana
Alenuihaha Channel
PACIFIC OCEAN
HAWAII
Upolu Pt
Hawi
Waimea
Honokaa
Mauna Kea 13796
Mauna Loa 13677
Hilo
Mountain View
Pahoa
Cape Kumukahi
Kailua
Captain Cook
Pahala
Ka Lae

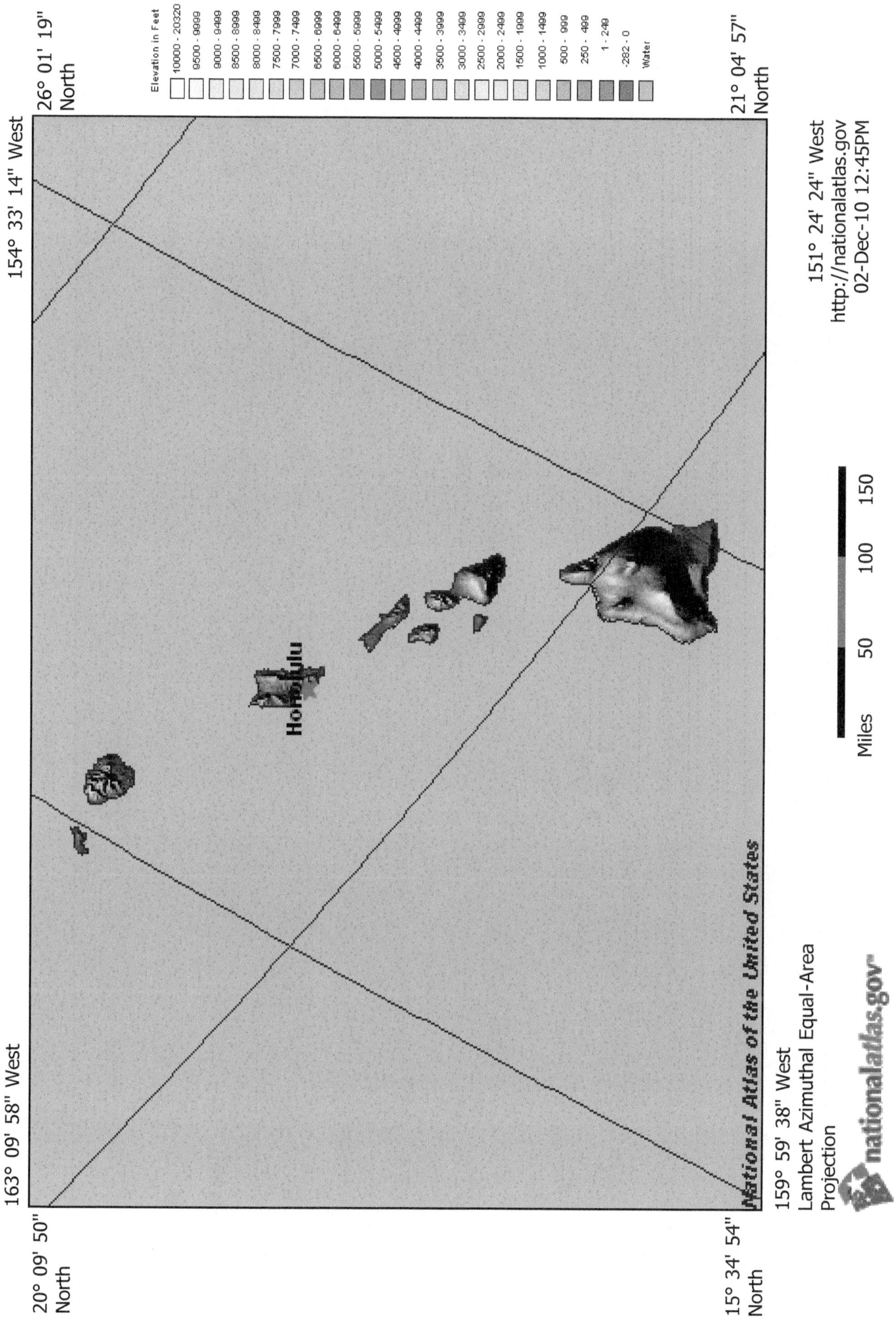
26° 01' 19" North
154° 33' 14" West
163° 09' 58" West
20° 09' 50" North
21° 04' 57" North
15° 34' 54" North
151° 24' 24" West
http://nationalatlas.gov
02-Dec-10 12:45PM
159° 59' 38" West
Lambert Azimuthal Equal-Area Projection
nationalatlas.gov
National Atlas of the United States
Honolulu
Miles 50 100 150
Elevation in Feet
10000 - 20320
9500 - 9999
9000 - 9499
8500 - 8999
8000 - 8499
7500 - 7999
7000 - 7499
6500 - 6999
6000 - 6499
5500 - 5999
5000 - 5499
4500 - 4999
4000 - 4499
3500 - 3999
3000 - 3499
2500 - 2999
2000 - 2499
1500 - 1999
1000 - 1499
500 - 999
250 - 499
1 - 249
-282 - 0
Water

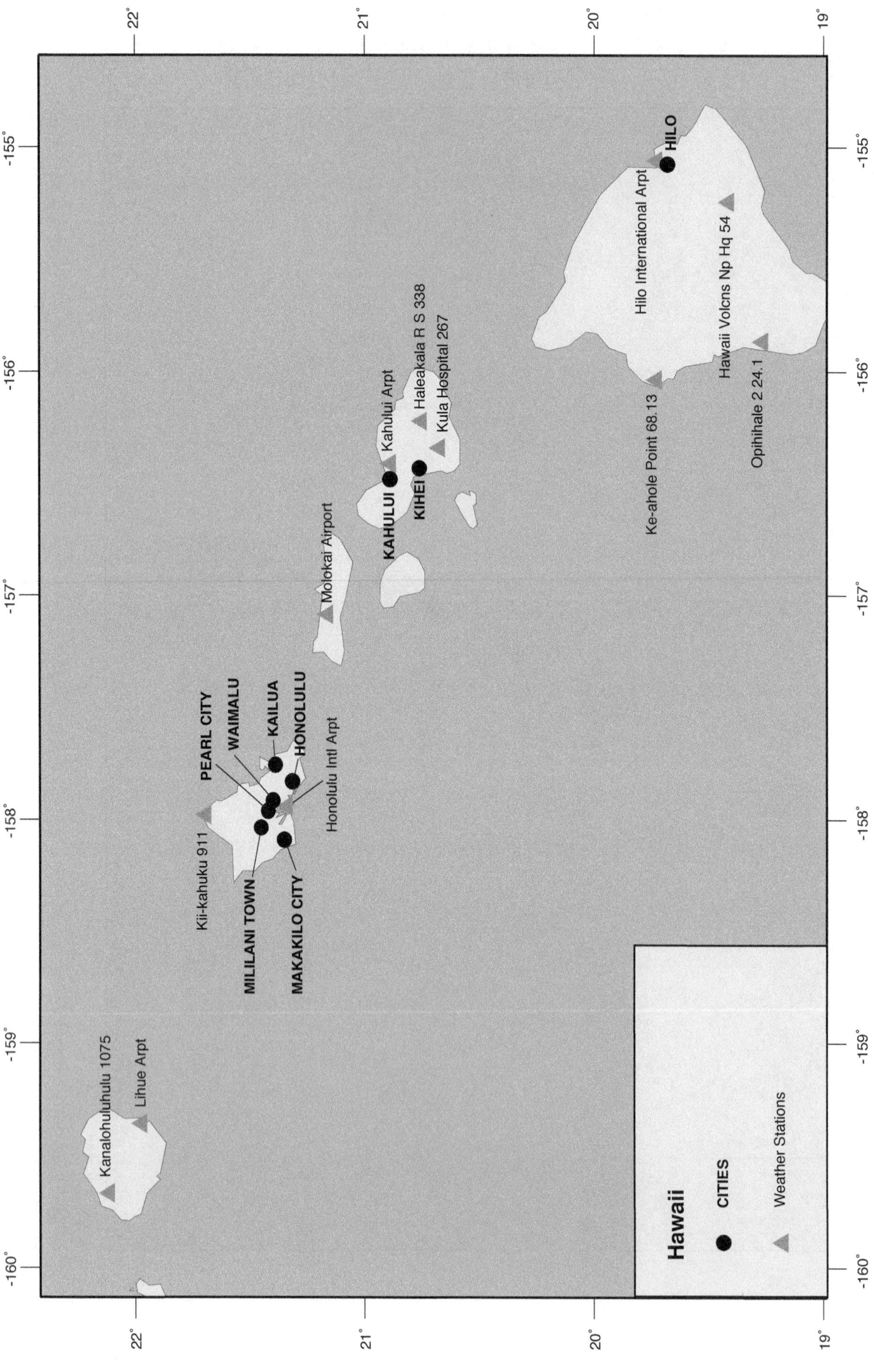
Hawaii
CITIES
Weather Stations
HILO
Hilo International Arpt
Hawaii Volcns Np Hq 54
Ke-ahole Point 68.13
Opihihale 2 24.1
Kahului Arpt
Haleakala R S 338
Kula Hospital 267
KAHULUI
KIHEI
Molokai Airport
PEARL CITY
WAIMALU
KAILUA
HONOLULU
Honolulu Intl Arpt
Kii-kahuku 911
MILILANI TOWN
MAKAKILO CITY
Kanalohuluhulu 1075
Lihue Arpt
22°
21°
20°
19°
-155°
-156°
-157°
-158°
-159°
-160°

Hawaii Weather Stations by County

County	Station Name
Hawaii	Hawaii Volcanos Np Hq 54
	Hilo International Arpt
	Ke-Ahole Point 68.13
	Opihihale 2 24.1
Honolulu	Honolulu Intl Arpt
	Kii-Kahuku 911
Kauai	Kanalohuluhulu 1075
	Lihue Arpt
Maui	Haleakala R S 338
	Kahului Arpt
	Kula Hospital 267
	Molokai Airport

Hawaii Weather Stations by City

City	Station Name	Miles
Hilo	Hawaii Volcanos Np Hq 54	21.5
	Hilo International Arpt	3.0
Honolulu	Honolulu Intl Arpt	6.6
Kahului	Haleakala R S 338	16.5
	Kahului Arpt	3.2
	Kula Hospital 267	14.2
Kailua	Honolulu Intl Arpt	13.6
Kaneohe	Honolulu Intl Arpt	10.9
	Kii-Kahuku 911	23.5
Kihei	Haleakala R S 338	13.1
	Kahului Arpt	10.0
	Kula Hospital 267	6.7
Makakilo City	Honolulu Intl Arpt	10.3
	Kii-Kahuku 911	24.8
Mililani Town	Honolulu Intl Arpt	10.4
	Kii-Kahuku 911	17.6
Pearl City	Honolulu Intl Arpt	6.4
	Kii-Kahuku 911	20.4
Wahiawa	Honolulu Intl Arpt	13.8
	Kii-Kahuku 911	14.0
Waimalu	Honolulu Intl Arpt	5.5
	Kii-Kahuku 911	21.2
Waipahu	Honolulu Intl Arpt	6.9
	Kii-Kahuku 911	21.7

Note: Miles is the distance between the geographic center of the city and the weather station.

See User Guide for station inclusion criteria.

Hawaii Weather Stations by Elevation

Feet	Station Name
6,959	Haleakala R S 338
3,971	Hawaii Volcanos Np Hq 54
3,600	Kanalohuluhulu 1075
3,003	Kula Hospital 267
1,359	Opihihale 2 24.1
450	Molokai Airport
103	Lihue Arpt
50	Kahului Arpt
29	Hilo International Arpt
20	Ke-Ahole Point 68.13
15	Kii-Kahuku 911
6	Honolulu Intl Arpt

Hilo International Airport

The city of Hilo is located near the midpoint of the eastern shore of the Island of Hawaii. This island is by far the largest of the Hawaiian group, with an area of 4,038 square miles, more than twice that of all the other islands combined. Its topography is dominated by the great volcanic masses of Mauna Loa (13,653 feet), Mauna Kea (13,796 feet), and of Haulalai, the Kohala Mountains, and Kilauea. In fact, the island consists entirely of the slopes of these mountains and of the broad saddles between them. Mauna Loa and Kilauea, which occupy the southern half of the island, are still active volcanoes.

Hawaii lies well within the belt of northeasterly trade winds generated by the semi-permanent Pacific high pressure cell to the north and east. The climate provides equable temperatures from day to day and season to season. In Hilo, July and August are the warmest months, with average daily highs and lows of 83 and 68 degrees. January and February, the coolest months, have highs of 80 degrees and lows of 63 degrees. Greater variations occur in localities with less rain and cloud, but temperatures in the mid-90s and low 50s are uncommon anywhere on the island near sea level.

Over the windward slopes of Hawaii , rainfall occurs principally as orographic showers within the ascending moist trade winds. Mean annual rainfall, except for the semi-sheltered Hamakua district, increases from 100 inches or more along the coasts to a maximum of over 300 inches at elevations of 2,000 to 3,000 feet, and then declines to about 15 inches at the summits of Mauna Kea and Mauna Loa. Leeward areas are topographically sheltered from the trades and are therefore drier, although sea breezes can cause afternoon and evening cloudiness and showers. The driest locality on the island, and in the State, with an annual rainfall of less than 10 inches, is the coastal strip just leeward of the southern portion of the Kohala Mountains and of the saddle between the Kohalas and Mauna Kea.

Within the city of Hilo, average rainfall varies from about 130 inches a year near the shore to as much as 200 upslope. The wettest part of the island, with a mean annual rainfall exceeding 300 inches, lies about six miles upslope from the city limits. Relative humidity at Hilo is in the moderate range, however.

The trade winds prevail throughout the year and profoundly influence the climate. The islands entire western coast is sheltered from the trades by high mountains, except that unusually strong trade winds may sweep through the saddle between the Kohala Mountains and Mauna Kea. Except for heavy rain, really severe weather seldom occurs. During the winter, cold fronts or the cyclonic storms of subtropical origin may bring blizzards to the upper slopes of Mauna Loa and Mauna Kea, with snow extending at times to 9,000 feet or below and icing nearer the summit.

Hilo International Airport *Hawaii County* Elevation: 29 ft. Latitude: 19° 43' N Longitude: 155° 03' W

	JAN	FEB	MAR	APR	MAY	JUN	JUL	AUG	SEP	OCT	NOV	DEC	YEAR
Mean Maximum Temp. (°F)	79.5	79.3	79.4	79.5	81.2	82.7	83.3	83.6	83.7	83.1	81.3	80.0	81.4
Mean Temp. (°F)	71.6	71.4	72.1	72.6	74.1	75.5	76.4	76.7	76.4	75.8	74.3	72.6	74.1
Mean Minimum Temp. (°F)	63.7	63.5	64.7	65.6	66.9	68.2	69.3	69.6	69.1	68.5	67.2	65.1	66.8
Extreme Maximum Temp. (°F)	92	91	89	87	91	88	91	90	91	90	92	93	93
Extreme Minimum Temp. (°F)	54	54	54	58	59	63	63	64	63	62	58	57	54
Days Maximum Temp. ≥ 90°F	0	0	0	0	0	0	0	0	0	0	0	0	0
Days Maximum Temp. ≤ 32°F	0	0	0	0	0	0	0	0	0	0	0	0	0
Days Minimum Temp. ≤ 32°F	0	0	0	0	0	0	0	0	0	0	0	0	0
Days Minimum Temp. ≤ 0°F	0	0	0	0	0	0	0	0	0	0	0	0	0
Heating Degree Days (base 65°F)	0	0	0	0	0	0	0	0	0	0	0	0	0
Cooling Degree Days (base 65°F)	211	188	227	234	288	322	359	368	350	342	286	242	3,417
Mean Precipitation (in.)	9.25	9.65	14.80	11.67	8.22	7.51	10.98	9.98	10.31	9.75	14.49	10.69	127.30
Maximum Precipitation (in.)*	32.2	45.5	49.9	43.2	25.0	13.3	28.6	26.9	21.8	26.1	45.8	50.8	211.
Minimum Precipitation (in.)*	0.4	0.6	0.9	2.9	2.7	1.8	3.8	2.7	1.6	2.4	1.0	0.3	68.1
Extreme Maximum Daily Precip. (in.)	12.20	10.81	15.66	7.82	7.89	3.39	5.91	9.64	8.67	4.97	16.17	10.12	16.17
Days With ≥ 0.1" Precipitation	11	11	15	18	15	17	20	18	17	17	17	14	190
Days With ≥ 0.5" Precipitation	5	5	7	7	4	5	6	5	6	6	8	6	70
Days With ≥ 1.0" Precipitation	3	2	4	3	2	1	2	2	2	2	4	3	30
Mean Snowfall (in.)	na	na	na	na	na	na	na	na	na	na	na	na	na
Maximum Snowfall (in.)*	0	0	0	0	0	0	0	0	0	0	0	0	0
Maximum 24-hr. Snowfall (in.)*	0	0	0	0	0	0	0	0	0	0	0	0	0
Maximum Snow Depth (in.)	na	na	na	na	na	na	na	na	na	na	na	na	na
Days With ≥ 1.0" Snow Depth	na	na	na	na	na	na	na	na	na	na	na	na	na
Thunderstorm Days*	1	1	2	1	1	< 1	< 1	< 1	1	1	1	1	10
Foggy Days*	< 1	< 1	< 1	< 1	0	< 1	< 1	< 1	< 1	< 1	< 1	< 1	1
Predominant Sky Cover*	OVR	OVR	OVR	OVR	OVR	OVR	OVR	OVR	OVR	OVR	OVR	OVR	OVR
Mean Relative Humidity 5am (%)*	82	82	85	88	88	87	88	88	86	86	86	84	86
Mean Relative Humidity 5pm (%)*	73	72	73	75	73	71	73	74	74	76	78	76	74
Mean Dewpoint (°F)*	63	63	63	65	66	67	68	69	68	68	67	64	66
Prevailing Wind Direction*	SW	SW	SW	SW	SW	SW	SW	SW	SW	SW	SW	SW	SW
Prevailing Wind Speed (mph)*	6	7	6	6	6	6	6	6	6	6	6	6	6
Maximum Wind Gust (mph)*	47	55	40	40	41	33	36	38	37	43	36	48	55

Note: (*) Period of record is 1949-1995

 The period of record for National Weather Service station data is 1980 – 2009 except where noted. See User Guide for detailed explanation of data.

Honolulu Int'l Airport

Oahu, on which Honolulu is located, is the third largest of the Hawaiian Islands. The Koolau Range, at an average elevation of 2,000 feet parallels the northeastern coast. The Waianae Mountains, somewhat higher in elevation, parallel the west coast. Honolulu Airport, the business and Waikiki districts, and a number of the residential areas of Honolulu lie along the southern coastal plain.

The climate of Hawaii is unusually pleasant for the tropics. Its outstanding features are the persistence of the trade winds, the remarkable variability in rainfall over short distances, the sunniness of the leeward lowlands in contrast to the persistent cloudiness over nearby mountain crests, the equable temperature, and the general infrequency of severe storms.

The prevailing wind throughout the year is the northeasterly trade wind, although its average frequency varies from more than 90 percent during the summer to only 50 percent in January.

Heavy mountain rainfall sustains extensive irrigation of cane fields and the water supply for Honolulu. Oahu is driest along the coast west of the Waianaes where rainfall drops to about 20 inches a year. Daytime showers, usually light, often occur while the sun continues to shine, a phenomenon referred to locally as liquid sunshine.

The moderate temperature range is associated with the small seasonal variation in the energy received from the sun and the tempering effect of the surrounding ocean. Honolulu Airport has recorded as high as the lower 90s and as low as the lower 50s.

Because of the trade winds, even the warmest months are usually comfortable. But when the trades diminish or give way to southerly winds, a situation known locally as kona weather, or kona storms when stormy, the humidity may become oppressively high.

Intense rains of the October to April winter season sometimes cause serious, flash flooding. Thunderstorms are infrequent and usually mild and hail seldom occurs. Infrequently, a small tornado or a waterspout may do some damage. Only a few tropical cyclones have struck Hawaii, although others have come near enough for their outlying winds, waves, clouds, and rain to affect the Islands.

Honolulu Int'l Airport *Honolulu County* Elevation: 6 ft. Latitude: 21° 19' N Longitude: 157° 56' W

	JAN	FEB	MAR	APR	MAY	JUN	JUL	AUG	SEP	OCT	NOV	DEC	YEAR
Mean Maximum Temp. (°F)	80.4	80.5	81.6	83.2	85.0	87.3	88.3	89.1	88.9	87.1	84.3	81.7	84.8
Mean Temp. (°F)	73.3	73.3	74.7	76.3	78.0	80.3	81.4	82.1	81.7	80.2	77.8	74.9	77.8
Mean Minimum Temp. (°F)	66.1	66.0	67.7	69.4	70.9	73.2	74.5	75.0	74.4	73.3	71.4	68.1	70.8
Extreme Maximum Temp. (°F)	88	88	88	91	93	92	94	96	95	94	93	89	96
Extreme Minimum Temp. (°F)	53	53	56	57	60	65	66	65	66	61	57	55	53
Days Maximum Temp. ≥ 90°F	0	0	0	0	1	2	7	13	11	5	0	0	39
Days Maximum Temp. ≤ 32°F	0	0	0	0	0	0	0	0	0	0	0	0	0
Days Minimum Temp. ≤ 32°F	0	0	0	0	0	0	0	0	0	0	0	0	0
Days Minimum Temp. ≤ 0°F	0	0	0	0	0	0	0	0	0	0	0	0	0
Heating Degree Days (base 65°F)	0	0	0	0	0	0	0	0	0	0	0	0	0
Cooling Degree Days (base 65°F)	263	241	307	346	409	466	515	538	508	479	392	314	4,778
Mean Precipitation (in.)	2.58	2.04	2.10	0.65	0.60	0.31	0.51	0.56	0.68	1.84	2.41	3.09	17.37
Maximum Precipitation (in.)*	13.3	13.7	20.8	8.9	7.2	2.5	2.3	3.1	2.1	11.1	14.7	17.3	42.8
Minimum Precipitation (in.)*	0.2	0.1	trace	trace	0.1	trace	trace	trace	0	0.1	trace	0.1	5.0
Extreme Maximum Daily Precip. (in.)	3.76	5.43	2.94	0.88	1.03	1.10	2.18	2.92	1.19	5.56	4.51	7.89	7.89
Days With ≥ 0.1" Precipitation	4	3	3	2	1	1	1	1	2	3	3	4	28
Days With ≥ 0.5" Precipitation	1	1	1	0	0	0	0	0	0	1	1	1	6
Days With ≥ 1.0" Precipitation	1	0	1	0	0	0	0	0	0	0	1	1	4
Mean Snowfall (in.)	na	na	na	na	na	na	na	na	na	na	na	na	na
Maximum Snowfall (in.)*	0	0	0	0	0	0	0	0	0	0	0	0	0
Maximum 24-hr. Snowfall (in.)*	0	0	0	0	0	0	0	0	0	0	0	0	0
Maximum Snow Depth (in.)	na	na	na	na	na	na	na	na	na	na	na	na	na
Days With ≥ 1.0" Snow Depth	na	na	na	na	na	na	na	na	na	na	na	na	na
Thunderstorm Days*	1	1	1	< 1	< 1	< 1	< 1	< 1	< 1	1	1	1	6
Foggy Days*	0	0	< 1	< 1	< 1	< 1	0	0	0	< 1	< 1	< 1	< 1
Predominant Sky Cover*	SCT	SCT	SCT	SCT	SCT	SCT	SCT	SCT	SCT	SCT	SCT	SCT	SCT
Mean Relative Humidity 5am (%)*	82	80	78	77	76	75	75	75	77	78	79	80	78
Mean Relative Humidity 5pm (%)*	66	64	62	61	60	58	58	58	60	63	66	66	62
Mean Dewpoint (°F)*	63	62	62	63	64	65	66	67	67	67	66	64	64
Prevailing Wind Direction*	ENE	ENE	ENE	ENE	ENE	ENE	ENE	ENE	ENE	ENE	ENE	ENE	ENE
Prevailing Wind Speed (mph)*	13	13	14	14	13	14	14	14	13	13	13	13	13
Maximum Wind Gust (mph)*	61	53	51	47	46	43	51	43	49	43	81	51	81

Note: (*) Period of record is 1949-1995

The period of record for National Weather Service station data is 1980 – 2009 except where noted. See User Guide for detailed explanation of data.

Kahului Airport

Kahului Airport is located in the relatively broad central valley of Maui near the northern coast of the island. Five miles to the west, the mountains of west Maui rise abruptly, reaching an elevation of 5,788 feet above sea level at the crest of Puu Kukui 10 miles west of the station. To the southeast the terrain rises gradually to the summit of Haleakala at 10,023 feet, located 17 miles from the airport.

The outstanding features of climate are the equable temperature marked seasonal variation in rainfall, persistent surface winds, and the rarity of severe storms.

The extremely equable temperatures at Kahului are associated with the tempering effect of the Pacific Ocean and the small seasonal variation in the amount of energy received from the sun. The range in normal temperature between the warmest month, August, and the coldest month, February, is 7.2 degrees.

Rainfall is relatively light. The contrast between the dry season, which extends from May through October, and the wet season, November through April, is quite pronounced. Major widespread rainstorms, which account for the bulk of the precipitation in the area, usually occur several times during each wet season, but are infrequent in the dry season. Approximately 50 percent of the normal annual rainfall occurs in the three months of December through February, and over 80 percent in the six months of the wet season.

Showers constitute the greatest number of rainfall occurrences and although most of these are light and short-lived, very heavy showers do occur at times. Thunderstorms, which are reported rather infrequently, are usually associated with major storms in the wet season.

Tropical storms, may produce heavy rain and strong wind at Kahului once every several years. The large Pacific semipermanent high pressure cell, produces a rather persistent flow of air from the northeast known as the Northeast Trades. Thus, surface wind at Kahului is predominantly from the northeast quadrant. The and flow is most prevalent during the dry season. Wind is more variable during the wet season although, on the average, the trades still blow more than 50 percent of the time during this period.

The normal trade winds, often attain a speed of 40 to 45 mph at the airport, but make living conditions in the nearby Kahului-Wailuku community pleasant and comfortable.

Humidity at Kahului is usually moderate to high, with wet season humidities averaging slightly higher than those in the dry season. However, due to the system of natural ventilation provided by the prevailing winds, the weather is seldom oppressive even during the warmer months of the year.

Kahului Airport *Maui County* Elevation: 50 ft. Latitude: 20° 54' N Longitude: 156° 26' W

	JAN	FEB	MAR	APR	MAY	JUN	JUL	AUG	SEP	OCT	NOV	DEC	YEAR
Mean Maximum Temp. (°F)	80.6	80.7	81.4	82.4	84.5	86.3	87.2	88.0	88.1	86.9	84.2	81.6	84.3
Mean Temp. (°F)	72.1	72.0	73.0	74.2	75.9	78.1	79.3	79.8	79.4	78.3	76.2	73.4	76.0
Mean Minimum Temp. (°F)	63.6	63.2	64.6	65.9	67.3	69.8	71.2	71.5	70.6	69.6	68.1	65.2	67.6
Extreme Maximum Temp. (°F)	90	89	90	91	92	94	95	97	96	95	93	90	97
Extreme Minimum Temp. (°F)	53	50	51	54	57	58	60	61	59	59	55	52	50
Days Maximum Temp. ≥ 90°F	0	0	0	0	1	2	4	6	7	5	1	0	26
Days Maximum Temp. ≤ 32°F	0	0	0	0	0	0	0	0	0	0	0	0	0
Days Minimum Temp. ≤ 32°F	0	0	0	0	0	0	0	0	0	0	0	0	0
Days Minimum Temp. ≤ 0°F	0	0	0	0	0	0	0	0	0	0	0	0	0
Heating Degree Days (base 65°F)	0	0	0	0	0	0	0	0	0	0	0	0	0
Cooling Degree Days (base 65°F)	228	203	257	282	346	400	450	465	438	419	342	269	4,099
Mean Precipitation (in.)	3.32	2.00	2.50	1.60	0.75	0.20	0.51	0.51	0.39	1.19	2.16	3.28	18.41
Maximum Precipitation (in.)*	14.5	8.3	10.9	14.3	4.4	2.5	1.6	1.5	1.4	5.7	9.3	10.2	40.6
Minimum Precipitation (in.)*	0.1	0.1	0.1	0.1	trace	trace	trace	trace	trace	trace	0.1	trace	8.6
Extreme Maximum Daily Precip. (in.)	4.70	4.76	2.89	3.95	2.41	0.33	1.04	1.13	0.81	3.26	3.14	4.63	4.76
Days With ≥ 0.1" Precipitation	5	4	5	3	2	0	2	1	1	2	4	5	34
Days With ≥ 0.5" Precipitation	2	1	2	1	0	0	0	0	0	0	1	2	9
Days With ≥ 1.0" Precipitation	1	0	1	0	0	0	0	0	0	0	1	1	4
Mean Snowfall (in.)	na	na	na	na	na	na	na	na	na	na	na	na	na
Maximum Snowfall (in.)*	0	0	0	0	0	0	0	0	0	0	0	0	0
Maximum 24-hr. Snowfall (in.)*	0	0	0	0	0	0	0	0	0	0	0	0	0
Maximum Snow Depth (in.)	na	na	na	na	na	na	na	na	na	na	na	na	na
Days With ≥ 1.0" Snow Depth	na	na	na	na	na	na	na	na	na	na	na	na	na
Thunderstorm Days*	1	1	< 1	< 1	< 1	< 1	< 1	< 1	< 1	< 1	< 1	< 1	2
Foggy Days*	< 1	0	< 1	0	0	0	0	0	0	0	0	0	< 1
Predominant Sky Cover*	SCT	SCT	SCT	SCT	SCT	SCT	SCT	SCT	SCT	SCT	SCT	SCT	SCT
Mean Relative Humidity 5am (%)*	84	83	82	82	82	81	80	81	81	82	82	83	82
Mean Relative Humidity 5pm (%)*	66	65	64	63	61	59	60	61	61	63	67	67	63
Mean Dewpoint (°F)*	63	62	63	64	65	66	67	68	67	67	66	64	65
Prevailing Wind Direction*	NE	NE	NE	NE	NE	NE	NE	NE	NE	NE	NE	NE	NE
Prevailing Wind Speed (mph)*	14	15	16	16	16	17	17	17	16	15	16	15	16
Maximum Wind Gust (mph)*	58	53	52	49	47	47	47	47	44	46	59	54	59

Note: (*) Period of record is 1958-1995

Lihue Airport

Lihue Airport, a little more than 100 feet above sea level, is located near the eastern shore of the island of Kauai. The island is 33 miles long and 25 miles wide and has an area of 555 square miles. The eastern one third of Kauai consists of broadly eroded valley lands, the western two thirds is mostly mountainous. Kawaikini, the highest elevation on the island, 5,170 feet above sea level, lies near the center of Kauai and is 20 miles northwest of the airport.

The outstanding features of the climate are the equable temperatures from day to day and season to season, the persistent northeasterly trade winds and the marked variation in rainfall from the wet to the dry season and place to place.

The equable temperatures are associated with the mid-ocean location of the island and to the small seasonal variation in the amount of energy received from the sun. The range in normal temperature from February to August is less than eight degrees.

The trade winds blow across the island during most of each year and the dominance of these winds has a marked influence on the climate of the area. Completely cloudless skies are quite rare. On the average, six tenths to seven tenths of the sky is covered by clouds during the daylight hours.

Trade-wind showers are relatively common. Although heavy at times, most of the showers are light and of short duration. The frequency and intensity of the showers increase toward the mountains to the west. Mt. Waialeale receives 486 inches annually, the highest recorded annual average in the world. Mt. Waialeale has recorded annual rainfalls over 620 inches.

Normal annual rainfall is over 40 inches. Three-fourths of this total, on the average, falls during the seven-month wet season which extends from October through April. Widespread rainstorms, which account for much of the precipitation, occur most frequently during this period. Normal precipitation in January, the wettest month, is over six inches.

The dry season includes the months of May through September. June, the driest month, receives only about one and a half inches of rain, on the average.

Hurricanes and other severe windstorms are quite rare. Strong winds do occur at times in connection with storm systems moving through the area, but seldom cause extensive damage.

Relative humidity, moderate to high in all seasons, is slightly higher in the wet season than in the dry. However, even during periods when the temperature and humidity are both high, the weather is seldom oppressive. This is due to the trade winds which provide a system of natural ventilation during most of each year.

Lihue Airport *Kauai County* Elevation: 103 ft. Latitude: 21° 59' N Longitude: 159° 20' W

	JAN	FEB	MAR	APR	MAY	JUN	JUL	AUG	SEP	OCT	NOV	DEC	YEAR
Mean Maximum Temp. (°F)	78.0	77.8	78.4	79.2	81.1	83.2	84.2	84.8	84.8	83.3	80.8	78.9	81.2
Mean Temp. (°F)	71.8	71.7	72.8	74.0	75.8	78.1	79.2	79.7	79.5	78.1	75.8	73.2	75.8
Mean Minimum Temp. (°F)	65.5	65.5	67.0	68.8	70.4	73.0	74.1	74.6	74.1	72.8	70.7	67.6	70.4
Extreme Maximum Temp. (°F)	86	86	88	88	88	88	89	90	90	89	89	87	90
Extreme Minimum Temp. (°F)	54	54	53	58	58	61	67	68	65	61	58	55	53
Days Maximum Temp. ≥ 90°F	0	0	0	0	0	0	0	0	0	0	0	0	0
Days Maximum Temp. ≤ 32°F	0	0	0	0	0	0	0	0	0	0	0	0	0
Days Minimum Temp. ≤ 32°F	0	0	0	0	0	0	0	0	0	0	0	0	0
Days Minimum Temp. ≤ 0°F	0	0	0	0	0	0	0	0	0	0	0	0	0
Heating Degree Days (base 65°F)	0	0	0	0	0	0	0	0	0	0	0	0	0
Cooling Degree Days (base 65°F)	217	196	247	277	340	400	447	464	441	413	331	263	4,036
Mean Precipitation (in.)	3.91	3.18	4.64	2.31	2.40	1.67	2.13	2.12	2.62	3.93	4.82	4.96	38.69
Maximum Precipitation (in.)*	17.6	11.3	14.5	10.6	12.6	4.8	8.8	8.1	10.9	18.0	18.4	22.9	74.4
Minimum Precipitation (in.)*	0.3	trace	0.3	0.3	0.4	0.4	0.8	0.7	0.4	1.0	0.6	0.5	16.4
Extreme Maximum Daily Precip. (in.)	6.06	5.31	6.71	3.07	3.65	2.09	4.68	2.21	7.15	6.31	9.75	8.55	9.75
Days With ≥ 0.1" Precipitation	5	5	7	6	5	5	6	6	5	7	7	7	71
Days With ≥ 0.5" Precipitation	2	1	2	1	1	0	1	1	1	2	2	2	16
Days With ≥ 1.0" Precipitation	1	1	1	0	0	0	0	0	0	1	1	1	6
Mean Snowfall (in.)	0.0	0.0	0.0	0.0	0.0	0.0	0.0	0.0	0.0	0.0	0.0	0.0	0.0
Maximum Snowfall (in.)*	0	0	0	0	0	0	0	0	0	0	0	0	0
Maximum 24-hr. Snowfall (in.)*	0	0	0	0	0	0	0	0	0	0	0	0	0
Maximum Snow Depth (in.)	0	0	0	0	0	0	0	0	0	0	0	0	0
Days With ≥ 1.0" Snow Depth	0	0	0	0	0	0	0	0	0	0	0	0	0
Thunderstorm Days*	1	1	1	< 1	1	< 1	< 1	< 1	< 1	1	1	1	7
Foggy Days*	< 1	< 1	< 1	< 1	< 1	< 1	< 1	0	0	< 1	< 1	< 1	1
Predominant Sky Cover*	SCT	SCT	BRK	BRK	BRK	BRK	BRK	BRK	SCT	SCT	BRK	BRK	BRK
Mean Relative Humidity 5am (%)*	82	82	81	81	81	80	80	81	82	83	82	81	81
Mean Relative Humidity 5pm (%)*	70	70	70	71	71	69	70	70	70	73	74	73	71
Mean Dewpoint (°F)*	63	62	63	65	66	68	69	70	69	69	67	64	66
Prevailing Wind Direction*	ENE	NE	ENE	NE	NE	ENE	ENE	ENE	ENE	ENE	ENE	NE	ENE
Prevailing Wind Speed (mph)*	14	15	15	15	14	14	15	14	13	14	14	15	14
Maximum Wind Gust (mph)*	84	60	54	47	43	39	41	38	115	41	85	55	115

Note: (*) Period of record is 1950-1995

Haleakala R S 338 *Maui County* Elevation: 6,959 ft. Latitude: 20° 46' N Longitude: 156° 15' W

	JAN	FEB	MAR	APR	MAY	JUN	JUL	AUG	SEP	OCT	NOV	DEC	YEAR
Mean Maximum Temp. (°F)	60.5	59.6	59.9	60.4	62.6	65.3	65.6	66.1	64.6	64.1	63.4	61.4	62.8
Mean Temp. (°F)	51.8	51.0	51.5	51.8	53.9	56.4	57.1	57.4	56.0	55.7	55.2	52.9	54.2
Mean Minimum Temp. (°F)	43.1	42.3	43.0	43.2	45.1	47.4	48.5	48.7	47.4	47.2	46.9	44.4	45.6
Extreme Maximum Temp. (°F)	74	74	71	72	78	78	76	76	76	75	76	74	78
Extreme Minimum Temp. (°F)	31	29	32	33	32	33	38	37	38	31	32	32	29
Days Maximum Temp. ≥ 90°F	0	0	0	0	0	0	0	0	0	0	0	0	0
Days Maximum Temp. ≤ 32°F	0	0	0	0	0	0	0	0	0	0	0	0	0
Days Minimum Temp. ≤ 32°F	0	0	0	0	0	0	0	0	0	0	0	0	0
Days Minimum Temp. ≤ 0°F	0	0	0	0	0	0	0	0	0	0	0	0	0
Heating Degree Days (base 65°F)	400	389	409	389	339	252	238	226	265	279	286	368	3,840
Cooling Degree Days (base 65°F)	0	0	0	0	1	0	0	1	0	0	0	0	2
Mean Precipitation (in.)	7.63	5.74	8.73	4.45	2.15	1.49	2.59	2.18	2.48	3.19	5.20	6.84	52.67
Extreme Maximum Daily Precip. (in.)	18.50	9.40	14.16	8.80	2.63	2.90	3.44	3.00	2.00	4.65	7.29	9.61	18.50
Days With ≥ 0.1" Precipitation	6	6	7	7	4	4	6	5	6	6	7	6	70
Days With ≥ 0.5" Precipitation	3	3	4	2	1	1	1	1	1	2	3	3	25
Days With ≥ 1.0" Precipitation	2	1	2	1	1	0	0	1	0	1	1	2	12
Mean Snowfall (in.)	0.0	0.0	0.0	0.0	0.0	0.0	0.0	0.0	0.0	0.0	0.0	0.0	0.0
Maximum Snow Depth (in.)	0	0	0	0	0	0	0	0	0	0	0	0	0
Days With ≥ 1.0" Snow Depth	0	0	0	0	0	0	0	0	0	0	0	0	0

Hawaii Volcanos Np Hq 54 *Hawaii County* Elevation: 3,971 ft. Latitude: 19° 26' N Longitude: 155° 16' W

	JAN	FEB	MAR	APR	MAY	JUN	JUL	AUG	SEP	OCT	NOV	DEC	YEAR
Mean Maximum Temp. (°F)	68.1	68.1	67.9	68.0	70.3	71.3	72.3	73.5	73.2	72.4	70.2	68.3	70.3
Mean Temp. (°F)	58.8	58.7	59.1	59.8	61.6	62.7	63.9	64.7	64.3	63.7	62.1	59.9	61.6
Mean Minimum Temp. (°F)	49.5	49.3	50.3	51.5	52.8	54.1	55.5	55.8	55.4	55.0	53.9	51.4	52.9
Extreme Maximum Temp. (°F)	79	80	80	80	81	93	87	84	82	81	80	89	93
Extreme Minimum Temp. (°F)	38	36	38	42	42	45	45	46	45	45	43	31	31
Days Maximum Temp. ≥ 90°F	0	0	0	0	0	0	0	0	0	0	0	0	0
Days Maximum Temp. ≤ 32°F	0	0	0	0	0	0	0	0	0	0	0	0	0
Days Minimum Temp. ≤ 32°F	0	0	0	0	0	0	0	0	0	0	0	0	0
Days Minimum Temp. ≤ 0°F	0	0	0	0	0	0	0	0	0	0	0	0	0
Heating Degree Days (base 65°F)	186	173	174	153	103	65	41	27	33	48	86	153	1,242
Cooling Degree Days (base 65°F)	0	0	0	1	4	4	15	23	17	15	5	1	85
Mean Precipitation (in.)	9.54	8.88	13.95	10.16	6.90	5.35	7.51	6.73	6.63	7.44	12.35	11.49	106.93
Extreme Maximum Daily Precip. (in.)	10.64	13.06	12.02	10.28	5.27	2.90	9.30	5.14	12.26	4.96	11.65	12.96	13.06
Days With ≥ 0.1" Precipitation	11	8	15	17	15	14	14	13	12	14	14	13	160
Days With ≥ 0.5" Precipitation	4	4	6	6	3	3	4	3	3	4	6	5	51
Days With ≥ 1.0" Precipitation	2	2	3	2	1	1	1	1	1	1	3	3	21
Mean Snowfall (in.)	0.0	0.0	0.0	0.0	0.0	0.0	0.0	0.0	0.0	0.0	0.0	0.0	0.0
Maximum Snow Depth (in.)	0	0	0	0	0	0	0	0	0	0	0	0	0
Days With ≥ 1.0" Snow Depth	0	0	0	0	0	0	0	0	0	0	0	0	0

Kanalohuluhulu 1075 *Kauai County* Elevation: 3,600 ft. Latitude: 22° 08' N Longitude: 159° 40' W

	JAN	FEB	MAR	APR	MAY	JUN	JUL	AUG	SEP	OCT	NOV	DEC	YEAR
Mean Maximum Temp. (°F)	62.8	62.9	63.7	64.8	66.5	68.8	69.9	70.7	70.4	68.9	66.4	63.5	66.6
Mean Temp. (°F)	54.5	54.6	55.8	57.2	58.5	61.1	62.5	62.9	62.0	61.1	58.7	55.9	58.7
Mean Minimum Temp. (°F)	46.1	46.0	47.8	49.5	50.4	53.4	55.1	55.2	53.6	53.3	51.0	48.2	50.8
Extreme Maximum Temp. (°F)	79	74	78	83	80	90	82	79	86	79	78	75	90
Extreme Minimum Temp. (°F)	30	31	29	32	35	40	37	39	39	35	32	31	29
Days Maximum Temp. ≥ 90°F	0	0	0	0	0	0	0	0	0	0	0	0	0
Days Maximum Temp. ≤ 32°F	0	0	0	0	0	0	0	0	0	0	0	0	0
Days Minimum Temp. ≤ 32°F	0	0	0	0	0	0	0	0	0	0	0	0	0
Days Minimum Temp. ≤ 0°F	0	0	0	0	0	0	0	0	0	0	0	0	0
Heating Degree Days (base 65°F)	***323***	***292***	285	233	201	***115***	80	68	92	***119***	***188***	***281***	***2,277***
Cooling Degree Days (base 65°F)	0	0	0	0	0	2	6	8	5	1	1	0	23
Mean Precipitation (in.)	9.74	7.30	7.29	3.97	3.15	1.77	2.07	***2.46***	***2.28***	4.75	***6.48***	***10.81***	***62.07***
Extreme Maximum Daily Precip. (in.)	11.97	7.00	9.06	5.40	4.50	2.00	3.50	2.95	1.98	6.37	6.25	9.50	11.97
Days With ≥ 0.1" Precipitation	9	9	10	9	7	5	6	5	6	7	9	10	92
Days With ≥ 0.5" Precipitation	5	4	4	2	2	1	0	1	1	2	3	4	29
Days With ≥ 1.0" Precipitation	3	2	2	1	1	0	0	0	0	1	2	3	15
Mean Snowfall (in.)	0.0	0.0	0.0	0.0	0.0	0.0	0.0	0.0	0.0	0.0	0.0	0.0	0.0
Maximum Snow Depth (in.)	0	0	0	0	0	0	0	0	0	0	0	0	0
Days With ≥ 1.0" Snow Depth	0	0	0	0	0	0	0	0	0	0	0	0	0

Ke-Ahole Point 68.13 *Hawaii County* Elevation: 20 ft. Latitude: 19° 44' N Longitude: 156° 04' W

	JAN	FEB	MAR	APR	MAY	JUN	JUL	AUG	SEP	OCT	NOV	DEC	YEAR
Mean Maximum Temp. (°F)	***82.0***	81.4	82.8	83.3	84.8	85.9	86.8	87.8	87.6	86.8	***85.6***	***82.9***	***84.8***
Mean Temp. (°F)	***74.3***	73.8	75.4	76.2	77.7	78.9	79.8	80.7	80.3	79.4	***78.0***	***75.2***	***77.5***
Mean Minimum Temp. (°F)	***66.5***	66.1	67.8	69.0	70.6	71.9	72.8	73.5	73.0	72.0	***70.5***	***67.6***	***70.1***
Extreme Maximum Temp. (°F)	90	90	91	94	92	94	94	95	94	94	93	92	95
Extreme Minimum Temp. (°F)	56	58	57	60	63	62	63	58	57	57	62	60	56
Days Maximum Temp. ≥ 90°F	0	0	0	0	0	2	4	7	6	5	1	0	25
Days Maximum Temp. ≤ 32°F	0	0	0	0	0	0	0	0	0	0	0	0	0
Days Minimum Temp. ≤ 32°F	0	0	0	0	0	0	0	0	0	0	0	0	0
Days Minimum Temp. ≤ 0°F	0	0	0	0	0	0	0	0	0	0	0	0	0
Heating Degree Days (base 65°F)	na	0	***0***	***0***	***0***	***0***	***0***	***0***	***0***	***0***	na	***0***	na
Cooling Degree Days (base 65°F)	***295***	254	***327***	344	401	424	466	492	466	453	***398***	***325***	***4,645***
Mean Precipitation (in.)	1.80	0.98	1.15	0.62	0.79	0.62	0.71	0.74	0.74	0.86	1.13	1.76	11.90
Extreme Maximum Daily Precip. (in.)	na	***2.96***	na	2.50	***2.09***	***1.20***	2.00	2.06	***1.27***	2.00	***2.75***	***5.10***	na
Days With ≥ 0.1" Precipitation	2	1	2	1	2	1	1	1	1	1	1	2	16
Days With ≥ 0.5" Precipitation	1	0	0	0	0	0	0	0	0	0	1	1	3
Days With ≥ 1.0" Precipitation	0	0	0	0	0	0	0	0	0	0	0	0	0
Mean Snowfall (in.)	0.0	0.0	0.0	0.0	0.0	0.0	0.0	0.0	0.0	0.0	0.0	0.0	0.0
Maximum Snow Depth (in.)	0	0	0	0	0	0	0	0	0	0	0	0	0
Days With ≥ 1.0" Snow Depth	0	0	0	0	0	0	0	0	0	0	0	0	0

The period of record for all cooperative weather station data is 1980 – 2009. See User Guide for detailed explanation of data.

Kii-Kahuku 911 *Honolulu County* Elevation: 15 ft. Latitude: 21° 42' N Longitude: 157° 59' W

	JAN	FEB	MAR	APR	MAY	JUN	JUL	AUG	SEP	OCT	NOV	DEC	YEAR
Mean Maximum Temp. (°F)	78.3	77.7	78.5	79.0	80.4	82.2	83.1	84.0	84.2	83.4	81.0	79.3	80.9
Mean Temp. (°F)	72.1	71.8	72.8	73.9	75.0	77.3	78.4	79.0	79.0	78.0	75.9	73.6	75.6
Mean Minimum Temp. (°F)	65.8	65.9	67.1	68.7	69.6	72.4	73.5	74.1	73.8	72.5	70.8	67.8	70.2
Extreme Maximum Temp. (°F)	91	90	88	89	88	89	91	92	94	95	91	91	95
Extreme Minimum Temp. (°F)	43	50	55	58	46	61	58	66	66	60	56	56	43
Days Maximum Temp. ≥ 90°F	0	0	0	0	0	0	0	1	2	1	0	0	4
Days Maximum Temp. ≤ 32°F	0	0	0	0	0	0	0	0	0	0	0	0	0
Days Minimum Temp. ≤ 32°F	0	0	0	0	0	0	0	0	0	0	0	0	0
Days Minimum Temp. ≤ 0°F	0	0	0	0	0	0	0	0	0	0	0	0	0
Heating Degree Days (base 65°F)	0	0	0	0	0	0	0	0	0	0	0	0	0
Cooling Degree Days (base 65°F)	226	200	249	273	318	376	422	441	426	409	334	273	3,947
Mean Precipitation (in.)	3.60	3.49	5.17	2.20	2.06	1.72	2.55	1.73	2.22	3.34	5.13	4.11	37.32
Extreme Maximum Daily Precip. (in.)	7.15	3.75	4.08	2.00	5.92	1.70	4.90	2.02	2.70	3.36	6.11	6.95	7.15
Days With ≥ 0.1" Precipitation	6	6	6	5	5	5	6	5	5	6	8	6	69
Days With ≥ 0.5" Precipitation	2	2	2	1	1	1	1	0	1	2	3	2	18
Days With ≥ 1.0" Precipitation	1	1	1	0	0	0	0	0	0	1	1	1	6
Mean Snowfall (in.)	0.0	0.0	0.0	0.0	0.0	0.0	0.0	0.0	0.0	0.0	0.0	0.0	0.0
Maximum Snow Depth (in.)	0	0	0	0	0	0	0	0	0	0	0	0	0
Days With ≥ 1.0" Snow Depth	0	0	0	0	0	0	0	0	0	0	0	0	0

Kula Hospital 267 *Maui County* Elevation: 3,003 ft. Latitude: 20° 42' N Longitude: 156° 22' W

	JAN	FEB	MAR	APR	MAY	JUN	JUL	AUG	SEP	OCT	NOV	DEC	YEAR
Mean Maximum Temp. (°F)	68.1	68.2	68.7	69.8	71.0	73.0	74.3	75.2	74.6	73.5	71.8	68.9	71.4
Mean Temp. (°F)	60.2	59.9	60.5	61.5	62.9	64.5	65.7	66.6	66.3	65.4	63.9	61.1	63.2
Mean Minimum Temp. (°F)	52.3	51.7	52.3	53.2	54.8	56.0	57.1	57.8	57.9	57.2	56.1	53.3	55.0
Extreme Maximum Temp. (°F)	78	81	82	77	78	81	80	82	81	83	81	80	83
Extreme Minimum Temp. (°F)	38	41	41	37	48	50	50	51	49	48	47	41	37
Days Maximum Temp. ≥ 90°F	0	0	0	0	0	0	0	0	0	0	0	0	0
Days Maximum Temp. ≤ 32°F	0	0	0	0	0	0	0	0	0	0	0	0	0
Days Minimum Temp. ≤ 32°F	0	0	0	0	0	0	0	0	0	0	0	0	0
Days Minimum Temp. ≤ 0°F	0	0	0	0	0	0	0	0	0	0	0	0	0
Heating Degree Days (base 65°F)	145	138	132	98	63	22	7	2	3	13	40	115	778
Cooling Degree Days (base 65°F)	2	1	1	1	6	15	38	58	48	32	14	2	218
Mean Precipitation (in.)	4.04	2.42	3.06	2.07	2.10	1.81	1.86	1.51	2.05	3.06	3.38	3.95	31.31
Extreme Maximum Daily Precip. (in.)	4.00	5.60	4.60	3.23	3.20	6.90	3.50	2.05	2.25	6.00	6.60	7.04	7.04
Days With ≥ 0.1" Precipitation	5	4	4	4	4	4	3	3	4	3	4	4	46
Days With ≥ 0.5" Precipitation	2	2	2	1	1	1	1	1	1	1	2	2	17
Days With ≥ 1.0" Precipitation	1	1	1	1	1	0	0	0	0	1	1	1	8
Mean Snowfall (in.)	0.0	0.0	0.0	0.0	0.0	0.0	0.0	0.0	0.0	0.0	0.0	0.0	0.0
Maximum Snow Depth (in.)	0	0	0	0	0	0	0	0	0	0	0	0	0
Days With ≥ 1.0" Snow Depth	0	0	0	0	0	0	0	0	0	0	0	0	0

Molokai Airport *Maui County* Elevation: 450 ft. Latitude: 21° 10' N Longitude: 157° 06' W

	JAN	FEB	MAR	APR	MAY	JUN	JUL	AUG	SEP	OCT	NOV	DEC	YEAR
Mean Maximum Temp. (°F)	77.8	78.0	79.0	80.1	81.9	83.8	84.8	85.7	85.9	84.8	81.9	79.2	81.9
Mean Temp. (°F)	70.5	70.4	71.4	72.7	74.3	76.6	77.8	78.5	78.5	77.4	75.0	72.3	74.6
Mean Minimum Temp. (°F)	63.1	62.8	63.8	65.4	66.7	69.4	70.7	71.3	71.0	70.0	68.1	65.3	67.3
Extreme Maximum Temp. (°F)	88	89	86	92	89	89	91	93	92	91	89	88	93
Extreme Minimum Temp. (°F)	52	48	46	48	52	57	52	56	60	60	57	50	46
Days Maximum Temp. ≥ 90°F	0	0	0	0	0	0	0	0	1	1	0	0	2
Days Maximum Temp. ≤ 32°F	0	0	0	0	0	0	0	0	0	0	0	0	0
Days Minimum Temp. ≤ 32°F	0	0	0	0	0	0	0	0	0	0	0	0	0
Days Minimum Temp. ≤ 0°F	0	0	0	0	0	0	0	0	0	0	0	0	0
Heating Degree Days (base 65°F)	1	1	0	0	0	0	0	0	0	0	0	0	2
Cooling Degree Days (base 65°F)	176	162	205	240	296	356	403	426	411	392	307	233	3,607
Mean Precipitation (in.)	3.98	3.08	2.41	1.99	1.31	0.55	0.67	0.66	0.83	2.00	3.29	4.24	25.01
Extreme Maximum Daily Precip. (in.)	7.02	9.03	3.48	4.12	2.20	1.32	0.76	1.40	1.68	3.20	5.30	4.35	9.03
Days With ≥ 0.1" Precipitation	6	5	5	4	3	2	2	2	2	3	5	6	45
Days With ≥ 0.5" Precipitation	2	1	2	1	1	0	0	0	0	1	2	2	12
Days With ≥ 1.0" Precipitation	1	1	0	0	0	0	0	0	0	1	1	1	5
Mean Snowfall (in.)	0.0	0.0	0.0	0.0	0.0	0.0	0.0	0.0	0.0	0.0	0.0	0.0	0.0
Maximum Snow Depth (in.)	0	0	0	0	0	0	0	0	0	0	0	0	0
Days With ≥ 1.0" Snow Depth	0	0	0	0	0	0	0	0	0	0	0	0	0

Opihihale 2 24.1 *Hawaii County* Elevation: 1,359 ft. Latitude: 19° 16' N Longitude: 155° 53' W

	JAN	FEB	MAR	APR	MAY	JUN	JUL	AUG	SEP	OCT	NOV	DEC	YEAR
Mean Maximum Temp. (°F)	76.9	76.9	77.1	77.6	78.2	79.0	80.0	80.9	80.8	80.7	79.4	77.9	78.8
Mean Temp. (°F)	67.3	67.2	67.9	68.6	69.9	71.0	71.9	72.5	72.1	71.6	70.3	68.3	69.9
Mean Minimum Temp. (°F)	57.5	57.4	58.6	59.5	61.5	63.0	63.7	64.1	63.4	62.5	61.0	58.6	60.9
Extreme Maximum Temp. (°F)	90	89	94	85	87	87	87	90	91	90	90	88	94
Extreme Minimum Temp. (°F)	50	50	51	53	50	57	57	57	56	55	49	50	49
Days Maximum Temp. ≥ 90°F	0	0	0	0	0	0	0	0	0	0	0	0	0
Days Maximum Temp. ≤ 32°F	0	0	0	0	0	0	0	0	0	0	0	0	0
Days Minimum Temp. ≤ 32°F	0	0	0	0	0	0	0	0	0	0	0	0	0
Days Minimum Temp. ≤ 0°F	0	0	0	0	0	0	0	0	0	0	0	0	0
Heating Degree Days (base 65°F)	4	4	3	1	0	0	0	0	0	0	0	1	13
Cooling Degree Days (base 65°F)	81	71	100	115	158	187	221	240	219	213	165	110	1,880
Mean Precipitation (in.)	2.95	2.44	3.53	2.75	2.70	2.91	3.64	3.47	4.08	3.66	2.79	2.80	37.72
Extreme Maximum Daily Precip. (in.)	3.89	5.26	5.23	4.57	3.33	2.16	6.22	5.13	6.28	3.24	6.09	5.58	6.28
Days With ≥ 0.1" Precipitation	4	4	6	6	6	7	7	8	8	7	5	4	72
Days With ≥ 0.5" Precipitation	2	1	2	1	1	1	2	2	2	2	1	2	19
Days With ≥ 1.0" Precipitation	1	0	1	1	0	0	1	1	1	1	1	1	9
Mean Snowfall (in.)	0.0	0.0	0.0	0.0	0.0	0.0	0.0	0.0	0.0	0.0	0.0	0.0	0.0
Maximum Snow Depth (in.)	0	0	0	0	0	0	0	0	0	0	0	0	0
Days With ≥ 1.0" Snow Depth	0	0	0	0	0	0	0	0	0	0	0	0	0

The period of record for all cooperative weather station data is 1980 – 2009. See User Guide for detailed explanation of data.

Hawaii Weather Station Rankings

Annual Extreme Maximum Temperature

Highest Rank	Station Name	°F	Lowest Rank	Station Name	°F
1	Kahului Arpt	97	1	Haleakala R S 338	78
2	Honolulu Intl Arpt	96	2	Kula Hospital 267	83
3	Ke-Ahole Point 68.13	95	3	Kanalohuluhulu 1075	90
3	Kii-Kahuku 911	95	3	Lihue Arpt	90
5	Opihihale 2 24.1	94	5	Hawaii Volcanos Np Hq 54	93
6	Hawaii Volcanos Np Hq 54	93	5	Hilo International Arpt	93
6	Hilo International Arpt	93	5	Molokai Airport	93
6	Molokai Airport	93	8	Opihihale 2 24.1	94
9	Kanalohuluhulu 1075	90	9	Ke-Ahole Point 68.13	95
9	Lihue Arpt	90	9	Kii-Kahuku 911	95
11	Kula Hospital 267	83	11	Honolulu Intl Arpt	96
12	Haleakala R S 338	78	12	Kahului Arpt	97

Annual Mean Maximum Temperature

Highest Rank	Station Name	°F	Lowest Rank	Station Name	°F
1	Honolulu Intl Arpt	84.8	1	Haleakala R S 338	62.8
1	Ke-Ahole Point 68.13	***84.8***	2	Kanalohuluhulu 1075	66.6
3	Kahului Arpt	84.3	3	Hawaii Volcanos Np Hq 54	70.3
4	Molokai Airport	81.9	4	Kula Hospital 267	71.4
5	Hilo International Arpt	81.4	5	Opihihale 2 24.1	78.8
6	Lihue Arpt	81.2	6	Kii-Kahuku 911	80.9
7	Kii-Kahuku 911	80.9	7	Lihue Arpt	81.2
8	Opihihale 2 24.1	78.8	8	Hilo International Arpt	81.4
9	Kula Hospital 267	71.4	9	Molokai Airport	81.9
10	Hawaii Volcanos Np Hq 54	70.3	10	Kahului Arpt	84.3
11	Kanalohuluhulu 1075	66.6	11	Honolulu Intl Arpt	84.8
12	Haleakala R S 338	62.8	11	Ke-Ahole Point 68.13	***84.8***

 Rankings include 25 highest/lowest stations. If state has less than 25 stations, all stations are included. The period of record is 1980–2009. See User Guide for detailed explanation of data.

Annual Mean Temperature

Rank	Station Name (Highest)	°F	Rank	Station Name (Lowest)	°F
1	Honolulu Intl Arpt	77.8	1	Haleakala R S 338	54.2
2	Ke-Ahole Point 68.13	*77.5*	2	Kanalohuluhulu 1075	58.7
3	Kahului Arpt	76.0	3	Hawaii Volcanos Np Hq 54	61.6
4	Lihue Arpt	75.8	4	Kula Hospital 267	63.2
5	Kii-Kahuku 911	*75.6*	5	Opihihale 2 24.1	69.9
6	Molokai Airport	74.6	6	Hilo International Arpt	74.1
7	Hilo International Arpt	74.1	7	Molokai Airport	74.6
8	Opihihale 2 24.1	69.9	8	Kii-Kahuku 911	*75.6*
9	Kula Hospital 267	63.2	9	Lihue Arpt	75.8
10	Hawaii Volcanos Np Hq 54	61.6	10	Kahului Arpt	76.0
11	Kanalohuluhulu 1075	58.7	11	Ke-Ahole Point 68.13	*77.5*
12	Haleakala R S 338	54.2	12	Honolulu Intl Arpt	77.8

Annual Mean Minimum Temperature

Rank	Station Name (Highest)	°F	Rank	Station Name (Lowest)	°F
1	Honolulu Intl Arpt	70.8	1	Haleakala R S 338	45.6
2	Lihue Arpt	70.4	2	Kanalohuluhulu 1075	50.8
3	Kii-Kahuku 911	*70.2*	3	Hawaii Volcanos Np Hq 54	52.9
4	Ke-Ahole Point 68.13	*70.1*	4	Kula Hospital 267	55.0
5	Kahului Arpt	67.6	5	Opihihale 2 24.1	60.9
6	Molokai Airport	67.3	6	Hilo International Arpt	66.8
7	Hilo International Arpt	66.8	7	Molokai Airport	67.3
8	Opihihale 2 24.1	60.9	8	Kahului Arpt	67.6
9	Kula Hospital 267	55.0	9	Ke-Ahole Point 68.13	*70.1*
10	Hawaii Volcanos Np Hq 54	52.9	10	Kii-Kahuku 911	*70.2*
11	Kanalohuluhulu 1075	50.8	11	Lihue Arpt	70.4
12	Haleakala R S 338	45.6	12	Honolulu Intl Arpt	70.8

Rankings include 25 highest/lowest stations. If state has less than 25 stations, all stations are included. The period of record is 1980–2009. See User Guide for detailed explanation of data.

Annual Extreme Minimum Temperature

Highest

Rank	Station Name	°F
1	Ke-Ahole Point 68.13	56
2	Hilo International Arpt	54
3	Honolulu Intl Arpt	53
3	Lihue Arpt	53
5	Kahului Arpt	50
6	Opihihale 2 24.1	49
7	Molokai Airport	46
8	Kii-Kahuku 911	43
9	Kula Hospital 267	37
10	Hawaii Volcanos Np Hq 54	31
11	Haleakala R S 338	29
11	Kanalohuluhulu 1075	29

Lowest

Rank	Station Name	°F
1	Haleakala R S 338	29
1	Kanalohuluhulu 1075	29
3	Hawaii Volcanos Np Hq 54	31
4	Kula Hospital 267	37
5	Kii-Kahuku 911	43
6	Molokai Airport	46
7	Opihihale 2 24.1	49
8	Kahului Arpt	50
9	Honolulu Intl Arpt	53
9	Lihue Arpt	53
11	Hilo International Arpt	54
12	Ke-Ahole Point 68.13	56

July Mean Maximum Temperature

Highest

Rank	Station Name	°F
1	Honolulu Intl Arpt	88.3
2	Kahului Arpt	87.2
3	Ke-Ahole Point 68.13	86.8
4	Molokai Airport	84.8
5	Lihue Arpt	84.2
6	Hilo International Arpt	83.3
7	Kii-Kahuku 911	83.1
8	Opihihale 2 24.1	80.1
9	Kula Hospital 267	74.3
10	Hawaii Volcanos Np Hq 54	72.3
11	Kanalohuluhulu 1075	69.9
12	Haleakala R S 338	65.6

Lowest

Rank	Station Name	°F
1	Haleakala R S 338	65.6
2	Kanalohuluhulu 1075	69.9
3	Hawaii Volcanos Np Hq 54	72.3
4	Kula Hospital 267	74.3
5	Opihihale 2 24.1	80.1
6	Kii-Kahuku 911	83.1
7	Hilo International Arpt	83.3
8	Lihue Arpt	84.2
9	Molokai Airport	84.8
10	Ke-Ahole Point 68.13	86.8
11	Kahului Arpt	87.2
12	Honolulu Intl Arpt	88.3

 Rankings include 25 highest/lowest stations. If state has less than 25 stations, all stations are included. The period of record is 1980–2009. See User Guide for detailed explanation of data.

January Mean Minimum Temperature

Highest			Lowest		
Rank	Station Name	°F	Rank	Station Name	°F
1	Ke-Ahole Point 68.13	***66.5***	1	Haleakala R S 338	43.1
2	Honolulu Intl Arpt	66.1	2	Kanalohuluhulu 1075	46.1
3	Kii-Kahuku 911	65.8	3	Hawaii Volcanos Np Hq 54	49.5
4	Lihue Arpt	65.5	4	Kula Hospital 267	52.3
5	Hilo International Arpt	63.7	5	Opihihale 2 24.1	57.5
6	Kahului Arpt	63.6	6	Molokai Airport	63.1
7	Molokai Airport	63.1	7	Kahului Arpt	63.6
8	Opihihale 2 24.1	57.5	8	Hilo International Arpt	63.7
9	Kula Hospital 267	52.3	9	Lihue Arpt	65.5
10	Hawaii Volcanos Np Hq 54	49.5	10	Kii-Kahuku 911	65.8
11	Kanalohuluhulu 1075	46.1	11	Honolulu Intl Arpt	66.1
12	Haleakala R S 338	43.1	12	Ke-Ahole Point 68.13	***66.5***

Number of Days Annually Maximum Temperature ≥ 90°F

Highest			Lowest		
Rank	Station Name	Days	Rank	Station Name	Days
1	Honolulu Intl Arpt	39	1	Haleakala R S 338	0
2	Kahului Arpt	26	1	Hawaii Volcanos Np Hq 54	0
3	Ke-Ahole Point 68.13	25	1	Hilo International Arpt	0
4	Kii-Kahuku 911	4	1	Kanalohuluhulu 1075	0
5	Molokai Airport	2	1	Kula Hospital 267	0
6	Haleakala R S 338	0	1	Lihue Arpt	0
6	Hawaii Volcanos Np Hq 54	0	1	Opihihale 2 24.1	0
6	Hilo International Arpt	0	8	Molokai Airport	2
6	Kanalohuluhulu 1075	0	9	Kii-Kahuku 911	4
6	Kula Hospital 267	0	10	Ke-Ahole Point 68.13	25
6	Lihue Arpt	0	11	Kahului Arpt	26
6	Opihihale 2 24.1	0	12	Honolulu Intl Arpt	39

Number of Days Annually Maximum Temperature ≤ 32°F

Highest

Rank	Station Name	Days
1	Haleakala R S 338	0
1	Hawaii Volcanos Np Hq 54	0
1	Hilo International Arpt	0
1	Honolulu Intl Arpt	0
1	Kahului Arpt	0
1	Kanalohuluhulu 1075	0
1	Ke-Ahole Point 68.13	0
1	Kii-Kahuku 911	0
1	Kula Hospital 267	0
1	Lihue Arpt	0
1	Molokai Airport	0
1	Opihihale 2 24.1	0

Lowest

Rank	Station Name	Days
1	Haleakala R S 338	0
1	Hawaii Volcanos Np Hq 54	0
1	Hilo International Arpt	0
1	Honolulu Intl Arpt	0
1	Kahului Arpt	0
1	Kanalohuluhulu 1075	0
1	Ke-Ahole Point 68.13	0
1	Kii-Kahuku 911	0
1	Kula Hospital 267	0
1	Lihue Arpt	0
1	Molokai Airport	0
1	Opihihale 2 24.1	0

Number of Days Annually Minimum Temperature ≤ 32°F

Highest

Rank	Station Name	Days
1	Haleakala R S 338	0
1	Hawaii Volcanos Np Hq 54	0
1	Hilo International Arpt	0
1	Honolulu Intl Arpt	0
1	Kahului Arpt	0
1	Kanalohuluhulu 1075	0
1	Ke-Ahole Point 68.13	0
1	Kii-Kahuku 911	0
1	Kula Hospital 267	0
1	Lihue Arpt	0
1	Molokai Airport	0
1	Opihihale 2 24.1	0

Lowest

Rank	Station Name	Days
1	Haleakala R S 338	0
1	Hawaii Volcanos Np Hq 54	0
1	Hilo International Arpt	0
1	Honolulu Intl Arpt	0
1	Kahului Arpt	0
1	Kanalohuluhulu 1075	0
1	Ke-Ahole Point 68.13	0
1	Kii-Kahuku 911	0
1	Kula Hospital 267	0
1	Lihue Arpt	0
1	Molokai Airport	0
1	Opihihale 2 24.1	0

Rankings include 25 highest/lowest stations. If state has less than 25 stations, all stations are included. The period of record is 1980–2009. See User Guide for detailed explanation of data.

Number of Days Annually Minimum Temperature ≤ 0°F

Highest			Lowest		
Rank	Station Name	Days	Rank	Station Name	Days
1	Haleakala R S 338	0	1	Haleakala R S 338	0
1	Hawaii Volcanos Np Hq 54	0	1	Hawaii Volcanos Np Hq 54	0
1	Hilo International Arpt	0	1	Hilo International Arpt	0
1	Honolulu Intl Arpt	0	1	Honolulu Intl Arpt	0
1	Kahului Arpt	0	1	Kahului Arpt	0
1	Kanalohuluhulu 1075	0	1	Kanalohuluhulu 1075	0
1	Ke-Ahole Point 68.13	0	1	Ke-Ahole Point 68.13	0
1	Kii-Kahuku 911	0	1	Kii-Kahuku 911	0
1	Kula Hospital 267	0	1	Kula Hospital 267	0
1	Lihue Arpt	0	1	Lihue Arpt	0
1	Molokai Airport	***0***	1	Molokai Airport	***0***
1	Opihihale 2 24.1	0	1	Opihihale 2 24.1	0

Number of Annual Heating Degree Days

Highest			Lowest		
Rank	Station Name	Num.	Rank	Station Name	Num.
1	Haleakala R S 338	3,840	1	Hilo International Arpt	0
2	Kanalohuluhulu 1075	***2,277***	1	Honolulu Intl Arpt	0
3	Hawaii Volcanos Np Hq 54	1,242	1	Kahului Arpt	0
4	Kula Hospital 267	778	1	Kii-Kahuku 911	***0***
5	Opihihale 2 24.1	13	1	Lihue Arpt	0
6	Molokai Airport	***2***	6	Molokai Airport	***2***
7	Hilo International Arpt	0	7	Opihihale 2 24.1	13
7	Honolulu Intl Arpt	0	8	Kula Hospital 267	778
7	Kahului Arpt	0	9	Hawaii Volcanos Np Hq 54	1,242
7	Kii-Kahuku 911	***0***	10	Kanalohuluhulu 1075	***2,277***
7	Lihue Arpt	0	11	Haleakala R S 338	3,840

Number of Annual Cooling Degree Days

Highest

Rank	Station Name	Num.
1	Honolulu Intl Arpt	4,778
2	Ke-Ahole Point 68.13	***4,645***
3	Kahului Arpt	4,099
4	Lihue Arpt	4,036
5	Kii-Kahuku 911	***3,947***
6	Molokai Airport	3,607
7	Hilo International Arpt	3,417
8	Opihihale 2 24.1	1,880
9	Kula Hospital 267	218
10	Hawaii Volcanos Np Hq 54	85
11	Kanalohuluhulu 1075	23
12	Haleakala R S 338	2

Lowest

Rank	Station Name	Num.
1	Haleakala R S 338	2
2	Kanalohuluhulu 1075	23
3	Hawaii Volcanos Np Hq 54	85
4	Kula Hospital 267	218
5	Opihihale 2 24.1	1,880
6	Hilo International Arpt	3,417
7	Molokai Airport	3,607
8	Kii-Kahuku 911	***3,947***
9	Lihue Arpt	4,036
10	Kahului Arpt	4,099
11	Ke-Ahole Point 68.13	***4,645***
12	Honolulu Intl Arpt	4,778

Annual Precipitation

Highest

Rank	Station Name	Inches
1	Hilo International Arpt	127.30
2	Hawaii Volcanos Np Hq 54	106.93
3	Kanalohuluhulu 1075	***62.07***
4	Haleakala R S 338	52.67
5	Lihue Arpt	38.69
6	Opihihale 2 24.1	37.72
7	Kii-Kahuku 911	***37.32***
8	Kula Hospital 267	31.31
9	Molokai Airport	25.01
10	Kahului Arpt	18.41
11	Honolulu Intl Arpt	17.37
12	Ke-Ahole Point 68.13	11.90

Lowest

Rank	Station Name	Inches
1	Ke-Ahole Point 68.13	11.90
2	Honolulu Intl Arpt	17.37
3	Kahului Arpt	18.41
4	Molokai Airport	25.01
5	Kula Hospital 267	31.31
6	Kii-Kahuku 911	***37.32***
7	Opihihale 2 24.1	37.72
8	Lihue Arpt	38.69
9	Haleakala R S 338	52.67
10	Kanalohuluhulu 1075	***62.07***
11	Hawaii Volcanos Np Hq 54	106.93
12	Hilo International Arpt	127.30

 Rankings include 25 highest/lowest stations. If state has less than 25 stations, all stations are included. The period of record is 1980–2009. See User Guide for detailed explanation of data.

Annual Extreme Maximum Daily Precipitation

Highest			Lowest		
Rank	Station Name	Inches	Rank	Station Name	Inches
1	Haleakala R S 338	18.50	1	Kahului Arpt	4.76
2	Hilo International Arpt	16.17	2	Opihihale 2 24.1	6.28
3	Hawaii Volcanos Np Hq 54	13.06	3	Kula Hospital 267	7.04
4	Kanalohuluhulu 1075	11.97	4	Kii-Kahuku 911	*7.15*
5	Lihue Arpt	9.75	5	Honolulu Intl Arpt	7.89
6	Molokai Airport	9.03	6	Molokai Airport	9.03
7	Honolulu Intl Arpt	7.89	7	Lihue Arpt	9.75
8	Kii-Kahuku 911	*7.15*	8	Kanalohuluhulu 1075	11.97
9	Kula Hospital 267	7.04	9	Hawaii Volcanos Np Hq 54	13.06
10	Opihihale 2 24.1	6.28	10	Hilo International Arpt	16.17
11	Kahului Arpt	4.76	11	Haleakala R S 338	18.50

Number of Days Annually With ≥ 0.1 Inches of Precipitation

Highest			Lowest		
Rank	Station Name	Days	Rank	Station Name	Days
1	Hilo International Arpt	190	1	Ke-Ahole Point 68.13	16
2	Hawaii Volcanos Np Hq 54	160	2	Honolulu Intl Arpt	28
3	Kanalohuluhulu 1075	92	3	Kahului Arpt	34
4	Opihihale 2 24.1	72	4	Molokai Airport	45
5	Lihue Arpt	71	5	Kula Hospital 267	46
6	Haleakala R S 338	70	6	Kii-Kahuku 911	69
7	Kii-Kahuku 911	69	7	Haleakala R S 338	70
8	Kula Hospital 267	46	8	Lihue Arpt	71
9	Molokai Airport	45	9	Opihihale 2 24.1	72
10	Kahului Arpt	34	10	Kanalohuluhulu 1075	92
11	Honolulu Intl Arpt	28	11	Hawaii Volcanos Np Hq 54	160
12	Ke-Ahole Point 68.13	16	12	Hilo International Arpt	190

Rankings include 25 highest/lowest stations. If state has less than 25 stations, all stations are included. The period of record is 1980–2009. See User Guide for detailed explanation of data.

Number of Days Annually With ≥ 0.5 Inches of Precipitation

Highest			Lowest		
Rank	Station Name	Days	Rank	Station Name	Days
1	Hilo International Arpt	70	1	Ke-Ahole Point 68.13	3
2	Hawaii Volcanos Np Hq 54	51	2	Honolulu Intl Arpt	6
3	Kanalohuluhulu 1075	29	3	Kahului Arpt	9
4	Haleakala R S 338	25	4	Molokai Airport	12
5	Opihihale 2 24.1	19	5	Lihue Arpt	16
6	Kii-Kahuku 911	18	6	Kula Hospital 267	17
7	Kula Hospital 267	17	7	Kii-Kahuku 911	18
8	Lihue Arpt	16	8	Opihihale 2 24.1	19
9	Molokai Airport	12	9	Haleakala R S 338	25
10	Kahului Arpt	9	10	Kanalohuluhulu 1075	29
11	Honolulu Intl Arpt	6	11	Hawaii Volcanos Np Hq 54	51
12	Ke-Ahole Point 68.13	3	12	Hilo International Arpt	70

Number of Days Annually With ≥ 1.0 Inches of Precipitation

Highest			Lowest		
Rank	Station Name	Days	Rank	Station Name	Days
1	Hilo International Arpt	30	1	Ke-Ahole Point 68.13	0
2	Hawaii Volcanos Np Hq 54	21	2	Honolulu Intl Arpt	4
3	Kanalohuluhulu 1075	15	2	Kahului Arpt	4
4	Haleakala R S 338	12	4	Molokai Airport	5
5	Opihihale 2 24.1	9	5	Kii-Kahuku 911	6
6	Kula Hospital 267	8	5	Lihue Arpt	6
7	Kii-Kahuku 911	6	7	Kula Hospital 267	8
7	Lihue Arpt	6	8	Opihihale 2 24.1	9
9	Molokai Airport	5	9	Haleakala R S 338	12
10	Honolulu Intl Arpt	4	10	Kanalohuluhulu 1075	15
10	Kahului Arpt	4	11	Hawaii Volcanos Np Hq 54	21
12	Ke-Ahole Point 68.13	0	12	Hilo International Arpt	30

Rankings include 25 highest/lowest stations. If state has less than 25 stations, all stations are included. The period of record is 1980–2009. See User Guide for detailed explanation of data.

Annual Snowfall

Highest			Lowest		
Rank	Station Name	Inches	Rank	Station Name	Inches
1	Haleakala R S 338	0.0	1	Haleakala R S 338	0.0
1	Hawaii Volcanos Np Hq 54	0.0	1	Hawaii Volcanos Np Hq 54	0.0
1	Kanalohuluhulu 1075	0.0	1	Kanalohuluhulu 1075	0.0
1	Ke-Ahole Point 68.13	0.0	1	Ke-Ahole Point 68.13	0.0
1	Kii-Kahuku 911	0.0	1	Kii-Kahuku 911	0.0
1	Kula Hospital 267	0.0	1	Kula Hospital 267	0.0
1	Lihue Arpt	0.0	1	Lihue Arpt	0.0
1	Molokai Airport	***0.0***	1	Molokai Airport	***0.0***
1	Opihihale 2 24.1	0.0	1	Opihihale 2 24.1	0.0

Annual Maximum Snow Depth

Highest			Lowest		
Rank	Station Name	Inches	Rank	Station Name	Inches
1	Haleakala R S 338	0	1	Haleakala R S 338	0
1	Hawaii Volcanos Np Hq 54	0	1	Hawaii Volcanos Np Hq 54	0
1	Kanalohuluhulu 1075	0	1	Kanalohuluhulu 1075	0
1	Ke-Ahole Point 68.13	0	1	Ke-Ahole Point 68.13	0
1	Kii-Kahuku 911	0	1	Kii-Kahuku 911	0
1	Kula Hospital 267	0	1	Kula Hospital 267	0
1	Lihue Arpt	0	1	Lihue Arpt	0
1	Molokai Airport	***0***	1	Molokai Airport	***0***
1	Opihihale 2 24.1	0	1	Opihihale 2 24.1	0

Number of Days Annually With ≥ 1.0 Inch Snow Depth

Highest			Lowest		
Rank	Station Name	Days	Rank	Station Name	Days
1	Haleakala R S 338	0	1	Haleakala R S 338	0
1	Hawaii Volcanos Np Hq 54	0	1	Hawaii Volcanos Np Hq 54	0
1	Kanalohuluhulu 1075	0	1	Kanalohuluhulu 1075	0
1	Ke-Ahole Point 68.13	0	1	Ke-Ahole Point 68.13	0
1	Kii-Kahuku 911	0	1	Kii-Kahuku 911	0
1	Kula Hospital 267	0	1	Kula Hospital 267	0
1	Lihue Arpt	0	1	Lihue Arpt	0
1	Molokai Airport	***0***	1	Molokai Airport	***0***
1	Opihihale 2 24.1	0	1	Opihihale 2 24.1	0

 Rankings include 25 highest/lowest stations. If state has less than 25 stations, all stations are included. The period of record is 1980–2009. See User Guide for detailed explanation of data.

Significant Storm Events in Hawaii: 2000 – 2009

Location or County	Date	Type	Mag.	Deaths	Injuries	Property Damage ($mil.)	Crop Damage ($mil.)
Hawaii	11/01/00	Flash Flood	na	0	0	70.0	0.0
Kauai, Niihau, and Oahu North Shores, and Waianae Coast	11/08/01	High Surf	na	1	0	0.0	0.0
Maui	01/29/02	Flash Flood	na	0	0	2.5	0.0
Kauai, Oahu, and Waianae Shores, and Koko Kai Beach	06/12/02	High Surf	na	1	1	0.0	0.0
Isle of Lihue, Niihau	11/15/02	Strong Wind	na	1	0	0.0	0.0
Kauai Leeward and Windward, Niihau, Oahu Shore, and Waianae Coast	01/02/03	Heavy Surf/High Surf	na	1	1	0.0	0.0
Maui	04/10/03	Flash Flood	na	2	0	0.0	0.0
Oahu, Kauai, Maui, and Big Island	01/14/04	High Wind	73 mph	1	0	0.0	0.0
North- and West-facing shores of Kauai, Oahu, Maui, and Molokai	02/27/04	Heavy Surf/High Surf	na	1	0	0.0	0.0
Honolulu	10/30/04	Flash Flood	na	0	0	80.0	0.0
Niihau, Oahu, Kauai, Maui, and Molokai Shores	12/16/04	Heavy Surf/High Surf	na	1	0	0.0	0.0
Niihau, Kauai, Kona, Oahu, Molokai, Lanaii, and Maui Shores	12/20/04	Heavy Surf/High Surf	na	1	0	0.0	0.0
Olomana, Oahu	12/18/05	Strong Wind	46 mph	1	1	0.0	0.0
Kauai	03/13/06	Flash Flood	na	7	0	0.0	0.0
Oahu South Shore	02/26/09	Strong Wind	49 mph	1	0	0.0	0.0
Maui	11/26/09	Heavy Rain	na	2	0	0.0	0.0

Note: Deaths, injuries, and damages are date and location specific.

IDAHO

PHYSICAL FEATURES. Idaho lies entirely west of the Continental Divide, which forms its boundary for some distance westward from Yellowstone National Park. With a maximum north-south extent of 7° of latitude, its east-west extent is 6° of longitude at latitude 42° N., but only 1° of longitude at 49° N. The northern part of the State averages lower in elevation than the much larger central and southern portions, where numerous mountain ranges form barriers to the free flow of air from all points of the compass. In the north the main barrier is the rugged chain of Bitterroot Mountains forming much of the boundary between Idaho and Montana. The extreme range of elevation in the State is from 738 feet at the confluence of the Clearwater and Snake Rivers to 12,655 feet at Mt. Borah in Custer County.

GENERAL CLIMATE. Comprising rugged mountain ranges, canyons, high grassy valleys, arid plains, and fertile lowlands, the State reflects in its topography and vegetation a wide range of climates. Located some 300 miles from the Pacific Ocean, Idaho is, nevertheless, influenced by maritime air borne eastward on the prevailing westerly winds. Particularly in winter, the maritime influence is noticeable in the greater average cloudiness, greater frequency of precipitation, and mean temperatures, which are above those at the same latitude and altitude in midcontinent. This maritime influence is most marked in the northern part of the State, where the air arrives via the Columbia River Gorge with a greater burden of moisture than at lower latitudes. Eastern Idaho's climate has a more continental character than the west and north, a fact quite evident not only in the somewhat greater range between winter and summer temperatures, but also in the reversal of the wet winter-dry summer patterns.

The pattern of average annual temperatures for the State indicates the effect both of latitude and altitude. The highest annual averages are found in the lower elevations of the Clearwater and Little Salmon River Basins, and in the stretch of the Snake River Valley from the vicinity of Bliss downstream to Lewiston, including the open valleys of the Boise, Payette, and Weiser Rivers. The diurnal range of temperature is, of course, most extreme in high valleys and in the semiarid plains of the Snake River Valley. The magnitude of diurnal range varies with the season, being lowest in winter when cloudiness is much more prevalent, and greatest in the warmer part of the year. In summer, periods of extreme heat extending beyond a week are quite rare, and the same can be said of periods of extremely low temperatures in winter. In both cases the normal progress of weather systems across the State usually results in a change at rather frequent intervals.

PRECIPITATION. To a large extent the source of moisture for precipitation in Idaho is the Pacific Ocean. In summer there are some exceptions to this when moisture-laden air is brought in from the south at high levels to produce thundershower activity, particularly in the eastern part of Idaho. The source of this moisture from the south is apparently the Gulf of Mexico and Caribbean region. The average precipitation map for Idaho is as complex as the physiography of the State. Partly because of the greater moisture supply in the west winds over the northern part of the State (less formidable barriers to the west) and partly because of greater frequency of cyclonic activity in the north, the average valley precipitation is considerably greater than in southern sections. Peaks on the average annual precipitation map are found, however, in nearly all parts of the State at higher elevations. Sizable areas in the Clearwater, Payette, and Boise River Basins receive an average of 40 to 50 inches per year, with a few points or small areas receiving in excess of 60 inches. Large areas including the northeastern valleys, much of the Upper Snake River Plains, Central Plains, and the lower elevations of the Southwestern Valleys receive less than 10 inches annually.

Seasonal distribution of precipitation shows a very marked pattern of winter maximum and midsummer minimum in the northern and western portions of the State. In the eastern part of the State, however, many reporting weather stations show maximum monthly amounts in summer and minimum amounts in winter. In the divisions called Northeastern Valleys and Eastern Highlands, more than 50 percent of the annual rainfall occurs during the period April through September. Over nearly all of the northern part of the State, however, less than 40 percent of the annual rainfall occurs in this same period, and in portions of the Boise, Payette, and Weiser River drainages less than 30 percent of the annual amount comes in that 6-month period.

SNOW. Snowfall distribution is affected both by availability of moisture and by elevation. The major mountain ranges of the State accumulate a deep snow cover during the winter months, and the release of water from a melting snowpack in late spring furnishes irrigation water for more than two million acres, mainly within the Snake River Basin above Weiser.

FLOODS. Floods in Idaho occur most often during the period of seasonal snowmelt in spring, particularly in April and May. A few areas in the State are actually flooded or threatened by flood waters nearly every year. So-called "out-of-season" floods do occur occasionally at a number of points in the State. Flash floods on small streams, or occasionally in ravines or dry gulches, occur a few times each year as the result of heavy rains associated with thunderstorms.

HUMIDITY. The diurnal range of relative humidity generally follows a pattern which is the reverse of the diurnal temperature curve. Precipitation or fog interferes with such a pattern, but the averages show maximum humidity at the time of minimum temperature and vice versa. In winter, average relative humidities are considerably higher than during hot weather. Comfort during the summer months is greatly affected by the moisture content of the air. In Idaho, where maximum temperatures above 90°F. are not uncommon in July and August, humidity at the time of maximum temperature is usually below 25 percent, and often down to 15 percent or lower. With any kind of air movement the higher temperatures are quite within the range of adjustment of the human system.

FOG. Fogs in Idaho are extremely variable. At Boise, heavy fog (visibility 1/4 mile or less) is experienced on an average of 17 days per year, with a maximum of six occurrences in December. The year-to-year variation is considerable, however.

STORMS. Windstorms are not uncommon in Idaho, but the State has no such destructive storms as hurricanes, and an extremely small incidence of tornadoes. Windstorms associated with cyclonic systems, and their cold fronts, do some damage each year. Storms of this type may occur at any time from October into June, while during the remaining 3 months of the year strong winds almost invariably come with thunderstorms. Hail damage in Idaho is very small in comparison with such damage in other areas of the central part of the United States. Often the hail that occurs does not grow to a size larger than 1/2 inch in diameter, and the areas affected are usually limited in size. Quite often hail comes in springtime storms, when it is mostly of the small, soft variety with a limited damaging effect. The incidence of summer thunderstorms is greatest in mountainous areas, with an important influence on the economy of the State, resulting from the lightning-caused forest and range fires.

SUNSHINE. The annual average percentage of possible sunshine ranges from about 50 in the north to about 70 in the south. Winter, with its frequent periods of cloudy weather, has about 40 percent of possible sunshine in the large open valleys of the south and less than 30 percent in the north, but in July and August the average percentage rises to the upper 80s in the southwest and to near 80 percent in the east and north.

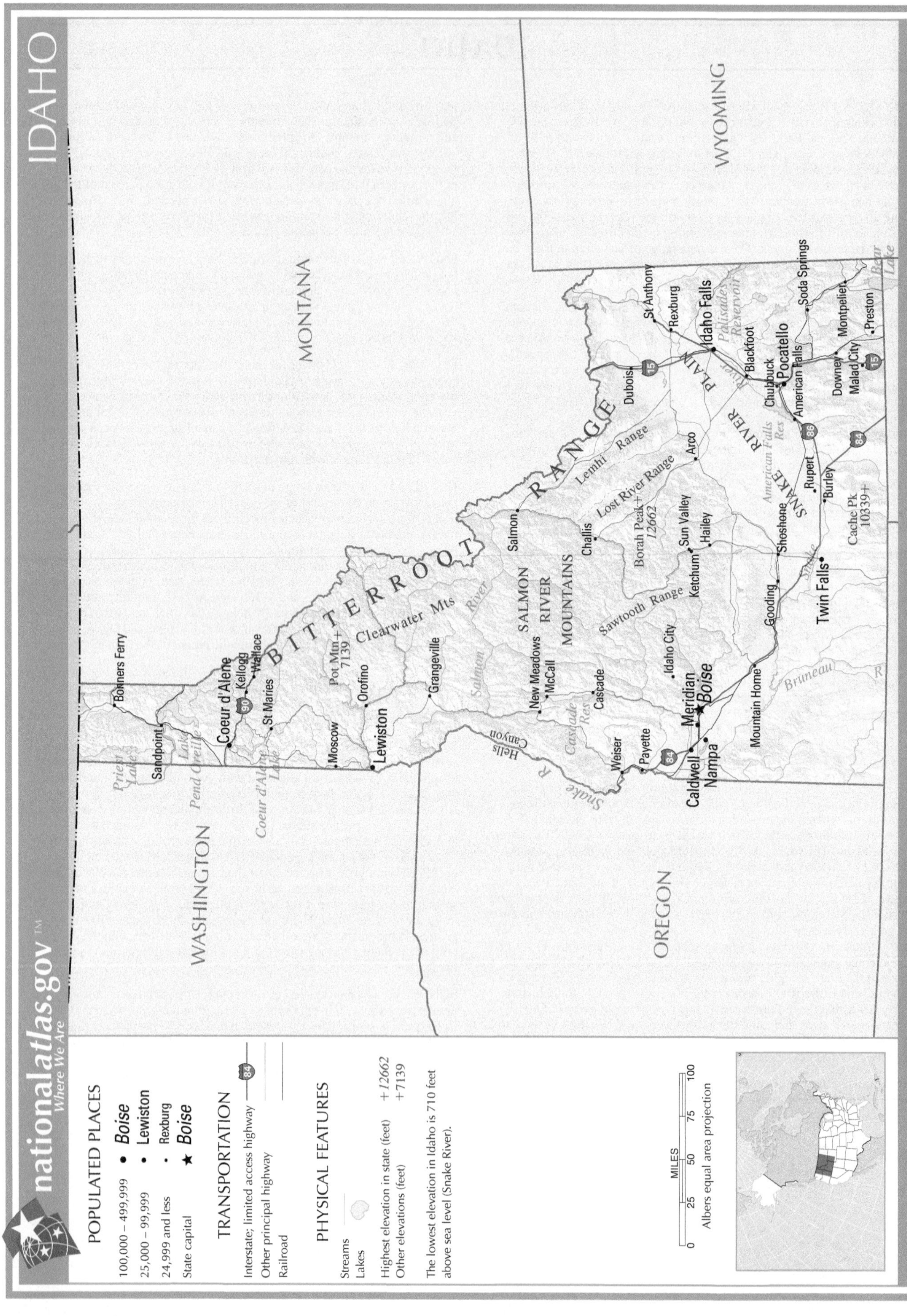
IDAHO
nationalatlas.gov™
Where We Are
POPULATED PLACES
100,000 – 499,999 ● Boise
25,000 – 99,999 • Lewiston
24,999 and less · Rexburg
State capital ★ Boise
TRANSPORTATION
Interstate; limited access highway 84
Other principal highway
Railroad
PHYSICAL FEATURES
Streams
Lakes
Highest elevation in state (feet) +12662
Other elevations (feet) +7139
The lowest elevation in Idaho is 710 feet above sea level (Snake River).
MILES
0 25 50 75 100
Albers equal area projection
U.S. Department of the Interior
U.S. Geological Survey
The National Atlas of the United States of America®
WASHINGTON
MONTANA
WYOMING
OREGON
BITTERROOT RANGE
SALMON RIVER MOUNTAINS
SNAKE RIVER PLAIN
Clearwater Mts
Lemhi Range
Lost River Range
Sawtooth Range
Borah Peak+ 12662
Pot Mtn+ 7139
Cache Pk 10339+
Bonners Ferry
Sandpoint
Priest Lakes
Lake Pend Oreille
Coeur d'Alene Lake
Coeur d'Alene
Kellogg
Wallace
St Maries
Moscow
Lewiston
Orofino
Grangeville
Salmon
Salmon River
Hells Canyon
Snake R
New Meadows
McCall
Cascade
Cascade Res
Weiser
Payette
Caldwell
Nampa
Meridian
Boise
Idaho City
Mountain Home
Bruneau
Challis
Sun Valley
Ketchum
Hailey
Arco
Gooding
Shoshone
Twin Falls
Rupert
Burley
American Falls Res
Dubois
St Anthony
Rexburg
Idaho Falls
Palisades Reservoir
Blackfoot
Chubbuck
Pocatello
American Falls
Soda Springs
Downey
Malad City
Montpelier
Preston
Bear Lake
15
84
86
90

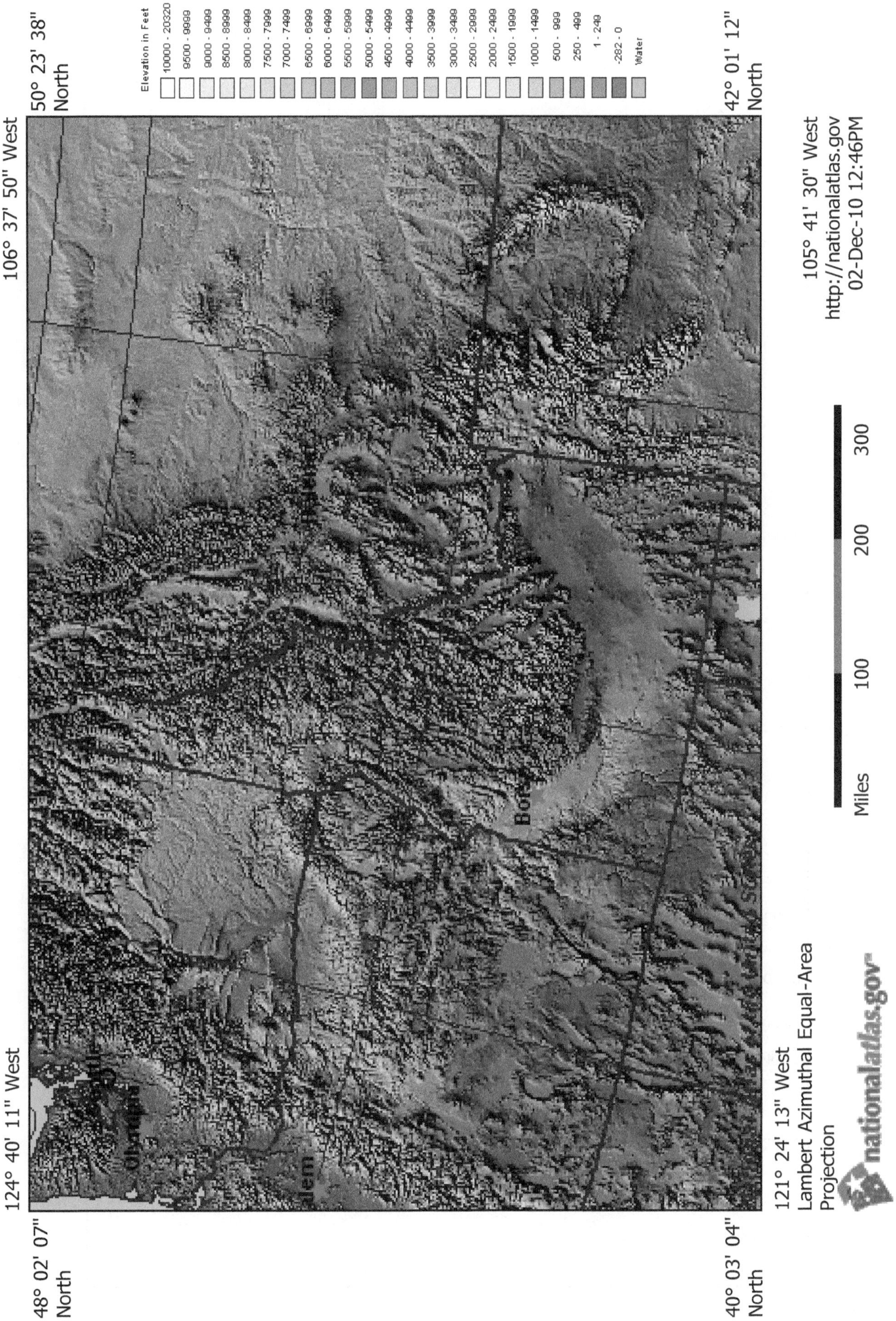

50° 23' 38" North
106° 37' 50" West
Elevation in Feet
10000 - 20320
9500 - 9999
9000 - 9499
8500 - 8999
8000 - 8499
7500 - 7999
7000 - 7499
6500 - 6999
6000 - 6499
5500 - 5999
5000 - 5499
4500 - 4999
4000 - 4499
3500 - 3999
3000 - 3499
2500 - 2999
2000 - 2499
1500 - 1999
1000 - 1499
500 - 999
250 - 499
1 - 249
-282 - 0
Water
42° 01' 12" North
105° 41' 30" West
http://nationalatlas.gov
02-Dec-10 12:46PM
Miles
100
200
300
124° 40' 11" West
48° 02' 07" North
121° 24' 13" West
Lambert Azimuthal Equal-Area Projection
nationalatlas.gov
40° 03' 04" North

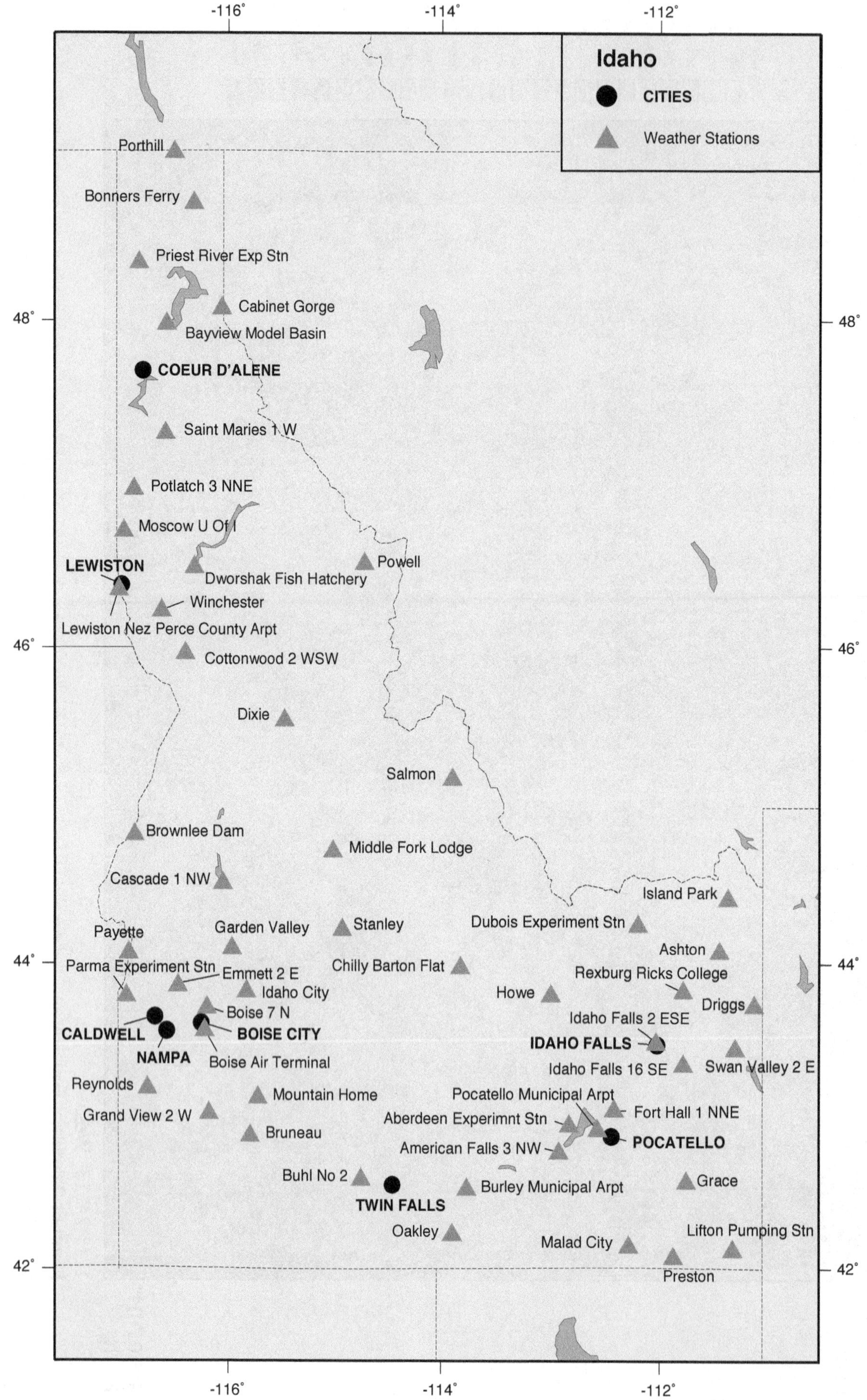
-116°
-114°
-112°
Idaho
CITIES
Weather Stations
48°
46°
44°
42°
Porthill
Bonners Ferry
Priest River Exp Stn
Cabinet Gorge
Bayview Model Basin
COEUR D'ALENE
Saint Maries 1 W
Potlatch 3 NNE
Moscow U Of I
LEWISTON
Powell
Dworshak Fish Hatchery
Winchester
Lewiston Nez Perce County Arpt
Cottonwood 2 WSW
Dixie
Salmon
Brownlee Dam
Middle Fork Lodge
Cascade 1 NW
Island Park
Payette
Garden Valley
Stanley
Dubois Experiment Stn
Ashton
Parma Experiment Stn
Emmett 2 E
Chilly Barton Flat
Rexburg Ricks College
Idaho City
Howe
Driggs
Boise 7 N
Idaho Falls 2 ESE
CALDWELL
BOISE CITY
IDAHO FALLS
NAMPA
Boise Air Terminal
Idaho Falls 16 SE
Swan Valley 2 E
Reynolds
Mountain Home
Pocatello Municipal Arpt
Grand View 2 W
Aberdeen Experimnt Stn
Fort Hall 1 NNE
Bruneau
POCATELLO
American Falls 3 NW
Buhl No 2
Burley Municipal Arpt
Grace
TWIN FALLS
Oakley
Lifton Pumping Stn
Malad City
Preston

Idaho Weather Stations by County

County	Station Name
Ada	Boise 7 N Boise Air Terminal
Adams	Brownlee Dam
Bear Lake	Lifton Pumping Stn
Benewah	Saint Maries 1 W
Bingham	Aberdeen Exp Station Fort Hall 1 NNE
Boise	Garden Valley Idaho City
Bonner	Cabinet Gorge Priest River Exp Stn
Bonneville	Idaho Falls 16 SE Idaho Falls 2 ESE Swan Valley 2 E
Boundary	Bonners Ferry Porthill
Butte	Howe
Canyon	Parma Experiment Stn
Caribou	Grace
Cassia	Burley Municipal Arpt Oakley
Clark	Dubois Experiment Stn
Clearwater	Dworshak Fish Hatchery
Custer	Chilly Barton Flat Middle Fork Lodge Stanley
Elmore	Mountain Home
Franklin	Preston
Fremont	Ashton Island Park
Gem	Emmett 2 E
Idaho	Cottonwood 2 WSW Dixie Powell
Kootenai	Bayview Model Basin
Latah	Moscow U of Idaho Potlatch 3 NNE
Lemhi	Salmon
Lewis	Winchester

County	Station Name
Madison	Rexburg Ricks College
Nez Perce	Lewiston Nez Perce County Arpt
Oneida	Malad City
Owyhee	Bruneau Grand View 2 W Reynolds
Payette	Payette
Power	American Falls 3 NW Pocatello Municipal Arpt
Teton	Driggs
Twin Falls	Buhl No 2
Valley	Cascade 1 NW

See User Guide for station inclusion criteria.

Idaho Weather Stations by City

City	Station Name	Miles
Ammon	Idaho Falls 2 ESE	2.4
	Idaho Falls 16 SE	12.8
Blackfoot	Fort Hall 1 NNE	10.2
	Pocatello Municipal Arpt	21.8
Boise City	Boise 7 N	7.3
	Boise Air Terminal	3.7
	Emmett 2 E	20.5
Caldwell	Boise 7 N	24.4
	Boise Air Terminal	24.0
	Emmett 2 E	18.1
	Parma Experiment Stn	16.7
Chubbuck	Aberdeen Exp Station	18.4
	American Falls 3 NW	24.6
	Fort Hall 1 NNE	9.1
	Pocatello Municipal Arpt	4.9
Coeur d'Alene	Bayview Model Basin	22.1
Eagle	Boise 7 N	7.2
	Boise Air Terminal	11.0
	Emmett 2 E	13.2
Garden City	Boise 7 N	5.3
	Boise Air Terminal	6.5
	Emmett 2 E	17.8
	Idaho City	24.7
Hayden	Bayview Model Basin	18.7
Idaho Falls	Idaho Falls 2 ESE	0.8
	Idaho Falls 16 SE	15.7
Lewiston	Lewiston Nez Perce County Arpt	2.0
	Moscow U of Idaho	23.8
	Winchester	20.9
Meridian	Boise 7 N	12.2
	Boise Air Terminal	9.8
	Emmett 2 E	17.6
Moscow	Moscow U of Idaho	1.4
	Potlatch 3 NNE	17.2
Mountain Home	Bruneau	18.3
	Mountain Home	1.2
Nampa	Boise 7 N	20.8
	Boise Air Terminal	17.5
	Emmett 2 E	20.9
	Parma Experiment Stn	24.7
Pocatello	Aberdeen Exp Station	20.3
	American Falls 3 NW	24.9
	Fort Hall 1 NNE	11.9
	Pocatello Municipal Arpt	6.8
Rexburg	Ashton	24.6
	Rexburg Ricks College	0.4
Twin Falls	Buhl No 2	14.8

Note: Miles is the distance between the geographic center of the city and the weather station.

See User Guide for station inclusion criteria.

Idaho Weather Stations by Elevation

Feet	Station Name
6,290	Island Park
6,271	Stanley
6,259	Chilly Barton Flat
6,116	Driggs
5,925	Lifton Pumping Stn
5,850	Idaho Falls 16 SE
5,620	Dixie
5,549	Grace
5,450	Dubois Experiment Stn
5,359	Swan Valley 2 E
5,211	Ashton
4,924	Rexburg Ricks College
4,896	Cascade 1 NW
4,819	Howe
4,799	Preston
4,765	Idaho Falls 2 ESE
4,560	Oakley
4,479	Middle Fork Lodge
4,470	Malad City
4,464	Fort Hall 1 NNE
4,439	Pocatello Municipal Arpt
4,404	Aberdeen Exp Station
4,404	American Falls 3 NW
4,157	Burley Municipal Arpt
3,964	Idaho City
3,950	Winchester
3,944	Cottonwood 2 WSW
3,931	Salmon
3,930	Reynolds
3,884	Boise 7 N
3,799	Buhl No 2
3,529	Powell
3,140	Mountain Home
3,100	Garden Valley
2,837	Boise Air Terminal
2,660	Moscow U of Idaho
2,600	Potlatch 3 NNE
2,529	Bruneau
2,399	Grand View 2 W
2,390	Emmett 2 E
2,379	Priest River Exp Stn
2,319	Saint Maries 1 W
2,290	Parma Experiment Stn
2,259	Cabinet Gorge
2,149	Payette
2,075	Bayview Model Basin
1,844	Brownlee Dam
1,774	Porthill
1,770	Bonners Ferry
1,436	Lewiston Nez Perce County Arpt
995	Dworshak Fish Hatchery

See User Guide for station inclusion criteria.

Boise Air Terminal

Boise is situated in the Boise River Valley about eight miles below the mouth of a mountain canyon where the valley proper begins. Sheltered by large shade trees and averaging 2,710 feet in elevation, the denser part of the city covers a gentle alluvial slope about two miles wide, stretching southwest from the foothills of the Boise Mountains to the river. The Boise Mountains immediately north of the city rise 5,000 to 6,000 feet above sea level in about eight miles, the slopes partly mantled with sagebrush and then chaparral giving way near the summit to ridges of fir, spruce, and pine.

Although air masses from the Pacific are considerably modified by the time they reach Boise, their influence, particularly in winter, alternates with that of atmospheric developments from other directions. The result is almost a typical upland continental type of climate in summer, while winters are usually tempered by periods of cloudy or stormy and mild weather. Autumns have prolonged periods of near ideal weather, while springtime is noted by changeable weather and varied temperatures.

Summer hot periods rarely last longer than a few days. Temperatures of 100 degrees or higher occur nearly every year.

Winter cold spells with temperatures of 10 degrees or lower generally last longer than the summer hot spells, but rarely include windy conditions.

The normal precipitation pattern in the Boise area shows a winter high and a very pronounced summer low. Total amounts and intensity are generally greatest near the foothills, dwindling to westward and southward.

Destructive force winds are rare. Northwesterly winds, drying and rather raw are common from March through May. Diurnal southeasterly winds, descending from nearby foothills at night, frequently have a moderating effect on winter temperatures. There is an occasional, but moderate, duststorm during the warmer months.

Relative humidity is low but widespread irrigation maintains humidity several percent above the general dryness of western arid conditions in summer. Thunderstorms occur primarily during spring and summer, with less frequency during fall and occasionally during winter. December and January are the months of heavy fog or low stratus cloud conditions. Winter has a moderate amount of sunshine but periods of clear, sunny weather are the rule in summer.

Based on the 1951-1980 period, the average first occurrence of 32 degrees Fahrenheit in the fall is October 9 and the average last occurrence in the spring is May 8.

Boise Air Terminal *Ada County* Elevation: 2,837 ft. Latitude: 43° 34' N Longitude: 116° 13' W

	JAN	FEB	MAR	APR	MAY	JUN	JUL	AUG	SEP	OCT	NOV	DEC	YEAR
Mean Maximum Temp. (°F)	37.6	44.7	54.5	62.5	71.8	81.2	91.2	89.6	78.6	64.8	48.3	37.5	63.5
Mean Temp. (°F)	30.5	36.0	43.9	50.4	58.7	66.9	75.2	74.0	64.2	52.2	39.6	30.2	51.8
Mean Minimum Temp. (°F)	23.4	27.3	33.2	38.3	45.6	52.5	59.2	58.3	49.8	39.5	30.9	22.9	40.1
Extreme Maximum Temp. (°F)	61	71	80	92	99	105	110	109	101	94	78	63	110
Extreme Minimum Temp. (°F)	-13	-15	13	20	22	31	35	34	28	13	-3	-25	-25
Days Maximum Temp. ≥ 90°F	0	0	0	0	2	7	20	17	4	0	0	0	50
Days Maximum Temp. ≤ 32°F	8	3	0	0	0	0	0	0	0	0	2	8	21
Days Minimum Temp. ≤ 32°F	26	21	14	7	2	0	0	0	0	5	17	26	118
Days Minimum Temp. ≤ 0°F	1	0	0	0	0	0	0	0	0	0	0	2	3
Heating Degree Days (base 65°F)	1,061	813	648	433	229	71	9	11	109	397	756	1,072	5,609
Cooling Degree Days (base 65°F)	0	0	0	3	41	133	332	296	92	6	0	0	903
Mean Precipitation (in.)	1.25	1.00	1.41	1.21	1.43	0.68	0.32	0.23	0.64	0.72	1.34	1.49	11.72
Maximum Precipitation (in.)*	3.9	3.7	3.5	3.0	4.1	2.9	1.6	2.4	2.9	2.3	3.4	4.2	18.8
Minimum Precipitation (in.)*	0.1	0.2	0.2	0.1	trace	trace	trace	trace	0	0	0.1	0.1	6.6
Extreme Maximum Daily Precip. (in.)	0.72	0.79	1.60	1.10	1.77	0.78	0.78	0.91	0.90	0.90	0.61	0.86	1.77
Days With ≥ 0.1" Precipitation	5	4	5	4	4	2	1	1	2	2	5	5	40
Days With ≥ 0.5" Precipitation	0	0	0	0	1	0	0	0	0	0	0	1	2
Days With ≥ 1.0" Precipitation	0	0	0	0	0	0	0	0	0	0	0	0	0
Mean Snowfall (in.)	5.1	2.9	1.3	0.3	trace	trace	trace	trace	trace	0.1	2.4	6.8	18.9
Maximum Snowfall (in.)*	21	25	12	8	4	trace	0	0	0	3	19	26	47
Maximum 24-hr. Snowfall (in.)*	7	7	6	7	4	trace	0	0	0	1	5	7	7
Maximum Snow Depth (in.)	12	5	2	1	trace	trace	trace	trace	trace	trace	11	13	13
Days With ≥ 1.0" Snow Depth	10	4	1	0	0	0	0	0	0	0	2	7	24
Thunderstorm Days*	< 1	< 1	1	1	3	3	2	3	1	< 1	< 1	< 1	14
Foggy Days*	14	8	3	2	1	1	< 1	< 1	1	2	7	13	52
Predominant Sky Cover*	OVR	OVR	OVR	OVR	OVR	CLR	CLR	CLR	CLR	CLR	OVR	OVR	OVR
Mean Relative Humidity 7am (%)*	81	80	75	69	65	59	48	50	58	67	77	81	68
Mean Relative Humidity 4pm (%)*	68	58	45	35	34	29	22	23	28	36	55	67	42
Mean Dewpoint (°F)*	21	26	28	31	38	42	44	42	38	33	28	24	33
Prevailing Wind Direction*	SE	SE	SE	NW	NW	NW	NW	NW	SE	SE	SE	SE	SE
Prevailing Wind Speed (mph)*	10	10	10	13	12	12	10	10	8	9	10	10	10
Maximum Wind Gust (mph)*	59	64	58	59	55	63	71	60	49	47	55	56	71

Note: (*) Period of record is 1948-1995

Lewiston Airport

Lewiston is located at the confluence of the Snake and Clearwater Rivers at an elevation of 738 feet above mean sea level. Lower Granite Lake extends from the confluence of the two rivers, 32 miles downstream in the Snake River channel, to Lower Granite Dam. The valley is rather narrow with a range of hills to the north sloping abruptly to about 2,000 feet above the valley floor. To the south the terrain rises more gradually to a more or less flat bench about 700 feet above the valley. The Weather Office is located on the bench at an elevation of 1,413 feet above sea level and about two miles south of Lewiston.

Considerable variations in the climate are to be found within relatively short distances from the valley itself. On the prairies surrounding the valley, winter temperatures are much lower and the precipitation is normally almost double that recorded in the valley and at the airport location.

Precipitation normally amounts to about 13 inches annually, which is rather evenly distributed through the year except for the months of July and August, which are characterized by infrequent thunderstorms that usually drop only small amounts of rain. Records show that several times during these two months not more than a trace of rain has been recorded. The thunderstorms on the prairie are, at times, accompanied by heavy hail and windstorms. Snowfall in the valley averages about 18 inches during the year, concentrated mostly in the three months of December, January, and February.

Temperatures show a wide range from more than 115 degrees to less than -20 degrees. Many winters have gone by without a temperature of zero being recorded in the valley, but the prairie sections usually experience lower temperatures. The summers experience hot and dry periods with as many as 10 consecutive days with afternoon temperatures reaching 100 degrees or more. Considerable cooling after sunset makes the nights very comfortable. Cold waves occur when arctic air, originating in the Yukon Territory, moves southward.

Winds are light, usually prevailing from the east, with occasional stronger winds accompanying the well-developed frontal systems from the west.

Relative humidity averages about 70 percent during the winter months and gradually lowers to about 40 percent during July and August.

The growing season of approximately 200 days in this part of the country, makes conditions favorable for the growing of many types of fruits, vegetables, and berries.

Lewiston Airport *Nez Perce County* Elevation: 1,436 ft. Latitude: 46° 22' N Longitude: 117° 01' W

	JAN	FEB	MAR	APR	MAY	JUN	JUL	AUG	SEP	OCT	NOV	DEC	YEAR
Mean Maximum Temp. (°F)	41.4	46.7	54.9	62.6	71.1	78.6	89.2	88.7	78.2	62.8	48.3	39.7	63.5
Mean Temp. (°F)	35.4	38.9	45.4	51.7	59.2	66.1	74.5	74.1	64.7	52.0	41.4	34.1	53.1
Mean Minimum Temp. (°F)	29.4	31.1	35.9	40.8	47.3	53.5	59.8	59.3	51.2	41.2	34.4	28.4	42.7
Extreme Maximum Temp. (°F)	62	72	78	93	100	105	110	108	102	89	77	65	110
Extreme Minimum Temp. (°F)	-5	-10	15	26	31	38	44	41	31	15	-1	-16	-16
Days Maximum Temp. ≥ 90°F	0	0	0	0	2	4	16	15	4	0	0	0	41
Days Maximum Temp. ≤ 32°F	5	2	0	0	0	0	0	0	0	0	1	6	14
Days Minimum Temp. ≤ 32°F	19	15	8	2	0	0	0	0	0	3	11	21	79
Days Minimum Temp. ≤ 0°F	0	0	0	0	0	0	0	0	0	0	0	0	0
Heating Degree Days (base 65°F)	910	731	600	395	207	66	6	7	92	400	701	952	5,067
Cooling Degree Days (base 65°F)	0	0	0	2	34	105	309	294	90	4	0	0	838
Mean Precipitation (in.)	1.07	0.82	1.16	1.29	1.61	1.19	0.66	0.70	0.68	0.94	1.17	0.94	12.23
Maximum Precipitation (in.)*	3.5	2.0	2.7	3.3	4.8	4.7	2.6	3.0	2.2	2.8	2.8	3.3	18.6
Minimum Precipitation (in.)*	0.1	0.2	0.3	0	0.3	0.2	trace	trace	trace	trace	0.2	0.1	8.4
Extreme Maximum Daily Precip. (in.)	0.91	0.72	0.88	0.77	1.32	1.46	1.80	1.17	0.94	0.87	1.22	0.60	1.80
Days With ≥ 0.1" Precipitation	3	3	4	4	5	4	2	2	2	3	4	4	40
Days With ≥ 0.5" Precipitation	0	0	0	0	1	0	0	0	0	0	0	0	1
Days With ≥ 1.0" Precipitation	0	0	0	0	0	0	0	0	0	0	0	0	0
Mean Snowfall (in.)	na	na	na	na	na	na	na	na	na	na	na	na	na
Maximum Snowfall (in.)*	26	15	10	1	trace	0	0	0	0	3	3	19	34
Maximum 24-hr. Snowfall (in.)*	9	7	5	1	trace	0	0	0	0	1	1	8	9
Maximum Snow Depth (in.)	na	na	na	na	na	na	na	na	na	na	na	na	na
Days With ≥ 1.0" Snow Depth	na	na	na	na	na	na	na	na	na	na	na	na	na
Thunderstorm Days*	0	< 1	< 1	2	3	6	7	5	2	< 1	0	< 1	25
Foggy Days*	10	9	4	1	1	1	< 1	1	1	6	8	13	55
Predominant Sky Cover*	OVR	OVR	OVR	OVR	OVR	OVR	CLR	CLR	CLR	OVR	OVR	OVR	OVR
Mean Relative Humidity 7am (%)*	81	80	77	71	68	64	55	55	66	80	83	82	72
Mean Relative Humidity 4pm (%)*	71	62	49	42	39	35	25	25	32	49	69	74	48
Mean Dewpoint (°F)*	25	29	31	34	41	46	46	44	42	38	33	28	36
Prevailing Wind Direction*	E	E	E	E	WNW	NW	NW	NW	E	E	E	E	E
Prevailing Wind Speed (mph)*	7	8	8	7	10	9	9	9	6	7	7	8	8
Maximum Wind Gust (mph)*	73	64	60	58	54	54	51	51	59	59	59	63	73

Note: (*) Period of record is 1948-1995

Pocatello Municipal Airport

Pocatello is located in the Snake River Valley at the mouth of Portneuf Canyon at an elevation of about 4,500 feet above sea level. A desert composed of sand, lava rock, and craters, extends to the west, while to the east the ground level rises steadily towards the crests of the Continental Divide.

Except in autumn, which is the season of the finest weather in Pocatello, the main feature of the climate is its variety. In winter there are frequent periods of persistent southwest wind, with a resulting mildness that matches the winters of the north Pacific Coast. There are also periods of several days when the temperature stays below freezing and approaches or falls below zero.

During cold periods, precipitation falling as snow occasionally accumulates to a depth of a foot or more. Cloudy and unsettled weather prevails throughout the winter, with measurable amounts of precipitation on about one-third of the days.

In the spring there is a gradual warming. Normally, spring months are the wettest and windiest. Winds of 20 to 30 mph for days at a time are common.

The summer season begins with a relatively sudden break in the disagreeable spring weather. Home heating, usually discontinued about the first of June, is sometimes needed intermittently until the first part of July. Suitable weather for outside evening activities is very uncertain during June, even though the afternoons may be mild. As night falls, the temperature often drops rapidly into the 40s, accompanied by a chilling wind from snows remaining on the nearby mountains. During the summer, precipitation usually falls as local showers, often accompanied by light to moderate thunderstorms and occasionally by hail. Damage by excessive precipitation, lightning, high winds, or hail is uncommon and quite localized. Long periods of extremely hot weather in July and August are also uncommon. Although afternoon temperatures may run into the 90s, nights are usually cool.

Exceptionally fine weather predominates during the autumn season. The sudden summer showers are gradually replaced by short periods of cloudy and unsettled weather with more general rains. Continuous home heating is not needed until mid-October. Evenings during September are ideal for outdoor activities, and pleasant afternoons are the rule until toward the end of November. The first cold wave may appear during late November but usually not until late December.

The average first occurrence of 32 degrees Fahrenheit in the fall is September 20 and the average last occurrence in the spring is May 20.

Pocatello Municipal Airport *Power County* Elevation: 4,439 ft. Latitude: 42° 55' N Longitude: 112° 34' W

	JAN	FEB	MAR	APR	MAY	JUN	JUL	AUG	SEP	OCT	NOV	DEC	YEAR
Mean Maximum Temp. (°F)	32.9	38.3	49.2	58.9	68.4	78.2	88.3	87.4	76.1	61.4	45.1	33.5	59.8
Mean Temp. (°F)	24.5	28.9	38.2	46.0	54.1	62.2	70.2	69.1	59.2	47.2	34.7	24.8	46.6
Mean Minimum Temp. (°F)	16.0	19.5	27.2	33.0	39.9	46.2	52.0	50.6	42.2	33.0	24.2	16.1	33.3
Extreme Maximum Temp. (°F)	60	65	75	86	97	103	104	104	97	91	75	64	104
Extreme Minimum Temp. (°F)	-28	-33	-12	13	20	28	34	30	19	7	-14	-29	-33
Days Maximum Temp. ≥ 90°F	0	0	0	0	0	4	15	14	2	0	0	0	35
Days Maximum Temp. ≤ 32°F	15	8	1	0	0	0	0	0	0	0	4	13	41
Days Minimum Temp. ≤ 32°F	29	25	24	14	4	0	0	0	4	15	25	29	169
Days Minimum Temp. ≤ 0°F	4	2	0	0	0	0	0	0	0	0	1	3	10
Heating Degree Days (base 65°F)	1,249	1,013	823	564	336	126	17	22	192	544	903	1,238	7,027
Cooling Degree Days (base 65°F)	0	0	0	0	7	50	184	154	24	0	0	0	419
Mean Precipitation (in.)	1.07	0.98	1.28	1.12	1.54	0.98	0.66	0.63	0.88	0.89	1.08	1.18	12.29
Maximum Precipitation (in.)*	3.2	2.6	2.9	3.3	3.3	3.3	2.3	4.0	3.4	2.6	2.8	3.4	20.3
Minimum Precipitation (in.)*	0.2	0.1	0.1	0.1	0.2	trace	trace	trace	0	0	trace	0.1	5.3
Extreme Maximum Daily Precip. (in.)	0.76	0.67	0.97	0.71	1.10	1.45	1.33	0.81	1.21	1.31	0.86	0.91	1.45
Days With ≥ 0.1" Precipitation	4	3	4	4	5	3	2	2	3	3	4	4	41
Days With ≥ 0.5" Precipitation	0	0	0	0	1	1	0	0	0	0	0	0	2
Days With ≥ 1.0" Precipitation	0	0	0	0	0	0	0	0	0	0	0	0	0
Mean Snowfall (in.)	8.9	7.0	5.4	3.1	0.8	trace	trace	trace	0.1	1.9	5.2	10.5	42.9
Maximum Snowfall (in.)*	30	21	17	16	6	trace	0	0	2	13	28	34	80
Maximum 24-hr. Snowfall (in.)*	8	6	8	9	5	trace	0	0	2	8	7	11	11
Maximum Snow Depth (in.)	17	13	10	8	4	trace	trace	trace	trace	8	10	16	17
Days With ≥ 1.0" Snow Depth	17	11	5	1	0	0	0	0	0	1	5	14	54
Thunderstorm Days*	< 1	< 1	< 1	1	4	5	6	5	3	1	< 1	< 1	25
Foggy Days*	12	8	5	2	1	1	< 1	< 1	1	2	6	11	49
Predominant Sky Cover*	OVR	OVR	OVR	OVR	OVR	CLR	CLR	CLR	CLR	CLR	OVR	OVR	OVR
Mean Relative Humidity 5am (%)*	80	80	77	70	71	70	62	60	64	70	77	81	72
Mean Relative Humidity 5pm (%)*	71	63	51	38	35	31	23	22	27	37	60	72	44
Mean Dewpoint (°F)*	17	21	24	27	34	40	43	40	35	29	24	19	29
Prevailing Wind Direction*	SW	SW	SW	WSW	SW	SW	SW	SW	SW	SW	SW	SW	SW
Prevailing Wind Speed (mph)*	13	13	13	16	13	12	10	10	12	12	13	13	13
Maximum Wind Gust (mph)*	68	60	64	61	61	62	82	68	74	53	60	77	82

Note: (*) Period of record is 1948-1995

Aberdeen Exp Station *Bingham County* Elevation: 4,404 ft. Latitude: 42° 57' N Longitude: 112° 50' W

	JAN	FEB	MAR	APR	MAY	JUN	JUL	AUG	SEP	OCT	NOV	DEC	YEAR
Mean Maximum Temp. (°F)	32.1	37.3	48.0	59.0	68.1	76.9	86.6	86.4	75.5	61.9	45.0	32.8	59.1
Mean Temp. (°F)	22.0	26.3	35.9	44.6	53.2	60.8	68.0	66.5	56.7	45.1	32.9	22.0	44.5
Mean Minimum Temp. (°F)	11.9	15.3	23.9	30.2	38.2	44.6	49.4	46.6	37.8	28.3	20.7	11.5	29.9
Extreme Maximum Temp. (°F)	54	63	76	86	96	100	104	103	98	89	73	62	104
Extreme Minimum Temp. (°F)	-33	-38	-17	13	19	26	31	29	17	2	-15	-30	-38
Days Maximum Temp. ≥ 90°F	0	0	0	0	0	3	12	11	2	0	0	0	28
Days Maximum Temp. ≤ 32°F	15	8	2	0	0	0	0	0	0	0	3	14	42
Days Minimum Temp. ≤ 32°F	30	27	28	19	6	1	0	0	7	22	27	30	197
Days Minimum Temp. ≤ 0°F	6	4	1	0	0	0	0	0	0	0	1	5	17
Heating Degree Days (base 65°F)	1,325	1,086	894	605	365	159	32	46	257	610	957	1,325	7,661
Cooling Degree Days (base 65°F)	0	0	0	0	5	39	132	100	13	0	0	0	289
Mean Precipitation (in.)	0.72	0.67	0.79	0.75	1.15	1.03	0.52	0.46	0.79	0.74	0.73	0.84	9.19
Extreme Maximum Daily Precip. (in.)	0.64	0.60	0.94	0.95	1.20	1.75	0.76	0.67	1.01	0.83	0.82	0.91	1.75
Days With ≥ 0.1" Precipitation	2	2	3	3	4	3	1	2	3	3	2	3	31
Days With ≥ 0.5" Precipitation	0	0	0	0	0	1	0	0	0	0	0	0	1
Days With ≥ 1.0" Precipitation	0	0	0	0	0	0	0	0	0	0	0	0	0
Mean Snowfall (in.)	***5.7***	***4.3***	1.3	0.3	0.1	0.0	0.0	0.0	trace	0.5	1.8	***6.5***	***20.5***
Maximum Snow Depth (in.)	28	20	20	1	3	0	0	0	trace	6	12	16	28
Days With ≥ 1.0" Snow Depth	19	13	5	0	0	0	0	0	0	0	4	16	57

American Falls 3 NW *Power County* Elevation: 4,404 ft. Latitude: 42° 47' N Longitude: 112° 55' W

	JAN	FEB	MAR	APR	MAY	JUN	JUL	AUG	SEP	OCT	NOV	DEC	YEAR
Mean Maximum Temp. (°F)	32.8	37.9	50.0	60.5	69.1	78.0	86.8	86.7	76.0	62.3	45.4	33.8	59.9
Mean Temp. (°F)	24.9	29.2	39.2	47.7	55.6	63.3	70.7	70.1	60.7	49.3	36.3	26.1	47.7
Mean Minimum Temp. (°F)	16.9	20.3	28.5	34.8	42.0	48.5	54.5	53.5	45.4	36.2	27.1	18.3	35.5
Extreme Maximum Temp. (°F)	59	65	78	87	92	103	101	103	95	87	72	72	103
Extreme Minimum Temp. (°F)	-28	-30	-11	15	22	31	36	33	23	8	-4	-23	-30
Days Maximum Temp. ≥ 90°F	0	0	0	0	0	3	12	11	1	0	0	0	27
Days Maximum Temp. ≤ 32°F	14	7	1	0	0	0	0	0	0	0	3	13	38
Days Minimum Temp. ≤ 32°F	29	24	21	11	2	0	0	0	1	10	22	29	149
Days Minimum Temp. ≤ 0°F	3	2	0	0	0	0	0	0	0	0	0	2	7
Heating Degree Days (base 65°F)	1,237	1,007	792	514	295	107	15	16	159	482	855	1,201	6,680
Cooling Degree Days (base 65°F)	0	0	0	0	11	62	198	182	37	1	0	0	491
Mean Precipitation (in.)	1.04	0.91	1.27	1.15	1.57	0.87	0.51	0.57	0.82	0.79	1.15	1.27	11.92
Extreme Maximum Daily Precip. (in.)	1.03	1.00	1.08	0.83	2.06	1.10	1.05	1.18	1.16	1.14	1.09	0.89	2.06
Days With ≥ 0.1" Precipitation	4	3	4	4	4	2	1	2	2	3	4	4	37
Days With ≥ 0.5" Precipitation	0	0	0	0	1	0	0	0	0	0	0	0	1
Days With ≥ 1.0" Precipitation	0	0	0	0	0	0	0	0	0	0	0	0	0
Mean Snowfall (in.)	9.0	5.7	3.0	1.6	0.5	0.0	0.0	0.0	0.1	1.0	3.3	8.6	32.8
Maximum Snow Depth (in.)	27	18	10	5	trace	0	0	0	trace	4	10	***19***	***27***
Days With ≥ 1.0" Snow Depth	19	12	3	0	0	0	0	0	0	0	3	15	52

Ashton *Fremont County* Elevation: 5,211 ft. Latitude: 44° 05' N Longitude: 111° 27' W

	JAN	FEB	MAR	APR	MAY	JUN	JUL	AUG	SEP	OCT	NOV	DEC	YEAR
Mean Maximum Temp. (°F)	28.6	32.6	41.7	53.6	64.4	72.6	82.4	81.8	71.6	57.5	39.7	28.8	54.6
Mean Temp. (°F)	20.0	23.7	32.2	41.9	51.1	58.0	65.5	64.3	55.5	43.9	30.4	20.4	42.2
Mean Minimum Temp. (°F)	11.5	14.7	22.6	30.0	37.7	43.4	48.6	46.8	39.4	30.2	21.0	11.9	29.8
Extreme Maximum Temp. (°F)	54	54	70	81	90	96	101	98	91	83	69	59	101
Extreme Minimum Temp. (°F)	-26	-28	-11	2	18	27	28	27	12	6	-16	-31	-31
Days Maximum Temp. ≥ 90°F	0	0	0	0	0	0	4	3	0	0	0	0	7
Days Maximum Temp. ≤ 32°F	20	13	3	0	0	0	0	0	0	0	7	20	63
Days Minimum Temp. ≤ 32°F	30	27	28	19	7	1	0	0	4	19	26	30	191
Days Minimum Temp. ≤ 0°F	5	4	1	0	0	0	0	0	0	0	2	6	18
Heating Degree Days (base 65°F)	1,387	1,162	1,010	688	428	217	55	68	283	648	1,032	1,378	8,356
Cooling Degree Days (base 65°F)	0	0	0	0	2	14	78	53	6	0	0	0	153
Mean Precipitation (in.)	2.20	1.46	1.49	1.49	2.36	1.76	0.89	0.89	1.11	1.61	1.95	2.09	19.30
Extreme Maximum Daily Precip. (in.)	2.61	1.27	1.36	1.52	***1.10***	***1.10***	1.14	0.90	***1.20***	***1.05***	***1.01***	***0.82***	***2.61***
Days With ≥ 0.1" Precipitation	7	5	5	5	6	5	2	3	3	4	5	6	56
Days With ≥ 0.5" Precipitation	1	1	1	0	1	1	1	0	1	1	1	1	10
Days With ≥ 1.0" Precipitation	0	0	0	0	0	0	0	0	0	0	0	0	0
Mean Snowfall (in.)	20.4	12.0	8.7	3.1	1.1	trace	0.0	trace	0.1	1.7	12.8	22.2	82.1
Maximum Snow Depth (in.)	54	50	48	24	4	0	0	1	trace	6	30	40	54
Days With ≥ 1.0" Snow Depth	30	27	25	6	0	0	0	0	0	1	14	27	130

Bayview Model Basin *Kootenai County* Elevation: 2,075 ft. Latitude: 47° 59' N Longitude: 116° 34' W

	JAN	FEB	MAR	APR	MAY	JUN	JUL	AUG	SEP	OCT	NOV	DEC	YEAR
Mean Maximum Temp. (°F)	36.0	38.9	46.3	55.4	64.4	71.6	80.1	79.6	69.1	55.2	42.9	35.0	56.2
Mean Temp. (°F)	29.5	31.3	36.9	43.9	51.3	58.1	64.4	63.6	54.8	44.0	35.5	28.5	45.1
Mean Minimum Temp. (°F)	22.9	23.6	27.4	32.4	38.2	44.5	48.8	47.5	40.4	32.6	28.1	22.0	34.0
Extreme Maximum Temp. (°F)	55	62	69	81	92	98	101	101	95	81	69	58	101
Extreme Minimum Temp. (°F)	-15	-10	-6	16	19	28	34	30	20	0	-6	-13	-15
Days Maximum Temp. ≥ 90°F	0	0	0	0	0	0	4	3	0	0	0	0	7
Days Maximum Temp. ≤ 32°F	8	4	1	0	0	0	0	0	0	0	2	10	25
Days Minimum Temp. ≤ 32°F	28	24	25	16	6	1	0	0	4	15	22	28	169
Days Minimum Temp. ≤ 0°F	1	1	0	0	0	0	0	0	0	0	0	1	3
Heating Degree Days (base 65°F)	1,094	945	863	626	420	216	82	90	304	646	878	1,125	7,289
Cooling Degree Days (base 65°F)	0	0	0	0	3	15	70	52	4	0	0	0	144
Mean Precipitation (in.)	2.63	1.84	2.19	1.98	2.31	1.81	1.06	0.97	1.18	1.83	3.43	3.03	24.26
Extreme Maximum Daily Precip. (in.)	1.37	1.10	1.04	1.70	1.48	1.55	1.61	1.48	1.03	1.05	2.00	1.50	2.00
Days With ≥ 0.1" Precipitation	8	6	7	6	6	5	3	3	4	5	9	8	70
Days With ≥ 0.5" Precipitation	1	1	1	1	1	1	1	0	0	1	2	2	12
Days With ≥ 1.0" Precipitation	0	0	0	0	0	0	0	0	0	0	0	0	0
Mean Snowfall (in.)	7.5	3.9	1.7	0.1	0.0	0.0	0.0	0.0	0.0	trace	1.9	8.6	23.7
Maximum Snow Depth (in.)	26	***18***	12	3	0	0	2	0	0	0	11	***28***	***28***
Days With ≥ 1.0" Snow Depth	11	***8***	3	0	0	0	0	0	0	0	2	7	***31***

The period of record for all cooperative weather station data is 1980 – 2009. See User Guide for detailed explanation of data.

Boise 7 N *Ada County* Elevation: 3,884 ft. Latitude: 43° 43' N Longitude: 116° 12' W

	JAN	FEB	MAR	APR	MAY	JUN	JUL	AUG	SEP	OCT	NOV	DEC	YEAR
Mean Maximum Temp. (°F)	36.5	42.1	50.9	58.8	68.1	77.4	88.0	86.9	75.8	61.7	46.0	36.2	60.7
Mean Temp. (°F)	29.7	34.1	41.6	47.6	55.4	63.2	72.5	72.1	62.6	50.8	38.1	29.3	49.7
Mean Minimum Temp. (°F)	22.9	26.1	32.2	36.5	42.6	49.0	57.0	57.2	49.3	39.8	30.2	22.3	38.7
Extreme Maximum Temp. (°F)	60	67	75	88	95	100	105	106	100	92	72	62	106
Extreme Minimum Temp. (°F)	-9	-16	9	18	20	28	36	34	27	12	-4	-23	-23
Days Maximum Temp. ≥ 90°F	0	0	0	0	1	3	14	13	2	0	0	0	33
Days Maximum Temp. ≤ 32°F	9	3	0	0	0	0	0	0	0	0	2	10	24
Days Minimum Temp. ≤ 32°F	27	21	16	9	3	0	0	0	1	5	18	27	127
Days Minimum Temp. ≤ 0°F	1	1	0	0	0	0	0	0	0	0	0	1	3
Heating Degree Days (base 65°F)	1,087	867	719	514	313	126	18	18	138	439	800	1,101	6,140
Cooling Degree Days (base 65°F)	0	0	0	1	21	79	259	243	72	5	0	0	680
Mean Precipitation (in.)	2.04	1.74	2.27	1.92	2.10	1.17	0.42	0.30	0.90	1.17	2.22	2.47	18.72
Extreme Maximum Daily Precip. (in.)	1.02	1.17	1.15	1.35	1.24	1.07	1.38	0.81	1.96	1.07	1.05	1.35	1.96
Days With ≥ 0.1" Precipitation	6	6	6	5	5	3	1	1	2	3	7	7	52
Days With ≥ 0.5" Precipitation	1	1	1	1	1	1	0	0	0	1	1	1	9
Days With ≥ 1.0" Precipitation	0	0	0	0	0	0	0	0	0	0	0	0	0
Mean Snowfall (in.)	13.0	8.7	6.9	2.2	0.3	0.0	0.0	trace	trace	0.3	7.4	15.6	54.4
Maximum Snow Depth (in.)	21	20	12	4	trace	trace	0	trace	trace	2	16	23	23
Days With ≥ 1.0" Snow Depth	19	13	5	0	0	0	0	0	0	0	6	16	59

Bonners Ferry *Boundary County* Elevation: 1,770 ft. Latitude: 48° 42' N Longitude: 116° 19' W

	JAN	FEB	MAR	APR	MAY	JUN	JUL	AUG	SEP	OCT	NOV	DEC	YEAR
Mean Maximum Temp. (°F)	33.8	39.1	49.5	61.0	69.8	75.7	84.2	84.0	72.9	56.8	41.5	32.6	58.4
Mean Temp. (°F)	27.8	31.4	39.2	47.7	55.5	61.6	67.5	66.7	57.4	45.4	35.1	27.1	46.9
Mean Minimum Temp. (°F)	21.8	23.8	29.0	34.4	41.3	47.5	50.8	49.4	41.9	33.9	28.7	21.5	35.3
Extreme Maximum Temp. (°F)	53	61	75	84	95	98	101	101	96	84	65	56	101
Extreme Minimum Temp. (°F)	-22	-15	-2	20	25	31	32	32	15	8	-8	-17	-22
Days Maximum Temp. ≥ 90°F	0	0	0	0	1	1	9	8	1	0	0	0	20
Days Maximum Temp. ≤ 32°F	11	5	1	0	0	0	0	0	0	0	3	13	33
Days Minimum Temp. ≤ 32°F	27	24	21	12	3	0	0	0	2	13	19	28	149
Days Minimum Temp. ≤ 0°F	1	1	0	0	0	0	0	0	0	0	0	1	3
Heating Degree Days (base 65°F)	1,146	943	791	512	294	131	37	43	230	601	889	1,168	6,785
Cooling Degree Days (base 65°F)	0	0	0	0	7	35	122	102	9	0	0	0	275
Mean Precipitation (in.)	2.40	1.42	1.56	1.40	1.74	1.62	0.81	0.81	1.05	1.62	2.80	2.87	20.10
Extreme Maximum Daily Precip. (in.)	2.80	1.31	***1.41***	1.08	2.08	1.42	0.71	1.01	0.94	***0.92***	1.25	1.55	***2.80***
Days With ≥ 0.1" Precipitation	7	4	5	4	5	4	3	2	3	5	7	8	57
Days With ≥ 0.5" Precipitation	1	1	0	1	1	1	0	0	0	1	1	2	9
Days With ≥ 1.0" Precipitation	0	0	0	0	0	0	0	0	0	0	0	0	0
Mean Snowfall (in.)	16.5	6.9	3.6	0.5	trace	trace	0.0	0.0	0.0	0.4	7.2	21.2	56.3
Maximum Snow Depth (in.)	41	34	31	3	trace	trace	0	0	0	***1***	29	55	***55***
Days With ≥ 1.0" Snow Depth	22	12	4	0	0	0	0	0	0	0	4	19	61

Brownlee Dam *Adams County* Elevation: 1,844 ft. Latitude: 44° 50' N Longitude: 116° 52' W

	JAN	FEB	MAR	APR	MAY	JUN	JUL	AUG	SEP	OCT	NOV	DEC	YEAR
Mean Maximum Temp. (°F)	38.7	44.6	55.7	65.5	74.6	83.2	94.8	93.9	82.3	66.7	49.5	39.7	65.8
Mean Temp. (°F)	32.4	36.6	45.7	53.8	62.1	69.9	79.2	78.5	68.5	55.4	42.0	33.4	54.8
Mean Minimum Temp. (°F)	25.9	28.4	35.7	42.1	49.5	56.5	63.6	63.0	54.6	44.0	34.6	27.0	43.7
Extreme Maximum Temp. (°F)	65	69	78	95	103	109	115	112	103	95	74	65	115
Extreme Minimum Temp. (°F)	-4	-9	16	27	34	39	44	45	35	24	2	-6	-9
Days Maximum Temp. ≥ 90°F	0	0	0	0	3	9	24	22	8	0	0	0	66
Days Maximum Temp. ≤ 32°F	5	2	0	0	0	0	0	0	0	0	1	4	12
Days Minimum Temp. ≤ 32°F	25	19	8	1	0	0	0	0	0	1	10	24	88
Days Minimum Temp. ≤ 0°F	0	0	0	0	0	0	0	0	0	0	0	0	0
Heating Degree Days (base 65°F)	1,005	796	590	335	150	40	3	3	52	304	682	974	4,934
Cooling Degree Days (base 65°F)	0	0	0	7	68	194	451	429	162	13	0	0	1,324
Mean Precipitation (in.)	1.98	1.48	1.57	1.38	1.92	1.31	0.47	0.45	0.72	1.04	1.78	1.94	16.04
Extreme Maximum Daily Precip. (in.)	0.95	1.01	0.85	1.16	1.70	1.20	1.08	0.89	1.26	1.18	0.98	1.30	1.70
Days With ≥ 0.1" Precipitation	6	5	5	4	5	4	1	1	2	3	6	6	48
Days With ≥ 0.5" Precipitation	1	1	0	0	1	1	0	0	0	0	1	1	6
Days With ≥ 1.0" Precipitation	0	0	0	0	0	0	0	0	0	0	0	0	0
Mean Snowfall (in.)	4.9	1.8	0.2	trace	trace	0.0	0.0	0.0	0.0	0.0	0.8	2.1	9.8
Maximum Snow Depth (in.)	16	19	8	trace	trace	0	0	0	0	0	10	16	19
Days With ≥ 1.0" Snow Depth	7	4	1	0	0	0	0	0	0	0	1	2	15

Bruneau *Owyhee County* Elevation: 2,529 ft. Latitude: 42° 53' N Longitude: 115° 48' W

	JAN	FEB	MAR	APR	MAY	JUN	JUL	AUG	SEP	OCT	NOV	DEC	YEAR
Mean Maximum Temp. (°F)	40.6	48.3	58.8	66.8	74.9	84.0	93.0	92.0	81.6	68.0	51.3	39.9	66.6
Mean Temp. (°F)	32.2	37.5	45.6	52.2	60.1	67.9	75.3	73.8	63.9	52.5	40.4	31.3	52.7
Mean Minimum Temp. (°F)	23.6	26.6	32.3	37.6	45.1	51.8	57.7	55.5	46.3	36.9	29.4	22.7	38.8
Extreme Maximum Temp. (°F)	67	74	84	94	104	104	113	108	103	95	83	68	113
Extreme Minimum Temp. (°F)	-16	-16	10	20	24	33	39	37	26	10	-4	-32	-32
Days Maximum Temp. ≥ 90°F	0	0	0	0	3	9	22	21	6	0	0	0	61
Days Maximum Temp. ≤ 32°F	5	2	0	0	0	0	0	0	0	0	1	6	14
Days Minimum Temp. ≤ 32°F	26	20	16	7	1	0	0	0	1	9	19	25	124
Days Minimum Temp. ≤ 0°F	1	0	0	0	0	0	0	0	0	0	0	1	2
Heating Degree Days (base 65°F)	1,011	770	594	381	191	50	4	6	100	384	732	1,037	5,260
Cooling Degree Days (base 65°F)	0	0	0	4	45	143	331	286	75	3	0	0	887
Mean Precipitation (in.)	0.75	0.53	0.83	0.75	0.97	0.65	0.12	0.16	0.43	0.53	0.86	0.85	7.43
Extreme Maximum Daily Precip. (in.)	0.68	0.76	0.80	0.74	1.20	0.95	0.29	0.54	1.67	0.73	0.85	0.83	1.67
Days With ≥ 0.1" Precipitation	3	2	3	3	3	2	0	1	1	2	3	3	26
Days With ≥ 0.5" Precipitation	0	0	0	0	0	0	0	0	0	0	0	0	0
Days With ≥ 1.0" Precipitation	0	0	0	0	0	0	0	0	0	0	0	0	0
Mean Snowfall (in.)	***0.5***	***0.4***	***0.1***	0.0	0.0	0.0	0.0	0.0	0.0	0.0	0.6	na	na
Maximum Snow Depth (in.)	***trace***	na	na	***trace***	***0***	***0***	***0***	***0***	***0***	***0***	***2***	na	na
Days With ≥ 1.0" Snow Depth	***0***	***0***	***0***	0	0	0	0	0	0	0	0	***0***	***0***

The period of record for all cooperative weather station data is 1980 – 2009. See User Guide for detailed explanation of data.

Buhl No 2 *Twin Falls County* Elevation: 3,799 ft. Latitude: 42° 36' N Longitude: 114° 45' W

	JAN	FEB	MAR	APR	MAY	JUN	JUL	AUG	SEP	OCT	NOV	DEC	YEAR
Mean Maximum Temp. (°F)	34.9	40.8	51.2	59.6	67.9	77.1	87.0	86.0	75.6	62.3	46.3	35.7	60.4
Mean Temp. (°F)	27.5	32.1	40.7	47.8	55.6	63.7	72.4	71.0	61.2	49.6	36.9	28.0	48.9
Mean Minimum Temp. (°F)	20.0	23.2	30.2	35.9	43.2	50.4	57.8	55.9	46.8	36.9	27.5	20.3	37.3
Extreme Maximum Temp. (°F)	59	67	75	90	100	96	106	102	98	93	77	63	106
Extreme Minimum Temp. (°F)	-19	-13	4	15	25	30	36	38	27	10	-4	-26	-26
Days Maximum Temp. ≥ 90°F	0	0	0	0	1	3	13	10	2	0	0	0	29
Days Maximum Temp. ≤ 32°F	12	5	1	0	0	0	0	0	0	0	3	12	33
Days Minimum Temp. ≤ 32°F	29	25	21	10	2	0	0	0	1	9	23	28	148
Days Minimum Temp. ≤ 0°F	1	1	0	0	0	0	0	0	0	0	0	1	3
Heating Degree Days (base 65°F)	1,157	924	748	512	304	111	17	17	160	474	835	1,139	6,398
Cooling Degree Days (base 65°F)	0	0	0	2	19	79	254	208	53	2	0	0	617
Mean Precipitation (in.)	0.97	0.74	1.00	1.05	1.19	0.82	0.26	0.26	0.38	0.74	1.01	1.20	9.62
Extreme Maximum Daily Precip. (in.)	0.83	1.23	0.87	1.12	1.38	1.14	0.61	0.69	1.14	1.07	0.85	0.96	1.38
Days With ≥ 0.1" Precipitation	3	3	3	3	4	3	1	1	1	2	4	3	31
Days With ≥ 0.5" Precipitation	0	0	0	0	0	0	0	0	0	0	0	0	0
Days With ≥ 1.0" Precipitation	0	0	0	0	0	0	0	0	0	0	0	0	0
Mean Snowfall (in.)	na	***0.0***	***0.0***	0.0	0.0	0.0	0.0	0.0	0.0	0.0	***0.0***	na	na
Maximum Snow Depth (in.)	na	na	na	na	na	***0***	na	***0***	***0***	na	na	na	na
Days With ≥ 1.0" Snow Depth	na	***0***	0	0	0	0	0	0	0	0	***0***	na	na

Burley Municipal Arpt *Cassia County* Elevation: 4,157 ft. Latitude: 42° 32' N Longitude: 113° 46' W

	JAN	FEB	MAR	APR	MAY	JUN	JUL	AUG	SEP	OCT	NOV	DEC	YEAR
Mean Maximum Temp. (°F)	36.4	41.8	52.1	60.5	69.2	78.2	87.2	86.4	76.0	62.8	47.5	36.6	61.2
Mean Temp. (°F)	28.1	32.3	40.8	47.8	55.9	63.6	71.0	69.7	60.2	49.2	37.2	28.1	48.7
Mean Minimum Temp. (°F)	19.8	22.7	29.5	35.0	42.6	49.0	54.8	52.9	44.4	35.6	26.9	19.5	36.1
Extreme Maximum Temp. (°F)	64	72	78	89	97	102	107	105	97	91	77	65	107
Extreme Minimum Temp. (°F)	-23	-26	-3	12	22	32	33	36	23	11	-6	-22	-26
Days Maximum Temp. ≥ 90°F	0	0	0	0	0	4	13	12	2	0	0	0	31
Days Maximum Temp. ≤ 32°F	10	5	1	0	0	0	0	0	0	0	3	10	29
Days Minimum Temp. ≤ 32°F	28	24	21	11	2	0	0	0	1	10	22	28	147
Days Minimum Temp. ≤ 0°F	2	1	0	0	0	0	0	0	0	0	0	2	5
Heating Degree Days (base 65°F)	1,135	918	742	511	289	104	14	20	172	484	827	1,138	6,354
Cooling Degree Days (base 65°F)	0	0	0	1	13	69	208	171	34	1	0	0	497
Mean Precipitation (in.)	0.97	0.74	1.02	1.04	1.38	0.87	0.32	0.41	0.58	0.72	0.94	1.09	10.08
Extreme Maximum Daily Precip. (in.)	0.85	1.72	1.13	0.81	1.34	0.87	0.66	0.70	0.73	0.73	1.04	0.80	1.72
Days With ≥ 0.1" Precipitation	3	2	3	4	4	3	1	1	2	3	4	4	34
Days With ≥ 0.5" Precipitation	0	0	0	0	1	0	0	0	0	0	0	0	1
Days With ≥ 1.0" Precipitation	0	0	0	0	0	0	0	0	0	0	0	0	0
Mean Snowfall (in.)	na	na	na	na	na	***trace***	na	na	na	na	na	na	na
Maximum Snow Depth (in.)	na	na	na	na	na	***trace***	na	na	na	na	na	na	na
Days With ≥ 1.0" Snow Depth	na	na	na	na	na	***0***	na	na	na	na	na	na	na

Cabinet Gorge *Bonner County* Elevation: 2,259 ft. Latitude: 48° 05' N Longitude: 116° 04' W

	JAN	FEB	MAR	APR	MAY	JUN	JUL	AUG	SEP	OCT	NOV	DEC	YEAR
Mean Maximum Temp. (°F)	34.0	39.1	47.3	57.0	66.2	72.7	82.0	81.6	71.3	56.2	41.5	33.2	56.8
Mean Temp. (°F)	28.7	31.6	37.8	45.3	53.3	59.5	66.2	65.7	57.3	46.0	35.8	28.3	46.3
Mean Minimum Temp. (°F)	23.3	24.0	28.3	33.5	40.4	46.3	50.4	49.8	43.3	35.8	30.1	23.3	35.7
Extreme Maximum Temp. (°F)	55	60	71	84	95	98	101	99	98	81	67	54	101
Extreme Minimum Temp. (°F)	-18	-14	-3	15	23	31	35	34	25	13	-3	-22	-22
Days Maximum Temp. ≥ 90°F	0	0	0	0	0	1	6	5	1	0	0	0	13
Days Maximum Temp. ≤ 32°F	11	4	1	0	0	0	0	0	0	0	3	12	31
Days Minimum Temp. ≤ 32°F	28	25	25	14	4	0	0	0	1	9	18	27	151
Days Minimum Temp. ≤ 0°F	1	1	0	0	0	0	0	0	0	0	0	1	3
Heating Degree Days (base 65°F)	1,119	937	836	584	360	182	51	55	232	582	868	1,131	6,937
Cooling Degree Days (base 65°F)	0	0	0	0	4	23	96	85	9	0	0	0	217
Mean Precipitation (in.)	3.95	2.68	2.91	2.16	2.56	2.53	1.23	1.02	1.53	2.64	4.36	4.03	31.60
Extreme Maximum Daily Precip. (in.)	1.62	2.13	***1.76***	1.24	2.64	2.77	1.08	1.59	1.38	2.00	2.27	2.50	***2.77***
Days With ≥ 0.1" Precipitation	10	7	7	7	7	6	3	3	4	7	10	9	80
Days With ≥ 0.5" Precipitation	2	1	1	1	1	2	1	1	1	1	3	2	17
Days With ≥ 1.0" Precipitation	1	0	0	0	0	0	0	0	0	0	1	0	2
Mean Snowfall (in.)	14.2	6.8	1.6	0.3	0.0	0.0	0.0	0.0	0.0	0.2	3.0	12.1	38.2
Maximum Snow Depth (in.)	34	30	17	trace	0	0	0	0	0	trace	22	***35***	***35***
Days With ≥ 1.0" Snow Depth	15	11	4	0	0	0	0	0	0	0	2	***12***	***44***

Cascade 1 NW *Valley County* Elevation: 4,896 ft. Latitude: 44° 31' N Longitude: 116° 03' W

	JAN	FEB	MAR	APR	MAY	JUN	JUL	AUG	SEP	OCT	NOV	DEC	YEAR
Mean Maximum Temp. (°F)	30.2	35.4	43.7	52.6	62.1	70.1	80.8	80.7	70.6	57.2	40.0	29.8	54.4
Mean Temp. (°F)	20.1	23.4	31.4	39.1	47.5	54.4	62.4	61.4	52.3	41.7	30.0	20.3	40.3
Mean Minimum Temp. (°F)	10.0	11.4	19.1	25.5	32.8	38.7	44.0	42.0	33.9	26.2	20.0	10.9	26.2
Extreme Maximum Temp. (°F)	49	56	70	81	88	92	103	97	91	84	67	52	103
Extreme Minimum Temp. (°F)	-25	-28	-11	2	15	21	27	24	14	1	-21	-35	-35
Days Maximum Temp. ≥ 90°F	0	0	0	0	0	0	4	3	0	0	0	0	7
Days Maximum Temp. ≤ 32°F	18	9	1	0	0	0	0	0	0	0	5	19	52
Days Minimum Temp. ≤ 32°F	31	28	30	27	15	5	1	2	12	26	28	30	235
Days Minimum Temp. ≤ 0°F	8	6	1	0	0	0	0	0	0	0	1	6	22
Heating Degree Days (base 65°F)	1,385	1,169	1,035	771	537	317	117	133	376	715	1,043	1,379	8,977
Cooling Degree Days (base 65°F)	0	0	0	0	1	5	43	27	1	0	0	0	77
Mean Precipitation (in.)	2.76	2.41	2.27	2.02	2.17	1.59	0.63	0.56	0.97	1.56	2.94	3.33	23.21
Extreme Maximum Daily Precip. (in.)	1.39	1.45	1.32	0.97	1.22	0.93	0.71	0.68	0.88	1.45	1.98	1.53	1.98
Days With ≥ 0.1" Precipitation	8	6	7	6	6	5	2	2	3	4	8	8	65
Days With ≥ 0.5" Precipitation	1	1	1	1	1	1	0	0	0	1	2	2	11
Days With ≥ 1.0" Precipitation	0	0	0	0	0	0	0	0	0	0	0	1	1
Mean Snowfall (in.)	21.3	14.8	8.3	2.9	0.3	0.1	0.0	trace	0.1	1.0	12.1	24.3	85.2
Maximum Snow Depth (in.)	44	50	37	26	3	1	0	trace	2	5	19	32	50
Days With ≥ 1.0" Snow Depth	30	27	23	5	0	0	0	0	0	1	12	27	125

The period of record for all cooperative weather station data is 1980 – 2009. See User Guide for detailed explanation of data.

Chilly Barton Flat *Custer County* Elevation: 6,259 ft. Latitude: 43° 59' N Longitude: 113° 50' W

	JAN	FEB	MAR	APR	MAY	JUN	JUL	AUG	SEP	OCT	NOV	DEC	YEAR
Mean Maximum Temp. (°F)	30.6	34.7	43.8	53.9	63.1	72.1	82.1	80.7	71.0	57.5	40.2	30.0	55.0
Mean Temp. (°F)	18.2	21.5	31.6	40.2	48.3	56.0	63.9	62.0	53.3	42.2	28.2	18.1	40.3
Mean Minimum Temp. (°F)	5.7	8.2	19.4	26.5	33.5	39.9	45.6	43.5	35.5	26.7	16.1	6.2	25.6
Extreme Maximum Temp. (°F)	54	55	68	78	88	94	100	100	91	80	65	53	100
Extreme Minimum Temp. (°F)	-32	-30	-12	2	15	21	25	24	13	-1	-21	-37	-37
Days Maximum Temp. ≥ 90°F	0	0	0	0	0	0	3	2	0	0	0	0	5
Days Maximum Temp. ≤ 32°F	18	11	3	0	0	0	0	0	0	0	6	18	56
Days Minimum Temp. ≤ 32°F	30	28	30	24	14	4	0	1	9	24	28	30	222
Days Minimum Temp. ≤ 0°F	10	7	1	0	0	0	0	0	0	0	2	10	30
Heating Degree Days (base 65°F)	1,445	1,222	1,028	738	511	269	79	108	346	700	1,097	1,448	8,991
Cooling Degree Days (base 65°F)	0	0	0	0	0	7	51	23	1	0	0	0	82
Mean Precipitation (in.)	0.33	0.28	0.49	0.67	1.25	1.35	0.77	0.73	0.71	0.66	0.39	0.37	8.00
Extreme Maximum Daily Precip. (in.)	0.66	0.44	1.03	0.51	0.88	1.15	0.64	1.08	1.03	0.85	0.47	0.60	1.15
Days With ≥ 0.1" Precipitation	1	1	1	2	4	4	3	2	2	2	1	1	24
Days With ≥ 0.5" Precipitation	0	0	0	0	0	1	0	0	0	0	0	0	1
Days With ≥ 1.0" Precipitation	0	0	0	0	0	0	0	0	0	0	0	0	0
Mean Snowfall (in.)	*4.3*	na	*1.6*	1.2	0.4	0.2	0.0	0.0	trace	0.4	1.4	na	na
Maximum Snow Depth (in.)	na	na	na	*3*	*trace*	*1*	*0*	*0*	*0*	*2*	*4*	na	na
Days With ≥ 1.0" Snow Depth	na	na	*8*	0	0	0	0	0	0	0	3	*16*	na

Cottonwood 2 WSW *Idaho County* Elevation: 3,944 ft. Latitude: 46° 02' N Longitude: 116° 24' W

	JAN	FEB	MAR	APR	MAY	JUN	JUL	AUG	SEP	OCT	NOV	DEC	YEAR
Mean Maximum Temp. (°F)	35.9	39.7	46.8	54.2	62.0	69.0	78.9	79.8	70.7	57.0	42.4	34.9	56.0
Mean Temp. (°F)	29.9	32.8	38.4	44.6	51.8	58.4	67.0	67.3	59.2	47.7	35.9	29.0	46.8
Mean Minimum Temp. (°F)	23.8	25.8	30.0	35.0	41.6	47.9	55.1	54.8	47.6	38.3	29.3	22.9	37.7
Extreme Maximum Temp. (°F)	56	64	71	81	86	92	99	98	94	87	68	58	99
Extreme Minimum Temp. (°F)	-11	-20	4	18	24	32	37	32	25	9	-5	-18	-20
Days Maximum Temp. ≥ 90°F	0	0	0	0	0	0	3	3	1	0	0	0	7
Days Maximum Temp. ≤ 32°F	9	5	1	0	0	0	0	0	0	0	4	11	30
Days Minimum Temp. ≤ 32°F	27	22	20	12	3	0	0	0	1	6	20	27	138
Days Minimum Temp. ≤ 0°F	1	1	0	0	0	0	0	0	0	0	0	1	3
Heating Degree Days (base 65°F)	1,083	903	816	606	411	218	63	54	207	532	864	1,111	6,868
Cooling Degree Days (base 65°F)	0	0	0	0	8	28	133	133	37	2	0	0	341
Mean Precipitation (in.)	1.91	1.42	1.95	2.35	3.14	2.54	1.43	1.13	1.15	1.57	2.15	1.67	22.41
Extreme Maximum Daily Precip. (in.)	2.10	1.26	0.86	1.07	1.98	1.23	1.50	1.39	2.00	1.01	1.00	0.95	2.10
Days With ≥ 0.1" Precipitation	6	5	7	8	8	7	4	3	3	5	7	6	69
Days With ≥ 0.5" Precipitation	1	0	1	1	2	2	1	1	1	1	1	0	12
Days With ≥ 1.0" Precipitation	0	0	0	0	0	0	0	0	0	0	0	0	0
Mean Snowfall (in.)	na	na	*6.8*	2.5	0.2	trace	0.0	0.0	trace	0.3	*5.0*	na	na
Maximum Snow Depth (in.)	na	na	na	na	na	na	na	na	na	na	na	na	na
Days With ≥ 1.0" Snow Depth	na	na	na	0	0	0	0	0	0	0	*1*	na	na

Dixie *Idaho County* Elevation: 5,620 ft. Latitude: 45° 33' N Longitude: 115° 28' W

	JAN	FEB	MAR	APR	MAY	JUN	JUL	AUG	SEP	OCT	NOV	DEC	YEAR
Mean Maximum Temp. (°F)	31.6	35.3	40.8	47.4	56.5	*65.5*	*75.2*	*75.5*	*66.5*	52.4	37.1	30.3	*51.2*
Mean Temp. (°F)	18.4	20.9	27.9	34.6	43.1	*50.4*	*56.8*	*55.7*	*47.9*	37.8	25.6	17.7	*36.4*
Mean Minimum Temp. (°F)	5.3	6.4	14.9	21.8	29.7	*35.3*	*38.3*	*35.8*	29.3	23.1	14.0	5.0	*21.6*
Extreme Maximum Temp. (°F)	54	59	64	78	86	*87*	*96*	*94*	90	80	64	53	*96*
Extreme Minimum Temp. (°F)	-35	-40	-18	-5	7	*19*	*24*	*19*	11	-6	-33	-49	*-49*
Days Maximum Temp. ≥ 90°F	0	0	0	0	0	*0*	*1*	*1*	0	0	0	0	*2*
Days Maximum Temp. ≤ 32°F	16	10	4	1	0	*0*	*0*	*0*	0	1	10	18	*60*
Days Minimum Temp. ≤ 32°F	30	27	30	28	22	*11*	*4*	*9*	22	29	29	30	*271*
Days Minimum Temp. ≤ 0°F	10	9	2	0	0	*0*	*0*	*0*	0	0	4	12	*37*
Heating Degree Days (base 65°F)	1,437	1,242	1,143	905	672	*432*	*255*	*285*	*505*	839	1,176	1,460	*10,351*
Cooling Degree Days (base 65°F)	0	0	0	0	0	*1*	*7*	*3*	*0*	0	0	0	*11*
Mean Precipitation (in.)	2.89	2.31	2.21	1.97	2.19	*2.24*	*1.15*	*1.16*	1.23	1.46	3.32	3.19	*25.32*
Extreme Maximum Daily Precip. (in.)	1.41	1.50	1.10	1.21	1.03	*1.60*	*1.00*	*1.43*	*1.15*	1.30	1.50	2.82	*2.82*
Days With ≥ 0.1" Precipitation	9	7	8	6	7	*6*	*4*	*3*	*4*	5	10	10	*79*
Days With ≥ 0.5" Precipitation	1	1	1	1	1	*1*	*1*	*1*	*0*	1	2	1	*12*
Days With ≥ 1.0" Precipitation	0	0	0	0	0	*0*	*0*	*0*	*0*	0	0	0	*0*
Mean Snowfall (in.)	37.2	26.6	25.4	14.4	4.6	*0.9*	*0.0*	*0.0*	*1.1*	4.1	*31.7*	36.2	*182.2*
Maximum Snow Depth (in.)	83	81	85	61	42	*4*	*0*	*0*	4	8	30	56	*85*
Days With ≥ 1.0" Snow Depth	29	28	29	25	7	*0*	*0*	*0*	*0*	3	*23*	30	*174*

Driggs *Teton County* Elevation: 6,116 ft. Latitude: 43° 44' N Longitude: 111° 07' W

	JAN	FEB	MAR	APR	MAY	JUN	JUL	AUG	SEP	OCT	NOV	DEC	YEAR
Mean Maximum Temp. (°F)	29.3	33.5	41.7	52.6	62.6	71.5	80.2	79.2	69.3	56.0	40.4	29.5	53.8
Mean Temp. (°F)	19.0	22.4	30.7	39.9	48.5	56.2	63.4	62.0	53.3	41.9	29.7	19.5	40.5
Mean Minimum Temp. (°F)	8.6	11.1	19.7	27.1	34.4	40.8	46.5	44.8	37.2	27.8	19.0	9.4	27.2
Extreme Maximum Temp. (°F)	55	58	69	79	86	92	93	93	89	81	71	55	93
Extreme Minimum Temp. (°F)	-34	-33	-20	0	12	23	29	24	9	-1	-20	-40	-40
Days Maximum Temp. ≥ 90°F	0	0	0	0	0	0	1	1	0	0	0	0	2
Days Maximum Temp. ≤ 32°F	19	12	4	0	0	0	0	0	0	1	7	19	62
Days Minimum Temp. ≤ 32°F	30	27	28	23	12	3	0	1	8	22	26	30	210
Days Minimum Temp. ≤ 0°F	9	6	1	0	0	0	0	0	0	0	2	9	27
Heating Degree Days (base 65°F)	1,421	1,199	1,056	746	504	263	84	106	346	710	1,051	1,405	8,891
Cooling Degree Days (base 65°F)	0	0	0	0	0	6	40	21	2	0	0	0	69
Mean Precipitation (in.)	1.21	0.84	1.04	1.38	2.01	1.38	1.18	0.97	1.13	1.28	1.10	1.37	14.89
Extreme Maximum Daily Precip. (in.)	*0.98*	*0.74*	*1.28*	*0.97*	*1.56*	*3.14*	*1.05*	*0.90*	*1.01*	*1.33*	*0.77*	*0.91*	*3.14*
Days With ≥ 0.1" Precipitation	4	3	3	5	6	4	4	3	3	3	4	4	46
Days With ≥ 0.5" Precipitation	0	0	0	0	1	1	1	0	1	1	0	0	5
Days With ≥ 1.0" Precipitation	0	0	0	0	0	0	0	0	0	0	0	0	0
Mean Snowfall (in.)	17.6	9.2	8.6	4.3	1.5	0.1	0.0	0.0	0.1	2.6	10.2	18.7	72.9
Maximum Snow Depth (in.)	36	39	38	25	6	trace	0	0	trace	6	17	26	39
Days With ≥ 1.0" Snow Depth	22	18	15	2	0	0	0	0	0	1	9	19	86

The period of record for all cooperative weather station data is 1980 – 2009. See User Guide for detailed explanation of data.

Dubois Experiment Stn *Clark County* Elevation: 5,450 ft. Latitude: 44° 15' N Longitude: 112° 12' W

	JAN	FEB	MAR	APR	MAY	JUN	JUL	AUG	SEP	OCT	NOV	DEC	YEAR
Mean Maximum Temp. (°F)	29.0	33.1	43.1	55.8	65.9	75.3	85.4	84.6	73.5	57.9	39.8	28.9	56.0
Mean Temp. (°F)	20.6	24.0	33.0	43.2	52.2	60.3	69.0	67.9	58.0	45.2	30.8	20.9	43.8
Mean Minimum Temp. (°F)	12.2	15.0	22.9	30.5	38.4	45.3	52.5	51.1	42.5	32.5	21.8	12.8	31.5
Extreme Maximum Temp. (°F)	53	52	71	81	92	98	103	101	92	83	66	53	103
Extreme Minimum Temp. (°F)	-21	-22	-8	6	20	27	32	33	15	5	-11	-31	-31
Days Maximum Temp. ≥ 90°F	0	0	0	0	0	2	9	7	0	0	0	0	18
Days Maximum Temp. ≤ 32°F	20	12	3	0	0	0	0	0	0	0	7	20	62
Days Minimum Temp. ≤ 32°F	31	28	28	18	7	1	0	0	3	14	27	31	188
Days Minimum Temp. ≤ 0°F	4	3	0	0	0	0	0	0	0	0	1	4	12
Heating Degree Days (base 65°F)	1,369	1,152	984	648	395	168	29	32	223	606	1,017	1,361	7,984
Cooling Degree Days (base 65°F)	0	0	0	0	4	34	158	128	21	0	0	0	345
Mean Precipitation (in.)	0.80	0.71	0.91	1.26	2.03	1.67	0.89	0.84	0.88	0.95	0.96	1.01	12.91
Extreme Maximum Daily Precip. (in.)	0.48	0.52	1.51	1.25	1.21	1.26	0.85	0.91	1.16	0.85	0.63	0.82	1.51
Days With ≥ 0.1" Precipitation	3	2	3	4	6	5	3	3	2	3	4	4	42
Days With ≥ 0.5" Precipitation	0	0	0	0	1	1	0	0	0	0	0	0	2
Days With ≥ 1.0" Precipitation	0	0	0	0	0	0	0	0	0	0	0	0	0
Mean Snowfall (in.)	9.9	7.6	4.8	2.9	1.2	0.2	0.0	0.0	trace	1.3	7.7	11.7	47.3
Maximum Snow Depth (in.)	35	37	33	23	8	0	0	0	trace	5	15	22	37
Days With ≥ 1.0" Snow Depth	30	28	19	2	0	0	0	0	0	1	9	27	116

Dworshak Fish Hatchery *Clearwater County* Elevation: 995 ft. Latitude: 46° 30' N Longitude: 116° 19' W

	JAN	FEB	MAR	APR	MAY	JUN	JUL	AUG	SEP	OCT	NOV	DEC	YEAR
Mean Maximum Temp. (°F)	40.1	46.5	55.6	64.3	72.3	79.1	89.5	89.8	80.1	64.2	47.9	38.9	64.0
Mean Temp. (°F)	33.9	37.8	44.6	51.6	58.8	65.3	72.7	72.1	63.8	51.5	40.5	33.2	52.2
Mean Minimum Temp. (°F)	27.7	29.0	33.6	38.8	45.3	51.4	55.8	54.4	47.4	38.7	33.1	27.5	40.2
Extreme Maximum Temp. (°F)	59	66	82	95	104	105	108	108	105	90	69	61	108
Extreme Minimum Temp. (°F)	-2	-9	12	27	28	35	41	39	28	16	1	-10	-10
Days Maximum Temp. ≥ 90°F	0	0	0	0	2	5	17	18	7	0	0	0	49
Days Maximum Temp. ≤ 32°F	4	1	0	0	0	0	0	0	0	0	1	4	10
Days Minimum Temp. ≤ 32°F	23	19	13	4	1	0	0	0	0	5	12	23	100
Days Minimum Temp. ≤ 0°F	0	0	0	0	0	0	0	0	0	0	0	0	0
Heating Degree Days (base 65°F)	956	764	625	397	216	77	8	13	106	414	727	979	5,282
Cooling Degree Days (base 65°F)	0	0	0	2	32	92	254	242	76	1	0	0	699
Mean Precipitation (in.)	2.88	2.25	2.47	2.31	2.56	1.73	1.03	0.82	1.17	1.71	3.25	2.74	24.92
Extreme Maximum Daily Precip. (in.)	1.54	1.55	0.92	1.20	1.99	1.07	1.53	1.10	1.12	1.94	1.75	1.40	1.99
Days With ≥ 0.1" Precipitation	9	7	9	7	7	5	3	2	3	5	10	9	76
Days With ≥ 0.5" Precipitation	1	1	1	1	1	1	0	0	1	1	2	1	11
Days With ≥ 1.0" Precipitation	0	0	0	0	0	0	0	0	0	0	0	0	0
Mean Snowfall (in.)	***6.2***	***1.1***	0.8	trace	0.0	0.0	0.0	0.0	0.0	trace	0.5	***5.1***	***13.7***
Maximum Snow Depth (in.)	na	na	na	na	***0***	***0***	***0***	***0***	***0***	na	***3***	na	na
Days With ≥ 1.0" Snow Depth	na	***1***	0	0	0	0	0	0	0	0	0	***4***	na

Emmett 2 E *Gem County* Elevation: 2,390 ft. Latitude: 43° 52' N Longitude: 116° 28' W

	JAN	FEB	MAR	APR	MAY	JUN	JUL	AUG	SEP	OCT	NOV	DEC	YEAR
Mean Maximum Temp. (°F)	37.9	45.2	55.7	63.5	72.4	81.2	90.7	89.4	78.9	65.6	49.0	38.2	64.0
Mean Temp. (°F)	30.2	35.5	43.7	50.0	58.0	65.8	73.8	72.4	62.9	51.6	39.1	30.3	51.1
Mean Minimum Temp. (°F)	22.3	25.8	31.7	36.3	43.5	50.4	56.7	55.3	46.9	37.5	29.2	22.4	38.2
Extreme Maximum Temp. (°F)	63	70	80	88	98	102	110	106	101	95	75	64	110
Extreme Minimum Temp. (°F)	-6	-15	14	20	23	32	37	36	27	12	-10	-20	-20
Days Maximum Temp. ≥ 90°F	0	0	0	0	2	6	20	17	4	0	0	0	49
Days Maximum Temp. ≤ 32°F	8	2	0	0	0	0	0	0	0	0	1	7	18
Days Minimum Temp. ≤ 32°F	28	23	17	9	2	0	0	0	1	7	20	27	134
Days Minimum Temp. ≤ 0°F	1	0	0	0	0	0	0	0	0	0	0	1	2
Heating Degree Days (base 65°F)	1,070	827	652	446	242	80	11	13	123	412	770	1,068	5,714
Cooling Degree Days (base 65°F)	0	0	0	0	2	31	110	289	249	68	3	0	752
Mean Precipitation (in.)	1.64	1.41	1.56	1.24	1.44	0.80	0.30	0.28	0.59	0.83	1.66	1.94	13.69
Extreme Maximum Daily Precip. (in.)	1.03	0.78	0.99	0.78	1.58	1.13	0.60	1.01	1.15	1.00	0.87	1.75	1.75
Days With ≥ 0.1" Precipitation	6	5	5	4	4	3	1	1	2	3	5	5	44
Days With ≥ 0.5" Precipitation	0	0	1	0	1	0	0	0	0	0	1	1	4
Days With ≥ 1.0" Precipitation	0	0	0	0	0	0	0	0	0	0	0	0	0
Mean Snowfall (in.)	***1.8***	***1.2***	0.1	0.1	0.0	0.0	0.0	0.0	0.0	0.0	0.9	***2.4***	***6.5***
Maximum Snow Depth (in.)	***14***	***4***	***1***	***trace***	***0***	***0***	***0***	***0***	***0***	***0***	***4***	***9***	***14***
Days With ≥ 1.0" Snow Depth	***4***	2	0	0	0	0	0	0	0	0	1	***2***	***9***

Fort Hall 1 NNE *Bingham County* Elevation: 4,464 ft. Latitude: 43° 03' N Longitude: 112° 25' W

	JAN	FEB	MAR	APR	MAY	JUN	JUL	AUG	SEP	OCT	NOV	DEC	YEAR
Mean Maximum Temp. (°F)	32.7	38.0	49.2	59.3	67.9	76.2	86.1	85.9	75.3	61.2	44.8	32.8	59.1
Mean Temp. (°F)	23.3	27.4	37.3	45.3	53.5	60.9	68.5	67.5	58.0	46.2	33.6	23.3	45.4
Mean Minimum Temp. (°F)	13.8	16.7	25.4	31.4	38.9	45.6	50.7	49.0	40.7	31.2	22.4	13.7	31.6
Extreme Maximum Temp. (°F)	55	69	76	85	93	99	101	103	96	90	74	63	103
Extreme Minimum Temp. (°F)	-29	-33	-11	10	17	25	35	27	14	8	-20	-30	-33
Days Maximum Temp. ≥ 90°F	0	0	0	0	0	2	10	10	2	0	0	0	24
Days Maximum Temp. ≤ 32°F	14	8	1	0	0	0	0	0	0	0	4	14	41
Days Minimum Temp. ≤ 32°F	30	27	25	17	5	1	0	0	4	17	25	29	180
Days Minimum Temp. ≤ 0°F	5	3	0	0	0	0	0	0	0	0	1	4	13
Heating Degree Days (base 65°F)	1,286	1,058	852	584	356	152	25	34	220	576	935	1,287	7,365
Cooling Degree Days (base 65°F)	0	0	0	0	5	36	140	118	18	0	0	0	317
Mean Precipitation (in.)	0.90	0.84	1.11	1.03	1.66	1.07	0.56	0.66	0.79	0.93	0.95	0.98	11.48
Extreme Maximum Daily Precip. (in.)	0.90	0.75	0.80	1.10	1.32	1.12	1.66	1.26	0.89	0.84	***0.94***	***0.63***	***1.66***
Days With ≥ 0.1" Precipitation	3	3	4	3	4	3	1	2	3	3	3	3	35
Days With ≥ 0.5" Precipitation	0	0	0	0	1	1	0	0	0	0	0	0	2
Days With ≥ 1.0" Precipitation	0	0	0	0	0	0	0	0	0	0	0	0	0
Mean Snowfall (in.)	6.8	4.5	3.1	0.8	0.4	trace	0.0	0.0	trace	1.5	2.6	8.4	28.1
Maximum Snow Depth (in.)	23	23	20	9	5	trace	0	0	0	5	13	21	23
Days With ≥ 1.0" Snow Depth	20	13	5	1	0	0	0	0	0	1	5	17	62

The period of record for all cooperative weather station data is 1980 – 2009. See User Guide for detailed explanation of data.

Garden Valley *Boise County* Elevation: 3,100 ft. Latitude: 44° 06' N Longitude: 115° 58' W

	JAN	FEB	MAR	APR	MAY	JUN	JUL	AUG	SEP	OCT	NOV	DEC	YEAR
Mean Maximum Temp. (°F)	35.3	42.3	52.9	62.0	71.6	79.6	89.8	89.7	79.4	65.3	45.0	34.3	62.3
Mean Temp. (°F)	26.8	31.3	39.8	47.0	54.8	61.5	68.4	67.2	58.4	47.7	35.1	26.4	47.0
Mean Minimum Temp. (°F)	18.3	20.2	26.6	31.7	37.9	43.3	47.0	44.5	37.5	30.1	25.1	18.4	31.7
Extreme Maximum Temp. (°F)	53	67	77	90	99	101	107	108	100	92	77	57	108
Extreme Minimum Temp. (°F)	-17	-21	0	16	17	26	29	26	19	10	-13	-21	-21
Days Maximum Temp. ≥ 90°F	0	0	0	0	1	5	18	18	5	0	0	0	47
Days Maximum Temp. ≤ 32°F	9	2	0	0	0	0	0	0	0	0	2	10	23
Days Minimum Temp. ≤ 32°F	28	26	24	16	7	1	0	0	7	20	23	27	179
Days Minimum Temp. ≤ 0°F	3	1	0	0	0	0	0	0	0	0	0	2	6
Heating Degree Days (base 65°F)	1,176	***951***	***779***	535	318	139	31	37	208	529	891	1,189	***6,783***
Cooling Degree Days (base 65°F)	0	0	0	0	8	40	144	111	18	0	0	0	321
Mean Precipitation (in.)	3.76	2.69	2.53	1.99	1.91	1.37	0.59	0.44	1.11	1.55	3.49	4.43	25.86
Extreme Maximum Daily Precip. (in.)	***1.67***	***1.33***	***1.54***	***1.40***	***1.57***	***1.10***	0.95	1.66	***1.63***	***2.19***	na	***1.89***	na
Days With ≥ 0.1" Precipitation	8	7	6	5	5	4	2	1	3	4	8	9	62
Days With ≥ 0.5" Precipitation	2	2	1	1	1	1	0	0	1	1	2	3	15
Days With ≥ 1.0" Precipitation	1	0	0	0	0	0	0	0	0	0	0	1	2
Mean Snowfall (in.)	***20.7***	***9.6***	***3.0***	***0.4***	trace	0.0	0.0	0.0	trace	0.2	***6.8***	***21.0***	***61.7***
Maximum Snow Depth (in.)	***35***	***40***	***19***	2	trace	0	0	0	trace	trace	***15***	***29***	***40***
Days With ≥ 1.0" Snow Depth	***26***	***20***	***11***	0	0	0	0	0	0	0	***3***	18	***78***

Grace *Caribou County* Elevation: 5,549 ft. Latitude: 42° 35' N Longitude: 111° 45' W

	JAN	FEB	MAR	APR	MAY	JUN	JUL	AUG	SEP	OCT	NOV	DEC	YEAR
Mean Maximum Temp. (°F)	32.4	36.6	46.8	57.3	66.7	76.4	86.5	85.5	75.1	61.4	44.4	33.5	58.5
Mean Temp. (°F)	21.7	24.7	34.6	43.2	51.4	59.2	67.1	65.8	56.7	45.4	32.7	23.0	43.8
Mean Minimum Temp. (°F)	11.1	12.8	22.4	29.0	36.1	42.0	47.7	46.1	38.3	29.4	21.0	12.4	29.0
Extreme Maximum Temp. (°F)	56	60	72	82	94	99	103	102	97	86	70	60	103
Extreme Minimum Temp. (°F)	-34	-36	-15	9	20	25	28	26	15	0	-20	-40	-40
Days Maximum Temp. ≥ 90°F	0	0	0	0	0	2	10	9	1	0	0	0	22
Days Maximum Temp. ≤ 32°F	15	8	1	0	0	0	0	0	0	0	4	13	41
Days Minimum Temp. ≤ 32°F	30	27	28	21	10	2	0	0	6	20	27	30	201
Days Minimum Temp. ≤ 0°F	7	6	1	0	0	0	0	0	0	0	1	6	21
Heating Degree Days (base 65°F)	1,335	1,133	935	649	417	188	35	47	251	601	962	1,297	7,850
Cooling Degree Days (base 65°F)	0	0	0	0	2	20	108	79	10	0	0	0	219
Mean Precipitation (in.)	1.15	1.01	1.32	1.41	2.38	1.36	0.97	1.21	1.31	1.43	1.10	1.11	15.76
Extreme Maximum Daily Precip. (in.)	0.94	0.87	0.80	0.96	1.44	1.37	1.02	1.73	1.30	1.22	0.80	0.61	1.73
Days With ≥ 0.1" Precipitation	3	4	5	4	6	4	3	3	4	4	4	4	48
Days With ≥ 0.5" Precipitation	0	0	0	0	1	1	0	1	1	1	0	0	5
Days With ≥ 1.0" Precipitation	0	0	0	0	0	0	0	0	0	0	0	0	0
Mean Snowfall (in.)	na	na	na	***0.3***	trace	0.0	0.0	0.0	0.0	0.1	na	na	na
Maximum Snow Depth (in.)	na	na	na	na	na	na	na	na	na	na	na	na	na
Days With ≥ 1.0" Snow Depth	na	na	na	1	0	0	0	0	0	0	na	na	na

Grand View 2 W *Owyhee County* Elevation: 2,399 ft. Latitude: 43° 01' N Longitude: 116° 11' W

	JAN	FEB	MAR	APR	MAY	JUN	JUL	AUG	SEP	OCT	NOV	DEC	YEAR
Mean Maximum Temp. (°F)	39.8	47.8	59.1	67.2	75.8	83.9	92.5	91.3	80.8	67.3	50.8	39.0	66.3
Mean Temp. (°F)	31.4	36.7	45.4	52.5	60.9	68.1	75.1	73.2	63.6	51.7	39.6	30.4	52.4
Mean Minimum Temp. (°F)	23.0	25.6	31.7	37.7	45.8	52.2	57.6	55.0	46.0	36.1	28.4	21.7	38.4
Extreme Maximum Temp. (°F)	67	76	82	91	102	106	110	109	101	93	84	68	110
Extreme Minimum Temp. (°F)	-21	-20	10	18	25	35	39	37	25	12	-5	-26	-26
Days Maximum Temp. ≥ 90°F	0	0	0	0	3	9	22	21	5	0	0	0	60
Days Maximum Temp. ≤ 32°F	6	2	0	0	0	0	0	0	0	0	1	6	15
Days Minimum Temp. ≤ 32°F	27	22	17	7	1	0	0	0	1	11	20	26	132
Days Minimum Temp. ≤ 0°F	1	0	0	0	0	0	0	0	0	0	0	1	2
Heating Degree Days (base 65°F)	1,034	793	600	372	170	44	4	7	96	407	754	1,068	5,349
Cooling Degree Days (base 65°F)	0	0	0	4	49	143	322	269	62	2	0	0	851
Mean Precipitation (in.)	0.59	0.52	0.74	0.66	0.95	0.62	0.23	0.19	0.43	0.46	0.76	0.71	6.86
Extreme Maximum Daily Precip. (in.)	0.44	0.81	0.85	1.04	1.04	1.60	0.79	0.63	0.93	0.60	***0.78***	0.72	***1.60***
Days With ≥ 0.1" Precipitation	2	2	3	2	3	2	1	1	1	1	2	2	22
Days With ≥ 0.5" Precipitation	0	0	0	0	0	0	0	0	0	0	0	0	0
Days With ≥ 1.0" Precipitation	0	0	0	0	0	0	0	0	0	0	0	0	0
Mean Snowfall (in.)	***0.8***	1.4	0.1	0.0	0.0	0.0	0.0	0.0	0.0	0.0	0.5	***0.8***	***3.6***
Maximum Snow Depth (in.)	***5***	***3***	na	***0***	***0***	***0***	***0***	***0***	***0***	***0***	***2***	na	na
Days With ≥ 1.0" Snow Depth	***0***	0	***0***	0	0	0	0	0	0	0	0	***1***	***1***

Howe *Butte County* Elevation: 4,819 ft. Latitude: 43° 48' N Longitude: 113° 00' W

	JAN	FEB	MAR	APR	MAY	JUN	JUL	AUG	SEP	OCT	NOV	DEC	YEAR
Mean Maximum Temp. (°F)	30.8	35.2	48.0	59.8	68.2	77.6	87.8	86.2	76.0	61.1	43.4	31.3	58.8
Mean Temp. (°F)	18.8	23.1	35.6	45.3	53.4	61.3	69.0	67.1	57.4	45.1	30.8	19.5	43.9
Mean Minimum Temp. (°F)	6.7	10.9	23.2	30.6	38.5	45.1	50.2	47.9	38.8	29.0	18.1	7.7	28.9
Extreme Maximum Temp. (°F)	54	58	74	86	96	102	103	101	94	85	68	58	103
Extreme Minimum Temp. (°F)	-35	-38	-16	8	20	28	33	28	19	7	-22	-36	-38
Days Maximum Temp. ≥ 90°F	0	0	0	0	0	3	13	10	1	0	0	0	27
Days Maximum Temp. ≤ 32°F	17	10	2	0	0	0	0	0	0	0	4	15	48
Days Minimum Temp. ≤ 32°F	29	27	27	17	6	1	0	0	6	20	27	29	189
Days Minimum Temp. ≤ 0°F	10	7	1	0	0	0	0	0	0	0	2	9	29
Heating Degree Days (base 65°F)	1,427	1,179	904	585	360	144	25	34	233	612	1,020	1,404	7,927
Cooling Degree Days (base 65°F)	0	0	0	0	6	39	157	106	11	0	0	0	319
Mean Precipitation (in.)	0.40	0.48	0.49	0.72	0.92	1.10	0.65	0.62	0.43	0.56	0.54	0.53	7.44
Extreme Maximum Daily Precip. (in.)	na	na	***0.68***	na	na	na	na	na	na	***1.23***	na	na	na
Days With ≥ 0.1" Precipitation	1	1	2	2	3	2	1	2	1	1	1	2	19
Days With ≥ 0.5" Precipitation	0	0	0	0	0	0	0	0	0	0	0	0	0
Days With ≥ 1.0" Precipitation	0	0	0	0	0	0	0	0	0	0	0	0	0
Mean Snowfall (in.)	2.8	1.5	0.6	0.5	trace	0.0	0.0	0.0	0.0	0.2	***0.7***	***3.8***	***10.1***
Maximum Snow Depth (in.)	***13***	***6***	8	5	trace	0	0	0	0	trace	8	***10***	***13***
Days With ≥ 1.0" Snow Depth	***5***	***2***	1	0	0	0	0	0	0	0	1	***4***	***13***

The period of record for all cooperative weather station data is 1980 – 2009. See User Guide for detailed explanation of data.

Idaho City *Boise County* Elevation: 3,964 ft. Latitude: 43° 50' N Longitude: 115° 50' W

	JAN	FEB	MAR	APR	MAY	JUN	JUL	AUG	SEP	OCT	NOV	DEC	YEAR
Mean Maximum Temp. (°F)	35.7	41.2	48.7	57.7	67.3	76.3	87.2	86.9	76.1	62.2	44.3	34.7	59.9
Mean Temp. (°F)	24.5	28.2	35.8	42.8	51.2	58.5	66.3	65.4	55.9	44.8	32.9	23.9	44.2
Mean Minimum Temp. (°F)	13.3	15.2	22.7	27.8	35.0	40.6	45.4	43.8	35.6	27.4	21.5	13.1	28.4
Extreme Maximum Temp. (°F)	52	65	73	88	96	100	107	104	100	90	74	54	107
Extreme Minimum Temp. (°F)	-20	-24	-6	9	17	26	27	25	17	6	-18	-32	-32
Days Maximum Temp. ≥ 90°F	0	0	0	0	0	3	13	13	2	0	0	0	31
Days Maximum Temp. ≤ 32°F	9	4	0	0	0	0	0	0	0	0	2	11	26
Days Minimum Temp. ≤ 32°F	30	27	29	23	11	3	0	1	10	24	28	30	216
Days Minimum Temp. ≤ 0°F	5	3	0	0	0	0	0	0	0	0	1	5	14
Heating Degree Days (base 65°F)	1,247	1,033	900	660	426	212	56	67	277	619	956	1,267	7,720
Cooling Degree Days (base 65°F)	0	0	0	0	4	23	104	84	10	0	0	0	225
Mean Precipitation (in.)	3.06	2.36	2.31	1.79	1.99	1.15	0.55	0.46	1.04	1.39	2.96	3.51	22.57
Extreme Maximum Daily Precip. (in.)	1.72	1.75	1.12	1.40	1.30	1.15	0.84	1.16	1.77	1.47	1.89	1.96	1.96
Days With ≥ 0.1" Precipitation	8	6	7	5	5	3	2	1	3	4	8	8	60
Days With ≥ 0.5" Precipitation	2	1	1	1	1	1	0	0	1	1	2	2	13
Days With ≥ 1.0" Precipitation	0	0	0	0	0	0	0	0	0	0	0	1	1
Mean Snowfall (in.)	20.8	10.2	4.4	1.2	0.1	0.0	0.0	0.0	trace	0.4	8.9	22.6	68.6
Maximum Snow Depth (in.)	46	46	37	16	trace	0	0	0	trace	3	22	39	46
Days With ≥ 1.0" Snow Depth	31	26	19	3	0	0	0	0	0	0	10	28	117

Idaho Falls 16 SE *Bonneville County* Elevation: 5,850 ft. Latitude: 43° 21' N Longitude: 111° 47' W

	JAN	FEB	MAR	APR	MAY	JUN	JUL	AUG	SEP	OCT	NOV	DEC	YEAR
Mean Maximum Temp. (°F)	31.2	34.9	42.6	52.6	62.3	71.2	80.9	79.6	69.8	56.5	41.2	30.9	54.5
Mean Temp. (°F)	21.6	24.5	32.5	40.5	48.9	56.3	64.1	62.8	53.8	42.7	30.7	21.3	41.6
Mean Minimum Temp. (°F)	12.0	14.0	22.3	28.4	35.5	41.4	47.3	45.9	37.8	28.8	20.2	11.7	28.8
Extreme Maximum Temp. (°F)	56	56	68	78	90	97	100	96	89	81	70	56	100
Extreme Minimum Temp. (°F)	-35	-40	-15	-6	11	21	28	19	7	-1	-25	-41	-41
Days Maximum Temp. ≥ 90°F	0	0	0	0	0	0	3	1	0	0	0	0	4
Days Maximum Temp. ≤ 32°F	17	10	3	0	0	0	0	0	0	0	6	17	53
Days Minimum Temp. ≤ 32°F	30	27	28	21	11	3	0	1	7	21	27	30	206
Days Minimum Temp. ≤ 0°F	6	4	1	0	0	0	0	0	0	0	1	6	18
Heating Degree Days (base 65°F)	1,338	1,140	1,002	728	491	263	78	98	334	685	1,021	1,348	8,526
Cooling Degree Days (base 65°F)	0	0	0	0	1	9	57	36	3	0	0	0	106
Mean Precipitation (in.)	1.46	1.09	1.32	1.31	2.01	1.38	1.08	0.89	1.11	1.21	1.57	1.55	15.98
Extreme Maximum Daily Precip. (in.)	1.20	0.86	1.21	0.85	2.19	1.53	1.04	0.93	1.33	0.95	2.10	1.53	2.19
Days With ≥ 0.1" Precipitation	5	4	4	5	6	5	3	3	3	4	5	5	52
Days With ≥ 0.5" Precipitation	0	0	0	0	1	0	0	0	1	0	1	1	4
Days With ≥ 1.0" Precipitation	0	0	0	0	0	0	0	0	0	0	0	0	0
Mean Snowfall (in.)	16.6	11.5	8.9	4.3	1.4	0.2	0.0	0.0	0.1	2.0	8.0	17.0	70.0
Maximum Snow Depth (in.)	29	30	28	16	6	trace	0	0	1	4	8	36	36
Days With ≥ 1.0" Snow Depth	29	26	16	3	0	0	0	0	0	1	9	24	108

Idaho Falls 2 ESE *Bonneville County* Elevation: 4,765 ft. Latitude: 43° 29' N Longitude: 112° 01' W

	JAN	FEB	MAR	APR	MAY	JUN	JUL	AUG	SEP	OCT	NOV	DEC	YEAR
Mean Maximum Temp. (°F)	30.6	36.8	49.0	59.6	68.9	78.2	87.3	86.8	75.8	61.6	43.6	30.9	59.1
Mean Temp. (°F)	22.2	27.2	37.7	46.2	54.7	62.8	70.3	68.9	59.1	47.1	33.6	22.5	46.0
Mean Minimum Temp. (°F)	13.7	17.6	26.3	32.7	40.5	47.3	53.2	51.0	42.3	32.4	23.6	14.0	32.9
Extreme Maximum Temp. (°F)	57	62	75	85	95	100	104	99	95	87	70	60	104
Extreme Minimum Temp. (°F)	-26	-34	-12	14	20	28	34	31	18	7	-12	-28	-34
Days Maximum Temp. ≥ 90°F	0	0	0	0	0	3	13	11	1	0	0	0	28
Days Maximum Temp. ≤ 32°F	17	8	1	0	0	0	0	0	0	0	4	16	46
Days Minimum Temp. ≤ 32°F	30	26	25	15	4	0	0	0	3	16	25	29	173
Days Minimum Temp. ≤ 0°F	5	3	0	0	0	0	0	0	0	0	1	4	13
Heating Degree Days (base 65°F)	1,321	1,061	840	559	321	121	19	21	194	550	935	1,312	7,254
Cooling Degree Days (base 65°F)	0	0	0	1	8	60	190	150	23	0	0	0	432
Mean Precipitation (in.)	1.24	1.05	1.27	1.30	2.05	1.27	0.61	0.68	0.95	1.12	1.22	1.21	13.97
Extreme Maximum Daily Precip. (in.)	1.60	1.35	1.49	1.25	1.67	1.68	1.00	0.90	1.73	1.36	0.83	1.10	1.73
Days With ≥ 0.1" Precipitation	4	4	4	4	5	3	2	2	2	3	4	4	41
Days With ≥ 0.5" Precipitation	0	0	0	1	1	1	0	0	1	0	0	0	4
Days With ≥ 1.0" Precipitation	0	0	0	0	0	0	0	0	0	0	0	0	0
Mean Snowfall (in.)	na	***5.6***	***3.1***	1.1	0.2	0.0	0.0	0.0	0.1	0.8	5.0	na	na
Maximum Snow Depth (in.)	na	na	na	***2***	***1***	***0***	***0***	***0***	***0***	***4***	***6***	na	na
Days With ≥ 1.0" Snow Depth	na	na	***1***	0	0	0	0	0	0	0	***2***	6	na

Island Park *Fremont County* Elevation: 6,290 ft. Latitude: 44° 25' N Longitude: 111° 22' W

	JAN	FEB	MAR	APR	MAY	JUN	JUL	AUG	SEP	OCT	NOV	DEC	YEAR
Mean Maximum Temp. (°F)	28.2	32.3	39.8	49.0	60.1	***70.0***	***79.4***	***79.7***	69.5	54.1	37.3	27.0	***52.2***
Mean Temp. (°F)	16.4	19.4	27.1	36.0	46.0	***54.1***	***61.2***	***60.1***	51.0	39.3	26.2	16.3	***37.8***
Mean Minimum Temp. (°F)	4.6	6.4	14.3	23.0	31.9	***38.1***	***43.0***	***40.5***	32.4	24.4	15.1	5.8	***23.3***
Extreme Maximum Temp. (°F)	49	53	61	76	84	***91***	***95***	***96***	89	80	68	51	***96***
Extreme Minimum Temp. (°F)	-46	-54	-32	-13	8	***20***	***25***	***20***	8	-4	-24	-41	***-54***
Days Maximum Temp. ≥ 90°F	0	0	0	0	0	***0***	1	***1***	0	0	0	0	***2***
Days Maximum Temp. ≤ 32°F	21	14	5	0	0	***0***	0	***0***	0	1	10	23	***74***
Days Minimum Temp. ≤ 32°F	30	28	30	27	17	***5***	***1***	***4***	16	27	28	30	***243***
Days Minimum Temp. ≤ 0°F	11	9	4	1	0	***0***	***0***	***0***	0	0	4	11	***40***
Heating Degree Days (base 65°F)	1,499	1,283	1,170	861	583	***323***	***133***	***158***	416	790	1,156	1,502	***9,874***
Cooling Degree Days (base 65°F)	0	0	0	0	0	***2***	***22***	***14***	1	0	0	0	***39***
Mean Precipitation (in.)	3.27	2.45	2.02	1.98	2.64	***2.42***	1.55	***1.28***	1.35	1.81	2.26	3.64	***26.67***
Extreme Maximum Daily Precip. (in.)	***3.12***	na	na	***1.50***	na	na	na	na	***1.46***	na	na	na	na
Days With ≥ 0.1" Precipitation	8	6	5	5	6	***6***	4	***4***	4	4	5	8	***65***
Days With ≥ 0.5" Precipitation	1	1	1	1	2	***1***	1	***0***	1	1	1	2	***13***
Days With ≥ 1.0" Precipitation	0	0	0	0	0	***0***	0	***0***	0	0	0	0	***0***
Mean Snowfall (in.)	49.8	35.3	27.6	15.7	4.3	***0.5***	***0.0***	***0.0***	0.1	7.0	***25.7***	56.0	***222.0***
Maximum Snow Depth (in.)	70	72	89	76	***37***	***0***	***0***	***0***	0	***18***	34	58	***89***
Days With ≥ 1.0" Snow Depth	28	26	28	25	6	***0***	0	***0***	0	2	13	28	***156***

The period of record for all cooperative weather station data is 1980 – 2009. See User Guide for detailed explanation of data.

Lifton Pumping Stn *Bear Lake County* Elevation: 5,925 ft. Latitude: 42° 07' N Longitude: 111° 19' W

	JAN	FEB	MAR	APR	MAY	JUN	JUL	AUG	SEP	OCT	NOV	DEC	YEAR
Mean Maximum Temp. (°F)	30.2	32.6	41.4	52.3	62.6	72.9	82.4	81.1	70.8	57.6	42.1	31.6	54.8
Mean Temp. (°F)	18.3	19.5	29.5	40.9	50.7	59.4	66.8	64.6	55.0	43.7	31.3	20.9	41.7
Mean Minimum Temp. (°F)	6.4	6.3	17.5	29.5	38.8	45.9	51.3	48.0	39.1	29.8	20.6	10.2	28.6
Extreme Maximum Temp. (°F)	52	55	69	77	90	94	98	96	89	81	66	58	98
Extreme Minimum Temp. (°F)	-37	-41	-22	-1	20	29	29	30	19	12	-12	-29	-41
Days Maximum Temp. ≥ 90°F	0	0	0	0	0	0	4	1	0	0	0	0	5
Days Maximum Temp. ≤ 32°F	18	12	4	0	0	0	0	0	0	0	5	16	55
Days Minimum Temp. ≤ 32°F	31	28	30	20	5	0	0	0	5	21	28	31	199
Days Minimum Temp. ≤ 0°F	9	10	2	0	0	0	0	0	0	0	1	6	28
Heating Degree Days (base 65°F)	1,442	1,282	1,094	716	438	181	34	59	297	652	1,003	1,360	8,558
Cooling Degree Days (base 65°F)	0	0	0	0	1	20	98	52	3	0	0	0	174
Mean Precipitation (in.)	0.83	0.79	0.79	1.07	1.64	0.93	0.78	0.76	1.15	1.12	0.86	0.63	11.35
Extreme Maximum Daily Precip. (in.)	0.83	1.47	0.76	0.87	1.86	0.90	1.54	1.30	1.64	0.97	0.65	0.55	1.86
Days With ≥ 0.1" Precipitation	3	3	3	4	5	3	2	2	3	3	3	2	36
Days With ≥ 0.5" Precipitation	0	0	0	0	1	0	0	0	1	1	0	0	3
Days With ≥ 1.0" Precipitation	0	0	0	0	0	0	0	0	0	0	0	0	0
Mean Snowfall (in.)	9.5	7.9	4.7	2.2	0.2	trace	trace	0.0	trace	1.0	5.2	7.1	37.8
Maximum Snow Depth (in.)	35	23	23	9	1	trace	trace	0	1	7	14	16	35
Days With ≥ 1.0" Snow Depth	29	27	17	3	0	0	0	0	0	1	8	21	106

Malad City *Oneida County* Elevation: 4,470 ft. Latitude: 42° 09' N Longitude: 112° 17' W

	JAN	FEB	MAR	APR	MAY	JUN	JUL	AUG	SEP	OCT	NOV	DEC	YEAR
Mean Maximum Temp. (°F)	33.1	38.7	50.4	60.7	69.6	79.8	89.9	89.1	78.5	64.2	***46.7***	***34.1***	***61.2***
Mean Temp. (°F)	23.1	27.0	37.6	45.6	53.7	61.8	69.5	68.7	59.1	47.0	***34.5***	***23.7***	***45.9***
Mean Minimum Temp. (°F)	13.0	15.2	24.7	30.4	37.8	43.7	49.2	48.3	39.6	29.9	22.1	***13.0***	***30.6***
Extreme Maximum Temp. (°F)	59	63	78	84	97	102	105	104	96	89	73	63	105
Extreme Minimum Temp. (°F)	-33	-35	-6	9	19	27	32	26	18	8	-10	-32	-35
Days Maximum Temp. ≥ 90°F	0	0	0	0	0	4	17	16	3	0	0	0	40
Days Maximum Temp. ≤ 32°F	14	7	1	0	0	0	0	0	0	0	2	12	36
Days Minimum Temp. ≤ 32°F	30	27	26	18	6	1	0	0	5	19	26	29	187
Days Minimum Temp. ≤ 0°F	6	4	0	0	0	0	0	0	0	0	1	4	15
Heating Degree Days (base 65°F)	1,293	1,068	842	579	344	132	***18***	19	190	***557***	***908***	***1,273***	***7,223***
Cooling Degree Days (base 65°F)	0	0	0	0	4	42	***157***	142	20	***0***	***0***	***0***	***365***
Mean Precipitation (in.)	1.16	1.11	1.03	1.21	2.21	1.05	0.96	0.89	0.96	1.21	0.90	1.18	13.87
Extreme Maximum Daily Precip. (in.)	1.05	0.84	0.83	1.16	1.23	1.14	1.85	1.31	1.00	1.50	0.73	***0.83***	***1.85***
Days With ≥ 0.1" Precipitation	4	3	3	4	6	3	2	2	3	3	3	4	40
Days With ≥ 0.5" Precipitation	0	0	0	0	1	0	0	0	0	1	0	0	2
Days With ≥ 1.0" Precipitation	0	0	0	0	0	0	0	0	0	0	0	0	0
Mean Snowfall (in.)	***10.1***	5.6	3.2	0.8	0.2	0.1	trace	trace	0.0	0.5	3.7	***9.2***	***33.4***
Maximum Snow Depth (in.)	***21***	22	22	5	2	trace	trace	trace	0	6	10	21	***22***
Days With ≥ 1.0" Snow Depth	***19***	15	5	0	0	0	0	0	0	0	4	***12***	***55***

Middle Fork Lodge *Custer County* Elevation: 4,479 ft. Latitude: 44° 43' N Longitude: 115° 01' W

	JAN	FEB	MAR	APR	MAY	JUN	JUL	AUG	SEP	OCT	NOV	DEC	YEAR
Mean Maximum Temp. (°F)	35.0	41.0	51.1	59.4	67.9	76.4	86.7	85.5	76.1	61.8	43.6	33.0	59.8
Mean Temp. (°F)	24.4	28.4	37.5	44.3	52.1	59.1	66.6	65.0	56.6	45.2	32.6	23.0	44.6
Mean Minimum Temp. (°F)	13.8	15.8	23.9	29.1	36.1	41.8	46.4	44.5	37.0	28.6	21.5	13.0	29.3
Extreme Maximum Temp. (°F)	53	62	74	87	95	100	103	104	98	92	68	56	104
Extreme Minimum Temp. (°F)	-19	-20	-1	10	18	26	28	28	18	4	-10	-28	-28
Days Maximum Temp. ≥ 90°F	0	0	0	0	0	2	13	10	2	0	0	0	27
Days Maximum Temp. ≤ 32°F	10	4	0	0	0	0	0	0	0	0	3	14	31
Days Minimum Temp. ≤ 32°F	31	28	29	22	8	1	0	0	7	23	28	31	208
Days Minimum Temp. ≤ 0°F	4	2	0	0	0	0	0	0	0	0	1	4	11
Heating Degree Days (base 65°F)	1,251	1,027	845	615	397	191	48	61	255	606	965	1,295	7,556
Cooling Degree Days (base 65°F)	0	0	0	0	2	21	103	69	8	0	0	0	203
Mean Precipitation (in.)	1.54	1.25	1.19	1.50	1.82	1.58	0.89	0.85	1.05	1.17	1.76	1.62	16.22
Extreme Maximum Daily Precip. (in.)	1.17	1.06	0.83	0.94	1.40	1.44	1.00	1.10	0.93	0.98	2.02	0.84	2.02
Days With ≥ 0.1" Precipitation	5	4	4	5	6	5	2	2	3	4	5	5	50
Days With ≥ 0.5" Precipitation	1	0	0	1	1	0	0	0	1	0	1	0	5
Days With ≥ 1.0" Precipitation	0	0	0	0	0	0	0	0	0	0	0	0	0
Mean Snowfall (in.)	12.5	6.9	3.2	1.5	0.1	0.0	trace	0.0	0.0	0.8	5.8	11.0	41.8
Maximum Snow Depth (in.)	26	21	13	8	1	0	trace	0	0	4	11	20	26
Days With ≥ 1.0" Snow Depth	28	25	13	1	0	0	0	0	0	1	7	23	98

Moscow U of Idaho *Latah County* Elevation: 2,660 ft. Latitude: 46° 44' N Longitude: 116° 58' W

	JAN	FEB	MAR	APR	MAY	JUN	JUL	AUG	SEP	OCT	NOV	DEC	YEAR
Mean Maximum Temp. (°F)	36.7	41.6	49.7	58.1	66.7	73.1	83.4	84.7	75.3	60.4	44.0	35.4	59.1
Mean Temp. (°F)	30.7	34.2	40.5	46.9	53.9	59.2	66.0	66.6	59.1	48.2	37.3	29.6	47.7
Mean Minimum Temp. (°F)	24.7	26.7	31.4	35.6	41.0	45.3	48.6	48.4	42.8	35.9	30.6	23.7	36.2
Extreme Maximum Temp. (°F)	57	66	73	88	92	97	103	103	99	88	73	59	103
Extreme Minimum Temp. (°F)	-20	-26	1	21	23	29	31	30	21	8	-11	-29	-29
Days Maximum Temp. ≥ 90°F	0	0	0	0	0	1	8	9	2	0	0	0	20
Days Maximum Temp. ≤ 32°F	8	3	0	0	0	0	0	0	0	0	2	10	23
Days Minimum Temp. ≤ 32°F	25	21	19	10	4	0	0	0	2	10	18	26	135
Days Minimum Temp. ≤ 0°F	1	1	0	0	0	0	0	0	0	0	0	1	3
Heating Degree Days (base 65°F)	1,057	864	751	537	348	188	58	55	200	515	825	1,092	6,490
Cooling Degree Days (base 65°F)	0	0	0	0	9	22	98	112	29	2	0	0	272
Mean Precipitation (in.)	3.16	2.34	2.71	2.45	2.59	1.84	0.99	1.03	1.18	2.14	3.65	2.99	27.07
Extreme Maximum Daily Precip. (in.)	1.94	1.08	1.28	1.19	1.43	1.12	1.22	2.21	1.35	2.19	1.87	2.51	2.51
Days With ≥ 0.1" Precipitation	9	7	8	7	6	5	3	2	3	5	10	8	73
Days With ≥ 0.5" Precipitation	2	1	1	1	2	1	1	1	1	1	2	1	15
Days With ≥ 1.0" Precipitation	0	0	0	0	0	0	0	0	0	0	0	0	0
Mean Snowfall (in.)	15.6	6.7	4.5	1.0	0.2	trace	trace	0.0	trace	0.1	5.6	14.7	48.4
Maximum Snow Depth (in.)	26	26	15	2	trace	0	0	0	trace	trace	9	24	26
Days With ≥ 1.0" Snow Depth	18	9	2	0	0	0	0	0	0	0	4	14	47

The period of record for all cooperative weather station data is 1980 – 2009. See User Guide for detailed explanation of data.

Mountain Home *Elmore County* Elevation: 3,140 ft. Latitude: 43° 08' N Longitude: 115° 43' W

	JAN	FEB	MAR	APR	MAY	JUN	JUL	AUG	SEP	OCT	NOV	DEC	YEAR
Mean Maximum Temp. (°F)	38.7	45.1	55.0	63.3	72.7	83.0	93.1	92.4	80.4	66.8	48.7	38.2	64.8
Mean Temp. (°F)	30.4	34.9	42.9	49.7	58.4	67.2	75.6	74.5	63.6	51.7	38.2	29.8	51.4
Mean Minimum Temp. (°F)	22.1	24.6	30.7	36.0	44.0	51.3	58.1	56.5	46.7	36.4	27.6	21.3	38.0
Extreme Maximum Temp. (°F)	60	70	82	92	101	105	115	109	104	94	80	60	115
Extreme Minimum Temp. (°F)	-10	-13	12	16	20	30	36	35	22	9	-3	-25	-25
Days Maximum Temp. ≥ 90°F	0	0	0	0	3	9	22	21	7	0	0	0	62
Days Maximum Temp. ≤ 32°F	7	3	0	0	0	0	0	0	0	0	2	7	19
Days Minimum Temp. ≤ 32°F	28	23	19	10	2	0	0	0	1	10	21	26	140
Days Minimum Temp. ≤ 0°F	1	1	0	0	0	0	0	0	0	0	0	1	3
Heating Degree Days (base 65°F)	1,065	844	679	456	242	73	10	9	122	413	798	1,087	5,798
Cooling Degree Days (base 65°F)	0	0	0	3	43	146	345	310	87	5	0	0	939
Mean Precipitation (in.)	1.14	0.89	1.19	0.93	1.11	0.55	0.21	0.13	0.61	0.69	1.29	1.41	10.15
Extreme Maximum Daily Precip. (in.)	0.98	***0.68***	1.04	0.98	1.33	0.81	1.13	0.37	1.68	0.73	***0.82***	1.06	***1.68***
Days With ≥ 0.1" Precipitation	4	3	4	3	3	2	1	1	2	2	4	4	33
Days With ≥ 0.5" Precipitation	0	0	0	0	1	0	0	0	0	0	0	1	2
Days With ≥ 1.0" Precipitation	0	0	0	0	0	0	0	0	0	0	0	0	0
Mean Snowfall (in.)	***2.4***	1.6	***0.3***	0.0	0.0	0.0	0.0	0.0	0.0	trace	***1.3***	***3.0***	***8.6***
Maximum Snow Depth (in.)	***12***	***6***	***1***	***0***	***0***	***0***	***0***	***0***	***0***	***1***	***10***	***11***	***12***
Days With ≥ 1.0" Snow Depth	***8***	4	***0***	0	0	0	0	0	0	0	***1***	***5***	***18***

Oakley *Cassia County* Elevation: 4,560 ft. Latitude: 42° 14' N Longitude: 113° 54' W

	JAN	FEB	MAR	APR	MAY	JUN	JUL	AUG	SEP	OCT	NOV	DEC	YEAR
Mean Maximum Temp. (°F)	38.7	43.4	52.2	60.0	68.0	76.6	84.7	84.7	75.4	63.5	48.1	38.2	61.1
Mean Temp. (°F)	29.6	33.5	40.7	47.0	54.6	62.3	70.1	69.7	60.6	50.1	38.0	29.2	48.8
Mean Minimum Temp. (°F)	20.5	23.4	29.3	34.0	41.1	48.1	55.4	54.6	45.7	36.7	27.8	20.1	36.4
Extreme Maximum Temp. (°F)	61	68	77	86	96	96	101	100	93	90	74	65	101
Extreme Minimum Temp. (°F)	-13	-18	4	14	18	28	33	34	20	9	-8	-24	-24
Days Maximum Temp. ≥ 90°F	0	0	0	0	0	2	8	7	1	0	0	0	18
Days Maximum Temp. ≤ 32°F	7	3	0	0	0	0	0	0	0	0	2	8	20
Days Minimum Temp. ≤ 32°F	28	23	21	12	4	0	0	0	2	9	20	28	147
Days Minimum Temp. ≤ 0°F	1	1	0	0	0	0	0	0	0	0	0	1	3
Heating Degree Days (base 65°F)	1,091	885	745	534	324	127	21	21	166	457	805	1,104	6,280
Cooling Degree Days (base 65°F)	0	0	0	0	9	54	186	173	39	1	0	0	462
Mean Precipitation (in.)	0.76	0.65	1.04	1.31	1.77	1.21	0.79	0.73	0.88	0.78	0.74	0.77	11.43
Extreme Maximum Daily Precip. (in.)	0.73	0.80	1.28	1.03	1.10	1.03	0.94	1.08	1.13	0.85	0.62	0.85	1.28
Days With ≥ 0.1" Precipitation	3	2	3	5	5	4	3	2	2	3	3	3	38
Days With ≥ 0.5" Precipitation	0	0	0	1	1	0	0	0	0	0	0	0	2
Days With ≥ 1.0" Precipitation	0	0	0	0	0	0	0	0	0	0	0	0	0
Mean Snowfall (in.)	7.1	4.5	3.2	1.4	0.1	0.0	0.0	0.0	0.1	0.6	2.7	6.2	25.9
Maximum Snow Depth (in.)	15	5	7	4	trace	0	0	0	trace	6	10	12	15
Days With ≥ 1.0" Snow Depth	4	2	0	0	0	0	0	0	0	0	2	4	12

Parma Experiment Stn *Canyon County* Elevation: 2,290 ft. Latitude: 43° 48' N Longitude: 116° 57' W

	JAN	FEB	MAR	APR	MAY	JUN	JUL	AUG	SEP	OCT	NOV	DEC	YEAR
Mean Maximum Temp. (°F)	36.2	44.5	56.5	64.9	73.3	81.6	91.4	90.8	80.4	66.3	48.6	37.3	64.3
Mean Temp. (°F)	28.3	34.5	43.6	50.5	59.0	66.2	73.5	71.9	62.3	50.3	37.9	29.1	50.6
Mean Minimum Temp. (°F)	20.3	24.5	30.8	36.1	44.6	50.7	55.5	52.9	44.2	34.2	27.1	20.8	36.8
Extreme Maximum Temp. (°F)	59	67	81	92	100	102	110	105	102	95	76	64	110
Extreme Minimum Temp. (°F)	-18	-25	2	19	26	32	37	34	24	12	-2	-21	-25
Days Maximum Temp. ≥ 90°F	0	0	0	0	2	7	21	20	6	0	0	0	56
Days Maximum Temp. ≤ 32°F	10	2	0	0	0	0	0	0	0	0	1	8	21
Days Minimum Temp. ≤ 32°F	29	24	19	9	1	0	0	0	1	13	23	28	147
Days Minimum Temp. ≤ 0°F	2	1	0	0	0	0	0	0	0	0	0	2	5
Heating Degree Days (base 65°F)	1,132	853	655	429	219	71	12	13	131	450	807	1,107	5,879
Cooling Degree Days (base 65°F)	0	0	0	2	38	113	282	234	58	2	0	0	729
Mean Precipitation (in.)	1.17	0.86	1.10	0.93	1.27	0.78	0.31	0.28	0.58	0.66	1.11	1.23	10.28
Extreme Maximum Daily Precip. (in.)	1.70	0.71	0.92	0.77	1.25	0.97	0.59	0.43	0.77	0.82	0.83	0.89	1.70
Days With ≥ 0.1" Precipitation	4	3	4	4	4	3	1	1	2	2	4	4	36
Days With ≥ 0.5" Precipitation	0	0	0	0	0	0	0	0	0	0	0	0	0
Days With ≥ 1.0" Precipitation	0	0	0	0	0	0	0	0	0	0	0	0	0
Mean Snowfall (in.)	5.0	1.9	0.3	trace	0.0	0.0	0.0	0.0	0.0	0.0	1.6	4.0	12.8
Maximum Snow Depth (in.)	19	13	5	trace	0	0	0	0	0	1	11	21	21
Days With ≥ 1.0" Snow Depth	12	4	1	0	0	0	0	0	0	0	2	7	26

Payette *Payette County* Elevation: 2,149 ft. Latitude: 44° 05' N Longitude: 116° 56' W

	JAN	FEB	MAR	APR	MAY	JUN	JUL	AUG	SEP	OCT	NOV	DEC	YEAR
Mean Maximum Temp. (°F)	37.7	46.6	58.6	66.7	75.0	82.7	92.3	90.6	81.1	68.2	51.6	39.5	65.9
Mean Temp. (°F)	29.3	35.6	45.3	51.8	60.2	67.4	75.1	73.4	64.1	52.3	40.2	30.8	52.1
Mean Minimum Temp. (°F)	20.9	24.6	31.9	37.0	45.3	52.0	58.0	56.1	47.2	36.4	28.7	21.9	38.3
Extreme Maximum Temp. (°F)	59	70	81	92	98	103	109	109	100	96	73	63	109
Extreme Minimum Temp. (°F)	-17	-23	8	19	24	33	38	37	25	13	-2	-21	-23
Days Maximum Temp. ≥ 90°F	0	0	0	0	2	8	21	19	5	0	0	0	55
Days Maximum Temp. ≤ 32°F	8	2	0	0	0	0	0	0	0	0	0	6	16
Days Minimum Temp. ≤ 32°F	27	24	17	8	2	0	0	0	1	9	20	27	135
Days Minimum Temp. ≤ 0°F	2	1	0	0	0	0	0	0	0	0	0	1	4
Heating Degree Days (base 65°F)	1,099	825	605	391	185	56	4	8	98	389	738	1,055	5,453
Cooling Degree Days (base 65°F)	0	0	0	2	42	134	325	275	78	3	0	0	859
Mean Precipitation (in.)	1.32	1.03	1.16	0.78	1.14	0.74	0.29	0.21	0.45	0.65	1.30	1.73	10.80
Extreme Maximum Daily Precip. (in.)	0.80	0.74	1.13	0.58	1.55	1.01	0.71	0.50	0.56	1.14	***0.83***	1.14	***1.55***
Days With ≥ 0.1" Precipitation	5	4	4	3	3	2	1	1	1	2	4	5	35
Days With ≥ 0.5" Precipitation	0	0	0	0	0	0	0	0	0	0	0	1	1
Days With ≥ 1.0" Precipitation	0	0	0	0	0	0	0	0	0	0	0	0	0
Mean Snowfall (in.)	na	***2.1***	0.2	trace	0.0	0.0	0.0	0.0	0.0	0.0	0.6	***5.4***	na
Maximum Snow Depth (in.)	na	7	***2***	***trace***	***0***	***0***	***0***	***0***	***0***	***0***	2	na	na
Days With ≥ 1.0" Snow Depth	na	1	***0***	0	0	0	0	0	0	0	0	***3***	na

The period of record for all cooperative weather station data is 1980 – 2009. See User Guide for detailed explanation of data.

Porthill *Boundary County* Elevation: 1,774 ft. Latitude: 49° 00' N Longitude: 116° 30' W

	JAN	FEB	MAR	APR	MAY	JUN	JUL	AUG	SEP	OCT	NOV	DEC	YEAR
Mean Maximum Temp. (°F)	33.8	38.3	48.5	59.4	68.0	73.9	82.5	82.4	71.5	56.7	42.1	33.0	57.5
Mean Temp. (°F)	26.7	29.9	38.0	46.7	54.8	60.9	67.2	65.7	56.2	44.7	34.5	26.2	46.0
Mean Minimum Temp. (°F)	19.6	21.5	27.5	34.0	41.5	47.9	51.7	49.0	40.8	32.5	26.9	19.3	34.4
Extreme Maximum Temp. (°F)	54	57	77	82	95	98	103	102	97	87	62	59	103
Extreme Minimum Temp. (°F)	-24	-15	-7	19	23	24	36	33	24	11	-11	-20	-24
Days Maximum Temp. ≥ 90°F	0	0	0	0	0	1	7	6	1	0	0	0	15
Days Maximum Temp. ≤ 32°F	12	5	1	0	0	0	0	0	0	0	3	14	35
Days Minimum Temp. ≤ 32°F	29	26	24	13	2	0	0	0	2	15	22	29	162
Days Minimum Temp. ≤ 0°F	2	1	0	0	0	0	0	0	0	0	0	2	5
Heating Degree Days (base 65°F)	1,180	986	829	542	317	151	49	61	266	625	908	1,197	7,111
Cooling Degree Days (base 65°F)	0	0	0	0	8	35	123	92	6	0	0	0	264
Mean Precipitation (in.)	2.06	1.44	1.60	1.42	2.05	2.04	1.24	0.95	1.20	1.52	2.78	2.47	20.77
Extreme Maximum Daily Precip. (in.)	1.12	1.18	1.18	0.95	1.97	1.10	0.90	1.10	0.88	0.78	1.23	1.05	1.97
Days With ≥ 0.1" Precipitation	7	5	5	5	6	6	4	3	4	5	9	7	66
Days With ≥ 0.5" Precipitation	1	1	1	0	1	1	1	0	0	1	1	1	9
Days With ≥ 1.0" Precipitation	0	0	0	0	0	0	0	0	0	0	0	0	0
Mean Snowfall (in.)	***10.6***	5.0	2.5	0.4	trace	0.0	0.0	0.0	0.0	0.3	***6.3***	***12.4***	***37.5***
Maximum Snow Depth (in.)	28	28	7	5	trace	0	0	0	0	2	22	35	35
Days With ≥ 1.0" Snow Depth	19	11	3	0	0	0	0	0	0	0	4	17	54

Potlatch 3 NNE *Latah County* Elevation: 2,600 ft. Latitude: 46° 58' N Longitude: 116° 53' W

	JAN	FEB	MAR	APR	MAY	JUN	JUL	AUG	SEP	OCT	NOV	DEC	YEAR
Mean Maximum Temp. (°F)	36.5	41.1	48.3	56.5	65.0	70.9	80.7	82.2	73.1	59.2	43.6	35.0	57.7
Mean Temp. (°F)	30.0	33.1	38.7	44.9	51.8	57.2	63.4	63.5	55.7	45.7	36.3	28.3	45.7
Mean Minimum Temp. (°F)	23.4	25.0	29.2	33.2	38.4	43.4	46.1	44.7	38.2	32.2	29.0	21.5	33.7
Extreme Maximum Temp. (°F)	58	65	73	89	95	93	102	102	101	90	70	57	102
Extreme Minimum Temp. (°F)	-30	-32	-5	18	21	26	31	25	16	13	-20	-29	-32
Days Maximum Temp. ≥ 90°F	0	0	0	0	0	0	5	7	1	0	0	0	13
Days Maximum Temp. ≤ 32°F	9	4	1	0	0	0	0	0	0	0	3	10	27
Days Minimum Temp. ≤ 32°F	26	23	23	15	6	1	0	1	5	15	20	27	162
Days Minimum Temp. ≤ 0°F	1	1	0	0	0	0	0	0	0	0	0	1	3
Heating Degree Days (base 65°F)	1,079	895	807	597	407	238	98	100	281	594	853	1,132	7,081
Cooling Degree Days (base 65°F)	0	0	0	0	4	9	55	60	9	1	0	0	138
Mean Precipitation (in.)	2.61	2.38	2.51	2.08	2.59	1.87	1.10	0.93	1.24	1.93	3.17	***2.97***	***25.38***
Extreme Maximum Daily Precip. (in.)	1.12	***1.65***	1.10	1.26	1.60	***0.94***	2.10	2.27	1.22	1.94	1.50	***1.92***	***2.27***
Days With ≥ 0.1" Precipitation	7	6	7	6	7	5	3	2	3	5	9	7	67
Days With ≥ 0.5" Precipitation	1	1	1	1	2	1	0	0	1	1	2	2	13
Days With ≥ 1.0" Precipitation	0	0	0	0	0	0	0	0	0	0	0	0	0
Mean Snowfall (in.)	***15.0***	6.2	***3.1***	0.9	0.2	trace	0.0	0.0	0.0	0.1	4.3	na	na
Maximum Snow Depth (in.)	na	na	na	***3***	***trace***	***trace***	***0***	***0***	***0***	na	na	na	na
Days With ≥ 1.0" Snow Depth	na	***4***	***1***	0	0	0	0	0	0	0	***1***	na	na

Powell *Idaho County* Elevation: 3,529 ft. Latitude: 46° 31' N Longitude: 114° 43' W

	JAN	FEB	MAR	APR	MAY	JUN	JUL	AUG	SEP	OCT	NOV	DEC	YEAR
Mean Maximum Temp. (°F)	33.3	38.9	46.9	55.4	64.9	72.6	82.9	82.8	72.0	56.6	39.4	31.1	56.4
Mean Temp. (°F)	24.8	28.1	35.4	42.1	49.8	57.0	63.9	62.8	53.8	42.8	31.6	23.5	43.0
Mean Minimum Temp. (°F)	16.3	17.2	23.8	28.7	34.7	41.3	44.9	42.8	35.7	29.0	23.8	15.8	29.5
Extreme Maximum Temp. (°F)	50	64	74	87	96	98	101	101	102	88	67	49	102
Extreme Minimum Temp. (°F)	-20	-25	-8	8	20	24	33	21	18	2	-12	-31	-31
Days Maximum Temp. ≥ 90°F	0	0	0	0	1	2	8	8	1	0	0	0	20
Days Maximum Temp. ≤ 32°F	11	4	1	0	0	0	0	0	0	0	4	15	35
Days Minimum Temp. ≤ 32°F	30	27	30	24	11	2	0	1	10	22	27	30	214
Days Minimum Temp. ≤ 0°F	3	2	0	0	0	0	0	0	0	0	0	3	8
Heating Degree Days (base 65°F)	1,240	1,037	911	680	465	250	90	107	333	680	995	1,280	8,068
Cooling Degree Days (base 65°F)	0	0	0	0	2	15	65	46	4	0	0	0	132
Mean Precipitation (in.)	4.80	3.54	3.22	2.70	3.15	2.99	1.43	1.33	2.11	2.85	5.05	4.45	37.62
Extreme Maximum Daily Precip. (in.)	***1.80***	2.63	1.58	1.96	1.73	2.00	1.25	1.30	1.62	1.75	***2.30***	***1.82***	***2.63***
Days With ≥ 0.1" Precipitation	11	8	9	8	8	8	5	4	5	6	11	10	93
Days With ≥ 0.5" Precipitation	3	2	1	1	2	2	1	1	1	2	3	3	22
Days With ≥ 1.0" Precipitation	1	0	0	0	0	0	0	0	0	0	1	0	2
Mean Snowfall (in.)	***36.5***	***20.0***	***13.6***	4.9	0.6	0.1	0.0	0.0	trace	1.1	***15.5***	***33.8***	***126.1***
Maximum Snow Depth (in.)	***54***	***62***	***64***	***37***	***5***	***3***	***0***	***0***	***1***	***7***	***22***	***64***	***64***
Days With ≥ 1.0" Snow Depth	***28***	***25***	23	9	0	0	0	0	0	1	***12***	***26***	***124***

Preston *Franklin County* Elevation: 4,799 ft. Latitude: 42° 05' N Longitude: 111° 52' W

	JAN	FEB	MAR	APR	MAY	JUN	JUL	AUG	SEP	OCT	NOV	DEC	YEAR
Mean Maximum Temp. (°F)	31.1	36.4	48.9	59.0	68.9	78.6	***88.3***	86.6	76.4	61.7	45.2	32.6	***59.5***
Mean Temp. (°F)	22.1	26.3	37.3	45.7	54.4	62.4	***70.5***	68.8	59.3	47.0	34.3	23.6	***46.0***
Mean Minimum Temp. (°F)	13.0	16.1	25.7	32.3	39.9	46.0	***52.5***	50.9	42.1	32.3	23.4	14.5	***32.4***
Extreme Maximum Temp. (°F)	58	62	76	83	93	96	***101***	100	94	84	70	65	***101***
Extreme Minimum Temp. (°F)	-25	-31	-3	13	23	30	***33***	30	20	12	-8	-31	***-31***
Days Maximum Temp. ≥ 90°F	0	0	0	0	0	3	***13***	11	1	0	0	0	***28***
Days Maximum Temp. ≤ 32°F	16	9	1	0	0	0	***0***	0	0	0	3	15	***44***
Days Minimum Temp. ≤ 32°F	30	27	26	15	4	0	***0***	0	3	15	26	30	***176***
Days Minimum Temp. ≤ 0°F	5	3	0	0	0	0	***0***	0	0	0	1	4	***13***
Heating Degree Days (base 65°F)	1,324	1,088	850	572	328	121	***14***	19	185	551	914	1,275	***7,241***
Cooling Degree Days (base 65°F)	0	0	0	0	6	50	***191***	144	20	0	0	0	***411***
Mean Precipitation (in.)	1.47	1.37	1.53	1.74	2.12	1.24	***0.95***	0.94	1.49	1.82	1.16	1.60	***17.43***
Extreme Maximum Daily Precip. (in.)	1.05	1.58	1.39	1.55	1.46	2.04	***1.09***	1.35	2.20	2.04	0.69	1.08	***2.20***
Days With ≥ 0.1" Precipitation	5	4	5	5	6	3	***2***	3	4	5	4	5	***51***
Days With ≥ 0.5" Precipitation	0	0	0	1	1	1	***0***	1	1	1	0	1	***7***
Days With ≥ 1.0" Precipitation	0	0	0	0	0	0	***0***	0	0	0	0	0	***0***
Mean Snowfall (in.)	***13.9***	na	***5.1***	***2.1***	0.1	0.1	***0.0***	0.0	trace	0.8	***2.8***	***13.9***	na
Maximum Snow Depth (in.)	na	na	na	na	na	na	na	na	na	na	na	na	na
Days With ≥ 1.0" Snow Depth	na	na	na	***0***	0	0	***0***	***0***	0	0	***0***	na	na

The period of record for all cooperative weather station data is 1980 – 2009. See User Guide for detailed explanation of data.

Priest River Exp Stn *Bonner County* Elevation: 2,379 ft. Latitude: 48° 21' N Longitude: 116° 50' W

	JAN	FEB	MAR	APR	MAY	JUN	JUL	AUG	SEP	OCT	NOV	DEC	YEAR
Mean Maximum Temp. (°F)	31.2	36.7	46.1	57.3	67.1	73.7	82.3	82.0	71.3	54.4	38.0	30.0	55.8
Mean Temp. (°F)	26.1	29.3	36.3	44.3	52.8	58.8	64.7	63.8	54.8	43.0	32.5	25.4	44.3
Mean Minimum Temp. (°F)	21.0	21.8	26.4	31.2	38.5	44.0	47.2	45.6	38.3	31.5	27.1	20.8	32.8
Extreme Maximum Temp. (°F)	50	56	71	85	92	96	100	100	97	81	59	54	100
Extreme Minimum Temp. (°F)	-22	-17	-10	15	20	30	31	30	18	3	-12	-25	-25
Days Maximum Temp. ≥ 90°F	0	0	0	0	0	1	6	6	1	0	0	0	14
Days Maximum Temp. ≤ 32°F	15	6	1	0	0	0	0	0	0	0	6	18	46
Days Minimum Temp. ≤ 32°F	30	27	27	19	7	0	0	0	6	17	23	30	186
Days Minimum Temp. ≤ 0°F	2	1	0	0	0	0	0	0	0	0	0	1	4
Heating Degree Days (base 65°F)	1,200	1,003	883	615	374	194	70	86	302	676	968	1,221	7,592
Cooling Degree Days (base 65°F)	0	0	0	0	3	16	69	56	4	0	0	0	148
Mean Precipitation (in.)	3.80	2.66	3.00	2.31	2.59	2.41	1.21	1.11	1.32	2.24	4.28	4.32	31.25
Extreme Maximum Daily Precip. (in.)	1.60	1.71	1.82	1.50	3.34	2.91	1.15	1.45	1.45	1.73	1.75	1.97	3.34
Days With ≥ 0.1" Precipitation	11	7	8	7	7	6	3	3	4	6	10	10	82
Days With ≥ 0.5" Precipitation	2	1	1	1	1	1	1	1	1	1	3	3	17
Days With ≥ 1.0" Precipitation	0	0	0	0	0	0	0	0	0	0	1	0	1
Mean Snowfall (in.)	20.5	11.1	5.1	0.3	trace	0.0	0.0	0.0	0.0	0.2	9.7	24.1	71.0
Maximum Snow Depth (in.)	48	48	50	24	trace	0	0	0	0	4	32	51	51
Days With ≥ 1.0" Snow Depth	29	27	20	2	0	0	0	0	0	0	8	26	112

Rexburg Ricks College *Madison County* Elevation: 4,924 ft. Latitude: 43° 49' N Longitude: 111° 47' W

	JAN	FEB	MAR	APR	MAY	JUN	JUL	AUG	SEP	OCT	NOV	DEC	YEAR
Mean Maximum Temp. (°F)	29.4	33.4	45.9	57.0	66.1	74.6	84.0	84.4	73.7	59.2	***41.9***	29.9	***56.6***
Mean Temp. (°F)	20.0	23.6	34.8	43.8	52.4	59.9	66.8	65.9	56.4	44.6	***31.5***	20.7	***43.4***
Mean Minimum Temp. (°F)	10.6	13.8	23.6	30.5	38.7	45.2	49.6	47.4	39.1	30.0	***21.0***	11.5	***30.1***
Extreme Maximum Temp. (°F)	52	60	72	84	91	102	102	99	94	87	***70***	61	***102***
Extreme Minimum Temp. (°F)	-32	-36	-12	12	16	29	32	27	14	6	***-13***	-31	***-36***
Days Maximum Temp. ≥ 90°F	0	0	0	0	0	1	7	8	1	0	***0***	0	***17***
Days Maximum Temp. ≤ 32°F	20	11	2	0	0	0	0	0	0	0	***6***	18	***57***
Days Minimum Temp. ≤ 32°F	31	27	28	18	6	1	0	0	5	20	***27***	30	***193***
Days Minimum Temp. ≤ 0°F	7	5	0	0	0	0	0	0	0	0	***1***	6	***19***
Heating Degree Days (base 65°F)	1,388	1,164	931	630	386	174	40	51	261	624	***999***	1,367	***8,015***
Cooling Degree Days (base 65°F)	0	0	0	0	3	28	103	86	11	0	***0***	0	***231***
Mean Precipitation (in.)	1.16	0.93	1.04	1.12	1.82	1.59	0.79	0.67	0.89	1.24	***1.08***	***1.08***	***13.41***
Extreme Maximum Daily Precip. (in.)	0.90	***0.67***	1.41	0.90	1.10	1.43	1.32	0.85	1.08	0.98	***1.40***	0.90	***1.43***
Days With ≥ 0.1" Precipitation	4	3	4	3	6	4	2	2	3	4	***4***	4	***43***
Days With ≥ 0.5" Precipitation	0	0	0	0	1	1	0	0	0	1	***0***	0	***3***
Days With ≥ 1.0" Precipitation	0	0	0	0	0	0	0	0	0	0	***0***	0	***0***
Mean Snowfall (in.)	12.6	10.4	3.5	2.1	0.3	trace	0.0	0.0	0.1	1.1	***6.6***	***14.4***	***51.1***
Maximum Snow Depth (in.)	***32***	***38***	***38***	21	***2***	***1***	***0***	***0***	***0***	***5***	na	***26***	na
Days With ≥ 1.0" Snow Depth	***27***	***21***	7	1	0	0	0	0	0	***0***	***6***	***18***	***80***

Reynolds *Owyhee County* Elevation: 3,930 ft. Latitude: 43° 12' N Longitude: 116° 45' W

	JAN	FEB	MAR	APR	MAY	JUN	JUL	AUG	SEP	OCT	NOV	DEC	YEAR
Mean Maximum Temp. (°F)	39.4	43.6	51.8	59.5	68.2	77.2	87.0	86.3	75.9	63.2	48.3	38.9	61.6
Mean Temp. (°F)	30.2	33.4	40.4	46.5	54.4	61.8	70.2	69.2	59.6	48.4	37.1	29.3	48.4
Mean Minimum Temp. (°F)	21.0	23.1	28.9	33.5	40.6	46.4	53.4	52.1	43.2	33.6	25.8	19.6	35.1
Extreme Maximum Temp. (°F)	62	66	78	87	97	102	107	105	98	93	77	61	107
Extreme Minimum Temp. (°F)	-16	-13	9	15	22	27	32	33	19	11	-7	-21	-21
Days Maximum Temp. ≥ 90°F	0	0	0	0	0	4	13	12	2	0	0	0	31
Days Maximum Temp. ≤ 32°F	7	3	0	0	0	0	0	0	0	0	1	7	18
Days Minimum Temp. ≤ 32°F	28	25	22	13	4	1	0	0	3	14	24	27	161
Days Minimum Temp. ≤ 0°F	1	1	0	0	0	0	0	0	0	0	0	2	4
Heating Degree Days (base 65°F)	1,070	887	757	547	334	147	29	31	192	507	830	1,100	6,431
Cooling Degree Days (base 65°F)	0	0	0	0	13	58	198	169	36	1	0	0	475
Mean Precipitation (in.)	1.07	0.79	1.00	0.92	1.53	0.88	0.36	0.28	0.49	0.62	1.08	1.21	10.23
Extreme Maximum Daily Precip. (in.)	1.25	0.77	0.66	1.23	1.59	1.00	0.74	0.71	1.36	0.57	0.74	1.25	1.59
Days With ≥ 0.1" Precipitation	3	3	3	3	4	3	1	1	2	2	4	4	33
Days With ≥ 0.5" Precipitation	0	0	0	0	1	0	0	0	0	0	0	0	1
Days With ≥ 1.0" Precipitation	0	0	0	0	0	0	0	0	0	0	0	0	0
Mean Snowfall (in.)	na	***2.0***	0.2	0.1	0.0	0.0	0.0	0.0	0.0	0.1	0.4	***1.0***	na
Maximum Snow Depth (in.)	na	na	***4***	***1***	***0***	***0***	***0***	***0***	***0***	***0***	***2***	na	na
Days With ≥ 1.0" Snow Depth	na	na	0	0	0	0	0	0	0	0	0	***3***	na

Saint Maries 1 W *Benewah County* Elevation: 2,319 ft. Latitude: 47° 19' N Longitude: 116° 35' W

	JAN	FEB	MAR	APR	MAY	JUN	JUL	AUG	SEP	OCT	NOV	DEC	YEAR
Mean Maximum Temp. (°F)	35.5	41.1	49.7	58.6	66.9	73.7	83.2	83.6	73.3	57.1	41.7	33.6	58.2
Mean Temp. (°F)	30.2	33.6	40.2	47.0	54.2	60.5	67.3	66.9	58.0	46.0	36.0	28.6	47.4
Mean Minimum Temp. (°F)	24.8	26.0	30.6	35.4	41.5	47.3	51.2	50.2	42.9	34.9	30.2	23.6	36.5
Extreme Maximum Temp. (°F)	59	66	79	95	95	100	105	106	104	87	68	55	106
Extreme Minimum Temp. (°F)	-15	-14	-4	21	25	30	36	30	21	9	-5	-20	-20
Days Maximum Temp. ≥ 90°F	0	0	0	0	1	2	8	9	2	0	0	0	22
Days Maximum Temp. ≤ 32°F	9	3	1	0	0	0	0	0	0	0	3	11	27
Days Minimum Temp. ≤ 32°F	25	22	19	11	3	0	0	0	2	11	18	27	138
Days Minimum Temp. ≤ 0°F	1	1	0	0	0	0	0	0	0	0	0	1	3
Heating Degree Days (base 65°F)	1,073	882	763	535	337	164	49	51	221	581	864	1,121	6,641
Cooling Degree Days (base 65°F)	0	0	0	1	9	35	125	117	19	0	0	0	306
Mean Precipitation (in.)	4.12	2.85	2.76	2.17	2.46	2.05	1.11	1.01	1.35	2.19	4.19	4.07	30.33
Extreme Maximum Daily Precip. (in.)	***1.83***	***1.53***	***1.65***	***1.47***	***1.89***	***1.67***	***1.38***	***1.72***	na	***2.33***	***1.61***	***2.26***	na
Days With ≥ 0.1" Precipitation	9	6	8	6	6	5	2	2	3	5	9	9	70
Days With ≥ 0.5" Precipitation	2	1	1	1	1	1	0	0	0	1	2	2	12
Days With ≥ 1.0" Precipitation	0	0	0	0	0	0	0	0	0	0	1	0	1
Mean Snowfall (in.)	***16.1***	7.3	3.9	0.6	0.1	trace	0.0	0.0	0.0	0.1	5.9	16.9	***50.9***
Maximum Snow Depth (in.)	59	31	26	4	trace	trace	0	0	0	1	13	33	59
Days With ≥ 1.0" Snow Depth	18	12	6	0	0	0	0	0	0	0	5	13	54

Salmon *Lemhi County* Elevation: 3,931 ft. Latitude: 45° 11' N Longitude: 113° 54' W

	JAN	FEB	MAR	APR	MAY	JUN	JUL	AUG	SEP	OCT	NOV	DEC	YEAR
Mean Maximum Temp. (°F)	30.1	37.5	51.4	61.3	70.1	77.7	87.6	86.2	75.5	60.1	42.2	29.6	59.1
Mean Temp. (°F)	21.5	27.3	39.2	47.1	55.1	62.2	69.7	67.8	58.3	45.9	32.8	21.5	45.7
Mean Minimum Temp. (°F)	12.9	17.1	26.8	32.9	40.2	46.6	51.7	49.2	41.0	31.7	23.4	13.3	32.2
Extreme Maximum Temp. (°F)	53	62	77	89	96	102	104	102	97	87	70	59	104
Extreme Minimum Temp. (°F)	-25	-26	-1	15	20	30	34	29	20	4	-12	-31	-31
Days Maximum Temp. ≥ 90°F	0	0	0	0	1	3	14	11	2	0	0	0	31
Days Maximum Temp. ≤ 32°F	17	7	0	0	0	0	0	0	0	0	4	18	46
Days Minimum Temp. ≤ 32°F	30	27	25	14	4	0	0	0	3	16	25	30	174
Days Minimum Temp. ≤ 0°F	4	2	0	0	0	0	0	0	0	0	0	4	10
Heating Degree Days (base 65°F)	1,342	1,059	794	529	306	125	21	30	209	584	958	1,342	7,299
Cooling Degree Days (base 65°F)	0	0	0	0	8	48	173	122	15	0	0	0	366
Mean Precipitation (in.)	0.57	0.43	0.50	0.77	1.40	1.41	0.97	0.73	0.77	0.63	0.71	0.66	9.55
Extreme Maximum Daily Precip. (in.)	0.65	0.55	0.71	0.77	1.14	1.02	1.42	0.85	0.94	0.96	0.78	0.68	1.42
Days With ≥ 0.1" Precipitation	2	2	2	3	5	5	3	2	2	2	2	3	33
Days With ≥ 0.5" Precipitation	0	0	0	0	0	0	0	0	0	0	0	0	0
Days With ≥ 1.0" Precipitation	0	0	0	0	0	0	0	0	0	0	0	0	0
Mean Snowfall (in.)	6.4	3.6	1.7	0.6	0.1	trace	trace	trace	trace	0.1	3.6	6.9	23.0
Maximum Snow Depth (in.)	17	15	11	1	trace	trace	trace	trace	trace	1	7	18	18
Days With ≥ 1.0" Snow Depth	23	16	2	0	0	0	0	0	0	0	3	18	62

Stanley *Custer County* Elevation: 6,271 ft. Latitude: 44° 13' N Longitude: 114° 56' W

	JAN	FEB	MAR	APR	MAY	JUN	JUL	AUG	SEP	OCT	NOV	DEC	YEAR
Mean Maximum Temp. (°F)	26.2	33.2	43.1	50.6	60.2	68.7	79.0	78.7	69.1	56.0	37.6	24.9	52.3
Mean Temp. (°F)	12.7	16.5	26.9	35.5	44.5	51.2	57.8	56.3	48.1	38.3	24.6	11.9	35.4
Mean Minimum Temp. (°F)	-0.8	-0.3	10.6	20.3	28.7	33.6	36.6	33.9	27.1	20.6	11.5	-1.1	18.4
Extreme Maximum Temp. (°F)	48	53	64	77	84	91	98	97	89	80	66	48	98
Extreme Minimum Temp. (°F)	-44	-47	-29	-16	8	18	21	16	9	-10	-26	-54	-54
Days Maximum Temp. ≥ 90°F	0	0	0	0	0	0	2	1	0	0	0	0	3
Days Maximum Temp. ≤ 32°F	22	12	3	1	0	0	0	0	0	0	9	23	70
Days Minimum Temp. ≤ 32°F	30	27	30	28	22	14	7	13	23	29	29	30	282
Days Minimum Temp. ≤ 0°F	16	14	6	1	0	0	0	0	0	0	6	17	60
Heating Degree Days (base 65°F)	1,616	1,368	1,174	879	630	408	224	265	499	820	1,207	1,641	10,731
Cooling Degree Days (base 65°F)	0	0	0	0	0	1	8	3	0	0	0	0	12
Mean Precipitation (in.)	***1.48***	1.38	1.03	0.93	1.11	0.93	0.45	0.40	0.54	***0.72***	1.43	1.75	***12.15***
Extreme Maximum Daily Precip. (in.)	***1.83***	***2.00***	***1.22***	***1.39***	***1.25***	***1.09***	***0.93***	***0.58***	***1.00***	na	***1.60***	na	na
Days With ≥ 0.1" Precipitation	4	***4***	3	3	3	3	2	1	2	***2***	4	***3***	***34***
Days With ≥ 0.5" Precipitation	1	***1***	0	0	0	0	0	0	0	***0***	1	***1***	***4***
Days With ≥ 1.0" Precipitation	0	0	0	0	0	0	0	0	0	***0***	0	***0***	***0***
Mean Snowfall (in.)	17.7	13.9	9.5	3.6	1.0	0.2	trace	trace	0.3	1.4	11.1	***15.2***	***73.9***
Maximum Snow Depth (in.)	na	na	***46***	49	***23***	1	***trace***	***trace***	3	***4***	***21***	***33***	na
Days With ≥ 1.0" Snow Depth	na	na	15	7	1	0	0	0	0	1	8	15	na

Swan Valley 2 E *Bonneville County* Elevation: 5,359 ft. Latitude: 43° 27' N Longitude: 111° 18' W

	JAN	FEB	MAR	APR	MAY	JUN	JUL	AUG	SEP	OCT	NOV	DEC	YEAR
Mean Maximum Temp. (°F)	30.5	35.3	44.7	56.3	65.4	74.8	84.6	83.6	73.4	59.1	42.0	30.5	56.7
Mean Temp. (°F)	21.3	24.8	33.6	42.6	50.8	58.4	65.6	64.5	55.7	44.2	31.9	21.7	42.9
Mean Minimum Temp. (°F)	12.0	14.3	22.6	28.9	36.1	42.0	46.5	45.4	37.9	29.4	21.8	12.9	29.2
Extreme Maximum Temp. (°F)	50	59	72	83	91	101	101	101	96	83	69	58	101
Extreme Minimum Temp. (°F)	-30	-36	-17	8	12	26	26	24	8	3	-20	-43	-43
Days Maximum Temp. ≥ 90°F	0	0	0	0	0	1	8	5	1	0	0	0	15
Days Maximum Temp. ≤ 32°F	17	10	2	0	0	0	0	0	0	0	5	18	52
Days Minimum Temp. ≤ 32°F	30	27	27	20	10	2	0	1	7	20	25	29	198
Days Minimum Temp. ≤ 0°F	6	5	1	0	0	0	0	0	0	0	1	5	18
Heating Degree Days (base 65°F)	1,349	1,129	965	665	435	206	56	65	281	637	986	1,337	8,111
Cooling Degree Days (base 65°F)	0	0	0	0	2	16	82	58	8	0	0	0	166
Mean Precipitation (in.)	1.55	1.02	1.36	1.65	2.83	1.79	1.35	1.29	1.48	1.53	1.56	1.32	18.73
Extreme Maximum Daily Precip. (in.)	1.40	0.83	1.20	0.80	1.82	2.30	1.83	1.34	1.87	1.00	1.05	1.00	2.30
Days With ≥ 0.1" Precipitation	5	4	5	6	8	5	4	4	4	5	5	5	60
Days With ≥ 0.5" Precipitation	1	0	0	0	1	1	1	1	1	1	0	0	7
Days With ≥ 1.0" Precipitation	0	0	0	0	0	0	0	0	0	0	0	0	0
Mean Snowfall (in.)	***9.7***	4.6	4.1	1.6	0.8	0.0	0.0	0.0	0.0	0.3	***5.0***	7.6	***33.7***
Maximum Snow Depth (in.)	na	na	***22***	***15***	***trace***	***0***	***trace***	***0***	***0***	***1***	***12***	na	na
Days With ≥ 1.0" Snow Depth	na	***11***	5	1	0	0	0	0	0	0	4	***9***	na

Winchester *Lewis County* Elevation: 3,950 ft. Latitude: 46° 14' N Longitude: 116° 37' W

	JAN	FEB	MAR	APR	MAY	JUN	JUL	AUG	SEP	OCT	NOV	DEC	YEAR
Mean Maximum Temp. (°F)	35.9	39.2	44.9	52.2	59.6	66.4	76.5	77.7	68.8	55.9	41.9	34.6	54.5
Mean Temp. (°F)	28.5	30.7	35.8	41.9	48.5	54.6	61.8	62.1	54.5	44.5	34.3	27.3	43.7
Mean Minimum Temp. (°F)	20.9	22.2	26.7	31.5	37.4	42.8	47.1	46.5	40.3	33.1	26.7	20.0	32.9
Extreme Maximum Temp. (°F)	56	67	70	84	93	90	96	97	95	88	67	60	97
Extreme Minimum Temp. (°F)	-18	-28	-9	12	23	23	28	25	17	4	-21	-33	-33
Days Maximum Temp. ≥ 90°F	0	0	0	0	0	0	1	2	0	0	0	0	3
Days Maximum Temp. ≤ 32°F	10	5	2	0	0	0	0	0	0	0	4	11	32
Days Minimum Temp. ≤ 32°F	28	25	25	18	8	1	0	0	4	15	23	29	176
Days Minimum Temp. ≤ 0°F	2	1	0	0	0	0	0	0	0	0	0	2	5
Heating Degree Days (base 65°F)	1,126	962	898	687	506	310	134	130	317	628	913	1,162	7,773
Cooling Degree Days (base 65°F)	0	0	0	0	2	6	43	48	9	0	0	0	108
Mean Precipitation (in.)	1.76	1.48	2.41	2.57	3.11	2.16	1.23	1.02	1.27	1.73	2.41	1.65	22.80
Extreme Maximum Daily Precip. (in.)	0.88	1.45	0.92	1.22	1.68	1.54	1.20	2.12	1.38	1.11	1.40	0.82	2.12
Days With ≥ 0.1" Precipitation	6	5	8	8	8	6	3	3	4	5	8	6	70
Days With ≥ 0.5" Precipitation	0	0	1	1	2	1	1	0	1	1	1	0	9
Days With ≥ 1.0" Precipitation	0	0	0	0	0	0	0	0	0	0	0	0	0
Mean Snowfall (in.)	16.6	11.3	15.0	7.6	1.4	0.2	0.0	0.0	0.1	1.4	13.2	16.1	82.9
Maximum Snow Depth (in.)	25	28	22	14	4	trace	0	0	trace	5	16	28	28
Days With ≥ 1.0" Snow Depth	23	18	12	3	0	0	0	0	0	1	9	21	87

The period of record for all cooperative weather station data is 1980 – 2009. See User Guide for detailed explanation of data.

Idaho Weather Station Rankings

Annual Extreme Maximum Temperature

Highest Rank	Highest Station Name	Highest °F	Lowest Rank	Lowest Station Name	Lowest °F
1	Brownlee Dam	115	1	Driggs	93
1	Mountain Home	115	2	Dixie	***96***
3	Bruneau	113	2	Island Park	***96***
4	Boise Air Terminal	110	4	Winchester	97
4	Emmett 2 E	110	5	Lifton Pumping Stn	98
4	Grand View 2 W	110	5	Stanley	98
4	Lewiston Nez Perce County Arpt	110	7	Cottonwood 2 WSW	99
4	Parma Experiment Stn	110	8	Chilly Barton Flat	100
9	Payette	109	8	Idaho Falls 16 SE	100
10	Dworshak Fish Hatchery	108	8	Priest River Exp Stn	100
10	Garden Valley	108	11	Ashton	101
12	Burley Municipal Arpt	107	11	Bayview Model Basin	101
12	Idaho City	107	11	Bonners Ferry	101
12	Reynolds	107	11	Cabinet Gorge	101
15	Boise 7 N	106	11	Oakley	101
15	Buhl No 2	106	11	Preston	***101***
15	Saint Maries 1 W	106	11	Swan Valley 2 E	101
18	Malad City	105	18	Potlatch 3 NNE	102
19	Aberdeen Exp Station	104	18	Powell	102
19	Idaho Falls 2 ESE	104	18	Rexburg Ricks College	***102***
19	Middle Fork Lodge	104	21	American Falls 3 NW	103
19	Pocatello Municipal Arpt	104	21	Cascade 1 NW	103
19	Salmon	104	21	Dubois Experiment Stn	103
24	American Falls 3 NW	103	21	Fort Hall 1 NNE	103
24	Cascade 1 NW	103	21	Grace	103

Annual Mean Maximum Temperature

Highest Rank	Highest Station Name	Highest °F	Lowest Rank	Lowest Station Name	Lowest °F
1	Bruneau	66.6	1	Dixie	***51.2***
2	Grand View 2 W	66.3	2	Island Park	***52.2***
3	Payette	65.9	3	Stanley	52.3
4	Brownlee Dam	65.8	4	Driggs	53.8
5	Mountain Home	64.8	5	Cascade 1 NW	54.4
6	Parma Experiment Stn	64.3	6	Idaho Falls 16 SE	54.5
7	Dworshak Fish Hatchery	64.0	6	Winchester	54.5
7	Emmett 2 E	64.0	8	Ashton	54.6
9	Boise Air Terminal	63.5	9	Lifton Pumping Stn	54.8
9	Lewiston Nez Perce County Arpt	63.5	10	Chilly Barton Flat	55.0
11	Garden Valley	62.3	11	Priest River Exp Stn	55.8
12	Reynolds	61.6	12	Cottonwood 2 WSW	56.0
13	Burley Municipal Arpt	61.2	12	Dubois Experiment Stn	56.0
13	Malad City	***61.2***	14	Bayview Model Basin	56.2
15	Oakley	61.1	15	Powell	56.4
16	Boise 7 N	60.7	16	Rexburg Ricks College	***56.6***
17	Buhl No 2	60.4	17	Swan Valley 2 E	56.7
18	American Falls 3 NW	59.9	18	Cabinet Gorge	56.9
18	Idaho City	59.9	19	Porthill	57.5
20	Middle Fork Lodge	59.8	20	Potlatch 3 NNE	57.7
20	Pocatello Municipal Arpt	59.8	21	Saint Maries 1 W	58.2
22	Preston	***59.5***	22	Bonners Ferry	58.4
23	Aberdeen Exp Station	59.1	23	Grace	58.5
23	Fort Hall 1 NNE	59.1	24	Howe	58.8
23	Idaho Falls 2 ESE	59.1	25	Aberdeen Exp Station	59.1

Rankings include 25 highest/lowest stations. If state has less than 25 stations, all stations are included. The period of record is 1980–2009. See User Guide for detailed explanation of data.

Annual Mean Temperature

Highest

Rank	Station Name	°F
1	Brownlee Dam	54.8
2	Lewiston Nez Perce County Arpt	53.1
3	Bruneau	52.7
4	Grand View 2 W	52.4
5	Dworshak Fish Hatchery	52.2
6	Payette	52.1
7	Boise Air Terminal	51.8
8	Mountain Home	51.4
9	Emmett 2 E	51.1
10	Parma Experiment Stn	50.6
11	Boise 7 N	49.8
12	Buhl No 2	48.9
13	Oakley	48.8
14	Burley Municipal Arpt	48.7
15	Reynolds	48.4
16	American Falls 3 NW	47.8
17	Moscow U of Idaho	47.7
18	Saint Maries 1 W	47.4
19	Garden Valley	47.0
20	Bonners Ferry	46.9
21	Cottonwood 2 WSW	46.8
22	Pocatello Municipal Arpt	46.6
23	Cabinet Gorge	46.3
24	Idaho Falls 2 ESE	46.0
24	Porthill	46.0

Lowest

Rank	Station Name	°F
1	Stanley	35.4
2	Dixie	***36.4***
3	Island Park	***37.8***
4	Cascade 1 NW	40.3
4	Chilly Barton Flat	40.3
6	Driggs	40.5
7	Idaho Falls 16 SE	41.6
8	Lifton Pumping Stn	41.7
9	Ashton	42.2
10	Swan Valley 2 E	42.9
11	Powell	43.0
12	Rexburg Ricks College	***43.4***
13	Winchester	43.7
14	Dubois Experiment Stn	43.8
14	Grace	43.8
16	Howe	43.9
17	Idaho City	44.2
18	Priest River Exp Stn	44.3
19	Aberdeen Exp Station	44.5
20	Middle Fork Lodge	44.6
21	Bayview Model Basin	45.1
22	Fort Hall 1 NNE	45.4
23	Potlatch 3 NNE	45.7
23	Salmon	45.7
25	Malad City	***45.9***

Annual Mean Minimum Temperature

Highest

Rank	Station Name	°F
1	Brownlee Dam	43.8
2	Lewiston Nez Perce County Arpt	42.7
3	Dworshak Fish Hatchery	40.2
4	Boise Air Terminal	40.1
5	Boise 7 N	38.8
5	Bruneau	38.8
7	Grand View 2 W	38.4
8	Payette	38.3
9	Emmett 2 E	38.2
10	Mountain Home	38.0
11	Cottonwood 2 WSW	37.7
12	Buhl No 2	37.3
13	Parma Experiment Stn	36.8
14	Saint Maries 1 W	36.6
15	Oakley	36.4
16	Moscow U of Idaho	36.2
17	Burley Municipal Arpt	36.1
18	Cabinet Gorge	35.7
19	American Falls 3 NW	35.5
20	Bonners Ferry	35.3
21	Reynolds	35.1
22	Porthill	34.4
23	Bayview Model Basin	34.0
24	Potlatch 3 NNE	33.7
25	Pocatello Municipal Arpt	33.3

Lowest

Rank	Station Name	°F
1	Stanley	18.4
2	Dixie	***21.6***
3	Island Park	***23.3***
4	Chilly Barton Flat	25.6
5	Cascade 1 NW	26.2
6	Driggs	27.2
7	Idaho City	28.5
8	Lifton Pumping Stn	28.6
9	Idaho Falls 16 SE	28.8
10	Howe	28.9
11	Grace	29.0
12	Swan Valley 2 E	29.2
13	Middle Fork Lodge	29.3
14	Powell	29.5
15	Ashton	29.8
16	Aberdeen Exp Station	29.9
17	Rexburg Ricks College	***30.1***
18	Malad City	***30.6***
19	Dubois Experiment Stn	31.5
20	Fort Hall 1 NNE	31.6
21	Garden Valley	31.7
22	Salmon	32.2
23	Preston	***32.4***
24	Priest River Exp Stn	32.8
25	Idaho Falls 2 ESE	32.9

Rankings include 25 highest/lowest stations. If state has less than 25 stations, all stations are included. The period of record is 1980–2009. See User Guide for detailed explanation of data.

Annual Extreme Minimum Temperature

Highest			Lowest		
Rank	Station Name	°F	Rank	Station Name	°F
1	Brownlee Dam	-9	1	Island Park	***-54***
2	Dworshak Fish Hatchery	-10	1	Stanley	-54
3	Bayview Model Basin	-15	3	Dixie	***-49***
4	Lewiston Nez Perce County Arpt	-16	4	Swan Valley 2 E	-43
5	Cottonwood 2 WSW	-20	5	Idaho Falls 16 SE	-41
5	Emmett 2 E	-20	5	Lifton Pumping Stn	-41
5	Saint Maries 1 W	-20	7	Driggs	-40
8	Garden Valley	-21	7	Grace	-40
8	Reynolds	-21	9	Aberdeen Exp Station	-38
10	Bonners Ferry	-22	9	Howe	-38
10	Cabinet Gorge	-22	11	Chilly Barton Flat	-37
12	Boise 7 N	-23	12	Rexburg Ricks College	***-36***
12	Payette	-23	13	Cascade 1 NW	-35
14	Oakley	-24	13	Malad City	-35
14	Porthill	-24	15	Idaho Falls 2 ESE	-34
16	Boise Air Terminal	-25	16	Fort Hall 1 NNE	-33
16	Mountain Home	-25	16	Pocatello Municipal Arpt	-33
16	Parma Experiment Stn	-25	16	Winchester	-33
16	Priest River Exp Stn	-25	19	Bruneau	-32
20	Buhl No 2	-26	19	Idaho City	-32
20	Burley Municipal Arpt	-26	19	Potlatch 3 NNE	-32
20	Grand View 2 W	-26	22	Ashton	-31
23	Middle Fork Lodge	-28	22	Dubois Experiment Stn	-31
24	Moscow U of Idaho	-29	22	Powell	-31
25	American Falls 3 NW	-30	22	Preston	***-31***

July Mean Maximum Temperature

Highest			Lowest		
Rank	Station Name	°F	Rank	Station Name	°F
1	Brownlee Dam	94.8	1	Dixie	***75.2***
2	Bruneau	93.1	2	Winchester	76.5
2	Mountain Home	93.1	3	Cottonwood 2 WSW	79.0
4	Grand View 2 W	92.5	3	Stanley	79.0
5	Payette	92.3	5	Island Park	***79.4***
6	Parma Experiment Stn	91.4	6	Bayview Model Basin	80.2
7	Boise Air Terminal	91.2	6	Driggs	80.2
8	Emmett 2 E	90.8	8	Potlatch 3 NNE	80.7
9	Malad City	89.9	9	Cascade 1 NW	80.8
10	Garden Valley	89.8	10	Idaho Falls 16 SE	80.9
11	Dworshak Fish Hatchery	89.6	11	Cabinet Gorge	82.0
12	Lewiston Nez Perce County Arpt	89.2	12	Chilly Barton Flat	82.1
13	Pocatello Municipal Arpt	88.3	13	Priest River Exp Stn	82.3
13	Preston	***88.3***	14	Ashton	82.4
15	Boise 7 N	88.0	14	Lifton Pumping Stn	82.4
16	Howe	87.8	16	Porthill	82.5
17	Salmon	87.6	17	Powell	82.9
18	Idaho Falls 2 ESE	87.3	18	Saint Maries 1 W	83.2
19	Burley Municipal Arpt	87.2	19	Moscow U of Idaho	83.4
19	Idaho City	87.2	20	Rexburg Ricks College	84.0
21	Buhl No 2	87.0	21	Bonners Ferry	84.2
21	Reynolds	87.0	22	Swan Valley 2 E	84.6
23	American Falls 3 NW	86.8	23	Oakley	84.7
24	Middle Fork Lodge	86.7	24	Dubois Experiment Stn	85.4
25	Aberdeen Exp Station	86.6	25	Fort Hall 1 NNE	86.1

Rankings include 25 highest/lowest stations. If state has less than 25 stations, all stations are included. The period of record is 1980–2009. See User Guide for detailed explanation of data.

January Mean Minimum Temperature

Highest Rank	Station Name	°F	Lowest Rank	Station Name	°F
1	Lewiston Nez Perce County Arpt	29.4	1	Stanley	-0.8
2	Dworshak Fish Hatchery	27.7	2	Island Park	4.6
3	Brownlee Dam	25.9	3	Dixie	5.3
4	Saint Maries 1 W	24.8	4	Chilly Barton Flat	5.7
5	Moscow U of Idaho	24.7	5	Lifton Pumping Stn	6.4
6	Cottonwood 2 WSW	23.8	6	Howe	6.7
7	Bruneau	23.6	7	Driggs	8.6
8	Boise Air Terminal	23.4	8	Cascade 1 NW	10.0
8	Potlatch 3 NNE	23.4	9	Rexburg Ricks College	10.6
10	Cabinet Gorge	23.3	10	Grace	11.1
11	Grand View 2 W	23.0	11	Ashton	11.5
12	Bayview Model Basin	22.9	12	Aberdeen Exp Station	11.9
12	Boise 7 N	22.9	13	Idaho Falls 16 SE	12.0
14	Emmett 2 E	22.3	13	Swan Valley 2 E	12.0
15	Mountain Home	22.1	15	Dubois Experiment Stn	12.2
16	Bonners Ferry	21.8	16	Salmon	12.9
17	Priest River Exp Stn	21.0	17	Malad City	13.0
17	Reynolds	21.0	17	Preston	13.0
19	Payette	20.9	19	Idaho City	13.3
19	Winchester	20.9	20	Idaho Falls 2 ESE	13.7
21	Oakley	20.5	21	Fort Hall 1 NNE	13.8
22	Parma Experiment Stn	20.3	21	Middle Fork Lodge	13.8
23	Buhl No 2	20.0	23	Pocatello Municipal Arpt	16.0
24	Burley Municipal Arpt	19.8	24	Powell	16.3
25	Porthill	19.6	25	American Falls 3 NW	16.9

Number of Days Annually Maximum Temperature ≥ 90°F

Highest Rank	Station Name	Days	Lowest Rank	Station Name	Days
1	Brownlee Dam	66	1	Dixie	*2*
2	Mountain Home	62	1	Driggs	2
3	Bruneau	61	1	Island Park	*2*
4	Grand View 2 W	60	4	Stanley	3
5	Parma Experiment Stn	56	4	Winchester	3
6	Payette	55	6	Idaho Falls 16 SE	4
7	Boise Air Terminal	50	7	Chilly Barton Flat	5
8	Dworshak Fish Hatchery	49	7	Lifton Pumping Stn	5
8	Emmett 2 E	49	9	Ashton	7
10	Garden Valley	47	9	Bayview Model Basin	7
11	Lewiston Nez Perce County Arpt	41	9	Cascade 1 NW	7
12	Malad City	40	9	Cottonwood 2 WSW	7
13	Pocatello Municipal Arpt	35	13	Cabinet Gorge	13
14	Boise 7 N	33	13	Potlatch 3 NNE	13
15	Burley Municipal Arpt	31	15	Priest River Exp Stn	14
15	Idaho City	31	16	Porthill	15
15	Reynolds	31	16	Swan Valley 2 E	15
15	Salmon	31	18	Rexburg Ricks College	*17*
19	Buhl No 2	29	19	Dubois Experiment Stn	18
20	Aberdeen Exp Station	28	19	Oakley	18
20	Idaho Falls 2 ESE	28	21	Bonners Ferry	20
20	Preston	*28*	21	Moscow U of Idaho	20
23	American Falls 3 NW	27	21	Powell	20
23	Howe	27	24	Grace	22
23	Middle Fork Lodge	27	24	Saint Maries 1 W	22

Rankings include 25 highest/lowest stations. If state has less than 25 stations, all stations are included. The period of record is 1980–2009. See User Guide for detailed explanation of data.

Number of Days Annually Maximum Temperature ≤ 32°F

Highest Rank	Station Name	Days	Lowest Rank	Station Name	Days
1	Island Park	***74***	1	Dworshak Fish Hatchery	10
2	Stanley	70	2	Brownlee Dam	12
3	Ashton	63	3	Bruneau	14
4	Driggs	62	3	Lewiston Nez Perce County Arpt	14
4	Dubois Experiment Stn	62	5	Grand View 2 W	15
6	Dixie	***60***	6	Payette	16
7	Rexburg Ricks College	***57***	7	Emmett 2 E	18
8	Chilly Barton Flat	56	7	Reynolds	18
9	Lifton Pumping Stn	55	9	Mountain Home	19
10	Idaho Falls 16 SE	53	10	Oakley	20
11	Cascade 1 NW	52	11	Boise Air Terminal	21
11	Swan Valley 2 E	52	11	Parma Experiment Stn	21
13	Howe	48	13	Garden Valley	23
14	Idaho Falls 2 ESE	46	13	Moscow U of Idaho	23
14	Priest River Exp Stn	46	15	Boise 7 N	24
14	Salmon	46	16	Bayview Model Basin	25
17	Preston	***44***	17	Idaho City	26
18	Aberdeen Exp Station	42	18	Potlatch 3 NNE	27
19	Fort Hall 1 NNE	41	18	Saint Maries 1 W	27
19	Grace	41	20	Burley Municipal Arpt	29
19	Pocatello Municipal Arpt	41	21	Cottonwood 2 WSW	30
22	American Falls 3 NW	38	22	Cabinet Gorge	31
23	Malad City	36	22	Middle Fork Lodge	31
24	Porthill	35	24	Winchester	32
24	Powell	35	25	Bonners Ferry	33

Number of Days Annually Minimum Temperature ≤ 32°F

Highest Rank	Station Name	Days	Lowest Rank	Station Name	Days
1	Stanley	282	1	Lewiston Nez Perce County Arpt	79
2	Dixie	***271***	2	Brownlee Dam	88
3	Island Park	***243***	3	Dworshak Fish Hatchery	100
4	Cascade 1 NW	235	4	Boise Air Terminal	118
5	Chilly Barton Flat	222	5	Bruneau	124
6	Idaho City	216	6	Boise 7 N	127
7	Powell	214	7	Grand View 2 W	132
8	Driggs	210	8	Emmett 2 E	134
9	Middle Fork Lodge	208	9	Moscow U of Idaho	135
10	Idaho Falls 16 SE	206	9	Payette	135
11	Grace	201	11	Cottonwood 2 WSW	138
12	Lifton Pumping Stn	199	11	Saint Maries 1 W	138
13	Swan Valley 2 E	198	13	Mountain Home	140
14	Aberdeen Exp Station	197	14	Burley Municipal Arpt	147
15	Rexburg Ricks College	***193***	14	Oakley	147
16	Ashton	191	14	Parma Experiment Stn	147
17	Howe	189	17	Buhl No 2	148
18	Dubois Experiment Stn	188	18	American Falls 3 NW	149
19	Malad City	187	18	Bonners Ferry	149
20	Priest River Exp Stn	186	20	Cabinet Gorge	151
21	Fort Hall 1 NNE	180	21	Reynolds	161
22	Garden Valley	179	22	Porthill	162
23	Preston	***176***	22	Potlatch 3 NNE	162
23	Winchester	176	24	Bayview Model Basin	169
25	Salmon	174	24	Pocatello Municipal Arpt	169

Rankings include 25 highest/lowest stations. If state has less than 25 stations, all stations are included. The period of record is 1980–2009. See User Guide for detailed explanation of data.

Number of Days Annually Minimum Temperature ≤ 0°F

Highest Rank	Station Name	Days	Lowest Rank	Station Name	Days
1	Stanley	60	1	Brownlee Dam	0
2	Island Park	*40*	1	Dworshak Fish Hatchery	0
3	Dixie	*37*	1	Lewiston Nez Perce County Arpt	0
4	Chilly Barton Flat	30	4	Bruneau	2
5	Howe	29	4	Emmett 2 E	2
6	Lifton Pumping Stn	28	4	Grand View 2 W	2
7	Driggs	27	7	Bayview Model Basin	3
8	Cascade 1 NW	22	7	Boise 7 N	3
9	Grace	21	7	Boise Air Terminal	3
10	Rexburg Ricks College	*19*	7	Bonners Ferry	3
11	Ashton	18	7	Buhl No 2	3
11	Idaho Falls 16 SE	18	7	Cabinet Gorge	3
11	Swan Valley 2 E	18	7	Cottonwood 2 WSW	3
14	Aberdeen Exp Station	17	7	Moscow U of Idaho	3
15	Malad City	15	7	Mountain Home	3
16	Idaho City	14	7	Oakley	3
17	Fort Hall 1 NNE	13	7	Potlatch 3 NNE	3
17	Idaho Falls 2 ESE	13	7	Saint Maries 1 W	3
17	Preston	*13*	19	Payette	4
20	Dubois Experiment Stn	12	19	Priest River Exp Stn	4
21	Middle Fork Lodge	11	19	Reynolds	4
22	Pocatello Municipal Arpt	10	22	Burley Municipal Arpt	5
22	Salmon	10	22	Parma Experiment Stn	5
24	Powell	8	22	Porthill	5
25	American Falls 3 NW	7	22	Winchester	5

Number of Annual Heating Degree Days

Highest Rank	Station Name	Num.	Lowest Rank	Station Name	Num.
1	Stanley	10,731	1	Brownlee Dam	4,934
2	Dixie	*10,351*	2	Lewiston Nez Perce County Arpt	5,067
3	Island Park	*9,874*	3	Bruneau	5,260
4	Chilly Barton Flat	8,991	4	Dworshak Fish Hatchery	5,282
5	Cascade 1 NW	8,977	5	Grand View 2 W	5,349
6	Driggs	8,891	6	Payette	5,453
7	Lifton Pumping Stn	8,558	7	Boise Air Terminal	5,609
8	Idaho Falls 16 SE	8,526	8	Emmett 2 E	5,714
9	Ashton	8,356	9	Mountain Home	5,798
10	Swan Valley 2 E	8,111	10	Parma Experiment Stn	5,879
11	Powell	8,068	11	Boise 7 N	6,140
12	Rexburg Ricks College	*8,015*	12	Oakley	6,280
13	Dubois Experiment Stn	7,984	13	Burley Municipal Arpt	6,354
14	Howe	7,927	14	Buhl No 2	6,398
15	Grace	7,850	15	Reynolds	6,431
16	Winchester	7,773	16	Moscow U of Idaho	6,490
17	Idaho City	7,720	17	Saint Maries 1 W	6,641
18	Aberdeen Exp Station	7,661	18	American Falls 3 NW	6,680
19	Priest River Exp Stn	7,592	19	Garden Valley	*6,783*
20	Middle Fork Lodge	7,556	20	Bonners Ferry	6,785
21	Fort Hall 1 NNE	7,365	21	Cottonwood 2 WSW	6,868
22	Salmon	7,299	22	Cabinet Gorge	6,937
23	Bayview Model Basin	7,289	23	Pocatello Municipal Arpt	7,027
24	Idaho Falls 2 ESE	7,254	24	Potlatch 3 NNE	7,081
25	Preston	*7,241*	25	Porthill	7,111

Rankings include 25 highest/lowest stations. If state has less than 25 stations, all stations are included. The period of record is 1980–2009. See User Guide for detailed explanation of data.

Number of Annual Cooling Degree Days

Highest Rank	Station Name	Num.	Lowest Rank	Station Name	Num.
1	Brownlee Dam	1,324	1	Dixie	***11***
2	Mountain Home	939	2	Stanley	12
3	Boise Air Terminal	903	3	Island Park	***39***
4	Bruneau	887	4	Driggs	69
5	Payette	859	5	Cascade 1 NW	77
6	Grand View 2 W	851	6	Chilly Barton Flat	82
7	Lewiston Nez Perce County Arpt	838	7	Idaho Falls 16 SE	106
8	Emmett 2 E	752	8	Winchester	108
9	Parma Experiment Stn	729	9	Powell	132
10	Dworshak Fish Hatchery	699	10	Potlatch 3 NNE	138
11	Boise 7 N	680	11	Bayview Model Basin	144
12	Buhl No 2	617	12	Priest River Exp Stn	148
13	Burley Municipal Arpt	497	13	Ashton	153
14	American Falls 3 NW	491	14	Swan Valley 2 E	166
15	Reynolds	475	15	Lifton Pumping Stn	174
16	Oakley	462	16	Middle Fork Lodge	203
17	Idaho Falls 2 ESE	432	17	Cabinet Gorge	217
18	Pocatello Municipal Arpt	419	18	Grace	219
19	Preston	***411***	19	Idaho City	225
20	Salmon	366	20	Rexburg Ricks College	***231***
21	Malad City	***365***	21	Porthill	264
22	Dubois Experiment Stn	345	22	Moscow U of Idaho	272
23	Cottonwood 2 WSW	341	23	Bonners Ferry	275
24	Garden Valley	321	24	Aberdeen Exp Station	289
25	Howe	319	25	Saint Maries 1 W	306

Annual Precipitation

Highest Rank	Station Name	Inches	Lowest Rank	Station Name	Inches
1	Powell	37.62	1	Grand View 2 W	6.86
2	Cabinet Gorge	31.60	2	Bruneau	7.43
3	Priest River Exp Stn	31.25	3	Howe	7.44
4	Saint Maries 1 W	30.33	4	Chilly Barton Flat	8.00
5	Moscow U of Idaho	27.07	5	Aberdeen Exp Station	9.19
6	Island Park	***26.67***	6	Salmon	9.55
7	Garden Valley	25.86	7	Buhl No 2	9.62
8	Potlatch 3 NNE	***25.38***	8	Burley Municipal Arpt	10.08
9	Dixie	***25.32***	9	Mountain Home	10.15
10	Dworshak Fish Hatchery	24.92	10	Reynolds	10.23
11	Bayview Model Basin	24.26	11	Parma Experiment Stn	10.28
12	Cascade 1 NW	23.21	12	Payette	10.80
13	Winchester	22.80	13	Lifton Pumping Stn	11.35
14	Idaho City	22.57	14	Oakley	11.43
15	Cottonwood 2 WSW	22.41	15	Fort Hall 1 NNE	11.48
16	Porthill	20.77	16	Boise Air Terminal	11.72
17	Bonners Ferry	20.10	17	American Falls 3 NW	11.92
18	Ashton	19.30	18	Stanley	***12.15***
19	Swan Valley 2 E	18.73	19	Lewiston Nez Perce County Arpt	12.23
20	Boise 7 N	18.72	20	Pocatello Municipal Arpt	12.29
21	Preston	***17.43***	21	Dubois Experiment Stn	12.91
22	Middle Fork Lodge	16.22	22	Rexburg Ricks College	***13.41***
23	Brownlee Dam	16.04	23	Emmett 2 E	13.69
24	Idaho Falls 16 SE	15.98	24	Malad City	13.87
25	Grace	15.76	25	Idaho Falls 2 ESE	13.97

Rankings include 25 highest/lowest stations. If state has less than 25 stations, all stations are included. The period of record is 1980–2009. See User Guide for detailed explanation of data.

Annual Extreme Maximum Daily Precipitation

Highest			Lowest		
Rank	Station Name	Inches	Rank	Station Name	Inches
1	Priest River Exp Stn	3.34	1	Chilly Barton Flat	1.15
2	Driggs	***3.14***	2	Oakley	1.28
3	Dixie	***2.82***	3	Buhl No 2	1.38
4	Bonners Ferry	***2.80***	4	Salmon	1.42
5	Cabinet Gorge	***2.77***	5	Rexburg Ricks College	***1.43***
6	Powell	***2.63***	6	Pocatello Municipal Arpt	1.45
7	Ashton	***2.61***	7	Dubois Experiment Stn	1.51
8	Moscow U of Idaho	2.51	8	Payette	***1.55***
9	Swan Valley 2 E	2.30	9	Reynolds	1.59
10	Potlatch 3 NNE	***2.27***	10	Grand View 2 W	***1.60***
11	Preston	***2.20***	11	Fort Hall 1 NNE	***1.66***
12	Idaho Falls 16 SE	2.19	12	Bruneau	1.67
13	Winchester	2.12	13	Mountain Home	***1.68***
14	Cottonwood 2 WSW	2.10	14	Brownlee Dam	1.70
15	American Falls 3 NW	2.06	14	Parma Experiment Stn	1.70
16	Middle Fork Lodge	2.02	16	Burley Municipal Arpt	1.72
17	Bayview Model Basin	2.00	17	Grace	1.73
18	Dworshak Fish Hatchery	1.99	17	Idaho Falls 2 ESE	1.73
19	Cascade 1 NW	1.98	19	Aberdeen Exp Station	1.75
20	Porthill	1.97	19	Emmett 2 E	1.75
21	Boise 7 N	1.96	21	Boise Air Terminal	1.77
21	Idaho City	1.96	22	Lewiston Nez Perce County Arpt	1.80
23	Lifton Pumping Stn	1.86	23	Malad City	***1.85***
24	Malad City	***1.85***	24	Lifton Pumping Stn	1.86
25	Lewiston Nez Perce County Arpt	1.80	25	Boise 7 N	1.96

Number of Days Annually With ≥ 0.1 Inches of Precipitation

Highest			Lowest		
Rank	Station Name	Days	Rank	Station Name	Days
1	Powell	93	1	Howe	19
2	Priest River Exp Stn	82	2	Grand View 2 W	22
3	Cabinet Gorge	80	3	Chilly Barton Flat	24
4	Dixie	***79***	4	Bruneau	26
5	Dworshak Fish Hatchery	76	5	Aberdeen Exp Station	31
6	Moscow U of Idaho	73	5	Buhl No 2	31
7	Bayview Model Basin	70	7	Mountain Home	33
7	Saint Maries 1 W	70	7	Reynolds	33
7	Winchester	70	7	Salmon	33
10	Cottonwood 2 WSW	69	10	Burley Municipal Arpt	34
11	Potlatch 3 NNE	67	10	Stanley	***34***
12	Porthill	66	12	Fort Hall 1 NNE	35
13	Cascade 1 NW	65	12	Payette	35
13	Island Park	***65***	14	Lifton Pumping Stn	36
15	Garden Valley	62	14	Parma Experiment Stn	36
16	Idaho City	60	16	American Falls 3 NW	37
16	Swan Valley 2 E	60	17	Oakley	38
18	Bonners Ferry	57	18	Boise Air Terminal	40
19	Ashton	56	18	Lewiston Nez Perce County Arpt	40
20	Boise 7 N	52	18	Malad City	40
20	Idaho Falls 16 SE	52	21	Idaho Falls 2 ESE	41
22	Preston	***51***	21	Pocatello Municipal Arpt	41
23	Middle Fork Lodge	50	23	Dubois Experiment Stn	42
24	Brownlee Dam	48	24	Rexburg Ricks College	***43***
24	Grace	48	25	Emmett 2 E	44

Rankings include 25 highest/lowest stations. If state has less than 25 stations, all stations are included. The period of record is 1980–2009. See User Guide for detailed explanation of data.

Number of Days Annually With ≥ 0.5 Inches of Precipitation

Highest Rank	Station Name	Days	Lowest Rank	Station Name	Days
1	Powell	22	1	Bruneau	0
2	Cabinet Gorge	17	1	Buhl No 2	0
2	Priest River Exp Stn	17	1	Grand View 2 W	0
4	Garden Valley	15	1	Howe	0
4	Moscow U of Idaho	15	1	Parma Experiment Stn	0
6	Idaho City	13	1	Salmon	0
6	Island Park	*13*	7	Aberdeen Exp Station	1
6	Potlatch 3 NNE	13	7	American Falls 3 NW	1
9	Bayview Model Basin	12	7	Burley Municipal Arpt	1
9	Cottonwood 2 WSW	12	7	Chilly Barton Flat	1
9	Dixie	*12*	7	Lewiston Nez Perce County Arpt	1
9	Saint Maries 1 W	12	7	Payette	1
13	Cascade 1 NW	11	7	Reynolds	1
13	Dworshak Fish Hatchery	11	14	Boise Air Terminal	2
15	Ashton	10	14	Dubois Experiment Stn	2
16	Boise 7 N	9	14	Fort Hall 1 NNE	2
16	Bonners Ferry	9	14	Malad City	2
16	Porthill	9	14	Mountain Home	2
16	Winchester	9	14	Oakley	2
20	Preston	*7*	14	Pocatello Municipal Arpt	2
20	Swan Valley 2 E	7	21	Lifton Pumping Stn	3
22	Brownlee Dam	6	21	Rexburg Ricks College	*3*
23	Driggs	5	23	Emmett 2 E	4
23	Grace	5	23	Idaho Falls 2 ESE	4
23	Middle Fork Lodge	5	23	Idaho Falls 16 SE	4

Number of Days Annually With ≥ 1.0 Inches of Precipitation

Highest Rank	Station Name	Days	Lowest Rank	Station Name	Days
1	Cabinet Gorge	2	1	Aberdeen Exp Station	0
1	Garden Valley	2	1	American Falls 3 NW	0
1	Powell	2	1	Ashton	0
4	Cascade 1 NW	1	1	Bayview Model Basin	0
4	Idaho City	1	1	Boise 7 N	0
4	Priest River Exp Stn	1	1	Boise Air Terminal	0
4	Saint Maries 1 W	1	1	Bonners Ferry	0
8	Aberdeen Exp Station	0	1	Brownlee Dam	0
8	American Falls 3 NW	0	1	Bruneau	0
8	Ashton	0	1	Buhl No 2	0
8	Bayview Model Basin	0	1	Burley Municipal Arpt	0
8	Boise 7 N	0	1	Chilly Barton Flat	0
8	Boise Air Terminal	0	1	Cottonwood 2 WSW	0
8	Bonners Ferry	0	1	Dixie	*0*
8	Brownlee Dam	0	1	Driggs	0
8	Bruneau	0	1	Dubois Experiment Stn	0
8	Buhl No 2	0	1	Dworshak Fish Hatchery	0
8	Burley Municipal Arpt	0	1	Emmett 2 E	0
8	Chilly Barton Flat	0	1	Fort Hall 1 NNE	0
8	Cottonwood 2 WSW	0	1	Grace	0
8	Dixie	*0*	1	Grand View 2 W	0
8	Driggs	0	1	Howe	0
8	Dubois Experiment Stn	0	1	Idaho Falls 2 ESE	0
8	Dworshak Fish Hatchery	0	1	Idaho Falls 16 SE	0
8	Emmett 2 E	0	1	Island Park	*0*

Annual Snowfall

Highest			Lowest		
Rank	Station Name	Inches	Rank	Station Name	Inches
1	Island Park	***222.0***	1	Grand View 2 W	***3.6***
2	Dixie	***182.2***	2	Emmett 2 E	***6.5***
3	Powell	***126.1***	3	Mountain Home	***8.6***
4	Cascade 1 NW	85.2	4	Brownlee Dam	9.8
5	Winchester	82.9	5	Howe	***10.1***
6	Ashton	82.1	6	Parma Experiment Stn	12.8
7	Stanley	***73.9***	7	Dworshak Fish Hatchery	***13.7***
8	Driggs	72.9	8	Boise Air Terminal	18.9
9	Priest River Exp Stn	71.0	9	Aberdeen Exp Station	***20.5***
10	Idaho Falls 16 SE	70.0	10	Salmon	23.0
11	Idaho City	68.6	11	Bayview Model Basin	23.7
12	Garden Valley	***61.7***	12	Oakley	25.9
13	Bonners Ferry	56.3	13	Fort Hall 1 NNE	28.1
14	Boise 7 N	54.4	14	American Falls 3 NW	32.8
15	Rexburg Ricks College	***51.1***	15	Malad City	***33.4***
16	Saint Maries 1 W	***50.9***	16	Swan Valley 2 E	***33.7***
17	Moscow U of Idaho	48.4	17	Porthill	***37.5***
18	Dubois Experiment Stn	47.3	18	Lifton Pumping Stn	37.8
19	Pocatello Municipal Arpt	42.9	19	Cabinet Gorge	38.2
20	Middle Fork Lodge	41.8	20	Middle Fork Lodge	41.8
21	Cabinet Gorge	38.2	21	Pocatello Municipal Arpt	42.9
22	Lifton Pumping Stn	37.8	22	Dubois Experiment Stn	47.3
23	Porthill	***37.5***	23	Moscow U of Idaho	48.4
24	Swan Valley 2 E	***33.7***	24	Saint Maries 1 W	***50.9***
25	Malad City	***33.4***	25	Rexburg Ricks College	***51.1***

Annual Maximum Snow Depth

Highest			Lowest		
Rank	Station Name	Inches	Rank	Station Name	Inches
1	Island Park	***89***	1	Mountain Home	***12***
2	Dixie	***85***	2	Boise Air Terminal	13
3	Powell	***64***	2	Howe	***13***
4	Saint Maries 1 W	59	4	Emmett 2 E	***14***
5	Bonners Ferry	***55***	5	Oakley	15
6	Ashton	54	6	Pocatello Municipal Arpt	17
7	Priest River Exp Stn	51	7	Salmon	18
8	Cascade 1 NW	50	8	Brownlee Dam	19
9	Idaho City	46	9	Parma Experiment Stn	21
10	Garden Valley	***40***	10	Malad City	***22***
11	Driggs	39	11	Boise 7 N	23
12	Dubois Experiment Stn	37	11	Fort Hall 1 NNE	23
13	Idaho Falls 16 SE	36	13	Middle Fork Lodge	26
14	Cabinet Gorge	***35***	13	Moscow U of Idaho	26
14	Lifton Pumping Stn	35	15	American Falls 3 NW	***27***
14	Porthill	35	16	Aberdeen Exp Station	28
17	Aberdeen Exp Station	28	16	Bayview Model Basin	***28***
17	Bayview Model Basin	***28***	16	Winchester	28
17	Winchester	28	19	Cabinet Gorge	***35***
20	American Falls 3 NW	***27***	19	Lifton Pumping Stn	35
21	Middle Fork Lodge	26	19	Porthill	35
21	Moscow U of Idaho	26	22	Idaho Falls 16 SE	36
23	Boise 7 N	23	23	Dubois Experiment Stn	37
23	Fort Hall 1 NNE	23	24	Driggs	39
25	Malad City	***22***	25	Garden Valley	***40***

Rankings include 25 highest/lowest stations. If state has less than 25 stations, all stations are included. The period of record is 1980–2009. See User Guide for detailed explanation of data.

Number of Days Annually With ≥ 1.0 Inch Snow Depth

Highest			Lowest		
Rank	**Station Name**	**Days**	**Rank**	**Station Name**	**Days**
1	Dixie	***174***	1	Bruneau	***0***
2	Island Park	***156***	2	Grand View 2 W	***1***
3	Ashton	130	3	Emmett 2 E	***9***
4	Cascade 1 NW	125	4	Oakley	12
5	Powell	***124***	5	Howe	***13***
6	Idaho City	117	6	Brownlee Dam	15
7	Dubois Experiment Stn	116	7	Mountain Home	***18***
8	Priest River Exp Stn	112	8	Boise Air Terminal	24
9	Idaho Falls 16 SE	108	9	Parma Experiment Stn	26
10	Lifton Pumping Stn	106	10	Bayview Model Basin	***31***
11	Middle Fork Lodge	98	11	Cabinet Gorge	***44***
12	Winchester	87	12	Moscow U of Idaho	47
13	Driggs	86	13	American Falls 3 NW	52
14	Rexburg Ricks College	***80***	14	Pocatello Municipal Arpt	54
15	Garden Valley	***78***	14	Porthill	54
16	Fort Hall 1 NNE	62	14	Saint Maries 1 W	54
16	Salmon	62	17	Malad City	***55***
18	Bonners Ferry	61	18	Aberdeen Exp Station	57
19	Boise 7 N	59	19	Boise 7 N	59
20	Aberdeen Exp Station	57	20	Bonners Ferry	61
21	Malad City	***55***	21	Fort Hall 1 NNE	62
22	Pocatello Municipal Arpt	54	21	Salmon	62
22	Porthill	54	23	Garden Valley	***78***
22	Saint Maries 1 W	54	24	Rexburg Ricks College	***80***
25	American Falls 3 NW	52	25	Driggs	86

Rankings include 25 highest/lowest stations. If state has less than 25 stations, all stations are included. The period of record is 1980–2009. See User Guide for detailed explanation of data.

Significant Storm Events in Idaho: 2000 – 2009

Location or County	Date	Type	Mag.	Deaths	Injuries	Property Damage ($mil.)	Crop Damage ($mil.)
Bingham	02/14/00	Thunderstorm Wind	85 mph	0	2	2.5	0.0
Bingham	02/14/00	Tornado	F1	0	0	2.2	0.0
Southeast Idaho	01/21/02	Winter Storm	na	1	0	0.0	0.0
Southeast Idaho	02/07/02	Winter Storm	na	2	0	0.0	0.0
Teton County-Upper Snake Highlands	03/12/02	Avalanche	na	1	0	0.0	0.0
Fremont County-Upper Snake Highlands	03/22/02	Avalanche	na	1	0	0.0	0.0
Southeast Idaho	04/15/02	Heavy Snow	na	2	0	0.0	0.0
Southeast Idaho	04/23/02	High Wind	70 mph	0	0	4.5	0.0
Canyon	07/07/02	Lightning	na	1	2	0.0	0.0
Northern Panhandle	02/22/03	Avalanche	na	2	3	0.0	0.0
Lemhi	07/22/03	Wildfire	na	2	0	0.0	0.0
Northern Panhandle	03/10/04	Avalanche	na	1	0	0.0	0.0
Snake River Plain and Eastern Magic Valley	11/27/04	Heavy Snow	na	2	0	0.0	0.0
North and Central Idaho	01/15/05	Heavy Snow	na	2	0	0.0	0.0
Nez Perce	05/06/05	Flash Flood	na	0	0	1.0	0.0
Latah	05/06/05	Flash Flood	na	0	0	1.0	0.0
Nez Perce	05/08/05	Flash Flood	na	0	0	4.0	0.0
Bonner	11/07/06	Flood	na	0	0	2.0	0.0
Ada County-Upper Treasure Valley	08/25/08	Wildfire	na	1	0	5.0	0.0
Bingham	06/06/09	Hail	0.50 in.	0	0	1.0	0.0

Note: Deaths, injuries, and damages are date and location specific.

ILLINOIS

PHYSICAL FEATURES. Illinois lies midway between the Continental Divide and the Atlantic Ocean and some 500 miles north of the Gulf of Mexico. Its climate is typically continental with cold winters, warm summers, and frequent short period fluctuations in temperature, humidity, cloudiness, and wind direction.

The irregular shape of the State has a width of less than 200 miles at most points, but extends for 385 miles in the north-south direction. Except for a few low hills in the extreme south and a small unglaciated area in the extreme northwest, the terrain is flat. Differences in elevation have no significant influence on the climate. River drainage is mainly toward the Mississippi River, which forms the entire western boundary of the State. From north to south the principal rivers entering the Mississippi are the Rock, Illinois, Kaskaskia, and the Big Muddy. Approximately one-seventh of the State area drains southeastward into the Wabash and Ohio Rivers. Only a small area drains into Lake Michigan.

GENERAL CLIMATE. Without the protection of natural barriers, such as mountain ranges, Illinois experiences the full sweep of the winds which are constantly bringing in the climates of other areas. Southeast and easterly winds bring mild and wet weather; southerly winds are warm and showery; westerly winds are dry with moderate temperatures; and winds from the northwest and north are cool and dry. Winds are controlled by the storm systems and weather fronts which move eastward and northeastward through this area.

Storm systems move through the State most frequently during the winter and spring months and cause a maximum of cloudiness during those seasons. Summer-season storm systems tend to be weaker and to stay farther north, leaving Illinois with much sunshine interspersed with thunderstorm situations of comparatively short duration. The retreat of the sun in autumn is associated with variable periods of pleasant dry weather of the Indian summer variety. This season ends rather abruptly with the returning storminess which usually begins in November.

TEMPERATURE. Because Illinois extends so far in a north-south direction, the contrasts in winter temperature conditions are rather strong. The extreme north has frequent snow and temperatures drop to below zero several times each winter. The soil freezes to a depth of about three feet and occasionally remains snow-covered for weeks at a time. In the extreme south snow falls only occasionally and leaves after a few days, while temperatures drop to zero on an average of only about one day each winter. The soil freezes, but only to a depth of eight to 12 inches, with great variation in the duration of soil-frost periods. The north-south range in winter mean temperatures is approximately 14°F.

During the summer season the sun heats the entire State quite strongly and uniformly. The north-south range of mean temperatures in July is only about 6°F. The annual average of days with temperatures of 90°F. or higher is near 20 in the north and near 50 in the south and west-central. Summer also brings periods of uncomfortably hot and humid weather, which are most persistent in the south. In the north the heat is usually broken after a few days by the arrival of cool air from Canada, but this cooling does not always penetrate to the southern portions of the State.

PRECIPITATION. Latitude is the principal control for both temperature and precipitation, with the northern counties averaging cooler and drier than the south. Distance from the Gulf of Mexico and lower airmass temperatures both tend to reduce the amounts of precipitation in the northern portion. Annual precipitation is approximately one and one-half times as great in the extreme south as in the extreme north, but most of the excess in the southern portion falls during winter and early spring. Mean total precipitation for the four-month period of December through March ranges from near seven inches in the extreme northwest to more than 14 inches in the extreme southeast. Precipitation during the warm season is more uniform. Totals for the six-month period of April through September range from 21 to 24 inches throughout the State. The driest month is February. The wettest months are May and June.

Precipitation during fall, winter, and spring tends to fall uniformly over large areas. In contrast, summer rainfall occurs principally as brief showers affecting relatively small areas. The erratic occurrence of summer showers results in uneven distribution. The high rates of summer rainfall also cause runoff and soil erosion. Summer showers are usually accompanied by thunder and, sometimes, by hail or destructive windstorms.

Floods occur nearly every year in at least some part of the State. The spring and early summer flood season results from a tendency for heavy general rainfall at that time of the year. The extreme north frequently has late winter or early spring flooding with the breakup of river ice, especially if there is an appreciable snow cover which is taken off by rain. River stages tend to decline during late summer, but local flash floods in minor streams, due to heavy thunderstorm rains, are common throughout the warm season. The interior rivers in the central and south have flat beds and sluggish currents so that they rise slowly and remain in flood conditions for relatively long periods.

SNOWFALL. The annual average of snowfall ranges from near 30 inches in the extreme north to only 10 inches in the extreme south. In the extreme north the most likely form of winter precipitation is snow. In contrast, more than 90% of Cairo's winter precipitation falls as rain. In a large number of winter storm situations, only a slight change in the temperature pattern would suffice to change rain to snow or vice versa. For this reason, Illinois snowfall records show great variability. Snowfalls of one inch or more occur on an average of 10 to 12 days per year in the extreme north and decrease to three or four in the far south. The two northern divisions average about 50 days annually when the ground is covered with one inch or more of snow, and this average decreases to about 15 days in the two southern divisions.

STORMS. Heavy snows of four to six inches or more average one or two per year in the north and less frequently in the south. Strong winds will drift snow and make driving hazardous. Moderate to heavy ice storms average about once every four or five years and can be quite damaging. Thunderstorms average about 35 to 50 annually, but most are quite harmless. On occasion they provide the source for hail, damaging winds, and tornadoes. Hail falls on an average of two or three days annually in the same locality, but usually causes little damage.

More than 65 percent of Illinois tornadoes occur during the months of March, April, May, and June. This "tornado season" is marked by a rapid increase in activity during March, a peak in April and May, and a decline during June. Tornadoes have occurred during each of the twelve months of the year.

INFLUENCE OF LAKE MICHIGAN. Because prevailing winds are westerly and storm systems move from the same direction, the influence of the lake on Illinois weather is not large. When the wind blows from the lake toward the shore, which it does for approximately one-fourth of the time during spring and summer and for about one-eighth of the time during fall and winter, the result is a moderation of temperature. In addition to the general occurrence of onshore winds, there is the local "sea breeze" effect on summer afternoons which is usually observable in a narrow strip near the lake shore.

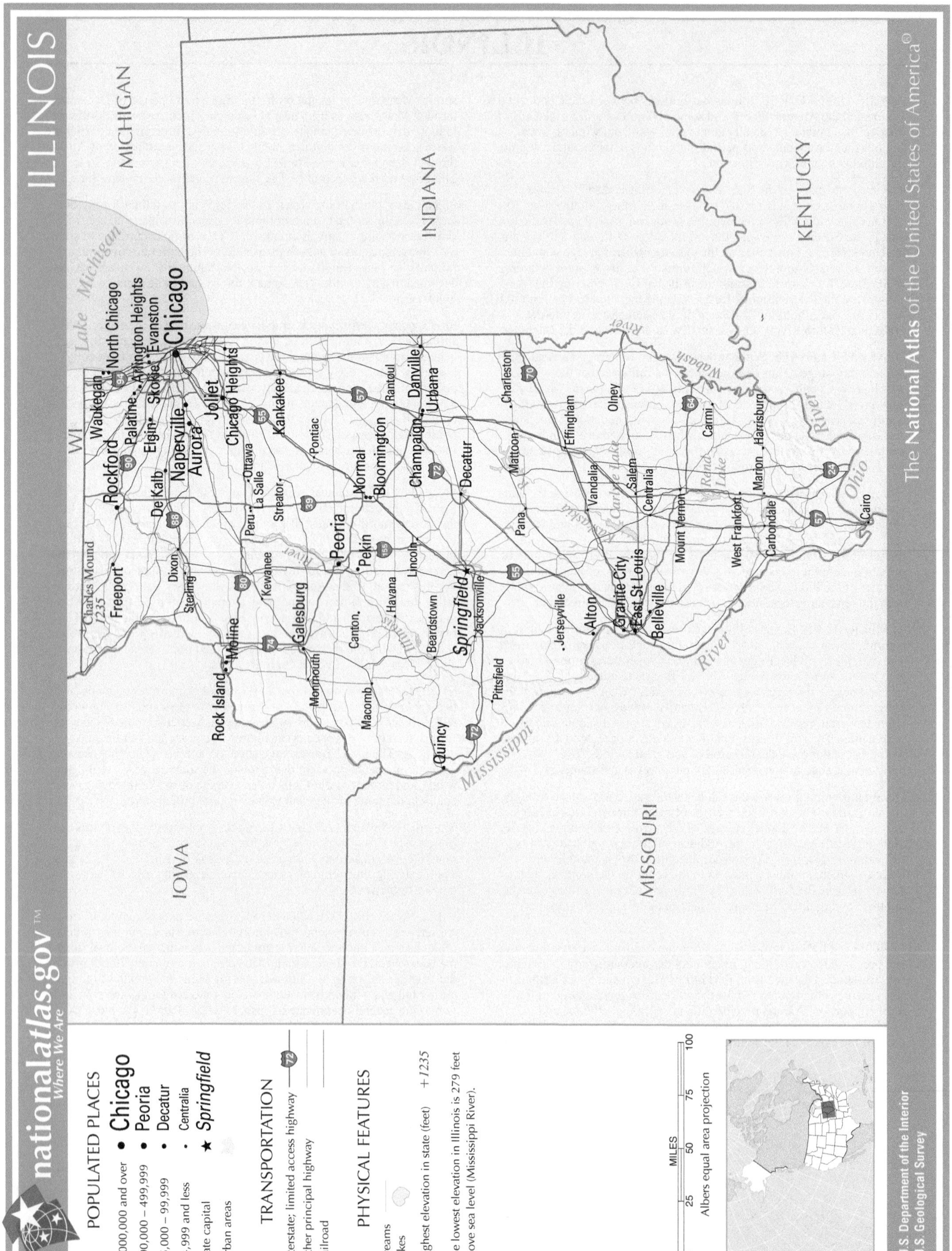
ILLINOIS
nationalatlas.gov™
Where We Are
POPULATED PLACES
1,000,000 and over • Chicago
100,000 – 499,999 • Peoria
25,000 – 99,999 • Decatur
24,999 and less • Centralia
State capital ★ Springfield
Urban areas
TRANSPORTATION
Interstate; limited access highway
Other principal highway
Railroad
PHYSICAL FEATURES
Streams
Lakes
Highest elevation in state (feet) +1235
The lowest elevation in Illinois is 279 feet above sea level (Mississippi River).
MILES
0 25 50 75 100
Albers equal area projection
U.S. Department of the Interior
U.S. Geological Survey
The National Atlas of the United States of America®
MICHIGAN
INDIANA
KENTUCKY
MISSOURI
IOWA
WI
Lake Michigan
Charles Mound 1235
Chicago
North Chicago
Arlington Heights
Evanston
Waukegan
Palatine
Skokie
Elgin
Naperville
Aurora
Joliet
Chicago Heights
Kankakee
Rockford
DeKalb
Freeport
Dixon
Sterling
Rock Island
Moline
Kewanee
Galesburg
Monmouth
Macomb
Quincy
Pittsfield
Ottawa
La Salle
Peru
Streator
Pontiac
Peoria
Pekin
Canton
Havana
Normal
Bloomington
Rantoul
Danville
Champaign
Urbana
Decatur
Lincoln
Beardstown
Springfield
Jacksonville
Charleston
Mattoon
Pana
Effingham
Olney
Vandalia
Salem
Centralia
Jerseyville
Alton
Granite City
East St Louis
Belleville
Mount Vernon
West Frankfort
Carbondale
Marion
Harrisburg
Carmi
Cairo
Carlyle Lake
Rend Lake
Illinois River
Mississippi River
Ohio River
Wabash River
Kaskaskia

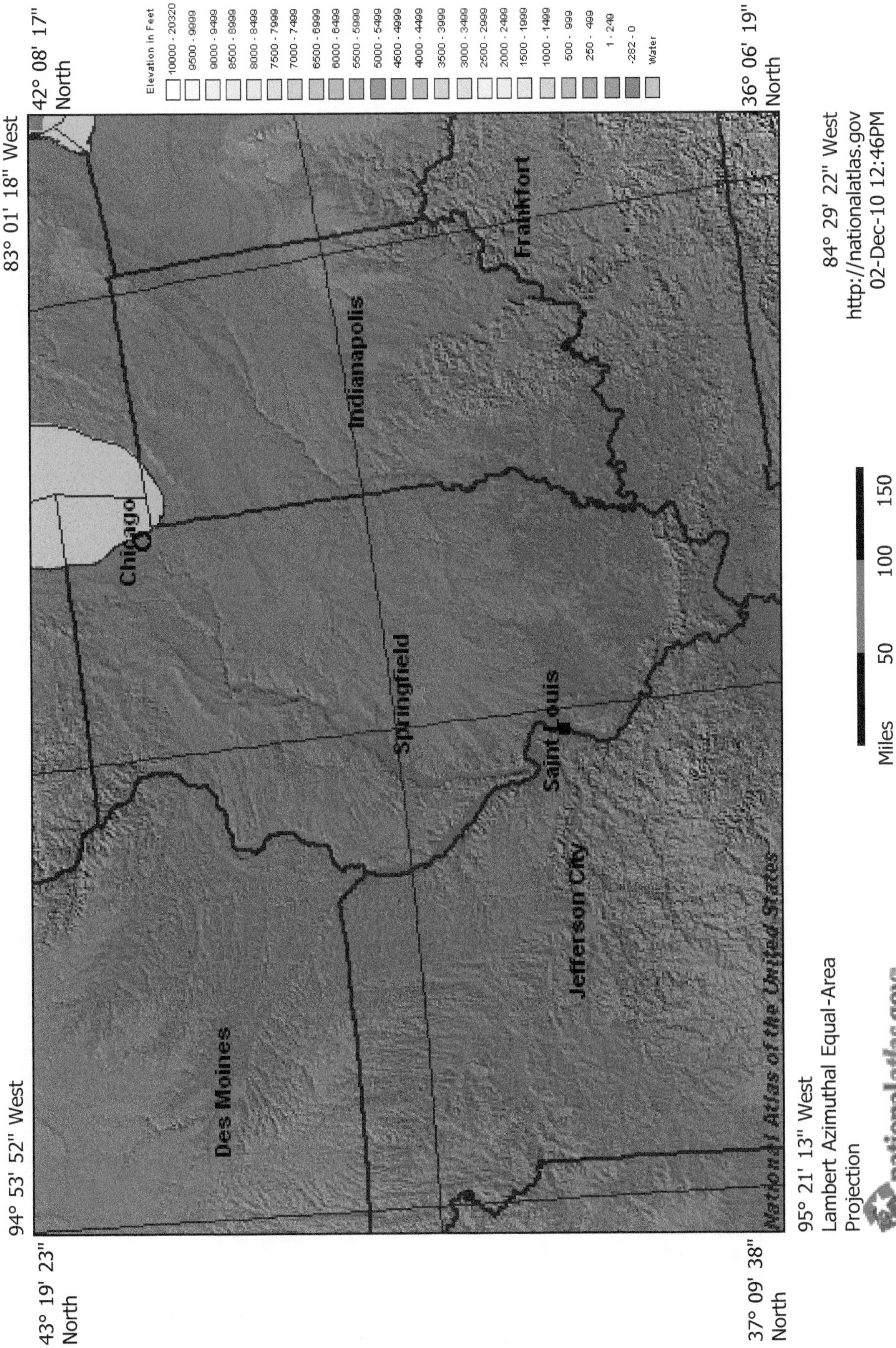
Elevation in Feet
10000 - 20320
9500 - 9999
9000 - 9499
8500 - 8999
8000 - 8499
7500 - 7999
7000 - 7499
6500 - 6999
6000 - 6499
5500 - 5999
5000 - 5499
4500 - 4999
4000 - 4499
3500 - 3999
3000 - 3499
2500 - 2999
2000 - 2499
1500 - 1999
1000 - 1499
500 - 999
250 - 499
1 - 249
-282 - 0
Water
42° 08' 17" North
83° 01' 18" West
36° 06' 19" North
84° 29' 22" West
http://nationalatlas.gov
02-Dec-10 12:46PM
43° 19' 23" North
94° 53' 52" West
37° 09' 38" North
95° 21' 13" West
Lambert Azimuthal Equal-Area
Projection
Chicago
Indianapolis
Frankfort
Springfield
Saint Louis
Jefferson City
Des Moines
National Atlas of the United States
Miles
50
100
150
nationalatlas.gov

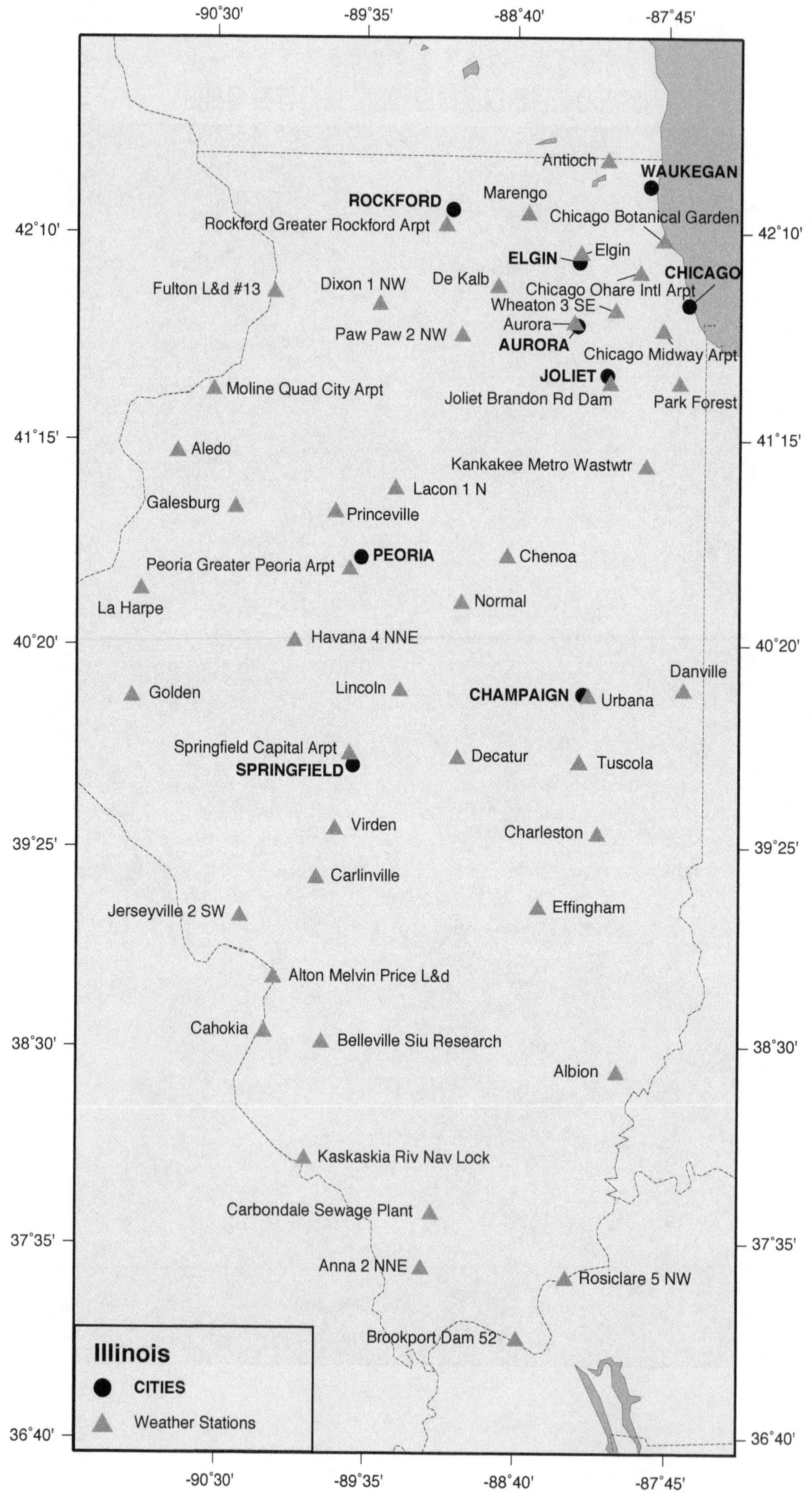
-90°30'
-89°35'
-88°40'
-87°45'
42°10'
41°15'
40°20'
39°25'
38°30'
37°35'
36°40'
Antioch
WAUKEGAN
Marengo
ROCKFORD
Rockford Greater Rockford Arpt
Chicago Botanical Garden
ELGIN
Elgin
CHICAGO
Fulton L&d #13
Dixon 1 NW
De Kalb
Chicago Ohare Intl Arpt
Wheaton 3 SE
Aurora
AURORA
Paw Paw 2 NW
Chicago Midway Arpt
JOLIET
Moline Quad City Arpt
Joliet Brandon Rd Dam
Park Forest
Aledo
Kankakee Metro Wastwtr
Lacon 1 N
Galesburg
Princeville
PEORIA
Chenoa
Peoria Greater Peoria Arpt
La Harpe
Normal
Havana 4 NNE
Danville
Golden
Lincoln
CHAMPAIGN
Urbana
Springfield Capital Arpt
SPRINGFIELD
Decatur
Tuscola
Virden
Charleston
Carlinville
Jerseyville 2 SW
Effingham
Alton Melvin Price L&d
Cahokia
Belleville Siu Research
Albion
Kaskaskia Riv Nav Lock
Carbondale Sewage Plant
Anna 2 NNE
Rosiclare 5 NW
Brookport Dam 52
Illinois
CITIES
Weather Stations

Illinois Weather Stations by County

County	Station Name
Adams	Golden
Champaign	Urbana
Coles	Charleston
Cook	Chicago Botanical Garden
	Chicago Midway Arpt
	Chicago Ohare Intl Arpt
	Park Forest
Dekalb	De Kalb
Douglas	Tuscola
Dupage	Wheaton 3 SE
Edwards	Albion
Effingham	Effingham
Hancock	La Harpe
Hardin	Rosiclare 5 NW
Jackson	Carbondale Sewage Plant
Jersey	Jerseyville 2 SW
Kane	Aurora
	Elgin
Kankakee	Kankakee Metro Wastwater
Knox	Galesburg
Lake	Antioch
Lee	Dixon 1 NW
	Paw Paw 2 NW
Logan	Lincoln
Macon	Decatur
Macoupin	Carlinville
	Virden
Madison	Alton Melvin Price L&D
Marshall	Lacon 1 N
Mason	Havana 4 NNE
Massac	Brookport Dam 52
Mchenry	Marengo
Mclean	Chenoa
	Normal
Mercer	Aledo
Peoria	Peoria Greater Peoria Arpt

County	Station Name
Peoria *(cont.)*	Princeville
Randolph	Kaskaskia River Nav Lock
Rock Island	Moline Quad City Arpt
Sangamon	Springfield Capital Arpt
St. Clair	Belleville Siu Research
	Cahokia
Union	Anna 2 NNE
Vermilion	Danville
Whiteside	Fulton L&D #13
Will	Joliet Brandon Rd Dam
Winnebago	Rockford Greater Rockford Arpt

See User Guide for station inclusion criteria.

Illinois Weather Stations by City

City	Station Name	Miles
Arlington Heights	Chicago Botanical Garden	10.5
	Chicago Ohare Intl Arpt	8.3
	Elgin	15.6
	Wheaton 3 SE	19.6
Aurora	Aurora	1.2
	Chicago Ohare Intl Arpt	24.9
	Elgin	21.3
	Joliet Brandon Rd Dam	20.5
	Wheaton 3 SE	12.5
Berwyn	Chicago Botanical Garden	19.9
	Chicago Ohare Intl Arpt	11.5
	Chicago Midway Arpt	7.8
	Park Forest	24.5
	Wheaton 3 SE	14.4
Bloomington	Chenoa	22.0
	Normal	2.9
Bolingbrook	Aurora	12.8
	Chicago Ohare Intl Arpt	21.3
	Chicago Midway Arpt	15.6
	Joliet Brandon Rd Dam	14.0
	Park Forest	24.9
	Wheaton 3 SE	8.0
Buffalo Grove	Antioch	23.4
	Chicago Botanical Garden	9.6
	Chicago Ohare Intl Arpt	12.7
	Elgin	17.6
	Wheaton 3 SE	24.5
Carol Stream	Aurora	14.1
	Chicago Botanical Garden	23.4
	Chicago Ohare Intl Arpt	12.1
	Chicago Midway Arpt	22.3
	Elgin	12.6
	Wheaton 3 SE	8.0
Champaign	Tuscola	21.5
	Urbana	1.6
Chicago	Chicago Botanical Garden	19.4
	Chicago Ohare Intl Arpt	14.6
	Chicago Midway Arpt	10.3
	Wheaton 3 SE	20.0
Cicero	Chicago Botanical Garden	19.8
	Chicago Ohare Intl Arpt	12.3
	Chicago Midway Arpt	8.0
	Park Forest	24.4
	Wheaton 3 SE	15.9
Crystal Lake	Antioch	21.3
	Elgin	11.1
	Marengo	13.5
DeKalb	De Kalb	1.2
	Marengo	23.2
	Paw Paw 2 NW	19.5
Decatur	Decatur	4.3

City	Station Name	Miles
Des Plaines	Chicago Botanical Garden	9.2
	Chicago Ohare Intl Arpt	3.6
	Chicago Midway Arpt	21.7
	Elgin	19.6
	Wheaton 3 SE	17.2
Downers Grove	Aurora	15.7
	Chicago Ohare Intl Arpt	14.5
	Chicago Midway Arpt	12.4
	Elgin	23.8
	Joliet Brandon Rd Dam	20.3
	Wheaton 3 SE	3.4
Elgin	Aurora	18.8
	Chicago Ohare Intl Arpt	19.4
	Elgin	2.0
	Marengo	21.7
	Wheaton 3 SE	19.1
Elmhurst	Aurora	21.1
	Chicago Botanical Garden	18.5
	Chicago Ohare Intl Arpt	6.4
	Chicago Midway Arpt	13.7
	Elgin	21.2
	Wheaton 3 SE	8.3
Evanston	Chicago Botanical Garden	7.8
	Chicago Ohare Intl Arpt	12.3
	Chicago Midway Arpt	22.0
	Wheaton 3 SE	24.9
Glenview	Chicago Botanical Garden	4.1
	Chicago Ohare Intl Arpt	8.3
	Chicago Midway Arpt	24.0
	Elgin	23.8
	Wheaton 3 SE	22.2
Hoffman Estates	Aurora	23.1
	Chicago Botanical Garden	17.5
	Chicago Ohare Intl Arpt	11.4
	Elgin	8.9
	Wheaton 3 SE	17.3
Joliet	Aurora	18.8
	Chicago Midway Arpt	22.1
	Joliet Brandon Rd Dam	2.8
	Park Forest	22.8
	Wheaton 3 SE	19.5
Lombard	Aurora	17.2
	Chicago Botanical Garden	21.5
	Chicago Ohare Intl Arpt	9.1
	Chicago Midway Arpt	15.3
	Elgin	19.2
	Wheaton 3 SE	4.7
Moline	Aledo	24.0
	Moline Quad City Arpt	2.0
	Clinton No 1, IA	24.4
	Le Claire L & D 14, IA	7.2
Mount Prospect	Chicago Botanical Garden	9.4
	Chicago Ohare Intl Arpt	5.5
	Chicago Midway Arpt	24.0

See User Guide for station inclusion criteria.

City	Station Name	Miles
Mt Prospect *(cont.)*	Elgin	17.6
	Wheaton 3 SE	18.1
Naperville	Aurora	8.4
	Chicago Ohare Intl Arpt	20.4
	Chicago Midway Arpt	19.2
	Elgin	23.0
	Joliet Brandon Rd Dam	17.3
	Wheaton 3 SE	6.6
Normal	Chenoa	20.7
	Normal	0.7
Oak Lawn	Chicago Ohare Intl Arpt	20.5
	Chicago Midway Arpt	2.1
	Joliet Brandon Rd Dam	23.3
	Park Forest	15.2
	Wheaton 3 SE	17.7
Oak Park	Chicago Botanical Garden	17.1
	Chicago Ohare Intl Arpt	9.4
	Chicago Midway Arpt	10.5
	Wheaton 3 SE	15.0
Orland Park	Chicago Midway Arpt	9.1
	Joliet Brandon Rd Dam	15.1
	Park Forest	11.5
	Wheaton 3 SE	18.1
Palatine	Chicago Botanical Garden	12.9
	Chicago Ohare Intl Arpt	11.5
	Elgin	13.3
	Wheaton 3 SE	21.3
Peoria	Lacon 1 N	23.9
	Peoria Greater Peoria Arpt	5.6
	Princeville	16.3
Rockford	Marengo	23.7
	Rockford Greater Rockford Arpt	5.6
	Beloit, WI	15.9
Schaumburg	Aurora	21.8
	Chicago Botanical Garden	17.0
	Chicago Ohare Intl Arpt	9.2
	Elgin	10.5
	Wheaton 3 SE	14.8
Skokie	Chicago Botanical Garden	7.1
	Chicago Ohare Intl Arpt	9.8
	Chicago Midway Arpt	21.1
	Wheaton 3 SE	22.6
Springfield	Springfield Capital Arpt	4.4
	Virden	20.8
Tinley Park	Chicago Midway Arpt	10.8
	Joliet Brandon Rd Dam	16.2
	Park Forest	8.3
	Wheaton 3 SE	21.3
Waukegan	Antioch	15.4
	Chicago Botanical Garden	16.7
	Kenosha, WI	13.8
	Racine, WI	23.2

City	Station Name	Miles
Wheaton	Aurora	12.5
	Chicago Ohare Intl Arpt	13.1
	Chicago Midway Arpt	18.6
	Elgin	17.2
	Joliet Brandon Rd Dam	24.6
	Wheaton 3 SE	3.4

Note: Miles is the distance between the geographic center of the city and the weather station.

Illinois Weather Stations by Elevation

Feet	Station Name
950	Paw Paw 2 NW
873	De Kalb
819	Marengo
785	Normal
771	Galesburg
763	Elgin
750	Antioch
743	Urbana
734	Princeville
725	Golden
720	Aledo
709	Chenoa
709	Park Forest
700	Dixon 1 NW
700	La Harpe
680	Charleston
680	Rockford Greater Rockford Arpt
680	Wheaton 3 SE
674	Virden
658	Chicago Ohare Intl Arpt
652	Tuscola
651	Peoria Greater Peoria Arpt
640	Aurora
640	Kankakee Metro Wastwater
629	Carlinville
629	Chicago Botanical Garden
629	Jerseyville 2 SW
620	Chicago Midway Arpt
620	Decatur
600	Anna 2 NNE
595	Effingham
591	Fulton L&D #13
591	Moline Quad City Arpt
585	Springfield Capital Arpt
583	Lincoln
558	Danville
542	Joliet Brandon Rd Dam
529	Albion
459	Havana 4 NNE
459	Lacon 1 N
450	Belleville Siu Research
430	Alton Melvin Price L&D
399	Cahokia
399	Rosiclare 5 NW
390	Carbondale Sewage Plant
379	Kaskaskia River Nav Lock
330	Brookport Dam 52

See User Guide for station inclusion criteria.

Chicago O'Hare Int'l Airport

Chicago is located along the southwest shore of Lake Michigan and occupies a plain which, for the most part, is only some tens of feet above the lake. Lake Michigan averages 579 feet above sea level. Natural water drainage over most of the city would be into Lake Michigan, and from areas west of the city is into the Mississippi River System. But actual drainage over most of the city is artificially channeled also into the Mississippi system.

Chicago is in a region of frequently changeable weather. The climate is predominately continental, ranging from relatively warm in summer to relatively cold in winter. In late autumn and winter however, air masses that are initially very cold often reach the city only after being tempered by passage over one or more of the lakes. Similarly, in late spring and summer, air masses reaching the city from the north, northeast, or east are cooler because of movement over the Great Lakes. Very low winter temperatures most often occur in air that flows southward to the west of Lake Superior before reaching the Chicago area. In summer the higher temperatures are with south or southwest flow and are therefore not influenced by the lakes, the only modifying effect being a local lake breeze.

During the warm season, when the lake is cold relative to land, there is frequently a lake breeze that reduces daytime temperature near the shore. When the breeze off the lake is light this effect usually reaches inland only a mile or two, but with stronger on-shore winds the whole city is cooled. On the other hand, temperatures at night are warmer near the lake.

At the O'Hare International Airport temperatures of 96 degrees or higher occur in about half the summers, while about half the winters have a minimum as low as -15 degrees. The average occurrence of the first temperature as low as 32 degrees in the fall is mid-October and the average occurrence of the last temperature as low as 32 degrees in the spring is late April.

Precipitation falls mostly from air that has passed over the Gulf of Mexico. But in winter there is sometimes snowfall, light inland but locally heavy near the lakeshore, with Lake Michigan as the principal moisture source. The effect of Lake Michigan, both on winter temperatures and lake-produced snowfall, is enhanced by non-freezing of much of the lake during the winter, even though areas and harbors are often ice-choked.

Summer thunderstorms are often locally heavy and variable, parts of the city may receive substantial rainfall and other parts none. Longer periods of continuous precipitation are mostly in autumn, winter, and spring.

Chicago O'Hare Int'l Airport *Cook County* Elevation: 658 ft. Latitude: 41° 59' N Longitude: 87° 55' W

	JAN	FEB	MAR	APR	MAY	JUN	JUL	AUG	SEP	OCT	NOV	DEC	YEAR
Mean Maximum Temp. (°F)	31.2	35.2	46.3	58.7	70.0	79.6	84.1	81.9	74.8	62.0	48.2	35.0	58.9
Mean Temp. (°F)	23.7	27.5	37.5	48.6	59.0	68.7	73.9	72.3	64.5	52.2	40.2	27.9	49.7
Mean Minimum Temp. (°F)	16.3	19.8	28.6	38.4	48.0	57.7	63.6	62.7	54.2	42.4	32.3	20.7	40.4
Extreme Maximum Temp. (°F)	65	72	88	91	92	104	104	101	99	88	75	71	104
Extreme Minimum Temp. (°F)	-27	-19	-7	7	27	37	45	42	29	17	6	-25	-27
Days Maximum Temp. ≥ 90°F	0	0	0	0	0	4	7	4	1	0	0	0	16
Days Maximum Temp. ≤ 32°F	16	11	4	0	0	0	0	0	0	0	2	12	45
Days Minimum Temp. ≤ 32°F	28	25	21	7	0	0	0	0	0	4	15	27	127
Days Minimum Temp. ≤ 0°F	4	2	0	0	0	0	0	0	0	0	0	2	8
Heating Degree Days (base 65°F)	1,272	1,054	848	495	224	48	4	8	102	399	737	1,144	6,335
Cooling Degree Days (base 65°F)	0	0	1	9	45	166	286	242	94	10	0	0	853
Mean Precipitation (in.)	1.72	1.77	2.51	3.39	3.62	3.37	3.52	5.12	3.30	3.19	3.10	2.29	36.90
Maximum Precipitation (in.)*	4.1	3.5	5.9	7.7	7.1	10.0	8.3	17.1	11.4	7.4	8.2	8.6	49.3
Minimum Precipitation (in.)*	0.1	0.1	0.6	1.0	0.3	0.9	1.2	0.5	trace	0.2	0.6	0.2	21.8
Extreme Maximum Daily Precip. (in.)	1.24	3.44	1.75	2.37	3.45	3.97	2.90	6.49	6.64	3.79	2.93	4.47	6.64
Days With ≥ 0.1" Precipitation	5	4	6	7	7	6	6	7	6	6	6	5	71
Days With ≥ 0.5" Precipitation	1	1	1	2	2	2	2	3	2	2	2	1	21
Days With ≥ 1.0" Precipitation	0	0	0	1	1	1	1	2	1	1	1	0	9
Mean Snowfall (in.)	11.4	8.6	5.9	1.4	trace	trace	trace	trace	trace	0.3	1.4	8.3	37.3
Maximum Snowfall (in.)*	34	26	25	11	2	0	0	0	0	7	10	35	75
Maximum 24-hr. Snowfall (in.)*	15	10	9	11	2	0	0	0	0	4	5	10	15
Maximum Snow Depth (in.)	18	15	12	6	trace	trace	trace	trace	trace	3	4	17	18
Days With ≥ 1.0" Snow Depth	17	11	4	1	0	0	0	0	0	0	1	9	43
Thunderstorm Days*	< 1	< 1	2	4	5	6	6	6	4	2	1	1	37
Foggy Days*	12	11	12	10	10	8	9	12	11	11	12	13	131
Predominant Sky Cover*	OVR	OVR	OVR	OVR	OVR	OVR	SCT	SCT	OVR	OVR	OVR	OVR	OVR
Mean Relative Humidity 6am (%)*	77	78	79	77	77	78	82	85	85	82	81	80	80
Mean Relative Humidity 3pm (%)*	66	63	59	53	51	52	54	55	55	53	62	68	58
Mean Dewpoint (°F)*	14	18	27	36	46	56	62	61	54	42	31	21	39
Prevailing Wind Direction*	W	W	W	NNE	NNE	SSW	SW	SSW	S	S	SSW	WNW	SSW
Prevailing Wind Speed (mph)*	12	10	12	13	12	10	9	9	9	10	13	12	10
Maximum Wind Gust (mph)*	58	54	84	69	58	63	76	64	58	58	62	62	84

Note: (*) Period of record is 1958-1995

Moline Quad City Airport

The locality is in the heart of the Corn Belt. Agricultural crops include many important staple products in addition to corn. Cattle, hogs, horses, and poultry produced in Iowa and Illinois rank high in the nation. Close to the Mississippi River there is large scale truck gardening and considerable dairying. Field production of grains and livestock attains greater development farther away from the large streams, where the countryside is rolling prairie. Damaging droughts are not common. This, together with the variety of agricultural products, has led to designating the section as the Bread Basket of America.

The climate is favorable for many industries as evidenced by the large number and variety of manufacturing and other enterprises which have located and developed in the community. Among these are some of the largest producers of agricultural machinery in the world.

This area has a temperate continental climate, with a wide temperature range throughout the year. There are some intensely hot, unusually humid, periods in summer and severely cold periods in winter. Maxima of 90 degrees or more have occurred in summer as frequently as 55 days and zero or lower readings have occurred during every winter.

Freezing temperatures have occurred as late in spring as late May and as early in autumn as late September. Precipitation is usually well distributed throughout the year with the greatest amounts falling during the 177-day average crop growing season. Substantial weather changes frequently occur at three or four day intervals, as a direct result of proximity to some of the most important storm tracks.

Moline Quad City Airport *Rock Island County* Elevation: 591 ft. Latitude: 41° 28' N Longitude: 90° 31' W

	JAN	FEB	MAR	APR	MAY	JUN	JUL	AUG	SEP	OCT	NOV	DEC	YEAR
Mean Maximum Temp. (°F)	31.4	35.9	48.7	62.2	73.2	82.4	85.9	83.7	76.8	63.7	49.1	34.8	60.6
Mean Temp. (°F)	23.2	27.4	38.9	51.0	61.7	71.2	75.3	73.2	65.2	52.7	40.1	26.9	50.6
Mean Minimum Temp. (°F)	14.8	18.9	29.1	39.8	50.2	60.0	64.7	62.7	53.5	41.7	31.1	19.0	40.5
Extreme Maximum Temp. (°F)	69	71	88	93	95	104	103	103	98	95	80	71	104
Extreme Minimum Temp. (°F)	-29	-28	-9	7	25	39	48	40	30	16	4	-24	-29
Days Maximum Temp. ≥ 90°F	0	0	0	0	1	5	9	6	2	0	0	0	23
Days Maximum Temp. ≤ 32°F	16	11	3	0	0	0	0	0	0	0	2	11	43
Days Minimum Temp. ≤ 32°F	29	24	20	7	0	0	0	0	0	6	17	27	130
Days Minimum Temp. ≤ 0°F	5	3	0	0	0	0	0	0	0	0	0	3	11
Heating Degree Days (base 65°F)	1,291	1,056	803	427	159	19	1	7	94	387	741	1,175	6,160
Cooling Degree Days (base 65°F)	0	0	2	14	63	213	328	268	106	14	0	0	1,008
Mean Precipitation (in.)	1.46	1.62	2.82	3.53	4.29	4.37	4.22	4.63	3.04	2.95	2.54	2.21	37.68
Maximum Precipitation (in.)*	4.4	2.8	7.4	11.3	11.4	13.2	11.8	15.2	14.2	8.5	6.8	5.0	56.4
Minimum Precipitation (in.)*	0.3	0.2	0.3	0.7	0.3	1.0	0.4	0.3	trace	trace	0.5	0.3	20.2
Extreme Maximum Daily Precip. (in.)	1.51	1.30	2.16	2.18	2.92	3.71	3.56	3.55	4.26	4.14	2.04	3.11	4.26
Days With ≥ 0.1" Precipitation	4	4	6	7	7	7	6	7	5	5	5	5	68
Days With ≥ 0.5" Precipitation	1	1	2	3	3	3	3	3	2	2	2	1	26
Days With ≥ 1.0" Precipitation	0	0	1	1	1	1	1	2	1	1	0	0	9
Mean Snowfall (in.)	9.2	6.7	4.1	1.2	trace	trace	trace	0.0	trace	0.1	1.2	8.8	31.3
Maximum Snowfall (in.)*	27	21	20	13	trace	0	0	0	0	7	16	22	63
Maximum 24-hr. Snowfall (in.)*	16	9	10	8	trace	0	0	0	0	7	8	9	16
Maximum Snow Depth (in.)	na	na	na	na	na	na	na	na	na	na	na	na	na
Days With ≥ 1.0" Snow Depth	na	na	na	na	na	na	na	na	na	na	na	na	na
Thunderstorm Days*	< 1	< 1	2	5	7	8	8	7	5	2	1	< 1	45
Foggy Days*	12	11	13	10	11	9	12	15	14	13	12	13	145
Predominant Sky Cover*	OVR	OVR	OVR	OVR	OVR	OVR	CLR	CLR	CLR	CLR	OVR	OVR	OVR
Mean Relative Humidity 6am (%)*	76	78	79	78	79	81	85	89	87	82	80	79	81
Mean Relative Humidity 3pm (%)*	66	63	57	50	49	50	54	55	52	49	59	67	56
Mean Dewpoint (°F)*	13	18	27	37	48	59	64	63	54	42	30	19	40
Prevailing Wind Direction*	WNW	WNW	WNW	WNW	S	S	S	S	S	S	WNW	WNW	WNW
Prevailing Wind Speed (mph)*	14	14	14	15	12	10	9	9	10	12	14	14	13
Maximum Wind Gust (mph)*	59	54	69	81	66	79	66	81	59	61	60	69	81

Note: (*) Period of record is 1943-1995

 The period of record for National Weather Service station data is 1980 – 2009 except where noted. See User Guide for detailed explanation of data.

Greater Peoria Airport

The airport station is situated on a rather level tableland surrounded by well-drained and gently rolling terrain. It is set back a mile from the rim of the Illinois River Valley and is almost 200 feet above the river bed. Exposures of all instruments are good. The climate of this area is typically continental as shown by its changeable weather and the wide range of temperature extremes.

June and September are usually the most pleasant months of the year. Then during October or the first of November, Indian Summer is often experienced with an extended period of warm, dry weather.

Precipitation is normally heaviest during the growing season and lowest during midwinter.

The earliest snowfalls have occurred in September and the latest in the spring have occurred as late as May. Heavy snowfalls have rarely exceeded 20 inches.

Based on the 1951-1980 period, the average first occurrence of 32 degrees Fahrenheit in the fall is October 20 and the average last occurrence in the spring is April 24.

Greater Peoria Airport *Peoria County* Elevation: 651 ft. Latitude: 40° 40' N Longitude: 89° 41' W

	JAN	FEB	MAR	APR	MAY	JUN	JUL	AUG	SEP	OCT	NOV	DEC	YEAR
Mean Maximum Temp. (°F)	32.9	37.6	50.0	62.7	73.2	82.1	85.6	83.8	77.1	64.2	50.2	36.3	61.3
Mean Temp. (°F)	25.1	29.3	40.4	52.0	62.4	71.6	75.6	73.8	66.2	53.8	41.5	28.8	51.7
Mean Minimum Temp. (°F)	17.1	20.9	30.7	41.2	51.5	61.1	65.5	63.8	55.2	43.3	32.8	21.2	42.0
Extreme Maximum Temp. (°F)	70	71	86	92	94	105	104	103	97	93	80	71	105
Extreme Minimum Temp. (°F)	-22	-19	-4	14	28	39	50	41	29	21	5	-23	-23
Days Maximum Temp. ≥ 90°F	0	0	0	0	1	5	9	6	2	0	0	0	23
Days Maximum Temp. ≤ 32°F	15	9	3	0	0	0	0	0	0	0	2	10	39
Days Minimum Temp. ≤ 32°F	28	24	18	5	0	0	0	0	0	4	15	26	120
Days Minimum Temp. ≤ 0°F	4	2	0	0	0	0	0	0	0	0	0	2	8
Heating Degree Days (base 65°F)	1,232	1,004	758	399	142	17	1	5	80	356	698	1,116	5,808
Cooling Degree Days (base 65°F)	0	0	2	14	69	222	336	285	121	15	0	0	1,064
Mean Precipitation (in.)	1.74	1.76	2.78	3.61	4.13	3.61	3.74	3.36	3.12	2.87	3.09	2.36	36.17
Maximum Precipitation (in.)*	8.1	4.9	6.9	8.7	11.5	11.7	10.1	8.6	13.1	10.5	7.6	6.3	55.3
Minimum Precipitation (in.)*	0.1	0.1	0.4	0.7	0.5	0.4	0.3	0.3	trace	trace	0.1	0.3	22.2
Extreme Maximum Daily Precip. (in.)	2.35	1.81	1.92	3.05	2.99	4.42	3.36	2.63	3.05	2.68	4.26	2.34	4.42
Days With ≥ 0.1" Precipitation	4	4	6	7	8	6	6	6	5	6	6	5	69
Days With ≥ 0.5" Precipitation	1	1	2	2	2	2	2	3	2	2	2	1	22
Days With ≥ 1.0" Precipitation	0	0	1	1	1	1	1	1	1	0	1	1	9
Mean Snowfall (in.)	6.8	5.9	2.9	0.9	trace	trace	trace	0.0	trace	trace	1.3	6.5	24.3
Maximum Snowfall (in.)*	25	15	18	13	trace	0	0	0	1	3	11	22	52
Maximum 24-hr. Snowfall (in.)*	12	9	9	6	trace	0	0	0	1	3	8	7	12
Maximum Snow Depth (in.)	16	10	7	10	trace	trace	trace	0	trace	trace	4	13	16
Days With ≥ 1.0" Snow Depth	14	9	3	0	0	0	0	0	0	0	1	9	36
Thunderstorm Days*	< 1	1	3	5	7	9	8	7	5	2	1	1	49
Foggy Days*	11	10	9	7	7	6	7	9	9	10	10	12	107
Predominant Sky Cover*	OVR	OVR	OVR	OVR	OVR	OVR	SCT	CLR	CLR	OVR	OVR	OVR	OVR
Mean Relative Humidity 6am (%)*	80	81	81	78	80	82	86	89	87	84	83	83	83
Mean Relative Humidity 3pm (%)*	67	64	58	52	52	52	55	56	52	52	61	69	57
Mean Dewpoint (°F)*	16	20	29	38	49	59	64	63	54	43	32	22	41
Prevailing Wind Direction*	S	S	S	S	S	S	S	S	S	S	S	S	S
Prevailing Wind Speed (mph)*	12	12	13	12	10	10	9	8	9	10	12	12	10
Maximum Wind Gust (mph)*	54	53	68	69	61	75	85	54	75	48	62	59	85

Note: (*) Period of record is 1948-1995

Rockford Greater Rockford Arpt.

The climate of Rockford is characterized by hot summers and cold winters.

When winter northeasterly winds blow across Lake Michigan, cloudiness often is increased in the Rockford area, and temperatures are somewhat higher than those westward around the Mississippi River. Conversely, in summer, the cooling effect of Lake Michigan sometimes is felt as far westward as Rockford.

While 34 percent of the precipitation occurs in the three summer months of June to August, and 64 percent in the six months, April to September, no month averages less than four percent of the annual total.

Though summers may be described as hot, seldom does oppressive heat prevail for extended periods. In general, the summers are pleasant.

Winters are cold. Snow cover is adequate for diversified winter sports, and usually is continuous from late December through February.

Based on the 1951-1980 period, the average first occurrence of 32 degrees Fahrenheit in the fall is October 11 and the average last occurrence in the spring is April 29.

Rockford Greater Rockford Arpt. *Winnebago County* Elevation: 680 ft. Latitude: 42° 12' N Longitude: 89° 07' W

	JAN	FEB	MAR	APR	MAY	JUN	JUL	AUG	SEP	OCT	NOV	DEC	YEAR
Mean Maximum Temp. (°F)	28.9	33.5	45.8	59.8	71.2	80.4	83.9	81.7	74.7	61.7	46.9	32.7	58.4
Mean Temp. (°F)	21.0	25.3	36.3	48.7	59.6	69.3	73.3	71.4	63.4	50.9	38.3	25.1	48.6
Mean Minimum Temp. (°F)	13.0	17.0	26.8	37.5	48.0	58.0	62.7	61.0	52.0	40.1	29.8	17.6	38.6
Extreme Maximum Temp. (°F)	63	70	85	91	93	101	102	104	95	90	76	67	104
Extreme Minimum Temp. (°F)	-27	-24	-11	5	26	37	47	41	27	18	1	-24	-27
Days Maximum Temp. ≥ 90°F	0	0	0	0	0	4	6	4	1	0	0	0	15
Days Maximum Temp. ≤ 32°F	19	13	4	0	0	0	0	0	0	0	3	14	53
Days Minimum Temp. ≤ 32°F	30	26	23	8	1	0	0	0	0	7	19	28	142
Days Minimum Temp. ≤ 0°F	6	4	0	0	0	0	0	0	0	0	0	4	14
Heating Degree Days (base 65°F)	1,358	1,117	882	491	206	34	3	12	120	437	793	1,229	6,682
Cooling Degree Days (base 65°F)	0	0	1	8	45	169	268	217	79	8	0	0	795
Mean Precipitation (in.)	1.37	1.43	2.30	3.34	3.90	4.65	3.75	4.70	3.49	2.61	2.55	2.01	36.10
Maximum Precipitation (in.)*	4.7	3.0	5.6	9.9	7.0	11.8	11.8	13.5	10.7	8.3	5.5	5.0	56.5
Minimum Precipitation (in.)*	0.2	trace	0.6	1.0	0.5	0.5	0.8	0.7	0	trace	0.4	0.4	23.3
Extreme Maximum Daily Precip. (in.)	1.34	1.39	2.15	1.71	4.77	4.20	3.87	5.70	3.26	2.18	2.06	2.00	5.70
Days With ≥ 0.1" Precipitation	4	4	5	6	7	7	6	7	5	5	5	5	66
Days With ≥ 0.5" Precipitation	1	1	1	2	2	3	3	3	2	2	2	1	23
Days With ≥ 1.0" Precipitation	0	0	0	1	1	1	1	1	1	0	0	0	6
Mean Snowfall (in.)	10.3	7.6	5.0	1.0	trace	trace	trace	trace	trace	0.1	1.7	10.8	36.5
Maximum Snowfall (in.)*	26	30	23	8	1	0	0	0	0	2	15	25	59
Maximum 24-hr. Snowfall (in.)*	10	8	10	6	1	0	0	0	0	2	7	11	11
Maximum Snow Depth (in.)	19	14	***9***	5	***trace***	***trace***	***trace***	trace	trace	***trace***	***7***	***18***	***19***
Days With ≥ 1.0" Snow Depth	21	15	***5***	1	***0***	***0***	***0***	0	0	***0***	***1***	***15***	***58***
Thunderstorm Days*	< 1	< 1	2	4	5	8	8	6	5	2	1	< 1	41
Foggy Days*	12	11	12	11	11	8	12	16	14	12	13	14	146
Predominant Sky Cover*	OVR	OVR	OVR	OVR	OVR	OVR	OVR	OVR	OVR	OVR	OVR	OVR	OVR
Mean Relative Humidity 6am (%)*	80	81	82	80	80	81	86	90	90	86	83	83	84
Mean Relative Humidity 3pm (%)*	69	64	60	51	50	51	53	56	54	53	63	70	58
Mean Dewpoint (°F)*	13	17	26	36	47	57	62	62	53	41	30	19	39
Prevailing Wind Direction*	WNW	WNW	WNW	ENE	S	S	S	S	S	S	S	WNW	S
Prevailing Wind Speed (mph)*	13	13	13	13	10	9	8	8	8	9	10	13	10
Maximum Wind Gust (mph)*	56	54	54	64	81	67	79	67	58	59	59	62	81

Note: (*) Period of record is 1951-1995

The period of record for National Weather Service station data is 1980 – 2009 except where noted. See User Guide for detailed explanation of data.

Springfield Capital Airport

The location of Springfield near the center of North America gives it a typical continental climate with warm summers and fairly cold winters. The surrounding country is nearly level. There are no large hills in the vicinity, but rolling terrain is found near the Sangamon River and Spring Creek.

Monthly temperatures range from the upper 20s for January to the upper 70s for July. Considerable variation may take place within the seasons. Temperatures of 70 degrees or higher may occur in winter and temperatures near 50 degrees are sometimes recorded during the summer months.

There are no wet and dry seasons. Monthly precipitation ranges from a little over four inches in May and June to about two inches in January. There is some variation in rainfall totals from year to year. Thunderstorms are common during hot weather, and these are sometimes locally severe with brief but heavy showers. The average year has about fifty thunderstorms of which two-thirds occur during the months of May through August. Damaging hail accompanies only a few of the thunderstorms and the areas affected are usually small.

Sunshine is particularly abundant during the summer months when days are long and not very cloudy. January is the cloudiest month, with only about a third as much sunshine as July or August. March is the windiest month, and August the month with the least wind. Velocities of more than 40 mph are not unusual for brief periods in most months of the year. The prevailing wind direction is southerly during most of the year with northwesterly winds during the late fall and early spring months.

An overall description of the climate of Springfield would be one indicating pleasant conditions with sharp seasonal changes, but no extended periods of severely cold weather. Summer weather is often uncomfortably warm and humid.

Based on the 1951-1980 period, the average first occurrence of 32 degrees Fahrenheit in the fall is October 19 and the average last occurrence in the spring is April 17.

Springfield Capital Airport *Sangamon County* Elevation: 585 ft. Latitude: 39° 51' N Longitude: 89° 41' W

	JAN	FEB	MAR	APR	MAY	JUN	JUL	AUG	SEP	OCT	NOV	DEC	YEAR
Mean Maximum Temp. (°F)	35.1	39.7	51.7	64.2	74.8	83.1	86.3	85.0	78.9	66.2	52.1	38.5	63.0
Mean Temp. (°F)	27.1	31.3	42.0	53.4	63.8	72.6	76.1	74.5	66.9	55.2	43.2	30.7	53.1
Mean Minimum Temp. (°F)	19.2	22.8	32.3	42.5	52.9	62.0	65.8	63.9	54.9	44.1	34.2	22.9	43.1
Extreme Maximum Temp. (°F)	69	74	87	90	94	101	102	102	101	93	81	74	102
Extreme Minimum Temp. (°F)	-21	-19	-2	19	30	39	49	43	32	19	1	-21	-21
Days Maximum Temp. ≥ 90°F	0	0	0	0	1	6	10	7	3	0	0	0	27
Days Maximum Temp. ≤ 32°F	13	8	2	0	0	0	0	0	0	0	1	9	33
Days Minimum Temp. ≤ 32°F	27	22	16	4	0	0	0	0	0	4	14	25	112
Days Minimum Temp. ≤ 0°F	3	2	0	0	0	0	0	0	0	0	0	2	7
Heating Degree Days (base 65°F)	1,167	947	708	362	118	14	0	4	72	322	648	1,055	5,417
Cooling Degree Days (base 65°F)	0	0	3	20	89	248	351	304	137	24	1	0	1,177
Mean Precipitation (in.)	1.80	1.78	2.69	3.46	4.02	4.30	3.82	3.22	2.80	3.16	3.16	2.53	36.74
Maximum Precipitation (in.)*	6.2	4.9	7.9	9.9	10.6	10.8	10.8	8.4	15.2	13.4	6.9	8.9	54.5
Minimum Precipitation (in.)*	trace	0.3	0.2	0.7	0.3	0.2	0.3	0.1	trace	0.1	trace	0.1	22.8
Extreme Maximum Daily Precip. (in.)	1.68	2.37	2.18	2.95	3.54	4.71	4.33	4.40	4.23	3.24	2.05	4.70	4.71
Days With ≥ 0.1" Precipitation	4	4	6	7	7	6	6	5	5	6	6	5	67
Days With ≥ 0.5" Precipitation	1	1	2	2	2	3	3	2	2	2	2	1	23
Days With ≥ 1.0" Precipitation	0	0	1	1	1	1	1	1	1	1	1	1	10
Mean Snowfall (in.)	6.3	5.6	2.7	0.5	trace	0.0	trace	0.0	0.0	trace	0.8	5.4	21.3
Maximum Snowfall (in.)*	21	18	23	8	1	0	0	0	0	3	9	23	48
Maximum 24-hr. Snowfall (in.)*	8	10	9	6	1	0	0	0	0	3	8	11	11
Maximum Snow Depth (in.)	12	11	6	4	trace	0	trace	0	0	trace	4	9	12
Days With ≥ 1.0" Snow Depth	10	8	2	0	0	0	0	0	0	0	0	7	27
Thunderstorm Days*	< 1	1	3	5	7	9	8	7	5	2	2	< 1	49
Foggy Days*	9	8	8	6	6	5	6	9	8	8	8	10	91
Predominant Sky Cover*	OVR	OVR	OVR	OVR	OVR	OVR	SCT	CLR	CLR	CLR	OVR	OVR	OVR
Mean Relative Humidity 6am (%)*	80	81	81	79	81	82	85	89	87	83	82	82	83
Mean Relative Humidity 3pm (%)*	67	65	59	52	51	51	54	56	50	50	60	69	57
Mean Dewpoint (°F)*	18	22	31	41	51	61	65	64	56	44	33	24	43
Prevailing Wind Direction*	S	S	S	S	S	S	S	S	S	S	S	S	S
Prevailing Wind Speed (mph)*	15	14	15	15	13	12	9	9	10	13	14	15	13
Maximum Wind Gust (mph)*	55	53	71	63	67	59	60	69	61	53	76	73	76

Note: (*) Period of record is 1948-1995

Albion *Edwards County* Elevation: 529 ft. Latitude: 38° 23' N Longitude: 88° 03' W

	JAN	FEB	MAR	APR	MAY	JUN	JUL	AUG	SEP	OCT	NOV	DEC	YEAR
Mean Maximum Temp. (°F)	39.4	45.0	54.8	67.3	76.9	85.5	89.9	88.5	82.0	70.6	55.3	42.6	66.5
Mean Temp. (°F)	31.5	36.3	45.1	56.5	66.4	75.1	79.2	77.6	70.4	59.1	46.2	34.5	56.5
Mean Minimum Temp. (°F)	23.9	27.3	35.3	45.7	55.8	64.6	68.4	66.5	58.8	47.5	37.2	26.4	46.5
Extreme Maximum Temp. (°F)	73	75	85	89	97	101	105	104	100	93	81	75	105
Extreme Minimum Temp. (°F)	-20	-11	2	23	32	42	50	47	31	24	11	-18	-20
Days Maximum Temp. ≥ 90°F	0	0	0	0	2	10	16	13	6	0	0	0	47
Days Maximum Temp. ≤ 32°F	7	5	1	0	0	0	0	0	0	0	0	6	19
Days Minimum Temp. ≤ 32°F	23	18	12	2	0	0	0	0	0	1	10	21	87
Days Minimum Temp. ≤ 0°F	1	0	0	0	0	0	0	0	0	0	0	1	2
Heating Degree Days (base 65°F)	1,032	806	612	280	76	6	0	1	36	218	559	937	4,563
Cooling Degree Days (base 65°F)	0	0	4	32	127	315	447	397	206	42	2	0	1,572
Mean Precipitation (in.)	2.62	2.47	4.03	4.86	5.43	3.66	3.55	3.17	2.76	3.66	4.07	3.04	43.32
Extreme Maximum Daily Precip. (in.)	2.90	na	3.80	4.50	na	na	4.20	6.80	4.50	3.20	4.20	4.90	na
Days With ≥ 0.1" Precipitation	4	4	5	7	7	6	4	4	4	5	5	5	60
Days With ≥ 0.5" Precipitation	2	2	3	3	4	2	2	2	2	3	3	2	30
Days With ≥ 1.0" Precipitation	1	1	1	1	1	1	1	1	1	1	1	1	12
Mean Snowfall (in.)	2.0	2.4	1.0	0.0	0.0	0.0	0.0	0.0	0.0	0.1	trace	2.6	8.1
Maximum Snow Depth (in.)	6	10	9	0	0	0	0	0	0	1	trace	7	10
Days With ≥ 1.0" Snow Depth	2	2	0	0	0	0	0	0	0	0	0	0	4

Aledo *Mercer County* Elevation: 720 ft. Latitude: 41° 12' N Longitude: 90° 45' W

	JAN	FEB	MAR	APR	MAY	JUN	JUL	AUG	SEP	OCT	NOV	DEC	YEAR
Mean Maximum Temp. (°F)	31.1	35.6	48.3	62.0	72.5	81.1	84.7	83.0	76.0	63.4	48.7	34.4	60.0
Mean Temp. (°F)	22.8	26.9	38.2	50.5	61.1	70.3	73.9	72.6	64.5	52.5	39.6	26.5	49.9
Mean Minimum Temp. (°F)	14.5	18.2	28.1	39.0	49.8	59.5	63.3	62.1	53.0	41.6	30.5	18.5	39.8
Extreme Maximum Temp. (°F)	69	68	87	91	93	103	103	102	97	91	78	70	103
Extreme Minimum Temp. (°F)	-25	-28	-8	10	23	42	49	45	30	18	0	-20	-28
Days Maximum Temp. ≥ 90°F	0	0	0	0	0	3	7	5	1	0	0	0	16
Days Maximum Temp. ≤ 32°F	16	11	4	0	0	0	0	0	0	0	2	12	45
Days Minimum Temp. ≤ 32°F	29	25	21	7	0	0	0	0	0	5	18	28	133
Days Minimum Temp. ≤ 0°F	5	3	0	0	0	0	0	0	0	0	0	3	11
Heating Degree Days (base 65°F)	1,300	1,072	825	440	167	23	2	7	102	390	755	1,189	6,272
Cooling Degree Days (base 65°F)	0	0	1	11	54	190	285	249	94	10	0	0	894
Mean Precipitation (in.)	1.35	1.53	2.44	3.70	4.34	4.47	3.95	4.53	3.28	2.98	2.34	2.01	36.92
Extreme Maximum Daily Precip. (in.)	2.10	1.75	1.78	1.72	4.80	3.12	3.10	6.27	4.15	3.40	1.60	2.70	6.27
Days With ≥ 0.1" Precipitation	4	4	5	7	8	7	6	7	5	6	5	5	69
Days With ≥ 0.5" Precipitation	1	1	2	3	3	3	3	3	2	2	1	1	25
Days With ≥ 1.0" Precipitation	0	0	1	1	1	1	1	1	1	1	0	0	8
Mean Snowfall (in.)	6.8	4.5	2.7	0.8	trace	0.0	0.0	0.0	0.0	0.1	0.6	5.2	20.7
Maximum Snow Depth (in.)	15	na	4	4	trace	0	0	0	0	trace	2	10	na
Days With ≥ 1.0" Snow Depth	5	3	1	0	0	0	0	0	0	0	0	3	12

Alton Melvin Price L&D *Madison County* Elevation: 430 ft. Latitude: 38° 49' N Longitude: 90° 09' W

	JAN	FEB	MAR	APR	MAY	JUN	JUL	AUG	SEP	OCT	NOV	DEC	YEAR
Mean Maximum Temp. (°F)	37.6	42.4	52.7	64.7	74.5	83.5	87.6	86.5	79.5	67.3	54.4	41.6	64.4
Mean Temp. (°F)	29.7	33.8	43.7	55.1	65.2	74.4	78.5	77.1	69.6	57.3	45.7	34.0	55.3
Mean Minimum Temp. (°F)	21.9	25.1	34.6	45.5	55.7	65.1	69.3	67.6	59.5	47.3	37.0	26.4	46.3
Extreme Maximum Temp. (°F)	71	76	85	90	93	98	106	103	98	97	81	73	106
Extreme Minimum Temp. (°F)	-16	-15	3	20	37	44	52	46	38	25	9	-16	-16
Days Maximum Temp. ≥ 90°F	0	0	0	0	0	6	12	10	3	0	0	0	31
Days Maximum Temp. ≤ 32°F	10	6	1	0	0	0	0	0	0	0	1	6	24
Days Minimum Temp. ≤ 32°F	26	21	13	2	0	0	0	0	0	1	9	21	93
Days Minimum Temp. ≤ 0°F	1	1	0	0	0	0	0	0	0	0	0	1	3
Heating Degree Days (base 65°F)	1,086	877	658	313	87	8	0	2	40	263	572	951	4,857
Cooling Degree Days (base 65°F)	0	0	4	22	99	296	425	382	183	25	1	0	1,437
Mean Precipitation (in.)	2.44	2.25	3.22	4.23	5.09	3.62	3.76	3.27	3.13	3.17	3.78	2.91	40.87
Extreme Maximum Daily Precip. (in.)	2.65	2.10	2.75	7.70	4.70	4.23	3.27	2.97	2.63	3.50	3.00	2.71	7.70
Days With ≥ 0.1" Precipitation	5	5	7	7	8	6	5	6	5	6	6	6	72
Days With ≥ 0.5" Precipitation	2	1	2	3	4	2	2	2	2	2	3	2	27
Days With ≥ 1.0" Precipitation	1	0	1	1	2	1	1	1	1	1	1	1	12
Mean Snowfall (in.)	1.4	1.8	0.8	0.2	0.0	0.0	0.0	0.0	0.0	trace	0.1	0.5	4.8
Maximum Snow Depth (in.)	10	21	6	5	0	0	0	0	0	0	7	5	21
Days With ≥ 1.0" Snow Depth	2	2	1	0	0	0	0	0	0	0	0	1	6

Anna 2 NNE *Union County* Elevation: 600 ft. Latitude: 37° 28' N Longitude: 89° 14' W

	JAN	FEB	MAR	APR	MAY	JUN	JUL	AUG	SEP	OCT	NOV	DEC	YEAR
Mean Maximum Temp. (°F)	43.1	48.4	58.5	69.1	77.2	85.3	88.7	88.6	81.4	70.4	57.8	45.6	67.8
Mean Temp. (°F)	34.0	38.3	47.2	57.2	65.9	74.2	78.1	77.2	69.4	58.3	47.5	36.7	57.0
Mean Minimum Temp. (°F)	24.8	28.1	35.9	45.3	54.5	63.1	67.3	65.7	57.4	46.2	37.1	27.7	46.1
Extreme Maximum Temp. (°F)	69	77	84	90	92	100	104	103	101	90	83	76	104
Extreme Minimum Temp. (°F)	-17	-10	5	20	31	44	49	46	32	20	10	-14	-17
Days Maximum Temp. ≥ 90°F	0	0	0	0	0	8	15	14	4	0	0	0	41
Days Maximum Temp. ≤ 32°F	5	3	0	0	0	0	0	0	0	0	0	4	12
Days Minimum Temp. ≤ 32°F	24	19	13	3	0	0	0	0	0	2	11	21	93
Days Minimum Temp. ≤ 0°F	1	0	0	0	0	0	0	0	0	0	0	1	2
Heating Degree Days (base 65°F)	954	750	548	256	73	4	0	1	38	231	520	872	4,247
Cooling Degree Days (base 65°F)	0	0	3	30	108	287	412	386	178	32	2	0	1,438
Mean Precipitation (in.)	3.66	3.48	4.58	4.50	5.87	4.37	3.36	3.23	3.32	4.29	4.76	4.48	49.90
Extreme Maximum Daily Precip. (in.)	6.70	2.34	7.74	3.22	4.76	4.86	3.26	3.71	4.45	3.42	6.24	4.43	7.74
Days With ≥ 0.1" Precipitation	6	6	7	8	8	6	6	5	5	7	7	7	78
Days With ≥ 0.5" Precipitation	2	3	3	3	4	3	2	2	2	3	3	3	33
Days With ≥ 1.0" Precipitation	1	1	1	1	2	1	1	1	1	1	1	1	13
Mean Snowfall (in.)	3.3	3.9	1.0	0.1	0.0	0.0	0.0	0.0	0.0	0.1	0.3	2.6	11.3
Maximum Snow Depth (in.)	7	10	6	trace	0	0	0	0	0	trace	4	14	14
Days With ≥ 1.0" Snow Depth	4	4	1	0	0	0	0	0	0	0	0	3	12

The period of record for all cooperative weather station data is 1980 – 2009. See User Guide for detailed explanation of data.

Antioch *Lake County* Elevation: 750 ft. Latitude: 42° 29' N Longitude: 88° 07' W

	JAN	FEB	MAR	APR	MAY	JUN	JUL	AUG	SEP	OCT	NOV	DEC	YEAR
Mean Maximum Temp. (°F)	29.6	***33.1***	43.6	57.0	***68.0***	***77.7***	***82.1***	80.9	73.6	61.0	46.7	***33.6***	***57.2***
Mean Temp. (°F)	21.5	***24.7***	34.8	47.0	***57.2***	***67.1***	***71.9***	70.9	63.1	50.9	38.5	***26.3***	***47.8***
Mean Minimum Temp. (°F)	13.5	***16.3***	25.9	36.8	***46.4***	***56.5***	***61.8***	60.9	52.7	40.7	30.3	***18.8***	***38.4***
Extreme Maximum Temp. (°F)	63	***70***	78	90	***91***	***96***	***102***	104	95	***89***	***74***	***68***	***104***
Extreme Minimum Temp. (°F)	-28	***-17***	-10	6	***27***	***36***	***42***	40	29	***18***	***4***	***-24***	***-28***
Days Maximum Temp. ≥ 90°F	0	***0***	0	0	***0***	***2***	***4***	3	1	0	0	***0***	***10***
Days Maximum Temp. ≤ 32°F	18	***13***	5	0	***0***	***0***	***0***	0	0	0	3	***13***	***52***
Days Minimum Temp. ≤ 32°F	29	***26***	23	9	***1***	***0***	***0***	0	0	6	17	***28***	***139***
Days Minimum Temp. ≤ 0°F	6	***5***	1	0	***0***	***0***	***0***	0	0	0	0	***3***	***15***
Heating Degree Days (base 65°F)	1,342	***1,132***	931	542	***267***	***61***	***10***	15	125	438	787	***1,193***	***6,843***
Cooling Degree Days (base 65°F)	0	***0***	1	7	***33***	***132***	***232***	206	77	7	0	***0***	***695***
Mean Precipitation (in.)	1.58	***1.54***	1.85	3.20	***4.08***	***4.05***	***3.80***	4.26	3.58	2.87	2.87	***2.09***	***35.77***
Extreme Maximum Daily Precip. (in.)	1.59	***1.62***	1.87	1.85	***2.60***	***4.64***	***8.10***	***3.31***	***3.81***	***2.30***	***1.64***	na	na
Days With ≥ 0.1" Precipitation	4	***4***	4	6	***7***	***7***	***6***	6	6	6	5	***5***	***66***
Days With ≥ 0.5" Precipitation	1	***1***	1	2	***3***	***2***	***3***	3	2	2	2	***1***	***23***
Days With ≥ 1.0" Precipitation	0	***0***	0	1	***1***	***1***	***1***	1	1	1	1	***0***	***8***
Mean Snowfall (in.)	11.1	***9.1***	5.6	1.5	***trace***	***0.0***	***0.0***	0.0	0.0	0.1	***1.7***	***10.1***	***39.2***
Maximum Snow Depth (in.)	21	***22***	16	8	***trace***	***0***	***0***	0	0	***1***	***4***	***17***	***22***
Days With ≥ 1.0" Snow Depth	18	***15***	6	1	***0***	***0***	***0***	0	0	***0***	***1***	***10***	***51***

Aurora *Kane County* Elevation: 640 ft. Latitude: 41° 46' N Longitude: 88° 19' W

	JAN	FEB	MAR	APR	MAY	JUN	JUL	AUG	SEP	OCT	NOV	DEC	YEAR
Mean Maximum Temp. (°F)	31.4	36.0	47.7	60.6	71.9	81.2	84.7	82.7	75.9	62.8	48.5	34.7	59.8
Mean Temp. (°F)	22.8	27.0	37.8	49.5	60.1	69.7	73.8	72.1	64.4	51.8	39.8	26.6	49.6
Mean Minimum Temp. (°F)	14.2	17.9	27.7	38.4	48.2	58.1	62.8	61.5	52.9	40.8	30.8	18.5	39.3
Extreme Maximum Temp. (°F)	66	72	83	91	94	103	102	101	95	89	77	69	103
Extreme Minimum Temp. (°F)	-26	-20	-8	8	26	39	42	43	28	15	5	-22	-26
Days Maximum Temp. ≥ 90°F	0	0	0	0	1	5	7	4	2	0	0	0	19
Days Maximum Temp. ≤ 32°F	16	10	3	0	0	0	0	0	0	0	2	11	42
Days Minimum Temp. ≤ 32°F	29	26	22	7	1	0	0	0	0	6	17	28	136
Days Minimum Temp. ≤ 0°F	5	3	0	0	0	0	0	0	0	0	0	3	11
Heating Degree Days (base 65°F)	1,303	1,066	838	466	196	34	3	8	105	414	751	1,186	6,370
Cooling Degree Days (base 65°F)	0	0	1	8	49	181	282	235	94	10	0	0	860
Mean Precipitation (in.)	1.64	1.74	2.34	3.67	3.88	4.02	4.20	4.26	3.57	3.04	3.27	2.27	37.90
Extreme Maximum Daily Precip. (in.)	1.82	3.26	2.47	2.09	3.59	4.38	16.91	3.01	4.00	2.81	2.74	2.83	16.91
Days With ≥ 0.1" Precipitation	4	4	5	7	7	7	6	7	5	6	6	5	69
Days With ≥ 0.5" Precipitation	1	1	1	3	3	2	2	3	2	2	2	1	23
Days With ≥ 1.0" Precipitation	0	0	0	1	1	1	1	1	1	1	1	0	8
Mean Snowfall (in.)	9.6	6.8	2.8	0.6	0.0	0.0	0.0	0.0	0.0	trace	0.9	7.6	28.3
Maximum Snow Depth (in.)	25	18	14	6	0	0	0	0	0	1	4	20	25
Days With ≥ 1.0" Snow Depth	18	13	3	0	0	0	0	0	0	0	1	10	45

Belleville Siu Research *St. Clair County* Elevation: 450 ft. Latitude: 38° 31' N Longitude: 89° 51' W

	JAN	FEB	MAR	APR	MAY	JUN	JUL	AUG	SEP	OCT	NOV	DEC	YEAR
Mean Maximum Temp. (°F)	41.9	47.1	57.8	68.9	77.6	86.0	89.5	88.5	81.9	71.0	57.4	44.3	67.7
Mean Temp. (°F)	32.9	37.3	46.8	57.1	66.2	74.6	78.3	76.6	69.1	58.3	47.3	35.7	56.7
Mean Minimum Temp. (°F)	23.9	27.4	35.6	45.2	54.8	63.2	67.1	64.7	56.3	45.6	37.1	27.0	45.7
Extreme Maximum Temp. (°F)	73	81	89	91	94	101	105	105	101	94	83	75	105
Extreme Minimum Temp. (°F)	-16	-21	2	18	32	41	49	39	26	20	2	-19	-21
Days Maximum Temp. ≥ 90°F	0	0	0	0	1	10	16	14	5	1	0	0	47
Days Maximum Temp. ≤ 32°F	7	4	1	0	0	0	0	0	0	0	0	5	17
Days Minimum Temp. ≤ 32°F	24	19	13	4	0	0	0	0	0	4	11	22	97
Days Minimum Temp. ≤ 0°F	1	1	0	0	0	0	0	0	0	0	0	1	3
Heating Degree Days (base 65°F)	988	779	565	266	76	5	0	2	45	239	529	903	4,397
Cooling Degree Days (base 65°F)	0	1	7	34	120	300	419	369	175	37	3	0	1,465
Mean Precipitation (in.)	2.25	2.20	3.23	3.85	4.79	4.18	3.81	3.19	3.27	3.50	3.83	2.82	40.92
Extreme Maximum Daily Precip. (in.)	2.17	4.48	2.68	4.58	4.57	3.22	3.48	3.00	3.75	3.45	3.23	3.97	4.58
Days With ≥ 0.1" Precipitation	4	4	6	7	8	7	5	5	5	6	6	5	68
Days With ≥ 0.5" Precipitation	1	1	2	3	3	3	3	2	2	3	3	2	28
Days With ≥ 1.0" Precipitation	1	1	1	1	1	1	1	1	1	1	1	1	12
Mean Snowfall (in.)	4.5	3.2	1.6	0.4	0.0	0.0	0.0	0.0	0.0	0.0	0.4	3.0	13.1
Maximum Snow Depth (in.)	15	19	8	30	0	0	0	0	0	0	3	8	30
Days With ≥ 1.0" Snow Depth	5	3	1	0	0	0	0	0	0	0	0	4	13

Brookport Dam 52 *Massac County* Elevation: 330 ft. Latitude: 37° 08' N Longitude: 88° 39' W

	JAN	FEB	MAR	APR	MAY	JUN	JUL	AUG	SEP	OCT	NOV	DEC	YEAR
Mean Maximum Temp. (°F)	43.6	48.2	58.1	68.9	77.4	85.5	89.3	88.8	81.7	70.3	58.1	46.1	68.0
Mean Temp. (°F)	35.0	39.0	47.7	57.9	66.8	74.9	79.0	77.8	70.4	58.9	48.3	37.6	57.8
Mean Minimum Temp. (°F)	26.3	29.7	37.3	46.7	56.2	64.3	68.6	66.8	58.9	47.3	38.4	29.0	47.5
Extreme Maximum Temp. (°F)	72	74	83	89	94	100	105	103	99	92	85	74	105
Extreme Minimum Temp. (°F)	-21	-9	9	21	34	43	52	42	29	18	9	-13	-21
Days Maximum Temp. ≥ 90°F	0	0	0	0	1	8	16	14	5	0	0	0	44
Days Maximum Temp. ≤ 32°F	5	3	0	0	0	0	0	0	0	0	0	4	12
Days Minimum Temp. ≤ 32°F	22	17	12	2	0	0	0	0	0	2	9	19	83
Days Minimum Temp. ≤ 0°F	1	0	0	0	0	0	0	0	0	0	0	0	1
Heating Degree Days (base 65°F)	924	730	532	238	60	3	0	1	34	223	498	844	4,087
Cooling Degree Days (base 65°F)	0	0	4	29	123	309	441	405	201	40	3	0	1,555
Mean Precipitation (in.)	3.49	3.92	4.14	4.64	4.97	4.13	4.15	2.82	3.49	3.97	4.16	4.56	48.44
Extreme Maximum Daily Precip. (in.)	2.60	5.32	3.88	5.20	3.66	3.20	3.60	2.93	3.88	3.50	3.40	3.50	5.32
Days With ≥ 0.1" Precipitation	6	6	7	8	8	6	5	4	5	6	7	7	75
Days With ≥ 0.5" Precipitation	2	3	2	3	3	3	3	2	3	3	3	4	34
Days With ≥ 1.0" Precipitation	1	1	1	1	1	1	1	1	1	1	1	1	12
Mean Snowfall (in.)	2.1	2.4	0.5	trace	0.0	0.0	0.0	0.0	0.0	0.0	0.0	1.7	6.7
Maximum Snow Depth (in.)	8	7	10	trace	0	0	0	0	0	0	0	13	13
Days With ≥ 1.0" Snow Depth	3	3	0	0	0	0	0	0	0	0	0	2	8

The period of record for all cooperative weather station data is 1980 – 2009. See User Guide for detailed explanation of data.

Cahokia *St. Clair County* Elevation: 399 ft. Latitude: 38° 34' N Longitude: 90° 12' W

	JAN	FEB	MAR	APR	MAY	JUN	JUL	AUG	SEP	OCT	NOV	DEC	YEAR
Mean Maximum Temp. (°F)	41.2	46.1	56.4	67.9	76.5	85.1	88.6	87.3	80.6	***69.6***	56.7	***43.6***	***66.6***
Mean Temp. (°F)	32.0	35.9	45.3	56.4	65.6	74.7	78.5	76.8	69.1	***57.6***	46.4	***34.5***	***56.1***
Mean Minimum Temp. (°F)	22.6	25.7	34.5	44.9	54.7	64.1	68.3	66.1	57.5	***45.5***	35.9	***25.4***	***45.4***
Extreme Maximum Temp. (°F)	78	81	89	93	***94***	102	106	***105***	102	***94***	85	***74***	***106***
Extreme Minimum Temp. (°F)	-17	-16	***4***	18	***32***	42	54	41	32	***22***	10	***-19***	***-19***
Days Maximum Temp. ≥ 90°F	0	0	0	0	1	9	15	11	4	***0***	0	0	***40***
Days Maximum Temp. ≤ 32°F	7	4	1	0	0	0	0	0	0	***0***	0	5	***17***
Days Minimum Temp. ≤ 32°F	26	21	14	3	0	0	0	0	0	***3***	12	23	***102***
Days Minimum Temp. ≤ 0°F	1	1	0	0	0	0	0	0	0	***0***	0	0	***2***
Heating Degree Days (base 65°F)	1,017	816	603	283	85	6	0	2	44	***257***	555	***939***	***4,607***
Cooling Degree Days (base 65°F)	0	0	6	31	111	302	427	374	173	***33***	3	***0***	***1,460***
Mean Precipitation (in.)	2.45	2.55	3.39	3.81	4.52	4.02	4.44	3.51	3.23	3.43	3.67	***2.99***	***42.01***
Extreme Maximum Daily Precip. (in.)	2.39	2.47	2.83	3.00	***4.37***	***2.68***	***3.47***	4.27	3.15	***2.52***	2.30	***2.55***	***4.37***
Days With ≥ 0.1" Precipitation	5	5	7	8	***8***	7	6	6	5	***6***	***7***	6	***76***
Days With ≥ 0.5" Precipitation	1	2	2	3	3	3	3	2	2	***3***	***3***	2	***29***
Days With ≥ 1.0" Precipitation	1	1	1	1	1	1	2	1	1	***1***	1	1	***13***
Mean Snowfall (in.)	5.0	3.8	1.9	0.2	0.0	0.0	0.0	0.0	0.0	***trace***	***0.6***	***3.9***	***15.4***
Maximum Snow Depth (in.)	***8***	***10***	11	3	***0***	0	0	0	0	***trace***	***4***	***9***	***11***
Days With ≥ 1.0" Snow Depth	***6***	***3***	1	0	0	0	0	0	0	***0***	***0***	***4***	***14***

Carbondale Sewage Plant *Jackson County* Elevation: 390 ft. Latitude: 37° 44' N Longitude: 89° 10' W

	JAN	FEB	MAR	APR	MAY	JUN	JUL	AUG	SEP	OCT	NOV	DEC	YEAR
Mean Maximum Temp. (°F)	41.5	46.4	56.1	67.2	76.3	84.8	88.4	88.3	81.2	69.3	56.9	44.9	66.8
Mean Temp. (°F)	32.4	36.2	45.1	55.5	65.0	73.9	77.6	76.2	68.2	56.1	46.2	35.5	55.7
Mean Minimum Temp. (°F)	23.2	25.9	34.1	43.7	53.7	62.9	66.8	64.1	55.2	42.9	35.4	26.1	44.5
Extreme Maximum Temp. (°F)	70	79	84	90	95	102	103	105	99	93	83	77	105
Extreme Minimum Temp. (°F)	-21	-11	5	21	31	41	51	43	30	18	10	-14	-21
Days Maximum Temp. ≥ 90°F	0	0	0	0	1	8	13	13	4	0	0	0	39
Days Maximum Temp. ≤ 32°F	7	4	1	0	0	0	0	0	0	0	0	4	16
Days Minimum Temp. ≤ 32°F	25	21	15	4	0	0	0	0	0	5	13	22	105
Days Minimum Temp. ≤ 0°F	1	1	0	0	0	0	0	0	0	0	0	1	3
Heating Degree Days (base 65°F)	1,006	809	612	305	90	7	0	2	53	293	559	908	4,644
Cooling Degree Days (base 65°F)	0	0	4	27	99	280	399	355	156	25	2	0	1,347
Mean Precipitation (in.)	3.15	3.06	4.25	4.47	5.47	4.60	3.68	3.10	3.10	3.72	4.43	4.07	47.10
Extreme Maximum Daily Precip. (in.)	3.52	3.75	6.10	4.96	4.14	6.90	4.35	3.19	4.22	3.47	5.35	3.57	6.90
Days With ≥ 0.1" Precipitation	6	6	7	8	8	6	5	5	5	5	7	6	74
Days With ≥ 0.5" Precipitation	2	2	3	3	4	3	2	2	2	3	3	3	32
Days With ≥ 1.0" Precipitation	1	1	1	1	2	1	1	1	1	1	1	1	13
Mean Snowfall (in.)	2.9	3.6	1.1	trace	0.0	0.0	0.0	0.0	0.0	0.1	0.3	2.7	10.7
Maximum Snow Depth (in.)	7	11	10	trace	0	0	0	0	0	2	7	13	13
Days With ≥ 1.0" Snow Depth	4	4	1	0	0	0	0	0	0	0	0	3	12

Carlinville *Macoupin County* Elevation: 629 ft. Latitude: 39° 17' N Longitude: 89° 53' W

	JAN	FEB	MAR	APR	MAY	JUN	JUL	AUG	SEP	OCT	NOV	DEC	YEAR
Mean Maximum Temp. (°F)	***36.5***	***42.4***	***53.4***	***65.4***	75.3	***83.7***	86.9	85.7	79.3	67.1	53.5	39.9	***64.1***
Mean Temp. (°F)	***28.5***	***33.6***	***43.4***	***54.3***	64.4	***73.2***	76.7	74.9	67.7	56.0	44.5	32.2	***54.1***
Mean Minimum Temp. (°F)	***20.6***	***24.8***	***33.4***	***43.2***	53.5	***62.7***	66.4	64.1	56.0	44.8	35.4	24.5	***44.1***
Extreme Maximum Temp. (°F)	***70***	***75***	***86***	***90***	92	***99***	***103***	***105***	***99***	***92***	***79***	***74***	***105***
Extreme Minimum Temp. (°F)	***-19***	***-17***	***-2***	***18***	30	***42***	***49***	***41***	***31***	***20***	***1***	***-15***	***-19***
Days Maximum Temp. ≥ 90°F	***0***	***0***	***0***	***0***	0	***6***	11	9	3	0	0	0	***29***
Days Maximum Temp. ≤ 32°F	***11***	***7***	***1***	***0***	0	***0***	0	0	0	0	1	7	***27***
Days Minimum Temp. ≤ 32°F	***27***	***21***	***15***	***4***	0	***0***	0	0	0	4	12	24	***107***
Days Minimum Temp. ≤ 0°F	***2***	***1***	***0***	***0***	0	***0***	0	0	0	0	0	1	***4***
Heating Degree Days (base 65°F)	***1,124***	***882***	***667***	***334***	103	***10***	1	4	60	296	610	1,009	***5,100***
Cooling Degree Days (base 65°F)	***0***	***0***	***4***	***20***	92	***263***	369	319	147	24	1	0	***1,239***
Mean Precipitation (in.)	***2.11***	***2.05***	***3.11***	***3.96***	3.98	***3.54***	3.57	3.19	3.22	3.24	3.70	2.82	***38.49***
Extreme Maximum Daily Precip. (in.)	***2.18***	***2.84***	***2.10***	***2.84***	2.74	***3.38***	***2.49***	***3.49***	***3.21***	***2.38***	***2.98***	***3.75***	***3.75***
Days With ≥ 0.1" Precipitation	***4***	***4***	***7***	***7***	7	***7***	6	5	5	6	6	5	***69***
Days With ≥ 0.5" Precipitation	***1***	***1***	***2***	***3***	3	***3***	3	2	2	2	3	2	***27***
Days With ≥ 1.0" Precipitation	***0***	***0***	***1***	***1***	1	***1***	1	1	1	1	1	1	***10***
Mean Snowfall (in.)	***5.9***	***4.4***	***2.7***	***0.4***	trace	***0.0***	0.0	0.0	0.0	trace	0.9	***3.4***	***17.7***
Maximum Snow Depth (in.)	***12***	***12***	7	***5***	0	***0***	***0***	***0***	***0***	***trace***	***4***	***8***	***12***
Days With ≥ 1.0" Snow Depth	***8***	***5***	***2***	***0***	0	***0***	0	0	0	***0***	0	5	***20***

Charleston *Coles County* Elevation: 680 ft. Latitude: 39° 29' N Longitude: 88° 10' W

	JAN	FEB	MAR	APR	MAY	JUN	JUL	AUG	SEP	OCT	NOV	DEC	YEAR
Mean Maximum Temp. (°F)	36.6	41.4	52.7	65.4	75.1	83.6	86.5	85.0	79.0	66.8	53.1	39.9	63.8
Mean Temp. (°F)	28.7	32.9	43.0	54.5	64.3	72.9	76.4	74.8	67.7	56.2	44.4	32.2	54.0
Mean Minimum Temp. (°F)	20.7	24.3	33.2	43.6	53.3	62.2	66.2	64.5	56.4	45.5	35.6	24.5	44.2
Extreme Maximum Temp. (°F)	69	74	84	89	94	102	101	102	97	91	80	71	102
Extreme Minimum Temp. (°F)	-27	-18	-1	17	29	38	50	42	32	20	6	-20	-27
Days Maximum Temp. ≥ 90°F	0	0	0	0	1	6	9	8	3	0	0	0	27
Days Maximum Temp. ≤ 32°F	11	7	1	0	0	0	0	0	0	0	1	7	27
Days Minimum Temp. ≤ 32°F	26	21	15	4	0	0	0	0	0	3	12	23	104
Days Minimum Temp. ≤ 0°F	2	1	0	0	0	0	0	0	0	0	0	1	4
Heating Degree Days (base 65°F)	1,120	900	678	329	106	11	0	3	59	293	613	1,010	5,122
Cooling Degree Days (base 65°F)	0	0	4	22	90	256	360	314	147	26	1	0	1,220
Mean Precipitation (in.)	2.35	2.39	3.02	4.15	4.47	3.86	4.18	3.31	3.22	3.85	3.96	3.09	41.85
Extreme Maximum Daily Precip. (in.)	1.76	2.70	2.24	3.55	4.66	3.23	3.46	2.75	4.95	3.61	2.49	2.87	4.95
Days With ≥ 0.1" Precipitation	5	5	7	8	8	6	6	5	5	6	7	6	74
Days With ≥ 0.5" Precipitation	1	1	2	3	3	3	3	2	2	3	3	2	28
Days With ≥ 1.0" Precipitation	1	0	0	1	1	1	1	1	1	1	1	1	10
Mean Snowfall (in.)	8.5	3.8	2.1	0.2	trace	0.0	0.0	0.0	0.0	trace	1.0	5.1	20.7
Maximum Snow Depth (in.)	24	21	9	2	trace	0	0	0	0	trace	8	9	24
Days With ≥ 1.0" Snow Depth	11	8	3	0	0	0	0	0	0	0	1	7	30

The period of record for all cooperative weather station data is 1980 – 2009. See User Guide for detailed explanation of data.

Chenoa *Mclean County* Elevation: 709 ft. Latitude: 40° 44' N Longitude: 88° 43' W

	JAN	FEB	MAR	APR	MAY	JUN	JUL	AUG	SEP	OCT	NOV	DEC	YEAR
Mean Maximum Temp. (°F)	33.4	38.0	50.2	63.7	74.5	83.0	85.2	83.6	78.0	65.2	50.5	36.6	61.8
Mean Temp. (°F)	25.0	29.2	40.0	52.0	62.8	71.8	74.6	72.8	66.0	54.1	41.7	28.8	51.6
Mean Minimum Temp. (°F)	16.6	20.4	29.7	40.4	50.9	60.5	64.0	61.9	53.9	43.0	32.8	21.0	41.3
Extreme Maximum Temp. (°F)	66	73	85	91	95	102	101	103	98	91	79	70	103
Extreme Minimum Temp. (°F)	-25	-19	-6	7	26	38	45	40	28	17	5	-26	-26
Days Maximum Temp. ≥ 90°F	0	0	0	0	1	6	7	5	2	0	0	0	21
Days Maximum Temp. ≤ 32°F	14	9	2	0	0	0	0	0	0	0	1	10	36
Days Minimum Temp. ≤ 32°F	29	25	20	6	0	0	0	0	0	4	16	26	126
Days Minimum Temp. ≤ 0°F	4	2	0	0	0	0	0	0	0	0	0	2	8
Heating Degree Days (base 65°F)	1,232	1,006	771	397	137	16	1	7	80	348	693	1,114	5,802
Cooling Degree Days (base 65°F)	0	0	2	15	74	227	307	255	117	17	0	0	1,014
Mean Precipitation (in.)	1.72	1.34	2.90	3.28	3.95	3.79	3.54	3.21	2.86	3.10	2.87	2.23	34.79
Extreme Maximum Daily Precip. (in.)	1.89	1.80	3.73	1.79	2.45	3.63	2.81	3.93	3.59	5.66	2.21	5.07	5.66
Days With ≥ 0.1" Precipitation	4	3	6	7	7	6	6	5	5	6	6	4	65
Days With ≥ 0.5" Precipitation	1	1	2	3	3	3	3	2	2	2	2	1	25
Days With ≥ 1.0" Precipitation	0	0	0	1	1	1	1	1	1	1	1	0	8
Mean Snowfall (in.)	5.0	5.5	1.8	0.9	trace	0.0	0.0	0.0	0.0	0.0	1.0	4.2	18.4
Maximum Snow Depth (in.)	14	20	5	5	0	0	0	0	0	trace	4	14	20
Days With ≥ 1.0" Snow Depth	9	9	2	0	0	0	0	0	0	0	1	6	27

Chicago Botanical Garden *Cook County* Elevation: 629 ft. Latitude: 42° 08' N Longitude: 87° 47' W

	JAN	FEB	MAR	APR	MAY	JUN	JUL	AUG	SEP	OCT	NOV	DEC	YEAR
Mean Maximum Temp. (°F)	31.9	35.7	45.2	56.3	67.3	77.7	82.5	81.2	74.5	62.4	48.5	35.8	58.3
Mean Temp. (°F)	24.1	27.5	36.7	47.1	57.3	67.3	72.8	71.7	64.2	52.4	40.7	28.2	49.2
Mean Minimum Temp. (°F)	16.2	19.2	28.2	37.8	47.2	56.8	63.0	62.2	53.8	42.3	32.8	20.6	40.0
Extreme Maximum Temp. (°F)	65	74	83	90	93	102	105	101	97	89	76	70	105
Extreme Minimum Temp. (°F)	-27	-20	-5	10	28	37	45	42	30	24	6	-20	-27
Days Maximum Temp. ≥ 90°F	0	0	0	0	1	4	6	4	1	0	0	0	16
Days Maximum Temp. ≤ 32°F	16	10	4	0	0	0	0	0	0	0	2	10	42
Days Minimum Temp. ≤ 32°F	28	25	21	8	0	0	0	0	0	4	14	27	127
Days Minimum Temp. ≤ 0°F	4	2	0	0	0	0	0	0	0	0	0	2	8
Heating Degree Days (base 65°F)	1,262	1,054	872	541	272	70	8	12	108	394	724	1,134	6,451
Cooling Degree Days (base 65°F)	0	0	1	10	40	145	257	228	90	10	0	0	781
Mean Precipitation (in.)	1.95	1.71	2.45	3.53	4.01	3.55	3.51	4.72	3.52	3.31	3.06	2.40	37.72
Extreme Maximum Daily Precip. (in.)	2.14	3.20	2.00	2.58	2.97	4.50	3.03	5.54	3.35	3.59	2.33	2.79	5.54
Days With ≥ 0.1" Precipitation	5	4	6	7	8	6	6	7	6	6	6	6	73
Days With ≥ 0.5" Precipitation	1	1	2	3	3	2	2	3	2	2	2	1	24
Days With ≥ 1.0" Precipitation	0	0	0	1	1	1	1	1	1	1	1	0	8
Mean Snowfall (in.)	10.2	8.1	5.2	0.9	trace	0.0	0.0	0.0	0.0	0.1	1.5	7.8	33.8
Maximum Snow Depth (in.)	15	15	13	9	trace	0	0	0	0	trace	5	18	18
Days With ≥ 1.0" Snow Depth	19	14	6	1	0	0	0	0	0	0	1	10	51

Chicago Midway Arpt *Cook County* Elevation: 620 ft. Latitude: 41° 44' N Longitude: 87° 47' W

	JAN	FEB	MAR	APR	MAY	JUN	JUL	AUG	SEP	OCT	NOV	DEC	YEAR
Mean Maximum Temp. (°F)	32.2	36.4	47.3	59.7	70.9	80.6	84.8	82.6	75.9	63.0	49.0	36.0	59.9
Mean Temp. (°F)	25.4	29.2	39.1	50.4	61.0	70.9	75.8	74.1	66.7	54.2	41.8	29.4	51.5
Mean Minimum Temp. (°F)	18.4	21.9	30.9	41.0	51.1	61.2	66.8	65.6	57.5	45.3	34.6	22.8	43.1
Extreme Maximum Temp. (°F)	67	73	86	91	94	104	106	102	98	89	77	69	106
Extreme Minimum Temp. (°F)	-25	-17	-4	10	28	39	48	46	34	20	7	-20	-25
Days Maximum Temp. ≥ 90°F	0	0	0	0	1	5	8	5	2	0	0	0	21
Days Maximum Temp. ≤ 32°F	15	10	3	0	0	0	0	0	0	0	2	11	41
Days Minimum Temp. ≤ 32°F	27	23	18	5	0	0	0	0	0	2	12	25	112
Days Minimum Temp. ≤ 0°F	3	1	0	0	0	0	0	0	0	0	0	1	5
Heating Degree Days (base 65°F)	1,222	1,008	797	446	182	29	1	4	71	346	689	1,097	5,892
Cooling Degree Days (base 65°F)	0	0	2	12	65	213	342	293	128	16	0	0	1,071
Mean Precipitation (in.)	2.04	1.92	2.70	3.60	4.13	3.91	3.85	4.09	3.42	3.26	3.38	2.57	38.87
Extreme Maximum Daily Precip. (in.)	1.59	3.25	2.02	1.84	2.80	3.16	5.72	3.90	4.16	3.80	3.49	2.78	5.72
Days With ≥ 0.1" Precipitation	5	5	6	7	7	6	6	6	5	6	6	5	70
Days With ≥ 0.5" Precipitation	1	1	2	2	3	3	3	3	2	2	2	1	25
Days With ≥ 1.0" Precipitation	0	0	0	1	1	1	1	1	1	1	1	1	9
Mean Snowfall (in.)	11.6	9.3	5.6	1.1	trace	0.0	trace	0.0	trace	0.1	1.4	8.5	37.6
Maximum Snow Depth (in.)	21	17	13	10	0	0	trace	0	trace	2	4	20	21
Days With ≥ 1.0" Snow Depth	18	13	5	1	0	0	0	0	0	0	1	10	48

Danville *Vermilion County* Elevation: 558 ft. Latitude: 40° 08' N Longitude: 87° 39' W

	JAN	FEB	MAR	APR	MAY	JUN	JUL	AUG	SEP	OCT	NOV	DEC	YEAR
Mean Maximum Temp. (°F)	35.4	40.2	51.7	64.8	75.0	83.2	85.7	84.2	78.5	66.2	52.3	38.7	63.0
Mean Temp. (°F)	27.4	31.4	41.6	53.3	63.1	71.9	75.2	73.7	66.8	54.9	43.4	31.1	52.8
Mean Minimum Temp. (°F)	19.3	22.6	31.5	41.7	51.2	60.4	64.6	63.1	55.0	43.6	34.5	23.5	42.6
Extreme Maximum Temp. (°F)	68	74	84	90	93	102	102	102	96	89	79	72	102
Extreme Minimum Temp. (°F)	-26	-22	-6	12	29	39	46	41	29	19	8	-25	-26
Days Maximum Temp. ≥ 90°F	0	0	0	0	1	5	7	5	2	0	0	0	20
Days Maximum Temp. ≤ 32°F	13	8	2	0	0	0	0	0	0	0	1	9	33
Days Minimum Temp. ≤ 32°F	26	23	17	6	0	0	0	0	0	4	14	24	114
Days Minimum Temp. ≤ 0°F	3	2	0	0	0	0	0	0	0	0	0	2	7
Heating Degree Days (base 65°F)	1,161	944	719	363	128	16	1	4	66	325	642	1,045	5,414
Cooling Degree Days (base 65°F)	0	0	2	18	76	228	324	279	126	20	1	0	1,074
Mean Precipitation (in.)	2.17	2.22	3.03	3.95	4.52	4.52	4.61	3.53	2.93	3.60	3.77	2.79	41.64
Extreme Maximum Daily Precip. (in.)	1.91	2.45	2.59	3.92	3.46	3.86	2.94	3.34	3.70	2.54	3.71	1.71	3.92
Days With ≥ 0.1" Precipitation	5	5	7	8	8	7	7	6	5	6	7	7	78
Days With ≥ 0.5" Precipitation	1	1	2	3	3	3	4	2	2	3	3	2	29
Days With ≥ 1.0" Precipitation	0	0	1	1	1	1	1	1	1	1	1	0	9
Mean Snowfall (in.)	4.5	4.4	2.1	0.2	trace	0.0	0.0	0.0	0.0	0.1	0.6	4.0	15.9
Maximum Snow Depth (in.)	13	14	7	2	trace	0	0	0	0	trace	5	11	14
Days With ≥ 1.0" Snow Depth	8	7	2	0	0	0	0	0	0	0	0	6	23

The period of record for all cooperative weather station data is 1980 – 2009. See User Guide for detailed explanation of data.

De Kalb *Dekalb County* Elevation: 873 ft. Latitude: 41° 56' N Longitude: 88° 47' W

	JAN	FEB	MAR	APR	MAY	JUN	JUL	AUG	SEP	OCT	NOV	DEC	YEAR
Mean Maximum Temp. (°F)	28.2	33.2	45.2	59.2	70.7	80.3	83.6	81.6	75.4	62.1	46.9	33.0	58.3
Mean Temp. (°F)	20.5	25.2	36.0	48.5	59.5	69.6	73.2	71.4	64.1	51.3	38.5	25.7	48.6
Mean Minimum Temp. (°F)	12.8	17.1	26.9	37.6	48.2	58.8	62.9	61.0	52.8	40.5	30.1	18.3	38.9
Extreme Maximum Temp. (°F)	62	69	81	91	95	101	102	103	94	89	76	65	103
Extreme Minimum Temp. (°F)	-27	-23	-13	8	24	34	46	42	27	13	5	-22	-27
Days Maximum Temp. ≥ 90°F	0	0	0	0	0	4	5	4	1	0	0	0	14
Days Maximum Temp. ≤ 32°F	20	13	5	0	0	0	0	0	0	0	3	14	55
Days Minimum Temp. ≤ 32°F	30	26	23	8	1	0	0	0	0	7	18	28	141
Days Minimum Temp. ≤ 0°F	6	4	0	0	0	0	0	0	0	0	0	3	13
Heating Degree Days (base 65°F)	1,373	1,121	892	498	209	36	4	14	111	427	787	1,213	6,685
Cooling Degree Days (base 65°F)	0	0	1	9	44	180	267	218	91	9	0	0	819
Mean Precipitation (in.)	1.43	1.55	2.25	3.27	4.48	4.09	4.27	4.67	3.38	2.90	2.67	2.19	37.15
Extreme Maximum Daily Precip. (in.)	1.46	2.60	1.72	2.08	2.81	2.79	8.09	***5.71***	3.47	2.82	2.20	2.03	***8.09***
Days With ≥ 0.1" Precipitation	4	4	5	7	8	7	6	6	6	6	5	5	69
Days With ≥ 0.5" Precipitation	0	1	1	2	3	3	2	3	2	2	2	1	22
Days With ≥ 1.0" Precipitation	0	0	0	1	1	1	1	1	1	1	1	0	8
Mean Snowfall (in.)	9.9	7.4	4.3	1.0	trace	0.0	0.0	0.0	0.0	0.1	1.2	9.6	33.5
Maximum Snow Depth (in.)	17	17	10	5	trace	0	0	***0***	0	1	5	***17***	***17***
Days With ≥ 1.0" Snow Depth	21	15	5	1	0	0	0	0	0	0	1	12	55

Decatur *Macon County* Elevation: 620 ft. Latitude: 39° 49' N Longitude: 89° 01' W

	JAN	FEB	MAR	APR	MAY	JUN	JUL	AUG	SEP	OCT	NOV	DEC	YEAR
Mean Maximum Temp. (°F)	36.2	41.4	52.8	65.7	75.9	84.5	87.6	86.1	80.1	67.5	53.1	39.9	64.2
Mean Temp. (°F)	27.7	32.3	42.5	54.1	64.0	73.0	76.5	74.9	67.9	55.9	43.8	31.8	53.7
Mean Minimum Temp. (°F)	19.2	23.2	32.3	42.5	52.0	61.5	65.4	63.6	55.7	44.3	34.5	23.6	43.2
Extreme Maximum Temp. (°F)	67	73	86	93	95	103	104	106	100	95	80	71	106
Extreme Minimum Temp. (°F)	-22	-20	-4	15	27	39	48	42	29	18	0	-22	-22
Days Maximum Temp. ≥ 90°F	0	0	0	0	1	7	11	8	4	0	0	0	31
Days Maximum Temp. ≤ 32°F	11	6	2	0	0	0	0	0	0	0	1	7	27
Days Minimum Temp. ≤ 32°F	27	23	16	5	0	0	0	0	0	4	13	24	112
Days Minimum Temp. ≤ 0°F	3	2	0	0	0	0	0	0	0	0	0	1	6
Heating Degree Days (base 65°F)	1,148	918	692	339	110	11	0	4	59	300	630	1,024	5,235
Cooling Degree Days (base 65°F)	0	0	2	20	86	258	363	317	153	25	1	0	1,225
Mean Precipitation (in.)	2.21	2.04	2.73	3.70	4.59	4.02	3.80	3.69	3.06	3.38	3.39	2.68	39.29
Extreme Maximum Daily Precip. (in.)	2.12	2.70	1.80	2.54	3.78	3.77	5.11	3.38	5.84	4.09	2.00	2.16	5.84
Days With ≥ 0.1" Precipitation	4	4	6	7	7	6	6	5	5	6	6	6	68
Days With ≥ 0.5" Precipitation	1	1	2	3	3	3	3	3	2	2	2	2	27
Days With ≥ 1.0" Precipitation	1	1	0	1	1	1	1	1	1	1	1	0	10
Mean Snowfall (in.)	6.0	4.3	1.9	0.2	trace	0.0	0.0	0.0	0.0	trace	0.7	5.0	18.1
Maximum Snow Depth (in.)	10	14	10	3	trace	0	0	0	0	trace	9	12	14
Days With ≥ 1.0" Snow Depth	10	7	2	0	0	0	0	0	0	0	1	5	25

Dixon 1 NW *Lee County* Elevation: 700 ft. Latitude: 41° 51' N Longitude: 89° 30' W

	JAN	FEB	MAR	APR	MAY	JUN	JUL	AUG	SEP	OCT	NOV	DEC	YEAR
Mean Maximum Temp. (°F)	29.1	33.7	45.9	60.1	70.8	79.5	82.9	81.4	74.7	62.3	47.6	33.2	58.4
Mean Temp. (°F)	20.4	24.6	36.3	48.9	59.7	68.9	72.7	71.0	63.0	50.8	38.5	25.1	48.3
Mean Minimum Temp. (°F)	11.6	15.5	26.6	37.6	48.5	58.2	62.4	60.5	51.3	39.3	29.3	17.0	38.2
Extreme Maximum Temp. (°F)	65	71	87	93	93	100	101	103	97	91	78	68	103
Extreme Minimum Temp. (°F)	-32	-26	-13	8	24	38	45	40	28	17	4	-25	-32
Days Maximum Temp. ≥ 90°F	0	0	0	0	0	2	5	4	1	0	0	0	12
Days Maximum Temp. ≤ 32°F	18	12	4	0	0	0	0	0	0	0	3	13	50
Days Minimum Temp. ≤ 32°F	30	26	23	9	1	0	0	0	0	8	19	28	144
Days Minimum Temp. ≤ 0°F	7	5	0	0	0	0	0	0	0	0	0	4	16
Heating Degree Days (base 65°F)	1,377	1,136	884	486	204	37	6	15	129	442	789	1,230	6,735
Cooling Degree Days (base 65°F)	0	0	1	9	47	161	251	207	75	10	0	0	761
Mean Precipitation (in.)	1.51	1.59	2.43	3.51	4.33	4.71	4.07	4.62	3.49	2.86	2.67	2.13	37.92
Extreme Maximum Daily Precip. (in.)	1.76	1.79	2.19	2.64	4.16	4.54	4.36	4.08	4.95	3.33	1.92	3.12	4.95
Days With ≥ 0.1" Precipitation	4	4	5	7	8	8	6	7	5	5	5	5	69
Days With ≥ 0.5" Precipitation	1	1	2	2	3	3	3	3	2	2	2	1	25
Days With ≥ 1.0" Precipitation	0	0	0	1	1	1	1	1	1	1	0	0	7
Mean Snowfall (in.)	10.3	6.9	3.7	0.8	0.0	0.0	0.0	0.0	0.0	0.1	1.3	8.5	31.6
Maximum Snow Depth (in.)	24	13	11	4	0	0	0	0	0	trace	7	19	24
Days With ≥ 1.0" Snow Depth	18	14	4	0	0	0	0	0	0	0	1	11	48

Effingham *Effingham County* Elevation: 595 ft. Latitude: 39° 08' N Longitude: 88° 32' W

	JAN	FEB	MAR	APR	MAY	JUN	JUL	AUG	SEP	OCT	NOV	DEC	YEAR
Mean Maximum Temp. (°F)	36.4	40.6	52.1	64.4	74.3	83.7	87.2	86.1	79.1	66.6	53.7	39.9	63.7
Mean Temp. (°F)	28.2	31.4	42.0	53.4	63.3	72.7	76.5	74.8	67.0	55.0	44.1	31.6	53.4
Mean Minimum Temp. (°F)	19.9	22.2	31.9	42.4	52.3	61.8	65.8	63.5	54.9	43.3	34.5	23.2	43.0
Extreme Maximum Temp. (°F)	69	74	84	89	94	102	102	103	98	93	81	71	103
Extreme Minimum Temp. (°F)	***-22***	-19	***-2***	21	30	39	50	44	33	20	***7***	-16	***-22***
Days Maximum Temp. ≥ 90°F	0	0	0	0	1	7	11	10	3	0	0	0	32
Days Maximum Temp. ≤ 32°F	11	7	2	0	0	0	0	0	0	0	1	8	29
Days Minimum Temp. ≤ 32°F	27	23	17	4	0	0	0	0	0	4	14	24	113
Days Minimum Temp. ≤ 0°F	2	2	0	0	0	0	0	0	0	0	0	2	6
Heating Degree Days (base 65°F)	1,134	943	708	360	122	14	1	4	70	325	621	1,029	5,331
Cooling Degree Days (base 65°F)	0	0	3	19	78	253	364	316	138	21	1	0	1,193
Mean Precipitation (in.)	2.43	2.72	3.23	3.87	5.07	4.21	4.34	2.88	3.09	3.74	4.05	3.30	42.93
Extreme Maximum Daily Precip. (in.)	2.24	2.78	2.50	2.61	3.79	5.70	5.25	2.90	3.39	4.45	3.17	3.27	5.70
Days With ≥ 0.1" Precipitation	5	5	7	8	9	7	7	5	5	6	7	6	77
Days With ≥ 0.5" Precipitation	2	2	2	2	4	3	3	2	2	3	3	2	30
Days With ≥ 1.0" Precipitation	1	1	1	1	1	1	1	1	1	1	1	1	12
Mean Snowfall (in.)	5.7	5.1	2.1	0.1	0.0	0.0	0.0	0.0	0.0	trace	1.0	3.8	17.8
Maximum Snow Depth (in.)	***10***	***16***	***8***	***trace***	***0***	***0***	***0***	***0***	***0***	***trace***	***10***	***8***	***16***
Days With ≥ 1.0" Snow Depth	***7***	***7***	2	0	0	0	0	0	0	0	1	5	***22***

The period of record for all cooperative weather station data is 1980 – 2009. See User Guide for detailed explanation of data.

Elgin *Kane County* Elevation: 763 ft. Latitude: 42° 04' N Longitude: 88° 17' W

	JAN	FEB	MAR	APR	MAY	JUN	JUL	AUG	SEP	OCT	NOV	DEC	YEAR
Mean Maximum Temp. (°F)	29.4	33.8	45.0	58.3	69.7	79.5	83.3	81.6	74.8	61.7	47.3	33.3	58.1
Mean Temp. (°F)	21.4	25.3	35.6	47.7	58.7	68.4	73.1	71.4	63.5	50.8	38.8	25.6	48.4
Mean Minimum Temp. (°F)	13.4	16.7	26.2	37.1	47.7	57.3	62.8	61.0	52.1	39.8	30.3	18.1	38.5
Extreme Maximum Temp. (°F)	63	70	82	91	92	101	101	98	95	88	75	67	101
Extreme Minimum Temp. (°F)	-27	-22	-8	11	28	36	45	40	29	18	4	-24	-27
Days Maximum Temp. ≥ 90°F	0	0	0	0	0	4	5	4	1	0	0	0	14
Days Maximum Temp. ≤ 32°F	18	12	5	0	0	0	0	0	0	0	3	13	51
Days Minimum Temp. ≤ 32°F	29	26	23	9	0	0	0	0	0	7	19	28	141
Days Minimum Temp. ≤ 0°F	5	4	0	0	0	0	0	0	0	0	0	3	12
Heating Degree Days (base 65°F)	1,346	1,116	904	520	228	47	6	12	117	442	779	1,214	6,731
Cooling Degree Days (base 65°F)	0	0	1	7	41	157	264	217	78	8	0	0	773
Mean Precipitation (in.)	1.51	1.47	2.08	3.70	4.19	3.83	3.70	5.08	3.53	2.95	3.09	2.10	37.23
Extreme Maximum Daily Precip. (in.)	1.63	3.17	1.81	2.14	2.35	3.25	3.11	4.93	3.75	3.02	2.25	2.60	4.93
Days With ≥ 0.1" Precipitation	4	4	5	7	8	7	6	7	6	6	6	5	71
Days With ≥ 0.5" Precipitation	1	1	1	3	3	3	3	3	2	2	2	1	25
Days With ≥ 1.0" Precipitation	0	0	0	1	1	1	1	2	1	1	1	0	9
Mean Snowfall (in.)	9.4	6.8	3.6	0.5	0.0	0.0	0.0	0.0	0.0	trace	0.7	8.1	29.1
Maximum Snow Depth (in.)	24	16	10	2	0	0	0	0	0	trace	4	19	24
Days With ≥ 1.0" Snow Depth	13	8	3	0	0	0	0	0	0	0	1	9	34

Fulton L&D #13 *Whiteside County* Elevation: 591 ft. Latitude: 41° 54' N Longitude: 90° 09' W

	JAN	FEB	MAR	APR	MAY	JUN	JUL	AUG	SEP	OCT	NOV	DEC	YEAR
Mean Maximum Temp. (°F)	29.5	33.2	44.8	59.0	70.3	79.5	83.5	81.9	74.6	62.2	47.3	32.9	58.2
Mean Temp. (°F)	21.2	24.8	36.0	49.2	60.2	69.6	73.7	72.2	64.2	52.1	39.2	25.4	49.0
Mean Minimum Temp. (°F)	13.0	16.3	27.2	39.3	50.0	59.6	63.8	62.5	53.7	41.9	30.9	17.8	39.7
Extreme Maximum Temp. (°F)	62	66	82	91	92	98	102	102	96	90	82	66	102
Extreme Minimum Temp. (°F)	-33	-26	-5	13	30	40	46	42	30	16	8	-22	-33
Days Maximum Temp. ≥ 90°F	0	0	0	0	0	3	6	4	1	0	0	0	14
Days Maximum Temp. ≤ 32°F	18	12	5	0	0	0	0	0	0	0	2	13	50
Days Minimum Temp. ≤ 32°F	30	26	23	6	0	0	0	0	0	4	17	28	134
Days Minimum Temp. ≤ 0°F	6	4	0	0	0	0	0	0	0	0	0	4	14
Heating Degree Days (base 65°F)	1,350	1,131	892	478	186	33	4	8	106	404	769	1,221	6,582
Cooling Degree Days (base 65°F)	0	0	0	10	44	177	280	238	88	10	0	0	847
Mean Precipitation (in.)	1.20	1.39	2.32	3.06	3.57	4.16	3.24	4.05	2.87	2.87	2.52	1.80	33.05
Extreme Maximum Daily Precip. (in.)	1.43	1.72	1.86	1.64	2.55	4.11	2.12	4.71	2.56	2.37	2.23	1.64	4.71
Days With ≥ 0.1" Precipitation	3	4	5	6	7	7	6	6	5	5	5	4	63
Days With ≥ 0.5" Precipitation	1	1	2	2	3	3	2	3	2	2	2	1	24
Days With ≥ 1.0" Precipitation	0	0	0	1	1	1	1	1	1	1	0	0	7
Mean Snowfall (in.)	3.1	1.7	0.4	0.5	0.0	0.0	0.0	0.0	0.0	0.0	0.1	1.5	7.3
Maximum Snow Depth (in.)	15	15	4	7	0	0	0	0	0	0	4	8	15
Days With ≥ 1.0" Snow Depth	6	7	2	0	0	0	0	0	0	0	0	3	18

Galesburg *Knox County* Elevation: 771 ft. Latitude: 40° 57' N Longitude: 90° 23' W

	JAN	FEB	MAR	APR	MAY	JUN	JUL	AUG	SEP	OCT	NOV	DEC	YEAR
Mean Maximum Temp. (°F)	31.2	35.8	48.6	61.9	72.6	81.4	84.7	82.6	75.8	63.0	48.7	34.4	60.1
Mean Temp. (°F)	23.5	27.8	39.2	51.4	62.2	71.4	75.2	73.2	65.5	53.1	40.2	27.1	50.8
Mean Minimum Temp. (°F)	15.7	19.7	29.7	40.9	51.7	61.4	65.7	63.8	55.2	43.1	31.6	19.7	41.5
Extreme Maximum Temp. (°F)	66	69	86	91	93	101	102	101	97	94	78	68	102
Extreme Minimum Temp. (°F)	-27	-24	-6	9	29	41	49	42	29	21	1	-21	-27
Days Maximum Temp. ≥ 90°F	0	0	0	0	1	4	7	5	1	0	0	0	18
Days Maximum Temp. ≤ 32°F	17	11	3	0	0	0	0	0	0	0	2	12	45
Days Minimum Temp. ≤ 32°F	29	25	20	6	0	0	0	0	0	4	17	27	128
Days Minimum Temp. ≤ 0°F	4	3	0	0	0	0	0	0	0	0	0	3	10
Heating Degree Days (base 65°F)	1,281	1,045	796	416	149	19	2	7	88	377	738	1,167	6,085
Cooling Degree Days (base 65°F)	0	0	2	14	68	218	325	268	111	14	0	0	1,020
Mean Precipitation (in.)	1.46	1.63	2.74	3.66	4.28	4.04	4.32	4.20	3.49	2.73	2.85	2.38	37.78
Extreme Maximum Daily Precip. (in.)	1.23	2.76	3.90	3.01	3.62	3.92	6.13	3.40	3.06	2.18	2.15	3.28	6.13
Days With ≥ 0.1" Precipitation	4	4	6	7	8	7	6	7	5	6	6	5	71
Days With ≥ 0.5" Precipitation	1	1	2	2	3	3	2	3	2	2	2	2	25
Days With ≥ 1.0" Precipitation	0	0	0	1	1	1	1	1	1	1	1	1	9
Mean Snowfall (in.)	7.4	5.2	2.0	1.3	trace	0.0	0.0	0.0	0.0	trace	0.8	6.0	22.7
Maximum Snow Depth (in.)	20	11	9	11	trace	0	0	0	0	1	6	13	20
Days With ≥ 1.0" Snow Depth	14	10	3	0	0	0	0	0	0	0	1	7	35

Golden *Adams County* Elevation: 725 ft. Latitude: 40° 06' N Longitude: 91° 01' W

	JAN	FEB	MAR	APR	MAY	JUN	JUL	AUG	SEP	OCT	NOV	DEC	YEAR
Mean Maximum Temp. (°F)	33.9	38.1	50.7	62.7	73.5	82.8	86.6	85.2	78.1	66.0	50.4	37.1	62.1
Mean Temp. (°F)	25.7	29.1	40.7	51.7	62.7	72.2	75.9	74.2	66.3	54.5	41.2	29.0	51.9
Mean Minimum Temp. (°F)	17.4	20.1	30.7	40.7	51.8	61.6	65.2	63.1	54.4	42.9	32.0	20.9	41.7
Extreme Maximum Temp. (°F)	68	73	84	93	93	101	102	103	98	95	78	71	103
Extreme Minimum Temp. (°F)	-23	-18	-5	13	31	43	50	43	30	20	-2	-22	-23
Days Maximum Temp. ≥ 90°F	0	0	0	0	1	5	10	9	3	0	0	0	28
Days Maximum Temp. ≤ 32°F	13	10	3	0	0	0	0	0	0	0	2	10	38
Days Minimum Temp. ≤ 32°F	28	24	19	6	0	0	0	0	0	4	17	27	125
Days Minimum Temp. ≤ 0°F	3	3	0	0	0	0	0	0	0	0	0	3	9
Heating Degree Days (base 65°F)	1,213	1,009	747	406	137	15	1	6	85	339	708	1,109	5,775
Cooling Degree Days (base 65°F)	0	0	2	14	73	239	346	298	129	19	0	0	1,120
Mean Precipitation (in.)	1.48	1.82	2.46	3.47	5.02	4.54	4.22	3.98	3.11	3.07	3.02	2.14	38.33
Extreme Maximum Daily Precip. (in.)	1.73	3.00	2.30	3.00	3.60	5.00	4.85	4.36	3.00	3.50	2.65	3.10	5.00
Days With ≥ 0.1" Precipitation	3	4	6	7	8	7	6	6	5	6	6	4	68
Days With ≥ 0.5" Precipitation	1	1	2	3	3	3	3	3	2	2	2	2	27
Days With ≥ 1.0" Precipitation	0	0	1	1	1	1	1	1	1	1	1	1	10
Mean Snowfall (in.)	5.1	4.2	1.4	0.5	0.0	0.0	0.0	0.0	0.0	trace	0.7	3.8	15.7
Maximum Snow Depth (in.)	9	8	3	2	0	0	0	0	0	trace	5	11	11
Days With ≥ 1.0" Snow Depth	2	2	0	0	0	0	0	0	0	0	0	3	7

The period of record for all cooperative weather station data is 1980 – 2009. See User Guide for detailed explanation of data.

Havana 4 NNE *Mason County* Elevation: 459 ft. Latitude: 40° 21' N Longitude: 90° 01' W

	JAN	FEB	MAR	APR	MAY	JUN	JUL	AUG	SEP	OCT	NOV	DEC	YEAR
Mean Maximum Temp. (°F)	34.0	38.9	50.7	63.7	74.1	83.5	88.2	86.1	79.5	67.0	51.7	37.7	62.9
Mean Temp. (°F)	25.1	29.3	40.2	51.9	62.5	72.1	76.5	74.1	66.0	53.8	41.5	28.8	51.8
Mean Minimum Temp. (°F)	16.2	19.7	29.6	40.1	50.9	60.5	64.7	62.1	52.4	40.6	31.2	19.8	40.7
Extreme Maximum Temp. (°F)	69	74	88	95	95	104	106	106	100	95	82	72	106
Extreme Minimum Temp. (°F)	-30	-19	-3	16	27	40	50	38	28	19	1	-23	-30
Days Maximum Temp. ≥ 90°F	0	0	0	0	1	7	13	9	4	0	0	0	34
Days Maximum Temp. ≤ 32°F	14	9	2	0	0	0	0	0	0	0	2	9	36
Days Minimum Temp. ≤ 32°F	29	25	20	6	0	0	0	0	0	7	18	27	132
Days Minimum Temp. ≤ 0°F	4	3	0	0	0	0	0	0	0	0	0	3	10
Heating Degree Days (base 65°F)	1,229	1,002	765	400	142	20	1	5	87	358	699	1,116	5,824
Cooling Degree Days (base 65°F)	0	0	2	14	72	239	364	296	124	17	0	0	1,128
Mean Precipitation (in.)	2.11	2.09	2.79	3.63	4.45	4.19	3.87	3.76	3.17	3.04	3.24	2.80	39.14
Extreme Maximum Daily Precip. (in.)	2.85	2.71	1.90	2.45	4.35	3.10	3.86	3.75	3.40	2.75	2.52	2.60	4.35
Days With ≥ 0.1" Precipitation	5	4	6	7	8	7	7	6	5	6	6	5	72
Days With ≥ 0.5" Precipitation	1	1	2	3	3	3	3	2	2	2	2	2	26
Days With ≥ 1.0" Precipitation	1	0	1	1	1	1	1	1	1	1	1	1	11
Mean Snowfall (in.)	9.3	7.5	3.1	1.1	trace	0.0	0.0	0.0	0.0	trace	1.0	7.5	29.5
Maximum Snow Depth (in.)	18	12	8	8	trace	0	0	0	0	trace	4	13	18
Days With ≥ 1.0" Snow Depth	14	8	2	0	0	0	0	0	0	0	1	7	32

Jerseyville 2 SW *Jersey County* Elevation: 629 ft. Latitude: 39° 06' N Longitude: 90° 21' W

	JAN	FEB	MAR	APR	MAY	JUN	JUL	AUG	SEP	OCT	NOV	DEC	YEAR
Mean Maximum Temp. (°F)	37.1	41.8	52.5	64.8	74.3	83.1	87.5	86.2	79.4	67.1	53.6	40.3	64.0
Mean Temp. (°F)	28.3	32.2	42.3	53.6	63.5	72.4	76.7	74.7	66.9	55.0	43.8	31.5	53.4
Mean Minimum Temp. (°F)	19.4	22.6	32.0	42.3	52.5	61.8	65.8	63.1	54.3	42.8	33.9	22.6	42.8
Extreme Maximum Temp. (°F)	71	76	86	91	92	100	104	104	101	92	80	73	104
Extreme Minimum Temp. (°F)	-20	-22	-3	20	29	42	48	38	27	17	-2	-19	-22
Days Maximum Temp. ≥ 90°F	0	0	0	0	0	5	12	10	3	0	0	0	30
Days Maximum Temp. ≤ 32°F	11	7	2	0	0	0	0	0	0	0	1	7	28
Days Minimum Temp. ≤ 32°F	28	23	17	5	0	0	0	0	0	5	14	25	117
Days Minimum Temp. ≤ 0°F	2	2	0	0	0	0	0	0	0	0	0	2	6
Heating Degree Days (base 65°F)	1,131	921	700	356	120	15	1	5	73	323	631	1,033	5,309
Cooling Degree Days (base 65°F)	0	0	3	20	80	244	369	312	135	20	1	0	1,184
Mean Precipitation (in.)	2.19	2.23	3.26	3.87	4.59	3.69	3.46	3.17	3.33	3.36	3.98	2.85	39.98
Extreme Maximum Daily Precip. (in.)	2.63	2.21	2.40	2.70	4.53	3.57	2.61	3.62	3.78	2.76	3.52	5.12	5.12
Days With ≥ 0.1" Precipitation	4	4	7	7	7	6	6	5	5	6	6	5	68
Days With ≥ 0.5" Precipitation	1	1	2	3	3	3	2	2	2	2	3	2	26
Days With ≥ 1.0" Precipitation	0	0	1	1	1	1	1	1	1	1	1	1	10
Mean Snowfall (in.)	4.0	3.4	2.0	0.2	0.0	0.0	0.0	0.0	0.0	trace	0.8	3.1	13.5
Maximum Snow Depth (in.)	15	16	12	4	0	0	0	0	0	trace	7	10	16
Days With ≥ 1.0" Snow Depth	8	5	2	0	0	0	0	0	0	0	1	5	21

Joliet Brandon Rd Dam *Will County* Elevation: 542 ft. Latitude: 41° 30' N Longitude: 88° 06' W

	JAN	FEB	MAR	APR	MAY	JUN	JUL	AUG	SEP	OCT	NOV	DEC	YEAR
Mean Maximum Temp. (°F)	31.4	35.8	47.0	60.2	71.1	80.9	84.3	82.5	76.3	63.5	49.3	35.5	59.8
Mean Temp. (°F)	23.6	27.6	37.8	49.7	60.0	70.0	74.0	72.5	65.2	52.9	40.9	28.0	50.2
Mean Minimum Temp. (°F)	15.8	19.3	28.5	39.1	48.8	59.1	63.6	62.4	54.1	42.4	32.4	20.4	40.5
Extreme Maximum Temp. (°F)	65	73	86	92	93	104	103	102	95	88	77	70	104
Extreme Minimum Temp. (°F)	-26	-19	-7	11	30	35	47	39	32	21	6	-20	-26
Days Maximum Temp. ≥ 90°F	0	0	0	0	1	4	6	4	2	0	0	0	17
Days Maximum Temp. ≤ 32°F	16	11	4	0	0	0	0	0	0	0	2	11	44
Days Minimum Temp. ≤ 32°F	28	25	22	7	0	0	0	0	0	4	16	27	129
Days Minimum Temp. ≤ 0°F	4	2	0	0	0	0	0	0	0	0	0	2	8
Heating Degree Days (base 65°F)	1,276	1,052	837	463	195	32	3	6	89	379	717	1,142	6,191
Cooling Degree Days (base 65°F)	0	0	1	10	47	189	288	245	103	12	0	0	895
Mean Precipitation (in.)	1.66	1.73	2.31	3.49	4.02	3.72	4.29	3.93	3.16	2.96	3.00	2.20	36.47
Extreme Maximum Daily Precip. (in.)	2.45	2.75	2.25	2.12	3.30	5.13	13.60	3.86	2.74	2.92	2.54	3.34	13.60
Days With ≥ 0.1" Precipitation	4	5	6	7	8	6	6	6	5	6	6	5	70
Days With ≥ 0.5" Precipitation	1	1	1	2	3	2	3	3	2	2	2	1	23
Days With ≥ 1.0" Precipitation	0	0	0	1	1	1	1	1	1	1	1	0	8
Mean Snowfall (in.)	na	na	*1.0*	0.1	0.0	0.0	0.0	0.0	0.0	0.0	0.1	*3.2*	na
Maximum Snow Depth (in.)	na	na	na	na	na	na	*0*	*0*	*0*	na	na	na	na
Days With ≥ 1.0" Snow Depth	na	na	*1*	0	0	0	0	0	0	0	0	*5*	na

Kankakee Metro Wastwater *Kankakee County* Elevation: 640 ft. Latitude: 41° 08' N Longitude: 87° 53' W

	JAN	FEB	MAR	APR	MAY	JUN	JUL	AUG	SEP	OCT	NOV	DEC	YEAR
Mean Maximum Temp. (°F)	32.6	36.8	48.3	61.2	72.5	82.3	85.3	83.5	77.7	64.8	50.5	36.7	61.0
Mean Temp. (°F)	23.9	27.6	38.2	49.8	60.8	70.6	74.4	72.3	65.1	52.7	41.1	28.3	50.4
Mean Minimum Temp. (°F)	15.1	18.4	28.0	38.3	49.0	58.8	63.4	61.1	52.4	40.6	31.6	19.9	39.7
Extreme Maximum Temp. (°F)	66	74	84	91	94	103	103	107	99	90	78	70	107
Extreme Minimum Temp. (°F)	-29	-19	-7	8	27	38	46	39	30	18	4	-26	-29
Days Maximum Temp. ≥ 90°F	0	0	0	0	1	6	8	5	2	0	0	0	22
Days Maximum Temp. ≤ 32°F	15	9	3	0	0	0	0	0	0	0	1	10	38
Days Minimum Temp. ≤ 32°F	29	26	22	7	0	0	0	0	0	5	16	27	132
Days Minimum Temp. ≤ 0°F	5	3	0	0	0	0	0	0	0	0	0	3	11
Heating Degree Days (base 65°F)	1,268	1,049	825	459	181	28	2	8	95	386	712	1,131	6,144
Cooling Degree Days (base 65°F)	0	0	1	8	56	202	300	243	105	12	0	0	927
Mean Precipitation (in.)	1.91	1.83	2.58	3.46	4.77	3.91	4.66	3.33	2.97	3.13	3.45	2.48	38.48
Extreme Maximum Daily Precip. (in.)	2.78	1.93	3.00	2.85	3.95	3.88	4.36	3.30	3.44	2.52	3.36	3.65	4.36
Days With ≥ 0.1" Precipitation	5	4	6	7	8	6	6	5	5	6	6	5	69
Days With ≥ 0.5" Precipitation	1	1	2	2	3	3	4	2	2	2	2	1	25
Days With ≥ 1.0" Precipitation	0	0	0	1	1	1	1	1	1	1	1	1	9
Mean Snowfall (in.)	7.7	6.5	2.8	0.9	trace	0.0	0.0	0.0	0.0	trace	0.7	5.5	24.1
Maximum Snow Depth (in.)	18	15	12	6	trace	0	0	0	0	1	4	13	18
Days With ≥ 1.0" Snow Depth	15	11	3	0	0	0	0	0	0	0	1	8	38

The period of record for all cooperative weather station data is 1980 – 2009. See User Guide for detailed explanation of data.

Kaskaskia River Nav Lock *Randolph County* Elevation: 379 ft. Latitude: 37° 59' N Longitude: 89° 57' W

	JAN	FEB	MAR	APR	MAY	JUN	JUL	AUG	SEP	OCT	NOV	DEC	YEAR
Mean Maximum Temp. (°F)	42.3	46.7	57.1	68.6	78.7	87.2	91.4	90.4	82.7	70.4	57.5	44.1	68.1
Mean Temp. (°F)	32.4	35.9	45.5	56.2	66.4	75.1	79.4	77.7	69.7	57.6	46.5	34.4	56.4
Mean Minimum Temp. (°F)	22.5	25.0	33.7	43.8	54.1	63.0	67.2	64.9	56.5	44.7	35.4	24.7	44.6
Extreme Maximum Temp. (°F)	74	83	89	99	98	105	108	109	105	96	87	77	109
Extreme Minimum Temp. (°F)	-18	-14	1	22	32	44	51	41	32	23	9	-18	-18
Days Maximum Temp. ≥ 90°F	0	0	0	0	3	12	20	18	8	1	0	0	62
Days Maximum Temp. ≤ 32°F	7	4	1	0	0	0	0	0	0	0	0	5	17
Days Minimum Temp. ≤ 32°F	27	22	14	3	0	0	0	0	0	3	13	24	106
Days Minimum Temp. ≤ 0°F	1	1	0	0	0	0	0	0	0	0	0	1	3
Heating Degree Days (base 65°F)	1,003	817	604	287	72	5	0	2	44	256	552	941	4,583
Cooling Degree Days (base 65°F)	0	0	4	31	123	317	452	402	191	33	2	0	1,555
Mean Precipitation (in.)	1.98	2.21	3.32	3.56	5.10	3.78	3.70	3.38	3.47	3.66	3.86	3.27	41.29
Extreme Maximum Daily Precip. (in.)	3.00	2.60	4.00	2.42	3.58	3.85	3.97	2.42	3.62	3.26	3.19	2.82	4.00
Days With ≥ 0.1" Precipitation	4	5	7	7	8	6	5	5	5	6	6	6	70
Days With ≥ 0.5" Precipitation	1	2	2	2	3	2	3	3	2	3	3	2	28
Days With ≥ 1.0" Precipitation	1	0	1	1	1	1	1	1	1	1	1	1	11
Mean Snowfall (in.)	1.5	2.1	0.2	0.1	0.0	0.0	0.0	0.0	0.0	0.0	0.4	1.6	5.9
Maximum Snow Depth (in.)	10	24	4	0	0	0	0	0	0	0	8	4	24
Days With ≥ 1.0" Snow Depth	1	2	0	0	0	0	0	0	0	0	0	1	4

La Harpe *Hancock County* Elevation: 700 ft. Latitude: 40° 35' N Longitude: 90° 58' W

	JAN	FEB	MAR	APR	MAY	JUN	JUL	AUG	SEP	OCT	NOV	DEC	YEAR
Mean Maximum Temp. (°F)	33.8	38.7	50.4	63.1	73.7	82.8	86.7	85.0	77.7	65.4	51.0	37.1	62.1
Mean Temp. (°F)	24.2	28.6	39.3	51.0	61.8	71.2	75.0	73.2	65.0	52.9	40.5	27.7	50.9
Mean Minimum Temp. (°F)	14.6	18.4	28.2	38.9	49.9	59.6	63.3	61.3	52.3	40.4	30.0	18.2	39.6
Extreme Maximum Temp. (°F)	66	72	87	92	95	105	104	105	99	96	80	72	105
Extreme Minimum Temp. (°F)	-23	-22	-8	13	28	40	49	40	29	18	-1	-23	-23
Days Maximum Temp. ≥ 90°F	0	0	0	0	1	6	11	8	3	0	0	0	29
Days Maximum Temp. ≤ 32°F	14	9	2	0	0	0	0	0	0	0	2	10	37
Days Minimum Temp. ≤ 32°F	30	25	22	7	0	0	0	0	0	7	19	28	138
Days Minimum Temp. ≤ 0°F	5	3	0	0	0	0	0	0	0	0	0	3	11
Heating Degree Days (base 65°F)	1,258	1,024	790	424	153	20	2	6	98	380	728	1,150	6,033
Cooling Degree Days (base 65°F)	0	0	1	12	60	212	320	266	106	13	0	0	990
Mean Precipitation (in.)	1.47	1.74	2.66	3.81	4.63	4.66	4.43	3.74	3.90	3.04	2.93	2.35	39.36
Extreme Maximum Daily Precip. (in.)	1.64	3.41	5.08	2.62	3.22	4.10	4.32	4.11	4.34	4.74	3.20	3.37	5.08
Days With ≥ 0.1" Precipitation	4	4	6	8	8	7	7	6	6	6	6	5	73
Days With ≥ 0.5" Precipitation	1	1	2	3	3	3	3	2	2	2	2	1	25
Days With ≥ 1.0" Precipitation	0	0	0	1	1	1	1	1	1	1	1	1	9
Mean Snowfall (in.)	6.0	3.7	2.7	0.8	0.0	0.0	0.0	0.0	0.0	trace	0.9	5.0	19.1
Maximum Snow Depth (in.)	17	9	8	5	0	0	0	0	0	trace	4	15	17
Days With ≥ 1.0" Snow Depth	15	10	3	0	0	0	0	0	0	0	1	10	39

Lacon 1 N *Marshall County* Elevation: 459 ft. Latitude: 41° 02' N Longitude: 89° 24' W

	JAN	FEB	MAR	APR	MAY	JUN	JUL	AUG	SEP	OCT	NOV	DEC	YEAR
Mean Maximum Temp. (°F)	33.6	38.5	50.6	64.3	74.8	83.7	87.1	85.5	78.8	66.3	51.5	37.5	62.7
Mean Temp. (°F)	26.2	29.9	40.6	52.8	62.9	72.1	75.9	74.3	66.6	54.8	42.4	29.7	52.3
Mean Minimum Temp. (°F)	18.2	21.2	30.5	41.2	50.9	60.4	64.6	62.9	54.4	43.2	33.1	21.9	41.9
Extreme Maximum Temp. (°F)	70	71	81	91	93	102	103	102	98	90	81	70	103
Extreme Minimum Temp. (°F)	-27	-19	-5	11	26	36	45	44	28	18	2	-24	-27
Days Maximum Temp. ≥ 90°F	0	0	0	0	1	6	11	8	3	0	0	0	29
Days Maximum Temp. ≤ 32°F	14	9	2	0	0	0	0	0	0	0	1	9	35
Days Minimum Temp. ≤ 32°F	27	24	19	6	0	0	0	0	0	4	15	26	121
Days Minimum Temp. ≤ 0°F	3	2	0	0	0	0	0	0	0	0	0	2	7
Heating Degree Days (base 65°F)	1,197	988	752	378	131	14	0	5	73	329	673	1,086	5,626
Cooling Degree Days (base 65°F)	0	0	2	18	71	232	345	298	129	20	0	0	1,115
Mean Precipitation (in.)	1.88	1.81	3.09	3.89	4.36	3.84	3.78	3.69	3.21	3.18	3.15	2.28	38.16
Extreme Maximum Daily Precip. (in.)	2.50	3.52	3.12	2.65	2.35	3.60	3.91	3.25	4.88	2.78	2.77	2.13	4.88
Days With ≥ 0.1" Precipitation	4	4	6	8	7	6	6	7	5	6	6	5	70
Days With ≥ 0.5" Precipitation	1	1	2	3	3	3	2	3	2	2	2	1	25
Days With ≥ 1.0" Precipitation	1	0	1	1	1	1	1	1	1	1	1	1	11
Mean Snowfall (in.)	6.5	5.0	2.8	0.8	trace	0.0	0.0	0.0	0.0	trace	0.8	6.1	22.0
Maximum Snow Depth (in.)	14	9	11	5	trace	0	0	0	0	trace	3	14	14
Days With ≥ 1.0" Snow Depth	14	11	3	1	0	0	0	0	0	0	1	9	39

Lincoln *Logan County* Elevation: 583 ft. Latitude: 40° 08' N Longitude: 89° 22' W

	JAN	FEB	MAR	APR	MAY	JUN	JUL	AUG	SEP	OCT	NOV	DEC	YEAR
Mean Maximum Temp. (°F)	34.0	38.9	50.9	63.8	74.5	83.2	86.2	84.5	79.0	66.1	51.8	38.4	62.6
Mean Temp. (°F)	25.6	29.9	40.5	52.2	62.9	72.1	75.2	73.2	66.1	53.8	42.1	30.0	52.0
Mean Minimum Temp. (°F)	17.1	20.8	30.1	40.5	51.3	60.8	64.2	61.8	53.1	41.5	32.3	21.5	41.2
Extreme Maximum Temp. (°F)	68	75	86	91	95	102	103	104	97	92	81	72	104
Extreme Minimum Temp. (°F)	-25	-20	-2	15	25	39	49	39	28	21	5	-19	-25
Days Maximum Temp. ≥ 90°F	0	0	0	0	1	6	9	7	3	0	0	0	26
Days Maximum Temp. ≤ 32°F	13	8	2	0	0	0	0	0	0	0	1	9	33
Days Minimum Temp. ≤ 32°F	28	24	19	6	0	0	0	0	0	6	16	26	125
Days Minimum Temp. ≤ 0°F	3	2	0	0	0	0	0	0	0	0	0	2	7
Heating Degree Days (base 65°F)	1,217	986	754	394	133	18	1	7	79	357	680	1,080	5,706
Cooling Degree Days (base 65°F)	0	0	2	15	76	236	324	267	118	17	0	0	1,055
Mean Precipitation (in.)	1.95	1.61	2.70	3.65	4.06	3.87	4.95	3.92	3.04	3.32	3.27	2.58	38.92
Extreme Maximum Daily Precip. (in.)	2.73	1.56	1.98	3.96	4.11	3.17	4.76	3.70	3.55	3.73	1.89	5.18	5.18
Days With ≥ 0.1" Precipitation	4	4	6	7	8	6	6	6	5	6	6	6	70
Days With ≥ 0.5" Precipitation	1	1	2	2	2	3	3	3	2	2	2	1	24
Days With ≥ 1.0" Precipitation	0	0	0	1	1	1	1	1	1	1	1	1	9
Mean Snowfall (in.)	6.1	4.9	1.8	0.5	0.0	0.0	0.0	0.0	0.0	trace	0.7	5.4	19.4
Maximum Snow Depth (in.)	14	11	4	5	0	0	0	0	0	trace	6	12	14
Days With ≥ 1.0" Snow Depth	10	6	1	0	0	0	0	0	0	0	0	6	23

The period of record for all cooperative weather station data is 1980 – 2009. See User Guide for detailed explanation of data.

Marengo *Mchenry County* Elevation: 819 ft. Latitude: 42° 15' N Longitude: 88° 36' W

	JAN	FEB	MAR	APR	MAY	JUN	JUL	AUG	SEP	OCT	NOV	DEC	YEAR
Mean Maximum Temp. (°F)	***29.5***	***33.0***	***44.8***	***58.7***	***70.8***	***81.1***	84.2	82.3	75.8	62.3	47.1	***33.1***	***58.6***
Mean Temp. (°F)	***20.6***	***23.6***	***35.0***	***47.4***	***58.5***	***68.7***	72.7	70.8	63.0	50.2	37.8	***24.9***	***47.8***
Mean Minimum Temp. (°F)	***11.8***	***14.2***	***25.2***	***36.0***	***46.2***	***56.3***	61.1	59.2	50.2	38.1	28.5	***16.6***	***36.9***
Extreme Maximum Temp. (°F)	61	***70***	84	***91***	***94***	***105***	105	103	98	90	76	64	***105***
Extreme Minimum Temp. (°F)	-28	***-23***	-10	***6***	***26***	***36***	43	39	26	14	1	-23	***-28***
Days Maximum Temp. ≥ 90°F	0	***0***	0	***0***	***1***	***5***	7	4	1	0	0	0	***18***
Days Maximum Temp. ≤ 32°F	17	***13***	4	***0***	***0***	***0***	0	0	0	0	2	13	***49***
Days Minimum Temp. ≤ 32°F	29	***27***	23	***11***	***1***	***0***	0	0	1	9	20	29	***150***
Days Minimum Temp. ≤ 0°F	7	***5***	1	***0***	***0***	***0***	0	0	0	0	0	4	***17***
Heating Degree Days (base 65°F)	***1,371***	***1,163***	***923***	***530***	***236***	***44***	7	18	130	460	808	***1,237***	***6,927***
Cooling Degree Days (base 65°F)	***0***	***0***	***0***	***8***	***42***	***163***	252	204	77	9	0	***0***	***755***
Mean Precipitation (in.)	1.30	***1.31***	2.03	3.23	***4.01***	***4.01***	3.70	4.81	2.97	2.85	2.58	1.87	***34.67***
Extreme Maximum Daily Precip. (in.)	2.90	***1.30***	1.94	1.94	***2.75***	5.15	3.30	8.20	3.34	2.32	1.96	2.21	***8.20***
Days With ≥ 0.1" Precipitation	3	3	4	7	***8***	6	6	7	6	6	6	4	***66***
Days With ≥ 0.5" Precipitation	1	1	1	2	***3***	3	2	3	2	2	2	1	***23***
Days With ≥ 1.0" Precipitation	0	0	0	1	***1***	1	1	1	1	1	0	0	***7***
Mean Snowfall (in.)	9.3	***8.0***	3.3	1.1	0.1	0.0	0.0	0.0	0.0	0.1	1.7	7.6	***31.2***
Maximum Snow Depth (in.)	17	***19***	14	6	2	0	0	0	0	1	5	12	***19***
Days With ≥ 1.0" Snow Depth	15	***13***	5	1	0	0	0	0	0	0	2	9	***45***

Normal *Mclean County* Elevation: 785 ft. Latitude: 40° 31' N Longitude: 89° 00' W

	JAN	FEB	MAR	APR	MAY	JUN	JUL	AUG	SEP	OCT	NOV	DEC	YEAR
Mean Maximum Temp. (°F)	33.7	38.9	49.7	62.9	73.9	83.2	85.9	84.4	78.2	65.7	50.8	37.1	62.0
Mean Temp. (°F)	25.3	29.8	39.5	51.4	62.5	72.0	75.4	73.5	66.2	54.2	41.6	28.9	51.7
Mean Minimum Temp. (°F)	16.9	20.6	29.3	39.9	51.0	60.9	64.8	62.6	54.1	42.7	32.4	20.7	41.3
Extreme Maximum Temp. (°F)	66	71	85	91	93	103	102	103	96	90	80	71	103
Extreme Minimum Temp. (°F)	-23	-20	-3	10	26	35	48	41	31	18	2	-22	-23
Days Maximum Temp. ≥ 90°F	0	0	0	0	1	6	9	7	2	0	0	0	25
Days Maximum Temp. ≤ 32°F	14	9	3	0	0	0	0	0	0	0	2	10	38
Days Minimum Temp. ≤ 32°F	28	24	20	7	0	0	0	0	0	5	16	27	127
Days Minimum Temp. ≤ 0°F	4	2	0	0	0	0	0	0	0	0	0	2	8
Heating Degree Days (base 65°F)	1,223	991	785	417	150	19	1	7	84	347	695	1,112	5,831
Cooling Degree Days (base 65°F)	0	0	2	15	79	237	330	278	126	19	0	0	1,086
Mean Precipitation (in.)	2.08	1.92	2.75	3.71	4.41	3.95	4.06	3.95	3.02	3.27	3.22	2.46	38.80
Extreme Maximum Daily Precip. (in.)	2.35	2.27	1.65	3.15	3.21	3.50	5.63	2.63	5.21	3.53	1.94	2.64	5.63
Days With ≥ 0.1" Precipitation	5	5	6	7	8	7	6	7	5	6	6	6	74
Days With ≥ 0.5" Precipitation	1	1	2	3	3	3	3	3	2	2	2	2	27
Days With ≥ 1.0" Precipitation	0	0	0	1	1	1	1	1	1	1	1	0	8
Mean Snowfall (in.)	6.1	5.3	1.8	0.8	trace	0.0	0.0	0.0	0.0	0.1	0.7	4.9	19.7
Maximum Snow Depth (in.)	18	11	7	4	trace	0	0	0	0	trace	6	12	18
Days With ≥ 1.0" Snow Depth	14	8	3	0	0	0	0	0	0	0	1	8	34

Park Forest *Cook County* Elevation: 709 ft. Latitude: 41° 30' N Longitude: 87° 41' W

	JAN	FEB	MAR	APR	MAY	JUN	JUL	AUG	SEP	OCT	NOV	DEC	YEAR
Mean Maximum Temp. (°F)	30.9	35.1	45.8	59.0	69.9	79.9	83.7	81.8	75.1	62.5	48.7	35.1	59.0
Mean Temp. (°F)	23.3	27.1	37.2	49.1	59.6	69.6	74.0	72.2	64.8	52.3	40.7	27.8	49.8
Mean Minimum Temp. (°F)	15.7	19.1	28.5	39.2	49.3	59.2	64.3	62.6	54.4	42.1	32.7	20.5	40.6
Extreme Maximum Temp. (°F)	65	71	83	89	94	102	102	103	95	89	75	70	103
Extreme Minimum Temp. (°F)	-27	-18	-6	9	28	37	46	41	29	18	4	-21	-27
Days Maximum Temp. ≥ 90°F	0	0	0	0	1	4	6	4	1	0	0	0	16
Days Maximum Temp. ≤ 32°F	17	11	4	0	0	0	0	0	0	0	2	11	45
Days Minimum Temp. ≤ 32°F	29	25	21	6	0	0	0	0	0	4	15	27	127
Days Minimum Temp. ≤ 0°F	4	2	0	0	0	0	0	0	0	0	0	2	8
Heating Degree Days (base 65°F)	1,287	1,063	857	480	212	41	5	10	100	398	721	1,146	6,320
Cooling Degree Days (base 65°F)	0	0	1	10	52	185	291	242	101	12	0	0	894
Mean Precipitation (in.)	2.06	1.81	2.57	3.78	4.41	4.35	4.27	4.11	3.27	3.25	3.52	2.56	39.96
Extreme Maximum Daily Precip. (in.)	3.48	2.27	1.97	3.88	6.43	3.61	6.55	3.13	4.04	3.18	3.40	3.87	6.55
Days With ≥ 0.1" Precipitation	5	4	6	7	7	6	6	6	6	6	6	6	71
Days With ≥ 0.5" Precipitation	1	1	1	3	3	3	3	3	2	2	2	1	25
Days With ≥ 1.0" Precipitation	0	0	0	1	1	1	1	2	1	1	1	0	9
Mean Snowfall (in.)	9.4	7.8	4.9	0.8	trace	0.0	0.0	0.0	0.0	0.3	0.9	6.7	30.8
Maximum Snow Depth (in.)	17	16	14	7	trace	0	0	0	0	2	4	17	17
Days With ≥ 1.0" Snow Depth	19	13	5	0	0	0	0	0	0	0	1	10	48

Paw Paw 2 NW *Lee County* Elevation: 950 ft. Latitude: 41° 43' N Longitude: 89° 00' W

	JAN	FEB	MAR	APR	MAY	JUN	JUL	AUG	SEP	OCT	NOV	DEC	YEAR
Mean Maximum Temp. (°F)	27.8	32.1	44.1	58.4	69.6	79.5	82.2	80.0	74.1	61.4	46.2	31.7	57.2
Mean Temp. (°F)	20.0	24.0	34.8	47.2	58.4	68.6	71.8	69.7	62.7	50.2	37.5	24.1	47.4
Mean Minimum Temp. (°F)	12.2	15.9	25.5	36.0	47.1	57.6	61.4	59.4	51.2	39.0	28.7	16.4	37.5
Extreme Maximum Temp. (°F)	62	66	83	92	91	101	100	99	92	90	75	65	101
Extreme Minimum Temp. (°F)	-25	-33	-16	9	24	38	41	37	29	17	3	-23	-33
Days Maximum Temp. ≥ 90°F	0	0	0	0	0	3	4	2	1	0	0	0	10
Days Maximum Temp. ≤ 32°F	20	14	5	0	0	0	0	0	0	0	4	15	58
Days Minimum Temp. ≤ 32°F	30	27	25	10	1	0	0	0	0	7	20	29	149
Days Minimum Temp. ≤ 0°F	7	4	0	0	0	0	0	0	0	0	0	4	15
Heating Degree Days (base 65°F)	1,388	1,152	930	532	234	40	9	19	129	458	818	1,262	6,971
Cooling Degree Days (base 65°F)	0	0	0	5	37	153	227	172	66	6	0	0	666
Mean Precipitation (in.)	1.28	1.42	2.07	3.07	4.45	4.00	4.14	4.25	3.62	2.78	2.96	1.98	36.02
Extreme Maximum Daily Precip. (in.)	1.43	2.95	1.86	2.02	2.95	6.92	5.46	3.15	5.24	2.94	2.55	3.77	6.92
Days With ≥ 0.1" Precipitation	3	3	5	7	8	7	6	6	6	5	6	5	67
Days With ≥ 0.5" Precipitation	1	1	1	2	3	2	3	3	2	2	2	1	23
Days With ≥ 1.0" Precipitation	0	0	0	0	1	1	1	1	1	1	1	0	7
Mean Snowfall (in.)	8.8	6.5	3.9	0.8	trace	0.0	0.0	0.0	0.0	0.2	1.2	8.5	29.9
Maximum Snow Depth (in.)	25	11	12	7	trace	0	0	0	0	3	3	24	25
Days With ≥ 1.0" Snow Depth	17	12	4	0	0	0	0	0	0	0	1	12	46

The period of record for all cooperative weather station data is 1980 – 2009. See User Guide for detailed explanation of data.

Princeville *Peoria County* Elevation: 734 ft. Latitude: 40° 56' N Longitude: 89° 46' W

	JAN	FEB	MAR	APR	MAY	JUN	JUL	AUG	SEP	OCT	NOV	DEC	YEAR
Mean Maximum Temp. (°F)	32.0	37.0	49.3	62.9	73.4	81.5	85.2	83.3	76.9	64.5	50.3	35.6	61.0
Mean Temp. (°F)	22.4	26.8	37.9	49.9	60.7	69.5	73.0	70.9	63.4	51.6	39.5	26.2	49.3
Mean Minimum Temp. (°F)	12.8	16.6	26.3	36.9	48.0	57.4	60.8	58.6	49.7	38.7	28.7	16.8	37.6
Extreme Maximum Temp. (°F)	66	72	87	93	95	101	104	105	99	92	82	70	105
Extreme Minimum Temp. (°F)	-26	-26	-8	5	22	35	44	36	26	12	0	-26	-26
Days Maximum Temp. ≥ 90°F	0	0	0	0	1	5	8	6	2	0	0	0	22
Days Maximum Temp. ≤ 32°F	15	10	3	0	0	0	0	0	0	0	2	11	41
Days Minimum Temp. ≤ 32°F	30	26	24	10	1	0	0	0	1	9	20	29	150
Days Minimum Temp. ≤ 0°F	6	4	0	0	0	0	0	0	0	0	0	4	14
Heating Degree Days (base 65°F)	1,314	1,072	836	457	179	34	5	17	124	419	759	1,194	6,410
Cooling Degree Days (base 65°F)	0	0	1	11	53	175	261	208	81	11	0	0	801
Mean Precipitation (in.)	2.08	1.85	2.92	3.55	4.46	3.71	3.86	3.87	3.39	2.77	3.01	2.35	37.82
Extreme Maximum Daily Precip. (in.)	5.00	1.84	3.02	1.71	4.60	3.74	4.45	3.15	3.50	3.95	2.81	3.10	5.00
Days With ≥ 0.1" Precipitation	4	4	6	8	8	7	6	7	5	6	6	5	72
Days With ≥ 0.5" Precipitation	1	1	2	3	3	3	3	3	2	2	2	2	27
Days With ≥ 1.0" Precipitation	1	0	1	1	1	1	1	1	1	0	1	0	9
Mean Snowfall (in.)	6.1	5.9	2.3	0.4	trace	0.0	0.0	0.0	0.0	trace	1.0	5.9	21.6
Maximum Snow Depth (in.)	14	11	5	12	trace	0	0	0	0	trace	3	***15***	***15***
Days With ≥ 1.0" Snow Depth	8	6	2	0	0	0	0	0	0	0	0	***5***	***21***

Rosiclare 5 NW *Hardin County* Elevation: 399 ft. Latitude: 37° 25' N Longitude: 88° 21' W

	JAN	FEB	MAR	APR	MAY	JUN	JUL	AUG	SEP	OCT	NOV	DEC	YEAR
Mean Maximum Temp. (°F)	42.7	47.9	58.1	68.8	76.6	84.2	87.7	87.8	81.3	70.2	58.1	45.8	67.4
Mean Temp. (°F)	32.8	36.9	46.1	55.8	64.3	72.8	76.6	75.8	68.2	56.7	46.6	35.9	55.7
Mean Minimum Temp. (°F)	22.8	25.9	34.1	42.8	52.4	61.3	65.5	63.9	55.2	43.2	35.1	25.9	44.0
Extreme Maximum Temp. (°F)	70	77	85	90	92	100	102	104	100	90	84	76	104
Extreme Minimum Temp. (°F)	-22	-12	6	16	31	39	47	36	32	18	3	-17	-22
Days Maximum Temp. ≥ 90°F	0	0	0	0	0	6	13	13	4	0	0	0	36
Days Maximum Temp. ≤ 32°F	6	3	1	0	0	0	0	0	0	0	0	4	14
Days Minimum Temp. ≤ 32°F	25	21	15	5	0	0	0	0	0	5	13	23	107
Days Minimum Temp. ≤ 0°F	1	1	0	0	0	0	0	0	0	0	0	0	2
Heating Degree Days (base 65°F)	992	788	586	292	100	8	0	2	51	275	546	896	4,536
Cooling Degree Days (base 65°F)	0	0	6	24	87	247	367	344	155	24	2	0	1,256
Mean Precipitation (in.)	3.58	3.81	4.61	4.63	5.51	4.36	4.32	3.18	3.46	3.80	4.19	4.46	49.91
Extreme Maximum Daily Precip. (in.)	2.66	3.31	5.87	3.55	3.38	2.65	4.42	6.14	3.02	4.60	2.87	4.96	6.14
Days With ≥ 0.1" Precipitation	6	6	8	7	8	6	6	4	5	5	7	7	75
Days With ≥ 0.5" Precipitation	2	3	3	3	4	3	3	2	3	3	3	4	36
Days With ≥ 1.0" Precipitation	1	1	1	1	2	1	1	1	1	1	1	1	13
Mean Snowfall (in.)	2.4	2.2	0.5	trace	0.0	0.0	0.0	0.0	0.0	0.2	trace	1.2	6.5
Maximum Snow Depth (in.)	8	10	7	trace	0	0	0	0	0	1	trace	8	10
Days With ≥ 1.0" Snow Depth	4	4	0	0	0	0	0	0	0	0	0	2	10

Tuscola *Douglas County* Elevation: 652 ft. Latitude: 39° 48' N Longitude: 88° 17' W

	JAN	FEB	MAR	APR	MAY	JUN	JUL	AUG	SEP	OCT	NOV	DEC	YEAR
Mean Maximum Temp. (°F)	35.5	39.8	51.7	65.1	75.6	84.5	87.3	85.6	80.1	67.2	52.6	39.7	63.7
Mean Temp. (°F)	27.2	30.9	41.6	53.4	64.2	73.2	76.2	74.3	67.6	55.4	43.2	31.8	53.3
Mean Minimum Temp. (°F)	19.0	22.0	31.4	41.8	52.6	61.9	65.1	62.9	55.1	43.5	33.9	23.9	42.7
Extreme Maximum Temp. (°F)	68	73	86	90	95	104	104	104	99	91	79	70	104
Extreme Minimum Temp. (°F)	-23	-18	0	15	30	39	49	43	31	20	1	-26	-26
Days Maximum Temp. ≥ 90°F	0	0	0	0	2	8	11	9	4	0	0	0	34
Days Maximum Temp. ≤ 32°F	12	8	2	0	0	0	0	0	0	0	1	7	30
Days Minimum Temp. ≤ 32°F	27	23	17	5	0	0	0	0	0	4	14	25	115
Days Minimum Temp. ≤ 0°F	3	2	0	0	0	0	0	0	0	0	0	1	6
Heating Degree Days (base 65°F)	1,165	956	721	357	111	13	0	4	59	314	647	1,021	5,368
Cooling Degree Days (base 65°F)	0	0	2	17	92	266	355	299	143	23	0	0	1,197
Mean Precipitation (in.)	2.22	2.20	2.75	4.01	4.14	4.08	4.47	3.37	3.15	3.35	3.83	2.88	40.45
Extreme Maximum Daily Precip. (in.)	1.68	2.30	2.02	2.40	3.75	3.72	3.89	4.07	3.72	2.60	3.02	3.00	4.07
Days With ≥ 0.1" Precipitation	5	5	6	8	8	7	6	5	5	6	7	6	74
Days With ≥ 0.5" Precipitation	2	1	2	3	3	3	3	2	2	2	3	2	28
Days With ≥ 1.0" Precipitation	0	0	0	1	1	1	1	1	1	1	1	1	9
Mean Snowfall (in.)	6.3	5.1	2.2	0.2	trace	0.0	0.0	0.0	0.0	trace	1.0	4.7	19.5
Maximum Snow Depth (in.)	15	19	7	2	trace	0	0	0	0	trace	8	10	19
Days With ≥ 1.0" Snow Depth	9	8	2	0	0	0	0	0	0	0	0	5	24

Urbana *Champaign County* Elevation: 743 ft. Latitude: 40° 06' N Longitude: 88° 14' W

	JAN	FEB	MAR	APR	MAY	JUN	JUL	AUG	SEP	OCT	NOV	DEC	YEAR
Mean Maximum Temp. (°F)	33.7	38.1	50.1	62.9	73.7	82.6	85.2	83.8	78.2	65.2	50.7	37.1	61.8
Mean Temp. (°F)	25.9	30.0	40.6	52.0	62.7	71.9	75.0	73.5	66.4	54.2	41.9	29.7	52.0
Mean Minimum Temp. (°F)	18.2	21.8	31.0	41.0	51.7	61.2	64.8	63.0	54.5	43.0	33.1	22.3	42.1
Extreme Maximum Temp. (°F)	67	72	84	91	94	103	101	102	97	92	79	71	103
Extreme Minimum Temp. (°F)	-25	-17	1	16	29	41	48	40	30	19	7	-20	-25
Days Maximum Temp. ≥ 90°F	0	0	0	0	1	6	7	6	2	0	0	0	22
Days Maximum Temp. ≤ 32°F	14	9	2	0	0	0	0	0	0	0	1	10	36
Days Minimum Temp. ≤ 32°F	28	24	18	5	0	0	0	0	0	4	15	26	120
Days Minimum Temp. ≤ 0°F	3	2	0	0	0	0	0	0	0	0	0	2	7
Heating Degree Days (base 65°F)	1,204	983	752	397	136	17	1	4	74	346	685	1,086	5,685
Cooling Degree Days (base 65°F)	0	0	1	12	72	231	319	274	123	17	0	0	1,049
Mean Precipitation (in.)	2.01	2.13	2.90	3.69	4.90	4.15	4.62	3.96	3.22	3.11	3.58	2.69	40.96
Extreme Maximum Daily Precip. (in.)	1.45	2.30	2.92	2.96	2.98	3.89	4.43	5.32	3.30	3.72	3.53	2.41	5.32
Days With ≥ 0.1" Precipitation	5	4	6	8	8	6	7	6	5	6	7	6	74
Days With ≥ 0.5" Precipitation	1	1	2	2	3	3	3	3	2	2	2	2	26
Days With ≥ 1.0" Precipitation	0	0	1	1	1	1	1	1	1	1	1	0	9
Mean Snowfall (in.)	6.8	5.9	2.5	0.5	trace	0.0	0.0	0.0	0.0	0.1	1.2	5.8	22.8
Maximum Snow Depth (in.)	17	19	10	3	trace	0	0	0	0	trace	8	13	19
Days With ≥ 1.0" Snow Depth	12	8	2	0	0	0	0	0	0	0	1	7	30

The period of record for all cooperative weather station data is 1980 – 2009. See User Guide for detailed explanation of data.

Virden *Macoupin County* Elevation: 674 ft. Latitude: 39° 30' N Longitude: 89° 46' W

	JAN	FEB	MAR	APR	MAY	JUN	JUL	AUG	SEP	OCT	NOV	DEC	YEAR
Mean Maximum Temp. (°F)	36.6	40.9	52.6	66.1	75.7	83.7	87.2	86.0	79.8	67.5	53.0	39.6	64.1
Mean Temp. (°F)	28.8	33.0	43.0	55.2	65.1	73.6	77.1	75.4	68.3	56.8	44.3	32.0	54.4
Mean Minimum Temp. (°F)	20.9	24.6	33.3	44.3	54.4	63.4	66.9	64.7	56.7	46.0	35.7	24.3	44.6
Extreme Maximum Temp. (°F)	70	72	85	90	93	100	102	105	99	91	81	72	105
Extreme Minimum Temp. (°F)	-19	-19	0	19	33	43	50	39	31	20	-1	-20	-20
Days Maximum Temp. ≥ 90°F	0	0	0	0	1	6	10	9	3	0	0	0	29
Days Maximum Temp. ≤ 32°F	11	7	1	0	0	0	0	0	0	0	1	8	28
Days Minimum Temp. ≤ 32°F	26	21	14	3	0	0	0	0	0	3	12	24	103
Days Minimum Temp. ≤ 0°F	2	1	0	0	0	0	0	0	0	0	0	1	4
Heating Degree Days (base 65°F)	1,117	899	679	313	92	9	0	2	55	277	614	1,017	5,074
Cooling Degree Days (base 65°F)	0	0	2	26	102	272	381	329	161	29	1	0	1,303
Mean Precipitation (in.)	1.85	2.11	2.77	3.52	4.16	3.84	3.51	2.74	2.94	3.11	3.45	2.53	36.53
Extreme Maximum Daily Precip. (in.)	2.24	1.72	1.92	3.98	3.77	4.30	4.30	2.27	4.38	3.05	2.63	4.25	4.38
Days With ≥ 0.1" Precipitation	4	4	6	6	7	6	5	5	5	6	6	4	64
Days With ≥ 0.5" Precipitation	1	1	2	2	3	2	2	2	2	2	2	2	23
Days With ≥ 1.0" Precipitation	0	0	0	1	1	1	1	1	1	1	1	1	9
Mean Snowfall (in.)	5.1	5.6	3.0	0.4	0.0	0.0	0.0	0.0	0.0	trace	0.8	4.6	19.5
Maximum Snow Depth (in.)	12	8	8	4	0	0	0	0	0	trace	4	12	12
Days With ≥ 1.0" Snow Depth	9	6	2	0	0	0	0	0	0	0	0	5	22

Wheaton 3 SE *Dupage County* Elevation: 680 ft. Latitude: 41° 49' N Longitude: 88° 04' W

	JAN	FEB	MAR	APR	MAY	JUN	JUL	AUG	SEP	OCT	NOV	DEC	YEAR
Mean Maximum Temp. (°F)	33.6	38.4	49.8	63.2	74.1	83.4	86.8	85.0	78.0	***65.7***	50.6	37.3	***62.2***
Mean Temp. (°F)	25.2	29.1	39.0	50.8	61.0	70.5	75.1	73.6	65.8	***53.7***	41.5	29.3	***51.2***
Mean Minimum Temp. (°F)	16.9	19.7	28.1	38.4	47.9	57.5	63.4	62.1	53.4	***41.7***	32.4	21.3	***40.2***
Extreme Maximum Temp. (°F)	65	74	85	90	94	103	105	100	96	***89***	77	70	***105***
Extreme Minimum Temp. (°F)	-26	-20	-7	4	26	34	44	42	28	***14***	5	-21	***-26***
Days Maximum Temp. ≥ 90°F	0	0	0	0	1	7	10	***7***	2	***0***	0	0	***27***
Days Maximum Temp. ≤ 32°F	14	8	2	0	0	0	0	0	0	***0***	1	9	***34***
Days Minimum Temp. ≤ 32°F	28	24	21	8	1	0	0	0	0	***6***	16	25	***129***
Days Minimum Temp. ≤ 0°F	4	3	0	0	0	0	0	0	0	***0***	0	2	***9***
Heating Degree Days (base 65°F)	1,226	1,010	801	433	178	29	2	5	85	***357***	697	1,098	***5,921***
Cooling Degree Days (base 65°F)	0	0	1	13	61	200	324	278	114	***15***	0	0	***1,006***
Mean Precipitation (in.)	1.88	1.66	2.37	3.52	4.00	3.98	4.10	4.44	3.36	***3.13***	3.49	2.13	***38.06***
Extreme Maximum Daily Precip. (in.)	1.75	2.85	2.58	2.00	3.79	3.22	9.24	6.01	3.35	***4.43***	2.98	3.04	***9.24***
Days With ≥ 0.1" Precipitation	5	4	6	7	7	7	6	***6***	6	***5***	6	5	***70***
Days With ≥ 0.5" Precipitation	1	1	1	2	3	3	3	***3***	2	***2***	2	1	***24***
Days With ≥ 1.0" Precipitation	0	0	0	1	1	1	1	***1***	1	***1***	1	0	***8***
Mean Snowfall (in.)	9.4	6.9	4.2	0.7	trace	0.0	0.0	0.0	0.0	***trace***	1.0	5.7	***27.9***
Maximum Snow Depth (in.)	***16***	***16***	***10***	***3***	***trace***	***0***	***0***	***0***	***0***	na	***4***	***21***	na
Days With ≥ 1.0" Snow Depth	***14***	***10***	3	0	0	0	0	0	0	***0***	1	7	***35***

The period of record for all cooperative weather station data is 1980 – 2009. See User Guide for detailed explanation of data.

Illinois Weather Station Rankings

Annual Extreme Maximum Temperature

Rank	Station Name (Highest)	°F	Rank	Station Name (Lowest)	°F
1	Kaskaskia River Nav Lock	***109***	1	Elgin	101
2	Kankakee Metro Wastwater	107	1	Paw Paw 2 NW	101
3	Alton Melvin Price L&D	***106***	3	Charleston	102
3	Cahokia	***106***	3	Danville	102
3	Chicago Midway Arpt	106	3	Fulton L&D #13	102
3	Decatur	106	3	Galesburg	102
3	Havana 4 NNE	106	3	Springfield Capital Arpt	102
8	Albion	***105***	8	Aledo	103
8	Belleville Siu Research	105	8	Aurora	103
8	Brookport Dam 52	105	8	Chenoa	103
8	Carbondale Sewage Plant	105	8	De Kalb	103
8	Carlinville	***105***	8	Dixon 1 NW	103
8	Chicago Botanical Garden	105	8	Effingham	103
8	La Harpe	105	8	Golden	***103***
8	Marengo	***105***	8	Lacon 1 N	103
8	Peoria Greater Peoria Arpt	105	8	Normal	103
8	Princeville	105	8	Park Forest	103
8	Virden	105	8	Urbana	103
8	Wheaton 3 SE	***105***	19	Anna 2 NNE	104
20	Anna 2 NNE	104	19	Antioch	***104***
20	Antioch	***104***	19	Chicago Ohare Intl Arpt	104
20	Chicago Ohare Intl Arpt	104	19	Jerseyville 2 SW	104
20	Jerseyville 2 SW	104	19	Joliet Brandon Rd Dam	104
20	Joliet Brandon Rd Dam	104	19	Lincoln	104
20	Lincoln	104	19	Moline Quad City Arpt	104

Annual Mean Maximum Temperature

Rank	Station Name (Highest)	°F	Rank	Station Name (Lowest)	°F
1	Kaskaskia River Nav Lock	***68.1***	1	Antioch	***57.3***
2	Brookport Dam 52	68.0	1	Paw Paw 2 NW	57.3
3	Anna 2 NNE	67.9	3	Elgin	***58.1***
4	Belleville Siu Research	67.7	4	Fulton L&D #13	58.2
5	Rosiclare 5 NW	67.4	5	Chicago Botanical Garden	58.3
6	Carbondale Sewage Plant	66.8	5	De Kalb	58.3
7	Cahokia	***66.6***	7	Dixon 1 NW	58.4
8	Albion	***66.5***	7	Rockford Greater Rockford Arpt	58.4
9	Alton Melvin Price L&D	64.4	9	Marengo	***58.6***
10	Decatur	64.2	10	Chicago Ohare Intl Arpt	58.9
11	Carlinville	***64.1***	11	Park Forest	59.0
11	Virden	64.1	12	Aurora	59.8
13	Jerseyville 2 SW	64.0	12	Joliet Brandon Rd Dam	59.8
14	Charleston	63.8	14	Chicago Midway Arpt	59.9
15	Effingham	63.7	15	Aledo	60.0
15	Tuscola	63.7	16	Galesburg	60.1
17	Danville	63.0	17	Moline Quad City Arpt	60.7
17	Springfield Capital Arpt	63.0	18	Kankakee Metro Wastwater	61.0
19	Havana 4 NNE	62.9	18	Princeville	61.0
20	Lacon 1 N	62.7	20	Peoria Greater Peoria Arpt	61.3
21	Lincoln	62.6	21	Chenoa	61.8
22	Wheaton 3 SE	***62.2***	21	Urbana	61.8
23	Golden	***62.1***	23	Normal	62.0
23	La Harpe	62.1	24	Golden	***62.1***
25	Normal	62.0	24	La Harpe	62.1

Rankings include 25 highest/lowest stations. If state has less than 25 stations, all stations are included. The period of record is 1980–2009. See User Guide for detailed explanation of data.

Annual Mean Temperature

Highest Rank	Highest Station Name	Highest °F	Lowest Rank	Lowest Station Name	Lowest °F
1	Brookport Dam 52	57.8	1	Paw Paw 2 NW	47.4
2	Anna 2 NNE	57.0	2	Antioch	***47.8***
3	Belleville Siu Research	56.7	2	Marengo	***47.8***
4	Albion	***56.5***	4	Dixon 1 NW	48.3
5	Kaskaskia River Nav Lock	***56.4***	5	Elgin	***48.4***
6	Cahokia	***56.1***	6	De Kalb	48.6
7	Carbondale Sewage Plant	55.7	6	Rockford Greater Rockford Arpt	48.6
7	Rosiclare 5 NW	55.7	8	Fulton L&D #13	49.0
9	Alton Melvin Price L&D	55.3	9	Chicago Botanical Garden	49.2
10	Virden	54.4	10	Princeville	49.3
11	Carlinville	***54.1***	11	Aurora	49.6
12	Charleston	54.0	12	Chicago Ohare Intl Arpt	49.7
13	Decatur	53.7	13	Park Forest	49.8
14	Effingham	53.4	14	Aledo	50.0
14	Jerseyville 2 SW	53.4	15	Joliet Brandon Rd Dam	50.2
16	Tuscola	53.3	16	Kankakee Metro Wastwater	50.4
17	Springfield Capital Arpt	53.1	17	Moline Quad City Arpt	50.6
18	Danville	52.8	18	Galesburg	50.8
19	Lacon 1 N	52.3	19	La Harpe	50.9
20	Lincoln	52.0	20	Wheaton 3 SE	***51.2***
20	Urbana	52.0	21	Chicago Midway Arpt	51.5
22	Golden	***51.9***	22	Chenoa	51.6
23	Havana 4 NNE	51.8	23	Normal	51.7
24	Normal	51.7	23	Peoria Greater Peoria Arpt	51.7
24	Peoria Greater Peoria Arpt	51.7	25	Havana 4 NNE	51.8

Annual Mean Minimum Temperature

Highest Rank	Highest Station Name	Highest °F	Lowest Rank	Lowest Station Name	Lowest °F
1	Brookport Dam 52	47.5	1	Marengo	***37.0***
2	Albion	***46.5***	2	Paw Paw 2 NW	37.5
3	Alton Melvin Price L&D	46.3	3	Princeville	37.6
4	Anna 2 NNE	46.1	4	Dixon 1 NW	38.2
5	Belleville Siu Research	45.7	5	Antioch	***38.4***
6	Cahokia	***45.5***	6	Elgin	38.5
7	Kaskaskia River Nav Lock	***44.6***	7	Rockford Greater Rockford Arpt	38.6
7	Virden	44.6	8	De Kalb	38.9
9	Carbondale Sewage Plant	44.5	9	Aurora	39.3
10	Charleston	44.2	10	La Harpe	39.6
11	Carlinville	***44.1***	11	Fulton L&D #13	39.7
12	Rosiclare 5 NW	44.0	11	Kankakee Metro Wastwater	39.7
13	Decatur	43.2	13	Aledo	39.8
14	Chicago Midway Arpt	43.1	14	Chicago Botanical Garden	40.0
14	Springfield Capital Arpt	43.1	15	Wheaton 3 SE	***40.2***
16	Effingham	43.0	16	Chicago Ohare Intl Arpt	40.4
17	Jerseyville 2 SW	42.8	17	Joliet Brandon Rd Dam	40.5
18	Tuscola	42.7	17	Moline Quad City Arpt	40.5
19	Danville	42.6	19	Park Forest	40.6
20	Urbana	42.1	20	Havana 4 NNE	40.7
21	Peoria Greater Peoria Arpt	42.0	21	Lincoln	41.2
22	Lacon 1 N	41.9	22	Chenoa	41.3
23	Golden	***41.7***	22	Normal	41.3
24	Galesburg	41.5	24	Galesburg	41.5
25	Chenoa	41.3	25	Golden	***41.7***

 Rankings include 25 highest/lowest stations. If state has less than 25 stations, all stations are included. The period of record is 1980–2009. See User Guide for detailed explanation of data.

Annual Extreme Minimum Temperature

Highest			Lowest		
Rank	**Station Name**	**°F**	**Rank**	**Station Name**	**°F**
1	Alton Melvin Price L&D	***-16***	1	Fulton L&D #13	-33
2	Anna 2 NNE	-17	1	Paw Paw 2 NW	-33
3	Kaskaskia River Nav Lock	***-18***	3	Dixon 1 NW	-32
4	Cahokia	***-19***	4	Havana 4 NNE	-30
4	Carlinville	***-19***	5	Kankakee Metro Wastwater	-29
6	Albion	***-20***	5	Moline Quad City Arpt	-29
6	Virden	-20	7	Aledo	-28
8	Belleville Siu Research	-21	7	Antioch	***-28***
8	Brookport Dam 52	-21	7	Marengo	***-28***
8	Carbondale Sewage Plant	-21	10	Charleston	-27
8	Springfield Capital Arpt	-21	10	Chicago Botanical Garden	-27
12	Decatur	-22	10	Chicago Ohare Intl Arpt	-27
12	Effingham	***-22***	10	De Kalb	-27
12	Jerseyville 2 SW	-22	10	Elgin	-27
12	Rosiclare 5 NW	-22	10	Galesburg	-27
16	Golden	***-23***	10	Lacon 1 N	-27
16	La Harpe	-23	10	Park Forest	-27
16	Normal	-23	10	Rockford Greater Rockford Arpt	-27
16	Peoria Greater Peoria Arpt	-23	19	Aurora	-26
20	Chicago Midway Arpt	-25	19	Chenoa	-26
20	Lincoln	-25	19	Danville	-26
20	Urbana	-25	19	Joliet Brandon Rd Dam	-26
23	Aurora	-26	19	Princeville	-26
23	Chenoa	-26	19	Tuscola	-26
23	Danville	-26	19	Wheaton 3 SE	***-26***

July Mean Maximum Temperature

Highest			Lowest		
Rank	**Station Name**	**°F**	**Rank**	**Station Name**	**°F**
1	Kaskaskia River Nav Lock	91.4	1	Antioch	***82.1***
2	Albion	***89.9***	2	Paw Paw 2 NW	82.2
3	Belleville Siu Research	89.5	3	Chicago Botanical Garden	82.5
4	Brookport Dam 52	89.3	4	Dixon 1 NW	82.9
5	Anna 2 NNE	88.7	5	Elgin	83.3
5	Cahokia	88.7	6	Fulton L&D #13	83.5
7	Carbondale Sewage Plant	88.4	7	De Kalb	83.6
8	Havana 4 NNE	88.2	8	Park Forest	83.7
9	Rosiclare 5 NW	87.7	9	Rockford Greater Rockford Arpt	83.9
10	Alton Melvin Price L&D	87.6	10	Chicago Ohare Intl Arpt	84.1
10	Decatur	87.6	11	Marengo	84.2
12	Jerseyville 2 SW	87.5	12	Joliet Brandon Rd Dam	84.3
13	Tuscola	87.3	13	Aledo	84.7
14	Effingham	87.2	13	Aurora	84.7
14	Virden	87.2	13	Galesburg	84.7
16	Lacon 1 N	87.1	16	Chicago Midway Arpt	84.8
17	Carlinville	86.9	17	Chenoa	85.2
18	Wheaton 3 SE	86.8	17	Princeville	85.2
19	La Harpe	86.7	19	Kankakee Metro Wastwater	85.3
20	Golden	***86.6***	19	Urbana	85.3
21	Charleston	86.5	21	Danville	85.7
22	Springfield Capital Arpt	86.3	21	Peoria Greater Peoria Arpt	85.7
23	Lincoln	86.2	23	Moline Quad City Arpt	85.9
24	Moline Quad City Arpt	85.9	23	Normal	85.9
24	Normal	85.9	25	Lincoln	86.2

Rankings include 25 highest/lowest stations. If state has less than 25 stations, all stations are included. The period of record is 1980–2009. See User Guide for detailed explanation of data.

January Mean Minimum Temperature

Highest

Rank	Station Name	°F
1	Brookport Dam 52	26.3
2	Anna 2 NNE	24.8
3	Albion	23.9
3	Belleville Siu Research	23.9
5	Carbondale Sewage Plant	23.2
6	Rosiclare 5 NW	22.8
7	Cahokia	22.6
8	Kaskaskia River Nav Lock	22.5
9	Alton Melvin Price L&D	21.9
10	Virden	20.9
11	Charleston	20.7
12	Carlinville	***20.6***
13	Effingham	19.9
14	Jerseyville 2 SW	19.4
15	Danville	19.3
16	Decatur	19.2
16	Springfield Capital Arpt	19.2
18	Tuscola	19.0
19	Chicago Midway Arpt	18.4
20	Lacon 1 N	18.2
20	Urbana	18.2
22	Golden	***17.4***
23	Lincoln	17.1
23	Peoria Greater Peoria Arpt	17.1
25	Normal	16.9

Lowest

Rank	Station Name	°F
1	Dixon 1 NW	11.6
2	Marengo	***11.8***
3	Paw Paw 2 NW	12.2
4	De Kalb	12.8
4	Princeville	12.8
6	Fulton L&D #13	13.0
6	Rockford Greater Rockford Arpt	13.0
8	Elgin	13.4
9	Antioch	13.5
10	Aurora	14.2
11	Aledo	14.5
12	La Harpe	14.6
13	Moline Quad City Arpt	14.8
14	Kankakee Metro Wastwater	15.1
15	Galesburg	15.7
15	Park Forest	15.7
17	Joliet Brandon Rd Dam	15.8
18	Chicago Botanical Garden	16.2
18	Havana 4 NNE	16.2
20	Chicago Ohare Intl Arpt	16.3
21	Chenoa	16.6
22	Normal	16.9
22	Wheaton 3 SE	16.9
24	Lincoln	17.1
24	Peoria Greater Peoria Arpt	17.1

Number of Days Annually Maximum Temperature ≥ 90°F

Highest

Rank	Station Name	Days
1	Kaskaskia River Nav Lock	***62***
2	Albion	***47***
2	Belleville Siu Research	47
4	Brookport Dam 52	44
5	Anna 2 NNE	41
6	Cahokia	***40***
7	Carbondale Sewage Plant	39
8	Rosiclare 5 NW	36
9	Havana 4 NNE	34
9	Tuscola	34
11	Effingham	32
12	Alton Melvin Price L&D	31
12	Decatur	31
14	Jerseyville 2 SW	30
15	Carlinville	***29***
15	La Harpe	29
15	Lacon 1 N	29
15	Virden	29
19	Golden	***28***
20	Charleston	27
20	Springfield Capital Arpt	27
20	Wheaton 3 SE	***27***
23	Lincoln	26
24	Normal	25
25	Moline Quad City Arpt	23

Lowest

Rank	Station Name	Days
1	Antioch	***10***
1	Paw Paw 2 NW	10
3	Dixon 1 NW	12
4	De Kalb	14
4	Elgin	14
4	Fulton L&D #13	14
7	Rockford Greater Rockford Arpt	15
8	Aledo	16
8	Chicago Botanical Garden	16
8	Chicago Ohare Intl Arpt	16
8	Park Forest	16
12	Joliet Brandon Rd Dam	17
13	Galesburg	18
13	Marengo	***18***
15	Aurora	19
16	Danville	20
17	Chenoa	21
17	Chicago Midway Arpt	21
19	Kankakee Metro Wastwater	22
19	Princeville	22
19	Urbana	22
22	Moline Quad City Arpt	23
22	Peoria Greater Peoria Arpt	23
24	Normal	25
25	Lincoln	26

Rankings include 25 highest/lowest stations. If state has less than 25 stations, all stations are included. The period of record is 1980–2009. See User Guide for detailed explanation of data.

Number of Days Annually Maximum Temperature ≤ 32°F

Highest			Lowest		
Rank	Station Name	Days	Rank	Station Name	Days
1	Paw Paw 2 NW	58	1	Anna 2 NNE	12
2	De Kalb	55	1	Brookport Dam 52	12
3	Rockford Greater Rockford Arpt	53	3	Rosiclare 5 NW	14
4	Antioch	***52***	4	Carbondale Sewage Plant	16
5	Elgin	51	5	Belleville Siu Research	17
6	Dixon 1 NW	50	5	Cahokia	***17***
6	Fulton L&D #13	50	5	Kaskaskia River Nav Lock	***17***
8	Marengo	***49***	8	Albion	***19***
9	Aledo	45	9	Alton Melvin Price L&D	24
9	Chicago Ohare Intl Arpt	45	10	Carlinville	***27***
9	Galesburg	45	10	Charleston	27
9	Park Forest	45	10	Decatur	27
13	Joliet Brandon Rd Dam	44	13	Jerseyville 2 SW	28
14	Moline Quad City Arpt	43	13	Virden	28
15	Aurora	42	15	Effingham	29
15	Chicago Botanical Garden	42	16	Tuscola	30
17	Chicago Midway Arpt	41	17	Danville	33
17	Princeville	41	17	Lincoln	33
19	Peoria Greater Peoria Arpt	39	17	Springfield Capital Arpt	33
20	Golden	***38***	20	Wheaton 3 SE	***34***
20	Kankakee Metro Wastwater	38	21	Lacon 1 N	35
20	Normal	38	22	Chenoa	36
23	La Harpe	37	22	Havana 4 NNE	36
24	Chenoa	36	22	Urbana	36
24	Havana 4 NNE	36	25	La Harpe	37

Number of Days Annually Minimum Temperature ≤ 32°F

Highest			Lowest		
Rank	Station Name	Days	Rank	Station Name	Days
1	Marengo	***150***	1	Brookport Dam 52	83
1	Princeville	150	2	Albion	***87***
3	Paw Paw 2 NW	149	3	Alton Melvin Price L&D	93
4	Dixon 1 NW	144	3	Anna 2 NNE	93
5	Rockford Greater Rockford Arpt	142	5	Belleville Siu Research	97
6	De Kalb	141	6	Cahokia	***102***
6	Elgin	141	7	Virden	103
8	Antioch	***139***	8	Charleston	104
9	La Harpe	138	9	Carbondale Sewage Plant	105
10	Aurora	136	10	Kaskaskia River Nav Lock	***106***
11	Fulton L&D #13	134	11	Carlinville	***107***
12	Aledo	133	11	Rosiclare 5 NW	107
13	Havana 4 NNE	132	13	Chicago Midway Arpt	112
13	Kankakee Metro Wastwater	132	13	Decatur	112
15	Moline Quad City Arpt	130	13	Springfield Capital Arpt	112
16	Joliet Brandon Rd Dam	129	16	Effingham	113
16	Wheaton 3 SE	***129***	17	Danville	114
18	Galesburg	128	18	Tuscola	115
19	Chicago Botanical Garden	127	19	Jerseyville 2 SW	117
19	Chicago Ohare Intl Arpt	127	20	Peoria Greater Peoria Arpt	120
19	Normal	127	20	Urbana	120
19	Park Forest	127	22	Lacon 1 N	121
23	Chenoa	126	23	Golden	***125***
24	Golden	***125***	23	Lincoln	125
24	Lincoln	125	25	Chenoa	126

Rankings include 25 highest/lowest stations. If state has less than 25 stations, all stations are included. The period of record is 1980–2009. See User Guide for detailed explanation of data.

Number of Days Annually Minimum Temperature ≤ 0°F

Highest			Lowest		
Rank	**Station Name**	**Days**	**Rank**	**Station Name**	**Days**
1	Marengo	***17***	1	Brookport Dam 52	1
2	Dixon 1 NW	16	2	Albion	***2***
3	Antioch	***15***	2	Anna 2 NNE	2
3	Paw Paw 2 NW	15	2	Cahokia	***2***
5	Fulton L&D #13	14	2	Rosiclare 5 NW	2
5	Princeville	14	6	Alton Melvin Price L&D	3
5	Rockford Greater Rockford Arpt	14	6	Belleville Siu Research	3
8	De Kalb	13	6	Carbondale Sewage Plant	3
9	Elgin	12	6	Kaskaskia River Nav Lock	***3***
10	Aledo	11	10	Carlinville	***4***
10	Aurora	11	10	Charleston	4
10	Kankakee Metro Wastwater	11	10	Virden	4
10	La Harpe	11	13	Chicago Midway Arpt	5
10	Moline Quad City Arpt	11	14	Decatur	6
15	Galesburg	10	14	Effingham	6
15	Havana 4 NNE	10	14	Jerseyville 2 SW	6
17	Golden	***9***	14	Tuscola	6
17	Wheaton 3 SE	***9***	18	Danville	7
19	Chenoa	8	18	Lacon 1 N	7
19	Chicago Botanical Garden	8	18	Lincoln	7
19	Chicago Ohare Intl Arpt	8	18	Springfield Capital Arpt	7
19	Joliet Brandon Rd Dam	8	18	Urbana	7
19	Normal	8	23	Chenoa	8
19	Park Forest	8	23	Chicago Botanical Garden	8
19	Peoria Greater Peoria Arpt	8	23	Chicago Ohare Intl Arpt	8

Number of Annual Heating Degree Days

Highest			Lowest		
Rank	**Station Name**	**Num.**	**Rank**	**Station Name**	**Num.**
1	Paw Paw 2 NW	6,971	1	Brookport Dam 52	4,087
2	Marengo	***6,927***	2	Anna 2 NNE	4,247
3	Antioch	***6,843***	3	Belleville Siu Research	4,397
4	Dixon 1 NW	6,735	4	Rosiclare 5 NW	4,536
5	Elgin	***6,731***	5	Albion	***4,563***
6	De Kalb	6,685	6	Kaskaskia River Nav Lock	***4,583***
7	Rockford Greater Rockford Arpt	6,682	7	Cahokia	***4,607***
8	Fulton L&D #13	6,582	8	Carbondale Sewage Plant	4,644
9	Chicago Botanical Garden	6,451	9	Alton Melvin Price L&D	***4,857***
10	Princeville	6,410	10	Virden	5,074
11	Aurora	6,370	11	Carlinville	***5,100***
12	Chicago Ohare Intl Arpt	6,335	12	Charleston	5,122
13	Park Forest	6,320	13	Decatur	5,235
14	Aledo	6,272	14	Jerseyville 2 SW	5,309
15	Joliet Brandon Rd Dam	6,191	15	Effingham	5,331
16	Moline Quad City Arpt	6,160	16	Tuscola	5,368
17	Kankakee Metro Wastwater	6,144	17	Danville	5,414
18	Galesburg	6,085	18	Springfield Capital Arpt	5,417
19	La Harpe	6,033	19	Lacon 1 N	5,626
20	Wheaton 3 SE	***5,921***	20	Urbana	5,685
21	Chicago Midway Arpt	5,892	21	Lincoln	5,706
22	Normal	5,831	22	Golden	***5,775***
23	Havana 4 NNE	5,824	23	Chenoa	5,802
24	Peoria Greater Peoria Arpt	5,808	24	Peoria Greater Peoria Arpt	5,808
25	Chenoa	5,802	25	Havana 4 NNE	5,824

Rankings include 25 highest/lowest stations. If state has less than 25 stations, all stations are included. The period of record is 1980–2009. See User Guide for detailed explanation of data.

Number of Annual Cooling Degree Days

Highest			Lowest		
Rank	Station Name	Num.	Rank	Station Name	Num.
1	Albion	***1,572***	1	Paw Paw 2 NW	666
2	Brookport Dam 52	1,555	2	Antioch	***695***
2	Kaskaskia River Nav Lock	***1,555***	3	Marengo	***755***
4	Belleville Siu Research	1,465	4	Dixon 1 NW	761
5	Cahokia	***1,460***	5	Elgin	***773***
6	Anna 2 NNE	1,438	6	Chicago Botanical Garden	781
7	Alton Melvin Price L&D	***1,437***	7	Rockford Greater Rockford Arpt	795
8	Carbondale Sewage Plant	1,347	8	Princeville	801
9	Virden	1,303	9	De Kalb	819
10	Rosiclare 5 NW	1,256	10	Fulton L&D #13	847
11	Carlinville	***1,239***	11	Chicago Ohare Intl Arpt	853
12	Decatur	1,225	12	Aurora	860
13	Charleston	1,220	13	Aledo	894
14	Tuscola	1,197	13	Park Forest	894
15	Effingham	1,193	15	Joliet Brandon Rd Dam	895
16	Jerseyville 2 SW	1,184	16	Kankakee Metro Wastwater	927
17	Springfield Capital Arpt	1,177	17	La Harpe	990
18	Havana 4 NNE	1,128	18	Wheaton 3 SE	***1,006***
19	Golden	***1,120***	19	Moline Quad City Arpt	1,008
20	Lacon 1 N	1,115	20	Chenoa	1,014
21	Normal	1,086	21	Galesburg	1,020
22	Danville	1,074	22	Urbana	1,049
23	Chicago Midway Arpt	1,071	23	Lincoln	1,055
24	Peoria Greater Peoria Arpt	1,064	24	Peoria Greater Peoria Arpt	1,064
25	Lincoln	1,055	25	Chicago Midway Arpt	1,071

Annual Precipitation

Highest			Lowest		
Rank	Station Name	Inches	Rank	Station Name	Inches
1	Rosiclare 5 NW	49.91	1	Fulton L&D #13	33.05
2	Anna 2 NNE	49.90	2	Marengo	***34.67***
3	Brookport Dam 52	48.44	3	Chenoa	34.79
4	Carbondale Sewage Plant	47.10	4	Antioch	***35.77***
5	Albion	***43.32***	5	Paw Paw 2 NW	36.02
6	Effingham	42.93	6	Rockford Greater Rockford Arpt	36.10
7	Cahokia	***42.01***	7	Peoria Greater Peoria Arpt	36.17
8	Charleston	41.85	8	Joliet Brandon Rd Dam	36.47
9	Danville	41.64	9	Virden	36.53
10	Kaskaskia River Nav Lock	***41.29***	10	Springfield Capital Arpt	36.74
11	Urbana	40.96	11	Chicago Ohare Intl Arpt	36.90
12	Belleville Siu Research	40.92	12	Aledo	36.92
13	Alton Melvin Price L&D	40.87	13	De Kalb	37.15
14	Tuscola	40.45	14	Elgin	37.23
15	Jerseyville 2 SW	39.98	15	Moline Quad City Arpt	37.68
16	Park Forest	39.96	16	Chicago Botanical Garden	37.72
17	La Harpe	39.36	17	Galesburg	37.78
18	Decatur	39.29	18	Princeville	37.82
19	Havana 4 NNE	39.14	19	Aurora	37.90
20	Lincoln	38.92	20	Dixon 1 NW	37.92
21	Chicago Midway Arpt	38.87	21	Wheaton 3 SE	***38.06***
22	Normal	38.80	22	Lacon 1 N	38.16
23	Carlinville	***38.49***	23	Golden	38.33
24	Kankakee Metro Wastwater	38.48	24	Kankakee Metro Wastwater	38.48
25	Golden	38.33	25	Carlinville	***38.49***

Rankings include 25 highest/lowest stations. If state has less than 25 stations, all stations are included. The period of record is 1980–2009. See User Guide for detailed explanation of data.

Annual Extreme Maximum Daily Precipitation

Highest			Lowest		
Rank	**Station Name**	**Inches**	**Rank**	**Station Name**	**Inches**
1	Aurora	16.91	1	Carlinville	***3.75***
2	Joliet Brandon Rd Dam	13.60	2	Danville	3.92
3	Wheaton 3 SE	***9.24***	3	Kaskaskia River Nav Lock	***4.00***
4	Marengo	***8.20***	4	Tuscola	4.07
5	De Kalb	***8.09***	5	Moline Quad City Arpt	4.26
6	Anna 2 NNE	7.74	6	Havana 4 NNE	4.35
7	Alton Melvin Price L&D	***7.70***	7	Kankakee Metro Wastwater	4.36
8	Paw Paw 2 NW	6.92	8	Cahokia	***4.37***
9	Carbondale Sewage Plant	6.90	9	Virden	4.38
10	Chicago Ohare Intl Arpt	6.64	10	Peoria Greater Peoria Arpt	4.42
11	Park Forest	6.55	11	Belleville Siu Research	4.58
12	Aledo	6.27	12	Fulton L&D #13	4.71
13	Rosiclare 5 NW	6.14	12	Springfield Capital Arpt	4.71
14	Galesburg	6.13	14	Lacon 1 N	4.88
15	Decatur	5.84	15	Elgin	***4.93***
16	Chicago Midway Arpt	5.72	16	Charleston	4.95
17	Effingham	5.70	16	Dixon 1 NW	4.95
17	Rockford Greater Rockford Arpt	5.70	18	Golden	5.00
19	Chenoa	5.66	18	Princeville	5.00
20	Normal	5.63	20	La Harpe	5.08
21	Chicago Botanical Garden	5.54	21	Jerseyville 2 SW	5.12
22	Brookport Dam 52	5.32	22	Lincoln	5.18
22	Urbana	5.32	23	Brookport Dam 52	5.32
24	Lincoln	5.18	23	Urbana	5.32
25	Jerseyville 2 SW	5.12	25	Chicago Botanical Garden	5.54

Number of Days Annually With ≥ 0.1 Inches of Precipitation

Highest			Lowest		
Rank	**Station Name**	**Days**	**Rank**	**Station Name**	**Days**
1	Anna 2 NNE	78	1	Albion	***60***
1	Danville	78	2	Fulton L&D #13	63
3	Effingham	77	3	Virden	64
4	Cahokia	***76***	4	Chenoa	65
5	Brookport Dam 52	75	5	Antioch	***66***
5	Rosiclare 5 NW	75	5	Marengo	***66***
7	Carbondale Sewage Plant	74	5	Rockford Greater Rockford Arpt	66
7	Charleston	74	8	Paw Paw 2 NW	67
7	Normal	74	8	Springfield Capital Arpt	67
7	Tuscola	74	10	Belleville Siu Research	68
7	Urbana	74	10	Decatur	68
12	Chicago Botanical Garden	73	10	Golden	68
12	La Harpe	73	10	Jerseyville 2 SW	68
14	Alton Melvin Price L&D	72	10	Moline Quad City Arpt	68
14	Havana 4 NNE	72	15	Aledo	69
14	Princeville	72	15	Aurora	69
17	Chicago Ohare Intl Arpt	71	15	Carlinville	***69***
17	Elgin	71	15	De Kalb	69
17	Galesburg	71	15	Dixon 1 NW	69
17	Park Forest	71	15	Kankakee Metro Wastwater	69
21	Chicago Midway Arpt	70	15	Peoria Greater Peoria Arpt	69
21	Joliet Brandon Rd Dam	70	22	Chicago Midway Arpt	70
21	Kaskaskia River Nav Lock	***70***	22	Joliet Brandon Rd Dam	70
21	Lacon 1 N	70	22	Kaskaskia River Nav Lock	***70***
21	Lincoln	70	22	Lacon 1 N	70

Rankings include 25 highest/lowest stations. If state has less than 25 stations, all stations are included. The period of record is 1980–2009. See User Guide for detailed explanation of data.

Number of Days Annually With ≥ 0.5 Inches of Precipitation

Highest Rank	Station Name	Days	Lowest Rank	Station Name	Days
1	Rosiclare 5 NW	36	1	Chicago Ohare Intl Arpt	21
2	Brookport Dam 52	34	2	De Kalb	22
3	Anna 2 NNE	33	2	Peoria Greater Peoria Arpt	22
4	Carbondale Sewage Plant	32	4	Antioch	***23***
5	Albion	***30***	4	Aurora	23
5	Effingham	30	4	Joliet Brandon Rd Dam	23
7	Cahokia	***29***	4	Marengo	***23***
7	Danville	29	4	Paw Paw 2 NW	23
9	Belleville Siu Research	28	4	Rockford Greater Rockford Arpt	23
9	Charleston	28	4	Springfield Capital Arpt	23
9	Kaskaskia River Nav Lock	***28***	4	Virden	23
9	Tuscola	28	12	Chicago Botanical Garden	24
13	Alton Melvin Price L&D	27	12	Fulton L&D #13	24
13	Carlinville	***27***	12	Lincoln	24
13	Decatur	27	12	Wheaton 3 SE	***24***
13	Golden	27	16	Aledo	25
13	Normal	27	16	Chenoa	25
13	Princeville	27	16	Chicago Midway Arpt	25
19	Havana 4 NNE	26	16	Dixon 1 NW	25
19	Jerseyville 2 SW	26	16	Elgin	25
19	Moline Quad City Arpt	26	16	Galesburg	25
19	Urbana	26	16	Kankakee Metro Wastwater	25
23	Aledo	25	16	La Harpe	25
23	Chenoa	25	16	Lacon 1 N	25
23	Chicago Midway Arpt	25	16	Park Forest	25

Number of Days Annually With ≥ 1.0 Inches of Precipitation

Highest Rank	Station Name	Days	Lowest Rank	Station Name	Days
1	Anna 2 NNE	13	1	Rockford Greater Rockford Arpt	6
1	Cahokia	***13***	2	Dixon 1 NW	7
1	Carbondale Sewage Plant	13	2	Fulton L&D #13	7
1	Rosiclare 5 NW	13	2	Marengo	***7***
5	Albion	***12***	2	Paw Paw 2 NW	7
5	Alton Melvin Price L&D	12	6	Aledo	8
5	Belleville Siu Research	12	6	Antioch	***8***
5	Brookport Dam 52	12	6	Aurora	8
5	Effingham	12	6	Chenoa	8
10	Havana 4 NNE	11	6	Chicago Botanical Garden	8
10	Kaskaskia River Nav Lock	***11***	6	De Kalb	8
10	Lacon 1 N	11	6	Joliet Brandon Rd Dam	8
13	Carlinville	***10***	6	Normal	8
13	Charleston	10	6	Wheaton 3 SE	***8***
13	Decatur	10	15	Chicago Midway Arpt	9
13	Golden	10	15	Chicago Ohare Intl Arpt	9
13	Jerseyville 2 SW	10	15	Danville	9
13	Springfield Capital Arpt	10	15	Elgin	9
19	Chicago Midway Arpt	9	15	Galesburg	9
19	Chicago Ohare Intl Arpt	9	15	Kankakee Metro Wastwater	9
19	Danville	9	15	La Harpe	9
19	Elgin	9	15	Lincoln	9
19	Galesburg	9	15	Moline Quad City Arpt	9
19	Kankakee Metro Wastwater	9	15	Park Forest	9
19	La Harpe	9	15	Peoria Greater Peoria Arpt	9

Rankings include 25 highest/lowest stations. If state has less than 25 stations, all stations are included. The period of record is 1980–2009. See User Guide for detailed explanation of data.

Annual Snowfall

Rank	Station Name (Highest)	Inches	Rank	Station Name (Lowest)	Inches
1	Antioch	***39.2***	1	Alton Melvin Price L&D	***4.8***
2	Chicago Midway Arpt	37.6	2	Kaskaskia River Nav Lock	***5.9***
3	Chicago Ohare Intl Arpt	37.3	3	Rosiclare 5 NW	6.5
4	Rockford Greater Rockford Arpt	36.5	4	Brookport Dam 52	6.7
5	Chicago Botanical Garden	33.8	5	Fulton L&D #13	***7.3***
6	De Kalb	33.5	6	Albion	***8.1***
7	Dixon 1 NW	31.6	7	Carbondale Sewage Plant	10.7
8	Moline Quad City Arpt	31.3	8	Anna 2 NNE	11.3
9	Marengo	***31.2***	9	Belleville Siu Research	13.1
10	Park Forest	30.8	10	Jerseyville 2 SW	13.5
11	Paw Paw 2 NW	29.9	11	Cahokia	***15.4***
12	Havana 4 NNE	29.5	12	Golden	***15.7***
13	Elgin	29.1	13	Danville	15.9
14	Aurora	28.3	14	Carlinville	***17.7***
15	Wheaton 3 SE	***27.9***	15	Effingham	17.8
16	Peoria Greater Peoria Arpt	24.3	16	Decatur	18.1
17	Kankakee Metro Wastwater	24.1	17	Chenoa	18.4
18	Urbana	22.8	18	La Harpe	19.1
19	Galesburg	22.7	19	Lincoln	19.4
20	Lacon 1 N	22.0	20	Tuscola	19.5
21	Princeville	21.6	20	Virden	19.5
22	Springfield Capital Arpt	21.3	22	Normal	19.7
23	Aledo	20.7	23	Aledo	20.7
23	Charleston	20.7	23	Charleston	20.7
25	Normal	19.7	25	Springfield Capital Arpt	21.3

Annual Maximum Snow Depth

Rank	Station Name (Highest)	Inches	Rank	Station Name (Lowest)	Inches
1	Belleville Siu Research	30	1	Albion	***10***
2	Aurora	25	1	Rosiclare 5 NW	10
2	Paw Paw 2 NW	25	3	Cahokia	***11***
4	Charleston	24	3	Golden	***11***
4	Dixon 1 NW	24	5	Carlinville	***12***
4	Elgin	***24***	5	Springfield Capital Arpt	12
4	Kaskaskia River Nav Lock	***24***	5	Virden	12
8	Antioch	***22***	8	Brookport Dam 52	13
9	Alton Melvin Price L&D	***21***	8	Carbondale Sewage Plant	13
9	Chicago Midway Arpt	21	10	Anna 2 NNE	14
11	Chenoa	20	10	Danville	14
11	Galesburg	20	10	Decatur	14
13	Marengo	***19***	10	Lacon 1 N	***14***
13	Rockford Greater Rockford Arpt	***19***	10	Lincoln	***14***
13	Tuscola	19	15	Fulton L&D #13	***15***
13	Urbana	19	15	Princeville	***15***
17	Chicago Botanical Garden	18	17	Effingham	***16***
17	Chicago Ohare Intl Arpt	18	17	Jerseyville 2 SW	16
17	Havana 4 NNE	18	17	Peoria Greater Peoria Arpt	16
17	Kankakee Metro Wastwater	18	20	De Kalb	***17***
17	Normal	18	20	La Harpe	17
22	De Kalb	***17***	20	Park Forest	17
22	La Harpe	17	23	Chicago Botanical Garden	18
22	Park Forest	17	23	Chicago Ohare Intl Arpt	18
25	Effingham	***16***	23	Havana 4 NNE	18

Rankings include 25 highest/lowest stations. If state has less than 25 stations, all stations are included. The period of record is 1980–2009. See User Guide for detailed explanation of data.

Number of Days Annually With ≥ 1.0 Inch Snow Depth

Highest			Lowest		
Rank	Station Name	Days	Rank	Station Name	Days
1	Rockford Greater Rockford Arpt	***58***	1	Albion	***4***
2	De Kalb	55	1	Kaskaskia River Nav Lock	***4***
3	Antioch	***51***	3	Alton Melvin Price L&D	***6***
3	Chicago Botanical Garden	51	4	Golden	*7*
5	Chicago Midway Arpt	48	5	Brookport Dam 52	8
5	Dixon 1 NW	48	6	Rosiclare 5 NW	10
5	Park Forest	48	7	Aledo	***12***
8	Paw Paw 2 NW	46	7	Anna 2 NNE	12
9	Aurora	45	7	Carbondale Sewage Plant	12
9	Marengo	***45***	10	Belleville Siu Research	13
11	Chicago Ohare Intl Arpt	43	11	Cahokia	***14***
12	La Harpe	39	12	Fulton L&D #13	***18***
12	Lacon 1 N	39	13	Carlinville	***20***
14	Kankakee Metro Wastwater	38	14	Jerseyville 2 SW	21
15	Peoria Greater Peoria Arpt	36	14	Princeville	***21***
16	Galesburg	35	16	Effingham	***22***
16	Wheaton 3 SE	***35***	16	Virden	22
18	Elgin	***34***	18	Danville	23
18	Normal	34	18	Lincoln	***23***
20	Havana 4 NNE	32	20	Tuscola	24
21	Charleston	30	21	Decatur	25
21	Urbana	30	22	Chenoa	27
23	Chenoa	27	22	Springfield Capital Arpt	27
23	Springfield Capital Arpt	27	24	Charleston	30
25	Decatur	25	24	Urbana	30

Rankings include 25 highest/lowest stations. If state has less than 25 stations, all stations are included. The period of record is 1980–2009. See User Guide for detailed explanation of data.

Significant Storm Events in Illinois: 2000 – 2009

Location or County	Date	Type	Mag.	Deaths	Injuries	Property Damage ($mil.)	Crop Damage ($mil.)
Vermilion	07/08/01	Thunderstorm Wind	85 mph	0	0	8.5	0.0
Cook County	07/21/01	Excessive Heat	na	10	0	0.0	0.0
Cook County	07/29/01	Excessive Heat	na	6	0	0.0	0.0
Cook	08/02/01	Flash Flood	na	0	0	37.0	0.0
Cook County	08/06/01	Excessive Heat	na	14	0	0.0	0.0
Wayne	04/21/02	Tornado	F3	1	42	4.0	0.0
Sangamon	05/27/02	Hail	2.00 in.	0	0	9.0	0.0
Cook County	06/21/02	Excessive Heat	na	7	0	0.0	0.0
Cook County	07/01/02	Excessive Heat	na	12	0	0.0	0.0
Cook County	07/15/02	Excessive Heat	na	11	0	0.0	0.0
Mercer	04/30/03	Flash Flood	na	0	0	10.0	0.0
Henry	04/30/03	Flash Flood	na	0	0	10.0	0.0
Massac	05/06/03	Tornado	F4	1	20	10.0	0.0
Pulaski	05/06/03	Tornado	F4	1	13	3.5	0.0
Henderson	05/08/03	Hail	4.00 in.	0	0	10.0	0.0
Tazewell	05/10/03	Tornado	F3	0	32	10.0	0.0
De Witt	05/30/03	Tornado	F2	0	4	9.3	0.0
Mercer	07/20/03	Thunderstorm Wind	81 mph	0	0	10.0	3.0
Henry	07/21/03	Thunderstorm Wind	92 mph	0	0	50.0	25.0
Will	07/27/03	Flash Flood	na	0	0	14.0	0.0
Coles	09/26/03	Tornado	F1	0	1	10.0	0.0
Putnam	04/20/04	Tornado	F2	0	5	8.0	0.0
La Salle	04/20/04	Tornado	F3	8	7	0.0	0.0
St. Clair	04/02/06	Tornado	F2	1	11	0.0	0.0
Cook County	07/15/06	Excessive Heat	na	9	0	0.0	0.0
Jefferson	07/21/06	Thunderstorm Wind	90 mph	0	5	13.0	0.0
Cook County	08/01/06	Excessive Heat	na	24	0	0.0	0.0
Winnebago	09/04/06	Flash Flood	na	0	0	20.0	0.0
Cook County	12/02/06	Extreme Cold/Wind Chill	na	7	5	0.0	0.0
Cook County	02/01/07	Extreme Cold/Wind Chill	na	10	0	0.0	0.0
Du Page	03/31/07	Thunderstorm Wind	96 mph	0	11	1.0	0.0
Cook County	01/22/08	Extreme Cold/Wind Chill	na	5	0	0.0	0.0
Saline	03/18/08	Flood	na	0	0	16.8	0.0
Cook	09/13/08	Flash Flood	na	1	0	35.0	0.0
Cook	09/14/08	Flash Flood	na	0	0	20.0	0.0
Du Page	09/14/08	Flash Flood	na	0	0	8.0	0.0
Cook County	12/21/08	Cold/Wind Chill	na	5	0	0.0	0.0
Williamson	05/08/09	Thunderstorm Wind	100 mph	0	1	175.0	0.0
Jackson	05/08/09	Thunderstorm Wind	106 mph	1	6	100.0	0.0
Sangamon	08/19/09	Tornado	F3	0	17	11.0	0.0
Logan	08/19/09	Tornado	F3	0	2	7.2	1.0

Note: Deaths, injuries, and damages are date and location specific.

INDIANA

PHYSICAL FEATURES AND GENERAL CLIMATE. Indiana has an invigorating climate of warm summers and cool winters, because of its location in the middle latitudes in the interior of a large continent. Imposed on the well-known daily and seasonal changes of temperature are changes occurring every few days as surges of polar air move southeastward or air of tropical origin moves northeastward. These outbreaks are more frequent and pronounced in the winter than in the summer. A winter may be unusually cold or a summer cool if the influence of polar air is rather continuous. Likewise, a summer may be unusually warm or a winter mild if air of tropical origin predominates. The action between these two air masses with a contrast in temperature and density fosters the development of low pressure centers which in moving generally eastward frequently pass through or near Indiana, resulting in normally abundant rain. The cyclones are least active and frequently pass north of Indiana in midsummer. Thunderstorms, often local in areal coverage, are important at such times when evaporation and loss of moisture from the soil and vegetation exceeds rainfall. Major climatological variations within the State are caused by differences of latitude, elevation, terrain, soil, and lakes.

The effect of the Great Lakes and more specifically, Lake Michigan, on the climate of northern Indiana is most pronounced just inland from the Lake Michigan shore and diminishes to insignificance in central Indiana. The result of cold air passing over the warmer lake water of Lake Michigan induces precipitation in the lee of Lake Michigan in fall and winter. Average daily minimum temperatures in the fall are higher and daily maximum temperatures in the spring are lower in northwestern Indiana than farther south. Winter precipitation, especially snowfall, is several times greater in the counties of Lake, Porter, and LaPorte as the result of this phenomena. Lake related snowfall and cloudiness often extends to central Indiana in the winter. Very local severe snowstorms have occurred just inland from Lake Michigan.

Another important variable in the composition of Indiana weather is the topography of the State. Elevations range from a little more than 300 feet at the mouth of the Wabash in the southwest corner of the State, to a little over 1,200 feet in the east-central portion (Randolph County) and northeastern section (Steuben County). Differences of terrain affect the climate considerably. South-central Indiana is unglaciated and has the most rugged relief. The Kankakee Valley in the northwest has but little slope to the west and drains what was formerly marshlands. Many small lakes abound in northeastern Indiana among numerous glacial moraines and hills. Most of the north, central, and southwest is rolling country.

TEMPERATURE. Variations of temperature and precipitation occur in short distances where terrain is hilly. On calm, clear nights the valley bottoms have lower temperatures than the slopes and tops of the surrounding hills. Mean maximum as well as mean minimum temperatures decrease from south to north with latitude and decrease from west to east with elevation. Near Lake Michigan temperatures average higher than expected for the latitude in the fall and winter, and lower than expected for the latitude in the spring and summer.

The average date of the last freezing temperature in the spring ranges from the first week of April in the Ohio River Valley of the southwest to the second week of May in the extreme northeast. The usual trend of a later date toward the north is reversed in extreme northwestern Indiana, where the average date is about April 30 near Lake Michigan. In the fall the average date of the first temperature of 32°F. or colder is from October 7 in the extreme northeast to October 26 along the Ohio River in the southwest.

Spring freezes are later in valleys and hollows and fall freezes are earlier. Longer freeze-free periods occur on ridges and hills. Southern Indiana has much of this type of terrain. The gradual slope upward from southwestern Indiana to northeastern Indiana results in lower minimum temperatures and shorter growing seasons in the east compared to the west at the same latitude. In the Kankakee Valley, peat or muck lands experience late spring and early fall frosts because of the radiative characteristic of the soil.

PRECIPITATION. Average annual rainfall ranges from 36 inches in northern Indiana to 43 inches in southern Indiana. July rainfall averages about the same in all areas. The greater precipitation in the south compared with the north comes in the winter months. Southern Indiana has the greatest rainfall in March and the least in October. The wettest month in northern and central Indiana is June and the driest is February. A drought occasionally occurs in the summer when evaporation is highest and dependence on rainfall is greatest.

Most of the state is drained by the Wabash River system. Other river basins are the Maumee in the extreme northeast, the St. Joseph (Lake Michigan) and Kankakee (Illinois River) in the north-central and northwest, and some Ohio River drainage in the extreme south and southeast. Floods occur in some part of the State nearly every year and have occurred in every month of the year. The season of greatest flood frequency is during the winter and spring months. The primary cause of floods is prolonged periods of heavy rains, although occasionally the rains falling on a snow cover and the formation of ice jams are an added factor. The most common type of flood-producing storm in the area is that having a quasi-stationary front oriented from west-southwest to east-northeast with a series of waves or perturbations moving to the east along the front.

Average annual snowfall increases from about 10 inches in southern Indiana to 40 inches in the northern portion of the State and higher in the three county areas along Lake Michigan. From year to year snowfall varies greatly, depending both on temperatures and the frequency of winter storms. At a given latitude in central and southern Indiana snowfall is greatest toward the east because of higher elevation.

OTHER CLIMATIC ELEMENTS. Cloudiness is least in the fall and greatest in the winter. The north is cloudier than the south, particularly in the winter when the Great Lakes have the greatest effect upon the weather.

Average relative humidity differs very little at night over Indiana. During the day relative humidity is usually lower in the south than in the north. This is true for all seasons. However, the simultaneous occurrence of high temperatures and high relative humidity is most frequent in the south.

Prevailing winds are from the southwest quadrant throughout most of the year. Winds from the northern quadrant occur in the winter and persist for a longer time in the north. Along the shore of Lake Michigan the sea-breeze effect is observed in the summer when winds in central United States are light or calm. Vertical currents from the heating of land during the day cause wind near the ground to flow from over water to land reducing the maximum temperature of the day. At night the breezes are in the opposite direction or from the land to water because of land cooling. These breezes are important in limiting extremely high temperatures of a summer day and account for rapid changes in short distances within a mile or so of the lake shore. Winds meet less friction passing over water so off-lake winds have a considerably higher speed than those off or over land.

Severe storms are most frequent in the spring. About one-half of the tornadoes occur between 2 p.m. and 6 p.m. and nearly three-fourths between 10 a.m. and 10 p.m. Hail falls occasionally in very local areas.

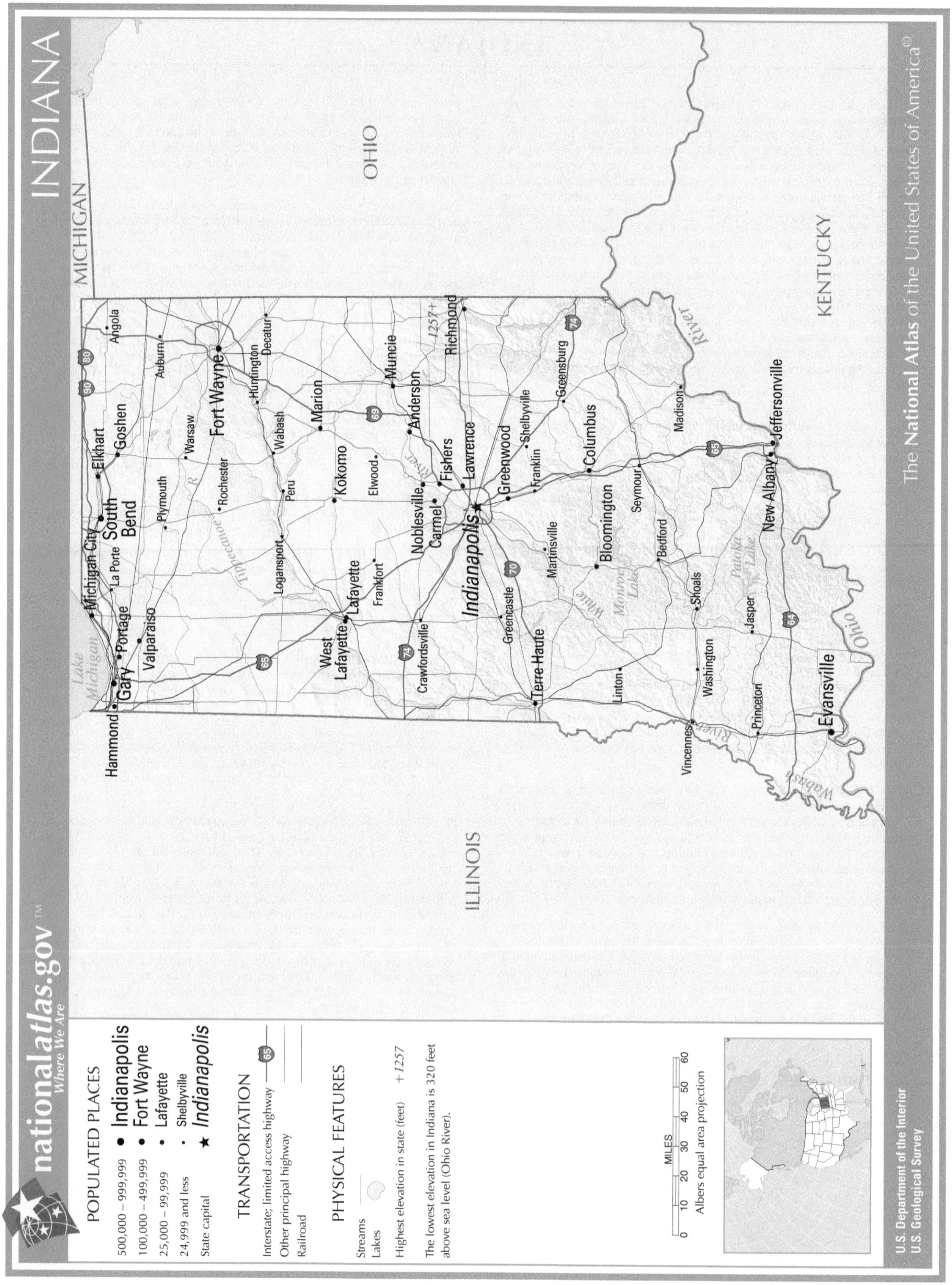
INDIANA
nationalatlas.gov™
Where We Are
POPULATED PLACES
500,000 – 999,999 Indianapolis
100,000 – 499,999 Fort Wayne
25,000 – 99,999 Lafayette
24,999 and less Shelbyville
State capital Indianapolis
TRANSPORTATION
Interstate; limited access highway
Other principal highway
Railroad
PHYSICAL FEATURES
Streams
Lakes
Highest elevation in state (feet) +1257
The lowest elevation in Indiana is 320 feet above sea level (Ohio River).
MILES
0 10 20 30 40 50 60
Albers equal area projection
U.S. Department of the Interior
U.S. Geological Survey
The National Atlas of the United States of America®
MICHIGAN
OHIO
KENTUCKY
ILLINOIS
Lake Michigan
Hammond
Gary
Portage
Valparaiso
Michigan City
La Porte
South Bend
Elkhart
Goshen
Angola
Auburn
Fort Wayne
Decatur
Huntington
Warsaw
Plymouth
Rochester
Wabash
Peru
Logansport
Marion
Kokomo
Elwood
Muncie
Anderson
Richmond
1257+
Noblesville
Fishers
Carmel
Lawrence
Indianapolis
Greenwood
Shelbyville
Franklin
Greensburg
Columbus
Madison
Lafayette
West Lafayette
Frankfort
Crawfordsville
Greencastle
Martinsville
Bloomington
Monroe Lake
Terre Haute
Seymour
Bedford
Shoals
Jasper
Patoka Lake
Jeffersonville
New Albany
Linton
Washington
Vincennes
Princeton
Evansville
Tippecanoe
White
Wabash
Ohio
River
90
80
69
65
70
74
64

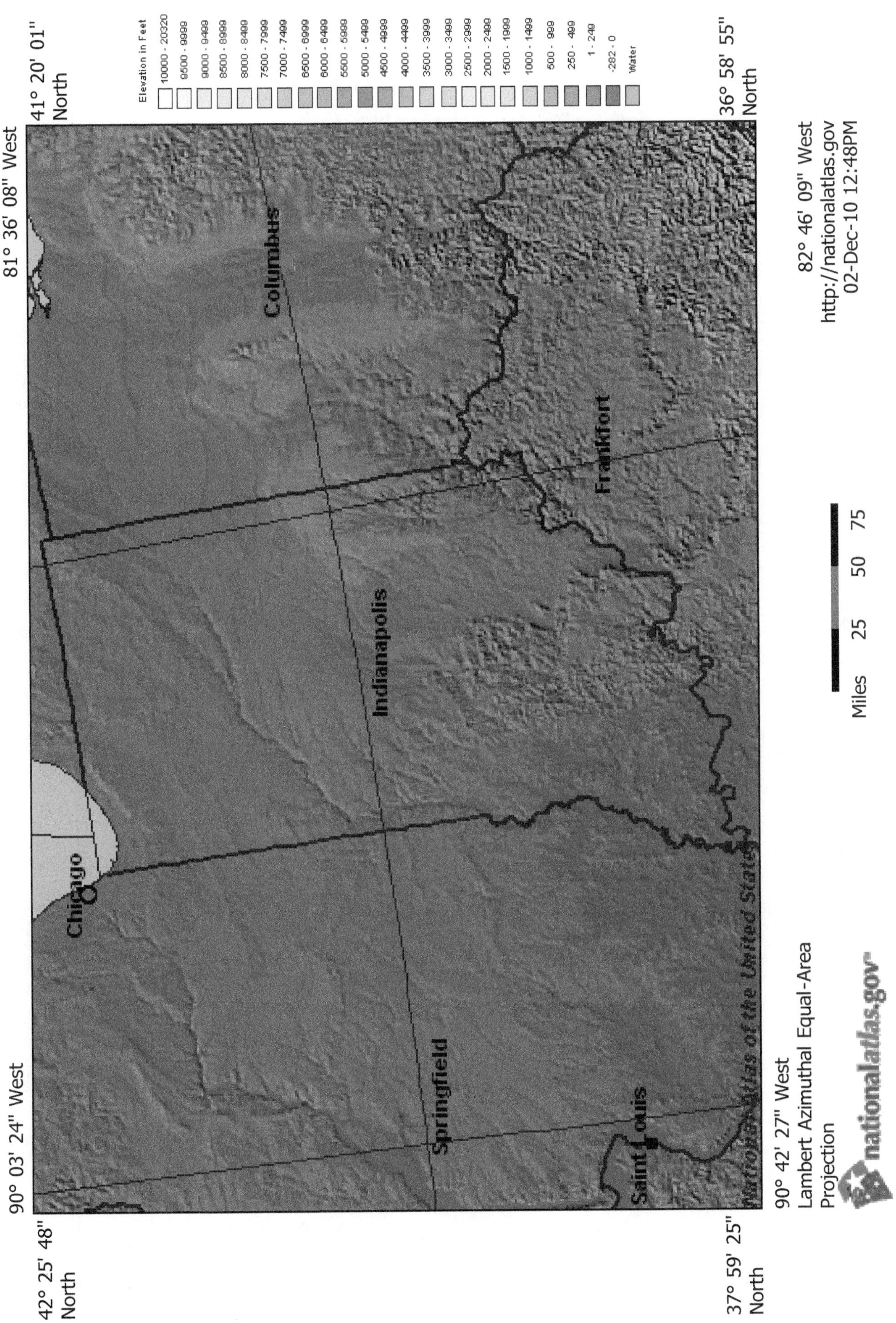
81° 36' 08" West
41° 20' 01" North
90° 03' 24" West
42° 25' 48" North
37° 59' 25" North
36° 58' 55" North
90° 42' 27" West
82° 46' 09" West
Elevation in Feet
10000 - 20320
9500 - 9999
9000 - 9499
8500 - 8999
8000 - 8499
7500 - 7999
7000 - 7499
6500 - 6999
6000 - 6499
5500 - 5999
5000 - 5499
4500 - 4999
4000 - 4499
3500 - 3999
3000 - 3499
2500 - 2999
2000 - 2499
1500 - 1999
1000 - 1499
500 - 999
250 - 499
1 - 249
-282 - 0
Water
Columbus
Chicago
Indianapolis
Frankfort
Springfield
Saint Louis
National Atlas of the United States
Miles 25 50 75
Lambert Azimuthal Equal-Area Projection
http://nationalatlas.gov
02-Dec-10 12:48PM
nationalatlas.gov

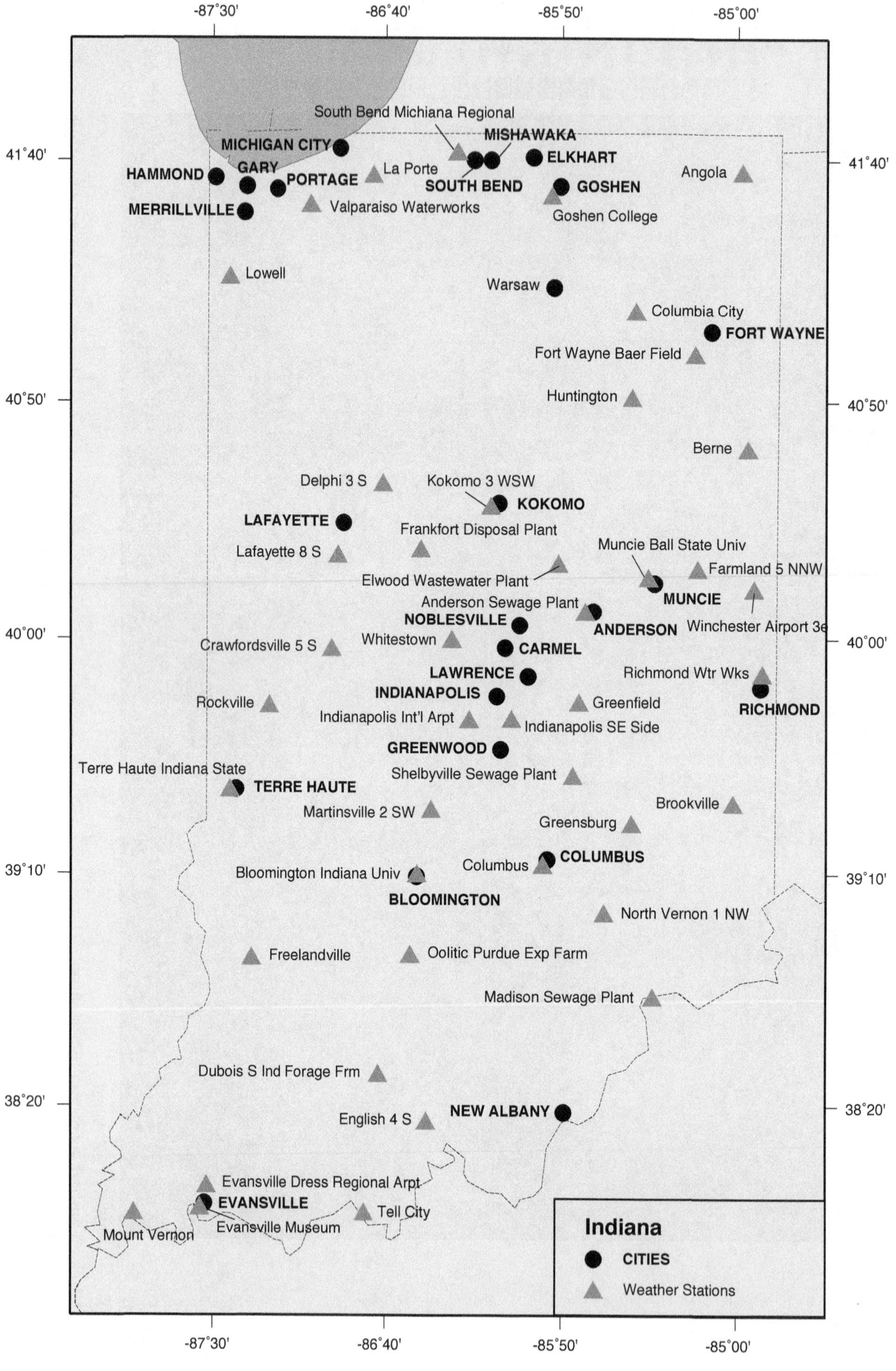
-87°30'
-86°40'
-85°50'
-85°00'
41°40'
40°50'
40°00'
39°10'
38°20'
South Bend Michiana Regional
MICHIGAN CITY
MISHAWAKA
ELKHART
HAMMOND
GARY
PORTAGE
La Porte
SOUTH BEND
GOSHEN
Angola
MERRILLVILLE
Valparaiso Waterworks
Goshen College
Lowell
Warsaw
Columbia City
FORT WAYNE
Fort Wayne Baer Field
Huntington
Berne
Delphi 3 S
Kokomo 3 WSW
KOKOMO
LAFAYETTE
Frankfort Disposal Plant
Lafayette 8 S
Muncie Ball State Univ
Farmland 5 NNW
Elwood Wastewater Plant
Anderson Sewage Plant
MUNCIE
NOBLESVILLE
ANDERSON
Winchester Airport 3e
Crawfordsville 5 S
Whitestown
CARMEL
LAWRENCE
Richmond Wtr Wks
INDIANAPOLIS
Rockville
Greenfield
RICHMOND
Indianapolis Int'l Arpt
Indianapolis SE Side
GREENWOOD
Terre Haute Indiana State
Shelbyville Sewage Plant
TERRE HAUTE
Martinsville 2 SW
Brookville
Greensburg
COLUMBUS
Columbus
Bloomington Indiana Univ
BLOOMINGTON
North Vernon 1 NW
Freelandville
Oolitic Purdue Exp Farm
Madison Sewage Plant
Dubois S Ind Forage Frm
NEW ALBANY
English 4 S
Evansville Dress Regional Arpt
EVANSVILLE
Tell City
Evansville Museum
Mount Vernon
Indiana
CITIES
Weather Stations
-87°30'
-86°40'
-85°50'
-85°00'
41°40'
40°50'
40°00'
39°10'
38°20'

Indiana Weather Stations by County

County	Station Name
Adams	Berne
Allen	Fort Wayne Baer Field
Bartholomew	Columbus
Boone	Whitestown
Carroll	Delphi 3 S
Clinton	Frankfort Disposal Plant
Crawford	English 4 S
Decatur	Greensburg
Delaware	Muncie Ball State Univ
Dubois	Dubois S Ind Forage Frm
Elkhart	Goshen College
Franklin	Brookville
Hancock	Greenfield
Howard	Kokomo 3 WSW
Huntington	Huntington
Jefferson	Madison Sewage Plant
Jennings	North Vernon 1 NW
Knox	Freelandville
Kosciusko	Warsaw
La Porte	La Porte
Lake	Lowell
Lawrence	Oolitic Purdue Exp Farm
Madison	Anderson Sewage Plant Elwood Wastewater Plant
Marion	Indianapolis Int'l Arpt Indianapolis SE Side
Monroe	Bloomington Indiana Univ
Montgomery	Crawfordsville 5 S
Morgan	Martinsville 2 SW
Parke	Rockville
Perry	Tell City
Porter	Valparaiso Waterworks
Posey	Mount Vernon

County	Station Name
Randolph	Farmland 5 NNW Winchester Airport 3E
Shelby	Shelbyville Sewage Plant
St. Joseph	South Bend Michiana Regional
Steuben	Angola
Tippecanoe	Lafayette 8 S
Vanderburgh	Evansville Dress Regional Arpt Evansville Museum
Vigo	Terre Haute Indiana State
Wayne	Richmond Water Works
Whitley	Columbia City

See User Guide for station inclusion criteria.

Indiana Weather Stations by City

City	Station Name	Miles
Anderson	Anderson Sewage Plant	1.9
	Elwood Wastewater Plant	14.6
	Greenfield	22.1
	Muncie Ball State Univ	16.2
Bloomington	Bloomington Indiana Univ	0.5
	Martinsville 2 SW	16.9
	Oolitic Purdue Exp Farm	19.3
Carmel	Anderson Sewage Plant	22.3
	Elwood Wastewater Plant	24.4
	Greenfield	22.9
	Indianapolis Int'l Arpt	19.6
	Indianapolis SE Side	17.8
	Whitestown	13.1
Columbus	Columbus	1.5
	Greensburg	23.4
	North Vernon 1 NW	19.3
	Shelbyville Sewage Plant	21.6
Elkhart	Goshen College	10.2
	South Bend Michiana Regional	18.9
	Three Rivers, MI	24.3
Evansville	Evansville Museum	1.5
	Evansville Dress Regional Arpt	5.1
	Mount Vernon	18.7
	Henderson 7 SSW, KY	16.4
Fishers	Anderson Sewage Plant	18.3
	Elwood Wastewater Plant	22.9
	Greenfield	18.3
	Indianapolis Int'l Arpt	21.5
	Indianapolis SE Side	17.0
	Whitestown	18.2
Fort Wayne	Columbia City	19.5
	Fort Wayne Baer Field	7.1
Gary	Park Forest, IL	18.5
	Lowell	21.9
	Valparaiso Waterworks	16.5
Goshen	Goshen College	3.2
	Warsaw	24.2
Greenwood	Greenfield	22.8
	Indianapolis Int'l Arpt	10.6
	Indianapolis SE Side	7.6
	Martinsville 2 SW	23.1
	Shelbyville Sewage Plant	19.1
Hammond	Chicago Midway Arpt, IL	17.4
	Park Forest, IL	12.3
	Lowell	23.8
	Valparaiso Waterworks	24.5
Indianapolis	Greenfield	20.9
	Indianapolis Int'l Arpt	8.5
	Indianapolis SE Side	6.8
	Whitestown	17.9
Kokomo	Elwood Wastewater Plant	20.9

City	Station Name	Miles
Kokomo *(cont.)*	Frankfort Disposal Plant	22.2
	Kokomo 3 WSW	1.9
Lafayette	Delphi 3 S	14.0
	Frankfort Disposal Plant	20.6
	Lafayette 8 S	7.6
Lawrence	Anderson Sewage Plant	21.8
	Greenfield	14.1
	Indianapolis Int'l Arpt	17.8
	Indianapolis SE Side	11.0
	Whitestown	21.1
Merrillville	Park Forest, IL	17.2
	Lowell	16.0
	Valparaiso Waterworks	16.5
Michigan City	La Porte	10.0
	Valparaiso Waterworks	15.1
Mishawaka	Goshen College	16.9
	South Bend Michiana Regional	8.7
Muncie	Anderson Sewage Plant	18.3
	Elwood Wastewater Plant	24.6
	Farmland 5 NNW	13.4
	Muncie Ball State Univ	1.9
New Albany	Louisville Standiford Field, KY	9.7
Noblesville	Anderson Sewage Plant	16.7
	Elwood Wastewater Plant	17.6
	Greenfield	23.5
	Indianapolis SE Side	23.1
	Whitestown	17.5
Portage	La Porte	23.6
	Lowell	24.2
	Valparaiso Waterworks	8.8
Richmond	Richmond Water Works	3.8
	Winchester Airport 3E	24.5
South Bend	Goshen College	20.8
	South Bend Michiana Regional	4.6
Terre Haute	Rockville	22.3
	Terre Haute Indiana State	1.4

Note: Miles is the distance between the geographic center of the city and the weather station.

See User Guide for station inclusion criteria.

Indiana Weather Stations by Elevation

Feet	Station Name
1,109	Winchester Airport 3E
1,015	Richmond Water Works
1,009	Angola
964	Farmland 5 NNW
939	Muncie Ball State Univ
935	Greensburg
935	Whitestown
875	Goshen College
865	Greenfield
859	Berne
850	Columbia City
845	Anderson Sewage Plant
845	Indianapolis SE Side
839	Elwood Wastewater Plant
834	Frankfort Disposal Plant
830	Bloomington Indiana Univ
819	Kokomo 3 WSW
810	La Porte
810	Warsaw
799	Valparaiso Waterworks
792	Indianapolis Int'l Arpt
791	Fort Wayne Baer Field
772	South Bend Michiana Regional
762	Crawfordsville 5 S
750	Shelbyville Sewage Plant
745	North Vernon 1 NW
732	Lafayette 8 S
725	Huntington
689	Dubois S Ind Forage Frm
689	Rockville
670	Delphi 3 S
665	Lowell
649	Oolitic Purdue Exp Farm
629	Brookville
621	Columbus
609	Martinsville 2 SW
549	Freelandville
509	English 4 S
506	Terre Haute Indiana State
459	Madison Sewage Plant
419	Mount Vernon
399	Tell City
380	Evansville Dress Regional Arpt
379	Evansville Museum

See User Guide for station inclusion criteria.

Evansville Regional Airport

Evansville, Indiana, is located on the Ohio River. The country around Evansville ranges from level to areas of rolling terrain near the river. Dress Regional Airport, where weather observations are taken, is located in a shallow valley with low hills to the east and west which parallel the valley, but slope down to the south. There are hills five miles to the north which are about 100 feet higher than the field. The open end of the valley slopes down and south toward the city of Evansville and the Ohio River.

Prevailing wind direction is from the south-southwest. The strongest winds occur during a deep winter storm passage through the Lower Ohio Valley. Strong and cold north to northwest winds occur from late autumn to early spring, most often, in January and February, as large domes of arctic high pressure moves into the midwest.

Geographically, Evansville lies in the path of moisture-bearing low pressure formations that move from the western Gulf region, northeastward over the Mississippi and Ohio Valleys to the Great Lakes and northern Atlantic Coast. Much of the precipitation results from these storm systems, especially in the cooler part of the year.

Both temperature and precipitation are closely related to the movement of the polar front and the storms which move along the front. This is especially true in the winter and spring months. In summer and early autumn changes are less severe and periods of polar air invasions are less prolonged. There is considerable variation in seasonal and monthly temperature and precipitation from year to year as these factors depend greatly on the frequency of storm and frontal passages.

Convective thunderstorms, developing in the maritime tropical air from the Gulf of Mexico and squall line activity, combine to supply the summer rainfall. The greatest precipitation intensities for short periods of time come in the months of greatest thunderstorm frequency. The greatest intensities for 24 hours or more are confined to the winter months.

Severe storms are rather infrequent but thunderstorms cause some wind damage each year. Hail often occurs with the stronger thunderstorms. Evansville is in tornado alley with the most frequent occurrence in early spring and late fall.

Snowfall varies greatly from season to season, as do rainfall and temperature. Snowfalls of two or more inches are very infrequent, and these amounts are usually melted within a day or two.

The growing season averages 199 days, but has been as long as 250 days and as short as 169 days.

Evansville Regional Airport *Vanderburgh County* Elevation: 380 ft. Latitude: 38° 03' N Longitude: 87° 32' W

	JAN	FEB	MAR	APR	MAY	JUN	JUL	AUG	SEP	OCT	NOV	DEC	YEAR
Mean Maximum Temp. (°F)	41.1	45.8	56.3	67.3	76.7	85.3	88.5	87.8	81.2	69.5	56.3	44.3	66.7
Mean Temp. (°F)	33.0	36.7	46.1	56.1	65.9	74.8	78.3	77.0	69.4	57.8	46.7	36.1	56.5
Mean Minimum Temp. (°F)	24.9	27.7	35.7	44.9	55.0	64.3	68.1	66.0	57.5	46.0	36.9	27.9	46.2
Extreme Maximum Temp. (°F)	71	77	84	91	94	101	102	104	100	93	82	77	104
Extreme Minimum Temp. (°F)	-18	-8	3	23	34	42	51	43	34	23	11	-15	-18
Days Maximum Temp. ≥ 90°F	0	0	0	0	1	9	14	12	5	0	0	0	41
Days Maximum Temp. ≤ 32°F	7	4	1	0	0	0	0	0	0	0	0	5	17
Days Minimum Temp. ≤ 32°F	24	19	13	3	0	0	0	0	0	2	11	21	93
Days Minimum Temp. ≤ 0°F	1	0	0	0	0	0	0	0	0	0	0	1	2
Heating Degree Days (base 65°F)	984	793	585	285	78	5	0	1	41	249	545	889	4,455
Cooling Degree Days (base 65°F)	0	0	4	26	113	307	420	378	179	32	1	0	1,460
Mean Precipitation (in.)	3.07	3.16	4.25	4.35	5.39	3.90	3.95	3.02	3.12	3.28	4.12	3.73	45.34
Maximum Precipitation (in.)*	13.5	7.3	12.8	10.3	13.5	6.9	9.7	8.4	7.0	7.9	8.5	8.2	63.1
Minimum Precipitation (in.)*	0.5	0.6	1.3	1.1	0.9	0.6	0.2	0.2	0.5	trace	0.9	0.6	27.9
Extreme Maximum Daily Precip. (in.)	3.72	3.38	6.40	6.04	4.92	3.67	2.95	3.03	2.83	2.45	3.48	2.30	6.40
Days With ≥ 0.1" Precipitation	6	5	7	7	8	6	6	5	5	6	6	7	74
Days With ≥ 0.5" Precipitation	2	2	3	3	4	3	3	2	2	2	3	3	32
Days With ≥ 1.0" Precipitation	1	1	1	1	1	1	1	1	1	1	1	1	12
Mean Snowfall (in.)	3.4	3.8	***1.3***	***0.2***	***trace***	***trace***	***0.0***	***0.0***	***trace***	***0.2***	***0.1***	2.4	***11.4***
Maximum Snowfall (in.)*	21	18	20	9	0	0	0	0	0	5	7	10	36
Maximum 24-hr. Snowfall (in.)*	8	11	8	9	0	0	0	0	0	4	7	7	11
Maximum Snow Depth (in.)	8	12	10	3	trace	trace	0	0	trace	2	***1***	7	***12***
Days With ≥ 1.0" Snow Depth	4	4	1	0	0	0	0	0	0	0	***0***	3	***12***
Thunderstorm Days*	1	1	4	5	6	7	7	5	3	2	2	1	44
Foggy Days*	12	12	12	9	11	11	13	16	15	12	11	13	147
Predominant Sky Cover*	OVR	OVR	OVR	OVR	OVR	OVR	SCT	CLR	CLR	CLR	OVR	OVR	OVR
Mean Relative Humidity 7am (%)*	80	80	78	73	75	75	78	82	83	83	80	81	79
Mean Relative Humidity 4pm (%)*	66	61	56	50	52	52	54	54	52	50	59	67	56
Mean Dewpoint (°F)*	24	27	35	44	54	63	67	66	58	46	36	28	46
Prevailing Wind Direction*	NW	NW	NW	SSW	S	SW	SW	SW	S	NW	S	NW	NW
Prevailing Wind Speed (mph)*	12	12	12	13	9	9	8	8	8	7	10	10	10
Maximum Wind Gust (mph)*	55	53	52	63	71	76	56	46	59	52	70	56	76

Note: (*) Period of record is 1948-1995

The period of record for National Weather Service station data is 1980 – 2009 except where noted. See User Guide for detailed explanation of data.

Fort Wayne Baer Field

Fort Wayne is located at the junction of the St. Marys, St. Joseph, and Maumee Rivers in northeastern Indiana. The surrounding area is generally level south and east of the city. Southwest and west, the terrain is somewhat rolling, while to the northwest and a few miles north from the city, it becomes quite hilly. The highest point in the general area is about 40 miles due north of Fort Wayne, near Angola, Indiana. At this point, the elevation rises to 1,060 feet above sea level.

The climate is representative of northeastern Indiana and is influenced to some extent by the Great Lakes. It does not differ greatly from the climates of other midwestern cities of the same general latitude. Temperature differences between daily highs and lows are invigorating and average about 20 degrees. The average occurrence of the last freeze in the spring is late April, and the first freeze in the fall is mid-October, making the average freeze-free period 173 days. The length of the growing season is favorable for the maturing of all crops and vegetables normally grown in the midwest.

Annual precipitation is well distributed, with somewhat larger monthly amounts falling in late spring and early summer. Damaging hailstorms occur at an average of about twice a year. One of the most notable storms caused severe damage to property, many thousands of trees, and power and telephone lines in the area. Severe flooding has also occurred in the area. Snow usually covers the ground for about 30 days during the winter months, but heavy snowstorms are not frequent.

Except for the considerable cloudiness that occurs during the winter months, Fort Wayne enjoys a good midwestern average sunshine. Heavy fog occurrence is infrequent.

Fort Wayne Baer Field *Allen County* Elevation: 791 ft. Latitude: 41° 00' N Longitude: 85° 12' W

	JAN	FEB	MAR	APR	MAY	JUN	JUL	AUG	SEP	OCT	NOV	DEC	YEAR
Mean Maximum Temp. (°F)	32.4	36.1	47.6	60.7	71.6	80.8	84.3	82.1	75.9	63.1	49.6	36.4	60.0
Mean Temp. (°F)	25.2	28.4	38.3	49.9	60.6	70.1	73.7	71.7	64.5	52.7	41.5	29.6	50.5
Mean Minimum Temp. (°F)	17.9	20.6	28.9	39.1	49.5	59.4	63.1	61.2	53.1	42.2	33.4	22.8	40.9
Extreme Maximum Temp. (°F)	66	73	82	88	94	106	102	99	97	89	77	71	106
Extreme Minimum Temp. (°F)	-22	-18	-7	7	27	38	45	40	29	19	10	-18	-22
Days Maximum Temp. ≥ 90°F	0	0	0	0	1	4	6	3	1	0	0	0	15
Days Maximum Temp. ≤ 32°F	15	11	3	0	0	0	0	0	0	0	1	11	41
Days Minimum Temp. ≤ 32°F	28	24	20	7	0	0	0	0	0	4	15	26	124
Days Minimum Temp. ≤ 0°F	4	2	0	0	0	0	0	0	0	0	0	2	8
Heating Degree Days (base 65°F)	1,229	1,029	823	455	183	27	2	9	94	387	697	1,091	6,026
Cooling Degree Days (base 65°F)	0	0	1	9	52	188	279	223	86	10	0	0	848
Mean Precipitation (in.)	2.26	2.08	2.76	3.50	4.13	4.15	4.28	3.68	2.83	2.88	2.98	2.82	38.35
Maximum Precipitation (in.)*	9.7	6.8	5.3	7.1	8.8	8.3	11.0	7.7	6.8	9.3	8.0	7.6	54.6
Minimum Precipitation (in.)*	0.4	0.3	0.7	1.3	1.0	0.8	0.4	0.4	0.3	0.1	0.6	0.4	24.4
Extreme Maximum Daily Precip. (in.)	1.79	3.03	1.96	2.57	4.35	4.40	2.83	3.40	2.13	2.69	2.44	1.79	4.40
Days With ≥ 0.1" Precipitation	5	5	6	8	8	7	7	6	5	6	7	7	77
Days With ≥ 0.5" Precipitation	1	1	2	2	3	3	3	3	2	2	2	2	26
Days With ≥ 1.0" Precipitation	0	0	0	1	1	1	1	1	1	1	1	0	8
Mean Snowfall (in.)	10.2	7.8	4.1	1.1	trace	trace	trace	trace	trace	0.4	2.0	8.2	33.8
Maximum Snowfall (in.)*	30	17	20	12	trace	0	0	0	0	8	14	20	62
Maximum 24-hr. Snowfall (in.)*	11	8	13	6	trace	0	0	0	0	6	6	11	13
Maximum Snow Depth (in.)	12	20	9	6	trace	trace	trace	trace	trace	3	4	9	20
Days With ≥ 1.0" Snow Depth	15	12	4	0	0	0	0	0	0	0	1	9	41
Thunderstorm Days*	< 1	1	2	4	5	7	7	6	4	2	1	< 1	39
Foggy Days*	14	13	13	11	12	10	14	17	14	14	13	15	160
Predominant Sky Cover*	OVR	OVR	OVR	OVR	OVR	OVR	SCT	SCT	OVR	OVR	OVR	OVR	OVR
Mean Relative Humidity 7am (%)*	81	81	80	78	77	78	82	86	87	85	83	83	82
Mean Relative Humidity 4pm (%)*	72	67	62	54	52	52	53	55	53	54	67	74	60
Mean Dewpoint (°F)*	18	20	28	38	48	57	62	61	54	43	33	23	41
Prevailing Wind Direction*	W	W	W	SW	SW	SW	SW	SW	SW	SW	SW	W	SW
Prevailing Wind Speed (mph)*	14	14	14	14	12	12	9	9	10	12	13	13	12
Maximum Wind Gust (mph)*	69	54	59	61	59	64	67	59	53	63	58	58	69

Note: (*) Period of record is 1948-1995

Indianapolis Int'l Airport

Indianapolis is located in the central part of the state and is situated on level or slightly rolling terrain. The greater part of the city lies east of the White River which flows in a general north to south direction.

The National Weather Service Forecast Office is located approximately seven miles southwest of the central part of the city at the Indianapolis International Airport. From a field elevation of 797 feet above sea level at the Indianapolis International Airport the terrain slopes gradually downward to a little below 645 feet at the White River, then upward to just over 910 feet in the northwest corner and eastern sections of the county. The street elevation at the former city office located in the Old Federal Building is 718 feet.

Indianapolis has a temperate climate, with very warm summers and without a dry season. Very cold temperatures may be produced by the invasion of continental polar air in the winter from northern latitudes. The polar air can be quite frigid with very low humidity. The arrival of maritime tropical air from the Gulf in the summer brings warm temperatures and moderate humidity. One of the longest and most severe heat waves brought temperatures of 100 degrees or more for nine consecutive days.

Precipitation is distributed fairly evenly throughout the year, and therefore there is no pronounced wet or dry season. Rainfall in the spring and summer is produced mostly by showers and thunderstorms. A rainfall of about two and a half inches in a 24-hour period can be expected about once a year. Snowfalls of three inches or more occur on an average of two or three times in the winter.

Local levees and/or channel improvements now protect some formerly flood-prone areas.

Based on the 1951-1980 period, the average first occurrence of 32 degrees Fahrenheit in the fall is October 20 and the average last occurrence in the spring is April 22.

Indianapolis Int'l Airport *Marion County* Elevation: 792 ft. Latitude: 39° 43' N Longitude: 86° 16' W

	JAN	FEB	MAR	APR	MAY	JUN	JUL	AUG	SEP	OCT	NOV	DEC	YEAR
Mean Maximum Temp. (°F)	36.0	40.5	51.5	63.3	73.1	82.0	85.3	84.1	77.8	65.3	52.3	39.4	62.5
Mean Temp. (°F)	28.3	32.2	42.0	52.9	62.8	72.0	75.5	74.2	67.0	55.0	43.7	32.0	53.1
Mean Minimum Temp. (°F)	20.5	23.8	32.4	42.4	52.5	61.9	65.8	64.3	56.2	44.5	35.0	24.6	43.7
Extreme Maximum Temp. (°F)	68	76	85	86	93	102	103	102	96	91	79	74	103
Extreme Minimum Temp. (°F)	-27	-21	-7	18	29	37	48	42	32	20	10	-23	-27
Days Maximum Temp. ≥ 90°F	0	0	0	0	0	3	7	6	2	0	0	0	18
Days Maximum Temp. ≤ 32°F	12	7	2	0	0	0	0	0	0	0	1	8	30
Days Minimum Temp. ≤ 32°F	26	22	16	4	0	0	0	0	0	3	13	23	107
Days Minimum Temp. ≤ 0°F	2	1	0	0	0	0	0	0	0	0	0	1	4
Heating Degree Days (base 65°F)	1,131	922	709	371	132	15	1	3	66	323	634	1,015	5,322
Cooling Degree Days (base 65°F)	0	0	2	15	72	231	334	296	133	18	0	0	1,101
Mean Precipitation (in.)	2.67	2.35	3.60	3.77	4.98	4.06	4.55	3.39	3.21	3.14	3.60	3.13	42.45
Maximum Precipitation (in.)*	12.7	5.3	10.7	8.1	9.3	7.4	11.8	8.3	8.1	7.8	8.5	7.7	55.8
Minimum Precipitation (in.)*	0.4	0.4	0.9	1.0	1.1	0.4	1.2	0.7	0.2	0.2	0.8	0.4	27.9
Extreme Maximum Daily Precip. (in.)	2.70	2.03	2.54	2.34	3.80	3.09	5.09	3.81	7.20	2.74	4.15	1.74	7.20
Days With ≥ 0.1" Precipitation	6	5	7	8	9	7	7	6	5	5	6	7	78
Days With ≥ 0.5" Precipitation	2	1	2	3	4	3	3	2	2	2	2	2	28
Days With ≥ 1.0" Precipitation	0	0	1	1	1	1	1	1	1	1	1	1	10
Mean Snowfall (in.)	8.5	6.4	2.7	0.3	trace	trace	0.0	trace	trace	0.4	0.8	6.4	25.5
Maximum Snowfall (in.)*	31	18	11	4	trace	0	0	0	0	9	8	28	45
Maximum 24-hr. Snowfall (in.)*	10	8	6	3	trace	0	0	0	0	8	8	10	10
Maximum Snow Depth (in.)	11	13	8	1	trace	trace	0	trace	trace	2	4	9	13
Days With ≥ 1.0" Snow Depth	10	8	2	0	0	0	0	0	0	0	0	6	26
Thunderstorm Days*	1	1	3	5	6	7	8	6	3	2	1	< 1	43
Foggy Days*	15	13	13	11	13	12	16	18	15	13	14	15	168
Predominant Sky Cover*	OVR	OVR	OVR	OVR	OVR	OVR	SCT	SCT	CLR	OVR	OVR	OVR	OVR
Mean Relative Humidity 7am (%)*	81	81	79	77	80	80	84	88	87	85	83	83	82
Mean Relative Humidity 4pm (%)*	69	64	59	54	53	53	56	56	53	53	63	70	59
Mean Dewpoint (°F)*	20	23	31	40	51	60	65	64	56	44	34	25	43
Prevailing Wind Direction*	WSW	WNW	WNW	SW	SW	SW	SW	SW	SW	SW	SW	SW	SW
Prevailing Wind Speed (mph)*	12	13	14	13	10	9	8	8	9	10	12	12	10
Maximum Wind Gust (mph)*	60	62	75	75	69	70	81	70	74	64	79	64	81

Note: (*) Period of record is 1948-1995

South Bend Michiana Regional

South Bend is located on the Saint Joseph River in the northern portion of Saint Joseph County, situated on mostly level to gently rolling terrain and some former marshland. Drainage for the area is through the Saint Joseph River and Kankakee River.

South Bend is under the climatic influence of Lake Michigan with its nearest shore 20 miles to the northwest. The lake has a moderating effect on the temperature. Temperatures of 100 degrees or higher are rare and cold waves are less severe than at many locations at the same latitude. This results in favorable conditions for orchard and vegetable growth.

Based on the 1951-1980 period, the average first occurrence of 32 degrees Fahrenheit in the fall is October 18 and the average last occurrence in the spring is May 1.

Precipitation is fairly evenly distributed throughout the year with the greatest amounts during the growing season. The predominant snow season is from November through March, although there are also generally lighter amounts in October and April.

Winter is marked by considerable cloudiness and rather high humidity along with frequent periods of snow. Heavy snowfalls, resulting from a cold northwest wind passing over Lake Michigan are not uncommon.

South Bend Michiana Regional *St. Joseph County* Elevation: 772 ft. Latitude: 41° 42' N Longitude: 86° 20' W

	JAN	FEB	MAR	APR	MAY	JUN	JUL	AUG	SEP	OCT	NOV	DEC	YEAR
Mean Maximum Temp. (°F)	31.9	35.6	46.7	59.6	70.5	79.8	83.3	81.2	74.5	61.8	48.5	35.8	59.1
Mean Temp. (°F)	25.0	28.1	37.7	49.2	59.6	69.3	73.3	71.6	64.2	52.3	41.0	29.3	50.1
Mean Minimum Temp. (°F)	18.0	20.6	28.6	38.8	48.7	58.8	63.3	61.9	53.9	42.8	33.5	22.7	41.0
Extreme Maximum Temp. (°F)	65	74	85	89	91	104	102	103	95	88	76	70	104
Extreme Minimum Temp. (°F)	-21	-13	-3	13	26	36	42	42	32	20	7	-15	-21
Days Maximum Temp. ≥ 90°F	0	0	0	0	1	4	6	3	1	0	0	0	15
Days Maximum Temp. ≤ 32°F	16	12	4	0	0	0	0	0	0	0	2	11	45
Days Minimum Temp. ≤ 32°F	28	24	21	8	0	0	0	0	0	3	15	26	125
Days Minimum Temp. ≤ 0°F	3	2	0	0	0	0	0	0	0	0	0	2	7
Heating Degree Days (base 65°F)	1,234	1,035	841	477	211	39	4	11	105	396	712	1,100	6,165
Cooling Degree Days (base 65°F)	0	0	1	10	51	175	270	223	89	10	0	0	829
Mean Precipitation (in.)	2.29	1.95	2.47	3.26	3.68	3.80	3.96	3.99	3.65	3.37	3.23	2.68	38.33
Maximum Precipitation (in.)*	5.3	4.5	8.0	6.0	6.9	10.9	7.5	8.3	9.0	9.8	6.7	5.5	55.6
Minimum Precipitation (in.)*	0.7	0.5	0.5	0.5	0.8	0.5	1.2	0.3	trace	0.4	1.4	0.7	25.1
Extreme Maximum Daily Precip. (in.)	1.80	1.70	1.41	2.48	2.79	3.51	3.64	3.96	6.58	3.47	3.92	2.45	6.58
Days With ≥ 0.1" Precipitation	6	5	6	7	7	7	7	7	6	7	7	7	79
Days With ≥ 0.5" Precipitation	1	1	1	2	3	2	3	3	2	2	2	1	23
Days With ≥ 1.0" Precipitation	0	0	0	1	1	1	1	1	1	1	1	0	8
Mean Snowfall (in.)	20.3	15.1	7.4	1.5	trace	trace	trace	trace	trace	0.5	5.0	17.5	67.3
Maximum Snowfall (in.)*	86	35	34	14	1	0	0	0	0	9	30	42	142
Maximum 24-hr. Snowfall (in.)*	16	12	9	8	1	0	0	0	0	7	15	11	16
Maximum Snow Depth (in.)	18	23	9	6	trace	trace	trace	trace	trace	6	8	14	23
Days With ≥ 1.0" Snow Depth	20	15	5	1	0	0	0	0	0	0	2	12	55
Thunderstorm Days*	< 1	< 1	2	4	5	8	7	6	4	2	1	< 1	39
Foggy Days*	15	14	15	13	13	12	14	18	16	16	15	17	178
Predominant Sky Cover*	OVR	OVR	OVR	OVR	OVR	OVR	OVR	OVR	OVR	OVR	OVR	OVR	OVR
Mean Relative Humidity 7am (%)*	82	82	80	77	76	78	82	86	86	84	83	83	82
Mean Relative Humidity 4pm (%)*	73	69	62	55	53	52	55	57	55	57	68	75	61
Mean Dewpoint (°F)*	18	20	28	37	47	57	62	62	54	43	33	23	41
Prevailing Wind Direction*	SW	SW	SW	NNW	SSW	SSW	SW	SW	SSW	SSW	SW	SW	SW
Prevailing Wind Speed (mph)*	13	13	13	13	12	10	9	9	10	12	12	13	12
Maximum Wind Gust (mph)*	67	58	55	66	86	71	66	59	63	59	74	69	86

Note: (*) Period of record is 1948-1995

Anderson Sewage Plant *Madison County* Elevation: 845 ft. Latitude: 40° 06' N Longitude: 85° 43' W

	JAN	FEB	MAR	APR	MAY	JUN	JUL	AUG	SEP	OCT	NOV	DEC	YEAR
Mean Maximum Temp. (°F)	34.4	39.0	49.2	61.6	71.9	80.7	83.8	82.3	76.2	63.9	50.8	37.9	61.0
Mean Temp. (°F)	27.1	31.2	40.3	51.4	61.7	70.7	74.0	72.5	65.4	53.8	42.8	31.0	51.8
Mean Minimum Temp. (°F)	19.8	23.3	31.4	41.2	51.3	60.6	64.2	62.6	54.7	43.6	34.8	24.0	42.6
Extreme Maximum Temp. (°F)	65	73	81	87	93	101	103	101	95	90	80	75	103
Extreme Minimum Temp. (°F)	-24	-12	-7	17	31	37	45	40	31	20	10	-22	-24
Days Maximum Temp. ≥ 90°F	0	0	0	0	0	4	6	4	1	0	0	0	15
Days Maximum Temp. ≤ 32°F	13	9	3	0	0	0	0	0	0	0	1	10	36
Days Minimum Temp. ≤ 32°F	27	22	18	5	0	0	0	0	0	4	14	24	114
Days Minimum Temp. ≤ 0°F	3	1	0	0	0	0	0	0	0	0	0	1	5
Heating Degree Days (base 65°F)	1,167	952	761	412	164	23	3	7	85	357	659	1,048	5,638
Cooling Degree Days (base 65°F)	0	0	2	12	67	200	289	246	105	17	1	0	939
Mean Precipitation (in.)	2.39	2.28	3.26	3.83	4.39	4.21	4.40	3.49	2.99	3.10	3.66	3.09	41.09
Extreme Maximum Daily Precip. (in.)	3.00	2.37	3.30	2.00	2.69	3.51	3.06	2.70	4.21	1.91	3.42	2.00	4.21
Days With ≥ 0.1" Precipitation	5	5	7	9	8	7	7	6	5	6	6	7	78
Days With ≥ 0.5" Precipitation	2	1	3	3	3	3	4	2	2	2	3	2	30
Days With ≥ 1.0" Precipitation	0	0	1	1	1	1	1	1	1	1	1	1	10
Mean Snowfall (in.)	7.2	4.2	1.6	0.2	0.0	0.0	0.0	0.0	0.0	0.1	0.5	4.1	17.9
Maximum Snow Depth (in.)	***18***	***12***	8	1	0	0	0	0	0	trace	3	***16***	***18***
Days With ≥ 1.0" Snow Depth	***7***	4	2	0	0	0	0	0	0	0	0	4	***17***

Angola *Steuben County* Elevation: 1,009 ft. Latitude: 41° 38' N Longitude: 84° 59' W

	JAN	FEB	MAR	APR	MAY	JUN	JUL	AUG	SEP	OCT	NOV	DEC	YEAR
Mean Maximum Temp. (°F)	30.3	33.9	44.3	57.7	68.8	78.2	81.8	80.1	73.3	60.4	47.4	34.4	57.5
Mean Temp. (°F)	22.5	25.1	34.4	46.7	57.8	67.5	71.3	69.4	61.8	49.6	38.8	27.3	47.7
Mean Minimum Temp. (°F)	14.7	16.3	24.5	35.7	46.7	56.6	60.7	58.6	50.2	38.7	30.1	20.1	37.7
Extreme Maximum Temp. (°F)	63	71	78	85	90	101	98	97	93	86	75	69	101
Extreme Minimum Temp. (°F)	-27	-14	-10	4	22	32	41	37	27	16	9	-19	-27
Days Maximum Temp. ≥ 90°F	0	0	0	0	0	2	3	2	0	0	0	0	7
Days Maximum Temp. ≤ 32°F	18	13	5	0	0	0	0	0	0	0	3	13	52
Days Minimum Temp. ≤ 32°F	29	27	25	12	1	0	0	0	0	9	19	28	150
Days Minimum Temp. ≤ 0°F	5	4	0	0	0	0	0	0	0	0	0	2	11
Heating Degree Days (base 65°F)	1,310	1,122	943	546	250	53	11	23	144	476	781	1,163	6,822
Cooling Degree Days (base 65°F)	0	0	1	6	33	134	212	166	54	4	0	0	610
Mean Precipitation (in.)	2.27	2.10	2.69	3.40	4.25	3.81	4.12	4.18	3.30	3.01	3.07	2.81	39.01
Extreme Maximum Daily Precip. (in.)	1.67	1.75	2.11	2.52	4.10	3.55	3.55	3.78	2.41	3.19	2.35	2.36	4.10
Days With ≥ 0.1" Precipitation	6	5	6	7	8	7	7	7	6	6	7	7	79
Days With ≥ 0.5" Precipitation	1	1	2	2	3	3	3	3	2	2	2	2	26
Days With ≥ 1.0" Precipitation	0	0	0	1	1	1	1	1	1	1	0	0	7
Mean Snowfall (in.)	10.6	8.4	4.8	1.0	trace	0.0	0.0	0.0	0.0	0.3	2.1	9.2	36.4
Maximum Snow Depth (in.)	23	22	13	6	trace	0	0	0	0	3	5	20	23
Days With ≥ 1.0" Snow Depth	18	15	6	1	0	0	0	0	0	0	2	11	53

Berne *Adams County* Elevation: 859 ft. Latitude: 40° 40' N Longitude: 84° 57' W

	JAN	FEB	MAR	APR	MAY	JUN	JUL	AUG	SEP	OCT	NOV	DEC	YEAR
Mean Maximum Temp. (°F)	33.7	37.5	48.4	61.1	71.8	81.0	84.6	82.8	76.6	63.7	50.3	37.2	60.7
Mean Temp. (°F)	26.6	29.5	39.0	50.7	61.3	70.9	74.6	72.8	65.7	53.7	42.3	30.4	51.5
Mean Minimum Temp. (°F)	19.4	21.5	29.5	40.2	50.7	60.7	64.6	62.6	54.9	43.7	34.1	23.5	42.1
Extreme Maximum Temp. (°F)	65	74	82	88	94	104	101	99	96	89	77	72	104
Extreme Minimum Temp. (°F)	-24	-13	-4	10	29	39	47	42	31	20	11	-19	-24
Days Maximum Temp. ≥ 90°F	0	0	0	0	0	4	7	4	1	0	0	0	16
Days Maximum Temp. ≤ 32°F	14	10	3	0	0	0	0	0	0	0	1	10	38
Days Minimum Temp. ≤ 32°F	27	23	20	6	0	0	0	0	0	3	14	25	118
Days Minimum Temp. ≤ 0°F	3	2	0	0	0	0	0	0	0	0	0	1	6
Heating Degree Days (base 65°F)	1,185	998	803	435	171	24	2	6	81	361	677	1,067	5,810
Cooling Degree Days (base 65°F)	0	0	2	11	62	207	306	253	109	16	0	0	966
Mean Precipitation (in.)	2.38	2.33	2.75	3.80	3.89	4.31	4.44	3.61	2.78	2.90	3.08	2.79	39.06
Extreme Maximum Daily Precip. (in.)	1.94	1.69	1.95	2.11	2.42	4.20	3.46	3.62	2.45	2.21	2.07	2.02	4.20
Days With ≥ 0.1" Precipitation	6	5	6	8	8	8	7	6	5	6	7	6	78
Days With ≥ 0.5" Precipitation	1	2	2	2	3	3	3	2	2	2	2	2	26
Days With ≥ 1.0" Precipitation	0	0	0	1	1	1	1	1	1	1	1	0	8
Mean Snowfall (in.)	8.2	7.3	4.1	0.8	0.0	0.0	0.0	0.0	0.0	0.3	1.6	5.9	28.2
Maximum Snow Depth (in.)	24	25	11	5	0	0	0	0	0	1	3	9	25
Days With ≥ 1.0" Snow Depth	13	10	4	0	0	0	0	0	0	0	1	8	36

Bloomington Indiana Univ *Monroe County* Elevation: 830 ft. Latitude: 39° 10' N Longitude: 86° 31' W

	JAN	FEB	MAR	APR	MAY	JUN	JUL	AUG	SEP	OCT	NOV	DEC	YEAR
Mean Maximum Temp. (°F)	37.4	42.2	52.2	63.9	73.6	81.8	85.4	84.9	78.2	66.0	53.9	40.8	63.4
Mean Temp. (°F)	29.4	33.0	42.1	53.3	63.2	71.9	75.7	74.6	67.2	55.3	44.9	32.9	53.6
Mean Minimum Temp. (°F)	21.2	23.9	31.9	42.6	52.8	62.0	65.8	64.2	56.1	44.5	35.9	25.0	43.8
Extreme Maximum Temp. (°F)	69	76	83	87	93	101	104	100	98	90	79	74	104
Extreme Minimum Temp. (°F)	-21	-13	-2	18	31	38	48	44	33	23	13	-20	-21
Days Maximum Temp. ≥ 90°F	0	0	0	0	0	3	7	7	2	0	0	0	19
Days Maximum Temp. ≤ 32°F	11	6	2	0	0	0	0	0	0	0	1	8	28
Days Minimum Temp. ≤ 32°F	27	22	17	5	0	0	0	0	0	2	13	23	109
Days Minimum Temp. ≤ 0°F	2	1	0	0	0	0	0	0	0	0	0	1	4
Heating Degree Days (base 65°F)	1,098	896	706	365	126	16	1	3	62	316	596	988	5,173
Cooling Degree Days (base 65°F)	0	0	3	20	78	232	338	307	134	21	1	0	1,134
Mean Precipitation (in.)	3.11	2.72	3.60	4.49	5.80	4.73	4.60	3.62	3.75	3.70	3.81	3.55	47.48
Extreme Maximum Daily Precip. (in.)	2.44	2.14	2.91	3.65	3.50	2.67	3.12	3.75	4.00	4.15	2.98	2.50	4.15
Days With ≥ 0.1" Precipitation	6	6	7	8	9	7	7	5	5	6	6	7	79
Days With ≥ 0.5" Precipitation	2	2	2	3	4	3	3	2	3	3	3	2	32
Days With ≥ 1.0" Precipitation	1	1	1	1	2	1	1	1	1	1	1	1	13
Mean Snowfall (in.)	***5.2***	2.7	0.9	trace	0.0	0.0	0.0	0.0	0.0	0.2	0.0	3.9	***12.9***
Maximum Snow Depth (in.)	***13***	***9***	***14***	1	0	0	0	0	0	2	trace	***15***	***15***
Days With ≥ 1.0" Snow Depth	***6***	4	1	0	0	0	0	0	0	0	0	4	***15***

The period of record for all cooperative weather station data is 1980 – 2009. See User Guide for detailed explanation of data.

Brookville *Franklin County* Elevation: 629 ft. Latitude: 39° 25' N Longitude: 85° 01' W

	JAN	FEB	MAR	APR	MAY	JUN	JUL	AUG	SEP	OCT	NOV	DEC	YEAR
Mean Maximum Temp. (°F)	37.9	42.0	52.6	65.0	74.7	83.3	86.8	86.0	79.6	66.9	54.7	41.3	64.2
Mean Temp. (°F)	28.9	31.8	41.0	52.3	62.1	71.0	74.8	73.8	66.2	53.9	43.8	32.5	52.7
Mean Minimum Temp. (°F)	19.8	21.5	29.3	39.5	49.6	58.6	62.8	61.5	52.8	40.8	32.9	23.7	41.1
Extreme Maximum Temp. (°F)	67	76	84	89	94	102	102	103	99	92	82	76	103
Extreme Minimum Temp. (°F)	-31	-15	-9	16	29	38	45	41	30	17	9	-20	-31
Days Maximum Temp. ≥ 90°F	0	0	0	0	0	6	10	9	3	0	0	0	28
Days Maximum Temp. ≤ 32°F	10	6	1	0	0	0	0	0	0	0	1	7	25
Days Minimum Temp. ≤ 32°F	27	24	20	7	1	0	0	0	0	7	16	24	126
Days Minimum Temp. ≤ 0°F	3	2	0	0	0	0	0	0	0	0	0	1	6
Heating Degree Days (base 65°F)	1,113	931	739	387	146	20	1	5	75	354	629	1,000	5,400
Cooling Degree Days (base 65°F)	0	0	2	12	65	206	312	284	120	18	1	0	1,020
Mean Precipitation (in.)	3.04	2.61	3.64	4.14	5.09	3.72	4.37	3.44	2.62	3.24	3.55	3.40	42.86
Extreme Maximum Daily Precip. (in.)	2.85	2.02	3.18	3.35	4.03	2.35	3.88	3.20	2.94	3.80	2.23	2.57	4.03
Days With ≥ 0.1" Precipitation	6	5	7	9	9	7	7	5	5	6	7	7	80
Days With ≥ 0.5" Precipitation	2	2	2	3	3	3	3	2	2	2	3	2	29
Days With ≥ 1.0" Precipitation	1	0	1	1	1	1	1	1	1	1	1	1	11
Mean Snowfall (in.)	***4.2***	***4.0***	1.5	0.1	trace	0.0	0.0	0.0	0.0	0.1	0.6	***3.7***	***14.2***
Maximum Snow Depth (in.)	***10***	***9***	***7***	***1***	***trace***	***0***	***0***	***0***	***0***	na	***6***	na	na
Days With ≥ 1.0" Snow Depth	***7***	***7***	1	0	0	0	0	0	0	0	0	4	***19***

Columbia City *Whitley County* Elevation: 850 ft. Latitude: 41° 09' N Longitude: 85° 29' W

	JAN	FEB	MAR	APR	MAY	JUN	JUL	AUG	SEP	OCT	NOV	DEC	YEAR
Mean Maximum Temp. (°F)	31.6	35.4	46.4	59.1	70.3	79.5	82.7	81.1	75.0	61.9	49.1	36.2	59.0
Mean Temp. (°F)	24.0	26.8	36.6	48.3	59.2	68.6	72.0	70.3	63.3	50.9	40.3	28.8	49.1
Mean Minimum Temp. (°F)	16.1	18.1	26.9	37.4	48.0	57.7	61.2	59.5	51.6	39.9	31.4	21.3	39.1
Extreme Maximum Temp. (°F)	66	72	80	88	92	103	101	98	95	89	77	70	103
Extreme Minimum Temp. (°F)	-24	-16	-6	7	24	36	44	36	27	17	8	-22	-24
Days Maximum Temp. ≥ 90°F	0	0	0	0	0	3	4	2	1	0	0	0	10
Days Maximum Temp. ≤ 32°F	16	11	4	0	0	0	0	0	0	0	2	11	44
Days Minimum Temp. ≤ 32°F	28	24	23	9	1	0	0	0	0	7	17	26	135
Days Minimum Temp. ≤ 0°F	4	3	0	0	0	0	0	0	0	0	0	2	9
Heating Degree Days (base 65°F)	1,264	1,073	873	503	214	41	7	17	117	437	733	1,117	6,396
Cooling Degree Days (base 65°F)	0	0	1	7	40	157	230	190	74	8	0	0	707
Mean Precipitation (in.)	2.34	1.85	2.79	3.52	4.13	4.41	4.03	3.91	3.33	3.05	3.26	2.85	39.47
Extreme Maximum Daily Precip. (in.)	2.58	1.39	2.14	2.54	2.52	4.48	3.09	4.30	3.20	2.39	3.57	1.70	4.48
Days With ≥ 0.1" Precipitation	6	5	6	7	8	7	7	6	6	6	7	7	78
Days With ≥ 0.5" Precipitation	1	1	2	2	3	3	3	3	2	2	2	2	26
Days With ≥ 1.0" Precipitation	0	0	1	1	1	1	1	1	1	1	1	0	9
Mean Snowfall (in.)	8.8	6.7	3.5	0.7	0.0	0.0	0.0	0.0	0.0	0.2	1.2	6.4	27.5
Maximum Snow Depth (in.)	11	16	7	6	0	0	0	0	0	1	4	11	16
Days With ≥ 1.0" Snow Depth	15	10	4	0	0	0	0	0	0	0	1	8	38

Columbus *Bartholomew County* Elevation: 621 ft. Latitude: 39° 12' N Longitude: 85° 55' W

	JAN	FEB	MAR	APR	MAY	JUN	JUL	AUG	SEP	OCT	NOV	DEC	YEAR
Mean Maximum Temp. (°F)	37.6	42.0	52.2	64.1	73.6	82.2	85.4	84.7	78.4	66.5	54.0	41.0	63.5
Mean Temp. (°F)	29.3	32.8	41.8	53.0	63.1	72.0	75.5	74.1	66.8	54.7	44.2	33.0	53.4
Mean Minimum Temp. (°F)	21.0	23.4	31.3	41.9	52.5	61.8	65.5	63.5	55.0	42.9	34.4	24.8	43.2
Extreme Maximum Temp. (°F)	68	76	83	86	91	100	103	103	97	91	80	73	103
Extreme Minimum Temp. (°F)	-26	-14	-6	18	31	41	51	43	34	21	11	-20	-26
Days Maximum Temp. ≥ 90°F	0	0	0	0	0	4	7	7	2	0	0	0	20
Days Maximum Temp. ≤ 32°F	10	6	1	0	0	0	0	0	0	0	1	7	25
Days Minimum Temp. ≤ 32°F	26	23	18	4	0	0	0	0	0	4	14	23	112
Days Minimum Temp. ≤ 0°F	2	1	0	0	0	0	0	0	0	0	0	1	4
Heating Degree Days (base 65°F)	1,099	905	715	367	125	15	1	3	64	329	616	987	5,226
Cooling Degree Days (base 65°F)	0	0	2	15	72	232	332	292	124	18	0	0	1,087
Mean Precipitation (in.)	2.85	2.63	3.71	4.54	5.25	3.87	4.10	3.67	3.05	3.24	3.66	3.45	44.02
Extreme Maximum Daily Precip. (in.)	2.76	2.17	2.67	3.99	3.01	2.72	6.37	4.11	2.72	3.20	2.30	2.25	6.37
Days With ≥ 0.1" Precipitation	5	5	7	8	9	7	6	6	5	5	6	7	76
Days With ≥ 0.5" Precipitation	2	2	3	3	4	3	3	3	2	2	3	3	33
Days With ≥ 1.0" Precipitation	1	0	1	1	1	1	1	1	1	1	1	1	11
Mean Snowfall (in.)	5.1	3.5	2.1	0.1	trace	0.0	0.0	0.0	0.0	0.1	0.1	3.4	14.4
Maximum Snow Depth (in.)	***16***	***9***	***10***	***1***	***trace***	***0***	***0***	0	***0***	***1***	***1***	***19***	***19***
Days With ≥ 1.0" Snow Depth	***6***	***4***	***1***	0	0	0	0	0	0	0	0	4	***15***

Crawfordsville 5 S *Montgomery County* Elevation: 762 ft. Latitude: 39° 58' N Longitude: 86° 56' W

	JAN	FEB	MAR	APR	MAY	JUN	JUL	AUG	SEP	OCT	NOV	DEC	YEAR
Mean Maximum Temp. (°F)	***34.7***	39.0	49.9	62.0	72.0	81.6	84.4	83.2	77.7	65.4	51.2	37.9	***61.6***
Mean Temp. (°F)	***25.8***	29.3	38.8	50.1	60.1	70.0	72.8	70.9	64.0	52.6	41.3	29.0	***50.4***
Mean Minimum Temp. (°F)	***16.9***	19.5	27.7	38.2	48.1	58.3	61.2	58.7	50.3	39.7	31.4	20.1	***39.2***
Extreme Maximum Temp. (°F)	65	74	83	87	93	102	99	101	96	89	80	74	102
Extreme Minimum Temp. (°F)	-31	-24	-12	3	28	32	41	36	23	18	3	-24	-31
Days Maximum Temp. ≥ 90°F	0	0	0	0	0	4	6	4	2	0	0	0	16
Days Maximum Temp. ≤ 32°F	13	9	3	0	0	0	0	0	0	0	1	10	36
Days Minimum Temp. ≤ 32°F	27	25	22	9	1	0	0	0	1	8	17	26	136
Days Minimum Temp. ≤ 0°F	4	3	0	0	0	0	0	0	0	0	0	3	10
Heating Degree Days (base 65°F)	***1,207***	1,002	806	449	193	31	7	15	109	390	702	1,110	***6,021***
Cooling Degree Days (base 65°F)	***0***	0	1	11	46	187	255	207	85	13	0	0	***805***
Mean Precipitation (in.)	***2.48***	2.46	2.94	4.01	4.66	4.53	4.44	3.70	3.20	3.33	4.16	3.10	***43.01***
Extreme Maximum Daily Precip. (in.)	2.70	2.98	2.10	2.75	3.50	***3.28***	2.71	4.35	2.25	3.76	2.65	3.20	***4.35***
Days With ≥ 0.1" Precipitation	5	5	6	8	9	8	7	5	5	6	7	***7***	***78***
Days With ≥ 0.5" Precipitation	2	2	2	3	3	3	3	3	2	2	3	***2***	***30***
Days With ≥ 1.0" Precipitation	0	1	0	1	1	1	1	1	1	1	1	***0***	***9***
Mean Snowfall (in.)	na	5.4	2.7	0.2	trace	0.0	0.0	0.0	0.0	trace	0.6	***4.7***	na
Maximum Snow Depth (in.)	na	na	na	***3***	***trace***	***0***	***0***	***0***	***0***	***1***	***5***	na	na
Days With ≥ 1.0" Snow Depth	na	na	***1***	0	0	0	0	0	0	0	0	***4***	na

Delphi 3 S *Carroll County* Elevation: 670 ft. Latitude: 40° 33' N Longitude: 86° 41' W

	JAN	FEB	MAR	APR	MAY	JUN	JUL	AUG	SEP	OCT	NOV	DEC	YEAR
Mean Maximum Temp. (°F)	34.6	39.0	50.7	64.0	74.2	82.8	85.4	83.8	78.3	65.5	52.1	38.3	62.4
Mean Temp. (°F)	26.9	30.5	40.9	52.3	62.5	71.4	74.3	72.6	65.9	54.1	43.4	31.0	52.1
Mean Minimum Temp. (°F)	19.3	22.1	30.9	40.5	50.7	59.9	63.2	61.5	53.5	42.7	34.6	23.6	41.9
Extreme Maximum Temp. (°F)	67	73	84	89	96	105	103	100	96	89	78	71	105
Extreme Minimum Temp. (°F)	-24	-16	0	10	30	36	44	38	27	18	9	-21	-24
Days Maximum Temp. ≥ 90°F	0	0	0	0	1	5	7	5	2	0	0	0	20
Days Maximum Temp. ≤ 32°F	13	8	2	0	0	0	0	0	0	0	1	8	32
Days Minimum Temp. ≤ 32°F	27	23	18	7	0	0	0	0	0	5	13	24	117
Days Minimum Temp. ≤ 0°F	3	2	0	0	0	0	0	0	0	0	0	2	7
Heating Degree Days (base 65°F)	1,174	968	744	389	142	19	2	7	75	347	643	1,048	5,558
Cooling Degree Days (base 65°F)	0	0	2	15	71	216	298	250	109	17	1	0	979
Mean Precipitation (in.)	2.15	2.05	2.76	3.49	4.37	4.00	4.57	3.68	2.74	2.98	3.12	2.61	38.52
Extreme Maximum Daily Precip. (in.)	2.07	2.42	2.03	2.59	3.00	3.00	3.55	2.64	4.78	2.78	2.50	2.44	4.78
Days With ≥ 0.1" Precipitation	5	4	6	7	8	6	7	6	5	6	6	6	72
Days With ≥ 0.5" Precipitation	1	1	2	3	3	3	3	3	2	2	2	2	27
Days With ≥ 1.0" Precipitation	1	0	1	1	1	1	1	1	1	1	1	0	10
Mean Snowfall (in.)	5.6	4.8	2.4	0.5	trace	0.0	0.0	0.0	0.0	0.2	0.5	4.6	18.6
Maximum Snow Depth (in.)	18	17	10	4	trace	0	0	0	0	4	2	9	18
Days With ≥ 1.0" Snow Depth	10	8	2	0	0	0	0	0	0	0	0	6	26

Dubois S Ind Forage Frm *Dubois County* Elevation: 689 ft. Latitude: 38° 27' N Longitude: 86° 42' W

	JAN	FEB	MAR	APR	MAY	JUN	JUL	AUG	SEP	OCT	NOV	DEC	YEAR
Mean Maximum Temp. (°F)	39.6	44.4	54.4	65.4	74.6	82.8	86.4	86.3	79.4	67.8	55.8	43.4	65.0
Mean Temp. (°F)	30.7	34.4	43.6	54.5	63.7	72.2	76.0	75.1	67.7	56.1	45.7	34.3	54.5
Mean Minimum Temp. (°F)	21.7	24.3	32.8	43.5	52.8	61.6	65.5	63.8	55.9	44.4	35.6	25.3	43.9
Extreme Maximum Temp. (°F)	70	76	83	88	92	101	102	102	99	92	81	75	102
Extreme Minimum Temp. (°F)	-25	-12	0	17	29	40	46	42	33	18	10	-20	-25
Days Maximum Temp. ≥ 90°F	0	0	0	0	0	5	9	10	3	0	0	0	27
Days Maximum Temp. ≤ 32°F	8	5	1	0	0	0	0	0	0	0	0	6	20
Days Minimum Temp. ≤ 32°F	26	22	16	4	0	0	0	0	0	4	13	23	108
Days Minimum Temp. ≤ 0°F	2	1	0	0	0	0	0	0	0	0	0	1	4
Heating Degree Days (base 65°F)	1,058	859	659	334	120	15	1	2	60	296	574	944	4,922
Cooling Degree Days (base 65°F)	0	0	4	24	87	238	348	322	147	28	2	0	1,200
Mean Precipitation (in.)	3.27	2.97	4.20	4.63	5.80	4.32	4.31	3.21	3.91	3.73	4.03	3.68	48.06
Extreme Maximum Daily Precip. (in.)	4.20	2.39	4.82	5.66	3.90	5.38	3.45	2.76	3.00	4.12	4.25	3.18	5.66
Days With ≥ 0.1" Precipitation	5	5	7	8	9	7	7	6	5	6	7	6	78
Days With ≥ 0.5" Precipitation	2	2	3	3	4	3	3	2	3	3	3	3	34
Days With ≥ 1.0" Precipitation	1	1	1	1	2	1	1	1	1	1	1	1	13
Mean Snowfall (in.)	2.4	2.7	***1.5***	trace	0.0	0.0	0.0	0.0	0.0	0.2	trace	***2.3***	***9.1***
Maximum Snow Depth (in.)	***8***	10	***14***	trace	0	0	0	***0***	0	0	1	***18***	***18***
Days With ≥ 1.0" Snow Depth	***4***	3	***1***	0	0	0	0	0	0	0	0	***3***	***11***

Elwood Wastewater Plant *Madison County* Elevation: 839 ft. Latitude: 40° 16' N Longitude: 85° 51' W

	JAN	FEB	MAR	APR	MAY	JUN	JUL	AUG	SEP	OCT	NOV	DEC	YEAR
Mean Maximum Temp. (°F)	33.5	38.1	48.8	61.6	72.3	81.3	84.7	83.3	77.5	64.5	51.2	37.6	61.2
Mean Temp. (°F)	25.2	29.1	38.5	50.0	60.9	70.1	73.5	71.7	64.9	52.4	41.7	29.4	50.6
Mean Minimum Temp. (°F)	16.8	20.0	28.2	38.2	49.4	58.8	62.4	60.1	52.2	40.3	32.2	21.3	40.0
Extreme Maximum Temp. (°F)	65	74	81	87	93	102	101	99	96	92	79	72	102
Extreme Minimum Temp. (°F)	-24	-23	-8	12	28	38	44	38	29	18	5	-20	-24
Days Maximum Temp. ≥ 90°F	0	0	0	0	0	4	6	5	2	0	0	0	17
Days Maximum Temp. ≤ 32°F	14	9	3	0	0	0	0	0	0	0	1	9	36
Days Minimum Temp. ≤ 32°F	28	24	21	8	0	0	0	0	0	7	17	26	131
Days Minimum Temp. ≤ 0°F	4	2	0	0	0	0	0	0	0	0	0	2	8
Heating Degree Days (base 65°F)	1,229	1,010	816	454	177	30	3	12	94	394	692	1,095	6,006
Cooling Degree Days (base 65°F)	0	0	1	9	57	189	275	227	96	11	0	0	865
Mean Precipitation (in.)	2.55	2.04	2.87	3.69	4.28	4.36	4.34	3.77	3.35	2.79	3.56	3.02	40.62
Extreme Maximum Daily Precip. (in.)	2.90	1.30	1.95	2.60	2.80	4.65	4.25	3.97	5.01	2.15	3.50	2.50	5.01
Days With ≥ 0.1" Precipitation	5	4	7	8	8	7	7	6	5	5	7	7	76
Days With ≥ 0.5" Precipitation	1	2	2	3	3	3	3	2	2	2	2	2	27
Days With ≥ 1.0" Precipitation	0	0	1	1	1	1	1	1	1	0	1	1	9
Mean Snowfall (in.)	na	na	0.8	trace	0.0	0.0	0.0	0.0	0.0	trace	0.1	***2.8***	na
Maximum Snow Depth (in.)	na	na	***10***	***4***	***0***	0	0	***0***	0	***trace***	***trace***	na	na
Days With ≥ 1.0" Snow Depth	na	na	1	0	0	0	0	0	0	0	0	***2***	na

English 4 S *Crawford County* Elevation: 509 ft. Latitude: 38° 17' N Longitude: 86° 28' W

	JAN	FEB	MAR	APR	MAY	JUN	JUL	AUG	SEP	OCT	NOV	DEC	YEAR
Mean Maximum Temp. (°F)	41.9	48.2	57.6	***68.3***	76.9	84.4	88.0	***87.1***	***80.8***	***69.8***	***57.5***	***45.1***	***67.1***
Mean Temp. (°F)	32.1	36.9	44.9	***54.7***	63.5	71.6	75.8	***74.2***	***66.8***	***55.5***	***45.9***	***35.2***	***54.7***
Mean Minimum Temp. (°F)	22.3	25.5	32.1	***40.9***	50.1	58.8	63.5	***61.3***	***52.7***	***41.1***	***34.3***	***25.2***	***42.3***
Extreme Maximum Temp. (°F)	72	76	85	91	93	102	104	***102***	***98***	***88***	***84***	***76***	***104***
Extreme Minimum Temp. (°F)	-30	-15	-2	15	26	36	41	***35***	***28***	***14***	***4***	***-21***	***-30***
Days Maximum Temp. ≥ 90°F	0	0	0	0	0	6	13	***11***	***3***	***0***	***0***	***0***	***33***
Days Maximum Temp. ≤ 32°F	6	3	0	0	0	0	0	***0***	***0***	***0***	***0***	***5***	***14***
Days Minimum Temp. ≤ 32°F	25	21	17	7	1	0	0	***0***	***0***	7	***14***	***22***	***114***
Days Minimum Temp. ≤ 0°F	2	1	0	0	0	0	0	***0***	***0***	***0***	***0***	***1***	***4***
Heating Degree Days (base 65°F)	1,012	789	620	***322***	113	14	1	***3***	***68***	***306***	***566***	***919***	***4,733***
Cooling Degree Days (base 65°F)	0	0	3	***18***	73	219	341	***295***	***127***	***17***	***1***	***1***	***1,095***
Mean Precipitation (in.)	3.53	3.54	4.45	4.45	5.66	4.45	4.00	***3.31***	***3.64***	***3.47***	***4.24***	***3.91***	***48.65***
Extreme Maximum Daily Precip. (in.)	5.50	4.30	3.01	3.82	4.06	3.29	***3.65***	***2.95***	***3.55***	***2.50***	***2.93***	***2.65***	***5.50***
Days With ≥ 0.1" Precipitation	6	7	8	8	9	7	6	***5***	***5***	***6***	***7***	***7***	***81***
Days With ≥ 0.5" Precipitation	2	2	3	3	4	3	3	***2***	***2***	***2***	***3***	***3***	***32***
Days With ≥ 1.0" Precipitation	1	1	1	1	2	1	1	***1***	***1***	***1***	***1***	***1***	***13***
Mean Snowfall (in.)	***1.0***	na	***0.1***	***trace***	0.0	0.0	0.0	***0.0***	***0.0***	***trace***	***trace***	***2.0***	na
Maximum Snow Depth (in.)	***10***	***15***	***14***	***trace***	***0***	***0***	***0***	***0***	***0***	***1***	***trace***	***22***	***22***
Days With ≥ 1.0" Snow Depth	***5***	3	***1***	0	0	0	0	***0***	***0***	***0***	***0***	***3***	***12***

The period of record for all cooperative weather station data is 1980 – 2009. See User Guide for detailed explanation of data.

Evansville Museum *Vanderburgh County* Elevation: 379 ft. Latitude: 37° 58' N Longitude: 87° 34' W

	JAN	FEB	MAR	APR	MAY	JUN	JUL	AUG	SEP	OCT	NOV	DEC	YEAR
Mean Maximum Temp. (°F)	42.9	47.8	59.1	70.2	78.7	87.4	90.0	90.0	83.3	71.6	58.9	46.1	68.8
Mean Temp. (°F)	35.2	38.7	48.5	59.1	68.0	76.7	80.0	79.6	72.2	60.6	49.7	38.2	58.9
Mean Minimum Temp. (°F)	27.2	29.5	38.2	47.9	57.2	66.1	70.0	69.1	61.1	49.4	40.6	30.2	48.9
Extreme Maximum Temp. (°F)	71	78	86	91	95	101	102	102	100	95	85	78	102
Extreme Minimum Temp. (°F)	-17	-8	5	24	36	45	47	46	37	22	13	-15	-17
Days Maximum Temp. ≥ 90°F	0	0	0	0	2	12	17	17	7	1	0	0	56
Days Maximum Temp. ≤ 32°F	5	3	0	0	0	0	0	0	0	0	0	3	11
Days Minimum Temp. ≤ 32°F	21	16	10	1	0	0	0	0	0	1	7	16	72
Days Minimum Temp. ≤ 0°F	1	0	0	0	0	0	0	0	0	0	0	0	1
Heating Degree Days (base 65°F)	917	738	509	216	52	2	0	0	26	186	455	824	3,925
Cooling Degree Days (base 65°F)	0	0	6	44	152	361	473	459	245	56	4	0	1,800
Mean Precipitation (in.)	2.97	3.35	4.48	4.34	4.96	3.55	4.25	3.31	3.57	3.55	4.17	3.79	46.29
Extreme Maximum Daily Precip. (in.)	2.81	2.83	3.84	5.47	2.97	3.77	5.74	4.00	5.34	2.57	4.10	3.15	5.74
Days With ≥ 0.1" Precipitation	5	6	7	7	8	6	6	5	5	6	6	6	73
Days With ≥ 0.5" Precipitation	2	2	3	3	3	2	3	2	2	2	3	2	29
Days With ≥ 1.0" Precipitation	0	1	1	1	1	1	1	1	1	1	1	1	11
Mean Snowfall (in.)	3.1	2.9	1.5	0.1	trace	0.0	0.0	0.0	0.0	trace	0.1	3.3	11.0
Maximum Snow Depth (in.)	6	9	6	trace	trace	0	0	0	0	trace	trace	22	22
Days With ≥ 1.0" Snow Depth	3	4	1	0	0	0	0	0	0	0	0	3	11

Farmland 5 NNW *Randolph County* Elevation: 964 ft. Latitude: 40° 15' N Longitude: 85° 09' W

	JAN	FEB	MAR	APR	MAY	JUN	JUL	AUG	SEP	OCT	NOV	DEC	YEAR
Mean Maximum Temp. (°F)	33.9	37.6	48.1	61.0	71.6	80.7	84.0	82.6	76.9	64.4	51.1	37.9	60.8
Mean Temp. (°F)	25.6	28.5	37.9	49.7	60.5	69.9	73.1	71.2	64.2	52.4	41.6	29.8	50.4
Mean Minimum Temp. (°F)	17.3	19.3	27.5	38.5	49.4	58.9	62.1	59.7	51.5	40.4	32.1	21.7	39.9
Extreme Maximum Temp. (°F)	66	74	81	85	94	102	100	98	95	90	79	72	102
Extreme Minimum Temp. (°F)	-25	-21	-16	10	28	37	40	38	27	17	5	-21	-25
Days Maximum Temp. ≥ 90°F	0	0	0	0	0	4	6	5	2	0	0	0	17
Days Maximum Temp. ≤ 32°F	14	10	4	0	0	0	0	0	0	0	1	10	39
Days Minimum Temp. ≤ 32°F	28	25	22	8	1	0	0	0	0	7	17	26	134
Days Minimum Temp. ≤ 0°F	4	2	0	0	0	0	0	0	0	0	0	2	8
Heating Degree Days (base 65°F)	1,214	1,026	836	460	187	33	5	15	106	397	695	1,084	6,058
Cooling Degree Days (base 65°F)	0	0	1	9	54	185	263	214	90	13	0	0	829
Mean Precipitation (in.)	2.11	1.94	2.83	3.65	4.28	4.23	4.77	3.60	2.98	2.95	3.26	2.61	39.21
Extreme Maximum Daily Precip. (in.)	3.31	2.09	2.24	2.36	2.51	3.73	4.40	3.02	3.18	2.73	3.01	2.40	4.40
Days With ≥ 0.1" Precipitation	5	5	7	8	8	7	7	5	5	6	6	6	75
Days With ≥ 0.5" Precipitation	1	1	2	2	3	3	3	3	2	2	2	2	26
Days With ≥ 1.0" Precipitation	0	0	0	1	1	1	1	1	1	1	1	0	8
Mean Snowfall (in.)	7.0	5.9	3.0	0.4	trace	0.0	0.0	0.0	0.0	0.3	1.0	4.8	22.4
Maximum Snow Depth (in.)	16	16	11	5	trace	0	0	0	0	3	4	7	16
Days With ≥ 1.0" Snow Depth	12	10	4	0	0	0	0	0	0	0	1	7	34

Frankfort Disposal Plant *Clinton County* Elevation: 834 ft. Latitude: 40° 19' N Longitude: 86° 30' W

	JAN	FEB	MAR	APR	MAY	JUN	JUL	AUG	SEP	OCT	NOV	DEC	YEAR
Mean Maximum Temp. (°F)	33.9	37.9	49.0	61.8	72.1	81.0	83.9	82.3	76.7	64.0	50.5	37.3	60.9
Mean Temp. (°F)	26.5	29.8	39.6	51.0	61.3	70.5	73.6	72.0	65.2	53.5	42.2	30.1	51.3
Mean Minimum Temp. (°F)	19.0	21.6	30.2	40.2	50.5	59.8	63.4	61.5	53.6	42.9	33.8	22.8	41.6
Extreme Maximum Temp. (°F)	66	73	83	87	92	101	105	98	95	90	77	72	105
Extreme Minimum Temp. (°F)	-25	-14	-13	16	30	36	44	38	28	20	9	-26	-26
Days Maximum Temp. ≥ 90°F	0	0	0	0	0	4	6	4	1	0	0	0	15
Days Maximum Temp. ≤ 32°F	14	9	3	0	0	0	0	0	0	0	1	10	37
Days Minimum Temp. ≤ 32°F	27	24	19	6	0	0	0	0	0	4	14	25	119
Days Minimum Temp. ≤ 0°F	3	2	0	0	0	0	0	0	0	0	0	2	7
Heating Degree Days (base 65°F)	1,188	989	782	422	167	24	3	9	87	364	678	1,076	5,789
Cooling Degree Days (base 65°F)	0	0	1	11	59	195	277	232	99	14	0	0	888
Mean Precipitation (in.)	2.29	2.21	3.01	3.66	4.25	4.42	4.34	3.91	2.96	3.08	3.53	2.94	40.60
Extreme Maximum Daily Precip. (in.)	1.90	3.12	2.80	2.74	3.47	4.30	3.38	4.25	3.50	3.30	3.15	2.27	4.30
Days With ≥ 0.1" Precipitation	5	5	7	8	9	7	7	6	5	6	7	7	79
Days With ≥ 0.5" Precipitation	1	1	2	2	3	3	3	3	2	2	2	2	26
Days With ≥ 1.0" Precipitation	0	0	1	1	1	1	1	1	1	1	1	0	9
Mean Snowfall (in.)	7.5	6.1	2.7	0.4	trace	0.0	0.0	0.0	0.0	0.4	0.5	5.0	22.6
Maximum Snow Depth (in.)	13	18	14	7	trace	0	0	0	0	7	3	7	18
Days With ≥ 1.0" Snow Depth	10	8	3	0	0	0	0	0	0	0	0	7	28

Freelandville *Knox County* Elevation: 549 ft. Latitude: 38° 52' N Longitude: 87° 19' W

	JAN	FEB	MAR	APR	MAY	JUN	JUL	AUG	SEP	OCT	NOV	DEC	YEAR
Mean Maximum Temp. (°F)	37.1	41.8	52.5	64.3	73.8	82.7	85.7	84.9	78.5	66.4	53.5	40.1	63.5
Mean Temp. (°F)	29.7	33.4	42.7	53.8	63.7	72.9	76.0	74.6	67.4	55.7	44.6	32.5	53.9
Mean Minimum Temp. (°F)	22.2	24.9	32.9	43.3	53.6	63.1	66.3	64.3	56.2	45.0	35.6	24.9	44.3
Extreme Maximum Temp. (°F)	69	75	82	86	92	101	101	99	97	90	80	72	101
Extreme Minimum Temp. (°F)	-21	-11	7	21	33	41	50	45	35	25	10	-23	-23
Days Maximum Temp. ≥ 90°F	0	0	0	0	0	4	7	6	2	0	0	0	19
Days Maximum Temp. ≤ 32°F	11	6	2	0	0	0	0	0	0	0	1	8	28
Days Minimum Temp. ≤ 32°F	25	22	16	4	0	0	0	0	0	2	12	23	104
Days Minimum Temp. ≤ 0°F	2	1	0	0	0	0	0	0	0	0	0	1	4
Heating Degree Days (base 65°F)	1,089	887	686	347	113	12	1	3	61	305	607	1,000	5,111
Cooling Degree Days (base 65°F)	0	0	3	19	81	257	349	309	139	24	1	0	1,182
Mean Precipitation (in.)	2.77	2.73	3.73	4.16	5.66	3.80	4.77	3.22	3.49	3.93	4.14	3.32	45.72
Extreme Maximum Daily Precip. (in.)	2.57	2.04	2.69	3.14	3.30	3.36	3.37	3.01	3.81	3.52	2.80	2.19	3.81
Days With ≥ 0.1" Precipitation	6	5	7	8	8	7	7	5	5	6	7	7	78
Days With ≥ 0.5" Precipitation	2	2	2	3	4	3	3	2	2	3	3	3	32
Days With ≥ 1.0" Precipitation	1	1	1	1	2	1	1	1	1	1	1	1	13
Mean Snowfall (in.)	4.5	3.5	1.5	trace	0.0	0.0	0.0	0.0	0.0	0.1	0.2	4.1	13.9
Maximum Snow Depth (in.)	11	7	8	trace	0	0	0	0	0	2	1	12	12
Days With ≥ 1.0" Snow Depth	5	3	1	0	0	0	0	0	0	0	0	4	13

Goshen College *Elkhart County* Elevation: 875 ft. Latitude: 41° 33' N Longitude: 85° 53' W

	JAN	FEB	MAR	APR	MAY	JUN	JUL	AUG	SEP	OCT	NOV	DEC	YEAR
Mean Maximum Temp. (°F)	32.2	36.0	47.5	60.6	71.6	80.5	83.6	81.6	75.2	62.5	49.2	35.9	59.7
Mean Temp. (°F)	25.2	28.3	38.2	49.9	60.4	69.8	73.3	71.4	64.4	52.6	41.5	29.5	50.4
Mean Minimum Temp. (°F)	18.2	20.5	28.9	39.1	49.2	58.9	62.8	61.3	53.6	42.7	33.7	23.0	41.0
Extreme Maximum Temp. (°F)	63	73	81	93	92	102	100	99	95	88	76	69	102
Extreme Minimum Temp. (°F)	-24	-14	-3	1	28	37	41	37	29	18	11	-18	-24
Days Maximum Temp. ≥ 90°F	0	0	0	0	0	4	5	3	1	0	0	0	13
Days Maximum Temp. ≤ 32°F	16	11	3	0	0	0	0	0	0	0	1	11	42
Days Minimum Temp. ≤ 32°F	28	24	20	7	0	0	0	0	0	4	14	26	123
Days Minimum Temp. ≤ 0°F	3	2	0	0	0	0	0	0	0	0	0	2	7
Heating Degree Days (base 65°F)	1,228	1,031	825	455	187	30	4	11	98	386	700	1,094	6,049
Cooling Degree Days (base 65°F)	0	0	1	8	52	179	266	217	86	9	0	0	818
Mean Precipitation (in.)	2.17	2.08	2.54	3.47	3.85	3.96	4.28	4.24	3.52	3.23	3.02	2.67	39.03
Extreme Maximum Daily Precip. (in.)	3.02	2.19	2.31	3.18	2.93	3.36	6.65	3.79	3.31	3.05	2.18	2.58	6.65
Days With ≥ 0.1" Precipitation	5	6	7	7	7	7	6	6	6	6	7	7	77
Days With ≥ 0.5" Precipitation	1	1	1	2	3	3	3	3	2	2	2	1	24
Days With ≥ 1.0" Precipitation	0	0	0	1	1	1	1	1	1	1	1	0	8
Mean Snowfall (in.)	10.9	9.0	5.0	1.3	trace	0.0	0.0	0.0	0.0	0.4	3.1	10.6	40.3
Maximum Snow Depth (in.)	17	14	8	4	trace	0	0	0	0	5	4	17	17
Days With ≥ 1.0" Snow Depth	16	12	4	0	0	0	0	0	0	0	1	10	43

Greenfield *Hancock County* Elevation: 865 ft. Latitude: 39° 47' N Longitude: 85° 45' W

	JAN	FEB	MAR	APR	MAY	JUN	JUL	AUG	SEP	OCT	NOV	DEC	YEAR
Mean Maximum Temp. (°F)	34.8	38.9	49.6	62.1	72.2	81.5	84.7	83.6	77.6	65.0	51.5	38.4	61.6
Mean Temp. (°F)	26.8	30.1	39.8	51.6	62.0	71.2	74.6	73.3	66.3	54.0	42.6	30.6	51.9
Mean Minimum Temp. (°F)	18.8	21.3	30.1	41.1	51.7	60.9	64.5	62.9	54.9	42.9	33.6	22.8	42.1
Extreme Maximum Temp. (°F)	65	73	84	87	93	103	102	101	95	90	79	72	103
Extreme Minimum Temp. (°F)	-29	-19	-6	16	30	39	48	41	31	20	10	-19	-29
Days Maximum Temp. ≥ 90°F	0	0	0	0	0	4	6	5	2	0	0	0	17
Days Maximum Temp. ≤ 32°F	13	8	3	0	0	0	0	0	0	0	1	9	34
Days Minimum Temp. ≤ 32°F	27	24	19	6	0	0	0	0	0	4	15	24	119
Days Minimum Temp. ≤ 0°F	3	2	0	0	0	0	0	0	0	0	0	2	7
Heating Degree Days (base 65°F)	1,178	979	774	408	156	23	2	6	74	352	666	1,060	5,678
Cooling Degree Days (base 65°F)	0	0	1	13	69	216	307	270	118	17	0	0	1,011
Mean Precipitation (in.)	2.69	2.36	3.56	4.32	5.48	4.59	5.11	3.86	3.47	3.42	3.82	3.22	45.90
Extreme Maximum Daily Precip. (in.)	2.43	1.67	2.41	3.80	3.41	3.85	4.37	4.71	3.13	4.10	3.00	3.41	4.71
Days With ≥ 0.1" Precipitation	6	5	7	8	9	8	7	6	6	6	7	7	82
Days With ≥ 0.5" Precipitation	2	2	2	3	4	3	4	3	2	2	3	2	32
Days With ≥ 1.0" Precipitation	1	0	1	1	2	1	2	1	1	1	1	0	12
Mean Snowfall (in.)	5.8	3.5	1.7	0.1	0.0	0.0	0.0	0.0	0.0	0.1	0.6	3.9	15.7
Maximum Snow Depth (in.)	15	12	8	3	0	0	0	0	0	3	5	10	15
Days With ≥ 1.0" Snow Depth	10	7	2	0	0	0	0	0	0	0	1	6	26

Greensburg *Decatur County* Elevation: 935 ft. Latitude: 39° 21' N Longitude: 85° 30' W

	JAN	FEB	MAR	APR	MAY	JUN	JUL	AUG	SEP	OCT	NOV	DEC	YEAR
Mean Maximum Temp. (°F)	35.8	40.5	50.6	62.8	72.8	81.6	84.8	83.8	77.4	65.2	52.4	39.7	62.3
Mean Temp. (°F)	28.4	32.0	41.3	52.8	63.0	71.8	75.2	73.9	66.9	54.8	43.8	32.3	53.0
Mean Minimum Temp. (°F)	20.9	23.5	32.0	42.9	53.2	62.0	65.6	63.8	56.2	44.4	35.1	24.8	43.7
Extreme Maximum Temp. (°F)	66	74	82	88	93	101	101	101	96	91	79	73	101
Extreme Minimum Temp. (°F)	-24	-14	-12	19	30	39	46	42	32	17	12	-21	-24
Days Maximum Temp. ≥ 90°F	0	0	0	0	0	4	6	6	1	0	0	0	17
Days Maximum Temp. ≤ 32°F	12	8	2	0	0	0	0	0	0	0	1	8	31
Days Minimum Temp. ≤ 32°F	26	22	17	4	0	0	0	0	0	4	13	24	110
Days Minimum Temp. ≤ 0°F	2	1	0	0	0	0	0	0	0	0	0	1	4
Heating Degree Days (base 65°F)	1,127	925	728	376	133	18	1	5	70	329	631	1,009	5,352
Cooling Degree Days (base 65°F)	0	0	3	18	79	230	324	285	132	21	1	0	1,093
Mean Precipitation (in.)	2.92	2.45	3.69	4.42	5.52	4.45	4.01	3.93	3.08	3.24	3.65	3.38	44.74
Extreme Maximum Daily Precip. (in.)	3.09	2.02	2.48	4.00	2.78	5.00	2.76	4.21	3.54	3.60	2.15	2.25	5.00
Days With ≥ 0.1" Precipitation	6	6	7	9	9	7	7	6	5	6	7	7	82
Days With ≥ 0.5" Precipitation	2	2	3	3	4	3	3	2	2	2	3	2	31
Days With ≥ 1.0" Precipitation	1	0	1	1	1	1	1	1	1	1	1	1	11
Mean Snowfall (in.)	5.5	3.8	2.2	0.3	trace	0.0	0.0	0.0	0.0	0.2	0.2	4.2	16.4
Maximum Snow Depth (in.)	16	8	10	3	0	0	0	0	0	1	1	21	21
Days With ≥ 1.0" Snow Depth	7	5	1	0	0	0	0	0	0	0	0	4	17

Huntington *Huntington County* Elevation: 725 ft. Latitude: 40° 51' N Longitude: 85° 30' W

	JAN	FEB	MAR	APR	MAY	JUN	JUL	AUG	SEP	OCT	NOV	DEC	YEAR
Mean Maximum Temp. (°F)	33.1	37.0	47.6	61.2	72.4	81.7	85.3	83.7	76.9	63.7	50.5	37.1	60.9
Mean Temp. (°F)	25.3	28.0	37.5	49.7	60.4	70.0	73.8	72.2	64.4	52.1	41.4	29.5	50.4
Mean Minimum Temp. (°F)	17.3	18.8	27.5	38.2	48.5	58.3	62.3	60.6	51.8	40.4	32.2	21.8	39.8
Extreme Maximum Temp. (°F)	66	75	82	89	94	105	105	103	96	92	79	71	105
Extreme Minimum Temp. (°F)	-28	-16	-11	6	26	37	43	38	28	16	9	-24	-28
Days Maximum Temp. ≥ 90°F	0	0	0	0	1	5	8	5	2	0	0	0	21
Days Maximum Temp. ≤ 32°F	15	9	3	0	0	0	0	0	0	0	1	10	38
Days Minimum Temp. ≤ 32°F	28	25	22	9	1	0	0	0	0	7	16	26	134
Days Minimum Temp. ≤ 0°F	4	2	0	0	0	0	0	0	0	0	0	2	8
Heating Degree Days (base 65°F)	1,226	1,040	846	462	188	32	3	10	101	404	703	1,094	6,109
Cooling Degree Days (base 65°F)	0	0	1	10	54	191	284	239	90	11	0	0	880
Mean Precipitation (in.)	2.25	2.00	2.62	3.50	4.33	4.17	4.05	3.74	2.99	3.07	3.02	2.69	38.43
Extreme Maximum Daily Precip. (in.)	1.65	2.41	1.94	2.33	2.80	3.08	5.53	4.15	2.80	3.36	3.07	2.21	5.53
Days With ≥ 0.1" Precipitation	6	5	6	8	8	7	6	6	6	6	6	7	77
Days With ≥ 0.5" Precipitation	1	1	2	2	3	3	3	2	2	2	2	2	25
Days With ≥ 1.0" Precipitation	0	0	0	1	1	1	1	1	1	1	1	0	8
Mean Snowfall (in.)	9.7	7.1	3.2	0.8	0.0	0.0	0.0	0.0	0.0	0.2	1.0	7.3	29.3
Maximum Snow Depth (in.)	*10*	15	*10*	9	0	0	0	0	0	3	4	*8*	*15*
Days With ≥ 1.0" Snow Depth	*7*	6	2	0	0	0	0	0	0	0	0	6	*21*

The period of record for all cooperative weather station data is 1980 – 2009. See User Guide for detailed explanation of data.

Indianapolis SE Side *Marion County* Elevation: 845 ft. Latitude: 39° 43' N Longitude: 86° 04' W

	JAN	FEB	MAR	APR	MAY	JUN	JUL	AUG	SEP	OCT	NOV	DEC	YEAR
Mean Maximum Temp. (°F)	35.0	39.2	49.6	61.9	72.2	81.2	84.3	83.3	77.1	64.7	51.6	38.6	61.6
Mean Temp. (°F)	27.2	30.6	40.0	51.6	61.9	71.2	74.5	73.1	66.0	54.1	42.8	30.9	52.0
Mean Minimum Temp. (°F)	19.4	21.9	30.3	41.4	51.6	61.2	64.7	63.0	54.9	43.4	33.8	23.1	42.4
Extreme Maximum Temp. (°F)	65	74	83	87	92	104	103	100	94	89	82	73	104
Extreme Minimum Temp. (°F)	-22	-12	2	18	29	35	44	45	30	20	8	-20	-22
Days Maximum Temp. ≥ 90°F	0	0	0	0	0	3	6	5	1	0	0	0	15
Days Maximum Temp. ≤ 32°F	13	8	3	0	0	0	0	0	0	0	1	9	34
Days Minimum Temp. ≤ 32°F	27	24	19	5	0	0	0	0	0	4	15	25	119
Days Minimum Temp. ≤ 0°F	3	1	0	0	0	0	0	0	0	0	0	2	6
Heating Degree Days (base 65°F)	1,166	966	772	407	154	22	3	6	78	347	661	1,050	5,632
Cooling Degree Days (base 65°F)	0	0	2	13	66	216	304	265	115	17	0	0	998
Mean Precipitation (in.)	2.33	2.09	3.25	4.10	4.99	4.33	4.71	3.38	2.95	3.24	3.63	3.11	42.11
Extreme Maximum Daily Precip. (in.)	1.94	1.96	2.25	2.80	2.55	3.57	4.16	3.90	4.03	3.04	3.11	2.73	4.16
Days With ≥ 0.1" Precipitation	5	5	7	8	8	7	7	5	5	5	6	7	75
Days With ≥ 0.5" Precipitation	2	1	2	3	4	3	3	2	2	2	3	2	29
Days With ≥ 1.0" Precipitation	1	0	1	1	1	1	1	1	1	1	1	1	11
Mean Snowfall (in.)	***5.0***	3.6	1.0	0.1	trace	0.0	0.0	0.0	0.0	0.2	0.2	3.3	***13.4***
Maximum Snow Depth (in.)	13	12	9	1	0	0	0	0	0	trace	3	15	15
Days With ≥ 1.0" Snow Depth	8	6	2	0	0	0	0	0	0	0	0	5	21

Kokomo 3 WSW *Howard County* Elevation: 819 ft. Latitude: 40° 28' N Longitude: 86° 10' W

	JAN	FEB	MAR	APR	MAY	JUN	JUL	AUG	SEP	OCT	NOV	DEC	YEAR
Mean Maximum Temp. (°F)	32.2	36.3	47.6	61.0	71.4	80.6	83.8	82.3	76.5	63.8	50.2	36.1	60.2
Mean Temp. (°F)	24.3	27.6	37.6	49.6	60.1	69.7	73.0	71.3	64.2	52.2	41.1	28.6	49.9
Mean Minimum Temp. (°F)	16.4	18.8	27.5	38.2	48.8	58.7	62.1	60.2	51.9	40.6	31.8	21.0	39.7
Extreme Maximum Temp. (°F)	65	74	82	88	92	104	102	100	95	91	81	71	104
Extreme Minimum Temp. (°F)	-26	-20	-10	8	28	34	43	37	27	17	3	-24	-26
Days Maximum Temp. ≥ 90°F	0	0	0	0	0	4	6	4	2	0	0	0	16
Days Maximum Temp. ≤ 32°F	16	11	4	0	0	0	0	0	0	0	2	11	44
Days Minimum Temp. ≤ 32°F	28	25	22	9	0	0	0	0	0	7	17	27	135
Days Minimum Temp. ≤ 0°F	5	3	0	0	0	0	0	0	0	0	0	2	10
Heating Degree Days (base 65°F)	1,256	1,051	845	466	194	35	6	14	106	402	712	1,123	6,210
Cooling Degree Days (base 65°F)	0	0	1	11	50	182	260	215	90	13	0	0	822
Mean Precipitation (in.)	2.61	2.48	2.99	3.87	4.47	4.41	4.78	3.98	3.51	3.27	3.56	3.19	43.12
Extreme Maximum Daily Precip. (in.)	1.94	2.66	2.40	2.40	3.54	4.90	8.82	3.56	6.37	3.54	2.83	3.00	8.82
Days With ≥ 0.1" Precipitation	6	6	7	8	9	8	7	6	6	6	7	8	84
Days With ≥ 0.5" Precipitation	1	1	2	3	3	3	3	3	2	2	3	2	28
Days With ≥ 1.0" Precipitation	1	0	0	1	1	1	1	1	1	1	1	1	10
Mean Snowfall (in.)	11.1	10.4	5.2	1.1	trace	0.0	0.0	0.0	0.0	0.4	1.3	8.8	38.3
Maximum Snow Depth (in.)	17	24	14	8	trace	0	0	0	0	7	3	9	24
Days With ≥ 1.0" Snow Depth	14	11	4	0	0	0	0	0	0	0	1	9	39

La Porte *La Porte County* Elevation: 810 ft. Latitude: 41° 37' N Longitude: 86° 44' W

	JAN	FEB	MAR	APR	MAY	JUN	JUL	AUG	SEP	OCT	NOV	DEC	YEAR
Mean Maximum Temp. (°F)	31.3	35.0	45.6	58.4	69.8	78.9	82.3	80.4	74.1	61.7	48.1	35.4	58.4
Mean Temp. (°F)	24.6	28.0	37.3	49.1	59.9	69.5	73.4	71.8	64.7	52.8	41.0	29.1	50.1
Mean Minimum Temp. (°F)	17.8	20.9	29.0	39.8	50.0	60.0	64.4	63.2	55.3	43.8	33.9	22.7	41.7
Extreme Maximum Temp. (°F)	64	71	82	90	91	101	101	100	95	89	75	72	101
Extreme Minimum Temp. (°F)	-23	-16	-6	16	30	38	47	44	35	24	10	-18	-23
Days Maximum Temp. ≥ 90°F	0	0	0	0	0	3	4	3	1	0	0	0	11
Days Maximum Temp. ≤ 32°F	17	12	4	0	0	0	0	0	0	0	2	11	46
Days Minimum Temp. ≤ 32°F	28	24	21	6	0	0	0	0	0	2	14	25	120
Days Minimum Temp. ≤ 0°F	3	2	0	0	0	0	0	0	0	0	0	2	7
Heating Degree Days (base 65°F)	1,247	1,040	852	480	204	37	3	9	94	383	713	1,106	6,168
Cooling Degree Days (base 65°F)	0	0	1	9	52	178	269	228	92	10	0	0	839
Mean Precipitation (in.)	2.63	2.28	2.94	3.55	3.82	4.21	4.26	4.40	3.68	3.75	3.86	3.18	42.56
Extreme Maximum Daily Precip. (in.)	2.34	1.70	1.77	2.56	3.23	3.62	4.59	3.49	6.73	2.81	5.00	2.13	6.73
Days With ≥ 0.1" Precipitation	8	6	7	8	8	7	7	7	6	7	8	8	87
Days With ≥ 0.5" Precipitation	1	1	2	3	3	3	3	3	2	2	2	2	27
Days With ≥ 1.0" Precipitation	0	0	1	1	1	1	1	1	1	1	1	1	10
Mean Snowfall (in.)	20.6	13.9	7.2	1.4	trace	0.0	0.0	0.0	0.0	0.4	3.8	14.9	62.2
Maximum Snow Depth (in.)	18	24	11	6	trace	0	0	0	0	1	10	14	24
Days With ≥ 1.0" Snow Depth	20	14	5	1	0	0	0	0	0	0	2	11	53

Lafayette 8 S *Tippecanoe County* Elevation: 732 ft. Latitude: 40° 18' N Longitude: 86° 54' W

	JAN	FEB	MAR	APR	MAY	JUN	JUL	AUG	SEP	OCT	NOV	DEC	YEAR
Mean Maximum Temp. (°F)	33.4	37.7	48.9	61.5	72.5	81.6	84.3	82.9	77.6	64.8	51.2	37.2	61.1
Mean Temp. (°F)	25.4	28.8	39.2	50.9	61.7	70.9	73.9	72.2	65.6	53.6	42.2	29.4	51.1
Mean Minimum Temp. (°F)	17.3	19.9	29.4	40.1	50.9	60.2	63.5	61.6	53.6	42.4	33.2	21.5	41.1
Extreme Maximum Temp. (°F)	65	74	82	89	93	104	102	98	96	91	80	71	104
Extreme Minimum Temp. (°F)	-25	-19	-8	4	29	36	44	37	26	19	7	-25	-25
Days Maximum Temp. ≥ 90°F	0	0	0	0	1	5	6	4	2	0	0	0	18
Days Maximum Temp. ≤ 32°F	14	10	3	0	0	0	0	0	0	0	1	10	38
Days Minimum Temp. ≤ 32°F	27	25	20	7	0	0	0	0	0	5	15	26	125
Days Minimum Temp. ≤ 0°F	4	3	0	0	0	0	0	0	0	0	0	2	9
Heating Degree Days (base 65°F)	1,221	1,017	796	431	165	27	3	10	87	363	676	1,098	5,894
Cooling Degree Days (base 65°F)	0	0	2	14	70	210	287	241	111	17	0	0	952
Mean Precipitation (in.)	2.07	1.96	2.73	3.37	4.60	4.44	4.08	3.76	2.79	2.81	3.24	2.59	38.44
Extreme Maximum Daily Precip. (in.)	2.30	2.26	3.30	3.44	4.14	4.51	2.50	3.66	3.72	2.19	2.35	2.02	4.51
Days With ≥ 0.1" Precipitation	5	4	6	7	8	7	7	6	5	5	6	6	72
Days With ≥ 0.5" Precipitation	1	1	2	2	3	3	3	2	2	2	2	2	25
Days With ≥ 1.0" Precipitation	0	0	0	0	1	1	1	1	1	1	1	0	7
Mean Snowfall (in.)	6.9	5.3	2.4	0.6	trace	0.0	0.0	0.0	0.0	0.5	0.5	5.1	21.3
Maximum Snow Depth (in.)	18	19	10	5	trace	0	0	0	0	5	4	9	19
Days With ≥ 1.0" Snow Depth	11	9	3	0	0	0	0	0	0	0	0	8	31

The period of record for all cooperative weather station data is 1980 – 2009. See User Guide for detailed explanation of data.

Lowell *Lake County* Elevation: 665 ft. Latitude: 41° 16' N Longitude: 87° 25' W

	JAN	FEB	MAR	APR	MAY	JUN	JUL	AUG	SEP	OCT	NOV	DEC	YEAR
Mean Maximum Temp. (°F)	31.5	35.9	47.5	60.6	71.8	81.0	84.0	82.1	76.5	63.6	49.4	35.4	59.9
Mean Temp. (°F)	23.3	27.0	37.5	49.3	60.0	69.6	73.1	71.2	64.2	52.0	40.4	27.2	49.6
Mean Minimum Temp. (°F)	15.0	18.1	27.6	37.9	48.2	58.2	62.1	60.2	51.9	40.3	31.3	19.3	39.2
Extreme Maximum Temp. (°F)	66	73	84	91	93	104	101	104	98	91	76	69	104
Extreme Minimum Temp. (°F)	-25	-21	-9	7	27	36	42	38	28	18	6	-20	-25
Days Maximum Temp. ≥ 90°F	0	0	0	0	1	5	7	3	2	0	0	0	18
Days Maximum Temp. ≤ 32°F	16	11	3	0	0	0	0	0	0	0	1	11	42
Days Minimum Temp. ≤ 32°F	29	25	23	9	1	0	0	0	0	6	17	27	137
Days Minimum Temp. ≤ 0°F	5	3	0	0	0	0	0	0	0	0	0	3	11
Heating Degree Days (base 65°F)	1,286	1,068	845	474	200	37	5	13	105	408	733	1,165	6,339
Cooling Degree Days (base 65°F)	0	0	1	9	52	182	261	211	88	11	0	0	815
Mean Precipitation (in.)	1.91	1.68	2.65	3.73	4.33	4.53	3.85	4.15	3.23	3.45	3.42	2.52	39.45
Extreme Maximum Daily Precip. (in.)	2.81	1.89	2.19	3.88	2.91	3.85	3.64	3.53	3.20	2.92	5.14	2.96	5.14
Days With ≥ 0.1" Precipitation	5	4	6	7	8	7	7	6	5	6	7	6	74
Days With ≥ 0.5" Precipitation	1	1	2	2	3	2	3	3	2	2	2	1	24
Days With ≥ 1.0" Precipitation	0	0	0	1	1	1	1	1	1	1	1	1	9
Mean Snowfall (in.)	9.4	9.1	3.6	0.3	trace	0.0	0.0	0.0	0.0	0.2	0.8	7.4	30.8
Maximum Snow Depth (in.)	na	na	9	1	trace	0	0	0	0	1	4	na	na
Days With ≥ 1.0" Snow Depth	na	7	2	0	0	0	0	0	0	0	0	8	na

Madison Sewage Plant *Jefferson County* Elevation: 459 ft. Latitude: 38° 44' N Longitude: 85° 24' W

	JAN	FEB	MAR	APR	MAY	JUN	JUL	AUG	SEP	OCT	NOV	DEC	YEAR
Mean Maximum Temp. (°F)	41.0	45.3	55.3	66.5	75.0	83.1	86.7	86.0	79.5	68.2	56.1	44.1	65.6
Mean Temp. (°F)	32.8	35.8	44.8	55.0	64.1	72.5	76.6	75.6	68.6	57.2	46.4	35.9	55.4
Mean Minimum Temp. (°F)	24.5	26.3	34.0	43.5	53.1	61.8	66.4	65.2	57.7	46.0	36.6	27.5	45.2
Extreme Maximum Temp. (°F)	68	76	84	91	93	103	103	104	99	93	84	77	104
Extreme Minimum Temp. (°F)	-17	-8	-2	19	31	40	51	43	33	23	11	-18	-18
Days Maximum Temp. ≥ 90°F	0	0	0	0	0	4	10	9	3	0	0	0	26
Days Maximum Temp. ≤ 32°F	6	4	0	0	0	0	0	0	0	0	0	5	15
Days Minimum Temp. ≤ 32°F	24	20	14	3	0	0	0	0	0	1	11	21	94
Days Minimum Temp. ≤ 0°F	1	0	0	0	0	0	0	0	0	0	0	1	2
Heating Degree Days (base 65°F)	991	820	623	305	105	11	0	1	44	260	553	897	4,610
Cooling Degree Days (base 65°F)	0	0	2	15	82	242	365	338	160	25	1	0	1,230
Mean Precipitation (in.)	3.40	2.96	4.19	4.33	5.32	4.21	4.55	4.11	3.23	3.79	3.69	3.76	47.54
Extreme Maximum Daily Precip. (in.)	4.00	2.60	3.10	2.20	2.80	2.90	3.65	4.97	5.16	5.00	2.80	2.60	5.16
Days With ≥ 0.1" Precipitation	6	6	8	9	9	8	7	6	5	6	7	7	84
Days With ≥ 0.5" Precipitation	2	2	3	3	4	3	3	3	2	3	3	2	33
Days With ≥ 1.0" Precipitation	1	1	1	1	2	1	2	1	1	1	1	1	14
Mean Snowfall (in.)	4.3	3.9	1.3	0.1	trace	0.0	0.0	0.0	0.0	0.1	trace	3.4	13.1
Maximum Snow Depth (in.)	10	16	8	1	trace	0	0	0	0	4	trace	15	16
Days With ≥ 1.0" Snow Depth	4	4	1	0	0	0	0	0	0	0	0	2	11

Martinsville 2 SW *Morgan County* Elevation: 609 ft. Latitude: 39° 24' N Longitude: 86° 27' W

	JAN	FEB	MAR	APR	MAY	JUN	JUL	AUG	SEP	OCT	NOV	DEC	YEAR
Mean Maximum Temp. (°F)	36.6	41.1	51.5	63.2	72.7	81.1	84.7	84.1	78.0	65.5	53.1	40.3	62.7
Mean Temp. (°F)	27.9	31.4	40.6	51.5	61.3	70.2	73.9	72.5	65.1	52.9	42.8	31.7	51.8
Mean Minimum Temp. (°F)	19.1	21.5	29.6	39.7	49.7	59.2	63.0	60.9	52.2	40.3	32.5	23.0	40.9
Extreme Maximum Temp. (°F)	67	75	83	88	92	101	101	100	95	89	81	75	101
Extreme Minimum Temp. (°F)	-35	-20	-15	12	29	35	45	38	28	19	9	-22	-35
Days Maximum Temp. ≥ 90°F	0	0	0	0	0	2	6	6	2	0	0	0	16
Days Maximum Temp. ≤ 32°F	11	7	2	0	0	0	0	0	0	0	1	8	29
Days Minimum Temp. ≤ 32°F	27	24	20	7	1	0	0	0	0	7	16	25	127
Days Minimum Temp. ≤ 0°F	3	2	0	0	0	0	0	0	0	0	0	2	7
Heating Degree Days (base 65°F)	1,145	945	753	411	162	25	3	8	90	380	659	1,027	5,608
Cooling Degree Days (base 65°F)	0	0	1	12	53	187	285	248	101	12	0	0	899
Mean Precipitation (in.)	2.65	2.42	3.42	4.41	5.29	4.57	4.31	3.83	3.50	3.42	3.64	3.23	44.69
Extreme Maximum Daily Precip. (in.)	2.16	2.34	2.20	3.50	2.83	8.02	3.85	5.82	4.12	4.76	3.40	2.92	8.02
Days With ≥ 0.1" Precipitation	5	5	7	8	9	7	7	5	5	5	6	7	76
Days With ≥ 0.5" Precipitation	2	2	2	3	4	3	3	3	2	2	3	2	31
Days With ≥ 1.0" Precipitation	1	0	1	1	1	1	1	1	1	1	1	1	11
Mean Snowfall (in.)	5.6	4.2	2.0	0.1	0.0	0.0	0.0	0.0	0.0	0.2	0.3	3.6	16.0
Maximum Snow Depth (in.)	16	9	10	1	0	0	0	0	0	0	4	13	16
Days With ≥ 1.0" Snow Depth	5	3	1	0	0	0	0	0	0	0	0	3	12

Mount Vernon *Posey County* Elevation: 419 ft. Latitude: 37° 57' N Longitude: 87° 53' W

	JAN	FEB	MAR	APR	MAY	JUN	JUL	AUG	SEP	OCT	NOV	DEC	YEAR
Mean Maximum Temp. (°F)	40.7	45.2	55.1	66.2	76.0	84.7	88.0	87.4	81.2	69.2	56.7	44.3	66.2
Mean Temp. (°F)	32.5	36.2	45.3	55.8	65.9	74.8	78.2	77.0	69.8	58.0	47.3	36.3	56.4
Mean Minimum Temp. (°F)	24.3	27.2	35.3	45.3	55.7	64.9	68.3	66.4	58.4	46.7	37.9	28.2	46.6
Extreme Maximum Temp. (°F)	71	76	83	90	93	101	102	104	99	90	82	77	104
Extreme Minimum Temp. (°F)	-16	-7	7	25	36	44	51	45	32	22	12	-16	-16
Days Maximum Temp. ≥ 90°F	0	0	0	0	1	8	13	12	4	0	0	0	38
Days Maximum Temp. ≤ 32°F	7	5	1	0	0	0	0	0	0	0	0	5	18
Days Minimum Temp. ≤ 32°F	24	19	12	2	0	0	0	0	0	1	10	20	88
Days Minimum Temp. ≤ 0°F	1	1	0	0	0	0	0	0	0	0	0	1	3
Heating Degree Days (base 65°F)	1,000	807	608	295	79	6	0	1	39	246	525	884	4,490
Cooling Degree Days (base 65°F)	0	0	3	26	113	307	416	379	191	34	2	0	1,471
Mean Precipitation (in.)	3.48	3.07	4.26	4.39	5.66	3.94	3.83	2.92	3.02	3.42	4.01	3.92	45.92
Extreme Maximum Daily Precip. (in.)	4.69	2.52	6.29	7.40	3.42	3.73	3.40	3.28	3.57	4.06	3.20	3.70	7.40
Days With ≥ 0.1" Precipitation	5	5	7	7	8	7	6	5	5	5	6	7	73
Days With ≥ 0.5" Precipitation	2	2	3	3	4	3	3	2	2	2	3	3	32
Days With ≥ 1.0" Precipitation	1	1	1	1	2	1	1	1	1	1	1	1	13
Mean Snowfall (in.)	2.3	3.2	1.3	0.1	0.0	0.0	0.0	0.0	0.0	0.1	0.0	1.8	8.8
Maximum Snow Depth (in.)	6	9	8	3	0	0	0	0	0	3	1	6	9
Days With ≥ 1.0" Snow Depth	4	3	1	0	0	0	0	0	0	0	0	2	10

The period of record for all cooperative weather station data is 1980 – 2009. See User Guide for detailed explanation of data.

Muncie Ball State Univ *Delaware County* Elevation: 939 ft. Latitude: 40° 13' N Longitude: 85° 25' W

	JAN	FEB	MAR	APR	MAY	JUN	JUL	AUG	SEP	OCT	NOV	DEC	YEAR
Mean Maximum Temp. (°F)	33.4	38.2	47.9	60.7	71.8	81.0	84.8	82.8	76.5	64.2	50.6	37.9	60.8
Mean Temp. (°F)	25.4	29.5	38.2	50.0	61.4	70.5	74.2	72.1	64.6	52.9	41.6	30.1	50.9
Mean Minimum Temp. (°F)	17.3	20.8	28.6	39.2	51.0	60.1	63.5	61.3	52.7	41.5	32.5	22.1	40.9
Extreme Maximum Temp. (°F)	64	74	80	86	90	102	100	99	96	88	79	71	102
Extreme Minimum Temp. (°F)	-29	-13	-8	10	25	36	40	39	27	18	9	-21	-29
Days Maximum Temp. ≥ 90°F	0	0	0	0	0	4	7	4	2	0	0	0	17
Days Maximum Temp. ≤ 32°F	14	9	4	0	0	0	0	0	0	0	2	9	38
Days Minimum Temp. ≤ 32°F	28	24	21	8	0	0	0	0	0	5	17	26	129
Days Minimum Temp. ≤ 0°F	4	2	0	0	0	0	0	0	0	0	0	2	8
Heating Degree Days (base 65°F)	1,222	997	824	454	170	29	3	9	103	382	696	1,076	5,965
Cooling Degree Days (base 65°F)	0	0	1	10	65	202	294	236	99	14	0	0	921
Mean Precipitation (in.)	1.88	2.12	2.91	3.45	4.56	4.51	4.59	3.14	3.25	2.70	3.52	2.86	39.49
Extreme Maximum Daily Precip. (in.)	1.38	2.05	1.83	na	2.52	4.74	3.10	2.92	4.14	2.13	2.69	3.09	na
Days With ≥ 0.1" Precipitation	5	5	7	7	8	7	7	5	5	5	7	7	75
Days With ≥ 0.5" Precipitation	1	1	2	2	3	3	3	2	2	2	3	2	26
Days With ≥ 1.0" Precipitation	0	0	0	1	1	1	1	1	1	1	1	0	8
Mean Snowfall (in.)	7.4	6.0	2.7	0.5	trace	0.0	0.0	0.0	0.0	0.3	1.0	6.1	24.0
Maximum Snow Depth (in.)	10	16	9	6	trace	0	0	0	0	3	4	10	16
Days With ≥ 1.0" Snow Depth	10	8	3	0	0	0	0	0	0	0	1	7	29

North Vernon 1 NW *Jennings County* Elevation: 745 ft. Latitude: 39° 02' N Longitude: 85° 38' W

	JAN	FEB	MAR	APR	MAY	JUN	JUL	AUG	SEP	OCT	NOV	DEC	YEAR
Mean Maximum Temp. (°F)	40.3	45.2	55.2	67.1	75.0	83.4	86.3	85.2	79.2	67.8	55.4	43.2	65.3
Mean Temp. (°F)	32.0	35.5	44.6	55.2	63.7	72.2	75.6	74.3	67.7	56.3	45.9	34.7	54.8
Mean Minimum Temp. (°F)	23.6	26.0	33.9	43.3	52.2	61.0	64.8	63.3	56.0	44.7	36.3	26.4	44.3
Extreme Maximum Temp. (°F)	67	75	85	87	90	101	102	103	96	91	80	74	103
Extreme Minimum Temp. (°F)	-22	-12	-6	19	30	39	47	40	33	23	8	-22	-22
Days Maximum Temp. ≥ 90°F	0	0	0	0	0	4	8	6	2	0	0	0	20
Days Maximum Temp. ≤ 32°F	7	5	1	0	0	0	0	0	0	0	0	5	18
Days Minimum Temp. ≤ 32°F	23	19	15	4	0	0	0	0	0	4	12	21	98
Days Minimum Temp. ≤ 0°F	1	1	0	0	0	0	0	0	0	0	0	1	3
Heating Degree Days (base 65°F)	1,015	826	630	311	113	11	0	3	55	288	569	932	4,753
Cooling Degree Days (base 65°F)	0	0	5	24	79	235	335	299	139	25	1	0	1,142
Mean Precipitation (in.)	2.40	2.63	3.70	4.49	5.03	3.96	4.44	4.60	3.20	3.69	3.88	3.59	45.61
Extreme Maximum Daily Precip. (in.)	2.09	2.10	3.92	4.00	2.90	3.63	3.47	4.55	3.51	4.02	2.27	2.14	4.55
Days With ≥ 0.1" Precipitation	5	5	6	8	8	6	6	5	4	5	6	7	71
Days With ≥ 0.5" Precipitation	2	2	3	3	3	2	3	3	2	2	3	2	30
Days With ≥ 1.0" Precipitation	1	0	1	1	1	1	1	1	1	1	1	1	11
Mean Snowfall (in.)	2.7	3.1	1.5	trace	trace	0.0	0.0	0.0	0.0	0.0	0.0	3.5	10.8
Maximum Snow Depth (in.)	11	7	12	trace	trace	0	0	0	0	0	1	na	na
Days With ≥ 1.0" Snow Depth	4	4	1	0	0	0	0	0	0	0	0	2	11

Oolitic Purdue Exp Farm *Lawrence County* Elevation: 649 ft. Latitude: 38° 53' N Longitude: 86° 33' W

	JAN	FEB	MAR	APR	MAY	JUN	JUL	AUG	SEP	OCT	NOV	DEC	YEAR
Mean Maximum Temp. (°F)	38.2	43.3	53.0	64.3	73.6	82.0	85.5	84.9	78.8	66.6	54.5	41.7	63.9
Mean Temp. (°F)	29.2	33.0	41.7	52.5	62.1	71.0	74.7	73.5	66.2	54.0	43.9	32.6	52.9
Mean Minimum Temp. (°F)	20.0	22.7	30.3	40.6	50.6	59.9	63.9	62.1	53.6	41.5	33.2	23.5	41.8
Extreme Maximum Temp. (°F)	68	75	82	88	91	102	102	102	99	91	81	75	102
Extreme Minimum Temp. (°F)	-29	-16	-4	15	29	38	47	41	31	16	8	-23	-29
Days Maximum Temp. ≥ 90°F	0	0	0	0	0	3	7	7	2	0	0	0	19
Days Maximum Temp. ≤ 32°F	10	6	1	0	0	0	0	0	0	0	1	7	25
Days Minimum Temp. ≤ 32°F	27	23	19	6	0	0	0	0	0	6	16	24	121
Days Minimum Temp. ≤ 0°F	3	1	0	0	0	0	0	0	0	0	0	2	6
Heating Degree Days (base 65°F)	1,103	898	718	383	144	18	1	4	75	347	628	996	5,315
Cooling Degree Days (base 65°F)	0	0	2	14	62	205	309	275	118	15	0	0	1,000
Mean Precipitation (in.)	2.92	2.74	3.83	4.43	5.76	4.07	4.53	3.65	3.17	3.70	3.70	3.51	46.01
Extreme Maximum Daily Precip. (in.)	3.06	2.67	2.90	4.80	3.18	4.05	3.78	4.61	2.57	3.80	2.83	2.48	4.80
Days With ≥ 0.1" Precipitation	6	5	7	9	8	7	7	6	5	6	7	6	79
Days With ≥ 0.5" Precipitation	2	2	3	3	4	3	3	2	2	3	2	3	32
Days With ≥ 1.0" Precipitation	1	0	1	1	2	1	1	1	1	1	1	1	12
Mean Snowfall (in.)	4.6	4.1	2.0	0.1	trace	0.0	0.0	0.0	0.0	0.1	0.1	3.9	14.9
Maximum Snow Depth (in.)	12	8	10	1	trace	0	0	0	0	1	1	16	16
Days With ≥ 1.0" Snow Depth	7	6	2	0	0	0	0	0	0	0	0	4	19

Richmond Water Works *Wayne County* Elevation: 1,015 ft. Latitude: 39° 53' N Longitude: 84° 53' W

	JAN	FEB	MAR	APR	MAY	JUN	JUL	AUG	SEP	OCT	NOV	DEC	YEAR
Mean Maximum Temp. (°F)	35.6	39.8	50.4	62.7	72.6	81.3	84.5	83.2	76.9	64.5	51.7	39.0	61.8
Mean Temp. (°F)	27.4	30.9	40.2	51.3	61.4	70.1	73.6	72.2	65.0	53.2	42.5	31.2	51.6
Mean Minimum Temp. (°F)	19.2	22.0	30.0	39.9	50.0	58.9	62.6	61.2	53.2	41.9	33.3	23.3	41.3
Extreme Maximum Temp. (°F)	66	74	82	94	92	99	100	100	96	90	78	72	100
Extreme Minimum Temp. (°F)	-27	-20	-9	14	29	37	43	41	32	18	10	-22	-27
Days Maximum Temp. ≥ 90°F	0	0	0	0	0	4	6	5	1	0	0	0	16
Days Maximum Temp. ≤ 32°F	12	8	2	0	0	0	0	0	0	0	1	9	32
Days Minimum Temp. ≤ 32°F	27	23	19	6	0	0	0	0	0	5	15	25	120
Days Minimum Temp. ≤ 0°F	3	2	0	0	0	0	0	0	0	0	0	1	6
Heating Degree Days (base 65°F)	1,159	958	763	412	163	25	2	7	88	372	667	1,041	5,657
Cooling Degree Days (base 65°F)	0	0	1	9	57	185	276	238	96	14	0	0	876
Mean Precipitation (in.)	2.73	2.25	3.19	3.84	4.72	4.30	4.02	3.49	2.75	3.15	3.36	2.90	40.70
Extreme Maximum Daily Precip. (in.)	3.19	1.80	2.12	2.79	2.41	3.12	3.38	2.86	2.41	4.53	2.41	2.27	4.53
Days With ≥ 0.1" Precipitation	6	5	7	8	9	8	6	5	5	6	6	6	77
Days With ≥ 0.5" Precipitation	2	1	2	2	3	3	3	2	2	2	2	2	26
Days With ≥ 1.0" Precipitation	1	0	1	1	1	1	1	1	1	1	1	1	11
Mean Snowfall (in.)	5.9	3.6	1.6	0.2	trace	0.0	0.0	0.0	0.0	0.2	0.4	3.8	15.7
Maximum Snow Depth (in.)	21	13	5	2	trace	0	0	0	0	2	5	20	21
Days With ≥ 1.0" Snow Depth	8	6	1	0	0	0	0	0	0	0	0	5	20

The period of record for all cooperative weather station data is 1980 – 2009. See User Guide for detailed explanation of data.

Rockville *Parke County* Elevation: 689 ft. Latitude: 39° 46' N Longitude: 87° 14' W

	JAN	FEB	MAR	APR	MAY	JUN	JUL	AUG	SEP	OCT	NOV	DEC	YEAR
Mean Maximum Temp. (°F)	36.9	42.0	53.5	66.0	75.7	84.1	86.9	85.5	79.2	67.2	53.6	40.1	64.2
Mean Temp. (°F)	28.8	32.9	43.2	54.4	63.9	72.7	76.0	74.5	67.3	55.8	44.6	32.4	53.9
Mean Minimum Temp. (°F)	20.5	23.8	32.8	42.7	52.1	61.2	64.9	63.5	55.4	44.4	35.5	24.6	43.5
Extreme Maximum Temp. (°F)	66	74	84	89	93	103	104	102	96	90	79	74	104
Extreme Minimum Temp. (°F)	-25	-18	-4	17	27	37	43	41	31	19	8	-21	-25
Days Maximum Temp. ≥ 90°F	0	0	0	0	1	7	10	7	2	0	0	0	27
Days Maximum Temp. ≤ 32°F	11	6	1	0	0	0	0	0	0	0	1	7	26
Days Minimum Temp. ≤ 32°F	26	22	16	5	0	0	0	0	0	4	13	23	109
Days Minimum Temp. ≤ 0°F	3	2	0	0	0	0	0	0	0	0	0	1	6
Heating Degree Days (base 65°F)	1,117	900	673	334	112	12	1	2	59	300	607	1,005	5,122
Cooling Degree Days (base 65°F)	0	0	3	22	86	250	347	304	135	23	1	0	1,171
Mean Precipitation (in.)	2.83	2.51	3.44	4.14	5.39	4.55	5.13	4.01	3.31	3.80	4.21	3.56	46.88
Extreme Maximum Daily Precip. (in.)	2.60	3.18	3.10	2.20	8.05	5.00	3.45	4.73	5.46	3.00	4.15	3.03	8.05
Days With ≥ 0.1" Precipitation	6	5	7	9	9	8	7	6	5	6	7	7	82
Days With ≥ 0.5" Precipitation	2	2	3	3	4	3	3	3	3	3	3	3	35
Days With ≥ 1.0" Precipitation	1	1	1	1	2	1	2	1	1	1	1	1	14
Mean Snowfall (in.)	5.1	2.9	1.6	0.0	trace	0.0	0.0	0.0	0.0	trace	0.1	3.9	13.6
Maximum Snow Depth (in.)	15	18	12	1	trace	0	0	0	0	1	4	12	18
Days With ≥ 1.0" Snow Depth	9	6	1	0	0	0	0	0	0	0	0	6	22

Shelbyville Sewage Plant *Shelby County* Elevation: 750 ft. Latitude: 39° 31' N Longitude: 85° 47' W

	JAN	FEB	MAR	APR	MAY	JUN	JUL	AUG	SEP	OCT	NOV	DEC	YEAR
Mean Maximum Temp. (°F)	36.2	40.4	51.3	63.2	73.1	82.3	85.3	83.7	78.3	66.0	***52.8***	39.4	***62.7***
Mean Temp. (°F)	28.0	31.2	41.0	52.4	62.6	71.9	74.9	72.9	66.4	54.3	***43.5***	31.4	***52.5***
Mean Minimum Temp. (°F)	19.7	22.0	30.7	41.6	52.1	61.4	64.4	62.0	54.4	42.6	***34.2***	23.5	***42.4***
Extreme Maximum Temp. (°F)	66	74	81	85	91	102	102	100	98	90	***80***	75	***102***
Extreme Minimum Temp. (°F)	-25	-16	0	17	31	41	48	46	32	20	***12***	-22	***-25***
Days Maximum Temp. ≥ 90°F	0	0	0	0	0	4	7	4	2	0	***0***	0	***17***
Days Maximum Temp. ≤ 32°F	11	7	2	0	0	0	0	0	0	0	***1***	8	***29***
Days Minimum Temp. ≤ 32°F	27	24	19	5	0	0	0	0	0	5	***14***	25	***119***
Days Minimum Temp. ≤ 0°F	3	2	0	0	0	0	0	0	0	0	***0***	1	***6***
Heating Degree Days (base 65°F)	1,141	950	737	386	137	16	1	6	71	343	***638***	1,036	***5,462***
Cooling Degree Days (base 65°F)	0	0	2	14	70	229	314	258	119	17	***0***	0	***1,023***
Mean Precipitation (in.)	2.80	2.35	3.28	4.20	4.99	4.11	4.00	3.27	2.99	2.93	3.23	3.00	41.15
Extreme Maximum Daily Precip. (in.)	2.58	2.03	1.84	3.62	3.49	***3.54***	3.35	3.96	3.15	4.43	***2.70***	2.50	***4.43***
Days With ≥ 0.1" Precipitation	6	5	7	8	8	7	7	6	5	5	***6***	6	***76***
Days With ≥ 0.5" Precipitation	2	2	3	3	4	3	3	2	2	2	***2***	2	***30***
Days With ≥ 1.0" Precipitation	1	0	1	1	1	1	1	1	1	1	1	1	11
Mean Snowfall (in.)	***2.4***	***1.7***	***0.8***	trace	0.0	0.0	0.0	0.0	0.0	trace	***trace***	***0.8***	***5.7***
Maximum Snow Depth (in.)	***8***	***11***	***7***	trace	0	***0***	0	***0***	0	***1***	***trace***	na	na
Days With ≥ 1.0" Snow Depth	***2***	***2***	1	0	0	0	0	0	0	0	***0***	***1***	***6***

Tell City *Perry County* Elevation: 399 ft. Latitude: 37° 57' N Longitude: 86° 46' W

	JAN	FEB	MAR	APR	MAY	JUN	JUL	AUG	SEP	OCT	NOV	DEC	YEAR
Mean Maximum Temp. (°F)	41.9	46.0	56.0	67.1	76.1	84.1	87.5	87.2	80.8	69.5	57.3	45.1	66.5
Mean Temp. (°F)	34.1	37.2	45.9	56.2	65.5	74.1	77.9	76.9	69.8	58.4	48.0	37.3	56.8
Mean Minimum Temp. (°F)	26.3	28.4	35.7	45.2	54.8	64.0	68.3	66.7	58.6	47.2	38.7	29.3	46.9
Extreme Maximum Temp. (°F)	71	74	84	89	91	99	103	100	100	92	83	77	103
Extreme Minimum Temp. (°F)	-17	-5	-1	22	34	43	52	46	36	22	14	-14	-17
Days Maximum Temp. ≥ 90°F	0	0	0	0	0	6	12	11	4	0	0	0	33
Days Maximum Temp. ≤ 32°F	6	4	1	0	0	0	0	0	0	0	0	4	15
Days Minimum Temp. ≤ 32°F	22	19	12	3	0	0	0	0	0	1	8	18	83
Days Minimum Temp. ≤ 0°F	1	0	0	0	0	0	0	0	0	0	0	0	1
Heating Degree Days (base 65°F)	950	779	591	286	85	7	0	1	39	235	505	854	4,332
Cooling Degree Days (base 65°F)	0	0	4	27	107	286	407	378	188	37	3	0	1,437
Mean Precipitation (in.)	3.31	3.18	4.25	4.25	5.78	4.38	4.47	3.35	3.59	3.40	3.78	4.10	47.84
Extreme Maximum Daily Precip. (in.)	3.51	3.09	4.75	3.34	3.93	4.37	3.20	3.27	4.43	2.72	3.10	2.25	4.75
Days With ≥ 0.1" Precipitation	6	6	7	7	9	7	7	5	5	5	6	7	77
Days With ≥ 0.5" Precipitation	2	2	3	3	4	3	3	2	2	2	3	3	32
Days With ≥ 1.0" Precipitation	1	1	1	1	2	1	1	1	1	1	1	1	13
Mean Snowfall (in.)	1.8	2.2	0.4	trace	0.0	0.0	0.0	0.0	0.0	0.0	0.1	0.8	5.3
Maximum Snow Depth (in.)	7	10	5	1	0	0	0	0	0	0	trace	21	21
Days With ≥ 1.0" Snow Depth	2	2	0	0	0	0	0	0	0	0	0	0	4

Terre Haute Indiana State *Vigo County* Elevation: 506 ft. Latitude: 39° 28' N Longitude: 87° 25' W

	JAN	FEB	MAR	APR	MAY	JUN	JUL	AUG	SEP	OCT	NOV	DEC	YEAR
Mean Maximum Temp. (°F)	***37.7***	42.1	53.3	65.3	75.8	84.4	***88.0***	***86.5***	***80.7***	***68.3***	***54.4***	***41.1***	***64.8***
Mean Temp. (°F)	***28.4***	32.2	42.6	54.0	64.0	73.0	***76.8***	***74.8***	***67.8***	***55.4***	***43.9***	***31.9***	***53.7***
Mean Minimum Temp. (°F)	***19.2***	22.2	32.3	42.6	52.2	61.4	***65.5***	***63.0***	***54.9***	***42.6***	***33.3***	***22.6***	***42.6***
Extreme Maximum Temp. (°F)	69	***76***	***84***	***89***	***99***	***102***	***102***	***102***	***100***	***91***	***82***	***74***	***102***
Extreme Minimum Temp. (°F)	-18	***-20***	***1***	***17***	***29***	***36***	***41***	***42***	***27***	***19***	***5***	***-22***	***-22***
Days Maximum Temp. ≥ 90°F	0	0	0	0	1	8	12	***10***	***4***	***0***	0	0	***35***
Days Maximum Temp. ≤ 32°F	10	6	1	0	0	0	0	***0***	***0***	***0***	1	6	***24***
Days Minimum Temp. ≤ 32°F	26	23	17	5	0	0	0	***0***	***0***	***5***	15	24	***115***
Days Minimum Temp. ≤ 0°F	***2***	2	0	0	0	0	0	***0***	***0***	***0***	0	1	***5***
Heating Degree Days (base 65°F)	***1,125***	922	688	346	113	13	***1***	***3***	***60***	***312***	***626***	***1,017***	***5,226***
Cooling Degree Days (base 65°F)	***0***	0	2	23	90	259	***372***	***314***	***149***	***23***	***0***	***0***	***1,232***
Mean Precipitation (in.)	***2.56***	2.53	3.49	4.49	5.04	4.50	4.42	3.36	***3.51***	***3.65***	3.57	3.12	***44.24***
Extreme Maximum Daily Precip. (in.)	***2.50***	***2.81***	***2.72***	***2.87***	***3.00***	***4.59***	na	***2.70***	***5.30***	na	***2.00***	***2.31***	na
Days With ≥ 0.1" Precipitation	5	5	6	8	8	6	7	5	***5***	***5***	6	5	***71***
Days With ≥ 0.5" Precipitation	2	2	2	3	3	3	3	2	***2***	***2***	2	2	***28***
Days With ≥ 1.0" Precipitation	1	1	1	1	1	1	1	1	***1***	***1***	1	1	***12***
Mean Snowfall (in.)	***3.9***	***3.3***	***1.0***	***0.0***	0.0	0.0	0.0	0.0	***0.0***	***0.0***	***0.3***	***2.9***	***11.4***
Maximum Snow Depth (in.)	***12***	na	***6***	***1***	***0***	***0***	***0***	***0***	***0***	***0***	***2***	na	na
Days With ≥ 1.0" Snow Depth	***6***	na	***1***	0	0	0	0	0	***0***	***0***	***0***	***4***	na

The period of record for all cooperative weather station data is 1980 – 2009. See User Guide for detailed explanation of data.

Valparaiso Waterworks *Porter County* Elevation: 799 ft. Latitude: 41° 31' N Longitude: 87° 02' W

	JAN	FEB	MAR	APR	MAY	JUN	JUL	AUG	SEP	OCT	NOV	DEC	YEAR
Mean Maximum Temp. (°F)	31.6	36.9	47.3	60.2	71.2	79.6	83.1	81.0	74.6	63.1	48.9	35.9	59.5
Mean Temp. (°F)	24.4	29.0	38.1	49.6	60.1	68.9	73.2	71.2	64.3	53.0	41.3	29.3	50.2
Mean Minimum Temp. (°F)	17.1	21.1	28.9	39.0	48.9	58.1	63.2	61.5	53.9	42.9	33.5	22.6	40.9
Extreme Maximum Temp. (°F)	63	71	83	88	90	100	99	99	93	85	74	68	100
Extreme Minimum Temp. (°F)	-25	-18	-5	14	30	35	44	39	32	20	8	-20	-25
Days Maximum Temp. ≥ 90°F	0	0	0	0	0	3	4	3	1	0	0	0	11
Days Maximum Temp. ≤ 32°F	17	10	3	0	0	0	0	0	0	0	1	11	42
Days Minimum Temp. ≤ 32°F	28	23	21	7	0	0	0	0	0	4	15	26	124
Days Minimum Temp. ≤ 0°F	4	2	0	0	0	0	0	0	0	0	0	2	8
Heating Degree Days (base 65°F)	1,253	1,011	828	465	197	40	4	12	104	374	706	1,100	6,094
Cooling Degree Days (base 65°F)	0	0	1	10	52	164	264	210	90	10	0	0	801
Mean Precipitation (in.)	2.16	1.91	2.56	3.54	4.13	4.51	4.24	3.91	3.29	3.22	3.81	2.64	39.92
Extreme Maximum Daily Precip. (in.)	1.76	1.59	1.99	2.07	2.20	5.28	7.34	4.42	2.52	2.64	4.05	2.33	7.34
Days With ≥ 0.1" Precipitation	5	5	6	7	8	7	7	6	7	6	7	6	77
Days With ≥ 0.5" Precipitation	1	1	2	2	3	3	3	2	2	2	2	2	25
Days With ≥ 1.0" Precipitation	0	0	0	1	1	1	1	1	1	1	1	1	9
Mean Snowfall (in.)	12.6	8.1	6.0	1.1	trace	0.0	0.0	0.0	0.0	0.2	2.2	9.5	39.7
Maximum Snow Depth (in.)	20	24	16	6	trace	0	0	0	0	3	6	22	24
Days With ≥ 1.0" Snow Depth	20	12	5	0	0	0	0	0	0	0	2	10	49

Warsaw *Kosciusko County* Elevation: 810 ft. Latitude: 41° 14' N Longitude: 85° 52' W

	JAN	FEB	MAR	APR	MAY	JUN	JUL	AUG	SEP	OCT	NOV	DEC	YEAR
Mean Maximum Temp. (°F)	32.3	36.1	47.1	59.7	70.8	79.9	82.9	81.2	74.7	62.3	49.3	36.1	59.4
Mean Temp. (°F)	24.9	28.1	37.9	49.5	59.9	69.3	72.8	71.3	64.0	52.2	41.1	29.3	50.0
Mean Minimum Temp. (°F)	17.5	20.1	28.7	39.2	49.0	58.8	62.7	61.3	53.3	42.1	32.7	22.0	40.6
Extreme Maximum Temp. (°F)	63	73	82	87	91	102	102	98	95	90	76	69	102
Extreme Minimum Temp. (°F)	-25	-13	-9	8	28	37	43	37	29	20	9	-20	-25
Days Maximum Temp. ≥ 90°F	0	0	0	0	0	3	4	2	1	0	0	0	10
Days Maximum Temp. ≤ 32°F	16	11	3	0	0	0	0	0	0	0	1	11	42
Days Minimum Temp. ≤ 32°F	28	24	21	7	0	0	0	0	0	5	16	26	127
Days Minimum Temp. ≤ 0°F	3	2	0	0	0	0	0	0	0	0	0	2	7
Heating Degree Days (base 65°F)	1,236	1,036	834	469	200	32	5	10	107	399	712	1,102	6,142
Cooling Degree Days (base 65°F)	0	0	1	9	49	168	252	213	83	9	0	0	784
Mean Precipitation (in.)	2.10	1.69	2.17	3.58	4.23	4.31	4.05	4.38	3.11	3.29	2.88	2.59	38.38
Extreme Maximum Daily Precip. (in.)	2.20	1.53	1.87	3.42	2.93	4.87	4.32	4.33	2.43	3.69	2.50	3.90	4.87
Days With ≥ 0.1" Precipitation	5	5	5	8	8	7	7	7	6	6	6	6	76
Days With ≥ 0.5" Precipitation	1	1	1	2	3	3	3	3	2	2	2	2	25
Days With ≥ 1.0" Precipitation	0	0	0	1	1	1	1	1	1	1	1	0	8
Mean Snowfall (in.)	na	na	1.7	0.3	0.0	0.0	0.0	0.0	0.0	trace	0.3	4.3	na
Maximum Snow Depth (in.)	na	na	6	4	0	0	0	0	0	trace	2	na	na
Days With ≥ 1.0" Snow Depth	na	na	1	0	0	0	0	0	0	0	0	6	na

Whitestown *Boone County* Elevation: 935 ft. Latitude: 40° 00' N Longitude: 86° 21' W

	JAN	FEB	MAR	APR	MAY	JUN	JUL	AUG	SEP	OCT	NOV	DEC	YEAR
Mean Maximum Temp. (°F)	35.1	40.2	51.4	64.4	74.3	83.0	85.7	84.3	78.5	66.0	52.1	38.6	62.8
Mean Temp. (°F)	27.1	31.2	41.1	52.8	62.8	71.6	74.6	73.0	66.2	54.7	43.2	31.1	52.4
Mean Minimum Temp. (°F)	19.0	22.2	30.8	41.2	51.2	60.2	63.5	61.6	53.9	43.3	34.3	23.5	42.0
Extreme Maximum Temp. (°F)	65	74	82	88	94	104	103	100	96	88	78	73	104
Extreme Minimum Temp. (°F)	-27	-20	-10	15	30	35	43	37	28	20	6	-22	-27
Days Maximum Temp. ≥ 90°F	0	0	0	0	1	5	8	6	2	0	0	0	22
Days Maximum Temp. ≤ 32°F	13	8	2	0	0	0	0	0	0	0	1	9	33
Days Minimum Temp. ≤ 32°F	27	23	18	6	0	0	0	0	0	5	14	24	117
Days Minimum Temp. ≤ 0°F	3	2	0	0	0	0	0	0	0	0	0	2	7
Heating Degree Days (base 65°F)	1,169	949	736	376	138	18	2	7	75	331	648	1,045	5,494
Cooling Degree Days (base 65°F)	0	0	2	17	75	223	307	261	118	19	0	0	1,022
Mean Precipitation (in.)	2.69	2.55	3.40	3.91	4.84	4.06	4.31	3.33	3.39	3.06	3.68	3.29	42.51
Extreme Maximum Daily Precip. (in.)	2.22	3.12	2.66	1.80	2.65	2.95	3.43	3.89	5.46	2.36	3.73	2.45	5.46
Days With ≥ 0.1" Precipitation	6	5	7	9	9	7	7	5	5	6	7	7	80
Days With ≥ 0.5" Precipitation	2	2	2	3	3	3	3	2	3	2	2	2	29
Days With ≥ 1.0" Precipitation	0	0	1	1	1	1	1	1	1	1	1	1	10
Mean Snowfall (in.)	8.0	6.4	2.4	0.3	0.0	0.0	0.0	0.0	0.0	0.3	0.7	5.8	23.9
Maximum Snow Depth (in.)	14	22	11	2	0	0	0	0	0	5	2	9	22
Days With ≥ 1.0" Snow Depth	11	8	2	0	0	0	0	0	0	0	0	7	28

Winchester Airport 3E *Randolph County* Elevation: 1,109 ft. Latitude: 40° 11' N Longitude: 84° 55' W

	JAN	FEB	MAR	APR	MAY	JUN	JUL	AUG	SEP	OCT	NOV	DEC	YEAR
Mean Maximum Temp. (°F)	33.0	36.9	47.4	60.4	70.8	79.7	82.9	81.5	75.7	63.1	49.9	37.0	59.9
Mean Temp. (°F)	25.4	28.5	38.2	50.3	60.9	69.9	73.0	71.3	64.8	53.0	41.5	29.7	50.5
Mean Minimum Temp. (°F)	17.8	20.1	28.9	40.1	50.9	60.1	63.1	61.1	53.9	42.7	33.0	22.3	41.2
Extreme Maximum Temp. (°F)	64	73	80	85	89	101	100	97	93	89	77	71	101
Extreme Minimum Temp. (°F)	-26	-15	-11	12	29	40	46	39	29	19	9	-22	-26
Days Maximum Temp. ≥ 90°F	0	0	0	0	0	2	4	2	1	0	0	0	9
Days Maximum Temp. ≤ 32°F	15	10	4	0	0	0	0	0	0	0	2	11	42
Days Minimum Temp. ≤ 32°F	28	25	21	6	0	0	0	0	0	4	16	26	126
Days Minimum Temp. ≤ 0°F	4	2	0	0	0	0	0	0	0	0	0	2	8
Heating Degree Days (base 65°F)	1,220	1,025	826	445	179	31	4	12	95	381	698	1,087	6,003
Cooling Degree Days (base 65°F)	0	0	1	11	58	185	260	216	96	15	0	0	842
Mean Precipitation (in.)	2.07	1.73	2.74	3.71	4.36	4.45	4.36	3.47	2.92	3.04	3.27	2.78	38.90
Extreme Maximum Daily Precip. (in.)	2.64	1.80	2.46	2.58	2.47	6.45	2.90	3.53	3.00	2.68	3.52	2.52	6.45
Days With ≥ 0.1" Precipitation	5	4	6	8	8	7	7	6	5	5	7	6	74
Days With ≥ 0.5" Precipitation	1	1	2	2	3	3	3	2	2	2	2	2	25
Days With ≥ 1.0" Precipitation	1	0	0	1	1	1	1	1	1	1	1	0	9
Mean Snowfall (in.)	5.9	5.4	2.5	0.3	0.0	0.0	0.0	0.0	0.0	0.1	0.5	3.8	18.5
Maximum Snow Depth (in.)	21	19	11	5	0	0	0	0	0	2	2	14	21
Days With ≥ 1.0" Snow Depth	11	10	3	0	0	0	0	0	0	0	1	6	31

The period of record for all cooperative weather station data is 1980 – 2009. See User Guide for detailed explanation of data.

Indiana Weather Station Rankings

Annual Extreme Maximum Temperature

Highest			Lowest		
Rank	Station Name	°F	Rank	Station Name	°F
1	Fort Wayne Baer Field	106	1	Richmond Water Works	100
2	Delphi 3 S	105	1	Valparaiso Waterworks	***100***
2	Frankfort Disposal Plant	105	3	Angola	101
2	Huntington	105	3	Freelandville	101
5	Berne	104	3	Greensburg	101
5	Bloomington Indiana Univ	104	3	La Porte	101
5	English 4 S	***104***	3	Martinsville 2 SW	101
5	Evansville Dress Regional Arpt	104	3	Winchester Airport 3E	101
5	Indianapolis SE Side	104	9	Crawfordsville 5 S	102
5	Kokomo 3 WSW	104	9	Dubois S Ind Forage Frm	102
5	Lafayette 8 S	104	9	Elwood Wastewater Plant	102
5	Lowell	104	9	Evansville Museum	***102***
5	Madison Sewage Plant	104	9	Farmland 5 NNW	102
5	Mount Vernon	104	9	Goshen College	102
5	Rockville	104	9	Muncie Ball State Univ	***102***
5	South Bend Michiana Regional	104	9	Oolitic Purdue Exp Farm	102
5	Whitestown	104	9	Shelbyville Sewage Plant	***102***
18	Anderson Sewage Plant	103	9	Terre Haute Indiana State	***102***
18	Brookville	103	9	Warsaw	102
18	Columbia City	103	20	Anderson Sewage Plant	103
18	Columbus	103	20	Brookville	103
18	Greenfield	103	20	Columbia City	103
18	Indianapolis Int'l Arpt	103	20	Columbus	103
18	North Vernon 1 NW	103	20	Greenfield	103
18	Tell City	103	20	Indianapolis Int'l Arpt	103

Annual Mean Maximum Temperature

Highest			Lowest		
Rank	Station Name	°F	Rank	Station Name	°F
1	Evansville Museum	***68.8***	1	Angola	57.5
2	English 4 S	***67.1***	2	La Porte	58.4
3	Evansville Dress Regional Arpt	66.7	3	Columbia City	59.0
4	Tell City	66.5	4	South Bend Michiana Regional	59.1
5	Mount Vernon	66.2	5	Warsaw	***59.4***
6	Madison Sewage Plant	65.6	6	Valparaiso Waterworks	***59.5***
7	North Vernon 1 NW	***65.3***	7	Goshen College	59.7
8	Dubois S Ind Forage Frm	65.0	8	Lowell	59.9
9	Terre Haute Indiana State	***64.8***	8	Winchester Airport 3E	59.9
10	Brookville	64.2	10	Fort Wayne Baer Field	60.0
10	Rockville	64.2	11	Kokomo 3 WSW	60.2
12	Oolitic Purdue Exp Farm	63.9	12	Berne	60.7
13	Columbus	63.5	13	Farmland 5 NNW	60.8
13	Freelandville	63.5	13	Muncie Ball State Univ	***60.8***
15	Bloomington Indiana Univ	63.4	15	Frankfort Disposal Plant	60.9
16	Whitestown	62.8	15	Huntington	60.9
17	Martinsville 2 SW	62.7	17	Anderson Sewage Plant	61.0
17	Shelbyville Sewage Plant	***62.7***	18	Lafayette 8 S	61.1
19	Indianapolis Int'l Arpt	62.6	19	Elwood Wastewater Plant	61.2
20	Delphi 3 S	62.4	20	Crawfordsville 5 S	***61.6***
21	Greensburg	62.3	20	Indianapolis SE Side	61.6
22	Richmond Water Works	61.8	22	Greenfield	61.7
23	Greenfield	61.7	23	Richmond Water Works	61.8
24	Crawfordsville 5 S	***61.6***	24	Greensburg	62.3
24	Indianapolis SE Side	61.6	25	Delphi 3 S	62.4

Rankings include 25 highest/lowest stations. If state has less than 25 stations, all stations are included. The period of record is 1980–2009. See User Guide for detailed explanation of data.

Annual Mean Temperature

Highest			Lowest		
Rank	Station Name	°F	Rank	Station Name	°F
1	Evansville Museum	***58.9***	1	Angola	47.7
2	Tell City	56.8	2	Columbia City	49.1
3	Evansville Dress Regional Arpt	56.5	3	Lowell	49.6
4	Mount Vernon	56.4	4	Kokomo 3 WSW	49.9
5	Madison Sewage Plant	55.4	5	Warsaw	***50.0***
6	English 4 S	***54.8***	6	La Porte	50.1
6	North Vernon 1 NW	***54.8***	6	South Bend Michiana Regional	50.1
8	Dubois S Ind Forage Frm	54.5	8	Valparaiso Waterworks	***50.2***
9	Freelandville	53.9	9	Crawfordsville 5 S	***50.4***
9	Rockville	53.9	9	Farmland 5 NNW	50.4
11	Terre Haute Indiana State	***53.7***	9	Goshen College	50.4
12	Bloomington Indiana Univ	53.6	9	Huntington	50.4
13	Columbus	53.4	13	Fort Wayne Baer Field	50.5
14	Indianapolis Int'l Arpt	53.1	13	Winchester Airport 3E	50.5
15	Greensburg	53.0	15	Elwood Wastewater Plant	50.6
16	Oolitic Purdue Exp Farm	52.9	16	Muncie Ball State Univ	***50.9***
17	Brookville	52.7	17	Lafayette 8 S	51.2
18	Shelbyville Sewage Plant	***52.5***	18	Frankfort Disposal Plant	51.3
18	Whitestown	52.5	19	Berne	51.5
20	Delphi 3 S	52.2	20	Richmond Water Works	51.6
21	Indianapolis SE Side	52.0	21	Anderson Sewage Plant	51.8
22	Greenfield	51.9	21	Martinsville 2 SW	51.8
23	Anderson Sewage Plant	51.8	23	Greenfield	51.9
23	Martinsville 2 SW	51.8	24	Indianapolis SE Side	52.0
25	Richmond Water Works	51.6	25	Delphi 3 S	52.2

Annual Mean Minimum Temperature

Highest			Lowest		
Rank	Station Name	°F	Rank	Station Name	°F
1	Evansville Museum	***48.9***	1	Angola	37.8
2	Tell City	46.9	2	Columbia City	39.1
3	Mount Vernon	46.6	3	Crawfordsville 5 S	***39.2***
4	Evansville Dress Regional Arpt	46.2	3	Lowell	39.2
5	Madison Sewage Plant	45.2	5	Kokomo 3 WSW	39.7
6	Freelandville	44.4	6	Huntington	39.8
7	North Vernon 1 NW	***44.3***	7	Farmland 5 NNW	39.9
8	Dubois S Ind Forage Frm	43.9	8	Elwood Wastewater Plant	40.0
9	Bloomington Indiana Univ	43.8	9	Warsaw	40.6
10	Greensburg	43.7	10	Fort Wayne Baer Field	40.9
10	Indianapolis Int'l Arpt	43.7	10	Martinsville 2 SW	40.9
12	Rockville	43.5	10	Muncie Ball State Univ	***40.9***
13	Columbus	43.2	10	Valparaiso Waterworks	***40.9***
14	Anderson Sewage Plant	42.6	14	Goshen College	41.0
14	Terre Haute Indiana State	***42.6***	14	South Bend Michiana Regional	41.0
16	Indianapolis SE Side	42.4	16	Brookville	41.1
16	Shelbyville Sewage Plant	***42.4***	16	Lafayette 8 S	41.1
18	English 4 S	***42.3***	18	Winchester Airport 3E	41.2
19	Berne	42.1	19	Richmond Water Works	41.3
19	Greenfield	42.1	20	Frankfort Disposal Plant	41.6
19	Whitestown	42.1	21	La Porte	41.7
22	Delphi 3 S	41.9	22	Oolitic Purdue Exp Farm	41.8
23	Oolitic Purdue Exp Farm	41.8	23	Delphi 3 S	41.9
24	La Porte	41.7	24	Berne	42.1
25	Frankfort Disposal Plant	41.6	24	Greenfield	42.1

Rankings include 25 highest/lowest stations. If state has less than 25 stations, all stations are included. The period of record is 1980–2009. See User Guide for detailed explanation of data.

Annual Extreme Minimum Temperature

Highest

Rank	Station Name	°F
1	Mount Vernon	-16
2	Evansville Museum	***-17***
2	Tell City	-17
4	Evansville Dress Regional Arpt	-18
4	Madison Sewage Plant	-18
6	Bloomington Indiana Univ	-21
6	South Bend Michiana Regional	-21
8	Fort Wayne Baer Field	-22
8	Indianapolis SE Side	-22
8	North Vernon 1 NW	-22
8	Terre Haute Indiana State	***-22***
12	Freelandville	-23
12	La Porte	-23
14	Anderson Sewage Plant	-24
14	Berne	-24
14	Columbia City	-24
14	Delphi 3 S	-24
14	Elwood Wastewater Plant	-24
14	Goshen College	-24
14	Greensburg	-24
21	Dubois S Ind Forage Frm	-25
21	Farmland 5 NNW	-25
21	Lafayette 8 S	-25
21	Lowell	-25
21	Rockville	-25

Lowest

Rank	Station Name	°F
1	Martinsville 2 SW	-35
2	Brookville	-31
2	Crawfordsville 5 S	-31
4	English 4 S	***-30***
5	Greenfield	-29
5	Muncie Ball State Univ	***-29***
5	Oolitic Purdue Exp Farm	-29
8	Huntington	-28
9	Angola	-27
9	Indianapolis Int'l Arpt	-27
9	Richmond Water Works	-27
9	Whitestown	-27
13	Columbus	-26
13	Frankfort Disposal Plant	-26
13	Kokomo 3 WSW	-26
13	Winchester Airport 3E	-26
17	Dubois S Ind Forage Frm	-25
17	Farmland 5 NNW	-25
17	Lafayette 8 S	-25
17	Lowell	-25
17	Rockville	-25
17	Shelbyville Sewage Plant	***-25***
17	Valparaiso Waterworks	***-25***
17	Warsaw	-25
25	Anderson Sewage Plant	-24

July Mean Maximum Temperature

Highest

Rank	Station Name	°F
1	Evansville Museum	***90.0***
2	Evansville Dress Regional Arpt	88.5
3	English 4 S	88.0
3	Mount Vernon	88.0
3	Terre Haute Indiana State	***88.0***
6	Tell City	87.5
7	Rockville	86.9
8	Brookville	86.8
9	Madison Sewage Plant	86.7
10	Dubois S Ind Forage Frm	86.4
11	North Vernon 1 NW	***86.3***
12	Freelandville	85.7
12	Whitestown	85.7
14	Oolitic Purdue Exp Farm	85.5
15	Bloomington Indiana Univ	85.4
15	Columbus	85.4
15	Delphi 3 S	85.4
18	Huntington	85.3
18	Indianapolis Int'l Arpt	85.3
18	Shelbyville Sewage Plant	85.3
21	Greensburg	84.8
21	Muncie Ball State Univ	***84.8***
23	Elwood Wastewater Plant	84.7
23	Greenfield	84.7
23	Martinsville 2 SW	84.7

Lowest

Rank	Station Name	°F
1	Angola	81.8
2	La Porte	82.3
3	Columbia City	82.7
4	Warsaw	82.9
4	Winchester Airport 3E	82.9
6	Valparaiso Waterworks	***83.1***
7	South Bend Michiana Regional	83.3
8	Goshen College	83.6
9	Anderson Sewage Plant	83.8
9	Kokomo 3 WSW	83.8
11	Frankfort Disposal Plant	83.9
12	Farmland 5 NNW	84.0
12	Lowell	84.0
14	Fort Wayne Baer Field	84.3
14	Indianapolis SE Side	84.3
14	Lafayette 8 S	84.3
17	Crawfordsville 5 S	84.4
18	Richmond Water Works	84.5
19	Berne	84.6
20	Elwood Wastewater Plant	84.7
20	Greenfield	84.7
20	Martinsville 2 SW	84.7
23	Greensburg	84.8
23	Muncie Ball State Univ	***84.8***
25	Huntington	85.3

Rankings include 25 highest/lowest stations. If state has less than 25 stations, all stations are included. The period of record is 1980–2009. See User Guide for detailed explanation of data.

January Mean Minimum Temperature

Highest Rank	Station Name	°F	Lowest Rank	Station Name	°F
1	Evansville Museum	*27.2*	1	Angola	14.7
2	Tell City	26.3	2	Lowell	15.0
3	Evansville Dress Regional Arpt	24.9	3	Columbia City	16.1
4	Madison Sewage Plant	24.5	4	Kokomo 3 WSW	16.4
5	Mount Vernon	24.4	5	Elwood Wastewater Plant	16.8
6	North Vernon 1 NW	*23.6*	6	Crawfordsville 5 S	*16.9*
7	English 4 S	22.3	7	Valparaiso Waterworks	17.1
8	Freelandville	22.2	8	Farmland 5 NNW	17.3
9	Dubois S Ind Forage Frm	21.7	8	Huntington	17.3
10	Bloomington Indiana Univ	21.2	8	Lafayette 8 S	17.3
11	Columbus	21.0	8	Muncie Ball State Univ	*17.3*
12	Greensburg	20.9	12	Warsaw	17.5
13	Indianapolis Int'l Arpt	20.5	13	La Porte	17.8
13	Rockville	20.5	13	Winchester Airport 3E	17.8
15	Oolitic Purdue Exp Farm	20.1	15	Fort Wayne Baer Field	17.9
16	Anderson Sewage Plant	19.8	16	South Bend Michiana Regional	18.0
16	Brookville	19.8	17	Goshen College	18.2
18	Shelbyville Sewage Plant	19.7	18	Greenfield	18.8
19	Berne	19.4	19	Frankfort Disposal Plant	19.0
19	Indianapolis SE Side	19.4	19	Whitestown	19.0
21	Delphi 3 S	19.3	21	Martinsville 2 SW	19.1
22	Richmond Water Works	19.2	22	Richmond Water Works	19.2
22	Terre Haute Indiana State	*19.2*	22	Terre Haute Indiana State	*19.2*
24	Martinsville 2 SW	19.1	24	Delphi 3 S	19.3
25	Frankfort Disposal Plant	19.0	25	Berne	19.4

Number of Days Annually Maximum Temperature ≥ 90°F

Highest Rank	Station Name	Days	Lowest Rank	Station Name	Days
1	Evansville Museum	*56*	1	Angola	7
2	Evansville Dress Regional Arpt	41	2	Winchester Airport 3E	9
3	Mount Vernon	38	3	Columbia City	10
4	Terre Haute Indiana State	*35*	3	Warsaw	10
5	English 4 S	*33*	5	La Porte	11
5	Tell City	33	5	Valparaiso Waterworks	*11*
7	Brookville	28	7	Goshen College	13
8	Dubois S Ind Forage Frm	27	8	Anderson Sewage Plant	15
8	Rockville	27	8	Frankfort Disposal Plant	15
10	Madison Sewage Plant	26	8	Fort Wayne Baer Field	15
11	Whitestown	22	8	Indianapolis SE Side	15
12	Huntington	21	8	South Bend Michiana Regional	15
13	Columbus	20	13	Berne	16
13	Delphi 3 S	20	13	Crawfordsville 5 S	16
13	North Vernon 1 NW	20	13	Kokomo 3 WSW	16
16	Bloomington Indiana Univ	19	13	Martinsville 2 SW	16
16	Freelandville	19	13	Richmond Water Works	16
16	Oolitic Purdue Exp Farm	19	18	Elwood Wastewater Plant	17
19	Indianapolis Int'l Arpt	18	18	Farmland 5 NNW	17
19	Lafayette 8 S	18	18	Greenfield	17
19	Lowell	18	18	Greensburg	17
22	Elwood Wastewater Plant	17	18	Muncie Ball State Univ	*17*
22	Farmland 5 NNW	17	18	Shelbyville Sewage Plant	*17*
22	Greenfield	17	24	Indianapolis Int'l Arpt	18
22	Greensburg	17	24	Lafayette 8 S	18

Rankings include 25 highest/lowest stations. If state has less than 25 stations, all stations are included. The period of record is 1980–2009. See User Guide for detailed explanation of data.

Number of Days Annually Maximum Temperature ≤ 32°F

Highest			Lowest		
Rank	Station Name	Days	Rank	Station Name	Days
1	Angola	52	1	Evansville Museum	*11*
2	La Porte	46	2	English 4 S	*14*
3	South Bend Michiana Regional	45	3	Madison Sewage Plant	15
4	Columbia City	44	3	Tell City	15
4	Kokomo 3 WSW	44	5	Evansville Dress Regional Arpt	17
6	Goshen College	42	6	Mount Vernon	18
6	Lowell	42	6	North Vernon 1 NW	18
6	Valparaiso Waterworks	*42*	8	Dubois S Ind Forage Frm	20
6	Warsaw	42	9	Terre Haute Indiana State	*24*
6	Winchester Airport 3E	42	10	Brookville	25
11	Fort Wayne Baer Field	41	10	Columbus	25
12	Farmland 5 NNW	39	10	Oolitic Purdue Exp Farm	25
13	Berne	38	13	Rockville	26
13	Huntington	38	14	Bloomington Indiana Univ	28
13	Lafayette 8 S	38	14	Freelandville	28
13	Muncie Ball State Univ	*38*	16	Martinsville 2 SW	29
17	Frankfort Disposal Plant	37	16	Shelbyville Sewage Plant	*29*
18	Anderson Sewage Plant	36	18	Indianapolis Int'l Arpt	30
18	Crawfordsville 5 S	36	19	Greensburg	31
18	Elwood Wastewater Plant	36	20	Delphi 3 S	32
21	Greenfield	34	20	Richmond Water Works	32
21	Indianapolis SE Side	34	22	Whitestown	33
23	Whitestown	33	23	Greenfield	34
24	Delphi 3 S	32	23	Indianapolis SE Side	34
24	Richmond Water Works	32	25	Anderson Sewage Plant	36

Number of Days Annually Minimum Temperature ≤ 32°F

Highest			Lowest		
Rank	Station Name	Days	Rank	Station Name	Days
1	Angola	150	1	Evansville Museum	*72*
2	Lowell	137	2	Tell City	83
3	Crawfordsville 5 S	136	3	Mount Vernon	88
4	Columbia City	135	4	Evansville Dress Regional Arpt	93
4	Kokomo 3 WSW	135	5	Madison Sewage Plant	94
6	Farmland 5 NNW	134	6	North Vernon 1 NW	98
6	Huntington	134	7	Freelandville	104
8	Elwood Wastewater Plant	131	8	Indianapolis Int'l Arpt	107
9	Muncie Ball State Univ	*129*	9	Dubois S Ind Forage Frm	108
10	Martinsville 2 SW	127	10	Bloomington Indiana Univ	109
10	Warsaw	127	10	Rockville	109
12	Brookville	126	12	Greensburg	110
12	Winchester Airport 3E	126	13	Columbus	112
14	Lafayette 8 S	125	14	Anderson Sewage Plant	114
14	South Bend Michiana Regional	125	14	English 4 S	*114*
16	Fort Wayne Baer Field	124	16	Terre Haute Indiana State	*115*
16	Valparaiso Waterworks	*124*	17	Delphi 3 S	117
18	Goshen College	123	17	Whitestown	117
19	Oolitic Purdue Exp Farm	121	19	Berne	118
20	La Porte	120	20	Frankfort Disposal Plant	119
20	Richmond Water Works	120	20	Greenfield	119
22	Frankfort Disposal Plant	119	20	Indianapolis SE Side	119
22	Greenfield	119	20	Shelbyville Sewage Plant	*119*
22	Indianapolis SE Side	119	24	La Porte	120
22	Shelbyville Sewage Plant	*119*	24	Richmond Water Works	120

Rankings include 25 highest/lowest stations. If state has less than 25 stations, all stations are included. The period of record is 1980–2009. See User Guide for detailed explanation of data.

Number of Days Annually Minimum Temperature ≤ 0°F

Highest			Lowest		
Rank	**Station Name**	**Days**	**Rank**	**Station Name**	**Days**
1	Angola	11	1	Evansville Museum	***1***
1	Lowell	11	1	Tell City	1
3	Crawfordsville 5 S	10	3	Evansville Dress Regional Arpt	2
3	Kokomo 3 WSW	10	3	Madison Sewage Plant	2
5	Columbia City	9	5	Mount Vernon	3
5	Lafayette 8 S	9	5	North Vernon 1 NW	3
7	Elwood Wastewater Plant	8	7	Bloomington Indiana Univ	4
7	Farmland 5 NNW	8	7	Columbus	4
7	Fort Wayne Baer Field	8	7	Dubois S Ind Forage Frm	4
7	Huntington	8	7	English 4 S	***4***
7	Muncie Ball State Univ	***8***	7	Freelandville	4
7	Valparaiso Waterworks	***8***	7	Greensburg	4
7	Winchester Airport 3E	8	7	Indianapolis Int'l Arpt	4
14	Delphi 3 S	7	14	Anderson Sewage Plant	5
14	Frankfort Disposal Plant	7	14	Terre Haute Indiana State	***5***
14	Goshen College	7	16	Berne	6
14	Greenfield	7	16	Brookville	6
14	La Porte	7	16	Indianapolis SE Side	6
14	Martinsville 2 SW	7	16	Oolitic Purdue Exp Farm	6
14	South Bend Michiana Regional	7	16	Richmond Water Works	6
14	Warsaw	7	16	Rockville	6
14	Whitestown	7	16	Shelbyville Sewage Plant	***6***
23	Berne	6	23	Delphi 3 S	7
23	Brookville	6	23	Frankfort Disposal Plant	7
23	Indianapolis SE Side	6	23	Goshen College	7

Number of Annual Heating Degree Days

Highest			Lowest		
Rank	**Station Name**	**Num.**	**Rank**	**Station Name**	**Num.**
1	Angola	6,822	1	Evansville Museum	***3,925***
2	Columbia City	6,396	2	Tell City	4,332
3	Lowell	6,339	3	Evansville Dress Regional Arpt	4,455
4	Kokomo 3 WSW	6,210	4	Mount Vernon	4,490
5	La Porte	6,168	5	Madison Sewage Plant	4,610
6	South Bend Michiana Regional	6,165	6	English 4 S	***4,733***
7	Warsaw	***6,142***	7	North Vernon 1 NW	***4,753***
8	Huntington	6,109	8	Dubois S Ind Forage Frm	4,922
9	Valparaiso Waterworks	***6,094***	9	Freelandville	5,111
10	Farmland 5 NNW	6,058	10	Rockville	5,122
11	Goshen College	6,049	11	Bloomington Indiana Univ	5,173
12	Fort Wayne Baer Field	6,026	12	Columbus	5,226
13	Crawfordsville 5 S	***6,021***	12	Terre Haute Indiana State	***5,226***
14	Elwood Wastewater Plant	6,006	14	Oolitic Purdue Exp Farm	5,315
15	Winchester Airport 3E	6,003	15	Indianapolis Int'l Arpt	5,322
16	Muncie Ball State Univ	***5,965***	16	Greensburg	5,352
17	Lafayette 8 S	5,894	17	Brookville	5,400
18	Berne	5,810	18	Shelbyville Sewage Plant	***5,462***
19	Frankfort Disposal Plant	5,789	19	Whitestown	5,494
20	Greenfield	5,678	20	Delphi 3 S	5,558
21	Richmond Water Works	5,657	21	Martinsville 2 SW	5,608
22	Anderson Sewage Plant	5,638	22	Indianapolis SE Side	5,632
23	Indianapolis SE Side	5,632	23	Anderson Sewage Plant	5,638
24	Martinsville 2 SW	5,608	24	Richmond Water Works	5,657
25	Delphi 3 S	5,558	25	Greenfield	5,678

Rankings include 25 highest/lowest stations. If state has less than 25 stations, all stations are included. The period of record is 1980–2009. See User Guide for detailed explanation of data.

Number of Annual Cooling Degree Days

Rank	Station Name (Highest)	Num.	Rank	Station Name (Lowest)	Num.
1	Evansville Museum	***1,800***	1	Angola	610
2	Mount Vernon	1,471	2	Columbia City	707
3	Evansville Dress Regional Arpt	1,460	3	Warsaw	***784***
4	Tell City	1,437	4	Valparaiso Waterworks	***801***
5	Terre Haute Indiana State	***1,232***	5	Crawfordsville 5 S	***805***
6	Madison Sewage Plant	1,230	6	Lowell	815
7	Dubois S Ind Forage Frm	1,200	7	Goshen College	818
8	Freelandville	1,182	8	Kokomo 3 WSW	822
9	Rockville	1,171	9	Farmland 5 NNW	829
10	North Vernon 1 NW	***1,142***	9	South Bend Michiana Regional	829
11	Bloomington Indiana Univ	1,134	11	La Porte	839
12	Indianapolis Int'l Arpt	1,101	12	Winchester Airport 3E	842
13	English 4 S	***1,095***	13	Fort Wayne Baer Field	848
14	Greensburg	1,093	14	Elwood Wastewater Plant	865
15	Columbus	1,087	15	Richmond Water Works	876
16	Shelbyville Sewage Plant	***1,023***	16	Huntington	880
17	Whitestown	1,022	17	Frankfort Disposal Plant	888
18	Brookville	1,020	18	Martinsville 2 SW	899
19	Greenfield	1,011	19	Muncie Ball State Univ	***921***
20	Oolitic Purdue Exp Farm	1,000	20	Anderson Sewage Plant	939
21	Indianapolis SE Side	998	21	Lafayette 8 S	952
22	Delphi 3 S	979	22	Berne	966
23	Berne	966	23	Delphi 3 S	979
24	Lafayette 8 S	952	24	Indianapolis SE Side	998
25	Anderson Sewage Plant	939	25	Oolitic Purdue Exp Farm	1,000

Annual Precipitation

Rank	Station Name (Highest)	Inches	Rank	Station Name (Lowest)	Inches
1	English 4 S	***48.65***	1	South Bend Michiana Regional	38.33
2	Dubois S Ind Forage Frm	48.06	2	Fort Wayne Baer Field	38.35
3	Tell City	47.84	3	Warsaw	38.38
4	Madison Sewage Plant	47.54	4	Huntington	38.43
5	Bloomington Indiana Univ	47.48	5	Lafayette 8 S	38.44
6	Rockville	46.88	6	Delphi 3 S	38.52
7	Evansville Museum	***46.29***	7	Winchester Airport 3E	38.90
8	Oolitic Purdue Exp Farm	46.01	8	Angola	39.01
9	Mount Vernon	45.92	9	Goshen College	39.03
10	Greenfield	45.90	10	Berne	39.06
11	Freelandville	45.72	11	Farmland 5 NNW	39.21
12	North Vernon 1 NW	45.61	12	Lowell	39.45
13	Evansville Dress Regional Arpt	45.34	13	Columbia City	39.47
14	Greensburg	44.74	14	Muncie Ball State Univ	***39.49***
15	Martinsville 2 SW	44.69	15	Valparaiso Waterworks	***39.92***
16	Terre Haute Indiana State	***44.24***	16	Frankfort Disposal Plant	40.60
17	Columbus	44.02	17	Elwood Wastewater Plant	40.62
18	Kokomo 3 WSW	43.12	18	Richmond Water Works	40.70
19	Crawfordsville 5 S	***43.01***	19	Anderson Sewage Plant	41.09
20	Brookville	42.86	20	Shelbyville Sewage Plant	41.15
21	La Porte	42.56	21	Indianapolis SE Side	42.11
22	Whitestown	42.51	22	Indianapolis Int'l Arpt	42.45
23	Indianapolis Int'l Arpt	42.45	23	Whitestown	42.51
24	Indianapolis SE Side	42.11	24	La Porte	42.56
25	Shelbyville Sewage Plant	41.15	25	Brookville	42.86

Rankings include 25 highest/lowest stations. If state has less than 25 stations, all stations are included. The period of record is 1980–2009. See User Guide for detailed explanation of data.

Annual Extreme Maximum Daily Precipitation

Highest Rank	Station Name	Inches	Lowest Rank	Station Name	Inches
1	Kokomo 3 WSW	8.82	1	Freelandville	3.81
2	Rockville	8.05	2	Brookville	4.03
3	Martinsville 2 SW	8.02	3	Angola	4.10
4	Mount Vernon	7.40	4	Bloomington Indiana Univ	4.15
5	Valparaiso Waterworks	*7.34*	5	Indianapolis SE Side	4.16
6	Indianapolis Int'l Arpt	7.20	6	Berne	4.20
7	La Porte	6.73	7	Anderson Sewage Plant	4.21
8	Goshen College	6.65	8	Frankfort Disposal Plant	4.30
9	South Bend Michiana Regional	6.58	9	Crawfordsville 5 S	*4.35*
10	Winchester Airport 3E	*6.45*	10	Farmland 5 NNW	4.40
11	Evansville Dress Regional Arpt	6.40	10	Fort Wayne Baer Field	4.40
12	Columbus	6.37	12	Shelbyville Sewage Plant	*4.43*
13	Evansville Museum	*5.74*	13	Columbia City	4.48
14	Dubois S Ind Forage Frm	5.66	14	Lafayette 8 S	4.51
15	Huntington	5.53	15	Richmond Water Works	4.53
16	English 4 S	*5.50*	16	North Vernon 1 NW	*4.55*
17	Whitestown	5.46	17	Greenfield	4.71
18	Madison Sewage Plant	5.16	18	Tell City	4.75
19	Lowell	5.14	19	Delphi 3 S	4.78
20	Elwood Wastewater Plant	5.01	20	Oolitic Purdue Exp Farm	4.80
21	Greensburg	5.00	21	Warsaw	4.87
22	Warsaw	4.87	22	Greensburg	5.00
23	Oolitic Purdue Exp Farm	4.80	23	Elwood Wastewater Plant	5.01
24	Delphi 3 S	4.78	24	Lowell	5.14
25	Tell City	4.75	25	Madison Sewage Plant	5.16

Number of Days Annually With ≥ 0.1 Inches of Precipitation

Highest Rank	Station Name	Days	Lowest Rank	Station Name	Days
1	La Porte	87	1	North Vernon 1 NW	71
2	Kokomo 3 WSW	84	1	Terre Haute Indiana State	*71*
2	Madison Sewage Plant	84	3	Delphi 3 S	72
4	Greenfield	82	3	Lafayette 8 S	72
4	Greensburg	82	5	Evansville Museum	*73*
4	Rockville	82	5	Mount Vernon	73
7	English 4 S	*81*	7	Evansville Dress Regional Arpt	74
8	Brookville	80	7	Lowell	74
8	Whitestown	80	7	Winchester Airport 3E	74
10	Angola	79	10	Farmland 5 NNW	75
10	Bloomington Indiana Univ	79	10	Indianapolis SE Side	75
10	Frankfort Disposal Plant	79	10	Muncie Ball State Univ	*75*
10	Oolitic Purdue Exp Farm	79	13	Columbus	76
10	South Bend Michiana Regional	79	13	Elwood Wastewater Plant	76
15	Anderson Sewage Plant	78	13	Martinsville 2 SW	76
15	Berne	78	13	Shelbyville Sewage Plant	*76*
15	Columbia City	78	13	Warsaw	76
15	Crawfordsville 5 S	*78*	18	Fort Wayne Baer Field	77
15	Dubois S Ind Forage Frm	78	18	Goshen College	77
15	Freelandville	78	18	Huntington	77
15	Indianapolis Int'l Arpt	78	18	Richmond Water Works	77
22	Fort Wayne Baer Field	77	18	Tell City	77
22	Goshen College	77	18	Valparaiso Waterworks	*77*
22	Huntington	77	24	Anderson Sewage Plant	78
22	Richmond Water Works	77	24	Berne	78

Rankings include 25 highest/lowest stations. If state has less than 25 stations, all stations are included. The period of record is 1980–2009. See User Guide for detailed explanation of data.

Number of Days Annually With ≥ 0.5 Inches of Precipitation

Highest			Lowest		
Rank	Station Name	Days	Rank	Station Name	Days
1	Rockville	35	1	South Bend Michiana Regional	23
2	Dubois S Ind Forage Frm	34	2	Goshen College	24
3	Columbus	33	2	Lowell	24
3	Madison Sewage Plant	33	4	Huntington	25
5	Bloomington Indiana Univ	32	4	Lafayette 8 S	25
5	English 4 S	***32***	4	Valparaiso Waterworks	***25***
5	Evansville Dress Regional Arpt	32	4	Warsaw	25
5	Freelandville	32	4	Winchester Airport 3E	25
5	Greenfield	32	9	Angola	26
5	Mount Vernon	32	9	Berne	26
5	Oolitic Purdue Exp Farm	32	9	Columbia City	26
5	Tell City	32	9	Farmland 5 NNW	26
13	Greensburg	31	9	Frankfort Disposal Plant	26
13	Martinsville 2 SW	31	9	Fort Wayne Baer Field	26
15	Anderson Sewage Plant	30	9	Muncie Ball State Univ	***26***
15	Crawfordsville 5 S	***30***	9	Richmond Water Works	26
15	North Vernon 1 NW	30	17	Delphi 3 S	27
15	Shelbyville Sewage Plant	***30***	17	Elwood Wastewater Plant	27
19	Brookville	29	17	La Porte	27
19	Evansville Museum	***29***	20	Indianapolis Int'l Arpt	28
19	Indianapolis SE Side	29	20	Kokomo 3 WSW	28
19	Whitestown	29	20	Terre Haute Indiana State	***28***
23	Indianapolis Int'l Arpt	28	23	Brookville	29
23	Kokomo 3 WSW	28	23	Evansville Museum	***29***
23	Terre Haute Indiana State	***28***	23	Indianapolis SE Side	29

Number of Days Annually With ≥ 1.0 Inches of Precipitation

Highest			Lowest		
Rank	Station Name	Days	Rank	Station Name	Days
1	Madison Sewage Plant	14	1	Angola	7
1	Rockville	14	1	Lafayette 8 S	7
3	Bloomington Indiana Univ	13	3	Berne	8
3	Dubois S Ind Forage Frm	13	3	Farmland 5 NNW	8
3	English 4 S	***13***	3	Fort Wayne Baer Field	8
3	Freelandville	13	3	Goshen College	8
3	Mount Vernon	13	3	Huntington	8
3	Tell City	13	3	Muncie Ball State Univ	***8***
9	Evansville Dress Regional Arpt	12	3	South Bend Michiana Regional	8
9	Greenfield	12	3	Warsaw	8
9	Oolitic Purdue Exp Farm	12	11	Columbia City	9
9	Terre Haute Indiana State	***12***	11	Crawfordsville 5 S	***9***
13	Brookville	11	11	Elwood Wastewater Plant	9
13	Columbus	11	11	Frankfort Disposal Plant	9
13	Evansville Museum	***11***	11	Lowell	9
13	Greensburg	11	11	Valparaiso Waterworks	***9***
13	Indianapolis SE Side	11	11	Winchester Airport 3E	9
13	Martinsville 2 SW	11	18	Anderson Sewage Plant	10
13	North Vernon 1 NW	11	18	Delphi 3 S	10
13	Richmond Water Works	11	18	Indianapolis Int'l Arpt	10
13	Shelbyville Sewage Plant	11	18	Kokomo 3 WSW	10
22	Anderson Sewage Plant	10	18	La Porte	10
22	Delphi 3 S	10	18	Whitestown	10
22	Indianapolis Int'l Arpt	10	24	Brookville	11
22	Kokomo 3 WSW	10	24	Columbus	11

Rankings include 25 highest/lowest stations. If state has less than 25 stations, all stations are included. The period of record is 1980–2009. See User Guide for detailed explanation of data.

Annual Snowfall

Rank	Station Name (Highest)	Inches	Rank	Station Name (Lowest)	Inches
1	South Bend Michiana Regional	67.3	1	Tell City	5.3
2	La Porte	62.2	2	Shelbyville Sewage Plant	*5.7*
3	Goshen College	40.3	3	Mount Vernon	8.8
4	Valparaiso Waterworks	*39.7*	4	Dubois S Ind Forage Frm	*9.1*
5	Kokomo 3 WSW	38.3	5	North Vernon 1 NW	*10.8*
6	Angola	36.4	6	Evansville Museum	*11.0*
7	Fort Wayne Baer Field	33.8	7	Evansville Dress Regional Arpt	*11.4*
8	Lowell	30.8	7	Terre Haute Indiana State	*11.4*
9	Huntington	29.3	9	Bloomington Indiana Univ	*12.9*
10	Berne	28.2	10	Madison Sewage Plant	13.1
11	Columbia City	27.5	11	Indianapolis SE Side	*13.4*
12	Indianapolis Int'l Arpt	25.5	12	Rockville	13.6
13	Muncie Ball State Univ	*24.0*	13	Freelandville	13.9
14	Whitestown	23.9	14	Brookville	*14.2*
15	Frankfort Disposal Plant	22.6	15	Columbus	14.4
16	Farmland 5 NNW	22.4	16	Oolitic Purdue Exp Farm	14.9
17	Lafayette 8 S	21.3	17	Greenfield	15.7
18	Delphi 3 S	18.6	17	Richmond Water Works	15.7
19	Winchester Airport 3E	18.5	19	Martinsville 2 SW	16.0
20	Anderson Sewage Plant	17.9	20	Greensburg	16.4
21	Greensburg	16.4	21	Anderson Sewage Plant	17.9
22	Martinsville 2 SW	16.0	22	Winchester Airport 3E	18.5
23	Greenfield	15.7	23	Delphi 3 S	18.6
23	Richmond Water Works	15.7	24	Lafayette 8 S	21.3
25	Oolitic Purdue Exp Farm	14.9	25	Farmland 5 NNW	22.4

Annual Maximum Snow Depth

Rank	Station Name (Highest)	Inches	Rank	Station Name (Lowest)	Inches
1	Berne	25	1	Mount Vernon	9
2	Kokomo 3 WSW	24	2	Evansville Dress Regional Arpt	*12*
2	La Porte	24	2	Freelandville	*12*
2	Valparaiso Waterworks	*24*	4	Indianapolis Int'l Arpt	13
5	Angola	23	5	Bloomington Indiana Univ	*15*
5	South Bend Michiana Regional	23	5	Greenfield	15
7	English 4 S	*22*	5	Huntington	*15*
7	Evansville Museum	*22*	5	Indianapolis SE Side	15
7	Whitestown	22	9	Columbia City	16
10	Greensburg	21	9	Farmland 5 NNW	16
10	Richmond Water Works	21	9	Madison Sewage Plant	*16*
10	Tell City	21	9	Martinsville 2 SW	*16*
10	Winchester Airport 3E	21	9	Muncie Ball State Univ	*16*
14	Fort Wayne Baer Field	20	9	Oolitic Purdue Exp Farm	16
15	Columbus	*19*	15	Goshen College	17
15	Lafayette 8 S	19	16	Anderson Sewage Plant	*18*
17	Anderson Sewage Plant	*18*	16	Delphi 3 S	18
17	Delphi 3 S	18	16	Dubois S Ind Forage Frm	*18*
17	Dubois S Ind Forage Frm	*18*	16	Frankfort Disposal Plant	18
17	Frankfort Disposal Plant	18	16	Rockville	18
17	Rockville	18	21	Columbus	*19*
22	Goshen College	17	21	Lafayette 8 S	19
23	Columbia City	16	23	Fort Wayne Baer Field	20
23	Farmland 5 NNW	16	24	Greensburg	21
23	Madison Sewage Plant	*16*	24	Richmond Water Works	21

Rankings include 25 highest/lowest stations. If state has less than 25 stations, all stations are included. The period of record is 1980–2009. See User Guide for detailed explanation of data.

Number of Days Annually With ≥ 1.0 Inch Snow Depth

Highest

Rank	Station Name	Days
1	South Bend Michiana Regional	55
2	Angola	53
2	La Porte	53
4	Valparaiso Waterworks	*49*
5	Goshen College	43
6	Fort Wayne Baer Field	41
7	Kokomo 3 WSW	39
8	Columbia City	38
9	Berne	36
10	Farmland 5 NNW	34
11	Lafayette 8 S	31
11	Winchester Airport 3E	31
13	Muncie Ball State Univ	*29*
14	Frankfort Disposal Plant	28
14	Whitestown	28
16	Delphi 3 S	26
16	Greenfield	26
16	Indianapolis Int'l Arpt	26
19	Rockville	22
20	Huntington	*21*
20	Indianapolis SE Side	21
22	Richmond Water Works	20
23	Brookville	*19*
23	Oolitic Purdue Exp Farm	19
25	Anderson Sewage Plant	*17*

Lowest

Rank	Station Name	Days
1	Tell City	4
2	Shelbyville Sewage Plant	*6*
3	Mount Vernon	10
4	Dubois S Ind Forage Frm	*11*
4	Evansville Museum	*11*
4	Madison Sewage Plant	*11*
4	North Vernon 1 NW	*11*
8	English 4 S	*12*
8	Evansville Dress Regional Arpt	*12*
8	Martinsville 2 SW	*12*
11	Freelandville	*13*
12	Bloomington Indiana Univ	*15*
12	Columbus	*15*
14	Anderson Sewage Plant	*17*
14	Greensburg	17
16	Brookville	*19*
16	Oolitic Purdue Exp Farm	19
18	Richmond Water Works	20
19	Huntington	*21*
19	Indianapolis SE Side	21
21	Rockville	22
22	Delphi 3 S	26
22	Greenfield	26
22	Indianapolis Int'l Arpt	26
25	Frankfort Disposal Plant	28

Rankings include 25 highest/lowest stations. If state has less than 25 stations, all stations are included. The period of record is 1980–2009. See User Guide for detailed explanation of data.

Significant Storm Events in Indiana: 2000 – 2009

Location or County	Date	Type	Mag.	Deaths	Injuries	Property Damage ($mil.)	Crop Damage ($mil.)
Kosciusko	10/24/01	Tornado	F1	0	14	2.5	0.0
Marion	09/20/02	Tornado	F2	0	97	40.0	0.0
Johnson	09/20/02	Tornado	F3	0	0	25.0	0.0
Morgan	09/20/02	Tornado	F3	0	28	15.0	0.0
Central Indiana	07/05/03	Flood	na	0	0	41.6	12.0
Carroll, Harold, and Tippecanoe Counties	07/05/03	Flood	na	0	0	24.0	9.0
Howard	07/05/03	Flash Flood	na	0	0	18.0	0.0
Central Indiana	09/01/03	Flood	na	0	0	22.0	0.0
Marion	05/30/04	Tornado	F2	0	26	19.0	0.0
Crawford	05/30/04	Tornado	F3	1	11	5.0	0.0
Warrick	11/06/05	Tornado	F3	4	30	65.0	0.0
Vanderburgh	11/06/05	Tornado	F3	20	200	15.0	0.0
Daviess	11/15/05	Tornado	F3	0	31	11.6	0.0
Marion	05/30/08	Tornado	F2	0	18	29.0	0.0
Vigo	06/01/08	Flood	na	0	0	50.0	50.0
Johnson	06/03/08	Tornado	F2	0	3	23.0	0.0
Morgan	06/04/08	Flood	na	0	0	80.0	100.0
Owen	06/04/08	Flood	na	0	0	50.0	60.0
Clay	06/04/08	Flood	na	0	0	45.0	45.0
Greene	06/04/08	Flood	na	0	0	20.0	60.0
Bartholomew	06/05/08	Flood	na	0	0	150.0	150.0
Jackson	06/05/08	Flood	na	0	0	30.0	30.0
Daviess	06/05/08	Flood	na	0	0	20.0	30.0
Bartholomew	06/07/08	Flash Flood	na	0	0	100.0	0.0
Johnson	06/07/08	Flash Flood	na	0	0	90.0	90.0

Note: Deaths, injuries, and damages are date and location specific.

IOWA

PHYSICAL FEATURES. The State of Iowa comprises 56,290 square miles, primarily of rolling prairie, located in the middle latitudes between the Upper Mississippi and the Missouri Rivers. The interior continental location is 800 to 1,000 miles distant from the Gulf of Mexico, North Atlantic, and Hudson Bay. The North Pacific Ocean is approximately 1,300 miles west and the Rocky Mountains shield is some 400 to 700 miles west of Iowa.

The extreme north-south distance across Iowa is 205 miles; the extreme east-west distance, 310 miles. Elevational changes are small across the State, varying from 1,675 feet on Ocheyedan Mound in the northwest to 477 feet at the mouth of the Des Moines River in the southeast. There is some rugged terrain, mostly of forest soils, in the northeast. Most of the State's lakes are located in the northwest.

GENERAL CLIMATE. Iowa's climate, because of latitude and interior continental location, is characterized by marked seasonal variations. During the six warm months of the year the prevailing moist, southerly flow from the Gulf of Mexico produces a summer rainfall maximum. The prevailing northwesterly flow of dry Canadian air in the winter causes this season to be cold and relatively dry. At intervals throughout the year, airmasses from the Pacific Ocean moving across the western United States reach Iowa, producing comparatively mild and dry weather. The autumnal "Indian Summers" are a result of the dominance of these modified Pacific airmasses. Hot, dry winds, originating in the desert southwest United States, occasionally sweep into Iowa during the summer, producing unusually high temperatures.

TEMPERATURE. The average annual temperatures range from 46°F. in the northern counties to 52°F. in the southeastern counties. In July, the hottest month, the average daily maximum is around 85°F. and the daily minima are mostly in the lower 60s. In January daily maxima range from 24 to 34°F., north to south, and the minima from 4 to 14°F.. In almost every year at some location in the State, a maximum exceeds 100°F. and a minimum of less than -20°F. occurs. In half the years the maximum exceeds 104°F. and the minimum -31°F. The average number of days with temperatures 90°F. or higher range from six to 47. The number of days with zero or lower temperatures range from about 10 per year in the south to 30 in the north.

PRECIPITATION. Precipitation averages around 31 inches per year for the State, ranging from 25 inches in the extreme northwest to about 34 inches in the East Central and Southeast Divisions. However, annual totals vary widely from year to year and locality to locality. Nearly two-thirds of the annual precipitation is measured during the six months of April through September. Measurable rain occurs on about 100 days per year; the frequency of a tenth of an inch or more increases southeastward across the State from 44 days per year to 69 days. Half an inch or more of rain per day varies from 15 days in the extreme northwest to near 25 in the southeast.

SNOWFALL. The average seasonal snowfall varies from near 20 inches at Keokuk to 35-45 inches over northern counties. The season normally extends from October or November to April but measurable snow has fallen as late in the season as May and as early as September. The average number of days with snow cover one inch or deeper per season varies from about 40 days along the southern border to around 90 in the northernmost counties. The average date of the first 1-inch snowfall varies from November 25 in the north to December 10 in the southeast. The first trace of snow occurs about one month earlier. In about half the years a daily snowfall of five inches or more occurs over southern Iowa, six or more over central counties, and seven or eight over northern counties. Late winter snowstorms have produced as much as 31 inches of snow in a single storm and 24-hour amounts have exceeded 20 inches.

STORMS. Around 80 percent of the 40 to 50 thunderstorms per year occur in the warm half of the state. Occasionally hail, high winds, heavy rains, and even tornadoes, are associated with the thunderstorms. The probability of occurrence is highest in late spring and early summer. Tornado frequency is highest in May and June in the afternoon and early evening. Tornado occurrences average about 15 per year on eight days. Damaging hailstorms, reaching a maximum in early summer, average 58 per year. Severe hailstorms are slightly more frequent over northwestern counties. In any locality hail usually occurs from two to six times a year.

Floods are most frequent in June at the normal maximum rainfall period, but also occur near the end of March, usually as a consequence of rain on frozen ground, or rain and rapid snowmelt. Ice jams often contribute to the spring flooding.

High winds at 15 feet above the ground (house-top level) reach 50 m.p.h. in about half the years. Winds to 75 m.p.h. at the 15-foot-level, excluding gusts, may be expected once in 50 years.

Drought occurs periodically in Iowa.

Sunshine increases from northeast to southwest. The percent of the possible sunshine varies from 40-52 in December, the cloudiest month, to 72-76 in July, the sunniest month. Available solar energy is four times as abundant in July as in December. The growing season for warm weather crops extends from mid-May to early October. The spring growing season, suitable for hardy crops, lasts approximately six weeks and the autumn season about seven weeks.

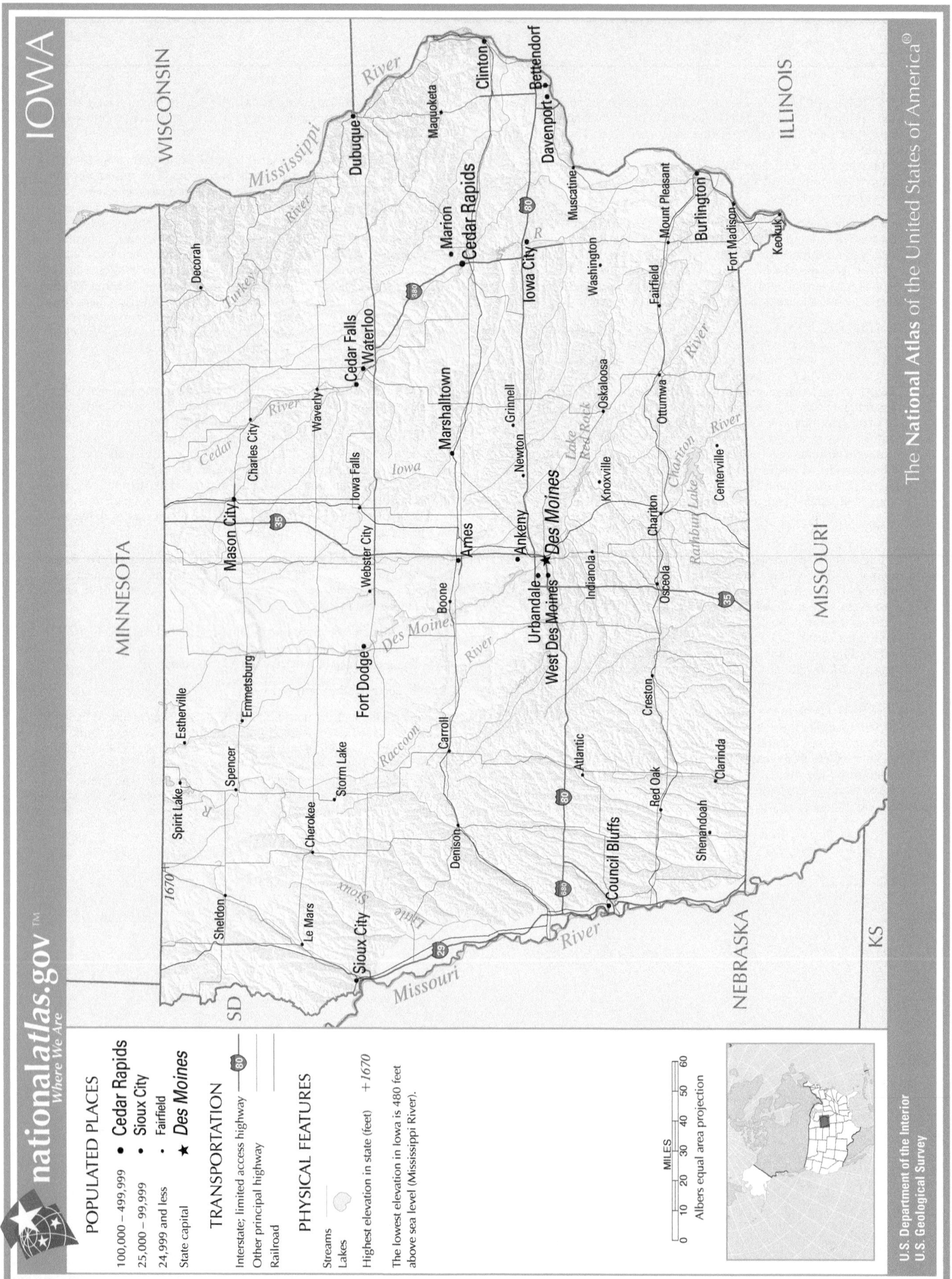
IOWA
nationalatlas.gov
Where We Are
POPULATED PLACES
100,000 – 499,999 Cedar Rapids
25,000 – 99,999 Sioux City
24,999 and less Fairfield
State capital Des Moines
TRANSPORTATION
Interstate; limited access highway
Other principal highway
Railroad
PHYSICAL FEATURES
Streams
Lakes
Highest elevation in state (feet) +1670
The lowest elevation in Iowa is 480 feet above sea level (Mississippi River).
MILES
0 10 20 30 40 50 60
Albers equal area projection
U.S. Department of the Interior
U.S. Geological Survey
The National Atlas of the United States of America®
MINNESOTA
WISCONSIN
ILLINOIS
MISSOURI
NEBRASKA
SD
KS
Mississippi River
Missouri River
Des Moines River
Cedar River
Iowa
Turkey River
Raccoon
Little Sioux
Chariton River
Lake Red Rock
Rathbun Lake
Decorah
Dubuque
Maquoketa
Clinton
Bettendorf
Davenport
Muscatine
Cedar Rapids
Marion
Iowa City
Washington
Mount Pleasant
Burlington
Fort Madison
Keokuk
Fairfield
Ottumwa
Oskaloosa
Centerville
Knoxville
Chariton
Osceola
Indianola
Des Moines
West Des Moines
Urbandale
Ankeny
Ames
Boone
Newton
Grinnell
Marshalltown
Cedar Falls
Waterloo
Waverly
Charles City
Mason City
Iowa Falls
Webster City
Fort Dodge
Estherville
Emmetsburg
Spencer
Spirit Lake
Storm Lake
Cherokee
Carroll
Denison
Sheldon
Le Mars
Sioux City
Council Bluffs
Atlantic
Creston
Red Oak
Clarinda
Shenandoah
1670
35
80
380
29
680

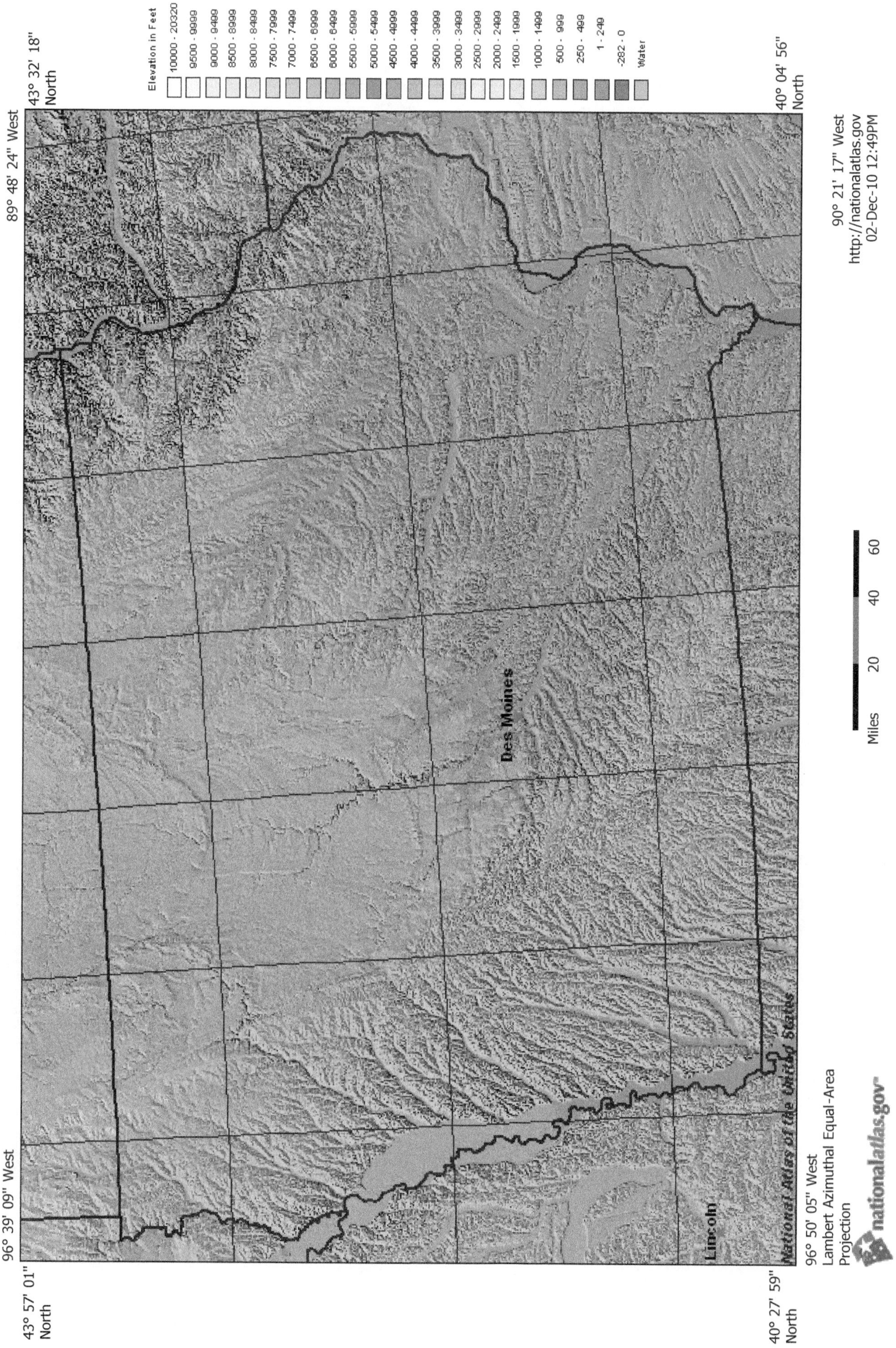
Elevation in Feet
10000 - 20320
9500 - 9999
9000 - 9499
8500 - 8999
8000 - 8499
7500 - 7999
7000 - 7499
6500 - 6999
6000 - 6499
5500 - 5999
5000 - 5499
4500 - 4999
4000 - 4499
3500 - 3999
3000 - 3499
2500 - 2999
2000 - 2499
1500 - 1999
1000 - 1499
500 - 999
250 - 499
1 - 249
-282 - 0
Water
43° 32' 18" North
89° 48' 24" West
40° 04' 56" North
90° 21' 17" West
http://nationalatlas.gov
02-Dec-10 12:49PM
Miles 20 40 60
Des Moines
Lincoln
National Atlas of the United States
96° 39' 09" West
43° 57' 01" North
40° 27' 59" North
96° 50' 05" West
Lambert Azimuthal Equal-Area Projection
nationalatlas.gov

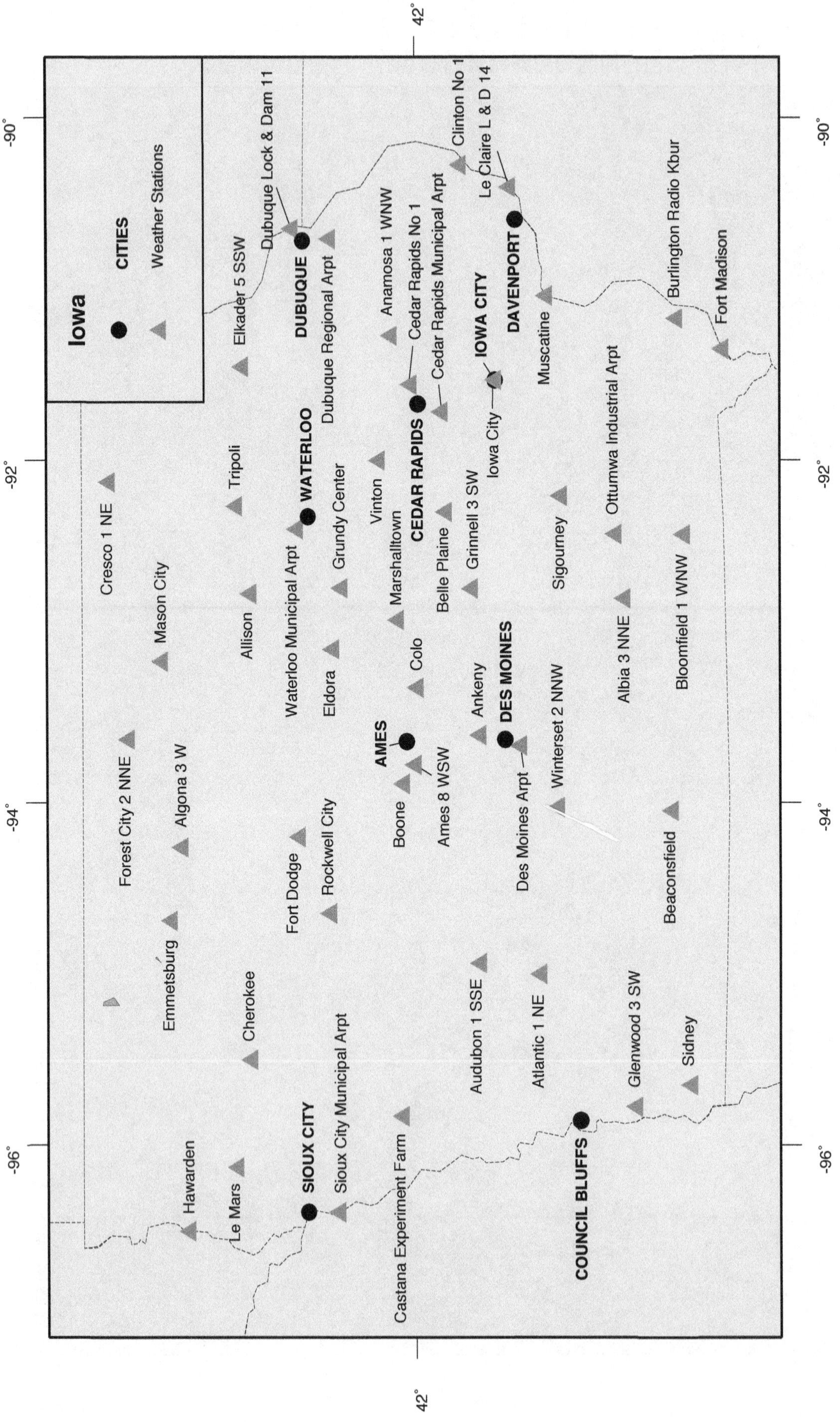
Iowa
CITIES
Weather Stations
-90°
-92°
-94°
-96°
42°
Cresco 1 NE
Mason City
Forest City 2 NNE
Algona 3 W
Emmetsburg
Hawarden
Le Mars
Cherokee
SIOUX CITY
Sioux City Municipal Arpt
Castana Experiment Farm
Elkader 5 SSW
Tripoli
Allison
WATERLOO
Waterloo Municipal Arpt
Fort Dodge
Rockwell City
Dubuque Lock & Dam 11
DUBUQUE
Dubuque Regional Arpt
Grundy Center
Eldora
Anamosa 1 WNW
Vinton
Marshalltown
Colo
AMES
Boone
Ames 8 WSW
Cedar Rapids No 1
Cedar Rapids Municipal Arpt
CEDAR RAPIDS
Belle Plaine
Grinnell 3 SW
Ankeny
Audubon 1 SSE
Clinton No 1
Le Claire L & D 14
IOWA CITY
Iowa City
DAVENPORT
DES MOINES
Des Moines Arpt
Winterset 2 NNW
Atlantic 1 NE
COUNCIL BLUFFS
Muscatine
Sigourney
Ottumwa Industrial Arpt
Albia 3 NNE
Glenwood 3 SW
Burlington Radio Kbur
Bloomfield 1 WNW
Beaconsfield
Sidney
Fort Madison

Iowa Weather Stations by County

County	Station Name
Audubon	Audubon 1 SSE
Benton	Belle Plaine Vinton
Black Hawk	Waterloo Municipal Arpt
Boone	Ames 8 WSW Boone
Bremer	Tripoli
Butler	Allison
Calhoun	Rockwell City
Cass	Atlantic 1 NE
Cerro Gordo	Mason City
Cherokee	Cherokee
Clayton	Elkader 5 SSW
Clinton	Clinton No 1
Davis	Bloomfield 1 WNW
Des Moines	Burlington Radio KBUR
Dubuque	Dubuque Lock & Dam 11 Dubuque Regional Arpt
Fremont	Sidney
Grundy	Grundy Center
Hardin	Eldora
Howard	Cresco 1 NE
Johnson	Iowa City
Jones	Anamosa 1 WNW
Keokuk	Sigourney
Kossuth	Algona 3 W
Lee	Fort Madison
Linn	Cedar Rapids Municipal Arpt Cedar Rapids No 1
Madison	Winterset 2 NNW
Marshall	Marshalltown
Mills	Glenwood 3 SW
Monona	Castana Experiment Farm
Monroe	Albia 3 NNE

County	Station Name
Muscatine	Muscatine
Palo Alto	Emmetsburg
Plymouth	Le Mars
Polk	Ankeny Des Moines Arpt
Poweshiek	Grinnell 3 SW
Ringgold	Beaconsfield
Scott	Le Claire L & D 14
Sioux	Hawarden
Story	Colo
Wapello	Ottumwa Industrial Arpt
Webster	Fort Dodge
Winnebago	Forest City 2 NNE
Woodbury	Sioux City Municipal Arpt

See User Guide for station inclusion criteria.

Iowa Weather Stations by City

City	Station Name	Miles
Ames	Ames 8 WSW	6.5
	Ankeny	21.8
	Boone	12.5
	Colo	16.7
Ankeny	Ames 8 WSW	21.3
	Ankeny	2.3
	Colo	24.7
	Des Moines Arpt	14.1
Bettendorf	Moline Quad City Arpt, IL	6.0
	Clinton No 1	20.8
	Le Claire L & D 14	5.0
Burlington	La Harpe, IL	17.3
	Burlington Radio KBUR	2.7
	Fort Madison	17.3
Cedar Falls	Allison	23.2
	Grundy Center	20.0
	Tripoli	22.5
	Waterloo Municipal Arpt	3.3
Cedar Rapids	Anamosa 1 WNW	21.1
	Cedar Rapids Municipal Arpt	7.6
	Cedar Rapids No 1	5.6
	Iowa City	24.4
	Vinton	20.8
Clinton	Fulton L&D #13, IL	4.4
	Clinton No 1	4.7
	Le Claire L & D 14	22.0
Council Bluffs	Glenwood 3 SW	18.5
	Omaha Eppley Airfield, NE	4.5
	Omaha WSFO, NE	11.0
Davenport	Moline Quad City Arpt, IL	6.8
	Clinton No 1	24.1
	Le Claire L & D 14	9.8
Des Moines	Ankeny	9.1
	Des Moines Arpt	4.6
Dubuque	Dubuque Lock & Dam 11	2.8
	Dubuque Regional Arpt	7.3
	Lancaster 4 WSW, WI	23.1
Fort Dodge	Fort Dodge	1.3
	Rockwell City	24.4
Iowa City	Cedar Rapids Municipal Arpt	18.5
	Iowa City	0.4
Marion	Anamosa 1 WNW	15.8
	Cedar Rapids Municipal Arpt	12.5
	Cedar Rapids No 1	0.4
	Vinton	22.8
Marshalltown	Colo	20.6
	Eldora	24.5
	Grinnell 3 SW	23.9
	Grundy Center	22.8
	Marshalltown	2.0

City	Station Name	Miles
Mason City	Forest City 2 NNE	23.8
	Mason City	1.2
Muscatine	Aledo, IL	22.3
	Muscatine	2.0
Ottumwa	Albia 3 NNE	19.4
	Bloomfield 1 WNW	17.3
	Ottumwa Industrial Arpt	6.0
	Sigourney	24.6
Sioux City	Le Mars	23.0
	Sioux City Municipal Arpt	8.2
	Walthill, NE	24.8
Urbandale	Ankeny	10.2
	Des Moines Arpt	7.8
	Winterset 2 NNW	24.2
Waterloo	Grundy Center	23.3
	Tripoli	23.1
	Waterloo Municipal Arpt	5.1
West Des Moines	Ankeny	13.6
	Des Moines Arpt	5.5
	Winterset 2 NNW	20.5

Note: Miles is the distance between the geographic center of the city and the weather station.

Iowa Weather Stations by Elevation

Feet	Station Name
1,450	Castana Experiment Farm
1,299	Forest City 2 NNE
1,290	Audubon 1 SSE
1,270	Emmetsburg
1,254	Cresco 1 NE
1,229	Algona 3 W
1,200	Beaconsfield
1,194	Le Mars
1,194	Rockwell City
1,189	Hawarden
1,180	Cherokee
1,160	Atlantic 1 NE
1,144	Eldora
1,129	Sidney
1,115	Fort Dodge
1,099	Ames 8 WSW
1,092	Sioux City Municipal Arpt
1,089	Mason City
1,069	Winterset 2 NNW
1,056	Dubuque Regional Arpt
1,050	Boone
1,049	Allison
1,020	Grundy Center
1,000	Colo
979	Glenwood 3 SW
959	Tripoli
957	Des Moines Arpt
939	Ankeny
904	Grinnell 3 SW
879	Albia 3 NNE
870	Marshalltown
865	Waterloo Municipal Arpt
850	Cedar Rapids No 1
850	Vinton
841	Ottumwa Industrial Arpt
839	Cedar Rapids Municipal Arpt
812	Bloomfield 1 WNW
810	Belle Plaine
805	Anamosa 1 WNW
799	Sigourney
770	Elkader 5 SSW
703	Burlington Radio KBUR
640	Iowa City
620	Dubuque Lock & Dam 11
584	Clinton No 1
577	Le Claire L & D 14
548	Muscatine
529	Fort Madison

See User Guide for station inclusion criteria.

Des Moines Airport

Located in the heart of North America, Des Moines has a climate which is continental in character. This results in a marked seasonal contrast in both temperature and precipitation. There is a gently rolling terrain in and around the Des Moines metropolitan area. Drainage of the area is generally to the southeast to the Des Moines River and its tributaries.

Since agriculture and services for it are the mainstay of the area, it is convenient to separate the year into arbitrary seasons corresponding to the growing seasons of the principal crops of the section. The winter season, when most plant life is dormant, is from mid-November to late March. The summer season, when corn and soybeans can be grown, lasts from early May to early October. The spring growing season, including part of the growing season of oats and forage crops, and the fall harvest season, each runs about 6 weeks. There is a large variation in annual precipitation from a minimum of about 17 inches to a maximum of about 56 inches. The average annual snowfall is 32 inches. Annual variation of snowfall is also large, ranging from a minimum of about eight inches to as much as 72 inches.

The winter is a season of cold dry air, interrupted by occasional storms of short duration. At the beginning and the end of the season, the precipitation may occur as rain, but during the major portion of the season it falls as snow. Drifting snow may be extensive and impede transportation. The average precipitation for this season is approximately 20 percent of the annual amount. Although occasional cold waves follow the storms, bitterly cold days on which the temperatures fail to rise above zero occur on an average of only three days in four years.

The average growing season with temperatures above 32 degrees normally spans 160 to 165 days between late April and mid-October. The growing season is characterized by prevailing southerly winds and precipitation falling primarily as showers and thunderstorms, occasionally with damaging wind, erosive downpours or hail. Some 60 percent of the annual precipitation falls during the crop season with the maximum rate normally in late May and June. The autumn is characteristically sunny with diminishing precipitation, a condition favorable for drying and harvesting crops.

Des Moines Airport *Polk County* Elevation: 957 ft. Latitude: 41° 32' N Longitude: 93° 40' W

	JAN	FEB	MAR	APR	MAY	JUN	JUL	AUG	SEP	OCT	NOV	DEC	YEAR
Mean Maximum Temp. (°F)	31.2	36.0	48.7	62.0	72.4	81.5	85.8	83.7	76.2	62.8	48.0	34.1	60.2
Mean Temp. (°F)	22.7	27.3	38.9	51.3	62.1	71.6	76.2	74.1	65.5	52.6	39.1	25.9	50.6
Mean Minimum Temp. (°F)	14.1	18.5	29.0	40.5	51.7	61.6	66.5	64.4	54.7	42.4	30.1	17.7	40.9
Extreme Maximum Temp. (°F)	67	70	91	93	93	103	104	108	98	92	81	69	108
Extreme Minimum Temp. (°F)	-22	-26	-9	10	30	41	50	41	28	18	-4	-22	-26
Days Maximum Temp. ≥ 90°F	0	0	0	0	0	4	9	6	2	0	0	0	21
Days Maximum Temp. ≤ 32°F	16	11	4	0	0	0	0	0	0	0	3	13	47
Days Minimum Temp. ≤ 32°F	30	24	20	6	0	0	0	0	0	5	18	28	131
Days Minimum Temp. ≤ 0°F	5	3	0	0	0	0	0	0	0	0	0	4	12
Heating Degree Days (base 65°F)	1,305	1,060	804	421	145	16	1	5	93	391	772	1,206	6,219
Cooling Degree Days (base 65°F)	0	0	2	15	61	221	354	294	115	13	0	0	1,075
Mean Precipitation (in.)	0.95	1.24	2.23	3.74	4.64	4.68	4.34	4.01	2.94	2.68	2.12	1.41	34.98
Maximum Precipitation (in.)*	4.4	3.0	5.8	7.8	7.9	9.5	10.5	13.7	10.2	6.9	6.5	3.4	55.9
Minimum Precipitation (in.)*	0.1	0.1	0.2	0.2	1.2	1.0	trace	0.3	0.4	trace	trace	0.1	17.1
Extreme Maximum Daily Precip. (in.)	1.51	1.58	2.11	2.68	3.23	4.23	3.18	3.45	3.29	2.23	3.55	1.48	4.23
Days With ≥ 0.1" Precipitation	3	3	5	7	9	7	7	6	5	5	4	4	65
Days With ≥ 0.5" Precipitation	0	1	1	3	3	3	3	3	2	2	1	1	23
Days With ≥ 1.0" Precipitation	0	0	0	1	1	1	1	1	1	1	0	0	7
Mean Snowfall (in.)	***8.6***	***8.3***	***4.8***	***1.9***	***trace***	***trace***	***trace***	***0.0***	***trace***	***0.5***	***3.4***	***8.4***	***35.9***
Maximum Snowfall (in.)*	19	21	19	16	trace	0	0	0	trace	7	15	24	76
Maximum 24-hr. Snowfall (in.)*	14	10	8	10	trace	0	0	0	trace	7	12	10	14
Maximum Snow Depth (in.)	19	14	14	6	trace	trace	trace	0	trace	5	9	16	19
Days With ≥ 1.0" Snow Depth	17	14	5	1	0	0	0	0	0	0	2	12	51
Thunderstorm Days*	< 1	< 1	2	4	7	9	8	7	5	3	1	< 1	46
Foggy Days*	10	10	11	10	9	7	7	10	9	8	10	12	113
Predominant Sky Cover*	OVR	OVR	OVR	OVR	OVR	OVR	CLR	CLR	CLR	CLR	OVR	OVR	OVR
Mean Relative Humidity 6am (%)*	77	79	80	78	79	81	84	86	85	80	79	80	81
Mean Relative Humidity 3pm (%)*	65	63	57	50	51	53	53	54	52	50	59	66	56
Mean Dewpoint (°F)*	12	17	26	37	48	59	64	62	53	41	29	18	39
Prevailing Wind Direction*	NW	NW	NW	NW	S	S	S	S	S	S	NW	NW	S
Prevailing Wind Speed (mph)*	15	15	15	16	12	12	9	9	10	10	15	15	13
Maximum Wind Gust (mph)*	59	62	58	67	59	76	83	73	54	61	62	56	83

Note: (*) Period of record is 1945-1995

The period of record for National Weather Service station data is 1980 – 2009 except where noted. See User Guide for detailed explanation of data.

Dubuque Regional Airport

The terrain around Dubuque varies from gently rolling, 10 to 15 miles to the south and west, to steep hills and bluffs around the city and along the Mississippi River.

The principal feature of the climate in Dubuque is its variety. The Dubuque area is subject to weather ranging from the cold, dry, arctic air masses in the winter, with readings as low as 32 degrees below zero, to the hot, dry weather of the desert southwest in the summer when the temperatures reach about 110. More often the area is covered by mild Pacific air that has lost considerable moisture in crossing the mountains far to the west, or by cool, dry Canadian air, or by warm, moist air from the Gulf regions. Most of the year the latter three types of air masses dominate Dubuque weather, with the invasions of Gulf air rarely occurring in the winter.

The seasons vary widely from year to year at Dubuque. For example, successive invasions of cold air from the north may bring a long, cold winter with snow-covered ground from mid November until March and many days of sub-zero temperatures. Another winter can be mild with bare ground most of the season and only a few sub-zero temperature readings. The summers, too, may vary from hot and humid with considerable thunderstorm activity when the Gulf air prevails, to relatively cool, dry weather when air of northerly origin dominates the season.

All seasons are marked by storms that accompany the changes from one type of air mass to another. In winter, rain changes to sleet and snow, and occasionally a peal of thunder is heard at the height of a snowstorm. In summer, thunderstorms are frequently heavy. They are occasionally accompanied by hail and on rare occasions by tornadoes. Thunderstorms have been sufficiently intense at times to raise the Mississippi River, which is about one-fourth mile wide at Debuque, nearly five feet overnight. Flash floods have drowned many people.

Most of the precipitation occurs during the spring and fall seasons. The last occurrence of snow and freezing rain can be in late May, and the first occurrence in late September.

While the climate of Dubuque does not lack for variety, there are times when a particular weather condition may persist for an extended period. Cold weather has lasted as long as 20 days in succession with sub-zero readings. Heat waves have persisted for 10 or more days with readings around 100 degrees each day. Hot, dry spells occasionally plague the crops and livestock in summer, but there are frequent periods of mild, dry weather in the spring and frequently in the autumn.

Dubuque Regional Airport *Dubuque County* Elevation: 1,056 ft. Latitude: 42° 24' N Longitude: 90° 42' W

	JAN	FEB	MAR	APR	MAY	JUN	JUL	AUG	SEP	OCT	NOV	DEC	YEAR
Mean Maximum Temp. (°F)	27.2	31.6	44.0	58.4	69.2	78.7	82.0	79.9	72.6	59.8	44.8	30.5	56.6
Mean Temp. (°F)	19.5	23.8	35.2	48.2	58.7	68.5	72.1	70.1	62.1	49.9	36.7	23.1	47.3
Mean Minimum Temp. (°F)	11.8	15.9	26.4	37.8	48.2	58.3	62.1	60.3	51.7	40.1	28.5	15.6	38.1
Extreme Maximum Temp. (°F)	60	66	85	93	91	100	101	100	95	90	75	67	101
Extreme Minimum Temp. (°F)	-30	-27	-13	13	21	37	44	40	28	19	1	-25	-30
Days Maximum Temp. ≥ 90°F	0	0	0	0	0	2	4	2	1	0	0	0	9
Days Maximum Temp. ≤ 32°F	20	14	5	0	0	0	0	0	0	0	4	16	59
Days Minimum Temp. ≤ 32°F	30	26	23	8	1	0	0	0	1	7	20	29	145
Days Minimum Temp. ≤ 0°F	7	4	1	0	0	0	0	0	0	0	0	5	17
Heating Degree Days (base 65°F)	1,404	1,160	917	505	222	36	7	18	145	467	843	1,293	7,017
Cooling Degree Days (base 65°F)	0	0	0	6	34	149	233	184	66	7	0	0	679
Mean Precipitation (in.)	1.15	1.48	2.36	3.58	4.13	4.50	3.89	4.62	3.59	2.73	2.36	1.82	36.21
Maximum Precipitation (in.)*	6.0	3.6	6.5	7.7	9.4	10.5	12.2	9.9	15.5	8.6	10.6	4.1	63.3
Minimum Precipitation (in.)*	0.3	0.1	0.4	0.8	0.7	0.7	0.9	0.1	0.1	trace	0.4	0.1	22.6
Extreme Maximum Daily Precip. (in.)	1.13	1.34	2.54	2.15	2.39	3.84	3.91	5.99	2.65	2.38	2.27	2.00	5.99
Days With ≥ 0.1" Precipitation	4	4	5	7	8	8	6	6	6	6	5	4	69
Days With ≥ 0.5" Precipitation	0	1	1	2	3	3	3	3	2	2	2	1	23
Days With ≥ 1.0" Precipitation	0	0	0	1	1	1	1	1	1	1	0	0	7
Mean Snowfall (in.)	10.0	9.0	6.4	2.2	trace	trace	0.0	trace	0.0	0.1	2.9	10.7	41.3
Maximum Snowfall (in.)*	29	25	30	20	3	0	0	0	0	2	14	26	74
Maximum 24-hr. Snowfall (in.)*	11	10	15	9	3	0	0	0	0	2	10	14	15
Maximum Snow Depth (in.)	na	na	na	na	na	na	na	na	na	na	na	na	na
Days With ≥ 1.0" Snow Depth	na	na	na	na	na	na	na	na	na	na	na	na	na
Thunderstorm Days*	< 1	< 1	2	3	5	6	6	6	3	2	1	< 1	34
Foggy Days*	12	11	11	9	9	8	11	13	11	9	11	13	128
Predominant Sky Cover*	OVR	OVR	OVR	OVR	OVR	OVR	OVR	OVR	OVR	OVR	OVR	OVR	OVR
Mean Relative Humidity 6am (%)*	78	79	80	77	78	82	86	88	87	82	82	82	82
Mean Relative Humidity 3pm (%)*	68	64	59	52	52	55	57	58	56	53	62	70	59
Mean Dewpoint (°F)*	10	15	24	35	46	57	62	61	52	40	27	17	37
Prevailing Wind Direction*	WNW	S	NW	S	S	S	SSW	S	S	S	S	S	S
Prevailing Wind Speed (mph)*	14	13	15	15	14	13	12	10	12	14	14	14	13
Maximum Wind Gust (mph)*	58	53	62	68	74	55	74	67	58	54	55	59	74

Note: (*) Period of record is 1951-1995

Sioux City Municipal Airport

Sioux City is located along the Missouri River at a point where Iowa boarders both Nebraska and South Dakota. Except for the river valleys, the countryside is rolling. The Sioux City business section lies in the river valley and the residential sections, for the most part, are spread over the hills which range from 100 to 200 feet higher than the valley. The local topography causes minor variations in wind and temperature.

Located in the midland of a continent and in the northern half of the Great Plains, the climate of Sioux City is typically continental and is largely determined by the movement and interaction of the large-scale weather systems. Under normal conditions, winters are cold and summers warm, and most of the precipitation comes during the warmer months from April to September. There is considerable fluctuation in temperature and precipitation from season to season and from year to year, as elsewhere in the northern plains. Except for an occasional dry year, the climate is quite favorable for agriculture with corn, the small grains, and grasses producing abundantly.

The grass usually starts to grow about the middle of April. The growing season averages about 160 days. Summers are sunny and most summer rains are associated with showers or thunderstorms. Winds are lightest in the summer months, except for occasional strong gusts with thunderstorms. Winds gradually increase in autumn and winter and usually reach their highest average velocities in April.

Sioux City Municipal Airport *Woodbury County* Elevation: 1,092 ft. Latitude: 42° 23' N Longitude: 96° 23' W

	JAN	FEB	MAR	APR	MAY	JUN	JUL	AUG	SEP	OCT	NOV	DEC	YEAR
Mean Maximum Temp. (°F)	30.8	35.1	47.4	62.1	73.0	82.0	85.8	83.3	76.3	63.0	46.5	32.3	59.8
Mean Temp. (°F)	21.0	25.6	36.7	49.7	61.2	70.6	74.8	72.4	63.8	50.8	36.1	23.1	48.8
Mean Minimum Temp. (°F)	11.1	16.0	25.9	37.3	49.4	59.2	63.8	61.5	51.2	38.5	25.8	13.8	37.8
Extreme Maximum Temp. (°F)	71	71	89	97	101	108	108	102	103	94	82	70	108
Extreme Minimum Temp. (°F)	-22	-23	-14	12	25	39	44	39	25	12	-9	-24	-24
Days Maximum Temp. ≥ 90°F	0	0	0	1	1	6	9	6	3	0	0	0	26
Days Maximum Temp. ≤ 32°F	16	12	4	0	0	0	0	0	0	0	4	14	50
Days Minimum Temp. ≤ 32°F	31	26	23	10	1	0	0	0	1	9	23	30	154
Days Minimum Temp. ≤ 0°F	7	4	1	0	0	0	0	0	0	0	0	5	17
Heating Degree Days (base 65°F)	1,360	1,108	871	465	170	25	2	10	123	444	859	1,295	6,732
Cooling Degree Days (base 65°F)	0	0	0	14	59	201	313	246	92	10	0	0	935
Mean Precipitation (in.)	0.59	0.65	1.99	2.95	3.82	3.71	3.15	3.27	2.91	2.14	1.29	0.78	27.25
Maximum Precipitation (in.)*	2.4	2.7	5.9	6.7	8.5	8.8	10.3	7.8	9.7	5.3	4.1	2.2	35.0
Minimum Precipitation (in.)*	0.1	0.1	trace	0.5	0.6	0.5	0.4	0.1	0.1	trace	trace	0.1	14.3
Extreme Maximum Daily Precip. (in.)	1.09	1.28	2.25	2.09	2.10	2.71	4.51	3.19	3.07	2.25	1.74	0.99	4.51
Days With ≥ 0.1" Precipitation	2	2	4	6	7	7	6	6	5	4	3	2	54
Days With ≥ 0.5" Precipitation	0	0	1	2	3	3	2	2	2	2	1	0	18
Days With ≥ 1.0" Precipitation	0	0	1	1	1	1	1	1	1	0	0	0	7
Mean Snowfall (in.)	7.1	6.6	6.6	1.8	trace	trace	trace	0.0	trace	1.2	4.2	7.6	35.1
Maximum Snowfall (in.)*	29	25	26	10	trace	0	0	0	trace	10	17	21	65
Maximum 24-hr. Snowfall (in.)*	17	14	12	7	trace	0	0	0	trace	9	12	9	17
Maximum Snow Depth (in.)	19	27	16	8	trace	trace	trace	0	trace	4	13	20	27
Days With ≥ 1.0" Snow Depth	17	12	6	1	0	0	0	0	0	0	4	14	54
Thunderstorm Days*	< 1	< 1	1	3	7	8	8	7	5	2	< 1	< 1	41
Foggy Days*	9	9	10	7	7	5	6	10	8	7	9	11	98
Predominant Sky Cover*	OVR	OVR	OVR	OVR	OVR	OVR	CLR	CLR	CLR	CLR	OVR	OVR	OVR
Mean Relative Humidity 6am (%)*	78	79	81	78	80	82	86	88	86	81	81	81	82
Mean Relative Humidity 3pm (%)*	64	62	58	46	48	50	53	54	50	46	56	65	54
Mean Dewpoint (°F)*	10	16	25	35	47	58	63	62	52	39	26	16	38
Prevailing Wind Direction*	NW	NW	NW	NW	SE	SSE	SSE	SE	SE	SE	NW	NW	NW
Prevailing Wind Speed (mph)*	15	15	15	16	12	13	12	9	9	10	16	15	13
Maximum Wind Gust (mph)*	66	66	62	71	64	75	68	60	76	53	69	60	76

Note: (*) Period of record is 1948-1995

Waterloo Municipal Airport

Waterloo is situated on the banks of the Cedar River in northeast Iowa, and has a continental humid climate. A wide variation is experienced in both temperature and precipitation during the four distinct seasons.

The distribution of precipitation through the year is very favorable for agriculture with an average 72 percent of the annual total falling in the April to September crop season. The annual temperature range is large. January, the coldest month, averages near 14 degrees and July, the warmest month, averages about 73 degrees. Extreme temperatures range from about -35 to 112 degrees.

It is sometimes convenient to divide the year into periods corresponding to the growing season of the area. Winter extends from November through March, based on a mean daily temperature of 40 degrees. The winter period is a season of cold, dry weather occasionally broken by storms of short duration. Precipitation during the winter is mainly snow with rain dominant at the beginning and end of the season. Annual snowfall varies considerably from year to year. Temperatures of zero degrees or below occur on average about 29 days per year. Bitterly cold days with high temperatures of zero degrees or lower average about three days per year. During the winter, prevailing winds are from the northwest.

The spring growing season is marked by an increase in both frequency and intensity of rainfall and by a rapid increase in the mean daily temperature. Spring extends from the first of April to mid May, when daily mean temperatures range between 40 and 59 degrees.

The summer growing season extends from mid May to mid September, based on a mean daily temperature of 60 degrees. Precipitation increases during the spring and reaches a maximum monthly amount in July. In summer, precipitation falls mainly from thunderstorms, three-fourths of which occur during the summer growing season. The prevailing summer wind is southerly, supplying moisture from the Gulf of Mexico. Daily temperatures reach their highest level in July or early August.

The fall growing season extends from mid September to the first part of November, by which time the mean daily temperature has fallen to 40 degrees. Precipitation declines and frequent periods of warm days, cool nights, and cloudless, but hazy, skies persist.

Waterloo Municipal Airport *Black Hawk County* Elevation: 865 ft. Latitude: 42° 33' N Longitude: 92° 24' W

	JAN	FEB	MAR	APR	MAY	JUN	JUL	AUG	SEP	OCT	NOV	DEC	YEAR
Mean Maximum Temp. (°F)	27.3	31.8	44.9	60.1	71.6	80.8	84.2	81.8	75.0	61.2	45.6	30.9	57.9
Mean Temp. (°F)	18.4	23.1	35.3	48.4	60.2	69.7	73.4	70.9	62.8	49.8	36.1	22.4	47.5
Mean Minimum Temp. (°F)	9.4	14.4	25.6	36.8	48.7	58.6	62.5	59.9	50.5	38.4	26.5	13.8	37.1
Extreme Maximum Temp. (°F)	65	66	87	100	93	103	105	105	98	95	80	67	105
Extreme Minimum Temp. (°F)	-34	-31	-12	-4	22	39	42	39	26	11	-4	-29	-34
Days Maximum Temp. ≥ 90°F	0	0	0	0	1	4	6	4	2	0	0	0	17
Days Maximum Temp. ≤ 32°F	20	13	5	0	0	0	0	0	0	0	4	16	58
Days Minimum Temp. ≤ 32°F	30	26	23	10	1	0	0	0	1	10	22	29	152
Days Minimum Temp. ≤ 0°F	8	6	1	0	0	0	0	0	0	0	0	6	21
Heating Degree Days (base 65°F)	1,440	1,179	915	499	189	27	4	16	138	473	861	1,315	7,056
Cooling Degree Days (base 65°F)	0	0	1	9	47	175	272	205	78	9	0	0	796
Mean Precipitation (in.)	0.81	0.98	2.06	3.57	4.56	5.00	4.62	4.27	2.68	2.52	1.97	1.18	34.22
Maximum Precipitation (in.)*	1.8	3.5	5.4	8.5	7.7	10.1	12.6	9.6	11.4	5.4	5.6	3.8	53.1
Minimum Precipitation (in.)*	0.1	trace	0.2	0.9	0.8	1.4	1.1	0.4	0.5	trace	0.1	0.2	19.0
Extreme Maximum Daily Precip. (in.)	0.91	1.32	1.95	3.05	3.41	4.35	5.50	3.62	2.35	2.33	3.00	1.68	5.50
Days With ≥ 0.1" Precipitation	2	3	5	7	8	8	7	6	5	5	4	3	63
Days With ≥ 0.5" Precipitation	0	0	1	2	3	4	3	3	2	2	1	0	21
Days With ≥ 1.0" Precipitation	0	0	0	1	1	1	1	1	1	1	0	0	7
Mean Snowfall (in.)	***8.6***	***7.0***	***4.6***	***2.0***	***0.0***	***trace***	***trace***	***0.0***	***0.0***	***0.2***	***3.3***	***9.1***	***34.8***
Maximum Snowfall (in.)*	18	24	16	10	trace	0	0	0	0	1	16	20	56
Maximum 24-hr. Snowfall (in.)*	13	8	8	6	trace	0	0	0	0	1	9	10	13
Maximum Snow Depth (in.)	***18***	***15***	***11***	***6***	***trace***	***trace***	***trace***	***0***	***0***	***trace***	***11***	***16***	***18***
Days With ≥ 1.0" Snow Depth	***20***	***18***	***7***	***1***	***0***	***0***	***0***	***0***	***0***	***0***	***3***	***17***	***66***
Thunderstorm Days*	< 1	< 1	2	4	6	8	8	7	5	2	< 1	< 1	42
Foggy Days*	10	11	13	11	10	8	10	13	12	10	13	13	134
Predominant Sky Cover*	OVR	OVR	OVR	OVR	OVR	OVR	SCT	CLR	OVR	OVR	OVR	OVR	OVR
Mean Relative Humidity 6am (%)*	77	80	82	81	81	83	87	90	89	84	83	82	83
Mean Relative Humidity 3pm (%)*	68	66	62	52	51	51	55	55	55	52	62	70	58
Mean Dewpoint (°F)*	8	14	25	35	47	57	63	61	52	39	28	15	37
Prevailing Wind Direction*	NW	NW	NW	NW	S	S	S	S	S	NW	NW	NW	NW
Prevailing Wind Speed (mph)*	14	14	15	15	12	12	10	10	10	13	14	14	13
Maximum Wind Gust (mph)*	58	52	59	76	68	86	105	51	53	49	59	53	105

Note: (*) Period of record is 1960-1995

Albia 3 NNE *Monroe County* Elevation: 879 ft. Latitude: 41° 04' N Longitude: 92° 47' W

	JAN	FEB	MAR	APR	MAY	JUN	JUL	AUG	SEP	OCT	NOV	DEC	YEAR
Mean Maximum Temp. (°F)	33.4	37.6	49.6	62.4	72.1	80.9	85.5	83.7	76.4	63.7	49.3	35.3	60.8
Mean Temp. (°F)	24.5	28.3	39.2	51.1	61.4	70.5	75.1	73.4	65.1	52.9	40.0	26.8	50.7
Mean Minimum Temp. (°F)	15.4	18.9	28.7	39.8	50.5	60.1	64.7	63.0	53.8	42.1	30.7	18.1	40.5
Extreme Maximum Temp. (°F)	71	71	86	89	90	101	106	105	98	91	79	71	106
Extreme Minimum Temp. (°F)	-24	-31	-8	16	26	40	48	41	30	16	-7	-26	-31
Days Maximum Temp. ≥ 90°F	0	0	0	0	0	2	8	6	2	0	0	0	18
Days Maximum Temp. ≤ 32°F	14	10	3	0	0	0	0	0	0	0	2	12	41
Days Minimum Temp. ≤ 32°F	28	24	20	7	0	0	0	0	0	5	17	28	129
Days Minimum Temp. ≤ 0°F	5	3	0	0	0	0	0	0	0	0	0	3	11
Heating Degree Days (base 65°F)	1,251	1,032	796	424	157	21	2	8	97	383	743	1,179	6,093
Cooling Degree Days (base 65°F)	0	0	2	14	52	194	324	274	107	15	0	0	982
Mean Precipitation (in.)	1.00	1.42	2.14	3.63	4.63	4.60	4.96	4.18	3.94	2.75	2.47	1.51	37.23
Extreme Maximum Daily Precip. (in.)	1.11	2.23	1.86	2.14	2.22	4.83	7.25	3.48	4.61	2.51	2.25	2.28	7.25
Days With ≥ 0.1" Precipitation	3	4	5	7	9	7	7	6	6	5	5	4	68
Days With ≥ 0.5" Precipitation	1	1	1	3	4	3	3	3	3	2	2	1	27
Days With ≥ 1.0" Precipitation	0	0	0	1	1	1	1	1	1	0	1	0	7
Mean Snowfall (in.)	6.2	6.6	4.0	1.5	0.0	0.0	0.0	0.0	0.0	0.6	1.7	6.8	27.4
Maximum Snow Depth (in.)	19	16	11	12	0	0	0	0	0	8	10	19	19
Days With ≥ 1.0" Snow Depth	13	12	4	1	0	0	0	0	0	0	2	10	42

Algona 3 W *Kossuth County* Elevation: 1,229 ft. Latitude: 43° 04' N Longitude: 94° 18' W

	JAN	FEB	MAR	APR	MAY	JUN	JUL	AUG	SEP	OCT	NOV	DEC	YEAR
Mean Maximum Temp. (°F)	25.3	29.7	42.5	58.7	70.7	79.7	82.6	80.0	73.7	60.4	43.2	27.9	56.2
Mean Temp. (°F)	16.5	21.1	33.3	47.2	59.3	68.8	72.2	69.7	62.1	49.3	34.1	19.7	46.1
Mean Minimum Temp. (°F)	7.6	12.4	24.1	35.7	47.9	57.8	61.7	59.3	50.4	38.1	24.9	11.5	35.9
Extreme Maximum Temp. (°F)	64	65	83	93	94	105	101	101	97	94	80	68	105
Extreme Minimum Temp. (°F)	-26	-29	-11	9	26	40	47	41	24	14	-11	-30	-30
Days Maximum Temp. ≥ 90°F	0	0	0	0	1	3	4	2	1	0	0	0	11
Days Maximum Temp. ≤ 32°F	22	16	6	0	0	0	0	0	0	0	6	19	69
Days Minimum Temp. ≤ 32°F	31	27	25	11	1	0	0	0	1	9	24	30	159
Days Minimum Temp. ≤ 0°F	10	6	1	0	0	0	0	0	0	0	1	7	25
Heating Degree Days (base 65°F)	1,499	1,236	976	533	210	36	7	20	147	488	921	1,398	7,471
Cooling Degree Days (base 65°F)	0	0	0	6	41	156	236	173	66	7	0	0	685
Mean Precipitation (in.)	0.69	0.71	1.69	3.16	4.23	5.10	4.32	4.06	2.89	2.34	1.58	0.98	31.75
Extreme Maximum Daily Precip. (in.)	0.83	1.24	1.77	2.11	3.00	5.09	2.49	6.90	3.24	1.68	2.42	1.03	6.90
Days With ≥ 0.1" Precipitation	2	2	4	6	8	8	7	6	5	5	3	3	59
Days With ≥ 0.5" Precipitation	0	0	1	3	3	4	3	3	2	2	1	0	22
Days With ≥ 1.0" Precipitation	0	0	0	1	1	1	1	1	1	1	0	0	7
Mean Snowfall (in.)	8.9	7.1	5.4	2.5	trace	0.0	0.0	0.0	0.0	0.4	4.5	9.2	38.0
Maximum Snow Depth (in.)	40	35	27	7	trace	0	0	0	0	trace	14	38	40
Days With ≥ 1.0" Snow Depth	22	19	8	1	0	0	0	0	0	0	5	18	73

Allison *Butler County* Elevation: 1,049 ft. Latitude: 42° 45' N Longitude: 92° 47' W

	JAN	FEB	MAR	APR	MAY	JUN	JUL	AUG	SEP	OCT	NOV	DEC	YEAR
Mean Maximum Temp. (°F)	27.0	31.6	44.5	60.2	71.9	80.9	83.8	81.3	74.7	61.4	44.9	29.7	57.7
Mean Temp. (°F)	18.4	23.1	35.1	48.7	60.5	70.0	73.2	70.8	63.3	50.6	36.0	21.9	47.6
Mean Minimum Temp. (°F)	9.8	14.6	25.6	37.1	49.1	58.9	62.6	60.3	51.9	39.9	27.1	14.0	37.6
Extreme Maximum Temp. (°F)	64	65	84	96	92	102	102	104	97	93	80	64	104
Extreme Minimum Temp. (°F)	-28	-31	-9	5	26	40	44	42	28	15	-4	-22	-31
Days Maximum Temp. ≥ 90°F	0	0	0	0	1	3	5	3	1	0	0	0	13
Days Maximum Temp. ≤ 32°F	20	14	5	0	0	0	0	0	0	0	5	17	61
Days Minimum Temp. ≤ 32°F	30	26	24	9	1	0	0	0	0	8	22	30	150
Days Minimum Temp. ≤ 0°F	8	5	1	0	0	0	0	0	0	0	0	5	19
Heating Degree Days (base 65°F)	1,438	1,178	920	491	178	24	4	13	121	447	862	1,331	7,007
Cooling Degree Days (base 65°F)	0	0	0	8	46	180	266	201	77	9	0	0	787
Mean Precipitation (in.)	0.76	0.78	1.63	3.38	4.54	4.98	4.53	4.31	3.09	2.37	1.76	1.15	33.28
Extreme Maximum Daily Precip. (in.)	0.95	0.88	1.95	4.00	3.86	4.49	2.90	5.24	4.12	2.30	2.58	1.63	5.24
Days With ≥ 0.1" Precipitation	3	2	4	6	8	7	7	6	5	5	4	3	60
Days With ≥ 0.5" Precipitation	0	0	1	2	3	3	3	3	2	2	1	1	21
Days With ≥ 1.0" Precipitation	0	0	0	1	1	1	1	1	1	0	0	0	6
Mean Snowfall (in.)	8.5	6.7	4.6	1.6	0.0	0.0	0.0	0.0	0.0	0.1	3.3	8.8	33.6
Maximum Snow Depth (in.)	19	15	12	5	0	0	0	0	0	2	12	17	19
Days With ≥ 1.0" Snow Depth	21	20	9	1	0	0	0	0	0	0	4	18	73

Ames 8 WSW *Boone County* Elevation: 1,099 ft. Latitude: 42° 01' N Longitude: 93° 46' W

	JAN	FEB	MAR	APR	MAY	JUN	JUL	AUG	SEP	OCT	NOV	DEC	YEAR
Mean Maximum Temp. (°F)	29.8	34.2	47.4	62.3	72.8	81.3	84.3	82.2	76.5	63.4	46.8	32.0	59.4
Mean Temp. (°F)	21.0	25.4	37.4	50.4	61.5	70.5	74.0	71.8	64.6	52.1	37.6	23.8	49.2
Mean Minimum Temp. (°F)	12.1	16.6	27.4	38.5	50.1	59.7	63.6	61.4	52.6	40.8	28.3	15.5	38.9
Extreme Maximum Temp. (°F)	67	67	90	97	95	101	99	102	98	95	80	66	102
Extreme Minimum Temp. (°F)	-25	-28	-11	8	29	41	47	42	29	15	-6	-24	-28
Days Maximum Temp. ≥ 90°F	0	0	0	0	1	3	6	4	2	0	0	0	16
Days Maximum Temp. ≤ 32°F	18	12	5	0	0	0	0	0	0	0	4	14	53
Days Minimum Temp. ≤ 32°F	30	26	22	8	0	0	0	0	0	7	20	30	143
Days Minimum Temp. ≤ 0°F	7	4	1	0	0	0	0	0	0	0	0	4	16
Heating Degree Days (base 65°F)	1,358	1,113	849	442	157	20	2	10	104	405	816	1,271	6,547
Cooling Degree Days (base 65°F)	0	0	1	13	56	191	288	227	98	12	0	0	886
Mean Precipitation (in.)	0.66	0.79	2.06	3.62	4.70	4.76	4.67	4.63	3.08	2.65	1.98	1.10	34.70
Extreme Maximum Daily Precip. (in.)	1.14	0.87	1.70	3.00	3.33	3.40	4.65	5.59	2.43	1.92	2.00	1.47	5.59
Days With ≥ 0.1" Precipitation	2	3	4	7	8	7	7	7	5	5	4	3	62
Days With ≥ 0.5" Precipitation	0	0	1	2	3	3	3	3	2	2	1	1	21
Days With ≥ 1.0" Precipitation	0	0	0	1	1	1	2	1	1	1	0	0	8
Mean Snowfall (in.)	7.4	6.9	5.2	1.6	0.0	0.0	0.0	0.0	0.0	0.5	2.3	7.8	31.7
Maximum Snow Depth (in.)	16	21	13	5	0	0	0	0	0	4	8	15	21
Days With ≥ 1.0" Snow Depth	17	14	5	1	0	0	0	0	0	0	2	14	53

The period of record for all cooperative weather station data is 1980 – 2009. See User Guide for detailed explanation of data.

Anamosa 1 WNW *Jones County* Elevation: 805 ft. Latitude: 42° 07' N Longitude: 91° 18' W

	JAN	FEB	MAR	APR	MAY	JUN	JUL	AUG	SEP	OCT	NOV	DEC	YEAR
Mean Maximum Temp. (°F)	29.0	33.7	46.4	61.3	72.3	81.4	84.6	82.5	75.6	62.6	46.8	32.7	59.1
Mean Temp. (°F)	19.9	24.3	36.1	49.1	59.7	69.1	73.0	70.8	62.8	50.7	37.4	24.1	48.1
Mean Minimum Temp. (°F)	10.7	14.8	25.7	36.8	47.0	56.7	61.4	59.1	50.0	38.7	27.9	15.4	37.0
Extreme Maximum Temp. (°F)	66	67	87	95	93	100	102	102	97	93	78	71	102
Extreme Minimum Temp. (°F)	-37	-37	-14	0	22	33	41	37	23	11	-2	-27	-37
Days Maximum Temp. ≥ 90°F	0	0	0	0	0	3	7	5	1	0	0	0	16
Days Maximum Temp. ≤ 32°F	18	12	4	0	0	0	0	0	0	0	3	14	51
Days Minimum Temp. ≤ 32°F	30	26	24	10	2	0	0	0	1	9	21	29	152
Days Minimum Temp. ≤ 0°F	8	5	1	0	0	0	0	0	0	0	0	5	19
Heating Degree Days (base 65°F)	1,392	1,145	890	481	200	34	6	18	136	446	822	1,261	6,831
Cooling Degree Days (base 65°F)	0	0	1	10	41	164	260	204	77	9	0	0	766
Mean Precipitation (in.)	1.11	1.32	2.18	3.56	4.37	4.72	4.78	4.73	3.39	2.94	2.55	1.68	37.33
Extreme Maximum Daily Precip. (in.)	1.53	3.35	2.32	1.75	2.80	3.90	6.52	4.64	3.35	2.65	1.98	1.63	6.52
Days With ≥ 0.1" Precipitation	3	3	5	7	8	8	7	7	6	5	5	4	68
Days With ≥ 0.5" Precipitation	0	1	2	3	3	3	3	3	2	2	2	1	25
Days With ≥ 1.0" Precipitation	0	0	0	1	1	1	1	1	1	1	1	0	8
Mean Snowfall (in.)	8.0	5.4	2.4	0.9	0.0	0.0	0.0	0.0	0.0	0.1	1.2	6.6	24.6
Maximum Snow Depth (in.)	18	13	8	8	0	0	0	0	0	3	6	17	18
Days With ≥ 1.0" Snow Depth	18	13	4	0	0	0	0	0	0	0	2	11	48

Ankeny *Polk County* Elevation: 939 ft. Latitude: 41° 43' N Longitude: 93° 34' W

	JAN	FEB	MAR	APR	MAY	JUN	JUL	AUG	SEP	OCT	NOV	DEC	YEAR
Mean Maximum Temp. (°F)	30.3	35.2	47.5	61.4	72.3	81.6	86.0	83.6	76.7	63.0	47.4	33.4	59.9
Mean Temp. (°F)	21.0	25.5	37.0	49.6	60.9	70.5	74.8	72.3	64.2	51.2	37.4	24.4	49.1
Mean Minimum Temp. (°F)	11.7	15.8	26.5	37.8	49.5	59.3	63.7	61.0	51.7	39.2	27.8	15.5	38.3
Extreme Maximum Temp. (°F)	66	69	90	93	94	102	103	106	98	93	80	70	106
Extreme Minimum Temp. (°F)	-28	-34	-9	8	26	40	46	42	22	12	-7	-25	-34
Days Maximum Temp. ≥ 90°F	0	0	0	0	0	4	9	6	2	0	0	0	21
Days Maximum Temp. ≤ 32°F	17	12	4	0	0	0	0	0	0	0	4	14	51
Days Minimum Temp. ≤ 32°F	30	26	23	9	1	0	0	0	1	8	21	29	148
Days Minimum Temp. ≤ 0°F	7	4	1	0	0	0	0	0	0	0	0	4	16
Heating Degree Days (base 65°F)	1,357	1,111	862	467	171	22	3	10	114	432	820	1,250	6,619
Cooling Degree Days (base 65°F)	0	0	1	13	52	193	315	245	97	10	0	0	926
Mean Precipitation (in.)	0.71	0.89	2.05	3.58	4.83	4.92	4.83	4.15	2.73	2.56	1.91	1.18	34.34
Extreme Maximum Daily Precip. (in.)	1.23	1.28	2.52	4.50	2.41	3.90	3.93	3.05	3.92	1.97	2.05	1.19	4.50
Days With ≥ 0.1" Precipitation	2	3	4	7	8	7	7	6	5	5	4	3	61
Days With ≥ 0.5" Precipitation	0	0	1	2	3	4	3	3	2	2	1	1	22
Days With ≥ 1.0" Precipitation	0	0	0	1	1	2	1	1	1	1	0	0	8
Mean Snowfall (in.)	6.3	7.1	4.3	1.2	trace	0.0	0.0	0.0	trace	0.4	1.2	6.7	27.2
Maximum Snow Depth (in.)	27	15	12	6	trace	0	0	0	trace	5	3	25	27
Days With ≥ 1.0" Snow Depth	17	15	6	0	0	0	0	0	0	0	2	11	51

Atlantic 1 NE *Cass County* Elevation: 1,160 ft. Latitude: 41° 25' N Longitude: 95° 00' W

	JAN	FEB	MAR	APR	MAY	JUN	JUL	AUG	SEP	OCT	NOV	DEC	YEAR
Mean Maximum Temp. (°F)	31.5	36.1	48.9	62.5	73.0	82.1	85.7	83.6	77.0	63.6	48.1	33.7	60.5
Mean Temp. (°F)	21.5	26.1	37.5	50.1	61.2	70.7	74.7	72.4	64.1	51.3	37.4	24.2	49.3
Mean Minimum Temp. (°F)	11.4	16.0	26.1	37.5	49.4	59.3	63.7	61.1	51.2	39.0	26.6	14.7	38.0
Extreme Maximum Temp. (°F)	67	72	90	93	95	102	102	103	101	95	83	67	103
Extreme Minimum Temp. (°F)	-28	-29	-21	6	23	33	44	39	20	9	-12	-33	-33
Days Maximum Temp. ≥ 90°F	0	0	0	0	1	5	9	6	3	0	0	0	24
Days Maximum Temp. ≤ 32°F	16	11	4	0	0	0	0	0	0	0	3	13	47
Days Minimum Temp. ≤ 32°F	30	26	23	10	1	0	0	0	1	9	22	30	152
Days Minimum Temp. ≤ 0°F	7	4	1	0	0	0	0	0	0	0	0	5	17
Heating Degree Days (base 65°F)	1,343	1,095	845	455	166	22	4	12	119	431	822	1,257	6,571
Cooling Degree Days (base 65°F)	0	0	1	14	55	200	312	248	99	13	0	0	942
Mean Precipitation (in.)	0.85	1.06	2.24	3.62	4.87	5.49	4.64	3.86	3.23	2.89	1.68	1.36	35.79
Extreme Maximum Daily Precip. (in.)	1.00	1.44	2.18	2.72	4.53	13.18	5.07	4.90	6.52	4.38	2.02	2.20	13.18
Days With ≥ 0.1" Precipitation	3	3	5	7	8	7	7	5	5	5	4	4	63
Days With ≥ 0.5" Precipitation	0	1	1	2	3	3	3	3	2	2	1	1	22
Days With ≥ 1.0" Precipitation	0	0	1	1	1	2	1	1	1	1	0	0	9
Mean Snowfall (in.)	6.4	6.1	4.3	0.7	0.0	0.0	0.0	0.0	0.0	0.6	2.3	6.6	27.0
Maximum Snow Depth (in.)	***11***	na	na	***2***	***0***	***0***	***0***	***0***	***0***	***4***	***7***	na	na
Days With ≥ 1.0" Snow Depth	***7***	na	1	0	0	0	0	0	0	0	1	6	na

Audubon 1 SSE *Audubon County* Elevation: 1,290 ft. Latitude: 41° 42' N Longitude: 94° 55' W

	JAN	FEB	MAR	APR	MAY	JUN	JUL	AUG	SEP	OCT	NOV	DEC	YEAR
Mean Maximum Temp. (°F)	30.5	34.9	48.0	62.0	72.5	81.4	84.7	82.5	75.8	62.9	47.0	32.6	59.6
Mean Temp. (°F)	20.8	25.1	36.8	49.4	60.5	69.9	73.7	71.3	63.2	50.8	36.7	23.5	48.5
Mean Minimum Temp. (°F)	11.1	15.2	25.5	36.6	48.4	58.3	62.7	60.1	50.5	38.6	26.4	14.4	37.3
Extreme Maximum Temp. (°F)	67	69	90	93	94	101	103	101	101	93	78	65	103
Extreme Minimum Temp. (°F)	-25	-27	-16	9	24	40	44	39	26	12	-12	-29	-29
Days Maximum Temp. ≥ 90°F	0	0	0	0	0	4	7	5	1	0	0	0	17
Days Maximum Temp. ≤ 32°F	16	12	4	0	0	0	0	0	0	0	4	14	50
Days Minimum Temp. ≤ 32°F	30	27	23	10	1	0	0	0	1	9	22	30	153
Days Minimum Temp. ≤ 0°F	7	5	1	0	0	0	0	0	0	0	0	5	18
Heating Degree Days (base 65°F)	1,363	1,123	867	474	182	27	6	15	132	444	842	1,279	6,754
Cooling Degree Days (base 65°F)	0	0	1	11	48	180	283	218	84	9	0	0	834
Mean Precipitation (in.)	0.66	0.74	1.92	3.47	4.87	4.58	4.41	3.78	2.96	2.79	1.61	1.10	32.89
Extreme Maximum Daily Precip. (in.)	1.28	1.70	2.10	2.69	6.00	3.10	3.27	3.50	4.23	3.44	2.11	1.27	6.00
Days With ≥ 0.1" Precipitation	2	3	4	7	9	7	6	6	5	5	4	3	61
Days With ≥ 0.5" Precipitation	0	0	1	2	3	3	3	3	2	2	1	0	20
Days With ≥ 1.0" Precipitation	0	0	0	1	1	1	1	1	1	1	0	0	7
Mean Snowfall (in.)	5.5	3.7	3.8	1.3	0.0	0.0	0.0	0.0	trace	0.6	1.9	5.9	22.7
Maximum Snow Depth (in.)	***14***	na	***14***	2	0	0	***0***	***0***	0	***trace***	***4***	na	na
Days With ≥ 1.0" Snow Depth	***8***	***9***	3	0	0	0	0	0	0	0	1	***6***	***27***

Beaconsfield *Ringgold County* Elevation: 1,200 ft. Latitude: 40° 49' N Longitude: 94° 03' W

	JAN	FEB	MAR	APR	MAY	JUN	JUL	AUG	SEP	OCT	NOV	DEC	YEAR
Mean Maximum Temp. (°F)	31.4	36.9	48.6	61.2	70.9	80.0	84.5	83.2	75.8	63.3	48.2	34.4	59.9
Mean Temp. (°F)	22.3	27.3	38.0	49.8	60.5	69.6	74.4	72.7	64.3	52.0	38.6	25.6	49.6
Mean Minimum Temp. (°F)	13.1	17.7	27.4	38.4	49.9	59.2	64.2	62.0	52.8	40.8	28.9	16.8	39.3
Extreme Maximum Temp. (°F)	65	72	87	89	92	105	105	104	97	90	79	67	105
Extreme Minimum Temp. (°F)	-24	-25	-10	8	25	37	49	41	26	15	-13	-21	-25
Days Maximum Temp. ≥ 90°F	0	0	0	0	0	2	7	6	2	0	0	0	17
Days Maximum Temp. ≤ 32°F	16	11	4	0	0	0	0	0	0	0	3	13	47
Days Minimum Temp. ≤ 32°F	30	25	22	9	0	0	0	0	1	6	19	29	141
Days Minimum Temp. ≤ 0°F	6	4	0	0	0	0	0	0	0	0	0	4	14
Heating Degree Days (base 65°F)	1,318	1,060	830	458	176	26	3	10	112	404	786	1,213	6,396
Cooling Degree Days (base 65°F)	0	0	1	9	42	171	301	254	98	10	0	0	886
Mean Precipitation (in.)	0.87	1.16	2.31	3.48	5.12	4.59	4.89	4.41	3.68	2.88	2.14	1.37	36.90
Extreme Maximum Daily Precip. (in.)	1.01	1.53	2.55	2.30	4.34	4.29	5.75	4.95	7.00	2.60	3.00	1.59	7.00
Days With ≥ 0.1" Precipitation	3	3	5	7	9	7	7	6	5	5	4	4	65
Days With ≥ 0.5" Precipitation	0	1	1	3	4	3	3	3	2	2	1	1	24
Days With ≥ 1.0" Precipitation	0	0	0	1	1	1	2	1	1	1	1	0	9
Mean Snowfall (in.)	5.8	5.5	3.5	1.1	trace	0.0	0.0	0.0	0.0	0.6	1.9	6.7	25.1
Maximum Snow Depth (in.)	15	15	9	10	0	0	0	0	0	10	5	13	15
Days With ≥ 1.0" Snow Depth	16	12	4	1	0	0	0	0	0	0	2	11	46

Belle Plaine *Benton County* Elevation: 810 ft. Latitude: 41° 53' N Longitude: 92° 18' W

	JAN	FEB	MAR	APR	MAY	JUN	JUL	AUG	SEP	OCT	NOV	DEC	YEAR
Mean Maximum Temp. (°F)	29.0	33.8	46.4	60.6	71.7	80.6	84.3	82.5	75.3	62.4	46.9	32.3	58.8
Mean Temp. (°F)	20.0	24.5	36.2	49.0	60.3	69.8	73.6	71.6	63.2	50.8	37.3	23.7	48.3
Mean Minimum Temp. (°F)	10.9	15.2	26.1	37.5	48.9	58.9	62.8	60.5	51.1	39.1	27.6	15.1	37.8
Extreme Maximum Temp. (°F)	65	70	88	95	92	102	103	105	99	91	80	69	105
Extreme Minimum Temp. (°F)	-38	-35	-11	8	22	38	46	41	26	11	-4	-30	-38
Days Maximum Temp. ≥ 90°F	0	0	0	0	0	3	7	5	1	0	0	0	16
Days Maximum Temp. ≤ 32°F	18	12	4	0	0	0	0	0	0	0	3	14	51
Days Minimum Temp. ≤ 32°F	30	26	23	9	1	0	0	0	1	9	21	29	149
Days Minimum Temp. ≤ 0°F	7	5	1	0	0	0	0	0	0	0	0	5	18
Heating Degree Days (base 65°F)	1,389	1,138	886	482	184	27	4	12	127	443	825	1,274	6,791
Cooling Degree Days (base 65°F)	0	0	1	10	46	176	277	223	81	9	0	0	823
Mean Precipitation (in.)	1.03	1.15	2.08	3.37	4.18	5.03	4.30	4.36	3.47	2.93	2.25	1.50	35.65
Extreme Maximum Daily Precip. (in.)	1.47	1.83	2.15	2.22	2.75	5.26	3.41	3.76	3.41	2.61	3.55	1.38	5.26
Days With ≥ 0.1" Precipitation	3	3	5	7	8	8	6	6	6	6	4	4	66
Days With ≥ 0.5" Precipitation	0	1	1	2	3	3	3	3	2	2	2	1	23
Days With ≥ 1.0" Precipitation	0	0	0	1	1	2	1	1	1	1	1	0	9
Mean Snowfall (in.)	7.7	6.3	3.6	1.3	trace	0.0	0.0	0.0	0.0	0.4	1.7	7.2	28.2
Maximum Snow Depth (in.)	17	15	9	8	trace	0	0	0	0	7	6	17	17
Days With ≥ 1.0" Snow Depth	18	15	5	1	0	0	0	0	0	0	2	13	54

Bloomfield 1 WNW *Davis County* Elevation: 812 ft. Latitude: 40° 46' N Longitude: 92° 26' W

	JAN	FEB	MAR	APR	MAY	JUN	JUL	AUG	SEP	OCT	NOV	DEC	YEAR
Mean Maximum Temp. (°F)	33.9	38.7	50.7	63.4	72.9	81.9	86.3	84.9	77.3	64.9	50.5	36.6	61.8
Mean Temp. (°F)	25.0	29.2	40.2	52.2	62.1	71.5	76.0	74.3	65.9	54.0	41.2	28.1	51.6
Mean Minimum Temp. (°F)	16.0	19.6	29.7	40.9	51.4	61.1	65.6	63.6	54.6	43.1	31.8	19.6	41.4
Extreme Maximum Temp. (°F)	70	71	86	89	93	101	105	106	100	90	77	70	106
Extreme Minimum Temp. (°F)	-22	-26	-4	10	30	42	49	40	30	18	-6	-23	-26
Days Maximum Temp. ≥ 90°F	0	0	0	0	0	4	9	8	2	0	0	0	23
Days Maximum Temp. ≤ 32°F	14	10	3	0	0	0	0	0	0	0	2	10	39
Days Minimum Temp. ≤ 32°F	29	24	19	5	0	0	0	0	0	4	16	27	124
Days Minimum Temp. ≤ 0°F	4	3	0	0	0	0	0	0	0	0	0	3	10
Heating Degree Days (base 65°F)	1,234	1,007	764	392	141	16	1	5	85	348	708	1,137	5,838
Cooling Degree Days (base 65°F)	0	0	1	15	59	217	348	299	121	15	0	0	1,075
Mean Precipitation (in.)	1.11	1.43	2.34	3.33	5.03	4.96	5.11	4.87	3.81	3.02	2.44	1.58	39.03
Extreme Maximum Daily Precip. (in.)	1.07	2.16	1.85	2.11	2.80	5.12	5.83	8.17	3.42	3.16	2.58	1.89	8.17
Days With ≥ 0.1" Precipitation	3	4	5	7	9	7	7	7	6	6	5	3	69
Days With ≥ 0.5" Precipitation	1	1	2	2	3	3	3	3	2	2	2	1	25
Days With ≥ 1.0" Precipitation	0	0	0	1	2	2	2	2	1	1	1	0	12
Mean Snowfall (in.)	6.5	6.4	3.5	1.7	trace	0.0	0.0	0.0	0.0	0.2	1.3	6.1	25.7
Maximum Snow Depth (in.)	15	13	9	22	trace	0	0	0	0	2	3	15	22
Days With ≥ 1.0" Snow Depth	16	12	4	1	0	0	0	0	0	0	1	9	43

Boone *Boone County* Elevation: 1,050 ft. Latitude: 42° 03' N Longitude: 93° 53' W

	JAN	FEB	MAR	APR	MAY	JUN	JUL	AUG	SEP	OCT	NOV	DEC	YEAR
Mean Maximum Temp. (°F)	29.4	34.3	46.4	60.5	71.6	80.7	84.8	82.7	76.0	63.0	46.5	32.2	59.0
Mean Temp. (°F)	19.1	23.8	35.8	48.5	59.7	68.9	73.3	71.2	63.2	50.5	36.5	22.8	47.8
Mean Minimum Temp. (°F)	8.6	13.2	25.1	36.5	47.6	57.0	61.8	59.7	50.3	37.9	26.2	13.3	36.4
Extreme Maximum Temp. (°F)	68	70	86	95	95	102	101	106	100	94	81	68	106
Extreme Minimum Temp. (°F)	-32	-35	-16	-1	25	35	45	37	23	15	-7	-25	-35
Days Maximum Temp. ≥ 90°F	0	0	0	0	0	4	8	5	2	0	0	0	19
Days Maximum Temp. ≤ 32°F	18	13	4	0	0	0	0	0	0	0	4	14	53
Days Minimum Temp. ≤ 32°F	31	27	24	10	1	0	0	0	1	10	23	30	157
Days Minimum Temp. ≤ 0°F	8	6	1	0	0	0	0	0	0	0	0	5	20
Heating Degree Days (base 65°F)	1,419	1,160	899	497	201	35	4	15	130	455	849	1,302	6,966
Cooling Degree Days (base 65°F)	0	0	1	10	42	159	270	215	81	10	0	0	788
Mean Precipitation (in.)	1.12	1.15	2.49	3.83	4.73	5.20	4.70	4.82	3.01	2.71	2.22	1.52	37.50
Extreme Maximum Daily Precip. (in.)	1.06	1.29	2.30	3.18	5.30	3.27	6.06	5.92	3.35	2.14	2.32	1.97	6.06
Days With ≥ 0.1" Precipitation	3	3	5	7	8	8	7	7	6	5	5	4	68
Days With ≥ 0.5" Precipitation	1	1	2	3	3	4	3	3	2	2	2	1	27
Days With ≥ 1.0" Precipitation	0	0	1	1	1	1	1	1	1	0	0	0	7
Mean Snowfall (in.)	8.1	7.2	5.4	1.3	trace	0.0	0.0	0.0	0.0	0.4	2.4	8.1	32.9
Maximum Snow Depth (in.)	17	20	16	5	trace	0	0	0	0	5	6	17	20
Days With ≥ 1.0" Snow Depth	19	17	6	1	0	0	0	0	0	0	3	16	62

The period of record for all cooperative weather station data is 1980 – 2009. See User Guide for detailed explanation of data.

Burlington Radio KBUR *Des Moines County* Elevation: 703 ft. Latitude: 40° 49' N Longitude: 91° 10' W

	JAN	FEB	MAR	APR	MAY	JUN	JUL	AUG	SEP	OCT	NOV	DEC	YEAR
Mean Maximum Temp. (°F)	32.7	37.3	49.7	62.3	72.7	81.7	85.6	83.6	76.5	64.1	49.4	35.8	61.0
Mean Temp. (°F)	24.7	29.0	40.3	52.3	62.8	72.1	76.3	74.3	66.4	54.3	40.9	28.1	51.8
Mean Minimum Temp. (°F)	16.6	20.7	30.9	42.1	52.8	62.4	66.9	65.0	56.2	44.5	32.4	20.4	42.6
Extreme Maximum Temp. (°F)	70	69	88	92	94	104	103	105	101	93	79	71	105
Extreme Minimum Temp. (°F)	-22	-26	-4	11	31	43	49	42	30	22	2	-20	-26
Days Maximum Temp. ≥ 90°F	0	0	0	0	1	4	9	6	2	0	0	0	22
Days Maximum Temp. ≤ 32°F	15	10	3	0	0	0	0	0	0	0	2	11	41
Days Minimum Temp. ≤ 32°F	29	24	18	5	0	0	0	0	0	3	15	26	120
Days Minimum Temp. ≤ 0°F	4	3	0	0	0	0	0	0	0	0	0	3	10
Heating Degree Days (base 65°F)	1,243	1,010	759	392	132	15	1	5	79	341	716	1,137	5,830
Cooling Degree Days (base 65°F)	0	0	2	16	71	234	357	302	127	17	0	0	1,126
Mean Precipitation (in.)	1.37	1.65	2.92	3.85	4.55	4.86	4.66	4.12	3.88	3.09	2.68	2.20	39.83
Extreme Maximum Daily Precip. (in.)	1.64	1.58	2.40	2.50	3.32	5.55	4.70	4.21	3.66	4.39	1.98	3.84	5.55
Days With ≥ 0.1" Precipitation	4	4	6	7	8	7	7	6	6	6	5	5	71
Days With ≥ 0.5" Precipitation	1	1	2	3	3	3	3	3	3	2	2	1	27
Days With ≥ 1.0" Precipitation	0	0	1	1	1	2	1	1	1	1	0	0	9
Mean Snowfall (in.)	7.5	5.7	2.6	1.0	0.0	0.0	0.0	0.0	0.0	0.1	0.9	6.8	24.6
Maximum Snow Depth (in.)	22	11	8	11	0	0	0	0	0	1	4	16	22
Days With ≥ 1.0" Snow Depth	14	9	2	0	0	0	0	0	0	0	1	8	34

Castana Experiment Farm *Monona County* Elevation: 1,450 ft. Latitude: 42° 04' N Longitude: 95° 50' W

	JAN	FEB	MAR	APR	MAY	JUN	JUL	AUG	SEP	OCT	NOV	DEC	YEAR
Mean Maximum Temp. (°F)	31.0	35.7	48.0	61.9	72.3	81.2	84.8	82.7	75.7	63.3	46.8	32.5	59.6
Mean Temp. (°F)	21.7	26.3	37.2	49.9	60.9	70.3	74.4	72.2	64.2	52.0	37.2	24.0	49.2
Mean Minimum Temp. (°F)	12.4	16.8	26.4	37.9	49.6	59.3	64.0	61.6	52.9	40.6	27.6	15.6	38.7
Extreme Maximum Temp. (°F)	67	71	87	94	93	104	104	104	101	89	81	68	104
Extreme Minimum Temp. (°F)	-24	-26	-10	12	25	39	49	38	24	15	-9	-26	-26
Days Maximum Temp. ≥ 90°F	0	0	0	0	0	3	6	5	2	0	0	0	16
Days Maximum Temp. ≤ 32°F	16	12	4	0	0	0	0	0	0	0	4	14	50
Days Minimum Temp. ≤ 32°F	30	26	23	9	1	0	0	0	0	7	21	30	147
Days Minimum Temp. ≤ 0°F	7	4	1	0	0	0	0	0	0	0	0	4	16
Heating Degree Days (base 65°F)	1,336	1,089	856	458	171	24	2	10	111	410	826	1,263	6,556
Cooling Degree Days (base 65°F)	0	0	1	13	52	189	301	240	95	12	0	0	903
Mean Precipitation (in.)	0.61	0.61	1.95	3.39	4.31	4.83	4.07	3.81	3.05	2.45	1.46	0.88	31.42
Extreme Maximum Daily Precip. (in.)	0.92	1.04	2.28	3.80	3.20	3.63	12.02	3.85	3.11	2.60	2.15	1.21	12.02
Days With ≥ 0.1" Precipitation	2	2	4	6	8	7	6	6	5	5	3	2	56
Days With ≥ 0.5" Precipitation	0	0	1	3	3	3	2	3	2	2	1	0	20
Days With ≥ 1.0" Precipitation	0	0	0	1	1	1	1	1	1	1	0	0	7
Mean Snowfall (in.)	6.3	5.7	6.1	1.9	trace	0.0	0.0	0.0	0.0	0.9	3.9	7.5	32.3
Maximum Snow Depth (in.)	15	26	17	14	0	0	0	0	0	4	11	22	26
Days With ≥ 1.0" Snow Depth	18	14	6	1	0	0	0	0	0	0	5	15	59

Cedar Rapids Municipal Arpt *Linn County* Elevation: 839 ft. Latitude: 41° 53' N Longitude: 91° 43' W

	JAN	FEB	MAR	APR	MAY	JUN	JUL	AUG	SEP	OCT	NOV	DEC	YEAR
Mean Maximum Temp. (°F)	28.8	32.7	46.2	60.6	71.7	80.5	83.9	81.7	74.6	61.4	47.2	31.8	58.4
Mean Temp. (°F)	20.5	24.1	36.7	49.5	60.7	69.9	73.6	71.4	63.1	50.6	38.1	23.6	48.5
Mean Minimum Temp. (°F)	12.1	15.4	27.2	38.4	49.7	59.3	63.3	61.1	51.6	39.8	28.9	15.3	38.5
Extreme Maximum Temp. (°F)	65	67	88	95	95	100	104	102	97	90	78	67	104
Extreme Minimum Temp. (°F)	-29	-18	-12	1	25	39	49	40	27	18	1	-22	-29
Days Maximum Temp. ≥ 90°F	0	0	0	0	0	3	6	4	1	0	0	0	14
Days Maximum Temp. ≤ 32°F	19	14	4	0	0	0	0	0	0	0	3	15	55
Days Minimum Temp. ≤ 32°F	30	26	22	8	0	0	0	0	0	8	20	29	143
Days Minimum Temp. ≤ 0°F	6	5	0	0	0	0	0	0	0	0	0	5	16
Heating Degree Days (base 65°F)	1,372	1,152	870	469	174	25	3	14	130	447	801	1,278	6,735
Cooling Degree Days (base 65°F)	0	0	1	11	48	179	277	220	79	9	0	0	824
Mean Precipitation (in.)	0.87	1.18	2.02	3.10	3.86	4.61	4.67	4.42	3.17	2.49	2.18	1.54	34.11
Extreme Maximum Daily Precip. (in.)	1.19	1.43	2.00	1.80	2.52	4.77	4.18	5.35	2.42	2.44	1.97	1.56	5.35
Days With ≥ 0.1" Precipitation	3	3	5	7	7	7	7	6	6	5	5	4	65
Days With ≥ 0.5" Precipitation	0	1	1	2	3	3	3	3	2	2	1	1	22
Days With ≥ 1.0" Precipitation	0	0	0	1	1	1	1	1	1	1	0	0	7
Mean Snowfall (in.)	na	na	***3.3***	***1.1***	na	na	na	na	na	na	na	***6.9***	na
Maximum Snow Depth (in.)	na	na	na	na	na	na	na	na	na	na	na	na	na
Days With ≥ 1.0" Snow Depth	na	na	na	na	na	na	na	na	na	na	na	na	na

Cedar Rapids No 1 *Linn County* Elevation: 850 ft. Latitude: 42° 02' N Longitude: 91° 35' W

	JAN	FEB	MAR	APR	MAY	JUN	JUL	AUG	SEP	OCT	NOV	DEC	YEAR
Mean Maximum Temp. (°F)	30.1	35.3	48.0	62.7	73.1	81.4	85.1	82.9	76.0	63.4	47.7	33.2	59.9
Mean Temp. (°F)	21.8	26.6	38.0	51.0	61.7	70.7	74.7	72.6	64.8	52.8	39.0	25.4	49.9
Mean Minimum Temp. (°F)	13.4	17.8	28.1	39.3	50.3	60.0	64.3	62.3	53.6	42.1	30.2	17.6	39.9
Extreme Maximum Temp. (°F)	68	68	88	94	93	101	105	102	98	94	80	69	105
Extreme Minimum Temp. (°F)	-33	-28	-6	3	25	38	46	41	26	15	1	-21	-33
Days Maximum Temp. ≥ 90°F	0	0	0	0	0	3	7	5	1	0	0	0	16
Days Maximum Temp. ≤ 32°F	18	11	4	0	0	0	0	0	0	0	3	13	49
Days Minimum Temp. ≤ 32°F	30	25	21	8	0	0	0	0	0	6	19	28	137
Days Minimum Temp. ≤ 0°F	6	4	1	0	0	0	0	0	0	0	0	4	15
Heating Degree Days (base 65°F)	1,334	1,081	831	426	153	20	2	8	99	385	774	1,220	6,333
Cooling Degree Days (base 65°F)	0	0	1	14	58	199	309	253	101	14	0	0	949
Mean Precipitation (in.)	1.09	1.23	1.95	3.34	4.73	4.91	4.41	4.81	3.67	2.89	2.41	1.61	37.05
Extreme Maximum Daily Precip. (in.)	1.29	1.78	2.61	2.43	3.40	4.76	6.63	4.48	2.95	2.41	2.05	1.86	6.63
Days With ≥ 0.1" Precipitation	3	3	5	7	8	8	7	7	6	6	5	4	69
Days With ≥ 0.5" Precipitation	0	1	1	2	3	3	3	3	3	2	2	1	24
Days With ≥ 1.0" Precipitation	0	0	0	1	1	1	1	1	1	1	0	0	7
Mean Snowfall (in.)	8.0	6.5	3.9	1.8	trace	0.0	0.0	0.0	0.0	0.3	2.0	8.2	30.7
Maximum Snow Depth (in.)	15	13	11	6	trace	0	0	0	0	6	8	16	16
Days With ≥ 1.0" Snow Depth	19	15	5	1	0	0	0	0	0	0	1	13	54

Cherokee *Cherokee County* Elevation: 1,180 ft. Latitude: 42° 45' N Longitude: 95° 32' W

	JAN	FEB	MAR	APR	MAY	JUN	JUL	AUG	SEP	OCT	NOV	DEC	YEAR
Mean Maximum Temp. (°F)	27.7	32.5	44.4	59.7	71.4	80.9	84.8	82.4	75.0	61.7	45.0	30.3	58.0
Mean Temp. (°F)	17.5	22.2	33.9	47.3	59.2	69.1	73.4	70.9	62.1	48.9	34.6	20.7	46.6
Mean Minimum Temp. (°F)	7.4	11.9	23.3	34.8	47.0	57.2	61.9	59.4	49.0	36.0	24.2	11.1	35.3
Extreme Maximum Temp. (°F)	67	68	86	94	95	103	104	102	100	91	80	68	104
Extreme Minimum Temp. (°F)	-33	-28	-12	4	21	34	43	37	25	9	-17	-26	-33
Days Maximum Temp. ≥ 90°F	0	0	0	0	1	4	7	5	2	0	0	0	19
Days Maximum Temp. ≤ 32°F	19	14	6	0	0	0	0	0	0	0	5	16	60
Days Minimum Temp. ≤ 32°F	31	27	25	12	1	0	0	0	2	12	25	30	165
Days Minimum Temp. ≤ 0°F	10	7	1	0	0	0	0	0	0	0	1	7	26
Heating Degree Days (base 65°F)	1,466	1,204	958	534	219	38	6	18	154	498	905	1,367	7,367
Cooling Degree Days (base 65°F)	0	0	0	9	46	168	274	208	73	7	0	0	785
Mean Precipitation (in.)	0.62	0.59	1.83	3.02	3.89	4.68	3.73	3.84	3.42	2.16	1.48	0.88	30.14
Extreme Maximum Daily Precip. (in.)	0.81	0.92	1.98	2.10	3.32	5.05	3.24	4.61	4.76	2.12	2.08	1.42	5.05
Days With ≥ 0.1" Precipitation	2	2	4	6	7	7	6	6	6	4	3	3	56
Days With ≥ 0.5" Precipitation	0	0	1	2	3	3	3	3	3	1	1	0	20
Days With ≥ 1.0" Precipitation	0	0	0	1	1	1	1	1	1	1	0	0	7
Mean Snowfall (in.)	6.9	5.6	5.7	1.9	trace	0.0	0.0	0.0	0.0	0.5	4.3	8.1	33.0
Maximum Snow Depth (in.)	***13***	***18***	12	7	trace	0	0	0	0	***1***	***12***	***23***	***23***
Days With ≥ 1.0" Snow Depth	***21***	***15***	6	1	0	0	0	0	0	0	4	***17***	***64***

Clinton No 1 *Clinton County* Elevation: 584 ft. Latitude: 41° 48' N Longitude: 90° 16' W

	JAN	FEB	MAR	APR	MAY	JUN	JUL	AUG	SEP	OCT	NOV	DEC	YEAR
Mean Maximum Temp. (°F)	30.5	35.3	48.4	62.8	73.3	81.7	85.0	82.7	76.0	63.4	48.4	33.9	60.1
Mean Temp. (°F)	22.5	26.9	38.6	51.4	62.1	71.0	74.8	72.8	65.0	52.9	39.8	26.5	50.4
Mean Minimum Temp. (°F)	14.4	18.5	28.9	39.9	50.8	60.4	64.6	62.7	53.9	42.3	31.2	19.0	40.6
Extreme Maximum Temp. (°F)	67	70	87	91	93	100	101	101	98	91	79	70	101
Extreme Minimum Temp. (°F)	-27	-29	-9	7	24	39	46	39	27	15	2	-22	-29
Days Maximum Temp. ≥ 90°F	0	0	0	0	0	4	7	5	1	0	0	0	17
Days Maximum Temp. ≤ 32°F	17	11	3	0	0	0	0	0	0	0	2	13	46
Days Minimum Temp. ≤ 32°F	29	25	20	6	0	0	0	0	0	5	17	28	130
Days Minimum Temp. ≤ 0°F	5	3	0	0	0	0	0	0	0	0	0	3	11
Heating Degree Days (base 65°F)	1,312	1,070	811	416	148	19	1	8	95	381	749	1,188	6,198
Cooling Degree Days (base 65°F)	0	0	2	14	65	206	313	255	102	13	0	0	970
Mean Precipitation (in.)	1.36	1.51	2.24	2.90	3.91	4.37	3.69	4.61	3.03	2.68	2.18	1.91	34.39
Extreme Maximum Daily Precip. (in.)	1.30	1.78	2.72	2.09	2.91	3.73	2.78	4.45	3.23	2.27	1.91	1.88	4.45
Days With ≥ 0.1" Precipitation	4	4	5	6	8	7	7	7	5	5	5	5	68
Days With ≥ 0.5" Precipitation	1	1	1	2	2	3	2	3	2	2	1	1	21
Days With ≥ 1.0" Precipitation	0	0	0	0	1	1	1	1	1	1	0	0	6
Mean Snowfall (in.)	9.0	6.8	3.3	1.0	trace	0.0	0.0	0.0	0.0	0.1	1.5	8.3	30.0
Maximum Snow Depth (in.)	14	13	11	7	trace	0	0	0	0	2	8	13	14
Days With ≥ 1.0" Snow Depth	19	14	4	0	0	0	0	0	0	0	1	12	50

Colo *Story County* Elevation: 1,000 ft. Latitude: 42° 01' N Longitude: 93° 19' W

	JAN	FEB	MAR	APR	MAY	JUN	JUL	AUG	SEP	OCT	NOV	DEC	YEAR
Mean Maximum Temp. (°F)	27.6	32.1	44.6	59.5	70.6	79.8	83.5	81.2	74.4	61.7	45.4	31.0	57.6
Mean Temp. (°F)	18.8	23.3	35.0	48.2	59.8	69.4	73.4	71.1	62.8	50.4	36.1	22.6	47.6
Mean Minimum Temp. (°F)	9.9	14.5	25.4	36.8	48.8	59.0	63.2	61.0	51.2	39.0	26.7	14.3	37.5
Extreme Maximum Temp. (°F)	65	66	89	96	92	101	100	104	98	93	80	68	104
Extreme Minimum Temp. (°F)	-25	-28	-7	4	24	40	47	40	26	14	-7	-23	-28
Days Maximum Temp. ≥ 90°F	0	0	0	0	0	3	6	3	1	0	0	0	13
Days Maximum Temp. ≤ 32°F	20	14	6	0	0	0	0	0	0	0	5	16	61
Days Minimum Temp. ≤ 32°F	31	27	24	10	1	0	0	0	1	8	23	30	155
Days Minimum Temp. ≤ 0°F	7	6	1	0	0	0	0	0	0	0	0	5	19
Heating Degree Days (base 65°F)	1,427	1,172	923	507	200	29	4	15	137	457	862	1,307	7,040
Cooling Degree Days (base 65°F)	0	0	1	9	44	170	271	211	78	10	0	0	794
Mean Precipitation (in.)	0.90	1.00	2.04	3.27	4.76	5.16	5.12	4.32	3.19	2.39	2.14	1.26	35.55
Extreme Maximum Daily Precip. (in.)	0.82	1.85	1.85	2.77	5.20	4.00	4.85	2.93	3.30	2.18	4.00	1.30	5.20
Days With ≥ 0.1" Precipitation	3	3	5	7	9	8	7	6	5	6	4	3	66
Days With ≥ 0.5" Precipitation	1	1	1	2	3	4	3	3	2	2	2	1	25
Days With ≥ 1.0" Precipitation	0	0	1	1	1	2	1	2	1	0	0	0	9
Mean Snowfall (in.)	6.6	6.2	4.8	1.6	0.0	0.0	0.0	0.0	0.0	0.6	2.1	6.9	28.8
Maximum Snow Depth (in.)	17	17	13	5	0	0	0	0	0	5	6	18	18
Days With ≥ 1.0" Snow Depth	19	16	7	1	0	0	0	0	0	0	3	16	62

Cresco 1 NE *Howard County* Elevation: 1,254 ft. Latitude: 43° 23' N Longitude: 92° 06' W

	JAN	FEB	MAR	APR	MAY	JUN	JUL	AUG	SEP	OCT	NOV	DEC	YEAR
Mean Maximum Temp. (°F)	23.5	28.1	40.5	56.5	68.7	77.9	81.7	79.5	72.0	58.6	42.2	27.3	54.7
Mean Temp. (°F)	14.4	18.8	31.0	45.1	56.8	66.5	70.5	68.3	59.9	47.0	33.1	18.7	44.2
Mean Minimum Temp. (°F)	5.3	9.4	21.5	33.6	44.9	55.1	59.2	57.0	47.7	35.5	23.8	10.0	33.6
Extreme Maximum Temp. (°F)	59	63	83	91	93	100	99	100	93	92	75	62	100
Extreme Minimum Temp. (°F)	-32	-36	-15	-1	21	34	40	36	26	10	-10	-30	-36
Days Maximum Temp. ≥ 90°F	0	0	0	0	0	2	3	2	0	0	0	0	7
Days Maximum Temp. ≤ 32°F	23	17	8	1	0	0	0	0	0	0	6	20	75
Days Minimum Temp. ≤ 32°F	31	28	27	14	2	0	0	0	1	13	24	30	170
Days Minimum Temp. ≤ 0°F	12	8	2	0	0	0	0	0	0	0	1	8	31
Heating Degree Days (base 65°F)	1,563	1,302	1,048	596	274	62	16	33	193	555	952	1,430	8,024
Cooling Degree Days (base 65°F)	0	0	0	5	26	115	192	142	47	5	0	0	532
Mean Precipitation (in.)	1.02	0.97	1.94	3.48	4.01	5.01	4.46	5.48	3.66	2.52	2.10	1.32	35.97
Extreme Maximum Daily Precip. (in.)	0.82	1.08	1.91	2.90	2.37	4.37	3.61	5.24	5.15	2.65	3.09	1.51	5.24
Days With ≥ 0.1" Precipitation	3	3	5	7	8	8	7	8	6	5	4	4	68
Days With ≥ 0.5" Precipitation	0	0	1	2	3	3	3	3	2	2	1	1	21
Days With ≥ 1.0" Precipitation	0	0	0	1	1	1	1	2	1	0	0	0	7
Mean Snowfall (in.)	10.2	8.1	6.3	2.1	trace	0.0	0.0	0.0	0.0	0.4	4.4	10.2	41.7
Maximum Snow Depth (in.)	na	na	na	na	na	na	na	na	na	na	na	na	na
Days With ≥ 1.0" Snow Depth	na	na	***3***	0	0	0	0	0	0	0	1	na	na

The period of record for all cooperative weather station data is 1980 – 2009. See User Guide for detailed explanation of data.

Dubuque Lock & Dam 11 *Dubuque County* Elevation: 620 ft. Latitude: 42° 32' N Longitude: 90° 39' W

	JAN	FEB	MAR	APR	MAY	JUN	JUL	AUG	SEP	OCT	NOV	DEC	YEAR
Mean Maximum Temp. (°F)	28.9	33.3	45.1	59.9	71.9	81.3	85.0	82.9	75.0	61.8	46.2	32.2	58.6
Mean Temp. (°F)	20.8	24.7	36.3	50.0	61.5	71.1	75.3	73.4	65.1	52.5	38.8	25.0	49.5
Mean Minimum Temp. (°F)	12.6	16.1	27.4	39.9	51.0	60.9	65.5	63.9	55.3	43.2	31.3	17.8	40.4
Extreme Maximum Temp. (°F)	61	65	87	93	95	101	108	104	97	92	75	66	108
Extreme Minimum Temp. (°F)	-27	-32	-8	11	29	43	46	43	29	19	4	-25	-32
Days Maximum Temp. ≥ 90°F	0	0	0	0	1	5	7	5	1	0	0	0	19
Days Maximum Temp. ≤ 32°F	19	12	4	0	0	0	0	0	0	0	3	13	51
Days Minimum Temp. ≤ 32°F	30	26	22	5	0	0	0	0	0	3	17	28	131
Days Minimum Temp. ≤ 0°F	6	5	1	0	0	0	0	0	0	0	0	4	16
Heating Degree Days (base 65°F)	1,366	1,133	884	455	161	20	1	5	94	392	780	1,233	6,524
Cooling Degree Days (base 65°F)	0	0	1	10	58	210	326	272	105	12	0	0	994
Mean Precipitation (in.)	1.12	1.21	2.04	3.34	4.27	4.78	4.53	4.19	3.61	2.77	2.36	1.61	35.83
Extreme Maximum Daily Precip. (in.)	1.06	1.78	2.22	1.90	3.10	4.86	3.86	3.98	3.25	2.23	3.57	1.29	4.86
Days With ≥ 0.1" Precipitation	4	4	5	7	8	7	6	6	6	5	5	4	67
Days With ≥ 0.5" Precipitation	0	1	1	2	3	3	3	3	3	2	1	1	23
Days With ≥ 1.0" Precipitation	0	0	0	1	1	1	1	1	1	1	0	0	7
Mean Snowfall (in.)	9.5	7.8	4.1	1.2	trace	0.0	0.0	0.0	0.0	trace	1.3	9.2	33.1
Maximum Snow Depth (in.)	32	25	17	8	trace	0	0	0	0	trace	8	31	32
Days With ≥ 1.0" Snow Depth	23	20	9	1	0	0	0	0	0	0	2	17	72

Eldora *Hardin County* Elevation: 1,144 ft. Latitude: 42° 22' N Longitude: 93° 06' W

	JAN	FEB	MAR	APR	MAY	JUN	JUL	AUG	SEP	OCT	NOV	DEC	YEAR
Mean Maximum Temp. (°F)	26.8	31.8	44.7	59.2	71.0	80.5	84.2	82.1	75.3	61.7	45.1	30.2	57.7
Mean Temp. (°F)	18.2	22.9	35.0	48.0	59.9	69.5	73.5	71.2	63.1	50.3	35.9	22.0	47.4
Mean Minimum Temp. (°F)	9.5	14.1	25.3	36.7	48.6	58.5	62.7	60.4	50.9	38.8	26.6	13.7	37.2
Extreme Maximum Temp. (°F)	66	66	87	98	93	104	103	108	98	94	80	66	108
Extreme Minimum Temp. (°F)	-24	-29	-6	6	26	40	46	41	28	17	-3	-23	-29
Days Maximum Temp. ≥ 90°F	0	0	0	0	1	4	7	5	2	0	0	0	19
Days Maximum Temp. ≤ 32°F	20	14	5	0	0	0	0	0	0	0	5	17	61
Days Minimum Temp. ≤ 32°F	31	27	24	10	1	0	0	0	1	9	22	30	155
Days Minimum Temp. ≤ 0°F	8	6	1	0	0	0	0	0	0	0	0	6	21
Heating Degree Days (base 65°F)	1,445	1,183	924	513	197	31	5	14	131	460	866	1,329	7,098
Cooling Degree Days (base 65°F)	0	0	0	8	46	173	274	214	80	11	0	0	806
Mean Precipitation (in.)	0.96	0.97	2.05	3.62	4.83	5.17	4.13	4.47	3.32	2.60	2.01	1.27	35.40
Extreme Maximum Daily Precip. (in.)	0.78	1.92	1.76	4.08	3.10	4.38	4.15	3.75	4.64	2.15	2.64	1.17	4.64
Days With ≥ 0.1" Precipitation	3	3	5	7	8	8	7	6	6	5	4	4	66
Days With ≥ 0.5" Precipitation	0	0	1	2	3	3	3	3	2	2	1	1	21
Days With ≥ 1.0" Precipitation	0	0	0	1	1	2	1	1	1	1	0	0	8
Mean Snowfall (in.)	8.6	6.7	4.0	1.8	0.0	0.0	0.0	0.0	0.0	0.2	2.4	8.1	31.8
Maximum Snow Depth (in.)	25	25	13	6	0	0	0	0	0	3	11	21	25
Days With ≥ 1.0" Snow Depth	22	19	8	1	0	0	0	0	0	0	3	18	71

Elkader 5 SSW *Clayton County* Elevation: 770 ft. Latitude: 42° 47' N Longitude: 91° 27' W

	JAN	FEB	MAR	APR	MAY	JUN	JUL	AUG	SEP	OCT	NOV	DEC	YEAR
Mean Maximum Temp. (°F)	28.2	33.0	45.3	60.6	71.5	80.4	84.2	82.0	74.9	62.0	45.8	31.3	58.3
Mean Temp. (°F)	18.3	22.8	34.2	47.9	58.5	67.6	72.0	70.0	61.8	49.5	35.9	22.2	46.7
Mean Minimum Temp. (°F)	8.3	12.5	23.1	35.2	45.5	54.8	59.7	57.9	48.5	36.9	25.9	13.2	35.1
Extreme Maximum Temp. (°F)	59	66	87	92	94	103	104	106	99	92	79	65	106
Extreme Minimum Temp. (°F)	-39	-33	-18	0	19	33	35	37	20	9	-11	-34	-39
Days Maximum Temp. ≥ 90°F	0	0	0	0	1	2	6	4	1	0	0	0	14
Days Maximum Temp. ≤ 32°F	19	13	4	0	0	0	0	0	0	0	3	15	54
Days Minimum Temp. ≤ 32°F	30	27	25	12	3	0	0	0	2	11	21	29	160
Days Minimum Temp. ≤ 0°F	10	6	1	0	0	0	0	0	0	0	0	6	23
Heating Degree Days (base 65°F)	1,442	1,186	947	513	229	47	9	22	156	481	867	1,318	7,217
Cooling Degree Days (base 65°F)	0	0	1	8	35	132	233	186	64	8	0	0	667
Mean Precipitation (in.)	1.05	1.12	1.87	3.65	4.32	4.86	4.04	4.62	3.15	2.58	2.34	1.34	34.94
Extreme Maximum Daily Precip. (in.)	0.86	1.48	3.23	3.01	4.50	3.36	2.92	4.36	3.23	2.50	3.50	1.36	4.50
Days With ≥ 0.1" Precipitation	3	3	4	7	8	7	6	7	6	5	5	4	65
Days With ≥ 0.5" Precipitation	0	0	1	3	3	3	3	3	2	2	1	1	22
Days With ≥ 1.0" Precipitation	0	0	0	1	1	1	1	1	1	0	0	0	6
Mean Snowfall (in.)	9.8	7.3	4.9	1.4	trace	0.0	0.0	0.0	0.0	0.2	2.7	9.3	35.6
Maximum Snow Depth (in.)	na	na	***12***	***5***	***trace***	***0***	***0***	***0***	***0***	***1***	na	***15***	na
Days With ≥ 1.0" Snow Depth	na	na	2	0	0	0	0	0	0	0	1	7	na

Emmetsburg *Palo Alto County* Elevation: 1,270 ft. Latitude: 43° 07' N Longitude: 94° 41' W

	JAN	FEB	MAR	APR	MAY	JUN	JUL	AUG	SEP	OCT	NOV	DEC	YEAR
Mean Maximum Temp. (°F)	26.7	30.8	43.0	59.3	71.4	81.0	84.3	81.6	74.4	61.7	43.5	29.4	57.3
Mean Temp. (°F)	17.8	22.1	33.6	47.9	60.0	69.8	73.7	71.0	62.7	49.9	34.4	21.0	47.0
Mean Minimum Temp. (°F)	8.9	13.3	24.3	36.5	48.5	58.5	63.0	60.4	50.9	38.2	25.1	12.6	36.7
Extreme Maximum Temp. (°F)	65	65	84	93	94	102	101	102	97	92	81	68	102
Extreme Minimum Temp. (°F)	-29	-29	-12	8	28	39	46	39	24	15	-7	-24	-29
Days Maximum Temp. ≥ 90°F	0	0	0	0	1	4	6	3	1	0	0	0	15
Days Maximum Temp. ≤ 32°F	20	15	6	1	0	0	0	0	0	0	6	17	65
Days Minimum Temp. ≤ 32°F	30	27	25	9	1	0	0	0	0	8	23	30	153
Days Minimum Temp. ≤ 0°F	9	6	1	0	0	0	0	0	0	0	1	6	23
Heating Degree Days (base 65°F)	1,458	1,208	964	514	195	29	4	14	138	468	913	1,357	7,262
Cooling Degree Days (base 65°F)	0	0	0	8	47	178	279	208	75	8	0	0	803
Mean Precipitation (in.)	0.66	0.62	1.78	3.24	4.02	4.64	4.11	4.43	2.98	2.26	1.60	0.86	31.20
Extreme Maximum Daily Precip. (in.)	1.38	0.82	2.79	2.33	4.00	4.28	3.01	9.00	5.75	3.75	2.08	1.45	9.00
Days With ≥ 0.1" Precipitation	2	2	4	6	8	7	6	6	5	4	4	2	56
Days With ≥ 0.5" Precipitation	0	0	1	3	3	3	3	3	2	1	1	1	21
Days With ≥ 1.0" Precipitation	0	0	0	1	1	1	1	1	1	0	0	0	6
Mean Snowfall (in.)	7.6	6.3	5.5	2.5	trace	0.0	0.0	0.0	0.0	0.2	4.7	7.3	34.1
Maximum Snow Depth (in.)	26	29	21	6	5	0	0	0	0	1	12	23	29
Days With ≥ 1.0" Snow Depth	20	18	9	1	0	0	0	0	0	0	5	15	68

The period of record for all cooperative weather station data is 1980 – 2009. See User Guide for detailed explanation of data.

Forest City 2 NNE *Winnebago County* Elevation: 1,299 ft. Latitude: 43° 17' N Longitude: 93° 38' W

	JAN	FEB	MAR	APR	MAY	JUN	JUL	AUG	SEP	OCT	NOV	DEC	YEAR
Mean Maximum Temp. (°F)	24.4	28.7	42.0	58.2	70.4	79.3	82.4	79.8	73.1	59.9	42.4	28.1	55.7
Mean Temp. (°F)	15.7	20.2	32.9	47.1	59.3	68.7	72.2	69.5	61.8	48.9	33.7	20.2	45.8
Mean Minimum Temp. (°F)	7.0	11.7	23.8	35.8	48.2	58.0	61.9	59.2	50.4	37.9	24.9	12.2	35.9
Extreme Maximum Temp. (°F)	62	65	83	92	92	100	101	99	93	92	80	69	101
Extreme Minimum Temp. (°F)	-27	-32	-10	6	25	38	45	38	28	15	-10	-25	-32
Days Maximum Temp. ≥ 90°F	0	0	0	0	1	3	4	2	1	0	0	0	11
Days Maximum Temp. ≤ 32°F	22	17	7	1	0	0	0	0	0	0	7	19	73
Days Minimum Temp. ≤ 32°F	31	27	25	11	1	0	0	0	1	10	24	30	160
Days Minimum Temp. ≤ 0°F	11	7	2	0	0	0	0	0	0	0	1	7	28
Heating Degree Days (base 65°F)	1,523	1,259	988	538	208	38	7	23	153	499	933	1,383	7,552
Cooling Degree Days (base 65°F)	0	0	0	6	40	154	237	169	62	7	0	0	675
Mean Precipitation (in.)	0.66	0.70	1.75	3.42	4.25	4.73	4.36	4.60	3.05	2.35	1.43	0.92	32.22
Extreme Maximum Daily Precip. (in.)	1.15	2.00	1.56	2.59	*3.04*	3.65	4.08	*4.40*	*5.66*	2.15	1.95	1.70	*5.66*
Days With ≥ 0.1" Precipitation	2	2	3	6	7	8	6	6	5	5	3	2	55
Days With ≥ 0.5" Precipitation	0	0	1	2	3	3	3	3	2	1	1	1	20
Days With ≥ 1.0" Precipitation	0	0	0	1	1	1	1	1	1	0	0	0	6
Mean Snowfall (in.)	9.9	6.9	5.6	2.1	trace	0.0	0.0	0.0	0.0	0.2	3.9	9.8	38.4
Maximum Snow Depth (in.)	21	18	19	11	trace	0	0	0	0	*1*	11	*27*	*27*
Days With ≥ 1.0" Snow Depth	15	13	6	1	0	0	0	0	0	0	3	13	51

Fort Dodge *Webster County* Elevation: 1,115 ft. Latitude: 42° 30' N Longitude: 94° 12' W

	JAN	FEB	MAR	APR	MAY	JUN	JUL	AUG	SEP	OCT	NOV	DEC	YEAR
Mean Maximum Temp. (°F)	27.3	32.1	44.9	60.4	71.6	81.2	84.6	81.9	75.2	61.6	45.0	30.1	58.0
Mean Temp. (°F)	18.2	22.8	34.8	48.5	60.1	69.9	73.9	71.3	63.2	50.1	35.6	21.6	47.5
Mean Minimum Temp. (°F)	9.1	13.4	24.6	36.5	48.5	58.7	63.1	60.6	51.1	38.7	26.1	13.1	36.9
Extreme Maximum Temp. (°F)	66	67	88	100	96	103	103	106	96	95	80	67	106
Extreme Minimum Temp. (°F)	-26	-30	-9	7	25	38	46	40	26	16	-8	-26	-30
Days Maximum Temp. ≥ 90°F	0	0	0	0	1	4	7	4	2	0	0	0	18
Days Maximum Temp. ≤ 32°F	20	14	5	0	0	0	0	0	0	0	5	16	60
Days Minimum Temp. ≤ 32°F	31	27	24	11	1	0	0	0	1	9	23	30	157
Days Minimum Temp. ≤ 0°F	9	6	1	0	0	0	0	0	0	0	1	6	23
Heating Degree Days (base 65°F)	1,445	1,187	930	499	195	28	5	14	130	462	876	1,338	7,109
Cooling Degree Days (base 65°F)	0	0	0	9	49	183	287	215	82	9	0	0	834
Mean Precipitation (in.)	0.84	0.92	1.95	3.62	4.70	5.23	4.41	4.52	2.87	2.41	1.73	1.17	34.37
Extreme Maximum Daily Precip. (in.)	0.80	1.13	1.95	2.81	3.28	6.50	3.85	4.40	2.32	2.45	2.00	1.48	6.50
Days With ≥ 0.1" Precipitation	3	3	4	7	9	8	6	6	5	5	4	4	64
Days With ≥ 0.5" Precipitation	0	0	1	3	3	3	3	3	2	2	1	1	22
Days With ≥ 1.0" Precipitation	0	0	0	1	1	2	1	1	1	0	0	0	7
Mean Snowfall (in.)	7.4	8.1	6.2	2.1	0.0	0.0	0.0	0.0	0.0	0.3	3.7	9.0	36.8
Maximum Snow Depth (in.)	na	na	*16*	*8*	*0*	*0*	*0*	*0*	*0*	*2*	*8*	na	na
Days With ≥ 1.0" Snow Depth	na	*10*	4	0	0	0	0	0	0	0	3	*9*	na

Fort Madison *Lee County* Elevation: 529 ft. Latitude: 40° 37' N Longitude: 91° 20' W

	JAN	FEB	MAR	APR	MAY	JUN	JUL	AUG	SEP	OCT	NOV	DEC	YEAR
Mean Maximum Temp. (°F)	34.0	37.9	50.1	62.6	72.8	81.9	86.1	84.5	77.1	64.4	50.3	36.8	61.5
Mean Temp. (°F)	25.8	29.6	40.8	52.8	63.3	72.7	77.0	75.3	67.2	54.8	42.0	29.1	52.5
Mean Minimum Temp. (°F)	17.5	21.3	31.5	42.9	53.9	63.5	68.0	66.2	57.3	45.2	33.7	21.4	43.5
Extreme Maximum Temp. (°F)	66	69	78	89	92	104	103	104	100	91	79	70	104
Extreme Minimum Temp. (°F)	-23	-20	-1	11	29	44	52	45	31	22	1	-19	-23
Days Maximum Temp. ≥ 90°F	0	0	0	0	0	3	9	7	2	0	0	0	21
Days Maximum Temp. ≤ 32°F	13	9	2	0	0	0	0	0	0	0	1	10	35
Days Minimum Temp. ≤ 32°F	28	24	16	4	0	0	0	0	0	2	14	26	114
Days Minimum Temp. ≤ 0°F	3	2	0	0	0	0	0	0	0	0	0	2	7
Heating Degree Days (base 65°F)	1,209	993	743	374	118	13	1	3	66	325	683	1,106	5,634
Cooling Degree Days (base 65°F)	0	0	0	13	72	251	378	328	140	16	0	0	1,198
Mean Precipitation (in.)	1.35	1.72	2.92	3.73	4.77	4.47	4.28	3.94	3.62	2.99	2.87	2.25	38.91
Extreme Maximum Daily Precip. (in.)	1.43	1.94	3.38	3.00	4.06	4.88	3.76	4.36	3.00	2.86	3.10	3.00	4.88
Days With ≥ 0.1" Precipitation	4	4	6	7	8	7	7	6	6	6	5	5	71
Days With ≥ 0.5" Precipitation	1	1	2	3	3	3	3	3	3	2	2	1	27
Days With ≥ 1.0" Precipitation	0	0	1	1	1	1	1	1	1	1	1	0	9
Mean Snowfall (in.)	6.1	4.9	1.9	0.4	0.0	0.0	0.0	0.0	0.0	trace	0.6	6.2	20.1
Maximum Snow Depth (in.)	*17*	na	*7*	*5*	*0*	*0*	*0*	*0*	*0*	*1*	*3*	*13*	na
Days With ≥ 1.0" Snow Depth	*11*	*5*	1	0	0	0	0	0	0	0	0	5	*22*

Glenwood 3 SW *Mills County* Elevation: 979 ft. Latitude: 41° 00' N Longitude: 95° 46' W

	JAN	FEB	MAR	APR	MAY	JUN	JUL	AUG	SEP	OCT	NOV	DEC	YEAR
Mean Maximum Temp. (°F)	34.1	38.5	51.1	64.0	74.6	83.4	87.4	85.5	79.0	66.5	50.1	36.3	62.5
Mean Temp. (°F)	23.6	27.7	39.3	51.3	62.5	71.9	76.2	74.0	65.7	53.2	38.9	26.6	50.9
Mean Minimum Temp. (°F)	13.1	16.8	27.5	38.6	50.3	60.3	64.9	62.4	52.4	39.9	27.7	16.8	39.2
Extreme Maximum Temp. (°F)	69	76	92	99	102	104	107	104	104	96	85	68	107
Extreme Minimum Temp. (°F)	-23	-23	-15	11	28	35	47	37	22	11	-7	-26	-26
Days Maximum Temp. ≥ 90°F	0	0	0	1	2	7	12	9	5	1	0	0	37
Days Maximum Temp. ≤ 32°F	13	10	3	0	0	0	0	0	0	0	3	11	40
Days Minimum Temp. ≤ 32°F	30	26	21	9	0	0	0	0	1	8	21	30	146
Days Minimum Temp. ≤ 0°F	5	4	1	0	0	0	0	0	0	0	0	3	13
Heating Degree Days (base 65°F)	1,277	1,049	790	423	143	17	2	7	101	375	775	1,185	6,144
Cooling Degree Days (base 65°F)	0	0	2	20	73	231	355	294	129	17	0	0	1,121
Mean Precipitation (in.)	0.63	0.87	2.08	3.50	5.26	5.19	4.29	3.73	2.82	2.09	1.48	1.01	32.95
Extreme Maximum Daily Precip. (in.)	0.85	1.57	2.17	3.77	4.98	5.02	6.48	3.21	6.00	2.20	1.48	2.50	6.48
Days With ≥ 0.1" Precipitation	2	3	5	6	8	7	6	6	5	4	3	3	58
Days With ≥ 0.5" Precipitation	0	0	2	2	4	3	3	2	2	1	1	0	20
Days With ≥ 1.0" Precipitation	0	0	0	1	1	2	1	1	1	0	0	0	7
Mean Snowfall (in.)	6.0	5.6	4.0	0.5	trace	0.0	0.0	0.0	0.0	0.3	1.5	4.5	22.4
Maximum Snow Depth (in.)	22	27	14	6	trace	0	0	0	0	7	7	20	27
Days With ≥ 1.0" Snow Depth	12	10	3	0	0	0	0	0	0	0	2	8	35

The period of record for all cooperative weather station data is 1980 – 2009. See User Guide for detailed explanation of data.

Grinnell 3 SW *Poweshiek County* Elevation: 904 ft. Latitude: 41° 43' N Longitude: 92° 45' W

	JAN	FEB	MAR	APR	MAY	JUN	JUL	AUG	SEP	OCT	NOV	DEC	YEAR
Mean Maximum Temp. (°F)	29.0	33.7	46.0	59.6	70.3	79.6	83.8	81.9	74.8	62.0	46.9	32.5	58.3
Mean Temp. (°F)	19.6	23.8	35.3	47.4	58.4	68.1	72.6	70.4	62.1	49.7	36.7	23.4	47.3
Mean Minimum Temp. (°F)	10.2	13.8	24.5	35.1	46.4	56.6	61.3	59.0	49.3	37.4	26.4	14.3	36.2
Extreme Maximum Temp. (°F)	64	68	88	92	91	100	102	103	96	91	79	69	103
Extreme Minimum Temp. (°F)	-32	-35	-11	1	19	35	44	37	21	10	-8	-32	-35
Days Maximum Temp. ≥ 90°F	0	0	0	0	0	2	6	4	1	0	0	0	13
Days Maximum Temp. ≤ 32°F	18	13	5	0	0	0	0	0	0	0	3	14	53
Days Minimum Temp. ≤ 32°F	30	26	24	13	2	0	0	0	1	11	22	29	158
Days Minimum Temp. ≤ 0°F	8	6	1	0	0	0	0	0	0	0	0	5	20
Heating Degree Days (base 65°F)	1,401	1,160	914	529	233	43	7	21	150	476	842	1,282	7,058
Cooling Degree Days (base 65°F)	0	0	0	7	34	144	249	195	68	9	0	0	706
Mean Precipitation (in.)	1.00	1.40	2.32	3.45	4.35	4.49	4.09	4.45	3.35	2.80	2.25	1.52	35.47
Extreme Maximum Daily Precip. (in.)	0.96	2.50	2.24	4.17	3.19	3.52	2.90	4.18	2.50	3.25	2.37	1.24	4.18
Days With ≥ 0.1" Precipitation	3	4	5	7	8	7	7	7	5	6	5	4	68
Days With ≥ 0.5" Precipitation	0	1	2	2	3	3	3	3	2	2	2	1	24
Days With ≥ 1.0" Precipitation	0	0	1	1	1	1	1	2	1	1	0	0	9
Mean Snowfall (in.)	7.6	7.1	4.4	1.1	trace	0.0	0.0	0.0	0.0	0.5	1.6	8.2	30.5
Maximum Snow Depth (in.)	20	19	16	7	trace	0	0	0	0	8	7	18	20
Days With ≥ 1.0" Snow Depth	17	13	4	1	0	0	0	0	0	0	1	11	47

Grundy Center *Grundy County* Elevation: 1,020 ft. Latitude: 42° 21' N Longitude: 92° 46' W

	JAN	FEB	MAR	APR	MAY	JUN	JUL	AUG	SEP	OCT	NOV	DEC	YEAR
Mean Maximum Temp. (°F)	26.6	31.3	43.9	58.7	70.4	79.6	83.0	81.0	74.3	61.2	45.3	30.1	57.1
Mean Temp. (°F)	17.7	22.3	34.2	47.2	59.1	69.0	72.6	70.3	62.2	49.6	35.6	21.6	46.8
Mean Minimum Temp. (°F)	8.8	13.3	24.5	35.7	47.8	58.4	62.1	59.6	50.1	38.0	25.9	13.0	36.4
Extreme Maximum Temp. (°F)	66	67	87	96	92	101	99	102	97	94	80	66	102
Extreme Minimum Temp. (°F)	-31	-29	-9	7	21	36	45	38	26	12	-3	-23	-31
Days Maximum Temp. ≥ 90°F	0	0	0	0	0	3	5	3	1	0	0	0	12
Days Maximum Temp. ≤ 32°F	21	15	5	0	0	0	0	0	0	0	5	17	63
Days Minimum Temp. ≤ 32°F	31	27	24	11	1	0	0	0	1	10	22	30	157
Days Minimum Temp. ≤ 0°F	9	6	1	0	0	0	0	0	0	0	0	6	22
Heating Degree Days (base 65°F)	1,459	1,201	947	533	214	34	7	20	147	479	874	1,341	7,256
Cooling Degree Days (base 65°F)	0	0	0	7	39	161	249	192	69	9	0	0	726
Mean Precipitation (in.)	0.83	0.93	2.12	3.67	4.61	5.20	4.32	4.29	2.93	2.53	2.13	1.21	34.77
Extreme Maximum Daily Precip. (in.)	0.93	1.42	1.75	4.42	2.94	2.94	6.25	3.01	3.37	2.19	3.00	1.33	6.25
Days With ≥ 0.1" Precipitation	3	3	5	7	8	8	7	7	5	5	5	4	67
Days With ≥ 0.5" Precipitation	0	0	1	2	3	4	3	3	2	2	1	1	22
Days With ≥ 1.0" Precipitation	0	0	0	1	1	2	1	1	1	0	0	0	7
Mean Snowfall (in.)	9.0	7.0	5.0	1.9	trace	0.0	trace	0.0	0.0	0.2	2.6	9.1	34.8
Maximum Snow Depth (in.)	29	19	16	7	trace	0	trace	0	0	4	11	26	29
Days With ≥ 1.0" Snow Depth	22	19	8	1	0	0	0	0	0	0	3	18	71

Hawarden *Sioux County* Elevation: 1,189 ft. Latitude: 43° 00' N Longitude: 96° 30' W

	JAN	FEB	MAR	APR	MAY	JUN	JUL	AUG	SEP	OCT	NOV	DEC	YEAR
Mean Maximum Temp. (°F)	28.4	33.1	45.1	60.4	71.8	81.1	85.0	83.1	75.5	62.0	44.7	30.6	58.4
Mean Temp. (°F)	18.3	22.9	34.3	47.8	59.7	69.5	73.7	71.5	62.6	49.4	34.4	21.0	47.1
Mean Minimum Temp. (°F)	8.2	12.6	23.5	35.1	47.6	57.8	62.4	60.0	49.7	36.8	24.0	11.4	35.8
Extreme Maximum Temp. (°F)	68	68	82	93	97	107	104	103	97	91	80	66	107
Extreme Minimum Temp. (°F)	-30	-33	-15	4	23	37	44	36	22	7	-19	-29	-33
Days Maximum Temp. ≥ 90°F	0	0	0	0	1	4	8	5	2	0	0	0	20
Days Maximum Temp. ≤ 32°F	18	13	5	0	0	0	0	0	0	0	5	16	57
Days Minimum Temp. ≤ 32°F	31	27	25	12	1	0	0	0	2	10	24	30	162
Days Minimum Temp. ≤ 0°F	9	6	2	0	0	0	0	0	0	0	1	6	24
Heating Degree Days (base 65°F)	1,441	1,185	945	519	205	33	6	14	143	484	911	1,358	7,244
Cooling Degree Days (base 65°F)	0	0	0	9	48	174	284	223	79	7	0	0	824
Mean Precipitation (in.)	0.59	0.62	1.86	3.13	3.49	3.92	3.43	3.10	3.14	2.29	1.53	0.83	27.93
Extreme Maximum Daily Precip. (in.)	1.09	1.06	2.03	2.27	2.00	6.01	3.30	4.78	3.33	2.62	2.56	1.09	6.01
Days With ≥ 0.1" Precipitation	2	2	4	6	7	7	5	6	5	4	3	2	53
Days With ≥ 0.5" Precipitation	0	0	1	2	2	2	2	2	2	1	1	0	15
Days With ≥ 1.0" Precipitation	0	0	0	1	1	1	1	1	1	1	0	0	7
Mean Snowfall (in.)	6.5	5.3	5.1	1.9	0.0	0.0	0.0	0.0	0.0	0.9	5.2	7.3	32.2
Maximum Snow Depth (in.)	20	17	12	7	0	0	0	0	0	7	13	20	20
Days With ≥ 1.0" Snow Depth	11	9	4	1	0	0	0	0	0	0	3	9	37

Iowa City *Johnson County* Elevation: 640 ft. Latitude: 41° 39' N Longitude: 91° 32' W

	JAN	FEB	MAR	APR	MAY	JUN	JUL	AUG	SEP	OCT	NOV	DEC	YEAR
Mean Maximum Temp. (°F)	32.2	37.1	49.9	64.3	74.9	83.5	87.3	85.1	78.3	65.4	49.8	35.3	61.9
Mean Temp. (°F)	23.8	28.4	40.0	52.7	63.5	72.7	76.7	74.6	66.7	54.5	40.9	27.4	51.8
Mean Minimum Temp. (°F)	15.4	19.6	30.0	41.1	52.0	61.8	66.1	64.1	55.1	43.5	31.9	19.5	41.7
Extreme Maximum Temp. (°F)	68	68	88	93	96	102	104	103	99	94	79	71	104
Extreme Minimum Temp. (°F)	-29	-26	-5	10	24	42	50	43	29	22	3	-20	-29
Days Maximum Temp. ≥ 90°F	0	0	0	0	1	5	11	7	3	0	0	0	27
Days Maximum Temp. ≤ 32°F	16	10	3	0	0	0	0	0	0	0	2	11	42
Days Minimum Temp. ≤ 32°F	29	24	18	5	0	0	0	0	0	4	16	28	124
Days Minimum Temp. ≤ 0°F	5	3	0	0	0	0	0	0	0	0	0	3	11
Heating Degree Days (base 65°F)	1,270	1,029	770	378	118	10	1	4	73	336	717	1,158	5,864
Cooling Degree Days (base 65°F)	0	0	1	16	79	249	370	310	130	17	0	0	1,172
Mean Precipitation (in.)	1.10	1.30	2.29	3.56	4.48	4.88	4.38	4.70	3.17	3.04	2.50	1.65	37.05
Extreme Maximum Daily Precip. (in.)	1.31	1.83	2.74	2.43	5.26	6.02	3.73	3.80	3.08	3.18	2.75	2.06	6.02
Days With ≥ 0.1" Precipitation	3	3	5	7	8	7	6	7	5	6	5	4	66
Days With ≥ 0.5" Precipitation	1	1	2	2	3	3	3	3	2	2	2	1	25
Days With ≥ 1.0" Precipitation	0	0	0	1	1	1	1	1	1	1	1	0	8
Mean Snowfall (in.)	7.8	6.0	3.3	1.0	trace	0.0	0.0	0.0	0.0	0.3	0.6	7.4	26.4
Maximum Snow Depth (in.)	24	18	8	7	trace	0	0	0	0	trace	6	23	24
Days With ≥ 1.0" Snow Depth	18	14	4	1	0	0	0	0	0	0	1	12	50

The period of record for all cooperative weather station data is 1980 – 2009. See User Guide for detailed explanation of data.

Le Claire L & D 14 *Scott County* Elevation: 577 ft. Latitude: 41° 34' N Longitude: 90° 24' W

	JAN	FEB	MAR	APR	MAY	JUN	JUL	AUG	SEP	OCT	NOV	DEC	YEAR
Mean Maximum Temp. (°F)	30.8	35.0	46.9	60.8	72.2	81.3	85.0	83.0	75.7	62.8	48.2	34.4	59.7
Mean Temp. (°F)	22.8	26.8	37.8	50.6	62.1	71.6	75.7	73.7	65.8	53.2	39.9	26.7	50.6
Mean Minimum Temp. (°F)	14.7	18.6	28.7	40.5	51.8	61.9	66.3	64.4	55.8	43.6	31.7	19.0	41.4
Extreme Maximum Temp. (°F)	63	67	83	88	93	100	102	103	97	91	78	69	103
Extreme Minimum Temp. (°F)	-24	-28	-10	11	28	43	50	43	32	20	4	-21	-28
Days Maximum Temp. ≥ 90°F	0	0	0	0	0	4	8	5	1	0	0	0	18
Days Maximum Temp. ≤ 32°F	17	11	4	0	0	0	0	0	0	0	2	12	46
Days Minimum Temp. ≤ 32°F	29	25	21	5	0	0	0	0	0	3	16	28	127
Days Minimum Temp. ≤ 0°F	5	3	0	0	0	0	0	0	0	0	0	3	11
Heating Degree Days (base 65°F)	1,304	1,075	836	435	148	17	1	6	82	372	746	1,181	6,203
Cooling Degree Days (base 65°F)	0	0	0	10	63	221	340	282	111	12	0	0	1,039
Mean Precipitation (in.)	1.19	1.44	2.44	3.23	3.90	4.54	3.81	4.45	3.09	2.62	2.31	2.16	35.18
Extreme Maximum Daily Precip. (in.)	1.80	1.55	3.00	2.69	2.60	7.53	3.62	4.26	3.45	3.43	1.80	1.95	7.53
Days With ≥ 0.1" Precipitation	3	3	5	6	7	7	6	6	5	5	5	5	63
Days With ≥ 0.5" Precipitation	0	1	1	2	3	3	2	3	2	2	2	1	22
Days With ≥ 1.0" Precipitation	0	0	1	1	1	1	1	1	1	1	0	0	8
Mean Snowfall (in.)	***3.1***	1.8	0.7	0.3	0.0	0.0	0.0	0.0	0.0	0.0	trace	1.7	***7.6***
Maximum Snow Depth (in.)	***13***	***11***	8	6	0	0	0	0	0	0	trace	12	***13***
Days With ≥ 1.0" Snow Depth	***9***	7	2	0	0	0	0	0	0	0	0	3	***21***

Le Mars *Plymouth County* Elevation: 1,194 ft. Latitude: 42° 47' N Longitude: 96° 09' W

	JAN	FEB	MAR	APR	MAY	JUN	JUL	AUG	SEP	OCT	NOV	DEC	YEAR
Mean Maximum Temp. (°F)	28.5	33.6	45.9	61.3	72.7	81.8	85.5	82.9	75.8	62.7	45.2	30.7	58.9
Mean Temp. (°F)	18.9	23.6	34.9	48.5	60.5	70.2	74.3	71.7	63.2	50.2	35.0	21.6	47.7
Mean Minimum Temp. (°F)	9.1	13.6	23.9	35.6	48.2	58.6	63.0	60.4	50.5	37.8	24.8	12.4	36.5
Extreme Maximum Temp. (°F)	69	70	86	96	98	105	106	103	99	92	80	68	106
Extreme Minimum Temp. (°F)	-29	-27	-13	7	26	37	46	38	25	11	-14	-28	-29
Days Maximum Temp. ≥ 90°F	0	0	0	0	1	5	8	5	2	0	0	0	21
Days Maximum Temp. ≤ 32°F	18	13	5	0	0	0	0	0	0	0	5	16	57
Days Minimum Temp. ≤ 32°F	31	27	25	11	1	0	0	0	1	9	24	30	159
Days Minimum Temp. ≤ 0°F	8	5	1	0	0	0	0	0	0	0	1	6	21
Heating Degree Days (base 65°F)	1,424	1,163	924	500	187	29	4	12	134	459	892	1,341	7,069
Cooling Degree Days (base 65°F)	0	0	0	11	55	192	300	227	87	8	0	0	880
Mean Precipitation (in.)	0.56	0.52	1.78	2.98	3.52	4.00	2.98	3.84	3.14	2.17	1.15	0.74	27.38
Extreme Maximum Daily Precip. (in.)	1.40	1.01	2.94	2.56	2.15	5.20	2.56	8.76	4.06	1.97	2.10	0.93	8.76
Days With ≥ 0.1" Precipitation	2	2	4	6	7	7	5	6	5	4	3	2	53
Days With ≥ 0.5" Precipitation	0	0	1	2	3	2	2	2	2	2	1	0	17
Days With ≥ 1.0" Precipitation	0	0	0	1	1	1	1	1	1	0	0	0	6
Mean Snowfall (in.)	5.8	4.5	5.3	1.6	0.0	0.0	0.0	trace	0.0	0.6	3.1	6.8	27.7
Maximum Snow Depth (in.)	***26***	na	13	9	0	0	0	trace	0	***3***	17	***23***	na
Days With ≥ 1.0" Snow Depth	***9***	***7***	4	1	0	0	0	0	0	1	2	7	***31***

Marshalltown *Marshall County* Elevation: 870 ft. Latitude: 42° 04' N Longitude: 92° 56' W

	JAN	FEB	MAR	APR	MAY	JUN	JUL	AUG	SEP	OCT	NOV	DEC	YEAR
Mean Maximum Temp. (°F)	28.4	33.2	45.7	60.0	71.2	80.5	84.2	82.0	75.1	61.9	46.5	31.8	58.4
Mean Temp. (°F)	19.0	23.7	35.7	48.6	60.0	69.6	73.4	71.0	62.7	50.1	36.6	22.8	47.8
Mean Minimum Temp. (°F)	9.5	14.2	25.6	37.1	48.7	58.7	62.7	60.0	50.3	38.2	26.6	13.9	37.1
Extreme Maximum Temp. (°F)	65	65	90	94	96	101	101	102	97	92	80	71	102
Extreme Minimum Temp. (°F)	-34	-35	-7	4	22	39	45	39	26	13	-3	-28	-35
Days Maximum Temp. ≥ 90°F	0	0	0	0	0	3	7	4	1	0	0	0	15
Days Maximum Temp. ≤ 32°F	19	13	4	0	0	0	0	0	0	0	4	15	55
Days Minimum Temp. ≤ 32°F	31	26	24	9	1	0	0	0	1	10	22	30	154
Days Minimum Temp. ≤ 0°F	8	5	1	0	0	0	0	0	0	0	0	6	20
Heating Degree Days (base 65°F)	1,422	1,163	904	494	194	31	4	16	137	465	846	1,301	6,977
Cooling Degree Days (base 65°F)	0	0	1	9	45	176	273	209	76	10	0	0	799
Mean Precipitation (in.)	0.89	1.00	2.27	3.52	4.62	5.53	4.85	4.44	3.54	2.70	2.10	1.24	36.70
Extreme Maximum Daily Precip. (in.)	0.84	1.96	2.31	2.69	4.15	4.20	4.43	3.82	2.59	2.47	3.78	1.58	4.43
Days With ≥ 0.1" Precipitation	3	3	5	7	9	8	7	6	5	5	4	4	66
Days With ≥ 0.5" Precipitation	0	0	1	2	3	4	3	3	2	2	1	1	22
Days With ≥ 1.0" Precipitation	0	0	1	1	1	2	2	1	1	1	0	0	10
Mean Snowfall (in.)	7.1	5.6	4.3	0.7	trace	0.0	0.0	0.0	0.0	0.3	1.7	7.4	27.1
Maximum Snow Depth (in.)	17	18	12	6	0	0	0	0	0	1	6	14	18
Days With ≥ 1.0" Snow Depth	17	14	5	1	0	0	0	0	0	0	2	13	52

Mason City *Cerro Gordo County* Elevation: 1,089 ft. Latitude: 43° 10' N Longitude: 93° 12' W

	JAN	FEB	MAR	APR	MAY	JUN	JUL	AUG	SEP	OCT	NOV	DEC	YEAR
Mean Maximum Temp. (°F)	25.2	29.7	41.8	57.8	69.9	79.3	82.8	80.4	73.4	60.0	43.2	28.4	56.0
Mean Temp. (°F)	16.0	20.6	32.3	46.3	58.2	67.8	71.9	69.4	61.3	48.5	34.1	20.1	45.5
Mean Minimum Temp. (°F)	6.8	11.5	22.7	34.8	46.4	56.4	61.0	58.2	49.2	37.0	24.8	11.7	35.1
Extreme Maximum Temp. (°F)	62	67	84	95	92	102	103	102	98	93	79	65	103
Extreme Minimum Temp. (°F)	-33	-32	-14	5	25	36	44	35	22	13	-7	-26	-33
Days Maximum Temp. ≥ 90°F	0	0	0	0	1	3	5	3	1	0	0	0	13
Days Maximum Temp. ≤ 32°F	22	16	7	1	0	0	0	0	0	0	6	19	71
Days Minimum Temp. ≤ 32°F	31	27	26	12	1	0	0	0	1	11	24	30	163
Days Minimum Temp. ≤ 0°F	11	7	1	0	0	0	0	0	0	0	0	6	25
Heating Degree Days (base 65°F)	1,513	1,249	1,007	560	240	47	9	23	162	510	921	1,386	7,627
Cooling Degree Days (base 65°F)	0	0	0	6	33	137	231	164	60	6	0	0	637
Mean Precipitation (in.)	0.89	0.86	1.99	3.48	5.00	5.30	4.66	4.68	3.23	2.42	1.80	1.10	35.41
Extreme Maximum Daily Precip. (in.)	1.09	1.54	2.40	2.90	4.88	4.34	4.00	6.25	5.02	2.07	2.73	1.50	6.25
Days With ≥ 0.1" Precipitation	3	2	4	7	8	8	6	7	6	5	4	3	63
Days With ≥ 0.5" Precipitation	0	0	1	3	3	4	3	3	2	2	1	1	23
Days With ≥ 1.0" Precipitation	0	0	1	1	2	2	2	1	1	0	0	0	10
Mean Snowfall (in.)	***8.2***	6.0	4.5	1.1	trace	0.0	0.0	0.0	0.0	0.1	2.1	***7.2***	***29.2***
Maximum Snow Depth (in.)	***23***	***17***	***23***	7	trace	***0***	0	0	0	***1***	***8***	na	na
Days With ≥ 1.0" Snow Depth	***19***	***19***	7	1	0	0	0	0	0	0	3	***19***	***68***

The period of record for all cooperative weather station data is 1980 – 2009. See User Guide for detailed explanation of data.

Muscatine *Muscatine County* Elevation: 548 ft. Latitude: 41° 24' N Longitude: 91° 04' W

	JAN	FEB	MAR	APR	MAY	JUN	JUL	AUG	SEP	OCT	NOV	DEC	YEAR
Mean Maximum Temp. (°F)	32.3	37.0	49.8	63.9	74.3	82.8	86.3	84.3	77.5	64.7	49.7	35.1	61.5
Mean Temp. (°F)	23.7	28.2	39.8	52.4	63.1	72.1	76.0	74.0	66.0	53.7	40.6	27.1	51.4
Mean Minimum Temp. (°F)	15.0	19.4	29.7	40.8	51.8	61.3	65.7	63.7	54.5	42.7	31.5	19.2	41.3
Extreme Maximum Temp. (°F)	69	69	89	91	94	104	105	105	99	96	80	72	105
Extreme Minimum Temp. (°F)	-28	-34	-9	10	26	39	47	39	26	17	2	-23	-34
Days Maximum Temp. ≥ 90°F	0	0	0	0	1	5	9	6	2	0	0	0	23
Days Maximum Temp. ≤ 32°F	15	10	3	0	0	0	0	0	0	0	2	11	41
Days Minimum Temp. ≤ 32°F	29	24	19	6	0	0	0	0	0	5	16	27	126
Days Minimum Temp. ≤ 0°F	5	3	0	0	0	0	0	0	0	0	0	3	11
Heating Degree Days (base 65°F)	1,274	1,033	776	389	129	14	1	5	80	358	726	1,169	5,954
Cooling Degree Days (base 65°F)	0	0	2	17	76	233	349	290	117	15	1	0	1,100
Mean Precipitation (in.)	1.33	1.55	2.64	3.43	4.54	4.82	3.92	4.57	3.40	3.04	2.42	2.07	37.73
Extreme Maximum Daily Precip. (in.)	2.12	1.93	2.55	1.89	3.45	4.12	2.29	4.06	3.34	3.13	1.80	1.76	4.12
Days With ≥ 0.1" Precipitation	3	4	6	7	8	8	6	7	5	5	5	5	69
Days With ≥ 0.5" Precipitation	1	1	2	2	3	3	2	3	2	2	2	1	24
Days With ≥ 1.0" Precipitation	0	0	1	1	1	2	1	1	1	1	0	0	9
Mean Snowfall (in.)	7.7	5.5	2.2	0.5	trace	0.0	0.0	0.0	0.0	0.1	0.5	6.7	23.2
Maximum Snow Depth (in.)	18	11	7	2	0	0	0	0	0	1	3	17	18
Days With ≥ 1.0" Snow Depth	14	11	2	0	0	0	0	0	0	0	1	9	37

Ottumwa Industrial Arpt *Wapello County* Elevation: 841 ft. Latitude: 41° 06' N Longitude: 92° 27' W

	JAN	FEB	MAR	APR	MAY	JUN	JUL	AUG	SEP	OCT	NOV	DEC	YEAR
Mean Maximum Temp. (°F)	32.0	36.5	48.7	62.1	72.4	81.6	85.8	83.8	76.2	63.3	48.9	35.0	60.5
Mean Temp. (°F)	23.6	27.9	39.0	51.4	62.1	71.7	75.9	73.8	65.2	53.0	40.0	26.9	50.9
Mean Minimum Temp. (°F)	15.1	19.3	29.2	40.6	51.8	61.7	66.0	63.7	54.1	42.6	31.0	18.8	41.2
Extreme Maximum Temp. (°F)	71	71	88	90	93	103	105	105	100	92	79	71	105
Extreme Minimum Temp. (°F)	-23	-27	-4	9	24	42	49	42	27	20	-5	-21	-27
Days Maximum Temp. ≥ 90°F	0	0	0	0	0	4	9	6	2	0	0	0	21
Days Maximum Temp. ≤ 32°F	16	11	3	0	0	0	0	0	0	0	2	12	44
Days Minimum Temp. ≤ 32°F	29	24	20	6	0	0	0	0	0	5	17	28	129
Days Minimum Temp. ≤ 0°F	5	3	0	0	0	0	0	0	0	0	0	3	11
Heating Degree Days (base 65°F)	1,277	1,042	800	416	146	16	1	7	98	380	743	1,174	6,100
Cooling Degree Days (base 65°F)	0	0	2	15	63	224	346	285	109	14	0	0	1,058
Mean Precipitation (in.)	0.91	1.29	2.39	3.33	4.70	5.04	4.09	4.42	3.57	2.88	2.36	1.42	36.40
Extreme Maximum Daily Precip. (in.)	0.98	1.93	2.08	2.10	4.43	3.41	3.78	3.45	5.32	2.26	2.54	1.90	5.32
Days With ≥ 0.1" Precipitation	3	3	5	7	8	7	7	6	6	5	5	3	65
Days With ≥ 0.5" Precipitation	0	1	1	2	3	3	2	3	3	2	2	1	23
Days With ≥ 1.0" Precipitation	0	0	0	1	1	2	1	1	1	1	0	0	8
Mean Snowfall (in.)	***6.5***	***5.9***	na	na	na	***trace***	***trace***	***trace***	na	***0.6***	***1.2***	***5.4***	na
Maximum Snow Depth (in.)	***14***	***11***	***11***	na	na	***trace***	***trace***	***trace***	na	***5***	***3***	***10***	na
Days With ≥ 1.0" Snow Depth	***15***	***12***	***4***	na	na	***0***	***0***	***0***	na	***0***	***1***	***8***	na

Rockwell City *Calhoun County* Elevation: 1,194 ft. Latitude: 42° 24' N Longitude: 94° 38' W

	JAN	FEB	MAR	APR	MAY	JUN	JUL	AUG	SEP	OCT	NOV	DEC	YEAR
Mean Maximum Temp. (°F)	28.2	32.9	45.5	60.6	71.6	80.9	83.9	81.7	75.2	62.1	45.2	30.6	58.2
Mean Temp. (°F)	19.1	23.6	35.3	48.6	60.2	69.8	73.3	71.0	63.2	50.5	35.7	22.2	47.7
Mean Minimum Temp. (°F)	10.0	14.4	25.0	36.6	48.7	58.7	62.7	60.3	51.1	38.9	26.1	13.6	37.2
Extreme Maximum Temp. (°F)	70	66	87	97	92	101	100	102	97	93	80	68	102
Extreme Minimum Temp. (°F)	-25	-26	-12	5	28	40	43	39	27	14	-7	-25	-26
Days Maximum Temp. ≥ 90°F	0	0	0	0	1	4	6	4	1	0	0	0	16
Days Maximum Temp. ≤ 32°F	19	13	5	0	0	0	0	0	0	0	5	16	58
Days Minimum Temp. ≤ 32°F	31	27	24	10	1	0	0	0	1	8	23	30	155
Days Minimum Temp. ≤ 0°F	8	5	1	0	0	0	0	0	0	0	0	5	19
Heating Degree Days (base 65°F)	1,416	1,164	916	494	189	26	4	13	128	452	872	1,322	6,996
Cooling Degree Days (base 65°F)	0	0	0	10	45	176	269	207	80	8	0	0	795
Mean Precipitation (in.)	0.74	0.70	1.85	3.34	4.73	4.60	3.93	4.53	2.92	2.43	1.49	1.05	32.31
Extreme Maximum Daily Precip. (in.)	0.99	0.86	2.04	2.35	5.87	3.86	3.58	5.29	2.62	2.53	1.21	1.10	5.87
Days With ≥ 0.1" Precipitation	2	2	4	6	8	7	7	6	5	5	4	3	59
Days With ≥ 0.5" Precipitation	0	0	1	2	3	3	3	3	2	2	1	1	21
Days With ≥ 1.0" Precipitation	0	0	0	1	1	1	1	1	1	1	0	0	7
Mean Snowfall (in.)	6.9	5.8	5.5	2.1	0.0	0.0	0.0	0.0	trace	0.7	3.4	7.7	32.1
Maximum Snow Depth (in.)	18	16	17	7	0	0	0	0	trace	4	8	17	18
Days With ≥ 1.0" Snow Depth	20	17	7	1	0	0	0	0	0	0	4	16	65

Sidney *Fremont County* Elevation: 1,129 ft. Latitude: 40° 45' N Longitude: 95° 39' W

	JAN	FEB	MAR	APR	MAY	JUN	JUL	AUG	SEP	OCT	NOV	DEC	YEAR
Mean Maximum Temp. (°F)	34.2	39.1	51.2	63.8	73.7	82.7	86.6	84.8	78.1	65.8	50.0	36.1	62.2
Mean Temp. (°F)	24.8	29.2	40.1	52.1	62.8	72.2	76.4	74.4	66.5	54.3	40.1	27.4	51.7
Mean Minimum Temp. (°F)	15.2	19.3	29.0	40.3	51.9	61.7	66.2	63.9	54.8	42.8	30.2	18.6	41.2
Extreme Maximum Temp. (°F)	69	76	91	96	100	105	106	103	102	93	83	68	106
Extreme Minimum Temp. (°F)	-21	-23	-10	16	32	41	52	45	28	14	-1	-25	-25
Days Maximum Temp. ≥ 90°F	0	0	0	1	1	5	10	8	3	0	0	0	28
Days Maximum Temp. ≤ 32°F	13	10	3	0	0	0	0	0	0	0	3	12	41
Days Minimum Temp. ≤ 32°F	30	24	20	7	0	0	0	0	0	4	18	29	132
Days Minimum Temp. ≤ 0°F	5	3	0	0	0	0	0	0	0	0	0	3	11
Heating Degree Days (base 65°F)	1,241	1,006	767	401	132	15	1	4	85	342	740	1,160	5,894
Cooling Degree Days (base 65°F)	0	0	2	20	72	237	362	302	135	19	0	0	1,149
Mean Precipitation (in.)	0.73	1.00	2.13	3.21	5.15	4.50	4.73	3.65	3.09	2.57	1.73	1.17	33.66
Extreme Maximum Daily Precip. (in.)	0.80	1.39	1.50	2.57	4.48	4.06	7.10	2.96	4.16	4.29	2.21	1.40	7.10
Days With ≥ 0.1" Precipitation	2	3	5	6	8	7	6	6	5	5	4	3	60
Days With ≥ 0.5" Precipitation	0	1	1	2	3	3	3	2	2	1	1	1	20
Days With ≥ 1.0" Precipitation	0	0	0	1	1	1	1	1	1	1	0	0	7
Mean Snowfall (in.)	5.5	5.9	5.1	1.5	trace	0.0	0.0	0.0	0.0	0.6	1.9	5.6	26.1
Maximum Snow Depth (in.)	13	12	10	12	trace	0	0	0	0	5	7	14	14
Days With ≥ 1.0" Snow Depth	13	11	4	1	0	0	0	0	0	0	2	10	41

The period of record for all cooperative weather station data is 1980 – 2009. See User Guide for detailed explanation of data.

Sigourney *Keokuk County* Elevation: 799 ft. Latitude: 41° 20' N Longitude: 92° 12' W

	JAN	FEB	MAR	APR	MAY	JUN	JUL	AUG	SEP	OCT	NOV	DEC	YEAR
Mean Maximum Temp. (°F)	31.0	35.9	48.1	61.6	71.8	80.9	85.2	83.5	76.0	63.3	48.5	34.3	60.0
Mean Temp. (°F)	22.1	26.6	37.9	50.3	61.2	70.5	74.8	72.9	64.5	52.3	39.1	25.8	49.8
Mean Minimum Temp. (°F)	13.2	17.3	27.6	38.9	50.5	59.9	64.2	62.3	52.9	41.3	29.7	17.3	39.6
Extreme Maximum Temp. (°F)	70	71	86	91	92	105	107	107	98	91	79	71	107
Extreme Minimum Temp. (°F)	-25	-27	-5	7	25	41	48	42	30	16	-2	-23	-27
Days Maximum Temp. ≥ 90°F	0	0	0	0	0	3	8	6	2	0	0	0	19
Days Maximum Temp. ≤ 32°F	17	11	4	0	0	0	0	0	0	0	3	13	48
Days Minimum Temp. ≤ 32°F	30	25	21	7	0	0	0	0	0	6	19	29	137
Days Minimum Temp. ≤ 0°F	6	4	0	0	0	0	0	0	0	0	0	4	14
Heating Degree Days (base 65°F)	1,323	1,079	835	447	166	24	2	9	107	398	770	1,209	6,369
Cooling Degree Days (base 65°F)	0	0	1	12	55	195	312	260	97	11	0	0	943
Mean Precipitation (in.)	1.02	1.19	2.45	3.40	4.36	4.55	4.04	4.78	3.42	2.88	2.42	1.46	35.97
Extreme Maximum Daily Precip. (in.)	1.42	1.66	2.25	4.51	3.61	3.24	3.85	3.85	3.52	2.42	1.45	1.26	4.51
Days With ≥ 0.1" Precipitation	3	3	5	7	8	7	6	7	6	6	5	4	67
Days With ≥ 0.5" Precipitation	0	1	2	3	3	3	3	3	2	2	2	1	25
Days With ≥ 1.0" Precipitation	0	0	0	1	1	1	1	1	1	1	1	0	8
Mean Snowfall (in.)	7.4	6.7	3.7	1.3	trace	0.0	0.0	0.0	0.0	0.4	1.1	6.8	27.4
Maximum Snow Depth (in.)	15	15	14	7	trace	0	0	0	0	8	5	16	16
Days With ≥ 1.0" Snow Depth	16	12	4	0	0	0	0	0	0	0	1	10	43

Tripoli *Bremer County* Elevation: 959 ft. Latitude: 42° 49' N Longitude: 92° 16' W

	JAN	FEB	MAR	APR	MAY	JUN	JUL	AUG	SEP	OCT	NOV	DEC	YEAR
Mean Maximum Temp. (°F)	25.2	29.6	43.2	58.4	70.6	79.5	82.9	80.7	73.8	60.4	44.0	29.0	56.4
Mean Temp. (°F)	16.2	21.0	33.8	47.2	59.1	68.5	72.0	69.7	61.7	48.9	35.0	20.7	46.1
Mean Minimum Temp. (°F)	7.2	12.3	24.3	35.9	47.6	57.4	61.1	58.6	49.6	37.4	25.9	12.3	35.8
Extreme Maximum Temp. (°F)	62	66	84	96	94	102	100	104	95	93	79	65	104
Extreme Minimum Temp. (°F)	-32	-32	-11	0	24	36	46	38	29	13	-5	-28	-32
Days Maximum Temp. ≥ 90°F	0	0	0	0	0	3	5	3	1	0	0	0	12
Days Maximum Temp. ≤ 32°F	22	15	6	0	0	0	0	0	0	0	5	18	66
Days Minimum Temp. ≤ 32°F	31	26	25	10	1	0	0	0	1	10	23	30	157
Days Minimum Temp. ≤ 0°F	10	7	1	0	0	0	0	0	0	0	1	***6***	***25***
Heating Degree Days (base 65°F)	1,507	1,238	962	534	212	39	9	22	154	498	894	1,369	7,438
Cooling Degree Days (base 65°F)	0	0	0	6	37	150	233	173	62	7	0	0	668
Mean Precipitation (in.)	0.96	0.86	1.85	3.76	4.60	5.24	4.63	5.23	3.13	2.55	2.14	1.22	36.17
Extreme Maximum Daily Precip. (in.)	0.91	1.05	1.83	5.13	5.53	3.81	3.50	***5.50***	***4.90***	2.51	***3.10***	***1.20***	***5.53***
Days With ≥ 0.1" Precipitation	3	3	5	7	8	8	7	7	6	5	4	4	67
Days With ≥ 0.5" Precipitation	0	0	1	3	3	4	3	3	2	2	1	0	22
Days With ≥ 1.0" Precipitation	0	0	0	1	1	2	1	2	1	1	1	0	10
Mean Snowfall (in.)	8.7	6.0	4.4	1.6	trace	0.0	0.0	0.0	0.0	0.3	3.4	9.5	33.9
Maximum Snow Depth (in.)	35	***21***	***10***	10	trace	0	0	***0***	***0***	***2***	***14***	***31***	***35***
Days With ≥ 1.0" Snow Depth	13	***13***	5	1	0	0	0	0	0	0	2	11	***45***

Vinton *Benton County* Elevation: 850 ft. Latitude: 42° 10' N Longitude: 92° 00' W

	JAN	FEB	MAR	APR	MAY	JUN	JUL	AUG	SEP	OCT	NOV	DEC	YEAR
Mean Maximum Temp. (°F)	28.9	33.8	47.1	62.2	72.4	81.0	84.4	82.1	75.3	62.4	46.6	31.8	59.0
Mean Temp. (°F)	20.4	25.1	37.2	50.5	60.8	70.0	73.7	71.5	63.7	51.5	37.7	23.8	48.8
Mean Minimum Temp. (°F)	11.5	16.4	27.2	38.3	49.2	58.7	62.8	60.7	51.8	40.4	28.6	16.0	38.5
Extreme Maximum Temp. (°F)	63	66	88	89	92	101	104	104	97	92	79	68	104
Extreme Minimum Temp. (°F)	-34	-30	-9	4	22	36	44	39	23	14	-4	-27	-34
Days Maximum Temp. ≥ 90°F	0	0	0	0	0	3	6	4	1	0	0	0	14
Days Maximum Temp. ≤ 32°F	18	12	4	0	0	0	0	0	0	0	3	15	52
Days Minimum Temp. ≤ 32°F	30	26	22	8	1	0	0	0	1	7	20	29	144
Days Minimum Temp. ≤ 0°F	7	4	1	0	0	0	0	0	0	0	0	4	16
Heating Degree Days (base 65°F)	1,377	1,120	854	440	172	24	3	11	120	420	812	1,272	6,625
Cooling Degree Days (base 65°F)	0	0	1	11	49	181	278	221	87	10	0	0	838
Mean Precipitation (in.)	1.10	1.14	2.07	3.39	4.68	4.90	4.28	4.29	3.50	2.85	2.31	1.46	35.97
Extreme Maximum Daily Precip. (in.)	0.82	1.20	1.98	2.81	4.25	4.00	3.30	3.20	2.45	2.37	3.56	1.46	4.25
Days With ≥ 0.1" Precipitation	3	3	5	7	8	8	7	7	6	6	5	4	69
Days With ≥ 0.5" Precipitation	0	1	1	2	3	4	3	3	2	2	1	1	23
Days With ≥ 1.0" Precipitation	0	0	0	1	1	2	1	1	1	1	1	0	9
Mean Snowfall (in.)	8.7	7.0	4.7	1.7	trace	0.0	0.0	0.0	0.0	0.3	2.2	8.3	32.9
Maximum Snow Depth (in.)	32	23	18	10	0	0	0	0	0	7	9	30	32
Days With ≥ 1.0" Snow Depth	20	17	6	1	0	0	0	0	0	0	2	12	58

Winterset 2 NNW *Madison County* Elevation: 1,069 ft. Latitude: 41° 22' N Longitude: 94° 02' W

	JAN	FEB	MAR	APR	MAY	JUN	JUL	AUG	SEP	OCT	NOV	DEC	YEAR
Mean Maximum Temp. (°F)	31.9	36.4	49.1	62.4	72.0	80.8	84.9	83.1	76.1	63.7	48.3	34.8	60.3
Mean Temp. (°F)	22.5	26.6	38.2	50.3	60.8	69.9	74.3	72.3	64.3	52.1	38.4	25.9	49.6
Mean Minimum Temp. (°F)	13.0	16.8	27.3	38.3	49.6	59.0	63.7	61.4	52.4	40.5	28.5	16.9	39.0
Extreme Maximum Temp. (°F)	67	70	89	92	94	101	104	106	100	93	80	67	106
Extreme Minimum Temp. (°F)	-25	-31	-11	10	24	40	47	38	29	12	-8	-25	-31
Days Maximum Temp. ≥ 90°F	0	0	0	0	0	3	8	5	2	0	0	0	18
Days Maximum Temp. ≤ 32°F	15	11	4	0	0	0	0	0	0	0	3	13	46
Days Minimum Temp. ≤ 32°F	30	26	21	9	1	0	0	0	1	8	20	29	145
Days Minimum Temp. ≤ 0°F	6	4	0	0	0	0	0	0	0	0	0	4	14
Heating Degree Days (base 65°F)	1,312	1,079	824	446	171	26	3	11	114	405	790	1,205	6,386
Cooling Degree Days (base 65°F)	0	0	1	13	49	180	300	243	98	12	0	0	896
Mean Precipitation (in.)	0.85	1.01	2.22	3.33	4.69	4.62	4.18	3.85	3.39	2.45	2.04	1.26	33.89
Extreme Maximum Daily Precip. (in.)	1.61	1.20	2.26	1.92	3.73	4.06	3.93	2.96	4.99	2.42	3.12	2.65	4.99
Days With ≥ 0.1" Precipitation	3	3	5	7	9	7	7	6	5	5	4	3	64
Days With ≥ 0.5" Precipitation	0	0	2	2	3	3	3	2	2	2	2	1	22
Days With ≥ 1.0" Precipitation	0	0	0	1	1	1	1	1	1	1	1	0	8
Mean Snowfall (in.)	7.0	7.8	4.5	1.1	0.1	0.0	0.0	0.0	0.0	0.6	2.2	7.5	30.8
Maximum Snow Depth (in.)	23	16	14	8	0	0	0	0	0	6	8	23	23
Days With ≥ 1.0" Snow Depth	16	14	5	1	0	0	0	0	0	0	2	11	49

The period of record for all cooperative weather station data is 1980 – 2009. See User Guide for detailed explanation of data.

Iowa Weather Station Rankings

Annual Extreme Maximum Temperature

Highest Rank	Station Name	°F	Lowest Rank	Station Name	°F
1	Des Moines Arpt	108	1	Cresco 1 NE	100
1	Dubuque Lock & Dam 11	108	2	Clinton No 1	101
1	Eldora	108	2	Dubuque Regional Arpt	101
1	Sioux City Municipal Arpt	108	2	Forest City 2 NNE	101
5	Glenwood 3 SW	107	5	Ames 8 WSW	102
5	Hawarden	107	5	Anamosa 1 WNW	102
5	Sigourney	107	5	Emmetsburg	102
8	Albia 3 NNE	106	5	Grundy Center	102
8	Ankeny	106	5	Marshalltown	102
8	Bloomfield 1 WNW	106	5	Rockwell City	102
8	Boone	106	11	Atlantic 1 NE	103
8	Elkader 5 SSW	106	11	Audubon 1 SSE	103
8	Fort Dodge	106	11	Grinnell 3 SW	103
8	Le Mars	106	11	Le Claire L & D 14	103
8	Sidney	106	11	Mason City	103
8	Winterset 2 NNW	106	16	Allison	104
17	Algona 3 W	105	16	Castana Experiment Farm	104
17	Beaconsfield	105	16	Cedar Rapids Municipal Arpt	104
17	Belle Plaine	105	16	Cherokee	104
17	Cedar Rapids No 1	105	16	Colo	104
17	Muscatine	105	16	Fort Madison	104
17	Ottumwa Industrial Arpt	105	16	Iowa City	104
17	Waterloo Municipal Arpt	105	16	Tripoli	104
17	Burlington Radio KBUR	105	16	Vinton	104
25	Allison	104	25	Algona 3 W	105

Annual Mean Maximum Temperature

Highest Rank	Station Name	°F	Lowest Rank	Station Name	°F
1	Glenwood 3 SW	62.5	1	Cresco 1 NE	54.7
2	Sidney	62.2	2	Forest City 2 NNE	55.7
3	Iowa City	61.9	3	Mason City	56.0
4	Bloomfield 1 WNW	61.8	4	Algona 3 W	56.2
5	Fort Madison	61.5	5	Tripoli	56.5
5	Muscatine	61.5	6	Dubuque Regional Arpt	56.6
7	Burlington Radio KBUR	61.0	7	Grundy Center	57.1
8	Albia 3 NNE	60.8	8	Emmetsburg	57.3
9	Atlantic 1 NE	60.5	9	Colo	57.6
9	Ottumwa Industrial Arpt	60.5	10	Allison	57.7
11	Winterset 2 NNW	60.3	10	Eldora	57.7
12	Des Moines Arpt	60.2	12	Waterloo Municipal Arpt	57.9
13	Clinton No 1	60.1	13	Cherokee	58.0
14	Sigourney	60.0	13	Fort Dodge	58.0
15	Ankeny	59.9	15	Rockwell City	58.2
15	Beaconsfield	59.9	16	Elkader 5 SSW	58.3
15	Cedar Rapids No 1	59.9	16	Grinnell 3 SW	58.3
18	Sioux City Municipal Arpt	59.8	18	Cedar Rapids Municipal Arpt	58.4
19	Le Claire L & D 14	59.7	18	Hawarden	58.4
20	Audubon 1 SSE	59.6	18	Marshalltown	58.4
20	Castana Experiment Farm	59.6	21	Dubuque Lock & Dam 11	58.6
22	Ames 8 WSW	59.4	22	Belle Plaine	58.8
23	Anamosa 1 WNW	59.1	23	Le Mars	58.9
24	Boone	59.0	24	Boone	59.0
24	Vinton	59.0	24	Vinton	59.0

Rankings include 25 highest/lowest stations. If state has less than 25 stations, all stations are included. The period of record is 1980–2009. See User Guide for detailed explanation of data.

Annual Mean Temperature

Highest

Rank	Station Name	°F
1	Fort Madison	52.5
2	Iowa City	51.8
2	Burlington Radio KBUR	51.8
4	Sidney	51.7
5	Bloomfield 1 WNW	51.6
6	Muscatine	51.4
7	Glenwood 3 SW	50.9
7	Ottumwa Industrial Arpt	50.9
9	Albia 3 NNE	50.7
10	Des Moines Arpt	50.6
10	Le Claire L & D 14	50.6
12	Clinton No 1	50.4
13	Cedar Rapids No 1	49.9
14	Sigourney	49.8
15	Beaconsfield	49.6
15	Winterset 2 NNW	49.6
17	Dubuque Lock & Dam 11	49.5
18	Atlantic 1 NE	49.3
19	Ames 8 WSW	49.2
19	Castana Experiment Farm	49.2
21	Ankeny	49.1
22	Sioux City Municipal Arpt	48.8
22	Vinton	48.8
24	Audubon 1 SSE	48.5
24	Cedar Rapids Municipal Arpt	48.5

Lowest

Rank	Station Name	°F
1	Cresco 1 NE	44.2
2	Mason City	45.6
3	Forest City 2 NNE	45.9
4	Algona 3 W	46.1
4	Tripoli	46.1
6	Cherokee	46.7
6	Elkader 5 SSW	46.7
8	Grundy Center	46.8
9	Emmetsburg	47.0
10	Hawarden	47.1
11	Dubuque Regional Arpt	47.3
11	Grinnell 3 SW	47.3
13	Eldora	47.5
13	Fort Dodge	47.5
13	Waterloo Municipal Arpt	47.5
16	Colo	47.6
17	Allison	47.7
17	Le Mars	47.7
17	Rockwell City	47.7
20	Boone	47.8
20	Marshalltown	47.8
22	Anamosa 1 WNW	48.1
23	Belle Plaine	48.3
24	Audubon 1 SSE	48.5
24	Cedar Rapids Municipal Arpt	48.5

Annual Mean Minimum Temperature

Highest

Rank	Station Name	°F
1	Fort Madison	43.5
2	Burlington Radio KBUR	42.6
3	Iowa City	41.7
4	Bloomfield 1 WNW	41.4
4	Le Claire L & D 14	41.4
6	Muscatine	41.3
7	Ottumwa Industrial Arpt	41.2
7	Sidney	41.2
9	Des Moines Arpt	41.0
10	Clinton No 1	40.6
11	Albia 3 NNE	40.5
12	Dubuque Lock & Dam 11	40.4
13	Cedar Rapids No 1	39.9
14	Sigourney	39.6
15	Beaconsfield	39.3
16	Glenwood 3 SW	39.2
17	Winterset 2 NNW	39.0
18	Ames 8 WSW	38.9
19	Castana Experiment Farm	38.7
20	Cedar Rapids Municipal Arpt	38.5
20	Vinton	38.5
22	Ankeny	38.3
23	Dubuque Regional Arpt	38.1
24	Atlantic 1 NE	38.0
25	Belle Plaine	37.8

Lowest

Rank	Station Name	°F
1	Cresco 1 NE	33.6
2	Elkader 5 SSW	35.1
2	Mason City	35.1
4	Cherokee	35.3
5	Hawarden	35.8
5	Tripoli	35.8
7	Algona 3 W	35.9
7	Forest City 2 NNE	35.9
9	Grinnell 3 SW	36.2
10	Boone	36.4
10	Grundy Center	36.4
12	Le Mars	36.5
13	Emmetsburg	36.7
14	Anamosa 1 WNW	37.0
14	Fort Dodge	37.0
16	Marshalltown	37.1
16	Waterloo Municipal Arpt	37.1
18	Eldora	37.2
18	Rockwell City	37.2
20	Audubon 1 SSE	37.3
21	Colo	37.5
22	Allison	37.6
23	Belle Plaine	37.8
23	Sioux City Municipal Arpt	37.8
25	Atlantic 1 NE	38.0

Rankings include 25 highest/lowest stations. If state has less than 25 stations, all stations are included. The period of record is 1980–2009. See User Guide for detailed explanation of data.

Annual Extreme Minimum Temperature

Highest Rank	Highest Station Name	°F	Lowest Rank	Lowest Station Name	°F
1	Fort Madison	-23	1	Elkader 5 SSW	-39
2	Sioux City Municipal Arpt	-24	2	Belle Plaine	-38
3	Beaconsfield	-25	3	Anamosa 1 WNW	-37
3	Sidney	-25	4	Cresco 1 NE	-36
5	Bloomfield 1 WNW	-26	5	Boone	-35
5	Castana Experiment Farm	-26	5	Grinnell 3 SW	-35
5	Des Moines Arpt	-26	5	Marshalltown	-35
5	Glenwood 3 SW	-26	8	Ankeny	-34
5	Rockwell City	-26	8	Muscatine	-34
5	Burlington Radio KBUR	-26	8	Vinton	-34
11	Ottumwa Industrial Arpt	-27	8	Waterloo Municipal Arpt	-34
11	Sigourney	-27	12	Atlantic 1 NE	-33
13	Ames 8 WSW	-28	12	Cedar Rapids No 1	-33
13	Colo	-28	12	Cherokee	-33
13	Le Claire L & D 14	-28	12	Hawarden	-33
16	Audubon 1 SSE	-29	12	Mason City	-33
16	Cedar Rapids Municipal Arpt	-29	17	Dubuque Lock & Dam 11	-32
16	Clinton No 1	-29	17	Forest City 2 NNE	-32
16	Eldora	-29	17	Tripoli	-32
16	Emmetsburg	-29	20	Albia 3 NNE	-31
16	Iowa City	-29	20	Allison	-31
16	Le Mars	-29	20	Grundy Center	-31
23	Algona 3 W	-30	20	Winterset 2 NNW	-31
23	Dubuque Regional Arpt	-30	24	Algona 3 W	-30
23	Fort Dodge	-30	24	Dubuque Regional Arpt	-30

July Mean Maximum Temperature

Highest Rank	Highest Station Name	°F	Lowest Rank	Lowest Station Name	°F
1	Glenwood 3 SW	87.4	1	Cresco 1 NE	81.7
2	Iowa City	87.3	2	Dubuque Regional Arpt	82.0
3	Sidney	86.6	3	Forest City 2 NNE	82.4
4	Bloomfield 1 WNW	86.3	4	Algona 3 W	82.6
4	Muscatine	86.3	5	Mason City	82.8
6	Fort Madison	86.1	6	Tripoli	82.9
7	Ankeny	86.0	7	Grundy Center	83.0
8	Des Moines Arpt	85.8	8	Colo	83.5
8	Ottumwa Industrial Arpt	85.8	9	Allison	83.8
8	Sioux City Municipal Arpt	85.8	9	Grinnell 3 SW	83.8
11	Atlantic 1 NE	85.7	11	Cedar Rapids Municipal Arpt	83.9
12	Burlington Radio KBUR	85.6	11	Rockwell City	83.9
13	Albia 3 NNE	85.5	13	Eldora	84.2
13	Le Mars	85.5	13	Elkader 5 SSW	84.2
15	Sigourney	85.2	13	Marshalltown	84.2
16	Cedar Rapids No 1	85.1	13	Waterloo Municipal Arpt	84.2
17	Clinton No 1	85.0	17	Ames 8 WSW	84.3
17	Dubuque Lock & Dam 11	85.0	17	Belle Plaine	84.3
17	Hawarden	85.0	17	Emmetsburg	84.3
17	Le Claire L & D 14	85.0	20	Vinton	84.4
21	Winterset 2 NNW	84.9	21	Beaconsfield	84.5
22	Boone	84.8	22	Anamosa 1 WNW	84.6
22	Castana Experiment Farm	84.8	22	Fort Dodge	84.6
22	Cherokee	84.8	24	Audubon 1 SSE	84.7
25	Audubon 1 SSE	84.7	25	Boone	84.8

Rankings include 25 highest/lowest stations. If state has less than 25 stations, all stations are included. The period of record is 1980–2009. See User Guide for detailed explanation of data.

January Mean Minimum Temperature

Highest			Lowest		
Rank	Station Name	°F	Rank	Station Name	°F
1	Fort Madison	17.5	1	Cresco 1 NE	5.3
2	Burlington Radio KBUR	16.6	2	Mason City	6.8
3	Bloomfield 1 WNW	16.0	3	Forest City 2 NNE	7.0
4	Albia 3 NNE	15.4	4	Tripoli	7.2
4	Iowa City	15.4	5	Cherokee	7.4
6	Sidney	15.2	6	Algona 3 W	7.6
7	Ottumwa Industrial Arpt	15.1	7	Hawarden	8.2
8	Muscatine	15.0	8	Elkader 5 SSW	8.3
9	Le Claire L & D 14	14.7	9	Boone	8.7
10	Clinton No 1	14.4	10	Grundy Center	8.8
11	Des Moines Arpt	14.1	11	Emmetsburg	8.9
12	Cedar Rapids No 1	13.4	12	Fort Dodge	9.1
13	Sigourney	13.2	12	Le Mars	9.1
14	Beaconsfield	13.1	14	Waterloo Municipal Arpt	9.4
14	Glenwood 3 SW	13.1	15	Eldora	9.5
16	Winterset 2 NNW	13.0	15	Marshalltown	9.5
17	Dubuque Lock & Dam 11	12.6	17	Allison	9.8
18	Castana Experiment Farm	12.4	18	Colo	9.9
19	Ames 8 WSW	12.1	19	Rockwell City	10.0
19	Cedar Rapids Municipal Arpt	12.1	20	Grinnell 3 SW	10.2
21	Dubuque Regional Arpt	11.8	21	Anamosa 1 WNW	10.7
22	Ankeny	11.7	22	Belle Plaine	10.9
23	Vinton	11.5	23	Audubon 1 SSE	11.1
24	Atlantic 1 NE	11.4	23	Sioux City Municipal Arpt	11.1
25	Audubon 1 SSE	11.1	25	Atlantic 1 NE	11.4

Number of Days Annually Maximum Temperature ≥ 90°F

Highest			Lowest		
Rank	Station Name	Days	Rank	Station Name	Days
1	Glenwood 3 SW	37	1	Cresco 1 NE	7
2	Sidney	28	2	Dubuque Regional Arpt	9
3	Iowa City	27	3	Algona 3 W	11
4	Sioux City Municipal Arpt	26	3	Forest City 2 NNE	11
5	Atlantic 1 NE	24	5	Grundy Center	12
6	Bloomfield 1 WNW	23	5	Tripoli	12
6	Muscatine	23	7	Allison	13
8	Burlington Radio KBUR	22	7	Colo	13
9	Ankeny	21	7	Grinnell 3 SW	13
9	Des Moines Arpt	21	7	Mason City	13
9	Fort Madison	21	11	Cedar Rapids Municipal Arpt	14
9	Le Mars	21	11	Elkader 5 SSW	14
9	Ottumwa Industrial Arpt	21	11	Vinton	14
14	Hawarden	20	14	Emmetsburg	15
15	Boone	19	14	Marshalltown	15
15	Cherokee	19	16	Ames 8 WSW	16
15	Dubuque Lock & Dam 11	19	16	Anamosa 1 WNW	16
15	Eldora	19	16	Belle Plaine	16
15	Sigourney	19	16	Castana Experiment Farm	16
20	Albia 3 NNE	18	16	Cedar Rapids No 1	16
20	Fort Dodge	18	16	Rockwell City	16
20	Le Claire L & D 14	18	22	Audubon 1 SSE	17
20	Winterset 2 NNW	18	22	Beaconsfield	17
24	Audubon 1 SSE	17	22	Clinton No 1	17
24	Beaconsfield	17	22	Waterloo Municipal Arpt	17

Rankings include 25 highest/lowest stations. If state has less than 25 stations, all stations are included. The period of record is 1980–2009. See User Guide for detailed explanation of data.

Number of Days Annually Maximum Temperature ≤ 32°F

Highest			Lowest		
Rank	Station Name	Days	Rank	Station Name	Days
1	Cresco 1 NE	75	1	Fort Madison	35
2	Forest City 2 NNE	73	2	Bloomfield 1 WNW	39
3	Mason City	71	3	Glenwood 3 SW	40
4	Algona 3 W	69	4	Albia 3 NNE	41
5	Tripoli	66	4	Muscatine	41
6	Emmetsburg	65	4	Sidney	41
7	Grundy Center	63	4	Burlington Radio KBUR	41
8	Allison	61	8	Iowa City	42
8	Colo	61	9	Ottumwa Industrial Arpt	44
8	Eldora	61	10	Clinton No 1	46
11	Cherokee	60	10	Le Claire L & D 14	46
11	Fort Dodge	60	10	Winterset 2 NNW	46
13	Dubuque Regional Arpt	59	13	Atlantic 1 NE	47
14	Rockwell City	58	13	Beaconsfield	47
14	Waterloo Municipal Arpt	58	13	Des Moines Arpt	47
16	Hawarden	57	16	Sigourney	48
16	Le Mars	57	17	Cedar Rapids No 1	49
18	Cedar Rapids Municipal Arpt	55	18	Audubon 1 SSE	50
18	Marshalltown	55	18	Castana Experiment Farm	50
20	Elkader 5 SSW	54	18	Sioux City Municipal Arpt	50
21	Ames 8 WSW	53	21	Anamosa 1 WNW	51
21	Boone	53	21	Ankeny	51
21	Grinnell 3 SW	53	21	Belle Plaine	51
24	Vinton	52	21	Dubuque Lock & Dam 11	51
25	Anamosa 1 WNW	51	25	Vinton	52

Number of Days Annually Minimum Temperature ≤ 32°F

Highest			Lowest		
Rank	Station Name	Days	Rank	Station Name	Days
1	Cresco 1 NE	170	1	Fort Madison	114
2	Cherokee	165	2	Burlington Radio KBUR	120
3	Mason City	163	3	Bloomfield 1 WNW	124
4	Hawarden	162	3	Iowa City	124
5	Elkader 5 SSW	160	5	Muscatine	126
5	Forest City 2 NNE	160	6	Le Claire L & D 14	127
7	Algona 3 W	159	7	Albia 3 NNE	129
7	Le Mars	159	7	Ottumwa Industrial Arpt	129
9	Grinnell 3 SW	158	9	Clinton No 1	130
10	Boone	157	10	Des Moines Arpt	131
10	Fort Dodge	157	10	Dubuque Lock & Dam 11	131
10	Grundy Center	157	12	Sidney	132
10	Tripoli	157	13	Cedar Rapids No 1	137
14	Colo	155	13	Sigourney	137
14	Eldora	155	15	Beaconsfield	141
14	Rockwell City	155	16	Ames 8 WSW	143
17	Marshalltown	154	16	Cedar Rapids Municipal Arpt	143
17	Sioux City Municipal Arpt	154	18	Vinton	144
19	Audubon 1 SSE	153	19	Dubuque Regional Arpt	145
19	Emmetsburg	153	19	Winterset 2 NNW	145
21	Anamosa 1 WNW	152	21	Glenwood 3 SW	146
21	Atlantic 1 NE	152	22	Castana Experiment Farm	147
21	Waterloo Municipal Arpt	152	23	Ankeny	148
24	Allison	150	24	Belle Plaine	149
25	Belle Plaine	149	25	Allison	150

Rankings include 25 highest/lowest stations. If state has less than 25 stations, all stations are included. The period of record is 1980–2009. See User Guide for detailed explanation of data.

Number of Days Annually Minimum Temperature ≤ 0°F

Highest			Lowest		
Rank	Station Name	Days	Rank	Station Name	Days
1	Cresco 1 NE	31	1	Fort Madison	7
2	Forest City 2 NNE	28	2	Bloomfield 1 WNW	10
3	Cherokee	26	2	Burlington Radio KBUR	10
4	Algona 3 W	25	4	Albia 3 NNE	11
4	Mason City	25	4	Clinton No 1	11
4	Tripoli	25	4	Iowa City	11
7	Hawarden	24	4	Le Claire L & D 14	11
8	Elkader 5 SSW	23	4	Muscatine	11
8	Emmetsburg	23	4	Ottumwa Industrial Arpt	11
8	Fort Dodge	23	4	Sidney	11
11	Grundy Center	22	11	Des Moines Arpt	12
12	Eldora	21	12	Glenwood 3 SW	13
12	Le Mars	21	13	Beaconsfield	14
12	Waterloo Municipal Arpt	21	13	Sigourney	14
15	Boone	20	13	Winterset 2 NNW	14
15	Grinnell 3 SW	20	16	Cedar Rapids No 1	15
15	Marshalltown	20	17	Ames 8 WSW	16
18	Allison	19	17	Ankeny	16
18	Anamosa 1 WNW	19	17	Castana Experiment Farm	16
18	Colo	19	17	Cedar Rapids Municipal Arpt	16
18	Rockwell City	19	17	Dubuque Lock & Dam 11	16
22	Audubon 1 SSE	18	17	Vinton	16
22	Belle Plaine	18	23	Atlantic 1 NE	17
24	Atlantic 1 NE	17	23	Dubuque Regional Arpt	17
24	Dubuque Regional Arpt	17	23	Sioux City Municipal Arpt	17

Number of Annual Heating Degree Days

Highest			Lowest		
Rank	Station Name	Num.	Rank	Station Name	Num.
1	Cresco 1 NE	8,024	1	Fort Madison	5,634
2	Mason City	7,627	2	Burlington Radio KBUR	5,830
3	Forest City 2 NNE	7,552	3	Bloomfield 1 WNW	5,838
4	Algona 3 W	7,471	4	Iowa City	5,864
5	Tripoli	7,438	5	Sidney	5,894
6	Cherokee	7,367	6	Muscatine	5,954
7	Emmetsburg	7,262	7	Albia 3 NNE	6,093
8	Grundy Center	7,256	8	Ottumwa Industrial Arpt	6,100
9	Hawarden	7,244	9	Glenwood 3 SW	6,144
10	Elkader 5 SSW	7,217	10	Clinton No 1	6,198
11	Fort Dodge	7,109	11	Le Claire L & D 14	6,203
12	Eldora	7,098	12	Des Moines Arpt	6,219
13	Le Mars	7,069	13	Cedar Rapids No 1	6,333
14	Grinnell 3 SW	7,058	14	Sigourney	6,369
15	Waterloo Municipal Arpt	7,056	15	Winterset 2 NNW	6,386
16	Colo	7,040	16	Beaconsfield	6,396
17	Dubuque Regional Arpt	7,017	17	Dubuque Lock & Dam 11	6,524
18	Allison	7,007	18	Ames 8 WSW	6,547
19	Rockwell City	6,996	19	Castana Experiment Farm	6,556
20	Marshalltown	6,977	20	Atlantic 1 NE	6,571
21	Boone	6,966	21	Ankeny	6,619
22	Anamosa 1 WNW	6,831	22	Vinton	6,625
23	Belle Plaine	6,791	23	Sioux City Municipal Arpt	6,732
24	Audubon 1 SSE	6,754	24	Cedar Rapids Municipal Arpt	6,735
25	Cedar Rapids Municipal Arpt	6,735	25	Audubon 1 SSE	6,754

Rankings include 25 highest/lowest stations. If state has less than 25 stations, all stations are included. The period of record is 1980–2009. See User Guide for detailed explanation of data.

Number of Annual Cooling Degree Days

Highest Rank	Station Name	Num.	Lowest Rank	Station Name	Num.
1	Fort Madison	1,198	1	Cresco 1 NE	532
2	Iowa City	1,172	2	Mason City	637
3	Sidney	1,149	3	Elkader 5 SSW	667
4	Burlington Radio KBUR	1,126	4	Tripoli	668
5	Glenwood 3 SW	1,121	5	Forest City 2 NNE	675
6	Muscatine	1,100	6	Dubuque Regional Arpt	679
7	Bloomfield 1 WNW	1,075	7	Algona 3 W	685
7	Des Moines Arpt	1,075	8	Grinnell 3 SW	706
9	Ottumwa Industrial Arpt	1,058	9	Grundy Center	726
10	Le Claire L & D 14	1,039	10	Anamosa 1 WNW	766
11	Dubuque Lock & Dam 11	994	11	Cherokee	785
12	Albia 3 NNE	982	12	Allison	787
13	Clinton No 1	970	13	Boone	788
14	Cedar Rapids No 1	949	14	Colo	794
15	Sigourney	943	15	Rockwell City	795
16	Atlantic 1 NE	942	16	Waterloo Municipal Arpt	796
17	Sioux City Municipal Arpt	935	17	Marshalltown	799
18	Ankeny	926	18	Emmetsburg	803
19	Castana Experiment Farm	903	19	Eldora	806
20	Winterset 2 NNW	896	20	Belle Plaine	823
21	Ames 8 WSW	886	21	Cedar Rapids Municipal Arpt	824
21	Beaconsfield	886	21	Hawarden	824
23	Le Mars	880	23	Audubon 1 SSE	834
24	Vinton	838	23	Fort Dodge	834
25	Audubon 1 SSE	834	25	Vinton	838

Annual Precipitation

Highest Rank	Station Name	Inches	Lowest Rank	Station Name	Inches
1	Burlington Radio KBUR	39.83	1	Sioux City Municipal Arpt	27.25
2	Bloomfield 1 WNW	39.03	2	Le Mars	27.38
3	Fort Madison	38.91	3	Hawarden	27.93
4	Muscatine	37.73	4	Cherokee	30.14
5	Boone	37.50	5	Emmetsburg	31.20
6	Anamosa 1 WNW	37.33	6	Castana Experiment Farm	31.42
7	Albia 3 NNE	37.23	7	Algona 3 W	31.75
8	Cedar Rapids No 1	37.05	8	Forest City 2 NNE	32.22
8	Iowa City	37.05	9	Rockwell City	32.31
10	Beaconsfield	36.90	10	Audubon 1 SSE	32.89
11	Marshalltown	36.70	11	Glenwood 3 SW	32.95
12	Ottumwa Industrial Arpt	36.40	12	Allison	33.28
13	Dubuque Regional Arpt	36.21	13	Sidney	33.66
14	Tripoli	36.17	14	Winterset 2 NNW	33.89
15	Cresco 1 NE	35.97	15	Cedar Rapids Municipal Arpt	34.11
15	Sigourney	35.97	16	Waterloo Municipal Arpt	34.22
15	Vinton	35.97	17	Ankeny	34.34
18	Dubuque Lock & Dam 11	35.83	18	Fort Dodge	34.37
19	Atlantic 1 NE	35.79	19	Clinton No 1	34.39
20	Belle Plaine	35.65	20	Ames 8 WSW	34.70
21	Colo	35.55	21	Grundy Center	34.77
22	Grinnell 3 SW	35.47	22	Elkader 5 SSW	34.94
23	Mason City	35.41	23	Des Moines Arpt	34.98
24	Eldora	35.40	24	Le Claire L & D 14	35.18
25	Le Claire L & D 14	35.18	25	Eldora	35.40

Rankings include 25 highest/lowest stations. If state has less than 25 stations, all stations are included. The period of record is 1980–2009. See User Guide for detailed explanation of data.

Annual Extreme Maximum Daily Precipitation

Highest

Rank	Station Name	Inches
1	Atlantic 1 NE	13.18
2	Castana Experiment Farm	12.02
3	Emmetsburg	9.00
4	Le Mars	8.76
5	Bloomfield 1 WNW	8.17
6	Le Claire L & D 14	7.53
7	Albia 3 NNE	7.25
8	Sidney	7.10
9	Beaconsfield	7.00
10	Algona 3 W	6.90
11	Cedar Rapids No 1	6.63
12	Anamosa 1 WNW	6.52
13	Fort Dodge	6.50
14	Glenwood 3 SW	6.48
15	Grundy Center	6.25
15	Mason City	6.25
17	Boone	6.06
18	Iowa City	6.02
19	Hawarden	6.01
20	Audubon 1 SSE	6.00
21	Dubuque Regional Arpt	5.99
22	Rockwell City	5.87
23	Forest City 2 NNE	***5.66***
24	Ames 8 WSW	5.59
25	Burlington Radio KBUR	5.55

Lowest

Rank	Station Name	Inches
1	Muscatine	4.12
2	Grinnell 3 SW	4.18
3	Des Moines Arpt	4.23
4	Vinton	4.25
5	Marshalltown	4.43
6	Clinton No 1	4.45
7	Ankeny	4.50
7	Elkader 5 SSW	4.50
9	Sigourney	4.51
9	Sioux City Municipal Arpt	4.51
11	Eldora	4.64
12	Dubuque Lock & Dam 11	4.86
13	Fort Madison	4.88
14	Winterset 2 NNW	4.99
15	Cherokee	5.05
16	Colo	5.20
17	Allison	5.24
17	Cresco 1 NE	5.24
19	Belle Plaine	5.26
20	Ottumwa Industrial Arpt	5.32
21	Cedar Rapids Municipal Arpt	5.35
22	Waterloo Municipal Arpt	5.50
23	Tripoli	***5.53***
24	Burlington Radio KBUR	5.55
25	Ames 8 WSW	5.59

Number of Days Annually With ≥ 0.1 Inches of Precipitation

Highest

Rank	Station Name	Days
1	Fort Madison	71
1	Burlington Radio KBUR	71
3	Bloomfield 1 WNW	69
3	Cedar Rapids No 1	69
3	Dubuque Regional Arpt	69
3	Muscatine	69
3	Vinton	69
8	Albia 3 NNE	68
8	Anamosa 1 WNW	68
8	Boone	68
8	Clinton No 1	68
8	Cresco 1 NE	68
8	Grinnell 3 SW	68
14	Dubuque Lock & Dam 11	67
14	Grundy Center	67
14	Sigourney	67
14	Tripoli	67
18	Belle Plaine	66
18	Colo	66
18	Eldora	66
18	Iowa City	66
18	Marshalltown	66
23	Beaconsfield	65
23	Cedar Rapids Municipal Arpt	65
23	Des Moines Arpt	65

Lowest

Rank	Station Name	Days
1	Hawarden	53
1	Le Mars	53
3	Sioux City Municipal Arpt	54
4	Forest City 2 NNE	55
5	Castana Experiment Farm	56
5	Cherokee	56
5	Emmetsburg	56
8	Glenwood 3 SW	58
9	Algona 3 W	59
9	Rockwell City	59
11	Allison	60
11	Sidney	60
13	Ankeny	61
13	Audubon 1 SSE	61
15	Ames 8 WSW	62
16	Atlantic 1 NE	63
16	Le Claire L & D 14	63
16	Mason City	63
16	Waterloo Municipal Arpt	63
20	Fort Dodge	64
20	Winterset 2 NNW	64
22	Beaconsfield	65
22	Cedar Rapids Municipal Arpt	65
22	Des Moines Arpt	65
22	Elkader 5 SSW	65

Rankings include 25 highest/lowest stations. If state has less than 25 stations, all stations are included. The period of record is 1980–2009. See User Guide for detailed explanation of data.

Number of Days Annually With ≥ 0.5 Inches of Precipitation

Highest Rank	Highest Station Name	Highest Days	Lowest Rank	Lowest Station Name	Lowest Days
1	Albia 3 NNE	27	1	Hawarden	15
1	Boone	27	2	Le Mars	17
1	Fort Madison	27	3	Sioux City Municipal Arpt	18
1	Burlington Radio KBUR	27	4	Audubon 1 SSE	20
5	Anamosa 1 WNW	25	4	Castana Experiment Farm	20
5	Bloomfield 1 WNW	25	4	Cherokee	20
5	Colo	25	4	Forest City 2 NNE	20
5	Iowa City	25	4	Glenwood 3 SW	20
5	Sigourney	25	4	Sidney	20
10	Beaconsfield	24	10	Allison	21
10	Cedar Rapids No 1	24	10	Ames 8 WSW	21
10	Grinnell 3 SW	24	10	Clinton No 1	21
10	Muscatine	24	10	Cresco 1 NE	21
14	Belle Plaine	23	10	Eldora	21
14	Des Moines Arpt	23	10	Emmetsburg	21
14	Dubuque Lock & Dam 11	23	10	Rockwell City	21
14	Dubuque Regional Arpt	23	10	Waterloo Municipal Arpt	21
14	Mason City	23	18	Algona 3 W	22
14	Ottumwa Industrial Arpt	23	18	Ankeny	22
14	Vinton	23	18	Atlantic 1 NE	22
21	Algona 3 W	22	18	Cedar Rapids Municipal Arpt	22
21	Ankeny	22	18	Elkader 5 SSW	22
21	Atlantic 1 NE	22	18	Fort Dodge	22
21	Cedar Rapids Municipal Arpt	22	18	Grundy Center	22
21	Elkader 5 SSW	22	18	Le Claire L & D 14	22

Number of Days Annually With ≥ 1.0 Inches of Precipitation

Highest Rank	Highest Station Name	Highest Days	Lowest Rank	Lowest Station Name	Lowest Days
1	Bloomfield 1 WNW	12	1	Allison	6
2	Marshalltown	10	1	Clinton No 1	6
2	Mason City	10	1	Elkader 5 SSW	6
2	Tripoli	10	1	Emmetsburg	6
5	Atlantic 1 NE	9	1	Forest City 2 NNE	6
5	Beaconsfield	9	1	Le Mars	6
5	Belle Plaine	9	7	Albia 3 NNE	7
5	Colo	9	7	Algona 3 W	7
5	Fort Madison	9	7	Audubon 1 SSE	7
5	Grinnell 3 SW	9	7	Boone	7
5	Muscatine	9	7	Castana Experiment Farm	7
5	Vinton	9	7	Cedar Rapids Municipal Arpt	7
5	Burlington Radio KBUR	9	7	Cedar Rapids No 1	7
14	Ames 8 WSW	8	7	Cherokee	7
14	Anamosa 1 WNW	8	7	Cresco 1 NE	7
14	Ankeny	8	7	Des Moines Arpt	7
14	Eldora	8	7	Dubuque Lock & Dam 11	7
14	Iowa City	8	7	Dubuque Regional Arpt	7
14	Le Claire L & D 14	8	7	Fort Dodge	7
14	Ottumwa Industrial Arpt	8	7	Glenwood 3 SW	7
14	Sigourney	8	7	Grundy Center	7
14	Winterset 2 NNW	8	7	Hawarden	7
23	Albia 3 NNE	7	7	Rockwell City	7
23	Algona 3 W	7	7	Sidney	7
23	Audubon 1 SSE	7	7	Sioux City Municipal Arpt	7

Annual Snowfall

Highest			Lowest		
Rank	Station Name	Inches	Rank	Station Name	Inches
1	Cresco 1 NE	41.7	1	Le Claire L & D 14	***7.6***
2	Dubuque Regional Arpt	41.3	2	Fort Madison	20.1
3	Forest City 2 NNE	38.4	3	Glenwood 3 SW	22.4
4	Algona 3 W	38.0	4	Audubon 1 SSE	22.7
5	Fort Dodge	36.8	5	Muscatine	23.2
6	Des Moines Arpt	***35.9***	6	Anamosa 1 WNW	24.6
7	Elkader 5 SSW	35.6	6	Burlington Radio KBUR	24.6
8	Sioux City Municipal Arpt	35.1	8	Beaconsfield	25.1
9	Grundy Center	34.8	9	Bloomfield 1 WNW	25.7
9	Waterloo Municipal Arpt	***34.8***	10	Sidney	26.1
11	Emmetsburg	34.1	11	Iowa City	26.4
12	Tripoli	33.9	12	Atlantic 1 NE	27.0
13	Allison	33.6	13	Marshalltown	27.1
14	Dubuque Lock & Dam 11	33.1	14	Ankeny	27.2
15	Cherokee	33.0	15	Albia 3 NNE	27.4
16	Boone	32.9	15	Sigourney	27.4
16	Vinton	32.9	17	Le Mars	27.7
18	Castana Experiment Farm	32.3	18	Belle Plaine	28.2
19	Hawarden	32.2	19	Colo	28.8
20	Rockwell City	32.1	20	Mason City	***29.2***
21	Eldora	31.8	21	Clinton No 1	30.0
22	Ames 8 WSW	31.7	22	Grinnell 3 SW	30.5
23	Winterset 2 NNW	30.8	23	Cedar Rapids No 1	30.7
24	Cedar Rapids No 1	30.7	24	Winterset 2 NNW	30.8
25	Grinnell 3 SW	30.5	25	Ames 8 WSW	31.7

Annual Maximum Snow Depth

Highest			Lowest		
Rank	Station Name	Inches	Rank	Station Name	Inches
1	Algona 3 W	40	1	Le Claire L & D 14	***13***
2	Tripoli	***35***	2	Clinton No 1	14
3	Dubuque Lock & Dam 11	32	2	Sidney	14
3	Vinton	32	4	Beaconsfield	15
5	Emmetsburg	29	5	Cedar Rapids No 1	16
5	Grundy Center	29	5	Sigourney	16
7	Ankeny	27	7	Belle Plaine	17
7	Forest City 2 NNE	***27***	8	Anamosa 1 WNW	18
7	Glenwood 3 SW	27	8	Colo	18
7	Sioux City Municipal Arpt	27	8	Marshalltown	18
11	Castana Experiment Farm	26	8	Muscatine	18
12	Eldora	25	8	Rockwell City	18
13	Iowa City	24	8	Waterloo Municipal Arpt	***18***
14	Cherokee	***23***	14	Albia 3 NNE	19
14	Winterset 2 NNW	23	14	Allison	19
16	Bloomfield 1 WNW	22	14	Des Moines Arpt	19
16	Burlington Radio KBUR	22	17	Boone	20
18	Ames 8 WSW	21	17	Grinnell 3 SW	20
19	Boone	20	17	Hawarden	20
19	Grinnell 3 SW	20	20	Ames 8 WSW	21
19	Hawarden	20	21	Bloomfield 1 WNW	22
22	Albia 3 NNE	19	21	Burlington Radio KBUR	22
22	Allison	19	23	Cherokee	***23***
22	Des Moines Arpt	19	23	Winterset 2 NNW	23
25	Anamosa 1 WNW	18	25	Iowa City	24

Rankings include 25 highest/lowest stations. If state has less than 25 stations, all stations are included. The period of record is 1980–2009. See User Guide for detailed explanation of data.

Number of Days Annually With ≥ 1.0 Inch Snow Depth

Highest Rank	Highest Station Name	Highest Days	Lowest Rank	Lowest Station Name	Lowest Days
1	Algona 3 W	73	1	Le Claire L & D 14	***21***
1	Allison	73	2	Fort Madison	***22***
3	Dubuque Lock & Dam 11	72	3	Audubon 1 SSE	***27***
4	Eldora	71	4	Le Mars	***31***
4	Grundy Center	71	5	Burlington Radio KBUR	34
6	Emmetsburg	68	6	Glenwood 3 SW	35
6	Mason City	***68***	7	Hawarden	37
8	Waterloo Municipal Arpt	***66***	7	Muscatine	37
9	Rockwell City	65	9	Sidney	41
10	Cherokee	***64***	10	Albia 3 NNE	42
11	Boone	62	11	Bloomfield 1 WNW	43
11	Colo	62	11	Sigourney	43
13	Castana Experiment Farm	59	13	Tripoli	***45***
14	Vinton	58	14	Beaconsfield	46
15	Belle Plaine	54	15	Grinnell 3 SW	47
15	Cedar Rapids No 1	54	16	Anamosa 1 WNW	48
15	Sioux City Municipal Arpt	54	17	Winterset 2 NNW	49
18	Ames 8 WSW	53	18	Clinton No 1	50
19	Marshalltown	52	18	Iowa City	50
20	Ankeny	51	20	Ankeny	51
20	Des Moines Arpt	51	20	Des Moines Arpt	51
20	Forest City 2 NNE	51	20	Forest City 2 NNE	51
23	Clinton No 1	50	23	Marshalltown	52
23	Iowa City	50	24	Ames 8 WSW	53
25	Winterset 2 NNW	49	25	Belle Plaine	54

Rankings include 25 highest/lowest stations. If state has less than 25 stations, all stations are included. The period of record is 1980–2009. See User Guide for detailed explanation of data.

Significant Storm Events in Iowa: 2000 – 2009

Location or County	Date	Type	Mag.	Deaths	Injuries	Property Damage ($mil.)	Crop Damage ($mil.)
Black Hawk	05/11/00	Tornado	F3	1	25	1.7	0.0
Allamakee and Clayton Counties	05/01/01	Flood	na	0	0	5.5	0.0
Polk	06/12/01	Hail	2.00 in.	0	0	9.5	0.0
Jackson	09/18/02	Hail	2.75 in.	0	0	20.0	0.0
Lee	05/08/03	Hail	2.00 in.	0	0	15.0	0.0
Des Moines	05/08/03	Hail	2.75 in.	0	0	10.0	0.0
Linn	07/20/03	Thunderstorm Wind	73 mph	0	0	5.0	0.0
Statewide	08/01/03	Drought	na	0	0	645.1	0.0
Humboldt	05/21/04	Tornado	F2	0	15	2.5	0.0
Statewide	05/22/04	Flood	na	0	0	5.1	15.2
Hamilton	11/12/05	Tornado	F3	1	3	11.7	0.0
Johnson	04/13/06	Tornado	F2	0	30	12.0	0.0
Harrison	05/05/07	Flash Flood	na	0	0	15.0	0.0
Muscatine	06/01/07	Tornado	F3	0	6	15.0	0.0
Butler	05/25/08	Tornado	F5	9	50	75.0	0.0
Black Hawk	05/25/08	Tornado	F2	0	20	25.0	0.1
Linn	06/01/08	Flood	na	0	0	750.0	0.0
Johnson	06/01/08	Flood	na	0	0	230.0	0.0
Polk	06/01/08	Flood	na	0	0	6.0	0.0
Monona	06/11/08	Tornado	F3	4	48	0.0	0.0
Polk	06/14/08	Flash Flood	na	0	0	7.0	0.0
Woodbury	07/20/08	Thunderstorm Wind	93 mph	0	1	5.0	0.0
Hardin	08/09/09	Hail	3.00 in.	0	22	20.0	55.0

Note: Deaths, injuries, and damages are date and location specific.

KANSAS

PHYSICAL FEATURES AND GENERAL CLIMATE. Located at the geographical center of the contiguous 48 states, Kansas has a distinctly continental climate with characteristically changeable temperature and precipitation.

Kansas weather is affected largely by two physical features, both some distance from the State: the Rocky Mountains to the west and the Gulf of Mexico to the south. The mountains on the west prevent the importation of moisture from the Pacific Ocean, while the Gulf is the feeding source for much of the State's precipitation.

A third factor, differences in elevation, also influences the climate. Elevation changes are quite gradual rising from 800 or 1,000 feet above sea level in a number of extreme eastern and southeastern counties to approximately 1,500 feet about the center of the State, north to south, and to 3,500 feet at the Colorado line. Quite coincident with these gradations is a change in climate.

PRECIPITATION. Average annual precipitation totals range from slightly more than 40 inches in the southeastern counties to 30 to 35 inches in the northeast, decreasing gradually westward to the Colorado line where the average is from 16 to 18 inches. Distribution of rainfall through the year favors crop production, with an average of about 75 percent of the year's total falling in the crop growing season, April to September. January, the month of least precipitation, has an average of one to two inches at the more eastern stations, decreasing to less than an inch over the western three-fourths of the State and to near a quarter inch in the extreme west. May and June, in contrast, are the months of greatest rain with between four and five inches on the average in the eastern three-fifths of the State to between two and three inches in the western counties. In addition to the seasonal changes of precipitation amounts over the State, there is a secondary fluctuation in the average rainfall which is quite pronounced in the east. In this area a noticeable decrease in the average rainfall occurs during the latter part of July and the forepart of August, with an increase again in September.

Precipitation is most frequent in the extreme east where on the average measurable amounts are recorded on 90 to 100 days of the year. The average annual number of days with an inch or more of precipitation is 60 to 80 over two-thirds of the central portion and about 70 in the northwestern portion, but decreases to near 50 in the southwestern section.

All parts of Kansas may receive 24-hour rainfalls of five to 10 inches, with the more frequent occurrence of heavy rains in the eastern area during the month of September. Almost one-half of the total rain falls in daily amounts of 0.75 inch or less. Monthly precipitation totals of 20 inches or more have been recorded at some eastern stations. Protracted periods of successive days with rain are occasionally recorded. On the other hand, all parts of the State have experienced from 50 to 75 successive days without more than 0.25 inch of rain on any day during the period April to September.

Snowfall averages near 10 inches a year in the south-central counties and increases gradually in other parts of the State to the largest average of 24 inches in the northwest. Snow has been recorded in all months except July and August. The greatest average fall is in February with March snows only slightly less. Falls of 12 to 24 inches in 24 hours have been recorded in most sections. Ordinarily snow remains on the ground only a short time, but during the winter the ground may be snow-covered from 10 to 15 days in the south and from 30 to 35 days in the north. In rare instances snow has covered the ground continuously in western and northern sections from 40 to 60 days.

Wet and dry trends or periods are noted in the longer records. Dry periods may persist for several years with an occasional interim of a month or two of above average rainfall. There appears to be some indication of recurring patterns of years with similar trends.

The river drainage in Kansas is about equally divided between the Missouri and Arkansas Rivers, the northern half of the State draining into the Missouri, the southern half into the Arkansas. The Kansas River basin, occupying the north half, has a total drainage area of more than 60,000 square miles above its confluence with the Missouri River at Kansas City. The Arkansas River above the Oklahoma line drains an area of over 45,000 square miles.

Floods in Kansas are generally due to torrential and often prolonged rains. They are seldom caused by melting snow, except in the case of the Arkansas River, where melting snow and heavy rains near its source in the mountains of Colorado have caused flooding. Overflows in the Kansas River and tributaries are practically unknown during the winter season, November to February, but they do occur in the Marias des Cygnes River and in the Arkansas River basin in southeastern Kansas during that period.

For the State as a whole the period of greatest flood frequency is during the spring and summer, from general heavy and prolonged rains. Intense local convective storms also cause damaging flash floods in the smaller streams during the warmer season.

TEMPERATURE. The annual mean temperature ranges from about 58°F. along the south-central and southeastern border to 52°F. in the extreme northwest. Monthly mean temperatures in the northwest range from about 28°F. in July, and in the southeast and south-central from 34°F. in January to 80 or 81°F. in July. Daily temperature ranges, on the average, increase from 20°F. in the east to 30°F. in the higher and drier elevations of the northwest.

Temperatures of 100°F. or higher occur on an average of 10 days per year in the east and west and about 15 days in the central portion. In some of the hotter summers the number of days with 100°F. or higher has totalled 50 to 60 in the central and south-central counties. The number of days with zero or lower averages two to four days per year at the southeastern stations and eight to 10 days in the northwest. Freezing temperatures have been recorded somewhere in the State all months of the year.

During much of the year there is a progressive increase in mean temperature from the higher northwestern counties to the southeastern area. The exception is during the warm summer months when the higher mean temperatures are found in the central and south-central counties.

WINDS AND STORMS. The prevailing winds are from a southerly direction with the exception of the cold months of December through March, which have considerable wind from the north or northwest. Generally the extreme winds are from a northerly direction. In the western part of the State wind speeds are higher and average about 15 m.p.h., approximately five m.p.h. faster than in the eastern sections.

Although storms occasionally result in considerable damage, they are for the most part of short duration. In dry periods duststorms may occur frequently in the west, and at intervals a blizzard or severe snowstorm lasts for 36 to 48 hours. The damaging winds, hail, and tornadoes, however, are generally of short duration, although very severe, and seldom cover great areas.

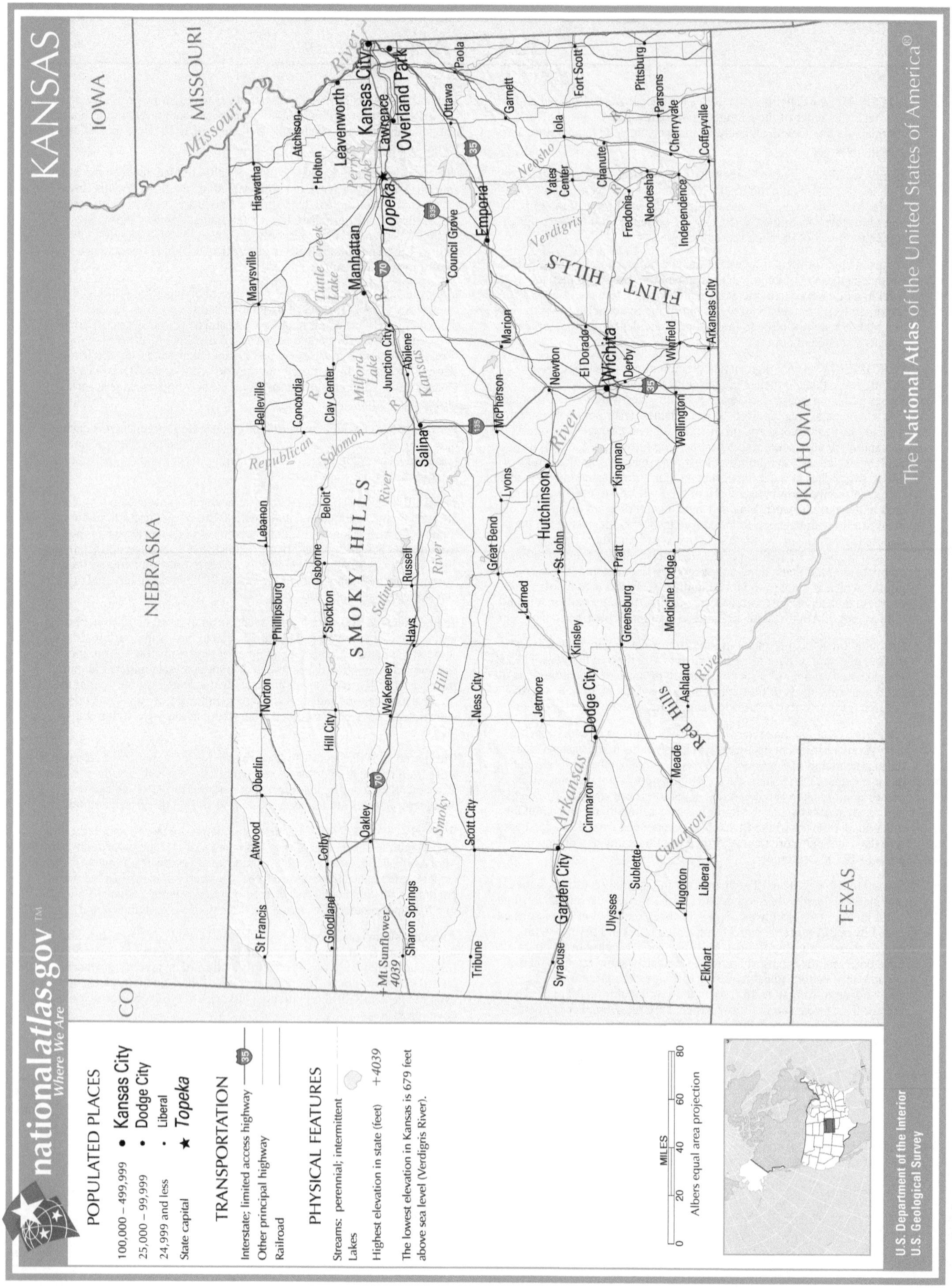
KANSAS
nationalatlas.gov™
Where We Are
POPULATED PLACES
100,000 – 499,999 • Kansas City
25,000 – 99,999 • Dodge City
24,999 and less · Liberal
State capital ★ Topeka
TRANSPORTATION
Interstate; limited access highway
Other principal highway
Railroad
PHYSICAL FEATURES
Streams: perennial; intermittent
Lakes
Highest elevation in state (feet) +4039
The lowest elevation in Kansas is 679 feet above sea level (Verdigris River).
MILES
0 20 40 60 80
Albers equal area projection
U.S. Department of the Interior
U.S. Geological Survey
The National Atlas of the United States of America®
IOWA
MISSOURI
NEBRASKA
CO
OKLAHOMA
TEXAS
SMOKY HILLS
FLINT HILLS
Red Hills
Missouri River
Republican R
Solomon River
Saline River
Smoky Hill River
Kansas R
Arkansas River
Cimarron
Neosho R
Verdigris R
Tuttle Creek Lake
Milford Lake
Perry Lake
+Mt Sunflower 4039
Kansas City
Overland Park
Topeka
Wichita
Lawrence
Leavenworth
Atchison
Holton
Hiawatha
Marysville
Manhattan
Junction City
Abilene
Clay Center
Concordia
Belleville
Salina
McPherson
Marion
Council Grove
Emporia
Ottawa
Paola
Garnett
Fort Scott
Iola
Yates Center
Chanute
Pittsburg
Parsons
Cherryvale
Coffeyville
Independence
Neodesha
Fredonia
El Dorado
Newton
Derby
Winfield
Arkansas City
Wellington
Hutchinson
Lyons
Kingman
Pratt
St John
Great Bend
Larned
Medicine Lodge
Greensburg
Kinsley
Ashland
Dodge City
Jetmore
Ness City
Hays
Russell
Osborne
Beloit
Lebanon
Stockton
Phillipsburg
Norton
Hill City
WaKeeney
Oberlin
Oakley
Atwood
Colby
St Francis
Goodland
Sharon Springs
Tribune
Scott City
Garden City
Cimarron
Meade
Sublette
Ulysses
Hugoton
Liberal
Syracuse
Elkhart
35
70
135
335

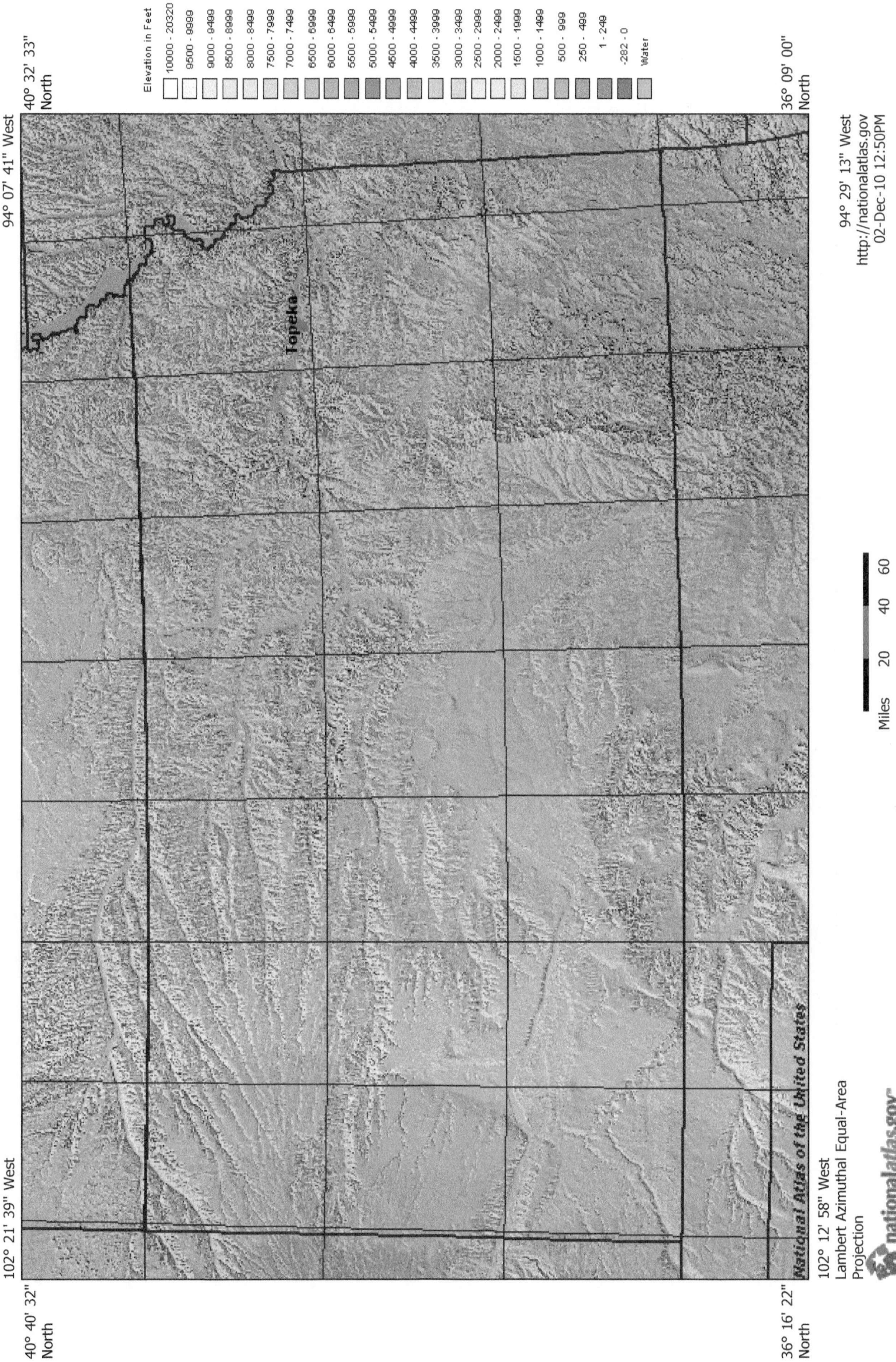
94° 07' 41" West
40° 32' 33" North
Elevation in Feet
10000 - 20320
9500 - 9999
9000 - 9499
8500 - 8999
8000 - 8499
7500 - 7999
7000 - 7499
6500 - 6999
6000 - 6499
5500 - 5999
5000 - 5499
4500 - 4999
4000 - 4499
3500 - 3999
3000 - 3499
2500 - 2999
2000 - 2499
1500 - 1999
1000 - 1499
500 - 999
250 - 499
1 - 249
-282 - 0
Water
36° 09' 00" North
94° 29' 13" West
http://nationalatlas.gov
02-Dec-10 12:50PM
Topeka
Miles 20 40 60
102° 21' 39" West
40° 40' 32" North
National Atlas of the United States
36° 16' 22" North
102° 12' 58" West
Lambert Azimuthal Equal-Area Projection
nationalatlas.gov

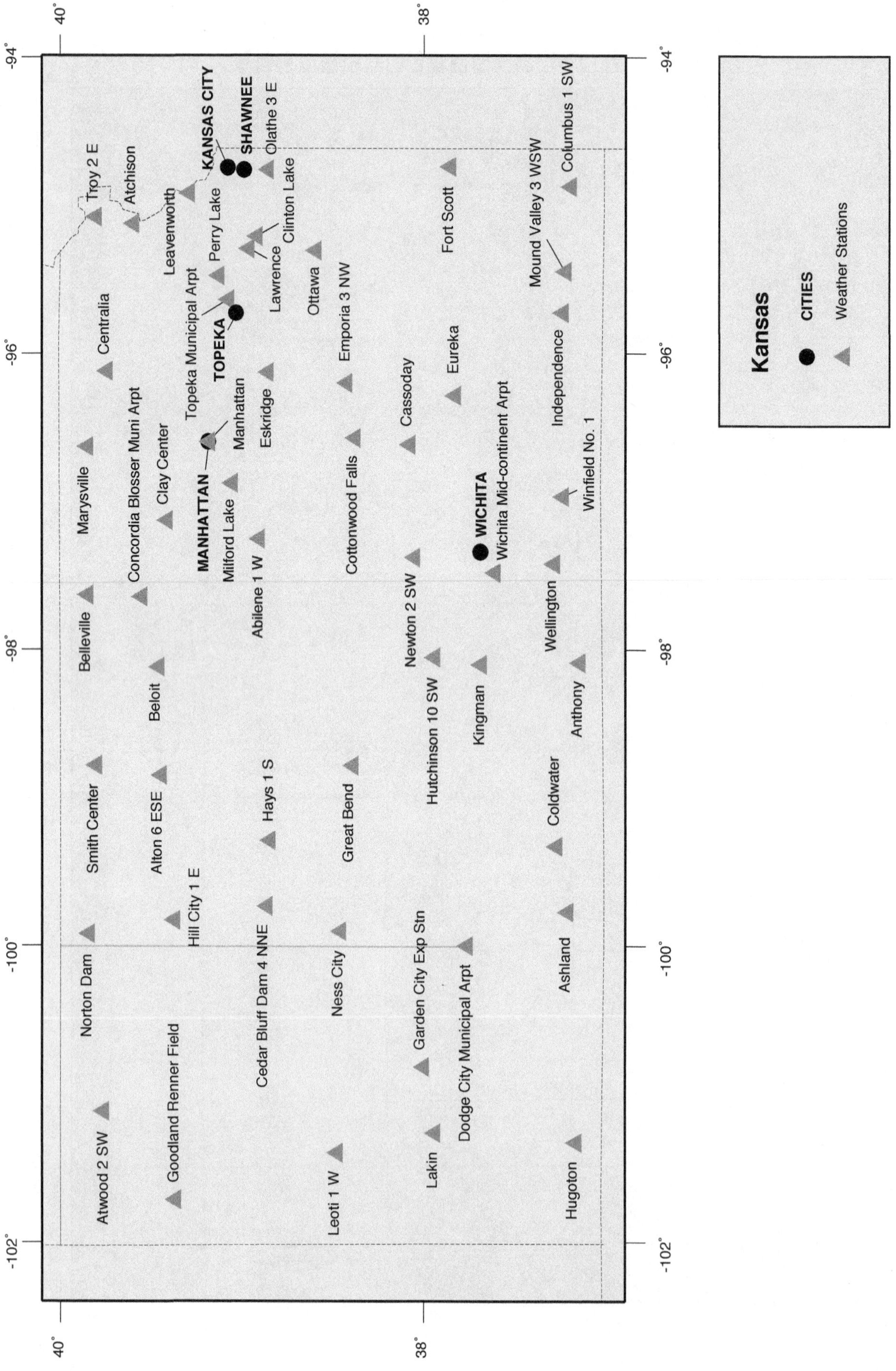
Kansas
CITIES
Weather Stations
KANSAS CITY
SHAWNEE
TOPEKA
MANHATTAN
WICHITA
Troy 2 E
Atchison
Leavenworth
Olathe 3 E
Perry Lake
Clinton Lake
Lawrence
Ottawa
Topeka Municipal Arpt
Fort Scott
Mound Valley 3 WSW
Columbus 1 SW
Centralia
Emporia 3 NW
Eureka
Independence
Marysville
Concordia Blosser Muni Arpt
Clay Center
Manhattan
Eskridge
Cassoday
Wichita Mid-continent Arpt
Winfield No. 1
Milford Lake
Abilene 1 W
Cottonwood Falls
Newton 2 SW
Wellington
Belleville
Beloit
Hutchinson 10 SW
Kingman
Anthony
Smith Center
Alton 6 ESE
Hays 1 S
Great Bend
Coldwater
Norton Dam
Hill City 1 E
Cedar Bluff Dam 4 NNE
Ness City
Garden City Exp Stn
Dodge City Municipal Arpt
Ashland
Atwood 2 SW
Goodland Renner Field
Leoti 1 W
Lakin
Hugoton
40°
38°
-94°
-96°
-98°
-100°
-102°

Kansas Weather Stations by County

County	Station Name
Atchison	Atchison
Barton	Great Bend
Bourbon	Fort Scott
Butler	Cassoday
Chase	Cottonwood Falls
Cherokee	Columbus 1 SW
Clark	Ashland
Clay	Clay Center
Cloud	Concordia Blosser Muni Arpt
Comanche	Coldwater
Cowley	Winfield No. 1
Dickinson	Abilene 1 W
Doniphan	Troy 2 E
Douglas	Clinton Lake Lawrence
Ellis	Hays 1 S
Finney	Garden City Exp Stn
Ford	Dodge City Municipal Arpt
Franklin	Ottawa
Geary	Milford Lake
Graham	Hill City 1 E
Greenwood	Eureka
Harper	Anthony
Harvey	Newton 2 SW
Jefferson	Perry Lake
Johnson	Olathe 3 E
Kearny	Lakin
Kingman	Kingman
Labette	Mound Valley 3 WSW
Leavenworth	Leavenworth
Lyon	Emporia 3 NW
Marshall	Marysville
Mitchell	Beloit

County	Station Name
Montgomery	Independence
Nemaha	Centralia
Ness	Ness City
Norton	Norton Dam
Osborne	Alton 6 ESE
Rawlins	Atwood 2 SW
Reno	Hutchinson 10 SW
Republic	Belleville
Riley	Manhattan
Sedgwick	Wichita Mid-Continent Arpt
Shawnee	Topeka Municipal Arpt
Sherman	Goodland Renner Field
Smith	Smith Center
Stevens	Hugoton
Sumner	Wellington
Trego	Cedar Bluff Dam 4 NNE
Wabaunsee	Eskridge
Wichita	Leoti 1 W

See User Guide for station inclusion criteria.

Kansas Weather Stations by City

City	Station Name	Miles
Derby	Wellington	21.5
	Wichita Mid-Continent Arpt	11.7
Dodge City	Dodge City Municipal Arpt	3.0
Emporia	Cottonwood Falls	19.8
	Emporia 3 NW	1.7
Garden City	Garden City Exp Stn	2.9
	Lakin	21.4
Hays	Cedar Bluff Dam 4 NNE	20.3
	Hays 1 S	1.1
Hutchinson	Hutchinson 10 SW	11.1
Junction City	Abilene 1 W	22.4
	Manhattan	18.3
	Milford Lake	4.4
Kansas City	Leavenworth	16.5
	Olathe 3 E	15.9
	Kansas City Int'l Arpt, MO	13.5
	Kansas City Muni Arpt, MO	5.7
	Lees Summit Reed Wlr, MO	24.5
Lawrence	Clinton Lake	4.3
	Lawrence	0.9
	Ottawa	23.5
	Perry Lake	14.0
	Topeka Municipal Arpt	21.5
Leavenworth	Atchison	20.2
	Leavenworth	3.3
	Kansas City Int'l Arpt, MO	11.3
	Kansas City Muni Arpt, MO	22.9
Leawood	Olathe 3 E	7.9
	Kansas City Muni Arpt, MO	14.1
	Lees Summit Reed Wlr, MO	15.9
Lenexa	Leavenworth	22.4
	Olathe 3 E	5.9
	Kansas City Int'l Arpt, MO	23.0
	Kansas City Muni Arpt, MO	13.7
	Lees Summit Reed Wlr, MO	23.3
Manhattan	Manhattan	0.7
	Milford Lake	17.4
Olathe	Olathe 3 E	1.4
	Kansas City Muni Arpt, MO	19.7
	Lees Summit Reed Wlr, MO	24.7
Overland Park	Olathe 3 E	5.5
	Kansas City Muni Arpt, MO	13.9
	Lees Summit Reed Wlr, MO	19.2
Prairie Village	Leavenworth	24.4
	Olathe 3 E	10.2
	Kansas City Int'l Arpt, MO	21.9
	Kansas City Muni Arpt, MO	9.2
	Lees Summit Reed Wlr, MO	17.8

City	Station Name	Miles
Salina	Abilene 1 W	21.2
Shawnee	Leavenworth	19.3
	Olathe 3 E	9.2
	Kansas City Int'l Arpt, MO	19.7
	Kansas City Muni Arpt, MO	11.6
	Lees Summit Reed Wlr, MO	24.5
Topeka	Clinton Lake	20.8
	Eskridge	24.4
	Lawrence	23.7
	Perry Lake	16.2
	Topeka Municipal Arpt	4.3
Wichita	Newton 2 SW	24.1
	Wichita Mid-Continent Arpt	5.7

Note: Miles is the distance between the geographic center of the city and the weather station.

See User Guide for station inclusion criteria.

Kansas Weather Stations by Elevation

Feet	Station Name
3,645	Goodland Renner Field
3,310	Leoti 1 W
3,109	Hugoton
2,998	Lakin
2,868	Garden City Exp Stn
2,861	Atwood 2 SW
2,576	Dodge City Municipal Arpt
2,339	Norton Dam
2,250	Ness City
2,229	Cedar Bluff Dam 4 NNE
2,146	Hill City 1 E
2,083	Coldwater
2,009	Hays 1 S
1,970	Ashland
1,859	Great Bend
1,779	Smith Center
1,620	Alton 6 ESE
1,569	Hutchinson 10 SW
1,560	Kingman
1,540	Belleville
1,469	Concordia Blosser Muni Arpt
1,461	Beloit
1,459	Cassoday
1,446	Newton 2 SW
1,414	Eskridge
1,339	Anthony
1,319	Centralia
1,319	Wichita Mid-Continent Arpt
1,240	Cottonwood Falls
1,220	Clay Center
1,220	Emporia 3 NW
1,220	Wellington
1,209	Milford Lake
1,180	Marysville
1,180	Winfield No. 1
1,169	Abilene 1 W
1,064	Manhattan
1,060	Troy 2 E
1,055	Olathe 3 E
1,040	Eureka
979	Lawrence
979	Clinton Lake
959	Perry Lake
944	Atchison
899	Columbus 1 SW
899	Ottawa
883	Topeka Municipal Arpt
870	Leavenworth
845	Fort Scott
805	Independence
799	Mound Valley 3 WSW

See User Guide for station inclusion criteria.

Concordia Blosser Muni Airport

A wide variety of weather occurs in the Concordia area which makes possible a great range in crop production. Wheat is ideally suited to the climate of north-central Kansas where a complete crop failure is unknown. Equally well suited to the climate are alfalfa, sweet clover, and sorghum. Corn is generally a successful crop although dry summers and hot winds occasionally prove disastrous. Adequate moisture throughout the year under normal conditions provides fine grazing conditions for a flourishing livestock industry.

Precipitation is light during the winter months, increasing in the spring until June and dropping off during the autumn months. Summer months with less than 1 inch of precipitation are common, even though monthly summer rainfall has exceeded 13 inches. Thunderstorms are frequent in May, June, July and August. Although heavy winter snowfalls are not uncommon, severe storms that paralyze industry and agriculture are very rare. Some periods have been distinguished by very dry

or very wet cycles. Sustained periods of hot, dry, and windy weather frequently occur in July and August with temperatures of 100 degrees or more recorded for a week or more at a time. The average last occurrence of temperatures as low as 32 degrees in the spring is mid April. The average first occurrence of 32 degrees in the autumn is late October.

Winds are southerly most of the year except for a short period of northerly winds during the winter. Velocities are nearly constant throughout the year except for a slight increase in the spring months.

The variety of weather in north-central Kansas is invigorating and healthful. Winters are usually mild, and summers are seldom oppressively hot. Spring and autumn, although very different in most respects, are very pleasant. A period of mild, dry Indian Summer weather usually occurs in October and early November before the winter snow and cold begin.

Concordia Blosser Muni Airport *Cloud County* Elevation: 1,469 ft. Latitude: 39° 33' N Longitude: 97° 39' W

	JAN	FEB	MAR	APR	MAY	JUN	JUL	AUG	SEP	OCT	NOV	DEC	YEAR
Mean Maximum Temp. (°F)	38.8	43.2	54.4	64.8	74.4	84.9	91.0	88.7	80.0	67.0	52.4	39.7	64.9
Mean Temp. (°F)	28.9	32.8	42.9	53.1	63.4	73.5	79.4	77.2	68.2	55.5	41.9	30.3	53.9
Mean Minimum Temp. (°F)	19.0	22.3	31.4	41.3	52.3	62.1	67.7	65.8	56.2	43.9	31.4	20.8	42.9
Extreme Maximum Temp. (°F)	74	80	88	98	102	109	109	108	109	94	85	70	109
Extreme Minimum Temp. (°F)	-17	-14	-5	15	28	43	50	44	29	14	2	-26	-26
Days Maximum Temp. ≥ 90°F	0	0	0	1	1	9	18	14	6	1	0	0	50
Days Maximum Temp. ≤ 32°F	10	7	2	0	0	0	0	0	0	0	2	9	30
Days Minimum Temp. ≤ 32°F	28	22	17	5	0	0	0	0	0	3	16	28	119
Days Minimum Temp. ≤ 0°F	2	2	0	0	0	0	0	0	0	0	0	2	6
Heating Degree Days (base 65°F)	1,112	904	680	369	121	12	0	2	67	312	687	1,069	5,335
Cooling Degree Days (base 65°F)	0	0	2	19	77	275	454	388	169	24	1	0	1,409
Mean Precipitation (in.)	0.64	0.85	2.07	2.43	4.13	3.88	3.75	3.07	2.79	1.87	1.04	0.95	27.47
Maximum Precipitation (in.)*	1.8	2.6	8.3	6.0	9.7	14.1	16.8	10.7	8.5	4.9	4.9	3.6	44.8
Minimum Precipitation (in.)*	0	trace	trace	0.4	0.3	1.3	0.1	0.4	0.2	trace	trace	trace	14.5
Extreme Maximum Daily Precip. (in.)	0.93	1.63	2.63	2.30	3.12	2.87	3.32	3.24	2.51	1.64	2.60	2.46	3.32
Days With ≥ 0.1" Precipitation	2	3	4	5	7	6	5	6	5	4	2	2	51
Days With ≥ 0.5" Precipitation	0	0	1	2	3	3	3	2	2	1	0	1	18
Days With ≥ 1.0" Precipitation	0	0	1	0	1	1	1	1	1	0	0	0	6
Mean Snowfall (in.)	***5.5***	na	na	na	na	na	na	na	na	na	na	na	na
Maximum Snowfall (in.)*	16	21	17	6	trace	0	0	0	trace	5	10	17	56
Maximum 24-hr. Snowfall (in.)*	9	13	9	3	trace	0	0	0	trace	5	7	12	13
Maximum Snow Depth (in.)	***16***	na	na	na	na	na	na	na	na	na	na	na	na
Days With ≥ 1.0" Snow Depth	***10***	***8***	na	***0***	na	na	na	na	na	na	***2***	***9***	na
Thunderstorm Days*	< 1	< 1	2	5	9	11	11	9	6	2	1	< 1	56
Foggy Days*	8	8	10	9	10	7	5	8	8	7	9	10	99
Predominant Sky Cover*	OVR	OVR	OVR	OVR	OVR	CLR	CLR	CLR	CLR	CLR	OVR	OVR	CLR
Mean Relative Humidity 6am (%)*	79	79	79	81	85	85	82	83	84	79	81	80	81
Mean Relative Humidity 3pm (%)*	59	56	50	49	53	49	45	47	48	45	54	59	51
Mean Dewpoint (°F)*	17	21	29	40	51	60	63	62	54	42	31	21	41
Prevailing Wind Direction*	N	N	N	S	S	S	S	S	S	S	S	N	S
Prevailing Wind Speed (mph)*	14	15	15	16	15	15	14	14	15	15	14	14	15
Maximum Wind Gust (mph)*	60	63	64	73	62	75	63	67	64	61	62	60	75

Note: (*) Period of record is 1948-1995

Dodge City Municipal Airport

The climate of Dodge City and southwestern Kansas is classified as semi-arid. Dodge City is nearly 300 miles east of the Rocky Mountains, but the weather reflects the influence of the mountains. The mountains form a barricade against all except high level moisture from the southwest, west, and northwest. Chinook winds occur occasionally but with less frequency and effect than at stations farther to the west. Relatively dry air predominating with an abundance of sunshine contribute to broad diurnal temperature ranges.

Thunderstorms during the growing season contribute most of the moisture. In general, the thunderstorms are widely scattered, occurring during the late afternoons and evenings. They are occasionally accompanied by hail and strong winds, but due to the local nature of the storms, damage to crops and buildings is spotty and variable. Winter is the dry season. However, the moisture accumulated during the winter months is important for the hard winter wheat. The duration of snow cover is generally brief due to mild temperatures and an abundance of sunshine. The exception results from the occasional blizzard that spreads across the flat treeless prairies of the high plains.

Afternoon temperatures in the 90s prevail during the summer months. Temperatures above 100 degrees are the exception. Due to low humidity and a continual breeze, these high temperatures are moderated. Temperatures normally drop sharply after sunset, allowing cool comfortable nights. During the winter months, large temperature changes are frequent, but the duration of extreme cold spells is brief.

The visibility at Dodge City is generally unrestricted as the terrain is favorable for unrestricted movement of air and air masses. Western Kansas is noted for clear skies and an abundance of sunshine.

Based on the 1951-1980 period, the average first occurrence of 32 degrees Fahrenheit in the fall is October 23 and the average last occurrence in the spring is April 21.

Dodge City Municipal Airport *Ford County* Elevation: 2,576 ft. Latitude: 37° 46' N Longitude: 99° 58' W

	JAN	FEB	MAR	APR	MAY	JUN	JUL	AUG	SEP	OCT	NOV	DEC	YEAR
Mean Maximum Temp. (°F)	44.0	48.4	57.6	67.3	76.8	86.7	93.2	90.9	82.3	69.6	56.0	44.8	68.1
Mean Temp. (°F)	32.2	36.1	44.4	54.0	64.3	74.0	79.9	78.3	69.3	56.6	43.3	33.3	55.5
Mean Minimum Temp. (°F)	20.3	23.6	31.1	40.5	51.8	61.3	66.7	65.6	56.3	43.5	30.6	21.7	42.7
Extreme Maximum Temp. (°F)	80	85	93	100	105	110	109	108	104	98	91	76	110
Extreme Minimum Temp. (°F)	-13	-13	-5	14	31	42	46	48	29	14	3	-21	-21
Days Maximum Temp. ≥ 90°F	0	0	0	1	3	13	22	19	8	1	0	0	67
Days Maximum Temp. ≤ 32°F	7	5	2	0	0	0	0	0	0	0	1	6	21
Days Minimum Temp. ≤ 32°F	29	23	18	5	0	0	0	0	0	4	17	28	124
Days Minimum Temp. ≤ 0°F	1	1	0	0	0	0	0	0	0	0	0	1	3
Heating Degree Days (base 65°F)	1,009	811	634	345	110	11	1	2	59	286	644	977	4,889
Cooling Degree Days (base 65°F)	0	0	2	21	96	288	471	419	195	31	1	0	1,524
Mean Precipitation (in.)	0.59	0.70	1.64	1.85	2.83	3.22	2.87	2.76	1.68	1.74	0.72	0.85	21.45
Maximum Precipitation (in.)*	2.0	2.9	8.8	6.3	8.7	7.9	9.1	7.4	6.8	4.9	3.8	2.4	32.8
Minimum Precipitation (in.)*	0	trace	trace	0.1	0.4	0.1	0.2	0.7	trace	trace	trace	trace	10.0
Extreme Maximum Daily Precip. (in.)	1.30	1.82	1.81	1.66	3.45	2.55	2.86	3.86	2.36	4.13	1.57	2.43	4.13
Days With ≥ 0.1" Precipitation	2	2	4	4	5	6	5	5	3	3	2	2	43
Days With ≥ 0.5" Precipitation	0	0	1	1	2	2	2	2	1	1	0	0	12
Days With ≥ 1.0" Precipitation	0	0	0	0	1	1	1	1	1	0	0	0	5
Mean Snowfall (in.)	4.7	4.1	5.2	1.1	trace	trace	trace	trace	0.1	0.4	1.8	3.9	21.3
Maximum Snowfall (in.)*	16	20	24	9	1	0	0	0	1	5	17	10	45
Maximum 24-hr. Snowfall (in.)*	11	12	9	6	1	0	0	0	1	4	12	7	12
Maximum Snow Depth (in.)	12	13	14	6	trace	trace	trace	trace	trace	1	14	12	14
Days With ≥ 1.0" Snow Depth	6	4	2	0	0	0	0	0	0	0	1	5	18
Thunderstorm Days*	< 1	< 1	1	3	8	10	10	9	4	2	1	< 1	48
Foggy Days*	8	9	9	7	8	5	4	6	7	6	7	8	84
Predominant Sky Cover*	CLR	OVR	OVR	OVR	OVR	SCT	SCT	CLR	CLR	CLR	CLR	CLR	CLR
Mean Relative Humidity 6am (%)*	77	78	76	76	82	80	77	79	78	74	76	76	77
Mean Relative Humidity 3pm (%)*	51	49	44	40	46	42	38	39	40	38	45	50	43
Mean Dewpoint (°F)*	18	22	27	36	49	57	60	59	51	39	28	21	39
Prevailing Wind Direction*	N	N	S	S	S	S	S	S	S	S	S	N	S
Prevailing Wind Speed (mph)*	16	16	16	17	17	17	15	14	16	15	15	16	16
Maximum Wind Gust (mph)*	61	71	82	69	68	67	71	74	56	60	74	56	82

Note: (*) Period of record is 1948-1995

Goodland Renner Field

Goodland is situated on an intermediate plain with few native trees. The terrain rises from east to west with only minor variations from north to south. The rate of rise is about 1,600 feet per 150 miles east of Goodland and about 2,500 feet per 150 miles west. This gradual slope in terrain makes conditions favorable for upslope fog, low clouds, and drizzle with easterly winds.

This is a typical steppe climate with wide variations in precipitation from year to year. Evaporation generally exceeds precipitation during the summer months. The number of subnormal years of precipitation nearly equals the above normal years. The mean monthly rainfall increases in the spring to a maximum in June. General storms provide the main source of precipitation during the spring months, while thunderstorms are the major factor during the summer months. Inadequate moisture received from March through June, often results in drought conditions throughout the summer months with thunderstorms providing only local relief. The frequency of thunderstorms increases to a maximum in July with a marked decrease in September. Hail is most frequent in May and June. Winds during thunderstorms have been recorded with gusts up to 80 mph.

Snow is an important factor in the production of winter wheat, and residual soil moisture often offsets the effects of subnormal spring precipitation. When snow is accompanied by strong winds it can become a dangerous enemy. As little as one inch of snow accompanied by strong winds can result in serious blocking of roads and highways. The heaviest snowfall is most likely to occur in March, although heavy snows have been recorded in every month from October through May. Snow may cover the ground about one third of the time from November through March.

Temperatures are typical of continental climates with January normally the coldest month and July the warmest. Winters are often modified by persistent foehn winds but polar outbreaks have been known to drop the temperature as much as 70 degrees in a 24-hour period. Low relative humidity during the summer months makes most nights comfortable even in the hottest weather.

Based on the 1951-1980 period, the average first occurrence of 32 degrees Fahrenheit in the fall is October 7 and the average last occurrence in the spring is May 4. The growing season is 156 days.

Goodland Renner Field *Sherman County* Elevation: 3,645 ft. Latitude: 39° 22' N Longitude: 101° 42' W

	JAN	FEB	MAR	APR	MAY	JUN	JUL	AUG	SEP	OCT	NOV	DEC	YEAR
Mean Maximum Temp. (°F)	42.1	45.3	54.3	63.4	72.9	83.9	90.1	87.5	79.0	66.1	52.4	43.0	65.0
Mean Temp. (°F)	29.6	32.6	40.4	49.2	59.5	69.8	75.9	73.8	64.7	51.9	39.2	30.4	51.4
Mean Minimum Temp. (°F)	17.0	19.7	26.5	34.9	46.0	55.7	61.5	60.1	50.3	37.6	25.9	17.8	37.8
Extreme Maximum Temp. (°F)	78	81	87	96	104	106	109	105	100	93	84	79	109
Extreme Minimum Temp. (°F)	-20	-22	-8	4	24	36	43	42	19	7	-3	-27	-27
Days Maximum Temp. ≥ 90°F	0	0	0	0	2	9	18	14	6	1	0	0	50
Days Maximum Temp. ≤ 32°F	8	6	2	0	0	0	0	0	0	0	2	7	25
Days Minimum Temp. ≤ 32°F	30	27	24	12	1	0	0	0	1	8	23	30	156
Days Minimum Temp. ≤ 0°F	2	2	0	0	0	0	0	0	0	0	0	2	6
Heating Degree Days (base 65°F)	1,092	910	755	474	202	33	3	7	107	410	767	1,066	5,826
Cooling Degree Days (base 65°F)	0	0	0	5	39	185	347	288	105	9	0	0	978
Mean Precipitation (in.)	0.39	0.48	1.10	1.60	2.94	3.20	3.58	2.72	1.24	1.38	0.71	0.46	19.80
Maximum Precipitation (in.)*	1.6	1.5	3.6	3.9	8.2	9.5	10.1	9.3	5.4	4.1	2.1	1.6	28.0
Minimum Precipitation (in.)*	0	trace	0.1	trace	0.5	0.1	1.0	0.1	trace	trace	trace	trace	9.2
Extreme Maximum Daily Precip. (in.)	1.02	0.67	1.73	2.98	2.52	4.15	3.65	3.10	1.90	1.99	1.14	1.36	4.15
Days With ≥ 0.1" Precipitation	1	2	3	4	6	6	6	5	3	3	2	1	42
Days With ≥ 0.5" Precipitation	0	0	1	1	2	2	2	2	1	1	0	0	12
Days With ≥ 1.0" Precipitation	0	0	0	0	1	1	1	1	0	0	0	0	4
Mean Snowfall (in.)	6.5	5.9	7.6	4.6	0.6	0.1	trace	trace	0.4	2.2	4.7	5.6	38.2
Maximum Snowfall (in.)*	19	24	27	22	7	0	0	0	6	18	23	17	86
Maximum 24-hr. Snowfall (in.)*	12	8	12	9	7	0	0	0	4	11	15	9	15
Maximum Snow Depth (in.)	18	12	15	15	1	trace	trace	trace	5	16	19	20	20
Days With ≥ 1.0" Snow Depth	9	8	4	2	0	0	0	0	0	1	3	7	34
Thunderstorm Days*	< 1	< 1	1	2	8	10	11	9	4	1	< 1	< 1	46
Foggy Days*	7	8	9	8	9	6	5	7	7	6	7	6	85
Predominant Sky Cover*	CLR	OVR	OVR	OVR	OVR	CLR	CLR	CLR	CLR	CLR	CLR	CLR	CLR
Mean Relative Humidity 6am (%)*	76	79	79	77	80	78	78	81	78	74	76	75	78
Mean Relative Humidity 3pm (%)*	51	49	44	39	44	39	36	38	36	35	44	50	42
Mean Dewpoint (°F)*	16	19	23	32	44	52	57	56	46	33	24	17	35
Prevailing Wind Direction*	WSW	NNW	NNW	SSE	SSE	SSE	SSE	SSE	SSE	SSE	NNW	WSW	SSE
Prevailing Wind Speed (mph)*	10	16	18	16	16	15	14	13	13	13	16	10	14
Maximum Wind Gust (mph)*	67	61	66	82	96	77	70	91	68	68	68	63	96

Note: (*) Period of record is 1949-1995

The period of record for National Weather Service station data is 1980 – 2009 except where noted. See User Guide for detailed explanation of data.

Topeka Municipal Airport

Topeka, is located near the geographical center of the United States, and the middle of the temperate zone. The city straddles the Kansas River about 60 miles above its junction with the Missouri River. The Kansas River flows in an easterly direction through northeastern Kansas. Near Topeka, the river valley ranges from two to four miles wide, and is bordered on both sides by rolling prairie uplands of some 200 to 300 feet. The city is built on both banks of the Kansas River and along two tributaries, Soldier Creek in north Topeka and Shunganunga Creek in the south and east part of town. Flooding is always a threat following periods of heavy rains but protective construction has reduced the problem.

Seventy percent of the annual precipitation normally falls during the six crop-growing months, April through September. The rains of this period are usually of short duration, predominantly of the thunderstorm type. They occur more frequently during the nighttime and early morning hours than at other times of the day. Excessive precipitation rates may occur with warm-season thunderstorms. Rainfall accumulations over eight inches in 24 hours have occurred in Topeka. Tornadoes have occurred in the area on several occasions and caused severe damage and numerous injuries.

Individual summers show wide departures from average conditions. Hottest summers may produce temperatures of 100 degrees or higher on more than 50 days. On the other hand, 25 percent of the summers pass with two or fewer 100 degree days. Similarly, precipitation has shown a wide range for June, July, and August, varying from under three inches to more than 27 inches during the three months. Summers are hot with low relative humidity and persistent southerly winds. Oppressively warm periods with high relative humidity are usually of short duration.

Winter temperatures average about 45 degrees cooler than summer. Cold spells are seldom prolonged. Winter precipitation is often in the form of snow, sleet, or glaze, but severe storms are not common.

In the transitional spring and fall seasons, the numerous days of fair weather are interspersed with short intervals of stormy weather. Strong, blustery winds are quite common in late winter and spring. Autumn is characteristically a season of warm days, cool nights, and infrequent precipitation, with cold air invasions gradually increasing in intensity as the season progresses.

Based on the 1951-1980 period, the average first occurrence of 32 degrees Fahrenheit in the fall is October 14 and the average last occurrence in the spring is April 21.

Topeka Municipal Airport *Shawnee County* Elevation: 883 ft. Latitude: 39° 04' N Longitude: 95° 38' W

	JAN	FEB	MAR	APR	MAY	JUN	JUL	AUG	SEP	OCT	NOV	DEC	YEAR
Mean Maximum Temp. (°F)	40.1	44.6	56.2	66.5	75.9	84.7	89.8	88.6	80.4	68.2	54.6	41.6	65.9
Mean Temp. (°F)	29.9	34.1	44.7	54.9	65.0	74.1	79.2	77.4	68.4	56.4	43.8	32.0	55.0
Mean Minimum Temp. (°F)	19.6	23.5	33.1	43.3	54.0	63.6	68.4	66.1	56.3	44.5	33.0	22.4	44.0
Extreme Maximum Temp. (°F)	74	81	89	95	97	106	110	110	109	96	85	73	110
Extreme Minimum Temp. (°F)	-15	-21	-6	19	30	43	48	41	29	19	4	-26	-26
Days Maximum Temp. ≥ 90°F	0	0	0	0	2	8	16	14	5	0	0	0	45
Days Maximum Temp. ≤ 32°F	9	6	1	0	0	0	0	0	0	0	1	7	24
Days Minimum Temp. ≤ 32°F	29	22	15	4	0	0	0	0	0	3	15	26	114
Days Minimum Temp. ≤ 0°F	2	2	0	0	0	0	0	0	0	0	0	1	5
Heating Degree Days (base 65°F)	1,081	868	626	323	93	6	0	1	64	287	630	1,016	4,995
Cooling Degree Days (base 65°F)	0	0	3	27	99	288	446	392	171	28	1	0	1,455
Mean Precipitation (in.)	0.89	1.34	2.58	3.46	4.85	5.10	3.69	4.38	3.55	3.23	1.81	1.46	36.34
Maximum Precipitation (in.)*	5.2	3.5	8.4	8.1	11.8	15.2	12.0	11.2	12.7	7.2	6.3	4.3	60.9
Minimum Precipitation (in.)*	trace	trace	0.1	0.6	0.4	0.6	0.6	0.3	0.7	trace	trace	0	19.1
Extreme Maximum Daily Precip. (in.)	1.26	1.65	2.47	3.19	5.10	4.15	2.99	3.60	5.61	3.48	3.40	2.55	5.61
Days With ≥ 0.1" Precipitation	2	3	5	6	8	7	6	6	5	5	4	3	60
Days With ≥ 0.5" Precipitation	0	1	2	3	3	3	2	3	3	2	1	1	24
Days With ≥ 1.0" Precipitation	0	0	1	1	1	2	1	1	1	1	0	0	9
Mean Snowfall (in.)	4.7	4.7	1.5	0.3	trace	trace	trace	0.0	trace	0.3	1.0	5.7	18.2
Maximum Snowfall (in.)*	23	22	22	7	0	0	0	0	0	1	9	19	49
Maximum 24-hr. Snowfall (in.)*	15	11	8	7	0	0	0	0	0	1	6	9	15
Maximum Snow Depth (in.)	14	10	7	1	trace	trace	trace	0	trace	4	4	9	14
Days With ≥ 1.0" Snow Depth	7	6	1	0	0	0	0	0	0	0	0	6	20
Thunderstorm Days*	< 1	1	3	5	9	10	9	8	6	3	1	< 1	55
Foggy Days*	10	11	11	9	10	8	8	8	10	9	9	11	114
Predominant Sky Cover*	OVR	OVR	OVR	OVR	OVR	OVR	CLR	CLR	CLR	CLR	OVR	OVR	OVR
Mean Relative Humidity 6am (%)*	78	79	79	80	85	87	86	87	87	83	80	80	83
Mean Relative Humidity 3pm (%)*	58	56	51	49	52	54	53	52	50	47	52	58	53
Mean Dewpoint (°F)*	18	23	30	41	53	63	67	65	56	44	32	23	43
Prevailing Wind Direction*	N	N	N	S	S	S	S	S	S	S	S	S	S
Prevailing Wind Speed (mph)*	13	13	14	15	14	13	12	10	12	13	12	12	13
Maximum Wind Gust (mph)*	53	59	62	64	67	82	77	67	61	59	58	54	82

Note: (*) Period of record is 1948-1995

Wichita Mid-Continent Airport

Wichita is in the Central Great Plains where masses of warm, moist air from the Gulf of Mexico collide with cold, dry air from the Arctic region to create a wide range of weather the year around. Summers are usually warm and humid, and can be very hot and dry. The winters are usually mild, with brief periods of very cold weather.

The elevation is just over 1,300 feet above sea level. The terrain is basically flat with natural tree areas mainly along the Arkansas River and its tributaries.

The temperature extremes for the period of weather records at Wichita range from more than 110 degrees to less than -20 degrees. Temperatures above 90 degrees occur an average of 63 days per year, while very cold temperatures below zero occur about two days per year.

Precipitation averages about 30 inches per year, with 70 percent of that falling from April through September during the growing season. The wettest years have recorded over 50 inches. The driest years less than 15 inches.

Thunderstorms occur mainly during the spring and early summer. They can be severe and cause damage from heavy rain, large hail, strong winds and tornadoes.

The city of Wichita is protected against floods from the Arkansas River and its local tributaries by the Wichita-Vally Center Flood Control Project, which is designed to protect against floods up to the 75 to 100 year frequency class.

Snowfall normally is 15 inches per year, falling from December through March. Monthly snowfalls in excess of 20 inches and 24-hour snowfalls of more than 13 inches have occurred.

The prevailing wind direction is south with the windiest months March and April. July has the least wind. Strong north winds often occur with the passage of cold fronts from late fall through early spring. Extremely low wind chill factors are experienced with very cold outbreaks during the mid winter. On rare occasions during the summer, strong, hot, dry southwest winds can do considerable damage to crops.

Wichita Mid-Continent Airport *Sedgwick County* Elevation: 1,319 ft. Latitude: 37° 39' N Longitude: 97° 26' W

	JAN	FEB	MAR	APR	MAY	JUN	JUL	AUG	SEP	OCT	NOV	DEC	YEAR
Mean Maximum Temp. (°F)	42.6	48.2	57.8	67.5	76.7	86.7	92.8	91.3	82.5	69.6	56.2	43.6	68.0
Mean Temp. (°F)	32.3	37.1	46.3	55.9	66.0	75.8	81.4	80.1	71.1	58.2	45.4	33.9	57.0
Mean Minimum Temp. (°F)	22.0	25.9	34.8	44.2	55.2	64.8	69.9	68.9	59.5	46.8	34.6	24.1	45.9
Extreme Maximum Temp. (°F)	75	87	89	96	100	110	112	110	108	97	86	73	112
Extreme Minimum Temp. (°F)	-10	-21	2	21	32	44	52	49	31	18	7	-16	-21
Days Maximum Temp. ≥ 90°F	0	0	0	0	2	12	21	19	8	1	0	0	63
Days Maximum Temp. ≤ 32°F	7	4	1	0	0	0	0	0	0	0	1	6	19
Days Minimum Temp. ≤ 32°F	28	21	12	3	0	0	0	0	0	1	13	26	104
Days Minimum Temp. ≤ 0°F	1	1	0	0	0	0	0	0	0	0	0	1	3
Heating Degree Days (base 65°F)	1,006	784	574	290	77	4	0	0	40	239	582	958	4,554
Cooling Degree Days (base 65°F)	0	0	2	24	113	334	514	475	229	37	1	0	1,729
Mean Precipitation (in.)	0.88	1.17	2.76	2.59	4.44	5.06	3.24	3.70	3.05	2.81	1.40	1.27	32.37
Maximum Precipitation (in.)*	6.3	3.3	9.2	6.3	9.6	10.5	13.4	7.9	9.5	6.1	5.9	4.7	50.5
Minimum Precipitation (in.)*	trace	trace	trace	0.2	0.5	0.9	0	0.3	trace	0	trace	trace	12.1
Extreme Maximum Daily Precip. (in.)	1.82	1.31	2.26	5.10	3.23	2.79	2.67	3.76	10.31	5.79	2.28	2.57	10.31
Days With ≥ 0.1" Precipitation	2	3	5	5	7	7	5	5	4	4	3	3	53
Days With ≥ 0.5" Precipitation	1	1	2	2	3	4	2	3	2	2	1	1	24
Days With ≥ 1.0" Precipitation	0	0	1	1	1	2	1	1	1	1	0	0	9
Mean Snowfall (in.)	3.6	3.5	2.2	0.2	trace	trace	trace	trace	trace	0.1	1.4	4.2	15.2
Maximum Snowfall (in.)*	20	17	17	5	0	0	0	0	0	2	8	14	45
Maximum 24-hr. Snowfall (in.)*	12	12	12	5	0	0	0	0	0	2	8	8	12
Maximum Snow Depth (in.)	11	11	7	2	trace	trace	trace	trace	trace	1	5	8	11
Days With ≥ 1.0" Snow Depth	4	4	1	0	0	0	0	0	0	0	1	5	15
Thunderstorm Days*	< 1	1	3	5	9	10	8	8	6	3	1	< 1	54
Foggy Days*	10	10	10	8	9	6	4	5	8	7	8	10	95
Predominant Sky Cover*	OVR	OVR	OVR	OVR	OVR	OVR	CLR	CLR	CLR	CLR	CLR	OVR	CLR
Mean Relative Humidity 6am (%)*	79	79	77	78	83	83	79	80	82	80	80	80	80
Mean Relative Humidity 3pm (%)*	57	54	48	47	52	47	42	43	47	46	52	57	49
Mean Dewpoint (°F)*	20	24	32	42	53	61	64	63	56	45	33	24	43
Prevailing Wind Direction*	N	N	S	S	S	S	S	S	S	S	S	S	S
Prevailing Wind Speed (mph)*	15	15	16	16	15	15	13	13	14	14	14	13	14
Maximum Wind Gust (mph)*	56	61	82	71	75	83	83	68	59	55	63	53	83

Note: (*) Period of record is 1948-1995

Abilene 1 W *Dickinson County* Elevation: 1,169 ft. Latitude: 38° 55' N Longitude: 97° 14' W

	JAN	FEB	MAR	APR	MAY	JUN	JUL	AUG	SEP	OCT	NOV	DEC	YEAR
Mean Maximum Temp. (°F)	42.8	48.0	58.2	68.7	77.9	87.5	93.8	91.9	83.1	70.4	56.3	43.8	68.5
Mean Temp. (°F)	31.9	36.4	46.1	56.3	66.2	75.7	81.6	79.7	70.6	58.1	45.1	33.7	56.8
Mean Minimum Temp. (°F)	20.9	24.5	33.9	43.8	54.5	63.9	69.2	67.4	58.0	45.7	33.8	23.6	44.9
Extreme Maximum Temp. (°F)	77	80	87	98	101	104	112	111	111	97	88	73	112
Extreme Minimum Temp. (°F)	-16	-19	-6	17	31	39	48	48	23	16	4	-24	-24
Days Maximum Temp. ≥ 90°F	0	0	0	1	3	13	22	19	8	1	0	0	67
Days Maximum Temp. ≤ 32°F	7	4	1	0	0	0	0	0	0	0	1	5	18
Days Minimum Temp. ≤ 32°F	28	22	14	4	0	0	0	0	0	3	14	26	111
Days Minimum Temp. ≤ 0°F	1	2	0	0	0	0	0	0	0	0	0	1	4
Heating Degree Days (base 65°F)	1,018	800	584	285	77	6	0	1	43	247	593	963	4,617
Cooling Degree Days (base 65°F)	0	0	3	33	122	334	521	462	217	39	2	0	1,733
Mean Precipitation (in.)	0.81	1.33	2.57	3.08	4.79	4.37	3.96	4.17	2.39	2.49	1.52	1.19	32.67
Extreme Maximum Daily Precip. (in.)	1.33	2.06	2.27	3.88	4.80	4.35	3.90	5.85	2.15	2.36	2.73	1.92	5.85
Days With ≥ 0.1" Precipitation	2	3	5	5	7	6	5	6	4	4	3	3	53
Days With ≥ 0.5" Precipitation	0	1	2	2	3	3	3	2	2	2	1	1	22
Days With ≥ 1.0" Precipitation	0	0	1	1	2	1	1	1	1	1	0	0	9
Mean Snowfall (in.)	4.1	3.5	1.8	0.1	0.0	0.0	0.0	0.0	0.0	0.1	0.7	3.6	13.9
Maximum Snow Depth (in.)	7	***12***	11	1	0	0	0	0	0	2	4	***6***	***12***
Days With ≥ 1.0" Snow Depth	3	2	0	0	0	0	0	0	0	0	0	***2***	***7***

Alton 6 ESE *Osborne County* Elevation: 1,620 ft. Latitude: 39° 26' N Longitude: 98° 51' W

	JAN	FEB	MAR	APR	MAY	JUN	JUL	AUG	SEP	OCT	NOV	DEC	YEAR
Mean Maximum Temp. (°F)	41.4	45.7	56.7	67.7	76.3	86.7	93.5	91.0	83.0	70.2	54.8	***44.2***	***67.6***
Mean Temp. (°F)	27.9	31.5	42.0	52.3	62.3	72.7	79.2	***76.7***	67.7	54.5	40.3	***30.7***	***53.1***
Mean Minimum Temp. (°F)	14.3	17.3	27.3	36.7	48.3	58.5	64.8	***62.4***	52.3	38.8	25.7	***17.2***	***38.6***
Extreme Maximum Temp. (°F)	80	86	90	106	104	113	***112***	***111***	111	100	***88***	***80***	***113***
Extreme Minimum Temp. (°F)	-24	-22	-8	***9***	23	33	***41***	***41***	26	6	***-5***	***-31***	***-31***
Days Maximum Temp. ≥ 90°F	0	0	0	1	3	12	***21***	***18***	10	1	0	***0***	***66***
Days Maximum Temp. ≤ 32°F	8	6	2	0	0	0	0	0	0	0	2	***5***	***23***
Days Minimum Temp. ≤ 32°F	30	26	21	10	2	0	0	0	1	8	23	***30***	***151***
Days Minimum Temp. ≤ 0°F	3	3	1	0	0	0	0	0	0	0	0	***2***	***9***
Heating Degree Days (base 65°F)	1,143	938	706	391	148	20	2	***4***	79	340	736	***1,056***	***5,563***
Cooling Degree Days (base 65°F)	0	0	1	16	71	258	448	***374***	167	22	0	0	***1,357***
Mean Precipitation (in.)	0.65	0.73	2.12	2.41	4.00	3.46	4.43	3.22	2.19	1.72	1.26	0.80	26.99
Extreme Maximum Daily Precip. (in.)	0.84	0.98	3.20	3.50	3.45	***3.30***	***4.16***	***3.40***	2.71	***2.94***	***3.33***	***1.01***	***4.16***
Days With ≥ 0.1" Precipitation	2	2	4	5	7	6	7	5	4	3	3	***2***	***50***
Days With ≥ 0.5" Precipitation	0	0	1	2	3	3	3	2	2	1	1	***1***	***19***
Days With ≥ 1.0" Precipitation	0	0	1	1	1	1	1	1	1	0	0	0	7
Mean Snowfall (in.)	4.4	5.0	2.6	0.9	0.0	0.0	0.0	0.0	0.1	0.2	1.9	***3.0***	***18.1***
Maximum Snow Depth (in.)	11	***11***	6	***11***	***0***	***0***	***0***	***0***	***0***	***5***	***8***	***8***	***11***
Days With ≥ 1.0" Snow Depth	7	8	3	0	0	0	0	***0***	0	0	1	***6***	***25***

Anthony *Harper County* Elevation: 1,339 ft. Latitude: 37° 09' N Longitude: 98° 02' W

	JAN	FEB	MAR	APR	MAY	JUN	JUL	AUG	SEP	OCT	NOV	DEC	YEAR
Mean Maximum Temp. (°F)	45.4	50.3	59.9	69.5	78.9	88.4	94.4	93.1	84.2	71.3	57.9	45.6	69.9
Mean Temp. (°F)	34.7	39.0	47.8	57.0	67.3	76.4	82.1	81.1	72.1	59.5	46.7	35.1	58.2
Mean Minimum Temp. (°F)	24.0	27.6	35.7	44.5	55.7	64.6	69.8	69.0	59.9	47.5	35.3	24.6	46.5
Extreme Maximum Temp. (°F)	74	90	92	99	103	108	110	110	107	95	88	77	110
Extreme Minimum Temp. (°F)	-12	-6	0	22	33	46	52	52	30	16	9	-15	-15
Days Maximum Temp. ≥ 90°F	0	0	0	1	3	14	24	22	9	1	0	0	74
Days Maximum Temp. ≤ 32°F	5	3	1	0	0	0	0	0	0	0	1	4	14
Days Minimum Temp. ≤ 32°F	25	20	11	2	0	0	0	0	0	1	11	25	95
Days Minimum Temp. ≤ 0°F	0	0	0	0	0	0	0	0	0	0	0	1	1
Heating Degree Days (base 65°F)	930	730	528	257	58	3	0	0	29	206	545	918	4,204
Cooling Degree Days (base 65°F)	0	0	3	24	138	353	538	506	248	43	1	0	1,854
Mean Precipitation (in.)	1.08	1.24	3.20	3.39	4.56	5.20	3.12	2.82	2.78	2.70	1.76	1.24	33.09
Extreme Maximum Daily Precip. (in.)	2.36	2.01	2.33	6.55	7.49	4.56	4.62	4.87	4.48	4.36	5.23	1.53	7.49
Days With ≥ 0.1" Precipitation	2	3	5	5	7	7	5	4	4	4	3	3	52
Days With ≥ 0.5" Precipitation	1	1	2	2	3	3	2	2	2	2	1	1	22
Days With ≥ 1.0" Precipitation	0	0	1	1	1	2	1	1	1	1	0	0	9
Mean Snowfall (in.)	3.0	3.3	***2.2***	0.1	0.0	0.0	0.0	0.0	0.0	0.1	0.6	3.5	***12.8***
Maximum Snow Depth (in.)	8	***14***	***9***	2	0	0	0	0	0	***2***	4	***9***	***14***
Days With ≥ 1.0" Snow Depth	2	***2***	***1***	0	0	0	0	0	0	0	0	3	***8***

Ashland *Clark County* Elevation: 1,970 ft. Latitude: 37° 12' N Longitude: 99° 46' W

	JAN	FEB	MAR	APR	MAY	JUN	JUL	AUG	SEP	OCT	NOV	DEC	YEAR
Mean Maximum Temp. (°F)	47.1	51.3	60.3	70.2	79.1	88.3	94.9	93.5	84.7	72.5	59.3	47.5	70.7
Mean Temp. (°F)	32.1	36.1	45.2	54.6	65.2	74.8	80.2	79.0	69.6	56.6	43.7	32.9	55.8
Mean Minimum Temp. (°F)	17.0	20.9	30.1	39.0	51.2	61.2	65.5	64.4	54.5	40.6	28.0	18.3	40.9
Extreme Maximum Temp. (°F)	84	90	93	102	105	112	113	111	109	99	90	77	113
Extreme Minimum Temp. (°F)	-19	-18	-3	14	27	40	46	43	24	11	4	-17	-19
Days Maximum Temp. ≥ 90°F	0	0	0	2	4	14	25	22	10	2	0	0	79
Days Maximum Temp. ≤ 32°F	5	4	1	0	0	0	0	0	0	0	1	5	16
Days Minimum Temp. ≤ 32°F	30	25	19	7	0	0	0	0	0	7	21	30	139
Days Minimum Temp. ≤ 0°F	1	1	0	0	0	0	0	0	0	0	0	1	3
Heating Degree Days (base 65°F)	1,013	810	608	324	97	8	0	2	52	281	634	989	4,818
Cooling Degree Days (base 65°F)	0	0	2	20	109	309	478	442	197	26	1	0	1,584
Mean Precipitation (in.)	0.57	0.70	1.64	1.91	3.34	4.02	2.66	2.72	1.75	1.86	0.85	0.94	22.96
Extreme Maximum Daily Precip. (in.)	1.05	1.25	2.41	2.90	3.30	4.40	2.50	3.55	1.95	2.52	1.90	2.98	4.40
Days With ≥ 0.1" Precipitation	2	2	4	4	5	6	4	5	4	3	2	2	43
Days With ≥ 0.5" Precipitation	0	0	1	1	2	3	2	2	1	1	1	0	14
Days With ≥ 1.0" Precipitation	0	0	0	0	1	1	1	1	0	1	0	0	5
Mean Snowfall (in.)	4.0	1.9	2.1	trace	0.0	0.0	0.0	0.0	0.0	0.1	0.5	3.1	11.7
Maximum Snow Depth (in.)	***14***	***9***	***16***	trace	0	0	0	0	0	***0***	***13***	***12***	***16***
Days With ≥ 1.0" Snow Depth	***2***	2	1	0	0	0	0	0	0	0	0	2	***7***

The period of record for all cooperative weather station data is 1980 – 2009. See User Guide for detailed explanation of data.

Atchison *Atchison County* Elevation: 944 ft. Latitude: 39° 34' N Longitude: 95° 07' W

	JAN	FEB	MAR	APR	MAY	JUN	JUL	AUG	SEP	OCT	NOV	DEC	YEAR
Mean Maximum Temp. (°F)	38.1	43.1	55.1	66.2	75.5	83.8	89.0	87.6	79.7	67.5	52.7	40.0	64.9
Mean Temp. (°F)	29.2	33.6	44.3	55.2	65.2	73.8	79.0	77.3	68.8	57.1	43.6	31.6	54.9
Mean Minimum Temp. (°F)	20.3	24.0	33.6	44.2	54.9	63.7	69.0	66.9	57.8	46.6	34.4	23.2	44.9
Extreme Maximum Temp. (°F)	72	77	86	94	95	105	109	109	105	94	84	71	109
Extreme Minimum Temp. (°F)	-16	-14	-6	19	34	44	53	48	32	20	2	-21	-21
Days Maximum Temp. ≥ 90°F	0	0	0	0	1	5	14	12	4	0	0	0	36
Days Maximum Temp. ≤ 32°F	10	7	1	0	0	0	0	0	0	0	1	8	27
Days Minimum Temp. ≤ 32°F	27	21	14	3	0	0	0	0	0	2	13	25	105
Days Minimum Temp. ≤ 0°F	2	1	0	0	0	0	0	0	0	0	0	1	4
Heating Degree Days (base 65°F)	1,103	883	636	312	83	7	0	1	55	267	637	1,028	5,012
Cooling Degree Days (base 65°F)	0	0	3	26	97	277	441	390	175	28	1	0	1,438
Mean Precipitation (in.)	0.93	1.11	2.13	3.33	5.23	5.10	4.60	4.05	3.69	3.13	1.83	1.53	36.66
Extreme Maximum Daily Precip. (in.)	0.95	1.70	2.35	2.85	4.45	4.07	3.60	3.62	3.83	3.77	2.05	2.45	4.45
Days With ≥ 0.1" Precipitation	3	3	5	6	8	7	6	6	6	5	4	3	62
Days With ≥ 0.5" Precipitation	0	1	1	3	3	3	3	3	3	2	1	1	24
Days With ≥ 1.0" Precipitation	0	0	0	1	2	2	2	1	1	1	0	0	10
Mean Snowfall (in.)	4.9	5.1	2.1	0.3	trace	0.0	0.0	0.0	0.0	0.2	0.7	5.3	18.6
Maximum Snow Depth (in.)	9	9	9	4	trace	0	0	0	0	1	4	11	11
Days With ≥ 1.0" Snow Depth	8	8	2	0	0	0	0	0	0	0	1	7	26

Atwood 2 SW *Rawlins County* Elevation: 2,861 ft. Latitude: 39° 47' N Longitude: 101° 05' W

	JAN	FEB	MAR	APR	MAY	JUN	JUL	AUG	SEP	OCT	NOV	DEC	YEAR
Mean Maximum Temp. (°F)	40.7	44.9	54.4	64.5	74.5	85.7	92.0	89.5	80.5	66.6	52.9	42.3	65.7
Mean Temp. (°F)	27.2	30.9	39.5	49.1	60.0	70.5	76.6	74.6	64.6	50.9	38.5	28.9	50.9
Mean Minimum Temp. (°F)	13.7	17.0	24.6	33.7	45.4	55.3	61.1	59.6	48.6	35.1	24.0	15.4	36.1
Extreme Maximum Temp. (°F)	77	79	89	96	104	108	111	110	104	96	86	75	111
Extreme Minimum Temp. (°F)	-25	-23	-8	9	21	32	40	40	21	8	-6	-26	-26
Days Maximum Temp. ≥ 90°F	0	0	0	1	3	12	20	17	8	1	0	0	62
Days Maximum Temp. ≤ 32°F	9	6	2	0	0	0	0	0	0	0	2	7	26
Days Minimum Temp. ≤ 32°F	31	27	25	14	2	0	0	0	1	12	25	30	167
Days Minimum Temp. ≤ 0°F	3	3	1	0	0	0	0	0	0	0	0	2	9
Heating Degree Days (base 65°F)	1,164	957	783	474	197	32	3	7	113	438	789	1,113	6,070
Cooling Degree Days (base 65°F)	0	0	0	5	48	205	369	311	108	7	0	0	1,053
Mean Precipitation (in.)	0.61	0.68	1.36	2.33	3.81	3.17	3.46	2.95	1.51	1.68	0.91	0.61	23.08
Extreme Maximum Daily Precip. (in.)	1.72	1.18	1.50	2.80	3.38	2.97	3.36	4.25	2.39	2.59	2.20	1.77	4.25
Days With ≥ 0.1" Precipitation	2	2	4	5	7	6	6	5	3	3	2	1	46
Days With ≥ 0.5" Precipitation	0	0	1	2	3	2	2	2	1	1	1	0	15
Days With ≥ 1.0" Precipitation	0	0	0	1	1	1	1	1	0	0	0	0	5
Mean Snowfall (in.)	6.9	5.6	*5.5*	3.5	0.1	0.0	0.0	0.0	0.3	1.4	4.1	4.3	*31.7*
Maximum Snow Depth (in.)	*19*	*10*	*11*	*6*	3	0	0	0	4	13	*11*	*19*	*19*
Days With ≥ 1.0" Snow Depth	*5*	*4*	*2*	1	0	0	0	0	0	0	1	*3*	*16*

Belleville *Republic County* Elevation: 1,540 ft. Latitude: 39° 50' N Longitude: 97° 38' W

	JAN	FEB	MAR	APR	MAY	JUN	JUL	AUG	SEP	OCT	NOV	DEC	YEAR
Mean Maximum Temp. (°F)	39.0	43.4	54.2	65.1	74.8	84.8	90.7	88.6	79.7	66.8	52.4	39.4	64.9
Mean Temp. (°F)	28.2	32.2	42.1	52.8	63.3	73.1	78.8	76.9	67.5	54.9	41.1	29.5	53.4
Mean Minimum Temp. (°F)	17.3	20.8	30.0	40.4	51.8	61.4	66.8	65.1	55.2	42.8	29.8	19.4	41.7
Extreme Maximum Temp. (°F)	78	77	87	97	99	106	111	109	105	94	85	73	111
Extreme Minimum Temp. (°F)	-18	-15	-9	14	29	40	50	47	25	14	0	-25	-25
Days Maximum Temp. ≥ 90°F	0	0	0	0	1	9	18	14	5	1	0	0	48
Days Maximum Temp. ≤ 32°F	10	7	2	0	0	0	0	0	0	0	2	9	30
Days Minimum Temp. ≤ 32°F	30	24	19	6	0	0	0	0	0	4	18	28	129
Days Minimum Temp. ≤ 0°F	3	2	0	0	0	0	0	0	0	0	0	2	7
Heating Degree Days (base 65°F)	1,134	922	703	378	121	13	1	2	72	328	711	1,095	5,480
Cooling Degree Days (base 65°F)	0	0	1	18	75	264	434	377	153	20	0	0	1,342
Mean Precipitation (in.)	0.65	0.81	2.03	2.91	4.34	4.25	4.01	3.79	3.14	2.34	1.12	1.00	30.39
Extreme Maximum Daily Precip. (in.)	1.02	1.30	2.75	2.95	4.80	6.50	3.61	4.30	4.75	3.95	2.21	2.25	6.50
Days With ≥ 0.1" Precipitation	2	2	4	6	8	6	5	5	5	4	3	2	52
Days With ≥ 0.5" Precipitation	0	0	1	2	3	3	3	2	2	2	1	1	20
Days With ≥ 1.0" Precipitation	0	0	0	1	1	1	1	1	1	0	0	0	6
Mean Snowfall (in.)	4.6	4.8	2.3	0.6	0.0	0.0	0.0	0.0	0.0	0.2	1.5	3.5	17.5
Maximum Snow Depth (in.)	*10*	na	*3*	0	0	0	0	0	0	5	3	na	na
Days With ≥ 1.0" Snow Depth	*1*	na	*0*	0	0	0	0	0	0	0	0	*1*	na

Beloit *Mitchell County* Elevation: 1,461 ft. Latitude: 39° 29' N Longitude: 98° 06' W

	JAN	FEB	MAR	APR	MAY	JUN	JUL	AUG	SEP	OCT	NOV	DEC	YEAR
Mean Maximum Temp. (°F)	39.8	44.6	55.2	66.3	75.5	86.4	92.6	90.2	81.4	68.2	53.7	40.7	66.2
Mean Temp. (°F)	28.7	33.0	42.7	53.4	63.6	74.3	80.2	78.2	68.9	55.8	41.9	30.1	54.2
Mean Minimum Temp. (°F)	17.7	21.3	30.1	40.4	51.7	62.1	67.8	66.2	56.3	43.3	30.1	19.5	42.2
Extreme Maximum Temp. (°F)	77	80	88	100	101	112	112	112	109	99	87	73	112
Extreme Minimum Temp. (°F)	-16	-15	-4	15	28	40	47	47	27	16	0	-26	-26
Days Maximum Temp. ≥ 90°F	0	0	0	1	2	11	20	17	7	1	0	0	59
Days Maximum Temp. ≤ 32°F	9	6	2	0	0	0	0	0	0	0	2	8	27
Days Minimum Temp. ≤ 32°F	30	24	19	6	0	0	0	0	0	4	18	29	130
Days Minimum Temp. ≤ 0°F	2	2	0	0	0	0	0	0	0	0	0	2	6
Heating Degree Days (base 65°F)	1,118	900	686	362	119	10	0	1	60	304	687	1,075	5,322
Cooling Degree Days (base 65°F)	0	0	1	20	83	297	480	419	184	25	1	0	1,510
Mean Precipitation (in.)	0.66	0.82	1.93	2.39	4.17	3.73	4.22	3.13	2.57	2.02	1.15	0.94	27.73
Extreme Maximum Daily Precip. (in.)	1.10	1.20	2.70	2.60	2.90	3.92	3.13	2.70	7.05	2.53	3.44	1.62	7.05
Days With ≥ 0.1" Precipitation	2	2	4	5	7	7	6	5	5	4	3	3	53
Days With ≥ 0.5" Precipitation	0	0	1	2	3	3	3	2	2	1	1	1	19
Days With ≥ 1.0" Precipitation	0	0	0	0	1	1	1	1	1	0	0	0	5
Mean Snowfall (in.)	4.7	5.4	2.5	0.7	0.0	0.0	0.0	0.0	0.0	0.2	1.1	4.7	19.3
Maximum Snow Depth (in.)	*8*	na	*8*	12	0	0	0	0	0	*3*	*5*	na	na
Days With ≥ 1.0" Snow Depth	*3*	*3*	1	0	0	0	0	0	0	0	1	*4*	*12*

The period of record for all cooperative weather station data is 1980 – 2009. See User Guide for detailed explanation of data.

Cassoday *Butler County* Elevation: 1,459 ft. Latitude: 38° 03' N Longitude: 96° 38' W

	JAN	FEB	MAR	APR	MAY	JUN	JUL	AUG	SEP	OCT	NOV	DEC	YEAR
Mean Maximum Temp. (°F)	41.7	46.8	57.0	67.2	75.4	84.0	90.2	89.6	81.5	69.0	55.8	42.9	66.7
Mean Temp. (°F)	30.4	34.7	44.3	54.8	64.1	73.1	78.9	77.8	69.3	56.8	44.1	32.2	55.0
Mean Minimum Temp. (°F)	18.9	22.5	31.5	42.3	52.8	62.2	67.5	66.0	57.0	44.5	32.5	21.5	43.3
Extreme Maximum Temp. (°F)	75	80	86	92	97	109	110	109	106	94	86	71	110
Extreme Minimum Temp. (°F)	-20	-18	-4	17	28	42	49	47	27	15	6	-22	-22
Days Maximum Temp. ≥ 90°F	0	0	0	0	1	6	16	16	6	0	0	0	45
Days Maximum Temp. ≤ 32°F	7	5	1	0	0	0	0	0	0	0	1	6	20
Days Minimum Temp. ≤ 32°F	28	23	17	5	0	0	0	0	0	3	15	27	118
Days Minimum Temp. ≤ 0°F	1	1	0	0	0	0	0	0	0	0	0	1	3
Heating Degree Days (base 65°F)	1,067	853	638	322	104	10	0	2	53	275	620	1,010	4,954
Cooling Degree Days (base 65°F)	0	0	2	22	84	260	437	405	188	27	1	0	1,426
Mean Precipitation (in.)	0.83	1.16	2.52	3.49	4.59	5.37	3.69	3.88	3.24	2.85	1.97	1.21	34.80
Extreme Maximum Daily Precip. (in.)	2.26	2.10	1.96	4.31	3.05	6.10	2.70	5.35	4.14	2.50	5.05	2.00	6.10
Days With ≥ 0.1" Precipitation	2	3	4	5	7	6	5	5	5	5	3	3	53
Days With ≥ 0.5" Precipitation	0	1	2	2	3	4	3	3	2	2	1	1	24
Days With ≥ 1.0" Precipitation	0	0	1	1	2	2	1	1	1	1	0	0	10
Mean Snowfall (in.)	2.4	3.0	1.1	0.3	0.0	0.0	0.0	0.0	0.0	trace	0.5	3.5	10.8
Maximum Snow Depth (in.)	9	na	7	4	0	0	0	0	0	0	4	9	na
Days With ≥ 1.0" Snow Depth	3	2	0	0	0	0	0	0	0	0	0	4	9

Cedar Bluff Dam 4 NNE *Trego County* Elevation: 2,229 ft. Latitude: 38° 52' N Longitude: 99° 42' W

	JAN	FEB	MAR	APR	MAY	JUN	JUL	AUG	SEP	OCT	NOV	DEC	YEAR
Mean Maximum Temp. (°F)	43.4	47.3	57.4	66.8	75.9	86.1	93.0	90.6	82.4	70.1	55.6	44.8	67.8
Mean Temp. (°F)	29.9	33.7	42.9	52.3	62.8	72.9	79.3	77.2	68.3	55.4	41.7	32.0	54.0
Mean Minimum Temp. (°F)	16.4	19.8	28.2	37.7	49.5	59.6	65.6	63.7	54.1	40.8	27.8	19.1	40.2
Extreme Maximum Temp. (°F)	79	85	95	103	105	108	110	110	110	102	87	79	110
Extreme Minimum Temp. (°F)	-14	-15	-1	12	27	39	47	45	26	12	-3	-24	-24
Days Maximum Temp. ≥ 90°F	0	0	0	1	3	12	21	17	8	1	0	0	63
Days Maximum Temp. ≤ 32°F	8	5	2	0	0	0	0	0	0	0	1	6	22
Days Minimum Temp. ≤ 32°F	30	26	21	9	1	0	0	0	0	6	21	30	144
Days Minimum Temp. ≤ 0°F	2	2	0	0	0	0	0	0	0	0	0	1	5
Heating Degree Days (base 65°F)	1,081	877	679	390	139	17	1	3	70	313	694	1,018	5,282
Cooling Degree Days (base 65°F)	0	0	1	15	76	260	451	386	175	23	0	0	1,387
Mean Precipitation (in.)	0.50	0.64	1.72	2.00	3.13	3.12	3.24	2.83	1.82	1.45	0.89	0.71	22.05
Extreme Maximum Daily Precip. (in.)	1.00	1.20	2.10	2.52	2.79	3.25	4.15	3.89	2.20	1.72	2.21	2.37	4.15
Days With ≥ 0.1" Precipitation	1	2	3	4	6	6	5	5	3	3	2	2	42
Days With ≥ 0.5" Precipitation	0	0	1	1	2	2	2	2	1	1	1	0	13
Days With ≥ 1.0" Precipitation	0	0	0	0	1	1	1	1	0	0	0	0	4
Mean Snowfall (in.)	4.2	4.0	3.6	1.0	0.0	0.0	0.0	0.0	0.1	0.4	1.8	3.3	18.4
Maximum Snow Depth (in.)	na	na	na	na	0	0	0	0	0	1	2	na	na
Days With ≥ 1.0" Snow Depth	na	3	1	0	0	0	0	0	0	0	0	3	na

Centralia *Nemaha County* Elevation: 1,319 ft. Latitude: 39° 43' N Longitude: 96° 07' W

	JAN	FEB	MAR	APR	MAY	JUN	JUL	AUG	SEP	OCT	NOV	DEC	YEAR
Mean Maximum Temp. (°F)	38.1	43.1	54.3	66.2	75.1	83.7	89.4	87.9	79.7	67.6	52.2	39.8	64.8
Mean Temp. (°F)	28.1	32.6	42.6	54.1	63.7	72.7	78.1	76.3	67.7	55.8	41.8	30.3	53.6
Mean Minimum Temp. (°F)	18.1	21.9	30.8	41.9	52.2	61.6	66.7	64.7	55.6	43.9	31.3	20.8	42.5
Extreme Maximum Temp. (°F)	72	77	87	94	97	109	110	107	107	92	82	70	110
Extreme Minimum Temp. (°F)	-18	-19	-15	17	27	40	47	44	26	13	2	-25	-25
Days Maximum Temp. ≥ 90°F	0	0	0	0	1	6	15	13	4	0	0	0	39
Days Maximum Temp. ≤ 32°F	10	7	2	0	0	0	0	0	0	0	2	8	29
Days Minimum Temp. ≤ 32°F	28	23	18	6	0	0	0	0	0	5	16	27	123
Days Minimum Temp. ≤ 0°F	3	2	0	0	0	0	0	0	0	0	0	2	7
Heating Degree Days (base 65°F)	1,138	911	690	346	113	12	1	3	75	303	690	1,068	5,350
Cooling Degree Days (base 65°F)	0	0	1	25	79	250	413	361	162	23	1	0	1,315
Mean Precipitation (in.)	0.82	1.08	2.45	3.10	4.59	4.87	5.15	3.97	3.50	2.41	1.70	1.06	34.70
Extreme Maximum Daily Precip. (in.)	0.89	1.44	3.35	2.82	3.50	4.90	5.15	3.27	3.30	2.64	2.79	3.15	5.15
Days With ≥ 0.1" Precipitation	2	3	4	6	7	7	6	6	5	5	4	3	58
Days With ≥ 0.5" Precipitation	0	0	2	2	3	3	3	3	2	2	1	1	22
Days With ≥ 1.0" Precipitation	0	0	1	1	1	1	2	1	1	0	0	0	8
Mean Snowfall (in.)	8.6	7.8	5.4	1.6	trace	trace	0.0	0.0	trace	0.6	3.1	7.2	34.3
Maximum Snow Depth (in.)	12	21	16	8	trace	trace	0	0	trace	7	7	12	21
Days With ≥ 1.0" Snow Depth	10	9	3	1	0	0	0	0	0	0	2	9	34

Clay Center *Clay County* Elevation: 1,220 ft. Latitude: 39° 24' N Longitude: 97° 08' W

	JAN	FEB	MAR	APR	MAY	JUN	JUL	AUG	SEP	OCT	NOV	DEC	YEAR
Mean Maximum Temp. (°F)	39.9	45.3	56.7	67.7	77.1	86.5	92.3	90.5	81.7	69.0	54.0	41.3	66.8
Mean Temp. (°F)	29.6	34.3	44.7	55.3	65.5	75.0	80.5	78.7	69.6	57.1	43.3	31.6	55.4
Mean Minimum Temp. (°F)	19.2	23.3	32.7	42.9	53.8	63.5	68.7	66.9	57.4	45.2	32.6	21.8	44.0
Extreme Maximum Temp. (°F)	77	79	89	99	98	109	111	109	109	96	84	71	111
Extreme Minimum Temp. (°F)	-17	-15	-6	17	30	41	50	47	28	14	4	-24	-24
Days Maximum Temp. ≥ 90°F	0	0	0	1	2	11	20	17	7	1	0	0	59
Days Maximum Temp. ≤ 32°F	9	6	1	0	0	0	0	0	0	0	1	7	24
Days Minimum Temp. ≤ 32°F	28	22	15	5	0	0	0	0	0	3	15	27	115
Days Minimum Temp. ≤ 0°F	2	1	0	0	0	0	0	0	0	0	0	2	5
Heating Degree Days (base 65°F)	1,091	860	625	313	88	6	0	1	54	268	645	1,028	4,979
Cooling Degree Days (base 65°F)	0	0	3	30	110	313	488	433	200	32	1	0	1,610
Mean Precipitation (in.)	0.73	1.05	2.25	2.67	4.58	4.03	3.66	3.55	3.26	2.18	1.38	1.11	30.45
Extreme Maximum Daily Precip. (in.)	0.80	1.36	1.86	1.97	4.20	3.28	3.20	2.60	4.97	2.10	2.37	2.41	4.97
Days With ≥ 0.1" Precipitation	2	3	4	5	7	7	5	5	5	4	3	3	53
Days With ≥ 0.5" Precipitation	0	1	2	2	3	3	2	2	2	2	1	1	21
Days With ≥ 1.0" Precipitation	0	0	1	1	1	1	1	1	1	0	0	0	7
Mean Snowfall (in.)	4.1	4.1	2.4	0.6	0.0	0.0	0.0	0.0	0.0	0.1	1.3	4.1	16.7
Maximum Snow Depth (in.)	12	18	7	2	0	0	0	0	0	1	5	13	18
Days With ≥ 1.0" Snow Depth	7	5	1	0	0	0	0	0	0	0	1	6	20

The period of record for all cooperative weather station data is 1980 – 2009. See User Guide for detailed explanation of data.

Clinton Lake *Douglas County* Elevation: 979 ft. Latitude: 38° 56' N Longitude: 95° 20' W

	JAN	FEB	MAR	APR	MAY	JUN	JUL	AUG	SEP	OCT	NOV	DEC	YEAR
Mean Maximum Temp. (°F)	38.9	43.4	54.7	64.9	74.2	82.8	88.5	88.0	79.6	67.4	53.6	40.3	64.7
Mean Temp. (°F)	28.6	32.9	43.5	53.8	63.7	72.9	78.3	77.1	68.1	55.8	43.4	30.9	54.1
Mean Minimum Temp. (°F)	18.4	22.3	32.2	42.7	53.2	62.9	68.1	66.2	56.5	44.2	33.2	21.5	43.4
Extreme Maximum Temp. (°F)	75	77	86	93	95	106	110	109	109	93	85	72	110
Extreme Minimum Temp. (°F)	-16	-15	-7	16	29	41	49	46	30	16	3	-25	-25
Days Maximum Temp. ≥ 90°F	0	0	0	0	0	5	13	13	4	0	0	0	35
Days Maximum Temp. ≤ 32°F	10	7	2	0	0	0	0	0	0	0	1	8	28
Days Minimum Temp. ≤ 32°F	29	23	16	4	0	0	0	0	0	3	15	26	116
Days Minimum Temp. ≤ 0°F	2	2	0	0	0	0	0	0	0	0	0	2	6
Heating Degree Days (base 65°F)	1,120	903	661	349	110	11	1	2	68	302	641	1,048	5,216
Cooling Degree Days (base 65°F)	0	0	2	21	78	254	420	385	167	24	1	0	1,352
Mean Precipitation (in.)	0.78	1.07	2.31	3.88	4.90	5.61	3.54	4.17	4.09	3.37	2.05	1.44	37.21
Extreme Maximum Daily Precip. (in.)	1.12	1.87	2.24	3.07	3.55	6.48	4.65	4.90	4.00	3.95	2.70	1.65	6.48
Days With ≥ 0.1" Precipitation	2	3	5	6	8	7	6	6	6	6	4	3	62
Days With ≥ 0.5" Precipitation	0	1	2	3	3	3	2	2	3	2	1	1	23
Days With ≥ 1.0" Precipitation	0	0	0	1	1	2	1	1	1	1	0	0	8
Mean Snowfall (in.)	2.9	3.8	0.9	trace	0.0	0.0	0.0	0.0	0.0	trace	0.1	2.1	9.8
Maximum Snow Depth (in.)	9	11	4	trace	0	0	0	0	0	3	1	11	11
Days With ≥ 1.0" Snow Depth	5	5	1	0	0	0	0	0	0	0	0	4	15

Coldwater *Comanche County* Elevation: 2,083 ft. Latitude: 37° 16' N Longitude: 99° 20' W

	JAN	FEB	MAR	APR	MAY	JUN	JUL	AUG	SEP	OCT	NOV	DEC	YEAR
Mean Maximum Temp. (°F)	47.7	52.8	61.2	70.9	79.0	87.6	93.6	92.3	84.1	72.5	59.4	47.7	70.7
Mean Temp. (°F)	35.5	39.8	48.0	57.6	66.8	75.7	81.3	80.0	71.5	59.7	46.8	36.1	58.2
Mean Minimum Temp. (°F)	23.0	26.5	34.6	44.0	54.4	63.6	68.8	67.7	58.8	46.9	34.2	24.3	45.6
Extreme Maximum Temp. (°F)	84	90	92	100	103	109	111	110	107	96	90	82	111
Extreme Minimum Temp. (°F)	-15	-14	-1	17	29	43	51	51	29	15	6	-17	-17
Days Maximum Temp. ≥ 90°F	0	0	0	1	3	12	23	21	9	1	0	0	70
Days Maximum Temp. ≤ 32°F	5	3	1	0	0	0	0	0	0	0	1	4	14
Days Minimum Temp. ≤ 32°F	27	19	13	3	0	0	0	0	0	2	13	26	103
Days Minimum Temp. ≤ 0°F	1	1	0	0	0	0	0	0	0	0	0	1	3
Heating Degree Days (base 65°F)	906	706	528	255	70	4	0	0	36	203	540	890	4,138
Cooling Degree Days (base 65°F)	0	0	6	39	131	333	511	474	237	47	2	0	1,780
Mean Precipitation (in.)	0.70	0.88	1.93	2.07	3.47	4.05	3.04	3.27	2.01	2.13	1.02	1.06	25.63
Extreme Maximum Daily Precip. (in.)	1.28	1.36	2.20	2.25	2.48	4.10	3.43	4.24	1.94	4.45	3.00	2.52	4.45
Days With ≥ 0.1" Precipitation	2	2	4	4	5	6	4	4	4	4	2	2	43
Days With ≥ 0.5" Precipitation	0	1	1	2	3	3	2	2	1	1	1	1	18
Days With ≥ 1.0" Precipitation	0	0	0	0	1	1	1	1	1	0	0	0	5
Mean Snowfall (in.)	3.7	3.7	4.0	0.6	0.0	trace	0.0	0.0	trace	0.1	1.6	4.5	18.2
Maximum Snow Depth (in.)	12	13	27	4	1	trace	0	0	trace	1	14	8	27
Days With ≥ 1.0" Snow Depth	2	2	1	0	0	0	0	0	0	0	1	2	8

Columbus 1 SW *Cherokee County* Elevation: 899 ft. Latitude: 37° 10' N Longitude: 94° 51' W

	JAN	FEB	MAR	APR	MAY	JUN	JUL	AUG	SEP	OCT	NOV	DEC	YEAR
Mean Maximum Temp. (°F)	43.1	48.5	57.8	67.3	76.1	84.3	89.9	89.9	81.4	70.1	57.5	45.3	67.6
Mean Temp. (°F)	33.5	38.0	46.7	56.0	65.9	74.3	79.5	78.9	70.0	58.7	47.2	35.9	57.1
Mean Minimum Temp. (°F)	23.8	27.5	35.7	44.6	55.7	64.2	69.0	67.8	58.7	47.3	36.9	26.4	46.5
Extreme Maximum Temp. (°F)	76	85	90	95	94	101	109	105	105	90	85	74	109
Extreme Minimum Temp. (°F)	-15	-7	1	22	35	46	53	47	32	19	10	-15	-15
Days Maximum Temp. ≥ 90°F	0	0	0	0	1	6	16	17	5	0	0	0	45
Days Maximum Temp. ≤ 32°F	7	4	1	0	0	0	0	0	0	0	0	5	17
Days Minimum Temp. ≤ 32°F	26	20	12	3	0	0	0	0	0	1	11	23	96
Days Minimum Temp. ≤ 0°F	1	0	0	0	0	0	0	0	0	0	0	1	2
Heating Degree Days (base 65°F)	971	757	563	290	74	6	0	1	45	227	530	897	4,361
Cooling Degree Days (base 65°F)	0	0	4	25	109	292	456	438	203	39	4	0	1,570
Mean Precipitation (in.)	1.67	2.22	3.42	4.57	6.10	5.49	3.84	3.50	4.40	3.97	3.35	2.56	45.09
Extreme Maximum Daily Precip. (in.)	2.62	5.58	2.70	5.57	4.31	6.10	4.95	7.45	7.58	5.08	3.47	2.84	7.58
Days With ≥ 0.1" Precipitation	4	4	6	7	8	8	5	4	6	6	5	5	68
Days With ≥ 0.5" Precipitation	1	1	2	3	4	4	2	2	2	2	2	2	27
Days With ≥ 1.0" Precipitation	0	1	1	1	2	2	1	1	1	1	1	1	13
Mean Snowfall (in.)	2.7	2.1	1.4	0.0	0.0	0.0	0.0	0.0	0.0	0.0	0.3	3.2	9.7
Maximum Snow Depth (in.)	7	14	9	0	0	0	0	0	0	0	3	10	14
Days With ≥ 1.0" Snow Depth	4	2	1	0	0	0	0	0	0	0	0	4	11

Cottonwood Falls *Chase County* Elevation: 1,240 ft. Latitude: 38° 22' N Longitude: 96° 33' W

	JAN	FEB	MAR	APR	MAY	JUN	JUL	AUG	SEP	OCT	NOV	DEC	YEAR
Mean Maximum Temp. (°F)	42.2	47.0	57.5	67.5	76.0	84.7	90.4	89.8	81.7	69.7	56.4	43.5	67.2
Mean Temp. (°F)	31.2	35.5	45.3	55.4	65.1	73.9	79.3	78.2	69.4	57.3	44.8	33.0	55.7
Mean Minimum Temp. (°F)	20.1	24.0	33.0	43.2	54.1	63.2	68.3	66.6	57.2	45.0	33.3	22.5	44.2
Extreme Maximum Temp. (°F)	77	81	85	95	97	111	113	111	105	96	87	73	113
Extreme Minimum Temp. (°F)	-14	-17	0	19	30	42	50	47	29	13	5	-22	-22
Days Maximum Temp. ≥ 90°F	0	0	0	1	1	7	17	16	6	1	0	0	49
Days Maximum Temp. ≤ 32°F	8	5	1	0	0	0	0	0	0	0	1	6	21
Days Minimum Temp. ≤ 32°F	28	22	16	4	0	0	0	0	0	3	14	26	113
Days Minimum Temp. ≤ 0°F	1	1	0	0	0	0	0	0	0	0	0	1	3
Heating Degree Days (base 65°F)	1,041	828	606	311	88	7	0	1	55	264	600	985	4,786
Cooling Degree Days (base 65°F)	0	0	3	30	98	282	452	418	195	34	2	0	1,514
Mean Precipitation (in.)	1.00	1.33	2.73	3.20	5.23	5.21	4.36	4.32	3.50	2.99	2.18	1.37	37.42
Extreme Maximum Daily Precip. (in.)	1.62	2.19	3.12	2.40	4.00	4.60	4.25	5.53	5.55	4.75	4.25	2.08	5.55
Days With ≥ 0.1" Precipitation	2	3	5	5	8	7	5	6	5	5	3	3	57
Days With ≥ 0.5" Precipitation	1	1	2	2	4	4	3	2	2	2	1	1	25
Days With ≥ 1.0" Precipitation	0	0	1	1	2	2	2	1	1	1	1	0	12
Mean Snowfall (in.)	2.7	2.6	0.8	0.3	0.0	0.0	0.0	0.0	0.0	0.2	0.5	3.2	10.3
Maximum Snow Depth (in.)	8	12	5	5	0	0	0	0	0	trace	3	7	12
Days With ≥ 1.0" Snow Depth	3	3	1	0	0	0	0	0	0	0	0	3	10

The period of record for all cooperative weather station data is 1980 – 2009. See User Guide for detailed explanation of data.

Emporia 3 NW *Lyon County* Elevation: 1,220 ft. Latitude: 38° 26' N Longitude: 96° 12' W

	JAN	FEB	MAR	APR	MAY	JUN	JUL	AUG	SEP	OCT	NOV	DEC	YEAR
Mean Maximum Temp. (°F)	40.4	45.4	55.7	65.5	75.0	83.6	89.1	88.5	80.3	68.1	54.5	41.5	65.6
Mean Temp. (°F)	30.1	34.4	43.9	53.9	64.4	73.5	78.5	77.3	68.5	56.4	43.7	31.6	54.7
Mean Minimum Temp. (°F)	19.7	23.3	32.0	42.3	53.8	63.3	67.8	66.1	56.7	44.7	32.8	21.7	43.7
Extreme Maximum Temp. (°F)	72	75	84	94	97	102	104	108	106	94	86	72	108
Extreme Minimum Temp. (°F)	-7	-11	0	18	31	44	51	49	29	15	5	-22	-22
Days Maximum Temp. ≥ 90°F	0	0	0	0	1	7	15	15	5	0	0	0	43
Days Maximum Temp. ≤ 32°F	9	5	2	0	0	0	0	0	0	0	1	7	24
Days Minimum Temp. ≤ 32°F	29	23	16	4	0	0	0	0	0	3	15	27	117
Days Minimum Temp. ≤ 0°F	1	1	0	0	0	0	0	0	0	0	0	1	3
Heating Degree Days (base 65°F)	1,076	860	650	345	99	9	0	2	63	285	633	1,028	5,050
Cooling Degree Days (base 65°F)	0	0	1	19	89	270	426	390	176	26	1	0	1,398
Mean Precipitation (in.)	0.91	1.23	2.55	3.40	5.06	5.51	4.56	4.36	3.27	3.05	2.09	1.30	37.29
Extreme Maximum Daily Precip. (in.)	1.72	1.75	2.10	2.88	4.61	4.08	3.98	5.51	5.22	4.49	4.89	1.75	5.51
Days With ≥ 0.1" Precipitation	2	3	5	5	8	7	6	5	5	5	3	3	57
Days With ≥ 0.5" Precipitation	1	1	2	2	4	4	3	3	2	2	1	1	26
Days With ≥ 1.0" Precipitation	0	0	1	1	1	2	2	1	1	1	0	0	10
Mean Snowfall (in.)	2.0	0.7	0.4	trace	0.0	0.0	0.0	0.0	0.0	trace	0.1	1.4	4.6
Maximum Snow Depth (in.)	na	na	na	na	na	na	na	na	0	na	trace	na	na
Days With ≥ 1.0" Snow Depth	na	na	0	0	0	0	0	0	0	0	0	1	na

Eskridge *Wabaunsee County* Elevation: 1,414 ft. Latitude: 38° 52' N Longitude: 96° 06' W

	JAN	FEB	MAR	APR	MAY	JUN	JUL	AUG	SEP	OCT	NOV	DEC	YEAR
Mean Maximum Temp. (°F)	38.3	42.7	54.8	64.6	73.4	82.5	88.1	87.0	78.6	66.4	52.8	39.9	64.1
Mean Temp. (°F)	28.2	31.8	43.0	52.9	62.9	72.1	77.1	75.7	66.9	54.9	42.2	30.1	53.2
Mean Minimum Temp. (°F)	18.1	20.9	31.1	41.2	52.4	61.7	66.0	64.3	55.2	43.3	31.5	20.4	42.2
Extreme Maximum Temp. (°F)	73	77	84	92	94	109	112	109	100	92	84	70	112
Extreme Minimum Temp. (°F)	-19	-16	-3	16	29	39	50	47	31	16	2	-25	-25
Days Maximum Temp. ≥ 90°F	0	0	0	0	0	4	12	12	3	0	0	0	31
Days Maximum Temp. ≤ 32°F	10	7	2	0	0	0	0	0	0	0	2	8	29
Days Minimum Temp. ≤ 32°F	29	24	18	5	0	0	0	0	0	3	16	27	122
Days Minimum Temp. ≤ 0°F	2	2	0	0	0	0	0	0	0	0	0	2	6
Heating Degree Days (base 65°F)	1,134	933	677	375	121	11	1	4	78	325	678	1,074	5,411
Cooling Degree Days (base 65°F)	0	0	1	19	63	232	383	342	141	18	1	0	1,200
Mean Precipitation (in.)	0.88	1.10	3.07	3.28	5.32	5.30	3.79	4.74	3.31	2.85	1.86	1.48	36.98
Extreme Maximum Daily Precip. (in.)	1.30	1.69	2.70	2.73	4.92	2.66	4.02	4.33	3.33	3.74	2.08	2.32	4.92
Days With ≥ 0.1" Precipitation	2	3	6	5	8	7	5	6	5	5	4	3	59
Days With ≥ 0.5" Precipitation	0	1	2	2	3	4	2	3	2	2	1	1	23
Days With ≥ 1.0" Precipitation	0	0	1	1	2	2	1	1	1	1	0	0	10
Mean Snowfall (in.)	5.3	5.2	2.1	0.6	0.0	0.0	0.0	0.0	trace	0.4	1.9	4.7	20.2
Maximum Snow Depth (in.)	9	11	6	4	0	0	0	0	trace	9	10	11	11
Days With ≥ 1.0" Snow Depth	8	6	1	0	0	0	0	0	0	0	1	6	22

Eureka *Greenwood County* Elevation: 1,040 ft. Latitude: 37° 49' N Longitude: 96° 17' W

	JAN	FEB	MAR	APR	MAY	JUN	JUL	AUG	SEP	OCT	NOV	DEC	YEAR
Mean Maximum Temp. (°F)	43.5	48.7	59.4	69.1	77.0	85.2	91.5	90.6	82.5	70.6	57.5	44.9	68.4
Mean Temp. (°F)	32.3	36.7	46.5	56.3	65.7	74.3	79.9	78.5	69.9	57.9	45.6	34.1	56.5
Mean Minimum Temp. (°F)	21.1	24.6	33.4	43.6	54.3	63.4	68.3	66.4	57.2	45.2	33.7	23.3	44.5
Extreme Maximum Temp. (°F)	75	83	87	94	96	110	112	111	109	97	87	76	112
Extreme Minimum Temp. (°F)	-13	-13	-1	19	31	44	52	46	28	15	5	-18	-18
Days Maximum Temp. ≥ 90°F	0	0	0	1	1	8	19	18	7	1	0	0	55
Days Maximum Temp. ≤ 32°F	7	4	1	0	0	0	0	0	0	0	1	5	18
Days Minimum Temp. ≤ 32°F	27	22	15	4	0	0	0	0	0	3	14	26	111
Days Minimum Temp. ≤ 0°F	1	1	0	0	0	0	0	0	0	0	0	1	3
Heating Degree Days (base 65°F)	1,005	795	572	284	76	5	0	1	45	246	577	951	4,557
Cooling Degree Days (base 65°F)	0	0	4	31	104	292	470	426	199	34	2	0	1,562
Mean Precipitation (in.)	1.07	1.60	2.77	3.38	5.22	5.85	3.99	4.39	3.27	3.44	2.58	1.67	39.23
Extreme Maximum Daily Precip. (in.)	1.58	2.85	3.60	3.12	5.59	6.96	6.96	5.95	6.35	3.51	4.83	1.65	6.96
Days With ≥ 0.1" Precipitation	3	4	5	5	7	7	5	6	5	5	4	3	59
Days With ≥ 0.5" Precipitation	1	1	2	2	4	4	2	3	2	2	2	1	26
Days With ≥ 1.0" Precipitation	0	0	1	1	2	2	1	1	1	1	1	0	11
Mean Snowfall (in.)	3.3	3.9	1.3	0.1	0.0	0.0	0.0	0.0	0.0	trace	0.7	3.9	13.2
Maximum Snow Depth (in.)	8	15	7	1	0	0	0	0	0	trace	1	10	15
Days With ≥ 1.0" Snow Depth	5	4	1	0	0	0	0	0	0	0	0	4	14

Fort Scott *Bourbon County* Elevation: 845 ft. Latitude: 37° 51' N Longitude: 94° 43' W

	JAN	FEB	MAR	APR	MAY	JUN	JUL	AUG	SEP	OCT	NOV	DEC	YEAR
Mean Maximum Temp. (°F)	42.0	47.4	57.8	67.9	77.1	85.7	91.0	90.5	81.9	69.8	56.6	43.9	67.6
Mean Temp. (°F)	32.2	36.9	46.6	56.4	66.4	75.4	80.4	79.3	70.2	58.2	46.4	34.6	56.9
Mean Minimum Temp. (°F)	22.3	26.3	35.3	44.9	55.8	65.0	69.8	68.1	58.5	46.6	36.2	25.1	46.2
Extreme Maximum Temp. (°F)	73	81	91	93	96	105	110	106	108	94	83	74	110
Extreme Minimum Temp. (°F)	-14	-10	1	20	33	44	53	48	30	18	8	-18	-18
Days Maximum Temp. ≥ 90°F	0	0	0	0	1	9	19	18	7	0	0	0	54
Days Maximum Temp. ≤ 32°F	7	5	1	0	0	0	0	0	0	0	1	6	20
Days Minimum Temp. ≤ 32°F	27	20	12	3	0	0	0	0	0	2	12	24	100
Days Minimum Temp. ≤ 0°F	1	1	0	0	0	0	0	0	0	0	0	1	3
Heating Degree Days (base 65°F)	1,011	788	569	285	71	5	0	1	47	241	554	938	4,510
Cooling Degree Days (base 65°F)	0	0	5	34	122	323	485	451	210	38	4	0	1,672
Mean Precipitation (in.)	1.46	1.92	3.07	4.58	5.45	5.91	4.59	3.60	4.37	4.34	2.93	2.18	44.40
Extreme Maximum Daily Precip. (in.)	2.17	3.13	2.85	4.10	3.70	4.49	4.50	4.50	12.50	8.60	2.80	2.90	12.50
Days With ≥ 0.1" Precipitation	3	4	6	6	8	7	6	5	5	6	5	4	65
Days With ≥ 0.5" Precipitation	1	1	2	3	4	4	3	2	3	3	2	2	30
Days With ≥ 1.0" Precipitation	0	1	1	2	1	2	1	1	1	1	1	1	13
Mean Snowfall (in.)	3.9	3.1	0.9	0.1	0.0	0.0	0.0	0.0	0.0	trace	0.6	2.8	11.4
Maximum Snow Depth (in.)	10	14	4	1	0	0	0	0	0	trace	4	9	14
Days With ≥ 1.0" Snow Depth	4	3	0	0	0	0	0	0	0	0	0	3	10

The period of record for all cooperative weather station data is 1980 – 2009. See User Guide for detailed explanation of data.

Garden City Exp Stn *Finney County* Elevation: 2,868 ft. Latitude: 38° 00' N Longitude: 100° 49' W

	JAN	FEB	MAR	APR	MAY	JUN	JUL	AUG	SEP	OCT	NOV	DEC	YEAR
Mean Maximum Temp. (°F)	44.2	47.9	57.1	66.9	76.4	86.4	92.3	89.8	82.3	69.9	56.2	45.2	67.9
Mean Temp. (°F)	30.3	33.7	42.6	52.0	62.6	72.6	78.0	76.2	67.6	54.6	41.6	31.5	53.6
Mean Minimum Temp. (°F)	16.4	19.5	28.1	36.9	48.8	58.7	63.7	62.6	52.9	39.3	26.9	17.7	39.3
Extreme Maximum Temp. (°F)	78	86	91	99	103	108	108	106	105	97	88	77	108
Extreme Minimum Temp. (°F)	-22	-19	-7	9	28	38	45	47	25	12	-5	-17	-22
Days Maximum Temp. ≥ 90°F	0	0	0	1	4	12	21	18	8	1	0	0	65
Days Maximum Temp. ≤ 32°F	7	5	2	0	0	0	0	0	0	0	1	6	21
Days Minimum Temp. ≤ 32°F	31	26	21	9	1	0	0	0	0	7	22	30	147
Days Minimum Temp. ≤ 0°F	2	2	0	0	0	0	0	0	0	0	0	2	6
Heating Degree Days (base 65°F)	1,069	876	689	397	144	20	1	3	72	332	695	1,032	5,330
Cooling Degree Days (base 65°F)	0	0	0	12	77	255	413	357	157	18	0	0	1,289
Mean Precipitation (in.)	0.47	0.55	1.32	1.73	3.09	3.11	2.77	2.52	1.41	1.19	0.54	0.60	19.30
Extreme Maximum Daily Precip. (in.)	0.93	1.00	1.94	2.17	2.73	2.80	2.70	2.58	2.10	1.92	1.26	2.12	2.80
Days With ≥ 0.1" Precipitation	1	2	3	4	6	6	5	5	3	3	1	2	41
Days With ≥ 0.5" Precipitation	0	0	1	1	2	2	2	2	1	1	0	0	12
Days With ≥ 1.0" Precipitation	0	0	0	0	1	1	1	1	0	0	0	0	4
Mean Snowfall (in.)	4.5	4.0	5.0	1.1	0.0	0.0	0.0	0.0	trace	0.6	1.8	3.2	20.2
Maximum Snow Depth (in.)	*8*	*9*	*9*	*6*	*0*	0	0	0	0	*11*	12	*8*	*12*
Days With ≥ 1.0" Snow Depth	5	4	*2*	0	0	0	0	0	0	0	1	3	*15*

Great Bend *Barton County* Elevation: 1,859 ft. Latitude: 38° 22' N Longitude: 98° 46' W

	JAN	FEB	MAR	APR	MAY	JUN	JUL	AUG	SEP	OCT	NOV	DEC	YEAR
Mean Maximum Temp. (°F)	44.6	49.6	59.0	69.7	78.3	88.1	93.9	91.7	83.4	71.0	56.9	44.7	69.2
Mean Temp. (°F)	33.1	37.2	46.1	56.3	66.1	75.7	81.0	79.3	70.5	58.2	44.8	33.8	56.8
Mean Minimum Temp. (°F)	21.5	24.8	33.1	42.9	53.9	63.2	68.1	66.8	57.5	45.4	32.7	22.9	44.4
Extreme Maximum Temp. (°F)	79	85	90	101	100	111	111	110	104	95	90	75	111
Extreme Minimum Temp. (°F)	-11	-16	-2	14	31	39	48	48	29	16	3	-21	-21
Days Maximum Temp. ≥ 90°F	0	0	0	1	4	14	23	20	8	1	0	0	71
Days Maximum Temp. ≤ 32°F	6	4	1	0	0	0	0	0	0	0	1	5	17
Days Minimum Temp. ≤ 32°F	27	21	15	4	0	0	0	0	0	3	15	27	112
Days Minimum Temp. ≤ 0°F	1	1	0	0	0	0	0	0	0	0	0	1	3
Heating Degree Days (base 65°F)	984	779	583	286	79	7	0	1	45	241	601	959	4,565
Cooling Degree Days (base 65°F)	0	0	3	32	121	334	505	450	215	38	1	0	1,699
Mean Precipitation (in.)	0.64	0.84	1.96	2.27	4.11	3.80	3.36	3.40	1.94	2.10	0.88	0.87	26.17
Extreme Maximum Daily Precip. (in.)	1.30	1.28	2.32	3.14	3.93	6.40	3.67	3.75	3.55	2.92	2.00	2.45	6.40
Days With ≥ 0.1" Precipitation	2	2	4	4	5	5	5	5	4	4	2	2	44
Days With ≥ 0.5" Precipitation	0	0	1	2	3	3	2	2	1	1	1	0	16
Days With ≥ 1.0" Precipitation	0	0	1	0	1	1	1	1	0	0	0	0	5
Mean Snowfall (in.)	4.8	4.0	2.7	0.6	0.0	0.0	0.0	0.0	0.0	0.1	1.0	3.7	16.9
Maximum Snow Depth (in.)	13	15	9	5	0	0	0	0	0	2	7	10	15
Days With ≥ 1.0" Snow Depth	8	6	2	0	0	0	0	0	0	0	1	6	23

Hays 1 S *Ellis County* Elevation: 2,009 ft. Latitude: 38° 52' N Longitude: 99° 20' W

	JAN	FEB	MAR	APR	MAY	JUN	JUL	AUG	SEP	OCT	NOV	DEC	YEAR
Mean Maximum Temp. (°F)	42.1	46.3	55.8	66.5	75.5	86.1	92.6	90.3	81.8	69.0	55.1	43.1	67.0
Mean Temp. (°F)	29.3	33.3	42.5	53.1	63.4	73.7	79.4	77.4	68.3	55.1	41.6	30.8	54.0
Mean Minimum Temp. (°F)	16.4	20.2	29.1	39.7	51.2	61.1	66.1	64.5	54.8	41.2	28.1	18.5	40.9
Extreme Maximum Temp. (°F)	79	84	90	107	103	110	113	111	107	101	90	79	113
Extreme Minimum Temp. (°F)	-17	-14	-6	11	27	36	46	44	25	9	-3	-20	-20
Days Maximum Temp. ≥ 90°F	0	0	0	1	3	12	21	17	8	1	0	0	63
Days Maximum Temp. ≤ 32°F	8	6	2	0	0	0	0	0	0	0	2	7	25
Days Minimum Temp. ≤ 32°F	31	25	20	6	0	0	0	0	0	5	20	30	137
Days Minimum Temp. ≤ 0°F	2	2	0	0	0	0	0	0	0	0	0	2	6
Heating Degree Days (base 65°F)	1,101	890	692	370	130	17	1	3	72	323	694	1,053	5,346
Cooling Degree Days (base 65°F)	0	0	1	20	86	284	454	396	178	25	0	0	1,444
Mean Precipitation (in.)	0.52	0.74	1.84	2.13	3.22	2.70	3.79	3.06	2.01	1.59	0.91	0.73	23.24
Extreme Maximum Daily Precip. (in.)	1.09	1.52	2.59	3.09	3.53	3.32	3.29	3.32	5.64	2.06	2.92	1.16	5.64
Days With ≥ 0.1" Precipitation	2	2	4	5	6	5	5	5	4	3	2	2	45
Days With ≥ 0.5" Precipitation	0	0	1	1	2	2	3	2	1	1	1	0	14
Days With ≥ 1.0" Precipitation	0	0	0	0	1	0	1	1	0	0	0	0	3
Mean Snowfall (in.)	4.3	4.2	3.4	0.7	0.0	0.0	0.0	0.0	0.1	0.3	1.4	4.2	18.6
Maximum Snow Depth (in.)	10	12	11	6	0	0	0	0	1	4	8	12	12
Days With ≥ 1.0" Snow Depth	7	8	2	0	0	0	0	0	0	0	1	7	25

Hill City 1 E *Graham County* Elevation: 2,146 ft. Latitude: 39° 22' N Longitude: 99° 50' W

	JAN	FEB	MAR	APR	MAY	JUN	JUL	AUG	SEP	OCT	NOV	DEC	YEAR
Mean Maximum Temp. (°F)	*42.8*	*47.2*	*56.5*	*66.6*	*76.0*	*86.6*	*92.6*	*90.0*	*81.5*	*68.8*	54.6	42.9	*67.2*
Mean Temp. (°F)	*29.0*	*32.8*	*41.4*	*51.4*	*62.1*	*72.4*	*78.3*	*75.9*	*66.5*	*53.4*	40.2	29.7	*52.7*
Mean Minimum Temp. (°F)	*15.2*	*18.4*	*26.2*	*36.2*	*48.1*	*58.1*	*64.0*	*61.7*	*51.5*	*37.9*	25.8	16.3	*38.3*
Extreme Maximum Temp. (°F)	*78*	*82*	*94*	*101*	*102*	*108*	*110*	*108*	*105*	*97*	88	76	*110*
Extreme Minimum Temp. (°F)	*-15*	*-17*	*-7*	*12*	*25*	*34*	*44*	*43*	*21*	*1*	-6	-26	*-26*
Days Maximum Temp. ≥ 90°F	*0*	*0*	*0*	*1*	*3*	*12*	*21*	*17*	*8*	*1*	0	0	*63*
Days Maximum Temp. ≤ 32°F	*8*	*5*	*2*	*0*	*0*	*0*	*0*	*0*	*0*	*0*	2	7	*24*
Days Minimum Temp. ≤ 32°F	*30*	*27*	*23*	*10*	*1*	*0*	*0*	*0*	*1*	*9*	24	30	*155*
Days Minimum Temp. ≤ 0°F	*3*	*2*	*1*	*0*	*0*	*0*	*0*	*0*	*0*	*0*	0	2	*8*
Heating Degree Days (base 65°F)	*1,109*	*904*	*727*	*413*	*153*	*21*	*2*	*5*	*90*	*371*	737	1,089	*5,621*
Cooling Degree Days (base 65°F)	*0*	*0*	*1*	*12*	*68*	*248*	*422*	*348*	*142*	*17*	0	0	*1,258*
Mean Precipitation (in.)	0.55	0.68	1.75	1.95	3.71	2.73	3.50	3.06	1.93	1.64	0.91	0.67	23.08
Extreme Maximum Daily Precip. (in.)	0.94	1.20	2.21	2.40	3.17	2.16	2.80	3.92	2.25	2.18	1.90	2.59	3.92
Days With ≥ 0.1" Precipitation	2	2	4	4	7	6	5	5	4	3	2	2	46
Days With ≥ 0.5" Precipitation	0	0	1	1	2	2	3	2	1	1	1	0	14
Days With ≥ 1.0" Precipitation	0	0	0	0	1	1	1	1	0	0	0	0	4
Mean Snowfall (in.)	4.3	4.6	4.1	0.6	0.0	0.0	0.0	0.0	0.2	0.5	2.2	3.5	20.0
Maximum Snow Depth (in.)	12	10	23	4	0	0	0	0	2	12	13	13	23
Days With ≥ 1.0" Snow Depth	4	*5*	2	0	0	0	0	0	0	0	1	5	*17*

The period of record for all cooperative weather station data is 1980 – 2009. See User Guide for detailed explanation of data.

Hugoton *Stevens County* Elevation: 3,109 ft. Latitude: 37° 10' N Longitude: 101° 20' W

	JAN	FEB	MAR	APR	MAY	JUN	JUL	AUG	SEP	OCT	NOV	DEC	YEAR
Mean Maximum Temp. (°F)	47.1	51.3	59.3	68.7	78.0	87.5	92.9	90.3	82.4	70.7	57.8	47.0	69.4
Mean Temp. (°F)	33.6	37.1	44.7	54.1	64.2	73.7	78.9	77.0	68.5	56.3	43.7	33.8	55.5
Mean Minimum Temp. (°F)	19.9	22.9	30.1	39.4	50.4	59.9	64.9	63.7	54.8	41.8	29.5	20.6	41.5
Extreme Maximum Temp. (°F)	82	86	89	99	104	112	108	107	104	96	90	79	112
Extreme Minimum Temp. (°F)	-18	-13	-3	15	31	42	51	48	29	13	-4	-13	-18
Days Maximum Temp. ≥ 90°F	0	0	0	1	4	14	22	18	8	1	0	0	68
Days Maximum Temp. ≤ 32°F	5	3	1	0	0	0	0	0	0	0	1	5	15
Days Minimum Temp. ≤ 32°F	30	24	18	6	0	0	0	0	0	4	20	29	131
Days Minimum Temp. ≤ 0°F	1	1	0	0	0	0	0	0	0	0	0	1	3
Heating Degree Days (base 65°F)	965	781	622	338	111	12	1	2	56	287	632	961	4,768
Cooling Degree Days (base 65°F)	0	0	1	17	93	281	439	381	170	23	0	0	1,405
Mean Precipitation (in.)	0.46	0.39	1.22	1.46	2.44	3.30	2.52	2.59	1.80	1.39	0.60	0.66	18.83
Extreme Maximum Daily Precip. (in.)	1.20	0.87	1.87	2.00	2.92	3.30	3.12	2.32	3.25	1.87	1.05	3.20	3.30
Days With ≥ 0.1" Precipitation	1	1	3	3	5	5	5	4	3	3	2	2	37
Days With ≥ 0.5" Precipitation	0	0	1	1	2	2	2	2	1	1	0	0	12
Days With ≥ 1.0" Precipitation	0	0	0	0	1	1	1	1	0	0	0	0	4
Mean Snowfall (in.)	***3.6***	***1.4***	***2.8***	0.5	0.0	0.0	0.0	0.0	0.0	0.2	0.7	***2.9***	***12.1***
Maximum Snow Depth (in.)	na	***3***	na	***5***	***0***	***0***	***0***	***0***	***0***	***0***	***2***	na	na
Days With ≥ 1.0" Snow Depth	na	***0***	***0***	0	0	0	0	0	0	0	0	***1***	na

Hutchinson 10 SW *Reno County* Elevation: 1,569 ft. Latitude: 37° 56' N Longitude: 98° 02' W

	JAN	FEB	MAR	APR	MAY	JUN	JUL	AUG	SEP	OCT	NOV	DEC	YEAR
Mean Maximum Temp. (°F)	42.5	47.1	56.5	66.4	75.7	86.4	92.3	91.1	82.4	69.5	55.8	43.3	67.4
Mean Temp. (°F)	30.9	35.2	44.5	54.0	64.4	74.5	79.9	78.7	69.5	56.6	43.8	32.4	55.4
Mean Minimum Temp. (°F)	19.3	23.3	32.5	41.7	53.0	62.6	67.5	66.3	56.6	43.7	31.7	21.5	43.3
Extreme Maximum Temp. (°F)	79	82	89	98	102	110	110	110	108	95	88	76	110
Extreme Minimum Temp. (°F)	-15	-19	-3	17	30	42	46	47	29	12	5	-18	-19
Days Maximum Temp. ≥ 90°F	0	0	0	1	2	11	21	18	8	1	0	0	62
Days Maximum Temp. ≤ 32°F	8	5	1	0	0	0	0	0	0	0	1	6	21
Days Minimum Temp. ≤ 32°F	30	23	16	5	0	0	0	0	0	4	17	28	123
Days Minimum Temp. ≤ 0°F	1	1	0	0	0	0	0	0	0	0	0	1	3
Heating Degree Days (base 65°F)	1,049	837	629	342	105	9	1	1	56	281	630	1,003	4,943
Cooling Degree Days (base 65°F)	0	0	1	20	92	301	470	434	199	28	1	0	1,546
Mean Precipitation (in.)	0.72	1.09	2.66	2.69	4.37	4.61	3.62	3.16	2.65	2.37	1.20	1.07	30.21
Extreme Maximum Daily Precip. (in.)	1.42	1.67	2.08	3.11	4.83	4.02	4.22	3.83	3.30	2.81	2.71	3.17	4.83
Days With ≥ 0.1" Precipitation	2	2	5	5	6	6	5	5	4	4	2	2	48
Days With ≥ 0.5" Precipitation	0	1	2	2	3	3	2	2	1	1	1	1	19
Days With ≥ 1.0" Precipitation	0	0	1	1	1	1	1	1	1	1	0	0	8
Mean Snowfall (in.)	3.6	3.4	2.8	0.5	0.0	0.0	0.0	0.0	0.0	0.1	0.6	2.8	13.8
Maximum Snow Depth (in.)	9	11	12	7	0	0	0	0	0	3	4	7	12
Days With ≥ 1.0" Snow Depth	6	4	2	0	0	0	0	0	0	0	1	5	18

Independence *Montgomery County* Elevation: 805 ft. Latitude: 37° 14' N Longitude: 95° 42' W

	JAN	FEB	MAR	APR	MAY	JUN	JUL	AUG	SEP	OCT	NOV	DEC	YEAR
Mean Maximum Temp. (°F)	45.1	50.1	59.9	69.4	77.3	85.6	91.4	91.5	82.9	71.4	58.9	46.4	69.2
Mean Temp. (°F)	34.3	38.5	47.8	57.4	66.6	75.3	80.5	79.9	71.1	59.3	47.6	35.9	57.8
Mean Minimum Temp. (°F)	23.4	26.8	35.7	45.4	55.8	64.9	69.6	68.2	59.2	47.2	36.2	25.5	46.5
Extreme Maximum Temp. (°F)	75	84	90	94	94	103	111	108	108	94	86	76	111
Extreme Minimum Temp. (°F)	-15	-9	-4	23	34	43	55	50	29	19	10	-16	-16
Days Maximum Temp. ≥ 90°F	0	0	0	1	1	8	19	20	8	1	0	0	58
Days Maximum Temp. ≤ 32°F	6	3	1	0	0	0	0	0	0	0	0	4	14
Days Minimum Temp. ≤ 32°F	26	20	12	2	0	0	0	0	0	2	12	23	97
Days Minimum Temp. ≤ 0°F	1	1	0	0	0	0	0	0	0	0	0	1	3
Heating Degree Days (base 65°F)	945	743	529	253	62	3	0	0	36	210	519	894	4,194
Cooling Degree Days (base 65°F)	0	0	5	34	118	318	488	468	224	41	4	0	1,700
Mean Precipitation (in.)	1.50	1.93	3.55	4.23	6.34	6.06	3.40	3.60	4.38	4.23	2.57	2.35	44.14
Extreme Maximum Daily Precip. (in.)	2.39	3.41	3.55	2.74	7.69	6.80	5.10	4.78	6.39	6.08	3.23	2.27	7.69
Days With ≥ 0.1" Precipitation	4	4	6	7	8	7	5	5	5	5	4	4	64
Days With ≥ 0.5" Precipitation	1	1	3	3	4	4	2	2	3	3	2	2	30
Days With ≥ 1.0" Precipitation	0	0	1	1	2	2	1	1	2	1	1	1	13
Mean Snowfall (in.)	3.3	2.8	1.5	trace	0.0	0.0	0.0	0.0	0.0	trace	0.3	4.2	12.1
Maximum Snow Depth (in.)	9	15	7	trace	0	0	0	0	0	trace	2	13	15
Days With ≥ 1.0" Snow Depth	5	3	1	0	0	0	0	0	0	0	0	4	13

Kingman *Kingman County* Elevation: 1,560 ft. Latitude: 37° 40' N Longitude: 98° 07' W

	JAN	FEB	MAR	APR	MAY	JUN	JUL	AUG	SEP	OCT	NOV	DEC	YEAR
Mean Maximum Temp. (°F)	44.4	48.8	58.6	68.5	77.8	87.8	93.9	92.4	83.3	70.4	57.0	44.7	69.0
Mean Temp. (°F)	33.1	37.0	46.1	55.8	65.9	75.7	81.3	80.0	70.6	57.8	45.0	34.0	56.8
Mean Minimum Temp. (°F)	21.7	25.1	33.6	43.1	53.9	63.4	68.6	67.5	57.8	45.2	32.9	23.1	44.7
Extreme Maximum Temp. (°F)	76	82	91	98	102	110	111	111	109	96	88	74	111
Extreme Minimum Temp. (°F)	-11	-16	0	17	27	43	47	49	24	14	6	-17	-17
Days Maximum Temp. ≥ 90°F	0	0	0	1	3	13	23	20	9	1	0	0	70
Days Maximum Temp. ≤ 32°F	6	4	1	0	0	0	0	0	0	0	1	5	17
Days Minimum Temp. ≤ 32°F	28	21	15	4	0	0	0	0	0	3	15	27	113
Days Minimum Temp. ≤ 0°F	1	1	0	0	0	0	0	0	0	0	0	1	3
Heating Degree Days (base 65°F)	984	786	582	296	80	5	0	1	44	248	595	956	4,577
Cooling Degree Days (base 65°F)	0	0	3	27	114	331	511	472	218	33	1	0	1,710
Mean Precipitation (in.)	0.80	1.16	2.94	2.68	4.28	4.68	3.21	3.33	2.87	3.02	1.41	1.19	31.57
Extreme Maximum Daily Precip. (in.)	1.80	1.72	2.20	2.64	3.56	3.67	2.95	3.80	3.57	4.94	2.00	1.75	4.94
Days With ≥ 0.1" Precipitation	2	3	5	5	6	6	5	5	4	4	3	3	51
Days With ≥ 0.5" Precipitation	1	1	2	2	3	3	2	2	2	2	1	1	22
Days With ≥ 1.0" Precipitation	0	0	1	1	1	2	1	1	1	1	0	0	9
Mean Snowfall (in.)	2.6	3.7	***2.5***	0.2	0.0	0.0	0.0	0.0	0.0	trace	0.8	3.2	***13.0***
Maximum Snow Depth (in.)	11	12	10	3	0	0	0	0	0	1	4	7	12
Days With ≥ 1.0" Snow Depth	3	3	1	0	0	0	0	0	0	0	1	2	10

Lakin *Kearny County* Elevation: 2,998 ft. Latitude: 37° 56' N Longitude: 101° 15' W

	JAN	FEB	MAR	APR	MAY	JUN	JUL	AUG	SEP	OCT	NOV	DEC	YEAR
Mean Maximum Temp. (°F)	45.0	49.1	57.9	66.9	77.4	87.7	93.7	91.2	82.9	70.6	56.9	45.8	68.7
Mean Temp. (°F)	31.6	35.2	43.4	52.1	63.4	73.4	79.1	77.2	68.4	55.7	42.5	32.5	54.5
Mean Minimum Temp. (°F)	18.1	21.3	28.9	37.2	49.3	59.0	64.5	63.2	53.9	40.8	28.0	19.2	40.3
Extreme Maximum Temp. (°F)	80	86	91	99	105	109	110	109	106	98	87	77	110
Extreme Minimum Temp. (°F)	-16	-13	-6	11	30	41	50	47	24	11	0	-15	-16
Days Maximum Temp. ≥ 90°F	0	0	0	1	4	14	23	20	9	2	0	0	73
Days Maximum Temp. ≤ 32°F	6	4	2	0	0	0	0	0	0	0	1	6	19
Days Minimum Temp. ≤ 32°F	30	25	20	8	0	0	0	0	0	5	21	30	139
Days Minimum Temp. ≤ 0°F	1	1	0	0	0	0	0	0	0	0	0	2	4
Heating Degree Days (base 65°F)	1,029	835	663	394	128	16	1	2	62	303	670	1,002	5,105
Cooling Degree Days (base 65°F)	0	0	0	12	85	274	445	387	172	23	0	0	1,398
Mean Precipitation (in.)	0.35	0.47	1.04	1.59	2.68	3.19	2.79	2.64	1.52	1.41	0.62	0.61	18.91
Extreme Maximum Daily Precip. (in.)	0.55	0.89	1.85	1.70	3.99	4.03	3.16	3.50	2.65	1.75	1.70	2.94	4.03
Days With ≥ 0.1" Precipitation	1	1	3	4	5	5	5	5	3	3	1	1	37
Days With ≥ 0.5" Precipitation	0	0	1	1	2	2	2	2	1	1	0	0	12
Days With ≥ 1.0" Precipitation	0	0	0	0	1	1	1	1	0	0	0	0	4
Mean Snowfall (in.)	4.9	3.6	4.3	1.1	0.0	0.0	0.0	0.0	trace	0.4	0.7	3.4	18.4
Maximum Snow Depth (in.)	12	***12***	***18***	12	0	0	0	0	trace	12	12	7	***18***
Days With ≥ 1.0" Snow Depth	4	3	2	0	0	0	0	0	0	0	1	3	13

Lawrence *Douglas County* Elevation: 979 ft. Latitude: 38° 58' N Longitude: 95° 16' W

	JAN	FEB	MAR	APR	MAY	JUN	JUL	AUG	SEP	OCT	NOV	DEC	YEAR
Mean Maximum Temp. (°F)	41.0	46.3	57.1	67.1	76.4	84.8	89.8	***89.1***	81.1	68.7	54.7	41.9	***66.5***
Mean Temp. (°F)	31.7	36.3	46.0	56.3	66.2	75.0	79.8	***78.7***	70.3	58.3	45.2	33.4	***56.4***
Mean Minimum Temp. (°F)	22.4	26.4	34.8	45.5	55.9	65.2	69.8	***68.3***	59.5	47.9	35.7	24.9	***46.4***
Extreme Maximum Temp. (°F)	71	77	86	94	95	107	107	107	107	93	84	71	107
Extreme Minimum Temp. (°F)	-16	-11	0	21	32	45	55	45	34	20	2	-21	-21
Days Maximum Temp. ≥ 90°F	0	0	0	0	1	8	16	15	5	0	0	0	45
Days Maximum Temp. ≤ 32°F	7	5	1	0	0	0	0	0	0	0	1	7	21
Days Minimum Temp. ≤ 32°F	25	19	13	3	0	0	0	0	0	1	11	23	95
Days Minimum Temp. ≤ 0°F	1	1	0	0	0	0	0	0	0	0	0	1	3
Heating Degree Days (base 65°F)	1,025	805	585	289	72	4	0	***1***	43	237	589	971	***4,621***
Cooling Degree Days (base 65°F)	0	0	3	35	116	313	467	***434***	208	37	2	0	***1,615***
Mean Precipitation (in.)	1.03	1.35	2.52	3.81	5.30	5.72	4.14	3.98	4.28	3.44	2.17	1.72	39.46
Extreme Maximum Daily Precip. (in.)	2.23	1.64	2.01	3.05	4.06	5.61	5.02	3.23	3.56	3.72	2.77	1.61	5.61
Days With ≥ 0.1" Precipitation	3	3	5	6	8	7	6	6	6	6	4	4	64
Days With ≥ 0.5" Precipitation	1	1	2	3	4	4	3	3	3	2	1	1	28
Days With ≥ 1.0" Precipitation	0	0	1	1	2	2	1	1	1	1	1	0	11
Mean Snowfall (in.)	3.9	4.1	0.8	0.2	0.0	0.0	0.0	0.0	0.0	0.2	0.8	3.9	13.9
Maximum Snow Depth (in.)	10	13	5	5	0	0	0	0	0	4	2	13	13
Days With ≥ 1.0" Snow Depth	5	4	1	0	0	0	0	0	0	0	0	4	14

Leavenworth *Leavenworth County* Elevation: 870 ft. Latitude: 39° 16' N Longitude: 94° 55' W

	JAN	FEB	MAR	APR	MAY	JUN	JUL	AUG	SEP	OCT	NOV	DEC	YEAR
Mean Maximum Temp. (°F)	39.8	44.8	56.1	67.5	76.5	85.1	90.2	88.6	80.0	68.0	54.1	41.2	66.0
Mean Temp. (°F)	30.2	34.4	44.8	55.7	65.4	74.3	79.4	77.5	68.5	56.8	43.9	32.1	55.2
Mean Minimum Temp. (°F)	20.3	23.9	33.3	43.7	54.2	63.4	68.5	66.4	56.9	45.5	33.6	22.9	44.4
Extreme Maximum Temp. (°F)	74	79	86	93	96	106	108	108	104	95	84	70	108
Extreme Minimum Temp. (°F)	-17	-16	-9	19	30	42	53	43	30	18	0	-27	-27
Days Maximum Temp. ≥ 90°F	0	0	0	0	1	8	17	13	4	0	0	0	43
Days Maximum Temp. ≤ 32°F	8	6	1	0	0	0	0	0	0	0	1	7	23
Days Minimum Temp. ≤ 32°F	27	21	14	4	0	0	0	0	0	3	14	25	108
Days Minimum Temp. ≤ 0°F	2	1	0	0	0	0	0	0	0	0	0	2	5
Heating Degree Days (base 65°F)	1,071	858	623	305	84	7	0	1	58	275	628	1,014	4,924
Cooling Degree Days (base 65°F)	0	0	3	32	101	291	453	397	169	28	1	0	1,475
Mean Precipitation (in.)	0.99	1.35	2.75	3.83	5.43	5.51	4.40	4.56	4.45	3.74	2.27	1.75	41.03
Extreme Maximum Daily Precip. (in.)	1.55	2.10	2.47	2.48	4.43	5.06	6.23	3.84	3.62	5.59	2.30	3.20	6.23
Days With ≥ 0.1" Precipitation	3	3	5	6	8	7	5	6	5	6	4	4	62
Days With ≥ 0.5" Precipitation	1	1	2	3	3	4	3	3	3	3	1	1	28
Days With ≥ 1.0" Precipitation	0	0	1	1	2	2	1	1	1	1	0	0	10
Mean Snowfall (in.)	***3.8***	***4.7***	1.3	trace	0.0	0.0	0.0	0.0	0.0	0.2	0.7	***3.9***	***14.6***
Maximum Snow Depth (in.)	na	na	***7***	***1***	***0***	***0***	***0***	***0***	***0***	7	***8***	na	na
Days With ≥ 1.0" Snow Depth	na	***4***	***1***	0	0	0	0	0	0	0	0	***4***	na

Leoti 1 W *Wichita County* Elevation: 3,310 ft. Latitude: 38° 29' N Longitude: 101° 22' W

	JAN	FEB	MAR	APR	MAY	JUN	JUL	AUG	SEP	OCT	NOV	DEC	YEAR
Mean Maximum Temp. (°F)	43.2	47.3	56.1	65.2	75.5	85.2	91.8	89.1	80.9	68.2	54.5	44.5	66.8
Mean Temp. (°F)	29.6	33.2	41.2	50.0	61.0	70.7	76.7	74.9	65.8	52.7	39.9	30.7	52.2
Mean Minimum Temp. (°F)	15.9	19.0	26.2	34.8	46.6	56.3	61.6	60.5	50.7	37.1	25.2	16.9	37.6
Extreme Maximum Temp. (°F)	78	83	90	96	101	107	107	105	105	96	86	80	107
Extreme Minimum Temp. (°F)	-20	-17	-7	8	23	32	42	43	24	9	-4	-16	-20
Days Maximum Temp. ≥ 90°F	0	0	0	0	3	11	20	16	7	1	0	0	58
Days Maximum Temp. ≤ 32°F	8	5	3	0	0	0	0	0	0	0	2	6	24
Days Minimum Temp. ≤ 32°F	31	27	23	12	1	0	0	0	1	9	24	29	157
Days Minimum Temp. ≤ 0°F	2	2	0	0	0	0	0	0	0	0	0	2	6
Heating Degree Days (base 65°F)	1,090	892	731	448	168	29	2	5	90	385	746	1,054	5,640
Cooling Degree Days (base 65°F)	0	0	0	6	53	207	372	318	121	8	0	0	1,085
Mean Precipitation (in.)	0.43	0.53	1.35	1.88	2.51	2.84	2.98	2.99	1.44	1.51	0.63	0.63	19.72
Extreme Maximum Daily Precip. (in.)	0.93	1.26	1.68	***3.69***	2.42	2.68	1.97	4.43	2.73	2.97	0.98	3.03	***4.43***
Days With ≥ 0.1" Precipitation	1	2	3	4	5	5	5	5	3	3	2	1	39
Days With ≥ 0.5" Precipitation	0	0	1	1	2	2	2	2	1	1	0	0	12
Days With ≥ 1.0" Precipitation	0	0	0	0	1	1	1	1	0	0	0	0	4
Mean Snowfall (in.)	6.0	4.7	5.4	2.9	0.0	trace	0.0	0.0	0.2	1.0	2.7	5.1	28.0
Maximum Snow Depth (in.)	19	14	***15***	***12***	0	trace	0	0	3	13	15	17	***19***
Days With ≥ 1.0" Snow Depth	9	5	3	1	0	0	0	0	0	1	2	6	27

The period of record for all cooperative weather station data is 1980 – 2009. See User Guide for detailed explanation of data.

Manhattan *Riley County* Elevation: 1,064 ft. Latitude: 39° 12' N Longitude: 96° 35' W

	JAN	FEB	MAR	APR	MAY	JUN	JUL	AUG	SEP	OCT	NOV	DEC	YEAR
Mean Maximum Temp. (°F)	41.8	47.1	58.0	68.3	77.1	86.5	92.0	90.7	82.1	70.0	55.4	42.8	67.7
Mean Temp. (°F)	30.5	35.0	45.1	55.5	65.1	74.6	79.9	78.3	69.2	57.0	43.6	32.0	55.5
Mean Minimum Temp. (°F)	19.0	22.8	32.1	42.7	53.1	62.6	67.8	65.9	56.2	43.9	31.9	21.1	43.3
Extreme Maximum Temp. (°F)	73	84	88	97	100	109	110	109	111	97	85	73	111
Extreme Minimum Temp. (°F)	-15	-15	-3	14	27	41	48	45	26	13	3	-22	-22
Days Maximum Temp. ≥ 90°F	0	0	0	1	2	11	20	17	7	1	0	0	59
Days Maximum Temp. ≤ 32°F	8	5	1	0	0	0	0	0	0	0	1	6	21
Days Minimum Temp. ≤ 32°F	28	22	17	6	0	0	0	0	0	4	16	27	120
Days Minimum Temp. ≤ 0°F	2	1	0	0	0	0	0	0	0	0	0	2	5
Heating Degree Days (base 65°F)	1,064	843	615	311	94	7	0	1	58	275	636	1,017	4,921
Cooling Degree Days (base 65°F)	0	0	4	34	104	301	470	421	190	34	1	0	1,559
Mean Precipitation (in.)	0.69	1.10	2.56	3.14	5.08	5.55	4.48	4.08	3.39	2.68	1.63	1.19	35.57
Extreme Maximum Daily Precip. (in.)	0.86	1.31	2.53	3.78	4.18	4.09	4.81	4.98	4.18	5.05	2.95	2.06	5.05
Days With ≥ 0.1" Precipitation	2	3	5	6	8	7	6	6	5	5	4	3	60
Days With ≥ 0.5" Precipitation	0	1	2	2	4	4	3	2	2	2	1	1	24
Days With ≥ 1.0" Precipitation	0	0	0	1	1	2	1	1	1	1	0	0	8
Mean Snowfall (in.)	4.6	4.6	2.1	0.1	0.0	0.0	0.0	0.0	0.0	trace	1.0	4.8	17.2
Maximum Snow Depth (in.)	9	14	15	1	0	0	0	0	0	1	3	9	15
Days With ≥ 1.0" Snow Depth	7	6	1	0	0	0	0	0	0	0	1	7	22

Marysville *Marshall County* Elevation: 1,180 ft. Latitude: 39° 50' N Longitude: 96° 38' W

	JAN	FEB	MAR	APR	MAY	JUN	JUL	AUG	SEP	OCT	NOV	DEC	YEAR
Mean Maximum Temp. (°F)	37.4	42.3	53.7	64.8	74.8	84.2	89.8	87.9	79.7	67.2	52.7	39.5	64.5
Mean Temp. (°F)	26.5	30.9	41.8	52.7	63.3	73.1	78.4	76.3	67.1	54.4	41.3	28.9	52.9
Mean Minimum Temp. (°F)	15.6	19.4	29.9	40.5	51.8	61.9	66.9	64.7	54.3	41.4	29.8	18.4	41.2
Extreme Maximum Temp. (°F)	71	79	92	97	99	108	110	107	109	95	84	71	110
Extreme Minimum Temp. (°F)	-18	-17	-18	15	27	40	49	44	27	11	-2	-27	-27
Days Maximum Temp. ≥ 90°F	0	0	0	1	2	8	16	13	5	1	0	0	46
Days Maximum Temp. ≤ 32°F	11	7	2	0	0	0	0	0	0	0	2	9	31
Days Minimum Temp. ≤ 32°F	30	25	19	6	0	0	0	0	0	6	19	29	134
Days Minimum Temp. ≤ 0°F	3	3	0	0	0	0	0	0	0	0	0	3	9
Heating Degree Days (base 65°F)	1,186	959	715	385	128	14	1	4	84	344	707	1,110	5,637
Cooling Degree Days (base 65°F)	0	0	2	23	83	262	422	361	152	21	1	0	1,327
Mean Precipitation (in.)	0.72	0.97	2.40	2.88	4.40	5.08	4.52	3.92	3.17	2.51	1.40	1.09	33.06
Extreme Maximum Daily Precip. (in.)	1.00	1.67	3.25	2.00	4.16	4.50	5.05	2.99	3.68	2.09	1.66	1.67	5.05
Days With ≥ 0.1" Precipitation	2	3	5	6	7	7	6	6	5	5	3	3	58
Days With ≥ 0.5" Precipitation	0	1	2	2	3	3	3	3	2	2	1	1	23
Days With ≥ 1.0" Precipitation	0	0	0	1	1	2	1	1	1	1	0	0	8
Mean Snowfall (in.)	3.7	2.6	1.7	0.6	0.0	0.0	0.0	0.0	0.0	trace	0.5	***2.1***	***11.2***
Maximum Snow Depth (in.)	***11***	***8***	5	12	0	0	***0***	0	0	***0***	5	***12***	***12***
Days With ≥ 1.0" Snow Depth	***1***	***1***	0	0	0	0	0	0	0	0	0	***4***	***6***

Milford Lake *Geary County* Elevation: 1,209 ft. Latitude: 39° 05' N Longitude: 96° 53' W

	JAN	FEB	MAR	APR	MAY	JUN	JUL	AUG	SEP	OCT	NOV	DEC	YEAR
Mean Maximum Temp. (°F)	39.8	43.9	55.0	65.5	74.8	84.1	90.3	89.2	80.5	68.0	54.5	41.0	65.6
Mean Temp. (°F)	29.0	32.7	43.2	53.6	63.6	73.1	78.9	77.5	68.3	55.8	43.3	31.0	54.2
Mean Minimum Temp. (°F)	18.2	21.4	31.3	41.6	52.4	62.0	67.4	65.6	55.9	43.6	32.0	20.8	42.7
Extreme Maximum Temp. (°F)	75	78	88	96	100	108	110	108	109	94	84	75	110
Extreme Minimum Temp. (°F)	-17	-15	-5	19	29	41	53	46	31	15	6	-21	-21
Days Maximum Temp. ≥ 90°F	0	0	0	1	1	8	16	14	5	0	0	0	45
Days Maximum Temp. ≤ 32°F	9	6	2	0	0	0	0	0	0	0	1	8	26
Days Minimum Temp. ≤ 32°F	29	24	17	5	0	0	0	0	0	4	16	28	123
Days Minimum Temp. ≤ 0°F	2	2	0	0	0	0	0	0	0	0	0	2	6
Heating Degree Days (base 65°F)	1,109	908	671	357	118	12	1	1	67	303	646	1,048	5,241
Cooling Degree Days (base 65°F)	0	0	2	21	82	261	438	396	172	25	1	0	1,398
Mean Precipitation (in.)	0.68	1.09	2.39	2.84	4.71	4.53	3.98	3.91	3.16	2.66	1.44	1.12	32.51
Extreme Maximum Daily Precip. (in.)	1.10	2.10	2.27	2.93	4.92	3.29	3.00	4.73	2.97	3.20	***3.03***	2.82	***4.92***
Days With ≥ 0.1" Precipitation	2	2	4	5	7	7	6	6	5	4	3	3	54
Days With ≥ 0.5" Precipitation	0	1	1	2	3	3	3	2	2	2	1	1	21
Days With ≥ 1.0" Precipitation	0	0	1	1	1	1	1	1	1	1	0	0	8
Mean Snowfall (in.)	1.7	1.4	0.3	trace	0.0	0.0	0.0	0.0	0.0	0.0	0.1	1.6	5.1
Maximum Snow Depth (in.)	12	15	5	3	0	0	0	0	0	1	3	14	15
Days With ≥ 1.0" Snow Depth	4	4	1	0	0	0	0	0	0	0	0	4	13

Mound Valley 3 WSW *Labette County* Elevation: 799 ft. Latitude: 37° 11' N Longitude: 95° 27' W

	JAN	FEB	MAR	APR	MAY	JUN	JUL	AUG	SEP	OCT	NOV	DEC	YEAR
Mean Maximum Temp. (°F)	43.3	48.6	58.2	67.8	76.2	84.7	90.3	90.8	81.8	70.3	57.4	45.0	67.9
Mean Temp. (°F)	32.3	36.9	46.2	55.6	65.4	74.2	79.1	78.5	69.5	57.5	45.8	34.3	56.3
Mean Minimum Temp. (°F)	21.2	24.9	34.1	43.3	54.4	63.7	68.0	66.2	57.1	44.6	34.1	23.5	44.6
Extreme Maximum Temp. (°F)	74	83	88	93	94	104	109	107	108	94	86	73	109
Extreme Minimum Temp. (°F)	-20	-11	-6	19	30	40	51	45	27	15	8	-18	-20
Days Maximum Temp. ≥ 90°F	0	0	0	0	1	6	18	19	7	0	0	0	51
Days Maximum Temp. ≤ 32°F	7	4	1	0	0	0	0	0	0	0	1	5	18
Days Minimum Temp. ≤ 32°F	28	22	14	4	0	0	0	0	0	4	14	26	112
Days Minimum Temp. ≤ 0°F	1	1	0	0	0	0	0	0	0	0	0	1	3
Heating Degree Days (base 65°F)	1,007	788	580	301	83	6	0	1	51	258	574	945	4,594
Cooling Degree Days (base 65°F)	0	0	3	25	101	290	445	427	192	31	3	0	1,517
Mean Precipitation (in.)	1.63	1.87	3.48	4.37	6.55	5.83	3.63	3.76	4.67	4.18	2.92	2.32	45.21
Extreme Maximum Daily Precip. (in.)	2.35	2.65	3.46	5.82	4.89	4.73	3.22	4.47	5.00	6.83	3.55	2.45	6.83
Days With ≥ 0.1" Precipitation	4	4	6	7	8	8	5	5	5	6	5	4	67
Days With ≥ 0.5" Precipitation	1	1	3	3	4	4	2	2	3	3	2	2	30
Days With ≥ 1.0" Precipitation	0	0	1	1	2	2	1	1	2	1	1	1	13
Mean Snowfall (in.)	***2.4***	1.9	1.1	trace	0.0	0.0	0.0	0.0	0.0	trace	0.2	3.6	***9.2***
Maximum Snow Depth (in.)	***8***	***12***	***4***	trace	0	0	0	0	0	***trace***	2	***12***	***12***
Days With ≥ 1.0" Snow Depth	***2***	1	0	0	0	0	0	0	0	0	0	***3***	***6***

The period of record for all cooperative weather station data is 1980 – 2009. See User Guide for detailed explanation of data.

Ness City *Ness County* Elevation: 2,250 ft. Latitude: 38° 27' N Longitude: 99° 54' W

	JAN	FEB	MAR	APR	MAY	JUN	JUL	AUG	SEP	OCT	NOV	DEC	YEAR
Mean Maximum Temp. (°F)	44.2	48.7	57.4	68.1	77.6	87.7	94.0	91.9	83.3	70.8	56.7	45.2	68.8
Mean Temp. (°F)	30.2	34.4	42.6	52.9	63.5	73.5	79.4	77.5	68.2	55.1	41.7	31.6	54.2
Mean Minimum Temp. (°F)	16.2	20.0	27.8	37.6	49.3	59.4	64.8	63.1	52.9	39.4	26.6	17.9	39.6
Extreme Maximum Temp. (°F)	81	85	91	103	105	114	113	108	105	100	89	80	114
Extreme Minimum Temp. (°F)	-16	-18	-8	10	28	37	41	45	20	13	-3	-25	-25
Days Maximum Temp. ≥ 90°F	0	0	0	1	4	14	23	20	10	2	0	0	74
Days Maximum Temp. ≤ 32°F	7	5	2	0	0	0	0	0	0	0	1	6	21
Days Minimum Temp. ≤ 32°F	30	25	20	8	1	0	0	0	1	7	22	29	143
Days Minimum Temp. ≤ 0°F	2	2	0	0	0	0	0	0	0	0	0	2	6
Heating Degree Days (base 65°F)	1,071	860	689	373	125	15	1	2	70	323	693	1,029	5,251
Cooling Degree Days (base 65°F)	0	0	1	17	85	279	455	396	171	23	0	0	1,427
Mean Precipitation (in.)	0.53	0.71	1.77	1.86	3.03	3.17	3.44	2.77	1.84	1.52	0.75	0.71	22.10
Extreme Maximum Daily Precip. (in.)	0.90	***1.46***	2.50	2.32	3.00	3.00	3.15	2.70	2.70	2.49	1.65	2.30	***3.15***
Days With ≥ 0.1" Precipitation	1	2	4	4	6	6	5	4	3	3	2	2	42
Days With ≥ 0.5" Precipitation	0	0	1	1	2	2	2	2	1	1	0	0	12
Days With ≥ 1.0" Precipitation	0	0	0	0	1	1	1	1	1	0	0	0	5
Mean Snowfall (in.)	4.9	***3.6***	4.1	0.8	0.0	0.0	0.0	0.0	0.1	0.1	1.3	3.2	***18.1***
Maximum Snow Depth (in.)	***13***	***10***	***20***	4	0	0	0	0	0	4	11	***8***	***20***
Days With ≥ 1.0" Snow Depth	***5***	***3***	1	0	0	0	0	0	0	0	1	4	***14***

Newton 2 SW *Harvey County* Elevation: 1,446 ft. Latitude: 38° 02' N Longitude: 97° 23' W

	JAN	FEB	MAR	APR	MAY	JUN	JUL	AUG	SEP	OCT	NOV	DEC	YEAR
Mean Maximum Temp. (°F)	41.8	47.2	57.1	67.0	76.5	86.6	92.7	91.4	82.6	69.3	55.6	42.7	67.5
Mean Temp. (°F)	31.6	36.4	45.5	55.4	65.6	75.4	81.0	79.7	70.8	57.9	44.8	33.1	56.4
Mean Minimum Temp. (°F)	21.4	25.5	33.9	43.7	54.6	64.3	69.3	68.0	58.9	46.5	33.9	23.3	45.3
Extreme Maximum Temp. (°F)	75	81	89	95	99	109	111	110	108	96	88	72	111
Extreme Minimum Temp. (°F)	-11	-9	-4	19	32	42	49	49	29	14	7	-20	-20
Days Maximum Temp. ≥ 90°F	0	0	0	0	2	12	21	19	8	0	0	0	62
Days Maximum Temp. ≤ 32°F	8	5	1	0	0	0	0	0	0	0	1	6	21
Days Minimum Temp. ≤ 32°F	27	21	14	3	0	0	0	0	0	2	14	27	108
Days Minimum Temp. ≤ 0°F	1	1	0	0	0	0	0	0	0	0	0	1	3
Heating Degree Days (base 65°F)	1,028	804	599	309	84	6	0	1	45	250	601	983	4,710
Cooling Degree Days (base 65°F)	0	0	2	26	109	325	503	463	225	37	1	0	1,691
Mean Precipitation (in.)	0.88	1.10	2.73	2.77	4.33	4.76	3.39	3.47	3.07	2.66	1.75	1.11	32.02
Extreme Maximum Daily Precip. (in.)	1.90	2.05	4.30	3.35	3.52	5.45	3.61	3.75	4.86	3.94	5.35	1.80	5.45
Days With ≥ 0.1" Precipitation	2	3	5	5	6	6	5	5	4	4	3	3	51
Days With ≥ 0.5" Precipitation	1	1	2	2	3	3	2	2	2	2	1	1	22
Days With ≥ 1.0" Precipitation	0	0	1	1	1	2	1	1	1	1	0	0	9
Mean Snowfall (in.)	3.2	2.9	0.7	0.4	0.0	0.0	0.0	0.0	0.0	0.1	0.5	***3.1***	***10.9***
Maximum Snow Depth (in.)	***10***	na	***6***	4	0	***0***	***0***	***0***	***0***	***1***	3	***10***	na
Days With ≥ 1.0" Snow Depth	***2***	***1***	0	0	0	0	0	0	0	0	0	***2***	***5***

Norton Dam *Norton County* Elevation: 2,339 ft. Latitude: 39° 49' N Longitude: 99° 56' W

	JAN	FEB	MAR	APR	MAY	JUN	JUL	AUG	SEP	OCT	NOV	DEC	YEAR
Mean Maximum Temp. (°F)	39.8	43.6	53.7	64.6	74.1	85.0	***91.7***	***89.1***	***80.2***	***66.9***	52.0	***40.9***	***65.1***
Mean Temp. (°F)	27.3	30.7	39.8	50.4	60.8	71.4	***77.8***	***75.6***	***65.8***	***52.6***	38.9	***28.8***	***51.7***
Mean Minimum Temp. (°F)	14.7	17.9	25.9	36.2	47.5	57.8	***63.9***	***62.2***	51.4	38.2	25.7	15.9	***38.1***
Extreme Maximum Temp. (°F)	78	80	***83***	94	101	***109***	***111***	108	102	95	88	77	***111***
Extreme Minimum Temp. (°F)	-20	-18	***-9***	11	24	31	***44***	43	20	6	-7	-28	***-28***
Days Maximum Temp. ≥ 90°F	0	0	0	1	2	10	***19***	15	7	1	0	0	***55***
Days Maximum Temp. ≤ 32°F	10	7	***3***	0	0	0	***0***	0	0	0	2	8	***30***
Days Minimum Temp. ≤ 32°F	29	26	***24***	11	1	0	***0***	0	0	8	23	29	***151***
Days Minimum Temp. ≤ 0°F	3	3	1	0	0	0	***0***	0	0	0	0	2	***9***
Heating Degree Days (base 65°F)	1,161	951	775	440	180	26	***2***	***4***	***96***	***391***	776	***1,116***	***5,918***
Cooling Degree Days (base 65°F)	0	0	0	9	58	225	***406***	***340***	***128***	***12***	0	***0***	***1,178***
Mean Precipitation (in.)	0.45	0.54	1.61	2.74	4.36	3.20	***3.77***	3.23	1.80	2.13	0.98	0.62	***25.43***
Extreme Maximum Daily Precip. (in.)	0.71	***0.89***	***1.96***	2.68	3.16	***2.23***	***2.52***	***2.80***	***2.91***	3.30	***1.82***	***2.04***	***3.30***
Days With ≥ 0.1" Precipitation	1	1	***3***	5	7	6	***6***	5	3	3	2	1	***43***
Days With ≥ 0.5" Precipitation	0	0	***1***	2	3	2	***3***	2	1	1	1	0	***16***
Days With ≥ 1.0" Precipitation	0	0	***0***	1	1	1	***1***	1	0	1	0	0	***6***
Mean Snowfall (in.)	***4.7***	***3.9***	***3.1***	1.1	0.0	0.0	***0.0***	0.0	0.0	0.8	1.2	***3.5***	***18.3***
Maximum Snow Depth (in.)	15	12	***15***	7	0	0	***0***	0	0	12	10	14	***15***
Days With ≥ 1.0" Snow Depth	10	8	***3***	1	0	0	***0***	0	0	0	2	9	***33***

Olathe 3 E *Johnson County* Elevation: 1,055 ft. Latitude: 38° 53' N Longitude: 94° 46' W

	JAN	FEB	MAR	APR	MAY	JUN	JUL	AUG	SEP	OCT	NOV	DEC	YEAR
Mean Maximum Temp. (°F)	39.7	44.7	55.7	65.8	74.9	83.3	88.5	87.5	79.5	67.9	54.0	41.7	65.3
Mean Temp. (°F)	30.7	35.0	45.1	55.3	65.0	73.7	78.9	77.5	69.0	57.6	44.7	33.1	55.5
Mean Minimum Temp. (°F)	21.5	25.3	34.4	44.8	55.1	64.2	69.1	67.4	58.4	47.2	35.4	24.4	45.6
Extreme Maximum Temp. (°F)	74	76	85	91	94	105	108	107	106	94	82	71	108
Extreme Minimum Temp. (°F)	-16	-12	-1	18	35	43	53	46	33	18	5	-22	-22
Days Maximum Temp. ≥ 90°F	0	0	0	0	0	5	13	12	3	0	0	0	33
Days Maximum Temp. ≤ 32°F	8	6	1	0	0	0	0	0	0	0	1	7	23
Days Minimum Temp. ≤ 32°F	27	20	14	3	0	0	0	0	0	2	12	24	102
Days Minimum Temp. ≤ 0°F	1	1	0	0	0	0	0	0	0	0	0	1	3
Heating Degree Days (base 65°F)	1,058	841	613	310	85	7	0	1	51	254	602	984	4,806
Cooling Degree Days (base 65°F)	0	0	2	26	93	276	437	395	178	32	1	0	1,440
Mean Precipitation (in.)	1.28	1.60	2.74	3.86	5.26	5.77	4.15	4.16	4.30	3.40	2.68	1.80	41.00
Extreme Maximum Daily Precip. (in.)	2.13	2.62	3.56	3.47	6.20	8.00	5.81	6.97	5.35	4.23	3.32	1.90	8.00
Days With ≥ 0.1" Precipitation	3	4	5	6	8	7	6	6	5	6	5	4	65
Days With ≥ 0.5" Precipitation	1	1	2	3	3	4	2	2	3	2	2	1	26
Days With ≥ 1.0" Precipitation	0	0	1	1	2	2	1	1	1	1	1	0	11
Mean Snowfall (in.)	4.5	4.6	1.6	0.2	0.0	0.0	0.0	0.0	0.0	0.2	1.1	4.0	16.2
Maximum Snow Depth (in.)	9	11	5	1	0	0	0	0	0	2	5	9	11
Days With ≥ 1.0" Snow Depth	9	7	1	0	0	0	0	0	0	0	1	7	25

The period of record for all cooperative weather station data is 1980 – 2009. See User Guide for detailed explanation of data.

Ottawa *Franklin County* Elevation: 899 ft. Latitude: 38° 37' N Longitude: 95° 17' W

	JAN	FEB	MAR	APR	MAY	JUN	JUL	AUG	SEP	OCT	NOV	DEC	YEAR
Mean Maximum Temp. (°F)	42.0	46.9	58.2	68.3	77.0	85.2	90.8	90.0	81.8	69.7	56.0	43.3	67.4
Mean Temp. (°F)	31.8	36.0	46.5	56.6	65.9	74.6	79.8	78.5	69.8	57.9	45.5	33.7	56.4
Mean Minimum Temp. (°F)	21.6	25.1	34.8	44.8	54.7	63.9	68.8	67.0	57.6	46.1	35.0	24.1	45.3
Extreme Maximum Temp. (°F)	74	84	86	95	101	108	109	109	109	94	86	74	109
Extreme Minimum Temp. (°F)	-15	-20	-6	18	31	42	51	45	28	17	6	-22	-22
Days Maximum Temp. ≥ 90°F	0	0	0	0	1	8	18	17	6	0	0	0	50
Days Maximum Temp. ≤ 32°F	7	5	1	0	0	0	0	0	0	0	1	6	20
Days Minimum Temp. ≤ 32°F	26	21	13	3	0	0	0	0	0	3	13	25	104
Days Minimum Temp. ≤ 0°F	1	1	0	0	0	0	0	0	0	0	0	1	3
Heating Degree Days (base 65°F)	1,021	813	570	280	75	5	0	1	46	248	580	962	4,601
Cooling Degree Days (base 65°F)	0	0	3	34	110	299	466	426	196	35	2	0	1,571
Mean Precipitation (in.)	1.26	1.44	2.80	3.70	5.28	5.56	3.86	4.14	3.96	3.42	2.65	1.82	39.89
Extreme Maximum Daily Precip. (in.)	2.60	2.86	2.54	3.34	3.66	5.46	5.54	5.12	5.76	4.41	2.90	1.60	5.76
Days With ≥ 0.1" Precipitation	3	4	5	6	8	7	6	6	5	6	4	4	64
Days With ≥ 0.5" Precipitation	0	1	2	3	3	4	3	3	2	2	2	1	26
Days With ≥ 1.0" Precipitation	0	0	1	1	1	2	1	1	1	1	1	0	10
Mean Snowfall (in.)	3.7	4.1	0.8	trace	0.0	0.0	0.0	0.0	0.0	trace	0.3	4.0	12.9
Maximum Snow Depth (in.)	***6***	na	***trace***	***trace***	***0***	***0***	***0***	***0***	***0***	***3***	***trace***	***8***	na
Days With ≥ 1.0" Snow Depth	***0***	***0***	0	0	0	0	0	0	0	0	0	1	***1***

Perry Lake *Jefferson County* Elevation: 959 ft. Latitude: 39° 07' N Longitude: 95° 25' W

	JAN	FEB	MAR	APR	MAY	JUN	JUL	AUG	SEP	OCT	NOV	DEC	YEAR
Mean Maximum Temp. (°F)	38.5	43.2	54.5	64.9	74.3	83.1	88.8	88.0	79.4	67.4	53.6	40.3	64.7
Mean Temp. (°F)	28.4	32.8	43.4	53.9	63.9	73.0	78.3	76.9	67.7	55.7	43.4	30.9	54.0
Mean Minimum Temp. (°F)	18.2	22.3	32.3	42.8	53.4	62.8	67.8	65.8	56.0	43.9	33.1	21.5	43.3
Extreme Maximum Temp. (°F)	72	78	88	93	96	110	111	112	108	94	84	74	112
Extreme Minimum Temp. (°F)	-16	-17	-9	19	31	41	49	45	28	13	2	-23	-23
Days Maximum Temp. ≥ 90°F	0	0	0	0	1	6	14	14	4	0	0	0	39
Days Maximum Temp. ≤ 32°F	10	7	2	0	0	0	0	0	0	0	1	8	28
Days Minimum Temp. ≤ 32°F	29	22	16	4	0	0	0	0	0	4	14	27	116
Days Minimum Temp. ≤ 0°F	2	2	0	0	0	0	0	0	0	0	0	2	6
Heating Degree Days (base 65°F)	1,128	905	664	350	109	11	1	2	71	305	644	1,049	5,239
Cooling Degree Days (base 65°F)	0	0	3	24	81	258	419	379	158	24	1	0	1,347
Mean Precipitation (in.)	0.95	1.12	2.55	3.74	5.28	5.66	4.14	4.31	4.15	3.22	2.00	1.60	38.72
Extreme Maximum Daily Precip. (in.)	1.49	2.05	2.25	2.55	3.78	5.30	5.25	4.15	6.59	3.85	3.24	2.20	6.59
Days With ≥ 0.1" Precipitation	2	2	4	6	8	8	6	6	6	6	3	3	60
Days With ≥ 0.5" Precipitation	0	1	2	3	4	4	3	3	3	2	1	1	27
Days With ≥ 1.0" Precipitation	0	0	1	1	2	2	1	1	1	1	1	0	11
Mean Snowfall (in.)	4.1	3.6	1.3	0.1	0.0	0.0	0.0	0.0	0.0	0.1	0.6	4.2	14.0
Maximum Snow Depth (in.)	10	11	7	2	0	0	0	0	0	trace	3	9	11
Days With ≥ 1.0" Snow Depth	6	5	1	0	0	0	0	0	0	0	0	6	18

Smith Center *Smith County* Elevation: 1,779 ft. Latitude: 39° 47' N Longitude: 98° 47' W

	JAN	FEB	MAR	APR	MAY	JUN	JUL	AUG	SEP	OCT	NOV	DEC	YEAR
Mean Maximum Temp. (°F)	40.1	44.7	55.6	67.2	76.4	87.0	93.0	90.4	82.0	68.4	52.9	40.5	66.5
Mean Temp. (°F)	28.8	33.0	42.8	53.7	63.9	74.2	79.9	77.7	68.7	55.5	41.3	30.0	54.1
Mean Minimum Temp. (°F)	17.5	21.2	30.0	40.1	51.4	61.4	66.8	65.1	55.4	42.5	29.6	19.5	41.7
Extreme Maximum Temp. (°F)	79	80	88	102	101	110	111	111	103	97	87	72	111
Extreme Minimum Temp. (°F)	-18	-17	-4	12	28	38	49	46	23	15	-3	-26	-26
Days Maximum Temp. ≥ 90°F	0	0	0	1	3	12	21	17	8	1	0	0	63
Days Maximum Temp. ≤ 32°F	9	6	2	0	0	0	0	0	0	0	2	8	27
Days Minimum Temp. ≤ 32°F	30	24	19	6	0	0	0	0	0	5	18	29	131
Days Minimum Temp. ≤ 0°F	2	2	0	0	0	0	0	0	0	0	0	2	6
Heating Degree Days (base 65°F)	1,114	898	681	353	113	10	0	2	62	309	705	1,079	5,326
Cooling Degree Days (base 65°F)	0	0	1	21	86	293	470	403	181	22	0	0	1,477
Mean Precipitation (in.)	0.53	0.58	1.87	2.23	3.87	3.43	3.74	3.18	2.01	1.93	1.18	0.67	25.22
Extreme Maximum Daily Precip. (in.)	0.77	0.94	2.12	2.38	3.16	3.54	3.68	2.77	2.68	3.00	3.20	0.81	3.68
Days With ≥ 0.1" Precipitation	2	2	4	5	7	6	6	5	4	4	3	2	50
Days With ≥ 0.5" Precipitation	0	0	1	1	3	2	3	2	2	1	1	0	16
Days With ≥ 1.0" Precipitation	0	0	0	1	1	1	1	1	0	1	0	0	6
Mean Snowfall (in.)	4.0	4.3	2.7	0.7	trace	0.0	0.0	0.0	0.2	0.5	1.8	3.3	17.5
Maximum Snow Depth (in.)	12	14	9	6	trace	0	0	0	4	11	8	10	14
Days With ≥ 1.0" Snow Depth	9	8	2	0	0	0	0	0	0	0	2	7	28

Troy 2 E *Doniphan County* Elevation: 1,060 ft. Latitude: 39° 47' N Longitude: 95° 05' W

	JAN	FEB	MAR	APR	MAY	JUN	JUL	AUG	SEP	OCT	NOV	DEC	YEAR
Mean Maximum Temp. (°F)	37.3	42.3	54.4	65.6	74.9	83.3	87.6	86.6	79.3	67.3	52.7	38.9	64.2
Mean Temp. (°F)	27.9	32.2	43.0	54.0	64.1	72.8	77.3	75.7	67.5	55.8	42.7	30.0	53.6
Mean Minimum Temp. (°F)	18.4	22.1	31.6	42.4	53.2	62.3	66.9	64.7	55.6	44.3	32.7	21.1	42.9
Extreme Maximum Temp. (°F)	71	78	89	92	94	103	105	106	100	95	83	70	106
Extreme Minimum Temp. (°F)	-18	-18	-13	18	26	42	48	44	30	17	-1	-22	-22
Days Maximum Temp. ≥ 90°F	0	0	0	0	1	5	12	11	3	0	0	0	32
Days Maximum Temp. ≤ 32°F	11	7	2	0	0	0	0	0	0	0	2	9	31
Days Minimum Temp. ≤ 32°F	28	22	17	5	0	0	0	0	0	4	15	27	118
Days Minimum Temp. ≤ 0°F	3	2	0	0	0	0	0	0	0	0	0	2	7
Heating Degree Days (base 65°F)	1,144	920	676	346	102	11	1	3	70	303	663	1,077	5,316
Cooling Degree Days (base 65°F)	0	0	3	24	80	252	389	341	150	25	1	0	1,265
Mean Precipitation (in.)	0.92	1.25	2.37	3.50	5.16	5.04	4.18	4.23	3.61	3.13	1.88	1.50	36.77
Extreme Maximum Daily Precip. (in.)	1.02	2.05	2.28	3.14	3.32	5.55	3.56	5.05	4.78	3.00	2.77	2.18	5.55
Days With ≥ 0.1" Precipitation	3	3	5	7	7	7	6	6	5	6	4	3	62
Days With ≥ 0.5" Precipitation	0	1	2	3	4	3	3	3	3	2	1	1	26
Days With ≥ 1.0" Precipitation	0	0	0	1	2	2	1	1	1	1	1	0	10
Mean Snowfall (in.)	5.0	4.7	2.5	0.5	0.0	0.0	0.0	0.0	0.0	0.2	1.1	5.2	19.2
Maximum Snow Depth (in.)	11	11	7	4	0	0	0	0	0	4	4	11	11
Days With ≥ 1.0" Snow Depth	10	8	2	0	0	0	0	0	0	0	1	8	29

The period of record for all cooperative weather station data is 1980 – 2009. See User Guide for detailed explanation of data.

Wellington *Sumner County* Elevation: 1,220 ft. Latitude: 37° 16' N Longitude: 97° 25' W

	JAN	FEB	MAR	APR	MAY	JUN	JUL	AUG	SEP	OCT	NOV	DEC	YEAR
Mean Maximum Temp. (°F)	43.5	48.3	58.2	68.1	77.1	86.9	93.3	92.4	83.7	70.8	57.4	44.6	68.7
Mean Temp. (°F)	32.5	36.7	46.3	55.8	65.9	75.5	81.3	80.3	71.2	58.4	45.9	34.1	57.0
Mean Minimum Temp. (°F)	21.4	25.0	34.3	43.5	54.6	64.1	69.2	68.2	58.7	45.9	34.2	23.6	45.2
Extreme Maximum Temp. (°F)	73	88	90	98	101	107	110	111	109	95	87	73	111
Extreme Minimum Temp. (°F)	-14	-10	1	19	33	43	49	47	28	14	9	-15	-15
Days Maximum Temp. ≥ 90°F	0	0	0	0	2	12	22	20	9	1	0	0	66
Days Maximum Temp. ≤ 32°F	7	4	1	0	0	0	0	0	0	0	1	5	18
Days Minimum Temp. ≤ 32°F	28	21	13	3	0	0	0	0	0	2	14	26	107
Days Minimum Temp. ≤ 0°F	1	1	0	0	0	0	0	0	0	0	0	1	3
Heating Degree Days (base 65°F)	1,000	794	576	294	79	6	0	1	41	236	569	950	4,546
Cooling Degree Days (base 65°F)	0	0	2	24	113	328	512	484	234	38	2	0	1,737
Mean Precipitation (in.)	1.08	1.39	3.00	3.00	4.64	5.45	3.33	3.69	2.63	3.09	1.82	1.32	34.44
Extreme Maximum Daily Precip. (in.)	2.99	2.12	2.06	3.44	4.68	4.84	2.90	4.79	3.36	4.31	2.83	1.51	4.84
Days With ≥ 0.1" Precipitation	2	3	5	5	7	7	5	5	5	5	3	3	55
Days With ≥ 0.5" Precipitation	1	1	2	2	3	4	2	3	2	2	1	1	24
Days With ≥ 1.0" Precipitation	0	0	1	1	1	2	1	1	1	1	1	0	10
Mean Snowfall (in.)	2.9	3.8	1.8	trace	0.0	0.0	0.0	0.0	0.0	trace	0.5	3.4	12.4
Maximum Snow Depth (in.)	14	14	9	trace	1	0	0	0	0	trace	4	8	14
Days With ≥ 1.0" Snow Depth	4	4	1	0	0	0	0	0	0	0	0	4	13

Winfield No. 1 *Cowley County* Elevation: 1,180 ft. Latitude: 37° 14' N Longitude: 96° 58' W

	JAN	FEB	MAR	APR	MAY	JUN	JUL	AUG	SEP	OCT	NOV	DEC	YEAR
Mean Maximum Temp. (°F)	44.5	49.8	59.6	69.2	77.6	86.1	92.2	92.0	83.1	71.1	57.9	45.8	69.1
Mean Temp. (°F)	33.4	37.9	47.2	56.7	66.3	74.9	80.7	79.9	70.9	58.7	46.4	35.3	57.4
Mean Minimum Temp. (°F)	22.3	25.9	34.8	44.2	55.0	63.7	69.1	67.6	58.8	46.3	34.8	24.6	45.6
Extreme Maximum Temp. (°F)	75	88	91	94	98	109	110	112	110	94	85	73	112
Extreme Minimum Temp. (°F)	-13	-12	0	20	31	40	51	45	31	12	6	-15	-15
Days Maximum Temp. ≥ 90°F	0	0	0	1	2	10	21	20	8	1	0	0	63
Days Maximum Temp. ≤ 32°F	6	3	1	0	0	0	0	0	0	0	1	4	15
Days Minimum Temp. ≤ 32°F	27	21	13	3	0	0	0	0	0	2	13	24	103
Days Minimum Temp. ≤ 0°F	1	1	0	0	0	0	0	0	0	0	0	1	3
Heating Degree Days (base 65°F)	971	761	549	273	69	5	0	0	39	227	554	915	4,363
Cooling Degree Days (base 65°F)	0	0	4	31	119	309	493	468	222	39	2	0	1,687
Mean Precipitation (in.)	1.23	1.82	3.24	3.54	5.75	5.97	3.61	3.85	3.17	3.60	2.37	1.76	39.91
Extreme Maximum Daily Precip. (in.)	3.87	4.00	3.02	6.10	5.35	3.97	3.86	3.55	5.05	4.77	3.16	1.77	6.10
Days With ≥ 0.1" Precipitation	3	4	5	5	8	8	5	5	5	5	4	4	61
Days With ≥ 0.5" Precipitation	1	1	2	2	4	4	2	2	2	2	2	1	25
Days With ≥ 1.0" Precipitation	0	0	1	1	2	2	1	1	1	1	1	0	11
Mean Snowfall (in.)	***1.8***	3.0	1.2	trace	0.0	0.0	0.0	0.0	0.0	trace	0.3	2.9	***9.2***
Maximum Snow Depth (in.)	***6***	na	***4***	***1***	***0***	***0***	***0***	***0***	***0***	***trace***	***trace***	***7***	na
Days With ≥ 1.0" Snow Depth	***2***	2	0	0	0	0	0	0	0	0	0	2	***6***

The period of record for all cooperative weather station data is 1980 – 2009. See User Guide for detailed explanation of data.

Kansas Weather Station Rankings

Annual Extreme Maximum Temperature

Highest			Lowest		
Rank	Station Name	°F	Rank	Station Name	°F
1	Ness City	114	1	Troy 2 E	106
2	Alton 6 ESE	***113***	2	Lawrence	107
2	Ashland	113	2	Leoti 1 W	107
2	Cottonwood Falls	113	4	Emporia 3 NW	***108***
2	Hays 1 S	113	4	Garden City Exp Stn	108
6	Abilene 1 W	112	4	Leavenworth	108
6	Beloit	112	4	Olathe 3 E	108
6	Eskridge	***112***	8	Atchison	109
6	Eureka	112	8	Columbus 1 SW	109
6	Hugoton	112	8	Concordia Blosser Muni Arpt	109
6	Perry Lake	112	8	Goodland Renner Field	109
6	Wichita Mid-Continent Arpt	112	8	Mound Valley 3 WSW	109
6	Winfield No. 1	112	8	Ottawa	109
14	Atwood 2 SW	111	14	Anthony	110
14	Belleville	111	14	Cassoday	110
14	Clay Center	111	14	Cedar Bluff Dam 4 NNE	110
14	Coldwater	111	14	Centralia	110
14	Great Bend	111	14	Clinton Lake	110
14	Independence	111	14	Dodge City Municipal Arpt	110
14	Kingman	111	14	Fort Scott	110
14	Manhattan	111	14	Hill City 1 E	***110***
14	Newton 2 SW	111	14	Hutchinson 10 SW	110
14	Norton Dam	***111***	14	Lakin	110
14	Smith Center	111	14	Marysville	110
14	Wellington	111	14	Milford Lake	110

Annual Mean Maximum Temperature

Highest			Lowest		
Rank	Station Name	°F	Rank	Station Name	°F
1	Ashland	70.7	1	Eskridge	***64.1***
1	Coldwater	70.7	2	Troy 2 E	64.2
3	Anthony	69.9	3	Marysville	64.5
4	Hugoton	69.4	4	Clinton Lake	64.7
5	Great Bend	69.2	4	Perry Lake	64.7
5	Independence	69.2	6	Centralia	64.8
7	Winfield No. 1	69.1	7	Atchison	64.9
8	Kingman	69.0	7	Belleville	64.9
9	Ness City	68.8	9	Concordia Blosser Muni Arpt	65.0
10	Lakin	68.7	9	Goodland Renner Field	65.0
10	Wellington	68.7	11	Norton Dam	***65.1***
12	Abilene 1 W	68.5	12	Olathe 3 E	65.3
13	Eureka	68.4	13	Emporia 3 NW	***65.6***
14	Dodge City Municipal Arpt	68.1	13	Milford Lake	65.6
15	Wichita Mid-Continent Arpt	68.0	15	Atwood 2 SW	65.7
16	Garden City Exp Stn	67.9	16	Topeka Municipal Arpt	65.9
16	Mound Valley 3 WSW	67.9	17	Leavenworth	66.0
18	Cedar Bluff Dam 4 NNE	67.8	18	Beloit	66.2
19	Manhattan	67.7	19	Lawrence	***66.5***
20	Alton 6 ESE	***67.6***	19	Smith Center	66.5
20	Columbus 1 SW	67.6	21	Cassoday	66.8
20	Fort Scott	67.6	21	Clay Center	66.8
23	Newton 2 SW	67.5	21	Leoti 1 W	66.8
24	Hutchinson 10 SW	67.4	24	Hays 1 S	67.0
24	Ottawa	67.4	25	Cottonwood Falls	67.2

Rankings include 25 highest/lowest stations. If state has less than 25 stations, all stations are included. The period of record is 1980–2009. See User Guide for detailed explanation of data.

Annual Mean Temperature

Highest Rank	Station Name	°F	Lowest Rank	Station Name	°F
1	Anthony	58.2	1	Atwood 2 SW	50.9
1	Coldwater	58.2	2	Goodland Renner Field	51.4
3	Independence	57.9	3	Norton Dam	***51.7***
4	Winfield No. 1	57.4	4	Leoti 1 W	52.2
5	Columbus 1 SW	57.1	5	Hill City 1 E	***52.8***
6	Wellington	57.0	6	Marysville	52.9
6	Wichita Mid-Continent Arpt	57.0	7	Alton 6 ESE	***53.2***
8	Fort Scott	56.9	7	Eskridge	***53.2***
8	Great Bend	56.9	9	Belleville	53.4
10	Abilene 1 W	56.8	10	Centralia	53.6
10	Kingman	56.8	10	Garden City Exp Stn	53.6
12	Eureka	56.5	10	Troy 2 E	53.6
12	Lawrence	***56.5***	13	Concordia Blosser Muni Arpt	53.9
14	Newton 2 SW	56.4	14	Cedar Bluff Dam 4 NNE	54.0
14	Ottawa	56.4	14	Hays 1 S	54.0
16	Mound Valley 3 WSW	56.3	14	Perry Lake	54.0
17	Ashland	55.8	17	Clinton Lake	54.1
18	Cottonwood Falls	55.7	17	Smith Center	54.1
19	Dodge City Municipal Arpt	55.5	19	Beloit	54.2
19	Hugoton	55.5	19	Milford Lake	54.2
19	Manhattan	55.5	19	Ness City	54.2
19	Olathe 3 E	55.5	22	Lakin	54.5
23	Clay Center	55.4	23	Emporia 3 NW	***54.7***
23	Hutchinson 10 SW	55.4	24	Atchison	54.9
25	Leavenworth	55.2	25	Cassoday	55.0

Annual Mean Minimum Temperature

Highest Rank	Station Name	°F	Lowest Rank	Station Name	°F
1	Anthony	46.5	1	Atwood 2 SW	36.1
1	Columbus 1 SW	46.5	2	Leoti 1 W	37.6
1	Independence	46.5	3	Goodland Renner Field	37.8
4	Lawrence	***46.4***	4	Norton Dam	***38.1***
5	Fort Scott	46.2	5	Hill City 1 E	***38.3***
6	Wichita Mid-Continent Arpt	45.9	6	Alton 6 ESE	***38.6***
7	Coldwater	45.6	7	Garden City Exp Stn	39.3
7	Olathe 3 E	45.6	8	Ness City	39.6
7	Winfield No. 1	45.6	9	Cedar Bluff Dam 4 NNE	40.2
10	Newton 2 SW	45.3	10	Lakin	40.3
10	Ottawa	45.3	11	Ashland	40.9
12	Wellington	45.2	11	Hays 1 S	40.9
13	Abilene 1 W	44.9	13	Marysville	41.2
13	Atchison	44.9	14	Hugoton	41.5
15	Kingman	44.7	15	Belleville	41.7
16	Mound Valley 3 WSW	44.6	15	Smith Center	41.7
17	Eureka	44.5	17	Beloit	42.2
18	Great Bend	44.4	17	Eskridge	***42.2***
18	Leavenworth	44.4	19	Centralia	42.5
20	Cottonwood Falls	44.2	20	Milford Lake	42.7
21	Clay Center	44.0	21	Dodge City Municipal Arpt	42.8
21	Topeka Municipal Arpt	44.0	22	Concordia Blosser Muni Arpt	42.9
23	Emporia 3 NW	***43.7***	22	Troy 2 E	42.9
24	Clinton Lake	43.4	24	Cassoday	43.3
25	Cassoday	43.3	24	Hutchinson 10 SW	43.3

 Rankings include 25 highest/lowest stations. If state has less than 25 stations, all stations are included. The period of record is 1980–2009. See User Guide for detailed explanation of data.

Annual Extreme Minimum Temperature

Highest

Rank	Station Name	°F
1	Anthony	-15
1	Columbus 1 SW	-15
1	Wellington	-15
1	Winfield No. 1	-15
5	Independence	-16
5	Lakin	-16
7	Coldwater	-17
7	Kingman	-17
9	Eureka	-18
9	Fort Scott	-18
9	Hugoton	-18
12	Ashland	-19
12	Hutchinson 10 SW	-19
14	Hays 1 S	-20
14	Leoti 1 W	-20
14	Mound Valley 3 WSW	-20
14	Newton 2 SW	-20
18	Atchison	-21
18	Dodge City Municipal Arpt	-21
18	Great Bend	-21
18	Lawrence	-21
18	Milford Lake	-21
18	Wichita Mid-Continent Arpt	-21
24	Cassoday	-22
24	Cottonwood Falls	-22

Lowest

Rank	Station Name	°F
1	Alton 6 ESE	***-31***
2	Norton Dam	***-28***
3	Goodland Renner Field	-27
3	Leavenworth	-27
3	Marysville	-27
6	Atwood 2 SW	-26
6	Beloit	-26
6	Concordia Blosser Muni Arpt	-26
6	Hill City 1 E	***-26***
6	Smith Center	-26
6	Topeka Municipal Arpt	-26
12	Belleville	-25
12	Centralia	-25
12	Clinton Lake	-25
12	Eskridge	***-25***
12	Ness City	-25
17	Abilene 1 W	-24
17	Cedar Bluff Dam 4 NNE	-24
17	Clay Center	-24
20	Perry Lake	-23
21	Cassoday	-22
21	Cottonwood Falls	-22
21	Emporia 3 NW	***-22***
21	Garden City Exp Stn	-22
21	Manhattan	-22

July Mean Maximum Temperature

Highest

Rank	Station Name	°F
1	Ashland	94.9
2	Anthony	94.4
3	Ness City	94.0
4	Great Bend	93.9
4	Kingman	93.9
6	Abilene 1 W	93.8
7	Coldwater	93.7
7	Lakin	93.7
9	Alton 6 ESE	93.5
10	Wellington	93.3
11	Dodge City Municipal Arpt	93.2
12	Cedar Bluff Dam 4 NNE	93.0
12	Smith Center	93.0
14	Hugoton	92.9
15	Wichita Mid-Continent Arpt	92.8
16	Newton 2 SW	92.7
17	Beloit	92.6
17	Hays 1 S	92.6
17	Hill City 1 E	***92.6***
20	Clay Center	92.3
20	Garden City Exp Stn	92.3
20	Hutchinson 10 SW	92.3
23	Winfield No. 1	92.2
24	Atwood 2 SW	92.0
24	Manhattan	92.0

Lowest

Rank	Station Name	°F
1	Troy 2 E	87.6
2	Eskridge	***88.1***
3	Clinton Lake	88.5
4	Olathe 3 E	88.6
5	Perry Lake	88.8
6	Atchison	89.0
7	Emporia 3 NW	89.1
8	Centralia	89.4
9	Lawrence	89.8
9	Marysville	89.8
9	Topeka Municipal Arpt	89.8
12	Columbus 1 SW	89.9
13	Goodland Renner Field	90.1
14	Cassoday	90.2
14	Leavenworth	90.2
16	Milford Lake	90.3
16	Mound Valley 3 WSW	90.3
18	Cottonwood Falls	90.4
19	Belleville	90.7
20	Ottawa	90.8
21	Concordia Blosser Muni Arpt	91.0
21	Fort Scott	91.0
23	Independence	91.4
24	Eureka	91.5
25	Norton Dam	***91.7***

Rankings include 25 highest/lowest stations. If state has less than 25 stations, all stations are included. The period of record is 1980–2009. See User Guide for detailed explanation of data.

January Mean Minimum Temperature

Highest Rank	Station Name	°F	Lowest Rank	Station Name	°F
1	Anthony	24.0	1	Atwood 2 SW	13.7
2	Columbus 1 SW	23.8	2	Alton 6 ESE	14.3
3	Independence	23.4	3	Norton Dam	14.7
4	Coldwater	23.0	4	Hill City 1 E	*15.2*
5	Lawrence	22.4	5	Marysville	15.6
6	Fort Scott	22.3	6	Leoti 1 W	15.9
6	Winfield No. 1	22.3	7	Ness City	16.2
8	Wichita Mid-Continent Arpt	22.0	8	Cedar Bluff Dam 4 NNE	16.4
9	Kingman	21.7	8	Garden City Exp Stn	16.4
10	Ottawa	21.6	8	Hays 1 S	16.4
11	Great Bend	21.5	11	Ashland	17.0
11	Olathe 3 E	21.5	11	Goodland Renner Field	17.0
13	Newton 2 SW	21.4	13	Belleville	17.3
13	Wellington	21.4	14	Smith Center	17.5
15	Mound Valley 3 WSW	21.2	15	Beloit	17.7
16	Eureka	21.1	16	Centralia	18.1
17	Abilene 1 W	20.9	16	Eskridge	*18.1*
18	Atchison	20.3	16	Lakin	18.1
18	Dodge City Municipal Arpt	20.3	19	Milford Lake	18.2
18	Leavenworth	20.3	19	Perry Lake	18.2
21	Cottonwood Falls	20.1	21	Clinton Lake	18.4
22	Hugoton	19.9	21	Troy 2 E	18.4
23	Emporia 3 NW	*19.7*	23	Cassoday	18.9
24	Topeka Municipal Arpt	19.6	24	Concordia Blosser Muni Arpt	19.0
25	Hutchinson 10 SW	19.3	24	Manhattan	19.0

Number of Days Annually Maximum Temperature ≥ 90°F

Highest Rank	Station Name	Days	Lowest Rank	Station Name	Days
1	Ashland	79	1	Eskridge	*31*
2	Anthony	74	2	Troy 2 E	32
2	Ness City	74	3	Olathe 3 E	33
4	Lakin	73	4	Clinton Lake	35
5	Great Bend	71	5	Atchison	36
6	Coldwater	70	6	Centralia	39
6	Kingman	70	6	Perry Lake	39
8	Hugoton	68	8	Emporia 3 NW	*43*
9	Abilene 1 W	67	8	Leavenworth	43
9	Dodge City Municipal Arpt	67	10	Cassoday	45
11	Alton 6 ESE	*66*	10	Columbus 1 SW	45
11	Wellington	66	10	Lawrence	45
13	Garden City Exp Stn	65	10	Milford Lake	45
14	Cedar Bluff Dam 4 NNE	63	10	Topeka Municipal Arpt	45
14	Hays 1 S	63	15	Marysville	46
14	Hill City 1 E	*63*	16	Belleville	48
14	Smith Center	63	17	Cottonwood Falls	49
14	Wichita Mid-Continent Arpt	63	18	Concordia Blosser Muni Arpt	50
14	Winfield No. 1	63	18	Goodland Renner Field	50
20	Atwood 2 SW	62	18	Ottawa	50
20	Hutchinson 10 SW	62	21	Mound Valley 3 WSW	51
20	Newton 2 SW	62	22	Fort Scott	54
23	Beloit	59	23	Eureka	55
23	Clay Center	59	23	Norton Dam	*55*
23	Manhattan	59	25	Independence	58

Rankings include 25 highest/lowest stations. If state has less than 25 stations, all stations are included. The period of record is 1980–2009. See User Guide for detailed explanation of data.

Number of Days Annually Maximum Temperature ≤ 32°F

Highest Rank	Highest Station Name	Highest Days	Lowest Rank	Lowest Station Name	Lowest Days
1	Marysville	31	1	Anthony	14
1	Troy 2 E	31	1	Coldwater	14
3	Belleville	30	1	Independence	14
3	Concordia Blosser Muni Arpt	30	4	Hugoton	15
3	Norton Dam	*30*	4	Winfield No. 1	15
6	Centralia	29	6	Ashland	16
6	Eskridge	*29*	7	Columbus 1 SW	17
8	Clinton Lake	28	7	Great Bend	17
8	Perry Lake	28	7	Kingman	17
10	Atchison	27	10	Abilene 1 W	18
10	Beloit	27	10	Eureka	18
10	Smith Center	27	10	Mound Valley 3 WSW	18
13	Atwood 2 SW	26	10	Wellington	18
13	Milford Lake	26	14	Lakin	19
15	Goodland Renner Field	25	14	Wichita Mid-Continent Arpt	19
15	Hays 1 S	25	16	Cassoday	20
17	Clay Center	24	16	Fort Scott	20
17	Emporia 3 NW	*24*	16	Ottawa	20
17	Hill City 1 E	*24*	19	Cottonwood Falls	21
17	Leoti 1 W	24	19	Dodge City Municipal Arpt	21
17	Topeka Municipal Arpt	24	19	Garden City Exp Stn	21
22	Alton 6 ESE	*23*	19	Hutchinson 10 SW	21
22	Leavenworth	23	19	Lawrence	21
22	Olathe 3 E	23	19	Manhattan	21
25	Cedar Bluff Dam 4 NNE	22	19	Ness City	21

Number of Days Annually Minimum Temperature ≤ 32°F

Highest Rank	Highest Station Name	Highest Days	Lowest Rank	Lowest Station Name	Lowest Days
1	Atwood 2 SW	167	1	Anthony	95
2	Leoti 1 W	157	1	Lawrence	95
3	Goodland Renner Field	156	3	Columbus 1 SW	96
4	Hill City 1 E	*155*	4	Independence	97
5	Alton 6 ESE	*151*	5	Fort Scott	100
5	Norton Dam	*151*	6	Olathe 3 E	102
7	Garden City Exp Stn	147	7	Coldwater	103
8	Cedar Bluff Dam 4 NNE	144	7	Winfield No. 1	103
9	Ness City	143	9	Ottawa	104
10	Ashland	139	9	Wichita Mid-Continent Arpt	104
10	Lakin	139	11	Atchison	105
12	Hays 1 S	137	12	Wellington	107
13	Marysville	134	13	Leavenworth	108
14	Hugoton	131	13	Newton 2 SW	108
14	Smith Center	131	15	Abilene 1 W	111
16	Beloit	130	15	Eureka	111
17	Belleville	129	17	Great Bend	112
18	Dodge City Municipal Arpt	124	17	Mound Valley 3 WSW	112
19	Centralia	123	19	Cottonwood Falls	113
19	Hutchinson 10 SW	123	19	Kingman	113
19	Milford Lake	123	21	Topeka Municipal Arpt	114
22	Eskridge	*122*	22	Clay Center	115
23	Manhattan	120	23	Clinton Lake	116
24	Concordia Blosser Muni Arpt	119	23	Perry Lake	116
25	Cassoday	118	25	Emporia 3 NW	*117*

Number of Days Annually Minimum Temperature ≤ 0°F

Highest Rank	Station Name	Days	Lowest Rank	Station Name	Days
1	Alton 6 ESE	*9*	1	Anthony	1
1	Atwood 2 SW	9	2	Columbus 1 SW	2
1	Marysville	9	3	Ashland	3
1	Norton Dam	*9*	3	Cassoday	3
5	Hill City 1 E	*8*	3	Coldwater	3
6	Belleville	7	3	Cottonwood Falls	3
6	Centralia	7	3	Dodge City Municipal Arpt	3
6	Troy 2 E	7	3	Emporia 3 NW	*3*
9	Beloit	6	3	Eureka	3
9	Clinton Lake	6	3	Fort Scott	3
9	Concordia Blosser Muni Arpt	6	3	Great Bend	3
9	Eskridge	*6*	3	Hugoton	3
9	Garden City Exp Stn	6	3	Hutchinson 10 SW	3
9	Goodland Renner Field	6	3	Independence	3
9	Hays 1 S	6	3	Kingman	3
9	Leoti 1 W	6	3	Lawrence	3
9	Milford Lake	6	3	Mound Valley 3 WSW	3
9	Ness City	6	3	Newton 2 SW	3
9	Perry Lake	6	3	Olathe 3 E	3
9	Smith Center	6	3	Ottawa	3
21	Cedar Bluff Dam 4 NNE	5	3	Wellington	3
21	Clay Center	5	3	Wichita Mid-Continent Arpt	3
21	Leavenworth	5	3	Winfield No. 1	3
21	Manhattan	5	24	Abilene 1 W	4
21	Topeka Municipal Arpt	5	24	Atchison	4

Number of Annual Heating Degree Days

Highest Rank	Station Name	Num.	Lowest Rank	Station Name	Num.
1	Atwood 2 SW	6,070	1	Coldwater	4,138
2	Norton Dam	*5,918*	2	Independence	4,194
3	Goodland Renner Field	5,826	3	Anthony	4,204
4	Leoti 1 W	5,640	4	Columbus 1 SW	4,361
5	Marysville	5,637	5	Winfield No. 1	4,363
6	Hill City 1 E	*5,621*	6	Fort Scott	4,510
7	Alton 6 ESE	*5,563*	7	Wellington	4,546
8	Belleville	5,480	8	Wichita Mid-Continent Arpt	4,554
9	Eskridge	*5,411*	9	Eureka	4,557
10	Centralia	5,350	10	Great Bend	4,565
11	Hays 1 S	5,346	11	Kingman	4,577
12	Concordia Blosser Muni Arpt	5,335	12	Mound Valley 3 WSW	4,594
13	Garden City Exp Stn	5,330	13	Ottawa	4,601
14	Smith Center	5,326	14	Abilene 1 W	4,617
15	Beloit	5,322	15	Lawrence	*4,621*
16	Troy 2 E	5,316	16	Newton 2 SW	4,710
17	Cedar Bluff Dam 4 NNE	5,282	17	Hugoton	4,768
18	Ness City	5,251	18	Cottonwood Falls	4,786
19	Milford Lake	5,241	19	Olathe 3 E	4,806
20	Perry Lake	5,239	20	Ashland	4,818
21	Clinton Lake	5,216	21	Dodge City Municipal Arpt	4,889
22	Lakin	5,105	22	Manhattan	4,921
23	Emporia 3 NW	*5,050*	23	Leavenworth	4,924
24	Atchison	5,012	24	Hutchinson 10 SW	4,943
25	Topeka Municipal Arpt	4,995	25	Cassoday	4,954

 Rankings include 25 highest/lowest stations. If state has less than 25 stations, all stations are included. The period of record is 1980–2009. See User Guide for detailed explanation of data.

Number of Annual Cooling Degree Days

Highest			Lowest		
Rank	Station Name	Num.	Rank	Station Name	Num.
1	Anthony	1,854	1	Goodland Renner Field	978
2	Coldwater	1,780	2	Atwood 2 SW	1,053
3	Wellington	1,737	3	Leoti 1 W	1,085
4	Abilene 1 W	1,733	4	Norton Dam	***1,178***
5	Wichita Mid-Continent Arpt	1,729	5	Eskridge	***1,200***
6	Kingman	1,710	6	Hill City 1 E	***1,258***
7	Independence	1,700	7	Troy 2 E	1,265
8	Great Bend	1,699	8	Garden City Exp Stn	1,289
9	Newton 2 SW	1,691	9	Centralia	1,315
10	Winfield No. 1	1,687	10	Marysville	1,327
11	Fort Scott	1,672	11	Belleville	1,342
12	Lawrence	***1,615***	12	Perry Lake	1,347
13	Clay Center	1,610	13	Clinton Lake	1,352
14	Ashland	1,584	14	Alton 6 ESE	***1,357***
15	Ottawa	1,571	15	Cedar Bluff Dam 4 NNE	1,387
16	Columbus 1 SW	1,570	16	Emporia 3 NW	***1,398***
17	Eureka	1,562	16	Lakin	1,398
18	Manhattan	1,559	16	Milford Lake	1,398
19	Hutchinson 10 SW	1,546	19	Hugoton	1,405
20	Dodge City Municipal Arpt	1,524	20	Concordia Blosser Muni Arpt	1,409
21	Mound Valley 3 WSW	1,517	21	Cassoday	1,426
22	Cottonwood Falls	1,514	22	Ness City	1,427
23	Beloit	1,510	23	Atchison	1,438
24	Smith Center	1,477	24	Olathe 3 E	1,440
25	Leavenworth	1,475	25	Hays 1 S	1,444

Annual Precipitation

Highest			Lowest		
Rank	Station Name	Inches	Rank	Station Name	Inches
1	Mound Valley 3 WSW	45.21	1	Hugoton	18.83
2	Columbus 1 SW	45.09	2	Lakin	18.91
3	Fort Scott	44.40	3	Garden City Exp Stn	19.30
4	Independence	44.14	4	Leoti 1 W	19.72
5	Leavenworth	41.03	5	Goodland Renner Field	19.80
6	Olathe 3 E	41.00	6	Dodge City Municipal Arpt	21.45
7	Winfield No. 1	39.91	7	Cedar Bluff Dam 4 NNE	22.05
8	Ottawa	39.89	8	Ness City	22.10
9	Lawrence	39.46	9	Ashland	22.96
10	Eureka	39.23	10	Atwood 2 SW	23.08
11	Perry Lake	38.72	10	Hill City 1 E	23.08
12	Cottonwood Falls	37.42	12	Hays 1 S	23.24
13	Emporia 3 NW	***37.29***	13	Smith Center	25.22
14	Clinton Lake	37.21	14	Norton Dam	***25.43***
15	Eskridge	***36.98***	15	Coldwater	25.63
16	Troy 2 E	36.77	16	Great Bend	26.17
17	Atchison	36.66	17	Alton 6 ESE	26.99
18	Topeka Municipal Arpt	36.34	18	Concordia Blosser Muni Arpt	27.47
19	Manhattan	35.57	19	Beloit	27.73
20	Cassoday	34.80	20	Hutchinson 10 SW	30.21
21	Centralia	34.70	21	Belleville	30.39
22	Wellington	34.44	22	Clay Center	30.45
23	Anthony	33.09	23	Kingman	31.57
24	Marysville	33.06	24	Newton 2 SW	32.02
25	Abilene 1 W	32.67	25	Wichita Mid-Continent Arpt	32.37

Rankings include 25 highest/lowest stations. If state has less than 25 stations, all stations are included. The period of record is 1980–2009. See User Guide for detailed explanation of data.

Annual Extreme Maximum Daily Precipitation

Highest Rank	Station Name	Inches	Lowest Rank	Station Name	Inches
1	Fort Scott	12.50	1	Garden City Exp Stn	2.80
2	Wichita Mid-Continent Arpt	10.31	2	Ness City	***3.15***
3	Olathe 3 E	8.00	3	Hugoton	3.30
4	Independence	7.69	3	Norton Dam	***3.30***
5	Columbus 1 SW	7.58	5	Concordia Blosser Muni Arpt	3.32
6	Anthony	7.49	6	Smith Center	3.68
7	Beloit	7.05	7	Hill City 1 E	3.92
8	Eureka	6.96	8	Lakin	4.03
9	Mound Valley 3 WSW	6.83	9	Dodge City Municipal Arpt	4.13
10	Perry Lake	6.59	10	Cedar Bluff Dam 4 NNE	4.15
11	Belleville	6.50	10	Goodland Renner Field	4.15
12	Clinton Lake	6.48	12	Alton 6 ESE	***4.16***
13	Great Bend	6.40	13	Atwood 2 SW	4.25
14	Leavenworth	6.23	14	Ashland	4.40
15	Cassoday	6.10	15	Leoti 1 W	***4.43***
15	Winfield No. 1	6.10	16	Atchison	4.45
17	Abilene 1 W	5.85	16	Coldwater	4.45
18	Ottawa	5.76	18	Hutchinson 10 SW	4.83
19	Hays 1 S	5.64	19	Wellington	4.84
20	Lawrence	5.61	20	Eskridge	***4.92***
20	Topeka Municipal Arpt	5.61	20	Milford Lake	***4.92***
22	Cottonwood Falls	5.55	22	Kingman	4.94
22	Troy 2 E	5.55	23	Clay Center	4.97
24	Emporia 3 NW	***5.51***	24	Manhattan	5.05
25	Newton 2 SW	5.45	24	Marysville	5.05

Number of Days Annually With ≥ 0.1 Inches of Precipitation

Highest Rank	Station Name	Days	Lowest Rank	Station Name	Days
1	Columbus 1 SW	68	1	Hugoton	37
2	Mound Valley 3 WSW	67	1	Lakin	37
3	Fort Scott	65	3	Leoti 1 W	39
3	Olathe 3 E	65	4	Garden City Exp Stn	41
5	Independence	64	5	Cedar Bluff Dam 4 NNE	42
5	Lawrence	64	5	Goodland Renner Field	42
5	Ottawa	64	5	Ness City	42
8	Atchison	62	8	Ashland	43
8	Clinton Lake	62	8	Coldwater	43
8	Leavenworth	62	8	Dodge City Municipal Arpt	43
8	Troy 2 E	62	8	Norton Dam	***43***
12	Winfield No. 1	61	12	Great Bend	44
13	Manhattan	60	13	Hays 1 S	45
13	Perry Lake	60	14	Atwood 2 SW	46
13	Topeka Municipal Arpt	60	14	Hill City 1 E	46
16	Eskridge	***59***	16	Hutchinson 10 SW	48
16	Eureka	59	17	Alton 6 ESE	***50***
18	Centralia	58	17	Smith Center	50
18	Marysville	58	19	Concordia Blosser Muni Arpt	51
20	Cottonwood Falls	57	19	Kingman	51
20	Emporia 3 NW	***57***	19	Newton 2 SW	51
22	Wellington	55	22	Anthony	52
23	Milford Lake	54	22	Belleville	52
24	Abilene 1 W	53	24	Abilene 1 W	53
24	Beloit	53	24	Beloit	53

 Rankings include 25 highest/lowest stations. If state has less than 25 stations, all stations are included. The period of record is 1980–2009. See User Guide for detailed explanation of data.

Number of Days Annually With ≥ 0.5 Inches of Precipitation					
Highest			Lowest		
Rank	Station Name	Days	Rank	Station Name	Days
1	Fort Scott	30	1	Dodge City Municipal Arpt	12
1	Independence	30	1	Garden City Exp Stn	12
1	Mound Valley 3 WSW	30	1	Goodland Renner Field	12
4	Lawrence	28	1	Hugoton	12
4	Leavenworth	28	1	Lakin	12
6	Columbus 1 SW	27	1	Leoti 1 W	12
6	Perry Lake	27	1	Ness City	12
8	Emporia 3 NW	*26*	8	Cedar Bluff Dam 4 NNE	13
8	Eureka	26	9	Ashland	14
8	Olathe 3 E	26	9	Hays 1 S	14
8	Ottawa	26	9	Hill City 1 E	14
8	Troy 2 E	26	12	Atwood 2 SW	15
13	Cottonwood Falls	25	13	Great Bend	16
13	Winfield No. 1	25	13	Norton Dam	*16*
15	Atchison	24	13	Smith Center	16
15	Cassoday	24	16	Coldwater	18
15	Manhattan	24	16	Concordia Blosser Muni Arpt	18
15	Topeka Municipal Arpt	24	18	Alton 6 ESE	*19*
15	Wellington	24	18	Beloit	19
15	Wichita Mid-Continent Arpt	24	18	Hutchinson 10 SW	19
21	Clinton Lake	23	21	Belleville	20
21	Eskridge	*23*	22	Clay Center	21
21	Marysville	23	22	Milford Lake	21
24	Abilene 1 W	22	24	Abilene 1 W	22
24	Anthony	22	24	Anthony	22

Number of Days Annually With ≥ 1.0 Inches of Precipitation					
Highest			Lowest		
Rank	Station Name	Days	Rank	Station Name	Days
1	Columbus 1 SW	13	1	Hays 1 S	3
1	Fort Scott	13	2	Cedar Bluff Dam 4 NNE	4
1	Independence	13	2	Garden City Exp Stn	4
1	Mound Valley 3 WSW	13	2	Goodland Renner Field	4
5	Cottonwood Falls	12	2	Hill City 1 E	4
6	Eureka	11	2	Hugoton	4
6	Lawrence	11	2	Lakin	4
6	Olathe 3 E	11	2	Leoti 1 W	4
6	Perry Lake	11	9	Ashland	5
6	Winfield No. 1	11	9	Atwood 2 SW	5
11	Atchison	10	9	Beloit	5
11	Cassoday	10	9	Coldwater	5
11	Emporia 3 NW	*10*	9	Dodge City Municipal Arpt	5
11	Eskridge	*10*	9	Great Bend	5
11	Leavenworth	10	9	Ness City	5
11	Ottawa	10	16	Belleville	6
11	Troy 2 E	10	16	Concordia Blosser Muni Arpt	6
11	Wellington	10	16	Norton Dam	*6*
19	Abilene 1 W	9	16	Smith Center	6
19	Anthony	9	20	Alton 6 ESE	7
19	Kingman	9	20	Clay Center	7
19	Newton 2 SW	9	22	Centralia	8
19	Topeka Municipal Arpt	9	22	Clinton Lake	8
19	Wichita Mid-Continent Arpt	9	22	Hutchinson 10 SW	8
25	Centralia	8	22	Manhattan	8

Rankings include 25 highest/lowest stations. If state has less than 25 stations, all stations are included. The period of record is 1980–2009. See User Guide for detailed explanation of data.

Annual Snowfall

Highest Rank	Station Name	Inches	Lowest Rank	Station Name	Inches
1	Goodland Renner Field	38.2	1	Emporia 3 NW	***4.6***
2	Centralia	34.3	2	Milford Lake	5.1
3	Atwood 2 SW	***31.7***	3	Mound Valley 3 WSW	***9.2***
4	Leoti 1 W	28.0	3	Winfield No. 1	***9.2***
5	Dodge City Municipal Arpt	21.3	5	Columbus 1 SW	9.7
6	Eskridge	***20.2***	6	Clinton Lake	9.8
6	Garden City Exp Stn	20.2	7	Cottonwood Falls	10.3
8	Hill City 1 E	20.0	8	Cassoday	10.8
9	Beloit	19.3	9	Newton 2 SW	***10.9***
10	Troy 2 E	19.2	10	Marysville	***11.2***
11	Atchison	18.6	11	Fort Scott	11.4
11	Hays 1 S	18.6	12	Ashland	11.7
13	Cedar Bluff Dam 4 NNE	18.4	13	Hugoton	***12.1***
13	Lakin	18.4	13	Independence	12.1
15	Norton Dam	***18.3***	15	Wellington	12.4
16	Coldwater	18.2	16	Anthony	***12.8***
16	Topeka Municipal Arpt	18.2	17	Ottawa	12.9
18	Alton 6 ESE	***18.1***	18	Kingman	***13.0***
18	Ness City	***18.1***	19	Eureka	13.2
20	Belleville	17.5	20	Hutchinson 10 SW	13.8
20	Smith Center	17.5	21	Abilene 1 W	13.9
22	Manhattan	17.2	21	Lawrence	13.9
23	Great Bend	16.9	23	Perry Lake	14.0
24	Clay Center	16.7	24	Leavenworth	***14.6***
25	Olathe 3 E	16.2	25	Wichita Mid-Continent Arpt	15.2

Annual Maximum Snow Depth

Highest Rank	Station Name	Inches	Lowest Rank	Station Name	Inches
1	Coldwater	27	1	Alton 6 ESE	***11***
2	Hill City 1 E	23	1	Atchison	11
3	Centralia	21	1	Clinton Lake	11
4	Goodland Renner Field	20	1	Eskridge	***11***
4	Ness City	***20***	1	Olathe 3 E	11
6	Atwood 2 SW	***19***	1	Perry Lake	11
6	Leoti 1 W	***19***	1	Troy 2 E	11
8	Clay Center	18	1	Wichita Mid-Continent Arpt	11
8	Lakin	***18***	9	Abilene 1 W	***12***
10	Ashland	***16***	9	Cottonwood Falls	12
11	Eureka	15	9	Garden City Exp Stn	***12***
11	Great Bend	15	9	Hays 1 S	12
11	Independence	15	9	Hutchinson 10 SW	12
11	Manhattan	15	9	Kingman	12
11	Milford Lake	15	9	Marysville	***12***
11	Norton Dam	***15***	9	Mound Valley 3 WSW	***12***
17	Anthony	***14***	17	Lawrence	13
17	Columbus 1 SW	14	18	Anthony	***14***
17	Dodge City Municipal Arpt	14	18	Columbus 1 SW	14
17	Fort Scott	14	18	Dodge City Municipal Arpt	14
17	Smith Center	14	18	Fort Scott	14
17	Topeka Municipal Arpt	14	18	Smith Center	14
17	Wellington	14	18	Topeka Municipal Arpt	14
24	Lawrence	13	18	Wellington	14
25	Abilene 1 W	***12***	25	Eureka	15

Rankings include 25 highest/lowest stations. If state has less than 25 stations, all stations are included. The period of record is 1980–2009. See User Guide for detailed explanation of data.

Number of Days Annually With ≥ 1.0 Inch Snow Depth

Highest			Lowest		
Rank	**Station Name**	**Days**	**Rank**	**Station Name**	**Days**
1	Centralia	34	1	Ottawa	***1***
1	Goodland Renner Field	34	2	Newton 2 SW	***5***
3	Norton Dam	***33***	3	Marysville	***6***
4	Troy 2 E	29	3	Mound Valley 3 WSW	***6***
5	Smith Center	28	3	Winfield No. 1	***6***
6	Leoti 1 W	27	6	Abilene 1 W	*7*
7	Atchison	26	6	Ashland	*7*
8	Alton 6 ESE	***25***	8	Anthony	***8***
8	Hays 1 S	25	8	Coldwater	8
8	Olathe 3 E	25	10	Cassoday	***9***
11	Great Bend	23	11	Cottonwood Falls	10
12	Eskridge	***22***	11	Fort Scott	10
12	Manhattan	22	11	Kingman	10
14	Clay Center	20	14	Columbus 1 SW	11
14	Topeka Municipal Arpt	20	15	Beloit	***12***
16	Dodge City Municipal Arpt	18	16	Independence	13
16	Hutchinson 10 SW	18	16	Lakin	13
16	Perry Lake	18	16	Milford Lake	13
19	Hill City 1 E	***17***	16	Wellington	13
20	Atwood 2 SW	***16***	20	Eureka	14
21	Clinton Lake	15	20	Lawrence	14
21	Garden City Exp Stn	***15***	20	Ness City	***14***
21	Wichita Mid-Continent Arpt	15	23	Clinton Lake	15
24	Eureka	14	23	Garden City Exp Stn	***15***
24	Lawrence	14	23	Wichita Mid-Continent Arpt	15

Rankings include 25 highest/lowest stations. If state has less than 25 stations, all stations are included. The period of record is 1980–2009. See User Guide for detailed explanation of data.

Significant Storm Events in Kansas: 2000 – 2009

Location or County	Date	Type	Mag.	Deaths	Injuries	Property Damage ($mil.)	Crop Damage ($mil.)
Labette	04/19/00	Tornado	F3	0	27	71.0	0.0
Barton	06/29/00	Hail	2.75 in.	0	5	20.0	0.0
Barton	04/21/01	Tornado	F4	1	28	43.0	0.0
Southeastern Kansas	01/30/02	Ice Storm	na	0	0	25.0	0.0
Pratt	05/07/02	Tornado	F2	0	0	20.0	0.0
Southeastern and South Central Kansas	02/23/03	Winter Storm	na	1	15	0.0	0.0
Wyandotte	05/04/03	Tornado	F4	2	30	15.5	0.0
Crawford	05/04/03	Tornado	F4	3	20	7.2	1.0
Cherokee	05/04/03	Tornado	F3	3	19	2.7	1.0
Chase	08/30/03	Flash Flood	na	6	0	0.2	0.0
Sumner	05/29/04	Tornado	F3	0	1	17.7	0.1
Central and South Central Kansas	01/04/05	Winter Storm	na	3	2	30.0	0.0
Barton	08/19/05	Thunderstorm Wind	75 mph	0	12	5.0	0.0
Sedgwick	04/24/06	Hail	3.00 in.	0	0	70.0	0.0
Central, South Central, and Southeast Kansas	07/16/06	Heat	na	5	0	0.0	0.0
Western Kansas	12/29/06	Winter Storm	na	0	0	21.0	0.0
Kiowa	05/04/07	Tornado	F5	11	63	250.0	0.0
Barton	05/05/07	Flash Flood	na	0	0	30.0	0.0
Montgomery	07/01/07	Flash Flood	na	1	0	81.1	0.0
Elk	07/01/07	Flash Flood	na	0	0	27.0	0.0
Wilson	07/01/07	Flash Flood	na	0	0	21.6	0.0
Miami	07/01/07	Flood	na	0	0	16.0	1.0
Reno County	12/10/07	Ice Storm	na	0	0	37.5	0.0
Marion County	12/10/07	Ice Storm	na	0	0	18.2	0.0
Dickinson	06/11/08	Tornado	F3	1	3	20.2	0.0
Butler	05/08/09	Thunderstorm Wind	81 mph	0	0	30.0	0.0
Sedgwick	07/08/09	Hail	2.75 in.	0	20	10.0	0.0

Note: Deaths, injuries, and damages are date and location specific.

KENTUCKY

PHYSICAL FEATURES. Kentucky has a land surface of 40,109 square miles. It is essentially an eroded plateau that slopes downward gradually to the southwest, with elevations ranging from about 400 feet above sea level at the western edge to 1,000 feet in the central districts, to above 4,000 feet near the southeastern border. There are seven major physiographic or natural regions.

The Bluegrass Region comprises about one-fifth of the State. The central area of this region is undulating to gently rolling. The outer area is more rolling and less uniform. Separating the two areas is a terrain that is hilly, with winding ridges and valleys and steep slopes.

The Knobs Region, named for its conical and flat-topped hills, comprises about one-tenth of the State. It forms a narrow crescent encircling the Bluegrass on the east, south, and west. Towards the Bluegrass the terrain is flat to rolling with scattered knobs and wide valleys, while the outer margin is rough.

The Eastern Mountains, also called the Cumberland Plateau, extends over the entire eastern fourth of the State. Ridges are high and sharp-crested there is little level land, and valleys are narrow. In the southeast the Pine and Cumberland Mountains comprise the highest and most rugged part of Kentucky.

The Pennyroyal Region or the Mississippean Plateaus Region is one of the three largest regions. Much of the surface is quite uniform, but as a whole is rather diverse. Much of the terrain is undulating to rolling. In some places it is hilly or cavernous. Subsurface drainage has created limestone sinks and karst terrain in much of the area.

The Western Coal Field is a small region. This area has extensive bottom lands in the valleys of the Ohio, Green, and Tradewater Rivers and many of their tributaries. There is also some undulating to gently rolling uplands.

The Cumberland-Tennessee Rivers Area is the smallest region. The topography is hilly and rough, except for the wide bottoms along the two major streams.

The Jackson Purchase is the extreme western area of Kentucky. In both elevation and relief it is lower than the other regions of the State, but it also has a varied surface. It is largely an upland plain which is mostly undulating to gently rolling, but is also level in places and hilly in others.

GENERAL CLIMATE. The climate of Kentucky is essentially continental in character, with rather wide extremes of temperature and precipitation. The State lies within the path of storms, in the belt of the westerly winds. The temperature generally varies as the storms move across the State. Thus in winter and summer, there are occasional cold and hot spells of short duration. In the spring and fall, the systems have a smaller frequency, temperatures are more consistent, and fewer extremes are experienced. Precipitation occurs with the systems which generally move from the west to east, or from summer thunderstorms. However, the greater portion of precipitation is due to the moisture-bearing low-pressure formations which move from southwest to northeast from the western Gulf of Mexico and frequently cross Kentucky. With warm moist tropical air predominating during the summer months, relative humidity remains consistently high during that season.

TEMPERATURE. The mean annual temperature ranges from 54°F. in the extreme north to 59°F. in the southwestern counties. July is usually the warmest month and January, the coldest. Extreme summer temperatures nearly always reach 100°F. or higher at most locations, but the frequencies of these high temperatures are low. Minimum temperatures of 0°F. or below can be expected during the months of December, January, and February at most locations, but the number of days with such temperatures is relatively small. Because of the State's geographic locations with reference to the center of the continent, the mid-winter cold waves from the Canadian Northwest usually have their intensity considerably modified by the time they reach Kentucky. In summer when the high pressure off the Florida coast is displaced westward from its normal position, extended periods of hot, sultry weather will occur. The spring and fall months are usually pleasant.

PRECIPITATION. Precipitation is generally plentiful. The fall season is generally the driest and the spring season the wettest. Approximately half of the average annual total occurs during the warm months of April to September. The average annual total in the State ranges from 36 inches in northern counties to 50 inches in the southern. Thunderstorms with high intensity rainfall are common during the spring and summer months, and rainfall during these storms in a 24-hour period frequently exceeds two to three inches, occasionally reaching five to six inches. Flash floods frequently result from the high intensity showers. Snowfall occurrence also varies from year to year but is common from November through March. Some snow has also been reported in the months of October and April. In some sections, the ground seldom remains covered with snow for more than a few days. The average annual snowfall for the State ranges from six to 10 inches in the southwest to 15 to 20 inches in the southeast.

WINDS. Winds in the State have an average velocity of seven to 12 m.p.h., and the prevailing direction is from south to southwest for the year. During the fall season some areas show a prevailing direction having a northerly component. The highest wind speeds usually range from 50 to 70 m.p.h., but in some storms (generally squalls attending thunderstorms), winds in gusts may occasionally exceed these speeds. A number of years may pass without a tornado, or several may visit the State in a single year. On the average, about one per year occurs somewhere in the State.

Thunderstorms may occur in any month, but they occur most frequently during the months March through September. The mean number of days with thunderstorms ranges approximately between 45 and 60. They are occasionally attended by damaging hail, but the area thus affected is nearly always small.

OTHER CLIMATIC ELEMENTS. Heavy fogs are rather rare in the State. The average number of days with heavy fogs varies between eight and 17 during the year with the majority occurring during the months of September through March inclusive.

The average date of the last spring freeze ranges from April 4 in the extreme west to May 5 in the mountain region in the extreme southeast; that of the first fall freeze, from October 11 in the Pennyroyal Region to October 30 near the lower Ohio River. The average length of the freeze-free period varies from 166 days on the southeastern plateau to 210 near the lower Ohio River.

The average number of days with clear and with partly cloudy skies is about the same and ranges between 115 and 120 days over the State. The number of days with cloudy skies averages about 130. The extreme northern section shows the greatest number of days with cloudy skies. The percentage of possible sunshine averages 35 to 50 for the winter months, 50 to 65 in the spring, 65 to 75 in the summer, and 55 to 65 in the fall. The largest percentage of possible sunshine is recorded in the extreme western section of the State.

The Ohio River forms the northern boundary and the Mississippi the western. All of the State is in the Ohio River Basin, except for a small section in the Jackson Purchase area that drains directly into the Mississippi. Kentucky lies in the path of rain producing lows moving from the west Gulf area northeastward. The flood season is in the winter and spring. Numerous flash floods occur from excessive rains and thunderstorms, particularly in the mountains of the eastern portion.

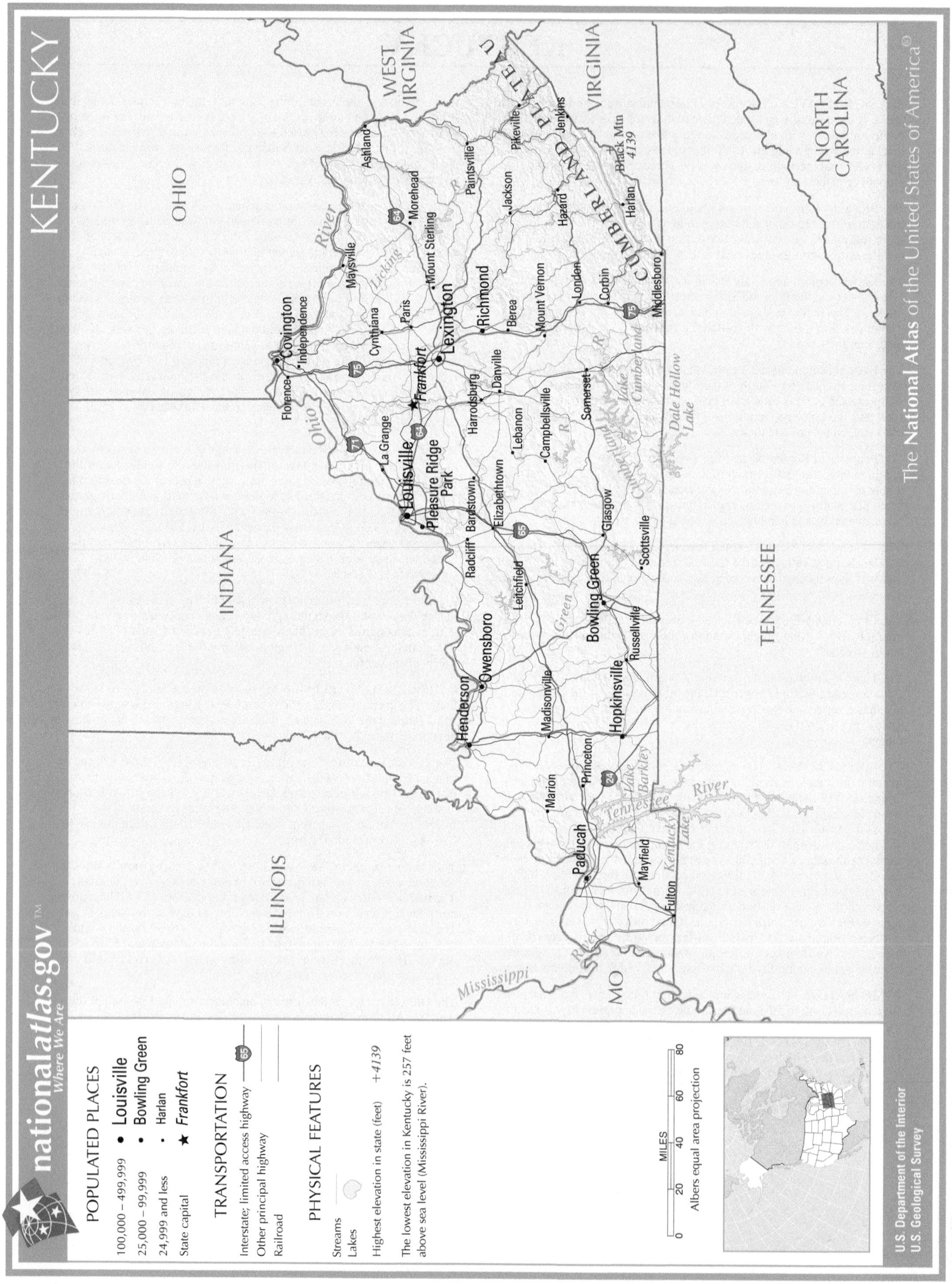
KENTUCKY
nationalatlas.gov™
Where We Are
POPULATED PLACES
100,000 – 499,999 • Louisville
25,000 – 99,999 • Bowling Green
24,999 and less • Harlan
State capital ★ Frankfort
TRANSPORTATION
Interstate; limited access highway 65
Other principal highway
Railroad
PHYSICAL FEATURES
Streams
Lakes
Highest elevation in state (feet) +4139
The lowest elevation in Kentucky is 257 feet above sea level (Mississippi River).
MILES
0 20 40 60 80
Albers equal area projection
U.S. Department of the Interior
U.S. Geological Survey
The National Atlas of the United States of America®
OHIO
INDIANA
ILLINOIS
MO
WEST VIRGINIA
VIRGINIA
NORTH CAROLINA
TENNESSEE
CUMBERLAND PLATEAU
Black Mtn 4139
Ohio River
Mississippi River
Tennessee River
Licking R
Green R
Cumberland R
Kentucky Lake
Lake Barkley
Lake Cumberland
Dale Hollow Lake
Covington
Independence
Florence
Ashland
Maysville
Morehead
Mount Sterling
Paintsville
Pikeville
Jenkins
Jackson
Hazard
Harlan
Cynthiana
Paris
Lexington
Frankfort
Richmond
Berea
Mount Vernon
London
Corbin
Middlesboro
Harrodsburg
Danville
Lebanon
Campbellsville
Somerset
La Grange
Louisville
Pleasure Ridge Park
Bardstown
Elizabethtown
Radcliff
Glasgow
Scottsville
Leitchfield
Bowling Green
Russellville
Owensboro
Henderson
Madisonville
Hopkinsville
Princeton
Marion
Paducah
Mayfield
Fulton

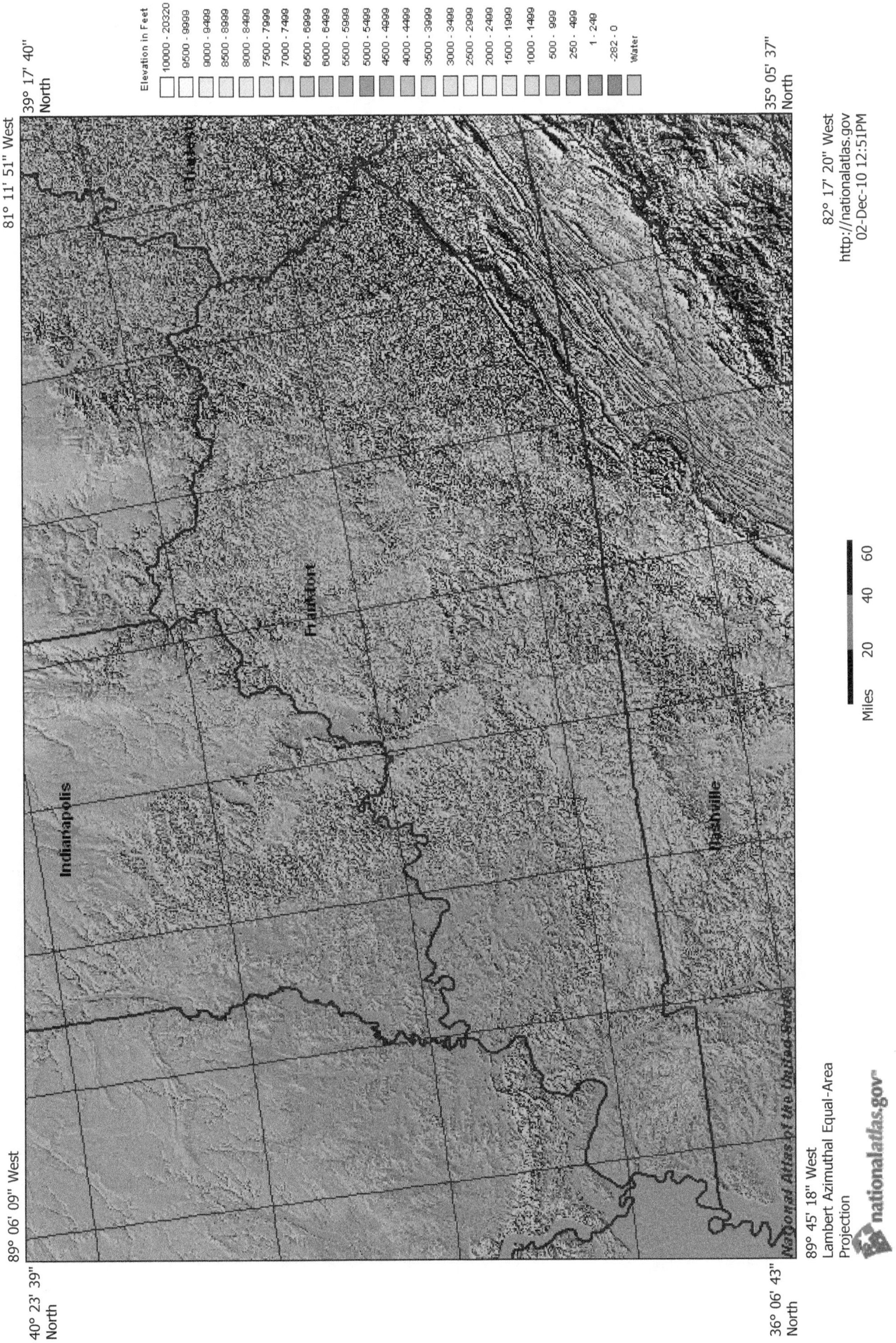

Elevation in Feet
10000 - 20320
9500 - 9999
9000 - 9499
8500 - 8999
8000 - 8499
7500 - 7999
7000 - 7499
6500 - 6999
6000 - 6499
5500 - 5999
5000 - 5499
4500 - 4999
4000 - 4499
3500 - 3999
3000 - 3499
2500 - 2999
2000 - 2499
1500 - 1999
1000 - 1499
500 - 999
250 - 499
1 - 249
-282 - 0
Water
81° 11' 51" West
39° 17' 40" North
35° 05' 37" North
82° 17' 20" West
http://nationalatlas.gov
02-Dec-10 12:51PM
Frankfort
Indianapolis
Nashville
Miles
20
40
60
89° 06' 09" West
40° 23' 39" North
36° 06' 43" North
89° 45' 18" West
Lambert Azimuthal Equal-Area
Projection
National Atlas of the United States
nationalatlas.gov

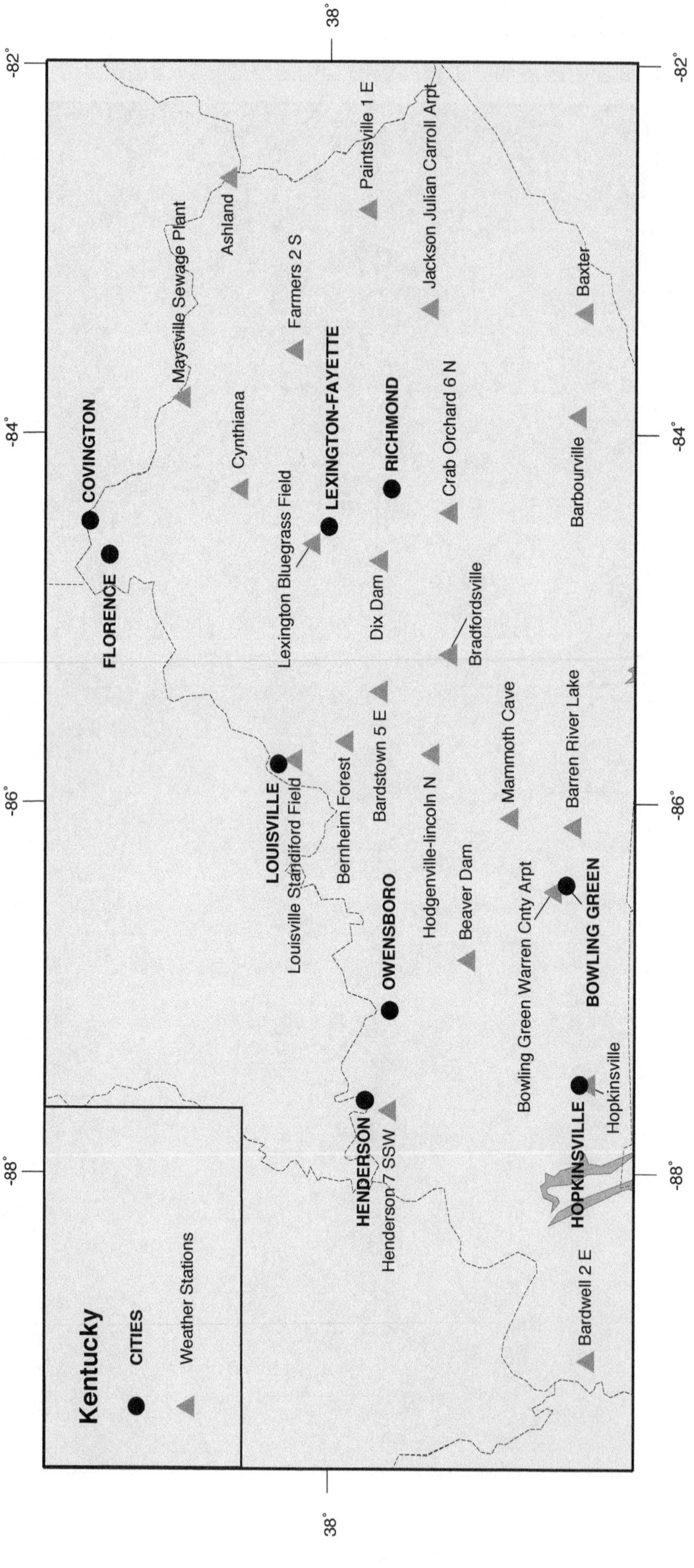
Kentucky
CITIES
Weather Stations
COVINGTON
FLORENCE
LEXINGTON-FAYETTE
RICHMOND
LOUISVILLE
OWENSBORO
HENDERSON
BOWLING GREEN
HOPKINSVILLE
Maysville Sewage Plant
Ashland
Farmers 2 S
Paintsville 1 E
Jackson Julian Carroll Arpt
Baxter
Cynthiana
Lexington Bluegrass Field
Crab Orchard 6 N
Barbourville
Dix Dam
Bradfordsville
Louisville Standiford Field
Bernheim Forest
Bardstown 5 E
Hodgenville-lincoln N
Mammoth Cave
Barren River Lake
Beaver Dam
Bowling Green Warren Cnty Arpt
Hopkinsville
Henderson 7 SSW
Bardwell 2 E
-82°
-84°
-86°
-88°
38°

Kentucky Weather Stations by County

County	Station Name
Allen	Barren River Lake
Boyd	Ashland
Breathitt	Jackson Julian Carroll Arpt
Bullitt	Bernheim Forest
Carlisle	Bardwell 2 E
Christian	Hopkinsville
Edmonson	Mammoth Cave
Fayette	Lexington Bluegrass Field
Garrard	Crab Orchard 6 N
Harlan	Baxter
Harrison	Cynthiana
Henderson	Henderson 7 SSW
Jefferson	Louisville Standiford Field
Johnson	Paintsville 1 E
Knox	Barbourville
Larue	Hodgenville-Lincoln Np
Marion	Bradfordsville
Mason	Maysville Sewage Plant
Mercer	Dix Dam
Nelson	Bardstown 5 E
Ohio	Beaver Dam
Rowan	Farmers 2 S
Warren	Bowling Green Warren Cnty Arpt

See User Guide for station inclusion criteria.

Kentucky Weather Stations by City

City	Station Name	Miles
Ashland	Ashland	1.6
	Portsmouth Sciotoville, OH	23.8
	Huntington Tri-State Arpt, WV	7.3
	Huntington Sewage Plant, WV	7.5
Bowling Green	Barren River Lake	18.2
	Bowling Green Warren Cnty Arpt	0.9
	Mammoth Cave	24.6
Covington	Cincinnati-Northern Kentucky, OH	8.4
	Fairfield, OH	20.8
	Milford, OH	15.1
Elizabethtown	Bernheim Forest	18.7
	Hodgenville-Lincoln Np	14.1
Florence	Cincinnati-Northern Kentucky, OH	4.3
	Fairfield, OH	25.0
	Milford, OH	23.3
Frankfort	Lexington Bluegrass Field	18.1
Georgetown	Cynthiana	18.6
	Lexington Bluegrass Field	12.3
Henderson	Evansville Museum, IN	8.7
	Evansville Dress Regional Arpt, IN	14.7
	Mount Vernon, IN	18.4
	Henderson 7 SSW	7.0
Hopkinsville	Hopkinsville	1.1
	Clarksville Sewage Plant, TN	22.7
Independence	Cincinnati-Northern Kentucky, OH	8.8
	Chilo Meldahl L&D, OH	23.6
	Milford, OH	21.7
Jeffersontown	Bernheim Forest	20.1
	Louisville Standiford Field	8.5
Lexington-Fayette	Dix Dam	19.3
	Lexington Bluegrass Field	5.7
Louisville	Bernheim Forest	21.9
	Louisville Standiford Field	2.9
Nicholasville	Dix Dam	9.5
	Lexington Bluegrass Field	10.7
Owensboro	Tell City, IN	23.6
Paducah	Brookport Dam 52, IL	4.4
	Bardwell 2 E	22.6
Pleasure Ridge Park	Bernheim Forest	19.7
	Louisville Standiford Field	6.9
Radcliff	Bernheim Forest	17.0
	Hodgenville-Lincoln Np	23.2
Richmond	Crab Orchard 6 N	19.7
	Dix Dam	23.1
Valley Station	Bernheim Forest	17.3
	Louisville Standiford Field	8.7

Note: Miles is the distance between the geographic center of the city and the weather station.

See User Guide for station inclusion criteria.

Kentucky Weather Stations by Elevation

Feet	Station Name
1,365	Jackson Julian Carroll Arpt
1,164	Baxter
1,100	Crab Orchard 6 N
990	Barbourville
964	Lexington Bluegrass Field
870	Dix Dam
790	Mammoth Cave
788	Hodgenville-Lincoln Np
779	Bardstown 5 E
700	Cynthiana
680	Farmers 2 S
660	Bradfordsville
629	Paintsville 1 E
620	Barren River Lake
560	Ashland
549	Bernheim Forest
527	Bowling Green Warren Cnty Arpt
520	Hopkinsville
515	Maysville Sewage Plant
480	Louisville Standiford Field
440	Beaver Dam
430	Henderson 7 SSW
410	Bardwell 2 E

See User Guide for station inclusion criteria.

Jackson Julian Carroll Airport

Jackson, County Seat of Breathitt County, is located on the leading edge of the Eastern Kentucky Coal Fields. The topography is mountainous, with 80 to 90 percent of the county area on a greater than 20 percent slope. The highest elevation is 1,547 feet above sea level. The terrain slopes gently westward into the Kentucky Bluegrass Region. To the east the mountains rise swiftly to heights of 4,000 to 5,000 feet above sea level.

The climate of Jackson and Eastern Kentucky is temperate and well suited to a variety of plant and animal life. The North Fork of the Kentucky River flows through Breathitt County westward into the Kentucky River and eventually into the Ohio River. There are numerous small creeks and streams in the county that are prone to flash flooding during periods of heavy rainfall.

Jackson is subject to sudden and large changes in temperature. Extremes of cold and heat are rare and usually of short duration. Temperatures above 100 degrees or below zero are extremely rare. Average daily temperatures range from about 32 degrees in the winter to the low 70s in the summer, and in the low 50s during the spring and fall months. January is the coldest month with an average temperature of 31 degrees. The warmest month is July, with an average temperature of 73 degrees.

Total annual precipitation for the Jackson area averages nearly 44 inches and is fairly evenly distributed throughout the year. The spring and summer seasons average nearly 12 inches each, while winter averages 11 inches and fall slightly over eight inches.

Jackson Julian Carroll Airport *Breathitt County* Elevation: 1,365 ft. Latitude: 37° 35' N Longitude: 83° 19' W

	JAN	FEB	MAR	APR	MAY	JUN	JUL	AUG	SEP	OCT	NOV	DEC	YEAR
Mean Maximum Temp. (°F)	43.4	48.2	57.6	67.9	74.6	81.5	84.6	84.0	77.9	68.0	57.3	46.4	65.9
Mean Temp. (°F)	35.1	39.2	47.5	57.3	64.6	72.0	75.4	74.5	68.1	58.1	48.4	38.5	56.6
Mean Minimum Temp. (°F)	26.9	30.2	37.3	46.6	54.5	62.5	66.1	64.9	58.3	48.1	39.4	30.5	47.1
Extreme Maximum Temp. (°F)	78	79	87	92	91	99	101	101	95	89	82	79	101
Extreme Minimum Temp. (°F)	-18	-8	7	20	32	44	52	45	34	26	13	-13	-18
Days Maximum Temp. ≥ 90°F	0	0	0	0	0	2	5	5	2	0	0	0	14
Days Maximum Temp. ≤ 32°F	7	4	1	0	0	0	0	0	0	0	0	5	17
Days Minimum Temp. ≤ 32°F	22	17	11	2	0	0	0	0	0	1	8	18	79
Days Minimum Temp. ≤ 0°F	0	0	0	0	0	0	0	0	0	0	0	0	0
Heating Degree Days (base 65°F)	919	722	545	266	100	10	0	2	48	239	495	816	4,162
Cooling Degree Days (base 65°F)	0	0	9	40	94	227	329	304	148	32	4	1	1,188
Mean Precipitation (in.)	3.55	3.77	4.17	3.87	5.10	4.66	4.69	3.69	3.50	3.24	3.89	4.22	48.35
Maximum Precipitation (in.)*	7.3	7.6	11.8	5.7	9.9	7.0	9.7	7.7	7.8	7.4	9.3	13.0	63.3
Minimum Precipitation (in.)*	0.8	2.0	1.6	0.8	2.3	1.4	1.8	1.5	1.4	0.5	1.4	1.7	37.6
Extreme Maximum Daily Precip. (in.)	2.04	2.38	2.72	2.10	3.56	3.04	2.77	3.84	3.20	2.32	3.45	3.13	3.84
Days With ≥ 0.1" Precipitation	7	8	9	8	10	8	8	6	6	6	7	8	91
Days With ≥ 0.5" Precipitation	2	2	3	3	3	3	3	2	2	2	3	3	31
Days With ≥ 1.0" Precipitation	1	1	1	1	1	1	1	1	1	1	1	1	12
Mean Snowfall (in.)	6.6	6.4	3.1	1.0	trace	trace	trace	trace	0.0	0.1	0.6	4.3	22.1
Maximum Snowfall (in.)*	26	21	22	18	1	0	0	0	0	2	5	12	44
Maximum 24-hr. Snowfall (in.)*	15	12	20	8	1	0	0	0	0	2	4	4	20
Maximum Snow Depth (in.)	17	14	20	11	trace	trace	trace	trace	0	trace	4	10	20
Days With ≥ 1.0" Snow Depth	6	5	1	0	0	0	0	0	0	0	0	4	16
Thunderstorm Days*	< 1	1	3	4	8	10	12	8	3	1	1	< 1	51
Foggy Days*	15	13	15	11	17	19	24	25	19	13	13	15	199
Predominant Sky Cover*	OVR	OVR	OVR	OVR	OVR	OVR	OVR	SCT	OVR	OVR	OVR	OVR	OVR
Mean Relative Humidity 7am (%)*	77	75	72	69	81	86	89	91	89	82	75	78	80
Mean Relative Humidity 4pm (%)*	59	56	49	44	57	59	62	60	59	52	54	62	56
Mean Dewpoint (°F)*	24	26	31	39	52	62	66	65	57	45	35	28	44
Prevailing Wind Direction*	SW	S	S	S	S	S	SSW	S	S	S	S	SW	S
Prevailing Wind Speed (mph)*	9	9	9	8	7	6	6	6	6	7	8	8	7
Maximum Wind Gust (mph)*	55	60	53	58	49	60	55	49	39	48	52	60	60

Note: (*) Period of record is 1981-1995

The period of record for National Weather Service station data is 1980 – 2009 except where noted. See User Guide for detailed explanation of data.

Lexington Bluegrass Field

Lexington, County Seat of Fayette County, is located in the heart of the famed Kentucky Blue Grass Region. Fayette County is a gently rolling plateau with the elevation varying between 900 and 1,050 feet above sea level. It is noted for its beauty, the fertility of its soil, excellent grass, stock farms, and burley tobacco. The soil has a high phosphorus content and this is very valuable in growing pasture grasses for the grazing of cattle and horses. Lexington has a decided continental climate with a rather large diurnal temperature range. The climate is temperate and well suited to a varied plant and animal life. There are no bodies of water close enough to have any effect on the climate. The closest river is the Kentucky which makes an arc about 15 to 20 miles to the southeast, south, and southwest on its course to the Ohio River. There are numerous small creeks that rise in the county and flow into the river. The reservoirs of the Lexington Water Company are about five miles southeast of the city and are the largest bodies of water in the area.

Lexington is subject to rather sudden and large changes in temperature with the spells generally of rather short duration. Temperatures above 100 degrees and below zero degrees are relatively rare. The average temperature for the winter is 35 degrees, spring 62 degrees, fall 50 degrees, and summer 74 degrees.

Precipitation is evenly distributed throughout the winter, spring, and summer, with about 12 inches recorded on the average for each of these seasons. The fall season averages nearly eight and a half inches. Snowfall amounts are variable and the ground does not retain snow cover more than a few days at a time.

The months of September and October are the most pleasant of the year. They have the least amount of precipitation, the greatest number of clear days, and generally comfortable temperatures are the rule during these months.

Based on the 1951-1980 period, the average first occurrence of 32 degrees Fahrenheit in the fall is October 25 and the average last occurrence in the spring is April 17.

Lexington Bluegrass Field *Fayette County* Elevation: 964 ft. Latitude: 38° 02' N Longitude: 84° 36' W

	JAN	FEB	MAR	APR	MAY	JUN	JUL	AUG	SEP	OCT	NOV	DEC	YEAR
Mean Maximum Temp. (°F)	41.0	45.5	55.1	65.4	74.3	82.7	86.1	85.5	78.7	67.3	55.2	44.3	65.1
Mean Temp. (°F)	33.0	36.7	45.2	55.0	64.2	72.6	76.3	75.4	68.3	56.9	46.2	36.3	55.5
Mean Minimum Temp. (°F)	25.0	27.9	35.3	44.5	54.1	62.5	66.5	65.2	57.8	46.5	37.2	28.2	45.9
Extreme Maximum Temp. (°F)	73	80	82	87	92	101	103	103	97	91	83	75	103
Extreme Minimum Temp. (°F)	-20	-10	0	18	32	42	50	45	34	24	12	-19	-20
Days Maximum Temp. ≥ 90°F	0	0	0	0	0	3	9	8	2	0	0	0	22
Days Maximum Temp. ≤ 32°F	8	5	1	0	0	0	0	0	0	0	0	5	19
Days Minimum Temp. ≤ 32°F	23	19	13	3	0	0	0	0	0	2	10	20	90
Days Minimum Temp. ≤ 0°F	1	0	0	0	0	0	0	0	0	0	0	0	1
Heating Degree Days (base 65°F)	985	793	610	313	107	10	0	2	48	271	559	885	4,583
Cooling Degree Days (base 65°F)	0	0	3	20	89	245	359	331	152	27	1	0	1,227
Mean Precipitation (in.)	3.15	3.18	4.24	3.61	5.00	4.35	4.63	3.40	2.97	3.16	3.44	3.90	45.03
Maximum Precipitation (in.)*	16.6	10.1	10.4	9.3	10.8	11.7	10.6	11.2	9.7	6.1	6.9	10.2	60.1
Minimum Precipitation (in.)*	0.4	0.7	1.0	1.2	1.2	0.6	0.8	0.6	0.2	0.3	0.4	0.6	32.1
Extreme Maximum Daily Precip. (in.)	2.05	3.10	5.56	2.95	3.36	5.04	4.38	2.88	4.76	4.33	2.49	3.32	5.56
Days With ≥ 0.1" Precipitation	6	6	8	7	8	7	7	6	5	5	7	7	79
Days With ≥ 0.5" Precipitation	2	2	3	2	4	3	3	2	2	2	2	3	30
Days With ≥ 1.0" Precipitation	1	1	1	1	1	1	2	1	1	1	1	1	13
Mean Snowfall (in.)	*4.3*	*4.4*	*1.7*	*0.4*	*trace*	*trace*	*trace*	*trace*	*0.0*	*trace*	*0.3*	*2.0*	*13.1*
Maximum Snowfall (in.)*	22	16	18	6	trace	0	0	0	0	trace	10	11	39
Maximum 24-hr. Snowfall (in.)*	10	7	7	5	trace	0	0	0	0	trace	8	8	10
Maximum Snow Depth (in.)	*12*	*9*	*7*	*1*	*trace*	*trace*	*trace*	*trace*	*0*	*trace*	*1*	*5*	*12*
Days With ≥ 1.0" Snow Depth	*4*	4	*1*	*0*	*0*	*0*	*0*	*0*	*0*	*0*	*0*	*2*	*11*
Thunderstorm Days*	1	1	3	4	6	8	9	7	3	1	1	< 1	44
Foggy Days*	14	12	12	9	12	13	16	18	15	12	12	13	158
Predominant Sky Cover*	OVR	OVR	OVR	OVR	OVR	OVR	SCT	SCT	CLR	CLR	OVR	OVR	OVR
Mean Relative Humidity 7am (%)*	81	80	77	75	79	81	84	86	86	83	81	81	81
Mean Relative Humidity 4pm (%)*	67	61	55	51	54	55	56	55	54	53	60	66	57
Mean Dewpoint (°F)*	25	26	33	42	52	61	65	64	57	45	35	28	45
Prevailing Wind Direction*	S	S	S	S	S	S	S	S	S	S	S	S	S
Prevailing Wind Speed (mph)*	12	10	12	12	9	8	7	7	8	8	10	12	9
Maximum Wind Gust (mph)*	78	56	53	61	59	64	63	51	52	52	56	58	78

Note: (*) Period of record is 1948-1995

Louisville Standiford Field

Louisville is located on the south bank of the Ohio River, 604 miles below Pittsburgh, Pennsylvania, and 377 miles above the mouth of the river at Cairo, Illinois. The city is divided by Beargrass Creek and its south fork into two topographical types. The eastern portion is rolling, containing several creeks, and consists of plateaus and rolling hillsides. The highest elevation in this area is 565 feet. The western portion is mostly flat with an average elevation about 100 feet lower than the eastern area. Much of the western section lies in the flood plain of the Ohio River. Nearly all of the industries in the city are located in the western portion, while the eastern portion is almost entirely residential. A range of low hills about five miles northwest of Louisville, on the Indiana side of the Ohio River, present a partial barrier to arctic blasts in the winter months. During colder months, snow is frequently observed on the summits of these hills.

The climate of Louisville, while continental in type, is of a variable nature because of its position with respect to the paths of high and low pressure systems and the occasional influx of warm moist air from the Gulf of Mexico. As a whole, winters are moderately cold and summers are quite warm. Temperatures of 100 degrees or more in summer and zero degrees or less in winter are rare.

Thunderstorms with high rainfall intensities are common during the spring and summer months. The precipitation in Louisville is nonseasonal and varies from year to year. The fall months are usually the driest. Snowfall usually occurs from November through March. As with rainfall, amounts vary from year to year and month to month. Relative humidity remains rather high throughout the summer months. Cloud cover is about equally distributed throughout the year with the winter months showing somewhat of an increase in amount. The percentage of possible sunshine at Louisville varies from month to month with the greatest amount during the summer months as a result of the decreasing sky cover during that season. Heavy fog occurs only an average of 10 days during the year, generally in the months of September through March.

Based on the 1951-1980 period, the average date for the last occurrence in the spring of temperatures as low as 32 degrees is mid-April, and the first occurrence in the fall is generally in late October.

The prevailing direction of the wind has a southerly component.

Louisville Standiford Field *Jefferson County* Elevation: 480 ft. Latitude: 38° 11' N Longitude: 85° 44' W

	JAN	FEB	MAR	APR	MAY	JUN	JUL	AUG	SEP	OCT	NOV	DEC	YEAR
Mean Maximum Temp. (°F)	42.6	47.2	57.1	67.9	76.5	84.6	88.2	87.6	80.8	69.3	57.2	45.6	67.0
Mean Temp. (°F)	34.6	38.4	47.2	57.3	66.5	75.0	78.9	77.9	70.6	58.9	48.2	37.7	57.6
Mean Minimum Temp. (°F)	26.6	29.5	37.2	46.7	56.5	65.3	69.5	68.2	60.3	48.4	39.1	29.9	48.1
Extreme Maximum Temp. (°F)	72	77	86	90	91	101	106	105	99	93	83	76	106
Extreme Minimum Temp. (°F)	-22	-5	1	22	35	45	54	46	37	24	15	-15	-22
Days Maximum Temp. ≥ 90°F	0	0	0	0	1	7	13	12	4	0	0	0	37
Days Maximum Temp. ≤ 32°F	6	4	1	0	0	0	0	0	0	0	0	4	15
Days Minimum Temp. ≤ 32°F	22	17	11	2	0	0	0	0	0	1	8	19	80
Days Minimum Temp. ≤ 0°F	1	0	0	0	0	0	0	0	0	0	0	0	1
Heating Degree Days (base 65°F)	936	746	551	257	70	5	0	0	31	223	500	839	4,158
Cooling Degree Days (base 65°F)	0	0	6	33	125	311	438	409	206	39	3	1	1,571
Mean Precipitation (in.)	3.20	3.15	4.28	3.96	5.14	3.77	4.10	3.39	3.15	3.30	3.47	3.81	44.72
Maximum Precipitation (in.)*	11.4	9.0	14.9	11.1	11.6	10.1	10.0	8.8	10.5	6.5	9.1	8.9	59.8
Minimum Precipitation (in.)*	0.4	0.8	1.0	0.8	1.4	0.5	1.0	0.2	0.3	0.4	0.7	0.6	30.4
Extreme Maximum Daily Precip. (in.)	3.64	3.66	7.22	2.55	3.31	2.74	4.60	4.53	4.28	4.24	2.21	2.44	7.22
Days With ≥ 0.1" Precipitation	6	6	8	8	8	7	7	6	5	5	6	7	79
Days With ≥ 0.5" Precipitation	2	2	3	3	4	3	3	2	2	2	3	3	32
Days With ≥ 1.0" Precipitation	1	1	1	1	1	1	1	1	1	1	1	1	12
Mean Snowfall (in.)	3.9	4.1	1.5	0.1	trace	trace	trace	trace	0.0	0.1	0.1	2.4	12.2
Maximum Snowfall (in.)*	28	16	23	2	trace	0	0	0	0	2	13	9	43
Maximum 24-hr. Snowfall (in.)*	16	11	12	1	trace	0	0	0	0	2	13	5	16
Maximum Snow Depth (in.)	16	11	9	2	trace	trace	trace	trace	0	1	trace	9	16
Days With ≥ 1.0" Snow Depth	4	3	1	0	0	0	0	0	0	0	0	3	11
Thunderstorm Days*	1	1	3	4	7	7	8	7	3	2	2	1	46
Foggy Days*	13	11	11	9	11	11	12	16	15	14	12	12	147
Predominant Sky Cover*	OVR	OVR	OVR	OVR	OVR	SCT	SCT	SCT	CLR	CLR	OVR	OVR	OVR
Mean Relative Humidity 7am (%)*	78	78	76	75	80	81	83	85	86	85	79	79	80
Mean Relative Humidity 4pm (%)*	63	58	53	49	52	53	54	53	53	51	57	63	55
Mean Dewpoint (°F)*	24	26	33	43	54	63	66	65	58	47	36	28	45
Prevailing Wind Direction*	S	WNW	WNW	S	S	S	S	S	S	S	S	S	S
Prevailing Wind Speed (mph)*	10	12	13	10	8	7	7	6	7	8	9	9	9
Maximum Wind Gust (mph)*	60	60	60	84	60	73	84	59	55	44	58	56	84

Note: (*) Period of record is 1948-1995

Ashland *Boyd County* Elevation: 560 ft. Latitude: 38° 27' N Longitude: 82° 37' W

	JAN	FEB	MAR	APR	MAY	JUN	JUL	AUG	SEP	OCT	NOV	DEC	YEAR
Mean Maximum Temp. (°F)	42.2	46.9	56.9	68.8	77.3	85.1	88.0	87.5	80.5	69.4	57.3	45.5	67.1
Mean Temp. (°F)	30.8	34.5	43.2	53.6	62.5	71.2	74.9	73.9	66.7	55.4	44.3	34.5	53.8
Mean Minimum Temp. (°F)	19.8	21.8	29.4	38.3	47.7	57.2	61.7	60.2	52.7	41.0	31.2	23.6	40.4
Extreme Maximum Temp. (°F)	79	80	88	92	94	102	104	105	99	90	84	82	105
Extreme Minimum Temp. (°F)	-25	-23	-8	16	22	30	34	33	31	18	6	-10	-25
Days Maximum Temp. ≥ 90°F	0	0	0	0	2	8	14	12	4	0	0	0	40
Days Maximum Temp. ≤ 32°F	7	4	1	0	0	0	0	0	0	0	0	4	16
Days Minimum Temp. ≤ 32°F	26	24	20	9	2	0	0	0	0	6	16	25	128
Days Minimum Temp. ≤ 0°F	2	1	0	0	0	0	0	0	0	0	0	1	4
Heating Degree Days (base 65°F)	1,053	858	670	353	138	17	1	4	66	309	614	939	5,022
Cooling Degree Days (base 65°F)	0	0	2	16	67	209	314	286	121	16	0	0	1,031
Mean Precipitation (in.)	2.95	3.19	3.90	3.56	4.52	4.02	4.62	3.63	3.01	2.90	3.43	3.55	43.28
Extreme Maximum Daily Precip. (in.)	1.61	2.60	4.00	1.90	2.87	2.38	4.00	3.00	3.72	2.30	2.95	2.80	4.00
Days With ≥ 0.1" Precipitation	6	7	8	8	9	8	7	6	5	6	7	7	84
Days With ≥ 0.5" Precipitation	2	2	3	2	3	3	3	2	2	2	2	2	28
Days With ≥ 1.0" Precipitation	0	1	1	1	1	1	1	1	1	1	1	1	11
Mean Snowfall (in.)	2.9	na	1.4	trace	0.0	0.0	0.0	0.0	0.0	0.0	trace	1.2	na
Maximum Snow Depth (in.)	11	12	24	14	0	0	0	0	0	0	1	3	24
Days With ≥ 1.0" Snow Depth	4	3	1	0	0	0	0	0	0	0	0	1	9

Barbourville *Knox County* Elevation: 990 ft. Latitude: 36° 53' N Longitude: 83° 53' W

	JAN	FEB	MAR	APR	MAY	JUN	JUL	AUG	SEP	OCT	NOV	DEC	YEAR
Mean Maximum Temp. (°F)	45.6	49.9	59.1	68.9	76.8	84.3	87.3	86.3	80.5	70.7	59.4	48.2	68.1
Mean Temp. (°F)	34.8	38.2	45.9	54.8	63.3	71.8	75.7	74.7	67.9	56.7	46.5	37.5	55.6
Mean Minimum Temp. (°F)	23.7	26.6	32.6	40.6	49.8	59.4	64.1	63.0	55.3	42.7	33.5	26.5	43.1
Extreme Maximum Temp. (°F)	76	77	86	91	92	100	101	102	96	92	82	78	102
Extreme Minimum Temp. (°F)	-22	-20	-5	17	30	38	46	44	34	19	11	-9	-22
Days Maximum Temp. ≥ 90°F	0	0	0	0	1	5	10	9	3	0	0	0	28
Days Maximum Temp. ≤ 32°F	4	2	1	0	0	0	0	0	0	0	0	3	10
Days Minimum Temp. ≤ 32°F	24	21	17	6	0	0	0	0	0	5	16	23	112
Days Minimum Temp. ≤ 0°F	1	0	0	0	0	0	0	0	0	0	0	0	1
Heating Degree Days (base 65°F)	930	750	588	314	115	11	0	2	45	277	551	847	4,430
Cooling Degree Days (base 65°F)	0	0	2	13	71	223	341	309	138	17	1	0	1,115
Mean Precipitation (in.)	3.86	3.77	4.30	4.27	4.88	4.23	4.97	3.90	3.48	2.91	4.16	4.54	49.27
Extreme Maximum Daily Precip. (in.)	2.06	2.09	3.08	3.22	4.25	3.62	3.07	2.46	3.20	2.58	2.60	3.65	4.25
Days With ≥ 0.1" Precipitation	7	7	8	8	8	8	8	6	6	5	7	8	86
Days With ≥ 0.5" Precipitation	3	2	3	3	4	3	4	3	2	2	3	3	35
Days With ≥ 1.0" Precipitation	1	1	1	1	1	1	1	1	1	1	1	1	12
Mean Snowfall (in.)	2.9	1.7	0.5	0.3	trace	0.0	0.0	0.0	0.0	0.0	trace	1.2	6.6
Maximum Snow Depth (in.)	***13***	***11***	***3***	***7***	***0***	***0***	***0***	0	0	***0***	***trace***	***4***	***13***
Days With ≥ 1.0" Snow Depth	***2***	***1***	0	0	0	0	0	0	0	0	0	1	***4***

Bardstown 5 E *Nelson County* Elevation: 779 ft. Latitude: 37° 49' N Longitude: 85° 23' W

	JAN	FEB	MAR	APR	MAY	JUN	JUL	AUG	SEP	OCT	NOV	DEC	YEAR
Mean Maximum Temp. (°F)	***43.4***	***49.0***	57.3	67.9	75.9	83.5	87.2	87.0	***80.9***	69.9	57.4	46.4	***67.2***
Mean Temp. (°F)	***34.7***	***39.1***	46.7	56.5	64.9	72.9	76.5	75.7	***68.9***	58.2	47.3	37.8	***56.6***
Mean Minimum Temp. (°F)	***26.0***	***29.3***	36.0	45.1	53.9	62.1	65.8	64.3	***56.9***	46.5	37.2	29.1	***46.0***
Extreme Maximum Temp. (°F)	71	***78***	***84***	***87***	***92***	***94***	***105***	***105***	***97***	***91***	***80***	***78***	***105***
Extreme Minimum Temp. (°F)	-26	***-9***	***3***	***19***	***32***	***41***	***50***	***47***	***33***	***20***	***10***	***-20***	***-26***
Days Maximum Temp. ≥ 90°F	0	***0***	0	0	0	4	10	10	***4***	0	0	0	***28***
Days Maximum Temp. ≤ 32°F	6	***3***	1	0	0	0	0	0	***0***	0	0	4	***14***
Days Minimum Temp. ≤ 32°F	22	***18***	13	4	0	0	0	0	***0***	3	10	19	***89***
Days Minimum Temp. ≤ 0°F	1	***0***	0	0	0	0	0	0	***0***	0	0	0	***1***
Heating Degree Days (base 65°F)	***930***	***724***	565	273	89	7	0	1	***44***	236	524	838	***4,231***
Cooling Degree Days (base 65°F)	***0***	***0***	4	25	94	249	364	339	***169***	32	2	0	***1,278***
Mean Precipitation (in.)	***3.63***	***3.92***	4.88	4.40	5.79	4.62	4.33	3.60	***3.32***	3.49	3.55	4.61	***50.14***
Extreme Maximum Daily Precip. (in.)	2.27	***3.42***	***5.72***	***3.73***	***3.25***	***3.13***	***4.00***	***3.37***	***4.12***	***3.55***	***2.15***	***2.52***	***5.72***
Days With ≥ 0.1" Precipitation	6	***7***	9	8	8	8	6	6	***5***	6	7	8	***84***
Days With ≥ 0.5" Precipitation	3	***3***	3	3	4	3	3	2	***2***	2	2	3	***33***
Days With ≥ 1.0" Precipitation	1	***1***	1	1	2	1	1	1	***1***	1	1	1	***13***
Mean Snowfall (in.)	***3.6***	na	***1.2***	trace	trace	0.0	0.0	0.0	***0.0***	trace	0.2	***2.4***	na
Maximum Snow Depth (in.)	na	na	***8***	***trace***	***trace***	***0***	***0***	***0***	***0***	***trace***	***3***	na	na
Days With ≥ 1.0" Snow Depth	na	na	***1***	0	0	0	0	0	***0***	***0***	0	***3***	na

Bardwell 2 E *Carlisle County* Elevation: 410 ft. Latitude: 36° 53' N Longitude: 88° 58' W

	JAN	FEB	MAR	APR	MAY	JUN	JUL	AUG	SEP	OCT	NOV	DEC	YEAR
Mean Maximum Temp. (°F)	44.5	49.3	59.7	70.1	78.7	86.9	90.2	89.2	82.5	71.4	58.9	47.6	69.1
Mean Temp. (°F)	35.2	39.4	48.6	***58.1***	67.1	75.5	79.3	77.6	70.2	58.9	48.3	38.2	***58.0***
Mean Minimum Temp. (°F)	25.8	29.6	37.5	***46.2***	55.4	64.2	68.3	66.1	57.8	46.4	37.6	28.7	***47.0***
Extreme Maximum Temp. (°F)	71	77	84	90	94	102	104	102	100	90	82	77	104
Extreme Minimum Temp. (°F)	-21	-6	10	***19***	33	42	51	41	30	21	11	-12	***-21***
Days Maximum Temp. ≥ 90°F	0	0	0	0	1	11	18	15	6	0	0	0	51
Days Maximum Temp. ≤ 32°F	5	3	0	0	0	0	0	0	0	0	0	3	11
Days Minimum Temp. ≤ 32°F	***23***	17	11	***3***	0	0	0	0	0	2	10	19	***85***
Days Minimum Temp. ≤ 0°F	1	0	0	***0***	0	0	0	0	0	0	0	0	***1***
Heating Degree Days (base 65°F)	918	717	509	***232***	58	2	0	1	30	217	497	826	***4,007***
Cooling Degree Days (base 65°F)	0	0	7	***30***	129	325	449	399	193	36	2	0	***1,570***
Mean Precipitation (in.)	***3.65***	4.10	5.12	5.12	5.74	4.62	4.80	3.27	3.67	4.82	4.89	4.88	***54.68***
Extreme Maximum Daily Precip. (in.)	***2.32***	***5.70***	6.05	***3.41***	7.01	2.90	3.92	3.30	7.68	4.55	5.05	***3.50***	***7.68***
Days With ≥ 0.1" Precipitation	6	6	8	8	8	7	6	5	5	6	7	7	79
Days With ≥ 0.5" Precipitation	2	3	3	3	4	3	4	2	2	3	3	3	35
Days With ≥ 1.0" Precipitation	1	1	1	2	2	2	2	1	1	1	1	2	17
Mean Snowfall (in.)	3.3	***3.2***	0.7	0.0	0.0	0.0	0.0	0.0	0.0	0.1	0.1	1.7	***9.1***
Maximum Snow Depth (in.)	12	***11***	3	0	0	0	0	0	0	trace	trace	7	***12***
Days With ≥ 1.0" Snow Depth	3	***3***	0	0	0	0	0	0	0	0	0	1	7

The period of record for all cooperative weather station data is 1980 – 2009. See User Guide for detailed explanation of data.

Barren River Lake *Allen County* Elevation: 620 ft. Latitude: 36° 54' N Longitude: 86° 08' W

	JAN	FEB	MAR	APR	MAY	JUN	JUL	AUG	SEP	OCT	NOV	DEC	YEAR
Mean Maximum Temp. (°F)	45.6	50.0	59.6	70.0	78.5	86.5	90.2	89.7	83.2	72.2	60.6	48.9	69.6
Mean Temp. (°F)	35.7	39.1	47.6	57.2	66.3	74.7	78.7	77.7	70.8	59.4	49.0	38.9	57.9
Mean Minimum Temp. (°F)	25.7	28.2	35.5	44.4	54.1	62.8	67.1	65.6	58.3	46.6	37.4	28.8	46.2
Extreme Maximum Temp. (°F)	76	82	90	94	94	104	106	105	102	96	88	80	106
Extreme Minimum Temp. (°F)	-19	-6	0	18	32	40	48	47	33	24	14	-15	-19
Days Maximum Temp. ≥ 90°F	0	0	0	0	2	12	19	17	7	1	0	0	58
Days Maximum Temp. ≤ 32°F	5	2	0	0	0	0	0	0	0	0	0	3	10
Days Minimum Temp. ≤ 32°F	22	19	14	4	0	0	0	0	0	3	10	19	91
Days Minimum Temp. ≤ 0°F	1	0	0	0	0	0	0	0	0	0	0	0	1
Heating Degree Days (base 65°F)	903	725	542	265	82	6	0	1	33	214	477	804	4,052
Cooling Degree Days (base 65°F)	0	0	8	38	128	304	430	401	213	47	5	1	1,575
Mean Precipitation (in.)	3.52	4.02	4.19	4.34	5.51	4.47	5.05	3.66	3.47	3.58	3.92	4.63	50.36
Extreme Maximum Daily Precip. (in.)	3.33	2.75	3.10	4.02	4.61	3.10	4.55	6.15	4.50	3.90	2.40	3.14	6.15
Days With ≥ 0.1" Precipitation	6	7	7	8	8	7	7	5	5	6	7	7	80
Days With ≥ 0.5" Precipitation	3	3	3	3	4	3	4	2	2	2	3	3	35
Days With ≥ 1.0" Precipitation	1	1	1	1	2	1	2	1	1	1	1	1	14
Mean Snowfall (in.)	2.2	2.2	0.9	trace	0.0	0.0	0.0	0.0	0.0	trace	trace	0.9	6.2
Maximum Snow Depth (in.)	6	9	5	1	0	0	0	0	0	trace	trace	4	9
Days With ≥ 1.0" Snow Depth	3	2	1	0	0	0	0	0	0	0	0	1	7

Baxter *Harlan County* Elevation: 1,164 ft. Latitude: 36° 51' N Longitude: 83° 20' W

	JAN	FEB	MAR	APR	MAY	JUN	JUL	AUG	SEP	OCT	NOV	DEC	YEAR
Mean Maximum Temp. (°F)	45.1	48.8	57.9	67.6	75.4	82.1	85.5	85.0	78.9	69.0	58.5	47.9	66.8
Mean Temp. (°F)	35.2	38.2	45.6	54.5	63.2	70.9	74.8	74.1	67.5	56.6	46.6	38.0	55.4
Mean Minimum Temp. (°F)	25.3	27.6	33.2	41.3	51.0	59.8	64.3	63.2	56.1	44.1	34.6	28.0	44.0
Extreme Maximum Temp. (°F)	74	77	85	89	90	96	99	101	94	92	83	78	101
Extreme Minimum Temp. (°F)	-19	-12	1	20	32	41	46	42	29	24	13	-7	-19
Days Maximum Temp. ≥ 90°F	0	0	0	0	0	2	6	6	1	0	0	0	15
Days Maximum Temp. ≤ 32°F	4	3	1	0	0	0	0	0	0	0	0	3	11
Days Minimum Temp. ≤ 32°F	24	20	16	6	0	0	0	0	0	3	14	22	105
Days Minimum Temp. ≤ 0°F	1	0	0	0	0	0	0	0	0	0	0	0	1
Heating Degree Days (base 65°F)	917	749	596	320	113	12	0	2	47	272	547	830	4,405
Cooling Degree Days (base 65°F)	0	0	1	11	65	197	312	291	130	17	0	0	1,024
Mean Precipitation (in.)	3.92	3.99	4.43	4.15	4.84	4.25	4.64	4.14	3.36	2.75	3.83	4.37	48.67
Extreme Maximum Daily Precip. (in.)	1.86	3.06	3.58	2.69	2.96	2.61	3.20	3.18	3.18	1.98	2.50	2.84	3.58
Days With ≥ 0.1" Precipitation	8	8	9	8	9	8	9	7	6	6	8	8	94
Days With ≥ 0.5" Precipitation	3	3	3	3	4	3	3	3	3	2	3	3	36
Days With ≥ 1.0" Precipitation	1	1	1	1	1	1	1	1	1	1	1	1	12
Mean Snowfall (in.)	2.8	2.6	1.1	0.7	0.0	0.0	0.0	0.0	0.0	trace	0.0	1.1	8.3
Maximum Snow Depth (in.)	9	***6***	16	***2***	0	***0***	***0***	0	0	***0***	trace	4	***16***
Days With ≥ 1.0" Snow Depth	***2***	***2***	1	0	0	0	0	0	0	0	0	1	***6***

Beaver Dam *Ohio County* Elevation: 440 ft. Latitude: 37° 25' N Longitude: 86° 52' W

	JAN	FEB	MAR	APR	MAY	JUN	JUL	AUG	SEP	OCT	NOV	DEC	YEAR
Mean Maximum Temp. (°F)	44.0	49.7	59.7	70.0	77.8	85.1	88.7	88.4	81.9	71.2	59.0	***47.4***	***68.6***
Mean Temp. (°F)	34.8	39.3	***48.1***	57.7	66.1	74.1	78.0	77.0	69.3	58.4	48.4	***38.4***	***57.5***
Mean Minimum Temp. (°F)	25.6	28.9	***36.5***	45.3	54.5	63.1	67.3	65.7	56.7	45.7	37.8	29.3	***46.3***
Extreme Maximum Temp. (°F)	71	81	87	90	92	100	104	103	100	94	82	78	104
Extreme Minimum Temp. (°F)	-23	-8	-2	21	33	40	47	42	32	20	9	-24	-24
Days Maximum Temp. ≥ 90°F	0	0	0	0	0	7	14	12	5	0	0	0	38
Days Maximum Temp. ≤ 32°F	5	3	0	0	0	0	0	0	0	0	0	3	11
Days Minimum Temp. ≤ 32°F	22	18	11	3	0	0	0	0	0	3	10	18	85
Days Minimum Temp. ≤ 0°F	1	0	0	0	0	0	0	0	0	0	0	0	1
Heating Degree Days (base 65°F)	928	720	***526***	250	74	5	0	1	40	233	494	***818***	***4,089***
Cooling Degree Days (base 65°F)	0	1	***7***	36	116	286	411	381	176	37	3	***1***	***1,455***
Mean Precipitation (in.)	3.22	4.29	4.38	4.53	5.26	3.68	3.91	3.14	3.58	3.61	4.18	4.61	48.39
Extreme Maximum Daily Precip. (in.)	3.50	4.20	5.70	5.95	4.48	3.61	3.40	2.52	***6.45***	***3.70***	3.34	3.80	***6.45***
Days With ≥ 0.1" Precipitation	6	6	7	7	8	6	6	5	5	5	7	7	75
Days With ≥ 0.5" Precipitation	2	3	3	3	4	2	3	2	2	2	3	3	32
Days With ≥ 1.0" Precipitation	1	1	1	1	2	1	1	1	1	1	1	1	13
Mean Snowfall (in.)	***3.9***	***3.0***	1.6	0.0	0.0	0.0	0.0	0.0	0.0	0.1	trace	2.0	***10.6***
Maximum Snow Depth (in.)	***6***	na	***4***	***0***	***0***	***0***	***0***	***0***	***0***	na	***trace***	na	na
Days With ≥ 1.0" Snow Depth	***1***	***1***	0	0	0	0	0	0	0	0	0	***0***	***2***

Bernheim Forest *Bullitt County* Elevation: 549 ft. Latitude: 37° 55' N Longitude: 85° 39' W

	JAN	FEB	MAR	APR	MAY	JUN	JUL	AUG	SEP	OCT	NOV	DEC	YEAR
Mean Maximum Temp. (°F)	45.0	50.2	60.1	70.8	78.5	85.9	89.4	89.5	83.1	72.2	59.8	48.4	69.4
Mean Temp. (°F)	35.5	39.3	47.8	57.6	66.1	73.7	77.7	77.0	70.1	59.1	48.8	38.8	57.6
Mean Minimum Temp. (°F)	25.9	28.4	35.5	44.4	53.7	61.5	66.0	64.6	57.1	46.1	37.8	29.1	45.8
Extreme Maximum Temp. (°F)	71	80	85	91	94	101	106	104	101	90	84	78	106
Extreme Minimum Temp. (°F)	-24	-10	4	17	31	41	47	42	34	18	10	-19	-24
Days Maximum Temp. ≥ 90°F	0	0	0	0	1	8	16	16	6	0	0	0	47
Days Maximum Temp. ≤ 32°F	4	3	0	0	0	0	0	0	0	0	0	2	9
Days Minimum Temp. ≤ 32°F	22	19	14	4	0	0	0	0	0	3	11	19	92
Days Minimum Temp. ≤ 0°F	1	0	0	0	0	0	0	0	0	0	0	0	1
Heating Degree Days (base 65°F)	908	720	532	251	75	6	0	1	33	216	484	803	4,029
Cooling Degree Days (base 65°F)	0	1	7	36	117	274	403	381	195	41	4	0	1,459
Mean Precipitation (in.)	3.15	3.66	4.41	4.18	5.39	4.50	4.25	3.00	3.21	3.45	4.02	4.19	47.41
Extreme Maximum Daily Precip. (in.)	***2.00***	2.76	6.60	4.80	3.30	2.44	3.25	3.02	4.50	3.42	2.23	***3.24***	***6.60***
Days With ≥ 0.1" Precipitation	5	6	8	8	8	7	6	6	5	5	7	6	77
Days With ≥ 0.5" Precipitation	2	2	3	3	4	4	3	2	2	2	4	3	34
Days With ≥ 1.0" Precipitation	1	1	1	1	2	1	1	1	1	1	1	1	13
Mean Snowfall (in.)	***1.0***	***1.9***	0.3	trace	0.0	0.0	0.0	0.0	0.0	0.0	0.1	***1.0***	***4.3***
Maximum Snow Depth (in.)	11	***8***	3	1	0	0	0	0	0	0	2	***4***	***11***
Days With ≥ 1.0" Snow Depth	2	***2***	0	0	0	0	0	0	0	0	0	1	***5***

The period of record for all cooperative weather station data is 1980 – 2009. See User Guide for detailed explanation of data.

Bowling Green Warren Cnty Arpt *Warren County* Elevation: 527 ft. Latitude: 36° 59' N Longitude: 86° 26' W

	JAN	FEB	MAR	APR	MAY	JUN	JUL	AUG	SEP	OCT	NOV	DEC	YEAR
Mean Maximum Temp. (°F)	44.1	***48.8***	59.0	69.1	77.0	85.3	89.0	88.4	81.2	70.1	58.9	47.4	***68.2***
Mean Temp. (°F)	35.3	***39.0***	48.0	57.5	65.9	74.4	78.5	77.4	69.6	58.2	48.3	38.3	***57.5***
Mean Minimum Temp. (°F)	26.4	***29.2***	37.0	45.9	54.8	63.5	68.0	66.3	58.1	46.2	37.7	29.1	***46.8***
Extreme Maximum Temp. (°F)	74	***79***	85	90	94	102	107	106	104	93	83	78	***107***
Extreme Minimum Temp. (°F)	-15	***-5***	1	23	33	45	48	43	33	23	15	-14	***-15***
Days Maximum Temp. ≥ 90°F	0	***0***	0	0	1	8	15	14	4	0	0	0	***42***
Days Maximum Temp. ≤ 32°F	5	***3***	0	0	0	0	0	0	0	0	0	3	***11***
Days Minimum Temp. ≤ 32°F	23	***19***	11	2	0	0	0	0	0	2	10	20	***87***
Days Minimum Temp. ≤ 0°F	1	***0***	0	0	0	0	0	0	0	0	0	0	***1***
Heating Degree Days (base 65°F)	912	***728***	525	248	74	4	0	1	37	236	497	823	***4,085***
Cooling Degree Days (base 65°F)	0	***0***	5	31	111	294	425	391	184	31	3	0	***1,475***
Mean Precipitation (in.)	3.36	***4.07***	4.07	4.05	5.47	3.78	4.25	3.47	3.95	3.53	4.20	4.75	***48.95***
Extreme Maximum Daily Precip. (in.)	2.86	***2.93***	3.00	2.32	3.22	3.28	4.91	3.48	3.66	3.99	2.71	2.96	***4.91***
Days With ≥ 0.1" Precipitation	6	***7***	7	8	8	7	6	5	6	6	7	8	***81***
Days With ≥ 0.5" Precipitation	2	***3***	3	3	4	3	3	2	2	2	3	3	***33***
Days With ≥ 1.0" Precipitation	1	***1***	1	1	2	1	1	1	1	1	1	1	***13***
Mean Snowfall (in.)	na	na	na	na	na	na	na	na	na	na	na	na	na
Maximum Snow Depth (in.)	na	na	na	na	na	na	na	na	na	na	na	na	na
Days With ≥ 1.0" Snow Depth	na	na	na	na	na	na	na	na	na	na	na	na	na

Bradfordsville *Marion County* Elevation: 660 ft. Latitude: 37° 29' N Longitude: 85° 09' W

	JAN	FEB	MAR	APR	MAY	JUN	JUL	AUG	SEP	OCT	NOV	DEC	YEAR
Mean Maximum Temp. (°F)	43.6	48.2	57.6	68.0	76.6	84.5	88.1	87.5	81.5	70.6	58.7	46.9	67.6
Mean Temp. (°F)	33.6	37.1	45.0	54.5	63.7	72.2	76.3	75.0	68.0	56.5	46.3	36.7	55.4
Mean Minimum Temp. (°F)	23.6	25.9	32.3	40.8	50.7	59.8	64.5	62.5	54.5	42.3	33.8	26.5	43.1
Extreme Maximum Temp. (°F)	75	82	85	90	93	100	105	105	99	92	84	78	105
Extreme Minimum Temp. (°F)	-22	-14	-7	17	29	39	45	38	32	20	11	-17	-22
Days Maximum Temp. ≥ 90°F	0	0	0	0	1	6	13	12	4	0	0	0	36
Days Maximum Temp. ≤ 32°F	6	3	1	0	0	0	0	0	0	0	0	4	14
Days Minimum Temp. ≤ 32°F	24	21	17	7	1	0	0	0	0	6	15	22	113
Days Minimum Temp. ≤ 0°F	1	1	0	0	0	0	0	0	0	0	0	1	3
Heating Degree Days (base 65°F)	966	783	617	328	116	11	0	2	51	282	556	871	4,583
Cooling Degree Days (base 65°F)	0	0	3	18	83	234	357	320	148	25	2	1	1,191
Mean Precipitation (in.)	3.75	4.09	4.79	4.16	5.33	4.54	4.79	3.56	3.81	3.23	3.84	4.51	50.40
Extreme Maximum Daily Precip. (in.)	2.68	4.22	4.07	2.05	3.17	3.15	4.20	3.02	4.31	3.14	3.25	3.19	4.31
Days With ≥ 0.1" Precipitation	7	7	8	8	9	7	6	6	5	5	7	8	83
Days With ≥ 0.5" Precipitation	2	3	3	3	4	3	3	2	2	2	3	3	33
Days With ≥ 1.0" Precipitation	1	1	1	1	1	1	2	1	1	1	1	1	13
Mean Snowfall (in.)	4.6	4.9	1.7	0.1	trace	0.0	0.0	0.0	0.0	trace	0.1	2.3	13.7
Maximum Snow Depth (in.)	9	14	6	1	trace	0	0	0	0	trace	trace	4	14
Days With ≥ 1.0" Snow Depth	5	4	1	0	0	0	0	0	0	0	0	2	12

Crab Orchard 6 N *Garrard County* Elevation: 1,100 ft. Latitude: 37° 29' N Longitude: 84° 26' W

	JAN	FEB	MAR	APR	MAY	JUN	JUL	AUG	SEP	OCT	NOV	DEC	YEAR
Mean Maximum Temp. (°F)	45.0	***49.0***	***58.5***	69.2	76.9	84.3	***87.6***	***87.3***	80.9	70.6	59.2	***47.5***	***68.0***
Mean Temp. (°F)	34.9	***38.1***	***46.1***	56.0	64.1	72.0	***75.4***	***74.4***	67.7	57.2	47.4	***37.3***	***55.9***
Mean Minimum Temp. (°F)	24.8	26.7	***33.4***	42.4	51.4	59.4	***63.2***	61.4	54.3	43.6	35.6	***27.1***	***43.6***
Extreme Maximum Temp. (°F)	76	***79***	85	***90***	92	99	103	104	98	91	82	77	***104***
Extreme Minimum Temp. (°F)	-24	-10	-8	17	29	38	45	36	29	19	8	-18	-24
Days Maximum Temp. ≥ 90°F	0	0	0	0	0	5	11	10	3	0	0	0	29
Days Maximum Temp. ≤ 32°F	5	***3***	0	0	0	0	0	0	0	0	0	2	***10***
Days Minimum Temp. ≤ 32°F	23	20	15	6	0	0	0	0	0	5	12	18	99
Days Minimum Temp. ≤ 0°F	1	1	0	0	0	0	0	0	0	0	0	1	3
Heating Degree Days (base 65°F)	925	***755***	***584***	285	107	10	***1***	***3***	55	261	522	***852***	***4,360***
Cooling Degree Days (base 65°F)	0	***0***	***3***	24	86	226	***331***	***302***	142	26	2	***0***	***1,142***
Mean Precipitation (in.)	3.13	3.57	4.11	3.87	5.23	4.38	4.51	3.59	3.30	3.26	3.68	3.90	46.53
Extreme Maximum Daily Precip. (in.)	***2.64***	***2.85***	***2.20***	***2.30***	2.90	4.15	***3.38***	***3.78***	***3.95***	2.50	2.04	2.75	***4.15***
Days With ≥ 0.1" Precipitation	6	***6***	7	7	8	7	6	5	5	5	7	6	***75***
Days With ≥ 0.5" Precipitation	2	2	3	3	4	3	3	3	2	2	3	3	33
Days With ≥ 1.0" Precipitation	1	1	1	1	2	1	1	1	1	1	1	1	13
Mean Snowfall (in.)	***3.0***	***2.3***	1.1	trace	0.0	0.0	0.0	0.0	0.0	trace	trace	1.5	***7.9***
Maximum Snow Depth (in.)	12	***15***	10	trace	0	0	0	0	0	trace	trace	4	***15***
Days With ≥ 1.0" Snow Depth	3	***2***	0	0	0	0	0	0	0	0	0	2	***7***

Cynthiana *Harrison County* Elevation: 700 ft. Latitude: 38° 23' N Longitude: 84° 18' W

	JAN	FEB	MAR	APR	MAY	JUN	JUL	AUG	SEP	OCT	NOV	DEC	YEAR
Mean Maximum Temp. (°F)	41.3	45.4	54.7	66.2	75.3	83.5	87.3	86.7	80.5	68.7	***56.7***	44.3	***65.9***
Mean Temp. (°F)	31.9	35.0	42.8	53.4	63.0	71.6	75.9	74.6	67.3	55.5	***45.5***	35.0	***54.3***
Mean Minimum Temp. (°F)	22.6	24.5	30.9	40.5	50.7	59.7	64.3	62.4	54.0	42.2	***34.2***	25.6	***42.6***
Extreme Maximum Temp. (°F)	74	77	84	91	92	102	104	106	100	92	83	77	106
Extreme Minimum Temp. (°F)	-33	-10	-6	14	27	42	47	38	33	18	12	-21	-33
Days Maximum Temp. ≥ 90°F	0	0	0	0	0	5	11	10	3	0	0	0	29
Days Maximum Temp. ≤ 32°F	7	5	1	0	0	0	0	0	0	0	0	5	18
Days Minimum Temp. ≤ 32°F	26	22	18	6	0	0	0	0	0	5	14	22	113
Days Minimum Temp. ≤ 0°F	1	1	0	0	0	0	0	0	0	0	0	1	3
Heating Degree Days (base 65°F)	1,018	842	683	355	129	16	1	3	60	304	***579***	924	***4,914***
Cooling Degree Days (base 65°F)	0	0	1	13	74	222	344	307	136	19	***1***	0	***1,117***
Mean Precipitation (in.)	2.94	2.92	4.03	3.73	4.84	3.94	4.03	2.93	2.93	3.27	3.56	3.59	42.71
Extreme Maximum Daily Precip. (in.)	2.10	4.41	2.32	2.24	2.37	2.71	2.74	2.42	3.10	3.44	2.15	2.38	4.41
Days With ≥ 0.1" Precipitation	6	5	8	8	8	7	7	6	5	6	7	7	80
Days With ≥ 0.5" Precipitation	2	2	3	3	4	3	3	2	2	2	3	2	31
Days With ≥ 1.0" Precipitation	1	1	1	1	1	1	1	1	1	1	1	1	12
Mean Snowfall (in.)	2.8	1.4	0.6	trace	0.0	0.0	0.0	0.0	0.0	trace	trace	1.7	6.5
Maximum Snow Depth (in.)	***5***	10	4	4	0	0	0	0	0	trace	***1***	***6***	***10***
Days With ≥ 1.0" Snow Depth	***1***	2	0	0	0	0	0	0	0	0	0	***0***	***3***

The period of record for all cooperative weather station data is 1980 – 2009. See User Guide for detailed explanation of data.

Dix Dam *Mercer County* Elevation: 870 ft. Latitude: 37° 48' N Longitude: 84° 43' W

	JAN	FEB	MAR	APR	MAY	JUN	JUL	AUG	SEP	OCT	NOV	DEC	YEAR
Mean Maximum Temp. (°F)	44.4	49.1	57.8	68.3	76.4	83.8	87.4	87.0	80.7	70.3	58.5	46.9	67.5
Mean Temp. (°F)	36.0	39.4	46.9	56.8	65.5	73.3	77.4	76.4	69.7	59.1	48.8	38.6	57.3
Mean Minimum Temp. (°F)	27.5	29.8	36.0	45.2	54.7	62.9	67.3	65.8	58.6	47.8	39.2	30.2	47.1
Extreme Maximum Temp. (°F)	74	***80***	83	89	92	101	104	103	97	***88***	82	76	***104***
Extreme Minimum Temp. (°F)	-18	-7	2	12	31	42	51	44	35	***24***	14	-17	***-18***
Days Maximum Temp. ≥ 90°F	0	0	0	0	0	4	10	11	3	0	0	0	28
Days Maximum Temp. ≤ 32°F	5	3	1	0	0	0	0	0	0	0	0	4	13
Days Minimum Temp. ≤ 32°F	21	18	13	3	0	0	0	0	0	2	9	19	85
Days Minimum Temp. ≤ 0°F	0	0	0	0	0	0	0	0	0	0	0	0	0
Heating Degree Days (base 65°F)	893	716	557	266	80	7	0	1	34	214	481	811	4,060
Cooling Degree Days (base 65°F)	0	0	3	25	104	262	390	362	183	36	2	0	1,367
Mean Precipitation (in.)	2.79	3.38	3.92	3.34	4.36	3.96	4.00	3.48	2.49	***2.76***	3.26	3.11	***40.85***
Extreme Maximum Daily Precip. (in.)	2.80	3.93	4.17	2.02	2.24	2.84	4.00	3.30	***2.34***	***3.94***	4.01	2.90	***4.17***
Days With ≥ 0.1" Precipitation	5	6	7	7	8	7	6	6	5	***6***	7	6	***76***
Days With ≥ 0.5" Precipitation	2	2	3	2	4	3	3	2	1	***2***	2	2	***28***
Days With ≥ 1.0" Precipitation	1	1	1	1	1	1	1	1	1	***1***	1	1	***12***
Mean Snowfall (in.)	***1.1***	na	***0.1***	0.0	0.0	0.0	0.0	0.0	0.0	0.0	trace	trace	na
Maximum Snow Depth (in.)	9	***12***	3	0	0	0	0	0	0	***0***	trace	2	***12***
Days With ≥ 1.0" Snow Depth	2	***1***	0	0	0	0	0	0	0	***0***	0	0	***3***

Farmers 2 S *Rowan County* Elevation: 680 ft. Latitude: 38° 07' N Longitude: 83° 33' W

	JAN	FEB	MAR	APR	MAY	JUN	JUL	AUG	SEP	OCT	NOV	DEC	YEAR
Mean Maximum Temp. (°F)	42.7	46.7	56.6	67.9	76.4	84.2	88.0	87.2	80.7	69.7	58.0	46.2	67.0
Mean Temp. (°F)	33.3	36.3	44.5	54.8	63.6	71.8	76.0	74.9	67.9	56.6	46.7	36.9	55.3
Mean Minimum Temp. (°F)	23.9	25.9	32.3	41.7	50.7	59.4	63.9	62.5	55.0	43.6	35.4	27.4	43.5
Extreme Maximum Temp. (°F)	77	80	89	92	95	101	105	103	99	96	85	79	105
Extreme Minimum Temp. (°F)	-26	-13	-7	17	28	37	45	35	32	20	10	-24	-26
Days Maximum Temp. ≥ 90°F	0	0	0	0	1	7	13	12	4	0	0	0	37
Days Maximum Temp. ≤ 32°F	6	4	1	0	0	0	0	0	0	0	0	4	15
Days Minimum Temp. ≤ 32°F	24	21	17	6	0	0	0	0	0	5	13	21	107
Days Minimum Temp. ≤ 0°F	1	1	0	0	0	0	0	0	0	0	0	0	2
Heating Degree Days (base 65°F)	975	805	634	323	121	16	1	3	54	279	544	865	4,620
Cooling Degree Days (base 65°F)	0	0	4	24	86	228	348	316	149	28	2	0	1,185
Mean Precipitation (in.)	3.20	3.35	4.24	3.90	4.94	4.30	5.38	3.61	3.12	3.26	3.71	3.88	46.89
Extreme Maximum Daily Precip. (in.)	2.24	2.73	4.32	2.15	3.60	3.25	3.39	4.12	4.03	3.64	3.36	3.10	4.32
Days With ≥ 0.1" Precipitation	7	7	8	8	9	8	8	6	5	6	7	8	87
Days With ≥ 0.5" Precipitation	2	2	3	3	3	3	4	2	2	2	3	3	32
Days With ≥ 1.0" Precipitation	1	1	1	1	1	1	2	1	1	1	1	1	13
Mean Snowfall (in.)	2.2	***1.7***	0.9	trace	0.0	0.0	0.0	0.0	0.0	0.0	trace	1.9	***6.7***
Maximum Snow Depth (in.)	12	12	10	trace	0	0	0	0	0	1	trace	5	12
Days With ≥ 1.0" Snow Depth	6	4	1	0	0	0	0	0	0	0	0	2	13

Henderson 7 SSW *Henderson County* Elevation: 430 ft. Latitude: 37° 45' N Longitude: 87° 38' W

	JAN	FEB	MAR	APR	MAY	JUN	JUL	AUG	SEP	OCT	NOV	DEC	YEAR
Mean Maximum Temp. (°F)	42.4	48.6	58.2	69.0	77.5	85.4	88.3	87.8	82.4	71.1	57.9	45.4	67.8
Mean Temp. (°F)	34.0	39.0	47.4	57.6	66.6	74.7	78.0	76.6	70.3	59.2	48.3	37.1	57.4
Mean Minimum Temp. (°F)	25.5	29.5	36.5	46.2	55.7	64.0	67.6	65.4	58.1	47.2	38.6	28.8	46.9
Extreme Maximum Temp. (°F)	72	78	84	89	93	99	101	102	99	93	84	77	102
Extreme Minimum Temp. (°F)	-20	-6	6	22	33	43	49	44	34	19	12	-15	-20
Days Maximum Temp. ≥ 90°F	0	0	0	0	1	7	13	12	5	0	0	0	38
Days Maximum Temp. ≤ 32°F	6	3	0	0	0	0	0	0	0	0	0	4	13
Days Minimum Temp. ≤ 32°F	23	16	12	2	0	0	0	0	0	2	9	20	84
Days Minimum Temp. ≤ 0°F	1	0	0	0	0	0	0	0	0	0	0	1	2
Heating Degree Days (base 65°F)	954	729	544	250	65	4	0	1	32	215	498	858	4,150
Cooling Degree Days (base 65°F)	0	0	5	33	123	302	409	368	197	42	3	0	1,482
Mean Precipitation (in.)	2.89	3.00	4.40	4.56	5.32	3.78	3.55	2.94	3.01	3.35	4.01	3.79	44.60
Extreme Maximum Daily Precip. (in.)	5.29	3.36	5.05	3.82	2.98	4.42	3.24	3.99	4.72	4.01	3.50	2.79	5.29
Days With ≥ 0.1" Precipitation	6	5	8	8	8	6	6	5	4	5	6	7	74
Days With ≥ 0.5" Precipitation	2	2	3	3	4	2	3	2	2	2	3	3	31
Days With ≥ 1.0" Precipitation	1	1	1	1	2	1	1	1	1	1	1	1	13
Mean Snowfall (in.)	3.9	4.2	1.4	0.1	0.0	0.0	0.0	0.0	0.0	0.1	0.1	2.9	12.7
Maximum Snow Depth (in.)	10	12	9	trace	0	0	0	0	0	2	trace	12	12
Days With ≥ 1.0" Snow Depth	4	4	0	0	0	0	0	0	0	0	0	3	11

Hodgenville-Lincoln Np *Larue County* Elevation: 788 ft. Latitude: 37° 32' N Longitude: 85° 44' W

	JAN	FEB	MAR	APR	MAY	JUN	JUL	AUG	SEP	OCT	NOV	DEC	YEAR
Mean Maximum Temp. (°F)	44.4	49.6	59.4	69.5	76.6	83.5	86.7	86.6	80.9	70.1	58.6	47.0	67.7
Mean Temp. (°F)	35.1	39.3	47.6	57.1	65.2	72.7	76.2	75.5	69.2	58.3	48.2	38.1	56.9
Mean Minimum Temp. (°F)	25.8	28.9	35.6	44.6	53.7	61.8	65.7	64.3	57.4	46.3	37.8	29.1	45.9
Extreme Maximum Temp. (°F)	71	77	90	88	90	99	107	104	99	97	82	78	107
Extreme Minimum Temp. (°F)	-25	-6	-3	20	32	42	49	43	35	21	13	-19	-25
Days Maximum Temp. ≥ 90°F	0	0	0	0	0	4	9	9	4	0	0	0	26
Days Maximum Temp. ≤ 32°F	5	3	0	0	0	0	0	0	0	0	0	3	11
Days Minimum Temp. ≤ 32°F	22	18	13	4	0	0	0	0	0	3	10	19	89
Days Minimum Temp. ≤ 0°F	1	0	0	0	0	0	0	0	0	0	0	0	1
Heating Degree Days (base 65°F)	920	721	540	257	87	9	0	2	39	235	499	825	4,134
Cooling Degree Days (base 65°F)	0	0	5	27	99	247	355	333	171	33	2	0	1,272
Mean Precipitation (in.)	3.22	3.99	4.33	4.18	5.82	4.03	4.60	3.33	3.83	3.65	4.12	4.51	49.61
Extreme Maximum Daily Precip. (in.)	***2.67***	***3.27***	***5.20***	***3.90***	***4.62***	***2.53***	3.60	4.00	***4.68***	3.30	***2.33***	***4.02***	***5.20***
Days With ≥ 0.1" Precipitation	5	5	7	6	8	6	6	5	5	5	6	6	70
Days With ≥ 0.5" Precipitation	2	2	3	3	4	3	3	2	3	3	3	3	34
Days With ≥ 1.0" Precipitation	1	1	1	1	2	1	2	1	1	1	1	1	14
Mean Snowfall (in.)	2.0	2.0	0.3	trace	0.0	0.0	0.0	0.0	0.0	0.0	trace	1.2	5.5
Maximum Snow Depth (in.)	9	9	5	1	0	0	0	0	0	0	trace	6	9
Days With ≥ 1.0" Snow Depth	2	1	0	0	0	0	0	0	0	0	0	1	4

The period of record for all cooperative weather station data is 1980 – 2009. See User Guide for detailed explanation of data.

Hopkinsville *Christian County* Elevation: 520 ft. Latitude: 36° 51' N Longitude: 87° 31' W

	JAN	FEB	MAR	APR	MAY	JUN	JUL	AUG	SEP	OCT	NOV	DEC	YEAR
Mean Maximum Temp. (°F)	43.6	47.8	58.9	69.2	77.4	85.7	89.4	89.0	82.1	70.4	59.0	46.6	68.2
Mean Temp. (°F)	34.3	37.4	47.4	56.9	65.8	74.2	78.1	77.1	69.9	58.0	48.0	37.1	57.0
Mean Minimum Temp. (°F)	24.5	26.9	35.8	44.6	54.1	62.7	66.8	65.2	57.6	45.6	37.0	27.7	45.7
Extreme Maximum Temp. (°F)	73	81	87	90	95	100	104	109	101	93	85	76	109
Extreme Minimum Temp. (°F)	-19	-3	3	21	34	44	53	48	32	20	15	-14	-19
Days Maximum Temp. ≥ 90°F	0	0	0	0	1	9	16	15	5	0	0	0	46
Days Maximum Temp. ≤ 32°F	5	4	0	0	0	0	0	0	0	0	0	4	13
Days Minimum Temp. ≤ 32°F	24	19	13	3	0	0	0	0	0	3	10	20	92
Days Minimum Temp. ≤ 0°F	1	0	0	0	0	0	0	0	0	0	0	0	1
Heating Degree Days (base 65°F)	947	776	545	268	79	6	0	1	39	244	505	855	4,265
Cooling Degree Days (base 65°F)	0	0	5	33	110	290	413	382	193	34	3	0	1,463
Mean Precipitation (in.)	3.62	4.43	4.34	4.52	5.51	3.67	4.28	3.37	3.67	3.93	4.61	5.00	50.95
Extreme Maximum Daily Precip. (in.)	3.54	4.07	2.95	3.25	3.57	3.28	3.91	6.47	6.08	4.67	3.15	4.34	6.47
Days With ≥ 0.1" Precipitation	6	6	8	8	8	6	6	4	5	5	7	7	76
Days With ≥ 0.5" Precipitation	2	3	3	3	4	2	3	2	2	3	3	3	33
Days With ≥ 1.0" Precipitation	1	1	1	1	2	1	1	1	1	1	1	1	13
Mean Snowfall (in.)	2.5	2.9	0.8	0.1	0.0	0.0	0.0	0.0	0.0	trace	trace	1.0	7.3
Maximum Snow Depth (in.)	7	9	5	0	0	0	0	0	0	trace	trace	3	9
Days With ≥ 1.0" Snow Depth	2	2	0	0	0	0	0	0	0	0	0	1	5

Mammoth Cave *Edmonson County* Elevation: 790 ft. Latitude: 37° 11' N Longitude: 86° 05' W

	JAN	FEB	MAR	APR	MAY	JUN	JUL	AUG	SEP	OCT	NOV	DEC	YEAR
Mean Maximum Temp. (°F)	45.4	51.3	60.1	70.9	78.6	85.3	88.9	87.9	82.0	71.3	59.5	48.1	69.1
Mean Temp. (°F)	35.9	40.7	48.3	58.1	66.1	73.4	77.4	76.2	69.6	58.9	49.0	38.7	57.7
Mean Minimum Temp. (°F)	26.4	30.0	36.3	45.2	53.6	61.4	65.9	64.3	57.1	46.4	38.5	29.3	46.2
Extreme Maximum Temp. (°F)	73	78	85	93	96	100	104	104	99	90	93	76	104
Extreme Minimum Temp. (°F)	-20	-10	-1	20	30	41	47	39	32	18	10	-18	-20
Days Maximum Temp. ≥ 90°F	0	0	0	0	1	7	15	13	4	0	0	0	40
Days Maximum Temp. ≤ 32°F	4	2	0	0	0	0	0	0	0	0	0	3	9
Days Minimum Temp. ≤ 32°F	22	17	12	4	0	0	0	0	0	3	9	19	86
Days Minimum Temp. ≤ 0°F	1	0	0	0	0	0	0	0	0	0	0	1	2
Heating Degree Days (base 65°F)	894	680	520	239	75	7	0	1	38	220	477	809	3,960
Cooling Degree Days (base 65°F)	0	0	7	38	116	265	392	354	181	37	5	0	1,395
Mean Precipitation (in.)	3.37	3.76	4.61	4.24	5.35	4.54	4.43	4.02	4.15	3.60	4.32	4.68	51.07
Extreme Maximum Daily Precip. (in.)	2.60	3.19	na	2.70	6.80	3.10	3.04	3.63	3.86	3.04	3.44	2.72	na
Days With ≥ 0.1" Precipitation	6	6	8	8	8	7	7	5	6	5	7	8	81
Days With ≥ 0.5" Precipitation	2	3	3	3	4	3	3	3	3	2	3	3	35
Days With ≥ 1.0" Precipitation	1	1	1	1	2	1	1	1	1	1	1	1	13
Mean Snowfall (in.)	2.2	2.3	0.9	0.1	0.0	0.0	0.0	0.0	0.0	0.0	trace	1.6	7.1
Maximum Snow Depth (in.)	10	9	na	trace	0	0	0	0	0	0	trace	5	na
Days With ≥ 1.0" Snow Depth	3	2	0	0	0	0	0	0	0	0	0	1	6

Maysville Sewage Plant *Mason County* Elevation: 515 ft. Latitude: 38° 41' N Longitude: 83° 47' W

	JAN	FEB	MAR	APR	MAY	JUN	JUL	AUG	SEP	OCT	NOV	DEC	YEAR
Mean Maximum Temp. (°F)	40.9	45.5	54.8	65.9	74.6	83.5	87.3	86.5	80.0	68.4	56.1	44.3	65.7
Mean Temp. (°F)	31.4	35.0	42.7	53.1	62.3	71.5	75.8	74.8	67.7	55.9	45.2	35.1	54.2
Mean Minimum Temp. (°F)	21.9	24.4	30.6	40.1	50.0	59.5	64.3	63.0	55.3	43.4	34.2	25.8	42.7
Extreme Maximum Temp. (°F)	74	75	83	90	92	100	105	103	100	89	84	78	105
Extreme Minimum Temp. (°F)	-25	-8	1	20	32	38	46	39	34	23	12	-17	-25
Days Maximum Temp. ≥ 90°F	0	0	0	0	0	5	10	9	3	0	0	0	27
Days Maximum Temp. ≤ 32°F	7	4	1	0	0	0	0	0	0	0	0	5	17
Days Minimum Temp. ≤ 32°F	25	21	18	6	0	0	0	0	0	3	13	22	108
Days Minimum Temp. ≤ 0°F	1	0	0	0	0	0	0	0	0	0	0	1	2
Heating Degree Days (base 65°F)	1,035	841	683	362	135	15	0	2	52	292	589	919	4,925
Cooling Degree Days (base 65°F)	0	0	1	11	59	218	342	314	141	19	1	0	1,106
Mean Precipitation (in.)	3.23	2.96	4.09	4.10	5.19	3.88	4.57	3.29	3.13	2.99	3.38	3.71	44.52
Extreme Maximum Daily Precip. (in.)	2.05	3.13	4.60	2.64	2.80	3.54	3.45	2.45	3.55	2.13	2.16	3.25	4.60
Days With ≥ 0.1" Precipitation	6	6	7	9	9	7	7	5	5	6	7	7	81
Days With ≥ 0.5" Precipitation	2	2	2	3	4	2	3	2	2	2	2	2	28
Days With ≥ 1.0" Precipitation	1	1	1	1	1	1	1	1	1	1	1	1	12
Mean Snowfall (in.)	1.5	trace	0.3	trace	trace	0.0	0.0	0.0	0.0	trace	trace	0.5	2.3
Maximum Snow Depth (in.)	23	7	3	trace	trace	0	0	0	0	trace	trace	6	23
Days With ≥ 1.0" Snow Depth	2	1	0	0	0	0	0	0	0	0	0	1	4

Paintsville 1 E *Johnson County* Elevation: 629 ft. Latitude: 37° 49' N Longitude: 82° 47' W

	JAN	FEB	MAR	APR	MAY	JUN	JUL	AUG	SEP	OCT	NOV	DEC	YEAR
Mean Maximum Temp. (°F)	45.1	48.8	58.8	69.4	77.4	84.9	88.3	87.7	81.0	71.1	60.2	47.8	68.4
Mean Temp. (°F)	35.2	37.9	46.0	55.6	64.9	73.2	77.1	76.3	68.9	57.3	47.3	37.5	56.4
Mean Minimum Temp. (°F)	25.1	27.0	33.2	41.7	52.3	61.4	65.9	64.8	56.8	43.6	34.3	27.2	44.5
Extreme Maximum Temp. (°F)	80	83	88	93	94	101	105	105	99	90	87	82	105
Extreme Minimum Temp. (°F)	-26	-16	-4	20	29	43	49	47	35	21	13	-10	-26
Days Maximum Temp. ≥ 90°F	0	0	0	0	2	8	12	12	4	0	0	0	38
Days Maximum Temp. ≤ 32°F	5	3	1	0	0	0	0	0	0	0	0	3	12
Days Minimum Temp. ≤ 32°F	23	20	15	5	0	0	0	0	0	4	13	22	102
Days Minimum Temp. ≤ 0°F	1	0	0	0	0	0	0	0	0	0	0	0	1
Heating Degree Days (base 65°F)	918	760	585	297	98	7	0	1	41	255	527	853	4,342
Cooling Degree Days (base 65°F)	0	0	3	21	102	260	381	357	161	25	2	0	1,312
Mean Precipitation (in.)	2.92	3.36	4.01	3.48	4.30	4.32	4.37	3.44	3.27	2.99	3.35	3.46	43.27
Extreme Maximum Daily Precip. (in.)	2.60	3.15	2.21	2.10	2.00	2.96	2.74	3.70	2.52	2.40	2.85	2.20	3.70
Days With ≥ 0.1" Precipitation	6	7	8	7	9	8	7	6	6	6	7	7	84
Days With ≥ 0.5" Precipitation	2	2	3	2	3	3	3	2	2	2	2	2	28
Days With ≥ 1.0" Precipitation	1	1	1	1	1	1	1	1	1	1	1	1	12
Mean Snowfall (in.)	4.7	3.5	1.8	trace	0.0	0.0	0.0	0.0	0.0	0.0	0.3	1.7	12.0
Maximum Snow Depth (in.)	8	7	27	trace	0	0	0	0	0	0	trace	4	27
Days With ≥ 1.0" Snow Depth	na	1	0	0	0	0	0	0	0	0	0	0	na

The period of record for all cooperative weather station data is 1980 – 2009. See User Guide for detailed explanation of data.

Kentucky Weather Station Rankings

Annual Extreme Maximum Temperature

Highest

Rank	Station Name	°F
1	Hopkinsville	***109***
2	Bowling Green Warren Cnty Arpt	***107***
2	Hodgenville-Lincoln Np	107
4	Barren River Lake	106
4	Bernheim Forest	106
4	Cynthiana	106
4	Louisville Standiford Field	106
8	Ashland	105
8	Bardstown 5 E	***105***
8	Bradfordsville	105
8	Farmers 2 S	105
8	Maysville Sewage Plant	105
8	Paintsville 1 E	105
14	Bardwell 2 E	104
14	Beaver Dam	104
14	Crab Orchard 6 N	***104***
14	Dix Dam	***104***
14	Mammoth Cave	***104***
19	Lexington Bluegrass Field	103
20	Barbourville	102
20	Henderson 7 SSW	102
22	Baxter	101
22	Jackson Julian Carroll Arpt	101

Lowest

Rank	Station Name	°F
1	Baxter	101
1	Jackson Julian Carroll Arpt	101
3	Barbourville	102
3	Henderson 7 SSW	102
5	Lexington Bluegrass Field	103
6	Bardwell 2 E	104
6	Beaver Dam	104
6	Crab Orchard 6 N	***104***
6	Dix Dam	***104***
6	Mammoth Cave	***104***
11	Ashland	105
11	Bardstown 5 E	***105***
11	Bradfordsville	105
11	Farmers 2 S	105
11	Maysville Sewage Plant	105
11	Paintsville 1 E	105
17	Barren River Lake	106
17	Bernheim Forest	106
17	Cynthiana	106
17	Louisville Standiford Field	106
21	Bowling Green Warren Cnty Arpt	***107***
21	Hodgenville-Lincoln Np	107
23	Hopkinsville	***109***

Annual Mean Maximum Temperature

Highest

Rank	Station Name	°F
1	Barren River Lake	69.6
2	Bernheim Forest	69.4
3	Bardwell 2 E	69.1
3	Mammoth Cave	***69.1***
5	Beaver Dam	***68.6***
6	Paintsville 1 E	68.4
7	Hopkinsville	***68.3***
8	Bowling Green Warren Cnty Arpt	***68.2***
9	Barbourville	68.1
10	Crab Orchard 6 N	***68.0***
11	Henderson 7 SSW	67.8
12	Bradfordsville	67.7
12	Hodgenville-Lincoln Np	67.7
14	Dix Dam	67.6
15	Bardstown 5 E	***67.2***
16	Ashland	67.1
16	Louisville Standiford Field	67.1
18	Farmers 2 S	67.0
19	Baxter	66.8
20	Jackson Julian Carroll Arpt	66.0
21	Cynthiana	***65.9***
22	Maysville Sewage Plant	65.7
23	Lexington Bluegrass Field	65.1

Lowest

Rank	Station Name	°F
1	Lexington Bluegrass Field	65.1
2	Maysville Sewage Plant	65.7
3	Cynthiana	***65.9***
4	Jackson Julian Carroll Arpt	66.0
5	Baxter	66.8
6	Farmers 2 S	67.0
7	Ashland	67.1
7	Louisville Standiford Field	67.1
9	Bardstown 5 E	***67.2***
10	Dix Dam	67.6
11	Bradfordsville	67.7
11	Hodgenville-Lincoln Np	67.7
13	Henderson 7 SSW	67.8
14	Crab Orchard 6 N	***68.0***
15	Barbourville	68.1
16	Bowling Green Warren Cnty Arpt	***68.2***
17	Hopkinsville	***68.3***
18	Paintsville 1 E	68.4
19	Beaver Dam	***68.6***
20	Bardwell 2 E	69.1
20	Mammoth Cave	***69.1***
22	Bernheim Forest	69.4
23	Barren River Lake	69.6

Rankings include 25 highest/lowest stations. If state has less than 25 stations, all stations are included. The period of record is 1980–2009. See User Guide for detailed explanation of data.

Annual Mean Temperature

Highest

Rank	Station Name	°F
1	Bardwell 2 E	***58.0***
2	Barren River Lake	57.9
3	Bernheim Forest	57.7
3	Mammoth Cave	***57.7***
5	Louisville Standiford Field	57.6
6	Beaver Dam	***57.5***
6	Bowling Green Warren Cnty Arpt	***57.5***
8	Henderson 7 SSW	57.4
9	Dix Dam	57.3
10	Hopkinsville	***57.0***
11	Hodgenville-Lincoln Np	56.9
12	Bardstown 5 E	***56.6***
12	Jackson Julian Carroll Arpt	56.6
14	Paintsville 1 E	***56.4***
15	Crab Orchard 6 N	***55.9***
16	Barbourville	55.7
17	Lexington Bluegrass Field	55.5
18	Baxter	55.4
18	Bradfordsville	55.4
20	Farmers 2 S	55.3
21	Cynthiana	***54.3***
22	Maysville Sewage Plant	54.2
23	Ashland	53.8

Lowest

Rank	Station Name	°F
1	Ashland	53.8
2	Maysville Sewage Plant	54.2
3	Cynthiana	***54.3***
4	Farmers 2 S	55.3
5	Baxter	55.4
5	Bradfordsville	55.4
7	Lexington Bluegrass Field	55.5
8	Barbourville	55.7
9	Crab Orchard 6 N	***55.9***
10	Paintsville 1 E	***56.4***
11	Bardstown 5 E	***56.6***
11	Jackson Julian Carroll Arpt	56.6
13	Hodgenville-Lincoln Np	56.9
14	Hopkinsville	***57.0***
15	Dix Dam	57.3
16	Henderson 7 SSW	57.4
17	Beaver Dam	***57.5***
17	Bowling Green Warren Cnty Arpt	***57.5***
19	Louisville Standiford Field	57.6
20	Bernheim Forest	57.7
20	Mammoth Cave	***57.7***
22	Barren River Lake	57.9
23	Bardwell 2 E	***58.0***

Annual Mean Minimum Temperature

Highest

Rank	Station Name	°F
1	Louisville Standiford Field	48.1
2	Dix Dam	47.1
2	Jackson Julian Carroll Arpt	47.1
4	Bardwell 2 E	***47.0***
5	Henderson 7 SSW	46.9
6	Bowling Green Warren Cnty Arpt	***46.8***
7	Beaver Dam	***46.4***
8	Barren River Lake	46.2
8	Mammoth Cave	***46.2***
10	Bardstown 5 E	***46.0***
11	Hodgenville-Lincoln Np	45.9
11	Lexington Bluegrass Field	45.9
13	Bernheim Forest	45.8
14	Hopkinsville	***45.7***
15	Paintsville 1 E	44.5
16	Baxter	44.0
17	Crab Orchard 6 N	***43.6***
18	Farmers 2 S	43.5
19	Barbourville	43.1
19	Bradfordsville	43.1
21	Maysville Sewage Plant	42.7
22	Cynthiana	***42.6***
23	Ashland	40.4

Lowest

Rank	Station Name	°F
1	Ashland	40.4
2	Cynthiana	***42.6***
3	Maysville Sewage Plant	42.7
4	Barbourville	43.1
4	Bradfordsville	43.1
6	Farmers 2 S	43.5
7	Crab Orchard 6 N	***43.6***
8	Baxter	44.0
9	Paintsville 1 E	44.5
10	Hopkinsville	***45.7***
11	Bernheim Forest	45.8
12	Hodgenville-Lincoln Np	45.9
12	Lexington Bluegrass Field	45.9
14	Bardstown 5 E	***46.0***
15	Barren River Lake	46.2
15	Mammoth Cave	***46.2***
17	Beaver Dam	***46.4***
18	Bowling Green Warren Cnty Arpt	***46.8***
19	Henderson 7 SSW	46.9
20	Bardwell 2 E	***47.0***
21	Dix Dam	47.1
21	Jackson Julian Carroll Arpt	47.1
23	Louisville Standiford Field	48.1

Rankings include 25 highest/lowest stations. If state has less than 25 stations, all stations are included. The period of record is 1980–2009. See User Guide for detailed explanation of data.

Annual Extreme Minimum Temperature

Highest

Rank	Station Name	°F
1	Bowling Green Warren Cnty Arpt	***-15***
2	Dix Dam	***-18***
2	Jackson Julian Carroll Arpt	-18
4	Barren River Lake	-19
4	Baxter	-19
4	Hopkinsville	***-19***
7	Henderson 7 SSW	-20
7	Lexington Bluegrass Field	-20
7	Mammoth Cave	***-20***
10	Bardwell 2 E	***-21***
11	Barbourville	-22
11	Bradfordsville	-22
11	Louisville Standiford Field	-22
14	Beaver Dam	-24
14	Bernheim Forest	-24
14	Crab Orchard 6 N	-24
17	Ashland	-25
17	Hodgenville-Lincoln Np	-25
17	Maysville Sewage Plant	-25
20	Bardstown 5 E	***-26***
20	Farmers 2 S	-26
20	Paintsville 1 E	-26
23	Cynthiana	-33

Lowest

Rank	Station Name	°F
1	Cynthiana	-33
2	Bardstown 5 E	***-26***
2	Farmers 2 S	-26
2	Paintsville 1 E	-26
5	Ashland	-25
5	Hodgenville-Lincoln Np	-25
5	Maysville Sewage Plant	-25
8	Beaver Dam	-24
8	Bernheim Forest	-24
8	Crab Orchard 6 N	-24
11	Barbourville	-22
11	Bradfordsville	-22
11	Louisville Standiford Field	-22
14	Bardwell 2 E	***-21***
15	Henderson 7 SSW	-20
15	Lexington Bluegrass Field	-20
15	Mammoth Cave	***-20***
18	Barren River Lake	-19
18	Baxter	-19
18	Hopkinsville	***-19***
21	Dix Dam	***-18***
21	Jackson Julian Carroll Arpt	-18
23	Bowling Green Warren Cnty Arpt	***-15***

July Mean Maximum Temperature

Highest

Rank	Station Name	°F
1	Bardwell 2 E	90.2
1	Barren River Lake	90.2
3	Bernheim Forest	89.4
3	Hopkinsville	***89.4***
5	Bowling Green Warren Cnty Arpt	89.0
6	Mammoth Cave	88.9
7	Beaver Dam	88.7
8	Henderson 7 SSW	88.3
8	Paintsville 1 E	88.3
10	Louisville Standiford Field	88.2
11	Bradfordsville	88.1
12	Ashland	88.0
12	Farmers 2 S	88.0
14	Crab Orchard 6 N	***87.6***
15	Dix Dam	87.4
16	Barbourville	87.3
16	Cynthiana	87.3
16	Maysville Sewage Plant	87.3
19	Bardstown 5 E	87.2
20	Hodgenville-Lincoln Np	86.7
21	Lexington Bluegrass Field	86.1
22	Baxter	85.5
23	Jackson Julian Carroll Arpt	84.6

Lowest

Rank	Station Name	°F
1	Jackson Julian Carroll Arpt	84.6
2	Baxter	85.5
3	Lexington Bluegrass Field	86.1
4	Hodgenville-Lincoln Np	86.7
5	Bardstown 5 E	87.2
6	Barbourville	87.3
6	Cynthiana	87.3
6	Maysville Sewage Plant	87.3
9	Dix Dam	87.4
10	Crab Orchard 6 N	***87.6***
11	Ashland	88.0
11	Farmers 2 S	88.0
13	Bradfordsville	88.1
14	Louisville Standiford Field	88.2
15	Henderson 7 SSW	88.3
15	Paintsville 1 E	88.3
17	Beaver Dam	88.7
18	Mammoth Cave	88.9
19	Bowling Green Warren Cnty Arpt	89.0
20	Bernheim Forest	89.4
20	Hopkinsville	***89.4***
22	Bardwell 2 E	90.2
22	Barren River Lake	90.2

Rankings include 25 highest/lowest stations. If state has less than 25 stations, all stations are included. The period of record is 1980–2009. See User Guide for detailed explanation of data.

January Mean Minimum Temperature

Highest

Rank	Station Name	°F
1	Dix Dam	27.5
2	Jackson Julian Carroll Arpt	26.9
3	Louisville Standiford Field	26.6
4	Bowling Green Warren Cnty Arpt	26.4
4	Mammoth Cave	26.4
6	Bardstown 5 E	***26.0***
7	Bernheim Forest	25.9
8	Bardwell 2 E	25.8
8	Hodgenville-Lincoln Np	25.8
10	Barren River Lake	25.7
11	Beaver Dam	25.6
12	Henderson 7 SSW	25.5
13	Baxter	25.3
14	Paintsville 1 E	25.1
15	Lexington Bluegrass Field	25.0
16	Crab Orchard 6 N	24.8
17	Hopkinsville	***24.5***
18	Farmers 2 S	23.9
19	Barbourville	23.7
20	Bradfordsville	23.6
21	Cynthiana	22.6
22	Maysville Sewage Plant	21.9
23	Ashland	19.8

Lowest

Rank	Station Name	°F
1	Ashland	19.8
2	Maysville Sewage Plant	21.9
3	Cynthiana	22.6
4	Bradfordsville	23.6
5	Barbourville	23.7
6	Farmers 2 S	23.9
7	Hopkinsville	***24.5***
8	Crab Orchard 6 N	24.8
9	Lexington Bluegrass Field	25.0
10	Paintsville 1 E	25.1
11	Baxter	25.3
12	Henderson 7 SSW	25.5
13	Beaver Dam	25.6
14	Barren River Lake	25.7
15	Bardwell 2 E	25.8
15	Hodgenville-Lincoln Np	25.8
17	Bernheim Forest	25.9
18	Bardstown 5 E	***26.0***
19	Bowling Green Warren Cnty Arpt	26.4
19	Mammoth Cave	26.4
21	Louisville Standiford Field	26.6
22	Jackson Julian Carroll Arpt	26.9
23	Dix Dam	27.5

Number of Days Annually Maximum Temperature ≥ 90°F

Highest

Rank	Station Name	Days
1	Barren River Lake	58
2	Bardwell 2 E	51
3	Bernheim Forest	47
4	Hopkinsville	***46***
5	Bowling Green Warren Cnty Arpt	***42***
6	Ashland	40
6	Mammoth Cave	***40***
8	Beaver Dam	38
8	Henderson 7 SSW	38
8	Paintsville 1 E	38
11	Farmers 2 S	37
11	Louisville Standiford Field	37
13	Bradfordsville	36
14	Crab Orchard 6 N	29
14	Cynthiana	29
16	Barbourville	28
16	Bardstown 5 E	***28***
16	Dix Dam	28
19	Maysville Sewage Plant	27
20	Hodgenville-Lincoln Np	26
21	Lexington Bluegrass Field	22
22	Baxter	15
23	Jackson Julian Carroll Arpt	14

Lowest

Rank	Station Name	Days
1	Jackson Julian Carroll Arpt	14
2	Baxter	15
3	Lexington Bluegrass Field	22
4	Hodgenville-Lincoln Np	26
5	Maysville Sewage Plant	27
6	Barbourville	28
6	Bardstown 5 E	***28***
6	Dix Dam	28
9	Crab Orchard 6 N	29
9	Cynthiana	29
11	Bradfordsville	36
12	Farmers 2 S	37
12	Louisville Standiford Field	37
14	Beaver Dam	38
14	Henderson 7 SSW	38
14	Paintsville 1 E	38
17	Ashland	40
17	Mammoth Cave	***40***
19	Bowling Green Warren Cnty Arpt	***42***
20	Hopkinsville	***46***
21	Bernheim Forest	47
22	Bardwell 2 E	51
23	Barren River Lake	58

Rankings include 25 highest/lowest stations. If state has less than 25 stations, all stations are included. The period of record is 1980–2009. See User Guide for detailed explanation of data.

Number of Days Annually Maximum Temperature ≤ 32°F

Highest

Rank	Station Name	Days
1	Lexington Bluegrass Field	19
2	Cynthiana	18
3	Jackson Julian Carroll Arpt	17
3	Maysville Sewage Plant	17
5	Ashland	16
6	Farmers 2 S	15
6	Louisville Standiford Field	15
8	Bardstown 5 E	*14*
8	Bradfordsville	14
10	Dix Dam	13
10	Henderson 7 SSW	13
10	Hopkinsville	*13*
13	Paintsville 1 E	12
14	Bardwell 2 E	11
14	Baxter	11
14	Beaver Dam	11
14	Bowling Green Warren Cnty Arpt	*11*
14	Hodgenville-Lincoln Np	11
19	Barbourville	10
19	Barren River Lake	10
19	Crab Orchard 6 N	*10*
22	Bernheim Forest	9
22	Mammoth Cave	*9*

Lowest

Rank	Station Name	Days
1	Bernheim Forest	9
1	Mammoth Cave	*9*
3	Barbourville	10
3	Barren River Lake	10
3	Crab Orchard 6 N	*10*
6	Bardwell 2 E	11
6	Baxter	11
6	Beaver Dam	11
6	Bowling Green Warren Cnty Arpt	*11*
6	Hodgenville-Lincoln Np	11
11	Paintsville 1 E	12
12	Dix Dam	13
12	Henderson 7 SSW	13
12	Hopkinsville	*13*
15	Bardstown 5 E	*14*
15	Bradfordsville	14
17	Farmers 2 S	15
17	Louisville Standiford Field	15
19	Ashland	16
20	Jackson Julian Carroll Arpt	17
20	Maysville Sewage Plant	17
22	Cynthiana	18
23	Lexington Bluegrass Field	19

Number of Days Annually Minimum Temperature ≤ 32°F

Highest

Rank	Station Name	Days
1	Ashland	128
2	Bradfordsville	113
2	Cynthiana	113
4	Barbourville	112
5	Maysville Sewage Plant	108
6	Farmers 2 S	107
7	Baxter	105
8	Paintsville 1 E	102
9	Crab Orchard 6 N	99
10	Bernheim Forest	92
10	Hopkinsville	*92*
12	Barren River Lake	91
13	Lexington Bluegrass Field	90
14	Bardstown 5 E	*89*
14	Hodgenville-Lincoln Np	89
16	Bowling Green Warren Cnty Arpt	*87*
17	Mammoth Cave	*86*
18	Bardwell 2 E	*85*
18	Beaver Dam	85
18	Dix Dam	85
21	Henderson 7 SSW	84
22	Louisville Standiford Field	80
23	Jackson Julian Carroll Arpt	79

Lowest

Rank	Station Name	Days
1	Jackson Julian Carroll Arpt	79
2	Louisville Standiford Field	80
3	Henderson 7 SSW	84
4	Bardwell 2 E	*85*
4	Beaver Dam	85
4	Dix Dam	85
7	Mammoth Cave	*86*
8	Bowling Green Warren Cnty Arpt	*87*
9	Bardstown 5 E	*89*
9	Hodgenville-Lincoln Np	89
11	Lexington Bluegrass Field	90
12	Barren River Lake	91
13	Bernheim Forest	92
13	Hopkinsville	*92*
15	Crab Orchard 6 N	99
16	Paintsville 1 E	102
17	Baxter	105
18	Farmers 2 S	107
19	Maysville Sewage Plant	108
20	Barbourville	112
21	Bradfordsville	113
21	Cynthiana	113
23	Ashland	128

Rankings include 25 highest/lowest stations. If state has less than 25 stations, all stations are included. The period of record is 1980–2009. See User Guide for detailed explanation of data.

Number of Days Annually Minimum Temperature ≤ 0°F

Highest

Rank	Station Name	Days
1	Ashland	4
2	Bradfordsville	3
2	Crab Orchard 6 N	3
2	Cynthiana	3
5	Farmers 2 S	2
5	Henderson 7 SSW	2
5	Mammoth Cave	*2*
5	Maysville Sewage Plant	2
9	Barbourville	1
9	Bardstown 5 E	*1*
9	Bardwell 2 E	*1*
9	Barren River Lake	1
9	Baxter	1
9	Beaver Dam	1
9	Bernheim Forest	1
9	Bowling Green Warren Cnty Arpt	*1*
9	Hodgenville-Lincoln Np	1
9	Hopkinsville	*1*
9	Lexington Bluegrass Field	1
9	Louisville Standiford Field	1
9	Paintsville 1 E	1
22	Dix Dam	0
22	Jackson Julian Carroll Arpt	0

Lowest

Rank	Station Name	Days
1	Dix Dam	0
1	Jackson Julian Carroll Arpt	0
3	Barbourville	1
3	Bardstown 5 E	*1*
3	Bardwell 2 E	*1*
3	Barren River Lake	1
3	Baxter	1
3	Beaver Dam	1
3	Bernheim Forest	1
3	Bowling Green Warren Cnty Arpt	*1*
3	Hodgenville-Lincoln Np	1
3	Hopkinsville	*1*
3	Lexington Bluegrass Field	1
3	Louisville Standiford Field	1
3	Paintsville 1 E	1
16	Farmers 2 S	2
16	Henderson 7 SSW	2
16	Mammoth Cave	*2*
16	Maysville Sewage Plant	2
20	Bradfordsville	3
20	Crab Orchard 6 N	3
20	Cynthiana	3
23	Ashland	4

Number of Annual Heating Degree Days

Highest

Rank	Station Name	Num.
1	Ashland	5,022
2	Maysville Sewage Plant	4,925
3	Cynthiana	*4,914*
4	Farmers 2 S	4,620
5	Bradfordsville	4,583
5	Lexington Bluegrass Field	4,583
7	Barbourville	4,430
8	Baxter	4,405
9	Crab Orchard 6 N	*4,360*
10	Paintsville 1 E	*4,342*
11	Hopkinsville	*4,265*
12	Bardstown 5 E	*4,231*
13	Jackson Julian Carroll Arpt	4,162
14	Louisville Standiford Field	4,158
15	Henderson 7 SSW	4,150
16	Hodgenville-Lincoln Np	4,134
17	Beaver Dam	*4,089*
18	Bowling Green Warren Cnty Arpt	*4,085*
19	Dix Dam	4,060
20	Barren River Lake	4,052
21	Bernheim Forest	4,029
22	Bardwell 2 E	*4,007*
23	Mammoth Cave	*3,960*

Lowest

Rank	Station Name	Num.
1	Mammoth Cave	*3,960*
2	Bardwell 2 E	*4,007*
3	Bernheim Forest	4,029
4	Barren River Lake	4,052
5	Dix Dam	4,060
6	Bowling Green Warren Cnty Arpt	*4,085*
7	Beaver Dam	*4,089*
8	Hodgenville-Lincoln Np	4,134
9	Henderson 7 SSW	4,150
10	Louisville Standiford Field	4,158
11	Jackson Julian Carroll Arpt	4,162
12	Bardstown 5 E	*4,231*
13	Hopkinsville	*4,265*
14	Paintsville 1 E	*4,342*
15	Crab Orchard 6 N	*4,360*
16	Baxter	4,405
17	Barbourville	4,430
18	Bradfordsville	4,583
18	Lexington Bluegrass Field	4,583
20	Farmers 2 S	4,620
21	Cynthiana	*4,914*
22	Maysville Sewage Plant	4,925
23	Ashland	5,022

Rankings include 25 highest/lowest stations. If state has less than 25 stations, all stations are included. The period of record is 1980–2009. See User Guide for detailed explanation of data.

Number of Annual Cooling Degree Days

Highest

Rank	Station Name	Num.
1	Barren River Lake	1,575
2	Louisville Standiford Field	1,571
3	Bardwell 2 E	*1,570*
4	Henderson 7 SSW	1,482
5	Bowling Green Warren Cnty Arpt	*1,475*
6	Hopkinsville	*1,463*
7	Bernheim Forest	1,459
8	Beaver Dam	*1,455*
9	Mammoth Cave	*1,395*
10	Dix Dam	1,367
11	Paintsville 1 E	*1,312*
12	Bardstown 5 E	*1,278*
13	Hodgenville-Lincoln Np	1,272
14	Lexington Bluegrass Field	1,227
15	Bradfordsville	1,191
16	Jackson Julian Carroll Arpt	1,188
17	Farmers 2 S	1,185
18	Crab Orchard 6 N	*1,142*
19	Cynthiana	*1,117*
20	Barbourville	1,115
21	Maysville Sewage Plant	1,106
22	Ashland	1,031
23	Baxter	1,024

Lowest

Rank	Station Name	Num.
1	Baxter	1,024
2	Ashland	1,031
3	Maysville Sewage Plant	1,106
4	Barbourville	1,115
5	Cynthiana	*1,117*
6	Crab Orchard 6 N	*1,142*
7	Farmers 2 S	1,185
8	Jackson Julian Carroll Arpt	1,188
9	Bradfordsville	1,191
10	Lexington Bluegrass Field	1,227
11	Hodgenville-Lincoln Np	1,272
12	Bardstown 5 E	*1,278*
13	Paintsville 1 E	*1,312*
14	Dix Dam	1,367
15	Mammoth Cave	*1,395*
16	Beaver Dam	*1,455*
17	Bernheim Forest	1,459
18	Hopkinsville	*1,463*
19	Bowling Green Warren Cnty Arpt	*1,475*
20	Henderson 7 SSW	1,482
21	Bardwell 2 E	*1,570*
22	Louisville Standiford Field	1,571
23	Barren River Lake	1,575

Annual Precipitation

Highest

Rank	Station Name	Inches
1	Bardwell 2 E	*54.68*
2	Mammoth Cave	*51.07*
3	Hopkinsville	50.95
4	Bradfordsville	50.40
5	Barren River Lake	50.36
6	Bardstown 5 E	*50.14*
7	Hodgenville-Lincoln Np	49.61
8	Barbourville	49.27
9	Bowling Green Warren Cnty Arpt	*48.95*
10	Baxter	48.67
11	Beaver Dam	48.39
12	Jackson Julian Carroll Arpt	48.35
13	Bernheim Forest	47.41
14	Farmers 2 S	46.89
15	Crab Orchard 6 N	46.53
16	Lexington Bluegrass Field	45.03
17	Louisville Standiford Field	44.72
18	Henderson 7 SSW	44.60
19	Maysville Sewage Plant	44.52
20	Ashland	43.28
21	Paintsville 1 E	43.27
22	Cynthiana	42.71
23	Dix Dam	*40.85*

Lowest

Rank	Station Name	Inches
1	Dix Dam	*40.85*
2	Cynthiana	42.71
3	Paintsville 1 E	43.27
4	Ashland	43.28
5	Maysville Sewage Plant	44.52
6	Henderson 7 SSW	44.60
7	Louisville Standiford Field	44.72
8	Lexington Bluegrass Field	45.03
9	Crab Orchard 6 N	46.53
10	Farmers 2 S	46.89
11	Bernheim Forest	47.41
12	Jackson Julian Carroll Arpt	48.35
13	Beaver Dam	48.39
14	Baxter	48.67
15	Bowling Green Warren Cnty Arpt	*48.95*
16	Barbourville	49.27
17	Hodgenville-Lincoln Np	49.61
18	Bardstown 5 E	*50.14*
19	Barren River Lake	50.36
20	Bradfordsville	50.40
21	Hopkinsville	50.95
22	Mammoth Cave	*51.07*
23	Bardwell 2 E	*54.68*

Rankings include 25 highest/lowest stations. If state has less than 25 stations, all stations are included. The period of record is 1980–2009. See User Guide for detailed explanation of data.

Annual Extreme Maximum Daily Precipitation

Highest			Lowest		
Rank	Station Name	Inches	Rank	Station Name	Inches
1	Bardwell 2 E	***7.68***	1	Baxter	3.58
2	Louisville Standiford Field	7.22	2	Paintsville 1 E	***3.70***
3	Bernheim Forest	***6.60***	3	Jackson Julian Carroll Arpt	3.84
4	Hopkinsville	***6.47***	4	Ashland	4.00
5	Beaver Dam	***6.45***	5	Crab Orchard 6 N	***4.15***
6	Barren River Lake	6.15	6	Dix Dam	***4.17***
7	Bardstown 5 E	***5.72***	7	Barbourville	4.25
8	Lexington Bluegrass Field	5.56	8	Bradfordsville	4.31
9	Henderson 7 SSW	5.29	9	Farmers 2 S	4.32
10	Hodgenville-Lincoln Np	***5.20***	10	Cynthiana	4.41
11	Bowling Green Warren Cnty Arpt	***4.91***	11	Maysville Sewage Plant	4.60
12	Maysville Sewage Plant	4.60	12	Bowling Green Warren Cnty Arpt	***4.91***
13	Cynthiana	4.41	13	Hodgenville-Lincoln Np	***5.20***
14	Farmers 2 S	4.32	14	Henderson 7 SSW	5.29
15	Bradfordsville	4.31	15	Lexington Bluegrass Field	5.56
16	Barbourville	4.25	16	Bardstown 5 E	***5.72***
17	Dix Dam	***4.17***	17	Barren River Lake	6.15
18	Crab Orchard 6 N	***4.15***	18	Beaver Dam	***6.45***
19	Ashland	4.00	19	Hopkinsville	***6.47***
20	Jackson Julian Carroll Arpt	3.84	20	Bernheim Forest	***6.60***
21	Paintsville 1 E	***3.70***	21	Louisville Standiford Field	7.22
22	Baxter	3.58	22	Bardwell 2 E	***7.68***

Number of Days Annually With ≥ 0.1 Inches of Precipitation

Highest			Lowest		
Rank	Station Name	Days	Rank	Station Name	Days
1	Baxter	94	1	Hodgenville-Lincoln Np	70
2	Jackson Julian Carroll Arpt	91	2	Henderson 7 SSW	74
3	Farmers 2 S	87	3	Beaver Dam	75
4	Barbourville	86	3	Crab Orchard 6 N	***75***
5	Ashland	84	5	Dix Dam	***76***
5	Bardstown 5 E	***84***	5	Hopkinsville	76
5	Paintsville 1 E	84	7	Bernheim Forest	77
8	Bradfordsville	83	8	Bardwell 2 E	79
9	Bowling Green Warren Cnty Arpt	***81***	8	Lexington Bluegrass Field	79
9	Mammoth Cave	***81***	8	Louisville Standiford Field	79
9	Maysville Sewage Plant	81	11	Barren River Lake	80
12	Barren River Lake	80	11	Cynthiana	80
12	Cynthiana	80	13	Bowling Green Warren Cnty Arpt	***81***
14	Bardwell 2 E	79	13	Mammoth Cave	***81***
14	Lexington Bluegrass Field	79	13	Maysville Sewage Plant	81
14	Louisville Standiford Field	79	16	Bradfordsville	83
17	Bernheim Forest	77	17	Ashland	84
18	Dix Dam	***76***	17	Bardstown 5 E	***84***
18	Hopkinsville	76	17	Paintsville 1 E	84
20	Beaver Dam	75	20	Barbourville	86
20	Crab Orchard 6 N	***75***	21	Farmers 2 S	87
22	Henderson 7 SSW	74	22	Jackson Julian Carroll Arpt	91
23	Hodgenville-Lincoln Np	70	23	Baxter	94

Rankings include 25 highest/lowest stations. If state has less than 25 stations, all stations are included. The period of record is 1980–2009. See User Guide for detailed explanation of data.

Number of Days Annually With ≥ 0.5 Inches of Precipitation

Highest Rank	Highest Station Name	Highest Days	Lowest Rank	Lowest Station Name	Lowest Days
1	Baxter	36	1	Ashland	28
2	Barbourville	35	1	Dix Dam	*28*
2	Bardwell 2 E	35	1	Maysville Sewage Plant	28
2	Barren River Lake	35	1	Paintsville 1 E	28
2	Mammoth Cave	*35*	5	Lexington Bluegrass Field	30
6	Bernheim Forest	34	6	Cynthiana	31
6	Hodgenville-Lincoln Np	34	6	Henderson 7 SSW	31
8	Bardstown 5 E	*33*	6	Jackson Julian Carroll Arpt	31
8	Bowling Green Warren Cnty Arpt	*33*	9	Beaver Dam	32
8	Bradfordsville	33	9	Farmers 2 S	32
8	Crab Orchard 6 N	33	9	Louisville Standiford Field	32
8	Hopkinsville	33	12	Bardstown 5 E	*33*
13	Beaver Dam	32	12	Bowling Green Warren Cnty Arpt	*33*
13	Farmers 2 S	32	12	Bradfordsville	33
13	Louisville Standiford Field	32	12	Crab Orchard 6 N	33
16	Cynthiana	31	12	Hopkinsville	33
16	Henderson 7 SSW	31	17	Bernheim Forest	34
16	Jackson Julian Carroll Arpt	31	17	Hodgenville-Lincoln Np	34
19	Lexington Bluegrass Field	30	19	Barbourville	35
20	Ashland	28	19	Bardwell 2 E	35
20	Dix Dam	*28*	19	Barren River Lake	35
20	Maysville Sewage Plant	28	19	Mammoth Cave	*35*
20	Paintsville 1 E	28	23	Baxter	36

Number of Days Annually With ≥ 1.0 Inches of Precipitation

Highest Rank	Highest Station Name	Highest Days	Lowest Rank	Lowest Station Name	Lowest Days
1	Bardwell 2 E	17	1	Ashland	11
2	Barren River Lake	14	2	Barbourville	12
2	Hodgenville-Lincoln Np	14	2	Baxter	12
4	Bardstown 5 E	*13*	2	Cynthiana	12
4	Beaver Dam	13	2	Dix Dam	*12*
4	Bernheim Forest	13	2	Jackson Julian Carroll Arpt	12
4	Bowling Green Warren Cnty Arpt	*13*	2	Louisville Standiford Field	12
4	Bradfordsville	13	2	Maysville Sewage Plant	12
4	Crab Orchard 6 N	13	2	Paintsville 1 E	12
4	Farmers 2 S	13	10	Bardstown 5 E	*13*
4	Henderson 7 SSW	13	10	Beaver Dam	13
4	Hopkinsville	13	10	Bernheim Forest	13
4	Lexington Bluegrass Field	13	10	Bowling Green Warren Cnty Arpt	*13*
4	Mammoth Cave	*13*	10	Bradfordsville	13
15	Barbourville	12	10	Crab Orchard 6 N	13
15	Baxter	12	10	Farmers 2 S	13
15	Cynthiana	12	10	Henderson 7 SSW	13
15	Dix Dam	*12*	10	Hopkinsville	13
15	Jackson Julian Carroll Arpt	12	10	Lexington Bluegrass Field	13
15	Louisville Standiford Field	12	10	Mammoth Cave	*13*
15	Maysville Sewage Plant	12	21	Barren River Lake	14
15	Paintsville 1 E	12	21	Hodgenville-Lincoln Np	14
23	Ashland	11	23	Bardwell 2 E	17

 Rankings include 25 highest/lowest stations. If state has less than 25 stations, all stations are included. The period of record is 1980–2009. See User Guide for detailed explanation of data.

Annual Snowfall

Highest Rank	Highest Station Name	Highest Inches	Lowest Rank	Lowest Station Name	Lowest Inches
1	Jackson Julian Carroll Arpt	22.1	1	Maysville Sewage Plant	*2.3*
2	Bradfordsville	13.7	2	Bernheim Forest	*4.3*
3	Lexington Bluegrass Field	*13.1*	3	Hodgenville-Lincoln Np	5.5
4	Henderson 7 SSW	12.7	4	Barren River Lake	6.2
5	Louisville Standiford Field	12.2	5	Cynthiana	6.5
6	Paintsville 1 E	12.0	6	Barbourville	6.6
7	Beaver Dam	*10.6*	7	Farmers 2 S	*6.7*
8	Bardwell 2 E	*9.1*	8	Mammoth Cave	*7.1*
9	Baxter	8.3	9	Hopkinsville	7.3
10	Crab Orchard 6 N	*7.9*	10	Crab Orchard 6 N	*7.9*
11	Hopkinsville	7.3	11	Baxter	8.3
12	Mammoth Cave	*7.1*	12	Bardwell 2 E	*9.1*
13	Farmers 2 S	*6.7*	13	Beaver Dam	*10.6*
14	Barbourville	6.6	14	Paintsville 1 E	12.0
15	Cynthiana	6.5	15	Louisville Standiford Field	12.2
16	Barren River Lake	6.2	16	Henderson 7 SSW	12.7
17	Hodgenville-Lincoln Np	5.5	17	Lexington Bluegrass Field	*13.1*
18	Bernheim Forest	*4.3*	18	Bradfordsville	13.7
19	Maysville Sewage Plant	*2.3*	19	Jackson Julian Carroll Arpt	22.1

Annual Maximum Snow Depth

Highest Rank	Highest Station Name	Highest Inches	Lowest Rank	Lowest Station Name	Lowest Inches
1	Paintsville 1 E	*27*	1	Barren River Lake	9
2	Ashland	24	1	Hodgenville-Lincoln Np	9
3	Maysville Sewage Plant	*23*	1	Hopkinsville	*9*
4	Jackson Julian Carroll Arpt	20	4	Cynthiana	*10*
5	Baxter	*16*	5	Bernheim Forest	*11*
5	Louisville Standiford Field	16	6	Bardwell 2 E	*12*
7	Crab Orchard 6 N	*15*	6	Dix Dam	*12*
8	Bradfordsville	14	6	Farmers 2 S	12
9	Barbourville	*13*	6	Henderson 7 SSW	12
10	Bardwell 2 E	*12*	6	Lexington Bluegrass Field	*12*
10	Dix Dam	*12*	11	Barbourville	*13*
10	Farmers 2 S	12	12	Bradfordsville	14
10	Henderson 7 SSW	12	13	Crab Orchard 6 N	*15*
10	Lexington Bluegrass Field	*12*	14	Baxter	*16*
15	Bernheim Forest	*11*	14	Louisville Standiford Field	16
16	Cynthiana	*10*	16	Jackson Julian Carroll Arpt	20
17	Barren River Lake	9	17	Maysville Sewage Plant	*23*
17	Hodgenville-Lincoln Np	9	18	Ashland	24
17	Hopkinsville	*9*	19	Paintsville 1 E	*27*

Rankings include 25 highest/lowest stations. If state has less than 25 stations, all stations are included. The period of record is 1980–2009. See User Guide for detailed explanation of data.

Number of Days Annually With ≥ 1.0 Inch Snow Depth

Highest			Lowest		
Rank	Station Name	Days	Rank	Station Name	Days
1	Jackson Julian Carroll Arpt	16	1	Beaver Dam	*2*
2	Farmers 2 S	13	2	Cynthiana	*3*
3	Bradfordsville	12	2	Dix Dam	*3*
4	Henderson 7 SSW	11	4	Barbourville	*4*
4	Lexington Bluegrass Field	*11*	4	Hodgenville-Lincoln Np	4
4	Louisville Standiford Field	11	4	Maysville Sewage Plant	*4*
7	Ashland	9	7	Bernheim Forest	*5*
8	Bardwell 2 E	*7*	7	Hopkinsville	5
8	Barren River Lake	7	9	Baxter	*6*
8	Crab Orchard 6 N	*7*	9	Mammoth Cave	*6*
11	Baxter	*6*	11	Bardwell 2 E	*7*
11	Mammoth Cave	*6*	11	Barren River Lake	7
13	Bernheim Forest	*5*	11	Crab Orchard 6 N	*7*
13	Hopkinsville	5	14	Ashland	9
15	Barbourville	*4*	15	Henderson 7 SSW	11
15	Hodgenville-Lincoln Np	4	15	Lexington Bluegrass Field	*11*
15	Maysville Sewage Plant	*4*	15	Louisville Standiford Field	11
18	Cynthiana	*3*	18	Bradfordsville	12
18	Dix Dam	*3*	19	Farmers 2 S	13
20	Beaver Dam	*2*	20	Jackson Julian Carroll Arpt	16

Rankings include 25 highest/lowest stations. If state has less than 25 stations, all stations are included. The period of record is 1980–2009. See User Guide for detailed explanation of data.

Significant Storm Events in Kentucky: 2000 – 2009

Location or County	Date	Type	Mag.	Deaths	Injuries	Property Damage ($mil.)	Crop Damage ($mil.)
Daviess	01/03/00	Tornado	F3	0	18	64.0	0.0
Grayson	05/23/00	Tornado	F3	0	16	50.0	0.0
Laurel	06/02/01	Tornado	F2	0	10	17.1	0.0
Cumberland River	03/17/02	Flood	na	0	0	26.5	0.0
Webster	04/28/02	Tornado	F3	0	26	15.0	0.0
Laurel	05/01/02	Hail	4.50 in.	0	0	30.0	2.0
North Central Kentucky	02/15/03	Ice Storm	na	1	0	26.3	0.0
Southeast Kentucky	02/16/03	Flood	na	0	0	19.6	0.0
Mccracken	05/04/03	Hail	2.50 in.	0	1	20.0	0.0
Lewis	05/10/03	Tornado	F3	0	17	5.0	0.0
Mercer	05/11/03	Tornado	F2	1	8	15.0	0.0
Eastern Kentucky	05/31/04	Flood	na	0	0	33.0	0.0
East Central Kentucky	06/01/04	Flood	na	0	0	17.5	0.0
Hopkins	11/15/05	Tornado	F4	0	40	31.0	0.0
Henderson	11/15/05	Flash Flood	na	0	0	17.5	0.0
Marshall	11/15/05	Tornado	F3	1	20	8.0	0.0
Christian	04/02/06	Tornado	F3	0	22	35.0	0.0
Muhlenberg	02/05/08	Tornado	F3	3	24	21.3	0.0
Allen	02/06/08	Tornado	F3	4	11	1.2	0.0
Kenton County	09/14/08	High Wind	69 mph	0	0	18.2	0.0
Henderson, Hopkins, Union, and Webster Counties	09/14/08	High Wind	73 mph	0	17	15.0	4.0
Boone County	09/14/08	High Wind	74 mph	0	0	12.9	0.0
Madison	05/08/09	Tornado	F3	2	15	0.0	0.0
Jefferson	08/04/09	Flash Flood	na	0	0	45.0	0.0

Note: Deaths, injuries, and damages are date and location specific.

LOUISIANA

PHYSICAL FEATURES. Louisiana extends roughly between latitudes 29.5° N. and 33° N. and from the 94th meridian eastward to the Mississippi River, and in the south to the Pearl River. Elevations increase gradually from the coast northward, rising to over 100 feet above sea level on uplands and 400 to 500 feet on some of the hills in the northwest.

Drainage in Louisiana is into the Gulf of Mexico. The Red River basin comprises the largest drainage area in the State. The Red joins with the Atchafalaya and Old Rivers, the latter forming an outlet to the Mississippi River. Southern Louisiana is mostly low and level with elevations generally less than 60 feet above mean Gulf level. The runoff is through numerous sluggish streams or bayous which flow through lakes and considerable marshland. The larger marshlands are mainly in the coastal area, extending farthest inland in the southeast. A great part of the southwestern region is drained through the Calcasieu River. The extreme southwestern part of the State drains into the Sabine River which forms more than half of the western boundary. The Pearl River drains a relatively small area in the southeast and forms the southeastern boundary.

GENERAL CLIMATE. The principal influences that determine the climate of Louisiana are its subtropical latitude and its proximity to the Gulf of Mexico. The marine tropical influence is evident from the fact that the average water temperatures of the Gulf along the Louisiana shore range from 64°F. in February to 84°F. in August.

In summer the prevailing southerly winds provide moist, semi-tropical weather often favorable for afternoon thundershowers. When westerly to northerly winds occur, periods of hotter and drier weather interrupt the prevailing moist condition. In the colder season the State is subjected alternately to tropical air and cold continental air, in periods of varying length. Although warmed by its southward journey, the cold air occasionally brings large and rather sudden drops in temperature, but conditions are usually less severe than farther west.

Louisiana is south of the usual track of winter storm centers, but occasionally one moves this far south. In some winters a succession of such centers will develop in the Gulf of Mexico and move over or near the State. The State is occasionally in the path of tropical storms or hurricanes.

From December to May the water of the Mississippi River is usually colder than the air temperature, which favors river fogs during this season, particularly with weak southerly winds. In the more southern sections, lakes also serve to modify the extremes of temperature and to increase fogginess over narrow strips along the shores.

PRECIPITATION. Mean annual precipitation ranges from 46 inches in Caddo Parish to as much as 66 inches in parts of St. Mary, Assumption, Terrebonne, and Lafourche Parishes. A median line of 56 inches per year runs from Hackberry northward to Leesville, Montgomery, Winona, Luna, and southward to Harrisonburg and Deerpark on the Mississippi River. This line separates areas of lower precipitation averages to the north from areas of higher precipitation to the south.

During the summer months, seasonal rainfall usually increases from the northwest toward the southeast. In the winter this pattern is reversed with the heaviest seasonal precipitation in the area extending from the Carroll Parishes southwestward to Winn and southward to St. Landry, with the least in the lower Delta. During the summer months the rich source of moist tropical air results in almost daily showers in the coastal parishes; however, shower frequency diminishes with distance from the Gulf coast toward the northern parishes. In the winter months the northern portion of the State is invaded by cold air which tends to stall and become stationary. This sometimes produces prolonged rains over that area, while clear weather continues in the southern parishes. The pattern of spring rains is similar to that of winter, while fall rains are distributed in the same manner as summer rains. However, fall (September, October, and November) is the driest season of the year, with precipitation ranging from nine inches in the north to 15 inches in the southeast. Spring precipitation ranges from 13 inches on the coast to 18 inches in the central interior.

The heaviest rains of short duration are associated with thunderstorms, although tropical storms sometimes cause prolonged heavy rains. Rains of as much as 20 inches in one month have occurred at most weather stations, and falls of as much as 10 inches in 24 hours are not rare. Although Louisiana is one of the wettest states, droughts are not unknown, especially during the summer and fall. Snow and sleet are of little importance in Louisiana.

FLOODS. Flood producing rains may occur during any month of the year in Louisiana, although they are less likely during September, October, and November, the drier months, and are most frequent during late winter and early spring. Floods on the lower Mississippi and Atchafalaya result from runoff upstream, and rainfall within the State has little influence on these stages. Major floods can occur on the lower Red River from heavy rains in Louisiana. Heavy rains cause several minor floods each year on the Sabine, Calcasieu, and Mermentau Rivers. A major flood on the Sabine occurs about once in four years. In the upper portions of the Calcasieu and Mermentau a major flood occurs about once in 10 years and in the lower portions not more than once in 25 years.

TEMPERATURE. The average annual temperature ranges from 66°F. in northern divisions to 69°F. in southern divisions. The lowest January average is 49°F. in the northwest and north-central ranging upward to 57°F. in the southeast. The highest July average is 83°F. in the northwest and north-central, ranging downward to 81°F. in the east-central. This reversal of temperature distribution with warmer summers in the northern portion than in the southern portion, is due to the almost daily showers in the parishes near or on the Gulf of Mexico. This is further shown by the number of days with temperatures 90°F. or above. While Shreveport and Alexandria average 102 such days, Lake Charles and New Orleans average 86 and 57, respectively. In other words, at New Orleans, where there is a 50 percent expectancy of showers on any day in July, the temperature reaches or exceeds 90°F. about half as often as at Shreveport where summer showers are much less frequent. Temperatures above 110°F. and below 0°F. are rare. The average number of days with freezing temperatures (32°F.) or lower ranges from 24 at Shreveport to four at New Orleans. Near the mouth of the Mississippi River a freeze can be expected only about once in seven years.

STORMS. Showers and thunderstorms occur on an average of 50 to 60 days a year in the northwest and north-central, 70 to 80 days a year in the south, and 60 to 70 days in central and northeast Louisiana. During fall, winter, and spring, these are often attended by high winds, but this is not the case during the summer. Thundershowers which move off Lake Pontchartrain at any season are usually attended by high winds. During late fall, winter, and early spring, thunder may occur at any time of day, but from late spring to early fall about 80 percent of all thundershowers occur between noon and midnight in the northern and between 6 a.m. and 6 p.m. in the southern half of the State.

Tropical cyclones are one of the hazards to life and property in Louisiana, especially in the parishes near the coast. About a third of the cyclones have been of hurricane intensity with winds of 74 miles per hour or more at some points. Most others are attended by gale winds. Almost one-half of all tropical cyclones and one-half of those reaching hurricane intensity have occurred in September.

Tornadoes have been reported in most years and in all months of the year. The largest number of tornadoes has occurred in April, followed by May, November, and March. Hurricanes and tornadoes affect only a relatively small area for a brief time and their frequency is quite low. Contrasting with these occasional adverse features are the mild and short winters, the abundant precipitation, the long growing (freeze-free) season, freedom from extreme summer heat, and the delightful spring and fall weather.

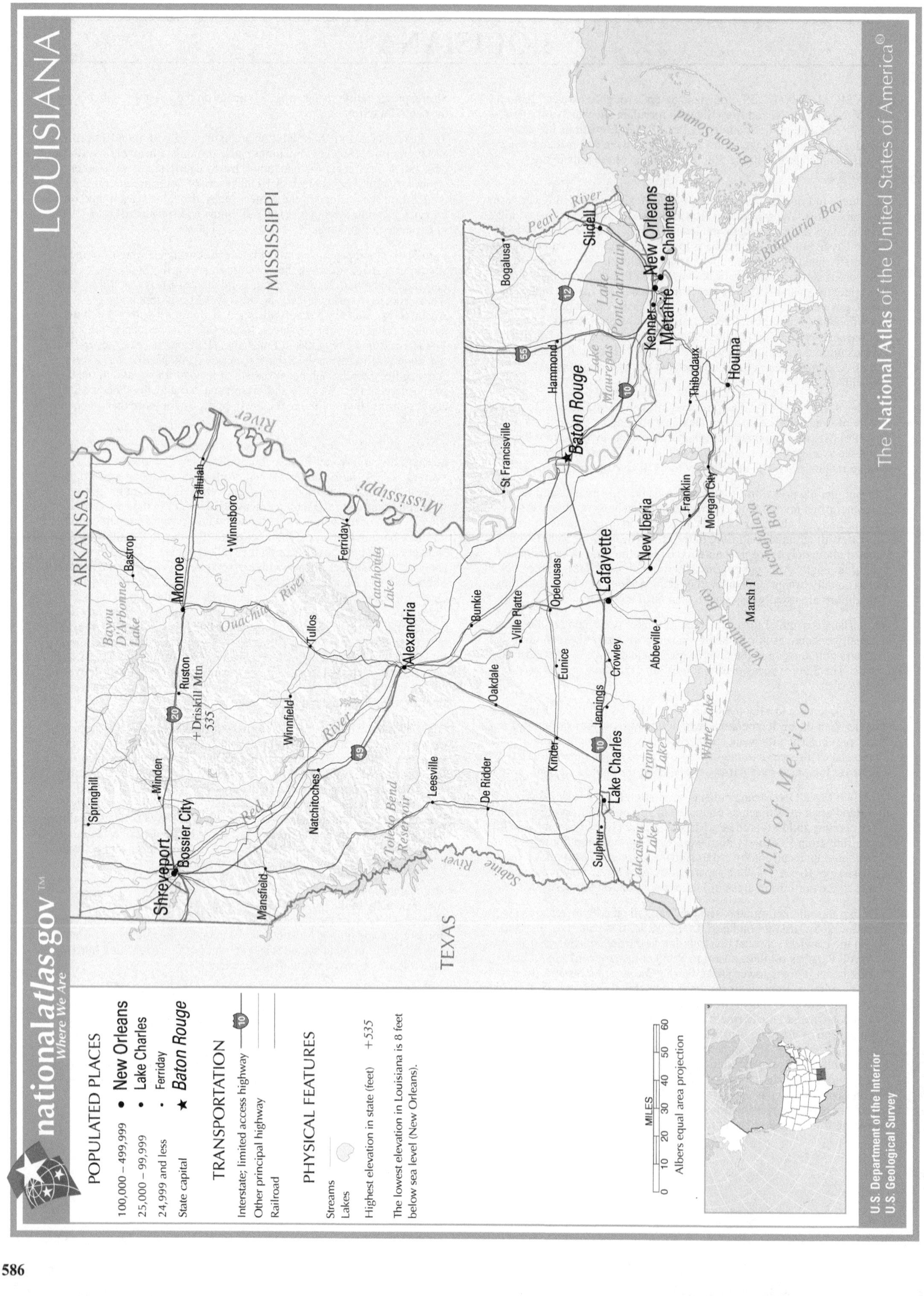
LOUISIANA
nationalatlas.gov™
Where We Are
POPULATED PLACES
100,000 – 499,999 New Orleans
25,000 – 99,999 Lake Charles
24,999 and less Ferriday
State capital Baton Rouge
TRANSPORTATION
Interstate; limited access highway
Other principal highway
Railroad
PHYSICAL FEATURES
Streams
Lakes
Highest elevation in state (feet) +535
The lowest elevation in Louisiana is 8 feet below sea level (New Orleans).
MILES
0 10 20 30 40 50 60
Albers equal area projection
U.S. Department of the Interior
U.S. Geological Survey
The National Atlas of the United States of America®
ARKANSAS
MISSISSIPPI
TEXAS
Gulf of Mexico
Shreveport
Bossier City
Springhill
Minden
Mansfield
Ruston
+ Driskill Mtn 535
Monroe
Bastrop
Bayou D'Arbonne Lake
Tallulah
Winnsboro
Ouachita River
Ferriday
Catahoula Lake
Tullos
Winnfield
Natchitoches
Red River
Toledo Bend Reservoir
Sabine River
Leesville
De Ridder
Alexandria
Bunkie
Oakdale
Kinder
Ville Platte
Eunice
Opelousas
Jennings
Crowley
Lafayette
Lake Charles
Sulphur
Calcasieu Lake
Grand Lake
White Lake
Abbeville
New Iberia
Franklin
Morgan City
Vermilion Bay
Marsh I
Atchafalaya Bay
St Francisville
Baton Rouge
Mississippi River
Hammond
Lake Maurepas
Lake Pontchartrain
Bogalusa
Slidell
Pearl River
Kenner
Metairie
New Orleans
Chalmette
Thibodaux
Houma
Barataria Bay
Breton Sound
10
12
20
49
55

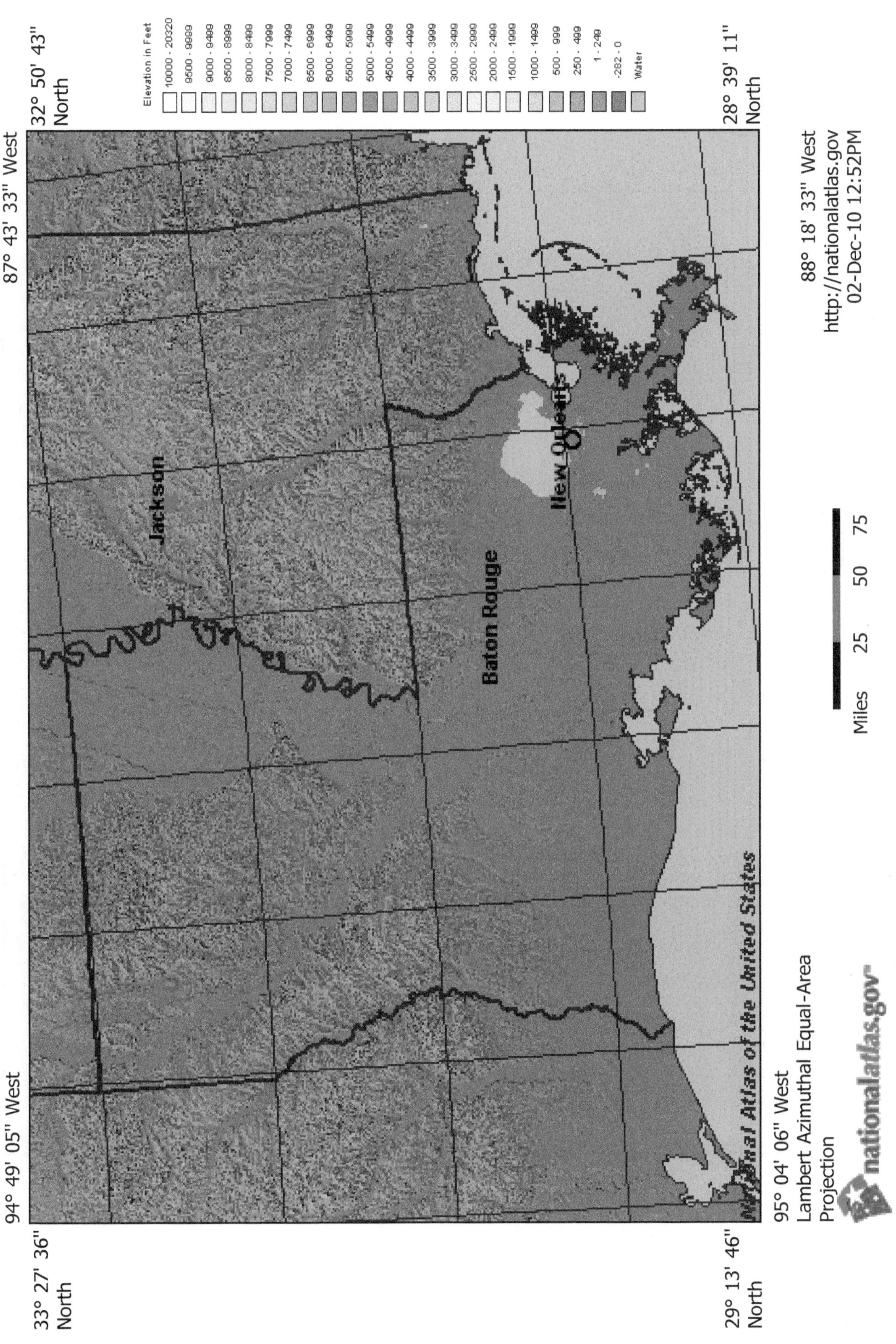
32° 50' 43" North
87° 43' 33" West
28° 39' 11" North
88° 18' 33" West
http://nationalatlas.gov
02-Dec-10 12:52PM
33° 27' 36" North
94° 49' 05" West
29° 13' 46" North
95° 04' 06" West
Lambert Azimuthal Equal-Area Projection
Elevation in Feet
10000 - 20320
9500 - 9999
9000 - 9499
8500 - 8999
8000 - 8499
7500 - 7999
7000 - 7499
6500 - 6999
6000 - 6499
5500 - 5999
5000 - 5499
4500 - 4999
4000 - 4499
3500 - 3999
3000 - 3499
2500 - 2999
2000 - 2499
1500 - 1999
1000 - 1499
500 - 999
250 - 499
1 - 249
-282 - 0
Water
Jackson
Baton Rouge
New Orleans
Miles 25 50 75
National Atlas of the United States
nationalatlas.gov

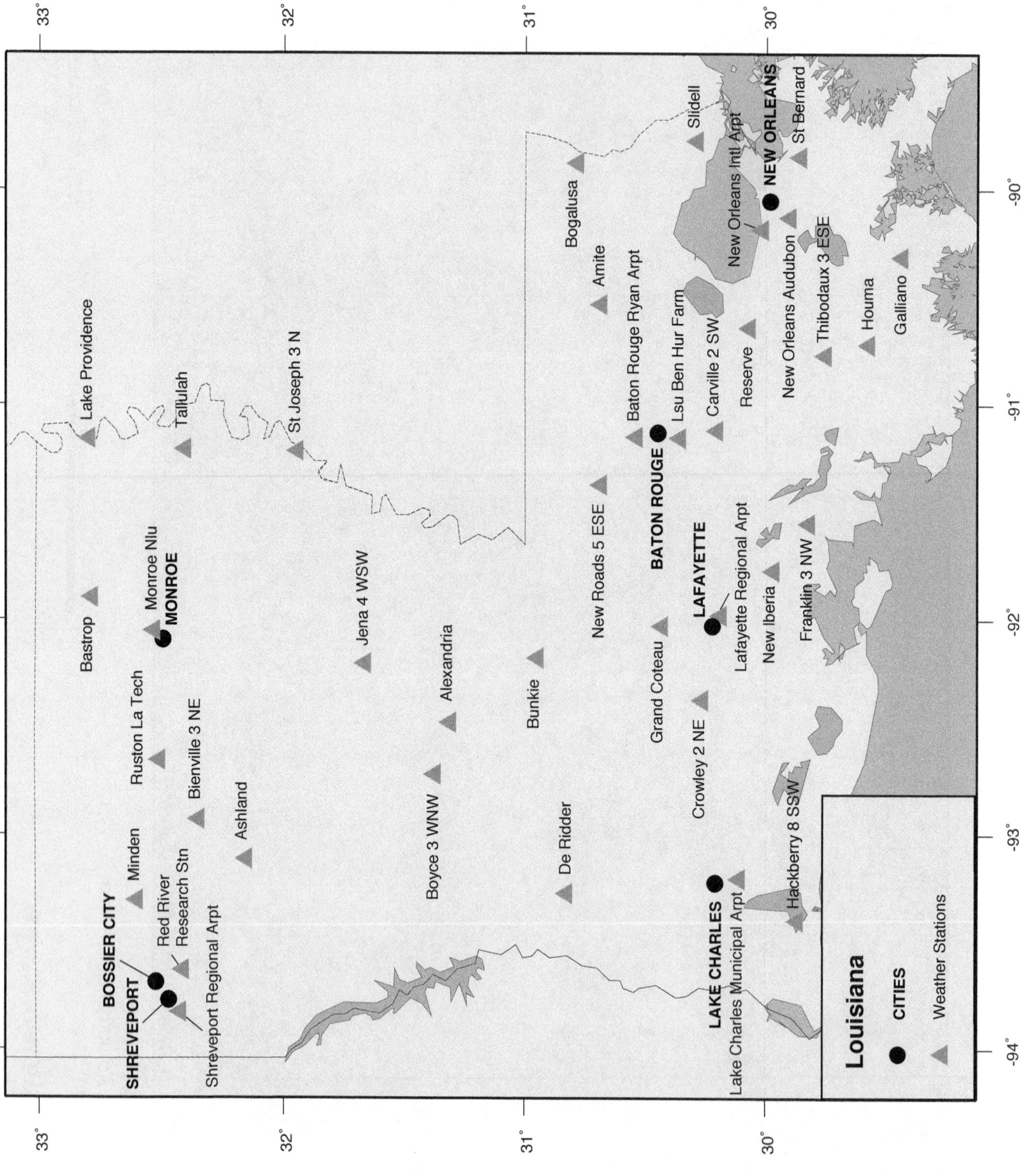
Louisiana
CITIES
Weather Stations
SHREVEPORT
BOSSIER CITY
MONROE
BATON ROUGE
LAFAYETTE
LAKE CHARLES
NEW ORLEANS
Shreveport Regional Arpt
Red River Research Stn
Minden
Ashland
Bienville 3 NE
Ruston La Tech
Bastrop
Monroe Nlu
Lake Providence
Tallulah
St Joseph 3 N
Jena 4 WSW
Alexandria
Boyce 3 WNW
Bunkie
De Ridder
New Roads 5 ESE
Amite
Bogalusa
Baton Rouge Ryan Arpt
Lsu Ben Hur Farm
Grand Coteau
Crowley 2 NE
Lake Charles Municipal Arpt
Lafayette Regional Arpt
Carville 2 SW
Slidell
Reserve
New Orleans Intl Arpt
New Iberia
Hackberry 8 SSW
Franklin 3 NW
New Orleans Audubon
St Bernard
Thibodaux 3 ESE
Houma
Galliano
33°
32°
31°
30°
-90°
-91°
-92°
-93°
-94°

Louisiana Weather Stations by Parish

Parish	Station Name
Acadia	Crowley 2 NE
Avoyelles	Bunkie
Beauregard	De Ridder
Bienville	Bienville 3 NE
Bossier	Red River Research Stn
Caddo	Shreveport Regional Arpt
Calcasieu	Lake Charles Municipal Arpt
Cameron	Hackberry 8 SSW
East Baton Rouge	Baton Rouge Ryan Arpt Lsu Ben Hur Farm
East Carroll	Lake Providence
Iberia	New Iberia
Iberville	Carville 2 SW
Jefferson	New Orleans Intl Arpt
La Salle	Jena 4 WSW
Lafayette	Lafayette Regional Arpt
Lafourche	Galliano Thibodaux 3 ESE
Lincoln	Ruston La Tech
Madison	Tallulah
Morehouse	Bastrop
Natchitoches	Ashland
Orleans	New Orleans Audubon
Ouachita	Monroe NLU
Pointe Coupee	New Roads 5 ESE
Rapides	Alexandria Boyce 3 WNW
St. Bernard	St Bernard
St. John The Baptist	Reserve
St. Landry	Grand Coteau
St. Mary	Franklin 3 NW
St. Tammany	Slidell
Tangipahoa	Amite
Tensas	St Joseph 3 N
Terrebonne	Houma
Washington	Bogalusa
Webster	Minden

See User Guide for station inclusion criteria.

Louisiana Weather Stations by City

City	Station Name	Miles
Alexandria	Alexandria	2.1
	Boyce 3 WNW	16.5
Baton Rouge	Baton Rouge Ryan Arpt	5.8
	Carville 2 SW	17.4
	Lsu Ben Hur Farm	6.3
	New Roads 5 ESE	21.5
Bossier City	Minden	23.3
	Red River Research Stn	7.6
	Shreveport Regional Arpt	8.8
Harvey	New Orleans Intl Arpt	13.7
	New Orleans Audubon	4.7
	St Bernard	13.8
Houma	Houma	1.1
	Thibodaux 3 ESE	13.0
Kenner	New Orleans Intl Arpt	1.2
	New Orleans Audubon	10.0
	Reserve	22.2
Lafayette	Crowley 2 NE	20.0
	Grand Coteau	15.4
	Lafayette Regional Arpt	3.1
	New Iberia	21.7
Lake Charles	Lake Charles Municipal Arpt	6.3
Laplace	New Orleans Intl Arpt	15.1
	New Orleans Audubon	23.9
	Reserve	7.8
Marrero	New Orleans Intl Arpt	11.6
	New Orleans Audubon	2.7
	St Bernard	16.7
Metairie	New Orleans Intl Arpt	4.2
	New Orleans Audubon	6.3
	St Bernard	22.6
Monroe	Bastrop	22.1
	Monroe NLU	2.4
New Iberia	Franklin 3 NW	20.7
	Lafayette Regional Arpt	16.7
	New Iberia	2.6
New Orleans	New Orleans Intl Arpt	12.0
	New Orleans Audubon	6.5
	St Bernard	15.1
Opelousas	Grand Coteau	7.3
	Lafayette Regional Arpt	23.6
Ruston	Bienville 3 NE	21.2
	Ruston La Tech	1.0
Shreveport	Red River Research Stn	8.8
	Shreveport Regional Arpt	2.5
Slidell	Slidell	1.1
	Bay St Louis Nasa, MS	12.8
	Waveland, MS	23.3
Terrytown	New Orleans Intl Arpt	14.9
	New Orleans Audubon	6.4
	St Bernard	11.9

Note: Miles is the distance between the geographic center of the city and the weather station.

See User Guide for station inclusion criteria.

Louisiana Weather Stations by Elevation

Feet	Station Name
307	Bienville 3 NE
279	Ruston La Tech
253	Shreveport Regional Arpt
240	Ashland
209	Jena 4 WSW
189	De Ridder
185	Minden
169	Amite
154	Red River Research Stn
149	Bastrop
109	Boyce 3 WNW
100	Bogalusa
100	Lake Providence
86	Alexandria
84	Tallulah
80	Bunkie
78	St Joseph 3 N
69	Monroe NLU
63	Baton Rouge Ryan Arpt
55	Grand Coteau
44	New Roads 5 ESE
38	Lafayette Regional Arpt
24	Carville 2 SW
24	Crowley 2 NE
24	New Iberia
21	Lsu Ben Hur Farm
15	Houma
15	Lake Charles Municipal Arpt
15	Reserve
15	Thibodaux 3 ESE
12	Franklin 3 NW
9	Slidell
5	Hackberry 8 SSW
5	New Orleans Audubon
4	Galliano
4	St Bernard
3	New Orleans Intl Arpt

See User Guide for station inclusion criteria.

Baton Rouge Ryan Airport

Baton Rouge, the capital city, is located on the east side of the Mississippi River in the southeast section of the state, some 65 miles inland from the coast. The area is near the first evident relief north of the deltaic coastal plains. The National Weather Service Office is located at Ryan Airport, some 8 miles north of the downtown area. Elevations in East Baton Rouge Parish range from near 25 feet to more than 100 feet above sea level.

The general climate of Baton Rouge is humid subtropical, but the city is subject to significant polar influences during winter. Prevailing wind flow is from the southerly direction during much of the year. This maritime air from the Gulf of Mexico helps to temper summer heat, shorten winter cold spells, and provides abundant moisture and rainfall. Winds are usually rather light.

Rainfall is heavy and amounts are substantial in all seasons, with an early autumn low in September and October. Almost all rainfall is from brief convective showers. Occasionally during winter, slow moving cold fronts may produce rains lasting for a few days.

The winter months are normally mild with short cold spells. The typical pattern shows cold with rain on the first day, colder with clear skies on the second day, and warming on the third day. Freezing or sub-freezing temperatures occur several times annually, but temperatures nearly always rise above freezing during the day. The average date of the first freeze in the autumn is late November, and the average date of the last freeze in spring is late February, producing a mean freeze-free period of 273 days. Annual total snowfall averages only a fraction of an inch and many years pass with no measurable snow.

The summer months are consistently quite warm, but high temperatures rarely exceed 100 degrees. Scattered showers normally fall in the area on about one-half of the days in June, July, and August.

Except for three or four days per month, point rainfall totals are usually less than 0.5 inch. Summer relative humidity exceeds 80 percent for about 12 hours per day. High humidity may be experienced at any hour, but occurs mainly at night. Readings of 50 percent or less occur about two hours per day, usually in the afternoons. Temperatures in the spring are usually mild and pleasant and in the autumn they are generally delightful for outdoor activities.

Thunderstorms occur each month, most frequently in July and August. Severe local storms are most frequent during the spring months. Large damaging hail very rarely occurs and tornadoes are unusual. Hurricane centers have occasionally passed very near Baton Rouge.

Baton Rouge Ryan Airport *East Baton Rouge Parish* Elevation: 63 ft. Latitude: 30° 32' N Longitude: 91° 09' W

	JAN	FEB	MAR	APR	MAY	JUN	JUL	AUG	SEP	OCT	NOV	DEC	YEAR
Mean Maximum Temp. (°F)	61.8	65.3	72.1	78.6	85.4	90.2	91.6	91.9	88.0	80.0	71.2	63.5	78.3
Mean Temp. (°F)	51.5	54.8	61.2	67.6	75.2	80.6	82.5	82.4	78.1	68.7	59.9	53.0	68.0
Mean Minimum Temp. (°F)	41.3	44.3	50.2	56.5	64.9	71.0	73.4	72.9	68.2	57.5	48.5	42.4	57.6
Extreme Maximum Temp. (°F)	84	85	88	93	97	101	102	105	104	97	87	85	105
Extreme Minimum Temp. (°F)	9	15	20	32	45	53	64	58	46	30	25	8	8
Days Maximum Temp. ≥ 90°F	0	0	0	0	6	19	24	24	14	2	0	0	89
Days Maximum Temp. ≤ 32°F	0	0	0	0	0	0	0	0	0	0	0	0	0
Days Minimum Temp. ≤ 32°F	7	4	1	0	0	0	0	0	0	0	1	6	19
Days Minimum Temp. ≤ 0°F	0	0	0	0	0	0	0	0	0	0	0	0	0
Heating Degree Days (base 65°F)	424	301	170	54	2	0	0	0	1	49	194	386	1,581
Cooling Degree Days (base 65°F)	14	19	58	137	324	476	550	547	403	172	48	21	2,769
Mean Precipitation (in.)	5.79	4.94	4.59	4.92	4.90	6.38	5.10	5.43	4.73	4.83	4.12	5.53	61.26
Maximum Precipitation (in.)*	11.4	14.5	12.7	14.8	14.7	23.2	11.6	14.5	13.9	14.5	13.5	15.9	88.3
Minimum Precipitation (in.)*	1.1	0.7	0.5	0.4	0.6	0.1	2.0	1.0	0.1	trace	0.1	1.9	38.3
Extreme Maximum Daily Precip. (in.)	9.01	4.25	3.46	5.57	4.75	9.35	2.73	7.94	5.09	4.73	6.16	7.22	9.35
Days With ≥ 0.1" Precipitation	7	6	6	5	6	8	9	7	6	5	5	7	77
Days With ≥ 0.5" Precipitation	3	3	3	3	3	4	4	3	3	3	3	3	38
Days With ≥ 1.0" Precipitation	2	2	2	2	2	2	1	1	2	2	1	2	21
Mean Snowfall (in.)	na	na	na	na	na	na	na	na	na	na	na	na	na
Maximum Snowfall (in.)*	2	3	trace	0	0	0	0	0	0	0	trace	trace	3
Maximum 24-hr. Snowfall (in.)*	2	3	trace	0	0	0	0	0	0	0	trace	trace	3
Maximum Snow Depth (in.)	na	na	na	na	na	na	na	na	na	na	na	na	na
Days With ≥ 1.0" Snow Depth	na	na	na	na	na	na	na	na	na	na	na	na	na
Thunderstorm Days*	2	3	4	5	7	10	15	13	7	2	3	2	73
Foggy Days*	17	14	16	17	19	17	16	18	18	17	16	17	202
Predominant Sky Cover*	OVR	OVR	OVR	OVR	OVR	SCT	SCT	SCT	CLR	CLR	CLR	OVR	OVR
Mean Relative Humidity 6am (%)*	85	85	86	89	91	91	92	93	91	89	88	86	89
Mean Relative Humidity 3pm (%)*	59	55	52	52	54	57	62	61	59	51	53	57	56
Mean Dewpoint (°F)*	42	44	49	57	64	70	72	72	68	57	49	44	57
Prevailing Wind Direction*	N	N	S	SE	SE	SE	W	E	NE	NE	N	N	SE
Prevailing Wind Speed (mph)*	10	10	12	10	9	8	7	7	7	7	9	10	9
Maximum Wind Gust (mph)*	54	48	52	52	59	49	59	73	64	60	47	52	73

Note: (*) Period of record is 1948-1995

The period of record for National Weather Service station data is 1980 – 2009 except where noted. See User Guide for detailed explanation of data.

Lake Charles Municipal Airport

Lake Charles is located on the east side of the lake of the same name. The Calcasieu River enters and exits Lake Charles and several other lakes in the area on its way to the Gulf of Mexico. The terrain is flat, level coastal plain. Extensive marshes begin some 10 to 15 miles south and extend to the coast. Area elevations range from near sea level to about 25 feet above sea level. The National Weather Service Office is at the Lake Charles Municipal Airport, about seven miles south of the downtown area. Calcasieu Lake is only six miles southwest of the airport.

The general classification of the Lake Charles climate is humid subtropical with a strong maritime character. The climate is influenced to a large degree by the amount of water surface in the immediate area and the proximity of the Gulf of Mexico.

Prevailing wind flow is southerly during much of the year. The flow of air from the Gulf of Mexico helps to temper extremes of summer heat, shorten the duration of winter cold spells and provide a source of abundant rain. Winds are usually rather light.

Rainfall is heavy, with the normal annual total more than 50 inches. Amounts are substantial in all seasons. Almost all rainfall occurs from brief convective showers, except occasionally during winter when nearly continuous frontal rains may persist for a few days. In spite of the large normal rainfall amounts, dry spells of two or three weeks duration are not uncommon.

The winter months are normally mild with cold spells usually of short duration. Temperatures of 20 degrees and below are extremely rare, occurring only about one year in five.

Snow is a negligible. Many years pass without measurable snowfall. However, on rare occasions, as much as 22 inches of snow have fallen at Lake Charles. Freezing rain and sleet are only a little less uncommon than snow.

The summer weather is consistently quite warm and humid but the temperature rarely reaches the 100 degree mark. The humidity is often above 90 percent at night and seldom falls below 50 percent during the afternoons.

The spring and fall seasons are very mild and pleasant with only brief rains interrupting long periods of dry sunny weather.

Severe local storms may occur during any season but are most frequent in the spring. The area weather is occasionally influenced by tropical storms or hurricanes. Some of these storms may be accompanied by tornadoes.

Lake Charles Municipal Airport *Calcasieu Parish* Elevation: 15 ft. Latitude: 30° 07' N Longitude: 93° 14' W

	JAN	FEB	MAR	APR	MAY	JUN	JUL	AUG	SEP	OCT	NOV	DEC	YEAR
Mean Maximum Temp. (°F)	61.5	64.8	71.4	77.8	84.5	89.3	91.2	91.8	88.1	80.6	71.4	63.5	78.0
Mean Temp. (°F)	52.0	55.2	61.5	67.9	75.5	81.0	82.9	82.9	78.7	70.0	61.0	53.8	68.5
Mean Minimum Temp. (°F)	42.5	45.6	51.4	58.1	66.5	72.6	74.6	74.0	69.1	59.3	50.5	44.0	59.0
Extreme Maximum Temp. (°F)	82	82	90	95	99	102	102	107	105	94	87	82	107
Extreme Minimum Temp. (°F)	15	17	23	35	49	56	63	59	48	30	28	11	11
Days Maximum Temp. ≥ 90°F	0	0	0	0	3	15	24	25	14	2	0	0	83
Days Maximum Temp. ≤ 32°F	0	0	0	0	0	0	0	0	0	0	0	0	0
Days Minimum Temp. ≤ 32°F	5	2	1	0	0	0	0	0	0	0	1	4	13
Days Minimum Temp. ≤ 0°F	0	0	0	0	0	0	0	0	0	0	0	0	0
Heating Degree Days (base 65°F)	406	286	157	44	1	0	0	0	1	35	169	361	1,460
Cooling Degree Days (base 65°F)	10	16	54	139	334	486	562	563	417	196	56	20	2,853
Mean Precipitation (in.)	5.30	3.39	3.90	3.38	5.81	6.76	5.68	4.82	5.42	4.95	4.39	4.65	58.45
Maximum Precipitation (in.)*	14.3	6.8	9.0	10.9	14.8	25.3	13.2	17.4	20.0	17.3	14.1	13.3	75.8
Minimum Precipitation (in.)*	0.8	0.6	0.3	0.5	0.3	0.8	0.5	0.8	0.4	trace	0.1	2.1	34.8
Extreme Maximum Daily Precip. (in.)	5.05	3.39	3.60	5.02	15.67	6.92	5.72	4.51	6.63	5.31	3.74	6.19	15.67
Days With ≥ 0.1" Precipitation	7	5	5	4	5	7	8	7	6	5	6	6	71
Days With ≥ 0.5" Precipitation	3	2	3	2	3	4	4	3	3	3	3	3	36
Days With ≥ 1.0" Precipitation	2	1	1	1	2	2	2	1	2	2	1	1	18
Mean Snowfall (in.)	na	na	na	na	na	na	na	na	na	na	na	na	na
Maximum Snowfall (in.)*	4	2	trace	0	0	0	0	0	0	0	trace	trace	4
Maximum 24-hr. Snowfall (in.)*	4	2	trace	0	0	0	0	0	0	0	trace	trace	4
Maximum Snow Depth (in.)	na	na	na	na	na	na	na	na	na	na	na	na	na
Days With ≥ 1.0" Snow Depth	na	na	na	na	na	na	na	na	na	na	na	na	na
Thunderstorm Days*	3	3	4	5	8	10	14	13	8	3	3	3	77
Foggy Days*	18	16	18	17	18	13	11	16	17	18	16	18	196
Predominant Sky Cover*	OVR	OVR	OVR	OVR	OVR	SCT	SCT	SCT	SCT	CLR	OVR	OVR	OVR
Mean Relative Humidity 6am (%)*	87	87	89	91	93	93	94	94	93	91	89	88	91
Mean Relative Humidity 3pm (%)*	64	59	59	59	60	62	64	62	60	52	57	63	60
Mean Dewpoint (°F)*	43	45	52	59	66	72	74	73	69	59	52	46	59
Prevailing Wind Direction*	N	N	S	S	S	S	S	ENE	ENE	NE	N	N	S
Prevailing Wind Speed (mph)*	12	12	12	12	12	9	8	7	7	8	10	12	10
Maximum Wind Gust (mph)*	51	62	59	70	61	61	66	56	59	62	69	53	70

Note: (*) Period of record is 1961-1995

New Orleans Int'l Airport

The New Orleans metropolitan area is virtually surrounded by water. Lake Pontchartrain borders the city on the north and is connected to the Gulf of Mexico through Lake Borgne on the east. In other directions there are bayous, lakes, and marshy delta land. The proximity of the Gulf of Mexico also has a great influence on the climate. Elevations in the city vary from a few feet below to a few feet above mean sea level. A massive levee system surrounding the city and along the Mississippi River offers protection against flooding from the river and tidal surges. The New Orleans International Airport is located 12 miles west of downtown New Orleans.

The climate of the city is humid with the surrounding water modifying the temperature. Almost daily sporadic afternoon thunderstorms from mid-June through September keep the temperature from rising much above 90 degrees. From about mid-November to mid-March, the area is subjected alternately to the southerly flow of warm tropical air and to the northerly flow of cold continental air in periods of varying lengths. The usual track of winter storms is to the north of New Orleans, but occasionally one moves this far south, bringing large and rather sudden drops in temperature. However, the cold spells seldom last over three or four days. The lowest temperatures observed are below 10 degrees.

During the winter and spring, the cold Mississippi River water enhances the formation of river fogs, particularly when light southerly winds bring warm, moist air into the area from the Gulf of Mexico. The nearby lakes and marshes also contribute to fog formation.

Rather frequent and sometimes very heavy rains are typical for this area. There are an average of 120 days of measurable rain per year and an annual average accumulation of over 60 inches. A fairly definite rainy period occurs from mid-December to mid-March. Precipitation during this period is most likely to be steady rain for two to three day periods. April, May, October, and November are generally dry, but there have been some extremely heavy showers in those months. Snowfall is rather infrequent and light.

While thunder occurs with most of the showers in the area, thunderstorms with damaging winds are infrequent. Damaging hail and tornadoes are extremely rare. However, waterspouts are observed quite often on nearby lakes. Hurricanes have effected the area.

The lower Mississippi River floods result from runoff upstream. Rainfall in the New Orleans area is pumped into the surrounding lakes and bayous. The average first occurrence of 32 degrees Fahrenheit in the fall is December 5 and the average last occurrence in the spring is February 20.

New Orleans Int'l Airport *Jefferson Parish* Elevation: 3 ft. Latitude: 30° 00' N Longitude: 90° 15' W

	JAN	FEB	MAR	APR	MAY	JUN	JUL	AUG	SEP	OCT	NOV	DEC	YEAR
Mean Maximum Temp. (°F)	62.3	65.5	71.8	78.0	85.1	89.4	91.2	91.2	87.4	79.8	71.5	64.4	78.1
Mean Temp. (°F)	53.2	56.4	62.4	68.5	76.2	81.0	82.8	82.8	79.3	70.7	62.1	55.3	69.2
Mean Minimum Temp. (°F)	44.1	47.3	52.9	59.0	67.2	72.6	74.5	74.4	71.2	61.6	52.6	46.1	60.3
Extreme Maximum Temp. (°F)	83	83	89	92	95	101	101	102	101	94	87	84	102
Extreme Minimum Temp. (°F)	14	16	25	37	48	50	65	62	52	35	28	11	11
Days Maximum Temp. ≥ 90°F	0	0	0	0	4	16	22	23	11	2	0	0	78
Days Maximum Temp. ≤ 32°F	0	0	0	0	0	0	0	0	0	0	0	0	0
Days Minimum Temp. ≤ 32°F	4	2	0	0	0	0	0	0	0	0	0	2	8
Days Minimum Temp. ≤ 0°F	0	0	0	0	0	0	0	0	0	0	0	0	0
Heating Degree Days (base 65°F)	374	259	138	37	0	0	0	0	0	27	145	322	1,302
Cooling Degree Days (base 65°F)	16	21	63	150	354	488	560	560	436	211	65	27	2,951
Mean Precipitation (in.)	5.27	5.18	4.74	5.02	4.34	7.74	5.93	5.79	5.34	3.75	4.16	5.29	62.55
Maximum Precipitation (in.)*	19.3	12.6	19.1	16.1	21.2	15.0	13.1	16.1	16.7	13.2	19.8	10.8	102.
Minimum Precipitation (in.)*	0.5	0.1	0.2	0.3	0.9	0.2	1.9	1.7	0.2	0	0.2	1.5	39.0
Extreme Maximum Daily Precip. (in.)	4.98	4.85	3.39	7.67	5.02	5.98	4.32	4.50	7.52	6.07	5.14	6.47	7.67
Days With ≥ 0.1" Precipitation	7	6	6	5	5	9	9	8	7	5	5	6	78
Days With ≥ 0.5" Precipitation	3	3	3	3	2	5	4	4	3	2	3	3	38
Days With ≥ 1.0" Precipitation	2	2	2	2	1	3	2	2	2	1	1	1	21
Mean Snowfall (in.)	na	na	na	na	na	na	na	na	na	na	na	na	na
Maximum Snowfall (in.)*	trace	2	trace	0	0	0	0	0	0	0	0	3	3
Maximum 24-hr. Snowfall (in.)*	trace	2	trace	0	0	0	0	0	0	0	0	3	3
Maximum Snow Depth (in.)	na	na	na	na	na	na	na	na	na	na	na	na	na
Days With ≥ 1.0" Snow Depth	na	na	na	na	na	na	na	na	na	na	na	na	na
Thunderstorm Days*	2	3	4	5	6	10	16	13	7	2	2	2	72
Foggy Days*	17	14	16	16	16	11	12	12	12	15	15	17	173
Predominant Sky Cover*	OVR	OVR	OVR	OVR	SCT	SCT	SCT	SCT	SCT	CLR	CLR	OVR	OVR
Mean Relative Humidity 6am (%)*	85	84	85	88	89	90	92	92	89	88	86	86	88
Mean Relative Humidity 3pm (%)*	63	59	57	57	58	61	66	65	63	56	59	62	60
Mean Dewpoint (°F)*	45	46	52	59	66	71	73	73	70	60	52	47	60
Prevailing Wind Direction*	N	N	S	S	S	S	SW	NE	NE	NE	N	N	S
Prevailing Wind Speed (mph)*	12	12	12	12	10	9	7	8	9	9	10	10	10
Maximum Wind Gust (mph)*	63	67	62	62	69	67	79	66	112	60	55	69	112

Note: (*) Period of record is 1948-1995

The period of record for National Weather Service station data is 1980 – 2009 except where noted. See User Guide for detailed explanation of data.

Shreveport Regional Airport

Shreveport is located in the northwestern section of Louisiana, some 30 miles south of Arkansas and 15 miles east of Texas. A portion of the city is situated in the Red River bottom lands and the remainder in gently rolling hills that begin about l mile west of the river. The NOAA National Weather Service Office is at the Shreveport Regional Airport, about seven miles southwest of the downtown area. Elevations in the Shreveport area range from about 170 to 280 feet above sea level. The climate of Shreveport is transitional between the subtropical humid type prevalent to the south and the con-tinental climates of the Great Plains and Middle West to the north. During winter, masses of moderate to severely cold air move periodically through the area. Rainfall is abundant with the normal annual total near 45 inches. Amounts are substantial from late autumn to spring and there is a sum-mer-early autumn low amount with monthly averages less than three inches in August, September, and October.

The winter months are normally mild with cold spells generally of short duration. Freezing temperatures are recorded on an average of 34 days during the year. The average first occurrence of 32 degrees in the autumn is mid-November, and the last occurrence in the spring is early March Although temperatures have fallen below zero degrees, they normally drop below about 15 degrees in about one-half the years. Temperatures recorded at the NWS Office at the airport on clear, calm nights are normally two to five degrees warmer than those experienced in the river bottom lands. The sum-mer months are consistently quite warm and humid with temperatures exceeding 100 degrees on about 10 days a year and exceeding 95 degrees about 45 days per year. Late afternoon humidity rarely drops below 55 percent.

Measurable snow occurs only once every other year on average. Many consecutive years may pass with no measurable snow. The heaviest snow-storms in the Shreveport area have produced more than 10 inches. More troublesome than the infrequent heavy snowfall are ice and sleet storms which may cause considerable damage to trees and utility lines, as well as make travel very difficult.

Thunderstorms occur each month, but are most frequent in spring and summer months. Severe local storms, including hailstorms, tornadoes, and local windstorms have occurred over small areas in all seasons, but are most frequent during the spring months, with a secondary peak from late November through early January. Large hail of a damaging nature is infrequent, although hail as large as grapefruit has fallen on a few occasions.

Shreveport Regional Airport *Caddo Parish* Elevation: 253 ft. Latitude: 32° 27' N Longitude: 93° 49' W

	JAN	FEB	MAR	APR	MAY	JUN	JUL	AUG	SEP	OCT	NOV	DEC	YEAR
Mean Maximum Temp. (°F)	57.4	61.8	69.5	76.8	83.6	90.1	93.6	94.1	88.2	78.0	67.5	58.6	76.6
Mean Temp. (°F)	47.1	51.0	58.2	65.3	73.4	80.0	83.4	83.3	77.2	66.5	56.6	48.4	65.9
Mean Minimum Temp. (°F)	36.9	40.2	46.8	53.8	63.1	69.9	73.1	72.5	66.1	55.0	45.6	38.1	55.1
Extreme Maximum Temp. (°F)	82	89	90	94	102	102	107	109	109	97	88	84	109
Extreme Minimum Temp. (°F)	5	14	17	31	44	53	60	53	42	28	22	5	5
Days Maximum Temp. ≥ 90°F	0	0	0	0	4	19	27	26	15	2	0	0	93
Days Maximum Temp. ≤ 32°F	0	0	0	0	0	0	0	0	0	0	0	1	1
Days Minimum Temp. ≤ 32°F	11	6	2	0	0	0	0	0	0	0	3	10	32
Days Minimum Temp. ≤ 0°F	0	0	0	0	0	0	0	0	0	0	0	0	0
Heating Degree Days (base 65°F)	552	397	239	82	6	0	0	0	5	77	272	517	2,147
Cooling Degree Days (base 65°F)	6	9	34	99	272	457	576	573	377	130	26	9	2,568
Mean Precipitation (in.)	4.25	4.74	4.16	4.26	5.02	5.39	3.51	2.71	3.21	5.01	4.49	4.78	51.53
Maximum Precipitation (in.)*	10.1	8.6	7.2	21.8	11.8	17.1	9.5	9.2	9.6	14.0	10.8	10.0	82.0
Minimum Precipitation (in.)*	0.3	0.8	0.6	0.4	0.4	0.1	0.1	0.3	0.1	0	0.4	0.6	30.0
Extreme Maximum Daily Precip. (in.)	4.34	3.20	3.14	10.44	6.71	7.27	4.40	3.30	5.52	5.88	3.50	2.83	10.44
Days With ≥ 0.1" Precipitation	6	6	6	5	7	7	5	4	4	6	6	6	68
Days With ≥ 0.5" Precipitation	3	3	3	3	3	3	2	2	2	3	3	4	34
Days With ≥ 1.0" Precipitation	1	2	1	1	1	2	1	1	1	2	2	2	17
Mean Snowfall (in.)	0.3	0.3	0.1	trace	trace	0.0	0.0	trace	0.0	trace	0.1	0.3	1.1
Maximum Snowfall (in.)*	12	4	4	trace	0	0	0	0	0	0	1	5	13
Maximum 24-hr. Snowfall (in.)*	8	4	4	trace	0	0	0	0	0	0	1	5	8
Maximum Snow Depth (in.)	6	3	1	trace	trace	0	0	trace	0	trace	1	2	6
Days With ≥ 1.0" Snow Depth	0	0	0	0	0	0	0	0	0	0	0	0	0
Thunderstorm Days*	2	3	5	6	7	7	8	6	4	3	3	2	56
Foggy Days*	13	10	9	9	9	6	5	7	9	11	11	12	111
Predominant Sky Cover*	OVR	OVR	OVR	OVR	OVR	SCT	SCT	SCT	CLR	CLR	OVR	OVR	OVR
Mean Relative Humidity 6am (%)*	84	83	83	87	90	91	91	91	90	89	86	85	88
Mean Relative Humidity 3pm (%)*	57	53	50	52	55	54	53	50	51	49	52	57	53
Mean Dewpoint (°F)*	36	39	45	54	62	69	71	70	65	55	45	39	54
Prevailing Wind Direction*	S	S	S	S	S	S	S	S	SE	SE	S	S	S
Prevailing Wind Speed (mph)*	12	12	13	12	10	9	8	8	7	8	10	10	10
Maximum Wind Gust (mph)*	69	66	73	81	83	74	66	86	66	54	87	67	87

Note: (*) Period of record is 1948-1995

Alexandria *Rapides Parish* Elevation: 86 ft. Latitude: 31° 19' N Longitude: 92° 28' W

	JAN	FEB	MAR	APR	MAY	JUN	JUL	AUG	SEP	OCT	NOV	DEC	YEAR
Mean Maximum Temp. (°F)	58.9	62.8	70.0	77.2	84.4	90.0	92.8	93.3	88.7	79.3	69.4	60.8	77.3
Mean Temp. (°F)	48.7	52.3	59.4	66.5	74.5	80.5	83.2	83.2	78.1	67.8	58.4	50.5	66.9
Mean Minimum Temp. (°F)	38.4	41.7	48.8	55.7	64.5	71.0	73.5	73.0	67.5	56.2	47.4	40.1	56.5
Extreme Maximum Temp. (°F)	82	85	87	94	99	102	103	108	109	96	87	83	109
Extreme Minimum Temp. (°F)	8	14	23	33	47	51	63	57	44	30	25	7	7
Days Maximum Temp. ≥ 90°F	0	0	0	0	5	18	25	26	15	2	0	0	91
Days Maximum Temp. ≤ 32°F	0	0	0	0	0	0	0	0	0	0	0	0	0
Days Minimum Temp. ≤ 32°F	9	5	1	0	0	0	0	0	0	0	2	8	25
Days Minimum Temp. ≤ 0°F	0	0	0	0	0	0	0	0	0	0	0	0	0
Heating Degree Days (base 65°F)	505	364	208	68	4	0	0	0	2	59	223	453	1,886
Cooling Degree Days (base 65°F)	6	11	42	119	305	471	571	570	402	153	33	11	2,694
Mean Precipitation (in.)	5.54	5.14	5.56	4.80	4.84	5.25	4.14	3.94	3.92	5.49	6.18	6.27	61.07
Extreme Maximum Daily Precip. (in.)	4.75	4.85	4.60	6.90	3.40	7.32	3.44	5.70	4.50	6.10	10.02	7.20	10.02
Days With ≥ 0.1" Precipitation	7	7	6	5	6	7	6	6	5	5	6	7	73
Days With ≥ 0.5" Precipitation	4	3	4	3	3	4	3	2	2	3	4	4	39
Days With ≥ 1.0" Precipitation	2	2	2	2	2	1	1	1	1	2	2	2	20
Mean Snowfall (in.)	0.1	trace	0.0	0.0	0.0	0.0	0.0	0.0	0.0	0.0	0.0	0.0	0.1
Maximum Snow Depth (in.)	1	trace	0	0	0	0	0	0	0	0	0	0	1
Days With ≥ 1.0" Snow Depth	0	0	0	0	0	0	0	0	0	0	0	0	0

Amite *Tangipahoa Parish* Elevation: 169 ft. Latitude: 30° 42' N Longitude: 90° 32' W

	JAN	FEB	MAR	APR	MAY	JUN	JUL	AUG	SEP	OCT	NOV	DEC	YEAR
Mean Maximum Temp. (°F)	61.2	65.1	72.2	78.5	85.5	90.5	92.1	92.5	89.0	80.8	71.5	63.1	78.5
Mean Temp. (°F)	49.8	53.3	60.1	66.1	73.7	79.4	81.5	81.5	77.3	67.8	59.0	51.3	66.7
Mean Minimum Temp. (°F)	38.3	41.5	47.9	53.6	61.9	68.3	70.8	70.4	65.6	54.7	46.5	39.5	54.9
Extreme Maximum Temp. (°F)	81	84	89	94	98	104	103	105	103	95	89	83	105
Extreme Minimum Temp. (°F)	7	13	20	30	40	49	60	54	43	29	25	5	5
Days Maximum Temp. ≥ 90°F	0	0	0	0	7	19	25	25	16	3	0	0	95
Days Maximum Temp. ≤ 32°F	0	0	0	0	0	0	0	0	0	0	0	0	0
Days Minimum Temp. ≤ 32°F	11	7	2	0	0	0	0	0	0	0	3	10	33
Days Minimum Temp. ≤ 0°F	0	0	0	0	0	0	0	0	0	0	0	0	0
Heating Degree Days (base 65°F)	473	337	191	70	5	0	0	0	2	62	215	429	1,784
Cooling Degree Days (base 65°F)	7	13	46	111	281	439	518	517	379	155	42	13	2,521
Mean Precipitation (in.)	5.74	5.61	5.96	5.19	5.16	5.75	5.88	5.79	4.14	4.67	4.21	5.32	63.42
Extreme Maximum Daily Precip. (in.)	5.43	4.60	3.69	8.77	7.35	5.66	3.96	7.48	4.07	5.41	3.86	7.07	8.77
Days With ≥ 0.1" Precipitation	7	6	6	5	6	8	9	8	6	5	6	6	78
Days With ≥ 0.5" Precipitation	4	4	4	3	3	4	4	4	3	3	3	3	42
Days With ≥ 1.0" Precipitation	2	2	2	2	2	2	2	2	1	2	2	2	23
Mean Snowfall (in.)	0.1	trace	trace	0.0	0.0	0.0	0.0	0.0	0.0	0.0	0.0	trace	0.1
Maximum Snow Depth (in.)	trace	1	0	0	0	0	0	0	0	0	0	8	8
Days With ≥ 1.0" Snow Depth	0	0	0	0	0	0	0	0	0	0	0	0	0

Ashland *Natchitoches Parish* Elevation: 240 ft. Latitude: 32° 10' N Longitude: 93° 08' W

	JAN	FEB	MAR	APR	MAY	JUN	JUL	AUG	SEP	OCT	NOV	DEC	YEAR
Mean Maximum Temp. (°F)	56.8	61.3	68.6	75.9	82.4	88.8	92.3	93.0	87.4	77.4	67.7	58.4	75.8
Mean Temp. (°F)	45.5	49.3	56.5	63.5	71.3	78.0	81.2	81.1	75.3	64.6	55.4	47.1	64.1
Mean Minimum Temp. (°F)	34.2	37.3	44.4	51.0	60.3	67.2	70.1	69.2	63.1	51.7	43.0	35.7	52.3
Extreme Maximum Temp. (°F)	80	86	89	92	97	101	105	108	110	94	89	83	110
Extreme Minimum Temp. (°F)	5	10	11	25	38	46	55	48	38	24	18	2	2
Days Maximum Temp. ≥ 90°F	0	0	0	0	2	14	24	24	13	2	0	0	79
Days Maximum Temp. ≤ 32°F	0	0	0	0	0	0	0	0	0	0	0	1	1
Days Minimum Temp. ≤ 32°F	15	10	5	1	0	0	0	0	0	1	5	14	51
Days Minimum Temp. ≤ 0°F	0	0	0	0	0	0	0	0	0	0	0	0	0
Heating Degree Days (base 65°F)	602	443	283	117	15	0	0	0	10	110	300	554	2,434
Cooling Degree Days (base 65°F)	4	6	26	78	219	397	509	507	325	104	18	6	2,199
Mean Precipitation (in.)	4.99	5.51	5.13	4.49	5.05	4.70	3.53	3.22	3.53	4.61	5.19	5.86	55.81
Extreme Maximum Daily Precip. (in.)	4.14	4.16	3.48	4.55	10.88	5.56	4.20	3.68	5.80	5.20	4.81	5.10	10.88
Days With ≥ 0.1" Precipitation	7	7	7	5	6	6	5	5	5	6	6	7	72
Days With ≥ 0.5" Precipitation	3	3	4	3	3	3	3	3	2	3	3	4	37
Days With ≥ 1.0" Precipitation	2	2	2	1	1	2	1	1	1	1	2	2	18
Mean Snowfall (in.)	0.5	0.2	trace	trace	0.0	0.0	0.0	0.0	0.0	0.0	0.0	0.1	0.8
Maximum Snow Depth (in.)	6	1	trace	trace	0	0	0	0	0	0	0	trace	6
Days With ≥ 1.0" Snow Depth	0	0	0	0	0	0	0	0	0	0	0	0	0

Bastrop *Morehouse Parish* Elevation: 149 ft. Latitude: 32° 47' N Longitude: 91° 54' W

	JAN	FEB	MAR	APR	MAY	JUN	JUL	AUG	SEP	OCT	NOV	DEC	YEAR
Mean Maximum Temp. (°F)	56.0	60.3	68.7	76.0	83.1	89.5	92.8	92.9	87.7	77.8	66.8	57.1	75.7
Mean Temp. (°F)	45.3	48.8	56.8	63.9	72.2	79.1	82.2	81.8	75.8	65.4	55.2	46.5	64.4
Mean Minimum Temp. (°F)	34.5	37.3	44.8	51.8	61.3	68.6	71.5	70.5	63.8	53.0	43.5	35.9	53.1
Extreme Maximum Temp. (°F)	81	85	90	94	98	101	105	107	106	94	86	83	107
Extreme Minimum Temp. (°F)	4	9	16	28	40	50	57	51	40	27	22	3	3
Days Maximum Temp. ≥ 90°F	0	0	0	0	4	17	25	24	14	2	0	0	86
Days Maximum Temp. ≤ 32°F	1	0	0	0	0	0	0	0	0	0	0	1	2
Days Minimum Temp. ≤ 32°F	15	10	4	0	0	0	0	0	0	1	4	13	47
Days Minimum Temp. ≤ 0°F	0	0	0	0	0	0	0	0	0	0	0	0	0
Heating Degree Days (base 65°F)	608	457	276	114	14	0	0	0	8	95	306	572	2,450
Cooling Degree Days (base 65°F)	3	6	27	86	245	431	540	526	338	116	19	6	2,343
Mean Precipitation (in.)	5.46	5.02	5.55	5.28	5.56	4.47	4.07	2.99	3.50	5.27	4.62	5.55	57.34
Extreme Maximum Daily Precip. (in.)	4.63	4.60	4.34	8.67	6.42	3.25	4.23	4.76	6.33	5.08	3.70	5.90	8.67
Days With ≥ 0.1" Precipitation	7	6	7	6	7	6	5	5	5	5	6	6	71
Days With ≥ 0.5" Precipitation	3	3	4	3	3	3	2	2	2	3	3	4	35
Days With ≥ 1.0" Precipitation	2	2	2	2	2	1	1	1	1	2	2	2	20
Mean Snowfall (in.)	0.2	0.1	0.1	0.0	0.0	0.0	0.0	0.0	0.0	0.0	trace	trace	0.4
Maximum Snow Depth (in.)	5	1	2	0	0	0	0	0	0	0	trace	trace	5
Days With ≥ 1.0" Snow Depth	0	0	0	0	0	0	0	0	0	0	0	0	0

The period of record for all cooperative weather station data is 1980 – 2009. See User Guide for detailed explanation of data.

Bienville 3 NE *Bienville Parish* Elevation: 307 ft. Latitude: 32° 22' N Longitude: 92° 57' W

	JAN	FEB	MAR	APR	MAY	JUN	JUL	AUG	SEP	OCT	NOV	DEC	YEAR
Mean Maximum Temp. (°F)	56.5	60.6	68.5	76.2	83.3	89.6	93.1	93.2	87.6	77.0	66.6	57.6	75.8
Mean Temp. (°F)	45.9	49.6	56.7	64.1	72.2	78.8	82.1	81.8	76.0	65.0	55.1	47.1	64.5
Mean Minimum Temp. (°F)	35.3	38.6	44.9	51.9	61.0	68.0	71.1	70.3	64.4	52.9	43.6	36.6	53.2
Extreme Maximum Temp. (°F)	80	85	90	93	101	102	106	109	109	98	85	82	109
Extreme Minimum Temp. (°F)	5	9	15	26	40	48	55	50	37	25	20	2	2
Days Maximum Temp. ≥ 90°F	0	0	0	0	4	16	25	24	13	2	0	0	84
Days Maximum Temp. ≤ 32°F	1	0	0	0	0	0	0	0	0	0	0	1	2
Days Minimum Temp. ≤ 32°F	14	9	3	1	0	0	0	0	0	0	5	13	45
Days Minimum Temp. ≤ 0°F	0	0	0	0	0	0	0	0	0	0	0	0	0
Heating Degree Days (base 65°F)	588	436	275	104	10	0	0	0	8	100	307	553	2,381
Cooling Degree Days (base 65°F)	4	6	25	84	239	421	538	528	344	107	18	6	2,320
Mean Precipitation (in.)	5.85	5.75	5.53	5.09	5.42	5.17	3.85	2.92	3.93	5.31	5.50	6.21	60.53
Extreme Maximum Daily Precip. (in.)	6.04	4.70	4.00	7.09	5.90	4.86	4.70	3.25	6.20	5.00	5.80	5.90	7.09
Days With ≥ 0.1" Precipitation	7	7	7	6	6	7	5	5	5	5	6	7	73
Days With ≥ 0.5" Precipitation	3	4	4	3	3	4	3	2	2	3	3	4	38
Days With ≥ 1.0" Precipitation	2	2	2	2	2	2	1	1	1	2	2	2	21
Mean Snowfall (in.)	0.2	trace	trace	0.0	0.0	0.0	0.0	0.0	0.0	0.0	trace	0.1	0.3
Maximum Snow Depth (in.)	5	3	trace	0	0	0	0	0	0	0	trace	2	5
Days With ≥ 1.0" Snow Depth	0	0	0	0	0	0	0	0	0	0	0	0	0

Bogalusa *Washington Parish* Elevation: 100 ft. Latitude: 30° 47' N Longitude: 89° 52' W

	JAN	FEB	MAR	APR	MAY	JUN	JUL	AUG	SEP	OCT	NOV	DEC	YEAR
Mean Maximum Temp. (°F)	60.8	64.3	71.2	77.9	85.1	89.9	92.0	91.9	87.9	79.5	70.6	62.7	77.8
Mean Temp. (°F)	49.7	53.0	59.6	65.9	73.9	79.7	82.1	81.8	77.1	67.5	58.8	51.3	66.7
Mean Minimum Temp. (°F)	38.6	41.7	47.8	54.1	62.7	69.4	72.1	71.6	66.3	55.4	46.8	39.9	55.5
Extreme Maximum Temp. (°F)	83	84	91	93	96	100	105	104	101	94	87	84	105
Extreme Minimum Temp. (°F)	6	14	20	31	44	48	61	57	45	31	26	6	6
Days Maximum Temp. ≥ 90°F	0	0	0	0	7	16	24	23	13	2	0	0	85
Days Maximum Temp. ≤ 32°F	0	0	0	0	0	0	0	0	0	0	0	0	0
Days Minimum Temp. ≤ 32°F	10	6	2	0	0	0	0	0	0	0	2	9	29
Days Minimum Temp. ≤ 0°F	0	0	0	0	0	0	0	0	0	0	0	0	0
Heating Degree Days (base 65°F)	477	346	206	75	5	0	0	0	3	65	221	431	1,829
Cooling Degree Days (base 65°F)	9	14	43	110	289	448	538	527	373	151	41	15	2,558
Mean Precipitation (in.)	5.49	5.61	6.01	4.68	4.71	6.82	5.65	4.93	4.45	4.01	5.03	4.86	62.25
Extreme Maximum Daily Precip. (in.)	5.00	4.67	5.08	4.95	4.22	9.15	5.51	3.71	6.00	7.35	4.40	9.06	9.15
Days With ≥ 0.1" Precipitation	7	6	6	5	6	9	8	7	6	5	6	6	77
Days With ≥ 0.5" Precipitation	3	4	4	3	3	4	4	3	3	2	3	3	39
Days With ≥ 1.0" Precipitation	2	2	2	2	1	2	1	2	1	1	2	2	20
Mean Snowfall (in.)	trace	trace	0.1	0.0	0.0	0.0	0.0	0.0	0.0	0.0	0.0	0.0	0.1
Maximum Snow Depth (in.)	trace	1	3	0	0	0	0	0	0	0	0	5	5
Days With ≥ 1.0" Snow Depth	0	0	0	0	0	0	0	0	0	0	0	0	0

Boyce 3 WNW *Rapides Parish* Elevation: 109 ft. Latitude: 31° 23' N Longitude: 92° 43' W

	JAN	FEB	MAR	APR	MAY	JUN	JUL	AUG	SEP	OCT	NOV	DEC	YEAR
Mean Maximum Temp. (°F)	58.9	62.8	70.2	77.6	84.4	89.6	92.6	92.7	87.4	78.3	68.4	60.1	76.9
Mean Temp. (°F)	49.5	53.1	59.9	67.2	74.8	80.6	83.3	83.2	77.7	68.0	58.6	50.9	67.2
Mean Minimum Temp. (°F)	40.1	43.4	49.5	56.7	65.2	71.4	74.0	73.6	67.9	57.6	48.8	41.7	57.5
Extreme Maximum Temp. (°F)	81	85	87	95	102	101	104	107	106	94	86	82	107
Extreme Minimum Temp. (°F)	9	15	23	31	43	55	59	56	43	30	25	7	7
Days Maximum Temp. ≥ 90°F	0	0	0	1	6	17	24	25	12	1	0	0	86
Days Maximum Temp. ≤ 32°F	0	0	0	0	0	0	0	0	0	0	0	0	0
Days Minimum Temp. ≤ 32°F	6	3	1	0	0	0	0	0	0	0	1	5	16
Days Minimum Temp. ≤ 0°F	0	0	0	0	0	0	0	0	0	0	0	0	0
Heating Degree Days (base 65°F)	479	341	193	56	3	0	0	0	2	53	216	439	1,782
Cooling Degree Days (base 65°F)	6	12	41	129	312	474	575	570	389	152	30	10	2,700
Mean Precipitation (in.)	5.43	4.71	5.34	4.83	4.78	4.91	4.06	3.40	4.42	5.16	6.18	6.00	59.22
Extreme Maximum Daily Precip. (in.)	6.50	3.82	4.00	5.40	5.00	5.45	3.50	3.48	9.75	8.00	8.50	5.03	9.75
Days With ≥ 0.1" Precipitation	7	6	6	5	6	7	6	5	5	5	6	7	71
Days With ≥ 0.5" Precipitation	3	3	4	3	3	3	3	2	3	3	4	4	38
Days With ≥ 1.0" Precipitation	2	2	2	2	1	1	1	1	1	2	2	2	19
Mean Snowfall (in.)	trace	trace	trace	0.0	0.0	0.0	0.0	0.0	0.0	0.0	0.0	0.0	trace
Maximum Snow Depth (in.)	2	trace	trace	0	0	0	0	0	0	0	0	0	2
Days With ≥ 1.0" Snow Depth	0	0	0	0	0	0	0	0	0	0	0	0	0

Bunkie *Avoyelles Parish* Elevation: 80 ft. Latitude: 30° 57' N Longitude: 92° 10' W

	JAN	FEB	MAR	APR	MAY	JUN	JUL	AUG	SEP	OCT	NOV	DEC	YEAR
Mean Maximum Temp. (°F)	58.8	62.7	70.2	77.5	84.7	89.8	92.1	92.5	88.0	79.6	69.7	60.9	77.2
Mean Temp. (°F)	49.1	52.7	59.8	66.8	74.7	80.3	82.5	82.2	77.1	67.7	58.9	51.0	66.9
Mean Minimum Temp. (°F)	39.3	42.7	49.4	56.1	64.7	70.6	72.9	71.9	66.0	55.8	48.0	41.1	56.5
Extreme Maximum Temp. (°F)	81	85	88	93	99	100	103	107	106	96	87	82	107
Extreme Minimum Temp. (°F)	10	16	23	33	44	50	60	56	44	29	28	8	8
Days Maximum Temp. ≥ 90°F	0	0	0	1	6	18	24	24	14	2	0	0	89
Days Maximum Temp. ≤ 32°F	0	0	0	0	0	0	0	0	0	0	0	0	0
Days Minimum Temp. ≤ 32°F	9	4	1	0	0	0	0	0	0	0	1	6	21
Days Minimum Temp. ≤ 0°F	0	0	0	0	0	0	0	0	0	0	0	0	0
Heating Degree Days (base 65°F)	493	354	201	64	4	0	0	0	4	63	216	440	1,839
Cooling Degree Days (base 65°F)	7	12	47	125	313	465	551	541	372	154	40	13	2,640
Mean Precipitation (in.)	5.90	5.12	5.41	4.95	5.51	5.49	3.82	3.49	4.79	5.49	5.55	5.79	61.31
Extreme Maximum Daily Precip. (in.)	5.99	3.80	6.51	13.15	4.81	8.00	3.46	3.58	8.44	4.55	5.35	4.10	13.15
Days With ≥ 0.1" Precipitation	7	7	6	5	6	8	6	6	5	5	6	7	74
Days With ≥ 0.5" Precipitation	4	3	3	3	3	4	3	2	2	3	4	4	38
Days With ≥ 1.0" Precipitation	2	2	2	2	2	2	1	1	1	2	2	2	21
Mean Snowfall (in.)	trace	trace	0.0	0.0	0.0	0.0	0.0	0.0	0.0	0.0	0.0	0.0	trace
Maximum Snow Depth (in.)	trace	trace	0	0	0	0	0	0	0	0	0	0	trace
Days With ≥ 1.0" Snow Depth	0	0	0	0	0	0	0	0	0	0	0	0	0

The period of record for all cooperative weather station data is 1980 – 2009. See User Guide for detailed explanation of data.

Carville 2 SW *Iberville Parish* Elevation: 24 ft. Latitude: 30° 12' N Longitude: 91° 07' W

	JAN	FEB	MAR	APR	MAY	JUN	JUL	AUG	SEP	OCT	NOV	DEC	YEAR
Mean Maximum Temp. (°F)	61.3	64.8	71.4	78.0	84.8	89.1	90.9	91.2	87.6	79.5	71.0	63.3	77.7
Mean Temp. (°F)	51.5	54.9	61.0	67.7	75.2	80.5	82.5	82.4	78.5	69.4	60.6	53.5	68.1
Mean Minimum Temp. (°F)	41.6	44.9	50.5	57.3	65.6	71.7	74.0	73.6	69.4	59.2	50.2	43.6	58.5
Extreme Maximum Temp. (°F)	83	84	85	91	95	98	100	104	102	95	87	82	104
Extreme Minimum Temp. (°F)	10	17	23	34	48	55	64	60	49	35	29	13	10
Days Maximum Temp. ≥ 90°F	0	0	0	0	4	15	22	23	12	1	0	0	77
Days Maximum Temp. ≤ 32°F	0	0	0	0	0	0	0	0	0	0	0	0	0
Days Minimum Temp. ≤ 32°F	5	2	1	0	0	0	0	0	0	0	1	4	13
Days Minimum Temp. ≤ 0°F	0	0	0	0	0	0	0	0	0	0	0	0	0
Heating Degree Days (base 65°F)	419	293	160	43	1	0	0	0	1	36	172	365	1,490
Cooling Degree Days (base 65°F)	7	12	42	131	325	470	549	547	413	179	47	16	2,738
Mean Precipitation (in.)	5.36	4.86	4.41	4.38	4.37	7.51	5.45	4.97	4.36	4.85	4.20	4.85	59.57
Extreme Maximum Daily Precip. (in.)	4.72	4.90	3.90	5.65	6.30	7.80	3.90	5.32	3.50	5.34	5.60	5.70	7.80
Days With ≥ 0.1" Precipitation	7	6	6	5	6	8	9	8	6	5	5	6	77
Days With ≥ 0.5" Precipitation	3	4	3	2	3	4	4	3	3	3	3	3	38
Days With ≥ 1.0" Precipitation	2	2	2	1	1	3	2	1	1	1	1	2	19
Mean Snowfall (in.)	trace	trace	0.0	0.0	0.0	0.0	0.0	0.0	0.0	0.0	0.0	0.0	trace
Maximum Snow Depth (in.)	trace	1	0	0	0	0	0	0	0	0	0	2	2
Days With ≥ 1.0" Snow Depth	0	0	0	0	0	0	0	0	0	0	0	0	0

Crowley 2 NE *Acadia Parish* Elevation: 24 ft. Latitude: 30° 15' N Longitude: 92° 22' W

	JAN	FEB	MAR	APR	MAY	JUN	JUL	AUG	SEP	OCT	NOV	DEC	YEAR
Mean Maximum Temp. (°F)	60.3	63.6	70.5	77.6	84.5	89.3	90.9	91.7	88.0	80.3	70.7	62.4	77.5
Mean Temp. (°F)	50.6	53.8	60.7	67.7	75.4	80.6	82.2	82.3	78.3	69.4	60.3	52.6	67.8
Mean Minimum Temp. (°F)	40.8	43.9	50.8	57.8	66.3	71.9	73.5	72.9	68.4	58.5	49.9	42.6	58.1
Extreme Maximum Temp. (°F)	80	83	87	94	97	102	102	105	106	96	87	82	106
Extreme Minimum Temp. (°F)	10	15	22	36	46	54	62	57	45	29	26	9	9
Days Maximum Temp. ≥ 90°F	0	0	0	0	4	16	22	24	13	2	0	0	81
Days Maximum Temp. ≤ 32°F	0	0	0	0	0	0	0	0	0	0	0	0	0
Days Minimum Temp. ≤ 32°F	7	3	1	0	0	0	0	0	0	0	1	5	17
Days Minimum Temp. ≤ 0°F	0	0	0	0	0	0	0	0	0	0	0	0	0
Heating Degree Days (base 65°F)	449	325	178	51	2	0	0	0	2	45	186	397	1,635
Cooling Degree Days (base 65°F)	8	14	50	140	331	475	540	542	406	189	52	19	2,766
Mean Precipitation (in.)	5.85	4.29	4.18	4.20	5.73	6.66	5.27	4.86	4.89	5.43	4.91	4.73	61.00
Extreme Maximum Daily Precip. (in.)	4.98	4.05	5.10	5.55	8.87	5.05	3.20	7.80	6.67	4.45	5.30	5.70	8.87
Days With ≥ 0.1" Precipitation	7	6	6	5	6	8	9	8	6	5	6	6	78
Days With ≥ 0.5" Precipitation	3	3	3	2	3	5	4	3	3	3	3	3	38
Days With ≥ 1.0" Precipitation	2	1	1	1	2	2	1	1	2	2	2	1	18
Mean Snowfall (in.)	trace	trace	0.0	0.0	0.0	0.0	0.0	0.0	0.0	0.0	0.0	trace	trace
Maximum Snow Depth (in.)	trace	trace	0	0	0	0	0	0	0	0	0	2	2
Days With ≥ 1.0" Snow Depth	0	0	0	0	0	0	0	0	0	0	0	0	0

De Ridder *Beauregard Parish* Elevation: 189 ft. Latitude: 30° 50' N Longitude: 93° 17' W

	JAN	FEB	MAR	APR	MAY	JUN	JUL	AUG	SEP	OCT	NOV	DEC	YEAR
Mean Maximum Temp. (°F)	60.3	64.3	71.3	77.8	84.6	89.6	92.1	92.6	88.1	79.3	70.0	61.9	77.7
Mean Temp. (°F)	49.5	52.9	59.9	66.4	74.1	79.7	82.2	82.3	77.2	67.7	58.6	50.8	66.8
Mean Minimum Temp. (°F)	38.6	41.5	48.4	54.9	63.6	69.8	72.3	71.8	66.3	55.9	47.2	39.7	55.8
Extreme Maximum Temp. (°F)	82	86	92	93	97	100	105	106	109	95	88	83	109
Extreme Minimum Temp. (°F)	10	15	21	30	45	50	62	54	41	28	25	7	7
Days Maximum Temp. ≥ 90°F	0	0	0	0	4	18	25	26	14	2	0	0	89
Days Maximum Temp. ≤ 32°F	0	0	0	0	0	0	0	0	0	0	0	0	0
Days Minimum Temp. ≤ 32°F	10	5	2	0	0	0	0	0	0	0	2	9	28
Days Minimum Temp. ≤ 0°F	0	0	0	0	0	0	0	0	0	0	0	0	0
Heating Degree Days (base 65°F)	481	347	196	68	4	0	0	0	3	61	221	445	1,826
Cooling Degree Days (base 65°F)	7	13	45	115	294	449	541	542	377	151	37	13	2,584
Mean Precipitation (in.)	5.46	5.07	5.11	4.39	5.08	6.37	5.05	4.30	5.37	5.42	6.03	6.86	64.51
Extreme Maximum Daily Precip. (in.)	6.45	6.58	4.00	6.35	4.40	5.32	3.83	3.80	13.60	7.70	7.31	8.40	13.60
Days With ≥ 0.1" Precipitation	8	6	7	5	6	8	7	6	6	6	6	7	78
Days With ≥ 0.5" Precipitation	3	3	3	3	3	4	3	3	3	3	3	4	38
Days With ≥ 1.0" Precipitation	2	2	2	2	2	2	2	1	1	2	2	2	22
Mean Snowfall (in.)	trace	trace	trace	0.0	0.0	0.0	0.0	0.0	0.0	0.0	0.0	trace	trace
Maximum Snow Depth (in.)	trace	trace	trace	0	0	0	0	0	0	0	0	3	3
Days With ≥ 1.0" Snow Depth	0	0	0	0	0	0	0	0	0	0	0	0	0

Franklin 3 NW *St. Mary Parish* Elevation: 12 ft. Latitude: 29° 49' N Longitude: 91° 33' W

	JAN	FEB	MAR	APR	MAY	JUN	JUL	AUG	SEP	OCT	NOV	DEC	YEAR
Mean Maximum Temp. (°F)	62.0	65.1	71.4	77.1	83.4	87.8	89.5	89.8	86.4	79.2	71.2	64.0	77.2
Mean Temp. (°F)	52.6	55.8	61.7	67.6	74.9	79.9	81.7	81.6	77.8	69.3	60.9	54.3	68.2
Mean Minimum Temp. (°F)	43.3	46.4	51.9	58.2	66.4	72.0	73.8	73.4	69.2	59.3	50.5	44.6	59.1
Extreme Maximum Temp. (°F)	80	82	86	92	94	97	100	98	98	93	89	82	100
Extreme Minimum Temp. (°F)	12	15	22	34	45	57	60	59	46	33	27	10	10
Days Maximum Temp. ≥ 90°F	0	0	0	0	1	9	17	18	8	0	0	0	53
Days Maximum Temp. ≤ 32°F	0	0	0	0	0	0	0	0	0	0	0	0	0
Days Minimum Temp. ≤ 32°F	4	2	1	0	0	0	0	0	0	0	0	3	10
Days Minimum Temp. ≤ 0°F	0	0	0	0	0	0	0	0	0	0	0	0	0
Heating Degree Days (base 65°F)	388	271	151	45	1	0	0	0	1	41	169	345	1,412
Cooling Degree Days (base 65°F)	12	16	55	130	316	454	524	522	392	180	53	20	2,674
Mean Precipitation (in.)	5.11	3.99	4.55	4.41	4.44	8.15	7.12	7.37	5.53	4.71	4.05	5.02	64.45
Extreme Maximum Daily Precip. (in.)	3.92	4.22	4.55	6.70	5.00	6.41	6.50	8.51	4.31	6.90	4.16	6.10	8.51
Days With ≥ 0.1" Precipitation	7	6	5	4	5	10	11	9	7	5	5	6	80
Days With ≥ 0.5" Precipitation	3	3	3	3	3	5	5	5	4	3	3	3	43
Days With ≥ 1.0" Precipitation	2	1	2	2	2	3	2	2	2	2	1	2	23
Mean Snowfall (in.)	trace	trace	0.0	0.0	0.0	0.0	0.0	0.0	0.0	0.0	0.0	0.1	0.1
Maximum Snow Depth (in.)	trace	trace	0	0	0	0	0	0	0	0	0	trace	trace
Days With ≥ 1.0" Snow Depth	0	0	0	0	0	0	0	0	0	0	0	0	0

The period of record for all cooperative weather station data is 1980 – 2009. See User Guide for detailed explanation of data.

Galliano *Lafourche Parish* Elevation: 4 ft. Latitude: 29° 27' N Longitude: 90° 18' W

	JAN	FEB	MAR	APR	MAY	JUN	JUL	AUG	SEP	OCT	NOV	DEC	YEAR
Mean Maximum Temp. (°F)	62.8	65.5	71.1	76.8	83.2	87.8	89.4	89.6	86.4	79.3	71.6	64.6	77.3
Mean Temp. (°F)	53.4	56.3	62.1	67.9	75.0	80.1	81.8	82.0	78.6	70.3	62.2	55.2	68.8
Mean Minimum Temp. (°F)	44.0	47.1	53.0	58.9	66.9	72.5	74.2	74.3	70.8	61.2	52.6	45.8	60.1
Extreme Maximum Temp. (°F)	82	81	86	91	94	98	100	100	97	94	86	82	100
Extreme Minimum Temp. (°F)	14	19	24	35	48	50	65	62	53	34	29	10	10
Days Maximum Temp. ≥ 90°F	0	0	0	0	1	8	16	17	6	0	0	0	48
Days Maximum Temp. ≤ 32°F	0	0	0	0	0	0	0	0	0	0	0	0	0
Days Minimum Temp. ≤ 32°F	4	2	0	0	0	0	0	0	0	0	0	3	9
Days Minimum Temp. ≤ 0°F	0	0	0	0	0	0	0	0	0	0	0	0	0
Heating Degree Days (base 65°F)	366	258	143	44	1	0	0	0	0	31	145	321	1,309
Cooling Degree Days (base 65°F)	14	20	59	137	319	461	529	532	415	203	67	25	2,781
Mean Precipitation (in.)	5.28	4.50	4.79	3.66	4.75	6.77	8.05	7.31	6.25	4.86	3.64	4.48	64.34
Extreme Maximum Daily Precip. (in.)	7.02	6.90	4.79	6.02	7.21	5.50	7.56	7.80	9.55	5.96	4.05	9.13	9.55
Days With ≥ 0.1" Precipitation	6	6	5	3	5	9	11	9	7	5	4	5	75
Days With ≥ 0.5" Precipitation	3	3	3	2	3	4	6	4	4	3	2	3	40
Days With ≥ 1.0" Precipitation	1	2	2	1	1	2	2	2	2	1	1	1	18
Mean Snowfall (in.)	trace	trace	0.0	0.0	0.0	0.0	0.0	0.0	0.0	0.0	0.0	trace	trace
Maximum Snow Depth (in.)	trace	trace	0	0	0	0	0	0	0	0	0	trace	trace
Days With ≥ 1.0" Snow Depth	0	0	0	0	0	0	0	0	0	0	0	0	0

Grand Coteau *St. Landry Parish* Elevation: 55 ft. Latitude: 30° 26' N Longitude: 92° 02' W

	JAN	FEB	MAR	APR	MAY	JUN	JUL	AUG	SEP	OCT	NOV	DEC	YEAR
Mean Maximum Temp. (°F)	62.9	65.9	72.9	79.4	86.0	90.5	92.2	93.0	88.6	80.8	72.0	64.4	79.1
Mean Temp. (°F)	52.3	55.2	61.6	68.0	75.3	80.3	82.4	82.7	78.0	69.1	60.7	53.7	68.3
Mean Minimum Temp. (°F)	41.6	44.5	50.2	56.5	64.5	70.1	72.5	72.1	67.2	57.4	49.3	42.9	57.4
Extreme Maximum Temp. (°F)	84	90	86	94	99	100	101	106	106	96	87	84	106
Extreme Minimum Temp. (°F)	10	13	20	30	44	53	61	58	44	29	25	8	8
Days Maximum Temp. ≥ 90°F	0	0	0	1	7	20	25	26	15	2	0	0	96
Days Maximum Temp. ≤ 32°F	0	0	0	0	0	0	0	0	0	0	0	0	0
Days Minimum Temp. ≤ 32°F	6	4	1	0	0	0	0	0	0	0	2	6	19
Days Minimum Temp. ≤ 0°F	0	0	0	0	0	0	0	0	0	0	0	0	0
Heating Degree Days (base 65°F)	401	289	156	46	2	0	0	0	1	44	175	366	1,480
Cooling Degree Days (base 65°F)	13	19	57	143	327	467	546	554	396	178	52	21	2,773
Mean Precipitation (in.)	6.25	4.61	4.10	4.31	5.65	6.94	4.50	4.53	4.75	5.86	5.02	5.21	61.73
Extreme Maximum Daily Precip. (in.)	8.40	6.17	3.57	4.23	8.25	6.05	10.00	4.08	7.80	7.76	6.00	8.67	10.00
Days With ≥ 0.1" Precipitation	7	6	6	5	6	9	7	7	6	6	6	6	77
Days With ≥ 0.5" Precipitation	4	3	3	3	3	5	3	3	3	3	3	4	40
Days With ≥ 1.0" Precipitation	2	2	2	1	2	2	1	1	1	2	2	2	20
Mean Snowfall (in.)	trace	trace	trace	0.0	0.0	0.0	0.0	0.0	0.0	0.0	0.0	trace	trace
Maximum Snow Depth (in.)	trace	1	trace	0	0	0	0	0	0	0	0	3	3
Days With ≥ 1.0" Snow Depth	0	0	0	0	0	0	0	0	0	0	0	0	0

Hackberry 8 SSW *Cameron Parish* Elevation: 5 ft. Latitude: 29° 53' N Longitude: 93° 25' W

	JAN	FEB	MAR	APR	MAY	JUN	JUL	AUG	SEP	OCT	NOV	DEC	YEAR
Mean Maximum Temp. (°F)	60.2	63.5	69.4	76.2	***82.8***	88.3	90.7	91.1	***87.7***	79.7	***70.9***	62.4	***76.9***
Mean Temp. (°F)	52.1	55.3	61.4	***68.6***	***76.0***	***81.7***	83.6	83.5	***79.6***	71.2	***62.4***	54.0	***69.1***
Mean Minimum Temp. (°F)	43.9	47.0	53.3	***60.8***	***69.2***	***74.9***	76.4	75.9	***71.5***	62.6	***53.9***	45.6	***61.3***
Extreme Maximum Temp. (°F)	82	80	84	93	96	98	99	103	106	98	***87***	81	***106***
Extreme Minimum Temp. (°F)	13	19	25	37	47	61	64	64	51	32	***30***	12	***12***
Days Maximum Temp. ≥ 90°F	0	0	0	0	1	11	22	23	11	1	***0***	0	***69***
Days Maximum Temp. ≤ 32°F	0	0	0	0	0	0	0	0	0	0	***0***	0	***0***
Days Minimum Temp. ≤ 32°F	3	1	0	0	0	0	0	0	0	0	***0***	2	***6***
Days Minimum Temp. ≤ 0°F	0	0	0	0	0	0	0	0	0	0	***0***	0	***0***
Heating Degree Days (base 65°F)	399	278	152	***33***	***1***	***0***	0	0	***1***	26	***137***	348	***1,375***
Cooling Degree Days (base 65°F)	5	10	46	***146***	***349***	***507***	582	581	***446***	224	***67***	15	***2,978***
Mean Precipitation (in.)	5.55	3.93	3.96	3.65	4.68	7.07	6.34	4.79	5.23	5.29	4.58	4.72	59.79
Extreme Maximum Daily Precip. (in.)	***3.96***	***3.80***	***4.75***	***5.50***	***6.26***	***6.00***	***4.48***	***4.55***	6.30	***5.75***	***4.93***	***5.42***	***6.30***
Days With ≥ 0.1" Precipitation	7	6	5	3	5	8	7	7	6	5	5	6	70
Days With ≥ 0.5" Precipitation	3	2	3	2	3	4	4	3	3	3	3	3	36
Days With ≥ 1.0" Precipitation	2	1	1	1	1	2	2	1	1	2	2	1	17
Mean Snowfall (in.)	trace	trace	0.0	0.0	0.0	0.0	0.0	0.0	0.0	0.0	0.0	0.0	trace
Maximum Snow Depth (in.)	trace	trace	0	0	0	0	0	0	0	0	0	0	trace
Days With ≥ 1.0" Snow Depth	0	0	0	0	0	0	0	0	0	0	0	0	0

Houma *Terrebonne Parish* Elevation: 15 ft. Latitude: 29° 35' N Longitude: 90° 44' W

	JAN	FEB	MAR	APR	MAY	JUN	JUL	AUG	SEP	OCT	NOV	DEC	YEAR
Mean Maximum Temp. (°F)	63.2	65.8	71.6	77.7	84.6	88.9	91.0	90.9	87.6	80.2	72.6	65.4	78.3
Mean Temp. (°F)	53.3	56.5	62.4	68.4	75.9	80.6	82.5	82.2	78.8	70.2	62.5	55.1	69.0
Mean Minimum Temp. (°F)	43.4	47.2	53.2	59.1	67.2	72.2	73.9	73.6	69.9	60.1	52.2	44.9	59.7
Extreme Maximum Temp. (°F)	82	82	86	92	94	98	99	101	100	97	89	84	101
Extreme Minimum Temp. (°F)	13	19	23	35	46	53	65	59	51	32	26	10	10
Days Maximum Temp. ≥ 90°F	0	0	0	0	4	14	23	22	12	1	0	0	76
Days Maximum Temp. ≤ 32°F	0	0	0	0	0	0	0	0	0	0	0	0	0
Days Minimum Temp. ≤ 32°F	5	2	1	0	0	0	0	0	0	0	0	3	11
Days Minimum Temp. ≤ 0°F	0	0	0	0	0	0	0	0	0	0	0	0	0
Heating Degree Days (base 65°F)	371	257	142	41	2	0	0	0	1	36	143	324	1,317
Cooling Degree Days (base 65°F)	16	23	67	150	346	474	548	542	419	204	74	26	2,889
Mean Precipitation (in.)	5.13	4.90	5.08	4.25	4.50	7.37	8.00	6.88	5.60	3.94	3.81	3.99	63.45
Extreme Maximum Daily Precip. (in.)	5.10	4.53	6.58	6.92	7.91	7.65	3.67	6.30	10.60	7.20	3.33	5.88	10.60
Days With ≥ 0.1" Precipitation	7	6	6	4	5	9	11	10	7	4	5	6	80
Days With ≥ 0.5" Precipitation	3	2	3	2	3	5	5	4	3	2	3	2	37
Days With ≥ 1.0" Precipitation	2	1	2	2	1	2	3	2	2	1	2	1	21
Mean Snowfall (in.)	trace	trace	0.0	0.0	0.0	0.0	0.0	0.0	0.0	0.0	0.0	0.1	0.1
Maximum Snow Depth (in.)	trace	trace	0	0	0	0	0	0	0	0	0	2	2
Days With ≥ 1.0" Snow Depth	0	0	0	0	0	0	0	0	0	0	0	0	0

Jena 4 WSW *La Salle Parish* Elevation: 209 ft. Latitude: 31° 40' N Longitude: 92° 12' W

	JAN	FEB	MAR	APR	MAY	JUN	JUL	AUG	SEP	OCT	NOV	DEC	YEAR
Mean Maximum Temp. (°F)	*57.8*	*62.1*	*68.9*	*76.3*	*83.4*	*89.2*	*91.8*	*92.4*	*87.8*	*78.0*	*68.1*	*58.7*	*76.2*
Mean Temp. (°F)	*47.1*	*50.8*	*57.2*	*64.2*	*72.4*	*78.5*	*81.3*	*81.0*	*76.0*	*65.1*	*56.4*	*48.0*	*64.8*
Mean Minimum Temp. (°F)	*36.4*	*39.6*	*45.5*	*52.1*	*61.3*	*67.8*	*70.8*	*69.7*	*64.2*	*52.1*	*44.6*	*37.2*	*53.4*
Extreme Maximum Temp. (°F)	*81*	*84*	*87*	*95*	*96*	*101*	*104*	*108*	*110*	*95*	*89*	*82*	*110*
Extreme Minimum Temp. (°F)	*13*	*9*	*16*	*26*	*38*	*49*	*57*	*51*	*41*	*27*	*20*	*6*	*6*
Days Maximum Temp. ≥ 90°F	*0*	*0*	*0*	*0*	*4*	*16*	*23*	*24*	*13*	*2*	*0*	*0*	*82*
Days Maximum Temp. ≤ 32°F	*0*	*0*	*0*	*0*	*0*	*0*	*0*	*0*	*0*	*0*	*0*	*0*	*0*
Days Minimum Temp. ≤ 32°F	*13*	*8*	*4*	*1*	*0*	*0*	*0*	*0*	*0*	*1*	*4*	*12*	*43*
Days Minimum Temp. ≤ 0°F	*0*	*0*	*0*	*0*	*0*	*0*	*0*	*0*	*0*	*0*	*0*	*0*	*0*
Heating Degree Days (base 65°F)	*552*	*403*	*267*	*109*	*14*	*0*	*0*	*0*	*6*	*99*	*276*	*526*	*2,252*
Cooling Degree Days (base 65°F)	*5*	*9*	*33*	*92*	*251*	*412*	*513*	*504*	*344*	*110*	*23*	*6*	*2,302*
Mean Precipitation (in.)	*5.70*	*5.23*	*5.57*	*4.73*	*4.68*	*5.36*	*4.82*	*3.03*	*3.93*	*5.10*	*5.86*	*5.76*	*59.77*
Extreme Maximum Daily Precip. (in.)	*4.10*	*4.38*	*4.20*	*4.00*	*4.41*	*4.10*	*5.60*	*4.05*	*6.00*	*6.38*	*12.96*	*4.40*	*12.96*
Days With ≥ 0.1" Precipitation	*7*	*7*	*6*	*4*	*6*	*7*	*7*	*5*	*4*	*5*	*6*	*7*	*71*
Days With ≥ 0.5" Precipitation	*4*	*3*	*4*	*3*	*3*	*4*	*3*	*2*	*2*	*3*	*3*	*4*	*38*
Days With ≥ 1.0" Precipitation	*2*	*2*	*2*	*2*	*2*	*2*	*1*	*1*	*1*	*2*	*2*	*2*	*21*
Mean Snowfall (in.)	*0.1*	*trace*	*trace*	*0.0*	*0.0*	*0.0*	*0.0*	*0.0*	*0.0*	*0.0*	*0.0*	*0.1*	*0.2*
Maximum Snow Depth (in.)	*1*	*trace*	*trace*	*0*	*0*	*0*	*0*	*0*	*0*	*0*	*0*	*1*	*1*
Days With ≥ 1.0" Snow Depth	*0*	*0*	*0*	*0*	*0*	*0*	*0*	*0*	*0*	*0*	*0*	*0*	*0*

Lafayette Regional Arpt *Lafayette Parish* Elevation: 38 ft. Latitude: 30° 12' N Longitude: 91° 59' W

	JAN	FEB	MAR	APR	MAY	JUN	JUL	AUG	SEP	OCT	NOV	DEC	YEAR
Mean Maximum Temp. (°F)	61.3	64.6	71.6	78.4	85.3	89.8	91.3	91.8	87.9	80.0	71.3	63.4	78.1
Mean Temp. (°F)	51.9	55.2	61.6	68.2	75.7	80.9	82.8	82.8	78.4	69.4	60.8	53.7	68.5
Mean Minimum Temp. (°F)	42.4	45.7	51.7	57.9	66.2	72.0	74.3	73.8	68.9	58.8	50.1	43.8	58.8
Extreme Maximum Temp. (°F)	82	81	86	93	98	102	100	104	103	94	86	82	104
Extreme Minimum Temp. (°F)	10	16	22	33	48	54	63	58	48	32	27	9	9
Days Maximum Temp. ≥ 90°F	0	0	0	0	5	17	23	24	14	2	0	0	85
Days Maximum Temp. ≤ 32°F	0	0	0	0	0	0	0	0	0	0	0	0	0
Days Minimum Temp. ≤ 32°F	5	2	1	0	0	0	0	0	0	0	1	4	13
Days Minimum Temp. ≤ 0°F	0	0	0	0	0	0	0	0	0	0	0	0	0
Heating Degree Days (base 65°F)	411	288	157	45	1	0	0	0	1	41	176	367	1,487
Cooling Degree Days (base 65°F)	13	17	60	147	341	483	559	560	410	186	56	22	2,854
Mean Precipitation (in.)	5.78	4.37	3.94	4.19	5.18	6.95	6.08	4.60	4.75	5.46	4.37	5.54	61.21
Extreme Maximum Daily Precip. (in.)	9.99	3.92	4.09	5.14	10.38	6.42	4.78	4.73	4.04	5.87	7.24	5.74	10.38
Days With ≥ 0.1" Precipitation	7	6	5	4	6	9	9	7	6	5	6	7	77
Days With ≥ 0.5" Precipitation	4	3	3	3	3	5	4	3	3	3	3	4	41
Days With ≥ 1.0" Precipitation	2	2	1	1	1	2	2	1	1	2	1	2	18
Mean Snowfall (in.)	na	na	na	na	na	na	na	na	na	na	na	na	na
Maximum Snow Depth (in.)	na	na	na	na	na	na	na	na	na	na	na	na	na
Days With ≥ 1.0" Snow Depth	na	na	na	na	na	na	na	na	na	na	na	na	na

Lake Providence *East Carroll Parish* Elevation: 100 ft. Latitude: 32° 48' N Longitude: 91° 10' W

	JAN	FEB	MAR	APR	MAY	JUN	JUL	AUG	SEP	OCT	NOV	DEC	YEAR
Mean Maximum Temp. (°F)	53.8	58.4	66.6	75.0	82.7	89.0	92.0	91.9	87.0	77.1	66.1	56.1	74.6
Mean Temp. (°F)	44.6	48.5	56.2	64.3	72.8	79.6	82.6	82.1	76.4	65.8	55.6	46.8	64.6
Mean Minimum Temp. (°F)	35.3	38.6	45.7	53.6	62.9	70.1	73.2	72.2	65.7	54.5	45.0	37.5	54.5
Extreme Maximum Temp. (°F)	79	83	88	94	95	102	104	106	106	97	86	80	106
Extreme Minimum Temp. (°F)	4	10	19	32	44	54	63	56	42	30	24	4	4
Days Maximum Temp. ≥ 90°F	0	0	0	0	4	15	23	23	12	1	0	0	78
Days Maximum Temp. ≤ 32°F	1	1	0	0	0	0	0	0	0	0	0	1	3
Days Minimum Temp. ≤ 32°F	13	7	2	0	0	0	0	0	0	0	3	10	35
Days Minimum Temp. ≤ 0°F	0	0	0	0	0	0	0	0	0	0	0	0	0
Heating Degree Days (base 65°F)	629	463	289	102	8	0	0	0	5	86	296	561	2,439
Cooling Degree Days (base 65°F)	3	4	23	88	257	444	554	537	353	119	20	5	2,407
Mean Precipitation (in.)	5.07	5.36	5.48	5.66	5.44	4.26	3.44	3.29	3.39	5.48	5.18	6.10	58.15
Extreme Maximum Daily Precip. (in.)	4.72	4.70	6.59	7.65	6.35	3.58	3.72	5.30	6.22	8.28	6.30	5.42	8.28
Days With ≥ 0.1" Precipitation	7	7	7	6	7	6	6	5	4	6	6	7	74
Days With ≥ 0.5" Precipitation	3	4	3	3	3	3	2	2	2	3	3	4	35
Days With ≥ 1.0" Precipitation	1	2	2	2	2	1	1	1	1	2	2	2	19
Mean Snowfall (in.)	0.1	0.1	trace	trace	0.0	0.0	0.0	0.0	0.0	0.0	0.0	0.1	0.3
Maximum Snow Depth (in.)	4	2	2	trace	0	0	0	0	0	0	0	trace	4
Days With ≥ 1.0" Snow Depth	0	0	0	0	0	0	0	0	0	0	0	0	0

Lsu Ben Hur Farm *East Baton Rouge Parish* Elevation: 21 ft. Latitude: 30° 22' N Longitude: 91° 10' W

	JAN	FEB	MAR	APR	MAY	JUN	JUL	AUG	SEP	OCT	NOV	DEC	YEAR
Mean Maximum Temp. (°F)	61.3	64.7	71.6	78.2	85.2	89.9	91.6	91.9	88.4	80.3	71.4	63.3	78.1
Mean Temp. (°F)	50.8	54.1	60.5	66.9	74.8	80.1	82.1	82.0	77.9	68.5	60.0	52.6	67.5
Mean Minimum Temp. (°F)	40.3	43.4	49.4	55.6	64.4	70.2	72.5	72.0	67.4	56.7	48.5	41.8	56.8
Extreme Maximum Temp. (°F)	82	84	88	93	96	100	100	105	103	95	87	84	105
Extreme Minimum Temp. (°F)	10	15	20	31	44	49	62	56	46	32	26	9	9
Days Maximum Temp. ≥ 90°F	0	0	0	1	6	19	25	24	15	2	0	0	92
Days Maximum Temp. ≤ 32°F	0	0	0	0	0	0	0	0	0	0	0	0	0
Days Minimum Temp. ≤ 32°F	8	4	1	0	0	0	0	0	0	0	1	6	20
Days Minimum Temp. ≤ 0°F	0	0	0	0	0	0	0	0	0	0	0	0	0
Heating Degree Days (base 65°F)	443	318	181	63	4	0	0	0	2	54	193	396	1,654
Cooling Degree Days (base 65°F)	9	15	49	128	315	460	537	532	397	170	49	17	2,678
Mean Precipitation (in.)	5.36	5.08	4.49	4.65	4.85	6.90	4.69	5.18	4.59	4.43	4.14	5.38	59.74
Extreme Maximum Daily Precip. (in.)	4.47	4.96	3.39	5.35	4.71	8.57	4.09	6.85	6.02	4.76	5.40	6.38	8.57
Days With ≥ 0.1" Precipitation	7	6	6	5	5	9	9	8	6	5	5	7	78
Days With ≥ 0.5" Precipitation	4	3	3	3	3	4	3	3	3	3	3	3	38
Days With ≥ 1.0" Precipitation	2	2	2	1	2	2	1	1	2	1	1	2	19
Mean Snowfall (in.)	trace	trace	0.0	0.0	0.0	0.0	0.0	0.0	0.0	0.0	0.0	0.0	trace
Maximum Snow Depth (in.)	1	1	0	0	0	0	0	0	0	0	0	0	1
Days With ≥ 1.0" Snow Depth	0	0	0	0	0	0	0	0	0	0	0	0	0

The period of record for all cooperative weather station data is 1980 – 2009. See User Guide for detailed explanation of data.

Minden *Webster Parish* Elevation: 185 ft. Latitude: 32° 36' N Longitude: 93° 18' W

	JAN	FEB	MAR	APR	MAY	JUN	JUL	AUG	SEP	OCT	NOV	DEC	YEAR
Mean Maximum Temp. (°F)	56.3	60.5	68.1	75.8	82.9	89.1	92.8	93.3	87.2	77.1	67.0	57.8	75.6
Mean Temp. (°F)	45.0	48.6	55.9	63.4	71.9	78.8	82.4	82.2	75.7	64.7	55.0	46.5	64.2
Mean Minimum Temp. (°F)	33.7	36.6	43.6	51.1	60.9	68.4	71.9	71.1	64.2	52.4	42.9	35.3	52.7
Extreme Maximum Temp. (°F)	81	85	91	94	97	102	107	106	108	95	86	83	108
Extreme Minimum Temp. (°F)	5	12	15	25	36	49	57	52	42	27	21	2	2
Days Maximum Temp. ≥ 90°F	0	0	0	0	3	16	25	24	12	2	0	0	82
Days Maximum Temp. ≤ 32°F	0	0	0	0	0	0	0	0	0	0	0	1	1
Days Minimum Temp. ≤ 32°F	16	11	4	0	0	0	0	0	0	0	5	15	51
Days Minimum Temp. ≤ 0°F	0	0	0	0	0	0	0	0	0	0	0	0	0
Heating Degree Days (base 65°F)	617	464	300	117	13	0	0	0	10	105	313	571	2,510
Cooling Degree Days (base 65°F)	4	5	24	76	236	421	546	541	338	105	19	6	2,321
Mean Precipitation (in.)	4.90	5.11	4.87	5.31	4.58	5.03	3.56	2.64	3.77	5.15	5.11	5.43	55.46
Extreme Maximum Daily Precip. (in.)	5.90	4.37	4.52	12.87	6.72	5.18	4.77	2.75	4.45	5.82	4.29	3.10	12.87
Days With ≥ 0.1" Precipitation	7	7	7	5	7	7	5	5	5	6	6	7	74
Days With ≥ 0.5" Precipitation	3	3	3	3	3	3	3	2	2	3	3	4	35
Days With ≥ 1.0" Precipitation	2	2	2	1	1	2	1	1	1	2	2	2	19
Mean Snowfall (in.)	0.2	0.1	trace	trace	0.0	0.0	0.0	0.0	0.0	0.0	trace	0.1	0.4
Maximum Snow Depth (in.)	5	2	1	trace	0	0	0	0	0	0	1	3	5
Days With ≥ 1.0" Snow Depth	0	0	0	0	0	0	0	0	0	0	0	0	0

Monroe NLU *Ouachita Parish* Elevation: 69 ft. Latitude: 32° 32' N Longitude: 92° 04' W

	JAN	FEB	MAR	APR	MAY	JUN	JUL	AUG	SEP	OCT	NOV	DEC	YEAR
Mean Maximum Temp. (°F)	56.4	60.5	68.3	76.3	83.9	90.2	93.6	93.7	88.2	78.3	67.7	58.6	76.3
Mean Temp. (°F)	45.5	49.2	56.7	64.4	72.8	79.4	82.7	82.2	75.8	65.1	55.6	47.5	64.8
Mean Minimum Temp. (°F)	34.4	37.9	45.2	52.5	61.6	68.6	71.8	70.7	63.4	51.9	43.4	36.4	53.2
Extreme Maximum Temp. (°F)	81	84	89	95	98	103	105	108	108	98	89	84	108
Extreme Minimum Temp. (°F)	4	10	17	32	43	51	59	52	41	28	20	3	3
Days Maximum Temp. ≥ 90°F	0	0	0	1	5	19	26	25	14	2	0	0	92
Days Maximum Temp. ≤ 32°F	1	0	0	0	0	0	0	0	0	0	0	1	2
Days Minimum Temp. ≤ 32°F	14	9	3	0	0	0	0	0	0	0	4	12	42
Days Minimum Temp. ≤ 0°F	0	0	0	0	0	0	0	0	0	0	0	0	0
Heating Degree Days (base 65°F)	602	446	275	101	11	0	0	0	9	99	296	542	2,381
Cooling Degree Days (base 65°F)	4	6	27	92	259	440	556	540	339	108	21	7	2,399
Mean Precipitation (in.)	5.17	5.18	5.45	5.07	5.59	4.48	3.62	2.98	3.53	5.04	4.90	5.56	56.57
Extreme Maximum Daily Precip. (in.)	4.65	4.52	4.51	5.98	11.50	2.71	3.50	3.75	6.69	5.30	5.30	6.82	11.50
Days With ≥ 0.1" Precipitation	7	7	7	5	7	7	6	4	4	5	6	6	71
Days With ≥ 0.5" Precipitation	3	3	4	3	4	3	2	2	2	3	3	3	35
Days With ≥ 1.0" Precipitation	1	2	2	2	2	1	1	1	1	2	1	2	18
Mean Snowfall (in.)	0.4	0.1	0.1	trace	trace	0.0	0.0	0.0	0.0	0.0	trace	trace	0.6
Maximum Snow Depth (in.)	5	3	2	trace	trace	0	0	0	0	0	trace	trace	5
Days With ≥ 1.0" Snow Depth	0	0	0	0	0	0	0	0	0	0	0	0	0

New Iberia *Iberia Parish* Elevation: 24 ft. Latitude: 29° 59' N Longitude: 91° 47' W

	JAN	FEB	MAR	APR	MAY	JUN	JUL	AUG	SEP	OCT	NOV	DEC	YEAR
Mean Maximum Temp. (°F)	62.2	65.4	72.3	78.9	84.9	89.6	91.5	91.6	88.1	80.4	72.1	64.5	78.5
Mean Temp. (°F)	52.4	55.5	62.1	68.6	75.6	80.8	82.7	82.6	78.6	69.9	61.5	54.3	68.7
Mean Minimum Temp. (°F)	42.4	45.5	51.8	58.3	66.2	72.0	73.8	73.5	69.1	59.3	50.8	44.0	58.9
Extreme Maximum Temp. (°F)	85	85	88	94	98	102	101	103	103	95	87	87	103
Extreme Minimum Temp. (°F)	11	17	19	36	45	54	66	61	48	32	26	9	9
Days Maximum Temp. ≥ 90°F	0	0	0	1	4	16	24	24	14	2	0	0	85
Days Maximum Temp. ≤ 32°F	0	0	0	0	0	0	0	0	0	0	0	0	0
Days Minimum Temp. ≤ 32°F	5	2	1	0	0	0	0	0	0	0	1	4	13
Days Minimum Temp. ≤ 0°F	0	0	0	0	0	0	0	0	0	0	0	0	0
Heating Degree Days (base 65°F)	397	282	146	39	2	0	0	0	1	36	161	348	1,412
Cooling Degree Days (base 65°F)	12	18	63	154	336	480	555	552	416	193	61	23	2,863
Mean Precipitation (in.)	4.75	4.33	3.84	4.17	4.56	7.27	6.90	5.96	5.59	5.07	4.03	4.57	61.04
Extreme Maximum Daily Precip. (in.)	4.19	4.42	4.10	4.87	***4.60***	4.06	4.87	5.20	***5.11***	7.95	3.30	5.12	***7.95***
Days With ≥ 0.1" Precipitation	7	6	5	4	5	9	9	8	6	5	5	6	75
Days With ≥ 0.5" Precipitation	3	3	2	2	3	5	4	4	3	3	3	3	38
Days With ≥ 1.0" Precipitation	1	1	1	1	2	3	2	2	1	2	1	1	18
Mean Snowfall (in.)	trace	trace	0.0	0.0	0.0	0.0	0.0	0.0	0.0	0.0	0.0	trace	trace
Maximum Snow Depth (in.)	trace	trace	0	0	0	0	0	0	0	0	0	0	trace
Days With ≥ 1.0" Snow Depth	0	0	0	0	0	0	0	0	0	0	0	0	0

New Orleans Audubon *Orleans Parish* Elevation: 5 ft. Latitude: 29° 55' N Longitude: 90° 08' W

	JAN	FEB	MAR	APR	MAY	JUN	JUL	AUG	SEP	OCT	NOV	DEC	YEAR
Mean Maximum Temp. (°F)	63.2	66.6	72.9	79.3	86.4	90.8	92.5	92.4	88.3	80.9	72.4	65.0	79.2
Mean Temp. (°F)	54.7	57.8	63.8	70.0	77.6	82.4	84.1	84.2	80.3	72.2	63.5	56.4	70.6
Mean Minimum Temp. (°F)	46.0	49.0	54.7	60.6	68.7	73.9	75.7	75.9	72.2	63.4	54.6	47.8	61.9
Extreme Maximum Temp. (°F)	82	85	88	93	96	104	101	103	101	97	87	84	104
Extreme Minimum Temp. (°F)	16	20	28	37	51	54	67	65	52	37	33	12	12
Days Maximum Temp. ≥ 90°F	0	0	0	1	8	20	25	25	14	2	0	0	95
Days Maximum Temp. ≤ 32°F	0	0	0	0	0	0	0	0	0	0	0	0	0
Days Minimum Temp. ≤ 32°F	2	1	0	0	0	0	0	0	0	0	0	1	4
Days Minimum Temp. ≤ 0°F	0	0	0	0	0	0	0	0	0	0	0	0	0
Heating Degree Days (base 65°F)	333	223	111	26	0	0	0	0	0	17	119	291	1,120
Cooling Degree Days (base 65°F)	18	27	81	182	392	528	600	601	466	247	81	32	3,255
Mean Precipitation (in.)	5.11	4.37	4.92	4.88	4.55	7.11	7.16	5.81	5.77	4.12	4.21	4.89	62.90
Extreme Maximum Daily Precip. (in.)	4.87	4.80	4.10	7.75	10.94	7.80	3.40	4.12	10.20	7.34	6.21	7.22	10.94
Days With ≥ 0.1" Precipitation	6	5	6	5	5	9	10	9	7	5	5	6	78
Days With ≥ 0.5" Precipitation	3	3	3	3	2	4	5	4	3	2	3	3	38
Days With ≥ 1.0" Precipitation	2	1	2	1	1	2	3	2	2	1	1	1	19
Mean Snowfall (in.)	trace	trace	trace	0.0	0.0	0.0	0.0	0.0	0.0	0.0	0.0	trace	trace
Maximum Snow Depth (in.)	trace	trace	0	0	0	0	0	0	0	0	0	2	2
Days With ≥ 1.0" Snow Depth	0	0	0	0	0	0	0	0	0	0	0	0	0

The period of record for all cooperative weather station data is 1980 – 2009. See User Guide for detailed explanation of data.

New Roads 5 ESE *Pointe Coupee Parish* Elevation: 44 ft. Latitude: 30° 41' N Longitude: 91° 22' W

	JAN	FEB	MAR	APR	MAY	JUN	JUL	AUG	SEP	OCT	NOV	DEC	YEAR
Mean Maximum Temp. (°F)	60.0	63.8	70.9	77.8	84.7	89.6	91.4	91.6	87.5	79.3	70.2	62.2	77.4
Mean Temp. (°F)	49.8	53.4	59.9	66.7	74.4	80.1	82.1	82.0	77.7	68.1	59.1	51.7	67.1
Mean Minimum Temp. (°F)	39.6	42.9	48.9	55.6	64.1	70.5	72.8	72.3	67.9	57.0	47.9	41.2	56.7
Extreme Maximum Temp. (°F)	85	85	89	94	97	101	100	105	105	94	87	85	105
Extreme Minimum Temp. (°F)	8	14	23	32	43	51	62	58	47	30	27	8	8
Days Maximum Temp. ≥ 90°F	0	0	0	1	5	16	23	23	12	2	0	0	82
Days Maximum Temp. ≤ 32°F	0	0	0	0	0	0	0	0	0	0	0	0	0
Days Minimum Temp. ≤ 32°F	8	4	1	0	0	0	0	0	0	0	2	7	22
Days Minimum Temp. ≤ 0°F	0	0	0	0	0	0	0	0	0	0	0	0	0
Heating Degree Days (base 65°F)	471	335	190	61	3	0	0	0	1	53	211	418	1,743
Cooling Degree Days (base 65°F)	7	13	39	118	302	459	537	532	390	157	40	12	2,606
Mean Precipitation (in.)	6.06	5.57	4.72	4.83	5.07	5.65	4.11	4.29	4.35	4.73	4.18	5.78	59.34
Extreme Maximum Daily Precip. (in.)	5.61	7.33	6.50	8.06	6.40	8.85	7.26	6.22	6.07	7.73	8.40	5.79	8.85
Days With ≥ 0.1" Precipitation	7	7	6	5	6	8	7	7	5	5	5	7	75
Days With ≥ 0.5" Precipitation	4	3	3	3	3	3	3	3	3	3	3	4	38
Days With ≥ 1.0" Precipitation	2	2	2	2	2	2	1	1	1	1	1	2	19
Mean Snowfall (in.)	trace	trace	0.0	0.0	0.0	0.0	0.0	0.0	0.0	0.0	0.0	trace	trace
Maximum Snow Depth (in.)	trace	1	0	0	0	0	0	0	0	0	0	3	3
Days With ≥ 1.0" Snow Depth	0	0	0	0	0	0	0	0	0	0	0	0	0

Red River Research Stn *Bossier Parish* Elevation: 154 ft. Latitude: 32° 25' N Longitude: 93° 38' W

	JAN	FEB	MAR	APR	MAY	JUN	JUL	AUG	SEP	OCT	NOV	DEC	YEAR
Mean Maximum Temp. (°F)	56.7	60.9	68.4	76.5	84.0	90.2	93.6	94.2	88.8	78.5	67.8	58.3	76.5
Mean Temp. (°F)	45.9	49.7	57.0	64.7	73.2	79.9	83.1	82.7	76.4	65.7	56.1	47.5	65.2
Mean Minimum Temp. (°F)	35.1	38.4	45.5	52.8	62.4	69.5	72.4	71.2	64.0	52.9	44.5	36.6	53.8
Extreme Maximum Temp. (°F)	81	87	88	95	99	103	105	108	108	97	87	83	108
Extreme Minimum Temp. (°F)	6	13	18	29	44	51	59	50	42	28	23	3	3
Days Maximum Temp. ≥ 90°F	0	0	0	1	6	19	27	26	16	2	0	0	97
Days Maximum Temp. ≤ 32°F	0	0	0	0	0	0	0	0	0	0	0	0	0
Days Minimum Temp. ≤ 32°F	14	8	2	0	0	0	0	0	0	0	4	13	41
Days Minimum Temp. ≤ 0°F	0	0	0	0	0	0	0	0	0	0	0	0	0
Heating Degree Days (base 65°F)	589	432	268	95	7	0	0	0	7	88	283	542	2,311
Cooling Degree Days (base 65°F)	4	6	26	93	269	454	567	556	356	117	24	5	2,477
Mean Precipitation (in.)	4.59	4.64	4.38	4.59	4.78	5.01	3.65	2.75	3.24	5.00	4.60	5.02	52.25
Extreme Maximum Daily Precip. (in.)	6.53	3.56	3.17	7.56	8.20	5.18	5.52	4.48	5.16	5.50	3.18	4.02	8.20
Days With ≥ 0.1" Precipitation	6	6	6	5	6	6	5	4	5	5	6	7	67
Days With ≥ 0.5" Precipitation	3	3	3	3	3	3	2	2	2	3	3	4	34
Days With ≥ 1.0" Precipitation	2	2	2	1	1	2	1	1	1	2	2	2	19
Mean Snowfall (in.)	0.1	trace	trace	0.0	0.0	0.0	0.0	0.0	0.0	0.0	0.1	trace	0.2
Maximum Snow Depth (in.)	2	trace	trace	0	0	0	0	0	0	0	trace	3	3
Days With ≥ 1.0" Snow Depth	0	0	0	0	0	0	0	0	0	0	0	0	0

Reserve *St. John The Baptist Parish* Elevation: 15 ft. Latitude: 30° 05' N Longitude: 90° 37' W

	JAN	FEB	MAR	APR	MAY	JUN	JUL	AUG	SEP	OCT	NOV	DEC	YEAR
Mean Maximum Temp. (°F)	62.1	65.3	71.8	78.1	84.7	89.4	91.4	91.3	87.7	79.9	71.9	64.2	78.1
Mean Temp. (°F)	51.9	55.0	61.3	67.3	74.7	80.2	82.3	82.1	78.2	69.3	61.2	53.8	68.1
Mean Minimum Temp. (°F)	41.8	44.7	50.7	56.6	64.5	70.9	73.1	72.9	68.7	58.7	50.4	43.3	58.0
Extreme Maximum Temp. (°F)	82	84	88	92	96	98	101	103	99	96	88	83	103
Extreme Minimum Temp. (°F)	11	16	23	34	42	53	62	58	45	33	28	9	9
Days Maximum Temp. ≥ 90°F	0	0	0	0	4	16	23	22	12	1	0	0	78
Days Maximum Temp. ≤ 32°F	0	0	0	0	0	0	0	0	0	0	0	0	0
Days Minimum Temp. ≤ 32°F	6	2	1	0	0	0	0	0	0	0	1	5	15
Days Minimum Temp. ≤ 0°F	0	0	0	0	0	0	0	0	0	0	0	0	0
Heating Degree Days (base 65°F)	406	291	159	49	2	0	0	0	1	39	161	360	1,468
Cooling Degree Days (base 65°F)	8	14	50	126	309	461	542	538	404	178	54	18	2,702
Mean Precipitation (in.)	5.75	5.24	5.39	5.06	4.77	8.23	6.90	5.33	5.40	4.21	4.32	4.34	64.94
Extreme Maximum Daily Precip. (in.)	4.30	3.56	5.77	6.72	7.40	7.10	4.62	6.00	5.70	4.97	5.30	5.69	7.40
Days With ≥ 0.1" Precipitation	7	6	6	5	6	9	10	8	6	5	5	6	79
Days With ≥ 0.5" Precipitation	3	3	4	3	3	5	4	4	3	2	3	3	40
Days With ≥ 1.0" Precipitation	2	2	2	2	2	3	2	1	2	1	2	1	22
Mean Snowfall (in.)	trace	trace	0.0	0.0	0.0	0.0	0.0	0.0	0.0	0.0	0.0	trace	trace
Maximum Snow Depth (in.)	trace	1	0	0	0	0	0	0	0	0	0	trace	1
Days With ≥ 1.0" Snow Depth	0	0	0	0	0	0	0	0	0	0	0	0	0

Ruston La Tech *Lincoln Parish* Elevation: 279 ft. Latitude: 32° 31' N Longitude: 92° 39' W

	JAN	FEB	MAR	APR	MAY	JUN	JUL	AUG	SEP	OCT	NOV	DEC	YEAR
Mean Maximum Temp. (°F)	56.2	60.3	68.2	76.1	82.9	89.4	93.0	93.2	87.1	76.8	66.9	57.7	75.6
Mean Temp. (°F)	45.2	49.0	55.9	63.6	71.7	78.5	81.8	81.4	75.3	64.6	55.2	46.8	64.1
Mean Minimum Temp. (°F)	34.1	37.4	43.7	51.1	60.4	67.5	70.5	69.7	63.4	52.3	43.5	35.9	52.5
Extreme Maximum Temp. (°F)	80	85	90	94	95	102	107	109	106	94	85	83	109
Extreme Minimum Temp. (°F)	4	9	16	28	39	52	56	49	42	25	20	0	0
Days Maximum Temp. ≥ 90°F	0	0	0	0	4	17	25	24	12	1	0	0	83
Days Maximum Temp. ≤ 32°F	1	0	0	0	0	0	0	0	0	0	0	1	2
Days Minimum Temp. ≤ 32°F	15	9	4	0	0	0	0	0	0	0	5	13	46
Days Minimum Temp. ≤ 0°F	0	0	0	0	0	0	0	0	0	0	0	0	0
Heating Degree Days (base 65°F)	611	450	297	114	14	0	0	0	10	103	305	563	2,467
Cooling Degree Days (base 65°F)	3	5	21	78	230	412	527	513	327	98	17	6	2,237
Mean Precipitation (in.)	5.11	5.27	5.08	4.68	5.23	4.46	3.30	3.02	3.51	4.96	4.81	5.57	55.00
Extreme Maximum Daily Precip. (in.)	5.06	4.77	3.69	4.09	11.84	3.48	3.60	2.60	4.45	4.70	4.28	5.96	11.84
Days With ≥ 0.1" Precipitation	7	7	7	5	6	7	5	5	5	6	6	7	73
Days With ≥ 0.5" Precipitation	3	3	3	3	3	3	2	2	2	3	3	4	34
Days With ≥ 1.0" Precipitation	2	2	2	2	2	1	1	1	1	2	2	2	20
Mean Snowfall (in.)	0.4	0.1	0.0	trace	0.0	0.0	0.0	0.0	0.0	0.0	trace	trace	0.5
Maximum Snow Depth (in.)	5	1	0	trace	0	0	0	0	0	0	trace	2	5
Days With ≥ 1.0" Snow Depth	0	0	0	0	0	0	0	0	0	0	0	0	0

The period of record for all cooperative weather station data is 1980 – 2009. See User Guide for detailed explanation of data.

Slidell *St. Tammany Parish* Elevation: 9 ft. Latitude: 30° 16' N Longitude: 89° 46' W

	JAN	FEB	MAR	APR	MAY	JUN	JUL	AUG	SEP	OCT	NOV	DEC	YEAR
Mean Maximum Temp. (°F)	61.5	64.6	71.0	77.4	84.4	89.1	91.0	91.0	87.5	79.8	71.3	63.4	77.7
Mean Temp. (°F)	51.3	54.4	60.7	67.1	74.7	80.1	82.1	82.0	78.0	69.0	60.4	53.1	67.7
Mean Minimum Temp. (°F)	41.0	44.2	50.3	56.7	65.0	71.1	73.2	72.9	68.6	58.1	49.4	42.7	57.8
Extreme Maximum Temp. (°F)	80	83	88	92	95	97	102	101	99	93	86	83	102
Extreme Minimum Temp. (°F)	8	15	22	32	42	50	65	58	46	31	28	9	8
Days Maximum Temp. ≥ 90°F	0	0	0	0	3	14	22	22	11	1	0	0	73
Days Maximum Temp. ≤ 32°F	0	0	0	0	0	0	0	0	0	0	0	0	0
Days Minimum Temp. ≤ 32°F	7	4	1	0	0	0	0	0	0	0	1	5	18
Days Minimum Temp. ≤ 0°F	0	0	0	0	0	0	0	0	0	0	0	0	0
Heating Degree Days (base 65°F)	426	305	174	55	3	0	0	0	1	45	181	379	1,569
Cooling Degree Days (base 65°F)	8	12	46	124	312	461	537	533	399	176	49	17	2,674
Mean Precipitation (in.)	5.73	4.71	5.59	4.90	5.43	5.19	6.86	6.58	5.09	3.96	4.48	4.92	63.44
Extreme Maximum Daily Precip. (in.)	4.89	4.30	5.29	7.26	13.42	8.20	6.29	6.10	6.82	6.20	5.37	4.68	13.42
Days With ≥ 0.1" Precipitation	7	6	6	5	5	7	8	9	6	4	5	6	74
Days With ≥ 0.5" Precipitation	3	3	3	3	3	3	4	4	3	2	3	3	37
Days With ≥ 1.0" Precipitation	2	2	2	2	2	2	2	2	2	1	2	2	23
Mean Snowfall (in.)	trace	0.1	0.1	0.0	trace	0.0	0.0	0.0	0.0	0.0	0.0	trace	0.2
Maximum Snow Depth (in.)	trace	1	2	0	trace	0	0	0	0	0	trace	2	2
Days With ≥ 1.0" Snow Depth	0	0	0	0	0	0	0	0	0	0	0	0	0

St Bernard *St. Bernard Parish* Elevation: 4 ft. Latitude: 29° 52' N Longitude: 89° 50' W

	JAN	FEB	MAR	APR	MAY	JUN	JUL	AUG	SEP	OCT	NOV	DEC	YEAR
Mean Maximum Temp. (°F)	62.6	65.9	71.8	77.8	84.9	88.7	90.7	90.6	86.6	79.4	71.5	64.6	77.9
Mean Temp. (°F)	52.9	56.6	61.9	68.5	76.0	80.5	82.4	82.4	78.6	70.4	62.3	55.0	69.0
Mean Minimum Temp. (°F)	43.1	47.2	52.2	59.1	67.1	72.3	74.1	74.2	70.6	61.4	52.9	45.4	60.0
Extreme Maximum Temp. (°F)	84	84	89	91	96	99	100	101	99	94	89	84	101
Extreme Minimum Temp. (°F)	11	17	22	37	49	54	65	62	50	35	30	10	10
Days Maximum Temp. ≥ 90°F	0	0	0	0	4	13	20	20	9	1	0	0	67
Days Maximum Temp. ≤ 32°F	0	0	0	0	0	0	0	0	0	0	0	0	0
Days Minimum Temp. ≤ 32°F	4	2	1	0	0	0	0	0	0	0	0	3	10
Days Minimum Temp. ≤ 0°F	0	0	0	0	0	0	0	0	0	0	0	0	0
Heating Degree Days (base 65°F)	381	253	148	35	1	0	0	0	0	26	146	325	1,315
Cooling Degree Days (base 65°F)	12	21	58	146	349	472	547	548	415	202	70	22	2,862
Mean Precipitation (in.)	4.52	4.80	6.06	5.32	4.21	7.34	7.02	5.53	5.85	3.45	4.87	3.96	62.93
Extreme Maximum Daily Precip. (in.)	3.52	8.80	6.20	8.88	6.00	6.40	9.00	na	9.20	4.28	12.38	na	na
Days With ≥ 0.1" Precipitation	6	5	6	4	5	9	8	8	7	4	5	5	72
Days With ≥ 0.5" Precipitation	3	3	4	2	2	5	4	3	4	2	3	3	38
Days With ≥ 1.0" Precipitation	2	2	2	2	2	3	2	2	2	1	2	1	23
Mean Snowfall (in.)	0.0	trace	0.0	0.0	0.0	0.0	0.0	0.0	0.0	0.0	0.0	trace	trace
Maximum Snow Depth (in.)	0	trace	0	0	0	0	0	0	0	0	0	trace	trace
Days With ≥ 1.0" Snow Depth	0	0	0	0	0	0	0	0	0	0	0	0	0

St Joseph 3 N *Tensas Parish* Elevation: 78 ft. Latitude: 31° 57' N Longitude: 91° 14' W

	JAN	FEB	MAR	APR	MAY	JUN	JUL	AUG	SEP	OCT	NOV	DEC	YEAR
Mean Maximum Temp. (°F)	57.5	61.6	69.4	77.3	84.9	90.6	93.1	93.2	88.8	79.5	69.6	60.0	77.1
Mean Temp. (°F)	47.2	50.9	58.3	65.8	74.3	80.3	82.7	82.2	77.1	66.8	57.9	49.5	66.1
Mean Minimum Temp. (°F)	36.8	40.2	47.2	54.4	63.6	69.9	72.4	71.2	65.2	54.1	46.1	39.0	55.0
Extreme Maximum Temp. (°F)	80	84	87	96	97	102	103	106	107	98	89	85	107
Extreme Minimum Temp. (°F)	6	12	18	30	41	52	58	51	41	29	23	5	5
Days Maximum Temp. ≥ 90°F	0	0	0	1	8	20	26	25	16	3	0	0	99
Days Maximum Temp. ≤ 32°F	0	0	0	0	0	0	0	0	0	0	0	1	1
Days Minimum Temp. ≤ 32°F	12	7	2	0	0	0	0	0	0	0	2	9	32
Days Minimum Temp. ≤ 0°F	0	0	0	0	0	0	0	0	0	0	0	0	0
Heating Degree Days (base 65°F)	549	400	234	81	6	0	0	0	6	79	240	483	2,078
Cooling Degree Days (base 65°F)	3	8	35	112	301	466	557	540	374	143	34	10	2,583
Mean Precipitation (in.)	5.46	5.26	5.77	4.67	4.92	4.23	4.38	3.71	3.55	4.12	5.35	5.41	56.83
Extreme Maximum Daily Precip. (in.)	4.01	4.33	5.77	5.35	7.37	5.22	4.50	4.52	5.92	4.71	6.30	4.76	7.37
Days With ≥ 0.1" Precipitation	7	6	7	5	6	6	6	6	5	5	6	7	72
Days With ≥ 0.5" Precipitation	3	4	4	3	3	3	3	2	2	3	3	4	37
Days With ≥ 1.0" Precipitation	2	2	2	2	2	1	1	1	1	1	2	2	19
Mean Snowfall (in.)	trace	trace	trace	0.0	0.0	0.0	0.0	0.0	0.0	0.0	0.0	0.0	trace
Maximum Snow Depth (in.)	2	1	trace	0	0	0	0	0	0	0	0	trace	2
Days With ≥ 1.0" Snow Depth	0	0	0	0	0	0	0	0	0	0	0	0	0

Tallulah *Madison Parish* Elevation: 84 ft. Latitude: 32° 24' N Longitude: 91° 13' W

	JAN	FEB	MAR	APR	MAY	JUN	JUL	AUG	SEP	OCT	NOV	DEC	YEAR
Mean Maximum Temp. (°F)	55.5	59.9	67.9	75.7	82.9	89.1	91.7	91.8	86.8	77.6	67.4	57.7	75.3
Mean Temp. (°F)	45.4	49.4	56.9	64.6	72.6	79.1	81.8	81.4	75.8	65.4	56.1	47.5	64.7
Mean Minimum Temp. (°F)	35.2	38.9	45.9	53.4	62.3	69.1	71.9	71.0	64.7	53.3	44.6	37.2	54.0
Extreme Maximum Temp. (°F)	81	84	89	92	94	100	103	106	105	95	88	83	106
Extreme Minimum Temp. (°F)	3	0	11	28	43	48	59	55	40	28	23	4	0
Days Maximum Temp. ≥ 90°F	0	0	0	0	3	16	23	23	11	1	0	0	77
Days Maximum Temp. ≤ 32°F	1	1	0	0	0	0	0	0	0	0	0	1	3
Days Minimum Temp. ≤ 32°F	14	8	2	0	0	0	0	0	0	0	4	12	40
Days Minimum Temp. ≤ 0°F	0	0	0	0	0	0	0	0	0	0	0	0	0
Heating Degree Days (base 65°F)	605	441	274	103	11	0	0	0	7	94	284	543	2,362
Cooling Degree Days (base 65°F)	3	7	29	97	254	431	529	517	337	115	23	7	2,349
Mean Precipitation (in.)	5.09	5.43	5.57	5.07	5.58	4.34	3.56	3.21	3.61	4.49	5.11	5.86	56.92
Extreme Maximum Daily Precip. (in.)	5.14	3.50	4.53	6.32	5.86	5.32	4.32	5.26	5.65	2.90	7.00	6.35	7.00
Days With ≥ 0.1" Precipitation	7	7	7	5	7	6	6	5	5	5	6	7	73
Days With ≥ 0.5" Precipitation	3	4	4	3	3	3	3	2	2	3	3	4	37
Days With ≥ 1.0" Precipitation	2	2	2	2	2	1	1	1	1	2	2	2	20
Mean Snowfall (in.)	0.0	trace	trace	0.0	0.0	0.0	0.0	0.0	0.0	0.0	0.0	trace	trace
Maximum Snow Depth (in.)	5	4	trace	0	0	0	0	0	0	0	0	2	5
Days With ≥ 1.0" Snow Depth	0	0	0	0	0	0	0	0	0	0	0	0	0

The period of record for all cooperative weather station data is 1980 – 2009. See User Guide for detailed explanation of data.

Thibodaux 3 ESE *Lafourche Parish* Elevation: 15 ft. Latitude: 29° 46' N Longitude: 90° 47' W

	JAN	FEB	MAR	APR	MAY	JUN	JUL	AUG	SEP	OCT	NOV	DEC	YEAR
Mean Maximum Temp. (°F)	63.6	66.4	72.9	78.9	85.4	89.6	91.3	91.4	88.0	80.8	73.0	65.7	78.9
Mean Temp. (°F)	53.4	56.4	62.3	68.3	75.5	80.4	82.2	82.2	78.4	69.7	62.3	55.2	68.9
Mean Minimum Temp. (°F)	43.2	46.4	51.7	57.6	65.5	71.1	73.1	72.8	68.8	58.6	51.5	44.6	58.8
Extreme Maximum Temp. (°F)	82	83	87	92	96	99	101	102	99	95	88	84	102
Extreme Minimum Temp. (°F)	12	19	23	34	46	51	63	59	48	31	28	9	9
Days Maximum Temp. ≥ 90°F	0	0	0	0	5	17	22	24	13	2	0	0	83
Days Maximum Temp. ≤ 32°F	0	0	0	0	0	0	0	0	0	0	0	0	0
Days Minimum Temp. ≤ 32°F	5	2	1	0	0	0	0	0	0	0	1	4	13
Days Minimum Temp. ≤ 0°F	0	0	0	0	0	0	0	0	0	0	0	0	0
Heating Degree Days (base 65°F)	369	260	140	41	1	0	0	0	1	36	145	324	1,317
Cooling Degree Days (base 65°F)	16	24	63	147	334	468	541	538	411	189	71	27	2,829
Mean Precipitation (in.)	5.84	5.07	5.36	4.97	5.56	8.90	8.28	7.34	5.80	4.77	4.19	5.32	71.40
Extreme Maximum Daily Precip. (in.)	5.21	3.69	4.06	11.80	10.32	15.16	3.71	5.09	7.51	4.82	4.02	7.83	15.16
Days With ≥ 0.1" Precipitation	8	7	6	5	6	10	12	10	8	6	5	6	89
Days With ≥ 0.5" Precipitation	4	3	3	3	3	5	6	4	3	2	3	3	42
Days With ≥ 1.0" Precipitation	2	2	2	1	2	3	3	2	2	1	1	2	23
Mean Snowfall (in.)	trace	trace	0.0	0.0	0.0	0.0	0.0	0.0	0.0	0.0	0.0	0.1	0.1
Maximum Snow Depth (in.)	trace	1	0	0	0	0	0	0	0	0	0	2	2
Days With ≥ 1.0" Snow Depth	0	0	0	0	0	0	0	0	0	0	0	0	0

The period of record for all cooperative weather station data is 1980 – 2009. See User Guide for detailed explanation of data.

Louisiana Weather Station Rankings

Annual Extreme Maximum Temperature

Highest			Lowest		
Rank	Station Name	°F	Rank	Station Name	°F
1	Ashland	110	1	Franklin 3 NW	100
1	Jena 4 WSW	***110***	1	Galliano	100
3	Alexandria	109	3	Houma	101
3	Bienville 3 NE	109	3	St Bernard	***101***
3	De Ridder	109	5	New Orleans Intl Arpt	102
3	Ruston La Tech	109	5	Slidell	102
3	Shreveport Regional Arpt	109	5	Thibodaux 3 ESE	102
8	Minden	108	8	New Iberia	103
8	Monroe NLU	108	8	Reserve	103
8	Red River Research Stn	108	10	Carville 2 SW	104
11	Bastrop	107	10	Lafayette Regional Arpt	104
11	Boyce 3 WNW	107	10	New Orleans Audubon	104
11	Bunkie	107	13	Amite	105
11	Lake Charles Municipal Arpt	107	13	Baton Rouge Ryan Arpt	105
11	St Joseph 3 N	107	13	Bogalusa	105
16	Crowley 2 NE	106	13	Lsu Ben Hur Farm	105
16	Grand Coteau	106	13	New Roads 5 ESE	105
16	Hackberry 8 SSW	***106***	18	Crowley 2 NE	106
16	Lake Providence	106	18	Grand Coteau	106
16	Tallulah	106	18	Hackberry 8 SSW	***106***
21	Amite	105	18	Lake Providence	106
21	Baton Rouge Ryan Arpt	105	18	Tallulah	106
21	Bogalusa	105	23	Bastrop	107
21	Lsu Ben Hur Farm	105	23	Boyce 3 WNW	107
21	New Roads 5 ESE	105	23	Bunkie	107

Annual Mean Maximum Temperature

Highest			Lowest		
Rank	Station Name	°F	Rank	Station Name	°F
1	New Orleans Audubon	79.2	1	Lake Providence	74.6
2	Grand Coteau	79.1	2	Tallulah	75.3
3	Thibodaux 3 ESE	78.9	3	Bastrop	75.7
4	Amite	78.5	3	Minden	75.7
4	New Iberia	78.5	3	Ruston La Tech	75.7
6	Baton Rouge Ryan Arpt	78.3	6	Ashland	75.8
6	Houma	78.3	6	Bienville 3 NE	75.8
8	Lsu Ben Hur Farm	78.2	8	Jena 4 WSW	***76.2***
9	Lafayette Regional Arpt	78.1	9	Monroe NLU	76.3
9	New Orleans Intl Arpt	78.1	10	Red River Research Stn	76.5
9	Reserve	78.1	11	Shreveport Regional Arpt	76.6
12	Lake Charles Municipal Arpt	78.0	12	Boyce 3 WNW	76.9
13	St Bernard	***77.9***	12	Hackberry 8 SSW	***76.9***
14	Bogalusa	77.8	14	St Joseph 3 N	77.1
15	Carville 2 SW	77.7	15	Bunkie	77.2
15	De Ridder	77.7	15	Franklin 3 NW	77.2
15	Slidell	77.7	17	Alexandria	77.3
18	Crowley 2 NE	77.5	18	Galliano	77.4
19	Galliano	77.4	18	New Roads 5 ESE	77.4
19	New Roads 5 ESE	77.4	20	Crowley 2 NE	77.5
21	Alexandria	77.3	21	Carville 2 SW	77.7
22	Bunkie	77.2	21	De Ridder	77.7
22	Franklin 3 NW	77.2	21	Slidell	77.7
24	St Joseph 3 N	77.1	24	Bogalusa	77.8
25	Boyce 3 WNW	76.9	25	St Bernard	***77.9***

Rankings include 25 highest/lowest stations. If state has less than 25 stations, all stations are included. The period of record is 1980–2009. See User Guide for detailed explanation of data.

Annual Mean Temperature

Highest			Lowest		
Rank	Station Name	°F	Rank	Station Name	°F
1	New Orleans Audubon	70.6	1	Ashland	64.1
2	New Orleans Intl Arpt	69.2	1	Ruston La Tech	64.1
3	Hackberry 8 SSW	***69.1***	3	Minden	64.2
4	Houma	69.0	4	Bastrop	64.4
4	St Bernard	***69.0***	5	Bienville 3 NE	64.5
6	Thibodaux 3 ESE	68.9	6	Lake Providence	64.6
7	Galliano	68.8	7	Tallulah	64.7
8	New Iberia	68.7	8	Monroe NLU	64.8
9	Lafayette Regional Arpt	68.5	9	Jena 4 WSW	***64.9***
9	Lake Charles Municipal Arpt	68.5	10	Red River Research Stn	65.2
11	Grand Coteau	68.3	11	Shreveport Regional Arpt	65.9
12	Franklin 3 NW	68.2	12	St Joseph 3 N	66.1
13	Carville 2 SW	68.1	13	Amite	66.7
13	Reserve	68.1	13	Bogalusa	66.7
15	Baton Rouge Ryan Arpt	68.0	15	De Ridder	66.8
16	Crowley 2 NE	67.8	16	Alexandria	66.9
17	Slidell	67.7	16	Bunkie	66.9
18	Lsu Ben Hur Farm	67.5	18	New Roads 5 ESE	67.1
19	Boyce 3 WNW	67.2	19	Boyce 3 WNW	67.2
20	New Roads 5 ESE	67.1	20	Lsu Ben Hur Farm	67.5
21	Alexandria	66.9	21	Slidell	67.7
21	Bunkie	66.9	22	Crowley 2 NE	67.8
23	De Ridder	66.8	23	Baton Rouge Ryan Arpt	68.0
24	Amite	66.7	24	Carville 2 SW	68.1
24	Bogalusa	66.7	24	Reserve	68.1

Annual Mean Minimum Temperature

Highest			Lowest		
Rank	Station Name	°F	Rank	Station Name	°F
1	New Orleans Audubon	61.9	1	Ashland	52.3
2	Hackberry 8 SSW	***61.3***	2	Ruston La Tech	52.5
3	New Orleans Intl Arpt	60.3	3	Minden	52.7
4	Galliano	60.1	4	Bastrop	53.1
5	St Bernard	***60.0***	5	Bienville 3 NE	53.2
6	Houma	59.7	5	Monroe NLU	53.2
7	Franklin 3 NW	59.1	7	Jena 4 WSW	***53.4***
8	Lake Charles Municipal Arpt	59.0	8	Red River Research Stn	53.8
9	New Iberia	58.9	9	Tallulah	54.0
10	Lafayette Regional Arpt	58.8	10	Lake Providence	54.5
10	Thibodaux 3 ESE	58.8	11	Amite	54.9
12	Carville 2 SW	58.5	12	St Joseph 3 N	55.0
13	Crowley 2 NE	58.1	13	Shreveport Regional Arpt	55.1
14	Reserve	58.0	14	Bogalusa	55.5
15	Slidell	57.8	15	De Ridder	55.8
16	Baton Rouge Ryan Arpt	57.6	16	Alexandria	56.5
17	Boyce 3 WNW	57.5	16	Bunkie	56.5
18	Grand Coteau	57.4	18	New Roads 5 ESE	56.7
19	Lsu Ben Hur Farm	56.8	19	Lsu Ben Hur Farm	56.8
20	New Roads 5 ESE	56.7	20	Grand Coteau	57.4
21	Alexandria	56.5	21	Boyce 3 WNW	57.5
21	Bunkie	56.5	22	Baton Rouge Ryan Arpt	57.6
23	De Ridder	55.8	23	Slidell	57.8
24	Bogalusa	55.5	24	Reserve	58.0
25	Shreveport Regional Arpt	55.1	25	Crowley 2 NE	58.1

Rankings include 25 highest/lowest stations. If state has less than 25 stations, all stations are included. The period of record is 1980–2009. See User Guide for detailed explanation of data.

Annual Extreme Minimum Temperature

Highest			Lowest		
Rank	Station Name	°F	Rank	Station Name	°F
1	Hackberry 8 SSW	***12***	1	Ruston La Tech	0
1	New Orleans Audubon	12	1	Tallulah	0
3	Lake Charles Municipal Arpt	11	3	Ashland	2
3	New Orleans Intl Arpt	11	3	Bienville 3 NE	2
5	Carville 2 SW	10	3	Minden	2
5	Franklin 3 NW	10	6	Bastrop	3
5	Galliano	10	6	Monroe NLU	3
5	Houma	10	6	Red River Research Stn	3
5	St Bernard	***10***	9	Lake Providence	4
10	Crowley 2 NE	9	10	Amite	5
10	Lafayette Regional Arpt	9	10	Shreveport Regional Arpt	5
10	Lsu Ben Hur Farm	9	10	St Joseph 3 N	5
10	New Iberia	9	13	Bogalusa	6
10	Reserve	9	13	Jena 4 WSW	***6***
10	Thibodaux 3 ESE	9	15	Alexandria	7
16	Baton Rouge Ryan Arpt	8	15	Boyce 3 WNW	7
16	Bunkie	8	15	De Ridder	7
16	Grand Coteau	8	18	Baton Rouge Ryan Arpt	8
16	New Roads 5 ESE	8	18	Bunkie	8
16	Slidell	8	18	Grand Coteau	8
21	Alexandria	7	18	New Roads 5 ESE	8
21	Boyce 3 WNW	7	18	Slidell	8
21	De Ridder	7	23	Crowley 2 NE	9
24	Bogalusa	6	23	Lafayette Regional Arpt	9
24	Jena 4 WSW	***6***	23	Lsu Ben Hur Farm	9

July Mean Maximum Temperature

Highest			Lowest		
Rank	Station Name	°F	Rank	Station Name	°F
1	Monroe NLU	93.6	1	Galliano	89.4
1	Red River Research Stn	93.6	2	Franklin 3 NW	89.5
1	Shreveport Regional Arpt	93.6	3	Hackberry 8 SSW	90.7
4	Bienville 3 NE	93.1	3	St Bernard	***90.7***
4	St Joseph 3 N	93.1	5	Carville 2 SW	90.9
6	Ruston La Tech	93.0	5	Crowley 2 NE	90.9
7	Alexandria	92.8	7	Houma	91.0
7	Bastrop	92.8	7	Slidell	91.0
7	Minden	92.8	9	Lake Charles Municipal Arpt	91.2
10	Boyce 3 WNW	92.6	9	New Orleans Intl Arpt	91.2
11	New Orleans Audubon	92.5	11	Lafayette Regional Arpt	91.3
12	Ashland	92.3	11	Thibodaux 3 ESE	91.3
13	Grand Coteau	92.2	13	New Roads 5 ESE	91.4
14	Amite	92.1	13	Reserve	91.4
14	Bunkie	92.1	15	New Iberia	91.5
14	De Ridder	92.1	16	Baton Rouge Ryan Arpt	91.6
17	Bogalusa	92.0	16	Lsu Ben Hur Farm	91.6
17	Lake Providence	92.0	18	Tallulah	91.7
19	Jena 4 WSW	***91.8***	19	Jena 4 WSW	***91.8***
20	Tallulah	91.7	20	Bogalusa	92.0
21	Baton Rouge Ryan Arpt	91.6	20	Lake Providence	92.0
21	Lsu Ben Hur Farm	91.6	22	Amite	92.1
23	New Iberia	91.5	22	Bunkie	92.1
24	New Roads 5 ESE	91.4	22	De Ridder	92.1
24	Reserve	91.4	25	Grand Coteau	92.2

Rankings include 25 highest/lowest stations. If state has less than 25 stations, all stations are included. The period of record is 1980–2009. See User Guide for detailed explanation of data.

January Mean Minimum Temperature

Highest			Lowest		
Rank	**Station Name**	**°F**	**Rank**	**Station Name**	**°F**
1	New Orleans Audubon	46.0	1	Minden	33.7
2	New Orleans Intl Arpt	44.1	2	Ruston La Tech	34.1
3	Galliano	44.0	3	Ashland	34.2
4	Hackberry 8 SSW	43.9	4	Monroe NLU	34.4
5	Houma	43.4	5	Bastrop	34.5
6	Franklin 3 NW	43.3	6	Red River Research Stn	35.1
7	Thibodaux 3 ESE	43.2	7	Tallulah	35.2
8	St Bernard	*43.1*	8	Bienville 3 NE	35.3
9	Lake Charles Municipal Arpt	42.5	8	Lake Providence	35.3
9	New Iberia	42.5	10	Jena 4 WSW	*36.4*
11	Lafayette Regional Arpt	42.4	11	St Joseph 3 N	36.8
12	Reserve	41.8	12	Shreveport Regional Arpt	36.9
13	Carville 2 SW	41.6	13	Amite	38.3
13	Grand Coteau	41.6	14	Alexandria	38.4
15	Baton Rouge Ryan Arpt	41.3	15	Bogalusa	38.6
16	Slidell	41.0	15	De Ridder	38.6
17	Crowley 2 NE	40.8	17	Bunkie	39.3
18	Lsu Ben Hur Farm	40.3	18	New Roads 5 ESE	39.6
19	Boyce 3 WNW	40.1	19	Boyce 3 WNW	40.1
20	New Roads 5 ESE	39.6	20	Lsu Ben Hur Farm	40.3
21	Bunkie	39.3	21	Crowley 2 NE	40.8
22	Bogalusa	38.6	22	Slidell	41.0
22	De Ridder	38.6	23	Baton Rouge Ryan Arpt	41.3
24	Alexandria	38.4	24	Carville 2 SW	41.6
25	Amite	38.3	24	Grand Coteau	41.6

Number of Days Annually Maximum Temperature ≥ 90°F

Highest			Lowest		
Rank	**Station Name**	**Days**	**Rank**	**Station Name**	**Days**
1	St Joseph 3 N	99	1	Galliano	48
2	Red River Research Stn	97	2	Franklin 3 NW	53
3	Grand Coteau	96	3	St Bernard	*67*
4	Amite	95	4	Hackberry 8 SSW	*69*
4	New Orleans Audubon	95	5	Slidell	73
6	Shreveport Regional Arpt	93	6	Houma	76
7	Lsu Ben Hur Farm	92	7	Carville 2 SW	77
7	Monroe NLU	92	7	Tallulah	77
9	Alexandria	91	9	Lake Providence	78
10	Baton Rouge Ryan Arpt	89	9	New Orleans Intl Arpt	78
10	Bunkie	89	9	Reserve	78
10	De Ridder	89	12	Ashland	79
13	Bastrop	86	13	Crowley 2 NE	81
13	Boyce 3 WNW	86	14	Jena 4 WSW	*82*
15	Bogalusa	85	14	Minden	82
15	Lafayette Regional Arpt	85	14	New Roads 5 ESE	82
15	New Iberia	85	17	Lake Charles Municipal Arpt	83
18	Bienville 3 NE	84	17	Ruston La Tech	83
19	Lake Charles Municipal Arpt	83	17	Thibodaux 3 ESE	83
19	Ruston La Tech	83	20	Bienville 3 NE	84
19	Thibodaux 3 ESE	83	21	Bogalusa	85
22	Jena 4 WSW	*82*	21	Lafayette Regional Arpt	85
22	Minden	82	21	New Iberia	85
22	New Roads 5 ESE	82	24	Bastrop	86
25	Crowley 2 NE	81	24	Boyce 3 WNW	86

Rankings include 25 highest/lowest stations. If state has less than 25 stations, all stations are included. The period of record is 1980–2009. See User Guide for detailed explanation of data.

Number of Days Annually Maximum Temperature ≤ 32°F

Highest Rank	Highest Station Name	Highest Days	Lowest Rank	Lowest Station Name	Lowest Days
1	Lake Providence	3	1	Alexandria	0
1	Tallulah	3	1	Amite	0
3	Bastrop	2	1	Baton Rouge Ryan Arpt	0
3	Bienville 3 NE	2	1	Bogalusa	0
3	Monroe NLU	2	1	Boyce 3 WNW	0
3	Ruston La Tech	2	1	Bunkie	0
7	Ashland	1	1	Carville 2 SW	0
7	Minden	1	1	Crowley 2 NE	0
7	Shreveport Regional Arpt	1	1	De Ridder	0
7	St Joseph 3 N	1	1	Franklin 3 NW	0
11	Alexandria	0	1	Galliano	0
11	Amite	0	1	Grand Coteau	0
11	Baton Rouge Ryan Arpt	0	1	Hackberry 8 SSW	*0*
11	Bogalusa	0	1	Houma	0
11	Boyce 3 WNW	0	1	Jena 4 WSW	*0*
11	Bunkie	0	1	Lafayette Regional Arpt	0
11	Carville 2 SW	0	1	Lake Charles Municipal Arpt	0
11	Crowley 2 NE	0	1	Lsu Ben Hur Farm	0
11	De Ridder	0	1	New Iberia	0
11	Franklin 3 NW	0	1	New Orleans Audubon	0
11	Galliano	0	1	New Orleans Intl Arpt	0
11	Grand Coteau	0	1	New Roads 5 ESE	0
11	Hackberry 8 SSW	*0*	1	Red River Research Stn	0
11	Houma	0	1	Reserve	0
11	Jena 4 WSW	*0*	1	Slidell	0

Number of Days Annually Minimum Temperature ≤ 32°F

Highest Rank	Highest Station Name	Highest Days	Lowest Rank	Lowest Station Name	Lowest Days
1	Ashland	51	1	New Orleans Audubon	4
1	Minden	51	2	Hackberry 8 SSW	*6*
3	Bastrop	47	3	New Orleans Intl Arpt	8
4	Ruston La Tech	46	4	Galliano	9
5	Bienville 3 NE	45	5	Franklin 3 NW	10
6	Jena 4 WSW	*43*	5	St Bernard	*10*
7	Monroe NLU	42	7	Houma	11
8	Red River Research Stn	41	8	Carville 2 SW	13
9	Tallulah	40	8	Lafayette Regional Arpt	13
10	Lake Providence	35	8	Lake Charles Municipal Arpt	13
11	Amite	33	8	New Iberia	13
12	Shreveport Regional Arpt	32	8	Thibodaux 3 ESE	13
12	St Joseph 3 N	32	13	Reserve	15
14	Bogalusa	29	14	Boyce 3 WNW	16
15	De Ridder	28	15	Crowley 2 NE	17
16	Alexandria	25	16	Slidell	18
17	New Roads 5 ESE	22	17	Baton Rouge Ryan Arpt	19
18	Bunkie	21	17	Grand Coteau	19
19	Lsu Ben Hur Farm	20	19	Lsu Ben Hur Farm	20
20	Baton Rouge Ryan Arpt	19	20	Bunkie	21
20	Grand Coteau	19	21	New Roads 5 ESE	22
22	Slidell	18	22	Alexandria	25
23	Crowley 2 NE	17	23	De Ridder	28
24	Boyce 3 WNW	16	24	Bogalusa	29
25	Reserve	15	25	Shreveport Regional Arpt	32

Number of Days Annually Minimum Temperature ≤ 0°F

Highest Rank	Highest Station Name	Highest Days	Lowest Rank	Lowest Station Name	Lowest Days
1	Alexandria	0	1	Alexandria	0
1	Amite	0	1	Amite	0
1	Ashland	0	1	Ashland	0
1	Bastrop	0	1	Bastrop	0
1	Baton Rouge Ryan Arpt	0	1	Baton Rouge Ryan Arpt	0
1	Bienville 3 NE	0	1	Bienville 3 NE	0
1	Bogalusa	0	1	Bogalusa	0
1	Boyce 3 WNW	0	1	Boyce 3 WNW	0
1	Bunkie	0	1	Bunkie	0
1	Carville 2 SW	0	1	Carville 2 SW	0
1	Crowley 2 NE	0	1	Crowley 2 NE	0
1	De Ridder	0	1	De Ridder	0
1	Franklin 3 NW	0	1	Franklin 3 NW	0
1	Galliano	0	1	Galliano	0
1	Grand Coteau	0	1	Grand Coteau	0
1	Hackberry 8 SSW	*0*	1	Hackberry 8 SSW	*0*
1	Houma	0	1	Houma	0
1	Jena 4 WSW	*0*	1	Jena 4 WSW	*0*
1	Lafayette Regional Arpt	0	1	Lafayette Regional Arpt	0
1	Lake Charles Municipal Arpt	0	1	Lake Charles Municipal Arpt	0
1	Lake Providence	0	1	Lake Providence	0
1	Lsu Ben Hur Farm	0	1	Lsu Ben Hur Farm	0
1	Minden	0	1	Minden	0
1	Monroe NLU	0	1	Monroe NLU	0
1	New Iberia	0	1	New Iberia	0

Number of Annual Heating Degree Days

Highest Rank	Highest Station Name	Highest Num.	Lowest Rank	Lowest Station Name	Lowest Num.
1	Minden	2,510	1	New Orleans Audubon	1,120
2	Ruston La Tech	2,467	2	New Orleans Intl Arpt	1,302
3	Bastrop	2,450	3	Galliano	1,309
4	Lake Providence	2,439	4	St Bernard	*1,315*
5	Ashland	2,434	5	Houma	1,317
6	Bienville 3 NE	2,381	5	Thibodaux 3 ESE	1,317
6	Monroe NLU	2,381	7	Hackberry 8 SSW	*1,375*
8	Tallulah	2,362	8	Franklin 3 NW	1,412
9	Red River Research Stn	2,311	8	New Iberia	1,412
10	Jena 4 WSW	*2,252*	10	Lake Charles Municipal Arpt	1,460
11	Shreveport Regional Arpt	2,147	11	Reserve	1,468
12	St Joseph 3 N	2,078	12	Grand Coteau	1,480
13	Alexandria	1,886	13	Lafayette Regional Arpt	1,487
14	Bunkie	1,839	14	Carville 2 SW	1,490
15	Bogalusa	1,829	15	Slidell	1,569
16	De Ridder	1,826	16	Baton Rouge Ryan Arpt	1,581
17	Amite	1,784	17	Crowley 2 NE	1,635
18	Boyce 3 WNW	1,782	18	Lsu Ben Hur Farm	1,654
19	New Roads 5 ESE	1,743	19	New Roads 5 ESE	1,743
20	Lsu Ben Hur Farm	1,654	20	Boyce 3 WNW	1,782
21	Crowley 2 NE	1,635	21	Amite	1,784
22	Baton Rouge Ryan Arpt	1,581	22	De Ridder	1,826
23	Slidell	1,569	23	Bogalusa	1,829
24	Carville 2 SW	1,490	24	Bunkie	1,839
25	Lafayette Regional Arpt	1,487	25	Alexandria	1,886

 Rankings include 25 highest/lowest stations. If state has less than 25 stations, all stations are included. The period of record is 1980–2009. See User Guide for detailed explanation of data.

Number of Annual Cooling Degree Days

Highest Rank	Highest Station Name	Highest Num.	Lowest Rank	Lowest Station Name	Lowest Num.
1	New Orleans Audubon	3,255	1	Ashland	2,199
2	Hackberry 8 SSW	***2,978***	2	Ruston La Tech	2,237
3	New Orleans Intl Arpt	2,951	3	Jena 4 WSW	***2,302***
4	Houma	2,889	4	Bienville 3 NE	2,320
5	New Iberia	2,863	5	Minden	2,321
6	St Bernard	***2,862***	6	Bastrop	2,343
7	Lafayette Regional Arpt	2,854	7	Tallulah	2,349
8	Lake Charles Municipal Arpt	2,853	8	Monroe NLU	2,399
9	Thibodaux 3 ESE	2,829	9	Lake Providence	2,407
10	Galliano	2,781	10	Red River Research Stn	2,477
11	Grand Coteau	2,773	11	Amite	2,521
12	Baton Rouge Ryan Arpt	2,769	12	Bogalusa	2,558
13	Crowley 2 NE	2,766	13	Shreveport Regional Arpt	2,568
14	Carville 2 SW	2,738	14	St Joseph 3 N	2,583
15	Reserve	2,702	15	De Ridder	2,584
16	Boyce 3 WNW	2,700	16	New Roads 5 ESE	2,606
17	Alexandria	2,694	17	Bunkie	2,640
18	Lsu Ben Hur Farm	2,678	18	Franklin 3 NW	2,674
19	Franklin 3 NW	2,674	18	Slidell	2,674
19	Slidell	2,674	20	Lsu Ben Hur Farm	2,678
21	Bunkie	2,640	21	Alexandria	2,694
22	New Roads 5 ESE	2,606	22	Boyce 3 WNW	2,700
23	De Ridder	2,584	23	Reserve	2,702
24	St Joseph 3 N	2,583	24	Carville 2 SW	2,738
25	Shreveport Regional Arpt	2,568	25	Crowley 2 NE	2,766

Annual Precipitation

Highest Rank	Highest Station Name	Highest Inches	Lowest Rank	Lowest Station Name	Lowest Inches
1	Thibodaux 3 ESE	71.40	1	Shreveport Regional Arpt	51.53
2	Reserve	64.94	2	Red River Research Stn	52.25
3	De Ridder	64.51	3	Ruston La Tech	55.00
4	Franklin 3 NW	64.45	4	Minden	55.46
5	Galliano	64.34	5	Ashland	55.81
6	Houma	63.45	6	Monroe NLU	56.57
7	Slidell	63.44	7	St Joseph 3 N	56.83
8	Amite	63.42	8	Tallulah	56.92
9	St Bernard	***62.93***	9	Bastrop	57.34
10	New Orleans Audubon	62.90	10	Lake Providence	58.15
11	New Orleans Intl Arpt	62.55	11	Lake Charles Municipal Arpt	58.45
12	Bogalusa	62.25	12	Boyce 3 WNW	59.22
13	Grand Coteau	61.73	13	New Roads 5 ESE	59.34
14	Bunkie	61.31	14	Carville 2 SW	59.57
15	Baton Rouge Ryan Arpt	61.26	15	Lsu Ben Hur Farm	59.74
16	Lafayette Regional Arpt	61.21	16	Jena 4 WSW	***59.77***
17	Alexandria	61.07	17	Hackberry 8 SSW	59.79
18	New Iberia	61.04	18	Bienville 3 NE	60.53
19	Crowley 2 NE	61.00	19	Crowley 2 NE	61.00
20	Bienville 3 NE	60.53	20	New Iberia	61.04
21	Hackberry 8 SSW	59.79	21	Alexandria	61.07
22	Jena 4 WSW	***59.77***	22	Lafayette Regional Arpt	61.21
23	Lsu Ben Hur Farm	59.74	23	Baton Rouge Ryan Arpt	61.26
24	Carville 2 SW	59.57	24	Bunkie	61.31
25	New Roads 5 ESE	59.34	25	Grand Coteau	61.73

Rankings include 25 highest/lowest stations. If state has less than 25 stations, all stations are included. The period of record is 1980–2009. See User Guide for detailed explanation of data.

Annual Extreme Maximum Daily Precipitation

Highest Rank	Station Name	Inches	Lowest Rank	Station Name	Inches
1	Lake Charles Municipal Arpt	15.67	1	Hackberry 8 SSW	*6.30*
2	Thibodaux 3 ESE	15.16	2	Tallulah	7.00
3	De Ridder	13.60	3	Bienville 3 NE	7.09
4	Slidell	13.42	4	St Joseph 3 N	7.37
5	Bunkie	13.15	5	Reserve	7.40
6	Jena 4 WSW	*12.96*	6	New Orleans Intl Arpt	7.67
7	Minden	12.87	7	Carville 2 SW	7.80
8	Ruston La Tech	11.84	8	New Iberia	*7.95*
9	Monroe NLU	11.50	9	Red River Research Stn	8.20
10	New Orleans Audubon	10.94	10	Lake Providence	8.28
11	Ashland	10.88	11	Franklin 3 NW	8.51
12	Houma	10.60	12	Lsu Ben Hur Farm	8.57
13	Shreveport Regional Arpt	10.44	13	Bastrop	8.67
14	Lafayette Regional Arpt	10.38	14	Amite	8.77
15	Alexandria	10.02	15	New Roads 5 ESE	8.85
16	Grand Coteau	10.00	16	Crowley 2 NE	8.87
17	Boyce 3 WNW	9.75	17	Bogalusa	9.15
18	Galliano	9.55	18	Baton Rouge Ryan Arpt	9.35
19	Baton Rouge Ryan Arpt	9.35	19	Galliano	9.55
20	Bogalusa	9.15	20	Boyce 3 WNW	9.75
21	Crowley 2 NE	8.87	21	Grand Coteau	10.00
22	New Roads 5 ESE	8.85	22	Alexandria	10.02
23	Amite	8.77	23	Lafayette Regional Arpt	10.38
24	Bastrop	8.67	24	Shreveport Regional Arpt	10.44
25	Lsu Ben Hur Farm	8.57	25	Houma	10.60

Number of Days Annually With ≥ 0.1 Inches of Precipitation

Highest Rank	Station Name	Days	Lowest Rank	Station Name	Days
1	Thibodaux 3 ESE	89	1	Red River Research Stn	67
2	Franklin 3 NW	80	2	Shreveport Regional Arpt	68
2	Houma	80	3	Hackberry 8 SSW	70
4	Reserve	79	4	Bastrop	71
5	Amite	78	4	Boyce 3 WNW	71
5	Crowley 2 NE	78	4	Jena 4 WSW	*71*
5	De Ridder	78	4	Lake Charles Municipal Arpt	71
5	Lsu Ben Hur Farm	78	4	Monroe NLU	71
5	New Orleans Audubon	78	9	Ashland	72
5	New Orleans Intl Arpt	78	9	St Bernard	*72*
11	Baton Rouge Ryan Arpt	77	9	St Joseph 3 N	72
11	Bogalusa	77	12	Alexandria	73
11	Carville 2 SW	77	12	Bienville 3 NE	73
11	Grand Coteau	77	12	Ruston La Tech	73
11	Lafayette Regional Arpt	77	12	Tallulah	73
16	Galliano	75	16	Bunkie	74
16	New Iberia	75	16	Lake Providence	74
16	New Roads 5 ESE	75	16	Minden	74
19	Bunkie	74	16	Slidell	74
19	Lake Providence	74	20	Galliano	75
19	Minden	74	20	New Iberia	75
19	Slidell	74	20	New Roads 5 ESE	75
23	Alexandria	73	23	Baton Rouge Ryan Arpt	77
23	Bienville 3 NE	73	23	Bogalusa	77
23	Ruston La Tech	73	23	Carville 2 SW	77

Rankings include 25 highest/lowest stations. If state has less than 25 stations, all stations are included. The period of record is 1980–2009. See User Guide for detailed explanation of data.

Number of Days Annually With ≥ 0.5 Inches of Precipitation

Highest			Lowest		
Rank	Station Name	Days	Rank	Station Name	Days
1	Franklin 3 NW	43	1	Red River Research Stn	34
2	Amite	42	1	Ruston La Tech	34
2	Thibodaux 3 ESE	42	1	Shreveport Regional Arpt	34
4	Lafayette Regional Arpt	41	4	Bastrop	35
5	Galliano	40	4	Lake Providence	35
5	Grand Coteau	40	4	Minden	35
5	Reserve	40	4	Monroe NLU	35
8	Alexandria	39	8	Hackberry 8 SSW	36
8	Bogalusa	39	8	Lake Charles Municipal Arpt	36
10	Baton Rouge Ryan Arpt	38	10	Ashland	37
10	Bienville 3 NE	38	10	Houma	37
10	Boyce 3 WNW	38	10	Slidell	37
10	Bunkie	38	10	St Joseph 3 N	37
10	Carville 2 SW	38	10	Tallulah	37
10	Crowley 2 NE	38	15	Baton Rouge Ryan Arpt	38
10	De Ridder	38	15	Bienville 3 NE	38
10	Jena 4 WSW	***38***	15	Boyce 3 WNW	38
10	Lsu Ben Hur Farm	38	15	Bunkie	38
10	New Iberia	38	15	Carville 2 SW	38
10	New Orleans Audubon	38	15	Crowley 2 NE	38
10	New Orleans Intl Arpt	38	15	De Ridder	38
10	New Roads 5 ESE	38	15	Jena 4 WSW	***38***
10	St Bernard	***38***	15	Lsu Ben Hur Farm	38
24	Ashland	37	15	New Iberia	38
24	Houma	37	15	New Orleans Audubon	38

Number of Days Annually With ≥ 1.0 Inches of Precipitation

Highest			Lowest		
Rank	Station Name	Days	Rank	Station Name	Days
1	Amite	23	1	Hackberry 8 SSW	17
1	Franklin 3 NW	23	1	Shreveport Regional Arpt	17
1	Slidell	23	3	Ashland	18
1	St Bernard	***23***	3	Crowley 2 NE	18
1	Thibodaux 3 ESE	23	3	Galliano	18
6	De Ridder	22	3	Lafayette Regional Arpt	18
6	Reserve	22	3	Lake Charles Municipal Arpt	18
8	Baton Rouge Ryan Arpt	21	3	Monroe NLU	18
8	Bienville 3 NE	21	3	New Iberia	18
8	Bunkie	21	10	Boyce 3 WNW	19
8	Houma	21	10	Carville 2 SW	19
8	Jena 4 WSW	***21***	10	Lake Providence	19
8	New Orleans Intl Arpt	21	10	Lsu Ben Hur Farm	19
14	Alexandria	20	10	Minden	19
14	Bastrop	20	10	New Orleans Audubon	19
14	Bogalusa	20	10	New Roads 5 ESE	19
14	Grand Coteau	20	10	Red River Research Stn	19
14	Ruston La Tech	20	10	St Joseph 3 N	19
14	Tallulah	20	19	Alexandria	20
20	Boyce 3 WNW	19	19	Bastrop	20
20	Carville 2 SW	19	19	Bogalusa	20
20	Lake Providence	19	19	Grand Coteau	20
20	Lsu Ben Hur Farm	19	19	Ruston La Tech	20
20	Minden	19	19	Tallulah	20
20	New Orleans Audubon	19	25	Baton Rouge Ryan Arpt	21

Rankings include 25 highest/lowest stations. If state has less than 25 stations, all stations are included. The period of record is 1980–2009. See User Guide for detailed explanation of data.

Annual Snowfall

Highest

Rank	Station Name	Inches
1	Shreveport Regional Arpt	1.1
2	Ashland	0.8
3	Monroe NLU	0.6
4	Ruston La Tech	0.5
5	Bastrop	0.4
5	Minden	0.4
7	Bienville 3 NE	0.3
7	Lake Providence	0.3
9	Jena 4 WSW	***0.2***
9	Red River Research Stn	0.2
9	Slidell	0.2
12	Alexandria	0.1
12	Amite	0.1
12	Bogalusa	0.1
12	Franklin 3 NW	0.1
12	Houma	0.1
12	Thibodaux 3 ESE	0.1
18	Boyce 3 WNW	Trace
18	Bunkie	Trace
18	Carville 2 SW	Trace
18	Crowley 2 NE	Trace
18	De Ridder	Trace
18	Galliano	Trace
18	Grand Coteau	Trace
18	Hackberry 8 SSW	Trace

Lowest

Rank	Station Name	Inches
1	Boyce 3 WNW	Trace
1	Bunkie	Trace
1	Carville 2 SW	Trace
1	Crowley 2 NE	Trace
1	De Ridder	Trace
1	Galliano	Trace
1	Grand Coteau	Trace
1	Hackberry 8 SSW	Trace
1	Lsu Ben Hur Farm	Trace
1	New Iberia	Trace
1	New Orleans Audubon	Trace
1	New Roads 5 ESE	Trace
1	Reserve	Trace
1	St Bernard	***Trace***
1	St Joseph 3 N	Trace
1	Tallulah	Trace
17	Alexandria	0.1
17	Amite	0.1
17	Bogalusa	0.1
17	Franklin 3 NW	0.1
17	Houma	0.1
17	Thibodaux 3 ESE	0.1
23	Jena 4 WSW	***0.2***
23	Red River Research Stn	0.2
23	Slidell	0.2

Annual Maximum Snow Depth

Highest

Rank	Station Name	Inches
1	Amite	8
2	Ashland	6
2	Shreveport Regional Arpt	6
4	Bastrop	5
4	Bienville 3 NE	5
4	Bogalusa	5
4	Minden	5
4	Monroe NLU	5
4	Ruston La Tech	5
4	Tallulah	5
11	Lake Providence	4
12	De Ridder	3
12	Grand Coteau	3
12	New Roads 5 ESE	3
12	Red River Research Stn	3
16	Boyce 3 WNW	2
16	Carville 2 SW	2
16	Crowley 2 NE	2
16	Houma	2
16	New Orleans Audubon	2
16	Slidell	2
16	St Joseph 3 N	2
16	Thibodaux 3 ESE	2
24	Alexandria	1
24	Jena 4 WSW	***1***

Lowest

Rank	Station Name	Inches
1	Bunkie	Trace
1	Franklin 3 NW	Trace
1	Galliano	Trace
1	Hackberry 8 SSW	Trace
1	New Iberia	Trace
1	St Bernard	Trace
7	Alexandria	1
7	Jena 4 WSW	***1***
7	Lsu Ben Hur Farm	1
7	Reserve	1
11	Boyce 3 WNW	2
11	Carville 2 SW	2
11	Crowley 2 NE	2
11	Houma	2
11	New Orleans Audubon	2
11	Slidell	2
11	St Joseph 3 N	2
11	Thibodaux 3 ESE	2
19	De Ridder	3
19	Grand Coteau	3
19	New Roads 5 ESE	3
19	Red River Research Stn	3
23	Lake Providence	4
24	Bastrop	5
24	Bienville 3 NE	5

Rankings include 25 highest/lowest stations. If state has less than 25 stations, all stations are included. The period of record is 1980–2009. See User Guide for detailed explanation of data.

Number of Days Annually With ≥ 1.0 Inch Snow Depth

Highest			Lowest		
Rank	Station Name	Days	Rank	Station Name	Days
1	Alexandria	0	1	Alexandria	0
1	Amite	0	1	Amite	0
1	Ashland	0	1	Ashland	0
1	Bastrop	0	1	Bastrop	0
1	Bienville 3 NE	0	1	Bienville 3 NE	0
1	Bogalusa	0	1	Bogalusa	0
1	Boyce 3 WNW	0	1	Boyce 3 WNW	0
1	Bunkie	0	1	Bunkie	0
1	Carville 2 SW	0	1	Carville 2 SW	0
1	Crowley 2 NE	0	1	Crowley 2 NE	0
1	De Ridder	0	1	De Ridder	0
1	Franklin 3 NW	0	1	Franklin 3 NW	0
1	Galliano	0	1	Galliano	0
1	Grand Coteau	0	1	Grand Coteau	0
1	Hackberry 8 SSW	0	1	Hackberry 8 SSW	0
1	Houma	0	1	Houma	0
1	Jena 4 WSW	*0*	1	Jena 4 WSW	*0*
1	Lake Providence	0	1	Lake Providence	0
1	Lsu Ben Hur Farm	0	1	Lsu Ben Hur Farm	0
1	Minden	0	1	Minden	0
1	Monroe NLU	0	1	Monroe NLU	0
1	New Iberia	0	1	New Iberia	0
1	New Orleans Audubon	0	1	New Orleans Audubon	0
1	New Roads 5 ESE	0	1	New Roads 5 ESE	0
1	Red River Research Stn	0	1	Red River Research Stn	0

Significant Storm Events in Louisiana: 2000 – 2009

Location or Parish	Date	Type	Mag.	Deaths	Injuries	Property Damage ($mil.)	Crop Damage ($mil.)
Jefferson	01/23/00	Hail	1.00 in.	0	0	65.0	0.0
Terrebonne	03/15/00	Tornado	F2	0	36	10.0	0.0
Caddo	07/14/00	Excessive Heat	na	5	0	0.0	0.0
Northwest Louisiana	12/24/00	Ice Storm	na	0	0	106.0	0.0
Southeast Louisiana	09/25/02	Tropical Storm	na	0	0	108.6	0.0
South Central Louisiana Coast	10/02/02	Hurricane Lili	na	0	0	149.5	0.0
Southwest and Central Louisiana	10/03/02	Hurricane Lili	na	0	3	368.0	168.0
Southeast Louisiana	06/30/03	Tropical Storm	na	0	0	34.0	0.0
La Salle	11/23/04	Tornado	F3	1	20	5.0	0.0
Claiborne	01/12/05	Tornado	F2	0	12	4.0	0.0
Southeast Louisiana	07/05/05	Hurricane Cindy	na	0	0	47.5	0.0
Southeast Louisiana	08/28/05	Hurricane Katrina	na	0	0	16,930.0	0.0
Southwest Louisiana	09/23/05	Hurricane Rita	na	1	0	4,000.0	0.0
Southeast Louisiana	09/23/05	Storm Surge	na	0	0	432.0	0.0
East and Southeast Louisiana	09/23/05	Tropical Storm	na	0	0	48.0	0.0
Lafayette	01/12/06	Dense Fog	na	1	22	0.1	0.0
Acadia	10/26/06	Flood	na	0	0	500.0	0.0
Jefferson Davis	10/26/06	Flood	na	0	0	100.0	0.0
Iberia	01/04/07	Tornado	F1	2	15	1.5	0.0
Orleans	02/13/07	Tornado	F2	0	15	2.0	0.0
Orleans	02/13/07	Tornado	F2	1	10	1.0	0.0
St. Mary	09/01/08	Hurricane Gustav	na	0	0	150.0	30.0
Calcasieu, Cameron, and Lafayette Parish	09/01/08	Hurricane Gustav	na	1	0	100.0	5.0
Iberia and Upper St. Martin Parish	09/01/08	Hurricane Gustav	na	0	0	100.0	30.0
Acadia and St. Landry Parish	09/01/08	Hurricane Gustav	na	0	0	100.0	25.0
Beauregard and Evangeline Parish	09/01/08	Hurricane Gustav	na	0	0	50.0	25.0
Acadia, Calcasieu, Cameron, and Iberia Parish	09/12/08	Storm Surge/Tide	na	0	0	75.0	0.0
East Carroll	05/10/09	Thunderstorm Wind	81 mph	0	0	700.0	0.2

Note: Deaths, injuries, and damages are date and location specific.

MAINE

PHYSICAL FEATURES. Maine occupies 33,215 square miles. From near the 43d parallel, the State extends northward over 300 miles, spanning a full 4.5° of latitude. Its width from the 67th meridian extends westward over 4° of longitude, a span of over 200 miles. The terrain is hilly. Elevations are generally less than 500 feet above sea level over the southeastern one-half of the State. The northwestern one-half is a plateau ranging in elevation from 1,000 to 1,500 feet, but sloping downward to 500 feet in the northeast from 1,000 feet in the north (Aroostook County). A number of mountain peaks, extensions of the Appalachian chain, rise to heights from 3,000 to 5,000 feet mostly in the western and central portions of the State. Mt. Katahdin is the highest point. Its summit, at 5,268 feet, rises nearly 4,500 feet from a relatively low base elevation.

The great glaciers of the ice age were all-important in the physical formation of the State. They left "horsebacks" or ridges of glacial deposits, some as long as 150 miles in length. These ridges furnish both natural highway routes and abundant material for roadbuilding. The glaciers formed or left over 1,600 lakes, spread abundantly over the entire State. The largest of these lakes is Moosehead. The total water area of the State exceeds 2,200 square miles. Some flatland is found near the coast, especially near the mouths of the Androscoggin and Kennebec Rivers. Other tracts of flatland, often marshy, lie near lakes.

The coastal portion of the State has many inlets, bays, channels, fine harbors, rocky islands, and promontories. The extreme irregularity of the coast stretches the total coastline to about 2,400 miles, more than 10 times the distance from Kittery to Eastport. The southwestern portion of the coast has many beaches. The mid-coastal portion has many rugged hills and small mountains, some of which rise abruptly from the water, such as Mount Desert Island.

GENERAL CLIMATE. Maine's chief climatic characteristics include: (1) changeableness of the weather, (2) large ranges of temperature, both diurnal and annual, (3) great differences between the same seasons in different years, (4) equable distribution of precipitation, and (5) considerable diversity from place to place. The regional climatic influences are modified in Maine by varying distances from the ocean, by elevations, and by types of terrain. These modifying factors divide the State into three natural climatological divisions. The Northern Division contains slightly more than one-half of the State's area, with its southern boundary nearly parallel to the coast. It represents that area of the State least affected by ocean influences and most affected by higher elevations. In contrast, the Coastal Division is a strip roughly 20 to 30 miles in width. It is most affected by maritime influences and has the lowest average elevation above sea level. The remainder, known conveniently as the Southern Interior Division, covers nearly one-third of the State's area.

Maine lies in the "prevailing westerlies"—the belt of generally eastward air movement which encircles the globe in the middle latitudes. Embedded in this circulation are extensive masses of air originating in higher or lower latitudes and interacting to produce storm systems. Relative to most other sections of the country, a large number of such storms pass over or near Maine. The majority of air masses affecting this State belong to three types: (1) cold, dry air pouring down from subarctic North America, (2) warm, moist air streaming up on a long overland journey from the Gulf of Mexico and from subtropical waters eastward, and (3) cool, damp air moving in from the North Atlantic. Because the atmospheric flow is usually offshore, Maine is influenced more by the first two types than it is by the third.

The procession of contrasting air masses and the relatively frequent passage of storms bring about a roughly twice-weekly alternation from fair to cloudy or stormy conditions, attended by often abrupt changes in temperature, moisture, sunshine, wind direction, and wind speed. There is no regular or persistent rhythm to this sequence. It is interrupted by periods of time during which the same weather patterns continue for several days, and infrequently for several weeks. Maine weather, however, is distinguished for variety rather than for monotony. Changeability is also one of its features on a longer time-scale; that is, the same month or season will exhibit varying characteristics over the years—sometimes in close alternation, sometimes arranged in similar groups for successive years.

TEMPERATURE. The average annual temperature ranges from near 40°F. in the Northern Division, to 44°F. in the Southern Interior Division, and to nearly 45°F. in the Coastal Division. Summer temperatures are delightfully cool and are reasonably uniform over the State. Average temperatures vary much more in winter than in summer.

PRECIPITATION. Maine has precipitation rather evenly distributed throughout the year. The distribution is most regular in the Southern Interior Division. Along the Atlantic coast, summer thunderstorm activity is somewhat suppressed by the effects of the cool ocean, while winter precipitation is increased by coastal storms or "northeasters." In the Northern Division, these effects are reversed with increased thunderstorm activity in summer and with very little effect of coastal storms in winter. Precipitation totals in this Division are greater in summer.

Storm systems are the principal year-round moisture producers. Such systems are less active in the summer, but bands or patches of thunderstorm or shower activity take over much of this function. Though brief and often covering small areas, thunderstorms produce the heaviest local rainfall rates for short intervals. Many weather stations have received from one to two inches in an hour. Winter precipitation occurs mostly as snow, except in the Coastal Division where considerable rain or wet snow falls; stations in this Division, more than stations farther inland, are subject to occasional glazing, or "ice storm" conditions. Freezing rain coats streets, roads, and all exposed surfaces; on rare occasions, a heavy load of ice builds on trees and wires.

SNOWFALL. As a rule, average seasonal snowfall amounts increase northwestward from the coast. The Coastal Division snowfall totals range from 50 to 80 inches. The Southern Interior Division receives from 60 to 90 inches. The Northern Division totals range on the average from 90 to 110 inches. Local topography has a marked influence on snowfall, causing large variations within a short distance. The snowfall season usually begins in late October or in November and lasts into April and sometimes into May. Seasonal totals in the north do not vary as markedly as along the coast. Snow cover lasts throughout the season in the north. Along the coast, however, the snow cover may melt entirely in midwinter and then be replaced by a new cover. Melting is usually gradual enough to prevent serious flooding.

OTHER CLIMATIC FEATURES. The amount of possible sunshine averages from 50 to 60 percent in most of the southern half of the State. This percentage varies along the coast from near 50 to 60 percent. At higher elevations and over much of northern Maine, the average is near 45 percent. The average annual number of clear days ranges from 80 to 120 days in the southern half and from about 50 to 90 days in the northern half of the State.

Heavy fog is frequent and sometimes persistent along the coast, particularly in the eastern portion of the coast where it may occur on an average of one day out of six. Fog frequency and duration diminish inland. But short-duration heavy ground fogs of early morning occur frequently at susceptible places inland.

Prolonged dry spells, quite frequent in late summer or fall, create serious forest-fire hazards. Low humidities and lack of precipitation during some late summers cause the forest litter to become extremely inflammable.

WINDS AND STORMS. On a yearly basis, the wind direction is mostly from the west. During winter, north to northwest winds tend to prevail. In the summer, they are more often from the southwest or south. Topography has a strong influence on the prevailing direction. Parts of a major river valley, for example, may have a prevailing wind paralleling the valley. Along the coast in spring and summer, the sea breeze is important. On-shore local winds, blowing from the cool ocean, may come as far inland as 10 miles. They tend to retard spring growth, but are pleasingly cooling in summer.

Coastal storms or "northeasters" sometimes seriously affect the Coastal Division. They generate very strong winds and heavy rain or snow. They can produce abnormally high wind-driven tides, affecting beaches and coastal installations. In winter, these storms produce some of the heavier snowfalls along the coast. Occasionally, in summer or fall, a storm of tropical origin affects Maine. Usually the storm will be similar to the northeasters. But a few such storms may retain near or full hurricane force. Tornadoes are a phenomena not common in Maine. It is likely that several occur on the average each year. Fortunately, most tornadoes are very small, affecting a very localized area. About 80 percent of Maine's tornadoes occur between May 15 and September 15. The peak month is July. Thunderstorms and hailstorms have a similar frequency maximum from midspring to early fall. Thunderstorms occur in a range from 10 to 20 days a year in the Coastal Division and from 15 to 30 days a year elsewhere. The most severe storms are attended by hail.

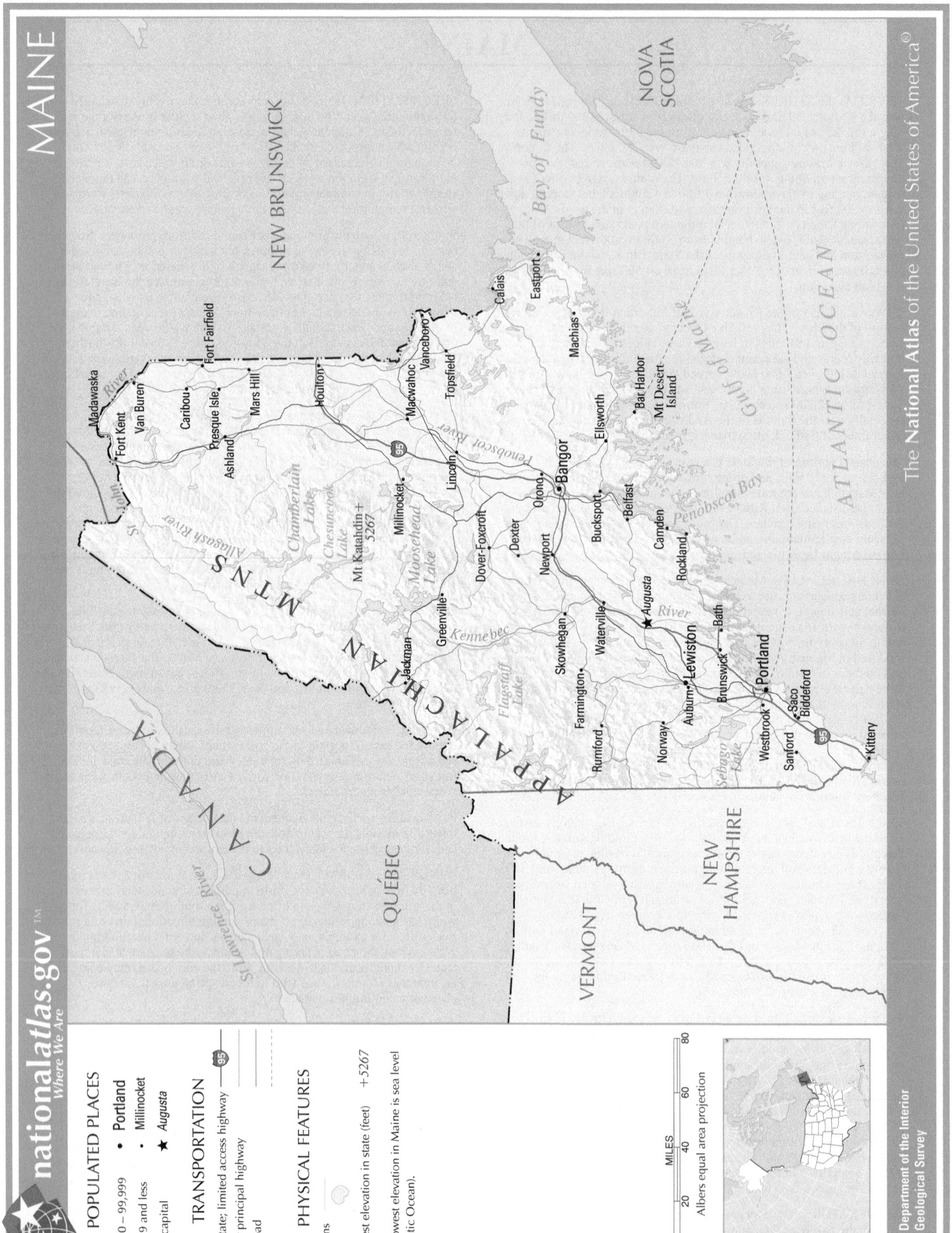
MAINE
nationalatlas.gov™
Where We Are
POPULATED PLACES
25,000 – 99,999 • Portland
24,999 and less · Millinocket
State capital ★ Augusta
TRANSPORTATION
Interstate; limited access highway 95
Other principal highway
Railroad
Ferry
PHYSICAL FEATURES
Streams
Lakes
Highest elevation in state (feet) +5267
The lowest elevation in Maine is sea level (Atlantic Ocean).
MILES
0 20 40 60 80
Albers equal area projection
U.S. Department of the Interior
U.S. Geological Survey
The National Atlas of the United States of America®
CANADA
QUÉBEC
NEW BRUNSWICK
NOVA SCOTIA
VERMONT
NEW HAMPSHIRE
ATLANTIC OCEAN
Bay of Fundy
Gulf of Maine
Penobscot Bay
St Lawrence River
St John River
Allagash River
Penobscot River
Kennebec River
APPALACHIAN MTNS
Chamberlain Lake
Chesuncook Lake
Moosehead Lake
Flagstaff Lake
Sebago Lake
Mt Katahdin +5267
Mt Desert Island
Madawaska
Fort Kent
Van Buren
Caribou
Presque Isle
Fort Fairfield
Mars Hill
Ashland
Houlton
Macwahoc
Vanceboro
Topsfield
Calais
Eastport
Machias
Bar Harbor
Ellsworth
Bangor
Orono
Lincoln
Millinocket
Dover-Foxcroft
Dexter
Newport
Bucksport
Belfast
Camden
Rockland
Augusta
Waterville
Skowhegan
Greenville
Jackman
Farmington
Rumford
Norway
Auburn
Lewiston
Brunswick
Bath
Portland
Westbrook
Saco
Biddeford
Sanford
Kittery

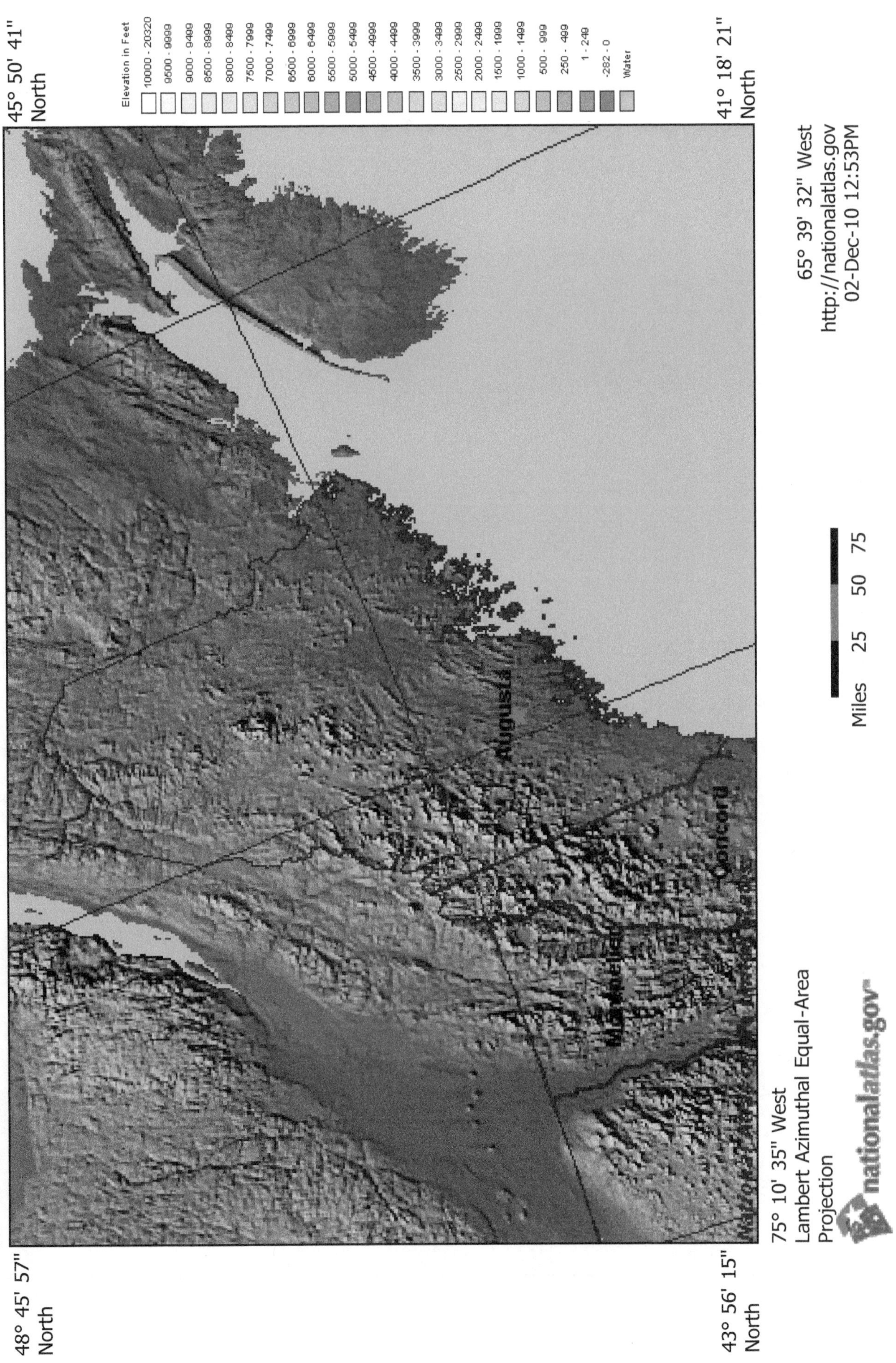
45° 50' 41" North
62° 36' 30" West
41° 18' 21" North
72° 45' 01" West
48° 45' 57" North
43° 56' 15" North
75° 10' 35" West
65° 39' 32" West
Lambert Azimuthal Equal-Area Projection
http://nationalatlas.gov
02-Dec-10 12:53PM
Elevation in Feet
10000 - 20320
9500 - 9999
9000 - 9499
8500 - 8999
8000 - 8499
7500 - 7999
7000 - 7499
6500 - 6999
6000 - 6499
5500 - 5999
5000 - 5499
4500 - 4999
4000 - 4499
3500 - 3999
3000 - 3499
2500 - 2999
2000 - 2499
1500 - 1999
1000 - 1499
500 - 999
250 - 499
1 - 249
-282 - 0
Water
Miles 25 50 75
Augusta
Concord
nationalatlas.gov

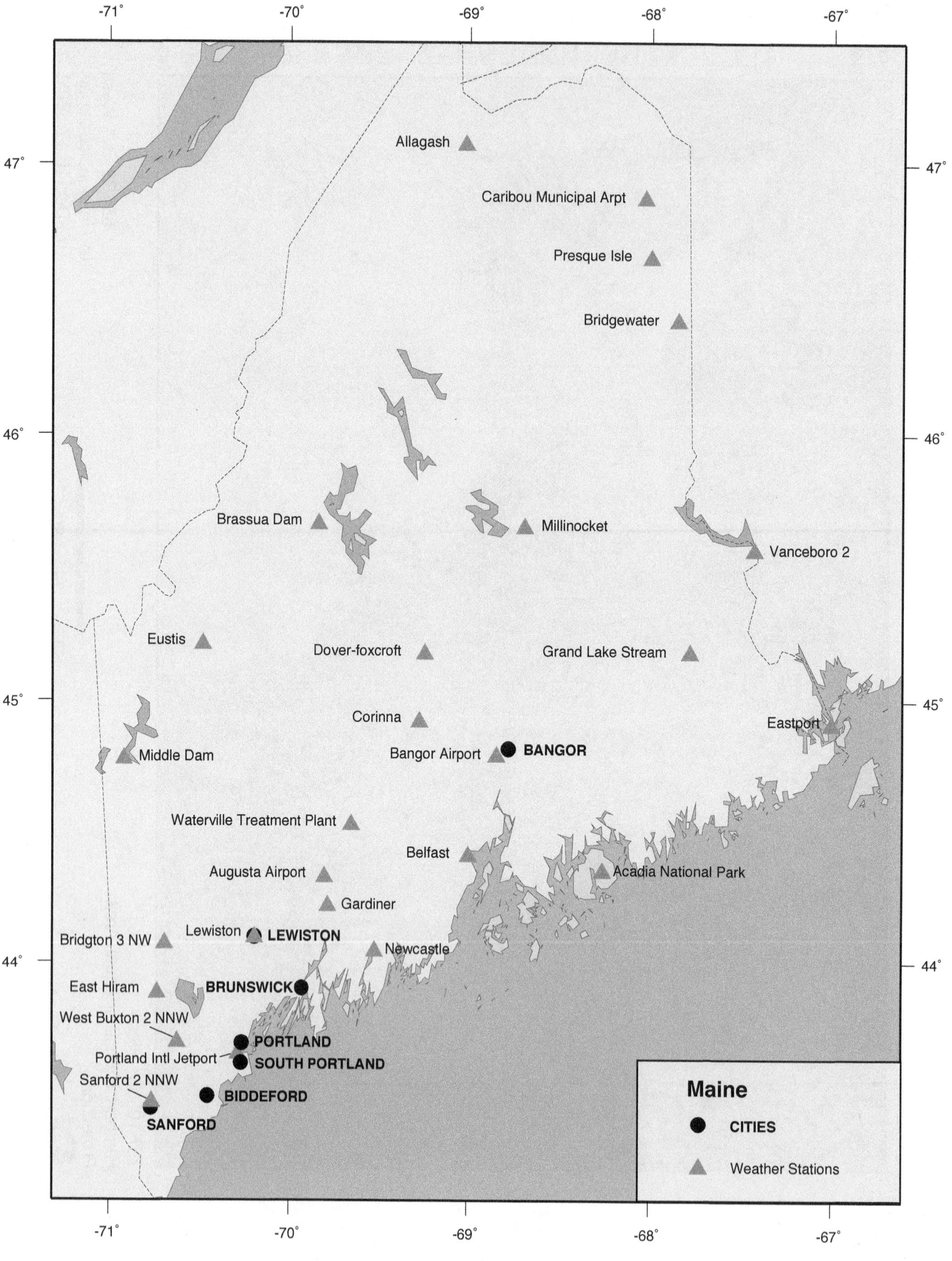
-71°
-70°
-69°
-68°
-67°
47°
46°
45°
44°
Allagash
Caribou Municipal Arpt
Presque Isle
Bridgewater
Brassua Dam
Millinocket
Vanceboro 2
Eustis
Dover-foxcroft
Grand Lake Stream
Corinna
Eastport
Middle Dam
Bangor Airport
BANGOR
Waterville Treatment Plant
Belfast
Augusta Airport
Acadia National Park
Gardiner
Bridgton 3 NW
Lewiston
LEWISTON
Newcastle
East Hiram
BRUNSWICK
West Buxton 2 NNW
PORTLAND
Portland Intl Jetport
SOUTH PORTLAND
Sanford 2 NNW
BIDDEFORD
SANFORD
Maine
CITIES
Weather Stations

Maine Weather Stations by County

County	Station Name
Androscoggin	Lewiston
Aroostook	Allagash Bridgewater Caribou Municipal Arpt Presque Isle
Cumberland	Bridgton 3 NW Portland Intl Jetport
Franklin	Eustis
Hancock	Acadia National Park
Kennebec	Augusta Airport Gardiner Waterville Treatment Plant
Lincoln	Newcastle
Oxford	East Hiram Middle Dam
Penobscot	Bangor Airport Corinna Millinocket
Piscataquis	Dover-Foxcroft
Somerset	Brassua Dam
Waldo	Belfast
Washington	Eastport Grand Lake Stream Vanceboro 2
York	Sanford 2 NNW West Buxton 2 NNW

See User Guide for station inclusion criteria.

Maine Weather Stations by City

City	Station Name	Miles
Auburn	Bridgton 3 NW	24.5
	Gardiner	24.2
	Lewiston	1.3
Augusta	Augusta Airport	1.8
	Gardiner	7.5
	Newcastle	22.1
	Waterville Treatment Plant	15.5
Bangor	Bangor Airport	2.0
	Corinna	24.6
Biddeford	Portland Intl Jetport	14.0
	Sanford 2 NNW	16.6
	West Buxton 2 NNW	17.2
Brunswick	Gardiner	23.4
	Lewiston	18.6
	Newcastle	23.5
	Portland Intl Jetport	24.4
Falmouth	Portland Intl Jetport	6.2
	West Buxton 2 NNW	17.7
Gorham	East Hiram	19.7
	Portland Intl Jetport	8.3
	Sanford 2 NNW	22.8
	West Buxton 2 NNW	8.1
Kennebunk	Portland Intl Jetport	22.0
	Sanford 2 NNW	12.9
	West Buxton 2 NNW	21.8
Kittery	Durham, NH	11.8
	Epping, NH	18.6
	Greenland, NH	7.8
Lewiston	Augusta Airport	24.5
	Gardiner	21.8
	Lewiston	1.3
Portland	Portland Intl Jetport	1.9
	West Buxton 2 NNW	17.0
Saco	Portland Intl Jetport	11.8
	Sanford 2 NNW	17.3
	West Buxton 2 NNW	15.4
Sanford	Sanford 2 NNW	2.2
	West Buxton 2 NNW	19.7
	Durham, NH	21.8
Scarborough	Portland Intl Jetport	5.2
	Sanford 2 NNW	23.3
	West Buxton 2 NNW	15.7
South Portland	Portland Intl Jetport	2.0
	West Buxton 2 NNW	18.0
Waterville	Augusta Airport	18.0
	Gardiner	24.1
	Waterville Treatment Plant	1.3

City	Station Name	Miles
Westbrook	East Hiram	23.9
	Portland Intl Jetport	3.8
	West Buxton 2 NNW	13.0
Windham	East Hiram	17.8
	Lewiston	22.8
	Portland Intl Jetport	11.8
	West Buxton 2 NNW	12.4
York	Sanford 2 NNW	21.9
	Durham, NH	15.0
	Epping, NH	23.6
	Greenland, NH	13.7

Note: Miles is the distance between the geographic center of the city and the weather station.

See User Guide for station inclusion criteria.

Maine Weather Stations by Elevation

Feet	Station Name
1,459	Middle Dam
1,259	Eustis
1,060	Brassua Dam
624	Caribou Municipal Arpt
599	Presque Isle
596	Allagash
560	Bridgton 3 NW
527	East Hiram
470	Acadia National Park
459	Dover-Foxcroft
419	Bridgewater
419	Vanceboro 2
359	Millinocket
350	Augusta Airport
290	Grand Lake Stream
279	Sanford 2 NNW
220	Corinna
189	Newcastle
185	Bangor Airport
180	Lewiston
149	West Buxton 2 NNW
140	Gardiner
84	Eastport
73	Waterville Treatment Plant
44	Portland Intl Jetport
29	Belfast

Caribou Municipal Airport

The Caribou Municipal Airport is located in Aroostook County, the largest and northernmost county in the state. The airport lies on top of high land which is about on the same level as most of the surrounding gently rolling hills. The Aroostook River, which runs about one mile to the east and southeast of the station, has little effect on the local weather. Even though Caribou is located only 150 miles from the Atlantic coast, its climate can be justly classed as a severe typical continental type. Winters are particularly long and windy, and seasonal snowfalls averaging over 100 inches are not unusual. While the extreme low temperatures may be less severe than one might expect, temperatures of zero or lower normally occur over 40 times per year. A study of heating degree day data will show the outstanding part that cold weather plays here.

Summers are cool and generally favored with abundant rainfall, which is one of the most important factors in the high yield of the potato and grain crops throughout the county. Caribou's location high up in the St. Lawrence Valley allows Aroostook County to come under the influence of the Summer Polar Front, resulting in practically no dry periods of more than 3 or 4 days in the growing season. The growing season at Caribou averages more than 120 days, with the average last freeze in the spring in mid-May and the average first freeze in autumn in late September.

Autumn climate is nearly ideal, with mostly sunny warm days and crisp cool nights predominating. Aroostook County, even with its relatively short growing season, provides profitable farming. The principal crops are potatoes, peas, a variety of grains, and some hardy vegetables.

Probably unknown to many victims of hay fever and similar afflictions, the immediate Caribou area offers sparkling visibility and relatively pollen-free air in the late summer months. This latter condition is principally due to the extremely high degree of cultivation of all available land.

Caribou Municipal Airport *Aroostook County* Elevation: 624 ft. Latitude: 46° 52' N Longitude: 68° 02' W

	JAN	FEB	MAR	APR	MAY	JUN	JUL	AUG	SEP	OCT	NOV	DEC	YEAR
Mean Maximum Temp. (°F)	19.5	23.7	33.7	47.7	62.4	71.5	75.9	74.3	65.3	51.9	38.2	25.8	49.1
Mean Temp. (°F)	10.0	13.7	24.3	38.6	51.5	60.7	65.5	63.6	54.8	43.3	31.4	17.7	39.6
Mean Minimum Temp. (°F)	0.5	3.7	14.9	29.5	40.5	49.8	55.0	52.9	44.2	34.6	24.6	9.6	30.0
Extreme Maximum Temp. (°F)	53	59	66	86	93	93	95	93	90	79	67	56	95
Extreme Minimum Temp. (°F)	-37	-28	-28	0	25	32	39	34	23	18	-8	-31	-37
Days Maximum Temp. ≥ 90°F	0	0	0	0	0	1	1	0	0	0	0	0	2
Days Maximum Temp. ≤ 32°F	26	22	13	1	0	0	0	0	0	0	9	22	93
Days Minimum Temp. ≤ 32°F	31	28	29	21	4	0	0	0	2	14	25	30	184
Days Minimum Temp. ≤ 0°F	17	12	5	0	0	0	0	0	0	0	0	8	42
Heating Degree Days (base 65°F)	1,701	1,445	1,255	785	417	162	56	94	311	667	1,000	1,459	9,352
Cooling Degree Days (base 65°F)	0	0	0	0	4	38	79	58	10	0	0	0	189
Mean Precipitation (in.)	2.70	2.19	2.51	2.67	3.32	3.31	4.11	3.79	3.26	3.47	3.60	3.19	38.12
Maximum Precipitation (in.)*	5.6	4.1	5.1	5.3	5.8	6.4	6.8	12.1	8.1	8.7	8.1	8.0	51.1
Minimum Precipitation (in.)*	0.3	0.3	0.7	0.5	0.5	0.9	1.0	0.9	0.9	0.6	1.2	0.7	27.9
Extreme Maximum Daily Precip. (in.)	1.58	2.10	2.29	1.67	1.67	1.70	2.42	6.67	2.60	3.00	2.22	2.77	6.67
Days With ≥ 0.1" Precipitation	6	5	6	7	8	8	9	8	7	7	8	7	86
Days With ≥ 0.5" Precipitation	2	1	2	1	2	2	3	2	2	2	2	2	23
Days With ≥ 1.0" Precipitation	0	0	0	0	0	0	1	1	1	1	1	0	5
Mean Snowfall (in.)	25.3	22.3	20.1	8.3	0.5	trace	trace	trace	0.1	1.6	10.7	24.0	112.9
Maximum Snowfall (in.)*	45	41	47	36	11	trace	0	0	3	12	35	60	167
Maximum 24-hr. Snowfall (in.)*	14	17	29	21	6	trace	0	0	2	9	21	19	29
Maximum Snow Depth (in.)	43	41	47	42	3	trace	trace	trace	1	7	22	33	47
Days With ≥ 1.0" Snow Depth	30	28	30	11	0	0	0	0	0	1	10	25	135
Thunderstorm Days*	< 1	0	< 1	< 1	2	5	7	5	1	1	0	0	21
Foggy Days*	8	6	8	11	10	12	14	15	14	13	12	9	132
Predominant Sky Cover*	OVR	OVR	OVR	OVR	OVR	OVR	OVR	OVR	OVR	OVR	OVR	OVR	OVR
Mean Relative Humidity 7am (%)*	75	74	76	75	74	78	83	86	87	86	84	80	80
Mean Relative Humidity 4pm (%)*	68	63	60	56	51	55	58	59	61	65	74	73	62
Mean Dewpoint (°F)*	4	5	15	27	38	50	56	54	46	36	25	11	31
Prevailing Wind Direction*	NW	NW	NW	NW	NW	S	S	WSW	S	WSW	NW	NW	NW
Prevailing Wind Speed (mph)*	16	16	17	16	16	10	9	10	10	12	15	16	14
Maximum Wind Gust (mph)*	28	38	31	41	37	33	35	35	37	44	53	48	53

Note: (*) Period of record is 1948-1995

The period of record for National Weather Service station data is 1980 – 2009 except where noted. See User Guide for detailed explanation of data.

Portland Int'l Jetport

The Portland International Jetport is located two and three fourths miles west of the site of the former city office. The surrounding country is mostly open, rolling and sloping generally toward the Fore River, a body of brackish water about 1,000 feet wide at a distance of about one half mile from the station and forming one boundary (north through east) of the field. The airport is about five and a half miles west-northwest of the open ocean. A slight rise reaching an elevation of 100 feet, lying northwest of the field, cuts down the wind slightly from that direction. The older portion of the city is situated on a hill rising abruptly from sea level to 170 feet, one and a half miles east of the airport and on the opposite side of the Fore River. A line of low hills southeast of the airport, near the ocean, which reach a maximum height of 160 feet, shuts off sight of the ocean from the airport. Sebago Lake with an area of 44 square miles is situated about 15 miles to the northwest and 45 miles farther are the White Mountains, averaging 3,000 to 5,000 feet in height.

As a rule, Portland has very pleasant summers and falls, cold winters with frequent thaws, and disagreeable springs. Autumn has the greatest number of sunny days and the least cloudiness. Winters are quite severe, but begin late and then extend deeply into the normal springtime.

Heavy seasonal snowfalls, over 100 inches, normally occur about each 10 years. True blizzards are very rare. The White Mountains, to the northwest, keep considerable snow from reaching the Portland area and also moderate the temperature.

Winds are generally quite light with the highest velocities being confined mostly to March and November. Even in these months the occasional north-easterly gales have usually lost much of their severity before reaching the coast of Maine.

Temperatures well below zero are recorded frequently each winter. Cold waves sometimes come in on strong winds, but extremely low temperatures are generally accompanied by light winds.

The average freeze-free season at the airport station is 139 days. Mid-May is the average occurrence of the last freeze in spring, and the average occurrence of the first freeze in fall is late September. The freeze-free period is longer in the city proper, but may be even shorter at susceptible places further inland.

Daily maximum temperatures at the present airport site agree closely with those near the former intown office, but minimum temperatures on clear, quiet mornings range as much as 15 degrees lower at the airport.

Portland Int'l Jetport *Cumberland County* Elevation: 44 ft. Latitude: 43° 39' N Longitude: 70° 18' W

	JAN	FEB	MAR	APR	MAY	JUN	JUL	AUG	SEP	OCT	NOV	DEC	YEAR
Mean Maximum Temp. (°F)	31.2	34.4	41.9	53.1	63.4	73.1	78.8	77.8	70.0	58.5	47.9	37.1	55.6
Mean Temp. (°F)	22.2	25.2	33.3	43.9	53.8	63.3	69.1	68.1	60.1	48.7	39.3	28.6	46.3
Mean Minimum Temp. (°F)	13.3	16.0	24.6	34.6	44.1	53.5	59.3	58.3	50.2	38.8	30.8	20.0	36.9
Extreme Maximum Temp. (°F)	67	63	88	92	94	98	98	97	95	83	74	71	98
Extreme Minimum Temp. (°F)	-19	-17	-6	15	28	37	46	39	30	21	3	-20	-20
Days Maximum Temp. ≥ 90°F	0	0	0	0	0	1	2	1	0	0	0	0	4
Days Maximum Temp. ≤ 32°F	17	11	4	0	0	0	0	0	0	0	1	10	43
Days Minimum Temp. ≤ 32°F	30	26	25	12	1	0	0	0	0	8	19	28	149
Days Minimum Temp. ≤ 0°F	4	2	0	0	0	0	0	0	0	0	0	1	7
Heating Degree Days (base 65°F)	1,318	1,118	977	627	349	104	15	28	169	500	763	1,122	7,090
Cooling Degree Days (base 65°F)	0	0	0	0	8	60	148	130	29	1	0	0	376
Mean Precipitation (in.)	3.32	3.09	4.01	4.46	4.01	3.78	3.54	3.11	3.59	4.73	4.92	3.92	46.48
Maximum Precipitation (in.)*	11.9	7.1	10.0	9.9	9.6	6.8	7.5	15.2	9.8	12.3	13.5	9.7	66.3
Minimum Precipitation (in.)*	0.8	trace	0.8	1.0	0.5	0.8	0.6	0.5	0.3	0.6	0.9	1.0	26.3
Extreme Maximum Daily Precip. (in.)	1.95	2.54	3.36	4.21	3.41	3.58	3.37	7.75	4.44	11.74	5.03	3.50	11.74
Days With ≥ 0.1" Precipitation	7	6	7	7	7	7	7	5	5	6	7	7	78
Days With ≥ 0.5" Precipitation	2	2	3	3	3	2	3	2	2	3	3	3	31
Days With ≥ 1.0" Precipitation	1	1	1	1	1	1	1	1	1	1	1	1	12
Mean Snowfall (in.)	18.7	13.7	12.8	2.8	0.0	0.0	trace	0.0	trace	trace	2.2	13.6	63.8
Maximum Snowfall (in.)*	62	61	49	16	2	0	0	0	trace	4	16	55	150
Maximum 24-hr. Snowfall (in.)*	16	17	17	14	1	0	0	0	trace	4	9	22	22
Maximum Snow Depth (in.)	31	30	34	16	0	0	trace	0	trace	trace	9	25	34
Days With ≥ 1.0" Snow Depth	21	20	14	1	0	0	0	0	0	0	1	12	69
Thunderstorm Days*	< 1	< 1	< 1	< 1	2	4	4	4	1	1	< 1	< 1	16
Foggy Days*	10	9	12	14	15	16	17	17	16	15	14	12	167
Predominant Sky Cover*	OVR	OVR	OVR	OVR	OVR	OVR	OVR	OVR	OVR	OVR	OVR	OVR	OVR
Mean Relative Humidity 7am (%)*	75	75	74	73	75	78	80	83	86	84	82	78	79
Mean Relative Humidity 4pm (%)*	62	59	60	58	61	63	62	63	64	64	66	65	62
Mean Dewpoint (°F)*	13	14	22	32	43	53	59	58	51	40	31	18	36
Prevailing Wind Direction*	N	NNW	N	S	S	S	S	S	S	N	W	N	S
Prevailing Wind Speed (mph)*	9	10	10	12	12	10	10	10	10	9	9	9	10
Maximum Wind Gust (mph)*	64	64	62	61	67	76	60	78	76	68	76	76	78

Note: (*) Period of record is 1948-1995

Acadia National Park *Hancock County* Elevation: 470 ft. Latitude: 44° 21' N Longitude: 68° 16' W

	JAN	FEB	MAR	APR	MAY	JUN	JUL	AUG	SEP	OCT	NOV	DEC	YEAR
Mean Maximum Temp. (°F)	31.5	34.0	40.8	52.6	64.3	73.8	78.7	78.0	70.0	58.0	47.3	37.1	55.5
Mean Temp. (°F)	21.8	24.4	31.7	42.9	53.4	62.9	68.2	67.7	60.0	49.1	39.1	28.2	45.8
Mean Minimum Temp. (°F)	12.1	14.6	22.6	33.2	42.5	51.9	57.6	57.3	50.0	40.2	31.0	19.3	36.0
Extreme Maximum Temp. (°F)	57	61	80	80	96	95	96	95	95	81	71	63	96
Extreme Minimum Temp. (°F)	-21	-18	-11	8	24	32	38	35	31	22	4	-16	-21
Days Maximum Temp. ≥ 90°F	0	0	0	0	0	1	1	1	0	0	0	0	3
Days Maximum Temp. ≤ 32°F	16	12	5	0	0	0	0	0	0	0	1	10	44
Days Minimum Temp. ≤ 32°F	29	26	26	14	1	0	0	0	0	5	17	27	145
Days Minimum Temp. ≤ 0°F	6	4	1	0	0	0	0	0	0	0	0	2	13
Heating Degree Days (base 65°F)	1,333	1,142	1,024	656	359	108	23	28	167	487	769	1,134	7,230
Cooling Degree Days (base 65°F)	0	0	0	0	7	52	129	118	24	1	0	0	331
Mean Precipitation (in.)	4.88	4.25	5.31	5.01	4.82	4.07	3.56	3.10	4.32	5.36	6.69	5.17	56.54
Extreme Maximum Daily Precip. (in.)	5.22	na	3.99	3.89	3.58	3.29	3.15	3.65	5.31	5.40	5.59	na	na
Days With ≥ 0.1" Precipitation	8	6	7	7	8	7	6	5	6	8	8	8	84
Days With ≥ 0.5" Precipitation	3	2	3	3	3	3	2	2	3	3	4	3	34
Days With ≥ 1.0" Precipitation	1	1	2	1	1	1	1	1	1	2	2	1	15
Mean Snowfall (in.)	19.0	14.0	15.1	5.1	trace	0.0	0.0	0.0	0.0	0.2	3.1	12.3	68.8
Maximum Snow Depth (in.)	32	35	45	22	0	0	0	0	0	6	12	24	45
Days With ≥ 1.0" Snow Depth	22	24	18	4	0	0	0	0	0	0	3	13	84

Allagash *Aroostook County* Elevation: 596 ft. Latitude: 47° 05' N Longitude: 69° 01' W

	JAN	FEB	MAR	APR	MAY	JUN	JUL	AUG	SEP	OCT	NOV	DEC	YEAR
Mean Maximum Temp. (°F)	19.3	23.3	34.3	47.2	62.6	72.3	76.4	75.1	66.4	52.0	38.4	25.6	49.4
Mean Temp. (°F)	5.5	7.2	19.4	35.6	48.8	58.5	63.4	61.5	52.8	40.9	29.5	14.8	36.5
Mean Minimum Temp. (°F)	-8.3	-9.0	4.6	23.9	35.0	44.7	50.4	47.7	39.2	29.8	20.5	3.9	23.5
Extreme Maximum Temp. (°F)	54	61	68	84	92	95	94	93	93	81	70	57	95
Extreme Minimum Temp. (°F)	-47	-43	-34	-4	13	25	33	29	20	9	-13	-36	-47
Days Maximum Temp. ≥ 90°F	0	0	0	0	0	1	1	0	0	0	0	0	2
Days Maximum Temp. ≤ 32°F	26	22	13	1	0	0	0	0	0	0	8	23	93
Days Minimum Temp. ≤ 32°F	31	28	31	27	12	2	0	1	7	21	27	30	217
Days Minimum Temp. ≤ 0°F	22	22	13	0	0	0	0	0	0	0	1	13	71
Heating Degree Days (base 65°F)	1,841	1,631	1,406	875	496	217	98	143	366	740	1,059	1,551	10,423
Cooling Degree Days (base 65°F)	0	0	0	0	2	29	55	40	7	0	0	0	133
Mean Precipitation (in.)	2.43	1.83	2.01	2.66	2.74	3.64	4.07	3.78	3.48	3.66	3.35	2.67	36.32
Extreme Maximum Daily Precip. (in.)	1.83	1.80	1.30	2.30	1.95	2.31	1.90	2.37	2.85	2.45	1.94	1.65	2.85
Days With ≥ 0.1" Precipitation	6	5	6	7	8	8	9	9	7	8	8	7	88
Days With ≥ 0.5" Precipitation	2	1	1	1	1	2	3	2	2	2	2	2	21
Days With ≥ 1.0" Precipitation	0	0	0	0	0	1	1	1	1	1	0	0	5
Mean Snowfall (in.)	20.6	19.5	16.1	6.1	0.4	0.0	0.0	0.0	trace	2.3	9.5	20.4	94.9
Maximum Snow Depth (in.)	39	41	52	46	3	0	0	0	trace	13	17	35	52
Days With ≥ 1.0" Snow Depth	31	28	31	14	0	0	0	0	0	2	12	28	146

Augusta Airport *Kennebec County* Elevation: 350 ft. Latitude: 44° 19' N Longitude: 69° 48' W

	JAN	FEB	MAR	APR	MAY	JUN	JUL	AUG	SEP	OCT	NOV	DEC	YEAR
Mean Maximum Temp. (°F)	27.7	31.7	40.3	53.1	65.1	74.0	79.2	78.1	69.7	57.3	45.2	33.5	54.6
Mean Temp. (°F)	19.5	23.1	31.9	44.0	55.0	64.2	69.7	68.5	60.2	48.6	38.1	26.0	45.7
Mean Minimum Temp. (°F)	11.3	14.4	23.6	34.9	44.9	54.5	60.2	58.9	50.6	39.8	30.9	18.5	36.9
Extreme Maximum Temp. (°F)	61	60	85	90	94	98	98	97	96	83	74	67	98
Extreme Minimum Temp. (°F)	-16	-18	-11	10	29	37	47	43	28	22	5	-12	-18
Days Maximum Temp. ≥ 90°F	0	0	0	0	0	1	2	1	0	0	0	0	4
Days Maximum Temp. ≤ 32°F	21	14	6	0	0	0	0	0	0	0	2	14	57
Days Minimum Temp. ≤ 32°F	30	26	25	11	0	0	0	0	0	6	18	28	144
Days Minimum Temp. ≤ 0°F	6	3	1	0	0	0	0	0	0	0	0	2	12
Heating Degree Days (base 65°F)	1,403	1,179	1,018	622	312	87	14	25	168	503	801	1,202	7,334
Cooling Degree Days (base 65°F)	0	0	0	0	9	71	168	141	30	1	0	0	420
Mean Precipitation (in.)	2.54	2.33	3.31	3.92	3.72	3.52	3.44	3.29	3.73	4.29	4.31	3.14	41.54
Extreme Maximum Daily Precip. (in.)	2.10	1.82	2.90	3.41	3.01	2.72	4.15	4.50	4.95	4.01	2.68	3.00	4.95
Days With ≥ 0.1" Precipitation	6	5	7	7	8	7	7	6	6	7	7	7	80
Days With ≥ 0.5" Precipitation	2	1	2	3	2	2	2	2	3	3	3	2	27
Days With ≥ 1.0" Precipitation	0	0	1	1	1	1	1	1	1	1	1	1	10
Mean Snowfall (in.)	na	na	na	na	trace	na	na	0.0	na	na	na	14.2	na
Maximum Snow Depth (in.)	39	na	na	na	trace	na	na	0	na	na	na	na	na
Days With ≥ 1.0" Snow Depth	24	na	na	na	0	na	na	0	na	na	na	na	na

Bangor Airport *Penobscot County* Elevation: 185 ft. Latitude: 44° 48' N Longitude: 68° 49' W

	JAN	FEB	MAR	APR	MAY	JUN	JUL	AUG	SEP	OCT	NOV	DEC	YEAR
Mean Maximum Temp. (°F)	26.9	30.6	39.5	52.9	65.0	73.9	79.1	78.0	69.7	57.2	45.4	33.2	54.3
Mean Temp. (°F)	17.3	20.5	30.3	43.0	54.1	63.4	68.7	67.6	59.0	47.5	37.5	24.4	44.4
Mean Minimum Temp. (°F)	7.5	10.3	21.0	33.1	43.2	52.8	58.3	57.1	48.3	37.7	29.5	15.6	34.5
Extreme Maximum Temp. (°F)	58	59	70	92	96	96	96	96	97	83	72	65	97
Extreme Minimum Temp. (°F)	-29	-27	-16	16	25	34	44	39	23	18	1	-23	-29
Days Maximum Temp. ≥ 90°F	0	0	0	0	0	1	1	1	0	0	0	0	3
Days Maximum Temp. ≤ 32°F	21	16	6	0	0	0	0	0	0	0	2	14	59
Days Minimum Temp. ≤ 32°F	30	27	27	14	1	0	0	0	1	9	20	29	158
Days Minimum Temp. ≤ 0°F	9	7	2	0	0	0	0	0	0	0	0	4	22
Heating Degree Days (base 65°F)	1,473	1,251	1,069	653	337	101	20	37	196	536	818	1,252	7,743
Cooling Degree Days (base 65°F)	0	0	0	0	7	59	142	123	22	1	0	0	354
Mean Precipitation (in.)	2.60	2.38	3.30	3.80	3.56	3.53	3.53	3.08	3.49	3.93	4.36	3.31	40.87
Extreme Maximum Daily Precip. (in.)	2.17	1.60	2.52	4.40	2.41	4.21	2.36	2.74	3.23	3.98	5.10	4.08	5.10
Days With ≥ 0.1" Precipitation	6	6	7	7	8	7	7	6	6	7	8	7	82
Days With ≥ 0.5" Precipitation	2	1	2	2	2	3	3	2	2	2	3	2	26
Days With ≥ 1.0" Precipitation	0	0	1	1	1	1	1	1	1	1	1	1	10
Mean Snowfall (in.)	18.2	14.9	11.9	3.7	trace	trace	trace	0.0	trace	0.1	2.9	13.5	65.2
Maximum Snow Depth (in.)	30	31	38	14	trace	trace	trace	0	trace	2	13	19	38
Days With ≥ 1.0" Snow Depth	25	24	18	3	0	0	0	0	0	0	2	16	88

The period of record for all cooperative weather station data is 1980 – 2009. See User Guide for detailed explanation of data.

Belfast *Waldo County* Elevation: 29 ft. Latitude: 44° 24' N Longitude: 69° 00' W

	JAN	FEB	MAR	APR	MAY	JUN	JUL	AUG	SEP	OCT	NOV	DEC	YEAR
Mean Maximum Temp. (°F)	31.0	34.5	41.9	53.5	64.7	73.6	78.6	77.7	70.2	58.4	47.1	36.2	55.6
Mean Temp. (°F)	20.7	23.8	31.8	43.0	53.4	62.4	67.8	66.7	59.3	48.4	38.8	27.1	45.3
Mean Minimum Temp. (°F)	10.4	13.1	21.7	32.6	42.0	51.2	56.9	55.7	48.3	38.3	30.4	18.0	34.9
Extreme Maximum Temp. (°F)	59	60	82	85	95	96	96	94	93	80	72	65	96
Extreme Minimum Temp. (°F)	-27	-25	-15	17	26	35	44	35	25	20	2	-27	-27
Days Maximum Temp. ≥ 90°F	0	0	0	0	0	1	1	1	0	0	0	0	3
Days Maximum Temp. ≤ 32°F	17	11	4	0	0	0	0	0	0	0	1	10	43
Days Minimum Temp. ≤ 32°F	30	27	28	15	2	0	0	0	0	8	19	29	158
Days Minimum Temp. ≤ 0°F	8	5	1	0	0	0	0	0	0	0	0	3	17
Heating Degree Days (base 65°F)	1,367	1,157	1,021	652	358	112	21	34	183	509	780	1,167	7,361
Cooling Degree Days (base 65°F)	0	0	0	0	5	43	114	94	18	0	0	0	274
Mean Precipitation (in.)	3.37	3.03	4.00	4.69	4.11	3.87	3.42	3.22	4.18	4.46	4.99	3.93	47.27
Extreme Maximum Daily Precip. (in.)	3.40	2.83	4.10	4.77	2.74	***3.80***	2.56	3.42	4.60	5.03	3.25	2.75	***5.03***
Days With ≥ 0.1" Precipitation	5	5	6	7	7	6	6	6	6	7	7	6	74
Days With ≥ 0.5" Precipitation	2	2	3	3	3	3	2	2	3	3	3	3	32
Days With ≥ 1.0" Precipitation	1	1	1	1	1	1	1	1	1	1	2	1	13
Mean Snowfall (in.)	***12.9***	***12.8***	***9.2***	1.3	0.0	0.0	0.0	0.0	0.0	0.1	1.3	***13.1***	***50.7***
Maximum Snow Depth (in.)	40	***35***	***34***	***10***	0	0	0	0	0	3	8	18	***40***
Days With ≥ 1.0" Snow Depth	10	8	***7***	1	0	0	0	0	0	0	1	7	***34***

Brassua Dam *Somerset County* Elevation: 1,060 ft. Latitude: 45° 40' N Longitude: 69° 49' W

	JAN	FEB	MAR	APR	MAY	JUN	JUL	AUG	SEP	OCT	NOV	DEC	YEAR
Mean Maximum Temp. (°F)	21.6	25.8	34.6	47.0	61.1	70.7	75.0	74.3	66.0	52.5	39.6	27.5	49.6
Mean Temp. (°F)	10.6	13.4	22.7	36.7	49.3	59.6	64.5	63.2	55.1	43.0	32.3	19.0	39.1
Mean Minimum Temp. (°F)	-0.4	0.9	10.8	26.2	37.6	48.5	54.0	52.1	44.1	33.6	24.9	10.4	28.6
Extreme Maximum Temp. (°F)	53	58	68	80	86	94	93	91	94	81	67	59	94
Extreme Minimum Temp. (°F)	-37	-33	-30	-2	21	29	37	33	20	16	-7	-30	-37
Days Maximum Temp. ≥ 90°F	0	0	0	0	0	0	0	0	0	0	0	0	0
Days Maximum Temp. ≤ 32°F	25	20	12	1	0	0	0	0	0	0	7	21	86
Days Minimum Temp. ≤ 32°F	31	28	30	25	9	0	0	0	2	15	24	30	194
Days Minimum Temp. ≤ 0°F	17	15	8	0	0	0	0	0	0	0	0	8	48
Heating Degree Days (base 65°F)	1,683	1,455	1,304	843	480	185	72	100	300	677	975	1,421	9,495
Cooling Degree Days (base 65°F)	0	0	0	0	2	30	64	52	9	0	0	0	157
Mean Precipitation (in.)	2.55	2.23	2.85	3.58	3.69	4.35	4.29	3.73	3.68	3.95	3.83	3.04	41.77
Extreme Maximum Daily Precip. (in.)	2.21	1.82	1.67	2.16	2.58	1.92	2.90	2.88	4.21	2.59	3.51	1.76	4.21
Days With ≥ 0.1" Precipitation	6	6	7	8	8	9	9	8	7	8	8	7	91
Days With ≥ 0.5" Precipitation	2	1	2	2	2	3	3	2	2	3	3	2	27
Days With ≥ 1.0" Precipitation	0	0	1	1	1	1	1	1	1	1	1	1	10
Mean Snowfall (in.)	21.8	21.3	19.2	8.5	0.2	trace	0.0	0.0	trace	2.0	7.9	21.8	102.7
Maximum Snow Depth (in.)	na	***43***	***46***	***44***	***9***	***0***	***0***	***0***	***0***	***14***	na	na	na
Days With ≥ 1.0" Snow Depth	na	***24***	***28***	17	0	0	0	0	0	1	***6***	na	na

Bridgewater *Aroostook County* Elevation: 419 ft. Latitude: 46° 25' N Longitude: 67° 51' W

	JAN	FEB	MAR	APR	MAY	JUN	JUL	AUG	SEP	OCT	NOV	DEC	YEAR
Mean Maximum Temp. (°F)	21.9	26.3	36.1	50.2	64.9	73.5	77.6	76.4	67.2	54.0	40.0	27.8	51.3
Mean Temp. (°F)	11.1	14.5	25.4	39.4	52.0	61.1	65.8	64.2	55.5	44.0	32.5	18.5	40.3
Mean Minimum Temp. (°F)	0.3	2.6	14.6	28.6	39.0	48.7	53.9	51.9	43.7	34.1	25.0	9.2	29.3
Extreme Maximum Temp. (°F)	54	61	67	86	95	94	95	95	92	80	67	56	95
Extreme Minimum Temp. (°F)	-43	-38	-35	-5	22	24	33	29	19	16	-9	-38	-43
Days Maximum Temp. ≥ 90°F	0	0	0	0	0	0	1	1	0	0	0	0	2
Days Maximum Temp. ≤ 32°F	25	20	10	1	0	0	0	0	0	0	6	20	82
Days Minimum Temp. ≤ 32°F	30	28	29	21	8	1	0	0	4	14	24	30	189
Days Minimum Temp. ≤ 0°F	16	13	5	0	0	0	0	0	0	0	0	8	42
Heating Degree Days (base 65°F)	1,669	1,423	1,221	761	401	149	50	86	291	645	969	1,435	9,100
Cooling Degree Days (base 65°F)	0	0	0	0	4	40	81	67	11	0	0	0	203
Mean Precipitation (in.)	3.25	2.43	2.85	3.12	3.58	3.79	3.93	3.97	3.51	3.86	4.17	3.46	41.92
Extreme Maximum Daily Precip. (in.)	2.30	1.78	2.25	1.47	1.58	2.57	3.11	5.90	3.62	3.25	2.62	2.43	5.90
Days With ≥ 0.1" Precipitation	7	5	6	7	8	8	8	7	7	7	8	7	85
Days With ≥ 0.5" Precipitation	2	2	2	2	3	3	3	2	3	3	3	2	30
Days With ≥ 1.0" Precipitation	1	1	1	1	0	1	1	1	1	1	1	1	11
Mean Snowfall (in.)	23.2	17.8	14.8	5.0	0.1	0.0	0.0	0.0	0.1	0.5	6.7	18.6	86.8
Maximum Snow Depth (in.)	39	45	50	45	1	0	0	0	trace	5	20	32	50
Days With ≥ 1.0" Snow Depth	30	28	29	8	0	0	0	0	0	0	7	24	126

Bridgton 3 NW *Cumberland County* Elevation: 560 ft. Latitude: 44° 05' N Longitude: 70° 44' W

	JAN	FEB	MAR	APR	MAY	JUN	JUL	AUG	SEP	OCT	NOV	DEC	YEAR
Mean Maximum Temp. (°F)	28.2	31.9	40.6	53.4	65.9	73.0	77.8	76.3	68.6	57.0	44.7	33.0	54.2
Mean Temp. (°F)	16.9	19.7	29.3	41.8	53.5	62.0	66.9	65.4	57.4	46.0	35.8	23.5	43.2
Mean Minimum Temp. (°F)	5.5	7.4	18.1	30.1	40.9	50.9	56.0	54.4	46.1	35.0	26.7	14.0	32.1
Extreme Maximum Temp. (°F)	64	63	76	91	93	95	95	95	95	82	74	68	95
Extreme Minimum Temp. (°F)	-26	-24	-19	8	23	28	36	29	19	18	-2	-25	-26
Days Maximum Temp. ≥ 90°F	0	0	0	0	0	1	1	1	0	0	0	0	3
Days Maximum Temp. ≤ 32°F	20	14	6	0	0	0	0	0	0	0	3	15	58
Days Minimum Temp. ≤ 32°F	31	28	29	20	4	0	0	0	1	13	23	30	179
Days Minimum Temp. ≤ 0°F	12	9	3	0	0	0	0	0	0	0	0	4	28
Heating Degree Days (base 65°F)	1,487	1,276	1,101	690	357	129	38	62	236	582	873	1,278	8,109
Cooling Degree Days (base 65°F)	0	0	0	0	6	44	105	81	15	1	0	0	252
Mean Precipitation (in.)	3.57	3.39	3.84	4.35	3.38	4.30	4.10	4.13	3.90	5.01	4.60	3.83	48.40
Extreme Maximum Daily Precip. (in.)	2.91	2.29	2.10	3.35	3.46	3.49	3.56	4.00	5.87	6.43	3.67	2.48	6.43
Days With ≥ 0.1" Precipitation	7	6	6	7	7	8	8	7	6	7	7	7	83
Days With ≥ 0.5" Precipitation	2	2	3	3	3	3	3	3	3	3	3	3	34
Days With ≥ 1.0" Precipitation	1	1	1	1	1	1	1	1	1	2	1	1	13
Mean Snowfall (in.)	20.6	17.5	15.2	3.9	trace	0.0	0.0	0.0	0.0	0.1	3.6	15.5	76.4
Maximum Snow Depth (in.)	***35***	***52***	***53***	39	trace	0	0	0	0	1	10	***29***	***53***
Days With ≥ 1.0" Snow Depth	***30***	***28***	***28***	7	0	0	0	0	0	0	4	***21***	***118***

The period of record for all cooperative weather station data is 1980 – 2009. See User Guide for detailed explanation of data.

Corinna *Penobscot County* Elevation: 220 ft. Latitude: 44° 55' N Longitude: 69° 16' W

	JAN	FEB	MAR	APR	MAY	JUN	JUL	AUG	SEP	OCT	NOV	DEC	YEAR
Mean Maximum Temp. (°F)	26.3	30.6	39.7	53.3	66.5	74.7	79.3	78.4	70.1	57.7	44.6	32.3	54.5
Mean Temp. (°F)	14.0	17.3	27.9	41.7	53.7	62.6	67.7	66.2	57.5	45.6	35.1	21.9	42.6
Mean Minimum Temp. (°F)	1.5	3.8	16.1	29.9	40.9	50.5	56.1	53.8	44.8	33.5	25.6	11.5	30.7
Extreme Maximum Temp. (°F)	58	59	72	92	96	96	95	95	93	83	71	63	96
Extreme Minimum Temp. (°F)	-38	-32	-28	6	22	33	37	31	21	15	-8	-31	-38
Days Maximum Temp. ≥ 90°F	0	0	0	0	0	1	1	1	0	0	0	0	3
Days Maximum Temp. ≤ 32°F	22	15	6	0	0	0	0	0	0	0	3	15	61
Days Minimum Temp. ≤ 32°F	30	28	29	19	4	0	0	0	2	15	23	30	180
Days Minimum Temp. ≤ 0°F	15	12	4	0	0	0	0	0	0	0	0	7	38
Heating Degree Days (base 65°F)	1,577	1,344	1,143	694	351	120	30	52	235	594	889	1,329	8,358
Cooling Degree Days (base 65°F)	0	0	0	0	7	56	122	95	16	0	0	0	296
Mean Precipitation (in.)	3.04	2.59	3.43	3.91	3.81	4.05	3.36	3.42	3.85	4.23	4.29	3.57	43.55
Extreme Maximum Daily Precip. (in.)	2.05	2.06	2.33	3.45	2.54	2.52	3.23	2.43	3.50	3.58	2.63	2.43	3.58
Days With ≥ 0.1" Precipitation	7	6	7	8	8	8	8	6	6	7	8	7	86
Days With ≥ 0.5" Precipitation	2	2	2	3	3	3	2	2	3	3	3	3	31
Days With ≥ 1.0" Precipitation	1	0	1	1	1	1	0	1	1	1	1	1	10
Mean Snowfall (in.)	17.8	15.1	13.8	3.6	0.0	0.0	0.0	0.0	0.0	0.3	4.0	15.7	70.3
Maximum Snow Depth (in.)	28	34	36	28	0	0	0	0	0	6	12	25	36
Days With ≥ 1.0" Snow Depth	28	27	27	5	0	0	0	0	0	0	4	20	111

Dover-Foxcroft *Piscataquis County* Elevation: 459 ft. Latitude: 45° 11' N Longitude: 69° 15' W

	JAN	FEB	MAR	APR	MAY	JUN	JUL	AUG	SEP	OCT	NOV	DEC	YEAR
Mean Maximum Temp. (°F)	23.5	28.1	36.4	49.4	63.4	72.6	77.7	76.5	68.0	55.0	41.7	29.4	51.8
Mean Temp. (°F)	12.9	16.9	25.9	39.0	51.3	60.7	66.0	64.6	55.9	44.3	33.5	20.5	41.0
Mean Minimum Temp. (°F)	2.3	5.6	15.4	28.6	39.1	48.8	54.3	52.6	43.7	33.6	25.1	11.7	30.1
Extreme Maximum Temp. (°F)	57	57	69	89	93	96	94	93	94	81	68	63	96
Extreme Minimum Temp. (°F)	-31	-29	-18	4	22	30	38	32	23	15	-3	-28	-31
Days Maximum Temp. ≥ 90°F	0	0	0	0	0	1	1	0	0	0	0	0	2
Days Maximum Temp. ≤ 32°F	25	18	10	1	0	0	0	0	0	0	4	19	77
Days Minimum Temp. ≤ 32°F	31	28	30	23	5	0	0	0	2	15	24	30	188
Days Minimum Temp. ≤ 0°F	15	11	4	0	0	0	0	0	0	0	0	6	36
Heating Degree Days (base 65°F)	1,611	1,356	1,204	773	422	159	50	76	277	634	939	1,372	8,873
Cooling Degree Days (base 65°F)	0	0	0	0	3	37	88	69	10	0	0	0	207
Mean Precipitation (in.)	3.17	2.69	3.09	3.62	3.60	3.76	3.56	3.18	3.86	4.12	4.24	3.47	42.36
Extreme Maximum Daily Precip. (in.)	2.43	2.17	2.27	3.09	2.80	2.48	2.88	3.74	3.45	3.30	3.47	1.75	3.74
Days With ≥ 0.1" Precipitation	7	6	6	7	8	8	8	7	6	7	8	7	85
Days With ≥ 0.5" Precipitation	2	1	2	2	2	2	2	2	3	3	3	2	26
Days With ≥ 1.0" Precipitation	1	0	1	1	0	1	1	1	1	1	1	1	10
Mean Snowfall (in.)	22.5	20.7	17.7	5.7	0.1	0.0	0.0	0.0	0.0	0.7	6.1	19.4	92.9
Maximum Snow Depth (in.)	48	60	57	38	1	0	0	0	0	6	15	30	60
Days With ≥ 1.0" Snow Depth	30	27	29	13	0	0	0	0	0	0	6	24	129

East Hiram *Oxford County* Elevation: 527 ft. Latitude: 43° 53' N Longitude: 70° 45' W

	JAN	FEB	MAR	APR	MAY	JUN	JUL	AUG	SEP	OCT	NOV	DEC	YEAR
Mean Maximum Temp. (°F)	28.5	32.2	40.7	54.0	65.9	74.1	79.1	78.0	69.6	57.3	44.8	33.6	54.8
Mean Temp. (°F)	16.8	19.3	29.0	42.0	53.1	62.2	67.1	65.6	57.3	45.6	35.4	23.5	43.1
Mean Minimum Temp. (°F)	5.1	6.4	17.3	29.9	40.3	50.2	55.1	53.2	45.0	33.8	26.0	13.4	31.3
Extreme Maximum Temp. (°F)	64	64	78	92	94	94	97	96	94	83	74	69	97
Extreme Minimum Temp. (°F)	-28	-26	-22	9	22	30	38	33	24	17	-4	-23	-28
Days Maximum Temp. ≥ 90°F	0	0	0	0	0	1	2	1	0	0	0	0	4
Days Maximum Temp. ≤ 32°F	20	14	7	0	0	0	0	0	0	0	3	14	58
Days Minimum Temp. ≤ 32°F	31	28	29	20	5	0	0	0	2	16	24	30	185
Days Minimum Temp. ≤ 0°F	12	10	3	0	0	0	0	0	0	0	0	5	30
Heating Degree Days (base 65°F)	1,489	1,285	1,108	684	368	131	38	61	242	595	882	1,279	8,162
Cooling Degree Days (base 65°F)	0	0	0	1	7	54	111	87	18	1	0	0	279
Mean Precipitation (in.)	3.30	3.08	4.30	4.81	4.13	4.24	4.03	3.57	4.00	4.86	4.90	3.98	49.20
Extreme Maximum Daily Precip. (in.)	2.52	2.88	3.68	3.90	2.95	3.69	3.24	3.91	6.82	5.40	4.14	2.75	6.82
Days With ≥ 0.1" Precipitation	6	6	7	8	8	8	7	7	6	7	8	8	86
Days With ≥ 0.5" Precipitation	2	2	3	3	3	3	2	2	2	3	3	3	31
Days With ≥ 1.0" Precipitation	1	1	1	1	1	1	1	1	1	1	1	1	12
Mean Snowfall (in.)	20.5	17.7	15.8	4.4	trace	0.0	0.0	0.0	0.0	trace	3.3	17.5	79.2
Maximum Snow Depth (in.)	43	45	49	46	trace	0	0	0	0	trace	10	28	49
Days With ≥ 1.0" Snow Depth	29	28	27	7	0	0	0	0	0	0	4	21	116

Eastport *Washington County* Elevation: 84 ft. Latitude: 44° 55' N Longitude: 67° 00' W

	JAN	FEB	MAR	APR	MAY	JUN	JUL	AUG	SEP	OCT	NOV	DEC	YEAR
Mean Maximum Temp. (°F)	***30.4***	***32.0***	38.6	49.5	60.1	68.8	73.9	73.9	66.6	55.6	45.8	***35.6***	***52.6***
Mean Temp. (°F)	***22.1***	***24.0***	30.9	41.5	50.6	58.5	63.7	64.1	57.7	47.9	39.1	***28.2***	***44.0***
Mean Minimum Temp. (°F)	***13.7***	***16.0***	23.2	33.4	41.1	48.1	53.5	54.3	48.8	40.2	32.4	***20.7***	***35.5***
Extreme Maximum Temp. (°F)	61	65	79	84	93	93	98	92	89	83	67	***60***	***98***
Extreme Minimum Temp. (°F)	-16	-14	-13	8	28	34	37	40	31	19	9	***-12***	***-16***
Days Maximum Temp. ≥ 90°F	0	0	0	0	0	0	0	0	0	0	0	***0***	***0***
Days Maximum Temp. ≤ 32°F	16	14	6	0	0	0	0	0	0	0	2	***10***	***48***
Days Minimum Temp. ≤ 32°F	28	25	26	13	1	0	0	0	0	4	16	***25***	***138***
Days Minimum Temp. ≤ 0°F	4	2	1	0	0	0	0	0	0	0	0	***1***	***8***
Heating Degree Days (base 65°F)	***1,324***	***1,152***	1,048	699	440	200	71	64	219	523	769	***1,135***	***7,644***
Cooling Degree Days (base 65°F)	***0***	***0***	0	0	1	12	38	43	7	0	0	***0***	***101***
Mean Precipitation (in.)	***3.74***	***3.19***	4.05	3.62	3.45	3.41	3.09	3.09	4.13	3.88	4.62	***4.20***	***44.47***
Extreme Maximum Daily Precip. (in.)	***3.06***	***2.28***	***2.50***	***3.93***	***2.32***	***2.67***	***4.14***	3.48	4.20	3.56	***3.65***	***2.62***	***4.20***
Days With ≥ 0.1" Precipitation	7	6	7	7	8	7	5	5	6	7	8	***8***	***81***
Days With ≥ 0.5" Precipitation	2	2	3	2	2	2	2	2	3	3	3	***3***	***29***
Days With ≥ 1.0" Precipitation	1	1	1	1	1	1	1	1	1	1	1	***1***	***12***
Mean Snowfall (in.)	***13.7***	***13.0***	12.3	3.9	trace	0.0	0.0	0.0	0.0	0.0	2.0	***12.6***	***57.5***
Maximum Snow Depth (in.)	na	***32***	***20***	***9***	***trace***	***0***	***0***	***0***	***0***	***trace***	***4***	na	na
Days With ≥ 1.0" Snow Depth	na	***17***	***15***	2	0	0	0	0	0	0	***1***	na	na

The period of record for all cooperative weather station data is 1980 – 2009. See User Guide for detailed explanation of data.

Eustis *Franklin County* Elevation: 1,259 ft. Latitude: 45° 13' N Longitude: 70° 29' W

	JAN	FEB	MAR	APR	MAY	JUN	JUL	AUG	SEP	OCT	NOV	DEC	YEAR
Mean Maximum Temp. (°F)	22.0	24.6	33.9	47.2	61.1	70.5	74.5	73.4	65.2	51.4	38.8	27.0	49.1
Mean Temp. (°F)	11.7	13.3	23.2	37.1	48.9	59.1	63.0	61.5	53.4	41.8	31.0	18.3	38.5
Mean Minimum Temp. (°F)	1.5	2.0	12.5	26.9	36.7	47.7	51.7	49.7	41.5	32.1	23.1	9.6	27.9
Extreme Maximum Temp. (°F)	57	59	69	84	90	94	95	92	91	79	68	63	95
Extreme Minimum Temp. (°F)	-34	-36	-23	-2	22	28	37	31	23	14	-12	-25	-36
Days Maximum Temp. ≥ 90°F	0	0	0	0	0	0	0	0	0	0	0	0	0
Days Maximum Temp. ≤ 32°F	25	21	14	2	0	0	0	0	0	0	8	21	91
Days Minimum Temp. ≤ 32°F	31	28	30	25	10	0	0	0	5	17	26	30	202
Days Minimum Temp. ≤ 0°F	15	14	7	0	0	0	0	0	0	0	0	8	44
Heating Degree Days (base 65°F)	1,647	1,457	1,289	832	494	202	104	138	349	714	1,014	1,443	9,683
Cooling Degree Days (base 65°F)	0	0	0	0	3	31	49	38	7	0	0	0	128
Mean Precipitation (in.)	2.53	2.32	2.67	3.26	3.58	4.35	4.07	3.59	3.41	3.88	3.61	2.87	40.14
Extreme Maximum Daily Precip. (in.)	1.68	2.37	2.15	3.05	2.19	2.53	2.55	3.90	4.56	2.73	2.53	1.65	4.56
Days With ≥ 0.1" Precipitation	6	6	6	7	8	9	9	7	7	7	7	7	86
Days With ≥ 0.5" Precipitation	1	1	2	2	2	3	3	2	2	3	3	2	26
Days With ≥ 1.0" Precipitation	0	0	0	1	0	1	1	1	1	1	1	0	7
Mean Snowfall (in.)	27.4	25.6	22.8	10.7	0.2	0.0	0.0	0.0	0.0	2.3	9.9	24.9	123.8
Maximum Snow Depth (in.)	38	45	51	50	13	0	0	0	0	12	17	40	51
Days With ≥ 1.0" Snow Depth	31	28	31	23	1	0	0	0	0	1	10	29	154

Gardiner *Kennebec County* Elevation: 140 ft. Latitude: 44° 13' N Longitude: 69° 47' W

	JAN	FEB	MAR	APR	MAY	JUN	JUL	AUG	SEP	OCT	NOV	DEC	YEAR
Mean Maximum Temp. (°F)	28.6	32.5	40.5	53.4	65.2	74.1	79.4	78.7	70.6	58.2	46.4	34.9	55.2
Mean Temp. (°F)	17.7	20.9	30.3	43.0	54.1	63.4	68.8	67.8	59.3	47.5	37.4	25.3	44.6
Mean Minimum Temp. (°F)	6.9	9.2	20.0	32.5	43.0	52.6	58.1	56.8	48.0	36.7	28.5	15.7	34.0
Extreme Maximum Temp. (°F)	58	62	75	90	94	96	96	97	95	82	73	67	97
Extreme Minimum Temp. (°F)	-34	-25	-15	9	27	36	40	35	23	17	-1	-24	-34
Days Maximum Temp. ≥ 90°F	0	0	0	0	0	1	2	1	0	0	0	0	4
Days Maximum Temp. ≤ 32°F	20	13	6	0	0	0	0	0	0	0	2	12	53
Days Minimum Temp. ≤ 32°F	31	27	28	16	2	0	0	0	0	10	21	30	165
Days Minimum Temp. ≤ 0°F	11	7	2	0	0	0	0	0	0	0	0	3	23
Heating Degree Days (base 65°F)	1,460	1,239	1,069	655	337	105	19	30	187	538	820	1,223	7,682
Cooling Degree Days (base 65°F)	0	0	0	0	7	62	143	124	22	1	0	0	359
Mean Precipitation (in.)	3.04	2.77	3.65	4.18	3.87	3.81	3.43	3.29	3.86	4.47	4.83	3.73	44.93
Extreme Maximum Daily Precip. (in.)	2.40	2.14	3.48	4.11	3.05	3.51	4.15	5.96	5.64	5.50	3.90	2.91	5.96
Days With ≥ 0.1" Precipitation	6	6	6	7	7	8	7	6	6	7	7	6	79
Days With ≥ 0.5" Precipitation	2	2	3	3	3	3	2	2	3	3	3	3	32
Days With ≥ 1.0" Precipitation	1	1	1	1	1	1	1	1	1	1	2	1	13
Mean Snowfall (in.)	17.3	14.5	11.8	2.4	trace	0.0	0.0	0.0	0.0	0.1	2.2	13.1	61.4
Maximum Snow Depth (in.)	33	30	27	11	trace	0	0	0	0	2	10	24	33
Days With ≥ 1.0" Snow Depth	25	25	17	2	0	0	0	0	0	0	2	16	87

Grand Lake Stream *Washington County* Elevation: 290 ft. Latitude: 45° 11' N Longitude: 67° 47' W

	JAN	FEB	MAR	APR	MAY	JUN	JUL	AUG	SEP	OCT	NOV	DEC	YEAR
Mean Maximum Temp. (°F)	26.7	30.8	39.0	51.4	64.3	73.1	78.4	77.7	69.6	57.2	44.9	32.8	53.8
Mean Temp. (°F)	14.8	18.2	27.4	39.9	51.6	60.8	66.4	65.4	56.8	45.2	35.0	22.4	42.0
Mean Minimum Temp. (°F)	2.9	5.6	15.8	28.3	38.8	48.4	54.3	53.0	44.0	33.2	25.0	11.9	30.1
Extreme Maximum Temp. (°F)	58	68	72	82	95	96	95	96	94	84	73	62	96
Extreme Minimum Temp. (°F)	-28	-24	-22	3	20	25	35	33	22	14	-6	-27	-28
Days Maximum Temp. ≥ 90°F	0	0	0	0	0	1	1	1	0	0	0	0	3
Days Maximum Temp. ≤ 32°F	21	16	7	0	0	0	0	0	0	0	2	14	60
Days Minimum Temp. ≤ 32°F	31	28	30	22	6	0	0	0	2	15	24	30	188
Days Minimum Temp. ≤ 0°F	14	10	3	0	0	0	0	0	0	0	0	6	33
Heating Degree Days (base 65°F)	1,550	1,316	1,159	748	412	154	45	60	250	606	894	1,315	8,509
Cooling Degree Days (base 65°F)	0	0	0	0	3	35	94	79	11	0	0	0	222
Mean Precipitation (in.)	3.64	3.09	4.04	3.60	3.54	3.27	3.47	3.09	3.71	4.13	4.54	4.15	44.27
Extreme Maximum Daily Precip. (in.)	2.67	2.13	3.63	2.74	1.96	2.98	3.00	2.58	3.40	3.44	2.95	3.27	3.63
Days With ≥ 0.1" Precipitation	7	6	8	7	7	7	7	6	6	7	8	8	84
Days With ≥ 0.5" Precipitation	3	2	3	2	3	2	2	2	3	3	3	3	31
Days With ≥ 1.0" Precipitation	1	1	1	1	1	1	1	1	1	1	1	1	12
Mean Snowfall (in.)	16.5	11.9	10.2	2.0	0.0	0.0	0.0	0.0	0.0	0.1	1.7	12.6	55.0
Maximum Snow Depth (in.)	na	na	na	na	na	na	na	na	na	na	na	na	na
Days With ≥ 1.0" Snow Depth	na	na	na	1	0	0	0	0	0	0	0	na	na

Lewiston *Androscoggin County* Elevation: 180 ft. Latitude: 44° 06' N Longitude: 70° 13' W

	JAN	FEB	MAR	APR	MAY	JUN	JUL	AUG	SEP	OCT	NOV	DEC	YEAR
Mean Maximum Temp. (°F)	29.7	33.6	41.7	53.9	66.7	75.8	81.1	79.7	70.5	58.4	45.7	34.7	56.0
Mean Temp. (°F)	20.9	24.3	32.9	44.6	56.3	65.6	71.1	69.9	61.1	49.3	38.6	27.3	46.8
Mean Minimum Temp. (°F)	12.0	15.0	24.0	35.2	45.8	55.3	61.1	60.1	51.7	40.2	31.5	19.7	37.6
Extreme Maximum Temp. (°F)	60	65	85	91	96	98	100	99	96	82	74	67	100
Extreme Minimum Temp. (°F)	-28	-15	-8	14	30	38	46	39	31	23	4	-17	-28
Days Maximum Temp. ≥ 90°F	0	0	0	0	1	2	4	3	1	0	0	0	11
Days Maximum Temp. ≤ 32°F	17	13	5	0	0	0	0	0	0	0	2	12	49
Days Minimum Temp. ≤ 32°F	29	26	25	10	0	0	0	0	0	5	17	28	140
Days Minimum Temp. ≤ 0°F	5	3	1	0	0	0	0	0	0	0	0	2	11
Heating Degree Days (base 65°F)	1,360	1,143	988	607	280	69	9	16	151	481	785	1,162	7,051
Cooling Degree Days (base 65°F)	0	0	0	0	15	93	206	176	42	1	0	0	533
Mean Precipitation (in.)	3.03	2.93	4.06	4.38	3.73	3.87	3.55	2.99	3.66	4.26	4.49	3.78	44.73
Extreme Maximum Daily Precip. (in.)	2.33	1.91	3.58	3.97	3.69	5.97	4.10	5.26	6.48	4.58	3.37	2.76	6.48
Days With ≥ 0.1" Precipitation	6	6	7	7	7	7	7	6	6	6	7	7	79
Days With ≥ 0.5" Precipitation	2	2	3	3	3	2	2	2	2	3	3	3	30
Days With ≥ 1.0" Precipitation	1	1	1	1	1	1	1	1	1	1	1	1	12
Mean Snowfall (in.)	17.9	14.1	13.5	3.3	trace	0.0	0.0	0.0	trace	trace	2.2	12.8	63.8
Maximum Snow Depth (in.)	27	na	na	22	trace	0	0	0	trace	trace	10	16	na
Days With ≥ 1.0" Snow Depth	21	na	14	1	0	0	0	0	0	0	2	12	na

The period of record for all cooperative weather station data is 1980 – 2009. See User Guide for detailed explanation of data.

Middle Dam *Oxford County* Elevation: 1,459 ft. Latitude: 44° 47' N Longitude: 70° 55' W

	JAN	FEB	MAR	APR	MAY	JUN	JUL	AUG	SEP	OCT	NOV	DEC	YEAR
Mean Maximum Temp. (°F)	23.8	27.5	36.0	48.0	61.5	70.9	75.4	74.4	66.1	53.3	40.6	28.9	50.5
Mean Temp. (°F)	12.4	14.9	24.3	37.6	50.1	60.0	64.6	63.2	55.0	43.3	32.4	19.3	39.8
Mean Minimum Temp. (°F)	1.1	2.3	12.6	27.2	38.6	49.0	53.6	52.0	43.9	33.3	24.1	9.8	29.0
Extreme Maximum Temp. (°F)	59	63	71	84	87	94	93	91	92	80	70	62	94
Extreme Minimum Temp. (°F)	-33	-31	-21	-1	21	28	39	32	22	16	-9	-28	-33
Days Maximum Temp. ≥ 90°F	0	0	0	0	0	0	0	0	0	0	0	0	0
Days Maximum Temp. ≤ 32°F	24	19	10	1	0	0	0	0	0	0	6	19	79
Days Minimum Temp. ≤ 32°F	30	28	30	23	7	0	0	0	2	15	25	30	190
Days Minimum Temp. ≤ 0°F	15	14	7	0	0	0	0	0	0	0	0	8	44
Heating Degree Days (base 65°F)	1,628	1,410	1,255	814	460	177	70	99	300	665	973	1,410	9,261
Cooling Degree Days (base 65°F)	0	0	0	0	2	32	63	51	8	0	0	0	156
Mean Precipitation (in.)	2.31	2.08	2.71	3.07	3.43	3.97	3.85	3.91	3.44	3.87	3.54	2.70	38.88
Extreme Maximum Daily Precip. (in.)	1.82	1.76	1.74	1.83	2.24	2.27	2.20	3.81	3.17	3.20	4.16	1.65	4.16
Days With ≥ 0.1" Precipitation	6	6	7	8	8	9	8	8	7	8	8	7	90
Days With ≥ 0.5" Precipitation	1	1	1	2	2	3	3	3	2	2	2	1	23
Days With ≥ 1.0" Precipitation	0	0	0	0	1	1	1	1	1	1	1	0	7
Mean Snowfall (in.)	18.1	na	15.8	4.3	0.1	0.0	0.0	0.0	trace	0.7	5.0	na	na
Maximum Snow Depth (in.)	na	na	na	40	2	0	0	0	trace	4	na	na	na
Days With ≥ 1.0" Snow Depth	na	na	na	8	0	0	0	0	0	0	5	22	na

Millinocket *Penobscot County* Elevation: 359 ft. Latitude: 45° 39' N Longitude: 68° 42' W

	JAN	FEB	MAR	APR	MAY	JUN	JUL	AUG	SEP	OCT	NOV	DEC	YEAR
Mean Maximum Temp. (°F)	23.9	27.9	37.0	50.7	64.3	73.6	78.5	77.3	67.7	54.9	42.2	29.6	52.3
Mean Temp. (°F)	13.8	16.7	26.4	40.4	52.9	62.7	67.8	66.2	57.0	45.2	34.6	21.2	42.1
Mean Minimum Temp. (°F)	3.5	5.4	15.8	30.0	41.1	51.7	57.1	55.0	46.2	35.6	26.9	12.7	31.7
Extreme Maximum Temp. (°F)	56	62	69	87	93	96	96	96	92	82	67	61	96
Extreme Minimum Temp. (°F)	-35	-31	-23	2	25	34	41	32	22	19	-5	-26	-35
Days Maximum Temp. ≥ 90°F	0	0	0	0	0	1	2	1	0	0	0	0	4
Days Maximum Temp. ≤ 32°F	24	19	10	1	0	0	0	0	0	0	4	18	76
Days Minimum Temp. ≤ 32°F	31	28	29	20	4	0	0	0	1	12	22	29	176
Days Minimum Temp. ≤ 0°F	14	11	4	0	0	0	0	0	0	0	0	6	35
Heating Degree Days (base 65°F)	1,584	1,360	1,190	731	375	120	30	53	249	606	906	1,352	8,556
Cooling Degree Days (base 65°F)	0	0	0	0	6	58	123	97	16	0	0	0	300
Mean Precipitation (in.)	3.05	2.44	2.89	3.67	3.77	4.11	3.97	3.73	3.76	4.35	4.17	3.21	43.12
Extreme Maximum Daily Precip. (in.)	1.93	1.83	2.91	3.21	2.73	2.39	3.50	3.27	3.35	3.83	2.99	2.13	3.83
Days With ≥ 0.1" Precipitation	6	6	6	8	8	8	9	7	7	7	8	7	87
Days With ≥ 0.5" Precipitation	2	2	2	2	2	3	3	2	2	3	3	2	28
Days With ≥ 1.0" Precipitation	1	0	0	1	1	1	1	1	1	1	1	1	10
Mean Snowfall (in.)	22.4	17.8	17.5	4.9	0.0	0.0	0.0	0.0	0.0	0.4	5.8	16.9	85.7
Maximum Snow Depth (in.)	na	na	na	na	na	na	na	na	na	na	na	na	na
Days With ≥ 1.0" Snow Depth	na	na	na	5	0	0	0	0	0	0	3	na	na

Newcastle *Lincoln County* Elevation: 189 ft. Latitude: 44° 03' N Longitude: 69° 32' W

	JAN	FEB	MAR	APR	MAY	JUN	JUL	AUG	SEP	OCT	NOV	DEC	YEAR
Mean Maximum Temp. (°F)	29.5	33.1	40.7	53.1	64.5	72.8	77.8	76.6	67.9	56.5	45.6	34.7	54.4
Mean Temp. (°F)	21.4	24.7	32.5	43.8	54.2	63.0	68.3	67.4	59.4	48.5	38.7	27.5	45.8
Mean Minimum Temp. (°F)	13.3	16.3	24.2	34.5	43.9	53.1	58.7	58.1	50.9	40.5	31.8	20.2	37.1
Extreme Maximum Temp. (°F)	57	60	85	82	94	93	96	95	93	77	71	64	96
Extreme Minimum Temp. (°F)	-20	-18	-9	12	27	36	45	40	29	24	3	-20	-20
Days Maximum Temp. ≥ 90°F	0	0	0	0	0	0	1	0	0	0	0	0	1
Days Maximum Temp. ≤ 32°F	19	13	5	0	0	0	0	0	0	0	2	13	52
Days Minimum Temp. ≤ 32°F	30	26	25	12	1	0	0	0	0	5	17	28	144
Days Minimum Temp. ≤ 0°F	5	2	1	0	0	0	0	0	0	0	0	1	9
Heating Degree Days (base 65°F)	1,345	1,132	1,000	629	334	104	18	30	181	506	781	1,155	7,215
Cooling Degree Days (base 65°F)	0	0	0	0	7	50	127	111	19	0	0	0	314
Mean Precipitation (in.)	3.62	3.25	4.29	4.40	4.07	3.75	3.33	3.05	4.01	4.27	5.02	4.31	47.37
Extreme Maximum Daily Precip. (in.)	2.13	2.21	3.13	4.16	2.37	3.06	3.05	3.21	5.45	4.02	4.27	3.75	5.45
Days With ≥ 0.1" Precipitation	7	6	7	8	8	7	7	5	6	7	8	8	84
Days With ≥ 0.5" Precipitation	3	2	3	3	3	2	2	2	3	3	3	3	32
Days With ≥ 1.0" Precipitation	1	1	1	1	1	1	1	1	1	1	1	1	12
Mean Snowfall (in.)	19.2	15.8	13.5	3.9	trace	0.0	0.0	0.0	0.0	0.2	3.1	16.1	71.8
Maximum Snow Depth (in.)	32	31	33	13	trace	0	0	0	0	trace	11	19	33
Days With ≥ 1.0" Snow Depth	24	24	18	2	0	0	0	0	0	0	3	16	87

Presque Isle *Aroostook County* Elevation: 599 ft. Latitude: 46° 39' N Longitude: 68° 00' W

	JAN	FEB	MAR	APR	MAY	JUN	JUL	AUG	SEP	OCT	NOV	DEC	YEAR
Mean Maximum Temp. (°F)	21.6	25.8	35.4	50.0	64.9	73.8	77.7	76.6	67.6	53.8	39.4	27.2	51.1
Mean Temp. (°F)	11.9	15.6	25.7	39.8	52.7	61.9	66.6	65.2	56.6	44.7	32.7	19.1	41.0
Mean Minimum Temp. (°F)	2.2	5.3	15.9	29.6	40.5	49.9	55.4	53.8	45.5	35.5	25.9	11.0	30.9
Extreme Maximum Temp. (°F)	54	59	67	84	94	94	96	93	90	79	68	55	96
Extreme Minimum Temp. (°F)	-35	-33	-29	-1	24	30	35	32	23	16	-6	-31	-35
Days Maximum Temp. ≥ 90°F	0	0	0	0	0	1	1	1	0	0	0	0	3
Days Maximum Temp. ≤ 32°F	26	21	11	1	0	0	0	0	0	0	7	21	87
Days Minimum Temp. ≤ 32°F	30	28	29	20	5	0	0	0	2	12	23	30	179
Days Minimum Temp. ≤ 0°F	14	11	5	0	0	0	0	0	0	0	0	7	37
Heating Degree Days (base 65°F)	1,642	1,392	1,213	748	380	138	43	70	263	624	963	1,418	8,894
Cooling Degree Days (base 65°F)	0	0	0	0	6	52	99	84	17	1	0	0	259
Mean Precipitation (in.)	2.28	1.60	2.10	2.45	3.36	3.33	3.82	3.72	3.32	3.82	3.16	2.59	35.55
Extreme Maximum Daily Precip. (in.)	1.98	0.99	2.10	1.73	1.67	1.93	2.30	2.40	3.16	3.79	2.44	1.69	3.79
Days With ≥ 0.1" Precipitation	6	5	5	7	8	8	9	7	7	8	7	6	83
Days With ≥ 0.5" Precipitation	1	1	1	1	2	2	2	2	2	3	2	1	20
Days With ≥ 1.0" Precipitation	0	0	0	0	0	1	1	1	1	1	1	0	6
Mean Snowfall (in.)	21.9	18.4	16.9	5.6	0.2	0.0	0.0	0.0	0.1	0.9	6.5	17.8	88.3
Maximum Snow Depth (in.)	47	na	58	39	1	0	0	0	0	5	20	43	na
Days With ≥ 1.0" Snow Depth	26	26	24	6	0	0	0	0	0	0	6	19	107

The period of record for all cooperative weather station data is 1980 – 2009. See User Guide for detailed explanation of data.

Sanford 2 NNW *York County* Elevation: 279 ft. Latitude: 43° 28' N Longitude: 70° 47' W

	JAN	FEB	MAR	APR	MAY	JUN	JUL	AUG	SEP	OCT	NOV	DEC	YEAR
Mean Maximum Temp. (°F)	32.6	36.8	45.2	58.2	69.3	77.7	82.3	81.2	73.3	61.4	48.8	37.5	58.7
Mean Temp. (°F)	22.7	25.9	34.4	46.0	56.5	65.5	70.5	69.5	61.6	49.8	39.7	28.6	47.6
Mean Minimum Temp. (°F)	12.7	15.0	23.5	33.8	43.7	53.2	58.6	57.7	49.7	38.2	30.5	19.6	36.4
Extreme Maximum Temp. (°F)	68	68	88	91	95	97	98	97	94	84	74	73	98
Extreme Minimum Temp. (°F)	-24	-18	-11	-10	22	31	43	36	28	19	-1	-18	-24
Days Maximum Temp. ≥ 90°F	0	0	0	0	1	2	3	2	0	0	0	0	8
Days Maximum Temp. ≤ 32°F	15	9	3	0	0	0	0	0	0	0	1	9	37
Days Minimum Temp. ≤ 32°F	30	27	26	14	2	0	0	0	1	9	19	28	156
Days Minimum Temp. ≤ 0°F	6	3	1	0	0	0	0	0	0	0	0	2	12
Heating Degree Days (base 65°F)	1,306	1,097	942	564	273	70	11	19	142	466	753	1,122	6,765
Cooling Degree Days (base 65°F)	0	0	0	2	17	91	187	165	46	2	0	0	510
Mean Precipitation (in.)	3.50	3.50	4.59	4.57	4.35	4.15	4.17	3.83	3.99	4.61	5.07	4.09	50.42
Extreme Maximum Daily Precip. (in.)	2.37	2.94	3.27	3.50	4.35	4.45	2.59	4.71	5.44	4.15	3.87	2.92	5.44
Days With ≥ 0.1" Precipitation	7	6	7	7	8	7	7	6	6	7	8	7	83
Days With ≥ 0.5" Precipitation	3	2	3	3	3	3	3	2	2	3	4	3	34
Days With ≥ 1.0" Precipitation	1	1	1	1	1	1	1	1	1	1	1	1	12
Mean Snowfall (in.)	*8.2*	*6.0*	*6.3*	0.6	trace	0.0	0.0	0.0	0.0	trace	0.7	*7.2*	*29.0*
Maximum Snow Depth (in.)	na	na	na	na	na	na	*0*	*0*	*0*	na	na	na	na
Days With ≥ 1.0" Snow Depth	na	na	na	0	0	0	0	0	0	0	0	na	na

Vanceboro 2 *Washington County* Elevation: 419 ft. Latitude: 45° 34' N Longitude: 67° 26' W

	JAN	FEB	MAR	APR	MAY	JUN	JUL	AUG	SEP	OCT	NOV	DEC	YEAR
Mean Maximum Temp. (°F)	26.0	30.1	38.5	51.4	65.4	74.8	79.3	78.6	69.8	57.3	43.2	31.6	53.8
Mean Temp. (°F)	14.9	18.3	27.7	40.5	52.5	61.8	67.1	66.1	57.4	45.9	34.8	21.9	42.4
Mean Minimum Temp. (°F)	3.9	6.5	16.9	29.5	39.5	48.9	54.8	53.5	45.0	34.5	26.3	12.3	31.0
Extreme Maximum Temp. (°F)	57	66	69	88	97	96	96	95	96	82	71	60	97
Extreme Minimum Temp. (°F)	-29	-25	-21	3	20	29	34	31	26	12	-5	-32	-32
Days Maximum Temp. ≥ 90°F	0	0	0	0	0	1	2	2	0	0	0	0	5
Days Maximum Temp. ≤ 32°F	22	17	8	0	0	0	0	0	0	0	3	17	67
Days Minimum Temp. ≤ 32°F	30	27	29	20	6	0	0	0	2	14	23	30	181
Days Minimum Temp. ≤ 0°F	14	10	3	0	0	0	0	0	0	0	0	6	33
Heating Degree Days (base 65°F)	1,547	1,314	1,148	730	385	134	35	54	236	586	899	1,328	8,396
Cooling Degree Days (base 65°F)	0	0	0	0	3	46	107	94	15	1	0	0	266
Mean Precipitation (in.)	3.17	2.46	3.29	3.48	4.08	3.57	3.98	3.41	4.02	4.09	4.73	3.45	43.73
Extreme Maximum Daily Precip. (in.)	1.98	2.53	3.00	2.33	2.10	3.52	3.30	2.50	2.90	3.10	3.42	2.34	3.52
Days With ≥ 0.1" Precipitation	6	6	7	7	8	7	8	6	7	7	8	7	84
Days With ≥ 0.5" Precipitation	2	2	2	2	3	2	3	2	3	3	3	2	29
Days With ≥ 1.0" Precipitation	1	0	1	1	1	1	1	1	1	1	1	1	11
Mean Snowfall (in.)	21.8	16.8	17.2	5.4	0.1	0.0	0.0	0.0	0.0	0.2	5.0	16.2	82.7
Maximum Snow Depth (in.)	36	42	43	33	trace	0	0	0	0	3	17	30	43
Days With ≥ 1.0" Snow Depth	26	25	24	5	0	0	0	0	0	0	4	17	101

Waterville Treatment Plant *Kennebec County* Elevation: 73 ft. Latitude: 44° 32' N Longitude: 69° 39' W

	JAN	FEB	MAR	APR	MAY	JUN	JUL	AUG	SEP	OCT	NOV	DEC	YEAR
Mean Maximum Temp. (°F)	29.6	33.9	42.1	55.1	67.3	75.9	80.9	80.1	71.8	59.3	46.8	35.0	56.5
Mean Temp. (°F)	18.5	21.9	31.0	43.4	54.6	64.0	69.3	68.2	59.8	48.1	37.6	25.3	45.1
Mean Minimum Temp. (°F)	7.3	9.8	20.0	31.7	41.9	51.9	57.6	56.2	47.8	36.8	28.4	15.6	33.7
Extreme Maximum Temp. (°F)	58	61	75	91	96	96	96	98	96	84	73	67	98
Extreme Minimum Temp. (°F)	-32	-28	-17	8	21	35	39	35	23	18	-1	-27	-32
Days Maximum Temp. ≥ 90°F	0	0	0	0	0	1	2	2	0	0	0	0	5
Days Maximum Temp. ≤ 32°F	18	11	5	0	0	0	0	0	0	0	2	11	47
Days Minimum Temp. ≤ 32°F	31	27	28	17	3	0	0	0	1	10	21	29	167
Days Minimum Temp. ≤ 0°F	10	7	2	0	0	0	0	0	0	0	0	4	23
Heating Degree Days (base 65°F)	1,435	1,212	1,046	642	322	89	16	28	175	518	814	1,223	7,520
Cooling Degree Days (base 65°F)	0	0	0	0	7	66	156	133	26	1	0	0	389
Mean Precipitation (in.)	2.55	2.33	3.33	3.61	3.61	4.03	3.62	3.41	3.77	4.33	4.02	3.03	41.64
Extreme Maximum Daily Precip. (in.)	2.30	2.12	2.55	3.30	2.40	2.58	3.20	3.10	5.68	3.48	2.70	2.13	5.68
Days With ≥ 0.1" Precipitation	5	5	6	7	7	8	7	7	6	7	7	6	78
Days With ≥ 0.5" Precipitation	2	2	2	2	3	3	2	2	3	3	3	2	29
Days With ≥ 1.0" Precipitation	0	0	1	1	1	1	1	1	1	1	1	1	10
Mean Snowfall (in.)	16.4	13.8	10.1	2.1	0.0	0.0	0.0	0.0	0.0	0.1	2.4	15.4	60.3
Maximum Snow Depth (in.)	26	30	30	18	0	0	0	0	0	4	9	19	30
Days With ≥ 1.0" Snow Depth	26	25	17	2	0	0	0	0	0	0	2	18	90

West Buxton 2 NNW *York County* Elevation: 149 ft. Latitude: 43° 42' N Longitude: 70° 37' W

	JAN	FEB	MAR	APR	MAY	JUN	JUL	AUG	SEP	OCT	NOV	DEC	YEAR
Mean Maximum Temp. (°F)	30.6	34.5	42.8	55.4	66.5	75.4	80.3	79.1	70.8	59.0	47.3	35.9	56.5
Mean Temp. (°F)	19.0	22.2	31.4	43.1	53.7	63.2	68.4	67.0	58.6	46.9	36.9	25.5	44.7
Mean Minimum Temp. (°F)	7.4	9.9	20.1	30.8	40.9	50.9	56.4	54.9	46.3	34.8	26.5	15.0	32.8
Extreme Maximum Temp. (°F)	69	63	88	94	94	95	98	96	94	83	74	70	98
Extreme Minimum Temp. (°F)	-33	-24	-18	11	20	32	38	32	23	15	-3	-31	-33
Days Maximum Temp. ≥ 90°F	0	0	0	0	0	2	2	2	0	0	0	0	6
Days Maximum Temp. ≤ 32°F	18	11	5	0	0	0	0	0	0	0	2	11	47
Days Minimum Temp. ≤ 32°F	31	28	28	18	5	0	0	0	2	13	23	30	178
Days Minimum Temp. ≤ 0°F	10	7	2	0	0	0	0	0	0	0	0	4	23
Heating Degree Days (base 65°F)	1,420	1,203	1,033	650	350	110	24	43	208	554	836	1,218	7,649
Cooling Degree Days (base 65°F)	0	0	0	1	8	62	135	113	22	0	0	0	341
Mean Precipitation (in.)	3.18	3.13	4.23	4.78	4.18	4.20	4.11	3.26	3.86	4.81	4.94	3.77	48.45
Extreme Maximum Daily Precip. (in.)	2.61	3.69	4.14	4.67	4.21	4.54	4.07	3.63	5.71	7.35	4.19	3.10	7.35
Days With ≥ 0.1" Precipitation	6	6	7	7	8	7	7	6	6	6	7	7	80
Days With ≥ 0.5" Precipitation	2	2	3	3	3	3	3	2	2	3	3	3	32
Days With ≥ 1.0" Precipitation	1	1	1	1	1	1	1	1	1	1	1	1	12
Mean Snowfall (in.)	na	na	na	*trace*	0.0	0.0	0.0	0.0	0.0	trace	*trace*	na	na
Maximum Snow Depth (in.)	na	na	na	*0*	*0*	*0*	*0*	*0*	*0*	*trace*	na	na	na
Days With ≥ 1.0" Snow Depth	na	na	na	0	0	0	0	0	0	0	*0*	*6*	na

The period of record for all cooperative weather station data is 1980 – 2009. See User Guide for detailed explanation of data.

Maine Weather Station Rankings

Annual Extreme Maximum Temperature

Highest			Lowest		
Rank	**Station Name**	**°F**	**Rank**	**Station Name**	**°F**
1	Lewiston	***100***	1	Brassua Dam	94
2	Augusta Airport	98	1	Middle Dam	94
2	Eastport	***98***	3	Allagash	***95***
2	Portland Intl Jetport	98	3	Bridgewater	95
2	Sanford 2 NNW	98	3	Bridgton 3 NW	95
2	Waterville Treatment Plant	98	3	Caribou Municipal Arpt	95
2	West Buxton 2 NNW	98	3	Eustis	***95***
8	Bangor Airport	***97***	8	Acadia National Park	96
8	East Hiram	97	8	Belfast	96
8	Gardiner	97	8	Corinna	96
8	Vanceboro 2	97	8	Dover-Foxcroft	96
12	Acadia National Park	96	8	Grand Lake Stream	96
12	Belfast	96	8	Millinocket	***96***
12	Corinna	96	8	Newcastle	96
12	Dover-Foxcroft	96	8	Presque Isle	96
12	Grand Lake Stream	96	16	Bangor Airport	***97***
12	Millinocket	***96***	16	East Hiram	97
12	Newcastle	96	16	Gardiner	97
12	Presque Isle	96	16	Vanceboro 2	97
20	Allagash	***95***	20	Augusta Airport	98
20	Bridgewater	95	20	Eastport	***98***
20	Bridgton 3 NW	95	20	Portland Intl Jetport	98
20	Caribou Municipal Arpt	95	20	Sanford 2 NNW	98
20	Eustis	***95***	20	Waterville Treatment Plant	98
25	Brassua Dam	94	20	West Buxton 2 NNW	98

Annual Mean Maximum Temperature

Highest			Lowest		
Rank	**Station Name**	**°F**	**Rank**	**Station Name**	**°F**
1	Sanford 2 NNW	58.7	1	Eustis	***49.1***
2	Waterville Treatment Plant	56.5	2	Caribou Municipal Arpt	49.2
2	West Buxton 2 NNW	56.5	3	Allagash	***49.4***
4	Lewiston	***56.0***	4	Brassua Dam	49.6
5	Belfast	55.6	5	Middle Dam	50.5
5	Portland Intl Jetport	55.6	6	Presque Isle	51.2
7	Acadia National Park	55.5	7	Bridgewater	51.3
8	Gardiner	55.2	8	Dover-Foxcroft	51.8
9	East Hiram	54.8	9	Millinocket	***52.3***
10	Augusta Airport	54.6	10	Eastport	***52.6***
11	Corinna	54.5	11	Grand Lake Stream	53.8
12	Newcastle	54.4	11	Vanceboro 2	53.8
13	Bangor Airport	***54.3***	13	Bridgton 3 NW	54.2
14	Bridgton 3 NW	54.2	14	Bangor Airport	***54.3***
15	Grand Lake Stream	53.8	15	Newcastle	54.4
15	Vanceboro 2	53.8	16	Corinna	54.5
17	Eastport	***52.6***	17	Augusta Airport	54.6
18	Millinocket	***52.3***	18	East Hiram	54.8
19	Dover-Foxcroft	51.8	19	Gardiner	55.2
20	Bridgewater	51.3	20	Acadia National Park	55.5
21	Presque Isle	51.2	21	Belfast	55.6
22	Middle Dam	50.5	21	Portland Intl Jetport	55.6
23	Brassua Dam	49.6	23	Lewiston	***56.0***
24	Allagash	***49.4***	24	Waterville Treatment Plant	56.5
25	Caribou Municipal Arpt	49.2	24	West Buxton 2 NNW	56.5

Rankings include 25 highest/lowest stations. If state has less than 25 stations, all stations are included. The period of record is 1980–2009. See User Guide for detailed explanation of data.

Annual Mean Temperature

Highest			Lowest		
Rank	Station Name	°F	Rank	Station Name	°F
1	Sanford 2 NNW	47.6	1	Allagash	***36.5***
2	Lewiston	***46.8***	2	Eustis	***38.5***
3	Portland Intl Jetport	46.3	3	Brassua Dam	39.1
4	Acadia National Park	45.8	4	Caribou Municipal Arpt	39.6
4	Newcastle	45.8	5	Middle Dam	39.8
6	Augusta Airport	45.7	6	Bridgewater	40.3
7	Belfast	45.3	7	Dover-Foxcroft	41.0
8	Waterville Treatment Plant	45.1	7	Presque Isle	41.0
9	West Buxton 2 NNW	44.7	9	Grand Lake Stream	42.0
10	Gardiner	44.6	10	Millinocket	***42.1***
11	Bangor Airport	***44.4***	11	Vanceboro 2	42.4
12	Eastport	***44.0***	12	Corinna	42.6
13	Bridgton 3 NW	43.2	13	East Hiram	43.1
14	East Hiram	43.1	14	Bridgton 3 NW	43.2
15	Corinna	42.6	15	Eastport	***44.0***
16	Vanceboro 2	42.4	16	Bangor Airport	***44.4***
17	Millinocket	***42.1***	17	Gardiner	44.6
18	Grand Lake Stream	42.0	18	West Buxton 2 NNW	44.7
19	Dover-Foxcroft	41.0	19	Waterville Treatment Plant	45.1
19	Presque Isle	41.0	20	Belfast	45.3
21	Bridgewater	40.3	21	Augusta Airport	45.7
22	Middle Dam	39.8	22	Acadia National Park	45.8
23	Caribou Municipal Arpt	39.6	22	Newcastle	45.8
24	Brassua Dam	39.1	24	Portland Intl Jetport	46.3
25	Eustis	***38.5***	25	Lewiston	***46.8***

Annual Mean Minimum Temperature

Highest			Lowest		
Rank	Station Name	°F	Rank	Station Name	°F
1	Lewiston	***37.6***	1	Allagash	***23.5***
2	Newcastle	37.1	2	Eustis	***27.9***
3	Portland Intl Jetport	37.0	3	Brassua Dam	28.6
4	Augusta Airport	36.9	4	Middle Dam	29.0
5	Sanford 2 NNW	36.4	5	Bridgewater	29.3
6	Acadia National Park	36.0	6	Caribou Municipal Arpt	30.0
7	Eastport	***35.5***	7	Dover-Foxcroft	30.1
8	Belfast	34.9	7	Grand Lake Stream	30.1
9	Bangor Airport	***34.5***	9	Corinna	30.7
10	Gardiner	34.0	10	Presque Isle	30.9
11	Waterville Treatment Plant	33.8	11	Vanceboro 2	31.0
12	West Buxton 2 NNW	32.8	12	East Hiram	31.3
13	Bridgton 3 NW	32.1	13	Millinocket	***31.8***
14	Millinocket	***31.8***	14	Bridgton 3 NW	32.1
15	East Hiram	31.3	15	West Buxton 2 NNW	32.8
16	Vanceboro 2	31.0	16	Waterville Treatment Plant	33.8
17	Presque Isle	30.9	17	Gardiner	34.0
18	Corinna	30.7	18	Bangor Airport	***34.5***
19	Dover-Foxcroft	30.1	19	Belfast	34.9
19	Grand Lake Stream	30.1	20	Eastport	***35.5***
21	Caribou Municipal Arpt	30.0	21	Acadia National Park	36.0
22	Bridgewater	29.3	22	Sanford 2 NNW	36.4
23	Middle Dam	29.0	23	Augusta Airport	36.9
24	Brassua Dam	28.6	24	Portland Intl Jetport	37.0
25	Eustis	***27.9***	25	Newcastle	37.1

Rankings include 25 highest/lowest stations. If state has less than 25 stations, all stations are included. The period of record is 1980–2009. See User Guide for detailed explanation of data.

Annual Extreme Minimum Temperature

Highest

Rank	Station Name	°F
1	Eastport	*-16*
2	Augusta Airport	-18
3	Newcastle	-20
3	Portland Intl Jetport	-20
5	Acadia National Park	-21
6	Sanford 2 NNW	-24
7	Bridgton 3 NW	-26
8	Belfast	-27
9	East Hiram	-28
9	Grand Lake Stream	-28
9	Lewiston	*-28*
12	Bangor Airport	*-29*
13	Dover-Foxcroft	-31
14	Vanceboro 2	-32
14	Waterville Treatment Plant	-32
16	Middle Dam	-33
16	West Buxton 2 NNW	-33
18	Gardiner	-34
19	Millinocket	*-35*
19	Presque Isle	-35
21	Eustis	*-36*
22	Brassua Dam	-37
22	Caribou Municipal Arpt	-37
24	Corinna	-38
25	Bridgewater	-43

Lowest

Rank	Station Name	°F
1	Allagash	*-47*
2	Bridgewater	-43
3	Corinna	-38
4	Brassua Dam	-37
4	Caribou Municipal Arpt	-37
6	Eustis	*-36*
7	Millinocket	*-35*
7	Presque Isle	-35
9	Gardiner	-34
10	Middle Dam	-33
10	West Buxton 2 NNW	-33
12	Vanceboro 2	-32
12	Waterville Treatment Plant	-32
14	Dover-Foxcroft	-31
15	Bangor Airport	*-29*
16	East Hiram	-28
16	Grand Lake Stream	-28
16	Lewiston	*-28*
19	Belfast	-27
20	Bridgton 3 NW	-26
21	Sanford 2 NNW	-24
22	Acadia National Park	-21
23	Newcastle	-20
23	Portland Intl Jetport	-20
25	Augusta Airport	-18

July Mean Maximum Temperature

Highest

Rank	Station Name	°F
1	Sanford 2 NNW	82.3
2	Lewiston	*81.1*
3	Waterville Treatment Plant	80.9
4	West Buxton 2 NNW	80.3
5	Gardiner	79.4
6	Corinna	79.3
6	Vanceboro 2	79.3
8	Augusta Airport	79.2
9	Bangor Airport	*79.1*
9	East Hiram	79.1
11	Portland Intl Jetport	78.8
12	Acadia National Park	78.7
12	Belfast	78.7
14	Millinocket	*78.5*
15	Grand Lake Stream	78.4
16	Bridgton 3 NW	77.8
16	Newcastle	77.8
18	Dover-Foxcroft	77.7
18	Presque Isle	77.7
20	Bridgewater	77.6
21	Allagash	*76.4*
22	Caribou Municipal Arpt	75.9
23	Middle Dam	75.4
24	Brassua Dam	75.0
25	Eustis	*74.5*

Lowest

Rank	Station Name	°F
1	Eastport	73.9
2	Eustis	*74.5*
3	Brassua Dam	75.0
4	Middle Dam	75.4
5	Caribou Municipal Arpt	75.9
6	Allagash	*76.4*
7	Bridgewater	77.6
8	Dover-Foxcroft	77.7
8	Presque Isle	77.7
10	Bridgton 3 NW	77.8
10	Newcastle	77.8
12	Grand Lake Stream	78.4
13	Millinocket	*78.5*
14	Acadia National Park	78.7
14	Belfast	78.7
16	Portland Intl Jetport	78.8
17	Bangor Airport	*79.1*
17	East Hiram	79.1
19	Augusta Airport	79.2
20	Corinna	79.3
20	Vanceboro 2	79.3
22	Gardiner	79.4
23	West Buxton 2 NNW	80.3
24	Waterville Treatment Plant	80.9
25	Lewiston	*81.1*

Rankings include 25 highest/lowest stations. If state has less than 25 stations, all stations are included. The period of record is 1980–2009. See User Guide for detailed explanation of data.

January Mean Minimum Temperature

Highest Rank	Station Name	°F	Lowest Rank	Station Name	°F
1	Eastport	*13.7*	1	Allagash	*-8.3*
2	Newcastle	13.3	2	Brassua Dam	-0.4
2	Portland Intl Jetport	13.3	3	Bridgewater	0.3
4	Sanford 2 NNW	12.7	4	Caribou Municipal Arpt	0.5
5	Acadia National Park	12.1	5	Middle Dam	1.1
6	Lewiston	*12.0*	6	Corinna	1.5
7	Augusta Airport	11.3	6	Eustis	*1.5*
8	Belfast	10.4	8	Presque Isle	2.2
9	Bangor Airport	*7.5*	9	Dover-Foxcroft	2.3
10	West Buxton 2 NNW	7.4	10	Grand Lake Stream	2.9
11	Waterville Treatment Plant	7.3	11	Millinocket	3.5
12	Gardiner	6.9	12	Vanceboro 2	3.9
13	Bridgton 3 NW	5.6	13	East Hiram	5.1
14	East Hiram	5.1	14	Bridgton 3 NW	5.6
15	Vanceboro 2	3.9	15	Gardiner	6.9
16	Millinocket	3.5	16	Waterville Treatment Plant	7.3
17	Grand Lake Stream	2.9	17	West Buxton 2 NNW	7.4
18	Dover-Foxcroft	2.3	18	Bangor Airport	*7.5*
19	Presque Isle	2.2	19	Belfast	10.4
20	Corinna	1.5	20	Augusta Airport	11.3
20	Eustis	*1.5*	21	Lewiston	*12.0*
22	Middle Dam	1.1	22	Acadia National Park	12.1
23	Caribou Municipal Arpt	0.5	23	Sanford 2 NNW	12.7
24	Bridgewater	0.3	24	Newcastle	13.3
25	Brassua Dam	-0.4	24	Portland Intl Jetport	13.3

Number of Days Annually Maximum Temperature ≥ 90°F

Highest Rank	Station Name	Days	Lowest Rank	Station Name	Days
1	Lewiston	*11*	1	Brassua Dam	0
2	Sanford 2 NNW	8	1	Eastport	*0*
3	West Buxton 2 NNW	6	1	Eustis	*0*
4	Vanceboro 2	5	1	Middle Dam	0
4	Waterville Treatment Plant	5	5	Newcastle	1
6	Augusta Airport	4	6	Allagash	*2*
6	East Hiram	4	6	Bridgewater	2
6	Gardiner	4	6	Caribou Municipal Arpt	2
6	Millinocket	*4*	6	Dover-Foxcroft	2
6	Portland Intl Jetport	4	10	Acadia National Park	3
11	Acadia National Park	3	10	Bangor Airport	*3*
11	Bangor Airport	*3*	10	Belfast	3
11	Belfast	3	10	Bridgton 3 NW	3
11	Bridgton 3 NW	3	10	Corinna	3
11	Corinna	3	10	Grand Lake Stream	3
11	Grand Lake Stream	3	10	Presque Isle	3
11	Presque Isle	3	17	Augusta Airport	4
18	Allagash	*2*	17	East Hiram	4
18	Bridgewater	2	17	Gardiner	4
18	Caribou Municipal Arpt	2	17	Millinocket	*4*
18	Dover-Foxcroft	2	17	Portland Intl Jetport	4
22	Newcastle	1	22	Vanceboro 2	5
23	Brassua Dam	0	22	Waterville Treatment Plant	5
23	Eastport	*0*	24	West Buxton 2 NNW	6
23	Eustis	*0*	25	Sanford 2 NNW	8

Rankings include 25 highest/lowest stations. If state has less than 25 stations, all stations are included. The period of record is 1980–2009. See User Guide for detailed explanation of data.

Number of Days Annually Maximum Temperature ≤ 32°F

Highest			Lowest		
Rank	Station Name	Days	Rank	Station Name	Days
1	Allagash	***93***	1	Sanford 2 NNW	37
1	Caribou Municipal Arpt	93	2	Belfast	43
3	Eustis	***91***	2	Portland Intl Jetport	43
4	Presque Isle	87	4	Acadia National Park	44
5	Brassua Dam	86	5	Waterville Treatment Plant	47
6	Bridgewater	82	5	West Buxton 2 NNW	47
7	Middle Dam	79	7	Eastport	***48***
8	Dover-Foxcroft	77	8	Lewiston	***49***
9	Millinocket	***76***	9	Newcastle	52
10	Vanceboro 2	67	10	Gardiner	53
11	Corinna	61	11	Augusta Airport	57
12	Grand Lake Stream	60	12	Bridgton 3 NW	58
13	Bangor Airport	***59***	12	East Hiram	58
14	Bridgton 3 NW	58	14	Bangor Airport	***59***
14	East Hiram	58	15	Grand Lake Stream	60
16	Augusta Airport	57	16	Corinna	61
17	Gardiner	53	17	Vanceboro 2	67
18	Newcastle	52	18	Millinocket	***76***
19	Lewiston	***49***	19	Dover-Foxcroft	77
20	Eastport	***48***	20	Middle Dam	79
21	Waterville Treatment Plant	47	21	Bridgewater	82
21	West Buxton 2 NNW	47	22	Brassua Dam	86
23	Acadia National Park	44	23	Presque Isle	87
24	Belfast	43	24	Eustis	***91***
24	Portland Intl Jetport	43	25	Allagash	***93***

Number of Days Annually Minimum Temperature ≤ 32°F

Highest			Lowest		
Rank	Station Name	Days	Rank	Station Name	Days
1	Allagash	***217***	1	Eastport	***138***
2	Eustis	***202***	2	Lewiston	***140***
3	Brassua Dam	194	3	Augusta Airport	144
4	Middle Dam	190	3	Newcastle	144
5	Bridgewater	189	5	Acadia National Park	145
6	Dover-Foxcroft	188	6	Portland Intl Jetport	149
6	Grand Lake Stream	188	7	Sanford 2 NNW	156
8	East Hiram	185	8	Bangor Airport	***158***
9	Caribou Municipal Arpt	184	8	Belfast	158
10	Vanceboro 2	181	10	Gardiner	165
11	Corinna	180	11	Waterville Treatment Plant	167
12	Bridgton 3 NW	179	12	Millinocket	***176***
12	Presque Isle	179	13	West Buxton 2 NNW	178
14	West Buxton 2 NNW	178	14	Bridgton 3 NW	179
15	Millinocket	***176***	14	Presque Isle	179
16	Waterville Treatment Plant	167	16	Corinna	180
17	Gardiner	165	17	Vanceboro 2	181
18	Bangor Airport	***158***	18	Caribou Municipal Arpt	184
18	Belfast	158	19	East Hiram	185
20	Sanford 2 NNW	156	20	Dover-Foxcroft	188
21	Portland Intl Jetport	149	20	Grand Lake Stream	188
22	Acadia National Park	145	22	Bridgewater	189
23	Augusta Airport	144	23	Middle Dam	190
23	Newcastle	144	24	Brassua Dam	194
25	Lewiston	***140***	25	Eustis	***202***

Rankings include 25 highest/lowest stations. If state has less than 25 stations, all stations are included. The period of record is 1980–2009. See User Guide for detailed explanation of data.

Number of Days Annually Minimum Temperature ≤ 0°F

Highest			Lowest		
Rank	Station Name	Days	Rank	Station Name	Days
1	Allagash	*71*	1	Portland Intl Jetport	7
2	Brassua Dam	48	2	Eastport	*8*
3	Eustis	*44*	3	Newcastle	9
3	Middle Dam	44	4	Lewiston	*11*
5	Bridgewater	42	5	Augusta Airport	12
5	Caribou Municipal Arpt	42	5	Sanford 2 NNW	12
7	Corinna	38	7	Acadia National Park	13
8	Presque Isle	37	8	Belfast	17
9	Dover-Foxcroft	36	9	Bangor Airport	*22*
10	Millinocket	*35*	10	Gardiner	23
11	Grand Lake Stream	33	10	Waterville Treatment Plant	23
11	Vanceboro 2	33	10	West Buxton 2 NNW	23
13	East Hiram	30	13	Bridgton 3 NW	28
14	Bridgton 3 NW	28	14	East Hiram	30
15	Gardiner	23	15	Grand Lake Stream	33
15	Waterville Treatment Plant	23	15	Vanceboro 2	33
15	West Buxton 2 NNW	23	17	Millinocket	*35*
18	Bangor Airport	*22*	18	Dover-Foxcroft	36
19	Belfast	17	19	Presque Isle	37
20	Acadia National Park	13	20	Corinna	38
21	Augusta Airport	12	21	Bridgewater	42
21	Sanford 2 NNW	12	21	Caribou Municipal Arpt	42
23	Lewiston	*11*	23	Eustis	*44*
24	Newcastle	9	23	Middle Dam	44
25	Eastport	*8*	25	Brassua Dam	48

Number of Annual Heating Degree Days

Highest			Lowest		
Rank	Station Name	Num.	Rank	Station Name	Num.
1	Allagash	*10,423*	1	Sanford 2 NNW	6,765
2	Eustis	*9,683*	2	Lewiston	*7,051*
3	Brassua Dam	9,495	3	Portland Intl Jetport	7,090
4	Caribou Municipal Arpt	9,352	4	Newcastle	7,215
5	Middle Dam	9,261	5	Acadia National Park	7,230
6	Bridgewater	9,100	6	Augusta Airport	7,334
7	Presque Isle	8,894	7	Belfast	7,361
8	Dover-Foxcroft	8,873	8	Waterville Treatment Plant	7,520
9	Millinocket	*8,556*	9	Eastport	*7,644*
10	Grand Lake Stream	8,509	10	West Buxton 2 NNW	7,649
11	Vanceboro 2	8,396	11	Gardiner	7,682
12	Corinna	8,358	12	Bangor Airport	*7,743*
13	East Hiram	8,162	13	Bridgton 3 NW	8,109
14	Bridgton 3 NW	8,109	14	East Hiram	8,162
15	Bangor Airport	*7,743*	15	Corinna	8,358
16	Gardiner	7,682	16	Vanceboro 2	8,396
17	West Buxton 2 NNW	7,649	17	Grand Lake Stream	8,509
18	Eastport	*7,644*	18	Millinocket	*8,556*
19	Waterville Treatment Plant	7,520	19	Dover-Foxcroft	8,873
20	Belfast	7,361	20	Presque Isle	8,894
21	Augusta Airport	7,334	21	Bridgewater	9,100
22	Acadia National Park	7,230	22	Middle Dam	9,261
23	Newcastle	7,215	23	Caribou Municipal Arpt	9,352
24	Portland Intl Jetport	7,090	24	Brassua Dam	9,495
25	Lewiston	*7,051*	25	Eustis	*9,683*

Rankings include 25 highest/lowest stations. If state has less than 25 stations, all stations are included. The period of record is 1980–2009. See User Guide for detailed explanation of data.

Number of Annual Cooling Degree Days

Highest Rank	Station Name	Num.	Lowest Rank	Station Name	Num.
1	Lewiston	***533***	1	Eastport	***101***
2	Sanford 2 NNW	510	2	Eustis	***128***
3	Augusta Airport	420	3	Allagash	***133***
4	Waterville Treatment Plant	389	4	Middle Dam	156
5	Portland Intl Jetport	376	5	Brassua Dam	157
6	Gardiner	359	6	Caribou Municipal Arpt	189
7	Bangor Airport	***354***	7	Bridgewater	203
8	West Buxton 2 NNW	341	8	Dover-Foxcroft	207
9	Acadia National Park	331	9	Grand Lake Stream	222
10	Newcastle	314	10	Bridgton 3 NW	252
11	Millinocket	***300***	11	Presque Isle	259
12	Corinna	296	12	Vanceboro 2	266
13	East Hiram	279	13	Belfast	274
14	Belfast	274	14	East Hiram	279
15	Vanceboro 2	266	15	Corinna	296
16	Presque Isle	259	16	Millinocket	***300***
17	Bridgton 3 NW	252	17	Newcastle	314
18	Grand Lake Stream	222	18	Acadia National Park	331
19	Dover-Foxcroft	207	19	West Buxton 2 NNW	341
20	Bridgewater	203	20	Bangor Airport	***354***
21	Caribou Municipal Arpt	189	21	Gardiner	359
22	Brassua Dam	157	22	Portland Intl Jetport	376
23	Middle Dam	156	23	Waterville Treatment Plant	389
24	Allagash	***133***	24	Augusta Airport	420
25	Eustis	***128***	25	Sanford 2 NNW	510

Annual Precipitation

Highest Rank	Station Name	Inches	Lowest Rank	Station Name	Inches
1	Acadia National Park	56.54	1	Presque Isle	35.55
2	Sanford 2 NNW	50.42	2	Allagash	***36.32***
3	East Hiram	49.20	3	Caribou Municipal Arpt	38.12
4	West Buxton 2 NNW	48.45	4	Middle Dam	38.88
5	Bridgton 3 NW	48.40	5	Eustis	***40.14***
6	Newcastle	47.37	6	Bangor Airport	***40.87***
7	Belfast	47.27	7	Augusta Airport	41.54
8	Portland Intl Jetport	46.48	8	Waterville Treatment Plant	41.64
9	Gardiner	44.93	9	Brassua Dam	41.77
10	Lewiston	44.73	10	Bridgewater	41.92
11	Eastport	***44.47***	11	Dover-Foxcroft	42.36
12	Grand Lake Stream	44.27	12	Millinocket	***43.12***
13	Vanceboro 2	43.73	13	Corinna	43.55
14	Corinna	43.55	14	Vanceboro 2	43.73
15	Millinocket	***43.12***	15	Grand Lake Stream	44.27
16	Dover-Foxcroft	42.36	16	Eastport	***44.47***
17	Bridgewater	41.92	17	Lewiston	44.73
18	Brassua Dam	41.77	18	Gardiner	44.93
19	Waterville Treatment Plant	41.64	19	Portland Intl Jetport	46.48
20	Augusta Airport	41.54	20	Belfast	47.27
21	Bangor Airport	***40.87***	21	Newcastle	47.37
22	Eustis	***40.14***	22	Bridgton 3 NW	48.40
23	Middle Dam	38.88	23	West Buxton 2 NNW	48.45
24	Caribou Municipal Arpt	38.12	24	East Hiram	49.20
25	Allagash	***36.32***	25	Sanford 2 NNW	50.42

Rankings include 25 highest/lowest stations. If state has less than 25 stations, all stations are included. The period of record is 1980–2009. See User Guide for detailed explanation of data.

Annual Extreme Maximum Daily Precipitation

Highest Rank	Station Name	Inches	Lowest Rank	Station Name	Inches
1	Portland Intl Jetport	11.74	1	Allagash	***2.85***
2	West Buxton 2 NNW	7.35	2	Vanceboro 2	3.52
3	East Hiram	6.82	3	Corinna	3.58
4	Caribou Municipal Arpt	6.67	4	Grand Lake Stream	3.63
5	Lewiston	6.48	5	Dover-Foxcroft	3.74
6	Bridgton 3 NW	6.43	6	Presque Isle	3.79
7	Gardiner	5.96	7	Millinocket	***3.83***
8	Bridgewater	5.90	8	Middle Dam	4.16
9	Waterville Treatment Plant	5.68	9	Eastport	***4.20***
10	Newcastle	5.45	10	Brassua Dam	4.21
11	Sanford 2 NNW	5.44	11	Eustis	***4.56***
12	Bangor Airport	***5.10***	12	Augusta Airport	4.95
13	Belfast	***5.03***	13	Belfast	***5.03***
14	Augusta Airport	4.95	14	Bangor Airport	***5.10***
15	Eustis	***4.56***	15	Sanford 2 NNW	5.44
16	Brassua Dam	4.21	16	Newcastle	5.45
17	Eastport	***4.20***	17	Waterville Treatment Plant	5.68
18	Middle Dam	4.16	18	Bridgewater	5.90
19	Millinocket	***3.83***	19	Gardiner	5.96
20	Presque Isle	3.79	20	Bridgton 3 NW	6.43
21	Dover-Foxcroft	3.74	21	Lewiston	6.48
22	Grand Lake Stream	3.63	22	Caribou Municipal Arpt	6.67
23	Corinna	3.58	23	East Hiram	6.82
24	Vanceboro 2	3.52	24	West Buxton 2 NNW	7.35
25	Allagash	***2.85***	25	Portland Intl Jetport	11.74

Number of Days Annually With ≥ 0.1 Inches of Precipitation

Highest Rank	Station Name	Days	Lowest Rank	Station Name	Days
1	Brassua Dam	91	1	Belfast	74
2	Middle Dam	90	2	Portland Intl Jetport	78
3	Allagash	***88***	2	Waterville Treatment Plant	78
4	Millinocket	***87***	4	Gardiner	79
5	Caribou Municipal Arpt	86	4	Lewiston	79
5	Corinna	86	6	Augusta Airport	80
5	East Hiram	86	6	West Buxton 2 NNW	80
5	Eustis	***86***	8	Eastport	***81***
9	Bridgewater	85	9	Bangor Airport	***82***
9	Dover-Foxcroft	85	10	Bridgton 3 NW	83
11	Acadia National Park	84	10	Presque Isle	83
11	Grand Lake Stream	84	10	Sanford 2 NNW	83
11	Newcastle	84	13	Acadia National Park	84
11	Vanceboro 2	84	13	Grand Lake Stream	84
15	Bridgton 3 NW	83	13	Newcastle	84
15	Presque Isle	83	13	Vanceboro 2	84
15	Sanford 2 NNW	83	17	Bridgewater	85
18	Bangor Airport	***82***	17	Dover-Foxcroft	85
19	Eastport	***81***	19	Caribou Municipal Arpt	86
20	Augusta Airport	80	19	Corinna	86
20	West Buxton 2 NNW	80	19	East Hiram	86
22	Gardiner	79	19	Eustis	***86***
22	Lewiston	79	23	Millinocket	***87***
24	Portland Intl Jetport	78	24	Allagash	***88***
24	Waterville Treatment Plant	78	25	Middle Dam	90

Rankings include 25 highest/lowest stations. If state has less than 25 stations, all stations are included. The period of record is 1980–2009. See User Guide for detailed explanation of data.

Number of Days Annually With ≥ 0.5 Inches of Precipitation

Highest

Rank	Station Name	Days
1	Acadia National Park	34
1	Bridgton 3 NW	34
1	Sanford 2 NNW	34
4	Belfast	32
4	Gardiner	32
4	Newcastle	32
4	West Buxton 2 NNW	32
8	Corinna	31
8	East Hiram	31
8	Grand Lake Stream	31
8	Portland Intl Jetport	31
12	Bridgewater	30
12	Lewiston	30
14	Eastport	***29***
14	Vanceboro 2	29
14	Waterville Treatment Plant	29
17	Millinocket	***28***
18	Augusta Airport	27
18	Brassua Dam	27
20	Bangor Airport	***26***
20	Dover-Foxcroft	26
20	Eustis	***26***
23	Caribou Municipal Arpt	23
23	Middle Dam	23
25	Allagash	***21***

Lowest

Rank	Station Name	Days
1	Presque Isle	20
2	Allagash	***21***
3	Caribou Municipal Arpt	23
3	Middle Dam	23
5	Bangor Airport	***26***
5	Dover-Foxcroft	26
5	Eustis	***26***
8	Augusta Airport	27
8	Brassua Dam	27
10	Millinocket	***28***
11	Eastport	***29***
11	Vanceboro 2	29
11	Waterville Treatment Plant	29
14	Bridgewater	30
14	Lewiston	30
16	Corinna	31
16	East Hiram	31
16	Grand Lake Stream	31
16	Portland Intl Jetport	31
20	Belfast	32
20	Gardiner	32
20	Newcastle	32
20	West Buxton 2 NNW	32
24	Acadia National Park	34
24	Bridgton 3 NW	34

Number of Days Annually With ≥ 1.0 Inches of Precipitation

Highest

Rank	Station Name	Days
1	Acadia National Park	15
2	Belfast	13
2	Bridgton 3 NW	13
2	Gardiner	13
5	East Hiram	12
5	Eastport	***12***
5	Grand Lake Stream	12
5	Lewiston	12
5	Newcastle	12
5	Portland Intl Jetport	12
5	Sanford 2 NNW	12
5	West Buxton 2 NNW	12
13	Bridgewater	11
13	Vanceboro 2	11
15	Augusta Airport	10
15	Bangor Airport	***10***
15	Brassua Dam	10
15	Corinna	10
15	Dover-Foxcroft	10
15	Millinocket	***10***
15	Waterville Treatment Plant	10
22	Eustis	***7***
22	Middle Dam	7
24	Presque Isle	6
25	Allagash	***5***

Lowest

Rank	Station Name	Days
1	Allagash	***5***
1	Caribou Municipal Arpt	5
3	Presque Isle	6
4	Eustis	***7***
4	Middle Dam	7
6	Augusta Airport	10
6	Bangor Airport	***10***
6	Brassua Dam	10
6	Corinna	10
6	Dover-Foxcroft	10
6	Millinocket	***10***
6	Waterville Treatment Plant	10
13	Bridgewater	11
13	Vanceboro 2	11
15	East Hiram	12
15	Eastport	***12***
15	Grand Lake Stream	12
15	Lewiston	12
15	Newcastle	12
15	Portland Intl Jetport	12
15	Sanford 2 NNW	12
15	West Buxton 2 NNW	12
23	Belfast	13
23	Bridgton 3 NW	13
23	Gardiner	13

Rankings include 25 highest/lowest stations. If state has less than 25 stations, all stations are included. The period of record is 1980–2009. See User Guide for detailed explanation of data.

Annual Snowfall

Highest Rank	Station Name	Inches	Lowest Rank	Station Name	Inches
1	Eustis	*123.8*	1	Sanford 2 NNW	*29.0*
2	Caribou Municipal Arpt	112.9	2	Belfast	*50.7*
3	Brassua Dam	102.7	3	Grand Lake Stream	*55.0*
4	Allagash	*94.9*	4	Eastport	*57.5*
5	Dover-Foxcroft	92.9	5	Waterville Treatment Plant	60.3
6	Presque Isle	88.3	6	Gardiner	61.4
7	Bridgewater	86.8	7	Lewiston	63.8
8	Millinocket	*85.7*	7	Portland Intl Jetport	63.8
9	Vanceboro 2	82.7	9	Bangor Airport	*65.2*
10	East Hiram	79.2	10	Acadia National Park	68.8
11	Bridgton 3 NW	76.4	11	Corinna	70.3
12	Newcastle	71.8	12	Newcastle	71.8
13	Corinna	70.3	13	Bridgton 3 NW	76.4
14	Acadia National Park	68.8	14	East Hiram	79.2
15	Bangor Airport	*65.2*	15	Vanceboro 2	82.7
16	Lewiston	63.8	16	Millinocket	*85.7*
16	Portland Intl Jetport	63.8	17	Bridgewater	86.8
18	Gardiner	61.4	18	Presque Isle	88.3
19	Waterville Treatment Plant	60.3	19	Dover-Foxcroft	92.9
20	Eastport	*57.5*	20	Allagash	*94.9*
21	Grand Lake Stream	*55.0*	21	Brassua Dam	102.7
22	Belfast	*50.7*	22	Caribou Municipal Arpt	112.9
23	Sanford 2 NNW	*29.0*	23	Eustis	*123.8*

Annual Maximum Snow Depth

Highest Rank	Station Name	Inches	Lowest Rank	Station Name	Inches
1	Dover-Foxcroft	60	1	Waterville Treatment Plant	30
2	Bridgton 3 NW	*53*	2	Gardiner	33
3	Allagash	*52*	2	Newcastle	33
4	Eustis	*51*	4	Portland Intl Jetport	34
5	Bridgewater	50	5	Corinna	36
6	East Hiram	49	6	Bangor Airport	*38*
7	Caribou Municipal Arpt	47	7	Belfast	*40*
8	Acadia National Park	45	8	Vanceboro 2	43
9	Vanceboro 2	43	9	Acadia National Park	45
10	Belfast	*40*	10	Caribou Municipal Arpt	47
11	Bangor Airport	*38*	11	East Hiram	49
12	Corinna	36	12	Bridgewater	50
13	Portland Intl Jetport	34	13	Eustis	*51*
14	Gardiner	33	14	Allagash	*52*
14	Newcastle	33	15	Bridgton 3 NW	*53*
16	Waterville Treatment Plant	30	16	Dover-Foxcroft	60

Number of Days Annually With ≥ 1.0 Inch Snow Depth

Highest

Rank	Station Name	Days
1	Eustis	***154***
2	Allagash	***146***
3	Caribou Municipal Arpt	135
4	Dover-Foxcroft	129
5	Bridgewater	126
6	Bridgton 3 NW	***118***
7	East Hiram	116
8	Corinna	111
9	Presque Isle	***107***
10	Vanceboro 2	101
11	Waterville Treatment Plant	90
12	Bangor Airport	***88***
13	Gardiner	87
13	Newcastle	87
15	Acadia National Park	84
16	Portland Intl Jetport	69
17	Belfast	***34***

Lowest

Rank	Station Name	Days
1	Belfast	***34***
2	Portland Intl Jetport	69
3	Acadia National Park	84
4	Gardiner	87
4	Newcastle	87
6	Bangor Airport	***88***
7	Waterville Treatment Plant	90
8	Vanceboro 2	101
9	Presque Isle	***107***
10	Corinna	111
11	East Hiram	116
12	Bridgton 3 NW	***118***
13	Bridgewater	126
14	Dover-Foxcroft	129
15	Caribou Municipal Arpt	135
16	Allagash	***146***
17	Eustis	***154***

Rankings include 25 highest/lowest stations. If state has less than 25 stations, all stations are included. The period of record is 1980–2009. See User Guide for detailed explanation of data.

Significant Storm Events in Maine: 2000 – 2009

Location or County	Date	Type	Mag.	Deaths	Injuries	Property Damage ($mil.)	Crop Damage ($mil.)
Hancock	07/04/00	Lightning	na	1	0	0.0	0.0
Somerset	07/17/00	Dam Break	na	0	0	1.0	0.0
Androscoggin, Cumberland, Sagadahoc, and York Counties	10/28/00	Strong Winds	na	0	0	1.2	0.0
Interior York County	03/16/01	Falling Snow/Ice	na	1	0	0.0	0.0
Southern Maine	04/03/05	Flood	na	0	0	1.3	0.0
Southern Maine	04/28/05	Flood	na	0	0	4.0	0.0
Cumberland and York County Coasts	05/23/05	Storm Surge	na	0	0	1.0	0.0
York	05/13/06	Flood	na	0	0	9.5	0.0
York	04/16/07	Flood	na	2	0	25.0	0.0
Knox, Lincoln, and Sagadahoc Counties and Cumberland, Waldo, and York County Coasts	04/16/07	Coastal Flood	na	0	0	15.0	0.0
Cumberland	04/16/07	Flood	na	0	0	8.0	0.0
Oxford	04/16/07	Flood	na	0	0	2.7	0.0
Kennebec	04/16/07	Flood	na	0	0	1.9	0.0
Lincoln	04/16/07	Flood	na	0	0	1.9	0.0
Androscoggin	04/16/07	Flood	na	0	0	1.3	0.0
Waldo	04/16/07	Flood	na	0	0	1.1	0.0
Oxford	07/11/07	Flash Flood	na	0	0	2.2	0.0
Androscoggin	08/16/08	Flash Flood	na	0	0	1.2	0.0
Franklin, Oxford, Somerset, and Interior York Counties	12/11/08	Ice Storm	na	0	0	4.9	0.0
Lincoln	07/02/09	Lightning	na	0	0	1.5	0.0
Hancock County Coast	08/23/09	High Surf	na	1	13	0.0	0.0

Note: Deaths, injuries, and damages are date and location specific.

MARYLAND

PHYSICAL FEATURES. The State of Maryland is on the east coast of the United States and lies in an east-west position between longitudes 75° and 79° W., spanning a distance of 240 miles. The latitude varies from about 38° to nearly 40° N., with a latitudinal width of approximately 125 miles in eastern portions which gradually narrows to about 1.5 miles in the Appalachian Mountain region near Hancock and increases again to 35 miles at the extreme western boundary. The total area of the State is 12,303 square miles, of which 9,887 square miles are land, 2,310 square miles are in the Chesapeake Bay and its tidal river waters, and 106 square miles are in Chincoteague Bay.

The Chesapeake Bay, elongated in a northerly direction, extends for about two-thirds of its length deep into Maryland. It virtually separates the State into two provinces except for a narrow neck of land about 10 miles wide in Cecil County, which bridges the gap between Chesapeake Bay and the State of Pennsylvania. That portion of the State east of Chesapeake Bay is commonly referred to as the Eastern Shore. The five southernmost counties between the Potomac River and Chesapeake Bay are commonly referred to as Southern Maryland. To the north and northwest of Southern Maryland, an area made up of six counties and located on the Piedmont, is an area commonly referred to as Northern-Central Maryland. The remainder of the State including roughly the Appalachian Mountain area or the three western counties is termed Western Maryland.

Although Maryland ranks as one of the smaller States with respect to size, it encompasses an extremely wide range of physiographic features which contribute to a comparatively wide range of climatic conditions. It extends across three well-defined physiographic belts which parallel the Atlantic coast in varying widths from New England to the southeastern United States. These physiographic provinces are the Coastal Plain, Piedmont province, and Appalachian province.

The land rises more or less gradually from the Atlantic Ocean across the Coastal Plain (which virtually includes the Eastern Shore and Southern Maryland) and then more rapidly across the Piedmont Plateau (northern-central Maryland) and the ridges of the Appalachian Mountains and finally reaches its highest point at 3,340 feet above mean sea level on Backbone Mountain in the Allegheny Plateau of Garrett County.

GENERAL CLIMATE. Since the general flow of the atmosphere in temperate latitudes is from west to east, the expansive North American Continent immediately to the west predisposes the Maryland area to a continental type of climate. This type of climate in middle latitudes is marked by well-defined seasons. Winter is the dormant season for plant growth based on low temperatures rather than drought. In spring and fall the changeableness of the weather is a striking feature. It is occasioned by a rapid succession of warm and cold fronts associated with cyclones and anticyclones which generally move from a westerly direction. Summers are warm to hot. The higher atmospheric humidity along the Atlantic coastal area causes the summer heat to be more oppressive and the winter cold more penetrating than for drier climates of the interior of the continent.

At times in winter the Appalachian Mountains afford a degree of protection from the icy blasts of cold Arctic air, particularly when a high pressure area attended by a coldwave approaches from the west. The modifying influences of the mountain barrier attending the passage of a storm area from the Ohio Valley is sometimes quite marked. The warming of the air as it descends the eastern slopes of the mountains may at times exceed 10°F.

The Allegheny Mountains contribute to the higher precipitation and heavy snowfall on the Allegheny Plateau. The formation of precipitation in the form of rain or snow is increased in storms or air masses which ascend the mountains from the Ohio Valley

TEMPERATURE. The winter climate on the Piedmont and Coastal plain sections of Maryland is intermediate between the cold of the Northeast and the mild weather of the South. Extremely cold air masses from the interior of the continent are moderated somewhat by passage over the Appalachian Mountains and in some instances by a short trajectory over the nearby ocean and bays. Weather on the Allegheny Plateau is frequently 10 to 15°F. colder than it is in eastern portions of the State and, at times, extremely low temperatures occur in winter. The average frost penetration ranges from about 5 inches or less in extreme southern portions of Maryland to more than 18 inches on the Allegheny Plateau.

Summer is characterized by considerable warm weather including at least several hot, humid periods. However, nights are usually quite comfortable. The average length of the freeze-free season based on a minimum temperature higher than 32°F. ranges from more than 225 days in extreme southern portions to fewer than 130 days on the Allegheny Plateau.

PRECIPITATION AND SNOWFALL. Although the heaviest precipitation occurs in the summer, this is the season when severe droughts are most frequent. Summer precipitation is less dependable and more variable than in winter. Average annual snowfall over Maryland ranges from a minimum of eight to 10 inches along the coastal areas of the Southern Eastern Shore division to a maximum well over 70 in the Garrett County area. Snow flurries fall as early as September on the Allegheny Plateau, and in October in extreme eastern portions of the State. The last snowfall in eastern portions usually occurs in April and on the Allegheny Plateau in May. Even in the warmest winters snow falls in Maryland; however, averages for a climatological division may be less than one inch for the season.

FLOODS. All of the State lies in the Atlantic drainage except for a portion of Garrett County in the western end of Maryland which drains into the Ohio Basin. The largest river in the State, the Potomac, forms the southern boundary through most of its length. The far eastern area is drained by many small streams and tidal estuaries into Chesapeake Bay and the Atlantic Ocean.

Minor or local flood damage can be expected every year in streams above the tidewater areas. Floods do occur in all months of the year, but the greatest frequency is in late winter and spring. Snow-melt at times is a factor. Intense convectional storms in summer occasionally cause local flash floods. Storms of tropical origin passing through the area in late summer and fall produce high water and occasionally damaging floods, mostly in tidewater areas. These are due to the heavy rains or strong easterly winds accompanying the storm, or a combination of both. Flooding from wind-driven tides at times extends upstream in the Potomac to the District of Columbia area. High water also results from persistent northeast winds along the coast caused by extra-tropical storms.

STORMS. Thunderstorms occur at a given station on an average of 30 days per year in extreme eastern portions of Maryland, and 40 days per year in western portions. They occur in all months of the year, but during the 4-month cold season from November through February, an average of less than one storm per month is observed. May, June, July, and August make up the thunderstorm season and include from 75 to 80 percent of the thunderstorms which occur annually. July is the peak of the season with about 25 percent of the annual total number of thunderstorms.

Hail at a given station occurs on an average of one day per year in extreme eastern portions and about two days per year in extreme western portions. The total number of days on which hail is observed at one or more weather stations in Maryland averages about 18 to 20 per year. Hail has been observed in all months of the year; however, occurrences in the 7-month period from September through March are infrequent. The number of days with hail at one or more weather stations increases from an average of one in April to about five in July, the peak of the hail season, and then decreases to an average of three in August. Although spring thunderstorms are much fewer in number than summer thunderstorms, they have a much greater tendency to occur with hail. Virtually all hailstorms occur between 2 p.m. and 9 p.m. Severe, devastating hailstorms occur somewhere in the State about once every five years on the average.

Tornadoes occur infrequently in Maryland, and of the ones that do occur most are small. Most tornadoes in Maryland tend to travel in the usual southwest to northeast direction, but few have been reported to travel southeastward or in a southerly direction. Usually paths are not more than a few miles in length; however, 10 to 15 percent of these storms maintain paths 20 miles or more in length.

RELATIVE HUMIDITY. Average relative humidity is lowest in the winter and early spring from February through April, and highest in the late summer and early from August through October.

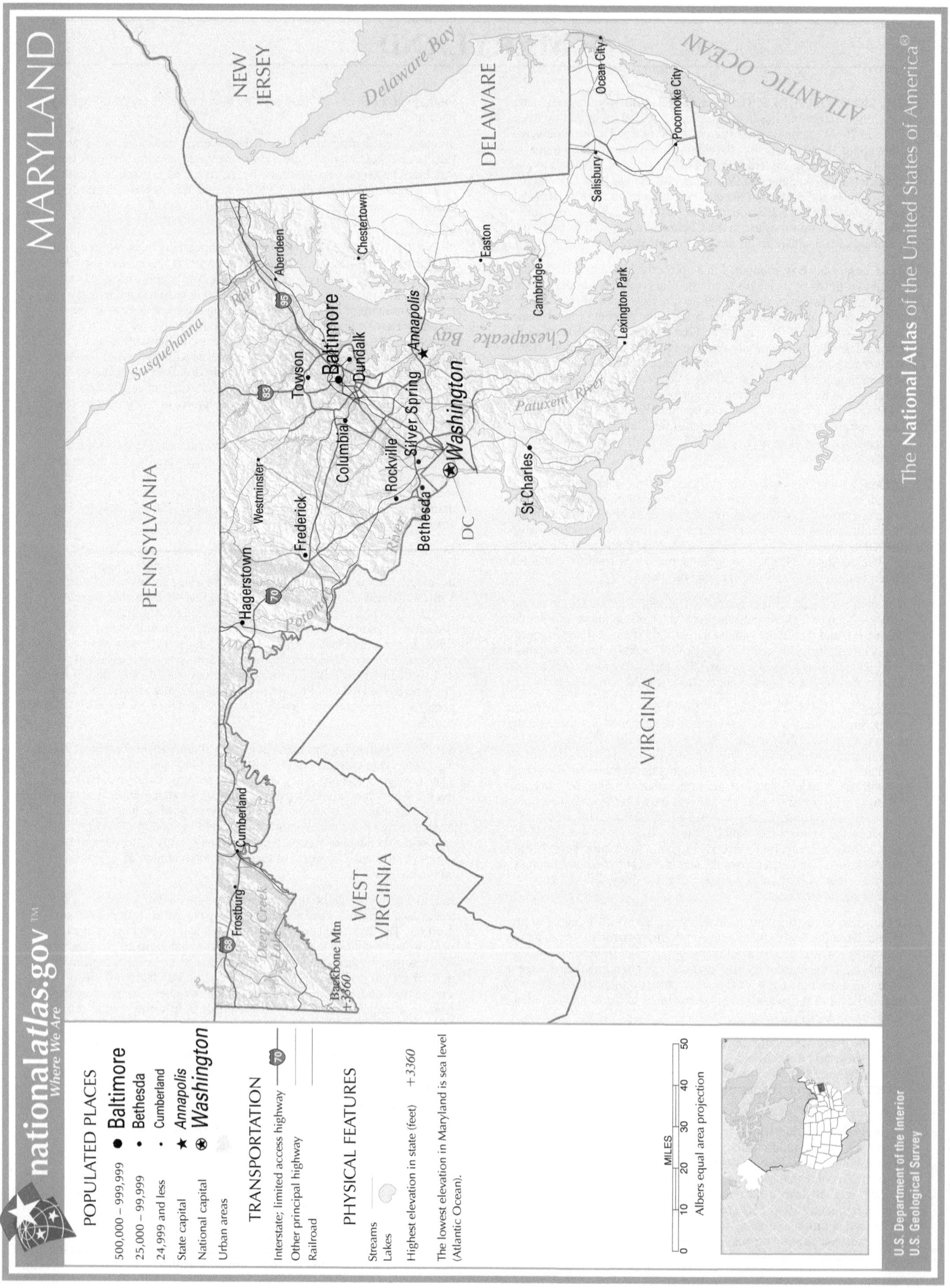
MARYLAND
nationalatlas.gov™
Where We Are
POPULATED PLACES
500,000 – 999,999 Baltimore
25,000 – 99,999 Bethesda
24,999 and less Cumberland
State capital Annapolis
National capital Washington
Urban areas
TRANSPORTATION
Interstate; limited access highway
Other principal highway
Railroad
PHYSICAL FEATURES
Streams
Lakes
Highest elevation in state (feet) +3360
The lowest elevation in Maryland is sea level (Atlantic Ocean).
MILES
0 10 20 30 40 50
Albers equal area projection
U.S. Department of the Interior
U.S. Geological Survey
The National Atlas of the United States of America®
PENNSYLVANIA
NEW JERSEY
DELAWARE
VIRGINIA
WEST VIRGINIA
DC
ATLANTIC OCEAN
Delaware Bay
Chesapeake Bay
Susquehanna River
Patuxent River
Potomac River
Deep Creek Lake
Backbone Mtn +3360
Frostburg
Cumberland
Hagerstown
Frederick
Westminster
Columbia
Rockville
Bethesda
Silver Spring
Washington
Towson
Baltimore
Dundalk
Annapolis
Aberdeen
Chestertown
Easton
Cambridge
Lexington Park
St Charles
Salisbury
Ocean City
Pocomoke City
68
70
83
95

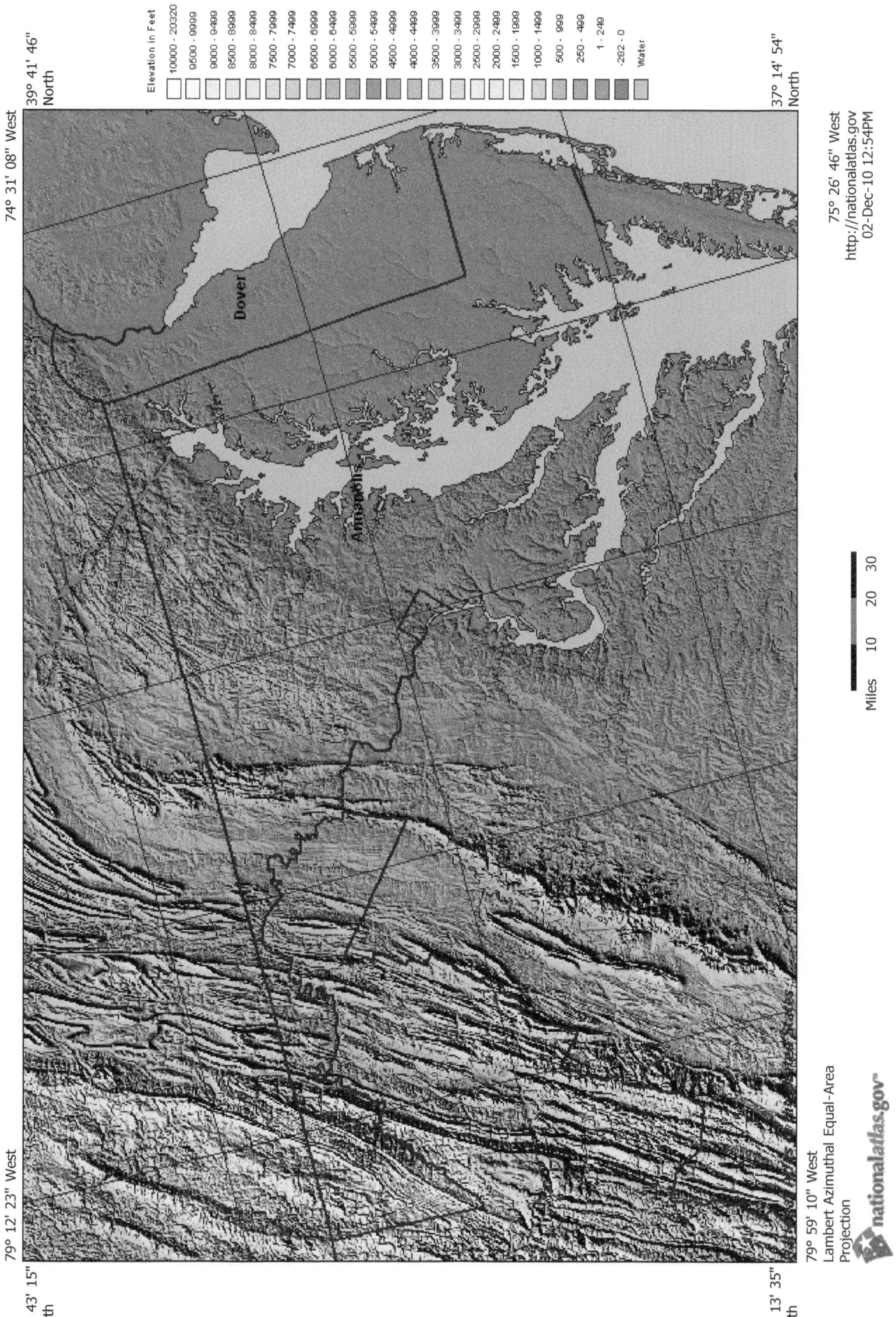
Elevation in Feet
10000 - 20320
9500 - 9999
9000 - 9499
8500 - 8999
8000 - 8499
7500 - 7999
7000 - 7499
6500 - 6999
6000 - 6499
5500 - 5999
5000 - 5499
4500 - 4999
4000 - 4499
3500 - 3999
3000 - 3499
2500 - 2999
2000 - 2499
1500 - 1999
1000 - 1499
500 - 999
250 - 499
1 - 249
-282 - 0
Water
39° 41' 46" North
74° 31' 08" West
37° 14' 54" North
75° 26' 46" West
http://nationalatlas.gov
02-Dec-10 12:54PM
Dover
Annapolis
Miles 10 20 30
40° 43' 15" North
79° 12' 23" West
38° 13' 35" North
79° 59' 10" West
Lambert Azimuthal Equal-Area Projection
nationalatlas.gov

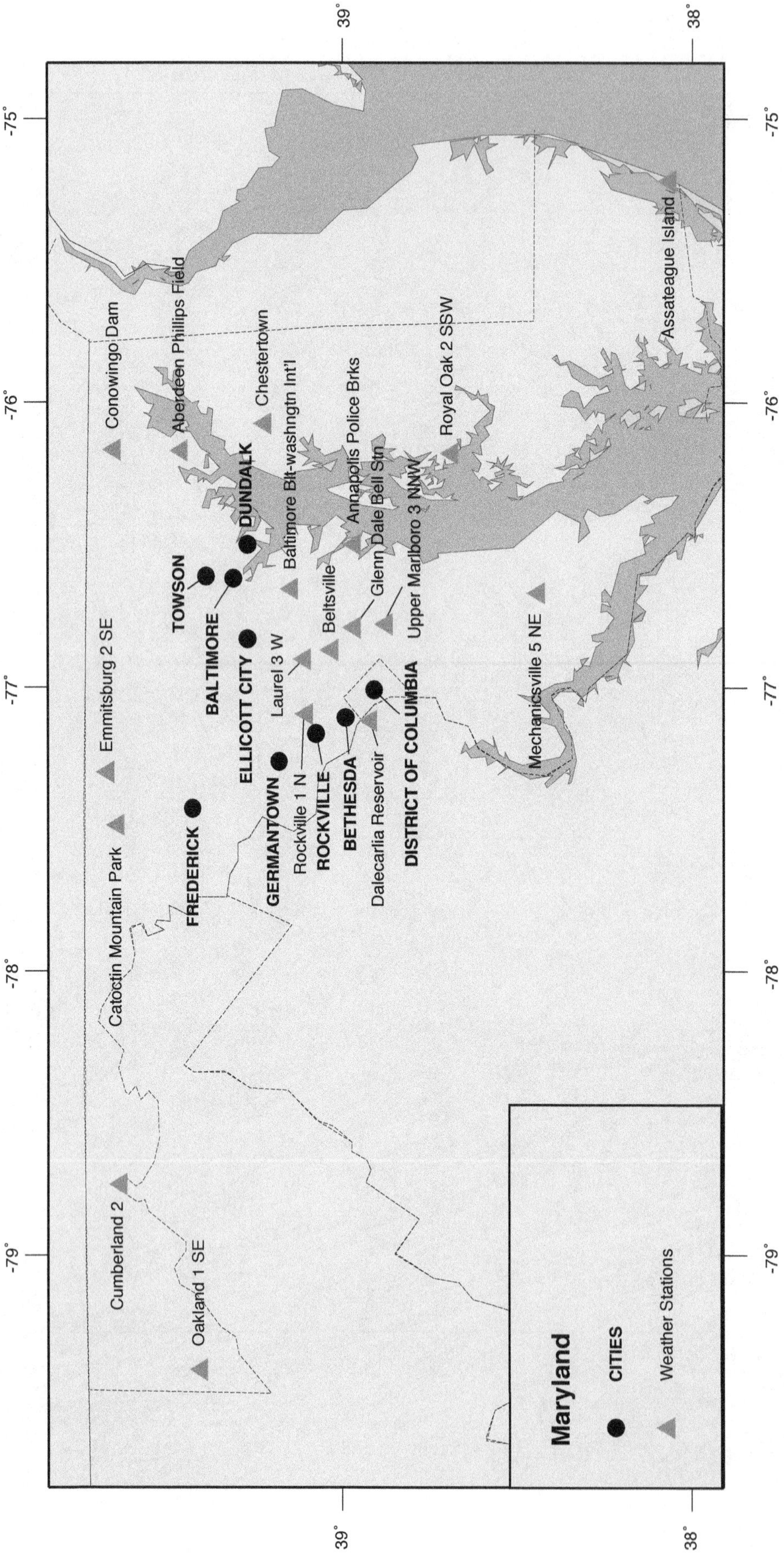
Maryland
CITIES
Weather Stations
Conowingo Dam
Aberdeen Phillips Field
Chestertown
Baltimore Blt-washngtn Int'l
Annapolis Police Brks
Glenn Dale Bell Stn
Upper Marlboro 3 NNW
Royal Oak 2 SSW
Assateague Island
Mechanicsville 5 NE
TOWSON
BALTIMORE
DUNDALK
ELLICOTT CITY
Laurel 3 W
Beltsville
Emmitsburg 2 SE
Catoctin Mountain Park
FREDERICK
GERMANTOWN
Rockville 1 N
ROCKVILLE
BETHESDA
Dalecarlia Reservoir
DISTRICT OF COLUMBIA
Cumberland 2
Oakland 1 SE
-75°
-76°
-77°
-78°
-79°
39°
38°

Maryland Weather Stations by County

County	Station Name
Allegany	Cumberland 2
Anne Arundel	Annapolis Police Brks Baltimore-Washngtn Int'l
District of Columbia	Dalecarlia Reservoir
Frederick	Catoctin Mountain Park Emmitsburg 2 SE
Garrett	Oakland 1 SE
Harford	Aberdeen Phillips Field Conowingo Dam
Kent	Chestertown
Montgomery	Rockville 1 NE
Prince George's	Beltsville Glenn Dale Bell Stn Laurel 3 W Upper Marlboro 3 NNW
St. Mary's	Mechanicsville 5 NE
Talbot	Royal Oak 2 SSW
Worcester	Assateague Island

Maryland Weather Stations by City

City	Station Name	Miles
Aspen Hill	Baltimore-Washngtn Int'l	21.7
	Beltsville	11.1
	Dalecarlia Reservoir	11.0
	Glenn Dale Bell Stn	17.1
	Laurel 3 W	9.5
	Rockville 1 NE	1.4
	Upper Marlboro 3 NNW	22.0
	Sterling RCS, VA	23.0
	Washington Dulles Int'l Arpt, VA	22.8
	Washington National Arpt, VA	15.6
Baltimore	Annapolis Police Brks	23.8
	Baltimore-Washngtn Int'l	10.8
	Beltsville	24.0
	Laurel 3 W	21.1
Bel Air South	Aberdeen Phillips Field	8.5
	Chestertown	23.8
	Conowingo Dam	13.1
Bethesda	Beltsville	12.8
	Dalecarlia Reservoir	3.6
	Glenn Dale Bell Stn	16.9
	Laurel 3 W	14.0
	Rockville 1 NE	7.9
	Upper Marlboro 3 NNW	19.6
	Sterling RCS, VA	19.8
	Washington Dulles Int'l Arpt, VA	18.4
	Washington National Arpt, VA	9.3
Bowie	Annapolis Police Brks	13.2
	Baltimore-Washngtn Int'l	15.0
	Beltsville	9.3
	Dalecarlia Reservoir	20.2
	Glenn Dale Bell Stn	3.2
	Laurel 3 W	13.1
	Rockville 1 NE	21.7
	Upper Marlboro 3 NNW	6.5
	Washington National Arpt, VA	16.8
Catonsville	Annapolis Police Brks	23.6
	Baltimore-Washngtn Int'l	7.8
	Beltsville	18.3
	Glenn Dale Bell Stn	21.4
	Laurel 3 W	14.8
	Rockville 1 NE	22.9
Columbia	Annapolis Police Brks	24.6
	Baltimore-Washngtn Int'l	9.9
	Beltsville	11.9
	Dalecarlia Reservoir	23.2
	Glenn Dale Bell Stn	16.7
	Laurel 3 W	7.5
	Rockville 1 NE	14.7
	Upper Marlboro 3 NNW	23.7
Dundalk	Aberdeen Phillips Field	22.6
	Annapolis Police Brks	19.7
	Baltimore-Washngtn Int'l	11.9
	Chestertown	23.7
	Laurel 3 W	24.2

City	Station Name	Miles
Ellicott City	Baltimore-Washngtn Int'l	10.6
	Beltsville	16.6
	Glenn Dale Bell Stn	21.0
	Laurel 3 W	12.3
	Rockville 1 NE	18.6
Frederick	Catoctin Mountain Park	15.7
	Emmitsburg 2 SE	19.0
Gaithersburg	Beltsville	18.1
	Dalecarlia Reservoir	13.9
	Glenn Dale Bell Stn	24.1
	Laurel 3 W	16.2
	Rockville 1 NE	5.7
	Sterling RCS, VA	18.0
	Washington Dulles Int'l Arpt, VA	18.7
	Washington National Arpt, VA	19.9
Germantown	Beltsville	22.6
	Dalecarlia Reservoir	18.5
	Laurel 3 W	20.1
	Rockville 1 NE	10.2
	Lincoln, VA	24.5
	Sterling RCS, VA	17.9
	Washington Dulles Int'l Arpt, VA	19.6
	Washington National Arpt, VA	24.7
Hagerstown	Catoctin Mountain Park	12.7
	Emmitsburg 2 SE	22.6
	Martinsburg E. WV Reg Arpt, WV	21.9
North Bethesda	Baltimore-Washngtn Int'l	24.8
	Beltsville	12.5
	Dalecarlia Reservoir	7.4
	Glenn Dale Bell Stn	17.7
	Laurel 3 W	12.3
	Rockville 1 NE	4.2
	Upper Marlboro 3 NNW	21.5
	Sterling RCS, VA	20.1
	Washington Dulles Int'l Arpt, VA	19.4
	Washington National Arpt, VA	12.8
Potomac	Beltsville	16.1
	Dalecarlia Reservoir	7.4
	Glenn Dale Bell Stn	21.0
	Laurel 3 W	16.0
	Rockville 1 NE	6.7
	Upper Marlboro 3 NNW	24.2
	Sterling RCS, VA	16.4
	Washington Dulles Int'l Arpt, VA	15.7
	Washington National Arpt, VA	13.7
Rockville	Beltsville	14.6
	Dalecarlia Reservoir	10.2
	Glenn Dale Bell Stn	20.3
	Laurel 3 W	13.4
	Rockville 1 NE	3.0
	Upper Marlboro 3 NNW	24.5
	Sterling RCS, VA	19.1
	Washington Dulles Int'l Arpt, VA	19.0
	Washington National Arpt, VA	16.0

See User Guide for station inclusion criteria.

City	Station Name	Miles
Silver Spring	Baltimore-Washngtn Int'l	21.1
	Beltsville	7.4
	Dalecarlia Reservoir	7.3
	Glenn Dale Bell Stn	11.8
	Laurel 3 W	9.1
	Rockville 1 NE	8.1
	Upper Marlboro 3 NNW	15.6
	Washington Dulles Int'l Arpt, VA	23.9
	Washington National Arpt, VA	9.5
Towson	Aberdeen Phillips Field	24.1
	Baltimore-Washngtn Int'l	16.2
Wheaton-Glenmont	Baltimore-Washngtn Int'l	21.5
	Beltsville	9.4
	Dalecarlia Reservoir	8.9
	Glenn Dale Bell Stn	15.1
	Laurel 3 W	9.0
	Rockville 1 NE	3.9
	Upper Marlboro 3 NNW	19.6
	Sterling RCS, VA	23.4
	Washington Dulles Int'l Arpt, VA	22.7
	Washington National Arpt, VA	13.0

Note: Miles is the distance between the geographic center of the city and the weather station.

Maryland Weather Stations by Elevation

Feet	Station Name
2,418	Oakland 1 SE
1,609	Catoctin Mountain Park
729	Cumberland 2
439	Rockville 1 NE
416	Emmitsburg 2 SE
399	Laurel 3 W
149	Dalecarlia Reservoir
149	Glenn Dale Bell Stn
147	Baltimore-Washngtn Int'l
145	Beltsville
100	Mechanicsville 5 NE
100	Upper Marlboro 3 NNW
57	Aberdeen Phillips Field
40	Chestertown
40	Conowingo Dam
24	Annapolis Police Brks
9	Assateague Island
9	Royal Oak 2 SSW

See User Guide for station inclusion criteria.

Baltimore-Washington Int'l Arpt.

Baltimore-Washington International Airport lies in a region about midway between the rigorous climates of the North and the mild climates of the South, and adjacent to the modifying influences of the Chesapeake Bay and Atlantic Ocean to the east and the Appalachian Mountains to the west. Since this region is near the average path of the low pressure systems which move across the country, changes in wind direction are frequent and contribute to the changeable character of the weather. The net effect of the mountains to the west and the bay and ocean to the east is to produce a more equable climate compared with other continental locations farther inland at the same latitude.

Rainfall distribution throughout the year is rather uniform, however, the greatest intensities are confined to the summer and early fall months, the season for hurricanes and severe thunderstorms. Moisture deficiencies for crops occur occasionally during the growing season, but severe droughts are rare. Rainfall during the growing season occurs principally in the form of thunderstorms, and rainfall totals during these months vary appreciably.

The average date for the last occurrence in spring of temperatures as low as 32 degrees is mid-April. The average date for the first occurrence in fall of temperatures as low as 32 degrees is late October. The freeze-free period is approximately 194 days.

In summer, the area is under the influence of the large semi-permanent high pressure system commonly known as the Bermuda High and centered over the Atlantic Ocean near 30 degrees N Latitude. This pressure system brings warm humid air to the area. The proximity of large water areas and the inflow of southerly winds contribute to high relative humidities during much of the year.

January is the coldest month, and July, the warmest. Snowfall occurs on about eleven days per year on the average, however, an average of only about six days annually produces snowfalls of one inch or greater. Snow is frequently mixed with rain and sleet, and snow seldom remains on the ground more than a few days.

Glaze or freezing rain which is hazardous to highway traffic occurs on an average of two to three times per year, generally in January or February. Some years pass without the occurrence of freezing rain, while in others it occurs on as many as eight to ten days. Sleet is observed on about five days annually with the greatest frequency of occurrence in January.

The annual prevailing wind direction is from the west. Winter and spring months have the highest average wind speed. Destructive velocities are rare and occur mostly during summer thunderstorms.

Baltimore-Washington Int'l Arpt. *Anne Arundel County* Elevation: 147 ft. Latitude: 39° 10' N Longitude: 76° 41' W

	JAN	FEB	MAR	APR	MAY	JUN	JUL	AUG	SEP	OCT	NOV	DEC	YEAR
Mean Maximum Temp. (°F)	42.0	45.6	54.0	65.1	74.5	83.4	87.6	85.7	78.5	67.2	56.8	45.9	65.5
Mean Temp. (°F)	33.6	36.4	44.0	54.2	63.5	72.8	77.5	75.8	68.4	56.6	47.0	37.4	55.6
Mean Minimum Temp. (°F)	25.2	27.2	33.9	43.3	52.5	62.2	67.3	65.8	58.3	46.0	37.0	28.8	45.6
Extreme Maximum Temp. (°F)	72	79	89	93	98	101	104	105	100	94	81	77	105
Extreme Minimum Temp. (°F)	-7	-1	8	22	33	44	50	45	39	26	17	0	-7
Days Maximum Temp. ≥ 90°F	0	0	0	0	2	6	12	8	2	0	0	0	30
Days Maximum Temp. ≤ 32°F	6	3	1	0	0	0	0	0	0	0	0	3	13
Days Minimum Temp. ≤ 32°F	24	21	14	3	0	0	0	0	0	1	10	21	94
Days Minimum Temp. ≤ 0°F	0	0	0	0	0	0	0	0	0	0	0	0	0
Heating Degree Days (base 65°F)	966	801	648	332	117	10	0	1	41	276	536	849	4,577
Cooling Degree Days (base 65°F)	0	0	3	15	79	251	395	342	151	23	1	0	1,260
Mean Precipitation (in.)	3.06	2.79	3.89	3.26	3.99	3.51	4.03	3.26	3.79	3.33	3.32	3.32	41.55
Maximum Precipitation (in.)*	7.8	7.2	8.6	8.1	8.7	9.9	8.2	18.3	8.6	8.1	7.7	7.4	59.0
Minimum Precipitation (in.)*	0.3	0.4	0.9	0.4	0.4	0.1	0.3	0.8	0.2	trace	0.3	0.2	27.9
Extreme Maximum Daily Precip. (in.)	2.51	3.26	2.56	2.52	2.40	2.75	4.45	3.23	5.02	4.37	2.65	2.73	5.02
Days With ≥ 0.1" Precipitation	6	5	7	7	7	6	7	6	5	5	6	6	73
Days With ≥ 0.5" Precipitation	2	2	3	2	3	2	3	2	2	2	3	3	29
Days With ≥ 1.0" Precipitation	1	1	1	1	1	1	1	1	1	1	1	1	12
Mean Snowfall (in.)	6.7	6.5	2.1	0.1	trace	trace	trace	0.0	0.0	trace	0.4	3.1	18.9
Maximum Snowfall (in.)*	25	33	22	1	trace	0	0	0	0	trace	8	20	53
Maximum 24-hr. Snowfall (in.)*	12	23	11	1	trace	0	0	0	0	trace	8	9	23
Maximum Snow Depth (in.)	25	23	9	trace	trace	trace	trace	0	0	trace	6	18	25
Days With ≥ 1.0" Snow Depth	5	5	1	0	0	0	0	0	0	0	0	3	14
Thunderstorm Days*	< 1	< 1	1	2	4	5	6	5	2	1	< 1	< 1	26
Foggy Days*	11	10	12	10	14	13	14	15	14	13	11	11	148
Predominant Sky Cover*	OVR	OVR	OVR	OVR	OVR	OVR	SCT	OVR	OVR	CLR	OVR	OVR	OVR
Mean Relative Humidity 7am (%)*	72	71	72	72	77	79	80	83	85	83	78	74	77
Mean Relative Humidity 4pm (%)*	56	52	49	47	52	53	53	55	55	54	55	57	53
Mean Dewpoint (°F)*	22	23	29	39	51	60	65	64	58	46	35	26	43
Prevailing Wind Direction*	WNW	WNW	WNW	WNW	W	W	W	W	W	W	WNW	WNW	WNW
Prevailing Wind Speed (mph)*	13	14	14	13	9	8	8	7	7	8	12	13	10
Maximum Wind Gust (mph)*	59	56	58	62	55	58	68	55	52	49	64	77	77

Note: (*) Period of record is 1950-1995

Aberdeen Phillips Field *Harford County* Elevation: 57 ft. Latitude: 39° 28' N Longitude: 76° 10' W

	JAN	FEB	MAR	APR	MAY	JUN	JUL	AUG	SEP	OCT	NOV	DEC	YEAR
Mean Maximum Temp. (°F)	na	46.4	53.9	65.6	74.2	83.1	87.5	85.6	79.2	na	na	na	na
Mean Temp. (°F)	na	37.9	44.4	55.0	63.8	72.9	na	76.2	69.4	na	na	na	na
Mean Minimum Temp. (°F)	na	29.3	34.8	44.4	53.1	62.6	na	66.5	59.2	na	na	na	na
Extreme Maximum Temp. (°F)	72	79	88	94	94	98	100	100	98	92	80	74	100
Extreme Minimum Temp. (°F)	-10	0	6	21	33	40	48	47	39	25	18	3	-10
Days Maximum Temp. ≥ 90°F	0	0	0	0	1	5	10	6	2	0	0	0	24
Days Maximum Temp. ≤ 32°F	4	2	0	0	0	0	0	0	0	0	0	2	8
Days Minimum Temp. ≤ 32°F	16	15	10	2	0	0	0	0	0	1	6	13	63
Days Minimum Temp. ≤ 0°F	0	0	0	0	0	0	0	0	0	0	0	0	0
Heating Degree Days (base 65°F)	na	760	632	309	110	9	na	1	30	na	na	na	na
Cooling Degree Days (base 65°F)	na	0	3	17	79	252	na	354	166	na	na	na	na
Mean Precipitation (in.)	2.93	2.48	3.73	3.44	4.02	4.11	4.37	3.60	4.47	3.63	3.33	3.45	43.56
Extreme Maximum Daily Precip. (in.)	2.16	na	na	na	na	na	na	na	na	na	na	2.28	na
Days With ≥ 0.1" Precipitation	4	3	4	4	5	5	5	4	4	4	4	4	50
Days With ≥ 0.5" Precipitation	1	1	2	2	2	2	2	2	2	2	2	2	22
Days With ≥ 1.0" Precipitation	1	0	1	0	1	1	1	1	1	1	0	1	9
Mean Snowfall (in.)	4.1	3.1	0.9	0.1	0.0	0.0	0.0	0.0	0.0	0.0	trace	2.3	10.5
Maximum Snow Depth (in.)	22	22	6	trace	0	0	0	0	0	0	trace	19	22
Days With ≥ 1.0" Snow Depth	3	3	0	0	0	0	0	0	0	0	0	1	7

Annapolis Police Brks *Anne Arundel County* Elevation: 24 ft. Latitude: 38° 59' N Longitude: 76° 30' W

	JAN	FEB	MAR	APR	MAY	JUN	JUL	AUG	SEP	OCT	NOV	DEC	YEAR
Mean Maximum Temp. (°F)	44.3	47.7	55.8	67.7	76.8	85.2	89.2	87.0	80.6	68.8	58.4	48.1	67.5
Mean Temp. (°F)	35.5	38.3	45.6	56.4	65.5	74.4	79.0	77.2	71.0	58.6	48.7	39.3	57.5
Mean Minimum Temp. (°F)	26.7	28.8	35.4	45.1	54.2	63.6	68.8	67.3	61.3	48.4	38.9	30.3	47.4
Extreme Maximum Temp. (°F)	75	80	92	98	98	101	103	103	99	91	81	78	103
Extreme Minimum Temp. (°F)	-8	2	10	22	34	42	50	46	37	26	14	-1	-8
Days Maximum Temp. ≥ 90°F	0	0	0	0	2	8	15	10	3	0	0	0	38
Days Maximum Temp. ≤ 32°F	4	1	0	0	0	0	0	0	0	0	0	2	7
Days Minimum Temp. ≤ 32°F	23	20	12	2	0	0	0	0	0	1	8	18	84
Days Minimum Temp. ≤ 0°F	0	0	0	0	0	0	0	0	0	0	0	0	0
Heating Degree Days (base 65°F)	909	750	598	271	81	5	0	0	21	221	487	792	4,135
Cooling Degree Days (base 65°F)	0	0	3	18	103	293	441	384	207	28	2	0	1,479
Mean Precipitation (in.)	2.97	2.79	4.67	3.58	4.28	3.88	4.23	3.85	4.65	3.32	3.74	3.50	45.46
Extreme Maximum Daily Precip. (in.)	2.50	2.51	3.75	1.94	4.70	2.52	3.00	4.39	na	2.90	3.04	2.42	na
Days With ≥ 0.1" Precipitation	6	5	7	7	7	6	7	6	5	5	5	6	72
Days With ≥ 0.5" Precipitation	2	2	3	2	3	3	3	3	3	2	3	2	31
Days With ≥ 1.0" Precipitation	1	1	1	1	1	1	1	1	1	1	1	1	12
Mean Snowfall (in.)	4.1	0.7	0.5	0.0	0.0	0.0	0.0	0.0	0.0	0.0	0.2	1.0	6.5
Maximum Snow Depth (in.)	22	na	9	0	0	0	0	0	0	0	5	7	na
Days With ≥ 1.0" Snow Depth	3	3	0	0	0	0	0	0	0	0	0	1	7

Assateague Island *Worcester County* Elevation: 9 ft. Latitude: 38° 04' N Longitude: 75° 13' W

	JAN	FEB	MAR	APR	MAY	JUN	JUL	AUG	SEP	OCT	NOV	DEC	YEAR
Mean Maximum Temp. (°F)	45.3	47.3	53.2	61.6	70.6	80.1	84.8	84.3	79.3	69.6	59.7	49.9	65.5
Mean Temp. (°F)	37.2	39.0	44.5	53.2	62.2	71.5	76.4	76.0	71.2	60.7	50.9	41.4	57.0
Mean Minimum Temp. (°F)	29.1	30.7	35.8	44.8	53.7	62.8	67.9	67.6	62.9	51.8	42.0	32.9	48.5
Extreme Maximum Temp. (°F)	74	78	89	88	99	102	102	101	96	94	81	76	102
Extreme Minimum Temp. (°F)	-2	7	10	22	35	42	49	48	42	29	19	2	-2
Days Maximum Temp. ≥ 90°F	0	0	0	0	1	3	6	5	1	0	0	0	16
Days Maximum Temp. ≤ 32°F	3	1	0	0	0	0	0	0	0	0	0	1	5
Days Minimum Temp. ≤ 32°F	20	17	10	1	0	0	0	0	0	0	4	15	67
Days Minimum Temp. ≤ 0°F	0	0	0	0	0	0	0	0	0	0	0	0	0
Heating Degree Days (base 65°F)	855	728	628	351	128	12	0	1	14	166	420	724	4,027
Cooling Degree Days (base 65°F)	0	0	1	4	47	213	359	349	206	41	2	0	1,222
Mean Precipitation (in.)	3.79	3.27	4.42	3.71	3.20	3.12	3.77	4.24	3.97	3.40	3.39	3.70	43.98
Extreme Maximum Daily Precip. (in.)	3.54	2.87	3.17	2.63	2.10	2.91	3.47	8.87	7.43	3.86	3.99	3.34	8.87
Days With ≥ 0.1" Precipitation	6	6	7	6	6	6	6	5	6	5	5	6	70
Days With ≥ 0.5" Precipitation	3	2	3	3	2	2	2	2	3	2	2	2	28
Days With ≥ 1.0" Precipitation	1	1	1	1	1	1	1	1	1	1	1	1	12
Mean Snowfall (in.)	1.7	1.6	0.4	0.0	0.0	0.0	0.0	0.0	0.0	0.0	trace	0.5	4.2
Maximum Snow Depth (in.)	6	3	4	0	0	0	0	0	0	0	0	7	7
Days With ≥ 1.0" Snow Depth	1	0	0	0	0	0	0	0	0	0	0	0	1

Beltsville *Prince George's County* Elevation: 145 ft. Latitude: 39° 02' N Longitude: 76° 53' W

	JAN	FEB	MAR	APR	MAY	JUN	JUL	AUG	SEP	OCT	NOV	DEC	YEAR
Mean Maximum Temp. (°F)	42.1	45.6	53.5	64.6	74.2	83.0	87.2	85.8	79.0	67.6	57.1	45.9	65.5
Mean Temp. (°F)	32.9	36.1	43.4	53.4	63.2	72.2	76.7	75.4	68.2	56.2	46.7	37.0	55.1
Mean Minimum Temp. (°F)	23.6	26.6	33.2	42.3	52.0	61.3	66.2	64.9	57.5	44.7	36.3	27.9	44.7
Extreme Maximum Temp. (°F)	73	79	88	93	96	99	103	102	98	93	82	78	103
Extreme Minimum Temp. (°F)	-12	-4	6	21	31	42	45	38	37	25	13	-1	-12
Days Maximum Temp. ≥ 90°F	0	0	0	0	1	6	11	9	2	0	0	0	29
Days Maximum Temp. ≤ 32°F	6	3	1	0	0	0	0	0	0	0	0	3	13
Days Minimum Temp. ≤ 32°F	25	22	15	4	0	0	0	0	0	2	11	23	102
Days Minimum Temp. ≤ 0°F	1	0	0	0	0	0	0	0	0	0	0	0	1
Heating Degree Days (base 65°F)	989	810	667	353	126	15	0	2	46	287	543	862	4,700
Cooling Degree Days (base 65°F)	0	0	3	13	75	237	370	331	149	21	1	0	1,200
Mean Precipitation (in.)	2.81	2.48	3.78	3.52	4.40	3.79	4.16	3.10	3.97	3.66	3.34	3.11	42.12
Extreme Maximum Daily Precip. (in.)	1.91	2.11	2.23	2.20	4.27	4.75	4.09	2.59	3.53	5.54	4.10	2.17	5.54
Days With ≥ 0.1" Precipitation	6	5	7	7	8	7	7	6	6	5	5	6	75
Days With ≥ 0.5" Precipitation	2	2	2	3	3	3	3	2	3	2	3	2	30
Days With ≥ 1.0" Precipitation	1	0	1	1	1	1	1	1	1	1	1	1	11
Mean Snowfall (in.)	6.0	4.7	1.7	0.1	0.0	0.0	0.0	0.0	0.0	0.0	0.6	2.6	15.7
Maximum Snow Depth (in.)	24	19	9	1	0	0	0	0	0	0	10	18	24
Days With ≥ 1.0" Snow Depth	5	4	1	0	0	0	0	0	0	0	0	3	13

The period of record for all cooperative weather station data is 1980 – 2009. See User Guide for detailed explanation of data.

Catoctin Mountain Park *Frederick County* Elevation: 1,609 ft. Latitude: 39° 39' N Longitude: 77° 29' W

	JAN	FEB	MAR	APR	MAY	JUN	JUL	AUG	SEP	OCT	NOV	DEC	YEAR
Mean Maximum Temp. (°F)	37.4	41.0	50.0	63.2	71.4	78.0	81.2	79.7	73.1	63.2	52.3	40.9	61.0
Mean Temp. (°F)	29.8	32.5	40.4	52.1	61.3	68.9	72.6	71.3	64.7	54.3	44.1	33.7	52.1
Mean Minimum Temp. (°F)	22.2	24.1	30.8	41.0	51.1	59.7	64.0	62.8	56.4	45.3	35.9	26.4	43.3
Extreme Maximum Temp. (°F)	69	75	86	91	92	94	96	94	91	87	82	75	96
Extreme Minimum Temp. (°F)	-18	-4	1	12	32	40	48	37	35	21	12	-11	-18
Days Maximum Temp. ≥ 90°F	0	0	0	0	0	0	2	2	0	0	0	0	4
Days Maximum Temp. ≤ 32°F	10	6	1	0	0	0	0	0	0	0	1	6	24
Days Minimum Temp. ≤ 32°F	26	23	18	5	0	0	0	0	0	2	11	22	107
Days Minimum Temp. ≤ 0°F	1	0	0	0	0	0	0	0	0	0	0	0	1
Heating Degree Days (base 65°F)	1,083	911	757	394	162	30	3	10	81	340	621	965	5,357
Cooling Degree Days (base 65°F)	0	0	3	13	54	154	246	211	80	12	0	0	773
Mean Precipitation (in.)	3.44	3.27	4.27	4.11	4.99	4.40	3.90	3.93	4.59	3.74	3.96	3.21	47.81
Extreme Maximum Daily Precip. (in.)	4.20	5.27	2.39	3.03	5.27	3.66	2.43	4.75	3.90	3.55	4.04	3.43	5.27
Days With ≥ 0.1" Precipitation	6	6	7	7	9	8	7	6	6	6	7	6	81
Days With ≥ 0.5" Precipitation	2	2	3	3	3	3	3	3	3	3	3	2	33
Days With ≥ 1.0" Precipitation	1	1	1	1	1	1	1	1	1	1	1	1	12
Mean Snowfall (in.)	9.3	8.4	3.6	0.9	0.0	0.0	0.0	0.0	0.0	trace	1.4	4.1	27.7
Maximum Snow Depth (in.)	42	31	28	5	0	0	0	0	0	trace	15	12	42
Days With ≥ 1.0" Snow Depth	13	11	6	0	0	0	0	0	0	0	1	7	38

Chestertown *Kent County* Elevation: 40 ft. Latitude: 39° 13' N Longitude: 76° 04' W

	JAN	FEB	MAR	APR	MAY	JUN	JUL	AUG	SEP	OCT	NOV	DEC	YEAR
Mean Maximum Temp. (°F)	41.9	45.4	54.1	65.5	75.1	83.8	88.0	86.6	79.6	68.2	57.3	46.1	66.0
Mean Temp. (°F)	33.5	36.4	43.9	54.5	64.0	73.1	77.6	76.1	68.8	57.3	47.3	37.5	55.8
Mean Minimum Temp. (°F)	25.1	27.2	33.8	43.4	52.9	62.3	67.2	65.5	58.0	46.3	37.2	28.8	45.6
Extreme Maximum Temp. (°F)	75	77	89	97	96	100	104	103	100	91	83	78	104
Extreme Minimum Temp. (°F)	-7	1	10	21	35	43	52	44	38	27	14	2	-7
Days Maximum Temp. ≥ 90°F	0	0	0	0	2	7	13	10	3	0	0	0	35
Days Maximum Temp. ≤ 32°F	6	3	1	0	0	0	0	0	0	0	0	3	13
Days Minimum Temp. ≤ 32°F	25	22	14	2	0	0	0	0	0	1	10	21	95
Days Minimum Temp. ≤ 0°F	0	0	0	0	0	0	0	0	0	0	0	0	0
Heating Degree Days (base 65°F)	969	804	648	324	107	10	0	1	36	259	526	846	4,530
Cooling Degree Days (base 65°F)	0	0	2	14	83	259	398	352	157	26	2	0	1,293
Mean Precipitation (in.)	3.15	2.81	4.09	3.62	4.16	4.11	3.95	3.14	4.32	3.39	3.34	3.50	43.58
Extreme Maximum Daily Precip. (in.)	2.20	2.25	3.21	2.55	3.60	4.40	2.51	4.45	11.06	2.95	2.65	3.15	11.06
Days With ≥ 0.1" Precipitation	6	6	7	7	7	7	6	5	6	6	6	7	76
Days With ≥ 0.5" Precipitation	2	2	3	3	3	3	3	2	3	2	3	3	32
Days With ≥ 1.0" Precipitation	1	1	1	1	1	1	1	1	1	1	1	1	12
Mean Snowfall (in.)	5.3	5.8	1.7	0.1	0.0	0.0	0.0	0.0	0.0	0.0	0.3	2.0	15.2
Maximum Snow Depth (in.)	13	18	7	trace	0	0	0	0	0	0	3	16	18
Days With ≥ 1.0" Snow Depth	6	4	1	0	0	0	0	0	0	0	0	2	13

Conowingo Dam *Harford County* Elevation: 40 ft. Latitude: 39° 39' N Longitude: 76° 10' W

	JAN	FEB	MAR	APR	MAY	JUN	JUL	AUG	SEP	OCT	NOV	DEC	YEAR
Mean Maximum Temp. (°F)	***41.5***	***44.3***	***53.0***	65.1	74.7	***84.4***	88.7	87.2	***79.9***	68.5	***56.1***	***45.5***	***65.7***
Mean Temp. (°F)	***31.7***	***34.4***	***42.2***	53.1	***63.0***	***72.8***	77.1	75.7	***68.2***	56.6	***45.6***	***36.3***	***54.7***
Mean Minimum Temp. (°F)	***22.2***	***24.5***	***31.3***	41.2	***51.1***	***61.1***	65.3	64.2	***56.5***	44.5	***34.8***	***27.0***	***43.6***
Extreme Maximum Temp. (°F)	73	76	90	95	99	109	106	***104***	***99***	94	***75***	77	***109***
Extreme Minimum Temp. (°F)	-9	-2	5	19	***31***	***42***	48	40	***35***	20	***11***	-1	***-9***
Days Maximum Temp. ≥ 90°F	0	0	0	0	1	***8***	14	12	3	0	***0***	0	***38***
Days Maximum Temp. ≤ 32°F	5	3	1	0	0	0	0	0	0	0	***0***	2	***11***
Days Minimum Temp. ≤ 32°F	26	22	16	4	***0***	***0***	0	0	0	3	***13***	23	***107***
Days Minimum Temp. ≤ 0°F	1	0	0	0	***0***	***0***	0	0	0	0	***0***	0	***1***
Heating Degree Days (base 65°F)	***1,025***	***859***	***701***	360	***120***	***10***	0	2	***39***	275	***578***	***881***	***4,850***
Cooling Degree Days (base 65°F)	***0***	***0***	***1***	10	***65***	***249***	380	341	***141***	20	***0***	***0***	***1,207***
Mean Precipitation (in.)	3.38	2.68	4.12	3.68	4.06	4.13	4.12	3.82	4.90	3.78	***3.72***	3.72	***46.11***
Extreme Maximum Daily Precip. (in.)	1.88	***2.15***	2.45	2.61	2.04	***3.65***	3.51	3.25	***8.25***	***3.16***	***2.54***	3.07	***8.25***
Days With ≥ 0.1" Precipitation	7	5	7	7	8	6	7	6	6	5	***7***	6	***77***
Days With ≥ 0.5" Precipitation	2	2	3	3	3	3	3	2	3	3	***2***	3	***32***
Days With ≥ 1.0" Precipitation	1	0	1	1	1	1	1	1	1	1	***1***	1	***11***
Mean Snowfall (in.)	***5.0***	***3.6***	0.7	trace	0.0	0.0	0.0	0.0	0.0	0.0	***0.3***	1.7	***11.3***
Maximum Snow Depth (in.)	***8***	***18***	7	***0***	***0***	***0***	***0***	***0***	***0***	***0***	na	***12***	na
Days With ≥ 1.0" Snow Depth	***3***	***3***	1	0	0	0	0	0	0	0	***0***	1	***8***

Cumberland 2 *Allegany County* Elevation: 729 ft. Latitude: 39° 38' N Longitude: 78° 45' W

	JAN	FEB	MAR	APR	MAY	JUN	JUL	AUG	SEP	OCT	NOV	DEC	YEAR
Mean Maximum Temp. (°F)	40.7	45.5	54.9	67.9	76.1	84.1	87.8	86.7	79.5	68.0	55.7	44.0	65.9
Mean Temp. (°F)	31.6	35.0	43.1	54.4	62.9	71.4	75.4	74.2	66.8	55.1	44.9	35.0	54.1
Mean Minimum Temp. (°F)	22.3	24.5	31.3	40.9	49.7	58.6	63.0	61.7	54.0	42.1	34.0	25.9	42.3
Extreme Maximum Temp. (°F)	75	78	90	96	98	100	104	105	98	93	87	80	105
Extreme Minimum Temp. (°F)	-14	-1	3	20	26	42	47	40	31	24	13	-8	-14
Days Maximum Temp. ≥ 90°F	0	0	0	0	2	7	12	10	3	0	0	0	34
Days Maximum Temp. ≤ 32°F	7	3	1	0	0	0	0	0	0	0	0	4	15
Days Minimum Temp. ≤ 32°F	26	23	18	5	0	0	0	0	0	4	13	24	113
Days Minimum Temp. ≤ 0°F	1	0	0	0	0	0	0	0	0	0	0	0	1
Heating Degree Days (base 65°F)	1,030	842	675	328	128	15	0	3	61	315	597	924	4,918
Cooling Degree Days (base 65°F)	0	0	3	16	71	212	331	297	121	15	0	0	1,066
Mean Precipitation (in.)	2.63	2.28	3.36	3.42	3.95	3.33	3.68	3.20	3.20	2.54	2.98	2.79	37.36
Extreme Maximum Daily Precip. (in.)	1.75	1.95	1.83	1.78	2.05	2.31	2.80	2.48	4.63	2.40	3.15	2.50	4.63
Days With ≥ 0.1" Precipitation	6	5	7	8	8	7	7	6	6	5	6	6	77
Days With ≥ 0.5" Precipitation	2	1	2	2	3	3	2	2	2	2	2	2	25
Days With ≥ 1.0" Precipitation	0	0	1	1	1	1	1	1	1	1	1	0	9
Mean Snowfall (in.)	10.1	7.4	5.8	0.2	0.0	0.0	0.0	0.0	0.0	0.0	1.0	5.4	29.9
Maximum Snow Depth (in.)	26	22	16	2	0	0	0	0	0	0	5	15	26
Days With ≥ 1.0" Snow Depth	12	8	4	0	0	0	0	0	0	0	1	7	32

The period of record for all cooperative weather station data is 1980 – 2009. See User Guide for detailed explanation of data.

Dalecarlia Reservoir *District Of Columbia County* Elevation: 149 ft. Latitude: 38° 56' N Longitude: 77° 07' W

	JAN	FEB	MAR	APR	MAY	JUN	JUL	AUG	SEP	OCT	NOV	DEC	YEAR
Mean Maximum Temp. (°F)	44.5	48.7	57.3	69.0	77.7	86.0	89.8	88.0	81.0	69.9	59.0	48.1	68.2
Mean Temp. (°F)	34.3	37.8	45.3	56.1	65.0	74.0	78.2	76.8	69.7	57.7	47.7	37.9	56.7
Mean Minimum Temp. (°F)	24.3	26.9	33.1	42.9	52.2	61.8	66.6	65.5	58.2	45.5	36.4	27.7	45.1
Extreme Maximum Temp. (°F)	74	81	91	95	98	100	103	105	99	95	85	82	105
Extreme Minimum Temp. (°F)	-11	-10	7	19	29	40	44	41	35	22	11	-2	-11
Days Maximum Temp. ≥ 90°F	0	0	0	1	3	9	17	12	3	0	0	0	45
Days Maximum Temp. ≤ 32°F	4	2	0	0	0	0	0	0	0	0	0	2	8
Days Minimum Temp. ≤ 32°F	25	21	15	3	0	0	0	0	0	2	11	22	99
Days Minimum Temp. ≤ 0°F	0	0	0	0	0	0	0	0	0	0	0	0	0
Heating Degree Days (base 65°F)	944	763	608	285	95	7	0	1	33	249	513	833	4,331
Cooling Degree Days (base 65°F)	0	0	4	24	102	282	417	375	180	29	2	0	1,415
Mean Precipitation (in.)	3.02	2.85	4.02	3.72	4.33	4.04	4.47	3.77	4.16	3.68	3.60	3.26	44.92
Extreme Maximum Daily Precip. (in.)	3.50	2.92	5.20	2.25	3.14	5.73	5.04	5.36	5.44	5.80	4.45	2.20	5.80
Days With ≥ 0.1" Precipitation	6	6	7	7	8	7	7	6	6	5	6	6	77
Days With ≥ 0.5" Precipitation	2	2	3	2	3	3	3	2	3	3	2	2	30
Days With ≥ 1.0" Precipitation	1	1	1	1	1	1	1	1	1	1	1	1	12
Mean Snowfall (in.)	3.2	2.2	0.7	0.0	0.0	0.0	0.0	0.0	0.0	0.0	trace	0.9	7.0
Maximum Snow Depth (in.)	21	18	11	0	0	0	0	0	0	0	8	11	21
Days With ≥ 1.0" Snow Depth	3	2	1	0	0	0	0	0	0	0	0	1	7

Emmitsburg 2 SE *Frederick County* Elevation: 416 ft. Latitude: 39° 41' N Longitude: 77° 18' W

	JAN	FEB	MAR	APR	MAY	JUN	JUL	AUG	SEP	OCT	NOV	DEC	YEAR
Mean Maximum Temp. (°F)	39.5	44.3	53.1	65.2	73.5	81.9	85.8	84.1	77.2	66.3	55.0	43.5	64.1
Mean Temp. (°F)	30.6	34.2	41.9	52.6	61.4	70.1	74.5	72.8	65.8	54.5	44.6	35.1	53.2
Mean Minimum Temp. (°F)	21.8	24.1	30.6	40.0	49.1	58.3	63.1	61.4	54.3	42.5	34.3	26.6	42.2
Extreme Maximum Temp. (°F)	73	78	85	92	92	97	101	103	98	90	80	77	103
Extreme Minimum Temp. (°F)	-27	-13	4	15	28	35	45	36	32	20	12	-4	-27
Days Maximum Temp. ≥ 90°F	0	0	0	0	0	4	8	5	2	0	0	0	19
Days Maximum Temp. ≤ 32°F	8	3	1	0	0	0	0	0	0	0	0	4	16
Days Minimum Temp. ≤ 32°F	26	23	19	6	1	0	0	0	0	5	14	23	117
Days Minimum Temp. ≤ 0°F	1	0	0	0	0	0	0	0	0	0	0	0	1
Heating Degree Days (base 65°F)	1,058	864	711	374	154	21	1	6	74	334	605	920	5,122
Cooling Degree Days (base 65°F)	0	0	1	9	48	181	302	255	103	14	0	0	913
Mean Precipitation (in.)	3.13	2.74	3.99	3.84	4.49	3.74	3.69	3.25	4.38	3.15	3.60	3.35	43.35
Extreme Maximum Daily Precip. (in.)	3.20	2.50	2.50	2.22	4.92	4.00	2.30	3.64	4.65	2.60	2.50	3.20	4.92
Days With ≥ 0.1" Precipitation	7	6	8	7	9	7	7	6	6	6	7	6	82
Days With ≥ 0.5" Precipitation	2	2	3	3	3	3	3	2	3	2	3	2	31
Days With ≥ 1.0" Precipitation	1	1	1	1	1	1	1	1	1	1	1	1	12
Mean Snowfall (in.)	10.7	9.0	4.8	0.7	0.0	0.0	0.0	0.0	0.0	0.0	0.8	5.3	31.3
Maximum Snow Depth (in.)	40	28	22	2	0	0	0	0	0	0	3	18	40
Days With ≥ 1.0" Snow Depth	9	8	3	0	0	0	0	0	0	0	0	4	24

Glenn Dale Bell Stn *Prince George's County* Elevation: 149 ft. Latitude: 38° 58' N Longitude: 76° 48' W

	JAN	FEB	MAR	APR	MAY	JUN	JUL	AUG	SEP	OCT	NOV	DEC	YEAR
Mean Maximum Temp. (°F)	44.3	48.1	56.7	67.5	76.1	84.1	88.6	86.9	80.1	68.9	58.8	48.1	67.4
Mean Temp. (°F)	33.8	36.7	44.2	54.1	63.1	71.8	76.6	75.0	67.9	56.1	46.8	37.5	55.3
Mean Minimum Temp. (°F)	23.2	25.1	31.6	40.6	50.1	59.4	64.6	63.1	55.6	43.1	34.7	26.8	43.1
Extreme Maximum Temp. (°F)	75	80	95	95	97	102	102	104	98	89	85	79	104
Extreme Minimum Temp. (°F)	-11	-10	2	20	28	38	40	38	34	21	9	-3	-11
Days Maximum Temp. ≥ 90°F	0	0	0	1	2	7	14	10	3	0	0	0	37
Days Maximum Temp. ≤ 32°F	4	2	0	0	0	0	0	0	0	0	0	2	8
Days Minimum Temp. ≤ 32°F	25	22	17	6	0	0	0	0	0	5	13	23	111
Days Minimum Temp. ≤ 0°F	1	0	0	0	0	0	0	0	0	0	0	0	1
Heating Degree Days (base 65°F)	962	795	642	337	127	16	1	3	51	289	543	848	4,614
Cooling Degree Days (base 65°F)	0	0	4	15	74	226	366	319	143	19	2	0	1,168
Mean Precipitation (in.)	2.99	2.76	3.90	3.41	4.52	4.21	4.12	3.58	3.96	3.50	3.63	3.10	43.68
Extreme Maximum Daily Precip. (in.)	***2.17***	1.60	2.28	2.75	2.31	5.87	3.84	3.40	***4.78***	5.80	***3.76***	***2.11***	***5.87***
Days With ≥ 0.1" Precipitation	6	5	6	7	7	6	7	6	5	5	5	6	71
Days With ≥ 0.5" Precipitation	2	2	3	3	3	3	3	3	2	2	2	2	30
Days With ≥ 1.0" Precipitation	1	1	1	1	1	1	1	1	1	1	1	1	12
Mean Snowfall (in.)	4.1	2.8	1.1	trace	0.0	0.0	0.0	0.0	0.0	0.0	0.8	1.5	10.3
Maximum Snow Depth (in.)	16	14	7	trace	0	0	0	0	0	0	10	8	16
Days With ≥ 1.0" Snow Depth	4	2	0	0	0	0	0	0	0	0	0	1	7

Laurel 3 W *Prince George's County* Elevation: 399 ft. Latitude: 39° 06' N Longitude: 76° 54' W

	JAN	FEB	MAR	APR	MAY	JUN	JUL	AUG	SEP	OCT	NOV	DEC	YEAR
Mean Maximum Temp. (°F)	***42.0***	***46.6***	***55.0***	66.1	***75.1***	***83.9***	***88.5***	***87.1***	79.2	68.2	57.2	46.2	***66.2***
Mean Temp. (°F)	***33.5***	***37.2***	***44.9***	55.4	***64.6***	***73.4***	***78.4***	***77.0***	69.2	57.8	47.7	37.9	***56.4***
Mean Minimum Temp. (°F)	***25.1***	27.8	34.6	44.6	***54.2***	***63.0***	68.1	***66.7***	59.2	47.4	38.3	29.6	***46.5***
Extreme Maximum Temp. (°F)	***73***	***80***	***89***	***95***	***97***	***101***	***104***	***102***	***99***	91	83	78	***104***
Extreme Minimum Temp. (°F)	***-12***	***3***	***8***	***22***	***35***	***41***	***52***	***47***	***38***	11	17	0	***-12***
Days Maximum Temp. ≥ 90°F	***0***	0	0	1	***2***	***7***	14	***10***	3	0	0	0	***37***
Days Maximum Temp. ≤ 32°F	***5***	3	0	0	***0***	***0***	0	***0***	0	0	0	3	***11***
Days Minimum Temp. ≤ 32°F	***24***	20	***13***	2	***0***	***0***	0	***0***	0	1	8	20	***88***
Days Minimum Temp. ≤ 0°F	***0***	0	0	0	***0***	***0***	0	***0***	0	0	0	0	***0***
Heating Degree Days (base 65°F)	***968***	***781***	***620***	303	***100***	***9***	***0***	***1***	34	244	512	833	***4,405***
Cooling Degree Days (base 65°F)	***0***	***0***	***4***	21	***94***	***269***	***421***	***378***	167	29	1	0	***1,384***
Mean Precipitation (in.)	3.14	2.78	4.12	3.88	4.58	4.06	4.08	3.22	4.41	3.90	4.08	3.53	45.78
Extreme Maximum Daily Precip. (in.)	2.33	2.15	2.48	2.97	3.10	3.89	3.40	3.40	3.80	4.47	3.55	2.50	4.47
Days With ≥ 0.1" Precipitation	6	5	7	7	8	7	7	5	6	5	6	6	75
Days With ≥ 0.5" Precipitation	2	2	3	3	3	3	3	3	3	3	3	3	34
Days With ≥ 1.0" Precipitation	1	0	1	1	1	1	1	1	1	1	1	1	11
Mean Snowfall (in.)	***4.0***	3.9	1.1	trace	0.0	0.0	0.0	0.0	0.0	0.0	0.7	0.8	***10.5***
Maximum Snow Depth (in.)	***12***	na	***trace***	trace	0	0	0	***0***	0	0	trace	***6***	na
Days With ≥ 1.0" Snow Depth	***0***	***0***	0	0	0	0	0	0	0	0	0	0	***0***

The period of record for all cooperative weather station data is 1980 – 2009. See User Guide for detailed explanation of data.

Mechanicsville 5 NE *St. Mary's County* Elevation: 100 ft. Latitude: 38° 27' N Longitude: 76° 41' W

	JAN	FEB	MAR	APR	MAY	JUN	JUL	AUG	SEP	OCT	NOV	DEC	YEAR
Mean Maximum Temp. (°F)	43.9	47.7	56.6	67.5	74.4	82.2	86.1	84.2	77.0	66.4	58.1	47.6	66.0
Mean Temp. (°F)	35.1	37.9	45.5	55.6	63.5	71.9	76.4	74.7	67.6	56.3	47.9	38.6	55.9
Mean Minimum Temp. (°F)	26.2	28.1	34.3	43.6	52.5	61.7	66.6	65.2	58.2	46.2	37.6	29.6	45.8
Extreme Maximum Temp. (°F)	81	81	91	94	94	98	103	101	100	88	82	80	103
Extreme Minimum Temp. (°F)	-7	-9	5	21	30	40	45	41	35	26	14	0	-9
Days Maximum Temp. ≥ 90°F	0	0	0	1	1	4	9	6	1	0	0	0	22
Days Maximum Temp. ≤ 32°F	4	2	0	0	0	0	0	0	0	0	0	2	8
Days Minimum Temp. ≤ 32°F	23	20	14	4	0	0	0	0	0	2	11	20	94
Days Minimum Temp. ≤ 0°F	0	0	0	0	0	0	0	0	0	0	0	0	0
Heating Degree Days (base 65°F)	921	761	603	299	115	12	0	2	48	282	510	811	4,364
Cooling Degree Days (base 65°F)	0	0	5	22	74	227	361	310	133	20	2	0	1,154
Mean Precipitation (in.)	3.36	3.03	4.46	3.55	4.05	4.08	4.08	3.70	4.18	3.75	3.65	3.52	45.41
Extreme Maximum Daily Precip. (in.)	3.11	2.33	3.52	2.12	4.71	2.44	3.23	4.21	8.10	2.95	3.41	3.20	8.10
Days With ≥ 0.1" Precipitation	6	6	7	7	7	7	7	6	6	5	6	6	76
Days With ≥ 0.5" Precipitation	3	2	3	3	3	3	3	2	3	2	3	3	33
Days With ≥ 1.0" Precipitation	1	1	1	1	1	1	1	1	1	1	1	1	12
Mean Snowfall (in.)	6.0	5.6	1.5	0.2	0.0	0.0	0.0	0.0	0.0	0.0	0.4	2.6	16.3
Maximum Snow Depth (in.)	23	14	10	1	0	0	0	0	0	0	5	16	23
Days With ≥ 1.0" Snow Depth	5	4	1	0	0	0	0	0	0	0	0	2	12

Oakland 1 SE *Garrett County* Elevation: 2,418 ft. Latitude: 39° 24' N Longitude: 79° 24' W

	JAN	FEB	MAR	APR	MAY	JUN	JUL	AUG	SEP	OCT	NOV	DEC	YEAR
Mean Maximum Temp. (°F)	36.6	39.8	48.8	60.8	69.0	76.2	79.5	78.7	72.3	62.3	51.0	40.3	59.6
Mean Temp. (°F)	27.5	29.7	37.5	48.2	56.8	64.7	68.7	67.5	60.8	50.0	40.5	31.3	48.6
Mean Minimum Temp. (°F)	18.4	19.7	26.1	35.6	44.6	53.1	57.8	56.3	49.2	37.7	30.0	22.2	37.5
Extreme Maximum Temp. (°F)	73	70	81	86	89	93	95	97	90	83	78	72	97
Extreme Minimum Temp. (°F)	-25	-20	-17	3	24	32	33	32	28	16	-3	-22	-25
Days Maximum Temp. ≥ 90°F	0	0	0	0	0	0	1	1	0	0	0	0	2
Days Maximum Temp. ≤ 32°F	12	9	3	0	0	0	0	0	0	0	2	9	35
Days Minimum Temp. ≤ 32°F	28	25	23	12	3	0	0	0	1	10	18	26	146
Days Minimum Temp. ≤ 0°F	3	1	0	0	0	0	0	0	0	0	0	1	5
Heating Degree Days (base 65°F)	1,155	990	847	498	260	74	20	30	152	459	726	1,038	6,249
Cooling Degree Days (base 65°F)	0	0	0	2	14	71	140	115	31	2	0	0	375
Mean Precipitation (in.)	3.30	2.97	4.06	4.00	4.93	4.64	5.47	3.98	3.50	2.99	3.75	3.60	47.19
Extreme Maximum Daily Precip. (in.)	1.87	3.30	2.19	2.20	2.68	2.26	4.16	3.82	3.48	2.15	2.62	2.25	4.16
Days With ≥ 0.1" Precipitation	8	7	9	9	11	10	10	8	8	7	8	9	104
Days With ≥ 0.5" Precipitation	2	2	3	2	3	3	4	3	2	2	3	2	31
Days With ≥ 1.0" Precipitation	0	0	1	0	1	1	1	1	1	1	1	0	8
Mean Snowfall (in.)	27.8	21.0	16.5	5.1	trace	0.0	0.0	0.0	0.0	0.7	6.8	20.1	98.0
Maximum Snow Depth (in.)	na	na	na	***13***	trace	***0***	***0***	***0***	***0***	***trace***	***9***	na	na
Days With ≥ 1.0" Snow Depth	na	na	***4***	1	0	0	0	0	0	0	1	***6***	na

Rockville 1 NE *Montgomery County* Elevation: 439 ft. Latitude: 39° 06' N Longitude: 77° 06' W

	JAN	FEB	MAR	APR	MAY	JUN	JUL	AUG	SEP	OCT	NOV	DEC	YEAR
Mean Maximum Temp. (°F)	42.1	45.1	54.2	66.0	74.3	82.3	86.4	***84.3***	***77.0***	66.2	56.1	45.7	***65.0***
Mean Temp. (°F)	33.8	36.1	44.1	55.0	63.7	72.2	76.7	***74.9***	***67.5***	56.0	46.6	37.3	***55.3***
Mean Minimum Temp. (°F)	25.4	27.1	34.1	44.0	53.1	62.0	67.0	***65.4***	***58.0***	45.7	37.1	29.0	***45.7***
Extreme Maximum Temp. (°F)	74	82	89	95	96	98	***101***	***100***	***96***	***87***	***84***	***78***	***101***
Extreme Minimum Temp. (°F)	-13	***-1***	5	19	30	38	***44***	***40***	***39***	***22***	***15***	***-1***	***-13***
Days Maximum Temp. ≥ 90°F	0	0	0	0	2	5	10	***6***	1	0	0	0	***24***
Days Maximum Temp. ≤ 32°F	6	3	1	0	0	0	0	***0***	0	0	0	3	***13***
Days Minimum Temp. ≤ 32°F	23	20	13	2	0	0	0	***0***	0	1	***10***	***20***	***89***
Days Minimum Temp. ≤ 0°F	0	0	0	0	0	0	0	***0***	0	0	0	0	***0***
Heating Degree Days (base 65°F)	962	810	644	312	116	15	1	***2***	***51***	290	***550***	852	***4,605***
Cooling Degree Days (base 65°F)	0	0	5	18	84	236	371	***316***	***134***	17	1	0	***1,182***
Mean Precipitation (in.)	2.89	2.52	3.72	3.06	4.03	3.49	3.65	***2.89***	3.77	3.17	3.54	2.73	***39.46***
Extreme Maximum Daily Precip. (in.)	1.55	1.92	2.75	1.90	3.15	5.15	***2.35***	***2.85***	***4.07***	***4.36***	***3.50***	***2.28***	***5.15***
Days With ≥ 0.1" Precipitation	6	5	7	6	8	6	7	***5***	6	5	***5***	6	***72***
Days With ≥ 0.5" Precipitation	2	2	2	2	3	2	3	***2***	2	2	2	2	***26***
Days With ≥ 1.0" Precipitation	1	1	1	0	1	1	1	***1***	1	1	1	1	***11***
Mean Snowfall (in.)	***8.1***	4.7	2.6	0.1	0.0	0.0	0.0	***0.0***	0.0	0.0	0.5	***2.2***	***18.2***
Maximum Snow Depth (in.)	30	***23***	***11***	***trace***	***0***	***0***	***0***	***0***	***0***	***0***	***5***	***7***	***30***
Days With ≥ 1.0" Snow Depth	7	6	1	0	0	0	0	***0***	***0***	***0***	0	3	***17***

Royal Oak 2 SSW *Talbot County* Elevation: 9 ft. Latitude: 38° 43' N Longitude: 76° 11' W

	JAN	FEB	MAR	APR	MAY	JUN	JUL	AUG	SEP	OCT	NOV	DEC	YEAR
Mean Maximum Temp. (°F)	44.1	47.4	55.5	66.3	75.1	83.6	87.7	86.3	79.8	69.1	58.5	48.0	66.8
Mean Temp. (°F)	36.3	38.9	46.2	56.2	65.3	74.2	78.6	76.9	70.3	59.5	49.8	40.2	57.7
Mean Minimum Temp. (°F)	28.5	30.4	36.9	46.1	55.5	64.9	69.4	67.6	60.7	49.9	41.2	32.4	48.6
Extreme Maximum Temp. (°F)	77	75	87	93	95	97	101	101	97	92	80	76	101
Extreme Minimum Temp. (°F)	-6	7	13	23	36	43	52	45	39	28	20	4	-6
Days Maximum Temp. ≥ 90°F	0	0	0	0	1	5	11	8	2	0	0	0	27
Days Maximum Temp. ≤ 32°F	4	1	0	0	0	0	0	0	0	0	0	2	7
Days Minimum Temp. ≤ 32°F	20	18	10	1	0	0	0	0	0	0	5	16	70
Days Minimum Temp. ≤ 0°F	0	0	0	0	0	0	0	0	0	0	0	0	0
Heating Degree Days (base 65°F)	881	732	577	275	81	5	0	1	24	201	451	760	3,988
Cooling Degree Days (base 65°F)	0	0	3	18	98	289	429	378	189	37	2	0	1,443
Mean Precipitation (in.)	3.62	3.07	4.35	3.97	4.17	3.85	4.22	4.16	4.01	3.63	3.54	3.66	46.25
Extreme Maximum Daily Precip. (in.)	2.68	2.24	3.09	3.60	3.64	5.61	4.05	3.31	7.90	2.69	2.54	2.68	7.90
Days With ≥ 0.1" Precipitation	7	6	7	7	7	7	7	6	5	5	6	7	77
Days With ≥ 0.5" Precipitation	3	2	3	3	3	3	3	3	3	2	3	3	34
Days With ≥ 1.0" Precipitation	1	1	1	1	1	1	1	1	1	1	1	1	12
Mean Snowfall (in.)	5.5	4.9	1.5	0.1	0.0	0.0	0.0	0.0	0.0	0.0	0.3	2.2	14.5
Maximum Snow Depth (in.)	17	14	11	trace	0	0	0	0	0	0	5	13	17
Days With ≥ 1.0" Snow Depth	4	3	1	0	0	0	0	0	0	0	0	2	10

The period of record for all cooperative weather station data is 1980 – 2009. See User Guide for detailed explanation of data.

Upper Marlboro 3 NNW *Prince George's County* Elevation: 100 ft. Latitude: 38° 52' N Longitude: 76° 47' W

	JAN	FEB	MAR	APR	MAY	JUN	JUL	AUG	SEP	OCT	NOV	DEC	YEAR
Mean Maximum Temp. (°F)	43.4	47.0	54.8	65.5	74.5	83.0	87.2	86.2	79.2	68.3	58.1	47.7	66.2
Mean Temp. (°F)	33.4	36.4	43.6	53.9	63.2	72.0	76.4	75.0	67.6	56.0	46.8	37.6	55.2
Mean Minimum Temp. (°F)	23.4	25.8	32.3	42.2	51.9	61.0	65.6	63.9	56.0	43.6	35.5	27.5	44.1
Extreme Maximum Temp. (°F)	75	80	89	95	97	100	102	102	99	93	84	80	102
Extreme Minimum Temp. (°F)	-12	-8	6	20	29	40	43	39	34	22	15	2	-12
Days Maximum Temp. ≥ 90°F	0	0	0	0	2	6	11	9	3	0	0	0	31
Days Maximum Temp. ≤ 32°F	6	2	0	0	0	0	0	0	0	0	0	2	10
Days Minimum Temp. ≤ 32°F	25	22	17	3	0	0	0	0	0	3	12	23	105
Days Minimum Temp. ≤ 0°F	1	0	0	0	0	0	0	0	0	0	0	0	1
Heating Degree Days (base 65°F)	971	802	660	343	127	15	1	3	53	294	541	843	4,653
Cooling Degree Days (base 65°F)	0	0	3	16	79	232	362	321	138	21	2	0	1,174
Mean Precipitation (in.)	2.83	2.60	3.64	3.72	4.42	4.01	4.06	3.51	3.82	3.62	3.53	3.16	42.92
Extreme Maximum Daily Precip. (in.)	2.00	2.98	2.14	2.40	5.15	2.96	2.50	2.78	5.00	3.19	***2.58***	2.42	***5.15***
Days With ≥ 0.1" Precipitation	6	6	7	7	8	7	7	6	6	5	5	6	76
Days With ≥ 0.5" Precipitation	2	2	3	3	3	3	3	2	3	2	3	2	31
Days With ≥ 1.0" Precipitation	1	1	1	1	1	1	1	1	1	1	1	1	12
Mean Snowfall (in.)	6.4	5.1	1.5	trace	0.0	0.0	0.0	0.0	0.0	0.0	0.3	2.0	15.3
Maximum Snow Depth (in.)	24	17	9	trace	0	0	0	0	0	0	9	16	24
Days With ≥ 1.0" Snow Depth	6	5	1	0	0	0	0	0	0	0	0	2	14

The period of record for all cooperative weather station data is 1980 – 2009. See User Guide for detailed explanation of data.

Maryland Weather Station Rankings

Annual Extreme Maximum Temperature

Highest Rank	Station Name	°F	Lowest Rank	Station Name	°F
1	Conowingo Dam	***109***	1	Catoctin Mountain Park	96
2	Baltimore Blt-Washngtn Int'l	105	2	Oakland 1 SE	97
2	Cumberland 2	105	3	Aberdeen Phillips Field	100
2	Dalecarlia Reservoir	105	4	Rockville 1 NE	***101***
5	Chestertown	104	4	Royal Oak 2 SSW	101
5	Glenn Dale Bell Stn	104	6	Assateague Island	***102***
5	Laurel 3 W	***104***	6	Upper Marlboro 3 NNW	102
8	Annapolis Police Brks	***103***	8	Annapolis Police Brks	***103***
8	Beltsville	103	8	Beltsville	103
8	Emmitsburg 2 SE	103	8	Emmitsburg 2 SE	103
8	Mechanicsville 5 NE	103	8	Mechanicsville 5 NE	103
12	Assateague Island	***102***	12	Chestertown	104
12	Upper Marlboro 3 NNW	102	12	Glenn Dale Bell Stn	104
14	Rockville 1 NE	***101***	12	Laurel 3 W	***104***
14	Royal Oak 2 SSW	101	15	Baltimore Blt-Washngtn Int'l	105
16	Aberdeen Phillips Field	100	15	Cumberland 2	105
17	Oakland 1 SE	97	15	Dalecarlia Reservoir	105
18	Catoctin Mountain Park	96	18	Conowingo Dam	***109***

Annual Mean Maximum Temperature

Highest Rank	Station Name	°F	Lowest Rank	Station Name	°F
1	Dalecarlia Reservoir	68.3	1	Oakland 1 SE	59.6
2	Annapolis Police Brks	***67.5***	2	Catoctin Mountain Park	61.0
3	Glenn Dale Bell Stn	67.4	3	Emmitsburg 2 SE	64.1
4	Royal Oak 2 SSW	66.8	4	Rockville 1 NE	***65.0***
5	Laurel 3 W	***66.2***	5	Assateague Island	***65.5***
5	Upper Marlboro 3 NNW	66.2	5	Baltimore Blt-Washngtn Int'l	65.5
7	Chestertown	66.0	5	Beltsville	65.5
7	Mechanicsville 5 NE	66.0	8	Conowingo Dam	***65.7***
9	Cumberland 2	65.9	9	Cumberland 2	65.9
10	Conowingo Dam	***65.7***	10	Chestertown	66.0
11	Assateague Island	***65.5***	10	Mechanicsville 5 NE	66.0
11	Baltimore Blt-Washngtn Int'l	65.5	12	Laurel 3 W	***66.2***
11	Beltsville	65.5	12	Upper Marlboro 3 NNW	66.2
14	Rockville 1 NE	***65.0***	14	Royal Oak 2 SSW	66.8
15	Emmitsburg 2 SE	64.1	15	Glenn Dale Bell Stn	67.4
16	Catoctin Mountain Park	61.0	16	Annapolis Police Brks	***67.5***
17	Oakland 1 SE	59.6	17	Dalecarlia Reservoir	68.3

Rankings include 25 highest/lowest stations. If state has less than 25 stations, all stations are included. The period of record is 1980–2009. See User Guide for detailed explanation of data.

Annual Mean Temperature

Highest			Lowest		
Rank	Station Name	°F	Rank	Station Name	°F
1	Royal Oak 2 SSW	57.7	1	Oakland 1 SE	48.6
2	Annapolis Police Brks	***57.5***	2	Catoctin Mountain Park	52.2
3	Assateague Island	***57.0***	3	Emmitsburg 2 SE	53.2
4	Dalecarlia Reservoir	56.7	4	Cumberland 2	54.1
5	Laurel 3 W	***56.4***	5	Conowingo Dam	***54.7***
6	Mechanicsville 5 NE	55.9	6	Beltsville	55.1
7	Chestertown	55.8	7	Upper Marlboro 3 NNW	55.2
8	Baltimore Blt-Washngtn Int'l	55.6	8	Glenn Dale Bell Stn	55.3
9	Glenn Dale Bell Stn	55.3	8	Rockville 1 NE	***55.3***
9	Rockville 1 NE	***55.3***	10	Baltimore Blt-Washngtn Int'l	55.6
11	Upper Marlboro 3 NNW	55.2	11	Chestertown	55.8
12	Beltsville	55.1	12	Mechanicsville 5 NE	55.9
13	Conowingo Dam	***54.7***	13	Laurel 3 W	***56.4***
14	Cumberland 2	54.1	14	Dalecarlia Reservoir	56.7
15	Emmitsburg 2 SE	53.2	15	Assateague Island	***57.0***
16	Catoctin Mountain Park	52.2	16	Annapolis Police Brks	***57.5***
17	Oakland 1 SE	48.6	17	Royal Oak 2 SSW	57.7

Annual Mean Minimum Temperature

Highest			Lowest		
Rank	Station Name	°F	Rank	Station Name	°F
1	Royal Oak 2 SSW	48.6	1	Oakland 1 SE	37.6
2	Assateague Island	***48.5***	2	Emmitsburg 2 SE	42.2
3	Annapolis Police Brks	***47.4***	3	Cumberland 2	42.3
4	Laurel 3 W	***46.6***	4	Glenn Dale Bell Stn	43.2
5	Mechanicsville 5 NE	45.8	5	Catoctin Mountain Park	43.3
6	Rockville 1 NE	***45.7***	6	Conowingo Dam	***43.7***
7	Baltimore Blt-Washngtn Int'l	45.6	7	Upper Marlboro 3 NNW	44.1
7	Chestertown	45.6	8	Beltsville	44.7
9	Dalecarlia Reservoir	45.1	9	Dalecarlia Reservoir	45.1
10	Beltsville	44.7	10	Baltimore Blt-Washngtn Int'l	45.6
11	Upper Marlboro 3 NNW	44.1	10	Chestertown	45.6
12	Conowingo Dam	***43.7***	12	Rockville 1 NE	***45.7***
13	Catoctin Mountain Park	43.3	13	Mechanicsville 5 NE	45.8
14	Glenn Dale Bell Stn	43.2	14	Laurel 3 W	***46.6***
15	Cumberland 2	42.3	15	Annapolis Police Brks	***47.4***
16	Emmitsburg 2 SE	42.2	16	Assateague Island	***48.5***
17	Oakland 1 SE	37.6	17	Royal Oak 2 SSW	48.6

Rankings include 25 highest/lowest stations. If state has less than 25 stations, all stations are included. The period of record is 1980–2009. See User Guide for detailed explanation of data.

Annual Extreme Minimum Temperature

Highest Rank	Highest Station Name	Highest °F	Lowest Rank	Lowest Station Name	Lowest °F
1	Assateague Island	***-2***	1	Emmitsburg 2 SE	-27
2	Royal Oak 2 SSW	-6	2	Oakland 1 SE	-25
3	Baltimore Blt-Washngtn Int'l	-7	3	Catoctin Mountain Park	-18
3	Chestertown	-7	4	Cumberland 2	-14
5	Annapolis Police Brks	***-8***	5	Rockville 1 NE	***-13***
6	Conowingo Dam	***-9***	6	Beltsville	-12
6	Mechanicsville 5 NE	-9	6	Laurel 3 W	***-12***
8	Aberdeen Phillips Field	-10	6	Upper Marlboro 3 NNW	-12
9	Dalecarlia Reservoir	-11	9	Dalecarlia Reservoir	-11
9	Glenn Dale Bell Stn	-11	9	Glenn Dale Bell Stn	-11
11	Beltsville	-12	11	Aberdeen Phillips Field	-10
11	Laurel 3 W	***-12***	12	Conowingo Dam	***-9***
11	Upper Marlboro 3 NNW	-12	12	Mechanicsville 5 NE	-9
14	Rockville 1 NE	***-13***	14	Annapolis Police Brks	***-8***
15	Cumberland 2	-14	15	Baltimore Blt-Washngtn Int'l	-7
16	Catoctin Mountain Park	-18	15	Chestertown	-7
17	Oakland 1 SE	-25	17	Royal Oak 2 SSW	-6
18	Emmitsburg 2 SE	-27	18	Assateague Island	***-2***

July Mean Maximum Temperature

Highest Rank	Highest Station Name	Highest °F	Lowest Rank	Lowest Station Name	Lowest °F
1	Dalecarlia Reservoir	89.8	1	Oakland 1 SE	79.5
2	Annapolis Police Brks	***89.2***	2	Catoctin Mountain Park	81.2
3	Conowingo Dam	88.7	3	Assateague Island	84.8
4	Glenn Dale Bell Stn	88.6	4	Emmitsburg 2 SE	85.8
5	Laurel 3 W	***88.5***	5	Mechanicsville 5 NE	86.1
6	Chestertown	88.0	6	Rockville 1 NE	86.4
7	Cumberland 2	87.8	7	Beltsville	87.2
8	Royal Oak 2 SSW	87.7	7	Upper Marlboro 3 NNW	87.2
9	Baltimore Blt-Washngtn Int'l	87.6	9	Aberdeen Phillips Field	***87.5***
10	Aberdeen Phillips Field	***87.5***	10	Baltimore Blt-Washngtn Int'l	87.6
11	Beltsville	87.2	11	Royal Oak 2 SSW	87.7
11	Upper Marlboro 3 NNW	87.2	12	Cumberland 2	87.8
13	Rockville 1 NE	86.4	13	Chestertown	88.0
14	Mechanicsville 5 NE	86.1	14	Laurel 3 W	***88.5***
15	Emmitsburg 2 SE	85.8	15	Glenn Dale Bell Stn	88.6
16	Assateague Island	84.8	16	Conowingo Dam	88.7
17	Catoctin Mountain Park	81.2	17	Annapolis Police Brks	***89.2***
18	Oakland 1 SE	79.5	18	Dalecarlia Reservoir	89.8

Rankings include 25 highest/lowest stations. If state has less than 25 stations, all stations are included. The period of record is 1980–2009. See User Guide for detailed explanation of data.

January Mean Minimum Temperature

Highest			Lowest		
Rank	Station Name	°F	Rank	Station Name	°F
1	Assateague Island	29.1	1	Oakland 1 SE	18.4
2	Royal Oak 2 SSW	28.6	2	Emmitsburg 2 SE	21.8
3	Annapolis Police Brks	*26.7*	3	Catoctin Mountain Park	22.2
4	Mechanicsville 5 NE	26.2	3	Conowingo Dam	*22.2*
5	Rockville 1 NE	25.4	5	Cumberland 2	22.3
6	Baltimore Blt-Washngtn Int'l	25.2	6	Glenn Dale Bell Stn	23.2
7	Chestertown	25.1	7	Upper Marlboro 3 NNW	23.4
7	Laurel 3 W	*25.1*	8	Beltsville	23.6
9	Dalecarlia Reservoir	24.3	9	Dalecarlia Reservoir	24.3
10	Beltsville	23.6	10	Chestertown	25.1
11	Upper Marlboro 3 NNW	23.4	10	Laurel 3 W	*25.1*
12	Glenn Dale Bell Stn	23.2	12	Baltimore Blt-Washngtn Int'l	25.2
13	Cumberland 2	22.3	13	Rockville 1 NE	25.4
14	Catoctin Mountain Park	22.2	14	Mechanicsville 5 NE	26.2
14	Conowingo Dam	*22.2*	15	Annapolis Police Brks	*26.7*
16	Emmitsburg 2 SE	21.8	16	Royal Oak 2 SSW	28.6
17	Oakland 1 SE	18.4	17	Assateague Island	29.1

Number of Days Annually Maximum Temperature ≥ 90°F

Highest			Lowest		
Rank	Station Name	Days	Rank	Station Name	Days
1	Dalecarlia Reservoir	45	1	Oakland 1 SE	2
2	Annapolis Police Brks	*38*	2	Catoctin Mountain Park	4
2	Conowingo Dam	*38*	3	Assateague Island	*16*
4	Glenn Dale Bell Stn	37	4	Emmitsburg 2 SE	19
4	Laurel 3 W	*37*	5	Mechanicsville 5 NE	22
6	Chestertown	35	6	Aberdeen Phillips Field	24
7	Cumberland 2	34	6	Rockville 1 NE	*24*
8	Upper Marlboro 3 NNW	31	8	Royal Oak 2 SSW	27
9	Baltimore Blt-Washngtn Int'l	30	9	Beltsville	29
10	Beltsville	29	10	Baltimore Blt-Washngtn Int'l	30
11	Royal Oak 2 SSW	27	11	Upper Marlboro 3 NNW	31
12	Aberdeen Phillips Field	24	12	Cumberland 2	34
12	Rockville 1 NE	*24*	13	Chestertown	35
14	Mechanicsville 5 NE	22	14	Glenn Dale Bell Stn	37
15	Emmitsburg 2 SE	19	14	Laurel 3 W	*37*
16	Assateague Island	*16*	16	Annapolis Police Brks	*38*
17	Catoctin Mountain Park	4	16	Conowingo Dam	*38*
18	Oakland 1 SE	2	18	Dalecarlia Reservoir	45

 Rankings include 25 highest/lowest stations. If state has less than 25 stations, all stations are included. The period of record is 1980–2009. See User Guide for detailed explanation of data.

Number of Days Annually Maximum Temperature ≤ 32°F

Highest Rank	Highest Station Name	Highest Days	Lowest Rank	Lowest Station Name	Lowest Days
1	Oakland 1 SE	35	1	Assateague Island	*5*
2	Catoctin Mountain Park	24	2	Annapolis Police Brks	*7*
3	Emmitsburg 2 SE	16	2	Royal Oak 2 SSW	7
4	Cumberland 2	15	4	Aberdeen Phillips Field	8
5	Baltimore Blt-Washngtn Int'l	13	4	Dalecarlia Reservoir	8
5	Beltsville	13	4	Glenn Dale Bell Stn	8
5	Chestertown	13	4	Mechanicsville 5 NE	8
5	Rockville 1 NE	*13*	8	Upper Marlboro 3 NNW	10
9	Conowingo Dam	*11*	9	Conowingo Dam	*11*
9	Laurel 3 W	*11*	9	Laurel 3 W	*11*
11	Upper Marlboro 3 NNW	10	11	Baltimore Blt-Washngtn Int'l	13
12	Aberdeen Phillips Field	8	11	Beltsville	13
12	Dalecarlia Reservoir	8	11	Chestertown	13
12	Glenn Dale Bell Stn	8	11	Rockville 1 NE	*13*
12	Mechanicsville 5 NE	8	15	Cumberland 2	15
16	Annapolis Police Brks	*7*	16	Emmitsburg 2 SE	16
16	Royal Oak 2 SSW	7	17	Catoctin Mountain Park	24
18	Assateague Island	*5*	18	Oakland 1 SE	35

Number of Days Annually Minimum Temperature ≤ 32°F

Highest Rank	Highest Station Name	Highest Days	Lowest Rank	Lowest Station Name	Lowest Days
1	Oakland 1 SE	146	1	Aberdeen Phillips Field	63
2	Emmitsburg 2 SE	117	2	Assateague Island	*67*
3	Cumberland 2	113	3	Royal Oak 2 SSW	70
4	Glenn Dale Bell Stn	111	4	Annapolis Police Brks	*84*
5	Catoctin Mountain Park	107	5	Laurel 3 W	*88*
5	Conowingo Dam	*107*	6	Rockville 1 NE	*89*
7	Upper Marlboro 3 NNW	105	7	Baltimore Blt-Washngtn Int'l	94
8	Beltsville	102	7	Mechanicsville 5 NE	94
9	Dalecarlia Reservoir	99	9	Chestertown	95
10	Chestertown	95	10	Dalecarlia Reservoir	99
11	Baltimore Blt-Washngtn Int'l	94	11	Beltsville	102
11	Mechanicsville 5 NE	94	12	Upper Marlboro 3 NNW	105
13	Rockville 1 NE	*89*	13	Catoctin Mountain Park	107
14	Laurel 3 W	*88*	13	Conowingo Dam	*107*
15	Annapolis Police Brks	*84*	15	Glenn Dale Bell Stn	111
16	Royal Oak 2 SSW	70	16	Cumberland 2	113
17	Assateague Island	*67*	17	Emmitsburg 2 SE	117
18	Aberdeen Phillips Field	63	18	Oakland 1 SE	146

Rankings include 25 highest/lowest stations. If state has less than 25 stations, all stations are included. The period of record is 1980–2009. See User Guide for detailed explanation of data.

Number of Days Annually Minimum Temperature ≤ 0°F

Highest			Lowest		
Rank	Station Name	Days	Rank	Station Name	Days
1	Oakland 1 SE	5	1	Aberdeen Phillips Field	0
2	Beltsville	1	1	Annapolis Police Brks	*0*
2	Catoctin Mountain Park	1	1	Assateague Island	*0*
2	Conowingo Dam	*1*	1	Baltimore Blt-Washngtn Int'l	0
2	Cumberland 2	1	1	Chestertown	0
2	Emmitsburg 2 SE	1	1	Dalecarlia Reservoir	0
2	Glenn Dale Bell Stn	1	1	Laurel 3 W	*0*
2	Upper Marlboro 3 NNW	1	1	Mechanicsville 5 NE	0
9	Aberdeen Phillips Field	0	1	Rockville 1 NE	*0*
9	Annapolis Police Brks	*0*	1	Royal Oak 2 SSW	0
9	Assateague Island	*0*	11	Beltsville	1
9	Baltimore Blt-Washngtn Int'l	0	11	Catoctin Mountain Park	1
9	Chestertown	0	11	Conowingo Dam	*1*
9	Dalecarlia Reservoir	0	11	Cumberland 2	1
9	Laurel 3 W	*0*	11	Emmitsburg 2 SE	1
9	Mechanicsville 5 NE	0	11	Glenn Dale Bell Stn	1
9	Rockville 1 NE	*0*	11	Upper Marlboro 3 NNW	1
9	Royal Oak 2 SSW	0	18	Oakland 1 SE	5

Number of Annual Heating Degree Days

Highest			Lowest		
Rank	Station Name	Num.	Rank	Station Name	Num.
1	Oakland 1 SE	6,249	1	Royal Oak 2 SSW	3,988
2	Catoctin Mountain Park	5,357	2	Assateague Island	*4,027*
3	Emmitsburg 2 SE	5,122	3	Annapolis Police Brks	*4,135*
4	Cumberland 2	4,918	4	Dalecarlia Reservoir	4,331
5	Conowingo Dam	*4,850*	5	Mechanicsville 5 NE	4,364
6	Beltsville	4,700	6	Laurel 3 W	*4,405*
7	Upper Marlboro 3 NNW	4,653	7	Chestertown	4,530
8	Glenn Dale Bell Stn	4,614	8	Baltimore Blt-Washngtn Int'l	4,577
9	Rockville 1 NE	*4,605*	9	Rockville 1 NE	*4,605*
10	Baltimore Blt-Washngtn Int'l	4,577	10	Glenn Dale Bell Stn	4,614
11	Chestertown	4,530	11	Upper Marlboro 3 NNW	4,653
12	Laurel 3 W	*4,405*	12	Beltsville	4,700
13	Mechanicsville 5 NE	4,364	13	Conowingo Dam	*4,850*
14	Dalecarlia Reservoir	4,331	14	Cumberland 2	4,918
15	Annapolis Police Brks	*4,135*	15	Emmitsburg 2 SE	5,122
16	Assateague Island	*4,027*	16	Catoctin Mountain Park	5,357
17	Royal Oak 2 SSW	3,988	17	Oakland 1 SE	6,249

 Rankings include 25 highest/lowest stations. If state has less than 25 stations, all stations are included. The period of record is 1980–2009. See User Guide for detailed explanation of data.

Number of Annual Cooling Degree Days

Highest			Lowest		
Rank	Station Name	Num.	Rank	Station Name	Num.
1	Annapolis Police Brks	***1,479***	1	Oakland 1 SE	375
2	Royal Oak 2 SSW	1,443	2	Catoctin Mountain Park	773
3	Dalecarlia Reservoir	1,415	3	Emmitsburg 2 SE	913
4	Laurel 3 W	***1,384***	4	Cumberland 2	1,066
5	Chestertown	1,293	5	Mechanicsville 5 NE	1,154
6	Baltimore Blt-Washngtn Int'l	1,260	6	Glenn Dale Bell Stn	1,168
7	Assateague Island	***1,222***	7	Upper Marlboro 3 NNW	1,174
8	Conowingo Dam	***1,207***	8	Rockville 1 NE	***1,182***
9	Beltsville	1,200	9	Beltsville	1,200
10	Rockville 1 NE	***1,182***	10	Conowingo Dam	***1,207***
11	Upper Marlboro 3 NNW	1,174	11	Assateague Island	***1,222***
12	Glenn Dale Bell Stn	1,168	12	Baltimore Blt-Washngtn Int'l	1,260
13	Mechanicsville 5 NE	1,154	13	Chestertown	1,293
14	Cumberland 2	1,066	14	Laurel 3 W	***1,384***
15	Emmitsburg 2 SE	913	15	Dalecarlia Reservoir	1,415
16	Catoctin Mountain Park	773	16	Royal Oak 2 SSW	1,443
17	Oakland 1 SE	375	17	Annapolis Police Brks	***1,479***

Annual Precipitation

Highest			Lowest		
Rank	Station Name	Inches	Rank	Station Name	Inches
1	Catoctin Mountain Park	47.81	1	Cumberland 2	37.36
2	Oakland 1 SE	47.19	2	Rockville 1 NE	***39.46***
3	Royal Oak 2 SSW	46.25	3	Baltimore Blt-Washngtn Int'l	41.55
4	Conowingo Dam	***46.11***	4	Beltsville	42.12
5	Laurel 3 W	45.78	5	Upper Marlboro 3 NNW	42.92
6	Annapolis Police Brks	***45.46***	6	Emmitsburg 2 SE	43.35
7	Mechanicsville 5 NE	45.41	7	Aberdeen Phillips Field	43.56
8	Dalecarlia Reservoir	44.92	8	Chestertown	43.58
9	Assateague Island	***43.98***	9	Glenn Dale Bell Stn	43.68
10	Glenn Dale Bell Stn	43.68	10	Assateague Island	***43.98***
11	Chestertown	43.58	11	Dalecarlia Reservoir	44.92
12	Aberdeen Phillips Field	43.56	12	Mechanicsville 5 NE	45.41
13	Emmitsburg 2 SE	43.35	13	Annapolis Police Brks	***45.46***
14	Upper Marlboro 3 NNW	42.92	14	Laurel 3 W	45.78
15	Beltsville	42.12	15	Conowingo Dam	***46.11***
16	Baltimore Blt-Washngtn Int'l	41.55	16	Royal Oak 2 SSW	46.25
17	Rockville 1 NE	***39.46***	17	Oakland 1 SE	47.19
18	Cumberland 2	37.36	18	Catoctin Mountain Park	47.81

Rankings include 25 highest/lowest stations. If state has less than 25 stations, all stations are included. The period of record is 1980–2009. See User Guide for detailed explanation of data.

Annual Extreme Maximum Daily Precipitation

Highest			Lowest		
Rank	Station Name	Inches	Rank	Station Name	Inches
1	Chestertown	11.06	1	Oakland 1 SE	4.16
2	Assateague Island	***8.87***	2	Laurel 3 W	4.47
3	Conowingo Dam	***8.25***	3	Cumberland 2	4.63
4	Mechanicsville 5 NE	8.10	4	Emmitsburg 2 SE	4.92
5	Royal Oak 2 SSW	7.90	5	Baltimore Blt-Washngtn Int'l	5.02
6	Glenn Dale Bell Stn	***5.87***	6	Rockville 1 NE	***5.15***
7	Dalecarlia Reservoir	5.80	6	Upper Marlboro 3 NNW	***5.15***
8	Beltsville	***5.54***	8	Catoctin Mountain Park	5.27
9	Catoctin Mountain Park	5.27	9	Beltsville	***5.54***
10	Rockville 1 NE	***5.15***	10	Dalecarlia Reservoir	5.80
10	Upper Marlboro 3 NNW	***5.15***	11	Glenn Dale Bell Stn	***5.87***
12	Baltimore Blt-Washngtn Int'l	5.02	12	Royal Oak 2 SSW	7.90
13	Emmitsburg 2 SE	4.92	13	Mechanicsville 5 NE	8.10
14	Cumberland 2	4.63	14	Conowingo Dam	***8.25***
15	Laurel 3 W	4.47	15	Assateague Island	***8.87***
16	Oakland 1 SE	4.16	16	Chestertown	11.06

Number of Days Annually With ≥ 0.1 Inches of Precipitation

Highest			Lowest		
Rank	Station Name	Days	Rank	Station Name	Days
1	Oakland 1 SE	104	1	Aberdeen Phillips Field	50
2	Emmitsburg 2 SE	82	2	Assateague Island	***70***
3	Catoctin Mountain Park	81	3	Glenn Dale Bell Stn	71
4	Conowingo Dam	***77***	4	Annapolis Police Brks	***72***
4	Cumberland 2	77	4	Rockville 1 NE	***72***
4	Dalecarlia Reservoir	77	6	Baltimore Blt-Washngtn Int'l	73
4	Royal Oak 2 SSW	77	7	Beltsville	75
8	Chestertown	76	7	Laurel 3 W	75
8	Mechanicsville 5 NE	76	9	Chestertown	76
8	Upper Marlboro 3 NNW	76	9	Mechanicsville 5 NE	76
11	Beltsville	75	9	Upper Marlboro 3 NNW	76
11	Laurel 3 W	75	12	Conowingo Dam	***77***
13	Baltimore Blt-Washngtn Int'l	73	12	Cumberland 2	77
14	Annapolis Police Brks	***72***	12	Dalecarlia Reservoir	77
14	Rockville 1 NE	***72***	12	Royal Oak 2 SSW	77
16	Glenn Dale Bell Stn	71	16	Catoctin Mountain Park	81
17	Assateague Island	***70***	17	Emmitsburg 2 SE	82
18	Aberdeen Phillips Field	50	18	Oakland 1 SE	104

 Rankings include 25 highest/lowest stations. If state has less than 25 stations, all stations are included. The period of record is 1980–2009. See User Guide for detailed explanation of data.

Number of Days Annually With ≥ 0.5 Inches of Precipitation

Highest			Lowest		
Rank	**Station Name**	**Days**	**Rank**	**Station Name**	**Days**
1	Laurel 3 W	34	1	Aberdeen Phillips Field	22
1	Royal Oak 2 SSW	34	2	Cumberland 2	25
3	Catoctin Mountain Park	33	3	Rockville 1 NE	***26***
3	Mechanicsville 5 NE	33	4	Assateague Island	***28***
5	Chestertown	32	5	Baltimore Blt-Washngtn Int'l	29
5	Conowingo Dam	***32***	6	Beltsville	30
7	Annapolis Police Brks	***31***	6	Dalecarlia Reservoir	30
7	Emmitsburg 2 SE	31	6	Glenn Dale Bell Stn	30
7	Oakland 1 SE	31	9	Annapolis Police Brks	***31***
7	Upper Marlboro 3 NNW	31	9	Emmitsburg 2 SE	31
11	Beltsville	30	9	Oakland 1 SE	31
11	Dalecarlia Reservoir	30	9	Upper Marlboro 3 NNW	31
11	Glenn Dale Bell Stn	30	13	Chestertown	32
14	Baltimore Blt-Washngtn Int'l	29	13	Conowingo Dam	***32***
15	Assateague Island	***28***	15	Catoctin Mountain Park	33
16	Rockville 1 NE	***26***	15	Mechanicsville 5 NE	33
17	Cumberland 2	25	17	Laurel 3 W	34
18	Aberdeen Phillips Field	22	17	Royal Oak 2 SSW	34

Number of Days Annually With ≥ 1.0 Inches of Precipitation

Highest			Lowest		
Rank	**Station Name**	**Days**	**Rank**	**Station Name**	**Days**
1	Annapolis Police Brks	***12***	1	Oakland 1 SE	8
1	Assateague Island	***12***	2	Aberdeen Phillips Field	9
1	Baltimore Blt-Washngtn Int'l	12	2	Cumberland 2	9
1	Catoctin Mountain Park	12	4	Beltsville	11
1	Chestertown	12	4	Conowingo Dam	***11***
1	Dalecarlia Reservoir	12	4	Laurel 3 W	11
1	Emmitsburg 2 SE	12	4	Rockville 1 NE	***11***
1	Glenn Dale Bell Stn	12	8	Annapolis Police Brks	***12***
1	Mechanicsville 5 NE	12	8	Assateague Island	***12***
1	Royal Oak 2 SSW	12	8	Baltimore Blt-Washngtn Int'l	12
1	Upper Marlboro 3 NNW	12	8	Catoctin Mountain Park	12
12	Beltsville	11	8	Chestertown	12
12	Conowingo Dam	***11***	8	Dalecarlia Reservoir	12
12	Laurel 3 W	11	8	Emmitsburg 2 SE	12
12	Rockville 1 NE	***11***	8	Glenn Dale Bell Stn	12
16	Aberdeen Phillips Field	9	8	Mechanicsville 5 NE	12
16	Cumberland 2	9	8	Royal Oak 2 SSW	12
18	Oakland 1 SE	8	8	Upper Marlboro 3 NNW	12

Annual Snowfall

Highest

Rank	Station Name	Inches
1	Oakland 1 SE	98.0
2	Emmitsburg 2 SE	31.3
3	Cumberland 2	29.9
4	Catoctin Mountain Park	27.7
5	Baltimore Blt-Washngtn Int'l	18.9
6	Rockville 1 NE	***18.2***
7	Mechanicsville 5 NE	16.3
8	Beltsville	15.7
9	Upper Marlboro 3 NNW	15.3
10	Chestertown	15.2
11	Royal Oak 2 SSW	14.5
12	Conowingo Dam	***11.3***
13	Aberdeen Phillips Field	10.5
13	Laurel 3 W	***10.5***
15	Glenn Dale Bell Stn	10.3
16	Dalecarlia Reservoir	7.0
17	Annapolis Police Brks	***6.5***
18	Assateague Island	***4.2***

Lowest

Rank	Station Name	Inches
1	Assateague Island	***4.2***
2	Annapolis Police Brks	***6.5***
3	Dalecarlia Reservoir	7.0
4	Glenn Dale Bell Stn	10.3
5	Aberdeen Phillips Field	10.5
5	Laurel 3 W	***10.5***
7	Conowingo Dam	***11.3***
8	Royal Oak 2 SSW	14.5
9	Chestertown	15.2
10	Upper Marlboro 3 NNW	15.3
11	Beltsville	15.7
12	Mechanicsville 5 NE	16.3
13	Rockville 1 NE	***18.2***
14	Baltimore Blt-Washngtn Int'l	18.9
15	Catoctin Mountain Park	27.7
16	Cumberland 2	29.9
17	Emmitsburg 2 SE	31.3
18	Oakland 1 SE	98.0

Annual Maximum Snow Depth

Highest

Rank	Station Name	Inches
1	Catoctin Mountain Park	42
2	Emmitsburg 2 SE	40
3	Rockville 1 NE	***30***
4	Cumberland 2	26
5	Baltimore Blt-Washngtn Int'l	25
6	Beltsville	24
6	Upper Marlboro 3 NNW	24
8	Mechanicsville 5 NE	23
9	Aberdeen Phillips Field	22
10	Dalecarlia Reservoir	21
11	Chestertown	18
12	Royal Oak 2 SSW	17
13	Glenn Dale Bell Stn	16
14	Assateague Island	*7*

Lowest

Rank	Station Name	Inches
1	Assateague Island	*7*
2	Glenn Dale Bell Stn	16
3	Royal Oak 2 SSW	17
4	Chestertown	18
5	Dalecarlia Reservoir	21
6	Aberdeen Phillips Field	22
7	Mechanicsville 5 NE	23
8	Beltsville	24
8	Upper Marlboro 3 NNW	24
10	Baltimore Blt-Washngtn Int'l	25
11	Cumberland 2	26
12	Rockville 1 NE	***30***
13	Emmitsburg 2 SE	40
14	Catoctin Mountain Park	42

Rankings include 25 highest/lowest stations. If state has less than 25 stations, all stations are included. The period of record is 1980–2009. See User Guide for detailed explanation of data.

Number of Days Annually With ≥ 1.0 Inch Snow Depth

Highest			Lowest		
Rank	Station Name	Days	Rank	Station Name	Days
1	Catoctin Mountain Park	38	1	Laurel 3 W	*0*
2	Cumberland 2	32	2	Assateague Island	*1*
3	Emmitsburg 2 SE	24	3	Aberdeen Phillips Field	7
4	Rockville 1 NE	*17*	3	Annapolis Police Brks	*7*
5	Baltimore Blt-Washngtn Int'l	14	3	Dalecarlia Reservoir	7
5	Upper Marlboro 3 NNW	14	3	Glenn Dale Bell Stn	7
7	Beltsville	13	7	Conowingo Dam	*8*
7	Chestertown	13	8	Royal Oak 2 SSW	10
9	Mechanicsville 5 NE	12	9	Mechanicsville 5 NE	12
10	Royal Oak 2 SSW	10	10	Beltsville	13
11	Conowingo Dam	*8*	10	Chestertown	13
12	Aberdeen Phillips Field	7	12	Baltimore Blt-Washngtn Int'l	14
12	Annapolis Police Brks	*7*	12	Upper Marlboro 3 NNW	14
12	Dalecarlia Reservoir	7	14	Rockville 1 NE	*17*
12	Glenn Dale Bell Stn	7	15	Emmitsburg 2 SE	24
16	Assateague Island	*1*	16	Cumberland 2	32
17	Laurel 3 W	*0*	17	Catoctin Mountain Park	38

Rankings include 25 highest/lowest stations. If state has less than 25 stations, all stations are included. The period of record is 1980–2009. See User Guide for detailed explanation of data.

Significant Storm Events in Maryland: 2000 – 2009

Location or County	Date	Type	Mag.	Deaths	Injuries	Property Damage ($mil.)	Crop Damage ($mil.)
Allegany	09/11/00	Flash Flood	na	0	0	2.0	0.0
Montgomery	06/20/01	Lightning	na	0	0	2.0	0.0
Prince George's	09/24/01	Tornado	F3	2	55	100.0	0.0
Charles	04/28/02	Tornado	F4	1	122	114.0	0.0
Calvert	04/28/02	Tornado	F2	2	0	10.0	0.0
Central Maryland	06/25/02	Excessive Heat	na	6	0	0.0	0.0
Northwest and Central Maryland	07/02/02	Excessive Heat	na	21	0	0.0	0.0
Northwest and Central Maryland	08/01/02	Excessive Heat	na	7	0	0.0	0.0
Western and North Central Maryland and Baltimore Metropolitan Area	02/14/03	Winter Storm	na	1	10	5.2	0.0
Western Shore Counties of Chesapeake Bay	09/18/03	Tropical Storm	na	1	200	530.4	0.1
Dorchester, Inland Worcester, Somerset, and Wicomico Counties	09/18/03	Tropical Storm	na	0	0	2.4	0.0
Allegany, Carroll, Frederick, Howard, Montgomery, and Washington Counties	09/18/03	High Wind	58 mph	0	3	1.8	0.2
Caroline, Cecil, Kent, Queen Anne's, and Talbot Counties	09/19/03	Storm Surge	na	0	0	50.0	0.0
Cecil	07/12/04	Flash Flood	na	0	0	2.0	0.0
Northwest and Central Maryland	01/14/06	High Wind	60 mph	0	0	1.5	0.0
Caroline	06/25/06	Flash Flood	na	0	0	4.0	1.0
Prince George's	06/25/06	Flash Flood	na	0	0	2.5	0.0
Montgomery	06/25/06	Flash Flood	na	0	0	1.6	0.0
Frederick	06/27/06	Flash Flood	na	5	1	0.5	0.0
Montgomery	07/02/06	Thunderstorm Wind	69 mph	0	0	5.0	0.0
Anne Arundel	07/02/06	Thunderstorm Wind	69 mph	0	0	1.5	0.0
Northwest and Central Maryland	08/01/06	Heat	na	6	5	0.0	0.0
Lower Maryland Eastern Shore	09/01/06	High Wind	67 mph	0	0	5.0	0.0
Calvert and St. Mary's Counties	09/01/06	High Wind	63 mph	0	0	3.4	0.0
Anne Arundel	09/28/06	Tornado	F1	0	0	6.0	0.0

Note: Deaths, injuries, and damages are date and location specific.

MASSACHUSETTS

PHYSICAL FEATURES. Massachusetts occupies 8,266 square miles, nearly one-eighth of New England's total area. Most of the State lies just above the 42nd parallel of latitude. Its north-south width is, roughly, 50 miles, except 100 miles in the eastern, Atlantic coast, portion. The east-west extension is barely 150 miles, excepting "the Cape." This is the familiar name of the long arm of land which reaches around the southern and eastern shores of Cape Cod Bay. Including the Cape, the State is nearly 200 miles in length.

The land surface is mountainous along the western border and generally hilly elsewhere. However, the Cape and some other sections of the coastal area consist of flat land with numerous marshes and some small lakes and ponds. In the west Mt. Greylock rises 3,491 feet above sea level, the highest peak in Massachusetts. The elevation is mostly over 1,000 feet west of the Connecticut River Valley. A number of peaks reach above 2,000 feet. Most of central Massachusetts lies between 500 and 1,000 feet. Eastern Massachusetts and the Connecticut River Valley are mostly less than 500 feet.

GENERAL CLIMATE. Climatic characteristics of Massachusetts includes: (1) changeableness in the weather, (2) large ranges of temperature, both daily and annual, (3) great differences between the same seasons in different years, (4) equable distribution of precipitation, and (5) considerable diversity from place to place. The regional New England climatic influences are modified in Massachusetts by varying distances from the ocean, elevations, and types of terrain. These modifying factors divide the State into three climatological divisions: (the Western Division, the Central Division, and the Coastal Division)

Massachusetts lies in the "prevailing westerlies," the belt of generally eastward air movement which encircles the globe in middle latitudes. Embedded in this circulation are extensive masses of air originating in higher or lower latitudes and interacting to produce storm systems. Relative to most other sections of the country, a large number of such storms pass over or near Massachusetts. The majority of air masses affecting this State belong to three types: (1) cold, dry air pouring down from subarctic North America, (2) warm, moist air streaming up on a long overland journey from the Gulf of Mexico and subtropical waters eastward, and (3) cool, damp air moving in from the North Atlantic. Because the atmospheric flow is usually offshore, Massachusetts is more influenced by the first two types than it is by the third. In other words, the adjacent ocean constitutes an important modifying factor, particularly on the immediate coast, but does not dominate the climate.

The procession of contrasting air masses and the relatively frequent passage of storm centers bring about a roughly twice-weekly alternation from fair to cloudy or stormy conditions, attended by often abrupt changes in temperature, moisture, sunshine, wind direction, and speed. There is no regular or persistent rhythm to this sequence, and it is interrupted by periods during which the weather patterns continue the same for several days, infrequently for several weeks. Massachusetts weather, however, is cited for variety rather than monotony. Changeability is also one of its features on a longer time-scale. That is, the same month or season will exhibit varying characteristics over the years, sometimes in close alternation, sometimes arranged in similar groups for successive years.

TEMPERATURE. Summer temperatures are delightfully comfortable for the most part, and summer averages are nearly uniform over the state. Hot days with maxima of 90°F. or higher generally average from five to 15 per year, varying not only from place to place but from year to year. They range, in frequency of occurrence, from only a few in cool summers to 25 or more in an occasional hot summer. The Cape and offshore islands are exceptions, averaging less than one day with a reading of 90°F. or higher per year.

Average temperatures vary from place to place more in winter than in summer. The diurnal temperature range in winter, though less than in summer, is still greater inland than along the coast. Days with subzero readings are rare on offshore islands. They average only a few per year near the coast, but increase in number of occurrences farther inland to from 5 to 15 annually.

PRECIPITATION. Massachusetts is fortunate in having its precipitation rather evenly distributed through the year. In this respect, the State is located in one of the relatively few areas of the world that does not have its "rainy" and "dry" seasons. Storm systems are the principal year-round moisture producers. But in the summer, when this activity ebbs, bands or patches of thunderstorms or showers tend to make up the difference. Though brief and often of small extent, the thunderstorms produce the heaviest local rainfall. Prolonged droughts are infrequent. Storms of a coastal nature make the Coastal Division the wettest in the winter season. Inland sections get the heavier rain in the warm season due, principally, to the higher frequency and greater intensity of convective showers and thunderstorms. The mountainous character of much of the Western Division is an additional cause for the heaviest annual totals being recorded in that part of the State.

SNOWFALL. Average annual amounts of snowfall increase rapidly from the coast westward. About 25 to 30 inches fall over Cape Cod, but up to 60 to 80 inches are recorded in the western part of the State. Topography has a marked influence on snowfall, causing much variation even in short distances. The average number of days with 1 inch or more of snowfall varies from about eight to 15 in the Coastal Division to mostly 20 to 30 in the Western Division. Most winters will have at least one snowstorm of five inches or more. The average number of days with snow on the ground also increases from shore to interior and with rise in elevation. There is little lasting snow cover in the coastal lowlands. In the Western Division the cover usually extends well into spring. Maximum snow depths usually occur in the middle part of February. Water stored in the snow over the watersheds makes an important contribution to the water supply. Melting is usually too gradual to threaten serious flooding.

FLOODS. The Connecticut River, the largest river system in New England, drains most of the western half of the State. Second in size in Massachusetts is the Merrimack River which occupies the northeast portion. The rest of the rivers are relatively small, most of them with headwaters in the State and flowing southward through Connecticut and Rhode Island, or directly to the coast in the east and southeast. Flooding occurs most often in spring, caused by combination of rain and melting snow. The Connecticut River shows a regular annual rise as the result of the melting of high elevation snow in northern and central New England, but extensive flooding does not occur unless the rise is accompanied by heavy rains. High flows and major floods occur from rainfall alone but less frequently. Some of the severest floods caused by heavy rains have been those associated with hurricanes or storms of tropical origin in late summer or fall, normally the low water season.

OTHER CLIMATIC FEATURES. The percentage of possible sunshine averages from 50 to 60 in most sections. Higher elevations are cloudier, reducing the Berkshire average to between 45 and 50 percent. The average annual number of clear days is between 90 and 120 for most of the State, with less in the Berkshires. Heavy fog is frequent and sometimes persistent south of Cape Cod. Nantucket Island has heavy fog on nearly 1 day out of 4. Fog frequency diminishes along the Massachusetts coast north of the Cape. Duration of fog also diminishes inland. But the shorter duration heavy ground fogs of early morning occur frequently at susceptible places inland. These, plus the fewer occurrences of other heavy fog, produce a frequency that also approaches this one day out of four in many localities. The number of days with fog varies from as low as about 15 up to nearly 100 per year over the State.

WINDS AND STORMS. The prevailing wind, on a yearly basis, comes from a westerly direction. It is more northwesterly in winter and southwesterly in summer. Along the coast in spring and summer the sea breeze is important. These onshore winds, blowing from the cool ocean, may come inland for 10 miles or so. They tend to retard the spring growth, but they are pleasantly cooling in summer. Coastal storms or "northeasters" are one of the State's most serious weather hazards. They generate very strong winds and heavy rain or snow. They can produce abnormally high, wind-driven tides. In winter, these storms produce the heaviest snow. Occasionally in summer or fall a storm of tropical origin affects Massachusetts. Often these will be similar to the northeasters. The few which retain full hurricane force cause widespread damage. Storms of tropical origin seriously affect Massachusetts about once in two years, on the average. Two such storms in the same year may be expected once in eight or 10 years.

Tornadoes are not common phenomena, yet, on a per unit area basis, Massachusetts ranks fairly high among the states. One or more may occur in Massachusetts each year. Four out of five tornadoes occur between May 15 and September 15. The peak month is July. Thunderstorms and hailstorms have a similar frequency maximum from midspring to early fall. Thunderstorms occur on about 20 to 30 days a year, and the most severe are attended by hail.

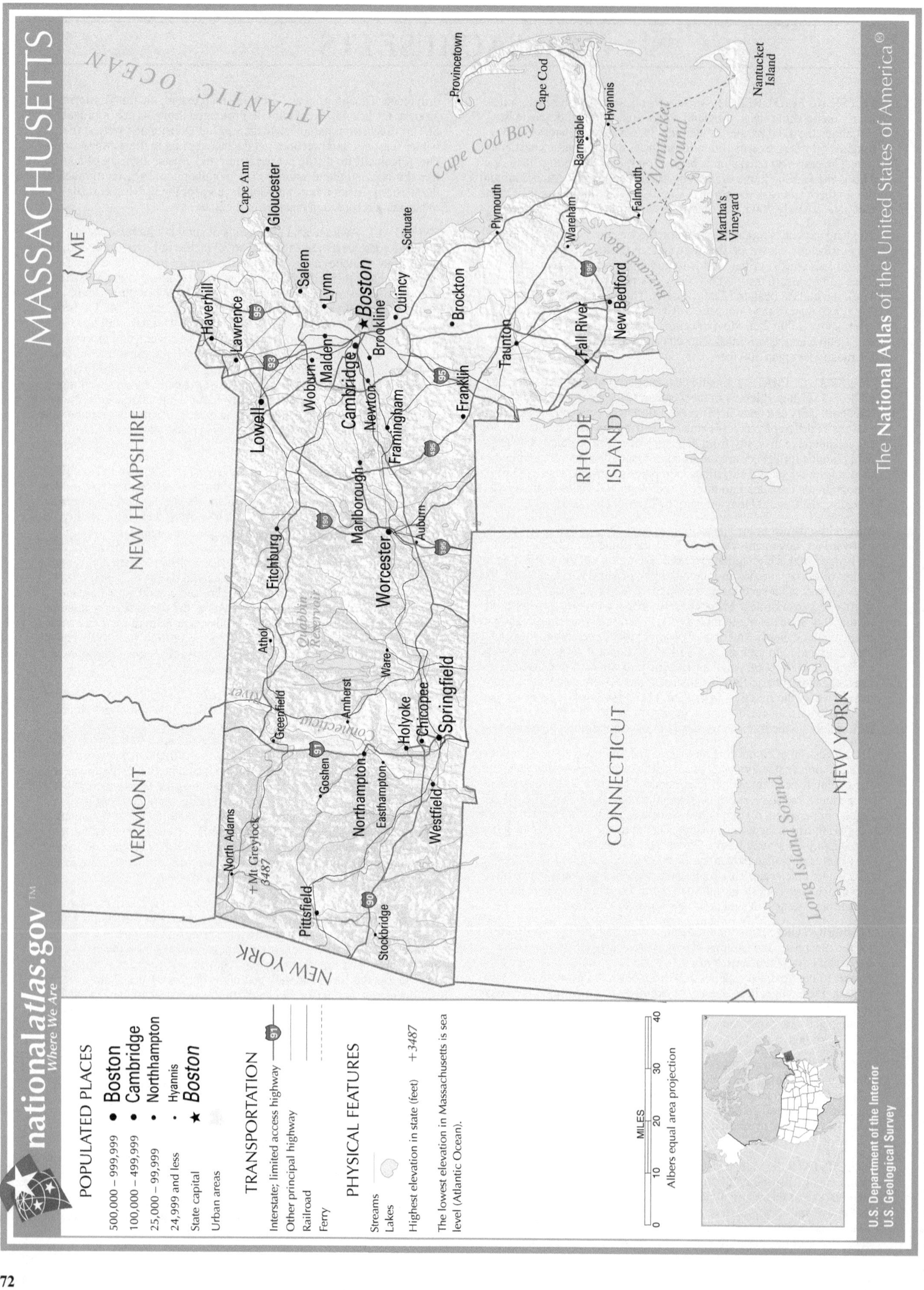
MASSACHUSETTS
nationalatlas.gov™
Where We Are
POPULATED PLACES
500,000 – 999,999 Boston
100,000 – 499,999 Cambridge
25,000 – 99,999 Northampton
24,999 and less Hyannis
State capital Boston
Urban areas
TRANSPORTATION
Interstate; limited access highway
Other principal highway
Railroad
Ferry
PHYSICAL FEATURES
Streams
Lakes
Highest elevation in state (feet) +3487
The lowest elevation in Massachusetts is sea level (Atlantic Ocean).
MILES
0 10 20 30 40
Albers equal area projection
U.S. Department of the Interior
U.S. Geological Survey
The National Atlas of the United States of America®
ATLANTIC OCEAN
ME
NEW HAMPSHIRE
VERMONT
NEW YORK
CONNECTICUT
RHODE ISLAND
Cape Ann
Gloucester
Salem
Lynn
Boston
Brookline
Quincy
Scituate
Haverhill
Lawrence
Lowell
Woburn
Malden
Cambridge
Newton
Framingham
Marlborough
Franklin
Brockton
Plymouth
Taunton
Fall River
New Bedford
Wareham
Buzzards Bay
Falmouth
Barnstable
Hyannis
Cape Cod Bay
Cape Cod
Provincetown
Nantucket Sound
Nantucket Island
Martha's Vineyard
Worcester
Auburn
Fitchburg
Athol
Quabbin Reservoir
Ware
Amherst
Greenfield
Connecticut River
Holyoke
Chicopee
Springfield
Westfield
Northampton
Easthampton
Goshen
North Adams
+Mt Greylock 3487
Pittsfield
Stockbridge
Long Island Sound

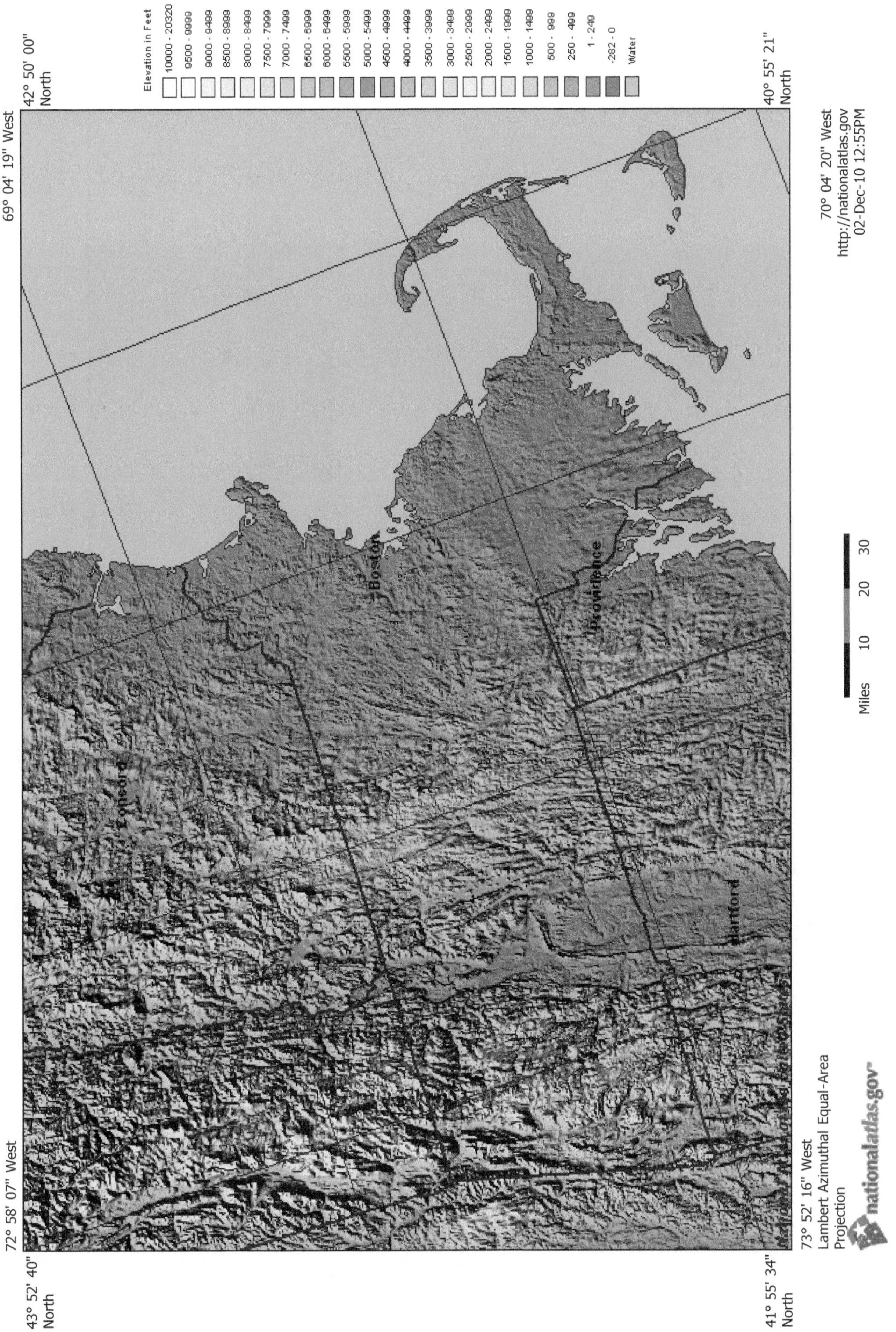
69° 04' 19" West
42° 50' 00" North
72° 58' 07" West
43° 52' 40" North
40° 55' 21" North
70° 04' 20" West
http://nationalatlas.gov
02-Dec-10 12:55PM
73° 52' 16" West
Lambert Azimuthal Equal-Area Projection
41° 55' 34" North
Elevation in Feet
10000 - 20320
9500 - 9999
9000 - 9499
8500 - 8999
8000 - 8499
7500 - 7999
7000 - 7499
6500 - 6999
6000 - 6499
5500 - 5999
5000 - 5499
4500 - 4999
4000 - 4499
3500 - 3999
3000 - 3499
2500 - 2999
2000 - 2499
1500 - 1999
1000 - 1499
500 - 999
250 - 499
1 - 249
-282 - 0
Water
Miles
10
20
30
Boston
Providence
Concord
Hartford
nationalatlas.gov

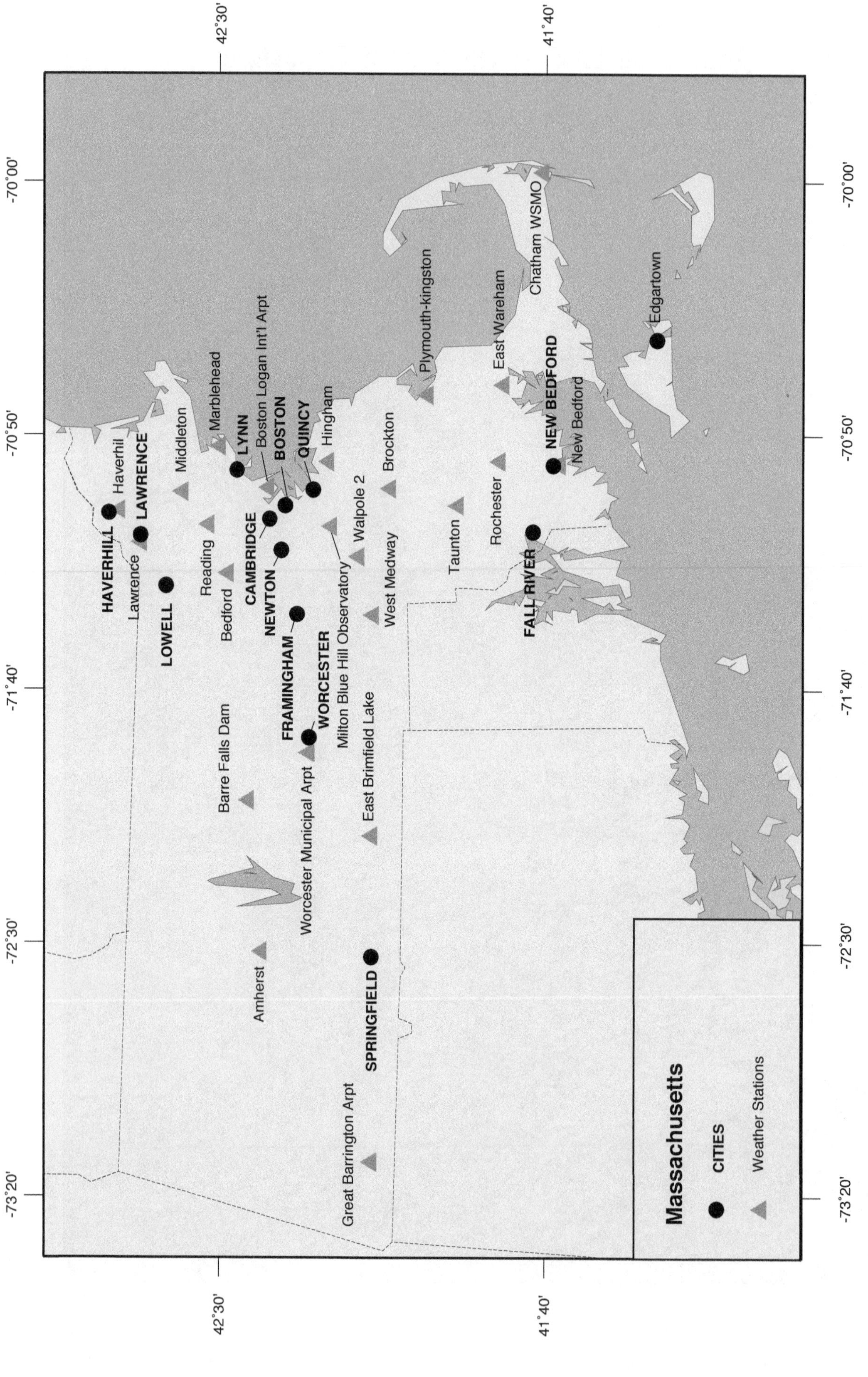
Massachusetts
CITIES
Weather Stations
42°30'
41°40'
-70°00'
-70°50'
-71°40'
-72°30'
-73°20'
HAVERHILL
Haverhil
LAWRENCE
Lawrence
LOWELL
Middleton
Marblehead
LYNN
Boston Logan Int'l Arpt
BOSTON
QUINCY
Hingham
Reading
Bedford
CAMBRIDGE
NEWTON
FRAMINGHAM
WORCESTER
Milton Blue Hill Observatory
Walpole 2
Brockton
West Medway
Worcester Municipal Arpt
East Brimfield Lake
Barre Falls Dam
Amherst
SPRINGFIELD
Great Barrington Arpt
Plymouth-kingston
Taunton
East Wareham
Rochester
Chatham WSMO
FALL RIVER
NEW BEDFORD
New Bedford
Edgartown

Massachusetts Weather Stations by County

County	Station Name
Barnstable	Chatham WSMO
Bristol	New Bedford
	Taunton
Dukes	Edgartown
Essex	Haverhill
	Lawrence
	Marblehead
	Middleton
Hampshire	Amherst
Middlesex	Bedford
	Reading
Norfolk	Milton Blue Hill Observatory
	Walpole 2
	West Medway
Plymouth	Brockton
	East Wareham
	Hingham
	Plymouth-Kingston
	Rochester
Suffolk	Boston Logan Int'l Arpt
Worcester	Barre Falls Dam
	East Brimfield Lake
	Worcester Municipal Arpt

See User Guide for station inclusion criteria.

Massachusetts Weather Stations by City

City	Station Name	Miles
Boston	Bedford	14.9
	Milton Blue Hill Observatory	7.4
	Boston Logan Int'l Arpt	4.9
	Brockton	19.3
	Hingham	10.8
	Marblehead	16.8
	Middleton	19.6
	Reading	13.6
	Walpole 2	13.5
	West Medway	21.8
Brockton	Milton Blue Hill Observatory	10.4
	Boston Logan Int'l Arpt	19.5
	Brockton	2.6
	Hingham	11.7
	Plymouth-Kingston	17.9
	Rochester	21.5
	Taunton	12.9
	Walpole 2	13.0
	West Medway	21.3
Brookline	Bedford	12.9
	Milton Blue Hill Observatory	8.2
	Boston Logan Int'l Arpt	6.1
	Brockton	20.8
	Hingham	12.9
	Marblehead	17.6
	Middleton	19.2
	Reading	12.5
	Walpole 2	13.2
	West Medway	20.9
Cambridge	Bedford	11.5
	Milton Blue Hill Observatory	10.9
	Boston Logan Int'l Arpt	4.9
	Brockton	23.1
	Hingham	14.0
	Lawrence	22.7
	Marblehead	15.3
	Middleton	16.4
	Reading	9.9
	Walpole 2	16.0
	West Medway	23.4
Chicopee	Hartford Bradley Int'l Arpt, CT	17.1
	Amherst	14.9
	East Brimfield Lake	23.6
Fall River	New Bedford	12.0
	Rochester	13.3
	Taunton	14.5
	Kingston, RI	24.8
	Providence T F Green State Arpt, RI	14.7
Framingham	Bedford	14.6
	Milton Blue Hill Observatory	16.8
	Boston Logan Int'l Arpt	21.4
	Reading	21.1
	Walpole 2	12.8
	West Medway	11.5
	Worcester Municipal Arpt	23.6
Haverhill	Bedford	22.6
	Haverhill	1.3

City	Station Name	Miles
Haverhill *(cont.)*	Lawrence	6.7
	Marblehead	22.2
	Middleton	12.8
	Reading	18.2
	Epping, NH	17.7
	Greenland, NH	21.0
	Massabesic Lake, NH	21.2
	Nashua 2 NNW, NH	20.0
Lawrence	Bedford	16.5
	Boston Logan Int'l Arpt	24.5
	Haverhill	6.5
	Lawrence	0.4
	Marblehead	20.7
	Middleton	10.4
	Reading	13.1
	Epping, NH	23.1
	Massabesic Lake, NH	22.6
	Nashua 2 NNW, NH	17.1
Lowell	Bedford	11.0
	Boston Logan Int'l Arpt	24.4
	Haverhill	15.5
	Lawrence	8.7
	Marblehead	25.0
	Middleton	15.6
	Reading	12.7
	Massabesic Lake, NH	24.0
	Nashua 2 NNW, NH	12.9
Lynn	Bedford	16.8
	Milton Blue Hill Observatory	19.5
	Boston Logan Int'l Arpt	7.9
	Haverhill	21.2
	Hingham	16.6
	Lawrence	19.1
	Marblehead	4.9
	Middleton	9.4
	Reading	9.7
Malden	Bedford	12.0
	Milton Blue Hill Observatory	15.0
	Boston Logan Int'l Arpt	4.9
	Haverhill	23.3
	Hingham	15.4
	Lawrence	19.5
	Marblehead	11.0
	Middleton	12.0
	Reading	7.1
	Walpole 2	20.6
Medford	Bedford	10.0
	Milton Blue Hill Observatory	13.9
	Boston Logan Int'l Arpt	5.8
	Haverhill	24.2
	Hingham	16.0
	Lawrence	19.8
	Marblehead	13.6
	Middleton	13.5
	Reading	7.0
	Walpole 2	18.8
New Bedford	East Wareham	15.9
	New Bedford	1.2

See User Guide for station inclusion criteria.

City	Station Name	Miles
New Bedford *(cont.)*	Rochester	9.2
	Taunton	18.5
Newton	Bedford	10.9
	Milton Blue Hill Observatory	9.5
	Boston Logan Int'l Arpt	9.9
	Brockton	22.4
	Hingham	16.4
	Marblehead	20.7
	Middleton	20.6
	Reading	13.0
	Walpole 2	11.9
	West Medway	18.2
Peabody	Bedford	16.8
	Milton Blue Hill Observatory	23.2
	Boston Logan Int'l Arpt	11.8
	Haverhill	17.1
	Hingham	20.8
	Lawrence	15.6
	Marblehead	5.3
	Middleton	5.5
	Reading	8.8
Plymouth	Brockton	21.4
	East Wareham	9.6
	New Bedford	24.2
	Plymouth-Kingston	6.5
	Rochester	16.8
	Taunton	22.3
Quincy	Bedford	20.9
	Milton Blue Hill Observatory	6.3
	Boston Logan Int'l Arpt	7.4
	Brockton	14.5
	Hingham	5.0
	Marblehead	18.1
	Middleton	23.5
	Plymouth-Kingston	24.8
	Reading	18.9
	Walpole 2	13.9
	West Medway	23.4
Revere	Bedford	15.0
	Milton Blue Hill Observatory	14.8
	Boston Logan Int'l Arpt	3.3
	Haverhill	24.6
	Hingham	13.3
	Lawrence	21.4
	Marblehead	9.2
	Middleton	12.9
	Reading	9.7
	Walpole 2	21.2
Somerville	Bedford	11.1
	Milton Blue Hill Observatory	12.1
	Boston Logan Int'l Arpt	4.8
	Brockton	24.2
	Hingham	14.6
	Lawrence	21.5
	Marblehead	14.3
	Middleton	15.1
	Reading	8.8
	Walpole 2	17.2
	West Medway	24.5

City	Station Name	Miles
Springfield	Hartford Bradley Int'l Arpt, CT	14.1
	Amherst	18.8
	East Brimfield Lake	21.4
Taunton	Milton Blue Hill Observatory	21.9
	Brockton	11.4
	East Wareham	23.9
	Hingham	24.7
	New Bedford	20.2
	Plymouth-Kingston	21.0
	Rochester	12.2
	Taunton	1.4
	Walpole 2	20.0
	West Medway	23.7
	Providence T F Green State Arpt, RI	21.6
Waltham	Bedford	7.4
	Milton Blue Hill Observatory	13.0
	Boston Logan Int'l Arpt	11.3
	Hingham	19.3
	Lawrence	22.2
	Marblehead	20.6
	Middleton	18.8
	Reading	10.7
	Walpole 2	14.9
	West Medway	19.9
Weymouth	Milton Blue Hill Observatory	8.8
	Boston Logan Int'l Arpt	11.8
	Brockton	11.0
	Hingham	2.5
	Marblehead	20.8
	Plymouth-Kingston	19.8
	Reading	23.6
	Taunton	21.9
	Walpole 2	15.8
Worcester	East Brimfield Lake	19.7
	West Medway	21.2
	Worcester Municipal Arpt	4.0

Note: Miles is the distance between the geographic center of the city and the weather station.

Massachusetts Weather Stations by Elevation

Feet	Station Name
985	Worcester Municipal Arpt
910	Barre Falls Dam
680	East Brimfield Lake
629	Milton Blue Hill Observatory
209	West Medway
165	Walpole 2
160	Bedford
149	Amherst
96	Marblehead
89	Middleton
89	Reading
80	Brockton
69	New Bedford
60	Lawrence
60	Rochester
46	Chatham WSMO
44	Plymouth-Kingston
29	Hingham
20	Boston Logan Int'l Arpt
20	East Wareham
20	Edgartown
20	Taunton
18	Haverhill

See User Guide for station inclusion criteria.

Boston Logan Int'l Airport

Three important influences are responsible for the main features of the Boston climate. First, the latitude places the city in the zone of prevailing west to east atmospheric flow. Both polar and tropical air masses influence the region. Secondly, Boston is situated on or near several tracks frequently followed by low pressure storm systems. The weather fluctuates regularly from fair to cloudy to stormy conditions and assures an adequate amount of precipitation. The third factor is the east-coast location of Boston. The ocean has a moderating influence on temperature extremes of winter and summer.

Hot summer afternoons are frequently relieved by the locally celebrated sea breeze, as air flows inland from the cool water surface to displace the warm air over the land. This refreshing east wind is more commonly experienced along the shore than in the interior of the city or the western suburbs. In winter, under appropriate conditions, the severity of cold waves is reduced by the nearness of the relatively warm ocean. The average last occurrence of freezing temperature in spring is early April and the first occurrence of freezing temperature in autumn is early November. In suburban areas, especially away from the coast, these dates are later in spring and earlier in autumn by up to one month in the more susceptible localities.

Boston has no dry season. Most growing seasons have several shorter dry spells during which irrigation for high-value crops may be useful. Much of the rainfall from June to September comes from showers and thunderstorms. During the rest of the year, low pressure systems pass more or less regularly and produce precipitation on an average of roughly one day in three. Coastal storms, or northeasters, are prolific producers of rain and snow. The main snow season extends from December through March. Periods when the ground is bare or nearly bare of snow may occur at any time in the winter.

Relative humidity has been known to fall as low as five percent but such desert dryness is very rare. Heavy fog occurs on an average of about two days per month with its prevalence increasing eastward from the interior of Boston Bay to the open waters beyond.

Although winds of 30 mph or higher may be expected on at least one day in every month of the year, gales are both more common and more severe in winter.

Boston Logan Int'l Airport *Suffolk County* Elevation: 20 ft. Latitude: 42° 22' N Longitude: 71° 01' W

	JAN	FEB	MAR	APR	MAY	JUN	JUL	AUG	SEP	OCT	NOV	DEC	YEAR
Mean Maximum Temp. (°F)	36.3	39.1	45.8	55.9	66.3	76.2	81.8	80.1	72.8	61.8	51.9	41.7	59.1
Mean Temp. (°F)	29.4	31.9	38.4	48.3	58.1	67.9	73.7	72.4	65.1	54.2	44.9	34.9	51.6
Mean Minimum Temp. (°F)	22.4	24.6	30.9	40.6	49.9	59.4	65.5	64.7	57.4	46.5	37.9	28.0	44.0
Extreme Maximum Temp. (°F)	69	70	89	93	93	98	100	101	99	86	79	76	101
Extreme Minimum Temp. (°F)	-7	-1	5	16	36	45	50	47	38	31	15	-7	-7
Days Maximum Temp. ≥ 90°F	0	0	0	0	1	3	6	4	1	0	0	0	15
Days Maximum Temp. ≤ 32°F	10	7	2	0	0	0	0	0	0	0	0	5	24
Days Minimum Temp. ≤ 32°F	26	22	16	2	0	0	0	0	0	0	7	21	94
Days Minimum Temp. ≤ 0°F	1	0	0	0	0	0	0	0	0	0	0	0	1
Heating Degree Days (base 65°F)	1,098	931	820	498	236	52	4	6	73	336	596	927	5,577
Cooling Degree Days (base 65°F)	0	0	1	3	29	144	279	244	84	8	1	0	793
Mean Precipitation (in.)	3.29	3.17	4.00	3.82	3.46	3.67	3.41	3.15	3.41	3.95	4.00	3.69	43.02
Maximum Precipitation (in.)*	10.5	7.8	11.0	9.5	13.4	13.2	8.1	17.1	8.3	8.7	8.9	9.7	62.3
Minimum Precipitation (in.)*	0.6	0.7	0.6	1.2	0.5	0.5	0.5	0.8	0.3	0.3	0.6	0.8	23.7
Extreme Maximum Daily Precip. (in.)	2.24	2.66	2.59	4.29	4.12	5.69	3.36	3.58	4.71	6.11	3.31	4.21	6.11
Days With ≥ 0.1" Precipitation	6	6	7	7	7	6	6	6	6	6	7	7	77
Days With ≥ 0.5" Precipitation	2	2	3	2	2	2	2	2	2	3	3	2	27
Days With ≥ 1.0" Precipitation	1	1	1	1	1	1	1	1	1	1	1	1	12
Mean Snowfall (in.)	12.9	11.5	8.0	1.0	0.0	trace	trace	trace	0.0	0.1	1.3	8.9	43.7
Maximum Snowfall (in.)*	36	41	39	13	1	0	0	0	0	trace	9	28	89
Maximum 24-hr. Snowfall (in.)*	21	19	13	11	1	0	0	0	0	trace	6	13	21
Maximum Snow Depth (in.)	***31***	***19***	***14***	***12***	***0***	***trace***	na	***trace***	na	***trace***	***6***	***17***	na
Days With ≥ 1.0" Snow Depth	***11***	***9***	***5***	***0***	***0***	***0***	na	***0***	na	***0***	***1***	***5***	na
Thunderstorm Days*	< 1	< 1	1	1	2	3	4	3	1	1	< 1	< 1	16
Foggy Days*	10	9	11	11	13	12	12	13	11	12	11	10	135
Predominant Sky Cover*	OVR	OVR	OVR	OVR	OVR	OVR	OVR	OVR	OVR	OVR	OVR	OVR	OVR
Mean Relative Humidity 7am (%)*	68	68	69	68	71	72	73	76	78	77	74	70	72
Mean Relative Humidity 4pm (%)*	58	56	57	56	58	58	57	60	61	59	61	60	58
Mean Dewpoint (°F)*	17	18	25	34	45	55	61	60	54	43	34	22	39
Prevailing Wind Direction*	WNW	WNW	WNW	WNW	SW	SW	SW	SW	SW	WNW	WNW	WNW	WNW
Prevailing Wind Speed (mph)*	16	16	16	15	14	13	12	12	13	13	15	15	14
Maximum Wind Gust (mph)*	69	79	81	76	70	84	60	100	87	58	86	78	100

Note: (*) Period of record is 1945-1995

Milton Blue Hill Observatory

The altitude of the Observatory and its proximity to Massachusetts Bay play major roles in determining the climate of Blue Hill. The elevation of 635 feet marks the summit as the highest point of a wooded range that extends east-northeast to west-southwest. The station lies at the southwest end of this range and has a three-quadrant unrestricted exposure, at approximately 400 feet above the surrounding terrain. The orographic effect created by this difference in elevation is responsible for lower temperatures, more precipitation, higher winds, more frequent occurrences of fog, and longer periods of snow cover than at nearby lower elevations. Eight miles to the northeast lies the nearest approach of Boston Harbor, and thus, the station is within range of the sea breeze.

Summer temperatures are generally comfortable. Winters at the summit are more severe than those experienced at surrounding areas. Average occurrence of last freezing temperature in the spring is late April and the first in the fall is late October. The freeze-free period is about 178 days. Records indicate that the freeze-free period at base stations is from six to seven weeks shorter than at the summit. This seeming paradox is due to temperature inversions, in which the colder air is found at lower elevations. This condition develops on clear, calm nights, and is responsible for the shorter freeze-free period in base areas.

Total precipitation is fairly evenly distributed throughout the year. Precipitation occurrences are most frequent January through March and least frequent August through October. Hourly precipitation occurrences indicate a coastal type distribution for the year as a whole, with maxima in the early morning and minima in the early afternoon. In the summer, however, convective action or the continental influence dominates, causing a late afternoon maximum. Coastal storms or northeasters are prolific producers of rain and snow.

The main snow season extends from November through early April. Nearly 14 percent of the annual total precipitation occurs as snow or sleet.

Wind velocities are higher in winter than in summer. Speeds average greatest from January through March and least in August. Surface contour is a factor in the stations, wind force, particularly from the southerly and westerly directions. These are the steepest slopes of the hill, and winds velocities increase. Peak winds have been recorded from these directions. Winds from the east-northeast and northeast are somewhat slowed by striking the lower range first.

Milton Blue Hill Observatory *Norfolk County* Elevation: 629 ft. Latitude: 42° 13' N Longitude: 71° 07' W

	JAN	FEB	MAR	APR	MAY	JUN	JUL	AUG	SEP	OCT	NOV	DEC	YEAR
Mean Maximum Temp. (°F)	34.0	36.9	44.5	56.0	66.6	75.3	80.8	79.1	71.3	60.2	49.9	39.0	57.8
Mean Temp. (°F)	26.3	28.9	36.0	46.8	56.8	65.8	71.6	70.3	62.7	51.8	42.2	31.6	49.2
Mean Minimum Temp. (°F)	18.6	20.8	27.4	37.6	47.0	56.2	62.3	61.5	54.0	43.3	34.6	24.3	40.6
Extreme Maximum Temp. (°F)	67	68	89	93	93	98	99	98	93	87	78	74	99
Extreme Minimum Temp. (°F)	-11	-7	1	13	30	39	44	41	31	25	11	-12	-12
Days Maximum Temp. ≥ 90°F	0	0	0	0	1	2	3	2	0	0	0	0	8
Days Maximum Temp. ≤ 32°F	14	10	3	0	0	0	0	0	0	0	1	9	37
Days Minimum Temp. ≤ 32°F	28	25	22	6	0	0	0	0	0	2	13	25	121
Days Minimum Temp. ≤ 0°F	2	1	0	0	0	0	0	0	0	0	0	0	3
Heating Degree Days (base 65°F)	1,193	1,015	893	541	268	74	9	18	117	408	676	1,027	6,239
Cooling Degree Days (base 65°F)	0	0	0	2	22	104	221	189	55	5	0	0	598
Mean Precipitation (in.)	4.25	4.03	5.16	4.61	4.08	4.38	4.00	3.81	4.10	4.64	4.73	4.79	52.58
Maximum Precipitation (in.)*	11.6	9.3	11.0	10.4	9.1	13.7	10.7	8.9	9.6	10.8	9.8	12.6	65.5
Minimum Precipitation (in.)*	1.0	0.7	0.6	1.4	0.6	0.9	0.7	0.5	0.7	0.4	0.5	1.1	27.0
Extreme Maximum Daily Precip. (in.)	2.15	2.74	3.48	3.47	5.02	6.07	3.54	3.13	5.60	7.10	3.10	3.94	7.10
Days With ≥ 0.1" Precipitation	7	6	9	8	8	7	7	6	6	7	7	8	86
Days With ≥ 0.5" Precipitation	3	3	3	3	2	2	3	3	2	3	3	3	33
Days With ≥ 1.0" Precipitation	1	1	1	1	1	1	1	1	1	1	1	2	13
Mean Snowfall (in.)	16.7	14.3	12.3	3.0	trace	trace	trace	0.0	0.0	0.2	2.6	13.3	62.4
Maximum Snowfall (in.)*	46	65	41	14	8	0	0	0	0	7	14	27	124
Maximum 24-hr. Snowfall (in.)*	19	27	14	12	5	0	0	0	0	7	11	15	27
Maximum Snow Depth (in.)	33	31	24	27	trace	trace	trace	0	0	2	10	23	33
Days With ≥ 1.0" Snow Depth	18	16	10	1	0	0	0	0	0	0	1	11	57
Thunderstorm Days*	< 1	< 1	1	3	2	4	5	4	1	1	< 1	0	21
Foggy Days*	12	8	17	13	9	12	15	14	14	13	11	12	150
Predominant Sky Cover*	na	na	na	na	na	na	na	na	na	na	na	na	na
Mean Relative Humidity 7am (%)*	na	na	na	na	na	na	na	na	na	na	na	na	na
Mean Relative Humidity 4pm (%)*	na	na	na	na	na	na	na	na	na	na	na	na	na
Mean Dewpoint (°F)*	na	na	na	na	na	na	na	na	na	na	na	na	na
Prevailing Wind Direction*	na	na	na	na	na	na	na	na	na	na	na	na	na
Prevailing Wind Speed (mph)*	na	na	na	na	na	na	na	na	na	na	na	na	na
Maximum Wind Gust (mph)*	na	na	na	na	na	na	na	na	na	na	na	na	na

Note: (*) Period of record is 1962-1995

The period of record for National Weather Service station data is 1980 – 2009 except where noted. See User Guide for detailed explanation of data.

Worcester Municipal Airport

Worcester Municipal Airport is located on the crest of a hill, 1,000 feet above sea level. It is about 500 feet above and three and a half miles northwest of the city proper. The airport is surrounded by ridges and valleys with many of the valleys containing reservoirs. Only two of the ridges extend above the airport elevation. One is 400 feet higher and two and a half miles to the northwest, and the other is 1,000 feet higher and 15 miles to the north.

The proximity to the Atlantic Ocean, Long Island Sound, and the Berkshire Hills plays an important part in determining the weather and, hence, the climate of Worcester. Rapid weather changes occur when storms move up the east coast after developing off the Carolina Coast. In the majority of these cases, they pass to the south and east, resulting in northeast and easterly winds with rain or snow and fog. Storms developing in the Texas-Oklahoma area normally travel up the St. Lawrence River Valley and, depending on the movement and intensity, usually deposit little precipitation over the area. However, they do bring an influx of warm air into the region. Wintertime cold snaps are quite frequent, but temperatures are usually modified by the passage of the air over land and mountains before reaching the county. Summertime thunderstorms develop over the hills to the west, with a majority moving toward the northeast.

Airport site temperatures are moderate. The normal mean for the warmest month, July, is around 70 degrees. Though winters are reasonably cold, prolonged periods of severe cold weather are extremely rare. The three coldest months, December through February, have an average temperature of over 25 degrees. A review of Worcester Cooperative records since 1901 shows maximum temperatures above 100 degrees and minimum temperatures below -24 degrees.

Precipitation is usually plentiful and well distributed throughout the year. The annual snowfall for all Worcester sites since 1901, averages slightly less than 60 inches. The airport location averages slightly higher.

Based on the 1951-1980 period, the average first occurrence of 32 degrees Fahrenheit in the fall is October 17 and the average last occurrence in the spring is April 27.

Worcester Municipal Airport *Worcester County* Elevation: 985 ft. Latitude: 42° 16' N Longitude: 71° 53' W

	JAN	FEB	MAR	APR	MAY	JUN	JUL	AUG	SEP	OCT	NOV	DEC	YEAR
Mean Maximum Temp. (°F)	31.5	34.7	42.9	55.1	66.1	74.0	79.0	77.6	69.7	58.5	47.6	36.4	56.1
Mean Temp. (°F)	24.1	26.8	34.5	45.9	56.3	64.8	70.1	69.0	61.1	50.1	40.1	29.4	47.7
Mean Minimum Temp. (°F)	16.7	18.9	26.0	36.7	46.5	55.6	61.2	60.3	52.5	41.6	32.6	22.2	39.2
Extreme Maximum Temp. (°F)	66	67	84	90	90	94	96	93	91	83	78	72	96
Extreme Minimum Temp. (°F)	-12	-9	-4	11	29	36	43	39	30	21	6	-11	-12
Days Maximum Temp. ≥ 90°F	0	0	0	0	0	1	1	1	0	0	0	0	3
Days Maximum Temp. ≤ 32°F	17	12	5	0	0	0	0	0	0	0	2	11	47
Days Minimum Temp. ≤ 32°F	29	26	24	8	0	0	0	0	0	4	16	27	134
Days Minimum Temp. ≤ 0°F	3	1	0	0	0	0	0	0	0	0	0	1	5
Heating Degree Days (base 65°F)	1,261	1,073	940	568	282	83	13	26	149	459	740	1,099	6,693
Cooling Degree Days (base 65°F)	0	0	0	2	20	85	178	156	40	3	0	0	484
Mean Precipitation (in.)	3.32	3.08	4.05	4.35	4.28	4.43	4.35	3.74	3.75	4.80	4.32	3.72	48.19
Maximum Precipitation (in.)*	11.2	8.4	8.6	8.8	9.9	12.2	7.9	9.2	13.1	10.2	10.4	9.8	71.7
Minimum Precipitation (in.)*	0.9	0.3	0.7	1.3	1.2	0.8	0.7	1.0	0.7	1.2	0.7	0.7	31.9
Extreme Maximum Daily Precip. (in.)	2.13	2.49	4.55	3.23	2.79	3.50	3.87	5.00	4.79	3.72	2.63	2.12	5.00
Days With ≥ 0.1" Precipitation	7	6	7	8	8	8	7	6	6	7	7	7	84
Days With ≥ 0.5" Precipitation	2	2	3	3	3	3	3	3	2	3	3	3	33
Days With ≥ 1.0" Precipitation	1	1	1	1	1	1	1	1	1	2	1	1	13
Mean Snowfall (in.)	***16.4***	***14.9***	***11.0***	***2.8***	***trace***	***trace***	***0.0***	***trace***	***trace***	***0.2***	***2.9***	***14.0***	***62.2***
Maximum Snowfall (in.)*	47	45	44	21	trace	0	0	0	trace	8	21	37	112
Maximum 24-hr. Snowfall (in.)*	18	20	15	15	trace	0	0	0	trace	8	15	17	20
Maximum Snow Depth (in.)	na	na	na	na	na	na	na	na	na	na	na	na	na
Days With ≥ 1.0" Snow Depth	na	na	na	na	na	na	na	na	na	na	na	na	na
Thunderstorm Days*	< 1	< 1	1	1	3	5	6	4	2	1	< 1	< 1	23
Foggy Days*	13	11	14	14	15	16	16	17	17	15	15	14	177
Predominant Sky Cover*	OVR	OVR	OVR	OVR	OVR	OVR	OVR	OVR	OVR	OVR	OVR	OVR	OVR
Mean Relative Humidity 7am (%)*	73	73	72	69	70	74	76	79	82	79	78	76	75
Mean Relative Humidity 4pm (%)*	61	58	56	50	52	57	58	60	62	58	63	65	58
Mean Dewpoint (°F)*	14	15	21	30	42	53	59	58	51	40	30	19	36
Prevailing Wind Direction*	WNW	WNW	WNW	WNW	W	W	WSW	W	W	W	W	WNW	W
Prevailing Wind Speed (mph)*	15	16	15	15	10	9	9	9	9	10	12	15	13
Maximum Wind Gust (mph)*	67	69	69	64	61	58	59	69	71	60	69	73	73

Note: (*) Period of record is 1949-1995

Amherst *Hampshire County* Elevation: 149 ft. Latitude: 42° 23' N Longitude: 72° 32' W

	JAN	FEB	MAR	APR	MAY	JUN	JUL	AUG	SEP	OCT	NOV	DEC	YEAR
Mean Maximum Temp. (°F)	34.5	38.2	46.1	59.2	70.1	78.6	83.3	81.9	74.4	62.5	50.7	39.2	59.9
Mean Temp. (°F)	23.9	27.1	35.2	46.9	57.5	66.5	71.3	69.7	61.8	50.0	40.2	29.5	48.3
Mean Minimum Temp. (°F)	13.2	15.9	24.2	34.6	44.7	54.4	59.2	57.6	49.1	37.5	29.5	19.7	36.6
Extreme Maximum Temp. (°F)	70	70	84	93	94	97	99	98	94	87	79	72	99
Extreme Minimum Temp. (°F)	-27	-15	-11	12	24	32	40	33	27	17	0	-20	-27
Days Maximum Temp. ≥ 90°F	0	0	0	0	0	2	5	3	1	0	0	0	11
Days Maximum Temp. ≤ 32°F	12	7	3	0	0	0	0	0	0	0	0	7	29
Days Minimum Temp. ≤ 32°F	29	26	25	12	2	0	0	0	1	11	20	28	154
Days Minimum Temp. ≤ 0°F	5	3	0	0	0	0	0	0	0	0	0	2	10
Heating Degree Days (base 65°F)	1,266	1,066	917	538	250	61	9	21	142	461	739	1,094	6,564
Cooling Degree Days (base 65°F)	0	0	0	3	23	112	210	176	53	4	0	0	581
Mean Precipitation (in.)	3.24	3.02	3.57	3.97	4.03	4.12	4.04	3.68	4.19	4.58	3.85	3.36	45.65
Extreme Maximum Daily Precip. (in.)	2.60	2.45	2.84	2.59	2.80	3.47	2.85	3.12	4.85	7.56	2.02	2.94	7.56
Days With ≥ 0.1" Precipitation	7	6	7	7	7	7	7	6	7	6	7	7	81
Days With ≥ 0.5" Precipitation	2	2	3	3	3	3	3	2	3	3	3	2	32
Days With ≥ 1.0" Precipitation	1	1	1	1	1	1	1	1	1	2	1	1	13
Mean Snowfall (in.)	12.0	8.6	7.3	1.3	0.0	0.0	0.0	0.0	0.0	trace	2.2	8.8	40.2
Maximum Snow Depth (in.)	22	23	24	14	0	0	0	0	0	trace	7	12	24
Days With ≥ 1.0" Snow Depth	20	17	9	1	0	0	0	0	0	0	2	11	60

Barre Falls Dam *Worcester County* Elevation: 910 ft. Latitude: 42° 26' N Longitude: 72° 02' W

	JAN	FEB	MAR	APR	MAY	JUN	JUL	AUG	SEP	OCT	NOV	DEC	YEAR
Mean Maximum Temp. (°F)	***32.2***	***35.6***	na	***55.4***	67.0	75.1	80.0	***78.5***	***70.8***	na	na	na	na
Mean Temp. (°F)	***21.9***	***24.7***	na	***43.5***	54.0	62.6	67.4	***65.7***	***57.8***	na	na	na	na
Mean Minimum Temp. (°F)	***11.5***	***13.8***	na	***31.4***	41.0	50.0	54.8	53.0	***44.8***	na	na	na	na
Extreme Maximum Temp. (°F)	64	67	80	91	91	94	95	98	92	84	77	69	98
Extreme Minimum Temp. (°F)	-25	-22	-16	8	21	29	34	30	25	13	-7	-16	-25
Days Maximum Temp. ≥ 90°F	0	0	0	0	0	1	2	1	0	0	0	0	4
Days Maximum Temp. ≤ 32°F	14	10	4	0	0	0	0	0	0	0	1	9	38
Days Minimum Temp. ≤ 32°F	27	24	25	16	5	0	0	0	3	13	19	24	156
Days Minimum Temp. ≤ 0°F	6	3	1	0	0	0	0	0	0	0	0	3	13
Heating Degree Days (base 65°F)	***1,329***	***1,133***	na	***638***	344	123	36	***66***	***232***	na	na	na	na
Cooling Degree Days (base 65°F)	***0***	***0***	na	***0***	10	58	115	***95***	***22***	na	na	na	na
Mean Precipitation (in.)	3.31	2.95	3.61	4.14	4.00	4.12	3.88	4.19	3.78	4.53	3.98	3.49	45.98
Extreme Maximum Daily Precip. (in.)	2.47	2.65	2.35	3.00	3.82	4.38	2.73	4.20	3.10	5.67	1.90	2.32	5.67
Days With ≥ 0.1" Precipitation	7	6	8	8	8	8	7	6	7	7	8	7	87
Days With ≥ 0.5" Precipitation	2	2	3	3	3	3	3	3	2	3	3	3	33
Days With ≥ 1.0" Precipitation	1	1	1	1	1	1	1	1	1	2	1	1	13
Mean Snowfall (in.)	14.9	11.9	10.5	3.5	0.1	0.0	0.0	0.0	0.0	trace	2.8	12.1	55.8
Maximum Snow Depth (in.)	30	30	26	22	1	0	0	0	0	trace	8	21	30
Days With ≥ 1.0" Snow Depth	20	20	14	2	0	0	0	0	0	0	2	14	72

Bedford *Middlesex County* Elevation: 160 ft. Latitude: 42° 29' N Longitude: 71° 17' W

	JAN	FEB	MAR	APR	MAY	JUN	JUL	AUG	SEP	OCT	NOV	DEC	YEAR
Mean Maximum Temp. (°F)	34.9	38.3	46.5	58.4	69.0	77.5	82.6	81.0	73.1	61.8	51.0	40.0	59.5
Mean Temp. (°F)	25.7	28.6	36.4	47.3	57.3	66.3	71.7	70.2	62.0	50.6	41.2	31.0	49.0
Mean Minimum Temp. (°F)	16.3	18.9	26.2	36.2	45.6	55.0	60.7	59.4	51.0	39.5	31.4	22.0	38.5
Extreme Maximum Temp. (°F)	70	72	90	94	94	98	99	98	95	85	79	77	99
Extreme Minimum Temp. (°F)	-19	-14	-5	14	27	36	42	40	29	20	-1	-15	-19
Days Maximum Temp. ≥ 90°F	0	0	0	0	1	2	5	3	1	0	0	0	12
Days Maximum Temp. ≤ 32°F	12	8	3	0	0	0	0	0	0	0	1	7	31
Days Minimum Temp. ≤ 32°F	29	26	24	10	1	0	0	0	0	7	18	27	142
Days Minimum Temp. ≤ 0°F	3	1	0	0	0	0	0	0	0	0	0	1	5
Heating Degree Days (base 65°F)	1,213	1,023	880	527	253	64	8	18	134	442	706	1,046	6,314
Cooling Degree Days (base 65°F)	0	0	1	3	22	109	221	186	52	4	0	0	598
Mean Precipitation (in.)	3.61	3.39	4.48	4.25	4.07	3.90	3.96	3.57	3.79	4.33	4.39	4.18	47.92
Extreme Maximum Daily Precip. (in.)	2.05	2.35	4.72	3.45	3.96	5.84	4.01	5.47	5.41	7.83	3.07	2.44	7.83
Days With ≥ 0.1" Precipitation	7	6	8	8	8	7	6	6	6	6	7	7	82
Days With ≥ 0.5" Precipitation	3	2	3	3	3	2	3	2	2	3	3	3	32
Days With ≥ 1.0" Precipitation	1	1	1	1	1	1	1	1	1	1	1	1	12
Mean Snowfall (in.)	15.6	11.8	10.4	2.6	trace	0.0	0.0	0.0	0.0	0.1	2.5	11.5	54.5
Maximum Snow Depth (in.)	32	24	22	21	trace	0	0	0	0	trace	7	20	32
Days With ≥ 1.0" Snow Depth	20	18	11	1	0	0	0	0	0	0	2	12	64

Brockton *Plymouth County* Elevation: 80 ft. Latitude: 42° 03' N Longitude: 71° 00' W

	JAN	FEB	MAR	APR	MAY	JUN	JUL	AUG	SEP	OCT	NOV	DEC	YEAR
Mean Maximum Temp. (°F)	37.8	40.6	47.8	58.4	68.7	77.9	83.3	81.7	74.2	63.3	53.0	42.6	60.8
Mean Temp. (°F)	28.3	30.5	37.6	47.5	57.1	66.5	72.4	71.0	62.9	51.9	42.9	33.2	50.1
Mean Minimum Temp. (°F)	18.6	20.5	27.4	36.6	45.4	55.1	61.3	60.2	51.5	40.4	32.8	23.7	39.5
Extreme Maximum Temp. (°F)	70	68	87	95	95	98	100	101	98	86	79	78	101
Extreme Minimum Temp. (°F)	-15	-7	-2	20	24	35	43	38	30	19	3	-10	-15
Days Maximum Temp. ≥ 90°F	0	0	0	0	1	3	5	4	0	0	0	0	13
Days Maximum Temp. ≤ 32°F	10	6	2	0	0	0	0	0	0	0	0	4	22
Days Minimum Temp. ≤ 32°F	28	25	22	9	1	0	0	0	0	6	16	26	133
Days Minimum Temp. ≤ 0°F	2	1	0	0	0	0	0	0	0	0	0	0	3
Heating Degree Days (base 65°F)	1,130	967	841	520	259	61	6	13	117	406	657	978	5,955
Cooling Degree Days (base 65°F)	0	0	0	2	21	114	240	205	60	6	0	0	648
Mean Precipitation (in.)	3.62	3.47	4.86	4.62	3.52	4.10	3.79	4.05	3.75	4.60	4.47	4.49	49.34
Extreme Maximum Daily Precip. (in.)	3.25	3.10	4.18	2.93	2.50	5.16	4.38	4.66	4.60	5.80	2.78	4.00	5.80
Days With ≥ 0.1" Precipitation	6	6	8	7	7	6	6	6	6	7	7	7	79
Days With ≥ 0.5" Precipitation	3	3	3	3	2	2	2	3	3	3	3	3	33
Days With ≥ 1.0" Precipitation	1	1	1	2	1	1	1	1	1	2	1	1	14
Mean Snowfall (in.)	na	***5.5***	***3.5***	0.8	trace	0.0	0.0	0.0	0.0	trace	0.5	4.2	na
Maximum Snow Depth (in.)	***46***	***21***	***10***	***18***	***trace***	***0***	***0***	***0***	***0***	***trace***	***5***	***16***	***46***
Days With ≥ 1.0" Snow Depth	***10***	***8***	***4***	1	0	0	0	0	0	0	0	***5***	***28***

The period of record for all cooperative weather station data is 1980 – 2009. See User Guide for detailed explanation of data.

Chatham WSMO *Barnstable County* Elevation: 46 ft. Latitude: 41° 40' N Longitude: 69° 58' W

	JAN	FEB	MAR	APR	MAY	JUN	JUL	AUG	SEP	OCT	NOV	DEC	YEAR
Mean Maximum Temp. (°F)	37.7	38.5	43.2	50.7	59.3	68.6	75.0	75.0	69.4	60.0	51.6	42.8	56.0
Mean Temp. (°F)	31.5	32.5	37.3	45.1	53.4	62.4	68.6	68.9	63.5	54.1	45.9	36.8	50.0
Mean Minimum Temp. (°F)	25.2	26.5	31.2	39.5	47.5	56.1	62.2	62.7	57.5	48.3	40.1	30.7	44.0
Extreme Maximum Temp. (°F)	61	57	77	80	88	89	95	90	***83***	80	68	69	***95***
Extreme Minimum Temp. (°F)	-6	0	7	19	35	44	51	49	***43***	31	19	0	***-6***
Days Maximum Temp. ≥ 90°F	0	0	0	0	0	0	0	0	0	0	0	0	0
Days Maximum Temp. ≤ 32°F	7	6	2	0	0	0	0	0	0	0	0	3	18
Days Minimum Temp. ≤ 32°F	23	20	16	2	0	0	0	0	0	0	4	17	82
Days Minimum Temp. ≤ 0°F	0	0	0	0	0	0	0	0	0	0	0	0	0
Heating Degree Days (base 65°F)	1,032	912	853	590	353	100	11	8	76	331	567	868	5,701
Cooling Degree Days (base 65°F)	0	0	0	0	1	29	130	135	37	2	0	0	334
Mean Precipitation (in.)	3.96	3.70	4.62	4.39	3.67	3.40	3.34	3.18	3.79	3.88	4.09	4.38	46.40
Extreme Maximum Daily Precip. (in.)	3.13	2.65	2.58	2.65	2.95	3.21	3.81	3.17	***4.52***	3.58	3.94	2.77	***4.52***
Days With ≥ 0.1" Precipitation	8	7	8	8	7	6	5	5	6	7	7	8	82
Days With ≥ 0.5" Precipitation	3	2	3	3	2	2	2	2	2	2	3	3	29
Days With ≥ 1.0" Precipitation	1	1	1	1	1	1	1	1	1	1	1	1	12
Mean Snowfall (in.)	7.3	11.2	3.4	0.9	trace	0.0	0.0	0.0	0.0	trace	0.5	4.3	27.6
Maximum Snow Depth (in.)	22	30	13	6	trace	0	0	0	***0***	trace	9	13	***30***
Days With ≥ 1.0" Snow Depth	8	7	3	0	0	0	0	0	0	0	0	3	21

East Brimfield Lake *Worcester County* Elevation: 680 ft. Latitude: 42° 07' N Longitude: 72° 08' W

	JAN	FEB	MAR	APR	MAY	JUN	JUL	AUG	SEP	OCT	NOV	DEC	YEAR
Mean Maximum Temp. (°F)	33.9	36.8	44.9	56.9	68.4	76.3	80.9	79.4	72.0	61.1	49.8	38.4	58.2
Mean Temp. (°F)	23.6	26.1	34.1	45.5	56.2	65.0	69.9	68.6	60.7	49.3	39.7	29.1	47.3
Mean Minimum Temp. (°F)	13.3	15.3	23.3	34.1	44.0	53.7	58.8	57.7	49.4	37.4	29.5	19.6	36.3
Extreme Maximum Temp. (°F)	68	68	83	93	92	94	96	95	94	86	78	72	96
Extreme Minimum Temp. (°F)	-27	-24	-11	12	26	35	43	38	28	19	-1	-14	-27
Days Maximum Temp. ≥ 90°F	0	0	0	0	0	1	2	1	0	0	0	0	4
Days Maximum Temp. ≤ 32°F	14	10	4	0	0	0	0	0	0	0	1	8	37
Days Minimum Temp. ≤ 32°F	29	26	26	13	2	0	0	0	0	10	20	28	154
Days Minimum Temp. ≤ 0°F	6	3	0	0	0	0	0	0	0	0	0	1	10
Heating Degree Days (base 65°F)	1,275	1,094	951	578	281	80	14	29	161	483	753	1,108	6,807
Cooling Degree Days (base 65°F)	0	0	0	1	16	86	172	147	38	3	0	0	463
Mean Precipitation (in.)	3.66	3.18	4.24	4.47	3.74	3.76	3.69	3.64	3.63	4.33	4.28	3.71	46.33
Extreme Maximum Daily Precip. (in.)	2.75	2.20	2.70	3.96	2.40	2.80	3.30	5.03	4.25	3.37	2.57	2.50	5.03
Days With ≥ 0.1" Precipitation	7	6	8	8	8	7	7	6	6	6	7	7	83
Days With ≥ 0.5" Precipitation	3	2	3	3	2	2	3	2	2	3	3	3	31
Days With ≥ 1.0" Precipitation	1	1	1	1	1	1	1	1	1	1	1	1	12
Mean Snowfall (in.)	15.2	12.1	11.4	3.4	trace	0.0	0.0	0.0	0.0	0.1	3.0	12.8	58.0
Maximum Snow Depth (in.)	26	26	27	24	trace	0	0	0	0	1	12	26	27
Days With ≥ 1.0" Snow Depth	19	17	10	1	0	0	0	0	0	0	2	12	61

East Wareham *Plymouth County* Elevation: 20 ft. Latitude: 41° 46' N Longitude: 70° 40' W

	JAN	FEB	MAR	APR	MAY	JUN	JUL	AUG	SEP	OCT	NOV	DEC	YEAR
Mean Maximum Temp. (°F)	37.2	39.1	45.2	54.4	64.6	73.4	79.5	78.7	72.0	61.6	52.4	42.7	58.4
Mean Temp. (°F)	28.9	30.7	37.0	45.9	55.9	65.2	71.4	70.7	63.2	52.6	43.8	34.4	50.0
Mean Minimum Temp. (°F)	20.6	22.4	28.7	37.4	47.1	56.9	63.2	62.6	54.3	43.4	35.3	26.0	41.5
Extreme Maximum Temp. (°F)	64	59	75	89	94	93	98	100	90	85	77	70	100
Extreme Minimum Temp. (°F)	-15	-3	4	13	30	41	45	40	35	23	5	-7	-15
Days Maximum Temp. ≥ 90°F	0	0	0	0	0	0	1	1	0	0	0	0	2
Days Maximum Temp. ≤ 32°F	9	6	2	0	0	0	0	0	0	0	0	4	21
Days Minimum Temp. ≤ 32°F	27	24	21	8	0	0	0	0	0	3	13	24	120
Days Minimum Temp. ≤ 0°F	1	0	0	0	0	0	0	0	0	0	0	0	1
Heating Degree Days (base 65°F)	1,110	962	862	567	284	65	6	12	104	384	628	942	5,926
Cooling Degree Days (base 65°F)	0	0	0	1	8	78	211	194	56	5	0	0	553
Mean Precipitation (in.)	4.02	3.48	5.13	4.67	3.71	3.78	3.21	3.82	4.25	4.11	4.66	4.51	49.35
Extreme Maximum Daily Precip. (in.)	2.94	2.25	4.10	2.54	3.00	4.13	2.48	4.82	5.27	4.12	2.85	4.13	5.27
Days With ≥ 0.1" Precipitation	7	6	8	7	7	7	6	6	5	6	7	8	80
Days With ≥ 0.5" Precipitation	3	2	3	3	3	3	2	2	2	3	3	3	32
Days With ≥ 1.0" Precipitation	1	1	1	1	1	1	1	1	1	1	2	1	13
Mean Snowfall (in.)	10.4	8.7	5.4	1.0	0.0	0.0	0.0	0.0	0.0	trace	1.0	6.6	33.1
Maximum Snow Depth (in.)	28	18	16	11	0	0	0	0	0	0	12	18	28
Days With ≥ 1.0" Snow Depth	10	7	4	0	0	0	0	0	0	0	0	4	25

Edgartown *Dukes County* Elevation: 20 ft. Latitude: 41° 23' N Longitude: 70° 31' W

	JAN	FEB	MAR	APR	MAY	JUN	JUL	AUG	SEP	OCT	NOV	DEC	YEAR
Mean Maximum Temp. (°F)	39.2	40.5	45.9	54.6	64.1	73.2	79.1	78.6	72.5	62.8	54.0	44.3	59.1
Mean Temp. (°F)	31.4	32.6	38.0	46.6	55.8	64.9	70.9	70.6	64.5	54.4	46.1	36.5	51.0
Mean Minimum Temp. (°F)	23.4	24.6	30.1	38.5	47.4	56.7	62.8	62.5	56.4	46.0	38.1	28.6	42.9
Extreme Maximum Temp. (°F)	62	62	79	90	91	93	95	96	87	80	74	67	96
Extreme Minimum Temp. (°F)	-6	1	4	16	28	39	45	41	34	25	14	-2	-6
Days Maximum Temp. ≥ 90°F	0	0	0	0	0	0	1	0	0	0	0	0	1
Days Maximum Temp. ≤ 32°F	7	5	1	0	0	0	0	0	0	0	0	3	16
Days Minimum Temp. ≤ 32°F	26	23	19	5	0	0	0	0	0	1	9	21	104
Days Minimum Temp. ≤ 0°F	0	0	0	0	0	0	0	0	0	0	0	0	0
Heating Degree Days (base 65°F)	1,037	909	830	546	286	62	6	8	73	327	561	878	5,523
Cooling Degree Days (base 65°F)	0	0	0	0	6	68	196	189	64	5	0	0	528
Mean Precipitation (in.)	3.83	3.10	4.82	4.33	3.51	3.70	2.98	3.91	3.45	3.90	4.32	4.26	46.11
Extreme Maximum Daily Precip. (in.)	1.95	2.38	3.29	2.54	2.55	4.62	3.74	6.04	3.72	2.92	2.82	3.36	6.04
Days With ≥ 0.1" Precipitation	7	6	7	7	7	6	4	6	5	7	7	8	77
Days With ≥ 0.5" Precipitation	3	2	3	3	2	2	2	3	2	3	3	3	31
Days With ≥ 1.0" Precipitation	1	1	1	1	1	1	1	1	1	1	1	1	12
Mean Snowfall (in.)	6.2	8.1	3.9	0.3	0.0	0.0	0.0	0.0	0.0	trace	0.3	4.0	22.8
Maximum Snow Depth (in.)	24	18	8	3	0	0	0	0	0	trace	7	11	24
Days With ≥ 1.0" Snow Depth	6	7	3	0	0	0	0	0	0	0	0	3	19

The period of record for all cooperative weather station data is 1980 – 2009. See User Guide for detailed explanation of data.

Haverhill *Essex County* Elevation: 18 ft. Latitude: 42° 46' N Longitude: 71° 04' W

	JAN	FEB	MAR	APR	MAY	JUN	JUL	AUG	SEP	OCT	NOV	DEC	YEAR
Mean Maximum Temp. (°F)	35.2	38.5	46.1	57.4	67.8	77.0	82.6	81.1	73.0	61.8	51.0	40.2	59.3
Mean Temp. (°F)	25.3	28.2	35.6	46.2	56.1	65.5	71.6	70.1	61.7	50.3	40.9	30.7	48.5
Mean Minimum Temp. (°F)	15.4	17.9	25.1	35.0	44.4	54.0	60.5	59.0	50.4	38.8	30.8	21.1	37.7
Extreme Maximum Temp. (°F)	68	73	90	95	94	101	100	99	98	87	82	76	101
Extreme Minimum Temp. (°F)	-21	-12	-3	15	24	36	41	36	29	21	-2	-12	-21
Days Maximum Temp. ≥ 90°F	0	0	0	0	1	3	5	4	1	0	0	0	14
Days Maximum Temp. ≤ 32°F	12	8	3	0	0	0	0	0	0	0	0	6	29
Days Minimum Temp. ≤ 32°F	29	26	25	12	1	0	0	0	0	8	18	27	146
Days Minimum Temp. ≤ 0°F	3	1	0	0	0	0	0	0	0	0	0	1	5
Heating Degree Days (base 65°F)	1,224	1,033	904	558	287	77	9	22	141	453	716	1,056	6,480
Cooling Degree Days (base 65°F)	0	0	1	2	18	98	219	185	49	4	0	0	576
Mean Precipitation (in.)	3.22	3.27	4.51	4.67	4.35	4.13	3.81	3.66	4.08	4.71	4.41	3.98	48.80
Extreme Maximum Daily Precip. (in.)	1.86	2.70	4.98	4.40	4.85	3.83	4.39	5.98	5.36	6.45	2.77	3.17	6.45
Days With ≥ 0.1" Precipitation	7	5	7	8	8	8	7	6	6	7	7	7	83
Days With ≥ 0.5" Precipitation	2	2	3	3	3	2	3	3	3	3	3	3	33
Days With ≥ 1.0" Precipitation	1	1	1	1	1	1	1	1	1	1	1	1	12
Mean Snowfall (in.)	16.2	11.6	10.2	2.1	0.0	0.0	0.0	0.0	0.0	trace	2.0	10.4	52.5
Maximum Snow Depth (in.)	27	28	28	21	0	0	0	0	0	trace	6	18	28
Days With ≥ 1.0" Snow Depth	15	11	7	1	0	0	0	0	0	0	1	7	42

Hingham *Plymouth County* Elevation: 29 ft. Latitude: 42° 14' N Longitude: 70° 55' W

	JAN	FEB	MAR	APR	MAY	JUN	JUL	AUG	SEP	OCT	NOV	DEC	YEAR
Mean Maximum Temp. (°F)	37.1	39.8	46.7	57.3	67.4	76.3	81.6	79.7	72.4	62.0	52.4	41.9	59.5
Mean Temp. (°F)	28.7	31.2	37.8	47.6	57.2	66.4	71.9	70.6	63.1	52.5	43.7	33.9	50.4
Mean Minimum Temp. (°F)	20.3	22.6	28.8	37.8	46.9	56.5	62.3	61.4	53.8	42.9	35.1	25.9	41.2
Extreme Maximum Temp. (°F)	68	69	89	95	93	100	99	100	96	88	78	77	100
Extreme Minimum Temp. (°F)	-13	-4	0	16	28	37	44	39	33	24	2	-8	-13
Days Maximum Temp. ≥ 90°F	0	0	0	0	1	2	4	3	0	0	0	0	10
Days Maximum Temp. ≤ 32°F	10	6	2	0	0	0	0	0	0	0	0	5	23
Days Minimum Temp. ≤ 32°F	27	24	21	7	1	0	0	0	0	3	13	24	120
Days Minimum Temp. ≤ 0°F	2	0	0	0	0	0	0	0	0	0	0	0	2
Heating Degree Days (base 65°F)	1,118	948	838	519	257	63	7	17	112	388	631	957	5,855
Cooling Degree Days (base 65°F)	0	0	1	3	22	113	230	197	62	6	1	0	635
Mean Precipitation (in.)	4.22	3.91	5.10	4.60	3.99	3.95	4.03	4.09	3.73	4.78	4.75	4.48	51.63
Extreme Maximum Daily Precip. (in.)	2.40	3.55	4.21	4.23	4.72	4.40	3.47	5.76	3.84	5.50	3.61	3.46	5.76
Days With ≥ 0.1" Precipitation	7	6	8	7	7	7	7	6	6	7	7	8	83
Days With ≥ 0.5" Precipitation	3	3	3	3	3	2	3	3	2	3	3	3	34
Days With ≥ 1.0" Precipitation	1	1	2	2	1	1	1	1	1	1	1	1	14
Mean Snowfall (in.)	13.6	11.7	8.5	1.7	trace	0.0	0.0	0.0	0.0	trace	1.5	9.0	46.0
Maximum Snow Depth (in.)	32	23	17	20	trace	0	0	0	0	trace	11	15	32
Days With ≥ 1.0" Snow Depth	16	13	8	1	0	0	0	0	0	0	1	8	47

Lawrence *Essex County* Elevation: 60 ft. Latitude: 42° 42' N Longitude: 71° 10' W

	JAN	FEB	MAR	APR	MAY	JUN	JUL	AUG	SEP	OCT	NOV	DEC	YEAR
Mean Maximum Temp. (°F)	34.6	38.1	45.6	57.3	68.1	77.5	82.7	81.8	73.7	62.1	51.6	40.3	59.5
Mean Temp. (°F)	25.4	28.7	36.3	47.5	57.7	67.1	72.5	71.5	63.3	51.5	42.2	31.7	49.6
Mean Minimum Temp. (°F)	16.1	19.3	27.0	37.6	47.3	56.7	62.2	61.1	52.7	40.9	32.8	23.2	39.7
Extreme Maximum Temp. (°F)	70	72	88	93	94	98	98	99	95	87	79	75	99
Extreme Minimum Temp. (°F)	-20	-7	2	15	28	35	46	43	30	21	4	-10	-20
Days Maximum Temp. ≥ 90°F	0	0	0	0	1	3	5	4	1	0	0	0	14
Days Maximum Temp. ≤ 32°F	13	8	3	0	0	0	0	0	0	0	0	7	31
Days Minimum Temp. ≤ 32°F	29	26	22	7	0	0	0	0	0	4	15	26	129
Days Minimum Temp. ≤ 0°F	3	1	0	0	0	0	0	0	0	0	0	1	5
Heating Degree Days (base 65°F)	1,220	1,019	882	522	243	55	6	11	108	416	677	1,024	6,183
Cooling Degree Days (base 65°F)	0	0	0	3	24	125	245	218	62	4	0	0	681
Mean Precipitation (in.)	3.41	2.71	4.04	4.11	4.13	3.79	3.64	3.25	3.72	4.24	4.05	3.28	44.37
Extreme Maximum Daily Precip. (in.)	2.92	2.16	2.60	3.73	4.70	3.30	2.65	6.05	4.45	6.72	3.00	3.00	6.72
Days With ≥ 0.1" Precipitation	6	5	7	7	8	7	6	6	6	6	7	6	77
Days With ≥ 0.5" Precipitation	2	2	3	3	3	2	3	2	2	3	3	3	31
Days With ≥ 1.0" Precipitation	1	1	1	1	1	1	1	1	1	1	1	1	12
Mean Snowfall (in.)	12.3	9.0	5.9	1.3	0.0	0.0	0.0	0.0	0.0	0.0	1.5	8.1	38.1
Maximum Snow Depth (in.)	37	23	20	11	0	0	0	0	0	0	8	17	37
Days With ≥ 1.0" Snow Depth	9	8	4	0	0	0	0	0	0	0	1	3	25

Marblehead *Essex County* Elevation: 96 ft. Latitude: 42° 30' N Longitude: 70° 52' W

	JAN	FEB	MAR	APR	MAY	JUN	JUL	AUG	SEP	OCT	NOV	DEC	YEAR
Mean Maximum Temp. (°F)	36.9	38.9	45.6	55.9	65.7	75.3	80.9	79.8	72.5	61.8	51.6	41.8	58.9
Mean Temp. (°F)	29.2	30.9	37.5	47.3	56.7	66.3	71.8	71.1	63.8	53.3	44.0	34.2	50.5
Mean Minimum Temp. (°F)	21.3	22.8	29.3	38.6	47.5	57.2	62.7	62.3	55.1	44.7	36.4	26.6	42.0
Extreme Maximum Temp. (°F)	71	70	91	94	97	98	100	97	96	84	78	77	100
Extreme Minimum Temp. (°F)	-9	-5	3	18	32	41	45	44	34	25	6	0	-9
Days Maximum Temp. ≥ 90°F	0	0	0	0	1	2	3	3	0	0	0	0	9
Days Maximum Temp. ≤ 32°F	10	7	2	0	0	0	0	0	0	0	0	5	24
Days Minimum Temp. ≤ 32°F	26	24	19	5	0	0	0	0	0	1	11	23	109
Days Minimum Temp. ≤ 0°F	1	0	0	0	0	0	0	0	0	0	0	0	1
Heating Degree Days (base 65°F)	1,104	957	846	528	272	65	7	10	91	363	623	949	5,815
Cooling Degree Days (base 65°F)	0	0	1	3	20	110	226	205	63	5	0	0	633
Mean Precipitation (in.)	3.82	3.26	4.34	4.45	3.88	3.57	3.74	3.48	3.95	4.36	4.34	4.16	47.35
Extreme Maximum Daily Precip. (in.)	4.00	2.87	3.98	4.90	5.58	2.95	3.04	3.11	4.15	3.85	4.68	3.20	5.58
Days With ≥ 0.1" Precipitation	8	6	7	8	8	7	7	6	7	7	7	7	85
Days With ≥ 0.5" Precipitation	3	2	3	3	2	2	3	2	2	3	3	3	31
Days With ≥ 1.0" Precipitation	1	1	1	1	1	1	1	1	1	1	1	1	12
Mean Snowfall (in.)	13.6	11.0	8.0	1.5	0.0	0.0	0.0	0.0	0.0	trace	1.8	7.6	43.5
Maximum Snow Depth (in.)	31	22	16	21	0	0	0	0	0	trace	10	21	31
Days With ≥ 1.0" Snow Depth	14	12	7	0	0	0	0	0	0	0	1	6	40

The period of record for all cooperative weather station data is 1980 – 2009. See User Guide for detailed explanation of data.

Middleton *Essex County* Elevation: 89 ft. Latitude: 42° 36' N Longitude: 71° 01' W

	JAN	FEB	MAR	APR	MAY	JUN	JUL	AUG	SEP	OCT	NOV	DEC	YEAR
Mean Maximum Temp. (°F)	37.4	40.5	47.3	58.3	68.7	77.8	82.8	81.8	74.9	64.0	53.1	42.2	60.7
Mean Temp. (°F)	27.5	30.3	37.2	47.7	57.9	67.1	72.4	71.4	64.0	52.9	43.6	33.0	50.4
Mean Minimum Temp. (°F)	17.6	19.9	27.0	37.0	47.0	56.3	62.0	60.8	53.0	41.9	34.1	23.7	40.0
Extreme Maximum Temp. (°F)	69	69	86	93	97	95	98	98	96	87	80	74	98
Extreme Minimum Temp. (°F)	-22	-15	-5	8	28	38	46	39	29	21	-3	-13	-22
Days Maximum Temp. ≥ 90°F	0	0	0	0	1	2	4	4	1	0	0	0	12
Days Maximum Temp. ≤ 32°F	9	5	1	0	0	0	0	0	0	0	0	4	19
Days Minimum Temp. ≤ 32°F	29	25	22	9	1	0	0	0	0	5	14	25	130
Days Minimum Temp. ≤ 0°F	3	1	0	0	0	0	0	0	0	0	0	1	5
Heating Degree Days (base 65°F)	1,154	976	857	516	240	56	6	13	98	374	636	984	5,910
Cooling Degree Days (base 65°F)	0	0	0	4	26	125	243	216	75	7	0	0	696
Mean Precipitation (in.)	3.29	3.12	4.20	4.61	4.04	4.00	3.99	3.23	3.74	4.36	4.51	4.00	47.09
Extreme Maximum Daily Precip. (in.)	2.73	2.39	4.83	4.15	6.47	4.70	3.40	3.98	4.65	6.55	3.27	3.44	6.55
Days With ≥ 0.1" Precipitation	7	6	7	7	8	7	7	6	6	7	7	6	81
Days With ≥ 0.5" Precipitation	3	2	3	3	2	3	3	2	2	3	3	3	32
Days With ≥ 1.0" Precipitation	1	1	1	1	1	1	1	1	1	1	1	1	12
Mean Snowfall (in.)	13.4	10.5	8.2	2.1	trace	0.0	0.0	0.0	0.0	trace	1.7	9.3	45.2
Maximum Snow Depth (in.)	29	27	25	23	trace	0	0	0	0	trace	7	25	29
Days With ≥ 1.0" Snow Depth	11	10	6	0	0	0	0	0	0	0	1	7	35

New Bedford *Bristol County* Elevation: 69 ft. Latitude: 41° 38' N Longitude: 70° 56' W

	JAN	FEB	MAR	APR	MAY	JUN	JUL	AUG	SEP	OCT	NOV	DEC	YEAR
Mean Maximum Temp. (°F)	37.6	39.5	45.7	55.6	66.5	76.3	82.0	80.8	73.5	62.9	52.6	42.4	59.6
Mean Temp. (°F)	29.9	31.9	38.0	47.7	57.8	67.6	73.7	72.8	65.5	54.7	45.1	34.9	51.6
Mean Minimum Temp. (°F)	22.2	24.2	30.3	39.7	49.0	58.9	65.4	64.8	57.4	46.5	37.5	27.3	43.6
Extreme Maximum Temp. (°F)	67	66	80	96	98	100	103	100	93	86	79	74	103
Extreme Minimum Temp. (°F)	-7	-6	6	16	34	44	50	44	36	28	11	-5	-7
Days Maximum Temp. ≥ 90°F	0	0	0	0	1	2	4	3	0	0	0	0	10
Days Maximum Temp. ≤ 32°F	9	7	2	0	0	0	0	0	0	0	0	5	23
Days Minimum Temp. ≤ 32°F	26	23	18	4	0	0	0	0	0	1	8	22	102
Days Minimum Temp. ≤ 0°F	1	0	0	0	0	0	0	0	0	0	0	0	1
Heating Degree Days (base 65°F)	1,080	931	830	515	238	44	3	5	72	321	592	929	5,560
Cooling Degree Days (base 65°F)	0	0	0	1	21	128	279	253	93	8	0	0	783
Mean Precipitation (in.)	4.14	3.80	5.35	4.39	3.53	4.07	3.70	4.56	3.63	3.85	4.66	4.33	50.01
Extreme Maximum Daily Precip. (in.)	2.88	3.53	5.92	3.24	2.78	3.51	2.65	7.28	3.77	3.25	3.19	2.43	7.28
Days With ≥ 0.1" Precipitation	7	6	8	7	7	6	6	6	6	6	7	8	80
Days With ≥ 0.5" Precipitation	3	3	4	3	3	3	3	3	2	3	3	3	36
Days With ≥ 1.0" Precipitation	1	1	2	1	1	1	1	1	1	1	2	1	14
Mean Snowfall (in.)	9.9	9.2	4.8	1.4	trace	0.0	0.0	0.0	0.0	0.0	1.1	5.5	31.9
Maximum Snow Depth (in.)	na	na	na	na	na	na	na	na	na	na	na	na	na
Days With ≥ 1.0" Snow Depth	na	na	na	0	0	0	0	0	0	na	0	na	na

Plymouth-Kingston *Plymouth County* Elevation: 44 ft. Latitude: 41° 59' N Longitude: 70° 42' W

	JAN	FEB	MAR	APR	MAY	JUN	JUL	AUG	SEP	OCT	NOV	DEC	YEAR
Mean Maximum Temp. (°F)	38.6	41.3	47.4	57.0	67.0	76.6	82.1	80.4	73.5	63.2	53.8	43.6	60.4
Mean Temp. (°F)	28.8	30.9	37.2	46.6	56.2	66.0	72.0	70.7	63.5	53.0	44.0	34.2	50.3
Mean Minimum Temp. (°F)	19.0	20.5	26.9	36.2	45.4	55.4	61.9	60.9	53.4	42.7	34.1	24.7	40.1
Extreme Maximum Temp. (°F)	70	69	85	94	95	98	101	101	95	87	78	77	101
Extreme Minimum Temp. (°F)	-17	-8	0	16	25	35	44	41	32	23	3	-14	-17
Days Maximum Temp. ≥ 90°F	0	0	0	0	0	2	4	3	0	0	0	0	9
Days Maximum Temp. ≤ 32°F	8	5	1	0	0	0	0	0	0	0	0	3	17
Days Minimum Temp. ≤ 32°F	28	25	23	9	1	0	0	0	0	3	14	24	127
Days Minimum Temp. ≤ 0°F	2	1	0	0	0	0	0	0	0	0	0	0	3
Heating Degree Days (base 65°F)	1,114	957	855	545	280	70	8	16	101	372	624	948	5,890
Cooling Degree Days (base 65°F)	0	0	0	1	15	107	231	198	62	7	0	0	621
Mean Precipitation (in.)	4.28	3.99	5.33	4.86	3.86	3.96	3.60	3.91	4.13	4.44	4.73	4.45	51.54
Extreme Maximum Daily Precip. (in.)	3.85	3.38	3.65	3.90	2.43	5.07	2.85	3.33	4.13	4.50	3.32	3.11	5.07
Days With ≥ 0.1" Precipitation	7	7	8	8	7	7	6	6	6	7	8	8	85
Days With ≥ 0.5" Precipitation	3	3	3	4	3	2	2	3	2	3	3	3	34
Days With ≥ 1.0" Precipitation	1	1	2	1	1	1	1	1	1	1	1	1	13
Mean Snowfall (in.)	12.3	10.0	6.2	1.0	trace	0.0	0.0	0.0	0.0	trace	0.8	5.9	36.2
Maximum Snow Depth (in.)	41	27	18	12	trace	0	0	0	0	trace	12	20	41
Days With ≥ 1.0" Snow Depth	10	9	4	0	0	0	0	0	0	0	0	5	28

Reading *Middlesex County* Elevation: 89 ft. Latitude: 42° 31' N Longitude: 71° 08' W

	JAN	FEB	MAR	APR	MAY	JUN	JUL	AUG	SEP	OCT	NOV	DEC	YEAR
Mean Maximum Temp. (°F)	35.3	38.4	46.3	57.9	68.3	76.4	81.6	80.0	72.3	61.4	51.3	40.1	59.1
Mean Temp. (°F)	26.2	28.9	36.3	46.9	57.0	66.0	71.4	70.1	62.1	50.8	41.7	31.4	49.1
Mean Minimum Temp. (°F)	17.1	19.4	26.3	35.9	45.6	55.5	61.2	60.2	51.7	40.2	32.1	22.6	39.0
Extreme Maximum Temp. (°F)	71	72	92	94	93	96	98	96	95	85	80	78	98
Extreme Minimum Temp. (°F)	-19	-11	-4	15	27	37	42	39	30	21	-2	-14	-19
Days Maximum Temp. ≥ 90°F	0	0	0	0	1	2	4	3	1	0	0	0	11
Days Maximum Temp. ≤ 32°F	12	8	3	0	0	0	0	0	0	0	0	7	30
Days Minimum Temp. ≤ 32°F	29	26	24	11	1	0	0	0	0	6	17	27	141
Days Minimum Temp. ≤ 0°F	3	1	0	0	0	0	0	0	0	0	0	0	4
Heating Degree Days (base 65°F)	1,196	1,014	883	538	264	70	9	19	134	436	692	1,035	6,290
Cooling Degree Days (base 65°F)	0	0	1	3	22	106	216	184	53	4	0	0	589
Mean Precipitation (in.)	3.83	3.56	4.71	4.56	4.18	4.01	4.38	3.54	3.83	4.60	4.55	4.42	50.17
Extreme Maximum Daily Precip. (in.)	2.10	2.45	4.83	4.87	4.59	5.62	3.80	3.83	5.00	7.67	3.40	2.69	7.67
Days With ≥ 0.1" Precipitation	7	6	8	8	8	7	7	6	6	7	7	7	84
Days With ≥ 0.5" Precipitation	3	3	3	3	3	2	3	2	3	3	3	3	34
Days With ≥ 1.0" Precipitation	1	1	1	1	1	1	1	1	1	1	1	1	12
Mean Snowfall (in.)	16.6	12.2	11.1	3.0	trace	0.0	0.0	0.0	0.0	0.1	2.4	12.4	57.8
Maximum Snow Depth (in.)	28	26	24	21	trace	0	0	0	0	1	6	20	28
Days With ≥ 1.0" Snow Depth	19	18	11	1	0	0	0	0	0	0	2	11	62

The period of record for all cooperative weather station data is 1980 – 2009. See User Guide for detailed explanation of data.

Rochester *Plymouth County* Elevation: 60 ft. Latitude: 41° 47' N Longitude: 70° 55' W

	JAN	FEB	MAR	APR	MAY	JUN	JUL	AUG	SEP	OCT	NOV	DEC	YEAR
Mean Maximum Temp. (°F)	37.4	40.0	46.7	56.7	67.5	76.9	82.3	80.8	73.7	62.5	52.9	42.5	60.0
Mean Temp. (°F)	28.7	31.1	37.9	47.5	57.4	66.8	72.4	71.3	64.0	52.9	44.4	34.2	50.7
Mean Minimum Temp. (°F)	20.0	22.2	29.0	38.2	47.2	56.7	62.6	61.6	54.2	43.3	35.9	25.9	41.4
Extreme Maximum Temp. (°F)	68	68	82	94	97	99	102	101	97	86	77	75	102
Extreme Minimum Temp. (°F)	-12	-7	4	11	30	40	46	42	34	26	8	-8	-12
Days Maximum Temp. ≥ 90°F	0	0	0	0	1	2	4	3	0	0	0	0	10
Days Maximum Temp. ≤ 32°F	10	7	2	0	0	0	0	0	0	0	0	5	24
Days Minimum Temp. ≤ 32°F	27	24	21	6	0	0	0	0	0	3	13	24	118
Days Minimum Temp. ≤ 0°F	2	0	0	0	0	0	0	0	0	0	0	0	2
Heating Degree Days (base 65°F)	1,118	952	834	520	250	55	6	11	93	375	611	947	5,772
Cooling Degree Days (base 65°F)	0	0	0	1	21	116	243	213	70	7	0	0	671
Mean Precipitation (in.)	3.86	3.22	4.92	4.97	3.59	4.12	3.82	4.19	4.23	4.31	4.76	4.71	50.70
Extreme Maximum Daily Precip. (in.)	2.30	2.85	3.57	3.96	2.60	3.64	6.75	4.10	3.96	3.80	3.86	4.01	6.75
Days With ≥ 0.1" Precipitation	7	6	7	7	7	7	6	6	6	7	7	8	81
Days With ≥ 0.5" Precipitation	3	2	4	3	3	3	3	3	3	3	3	3	36
Days With ≥ 1.0" Precipitation	1	1	1	2	1	1	1	1	1	1	1	1	13
Mean Snowfall (in.)	8.0	6.2	3.2	0.6	0.0	0.0	0.0	0.0	0.0	trace	0.7	6.1	24.8
Maximum Snow Depth (in.)	25	22	13	10	0	0	0	0	0	0	1	22	25
Days With ≥ 1.0" Snow Depth	10	8	4	0	0	0	0	0	0	0	0	5	27

Taunton *Bristol County* Elevation: 20 ft. Latitude: 41° 54' N Longitude: 71° 04' W

	JAN	FEB	MAR	APR	MAY	JUN	JUL	AUG	SEP	OCT	NOV	DEC	YEAR
Mean Maximum Temp. (°F)	37.8	39.6	47.4	58.2	69.1	78.0	83.0	81.9	74.3	62.5	52.7	42.0	60.5
Mean Temp. (°F)	28.4	30.3	37.5	47.5	57.7	66.9	72.1	71.2	63.2	51.5	43.1	32.8	50.2
Mean Minimum Temp. (°F)	18.9	20.9	27.6	36.7	46.1	55.8	61.2	60.5	52.1	40.5	33.4	23.6	39.8
Extreme Maximum Temp. (°F)	66	65	82	94	96	96	100	100	97	84	77	76	100
Extreme Minimum Temp. (°F)	-20	-12	-2	14	25	37	42	36	30	18	5	-13	-20
Days Maximum Temp. ≥ 90°F	0	0	0	0	1	2	4	4	0	0	0	0	11
Days Maximum Temp. ≤ 32°F	9	7	2	0	0	0	0	0	0	0	0	5	23
Days Minimum Temp. ≤ 32°F	27	25	22	9	1	0	0	0	0	6	16	26	132
Days Minimum Temp. ≤ 0°F	2	0	0	0	0	0	0	0	0	0	0	0	2
Heating Degree Days (base 65°F)	1,129	975	844	521	244	55	8	15	114	417	653	992	5,967
Cooling Degree Days (base 65°F)	0	0	0	1	21	118	235	214	66	5	0	0	660
Mean Precipitation (in.)	3.77	3.21	4.56	4.56	4.20	3.72	3.72	3.52	3.75	3.94	4.56	3.95	47.46
Extreme Maximum Daily Precip. (in.)	3.25	3.08	3.43	3.40	8.01	4.56	4.67	4.20	3.10	4.30	2.60	2.38	8.01
Days With ≥ 0.1" Precipitation	6	6	7	7	8	6	6	6	6	6	7	7	78
Days With ≥ 0.5" Precipitation	3	2	3	3	3	2	2	2	2	3	3	3	31
Days With ≥ 1.0" Precipitation	1	1	1	2	1	1	1	1	1	1	1	1	13
Mean Snowfall (in.)	8.3	7.6	5.0	1.3	0.0	0.0	0.0	0.0	0.0	0.0	1.0	4.9	28.1
Maximum Snow Depth (in.)	27	20	14	17	0	0	0	0	0	0	3	15	27
Days With ≥ 1.0" Snow Depth	12	11	5	1	0	0	0	0	0	0	0	4	33

Walpole 2 *Norfolk County* Elevation: 165 ft. Latitude: 42° 10' N Longitude: 71° 15' W

	JAN	FEB	MAR	APR	MAY	JUN	JUL	AUG	SEP	OCT	NOV	DEC	YEAR
Mean Maximum Temp. (°F)	36.4	39.7	47.5	58.8	69.3	77.7	82.7	81.0	73.3	62.1	51.7	41.0	60.1
Mean Temp. (°F)	27.3	30.3	37.5	47.9	58.1	67.1	72.5	71.1	63.2	51.8	42.6	32.4	50.1
Mean Minimum Temp. (°F)	18.3	20.9	27.4	37.1	46.8	56.5	62.3	61.2	53.0	41.4	33.4	23.7	40.1
Extreme Maximum Temp. (°F)	68	70	90	93	95	97	100	100	97	87	78	76	100
Extreme Minimum Temp. (°F)	-19	-16	-4	14	28	37	42	39	30	21	4	-14	-19
Days Maximum Temp. ≥ 90°F	0	0	0	0	1	3	4	3	1	0	0	0	12
Days Maximum Temp. ≤ 32°F	11	6	2	0	0	0	0	0	0	0	0	6	25
Days Minimum Temp. ≤ 32°F	28	25	22	9	1	0	0	0	0	6	15	26	132
Days Minimum Temp. ≤ 0°F	3	1	0	0	0	0	0	0	0	0	0	1	5
Heating Degree Days (base 65°F)	1,161	975	847	508	234	53	5	14	113	409	667	1,004	5,990
Cooling Degree Days (base 65°F)	0	0	1	3	26	123	244	211	64	6	0	0	678
Mean Precipitation (in.)	3.66	3.40	4.43	4.50	3.60	4.06	3.99	3.79	3.61	4.32	4.44	4.37	48.17
Extreme Maximum Daily Precip. (in.)	2.87	2.43	3.06	3.14	2.34	7.00	3.08	4.00	3.32	5.66	2.54	3.43	7.00
Days With ≥ 0.1" Precipitation	7	6	8	7	8	7	7	7	6	6	7	7	83
Days With ≥ 0.5" Precipitation	3	2	3	3	2	2	3	3	2	3	3	3	32
Days With ≥ 1.0" Precipitation	1	1	1	1	1	1	1	1	1	1	1	1	12
Mean Snowfall (in.)	13.4	11.4	9.6	2.6	trace	0.0	0.0	0.0	0.0	0.2	2.3	11.0	50.5
Maximum Snow Depth (in.)	33	25	22	25	trace	0	0	0	0	1	10	21	33
Days With ≥ 1.0" Snow Depth	18	15	10	1	0	0	0	0	0	0	2	11	57

West Medway *Norfolk County* Elevation: 209 ft. Latitude: 42° 08' N Longitude: 71° 26' W

	JAN	FEB	MAR	APR	MAY	JUN	JUL	AUG	SEP	OCT	NOV	DEC	YEAR
Mean Maximum Temp. (°F)	37.1	40.8	48.2	58.7	70.0	78.5	83.8	82.4	74.9	63.8	52.8	41.8	61.1
Mean Temp. (°F)	25.5	29.0	36.5	46.7	57.2	66.1	71.4	70.1	61.7	50.1	41.1	31.0	48.9
Mean Minimum Temp. (°F)	13.8	17.1	24.8	34.6	44.4	53.7	59.1	57.6	48.5	36.4	29.3	20.2	36.6
Extreme Maximum Temp. (°F)	68	70	87	94	97	97	102	101	96	87	82	76	102
Extreme Minimum Temp. (°F)	-23	-20	-6	15	25	34	38	33	26	17	-2	-16	-23
Days Maximum Temp. ≥ 90°F	0	0	0	0	1	3	6	5	1	0	0	0	16
Days Maximum Temp. ≤ 32°F	9	6	1	0	0	0	0	0	0	0	0	5	21
Days Minimum Temp. ≤ 32°F	29	26	25	12	2	0	0	0	2	12	20	28	156
Days Minimum Temp. ≤ 0°F	5	2	0	0	0	0	0	0	0	0	0	1	8
Heating Degree Days (base 65°F)	1,219	1,012	876	545	256	68	10	22	144	458	710	1,046	6,366
Cooling Degree Days (base 65°F)	0	0	0	1	22	109	216	186	54	4	0	0	592
Mean Precipitation (in.)	3.78	3.32	4.40	4.75	3.50	4.39	3.77	4.11	3.91	4.14	4.56	3.97	48.60
Extreme Maximum Daily Precip. (in.)	2.46	2.07	3.02	3.14	2.44	4.61	3.95	5.09	5.81	6.39	3.87	3.67	6.39
Days With ≥ 0.1" Precipitation	6	6	7	7	7	7	6	6	6	6	7	6	77
Days With ≥ 0.5" Precipitation	3	2	3	3	2	2	2	3	2	3	3	3	31
Days With ≥ 1.0" Precipitation	1	1	1	1	1	1	1	1	1	1	1	1	12
Mean Snowfall (in.)	12.9	9.6	7.5	2.7	trace	0.0	0.0	0.0	0.0	0.1	2.0	8.3	43.1
Maximum Snow Depth (in.)	31	27	17	22	trace	0	0	0	0	trace	7	22	31
Days With ≥ 1.0" Snow Depth	15	11	6	1	0	0	0	0	0	0	2	8	43

The period of record for all cooperative weather station data is 1980 – 2009. See User Guide for detailed explanation of data.

Massachusetts Weather Station Rankings

Annual Extreme Maximum Temperature

Highest

Rank	Station Name	°F
1	New Bedford	***103***
2	Rochester	102
2	West Medway	***102***
4	Boston Logan Int'l Arpt	101
4	Brockton	101
4	Haverhill	101
4	Plymouth-Kingston	101
8	East Wareham	100
8	Hingham	100
8	Marblehead	***100***
8	Taunton	100
8	Walpole 2	100
13	Amherst	99
13	Bedford	99
13	Milton Blue Hill Observatory	99
13	Lawrence	99
17	Barre Falls Dam	98
17	Middleton	98
17	Reading	98
20	East Brimfield Lake	96
20	Edgartown	96
20	Worcester Municipal Arpt	96
23	Chatham WSMO	***95***

Lowest

Rank	Station Name	°F
1	Chatham WSMO	***95***
2	East Brimfield Lake	96
2	Edgartown	96
2	Worcester Municipal Arpt	96
5	Barre Falls Dam	98
5	Middleton	98
5	Reading	98
8	Amherst	99
8	Bedford	99
8	Milton Blue Hill Observatory	99
8	Lawrence	99
12	East Wareham	100
12	Hingham	100
12	Marblehead	***100***
12	Taunton	100
12	Walpole 2	100
17	Boston Logan Int'l Arpt	101
17	Brockton	101
17	Haverhill	101
17	Plymouth-Kingston	101
21	Rochester	102
21	West Medway	***102***
23	New Bedford	***103***

Annual Mean Maximum Temperature

Highest

Rank	Station Name	°F
1	West Medway	***61.1***
2	Brockton	60.8
2	Middleton	60.8
4	Taunton	60.5
5	Plymouth-Kingston	60.4
6	Walpole 2	60.1
7	Rochester	60.0
8	Amherst	59.9
9	New Bedford	***59.6***
10	Bedford	59.5
10	Hingham	59.5
10	Lawrence	59.5
13	Haverhill	59.3
14	Boston Logan Int'l Arpt	59.1
14	Edgartown	59.1
14	Reading	59.1
17	Marblehead	***58.9***
18	East Wareham	58.4
19	East Brimfield Lake	58.2
20	Milton Blue Hill Observatory	57.8
21	Worcester Municipal Arpt	56.1
22	Chatham WSMO	56.0

Lowest

Rank	Station Name	°F
1	Chatham WSMO	56.0
2	Worcester Municipal Arpt	56.1
3	Milton Blue Hill Observatory	57.8
4	East Brimfield Lake	58.2
5	East Wareham	58.4
6	Marblehead	***58.9***
7	Boston Logan Int'l Arpt	59.1
7	Edgartown	59.1
7	Reading	59.1
10	Haverhill	59.3
11	Bedford	59.5
11	Hingham	59.5
11	Lawrence	59.5
14	New Bedford	***59.6***
15	Amherst	59.9
16	Rochester	60.0
17	Walpole 2	60.1
18	Plymouth-Kingston	60.4
19	Taunton	60.5
20	Brockton	60.8
20	Middleton	60.8
22	West Medway	***61.1***

Rankings include 25 highest/lowest stations. If state has less than 25 stations, all stations are included. The period of record is 1980–2009. See User Guide for detailed explanation of data.

Annual Mean Temperature

Highest

Rank	Station Name	°F
1	Boston Logan Int'l Arpt	51.6
1	New Bedford	***51.6***
3	Edgartown	51.0
4	Rochester	50.7
5	Marblehead	***50.5***
6	Hingham	50.4
6	Middleton	50.4
8	Plymouth-Kingston	50.3
9	Brockton	50.2
9	Taunton	50.2
11	Walpole 2	50.1
12	Chatham WSMO	50.0
12	East Wareham	50.0
14	Lawrence	49.6
15	Milton Blue Hill Observatory	49.2
16	Reading	49.1
17	Bedford	49.0
18	West Medway	***48.9***
19	Haverhill	48.5
20	Amherst	48.3
21	Worcester Municipal Arpt	47.7
22	East Brimfield Lake	47.3

Lowest

Rank	Station Name	°F
1	East Brimfield Lake	47.3
2	Worcester Municipal Arpt	47.7
3	Amherst	48.3
4	Haverhill	48.5
5	West Medway	***48.9***
6	Bedford	49.0
7	Reading	49.1
8	Milton Blue Hill Observatory	49.2
9	Lawrence	49.6
10	Chatham WSMO	50.0
10	East Wareham	50.0
12	Walpole 2	50.1
13	Brockton	50.2
13	Taunton	50.2
15	Plymouth-Kingston	50.3
16	Hingham	50.4
16	Middleton	50.4
18	Marblehead	***50.5***
19	Rochester	50.7
20	Edgartown	51.0
21	Boston Logan Int'l Arpt	51.6
21	New Bedford	***51.6***

Annual Mean Minimum Temperature

Highest

Rank	Station Name	°F
1	Boston Logan Int'l Arpt	44.0
1	Chatham WSMO	44.0
3	New Bedford	***43.6***
4	Edgartown	42.9
5	Marblehead	***42.1***
6	East Wareham	41.5
7	Rochester	41.4
8	Hingham	41.2
9	Milton Blue Hill Observatory	40.6
10	Walpole 2	40.2
11	Plymouth-Kingston	40.1
12	Middleton	40.0
13	Taunton	39.8
14	Lawrence	39.7
15	Brockton	39.5
16	Worcester Municipal Arpt	39.2
17	Reading	39.0
18	Bedford	38.5
19	Haverhill	37.7
20	Amherst	36.6
20	West Medway	***36.6***
22	East Brimfield Lake	36.3

Lowest

Rank	Station Name	°F
1	East Brimfield Lake	36.3
2	Amherst	36.6
2	West Medway	***36.6***
4	Haverhill	37.7
5	Bedford	38.5
6	Reading	39.0
7	Worcester Municipal Arpt	39.2
8	Brockton	39.5
9	Lawrence	39.7
10	Taunton	39.8
11	Middleton	40.0
12	Plymouth-Kingston	40.1
13	Walpole 2	40.2
14	Milton Blue Hill Observatory	40.6
15	Hingham	41.2
16	Rochester	41.4
17	East Wareham	41.5
18	Marblehead	***42.1***
19	Edgartown	42.9
20	New Bedford	***43.6***
21	Boston Logan Int'l Arpt	44.0
21	Chatham WSMO	44.0

Rankings include 25 highest/lowest stations. If state has less than 25 stations, all stations are included. The period of record is 1980–2009. See User Guide for detailed explanation of data.

Annual Extreme Minimum Temperature

Highest			Lowest		
Rank	Station Name	°F	Rank	Station Name	°F
1	Chatham WSMO	***-6***	1	Amherst	-27
1	Edgartown	-6	1	East Brimfield Lake	-27
3	Boston Logan Int'l Arpt	-7	3	Barre Falls Dam	-25
3	New Bedford	***-7***	4	West Medway	***-23***
5	Marblehead	***-9***	5	Middleton	-22
6	Milton Blue Hill Observatory	-12	6	Haverhill	-21
6	Rochester	-12	7	Lawrence	-20
6	Worcester Municipal Arpt	-12	7	Taunton	-20
9	Hingham	-13	9	Bedford	-19
10	Brockton	-15	9	Reading	-19
10	East Wareham	-15	9	Walpole 2	-19
12	Plymouth-Kingston	-17	12	Plymouth-Kingston	-17
13	Bedford	-19	13	Brockton	-15
13	Reading	-19	13	East Wareham	-15
13	Walpole 2	-19	15	Hingham	-13
16	Lawrence	-20	16	Milton Blue Hill Observatory	-12
16	Taunton	-20	16	Rochester	-12
18	Haverhill	-21	16	Worcester Municipal Arpt	-12
19	Middleton	-22	19	Marblehead	***-9***
20	West Medway	***-23***	20	Boston Logan Int'l Arpt	-7
21	Barre Falls Dam	-25	20	New Bedford	***-7***
22	Amherst	-27	22	Chatham WSMO	***-6***
22	East Brimfield Lake	-27	22	Edgartown	-6

July Mean Maximum Temperature

Highest			Lowest		
Rank	Station Name	°F	Rank	Station Name	°F
1	West Medway	***83.8***	1	Chatham WSMO	75.0
2	Amherst	83.3	2	Worcester Municipal Arpt	79.0
2	Brockton	83.3	3	Edgartown	79.1
4	Taunton	83.0	4	East Wareham	79.5
5	Middleton	82.8	5	Barre Falls Dam	80.0
6	Lawrence	82.7	6	Milton Blue Hill Observatory	80.8
6	Walpole 2	82.7	7	Marblehead	***80.9***
8	Bedford	82.6	8	East Brimfield Lake	81.0
8	Haverhill	82.6	9	Hingham	81.6
10	Rochester	82.3	9	Reading	81.6
11	Plymouth-Kingston	82.1	11	Boston Logan Int'l Arpt	81.8
12	New Bedford	***82.0***	12	New Bedford	***82.0***
13	Boston Logan Int'l Arpt	81.8	13	Plymouth-Kingston	82.1
14	Hingham	81.6	14	Rochester	82.3
14	Reading	81.6	15	Bedford	82.6
16	East Brimfield Lake	81.0	15	Haverhill	82.6
17	Marblehead	***80.9***	17	Lawrence	82.7
18	Milton Blue Hill Observatory	80.8	17	Walpole 2	82.7
19	Barre Falls Dam	80.0	19	Middleton	82.8
20	East Wareham	79.5	20	Taunton	83.0
21	Edgartown	79.1	21	Amherst	83.3
22	Worcester Municipal Arpt	79.0	21	Brockton	83.3
23	Chatham WSMO	75.0	23	West Medway	***83.8***

Rankings include 25 highest/lowest stations. If state has less than 25 stations, all stations are included. The period of record is 1980–2009. See User Guide for detailed explanation of data.

January Mean Minimum Temperature

Highest

Rank	Station Name	°F
1	Chatham WSMO	25.2
2	Edgartown	23.4
3	Boston Logan Int'l Arpt	22.4
4	New Bedford	*22.2*
5	Marblehead	*21.3*
6	East Wareham	20.6
7	Hingham	20.3
8	Rochester	20.0
9	Plymouth-Kingston	19.0
10	Taunton	18.9
11	Milton Blue Hill Observatory	18.6
11	Brockton	18.6
13	Walpole 2	18.3
14	Middleton	17.6
15	Reading	17.1
16	Worcester Municipal Arpt	16.7
17	Bedford	16.3
18	Lawrence	16.1
19	Haverhill	15.4
20	West Medway	*13.8*
21	Amherst	13.3
21	East Brimfield Lake	13.3
23	Barre Falls Dam	*11.5*

Lowest

Rank	Station Name	°F
1	Barre Falls Dam	*11.5*
2	Amherst	13.3
2	East Brimfield Lake	13.3
4	West Medway	*13.8*
5	Haverhill	15.4
6	Lawrence	16.1
7	Bedford	16.3
8	Worcester Municipal Arpt	16.7
9	Reading	17.1
10	Middleton	17.6
11	Walpole 2	18.3
12	Milton Blue Hill Observatory	18.6
12	Brockton	18.6
14	Taunton	18.9
15	Plymouth-Kingston	19.0
16	Rochester	20.0
17	Hingham	20.3
18	East Wareham	20.6
19	Marblehead	*21.3*
20	New Bedford	*22.2*
21	Boston Logan Int'l Arpt	22.4
22	Edgartown	23.4
23	Chatham WSMO	25.2

Number of Days Annually Maximum Temperature ≥ 90°F

Highest

Rank	Station Name	Days
1	West Medway	*16*
2	Boston Logan Int'l Arpt	15
3	Haverhill	14
3	Lawrence	14
5	Brockton	13
6	Bedford	12
6	Middleton	12
6	Walpole 2	12
9	Amherst	11
9	Reading	11
9	Taunton	11
12	Hingham	10
12	New Bedford	*10*
12	Rochester	10
15	Marblehead	*9*
15	Plymouth-Kingston	9
17	Milton Blue Hill Observatory	8
18	Barre Falls Dam	4
18	East Brimfield Lake	4
20	Worcester Municipal Arpt	3
21	East Wareham	2
22	Edgartown	1
23	Chatham WSMO	0

Lowest

Rank	Station Name	Days
1	Chatham WSMO	0
2	Edgartown	1
3	East Wareham	2
4	Worcester Municipal Arpt	3
5	Barre Falls Dam	4
5	East Brimfield Lake	4
7	Milton Blue Hill Observatory	8
8	Marblehead	*9*
8	Plymouth-Kingston	9
10	Hingham	10
10	New Bedford	*10*
10	Rochester	10
13	Amherst	11
13	Reading	11
13	Taunton	11
16	Bedford	12
16	Middleton	12
16	Walpole 2	12
19	Brockton	13
20	Haverhill	14
20	Lawrence	14
22	Boston Logan Int'l Arpt	15
23	West Medway	*16*

Rankings include 25 highest/lowest stations. If state has less than 25 stations, all stations are included. The period of record is 1980–2009. See User Guide for detailed explanation of data.

Number of Days Annually Maximum Temperature ≤ 32°F

Highest Rank	Station Name	Days	Lowest Rank	Station Name	Days
1	Worcester Municipal Arpt	47	1	Edgartown	16
2	Barre Falls Dam	38	2	Plymouth-Kingston	17
3	Milton Blue Hill Observatory	37	3	Chatham WSMO	18
3	East Brimfield Lake	37	4	Middleton	19
5	Bedford	31	5	East Wareham	21
5	Lawrence	31	5	West Medway	***21***
7	Reading	30	7	Brockton	22
8	Amherst	29	8	Hingham	23
8	Haverhill	29	8	New Bedford	***23***
10	Walpole 2	25	8	Taunton	23
11	Boston Logan Int'l Arpt	24	11	Boston Logan Int'l Arpt	24
11	Marblehead	***24***	11	Marblehead	***24***
11	Rochester	24	11	Rochester	24
14	Hingham	23	14	Walpole 2	25
14	New Bedford	***23***	15	Amherst	29
14	Taunton	23	15	Haverhill	29
17	Brockton	22	17	Reading	30
18	East Wareham	21	18	Bedford	31
18	West Medway	***21***	18	Lawrence	31
20	Middleton	19	20	Milton Blue Hill Observatory	37
21	Chatham WSMO	18	20	East Brimfield Lake	37
22	Plymouth-Kingston	17	22	Barre Falls Dam	38
23	Edgartown	16	23	Worcester Municipal Arpt	47

Number of Days Annually Minimum Temperature ≤ 32°F

Highest Rank	Station Name	Days	Lowest Rank	Station Name	Days
1	Barre Falls Dam	156	1	Chatham WSMO	82
1	West Medway	***156***	2	Boston Logan Int'l Arpt	94
3	Amherst	154	3	New Bedford	***102***
3	East Brimfield Lake	154	4	Edgartown	104
5	Haverhill	146	5	Marblehead	***109***
6	Bedford	142	6	Rochester	118
7	Reading	141	7	East Wareham	120
8	Worcester Municipal Arpt	134	7	Hingham	120
9	Brockton	133	9	Milton Blue Hill Observatory	121
10	Taunton	132	10	Plymouth-Kingston	127
10	Walpole 2	132	11	Lawrence	129
12	Middleton	130	12	Middleton	130
13	Lawrence	129	13	Taunton	132
14	Plymouth-Kingston	127	13	Walpole 2	132
15	Milton Blue Hill Observatory	121	15	Brockton	133
16	East Wareham	120	16	Worcester Municipal Arpt	134
16	Hingham	120	17	Reading	141
18	Rochester	118	18	Bedford	142
19	Marblehead	***109***	19	Haverhill	146
20	Edgartown	104	20	Amherst	154
21	New Bedford	***102***	20	East Brimfield Lake	154
22	Boston Logan Int'l Arpt	94	22	Barre Falls Dam	156
23	Chatham WSMO	82	22	West Medway	***156***

Rankings include 25 highest/lowest stations. If state has less than 25 stations, all stations are included. The period of record is 1980–2009. See User Guide for detailed explanation of data.

Number of Days Annually Minimum Temperature ≤ 0°F

Highest

Rank	Station Name	Days
1	Barre Falls Dam	13
2	Amherst	10
2	East Brimfield Lake	10
4	West Medway	*8*
5	Bedford	5
5	Haverhill	5
5	Lawrence	5
5	Middleton	5
5	Walpole 2	5
5	Worcester Municipal Arpt	5
11	Reading	4
12	Milton Blue Hill Observatory	3
12	Brockton	3
12	Plymouth-Kingston	3
15	Hingham	2
15	Rochester	2
15	Taunton	2
18	Boston Logan Int'l Arpt	1
18	East Wareham	1
18	Marblehead	*1*
18	New Bedford	*1*
22	Chatham WSMO	0
22	Edgartown	0

Lowest

Rank	Station Name	Days
1	Chatham WSMO	0
1	Edgartown	0
3	Boston Logan Int'l Arpt	1
3	East Wareham	1
3	Marblehead	*1*
3	New Bedford	*1*
7	Hingham	2
7	Rochester	2
7	Taunton	2
10	Milton Blue Hill Observatory	3
10	Brockton	3
10	Plymouth-Kingston	3
13	Reading	4
14	Bedford	5
14	Haverhill	5
14	Lawrence	5
14	Middleton	5
14	Walpole 2	5
14	Worcester Municipal Arpt	5
20	West Medway	*8*
21	Amherst	10
21	East Brimfield Lake	10
23	Barre Falls Dam	13

Number of Annual Heating Degree Days

Highest

Rank	Station Name	Num.
1	East Brimfield Lake	6,807
2	Worcester Municipal Arpt	6,693
3	Amherst	6,564
4	Haverhill	6,480
5	West Medway	***6,366***
6	Bedford	6,314
7	Reading	6,290
8	Milton Blue Hill Observatory	6,239
9	Lawrence	6,183
10	Walpole 2	5,990
11	Taunton	5,967
12	Brockton	5,955
13	East Wareham	5,926
14	Middleton	5,910
15	Plymouth-Kingston	5,890
16	Hingham	5,855
17	Marblehead	***5,815***
18	Rochester	5,772
19	Chatham WSMO	5,701
20	Boston Logan Int'l Arpt	5,577
21	New Bedford	***5,560***
22	Edgartown	5,523

Lowest

Rank	Station Name	Num.
1	Edgartown	5,523
2	New Bedford	***5,560***
3	Boston Logan Int'l Arpt	5,577
4	Chatham WSMO	5,701
5	Rochester	5,772
6	Marblehead	***5,815***
7	Hingham	5,855
8	Plymouth-Kingston	5,890
9	Middleton	5,910
10	East Wareham	5,926
11	Brockton	5,955
12	Taunton	5,967
13	Walpole 2	5,990
14	Lawrence	6,183
15	Milton Blue Hill Observatory	6,239
16	Reading	6,290
17	Bedford	6,314
18	West Medway	***6,366***
19	Haverhill	6,480
20	Amherst	6,564
21	Worcester Municipal Arpt	6,693
22	East Brimfield Lake	6,807

Rankings include 25 highest/lowest stations. If state has less than 25 stations, all stations are included. The period of record is 1980–2009. See User Guide for detailed explanation of data.

Number of Annual Cooling Degree Days

Highest Rank	Station Name	Num.	Lowest Rank	Station Name	Num.
1	Boston Logan Int'l Arpt	793	1	Chatham WSMO	334
2	New Bedford	***783***	2	East Brimfield Lake	463
3	Middleton	696	3	Worcester Municipal Arpt	484
4	Lawrence	681	4	Edgartown	528
5	Walpole 2	678	5	East Wareham	553
6	Rochester	671	6	Haverhill	576
7	Taunton	660	7	Amherst	581
8	Brockton	648	8	Reading	589
9	Hingham	635	9	West Medway	***592***
10	Marblehead	***633***	10	Bedford	598
11	Plymouth-Kingston	621	10	Milton Blue Hill Observatory	598
12	Bedford	598	12	Plymouth-Kingston	621
12	Milton Blue Hill Observatory	598	13	Marblehead	***633***
14	West Medway	***592***	14	Hingham	635
15	Reading	589	15	Brockton	648
16	Amherst	581	16	Taunton	660
17	Haverhill	576	17	Rochester	671
18	East Wareham	553	18	Walpole 2	678
19	Edgartown	528	19	Lawrence	681
20	Worcester Municipal Arpt	484	20	Middleton	696
21	East Brimfield Lake	463	21	New Bedford	***783***
22	Chatham WSMO	334	22	Boston Logan Int'l Arpt	793

Annual Precipitation

Highest Rank	Station Name	Inches	Lowest Rank	Station Name	Inches
1	Milton Blue Hill Observatory	52.58	1	Boston Logan Int'l Arpt	43.02
2	Hingham	51.63	2	Lawrence	44.37
3	Plymouth-Kingston	51.54	3	Amherst	45.65
4	Rochester	50.70	4	Barre Falls Dam	45.98
5	Reading	50.17	5	Edgartown	46.11
6	New Bedford	***50.01***	6	East Brimfield Lake	46.33
7	East Wareham	49.35	7	Chatham WSMO	46.40
8	Brockton	49.34	8	Middleton	47.09
9	Haverhill	48.80	9	Marblehead	***47.35***
10	West Medway	***48.60***	10	Taunton	47.46
11	Worcester Municipal Arpt	48.19	11	Bedford	47.92
12	Walpole 2	48.17	12	Walpole 2	48.17
13	Bedford	47.92	13	Worcester Municipal Arpt	48.19
14	Taunton	47.46	14	West Medway	***48.60***
15	Marblehead	***47.35***	15	Haverhill	48.80
16	Middleton	47.09	16	Brockton	49.34
17	Chatham WSMO	46.40	17	East Wareham	49.35
18	East Brimfield Lake	46.33	18	New Bedford	***50.01***
19	Edgartown	46.11	19	Reading	50.17
20	Barre Falls Dam	45.98	20	Rochester	50.70
21	Amherst	45.65	21	Plymouth-Kingston	51.54
22	Lawrence	44.37	22	Hingham	51.63
23	Boston Logan Int'l Arpt	43.02	23	Milton Blue Hill Observatory	52.58

Rankings include 25 highest/lowest stations. If state has less than 25 stations, all stations are included. The period of record is 1980–2009. See User Guide for detailed explanation of data.

Annual Extreme Maximum Daily Precipitation

Highest			Lowest		
Rank	Station Name	Inches	Rank	Station Name	Inches
1	Taunton	***8.01***	1	Chatham WSMO	***4.52***
2	Bedford	7.83	2	Worcester Municipal Arpt	5.00
3	Reading	7.67	3	East Brimfield Lake	5.03
4	Amherst	7.56	4	Plymouth-Kingston	5.07
5	New Bedford	***7.28***	5	East Wareham	5.27
6	Milton Blue Hill Observatory	7.10	6	Marblehead	***5.58***
7	Walpole 2	7.00	7	Barre Falls Dam	5.67
8	Rochester	6.75	8	Hingham	5.76
9	Lawrence	***6.72***	9	Brockton	5.80
10	Middleton	6.55	10	Edgartown	6.04
11	Haverhill	6.45	11	Boston Logan Int'l Arpt	6.11
12	West Medway	***6.39***	12	West Medway	***6.39***
13	Boston Logan Int'l Arpt	6.11	13	Haverhill	6.45
14	Edgartown	6.04	14	Middleton	6.55
15	Brockton	5.80	15	Lawrence	***6.72***
16	Hingham	5.76	16	Rochester	6.75
17	Barre Falls Dam	5.67	17	Walpole 2	7.00
18	Marblehead	***5.58***	18	Milton Blue Hill Observatory	7.10
19	East Wareham	5.27	19	New Bedford	***7.28***
20	Plymouth-Kingston	5.07	20	Amherst	7.56
21	East Brimfield Lake	5.03	21	Reading	7.67
22	Worcester Municipal Arpt	5.00	22	Bedford	7.83
23	Chatham WSMO	***4.52***	23	Taunton	***8.01***

Number of Days Annually With ≥ 0.1 Inches of Precipitation

Highest			Lowest		
Rank	Station Name	Days	Rank	Station Name	Days
1	Barre Falls Dam	87	1	Boston Logan Int'l Arpt	77
2	Milton Blue Hill Observatory	86	1	Edgartown	77
3	Marblehead	***85***	1	Lawrence	77
3	Plymouth-Kingston	85	1	West Medway	***77***
5	Reading	84	5	Taunton	78
5	Worcester Municipal Arpt	84	6	Brockton	79
7	East Brimfield Lake	83	7	East Wareham	80
7	Haverhill	83	7	New Bedford	***80***
7	Hingham	83	9	Amherst	81
7	Walpole 2	83	9	Middleton	81
11	Bedford	82	9	Rochester	81
11	Chatham WSMO	82	12	Bedford	82
13	Amherst	81	12	Chatham WSMO	82
13	Middleton	81	14	East Brimfield Lake	83
13	Rochester	81	14	Haverhill	83
16	East Wareham	80	14	Hingham	83
16	New Bedford	***80***	14	Walpole 2	83
18	Brockton	79	18	Reading	84
19	Taunton	78	18	Worcester Municipal Arpt	84
20	Boston Logan Int'l Arpt	77	20	Marblehead	***85***
20	Edgartown	77	20	Plymouth-Kingston	85
20	Lawrence	77	22	Milton Blue Hill Observatory	86
20	West Medway	***77***	23	Barre Falls Dam	87

 Rankings include 25 highest/lowest stations. If state has less than 25 stations, all stations are included. The period of record is 1980–2009. See User Guide for detailed explanation of data.

Number of Days Annually With ≥ 0.5 Inches of Precipitation

Highest Rank	Station Name	Days	Lowest Rank	Station Name	Days
1	New Bedford	***36***	1	Boston Logan Int'l Arpt	27
1	Rochester	36	2	Chatham WSMO	29
3	Hingham	34	3	East Brimfield Lake	31
3	Plymouth-Kingston	34	3	Edgartown	31
3	Reading	34	3	Lawrence	31
6	Barre Falls Dam	33	3	Marblehead	***31***
6	Milton Blue Hill Observatory	33	3	Taunton	31
6	Brockton	33	3	West Medway	***31***
6	Haverhill	33	9	Amherst	32
6	Worcester Municipal Arpt	33	9	Bedford	32
11	Amherst	32	9	East Wareham	32
11	Bedford	32	9	Middleton	32
11	East Wareham	32	9	Walpole 2	32
11	Middleton	32	14	Barre Falls Dam	33
11	Walpole 2	32	14	Milton Blue Hill Observatory	33
16	East Brimfield Lake	31	14	Brockton	33
16	Edgartown	31	14	Haverhill	33
16	Lawrence	31	14	Worcester Municipal Arpt	33
16	Marblehead	***31***	19	Hingham	34
16	Taunton	31	19	Plymouth-Kingston	34
16	West Medway	***31***	19	Reading	34
22	Chatham WSMO	29	22	New Bedford	***36***
23	Boston Logan Int'l Arpt	27	22	Rochester	36

Number of Days Annually With ≥ 1.0 Inches of Precipitation

Highest Rank	Station Name	Days	Lowest Rank	Station Name	Days
1	Brockton	14	1	Bedford	12
1	Hingham	14	1	Boston Logan Int'l Arpt	12
1	New Bedford	***14***	1	Chatham WSMO	12
4	Amherst	13	1	East Brimfield Lake	12
4	Barre Falls Dam	13	1	Edgartown	12
4	Milton Blue Hill Observatory	13	1	Haverhill	12
4	East Wareham	13	1	Lawrence	12
4	Plymouth-Kingston	13	1	Marblehead	***12***
4	Rochester	13	1	Middleton	12
4	Taunton	13	1	Reading	12
4	Worcester Municipal Arpt	13	1	Walpole 2	12
12	Bedford	12	1	West Medway	***12***
12	Boston Logan Int'l Arpt	12	13	Amherst	13
12	Chatham WSMO	12	13	Barre Falls Dam	13
12	East Brimfield Lake	12	13	Milton Blue Hill Observatory	13
12	Edgartown	12	13	East Wareham	13
12	Haverhill	12	13	Plymouth-Kingston	13
12	Lawrence	12	13	Rochester	13
12	Marblehead	***12***	13	Taunton	13
12	Middleton	12	13	Worcester Municipal Arpt	13
12	Reading	12	21	Brockton	14
12	Walpole 2	12	21	Hingham	14
12	West Medway	***12***	21	New Bedford	***14***

Rankings include 25 highest/lowest stations. If state has less than 25 stations, all stations are included. The period of record is 1980–2009. See User Guide for detailed explanation of data.

Annual Snowfall

Highest			Lowest		
Rank	**Station Name**	**Inches**	**Rank**	**Station Name**	**Inches**
1	Milton Blue Hill Observatory	62.4	1	Edgartown	22.8
2	Worcester Municipal Arpt	***62.2***	2	Rochester	***24.8***
3	East Brimfield Lake	58.0	3	Chatham WSMO	27.6
4	Reading	57.8	4	Taunton	***28.1***
5	Barre Falls Dam	55.8	5	New Bedford	***31.9***
6	Bedford	54.5	6	East Wareham	33.1
7	Haverhill	52.5	7	Plymouth-Kingston	36.2
8	Walpole 2	50.5	8	Lawrence	38.1
9	Hingham	46.0	9	Amherst	40.2
10	Middleton	45.2	10	West Medway	***43.1***
11	Boston Logan Int'l Arpt	43.7	11	Marblehead	***43.5***
12	Marblehead	***43.5***	12	Boston Logan Int'l Arpt	43.7
13	West Medway	***43.1***	13	Middleton	45.2
14	Amherst	40.2	14	Hingham	46.0
15	Lawrence	38.1	15	Walpole 2	50.5
16	Plymouth-Kingston	36.2	16	Haverhill	52.5
17	East Wareham	33.1	17	Bedford	54.5
18	New Bedford	***31.9***	18	Barre Falls Dam	55.8
19	Taunton	***28.1***	19	Reading	57.8
20	Chatham WSMO	27.6	20	East Brimfield Lake	58.0
21	Rochester	***24.8***	21	Worcester Municipal Arpt	***62.2***
22	Edgartown	22.8	22	Milton Blue Hill Observatory	62.4

Annual Maximum Snow Depth

Highest			Lowest		
Rank	**Station Name**	**Inches**	**Rank**	**Station Name**	**Inches**
1	Brockton	***46***	1	Amherst	24
2	Plymouth-Kingston	41	1	Edgartown	24
3	Lawrence	***37***	3	Rochester	***25***
4	Milton Blue Hill Observatory	33	4	East Brimfield Lake	27
4	Walpole 2	33	4	Taunton	***27***
6	Bedford	32	6	East Wareham	28
6	Hingham	32	6	Haverhill	28
8	Marblehead	***31***	6	Reading	28
8	West Medway	***31***	9	Middleton	29
10	Barre Falls Dam	30	10	Barre Falls Dam	30
10	Chatham WSMO	***30***	10	Chatham WSMO	***30***
12	Middleton	29	12	Marblehead	***31***
13	East Wareham	28	12	West Medway	***31***
13	Haverhill	28	14	Bedford	32
13	Reading	28	14	Hingham	32
16	East Brimfield Lake	27	16	Milton Blue Hill Observatory	33
16	Taunton	***27***	16	Walpole 2	33
18	Rochester	***25***	18	Lawrence	***37***
19	Amherst	24	19	Plymouth-Kingston	41
19	Edgartown	24	20	Brockton	***46***

Rankings include 25 highest/lowest stations. If state has less than 25 stations, all stations are included. The period of record is 1980–2009. See User Guide for detailed explanation of data.

Number of Days Annually With ≥ 1.0 Inch Snow Depth

Highest Rank	Station Name	Days	Lowest Rank	Station Name	Days
1	Barre Falls Dam	72	1	Edgartown	19
2	Bedford	64	2	Chatham WSMO	21
3	Reading	62	3	East Wareham	25
4	East Brimfield Lake	61	3	Lawrence	***25***
5	Amherst	60	5	Rochester	***27***
6	Milton Blue Hill Observatory	57	6	Brockton	***28***
6	Walpole 2	57	6	Plymouth-Kingston	28
8	Hingham	47	8	Taunton	***33***
9	West Medway	***43***	9	Middleton	35
10	Haverhill	42	10	Marblehead	***40***
11	Marblehead	***40***	11	Haverhill	42
12	Middleton	35	12	West Medway	***43***
13	Taunton	***33***	13	Hingham	47
14	Brockton	***28***	14	Milton Blue Hill Observatory	57
14	Plymouth-Kingston	28	14	Walpole 2	57
16	Rochester	***27***	16	Amherst	60
17	East Wareham	25	17	East Brimfield Lake	61
17	Lawrence	***25***	18	Reading	62
19	Chatham WSMO	21	19	Bedford	64
20	Edgartown	19	20	Barre Falls Dam	72

Significant Storm Events in Massachusetts: 2000 – 2009

Location or County	Date	Type	Mag.	Deaths	Injuries	Property Damage ($mil.)	Crop Damage ($mil.)
Eastern Massachusetts	03/05/01	Coastal Flooding	na	0	0	15.0	0.0
Central and Northeast Massachusetts	03/09/01	Heavy Snow	na	0	0	3.0	0.0
Essex	03/22/01	Flood	na	0	0	10.0	0.0
Central Massachusetts	03/30/01	Heavy Snow	na	0	0	8.0	0.0
Barnstable	08/16/03	Lightning	na	0	0	2.5	0.0
Eastern Franklin, Western Hampshire, and Hampden Counties	10/08/05	Flood	na	0	0	4.1	0.0
Southern Massachusetts and South Coasts	10/15/05	Flood	na	0	0	5.9	0.0
Southeast Massachusetts	12/09/05	High Wind	75 mph	0	0	2.3	0.0
Essex	05/13/06	Flood	na	2	0	7.0	0.0
Middlesex	05/13/06	Flood	na	0	0	5.0	0.0
Suffolk	06/27/08	Lightning	na	0	0	5.0	0.0
Northern Worcester County	12/11/08	Ice Storm	na	0	0	20.0	0.0
Western Middlesex County	12/11/08	Ice Storm	na	0	0	3.0	0.0
Eastern Franklin County	12/11/08	Ice Storm	na	0	0	3.0	0.0
Eastern Hampshire County	12/11/08	Ice Storm	na	0	0	3.0	0.0
Northwest Middlesex County	12/11/08	Ice Storm	na	0	0	3.0	0.0
Western Franklin County	12/11/08	Ice Storm	na	0	0	3.0	0.0
Southern Worcester County	12/11/08	Ice Storm	na	0	0	3.0	0.0
Western Hampshire County	12/11/08	Ice Storm	na	0	0	3.0	0.0
Western Essex County	12/11/08	Ice Storm	na	0	0	2.0	0.0

Note: Deaths, injuries, and damages are date and location specific.

MICHIGAN

PHYSICAL FEATURES. Michigan is located in the heart of the Great Lakes region and is composed of two large peninsulas. Many smaller peninsulas jut from these two peninsulas into the world's largest bodies of fresh water to give most of Michigan a quasi-marine type climate in spite of its midcontinent location.

The Upper Peninsula is long and narrow, lying primarily between 45° and 47° N. latitude. It averages only 75 miles in width and extends from Northern Wisconsin eastward over 300 miles into Northern Lake Huron. Lake Superior lies to the north while the northern portion of Lake Michigan forms the boundary to the southeast. Isle Royale, separated from the mainland, is located in Lake Superior about 50 miles northwest of the tip of the Keweenaw Peninsula. The Lower Peninsula, shaped like a mitten and occupying about 70 percent of Michigan's total land area, extends northward nearly 300 miles from the Indiana and Ohio border or about 42° N. latitude to the eastern end of the Upper Peninsula. Lake Michigan extends the entire length of the Lower Peninsula on the west while Lakes Huron, St. Clair and Erie form the eastern boundary. The total coastline for the state exceeds 3,100 miles. In addition, Michigan has over 11,000 smaller lakes with a total surface area of over 1,000 square miles. These lakes are scattered throughout 81 of the 83 counties while more than 36,000 miles of streams wind their way across the state.

While latitude, by determining the amount of solar insolation, is the major climatic control, the Great Lakes and variations in elevation play an important role in the amelioration of Michigan's climate. Because of its mid-latitude location, prevailing winds are from a westerly direction. During the summer months winds are predominantly from the southwest when the semi-permanent Bermuda High Pressure Center is located over the southeastern United States. During the winter months the prevailing winds are west to northwest, but change quite frequently for short periods as migrating cyclones and anticyclones move through the area.

The eastern half of the Upper Peninsula varies from level to gently rolling hills with elevation generally between 600 and 1,000 feet above sea level. The western tablelands rise to elevations generally between 1,400 and 1,600 feet with Porcupine Mountain, the State's highest point, 2,023 feet, located in Ontonagan County overlooking Lake Superior. The rugged hills extend northeastward from Ontonagan County through the center of the Keweenaw Peninsula and play an important role in the larger precipitation amounts received in this area.

The Lower Peninsula features range from quite level terrain in the southeast to gently rolling hills in the southwest with elevations generally between 800 and 1,000 feet. A series of sand dunes along the Lake Michigan shoreline rise to heights of nearly 400 feet above the lake level. These are the result of the prevailing westerly winds which blow across the lake. Tablelands cover the northern part of the Lower Peninsula and reach a maximum elevation of 1,700 feet in Osecola County near Cadillac. In the northwestern section of the Lower Peninsula a number of finger-like peninsulas extend into Grand Traverse Bay and Lake Michigan.

GENERAL CLIMATE. The lake effect imparts many interesting departures to Michigan's climate which one would not ordinarily expect to find at a midcontinental location. Because of the lake waters' slow response to temperature changes and the dominating westerly winds, the arrival of both summer and winter are retarded. In the spring, the cooler temperatures slow the development of vegetation until the danger of frost is past. In the fall, the warmer lake waters temper the first outbreaks of cold air allowing additional time for crops to mature. With the first cold air outbreaks in the fall, Michigan experiences a considerable increase in cloudiness. When cold air passes over the warmer lake water, a shallow layer of unstable, moisture-laden air develops in the lower levels of the atmosphere. This air, when forced to rise, produces the increased cloudiness and frequent snow flurry activity observed in the fall and early winter months.

On warm, summer days when prevailing winds are generally light, the lake's shore area frequently develops a localized wind pattern which may extend inland for only a few miles. This is frequently referred to as the "lake breeze." It develops when the much warmer air over the land masses begins to rise, allowing the cooler air over the lakes to move inland. At night this pattern may be reversed creating what is known as a "land breeze". A wind of this type may also be observed, but on a much smaller scale, along the shores of the larger inland lakes.

The length of Michigan's growing season or freeze-free period does not decrease in the normal manner from south to north. Instead, isolines for the length of the growing season follow closely the contours of the lake shores. The shortest average growing season, about 60 days, occurs in the interior section of the Western Upper Peninsula. The growing season increases to between 140 and 160 days, as one goes towards the lake shores. A similar pattern exists in the Lower Peninsula where the growing season in the northern tablelands averages only 70 days, but increases rapidly to 140 days near the lakes. Michigan's maximum average growing season, 170 days, is found in the southwest and southeastern corners of the state.

PRECIPITATION. Michigan averages about 31 inches of precipitation per year. About 55-60 percent of the annual total is recorded during the normal growing season. Summer precipitation falls primarily in the form of showers or thunderstorms, while a more steady type of precipitation of lighter intensity dominates the winter months. The annual number of thunderstorms observed decreases from about 40 in the south to around 25 in the Upper Peninsula area with nearly 50 percent of these recorded during the summer months, June through August.

The frequency of floods is quite low in Michigan with the greatest likelihood occurring in late winter or early spring when sudden warming and rain may be combined with snowmelt. Mild meteorological drought conditions are not uncommon in Michigan, but meteorological droughts reaching severe conditions are infrequent and generally of short duration. The normally even distribution of precipitation and higher humidities observed in Michigan are helpful in reducing the high demands for moisture.

SNOWFALL. Michigan receives some of the heaviest snowfall totals east of the Rockies except for isolated points in the New England States. The maximum average annual snowfall amounts of over 170 inches are located along the escarpment which rises abruptly to an elevation of over 1,400 feet above Lake Superior, at the western end of the Upper Peninsula. Another area with amounts exceeding 120 inches is centered in the western section of the tableland region of the Lower Peninsula. The prevailing westerlies, passing over the Great Lakes, become moisture laden in the lower levels and when forced upward by the land masses, drop much of their excessive moisture in the form of snow squalls in these areas.

STORMS. Damaging or dangerous storms do not occur as frequently in Michigan as in the states to the south and west. Recorded tornado occurrences have averaged four per year. About 90 percent of these tornadoes occurred in the southern one-half of the Lower Peninsula. Damaging wind storms and blizzards are not as frequent but do cause considerable damage from time to time. Hail is most frequently observed in the spring months. A higher frequency of hail is noted in the fall months over the northwestern section of the Lower Peninsula. This is attributed mainly to the strong lake influence in this region.

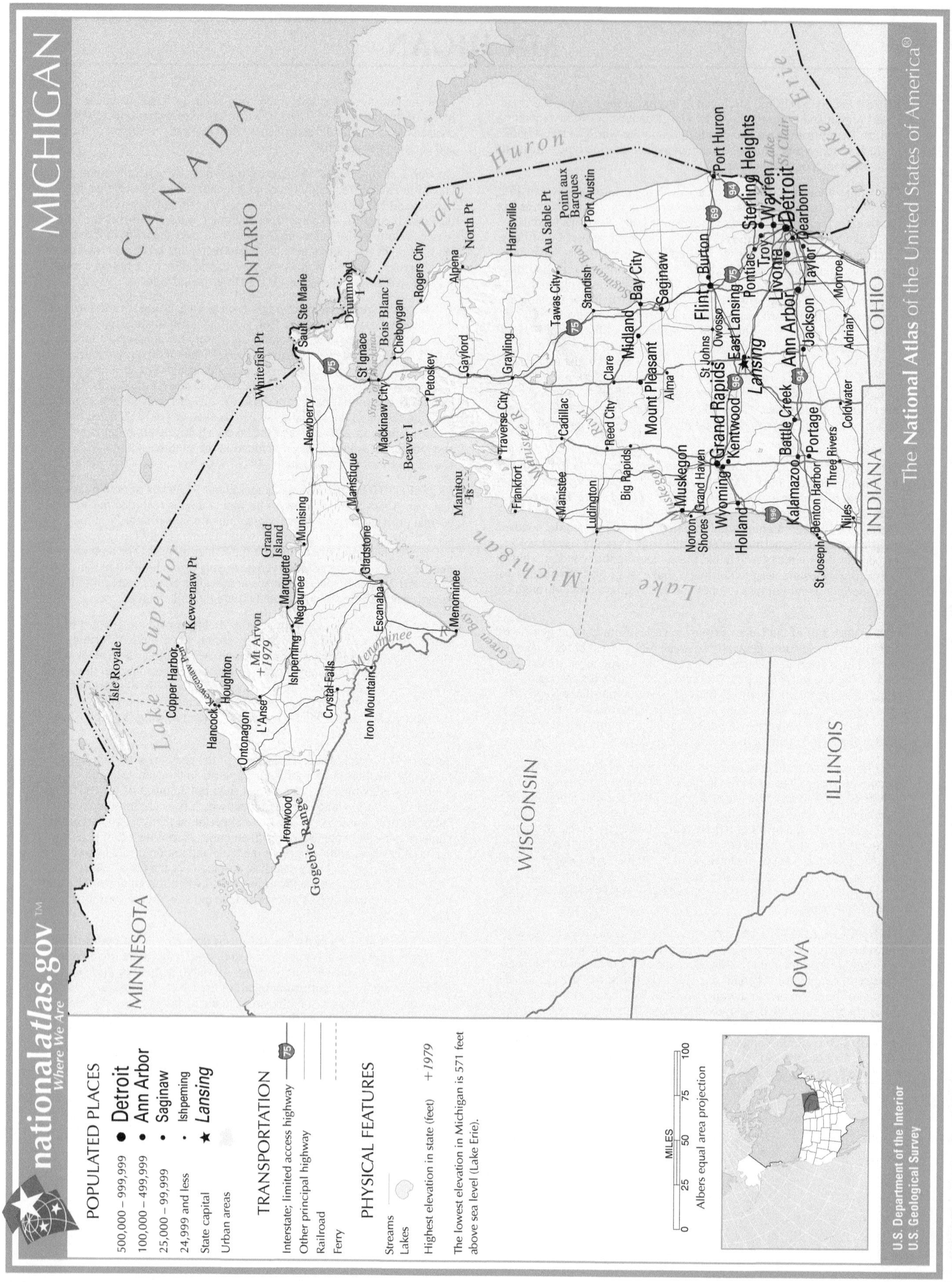
MICHIGAN
nationalatlas.gov™
Where We Are
The National Atlas of the United States of America®
POPULATED PLACES
500,000 – 999,999 Detroit
100,000 – 499,999 Ann Arbor
25,000 – 99,999 Saginaw
24,999 and less Ishpeming
State capital Lansing
Urban areas
TRANSPORTATION
Interstate; limited access highway
Other principal highway
Railroad
Ferry
PHYSICAL FEATURES
Streams
Lakes
Highest elevation in state (feet) +1979
The lowest elevation in Michigan is 571 feet above sea level (Lake Erie).
MILES
0 25 50 75 100
Albers equal area projection
U.S. Department of the Interior
U.S. Geological Survey
CANADA
ONTARIO
MINNESOTA
WISCONSIN
IOWA
ILLINOIS
INDIANA
OHIO
Lake Superior
Lake Michigan
Lake Huron
Lake Erie
Lake St Clair
Green Bay
Saginaw Bay
Isle Royale
Keweenaw Pt
Copper Harbor
Keweenaw Pen
Hancock
Houghton
Ontonagon
L'Anse
Mt Arvon +1979
Ironwood
Gogebic Range
Ishpeming
Negaunee
Marquette
Grand Island
Munising
Crystal Falls
Iron Mountain
Menominee
Escanaba
Gladstone
Manistique
Newberry
Whitefish Pt
Sault Ste Marie
St Ignace
Drummond I
Bois Blanc I
Mackinaw City
Cheboygan
Beaver I
Rogers City
Alpena
North Pt
Petoskey
Gaylord
Grayling
Harrisville
Au Sable Pt
Point aux Barques
Port Austin
Tawas City
Standish
Traverse City
Manitou Is
Frankfort
Manistee
Cadillac
Reed City
Clare
Midland
Bay City
Saginaw
Mount Pleasant
Alma
Ludington
Big Rapids
Muskegon
Norton Shores
Grand Haven
Holland
Wyoming
Grand Rapids
Kentwood
St Johns
Owosso
Flint
Burton
East Lansing
Lansing
Pontiac
Troy
Sterling Heights
Warren
Port Huron
Livonia
Detroit
Dearborn
Taylor
Ann Arbor
Jackson
Battle Creek
Portage
Kalamazoo
Benton Harbor
St Joseph
Niles
Three Rivers
Coldwater
Adrian
Monroe
Manistee R
Muskegon River
Menominee
75
69
94
96
196

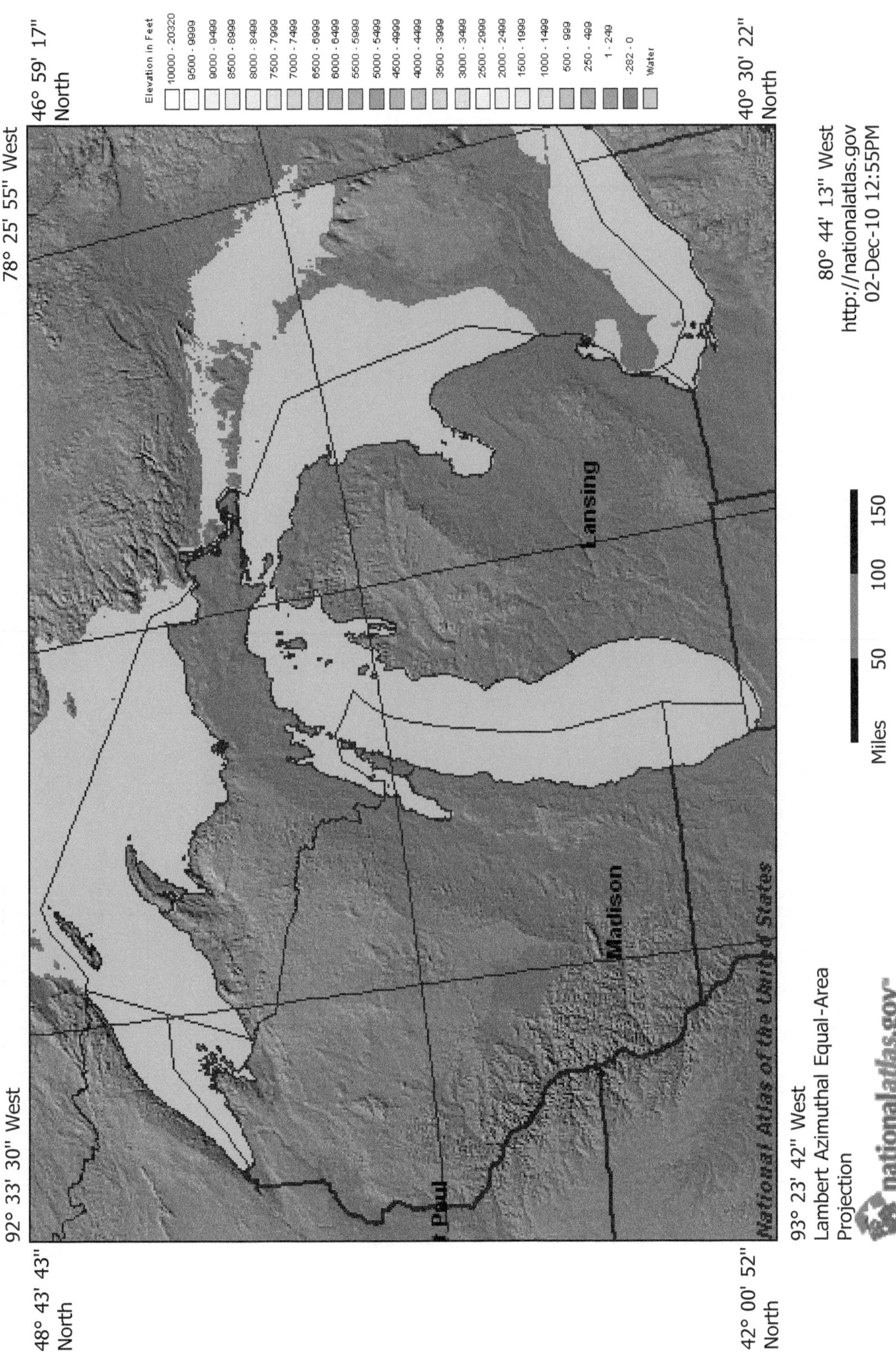

Elevation in Feet
10000 - 20320
9500 - 9999
9000 - 9499
8500 - 8999
8000 - 8499
7500 - 7999
7000 - 7499
6500 - 6999
6000 - 6499
5500 - 5999
5000 - 5499
4500 - 4999
4000 - 4499
3500 - 3999
3000 - 3499
2500 - 2999
2000 - 2499
1500 - 1999
1000 - 1499
500 - 999
250 - 499
1 - 249
-282 - 0
Water
46° 59' 17" North
78° 25' 55" West
40° 30' 22" North
80° 44' 13" West
http://nationalatlas.gov
02-Dec-10 12:55PM
Lansing
Madison
Miles
50
100
150
National Atlas of the United States
92° 33' 30" West
48° 43' 43" North
42° 00' 52" North
93° 23' 42" West
Lambert Azimuthal Equal-Area
Projection
nationalatlas.gov

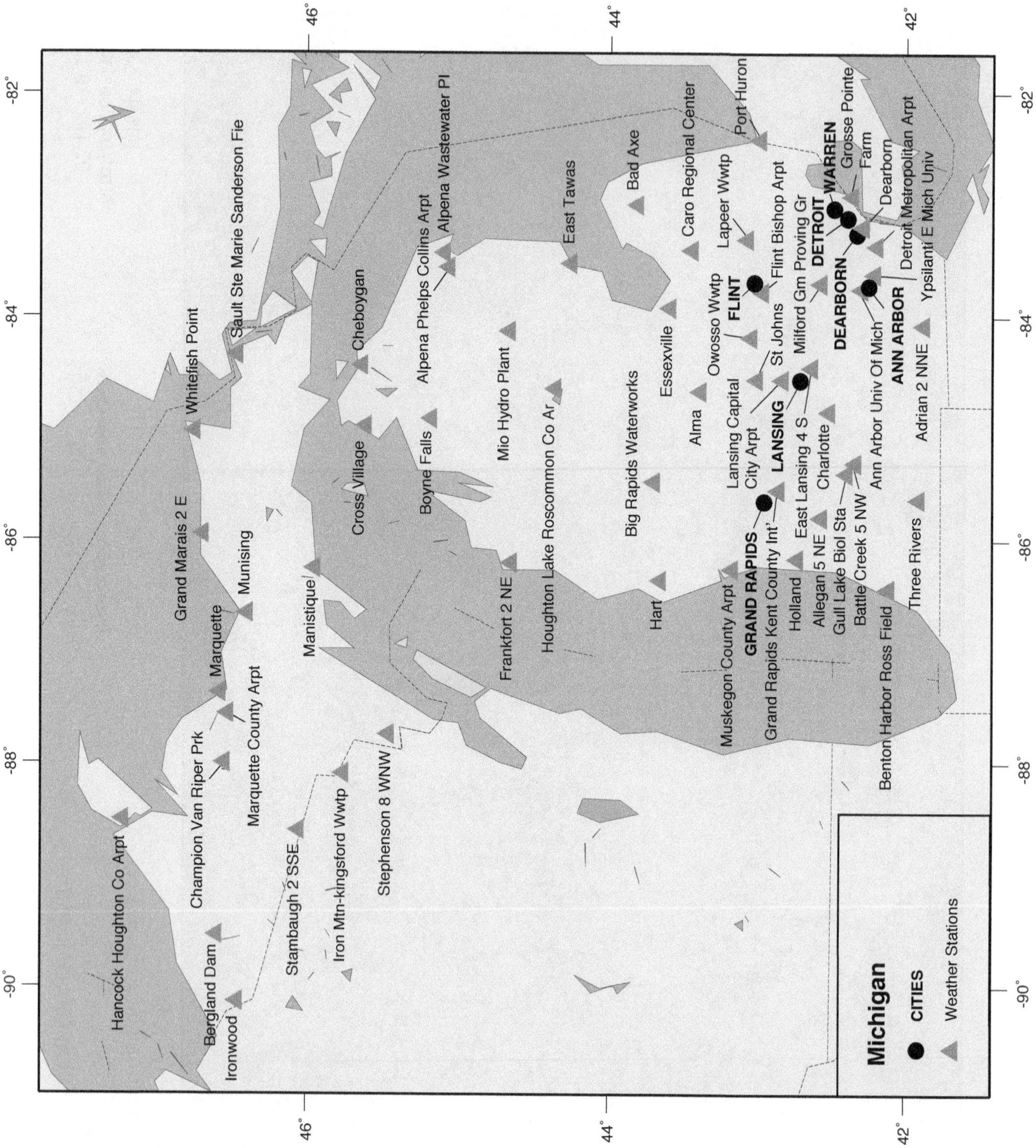
Michigan
CITIES
Weather Stations
-82°
-84°
-86°
-88°
-90°
46°
44°
42°
Hancock Houghton Co Arpt
Bergland Dam
Ironwood
Champion Van Riper Prk
Marquette County Arpt
Marquette
Stambaugh 2 SSE
Iron Mtn-kingsford Wwtp
Stephenson 8 WNW
Grand Marais 2 E
Munising
Whitefish Point
Sault Ste Marie Sanderson Fie
Manistique
Cheboygan
Cross Village
Boyne Falls
Alpena Phelps Collins Arpt
Alpena Wastewater Pl
Frankfort 2 NE
Mio Hydro Plant
Houghton Lake Roscommon Co Ar
East Tawas
Big Rapids Waterworks
Hart
Bad Axe
Essexville
Caro Regional Center
Alma
Muskegon County Arpt
GRAND RAPIDS
Grand Rapids Kent County Int'
Holland
Allegan 5 NE
Gull Lake Biol Sta
Battle Creek 5 NW
Benton Harbor Ross Field
Three Rivers
Lansing Capital City Arpt
LANSING
East Lansing 4 S
Charlotte
Owosso Wwtp
FLINT
St Johns
Flint Bishop Arpt
Lapeer Wwtp
Port Huron
Milford Gm Proving Gr
DETROIT
WARREN
Grosse Pointe Farm
Dearborn
DEARBORN
Detroit Metropolitan Arpt
Ypsilanti E Mich Univ
Ann Arbor Univ Of Mich
ANN ARBOR
Adrian 2 NNE

Michigan Weather Stations by County

County	Station Name
Alger	Grand Marais 2 E Munising
Allegan	Allegan 5 NE
Alpena	Alpena Phelps Collins Arpt Alpena Wastewater Pl
Bay	Essexville
Benzie	Frankfort 2 NE
Berrien	Benton Harbor Ross Field
Calhoun	Battle Creek 5 NW
Charlevoix	Boyne Falls
Cheboygan	Cheboygan
Chippewa	Sault Ste Marie Sanderson Field Whitefish Point
Clinton	Lansing Capital City Arpt St Johns
Dickinson	Iron Mtn-Kingsford WWTP
Eaton	Charlotte
Emmet	Cross Village
Genesee	Flint Bishop Arpt
Gogebic	Ironwood
Gratiot	Alma
Houghton	Hancock Houghton Co Arpt
Huron	Bad Axe
Ingham	East Lansing 4 S
Iosco	East Tawas
Iron	Stambaugh 2 SSE
Kalamazoo	Gull Lake Biol Sta
Kent	Grand Rapids Kent County Intl
Lapeer	Lapeer WWTP
Lenawee	Adrian 2 NNE
Livingston	Milford Gm Proving Ground
Marquette	Champion Van Riper Prk Marquette Marquette County Arpt
Mecosta	Big Rapids Waterworks

County	Station Name
Menominee	Stephenson 8 WNW
Muskegon	Muskegon County Arpt
Oceana	Hart
Ontonagon	Bergland Dam
Oscoda	Mio Hydro Plant
Ottawa	Holland
Roscommon	Houghton Lake Roscommon Co Arpt
Schoolcraft	Manistique
Shiawassee	Owosso Wwtp
St. Clair	Port Huron
St. Joseph	Three Rivers
Tuscola	Caro Regional Center
Washtenaw	Ann Arbor Univ of Mich Ypsilanti E Mich Univ
Wayne	Dearborn Detroit Metropolitan Arpt Grosse Pointe Farms

See User Guide for station inclusion criteria.

Michigan Weather Stations by City

City	Station Name	Miles
Ann Arbor	Ann Arbor Univ of Mich	1.9
	Detroit Metropolitan Arpt	20.0
	Milford Gm Proving Ground	21.4
	Ypsilanti E Mich Univ	6.6
Battle Creek	Battle Creek 5 NW	5.3
	Charlotte	24.9
	Gull Lake Biol Sta	11.4
Canton	Ann Arbor Univ of Mich	12.5
	Dearborn	12.2
	Detroit Metropolitan Arpt	9.3
	Milford Gm Proving Ground	21.8
	Ypsilanti E Mich Univ	9.3
Clinton	Dearborn	24.3
	Grosse Pointe Farms	13.8
Dearborn	Dearborn	1.0
	Detroit Metropolitan Arpt	9.9
	Grosse Pointe Farms	16.6
	Ypsilanti E Mich Univ	21.4
Detroit	Dearborn	8.2
	Detroit Metropolitan Arpt	17.2
	Grosse Pointe Farms	10.6
Farmington Hills	Ann Arbor Univ of Mich	21.5
	Dearborn	13.8
	Detroit Metropolitan Arpt	18.6
	Milford Gm Proving Ground	17.8
	Ypsilanti E Mich Univ	21.2
Flint	Flint Bishop Arpt	5.2
	Lapeer WWTP	20.1
	Owosso Wwtp	24.7
Grand Rapids	Grand Rapids Kent County Intl	8.7
Kalamazoo	Allegan 5 NE	23.2
	Battle Creek 5 NW	17.8
	Gull Lake Biol Sta	13.6
	Three Rivers	23.9
Lansing	Charlotte	17.9
	East Lansing 4 S	4.9
	Lansing Capital City Arpt	5.1
	St Johns	21.1
Livonia	Ann Arbor Univ of Mich	18.9
	Dearborn	8.9
	Detroit Metropolitan Arpt	12.4
	Grosse Pointe Farms	24.0
	Milford Gm Proving Ground	21.2
	Ypsilanti E Mich Univ	16.9
Macomb Twp	Grosse Pointe Farms	18.9
Novi	Ann Arbor Univ of Mich	17.1
	Dearborn	16.6
	Detroit Metropolitan Arpt	19.0
	Milford Gm Proving Ground	13.6
	Ypsilanti E Mich Univ	18.1

City	Station Name	Miles
Pontiac	Dearborn	23.2
	Milford Gm Proving Ground	21.3
Rochester Hills	Dearborn	24.5
	Grosse Pointe Farms	23.6
Royal Oak	Dearborn	13.8
	Detroit Metropolitan Arpt	22.5
	Grosse Pointe Farms	15.4
Saginaw	Essexville	14.3
Shelby	Grosse Pointe Farms	20.6
Southfield	Dearborn	11.4
	Detroit Metropolitan Arpt	19.0
	Grosse Pointe Farms	19.2
	Milford Gm Proving Ground	23.9
St. Clair Shores	Dearborn	21.0
	Grosse Pointe Farms	7.5
Sterling Heights	Dearborn	20.9
	Grosse Pointe Farms	15.1
Taylor	Ann Arbor Univ of Mich	23.5
	Dearborn	6.2
	Detroit Metropolitan Arpt	4.3
	Grosse Pointe Farms	21.5
	Ypsilanti E Mich Univ	17.9
Troy	Dearborn	18.9
	Grosse Pointe Farms	18.5
Warren	Dearborn	16.1
	Grosse Pointe Farms	10.0
Waterford	Dearborn	24.8
	Milford Gm Proving Ground	17.0
West Bloomfield Twp	Ann Arbor Univ of Mich	24.9
	Dearborn	18.8
	Detroit Metropolitan Arpt	24.1
	Milford Gm Proving Ground	16.1
Westland	Ann Arbor Univ of Mich	17.2
	Dearborn	7.5
	Detroit Metropolitan Arpt	7.3
	Grosse Pointe Farms	24.9
	Milford Gm Proving Ground	24.5
	Ypsilanti E Mich Univ	13.4
Wyoming	Allegan 5 NE	22.2
	Grand Rapids Kent County Intl	9.5
	Holland	22.5
Ypsilanti Twp	Ann Arbor Univ of Mich	8.5
	Dearborn	20.0
	Detroit Metropolitan Arpt	12.7
	Ypsilanti E Mich Univ	1.7

Note: Miles is the distance between the geographic center of the city and the weather station.

See User Guide for station inclusion criteria.

Michigan Weather Stations by Elevation

Feet	Station Name
1,564	Champion Van Riper Prk
1,560	Stambaugh 2 SSE
1,430	Ironwood
1,415	Marquette County Arpt
1,299	Bergland Dam
1,149	Houghton Lake Roscommon Co Arpt
1,074	Hancock Houghton Co Arpt
1,060	Iron Mtn-Kingsford WWTP
990	Milford Gm Proving Ground
959	Mio Hydro Plant
930	Battle Creek 5 NW
930	Big Rapids Waterworks
910	Gull Lake Biol Sta
901	Charlotte
899	Ann Arbor Univ of Mich
879	East Lansing 4 S
865	Frankfort 2 NE
840	Lansing Capital City Arpt
819	Lapeer WWTP
810	Three Rivers
784	Grand Rapids Kent County Intl
779	Ypsilanti E Mich Univ
766	Flint Bishop Arpt
759	Adrian 2 NNE
759	Alma
750	Allegan 5 NE
743	Cross Village
743	St Johns
734	Boyne Falls
729	Owosso Wwtp
717	Sault Ste Marie Sanderson Field
714	Bad Axe
709	Stephenson 8 WNW
700	Hart
688	Alpena Phelps Collins Arpt
680	Munising
669	Caro Regional Center
665	Marquette
632	Detroit Metropolitan Arpt
627	Benton Harbor Ross Field
625	Muskegon County Arpt
624	Grand Marais 2 E
620	Manistique
612	Grosse Pointe Farms
609	Holland
604	Dearborn
604	Whitefish Point
589	Alpena Wastewater Pl
589	Cheboygan
589	Port Huron
587	Essexville
585	East Tawas

Alpena Phelps Collins Airport

The city of Alpena lies on the northwest shore of Thunder Bay, eight miles from the open waters of Lake Huron. Lake Huron and Thunder Bay lie at an elevation of 580 feet above sea level. Generally, the land slopes up westward from the lakeshore to 689 feet at the airport. Farther to the west and southwest the land becomes higher and more rolling. A range of hills with tops 1,000 to 1,350 feet lies northwest to southeast about 25 miles southwest of the station.

Summer showers moving from the southwest weaken and sometimes dissipate as they approach Alpena. Winter storms often bring winds with an easterly component. Precipitation from these is increased by moisture and instability picked up from Lake Huron and by forced upslope flow.

The normal wintertime storm track is south of the city, and most passing storms bring snow. Rain, freezing rain, and sleet are uncommon, but not unknown, in winter. In summer, most storms pass to the north, often bringing brief showers to the area, but occasionally, heavy thunderstorms with damaging winds occur. The Great Lakes modify most climatic extremes. Precipitation amounts are distributed evenly throughout the year. The lake effect is most pronounced in early winter, before ice forms. Minimum temperatures during this season are higher than would be expected at this latitude.

Summers in Alpena are warm and sunny. Brief showers usually occur every few days, often falling on only part of the area. Hailstorms average less than one a year. During prolonged heat waves the highest temperatures in Michigan often occur in the forest area southwest of Alpena. Winter months are cloudy and marked by frequent snow flurries. Storms bring heavier snowfall. Snow cover is sufficiently deep and persistent to provide good protection for grasses and winter grains.

The climate along the immediate Lake Huron shore is semi-maritime and lacks the temperature extremes experienced just a few miles inland. Maximum temperatures near the lake shore average 1.6 degrees lower than those at the airport, minimum temperatures average five degrees higher. Afternoon lake breezes which are strongest in the late spring and early summer cause lake shore maximum temperatures to average 3.6 degrees lower during the month of May.

Freezing temperatures have occurred as late as late June and as early as late August. Principal crops in the area are hay, potatoes, berries, and apples.

Prevailing winds are from the northwest except during May and June when southeast winds predominate. Southeast winds are common in the afternoon during all the summer months.

Alpena Phelps Collins Airport *Alpena County* Elevation: 688 ft. Latitude: 45° 04' N Longitude: 83° 35' W

	JAN	FEB	MAR	APR	MAY	JUN	JUL	AUG	SEP	OCT	NOV	DEC	YEAR
Mean Maximum Temp. (°F)	27.3	29.6	38.3	52.5	64.9	74.9	79.8	77.4	69.4	56.2	43.4	32.1	53.8
Mean Temp. (°F)	19.4	20.4	28.7	41.7	52.6	62.2	67.5	65.6	57.9	46.3	35.8	25.1	43.6
Mean Minimum Temp. (°F)	11.3	11.2	19.0	30.9	40.3	49.5	55.3	53.7	46.5	36.4	28.3	18.1	33.4
Extreme Maximum Temp. (°F)	52	65	80	90	93	103	102	102	94	90	75	65	103
Extreme Minimum Temp. (°F)	-28	-25	-17	-7	21	29	37	30	25	16	-6	-18	-28
Days Maximum Temp. ≥ 90°F	0	0	0	0	0	2	3	1	0	0	0	0	6
Days Maximum Temp. ≤ 32°F	21	18	9	1	0	0	0	0	0	0	4	15	68
Days Minimum Temp. ≤ 32°F	30	27	28	18	5	0	0	0	1	11	21	29	170
Days Minimum Temp. ≤ 0°F	7	6	3	0	0	0	0	0	0	0	0	2	18
Heating Degree Days (base 65°F)	1,409	1,254	1,120	694	389	137	40	65	230	574	868	1,229	8,009
Cooling Degree Days (base 65°F)	0	0	0	2	13	61	125	91	25	3	0	0	320
Mean Precipitation (in.)	1.65	1.30	1.87	2.46	2.63	2.55	2.95	3.25	2.86	2.58	2.10	1.76	27.96
Maximum Precipitation (in.)*	3.3	3.2	4.4	4.1	8.3	8.4	7.2	6.3	7.1	6.5	7.4	4.4	35.2
Minimum Precipitation (in.)*	0.2	0.1	0.3	1.2	1.0	0.2	0.2	0.9	0.3	0.6	0.6	0.4	21.4
Extreme Maximum Daily Precip. (in.)	1.41	1.51	1.85	1.22	2.11	1.55	2.59	2.01	1.54	3.44	1.58	1.28	3.44
Days With ≥ 0.1" Precipitation	5	4	5	6	6	6	6	6	6	6	6	5	67
Days With ≥ 0.5" Precipitation	0	1	1	2	2	2	2	2	2	1	1	1	17
Days With ≥ 1.0" Precipitation	0	0	0	0	0	0	1	1	1	0	0	0	3
Mean Snowfall (in.)	***21.4***	***18.0***	***11.0***	na	na	na	na	na	***trace***	***0.4***	***8.0***	***19.3***	na
Maximum Snowfall (in.)*	44	33	36	13	4	0	0	0	trace	4	35	46	146
Maximum 24-hr. Snowfall (in.)*	16	11	17	11	4	0	0	0	trace	2	15	16	17
Maximum Snow Depth (in.)	***28***	***37***	***28***	na	na	na	na	na	***trace***	***1***	***12***	***26***	na
Days With ≥ 1.0" Snow Depth	***29***	***27***	***21***	na	na	na	na	na	***0***	***0***	***7***	***20***	na
Thunderstorm Days*	< 1	< 1	1	2	4	5	7	6	4	1	< 1	< 1	30
Foggy Days*	10	9	13	12	13	14	14	17	16	14	14	12	158
Predominant Sky Cover*	OVR	OVR	OVR	OVR	OVR	OVR	OVR	OVR	OVR	OVR	OVR	OVR	OVR
Mean Relative Humidity 7am (%)*	81	80	82	80	78	81	85	90	91	86	84	83	83
Mean Relative Humidity 4pm (%)*	67	62	59	53	51	53	54	59	61	62	68	72	60
Mean Dewpoint (°F)*	13	12	20	29	40	51	57	56	50	39	29	19	35
Prevailing Wind Direction*	WNW	WNW	WNW	WNW	ESE	SE	WNW	SW	W	WSW	WNW	SW	WNW
Prevailing Wind Speed (mph)*	10	9	10	10	9	8	8	7	7	8	9	8	9
Maximum Wind Gust (mph)*	53	54	54	60	53	58	53	60	45	47	56	54	60

Note: (*) Period of record is 1959-1995

Detroit Metropolitan Airport

Detroit and the immediate suburbs, including nearby urban areas in Canada, occupy an area approximately 25 miles in radius. The waterway, consisting of the Detroit and St. Clair Rivers, Lake St. Clair, and the west end of Lake Erie, lies at an elevation of 568 to 580 feet above sea level. Nearly flat land slopes up gently from the waters edge northwestward for about 10 miles and then gives way to increasingly rolling terrain. The Irish Hills, parallel to and about 40 miles northwest of the waterway, have tops 1,000 to 1,250 feet above sea level. On the Canadian side of the waterway the land is relatively level.

Northwest winds in winter bring snow flurry accumulations to all of Michigan except in the Detroit Metropolitan area while summer showers moving from the northwest weaken and sometimes dissipate as they approach Detroit. On the other hand, much of the heaviest precipitation in winter comes from southeast winds, especially to the northwest suburbs of the city.

The climate of Detroit is influenced by its location with respect to major storm tracks and the influence of the Great Lakes. The normal wintertime storm track is south of the city, which brings on the average, about three inch snowfalls. Winter storms can bring combinations of rain, snow, freezing rain, and sleet with heavy snowfall accumulations possible at times. In summer, most storms pass to the north allowing for intervals of warm, humid, sunny skies with occasional thunderstorms followed by days of mild, dry, and fair weather. Temperatures of 90 degrees or higher are reached during each summer.

Local climatic variations are due largely to the immediate effect of Lake St. Clair and the urban heat island. On warm days in late spring or early summer, lake breezes often lower temperatures by 10 to 15 degrees in the eastern part of the city and the northeastern suburbs. The urban heat island effect shows up mainly at night where minimum temperatures at the Metropolitan Airport average four degrees lower than downtown Detroit. On humid summer nights or on very cold winter nights, this difference can exceed 10 degrees.

The growing season averages 180 days and has ranged from 145 days to 205 days. On average, the last freezing temperature occurs in late April while the average first freezing temperature occurs in late October. A freeze has occurred as late as mid-May and as early as late September.

Detroit Metropolitan Airport *Wayne County* Elevation: 632 ft. Latitude: 42° 13' N Longitude: 83° 21' W

	JAN	FEB	MAR	APR	MAY	JUN	JUL	AUG	SEP	OCT	NOV	DEC	YEAR
Mean Maximum Temp. (°F)	32.1	35.1	45.4	58.7	69.9	79.2	83.3	81.3	74.1	61.2	48.6	36.3	58.7
Mean Temp. (°F)	25.3	27.7	36.6	48.7	59.4	69.0	73.3	71.8	64.2	51.9	41.1	29.9	49.9
Mean Minimum Temp. (°F)	18.4	20.3	27.8	38.7	48.8	58.7	63.3	62.2	54.2	42.5	33.6	23.5	41.0
Extreme Maximum Temp. (°F)	64	70	81	87	93	104	102	100	94	90	75	69	104
Extreme Minimum Temp. (°F)	-21	-15	-4	10	29	38	44	38	33	20	12	-10	-21
Days Maximum Temp. ≥ 90°F	0	0	0	0	0	3	5	3	1	0	0	0	12
Days Maximum Temp. ≤ 32°F	16	12	4	0	0	0	0	0	0	0	1	10	43
Days Minimum Temp. ≤ 32°F	28	25	22	7	0	0	0	0	0	3	14	25	124
Days Minimum Temp. ≤ 0°F	2	1	0	0	0	0	0	0	0	0	0	1	4
Heating Degree Days (base 65°F)	1,224	1,048	874	488	210	36	3	8	102	408	709	1,081	6,191
Cooling Degree Days (base 65°F)	0	0	0	7	41	162	267	225	83	8	0	0	793
Mean Precipitation (in.)	1.95	1.98	2.37	2.96	3.31	3.55	3.31	3.18	3.25	2.53	2.70	2.49	33.58
Maximum Precipitation (in.)*	3.9	5.0	4.5	5.4	6.2	7.0	6.0	7.8	7.5	4.9	5.7	6.0	42.6
Minimum Precipitation (in.)*	0.3	0.1	0.8	0.9	0.9	1.0	0.6	0.7	0.4	0.3	0.8	0.5	21.0
Extreme Maximum Daily Precip. (in.)	1.59	2.28	1.69	3.58	1.78	2.59	4.34	2.51	3.71	2.02	2.30	1.45	4.34
Days With ≥ 0.1" Precipitation	6	5	6	7	7	6	7	6	6	5	6	6	73
Days With ≥ 0.5" Precipitation	1	1	1	2	2	2	2	2	2	2	2	1	20
Days With ≥ 1.0" Precipitation	0	0	0	0	1	1	1	1	1	0	0	0	5
Mean Snowfall (in.)	12.3	10.1	7.3	1.8	trace	trace	0.0	0.0	trace	0.3	1.5	9.8	43.1
Maximum Snowfall (in.)*	30	21	16	9	trace	0	0	0	0	3	12	35	75
Maximum 24-hr. Snowfall (in.)*	11	8	8	5	trace	0	0	0	0	3	6	18	18
Maximum Snow Depth (in.)	24	18	9	6	trace	trace	0	0	trace	1	3	12	24
Days With ≥ 1.0" Snow Depth	17	12	6	1	0	0	0	0	0	0	1	8	45
Thunderstorm Days*	< 1	< 1	2	3	4	6	6	5	4	1	1	< 1	32
Foggy Days*	12	11	13	11	12	12	13	17	15	15	14	14	159
Predominant Sky Cover*	OVR	OVR	OVR	OVR	OVR	OVR	SCT	OVR	OVR	OVR	OVR	OVR	OVR
Mean Relative Humidity 7am (%)*	80	79	79	78	78	79	82	86	87	84	82	81	81
Mean Relative Humidity 4pm (%)*	67	63	58	53	51	52	52	54	54	55	64	69	58
Mean Dewpoint (°F)*	17	18	26	35	46	56	61	60	53	42	32	22	39
Prevailing Wind Direction*	WSW	SW	WNW	WSW	WSW	SW	SW	SW	SW	SW	SW	SW	SW
Prevailing Wind Speed (mph)*	14	14	14	14	13	10	9	9	10	12	13	13	12
Maximum Wind Gust (mph)*	66	64	64	66	61	94	71	69	54	52	58	61	94

Note: (*) Period of record is 1958-1995

Flint Bishop Airport

Flint, Michigan, is located in the Flint River Valley, in the center of Genesee County. Lake Huron lies approximately 65 miles to the east, while Saginaw Bay is about 40 miles to the north. The surrounding terrain is generally level with a slight rising tendency to a range of hills 15 to 20 miles southeast of the city.

Flint is generally under the climatic influence of the Great Lakes. Temperatures of 100 degrees or higher are rare and cold waves are less severe then expected. During the winter months, snow showers occur with strong northwesterly winds, and Lake Michigan, lying 120 miles to the west, causes a tempering effect upon cold waves coming from the northwest. The lake effect also results in delaying the coming of spring and prolonging warmer weather in late autumn. This results in conditions favorable for orchards and small fruit.

Precipitation is usually ample for growth and development of vegetation. The wettest periods normally occur in the late spring, early summer, and early fall. The driest period is normally during the winter, and although there is an occasional heavy snowfall, most of the snow occurs in the form of frequent light flurries.

Winter months are marked by considerable cloudiness and rather high relative humidity, while during the summer relative humidity is usually not excessive and sunshine is plentiful.

Violent windstorms associated with thunderstorms and squall lines occasionally hit this area. Tornadoes are infrequent but have caused extensive property damage and loss of life.

Weather changes are frequent throughout the year, since a majority of atmospheric disturbances moving eastward across the country pass near enough to affect the weather in Flint.

Flint Bishop Airport *Genesee County* Elevation: 766 ft. Latitude: 42° 58' N Longitude: 83° 45' W

	JAN	FEB	MAR	APR	MAY	JUN	JUL	AUG	SEP	OCT	NOV	DEC	YEAR
Mean Maximum Temp. (°F)	30.2	33.2	43.5	57.3	68.9	78.2	82.2	79.9	72.7	59.7	46.9	34.5	57.3
Mean Temp. (°F)	23.0	25.2	34.4	46.7	57.3	66.9	71.0	69.2	61.6	49.7	39.2	27.9	47.7
Mean Minimum Temp. (°F)	15.8	17.3	25.1	36.0	45.8	55.4	59.7	58.5	50.4	39.8	31.5	21.2	38.0
Extreme Maximum Temp. (°F)	61	68	80	87	93	101	101	98	94	89	75	70	101
Extreme Minimum Temp. (°F)	-21	-19	-11	6	23	33	40	37	26	20	9	-13	-21
Days Maximum Temp. ≥ 90°F	0	0	0	0	0	2	4	2	1	0	0	0	9
Days Maximum Temp. ≤ 32°F	18	14	5	0	0	0	0	0	0	0	2	12	51
Days Minimum Temp. ≤ 32°F	29	25	24	11	1	0	0	0	0	7	17	27	141
Days Minimum Temp. ≤ 0°F	4	3	1	0	0	0	0	0	0	0	0	2	10
Heating Degree Days (base 65°F)	1,294	1,117	944	549	264	59	12	25	151	472	766	1,142	6,795
Cooling Degree Days (base 65°F)	0	0	1	6	33	121	203	162	55	6	0	0	587
Mean Precipitation (in.)	1.64	1.46	1.96	2.94	3.01	3.04	3.42	3.28	3.78	2.46	2.63	1.96	31.58
Maximum Precipitation (in.)*	3.2	5.3	4.2	5.6	6.8	6.5	7.9	11.0	10.9	4.2	4.9	4.7	45.4
Minimum Precipitation (in.)*	0.3	0.2	0.3	1.0	0.3	0.6	0.7	0.4	0.3	0.4	0.7	0.4	18.1
Extreme Maximum Daily Precip. (in.)	1.17	1.49	1.37	2.25	2.23	3.46	2.72	3.89	3.62	1.90	1.87	0.96	3.89
Days With ≥ 0.1" Precipitation	5	4	5	7	6	6	6	6	6	6	6	6	69
Days With ≥ 0.5" Precipitation	1	1	1	1	2	2	3	2	2	2	1	1	19
Days With ≥ 1.0" Precipitation	0	0	0	0	1	1	1	1	1	0	0	0	5
Mean Snowfall (in.)	13.0	10.3	6.8	2.6	trace	trace	trace	trace	0.0	0.4	2.5	11.8	47.4
Maximum Snowfall (in.)*	29	21	19	17	1	0	0	0	trace	4	16	25	84
Maximum 24-hr. Snowfall (in.)*	15	10	13	12	1	0	0	0	trace	4	11	9	15
Maximum Snow Depth (in.)	18	12	10	7	trace	trace	trace	trace	0	2	6	20	20
Days With ≥ 1.0" Snow Depth	21	17	8	1	0	0	0	0	0	0	2	13	62
Thunderstorm Days*	< 1	< 1	1	3	4	6	6	6	4	1	1	< 1	32
Foggy Days*	11	10	12	11	10	10	12	16	14	14	13	13	146
Predominant Sky Cover*	OVR	OVR	OVR	OVR	OVR	OVR	OVR	OVR	OVR	OVR	OVR	OVR	OVR
Mean Relative Humidity 6am (%)*	81	81	81	80	81	85	88	91	90	86	83	83	84
Mean Relative Humidity 3pm (%)*	70	67	60	53	51	53	52	55	56	57	65	72	59
Mean Dewpoint (°F)*	17	18	25	34	45	55	60	59	52	42	31	22	38
Prevailing Wind Direction*	SW	WSW	WNW	WSW	WSW	WSW	SW	SW	S	S	SW	SW	SW
Prevailing Wind Speed (mph)*	12	12	14	13	12	10	9	8	9	10	13	12	12
Maximum Wind Gust (mph)*	61	54	69	68	56	76	73	71	63	49	63	69	76

Note: (*) Period of record is 1949-1995

The period of record for National Weather Service station data is 1980 – 2009 except where noted. See User Guide for detailed explanation of data.

Grand Rapids Int'l Airport

Grand Rapids, Michigan, is located in the west-central part of Kent County, in the picturesque Grand River valley about 30 air miles east of Lake Michigan. The Grand River, the longest stream in Michigan, flows through the city and bisects it into east and west sections. High hills rise on either side of the valley. Elevations range from 602 feet on the valley floor to 1,020 feet in the extreme southern part of Kent County, southwest of the airport.

Grand Rapids is under the natural climatic influence of Lake Michigan. In spring the cooling effect of Lake Michigan helps retard the growth of vegetation until the danger of frost has passed. The warming effect in the fall retards frost until most of the crops have matured. Fall is a colorful time of year in western Michigan, compensating for the late spring. During the winter, excessive cloudiness and numerous snow flurries occur with strong westerly winds. The tempering effect of Lake Michigan on cold waves coming in from the west and northwest is quite evident.

The tempering effect of the lake promotes the growth of a great variety of fruit trees and berries, especially apples, peaches, cherries, and blueberries. The intense cold of winter is modified, thus reducing winter kill of fruit trees. Summer days are pleasantly warm and most summer nights are quite comfortable, although there are about three weeks of hot, humid weather during most summers. Prolonged severe cold waves with below-zero temperatures are infrequent. The temperature usually rises to above zero during the daytime hours regardless of early morning readings.

July is the sunniest month and December is the month with the least sunshine. November through January is usually a period of excessive cloudiness and minimal sunshine.

Precipitation is usually ample for the growth and development of all vegetation. About one-half of the annual precipitation falls during the growing season, May through September. Droughts occur occasionally, but are seldom of protracted length. The snowfall season extends from mid-November to mid-March. Some winters have had continuous snow cover throughout this period, although there is usually a mid-winter thaw. The Grand River flows through the city and reaches critical heights a couple of times each year. Overflow is generally limited to the lowlands of the flood plain.

November is one of the windiest months and although violent windstorms are infrequent, gusts have on occasion exceeded 65 mph. Summer thunderstorms occasionally produce gusty winds over 60 mph.

Grand Rapids Int'l Airport *Kent County* Elevation: 784 ft. Latitude: 42° 53' N Longitude: 85° 31' W

	JAN	FEB	MAR	APR	MAY	JUN	JUL	AUG	SEP	OCT	NOV	DEC	YEAR
Mean Maximum Temp. (°F)	30.4	33.2	43.6	57.5	69.2	78.5	82.4	80.1	72.6	59.6	46.6	34.4	57.3
Mean Temp. (°F)	23.8	26.0	34.7	47.1	58.0	67.6	71.8	70.1	62.2	50.1	39.3	28.4	48.3
Mean Minimum Temp. (°F)	17.1	18.7	25.8	36.6	46.8	56.6	61.1	60.0	51.7	40.6	32.0	22.4	39.1
Extreme Maximum Temp. (°F)	63	69	78	86	91	98	100	98	92	88	74	69	100
Extreme Minimum Temp. (°F)	-22	-17	-7	3	26	35	41	41	27	18	9	-18	-22
Days Maximum Temp. ≥ 90°F	0	0	0	0	0	3	4	2	0	0	0	0	9
Days Maximum Temp. ≤ 32°F	18	14	5	0	0	0	0	0	0	0	2	13	52
Days Minimum Temp. ≤ 32°F	28	26	23	10	1	0	0	0	0	5	17	27	137
Days Minimum Temp. ≤ 0°F	3	2	0	0	0	0	0	0	0	0	0	1	6
Heating Degree Days (base 65°F)	1,272	1,096	933	537	246	50	8	18	140	460	763	1,127	6,650
Cooling Degree Days (base 65°F)	0	0	1	7	36	134	225	182	61	6	0	0	652
Mean Precipitation (in.)	2.11	1.77	2.39	3.33	3.92	3.63	3.81	3.63	4.33	3.23	3.44	2.53	38.12
Maximum Precipitation (in.)*	4.4	3.3	5.8	6.1	8.3	8.2	8.8	8.5	11.8	8.3	7.8	6.6	47.5
Minimum Precipitation (in.)*	0.3	0.3	0.7	1.8	0.9	0.3	0.6	0.1	trace	trace	0.6	0.7	22.8
Extreme Maximum Daily Precip. (in.)	2.15	2.96	1.36	2.35	4.15	3.17	3.56	3.61	3.21	2.83	2.94	1.51	4.15
Days With ≥ 0.1" Precipitation	6	5	6	7	7	6	6	6	7	7	7	7	77
Days With ≥ 0.5" Precipitation	1	1	1	2	2	3	3	3	3	2	2	1	24
Days With ≥ 1.0" Precipitation	0	0	0	1	1	1	1	1	1	1	1	0	8
Mean Snowfall (in.)	20.8	14.2	8.3	2.0	trace	trace	trace	trace	trace	0.6	6.8	21.9	74.6
Maximum Snowfall (in.)*	46	30	36	16	2	0	0	0	trace	8	27	51	118
Maximum 24-hr. Snowfall (in.)*	16	9	10	12	1	0	0	0	trace	8	10	10	16
Maximum Snow Depth (in.)	20	21	14	7	trace	trace	trace	trace	trace	1	11	17	21
Days With ≥ 1.0" Snow Depth	23	17	8	1	0	0	0	0	0	0	3	16	68
Thunderstorm Days*	< 1	< 1	2	4	4	6	6	5	4	2	1	< 1	34
Foggy Days*	11	11	12	11	10	10	12	15	13	13	12	13	143
Predominant Sky Cover*	OVR	OVR	OVR	OVR	OVR	OVR	OVR	OVR	OVR	OVR	OVR	OVR	OVR
Mean Relative Humidity 7am (%)*	82	81	81	79	79	81	84	89	89	85	83	83	83
Mean Relative Humidity 4pm (%)*	72	66	61	54	50	51	53	56	58	59	68	74	60
Mean Dewpoint (°F)*	17	17	25	34	45	55	60	60	53	41	31	22	39
Prevailing Wind Direction*	WSW	WSW	ENE	WSW	WSW	WSW	WSW	WSW	S	S	WSW	WSW	WSW
Prevailing Wind Speed (mph)*	14	13	12	13	12	10	10	10	8	9	13	13	12
Maximum Wind Gust (mph)*	62	62	71	68	68	63	61	61	61	48	78	62	78

Note: (*) Period of record is 1948-1995

Houghton Lake Airport

Houghton Lake is located in north-central lower Michigan. The present station is on the northeast shore of Houghton Lake, the largest inland lake in Michigan, with a circumference of about 32 miles. The Muskegon River source is Higgins Lake, eight miles to the north. It flows through Houghton Lake, then southwestward to Lake Michigan. The station lies within an elongated bowl shaped 1,000-foot plateau, which extends roughly 50 miles north, 75 miles southwest, and about 20 miles southeast of Houghton Lake. In the immediate area, the land is level to rolling, but there are hills and ridges from 100 to 300 feet higher in elevation surrounding the station. Soils are generally sand, or sandy loam supporting little agricultural production, but the area is rich in natural resources of forests, lakes, and streams.

The interior location diminishes the influence of the larger Great Lakes, which lie 70 to 80 miles east and west of Houghton Lake. Hence, the daily temperature range is larger, especially in summer, and temperature extremes are greater than are found nearer the shores of either Lake Michigan or Lake Huron. Temperatures reach the 100 degree mark about one summer out of ten, and at the other extreme, fall below zero an average of 22 times during the winter season.

Precipitation is normally a little heavier during the summer season. About 60 percent of the annual total falls in the six-month period from April through September. The heaviest precipitation occurs with summertime thunderstorms.

Snowfall averages above 80 inches per year at Houghton Lake, with considerable variation from year to year. Much heavier snows, averaging over 100 inches a season, fall within a 30- to 60-mile radius to the north and west of Houghton Lake. Seasonal totals have ranged from 24 inches to over 124 inches. Measurable amounts of snow have occurred in nine of the 12 months, and the average number of months with measurable snowfall is six.

Cloudiness is greatest in the late fall and early winter, while sunshine percentage is highest in the spring and summer. Cloudiness is increased in the late fall due to the moisture and warmth picked up by the westerly and northwesterly winds while crossing Lake Michigan.

The growing season is normally quite short, averaging about 90 days between spring and fall freezes.

Houghton Lake Airport *Roscommon County* Elevation: 1,149 ft. Latitude: 44° 22' N Longitude: 84° 41' W

	JAN	FEB	MAR	APR	MAY	JUN	JUL	AUG	SEP	OCT	NOV	DEC	YEAR
Mean Maximum Temp. (°F)	26.5	29.6	39.5	54.0	66.5	75.7	79.9	77.3	69.2	55.7	42.5	30.8	54.0
Mean Temp. (°F)	18.7	20.5	29.5	43.0	54.5	63.4	67.7	65.6	57.9	46.4	35.5	24.5	43.9
Mean Minimum Temp. (°F)	10.9	11.4	19.4	31.9	42.4	51.1	55.4	53.8	46.6	37.0	28.5	18.1	33.9
Extreme Maximum Temp. (°F)	54	59	76	86	90	103	98	96	92	85	70	64	103
Extreme Minimum Temp. (°F)	-26	-31	-20	2	22	29	34	29	21	18	-5	-18	-31
Days Maximum Temp. ≥ 90°F	0	0	0	0	0	1	2	1	0	0	0	0	4
Days Maximum Temp. ≤ 32°F	23	18	8	1	0	0	0	0	0	0	4	17	71
Days Minimum Temp. ≤ 32°F	30	27	28	16	4	0	0	0	2	10	22	29	168
Days Minimum Temp. ≤ 0°F	7	6	3	0	0	0	0	0	0	0	0	2	18
Heating Degree Days (base 65°F)	1,428	1,252	1,095	656	336	111	40	68	231	573	878	1,249	7,917
Cooling Degree Days (base 65°F)	0	0	0	3	18	70	129	93	26	2	0	0	341
Mean Precipitation (in.)	1.55	1.22	1.85	2.51	2.79	3.05	2.63	3.41	3.13	2.57	2.32	1.67	28.70
Maximum Precipitation (in.)*	3.1	3.4	5.7	4.7	6.0	6.7	5.3	7.2	9.5	8.1	5.1	4.5	37.7
Minimum Precipitation (in.)*	0.6	0.3	0.6	1.0	0.4	0.8	0.5	0.8	trace	0.5	0.4	0.5	20.2
Extreme Maximum Daily Precip. (in.)	0.93	1.45	1.55	1.81	1.85	2.84	3.55	3.12	2.30	3.47	1.65	1.20	3.55
Days With ≥ 0.1" Precipitation	5	4	5	6	6	6	5	7	6	6	6	5	67
Days With ≥ 0.5" Precipitation	1	0	1	1	2	2	2	2	2	1	1	1	16
Days With ≥ 1.0" Precipitation	0	0	0	0	0	1	1	1	1	0	0	0	4
Mean Snowfall (in.)	***18.0***	***12.0***	***8.7***	na	na	na	na	***trace***	***trace***	***0.7***	***9.2***	***16.4***	na
Maximum Snowfall (in.)*	38	24	29	12	2	0	0	0	trace	4	42	30	117
Maximum 24-hr. Snowfall (in.)*	15	7	12	6	2	0	0	0	trace	4	14	13	15
Maximum Snow Depth (in.)	***21***	***20***	***18***	na	na	na	na	***trace***	***trace***	***1***	***17***	***22***	na
Days With ≥ 1.0" Snow Depth	***29***	***27***	***18***	na	na	na	na	***0***	***0***	***0***	***7***	***22***	na
Thunderstorm Days*	< 1	< 1	1	2	4	5	6	6	4	1	1	< 1	30
Foggy Days*	11	10	12	10	11	12	12	17	16	14	14	13	152
Predominant Sky Cover*	OVR	OVR	OVR	OVR	OVR	OVR	OVR	OVR	OVR	OVR	OVR	OVR	OVR
Mean Relative Humidity 7am (%)*	83	82	84	80	78	81	85	91	91	88	87	85	85
Mean Relative Humidity 4pm (%)*	72	66	61	53	47	51	52	58	61	62	72	76	61
Mean Dewpoint (°F)*	13	13	21	30	41	52	58	57	50	39	29	19	35
Prevailing Wind Direction*	W	W	W	NW	W	W	SW	WSW	SW	SW	W	W	W
Prevailing Wind Speed (mph)*	12	9	9	12	9	9	8	8	9	10	13	12	10
Maximum Wind Gust (mph)*	62	48	61	61	60	58	58	59	48	54	61	43	62

Note: (*) Period of record is 1964-1995

The period of record for National Weather Service station data is 1980 – 2009 except where noted. See User Guide for detailed explanation of data.

Lansing Capital City Airport

The climate at Lansing alternates between continental and semi-marine, depending on meteorological conditions. The marine type is due to the influence of the Great Lakes and is governed by the force and direction of the wind. When there is little or no wind, the weather becomes continental in character, which means pronounced fluctuation in temperature, hot weather in summer and severe cold in winter. On the other hand, a strong wind from the Lakes may immediately transform the weather into a semi-marine type.

Since large bodies of water are less responsive to temperature changes, the Great Lakes hold the winter cold longer in the spring and the summer heat longer in the fall than do the land areas. This fact is illustrated by looking at some monthly mean temperatures at Lansing as compared to similar latitudes west of the Lakes. Such a comparison shows cooler summers and milder winters in Lansing because of the lake effect.

Based on the 1951-1980 period, the average first occurrence of 32 degrees Fahrenheit in the fall is September 30 and the average last occurrence in the spring is May 13.

Precipitation is fairly well distributed through the year, and no conspicuous annual variation is noted, although there is about one inch less per month in winter than in summer. The heavier amounts in summer occur in thunderstorms. The wettest months are May and June. Snowfall for Lansing is moderate, averaging about 52 inches per year.

There are almost twice as many cloudy days as clear days throughout the year. Much cloudiness prevails during the winter season, but sunshine is abundant during the summer months. Similarly, relative humidity remains rather high during the winter, but is only moderate in summer.

Tornadoes sometimes occur in this area, but their frequency is less than in states farther to the south and west. Destructive thunder and wind storms are not uncommon. Flooding of streams and rivers in the upper grand Basin occurs in about one year out of three, with floods causing considerable damage in about one year out of ten.

Lansing Capital City Airport *Clinton County* Elevation: 840 ft. Latitude: 42° 47' N Longitude: 84° 35' W

	JAN	FEB	MAR	APR	MAY	JUN	JUL	AUG	SEP	OCT	NOV	DEC	YEAR
Mean Maximum Temp. (°F)	30.1	33.1	43.7	57.5	68.9	78.3	82.3	80.0	72.7	59.6	46.6	34.3	57.3
Mean Temp. (°F)	22.8	25.0	34.1	46.5	57.0	66.7	70.8	69.1	61.3	49.4	38.8	27.6	47.4
Mean Minimum Temp. (°F)	15.3	16.8	24.4	35.4	45.2	55.1	59.2	58.0	49.8	39.2	30.9	20.8	37.5
Extreme Maximum Temp. (°F)	62	69	79	86	91	99	100	100	93	87	74	69	100
Extreme Minimum Temp. (°F)	-29	-25	-13	-2	23	33	38	36	22	19	8	-18	-29
Days Maximum Temp. ≥ 90°F	0	0	0	0	0	2	4	2	1	0	0	0	9
Days Maximum Temp. ≤ 32°F	18	14	6	1	0	0	0	0	0	0	2	13	54
Days Minimum Temp. ≤ 32°F	29	26	25	12	2	0	0	0	1	8	18	27	148
Days Minimum Temp. ≤ 0°F	5	3	1	0	0	0	0	0	0	0	0	2	11
Heating Degree Days (base 65°F)	1,303	1,124	952	555	272	62	14	29	160	483	780	1,153	6,887
Cooling Degree Days (base 65°F)	0	0	1	6	32	120	200	162	55	6	0	0	582
Mean Precipitation (in.)	1.64	1.46	2.11	3.02	3.28	3.45	2.89	3.37	3.44	2.50	2.73	1.92	31.81
Maximum Precipitation (in.)*	3.6	4.2	4.4	5.2	6.6	10.2	6.4	9.8	8.3	5.6	5.4	4.7	39.6
Minimum Precipitation (in.)*	0.4	0.2	0.9	1.1	0.6	0.2	0.5	0.2	trace	0.3	0.5	0.4	21.2
Extreme Maximum Daily Precip. (in.)	1.59	2.14	1.24	2.10	3.22	4.95	2.12	2.70	3.43	1.43	2.16	1.02	4.95
Days With ≥ 0.1" Precipitation	4	4	5	8	7	6	6	6	6	6	6	6	70
Days With ≥ 0.5" Precipitation	1	1	1	2	2	2	2	2	2	2	2	1	20
Days With ≥ 1.0" Precipitation	0	0	0	0	1	1	1	1	1	0	1	0	6
Mean Snowfall (in.)	13.7	11.0	***7.3***	***2.1***	***trace***	***trace***	***trace***	***0.0***	***trace***	***0.4***	***3.5***	***13.2***	***51.2***
Maximum Snowfall (in.)*	34	24	20	17	trace	0	0	0	trace	8	17	28	80
Maximum 24-hr. Snowfall (in.)*	15	8	14	10	trace	0	0	0	trace	8	8	9	15
Maximum Snow Depth (in.)	23	17	13	***6***	***trace***	***trace***	***trace***	***0***	***trace***	***1***	***7***	***16***	***23***
Days With ≥ 1.0" Snow Depth	23	17	8	***1***	***0***	***0***	***0***	***0***	***0***	***0***	***2***	***15***	***66***
Thunderstorm Days*	< 1	< 1	1	3	4	6	6	6	4	1	1	< 1	32
Foggy Days*	13	12	13	12	11	11	12	16	14	14	14	14	156
Predominant Sky Cover*	OVR	OVR	OVR	OVR	OVR	OVR	SCT	OVR	OVR	OVR	OVR	OVR	OVR
Mean Relative Humidity 7am (%)*	83	82	83	80	79	81	85	90	90	87	85	84	84
Mean Relative Humidity 4pm (%)*	72	67	62	55	52	53	53	56	58	59	68	74	61
Mean Dewpoint (°F)*	17	17	25	35	45	56	60	60	53	41	32	22	39
Prevailing Wind Direction*	W	W	W	W	W	W	W	W	SSW	SW	SSW	SW	W
Prevailing Wind Speed (mph)*	14	14	14	14	12	10	10	9	10	12	12	13	12
Maximum Wind Gust (mph)*	60	52	64	70	62	69	64	54	48	55	60	62	70

Note: (*) Period of record is 1948-1995

Marquette County Airport

The Marquette County Airport lies about 7.5 miles southwest of the nearest shoreline of Lake Superior and about eight miles west of the city of Marquette. Lake Superior is the largest body of fresh water in the world and the deepest and coldest of the Great Lakes. An irregular northwest-southeast ridge line lies just to the east of the airport. There are several water storage basins in the vicinity of the station. One basin, about 20 miles long, is three miles northwest and another, about eight miles in diameter, is three miles west.

The climate is influenced considerably by the proximity of Lake Superior. As a consequence of the cool expanse of water in the summer, there is rarely a long period of sweltering hot weather. Periods of drought are extremely rare. In the winter, cold outbreaks are tempered considerably by the waters of Lake Superior if the lake is unfrozen. However, winds blowing across these relatively warmer waters pick up moisture and cause cloudy weather throughout the winter, as well as frequent periods of light snow. Lake-formed snow showers and snow squalls are intensified near the station by upslope winds, especially from the northwest through northeast. With a northeast through east wind, especially in autumn, the upslope condition will cause light snow at the airport, while along the lakeshore, only drizzle or no precipitation may occur.

The growing season averages 117 days. Precipitation is rather evenly distributed throughout the year, with an average precipitation of four inches or more in June and September and less than two inch averages only in January and February. One hundred inches or more of snow occur in nine of ten winter seasons.

Marquette County Airport *Marquette County* Elevation: 1,415 ft. Latitude: 46° 32' N Longitude: 87° 33' W

	JAN	FEB	MAR	APR	MAY	JUN	JUL	AUG	SEP	OCT	NOV	DEC	YEAR
Mean Maximum Temp. (°F)	22.2	25.9	34.6	48.0	62.2	71.9	76.4	74.2	65.8	51.8	37.5	26.0	49.7
Mean Temp. (°F)	14.1	16.3	24.5	38.0	50.8	60.4	65.2	63.5	55.7	43.1	30.6	18.9	40.1
Mean Minimum Temp. (°F)	6.0	6.6	14.3	27.9	39.3	48.8	54.0	52.8	45.5	34.4	23.6	11.8	30.4
Extreme Maximum Temp. (°F)	49	61	71	92	93	96	99	96	93	87	73	59	99
Extreme Minimum Temp. (°F)	-27	-32	-30	-9	17	28	36	34	24	14	-8	-28	-32
Days Maximum Temp. ≥ 90°F	0	0	0	0	0	1	2	1	0	0	0	0	4
Days Maximum Temp. ≤ 32°F	26	21	13	3	0	0	0	0	0	0	10	23	96
Days Minimum Temp. ≤ 32°F	31	28	29	22	8	0	0	0	2	15	26	30	191
Days Minimum Temp. ≤ 0°F	10	10	5	0	0	0	0	0	0	0	0	7	32
Heating Degree Days (base 65°F)	1,571	1,373	1,250	806	447	182	80	106	295	673	1,026	1,424	9,233
Cooling Degree Days (base 65°F)	0	0	0	2	12	51	95	68	22	2	0	0	252
Mean Precipitation (in.)	2.43	2.07	3.00	3.09	3.06	2.71	2.77	3.10	3.72	3.85	3.18	2.53	35.51
Maximum Precipitation (in.)*	4.5	3.6	6.1	6.6	7.9	12.3	5.6	8.6	7.6	7.6	8.3	6.9	51.6
Minimum Precipitation (in.)*	0.6	0.5	0.3	0.9	0.1	0.6	0.6	0.6	1.2	0.9	1.0	0.4	22.7
Extreme Maximum Daily Precip. (in.)	2.21	1.53	2.42	3.09	3.15	1.87	2.46	2.30	4.29	2.89	2.18	2.30	4.29
Days With ≥ 0.1" Precipitation	7	5	7	7	6	7	7	6	8	8	7	7	82
Days With ≥ 0.5" Precipitation	1	1	1	2	2	2	2	2	2	2	2	1	20
Days With ≥ 1.0" Precipitation	0	0	1	1	1	0	0	1	1	1	1	0	7
Mean Snowfall (in.)	43.4	35.8	34.8	14.5	1.3	trace	trace	trace	0.1	6.4	24.5	42.2	203.0
Maximum Snowfall (in.)*	69	64	61	29	23	trace	0	0	2	19	49	83	269
Maximum 24-hr. Snowfall (in.)*	23	18	21	16	14	trace	0	0	2	11	18	24	24
Maximum Snow Depth (in.)	45	44	63	41	17	trace	trace	trace	trace	10	24	47	63
Days With ≥ 1.0" Snow Depth	31	28	30	14	1	0	0	0	0	3	16	29	152
Thunderstorm Days*	< 1	< 1	1	1	3	6	6	5	4	2	< 1	< 1	28
Foggy Days*	7	7	9	9	10	11	10	13	14	12	11	9	122
Predominant Sky Cover*	na	na	na	na	na	na	na	na	na	na	na	na	na
Mean Relative Humidity 7am (%)*	na	na	na	na	na	na	na	na	na	na	na	na	na
Mean Relative Humidity 4pm (%)*	na	na	na	na	na	na	na	na	na	na	na	na	na
Mean Dewpoint (°F)*	na	na	na	na	na	na	na	na	na	na	na	na	na
Prevailing Wind Direction*	na	na	na	na	na	na	na	na	na	na	na	na	na
Prevailing Wind Speed (mph)*	na	na	na	na	na	na	na	na	na	na	na	na	na
Maximum Wind Gust (mph)*	na	na	na	na	na	na	na	na	na	na	na	na	na

Note: (*) Period of record is 1963-1995

The period of record for National Weather Service station data is 1980 – 2009 except where noted. See User Guide for detailed explanation of data.

Muskegon County Airport

Muskegon is located on the eastern shore of Lake Michigan approximately 100 miles north of the southern tip of the lake. The terrain is generally level with several sand dunes along the shoreline. Much of the soil is sandy and vegetation grows well, as evidenced by the trees and grass which grow on the dunes. Many crops grow in the area. Asparagus and celery are the principal truck- garden vegetables. A variety of fruits is raised and blueberries lead as a principal product. The main industry in this area is manufacturing with emphasis on foundry and machined products. The area is also a resort center due to features such as extensive sandy beaches, both on Lake Michigan and inland lakes.

Lake Michigan has a very decided effect upon the weather and climate of this area. The prevailing westerly winds tend to moderate the temperatures, resulting in warmer winters than further inland. In the summer the effect is just the opposite. The air temperature usually remains below the uncomfortable readings of the high 90s. Spring arrives about three to four weeks later than normal for this latitude. Autumn is also delayed, as is the cold of early winter.

Precipitation is fairly moderate, but snowfall is moderate to heavy. The heaviest snows occur during late December, January, and February. Precipitation is also influenced by the lake, especially during the winter. Instability in snow showers along the lakeshore vary enormously in intensity, resulting in traces of snow to more than a foot in 24 hours. The heavier snow squalls tend to concentrate over small sections of the shoreline, depending on their intensity and the direction of the wind. With strong winds most snowshowers will fall further inland, sometimes as much as 30 to 40 miles. Snowfall is likely to occur every day for weeks at a time. The daily accumulation of lake effect snow varies greatly. However, due to low water content of most of the storms, the snow settles rapidly.

Summertime thunderstorms have a tendency, as they move inland, to follow the Muskegon and Grand River Valleys. Thus, these areas are more often frequented by severe electrical storms which will pass without a drop of rain two to three miles from the immediate river valleys. Thunderstorms near the shoreline are most frequent at night. The afternoon convection-type storms seldom occur within five miles of the lake. Lake Michigan-spawned thunderstorms give shoreline areas a surprising number of occurrences.

Based on the 1951-1980 period, the average first occurrence of 32 degrees Fahrenheit in the fall is October 11 and the average last occurrence in the spring is May 8.

Muskegon County Airport *Muskegon County* Elevation: 625 ft. Latitude: 43° 10' N Longitude: 86° 14' W

	JAN	FEB	MAR	APR	MAY	JUN	JUL	AUG	SEP	OCT	NOV	DEC	YEAR
Mean Maximum Temp. (°F)	30.7	33.0	42.6	55.5	66.8	75.8	80.3	78.6	71.3	58.5	46.2	35.0	56.2
Mean Temp. (°F)	24.9	26.5	34.2	45.9	56.3	65.6	70.5	69.3	61.5	49.9	39.6	29.6	47.8
Mean Minimum Temp. (°F)	18.9	19.9	25.8	36.2	45.7	55.4	60.7	59.8	51.7	41.3	32.9	24.1	39.4
Extreme Maximum Temp. (°F)	61	67	80	84	89	98	96	95	91	83	72	64	98
Extreme Minimum Temp. (°F)	-11	-19	-6	1	25	32	39	38	27	21	10	-8	-19
Days Maximum Temp. ≥ 90°F	0	0	0	0	0	1	1	1	0	0	0	0	3
Days Maximum Temp. ≤ 32°F	17	14	6	0	0	0	0	0	0	0	2	11	50
Days Minimum Temp. ≤ 32°F	28	26	24	10	1	0	0	0	0	5	15	26	135
Days Minimum Temp. ≤ 0°F	2	1	0	0	0	0	0	0	0	0	0	0	3
Heating Degree Days (base 65°F)	1,237	1,082	947	570	286	72	13	22	149	465	756	1,090	6,689
Cooling Degree Days (base 65°F)	0	0	0	4	23	97	191	161	51	4	0	0	531
Mean Precipitation (in.)	2.05	1.78	2.37	2.98	3.21	2.55	2.37	3.52	3.82	3.11	3.37	2.59	33.72
Maximum Precipitation (in.)*	4.5	2.8	6.6	6.1	6.5	5.5	6.6	9.9	13.5	7.3	6.6	5.4	42.3
Minimum Precipitation (in.)*	0.4	0.4	0.5	0.7	0.3	0.2	0.5	0.1	0.2	0.5	0.6	0.9	23.1
Extreme Maximum Daily Precip. (in.)	1.18	1.65	4.00	2.66	2.30	2.52	1.57	3.45	4.33	2.58	2.12	2.58	4.33
Days With ≥ 0.1" Precipitation	6	5	6	7	6	5	5	6	7	7	7	7	74
Days With ≥ 0.5" Precipitation	1	1	1	2	2	2	2	2	3	2	2	1	21
Days With ≥ 1.0" Precipitation	0	0	0	0	1	1	0	1	1	1	1	0	6
Mean Snowfall (in.)	29.2	18.8	9.2	2.5	***trace***	***trace***	***trace***	***trace***	***trace***	***0.2***	6.3	28.9	***95.1***
Maximum Snowfall (in.)*	102	46	36	20	trace	0	0	0	trace	5	26	83	182
Maximum 24-hr. Snowfall (in.)*	22	14	9	12	trace	0	0	0	trace	5	9	15	22
Maximum Snow Depth (in.)	30	30	15	13	trace	***trace***	***trace***	***trace***	***trace***	***1***	11	24	***30***
Days With ≥ 1.0" Snow Depth	24	20	9	1	0	***0***	***0***	***0***	***0***	***0***	3	17	***74***
Thunderstorm Days*	< 1	< 1	2	3	4	6	6	6	5	2	1	< 1	35
Foggy Days*	11	10	12	11	11	11	11	14	12	13	12	12	140
Predominant Sky Cover*	OVR	OVR	OVR	OVR	OVR	OVR	CLR	OVR	OVR	OVR	OVR	OVR	OVR
Mean Relative Humidity 7am (%)*	81	81	80	78	76	80	84	88	88	84	80	81	82
Mean Relative Humidity 4pm (%)*	75	70	63	55	52	55	56	59	61	62	70	75	63
Mean Dewpoint (°F)*	18	18	25	33	43	54	60	60	53	42	32	23	38
Prevailing Wind Direction*	WNW	WNW	E	WNW	SW	SW	SW	SW	SSW	SSW	WNW	WNW	WNW
Prevailing Wind Speed (mph)*	14	13	12	13	13	12	12	12	13	15	15	14	13
Maximum Wind Gust (mph)*	62	67	59	63	54	55	58	63	54	55	59	56	67

Note: (*) Period of record is 1948-1995

The period of record for National Weather Service station data is 1980 – 2009 except where noted. See User Guide for detailed explanation of data.

Sault Ste Marie Sanderson Field

Sault Ste. Marie is located at the extreme eastern tip of the Upper Peninsula of Michigan at the intersection of Lake Superior, Michigan, and Huron. Consequently, the regional climate is essentially maritime during ice-free periods of the year. Lake ice development usually begins in December and progresses to maximum coverage in February. As ice cover develops, the character of the regional climate gradually changes to continental polar by the time of maximum lake ice development. Lake Superior, to the northwest, is the largest, deepest, and coldest of the Great Lakes and is the dominant climatic control for the area. Water in the northern Great Lakes remains relatively cool during the summer and seldom freezes over during the winter. Therefore, temperatures are moderated throughout most of the year, whereas cloudiness and precipitation are increased.

Terrain on the Michigan side of the international border is nearly flat and lies 700 to 800 feet above sea level. Very little climatological influence is related to Michigan terrain. However, terrain on the Canadian side of the border rises rather abruptly to about 1,500 feet above sea level and this definite topographic influence increases the rain and snow shower activity over the Canadian hills.

Heavy fog occurrences reach a maximum in August, September, and October and form in response to the passage of relatively cold air masses over the warmer waters of the northern Great Lakes. Destructive tornadoes and thunderstorms have occurred on rare occasions.

Most summers pass without a temperature reaching 90 degrees. Winters are cold and snowy with total seasonal snowfall ranging from about 30 inches to more than 175 inches. November 21 is the average date for the appearance of the permanent winter snow cover which normally lasts until April 7.

Annual percent of possible sunshine is low but is especially low during late fall and early winter because of cloud cover produced by lake moisture evaporated into the cold air. Sunshine amounts increase as ice development increases in the winter season. Daylight during most of June and July lasts almost 16 hours, whereas winter daylight reaches a minimum of less than 9 hours a day in late December.

Based on the 1951-1980 period, the average first occurrence of 32 degrees Fahrenheit in the fall is September 27 and the average last occurrence in the spring is May 26.

Sault Ste Marie Sanderson Field *Chippewa County* Elevation: 717 ft. Latitude: 46° 28' N Longitude: 84° 21' W

	JAN	FEB	MAR	APR	MAY	JUN	JUL	AUG	SEP	OCT	NOV	DEC	YEAR
Mean Maximum Temp. (°F)	22.7	25.4	33.8	48.7	62.5	71.0	75.8	74.4	66.2	52.7	39.7	28.2	50.1
Mean Temp. (°F)	14.6	16.8	25.1	39.3	51.1	59.2	64.5	63.9	56.4	44.7	33.4	21.4	40.9
Mean Minimum Temp. (°F)	6.5	8.1	16.3	29.9	39.7	47.5	53.1	53.4	46.6	36.5	27.0	14.6	31.6
Extreme Maximum Temp. (°F)	44	49	63	85	89	93	97	94	90	81	68	62	97
Extreme Minimum Temp. (°F)	-36	-28	-21	-2	24	26	36	29	25	16	-4	-31	-36
Days Maximum Temp. ≥ 90°F	0	0	0	0	0	0	1	0	0	0	0	0	1
Days Maximum Temp. ≤ 32°F	25	21	13	2	0	0	0	0	0	0	6	19	86
Days Minimum Temp. ≤ 32°F	31	28	29	19	6	1	0	0	1	10	22	29	176
Days Minimum Temp. ≤ 0°F	10	9	4	0	0	0	0	0	0	0	0	5	28
Heating Degree Days (base 65°F)	1,558	1,358	1,230	764	428	193	78	85	268	624	942	1,345	8,873
Cooling Degree Days (base 65°F)	0	0	0	0	5	27	70	58	17	1	0	0	178
Mean Precipitation (in.)	2.26	1.35	1.92	2.47	2.56	2.65	2.88	3.10	3.64	3.79	3.34	2.87	32.83
Maximum Precipitation (in.)*	4.5	3.7	5.0	5.2	5.3	7.3	6.0	9.5	7.8	6.5	7.7	6.2	45.8
Minimum Precipitation (in.)*	0.5	0.2	0.3	0.6	0.8	0.5	0.6	0.5	1.0	0.2	0.9	0.6	25.5
Extreme Maximum Daily Precip. (in.)	1.21	0.90	1.08	1.63	1.63	1.91	1.75	3.15	2.20	1.65	2.33	1.46	3.15
Days With ≥ 0.1" Precipitation	7	4	5	6	6	6	6	7	8	10	9	9	83
Days With ≥ 0.5" Precipitation	1	0	1	1	2	2	2	2	2	2	2	1	18
Days With ≥ 1.0" Precipitation	0	0	0	0	0	0	0	1	1	1	0	0	3
Mean Snowfall (in.)	***32.5***	***18.2***	***13.2***	na	na	na	na	***trace***	***trace***	***2.1***	***16.5***	***37.8***	na
Maximum Snowfall (in.)*	71	40	35	26	5	0	0	0	3	12	47	99	209
Maximum 24-hr. Snowfall (in.)*	15	12	12	9	3	0	0	0	3	7	11	27	27
Maximum Snow Depth (in.)	***38***	***36***	***37***	na	na	na	na	***trace***	***trace***	***4***	***14***	***49***	na
Days With ≥ 1.0" Snow Depth	***29***	***28***	***29***	na	na	na	na	***0***	***0***	***1***	***10***	***27***	na
Thunderstorm Days*	< 1	< 1	1	1	3	6	6	5	4	2	< 1	< 1	28
Foggy Days*	8	7	11	10	10	14	15	18	18	15	12	11	149
Predominant Sky Cover*	OVR	OVR	OVR	OVR	OVR	OVR	OVR	OVR	OVR	OVR	OVR	OVR	OVR
Mean Relative Humidity 7am (%)*	80	80	82	80	80	85	89	92	92	89	86	84	85
Mean Relative Humidity 4pm (%)*	74	70	67	59	53	59	60	62	67	68	76	78	66
Mean Dewpoint (°F)*	8	9	17	28	39	50	56	56	49	39	27	16	33
Prevailing Wind Direction*	E	NW	NW	NW	WNW	WNW	WNW	NW	NW	ESE	ESE	E	NW
Prevailing Wind Speed (mph)*	8	13	13	13	12	10	9	10	12	9	9	8	10
Maximum Wind Gust (mph)*	61	56	59	58	55	52	54	56	55	61	71	60	71

Note: (*) Period of record is 1947-1995

The period of record for National Weather Service station data is 1980 – 2009 except where noted. See User Guide for detailed explanation of data.

Adrian 2 NNE *Lenawee County* Elevation: 759 ft. Latitude: 41° 55' N Longitude: 84° 01' W

	JAN	FEB	MAR	APR	MAY	JUN	JUL	AUG	SEP	OCT	NOV	DEC	YEAR
Mean Maximum Temp. (°F)	32.5	35.3	46.2	59.5	70.6	80.0	83.6	81.5	74.5	61.6	48.6	36.1	59.2
Mean Temp. (°F)	24.4	26.6	36.0	47.8	58.1	67.7	71.5	69.7	62.2	50.2	39.6	28.6	48.5
Mean Minimum Temp. (°F)	16.2	17.9	25.7	36.1	45.6	55.3	59.4	57.8	49.8	38.8	30.5	21.0	37.8
Extreme Maximum Temp. (°F)	62	70	80	88	94	104	100	100	94	88	76	69	104
Extreme Minimum Temp. (°F)	-22	-16	-6	8	25	35	41	32	27	15	7	-14	-22
Days Maximum Temp. ≥ 90°F	0	0	0	0	1	3	5	3	1	0	0	0	13
Days Maximum Temp. ≤ 32°F	15	11	3	0	0	0	0	0	0	0	1	11	41
Days Minimum Temp. ≤ 32°F	29	26	24	11	1	0	0	0	1	7	19	28	146
Days Minimum Temp. ≤ 0°F	4	2	0	0	0	0	0	0	0	0	0	2	8
Heating Degree Days (base 65°F)	1,252	1,080	894	515	238	47	8	21	135	457	757	1,122	6,526
Cooling Degree Days (base 65°F)	0	0	0	6	30	133	218	173	57	5	0	0	622
Mean Precipitation (in.)	2.05	1.95	2.48	3.22	3.68	3.93	3.19	3.92	3.63	2.77	2.91	2.58	36.31
Extreme Maximum Daily Precip. (in.)	2.25	2.35	1.61	2.06	3.00	3.25	2.90	4.20	4.74	1.88	2.00	1.79	4.74
Days With ≥ 0.1" Precipitation	6	5	7	7	8	7	6	6	7	6	7	7	79
Days With ≥ 0.5" Precipitation	1	1	1	2	2	3	2	2	2	2	2	2	22
Days With ≥ 1.0" Precipitation	0	0	0	1	1	1	1	1	1	1	1	0	8
Mean Snowfall (in.)	8.9	6.8	4.5	0.7	0.0	0.0	0.0	0.0	0.0	0.1	1.6	7.0	29.6
Maximum Snow Depth (in.)	21	16	11	8	0	0	0	0	0	3	7	10	21
Days With ≥ 1.0" Snow Depth	18	15	6	0	0	0	0	0	0	0	2	10	51

Allegan 5 NE *Allegan County* Elevation: 750 ft. Latitude: 42° 35' N Longitude: 85° 47' W

	JAN	FEB	MAR	APR	MAY	JUN	JUL	AUG	SEP	OCT	NOV	DEC	YEAR
Mean Maximum Temp. (°F)	30.9	33.9	43.8	***57.9***	69.2	***78.2***	***82.5***	***80.3***	73.1	60.3	47.8	34.8	***57.7***
Mean Temp. (°F)	23.3	25.5	33.8	***46.4***	57.2	***66.2***	***70.5***	***68.7***	***61.3***	49.5	39.4	28.1	***47.5***
Mean Minimum Temp. (°F)	15.7	17.1	23.8	***34.9***	45.0	***54.2***	***58.5***	***57.2***	***49.6***	38.7	30.9	21.3	***37.2***
Extreme Maximum Temp. (°F)	60	70	79	***88***	91	***97***	***100***	***97***	93	84	75	70	***100***
Extreme Minimum Temp. (°F)	-21	-25	-10	***0***	23	***32***	***39***	***36***	26	18	6	-18	***-25***
Days Maximum Temp. ≥ 90°F	0	0	0	***0***	0	***2***	***4***	***2***	1	0	0	0	***9***
Days Maximum Temp. ≤ 32°F	17	13	5	***0***	0	***0***	***0***	***0***	0	0	2	11	***48***
Days Minimum Temp. ≤ 32°F	29	25	25	***13***	3	***0***	***0***	***0***	1	8	19	26	***149***
Days Minimum Temp. ≤ 0°F	4	2	1	***0***	0	***0***	***0***	***0***	0	0	0	1	***8***
Heating Degree Days (base 65°F)	1,285	1,110	960	***559***	268	***68***	***17***	***28***	***157***	478	762	1,137	***6,829***
Cooling Degree Days (base 65°F)	0	0	1	***7***	32	***110***	***194***	***150***	***53***	5	0	0	***552***
Mean Precipitation (in.)	2.98	2.14	2.48	***3.41***	4.55	***3.55***	***3.86***	***3.85***	3.95	3.25	***3.79***	3.17	***40.98***
Extreme Maximum Daily Precip. (in.)	1.90	1.36	1.75	***2.12***	3.73	***5.80***	***4.79***	***3.52***	3.40	2.52	***3.28***	2.23	***5.80***
Days With ≥ 0.1" Precipitation	8	7	6	***7***	8	***6***	***6***	***7***	7	7	7	9	***85***
Days With ≥ 0.5" Precipitation	2	1	1	***2***	3	***2***	***3***	***3***	3	2	2	1	***25***
Days With ≥ 1.0" Precipitation	0	0	0	***1***	1	***1***	***1***	***1***	1	0	1	0	***7***
Mean Snowfall (in.)	25.6	17.3	8.5	***2.6***	trace	***0.0***	***0.0***	***0.0***	0.0	0.4	7.4	24.8	***86.6***
Maximum Snow Depth (in.)	27	25	23	***10***	trace	***0***	***0***	***0***	0	***5***	20	22	***27***
Days With ≥ 1.0" Snow Depth	25	21	10	***1***	0	***0***	***0***	***0***	0	***0***	4	17	***78***

Alma *Gratiot County* Elevation: 759 ft. Latitude: 43° 23' N Longitude: 84° 40' W

	JAN	FEB	MAR	APR	MAY	JUN	JUL	AUG	SEP	OCT	NOV	DEC	YEAR
Mean Maximum Temp. (°F)	29.8	32.8	42.8	56.7	69.0	78.6	82.9	80.7	72.9	59.6	46.1	34.0	57.2
Mean Temp. (°F)	21.9	24.0	32.8	45.4	56.8	66.5	70.7	68.7	60.7	48.6	37.6	26.9	46.7
Mean Minimum Temp. (°F)	14.0	15.2	22.7	34.0	44.6	54.3	58.4	56.8	48.5	37.6	29.0	19.7	36.2
Extreme Maximum Temp. (°F)	59	67	79	88	94	100	103	101	93	90	76	68	103
Extreme Minimum Temp. (°F)	-22	-15	-8	5	24	34	41	36	27	20	6	-8	-22
Days Maximum Temp. ≥ 90°F	0	0	0	0	0	3	5	3	1	0	0	0	12
Days Maximum Temp. ≤ 32°F	19	14	5	0	0	0	0	0	0	0	2	13	53
Days Minimum Temp. ≤ 32°F	30	27	27	14	2	0	0	0	1	9	22	29	161
Days Minimum Temp. ≤ 0°F	5	3	1	0	0	0	0	0	0	0	0	1	10
Heating Degree Days (base 65°F)	1,329	1,152	993	587	275	66	14	28	167	506	816	1,176	7,109
Cooling Degree Days (base 65°F)	0	0	0	5	29	117	198	151	46	4	0	0	550
Mean Precipitation (in.)	1.90	1.63	2.11	3.05	3.46	3.33	2.78	3.42	3.52	2.96	2.84	2.13	33.13
Extreme Maximum Daily Precip. (in.)	1.28	1.86	1.39	3.40	3.22	3.22	2.38	2.51	9.33	4.04	3.00	1.80	9.33
Days With ≥ 0.1" Precipitation	5	4	5	7	7	6	5	6	6	6	6	6	69
Days With ≥ 0.5" Precipitation	1	1	1	2	2	2	2	2	2	2	2	1	20
Days With ≥ 1.0" Precipitation	0	0	0	0	1	1	1	1	1	0	1	0	6
Mean Snowfall (in.)	11.0	8.3	6.0	1.8	trace	0.0	0.0	0.0	0.0	0.3	2.8	9.8	40.0
Maximum Snow Depth (in.)	17	22	15	5	trace	0	0	0	0	2	8	16	22
Days With ≥ 1.0" Snow Depth	23	21	11	1	0	0	0	0	0	0	2	15	73

Alpena Wastewater Pl *Alpena County* Elevation: 589 ft. Latitude: 45° 04' N Longitude: 83° 26' W

	JAN	FEB	MAR	APR	MAY	JUN	JUL	AUG	SEP	OCT	NOV	DEC	YEAR
Mean Maximum Temp. (°F)	27.7	29.5	37.2	50.2	61.4	71.6	77.2	76.1	68.6	55.7	43.2	33.2	52.6
Mean Temp. (°F)	20.6	21.7	29.5	41.8	52.5	62.6	68.2	67.2	59.8	47.7	36.7	26.9	44.6
Mean Minimum Temp. (°F)	13.3	13.8	21.7	33.4	43.6	53.6	59.2	58.2	50.9	39.7	30.2	20.6	36.5
Extreme Maximum Temp. (°F)	55	62	75	88	92	100	100	100	92	87	75	65	100
Extreme Minimum Temp. (°F)	-21	-18	-12	6	21	36	39	36	29	22	4	-12	-21
Days Maximum Temp. ≥ 90°F	0	0	0	0	0	1	2	1	0	0	0	0	4
Days Maximum Temp. ≤ 32°F	21	17	9	1	0	0	0	0	0	0	3	13	64
Days Minimum Temp. ≤ 32°F	30	27	26	13	2	0	0	0	0	5	18	28	149
Days Minimum Temp. ≤ 0°F	4	4	1	0	0	0	0	0	0	0	0	1	10
Heating Degree Days (base 65°F)	1,371	1,219	1,095	690	391	125	31	40	183	531	842	1,174	7,692
Cooling Degree Days (base 65°F)	0	0	0	2	10	61	138	116	32	3	0	0	362
Mean Precipitation (in.)	1.83	1.52	1.73	2.46	2.94	2.62	3.14	3.48	3.27	2.72	2.15	1.93	29.79
Extreme Maximum Daily Precip. (in.)	1.60	1.58	***1.61***	1.86	2.04	2.05	2.97	2.22	2.50	2.31	1.52	1.06	***2.97***
Days With ≥ 0.1" Precipitation	5	4	4	6	7	6	6	7	7	7	6	6	71
Days With ≥ 0.5" Precipitation	1	1	1	2	2	2	2	2	2	2	1	1	19
Days With ≥ 1.0" Precipitation	0	0	0	0	1	0	1	1	1	0	0	0	4
Mean Snowfall (in.)	***15.3***	***11.8***	***6.3***	2.4	trace	0.0	0.0	0.0	0.0	0.3	3.2	13.1	***52.4***
Maximum Snow Depth (in.)	34	50	53	17	trace	0	0	0	0	4	10	34	53
Days With ≥ 1.0" Snow Depth	26	25	18	2	0	0	0	0	0	0	3	15	89

The period of record for all cooperative weather station data is 1980 – 2009. See User Guide for detailed explanation of data.

Ann Arbor Univ of Mich *Washtenaw County* Elevation: 899 ft. Latitude: 42° 18' N Longitude: 83° 43' W

	JAN	FEB	MAR	APR	MAY	JUN	JUL	AUG	SEP	OCT	NOV	DEC	YEAR
Mean Maximum Temp. (°F)	31.5	35.1	45.8	59.6	70.9	79.8	83.3	81.3	74.5	61.5	48.0	35.2	58.9
Mean Temp. (°F)	24.8	27.4	36.4	48.8	59.5	68.8	72.7	71.2	64.0	51.9	40.5	29.1	49.6
Mean Minimum Temp. (°F)	17.9	19.7	26.9	37.9	48.1	57.7	62.1	61.0	53.4	42.2	33.0	22.9	40.2
Extreme Maximum Temp. (°F)	62	67	80	87	92	101	100	98	94	89	75	67	101
Extreme Minimum Temp. (°F)	-22	-13	-8	7	27	36	43	39	30	21	10	-12	-22
Days Maximum Temp. ≥ 90°F	0	0	0	0	0	3	5	2	1	0	0	0	11
Days Maximum Temp. ≤ 32°F	17	12	4	0	0	0	0	0	0	0	2	12	47
Days Minimum Temp. ≤ 32°F	28	25	23	9	1	0	0	0	0	4	15	27	132
Days Minimum Temp. ≤ 0°F	2	1	0	0	0	0	0	0	0	0	0	1	4
Heating Degree Days (base 65°F)	1,241	1,056	881	489	206	37	5	12	106	408	728	1,106	6,275
Cooling Degree Days (base 65°F)	0	0	1	8	44	156	251	211	82	8	0	0	761
Mean Precipitation (in.)	2.58	2.36	2.75	3.31	3.31	3.56	3.51	3.84	3.50	2.86	3.00	2.94	37.52
Extreme Maximum Daily Precip. (in.)	1.57	1.88	1.65	2.09	2.19	3.17	2.58	4.54	2.66	2.23	1.90	1.46	4.54
Days With ≥ 0.1" Precipitation	7	6	6	8	7	7	7	7	6	6	7	7	81
Days With ≥ 0.5" Precipitation	1	1	2	2	2	3	2	3	3	2	2	2	25
Days With ≥ 1.0" Precipitation	0	0	0	0	1	1	1	1	1	1	0	0	6
Mean Snowfall (in.)	16.2	12.1	9.0	2.7	trace	0.0	0.0	0.0	trace	0.3	3.2	13.5	57.0
Maximum Snow Depth (in.)	18	19	22	6	trace	0	trace	0	trace	1	4	16	22
Days With ≥ 1.0" Snow Depth	21	17	7	1	0	0	0	0	0	0	1	13	60

Bad Axe *Huron County* Elevation: 714 ft. Latitude: 43° 49' N Longitude: 83° 00' W

	JAN	FEB	MAR	APR	MAY	JUN	JUL	AUG	SEP	OCT	NOV	DEC	YEAR
Mean Maximum Temp. (°F)	28.4	30.8	39.7	53.3	65.7	75.8	80.3	78.3	71.0	58.3	45.2	32.7	55.0
Mean Temp. (°F)	21.5	23.1	31.2	43.4	54.6	64.6	69.2	67.6	60.4	49.1	38.1	26.8	45.8
Mean Minimum Temp. (°F)	14.7	15.4	22.6	33.4	43.5	53.3	58.1	56.9	49.8	39.9	31.0	20.9	36.6
Extreme Maximum Temp. (°F)	61	66	80	88	92	97	101	98	92	89	74	68	101
Extreme Minimum Temp. (°F)	-20	-18	-9	14	25	32	42	34	27	23	6	-6	-20
Days Maximum Temp. ≥ 90°F	0	0	0	0	0	2	3	1	0	0	0	0	6
Days Maximum Temp. ≤ 32°F	20	16	9	1	0	0	0	0	0	0	2	14	62
Days Minimum Temp. ≤ 32°F	30	27	27	15	2	0	0	0	0	6	19	28	154
Days Minimum Temp. ≤ 0°F	4	3	1	0	0	0	0	0	0	0	0	1	9
Heating Degree Days (base 65°F)	1,341	1,178	1,043	646	335	97	25	41	173	491	801	1,176	7,347
Cooling Degree Days (base 65°F)	0	0	0	4	20	92	163	129	43	6	0	0	457
Mean Precipitation (in.)	1.81	1.81	1.97	2.91	3.16	2.92	3.20	3.64	3.95	2.66	2.80	2.10	32.93
Extreme Maximum Daily Precip. (in.)	1.68	2.02	1.99	1.62	2.87	2.01	2.85	2.63	6.46	1.56	2.25	0.96	6.46
Days With ≥ 0.1" Precipitation	5	5	5	7	7	6	6	6	7	7	6	6	73
Days With ≥ 0.5" Precipitation	1	1	1	2	2	2	2	2	2	2	2	1	20
Days With ≥ 1.0" Precipitation	0	0	0	1	1	1	1	1	1	0	0	0	6
Mean Snowfall (in.)	12.3	9.7	7.2	2.2	0.1	0.0	0.0	0.0	0.0	0.4	3.4	10.8	46.1
Maximum Snow Depth (in.)	24	31	10	7	trace	0	0	0	0	1	6	21	31
Days With ≥ 1.0" Snow Depth	23	22	11	1	0	0	0	0	0	0	3	15	75

Battle Creek 5 NW *Calhoun County* Elevation: 930 ft. Latitude: 42° 22' N Longitude: 85° 16' W

	JAN	FEB	MAR	APR	MAY	JUN	JUL	AUG	SEP	OCT	NOV	DEC	YEAR
Mean Maximum Temp. (°F)	31.9	35.5	46.4	59.8	70.9	79.3	82.7	***80.9***	***73.3***	60.8	***47.2***	35.6	***58.7***
Mean Temp. (°F)	24.2	26.8	36.1	48.2	58.8	67.7	71.3	***69.7***	***61.8***	50.5	***39.1***	28.5	***48.6***
Mean Minimum Temp. (°F)	16.5	18.0	25.7	36.6	46.7	55.9	59.9	***58.4***	***50.5***	40.1	***30.8***	21.2	***38.4***
Extreme Maximum Temp. (°F)	62	72	79	87	94	97	100	99	95	87	75	69	100
Extreme Minimum Temp. (°F)	-20	-19	-6	5	22	30	40	37	25	16	7	-18	-20
Days Maximum Temp. ≥ 90°F	0	0	0	0	0	2	4	2	0	0	0	0	8
Days Maximum Temp. ≤ 32°F	17	12	3	0	0	0	0	0	0	0	2	12	46
Days Minimum Temp. ≤ 32°F	29	26	24	11	2	0	0	0	1	7	18	27	145
Days Minimum Temp. ≤ 0°F	3	2	0	0	0	0	0	0	0	0	0	1	6
Heating Degree Days (base 65°F)	1,257	1,075	892	506	225	50	12	***23***	***150***	447	***772***	1,125	***6,534***
Cooling Degree Days (base 65°F)	0	0	1	8	39	136	214	***175***	***61***	5	***0***	0	***639***
Mean Precipitation (in.)	1.74	1.49	2.06	2.93	3.76	3.17	3.51	3.75	3.93	3.38	2.80	2.15	34.67
Extreme Maximum Daily Precip. (in.)	1.54	2.24	1.88	1.96	2.43	2.65	3.35	2.75	***3.83***	2.80	2.46	1.25	***3.83***
Days With ≥ 0.1" Precipitation	5	4	5	7	8	6	6	7	7	7	5	6	73
Days With ≥ 0.5" Precipitation	1	1	1	2	3	2	2	3	2	2	2	1	22
Days With ≥ 1.0" Precipitation	0	0	0	0	1	1	1	1	1	1	1	0	7
Mean Snowfall (in.)	16.3	11.7	6.3	2.1	trace	0.0	0.0	0.0	trace	0.6	5.2	17.0	59.2
Maximum Snow Depth (in.)	18	24	21	5	trace	0	0	0	1	3	***11***	20	***24***
Days With ≥ 1.0" Snow Depth	22	17	7	0	0	0	0	0	0	0	***3***	15	***64***

Benton Harbor Ross Field *Berrien County* Elevation: 627 ft. Latitude: 42° 08' N Longitude: 86° 26' W

	JAN	FEB	MAR	APR	MAY	JUN	JUL	AUG	SEP	OCT	NOV	DEC	YEAR
Mean Maximum Temp. (°F)	33.1	36.3	46.4	58.8	69.6	79.0	83.4	81.5	75.2	63.1	49.5	36.9	59.4
Mean Temp. (°F)	26.2	28.4	36.8	47.9	57.9	67.6	72.2	70.4	63.5	52.4	41.3	30.1	49.6
Mean Minimum Temp. (°F)	19.0	20.5	27.1	36.9	46.3	56.2	60.9	59.3	51.7	41.7	33.1	23.2	39.7
Extreme Maximum Temp. (°F)	66	70	84	89	97	100	104	101	98	92	76	69	104
Extreme Minimum Temp. (°F)	-17	-12	-3	9	24	31	37	37	23	15	8	-15	-17
Days Maximum Temp. ≥ 90°F	0	0	0	0	1	4	6	4	1	0	0	0	16
Days Maximum Temp. ≤ 32°F	15	10	3	0	0	0	0	0	0	0	2	10	40
Days Minimum Temp. ≤ 32°F	28	25	23	10	2	0	0	0	1	5	15	26	135
Days Minimum Temp. ≤ 0°F	2	1	0	0	0	0	0	0	0	0	0	1	4
Heating Degree Days (base 65°F)	1,197	1,028	870	517	256	63	13	22	121	397	705	1,076	6,265
Cooling Degree Days (base 65°F)	0	0	2	11	45	148	241	197	82	12	0	0	738
Mean Precipitation (in.)	1.97	1.60	2.08	3.27	3.52	3.24	3.22	4.05	4.07	3.51	3.32	2.28	36.13
Extreme Maximum Daily Precip. (in.)	1.80	2.37	2.20	1.88	1.87	2.10	3.14	3.25	2.42	2.81	2.78	2.37	3.25
Days With ≥ 0.1" Precipitation	5	4	6	8	7	6	6	6	7	8	7	7	77
Days With ≥ 0.5" Precipitation	1	1	1	2	3	2	2	3	3	2	2	1	23
Days With ≥ 1.0" Precipitation	0	0	0	1	1	1	1	1	1	1	1	0	8
Mean Snowfall (in.)	29.6	20.0	7.6	0.8	trace	0.0	0.0	0.0	trace	0.4	3.5	23.8	85.7
Maximum Snow Depth (in.)	61	80	12	4	trace	0	0	0	trace	4	12	72	80
Days With ≥ 1.0" Snow Depth	15	10	4	0	0	0	0	0	0	0	2	10	41

The period of record for all cooperative weather station data is 1980 – 2009. See User Guide for detailed explanation of data.

Bergland Dam *Ontonagon County* Elevation: 1,299 ft. Latitude: 46° 35' N Longitude: 89° 33' W

	JAN	FEB	MAR	APR	MAY	JUN	JUL	AUG	SEP	OCT	NOV	DEC	YEAR
Mean Maximum Temp. (°F)	21.3	25.8	35.7	50.3	64.5	73.3	77.5	76.0	67.1	53.1	37.9	25.2	50.6
Mean Temp. (°F)	11.7	13.9	23.0	38.0	51.0	60.5	64.8	63.3	55.3	42.7	30.0	16.8	39.2
Mean Minimum Temp. (°F)	1.9	1.9	10.3	25.7	37.4	47.6	52.0	50.6	43.4	32.2	22.1	8.3	27.8
Extreme Maximum Temp. (°F)	53	58	70	89	93	96	97	96	91	86	73	59	97
Extreme Minimum Temp. (°F)	-38	-39	-31	-11	15	27	35	32	21	13	-10	-30	-39
Days Maximum Temp. ≥ 90°F	0	0	0	0	0	0	1	1	0	0	0	0	2
Days Maximum Temp. ≤ 32°F	26	20	11	2	0	0	0	0	0	1	10	23	93
Days Minimum Temp. ≤ 32°F	31	28	29	25	10	1	0	0	3	18	26	31	202
Days Minimum Temp. ≤ 0°F	14	13	8	0	0	0	0	0	0	0	1	9	45
Heating Degree Days (base 65°F)	1,650	1,440	1,295	804	438	174	80	103	304	685	1,043	1,489	9,505
Cooling Degree Days (base 65°F)	0	0	0	1	10	44	81	57	18	1	0	0	212
Mean Precipitation (in.)	2.99	1.91	2.46	2.74	3.38	3.71	3.97	3.58	3.90	4.05	3.22	3.44	39.35
Extreme Maximum Daily Precip. (in.)	1.36	1.41	2.43	2.24	2.12	4.52	2.26	3.07	2.04	2.06	1.88	1.75	4.52
Days With ≥ 0.1" Precipitation	9	6	6	7	7	8	8	7	9	10	9	10	96
Days With ≥ 0.5" Precipitation	1	1	1	1	2	2	3	3	3	3	1	1	22
Days With ≥ 1.0" Precipitation	0	0	0	0	1	1	1	1	1	1	0	0	6
Mean Snowfall (in.)	41.9	25.8	26.0	9.7	1.2	0.0	0.0	0.0	0.2	5.2	25.1	42.7	177.8
Maximum Snow Depth (in.)	49	43	49	33	16	0	0	0	3	14	41	42	49
Days With ≥ 1.0" Snow Depth	31	28	29	14	1	0	0	0	0	3	16	29	151

Big Rapids Waterworks *Mecosta County* Elevation: 930 ft. Latitude: 43° 42' N Longitude: 85° 29' W

	JAN	FEB	MAR	APR	MAY	JUN	JUL	AUG	SEP	OCT	NOV	DEC	YEAR
Mean Maximum Temp. (°F)	29.4	33.0	42.6	56.4	68.6	78.0	82.0	79.5	71.7	58.2	44.9	33.2	56.4
Mean Temp. (°F)	20.9	23.4	31.5	44.3	55.7	65.3	69.5	67.3	59.3	47.2	36.3	25.7	45.5
Mean Minimum Temp. (°F)	12.4	13.7	20.4	32.3	42.9	52.5	56.9	55.1	46.8	36.2	27.8	18.2	34.6
Extreme Maximum Temp. (°F)	58	64	76	89	93	98	100	101	92	87	75	66	101
Extreme Minimum Temp. (°F)	-25	-29	-15	1	19	30	37	32	24	16	3	-15	-29
Days Maximum Temp. ≥ 90°F	0	0	0	0	0	2	4	2	0	0	0	0	8
Days Maximum Temp. ≤ 32°F	19	14	6	1	0	0	0	0	0	0	3	14	57
Days Minimum Temp. ≤ 32°F	30	27	28	16	4	0	0	0	1	11	22	29	168
Days Minimum Temp. ≤ 0°F	6	4	2	0	0	0	0	0	0	0	0	2	14
Heating Degree Days (base 65°F)	1,359	1,170	1,031	617	303	80	23	42	197	547	853	1,212	7,434
Cooling Degree Days (base 65°F)	0	0	0	2	22	95	168	121	33	3	0	0	444
Mean Precipitation (in.)	2.16	1.71	2.43	3.26	3.42	3.31	3.20	4.02	4.02	3.30	3.17	2.41	36.41
Extreme Maximum Daily Precip. (in.)	1.80	1.66	2.22	1.70	1.93	3.24	3.94	3.53	7.64	2.73	1.90	2.13	7.64
Days With ≥ 0.1" Precipitation	6	5	6	7	7	6	6	7	8	7	7	7	79
Days With ≥ 0.5" Precipitation	1	1	2	2	2	2	2	3	2	2	2	1	22
Days With ≥ 1.0" Precipitation	0	0	0	1	1	1	1	1	1	1	1	0	8
Mean Snowfall (in.)	18.1	12.6	8.1	2.0	trace	0.0	0.0	0.0	trace	0.3	5.0	16.4	62.5
Maximum Snow Depth (in.)	18	26	14	8	trace	0	0	0	trace	4	12	16	26
Days With ≥ 1.0" Snow Depth	27	23	11	1	0	0	0	0	0	0	4	20	86

Boyne Falls *Charlevoix County* Elevation: 734 ft. Latitude: 45° 10' N Longitude: 84° 55' W

	JAN	FEB	MAR	APR	MAY	JUN	JUL	AUG	SEP	OCT	NOV	DEC	YEAR
Mean Maximum Temp. (°F)	28.3	31.8	41.8	56.9	69.7	78.6	82.7	80.6	72.6	58.9	44.6	32.7	56.6
Mean Temp. (°F)	20.7	22.4	30.8	44.3	55.7	65.1	69.5	68.0	60.8	48.8	37.2	26.3	45.8
Mean Minimum Temp. (°F)	13.1	12.8	19.7	31.7	41.7	51.6	56.3	55.4	49.0	38.6	29.8	19.8	35.0
Extreme Maximum Temp. (°F)	56	65	82	89	94	97	101	100	95	91	76	66	101
Extreme Minimum Temp. (°F)	-32	-32	-23	-6	20	28	33	30	24	19	-3	-17	-32
Days Maximum Temp. ≥ 90°F	0	0	0	0	0	3	5	2	1	0	0	0	11
Days Maximum Temp. ≤ 32°F	21	16	6	0	0	0	0	0	0	0	3	15	61
Days Minimum Temp. ≤ 32°F	30	27	27	17	7	1	0	0	1	9	20	29	168
Days Minimum Temp. ≤ 0°F	6	6	3	0	0	0	0	0	0	0	0	2	17
Heating Degree Days (base 65°F)	1,366	1,200	1,053	619	308	93	26	39	174	504	826	1,194	7,402
Cooling Degree Days (base 65°F)	0	0	0	5	27	102	172	140	56	8	0	0	510
Mean Precipitation (in.)	2.39	1.57	1.84	2.49	2.89	2.84	2.64	3.58	3.76	3.89	3.04	2.69	33.62
Extreme Maximum Daily Precip. (in.)	1.76	0.83	2.03	1.69	1.86	2.20	2.11	3.15	2.55	1.95	1.81	1.24	3.15
Days With ≥ 0.1" Precipitation	8	5	6	6	7	6	6	7	8	9	9	9	86
Days With ≥ 0.5" Precipitation	1	1	1	2	2	2	2	2	2	2	1	1	19
Days With ≥ 1.0" Precipitation	0	0	0	0	1	1	1	1	1	1	0	0	6
Mean Snowfall (in.)	31.1	21.3	11.0	4.5	0.3	0.0	0.0	0.0	trace	0.8	12.7	32.4	114.1
Maximum Snow Depth (in.)	29	33	25	13	trace	0	0	0	trace	4	16	26	33
Days With ≥ 1.0" Snow Depth	29	27	20	2	0	0	0	0	0	0	7	23	108

Caro Regional Center *Tuscola County* Elevation: 669 ft. Latitude: 43° 27' N Longitude: 83° 24' W

	JAN	FEB	MAR	APR	MAY	JUN	JUL	AUG	SEP	OCT	NOV	DEC	YEAR
Mean Maximum Temp. (°F)	30.1	32.7	43.3	57.8	69.7	***79.1***	***83.2***	***80.8***	***73.2***	60.4	46.7	33.9	***57.6***
Mean Temp. (°F)	22.6	24.1	33.7	46.2	56.9	***66.3***	***70.9***	***68.9***	***61.4***	49.9	38.9	27.3	***47.3***
Mean Minimum Temp. (°F)	15.0	15.5	23.9	34.5	44.0	***53.5***	***58.6***	***56.9***	***49.5***	39.4	31.0	20.7	***36.9***
Extreme Maximum Temp. (°F)	61	65	80	88	94	***100***	***101***	***101***	92	89	76	69	***101***
Extreme Minimum Temp. (°F)	-24	-24	-15	9	23	***31***	***38***	***32***	25	16	1	-18	***-24***
Days Maximum Temp. ≥ 90°F	0	0	0	0	1	***3***	***5***	***3***	1	0	0	0	***13***
Days Maximum Temp. ≤ 32°F	18	14	6	1	0	***0***	***0***	***0***	0	0	2	13	***54***
Days Minimum Temp. ≤ 32°F	29	26	25	14	3	***0***	***0***	***0***	1	8	18	27	***151***
Days Minimum Temp. ≤ 0°F	5	4	1	0	0	***0***	***0***	***0***	0	0	0	2	***12***
Heating Degree Days (base 65°F)	1,308	1,150	965	564	278	***69***	***14***	***30***	***155***	467	778	1,162	***6,940***
Cooling Degree Days (base 65°F)	0	0	1	6	33	***115***	***205***	***157***	***52***	6	0	0	***575***
Mean Precipitation (in.)	1.86	1.38	2.00	3.15	3.01	***3.52***	***3.13***	***3.07***	4.33	3.01	2.79	2.07	***33.32***
Extreme Maximum Daily Precip. (in.)	1.22	1.98	1.53	2.40	1.71	***4.02***	***2.61***	***2.55***	7.28	1.75	2.34	2.60	***7.28***
Days With ≥ 0.1" Precipitation	6	4	6	8	7	***7***	***6***	***6***	7	7	6	6	***76***
Days With ≥ 0.5" Precipitation	1	1	1	2	2	***2***	***2***	***2***	3	2	2	1	***21***
Days With ≥ 1.0" Precipitation	0	0	0	0	1	***1***	***1***	***1***	1	0	0	0	***5***
Mean Snowfall (in.)	11.6	7.3	5.2	1.0	trace	***0.0***	***0.0***	***0.0***	0.0	0.1	2.0	9.6	***36.8***
Maximum Snow Depth (in.)	16	18	12	4	trace	***0***	***0***	***0***	0	1	6	***16***	***18***
Days With ≥ 1.0" Snow Depth	21	18	7	1	0	***0***	***0***	***0***	0	0	2	14	***63***

Champion Van Riper Prk *Marquette County* Elevation: 1,564 ft. Latitude: 46° 31' N Longitude: 87° 59' W

	JAN	FEB	MAR	APR	MAY	JUN	JUL	AUG	SEP	OCT	NOV	DEC	YEAR
Mean Maximum Temp. (°F)	22.9	27.4	37.8	51.9	65.6	74.3	78.8	76.4	67.4	54.3	37.8	25.6	51.7
Mean Temp. (°F)	12.3	14.7	24.2	38.0	50.2	59.4	64.4	62.6	54.7	42.9	29.3	16.6	39.1
Mean Minimum Temp. (°F)	1.5	2.0	10.5	24.0	34.7	44.5	49.9	48.8	41.9	31.5	20.8	7.6	26.5
Extreme Maximum Temp. (°F)	50	61	69	92	91	95	98	96	94	85	72	60	98
Extreme Minimum Temp. (°F)	-38	-40	-33	-16	12	17	26	27	15	10	-11	-38	-40
Days Maximum Temp. ≥ 90°F	0	0	0	0	0	1	1	0	0	0	0	0	2
Days Maximum Temp. ≤ 32°F	24	18	9	1	0	0	0	0	0	0	9	22	83
Days Minimum Temp. ≤ 32°F	30	26	29	24	14	3	0	1	5	18	26	29	205
Days Minimum Temp. ≤ 0°F	14	12	8	1	0	0	0	0	0	0	1	9	45
Heating Degree Days (base 65°F)	1,630	1,417	1,258	805	462	195	89	119	315	679	1,064	1,494	9,527
Cooling Degree Days (base 65°F)	0	0	0	1	7	35	76	53	15	1	0	0	188
Mean Precipitation (in.)	1.81	1.23	2.07	2.40	3.01	3.34	3.75	3.29	3.54	3.54	2.23	1.85	32.06
Extreme Maximum Daily Precip. (in.)	***1.52***	***1.27***	2.13	***2.49***	2.40	***2.96***	***3.61***	2.55	2.30	***1.92***	1.49	1.15	***3.61***
Days With ≥ 0.1" Precipitation	5	3	5	5	5	6	7	6	8	7	6	5	68
Days With ≥ 0.5" Precipitation	1	0	1	1	2	2	2	2	2	2	1	1	17
Days With ≥ 1.0" Precipitation	0	0	0	0	0	1	1	1	1	1	0	0	5
Mean Snowfall (in.)	25.9	16.1	19.3	6.8	0.5	0.0	0.0	0.0	0.1	4.2	***15.6***	26.1	***114.6***
Maximum Snow Depth (in.)	54	60	53	44	19	0	0	0	trace	7	24	31	60
Days With ≥ 1.0" Snow Depth	27	25	26	12	1	0	0	0	0	2	14	24	131

Charlotte *Eaton County* Elevation: 901 ft. Latitude: 42° 33' N Longitude: 84° 50' W

	JAN	FEB	MAR	APR	MAY	JUN	JUL	AUG	SEP	OCT	NOV	DEC	YEAR
Mean Maximum Temp. (°F)	30.1	33.2	43.1	56.7	68.1	77.8	81.2	79.4	72.2	59.5	46.5	34.1	56.8
Mean Temp. (°F)	22.4	24.6	33.4	45.8	56.8	66.5	70.0	68.4	60.7	49.0	38.3	27.2	46.9
Mean Minimum Temp. (°F)	14.7	16.0	23.7	34.8	45.4	55.1	58.7	57.3	49.1	38.5	30.0	20.2	37.0
Extreme Maximum Temp. (°F)	60	70	79	88	91	99	100	101	93	87	73	69	101
Extreme Minimum Temp. (°F)	-21	-17	-8	3	25	31	41	36	27	18	6	-15	-21
Days Maximum Temp. ≥ 90°F	0	0	0	0	0	2	3	2	0	0	0	0	7
Days Maximum Temp. ≤ 32°F	18	14	6	0	0	0	0	0	0	0	3	13	54
Days Minimum Temp. ≤ 32°F	29	27	25	13	2	0	0	0	0	9	20	28	153
Days Minimum Temp. ≤ 0°F	4	3	1	0	0	0	0	0	0	0	0	2	10
Heating Degree Days (base 65°F)	1,313	1,135	972	575	278	65	18	32	170	493	794	1,165	7,010
Cooling Degree Days (base 65°F)	0	0	1	5	30	115	178	143	47	4	0	0	523
Mean Precipitation (in.)	1.78	1.46	2.13	3.14	3.65	3.30	3.04	3.59	3.68	3.18	2.88	2.18	34.01
Extreme Maximum Daily Precip. (in.)	1.80	1.55	1.60	2.42	2.45	3.15	2.46	3.18	3.60	2.31	2.26	1.37	3.60
Days With ≥ 0.1" Precipitation	5	4	5	7	7	6	7	7	6	7	7	6	74
Days With ≥ 0.5" Precipitation	1	1	1	2	2	2	2	2	3	2	2	1	21
Days With ≥ 1.0" Precipitation	0	0	0	0	1	1	1	1	1	1	0	0	6
Mean Snowfall (in.)	13.3	8.7	6.4	1.2	0.0	0.0	0.0	0.0	0.0	0.5	1.9	10.9	42.9
Maximum Snow Depth (in.)	27	18	16	8	0	0	0	0	0	5	6	28	28
Days With ≥ 1.0" Snow Depth	22	17	8	1	0	0	0	0	0	0	2	14	64

Cheboygan *Cheboygan County* Elevation: 589 ft. Latitude: 45° 39' N Longitude: 84° 28' W

	JAN	FEB	MAR	APR	MAY	JUN	JUL	AUG	SEP	OCT	NOV	DEC	YEAR
Mean Maximum Temp. (°F)	27.1	29.2	37.3	49.9	62.2	72.0	77.5	76.2	68.8	55.7	43.4	32.3	52.6
Mean Temp. (°F)	18.7	19.5	27.5	40.4	51.6	61.7	67.5	66.4	59.0	46.9	36.3	25.3	43.4
Mean Minimum Temp. (°F)	10.2	9.7	17.5	30.8	40.9	51.3	57.5	56.6	49.1	38.0	29.2	18.3	34.1
Extreme Maximum Temp. (°F)	55	62	74	86	90	96	98	98	92	88	72	64	98
Extreme Minimum Temp. (°F)	-27	-28	-18	-2	17	32	41	36	26	19	8	-15	-28
Days Maximum Temp. ≥ 90°F	0	0	0	0	0	1	1	1	0	0	0	0	3
Days Maximum Temp. ≤ 32°F	22	18	9	1	0	0	0	0	0	0	3	15	68
Days Minimum Temp. ≤ 32°F	30	28	29	18	3	0	0	0	0	7	20	29	164
Days Minimum Temp. ≤ 0°F	7	7	3	0	0	0	0	0	0	0	0	2	19
Heating Degree Days (base 65°F)	1,429	1,281	1,155	733	412	143	39	50	206	558	854	1,223	8,083
Cooling Degree Days (base 65°F)	0	0	0	1	4	49	124	101	32	3	0	0	314
Mean Precipitation (in.)	1.72	1.32	1.76	2.58	2.75	2.62	3.05	3.40	3.35	3.45	2.48	2.04	30.52
Extreme Maximum Daily Precip. (in.)	2.20	1.13	1.64	2.88	2.14	2.51	3.21	4.48	2.70	2.09	1.51	1.67	4.48
Days With ≥ 0.1" Precipitation	5	4	5	6	6	5	5	6	7	8	7	6	70
Days With ≥ 0.5" Precipitation	1	1	1	1	2	2	2	2	2	2	1	1	18
Days With ≥ 1.0" Precipitation	0	0	0	0	0	1	1	1	1	1	0	0	5
Mean Snowfall (in.)	25.4	19.3	12.1	4.0	0.1	0.0	0.0	0.0	0.0	0.6	7.0	24.3	92.8
Maximum Snow Depth (in.)	32	41	30	18	2	0	0	0	0	11	11	30	41
Days With ≥ 1.0" Snow Depth	28	27	21	3	0	0	0	0	0	0	7	21	107

Cross Village *Emmet County* Elevation: 743 ft. Latitude: 45° 38' N Longitude: 85° 02' W

	JAN	FEB	MAR	APR	MAY	JUN	JUL	AUG	SEP	OCT	NOV	DEC	YEAR
Mean Maximum Temp. (°F)	27.3	29.6	38.3	51.8	63.6	71.5	76.0	74.9	68.2	55.4	43.4	32.3	52.7
Mean Temp. (°F)	20.2	21.0	28.7	41.4	52.4	61.2	66.5	65.9	59.6	47.8	37.3	26.7	44.1
Mean Minimum Temp. (°F)	13.1	12.3	19.0	31.1	41.2	50.9	57.0	56.9	50.9	40.2	31.2	21.1	35.4
Extreme Maximum Temp. (°F)	55	61	76	89	90	90	95	93	90	82	73	65	95
Extreme Minimum Temp. (°F)	-27	-23	-19	-4	22	31	36	38	25	18	6	-12	-27
Days Maximum Temp. ≥ 90°F	0	0	0	0	0	0	0	0	0	0	0	0	0
Days Maximum Temp. ≤ 32°F	22	18	9	1	0	0	0	0	0	0	3	15	68
Days Minimum Temp. ≤ 32°F	30	27	28	18	5	0	0	0	0	5	17	28	158
Days Minimum Temp. ≤ 0°F	5	5	2	0	0	0	0	0	0	0	0	1	13
Heating Degree Days (base 65°F)	1,382	1,239	1,120	702	392	150	48	53	188	528	823	1,179	7,804
Cooling Degree Days (base 65°F)	0	0	0	2	8	43	102	88	31	3	0	0	277
Mean Precipitation (in.)	1.78	1.19	1.77	2.61	2.71	2.55	2.09	3.20	3.38	3.56	2.62	2.12	29.58
Extreme Maximum Daily Precip. (in.)	1.10	1.24	1.55	2.17	1.94	1.98	1.56	2.72	2.08	2.01	1.66	1.50	2.72
Days With ≥ 0.1" Precipitation	5	4	5	6	6	6	5	6	7	8	7	7	72
Days With ≥ 0.5" Precipitation	1	0	1	2	2	1	1	2	2	2	1	1	16
Days With ≥ 1.0" Precipitation	0	0	0	0	0	0	0	1	1	1	0	0	3
Mean Snowfall (in.)	21.4	16.3	10.5	4.9	0.1	0.0	0.0	0.0	trace	0.3	5.8	20.5	79.8
Maximum Snow Depth (in.)	35	30	27	19	trace	0	0	0	trace	4	14	26	35
Days With ≥ 1.0" Snow Depth	28	28	22	5	0	0	0	0	0	0	6	21	110

The period of record for all cooperative weather station data is 1980 – 2009. See User Guide for detailed explanation of data.

Dearborn *Wayne County* Elevation: 604 ft. Latitude: 42° 19' N Longitude: 83° 14' W

	JAN	FEB	MAR	APR	MAY	JUN	JUL	AUG	SEP	OCT	NOV	DEC	YEAR
Mean Maximum Temp. (°F)	32.9	36.1	45.8	59.1	70.7	80.3	84.5	82.9	76.0	62.4	49.4	37.1	59.8
Mean Temp. (°F)	25.1	27.5	36.2	48.2	58.9	68.5	73.1	71.6	64.2	51.6	40.9	29.5	49.6
Mean Minimum Temp. (°F)	17.3	18.9	26.4	37.2	47.0	56.7	61.6	60.2	52.4	40.8	32.3	22.2	39.4
Extreme Maximum Temp. (°F)	65	71	83	90	95	104	102	102	100	91	76	69	104
Extreme Minimum Temp. (°F)	-20	-12	-9	10	25	36	41	40	29	19	11	-9	-20
Days Maximum Temp. ≥ 90°F	0	0	0	0	0	4	6	4	1	0	0	0	15
Days Maximum Temp. ≤ 32°F	15	10	3	0	0	0	0	0	0	0	1	10	39
Days Minimum Temp. ≤ 32°F	28	25	23	9	1	0	0	0	0	5	16	26	133
Days Minimum Temp. ≤ 0°F	3	1	0	0	0	0	0	0	0	0	0	1	5
Heating Degree Days (base 65°F)	1,229	1,052	888	504	223	43	5	12	105	415	716	1,092	6,284
Cooling Degree Days (base 65°F)	0	0	1	7	41	156	261	222	88	8	0	0	784
Mean Precipitation (in.)	2.04	2.04	2.41	2.98	3.06	3.34	3.31	2.80	3.39	2.95	2.76	2.53	33.61
Extreme Maximum Daily Precip. (in.)	1.85	1.85	1.79	2.05	2.39	2.95	2.22	2.32	3.93	2.64	1.95	1.19	3.93
Days With ≥ 0.1" Precipitation	5	5	6	7	6	7	6	6	6	6	7	7	74
Days With ≥ 0.5" Precipitation	1	1	2	2	2	2	2	2	2	2	2	2	22
Days With ≥ 1.0" Precipitation	0	0	0	0	1	1	1	1	1	1	0	0	6
Mean Snowfall (in.)	10.6	8.0	5.3	0.7	0.0	0.0	0.0	0.0	0.0	0.1	1.0	7.1	32.8
Maximum Snow Depth (in.)	24	24	16	5	0	0	0	0	0	1	5	14	24
Days With ≥ 1.0" Snow Depth	19	16	7	0	0	0	0	0	0	0	1	9	52

East Lansing 4 S *Ingham County* Elevation: 879 ft. Latitude: 42° 40' N Longitude: 84° 29' W

	JAN	FEB	MAR	APR	MAY	JUN	JUL	AUG	SEP	OCT	NOV	DEC	YEAR
Mean Maximum Temp. (°F)	30.4	33.3	43.4	57.0	68.7	78.3	82.2	80.7	***73.6***	60.0	47.2	34.5	***57.4***
Mean Temp. (°F)	22.7	24.7	33.9	46.3	57.2	66.7	70.5	69.2	***61.5***	49.2	38.9	27.4	***47.3***
Mean Minimum Temp. (°F)	14.9	16.1	24.4	35.5	45.7	55.2	58.9	57.6	***49.3***	38.4	30.6	20.2	***37.2***
Extreme Maximum Temp. (°F)	62	63	80	87	92	98	101	100	94	88	75	67	101
Extreme Minimum Temp. (°F)	-20	-19	-8	3	25	34	39	33	26	19	9	-12	-20
Days Maximum Temp. ≥ 90°F	0	0	0	0	0	2	3	3	1	0	0	0	9
Days Maximum Temp. ≤ 32°F	18	13	6	1	0	0	0	0	0	0	2	13	53
Days Minimum Temp. ≤ 32°F	29	26	25	12	2	0	0	0	0	8	19	28	149
Days Minimum Temp. ≤ 0°F	4	3	1	0	0	0	0	0	0	0	0	2	10
Heating Degree Days (base 65°F)	1,306	1,133	957	560	268	64	16	29	***156***	488	776	1,160	***6,913***
Cooling Degree Days (base 65°F)	0	0	1	5	33	123	195	166	***57***	5	0	0	***585***
Mean Precipitation (in.)	1.61	1.42	1.70	2.83	3.26	3.37	3.12	3.31	3.59	2.64	2.58	1.64	31.07
Extreme Maximum Daily Precip. (in.)	1.63	1.42	1.60	2.20	3.10	2.87	2.11	3.56	***4.50***	2.82	2.17	1.17	***4.50***
Days With ≥ 0.1" Precipitation	5	4	5	7	7	6	6	6	6	6	5	5	68
Days With ≥ 0.5" Precipitation	1	1	1	2	2	2	2	2	3	2	2	1	21
Days With ≥ 1.0" Precipitation	0	0	0	0	1	1	1	1	1	0	0	0	5
Mean Snowfall (in.)	12.0	8.7	4.9	1.0	0.0	0.0	0.0	0.0	0.0	0.3	1.7	9.7	38.3
Maximum Snow Depth (in.)	14	24	17	6	0	0	0	0	0	4	5	13	24
Days With ≥ 1.0" Snow Depth	20	17	8	1	0	0	0	0	0	0	2	13	61

East Tawas *Iosco County* Elevation: 585 ft. Latitude: 44° 17' N Longitude: 83° 30' W

	JAN	FEB	MAR	APR	MAY	JUN	JUL	AUG	SEP	OCT	NOV	DEC	YEAR
Mean Maximum Temp. (°F)	29.8	32.2	40.6	53.0	65.1	75.1	80.1	78.4	71.1	58.1	45.5	34.3	55.3
Mean Temp. (°F)	21.5	22.9	31.0	43.1	54.2	63.9	68.9	67.5	60.2	48.2	37.7	27.1	45.5
Mean Minimum Temp. (°F)	13.2	13.5	21.4	33.1	43.3	52.7	57.6	56.5	49.2	38.3	29.8	20.0	35.7
Extreme Maximum Temp. (°F)	58	59	78	91	92	101	102	100	95	93	76	65	102
Extreme Minimum Temp. (°F)	-18	-21	-18	6	26	32	39	31	26	19	1	-19	-21
Days Maximum Temp. ≥ 90°F	0	0	0	0	0	1	2	1	0	0	0	0	4
Days Maximum Temp. ≤ 32°F	18	14	6	1	0	0	0	0	0	0	1	12	52
Days Minimum Temp. ≤ 32°F	30	27	27	14	3	0	0	0	1	8	19	28	157
Days Minimum Temp. ≤ 0°F	6	5	1	0	0	0	0	0	0	0	0	1	13
Heating Degree Days (base 65°F)	1,341	1,183	1,047	652	341	102	25	40	172	517	813	1,167	7,400
Cooling Degree Days (base 65°F)	0	0	0	1	15	77	151	123	35	3	0	0	405
Mean Precipitation (in.)	2.04	1.69	2.10	2.83	3.00	3.03	2.69	3.37	3.45	2.75	2.62	2.06	31.63
Extreme Maximum Daily Precip. (in.)	1.41	1.51	1.54	3.52	1.94	2.40	3.07	2.20	2.62	3.06	1.56	1.77	3.52
Days With ≥ 0.1" Precipitation	5	5	5	6	7	6	6	6	6	6	6	6	70
Days With ≥ 0.5" Precipitation	1	1	1	2	2	2	2	2	3	2	2	1	21
Days With ≥ 1.0" Precipitation	0	0	0	1	1	1	0	1	1	0	0	0	5
Mean Snowfall (in.)	16.8	12.7	8.1	1.9	0.1	0.0	0.0	0.0	trace	0.1	2.7	11.2	53.6
Maximum Snow Depth (in.)	24	23	21	9	2	0	0	0	trace	2	14	16	24
Days With ≥ 1.0" Snow Depth	25	25	17	2	0	0	0	0	0	0	3	15	87

Essexville *Bay County* Elevation: 587 ft. Latitude: 43° 37' N Longitude: 83° 52' W

	JAN	FEB	MAR	APR	MAY	JUN	JUL	AUG	SEP	OCT	NOV	DEC	YEAR
Mean Maximum Temp. (°F)	29.3	31.7	41.0	54.8	66.9	77.0	81.5	79.3	72.1	58.9	46.0	33.9	56.0
Mean Temp. (°F)	22.5	24.4	33.0	45.7	57.4	67.3	71.7	69.9	62.3	50.1	39.1	27.9	47.6
Mean Minimum Temp. (°F)	15.6	17.0	24.9	36.7	47.9	57.4	61.8	60.3	52.4	41.3	32.1	21.8	39.1
Extreme Maximum Temp. (°F)	60	68	81	90	95	101	99	100	92	90	75	68	101
Extreme Minimum Temp. (°F)	-18	-13	-7	14	28	37	42	39	32	23	7	-5	-18
Days Maximum Temp. ≥ 90°F	0	0	0	0	0	3	4	2	1	0	0	0	10
Days Maximum Temp. ≤ 32°F	19	15	7	1	0	0	0	0	0	0	2	13	57
Days Minimum Temp. ≤ 32°F	29	27	25	10	0	0	0	0	0	4	16	28	139
Days Minimum Temp. ≤ 0°F	3	2	0	0	0	0	0	0	0	0	0	1	6
Heating Degree Days (base 65°F)	1,312	1,142	987	578	263	57	10	21	134	462	772	1,144	6,882
Cooling Degree Days (base 65°F)	0	0	0	6	35	131	224	177	59	7	0	0	639
Mean Precipitation (in.)	1.67	1.46	1.80	3.09	3.33	3.19	2.60	3.40	4.18	2.90	2.66	1.83	32.11
Extreme Maximum Daily Precip. (in.)	1.21	1.68	1.40	1.81	2.48	2.50	2.81	2.47	7.72	2.05	1.85	1.42	7.72
Days With ≥ 0.1" Precipitation	5	4	5	7	7	6	6	6	6	6	6	6	70
Days With ≥ 0.5" Precipitation	1	1	1	2	2	2	2	2	3	2	2	1	21
Days With ≥ 1.0" Precipitation	0	0	0	1	1	1	0	1	1	1	1	0	7
Mean Snowfall (in.)	12.6	8.4	5.3	0.9	0.0	0.0	0.0	0.0	0.0	trace	1.4	9.9	38.5
Maximum Snow Depth (in.)	***16***	***21***	9	3	0	0	0	0	0	0	5	32	***32***
Days With ≥ 1.0" Snow Depth	***14***	***12***	5	0	0	0	0	0	0	0	1	7	***39***

Frankfort 2 NE *Benzie County* Elevation: 865 ft. Latitude: 44° 39' N Longitude: 86° 12' W

	JAN	FEB	MAR	APR	MAY	JUN	JUL	AUG	SEP	OCT	NOV	DEC	YEAR
Mean Maximum Temp. (°F)	29.1	31.1	39.3	52.7	64.0	73.2	77.7	76.1	69.0	56.6	44.3	33.1	53.9
Mean Temp. (°F)	23.8	25.1	32.0	43.8	54.1	63.3	68.5	67.9	61.0	49.3	38.5	28.1	46.3
Mean Minimum Temp. (°F)	18.5	19.0	24.7	35.0	44.1	53.3	59.3	59.6	52.9	41.9	32.5	23.0	38.6
Extreme Maximum Temp. (°F)	56	63	73	85	88	91	93	95	91	84	79	62	95
Extreme Minimum Temp. (°F)	-15	-11	-10	11	25	34	39	40	31	24	10	-3	-15
Days Maximum Temp. ≥ 90°F	0	0	0	0	0	0	1	0	0	0	0	0	1
Days Maximum Temp. ≤ 32°F	19	16	8	1	0	0	0	0	0	0	2	13	59
Days Minimum Temp. ≤ 32°F	29	26	25	12	2	0	0	0	0	3	16	27	140
Days Minimum Temp. ≤ 0°F	1	1	0	0	0	0	0	0	0	0	0	0	2
Heating Degree Days (base 65°F)	1,270	1,122	1,015	629	342	112	23	27	158	484	790	1,138	7,110
Cooling Degree Days (base 65°F)	0	0	0	2	11	68	138	123	43	4	0	0	389
Mean Precipitation (in.)	2.49	1.83	1.98	2.72	3.04	3.09	2.97	3.34	4.02	3.51	3.04	2.67	34.70
Extreme Maximum Daily Precip. (in.)	1.34	1.15	2.45	1.74	2.08	2.81	2.40	4.08	3.20	2.20	2.02	1.56	4.08
Days With ≥ 0.1" Precipitation	8	6	6	6	6	6	5	6	7	8	8	9	81
Days With ≥ 0.5" Precipitation	1	1	1	2	2	2	2	2	2	2	2	1	20
Days With ≥ 1.0" Precipitation	0	0	0	0	1	1	1	1	1	1	0	0	6
Mean Snowfall (in.)	30.6	20.3	13.9	4.0	0.1	0.0	0.0	0.0	trace	0.3	8.0	27.7	104.9
Maximum Snow Depth (in.)	42	48	27	9	trace	0	0	0	trace	2	10	35	48
Days With ≥ 1.0" Snow Depth	27	26	21	2	0	0	0	0	0	0	7	21	104

Grand Marais 2 E *Alger County* Elevation: 624 ft. Latitude: 46° 40' N Longitude: 85° 57' W

	JAN	FEB	MAR	APR	MAY	JUN	JUL	AUG	SEP	OCT	NOV	DEC	YEAR
Mean Maximum Temp. (°F)	26.3	29.4	37.6	49.9	62.4	71.4	76.4	76.3	68.6	55.2	41.3	30.8	52.1
Mean Temp. (°F)	18.8	20.6	27.4	39.0	49.7	58.3	63.8	64.4	57.6	45.4	34.1	23.9	41.9
Mean Minimum Temp. (°F)	11.2	11.7	17.2	28.0	37.0	45.3	51.1	52.5	46.6	35.6	26.8	16.9	31.7
Extreme Maximum Temp. (°F)	48	56	73	87	92	97	99	97	94	84	71	57	99
Extreme Minimum Temp. (°F)	-25	-31	-23	4	17	26	30	31	24	16	-4	-17	-31
Days Maximum Temp. ≥ 90°F	0	0	0	0	0	1	2	1	0	0	0	0	4
Days Maximum Temp. ≤ 32°F	23	18	9	0	0	0	0	0	0	0	5	17	72
Days Minimum Temp. ≤ 32°F	31	28	29	23	10	2	0	0	1	11	24	30	189
Days Minimum Temp. ≤ 0°F	5	5	2	0	0	0	0	0	0	0	0	2	14
Heating Degree Days (base 65°F)	1,427	1,250	1,158	774	475	231	106	82	240	601	921	1,266	8,531
Cooling Degree Days (base 65°F)	0	0	0	1	8	38	76	71	26	1	0	0	221
Mean Precipitation (in.)	2.23	1.18	1.31	1.21	2.41	2.60	2.97	2.61	3.58	3.42	2.22	2.05	27.79
Extreme Maximum Daily Precip. (in.)	0.97	0.98	1.43	1.36	1.71	2.00	3.00	2.88	2.32	1.90	***1.03***	***0.97***	***3.00***
Days With ≥ 0.1" Precipitation	8	4	4	3	6	6	6	5	8	9	7	8	74
Days With ≥ 0.5" Precipitation	1	0	1	0	1	2	2	2	2	2	1	0	14
Days With ≥ 1.0" Precipitation	0	0	0	0	0	0	1	1	1	0	0	0	3
Mean Snowfall (in.)	40.9	24.6	15.1	4.1	0.3	0.0	0.0	0.0	trace	0.6	11.6	***35.7***	***132.9***
Maximum Snow Depth (in.)	36	42	40	26	8	0	0	0	trace	***5***	12	33	***42***
Days With ≥ 1.0" Snow Depth	30	27	28	10	0	0	0	0	0	***0***	10	26	***131***

Grosse Pointe Farms *Wayne County* Elevation: 612 ft. Latitude: 42° 23' N Longitude: 82° 54' W

	JAN	FEB	MAR	APR	MAY	JUN	JUL	AUG	SEP	OCT	NOV	DEC	YEAR
Mean Maximum Temp. (°F)	32.7	35.2	44.4	57.6	68.9	78.5	83.0	80.9	73.8	61.1	48.8	36.5	58.5
Mean Temp. (°F)	26.0	27.9	36.0	48.0	58.9	68.5	73.3	72.0	64.6	52.6	41.6	30.4	50.0
Mean Minimum Temp. (°F)	19.3	20.6	27.6	38.3	48.8	58.3	63.6	63.1	55.4	44.0	34.4	24.2	41.5
Extreme Maximum Temp. (°F)	60	69	81	90	93	105	102	101	92	88	75	69	105
Extreme Minimum Temp. (°F)	-17	-7	-6	12	29	38	43	40	33	19	14	-7	-17
Days Maximum Temp. ≥ 90°F	0	0	0	0	0	3	6	3	0	0	0	0	12
Days Maximum Temp. ≤ 32°F	15	11	4	0	0	0	0	0	0	0	1	10	41
Days Minimum Temp. ≤ 32°F	28	25	22	7	0	0	0	0	0	2	13	24	121
Days Minimum Temp. ≤ 0°F	1	1	0	0	0	0	0	0	0	0	0	1	3
Heating Degree Days (base 65°F)	1,202	1,041	892	511	223	42	5	9	93	385	694	1,068	6,165
Cooling Degree Days (base 65°F)	0	0	1	6	40	153	269	233	88	8	0	0	798
Mean Precipitation (in.)	1.94	1.96	2.37	3.09	3.26	3.64	3.51	3.47	3.47	2.90	2.81	2.57	34.99
Extreme Maximum Daily Precip. (in.)	1.42	1.95	2.08	1.72	2.16	3.31	2.91	2.21	3.48	4.30	1.91	1.98	4.30
Days With ≥ 0.1" Precipitation	6	5	6	8	7	7	6	6	7	6	7	6	77
Days With ≥ 0.5" Precipitation	1	1	1	2	2	2	2	2	2	2	2	2	21
Days With ≥ 1.0" Precipitation	0	0	0	0	1	1	1	1	1	0	0	0	5
Mean Snowfall (in.)	8.7	6.9	3.6	0.6	0.0	0.0	0.0	0.0	0.0	trace	0.6	6.5	26.9
Maximum Snow Depth (in.)	23	18	12	5	0	0	0	0	0	0	4	13	23
Days With ≥ 1.0" Snow Depth	18	15	7	0	0	0	0	0	0	0	1	8	49

Gull Lake Biol Sta *Kalamazoo County* Elevation: 910 ft. Latitude: 42° 24' N Longitude: 85° 23' W

	JAN	FEB	MAR	APR	MAY	JUN	JUL	AUG	SEP	OCT	NOV	DEC	YEAR
Mean Maximum Temp. (°F)	32.4	36.3	47.4	60.8	72.6	81.6	85.0	82.7	75.5	62.8	48.9	36.4	60.2
Mean Temp. (°F)	24.9	27.6	37.0	49.1	60.2	69.3	73.1	71.5	64.0	52.3	41.0	29.4	50.0
Mean Minimum Temp. (°F)	17.4	18.8	26.6	37.3	47.8	57.0	61.3	60.2	52.5	41.7	33.0	22.4	39.7
Extreme Maximum Temp. (°F)	61	70	79	88	94	98	101	98	***95***	***88***	74	69	***101***
Extreme Minimum Temp. (°F)	-20	-19	-7	4	25	34	40	39	***29***	***22***	10	-13	***-20***
Days Maximum Temp. ≥ 90°F	0	0	0	0	1	5	6	3	1	0	0	0	16
Days Maximum Temp. ≤ 32°F	16	10	3	0	0	0	0	0	0	0	1	10	40
Days Minimum Temp. ≤ 32°F	28	25	22	10	1	0	0	0	0	5	15	27	133
Days Minimum Temp. ≤ 0°F	3	2	0	0	0	0	0	0	0	0	0	1	6
Heating Degree Days (base 65°F)	1,236	1,052	861	480	193	34	4	13	109	395	714	1,096	6,187
Cooling Degree Days (base 65°F)	0	0	1	9	51	170	263	221	85	7	0	0	807
Mean Precipitation (in.)	2.17	1.88	2.61	3.57	3.89	3.67	3.70	4.17	4.69	3.44	3.28	2.77	39.84
Extreme Maximum Daily Precip. (in.)	1.63	2.10	1.77	2.70	3.20	3.23	4.18	2.31	***6.05***	***2.05***	***2.35***	1.32	***6.05***
Days With ≥ 0.1" Precipitation	6	5	6	8	8	7	6	7	7	7	7	7	81
Days With ≥ 0.5" Precipitation	1	1	2	2	3	3	3	3	3	2	2	1	26
Days With ≥ 1.0" Precipitation	0	0	0	1	1	1	1	1	1	1	1	0	8
Mean Snowfall (in.)	17.1	10.9	5.5	0.9	trace	0.0	0.0	0.0	0.0	***0.4***	3.9	16.9	***55.6***
Maximum Snow Depth (in.)	20	25	17	7	0	0	0	0	***0***	***3***	17	24	***25***
Days With ≥ 1.0" Snow Depth	22	19	7	1	0	0	0	0	0	***0***	2	15	***66***

The period of record for all cooperative weather station data is 1980 – 2009. See User Guide for detailed explanation of data.

Hancock Houghton Co Arpt *Houghton County* Elevation: 1,074 ft. Latitude: 47° 10' N Longitude: 88° 30' W

	JAN	FEB	MAR	APR	MAY	JUN	JUL	AUG	SEP	OCT	NOV	DEC	YEAR
Mean Maximum Temp. (°F)	22.4	24.6	32.8	46.9	61.1	70.4	75.4	73.8	64.5	50.9	37.3	26.2	48.9
Mean Temp. (°F)	16.4	17.5	25.2	38.6	51.0	60.1	65.5	64.6	56.1	43.9	31.9	20.8	41.0
Mean Minimum Temp. (°F)	10.4	10.3	17.6	30.2	40.8	49.8	55.6	55.3	47.7	36.7	26.4	15.4	33.0
Extreme Maximum Temp. (°F)	50	56	65	88	90	96	102	95	90	83	71	53	102
Extreme Minimum Temp. (°F)	-26	-23	-23	-4	22	32	37	35	24	17	-6	-13	-26
Days Maximum Temp. ≥ 90°F	0	0	0	0	0	1	1	0	0	0	0	0	2
Days Maximum Temp. ≤ 32°F	26	21	15	3	0	0	0	0	0	0	10	22	97
Days Minimum Temp. ≤ 32°F	30	27	29	19	4	0	0	0	1	9	24	30	173
Days Minimum Temp. ≤ 0°F	6	6	3	0	0	0	0	0	0	0	0	3	18
Heating Degree Days (base 65°F)	1,499	1,338	1,226	787	439	180	69	80	279	649	986	1,364	8,896
Cooling Degree Days (base 65°F)	0	0	0	1	10	40	93	73	19	1	0	0	237
Mean Precipitation (in.)	2.82	1.54	1.78	1.88	2.48	2.64	2.77	2.37	3.32	3.07	2.29	2.59	29.55
Extreme Maximum Daily Precip. (in.)	1.82	1.79	2.49	1.49	1.80	2.07	2.99	3.23	3.58	2.03	1.36	1.53	3.58
Days With ≥ 0.1" Precipitation	9	5	5	5	6	6	6	5	7	8	6	8	76
Days With ≥ 0.5" Precipitation	1	1	1	1	1	2	2	1	2	2	1	1	16
Days With ≥ 1.0" Precipitation	0	0	0	0	0	0	1	1	1	0	0	0	3
Mean Snowfall (in.)	na	na	na	na	na	na	na	na	na	na	na	na	na
Maximum Snow Depth (in.)	na	na	na	na	na	na	na	na	na	na	na	na	na
Days With ≥ 1.0" Snow Depth	na	na	na	na	na	na	na	na	na	na	na	na	na

Hart *Oceana County* Elevation: 700 ft. Latitude: 43° 41' N Longitude: 86° 21' W

	JAN	FEB	MAR	APR	MAY	JUN	JUL	AUG	SEP	OCT	NOV	DEC	YEAR
Mean Maximum Temp. (°F)	29.6	32.3	40.9	54.6	66.2	75.2	***79.8***	77.8	70.5	57.5	45.6	34.1	***55.3***
Mean Temp. (°F)	23.0	24.9	32.1	44.6	55.0	64.3	***69.1***	67.7	60.2	48.4	38.3	28.1	***46.3***
Mean Minimum Temp. (°F)	16.4	17.4	23.3	34.5	43.8	53.5	***58.3***	57.6	49.8	39.2	31.0	22.1	***37.2***
Extreme Maximum Temp. (°F)	59	65	77	84	88	98	***97***	94	89	87	71	68	***98***
Extreme Minimum Temp. (°F)	-14	-19	-6	1	24	33	***39***	37	26	22	7	-7	***-19***
Days Maximum Temp. ≥ 90°F	0	0	0	0	0	1	***1***	1	0	0	0	0	***3***
Days Maximum Temp. ≤ 32°F	19	14	7	1	0	0	***0***	0	0	0	2	12	***55***
Days Minimum Temp. ≤ 32°F	29	26	25	13	3	0	***0***	0	1	8	19	27	***151***
Days Minimum Temp. ≤ 0°F	2	2	1	0	0	0	***0***	0	0	0	0	1	***6***
Heating Degree Days (base 65°F)	1,294	1,128	1,012	610	322	95	***26***	35	180	511	793	1,137	***7,143***
Cooling Degree Days (base 65°F)	0	0	0	3	19	82	***160***	127	42	3	0	0	***436***
Mean Precipitation (in.)	2.59	1.89	2.13	2.95	3.71	3.22	***3.01***	3.81	3.88	3.57	3.33	2.68	***36.77***
Extreme Maximum Daily Precip. (in.)	1.70	1.51	1.28	1.80	4.65	3.75	***4.60***	4.83	5.43	2.50	3.45	1.90	***5.43***
Days With ≥ 0.1" Precipitation	8	5	5	6	6	6	***6***	6	7	8	7	8	***78***
Days With ≥ 0.5" Precipitation	1	1	1	2	3	2	***2***	3	3	3	2	1	***24***
Days With ≥ 1.0" Precipitation	0	0	0	1	1	1	***1***	1	1	1	1	0	***8***
Mean Snowfall (in.)	25.7	17.3	6.7	1.8	trace	0.0	***0.0***	0.0	0.0	trace	3.9	22.7	***78.1***
Maximum Snow Depth (in.)	***39***	***35***	***15***	***8***	trace	0	***0***	0	***0***	***1***	10	***31***	***39***
Days With ≥ 1.0" Snow Depth	***20***	***18***	8	1	0	0	***0***	0	0	0	2	***13***	***62***

Holland *Ottawa County* Elevation: 609 ft. Latitude: 42° 47' N Longitude: 86° 07' W

	JAN	FEB	MAR	APR	MAY	JUN	JUL	AUG	SEP	OCT	NOV	DEC	YEAR
Mean Maximum Temp. (°F)	33.0	35.9	45.3	58.3	69.7	79.2	83.3	81.8	74.4	61.3	48.6	36.8	59.0
Mean Temp. (°F)	26.0	28.1	36.0	47.7	58.2	67.6	72.2	70.9	63.2	51.4	40.9	30.2	49.4
Mean Minimum Temp. (°F)	18.8	20.4	26.4	37.0	46.8	56.1	61.0	59.9	52.1	41.5	33.1	23.5	39.7
Extreme Maximum Temp. (°F)	65	72	80	91	93	101	100	97	93	86	75	70	101
Extreme Minimum Temp. (°F)	-11	-11	-4	5	25	33	41	40	27	22	11	-9	-11
Days Maximum Temp. ≥ 90°F	0	0	0	0	0	3	5	2	0	0	0	0	10
Days Maximum Temp. ≤ 32°F	14	10	3	0	0	0	0	0	0	0	1	9	37
Days Minimum Temp. ≤ 32°F	28	26	23	10	1	0	0	0	0	4	14	26	132
Days Minimum Temp. ≤ 0°F	1	1	0	0	0	0	0	0	0	0	0	0	2
Heating Degree Days (base 65°F)	1,203	1,038	894	521	245	54	9	14	117	422	716	1,074	6,307
Cooling Degree Days (base 65°F)	0	0	0	9	40	139	238	203	71	8	0	0	708
Mean Precipitation (in.)	na	***1.32***	1.71	3.00	3.85	3.53	3.40	3.53	3.83	3.71	3.31	***2.60***	na
Extreme Maximum Daily Precip. (in.)	2.00	***2.00***	1.50	2.37	4.10	6.87	7.99	***3.00***	2.97	3.20	***2.50***	2.50	***7.99***
Days With ≥ 0.1" Precipitation	4	4	4	6	7	6	5	5	7	7	6	5	66
Days With ≥ 0.5" Precipitation	1	1	1	2	3	2	2	2	3	2	2	1	22
Days With ≥ 1.0" Precipitation	0	0	0	1	1	1	1	1	1	1	1	0	8
Mean Snowfall (in.)	20.8	13.7	5.2	1.1	trace	0.0	0.0	0.0	0.0	0.2	3.3	20.4	64.7
Maximum Snow Depth (in.)	36	23	14	12	trace	0	0	0	0	2	7	22	36
Days With ≥ 1.0" Snow Depth	15	12	5	1	0	0	0	0	0	0	2	10	45

Iron Mtn-Kingsford WWTP *Dickinson County* Elevation: 1,060 ft. Latitude: 45° 47' N Longitude: 88° 05' W

	JAN	FEB	MAR	APR	MAY	JUN	JUL	AUG	SEP	OCT	NOV	DEC	YEAR
Mean Maximum Temp. (°F)	24.5	29.1	38.9	53.7	66.8	76.2	80.4	78.1	69.6	55.6	40.7	28.2	53.5
Mean Temp. (°F)	13.7	17.6	27.7	41.7	53.9	63.6	68.1	66.3	57.8	44.9	32.2	19.4	42.2
Mean Minimum Temp. (°F)	2.9	6.1	16.5	29.7	40.9	51.0	55.7	54.5	46.0	34.1	23.7	10.6	31.0
Extreme Maximum Temp. (°F)	53	60	77	94	95	100	100	98	98	88	75	64	100
Extreme Minimum Temp. (°F)	-33	-39	-24	0	16	29	37	35	22	13	-8	-23	-39
Days Maximum Temp. ≥ 90°F	0	0	0	0	0	2	3	1	0	0	0	0	6
Days Maximum Temp. ≤ 32°F	24	18	9	1	0	0	0	0	0	0	6	20	78
Days Minimum Temp. ≤ 32°F	31	28	29	19	5	0	0	0	2	15	26	30	185
Days Minimum Temp. ≤ 0°F	14	10	4	0	0	0	0	0	0	0	0	8	36
Heating Degree Days (base 65°F)	1,585	1,334	1,149	693	354	112	37	56	236	618	978	1,407	8,559
Cooling Degree Days (base 65°F)	0	0	0	1	17	77	139	103	26	1	0	0	364
Mean Precipitation (in.)	1.29	1.00	1.59	2.30	3.04	3.30	3.37	3.52	3.45	3.07	1.89	1.53	29.35
Extreme Maximum Daily Precip. (in.)	1.55	1.17	2.38	1.61	2.00	2.82	4.05	2.68	1.91	2.72	1.84	1.02	4.05
Days With ≥ 0.1" Precipitation	4	3	5	6	7	8	7	7	7	6	5	5	70
Days With ≥ 0.5" Precipitation	0	0	1	2	2	2	2	3	2	2	1	1	18
Days With ≥ 1.0" Precipitation	0	0	0	0	1	1	0	1	1	1	0	0	5
Mean Snowfall (in.)	14.2	9.4	10.6	4.6	0.6	0.0	0.0	0.0	trace	0.7	5.8	13.8	59.7
Maximum Snow Depth (in.)	34	34	31	18	8	0	0	0	trace	8	10	27	34
Days With ≥ 1.0" Snow Depth	30	28	23	3	0	0	0	0	0	0	6	24	114

The period of record for all cooperative weather station data is 1980 – 2009. See User Guide for detailed explanation of data.

Ironwood *Gogebic County* Elevation: 1,430 ft. Latitude: 46° 28' N Longitude: 90° 11' W

	JAN	FEB	MAR	APR	MAY	JUN	JUL	AUG	SEP	OCT	NOV	DEC	YEAR
Mean Maximum Temp. (°F)	20.6	25.5	35.3	49.9	63.2	72.3	76.5	74.7	66.2	52.3	37.5	24.5	49.9
Mean Temp. (°F)	11.5	15.0	24.6	39.2	51.9	61.3	65.8	64.0	55.8	43.1	30.0	16.6	39.9
Mean Minimum Temp. (°F)	2.3	4.4	13.9	28.4	40.4	50.2	55.0	53.3	45.4	33.9	22.3	8.6	29.8
Extreme Maximum Temp. (°F)	55	60	72	84	92	94	97	96	90	86	72	59	97
Extreme Minimum Temp. (°F)	-41	-37	-34	-12	16	26	35	32	22	5	-10	-36	-41
Days Maximum Temp. ≥ 90°F	0	0	0	0	0	0	1	1	0	0	0	0	2
Days Maximum Temp. ≤ 32°F	26	20	13	2	0	0	0	0	0	1	10	24	96
Days Minimum Temp. ≤ 32°F	31	28	29	21	7	1	0	0	2	15	26	31	191
Days Minimum Temp. ≤ 0°F	13	11	5	0	0	0	0	0	0	0	1	9	39
Heating Degree Days (base 65°F)	1,656	1,409	1,246	770	414	159	70	93	292	673	1,042	1,495	9,319
Cooling Degree Days (base 65°F)	0	0	0	2	14	56	102	70	22	1	0	0	267
Mean Precipitation (in.)	1.96	1.25	1.98	2.63	3.08	3.51	4.14	3.42	4.02	3.92	2.65	2.11	34.67
Extreme Maximum Daily Precip. (in.)	1.46	1.12	1.64	2.26	4.09	2.25	2.82	2.06	2.54	2.10	2.26	1.13	4.09
Days With ≥ 0.1" Precipitation	6	4	5	7	7	8	7	7	8	8	7	7	81
Days With ≥ 0.5" Precipitation	1	0	1	2	2	2	3	2	3	2	1	1	20
Days With ≥ 1.0" Precipitation	0	0	0	0	1	1	1	1	1	1	0	0	6
Mean Snowfall (in.)	45.2	26.7	24.6	11.4	1.8	0.0	0.0	0.0	0.3	6.8	24.9	45.5	187.2
Maximum Snow Depth (in.)	47	44	42	27	13	0	0	0	6	15	27	32	47
Days With ≥ 1.0" Snow Depth	31	28	27	9	1	0	0	0	0	3	16	30	145

Lapeer WWTP *Lapeer County* Elevation: 819 ft. Latitude: 43° 04' N Longitude: 83° 18' W

	JAN	FEB	MAR	APR	MAY	JUN	JUL	AUG	SEP	OCT	NOV	DEC	YEAR
Mean Maximum Temp. (°F)	30.2	33.1	43.3	57.2	68.9	77.9	82.1	79.9	73.1	60.0	47.1	34.3	57.3
Mean Temp. (°F)	22.7	24.5	33.6	46.1	57.0	66.1	70.7	68.7	61.5	49.7	39.0	27.5	47.3
Mean Minimum Temp. (°F)	15.1	15.9	23.8	35.1	45.1	54.4	59.2	57.5	49.8	39.3	30.9	20.7	37.2
Extreme Maximum Temp. (°F)	61	68	81	87	92	100	100	99	94	***86***	75	69	***100***
Extreme Minimum Temp. (°F)	-26	-24	-16	7	24	32	36	32	26	***17***	8	-10	***-26***
Days Maximum Temp. ≥ 90°F	0	0	0	0	0	2	4	2	0	0	0	0	8
Days Maximum Temp. ≤ 32°F	18	14	6	1	0	0	0	0	0	0	2	13	54
Days Minimum Temp. ≤ 32°F	29	27	26	13	2	0	0	0	1	7	18	28	151
Days Minimum Temp. ≤ 0°F	5	4	1	0	0	0	0	0	0	0	0	2	12
Heating Degree Days (base 65°F)	1,304	1,140	968	565	274	69	15	29	154	472	774	1,155	6,919
Cooling Degree Days (base 65°F)	0	0	1	6	34	110	198	151	54	4	0	0	558
Mean Precipitation (in.)	1.59	1.50	1.75	2.73	3.12	3.02	3.74	3.34	3.85	2.86	2.64	1.76	31.90
Extreme Maximum Daily Precip. (in.)	1.22	1.18	1.36	2.14	1.95	2.32	3.60	2.39	3.72	***3.53***	1.70	1.34	***3.72***
Days With ≥ 0.1" Precipitation	5	4	5	6	6	6	6	7	6	6	6	5	68
Days With ≥ 0.5" Precipitation	1	1	1	2	2	2	3	2	3	2	2	1	22
Days With ≥ 1.0" Precipitation	0	0	0	0	1	1	1	1	1	0	0	0	5
Mean Snowfall (in.)	***10.0***	7.8	4.7	1.3	0.0	0.0	0.0	0.0	0.0	***0.1***	1.4	8.1	***33.4***
Maximum Snow Depth (in.)	***19***	***14***	12	6	0	0	0	0	0	***1***	5	***17***	***19***
Days With ≥ 1.0" Snow Depth	***18***	***17***	7	1	0	0	0	0	0	***0***	1	12	***56***

Manistique *Schoolcraft County* Elevation: 620 ft. Latitude: 45° 57' N Longitude: 86° 15' W

	JAN	FEB	MAR	APR	MAY	JUN	JUL	AUG	SEP	OCT	NOV	DEC	YEAR
Mean Maximum Temp. (°F)	25.6	27.5	34.9	46.9	57.8	67.7	73.3	73.6	65.7	52.9	41.1	30.3	49.8
Mean Temp. (°F)	17.6	19.1	26.7	38.9	49.4	59.1	64.8	64.8	57.2	45.4	34.5	23.4	41.7
Mean Minimum Temp. (°F)	9.6	10.7	18.3	30.8	40.8	50.5	56.2	56.0	48.6	37.7	27.8	16.3	33.6
Extreme Maximum Temp. (°F)	46	47	69	84	87	96	93	94	87	74	65	59	96
Extreme Minimum Temp. (°F)	-25	-25	-19	3	25	34	39	38	19	20	3	-15	-25
Days Maximum Temp. ≥ 90°F	0	0	0	0	0	0	0	0	0	0	0	0	0
Days Maximum Temp. ≤ 32°F	23	19	11	1	0	0	0	0	0	0	5	17	76
Days Minimum Temp. ≤ 32°F	31	28	28	17	3	0	0	0	1	9	22	29	168
Days Minimum Temp. ≤ 0°F	8	6	2	0	0	0	0	0	0	0	0	4	20
Heating Degree Days (base 65°F)	1,461	1,289	1,182	776	479	188	64	63	241	602	909	1,284	8,538
Cooling Degree Days (base 65°F)	0	0	0	1	1	18	64	64	13	0	0	0	161
Mean Precipitation (in.)	na	***0.66***	1.33	2.35	2.58	2.90	2.93	2.94	3.36	3.30	2.38	***1.45***	na
Extreme Maximum Daily Precip. (in.)	***0.84***	***0.58***	***1.30***	***3.86***	***2.46***	***1.61***	***3.70***	***2.41***	***3.85***	***2.71***	***1.43***	***1.50***	***3.86***
Days With ≥ 0.1" Precipitation	2	2	3	5	6	6	6	6	7	7	5	3	58
Days With ≥ 0.5" Precipitation	0	0	1	1	2	2	1	2	2	2	2	1	16
Days With ≥ 1.0" Precipitation	0	0	0	0	0	1	0	1	1	1	0	0	4
Mean Snowfall (in.)	***21.6***	14.3	11.0	2.7	trace	0.0	0.0	0.0	0.0	0.2	4.7	19.6	***74.1***
Maximum Snow Depth (in.)	55	61	48	19	1	0	0	0	0	***1***	13	42	***61***
Days With ≥ 1.0" Snow Depth	26	27	23	3	0	0	0	0	0	0	4	18	101

Marquette *Marquette County* Elevation: 665 ft. Latitude: 46° 33' N Longitude: 87° 23' W

	JAN	FEB	MAR	APR	MAY	JUN	JUL	AUG	SEP	OCT	NOV	DEC	YEAR
Mean Maximum Temp. (°F)	26.1	29.1	36.9	48.2	60.3	69.2	75.1	74.9	67.4	54.4	41.0	30.0	51.0
Mean Temp. (°F)	19.3	21.5	29.2	40.1	50.8	59.8	66.1	66.4	59.1	47.0	35.1	23.9	43.2
Mean Minimum Temp. (°F)	12.5	13.8	21.5	32.0	41.2	50.3	57.1	57.9	50.7	39.5	29.2	17.8	35.3
Extreme Maximum Temp. (°F)	52	59	77	91	91	99	102	99	97	85	74	60	102
Extreme Minimum Temp. (°F)	-22	-24	-11	4	23	31	41	42	30	19	1	-17	-24
Days Maximum Temp. ≥ 90°F	0	0	0	0	0	1	1	1	0	0	0	0	3
Days Maximum Temp. ≤ 32°F	23	18	10	1	0	0	0	0	0	0	5	18	75
Days Minimum Temp. ≤ 32°F	31	27	27	16	3	0	0	0	0	5	20	29	158
Days Minimum Temp. ≤ 0°F	5	4	1	0	0	0	0	0	0	0	0	2	12
Heating Degree Days (base 65°F)	1,409	1,223	1,103	742	444	193	62	52	204	553	889	1,267	8,141
Cooling Degree Days (base 65°F)	0	0	0	2	9	43	104	103	33	2	0	0	296
Mean Precipitation (in.)	1.86	1.30	2.01	2.38	2.57	2.54	2.57	2.64	3.33	3.16	2.64	1.93	28.93
Extreme Maximum Daily Precip. (in.)	1.28	1.28	1.12	1.88	5.12	2.13	2.48	2.76	2.53	2.25	1.95	1.11	5.12
Days With ≥ 0.1" Precipitation	6	4	5	6	6	6	6	6	7	8	7	6	73
Days With ≥ 0.5" Precipitation	0	0	1	1	1	2	2	2	2	2	1	1	15
Days With ≥ 1.0" Precipitation	0	0	0	0	0	0	0	0	1	0	0	0	1
Mean Snowfall (in.)	28.3	21.2	20.7	7.6	0.6	0.0	0.0	0.0	0.0	1.0	10.8	25.1	115.3
Maximum Snow Depth (in.)	37	33	41	23	9	0	0	0	trace	4	15	26	41
Days With ≥ 1.0" Snow Depth	30	28	28	8	0	0	0	0	0	1	9	26	130

The period of record for all cooperative weather station data is 1980 – 2009. See User Guide for detailed explanation of data.

Milford Gm Proving Ground *Livingston County* Elevation: 990 ft. Latitude: 42° 35' N Longitude: 83° 42' W

	JAN	FEB	MAR	APR	MAY	JUN	JUL	AUG	SEP	OCT	NOV	DEC	YEAR
Mean Maximum Temp. (°F)	30.2	32.8	43.0	56.3	67.9	76.8	80.9	78.9	71.3	58.7	46.4	33.6	56.4
Mean Temp. (°F)	22.6	24.6	33.5	45.9	56.9	66.2	70.3	68.9	61.2	49.2	38.5	26.7	47.0
Mean Minimum Temp. (°F)	15.2	16.1	23.9	35.4	46.0	55.5	59.6	58.7	51.1	39.7	30.5	19.9	37.6
Extreme Maximum Temp. (°F)	61	67	79	86	92	94	97	97	93	84	75	64	97
Extreme Minimum Temp. (°F)	-23	-16	-8	12	24	35	41	39	26	20	8	-18	-23
Days Maximum Temp. ≥ 90°F	0	0	0	0	0	1	2	1	0	0	0	0	4
Days Maximum Temp. ≤ 32°F	18	14	6	1	0	0	0	0	0	0	3	14	56
Days Minimum Temp. ≤ 32°F	28	26	25	12	2	0	0	0	0	7	18	27	145
Days Minimum Temp. ≤ 0°F	4	3	1	0	0	0	0	0	0	0	0	2	10
Heating Degree Days (base 65°F)	1,307	1,138	970	572	275	65	14	27	156	485	789	1,180	6,978
Cooling Degree Days (base 65°F)	0	0	0	4	30	108	185	154	50	4	0	0	535
Mean Precipitation (in.)	1.59	1.91	1.78	2.46	3.17	3.29	2.82	3.03	2.99	2.43	2.45	1.98	29.90
Extreme Maximum Daily Precip. (in.)	1.75	2.67	1.53	2.36	na	na	2.52	2.56	5.08	2.00	1.70	1.34	na
Days With ≥ 0.1" Precipitation	4	4	5	6	6	6	5	6	6	5	5	5	63
Days With ≥ 0.5" Precipitation	1	1	1	1	2	2	2	2	2	1	2	1	18
Days With ≥ 1.0" Precipitation	0	0	0	0	1	1	1	1	1	0	0	0	5
Mean Snowfall (in.)	11.0	7.6	3.5	1.2	trace	0.0	0.0	0.0	0.0	0.1	1.6	8.4	33.4
Maximum Snow Depth (in.)	18	12	13	5	trace	0	0	0	0	trace	4	14	18
Days With ≥ 1.0" Snow Depth	18	16	5	0	0	0	0	0	0	0	1	11	51

Mio Hydro Plant *Oscoda County* Elevation: 959 ft. Latitude: 44° 40' N Longitude: 84° 08' W

	JAN	FEB	MAR	APR	MAY	JUN	JUL	AUG	SEP	OCT	NOV	DEC	YEAR
Mean Maximum Temp. (°F)	28.3	31.9	41.0	54.6	67.2	76.9	81.9	79.3	71.0	57.5	44.2	33.0	55.6
Mean Temp. (°F)	19.2	21.1	29.6	42.7	54.1	63.8	68.9	66.6	58.6	46.6	36.0	25.1	44.3
Mean Minimum Temp. (°F)	10.0	10.3	18.1	30.8	41.0	50.7	55.8	53.7	46.0	35.6	27.7	17.1	33.1
Extreme Maximum Temp. (°F)	55	61	78	88	95	103	101	101	94	85	74	66	103
Extreme Minimum Temp. (°F)	-29	-31	-22	-1	22	30	37	24	25	17	-8	-21	-31
Days Maximum Temp. ≥ 90°F	0	0	0	0	0	2	4	2	0	0	0	0	8
Days Maximum Temp. ≤ 32°F	21	15	7	1	0	0	0	0	0	0	3	14	61
Days Minimum Temp. ≤ 32°F	30	27	28	18	6	0	0	0	2	12	22	29	174
Days Minimum Temp. ≤ 0°F	8	7	3	0	0	0	0	0	0	0	0	4	22
Heating Degree Days (base 65°F)	1,412	1,235	1,091	664	351	108	28	53	217	566	864	1,231	7,820
Cooling Degree Days (base 65°F)	0	0	0	3	20	79	156	108	29	2	0	0	397
Mean Precipitation (in.)	1.42	1.10	1.46	2.22	2.62	2.73	2.83	3.26	2.83	2.56	2.14	1.42	26.59
Extreme Maximum Daily Precip. (in.)	1.00	1.05	2.12	1.30	1.58	2.39	3.75	3.13	2.31	2.10	1.62	1.06	3.75
Days With ≥ 0.1" Precipitation	5	4	4	6	7	6	6	7	7	6	6	4	68
Days With ≥ 0.5" Precipitation	1	1	1	1	2	2	2	2	2	2	1	1	18
Days With ≥ 1.0" Precipitation	0	0	0	0	0	0	1	0	1	0	0	0	2
Mean Snowfall (in.)	na	4.7	na	1.4	trace	0.0	0.0	0.0	0.0	0.1	2.0	na	na
Maximum Snow Depth (in.)	29	32	27	7	4	0	0	0	0	3	14	14	32
Days With ≥ 1.0" Snow Depth	25	23	16	3	0	0	0	0	0	0	6	18	91

Munising *Alger County* Elevation: 680 ft. Latitude: 46° 25' N Longitude: 86° 40' W

	JAN	FEB	MAR	APR	MAY	JUN	JUL	AUG	SEP	OCT	NOV	DEC	YEAR
Mean Maximum Temp. (°F)	24.9	27.1	35.2	47.5	60.9	69.6	74.7	74.0	66.1	53.4	40.6	29.4	50.3
Mean Temp. (°F)	18.0	19.2	27.6	38.8	50.2	59.0	64.9	64.7	57.5	45.8	34.4	23.2	42.0
Mean Minimum Temp. (°F)	11.0	11.3	19.8	30.1	39.5	48.4	55.0	55.4	48.9	38.0	28.2	17.0	33.6
Extreme Maximum Temp. (°F)	47	57	71	89	92	93	101	98	90	83	70	57	101
Extreme Minimum Temp. (°F)	-27	-21	-18	3	20	29	35	33	28	13	5	-21	-27
Days Maximum Temp. ≥ 90°F	0	0	0	0	0	0	1	1	0	0	0	0	2
Days Maximum Temp. ≤ 32°F	24	20	12	2	0	0	0	0	0	0	5	19	82
Days Minimum Temp. ≤ 32°F	31	28	28	19	6	1	0	0	0	7	21	30	171
Days Minimum Temp. ≤ 0°F	6	5	1	0	0	0	0	0	0	0	0	3	15
Heating Degree Days (base 65°F)	1,451	1,288	1,151	780	458	210	81	76	240	591	910	1,289	8,525
Cooling Degree Days (base 65°F)	0	0	0	1	7	37	85	75	22	1	0	0	228
Mean Precipitation (in.)	3.30	2.11	2.21	2.18	2.83	2.77	3.24	3.04	3.92	4.22	3.08	3.61	36.51
Extreme Maximum Daily Precip. (in.)	1.40	1.16	1.86	1.22	1.76	1.64	3.12	3.16	2.13	2.00	2.14	1.41	3.16
Days With ≥ 0.1" Precipitation	12	7	7	7	7	7	7	6	9	10	9	12	100
Days With ≥ 0.5" Precipitation	1	1	1	1	2	2	2	2	3	3	2	1	21
Days With ≥ 1.0" Precipitation	0	0	0	0	0	1	1	1	1	1	0	0	5
Mean Snowfall (in.)	42.4	28.2	19.3	7.2	0.4	0.0	0.0	0.0	trace	1.8	12.9	39.5	151.7
Maximum Snow Depth (in.)	na	na	na	na	1	0	0	0	trace	4	19	na	na
Days With ≥ 1.0" Snow Depth	na	na	na	11	0	0	0	0	0	1	9	23	na

Owosso Wwtp *Shiawassee County* Elevation: 729 ft. Latitude: 43° 01' N Longitude: 84° 11' W

	JAN	FEB	MAR	APR	MAY	JUN	JUL	AUG	SEP	OCT	NOV	DEC	YEAR
Mean Maximum Temp. (°F)	29.7	32.5	43.1	56.9	68.5	78.0	81.9	79.8	72.8	59.8	47.4	34.8	57.1
Mean Temp. (°F)	22.1	24.3	33.4	45.8	56.8	66.3	70.3	68.8	61.6	49.7	39.3	28.0	47.2
Mean Minimum Temp. (°F)	14.4	16.0	23.7	34.7	45.0	54.6	58.7	57.7	50.4	39.5	31.3	21.2	37.3
Extreme Maximum Temp. (°F)	62	67	80	88	91	99	101	97	92	89	76	69	101
Extreme Minimum Temp. (°F)	-20	-17	-8	3	25	33	40	37	26	21	9	-10	-20
Days Maximum Temp. ≥ 90°F	0	0	0	0	0	2	3	2	0	0	0	0	7
Days Maximum Temp. ≤ 32°F	19	14	6	1	0	0	0	0	0	0	2	12	54
Days Minimum Temp. ≤ 32°F	29	26	25	14	2	0	0	0	0	8	18	28	150
Days Minimum Temp. ≤ 0°F	5	3	1	0	0	0	0	0	0	0	0	1	10
Heating Degree Days (base 65°F)	1,324	1,144	973	573	277	66	17	30	151	474	763	1,138	6,930
Cooling Degree Days (base 65°F)	0	0	1	4	30	113	189	154	57	6	0	0	554
Mean Precipitation (in.)	1.59	1.48	1.77	3.02	3.46	3.16	3.05	3.26	3.66	2.86	2.58	2.06	31.95
Extreme Maximum Daily Precip. (in.)	1.56	1.63	1.60	1.88	2.54	2.44	1.95	3.62	3.00	4.67	1.68	1.81	4.67
Days With ≥ 0.1" Precipitation	5	4	5	7	6	6	6	6	6	7	6	6	70
Days With ≥ 0.5" Precipitation	1	1	1	2	2	2	2	2	3	2	2	1	21
Days With ≥ 1.0" Precipitation	0	0	0	0	1	1	1	1	1	0	0	0	5
Mean Snowfall (in.)	10.3	7.7	4.3	0.9	trace	0.0	0.0	0.0	0.0	0.2	1.6	10.6	35.6
Maximum Snow Depth (in.)	19	22	10	5	trace	0	0	0	0	3	5	16	22
Days With ≥ 1.0" Snow Depth	18	13	6	0	0	0	0	0	0	0	1	12	50

The period of record for all cooperative weather station data is 1980 – 2009. See User Guide for detailed explanation of data.

Port Huron *St. Clair County* Elevation: 589 ft. Latitude: 42° 59' N Longitude: 82° 25' W

	JAN	FEB	MAR	APR	MAY	JUN	JUL	AUG	SEP	OCT	NOV	DEC	YEAR
Mean Maximum Temp. (°F)	31.4	33.6	42.4	55.2	67.0	77.1	81.9	80.5	73.4	60.4	47.6	35.3	57.2
Mean Temp. (°F)	24.4	26.0	34.1	45.7	56.7	66.8	72.2	71.1	63.8	51.4	40.4	28.8	48.5
Mean Minimum Temp. (°F)	17.3	18.4	25.7	36.1	46.4	56.3	62.5	61.7	54.2	42.4	33.1	22.2	39.7
Extreme Maximum Temp. (°F)	60	69	80	87	96	102	101	102	95	90	75	66	102
Extreme Minimum Temp. (°F)	-19	-8	-7	13	28	35	43	41	32	20	12	-7	-19
Days Maximum Temp. ≥ 90°F	0	0	0	0	1	3	4	2	1	0	0	0	11
Days Maximum Temp. ≤ 32°F	17	13	6	0	0	0	0	0	0	0	1	11	48
Days Minimum Temp. ≤ 32°F	29	26	25	9	0	0	0	0	0	2	15	26	132
Days Minimum Temp. ≤ 0°F	2	1	0	0	0	0	0	0	0	0	0	1	4
Heating Degree Days (base 65°F)	1,252	1,096	950	577	278	63	6	12	106	421	732	1,115	6,608
Cooling Degree Days (base 65°F)	0	0	0	3	29	122	237	209	78	7	0	0	685
Mean Precipitation (in.)	1.94	1.93	2.13	2.90	3.07	3.42	3.22	3.27	3.76	2.75	3.03	2.21	33.63
Extreme Maximum Daily Precip. (in.)	1.45	1.80	1.65	1.95	2.98	2.61	3.72	2.74	3.97	2.87	2.06	1.52	3.97
Days With ≥ 0.1" Precipitation	5	5	6	8	7	7	7	6	7	6	7	6	77
Days With ≥ 0.5" Precipitation	1	1	1	1	2	2	2	2	2	2	2	1	19
Days With ≥ 1.0" Precipitation	0	0	0	0	1	1	1	1	1	0	1	0	6
Mean Snowfall (in.)	10.9	9.0	4.7	0.7	0.0	0.0	0.0	0.0	0.0	0.0	1.3	8.3	34.9
Maximum Snow Depth (in.)	16	18	11	8	0	0	0	0	0	0	12	19	19
Days With ≥ 1.0" Snow Depth	17	16	6	0	0	0	0	0	0	0	1	11	51

St Johns *Clinton County* Elevation: 743 ft. Latitude: 43° 01' N Longitude: 84° 33' W

	JAN	FEB	MAR	APR	MAY	JUN	JUL	AUG	SEP	OCT	NOV	DEC	YEAR
Mean Maximum Temp. (°F)	30.2	33.2	43.8	57.5	69.5	78.9	82.9	80.7	73.8	60.5	47.0	34.6	57.7
Mean Temp. (°F)	22.7	25.0	34.1	46.4	57.7	67.2	71.3	69.4	62.1	50.1	38.8	27.7	47.7
Mean Minimum Temp. (°F)	15.0	16.7	24.4	35.2	45.8	55.6	59.6	58.1	50.3	39.7	30.6	20.8	37.6
Extreme Maximum Temp. (°F)	61	69	79	89	93	98	100	100	92	88	75	69	100
Extreme Minimum Temp. (°F)	-19	-12	-10	7	25	34	41	38	27	20	0	-13	-19
Days Maximum Temp. ≥ 90°F	0	0	0	0	0	3	5	2	1	0	0	0	11
Days Maximum Temp. ≤ 32°F	18	14	5	1	0	0	0	0	0	0	2	12	52
Days Minimum Temp. ≤ 32°F	29	26	25	13	2	0	0	0	0	7	19	28	149
Days Minimum Temp. ≤ 0°F	4	3	0	0	0	0	0	0	0	0	0	1	8
Heating Degree Days (base 65°F)	1,306	1,126	952	558	254	55	12	24	142	461	781	1,149	6,820
Cooling Degree Days (base 65°F)	0	0	1	6	35	130	212	167	61	6	0	0	618
Mean Precipitation (in.)	1.79	1.50	2.10	3.26	3.58	3.23	3.23	3.35	3.73	2.97	2.67	1.73	33.14
Extreme Maximum Daily Precip. (in.)	1.50	2.40	1.80	4.50	4.86	3.45	3.36	2.80	3.82	6.50	2.18	1.18	6.50
Days With ≥ 0.1" Precipitation	5	4	5	8	7	6	6	6	6	7	6	5	71
Days With ≥ 0.5" Precipitation	1	1	1	2	2	2	2	2	3	2	2	1	21
Days With ≥ 1.0" Precipitation	0	0	0	0	1	1	1	1	1	0	1	0	6
Mean Snowfall (in.)	13.5	9.5	5.8	1.3	trace	0.0	0.0	0.0	0.0	0.3	2.1	9.7	42.2
Maximum Snow Depth (in.)	24	27	10	6	trace	0	0	0	0	3	5	14	27
Days With ≥ 1.0" Snow Depth	18	15	6	1	0	0	0	0	0	0	1	10	51

Stambaugh 2 SSE *Iron County* Elevation: 1,560 ft. Latitude: 46° 03' N Longitude: 88° 37' W

	JAN	FEB	MAR	APR	MAY	JUN	JUL	AUG	SEP	OCT	NOV	DEC	YEAR
Mean Maximum Temp. (°F)	22.0	26.5	36.5	51.5	64.6	73.4	77.2	75.3	66.5	53.1	37.9	25.5	50.8
Mean Temp. (°F)	10.9	13.7	23.7	38.7	50.8	59.9	63.8	61.9	53.5	41.7	29.2	16.2	38.7
Mean Minimum Temp. (°F)	-0.3	0.8	10.8	25.8	37.0	46.3	50.3	48.6	40.6	30.4	20.4	6.9	26.5
Extreme Maximum Temp. (°F)	55	60	73	92	90	97	96	96	94	84	72	59	97
Extreme Minimum Temp. (°F)	-40	-45	-31	-11	16	25	32	29	20	10	-11	-41	-45
Days Maximum Temp. ≥ 90°F	0	0	0	0	0	0	1	0	0	0	0	0	1
Days Maximum Temp. ≤ 32°F	26	20	11	2	0	0	0	0	0	0	10	23	92
Days Minimum Temp. ≤ 32°F	31	28	30	24	11	2	0	1	6	20	27	31	211
Days Minimum Temp. ≤ 0°F	16	14	8	0	0	0	0	0	0	0	1	10	49
Heating Degree Days (base 65°F)	1,675	1,447	1,275	784	439	184	97	133	348	715	1,069	1,507	9,673
Cooling Degree Days (base 65°F)	0	0	0	1	8	37	67	45	11	1	0	0	170
Mean Precipitation (in.)	1.03	0.84	1.35	2.24	3.03	3.61	4.08	3.13	3.54	3.07	1.91	1.29	29.12
Extreme Maximum Daily Precip. (in.)	0.96	0.87	1.21	1.78	1.74	3.70	5.20	1.96	2.94	2.94	1.84	0.88	5.20
Days With ≥ 0.1" Precipitation	4	3	4	6	7	8	8	7	8	7	5	4	71
Days With ≥ 0.5" Precipitation	0	0	1	1	2	2	3	2	2	2	1	0	16
Days With ≥ 1.0" Precipitation	0	0	0	0	1	1	1	1	1	1	0	0	6
Mean Snowfall (in.)	14.9	10.6	11.5	5.8	0.4	0.0	0.0	trace	trace	2.0	8.7	15.2	69.1
Maximum Snow Depth (in.)	39	32	34	34	7	0	0	trace	trace	6	11	39	39
Days With ≥ 1.0" Snow Depth	31	28	27	6	0	0	0	0	0	1	10	27	130

Stephenson 8 WNW *Menominee County* Elevation: 709 ft. Latitude: 45° 27' N Longitude: 87° 45' W

	JAN	FEB	MAR	APR	MAY	JUN	JUL	AUG	SEP	OCT	NOV	DEC	YEAR
Mean Maximum Temp. (°F)	26.3	29.6	40.2	54.2	67.0	76.3	***80.2***	78.2	69.6	57.0	42.0	30.1	***54.2***
Mean Temp. (°F)	15.5	17.6	28.6	41.9	53.4	62.9	***67.0***	65.5	57.1	45.4	32.9	21.0	***42.4***
Mean Minimum Temp. (°F)	4.6	5.5	16.9	29.6	39.8	49.4	***53.8***	52.8	44.6	33.6	23.7	11.7	***30.5***
Extreme Maximum Temp. (°F)	56	58	78	91	93	96	99	***99***	***93***	88	***76***	62	***99***
Extreme Minimum Temp. (°F)	-39	-45	-21	0	19	28	35	***30***	***21***	13	***-12***	-24	***-45***
Days Maximum Temp. ≥ 90°F	0	0	0	0	0	2	3	1	0	0	0	0	6
Days Maximum Temp. ≤ 32°F	23	17	7	1	0	0	0	0	0	0	5	17	70
Days Minimum Temp. ≤ 32°F	31	27	28	20	7	1	0	0	3	15	25	30	187
Days Minimum Temp. ≤ 0°F	12	11	4	0	0	0	0	0	0	0	0	7	34
Heating Degree Days (base 65°F)	1,530	1,335	1,122	686	366	124	***46***	63	250	604	955	1,359	***8,440***
Cooling Degree Days (base 65°F)	0	0	0	2	14	67	***116***	87	21	2	0	0	***309***
Mean Precipitation (in.)	1.14	0.75	1.55	2.38	3.01	3.36	3.44	3.42	3.47	2.92	2.30	1.42	29.16
Extreme Maximum Daily Precip. (in.)	1.69	1.08	1.70	2.05	2.18	2.83	3.35	***2.95***	***2.40***	***2.13***	***2.35***	1.00	***3.35***
Days With ≥ 0.1" Precipitation	4	2	4	6	7	7	6	6	7	6	5	4	64
Days With ≥ 0.5" Precipitation	0	0	1	1	2	2	2	2	3	2	1	1	17
Days With ≥ 1.0" Precipitation	0	0	0	0	1	1	1	1	1	1	0	0	6
Mean Snowfall (in.)	15.0	8.2	9.5	3.8	0.4	0.0	0.0	0.0	trace	0.6	4.3	12.1	53.9
Maximum Snow Depth (in.)	36	37	24	12	7	0	0	***0***	***0***	2	***10***	28	***37***
Days With ≥ 1.0" Snow Depth	26	26	20	3	0	0	0	0	0	0	4	18	97

The period of record for all cooperative weather station data is 1980 – 2009. See User Guide for detailed explanation of data.

Three Rivers *St. Joseph County* Elevation: 810 ft. Latitude: 41° 56' N Longitude: 85° 38' W

	JAN	FEB	MAR	APR	MAY	JUN	JUL	AUG	SEP	OCT	NOV	DEC	YEAR
Mean Maximum Temp. (°F)	32.5	36.2	46.6	59.8	71.1	80.5	83.9	82.0	75.2	62.5	49.2	36.4	59.7
Mean Temp. (°F)	24.4	27.0	36.1	48.1	58.8	68.4	72.0	70.3	62.8	50.9	40.2	28.8	49.0
Mean Minimum Temp. (°F)	16.2	17.9	25.5	36.4	46.5	56.3	60.0	58.5	50.3	39.3	31.1	21.2	38.3
Extreme Maximum Temp. (°F)	66	72	80	88	93	103	102	100	96	88	79	72	103
Extreme Minimum Temp. (°F)	-23	-14	-4	7	25	35	41	38	28	18	9	-15	-23
Days Maximum Temp. ≥ 90°F	0	0	0	0	1	4	6	3	1	0	0	0	15
Days Maximum Temp. ≤ 32°F	16	10	4	0	0	0	0	0	0	0	1	11	42
Days Minimum Temp. ≤ 32°F	29	26	24	11	1	0	0	0	0	8	18	27	144
Days Minimum Temp. ≤ 0°F	4	2	0	0	0	0	0	0	0	0	0	1	7
Heating Degree Days (base 65°F)	1,252	1,067	891	506	227	44	8	17	128	436	737	1,114	6,427
Cooling Degree Days (base 65°F)	0	0	1	8	42	153	231	187	69	6	0	0	697
Mean Precipitation (in.)	2.27	1.79	2.37	3.18	4.13	3.52	4.31	4.23	3.88	3.40	3.18	2.59	38.85
Extreme Maximum Daily Precip. (in.)	2.33	1.37	1.66	2.31	2.31	4.35	4.08	3.30	5.05	3.19	3.17	1.46	5.05
Days With ≥ 0.1" Precipitation	6	5	6	7	8	6	7	7	6	7	7	7	79
Days With ≥ 0.5" Precipitation	1	1	1	2	3	2	3	3	2	2	2	1	23
Days With ≥ 1.0" Precipitation	0	0	0	1	1	1	1	1	1	1	1	0	8
Mean Snowfall (in.)	9.6	6.4	4.8	0.9	trace	0.0	0.0	0.0	0.0	0.4	2.5	9.5	34.1
Maximum Snow Depth (in.)	18	18	16	4	trace	0	0	0	0	3	5	19	19
Days With ≥ 1.0" Snow Depth	19	16	7	1	0	0	0	0	0	0	2	14	59

Whitefish Point *Chippewa County* Elevation: 604 ft. Latitude: 46° 45' N Longitude: 84° 59' W

	JAN	FEB	MAR	APR	MAY	JUN	JUL	AUG	SEP	OCT	NOV	DEC	YEAR
Mean Maximum Temp. (°F)	24.8	26.8	34.4	45.6	57.7	66.8	72.4	73.4	66.3	52.9	40.4	29.8	49.3
Mean Temp. (°F)	18.4	18.9	25.6	37.3	47.7	56.3	62.2	64.1	57.8	46.0	34.9	24.3	41.1
Mean Minimum Temp. (°F)	12.0	10.9	16.8	28.9	37.6	45.7	52.1	54.9	49.3	39.1	29.4	18.8	32.9
Extreme Maximum Temp. (°F)	43	50	61	78	85	89	96	94	90	74	68	57	96
Extreme Minimum Temp. (°F)	-23	-26	-22	0	23	29	33	33	26	19	6	-14	-26
Days Maximum Temp. ≥ 90°F	0	0	0	0	0	0	0	0	0	0	0	0	0
Days Maximum Temp. ≤ 32°F	25	20	11	1	0	0	0	0	0	0	5	18	80
Days Minimum Temp. ≤ 32°F	30	28	29	20	7	1	0	0	0	6	20	29	170
Days Minimum Temp. ≤ 0°F	5	6	3	0	0	0	0	0	0	0	0	1	15
Heating Degree Days (base 65°F)	1,438	1,298	1,214	825	531	265	121	76	226	582	895	1,254	8,725
Cooling Degree Days (base 65°F)	0	0	0	0	1	11	43	56	17	0	0	0	128
Mean Precipitation (in.)	2.27	1.49	1.84	2.17	2.48	2.72	3.19	3.05	3.51	3.72	2.82	2.78	32.04
Extreme Maximum Daily Precip. (in.)	0.79	0.87	1.60	1.20	1.83	1.76	3.00	2.20	2.12	2.30	1.45	2.20	3.00
Days With ≥ 0.1" Precipitation	9	5	5	6	6	6	7	6	8	10	8	10	86
Days With ≥ 0.5" Precipitation	0	0	1	1	2	2	2	2	2	2	1	1	16
Days With ≥ 1.0" Precipitation	0	0	0	0	0	0	1	1	0	0	0	0	2
Mean Snowfall (in.)	36.0	21.7	12.7	4.7	0.1	0.0	0.0	0.0	trace	1.1	11.6	34.7	122.6
Maximum Snow Depth (in.)	34	38	39	36	7	0	0	0	trace	3	12	28	39
Days With ≥ 1.0" Snow Depth	31	28	30	16	0	0	0	0	0	1	8	25	139

Ypsilanti E Mich Univ *Washtenaw County* Elevation: 779 ft. Latitude: 42° 14' N Longitude: 83° 37' W

	JAN	FEB	MAR	APR	MAY	JUN	JUL	AUG	SEP	OCT	NOV	DEC	YEAR
Mean Maximum Temp. (°F)	32.6	36.4	46.7	60.8	71.9	81.1	***84.8***	82.4	75.3	62.8	48.8	36.6	***60.0***
Mean Temp. (°F)	25.7	28.6	37.4	50.0	60.7	69.9	***74.0***	72.1	64.6	52.9	41.1	***30.2***	***50.6***
Mean Minimum Temp. (°F)	19.0	20.8	28.1	39.1	49.4	58.7	***63.1***	61.7	53.9	43.0	33.4	***24.0***	***41.2***
Extreme Maximum Temp. (°F)	64	69	82	87	96	102	100	99	95	90	74	68	102
Extreme Minimum Temp. (°F)	-20	-11	-6	10	29	38	38	38	33	22	9	-10	-20
Days Maximum Temp. ≥ 90°F	0	0	0	0	1	4	7	4	1	0	0	0	17
Days Maximum Temp. ≤ 32°F	15	10	3	0	0	0	0	0	0	0	1	10	39
Days Minimum Temp. ≤ 32°F	27	24	21	7	0	0	0	0	0	3	15	25	122
Days Minimum Temp. ≤ 0°F	2	1	0	0	0	0	0	0	0	0	0	1	4
Heating Degree Days (base 65°F)	1,211	1,021	849	452	181	29	***2***	8	97	377	709	***1,072***	***6,008***
Cooling Degree Days (base 65°F)	0	0	1	8	53	185	***288***	234	92	10	0	***0***	***871***
Mean Precipitation (in.)	1.93	1.76	2.30	3.00	3.60	3.19	3.27	3.46	3.50	2.73	2.86	2.34	33.94
Extreme Maximum Daily Precip. (in.)	1.57	2.10	1.51	1.87	3.34	2.17	***2.06***	4.07	2.17	2.43	1.96	***1.47***	***4.07***
Days With ≥ 0.1" Precipitation	5	4	6	7	7	6	6	6	6	5	6	5	69
Days With ≥ 0.5" Precipitation	1	1	1	2	2	2	2	2	3	2	2	1	21
Days With ≥ 1.0" Precipitation	0	0	0	0	1	1	1	1	1	1	0	0	6
Mean Snowfall (in.)	10.8	6.8	5.1	1.0	trace	0.0	0.0	0.0	0.0	0.1	1.3	***8.3***	***33.4***
Maximum Snow Depth (in.)	23	24	10	5	trace	0	0	0	0	1	6	20	24
Days With ≥ 1.0" Snow Depth	18	14	7	1	0	0	0	0	0	0	1	10	51

Michigan Weather Station Rankings

Annual Extreme Maximum Temperature

Highest Rank	Station Name	°F	Lowest Rank	Station Name	°F
1	Grosse Pointe Farms	105	1	Cross Village	95
2	Adrian 2 NNE	104	1	Frankfort 2 NE	95
2	Benton Harbor Ross Field	104	3	Manistique	96
2	Dearborn	104	3	Whitefish Point	96
2	Detroit Metropolitan Arpt	104	5	Bergland Dam	97
6	Alma	103	5	Ironwood	97
6	Alpena Phelps Collins Arpt	103	5	Milford Gm Proving Ground	*97*
6	Houghton Lake Roscommon Co Arpt	103	5	Sault Ste Marie Sanderson Field	97
6	Mio Hydro Plant	*103*	5	Stambaugh 2 SSE	97
6	Three Rivers	103	10	Champion Van Riper Prk	98
11	East Tawas	102	10	Cheboygan	98
11	Hancock Houghton Co Arpt	102	10	Hart	*98*
11	Marquette	102	10	Muskegon County Arpt	98
11	Port Huron	102	14	Grand Marais 2 E	99
11	Ypsilanti E Mich Univ	102	14	Marquette County Arpt	99
16	Ann Arbor Univ of Mich	101	14	Stephenson 8 WNW	*99*
16	Bad Axe	101	17	Allegan 5 NE	*100*
16	Big Rapids Waterworks	101	17	Alpena Wastewater Pl	100
16	Boyne Falls	101	17	Battle Creek 5 NW	100
16	Caro Regional Center	*101*	17	Grand Rapids Kent County Intl	100
16	Charlotte	101	17	Iron Mtn-Kingsford WWTP	100
16	East Lansing 4 S	101	17	Lansing Capital City Arpt	100
16	Essexville	101	17	Lapeer WWTP	*100*
16	Flint Bishop Arpt	101	17	St Johns	100
16	Gull Lake Biol Sta	*101*	25	Ann Arbor Univ of Mich	101

Annual Mean Maximum Temperature

Highest Rank	Station Name	°F	Lowest Rank	Station Name	°F
1	Gull Lake Biol Sta	60.2	1	Hancock Houghton Co Arpt	48.9
2	Ypsilanti E Mich Univ	*60.0*	2	Whitefish Point	49.3
3	Dearborn	59.8	3	Marquette County Arpt	49.7
4	Three Rivers	59.7	4	Manistique	49.8
5	Benton Harbor Ross Field	59.4	5	Ironwood	49.9
6	Adrian 2 NNE	59.2	6	Sault Ste Marie Sanderson Field	50.1
7	Holland	59.0	7	Munising	50.3
8	Ann Arbor Univ of Mich	58.9	8	Bergland Dam	50.6
9	Detroit Metropolitan Arpt	58.8	9	Stambaugh 2 SSE	50.8
10	Battle Creek 5 NW	*58.7*	10	Marquette	51.1
11	Grosse Pointe Farms	58.5	11	Champion Van Riper Prk	51.7
12	Allegan 5 NE	*57.7*	12	Grand Marais 2 E	52.1
12	St Johns	57.7	13	Alpena Wastewater Pl	52.6
14	Caro Regional Center	*57.6*	13	Cheboygan	52.6
15	East Lansing 4 S	*57.4*	15	Cross Village	52.7
15	Grand Rapids Kent County Intl	57.4	16	Iron Mtn-Kingsford WWTP	53.5
17	Flint Bishop Arpt	57.3	17	Alpena Phelps Collins Arpt	53.8
17	Lansing Capital City Arpt	57.3	18	Frankfort 2 NE	53.9
17	Lapeer WWTP	57.3	19	Houghton Lake Roscommon Co Arpt	54.0
20	Alma	57.2	20	Stephenson 8 WNW	*54.2*
20	Port Huron	57.2	21	Bad Axe	55.0
22	Owosso Wwtp	57.1	22	East Tawas	55.3
23	Charlotte	56.8	23	Hart	*55.4*
24	Boyne Falls	56.6	24	Mio Hydro Plant	*55.6*
25	Big Rapids Waterworks	56.5	25	Essexville	56.0

Rankings include 25 highest/lowest stations. If state has less than 25 stations, all stations are included. The period of record is 1980–2009. See User Guide for detailed explanation of data.

Annual Mean Temperature

Highest Rank	Station Name	°F	Lowest Rank	Station Name	°F
1	Ypsilanti E Mich Univ	***50.6***	1	Stambaugh 2 SSE	38.7
2	Grosse Pointe Farms	50.0	2	Champion Van Riper Prk	39.1
2	Gull Lake Biol Sta	50.0	3	Bergland Dam	39.2
4	Detroit Metropolitan Arpt	49.9	4	Ironwood	39.9
5	Ann Arbor Univ of Mich	49.6	5	Marquette County Arpt	40.1
5	Benton Harbor Ross Field	49.6	6	Sault Ste Marie Sanderson Field	40.9
5	Dearborn	49.6	7	Hancock Houghton Co Arpt	41.0
8	Holland	49.4	8	Whitefish Point	41.1
9	Three Rivers	49.0	9	Manistique	41.7
10	Battle Creek 5 NW	***48.6***	10	Grand Marais 2 E	41.9
11	Adrian 2 NNE	48.5	11	Munising	***42.0***
11	Port Huron	48.5	12	Iron Mtn-Kingsford WWTP	42.3
13	Grand Rapids Kent County Intl	48.3	13	Stephenson 8 WNW	***42.4***
14	Muskegon County Arpt	47.8	14	Marquette	43.2
15	Flint Bishop Arpt	47.7	15	Cheboygan	43.4
15	St Johns	47.7	16	Alpena Phelps Collins Arpt	43.6
17	Essexville	47.6	17	Houghton Lake Roscommon Co Arpt	43.9
18	Allegan 5 NE	***47.5***	18	Cross Village	44.1
19	East Lansing 4 S	***47.4***	19	Mio Hydro Plant	***44.4***
19	Lansing Capital City Arpt	47.4	20	Alpena Wastewater Pl	44.6
21	Caro Regional Center	***47.3***	21	Big Rapids Waterworks	45.5
21	Lapeer WWTP	47.3	21	East Tawas	45.5
23	Owosso Wwtp	47.2	23	Bad Axe	45.8
24	Milford Gm Proving Ground	***47.0***	23	Boyne Falls	45.8
25	Charlotte	46.9	25	Frankfort 2 NE	46.3

Annual Mean Minimum Temperature

Highest Rank	Station Name	°F	Lowest Rank	Station Name	°F
1	Grosse Pointe Farms	41.5	1	Champion Van Riper Prk	26.5
2	Ypsilanti E Mich Univ	***41.2***	1	Stambaugh 2 SSE	26.5
3	Detroit Metropolitan Arpt	41.0	3	Bergland Dam	27.8
4	Ann Arbor Univ of Mich	40.2	4	Ironwood	29.8
5	Benton Harbor Ross Field	39.7	5	Marquette County Arpt	30.4
5	Gull Lake Biol Sta	39.7	6	Stephenson 8 WNW	***30.5***
5	Holland	39.7	7	Iron Mtn-Kingsford WWTP	31.0
5	Port Huron	39.7	8	Sault Ste Marie Sanderson Field	31.6
9	Dearborn	39.4	9	Grand Marais 2 E	31.7
9	Muskegon County Arpt	39.4	10	Hancock Houghton Co Arpt	33.0
11	Essexville	39.1	10	Whitefish Point	33.0
11	Grand Rapids Kent County Intl	39.1	12	Mio Hydro Plant	***33.1***
13	Frankfort 2 NE	38.6	13	Alpena Phelps Collins Arpt	33.4
14	Battle Creek 5 NW	***38.4***	14	Manistique	33.6
15	Three Rivers	38.3	14	Munising	***33.6***
16	Flint Bishop Arpt	38.0	16	Houghton Lake Roscommon Co Arpt	33.9
17	Adrian 2 NNE	37.8	17	Cheboygan	34.1
18	Milford Gm Proving Ground	***37.6***	18	Big Rapids Waterworks	34.6
18	St Johns	37.6	19	Boyne Falls	35.0
20	Lansing Capital City Arpt	37.5	20	Marquette	35.3
21	Owosso Wwtp	37.3	21	Cross Village	35.4
22	Allegan 5 NE	***37.2***	22	East Tawas	35.7
22	East Lansing 4 S	***37.2***	23	Alma	36.2
22	Hart	***37.2***	24	Alpena Wastewater Pl	36.5
22	Lapeer WWTP	37.2	25	Bad Axe	36.6

Rankings include 25 highest/lowest stations. If state has less than 25 stations, all stations are included. The period of record is 1980–2009. See User Guide for detailed explanation of data.

Annual Extreme Minimum Temperature

Highest			Lowest		
Rank	Station Name	°F	Rank	Station Name	°F
1	Holland	-11	1	Stambaugh 2 SSE	-45
2	Frankfort 2 NE	-15	1	Stephenson 8 WNW	***-45***
3	Benton Harbor Ross Field	-17	3	Ironwood	-41
3	Grosse Pointe Farms	-17	4	Champion Van Riper Prk	-40
5	Essexville	-18	5	Bergland Dam	-39
6	Hart	***-19***	5	Iron Mtn-Kingsford WWTP	-39
6	Muskegon County Arpt	-19	7	Sault Ste Marie Sanderson Field	-36
6	Port Huron	-19	8	Boyne Falls	-32
6	St Johns	-19	8	Marquette County Arpt	-32
10	Bad Axe	-20	10	Grand Marais 2 E	-31
10	Battle Creek 5 NW	-20	10	Houghton Lake Roscommon Co Arpt	-31
10	Dearborn	-20	10	Mio Hydro Plant	***-31***
10	East Lansing 4 S	-20	13	Big Rapids Waterworks	-29
10	Gull Lake Biol Sta	***-20***	13	Lansing Capital City Arpt	-29
10	Owosso Wwtp	***-20***	15	Alpena Phelps Collins Arpt	-28
10	Ypsilanti E Mich Univ	-20	15	Cheboygan	-28
17	Alpena Wastewater Pl	-21	17	Cross Village	-27
17	Charlotte	-21	17	Munising	***-27***
17	Detroit Metropolitan Arpt	-21	19	Hancock Houghton Co Arpt	-26
17	East Tawas	-21	19	Lapeer WWTP	***-26***
17	Flint Bishop Arpt	-21	19	Whitefish Point	-26
22	Adrian 2 NNE	-22	22	Allegan 5 NE	***-25***
22	Alma	-22	22	Manistique	-25
22	Ann Arbor Univ of Mich	-22	24	Caro Regional Center	***-24***
22	Grand Rapids Kent County Intl	-22	24	Marquette	-24

July Mean Maximum Temperature

Highest			Lowest		
Rank	Station Name	°F	Rank	Station Name	°F
1	Gull Lake Biol Sta	85.0	1	Whitefish Point	72.4
2	Ypsilanti E Mich Univ	***84.8***	2	Manistique	73.3
3	Dearborn	84.5	3	Munising	74.7
4	Three Rivers	83.9	4	Marquette	75.1
5	Adrian 2 NNE	83.6	5	Hancock Houghton Co Arpt	75.4
6	Benton Harbor Ross Field	83.4	6	Sault Ste Marie Sanderson Field	75.8
7	Ann Arbor Univ of Mich	83.3	7	Cross Village	76.0
7	Detroit Metropolitan Arpt	83.3	8	Grand Marais 2 E	76.4
7	Holland	83.3	8	Marquette County Arpt	76.4
10	Caro Regional Center	***83.2***	10	Ironwood	76.5
11	Grosse Pointe Farms	83.0	11	Alpena Wastewater Pl	77.2
12	Alma	82.9	11	Stambaugh 2 SSE	77.2
12	St Johns	82.9	13	Bergland Dam	77.5
14	Battle Creek 5 NW	82.7	13	Cheboygan	77.5
14	Boyne Falls	82.7	15	Frankfort 2 NE	77.7
16	Allegan 5 NE	***82.5***	16	Champion Van Riper Prk	78.8
17	Grand Rapids Kent County Intl	82.4	17	Alpena Phelps Collins Arpt	79.8
18	Lansing Capital City Arpt	82.3	18	Hart	***79.9***
19	East Lansing 4 S	82.2	18	Houghton Lake Roscommon Co Arpt	79.9
19	Flint Bishop Arpt	82.2	20	East Tawas	80.1
21	Lapeer WWTP	82.1	21	Stephenson 8 WNW	***80.2***
22	Big Rapids Waterworks	82.0	22	Bad Axe	80.3
23	Mio Hydro Plant	81.9	22	Muskegon County Arpt	80.3
23	Owosso Wwtp	81.9	24	Iron Mtn-Kingsford WWTP	80.4
23	Port Huron	81.9	25	Milford Gm Proving Ground	80.9

Rankings include 25 highest/lowest stations. If state has less than 25 stations, all stations are included. The period of record is 1980–2009. See User Guide for detailed explanation of data.

January Mean Minimum Temperature

Rank	Station Name (Highest)	°F	Rank	Station Name (Lowest)	°F
1	Grosse Pointe Farms	19.3	1	Stambaugh 2 SSE	-0.3
2	Benton Harbor Ross Field	19.0	2	Champion Van Riper Prk	1.5
2	Ypsilanti E Mich Univ	19.0	3	Bergland Dam	1.9
4	Muskegon County Arpt	18.9	4	Ironwood	2.3
5	Holland	18.8	5	Iron Mtn-Kingsford WWTP	2.9
6	Frankfort 2 NE	18.5	6	Stephenson 8 WNW	4.6
7	Detroit Metropolitan Arpt	18.4	7	Marquette County Arpt	6.0
8	Ann Arbor Univ of Mich	17.9	8	Sault Ste Marie Sanderson Field	6.5
9	Gull Lake Biol Sta	17.4	9	Manistique	9.6
10	Dearborn	17.3	10	Mio Hydro Plant	10.0
10	Port Huron	17.3	11	Cheboygan	10.2
12	Grand Rapids Kent County Intl	17.1	12	Hancock Houghton Co Arpt	10.4
13	Battle Creek 5 NW	16.5	13	Houghton Lake Roscommon Co Arpt	10.9
14	Hart	16.4	14	Munising	11.0
15	Adrian 2 NNE	16.2	15	Grand Marais 2 E	11.2
15	Three Rivers	16.2	16	Alpena Phelps Collins Arpt	11.3
17	Flint Bishop Arpt	15.8	17	Whitefish Point	12.0
18	Allegan 5 NE	15.7	18	Big Rapids Waterworks	12.5
19	Essexville	15.6	18	Marquette	12.5
20	Lansing Capital City Arpt	15.3	20	Boyne Falls	13.1
21	Lapeer WWTP	15.2	20	Cross Village	13.1
21	Milford Gm Proving Ground	15.2	22	East Tawas	13.2
23	Caro Regional Center	15.0	23	Alpena Wastewater Pl	13.4
23	St Johns	15.0	24	Alma	14.0
25	East Lansing 4 S	14.9	25	Owosso Wwtp	14.4

Number of Days Annually Maximum Temperature ≥ 90°F

Rank	Station Name (Highest)	Days	Rank	Station Name (Lowest)	Days
1	Ypsilanti E Mich Univ	17	1	Cross Village	0
2	Benton Harbor Ross Field	16	1	Manistique	0
2	Gull Lake Biol Sta	16	1	Whitefish Point	0
4	Dearborn	15	4	Frankfort 2 NE	1
4	Three Rivers	15	4	Sault Ste Marie Sanderson Field	1
6	Adrian 2 NNE	13	4	Stambaugh 2 SSE	1
6	Caro Regional Center	*13*	7	Bergland Dam	2
8	Alma	12	7	Champion Van Riper Prk	2
8	Detroit Metropolitan Arpt	12	7	Hancock Houghton Co Arpt	2
8	Grosse Pointe Farms	12	7	Ironwood	2
11	Ann Arbor Univ of Mich	11	7	Munising	2
11	Boyne Falls	11	12	Cheboygan	3
11	Port Huron	11	12	Hart	*3*
11	St Johns	11	12	Marquette	3
15	Essexville	10	12	Muskegon County Arpt	3
15	Holland	10	16	Alpena Wastewater Pl	4
17	Allegan 5 NE	*9*	16	East Tawas	4
17	East Lansing 4 S	9	16	Grand Marais 2 E	4
17	Flint Bishop Arpt	9	16	Houghton Lake Roscommon Co Arpt	4
17	Grand Rapids Kent County Intl	9	16	Marquette County Arpt	4
17	Lansing Capital City Arpt	9	16	Milford Gm Proving Ground	4
22	Battle Creek 5 NW	8	22	Alpena Phelps Collins Arpt	6
22	Big Rapids Waterworks	8	22	Bad Axe	6
22	Lapeer WWTP	8	22	Iron Mtn-Kingsford WWTP	6
22	Mio Hydro Plant	*8*	22	Stephenson 8 WNW	6

Rankings include 25 highest/lowest stations. If state has less than 25 stations, all stations are included. The period of record is 1980–2009. See User Guide for detailed explanation of data.

Number of Days Annually Maximum Temperature ≤ 32°F

Highest

Rank	Station Name	Days
1	Hancock Houghton Co Arpt	97
2	Ironwood	96
2	Marquette County Arpt	96
4	Bergland Dam	93
5	Stambaugh 2 SSE	92
6	Sault Ste Marie Sanderson Field	86
7	Champion Van Riper Prk	83
8	Munising	82
9	Whitefish Point	80
10	Iron Mtn-Kingsford WWTP	78
11	Manistique	76
12	Marquette	75
13	Grand Marais 2 E	72
14	Houghton Lake Roscommon Co Arpt	71
15	Stephenson 8 WNW	70
16	Alpena Phelps Collins Arpt	68
16	Cheboygan	68
16	Cross Village	68
19	Alpena Wastewater Pl	64
20	Bad Axe	62
21	Boyne Falls	61
21	Mio Hydro Plant	***61***
23	Frankfort 2 NE	59
24	Big Rapids Waterworks	57
24	Essexville	57

Lowest

Rank	Station Name	Days
1	Holland	37
2	Dearborn	39
2	Ypsilanti E Mich Univ	39
4	Benton Harbor Ross Field	40
4	Gull Lake Biol Sta	40
6	Adrian 2 NNE	41
6	Grosse Pointe Farms	41
8	Three Rivers	42
9	Detroit Metropolitan Arpt	43
10	Battle Creek 5 NW	46
11	Ann Arbor Univ of Mich	47
12	Allegan 5 NE	***48***
12	Port Huron	48
14	Muskegon County Arpt	50
15	Flint Bishop Arpt	51
16	East Tawas	52
16	Grand Rapids Kent County Intl	52
16	St Johns	52
19	Alma	53
19	East Lansing 4 S	53
21	Caro Regional Center	***54***
21	Charlotte	54
21	Lansing Capital City Arpt	54
21	Lapeer WWTP	54
21	Owosso Wwtp	54

Number of Days Annually Minimum Temperature ≤ 32°F

Highest

Rank	Station Name	Days
1	Stambaugh 2 SSE	211
2	Champion Van Riper Prk	205
3	Bergland Dam	202
4	Ironwood	191
4	Marquette County Arpt	191
6	Grand Marais 2 E	189
7	Stephenson 8 WNW	187
8	Iron Mtn-Kingsford WWTP	185
9	Sault Ste Marie Sanderson Field	176
10	Mio Hydro Plant	***174***
11	Hancock Houghton Co Arpt	173
12	Munising	171
13	Alpena Phelps Collins Arpt	170
13	Whitefish Point	170
15	Big Rapids Waterworks	168
15	Boyne Falls	168
15	Houghton Lake Roscommon Co Arpt	168
15	Manistique	168
19	Cheboygan	164
20	Alma	161
21	Cross Village	158
21	Marquette	158
23	East Tawas	157
24	Bad Axe	154
25	Charlotte	153

Lowest

Rank	Station Name	Days
1	Grosse Pointe Farms	121
2	Ypsilanti E Mich Univ	122
3	Detroit Metropolitan Arpt	124
4	Ann Arbor Univ of Mich	132
4	Holland	132
4	Port Huron	132
7	Dearborn	133
7	Gull Lake Biol Sta	133
9	Benton Harbor Ross Field	135
9	Muskegon County Arpt	135
11	Grand Rapids Kent County Intl	137
12	Essexville	139
13	Frankfort 2 NE	140
14	Flint Bishop Arpt	141
15	Three Rivers	144
16	Battle Creek 5 NW	145
16	Milford Gm Proving Ground	145
18	Adrian 2 NNE	146
19	Lansing Capital City Arpt	148
20	Allegan 5 NE	***149***
20	Alpena Wastewater Pl	149
20	East Lansing 4 S	149
20	St Johns	149
24	Owosso Wwtp	150
25	Caro Regional Center	***151***

Rankings include 25 highest/lowest stations. If state has less than 25 stations, all stations are included. The period of record is 1980–2009. See User Guide for detailed explanation of data.

Number of Days Annually Minimum Temperature ≤ 0°F

Highest Rank	Station Name	Days	Lowest Rank	Station Name	Days
1	Stambaugh 2 SSE	49	1	Frankfort 2 NE	2
2	Bergland Dam	45	1	Holland	2
2	Champion Van Riper Prk	45	3	Grosse Pointe Farms	3
4	Ironwood	39	3	Muskegon County Arpt	3
5	Iron Mtn-Kingsford WWTP	36	5	Ann Arbor Univ of Mich	4
6	Stephenson 8 WNW	34	5	Benton Harbor Ross Field	4
7	Marquette County Arpt	32	5	Detroit Metropolitan Arpt	4
8	Sault Ste Marie Sanderson Field	28	5	Port Huron	4
9	Mio Hydro Plant	***22***	5	Ypsilanti E Mich Univ	4
10	Manistique	20	10	Dearborn	5
11	Cheboygan	19	11	Battle Creek 5 NW	6
12	Alpena Phelps Collins Arpt	18	11	Essexville	6
12	Hancock Houghton Co Arpt	18	11	Grand Rapids Kent County Intl	6
12	Houghton Lake Roscommon Co Arpt	18	11	Gull Lake Biol Sta	6
15	Boyne Falls	17	11	Hart	***6***
16	Munising	15	16	Three Rivers	7
16	Whitefish Point	15	17	Adrian 2 NNE	8
18	Big Rapids Waterworks	14	17	Allegan 5 NE	***8***
18	Grand Marais 2 E	14	17	St Johns	8
20	Cross Village	13	20	Bad Axe	9
20	East Tawas	13	21	Alma	10
22	Caro Regional Center	***12***	21	Alpena Wastewater Pl	10
22	Lapeer WWTP	12	21	Charlotte	10
22	Marquette	12	21	East Lansing 4 S	10
25	Lansing Capital City Arpt	11	21	Flint Bishop Arpt	10

Number of Annual Heating Degree Days

Highest Rank	Station Name	Num.	Lowest Rank	Station Name	Num.
1	Stambaugh 2 SSE	9,673	1	Ypsilanti E Mich Univ	***6,008***
2	Champion Van Riper Prk	9,527	2	Grosse Pointe Farms	6,165
3	Bergland Dam	9,505	3	Gull Lake Biol Sta	6,187
4	Ironwood	9,319	4	Detroit Metropolitan Arpt	6,191
5	Marquette County Arpt	9,233	5	Benton Harbor Ross Field	6,265
6	Hancock Houghton Co Arpt	8,896	6	Ann Arbor Univ of Mich	6,275
7	Sault Ste Marie Sanderson Field	8,873	7	Dearborn	6,284
8	Whitefish Point	8,725	8	Holland	6,307
9	Iron Mtn-Kingsford WWTP	8,559	9	Three Rivers	6,427
10	Manistique	8,538	10	Adrian 2 NNE	6,526
11	Grand Marais 2 E	8,531	11	Battle Creek 5 NW	***6,534***
12	Munising	***8,525***	12	Port Huron	6,608
13	Stephenson 8 WNW	***8,440***	13	Grand Rapids Kent County Intl	6,650
14	Marquette	8,141	14	Muskegon County Arpt	6,689
15	Cheboygan	8,083	15	Flint Bishop Arpt	6,795
16	Alpena Phelps Collins Arpt	8,009	16	St Johns	6,820
17	Houghton Lake Roscommon Co Arpt	7,917	17	Allegan 5 NE	***6,829***
18	Mio Hydro Plant	***7,820***	18	Essexville	6,882
19	Cross Village	7,804	19	Lansing Capital City Arpt	6,887
20	Alpena Wastewater Pl	7,692	20	East Lansing 4 S	***6,913***
21	Big Rapids Waterworks	7,434	21	Lapeer WWTP	6,919
22	Boyne Falls	7,402	22	Owosso Wwtp	6,930
23	East Tawas	7,400	23	Caro Regional Center	***6,940***
24	Bad Axe	7,347	24	Milford Gm Proving Ground	***6,978***
25	Hart	***7,143***	25	Charlotte	7,010

Rankings include 25 highest/lowest stations. If state has less than 25 stations, all stations are included. The period of record is 1980–2009. See User Guide for detailed explanation of data.

Number of Annual Cooling Degree Days

Highest

Rank	Station Name	Num.
1	Ypsilanti E Mich Univ	***871***
2	Gull Lake Biol Sta	807
3	Grosse Pointe Farms	798
4	Detroit Metropolitan Arpt	793
5	Dearborn	784
6	Ann Arbor Univ of Mich	761
7	Benton Harbor Ross Field	738
8	Holland	708
9	Three Rivers	697
10	Port Huron	685
11	Grand Rapids Kent County Intl	652
12	Battle Creek 5 NW	***639***
12	Essexville	639
14	Adrian 2 NNE	622
15	St Johns	618
16	Flint Bishop Arpt	587
17	East Lansing 4 S	***585***
18	Lansing Capital City Arpt	582
19	Caro Regional Center	***575***
20	Lapeer WWTP	558
21	Owosso Wwtp	554
22	Allegan 5 NE	***552***
23	Alma	550
24	Milford Gm Proving Ground	***535***
25	Muskegon County Arpt	531

Lowest

Rank	Station Name	Num.
1	Whitefish Point	128
2	Manistique	161
3	Stambaugh 2 SSE	170
4	Sault Ste Marie Sanderson Field	178
5	Champion Van Riper Prk	188
6	Bergland Dam	212
7	Grand Marais 2 E	221
8	Munising	***228***
9	Hancock Houghton Co Arpt	237
10	Marquette County Arpt	252
11	Ironwood	267
12	Cross Village	277
13	Marquette	296
14	Stephenson 8 WNW	***309***
15	Cheboygan	314
16	Alpena Phelps Collins Arpt	320
17	Houghton Lake Roscommon Co Arpt	341
18	Alpena Wastewater Pl	362
19	Iron Mtn-Kingsford WWTP	364
20	Frankfort 2 NE	389
21	Mio Hydro Plant	***397***
22	East Tawas	405
23	Hart	***436***
24	Big Rapids Waterworks	444
25	Bad Axe	457

Annual Precipitation

Highest

Rank	Station Name	Inches
1	Allegan 5 NE	***40.98***
2	Gull Lake Biol Sta	39.84
3	Bergland Dam	39.35
4	Three Rivers	38.85
5	Grand Rapids Kent County Intl	38.12
6	Ann Arbor Univ of Mich	37.52
7	Hart	***36.77***
8	Munising	***36.51***
9	Big Rapids Waterworks	36.41
10	Adrian 2 NNE	36.31
11	Benton Harbor Ross Field	36.13
12	Marquette County Arpt	35.51
13	Grosse Pointe Farms	34.99
14	Frankfort 2 NE	34.70
15	Battle Creek 5 NW	34.67
15	Ironwood	34.67
17	Charlotte	34.01
18	Ypsilanti E Mich Univ	33.94
19	Muskegon County Arpt	33.72
20	Port Huron	33.63
21	Boyne Falls	33.62
22	Dearborn	33.61
23	Detroit Metropolitan Arpt	33.58
24	Caro Regional Center	***33.32***
25	St Johns	33.14

Lowest

Rank	Station Name	Inches
1	Mio Hydro Plant	***26.59***
2	Grand Marais 2 E	27.79
3	Alpena Phelps Collins Arpt	27.96
4	Houghton Lake Roscommon Co Arpt	28.70
5	Marquette	28.93
6	Stambaugh 2 SSE	29.12
7	Stephenson 8 WNW	29.16
8	Iron Mtn-Kingsford WWTP	29.35
9	Hancock Houghton Co Arpt	29.55
10	Cross Village	29.58
11	Alpena Wastewater Pl	29.79
12	Milford Gm Proving Ground	***29.90***
13	Cheboygan	30.52
14	East Lansing 4 S	31.07
15	Flint Bishop Arpt	31.58
16	East Tawas	31.63
17	Lansing Capital City Arpt	31.81
18	Lapeer WWTP	31.90
19	Owosso Wwtp	31.95
20	Whitefish Point	32.04
21	Champion Van Riper Prk	32.06
22	Essexville	32.11
23	Sault Ste Marie Sanderson Field	32.83
24	Bad Axe	32.93
25	Alma	33.13

Rankings include 25 highest/lowest stations. If state has less than 25 stations, all stations are included. The period of record is 1980–2009. See User Guide for detailed explanation of data.

Annual Extreme Maximum Daily Precipitation

Highest			Lowest		
Rank	**Station Name**	**Inches**	**Rank**	**Station Name**	**Inches**
1	Alma	9.33	1	Cross Village	2.72
2	Holland	***7.99***	2	Alpena Wastewater Pl	***2.97***
3	Essexville	7.72	3	Grand Marais 2 E	***3.00***
4	Big Rapids Waterworks	7.64	3	Whitefish Point	3.00
5	Caro Regional Center	***7.28***	5	Boyne Falls	3.15
6	St Johns	6.50	5	Sault Ste Marie Sanderson Field	3.15
7	Bad Axe	6.46	7	Munising	***3.16***
8	Gull Lake Biol Sta	***6.05***	8	Benton Harbor Ross Field	3.25
9	Allegan 5 NE	***5.80***	9	Stephenson 8 WNW	***3.35***
10	Hart	***5.43***	10	Alpena Phelps Collins Arpt	3.44
11	Stambaugh 2 SSE	5.20	11	East Tawas	3.52
12	Marquette	5.12	12	Houghton Lake Roscommon Co Arpt	3.55
13	Three Rivers	5.05	13	Hancock Houghton Co Arpt	3.58
14	Lansing Capital City Arpt	4.95	14	Charlotte	3.60
15	Adrian 2 NNE	4.74	15	Champion Van Riper Prk	***3.61***
16	Owosso Wwtp	***4.67***	16	Lapeer WWTP	***3.72***
17	Ann Arbor Univ of Mich	4.54	17	Mio Hydro Plant	***3.75***
18	Bergland Dam	4.52	18	Battle Creek 5 NW	***3.83***
19	East Lansing 4 S	***4.50***	19	Manistique	***3.86***
20	Cheboygan	4.48	20	Flint Bishop Arpt	3.89
21	Detroit Metropolitan Arpt	4.34	21	Dearborn	3.93
22	Muskegon County Arpt	4.33	22	Port Huron	3.97
23	Grosse Pointe Farms	4.30	23	Iron Mtn-Kingsford WWTP	4.05
24	Marquette County Arpt	4.29	24	Ypsilanti E Mich Univ	***4.07***
25	Grand Rapids Kent County Intl	4.15	25	Frankfort 2 NE	4.08

Number of Days Annually With ≥ 0.1 Inches of Precipitation

Highest			Lowest		
Rank	**Station Name**	**Days**	**Rank**	**Station Name**	**Days**
1	Munising	***100***	1	Manistique	58
2	Bergland Dam	96	2	Milford Gm Proving Ground	***63***
3	Boyne Falls	86	3	Stephenson 8 WNW	64
3	Whitefish Point	86	4	Holland	66
5	Allegan 5 NE	***85***	5	Alpena Phelps Collins Arpt	67
6	Sault Ste Marie Sanderson Field	83	5	Houghton Lake Roscommon Co Arpt	67
7	Marquette County Arpt	82	7	Champion Van Riper Prk	68
8	Ann Arbor Univ of Mich	81	7	East Lansing 4 S	68
8	Frankfort 2 NE	81	7	Lapeer WWTP	68
8	Gull Lake Biol Sta	81	7	Mio Hydro Plant	***68***
8	Ironwood	81	11	Alma	69
12	Adrian 2 NNE	79	11	Flint Bishop Arpt	69
12	Big Rapids Waterworks	79	11	Ypsilanti E Mich Univ	69
12	Three Rivers	79	14	Cheboygan	70
15	Hart	***78***	14	East Tawas	70
16	Benton Harbor Ross Field	77	14	Essexville	70
16	Grand Rapids Kent County Intl	77	14	Iron Mtn-Kingsford WWTP	70
16	Grosse Pointe Farms	77	14	Lansing Capital City Arpt	70
16	Port Huron	77	14	Owosso Wwtp	70
20	Caro Regional Center	***76***	20	Alpena Wastewater Pl	71
20	Hancock Houghton Co Arpt	76	20	St Johns	71
22	Charlotte	74	20	Stambaugh 2 SSE	71
22	Dearborn	74	23	Cross Village	72
22	Grand Marais 2 E	74	24	Bad Axe	73
22	Muskegon County Arpt	74	24	Battle Creek 5 NW	73

Rankings include 25 highest/lowest stations. If state has less than 25 stations, all stations are included. The period of record is 1980–2009. See User Guide for detailed explanation of data.

Number of Days Annually With ≥ 0.5 Inches of Precipitation

Highest Rank	Highest Station Name	Highest Days	Lowest Rank	Lowest Station Name	Lowest Days
1	Gull Lake Biol Sta	26	1	Grand Marais 2 E	14
2	Allegan 5 NE	*25*	2	Marquette	15
2	Ann Arbor Univ of Mich	25	3	Cross Village	16
4	Grand Rapids Kent County Intl	24	3	Hancock Houghton Co Arpt	16
4	Hart	*24*	3	Houghton Lake Roscommon Co Arpt	16
6	Benton Harbor Ross Field	23	3	Manistique	16
6	Three Rivers	23	3	Stambaugh 2 SSE	16
8	Adrian 2 NNE	22	3	Whitefish Point	16
8	Battle Creek 5 NW	22	9	Alpena Phelps Collins Arpt	17
8	Bergland Dam	22	9	Champion Van Riper Prk	17
8	Big Rapids Waterworks	22	9	Stephenson 8 WNW	17
8	Dearborn	22	12	Cheboygan	18
8	Holland	22	12	Iron Mtn-Kingsford WWTP	18
8	Lapeer WWTP	22	12	Milford Gm Proving Ground	*18*
15	Caro Regional Center	*21*	12	Mio Hydro Plant	*18*
15	Charlotte	21	12	Sault Ste Marie Sanderson Field	18
15	East Lansing 4 S	21	17	Alpena Wastewater Pl	19
15	East Tawas	21	17	Boyne Falls	19
15	Essexville	21	17	Flint Bishop Arpt	19
15	Grosse Pointe Farms	21	17	Port Huron	19
15	Munising	*21*	21	Alma	20
15	Muskegon County Arpt	21	21	Bad Axe	20
15	Owosso Wwtp	21	21	Detroit Metropolitan Arpt	20
15	St Johns	21	21	Frankfort 2 NE	20
15	Ypsilanti E Mich Univ	21	21	Ironwood	20

Number of Days Annually With ≥ 1.0 Inches of Precipitation

Highest Rank	Highest Station Name	Highest Days	Lowest Rank	Lowest Station Name	Lowest Days
1	Adrian 2 NNE	8	1	Marquette	1
1	Benton Harbor Ross Field	8	2	Mio Hydro Plant	*2*
1	Big Rapids Waterworks	8	2	Whitefish Point	2
1	Grand Rapids Kent County Intl	8	4	Alpena Phelps Collins Arpt	3
1	Gull Lake Biol Sta	8	4	Cross Village	3
1	Hart	*8*	4	Grand Marais 2 E	3
1	Holland	8	4	Hancock Houghton Co Arpt	3
1	Three Rivers	8	4	Sault Ste Marie Sanderson Field	3
9	Allegan 5 NE	*7*	9	Alpena Wastewater Pl	4
9	Battle Creek 5 NW	7	9	Houghton Lake Roscommon Co Arpt	4
9	Essexville	7	9	Manistique	4
9	Marquette County Arpt	7	12	Caro Regional Center	*5*
13	Alma	6	12	Champion Van Riper Prk	5
13	Ann Arbor Univ of Mich	6	12	Cheboygan	5
13	Bad Axe	6	12	Detroit Metropolitan Arpt	5
13	Bergland Dam	6	12	East Lansing 4 S	5
13	Boyne Falls	6	12	East Tawas	5
13	Charlotte	6	12	Flint Bishop Arpt	5
13	Dearborn	6	12	Grosse Pointe Farms	5
13	Frankfort 2 NE	6	12	Iron Mtn-Kingsford WWTP	5
13	Ironwood	6	12	Lapeer WWTP	5
13	Lansing Capital City Arpt	6	12	Milford Gm Proving Ground	*5*
13	Muskegon County Arpt	6	12	Munising	*5*
13	Port Huron	6	12	Owosso Wwtp	5
13	St Johns	6	25	Alma	6

Rankings include 25 highest/lowest stations. If state has less than 25 stations, all stations are included. The period of record is 1980–2009. See User Guide for detailed explanation of data.

Annual Snowfall

Highest			Lowest		
Rank	Station Name	Inches	Rank	Station Name	Inches
1	Marquette County Arpt	203.0	1	Grosse Pointe Farms	26.9
2	Ironwood	187.2	2	Adrian 2 NNE	29.6
3	Bergland Dam	177.8	3	Dearborn	32.8
4	Munising	***151.7***	4	Lapeer WWTP	***33.4***
5	Grand Marais 2 E	***132.9***	4	Milford Gm Proving Ground	***33.4***
6	Whitefish Point	122.6	4	Ypsilanti E Mich Univ	***33.4***
7	Marquette	115.3	7	Three Rivers	34.1
8	Champion Van Riper Prk	***114.6***	8	Port Huron	34.9
9	Boyne Falls	114.1	9	Owosso Wwtp	***35.6***
10	Frankfort 2 NE	104.9	10	Caro Regional Center	***36.8***
11	Muskegon County Arpt	***95.1***	11	East Lansing 4 S	38.3
12	Cheboygan	92.8	12	Essexville	38.5
13	Allegan 5 NE	***86.6***	13	Alma	40.0
14	Benton Harbor Ross Field	85.7	14	St Johns	42.2
15	Cross Village	79.8	15	Charlotte	42.9
16	Hart	***78.1***	16	Detroit Metropolitan Arpt	43.1
17	Grand Rapids Kent County Intl	74.6	17	Bad Axe	46.1
18	Manistique	***74.1***	18	Flint Bishop Arpt	47.4
19	Stambaugh 2 SSE	69.1	19	Lansing Capital City Arpt	***51.2***
20	Holland	64.7	20	Alpena Wastewater Pl	***52.4***
21	Big Rapids Waterworks	62.5	21	East Tawas	53.6
22	Iron Mtn-Kingsford WWTP	59.7	22	Stephenson 8 WNW	53.9
23	Battle Creek 5 NW	59.2	23	Gull Lake Biol Sta	***55.6***
24	Ann Arbor Univ of Mich	57.0	24	Ann Arbor Univ of Mich	57.0
25	Gull Lake Biol Sta	***55.6***	25	Battle Creek 5 NW	59.2

Annual Maximum Snow Depth

Highest			Lowest		
Rank	Station Name	Inches	Rank	Station Name	Inches
1	Benton Harbor Ross Field	80	1	Caro Regional Center	***18***
2	Marquette County Arpt	63	1	Milford Gm Proving Ground	***18***
3	Manistique	***61***	3	Lapeer WWTP	***19***
4	Champion Van Riper Prk	60	3	Port Huron	19
5	Alpena Wastewater Pl	53	3	Three Rivers	19
6	Bergland Dam	49	6	Flint Bishop Arpt	20
7	Frankfort 2 NE	48	7	Adrian 2 NNE	21
8	Ironwood	47	7	Grand Rapids Kent County Intl	21
9	Grand Marais 2 E	***42***	9	Alma	22
10	Cheboygan	41	9	Ann Arbor Univ of Mich	22
10	Marquette	41	9	Owosso Wwtp	***22***
12	Hart	***39***	12	Grosse Pointe Farms	23
12	Stambaugh 2 SSE	39	12	Lansing Capital City Arpt	***23***
12	Whitefish Point	39	14	Battle Creek 5 NW	***24***
15	Stephenson 8 WNW	***37***	14	Dearborn	24
16	Holland	36	14	Detroit Metropolitan Arpt	24
17	Cross Village	35	14	East Lansing 4 S	24
18	Iron Mtn-Kingsford WWTP	34	14	East Tawas	24
19	Boyne Falls	33	14	Ypsilanti E Mich Univ	24
20	Essexville	***32***	20	Gull Lake Biol Sta	***25***
20	Mio Hydro Plant	***32***	21	Big Rapids Waterworks	26
22	Bad Axe	31	22	Allegan 5 NE	***27***
23	Muskegon County Arpt	***30***	22	St Johns	27
24	Charlotte	28	24	Charlotte	28
25	Allegan 5 NE	***27***	25	Muskegon County Arpt	***30***

Rankings include 25 highest/lowest stations. If state has less than 25 stations, all stations are included. The period of record is 1980–2009. See User Guide for detailed explanation of data.

Number of Days Annually With ≥ 1.0 Inch Snow Depth

Highest

Rank	Station Name	Days
1	Marquette County Arpt	152
2	Bergland Dam	151
3	Ironwood	145
4	Whitefish Point	139
5	Champion Van Riper Prk	131
5	Grand Marais 2 E	***131***
7	Marquette	130
7	Stambaugh 2 SSE	130
9	Iron Mtn-Kingsford WWTP	114
10	Cross Village	110
11	Boyne Falls	108
12	Cheboygan	107
13	Frankfort 2 NE	104
14	Manistique	101
15	Stephenson 8 WNW	97
16	Mio Hydro Plant	***91***
17	Alpena Wastewater Pl	89
18	East Tawas	87
19	Big Rapids Waterworks	86
20	Allegan 5 NE	***78***
21	Bad Axe	75
22	Muskegon County Arpt	***74***
23	Alma	73
24	Grand Rapids Kent County Intl	68
25	Gull Lake Biol Sta	***66***

Lowest

Rank	Station Name	Days
1	Essexville	***39***
2	Benton Harbor Ross Field	41
3	Detroit Metropolitan Arpt	45
3	Holland	45
5	Grosse Pointe Farms	49
6	Owosso Wwtp	***50***
7	Adrian 2 NNE	51
7	Milford Gm Proving Ground	***51***
7	Port Huron	51
7	St Johns	51
7	Ypsilanti E Mich Univ	51
12	Dearborn	52
13	Lapeer WWTP	***56***
14	Three Rivers	59
15	Ann Arbor Univ of Mich	60
16	East Lansing 4 S	61
17	Flint Bishop Arpt	62
17	Hart	***62***
19	Caro Regional Center	***63***
20	Battle Creek 5 NW	***64***
20	Charlotte	64
22	Gull Lake Biol Sta	***66***
22	Lansing Capital City Arpt	***66***
24	Grand Rapids Kent County Intl	68
25	Alma	73

 Rankings include 25 highest/lowest stations. If state has less than 25 stations, all stations are included. The period of record is 1980–2009. See User Guide for detailed explanation of data.

Significant Storm Events in Michigan: 2000 – 2009

Location or County	Date	Type	Mag.	Deaths	Injuries	Property Damage ($mil.)	Crop Damage ($mil.)
Wayne	09/11/00	Flood	na	0	0	20.0	0.0
Southeast Lower Michigan	08/06/01	Excessive Heat	na	1	200	0.0	0.0
Eaton	09/09/01	Tornado	F1	0	1	10.0	0.1
Northwest Upper Michigan	04/12/02	Flood	na	0	0	18.5	0.0
Dickinson	09/30/02	Tornado	F1	0	0	7.0	0.0
Southeast Lower Michigan	04/03/03	Ice Storm	na	1	2	161.1	0.0
Marquette County	05/15/03	Flood	na	0	0	14.0	0.0
Southeast Michigan	11/12/03	High Wind	87 mph	0	0	21.0	0.0
Southwestern and South Central Lower Michigan	05/21/04	Flood	na	0	0	25.0	4.6
Southeast Michigan	05/23/04	Flood	na	0	0	100.0	0.0
Southeast Lower Michigan	11/15/05	Strong Wind	55 mph	0	0	7.2	0.0
Marquette	06/20/07	Hail	1.75 in.	0	0	20.0	0.0
Marquette	06/20/07	Hail	1.50 in.	0	0	18.0	0.0
Eaton	08/24/07	Tornado	F3	0	5	40.0	0.0
Genesee	08/24/07	Tornado	F2	0	1	13.0	0.0
Livingston	08/24/07	Tornado	F2	0	0	7.0	0.0
Ingham	10/18/07	Tornado	F2	2	0	15.0	0.0
Kalamazoo	09/13/08	Flood	na	0	0	11.0	0.0
Ottawa	06/19/09	Flash Flood	na	0	0	34.0	0.0

Note: Deaths, injuries, and damages are date and location specific.

MINNESOTA

PHYSICAL FEATURES. The State of Minnesota covers 84,068 square miles, of which 4,059 square miles is water (15,291 lakes greater than 10 acres). It extends about 400 miles south to north between latitudes 43° 30' and 49° N., and averages 275 miles east to west between longitudes 89° 30' and 97° W.

Elevations are less than 1,200 feet near each of the three major rivers—the Red, the Minnesota, and the Mississippi (except in the northern part). There are three areas at elevations greater than 1,600 feet: the Iron Range, paralleling the north shore of Lake Superior; the Coteau Des Prairies (also known as Buffalo Ridge), extending out of South Dakota across the southwest portion of the State; and a small area in the Lake Itasca region. The highest point above sea level is at 2,301 feet, Eagle Mountain, in the extreme northeast; and the lowest is at 602 feet, the surface of Lake Superior. Minnesota can be considered to have a continental divide in three directions; drainage is toward Hudson Bay to the north; toward the Atlantic Ocean to the east; and toward the Gulf of Mexico to the south.

GENERAL CLIMATE. Minnesota has a continental-type climate. The State is subject to frequent outbreaks of continental polar air throughout the year, with occasional Arctic outbreaks during the cold season. Occasional periods of prolonged heat occur during summer, particularly in the southern portion when warm air pushes northward from the Gulf of Mexico and the southwestern United States. Pacific Ocean air masses that move across the Western United States produce comparatively mild and dry weather at all seasons.

PRECIPITATION. Although the total precipitation is important, its distribution during the growing season is even more significant. For the most part, native vegetation grows for seven months (April to October) and row crops grow for five months (May through September). During the latter five-month period, approximately two-thirds of the annual precipitation occurs. Mean annual precipitation is 32 inches in extreme southeast Minnesota, an amount which gradually decreases to 19 inches in the extreme northwest portion of the State.

SNOWFALL. Seasonal snowfall averages near 70 inches along the north shore of Lake Superior in northeast Minnesota, gradually decreases to 40 inches along the Iowa border in the south, and measures 30 inches along the North Dakota and South Dakota borders in the west.

DROUGHT. Conditions of moderate droughts or worse are expected on the average at least once in four to five years, except in southwest Minnesota when they occur about once in every three years. Severe or extreme drought conditions occur on the average about once in every eight to nine years, except in the western divisions where they occur about once in every six years. Generally, the more severe droughts tend to persist or recur several years in succession.

STORMS. Thunderstorm winds generally cause more damage to property than any other weather factor. The annual frequency of thunderstorm days is about 45 days in southern Minnesota, decreasing to about 30 days along the Canadian border. Generally, 80 percent or more of these storms occur during the heavier rainfall months—from May through September. Damaging local windstorms, tornadoes, hail, and heavy rains generally occur with the stronger and more well-developed thunderstorms.

The month with the greatest frequency of tornadoes is June, followed by July, and then May. During these 3 months, nearly 75 percent of all tornadoes occur. Tornadoes have never been reported in December, January, and February. The southern one-half of Minnesota has three to four times as many tornadoes as does the northern one-half of the State.

The frequency of hailstorms shows a high of four to five days annually in southwestern Minnesota, decreasing to near two days in the northern portion of the State. The month with the most hail is July, with June next, and then August. During these three months, over 80 percent of the hail occurs. The size of the hail reported is generally in the marble-to-golfball category, with several reports annually of baseball-size and larger.

Heavy snowfalls of greater than four inches are common any time from mid-November through mid-April. Heavy snowfalls with blizzard conditions affect the State on the average about two times each winter. (Blizzard conditions involve snow, temperatures of 20°F. or less, and wind velocities of 35 m.p.h. and greater.)

Freezing rain and glaze storms are not numerous, but do coat the roads several times each season in Minnesota. The more severe ice storms cause extensive damage; such storms are not as common in the far north as they are in southern and southeastern portions of the State.

FLOODS. Major floods on the larger rivers occur on the average one or two years out of 10. Floods show the greatest frequency in April during the spring breakup of snow cover and frozen ground. Local flash flooding is most common in the hilly terrain and narrow valleys of southeast Minnesota, partly because of the intensive rainstorms in the southern portion of the State.

SUNSHINE. Sunshine amounts vary from a low in November of nearly 40 percent of possible sunshine hours to a high of about 70 percent in July, with an annual average of 58 percent. Hours of sunlight varies from near 8.5 hours in December to about 16 hours in June.

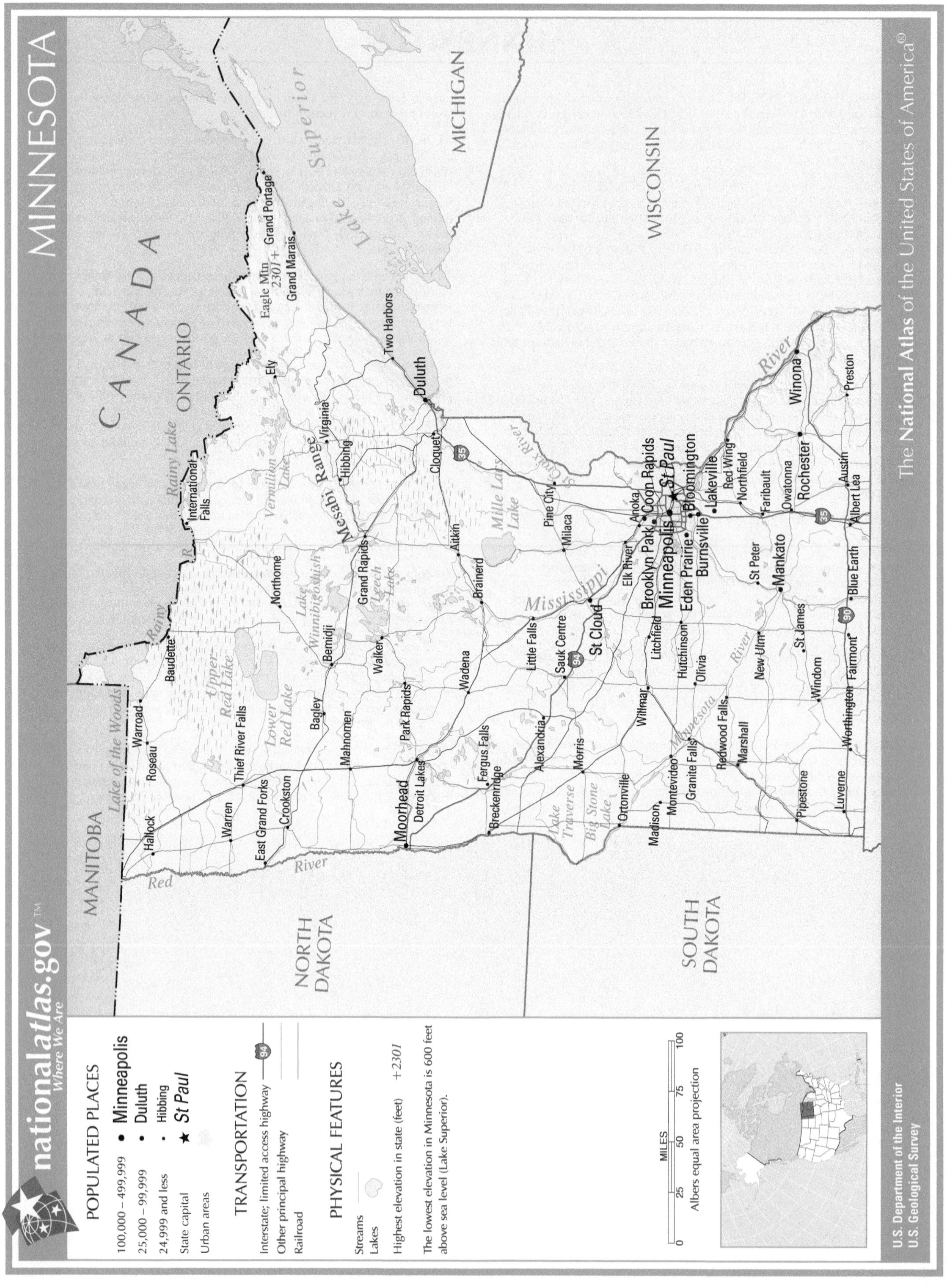
MINNESOTA
nationalatlas.gov™
Where We Are
POPULATED PLACES
100,000 – 499,999 • Minneapolis
25,000 – 99,999 • Duluth
24,999 and less • Hibbing
State capital ★ St Paul
Urban areas
TRANSPORTATION
Interstate; limited access highway 94
Other principal highway
Railroad
PHYSICAL FEATURES
Streams
Lakes
Highest elevation in state (feet) +2301
The lowest elevation in Minnesota is 600 feet above sea level (Lake Superior).
MILES
0 25 50 75 100
Albers equal area projection
U.S. Department of the Interior
U.S. Geological Survey
The National Atlas of the United States of America®
CANADA
ONTARIO
MANITOBA
NORTH DAKOTA
SOUTH DAKOTA
WISCONSIN
MICHIGAN
Lake Superior
Lake of the Woods
Rainy Lake
Rainy R.
Red River
Upper Red Lake
Lower Red Lake
Lake Winnibigoshish
Leech Lake
Vermilion Lake
Mille Lacs Lake
Mesabi Range
Mississippi
Minnesota River
Mississippi River
St Croix River
Lake Traverse
Big Stone Lake
Eagle Mtn 2301+
Grand Portage
Grand Marais
Two Harbors
Duluth
Ely
Virginia
Hibbing
International Falls
Cloquet
Grand Rapids
Aitkin
Northome
Baudette
Warroad
Roseau
Hallock
Warren
Thief River Falls
East Grand Forks
Crookston
Bagley
Bemidji
Walker
Mahnomen
Park Rapids
Moorhead
Detroit Lakes
Wadena
Brainerd
Pine City
Milaca
Little Falls
Fergus Falls
Breckenridge
Alexandria
Sauk Centre
St Cloud
Elk River
Anoka
Coon Rapids
Brooklyn Park
Minneapolis
St Paul
Bloomington
Eden Prairie
Burnsville
Lakeville
Red Wing
Northfield
Faribault
Owatonna
Rochester
Winona
Preston
Austin
Albert Lea
Mankato
St Peter
Blue Earth
Litchfield
Hutchinson
Olivia
Willmar
Morris
Ortonville
Madison
Montevideo
Granite Falls
Redwood Falls
Marshall
New Ulm
St James
Windom
Fairmont
Worthington
Pipestone
Luverne
35
94
90

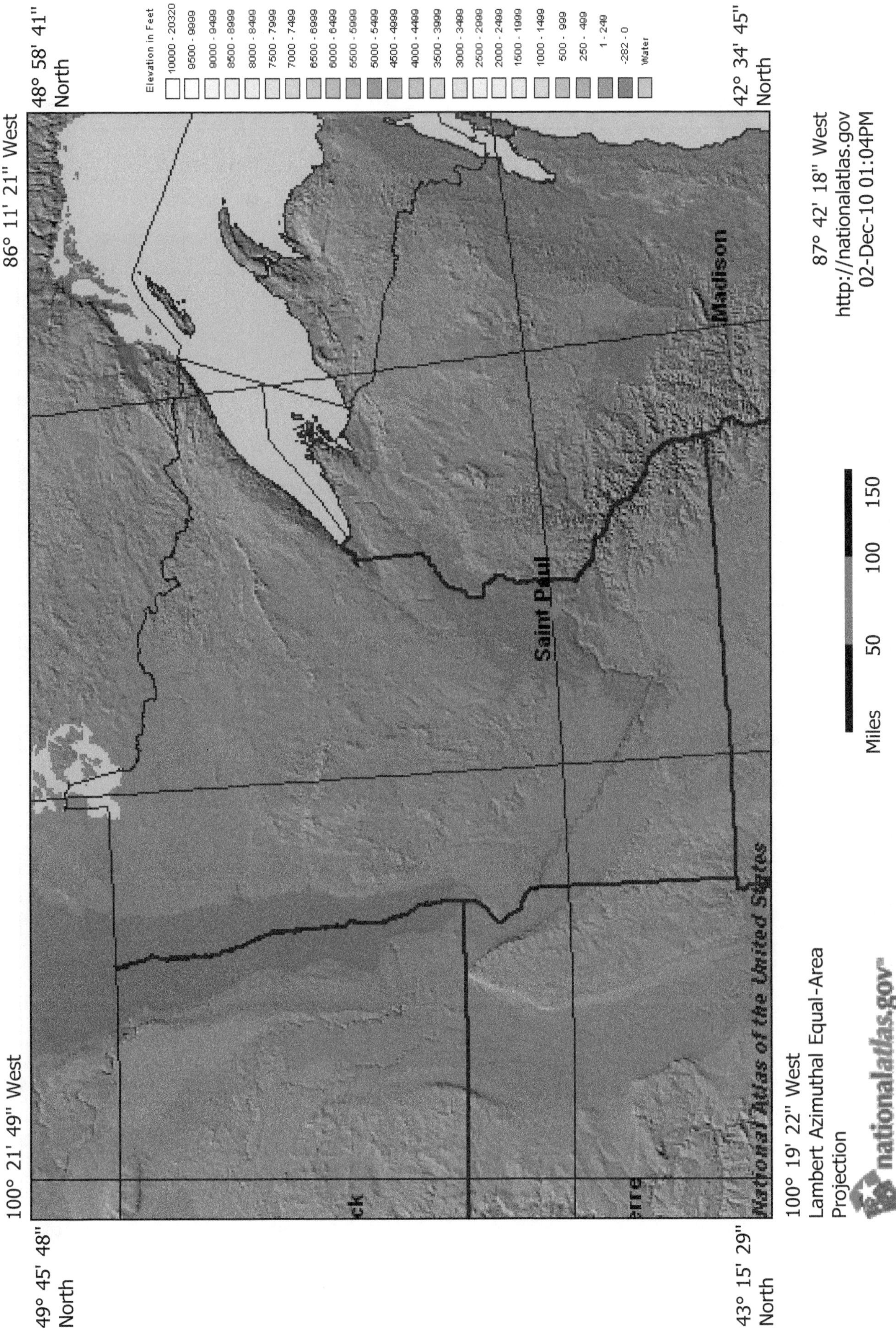
49° 45' 48" North
100° 21' 49" West
86° 11' 21" West
48° 58' 41" North
Elevation in Feet
10000 - 20320
9500 - 9999
9000 - 9499
8500 - 8999
8000 - 8499
7500 - 7999
7000 - 7499
6500 - 6999
6000 - 6499
5500 - 5999
5000 - 5499
4500 - 4999
4000 - 4499
3500 - 3999
3000 - 3499
2500 - 2999
2000 - 2499
1500 - 1999
1000 - 1499
500 - 999
250 - 499
1 - 249
-282 - 0
Water
42° 34' 45" North
87° 42' 18" West
http://nationalatlas.gov
02-Dec-10 01:04PM
Madison
Saint Paul
Miles 50 100 150
National Atlas of the United States
43° 15' 29" North
100° 19' 22" West
Lambert Azimuthal Equal-Area
Projection
nationalatlas.gov

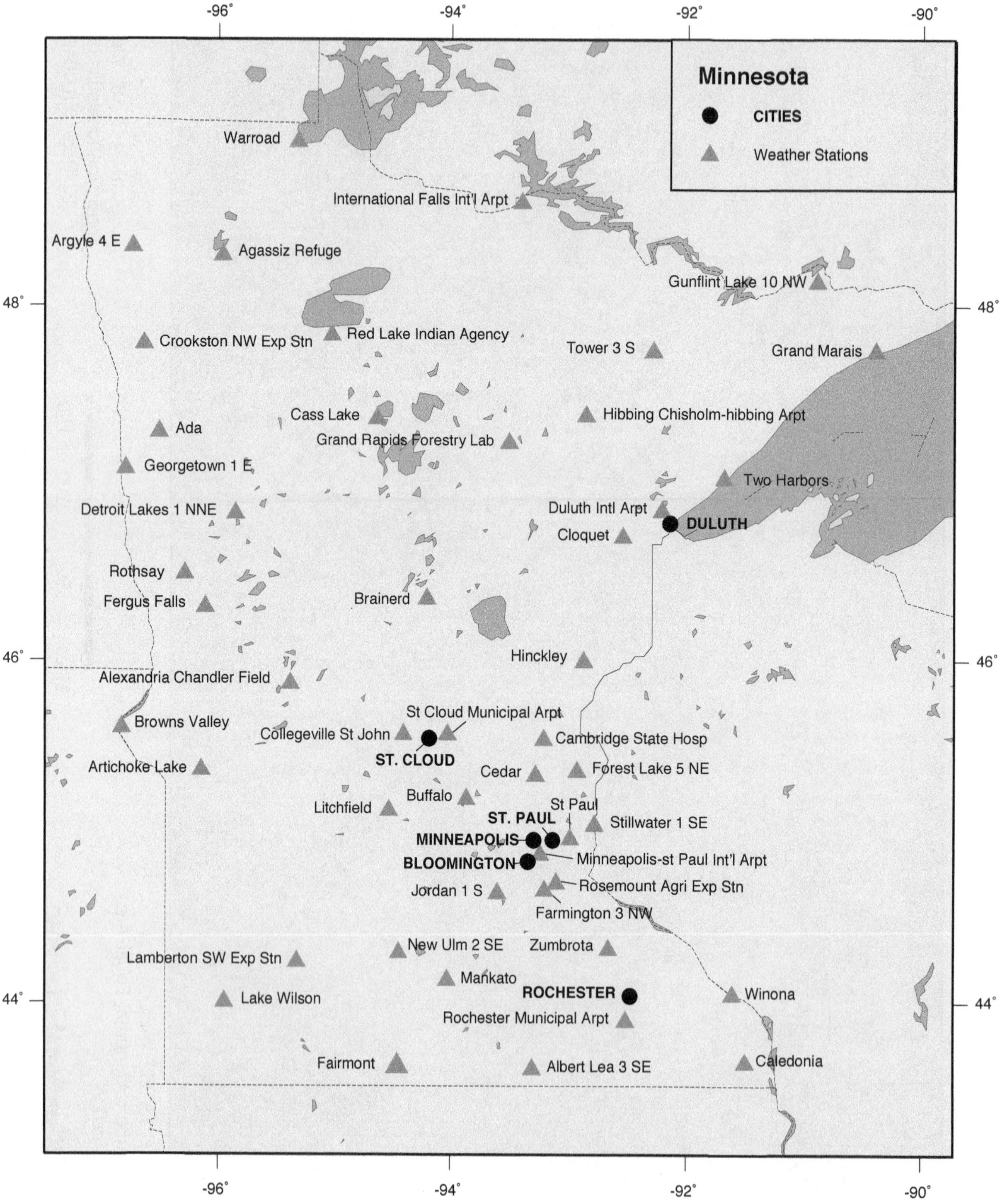
-96°
-94°
-92°
-90°
48°
46°
44°
Minnesota
CITIES
Weather Stations
Warroad
International Falls Int'l Arpt
Argyle 4 E
Agassiz Refuge
Gunflint Lake 10 NW
Crookston NW Exp Stn
Red Lake Indian Agency
Tower 3 S
Grand Marais
Ada
Cass Lake
Hibbing Chisholm-hibbing Arpt
Grand Rapids Forestry Lab
Georgetown 1 E
Two Harbors
Detroit Lakes 1 NNE
Duluth Intl Arpt
DULUTH
Cloquet
Rothsay
Fergus Falls
Brainerd
Hinckley
Alexandria Chandler Field
St Cloud Municipal Arpt
Browns Valley
Collegeville St John
Cambridge State Hosp
ST. CLOUD
Artichoke Lake
Cedar
Forest Lake 5 NE
Buffalo
St Paul
Litchfield
ST. PAUL
Stillwater 1 SE
MINNEAPOLIS
Minneapolis-st Paul Int'l Arpt
BLOOMINGTON
Rosemount Agri Exp Stn
Jordan 1 S
Farmington 3 NW
New Ulm 2 SE
Zumbrota
Lamberton SW Exp Stn
Mankato
ROCHESTER
Winona
Lake Wilson
Rochester Municipal Arpt
Fairmont
Albert Lea 3 SE
Caledonia

Minnesota Weather Stations by County

County	Station Name
Anoka	Cedar
Becker	Detroit Lakes 1 NNE
Beltrami	Red Lake Indian Agency
Big Stone	Artichoke Lake
Blue Earth	Mankato
Brown	New Ulm 2 SE
Carlton	Cloquet
Cass	Cass Lake
Chisago	Forest Lake 5 NE
Clay	Georgetown 1 E
Cook	Grand Marais Gunflint Lake 10 NW
Crow Wing	Brainerd
Dakota	Farmington 3 NW Rosemount Agri Exp Stn
Douglas	Alexandria Chandler Field
Freeborn	Albert Lea 3 SE
Goodhue	Zumbrota
Hennepin	Minneapolis-St Paul Int'l Arpt
Houston	Caledonia
Isanti	Cambridge State Hosp
Itasca	Grand Rapids Forestry Lab
Koochiching	International Falls Int'l Arpt
Lake	Two Harbors
Marshall	Agassiz Refuge Argyle 4 E
Martin	Fairmont
Meeker	Litchfield
Murray	Lake Wilson
Norman	Ada
Olmsted	Rochester Municipal Arpt
Otter Tail	Fergus Falls
Pine	Hinckley
Polk	Crookston NW Exp Stn

County	Station Name
Ramsey	St Paul
Redwood	Lamberton SW Exp Stn
Roseau	Warroad
Scott	Jordan 1 S
Sherburne	St Cloud Municipal Arpt
St. Louis	Duluth Intl Arpt Hibbing Chisholm-Hibbing Arpt Tower 3 S
Stearns	Collegeville St John
Traverse	Browns Valley
Washington	Stillwater 1 SE
Wilkin	Rothsay
Winona	Winona
Wright	Buffalo

Minnesota Weather Stations by City

City	Station Name	Miles
Andover	Cambridge State Hosp	23.0
	Cedar	5.7
	Forest Lake 5 NE	21.4
Apple Valley	Farmington 3 NW	5.5
	Jordan 1 S	21.2
	Minneapolis-St Paul Int'l Arpt	9.7
	Rosemount Agri Exp Stn	5.5
	St Paul	17.9
Blaine	Cedar	10.7
	Forest Lake 5 NE	19.8
	Minneapolis-St Paul Int'l Arpt	19.6
	St Paul	19.2
	Stillwater 1 SE	23.6
Bloomington	Farmington 3 NW	13.1
	Jordan 1 S	19.2
	Minneapolis-St Paul Int'l Arpt	5.5
	Rosemount Agri Exp Stn	13.2
	St Paul	18.3
Brooklyn Center	Cedar	17.2
	Minneapolis-St Paul Int'l Arpt	13.5
	St Paul	18.3
Brooklyn Park	Cedar	15.3
	Minneapolis-St Paul Int'l Arpt	15.9
	St Paul	20.4
Burnsville	Farmington 3 NW	7.9
	Jordan 1 S	18.4
	Minneapolis-St Paul Int'l Arpt	8.8
	Rosemount Agri Exp Stn	9.1
	St Paul	19.4
Coon Rapids	Cedar	9.8
	Forest Lake 5 NE	22.7
	Minneapolis-St Paul Int'l Arpt	20.6
	St Paul	22.4
Cottage Grove	Farmington 3 NW	16.6
	Minneapolis-St Paul Int'l Arpt	15.0
	Rosemount Agri Exp Stn	11.2
	St Paul	8.6
	Stillwater 1 SE	15.9
	Ellsworth 1 E, WI	24.0
	River Falls, WI	15.7
Duluth	Cloquet	20.8
	Duluth Intl Arpt	5.7
	Foxboro, WI	22.7
	Superior, WI	7.7
Eagan	Farmington 3 NW	10.0
	Jordan 1 S	24.7
	Minneapolis-St Paul Int'l Arpt	6.0
	Rosemount Agri Exp Stn	7.3
	St Paul	13.2
	Stillwater 1 SE	24.3
Eden Prairie	Farmington 3 NW	18.8
	Jordan 1 S	16.1
	Minneapolis-St Paul Int'l Arpt	11.3
Eden Prairie *(cont.)*	Rosemount Agri Exp Stn	20.1
	St Paul	24.3
Edina	Farmington 3 NW	17.7
	Jordan 1 S	21.2
	Minneapolis-St Paul Int'l Arpt	5.9
	Rosemount Agri Exp Stn	17.4
	St Paul	18.5
Fridley	Cedar	16.0
	Forest Lake 5 NE	24.6
	Minneapolis-St Paul Int'l Arpt	14.1
	St Paul	16.3
	Stillwater 1 SE	23.3
Inver Grove Heights	Farmington 3 NW	13.7
	Minneapolis-St Paul Int'l Arpt	9.3
	Rosemount Agri Exp Stn	9.0
	St Paul	8.2
	Stillwater 1 SE	18.6
	River Falls, WI	21.3
Lakeville	Farmington 3 NW	3.4
	Jordan 1 S	18.6
	Minneapolis-St Paul Int'l Arpt	13.2
	Rosemount Agri Exp Stn	7.2
	St Paul	21.9
Mankato	Mankato	1.3
	New Ulm 2 SE	24.7
Maple Grove	Buffalo	20.8
	Cedar	16.7
	Minneapolis-St Paul Int'l Arpt	18.8
Maplewood	Cedar	24.1
	Farmington 3 NW	24.6
	Forest Lake 5 NE	24.4
	Minneapolis-St Paul Int'l Arpt	12.5
	Rosemount Agri Exp Stn	20.4
	St Paul	5.3
	Stillwater 1 SE	13.2
	River Falls, WI	23.9
Minneapolis	Cedar	24.5
	Farmington 3 NW	20.8
	Minneapolis-St Paul Int'l Arpt	5.7
	Rosemount Agri Exp Stn	18.9
	St Paul	14.0
	Stillwater 1 SE	24.2
Minnetonka	Farmington 3 NW	22.7
	Jordan 1 S	20.9
	Minneapolis-St Paul Int'l Arpt	11.5
	Rosemount Agri Exp Stn	23.0
	St Paul	23.3
Moorhead	Georgetown 1 E	15.3
	Fargo Hector Field, ND	5.6
Oakdale	Farmington 3 NW	24.6
	Minneapolis-St Paul Int'l Arpt	14.9
	Rosemount Agri Exp Stn	19.8
	St Paul	2.7

See User Guide for station inclusion criteria.

City	Station Name	Miles
Oakdale *(cont.)*	Stillwater 1 SE	9.5
	River Falls, WI	19.5
Plymouth	Buffalo	22.9
	Cedar	22.2
	Minneapolis-St Paul Int'l Arpt	14.5
	St Paul	23.7
Richfield	Farmington 3 NW	15.2
	Jordan 1 S	22.6
	Minneapolis-St Paul Int'l Arpt	2.5
	Rosemount Agri Exp Stn	14.2
	St Paul	15.5
Rochester	Rochester Municipal Arpt	9.3
	Zumbrota	20.8
Roseville	Cedar	21.9
	Farmington 3 NW	24.2
	Minneapolis-St Paul Int'l Arpt	10.1
	Rosemount Agri Exp Stn	20.7
	St Paul	9.1
	Stillwater 1 SE	17.7
Savage	Farmington 3 NW	10.2
	Jordan 1 S	14.8
	Minneapolis-St Paul Int'l Arpt	10.8
	Rosemount Agri Exp Stn	12.6
	St Paul	22.7
Shakopee	Farmington 3 NW	18.1
	Jordan 1 S	10.6
	Minneapolis-St Paul Int'l Arpt	15.3
	Rosemount Agri Exp Stn	20.8
St. Cloud	Collegeville St John	11.1
	St Cloud Municipal Arpt	6.0
St. Louis Park	Farmington 3 NW	21.5
	Jordan 1 S	24.1
	Minneapolis-St Paul Int'l Arpt	7.9
	Rosemount Agri Exp Stn	20.6
	St Paul	18.6
St. Paul	Farmington 3 NW	20.2
	Minneapolis-St Paul Int'l Arpt	7.8
	Rosemount Agri Exp Stn	16.4
	St Paul	6.2
	Stillwater 1 SE	16.8
Winona	Winona	1.0
	Alma Dam 4, WI	24.3
	La Crosse Municipal Arpt, WI	23.4
Woodbury	Farmington 3 NW	21.0
	Minneapolis-St Paul Int'l Arpt	14.6
	Rosemount Agri Exp Stn	15.9
	St Paul	3.2
	Stillwater 1 SE	11.1
	River Falls, WI	16.4

Note: Miles is the distance between the geographic center of the city and the weather station.

Minnesota Weather Stations by Elevation

Feet	Station Name
1,649	Lake Wilson
1,460	Gunflint Lake 10 NW
1,459	Tower 3 S
1,433	Duluth Intl Arpt
1,416	Alexandria Chandler Field
1,375	Detroit Lakes 1 NNE
1,347	Hibbing Chisholm-Hibbing Arpt
1,310	Grand Rapids Forestry Lab
1,296	Rochester Municipal Arpt
1,295	Cass Lake
1,265	Cloquet
1,250	Fergus Falls
1,229	Albert Lea 3 SE
1,225	Collegeville St John
1,220	Red Lake Indian Agency
1,206	Rothsay
1,187	Fairmont
1,180	Brainerd
1,179	International Falls Int'l Arpt
1,174	Caledonia
1,144	Lamberton SW Exp Stn
1,142	Agassiz Refuge
1,131	Litchfield
1,075	Artichoke Lake
1,068	Warroad
1,035	Hinckley
1,027	St Cloud Municipal Arpt
984	Browns Valley
984	Zumbrota
979	Buffalo
979	Farmington 3 NW
959	Cambridge State Hosp
959	Forest Lake 5 NE
950	Rosemount Agri Exp Stn
930	Jordan 1 S
910	Ada
907	Cedar
899	St Paul
888	Crookston NW Exp Stn
884	Georgetown 1 E
870	Argyle 4 E
859	New Ulm 2 SE
850	Mankato
833	Minneapolis-St Paul Int'l Arpt
711	Stillwater 1 SE
651	Winona
625	Two Harbors
611	Grand Marais

See User Guide for station inclusion criteria.

Duluth Int'l Airport

Duluth, Minnesota is located at the western tip of Lake Superior. The city, about 20 miles long, lies at the base of a range of hills that rise abruptly to 600 - 800 feet above the level of Lake Superior. The range runs in a northeast and southwest direction. Two or three miles from the lake the land becomes a slightly rolling plateau.

Duluth in the summer is known as the Air Conditioned City. Being situated below high terrain and along the lake, any easterly component winds automatically cool the city. However, with westerly flow in the summer, the wind generally abates at night, thus, allowing cool lake air to move back into the city area near the lake.

An important influence on the climate is the passage of a succession of high and low pressure systems west and east. The proximity of Lake Superior, which is the largest and coldest of the Great Lakes, modifies the local weather. Summer temperatures are cooler and winter temperatures are warmer. The lake effect at Duluth is most prevalent when low pressure systems pass to the south creating easterly winds. In the summer, warm, moist air flowing over the cold lake surface has a stabilizing effect that results in cool, cloudy weather over Duluth. However, during the winter cold air flowing over the warm open lake surface absorbs moisture that is later precipitated over Duluth as snow. The lake effect is further reflected from the low frequency of severe storms such as wind, hail, tornadoes, freezing rain (glaze), and blizzards when compared to other areas that are a further distance from the lake.

Easterly component winds at Duluth occur 40 to 50 percent of the time from March through August and 20 to 25 percent of the time from November through February. During the winter 60 to 70 percent of the winds are from a westerly component.

The climate of Duluth is predominantly continental with significant local Lake Superior effects. Duluth averages 143 days between the last occurrence of 32 degrees in mid-May and the first in early October. At the Duluth Airport about six miles away from the lake, the average first and last occurrences of 32 degrees are late May and late September, giving a freeze-free period of 123 days.

Ice in the harbor forms about mid-November and generally is gone by mid-April. The shipping season can vary from year to year depending on temperatures and the winds that move the ice around. In most years there is little or no shipping during February and March on Lake Superior.

Duluth Int'l Airport *St. Louis County* Elevation: 1,433 ft. Latitude: 46° 50' N Longitude: 92° 13' W

	JAN	FEB	MAR	APR	MAY	JUN	JUL	AUG	SEP	OCT	NOV	DEC	YEAR
Mean Maximum Temp. (°F)	18.9	23.7	33.8	49.0	62.3	70.9	76.3	74.1	65.0	51.2	35.6	22.3	48.6
Mean Temp. (°F)	10.2	14.9	25.4	39.5	51.5	60.1	65.8	64.2	55.6	42.9	28.8	14.8	39.5
Mean Minimum Temp. (°F)	1.5	6.0	16.9	29.9	40.6	49.3	55.2	54.3	46.1	34.6	21.9	7.3	30.3
Extreme Maximum Temp. (°F)	48	55	72	82	90	94	97	93	92	84	71	53	97
Extreme Minimum Temp. (°F)	-38	-39	-29	-1	19	30	35	32	24	10	-18	-34	-39
Days Maximum Temp. ≥ 90°F	0	0	0	0	0	0	1	1	0	0	0	0	2
Days Maximum Temp. ≤ 32°F	27	21	14	2	0	0	0	0	0	1	12	25	102
Days Minimum Temp. ≤ 32°F	31	28	29	19	5	0	0	0	2	13	26	31	184
Days Minimum Temp. ≤ 0°F	15	11	4	0	0	0	0	0	0	0	1	11	42
Heating Degree Days (base 65°F)	1,694	1,412	1,222	759	419	174	62	84	291	678	1,080	1,551	9,426
Cooling Degree Days (base 65°F)	0	0	0	0	6	33	94	67	15	0	0	0	215
Mean Precipitation (in.)	0.97	0.81	1.49	2.41	3.06	4.13	3.88	3.66	4.21	2.77	2.03	1.15	30.57
Maximum Precipitation (in.)*	4.7	2.4	5.1	5.8	7.7	8.0	8.5	10.3	9.4	7.5	5.0	3.7	43.4
Minimum Precipitation (in.)*	0.1	0.1	0.2	0.2	0.1	0.5	1.1	0.7	0.2	0.3	0.2	0.2	19.8
Extreme Maximum Daily Precip. (in.)	0.88	1.16	1.76	1.86	1.96	3.33	3.25	3.11	3.57	2.66	2.26	1.65	3.57
Days With ≥ 0.1" Precipitation	2	3	4	5	7	8	7	7	7	6	5	3	64
Days With ≥ 0.5" Precipitation	0	0	1	2	2	3	2	2	3	2	1	0	18
Days With ≥ 1.0" Precipitation	0	0	0	0	0	1	1	1	1	0	0	0	4
Mean Snowfall (in.)	18.7	12.3	13.6	6.8	0.2	trace	trace	trace	0.1	2.1	14.5	17.2	85.5
Maximum Snowfall (in.)*	47	32	46	32	8	0	0	0	2	10	50	44	169
Maximum 24-hr. Snowfall (in.)*	16	13	17	12	4	0	0	0	2	8	24	23	24
Maximum Snow Depth (in.)	42	34	37	24	1	trace	trace	trace	trace	4	30	34	42
Days With ≥ 1.0" Snow Depth	31	28	28	10	0	0	0	0	0	1	12	27	137
Thunderstorm Days*	< 1	< 1	1	2	4	7	8	7	4	1	< 1	< 1	34
Foggy Days*	10	9	10	9	10	12	11	14	13	12	10	12	132
Predominant Sky Cover*	OVR	OVR	OVR	OVR	OVR	OVR	OVR	OVR	OVR	OVR	OVR	OVR	OVR
Mean Relative Humidity 6am (%)*	77	77	79	77	76	82	86	89	89	83	82	80	81
Mean Relative Humidity 3pm (%)*	66	62	61	53	50	56	56	59	60	58	67	70	60
Mean Dewpoint (°F)*	1	5	15	26	37	49	55	54	46	34	21	8	29
Prevailing Wind Direction*	NW	NW	E	E	E	ESE	WNW	ESE	WNW	WNW	WNW	NW	NW
Prevailing Wind Speed (mph)*	14	13	15	15	13	10	10	9	12	13	14	13	13
Maximum Wind Gust (mph)*	58	55	71	60	71	69	64	56	60	70	55	54	71

Note: (*) Period of record is 1948-1995

International Falls Int'l Arpt.

Situated on the Canadian border, International Falls is subjected to frequent outbreaks of continental polar air throughout most of the year. These are tempered to mildness during June, July, and August, when the land and lake areas to the north and northwest have been warmed by long days of sunshine. Periods of fine, mild weather occur, interspersed with showers and an occasional three or four day period of cloudy, rainy weather. The area of small lakes, covering up to 30 percent of the area to the north and northwest, supplies a good deal of the moisture for the late afternoon and evening showers and stores heat that tempers southward flow of cold air during September and October. This prolongs the fall season until early November. In November the water surfaces freeze and snow returns to International Falls. From December through February, temperatures fall below zero on most days and occasionally fail to rise above zero for a week or more.

In winter, frost penetrates into the ground to depths of 36 to 60 inches. If winter begins abruptly so that a heavy blanket of snow covers the ground before protracted freezing occurs, it may freeze to only a few inches deep. This is very important to loggers, who depend upon deep soil freezing for road foundations into otherwise inaccessible places. The wide expanse of deep snow and ice prolongs winter. The transition to summer is rapid after the spring thaw. Spring lasts only about a month.

By June 1st, the ground generally is warm enough for successful planting, but vigilance against freezing temperatures is required through most of June. Crops that do not mature by September 1st have little chance of providing a harvest. Heaviest precipitation coincides with the growing season.

Based on the 1951-1980 period, the average first occurrence of 32 degrees Fahrenheit in the fall is September 15 and the average last occurrence in the spring is May 26.

Heavy deposits of glaze occur only about once a year at International Falls. Occasional storms that intensify over the southern plateau or plains states and move rapidly northeastward, drawing up moist gulf air, bring the most violent weather changes. They often produce severe thunderstorms and windstorms in early fall and blizzards with heavy snowfall and drifting in winter. Quite often such a storm brings an abrupt end to fall weather. During winter, a variation of 100 miles in the paths of such storms as they approach the border is of tremendous importance to local transportation and road maintenance.

Surrounding terrain is generally level. Forests of varying density and swampland surround the station for many miles to the east, south, and west. Rainy Lake, approximately 300 square miles in area, lies to the north. The lake is five miles from the station at its closest point.

International Falls Int'l Arpt. *Koochiching County* Elevation: 1,179 ft. Latitude: 48° 34' N Longitude: 93° 24' W

	JAN	FEB	MAR	APR	MAY	JUN	JUL	AUG	SEP	OCT	NOV	DEC	YEAR
Mean Maximum Temp. (°F)	15.3	21.8	34.2	51.5	65.1	73.3	77.9	75.8	65.5	50.8	33.6	19.0	48.6
Mean Temp. (°F)	4.8	10.8	23.5	39.7	52.5	61.3	65.7	63.7	54.2	41.3	25.9	10.1	37.8
Mean Minimum Temp. (°F)	-5.8	-0.3	12.7	27.9	39.8	49.3	53.6	51.6	42.8	31.8	18.2	1.1	26.9
Extreme Maximum Temp. (°F)	47	58	67	90	92	99	98	95	92	83	72	48	99
Extreme Minimum Temp. (°F)	-45	-45	-30	-11	18	27	34	30	23	2	-32	-40	-45
Days Maximum Temp. ≥ 90°F	0	0	0	0	0	1	1	1	0	0	0	0	3
Days Maximum Temp. ≤ 32°F	28	22	13	2	0	0	0	0	0	1	14	26	106
Days Minimum Temp. ≤ 32°F	31	28	29	21	7	0	0	0	4	18	28	31	197
Days Minimum Temp. ≤ 0°F	20	15	7	0	0	0	0	0	0	0	3	15	60
Heating Degree Days (base 65°F)	1,865	1,529	1,281	752	395	150	60	98	331	728	1,167	1,699	10,055
Cooling Degree Days (base 65°F)	0	0	0	1	13	46	89	66	13	1	0	0	229
Mean Precipitation (in.)	0.70	0.55	0.95	1.48	2.78	3.87	3.48	2.82	2.92	2.10	1.36	0.77	23.78
Maximum Precipitation (in.)*	3.0	1.8	3.1	3.3	6.7	7.4	9.5	6.7	7.4	4.8	3.5	1.7	32.6
Minimum Precipitation (in.)*	0.1	0.1	0.2	0.1	0.2	0.7	1.1	0.6	0.3	0.1	0.2	0.2	17.2
Extreme Maximum Daily Precip. (in.)	2.70	0.58	1.21	1.50	2.67	3.10	3.98	2.51	1.97	1.65	1.37	0.75	3.98
Days With ≥ 0.1" Precipitation	2	2	3	4	6	8	7	6	6	5	4	2	55
Days With ≥ 0.5" Precipitation	0	0	0	1	2	2	2	2	2	1	1	0	13
Days With ≥ 1.0" Precipitation	0	0	0	0	0	1	1	1	1	0	0	0	4
Mean Snowfall (in.)	15.0	11.0	8.4	6.6	0.2	trace	trace	trace	0.2	2.3	13.3	16.0	73.0
Maximum Snowfall (in.)*	43	32	32	23	13	trace	0	0	2	9	30	44	132
Maximum 24-hr. Snowfall (in.)*	14	10	13	14	7	trace	0	0	1	5	12	9	14
Maximum Snow Depth (in.)	38	34	30	19	1	trace	trace	trace	trace	5	18	25	38
Days With ≥ 1.0" Snow Depth	31	28	24	6	0	0	0	0	0	1	14	29	133
Thunderstorm Days*	< 1	0	< 1	1	4	7	9	7	4	1	< 1	< 1	33
Foggy Days*	7	6	6	6	7	8	7	10	10	8	7	8	90
Predominant Sky Cover*	OVR	OVR	OVR	OVR	OVR	OVR	OVR	OVR	OVR	OVR	OVR	OVR	OVR
Mean Relative Humidity 7am (%)*	74	75	77	74	72	77	84	88	89	85	84	79	80
Mean Relative Humidity 4pm (%)*	65	60	55	47	45	52	54	56	59	58	69	70	58
Mean Dewpoint (°F)*	-3	2	14	25	38	50	56	55	45	33	19	3	28
Prevailing Wind Direction*	W	W	WNW	NW	NW	S	WNW	S	S	S	WNW	WNW	WNW
Prevailing Wind Speed (mph)*	9	9	12	12	12	9	9	8	9	9	12	10	10
Maximum Wind Gust (mph)*	55	46	52	60	59	58	63	67	48	46	49	44	67

Note: (*) Period of record is 1948-1995

The period of record for National Weather Service station data is 1980 – 2009 except where noted. See User Guide for detailed explanation of data.

Minneapolis-St Paul Int'l Arpt.

The Twin Cities of Minneapolis and St. Paul are located at the confluence of the Mississippi and Minnesota Rivers over the heart of an artesian water basin. Its flat or gently rolling terrain varies little in elevation from that of the official observation station at International Airport. Numerous lakes dot the surrounding area. Minneapolis alone boasts of 22 lakes within the city park system. The largest body of water, nearly 15,000 acres, is Lake Minnetonka, located about 15 miles west of the airport. Most bodies of water are relatively small and shallow and are ice covered during winter.

The climate of the Minneapolis-St. Paul area is predominantly continental. Seasonal temperature variations are quite large. Temperatures range from less than -30 degrees to over 100 degrees. The growing season is 166 days. Because of this favorable growing season, all crops generally mature before the autumn freeze occurs.

The Twin Cities lie near the northern edge of the influx of moisture from the Gulf of Mexico. Severe storms such as blizzards, freezing rain (glaze), tornadoes, wind and hail storms do occur. The total annual precipitation is important. Even more significant is its proper distribution during the growing season. During the five month growing season, May through September, the major crops produced are corn, soybeans, small grains, and hay. During this period, the normal rainfall is over 16 inches, approximately 65 percent of the annual precipitation. Winter snowfall is nearly 48 inches. Winter recreational weather is excellent because of the dry snow. These conditions exist from about Christmas into early March. Snow depths average six to eight inches in the city and eight to 10 inches in the suburbs during this period.

Floods occur along the Mississippi River due to spring snow melt, excessive rainfall, or both. Occasionally an ice jam forms and creates a local flood condition. The flood problem at St. Paul is complicated because the Minnesota River empties into the Mississippi River between the two cities. Consequently, high water or flooding on the Minnesota River creates a greater flood potential at St. Paul. Flood stage at St. Paul can be expected on the average once in every eight years.

Minneapolis-St Paul Int'l Arpt. *Hennepin County* Elevation: 833 ft. Latitude: 44° 53' N Longitude: 93° 14' W

	JAN	FEB	MAR	APR	MAY	JUN	JUL	AUG	SEP	OCT	NOV	DEC	YEAR
Mean Maximum Temp. (°F)	23.8	28.7	40.8	57.6	69.5	78.8	83.5	80.3	71.7	57.7	41.3	27.3	55.1
Mean Temp. (°F)	15.7	20.7	32.3	47.3	59.2	68.7	73.7	70.9	62.0	48.6	33.8	19.8	46.0
Mean Minimum Temp. (°F)	7.5	12.6	23.7	37.0	48.8	58.5	63.9	61.5	52.2	39.4	26.2	12.3	37.0
Extreme Maximum Temp. (°F)	57	61	83	95	97	102	105	101	93	90	77	68	105
Extreme Minimum Temp. (°F)	-27	-32	-10	5	25	35	46	44	28	13	-12	-29	-32
Days Maximum Temp. ≥ 90°F	0	0	0	0	1	3	6	3	1	0	0	0	14
Days Maximum Temp. ≤ 32°F	22	16	7	0	0	0	0	0	0	0	7	19	71
Days Minimum Temp. ≤ 32°F	31	27	24	10	1	0	0	0	0	7	22	30	152
Days Minimum Temp. ≤ 0°F	10	6	1	0	0	0	0	0	0	0	1	6	24
Heating Degree Days (base 65°F)	1,524	1,247	1,006	530	213	42	5	14	153	508	931	1,396	7,569
Cooling Degree Days (base 65°F)	0	0	0	6	40	160	282	205	70	6	0	0	769
Mean Precipitation (in.)	0.91	0.76	1.90	2.60	3.35	4.23	4.01	4.24	3.01	2.40	1.70	1.07	30.18
Maximum Precipitation (in.)*	3.6	2.1	4.8	5.9	8.0	9.8	17.9	9.3	6.9	5.7	5.3	4.3	39.9
Minimum Precipitation (in.)*	0.1	0.1	0.3	0.2	0.6	0.2	0.6	0.4	0.4	trace	0.1	0.2	16.2
Extreme Maximum Daily Precip. (in.)	0.90	1.01	1.52	2.58	1.84	2.95	9.15	3.19	2.59	4.61	1.85	1.35	9.15
Days With ≥ 0.1" Precipitation	3	3	5	6	8	7	6	6	6	5	4	3	62
Days With ≥ 0.5" Precipitation	0	0	1	2	2	3	2	3	2	1	1	0	17
Days With ≥ 1.0" Precipitation	0	0	0	0	1	1	1	1	1	0	0	0	5
Mean Snowfall (in.)	11.5	***7.6***	***10.7***	***2.8***	trace	trace	trace	trace	trace	0.6	***9.2***	***10.5***	***52.9***
Maximum Snowfall (in.)*	46	27	40	22	3	0	0	0	trace	8	47	33	102
Maximum 24-hr. Snowfall (in.)*	17	9	15	14	3	0	0	0	trace	8	19	12	19
Maximum Snow Depth (in.)	38	21	16	***10***	2	trace	trace	trace	trace	1	***23***	***21***	***38***
Days With ≥ 1.0" Snow Depth	26	22	13	***1***	0	0	0	0	0	0	***7***	***21***	***90***
Thunderstorm Days*	< 1	< 1	1	3	5	8	7	7	4	2	1	< 1	38
Foggy Days*	10	9	9	7	7	5	5	8	8	8	9	11	96
Predominant Sky Cover*	OVR	OVR	OVR	OVR	OVR	OVR	SCT	CLR	OVR	OVR	OVR	OVR	OVR
Mean Relative Humidity 6am (%)*	75	76	77	75	75	79	82	84	85	81	80	79	79
Mean Relative Humidity 3pm (%)*	65	62	58	48	47	50	50	52	53	52	63	68	56
Mean Dewpoint (°F)*	5	10	21	32	43	55	60	59	50	38	24	12	34
Prevailing Wind Direction*	NW	NW	NW	NW	SE	SE	S	SE	S	NW	NW	NW	NW
Prevailing Wind Speed (mph)*	14	14	13	14	10	10	10	9	12	14	14	13	13
Maximum Wind Gust (mph)*	67	55	60	61	67	66	63	71	54	53	66	48	71

Note: (*) Period of record is 1945-1995

Rochester Municipal Airport

Rochester, Minnesota, is in the Zumbro River Valley. The south branch of the Zumbro flows through Rochester. Within the city of Rochester three creeks flow into the south branch. Terrain around Rochester is rolling, and the elevation ranges from 1,000 to 1,300 feet above sea level.

The National Weather Service station is located eight miles south of Rochester on a ridge 300 feet above the city elevation. Temperatures from radiation cooling on clear, calm nights can sometimes be much lower in the city.

The succession of high and low pressure systems over Rochester brings a variety of weather that is changeable and stimulating. The weather pattern is continental with four definite seasons. Winters are cold, but summers are pleasant.

The season-to-season temperature variation is quite large. The average temperature for a warm winter is 20 degrees and for a cold winter it is 12 degrees. The average temperature for a warm summer is 70 degrees and a cold summer is 67 degrees, which indicates that summer temperatures are not as variable as those during the winter. The average growing season is about 140 days.

Rochester lies near the northern edge of the influx of moisture from the Gulf of Mexico. Severe storms such as blizzards, freezing rain (glaze), tornadoes, wind, and hail storms do occur. During the five month growing season, May through September, the major crops of corn, soybeans, small grains, and hay are produced. During this period, the normal rainfall is over 18 inches, approximately 65 percent of the annual precipitation.

Snowfall averages above 45 inches per season. The snow season usually begins in November. About one year in ten the first one inch or more of snow will occur the latter part of October.

Rolling terrain and the thunderstorm probability make the south branch of the Zumbro River and its tributaries susceptible to flash flooding. Some flooding can occur with the spring snowmelt. In some instances the snowmelt is complicated with moderate spring rainfall.

Rochester Municipal Airport *Olmsted County* Elevation: 1,296 ft. Latitude: 43° 54' N Longitude: 92° 30' W

	JAN	FEB	MAR	APR	MAY	JUN	JUL	AUG	SEP	OCT	NOV	DEC	YEAR
Mean Maximum Temp. (°F)	22.9	27.2	39.2	55.9	68.0	77.2	80.7	78.0	70.6	57.1	40.8	26.4	53.7
Mean Temp. (°F)	15.0	19.3	31.1	45.6	57.3	66.7	70.5	68.1	60.1	47.2	32.9	18.9	44.4
Mean Minimum Temp. (°F)	6.9	11.5	23.0	35.2	46.5	56.2	60.3	58.2	49.5	37.3	25.0	11.5	35.1
Extreme Maximum Temp. (°F)	55	63	79	92	95	101	102	99	91	93	75	62	102
Extreme Minimum Temp. (°F)	-29	-35	-11	5	22	35	44	39	27	11	-12	-33	-35
Days Maximum Temp. ≥ 90°F	0	0	0	0	0	2	2	1	0	0	0	0	5
Days Maximum Temp. ≤ 32°F	24	18	8	1	0	0	0	0	0	0	7	21	79
Days Minimum Temp. ≤ 32°F	31	27	25	11	1	0	0	0	1	10	24	30	160
Days Minimum Temp. ≤ 0°F	10	7	2	0	0	0	0	0	0	0	1	8	28
Heating Degree Days (base 65°F)	1,547	1,285	1,043	580	261	60	13	32	189	550	955	1,423	7,938
Cooling Degree Days (base 65°F)	0	0	0	4	28	119	192	136	48	5	0	0	532
Mean Precipitation (in.)	0.86	0.83	1.87	3.22	3.69	4.47	4.47	4.66	3.21	2.27	1.82	1.11	32.48
Maximum Precipitation (in.)*	2.5	2.2	4.0	6.5	8.4	9.3	12.3	9.5	10.5	6.1	5.9	2.8	43.9
Minimum Precipitation (in.)*	0.1	trace	0.2	0.9	1.2	0.9	0.5	0.6	0.3	trace	0.1	0.2	15.4
Extreme Maximum Daily Precip. (in.)	1.10	0.94	1.81	3.81	4.02	4.80	7.47	5.16	4.04	1.88	2.30	1.00	7.47
Days With ≥ 0.1" Precipitation	3	2	5	7	7	7	7	7	6	5	4	3	63
Days With ≥ 0.5" Precipitation	0	0	1	2	2	3	3	3	2	1	1	0	18
Days With ≥ 1.0" Precipitation	0	0	0	1	1	1	1	1	1	0	0	0	6
Mean Snowfall (in.)	11.0	8.8	9.1	4.0	trace	***trace***	***trace***	***trace***	***trace***	***1.0***	6.3	11.7	***51.9***
Maximum Snowfall (in.)*	27	19	35	16	1	0	0	0	1	5	23	31	89
Maximum 24-hr. Snowfall (in.)*	15	9	11	13	1	0	0	0	1	5	11	10	15
Maximum Snow Depth (in.)	29	20	20	11	trace	trace	trace	trace	trace	2	11	19	29
Days With ≥ 1.0" Snow Depth	25	23	15	2	0	0	0	0	0	0	6	22	93
Thunderstorm Days*	< 1	< 1	1	3	6	8	8	7	5	2	1	< 1	41
Foggy Days*	11	10	12	10	10	8	9	11	11	9	12	13	126
Predominant Sky Cover*	OVR	OVR	OVR	OVR	OVR	OVR	OVR	OVR	OVR	OVR	OVR	OVR	OVR
Mean Relative Humidity 6am (%)*	80	81	82	80	80	82	86	88	87	82	83	83	83
Mean Relative Humidity 3pm (%)*	72	68	65	54	52	53	56	57	56	54	66	74	61
Mean Dewpoint (°F)*	7	12	22	33	45	55	60	59	50	38	25	14	35
Prevailing Wind Direction*	NW	NW	NW	NW	S	S	S	S	S	S	WNW	NW	S
Prevailing Wind Speed (mph)*	15	15	15	15	14	14	12	12	13	14	15	15	14
Maximum Wind Gust (mph)*	69	56	90	85	76	82	74	78	64	62	67	56	90

Note: (*) Period of record is 1948-1995

The period of record for National Weather Service station data is 1980 – 2009 except where noted. See User Guide for detailed explanation of data.

Saint Cloud Municipal Airport

St. Cloud is located in central Minnesota on the banks of the Mississippi River. The topography is gently rolling terrain with numerous lakes and wooded areas.

The climate is influenced by atmospheric moisture flowing into the state from the Gulf of Mexico and the Pacific coast. Air masses carrying moisture which is eventually released as precipitation may travel nearly 1,500 miles. Due to this long trek, a minor change in the wind system can result in the area receiving well below or well above the normal precipitation. Rainfall is generally ample for farm and garden crops. Although the total amount is important, its distribution during the average 140 day growing season from mid-May to the end of September is even more significant. Thunderstorms are the principal source of rainfall during this period.

Spring, summer, and fall are very pleasant. Prolonged periods of hot and humid weather are infrequent. Extremely hot days with temperatures of 100 degrees or higher occur only once every five to ten years and rarely are temperatures this high recorded on successive days. Tornadoes and severe local storms are common.

Winter is cold, but not unpleasant, since strong winds and high humidities are generally absent on the coldest days. Cold Canadian air masses are prevalent throughout the winter season. The normal winter will have five to ten days with temperatures in the -20 to -30 degree range. Heavy snowfalls do occur, but the northern location limits the numerous heavy snowfalls that occur just a short distance to the south. Snowfalls of three inches or more in a 24 hour period occur only on an average of four times per year. Snow generally remains on the ground from the onset of the winter season until spring. Blizzards occur on the average of once per year with a severe blizzard once every three or four years. Ice storms are infrequent because temperatures are usually too cold and the transition period from season to season is rather abrupt.

Saint Cloud Municipal Airport *Sherburne County* Elevation: 1,027 ft. Latitude: 45° 33' N Longitude: 94° 03' W

	JAN	FEB	MAR	APR	MAY	JUN	JUL	AUG	SEP	OCT	NOV	DEC	YEAR
Mean Maximum Temp. (°F)	21.5	26.7	38.5	56.2	69.0	77.5	82.3	79.4	70.4	56.3	39.2	24.9	53.5
Mean Temp. (°F)	11.7	16.9	29.0	44.4	56.6	65.5	70.3	67.6	58.6	45.5	30.4	16.1	42.7
Mean Minimum Temp. (°F)	1.8	7.0	19.3	32.5	44.2	53.5	58.3	55.8	46.8	34.7	21.7	7.2	31.9
Extreme Maximum Temp. (°F)	56	57	79	96	98	102	102	99	94	90	75	61	102
Extreme Minimum Temp. (°F)	-40	-40	-20	3	21	32	41	33	22	11	-16	-41	-41
Days Maximum Temp. ≥ 90°F	0	0	0	0	1	2	4	2	0	0	0	0	9
Days Maximum Temp. ≤ 32°F	25	18	8	1	0	0	0	0	0	0	9	22	83
Days Minimum Temp. ≤ 32°F	31	27	27	15	3	0	0	0	2	13	26	31	175
Days Minimum Temp. ≤ 0°F	14	10	3	0	0	0	0	0	0	0	2	10	39
Heating Degree Days (base 65°F)	1,649	1,356	1,110	614	279	76	16	39	223	599	1,031	1,512	8,504
Cooling Degree Days (base 65°F)	0	0	0	3	26	99	188	128	38	2	0	0	484
Mean Precipitation (in.)	0.66	0.59	1.53	2.54	2.94	4.21	3.25	3.81	3.42	2.43	1.35	0.74	27.47
Maximum Precipitation (in.)*	2.5	2.8	3.4	5.5	8.0	10.5	8.0	7.5	9.5	6.2	3.7	2.0	39.3
Minimum Precipitation (in.)*	0.1	trace	0.1	0	0.3	0	0.2	0.5	0.1	0.1	0.1	0.1	14.9
Extreme Maximum Daily Precip. (in.)	0.75	1.00	2.49	3.52	1.63	3.46	2.08	3.43	3.62	3.42	1.49	0.78	3.62
Days With ≥ 0.1" Precipitation	2	2	4	5	7	8	6	6	6	5	4	2	57
Days With ≥ 0.5" Precipitation	0	0	1	2	2	2	2	3	2	1	1	0	16
Days With ≥ 1.0" Precipitation	0	0	0	0	1	1	1	1	1	1	0	0	6
Mean Snowfall (in.)	***8.7***	***7.1***	***8.6***	***3.0***	***trace***	***0.0***	***0.0***	***trace***	***trace***	***0.8***	***8.6***	***9.6***	***46.4***
Maximum Snowfall (in.)*	30	22	52	11	3	0	0	0	trace	6	25	25	82
Maximum 24-hr. Snowfall (in.)*	9	12	15	7	3	0	0	0	trace	5	11	10	15
Maximum Snow Depth (in.)	***25***	***23***	***20***	***7***	***trace***	***0***	***0***	***trace***	***trace***	***1***	***14***	***18***	***25***
Days With ≥ 1.0" Snow Depth	***26***	***25***	***15***	***2***	***0***	***0***	***0***	***0***	***0***	***0***	***7***	***23***	***98***
Thunderstorm Days*	0	< 1	1	3	6	9	9	9	4	2	< 1	0	43
Foggy Days*	11	10	11	9	9	9	10	14	12	12	11	14	132
Predominant Sky Cover*	OVR	OVR	OVR	OVR	OVR	OVR	CLR	OVR	OVR	OVR	OVR	OVR	OVR
Mean Relative Humidity 6am (%)*	77	79	81	81	81	85	88	91	90	85	83	80	84
Mean Relative Humidity 3pm (%)*	66	63	60	48	46	51	51	54	54	53	64	69	57
Mean Dewpoint (°F)*	2	8	19	30	42	54	59	58	48	37	23	10	32
Prevailing Wind Direction*	WNW	NW	NW	NW	NW	S	S	S	S	NW	WNW	WNW	NW
Prevailing Wind Speed (mph)*	10	10	12	13	12	10	9	9	9	12	12	10	10
Maximum Wind Gust (mph)*	58	46	46	78	51	63	63	48	51	46	53	46	78

Note: (*) Period of record is 1948-1995

Ada *Norman County* Elevation: 910 ft. Latitude: 47° 18' N Longitude: 96° 31' W

	JAN	FEB	MAR	APR	MAY	JUN	JUL	AUG	SEP	OCT	NOV	DEC	YEAR
Mean Maximum Temp. (°F)	17.8	23.4	35.9	55.4	69.6	77.4	82.3	81.0	71.0	55.7	37.0	22.0	52.4
Mean Temp. (°F)	8.0	13.4	26.5	43.7	56.6	65.9	70.5	68.6	59.0	44.9	28.5	13.4	41.6
Mean Minimum Temp. (°F)	-1.9	3.3	17.1	31.9	43.6	54.3	58.6	56.1	46.9	34.1	19.9	4.9	30.7
Extreme Maximum Temp. (°F)	53	54	75	100	96	98	105	103	95	90	73	55	105
Extreme Minimum Temp. (°F)	-43	-43	-30	4	19	34	40	33	23	8	-28	-32	-43
Days Maximum Temp. ≥ 90°F	0	0	0	0	1	2	4	4	1	0	0	0	12
Days Maximum Temp. ≤ 32°F	26	19	11	1	0	0	0	0	0	1	11	23	92
Days Minimum Temp. ≤ 32°F	31	28	28	17	4	0	0	0	2	14	26	31	181
Days Minimum Temp. ≤ 0°F	17	12	4	0	0	0	0	0	0	0	2	13	48
Heating Degree Days (base 65°F)	1,765	1,457	1,187	633	282	70	19	37	217	618	1,090	1,595	8,970
Cooling Degree Days (base 65°F)	0	0	0	3	29	103	195	155	43	2	0	0	530
Mean Precipitation (in.)	0.72	0.62	1.01	1.36	3.06	4.55	3.42	2.82	2.47	2.16	0.95	0.82	23.96
Extreme Maximum Daily Precip. (in.)	0.66	0.60	1.18	1.96	4.51	3.50	3.40	3.20	2.35	2.16	0.85	1.36	4.51
Days With ≥ 0.1" Precipitation	2	3	3	3	6	7	6	5	5	4	3	3	50
Days With ≥ 0.5" Precipitation	0	0	1	1	2	3	2	2	2	1	0	0	14
Days With ≥ 1.0" Precipitation	0	0	0	0	1	1	1	1	1	1	0	0	6
Mean Snowfall (in.)	***11.2***	6.6	***7.4***	2.0	trace	0.0	0.0	0.0	0.0	0.6	5.7	***10.5***	***44.0***
Maximum Snow Depth (in.)	na	na	na	***15***	***trace***	***0***	***0***	***0***	***0***	***5***	***14***	na	na
Days With ≥ 1.0" Snow Depth	na	na	***7***	0	0	0	0	0	0	0	4	***10***	na

Agassiz Refuge *Marshall County* Elevation: 1,142 ft. Latitude: 48° 18' N Longitude: 95° 59' W

	JAN	FEB	MAR	APR	MAY	JUN	JUL	AUG	SEP	OCT	NOV	DEC	YEAR
Mean Maximum Temp. (°F)	16.4	22.8	35.4	54.7	68.3	75.7	80.4	79.0	69.0	54.4	34.4	20.6	50.9
Mean Temp. (°F)	6.5	12.4	25.1	42.5	55.8	64.2	68.9	66.8	57.1	43.8	26.3	11.8	40.1
Mean Minimum Temp. (°F)	-3.5	2.0	14.8	30.2	43.2	52.6	57.2	54.6	45.2	33.2	18.1	3.1	29.2
Extreme Maximum Temp. (°F)	44	56	70	94	94	98	99	97	94	86	70	52	99
Extreme Minimum Temp. (°F)	-43	-46	-31	-3	21	32	38	31	20	4	-29	-35	-46
Days Maximum Temp. ≥ 90°F	0	0	0	0	0	1	2	2	0	0	0	0	5
Days Maximum Temp. ≤ 32°F	28	20	11	1	0	0	0	0	0	1	13	25	99
Days Minimum Temp. ≤ 32°F	31	28	29	18	4	0	0	0	3	15	27	31	186
Days Minimum Temp. ≤ 0°F	18	13	5	0	0	0	0	0	0	0	3	13	52
Heating Degree Days (base 65°F)	1,812	1,483	1,230	671	302	93	25	54	260	652	1,156	1,645	9,383
Cooling Degree Days (base 65°F)	0	0	0	2	24	75	152	117	28	1	0	0	399
Mean Precipitation (in.)	0.53	0.46	0.83	1.18	2.99	3.89	3.49	3.22	2.48	1.84	1.05	0.60	22.56
Extreme Maximum Daily Precip. (in.)	0.39	0.50	1.06	1.65	3.70	6.05	2.83	2.84	2.24	1.70	1.20	0.57	6.05
Days With ≥ 0.1" Precipitation	2	1	2	3	6	7	6	6	5	4	3	2	47
Days With ≥ 0.5" Precipitation	0	0	0	1	2	3	2	2	2	1	1	0	14
Days With ≥ 1.0" Precipitation	0	0	0	0	1	1	1	1	1	0	0	0	5
Mean Snowfall (in.)	8.4	5.1	5.8	2.7	0.1	0.0	0.0	0.0	0.1	1.4	7.4	8.0	39.0
Maximum Snow Depth (in.)	24	24	30	24	1	0	0	0	trace	8	15	20	30
Days With ≥ 1.0" Snow Depth	31	27	24	5	0	0	0	0	0	1	16	29	133

Albert Lea 3 SE *Freeborn County* Elevation: 1,229 ft. Latitude: 43° 37' N Longitude: 93° 18' W

	JAN	FEB	MAR	APR	MAY	JUN	JUL	AUG	SEP	OCT	NOV	DEC	YEAR
Mean Maximum Temp. (°F)	23.2	27.7	39.7	55.8	68.8	78.4	82.2	79.5	72.2	58.4	41.6	26.8	54.5
Mean Temp. (°F)	14.3	18.9	31.1	45.6	58.2	68.0	72.0	69.4	60.9	47.6	33.1	18.7	44.8
Mean Minimum Temp. (°F)	5.4	10.1	22.5	35.3	47.6	57.6	61.7	59.2	49.6	36.7	24.5	10.5	35.1
Extreme Maximum Temp. (°F)	58	64	82	92	94	102	101	101	93	94	79	67	102
Extreme Minimum Temp. (°F)	-28	-33	-16	6	25	38	44	37	27	13	-11	-29	-33
Days Maximum Temp. ≥ 90°F	0	0	0	0	1	3	4	2	1	0	0	0	11
Days Maximum Temp. ≤ 32°F	23	17	9	1	0	0	0	0	0	0	7	20	77
Days Minimum Temp. ≤ 32°F	31	28	26	11	1	0	0	0	1	11	24	30	163
Days Minimum Temp. ≤ 0°F	12	8	2	0	0	0	0	0	0	0	1	8	31
Heating Degree Days (base 65°F)	1,566	1,297	1,044	582	237	47	9	24	171	538	951	1,431	7,897
Cooling Degree Days (base 65°F)	0	0	0	5	35	144	232	166	55	5	0	0	642
Mean Precipitation (in.)	0.72	0.66	1.86	3.65	4.52	4.62	4.41	4.78	3.35	2.57	1.66	1.01	33.81
Extreme Maximum Daily Precip. (in.)	1.02	1.01	1.54	3.82	4.20	2.35	3.70	5.06	6.97	2.37	2.02	1.47	6.97
Days With ≥ 0.1" Precipitation	2	2	4	6	8	8	7	7	6	5	4	3	62
Days With ≥ 0.5" Precipitation	0	0	1	3	3	3	3	3	2	2	1	0	21
Days With ≥ 1.0" Precipitation	0	0	0	1	1	1	1	2	1	1	0	0	8
Mean Snowfall (in.)	9.0	6.5	6.3	3.1	0.0	0.0	0.0	0.0	0.0	0.4	3.9	9.2	38.4
Maximum Snow Depth (in.)	32	35	22	13	0	0	0	0	0	4	13	37	37
Days With ≥ 1.0" Snow Depth	22	19	11	2	0	0	0	0	0	0	5	18	77

Alexandria Chandler Field *Douglas County* Elevation: 1,416 ft. Latitude: 45° 52' N Longitude: 95° 23' W

	JAN	FEB	MAR	APR	MAY	JUN	JUL	AUG	SEP	OCT	NOV	DEC	YEAR
Mean Maximum Temp. (°F)	20.1	24.0	36.8	54.3	67.5	75.5	81.1	78.4	68.6	54.0	37.8	22.7	51.7
Mean Temp. (°F)	***11.1***	15.2	28.2	44.0	56.9	65.6	71.1	68.5	58.8	45.2	30.3	14.9	***42.5***
Mean Minimum Temp. (°F)	***2.1***	6.4	19.6	33.7	46.2	55.7	61.1	58.6	49.0	36.2	22.8	7.1	***33.2***
Extreme Maximum Temp. (°F)	58	58	71	95	95	102	100	104	94	86	76	55	104
Extreme Minimum Temp. (°F)	-35	-33	-19	3	25	39	47	39	26	14	-15	-32	-35
Days Maximum Temp. ≥ 90°F	0	0	0	0	0	2	3	2	0	0	0	0	7
Days Maximum Temp. ≤ 32°F	26	20	10	1	0	0	0	0	0	1	10	24	92
Days Minimum Temp. ≤ 32°F	30	28	27	14	1	0	0	0	1	10	25	31	167
Days Minimum Temp. ≤ 0°F	14	11	3	0	0	0	0	0	0	0	1	10	39
Heating Degree Days (base 65°F)	***1,667***	1,402	1,134	626	272	73	13	32	216	610	1,035	1,547	***8,627***
Cooling Degree Days (base 65°F)	***0***	0	0	3	27	100	209	148	38	2	0	0	***527***
Mean Precipitation (in.)	0.64	0.45	1.33	2.18	2.81	4.04	3.23	3.53	2.92	2.10	1.01	***0.46***	***24.70***
Extreme Maximum Daily Precip. (in.)	1.04	0.66	1.23	2.07	2.48	4.22	3.30	3.45	3.19	2.64	2.11	1.10	4.22
Days With ≥ 0.1" Precipitation	2	1	3	4	6	7	6	5	5	4	3	1	47
Days With ≥ 0.5" Precipitation	0	0	1	1	2	3	2	2	2	1	0	0	14
Days With ≥ 1.0" Precipitation	0	0	0	0	1	1	1	1	1	0	0	0	5
Mean Snowfall (in.)	na	na	na	na	na	na	na	na	na	na	na	na	na
Maximum Snow Depth (in.)	na	na	na	na	na	na	na	na	na	na	na	na	na
Days With ≥ 1.0" Snow Depth	na	na	na	na	na	na	na	na	na	na	na	na	na

The period of record for all cooperative weather station data is 1980 – 2009. See User Guide for detailed explanation of data.

Argyle 4 E *Marshall County* Elevation: 870 ft. Latitude: 48° 20' N Longitude: 96° 44' W

	JAN	FEB	MAR	APR	MAY	JUN	JUL	AUG	SEP	OCT	NOV	DEC	YEAR
Mean Maximum Temp. (°F)	15.1	21.1	33.8	53.8	68.1	76.1	80.9	80.2	70.0	54.4	35.3	20.1	50.7
Mean Temp. (°F)	4.9	10.2	23.5	41.4	54.3	63.6	67.9	66.3	56.7	42.9	26.3	11.0	39.1
Mean Minimum Temp. (°F)	-5.4	-0.8	13.3	29.0	40.4	51.0	54.9	52.4	43.3	31.4	17.2	2.0	27.4
Extreme Maximum Temp. (°F)	45	60	68	98	98	100	105	104	100	92	75	54	105
Extreme Minimum Temp. (°F)	-43	-48	-29	-3	19	31	37	30	22	6	-34	-35	-48
Days Maximum Temp. ≥ 90°F	0	0	0	0	1	2	3	3	1	0	0	0	10
Days Maximum Temp. ≤ 32°F	28	22	13	1	0	0	0	0	0	1	13	25	103
Days Minimum Temp. ≤ 32°F	31	28	29	20	7	0	0	0	3	17	28	31	194
Days Minimum Temp. ≤ 0°F	19	15	6	0	0	0	0	0	0	0	3	14	57
Heating Degree Days (base 65°F)	1,862	1,548	1,279	702	346	107	35	60	270	678	1,155	1,670	9,712
Cooling Degree Days (base 65°F)	0	0	0	2	20	71	132	109	27	1	0	0	362
Mean Precipitation (in.)	0.66	0.58	0.87	0.94	2.55	3.59	2.71	2.95	2.26	1.92	1.02	0.76	20.81
Extreme Maximum Daily Precip. (in.)	0.72	0.97	1.13	1.29	4.26	2.58	2.89	5.61	2.61	1.97	1.43	0.84	5.61
Days With ≥ 0.1" Precipitation	2	2	3	3	5	7	6	5	5	4	3	3	48
Days With ≥ 0.5" Precipitation	0	0	0	0	1	2	1	2	1	1	0	0	8
Days With ≥ 1.0" Precipitation	0	0	0	0	1	1	1	1	1	1	0	0	6
Mean Snowfall (in.)	9.0	6.1	5.6	1.6	0.1	0.0	0.0	0.0	trace	1.3	5.9	9.1	38.7
Maximum Snow Depth (in.)	31	31	32	17	1	0	0	0	trace	14	13	22	32
Days With ≥ 1.0" Snow Depth	26	22	17	2	0	0	0	0	0	1	8	20	96

Artichoke Lake *Big Stone County* Elevation: 1,075 ft. Latitude: 45° 23' N Longitude: 96° 09' W

	JAN	FEB	MAR	APR	MAY	JUN	JUL	AUG	SEP	OCT	NOV	DEC	YEAR
Mean Maximum Temp. (°F)	21.5	26.3	37.3	55.2	68.5	76.3	80.8	78.4	70.3	56.2	38.9	24.9	52.9
Mean Temp. (°F)	12.4	17.3	28.9	44.9	58.1	66.8	71.3	69.0	60.3	46.7	30.9	16.9	43.6
Mean Minimum Temp. (°F)	3.2	8.4	20.4	34.6	47.7	57.2	61.8	59.5	50.2	37.1	22.8	8.7	34.3
Extreme Maximum Temp. (°F)	63	60	76	97	95	106	108	103	97	91	75	60	108
Extreme Minimum Temp. (°F)	-30	-36	-17	6	24	37	46	36	25	11	-17	-31	-36
Days Maximum Temp. ≥ 90°F	0	0	0	0	0	2	3	2	1	0	0	0	8
Days Maximum Temp. ≤ 32°F	24	18	10	1	0	0	0	0	0	0	9	21	83
Days Minimum Temp. ≤ 32°F	31	27	27	13	1	0	0	0	0	10	25	30	164
Days Minimum Temp. ≤ 0°F	14	9	3	0	0	0	0	0	0	0	1	9	36
Heating Degree Days (base 65°F)	1,628	1,344	1,114	601	242	59	11	28	185	563	1,018	1,487	8,280
Cooling Degree Days (base 65°F)	0	0	0	4	35	118	214	159	50	3	0	0	583
Mean Precipitation (in.)	0.79	0.72	1.44	2.22	2.60	3.60	4.03	2.95	2.54	2.21	1.11	0.59	24.80
Extreme Maximum Daily Precip. (in.)	2.30	0.86	1.84	2.60	2.09	3.22	3.58	2.56	2.02	2.36	1.47	0.86	3.58
Days With ≥ 0.1" Precipitation	2	2	4	5	6	7	6	5	5	5	3	2	52
Days With ≥ 0.5" Precipitation	0	0	1	1	2	3	3	2	2	2	1	0	17
Days With ≥ 1.0" Precipitation	0	0	0	0	0	1	1	1	0	1	0	0	4
Mean Snowfall (in.)	9.0	7.5	8.3	2.8	trace	0.0	0.0	0.0	trace	0.8	6.1	6.7	41.2
Maximum Snow Depth (in.)	26	27	27	15	trace	0	0	0	trace	2	14	19	27
Days With ≥ 1.0" Snow Depth	24	22	16	2	0	0	0	0	0	0	7	19	90

Brainerd *Crow Wing County* Elevation: 1,180 ft. Latitude: 46° 22' N Longitude: 94° 12' W

	JAN	FEB	MAR	APR	MAY	JUN	JUL	AUG	SEP	OCT	NOV	DEC	YEAR
Mean Maximum Temp. (°F)	20.7	26.3	37.9	54.5	67.8	75.9	80.6	78.6	69.0	55.3	38.0	23.9	52.4
Mean Temp. (°F)	9.1	14.2	26.7	42.3	55.3	64.2	68.8	66.5	57.0	44.3	29.1	14.3	41.0
Mean Minimum Temp. (°F)	-2.8	1.7	15.4	30.1	42.8	52.3	57.0	54.2	45.0	33.2	20.2	4.7	29.5
Extreme Maximum Temp. (°F)	56	57	78	94	95	100	102	100	96	88	71	57	102
Extreme Minimum Temp. (°F)	-47	-54	-33	-3	21	33	39	32	21	11	-19	-43	-54
Days Maximum Temp. ≥ 90°F	0	0	0	0	0	1	3	2	0	0	0	0	6
Days Maximum Temp. ≤ 32°F	26	19	9	1	0	0	0	0	0	0	10	24	89
Days Minimum Temp. ≤ 32°F	31	28	29	19	3	0	0	0	3	16	27	31	187
Days Minimum Temp. ≤ 0°F	17	13	4	0	0	0	0	0	0	0	2	12	48
Heating Degree Days (base 65°F)	1,731	1,432	1,180	675	311	95	27	53	259	637	1,070	1,567	9,037
Cooling Degree Days (base 65°F)	0	0	0	2	18	77	153	104	27	1	0	0	382
Mean Precipitation (in.)	0.80	0.66	1.44	2.32	3.30	4.41	3.74	3.00	3.18	2.85	1.44	0.76	27.90
Extreme Maximum Daily Precip. (in.)	0.97	1.12	1.30	3.04	2.11	3.92	4.76	2.25	2.38	3.14	1.45	0.75	4.76
Days With ≥ 0.1" Precipitation	3	2	4	5	7	8	7	6	6	5	4	2	59
Days With ≥ 0.5" Precipitation	0	0	1	2	2	3	3	2	2	2	1	0	18
Days With ≥ 1.0" Precipitation	0	0	0	0	1	1	1	1	1	1	0	0	6
Mean Snowfall (in.)	11.2	6.6	8.9	3.2	trace	0.0	0.0	0.0	0.0	0.5	7.2	9.3	46.9
Maximum Snow Depth (in.)	34	30	32	15	trace	0	0	0	0	2	15	20	34
Days With ≥ 1.0" Snow Depth	29	27	20	3	0	0	0	0	0	0	10	26	115

Browns Valley *Traverse County* Elevation: 984 ft. Latitude: 45° 36' N Longitude: 96° 50' W

	JAN	FEB	MAR	APR	MAY	JUN	JUL	AUG	SEP	OCT	NOV	DEC	YEAR
Mean Maximum Temp. (°F)	22.6	27.7	39.0	56.8	70.3	78.5	84.1	82.2	72.6	57.9	40.6	26.3	54.9
Mean Temp. (°F)	12.7	17.7	29.4	44.7	58.0	66.9	72.2	69.9	60.1	46.5	31.2	17.1	43.8
Mean Minimum Temp. (°F)	2.7	7.7	19.6	32.6	45.6	55.3	60.3	57.5	47.5	35.1	21.7	7.9	32.8
Extreme Maximum Temp. (°F)	63	65	79	100	96	107	109	105	100	91	79	67	109
Extreme Minimum Temp. (°F)	-33	-41	-19	5	18	35	44	34	25	11	-19	-32	-41
Days Maximum Temp. ≥ 90°F	0	0	0	0	1	3	7	5	2	0	0	0	18
Days Maximum Temp. ≤ 32°F	22	17	9	1	0	0	0	0	0	0	8	20	77
Days Minimum Temp. ≤ 32°F	31	28	27	16	2	0	0	0	1	12	26	30	173
Days Minimum Temp. ≤ 0°F	14	10	3	0	0	0	0	0	0	0	1	10	38
Heating Degree Days (base 65°F)	1,618	1,333	1,098	608	247	60	12	27	195	569	1,008	1,482	8,257
Cooling Degree Days (base 65°F)	0	0	0	4	36	125	241	185	53	4	0	0	648
Mean Precipitation (in.)	0.75	0.67	1.53	2.25	2.55	3.93	3.45	2.78	2.60	2.12	1.03	0.62	24.28
Extreme Maximum Daily Precip. (in.)	1.87	0.82	2.12	2.10	1.60	4.18	3.40	2.95	3.30	2.20	1.46	0.95	4.18
Days With ≥ 0.1" Precipitation	2	2	3	5	6	7	6	5	4	4	3	2	49
Days With ≥ 0.5" Precipitation	0	0	1	2	2	2	2	2	2	1	0	0	14
Days With ≥ 1.0" Precipitation	0	0	0	0	0	1	1	1	1	0	0	0	4
Mean Snowfall (in.)	8.7	7.4	8.3	3.8	trace	0.0	0.0	0.0	0.0	0.5	6.6	7.1	42.4
Maximum Snow Depth (in.)	na	na	na	na	na	na	na	na	na	na	na	na	na
Days With ≥ 1.0" Snow Depth	na	na	na	1	0	0	0	0	0	0	1	na	na

The period of record for all cooperative weather station data is 1980 – 2009. See User Guide for detailed explanation of data.

Buffalo *Wright County* Elevation: 979 ft. Latitude: 45° 11' N Longitude: 93° 52' W

	JAN	FEB	MAR	APR	MAY	JUN	JUL	AUG	SEP	OCT	NOV	DEC	YEAR
Mean Maximum Temp. (°F)	22.8	27.8	39.3	56.6	69.5	77.6	82.3	79.8	71.3	57.3	40.0	25.3	54.1
Mean Temp. (°F)	13.4	18.3	29.9	45.4	58.2	67.0	71.9	69.5	60.5	47.3	32.1	17.1	44.2
Mean Minimum Temp. (°F)	4.0	8.9	20.4	34.2	46.9	56.4	61.5	59.2	49.5	37.3	24.1	9.0	34.3
Extreme Maximum Temp. (°F)	56	60	80	94	95	102	105	102	92	89	77	64	105
Extreme Minimum Temp. (°F)	-30	-36	-15	3	24	37	43	39	27	15	-14	-33	-36
Days Maximum Temp. ≥ 90°F	0	0	0	0	1	2	4	2	0	0	0	0	9
Days Maximum Temp. ≤ 32°F	24	17	7	0	0	0	0	0	0	0	8	20	76
Days Minimum Temp. ≤ 32°F	31	27	26	13	1	0	0	0	1	10	25	30	164
Days Minimum Temp. ≤ 0°F	13	9	2	0	0	0	0	0	0	0	1	8	33
Heating Degree Days (base 65°F)	1,594	1,315	1,082	583	237	57	10	21	179	546	981	1,478	8,083
Cooling Degree Days (base 65°F)	0	0	0	4	33	126	231	168	50	4	0	0	616
Mean Precipitation (in.)	0.68	0.64	1.44	2.62	2.97	4.58	3.59	4.47	3.54	2.41	1.48	0.87	29.29
Extreme Maximum Daily Precip. (in.)	1.12	0.94	1.31	2.88	1.73	6.35	4.89	4.58	6.31	3.23	1.83	1.12	6.35
Days With ≥ 0.1" Precipitation	2	2	4	5	7	7	6	6	6	5	4	3	57
Days With ≥ 0.5" Precipitation	0	0	1	2	2	3	3	3	2	1	1	0	18
Days With ≥ 1.0" Precipitation	0	0	0	1	1	1	1	1	1	1	0	0	7
Mean Snowfall (in.)	8.0	7.1	8.0	2.9	trace	0.0	0.0	0.0	trace	0.3	6.8	9.2	42.3
Maximum Snow Depth (in.)	32	27	24	11	trace	0	0	0	trace	2	20	25	32
Days With ≥ 1.0" Snow Depth	25	24	15	2	0	0	0	0	0	0	8	20	94

Caledonia *Houston County* Elevation: 1,174 ft. Latitude: 43° 38' N Longitude: 91° 30' W

	JAN	FEB	MAR	APR	MAY	JUN	JUL	AUG	SEP	OCT	NOV	DEC	YEAR
Mean Maximum Temp. (°F)	24.1	28.6	40.5	56.2	67.5	77.0	81.0	78.7	71.0	57.9	41.8	27.7	54.3
Mean Temp. (°F)	15.2	19.2	31.3	45.5	56.7	66.7	70.7	68.5	60.1	47.7	33.6	19.6	44.6
Mean Minimum Temp. (°F)	6.4	10.2	22.1	34.8	46.1	56.3	60.4	58.4	49.1	37.4	25.3	11.5	34.8
Extreme Maximum Temp. (°F)	57	58	82	93	90	97	101	102	91	91	74	62	102
Extreme Minimum Temp. (°F)	-33	-35	-13	2	23	38	45	39	27	13	-6	-28	-35
Days Maximum Temp. ≥ 90°F	0	0	0	0	0	2	3	2	0	0	0	0	7
Days Maximum Temp. ≤ 32°F	23	16	7	1	0	0	0	0	0	0	6	19	72
Days Minimum Temp. ≤ 32°F	30	27	25	12	1	0	0	0	1	10	24	30	160
Days Minimum Temp. ≤ 0°F	10	7	2	0	0	0	0	0	0	0	1	7	27
Heating Degree Days (base 65°F)	1,536	1,289	1,034	584	276	59	15	30	187	535	935	1,401	7,881
Cooling Degree Days (base 65°F)	0	0	0	5	24	117	199	146	45	5	0	0	541
Mean Precipitation (in.)	0.87	0.84	1.76	3.86	3.98	4.93	4.51	5.23	3.56	2.51	2.22	1.28	35.55
Extreme Maximum Daily Precip. (in.)	1.22	1.70	2.20	2.92	3.96	3.82	3.82	5.56	3.88	2.37	1.97	2.51	5.56
Days With ≥ 0.1" Precipitation	3	2	4	7	8	8	7	7	6	5	5	4	66
Days With ≥ 0.5" Precipitation	0	0	1	3	3	3	3	3	2	1	1	0	20
Days With ≥ 1.0" Precipitation	0	0	0	1	1	2	1	1	1	1	1	0	9
Mean Snowfall (in.)	10.1	8.8	8.1	2.9	trace	0.0	0.0	0.0	0.0	0.3	4.7	10.4	45.3
Maximum Snow Depth (in.)	25	25	25	9	trace	0	0	0	0	2	9	24	25
Days With ≥ 1.0" Snow Depth	17	18	9	1	0	0	0	0	0	0	3	19	67

Cambridge State Hosp *Isanti County* Elevation: 959 ft. Latitude: 45° 34' N Longitude: 93° 14' W

	JAN	FEB	MAR	APR	MAY	JUN	JUL	AUG	SEP	OCT	NOV	DEC	YEAR
Mean Maximum Temp. (°F)	21.6	26.7	37.6	54.9	69.0	76.6	80.6	78.1	68.6	55.8	38.5	24.7	52.7
Mean Temp. (°F)	11.9	17.0	28.0	43.9	57.3	65.4	69.7	67.7	57.9	45.8	30.4	16.4	42.6
Mean Minimum Temp. (°F)	2.1	7.3	18.3	32.8	45.3	54.1	59.0	57.2	47.2	35.7	22.2	8.1	32.4
Extreme Maximum Temp. (°F)	52	58	71	92	99	99	102	100	93	85	72	60	102
Extreme Minimum Temp. (°F)	-37	-41	-24	2	22	32	42	39	19	10	-10	-41	-41
Days Maximum Temp. ≥ 90°F	0	0	0	0	1	1	3	1	0	0	0	0	6
Days Maximum Temp. ≤ 32°F	24	18	10	0	0	0	0	0	0	0	9	23	84
Days Minimum Temp. ≤ 32°F	31	27	28	15	2	0	0	0	2	11	26	31	173
Days Minimum Temp. ≤ 0°F	14	9	3	0	0	0	0	0	0	0	1	10	37
Heating Degree Days (base 65°F)	1,643	1,351	1,141	631	263	74	19	38	236	590	1,032	1,501	8,519
Cooling Degree Days (base 65°F)	0	0	0	3	31	92	172	127	30	2	0	0	457
Mean Precipitation (in.)	0.91	0.59	1.20	2.49	2.99	4.30	4.19	4.05	3.25	2.54	1.84	0.99	29.34
Extreme Maximum Daily Precip. (in.)	1.51	0.56	1.38	2.40	2.22	4.05	2.96	3.50	4.60	5.20	na	1.08	na
Days With ≥ 0.1" Precipitation	3	2	3	5	6	8	6	6	6	5	4	3	57
Days With ≥ 0.5" Precipitation	0	0	1	2	2	3	3	3	2	2	1	1	20
Days With ≥ 1.0" Precipitation	0	0	0	0	1	1	1	1	1	0	0	0	5
Mean Snowfall (in.)	na	4.2	6.4	1.7	trace	0.0	0.0	0.0	0.0	0.5	5.8	7.8	na
Maximum Snow Depth (in.)	32	30	31	7	trace	0	0	na	0	5	na	31	na
Days With ≥ 1.0" Snow Depth	27	24	18	2	0	0	0	0	0	0	7	21	99

Cass Lake *Cass County* Elevation: 1,295 ft. Latitude: 47° 23' N Longitude: 94° 37' W

	JAN	FEB	MAR	APR	MAY	JUN	JUL	AUG	SEP	OCT	NOV	DEC	YEAR
Mean Maximum Temp. (°F)	18.6	24.1	36.4	52.4	66.0	74.7	79.4	77.4	67.2	52.4	35.7	22.1	50.5
Mean Temp. (°F)	6.7	11.6	25.1	40.3	53.5	63.0	67.8	65.8	56.3	42.6	27.0	12.0	39.3
Mean Minimum Temp. (°F)	-5.3	-1.1	13.8	28.2	40.9	51.2	56.1	54.2	45.4	32.8	18.3	1.9	28.0
Extreme Maximum Temp. (°F)	51	59	73	96	93	98	104	101	98	86	72	53	104
Extreme Minimum Temp. (°F)	-48	-48	-32	-11	16	27	33	26	21	5	-30	-46	-48
Days Maximum Temp. ≥ 90°F	0	0	0	0	0	1	2	2	0	0	0	0	5
Days Maximum Temp. ≤ 32°F	26	20	11	1	0	0	0	0	0	1	13	23	95
Days Minimum Temp. ≤ 32°F	30	28	28	20	7	1	0	0	3	16	27	30	190
Days Minimum Temp. ≤ 0°F	19	15	6	0	0	0	0	0	0	0	3	14	57
Heating Degree Days (base 65°F)	1,806	1,507	1,230	736	366	123	42	70	278	687	1,133	1,639	9,617
Cooling Degree Days (base 65°F)	0	0	0	1	15	70	135	102	24	1	0	0	348
Mean Precipitation (in.)	0.72	0.67	1.27	1.87	2.92	3.89	4.02	2.99	3.00	2.80	1.38	0.78	26.31
Extreme Maximum Daily Precip. (in.)	0.92	1.30	1.55	1.66	1.90	3.72	3.48	2.58	2.79	2.76	1.70	0.65	3.72
Days With ≥ 0.1" Precipitation	2	2	3	4	7	7	7	6	6	5	4	2	55
Days With ≥ 0.5" Precipitation	0	0	1	1	2	2	2	2	2	2	1	0	15
Days With ≥ 1.0" Precipitation	0	0	0	0	0	1	1	1	0	1	0	0	4
Mean Snowfall (in.)	9.2	7.2	7.5	3.7	0.1	0.0	0.0	0.0	0.0	1.0	7.5	9.2	45.4
Maximum Snow Depth (in.)	na	na	na	na	na	na	na	na	na	na	na	na	na
Days With ≥ 1.0" Snow Depth	na	na	na	1	0	0	0	0	0	1	3	na	na

The period of record for all cooperative weather station data is 1980 – 2009. See User Guide for detailed explanation of data.

Cedar *Anoka County* Elevation: 907 ft. Latitude: 45° 19' N Longitude: 93° 17' W

	JAN	FEB	MAR	APR	MAY	JUN	JUL	AUG	SEP	OCT	NOV	DEC	YEAR
Mean Maximum Temp. (°F)	*23.0*	*29.2*	*40.9*	*58.7*	*70.4*	*77.8*	*81.6*	*78.9*	*70.9*	*58.0*	*39.8*	*26.9*	*54.7*
Mean Temp. (°F)	*13.7*	*19.7*	*31.0*	*46.7*	*58.4*	*66.6*	*71.1*	*68.7*	*60.5*	*47.7*	*31.9*	*18.8*	*44.6*
Mean Minimum Temp. (°F)	*4.2*	*10.1*	*21.1*	*34.6*	*46.3*	*55.4*	*60.7*	*58.4*	*50.0*	*37.4*	*23.9*	*10.6*	*34.4*
Extreme Maximum Temp. (°F)	*55*	*60*	*83*	*93*	*92*	*99*	*103*	*98*	*92*	*86*	*76*	*64*	*103*
Extreme Minimum Temp. (°F)	*-36*	*-39*	*-17*	*3*	*23*	*31*	*42*	*36*	*28*	*11*	*-18*	*-28*	*-39*
Days Maximum Temp. ≥ 90°F	*0*	*0*	*0*	*0*	*1*	*2*	*3*	*2*	*0*	*0*	*0*	*0*	*8*
Days Maximum Temp. ≤ 32°F	*24*	*16*	*7*	*0*	*0*	*0*	*0*	*0*	*0*	*0*	*8*	*20*	*75*
Days Minimum Temp. ≤ 32°F	*31*	*27*	*26*	*13*	*2*	*0*	*0*	*0*	*1*	*10*	*24*	*31*	*165*
Days Minimum Temp. ≤ 0°F	*12*	*8*	*2*	*0*	*0*	*0*	*0*	*0*	*0*	*0*	*1*	*8*	*31*
Heating Degree Days (base 65°F)	*1,588*	*1,276*	*1,046*	*550*	*233*	*61*	*12*	*29*	*181*	*532*	*987*	*1,427*	*7,922*
Cooling Degree Days (base 65°F)	*0*	*0*	*0*	*7*	*35*	*117*	*209*	*150*	*52*	*4*	*0*	*0*	*574*
Mean Precipitation (in.)	*1.02*	*0.84*	*1.83*	*2.89*	*3.87*	*4.44*	*4.49*	*4.35*	*3.88*	*2.59*	*2.08*	*0.86*	*33.14*
Extreme Maximum Daily Precip. (in.)	*1.23*	*0.77*	*1.25*	*2.14*	*2.51*	*4.60*	*3.48*	*3.07*	*2.86*	*4.75*	*2.07*	*1.25*	*4.75*
Days With ≥ 0.1" Precipitation	*3*	*3*	*4*	*6*	*8*	*8*	*8*	*7*	*7*	*5*	*5*	*3*	*67*
Days With ≥ 0.5" Precipitation	*0*	*0*	*1*	*2*	*2*	*3*	*3*	*3*	*2*	*2*	*1*	*0*	*19*
Days With ≥ 1.0" Precipitation	*0*	*0*	*0*	*1*	*1*	*1*	*1*	*1*	*1*	*0*	*0*	*0*	*6*
Mean Snowfall (in.)	*12.9*	*9.6*	*11.6*	*3.5*	*trace*	*0.0*	*0.0*	*0.0*	*trace*	*0.7*	*11.1*	*10.0*	*59.4*
Maximum Snow Depth (in.)	*27*	*27*	*30*	*12*	*trace*	*0*	*0*	*0*	*trace*	*3*	*23*	*21*	*30*
Days With ≥ 1.0" Snow Depth	*26*	*24*	*19*	*2*	*0*	*0*	*0*	*0*	*0*	*0*	*9*	*23*	*103*

Cloquet *Carlton County* Elevation: 1,265 ft. Latitude: 46° 42' N Longitude: 92° 32' W

	JAN	FEB	MAR	APR	MAY	JUN	JUL	AUG	SEP	OCT	NOV	DEC	YEAR
Mean Maximum Temp. (°F)	21.3	26.9	38.0	54.0	67.7	76.1	80.9	78.1	68.7	53.8	37.0	23.9	52.2
Mean Temp. (°F)	11.4	16.1	26.9	41.3	53.2	61.9	67.6	65.7	57.0	44.0	29.4	15.4	40.8
Mean Minimum Temp. (°F)	1.6	5.3	15.9	28.5	38.7	47.7	54.1	53.3	45.4	34.1	21.7	6.9	29.4
Extreme Maximum Temp. (°F)	50	55	73	84	92	96	103	97	91	86	68	54	103
Extreme Minimum Temp. (°F)	-42	-41	-30	-2	16	25	34	33	23	9	-19	-35	-42
Days Maximum Temp. ≥ 90°F	0	0	0	0	0	1	4	1	0	0	0	0	6
Days Maximum Temp. ≤ 32°F	26	18	8	1	0	0	0	0	0	0	10	23	86
Days Minimum Temp. ≤ 32°F	31	28	29	21	7	1	0	0	3	14	26	31	191
Days Minimum Temp. ≤ 0°F	14	11	5	0	0	0	0	0	0	0	1	11	42
Heating Degree Days (base 65°F)	1,657	1,378	1,173	706	367	131	36	62	254	645	1,062	1,532	9,003
Cooling Degree Days (base 65°F)	0	0	0	0	8	45	124	91	22	0	0	0	290
Mean Precipitation (in.)	0.98	0.84	1.50	2.30	3.19	4.17	4.15	3.90	4.22	2.97	1.92	1.10	31.24
Extreme Maximum Daily Precip. (in.)	1.03	0.88	1.63	2.19	2.26	3.14	3.56	3.21	8.44	3.09	3.08	1.54	8.44
Days With ≥ 0.1" Precipitation	3	2	4	5	7	8	7	7	7	6	4	3	63
Days With ≥ 0.5" Precipitation	0	0	1	1	2	3	3	2	3	2	1	0	18
Days With ≥ 1.0" Precipitation	0	0	0	0	1	1	1	1	1	1	0	0	6
Mean Snowfall (in.)	14.6	11.3	10.4	3.9	0.1	0.0	0.0	0.0	trace	1.2	10.2	14.3	66.0
Maximum Snow Depth (in.)	35	37	34	20	trace	0	0	0	0	4	20	28	37
Days With ≥ 1.0" Snow Depth	31	28	27	7	0	0	0	0	0	1	14	28	136

Collegeville St John *Stearns County* Elevation: 1,225 ft. Latitude: 45° 35' N Longitude: 94° 24' W

	JAN	FEB	MAR	APR	MAY	JUN	JUL	AUG	SEP	OCT	NOV	DEC	YEAR
Mean Maximum Temp. (°F)	22.7	28.2	39.9	57.4	70.1	78.4	83.0	80.3	71.5	57.5	39.9	25.8	54.6
Mean Temp. (°F)	13.8	19.1	30.6	46.3	58.8	67.5	72.4	70.0	61.3	48.0	32.4	17.9	44.8
Mean Minimum Temp. (°F)	4.8	9.9	21.2	35.0	47.4	56.6	61.7	59.7	51.0	38.5	24.7	10.1	35.1
Extreme Maximum Temp. (°F)	54	56	79	95	96	101	103	100	93	89	78	61	103
Extreme Minimum Temp. (°F)	-35	-37	-16	3	25	37	46	42	30	14	-11	-35	-37
Days Maximum Temp. ≥ 90°F	0	0	0	0	1	2	5	3	1	0	0	0	12
Days Maximum Temp. ≤ 32°F	24	17	7	0	0	0	0	0	0	0	8	21	77
Days Minimum Temp. ≤ 32°F	31	27	26	12	1	0	0	0	0	8	23	31	159
Days Minimum Temp. ≤ 0°F	12	8	2	0	0	0	0	0	0	0	1	8	31
Heating Degree Days (base 65°F)	1,584	1,292	1,060	560	223	49	7	19	162	523	973	1,454	7,906
Cooling Degree Days (base 65°F)	0	0	0	4	38	132	243	181	57	4	0	0	659
Mean Precipitation (in.)	0.78	0.73	1.78	2.66	3.39	4.73	3.60	3.80	3.53	2.68	1.61	0.81	30.10
Extreme Maximum Daily Precip. (in.)	1.40	0.95	2.58	2.57	3.21	3.49	4.67	3.39	3.10	3.05	1.58	0.90	4.67
Days With ≥ 0.1" Precipitation	2	2	4	5	6	8	6	6	6	5	4	2	56
Days With ≥ 0.5" Precipitation	0	0	1	2	2	3	2	3	3	2	1	0	19
Days With ≥ 1.0" Precipitation	0	0	0	1	1	1	1	1	1	1	0	0	7
Mean Snowfall (in.)	10.9	8.2	10.3	4.0	trace	trace	0.0	0.0	trace	0.8	9.1	9.6	52.9
Maximum Snow Depth (in.)	28	26	27	10	trace	trace	0	0	trace	4	18	18	28
Days With ≥ 1.0" Snow Depth	27	25	16	2	0	0	0	0	0	0	9	22	101

Crookston NW Exp Stn *Polk County* Elevation: 888 ft. Latitude: 47° 48' N Longitude: 96° 36' W

	JAN	FEB	MAR	APR	MAY	JUN	JUL	AUG	SEP	OCT	NOV	DEC	YEAR
Mean Maximum Temp. (°F)	16.1	21.5	33.9	53.5	67.6	75.8	80.9	79.8	69.1	53.9	35.4	20.5	50.7
Mean Temp. (°F)	6.3	11.6	24.9	42.3	55.5	64.7	69.4	67.5	57.1	43.3	27.0	11.9	40.1
Mean Minimum Temp. (°F)	-3.5	1.6	15.9	31.1	43.3	53.6	57.7	55.2	45.1	32.7	18.5	3.3	29.5
Extreme Maximum Temp. (°F)	49	53	70	96	95	99	104	104	98	88	73	56	104
Extreme Minimum Temp. (°F)	-41	-45	-31	2	18	34	39	33	22	5	-30	-35	-45
Days Maximum Temp. ≥ 90°F	0	0	0	0	1	2	3	3	1	0	0	0	10
Days Maximum Temp. ≤ 32°F	27	22	13	2	0	0	0	0	0	1	13	25	103
Days Minimum Temp. ≤ 32°F	31	28	28	18	4	0	0	0	2	15	27	31	184
Days Minimum Temp. ≤ 0°F	18	14	5	0	0	0	0	0	0	0	2	13	52
Heating Degree Days (base 65°F)	1,817	1,507	1,237	676	315	88	26	46	261	665	1,133	1,643	9,414
Cooling Degree Days (base 65°F)	0	0	0	2	27	88	168	132	32	1	0	0	450
Mean Precipitation (in.)	0.46	0.50	0.72	1.16	2.75	3.79	3.02	3.29	2.28	2.04	0.92	0.62	21.55
Extreme Maximum Daily Precip. (in.)	0.64	1.24	0.92	2.00	2.52	3.28	4.04	3.26	1.88	2.70	1.90	1.20	4.04
Days With ≥ 0.1" Precipitation	1	2	2	3	6	7	6	6	5	4	3	2	47
Days With ≥ 0.5" Precipitation	0	0	0	1	2	2	2	2	2	1	0	0	12
Days With ≥ 1.0" Precipitation	0	0	0	0	1	1	1	1	0	0	0	0	4
Mean Snowfall (in.)	8.4	6.3	5.7	1.9	0.1	0.0	0.0	0.0	0.0	0.6	5.2	9.8	38.0
Maximum Snow Depth (in.)	38	36	31	22	0	0	0	0	0	6	20	38	38
Days With ≥ 1.0" Snow Depth	28	23	16	2	0	0	0	0	0	0	10	25	104

The period of record for all cooperative weather station data is 1980 – 2009. See User Guide for detailed explanation of data.

Detroit Lakes 1 NNE *Becker County* Elevation: 1,375 ft. Latitude: 46° 50' N Longitude: 95° 51' W

	JAN	FEB	MAR	APR	MAY	JUN	JUL	AUG	SEP	OCT	NOV	DEC	YEAR
Mean Maximum Temp. (°F)	20.2	***25.6***	37.6	56.4	69.5	76.9	81.7	79.9	70.6	55.5	37.5	22.7	***52.8***
Mean Temp. (°F)	9.7	***14.9***	27.2	43.7	56.2	64.7	69.4	67.6	58.7	45.0	28.9	13.7	***41.6***
Mean Minimum Temp. (°F)	-0.9	***4.1***	16.7	30.8	42.9	52.4	57.0	55.4	46.8	34.4	20.4	4.8	***30.4***
Extreme Maximum Temp. (°F)	53	***57***	72	98	95	100	100	***101***	95	***88***	70	53	***101***
Extreme Minimum Temp. (°F)	-44	***-45***	-35	0	16	29	38	***32***	20	***6***	-23	-39	***-45***
Days Maximum Temp. ≥ 90°F	0	***0***	0	0	0	2	4	2	1	0	0	0	***9***
Days Maximum Temp. ≤ 32°F	26	***18***	10	1	0	0	0	0	0	0	11	24	***90***
Days Minimum Temp. ≤ 32°F	31	***28***	28	18	5	0	0	0	3	13	26	31	***183***
Days Minimum Temp. ≤ 0°F	16	***11***	5	0	0	0	0	0	0	0	2	12	***46***
Heating Degree Days (base 65°F)	1,711	***1,411***	1,165	636	288	90	25	47	223	615	1,075	1,585	***8,871***
Cooling Degree Days (base 65°F)	0	***0***	0	3	23	87	169	136	42	1	0	0	***461***
Mean Precipitation (in.)	0.61	***0.56***	1.20	1.69	3.40	4.46	3.61	3.35	3.30	3.08	1.09	0.75	***27.10***
Extreme Maximum Daily Precip. (in.)	0.90	***0.58***	***1.05***	2.25	3.55	***2.58***	***3.36***	***2.25***	***3.18***	***2.00***	***1.08***	***0.75***	***3.55***
Days With ≥ 0.1" Precipitation	2	***2***	3	4	7	8	7	6	6	6	3	2	***56***
Days With ≥ 0.5" Precipitation	0	***0***	1	1	2	3	2	2	2	2	1	0	***16***
Days With ≥ 1.0" Precipitation	0	***0***	0	0	1	1	1	1	1	1	0	0	***6***
Mean Snowfall (in.)	9.8	***6.9***	7.8	3.7	trace	0.0	0.0	0.0	0.0	1.1	6.6	9.4	***45.3***
Maximum Snow Depth (in.)	na	na	na	***12***	***trace***	***0***	***0***	***0***	***0***	***4***	***16***	na	na
Days With ≥ 1.0" Snow Depth	na	na	na	1	0	0	0	0	0	0	5	na	na

Fairmont *Martin County* Elevation: 1,187 ft. Latitude: 43° 38' N Longitude: 94° 28' W

	JAN	FEB	MAR	APR	MAY	JUN	JUL	AUG	SEP	OCT	NOV	DEC	YEAR
Mean Maximum Temp. (°F)	24.6	29.1	40.8	57.0	69.8	79.3	82.8	80.2	73.0	59.0	42.0	27.7	55.4
Mean Temp. (°F)	16.0	20.6	32.1	46.9	59.5	69.2	73.0	70.5	62.3	49.1	33.9	20.0	46.1
Mean Minimum Temp. (°F)	7.4	12.1	23.4	36.8	49.1	59.1	63.2	60.8	51.6	39.1	25.7	12.3	36.7
Extreme Maximum Temp. (°F)	64	63	79	93	93	100	100	100	94	91	79	65	100
Extreme Minimum Temp. (°F)	-29	-28	-17	9	27	39	48	41	27	17	-13	-24	-29
Days Maximum Temp. ≥ 90°F	0	0	0	0	0	3	5	2	1	0	0	0	11
Days Maximum Temp. ≤ 32°F	22	16	8	1	0	0	0	0	0	0	7	19	73
Days Minimum Temp. ≤ 32°F	31	27	26	9	0	0	0	0	1	7	23	30	154
Days Minimum Temp. ≤ 0°F	10	7	2	0	0	0	0	0	0	0	1	6	26
Heating Degree Days (base 65°F)	1,513	1,250	1,013	541	207	34	5	16	143	493	927	1,388	7,530
Cooling Degree Days (base 65°F)	0	0	0	5	42	167	261	194	68	7	0	0	744
Mean Precipitation (in.)	0.80	0.77	1.87	3.49	3.93	4.37	4.07	4.20	3.09	2.33	1.75	1.16	31.83
Extreme Maximum Daily Precip. (in.)	1.25	1.25	1.44	3.35	3.73	4.68	3.77	5.03	6.20	2.79	1.95	2.11	6.20
Days With ≥ 0.1" Precipitation	2	2	4	6	7	7	6	6	5	4	4	3	56
Days With ≥ 0.5" Precipitation	0	0	1	2	3	3	3	2	2	2	1	1	20
Days With ≥ 1.0" Precipitation	0	0	0	1	1	1	1	1	1	1	0	0	7
Mean Snowfall (in.)	9.1	6.8	7.6	3.4	trace	0.0	0.0	0.0	0.0	0.5	5.5	10.0	42.9
Maximum Snow Depth (in.)	25	26	28	7	trace	0	0	0	0	2	14	25	28
Days With ≥ 1.0" Snow Depth	23	19	11	2	0	0	0	0	0	0	6	19	80

Farmington 3 NW *Dakota County* Elevation: 979 ft. Latitude: 44° 40' N Longitude: 93° 11' W

	JAN	FEB	MAR	APR	MAY	JUN	JUL	AUG	SEP	OCT	NOV	DEC	YEAR
Mean Maximum Temp. (°F)	24.2	29.2	41.1	58.4	70.6	79.1	82.9	80.2	72.2	58.7	41.7	26.9	55.4
Mean Temp. (°F)	15.8	20.7	32.2	47.5	59.4	68.4	72.3	69.8	61.6	48.7	33.9	19.2	45.8
Mean Minimum Temp. (°F)	7.4	12.2	23.3	36.4	48.1	57.6	61.7	59.4	50.9	38.7	25.9	11.4	36.1
Extreme Maximum Temp. (°F)	59	59	79	93	94	102	104	101	94	91	77	67	104
Extreme Minimum Temp. (°F)	-30	-33	-11	5	24	38	40	42	25	14	-15	-35	-35
Days Maximum Temp. ≥ 90°F	0	0	0	0	1	3	4	2	0	0	0	0	10
Days Maximum Temp. ≤ 32°F	23	16	6	0	0	0	0	0	0	0	7	20	72
Days Minimum Temp. ≤ 32°F	31	27	25	10	1	0	0	0	1	8	23	30	156
Days Minimum Temp. ≤ 0°F	10	7	2	0	0	0	0	0	0	0	1	7	27
Heating Degree Days (base 65°F)	1,518	1,247	1,010	526	208	41	6	17	156	504	928	1,414	7,575
Cooling Degree Days (base 65°F)	0	0	0	6	42	150	240	173	61	6	0	0	678
Mean Precipitation (in.)	0.74	0.57	1.70	2.64	3.49	4.44	3.83	4.76	3.30	2.47	1.73	***0.94***	***30.61***
Extreme Maximum Daily Precip. (in.)	1.35	1.05	1.62	1.70	2.20	4.54	4.24	4.65	6.05	2.84	1.47	1.82	6.05
Days With ≥ 0.1" Precipitation	3	2	4	6	8	8	6	7	6	5	4	2	61
Days With ≥ 0.5" Precipitation	0	0	1	2	2	3	3	3	2	1	1	0	18
Days With ≥ 1.0" Precipitation	0	0	0	0	1	1	1	1	1	1	0	0	6
Mean Snowfall (in.)	9.6	6.9	8.7	3.1	trace	0.0	0.0	0.0	trace	0.2	6.7	9.1	44.3
Maximum Snow Depth (in.)	***40***	***29***	27	16	trace	0	0	0	trace	4	29	***46***	***46***
Days With ≥ 1.0" Snow Depth	***25***	***21***	13	1	0	0	0	0	0	0	7	***19***	***86***

Fergus Falls *Otter Tail County* Elevation: 1,250 ft. Latitude: 46° 18' N Longitude: 96° 07' W

	JAN	FEB	MAR	APR	MAY	JUN	JUL	AUG	SEP	OCT	NOV	DEC	YEAR
Mean Maximum Temp. (°F)	18.5	23.8	35.4	54.2	67.4	75.5	80.5	79.1	69.4	55.1	36.6	23.2	51.6
Mean Temp. (°F)	9.1	14.4	26.6	43.5	56.5	65.6	70.4	68.6	58.6	45.0	28.6	14.9	41.8
Mean Minimum Temp. (°F)	-0.4	4.9	17.7	32.9	45.7	55.5	60.3	57.9	47.9	34.9	20.7	6.6	32.0
Extreme Maximum Temp. (°F)	55	56	73	94	95	99	102	102	96	89	74	54	102
Extreme Minimum Temp. (°F)	-37	-40	-23	3	23	31	44	38	26	10	-20	-35	-40
Days Maximum Temp. ≥ 90°F	0	0	0	0	0	2	3	2	1	0	0	0	8
Days Maximum Temp. ≤ 32°F	26	19	11	1	0	0	0	0	0	1	12	23	93
Days Minimum Temp. ≤ 32°F	31	28	28	15	2	0	0	0	1	12	26	31	174
Days Minimum Temp. ≤ 0°F	16	12	4	0	0	0	0	0	0	0	1	11	44
Heating Degree Days (base 65°F)	1,729	1,426	1,184	640	282	76	19	36	227	615	1,085	1,547	8,866
Cooling Degree Days (base 65°F)	0	0	0	3	27	100	195	153	42	2	0	0	522
Mean Precipitation (in.)	0.91	0.53	1.31	1.48	3.08	3.95	3.37	3.20	2.68	2.03	1.12	0.49	24.15
Extreme Maximum Daily Precip. (in.)	***1.85***	***0.92***	***1.09***	***1.57***	***2.90***	***3.84***	***3.40***	***4.30***	***2.08***	***2.26***	***1.50***	***0.50***	***4.30***
Days With ≥ 0.1" Precipitation	2	2	3	3	6	7	6	5	5	4	3	2	48
Days With ≥ 0.5" Precipitation	0	0	1	1	2	3	2	2	2	1	1	0	15
Days With ≥ 1.0" Precipitation	0	0	0	0	0	1	1	1	1	1	0	0	5
Mean Snowfall (in.)	***11.9***	***6.1***	7.4	***1.7***	trace	0.0	0.0	0.0	0.0	0.6	***7.3***	7.4	***42.4***
Maximum Snow Depth (in.)	***62***	***64***	68	30	trace	0	0	0	trace	4	***22***	32	***68***
Days With ≥ 1.0" Snow Depth	***26***	***21***	15	1	0	0	0	0	0	1	***8***	17	***89***

The period of record for all cooperative weather station data is 1980 – 2009. See User Guide for detailed explanation of data.

Forest Lake 5 NE *Chisago County* Elevation: 959 ft. Latitude: 45° 21' N Longitude: 92° 55' W

	JAN	FEB	MAR	APR	MAY	JUN	JUL	AUG	SEP	OCT	NOV	DEC	YEAR
Mean Maximum Temp. (°F)	25.3	30.9	42.5	59.4	71.4	79.5	83.7	81.5	73.2	59.6	42.6	28.2	56.5
Mean Temp. (°F)	15.3	20.5	31.8	47.1	59.3	68.1	72.5	70.6	62.1	49.1	33.9	19.5	45.8
Mean Minimum Temp. (°F)	5.2	10.1	21.1	34.8	47.1	56.6	61.3	59.6	50.9	38.5	25.2	10.8	35.1
Extreme Maximum Temp. (°F)	57	65	81	89	95	99	104	102	93	88	75	65	104
Extreme Minimum Temp. (°F)	-33	-37	-17	3	22	37	45	41	29	13	-14	-37	-37
Days Maximum Temp. ≥ 90°F	0	0	0	0	1	3	5	3	1	0	0	0	13
Days Maximum Temp. ≤ 32°F	21	14	5	0	0	0	0	0	0	0	6	18	64
Days Minimum Temp. ≤ 32°F	31	27	26	12	1	0	0	0	0	8	23	31	159
Days Minimum Temp. ≤ 0°F	12	8	2	0	0	0	0	0	0	0	1	8	31
Heating Degree Days (base 65°F)	1,539	1,252	1,021	534	210	44	6	16	150	492	926	1,405	7,595
Cooling Degree Days (base 65°F)	0	0	0	5	39	143	245	196	68	6	0	0	702
Mean Precipitation (in.)	0.89	0.86	1.60	2.84	3.66	4.40	4.32	4.10	3.48	2.83	1.75	1.08	31.81
Extreme Maximum Daily Precip. (in.)	1.28	1.40	1.26	2.84	2.76	4.01	3.99	2.79	2.81	3.52	1.84	1.65	4.01
Days With ≥ 0.1" Precipitation	3	3	4	6	7	8	7	7	6	6	4	3	64
Days With ≥ 0.5" Precipitation	0	0	1	2	2	3	3	3	2	2	1	1	20
Days With ≥ 1.0" Precipitation	0	0	0	1	1	1	1	1	1	1	0	0	7
Mean Snowfall (in.)	9.8	8.4	9.7	3.3	trace	0.0	0.0	0.0	trace	0.5	8.1	10.5	50.3
Maximum Snow Depth (in.)	24	22	25	11	trace	0	0	0	trace	4	21	20	25
Days With ≥ 1.0" Snow Depth	28	26	19	2	0	0	0	0	0	0	8	23	106

Georgetown 1 E *Clay County* Elevation: 884 ft. Latitude: 47° 05' N Longitude: 96° 47' W

	JAN	FEB	MAR	APR	MAY	JUN	JUL	AUG	SEP	OCT	NOV	DEC	YEAR
Mean Maximum Temp. (°F)	18.2	23.9	36.6	57.0	70.5	78.0	82.6	81.2	71.0	56.2	36.6	22.7	52.9
Mean Temp. (°F)	8.6	14.3	27.6	44.7	57.5	66.3	70.7	68.9	59.0	45.7	28.2	14.1	42.1
Mean Minimum Temp. (°F)	-1.0	4.8	18.6	32.3	44.5	54.6	58.8	56.6	46.9	35.2	19.7	5.5	31.4
Extreme Maximum Temp. (°F)	52	54	73	100	97	100	107	102	100	90	72	54	107
Extreme Minimum Temp. (°F)	-37	-42	-24	4	19	31	39	30	22	8	-26	-32	-42
Days Maximum Temp. ≥ 90°F	0	0	0	0	1	3	5	4	1	0	0	0	14
Days Maximum Temp. ≤ 32°F	26	19	10	1	0	0	0	0	0	0	11	23	90
Days Minimum Temp. ≤ 32°F	31	28	27	16	3	0	0	0	2	12	26	30	175
Days Minimum Temp. ≤ 0°F	17	11	4	0	0	0	0	0	0	0	2	12	46
Heating Degree Days (base 65°F)	1,744	1,430	1,152	613	259	65	16	31	217	593	1,098	1,574	8,792
Cooling Degree Days (base 65°F)	0	0	0	4	35	111	202	159	44	2	0	0	557
Mean Precipitation (in.)	0.60	0.53	1.07	1.29	2.71	3.77	3.30	3.02	2.49	2.14	0.86	0.72	22.50
Extreme Maximum Daily Precip. (in.)	1.17	0.62	0.99	1.37	3.95	5.93	3.94	5.57	4.07	2.70	0.75	0.82	5.93
Days With ≥ 0.1" Precipitation	2	2	3	3	5	7	6	5	5	4	2	2	46
Days With ≥ 0.5" Precipitation	0	0	1	1	2	2	2	2	2	2	0	0	14
Days With ≥ 1.0" Precipitation	0	0	0	0	1	1	1	1	1	1	0	0	6
Mean Snowfall (in.)	9.5	5.5	***7.1***	2.6	trace	0.0	0.0	0.0	0.0	0.5	5.5	***8.2***	***38.9***
Maximum Snow Depth (in.)	***63***	na	***38***	***24***	***0***	***0***	***0***	***0***	***0***	***6***	***26***	na	na
Days With ≥ 1.0" Snow Depth	na	na	***5***	1	0	0	0	0	0	0	3	7	na

Grand Marais *Cook County* Elevation: 611 ft. Latitude: 47° 44' N Longitude: 90° 22' W

	JAN	FEB	MAR	APR	MAY	JUN	JUL	AUG	SEP	OCT	NOV	DEC	YEAR
Mean Maximum Temp. (°F)	24.5	28.0	35.7	47.0	56.1	63.5	70.8	71.9	64.2	51.7	39.0	28.0	48.4
Mean Temp. (°F)	15.6	18.9	27.3	38.7	47.0	53.8	61.3	63.1	55.9	44.1	32.3	20.1	39.8
Mean Minimum Temp. (°F)	6.7	9.9	18.8	30.3	37.9	43.9	51.8	54.4	47.7	36.5	25.5	12.1	31.3
Extreme Maximum Temp. (°F)	56	53	67	81	87	91	94	92	87	79	67	51	94
Extreme Minimum Temp. (°F)	-33	-32	-21	-1	21	31	40	35	28	13	-10	-24	-33
Days Maximum Temp. ≥ 90°F	0	0	0	0	0	0	0	0	0	0	0	0	0
Days Maximum Temp. ≤ 32°F	23	18	9	1	0	0	0	0	0	0	6	18	75
Days Minimum Temp. ≤ 32°F	31	28	28	18	4	0	0	0	1	10	23	29	172
Days Minimum Temp. ≤ 0°F	11	8	2	0	0	0	0	0	0	0	0	7	28
Heating Degree Days (base 65°F)	1,526	1,296	1,163	783	551	333	139	93	271	641	975	1,386	9,157
Cooling Degree Days (base 65°F)	0	0	0	0	0	2	33	42	6	0	0	0	83
Mean Precipitation (in.)	0.64	0.48	0.89	1.60	2.51	3.47	3.18	2.90	3.03	2.96	1.69	1.05	24.40
Extreme Maximum Daily Precip. (in.)	0.55	0.86	2.00	1.95	1.93	5.43	3.60	2.93	2.25	2.47	1.56	1.78	5.43
Days With ≥ 0.1" Precipitation	3	2	2	4	6	6	6	6	6	6	4	3	54
Days With ≥ 0.5" Precipitation	0	0	0	1	2	2	2	2	2	2	1	0	14
Days With ≥ 1.0" Precipitation	0	0	0	0	0	1	1	0	1	1	0	0	4
Mean Snowfall (in.)	16.7	6.9	6.3	1.8	trace	0.0	0.0	0.0	0.0	0.1	3.6	13.0	48.4
Maximum Snow Depth (in.)	52	47	40	22	1	0	0	0	0	2	17	32	52
Days With ≥ 1.0" Snow Depth	29	28	27	7	0	0	0	0	0	0	5	21	117

Grand Rapids Forestry Lab *Itasca County* Elevation: 1,310 ft. Latitude: 47° 15' N Longitude: 93° 30' W

	JAN	FEB	MAR	APR	MAY	JUN	JUL	AUG	SEP	OCT	NOV	DEC	YEAR
Mean Maximum Temp. (°F)	19.9	26.2	38.1	54.3	67.4	75.7	80.4	78.2	68.1	53.6	36.6	22.7	51.8
Mean Temp. (°F)	9.1	14.5	26.8	41.9	54.3	63.4	68.1	66.0	56.5	43.5	28.5	13.6	40.5
Mean Minimum Temp. (°F)	-1.8	2.7	15.5	29.5	41.2	50.9	55.7	53.7	44.8	33.3	20.3	4.5	29.2
Extreme Maximum Temp. (°F)	51	57	74	93	94	96	100	99	94	86	71	53	100
Extreme Minimum Temp. (°F)	-41	-41	-29	-2	19	30	40	31	23	10	-22	-40	-41
Days Maximum Temp. ≥ 90°F	0	0	0	0	0	1	3	2	0	0	0	0	6
Days Maximum Temp. ≤ 32°F	26	19	9	1	0	0	0	0	0	1	11	24	91
Days Minimum Temp. ≤ 32°F	31	28	29	19	5	0	0	0	2	15	27	31	187
Days Minimum Temp. ≤ 0°F	17	13	5	0	0	0	0	0	0	0	2	13	50
Heating Degree Days (base 65°F)	1,732	1,423	1,176	687	340	111	34	60	271	661	1,090	1,588	9,173
Cooling Degree Days (base 65°F)	0	0	0	1	16	68	137	98	22	1	0	0	343
Mean Precipitation (in.)	0.96	0.64	1.33	2.06	2.99	4.30	4.14	3.46	3.29	2.77	1.60	1.01	28.55
Extreme Maximum Daily Precip. (in.)	1.25	0.55	2.26	1.89	2.42	4.50	3.01	4.37	3.40	2.69	1.62	0.99	4.50
Days With ≥ 0.1" Precipitation	3	2	4	5	7	8	7	6	7	6	4	3	62
Days With ≥ 0.5" Precipitation	0	0	1	1	2	3	3	2	2	2	1	0	17
Days With ≥ 1.0" Precipitation	0	0	0	0	0	1	1	1	1	1	0	0	5
Mean Snowfall (in.)	13.2	7.3	8.2	3.8	0.1	0.0	0.0	0.0	trace	1.5	9.4	11.7	55.2
Maximum Snow Depth (in.)	***34***	35	36	23	1	0	0	0	trace	5	13	22	***36***
Days With ≥ 1.0" Snow Depth	***24***	22	19	4	0	0	0	0	0	1	11	23	***104***

The period of record for all cooperative weather station data is 1980 – 2009. See User Guide for detailed explanation of data.

Gunflint Lake 10 NW *Cook County* Elevation: 1,460 ft. Latitude: 48° 09' N Longitude: 90° 53' W

	JAN	FEB	MAR	APR	MAY	JUN	JUL	AUG	SEP	OCT	NOV	DEC	YEAR
Mean Maximum Temp. (°F)	17.2	23.5	35.4	50.8	65.0	72.4	78.6	75.6	65.0	49.4	34.5	20.2	49.0
Mean Temp. (°F)	6.1	11.4	22.2	38.0	51.2	60.1	66.2	63.9	54.7	40.8	27.3	10.7	37.7
Mean Minimum Temp. (°F)	-5.1	-0.7	9.2	25.2	37.3	47.8	53.8	52.1	44.4	32.2	20.0	1.0	26.4
Extreme Maximum Temp. (°F)	47	54	65	81	91	95	97	98	92	77	65	52	98
Extreme Minimum Temp. (°F)	-44	-38	-35	-17	15	30	38	35	26	8	-26	-40	-44
Days Maximum Temp. ≥ 90°F	0	0	0	0	0	1	2	1	0	0	0	0	4
Days Maximum Temp. ≤ 32°F	28	21	12	1	0	0	0	0	0	1	12	25	100
Days Minimum Temp. ≤ 32°F	31	28	30	24	10	0	0	0	2	17	26	30	198
Days Minimum Temp. ≤ 0°F	19	15	9	1	0	0	0	0	0	0	2	14	60
Heating Degree Days (base 65°F)	1,826	1,513	1,323	803	429	173	55	95	315	742	1,122	1,682	10,078
Cooling Degree Days (base 65°F)	0	0	0	0	9	33	99	67	13	0	0	0	221
Mean Precipitation (in.)	0.93	0.81	0.91	1.89	2.80	3.76	3.59	3.85	3.41	2.52	1.56	1.00	27.03
Extreme Maximum Daily Precip. (in.)	0.88	1.40	0.64	2.05	1.42	2.42	4.60	4.05	2.95	1.32	1.95	2.57	4.60
Days With ≥ 0.1" Precipitation	3	3	3	4	7	8	7	7	7	7	4	3	63
Days With ≥ 0.5" Precipitation	0	0	0	1	2	3	2	2	2	1	1	0	14
Days With ≥ 1.0" Precipitation	0	0	0	0	0	0	1	1	1	0	0	0	3
Mean Snowfall (in.)	13.4	8.6	7.2	6.0	0.5	trace	0.0	0.0	trace	2.3	10.8	10.7	59.5
Maximum Snow Depth (in.)	na	na	na	na	na	na	na	na	na	na	na	na	na
Days With ≥ 1.0" Snow Depth	na	17	17	na	0	0	0	0	0	1	7	na	na

Hibbing Chisholm-Hibbing Arpt *St. Louis County* Elevation: 1,347 ft. Latitude: 47° 23' N Longitude: 92° 51' W

	JAN	FEB	MAR	APR	MAY	JUN	JUL	AUG	SEP	OCT	NOV	DEC	YEAR
Mean Maximum Temp. (°F)	17.9	23.5	34.9	51.5	64.8	72.9	77.5	75.5	65.5	51.6	34.4	21.5	49.3
Mean Temp. (°F)	7.4	12.6	24.4	39.5	51.5	60.2	65.2	63.0	53.7	41.4	26.3	12.5	38.1
Mean Minimum Temp. (°F)	-3.2	1.6	13.8	27.5	38.1	47.5	52.9	50.6	41.9	31.1	18.3	3.4	26.9
Extreme Maximum Temp. (°F)	47	55	72	89	92	97	100	94	91	83	70	53	100
Extreme Minimum Temp. (°F)	-50	-44	-37	0	16	28	32	27	20	6	-27	-38	-50
Days Maximum Temp. ≥ 90°F	0	0	0	0	0	1	1	1	0	0	0	0	3
Days Maximum Temp. ≤ 32°F	28	21	12	1	0	0	0	0	0	1	13	25	101
Days Minimum Temp. ≤ 32°F	30	28	29	22	8	1	0	0	5	19	28	31	201
Days Minimum Temp. ≤ 0°F	18	13	5	0	0	0	0	0	0	0	3	13	52
Heating Degree Days (base 65°F)	1,785	1,478	1,252	759	419	171	67	108	344	726	1,153	1,625	9,887
Cooling Degree Days (base 65°F)	0	0	0	0	7	34	81	54	11	0	0	0	187
Mean Precipitation (in.)	0.66	0.46	0.90	1.62	2.49	4.14	4.35	3.11	3.14	2.37	1.20	0.71	25.15
Extreme Maximum Daily Precip. (in.)	0.87	0.54	1.35	1.57	1.78	3.66	4.50	5.75	3.21	2.10	1.27	0.93	5.75
Days With ≥ 0.1" Precipitation	2	2	3	4	6	8	7	6	6	5	3	2	54
Days With ≥ 0.5" Precipitation	0	0	0	1	2	3	3	2	2	1	0	0	14
Days With ≥ 1.0" Precipitation	0	0	0	0	0	1	1	1	1	0	0	0	4
Mean Snowfall (in.)	na	na	na	na	na	na	na	na	na	na	na	na	na
Maximum Snow Depth (in.)	na	na	na	na	na	na	na	na	na	na	na	na	na
Days With ≥ 1.0" Snow Depth	na	na	na	na	na	na	na	na	na	na	na	na	na

Hinckley *Pine County* Elevation: 1,035 ft. Latitude: 45° 59' N Longitude: 92° 53' W

	JAN	FEB	MAR	APR	MAY	JUN	JUL	AUG	SEP	OCT	NOV	DEC	YEAR
Mean Maximum Temp. (°F)	20.8	26.8	38.1	54.4	67.0	75.7	80.4	78.4	69.0	54.6	38.8	24.0	52.3
Mean Temp. (°F)	10.1	15.2	27.8	42.6	54.3	63.3	68.4	66.1	56.6	43.8	29.7	14.6	41.0
Mean Minimum Temp. (°F)	-0.6	3.6	17.4	30.6	41.6	51.0	56.2	53.7	44.1	33.0	20.5	5.1	29.7
Extreme Maximum Temp. (°F)	53	58	78	94	91	99	102	100	91	88	70	59	102
Extreme Minimum Temp. (°F)	-38	-35	-27	-2	19	32	38	34	21	10	-13	-40	-40
Days Maximum Temp. ≥ 90°F	0	0	0	0	0	1	3	1	0	0	0	0	5
Days Maximum Temp. ≤ 32°F	24	17	9	1	0	0	0	0	0	0	9	21	81
Days Minimum Temp. ≤ 32°F	29	25	27	18	4	0	0	0	2	15	25	28	173
Days Minimum Temp. ≤ 0°F	15	11	4	0	0	0	0	0	0	0	1	11	42
Heating Degree Days (base 65°F)	1,697	1,404	1,147	669	338	108	29	56	267	650	1,052	1,559	8,976
Cooling Degree Days (base 65°F)	0	0	0	1	14	65	143	96	20	1	0	0	340
Mean Precipitation (in.)	0.94	0.85	1.55	2.80	3.29	4.36	3.97	4.15	3.49	3.05	1.82	1.08	31.35
Extreme Maximum Daily Precip. (in.)	1.63	1.32	1.02	3.15	3.07	4.20	4.23	4.76	3.05	5.43	1.74	1.31	5.43
Days With ≥ 0.1" Precipitation	3	2	4	6	7	8	7	7	6	6	4	3	63
Days With ≥ 0.5" Precipitation	0	0	1	2	2	3	3	3	2	2	1	0	19
Days With ≥ 1.0" Precipitation	0	0	0	0	1	1	1	1	1	1	0	0	6
Mean Snowfall (in.)	10.0	7.8	9.9	3.2	trace	0.0	0.0	0.0	0.0	0.9	9.5	10.2	51.5
Maximum Snow Depth (in.)	30	38	38	13	trace	0	0	0	0	4	22	24	38
Days With ≥ 1.0" Snow Depth	18	16	14	2	0	0	0	0	0	0	7	17	74

Jordan 1 S *Scott County* Elevation: 930 ft. Latitude: 44° 39' N Longitude: 93° 37' W

	JAN	FEB	MAR	APR	MAY	JUN	JUL	AUG	SEP	OCT	NOV	DEC	YEAR
Mean Maximum Temp. (°F)	24.2	28.5	40.6	58.0	70.2	78.8	82.5	79.3	71.6	58.5	41.2	27.2	55.1
Mean Temp. (°F)	14.2	18.8	30.6	45.8	57.9	66.9	71.1	67.9	59.6	46.9	31.9	17.7	44.1
Mean Minimum Temp. (°F)	4.1	9.0	20.5	33.5	45.5	54.9	59.6	56.4	47.6	35.3	22.6	8.3	33.1
Extreme Maximum Temp. (°F)	59	61	80	93	95	102	105	101	92	90	77	67	105
Extreme Minimum Temp. (°F)	-33	-36	-21	5	18	34	39	33	20	3	-17	-41	-41
Days Maximum Temp. ≥ 90°F	0	0	0	0	1	2	4	1	0	0	0	0	8
Days Maximum Temp. ≤ 32°F	22	16	7	0	0	0	0	0	0	0	7	19	71
Days Minimum Temp. ≤ 32°F	30	27	27	14	2	0	0	0	2	12	25	30	169
Days Minimum Temp. ≤ 0°F	12	8	3	0	0	0	0	0	0	0	1	10	34
Heating Degree Days (base 65°F)	1,572	1,303	1,059	575	244	56	10	35	199	557	988	1,460	8,058
Cooling Degree Days (base 65°F)	0	0	0	5	31	119	205	131	44	4	0	0	539
Mean Precipitation (in.)	0.71	0.49	1.54	2.56	3.67	4.37	3.60	5.10	3.20	2.30	1.54	0.83	29.91
Extreme Maximum Daily Precip. (in.)	2.28	1.05	2.50	1.55	2.35	4.17	4.14	4.15	6.04	2.70	1.98	1.25	6.04
Days With ≥ 0.1" Precipitation	2	1	4	6	7	7	6	7	5	4	3	2	54
Days With ≥ 0.5" Precipitation	0	0	1	2	3	3	2	4	2	2	1	0	20
Days With ≥ 1.0" Precipitation	0	0	0	1	1	1	1	2	1	0	0	0	7
Mean Snowfall (in.)	na	1.9	2.8	1.5	0.0	0.0	0.0	0.0	trace	0.2	1.4	4.8	na
Maximum Snow Depth (in.)	na	na	na	na	na	na	na	na	na	na	na	na	na
Days With ≥ 1.0" Snow Depth	na	na	na	0	0	0	0	0	0	0	2	na	na

The period of record for all cooperative weather station data is 1980 – 2009. See User Guide for detailed explanation of data.

Lake Wilson *Murray County* Elevation: 1,649 ft. Latitude: 44° 00' N Longitude: 95° 57' W

	JAN	FEB	MAR	APR	MAY	JUN	JUL	AUG	SEP	OCT	NOV	DEC	YEAR
Mean Maximum Temp. (°F)	24.6	29.0	40.5	56.9	69.9	78.7	82.9	80.2	72.9	58.9	41.5	26.8	55.2
Mean Temp. (°F)	15.4	19.8	31.0	45.4	58.3	67.5	71.9	69.2	61.0	47.5	32.4	18.3	44.8
Mean Minimum Temp. (°F)	6.2	10.5	21.5	33.8	46.6	56.2	60.8	58.1	49.0	36.0	23.4	9.8	34.3
Extreme Maximum Temp. (°F)	64	70	78	91	96	105	104	100	93	92	79	64	105
Extreme Minimum Temp. (°F)	-30	-26	-17	5	22	36	44	34	25	11	-12	-28	-30
Days Maximum Temp. ≥ 90°F	0	0	0	0	1	2	5	2	1	0	0	0	11
Days Maximum Temp. ≤ 32°F	22	16	8	1	0	0	0	0	0	0	8	20	75
Days Minimum Temp. ≤ 32°F	31	27	26	14	2	0	0	0	2	11	25	31	169
Days Minimum Temp. ≤ 0°F	11	8	2	0	0	0	0	0	0	0	1	8	30
Heating Degree Days (base 65°F)	1,532	1,272	1,047	588	238	52	12	28	175	540	970	1,441	7,895
Cooling Degree Days (base 65°F)	0	0	0	5	36	133	233	165	61	4	0	0	637
Mean Precipitation (in.)	0.56	0.72	1.97	3.12	3.14	4.19	2.99	3.36	2.84	1.97	1.60	0.79	27.25
Extreme Maximum Daily Precip. (in.)	1.00	1.00	2.00	3.15	3.30	***3.05***	2.29	4.40	4.03	1.82	2.50	***0.97***	***4.40***
Days With ≥ 0.1" Precipitation	1	2	4	6	7	7	5	5	5	4	3	2	51
Days With ≥ 0.5" Precipitation	0	0	1	2	2	3	2	2	2	1	1	0	16
Days With ≥ 1.0" Precipitation	0	0	0	1	1	1	1	1	1	1	0	0	7
Mean Snowfall (in.)	7.4	6.8	9.5	3.9	trace	0.0	0.0	0.0	trace	1.0	7.1	8.6	44.3
Maximum Snow Depth (in.)	***26***	na	***21***	8	trace	0	0	0	0	5	16	***19***	na
Days With ≥ 1.0" Snow Depth	***13***	na	***7***	1	0	0	0	0	0	0	4	***10***	na

Lamberton SW Exp Stn *Redwood County* Elevation: 1,144 ft. Latitude: 44° 15' N Longitude: 95° 19' W

	JAN	FEB	MAR	APR	MAY	JUN	JUL	AUG	SEP	OCT	NOV	DEC	YEAR
Mean Maximum Temp. (°F)	24.6	29.0	40.1	57.1	70.6	79.9	83.3	80.6	73.6	59.9	42.2	27.6	55.7
Mean Temp. (°F)	14.7	19.3	30.6	45.3	58.5	68.4	71.9	69.1	60.7	47.5	32.3	18.4	44.7
Mean Minimum Temp. (°F)	4.8	9.5	21.1	33.4	46.3	56.7	60.4	57.5	47.9	35.1	22.5	9.1	33.7
Extreme Maximum Temp. (°F)	66	65	81	95	99	105	104	106	96	91	81	68	106
Extreme Minimum Temp. (°F)	-30	-30	-23	3	22	35	40	35	24	10	-15	-31	-31
Days Maximum Temp. ≥ 90°F	0	0	0	0	2	4	6	3	1	0	0	0	16
Days Maximum Temp. ≤ 32°F	21	16	9	1	0	0	0	0	0	0	7	19	73
Days Minimum Temp. ≤ 32°F	31	28	27	14	2	0	0	0	2	13	24	31	172
Days Minimum Temp. ≤ 0°F	12	9	2	0	0	0	0	0	0	0	1	9	33
Heating Degree Days (base 65°F)	1,555	1,288	1,060	590	240	46	11	29	180	541	973	1,440	7,953
Cooling Degree Days (base 65°F)	0	0	0	5	43	154	232	163	60	6	0	0	663
Mean Precipitation (in.)	0.56	0.50	1.59	2.90	3.36	4.13	3.67	3.72	3.00	2.01	1.30	0.66	27.40
Extreme Maximum Daily Precip. (in.)	1.22	0.56	1.54	3.60	3.48	4.30	3.77	3.63	3.21	2.60	1.94	0.96	4.30
Days With ≥ 0.1" Precipitation	2	2	4	6	7	7	6	6	5	4	3	2	54
Days With ≥ 0.5" Precipitation	0	0	1	2	2	3	2	3	2	1	1	0	17
Days With ≥ 1.0" Precipitation	0	0	0	1	1	1	1	1	1	0	0	0	6
Mean Snowfall (in.)	8.3	6.4	8.8	3.2	0.0	0.0	0.0	0.0	0.0	0.3	6.9	8.1	42.0
Maximum Snow Depth (in.)	27	32	32	7	0	0	0	0	0	4	14	28	32
Days With ≥ 1.0" Snow Depth	21	19	11	2	0	0	0	0	0	0	7	17	77

Litchfield *Meeker County* Elevation: 1,131 ft. Latitude: 45° 08' N Longitude: 94° 32' W

	JAN	FEB	MAR	APR	MAY	JUN	JUL	AUG	SEP	OCT	NOV	DEC	YEAR
Mean Maximum Temp. (°F)	22.4	27.2	39.0	57.1	69.8	78.6	82.8	80.1	72.0	58.1	40.0	25.5	54.4
Mean Temp. (°F)	13.0	18.0	29.8	45.9	58.5	67.7	72.2	69.5	60.7	47.6	31.8	17.4	44.3
Mean Minimum Temp. (°F)	3.7	8.7	20.6	34.7	47.1	56.8	61.5	58.9	49.3	37.0	23.5	9.2	34.3
Extreme Maximum Temp. (°F)	60	58	77	93	97	101	104	104	93	87	78	62	104
Extreme Minimum Temp. (°F)	-34	-37	-17	4	24	30	45	37	24	13	-14	-34	-37
Days Maximum Temp. ≥ 90°F	0	0	0	0	1	3	4	2	1	0	0	0	11
Days Maximum Temp. ≤ 32°F	24	17	8	1	0	0	0	0	0	0	8	21	79
Days Minimum Temp. ≤ 32°F	31	27	26	13	1	0	0	0	1	10	25	31	165
Days Minimum Temp. ≤ 0°F	13	9	3	0	0	0	0	0	0	0	1	9	35
Heating Degree Days (base 65°F)	1,606	1,324	1,083	571	234	52	7	24	174	537	990	1,471	8,073
Cooling Degree Days (base 65°F)	0	0	0	5	39	141	235	171	51	4	0	0	646
Mean Precipitation (in.)	***0.74***	0.61	1.57	2.38	3.24	5.02	3.83	4.05	3.42	2.39	1.28	0.81	***29.34***
Extreme Maximum Daily Precip. (in.)	***0.92***	1.12	***1.65***	na	***2.58***	***4.31***	***2.95***	***3.40***	na	***3.28***	***1.33***	***1.31***	na
Days With ≥ 0.1" Precipitation	2	2	3	4	5	6	6	5	5	4	3	2	47
Days With ≥ 0.5" Precipitation	0	0	1	1	2	3	2	2	2	1	1	0	15
Days With ≥ 1.0" Precipitation	0	0	0	1	1	1	1	1	1	1	0	0	7
Mean Snowfall (in.)	***9.2***	***6.2***	***8.6***	***3.0***	***trace***	***0.0***	***0.0***	***0.0***	***0.0***	***0.3***	***8.0***	***8.5***	***43.8***
Maximum Snow Depth (in.)	na	na	na	na	na	na	na	na	na	na	na	na	na
Days With ≥ 1.0" Snow Depth	na	12	***9***	***0***	***0***	***0***	***0***	***0***	***0***	***0***	***3***	na	na

Mankato *Blue Earth County* Elevation: 850 ft. Latitude: 44° 09' N Longitude: 94° 01' W

	JAN	FEB	MAR	APR	MAY	JUN	JUL	AUG	SEP	OCT	NOV	DEC	YEAR
Mean Maximum Temp. (°F)	***24.8***	***29.4***	***41.7***	***58.0***	***70.4***	***79.6***	***82.7***	***80.1***	73.2	60.0	42.5	28.6	***55.9***
Mean Temp. (°F)	***15.3***	***19.6***	***31.9***	***46.3***	***58.6***	***68.2***	***71.9***	***69.3***	61.2	48.3	33.3	19.9	***45.3***
Mean Minimum Temp. (°F)	***5.8***	***9.9***	***22.0***	***34.5***	***46.6***	***56.7***	***61.1***	***58.4***	49.2	36.5	24.0	11.1	***34.7***
Extreme Maximum Temp. (°F)	***58***	***63***	***83***	***93***	***96***	***105***	***104***	***107***	***96***	***92***	***83***	***69***	***107***
Extreme Minimum Temp. (°F)	***-30***	***-35***	***-12***	***8***	***26***	***35***	***44***	***38***	***25***	***13***	***-14***	***-26***	***-35***
Days Maximum Temp. ≥ 90°F	***0***	***0***	***0***	***0***	***1***	***4***	***5***	***3***	1	0	0	0	***14***
Days Maximum Temp. ≤ 32°F	***21***	***16***	***7***	***1***	***0***	***0***	***0***	***0***	0	0	6	18	***69***
Days Minimum Temp. ≤ 32°F	***31***	***27***	***26***	***12***	***1***	***0***	***0***	***0***	1	11	24	30	***163***
Days Minimum Temp. ≤ 0°F	***11***	***7***	***2***	***0***	***0***	***0***	***0***	***0***	0	0	1	8	***29***
Heating Degree Days (base 65°F)	***1,535***	***1,275***	***1,020***	***560***	***234***	***50***	***8***	***26***	168	518	946	1,392	***7,732***
Cooling Degree Days (base 65°F)	***0***	***0***	***0***	***7***	***41***	***153***	***229***	***165***	62	8	0	0	***665***
Mean Precipitation (in.)	***0.99***	***0.67***	***1.97***	***3.23***	***3.46***	***5.13***	***4.35***	***4.37***	3.16	2.34	***1.72***	1.02	***32.41***
Extreme Maximum Daily Precip. (in.)	***1.51***	***1.19***	***1.37***	***2.28***	***1.87***	***6.23***	***2.85***	***4.61***	***5.44***	***1.92***	***1.77***	***0.79***	***6.23***
Days With ≥ 0.1" Precipitation	***3***	***2***	***5***	***6***	***8***	***8***	***7***	***6***	6	5	4	3	***63***
Days With ≥ 0.5" Precipitation	***0***	***0***	***1***	***2***	***3***	***3***	***3***	***3***	2	2	1	0	***20***
Days With ≥ 1.0" Precipitation	***0***	***0***	***0***	***1***	***1***	***1***	***1***	***1***	1	1	0	0	***7***
Mean Snowfall (in.)	***8.7***	***6.3***	***7.8***	***1.6***	***0.0***	***0.0***	***0.0***	***0.0***	trace	0.2	5.6	9.3	***39.5***
Maximum Snow Depth (in.)	***33***	***39***	***49***	***5***	***trace***	***0***	***0***	***0***	***trace***	***1***	***14***	***23***	***49***
Days With ≥ 1.0" Snow Depth	***22***	***17***	***10***	***1***	***0***	***0***	***0***	***0***	0	***0***	6	***18***	***74***

The period of record for all cooperative weather station data is 1980 – 2009. See User Guide for detailed explanation of data.

New Ulm 2 SE *Brown County* Elevation: 859 ft. Latitude: 44° 18' N Longitude: 94° 27' W

	JAN	FEB	MAR	APR	MAY	JUN	JUL	AUG	SEP	OCT	NOV	DEC	YEAR
Mean Maximum Temp. (°F)	24.8	29.8	42.0	58.9	71.0	79.5	82.9	80.1	73.0	59.7	42.2	27.5	55.9
Mean Temp. (°F)	15.8	20.8	32.9	47.6	59.5	68.6	72.5	69.8	62.0	49.0	33.7	19.3	46.0
Mean Minimum Temp. (°F)	6.8	11.8	23.7	36.2	48.1	57.7	62.1	59.5	50.9	38.3	25.2	11.1	35.9
Extreme Maximum Temp. (°F)	65	63	82	95	96	103	105	100	96	89	83	67	105
Extreme Minimum Temp. (°F)	-37	-33	-18	6	24	35	45	35	24	13	-15	-36	-37
Days Maximum Temp. ≥ 90°F	0	0	0	0	1	3	5	2	1	0	0	0	12
Days Maximum Temp. ≤ 32°F	22	16	7	1	0	0	0	0	0	0	7	19	72
Days Minimum Temp. ≤ 32°F	31	27	24	11	1	0	0	0	1	9	23	30	157
Days Minimum Temp. ≤ 0°F	11	7	2	0	0	0	0	0	0	0	1	7	28
Heating Degree Days (base 65°F)	1,520	1,244	990	523	206	40	8	21	150	494	932	1,410	7,538
Cooling Degree Days (base 65°F)	0	0	0	7	44	156	247	178	66	7	0	0	705
Mean Precipitation (in.)	0.66	0.65	1.88	2.81	3.45	4.64	3.88	4.17	3.01	2.23	1.57	0.82	29.77
Extreme Maximum Daily Precip. (in.)	1.30	0.91	1.50	1.90	2.34	2.50	2.92	5.42	3.37	2.47	1.97	1.41	5.42
Days With ≥ 0.1" Precipitation	2	2	4	6	7	8	6	6	5	4	4	2	56
Days With ≥ 0.5" Precipitation	0	0	1	2	2	3	3	3	2	1	1	0	18
Days With ≥ 1.0" Precipitation	0	0	0	1	1	1	1	1	1	1	0	0	7
Mean Snowfall (in.)	7.7	6.0	8.1	1.8	0.0	0.0	0.0	0.0	trace	0.4	6.4	8.6	39.0
Maximum Snow Depth (in.)	23	***23***	14	5	trace	0	0	0	trace	4	***17***	20	***23***
Days With ≥ 1.0" Snow Depth	22	18	10	1	0	0	0	0	0	0	6	17	74

Red Lake Indian Agency *Beltrami County* Elevation: 1,220 ft. Latitude: 47° 53' N Longitude: 95° 01' W

	JAN	FEB	MAR	APR	MAY	JUN	JUL	AUG	SEP	OCT	NOV	DEC	YEAR
Mean Maximum Temp. (°F)	16.3	22.3	34.3	50.9	64.8	73.0	77.8	76.6	65.7	***52.0***	34.4	21.5	***49.1***
Mean Temp. (°F)	6.2	11.5	23.9	39.7	53.5	62.8	67.6	***66.2***	55.5	***42.6***	26.3	12.4	***39.0***
Mean Minimum Temp. (°F)	-3.9	0.7	13.5	28.5	42.3	52.5	57.4	***55.8***	45.2	***33.2***	18.2	3.2	***28.9***
Extreme Maximum Temp. (°F)	51	59	71	95	93	100	101	100	90	***85***	73	55	***101***
Extreme Minimum Temp. (°F)	-43	-44	-30	-4	17	32	36	***35***	13	***-3***	-23	-38	***-44***
Days Maximum Temp. ≥ 90°F	0	0	0	0	0	1	2	1	0	***0***	0	0	***4***
Days Maximum Temp. ≤ 32°F	27	21	13	2	0	0	0	0	0	***1***	14	23	***101***
Days Minimum Temp. ≤ 32°F	31	28	29	21	5	0	0	***0***	3	***15***	28	30	***190***
Days Minimum Temp. ≤ 0°F	19	14	6	0	0	0	0	***0***	0	***0***	2	13	***54***
Heating Degree Days (base 65°F)	1,820	1,507	1,268	754	367	122	40	***58***	300	***687***	1,153	1,628	***9,704***
Cooling Degree Days (base 65°F)	0	0	0	2	18	62	128	***101***	20	***1***	0	0	***332***
Mean Precipitation (in.)	***0.65***	0.48	0.79	1.22	2.97	3.85	3.61	3.37	2.28	***2.27***	0.96	***0.30***	***22.75***
Extreme Maximum Daily Precip. (in.)	***1.00***	1.50	***0.95***	***3.00***	***3.20***	***3.07***	na	***4.07***	***1.64***	***1.96***	***0.95***	***0.50***	na
Days With ≥ 0.1" Precipitation	2	1	3	3	6	6	***6***	6	5	***4***	3	***1***	***46***
Days With ≥ 0.5" Precipitation	0	0	0	1	2	2	***3***	2	1	***1***	1	***0***	***13***
Days With ≥ 1.0" Precipitation	0	0	0	0	1	1	***1***	1	0	***0***	0	***0***	***4***
Mean Snowfall (in.)	***8.7***	4.8	4.7	1.0	trace	0.0	0.0	0.0	0.0	***0.4***	***6.0***	***5.6***	***31.2***
Maximum Snow Depth (in.)	37	30	26	9	trace	0	***0***	***0***	0	***3***	19	20	***37***
Days With ≥ 1.0" Snow Depth	28	25	19	2	0	0	0	0	0	***0***	10	22	***106***

Rosemount Agri Exp Stn *Dakota County* Elevation: 950 ft. Latitude: 44° 43' N Longitude: 93° 06' W

	JAN	FEB	MAR	APR	MAY	JUN	JUL	AUG	SEP	OCT	NOV	DEC	YEAR
Mean Maximum Temp. (°F)	24.3	29.0	41.2	58.7	70.5	79.1	83.0	80.4	72.8	59.2	42.0	27.8	55.7
Mean Temp. (°F)	14.9	19.5	31.6	46.9	58.8	68.1	72.1	69.8	61.7	48.5	33.4	19.5	45.4
Mean Minimum Temp. (°F)	5.6	10.0	22.0	35.0	47.1	57.0	61.2	59.1	50.6	37.8	24.7	11.2	35.1
Extreme Maximum Temp. (°F)	57	61	81	93	96	100	105	103	92	91	77	66	105
Extreme Minimum Temp. (°F)	-32	-37	-15	4	24	36	44	39	27	14	-16	-31	-37
Days Maximum Temp. ≥ 90°F	0	0	0	0	1	3	5	2	0	0	0	0	11
Days Maximum Temp. ≤ 32°F	23	16	6	0	0	0	0	0	0	0	7	19	71
Days Minimum Temp. ≤ 32°F	31	27	26	12	1	0	0	0	1	10	23	30	161
Days Minimum Temp. ≤ 0°F	11	8	2	0	0	0	0	0	0	0	1	8	30
Heating Degree Days (base 65°F)	1,547	1,280	1,028	541	222	45	7	18	153	511	941	1,404	7,697
Cooling Degree Days (base 65°F)	0	0	0	4	37	144	235	172	62	6	0	0	660
Mean Precipitation (in.)	1.10	0.87	2.13	2.99	4.13	4.42	4.27	4.83	3.58	2.86	1.96	1.15	34.29
Extreme Maximum Daily Precip. (in.)	1.44	1.05	1.51	1.64	2.55	5.47	5.80	***4.02***	4.35	3.40	2.06	***1.40***	***5.80***
Days With ≥ 0.1" Precipitation	3	3	5	6	8	7	6	6	5	6	4	3	62
Days With ≥ 0.5" Precipitation	0	0	1	2	3	3	2	3	2	2	1	0	19
Days With ≥ 1.0" Precipitation	0	0	0	0	1	1	1	1	1	1	0	0	6
Mean Snowfall (in.)	8.6	5.3	6.8	2.0	0.0	0.0	0.0	0.0	0.0	0.2	5.5	***6.7***	***35.1***
Maximum Snow Depth (in.)	32	26	20	10	0	0	0	0	0	3	14	19	32
Days With ≥ 1.0" Snow Depth	22	20	10	1	0	0	0	0	0	0	6	17	76

Rothsay *Wilkin County* Elevation: 1,206 ft. Latitude: 46° 29' N Longitude: 96° 16' W

	JAN	FEB	MAR	APR	MAY	JUN	JUL	AUG	SEP	OCT	NOV	DEC	YEAR
Mean Maximum Temp. (°F)	18.2	24.1	36.5	55.2	68.7	76.5	81.0	79.4	70.2	55.0	37.4	22.1	52.0
Mean Temp. (°F)	9.1	15.1	27.9	44.1	57.2	66.1	70.5	68.7	59.4	45.4	29.4	14.0	42.2
Mean Minimum Temp. (°F)	0.0	6.1	19.2	33.1	45.6	55.7	59.8	58.1	48.5	35.8	21.3	5.8	32.4
Extreme Maximum Temp. (°F)	55	53	73	98	93	97	102	101	98	88	73	55	102
Extreme Minimum Temp. (°F)	-38	-37	-24	3	22	35	41	35	21	10	-21	-32	-38
Days Maximum Temp. ≥ 90°F	0	0	0	0	0	2	3	3	1	0	0	0	9
Days Maximum Temp. ≤ 32°F	26	19	10	1	0	0	0	0	0	1	11	24	92
Days Minimum Temp. ≤ 32°F	31	28	27	14	2	0	0	0	1	11	25	31	170
Days Minimum Temp. ≤ 0°F	16	11	3	0	0	0	0	0	0	0	2	12	44
Heating Degree Days (base 65°F)	1,732	1,406	1,144	622	267	66	18	33	210	601	1,063	1,578	8,740
Cooling Degree Days (base 65°F)	0	0	0	3	31	107	194	156	48	2	0	0	541
Mean Precipitation (in.)	0.56	0.49	1.21	1.67	3.16	3.75	3.46	2.83	2.56	2.54	0.88	0.63	23.74
Extreme Maximum Daily Precip. (in.)	1.78	0.52	1.50	2.25	3.27	2.86	4.75	3.50	2.38	2.00	1.77	0.98	4.75
Days With ≥ 0.1" Precipitation	2	2	3	4	6	7	6	5	5	5	2	2	49
Days With ≥ 0.5" Precipitation	0	0	1	1	2	3	2	2	2	2	1	0	16
Days With ≥ 1.0" Precipitation	0	0	0	0	1	1	1	1	1	1	0	0	6
Mean Snowfall (in.)	10.1	6.6	7.9	3.4	trace	0.0	0.0	0.0	trace	***1.2***	6.1	8.4	***43.7***
Maximum Snow Depth (in.)	***42***	na	***41***	19	trace	0	0	0	trace	***4***	17	***23***	na
Days With ≥ 1.0" Snow Depth	***20***	***16***	***10***	1	0	0	0	0	0	0	6	***13***	***66***

The period of record for all cooperative weather station data is 1980 – 2009. See User Guide for detailed explanation of data.

St Paul *Ramsey County* Elevation: 899 ft. Latitude: 44° 57' N Longitude: 92° 59' W

	JAN	FEB	MAR	APR	MAY	JUN	JUL	AUG	SEP	OCT	NOV	DEC	YEAR
Mean Maximum Temp. (°F)	24.3	29.7	41.4	58.4	70.1	78.5	83.3	80.9	72.0	58.3	40.3	26.9	55.3
Mean Temp. (°F)	16.1	21.1	32.3	47.4	59.1	68.1	73.2	71.0	61.9	48.7	33.0	19.6	45.9
Mean Minimum Temp. (°F)	7.8	12.6	23.2	36.4	48.0	57.6	62.9	61.0	51.8	39.0	25.6	12.1	36.5
Extreme Maximum Temp. (°F)	57	61	83	93	93	100	105	103	94	88	72	66	105
Extreme Minimum Temp. (°F)	-29	-32	-12	3	24	36	47	42	28	15	-10	-29	-32
Days Maximum Temp. ≥ 90°F	0	0	0	0	1	2	5	3	1	0	0	0	12
Days Maximum Temp. ≤ 32°F	23	16	6	0	0	0	0	0	0	0	8	20	73
Days Minimum Temp. ≤ 32°F	31	26	25	10	1	0	0	0	0	8	23	30	154
Days Minimum Temp. ≤ 0°F	10	6	1	0	0	0	0	0	0	0	0	7	24
Heating Degree Days (base 65°F)	1,512	1,234	1,007	527	218	48	5	13	153	504	954	1,404	7,579
Cooling Degree Days (base 65°F)	0	0	0	6	41	146	264	206	66	5	0	0	734
Mean Precipitation (in.)	0.97	0.78	1.91	2.69	3.87	4.96	4.53	4.39	3.66	2.81	2.02	1.04	33.63
Extreme Maximum Daily Precip. (in.)	1.05	0.76	1.66	1.84	2.06	4.36	5.47	na	3.90	4.59	na	na	na
Days With ≥ 0.1" Precipitation	3	3	5	6	8	7	7	6	6	5	4	3	63
Days With ≥ 0.5" Precipitation	0	0	1	2	3	3	3	3	2	2	1	0	20
Days With ≥ 1.0" Precipitation	0	0	0	0	1	1	1	1	1	1	0	0	6
Mean Snowfall (in.)	10.4	7.6	10.0	3.1	trace	0.0	0.0	0.0	trace	0.4	9.2	9.7	50.4
Maximum Snow Depth (in.)	32	25	24	11	2	0	0	0	trace	4	17	24	32
Days With ≥ 1.0" Snow Depth	26	25	15	1	0	0	0	0	0	0	8	21	96

Stillwater 1 SE *Washington County* Elevation: 711 ft. Latitude: 45° 02' N Longitude: 92° 47' W

	JAN	FEB	MAR	APR	MAY	JUN	JUL	AUG	SEP	OCT	NOV	DEC	YEAR
Mean Maximum Temp. (°F)	26.4	32.0	43.0	59.7	71.6	80.4	85.2	82.8	73.8	60.3	43.0	29.2	57.3
Mean Temp. (°F)	16.9	22.1	32.8	48.0	59.9	69.0	74.1	71.7	62.7	49.9	34.6	20.9	46.9
Mean Minimum Temp. (°F)	7.4	12.0	22.6	36.2	48.1	57.6	62.8	60.5	51.6	39.5	26.2	12.4	36.4
Extreme Maximum Temp. (°F)	57	62	83	94	94	101	106	104	95	90	78	67	106
Extreme Minimum Temp. (°F)	-32	-36	-13	6	22	34	46	42	27	16	-10	-39	-39
Days Maximum Temp. ≥ 90°F	0	0	0	0	1	3	8	5	1	0	0	0	18
Days Maximum Temp. ≤ 32°F	20	13	5	0	0	0	0	0	0	0	5	17	60
Days Minimum Temp. ≤ 32°F	31	27	25	10	1	0	0	0	0	7	23	30	154
Days Minimum Temp. ≤ 0°F	9	7	2	0	0	0	0	0	0	0	1	7	26
Heating Degree Days (base 65°F)	1,485	1,209	992	512	195	36	3	10	139	467	906	1,362	7,316
Cooling Degree Days (base 65°F)	0	0	0	7	43	164	290	225	80	6	0	0	815
Mean Precipitation (in.)	0.98	0.78	1.70	3.10	3.89	5.15	4.64	4.39	3.81	2.93	2.12	0.93	34.42
Extreme Maximum Daily Precip. (in.)	1.77	0.76	1.16	2.35	2.70	4.09	5.14	4.50	3.56	5.04	1.80	1.81	5.14
Days With ≥ 0.1" Precipitation	3	3	4	6	8	8	7	6	6	6	5	3	65
Days With ≥ 0.5" Precipitation	0	0	1	2	3	3	3	3	2	1	1	0	19
Days With ≥ 1.0" Precipitation	0	0	0	1	1	1	1	2	1	1	0	0	8
Mean Snowfall (in.)	10.0	na	na	1.5	trace	0.0	0.0	0.0	0.0	trace	na	na	na
Maximum Snow Depth (in.)	na	na	na	na	na	na	na	na	na	na	na	na	na
Days With ≥ 1.0" Snow Depth	na	na	na	1	0	0	0	0	0	0	na	na	na

Tower 3 S *St. Louis County* Elevation: 1,459 ft. Latitude: 47° 45' N Longitude: 92° 17' W

	JAN	FEB	MAR	APR	MAY	JUN	JUL	AUG	SEP	OCT	NOV	DEC	YEAR
Mean Maximum Temp. (°F)	17.6	24.1	36.3	51.5	64.9	73.4	78.1	75.8	65.8	51.6	34.6	21.6	49.6
Mean Temp. (°F)	4.3	9.5	22.4	37.4	49.7	58.7	63.3	61.1	52.2	39.9	24.8	10.1	36.1
Mean Minimum Temp. (°F)	-9.1	-5.2	8.5	23.3	34.4	43.9	48.5	46.3	38.6	28.2	14.9	-1.4	22.6
Extreme Maximum Temp. (°F)	49	58	71	86	95	97	98	96	93	82	75	52	98
Extreme Minimum Temp. (°F)	-57	-60	-42	-22	10	21	24	21	15	-2	-31	-52	-60
Days Maximum Temp. ≥ 90°F	0	0	0	0	0	1	2	1	0	0	0	0	4
Days Maximum Temp. ≤ 32°F	27	21	11	2	0	0	0	0	0	1	14	24	100
Days Minimum Temp. ≤ 32°F	31	28	30	26	15	5	1	2	9	21	28	30	226
Days Minimum Temp. ≤ 0°F	21	17	10	1	0	0	0	0	0	0	5	15	69
Heating Degree Days (base 65°F)	1,881	1,568	1,314	821	476	212	109	153	389	772	1,199	1,698	10,592
Cooling Degree Days (base 65°F)	0	0	0	1	7	29	62	39	11	0	0	0	149
Mean Precipitation (in.)	0.58	0.60	0.76	1.77	3.06	4.03	4.05	3.93	4.31	2.83	1.37	0.58	27.87
Extreme Maximum Daily Precip. (in.)	0.80	1.54	0.74	1.73	2.00	2.25	2.73	3.22	8.70	4.00	3.21	0.76	8.70
Days With ≥ 0.1" Precipitation	2	2	2	4	7	8	8	8	8	6	3	2	60
Days With ≥ 0.5" Precipitation	0	0	0	1	2	3	3	3	2	2	1	0	17
Days With ≥ 1.0" Precipitation	0	0	0	0	0	1	1	1	1	0	0	0	4
Mean Snowfall (in.)	13.5	9.6	8.9	7.3	0.3	0.0	0.0	0.0	trace	2.9	13.4	11.5	67.4
Maximum Snow Depth (in.)	53	65	49	32	2	0	0	0	trace	12	34	42	65
Days With ≥ 1.0" Snow Depth	18	18	16	6	0	0	0	0	0	1	10	17	86

Two Harbors *Lake County* Elevation: 625 ft. Latitude: 47° 02' N Longitude: 91° 40' W

	JAN	FEB	MAR	APR	MAY	JUN	JUL	AUG	SEP	OCT	NOV	DEC	YEAR
Mean Maximum Temp. (°F)	24.4	28.3	36.5	48.9	58.5	67.3	74.7	74.3	66.3	53.6	39.8	27.9	50.0
Mean Temp. (°F)	15.9	19.7	28.7	40.2	48.8	56.6	64.6	65.3	57.6	45.6	33.2	20.5	41.4
Mean Minimum Temp. (°F)	7.3	11.1	20.9	31.5	39.1	45.8	54.5	56.4	48.8	37.6	26.5	13.1	32.7
Extreme Maximum Temp. (°F)	52	59	69	81	87	96	98	98	87	86	71	57	98
Extreme Minimum Temp. (°F)	-33	-36	-15	1	23	33	41	39	29	10	-13	-26	-36
Days Maximum Temp. ≥ 90°F	0	0	0	0	0	0	1	0	0	0	0	0	1
Days Maximum Temp. ≤ 32°F	24	18	9	1	0	0	0	0	0	0	6	20	78
Days Minimum Temp. ≤ 32°F	30	27	27	15	3	0	0	0	1	8	21	29	161
Days Minimum Temp. ≤ 0°F	10	7	2	0	0	0	0	0	0	0	0	6	25
Heating Degree Days (base 65°F)	1,519	1,275	1,118	736	496	255	78	59	228	595	948	1,373	8,680
Cooling Degree Days (base 65°F)	0	0	0	0	1	9	73	76	13	0	0	0	172
Mean Precipitation (in.)	0.98	0.91	1.41	2.55	3.05	3.94	3.90	3.68	4.14	2.80	2.10	1.28	30.74
Extreme Maximum Daily Precip. (in.)	1.36	1.84	1.25	2.76	1.87	4.80	4.13	3.82	3.34	2.55	1.90	2.12	4.80
Days With ≥ 0.1" Precipitation	3	3	4	5	7	8	7	6	7	6	5	3	64
Days With ≥ 0.5" Precipitation	0	0	1	1	2	3	3	2	3	2	1	1	19
Days With ≥ 1.0" Precipitation	0	0	0	1	1	1	1	1	1	1	0	0	7
Mean Snowfall (in.)	17.3	10.0	8.9	2.7	0.0	0.0	0.0	0.0	0.0	0.1	5.6	14.2	58.8
Maximum Snow Depth (in.)	38	39	27	37	1	0	0	0	0	2	36	46	46
Days With ≥ 1.0" Snow Depth	20	19	16	3	0	0	0	0	0	0	5	16	79

The period of record for all cooperative weather station data is 1980 – 2009. See User Guide for detailed explanation of data.

Warroad *Roseau County* Elevation: 1,068 ft. Latitude: 48° 55' N Longitude: 95° 19' W

	JAN	FEB	MAR	APR	MAY	JUN	JUL	AUG	SEP	OCT	NOV	DEC	YEAR
Mean Maximum Temp. (°F)	14.0	20.3	32.5	50.2	63.9	73.2	78.3	76.6	66.2	51.2	33.5	18.6	48.2
Mean Temp. (°F)	3.7	9.2	22.1	39.1	52.8	62.7	67.5	65.4	55.1	41.7	25.6	9.7	37.9
Mean Minimum Temp. (°F)	-6.7	-1.9	11.7	27.8	41.6	52.1	56.7	54.2	44.2	32.0	17.7	0.8	27.5
Extreme Maximum Temp. (°F)	46	50	64	93	93	98	100	101	93	85	69	50	101
Extreme Minimum Temp. (°F)	-43	-46	-31	-2	20	31	37	32	24	2	-29	-36	-46
Days Maximum Temp. ≥ 90°F	0	0	0	0	0	1	2	1	0	0	0	0	4
Days Maximum Temp. ≤ 32°F	28	22	14	2	0	0	0	0	0	1	14	26	107
Days Minimum Temp. ≤ 32°F	31	28	29	21	5	0	0	0	2	16	28	31	191
Days Minimum Temp. ≤ 0°F	20	16	8	0	0	0	0	0	0	0	3	15	62
Heating Degree Days (base 65°F)	1,899	1,576	1,324	772	387	124	40	70	305	718	1,174	1,712	10,101
Cooling Degree Days (base 65°F)	0	0	0	1	15	63	125	91	15	0	0	0	310
Mean Precipitation (in.)	0.63	0.57	0.84	1.18	2.90	4.37	3.74	3.35	2.71	2.11	1.09	0.78	24.27
Extreme Maximum Daily Precip. (in.)	0.61	***0.94***	1.03	1.30	4.48	5.16	2.41	2.84	3.05	1.92	1.27	0.91	***5.16***
Days With ≥ 0.1" Precipitation	2	2	3	3	6	8	7	6	6	5	3	3	54
Days With ≥ 0.5" Precipitation	0	0	0	1	2	3	2	2	1	1	1	0	13
Days With ≥ 1.0" Precipitation	0	0	0	0	1	1	1	1	0	0	0	0	4
Mean Snowfall (in.)	8.2	***4.2***	***5.7***	2.1	0.0	0.0	0.0	0.0	0.0	0.9	***5.4***	***8.2***	***34.7***
Maximum Snow Depth (in.)	31	na	na	***25***	0	0	0	0	0	***5***	***16***	29	na
Days With ≥ 1.0" Snow Depth	9	na	na	1	0	0	0	0	0	0	***2***	9	na

Winona *Winona County* Elevation: 651 ft. Latitude: 44° 03' N Longitude: 91° 38' W

	JAN	FEB	MAR	APR	MAY	JUN	JUL	AUG	SEP	OCT	NOV	DEC	YEAR
Mean Maximum Temp. (°F)	26.9	32.4	44.1	60.7	71.3	80.5	84.6	81.7	73.9	60.9	44.5	30.2	57.7
Mean Temp. (°F)	18.5	23.5	34.7	49.8	60.5	70.0	74.6	71.9	63.6	51.1	36.6	22.6	48.1
Mean Minimum Temp. (°F)	10.0	14.5	25.3	38.9	49.5	59.3	64.4	62.1	53.3	41.2	28.8	14.9	38.5
Extreme Maximum Temp. (°F)	57	68	82	93	94	104	104	102	94	93	77	65	104
Extreme Minimum Temp. (°F)	-28	-31	-6	4	***26***	39	45	41	27	18	-5	-28	***-31***
Days Maximum Temp. ≥ 90°F	0	0	0	0	1	4	6	3	1	0	0	0	15
Days Maximum Temp. ≤ 32°F	20	14	5	0	0	0	0	0	0	0	4	16	59
Days Minimum Temp. ≤ 32°F	30	26	23	7	0	0	0	0	0	5	19	29	139
Days Minimum Temp. ≤ 0°F	8	5	1	0	0	0	0	0	0	0	0	5	19
Heating Degree Days (base 65°F)	1,436	1,169	934	460	183	29	2	10	120	435	844	1,309	6,931
Cooling Degree Days (base 65°F)	0	0	0	12	49	184	307	232	84	10	0	0	878
Mean Precipitation (in.)	***1.13***	0.79	1.75	3.58	4.12	4.22	4.16	5.31	3.74	2.11	2.04	1.19	***34.14***
Extreme Maximum Daily Precip. (in.)	***2.25***	***1.59***	***2.00***	***3.00***	***2.54***	***2.74***	***3.25***	na	***3.70***	***2.64***	***3.28***	***1.50***	na
Days With ≥ 0.1" Precipitation	***3***	2	4	6	8	7	7	***7***	6	5	4	4	***63***
Days With ≥ 0.5" Precipitation	***0***	0	1	2	3	3	3	***4***	2	1	1	0	***20***
Days With ≥ 1.0" Precipitation	***0***	0	0	1	1	1	1	***1***	1	0	0	0	***6***
Mean Snowfall (in.)	10.0	6.9	6.8	1.2	0.0	0.0	0.0	0.0	0.0	0.3	***2.6***	8.9	***36.7***
Maximum Snow Depth (in.)	na	na	na	na	na	na	na	na	na	na	na	na	na
Days With ≥ 1.0" Snow Depth	na	na	***6***	0	0	0	0	0	0	0	***1***	na	na

Zumbrota *Goodhue County* Elevation: 984 ft. Latitude: 44° 18' N Longitude: 92° 40' W

	JAN	FEB	MAR	APR	MAY	JUN	JUL	AUG	SEP	OCT	NOV	DEC	YEAR
Mean Maximum Temp. (°F)	25.0	29.9	42.4	59.0	70.6	79.4	83.1	80.7	73.4	60.3	43.2	28.7	56.3
Mean Temp. (°F)	15.3	20.1	32.3	46.8	58.3	67.5	71.4	69.2	61.3	48.8	34.2	20.1	45.4
Mean Minimum Temp. (°F)	5.5	10.3	22.2	34.6	45.9	55.4	59.8	57.7	49.2	37.2	25.1	11.4	34.5
Extreme Maximum Temp. (°F)	57	63	82	92	93	102	103	103	93	92	78	65	103
Extreme Minimum Temp. (°F)	-37	-37	-17	-1	20	33	40	36	25	11	-11	-40	-40
Days Maximum Temp. ≥ 90°F	0	0	0	0	1	2	4	3	1	0	0	0	11
Days Maximum Temp. ≤ 32°F	22	15	6	0	0	0	0	0	0	0	5	18	66
Days Minimum Temp. ≤ 32°F	31	27	25	13	2	0	0	0	1	11	23	30	163
Days Minimum Temp. ≤ 0°F	12	8	2	0	0	0	0	0	0	0	1	8	31
Heating Degree Days (base 65°F)	1,536	1,264	1,007	544	238	55	11	25	165	501	918	1,385	7,649
Cooling Degree Days (base 65°F)	0	0	0	6	37	135	219	163	61	6	0	0	627
Mean Precipitation (in.)	0.94	0.82	1.95	3.36	3.81	4.67	4.09	4.94	3.55	2.47	2.08	1.04	33.72
Extreme Maximum Daily Precip. (in.)	1.33	0.93	1.72	2.65	2.28	6.46	4.84	4.79	3.92	2.45	2.17	1.48	6.46
Days With ≥ 0.1" Precipitation	3	3	5	7	8	7	6	6	6	5	4	3	63
Days With ≥ 0.5" Precipitation	0	0	1	2	3	3	3	3	2	2	1	0	20
Days With ≥ 1.0" Precipitation	0	0	0	1	1	1	1	1	1	1	0	0	7
Mean Snowfall (in.)	***10.8***	***6.7***	***8.3***	***3.4***	***0.0***	***0.0***	na	na	***0.0***	na	***5.9***	***10.4***	na
Maximum Snow Depth (in.)	***30***	***28***	***15***	***11***	na	na	na	na	na	na	***15***	22	na
Days With ≥ 1.0" Snow Depth	***10***	8	5	1	***0***	***0***	na	na	***0***	***0***	***3***	9	na

The period of record for all cooperative weather station data is 1980 – 2009. See User Guide for detailed explanation of data.

Minnesota Weather Station Rankings

Annual Extreme Maximum Temperature

Highest			Lowest		
Rank	Station Name	°F	Rank	Station Name	°F
1	Browns Valley	109	1	Grand Marais	94
2	Artichoke Lake	108	2	Duluth Intl Arpt	97
3	Georgetown 1 E	107	3	Gunflint Lake 10 NW	***98***
3	Mankato	***107***	3	Tower 3 S	98
5	Lamberton SW Exp Stn	106	3	Two Harbors	98
5	Stillwater 1 SE	***106***	6	Agassiz Refuge	99
7	Ada	105	6	International Falls Int'l Arpt	99
7	Argyle 4 E	105	8	Fairmont	100
7	Buffalo	105	8	Grand Rapids Forestry Lab	100
7	Jordan 1 S	105	8	Hibbing Chisholm-Hibbing Arpt	100
7	Lake Wilson	105	11	Detroit Lakes 1 NNE	***101***
7	Minneapolis-St Paul Int'l Arpt	105	11	Red Lake Indian Agency	***101***
7	New Ulm 2 SE	105	11	Warroad	101
7	Rosemount Agri Exp Stn	105	14	Albert Lea 3 SE	102
7	St Paul	***105***	14	Brainerd	102
16	Alexandria Chandler Field	104	14	Caledonia	102
16	Cass Lake	104	14	Cambridge State Hosp	***102***
16	Crookston NW Exp Stn	104	14	Fergus Falls	102
16	Farmington 3 NW	104	14	Hinckley	102
16	Forest Lake 5 NE	104	14	Rochester Municipal Arpt	102
16	Litchfield	104	14	Rothsay	102
16	Winona	104	14	St Cloud Municipal Arpt	102
23	Cedar	***103***	23	Cedar	***103***
23	Cloquet	103	23	Cloquet	103
23	Collegeville St John	103	23	Collegeville St John	103

Annual Mean Maximum Temperature

Highest			Lowest		
Rank	Station Name	°F	Rank	Station Name	°F
1	Winona	57.7	1	Warroad	48.2
2	Stillwater 1 SE	***57.3***	2	Grand Marais	48.4
3	Forest Lake 5 NE	56.5	3	Duluth Intl Arpt	48.6
4	Zumbrota	56.3	3	International Falls Int'l Arpt	48.6
5	New Ulm 2 SE	56.0	5	Gunflint Lake 10 NW	***49.0***
6	Mankato	***55.9***	6	Red Lake Indian Agency	***49.1***
7	Lamberton SW Exp Stn	55.7	7	Hibbing Chisholm-Hibbing Arpt	49.3
7	Rosemount Agri Exp Stn	55.7	8	Tower 3 S	49.6
9	Fairmont	55.4	9	Two Harbors	50.0
9	Farmington 3 NW	55.4	10	Cass Lake	50.5
9	St Paul	***55.4***	11	Argyle 4 E	50.7
12	Lake Wilson	55.2	11	Crookston NW Exp Stn	50.7
13	Jordan 1 S	***55.1***	13	Agassiz Refuge	50.9
13	Minneapolis-St Paul Int'l Arpt	55.1	14	Fergus Falls	51.6
15	Browns Valley	54.9	15	Alexandria Chandler Field	51.7
16	Cedar	***54.7***	16	Grand Rapids Forestry Lab	51.8
17	Collegeville St John	54.6	17	Rothsay	52.0
18	Albert Lea 3 SE	54.5	18	Cloquet	52.2
19	Litchfield	54.4	19	Hinckley	***52.3***
20	Caledonia	54.3	20	Ada	52.4
21	Buffalo	***54.1***	20	Brainerd	52.4
22	Rochester Municipal Arpt	53.7	22	Cambridge State Hosp	***52.7***
23	St Cloud Municipal Arpt	53.5	23	Detroit Lakes 1 NNE	***52.8***
24	Artichoke Lake	52.9	24	Artichoke Lake	52.9
24	Georgetown 1 E	52.9	24	Georgetown 1 E	52.9

Rankings include 25 highest/lowest stations. If state has less than 25 stations, all stations are included. The period of record is 1980–2009. See User Guide for detailed explanation of data.

Annual Mean Temperature

Highest

Rank	Station Name	°F
1	Winona	48.1
2	Stillwater 1 SE	***46.9***
3	Fairmont	46.1
3	Minneapolis-St Paul Int'l Arpt	46.1
5	New Ulm 2 SE	46.0
5	St Paul	***46.0***
7	Farmington 3 NW	45.8
7	Forest Lake 5 NE	45.8
9	Zumbrota	45.5
10	Rosemount Agri Exp Stn	45.4
11	Mankato	***45.3***
12	Albert Lea 3 SE	44.8
12	Collegeville St John	44.8
12	Lake Wilson	44.8
15	Lamberton SW Exp Stn	44.7
16	Caledonia	44.6
16	Cedar	***44.6***
18	Rochester Municipal Arpt	44.4
19	Litchfield	44.3
20	Buffalo	***44.2***
21	Jordan 1 S	***44.1***
22	Browns Valley	43.9
23	Artichoke Lake	43.6
24	St Cloud Municipal Arpt	42.7
25	Cambridge State Hosp	***42.6***

Lowest

Rank	Station Name	°F
1	Tower 3 S	36.1
2	Gunflint Lake 10 NW	***37.7***
3	International Falls Int'l Arpt	37.8
4	Warroad	37.9
5	Hibbing Chisholm-Hibbing Arpt	38.1
6	Red Lake Indian Agency	***39.0***
7	Argyle 4 E	39.1
8	Cass Lake	39.3
9	Duluth Intl Arpt	39.5
10	Grand Marais	39.9
11	Agassiz Refuge	40.1
11	Crookston NW Exp Stn	40.1
13	Grand Rapids Forestry Lab	40.5
14	Cloquet	40.8
15	Brainerd	41.0
15	Hinckley	***41.0***
17	Two Harbors	41.4
18	Ada	41.6
18	Detroit Lakes 1 NNE	***41.6***
20	Fergus Falls	41.8
21	Georgetown 1 E	42.2
21	Rothsay	42.2
23	Alexandria Chandler Field	***42.5***
24	Cambridge State Hosp	***42.6***
25	St Cloud Municipal Arpt	42.7

Annual Mean Minimum Temperature

Highest

Rank	Station Name	°F
1	Winona	38.5
2	Minneapolis-St Paul Int'l Arpt	37.0
3	Fairmont	36.7
4	St Paul	***36.5***
5	Stillwater 1 SE	***36.4***
6	Farmington 3 NW	36.1
7	New Ulm 2 SE	35.9
8	Albert Lea 3 SE	35.1
8	Collegeville St John	35.1
8	Forest Lake 5 NE	35.1
8	Rochester Municipal Arpt	35.1
8	Rosemount Agri Exp Stn	35.1
13	Caledonia	34.8
14	Mankato	***34.7***
15	Zumbrota	34.5
16	Cedar	***34.4***
17	Artichoke Lake	34.3
17	Buffalo	***34.3***
17	Lake Wilson	34.3
17	Litchfield	34.3
21	Lamberton SW Exp Stn	33.7
22	Alexandria Chandler Field	***33.2***
23	Jordan 1 S	***33.1***
24	Browns Valley	32.8
25	Two Harbors	32.7

Lowest

Rank	Station Name	°F
1	Tower 3 S	22.6
2	Gunflint Lake 10 NW	***26.4***
3	International Falls Int'l Arpt	26.9
4	Hibbing Chisholm-Hibbing Arpt	27.0
5	Argyle 4 E	27.4
6	Warroad	27.5
7	Cass Lake	28.0
8	Red Lake Indian Agency	***28.9***
9	Agassiz Refuge	29.2
9	Grand Rapids Forestry Lab	29.2
11	Cloquet	29.4
12	Brainerd	29.5
13	Crookston NW Exp Stn	29.6
14	Hinckley	***29.7***
15	Duluth Intl Arpt	30.3
16	Detroit Lakes 1 NNE	***30.4***
17	Ada	30.7
18	Grand Marais	31.3
19	Georgetown 1 E	31.4
20	St Cloud Municipal Arpt	31.9
21	Fergus Falls	32.0
22	Cambridge State Hosp	***32.4***
22	Rothsay	32.4
24	Two Harbors	32.7
25	Browns Valley	32.8

Rankings include 25 highest/lowest stations. If state has less than 25 stations, all stations are included. The period of record is 1980–2009. See User Guide for detailed explanation of data.

Annual Extreme Minimum Temperature

Highest Rank	Station Name	°F	Lowest Rank	Station Name	°F
1	Fairmont	-29	1	Tower 3 S	-60
2	Lake Wilson	-30	2	Brainerd	-54
3	Lamberton SW Exp Stn	-31	3	Hibbing Chisholm-Hibbing Arpt	-50
3	Winona	***-31***	4	Argyle 4 E	-48
5	Minneapolis-St Paul Int'l Arpt	-32	4	Cass Lake	-48
5	St Paul	***-32***	6	Agassiz Refuge	-46
7	Albert Lea 3 SE	-33	6	Warroad	-46
7	Grand Marais	-33	8	Crookston NW Exp Stn	-45
9	Alexandria Chandler Field	-35	8	Detroit Lakes 1 NNE	***-45***
9	Caledonia	-35	8	International Falls Int'l Arpt	-45
9	Farmington 3 NW	-35	11	Gunflint Lake 10 NW	***-44***
9	Mankato	***-35***	11	Red Lake Indian Agency	***-44***
9	Rochester Municipal Arpt	-35	13	Ada	-43
14	Artichoke Lake	-36	14	Cloquet	-42
14	Buffalo	-36	14	Georgetown 1 E	-42
14	Two Harbors	-36	16	Browns Valley	-41
17	Collegeville St John	-37	16	Cambridge State Hosp	***-41***
17	Forest Lake 5 NE	-37	16	Grand Rapids Forestry Lab	-41
17	Litchfield	-37	16	Jordan 1 S	-41
17	New Ulm 2 SE	-37	16	St Cloud Municipal Arpt	-41
17	Rosemount Agri Exp Stn	-37	21	Fergus Falls	-40
22	Rothsay	-38	21	Hinckley	-40
23	Cedar	***-39***	21	Zumbrota	-40
23	Duluth Intl Arpt	-39	24	Cedar	***-39***
23	Stillwater 1 SE	***-39***	24	Duluth Intl Arpt	-39

July Mean Maximum Temperature

Highest Rank	Station Name	°F	Lowest Rank	Station Name	°F
1	Stillwater 1 SE	***85.2***	1	Grand Marais	70.8
2	Winona	84.7	2	Two Harbors	74.7
3	Browns Valley	84.1	3	Duluth Intl Arpt	76.3
4	Forest Lake 5 NE	83.7	4	Hibbing Chisholm-Hibbing Arpt	77.5
5	Minneapolis-St Paul Int'l Arpt	83.5	5	Red Lake Indian Agency	77.8
6	Lamberton SW Exp Stn	83.3	6	International Falls Int'l Arpt	77.9
6	St Paul	***83.3***	7	Tower 3 S	78.1
8	Collegeville St John	83.1	8	Warroad	78.3
8	Zumbrota	83.1	9	Gunflint Lake 10 NW	***78.6***
10	Rosemount Agri Exp Stn	83.0	10	Cass Lake	79.4
11	Farmington 3 NW	82.9	11	Agassiz Refuge	80.4
11	Lake Wilson	82.9	11	Hinckley	80.4
11	New Ulm 2 SE	82.9	13	Fergus Falls	80.5
14	Fairmont	82.8	13	Grand Rapids Forestry Lab	80.5
14	Litchfield	82.8	15	Brainerd	80.6
16	Mankato	***82.7***	15	Cambridge State Hosp	***80.6***
17	Georgetown 1 E	82.6	17	Rochester Municipal Arpt	80.7
18	Jordan 1 S	82.5	18	Artichoke Lake	80.8
19	Ada	82.3	19	Argyle 4 E	80.9
19	Buffalo	82.3	19	Cloquet	80.9
19	St Cloud Municipal Arpt	82.3	19	Crookston NW Exp Stn	80.9
22	Albert Lea 3 SE	82.2	22	Caledonia	81.0
23	Detroit Lakes 1 NNE	81.7	22	Rothsay	81.0
24	Cedar	***81.6***	24	Alexandria Chandler Field	81.1
25	Alexandria Chandler Field	81.1	25	Cedar	***81.6***

Rankings include 25 highest/lowest stations. If state has less than 25 stations, all stations are included. The period of record is 1980–2009. See User Guide for detailed explanation of data.

January Mean Minimum Temperature

Highest

Rank	Station Name	°F
1	Winona	10.1
2	St Paul	7.8
3	Minneapolis-St Paul Int'l Arpt	7.5
3	Stillwater 1 SE	7.5
5	Fairmont	7.4
5	Farmington 3 NW	7.4
7	Two Harbors	7.3
8	Rochester Municipal Arpt	6.9
9	New Ulm 2 SE	6.8
10	Grand Marais	6.7
11	Caledonia	6.4
12	Lake Wilson	6.2
13	Mankato	***5.8***
14	Rosemount Agri Exp Stn	5.6
15	Zumbrota	5.5
16	Albert Lea 3 SE	5.4
17	Forest Lake 5 NE	5.2
18	Collegeville St John	4.8
18	Lamberton SW Exp Stn	4.8
20	Cedar	***4.2***
21	Buffalo	4.1
21	Jordan 1 S	4.1
23	Litchfield	3.7
24	Artichoke Lake	3.2
25	Browns Valley	2.7

Lowest

Rank	Station Name	°F
1	Tower 3 S	-9.1
2	Warroad	-6.7
3	International Falls Int'l Arpt	-5.8
4	Argyle 4 E	-5.4
5	Cass Lake	-5.3
6	Gunflint Lake 10 NW	-5.1
7	Red Lake Indian Agency	-3.9
8	Agassiz Refuge	-3.5
8	Crookston NW Exp Stn	-3.5
10	Hibbing Chisholm-Hibbing Arpt	-3.2
11	Brainerd	-2.8
12	Ada	-1.9
13	Grand Rapids Forestry Lab	-1.8
14	Georgetown 1 E	-1.0
15	Detroit Lakes 1 NNE	-0.9
16	Hinckley	***-0.6***
17	Fergus Falls	-0.4
18	Rothsay	0.0
19	Duluth Intl Arpt	1.5
20	Cloquet	1.6
21	St Cloud Municipal Arpt	1.8
22	Cambridge State Hosp	***2.1***
23	Alexandria Chandler Field	***2.2***
24	Browns Valley	2.7
25	Artichoke Lake	3.2

Number of Days Annually Maximum Temperature ≥ 90°F

Highest

Rank	Station Name	Days
1	Browns Valley	18
1	Stillwater 1 SE	***18***
3	Lamberton SW Exp Stn	16
4	Winona	15
5	Georgetown 1 E	14
5	Mankato	***14***
5	Minneapolis-St Paul Int'l Arpt	14
8	Forest Lake 5 NE	13
9	Ada	12
9	Collegeville St John	12
9	New Ulm 2 SE	12
9	St Paul	***12***
13	Albert Lea 3 SE	11
13	Fairmont	11
13	Lake Wilson	11
13	Litchfield	11
13	Rosemount Agri Exp Stn	11
13	Zumbrota	11
19	Argyle 4 E	10
19	Crookston NW Exp Stn	10
19	Farmington 3 NW	10
22	Buffalo	9
22	Detroit Lakes 1 NNE	***9***
22	Rothsay	9
22	St Cloud Municipal Arpt	9

Lowest

Rank	Station Name	Days
1	Grand Marais	0
2	Two Harbors	1
3	Duluth Intl Arpt	2
4	Hibbing Chisholm-Hibbing Arpt	3
4	International Falls Int'l Arpt	3
6	Gunflint Lake 10 NW	***4***
6	Red Lake Indian Agency	***4***
6	Tower 3 S	4
6	Warroad	4
10	Agassiz Refuge	5
10	Cass Lake	5
10	Hinckley	5
10	Rochester Municipal Arpt	5
14	Brainerd	6
14	Cambridge State Hosp	***6***
14	Cloquet	6
14	Grand Rapids Forestry Lab	6
18	Alexandria Chandler Field	7
18	Caledonia	7
20	Artichoke Lake	8
20	Cedar	***8***
20	Fergus Falls	8
20	Jordan 1 S	8
24	Buffalo	9
24	Detroit Lakes 1 NNE	***9***

Rankings include 25 highest/lowest stations. If state has less than 25 stations, all stations are included. The period of record is 1980–2009. See User Guide for detailed explanation of data.

Number of Days Annually Maximum Temperature ≤ 32°F

Highest Rank	Highest Station Name	Highest Days	Lowest Rank	Lowest Station Name	Lowest Days
1	Warroad	107	1	Winona	59
2	International Falls Int'l Arpt	106	2	Stillwater 1 SE	***60***
3	Argyle 4 E	103	3	Forest Lake 5 NE	64
3	Crookston NW Exp Stn	103	4	Zumbrota	66
5	Duluth Intl Arpt	102	5	Mankato	***69***
6	Hibbing Chisholm-Hibbing Arpt	101	6	Jordan 1 S	71
6	Red Lake Indian Agency	***101***	6	Minneapolis-St Paul Int'l Arpt	71
8	Gunflint Lake 10 NW	***100***	6	Rosemount Agri Exp Stn	71
8	Tower 3 S	100	9	Caledonia	72
10	Agassiz Refuge	99	9	Farmington 3 NW	72
11	Cass Lake	95	9	New Ulm 2 SE	72
12	Fergus Falls	93	12	Fairmont	73
13	Ada	92	12	Lamberton SW Exp Stn	73
13	Alexandria Chandler Field	92	12	St Paul	***73***
13	Rothsay	92	15	Cedar	***75***
16	Grand Rapids Forestry Lab	91	15	Grand Marais	75
17	Detroit Lakes 1 NNE	***90***	15	Lake Wilson	75
17	Georgetown 1 E	90	18	Buffalo	76
19	Brainerd	89	19	Albert Lea 3 SE	77
20	Cloquet	86	19	Browns Valley	77
21	Cambridge State Hosp	***84***	19	Collegeville St John	77
22	Artichoke Lake	83	22	Two Harbors	78
22	St Cloud Municipal Arpt	83	23	Litchfield	79
24	Hinckley	81	23	Rochester Municipal Arpt	79
25	Litchfield	79	25	Hinckley	81

Number of Days Annually Minimum Temperature ≤ 32°F

Highest Rank	Highest Station Name	Highest Days	Lowest Rank	Lowest Station Name	Lowest Days
1	Tower 3 S	226	1	Winona	139
2	Hibbing Chisholm-Hibbing Arpt	201	2	Minneapolis-St Paul Int'l Arpt	152
3	Gunflint Lake 10 NW	***198***	3	Fairmont	154
4	International Falls Int'l Arpt	197	3	St Paul	***154***
5	Argyle 4 E	194	3	Stillwater 1 SE	***154***
6	Cloquet	191	6	Farmington 3 NW	156
6	Warroad	191	7	New Ulm 2 SE	157
8	Cass Lake	190	8	Collegeville St John	159
8	Red Lake Indian Agency	***190***	8	Forest Lake 5 NE	159
10	Brainerd	187	10	Caledonia	160
10	Grand Rapids Forestry Lab	187	10	Rochester Municipal Arpt	160
12	Agassiz Refuge	186	12	Rosemount Agri Exp Stn	161
13	Crookston NW Exp Stn	184	12	Two Harbors	161
13	Duluth Intl Arpt	184	14	Albert Lea 3 SE	163
15	Detroit Lakes 1 NNE	***183***	14	Mankato	***163***
16	Ada	181	14	Zumbrota	163
17	Georgetown 1 E	175	17	Artichoke Lake	164
17	St Cloud Municipal Arpt	175	17	Buffalo	164
19	Fergus Falls	174	19	Cedar	***165***
20	Browns Valley	173	19	Litchfield	165
20	Cambridge State Hosp	***173***	21	Alexandria Chandler Field	167
20	Hinckley	173	22	Jordan 1 S	169
23	Grand Marais	172	22	Lake Wilson	169
23	Lamberton SW Exp Stn	172	24	Rothsay	170
25	Rothsay	170	25	Grand Marais	172

Rankings include 25 highest/lowest stations. If state has less than 25 stations, all stations are included. The period of record is 1980–2009. See User Guide for detailed explanation of data.

Number of Days Annually Minimum Temperature ≤ 0°F

Highest Rank	Station Name	Days	Lowest Rank	Station Name	Days
1	Tower 3 S	69	1	Winona	19
2	Warroad	62	2	Minneapolis-St Paul Int'l Arpt	24
3	Gunflint Lake 10 NW	*60*	2	St Paul	*24*
3	International Falls Int'l Arpt	60	4	Two Harbors	25
5	Argyle 4 E	57	5	Fairmont	26
5	Cass Lake	57	5	Stillwater 1 SE	*26*
7	Red Lake Indian Agency	*54*	7	Caledonia	27
8	Agassiz Refuge	52	7	Farmington 3 NW	27
8	Crookston NW Exp Stn	52	9	Grand Marais	28
8	Hibbing Chisholm-Hibbing Arpt	52	9	New Ulm 2 SE	28
11	Grand Rapids Forestry Lab	50	9	Rochester Municipal Arpt	28
12	Ada	48	12	Mankato	*29*
12	Brainerd	48	13	Lake Wilson	30
14	Detroit Lakes 1 NNE	*46*	13	Rosemount Agri Exp Stn	30
14	Georgetown 1 E	46	15	Albert Lea 3 SE	31
16	Fergus Falls	44	15	Cedar	*31*
16	Rothsay	44	15	Collegeville St John	31
18	Cloquet	42	15	Forest Lake 5 NE	31
18	Duluth Intl Arpt	42	15	Zumbrota	31
18	Hinckley	42	20	Buffalo	33
21	Alexandria Chandler Field	39	20	Lamberton SW Exp Stn	33
21	St Cloud Municipal Arpt	39	22	Jordan 1 S	34
23	Browns Valley	38	23	Litchfield	35
24	Cambridge State Hosp	*37*	24	Artichoke Lake	36
25	Artichoke Lake	36	25	Cambridge State Hosp	*37*

Number of Annual Heating Degree Days

Highest Rank	Station Name	Num.	Lowest Rank	Station Name	Num.
1	Tower 3 S	10,592	1	Winona	6,931
2	Warroad	10,101	2	Stillwater 1 SE	*7,316*
3	Gunflint Lake 10 NW	*10,078*	3	Fairmont	7,530
4	International Falls Int'l Arpt	10,055	4	New Ulm 2 SE	7,538
5	Hibbing Chisholm-Hibbing Arpt	9,887	5	Minneapolis-St Paul Int'l Arpt	7,569
6	Argyle 4 E	9,712	6	Farmington 3 NW	7,575
7	Red Lake Indian Agency	*9,704*	7	St Paul	*7,579*
8	Cass Lake	9,617	8	Forest Lake 5 NE	7,595
9	Duluth Intl Arpt	9,426	9	Zumbrota	7,649
10	Crookston NW Exp Stn	9,414	10	Rosemount Agri Exp Stn	7,697
11	Agassiz Refuge	9,383	11	Mankato	*7,732*
12	Grand Rapids Forestry Lab	9,173	12	Caledonia	7,881
13	Grand Marais	9,157	13	Lake Wilson	7,895
14	Brainerd	9,037	14	Albert Lea 3 SE	7,897
15	Cloquet	9,003	15	Collegeville St John	7,906
16	Hinckley	*8,976*	16	Cedar	*7,922*
17	Ada	8,970	17	Rochester Municipal Arpt	7,938
18	Detroit Lakes 1 NNE	*8,871*	18	Lamberton SW Exp Stn	7,953
19	Fergus Falls	8,866	19	Jordan 1 S	*8,058*
20	Georgetown 1 E	8,792	20	Litchfield	8,073
21	Rothsay	8,740	21	Buffalo	*8,083*
22	Two Harbors	8,680	22	Browns Valley	8,257
23	Alexandria Chandler Field	*8,627*	23	Artichoke Lake	8,280
24	Cambridge State Hosp	*8,519*	24	St Cloud Municipal Arpt	8,504
25	St Cloud Municipal Arpt	8,504	25	Cambridge State Hosp	*8,519*

Rankings include 25 highest/lowest stations. If state has less than 25 stations, all stations are included. The period of record is 1980–2009. See User Guide for detailed explanation of data.

Number of Annual Cooling Degree Days

Highest Rank	Highest Station Name	Highest Num.	Lowest Rank	Lowest Station Name	Lowest Num.
1	Winona	878	1	Grand Marais	83
2	Stillwater 1 SE	***815***	2	Tower 3 S	149
3	Minneapolis-St Paul Int'l Arpt	769	3	Two Harbors	172
4	Fairmont	744	4	Hibbing Chisholm-Hibbing Arpt	187
5	St Paul	***734***	5	Duluth Intl Arpt	215
6	New Ulm 2 SE	705	6	Gunflint Lake 10 NW	***221***
7	Forest Lake 5 NE	702	7	International Falls Int'l Arpt	229
8	Farmington 3 NW	678	8	Cloquet	290
9	Mankato	***665***	9	Warroad	310
10	Lamberton SW Exp Stn	663	10	Red Lake Indian Agency	***332***
11	Rosemount Agri Exp Stn	660	11	Hinckley	***340***
12	Collegeville St John	659	12	Grand Rapids Forestry Lab	343
13	Browns Valley	648	13	Cass Lake	348
14	Litchfield	646	14	Argyle 4 E	362
15	Albert Lea 3 SE	642	15	Brainerd	382
16	Lake Wilson	637	16	Agassiz Refuge	399
17	Zumbrota	627	17	Crookston NW Exp Stn	450
18	Buffalo	***616***	18	Cambridge State Hosp	***457***
19	Artichoke Lake	583	19	Detroit Lakes 1 NNE	***461***
20	Cedar	***574***	20	St Cloud Municipal Arpt	484
21	Georgetown 1 E	557	21	Fergus Falls	522
22	Caledonia	541	22	Alexandria Chandler Field	***527***
22	Rothsay	541	23	Ada	530
24	Jordan 1 S	***539***	24	Rochester Municipal Arpt	532
25	Rochester Municipal Arpt	532	25	Jordan 1 S	***539***

Annual Precipitation

Highest Rank	Highest Station Name	Highest Inches	Lowest Rank	Lowest Station Name	Lowest Inches
1	Caledonia	35.55	1	Argyle 4 E	20.81
2	Stillwater 1 SE	***34.42***	2	Crookston NW Exp Stn	21.55
3	Rosemount Agri Exp Stn	34.29	3	Georgetown 1 E	22.50
4	Winona	***34.14***	4	Agassiz Refuge	22.56
5	Albert Lea 3 SE	33.81	5	Red Lake Indian Agency	***22.75***
6	Zumbrota	33.72	6	Rothsay	23.74
7	St Paul	***33.63***	7	International Falls Int'l Arpt	23.78
8	Cedar	***33.14***	8	Ada	23.96
9	Rochester Municipal Arpt	32.48	9	Fergus Falls	24.15
10	Mankato	***32.41***	10	Warroad	24.27
11	Fairmont	31.83	11	Browns Valley	24.28
12	Forest Lake 5 NE	31.81	12	Grand Marais	24.40
13	Hinckley	31.35	13	Alexandria Chandler Field	***24.70***
14	Cloquet	31.24	14	Artichoke Lake	24.80
15	Two Harbors	30.74	15	Hibbing Chisholm-Hibbing Arpt	25.15
16	Farmington 3 NW	***30.61***	16	Cass Lake	26.31
17	Duluth Intl Arpt	30.57	17	Gunflint Lake 10 NW	***27.03***
18	Minneapolis-St Paul Int'l Arpt	30.18	18	Detroit Lakes 1 NNE	***27.10***
19	Collegeville St John	30.10	19	Lake Wilson	27.25
20	Jordan 1 S	29.91	20	Lamberton SW Exp Stn	27.40
21	New Ulm 2 SE	29.77	21	St Cloud Municipal Arpt	27.47
22	Cambridge State Hosp	***29.34***	22	Tower 3 S	27.87
22	Litchfield	***29.34***	23	Brainerd	27.90
24	Buffalo	***29.29***	24	Grand Rapids Forestry Lab	28.55
25	Grand Rapids Forestry Lab	28.55	25	Buffalo	***29.29***

Rankings include 25 highest/lowest stations. If state has less than 25 stations, all stations are included. The period of record is 1980–2009. See User Guide for detailed explanation of data.

Annual Extreme Maximum Daily Precipitation

Highest

Rank	Station Name	Inches
1	Minneapolis-St Paul Int'l Arpt	9.15
2	Tower 3 S	8.70
3	Cloquet	8.44
4	Rochester Municipal Arpt	7.47
5	Albert Lea 3 SE	6.97
6	Zumbrota	6.46
7	Buffalo	6.35
8	Mankato	*6.23*
9	Fairmont	6.20
10	Agassiz Refuge	6.05
10	Farmington 3 NW	6.05
12	Jordan 1 S	*6.04*
13	Georgetown 1 E	5.93
14	Rosemount Agri Exp Stn	*5.80*
15	Hibbing Chisholm-Hibbing Arpt	5.75
16	Argyle 4 E	5.61
17	Caledonia	5.56
18	Grand Marais	5.43
18	Hinckley	5.43
20	New Ulm 2 SE	5.42
21	Warroad	*5.16*
22	Stillwater 1 SE	*5.14*
23	Two Harbors	4.80
24	Brainerd	4.76
25	Cedar	*4.75*

Lowest

Rank	Station Name	Inches
1	Detroit Lakes 1 NNE	*3.55*
2	Duluth Intl Arpt	3.57
3	Artichoke Lake	3.58
4	St Cloud Municipal Arpt	3.62
5	Cass Lake	3.72
6	International Falls Int'l Arpt	3.98
7	Forest Lake 5 NE	4.01
8	Crookston NW Exp Stn	4.04
9	Browns Valley	4.18
10	Alexandria Chandler Field	4.22
11	Fergus Falls	*4.30*
11	Lamberton SW Exp Stn	4.30
13	Lake Wilson	*4.40*
14	Grand Rapids Forestry Lab	4.50
15	Ada	4.51
16	Gunflint Lake 10 NW	*4.60*
17	Collegeville St John	4.67
18	Cedar	*4.75*
18	Rothsay	4.75
20	Brainerd	4.76
21	Two Harbors	4.80
22	Stillwater 1 SE	*5.14*
23	Warroad	*5.16*
24	New Ulm 2 SE	5.42
25	Grand Marais	5.43

Number of Days Annually With ≥ 0.1 Inches of Precipitation

Highest

Rank	Station Name	Days
1	Cedar	*67*
2	Caledonia	66
3	Stillwater 1 SE	*65*
4	Duluth Intl Arpt	64
4	Forest Lake 5 NE	64
4	Two Harbors	64
7	Cloquet	63
7	Gunflint Lake 10 NW	*63*
7	Hinckley	63
7	Mankato	*63*
7	Rochester Municipal Arpt	63
7	St Paul	*63*
7	Winona	*63*
7	Zumbrota	63
15	Albert Lea 3 SE	62
15	Grand Rapids Forestry Lab	62
15	Minneapolis-St Paul Int'l Arpt	62
15	Rosemount Agri Exp Stn	62
19	Farmington 3 NW	61
20	Tower 3 S	60
21	Brainerd	59
22	Buffalo	57
22	Cambridge State Hosp	*57*
22	St Cloud Municipal Arpt	57
25	Collegeville St John	56

Lowest

Rank	Station Name	Days
1	Georgetown 1 E	46
1	Red Lake Indian Agency	*46*
3	Agassiz Refuge	47
3	Alexandria Chandler Field	47
3	Crookston NW Exp Stn	47
3	Litchfield	47
7	Argyle 4 E	48
7	Fergus Falls	48
9	Browns Valley	49
9	Rothsay	49
11	Ada	50
12	Lake Wilson	51
13	Artichoke Lake	52
14	Grand Marais	54
14	Hibbing Chisholm-Hibbing Arpt	54
14	Jordan 1 S	54
14	Lamberton SW Exp Stn	54
14	Warroad	54
19	Cass Lake	55
19	International Falls Int'l Arpt	55
21	Collegeville St John	56
21	Detroit Lakes 1 NNE	*56*
21	Fairmont	56
21	New Ulm 2 SE	56
25	Buffalo	57

 Rankings include 25 highest/lowest stations. If state has less than 25 stations, all stations are included. The period of record is 1980–2009. See User Guide for detailed explanation of data.

Number of Days Annually With ≥ 0.5 Inches of Precipitation

Highest

Rank	Station Name	Days
1	Albert Lea 3 SE	21
2	Caledonia	20
2	Cambridge State Hosp	***20***
2	Fairmont	20
2	Forest Lake 5 NE	20
2	Jordan 1 S	20
2	Mankato	***20***
2	St Paul	***20***
2	Winona	***20***
2	Zumbrota	20
11	Cedar	***19***
11	Collegeville St John	19
11	Hinckley	19
11	Rosemount Agri Exp Stn	19
11	Stillwater 1 SE	***19***
11	Two Harbors	19
17	Brainerd	18
17	Buffalo	18
17	Cloquet	18
17	Duluth Intl Arpt	18
17	Farmington 3 NW	18
17	New Ulm 2 SE	18
17	Rochester Municipal Arpt	18
24	Artichoke Lake	17
24	Grand Rapids Forestry Lab	17

Lowest

Rank	Station Name	Days
1	Argyle 4 E	8
2	Crookston NW Exp Stn	12
3	International Falls Int'l Arpt	13
3	Red Lake Indian Agency	***13***
3	Warroad	13
6	Ada	14
6	Agassiz Refuge	14
6	Alexandria Chandler Field	14
6	Browns Valley	14
6	Georgetown 1 E	14
6	Grand Marais	14
6	Gunflint Lake 10 NW	***14***
6	Hibbing Chisholm-Hibbing Arpt	14
14	Cass Lake	15
14	Fergus Falls	15
14	Litchfield	15
17	Detroit Lakes 1 NNE	***16***
17	Lake Wilson	16
17	Rothsay	16
17	St Cloud Municipal Arpt	16
21	Artichoke Lake	17
21	Grand Rapids Forestry Lab	17
21	Lamberton SW Exp Stn	17
21	Minneapolis-St Paul Int'l Arpt	17
21	Tower 3 S	17

Number of Days Annually With ≥ 1.0 Inches of Precipitation

Highest

Rank	Station Name	Days
1	Caledonia	9
2	Albert Lea 3 SE	8
2	Stillwater 1 SE	***8***
4	Buffalo	7
4	Collegeville St John	7
4	Fairmont	7
4	Forest Lake 5 NE	7
4	Jordan 1 S	7
4	Lake Wilson	7
4	Litchfield	7
4	Mankato	***7***
4	New Ulm 2 SE	7
4	Two Harbors	7
4	Zumbrota	7
15	Ada	6
15	Argyle 4 E	6
15	Brainerd	6
15	Cedar	***6***
15	Cloquet	6
15	Detroit Lakes 1 NNE	***6***
15	Farmington 3 NW	6
15	Georgetown 1 E	6
15	Hinckley	6
15	Lamberton SW Exp Stn	6
15	Rochester Municipal Arpt	6

Lowest

Rank	Station Name	Days
1	Gunflint Lake 10 NW	***3***
2	Artichoke Lake	4
2	Browns Valley	4
2	Cass Lake	4
2	Crookston NW Exp Stn	4
2	Duluth Intl Arpt	4
2	Grand Marais	4
2	Hibbing Chisholm-Hibbing Arpt	4
2	International Falls Int'l Arpt	4
2	Red Lake Indian Agency	***4***
2	Tower 3 S	4
2	Warroad	4
13	Agassiz Refuge	5
13	Alexandria Chandler Field	5
13	Cambridge State Hosp	***5***
13	Fergus Falls	5
13	Grand Rapids Forestry Lab	5
13	Minneapolis-St Paul Int'l Arpt	5
19	Ada	6
19	Argyle 4 E	6
19	Brainerd	6
19	Cedar	***6***
19	Cloquet	6
19	Detroit Lakes 1 NNE	***6***
19	Farmington 3 NW	6

Rankings include 25 highest/lowest stations. If state has less than 25 stations, all stations are included. The period of record is 1980–2009. See User Guide for detailed explanation of data.

Annual Snowfall

Rank	Station Name (Highest)	Inches	Rank	Station Name (Lowest)	Inches
1	Duluth Intl Arpt	85.5	1	Red Lake Indian Agency	***31.2***
2	International Falls Int'l Arpt	73.0	2	Warroad	***34.7***
3	Tower 3 S	67.4	3	Rosemount Agri Exp Stn	***35.1***
4	Cloquet	66.0	4	Winona	***36.7***
5	Gunflint Lake 10 NW	***59.5***	5	Crookston NW Exp Stn	38.0
6	Cedar	***59.4***	6	Albert Lea 3 SE	38.4
7	Two Harbors	***58.8***	7	Argyle 4 E	38.7
8	Grand Rapids Forestry Lab	55.2	8	Georgetown 1 E	***38.9***
9	Collegeville St John	52.9	9	Agassiz Refuge	39.0
9	Minneapolis-St Paul Int'l Arpt	***52.9***	9	New Ulm 2 SE	39.0
11	Rochester Municipal Arpt	***51.9***	11	Mankato	***39.5***
12	Hinckley	***51.5***	12	Artichoke Lake	41.2
13	St Paul	***50.4***	13	Lamberton SW Exp Stn	42.0
14	Forest Lake 5 NE	50.3	14	Buffalo	***42.3***
15	Grand Marais	48.4	15	Browns Valley	42.4
16	Brainerd	46.9	15	Fergus Falls	***42.4***
17	St Cloud Municipal Arpt	***46.4***	17	Fairmont	42.9
18	Cass Lake	45.4	18	Rothsay	***43.7***
19	Caledonia	45.3	19	Litchfield	***43.8***
19	Detroit Lakes 1 NNE	***45.3***	20	Ada	***44.0***
21	Farmington 3 NW	44.3	21	Farmington 3 NW	44.3
21	Lake Wilson	44.3	21	Lake Wilson	44.3
23	Ada	***44.0***	23	Caledonia	45.3
24	Litchfield	***43.8***	23	Detroit Lakes 1 NNE	***45.3***
25	Rothsay	***43.7***	25	Cass Lake	45.4

Annual Maximum Snow Depth

Rank	Station Name (Highest)	Inches	Rank	Station Name (Lowest)	Inches
1	Fergus Falls	***68***	1	New Ulm 2 SE	***23***
2	Tower 3 S	***65***	2	Caledonia	***25***
3	Grand Marais	52	2	Forest Lake 5 NE	25
4	Mankato	***49***	2	St Cloud Municipal Arpt	***25***
5	Farmington 3 NW	***46***	5	Artichoke Lake	27
5	Two Harbors	46	6	Collegeville St John	28
7	Duluth Intl Arpt	42	6	Fairmont	28
8	Crookston NW Exp Stn	38	8	Rochester Municipal Arpt	29
8	Hinckley	38	9	Agassiz Refuge	30
8	International Falls Int'l Arpt	38	9	Cedar	***30***
8	Minneapolis-St Paul Int'l Arpt	***38***	11	Argyle 4 E	32
12	Albert Lea 3 SE	37	11	Buffalo	***32***
12	Cloquet	37	11	Lamberton SW Exp Stn	32
12	Red Lake Indian Agency	***37***	11	Rosemount Agri Exp Stn	32
15	Grand Rapids Forestry Lab	***36***	11	St Paul	***32***
16	Brainerd	34	16	Brainerd	34
17	Argyle 4 E	32	17	Grand Rapids Forestry Lab	***36***
17	Buffalo	***32***	18	Albert Lea 3 SE	37
17	Lamberton SW Exp Stn	32	18	Cloquet	37
17	Rosemount Agri Exp Stn	32	18	Red Lake Indian Agency	***37***
17	St Paul	***32***	21	Crookston NW Exp Stn	38
22	Agassiz Refuge	30	21	Hinckley	38
22	Cedar	***30***	21	International Falls Int'l Arpt	38
24	Rochester Municipal Arpt	29	21	Minneapolis-St Paul Int'l Arpt	***38***
25	Collegeville St John	28	25	Duluth Intl Arpt	42

Rankings include 25 highest/lowest stations. If state has less than 25 stations, all stations are included. The period of record is 1980–2009. See User Guide for detailed explanation of data.

Number of Days Annually With ≥ 1.0 Inch Snow Depth

Highest Rank	Station Name	Days	Lowest Rank	Station Name	Days
1	Duluth Intl Arpt	137	1	Rothsay	***66***
2	Cloquet	136	2	Caledonia	***67***
3	Agassiz Refuge	133	3	Hinckley	74
3	International Falls Int'l Arpt	133	3	Mankato	***74***
5	Grand Marais	117	3	New Ulm 2 SE	74
6	Brainerd	115	6	Rosemount Agri Exp Stn	76
7	Forest Lake 5 NE	106	7	Albert Lea 3 SE	77
7	Red Lake Indian Agency	***106***	7	Lamberton SW Exp Stn	77
9	Crookston NW Exp Stn	104	9	Two Harbors	79
9	Grand Rapids Forestry Lab	***104***	10	Fairmont	80
11	Cedar	***103***	11	Farmington 3 NW	***86***
12	Collegeville St John	101	11	Tower 3 S	***86***
13	Cambridge State Hosp	***99***	13	Fergus Falls	***89***
14	St Cloud Municipal Arpt	***98***	14	Artichoke Lake	90
15	Argyle 4 E	96	14	Minneapolis-St Paul Int'l Arpt	***90***
15	St Paul	***96***	16	Rochester Municipal Arpt	93
17	Buffalo	94	17	Buffalo	94
18	Rochester Municipal Arpt	93	18	Argyle 4 E	96
19	Artichoke Lake	90	18	St Paul	***96***
19	Minneapolis-St Paul Int'l Arpt	***90***	20	St Cloud Municipal Arpt	***98***
21	Fergus Falls	***89***	21	Cambridge State Hosp	***99***
22	Farmington 3 NW	***86***	22	Collegeville St John	101
22	Tower 3 S	***86***	23	Cedar	***103***
24	Fairmont	80	24	Crookston NW Exp Stn	104
25	Two Harbors	79	24	Grand Rapids Forestry Lab	***104***

Significant Storm Events in Minnesota: 2000 – 2009

Location or County	Date	Type	Mag.	Deaths	Injuries	Property Damage ($mil.)	Crop Damage ($mil.)
Yellow Medicine	07/25/00	Tornado	F4	1	15	20.0	0.0
Central and South Central Minnesota	04/01/01	Flood	na	3	1	200.0	0.0
Freeborn	05/01/01	Tornado	F2	0	0	20.0	0.0
Hennepin	06/11/01	Hail	3.00 in.	0	0	25.0	0.0
Southern Minnesota	08/04/01	Excessive Heat	na	5	0	0.0	0.0
Carlton and Southern St. Louis Counties	08/07/01	Excessive Heat	na	5	0	0.0	0.0
Roseau Co.	06/10/02	Flood	na	0	0	200.0	0.0
Wright	06/24/02	Flash Flood	na	0	0	25.0	0.0
Hennepin	09/21/05	Thunderstorm Wind	81 mph	1	0	130.0	0.0
Anoka	09/21/05	Thunderstorm Wind	98 mph	0	0	85.0	0.0
Sherburne	09/21/05	Hail	1.75 in.	0	0	25.0	0.0
Wright	09/21/05	Hail	1.50 in.	0	0	25.0	0.0
Ramsey	09/21/05	Thunderstorm Wind	75 mph	0	1	25.0	0.0
Roseau	08/05/06	Tornado	F3	0	0	20.0	0.0
Rice	08/24/06	Hail	2.75 in.	0	0	50.0	2.3
Le Sueur	08/24/06	Tornado	F3	1	30	20.0	4.0
Anoka	08/24/06	Hail	2.00 in.	0	0	20.0	0.0
Hennepin	09/16/06	Tornado	F2	1	0	30.0	0.0
Stearns	06/20/07	Hail	3.50 in.	0	20	7.0	0.0
Fillmore	08/18/07	Flash Flood	na	0	0	38.0	0.3
Olmsted	08/18/07	Flash Flood	na	0	0	35.0	0.0
Houston	08/18/07	Flash Flood	na	0	30	27.0	0.7
Winona	08/18/07	Flash Flood	na	0	0	22.0	0.2
Winona	08/18/07	Flash Flood	na	5	0	0.3	0.1
Washington	05/25/08	Tornado	F3	1	17	25.0	0.0

Note: Deaths, injuries, and damages are date and location specific.

MISSISSIPPI

PHYSICAL FEATURES. The State of Mississippi extends on the west from the Mississippi River to about longitude 88° W., between latitude 31° and 35° N; and from the Pearl River on the west to about 88.5° W. longitude below latitude 31° N. The southern boundary of this area, a sort of "panhandle," is Mississippi Sound, which is an arm of the Gulf of Mexico. Land areas near the coast line, in contrast to those of Louisiana, are sharply defined, with the land rising to elevations of 10 to 20 feet behind the beaches. The coast is cut by numerous bays. A string of islands parallels the coast a few miles offshore. The waters of Mississippi Sound provide a natural air conditioning to ameliorate the summer heat. Thus Biloxi has an average of only 55 days with temperature 90°F. or higher, while only 40 miles inland Wiggins averages 105 such days.

A triangular area comprising nearly one-third of the State, with its apex in Rankin County and its base on the coast, is composed of rolling hills at from 200 to 500 feet above sea level. The "Delta" region in the northwest extends from the Yazoo-Tallahatchie River system westward to the Mississippi River. Between the Delta and the upland prairie the land is broken by a series of ridges and valleys which are oriented in a general southwest-northeast direction. These extend from the Tennessee border to the lower Mississippi River. From Vicksburg to Natchez these ridges stop abruptly at the river forming high bluffs along its left bank. The valleys form natural paths for the northeastward passage of tornadoes and for southward drainage of cold winter air. On clear, cold nights temperatures in these valleys are lower, sometimes as much as 20°F., than on the nearby hilltops.

GENERAL CLIMATE. In its broader aspects the climate of Mississippi is determined by the huge land mass to the north, its subtropical latitude, and the Gulf of Mexico to the south, but modifications are introduced by the varied topography.

The prevailing southerly winds provide a moist, semitropical climate, with conditions often favorable for afternoon thundershowers. When the pressure distribution is altered so as to bring westerly or northerly winds, periods of hotter and drier weather interrupt the prevailing moist condition. The high humidity, combined with hot days and nights in the interior from May to September, produces discomfort at times. The principal relief is by thunderstorms, sometimes accompanied by locally violent and destructive winds.

In the colder season the State is alternately subjected to warm tropical air and cold continental air, in periods of varying length. However, cold spells seldom last over three or four days. The ground rarely freezes, and then mostly only in the extreme north and only a few inches deep. Although slowly warmed by its southward journey, the cold air occasionally brings large and rather sudden drops in temperature. In winter the Atlantic High is also sometimes located far enough west to serve as a barrier to cold air approaching the State. Most frequently this produces a pattern of warm, clear weather over the southern part of the State with cold, rainy weather to the north of the "front," but occasionally the entire State will be under the balmy influence of this subtropical anticyclone.

Mississippi is south of the average track of winter cyclones, but occasionally one moves over the State. In some winters a succession of such cyclones will develop in the Gulf of Mexico or in Texas and move over or near the State. The State is also occasionally in the path of tropical storms or hurricanes.

FLOODS. All of the State is in the Gulf of Mexico drainage. Main rivers which flow directly into the Gulf include the Tombigbee in the northeast portion, and the Pascagoula and Pearl which forms the southwestern boundary. The Mississippi River forms most of the western boundary. The flood season in Mississippi is from November through June (the period of greatest rainfall), with March and April being the months of greatest frequency. The season of high flows in the main Mississippi River is during the first six months of the year. In other streams flooding sometimes occurs during the summer from persistent thundershower rains, or during the late summer and early fall from heavy rains associated with tropical storms originating in the Gulf of Mexico.

PRECIPITATION. Mean annual precipitation ranges from about 50 inches in the northwest to 65 inches in the southeast. During the freeze-free season rainfall ranges from 23 to 25 inches in the Delta districts to 36 to 38 inches in the southeast. During the winter the precipitation maximum is centered over the northern and western counties (16 to 18 inches) with the minimum (13 inches) on the coast. In summer the maximum shifts to the coastal counties (19 to 21 inches) and the minimum to the Delta counties (nine to 11 inches). The spring and fall patterns are very similar to the summer pattern. The fall months are the driest of the year, precipitation ranging from about eight to 13 inches. Fall is the most agreeable season of the year, with cool nights and mild, clear, sunny days persisting for several days, and even weeks, at a time.

While snowfall is not of much economic importance, it is not such a rare event in Mississippi as is generally believed. Measurable snow or sleet falls on some part of the State most years.

TEMPERATURE. The normal annual temperature ranges from 62°F. in the northern border counties to 68°F. in the coastal counties. The lowest January normal is 43°F. in the north-central area, ranging upward to 54°F. in the coastal district. The highest July normal is 84°F. in the upper Delta, ranging downward to 80 to 81°F. in parts of central and north-central districts. Temperatures of 90°F. or higher occur on an average of 55 days per year on the immediate Gulf coast under the ameliorating effect of the relatively cooler Gulf waters. There is a rapid increase in number of days 90°F. or higher inland from the coast, reaching a maximum of 105 such days in Stone County. Temperatures of 32°F. (freezing) or lower occur on an average of 11 days a year on the immediate Gulf coast, increasing to a maximum of 60 days in Panola County. Temperatures exceed 100°F. at one or more weather stations each summer. They drop to zero or lower in Mississippi on an average of once in five years and to 32°F. or lower on the Gulf coast almost every winter.

STORMS. Thunderstorms occur on an average of 50 to 60 days a year in the northern districts and 70 to 80 days a year near the coast. Thundershowers occur more frequently in July than any other month, with the least in December. Those in late fall, winter, and early spring are more apt to be attended by high winds than in summer. However, in the interior in summer after a spell of unusually high temperatures, thunderstorms may develop with local violence.

A hazard to life and property in Mississippi is the tropical cyclone which occurs from June to November. While these storms generally move into the State on the coast, they have on occasion entered as far north as Meridian and Greenville after crossing part of Alabama or Louisiana. These latter storms are usually weakened considerably by passage over land. Hurricanes which move inland over southeast Louisiana may be as damaging on the Mississippi coast as those which cross the coast line. This is especially true of those moving from the southeast because of the usually more severe winds in the northeast quadrant and because of the high seas which move across Mississippi Sound and pile up on the shore. Those which move westward offshore often cause tide and wind damage on the coast. Those which move northeastward across or south of the Louisiana Delta and move inland between Mobile and Panama City are usually less damaging because winds are offshore and tides are subnormal. Hurricanes which move inland on the Alabama coast may affect Mississippi only slightly because of less intense and offshore winds in their western portions.

About a fourth of the tropical cyclones which affect Mississippi are of hurricane intensity with winds of 74 m.p.h. or higher at some point. One-half of all hurricanes occur in September and twice as many tropical cyclones occur in August and September as during June, July, October, and November combined.

Tornadoes occur in all months in Mississippi, but the largest number of reported tornadoes occur in March, while April, February, and May rank high. Tornadoes may occur at any place in Mississippi, but are least likely in the tier of counties within the "panhandle" below 31 N. latitude; this, however, is the area where hurricanes are most likely to occur.

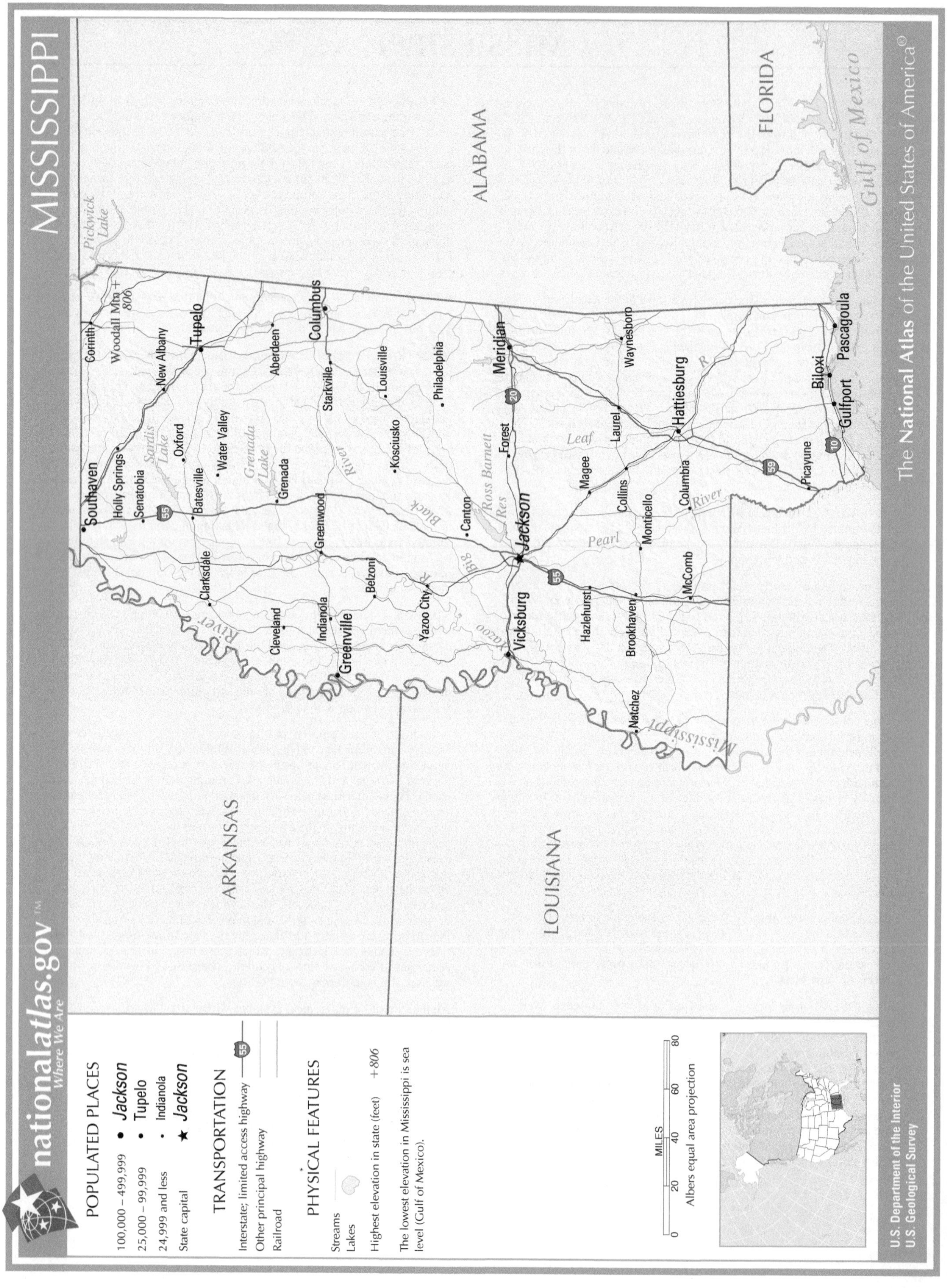
MISSISSIPPI
nationalatlas.gov™
Where We Are
POPULATED PLACES
100,000 – 499,999 Jackson
25,000 – 99,999 Tupelo
24,999 and less Indianola
State capital Jackson
TRANSPORTATION
Interstate; limited access highway 55
Other principal highway
Railroad
PHYSICAL FEATURES
Streams
Lakes
Highest elevation in state (feet) +806
The lowest elevation in Mississippi is sea level (Gulf of Mexico).
MILES
0 20 40 60 80
Albers equal area projection
U.S. Department of the Interior
U.S. Geological Survey
The National Atlas of the United States of America®
ALABAMA
ARKANSAS
LOUISIANA
FLORIDA
Gulf of Mexico
Pickwick Lake
Woodall Mtn + 806
Corinth
Southaven
Holly Springs
Senatobia
New Albany
Tupelo
Sardis Lake
Oxford
Batesville
Water Valley
Grenada Lake
Grenada
Aberdeen
Columbus
Starkville
Louisville
Clarksdale
Cleveland
Greenwood
Kosciusko
Philadelphia
Meridian
Indianola
Greenville
Belzoni
Yazoo City
Canton
Ross Barnett Res
Forest
Jackson
Vicksburg
Hazlehurst
Brookhaven
Natchez
Magee
Collins
Monticello
McComb
Columbia
Laurel
Waynesboro
Hattiesburg
Picayune
Gulfport
Biloxi
Pascagoula
Mississippi River
Yazoo R
Big Black River
Pearl River
Leaf R
55
20
59
10

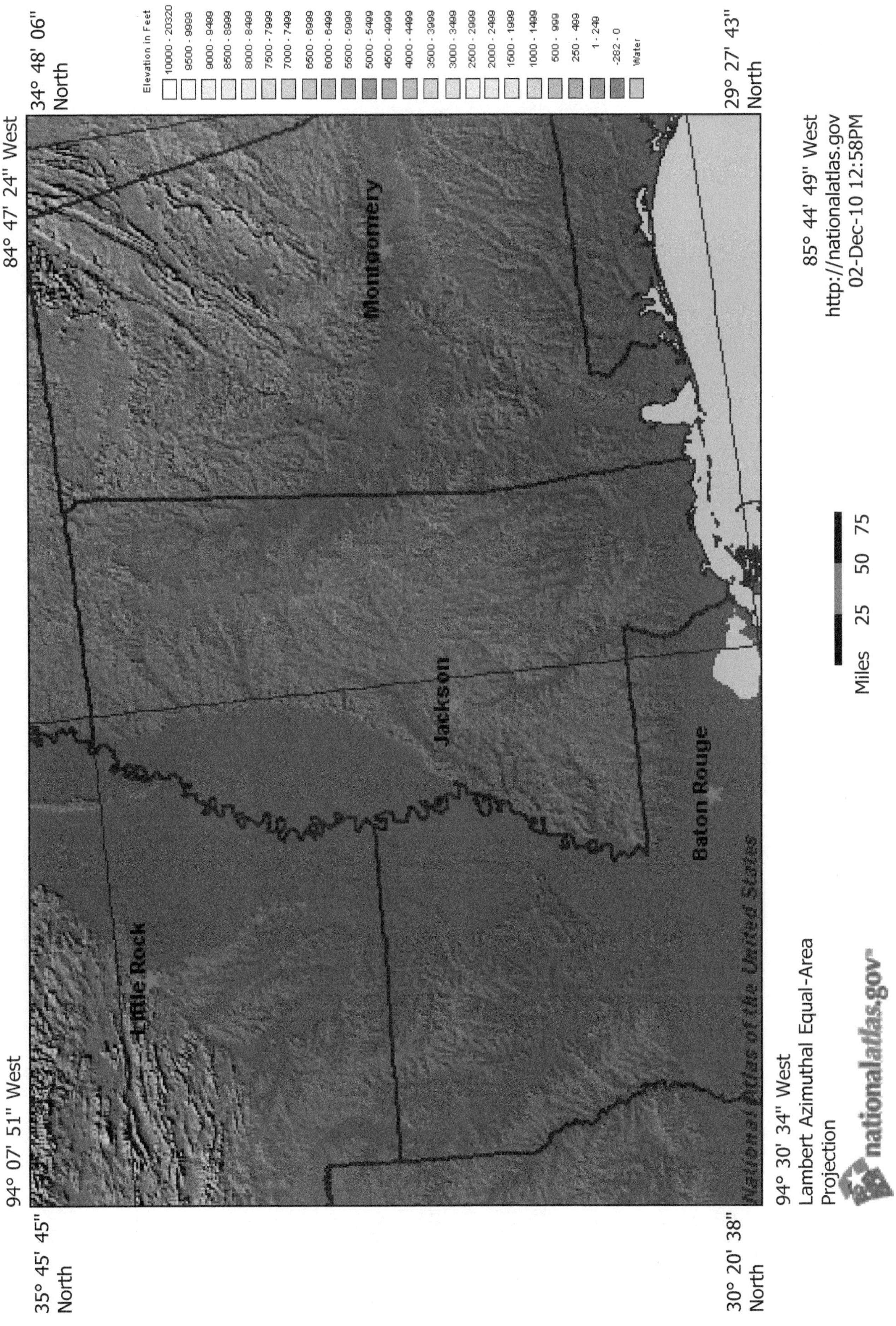
84° 47' 24" West
34° 48' 06" North
Elevation in Feet
10000 - 20320
9500 - 9999
9000 - 9499
8500 - 8999
8000 - 8499
7500 - 7999
7000 - 7499
6500 - 6999
6000 - 6499
5500 - 5999
5000 - 5499
4500 - 4999
4000 - 4499
3500 - 3999
3000 - 3499
2500 - 2999
2000 - 2499
1500 - 1999
1000 - 1499
500 - 999
250 - 499
1 - 249
-282 - 0
Water
Montgomery
Jackson
Baton Rouge
Little Rock
National Atlas of the United States
29° 27' 43" North
85° 44' 49" West
http://nationalatlas.gov
02-Dec-10 12:58PM
Miles 25 50 75
94° 07' 51" West
35° 45' 45" North
30° 20' 38" North
94° 30' 34" West
Lambert Azimuthal Equal-Area Projection
nationalatlas.gov

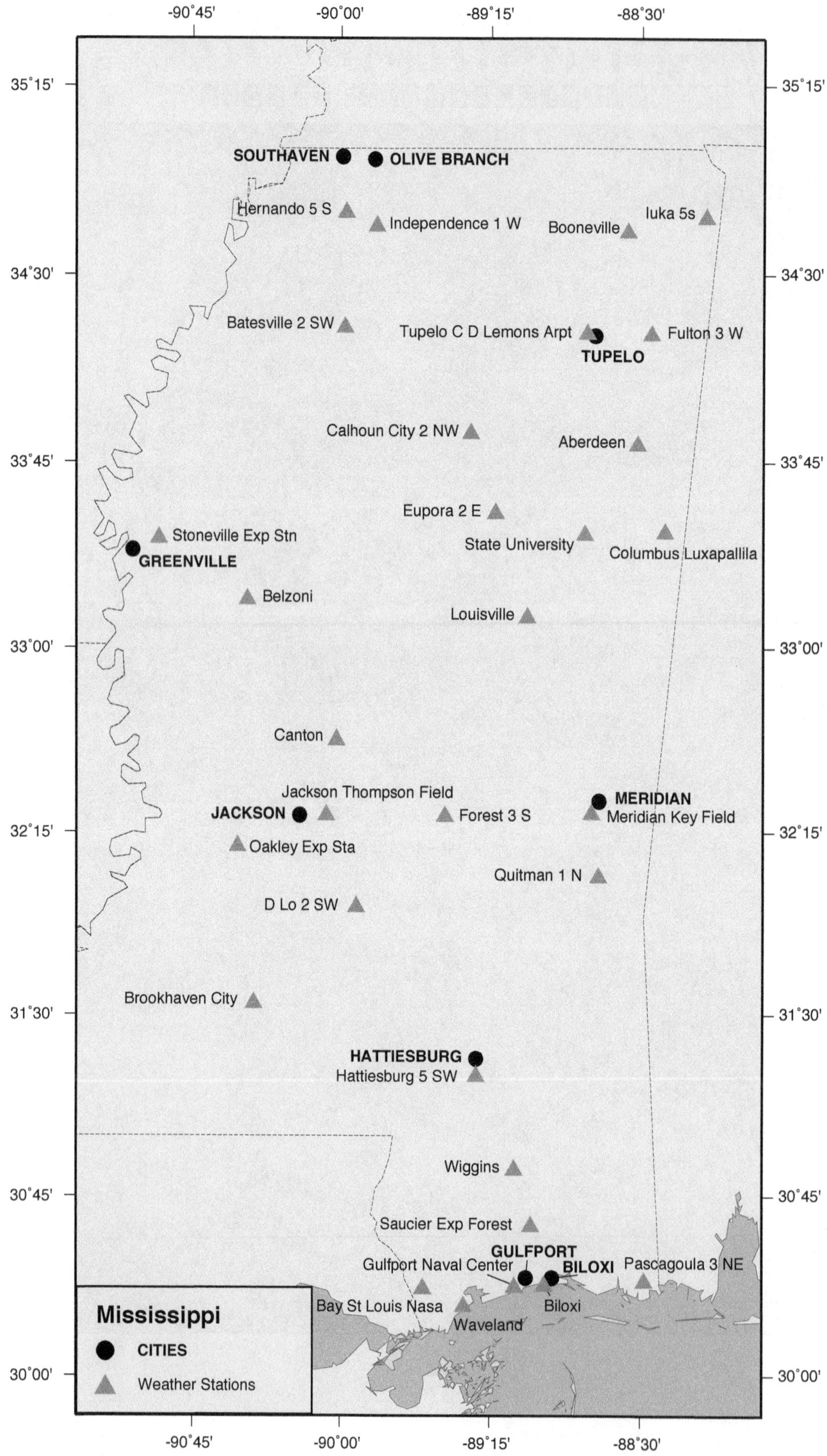
-90°45'
-90°00'
-89°15'
-88°30'
35°15'
34°30'
33°45'
33°00'
32°15'
31°30'
30°45'
30°00'
SOUTHAVEN
OLIVE BRANCH
Hernando 5 S
Independence 1 W
Booneville
Iuka 5s
Batesville 2 SW
Tupelo C D Lemons Arpt
Fulton 3 W
TUPELO
Calhoun City 2 NW
Aberdeen
Eupora 2 E
Stoneville Exp Stn
GREENVILLE
State University
Columbus Luxapallila
Belzoni
Louisville
Canton
Jackson Thompson Field
JACKSON
Forest 3 S
MERIDIAN
Meridian Key Field
Oakley Exp Sta
Quitman 1 N
D Lo 2 SW
Brookhaven City
HATTIESBURG
Hattiesburg 5 SW
Wiggins
Saucier Exp Forest
GULFPORT
Gulfport Naval Center
BILOXI
Pascagoula 3 NE
Bay St Louis Nasa
Waveland
Biloxi
Mississippi
CITIES
Weather Stations

Mississippi Weather Stations by County

County	Station Name
Calhoun	Calhoun City 2 NW
Clarke	Quitman 1 N
De Soto	Hernando 5 S
Forrest	Hattiesburg 5 SW
Hancock	Bay St Louis Nasa Waveland
Harrison	Biloxi Gulfport Naval Center Saucier Exp Forest
Hinds	Oakley Exp Station
Humphreys	Belzoni
Itawamba	Fulton 3 W
Jackson	Pascagoula 3 NE
Lauderdale	Meridian Key Field
Lee	Tupelo C D Lemons Arpt
Lincoln	Brookhaven City
Lowndes	Columbus Luxapallila
Madison	Canton
Monroe	Aberdeen
Oktibbeha	State University
Panola	Batesville 2 SW
Prentiss	Booneville
Rankin	Jackson Thompson Field
Scott	Forest 3 S
Simpson	D Lo 2 SW
Stone	Wiggins
Tate	Independence 1 W
Tishomingo	Iuka 5s
Washington	Stoneville Exp Stn
Webster	Eupora 2 E
Winston	Louisville

See User Guide for station inclusion criteria.

Mississippi Weather Stations by City

City	Station Name	Miles
Biloxi	Biloxi	3.3
	Gulfport Naval Center	11.7
	Saucier Exp Forest	16.4
Brandon	Canton	24.3
	D Lo 2 SW	23.3
	Jackson Thompson Field	5.1
Clinton	Jackson Thompson Field	14.0
	Oakley Exp Station	14.8
Columbus	Aberdeen	23.5
	Columbus Luxapallila	3.0
	State University	21.7
Greenville	Eudora, AR	23.1
	Stoneville Exp Stn	8.3
Gulfport	Biloxi	5.6
	Gulfport Naval Center	4.3
	Saucier Exp Forest	15.3
	Waveland	20.2
Hattiesburg	Hattiesburg 5 SW	4.9
Jackson	Canton	24.1
	Jackson Thompson Field	7.2
	Oakley Exp Station	20.0
Meridian	Meridian Key Field	4.2
	Quitman 1 N	21.8
Olive Branch	West Memphis, AR	22.5
	Hernando 5 S	16.8
	Independence 1 W	18.0
	Memphis Intl Arpt, TN	11.2
	Moscow, TN	24.7
Pascagoula	Coden, AL	17.9
	Pascagoula 3 NE	3.9
Pearl	D Lo 2 SW	24.5
	Jackson Thompson Field	3.2
	Oakley Exp Station	24.6
Ridgeland	Canton	16.2
	Jackson Thompson Field	7.2
Southaven	West Memphis, AR	14.8
	Hernando 5 S	15.1
	Independence 1 W	21.1
	Memphis Intl Arpt, TN	5.7
Starkville	Eupora 2 E	24.7
	State University	2.2
Tupelo	Fulton 3 W	16.0
	Tupelo C D Lemons Arpt	2.2
Vicksburg	Tallulah, LA	20.6
	Oakley Exp Station	22.7

Note: Miles is the distance between the geographic center of the city and the weather station.

See User Guide for station inclusion criteria.

Mississippi Weather Stations by Elevation

Feet	Station Name
581	Louisville
490	Booneville
479	Forest 3 S
470	Iuka 5s
439	Eupora 2 E
435	Brookhaven City
384	Hattiesburg 5 SW
379	Hernando 5 S
360	Tupelo C D Lemons Arpt
350	Fulton 3 W
345	Independence 1 W
334	D Lo 2 SW
310	Jackson Thompson Field
299	Quitman 1 N
293	Meridian Key Field
268	Calhoun City 2 NW
229	Saucier Exp Forest
225	Canton
220	Batesville 2 SW
205	Oakley Exp Station
198	Aberdeen
185	State University
160	Wiggins
145	Columbus Luxapallila
126	Stoneville Exp Stn
109	Belzoni
35	Gulfport Naval Center
29	Bay St Louis Nasa
11	Pascagoula 3 NE
9	Biloxi
7	Waveland

See User Guide for station inclusion criteria.

Jackson Thompson Field

Jackson is located on the west bank of the Pearl River, about 45 miles east of the Mississippi River and 150 miles north of the Gulf of Mexico. The nearby terrain is gently rolling with no topographic features that appreciably influence the weather. The National Weather Service Office is nearly seven miles east-northeast of the Jackson Post Office and over five miles southwest of the Ross Barnett Reservoir.

The climate is significantly humid during most of the year, with relatively short mild winters and long warm summers. The Gulf of Mexico has a moderating effect on the climate. Cold spells are fairly frequent in winter, but are usually of short duration. Temperatures occasionally exceed 80 degrees in mid-winter. In summer, temperatures reach 90 degrees or higher on about two-thirds of the days, 100 degree readings are infrequent. Extended periods of very hot weather are rare.

Snowfall averages less than two inches per season. Rainfall is abundant and fairly well-distributed throughout the year.

Thunderstorms can be expected on an average of 65 days a year, usually occurring in each month. They are most frequent in summer when they occur on about one-third of the days.

Jackson Thompson Field *Rankin County* Elevation: 310 ft. Latitude: 32° 19' N Longitude: 90° 05' W

	JAN	FEB	MAR	APR	MAY	JUN	JUL	AUG	SEP	OCT	NOV	DEC	YEAR
Mean Maximum Temp. (°F)	57.0	61.4	69.2	76.4	83.7	90.1	92.4	92.4	87.4	77.6	67.9	59.0	76.2
Mean Temp. (°F)	46.2	50.0	57.3	64.3	72.6	79.3	82.0	81.6	76.1	65.3	55.9	48.2	64.9
Mean Minimum Temp. (°F)	35.5	38.6	45.3	52.1	61.5	68.4	71.6	70.8	64.8	52.9	43.8	37.3	53.6
Extreme Maximum Temp. (°F)	83	85	89	94	95	105	106	107	104	95	86	83	107
Extreme Minimum Temp. (°F)	2	10	15	27	41	47	60	54	41	26	23	4	2
Days Maximum Temp. ≥ 90°F	0	0	0	0	4	18	24	24	12	1	0	0	83
Days Maximum Temp. ≤ 32°F	0	0	0	0	0	0	0	0	0	0	0	0	0
Days Minimum Temp. ≤ 32°F	14	9	4	0	0	0	0	0	0	0	5	13	45
Days Minimum Temp. ≤ 0°F	0	0	0	0	0	0	0	0	0	0	0	0	0
Heating Degree Days (base 65°F)	579	425	264	103	9	0	0	0	6	96	289	524	2,295
Cooling Degree Days (base 65°F)	5	8	31	88	252	436	534	522	346	112	23	9	2,366
Mean Precipitation (in.)	5.05	4.73	5.37	5.38	4.48	3.97	4.79	4.01	3.14	3.96	4.70	5.05	54.63
Maximum Precipitation (in.)*	14.1	10.3	15.1	15.9	10.8	8.2	13.3	8.3	9.6	9.1	10.0	17.7	92.8
Minimum Precipitation (in.)*	0.8	1.4	2.0	1.2	0.3	0.1	1.0	0.6	0.6	0	0.5	0.9	38.9
Extreme Maximum Daily Precip. (in.)	4.72	4.62	3.83	7.38	3.58	6.49	5.45	4.07	3.39	4.15	3.49	4.92	7.38
Days With ≥ 0.1" Precipitation	7	6	7	6	6	6	7	6	5	5	6	7	74
Days With ≥ 0.5" Precipitation	3	3	4	3	3	3	3	2	2	3	3	4	36
Days With ≥ 1.0" Precipitation	2	1	2	2	2	1	1	1	1	1	2	2	18
Mean Snowfall (in.)	*0.3*	*0.1*	*0.1*	*0.1*	*0.0*	*0.0*	*0.0*	*trace*	*0.0*	na	na	na	na
Maximum Snowfall (in.)*	6	4	5	1	0	0	0	0	0	0	trace	3	9
Maximum 24-hr. Snowfall (in.)*	6	4	5	1	0	0	0	0	0	0	trace	2	6
Maximum Snow Depth (in.)	*6*	*1*	*2*	*1*	*0*	*0*	*0*	*trace*	*0*	na	na	na	na
Days With ≥ 1.0" Snow Depth	*0*	*0*	*0*	*0*	*0*	*0*	*0*	*0*	*0*	na	na	na	na
Thunderstorm Days*	2	3	6	6	7	9	13	10	5	2	3	2	68
Foggy Days*	16	13	16	15	18	18	18	22	20	17	15	16	204
Predominant Sky Cover*	OVR	OVR	OVR	OVR	OVR	SCT	SCT	SCT	CLR	CLR	OVR	OVR	OVR
Mean Relative Humidity 6am (%)*	87	87	87	91	92	92	94	95	94	93	90	87	91
Mean Relative Humidity 3pm (%)*	59	54	51	50	53	53	57	55	54	49	52	58	54
Mean Dewpoint (°F)*	37	38	46	54	62	68	72	71	66	54	46	40	55
Prevailing Wind Direction*	N	N	S	SSE	SSE	S	SSW	SE	SE	SE	SSE	SSE	SSE
Prevailing Wind Speed (mph)*	10	10	10	10	9	8	7	7	8	8	9	10	9
Maximum Wind Gust (mph)*	59	53	68	63	60	63	67	56	52	51	69	48	69

Note: (*) Period of record is 1963-1995

The period of record for National Weather Service station data is 1980 – 2009 except where noted. See User Guide for detailed explanation of data.

Meridian Key Field

Mild winters and warm summers describe the general temperature pattern for Meridian. However, the terrain features exert a pronounced influence, particularly during the winter months. The hills to the north, east, and west leave Meridian in a valley. During periods of near calm winds, cold air drainage brings temperatures which may be as much as 10 degrees lower than for other locations in the area. January is usually the coldest month, followed closely by December and February. Sub-zero temperatures are very rare. Summer temperatures are consistently warm. Prolonged periods with above 100 degrees readings are rare.

Precipitation is distributed evenly throughout the year. The widespread rains of the winter months reach a maximum in March. Spring showers reach a minimum in May, followed by localized summer thunderstorms in July and August. The driest period of the year is in late September and October, followed by the onset of winter-type precipitation in late November. This pattern is ideally suited to agricultural operations since the spring rains are conducive to crop growth in the early stages and the dry period in the fall is ideal for harvesting operations. Summer thunderstorms are highly localized and occur on one in three days during July and August.

The long growing season averages 235 days, nearly eight months. The average date of the first occurrence of a temperature as low as 32 degrees in autumn is November 7, and the occurrence of 32 degrees before October 20 is very rare. The average date of the last occurrence of 32 degrees in spring is March 19, although 32 degrees has been recorded in late April. Some portions of the area not affected by cold air drainage may have slightly longer average growing seasons.

The nearby Gulf of Mexico provides an abundant supply of moisture to the Meridian area and results in high humidities for prolonged periods. Humidities of greater than 90 percent occur nightly during every month except for short periods during the autumn and winter when cool continental air is flowing from the north. Lowest humidities are observed during the early afternoons, but seldom reach below 40 percent except for short periods.

March is generally the windiest month of the year due to the frequent occurrence of late winter and spring storms across the Gulf States. October has the lowest average wind speed. Prevailing winds are from the north and northeast during the autumn and winter months, and from the south and southwest during the spring and summer. Local thunderstorms produce short periods of high winds during the spring and summer months and can be quite destructive. Severe thunderstorms and tornadoes have caused considerable loss of life and property in this area. The highest sustained wind speed recorded was 50 mph, but there have been short periods with winds in excess of 50 mph.

Fifty years of record show that December, January, and February receive the smallest amount of possible sunshine. About 40 to 45 percent of the days during these months are cloudy. Sunshine reaches a maximum during the dry period in the fall, September and October. These months are characterized by long periods of cloudless skies.

Thunderstorms normally occur during every month in the year, but most occur during the summer months. These summer thunderstorms provide most of the precipitation during the crop growing season.

Meridian Key Field *Lauderdale County* Elevation: 293 ft. Latitude: 32° 20' N Longitude: 88° 45' W

	JAN	FEB	MAR	APR	MAY	JUN	JUL	AUG	SEP	OCT	NOV	DEC	YEAR
Mean Maximum Temp. (°F)	57.7	62.3	70.0	77.0	83.9	89.9	92.5	92.3	87.4	77.7	68.4	59.8	76.6
Mean Temp. (°F)	46.3	50.2	57.1	63.8	71.8	78.5	81.4	81.1	75.7	64.8	55.6	48.3	64.6
Mean Minimum Temp. (°F)	34.8	38.0	44.2	50.6	59.7	67.0	70.3	69.8	63.8	51.9	42.8	36.8	52.5
Extreme Maximum Temp. (°F)	82	85	89	95	96	104	107	106	105	96	87	84	107
Extreme Minimum Temp. (°F)	5	8	15	28	39	42	57	51	40	28	20	2	2
Days Maximum Temp. ≥ 90°F	0	0	0	0	5	18	24	24	12	1	0	0	84
Days Maximum Temp. ≤ 32°F	0	0	0	0	0	0	0	0	0	0	0	0	0
Days Minimum Temp. ≤ 32°F	15	10	4	1	0	0	0	0	0	1	6	13	50
Days Minimum Temp. ≤ 0°F	0	0	0	0	0	0	0	0	0	0	0	0	0
Heating Degree Days (base 65°F)	576	420	265	107	12	0	0	0	5	102	295	518	2,300
Cooling Degree Days (base 65°F)	4	7	26	78	231	410	516	505	332	103	20	8	2,240
Mean Precipitation (in.)	5.23	5.56	5.70	5.02	4.68	4.29	5.19	3.89	3.54	3.93	4.90	5.05	56.98
Maximum Precipitation (in.)*	11.4	15.9	16.5	16.8	9.8	8.9	15.3	10.3	10.2	10.6	13.9	14.8	79.0
Minimum Precipitation (in.)*	1.2	1.7	1.3	0.9	0.3	0.7	1.1	0.7	0.1	0	0.4	1.1	35.3
Extreme Maximum Daily Precip. (in.)	5.25	7.48	4.23	4.27	3.41	2.79	3.95	4.75	4.42	5.34	4.93	4.60	7.48
Days With ≥ 0.1" Precipitation	8	7	7	6	6	7	8	6	5	5	6	7	78
Days With ≥ 0.5" Precipitation	3	4	4	3	3	3	4	3	2	2	3	4	38
Days With ≥ 1.0" Precipitation	1	2	2	2	2	1	2	1	1	1	2	2	19
Mean Snowfall (in.)	na	na	na	na	na	na	na	na	na	na	na	na	na
Maximum Snowfall (in.)*	7	3	6	3	0	0	0	0	0	0	trace	18	20
Maximum 24-hr. Snowfall (in.)*	5	3	5	2	0	0	0	0	0	0	trace	14	14
Maximum Snow Depth (in.)	na	na	na	na	na	na	na	na	na	na	na	na	na
Days With ≥ 1.0" Snow Depth	na	na	na	na	na	na	na	na	na	na	na	na	na
Thunderstorm Days*	2	3	5	6	6	8	12	9	4	2	2	2	61
Foggy Days*	15	13	14	15	17	16	18	20	18	17	15	15	193
Predominant Sky Cover*	OVR	OVR	OVR	OVR	OVR	SCT	BRK	SCT	CLR	CLR	CLR	OVR	OVR
Mean Relative Humidity 6am (%)*	87	86	87	90	91	91	93	93	92	91	88	87	90
Mean Relative Humidity 3pm (%)*	56	51	47	46	50	52	57	54	53	48	49	55	52
Mean Dewpoint (°F)*	37	39	44	52	61	67	71	70	65	54	45	39	54
Prevailing Wind Direction*	S	S	S	S	S	S	S	S	N	N	S	S	S
Prevailing Wind Speed (mph)*	8	9	10	9	8	7	6	6	7	8	8	9	8
Maximum Wind Gust (mph)*	49	55	64	52	51	64	66	56	69	44	55	68	69

Note: (*) Period of record is 1948-1995

Tupelo C D Lemons Airport

Tupelo is located in the Black Prairie physiographic region of Mississippi. The surface is flat to gently undulating, underlain by soft limestone which has weathered into dark, fertile soils. The Black Prairie is largely devoid of trees, although precipitation in the region is more than sufficient for forest growth. The Black Prairie is bordered by the Fall Line Hills on the east and the Pontotoc Ridge on the west, thus being situated as a low, flat region from 20 to 25 miles wide trending northwest-southeast in the northeastern corner of Mississippi.

Agricultural interests are varied, but the region is a major producer of soybeans and livestock. Tupelo is the dominant urban center of the region, and population is projected to continue to increase in the future. Manufacturing and industry are growing rapidly in the area, enhanced by recent completion of the Tenn-Tom Waterway. Water supply for the growing municipal and industrial demand has been identified as a potential problem in the region as ground water is being used faster than it can be replenished by natural processes.

Average annual precipitation of over 50 inches is well distributed throughout the year. On average, about half the annual total falls between April and September, with March being the wettest month and October the driest month. There is a 90 percent probability that the freeze-free period will be longer than six months, with a 50 percent chance for a freeze before the end of October and after the first of April. Maximum temperatures over 90 degrees are expected on 78 days between May and September, with freezes expected on 66 days between October and March.

Record temperatures of over 105 degrees and below -10 degrees have been observed at Tupelo. Snow is not infrequent during the winter, although amounts average less than two and one-half inches each year. However, accumulations greater than 10 inches have been recorded. Frontal passages are common features of the climate from fall through spring, and there are seasonal occurrences of thunderstorms. Tornadoes, though quite rare, have occurred in the region, particularly during late spring. Precipitation amounts of one-half inch or more are expected on 37 days each year, with one-tenth inch or more expected on 73 days. Daily totals of precipitation have exceeded six inches on several occasions.

Tupelo C D Lemons Airport *Lee County* Elevation: 360 ft. Latitude: 34° 16' N Longitude: 88° 46' W

	JAN	FEB	MAR	APR	MAY	JUN	JUL	AUG	SEP	OCT	NOV	DEC	YEAR
Mean Maximum Temp. (°F)	51.6	56.5	65.1	73.7	81.4	88.3	91.5	91.3	85.3	74.7	63.7	53.9	73.1
Mean Temp. (°F)	41.9	45.9	53.8	61.8	70.3	77.7	81.2	80.5	74.0	62.7	52.7	44.2	62.2
Mean Minimum Temp. (°F)	32.1	35.3	42.5	49.9	59.2	67.1	70.9	69.7	62.6	50.7	41.6	34.5	51.3
Extreme Maximum Temp. (°F)	77	84	86	93	95	101	105	107	104	92	87	79	107
Extreme Minimum Temp. (°F)	-6	4	7	28	38	45	54	52	35	24	16	-3	-6
Days Maximum Temp. ≥ 90°F	0	0	0	0	3	14	21	20	9	1	0	0	68
Days Maximum Temp. ≤ 32°F	1	1	0	0	0	0	0	0	0	0	0	1	3
Days Minimum Temp. ≤ 32°F	17	11	5	1	0	0	0	0	0	1	7	15	57
Days Minimum Temp. ≤ 0°F	0	0	0	0	0	0	0	0	0	0	0	0	0
Heating Degree Days (base 65°F)	712	535	354	149	23	0	0	0	12	137	373	639	2,934
Cooling Degree Days (base 65°F)	1	1	14	59	195	389	510	488	288	74	9	2	2,030
Mean Precipitation (in.)	4.30	4.95	5.39	4.99	5.37	4.57	3.72	3.42	3.58	4.14	4.69	6.39	55.51
Maximum Precipitation (in.)*	7.0	10.9	9.3	12.2	17.6	11.1	6.5	6.2	6.3	7.9	9.6	14.5	81.0
Minimum Precipitation (in.)*	0.3	2.3	2.1	0.5	1.3	0.2	0.5	0.6	0.6	0.4	1.5	1.6	37.6
Extreme Maximum Daily Precip. (in.)	3.75	4.53	4.85	4.16	7.89	3.67	3.60	6.15	6.83	4.15	3.76	5.62	7.89
Days With ≥ 0.1" Precipitation	7	7	7	7	7	7	6	5	5	6	6	8	78
Days With ≥ 0.5" Precipitation	3	3	4	3	3	3	3	2	2	3	3	4	36
Days With ≥ 1.0" Precipitation	1	2	2	2	2	1	1	1	1	1	1	2	17
Mean Snowfall (in.)	na	na	na	***trace***	***trace***	***0.0***	***trace***	***0.0***	***0.0***	***trace***	***trace***	***0.2***	na
Maximum Snowfall (in.)*	7	5	2	trace	0	0	0	0	0	trace	trace	2	10
Maximum 24-hr. Snowfall (in.)*	5	3	2	trace	0	0	0	0	0	trace	trace	2	5
Maximum Snow Depth (in.)	na	na	na	***trace***	***trace***	***0***	***trace***	***0***	***0***	***trace***	***trace***	***2***	na
Days With ≥ 1.0" Snow Depth	na	na	na	***0***	***0***	***0***	***0***	***0***	***0***	***0***	***0***	***0***	na
Thunderstorm Days*	1	2	4	5	8	9	9	7	4	3	3	2	57
Foggy Days*	15	14	14	12	19	20	19	22	19	19	15	15	203
Predominant Sky Cover*	OVR	OVR	OVR	OVR	OVR	SCT	SCT	SCT	SCT	CLR	OVR	OVR	OVR
Mean Relative Humidity 6am (%)*	82	82	81	85	88	89	91	92	91	89	84	82	86
Mean Relative Humidity 3pm (%)*	57	55	49	47	54	54	54	53	52	50	53	59	53
Mean Dewpoint (°F)*	32	35	41	49	59	67	70	69	63	52	42	35	51
Prevailing Wind Direction*	N	N	S	S	S	S	S	N	N	N	SSE	S	S
Prevailing Wind Speed (mph)*	9	9	9	9	8	7	7	7	7	7	9	8	8
Maximum Wind Gust (mph)*	48	51	51	51	47	58	45	52	45	79	56	47	79

Note: (*) Period of record is 1983-1995

The period of record for National Weather Service station data is 1980 – 2009 except where noted. See User Guide for detailed explanation of data.

Aberdeen *Monroe County* Elevation: 198 ft. Latitude: 33° 50' N Longitude: 88° 31' W

	JAN	FEB	MAR	APR	MAY	JUN	JUL	AUG	SEP	OCT	NOV	DEC	YEAR
Mean Maximum Temp. (°F)	53.2	57.4	66.5	74.3	82.0	88.2	91.6	91.1	85.2	75.1	64.8	55.4	73.7
Mean Temp. (°F)	42.9	46.5	54.6	62.2	70.7	77.6	81.3	80.7	74.5	63.5	53.5	45.1	62.8
Mean Minimum Temp. (°F)	32.6	35.7	42.7	50.0	59.3	67.0	71.0	70.2	63.8	51.8	42.2	34.8	51.8
Extreme Maximum Temp. (°F)	78	87	87	94	96	102	104	106	100	92	87	84	106
Extreme Minimum Temp. (°F)	0	5	14	28	36	49	57	50	40	29	22	-5	-5
Days Maximum Temp. ≥ 90°F	0	0	0	0	3	13	21	20	7	1	0	0	65
Days Maximum Temp. ≤ 32°F	1	0	0	0	0	0	0	0	0	0	0	1	2
Days Minimum Temp. ≤ 32°F	16	11	5	1	0	0	0	0	0	1	6	15	55
Days Minimum Temp. ≤ 0°F	0	0	0	0	0	0	0	0	0	0	0	0	0
Heating Degree Days (base 65°F)	678	518	331	141	19	0	0	0	9	121	349	612	2,778
Cooling Degree Days (base 65°F)	1	3	16	64	201	386	513	493	300	81	11	3	2,072
Mean Precipitation (in.)	4.87	4.87	5.00	4.87	5.26	4.37	3.64	3.14	3.95	4.17	4.52	5.46	54.12
Extreme Maximum Daily Precip. (in.)	4.40	5.25	3.20	4.02	5.40	6.02	3.90	6.13	4.86	4.05	5.10	5.80	6.13
Days With ≥ 0.1" Precipitation	7	7	7	6	7	7	6	5	5	6	7	7	77
Days With ≥ 0.5" Precipitation	3	3	4	3	3	3	3	2	3	3	3	3	36
Days With ≥ 1.0" Precipitation	2	1	2	2	2	1	1	1	1	1	1	2	17
Mean Snowfall (in.)	0.4	0.1	0.1	trace	0.0	0.0	0.0	0.0	0.0	0.0	0.0	trace	0.6
Maximum Snow Depth (in.)	4	5	1	trace	0	0	0	0	0	0	0	trace	5
Days With ≥ 1.0" Snow Depth	0	0	0	0	0	0	0	0	0	0	0	0	0

Batesville 2 SW *Panola County* Elevation: 220 ft. Latitude: 34° 18' N Longitude: 89° 59' W

	JAN	FEB	MAR	APR	MAY	JUN	JUL	AUG	SEP	OCT	NOV	DEC	YEAR
Mean Maximum Temp. (°F)	50.6	55.3	63.9	72.8	81.1	87.8	90.8	91.1	85.5	75.2	64.0	53.2	72.6
Mean Temp. (°F)	40.6	44.3	52.3	60.8	69.9	77.1	80.2	79.3	73.0	62.1	52.0	42.9	61.2
Mean Minimum Temp. (°F)	30.6	33.2	40.6	48.9	58.6	66.3	69.5	67.5	60.5	49.0	40.0	32.5	49.8
Extreme Maximum Temp. (°F)	79	79	86	93	95	102	106	107	105	96	86	82	107
Extreme Minimum Temp. (°F)	-8	3	13	26	35	45	53	49	38	22	18	-2	-8
Days Maximum Temp. ≥ 90°F	0	0	0	0	2	12	20	20	9	1	0	0	64
Days Maximum Temp. ≤ 32°F	2	1	0	0	0	0	0	0	0	0	0	1	4
Days Minimum Temp. ≤ 32°F	19	15	7	1	0	0	0	0	0	2	8	18	70
Days Minimum Temp. ≤ 0°F	0	0	0	0	0	0	0	0	0	0	0	0	0
Heating Degree Days (base 65°F)	749	581	400	175	31	1	0	0	19	155	392	681	3,184
Cooling Degree Days (base 65°F)	1	1	12	57	189	369	478	451	265	72	11	2	1,908
Mean Precipitation (in.)	4.16	4.56	4.97	4.88	5.19	4.54	3.74	2.75	3.52	4.20	5.13	6.01	53.65
Extreme Maximum Daily Precip. (in.)	3.90	4.72	4.36	4.93	5.90	4.32	4.40	3.20	6.65	8.85	8.51	5.14	8.85
Days With ≥ 0.1" Precipitation	6	6	6	6	6	6	5	4	4	5	6	6	66
Days With ≥ 0.5" Precipitation	3	3	3	3	3	3	2	2	2	2	3	4	33
Days With ≥ 1.0" Precipitation	1	2	2	2	2	2	1	1	1	1	1	2	18
Mean Snowfall (in.)	0.8	0.2	trace	0.0	0.0	0.0	0.0	0.0	0.0	0.0	0.0	trace	1.0
Maximum Snow Depth (in.)	6	3	trace	0	0	0	0	0	0	0	0	1	6
Days With ≥ 1.0" Snow Depth	0	0	0	0	0	0	0	0	0	0	0	0	0

Bay St Louis Nasa *Hancock County* Elevation: 29 ft. Latitude: 30° 22' N Longitude: 89° 35' W

	JAN	FEB	MAR	APR	MAY	JUN	JUL	AUG	SEP	OCT	NOV	DEC	YEAR
Mean Maximum Temp. (°F)	62.0	65.3	71.3	77.4	84.4	89.5	91.8	91.6	87.8	80.0	71.8	63.9	78.1
Mean Temp. (°F)	50.5	53.5	59.8	65.8	73.5	79.3	81.7	81.5	77.2	67.7	59.6	52.2	66.9
Mean Minimum Temp. (°F)	38.9	41.7	48.3	54.1	62.5	69.1	71.5	71.3	66.6	55.3	47.4	40.5	55.6
Extreme Maximum Temp. (°F)	83	85	88	94	98	101	104	104	103	97	88	83	104
Extreme Minimum Temp. (°F)	5	9	20	28	41	48	62	54	44	30	24	10	5
Days Maximum Temp. ≥ 90°F	0	0	0	0	4	15	23	23	12	1	0	0	78
Days Maximum Temp. ≤ 32°F	0	0	0	0	0	0	0	0	0	0	0	0	0
Days Minimum Temp. ≤ 32°F	10	6	2	0	0	0	0	0	0	0	3	9	30
Days Minimum Temp. ≤ 0°F	0	0	0	0	0	0	0	0	0	0	0	0	0
Heating Degree Days (base 65°F)	449	332	194	71	5	0	0	0	1	59	198	403	1,712
Cooling Degree Days (base 65°F)	6	12	40	101	274	437	524	518	376	149	44	15	2,496
Mean Precipitation (in.)	5.70	4.89	5.97	5.04	5.06	5.58	6.68	6.05	4.91	3.74	4.89	4.25	62.76
Extreme Maximum Daily Precip. (in.)	6.00	4.20	5.54	9.10	11.81	4.96	3.68	4.96	5.30	15.32	***5.07***	***4.32***	***15.32***
Days With ≥ 0.1" Precipitation	7	5	6	5	5	8	9	8	6	4	5	5	73
Days With ≥ 0.5" Precipitation	3	3	3	2	3	4	5	4	3	2	3	3	38
Days With ≥ 1.0" Precipitation	2	1	2	2	1	2	2	2	1	1	1	1	18
Mean Snowfall (in.)	0.0	0.0	trace	0.0	0.0	0.0	0.0	0.0	0.0	0.0	0.0	0.0	trace
Maximum Snow Depth (in.)	0	0	0	0	0	0	0	0	0	0	0	2	2
Days With ≥ 1.0" Snow Depth	0	0	0	0	0	0	0	0	0	0	0	0	0

Belzoni *Humphreys County* Elevation: 109 ft. Latitude: 33° 12' N Longitude: 90° 29' W

	JAN	FEB	MAR	APR	MAY	JUN	JUL	AUG	SEP	OCT	NOV	DEC	YEAR
Mean Maximum Temp. (°F)	53.4	57.7	66.5	75.2	83.7	90.3	92.7	93.0	87.9	77.6	66.3	55.6	75.0
Mean Temp. (°F)	44.0	47.9	56.0	64.0	73.1	80.0	82.4	81.9	76.0	65.6	55.4	46.0	64.3
Mean Minimum Temp. (°F)	34.5	37.9	45.5	52.7	62.4	69.6	72.0	70.8	64.1	53.4	44.5	36.4	53.7
Extreme Maximum Temp. (°F)	78	***82***	88	95	97	103	107	105	106	97	90	82	***107***
Extreme Minimum Temp. (°F)	5	6	14	30	44	53	55	53	41	26	22	1	1
Days Maximum Temp. ≥ 90°F	0	0	0	1	6	19	24	24	14	2	0	0	90
Days Maximum Temp. ≤ 32°F	1	1	0	0	0	0	0	0	0	0	0	1	3
Days Minimum Temp. ≤ 32°F	***13***	***8***	3	0	0	0	0	0	0	0	3	11	***38***
Days Minimum Temp. ≤ 0°F	0	0	0	0	0	0	0	0	0	0	0	0	0
Heating Degree Days (base 65°F)	***642***	481	297	111	9	0	0	0	8	95	296	587	***2,526***
Cooling Degree Days (base 65°F)	2	3	25	88	265	455	546	531	345	119	20	5	2,404
Mean Precipitation (in.)	4.80	***5.11***	5.28	5.43	5.91	3.70	4.56	3.28	3.16	4.61	4.71	5.86	***56.41***
Extreme Maximum Daily Precip. (in.)	4.45	***3.55***	5.85	***6.50***	***6.35***	4.50	7.30	3.50	3.75	5.39	4.10	5.35	***7.30***
Days With ≥ 0.1" Precipitation	7	***6***	7	6	***6***	5	6	5	4	5	5	7	***69***
Days With ≥ 0.5" Precipitation	4	***4***	3	3	***3***	2	3	2	2	3	3	3	***35***
Days With ≥ 1.0" Precipitation	1	2	2	2	***2***	1	2	1	1	2	2	2	***20***
Mean Snowfall (in.)	trace	***trace***	trace	0.0	0.0	0.0	0.0	0.0	0.0	0.0	0.0	0.0	***trace***
Maximum Snow Depth (in.)	trace	***trace***	***1***	0	***0***	0	0	0	0	0	0	0	***1***
Days With ≥ 1.0" Snow Depth	0	***0***	0	0	0	0	0	0	0	0	0	0	***0***

The period of record for all cooperative weather station data is 1980 – 2009. See User Guide for detailed explanation of data.

Biloxi *Harrison County* Elevation: 9 ft. Latitude: 30° 23' N Longitude: 88° 59' W

	JAN	FEB	MAR	APR	MAY	JUN	JUL	AUG	SEP	OCT	NOV	DEC	YEAR
Mean Maximum Temp. (°F)	60.3	63.2	68.8	75.7	83.0	88.1	90.2	90.2	87.0	79.1	70.3	62.6	76.5
Mean Temp. (°F)	51.9	54.8	60.5	67.6	75.4	80.8	82.7	82.7	78.9	70.2	61.2	54.0	68.4
Mean Minimum Temp. (°F)	43.5	46.3	52.3	59.5	67.8	73.5	75.3	75.2	70.8	61.3	52.1	45.4	60.2
Extreme Maximum Temp. (°F)	81	80	85	90	96	100	103	104	98	94	86	80	104
Extreme Minimum Temp. (°F)	10	15	22	35	47	59	65	61	49	32	29	11	10
Days Maximum Temp. ≥ 90°F	0	0	0	0	1	8	17	17	7	0	0	0	50
Days Maximum Temp. ≤ 32°F	0	0	0	0	0	0	0	0	0	0	0	0	0
Days Minimum Temp. ≤ 32°F	5	2	1	0	0	0	0	0	0	0	0	3	11
Days Minimum Temp. ≤ 0°F	0	0	0	0	0	0	0	0	0	0	0	0	0
Heating Degree Days (base 65°F)	402	289	167	42	1	0	0	0	0	30	155	343	1,429
Cooling Degree Days (base 65°F)	3	5	35	127	331	482	557	556	425	200	48	9	2,778
Mean Precipitation (in.)	5.17	4.95	6.17	5.14	4.64	6.45	7.33	6.51	5.53	3.95	4.59	4.65	65.08
Extreme Maximum Daily Precip. (in.)	4.25	4.65	7.28	7.73	7.09	7.17	9.49	10.46	11.30	7.13	7.19	6.35	11.30
Days With ≥ 0.1" Precipitation	6	6	6	5	5	7	10	9	6	4	6	6	76
Days With ≥ 0.5" Precipitation	3	3	3	3	3	4	4	4	3	2	3	3	38
Days With ≥ 1.0" Precipitation	2	2	2	2	1	2	2	2	1	1	1	2	20
Mean Snowfall (in.)	0.0	trace	0.1	0.0	0.0	0.0	0.0	0.0	0.0	0.0	0.0	trace	0.1
Maximum Snow Depth (in.)	0	trace	0	0	0	0	0	0	0	0	0	1	1
Days With ≥ 1.0" Snow Depth	0	0	0	0	0	0	0	0	0	0	0	0	0

Booneville *Prentiss County* Elevation: 490 ft. Latitude: 34° 40' N Longitude: 88° 34' W

	JAN	FEB	MAR	APR	MAY	JUN	JUL	AUG	SEP	OCT	NOV	DEC	YEAR
Mean Maximum Temp. (°F)	49.3	53.6	62.8	71.4	79.0	85.7	89.4	89.1	83.2	72.6	62.1	51.7	70.8
Mean Temp. (°F)	39.8	43.4	51.9	60.1	68.6	76.1	79.9	79.0	72.4	61.2	51.4	42.2	60.5
Mean Minimum Temp. (°F)	30.2	33.1	40.8	48.8	58.1	66.3	70.4	68.9	61.6	49.8	40.6	32.7	50.1
Extreme Maximum Temp. (°F)	75	83	85	93	98	100	106	106	98	92	86	79	106
Extreme Minimum Temp. (°F)	-8	1	11	25	38	48	56	50	40	28	18	-6	-8
Days Maximum Temp. ≥ 90°F	0	0	0	0	1	8	16	14	5	0	0	0	44
Days Maximum Temp. ≤ 32°F	2	1	0	0	0	0	0	0	0	0	0	2	5
Days Minimum Temp. ≤ 32°F	18	14	7	1	0	0	0	0	0	1	7	17	65
Days Minimum Temp. ≤ 0°F	0	0	0	0	0	0	0	0	0	0	0	0	0
Heating Degree Days (base 65°F)	776	604	410	186	38	1	0	0	19	166	409	699	3,308
Cooling Degree Days (base 65°F)	0	0	10	47	156	340	469	441	249	56	6	1	1,775
Mean Precipitation (in.)	4.94	4.96	5.27	5.12	5.61	4.45	3.69	3.84	3.91	4.12	5.09	6.43	57.43
Extreme Maximum Daily Precip. (in.)	4.10	4.86	4.42	3.80	7.29	4.10	3.91	6.30	8.13	5.52	4.38	7.59	8.13
Days With ≥ 0.1" Precipitation	7	7	7	7	7	7	7	6	5	6	7	8	81
Days With ≥ 0.5" Precipitation	4	4	4	4	4	3	3	2	3	3	3	4	41
Days With ≥ 1.0" Precipitation	1	1	2	2	2	1	1	1	1	1	2	2	17
Mean Snowfall (in.)	0.9	0.9	trace	trace	trace	0.0	0.0	0.0	0.0	trace	trace	0.3	2.1
Maximum Snow Depth (in.)	8	5	1	trace	trace	0	0	0	0	trace	trace	2	8
Days With ≥ 1.0" Snow Depth	1	1	0	0	0	0	0	0	0	0	0	0	2

Brookhaven City *Lincoln County* Elevation: 435 ft. Latitude: 31° 33' N Longitude: 90° 27' W

	JAN	FEB	MAR	APR	MAY	JUN	JUL	AUG	SEP	OCT	NOV	DEC	YEAR
Mean Maximum Temp. (°F)	57.9	61.9	69.2	76.1	82.8	88.7	91.0	91.3	86.9	77.8	68.6	60.3	76.0
Mean Temp. (°F)	46.3	49.9	56.9	63.4	71.3	77.8	80.3	79.9	74.9	64.6	56.0	48.6	64.2
Mean Minimum Temp. (°F)	34.6	37.8	44.4	50.6	59.6	66.8	69.5	68.5	62.9	51.4	43.4	36.9	52.2
Extreme Maximum Temp. (°F)	80	83	89	91	93	102	103	106	105	94	88	81	106
Extreme Minimum Temp. (°F)	3	10	14	26	39	44	58	50	40	27	22	5	3
Days Maximum Temp. ≥ 90°F	0	0	0	0	2	14	21	21	11	1	0	0	70
Days Maximum Temp. ≤ 32°F	0	0	0	0	0	0	0	0	0	0	0	0	0
Days Minimum Temp. ≤ 32°F	15	9	4	1	0	0	0	0	0	1	5	13	48
Days Minimum Temp. ≤ 0°F	0	0	0	0	0	0	0	0	0	0	0	0	0
Heating Degree Days (base 65°F)	576	428	272	117	15	0	0	0	7	106	285	508	2,314
Cooling Degree Days (base 65°F)	3	6	26	75	216	390	480	470	312	102	21	8	2,109
Mean Precipitation (in.)	6.12	6.34	5.92	5.26	4.87	4.33	4.88	4.36	4.37	3.99	4.32	5.68	60.44
Extreme Maximum Daily Precip. (in.)	6.74	7.11	4.70	6.80	8.08	4.30	3.20	6.70	6.40	3.30	4.36	7.75	8.08
Days With ≥ 0.1" Precipitation	7	7	7	5	6	7	8	6	5	5	5	7	75
Days With ≥ 0.5" Precipitation	4	4	4	3	3	3	3	3	3	3	3	4	40
Days With ≥ 1.0" Precipitation	2	2	2	2	2	1	2	1	1	2	2	2	21
Mean Snowfall (in.)	0.0	trace	0.1	0.0	0.0	0.0	0.0	0.0	0.0	0.0	0.0	0.0	0.1
Maximum Snow Depth (in.)	0	trace	0	0	0	0	0	0	0	0	0	3	3
Days With ≥ 1.0" Snow Depth	0	0	0	0	0	0	0	0	0	0	0	0	0

Calhoun City 2 NW *Calhoun County* Elevation: 268 ft. Latitude: 33° 52' N Longitude: 89° 21' W

	JAN	FEB	MAR	APR	MAY	JUN	JUL	AUG	SEP	OCT	NOV	DEC	YEAR
Mean Maximum Temp. (°F)	53.9	58.4	67.1	74.6	81.4	87.3	90.8	90.7	85.3	75.9	65.4	55.7	73.9
Mean Temp. (°F)	42.9	46.7	54.6	61.9	69.8	76.6	80.3	79.6	73.4	62.9	53.5	45.0	62.3
Mean Minimum Temp. (°F)	31.9	35.1	42.1	49.4	58.1	65.8	69.6	68.4	61.4	49.8	41.5	34.2	50.6
Extreme Maximum Temp. (°F)	78	86	87	92	95	101	104	106	104	95	85	79	106
Extreme Minimum Temp. (°F)	-6	-8	10	26	37	44	54	50	37	27	17	-8	-8
Days Maximum Temp. ≥ 90°F	0	0	0	0	1	10	20	19	8	0	0	0	58
Days Maximum Temp. ≤ 32°F	1	0	0	0	0	0	0	0	0	0	0	1	2
Days Minimum Temp. ≤ 32°F	17	13	7	1	0	0	0	0	0	1	7	16	62
Days Minimum Temp. ≤ 0°F	0	0	0	0	0	0	0	0	0	0	0	0	0
Heating Degree Days (base 65°F)	679	513	331	146	26	0	0	0	12	131	349	617	2,804
Cooling Degree Days (base 65°F)	1	3	18	58	180	354	479	458	271	73	10	3	1,908
Mean Precipitation (in.)	4.64	4.76	5.05	5.74	5.51	4.90	3.76	3.42	3.73	3.75	4.31	5.98	55.55
Extreme Maximum Daily Precip. (in.)	5.80	4.90	3.83	5.75	5.83	5.16	2.76	4.83	5.02	4.05	3.78	7.62	7.62
Days With ≥ 0.1" Precipitation	6	6	6	6	6	6	5	5	4	4	6	7	67
Days With ≥ 0.5" Precipitation	3	3	3	3	4	3	2	2	3	2	3	4	35
Days With ≥ 1.0" Precipitation	1	2	2	2	2	2	1	1	1	1	2	2	19
Mean Snowfall (in.)	0.8	0.3	trace	0.0	0.0	0.0	0.0	0.0	0.0	0.0	trace	0.1	1.2
Maximum Snow Depth (in.)	5	3	trace	0	0	0	0	0	0	0	trace	1	5
Days With ≥ 1.0" Snow Depth	0	0	0	0	0	0	0	0	0	0	0	0	0

The period of record for all cooperative weather station data is 1980 – 2009. See User Guide for detailed explanation of data.

Canton *Madison County* Elevation: 225 ft. Latitude: 32° 38' N Longitude: 90° 01' W

	JAN	FEB	MAR	APR	MAY	JUN	JUL	AUG	SEP	OCT	NOV	DEC	YEAR
Mean Maximum Temp. (°F)	56.2	59.3	68.3	75.4	83.1	89.7	92.4	92.7	87.2	77.3	67.9	57.8	75.6
Mean Temp. (°F)	45.1	48.1	56.2	63.1	71.7	78.4	81.2	81.0	74.9	64.2	55.4	46.4	63.8
Mean Minimum Temp. (°F)	33.9	36.8	44.1	50.7	60.3	67.0	70.0	69.3	62.5	51.0	42.7	35.1	51.9
Extreme Maximum Temp. (°F)	81	84	89	95	95	103	104	107	107	93	89	83	107
Extreme Minimum Temp. (°F)	2	9	15	28	40	46	56	52	37	26	21	2	2
Days Maximum Temp. ≥ 90°F	0	0	0	0	4	17	24	23	11	1	0	0	80
Days Maximum Temp. ≤ 32°F	1	0	0	0	0	0	0	0	0	0	0	1	2
Days Minimum Temp. ≤ 32°F	15	11	4	1	0	0	0	0	0	1	6	15	53
Days Minimum Temp. ≤ 0°F	0	0	0	0	0	0	0	0	0	0	0	0	0
Heating Degree Days (base 65°F)	613	478	292	123	16	0	0	0	10	117	301	575	2,525
Cooling Degree Days (base 65°F)	4	6	27	73	230	408	508	504	313	98	20	6	2,197
Mean Precipitation (in.)	4.84	5.24	5.17	5.23	5.22	3.68	3.91	3.52	3.46	4.50	4.80	5.36	54.93
Extreme Maximum Daily Precip. (in.)	3.10	4.65	4.15	5.03	5.06	4.18	3.30	4.94	4.37	5.82	4.12	5.35	5.82
Days With ≥ 0.1" Precipitation	7	7	7	5	6	5	6	5	5	5	6	7	71
Days With ≥ 0.5" Precipitation	4	4	3	3	3	2	3	2	2	3	4	4	37
Days With ≥ 1.0" Precipitation	2	2	2	2	2	1	1	1	1	2	2	2	20
Mean Snowfall (in.)	0.0	trace	trace	0.0	0.0	0.0	0.0	0.0	0.0	0.0	0.0	0.3	0.3
Maximum Snow Depth (in.)	0	trace	trace	0	0	0	0	0	0	0	0	trace	trace
Days With ≥ 1.0" Snow Depth	0	0	0	0	0	0	0	0	0	0	0	0	0

Columbus Luxapallila *Lowndes County* Elevation: 145 ft. Latitude: 33° 28' N Longitude: 88° 23' W

	JAN	FEB	MAR	APR	MAY	JUN	JUL	AUG	SEP	OCT	NOV	DEC	YEAR
Mean Maximum Temp. (°F)	54.0	58.9	67.4	74.8	83.0	88.9	92.0	91.8	86.3	76.2	65.9	56.0	74.6
Mean Temp. (°F)	43.9	47.9	55.6	62.6	71.6	78.1	81.5	81.1	75.0	64.1	54.1	45.8	63.4
Mean Minimum Temp. (°F)	33.7	36.7	43.8	50.3	60.1	67.3	70.9	70.2	63.7	52.0	42.3	35.5	52.2
Extreme Maximum Temp. (°F)	79	89	90	93	98	101	105	108	104	94	87	79	108
Extreme Minimum Temp. (°F)	-1	7	17	30	41	48	55	52	42	28	18	-4	-4
Days Maximum Temp. ≥ 90°F	0	0	0	0	5	15	21	22	10	1	0	0	74
Days Maximum Temp. ≤ 32°F	1	0	0	0	0	0	0	0	0	0	0	1	2
Days Minimum Temp. ≤ 32°F	15	10	4	1	0	0	0	0	0	1	6	14	51
Days Minimum Temp. ≤ 0°F	0	0	0	0	0	0	0	0	0	0	0	0	0
Heating Degree Days (base 65°F)	647	482	306	132	15	0	0	0	7	112	332	593	2,626
Cooling Degree Days (base 65°F)	2	4	21	66	226	401	517	504	315	91	12	3	2,162
Mean Precipitation (in.)	5.46	5.75	4.79	5.00	4.23	5.06	4.40	4.00	3.71	4.04	4.73	5.29	56.46
Extreme Maximum Daily Precip. (in.)	4.71	6.00	3.82	4.46	4.65	3.98	4.25	5.50	2.89	3.45	3.82	7.92	7.92
Days With ≥ 0.1" Precipitation	8	7	7	6	6	7	7	6	5	5	6	7	77
Days With ≥ 0.5" Precipitation	4	4	3	3	3	3	3	3	2	3	3	3	37
Days With ≥ 1.0" Precipitation	2	2	1	1	1	1	1	1	1	2	2	2	17
Mean Snowfall (in.)	0.3	trace	trace	trace	0.0	0.0	0.0	0.0	0.0	0.0	0.0	trace	0.3
Maximum Snow Depth (in.)	trace	trace	trace	0	0	0	0	0	0	0	0	trace	trace
Days With ≥ 1.0" Snow Depth	0	0	0	0	0	0	0	0	0	0	0	0	0

D Lo 2 SW *Simpson County* Elevation: 334 ft. Latitude: 31° 57' N Longitude: 89° 56' W

	JAN	FEB	MAR	APR	MAY	JUN	JUL	AUG	SEP	OCT	NOV	DEC	YEAR
Mean Maximum Temp. (°F)	57.2	61.4	69.0	75.9	83.0	88.9	91.3	91.3	86.8	77.6	68.3	59.3	75.8
Mean Temp. (°F)	45.1	48.7	55.9	62.6	70.9	77.4	80.2	79.8	74.4	63.6	54.6	47.0	63.3
Mean Minimum Temp. (°F)	33.0	36.0	42.7	49.2	58.7	65.8	69.1	68.3	61.8	49.4	40.9	34.6	50.8
Extreme Maximum Temp. (°F)	81	85	90	92	95	103	104	105	105	95	89	83	105
Extreme Minimum Temp. (°F)	0	9	14	25	38	44	56	49	37	27	18	3	0
Days Maximum Temp. ≥ 90°F	0	0	0	0	2	15	22	22	10	1	0	0	72
Days Maximum Temp. ≤ 32°F	0	0	0	0	0	0	0	0	0	0	0	1	1
Days Minimum Temp. ≤ 32°F	17	13	6	1	0	0	0	0	0	2	8	16	63
Days Minimum Temp. ≤ 0°F	0	0	0	0	0	0	0	0	0	0	0	0	0
Heating Degree Days (base 65°F)	612	460	301	133	20	0	0	0	11	129	324	560	2,550
Cooling Degree Days (base 65°F)	3	5	24	68	208	379	479	466	298	91	18	8	2,047
Mean Precipitation (in.)	5.38	5.57	5.59	5.18	4.39	4.37	5.26	4.51	3.23	3.52	4.86	5.50	57.36
Extreme Maximum Daily Precip. (in.)	4.16	6.26	4.09	6.05	5.15	3.21	5.62	4.80	4.17	3.90	6.32	5.00	6.32
Days With ≥ 0.1" Precipitation	7	7	7	6	6	7	8	7	5	5	6	7	78
Days With ≥ 0.5" Precipitation	4	4	4	3	3	3	4	3	2	3	3	4	40
Days With ≥ 1.0" Precipitation	2	2	2	2	2	1	2	1	1	1	2	2	20
Mean Snowfall (in.)	0.2	trace	0.1	trace	0.0	0.0	0.0	0.0	0.0	0.0	0.0	0.3	0.6
Maximum Snow Depth (in.)	4	1	3	1	0	0	0	0	0	0	0	1	4
Days With ≥ 1.0" Snow Depth	0	0	0	0	0	0	0	0	0	0	0	0	0

Eupora 2 E *Webster County* Elevation: 439 ft. Latitude: 33° 33' N Longitude: 89° 14' W

	JAN	FEB	MAR	APR	MAY	JUN	JUL	AUG	SEP	OCT	NOV	DEC	YEAR
Mean Maximum Temp. (°F)	54.4	59.1	67.6	75.4	82.1	88.4	91.3	91.2	86.0	76.1	66.0	56.6	74.5
Mean Temp. (°F)	43.2	47.0	54.7	62.1	70.0	76.8	80.1	79.4	73.6	62.6	53.5	45.5	62.4
Mean Minimum Temp. (°F)	32.0	34.8	41.6	48.8	57.9	65.3	68.8	67.6	61.1	49.2	40.9	34.4	50.2
Extreme Maximum Temp. (°F)	79	85	87	92	95	102	104	106	105	96	87	81	106
Extreme Minimum Temp. (°F)	-4	3	11	25	37	42	54	50	37	26	17	-4	-4
Days Maximum Temp. ≥ 90°F	0	0	0	0	2	13	21	20	9	1	0	0	66
Days Maximum Temp. ≤ 32°F	1	0	0	0	0	0	0	0	0	0	0	1	2
Days Minimum Temp. ≤ 32°F	17	13	7	2	0	0	0	0	0	2	8	15	64
Days Minimum Temp. ≤ 0°F	0	0	0	0	0	0	0	0	0	0	0	0	0
Heating Degree Days (base 65°F)	670	506	331	145	24	0	0	0	12	138	351	599	2,776
Cooling Degree Days (base 65°F)	1	3	18	65	187	362	474	453	277	71	12	3	1,926
Mean Precipitation (in.)	5.14	4.95	5.66	5.17	5.22	4.40	4.12	3.35	4.02	4.10	4.94	5.97	57.04
Extreme Maximum Daily Precip. (in.)	4.60	7.35	3.61	4.87	7.58	3.30	4.69	5.83	6.10	5.53	4.01	7.89	7.89
Days With ≥ 0.1" Precipitation	7	7	7	6	6	7	6	5	5	4	6	7	73
Days With ≥ 0.5" Precipitation	3	4	4	3	3	3	3	2	2	3	3	4	37
Days With ≥ 1.0" Precipitation	2	2	2	2	2	1	1	1	1	2	2	2	20
Mean Snowfall (in.)	0.7	0.1	0.1	trace	0.0	0.0	0.0	0.0	0.0	trace	0.0	trace	0.9
Maximum Snow Depth (in.)	6	trace	3	trace	0	0	0	0	0	trace	0	1	6
Days With ≥ 1.0" Snow Depth	0	0	0	0	0	0	0	0	0	0	0	0	0

The period of record for all cooperative weather station data is 1980 – 2009. See User Guide for detailed explanation of data.

Forest 3 S *Scott County* Elevation: 479 ft. Latitude: 32° 19' N Longitude: 89° 29' W

	JAN	FEB	MAR	APR	MAY	JUN	JUL	AUG	SEP	OCT	NOV	DEC	YEAR
Mean Maximum Temp. (°F)	57.6	62.4	70.1	76.6	83.3	89.2	91.5	91.5	87.1	77.8	68.6	59.7	76.3
Mean Temp. (°F)	45.8	50.0	56.8	63.4	71.1	77.3	80.1	79.9	74.7	64.3	55.5	48.1	63.9
Mean Minimum Temp. (°F)	33.9	37.5	43.4	50.1	58.8	65.3	68.7	68.2	62.3	50.9	42.5	36.4	51.5
Extreme Maximum Temp. (°F)	80	83	87	93	94	104	103	104	102	96	89	87	104
Extreme Minimum Temp. (°F)	-1	6	7	26	38	43	52	52	38	28	19	0	-1
Days Maximum Temp. ≥ 90°F	0	0	0	0	2	15	23	21	11	1	0	0	73
Days Maximum Temp. ≤ 32°F	0	0	0	0	0	0	0	0	0	0	0	0	0
Days Minimum Temp. ≤ 32°F	15	11	6	1	0	0	0	0	0	1	7	13	54
Days Minimum Temp. ≤ 0°F	0	0	0	0	0	0	0	0	0	0	0	0	0
Heating Degree Days (base 65°F)	592	422	274	112	13	0	0	0	7	107	295	524	2,346
Cooling Degree Days (base 65°F)	2	5	25	69	209	376	476	467	304	93	18	7	2,051
Mean Precipitation (in.)	5.14	5.95	5.54	5.41	4.47	4.61	5.45	4.51	3.56	4.23	4.73	5.53	59.13
Extreme Maximum Daily Precip. (in.)	4.19	4.85	***5.05***	4.16	3.07	***3.58***	5.00	6.80	5.00	3.90	5.65	5.50	***6.80***
Days With ≥ 0.1" Precipitation	6	7	7	5	6	6	8	6	5	5	6	7	74
Days With ≥ 0.5" Precipitation	3	4	4	3	3	3	4	3	2	3	3	4	39
Days With ≥ 1.0" Precipitation	1	2	2	2	2	1	2	2	1	1	2	2	20
Mean Snowfall (in.)	0.2	0.0	trace	0.0	0.0	0.0	0.0	0.0	0.0	0.0	0.0	0.1	0.3
Maximum Snow Depth (in.)	4	0	0	0	0	0	0	0	0	0	0	0	4
Days With ≥ 1.0" Snow Depth	0	0	0	0	0	0	0	0	0	0	0	0	0

Fulton 3 W *Itawamba County* Elevation: 350 ft. Latitude: 34° 16' N Longitude: 88° 27' W

	JAN	FEB	MAR	APR	MAY	JUN	JUL	AUG	SEP	OCT	NOV	DEC	YEAR
Mean Maximum Temp. (°F)	52.5	57.6	66.5	74.6	81.6	87.9	91.1	91.4	85.4	75.0	64.3	54.4	73.5
Mean Temp. (°F)	42.3	46.3	54.2	61.8	69.9	76.7	80.1	79.6	73.5	62.5	52.9	44.5	62.0
Mean Minimum Temp. (°F)	32.0	35.0	41.8	49.0	58.0	65.5	69.1	67.6	61.4	50.0	41.4	34.5	50.4
Extreme Maximum Temp. (°F)	78	85	87	94	95	102	108	108	101	92	85	78	108
Extreme Minimum Temp. (°F)	-9	4	9	25	37	42	51	48	36	27	16	-4	-9
Days Maximum Temp. ≥ 90°F	0	0	0	0	2	12	20	20	8	0	0	0	62
Days Maximum Temp. ≤ 32°F	1	1	0	0	0	0	0	0	0	0	0	1	3
Days Minimum Temp. ≤ 32°F	17	13	7	2	0	0	0	0	0	2	7	15	63
Days Minimum Temp. ≤ 0°F	0	0	0	0	0	0	0	0	0	0	0	0	0
Heating Degree Days (base 65°F)	698	524	345	148	26	1	0	0	12	141	366	632	2,893
Cooling Degree Days (base 65°F)	1	2	17	59	183	358	476	458	272	70	9	3	1,908
Mean Precipitation (in.)	4.86	5.37	5.51	5.29	6.15	4.69	4.18	4.06	4.08	4.09	5.14	6.61	60.03
Extreme Maximum Daily Precip. (in.)	4.29	5.96	4.42	4.40	4.67	5.34	3.35	5.60	5.75	3.36	3.96	6.28	6.28
Days With ≥ 0.1" Precipitation	7	8	7	7	8	7	7	5	5	5	7	8	81
Days With ≥ 0.5" Precipitation	4	4	4	3	4	3	3	3	2	3	3	4	40
Days With ≥ 1.0" Precipitation	2	2	2	2	2	2	1	1	1	2	2	2	21
Mean Snowfall (in.)	0.6	0.7	0.2	trace	0.0	0.0	0.0	0.0	0.0	0.0	trace	0.1	1.6
Maximum Snow Depth (in.)	5	3	2	0	0	0	0	0	0	0	0	1	5
Days With ≥ 1.0" Snow Depth	0	0	0	0	0	0	0	0	0	0	0	0	0

Gulfport Naval Center *Harrison County* Elevation: 35 ft. Latitude: 30° 23' N Longitude: 89° 08' W

	JAN	FEB	MAR	APR	MAY	JUN	JUL	AUG	SEP	OCT	NOV	DEC	YEAR
Mean Maximum Temp. (°F)	60.6	63.7	69.8	76.1	83.2	87.9	90.5	90.3	86.9	79.0	70.1	62.4	76.7
Mean Temp. (°F)	51.6	54.8	60.8	67.3	75.0	79.9	82.3	82.1	78.2	69.4	60.6	53.5	68.0
Mean Minimum Temp. (°F)	42.7	45.9	51.7	58.4	66.7	71.8	74.0	73.7	69.5	59.9	51.1	44.5	59.2
Extreme Maximum Temp. (°F)	80	79	87	94	95	99	103	102	100	92	84	81	103
Extreme Minimum Temp. (°F)	4	15	22	34	46	52	66	59	46	35	27	9	4
Days Maximum Temp. ≥ 90°F	0	0	0	0	2	9	17	19	8	0	0	0	55
Days Maximum Temp. ≤ 32°F	0	0	0	0	0	0	0	0	0	0	0	0	0
Days Minimum Temp. ≤ 32°F	6	3	1	0	0	0	0	0	0	0	1	4	15
Days Minimum Temp. ≤ 0°F	0	0	0	0	0	0	0	0	0	0	0	0	0
Heating Degree Days (base 65°F)	412	289	165	47	2	0	0	0	1	37	171	361	1,485
Cooling Degree Days (base 65°F)	4	8	41	123	318	453	542	536	403	182	47	11	2,668
Mean Precipitation (in.)	5.78	5.15	5.75	5.38	5.22	6.47	7.37	6.09	5.82	3.40	4.79	4.47	65.69
Extreme Maximum Daily Precip. (in.)	8.00	5.53	5.21	8.00	7.92	7.95	6.86	7.30	8.85	2.80	6.20	5.80	8.85
Days With ≥ 0.1" Precipitation	7	6	6	5	5	8	9	9	6	4	5	6	76
Days With ≥ 0.5" Precipitation	3	3	4	3	3	4	4	4	3	2	3	3	39
Days With ≥ 1.0" Precipitation	2	2	2	2	2	2	2	2	1	1	2	2	22
Mean Snowfall (in.)	0.0	0.0	0.1	0.0	0.0	0.0	0.0	0.0	0.0	0.0	0.0	trace	0.1
Maximum Snow Depth (in.)	0	0	0	0	0	0	0	0	0	0	0	0	0
Days With ≥ 1.0" Snow Depth	0	0	0	0	0	0	0	0	0	0	0	0	0

Hattiesburg 5 SW *Forrest County* Elevation: 384 ft. Latitude: 31° 15' N Longitude: 89° 20' W

	JAN	FEB	MAR	APR	MAY	JUN	JUL	AUG	SEP	OCT	NOV	DEC	YEAR
Mean Maximum Temp. (°F)	59.4	63.5	70.9	77.4	84.3	89.6	91.7	91.6	87.6	78.7	69.8	61.4	77.2
Mean Temp. (°F)	48.2	51.9	59.0	65.4	73.2	79.1	81.6	81.4	76.8	66.7	57.8	50.2	65.9
Mean Minimum Temp. (°F)	37.0	40.3	47.1	53.4	62.0	68.6	71.3	71.2	66.0	54.6	45.8	38.9	54.7
Extreme Maximum Temp. (°F)	80	84	89	93	97	101	105	104	102	95	90	83	105
Extreme Minimum Temp. (°F)	4	15	17	31	40	49	62	56	44	32	26	4	4
Days Maximum Temp. ≥ 90°F	0	0	0	0	4	17	23	23	13	2	0	0	82
Days Maximum Temp. ≤ 32°F	0	0	0	0	0	0	0	0	0	0	0	0	0
Days Minimum Temp. ≤ 32°F	12	7	2	0	0	0	0	0	0	0	3	10	34
Days Minimum Temp. ≤ 0°F	0	0	0	0	0	0	0	0	0	0	0	0	0
Heating Degree Days (base 65°F)	518	375	216	81	7	0	0	0	3	77	238	464	1,979
Cooling Degree Days (base 65°F)	5	10	38	101	267	431	520	515	365	136	30	11	2,429
Mean Precipitation (in.)	6.42	5.68	5.73	5.17	4.69	4.81	5.52	5.64	4.61	3.88	4.77	5.52	62.44
Extreme Maximum Daily Precip. (in.)	9.85	4.08	5.05	10.68	6.70	5.11	6.10	9.00	7.78	4.30	4.02	4.48	10.68
Days With ≥ 0.1" Precipitation	8	7	7	5	6	7	8	8	6	5	6	7	80
Days With ≥ 0.5" Precipitation	4	4	4	3	3	3	4	4	3	2	3	4	41
Days With ≥ 1.0" Precipitation	2	2	2	2	1	1	2	2	1	1	2	2	20
Mean Snowfall (in.)	0.1	trace	0.1	0.0	0.0	0.0	0.0	0.0	0.0	0.0	0.0	0.1	0.3
Maximum Snow Depth (in.)	trace	trace	0	0	0	0	0	0	0	0	0	3	3
Days With ≥ 1.0" Snow Depth	0	0	0	0	0	0	0	0	0	0	0	0	0

The period of record for all cooperative weather station data is 1980 – 2009. See User Guide for detailed explanation of data.

Hernando 5 S *De Soto County* Elevation: 379 ft. Latitude: 34° 45' N Longitude: 89° 59' W

	JAN	FEB	MAR	APR	MAY	JUN	JUL	AUG	SEP	OCT	NOV	DEC	YEAR
Mean Maximum Temp. (°F)	50.3	55.2	64.1	73.3	81.3	88.6	91.3	91.3	85.4	74.5	63.1	52.3	72.6
Mean Temp. (°F)	40.9	45.1	53.3	61.9	70.5	78.0	81.1	80.5	73.9	62.9	52.8	43.1	62.0
Mean Minimum Temp. (°F)	31.4	35.0	42.4	50.6	59.7	67.4	70.8	69.5	62.4	51.2	42.3	33.9	51.4
Extreme Maximum Temp. (°F)	80	80	91	97	97	103	106	112	103	99	87	81	112
Extreme Minimum Temp. (°F)	-6	3	14	27	36	49	56	51	39	27	18	-5	-6
Days Maximum Temp. ≥ 90°F	0	0	0	0	3	13	21	19	9	1	0	0	66
Days Maximum Temp. ≤ 32°F	2	1	0	0	0	0	0	0	0	0	0	2	5
Days Minimum Temp. ≤ 32°F	17	12	6	1	0	0	0	0	0	1	6	15	58
Days Minimum Temp. ≤ 0°F	0	0	0	0	0	0	0	0	0	0	0	0	0
Heating Degree Days (base 65°F)	741	557	372	151	21	1	0	0	14	138	370	673	3,038
Cooling Degree Days (base 65°F)	1	1	16	66	200	398	506	486	289	79	10	2	2,054
Mean Precipitation (in.)	4.26	4.41	5.28	5.76	5.61	4.80	3.76	3.42	2.92	4.21	4.64	5.66	54.73
Extreme Maximum Daily Precip. (in.)	3.46	3.30	3.73	3.05	***4.35***	4.99	4.06	3.70	3.21	4.20	4.70	***3.58***	***4.99***
Days With ≥ 0.1" Precipitation	7	6	7	7	7	6	6	4	4	5	6	7	72
Days With ≥ 0.5" Precipitation	3	3	4	4	3	3	3	2	2	3	3	3	36
Days With ≥ 1.0" Precipitation	1	1	1	2	2	2	1	1	1	2	2	2	18
Mean Snowfall (in.)	1.6	0.7	0.4	0.0	0.0	0.0	0.0	0.0	0.0	trace	0.1	0.2	3.0
Maximum Snow Depth (in.)	10	7	6	0	0	0	0	0	0	trace	trace	2	10
Days With ≥ 1.0" Snow Depth	1	1	0	0	0	0	0	0	0	0	0	0	2

Independence 1 W *Tate County* Elevation: 345 ft. Latitude: 34° 42' N Longitude: 89° 49' W

	JAN	FEB	MAR	APR	MAY	JUN	JUL	AUG	SEP	OCT	NOV	DEC	YEAR
Mean Maximum Temp. (°F)	48.7	53.5	62.1	71.2	79.1	86.2	89.2	89.6	83.7	73.1	62.1	51.4	70.8
Mean Temp. (°F)	39.1	43.0	51.1	59.7	68.3	75.8	79.1	78.5	71.9	60.6	50.9	41.6	60.0
Mean Minimum Temp. (°F)	29.5	32.5	40.1	48.1	57.5	65.4	68.9	67.4	60.0	48.1	39.6	31.8	49.1
Extreme Maximum Temp. (°F)	76	80	85	93	94	101	105	106	104	93	86	77	106
Extreme Minimum Temp. (°F)	-8	-1	11	24	35	45	53	46	36	23	15	-5	-8
Days Maximum Temp. ≥ 90°F	0	0	0	0	1	8	16	16	6	0	0	0	47
Days Maximum Temp. ≤ 32°F	3	1	0	0	0	0	0	0	0	0	0	2	6
Days Minimum Temp. ≤ 32°F	20	15	8	2	0	0	0	0	0	2	9	17	73
Days Minimum Temp. ≤ 0°F	0	0	0	0	0	0	0	0	0	0	0	0	0
Heating Degree Days (base 65°F)	796	615	433	202	44	2	0	1	24	185	426	720	3,448
Cooling Degree Days (base 65°F)	1	1	10	47	153	333	444	426	236	55	8	1	1,715
Mean Precipitation (in.)	4.05	4.21	5.01	4.80	5.27	4.44	4.23	3.26	3.50	4.13	4.44	5.50	52.84
Extreme Maximum Daily Precip. (in.)	3.59	3.35	4.11	2.82	3.95	4.59	5.68	4.13	4.47	4.37	3.92	4.78	5.68
Days With ≥ 0.1" Precipitation	6	7	7	7	7	6	6	4	5	5	6	7	73
Days With ≥ 0.5" Precipitation	3	3	4	4	3	3	3	2	2	3	3	3	36
Days With ≥ 1.0" Precipitation	1	1	1	2	2	1	1	1	1	2	1	2	16
Mean Snowfall (in.)	1.1	0.8	0.3	0.0	0.0	0.0	0.0	0.0	0.0	0.0	trace	0.1	2.3
Maximum Snow Depth (in.)	8	3	3	0	0	0	0	0	0	0	0	2	8
Days With ≥ 1.0" Snow Depth	0	0	0	0	0	0	0	0	0	0	0	0	0

Iuka 5s *Tishomingo County* Elevation: 470 ft. Latitude: 34° 44' N Longitude: 88° 11' W

	JAN	FEB	MAR	APR	MAY	JUN	JUL	AUG	SEP	OCT	NOV	DEC	YEAR
Mean Maximum Temp. (°F)	49.6	53.9	62.6	71.8	79.2	85.8	89.1	89.5	***83.7***	73.2	62.6	51.8	***71.1***
Mean Temp. (°F)	38.5	41.9	49.8	58.1	66.5	73.9	77.7	77.1	***70.3***	59.0	49.6	40.6	***58.6***
Mean Minimum Temp. (°F)	27.4	29.9	36.9	44.2	53.9	62.0	66.2	64.6	56.9	44.7	36.6	29.3	46.0
Extreme Maximum Temp. (°F)	75	82	86	94	94	100	105	106	100	92	87	77	106
Extreme Minimum Temp. (°F)	-12	-2	7	21	32	40	52	43	34	23	14	-6	-12
Days Maximum Temp. ≥ 90°F	0	0	0	0	1	9	15	14	6	0	0	0	45
Days Maximum Temp. ≤ 32°F	2	2	0	0	0	0	0	0	0	0	0	2	6
Days Minimum Temp. ≤ 32°F	21	18	12	4	0	0	0	0	0	4	13	20	92
Days Minimum Temp. ≤ 0°F	0	0	0	0	0	0	0	0	0	0	0	0	0
Heating Degree Days (base 65°F)	815	646	471	232	62	4	0	1	***32***	215	462	751	***3,691***
Cooling Degree Days (base 65°F)	0	0	6	31	117	278	400	383	***199***	35	4	1	***1,454***
Mean Precipitation (in.)	5.04	5.23	5.81	5.07	5.47	4.24	4.19	3.98	4.06	3.90	5.45	6.87	59.31
Extreme Maximum Daily Precip. (in.)	5.95	6.40	4.62	3.68	5.70	4.08	4.10	7.12	6.35	3.35	4.70	8.00	8.00
Days With ≥ 0.1" Precipitation	7	7	8	7	8	6	7	6	5	5	7	9	82
Days With ≥ 0.5" Precipitation	3	4	4	3	4	3	3	2	2	2	4	5	39
Days With ≥ 1.0" Precipitation	2	1	2	1	2	1	1	1	1	1	2	2	17
Mean Snowfall (in.)	1.0	0.8	0.2	trace	0.0	0.0	0.0	0.0	0.0	0.0	trace	0.3	2.3
Maximum Snow Depth (in.)	4	4	2	trace	0	0	0	0	0	***0***	trace	1	***4***
Days With ≥ 1.0" Snow Depth	0	1	0	0	0	0	0	0	0	0	0	0	1

Louisville *Winston County* Elevation: 581 ft. Latitude: 33° 08' N Longitude: 89° 04' W

	JAN	FEB	MAR	APR	MAY	JUN	JUL	AUG	SEP	OCT	NOV	DEC	YEAR
Mean Maximum Temp. (°F)	53.2	57.6	66.6	73.7	80.9	87.5	90.2	89.6	84.6	74.5	64.6	55.7	73.2
Mean Temp. (°F)	43.0	46.6	54.9	61.7	70.2	77.0	79.9	79.4	73.8	63.1	53.7	45.3	62.4
Mean Minimum Temp. (°F)	32.7	35.5	43.2	49.6	59.4	66.5	69.6	69.1	63.0	51.7	42.7	35.0	51.5
Extreme Maximum Temp. (°F)	79	87	88	92	96	101	104	107	100	97	85	81	107
Extreme Minimum Temp. (°F)	-3	3	12	26	40	47	52	49	41	28	21	-3	-3
Days Maximum Temp. ≥ 90°F	0	0	0	0	1	12	18	17	7	1	0	0	56
Days Maximum Temp. ≤ 32°F	1	1	0	0	0	0	0	0	0	0	0	1	3
Days Minimum Temp. ≤ 32°F	16	11	5	1	0	0	0	0	0	0	5	14	52
Days Minimum Temp. ≤ 0°F	0	0	0	0	0	0	0	0	0	0	0	0	0
Heating Degree Days (base 65°F)	676	518	321	150	24	1	0	0	12	129	346	605	2,782
Cooling Degree Days (base 65°F)	1	3	17	56	192	367	470	452	284	79	13	3	1,937
Mean Precipitation (in.)	4.82	***5.62***	5.48	5.02	5.17	4.31	4.99	3.98	3.68	4.53	4.42	5.35	***57.37***
Extreme Maximum Daily Precip. (in.)	3.03	3.39	3.98	4.74	5.44	3.44	3.50	6.81	3.45	6.72	2.87	5.95	6.81
Days With ≥ 0.1" Precipitation	7	7	7	6	7	6	7	6	5	5	6	7	76
Days With ≥ 0.5" Precipitation	3	4	4	3	4	3	4	3	2	3	3	3	39
Days With ≥ 1.0" Precipitation	1	2	2	2	2	1	2	1	1	2	2	2	20
Mean Snowfall (in.)	0.2	0.1	trace	0.1	0.0	0.0	0.0	0.0	0.0	0.0	0.0	0.2	0.6
Maximum Snow Depth (in.)	trace	trace	0	3	0	0	0	0	0	0	0	0	3
Days With ≥ 1.0" Snow Depth	0	0	0	0	0	0	0	0	0	0	0	0	0

The period of record for all cooperative weather station data is 1980 – 2009. See User Guide for detailed explanation of data.

Oakley Exp Station *Hinds County* Elevation: 205 ft. Latitude: 32° 12' N Longitude: 90° 31' W

	JAN	FEB	MAR	APR	MAY	JUN	JUL	AUG	SEP	OCT	NOV	DEC	YEAR
Mean Maximum Temp. (°F)	56.9	61.5	69.1	76.2	83.5	89.5	92.8	92.5	87.9	78.7	68.5	59.0	76.3
Mean Temp. (°F)	45.4	49.4	56.9	63.9	72.2	78.4	81.7	80.8	75.2	65.0	55.6	48.0	64.4
Mean Minimum Temp. (°F)	33.8	37.2	44.7	51.5	60.7	67.4	70.5	69.0	62.4	51.3	42.6	36.6	52.3
Extreme Maximum Temp. (°F)	84	85	88	92	95	101	105	110	109	96	90	83	110
Extreme Minimum Temp. (°F)	2	9	12	27	39	48	56	50	37	26	18	1	1
Days Maximum Temp. ≥ 90°F	0	0	0	0	5	17	24	23	14	2	0	0	85
Days Maximum Temp. ≤ 32°F	1	0	0	0	0	0	0	0	0	0	0	0	1
Days Minimum Temp. ≤ 32°F	15	10	4	1	0	0	0	0	0	1	6	12	49
Days Minimum Temp. ≤ 0°F	0	0	0	0	0	0	0	0	0	0	0	0	0
Heating Degree Days (base 65°F)	606	442	273	112	15	0	0	0	10	105	300	529	2,392
Cooling Degree Days (base 65°F)	5	7	29	87	243	410	524	496	322	112	24	8	2,267
Mean Precipitation (in.)	5.53	5.03	5.81	5.25	4.68	5.07	4.19	4.43	3.68	4.34	5.17	5.39	58.57
Extreme Maximum Daily Precip. (in.)	5.06	3.20	4.76	6.42	3.71	4.00	7.20	5.01	5.35	4.59	4.53	4.80	7.20
Days With ≥ 0.1" Precipitation	7	6	7	5	6	7	6	6	5	5	5	6	71
Days With ≥ 0.5" Precipitation	3	3	4	3	3	3	3	2	2	3	3	4	36
Days With ≥ 1.0" Precipitation	2	2	2	2	2	1	1	1	1	1	2	2	19
Mean Snowfall (in.)	0.2	trace	0.0	trace	0.0	0.0	0.0	0.0	0.0	0.0	0.0	trace	0.2
Maximum Snow Depth (in.)	5	trace	0	trace	0	0	0	0	0	0	0	0	5
Days With ≥ 1.0" Snow Depth	0	0	0	0	0	0	0	0	0	0	0	0	0

Pascagoula 3 NE *Jackson County* Elevation: 11 ft. Latitude: 30° 24' N Longitude: 88° 29' W

	JAN	FEB	MAR	APR	MAY	JUN	JUL	AUG	SEP	OCT	NOV	DEC	YEAR
Mean Maximum Temp. (°F)	60.5	63.1	68.9	75.2	81.8	86.7	89.3	89.3	86.2	78.5	70.3	62.6	76.0
Mean Temp. (°F)	50.5	53.2	59.2	65.5	73.0	78.8	81.3	81.1	77.2	68.0	59.5	52.2	66.6
Mean Minimum Temp. (°F)	40.3	43.3	49.6	55.8	64.1	70.8	73.2	72.9	68.3	57.5	48.6	41.7	57.2
Extreme Maximum Temp. (°F)	77	80	85	92	93	101	104	101	99	92	85	81	104
Extreme Minimum Temp. (°F)	6	14	22	32	41	55	64	58	47	32	26	6	6
Days Maximum Temp. ≥ 90°F	0	0	0	0	1	6	14	14	6	0	0	0	41
Days Maximum Temp. ≤ 32°F	0	0	0	0	0	0	0	0	0	0	0	0	0
Days Minimum Temp. ≤ 32°F	8	4	1	0	0	0	0	0	0	0	2	7	22
Days Minimum Temp. ≤ 0°F	0	0	0	0	0	0	0	0	0	0	0	0	0
Heating Degree Days (base 65°F)	446	333	198	70	5	0	0	0	1	53	198	404	1,708
Cooling Degree Days (base 65°F)	3	6	27	93	259	420	512	507	375	154	38	12	2,406
Mean Precipitation (in.)	5.42	5.30	5.52	4.67	4.83	5.98	7.08	6.98	6.16	4.44	4.56	4.28	65.22
Extreme Maximum Daily Precip. (in.)	5.60	8.34	6.12	8.48	6.62	4.51	6.00	7.23	8.40	6.04	4.37	3.28	8.48
Days With ≥ 0.1" Precipitation	6	6	5	4	5	7	9	8	6	4	5	5	70
Days With ≥ 0.5" Precipitation	3	3	3	2	3	4	4	4	3	2	3	3	37
Days With ≥ 1.0" Precipitation	2	2	2	1	2	2	2	2	2	1	2	1	21
Mean Snowfall (in.)	0.0	0.0	trace	0.0	0.0	0.0	0.0	0.0	0.0	0.0	0.0	0.0	trace
Maximum Snow Depth (in.)	0	0	0	0	0	0	0	0	0	0	0	0	0
Days With ≥ 1.0" Snow Depth	0	0	0	0	0	0	0	0	0	0	0	0	0

Quitman 1 N *Clarke County* Elevation: 299 ft. Latitude: 32° 04' N Longitude: 88° 43' W

	JAN	FEB	MAR	APR	MAY	JUN	JUL	AUG	SEP	OCT	NOV	DEC	YEAR
Mean Maximum Temp. (°F)	57.0	62.2	69.4	76.6	83.8	89.2	91.6	91.4	86.7	76.9	67.9	59.3	76.0
Mean Temp. (°F)	45.4	49.8	56.4	63.1	71.4	77.6	80.4	79.8	74.4	63.3	55.0	47.8	63.7
Mean Minimum Temp. (°F)	33.8	37.4	43.3	49.6	58.9	66.0	69.1	68.2	62.0	49.6	42.1	36.2	51.3
Extreme Maximum Temp. (°F)	80	84	89	94	96	104	104	105	102	93	87	83	105
Extreme Minimum Temp. (°F)	0	7	11	27	39	42	58	54	39	22	20	2	0
Days Maximum Temp. ≥ 90°F	0	0	0	0	4	15	21	20	11	1	0	0	72
Days Maximum Temp. ≤ 32°F	0	0	0	0	0	0	0	0	0	0	0	0	0
Days Minimum Temp. ≤ 32°F	15	10	5	1	0	0	0	0	0	1	6	13	51
Days Minimum Temp. ≤ 0°F	0	0	0	0	0	0	0	0	0	0	0	0	0
Heating Degree Days (base 65°F)	604	429	286	123	14	0	0	0	10	129	311	535	2,441
Cooling Degree Days (base 65°F)	2	6	25	72	219	385	483	466	298	79	17	7	2,059
Mean Precipitation (in.)	5.77	4.86	5.77	5.09	3.93	4.44	4.69	3.40	3.53	3.75	4.57	4.74	54.54
Extreme Maximum Daily Precip. (in.)	5.75	3.09	3.84	5.06	3.79	3.93	3.91	5.42	4.46	na	3.53	4.34	na
Days With ≥ 0.1" Precipitation	7	6	6	6	5	6	7	6	4	4	5	5	67
Days With ≥ 0.5" Precipitation	3	3	4	3	2	3	3	2	2	2	3	3	33
Days With ≥ 1.0" Precipitation	2	2	2	2	2	1	1	1	1	1	2	2	19
Mean Snowfall (in.)	0.1	trace	0.1	0.1	0.0	0.0	0.0	0.0	0.0	0.0	0.0	trace	0.3
Maximum Snow Depth (in.)	trace	trace	3	0	0	0	0	0	0	0	0	trace	3
Days With ≥ 1.0" Snow Depth	0	0	0	0	0	0	0	0	0	0	0	0	0

Saucier Exp Forest *Harrison County* Elevation: 229 ft. Latitude: 30° 38' N Longitude: 89° 03' W

	JAN	FEB	MAR	APR	MAY	JUN	JUL	AUG	SEP	OCT	NOV	DEC	YEAR
Mean Maximum Temp. (°F)	62.6	66.2	72.4	78.4	84.9	89.8	91.6	91.2	87.4	80.1	71.4	64.2	78.4
Mean Temp. (°F)	52.0	55.3	61.1	67.1	74.2	79.6	81.8	81.5	77.5	69.0	60.4	53.7	67.8
Mean Minimum Temp. (°F)	41.4	44.3	49.6	55.7	63.5	69.4	71.8	71.7	67.5	57.9	49.4	43.1	57.1
Extreme Maximum Temp. (°F)	81	83	87	94	96	102	104	102	98	93	86	82	104
Extreme Minimum Temp. (°F)	4	11	19	30	44	52	62	58	45	29	25	7	4
Days Maximum Temp. ≥ 90°F	0	0	0	0	4	17	23	23	11	1	0	0	79
Days Maximum Temp. ≤ 32°F	0	0	0	0	0	0	0	0	0	0	0	0	0
Days Minimum Temp. ≤ 32°F	7	4	2	0	0	0	0	0	0	0	1	5	19
Days Minimum Temp. ≤ 0°F	0	0	0	0	0	0	0	0	0	0	0	0	0
Heating Degree Days (base 65°F)	404	284	162	50	2	0	0	0	1	42	174	361	1,480
Cooling Degree Days (base 65°F)	9	14	47	119	295	446	526	517	382	173	44	17	2,589
Mean Precipitation (in.)	5.70	5.42	6.59	5.31	5.69	6.18	7.45	7.00	5.62	3.95	4.91	5.43	69.25
Extreme Maximum Daily Precip. (in.)	6.54	6.31	6.40	8.24	10.77	7.35	4.82	8.68	14.05	4.04	6.13	7.13	14.05
Days With ≥ 0.1" Precipitation	7	6	6	5	6	8	10	10	7	5	6	6	82
Days With ≥ 0.5" Precipitation	3	3	4	3	3	4	5	4	3	2	3	3	40
Days With ≥ 1.0" Precipitation	2	2	2	2	2	2	2	2	1	2	2	2	23
Mean Snowfall (in.)	trace	trace	0.1	0.0	0.0	0.0	0.0	0.0	0.0	0.0	0.0	0.0	0.1
Maximum Snow Depth (in.)	trace	0	0	0	0	0	0	0	0	0	0	0	trace
Days With ≥ 1.0" Snow Depth	0	0	0	0	0	0	0	0	0	0	0	0	0

The period of record for all cooperative weather station data is 1980 – 2009. See User Guide for detailed explanation of data.

State University *Oktibbeha County* Elevation: 185 ft. Latitude: 33° 28' N Longitude: 88° 47' W

	JAN	FEB	MAR	APR	MAY	JUN	JUL	AUG	SEP	OCT	NOV	DEC	YEAR
Mean Maximum Temp. (°F)	53.1	57.6	66.4	74.2	81.7	88.3	91.6	91.6	86.0	75.7	65.5	55.6	73.9
Mean Temp. (°F)	42.4	46.3	54.5	62.1	70.6	77.8	81.2	80.5	74.3	63.0	53.8	44.9	62.6
Mean Minimum Temp. (°F)	32.0	35.0	42.6	50.0	59.5	67.1	70.8	69.3	62.4	50.3	42.0	34.0	51.3
Extreme Maximum Temp. (°F)	79	88	88	93	95	99	108	106	109	94	87	81	109
Extreme Minimum Temp. (°F)	-6	4	13	26	40	41	56	52	40	27	15	-8	-8
Days Maximum Temp. ≥ 90°F	0	0	0	0	3	14	21	21	9	1	0	0	69
Days Maximum Temp. ≤ 32°F	1	0	0	0	0	0	0	0	0	0	0	1	2
Days Minimum Temp. ≤ 32°F	17	12	5	1	0	0	0	0	0	1	6	15	57
Days Minimum Temp. ≤ 0°F	0	0	0	0	0	0	0	0	0	0	0	0	0
Heating Degree Days (base 65°F)	695	525	335	143	20	0	0	0	10	130	342	619	2,819
Cooling Degree Days (base 65°F)	1	3	17	64	202	390	510	487	295	74	13	2	2,058
Mean Precipitation (in.)	5.09	5.79	5.30	5.15	4.64	4.34	4.08	3.91	3.55	4.32	4.57	5.28	56.02
Extreme Maximum Daily Precip. (in.)	3.75	8.28	3.73	3.60	4.15	3.16	2.37	2.96	3.54	6.00	3.25	5.90	8.28
Days With ≥ 0.1" Precipitation	8	7	7	6	7	7	7	6	5	5	7	7	79
Days With ≥ 0.5" Precipitation	4	4	3	3	3	3	3	3	2	3	3	4	38
Days With ≥ 1.0" Precipitation	1	2	2	2	2	1	1	1	1	2	2	2	19
Mean Snowfall (in.)	0.2	0.1	trace	0.0	0.0	0.0	0.0	0.0	0.0	0.0	trace	trace	0.3
Maximum Snow Depth (in.)	4	trace	1	0	0	0	0	0	0	0	trace	trace	4
Days With ≥ 1.0" Snow Depth	0	0	0	0	0	0	0	0	0	0	0	0	0

Stoneville Exp Stn *Washington County* Elevation: 126 ft. Latitude: 33° 27' N Longitude: 90° 55' W

	JAN	FEB	MAR	APR	MAY	JUN	JUL	AUG	SEP	OCT	NOV	DEC	YEAR
Mean Maximum Temp. (°F)	51.5	56.0	65.0	74.3	82.9	89.4	91.7	91.8	86.2	76.3	64.4	53.9	73.6
Mean Temp. (°F)	42.4	46.4	54.6	63.6	72.7	79.5	82.0	81.2	74.7	64.3	53.8	44.7	63.3
Mean Minimum Temp. (°F)	33.2	36.8	44.1	52.8	62.5	69.7	72.4	70.6	63.1	52.2	43.1	35.5	53.0
Extreme Maximum Temp. (°F)	78	83	90	94	96	101	104	105	104	96	87	82	105
Extreme Minimum Temp. (°F)	3	12	16	32	45	52	58	52	42	28	23	4	3
Days Maximum Temp. ≥ 90°F	0	0	0	0	5	17	23	22	11	2	0	0	80
Days Maximum Temp. ≤ 32°F	2	1	0	0	0	0	0	0	0	0	0	1	4
Days Minimum Temp. ≤ 32°F	16	10	3	0	0	0	0	0	0	0	4	13	46
Days Minimum Temp. ≤ 0°F	0	0	0	0	0	0	0	0	0	0	0	0	0
Heating Degree Days (base 65°F)	696	522	334	124	12	0	0	0	12	115	342	625	2,782
Cooling Degree Days (base 65°F)	2	2	19	88	258	444	535	511	309	100	13	4	2,285
Mean Precipitation (in.)	4.74	4.42	4.87	4.90	4.87	3.56	3.67	2.48	3.60	4.30	4.92	5.47	51.80
Extreme Maximum Daily Precip. (in.)	4.07	2.29	3.38	6.33	4.38	3.69	2.97	2.70	7.43	5.70	6.44	5.30	7.43
Days With ≥ 0.1" Precipitation	7	6	7	6	7	5	6	4	5	5	6	7	71
Days With ≥ 0.5" Precipitation	3	3	3	3	3	2	2	2	2	3	3	3	32
Days With ≥ 1.0" Precipitation	1	1	2	2	1	1	1	1	1	2	2	2	17
Mean Snowfall (in.)	0.5	0.1	trace	trace	0.0	0.0	0.0	0.0	0.0	0.0	0.0	0.1	0.7
Maximum Snow Depth (in.)	4	trace	1	trace	0	0	0	0	0	0	0	trace	4
Days With ≥ 1.0" Snow Depth	0	0	0	0	0	0	0	0	0	0	0	0	0

Waveland *Hancock County* Elevation: 7 ft. Latitude: 30° 18' N Longitude: 89° 23' W

	JAN	FEB	MAR	APR	MAY	JUN	JUL	AUG	SEP	OCT	NOV	DEC	YEAR
Mean Maximum Temp. (°F)	59.8	63.2	68.7	75.5	82.8	87.6	89.9	89.9	86.2	78.3	69.5	61.7	76.1
Mean Temp. (°F)	49.9	53.2	58.8	65.6	73.7	79.0	81.2	81.1	77.0	68.0	59.1	51.7	66.5
Mean Minimum Temp. (°F)	39.9	43.2	48.9	55.6	64.6	70.4	72.4	72.3	67.8	57.6	48.7	41.8	56.9
Extreme Maximum Temp. (°F)	79	88	85	94	95	99	103	104	95	92	85	81	104
Extreme Minimum Temp. (°F)	6	15	22	28	42	44	61	59	43	33	26	8	6
Days Maximum Temp. ≥ 90°F	0	0	0	0	1	9	17	17	6	1	0	0	51
Days Maximum Temp. ≤ 32°F	0	0	0	0	0	0	0	0	0	0	0	0	0
Days Minimum Temp. ≤ 32°F	8	4	2	0	0	0	0	0	0	0	2	7	23
Days Minimum Temp. ≤ 0°F	0	0	0	0	0	0	0	0	0	0	0	0	0
Heating Degree Days (base 65°F)	464	332	211	74	4	0	0	0	2	58	204	412	1,761
Cooling Degree Days (base 65°F)	2	5	25	98	281	427	508	507	368	157	35	8	2,421
Mean Precipitation (in.)	6.18	4.97	5.85	5.19	5.37	6.38	6.68	5.26	6.20	3.75	5.05	4.79	65.67
Extreme Maximum Daily Precip. (in.)	9.35	4.80	5.38	5.65	9.08	7.75	7.24	3.35	7.72	5.10	6.68	5.75	9.35
Days With ≥ 0.1" Precipitation	7	6	6	4	5	8	9	8	7	5	5	6	76
Days With ≥ 0.5" Precipitation	3	3	3	3	3	4	4	3	4	2	3	3	38
Days With ≥ 1.0" Precipitation	2	1	2	2	2	2	2	2	2	1	2	2	22
Mean Snowfall (in.)	trace	trace	trace	0.0	0.0	0.0	0.0	0.0	0.0	0.0	0.0	trace	trace
Maximum Snow Depth (in.)	trace	1	1	0	0	0	0	0	0	0	0	trace	1
Days With ≥ 1.0" Snow Depth	0	0	0	0	0	0	0	0	0	0	0	0	0

Wiggins *Stone County* Elevation: 160 ft. Latitude: 30° 52' N Longitude: 89° 08' W

	JAN	FEB	MAR	APR	MAY	JUN	JUL	AUG	SEP	OCT	NOV	DEC	YEAR
Mean Maximum Temp. (°F)	60.5	64.7	72.0	78.0	84.6	89.8	91.8	91.5	87.6	80.1	70.4	63.6	77.9
Mean Temp. (°F)	48.5	51.9	58.9	65.3	72.8	78.7	81.1	81.0	76.5	67.6	57.9	51.4	66.0
Mean Minimum Temp. (°F)	36.4	39.0	45.7	52.6	61.0	67.6	70.4	70.4	65.3	55.1	45.3	39.1	54.0
Extreme Maximum Temp. (°F)	80	82	89	91	97	102	105	108	101	94	86	82	108
Extreme Minimum Temp. (°F)	1	10	20	30	42	53	57	58	46	31	21	8	1
Days Maximum Temp. ≥ 90°F	0	0	0	0	5	16	23	23	10	2	0	0	79
Days Maximum Temp. ≤ 32°F	0	0	0	0	0	0	0	0	0	0	0	0	0
Days Minimum Temp. ≤ 32°F	13	8	3	0	0	0	0	0	0	0	3	9	36
Days Minimum Temp. ≤ 0°F	0	0	0	0	0	0	0	0	0	0	0	0	0
Heating Degree Days (base 65°F)	509	373	215	73	4	0	0	0	2	60	237	424	1,897
Cooling Degree Days (base 65°F)	5	8	31	90	254	419	507	501	353	148	31	8	2,355
Mean Precipitation (in.)	5.10	5.43	6.47	5.49	4.50	5.25	6.41	4.94	5.49	3.95	4.51	5.95	63.49
Extreme Maximum Daily Precip. (in.)	7.30	8.20	7.30	7.90	na	6.55	5.10	5.28	na	6.40	4.25	7.90	na
Days With ≥ 0.1" Precipitation	6	6	6	5	5	7	9	7	5	4	5	5	70
Days With ≥ 0.5" Precipitation	3	3	4	3	3	3	4	3	2	2	3	3	36
Days With ≥ 1.0" Precipitation	2	2	2	2	1	1	2	1	1	1	2	2	19
Mean Snowfall (in.)	0.0	0.0	0.1	0.0	0.0	0.0	0.0	0.0	0.0	0.0	0.0	0.0	0.1
Maximum Snow Depth (in.)	0	0	3	0	0	0	0	0	0	0	0	0	3
Days With ≥ 1.0" Snow Depth	0	0	0	0	0	0	0	0	0	0	0	0	0

The period of record for all cooperative weather station data is 1980 – 2009. See User Guide for detailed explanation of data.

Mississippi Weather Station Rankings

Annual Extreme Maximum Temperature

Highest Rank	Highest Station Name	Highest °F	Lowest Rank	Lowest Station Name	Lowest °F
1	Hernando 5 S	112	1	Gulfport Naval Center	103
2	Oakley Exp Station	110	2	Bay St Louis Nasa	104
3	State University	109	2	Biloxi	***104***
4	Columbus Luxapallila	108	2	Forest 3 S	104
4	Fulton 3 W	108	2	Pascagoula 3 NE	104
4	Wiggins	***108***	2	Saucier Exp Forest	104
7	Batesville 2 SW	107	2	Waveland	***104***
7	Belzoni	***107***	8	D Lo 2 SW	105
7	Canton	***107***	8	Hattiesburg 5 SW	105
7	Jackson Thompson Field	107	8	Quitman 1 N	***105***
7	Louisville	107	8	Stoneville Exp Stn	***105***
7	Meridian Key Field	107	12	Aberdeen	106
7	Tupelo C D Lemons Arpt	107	12	Booneville	106
14	Aberdeen	106	12	Brookhaven City	106
14	Booneville	106	12	Calhoun City 2 NW	106
14	Brookhaven City	106	12	Eupora 2 E	106
14	Calhoun City 2 NW	106	12	Independence 1 W	106
14	Eupora 2 E	106	12	Iuka 5s	106
14	Independence 1 W	106	19	Batesville 2 SW	107
14	Iuka 5s	106	19	Belzoni	***107***
21	D Lo 2 SW	105	19	Canton	***107***
21	Hattiesburg 5 SW	105	19	Jackson Thompson Field	107
21	Quitman 1 N	***105***	19	Louisville	107
21	Stoneville Exp Stn	***105***	19	Meridian Key Field	107
25	Bay St Louis Nasa	104	19	Tupelo C D Lemons Arpt	107

Annual Mean Maximum Temperature

Highest Rank	Highest Station Name	Highest °F	Lowest Rank	Lowest Station Name	Lowest °F
1	Saucier Exp Forest	78.4	1	Booneville	70.8
2	Bay St Louis Nasa	78.1	1	Independence 1 W	70.8
3	Wiggins	***77.9***	3	Iuka 5s	***71.1***
4	Hattiesburg 5 SW	77.2	4	Batesville 2 SW	72.6
5	Gulfport Naval Center	76.7	4	Hernando 5 S	72.6
6	Meridian Key Field	76.6	6	Tupelo C D Lemons Arpt	73.1
7	Biloxi	***76.5***	7	Louisville	73.2
8	Oakley Exp Station	***76.4***	8	Fulton 3 W	73.5
9	Forest 3 S	76.3	9	Stoneville Exp Stn	73.6
10	Jackson Thompson Field	76.2	10	Aberdeen	73.7
11	Waveland	***76.1***	11	Calhoun City 2 NW	73.9
12	Brookhaven City	76.0	11	State University	73.9
12	Pascagoula 3 NE	76.0	13	Eupora 2 E	74.5
12	Quitman 1 N	***76.0***	14	Columbus Luxapallila	74.6
15	D Lo 2 SW	75.8	15	Belzoni	75.0
16	Canton	***75.6***	16	Canton	***75.6***
17	Belzoni	75.0	17	D Lo 2 SW	75.8
18	Columbus Luxapallila	74.6	18	Brookhaven City	76.0
19	Eupora 2 E	74.5	18	Pascagoula 3 NE	76.0
20	Calhoun City 2 NW	73.9	18	Quitman 1 N	***76.0***
20	State University	73.9	21	Waveland	***76.1***
22	Aberdeen	73.7	22	Jackson Thompson Field	76.2
23	Stoneville Exp Stn	73.6	23	Forest 3 S	76.3
24	Fulton 3 W	73.5	24	Oakley Exp Station	***76.4***
25	Louisville	73.2	25	Biloxi	***76.5***

Rankings include 25 highest/lowest stations. If state has less than 25 stations, all stations are included. The period of record is 1980–2009. See User Guide for detailed explanation of data.

Annual Mean Temperature

Highest

Rank	Station Name	°F
1	Biloxi	***68.4***
2	Gulfport Naval Center	68.0
3	Saucier Exp Forest	67.8
4	Bay St Louis Nasa	66.9
5	Pascagoula 3 NE	66.6
6	Waveland	***66.5***
7	Hattiesburg 5 SW	66.0
7	Wiggins	***66.0***
9	Jackson Thompson Field	64.9
10	Meridian Key Field	64.6
11	Belzoni	64.4
11	Oakley Exp Station	***64.4***
13	Brookhaven City	64.2
14	Forest 3 S	63.9
15	Canton	***63.8***
16	Quitman 1 N	***63.7***
17	Columbus Luxapallila	63.4
18	D Lo 2 SW	63.3
18	Stoneville Exp Stn	63.3
20	Aberdeen	62.8
21	State University	62.6
22	Eupora 2 E	62.4
22	Louisville	62.4
24	Calhoun City 2 NW	62.3
25	Tupelo C D Lemons Arpt	62.2

Lowest

Rank	Station Name	°F
1	Iuka 5s	***58.6***
2	Independence 1 W	60.0
3	Booneville	60.5
4	Batesville 2 SW	61.2
5	Fulton 3 W	62.0
5	Hernando 5 S	62.0
7	Tupelo C D Lemons Arpt	62.2
8	Calhoun City 2 NW	62.3
9	Eupora 2 E	62.4
9	Louisville	62.4
11	State University	62.6
12	Aberdeen	62.8
13	D Lo 2 SW	63.3
13	Stoneville Exp Stn	63.3
15	Columbus Luxapallila	63.4
16	Quitman 1 N	***63.7***
17	Canton	***63.8***
18	Forest 3 S	63.9
19	Brookhaven City	64.2
20	Belzoni	64.4
20	Oakley Exp Station	***64.4***
22	Meridian Key Field	64.6
23	Jackson Thompson Field	64.9
24	Hattiesburg 5 SW	66.0
24	Wiggins	***66.0***

Annual Mean Minimum Temperature

Highest

Rank	Station Name	°F
1	Biloxi	***60.2***
2	Gulfport Naval Center	59.2
3	Pascagoula 3 NE	57.2
4	Saucier Exp Forest	57.1
5	Waveland	***56.9***
6	Bay St Louis Nasa	55.6
7	Hattiesburg 5 SW	54.7
8	Wiggins	***54.0***
9	Belzoni	53.7
10	Jackson Thompson Field	53.6
11	Stoneville Exp Stn	53.0
12	Meridian Key Field	52.5
13	Oakley Exp Station	***52.3***
14	Brookhaven City	52.2
14	Columbus Luxapallila	52.2
16	Canton	***51.9***
17	Aberdeen	51.8
18	Forest 3 S	51.5
18	Louisville	51.5
20	Hernando 5 S	51.4
21	Quitman 1 N	***51.3***
21	State University	51.3
21	Tupelo C D Lemons Arpt	51.3
24	D Lo 2 SW	50.8
25	Calhoun City 2 NW	50.6

Lowest

Rank	Station Name	°F
1	Iuka 5s	46.0
2	Independence 1 W	49.1
3	Batesville 2 SW	49.8
4	Booneville	50.1
5	Eupora 2 E	50.2
6	Fulton 3 W	50.4
7	Calhoun City 2 NW	50.6
8	D Lo 2 SW	50.8
9	Quitman 1 N	***51.3***
9	State University	51.3
9	Tupelo C D Lemons Arpt	51.3
12	Hernando 5 S	51.4
13	Forest 3 S	51.5
13	Louisville	51.5
15	Aberdeen	51.8
16	Canton	***51.9***
17	Brookhaven City	52.2
17	Columbus Luxapallila	52.2
19	Oakley Exp Station	***52.3***
20	Meridian Key Field	52.5
21	Stoneville Exp Stn	53.0
22	Jackson Thompson Field	53.6
23	Belzoni	53.7
24	Wiggins	***54.0***
25	Hattiesburg 5 SW	54.7

Rankings include 25 highest/lowest stations. If state has less than 25 stations, all stations are included. The period of record is 1980–2009. See User Guide for detailed explanation of data.

Annual Extreme Minimum Temperature

Highest

Rank	Station Name	°F
1	Biloxi	***10***
2	Pascagoula 3 NE	6
2	Waveland	***6***
4	Bay St Louis Nasa	5
5	Gulfport Naval Center	4
5	Hattiesburg 5 SW	4
5	Saucier Exp Forest	4
8	Brookhaven City	3
8	Stoneville Exp Stn	***3***
10	Canton	***2***
10	Jackson Thompson Field	2
10	Meridian Key Field	2
13	Belzoni	1
13	Oakley Exp Station	1
13	Wiggins	***1***
16	D Lo 2 SW	0
16	Quitman 1 N	***0***
18	Forest 3 S	-1
19	Louisville	-3
20	Columbus Luxapallila	-4
20	Eupora 2 E	-4
22	Aberdeen	-5
23	Hernando 5 S	-6
23	Tupelo C D Lemons Arpt	-6
25	Batesville 2 SW	-8

Lowest

Rank	Station Name	°F
1	Iuka 5s	-12
2	Fulton 3 W	-9
3	Batesville 2 SW	-8
3	Booneville	-8
3	Calhoun City 2 NW	-8
3	Independence 1 W	-8
3	State University	-8
8	Hernando 5 S	-6
8	Tupelo C D Lemons Arpt	-6
10	Aberdeen	-5
11	Columbus Luxapallila	-4
11	Eupora 2 E	-4
13	Louisville	-3
14	Forest 3 S	-1
15	D Lo 2 SW	0
15	Quitman 1 N	***0***
17	Belzoni	1
17	Oakley Exp Station	1
17	Wiggins	***1***
20	Canton	***2***
20	Jackson Thompson Field	2
20	Meridian Key Field	2
23	Brookhaven City	3
23	Stoneville Exp Stn	***3***
25	Gulfport Naval Center	4

July Mean Maximum Temperature

Highest

Rank	Station Name	°F
1	Oakley Exp Station	92.8
2	Belzoni	92.7
3	Meridian Key Field	92.5
4	Canton	92.4
4	Jackson Thompson Field	92.4
6	Columbus Luxapallila	92.0
7	Bay St Louis Nasa	91.8
7	Wiggins	***91.8***
9	Hattiesburg 5 SW	91.7
9	Stoneville Exp Stn	91.7
11	Aberdeen	91.6
11	Quitman 1 N	***91.6***
11	Saucier Exp Forest	91.6
11	State University	91.6
15	Forest 3 S	91.5
15	Tupelo C D Lemons Arpt	91.5
17	D Lo 2 SW	91.3
17	Eupora 2 E	91.3
17	Hernando 5 S	91.3
20	Fulton 3 W	91.1
21	Brookhaven City	91.0
22	Batesville 2 SW	90.8
22	Calhoun City 2 NW	90.8
24	Gulfport Naval Center	90.5
25	Biloxi	***90.2***

Lowest

Rank	Station Name	°F
1	Independence 1 W	89.2
1	Iuka 5s	89.2
3	Pascagoula 3 NE	89.3
4	Booneville	89.4
5	Waveland	89.9
6	Biloxi	***90.2***
6	Louisville	90.2
8	Gulfport Naval Center	90.5
9	Batesville 2 SW	90.8
9	Calhoun City 2 NW	90.8
11	Brookhaven City	91.0
12	Fulton 3 W	91.1
13	D Lo 2 SW	91.3
13	Eupora 2 E	91.3
13	Hernando 5 S	91.3
16	Forest 3 S	91.5
16	Tupelo C D Lemons Arpt	91.5
18	Aberdeen	91.6
18	Quitman 1 N	***91.6***
18	Saucier Exp Forest	91.6
18	State University	91.6
22	Hattiesburg 5 SW	91.7
22	Stoneville Exp Stn	91.7
24	Bay St Louis Nasa	91.8
24	Wiggins	***91.8***

Rankings include 25 highest/lowest stations. If state has less than 25 stations, all stations are included. The period of record is 1980–2009. See User Guide for detailed explanation of data.

January Mean Minimum Temperature

Highest			Lowest		
Rank	Station Name	°F	Rank	Station Name	°F
1	Biloxi	***43.5***	1	Iuka 5s	27.4
2	Gulfport Naval Center	42.7	2	Independence 1 W	29.5
3	Saucier Exp Forest	41.4	3	Booneville	30.2
4	Pascagoula 3 NE	40.3	4	Batesville 2 SW	30.6
5	Waveland	39.9	5	Hernando 5 S	31.5
6	Bay St Louis Nasa	38.9	6	Calhoun City 2 NW	31.9
7	Hattiesburg 5 SW	37.0	7	Eupora 2 E	32.0
8	Wiggins	***36.4***	7	Fulton 3 W	32.0
9	Jackson Thompson Field	35.5	7	State University	32.0
10	Meridian Key Field	34.8	10	Tupelo C D Lemons Arpt	32.1
11	Brookhaven City	34.6	11	Aberdeen	32.6
12	Belzoni	34.5	12	Louisville	32.7
13	Canton	***33.9***	13	D Lo 2 SW	33.0
13	Forest 3 S	33.9	14	Stoneville Exp Stn	33.2
15	Oakley Exp Station	33.8	15	Columbus Luxapallila	33.7
15	Quitman 1 N	***33.8***	16	Oakley Exp Station	33.8
17	Columbus Luxapallila	33.7	16	Quitman 1 N	***33.8***
18	Stoneville Exp Stn	33.2	18	Canton	***33.9***
19	D Lo 2 SW	33.0	18	Forest 3 S	33.9
20	Louisville	32.7	20	Belzoni	34.5
21	Aberdeen	32.6	21	Brookhaven City	34.6
22	Tupelo C D Lemons Arpt	32.1	22	Meridian Key Field	34.8
23	Eupora 2 E	32.0	23	Jackson Thompson Field	35.5
23	Fulton 3 W	32.0	24	Wiggins	***36.4***
23	State University	32.0	25	Hattiesburg 5 SW	37.0

Number of Days Annually Maximum Temperature ≥ 90°F

Highest			Lowest		
Rank	Station Name	Days	Rank	Station Name	Days
1	Belzoni	90	1	Pascagoula 3 NE	41
2	Oakley Exp Station	85	2	Booneville	44
3	Meridian Key Field	84	3	Iuka 5s	45
4	Jackson Thompson Field	83	4	Independence 1 W	47
5	Hattiesburg 5 SW	82	5	Biloxi	***50***
6	Canton	***80***	6	Waveland	***51***
6	Stoneville Exp Stn	80	7	Gulfport Naval Center	55
8	Saucier Exp Forest	79	8	Louisville	56
8	Wiggins	***79***	9	Calhoun City 2 NW	58
10	Bay St Louis Nasa	78	10	Fulton 3 W	62
11	Columbus Luxapallila	74	11	Batesville 2 SW	64
12	Forest 3 S	73	12	Aberdeen	65
13	D Lo 2 SW	72	13	Eupora 2 E	66
13	Quitman 1 N	***72***	13	Hernando 5 S	66
15	Brookhaven City	70	15	Tupelo C D Lemons Arpt	68
16	State University	69	16	State University	69
17	Tupelo C D Lemons Arpt	68	17	Brookhaven City	70
18	Eupora 2 E	66	18	D Lo 2 SW	72
18	Hernando 5 S	66	18	Quitman 1 N	***72***
20	Aberdeen	65	20	Forest 3 S	73
21	Batesville 2 SW	64	21	Columbus Luxapallila	74
22	Fulton 3 W	62	22	Bay St Louis Nasa	78
23	Calhoun City 2 NW	58	23	Saucier Exp Forest	79
24	Louisville	56	23	Wiggins	***79***
25	Gulfport Naval Center	55	25	Canton	***80***

Rankings include 25 highest/lowest stations. If state has less than 25 stations, all stations are included. The period of record is 1980–2009. See User Guide for detailed explanation of data.

Number of Days Annually Maximum Temperature ≤ 32°F

Highest			Lowest		
Rank	Station Name	Days	Rank	Station Name	Days
1	Independence 1 W	6	1	Bay St Louis Nasa	0
1	Iuka 5s	6	1	Biloxi	***0***
3	Booneville	5	1	Brookhaven City	0
3	Hernando 5 S	5	1	Forest 3 S	0
5	Batesville 2 SW	4	1	Gulfport Naval Center	0
5	Stoneville Exp Stn	4	1	Hattiesburg 5 SW	0
7	Belzoni	3	1	Jackson Thompson Field	0
7	Fulton 3 W	3	1	Meridian Key Field	0
7	Louisville	3	1	Pascagoula 3 NE	0
7	Tupelo C D Lemons Arpt	3	1	Quitman 1 N	***0***
11	Aberdeen	2	1	Saucier Exp Forest	0
11	Calhoun City 2 NW	2	1	Waveland	***0***
11	Canton	***2***	1	Wiggins	***0***
11	Columbus Luxapallila	2	14	D Lo 2 SW	1
11	Eupora 2 E	2	14	Oakley Exp Station	1
11	State University	2	16	Aberdeen	2
17	D Lo 2 SW	1	16	Calhoun City 2 NW	2
17	Oakley Exp Station	1	16	Canton	***2***
19	Bay St Louis Nasa	0	16	Columbus Luxapallila	2
19	Biloxi	***0***	16	Eupora 2 E	2
19	Brookhaven City	0	16	State University	2
19	Forest 3 S	0	22	Belzoni	3
19	Gulfport Naval Center	0	22	Fulton 3 W	3
19	Hattiesburg 5 SW	0	22	Louisville	3
19	Jackson Thompson Field	0	22	Tupelo C D Lemons Arpt	3

Number of Days Annually Minimum Temperature ≤ 32°F

Highest			Lowest		
Rank	Station Name	Days	Rank	Station Name	Days
1	Iuka 5s	92	1	Biloxi	***11***
2	Independence 1 W	73	2	Gulfport Naval Center	15
3	Batesville 2 SW	70	3	Saucier Exp Forest	19
4	Booneville	65	4	Pascagoula 3 NE	22
5	Eupora 2 E	64	5	Waveland	***23***
6	D Lo 2 SW	63	6	Bay St Louis Nasa	30
6	Fulton 3 W	63	7	Hattiesburg 5 SW	34
8	Calhoun City 2 NW	62	8	Wiggins	***36***
9	Hernando 5 S	58	9	Belzoni	***38***
10	State University	57	10	Jackson Thompson Field	45
10	Tupelo C D Lemons Arpt	57	11	Stoneville Exp Stn	46
12	Aberdeen	55	12	Brookhaven City	48
13	Forest 3 S	54	13	Oakley Exp Station	49
14	Canton	***53***	14	Meridian Key Field	50
15	Louisville	52	15	Columbus Luxapallila	51
16	Columbus Luxapallila	51	15	Quitman 1 N	***51***
16	Quitman 1 N	***51***	17	Louisville	52
18	Meridian Key Field	50	18	Canton	***53***
19	Oakley Exp Station	49	19	Forest 3 S	54
20	Brookhaven City	48	20	Aberdeen	55
21	Stoneville Exp Stn	46	21	State University	57
22	Jackson Thompson Field	45	21	Tupelo C D Lemons Arpt	57
23	Belzoni	***38***	23	Hernando 5 S	58
24	Wiggins	***36***	24	Calhoun City 2 NW	62
25	Hattiesburg 5 SW	34	25	D Lo 2 SW	63

Rankings include 25 highest/lowest stations. If state has less than 25 stations, all stations are included. The period of record is 1980–2009. See User Guide for detailed explanation of data.

Number of Days Annually Minimum Temperature ≤ 0°F

Highest

Rank	Station Name	Days
1	Aberdeen	0
1	Batesville 2 SW	0
1	Bay St Louis Nasa	0
1	Belzoni	0
1	Biloxi	***0***
1	Booneville	0
1	Brookhaven City	0
1	Calhoun City 2 NW	0
1	Canton	***0***
1	Columbus Luxapallila	0
1	D Lo 2 SW	0
1	Eupora 2 E	0
1	Forest 3 S	0
1	Fulton 3 W	0
1	Gulfport Naval Center	0
1	Hattiesburg 5 SW	0
1	Hernando 5 S	0
1	Independence 1 W	0
1	Iuka 5s	0
1	Jackson Thompson Field	0
1	Louisville	0
1	Meridian Key Field	0
1	Oakley Exp Station	0
1	Pascagoula 3 NE	0
1	Quitman 1 N	***0***

Lowest

Rank	Station Name	Days
1	Aberdeen	0
1	Batesville 2 SW	0
1	Bay St Louis Nasa	0
1	Belzoni	0
1	Biloxi	***0***
1	Booneville	0
1	Brookhaven City	0
1	Calhoun City 2 NW	0
1	Canton	***0***
1	Columbus Luxapallila	0
1	D Lo 2 SW	0
1	Eupora 2 E	0
1	Forest 3 S	0
1	Fulton 3 W	0
1	Gulfport Naval Center	0
1	Hattiesburg 5 SW	0
1	Hernando 5 S	0
1	Independence 1 W	0
1	Iuka 5s	0
1	Jackson Thompson Field	0
1	Louisville	0
1	Meridian Key Field	0
1	Oakley Exp Station	0
1	Pascagoula 3 NE	0
1	Quitman 1 N	***0***

Number of Annual Heating Degree Days

Highest

Rank	Station Name	Num.
1	Iuka 5s	***3,691***
2	Independence 1 W	3,448
3	Booneville	3,308
4	Batesville 2 SW	3,184
5	Hernando 5 S	3,038
6	Tupelo C D Lemons Arpt	2,934
7	Fulton 3 W	2,893
8	State University	2,819
9	Calhoun City 2 NW	2,804
10	Louisville	2,782
10	Stoneville Exp Stn	2,782
12	Aberdeen	2,778
13	Eupora 2 E	2,776
14	Columbus Luxapallila	2,626
15	D Lo 2 SW	2,550
16	Belzoni	***2,526***
17	Canton	***2,525***
18	Quitman 1 N	***2,441***
19	Oakley Exp Station	***2,392***
20	Forest 3 S	2,346
21	Brookhaven City	2,314
22	Meridian Key Field	2,300
23	Jackson Thompson Field	2,295
24	Hattiesburg 5 SW	1,979
25	Wiggins	***1,897***

Lowest

Rank	Station Name	Num.
1	Biloxi	***1,429***
2	Saucier Exp Forest	1,480
3	Gulfport Naval Center	1,485
4	Pascagoula 3 NE	1,708
5	Bay St Louis Nasa	1,712
6	Waveland	***1,761***
7	Wiggins	***1,897***
8	Hattiesburg 5 SW	1,979
9	Jackson Thompson Field	2,295
10	Meridian Key Field	2,300
11	Brookhaven City	2,314
12	Forest 3 S	2,346
13	Oakley Exp Station	***2,392***
14	Quitman 1 N	***2,441***
15	Canton	***2,525***
16	Belzoni	***2,526***
17	D Lo 2 SW	2,550
18	Columbus Luxapallila	2,626
19	Eupora 2 E	2,776
20	Aberdeen	2,778
21	Louisville	2,782
21	Stoneville Exp Stn	2,782
23	Calhoun City 2 NW	2,804
24	State University	2,819
25	Fulton 3 W	2,893

Rankings include 25 highest/lowest stations. If state has less than 25 stations, all stations are included. The period of record is 1980–2009. See User Guide for detailed explanation of data.

Number of Annual Cooling Degree Days

Highest

Rank	Station Name	Num.
1	Biloxi	***2,778***
2	Gulfport Naval Center	2,668
3	Saucier Exp Forest	2,589
4	Bay St Louis Nasa	2,496
5	Hattiesburg 5 SW	2,429
6	Waveland	***2,421***
7	Pascagoula 3 NE	2,406
8	Belzoni	2,404
9	Jackson Thompson Field	2,366
10	Wiggins	***2,355***
11	Stoneville Exp Stn	2,285
12	Oakley Exp Station	***2,267***
13	Meridian Key Field	2,240
14	Canton	***2,197***
15	Columbus Luxapallila	2,162
16	Brookhaven City	2,109
17	Aberdeen	2,072
18	Quitman 1 N	***2,059***
19	State University	2,058
20	Hernando 5 S	2,054
21	Forest 3 S	2,051
22	D Lo 2 SW	2,047
23	Tupelo C D Lemons Arpt	2,030
24	Louisville	1,937
25	Eupora 2 E	1,926

Lowest

Rank	Station Name	Num.
1	Iuka 5s	***1,454***
2	Independence 1 W	1,715
3	Booneville	1,775
4	Batesville 2 SW	1,908
4	Calhoun City 2 NW	1,908
4	Fulton 3 W	1,908
7	Eupora 2 E	1,926
8	Louisville	1,937
9	Tupelo C D Lemons Arpt	2,030
10	D Lo 2 SW	2,047
11	Forest 3 S	2,051
12	Hernando 5 S	2,054
13	State University	2,058
14	Quitman 1 N	***2,059***
15	Aberdeen	2,072
16	Brookhaven City	2,109
17	Columbus Luxapallila	2,162
18	Canton	***2,197***
19	Meridian Key Field	2,240
20	Oakley Exp Station	***2,267***
21	Stoneville Exp Stn	2,285
22	Wiggins	***2,355***
23	Jackson Thompson Field	2,366
24	Belzoni	2,404
25	Pascagoula 3 NE	2,406

Annual Precipitation

Highest

Rank	Station Name	Inches
1	Saucier Exp Forest	69.25
2	Gulfport Naval Center	65.69
3	Waveland	***65.67***
4	Pascagoula 3 NE	65.22
5	Biloxi	***65.08***
6	Wiggins	***63.49***
7	Bay St Louis Nasa	62.76
8	Hattiesburg 5 SW	62.44
9	Brookhaven City	60.44
10	Fulton 3 W	60.03
11	Iuka 5s	59.31
12	Forest 3 S	59.13
13	Oakley Exp Station	58.57
14	Booneville	57.43
15	Louisville	***57.37***
16	D Lo 2 SW	57.36
17	Eupora 2 E	57.04
18	Meridian Key Field	56.98
19	Columbus Luxapallila	56.46
20	Belzoni	***56.41***
21	State University	56.02
22	Calhoun City 2 NW	55.55
23	Tupelo C D Lemons Arpt	55.51
24	Canton	***54.93***
25	Hernando 5 S	54.73

Lowest

Rank	Station Name	Inches
1	Stoneville Exp Stn	51.80
2	Independence 1 W	52.84
3	Batesville 2 SW	53.65
4	Aberdeen	54.12
5	Quitman 1 N	***54.54***
6	Jackson Thompson Field	54.63
7	Hernando 5 S	54.73
8	Canton	***54.93***
9	Tupelo C D Lemons Arpt	55.51
10	Calhoun City 2 NW	55.55
11	State University	56.02
12	Belzoni	***56.41***
13	Columbus Luxapallila	56.46
14	Meridian Key Field	56.98
15	Eupora 2 E	57.04
16	D Lo 2 SW	57.36
17	Louisville	***57.37***
18	Booneville	57.43
19	Oakley Exp Station	58.57
20	Forest 3 S	59.13
21	Iuka 5s	59.31
22	Fulton 3 W	60.03
23	Brookhaven City	60.44
24	Hattiesburg 5 SW	62.44
25	Bay St Louis Nasa	62.76

Rankings include 25 highest/lowest stations. If state has less than 25 stations, all stations are included. The period of record is 1980–2009. See User Guide for detailed explanation of data.

Annual Extreme Maximum Daily Precipitation

Highest

Rank	Station Name	Inches
1	Bay St Louis Nasa	***15.32***
2	Saucier Exp Forest	14.05
3	Biloxi	***11.30***
4	Hattiesburg 5 SW	10.68
5	Waveland	***9.35***
6	Batesville 2 SW	8.85
6	Gulfport Naval Center	8.85
8	Pascagoula 3 NE	***8.48***
9	State University	8.28
10	Booneville	8.13
11	Brookhaven City	8.08
12	Iuka 5s	8.00
13	Columbus Luxapallila	7.92
14	Eupora 2 E	7.89
14	Tupelo C D Lemons Arpt	7.89
16	Calhoun City 2 NW	7.62
17	Meridian Key Field	7.48
18	Stoneville Exp Stn	***7.43***
19	Jackson Thompson Field	7.38
20	Belzoni	***7.30***
21	Oakley Exp Station	***7.20***
22	Louisville	6.81
23	Forest 3 S	***6.80***
24	D Lo 2 SW	6.32
25	Fulton 3 W	6.28

Lowest

Rank	Station Name	Inches
1	Hernando 5 S	***4.99***
2	Independence 1 W	5.68
3	Canton	***5.82***
4	Aberdeen	6.13
5	Fulton 3 W	6.28
6	D Lo 2 SW	6.32
7	Forest 3 S	***6.80***
8	Louisville	6.81
9	Oakley Exp Station	***7.20***
10	Belzoni	***7.30***
11	Jackson Thompson Field	7.38
12	Stoneville Exp Stn	***7.43***
13	Meridian Key Field	7.48
14	Calhoun City 2 NW	7.62
15	Eupora 2 E	7.89
15	Tupelo C D Lemons Arpt	7.89
17	Columbus Luxapallila	7.92
18	Iuka 5s	8.00
19	Brookhaven City	8.08
20	Booneville	8.13
21	State University	8.28
22	Pascagoula 3 NE	***8.48***
23	Batesville 2 SW	8.85
23	Gulfport Naval Center	8.85
25	Waveland	***9.35***

Number of Days Annually With ≥ 0.1 Inches of Precipitation

Highest

Rank	Station Name	Days
1	Iuka 5s	82
1	Saucier Exp Forest	82
3	Booneville	81
3	Fulton 3 W	81
5	Hattiesburg 5 SW	80
6	State University	79
7	D Lo 2 SW	78
7	Meridian Key Field	78
7	Tupelo C D Lemons Arpt	78
10	Aberdeen	77
10	Columbus Luxapallila	77
12	Biloxi	***76***
12	Gulfport Naval Center	76
12	Louisville	76
12	Waveland	***76***
16	Brookhaven City	75
17	Forest 3 S	74
17	Jackson Thompson Field	74
19	Bay St Louis Nasa	73
19	Eupora 2 E	73
19	Independence 1 W	73
22	Hernando 5 S	72
23	Canton	***71***
23	Oakley Exp Station	71
23	Stoneville Exp Stn	71

Lowest

Rank	Station Name	Days
1	Batesville 2 SW	66
2	Calhoun City 2 NW	67
2	Quitman 1 N	***67***
4	Belzoni	***69***
5	Pascagoula 3 NE	70
5	Wiggins	***70***
7	Canton	***71***
7	Oakley Exp Station	71
7	Stoneville Exp Stn	71
10	Hernando 5 S	72
11	Bay St Louis Nasa	73
11	Eupora 2 E	73
11	Independence 1 W	73
14	Forest 3 S	74
14	Jackson Thompson Field	74
16	Brookhaven City	75
17	Biloxi	***76***
17	Gulfport Naval Center	76
17	Louisville	76
17	Waveland	***76***
21	Aberdeen	77
21	Columbus Luxapallila	77
23	D Lo 2 SW	78
23	Meridian Key Field	78
23	Tupelo C D Lemons Arpt	78

Rankings include 25 highest/lowest stations. If state has less than 25 stations, all stations are included. The period of record is 1980–2009. See User Guide for detailed explanation of data.

Number of Days Annually With ≥ 0.5 Inches of Precipitation

Highest

Rank	Station Name	Days
1	Booneville	41
1	Hattiesburg 5 SW	41
3	Brookhaven City	40
3	D Lo 2 SW	40
3	Fulton 3 W	40
3	Saucier Exp Forest	40
7	Forest 3 S	39
7	Gulfport Naval Center	39
7	Iuka 5s	39
7	Louisville	39
11	Bay St Louis Nasa	38
11	Biloxi	***38***
11	Meridian Key Field	38
11	State University	38
11	Waveland	***38***
16	Canton	***37***
16	Columbus Luxapallila	37
16	Eupora 2 E	37
16	Pascagoula 3 NE	37
20	Aberdeen	36
20	Hernando 5 S	36
20	Independence 1 W	36
20	Jackson Thompson Field	36
20	Oakley Exp Station	36
20	Tupelo C D Lemons Arpt	36

Lowest

Rank	Station Name	Days
1	Stoneville Exp Stn	32
2	Batesville 2 SW	33
2	Quitman 1 N	***33***
4	Belzoni	***35***
4	Calhoun City 2 NW	35
6	Aberdeen	36
6	Hernando 5 S	36
6	Independence 1 W	36
6	Jackson Thompson Field	36
6	Oakley Exp Station	36
6	Tupelo C D Lemons Arpt	36
6	Wiggins	***36***
13	Canton	***37***
13	Columbus Luxapallila	37
13	Eupora 2 E	37
13	Pascagoula 3 NE	37
17	Bay St Louis Nasa	38
17	Biloxi	***38***
17	Meridian Key Field	38
17	State University	38
17	Waveland	***38***
22	Forest 3 S	39
22	Gulfport Naval Center	39
22	Iuka 5s	39
22	Louisville	39

Number of Days Annually With ≥ 1.0 Inches of Precipitation

Highest

Rank	Station Name	Days
1	Saucier Exp Forest	23
2	Gulfport Naval Center	22
2	Waveland	***22***
4	Brookhaven City	21
4	Fulton 3 W	21
4	Pascagoula 3 NE	21
7	Belzoni	***20***
7	Biloxi	***20***
7	Canton	***20***
7	D Lo 2 SW	20
7	Eupora 2 E	20
7	Forest 3 S	20
7	Hattiesburg 5 SW	20
7	Louisville	20
15	Calhoun City 2 NW	19
15	Meridian Key Field	19
15	Oakley Exp Station	19
15	Quitman 1 N	***19***
15	State University	19
15	Wiggins	***19***
21	Batesville 2 SW	18
21	Bay St Louis Nasa	18
21	Hernando 5 S	18
21	Jackson Thompson Field	18
25	Aberdeen	17

Lowest

Rank	Station Name	Days
1	Independence 1 W	16
2	Aberdeen	17
2	Booneville	17
2	Columbus Luxapallila	17
2	Iuka 5s	17
2	Stoneville Exp Stn	17
2	Tupelo C D Lemons Arpt	17
8	Batesville 2 SW	18
8	Bay St Louis Nasa	18
8	Hernando 5 S	18
8	Jackson Thompson Field	18
12	Calhoun City 2 NW	19
12	Meridian Key Field	19
12	Oakley Exp Station	19
12	Quitman 1 N	***19***
12	State University	19
12	Wiggins	***19***
18	Belzoni	***20***
18	Biloxi	***20***
18	Canton	***20***
18	D Lo 2 SW	20
18	Eupora 2 E	20
18	Forest 3 S	20
18	Hattiesburg 5 SW	20
18	Louisville	20

Rankings include 25 highest/lowest stations. If state has less than 25 stations, all stations are included. The period of record is 1980–2009. See User Guide for detailed explanation of data.

Annual Snowfall

Highest Rank	Station Name	Inches	Lowest Rank	Station Name	Inches
1	Hernando 5 S	3.0	1	Bay St Louis Nasa	Trace
2	Independence 1 W	2.3	1	Belzoni	*Trace*
2	Iuka 5s	2.3	1	Pascagoula 3 NE	Trace
4	Booneville	2.1	1	Waveland	*Trace*
5	Fulton 3 W	1.6	5	Biloxi	*0.1*
6	Calhoun City 2 NW	1.2	5	Brookhaven City	0.1
7	Batesville 2 SW	1.0	5	Gulfport Naval Center	0.1
8	Eupora 2 E	0.9	5	Saucier Exp Forest	0.1
9	Stoneville Exp Stn	*0.7*	5	Wiggins	*0.1*
10	Aberdeen	0.6	10	Oakley Exp Station	0.2
10	D Lo 2 SW	0.6	11	Canton	*0.3*
10	Louisville	0.6	11	Columbus Luxapallila	0.3
13	Canton	*0.3*	11	Forest 3 S	0.3
13	Columbus Luxapallila	0.3	11	Hattiesburg 5 SW	0.3
13	Forest 3 S	0.3	11	Quitman 1 N	*0.3*
13	Hattiesburg 5 SW	0.3	11	State University	0.3
13	Quitman 1 N	*0.3*	17	Aberdeen	0.6
13	State University	0.3	17	D Lo 2 SW	0.6
19	Oakley Exp Station	0.2	17	Louisville	0.6
20	Biloxi	*0.1*	20	Stoneville Exp Stn	*0.7*
20	Brookhaven City	0.1	21	Eupora 2 E	0.9
20	Gulfport Naval Center	0.1	22	Batesville 2 SW	1.0
20	Saucier Exp Forest	0.1	23	Calhoun City 2 NW	1.2
20	Wiggins	*0.1*	24	Fulton 3 W	1.6
25	Bay St Louis Nasa	Trace	25	Booneville	2.1

Annual Maximum Snow Depth

Highest Rank	Station Name	Inches	Lowest Rank	Station Name	Inches
1	Hernando 5 S	10	1	Gulfport Naval Center	0
2	Booneville	8	1	Pascagoula 3 NE	0
2	Independence 1 W	8	3	Canton	Trace
4	Batesville 2 SW	6	3	Columbus Luxapallila	Trace
4	Eupora 2 E	6	3	Saucier Exp Forest	Trace
6	Aberdeen	5	6	Belzoni	*1*
6	Calhoun City 2 NW	5	6	Biloxi	*1*
6	Fulton 3 W	5	6	Waveland	*1*
6	Oakley Exp Station	5	9	Bay St Louis Nasa	2
10	D Lo 2 SW	4	10	Brookhaven City	3
10	Forest 3 S	4	10	Hattiesburg 5 SW	3
10	Iuka 5s	*4*	10	Louisville	3
10	State University	*4*	10	Quitman 1 N	*3*
10	Stoneville Exp Stn	*4*	10	Wiggins	*3*
15	Brookhaven City	3	15	D Lo 2 SW	4
15	Hattiesburg 5 SW	3	15	Forest 3 S	4
15	Louisville	3	15	Iuka 5s	*4*
15	Quitman 1 N	*3*	15	State University	*4*
15	Wiggins	*3*	15	Stoneville Exp Stn	*4*
20	Bay St Louis Nasa	2	20	Aberdeen	5
21	Belzoni	*1*	20	Calhoun City 2 NW	5
21	Biloxi	*1*	20	Fulton 3 W	5
21	Waveland	*1*	20	Oakley Exp Station	5
24	Canton	Trace	24	Batesville 2 SW	6
24	Columbus Luxapallila	Trace	24	Eupora 2 E	6

Rankings include 25 highest/lowest stations. If state has less than 25 stations, all stations are included. The period of record is 1980–2009. See User Guide for detailed explanation of data.

Number of Days Annually With ≥ 1.0 Inch Snow Depth

Highest

Rank	Station Name	Days
1	Booneville	2
1	Hernando 5 S	2
3	Iuka 5s	1
4	Aberdeen	0
4	Batesville 2 SW	0
4	Bay St Louis Nasa	0
4	Belzoni	*0*
4	Biloxi	*0*
4	Brookhaven City	0
4	Calhoun City 2 NW	0
4	Canton	*0*
4	Columbus Luxapallila	0
4	D Lo 2 SW	0
4	Eupora 2 E	0
4	Forest 3 S	0
4	Fulton 3 W	0
4	Gulfport Naval Center	0
4	Hattiesburg 5 SW	0
4	Independence 1 W	0
4	Louisville	0
4	Oakley Exp Station	0
4	Pascagoula 3 NE	0
4	Quitman 1 N	*0*
4	Saucier Exp Forest	0
4	State University	0

Lowest

Rank	Station Name	Days
1	Aberdeen	0
1	Batesville 2 SW	0
1	Bay St Louis Nasa	0
1	Belzoni	*0*
1	Biloxi	*0*
1	Brookhaven City	0
1	Calhoun City 2 NW	0
1	Canton	*0*
1	Columbus Luxapallila	0
1	D Lo 2 SW	0
1	Eupora 2 E	0
1	Forest 3 S	0
1	Fulton 3 W	0
1	Gulfport Naval Center	0
1	Hattiesburg 5 SW	0
1	Independence 1 W	0
1	Louisville	0
1	Oakley Exp Station	0
1	Pascagoula 3 NE	0
1	Quitman 1 N	*0*
1	Saucier Exp Forest	0
1	State University	0
1	Stoneville Exp Stn	*0*
1	Waveland	*0*
1	Wiggins	*0*

Rankings include 25 highest/lowest stations. If state has less than 25 stations, all stations are included. The period of record is 1980–2009. See User Guide for detailed explanation of data.

Significant Storm Events in Mississippi: 2000 – 2009

Location or County	Date	Type	Mag.	Deaths	Injuries	Property Damage ($mil.)	Crop Damage ($mil.)
Lauderdale	12/16/00	Tornado	F2	0	17	2.1	0.0
Lowndes	02/16/01	Thunderstorm Wind	na	0	0	11.0	0.0
Pontotoc	02/24/01	Tornado	F3	6	43	28.0	0.0
Prentiss	02/24/01	Tornado	F3	0	30	2.0	0.0
Madison	11/24/01	Tornado	F4	2	21	12.0	0.0
Bolivar	11/24/01	Tornado	F4	0	36	6.0	0.0
Quitman	11/24/01	Tornado	F2	2	16	5.0	0.0
Washington	11/24/01	Tornado	F4	0	12	3.5	0.0
Panola	11/24/01	Tornado	F2	1	12	2.0	0.0
Hancock, Harrison, Jackson and Pearl River Counties	09/25/02	Tropical Storm	na	1	0	25.0	0.0
Southern Mississippi	10/02/02	Tropical Storm	na	0	0	13.3	0.0
Lowndes	11/10/02	Tornado	F3	0	55	60.0	0.0
Scott	04/06/03	Flash Flood	na	1	0	50.0	0.0
Madison	04/06/03	Flash Flood	na	0	0	50.0	0.0
Newton	04/06/03	Flash Flood	na	0	0	30.0	0.0
Rankin	04/06/03	Flash Flood	na	0	0	30.0	0.0
Hinds	04/06/03	Flash Flood	na	0	0	20.0	0.0
Lauderdale	04/07/03	Flash Flood	na	0	0	50.0	0.0
Rankin	04/24/03	Tornado	F3	0	6	50.0	0.0
Warren	03/13/05	Hail	2.75 in.	0	1	20.0	0.0
Southeast Mississippi	08/27/05	Hurricane Katrina	na	0	0	250.0	0.0
Mississippi Coast	08/28/05	Hurricane Katrina	na	0	0	7,350.0	0.0
Mississippi Gulf Coast	08/29/05	Hurricane Katrina	na	15	104	5,880.0	1,510.0
Lowndes	03/09/06	Thunderstorm Wind	92 mph	0	3	15.0	0.0
Lowndes	01/10/08	Tornado	F3	0	11	7.0	0.0
Lafayette	02/05/08	Tornado	F3	0	14	35.0	0.0
De Soto	02/05/08	Tornado	F2	0	0	28.4	0.0
Forrest	03/03/08	Tornado	F1	0	14	1.5	0.0
Simpson	03/26/09	Tornado	F3	0	25	5.0	0.0

Note: Deaths, injuries, and damages are date and location specific.

MISSOURI

PHYSICAL FEATURES. Missouri's three main terrain features are the rolling prairies of the area north of the Missouri River and in the west-central counties, the Ozarks, and the southeast lowlands, commonly called the "Bootheel." The flat lowlands of the Bootheel counties are about 250 feet above sea level. The highest elevation in the State is 1,772 feet above sea level on Taum Sauk Mountain in Iron County, in the eastern Ozarks, but the largest area of high elevation is in the central Ozarks, in Webster County, where elevations of 1,600 to 1,700 feet are common. The northwestern part of Missouri has extensive areas above 1,000 feet and some over 1,200. The northeastern part of the State slopes down to about 700 feet above sea level near the Mississippi River. The terrain varies from rugged areas bordering some of the larger streams, with deep valleys and steep hills, to broad, rolling uplands.

GENERAL CLIMATE. Missouri is an inland state, thus its climate is essentially continental. There are frequent changes in the weather, both from day to day and from season to season. Missouri is in the path of cold air moving down out of Canada, warm, moist air coming up from the Gulf of Mexico, and dry air from the west.

Annual precipitation in Missouri averages from near 50 inches in the southeastern corner to about 32 inches in the northwest. In the southeastern counties much of the precipitation comes during the fall, winter, and early spring months. In most of the western and northern counties the winter months are comparatively dry, with most of the precipitation coming in the spring, summer, and fall months.

Snow has been known to fall in Missouri as early as October, and as late as May. However, most of it falls in December, January, and February. As one would expect, the northern counties usually get the most snow. North of the Missouri River the winter snowfall averages 18 to 22 inches. This average figure tapers off to eight to 12 inches in the southernmost counties. It is unusual for snow to stay on the ground for more than a week or two before it melts. Winter precipitation usually is in the form of rain or snow, or both. Conditions sometimes are on the borderline between rain and snow, and in these situations freezing drizzle or freezing rain occurs. This does not usually happen more than twice in a winter season.

Spring, summer, and early fall precipitation comes largely in the form of showers or thunderstorms. Thunderstorms have been observed in Missouri during the winter months, but they are most frequent from April to July. Occasionally, these produce some very heavy rains. Measurable precipitation occurs on an average of about 100 days a year. About half of these will be days with thunderstorms.

The river drainage in Missouri is wholly, either directly or indirectly, into the Mississippi River which forms the eastern boundary of the State. The northern part of the western boundary is formed by the Missouri River which then flows eastward across the State from Kansas City, entering the Mississippi just above St. Louis. Most of northern Missouri is drained by tributaries of the Missouri River, the principal ones being the Grand, Charlton, One Hundred and Two, and the Nodaway Rivers. The principal southern tributaries of the Missouri are the Osage and the Gasconade. Important tributaries which drain directly into the Mississippi within the borders of the State are the Fox, Wyaconda, Fabius, and Salt Rivers in the northeast, and the Meramec River which enters the Mississippi just below St. Louis.

Tributary flooding resulting from heavy rains may be expected once or twice in most years, and flash flooding along minor streams following heavy thunderstorm rains, occur most frequently in the spring and early summer, April to July, but may occur during any month. Serious flooding occurs less frequently along the main stems of the Missouri and Mississippi Rivers and usually occurs during the spring and early summer. Main stem flooding may be caused by prolonged periods of heavy rains, ice jams, or upstream flood crests synchronized with high tributary discharge.

On the average the amount of water that falls in Missouri on a square mile in a year varies from near 600 million gallons in the northwest corner to over 800 million gallons in the southeast. Some of this water runs off into the rivers and streams, some is consumed by animal life, and large amounts are evaporated back into the atmosphere, or transpired by growing vegetation. During years when precipitation comes in a fairly normal manner, moisture is stored in the top layers of the soil during the winter and early spring, when evaporation and transpiration are low. During the summer months the loss of water by evaporation and transpiration is high, and if rainfall fails to occur at frequent intervals, drought will result. Nearly every year some areas have short periods of drought in Missouri.

Tornadoes have been observed during every month of the year, with about 70 percent occurring during the four months, March through June. Over 25 percent of the total number were reported during May for the month of greatest frequency. Paths of the Missouri tornadoes have been short, averaging only nine and a half miles. The width of tornado paths averages slightly less than 300 yards.

TEMPERATURE. Because of its inland location, Missouri is subject to frequent changes in temperature. While winters are cold and summers are hot, prolonged periods of very cold or very hot weather are unusual. Occasional periods of mild, above freezing temperatures are noted almost every winter. Conversely, during the peak of the summer season, occasional periods of dry, cool weather break up stretches of hot, humid weather.

Temperatures over 100°F. are rare, but they have occurred in every section of the State. In the summer, temperatures rise to 90°F. or higher on an average of 40 to 50 days in the west and north, and 55 to 60 days in the southeast. Temperatures below zero are infrequent, but have occurred in every county in Missouri. On the average there are two to five days a year with below zero temperatures in the northern counties, and one to two days in the southern counties, although there are some winters when temperatures do not go below zero at all.

In winter there is an average of about 110 days with temperatures below 32°F. in the northern half, the West Central Plains, and East Ozarks, about 100 days in the West Ozarks, and about 70 such days in the Bootheel counties. The average date of the first occurrence of temperatures 28 to 32°F. in the fall would come as early as mid-October in the northernmost counties and high elevations of the Ozarks, and as early as the third week in October over much of the rest of the State, except the Bootheel where the average date of the first freeze is in early November. About one year in 20, the first freeze would come as early as mid-September in the northern counties and late September in the rest of the State, except the Bootheel where it would occur as early as the third week in October.

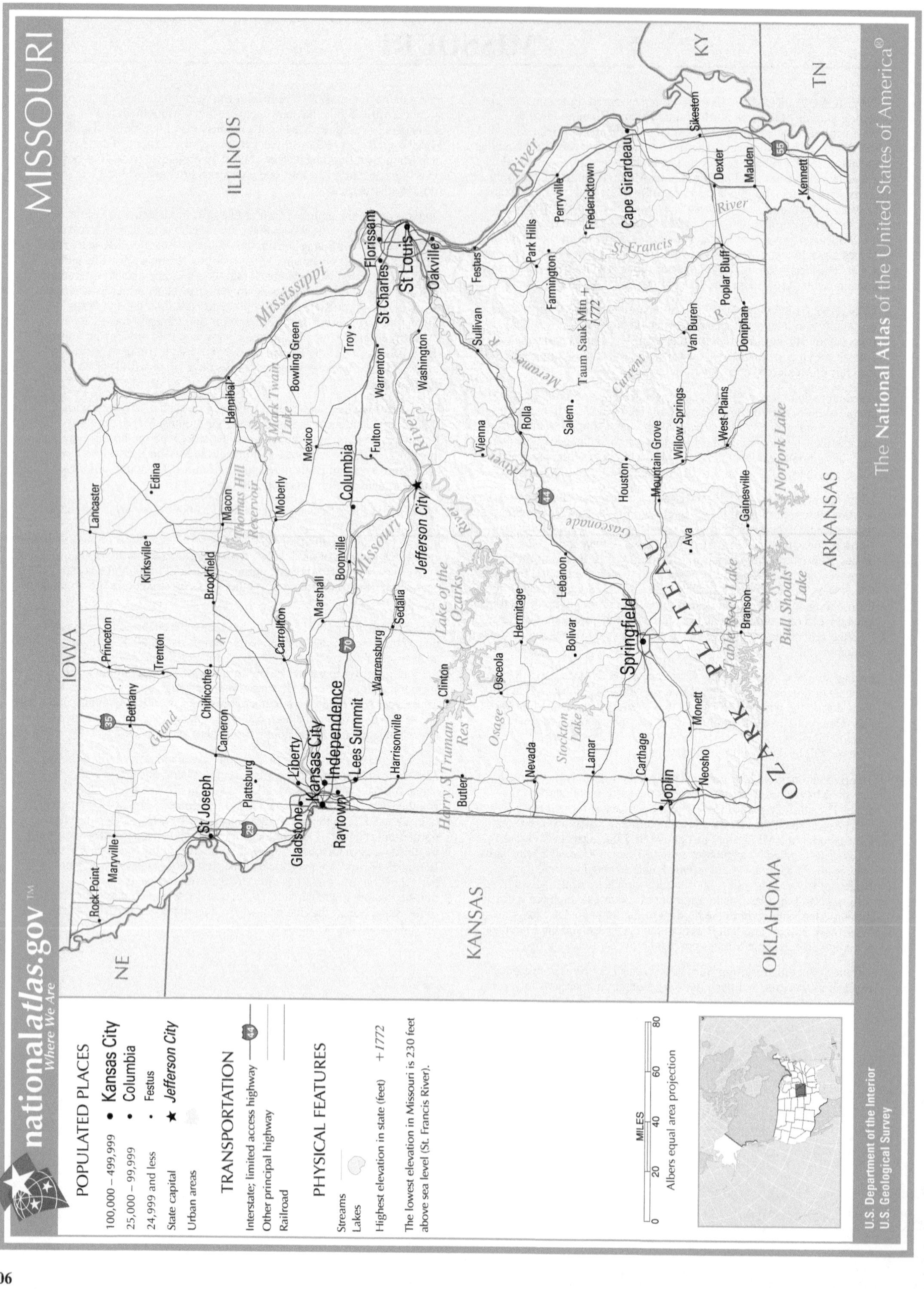
MISSOURI
nationalatlas.gov™
Where We Are
POPULATED PLACES
100,000 – 499,999 • Kansas City
25,000 – 99,999 • Columbia
24,999 and less • Festus
State capital ★ Jefferson City
Urban areas
TRANSPORTATION
Interstate; limited access highway 44
Other principal highway
Railroad
PHYSICAL FEATURES
Streams
Lakes
Highest elevation in state (feet) +1772
The lowest elevation in Missouri is 230 feet above sea level (St. Francis River).
MILES
0 20 40 60 80
Albers equal area projection
U.S. Department of the Interior
U.S. Geological Survey
The National Atlas of the United States of America®
IOWA
ILLINOIS
KANSAS
NE
OKLAHOMA
ARKANSAS
KY
TN
OZARK PLATEAU
Mississippi River
Missouri River
Grand R
Osage
Gasconade River
Meramec R
Current R
St Francis River
Mark Twain Lake
Thomas Hill Reservoir
Lake of the Ozarks
Harry S Truman Res
Stockton Lake
Table Rock Lake
Bull Shoals Lake
Norfork Lake
Taum Sauk Mtn + 1772
Rock Point
Maryville
St Joseph
Plattsburg
Gladstone
Kansas City
Liberty
Raytown
Independence
Lees Summit
Harrisonville
Butler
Nevada
Lamar
Carthage
Joplin
Neosho
Monett
Springfield
Branson
Bethany
Princeton
Trenton
Chillicothe
Cameron
Lancaster
Kirksville
Edina
Brookfield
Macon
Hannibal
Moberly
Carrollton
Marshall
Warrensburg
Clinton
Osceola
Bolivar
Hermitage
Sedalia
Boonville
Columbia
Jefferson City
Mexico
Fulton
Bowling Green
Troy
Warrenton
Washington
St Charles
Florissant
St Louis
Oakville
Festus
Sullivan
Vienna
Rolla
Lebanon
Ava
Gainesville
Houston
Mountain Grove
Willow Springs
West Plains
Salem
Van Buren
Doniphan
Poplar Bluff
Farmington
Park Hills
Fredericktown
Perryville
Cape Girardeau
Sikeston
Dexter
Malden
Kennett
35
29
70
44
55

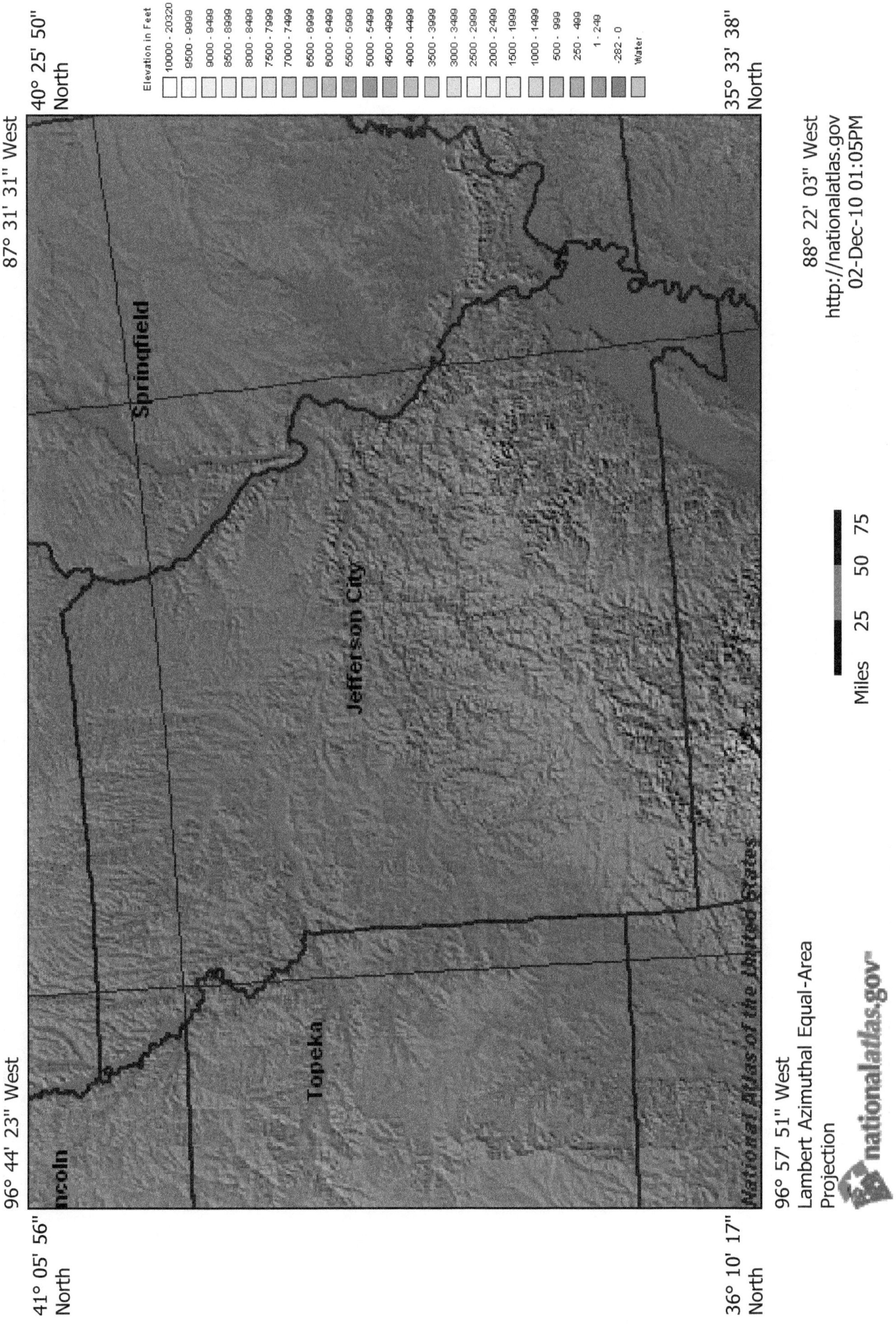
40° 25' 50" North
87° 31' 31" West
41° 05' 56" North
96° 44' 23" West
36° 10' 17" North
96° 57' 51" West
35° 33' 38" North
88° 22' 03" West
Elevation in Feet
10000 - 20320
9500 - 9999
9000 - 9499
8500 - 8999
8000 - 8499
7500 - 7999
7000 - 7499
6500 - 6999
6000 - 6499
5500 - 5999
5000 - 5499
4500 - 4999
4000 - 4499
3500 - 3999
3000 - 3499
2500 - 2999
2000 - 2499
1500 - 1999
1000 - 1499
500 - 999
250 - 499
1 - 249
-282 - 0
Water
Springfield
Jefferson City
Topeka
ncoln
National Atlas of the United States
Miles 25 50 75
Lambert Azimuthal Equal-Area Projection
http://nationalatlas.gov
02-Dec-10 01:05PM
nationalatlas.gov

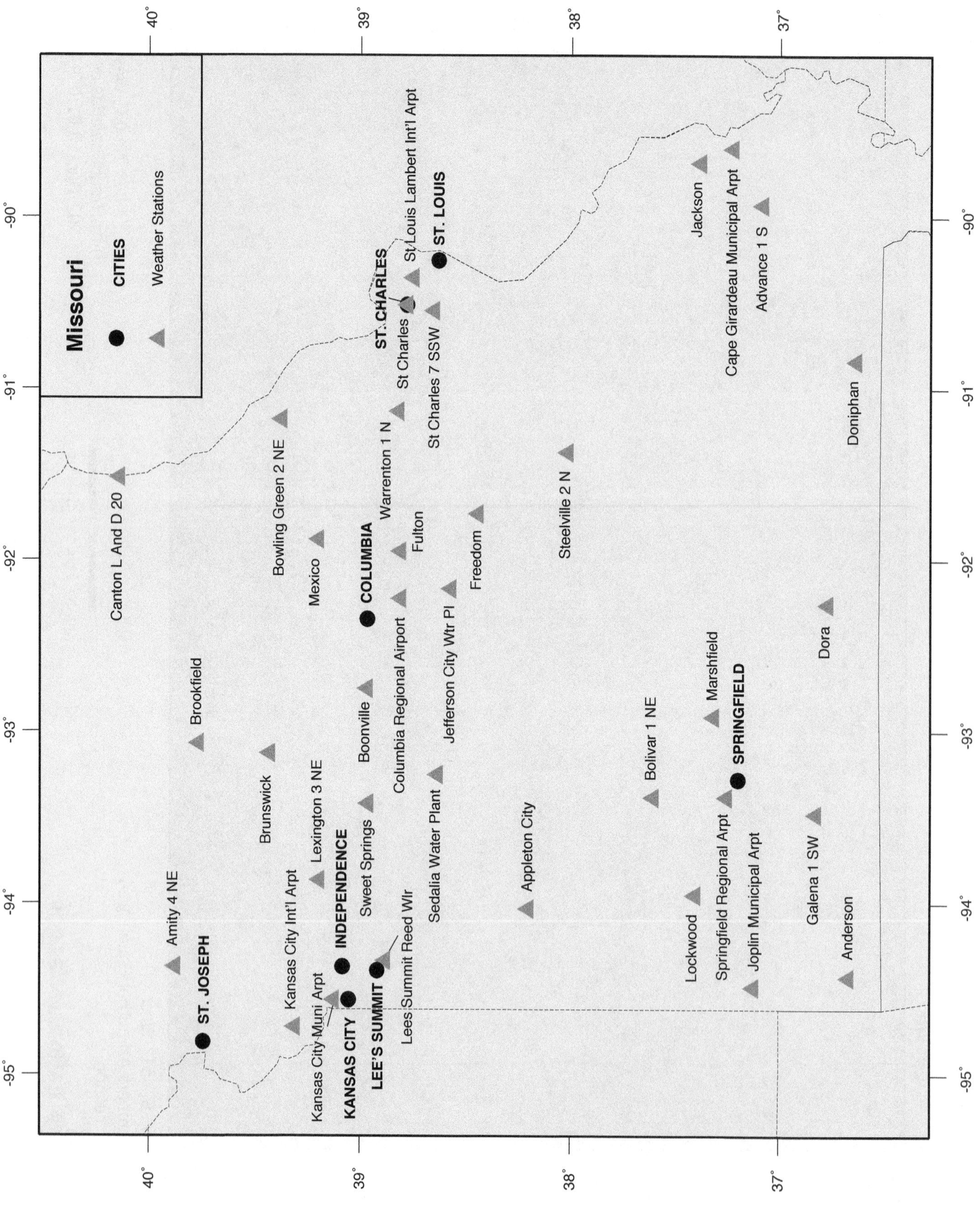
Missouri
CITIES
Weather Stations
ST. JOSEPH
KANSAS CITY
INDEPENDENCE
LEE'S SUMMIT
COLUMBIA
ST. CHARLES
ST. LOUIS
SPRINGFIELD
Amity 4 NE
Brookfield
Canton L And D 20
Brunswick
Bowling Green 2 NE
Kansas City Int'l Arpt
Kansas City Muni Arpt
Lexington 3 NE
Mexico
Sweet Springs
Boonville
Warrenton 1 N
St Charles
St Louis Lambert Int'l Arpt
Lees Summit Reed Wlr
Columbia Regional Airport
Fulton
St Charles 7 SSW
Sedalia Water Plant
Jefferson City Wtr Pl
Freedom
Appleton City
Steelville 2 N
Bolivar 1 NE
Lockwood
Springfield Regional Arpt
Marshfield
Jackson
Cape Girardeau Municipal Arpt
Joplin Municipal Arpt
Advance 1 S
Galena 1 SW
Dora
Anderson
Doniphan
40°
39°
38°
37°
-90°
-91°
-92°
-93°
-94°
-95°

Missouri Weather Stations by County

County	Station Name
Audrain	Mexico
Boone	Columbia Regional Airport
Callaway	Fulton
Cape Girardeau	Jackson
Chariton	Brunswick
Cole	Jefferson City Wtr Plant
Cooper	Boonville
Crawford	Steelville 2 N
Dade	Lockwood
Dekalb	Amity 4 NE
Greene	Springfield Regional Arpt
Jackson	Kansas City Muni Arpt Lees Summit Reed Wlr
Jasper	Joplin Municipal Arpt
Lafayette	Lexington 3 NE
Lewis	Canton L and D 20
Linn	Brookfield
Mcdonald	Anderson
Osage	Freedom
Ozark	Dora
Pettis	Sedalia Water Plant
Pike	Bowling Green 2 NE
Platte	Kansas City Int'l Arpt
Polk	Bolivar 1 NE
Ripley	Doniphan
Saline	Sweet Springs
Scott	Cape Girardeau Municipal Arpt
St. Charles	St Charles
St. Clair	Appleton City
St. Louis	St Charles 7 SSW St Louis Lambert Int'l Arpt
Stoddard	Advance 1 S
Stone	Galena 1 SW

County	Station Name
Warren	Warrenton 1 N
Webster	Marshfield

See User Guide for station inclusion criteria.

Missouri Weather Stations by City

City	Station Name	Miles
Arnold	Cahokia, IL	13.2
	St Charles 7 SSW	18.9
	St Louis Lambert Int'l Arpt	21.9
Ballwin	Cahokia, IL	19.0
	St Charles	13.4
	St Charles 7 SSW	6.5
	St Louis Lambert Int'l Arpt	14.7
Belton	Olathe 3 E, KS	13.6
	Kansas City Muni Arpt	20.8
	Lees Summit Reed Wlr	11.4
Blue Springs	Kansas City Muni Arpt	17.8
	Lees Summit Reed Wlr	9.8
Cape Girardeau	Anna 2 NNE, IL	20.2
	Advance 1 S	24.5
	Cape Girardeau Municipal Arpt	6.0
	Jackson	7.4
Chesterfield	Alton Melvin Price L&D, IL	24.4
	Cahokia, IL	19.6
	St Charles	9.7
	St Charles 7 SSW	2.9
	St Louis Lambert Int'l Arpt	12.0
Columbia	Boonville	22.3
	Columbia Regional Airport	11.0
	Fulton	22.6
Ferguson	Alton Melvin Price L&D, IL	9.2
	Cahokia, IL	13.4
	Jerseyville 2 SW, IL	24.6
	St Charles	11.3
	St Charles 7 SSW	12.7
	St Louis Lambert Int'l Arpt	3.8
Florissant	Alton Melvin Price L&D, IL	9.6
	Cahokia, IL	17.4
	Jerseyville 2 SW, IL	20.9
	St Charles	9.4
	St Charles 7 SSW	13.0
	St Louis Lambert Int'l Arpt	4.0
Gladstone	Leavenworth, KS	19.5
	Kansas City Int'l Arpt	10.4
	Kansas City Muni Arpt	6.8
Grandview	Olathe 3 E, KS	13.2
	Kansas City Muni Arpt	16.5
	Lees Summit Reed Wlr	10.1
Hazelwood	Alton Melvin Price L&D, IL	11.8
	Cahokia, IL	17.5
	Jerseyville 2 SW, IL	21.8
	St Charles	7.3
	St Charles 7 SSW	10.8
	St Louis Lambert Int'l Arpt	2.4
Independence	Olathe 3 E, KS	23.8
	Kansas City Int'l Arpt	22.7
	Kansas City Muni Arpt	10.0
	Lees Summit Reed Wlr	14.1

City	Station Name	Miles
Jefferson City	Columbia Regional Airport	17.0
	Fulton	23.7
	Jefferson City Wtr Plant	0.9
Joplin	Columbus 1 SW, KS	19.9
	Joplin Municipal Arpt	5.1
Kansas City	Leavenworth, KS	23.5
	Olathe 3 E, KS	17.5
	Kansas City Int'l Arpt	17.8
	Kansas City Muni Arpt	3.3
	Lees Summit Reed Wlr	17.8
Kirkwood	Alton Melvin Price L&D, IL	21.6
	Cahokia, IL	11.8
	St Charles	14.6
	St Charles 7 SSW	8.8
	St Louis Lambert Int'l Arpt	11.9
Lee's Summit	Olathe 3 E, KS	21.4
	Kansas City Muni Arpt	17.6
	Lees Summit Reed Wlr	3.4
Liberty	Kansas City Int'l Arpt	16.0
	Kansas City Muni Arpt	12.0
Maryland Heights	Alton Melvin Price L&D, IL	17.5
	Cahokia, IL	17.1
	St Charles	5.2
	St Charles 7 SSW	4.4
	St Louis Lambert Int'l Arpt	4.9
Mehlville	Alton Melvin Price L&D, IL	23.5
	Cahokia, IL	7.8
	St Charles	21.8
	St Charles 7 SSW	16.5
	St Louis Lambert Int'l Arpt	17.3
O'Fallon	St Charles	11.0
	St Charles 7 SSW	12.3
	St Louis Lambert Int'l Arpt	18.4
	Warrenton 1 N	23.2
Oakville	Cahokia, IL	9.9
	St Charles	24.5
	St Charles 7 SSW	18.9
	St Louis Lambert Int'l Arpt	20.4
Raytown	Olathe 3 E, KS	17.9
	Kansas City Muni Arpt	10.6
	Lees Summit Reed Wlr	10.4
Sedalia	Sedalia Water Plant	2.6
	Sweet Springs	20.8
Spanish Lake	Alton Melvin Price L&D, IL	4.0
	Cahokia, IL	15.2
	Jerseyville 2 SW, IL	22.9
	St Charles	15.5
	St Charles 7 SSW	17.9
	St Louis Lambert Int'l Arpt	8.7
Springfield	Marshfield	22.4
	Springfield Regional Arpt	6.1

See User Guide for station inclusion criteria.

City	Station Name	Miles
St. Charles	Alton Melvin Price L&D, IL	19.8
	Cahokia, IL	22.9
	Jerseyville 2 SW, IL	23.3
	St Charles	0.9
	St Charles 7 SSW	7.2
	St Louis Lambert Int'l Arpt	8.4
St. Joseph	Atchison, KS	20.6
	Troy 2 E, KS	13.7
St. Louis	Alton Melvin Price L&D, IL	14.4
	Belleville Siu Research, IL	23.1
	Cahokia, IL	5.0
	St Charles	17.2
	St Charles 7 SSW	14.7
	St Louis Lambert Int'l Arpt	10.6
St. Peters	Alton Melvin Price L&D, IL	24.7
	St Charles	5.7
	St Charles 7 SSW	7.8
	St Louis Lambert Int'l Arpt	12.9
University City	Alton Melvin Price L&D, IL	14.2
	Cahokia, IL	9.7
	St Charles	12.4
	St Charles 7 SSW	10.2
	St Louis Lambert Int'l Arpt	6.2
Webster Groves	Alton Melvin Price L&D, IL	19.3
	Cahokia, IL	8.4
	St Charles	15.7
	St Charles 7 SSW	11.1
	St Louis Lambert Int'l Arpt	11.3
Wildwood	Cahokia, IL	23.6
	St Charles	15.2
	St Charles 7 SSW	9.1
	St Louis Lambert Int'l Arpt	18.2

Note: Miles is the distance between the geographic center of the city and the weather station.

Missouri Weather Stations by Elevation

Feet	Station Name
1,490	Marshfield
1,258	Springfield Regional Arpt
1,100	Galena 1 SW
1,080	Lockwood
1,049	Anderson
1,034	Bolivar 1 NE
1,000	Lees Summit Reed Wlr
990	Dora
979	Joplin Municipal Arpt
974	Amity 4 NE
973	Kansas City Int'l Arpt
889	Columbia Regional Airport
870	Fulton
850	Warrenton 1 N
825	Lexington 3 NE
801	Mexico
799	Appleton City
779	Sedalia Water Plant
767	Brookfield
745	Freedom
709	Bowling Green 2 NE
700	Steelville 2 N
680	Sweet Springs
669	Boonville
669	Jefferson City Wtr Plant
660	Brunswick
575	Kansas City Muni Arpt
567	St Louis Lambert Int'l Arpt
490	Canton L and D 20
466	St Charles
450	St Charles 7 SSW
439	Jackson
359	Advance 1 S
336	Cape Girardeau Municipal Arpt
330	Doniphan

See User Guide for station inclusion criteria.

Columbia Regional Airport

Columbia, Missouri, with its interior continental location, experiences moderately cold winters and warm summers that are often humid.

There are usually a few days of temperatures below zero during the winter months, but there have been several winters when this did not occur. Periods of cold weather are usually interrupted by periods of at least a few mild days. It is not uncommon to find some days with temperatures in the 60s in the midst of the winter months. Some snow falls each winter, but it is very unlikely that a snow cover will persist for more than three weeks. Most of the time when snow does fall, it stays on the ground for less than a week. March is the month in which substantial amounts of snowfall are most likely.

Temperatures of 100 degrees or more occur in most summers, but there have been several summers when temperatures failed to reach this high. The late spring and early summer months produce more frequent and larger amounts of rain than the other months of the year. Thus, in addition to being warm, these months are often quite humid. By late summer smaller amounts of rain fall and rains occur less frequently, so by mid-August, the moisture in the top two feet of soil is often depleted.

Based on the 1951-1980 period, the average occurrence of the last temperature as cold as 32 degrees in spring is early April, and the first 32 degree temperature in the fall occurs in late October.

Columbia Regional Airport *Boone County* Elevation: 889 ft. Latitude: 38° 49' N Longitude: 92° 13' W

	JAN	FEB	MAR	APR	MAY	JUN	JUL	AUG	SEP	OCT	NOV	DEC	YEAR
Mean Maximum Temp. (°F)	38.7	43.9	54.9	65.8	74.5	83.1	88.1	87.2	78.9	66.9	53.8	41.3	64.8
Mean Temp. (°F)	29.9	34.4	44.4	54.8	64.1	72.8	77.6	76.3	67.7	56.0	44.4	32.7	54.6
Mean Minimum Temp. (°F)	21.0	24.9	33.8	43.8	53.5	62.6	67.1	65.4	56.4	45.1	34.8	24.0	44.4
Extreme Maximum Temp. (°F)	74	77	85	90	92	103	111	110	99	94	82	76	111
Extreme Minimum Temp. (°F)	-19	-14	-4	19	34	40	51	42	32	22	0	-20	-20
Days Maximum Temp. ≥ 90°F	0	0	0	0	0	5	13	12	3	0	0	0	33
Days Maximum Temp. ≤ 32°F	10	6	1	0	0	0	0	0	0	0	1	7	25
Days Minimum Temp. ≤ 32°F	27	21	15	3	0	0	0	0	0	3	13	24	106
Days Minimum Temp. ≤ 0°F	2	1	0	0	0	0	0	0	0	0	0	1	4
Heating Degree Days (base 65°F)	1,082	859	635	322	103	10	0	3	62	294	614	995	4,979
Cooling Degree Days (base 65°F)	0	0	3	24	81	253	399	361	149	22	1	0	1,293
Mean Precipitation (in.)	1.86	2.22	2.90	4.34	4.95	4.35	4.16	4.31	3.70	3.44	3.22	2.39	41.84
Maximum Precipitation (in.)*	4.8	6.2	10.1	11.7	12.3	10.3	12.1	9.0	12.1	6.1	10.4	7.0	62.5
Minimum Precipitation (in.)*	0	0.1	0.8	1.4	1.6	0.3	0.2	0.2	0.4	1.0	0.4	0.6	23.3
Extreme Maximum Daily Precip. (in.)	1.76	2.40	3.93	4.50	4.78	3.21	5.94	4.27	2.80	4.88	2.77	2.71	5.94
Days With ≥ 0.1" Precipitation	4	4	6	7	8	6	6	6	5	6	6	5	69
Days With ≥ 0.5" Precipitation	1	1	2	3	3	3	2	3	3	2	2	2	27
Days With ≥ 1.0" Precipitation	0	1	0	1	1	1	1	1	1	1	1	1	10
Mean Snowfall (in.)	5.3	5.3	1.9	0.5	***trace***	trace	***trace***	***trace***	***0.0***	***trace***	***1.3***	***4.8***	***19.1***
Maximum Snowfall (in.)*	24	20	18	7	0	0	0	0	0	trace	8	18	49
Maximum 24-hr. Snowfall (in.)*	18	12	6	7	0	0	0	0	0	trace	8	11	18
Maximum Snow Depth (in.)	13	14	9	5	trace	trace	***trace***	***trace***	***0***	***trace***	***5***	***15***	***15***
Days With ≥ 1.0" Snow Depth	8	6	1	0	0	0	***0***	0	***0***	***0***	***1***	***5***	***21***
Thunderstorm Days*	1	1	3	5	8	8	8	7	5	3	2	1	52
Foggy Days*	11	11	11	9	11	9	8	12	12	10	11	13	128
Predominant Sky Cover*	OVR	OVR	OVR	OVR	OVR	OVR	CLR	CLR	CLR	OVR	OVR	OVR	OVR
Mean Relative Humidity 6am (%)*	80	80	79	79	85	86	87	89	88	84	82	81	83
Mean Relative Humidity 3pm (%)*	62	59	53	52	57	56	53	52	54	53	59	64	56
Mean Dewpoint (°F)*	19	23	32	42	53	62	66	64	57	45	34	24	43
Prevailing Wind Direction*	WNW	WNW	S	S	S	S	S	S	S	S	S	WNW	S
Prevailing Wind Speed (mph)*	13	12	13	12	10	9	8	8	9	10	10	12	10
Maximum Wind Gust (mph)*	53	63	66	69	70	96	73	62	58	48	61	71	96

Note: (*) Period of record is 1969-1995

Kansas City Int'l Airport

The National Weather Service Office at Kansas City is very near the geographical center of the United States. The surrounding terrain is gently rolling. It has a modified continental climate. There are no natural topographic obstructions to prevent the free sweep of air from all directions. The influx of moist air from the Gulf of Mexico, or dry air from the semi-arid regions of the southwest, determine whether wet or dry conditions will prevail. There is often conflict between the warm moist gulf air and the cold polar continental air from the north in this area.

Early spring brings a period of frequent and rapid fluctuations in weather, with the fluctuations generally less frequent as spring progresses. The summer season is characterized by warm days and mild nights, with moderate humidities. July is the warmest month. The fall season is normally mild and usually includes a period near the middle of the season characterized by mild, sunny days, and cool nights. Winters are not severely cold. January is the coldest month. Falls of snow to a depth of 10 inches or more are comparatively rare. The distribution of measurable snow normally extends from November to April.

Nearly 60 percent of the annual precipitation occurs during the six months from April through September. More than 75 percent of the annual moisture normally falls during the growing season. The frequency and distribution of precipitation over a normal day is also important. The maximum frequency of precipitation, from April through October, occurs during the six hours following midnight and the minimum frequency occurs during the six hours following noon.

Kansas City Int'l Airport *Platte County* Elevation: 973 ft. Latitude: 39° 18' N Longitude: 94° 43' W

	JAN	FEB	MAR	APR	MAY	JUN	JUL	AUG	SEP	OCT	NOV	DEC	YEAR
Mean Maximum Temp. (°F)	38.1	43.2	54.7	65.4	74.8	83.4	88.5	87.3	79.0	66.7	53.1	40.3	64.5
Mean Temp. (°F)	29.0	33.4	44.0	54.6	64.5	73.4	78.5	77.0	68.2	56.2	43.6	31.6	54.5
Mean Minimum Temp. (°F)	19.8	23.7	33.2	43.8	54.2	63.4	68.4	66.7	57.3	45.7	34.1	22.8	44.4
Extreme Maximum Temp. (°F)	71	78	86	93	95	105	106	109	106	95	82	74	109
Extreme Minimum Temp. (°F)	-17	-19	-7	18	31	42	51	43	31	17	1	-23	-23
Days Maximum Temp. ≥ 90°F	0	0	0	0	1	6	14	12	4	0	0	0	37
Days Maximum Temp. ≤ 32°F	10	7	1	0	0	0	0	0	0	0	1	8	27
Days Minimum Temp. ≤ 32°F	28	22	15	4	0	0	0	0	0	2	13	25	109
Days Minimum Temp. ≤ 0°F	2	1	0	0	0	0	0	0	0	0	0	2	5
Heating Degree Days (base 65°F)	1,109	886	649	331	99	8	0	2	63	293	637	1,031	5,108
Cooling Degree Days (base 65°F)	0	0	3	27	91	268	424	382	165	27	1	0	1,388
Mean Precipitation (in.)	1.11	1.46	2.40	3.60	5.12	5.13	4.29	3.93	4.42	3.26	2.10	1.69	38.51
Maximum Precipitation (in.)*	5.5	6.8	6.7	10.6	11.0	11.0	11.4	11.6	16.2	11.9	9.5	4.1	60.3
Minimum Precipitation (in.)*	trace	trace	0.1	0.5	0.7	0.3	0.4	0.3	0.2	0.2	trace	trace	19.2
Extreme Maximum Daily Precip. (in.)	1.82	1.38	2.56	2.50	3.35	3.97	5.08	4.63	4.59	3.29	1.98	2.82	5.08
Days With ≥ 0.1" Precipitation	3	4	5	7	8	7	6	6	6	6	4	3	65
Days With ≥ 0.5" Precipitation	1	1	2	3	4	4	3	2	3	2	1	1	27
Days With ≥ 1.0" Precipitation	0	0	0	1	1	2	1	1	1	1	0	0	8
Mean Snowfall (in.)	4.5	5.2	1.9	0.6	trace	trace	trace	trace	trace	0.3	1.2	4.9	18.6
Maximum Snowfall (in.)*	31	21	40	7	2	0	0	0	0	3	9	17	63
Maximum 24-hr. Snowfall (in.)*	12	12	21	7	2	0	0	0	0	3	9	9	21
Maximum Snow Depth (in.)	11	9	9	2	trace	trace	trace	trace	trace	trace	5	11	11
Days With ≥ 1.0" Snow Depth	8	6	2	0	0	0	0	0	0	0	1	6	23
Thunderstorm Days*	< 1	1	3	5	8	9	8	8	6	3	1	< 1	52
Foggy Days*	8	7	6	5	6	4	4	4	6	7	6	8	71
Predominant Sky Cover*	OVR	OVR	OVR	OVR	OVR	OVR	CLR	CLR	CLR	CLR	OVR	OVR	OVR
Mean Relative Humidity 6am (%)*	74	74	73	73	77	79	78	79	80	75	74	75	76
Mean Relative Humidity 3pm (%)*	57	55	49	47	49	51	49	49	48	46	51	57	51
Mean Dewpoint (°F)*	18	23	29	41	53	62	66	64	56	44	32	24	43
Prevailing Wind Direction*	SSW	SSW	S	S	S	S	S	S	S	S	S	SSW	S
Prevailing Wind Speed (mph)*	10	10	13	14	13	12	12	10	12	12	12	10	12
Maximum Wind Gust (mph)*	55	52	33	54	49	58	54	55	44	45	53	35	58

Note: (*) Period of record is 1948-1988

The period of record for National Weather Service station data is 1980 – 2009 except where noted. See User Guide for detailed explanation of data.

Springfield Regional Airport

The entire metropolitan area, airport, and surrounding territory consists of comparatively flat or very gently rolling tableland, practically atop the crest of the Missouri Ozark Mountain plateau. The average elevation of the city proper is slightly over 1,300 feet above sea level. There are no serious problems of instrumental exposure.

As a result of this advantageous location, the city and surrounding territory enjoy what is described as a plateau climate. The winter season in the Ozarks has temperatures considerably milder than in the upland, plain or prairie, and in the summer the Ozarks are appreciably cooler.

The city of Springfield also occupies a unique location with regard to natural water drainage. The line separating two major water sheds crosses the north-central part of the city. Drainage north of this line flows north into the Gasconade and Missouri Rivers. To the south of the line, drainage is to the south into the White and Mississippi Rivers.

The average annual temperature range is over 140 degrees with lowest temperatures below -25 and and highest temperatures above 115 degrees.

The growing season extends over a period of 199 days. Agriculture is greatly diversified, practically every farm product of the temperate zone is grown in this area. It is a noted livestock and poultry production and distribution center. The climate permits green pasturage the year around in varying quantity, resulting in ever increasing cattle production for both meat and dairy products.

The air is remarkably free from palls of industrial smoke, and the altitude of the city also tends to prevent other than few amounts of either radiation or advection fogs.

Springfield Regional Airport *Greene County* Elevation: 1,258 ft. Latitude: 37° 14' N Longitude: 93° 23' W

	JAN	FEB	MAR	APR	MAY	JUN	JUL	AUG	SEP	OCT	NOV	DEC	YEAR
Mean Maximum Temp. (°F)	43.3	48.4	57.7	67.2	75.3	83.8	88.9	88.8	80.1	68.7	56.6	45.0	67.0
Mean Temp. (°F)	33.4	37.9	46.6	55.9	64.9	73.5	78.4	77.8	69.0	57.7	46.4	35.5	56.4
Mean Minimum Temp. (°F)	23.5	27.4	35.5	44.6	54.5	63.1	67.8	66.7	57.9	46.7	36.2	26.0	45.8
Extreme Maximum Temp. (°F)	73	79	86	92	91	99	108	106	102	93	83	77	108
Extreme Minimum Temp. (°F)	-13	-10	-2	20	31	43	49	46	31	18	5	-16	-16
Days Maximum Temp. ≥ 90°F	0	0	0	0	0	5	15	15	4	0	0	0	39
Days Maximum Temp. ≤ 32°F	6	4	1	0	0	0	0	0	0	0	0	5	16
Days Minimum Temp. ≤ 32°F	25	20	12	3	0	0	0	0	0	2	11	23	96
Days Minimum Temp. ≤ 0°F	1	1	0	0	0	0	0	0	0	0	0	1	3
Heating Degree Days (base 65°F)	972	760	566	291	90	8	1	2	52	250	552	908	4,452
Cooling Degree Days (base 65°F)	0	0	4	25	95	268	422	405	180	30	2	0	1,431
Mean Precipitation (in.)	2.40	2.53	3.63	4.28	4.94	4.89	3.49	3.54	4.28	3.47	4.21	3.12	44.78
Maximum Precipitation (in.)*	6.8	5.7	9.0	10.6	13.4	11.3	18.8	8.6	17.5	8.7	12.2	8.8	63.2
Minimum Precipitation (in.)*	0.1	0.4	0.5	0.1	1.5	0.2	0.3	0.5	0.2	0.4	0.2	0.1	25.2
Extreme Maximum Daily Precip. (in.)	2.55	2.26	3.93	3.09	4.21	3.88	4.52	3.26	5.03	2.84	6.27	3.67	6.27
Days With ≥ 0.1" Precipitation	4	5	7	7	8	8	6	5	5	6	6	5	72
Days With ≥ 0.5" Precipitation	2	2	2	3	3	4	3	2	2	2	3	2	30
Days With ≥ 1.0" Precipitation	1	1	1	1	1	1	1	1	1	1	1	1	12
Mean Snowfall (in.)	5.3	4.2	2.4	0.1	trace	trace	trace	trace	0.0	0.1	1.0	4.7	17.8
Maximum Snowfall (in.)*	23	19	24	7	0	0	0	0	0	1	20	15	35
Maximum 24-hr. Snowfall (in.)*	9	12	16	7	0	0	0	0	0	1	11	6	16
Maximum Snow Depth (in.)	14	16	14	2	trace	trace	trace	trace	0	1	7	13	16
Days With ≥ 1.0" Snow Depth	7	4	1	0	0	0	0	0	0	0	0	5	17
Thunderstorm Days*	1	1	4	6	8	9	8	8	5	3	2	1	56
Foggy Days*	12	12	11	9	10	9	8	10	11	10	10	12	124
Predominant Sky Cover*	OVR	OVR	OVR	OVR	OVR	OVR	CLR	CLR	CLR	CLR	OVR	OVR	OVR
Mean Relative Humidity 6am (%)*	79	80	79	79	85	87	87	88	87	82	80	80	83
Mean Relative Humidity 3pm (%)*	59	55	52	50	56	56	53	50	52	50	54	59	54
Mean Dewpoint (°F)*	22	26	33	43	54	63	66	64	57	46	34	26	45
Prevailing Wind Direction*	SSE	SSE	SSE	SSE	SSE	SSE	SSE	SSE	SSE	SSE	SSE	SSE	SSE
Prevailing Wind Speed (mph)*	13	13	14	13	12	10	9	9	10	12	13	13	12
Maximum Wind Gust (mph)*	52	52	52	56	60	55	73	59	52	68	53	115	115

Note: (*) Period of record is 1948-1995

Saint Louis Lambert Int'l Arpt.

Saint Louis is located at the confluence of the Missouri and Mississippi Rivers and near the geographical center of the United States. Thus, with a somewhat modified continental climate, it is in the enviable position of being able to enjoy the changes of a four-season climate without the undue hardship of prolonged periods of extreme heat or high humidity. To the south is the warm, moist air of the Gulf of Mexico, and to the north, in Canada, is a favored region of cold air masses. The alternate invasion of Saint Louis by air masses from these sources, and the conflict along the frontal zones where they come together, produce a variety of weather conditions, none of which are likely to persist to the point of monotony.

Winters are brisk and stimulating, seldom severe. Records since 1870 show that temperatures drop to zero or below an average of two or three days per year. Temperatures remain as cold as 32 degrees or lower less than 25 days in most years. Snowfall has averaged a little over 18 inches per winter season. Snowfall of an inch or more is received on five to ten days in most years.

The long-term record for Saint Louis (since 1870) indicates that temperatures of 90 degrees or higher occur on about 35-40 days a year. Extremely hot days of 100 degrees or more are expected on no more than five days per year.

Normal annual precipitation for the Saint Louis area, is a little less than 34 inches. The three winter months are the driest, with an average total of about six inches of precipitation. The spring months of March through May are normally the wettest with normal total precipitation of just under 10 and a half inches. It is not unusual to have extended dry periods of one to two weeks during the growing season.

Thunderstorms occur normally on between 40 and 50 days per year. During any year, there are usually a few of these that can be classified as severe storms with hail and damaging winds. Tornadoes have produced extensive damage and loss of life in the Saint Louis area.

Saint Louis Lambert Int'l Arpt. *St. Louis County* Elevation: 567 ft. Latitude: 38° 45' N Longitude: 90° 22' W

	JAN	FEB	MAR	APR	MAY	JUN	JUL	AUG	SEP	OCT	NOV	DEC	YEAR
Mean Maximum Temp. (°F)	40.0	45.0	55.6	67.1	76.3	84.9	89.2	88.0	80.3	68.3	55.3	42.8	66.1
Mean Temp. (°F)	32.0	36.2	46.0	57.0	66.8	75.8	80.1	78.7	70.4	58.6	46.7	35.0	56.9
Mean Minimum Temp. (°F)	23.9	27.5	36.4	46.9	57.1	66.5	71.0	69.4	60.6	48.8	38.1	27.2	47.8
Extreme Maximum Temp. (°F)	75	80	89	93	94	102	107	107	104	94	85	74	107
Extreme Minimum Temp. (°F)	-18	-12	2	23	38	48	54	47	37	25	8	-16	-18
Days Maximum Temp. ≥ 90°F	0	0	0	0	1	9	15	13	4	0	0	0	42
Days Maximum Temp. ≤ 32°F	9	5	1	0	0	0	0	0	0	0	0	6	21
Days Minimum Temp. ≤ 32°F	25	19	11	2	0	0	0	0	0	1	9	21	88
Days Minimum Temp. ≤ 0°F	1	0	0	0	0	0	0	0	0	0	0	1	2
Heating Degree Days (base 65°F)	1,016	808	587	273	69	5	0	1	38	235	545	925	4,502
Cooling Degree Days (base 65°F)	0	0	7	40	130	334	477	433	207	42	4	0	1,674
Mean Precipitation (in.)	2.37	2.22	3.37	3.64	4.67	4.22	4.00	2.96	3.11	3.39	3.77	2.82	40.54
Maximum Precipitation (in.)*	8.0	5.0	6.7	10.3	12.9	10.5	12.7	14.8	10.0	7.1	9.9	7.8	55.0
Minimum Precipitation (in.)*	0.1	0.3	0.8	1.0	1.0	0.4	0.6	0.1	trace	0.2	0.1	trace	20.6
Extreme Maximum Daily Precip. (in.)	2.20	2.36	2.46	4.46	5.59	3.31	3.37	2.68	4.58	2.67	3.15	2.76	5.59
Days With ≥ 0.1" Precipitation	4	5	7	7	8	6	6	5	4	6	6	5	69
Days With ≥ 0.5" Precipitation	2	1	2	3	3	3	3	2	2	2	3	2	28
Days With ≥ 1.0" Precipitation	1	0	1	1	1	1	1	1	1	1	1	1	11
Mean Snowfall (in.)	5.6	4.3	2.6	0.6	trace	trace	trace	0.0	0.0	trace	1.0	4.1	18.2
Maximum Snowfall (in.)*	24	21	22	7	0	0	0	0	0	trace	11	26	49
Maximum 24-hr. Snowfall (in.)*	11	10	10	5	0	0	0	0	0	trace	8	12	12
Maximum Snow Depth (in.)	10	20	11	3	trace	trace	trace	0	0	trace	7	8	20
Days With ≥ 1.0" Snow Depth	7	5	2	0	0	0	0	0	0	0	1	5	20
Thunderstorm Days*	1	1	3	6	7	8	7	6	4	2	2	1	48
Foggy Days*	13	13	13	11	11	9	9	13	13	12	12	14	143
Predominant Sky Cover*	OVR	OVR	OVR	OVR	OVR	OVR	SCT	CLR	CLR	CLR	OVR	OVR	OVR
Mean Relative Humidity 6am (%)*	80	80	80	77	81	82	83	86	86	82	80	81	82
Mean Relative Humidity 3pm (%)*	62	58	54	49	51	51	51	51	50	50	56	63	54
Mean Dewpoint (°F)*	22	25	33	42	53	62	66	65	57	46	35	26	44
Prevailing Wind Direction*	WNW	WNW	WNW	WNW	S	S	S	S	S	S	WNW	WNW	S
Prevailing Wind Speed (mph)*	13	13	14	14	10	10	9	8	9	10	13	13	12
Maximum Wind Gust (mph)*	62	66	66	83	59	76	62	63	56	78	64	56	83

Note: (*) Period of record is 1945-1995

The period of record for National Weather Service station data is 1980 – 2009 except where noted. See User Guide for detailed explanation of data.

Advance 1 S *Stoddard County* Elevation: 359 ft. Latitude: 37° 06' N Longitude: 89° 54' W

	JAN	FEB	MAR	APR	MAY	JUN	JUL	AUG	SEP	OCT	NOV	DEC	YEAR
Mean Maximum Temp. (°F)	41.5	48.0	56.9	67.9	77.2	85.6	89.8	88.7	81.6	70.5	57.6	44.8	67.5
Mean Temp. (°F)	32.4	37.7	45.9	56.2	65.9	74.5	78.7	76.7	68.7	57.2	46.7	35.7	56.3
Mean Minimum Temp. (°F)	23.3	27.4	34.9	44.5	54.6	63.3	67.6	64.7	55.6	43.8	35.7	26.4	45.1
Extreme Maximum Temp. (°F)	72	77	82	90	95	102	105	103	101	91	85	75	105
Extreme Minimum Temp. (°F)	-20	-13	9	25	34	41	52	40	32	22	11	-11	-20
Days Maximum Temp. ≥ 90°F	0	0	0	0	1	9	18	15	5	0	0	0	48
Days Maximum Temp. ≤ 32°F	6	4	1	0	0	0	0	0	0	0	0	5	16
Days Minimum Temp. ≤ 32°F	26	20	14	3	0	0	0	0	0	5	13	22	103
Days Minimum Temp. ≤ 0°F	1	0	0	0	0	0	0	0	0	0	0	1	2
Heating Degree Days (base 65°F)	1,003	765	587	282	73	5	0	2	50	260	545	903	4,475
Cooling Degree Days (base 65°F)	0	0	3	26	108	296	432	371	166	23	2	0	1,427
Mean Precipitation (in.)	3.29	3.35	4.18	4.69	5.13	3.98	3.65	3.01	2.96	3.72	4.64	4.10	46.70
Extreme Maximum Daily Precip. (in.)	5.40	2.70	4.40	5.60	3.50	4.10	2.62	4.10	4.75	4.50	5.05	3.56	5.60
Days With ≥ 0.1" Precipitation	5	5	7	7	8	7	6	5	5	6	7	6	74
Days With ≥ 0.5" Precipitation	2	2	3	3	4	3	2	2	2	3	3	3	32
Days With ≥ 1.0" Precipitation	1	1	1	1	2	1	1	1	1	1	2	1	14
Mean Snowfall (in.)	2.5	3.8	1.0	0.0	0.0	0.0	0.0	0.0	0.0	0.1	0.3	1.8	9.5
Maximum Snow Depth (in.)	6	na	9	0	0	0	0	0	0	0	5	8	na
Days With ≥ 1.0" Snow Depth	4	na	1	0	0	0	0	0	0	0	0	3	na

Amity 4 NE *Dekalb County* Elevation: 974 ft. Latitude: 39° 53' N Longitude: 94° 22' W

	JAN	FEB	MAR	APR	MAY	JUN	JUL	AUG	SEP	OCT	NOV	DEC	YEAR
Mean Maximum Temp. (°F)	34.9	40.4	52.2	63.4	73.0	81.8	86.3	85.4	77.6	65.2	51.2	37.5	62.4
Mean Temp. (°F)	25.5	30.3	41.1	52.2	62.3	71.4	76.0	74.5	66.1	53.9	41.3	28.7	51.9
Mean Minimum Temp. (°F)	16.1	20.1	29.9	40.9	51.5	61.0	65.6	63.7	54.6	42.6	31.4	19.7	41.4
Extreme Maximum Temp. (°F)	69	77	85	90	92	99	104	105	99	93	82	71	105
Extreme Minimum Temp. (°F)	-19	-19	-12	12	27	39	49	40	27	18	-7	-32	-32
Days Maximum Temp. ≥ 90°F	0	0	0	0	0	4	10	9	3	0	0	0	26
Days Maximum Temp. ≤ 32°F	12	8	2	0	0	0	0	0	0	0	2	10	34
Days Minimum Temp. ≤ 32°F	29	24	19	6	0	0	0	0	0	5	17	28	128
Days Minimum Temp. ≤ 0°F	4	3	0	0	0	0	0	0	0	0	0	3	10
Heating Degree Days (base 65°F)	1,218	976	737	395	139	17	1	6	88	352	705	1,121	5,755
Cooling Degree Days (base 65°F)	0	0	2	17	60	216	349	309	127	16	0	0	1,096
Mean Precipitation (in.)	0.90	1.27	2.25	3.60	5.16	5.01	4.54	4.34	4.24	3.23	1.86	1.63	38.03
Extreme Maximum Daily Precip. (in.)	1.01	1.82	1.75	3.10	5.05	6.00	2.97	6.20	6.70	3.85	2.18	2.18	6.70
Days With ≥ 0.1" Precipitation	3	3	5	7	8	7	6	6	5	6	4	4	64
Days With ≥ 0.5" Precipitation	0	1	1	2	3	3	3	3	3	2	1	1	23
Days With ≥ 1.0" Precipitation	0	0	0	1	2	2	2	2	2	1	0	0	12
Mean Snowfall (in.)	4.1	4.7	2.2	0.6	0.0	0.0	0.0	0.0	0.0	0.1	0.6	5.4	17.7
Maximum Snow Depth (in.)	9	***10***	***10***	5	0	0	0	0	0	3	4	12	***12***
Days With ≥ 1.0" Snow Depth	7	***6***	2	0	0	0	0	0	0	0	0	6	***21***

Anderson *Mcdonald County* Elevation: 1,049 ft. Latitude: 36° 39' N Longitude: 94° 26' W

	JAN	FEB	MAR	APR	MAY	JUN	JUL	AUG	SEP	OCT	NOV	DEC	YEAR
Mean Maximum Temp. (°F)	46.2	51.2	60.7	70.1	76.2	83.0	88.5	88.7	80.4	70.4	59.2	48.1	68.6
Mean Temp. (°F)	35.2	39.3	48.2	57.3	65.0	72.5	77.5	76.9	68.7	58.1	47.5	37.2	56.9
Mean Minimum Temp. (°F)	24.1	27.3	35.5	44.4	53.6	62.0	66.4	65.1	56.9	45.7	35.8	26.3	45.3
Extreme Maximum Temp. (°F)	76	86	88	93	90	98	107	104	104	92	86	76	107
Extreme Minimum Temp. (°F)	-21	-21	-4	17	29	42	49	42	27	17	6	-18	-21
Days Maximum Temp. ≥ 90°F	0	0	0	0	0	3	13	15	4	0	0	0	35
Days Maximum Temp. ≤ 32°F	4	2	0	0	0	0	0	0	0	0	0	3	9
Days Minimum Temp. ≤ 32°F	24	20	13	4	0	0	0	0	0	3	13	22	99
Days Minimum Temp. ≤ 0°F	1	0	0	0	0	0	0	0	0	0	0	1	2
Heating Degree Days (base 65°F)	918	721	521	255	84	7	0	2	53	238	521	854	4,174
Cooling Degree Days (base 65°F)	0	0	6	31	89	240	394	378	170	30	3	0	1,341
Mean Precipitation (in.)	2.15	2.13	3.44	4.16	5.43	4.78	3.08	3.17	4.12	3.51	4.11	2.92	43.00
Extreme Maximum Daily Precip. (in.)	3.77	3.04	4.13	3.71	3.10	5.48	4.35	4.00	5.14	3.80	5.22	2.64	5.48
Days With ≥ 0.1" Precipitation	3	4	6	6	8	7	4	5	5	6	5	5	64
Days With ≥ 0.5" Precipitation	1	1	3	3	4	3	2	2	3	3	3	2	30
Days With ≥ 1.0" Precipitation	1	0	1	1	2	2	1	1	1	1	1	1	13
Mean Snowfall (in.)	2.9	2.9	1.9	trace	0.0	0.0	0.0	0.0	0.0	trace	0.4	3.2	11.3
Maximum Snow Depth (in.)	7	8	15	trace	0	0	0	0	0	1	3	13	15
Days With ≥ 1.0" Snow Depth	4	3	1	0	0	0	0	0	0	0	0	3	11

Appleton City *St. Clair County* Elevation: 799 ft. Latitude: 38° 11' N Longitude: 94° 02' W

	JAN	FEB	MAR	APR	MAY	JUN	JUL	AUG	SEP	OCT	NOV	DEC	YEAR
Mean Maximum Temp. (°F)	41.0	46.2	56.9	66.9	75.8	84.0	89.3	88.9	80.2	68.3	55.4	43.1	66.3
Mean Temp. (°F)	31.0	35.5	45.3	55.2	64.8	73.5	78.3	77.3	68.5	56.7	45.1	33.4	55.4
Mean Minimum Temp. (°F)	20.9	24.8	33.7	43.4	53.7	62.8	67.3	65.6	56.7	45.1	34.7	23.7	44.4
Extreme Maximum Temp. (°F)	72	79	86	93	94	104	112	111	105	95	83	73	112
Extreme Minimum Temp. (°F)	-17	-13	-1	20	33	44	51	44	31	19	4	-22	-22
Days Maximum Temp. ≥ 90°F	0	0	0	0	0	6	15	15	4	0	0	0	40
Days Maximum Temp. ≤ 32°F	7	5	1	0	0	0	0	0	0	0	1	6	20
Days Minimum Temp. ≤ 32°F	27	21	15	4	0	0	0	0	0	3	13	25	108
Days Minimum Temp. ≤ 0°F	1	1	0	0	0	0	0	0	0	0	0	1	3
Heating Degree Days (base 65°F)	1,048	826	605	312	90	8	0	2	57	275	593	974	4,790
Cooling Degree Days (base 65°F)	0	0	3	24	90	268	420	390	167	26	2	0	1,390
Mean Precipitation (in.)	1.57	1.94	3.13	4.33	5.20	4.98	4.02	3.80	4.13	4.07	3.22	2.33	42.72
Extreme Maximum Daily Precip. (in.)	2.47	2.55	3.73	4.82	5.12	4.25	5.86	5.38	6.39	9.10	3.34	3.17	9.10
Days With ≥ 0.1" Precipitation	4	4	6	6	8	7	6	5	6	6	5	4	67
Days With ≥ 0.5" Precipitation	1	1	2	3	4	4	3	3	3	2	2	2	30
Days With ≥ 1.0" Precipitation	0	1	1	1	1	1	1	1	1	1	1	1	11
Mean Snowfall (in.)	4.1	3.4	1.4	trace	0.0	0.0	0.0	0.0	0.0	trace	0.3	3.1	12.3
Maximum Snow Depth (in.)	9	9	7	trace	0	0	0	0	0	trace	2	12	12
Days With ≥ 1.0" Snow Depth	7	4	1	0	0	0	0	0	0	0	0	5	17

The period of record for all cooperative weather station data is 1980 – 2009. See User Guide for detailed explanation of data.

Bolivar 1 NE *Polk County* Elevation: 1,034 ft. Latitude: 37° 37' N Longitude: 93° 23' W

	JAN	FEB	MAR	APR	MAY	JUN	JUL	AUG	SEP	OCT	NOV	DEC	YEAR
Mean Maximum Temp. (°F)	42.9	47.4	57.1	67.2	75.6	83.9	89.1	89.1	80.9	69.8	57.0	45.6	67.1
Mean Temp. (°F)	31.8	35.8	45.2	55.1	64.2	72.9	77.6	76.9	68.0	56.6	45.5	34.9	55.4
Mean Minimum Temp. (°F)	20.6	24.2	33.1	42.9	52.8	62.0	66.1	64.5	55.0	43.4	33.9	24.1	43.5
Extreme Maximum Temp. (°F)	73	80	86	93	95	102	107	105	104	93	83	75	107
Extreme Minimum Temp. (°F)	-18	-12	-4	16	28	40	48	36	19	18	-1	-19	-19
Days Maximum Temp. ≥ 90°F	0	0	0	0	0	6	16	16	5	0	0	0	43
Days Maximum Temp. ≤ 32°F	7	4	1	0	0	0	0	0	0	0	0	5	17
Days Minimum Temp. ≤ 32°F	27	22	15	5	0	0	0	0	1	5	15	24	114
Days Minimum Temp. ≤ 0°F	1	1	0	0	0	0	0	0	0	0	0	1	3
Heating Degree Days (base 65°F)	1,024	819	612	318	103	10	1	3	66	279	581	927	4,743
Cooling Degree Days (base 65°F)	0	0	4	25	87	255	399	378	162	25	2	0	1,337
Mean Precipitation (in.)	2.16	2.39	3.75	4.60	5.55	5.19	4.19	3.61	4.15	4.35	3.87	2.96	46.77
Extreme Maximum Daily Precip. (in.)	3.47	4.54	3.32	3.00	5.41	5.46	5.50	3.63	4.80	4.57	3.52	3.04	5.50
Days With ≥ 0.1" Precipitation	4	4	7	7	8	8	5	5	5	6	6	5	70
Days With ≥ 0.5" Precipitation	1	2	3	3	4	3	3	2	3	3	3	2	32
Days With ≥ 1.0" Precipitation	1	1	1	1	2	2	1	1	1	1	1	1	14
Mean Snowfall (in.)	0.7	na	trace	0.0	0.0	0.0	0.0	0.0	0.0	0.0	0.0	0.0	na
Maximum Snow Depth (in.)	na	na	trace	0	0	0	0	0	0	0	0	na	na
Days With ≥ 1.0" Snow Depth	na	na	0	0	0	0	0	0	0	0	0	0	na

Boonville *Cooper County* Elevation: 669 ft. Latitude: 38° 58' N Longitude: 92° 45' W

	JAN	FEB	MAR	APR	MAY	JUN	JUL	AUG	SEP	OCT	NOV	DEC	YEAR
Mean Maximum Temp. (°F)	38.1	43.5	54.7	66.3	75.9	84.5	89.8	88.6	80.5	68.4	54.2	41.5	65.5
Mean Temp. (°F)	29.1	33.7	44.0	55.2	65.1	74.2	79.2	77.4	68.6	56.7	44.2	32.6	55.0
Mean Minimum Temp. (°F)	20.1	23.8	33.2	44.1	54.3	63.8	68.5	66.2	56.6	44.9	34.2	23.6	44.4
Extreme Maximum Temp. (°F)	74	78	86	92	95	103	110	108	104	97	84	74	110
Extreme Minimum Temp. (°F)	-18	-12	-2	19	34	43	53	45	32	24	0	-22	-22
Days Maximum Temp. ≥ 90°F	0	0	0	0	1	8	17	15	5	0	0	0	46
Days Maximum Temp. ≤ 32°F	10	6	2	0	0	0	0	0	0	0	1	7	26
Days Minimum Temp. ≤ 32°F	28	22	15	3	0	0	0	0	0	3	13	25	109
Days Minimum Temp. ≤ 0°F	2	1	0	0	0	0	0	0	0	0	0	1	4
Heating Degree Days (base 65°F)	1,107	880	649	318	93	8	1	2	62	283	619	999	5,021
Cooling Degree Days (base 65°F)	0	0	4	30	101	290	446	393	174	30	2	0	1,470
Mean Precipitation (in.)	1.69	2.03	2.88	4.08	5.36	5.23	3.84	4.69	3.91	3.39	3.92	2.47	43.49
Extreme Maximum Daily Precip. (in.)	2.54	3.46	2.30	4.10	4.88	6.00	3.96	5.50	4.80	4.54	4.24	3.90	6.00
Days With ≥ 0.1" Precipitation	3	4	6	7	8	6	6	6	5	6	6	4	67
Days With ≥ 0.5" Precipitation	1	1	2	3	3	3	3	3	2	2	2	1	26
Days With ≥ 1.0" Precipitation	0	1	1	1	1	2	1	2	1	1	1	0	12
Mean Snowfall (in.)	5.9	4.6	1.7	0.1	0.0	0.0	0.0	0.0	0.0	trace	0.6	4.6	17.5
Maximum Snow Depth (in.)	12	12	7	trace	0	0	0	0	0	trace	4	13	13
Days With ≥ 1.0" Snow Depth	7	5	1	0	0	0	0	0	0	0	0	4	17

Bowling Green 2 NE *Pike County* Elevation: 709 ft. Latitude: 39° 22' N Longitude: 91° 11' W

	JAN	FEB	MAR	APR	MAY	JUN	JUL	AUG	SEP	OCT	NOV	DEC	YEAR
Mean Maximum Temp. (°F)	37.0	43.0	52.7	65.2	74.3	83.2	87.9	86.1	79.1	67.7	53.2	40.0	64.1
Mean Temp. (°F)	27.2	32.0	41.1	53.3	62.2	71.4	76.3	74.4	66.2	54.8	42.8	30.5	52.7
Mean Minimum Temp. (°F)	17.4	21.0	29.3	41.3	50.1	59.6	64.7	62.6	53.3	41.8	32.3	20.9	41.2
Extreme Maximum Temp. (°F)	72	74	85	92	96	104	104	106	102	92	80	78	106
Extreme Minimum Temp. (°F)	-25	-22	-9	17	26	39	42	37	28	18	-8	-21	-25
Days Maximum Temp. ≥ 90°F	0	0	0	0	1	5	12	10	4	0	0	0	32
Days Maximum Temp. ≤ 32°F	11	6	2	0	0	0	0	0	0	0	1	7	27
Days Minimum Temp. ≤ 32°F	27	22	18	6	1	0	0	0	0	7	16	25	122
Days Minimum Temp. ≤ 0°F	3	3	0	0	0	0	0	0	0	0	0	2	8
Heating Degree Days (base 65°F)	1,166	925	741	366	150	21	1	8	89	330	662	1,068	5,527
Cooling Degree Days (base 65°F)	0	0	3	21	69	219	361	304	132	20	1	0	1,130
Mean Precipitation (in.)	1.74	1.89	2.69	3.92	4.36	3.63	3.89	3.64	3.37	2.88	3.61	2.54	38.16
Extreme Maximum Daily Precip. (in.)	3.05	1.66	1.60	2.25	3.63	3.10	3.80	3.70	4.00	2.20	3.03	3.19	4.00
Days With ≥ 0.1" Precipitation	3	3	5	6	7	6	5	5	5	5	6	4	60
Days With ≥ 0.5" Precipitation	1	1	2	2	3	3	2	3	2	2	3	1	25
Days With ≥ 1.0" Precipitation	1	1	1	1	1	1	1	1	1	1	1	1	12
Mean Snowfall (in.)	2.4	3.6	1.9	trace	0.0	0.0	0.0	0.0	0.0	0.0	0.7	1.6	10.2
Maximum Snow Depth (in.)	11	na	7	trace	0	0	0	0	0	0	2	9	na
Days With ≥ 1.0" Snow Depth	2	3	1	0	0	0	0	0	0	0	0	2	8

Brookfield *Linn County* Elevation: 767 ft. Latitude: 39° 46' N Longitude: 93° 04' W

	JAN	FEB	MAR	APR	MAY	JUN	JUL	AUG	SEP	OCT	NOV	DEC	YEAR
Mean Maximum Temp. (°F)	36.5	41.8	53.7	65.3	74.3	82.8	87.4	86.2	78.9	66.9	52.5	38.9	63.8
Mean Temp. (°F)	27.3	31.9	42.7	53.8	63.6	72.6	77.2	75.7	67.6	55.7	42.7	30.2	53.4
Mean Minimum Temp. (°F)	18.2	22.0	31.6	42.3	52.9	62.4	66.9	65.1	56.3	44.4	33.0	21.5	43.0
Extreme Maximum Temp. (°F)	72	74	86	91	91	103	109	108	99	94	81	71	109
Extreme Minimum Temp. (°F)	-21	-16	-7	17	31	41	50	43	30	16	-6	-24	-24
Days Maximum Temp. ≥ 90°F	0	0	0	0	0	4	11	10	3	0	0	0	28
Days Maximum Temp. ≤ 32°F	11	7	2	0	0	0	0	0	0	0	1	9	30
Days Minimum Temp. ≤ 32°F	28	23	17	5	0	0	0	0	0	3	15	26	117
Days Minimum Temp. ≤ 0°F	3	2	0	0	0	0	0	0	0	0	0	2	7
Heating Degree Days (base 65°F)	1,161	929	689	352	112	13	1	3	66	305	662	1,071	5,364
Cooling Degree Days (base 65°F)	0	0	3	22	76	247	386	340	152	23	1	0	1,250
Mean Precipitation (in.)	1.47	1.66	2.81	3.55	4.92	4.99	5.02	4.47	4.12	3.62	2.78	2.15	41.56
Extreme Maximum Daily Precip. (in.)	2.71	2.43	2.02	2.73	4.59	5.47	4.22	4.58	4.38	5.06	3.27	3.40	5.47
Days With ≥ 0.1" Precipitation	3	4	6	7	8	8	7	6	6	6	5	5	71
Days With ≥ 0.5" Precipitation	1	1	2	2	3	3	3	3	2	2	2	1	25
Days With ≥ 1.0" Precipitation	0	0	1	1	1	2	2	2	1	1	1	0	12
Mean Snowfall (in.)	3.7	2.7	1.1	0.2	0.0	0.0	0.0	0.0	0.0	0.1	1.1	3.6	12.5
Maximum Snow Depth (in.)	12	14	11	2	0	0	0	0	0	2	5	14	14
Days With ≥ 1.0" Snow Depth	11	8	2	0	0	0	0	0	0	0	1	8	30

The period of record for all cooperative weather station data is 1980 – 2009. See User Guide for detailed explanation of data.

Brunswick *Chariton County* Elevation: 660 ft. Latitude: 39° 26' N Longitude: 93° 07' W

	JAN	FEB	MAR	APR	MAY	JUN	JUL	AUG	SEP	OCT	NOV	DEC	YEAR
Mean Maximum Temp. (°F)	36.2	41.5	53.2	64.5	73.5	81.8	86.3	85.2	77.5	66.2	52.5	39.4	63.1
Mean Temp. (°F)	26.9	31.6	42.2	53.1	63.1	71.9	76.5	74.7	66.2	54.9	42.8	30.4	52.9
Mean Minimum Temp. (°F)	17.6	21.7	31.1	41.7	52.6	61.9	66.6	64.3	54.9	43.6	32.9	21.4	42.5
Extreme Maximum Temp. (°F)	70	76	86	91	94	102	108	106	100	94	83	71	108
Extreme Minimum Temp. (°F)	-22	-17	-3	18	31	40	49	42	30	20	-7	-25	-25
Days Maximum Temp. ≥ 90°F	0	0	0	0	0	3	9	9	2	0	0	0	23
Days Maximum Temp. ≤ 32°F	12	7	2	0	0	0	0	0	0	0	1	8	30
Days Minimum Temp. ≤ 32°F	29	23	17	5	0	0	0	0	0	4	15	26	119
Days Minimum Temp. ≤ 0°F	3	2	0	0	0	0	0	0	0	0	0	2	7
Heating Degree Days (base 65°F)	1,175	939	704	370	122	15	1	5	85	323	661	1,066	5,466
Cooling Degree Days (base 65°F)	0	0	3	20	69	229	363	313	128	18	1	0	1,144
Mean Precipitation (in.)	1.44	1.74	2.40	3.36	5.41	4.99	4.25	3.96	3.40	3.31	2.71	1.94	38.91
Extreme Maximum Daily Precip. (in.)	3.12	2.55	2.44	2.34	4.22	5.36	2.86	5.81	3.96	3.17	2.71	3.58	5.81
Days With ≥ 0.1" Precipitation	3	3	5	7	8	7	6	5	5	5	5	4	63
Days With ≥ 0.5" Precipitation	1	1	1	2	4	3	3	3	2	2	2	1	25
Days With ≥ 1.0" Precipitation	0	0	0	1	1	2	1	1	1	1	1	0	9
Mean Snowfall (in.)	3.2	2.5	1.3	0.1	0.0	0.0	0.0	0.0	0.0	trace	0.6	2.8	10.5
Maximum Snow Depth (in.)	*7*	*10*	6	trace	0	0	0	0	0	trace	4	10	*10*
Days With ≥ 1.0" Snow Depth	*6*	*4*	1	0	0	0	0	0	0	0	0	3	*14*

Canton L and D 20 *Lewis County* Elevation: 490 ft. Latitude: 40° 09' N Longitude: 91° 31' W

	JAN	FEB	MAR	APR	MAY	JUN	JUL	AUG	SEP	OCT	NOV	DEC	YEAR
Mean Maximum Temp. (°F)	35.3	39.8	51.6	63.9	74.0	83.0	87.3	85.7	78.4	66.5	52.4	38.4	63.0
Mean Temp. (°F)	26.7	30.5	41.2	53.1	63.6	72.7	77.0	75.3	67.1	55.2	42.8	29.9	52.9
Mean Minimum Temp. (°F)	18.1	21.2	30.9	42.1	53.1	62.5	66.7	64.9	55.7	43.9	33.1	21.3	42.8
Extreme Maximum Temp. (°F)	70	76	89	95	96	103	110	108	104	95	82	73	110
Extreme Minimum Temp. (°F)	-20	-16	-4	17	30	42	52	44	32	24	-6	-18	-20
Days Maximum Temp. ≥ 90°F	0	0	0	0	1	6	11	9	3	0	0	0	30
Days Maximum Temp. ≤ 32°F	12	8	2	0	0	0	0	0	0	0	1	9	32
Days Minimum Temp. ≤ 32°F	28	24	18	5	0	0	0	0	0	3	15	26	119
Days Minimum Temp. ≤ 0°F	3	2	0	0	0	0	0	0	0	0	0	2	7
Heating Degree Days (base 65°F)	1,181	969	732	371	118	12	0	3	71	318	661	1,081	5,517
Cooling Degree Days (base 65°F)	0	0	3	19	80	251	379	329	140	20	1	0	1,222
Mean Precipitation (in.)	1.44	1.71	2.68	3.61	5.11	4.05	4.05	3.98	3.91	3.14	3.07	2.13	38.88
Extreme Maximum Daily Precip. (in.)	1.90	2.10	4.35	2.48	4.00	4.48	4.98	4.26	6.57	2.66	3.01	3.07	6.57
Days With ≥ 0.1" Precipitation	3	4	5	7	8	7	6	6	5	6	5	4	66
Days With ≥ 0.5" Precipitation	1	1	2	2	3	3	3	3	3	2	2	1	26
Days With ≥ 1.0" Precipitation	0	0	0	1	1	1	1	1	1	1	1	0	8
Mean Snowfall (in.)	*0.6*	*0.7*	trace	0.0	0.0	0.0	0.0	0.0	0.0	0.0	trace	*1.3*	*2.6*
Maximum Snow Depth (in.)	na	na	*trace*	*0*	*0*	*0*	*0*	*0*	*0*	*0*	*trace*	na	na
Days With ≥ 1.0" Snow Depth	na	*1*	0	0	0	0	0	0	0	0	0	*1*	na

Cape Girardeau Municipal Arpt *Scott County* Elevation: 336 ft. Latitude: 37° 14' N Longitude: 89° 35' W

	JAN	FEB	MAR	APR	MAY	JUN	JUL	AUG	SEP	OCT	NOV	DEC	YEAR
Mean Maximum Temp. (°F)	42.3	47.3	58.0	68.8	77.7	86.3	89.7	88.9	81.2	70.0	57.3	45.1	67.7
Mean Temp. (°F)	33.7	38.1	47.6	57.8	67.2	75.8	79.4	77.9	69.4	58.2	47.4	36.7	57.4
Mean Minimum Temp. (°F)	25.1	28.8	37.1	46.8	56.7	65.2	69.0	66.8	57.7	46.3	37.5	28.2	47.1
Extreme Maximum Temp. (°F)	72	76	94	91	97	103	105	104	99	92	82	76	105
Extreme Minimum Temp. (°F)	-15	-8	7	18	35	45	51	45	33	23	12	-11	-15
Days Maximum Temp. ≥ 90°F	0	0	0	0	1	10	17	15	4	0	0	0	47
Days Maximum Temp. ≤ 32°F	6	4	0	0	0	0	0	0	0	0	0	4	14
Days Minimum Temp. ≤ 32°F	24	18	12	2	0	0	0	0	0	2	11	21	90
Days Minimum Temp. ≤ 0°F	1	0	0	0	0	0	0	0	0	0	0	1	2
Heating Degree Days (base 65°F)	963	755	539	243	57	2	0	1	42	238	522	872	4,234
Cooling Degree Days (base 65°F)	0	0	5	34	133	332	453	408	182	33	2	0	1,582
Mean Precipitation (in.)	3.24	3.42	4.35	4.15	5.35	3.49	3.26	3.09	3.31	3.97	4.47	4.25	46.35
Extreme Maximum Daily Precip. (in.)	4.81	3.16	11.49	5.54	6.64	3.63	5.81	4.93	4.66	3.16	6.05	3.92	11.49
Days With ≥ 0.1" Precipitation	6	6	7	7	8	6	6	5	5	6	7	7	76
Days With ≥ 0.5" Precipitation	2	2	3	3	3	3	2	2	2	3	3	3	31
Days With ≥ 1.0" Precipitation	1	1	1	1	1	1	1	1	1	1	1	1	12
Mean Snowfall (in.)	na	na	na	na	na	na	na	na	na	na	na	na	na
Maximum Snow Depth (in.)	na	na	na	na	na	na	na	na	na	na	na	na	na
Days With ≥ 1.0" Snow Depth	na	na	na	na	na	na	na	na	na	na	na	na	na

Doniphan *Ripley County* Elevation: 330 ft. Latitude: 36° 37' N Longitude: 90° 49' W

	JAN	FEB	MAR	APR	MAY	JUN	JUL	AUG	SEP	OCT	NOV	DEC	YEAR
Mean Maximum Temp. (°F)	45.6	51.1	60.3	70.8	78.7	86.7	91.1	90.4	83.0	71.9	59.6	47.2	69.7
Mean Temp. (°F)	33.7	38.0	46.5	56.5	65.3	74.0	78.4	77.3	69.0	57.0	46.4	35.6	56.5
Mean Minimum Temp. (°F)	21.7	24.9	32.7	42.1	52.0	61.2	65.6	64.2	54.9	42.1	33.2	23.9	43.2
Extreme Maximum Temp. (°F)	74	84	87	94	94	105	110	108	102	93	85	75	110
Extreme Minimum Temp. (°F)	-19	-11	6	17	30	35	49	38	32	17	11	-14	-19
Days Maximum Temp. ≥ 90°F	0	0	0	0	2	11	20	18	7	0	0	0	58
Days Maximum Temp. ≤ 32°F	3	2	0	0	0	0	0	0	0	0	0	3	8
Days Minimum Temp. ≤ 32°F	26	21	16	6	0	0	0	0	0	7	15	24	115
Days Minimum Temp. ≤ 0°F	1	1	0	0	0	0	0	0	0	0	0	1	3
Heating Degree Days (base 65°F)	965	756	571	274	83	5	0	1	44	265	553	905	4,422
Cooling Degree Days (base 65°F)	0	0	4	25	100	281	423	390	171	25	1	0	1,420
Mean Precipitation (in.)	3.49	3.57	4.46	4.73	5.01	3.01	4.20	3.30	3.76	4.26	4.92	4.40	49.11
Extreme Maximum Daily Precip. (in.)	4.28	3.27	6.67	3.52	5.03	1.80	4.86	7.12	7.23	3.38	4.82	5.38	7.23
Days With ≥ 0.1" Precipitation	5	6	7	7	8	6	6	5	5	6	7	6	74
Days With ≥ 0.5" Precipitation	2	3	3	3	3	2	3	2	2	3	3	3	32
Days With ≥ 1.0" Precipitation	1	1	1	1	1	1	1	1	1	1	2	1	13
Mean Snowfall (in.)	2.6	3.3	1.6	0.0	0.0	0.0	0.0	0.0	0.0	0.1	0.2	1.4	9.2
Maximum Snow Depth (in.)	7	12	17	0	0	0	0	0	0	2	6	6	17
Days With ≥ 1.0" Snow Depth	3	3	1	0	0	0	0	0	0	0	0	2	9

The period of record for all cooperative weather station data is 1980 – 2009. See User Guide for detailed explanation of data.

Dora *Ozark County* Elevation: 990 ft. Latitude: 36° 47' N Longitude: 92° 14' W

	JAN	FEB	MAR	APR	MAY	JUN	JUL	AUG	SEP	OCT	NOV	DEC	YEAR
Mean Maximum Temp. (°F)	45.2	50.4	59.6	69.8	76.2	83.4	88.6	89.1	81.1	70.2	58.6	46.5	68.2
Mean Temp. (°F)	34.0	38.3	46.7	56.5	64.5	72.4	77.3	76.9	68.7	57.1	46.7	35.6	56.2
Mean Minimum Temp. (°F)	22.7	26.0	33.8	43.1	52.8	61.4	66.0	64.7	56.2	43.8	34.8	24.9	44.2
Extreme Maximum Temp. (°F)	76	82	87	94	93	102	109	107	103	92	88	78	109
Extreme Minimum Temp. (°F)	-16	-9	2	14	26	40	50	41	26	16	5	-21	-21
Days Maximum Temp. ≥ 90°F	0	0	0	0	0	3	15	15	5	0	0	0	38
Days Maximum Temp. ≤ 32°F	5	2	0	0	0	0	0	0	0	0	0	3	10
Days Minimum Temp. ≤ 32°F	26	20	14	4	0	0	0	0	0	4	12	23	103
Days Minimum Temp. ≤ 0°F	1	1	0	0	0	0	0	0	0	0	0	1	3
Heating Degree Days (base 65°F)	954	749	565	275	91	8	1	2	52	259	542	905	4,403
Cooling Degree Days (base 65°F)	0	0	4	26	83	236	390	378	168	22	2	0	1,309
Mean Precipitation (in.)	2.25	2.70	3.90	4.53	5.00	4.20	3.20	2.79	3.89	3.92	4.45	3.47	44.30
Extreme Maximum Daily Precip. (in.)	2.65	4.89	4.45	3.23	4.09	2.90	3.40	3.38	3.53	4.15	6.40	4.25	6.40
Days With ≥ 0.1" Precipitation	4	4	6	6	8	6	5	4	5	5	6	4	63
Days With ≥ 0.5" Precipitation	2	2	3	3	4	3	2	2	2	3	3	2	31
Days With ≥ 1.0" Precipitation	1	1	1	1	1	1	1	1	1	1	1	1	12
Mean Snowfall (in.)	2.8	2.6	1.0	0.2	0.0	0.0	0.0	0.0	0.0	trace	0.2	2.1	8.9
Maximum Snow Depth (in.)	9	18	13	4	0	0	0	0	0	trace	6	9	18
Days With ≥ 1.0" Snow Depth	4	4	1	0	0	0	0	0	0	0	0	3	12

Freedom *Osage County* Elevation: 745 ft. Latitude: 38° 28' N Longitude: 91° 42' W

	JAN	FEB	MAR	APR	MAY	JUN	JUL	AUG	SEP	OCT	NOV	DEC	YEAR
Mean Maximum Temp. (°F)	40.7	45.8	56.4	67.0	75.2	83.1	88.2	87.8	79.7	68.4	55.7	43.1	65.9
Mean Temp. (°F)	30.5	34.7	44.4	54.6	63.5	71.9	76.7	75.6	67.2	55.8	45.0	33.2	54.4
Mean Minimum Temp. (°F)	20.2	23.6	32.4	42.2	51.8	60.7	65.2	63.3	54.6	43.2	34.3	23.4	42.9
Extreme Maximum Temp. (°F)	75	78	87	94	93	106	111	109	103	92	85	77	111
Extreme Minimum Temp. (°F)	-20	-17	-3	17	27	38	47	37	28	17	2	-21	-21
Days Maximum Temp. ≥ 90°F	0	0	0	0	1	5	14	13	4	0	0	0	37
Days Maximum Temp. ≤ 32°F	8	6	1	0	0	0	0	0	0	0	1	6	22
Days Minimum Temp. ≤ 32°F	27	22	16	5	0	0	0	0	0	5	13	24	112
Days Minimum Temp. ≤ 0°F	2	1	0	0	0	0	0	0	0	0	0	1	4
Heating Degree Days (base 65°F)	1,064	850	636	331	113	16	2	5	69	302	595	977	4,960
Cooling Degree Days (base 65°F)	0	0	6	26	76	231	372	339	142	23	2	0	1,217
Mean Precipitation (in.)	1.79	2.17	3.30	3.98	5.24	4.34	3.79	4.10	3.95	3.93	3.71	2.78	43.08
Extreme Maximum Daily Precip. (in.)	2.65	3.00	3.25	3.00	3.38	3.40	6.72	3.15	5.13	3.52	2.60	4.80	6.72
Days With ≥ 0.1" Precipitation	4	4	7	7	8	7	6	5	6	6	6	5	71
Days With ≥ 0.5" Precipitation	1	1	2	3	4	3	2	3	3	3	3	2	30
Days With ≥ 1.0" Precipitation	0	1	1	1	2	1	1	1	1	1	1	1	12
Mean Snowfall (in.)	3.3	3.4	1.2	trace	0.0	0.0	0.0	0.0	0.0	0.0	0.9	*2.7*	*11.5*
Maximum Snow Depth (in.)	*12*	*4*	6	trace	0	0	0	0	0	0	6	*8*	*12*
Days With ≥ 1.0" Snow Depth	*1*	*1*	0	0	0	0	0	0	0	0	0	*1*	*3*

Fulton *Callaway County* Elevation: 870 ft. Latitude: 38° 51' N Longitude: 91° 56' W

	JAN	FEB	MAR	APR	MAY	JUN	JUL	AUG	SEP	OCT	NOV	DEC	YEAR
Mean Maximum Temp. (°F)	37.8	43.2	53.9	65.2	73.9	82.2	87.2	86.4	78.4	66.9	53.8	40.9	64.1
Mean Temp. (°F)	28.7	33.2	42.9	53.8	63.1	71.9	76.6	75.4	66.9	55.3	43.8	31.8	53.6
Mean Minimum Temp. (°F)	19.6	23.2	31.9	42.4	52.1	61.5	66.1	64.3	55.3	43.7	33.7	22.8	43.0
Extreme Maximum Temp. (°F)	73	78	85	91	92	101	108	106	99	94	82	76	108
Extreme Minimum Temp. (°F)	-19	-15	-2	19	33	42	51	43	31	22	0	-21	-21
Days Maximum Temp. ≥ 90°F	0	0	0	0	0	4	11	11	3	0	0	0	29
Days Maximum Temp. ≤ 32°F	11	7	2	0	0	0	0	0	0	0	1	7	28
Days Minimum Temp. ≤ 32°F	28	23	17	4	0	0	0	0	0	4	14	26	116
Days Minimum Temp. ≤ 0°F	2	1	0	0	0	0	0	0	0	0	0	1	4
Heating Degree Days (base 65°F)	1,118	892	679	351	121	15	1	4	73	312	631	1,021	5,218
Cooling Degree Days (base 65°F)	0	0	3	22	68	229	369	333	136	18	1	0	1,179
Mean Precipitation (in.)	2.11	2.31	3.03	4.24	4.94	4.54	4.43	4.09	4.02	3.74	3.63	2.75	43.83
Extreme Maximum Daily Precip. (in.)	2.00	2.03	2.97	2.82	4.83	4.00	4.31	5.37	4.82	3.76	2.41	2.47	5.37
Days With ≥ 0.1" Precipitation	5	4	6	7	8	7	6	6	5	6	6	5	71
Days With ≥ 0.5" Precipitation	1	2	2	3	3	3	3	3	3	3	3	2	31
Days With ≥ 1.0" Precipitation	0	1	1	1	1	1	1	1	1	1	1	1	11
Mean Snowfall (in.)	6.1	4.9	2.4	0.4	0.0	0.0	0.0	0.0	0.0	trace	1.0	4.9	19.7
Maximum Snow Depth (in.)	14	12	8	3	0	0	0	0	0	trace	5	14	14
Days With ≥ 1.0" Snow Depth	9	6	2	0	0	0	0	0	0	0	1	6	24

Galena 1 SW *Stone County* Elevation: 1,100 ft. Latitude: 36° 48' N Longitude: 93° 29' W

	JAN	FEB	MAR	APR	MAY	JUN	JUL	AUG	SEP	OCT	NOV	DEC	YEAR
Mean Maximum Temp. (°F)	45.3	50.2	59.5	69.4	76.4	84.0	89.0	89.3	81.0	70.5	58.7	47.5	68.4
Mean Temp. (°F)	33.7	37.7	46.7	56.0	64.5	72.5	77.2	76.7	68.2	57.1	46.3	36.2	56.1
Mean Minimum Temp. (°F)	22.1	25.2	33.9	42.5	52.6	61.0	65.2	64.0	55.4	43.6	34.0	24.8	43.7
Extreme Maximum Temp. (°F)	76	79	88	96	92	99	106	105	105	92	86	77	106
Extreme Minimum Temp. (°F)	-21	-16	2	16	28	41	47	40	28	17	5	-18	-21
Days Maximum Temp. ≥ 90°F	0	0	0	0	0	5	16	16	5	0	0	0	42
Days Maximum Temp. ≤ 32°F	5	3	1	0	0	0	0	0	0	0	0	3	12
Days Minimum Temp. ≤ 32°F	26	21	15	5	0	0	0	0	0	5	13	24	109
Days Minimum Temp. ≤ 0°F	1	1	0	0	0	0	0	0	0	0	0	1	3
Heating Degree Days (base 65°F)	964	764	565	289	96	10	1	3	57	263	555	888	4,455
Cooling Degree Days (base 65°F)	0	0	5	25	88	242	385	371	160	24	2	0	1,302
Mean Precipitation (in.)	2.46	2.74	4.06	4.29	4.68	4.89	3.95	2.90	4.42	3.53	4.20	3.16	45.28
Extreme Maximum Daily Precip. (in.)	3.35	2.88	3.20	3.30	3.00	4.60	4.22	2.91	4.50	5.05	3.45	4.87	5.05
Days With ≥ 0.1" Precipitation	4	4	7	6	8	7	5	4	5	5	6	5	66
Days With ≥ 0.5" Precipitation	2	2	3	3	3	3	2	2	3	2	3	2	30
Days With ≥ 1.0" Precipitation	1	1	1	1	1	1	1	1	1	1	1	1	12
Mean Snowfall (in.)	1.9	*2.0*	0.8	trace	0.0	0.0	0.0	0.0	0.0	0.0	0.2	1.8	*6.7*
Maximum Snow Depth (in.)	9	12	12	trace	0	0	0	0	0	1	3	9	12
Days With ≥ 1.0" Snow Depth	1	1	1	0	0	0	0	0	0	0	0	1	4

The period of record for all cooperative weather station data is 1980 – 2009. See User Guide for detailed explanation of data.

Jackson *Cape Girardeau County* Elevation: 439 ft. Latitude: 37° 22' N Longitude: 89° 40' W

	JAN	FEB	MAR	APR	MAY	JUN	JUL	AUG	SEP	OCT	NOV	DEC	YEAR
Mean Maximum Temp. (°F)	43.0	48.4	58.9	70.4	79.1	87.9	91.2	90.3	82.8	71.1	57.4	44.8	68.8
Mean Temp. (°F)	33.9	38.5	47.7	58.3	67.4	76.3	79.7	78.2	70.4	58.8	47.5	36.1	57.7
Mean Minimum Temp. (°F)	24.8	28.5	36.4	46.1	55.6	64.7	68.3	66.3	58.1	46.4	37.5	27.3	46.7
Extreme Maximum Temp. (°F)	71	77	85	92	95	103	106	105	100	91	87	71	106
Extreme Minimum Temp. (°F)	-21	-16	7	21	29	45	52	40	32	22	6	-16	-21
Days Maximum Temp. ≥ 90°F	0	0	0	0	2	13	20	17	6	0	0	0	58
Days Maximum Temp. ≤ 32°F	6	3	0	0	0	0	0	0	0	0	0	4	13
Days Minimum Temp. ≤ 32°F	24	18	12	3	0	0	0	0	0	3	10	21	91
Days Minimum Temp. ≤ 0°F	1	0	0	0	0	0	0	0	0	0	0	1	2
Heating Degree Days (base 65°F)	957	744	535	233	60	1	0	1	33	225	521	890	4,200
Cooling Degree Days (base 65°F)	0	0	4	38	141	347	464	418	204	38	2	0	1,656
Mean Precipitation (in.)	3.01	3.66	4.76	4.72	5.19	4.11	4.05	3.03	3.35	4.12	4.68	3.96	48.64
Extreme Maximum Daily Precip. (in.)	3.45	3.37	9.21	3.67	5.80	3.70	4.35	5.70	2.77	3.79	5.97	3.10	9.21
Days With ≥ 0.1" Precipitation	6	6	7	7	8	6	6	5	5	6	7	6	75
Days With ≥ 0.5" Precipitation	2	3	3	3	4	3	3	2	2	3	4	3	35
Days With ≥ 1.0" Precipitation	1	1	1	1	1	1	1	1	1	1	1	1	12
Mean Snowfall (in.)	2.1	2.5	1.0	trace	0.0	0.0	0.0	0.0	0.0	0.1	0.4	1.7	7.8
Maximum Snow Depth (in.)	8	12	7	trace	0	0	0	0	0	0	1	8	12
Days With ≥ 1.0" Snow Depth	0	0	0	0	0	0	0	0	0	0	0	0	0

Jefferson City Wtr Plant *Cole County* Elevation: 669 ft. Latitude: 38° 35' N Longitude: 92° 11' W

	JAN	FEB	MAR	APR	MAY	JUN	JUL	AUG	SEP	OCT	NOV	DEC	YEAR
Mean Maximum Temp. (°F)	39.9	45.2	55.4	66.3	75.1	83.5	88.7	88.0	80.1	68.3	55.4	42.4	65.7
Mean Temp. (°F)	30.0	34.4	43.9	54.5	64.1	73.1	78.0	76.7	68.1	56.2	44.7	32.8	54.7
Mean Minimum Temp. (°F)	20.2	23.5	32.3	42.7	53.1	62.6	67.3	65.4	56.2	44.1	33.9	23.1	43.7
Extreme Maximum Temp. (°F)	73	81	87	93	93	103	110	110	100	93	84	78	110
Extreme Minimum Temp. (°F)	-17	-13	-1	17	34	44	50	42	30	14	3	-21	-21
Days Maximum Temp. ≥ 90°F	0	0	0	0	1	6	14	14	4	0	0	0	39
Days Maximum Temp. ≤ 32°F	9	6	1	0	0	0	0	0	0	0	1	7	24
Days Minimum Temp. ≤ 32°F	27	23	17	4	0	0	0	0	0	3	14	25	113
Days Minimum Temp. ≤ 0°F	2	1	0	0	0	0	0	0	0	0	0	1	4
Heating Degree Days (base 65°F)	1,077	859	652	333	105	10	1	2	58	290	603	992	4,982
Cooling Degree Days (base 65°F)	0	0	4	25	85	259	412	372	159	25	1	0	1,342
Mean Precipitation (in.)	1.85	2.22	3.00	4.10	5.07	4.26	4.17	3.99	3.94	3.54	3.54	2.68	42.36
Extreme Maximum Daily Precip. (in.)	2.21	2.80	2.12	3.19	4.17	3.70	7.41	5.55	4.98	3.85	3.25	2.22	7.41
Days With ≥ 0.1" Precipitation	4	4	6	7	8	7	6	5	5	6	6	5	69
Days With ≥ 0.5" Precipitation	1	2	2	3	3	3	3	3	3	2	2	2	29
Days With ≥ 1.0" Precipitation	0	1	1	1	1	1	1	1	1	1	1	1	11
Mean Snowfall (in.)	4.4	3.1	1.2	0.1	0.0	0.0	0.0	0.0	0.0	0.0	0.4	3.1	12.3
Maximum Snow Depth (in.)	4	7	6	3	0	0	0	0	0	0	4	12	12
Days With ≥ 1.0" Snow Depth	1	2	0	0	0	0	0	0	0	0	0	2	5

Joplin Municipal Arpt *Jasper County* Elevation: 979 ft. Latitude: 37° 09' N Longitude: 94° 30' W

	JAN	FEB	MAR	APR	MAY	JUN	JUL	AUG	SEP	OCT	NOV	DEC	YEAR
Mean Maximum Temp. (°F)	44.7	49.6	59.8	69.5	77.2	85.1	90.6	90.6	81.9	71.0	58.1	46.7	68.7
Mean Temp. (°F)	35.1	39.3	48.7	58.2	66.7	75.1	80.4	79.6	70.5	59.7	47.9	37.2	58.2
Mean Minimum Temp. (°F)	25.4	28.9	37.6	46.9	56.1	65.0	70.1	68.6	59.2	48.3	37.6	27.7	47.6
Extreme Maximum Temp. (°F)	77	87	90	95	94	100	108	105	105	93	87	75	108
Extreme Minimum Temp. (°F)	-12	-8	0	19	32	44	51	47	30	18	8	-15	-15
Days Maximum Temp. ≥ 90°F	0	0	0	0	1	7	19	18	6	0	0	0	51
Days Maximum Temp. ≤ 32°F	6	3	0	0	0	0	0	0	0	0	0	4	13
Days Minimum Temp. ≤ 32°F	23	18	10	2	0	0	0	0	0	2	11	21	87
Days Minimum Temp. ≤ 0°F	1	0	0	0	0	0	0	0	0	0	0	1	2
Heating Degree Days (base 65°F)	920	722	505	241	66	4	0	1	43	210	513	854	4,079
Cooling Degree Days (base 65°F)	0	0	8	45	125	315	483	462	216	51	6	0	1,711
Mean Precipitation (in.)	2.03	2.38	3.33	4.56	5.67	5.82	3.53	3.46	4.64	3.83	3.78	2.92	45.95
Extreme Maximum Daily Precip. (in.)	2.14	4.69	3.22	3.45	5.71	3.86	3.08	4.91	7.12	4.35	3.35	3.59	7.12
Days With ≥ 0.1" Precipitation	4	4	6	7	8	8	5	5	6	6	5	5	69
Days With ≥ 0.5" Precipitation	1	2	2	3	4	4	2	2	3	2	3	2	30
Days With ≥ 1.0" Precipitation	0	0	1	1	2	2	1	1	2	1	1	1	13
Mean Snowfall (in.)	na	na	na	na	na	na	na	na	na	na	na	na	na
Maximum Snow Depth (in.)	na	na	na	na	na	na	na	na	na	na	na	na	na
Days With ≥ 1.0" Snow Depth	na	na	na	na	na	na	na	na	na	na	na	na	na

Kansas City Muni Arpt *Jackson County* Elevation: 575 ft. Latitude: 39° 07' N Longitude: 94° 35' W

	JAN	FEB	MAR	APR	MAY	JUN	JUL	AUG	SEP	OCT	NOV	DEC	YEAR
Mean Maximum Temp. (°F)	39.6	45.3	55.8	66.0	75.9	84.5	90.5	88.6	79.9	67.8	54.1	41.1	65.7
Mean Temp. (°F)	31.0	36.2	46.0	56.3	66.6	75.5	81.4	79.6	70.4	58.4	45.3	33.1	56.7
Mean Minimum Temp. (°F)	22.4	27.2	36.1	46.5	57.3	66.5	72.3	70.5	60.9	49.0	36.5	25.0	47.5
Extreme Maximum Temp. (°F)	72	79	86	93	96	108	109	110	106	94	82	73	110
Extreme Minimum Temp. (°F)	-14	-12	2	20	36	46	57	48	34	22	7	-13	-14
Days Maximum Temp. ≥ 90°F	0	0	0	0	1	7	17	14	4	0	0	0	43
Days Maximum Temp. ≤ 32°F	8	5	1	0	0	0	0	0	0	0	1	7	22
Days Minimum Temp. ≤ 32°F	26	19	12	2	0	0	0	0	0	1	11	23	94
Days Minimum Temp. ≤ 0°F	1	1	0	0	0	0	0	0	0	0	0	1	3
Heating Degree Days (base 65°F)	1,046	808	589	288	66	4	0	0	44	238	585	983	4,651
Cooling Degree Days (base 65°F)	0	0	5	33	124	328	516	459	214	41	2	0	1,722
Mean Precipitation (in.)	1.07	1.43	2.25	3.52	5.06	5.76	4.05	4.50	4.16	3.77	2.01	1.57	39.15
Extreme Maximum Daily Precip. (in.)	3.50	2.50	2.40	2.09	4.73	5.25	6.45	5.60	4.84	4.95	1.82	2.60	6.45
Days With ≥ 0.1" Precipitation	2	3	5	7	8	8	6	6	6	6	4	3	64
Days With ≥ 0.5" Precipitation	0	1	2	2	4	4	2	3	3	2	1	1	25
Days With ≥ 1.0" Precipitation	0	0	0	1	1	2	1	1	1	1	1	0	9
Mean Snowfall (in.)	3.9	2.8	1.0	0.2	trace	0.0	0.0	0.0	0.0	0.3	0.3	4.2	12.7
Maximum Snow Depth (in.)	na	na	na	na	na	na	na	na	na	na	na	na	na
Days With ≥ 1.0" Snow Depth	na	na	na	na	na	na	0	0	0	0	0	na	na

Lees Summit Reed Wlr *Jackson County* Elevation: 1,000 ft. Latitude: 38° 53' N Longitude: 94° 20' W

	JAN	FEB	MAR	APR	MAY	JUN	JUL	AUG	SEP	OCT	NOV	DEC	YEAR
Mean Maximum Temp. (°F)	39.6	44.7	55.8	66.2	75.1	83.6	88.4	87.7	79.6	67.9	54.1	41.3	65.3
Mean Temp. (°F)	29.5	34.0	44.1	54.6	64.0	72.7	77.4	76.2	67.7	56.0	43.7	31.7	54.3
Mean Minimum Temp. (°F)	19.2	23.2	32.3	43.0	52.8	61.8	66.4	64.7	55.7	44.1	33.5	22.0	43.2
Extreme Maximum Temp. (°F)	73	75	85	91	91	103	108	107	105	94	82	72	108
Extreme Minimum Temp. (°F)	-19	-15	-2	17	30	35	49	43	29	7	0	-25	-25
Days Maximum Temp. ≥ 90°F	0	0	0	0	1	5	14	13	4	0	0	0	37
Days Maximum Temp. ≤ 32°F	9	6	1	0	0	0	0	0	0	0	1	7	24
Days Minimum Temp. ≤ 32°F	27	22	16	4	0	0	0	0	0	4	14	26	113
Days Minimum Temp. ≤ 0°F	2	1	0	0	0	0	0	0	0	0	0	2	5
Heating Degree Days (base 65°F)	1,095	870	642	327	102	11	1	4	68	293	632	1,025	5,070
Cooling Degree Days (base 65°F)	0	0	2	22	78	249	393	359	154	22	1	0	1,280
Mean Precipitation (in.)	1.28	1.79	2.66	3.98	5.55	6.09	4.34	4.58	4.49	3.92	2.59	1.77	43.04
Extreme Maximum Daily Precip. (in.)	2.30	2.40	1.97	3.10	6.90	5.30	2.98	8.02	7.50	5.00	2.80	2.28	8.02
Days With ≥ 0.1" Precipitation	3	3	5	7	8	7	6	6	6	6	5	4	66
Days With ≥ 0.5" Precipitation	1	1	2	3	4	4	3	3	3	3	2	1	30
Days With ≥ 1.0" Precipitation	0	0	1	1	1	2	1	1	2	1	1	0	11
Mean Snowfall (in.)	3.8	3.9	1.2	0.1	0.0	0.0	0.0	0.0	0.0	trace	0.5	3.0	12.5
Maximum Snow Depth (in.)	9	13	4	1	0	0	0	0	0	0	4	9	13
Days With ≥ 1.0" Snow Depth	4	4	1	0	0	0	0	0	0	0	0	4	13

Lexington 3 NE *Lafayette County* Elevation: 825 ft. Latitude: 39° 12' N Longitude: 93° 52' W

	JAN	FEB	MAR	APR	MAY	JUN	JUL	AUG	SEP	OCT	NOV	DEC	YEAR
Mean Maximum Temp. (°F)	38.6	43.2	55.0	65.8	75.1	83.9	88.3	87.2	79.9	67.9	53.7	41.7	65.0
Mean Temp. (°F)	28.7	32.8	43.4	54.3	63.8	73.0	77.4	75.8	67.5	55.8	43.2	32.1	54.0
Mean Minimum Temp. (°F)	18.7	22.4	31.8	42.5	52.4	61.8	66.5	64.4	54.9	43.7	32.6	22.3	42.8
Extreme Maximum Temp. (°F)	70	77	86	91	96	102	109	***108***	105	95	82	74	***109***
Extreme Minimum Temp. (°F)	-18	-14	-2	16	29	42	49	***41***	30	20	-5	-22	***-22***
Days Maximum Temp. ≥ 90°F	0	0	0	0	1	6	13	13	4	0	0	0	37
Days Maximum Temp. ≤ 32°F	9	6	1	0	0	0	0	0	0	0	1	7	24
Days Minimum Temp. ≤ 32°F	28	23	16	4	0	0	0	0	0	4	15	26	116
Days Minimum Temp. ≤ 0°F	2	1	0	0	0	0	0	0	0	0	0	2	5
Heating Degree Days (base 65°F)	1,119	903	666	339	111	10	1	4	69	300	649	1,014	5,185
Cooling Degree Days (base 65°F)	0	0	3	23	80	255	393	344	149	22	1	0	1,270
Mean Precipitation (in.)	1.49	1.80	2.68	3.57	5.19	5.12	4.62	4.20	4.56	3.47	2.51	2.04	41.25
Extreme Maximum Daily Precip. (in.)	2.41	2.28	2.57	2.68	3.96	***4.03***	3.74	***4.21***	***6.17***	5.64	2.08	1.73	***6.17***
Days With ≥ 0.1" Precipitation	3	4	5	6	8	7	6	6	6	6	4	4	65
Days With ≥ 0.5" Precipitation	1	1	2	3	3	3	3	3	3	2	2	1	27
Days With ≥ 1.0" Precipitation	0	0	1	1	1	2	1	1	2	1	1	1	12
Mean Snowfall (in.)	4.8	4.0	1.2	0.1	0.0	0.0	0.0	0.0	0.0	trace	0.6	3.8	14.5
Maximum Snow Depth (in.)	8	13	8	2	0	0	0	***0***	***0***	***trace***	3	11	***13***
Days With ≥ 1.0" Snow Depth	7	5	1	0	0	0	0	0	0	0	0	5	18

Lockwood *Dade County* Elevation: 1,080 ft. Latitude: 37° 23' N Longitude: 93° 57' W

	JAN	FEB	MAR	APR	MAY	JUN	JUL	AUG	SEP	OCT	NOV	DEC	YEAR
Mean Maximum Temp. (°F)	43.0	48.2	57.7	67.5	75.8	84.0	89.3	89.5	81.1	69.7	57.0	45.1	67.3
Mean Temp. (°F)	33.0	37.6	46.5	55.8	65.2	73.7	78.8	78.1	69.5	58.2	46.7	35.4	56.5
Mean Minimum Temp. (°F)	23.1	26.9	35.1	44.1	54.5	63.4	68.3	66.7	57.8	46.5	36.2	25.7	45.7
Extreme Maximum Temp. (°F)	74	80	86	93	92	101	108	105	105	93	87	75	108
Extreme Minimum Temp. (°F)	-16	-9	0	21	33	45	50	45	32	18	6	-17	-17
Days Maximum Temp. ≥ 90°F	0	0	0	0	1	6	16	17	5	0	0	0	45
Days Maximum Temp. ≤ 32°F	6	4	1	0	0	0	0	0	0	0	1	5	17
Days Minimum Temp. ≤ 32°F	26	20	13	3	0	0	0	0	0	2	11	23	98
Days Minimum Temp. ≤ 0°F	1	1	0	0	0	0	0	0	0	0	0	1	3
Heating Degree Days (base 65°F)	984	769	572	296	87	8	0	2	50	241	547	911	4,467
Cooling Degree Days (base 65°F)	0	0	4	26	99	276	436	416	190	36	3	0	1,486
Mean Precipitation (in.)	2.13	2.45	3.61	4.44	5.57	5.48	4.35	3.57	4.64	4.02	3.89	2.79	46.94
Extreme Maximum Daily Precip. (in.)	3.35	5.28	2.89	3.05	4.61	3.77	3.75	4.76	6.04	5.37	4.05	2.15	6.04
Days With ≥ 0.1" Precipitation	4	4	7	7	8	8	5	5	5	6	5	5	69
Days With ≥ 0.5" Precipitation	1	2	3	3	4	4	3	2	3	2	3	2	32
Days With ≥ 1.0" Precipitation	1	1	1	1	2	2	2	1	1	1	1	1	15
Mean Snowfall (in.)	4.3	3.6	2.4	trace	0.0	0.0	0.0	0.0	0.0	trace	0.4	3.9	14.6
Maximum Snow Depth (in.)	9	16	15	trace	0	0	0	0	0	trace	5	11	16
Days With ≥ 1.0" Snow Depth	6	4	1	0	0	0	0	0	0	0	0	4	15

Marshfield *Webster County* Elevation: 1,490 ft. Latitude: 37° 20' N Longitude: 92° 55' W

	JAN	FEB	MAR	APR	MAY	JUN	JUL	AUG	SEP	OCT	NOV	DEC	YEAR
Mean Maximum Temp. (°F)	42.6	47.5	57.4	67.3	75.4	83.1	87.9	87.9	79.6	68.2	56.2	44.6	66.5
Mean Temp. (°F)	33.0	37.4	46.4	56.2	65.0	73.1	77.9	77.4	69.0	57.7	46.4	35.4	56.2
Mean Minimum Temp. (°F)	23.4	27.1	35.4	45.0	54.7	63.0	67.8	66.8	58.3	47.2	36.6	26.1	46.0
Extreme Maximum Temp. (°F)	74	79	84	91	92	100	105	103	102	91	84	75	105
Extreme Minimum Temp. (°F)	-20	-11	1	19	32	43	51	47	31	19	4	-18	-20
Days Maximum Temp. ≥ 90°F	0	0	0	0	0	4	13	13	3	0	0	0	33
Days Maximum Temp. ≤ 32°F	7	4	1	0	0	0	0	0	0	0	0	5	17
Days Minimum Temp. ≤ 32°F	25	19	13	3	0	0	0	0	0	2	11	22	95
Days Minimum Temp. ≤ 0°F	1	1	0	0	0	0	0	0	0	0	0	1	3
Heating Degree Days (base 65°F)	985	775	572	286	86	9	0	2	50	250	552	911	4,478
Cooling Degree Days (base 65°F)	0	0	4	29	95	259	407	393	177	30	2	0	1,396
Mean Precipitation (in.)	2.50	2.46	3.59	4.16	4.83	4.58	3.81	2.86	3.91	3.80	4.03	2.99	43.52
Extreme Maximum Daily Precip. (in.)	3.80	2.40	3.50	2.73	3.90	3.77	4.28	2.85	4.55	6.17	5.30	3.40	6.17
Days With ≥ 0.1" Precipitation	4	5	6	7	8	7	6	5	5	6	6	5	70
Days With ≥ 0.5" Precipitation	2	2	2	3	3	3	2	2	2	2	3	2	28
Days With ≥ 1.0" Precipitation	1	1	1	1	1	1	1	1	1	1	1	1	12
Mean Snowfall (in.)	2.7	3.1	0.6	0.1	0.0	0.0	0.0	0.0	0.0	0.0	0.3	2.0	8.8
Maximum Snow Depth (in.)	***8***	***10***	2	0	0	0	0	0	0	0	trace	6	***10***
Days With ≥ 1.0" Snow Depth	***2***	1	0	0	0	0	0	0	0	0	0	0	***3***

The period of record for all cooperative weather station data is 1980 – 2009. See User Guide for detailed explanation of data.

Mexico *Audrain County* Elevation: 801 ft. Latitude: 39° 11' N Longitude: 91° 53' W

	JAN	FEB	MAR	APR	MAY	JUN	JUL	AUG	SEP	OCT	NOV	DEC	YEAR
Mean Maximum Temp. (°F)	37.8	42.3	53.7	65.7	74.9	83.7	88.3	87.2	***79.4***	***67.5***	54.5	40.4	***64.6***
Mean Temp. (°F)	28.3	31.8	42.3	53.8	63.7	72.9	77.5	75.9	***67.3***	***55.5***	44.1	31.0	***53.7***
Mean Minimum Temp. (°F)	18.8	21.3	30.9	42.0	52.4	62.0	66.6	64.5	***55.1***	***43.4***	33.6	21.6	***42.7***
Extreme Maximum Temp. (°F)	73	75	86	93	94	103	109	***108***	***99***	***93***	83	73	***109***
Extreme Minimum Temp. (°F)	-20	-18	-1	18	33	42	49	***41***	***30***	***22***	4	-25	***-25***
Days Maximum Temp. ≥ 90°F	0	0	0	0	1	6	14	12	***4***	***0***	0	0	***37***
Days Maximum Temp. ≤ 32°F	10	7	2	0	0	0	0	0	***0***	***0***	1	8	***28***
Days Minimum Temp. ≤ 32°F	29	23	18	5	0	0	0	0	***0***	***4***	14	26	***119***
Days Minimum Temp. ≤ 0°F	2	2	0	0	0	0	0	0	***0***	***0***	0	2	***6***
Heating Degree Days (base 65°F)	1,130	933	700	352	114	12	0	4	***71***	***309***	623	1,048	***5,296***
Cooling Degree Days (base 65°F)	0	0	3	24	79	255	394	349	***147***	***20***	1	0	***1,272***
Mean Precipitation (in.)	1.99	1.99	2.85	4.01	5.18	4.85	4.18	3.91	3.78	3.33	3.53	2.71	42.31
Extreme Maximum Daily Precip. (in.)	2.79	1.85	2.07	3.90	3.67	***4.80***	4.65	***5.37***	***6.28***	***3.58***	2.08	***1.94***	***6.28***
Days With ≥ 0.1" Precipitation	4	4	7	7	9	7	6	6	5	6	6	5	72
Days With ≥ 0.5" Precipitation	1	1	2	3	3	3	3	3	2	3	3	2	29
Days With ≥ 1.0" Precipitation	1	0	0	1	2	1	1	1	1	1	1	1	11
Mean Snowfall (in.)	5.7	4.6	2.3	0.2	0.0	0.0	0.0	0.0	0.0	trace	0.7	5.0	18.5
Maximum Snow Depth (in.)	***11***	na	na	***3***	***0***	***0***	***0***	na	na	na	***6***	na	na
Days With ≥ 1.0" Snow Depth	***4***	3	1	0	0	0	0	0	0	***0***	0	***4***	***12***

Sedalia Water Plant *Pettis County* Elevation: 779 ft. Latitude: 38° 40' N Longitude: 93° 13' W

	JAN	FEB	MAR	APR	MAY	JUN	JUL	AUG	SEP	OCT	NOV	DEC	YEAR
Mean Maximum Temp. (°F)	38.8	43.8	54.4	65.1	74.3	82.9	87.9	87.2	79.0	67.4	54.3	41.5	64.7
Mean Temp. (°F)	28.6	32.8	42.7	53.1	62.9	72.1	76.9	75.3	66.5	54.9	43.3	31.6	53.4
Mean Minimum Temp. (°F)	18.4	21.8	31.0	41.1	51.5	61.3	65.8	63.4	54.1	42.4	32.3	21.7	42.1
Extreme Maximum Temp. (°F)	71	77	84	91	91	105	107	107	103	93	81	74	107
Extreme Minimum Temp. (°F)	-18	-18	-9	18	28	41	50	39	28	20	-6	-28	-28
Days Maximum Temp. ≥ 90°F	0	0	0	0	0	5	13	12	3	0	0	0	33
Days Maximum Temp. ≤ 32°F	9	6	1	0	0	0	0	0	0	0	1	7	24
Days Minimum Temp. ≤ 32°F	28	24	18	6	0	0	0	0	1	6	16	26	125
Days Minimum Temp. ≤ 0°F	2	2	0	0	0	0	0	0	0	0	0	2	6
Heating Degree Days (base 65°F)	1,121	903	686	370	128	15	1	5	81	325	644	1,028	5,307
Cooling Degree Days (base 65°F)	0	0	3	21	70	236	376	330	134	20	1	0	1,191
Mean Precipitation (in.)	1.57	2.00	2.78	4.16	5.25	5.60	4.78	3.81	3.87	3.73	3.18	2.40	43.13
Extreme Maximum Daily Precip. (in.)	2.10	6.00	2.05	2.98	3.41	4.81	6.50	3.90	4.70	5.20	2.51	3.55	6.50
Days With ≥ 0.1" Precipitation	3	4	6	7	8	7	6	5	5	6	5	4	66
Days With ≥ 0.5" Precipitation	1	1	2	3	4	4	3	3	2	2	2	2	29
Days With ≥ 1.0" Precipitation	0	0	0	1	2	2	1	1	1	1	1	1	11
Mean Snowfall (in.)	3.1	2.6	1.0	0.2	0.0	0.0	0.0	0.0	0.0	0.0	0.3	2.3	9.5
Maximum Snow Depth (in.)	10	6	6	3	0	0	0	0	0	0	trace	16	16
Days With ≥ 1.0" Snow Depth	2	3	1	0	0	0	0	0	0	0	0	2	8

St Charles *St. Charles County* Elevation: 466 ft. Latitude: 38° 47' N Longitude: 90° 30' W

	JAN	FEB	MAR	APR	MAY	JUN	JUL	AUG	SEP	OCT	NOV	DEC	YEAR
Mean Maximum Temp. (°F)	39.5	44.6	54.7	66.7	75.4	83.8	87.8	86.9	79.7	68.0	***54.9***	42.4	***65.4***
Mean Temp. (°F)	30.5	35.0	44.3	55.2	64.5	73.3	77.5	75.8	67.6	56.1	***44.9***	33.4	***54.8***
Mean Minimum Temp. (°F)	21.5	25.1	33.6	43.5	53.4	62.6	67.1	64.5	55.4	44.0	35.0	24.4	44.2
Extreme Maximum Temp. (°F)	74	79	88	94	94	102	107	107	101	92	***85***	75	***107***
Extreme Minimum Temp. (°F)	-19	-14	3	22	34	45	50	43	31	21	4	-18	-19
Days Maximum Temp. ≥ 90°F	0	0	0	0	1	6	12	11	3	0	***0***	0	***33***
Days Maximum Temp. ≤ 32°F	9	5	1	0	0	0	0	0	0	0	***1***	6	***22***
Days Minimum Temp. ≤ 32°F	26	22	15	3	0	0	0	0	0	3	13	24	106
Days Minimum Temp. ≤ 0°F	1	1	0	0	0	0	0	0	0	0	0	1	3
Heating Degree Days (base 65°F)	1,063	839	641	316	102	10	0	3	61	296	***598***	970	***4,899***
Cooling Degree Days (base 65°F)	0	0	5	29	94	264	394	344	147	26	2	0	1,305
Mean Precipitation (in.)	2.52	2.58	3.33	4.21	4.96	3.79	4.18	3.32	3.12	3.63	3.63	3.03	42.30
Extreme Maximum Daily Precip. (in.)	2.66	2.81	2.24	3.87	4.79	3.87	5.88	2.73	3.52	4.01	3.27	3.40	5.88
Days With ≥ 0.1" Precipitation	5	4	7	8	8	6	6	6	5	6	6	5	72
Days With ≥ 0.5" Precipitation	2	2	2	3	3	2	3	2	2	2	3	2	28
Days With ≥ 1.0" Precipitation	1	1	1	1	1	1	1	1	1	1	1	1	12
Mean Snowfall (in.)	***3.9***	***3.5***	0.8	0.0	0.0	0.0	0.0	0.0	0.0	0.0	0.4	2.3	***10.9***
Maximum Snow Depth (in.)	***9***	***10***	6	0	0	0	0	0	0	***0***	***1***	***5***	***10***
Days With ≥ 1.0" Snow Depth	***1***	***1***	0	0	0	0	0	0	0	0	0	***1***	***3***

St Charles 7 SSW *St. Louis County* Elevation: 450 ft. Latitude: 38° 41' N Longitude: 90° 31' W

	JAN	FEB	MAR	APR	MAY	JUN	JUL	AUG	SEP	OCT	NOV	DEC	YEAR
Mean Maximum Temp. (°F)	39.8	44.9	54.8	66.5	75.9	84.5	88.7	87.4	80.1	68.4	55.8	42.9	65.8
Mean Temp. (°F)	30.0	34.2	43.8	55.1	65.0	73.9	78.0	76.3	68.0	56.3	45.2	33.1	54.9
Mean Minimum Temp. (°F)	20.1	23.4	32.8	43.7	54.1	63.1	67.2	65.0	55.8	44.1	34.6	23.3	43.9
Extreme Maximum Temp. (°F)	75	81	88	92	95	101	106	106	101	94	85	75	106
Extreme Minimum Temp. (°F)	-18	-18	-1	20	30	41	50	43	29	22	-2	-20	-20
Days Maximum Temp. ≥ 90°F	0	0	0	0	1	9	14	12	4	0	0	0	40
Days Maximum Temp. ≤ 32°F	9	5	1	0	0	0	0	0	0	0	0	6	21
Days Minimum Temp. ≤ 32°F	27	22	16	4	0	0	0	0	0	4	13	25	111
Days Minimum Temp. ≤ 0°F	2	1	0	0	0	0	0	0	0	0	0	1	4
Heating Degree Days (base 65°F)	1,079	865	655	320	95	9	0	3	61	290	590	982	4,949
Cooling Degree Days (base 65°F)	0	0	5	31	102	284	410	359	158	27	3	0	1,379
Mean Precipitation (in.)	2.00	2.35	3.16	3.62	4.97	4.08	3.83	3.17	3.42	3.41	3.78	2.77	40.56
Extreme Maximum Daily Precip. (in.)	2.96	3.50	2.47	2.00	3.80	3.30	3.93	2.84	3.25	2.97	3.30	2.86	3.93
Days With ≥ 0.1" Precipitation	4	5	6	7	8	6	5	5	5	6	6	5	68
Days With ≥ 0.5" Precipitation	1	2	2	3	3	3	2	2	2	2	3	2	27
Days With ≥ 1.0" Precipitation	1	0	0	1	1	1	1	1	1	1	1	1	10
Mean Snowfall (in.)	2.3	***2.0***	***0.2***	0.1	0.0	0.0	0.0	0.0	0.0	0.0	0.3	2.1	***7.0***
Maximum Snow Depth (in.)	***6***	***8***	***6***	trace	0	0	0	0	0	0	***1***	***5***	***8***
Days With ≥ 1.0" Snow Depth	***1***	***0***	0	0	0	0	0	0	0	0	0	***1***	***2***

The period of record for all cooperative weather station data is 1980 – 2009. See User Guide for detailed explanation of data.

Steelville 2 N *Crawford County* Elevation: 700 ft. Latitude: 38° 00' N Longitude: 91° 22' W

	JAN	FEB	MAR	APR	MAY	JUN	JUL	AUG	SEP	OCT	NOV	DEC	YEAR
Mean Maximum Temp. (°F)	41.8	48.0	57.1	68.8	76.8	83.9	89.1	88.3	80.0	69.6	56.7	44.2	67.0
Mean Temp. (°F)	29.4	34.5	42.7	53.5	62.3	70.6	75.8	74.4	65.4	54.1	43.0	32.0	53.1
Mean Minimum Temp. (°F)	17.0	20.9	28.2	38.1	47.7	57.2	62.5	60.4	50.7	38.7	29.3	19.8	39.2
Extreme Maximum Temp. (°F)	77	84	89	95	94	102	111	110	100	92	85	76	111
Extreme Minimum Temp. (°F)	-23	-22	-10	13	25	32	46	37	24	13	3	-29	-29
Days Maximum Temp. ≥ 90°F	0	0	0	1	1	6	16	13	5	0	0	0	42
Days Maximum Temp. ≤ 32°F	7	4	1	0	0	0	0	0	0	0	1	6	19
Days Minimum Temp. ≤ 32°F	28	24	21	10	2	0	0	0	1	10	19	26	141
Days Minimum Temp. ≤ 0°F	3	2	0	0	0	0	0	0	0	0	0	2	7
Heating Degree Days (base 65°F)	1,097	858	688	361	140	23	2	6	99	343	653	1,015	5,285
Cooling Degree Days (base 65°F)	0	0	3	21	61	199	345	304	117	13	1	0	1,064
Mean Precipitation (in.)	2.04	2.23	3.75	4.35	4.90	4.50	4.01	3.77	3.95	3.67	4.00	2.84	44.01
Extreme Maximum Daily Precip. (in.)	2.47	2.20	4.00	3.92	2.77	3.83	2.87	6.47	3.49	3.63	3.55	4.42	6.47
Days With ≥ 0.1" Precipitation	4	4	7	7	8	7	6	5	5	6	7	5	71
Days With ≥ 0.5" Precipitation	1	2	3	3	3	3	3	2	3	3	3	2	31
Days With ≥ 1.0" Precipitation	1	0	1	1	2	1	1	1	1	1	1	1	12
Mean Snowfall (in.)	3.7	3.3	1.3	0.1	0.0	0.0	0.0	0.0	0.0	trace	0.6	3.5	12.5
Maximum Snow Depth (in.)	12	13	11	2	0	0	0	0	0	trace	7	12	13
Days With ≥ 1.0" Snow Depth	5	4	1	0	0	0	0	0	0	0	1	4	15

Sweet Springs *Saline County* Elevation: 680 ft. Latitude: 38° 58' N Longitude: 93° 25' W

	JAN	FEB	MAR	APR	MAY	JUN	JUL	AUG	SEP	OCT	NOV	DEC	YEAR
Mean Maximum Temp. (°F)	39.4	44.6	56.1	67.0	76.2	84.3	89.2	88.2	80.1	68.1	54.7	41.8	65.8
Mean Temp. (°F)	30.0	34.5	45.0	55.4	65.1	73.7	78.5	77.0	68.2	56.5	44.7	32.7	55.1
Mean Minimum Temp. (°F)	20.6	24.3	33.9	43.8	54.0	63.1	67.7	65.7	56.3	44.8	34.7	23.7	44.4
Extreme Maximum Temp. (°F)	72	77	88	93	92	106	110	109	103	93	82	73	110
Extreme Minimum Temp. (°F)	-17	-18	-7	20	30	43	50	42	30	21	-8	-23	-23
Days Maximum Temp. ≥ 90°F	0	0	0	0	1	7	15	14	4	0	0	0	41
Days Maximum Temp. ≤ 32°F	9	6	1	0	0	0	0	0	0	0	1	7	24
Days Minimum Temp. ≤ 32°F	26	22	14	4	0	0	0	0	0	4	13	24	107
Days Minimum Temp. ≤ 0°F	2	1	0	0	0	0	0	0	0	0	0	1	4
Heating Degree Days (base 65°F)	1,079	857	616	309	86	8	1	2	59	282	604	993	4,896
Cooling Degree Days (base 65°F)	0	0	4	29	97	277	426	379	163	25	2	0	1,402
Mean Precipitation (in.)	1.48	1.95	2.85	4.07	5.27	4.69	4.50	4.33	4.15	3.70	2.81	2.39	42.19
Extreme Maximum Daily Precip. (in.)	1.97	3.19	2.50	3.36	3.60	3.78	7.03	3.80	5.07	3.55	2.61	4.85	7.03
Days With ≥ 0.1" Precipitation	3	4	6	7	8	7	6	6	6	6	5	4	68
Days With ≥ 0.5" Precipitation	1	1	2	3	3	3	3	3	3	3	2	1	28
Days With ≥ 1.0" Precipitation	0	1	1	1	1	1	1	1	1	1	1	1	11
Mean Snowfall (in.)	4.8	4.5	2.0	0.3	trace	trace	0.0	0.0	0.0	0.1	0.6	4.2	16.5
Maximum Snow Depth (in.)	9	10	4	3	trace	trace	0	0	0	trace	3	11	11
Days With ≥ 1.0" Snow Depth	7	5	1	0	0	0	0	0	0	0	0	5	18

Warrenton 1 N *Warren County* Elevation: 850 ft. Latitude: 38° 49' N Longitude: 91° 08' W

	JAN	FEB	MAR	APR	MAY	JUN	JUL	AUG	SEP	OCT	NOV	DEC	YEAR
Mean Maximum Temp. (°F)	39.9	43.3	54.2	65.8	74.7	83.2	87.8	87.1	79.3	66.7	55.0	41.5	64.9
Mean Temp. (°F)	30.4	33.4	43.1	54.7	63.4	72.8	77.3	76.1	67.3	55.2	44.9	33.0	54.3
Mean Minimum Temp. (°F)	21.0	23.5	32.0	43.4	52.2	62.3	66.8	65.1	55.2	43.6	34.8	24.0	43.7
Extreme Maximum Temp. (°F)	71	78	85	90	93	102	107	107	99	91	81	74	107
Extreme Minimum Temp. (°F)	-15	-12	-1	19	31	40	50	42	31	22	3	-21	-21
Days Maximum Temp. ≥ 90°F	0	0	0	0	0	5	12	11	3	0	0	0	31
Days Maximum Temp. ≤ 32°F	9	6	1	0	0	0	0	0	0	0	1	6	23
Days Minimum Temp. ≤ 32°F	25	23	16	4	0	0	0	0	0	4	11	24	107
Days Minimum Temp. ≤ 0°F	1	1	0	0	0	0	0	0	0	0	0	1	3
Heating Degree Days (base 65°F)	1,064	889	675	326	115	11	1	3	63	320	595	985	5,047
Cooling Degree Days (base 65°F)	0	0	4	24	73	251	389	355	139	20	2	0	1,257
Mean Precipitation (in.)	1.95	1.68	2.81	3.57	4.87	4.32	4.08	2.79	2.85	3.14	3.52	1.96	37.54
Extreme Maximum Daily Precip. (in.)	2.80	2.15	2.40	3.41	5.48	3.60	5.85	2.83	4.43	na	na	1.94	na
Days With ≥ 0.1" Precipitation	3	3	5	5	7	5	5	4	4	4	4	3	52
Days With ≥ 0.5" Precipitation	1	1	2	3	3	3	3	2	2	2	2	1	25
Days With ≥ 1.0" Precipitation	1	0	1	1	1	1	1	1	1	1	1	1	11
Mean Snowfall (in.)	2.9	2.9	1.2	0.4	0.0	0.0	0.0	0.0	0.0	trace	0.7	2.6	10.7
Maximum Snow Depth (in.)	na	na	1	0	0	0	0	0	0	na	na	10	na
Days With ≥ 1.0" Snow Depth	na	1	0	0	0	0	0	0	0	0	0	1	na

The period of record for all cooperative weather station data is 1980 – 2009. See User Guide for detailed explanation of data.

Missouri Weather Station Rankings

Annual Extreme Maximum Temperature

Highest Rank	Station Name	°F	Lowest Rank	Station Name	°F
1	Appleton City	112	1	Advance 1 S	***105***
2	Columbia Regional Airport	111	1	Amity 4 NE	105
2	Freedom	111	1	Cape Girardeau Municipal Arpt	105
2	Steelville 2 N	***111***	1	Marshfield	105
5	Boonville	110	5	Bowling Green 2 NE	***106***
5	Canton L and D 20	110	5	Galena 1 SW	106
5	Doniphan	110	5	Jackson	106
5	Jefferson City Wtr Plant	110	5	St Charles 7 SSW	106
5	Kansas City Muni Arpt	***110***	9	Anderson	107
5	Sweet Springs	110	9	Bolivar 1 NE	107
11	Brookfield	109	9	Sedalia Water Plant	107
11	Dora	109	9	St Charles	***107***
11	Kansas City Int'l Arpt	109	9	St Louis Lambert Int'l Arpt	107
11	Lexington 3 NE	***109***	9	Warrenton 1 N	***107***
11	Mexico	***109***	15	Brunswick	108
16	Brunswick	108	15	Fulton	108
16	Fulton	108	15	Joplin Municipal Arpt	108
16	Joplin Municipal Arpt	108	15	Lees Summit Reed Wlr	108
16	Lees Summit Reed Wlr	108	15	Lockwood	108
16	Lockwood	108	15	Springfield Regional Arpt	108
16	Springfield Regional Arpt	108	21	Brookfield	109
22	Anderson	107	21	Dora	109
22	Bolivar 1 NE	107	21	Kansas City Int'l Arpt	109
22	Sedalia Water Plant	107	21	Lexington 3 NE	***109***
22	St Charles	***107***	21	Mexico	***109***

Annual Mean Maximum Temperature

Highest Rank	Station Name	°F	Lowest Rank	Station Name	°F
1	Doniphan	69.7	1	Amity 4 NE	62.4
2	Jackson	68.8	2	Canton L and D 20	63.0
3	Joplin Municipal Arpt	68.7	3	Brunswick	63.2
4	Anderson	68.6	4	Brookfield	63.8
5	Galena 1 SW	68.4	5	Bowling Green 2 NE	***64.1***
6	Dora	68.2	5	Fulton	64.1
7	Cape Girardeau Municipal Arpt	67.7	7	Kansas City Int'l Arpt	64.5
8	Advance 1 S	***67.5***	8	Mexico	***64.6***
9	Lockwood	67.3	9	Sedalia Water Plant	64.7
10	Bolivar 1 NE	67.1	10	Columbia Regional Airport	64.8
11	Springfield Regional Arpt	67.0	11	Warrenton 1 N	***64.9***
11	Steelville 2 N	***67.0***	12	Lexington 3 NE	65.0
13	Marshfield	66.5	13	Lees Summit Reed Wlr	65.3
14	Appleton City	66.3	14	St Charles	***65.4***
15	St Louis Lambert Int'l Arpt	66.1	15	Boonville	65.5
16	Freedom	65.9	16	Jefferson City Wtr Plant	65.7
17	St Charles 7 SSW	65.8	16	Kansas City Muni Arpt	***65.7***
17	Sweet Springs	65.8	18	St Charles 7 SSW	65.8
19	Jefferson City Wtr Plant	65.7	18	Sweet Springs	65.8
19	Kansas City Muni Arpt	***65.7***	20	Freedom	65.9
21	Boonville	65.5	21	St Louis Lambert Int'l Arpt	66.1
22	St Charles	***65.4***	22	Appleton City	66.3
23	Lees Summit Reed Wlr	65.3	23	Marshfield	66.5
24	Lexington 3 NE	65.0	24	Springfield Regional Arpt	67.0
25	Warrenton 1 N	***64.9***	24	Steelville 2 N	***67.0***

Rankings include 25 highest/lowest stations. If state has less than 25 stations, all stations are included. The period of record is 1980–2009. See User Guide for detailed explanation of data.

Annual Mean Temperature

Highest			Lowest		
Rank	Station Name	°F	Rank	Station Name	°F
1	Joplin Municipal Arpt	58.2	1	Amity 4 NE	51.9
2	Jackson	57.7	2	Bowling Green 2 NE	***52.7***
3	Cape Girardeau Municipal Arpt	57.4	3	Brunswick	52.9
4	St Louis Lambert Int'l Arpt	57.0	3	Canton L and D 20	52.9
5	Anderson	56.9	5	Steelville 2 N	***53.1***
6	Kansas City Muni Arpt	***56.7***	6	Brookfield	53.4
7	Doniphan	56.5	6	Sedalia Water Plant	53.4
7	Lockwood	56.5	8	Fulton	53.6
9	Advance 1 S	***56.4***	9	Mexico	***53.7***
9	Springfield Regional Arpt	56.4	10	Lexington 3 NE	54.0
11	Marshfield	56.3	11	Lees Summit Reed Wlr	54.3
12	Dora	56.2	11	Warrenton 1 N	***54.3***
13	Galena 1 SW	56.1	13	Freedom	54.4
14	Appleton City	55.4	14	Kansas City Int'l Arpt	54.5
14	Bolivar 1 NE	55.4	15	Columbia Regional Airport	54.6
16	Sweet Springs	55.1	16	Jefferson City Wtr Plant	54.7
17	Boonville	55.0	17	St Charles	***54.8***
18	St Charles 7 SSW	54.9	18	St Charles 7 SSW	54.9
19	St Charles	***54.8***	19	Boonville	55.0
20	Jefferson City Wtr Plant	54.7	20	Sweet Springs	55.1
21	Columbia Regional Airport	54.6	21	Appleton City	55.4
22	Kansas City Int'l Arpt	54.5	21	Bolivar 1 NE	55.4
23	Freedom	54.4	23	Galena 1 SW	56.1
24	Lees Summit Reed Wlr	54.3	24	Dora	56.2
24	Warrenton 1 N	***54.3***	25	Marshfield	56.3

Annual Mean Minimum Temperature

Highest			Lowest		
Rank	Station Name	°F	Rank	Station Name	°F
1	St Louis Lambert Int'l Arpt	47.8	1	Steelville 2 N	***39.2***
2	Joplin Municipal Arpt	47.6	2	Bowling Green 2 NE	***41.2***
3	Kansas City Muni Arpt	***47.5***	3	Amity 4 NE	41.4
4	Cape Girardeau Municipal Arpt	47.1	4	Sedalia Water Plant	42.1
5	Jackson	46.7	5	Brunswick	42.5
6	Marshfield	46.0	6	Mexico	***42.7***
7	Springfield Regional Arpt	45.8	7	Canton L and D 20	42.8
8	Lockwood	45.7	7	Lexington 3 NE	42.8
9	Anderson	45.3	9	Freedom	42.9
10	Advance 1 S	***45.1***	10	Brookfield	43.0
11	Boonville	44.5	10	Fulton	43.0
12	Appleton City	44.4	12	Doniphan	43.2
12	Columbia Regional Airport	44.4	12	Lees Summit Reed Wlr	43.2
12	Kansas City Int'l Arpt	44.4	14	Bolivar 1 NE	43.5
12	Sweet Springs	44.4	15	Galena 1 SW	43.7
16	Dora	44.2	15	Jefferson City Wtr Plant	43.7
16	St Charles	44.2	15	Warrenton 1 N	***43.7***
18	St Charles 7 SSW	43.9	18	St Charles 7 SSW	43.9
19	Galena 1 SW	43.7	19	Dora	44.2
19	Jefferson City Wtr Plant	43.7	19	St Charles	44.2
19	Warrenton 1 N	***43.7***	21	Appleton City	44.4
22	Bolivar 1 NE	43.5	21	Columbia Regional Airport	44.4
23	Doniphan	43.2	21	Kansas City Int'l Arpt	44.4
23	Lees Summit Reed Wlr	43.2	21	Sweet Springs	44.4
25	Brookfield	43.0	25	Boonville	44.5

Rankings include 25 highest/lowest stations. If state has less than 25 stations, all stations are included. The period of record is 1980–2009. See User Guide for detailed explanation of data.

Annual Extreme Minimum Temperature

Highest			Lowest		
Rank	Station Name	°F	Rank	Station Name	°F
1	Kansas City Muni Arpt	***-14***	1	Amity 4 NE	-32
2	Cape Girardeau Municipal Arpt	-15	2	Steelville 2 N	***-29***
2	Joplin Municipal Arpt	-15	3	Sedalia Water Plant	-28
4	Springfield Regional Arpt	-16	4	Bowling Green 2 NE	***-25***
5	Lockwood	-17	4	Brunswick	-25
6	St Louis Lambert Int'l Arpt	-18	4	Lees Summit Reed Wlr	-25
7	Bolivar 1 NE	-19	4	Mexico	***-25***
7	Doniphan	-19	8	Brookfield	-24
7	St Charles	-19	9	Kansas City Int'l Arpt	-23
10	Advance 1 S	***-20***	9	Sweet Springs	-23
10	Canton L and D 20	-20	11	Appleton City	-22
10	Columbia Regional Airport	-20	11	Boonville	-22
10	Marshfield	-20	11	Lexington 3 NE	***-22***
10	St Charles 7 SSW	-20	14	Anderson	-21
15	Anderson	-21	14	Dora	-21
15	Dora	-21	14	Freedom	-21
15	Freedom	-21	14	Fulton	-21
15	Fulton	-21	14	Galena 1 SW	-21
15	Galena 1 SW	-21	14	Jackson	-21
15	Jackson	-21	14	Jefferson City Wtr Plant	-21
15	Jefferson City Wtr Plant	-21	14	Warrenton 1 N	***-21***
15	Warrenton 1 N	***-21***	22	Advance 1 S	***-20***
23	Appleton City	-22	22	Canton L and D 20	-20
23	Boonville	-22	22	Columbia Regional Airport	-20
23	Lexington 3 NE	***-22***	22	Marshfield	-20

July Mean Maximum Temperature

Highest			Lowest		
Rank	Station Name	°F	Rank	Station Name	°F
1	Jackson	91.2	1	Amity 4 NE	86.3
2	Doniphan	91.1	1	Brunswick	86.3
3	Joplin Municipal Arpt	90.6	3	Fulton	87.2
4	Kansas City Muni Arpt	90.5	4	Canton L and D 20	87.3
5	Advance 1 S	***89.8***	5	Brookfield	87.4
5	Boonville	89.8	6	St Charles	87.8
7	Cape Girardeau Municipal Arpt	89.7	6	Warrenton 1 N	***87.8***
8	Appleton City	89.3	8	Bowling Green 2 NE	***87.9***
8	Lockwood	89.3	8	Marshfield	87.9
10	St Louis Lambert Int'l Arpt	89.2	8	Sedalia Water Plant	87.9
10	Sweet Springs	89.2	11	Columbia Regional Airport	88.1
12	Bolivar 1 NE	89.1	12	Freedom	88.2
12	Steelville 2 N	***89.1***	13	Lexington 3 NE	88.3
14	Galena 1 SW	89.0	13	Mexico	88.3
15	Springfield Regional Arpt	88.9	15	Lees Summit Reed Wlr	88.4
16	Jefferson City Wtr Plant	88.7	16	Anderson	88.5
16	St Charles 7 SSW	88.7	16	Kansas City Int'l Arpt	88.5
18	Dora	88.6	18	Dora	88.6
19	Anderson	88.5	19	Jefferson City Wtr Plant	88.7
19	Kansas City Int'l Arpt	88.5	19	St Charles 7 SSW	88.7
21	Lees Summit Reed Wlr	88.4	21	Springfield Regional Arpt	88.9
22	Lexington 3 NE	88.3	22	Galena 1 SW	89.0
22	Mexico	88.3	23	Bolivar 1 NE	89.1
24	Freedom	88.2	23	Steelville 2 N	***89.1***
25	Columbia Regional Airport	88.1	25	St Louis Lambert Int'l Arpt	89.2

Rankings include 25 highest/lowest stations. If state has less than 25 stations, all stations are included. The period of record is 1980–2009. See User Guide for detailed explanation of data.

January Mean Minimum Temperature

Highest

Rank	Station Name	°F
1	Joplin Municipal Arpt	25.4
2	Cape Girardeau Municipal Arpt	25.1
3	Jackson	24.8
4	Anderson	24.1
5	St Louis Lambert Int'l Arpt	23.9
6	Springfield Regional Arpt	23.5
7	Marshfield	23.4
8	Advance 1 S	***23.3***
9	Lockwood	23.1
10	Dora	22.7
11	Kansas City Muni Arpt	***22.4***
12	Galena 1 SW	22.1
13	Doniphan	21.7
14	St Charles	21.5
15	Appleton City	21.0
15	Columbia Regional Airport	21.0
15	Warrenton 1 N	***21.0***
18	Bolivar 1 NE	20.6
18	Sweet Springs	20.6
20	Freedom	20.2
20	Jefferson City Wtr Plant	20.2
22	Boonville	20.1
22	St Charles 7 SSW	20.1
24	Kansas City Int'l Arpt	19.8
25	Fulton	19.6

Lowest

Rank	Station Name	°F
1	Amity 4 NE	16.1
2	Steelville 2 N	***17.0***
3	Bowling Green 2 NE	***17.4***
4	Brunswick	17.6
5	Canton L and D 20	18.1
6	Brookfield	18.2
7	Sedalia Water Plant	18.4
8	Lexington 3 NE	18.7
9	Mexico	18.8
10	Lees Summit Reed Wlr	19.2
11	Fulton	19.6
12	Kansas City Int'l Arpt	19.8
13	Boonville	20.1
13	St Charles 7 SSW	20.1
15	Freedom	20.2
15	Jefferson City Wtr Plant	20.2
17	Bolivar 1 NE	20.6
17	Sweet Springs	20.6
19	Appleton City	21.0
19	Columbia Regional Airport	21.0
19	Warrenton 1 N	***21.0***
22	St Charles	21.5
23	Doniphan	21.7
24	Galena 1 SW	22.1
25	Kansas City Muni Arpt	***22.4***

Number of Days Annually Maximum Temperature ≥ 90°F

Highest

Rank	Station Name	Days
1	Doniphan	58
1	Jackson	58
3	Joplin Municipal Arpt	51
4	Advance 1 S	***48***
5	Cape Girardeau Municipal Arpt	47
6	Boonville	46
7	Lockwood	45
8	Bolivar 1 NE	43
8	Kansas City Muni Arpt	***43***
10	Galena 1 SW	42
10	St Louis Lambert Int'l Arpt	42
10	Steelville 2 N	***42***
13	Sweet Springs	41
14	Appleton City	40
14	St Charles 7 SSW	40
16	Jefferson City Wtr Plant	39
16	Springfield Regional Arpt	39
18	Dora	38
19	Freedom	37
19	Kansas City Int'l Arpt	37
19	Lees Summit Reed Wlr	37
19	Lexington 3 NE	37
19	Mexico	***37***
24	Anderson	35
25	Columbia Regional Airport	33

Lowest

Rank	Station Name	Days
1	Brunswick	23
2	Amity 4 NE	26
3	Brookfield	28
4	Fulton	29
5	Canton L and D 20	30
6	Warrenton 1 N	***31***
7	Bowling Green 2 NE	***32***
8	Columbia Regional Airport	33
8	Marshfield	33
8	Sedalia Water Plant	33
8	St Charles	***33***
12	Anderson	35
13	Freedom	37
13	Kansas City Int'l Arpt	37
13	Lees Summit Reed Wlr	37
13	Lexington 3 NE	37
13	Mexico	***37***
18	Dora	38
19	Jefferson City Wtr Plant	39
19	Springfield Regional Arpt	39
21	Appleton City	40
21	St Charles 7 SSW	40
23	Sweet Springs	41
24	Galena 1 SW	42
24	St Louis Lambert Int'l Arpt	42

Rankings include 25 highest/lowest stations. If state has less than 25 stations, all stations are included. The period of record is 1980–2009. See User Guide for detailed explanation of data.

Number of Days Annually Maximum Temperature ≤ 32°F

Highest			Lowest		
Rank	**Station Name**	**Days**	**Rank**	**Station Name**	**Days**
1	Amity 4 NE	34	1	Doniphan	8
2	Canton L and D 20	32	2	Anderson	9
3	Brookfield	30	3	Dora	10
3	Brunswick	30	4	Galena 1 SW	12
5	Fulton	28	5	Jackson	13
5	Mexico	***28***	5	Joplin Municipal Arpt	13
7	Bowling Green 2 NE	***27***	7	Cape Girardeau Municipal Arpt	14
7	Kansas City Int'l Arpt	27	8	Advance 1 S	***16***
9	Boonville	26	8	Springfield Regional Arpt	16
10	Columbia Regional Airport	25	10	Bolivar 1 NE	17
11	Jefferson City Wtr Plant	24	10	Lockwood	17
11	Lees Summit Reed Wlr	24	10	Marshfield	17
11	Lexington 3 NE	24	13	Steelville 2 N	***19***
11	Sedalia Water Plant	24	14	Appleton City	20
11	Sweet Springs	24	15	St Charles 7 SSW	21
16	Warrenton 1 N	***23***	15	St Louis Lambert Int'l Arpt	21
17	Freedom	22	17	Freedom	22
17	Kansas City Muni Arpt	***22***	17	Kansas City Muni Arpt	***22***
17	St Charles	***22***	17	St Charles	***22***
20	St Charles 7 SSW	21	20	Warrenton 1 N	***23***
20	St Louis Lambert Int'l Arpt	21	21	Jefferson City Wtr Plant	24
22	Appleton City	20	21	Lees Summit Reed Wlr	24
23	Steelville 2 N	***19***	21	Lexington 3 NE	24
24	Bolivar 1 NE	17	21	Sedalia Water Plant	24
24	Lockwood	17	21	Sweet Springs	24

Number of Days Annually Minimum Temperature ≤ 32°F

Highest			Lowest		
Rank	**Station Name**	**Days**	**Rank**	**Station Name**	**Days**
1	Steelville 2 N	***141***	1	Joplin Municipal Arpt	87
2	Amity 4 NE	128	2	St Louis Lambert Int'l Arpt	88
3	Sedalia Water Plant	125	3	Cape Girardeau Municipal Arpt	90
4	Bowling Green 2 NE	***122***	4	Jackson	91
5	Brunswick	119	5	Kansas City Muni Arpt	***94***
5	Canton L and D 20	119	6	Marshfield	95
5	Mexico	***119***	7	Springfield Regional Arpt	96
8	Brookfield	117	8	Lockwood	98
9	Fulton	116	9	Anderson	99
9	Lexington 3 NE	116	10	Advance 1 S	***103***
11	Doniphan	115	10	Dora	103
12	Bolivar 1 NE	114	12	Columbia Regional Airport	106
13	Jefferson City Wtr Plant	113	12	St Charles	106
13	Lees Summit Reed Wlr	113	14	Sweet Springs	107
15	Freedom	112	14	Warrenton 1 N	***107***
16	St Charles 7 SSW	111	16	Appleton City	108
17	Boonville	109	17	Boonville	109
17	Galena 1 SW	109	17	Galena 1 SW	109
17	Kansas City Int'l Arpt	109	17	Kansas City Int'l Arpt	109
20	Appleton City	108	20	St Charles 7 SSW	111
21	Sweet Springs	107	21	Freedom	112
21	Warrenton 1 N	***107***	22	Jefferson City Wtr Plant	113
23	Columbia Regional Airport	106	22	Lees Summit Reed Wlr	113
23	St Charles	106	24	Bolivar 1 NE	114
25	Advance 1 S	***103***	25	Doniphan	115

Rankings include 25 highest/lowest stations. If state has less than 25 stations, all stations are included. The period of record is 1980–2009. See User Guide for detailed explanation of data.

Number of Days Annually Minimum Temperature ≤ 0°F

Highest

Rank	Station Name	Days
1	Amity 4 NE	10
2	Bowling Green 2 NE	***8***
3	Brookfield	7
3	Brunswick	7
3	Canton L and D 20	7
3	Steelville 2 N	***7***
7	Mexico	***6***
7	Sedalia Water Plant	6
9	Kansas City Int'l Arpt	5
9	Lees Summit Reed Wlr	5
9	Lexington 3 NE	5
12	Boonville	4
12	Columbia Regional Airport	4
12	Freedom	4
12	Fulton	4
12	Jefferson City Wtr Plant	4
12	St Charles 7 SSW	4
12	Sweet Springs	4
19	Appleton City	3
19	Bolivar 1 NE	3
19	Doniphan	3
19	Dora	3
19	Galena 1 SW	3
19	Kansas City Muni Arpt	***3***
19	Lockwood	3

Lowest

Rank	Station Name	Days
1	Advance 1 S	***2***
1	Anderson	2
1	Cape Girardeau Municipal Arpt	2
1	Jackson	2
1	Joplin Municipal Arpt	2
1	St Louis Lambert Int'l Arpt	2
7	Appleton City	3
7	Bolivar 1 NE	3
7	Doniphan	3
7	Dora	3
7	Galena 1 SW	3
7	Kansas City Muni Arpt	***3***
7	Lockwood	3
7	Marshfield	3
7	Springfield Regional Arpt	3
7	St Charles	3
7	Warrenton 1 N	***3***
18	Boonville	4
18	Columbia Regional Airport	4
18	Freedom	4
18	Fulton	4
18	Jefferson City Wtr Plant	4
18	St Charles 7 SSW	4
18	Sweet Springs	4
25	Kansas City Int'l Arpt	5

Number of Annual Heating Degree Days

Highest

Rank	Station Name	Num.
1	Amity 4 NE	5,755
2	Bowling Green 2 NE	***5,527***
3	Canton L and D 20	5,517
4	Brunswick	5,466
5	Brookfield	5,364
6	Sedalia Water Plant	5,307
7	Mexico	***5,296***
8	Steelville 2 N	***5,285***
9	Fulton	5,218
10	Lexington 3 NE	5,185
11	Kansas City Int'l Arpt	5,108
12	Lees Summit Reed Wlr	5,070
13	Warrenton 1 N	***5,047***
14	Boonville	5,021
15	Jefferson City Wtr Plant	4,982
16	Columbia Regional Airport	4,979
17	Freedom	4,960
18	St Charles 7 SSW	4,949
19	St Charles	***4,899***
20	Sweet Springs	4,896
21	Appleton City	4,790
22	Bolivar 1 NE	4,743
23	Kansas City Muni Arpt	***4,651***
24	St Louis Lambert Int'l Arpt	4,502
25	Marshfield	4,478

Lowest

Rank	Station Name	Num.
1	Joplin Municipal Arpt	4,079
2	Anderson	4,174
3	Jackson	4,200
4	Cape Girardeau Municipal Arpt	4,234
5	Dora	4,403
6	Doniphan	4,422
7	Springfield Regional Arpt	4,452
8	Galena 1 SW	4,455
9	Lockwood	4,467
10	Advance 1 S	***4,475***
11	Marshfield	4,478
12	St Louis Lambert Int'l Arpt	4,502
13	Kansas City Muni Arpt	***4,651***
14	Bolivar 1 NE	4,743
15	Appleton City	4,790
16	Sweet Springs	4,896
17	St Charles	***4,899***
18	St Charles 7 SSW	4,949
19	Freedom	4,960
20	Columbia Regional Airport	4,979
21	Jefferson City Wtr Plant	4,982
22	Boonville	5,021
23	Warrenton 1 N	***5,047***
24	Lees Summit Reed Wlr	5,070
25	Kansas City Int'l Arpt	5,108

Rankings include 25 highest/lowest stations. If state has less than 25 stations, all stations are included. The period of record is 1980–2009. See User Guide for detailed explanation of data.

Number of Annual Cooling Degree Days

Highest Rank	Station Name	Num.	Lowest Rank	Station Name	Num.
1	Kansas City Muni Arpt	***1,722***	1	Steelville 2 N	***1,064***
2	Joplin Municipal Arpt	1,711	2	Amity 4 NE	1,096
3	St Louis Lambert Int'l Arpt	1,674	3	Bowling Green 2 NE	***1,130***
4	Jackson	1,656	4	Brunswick	1,144
5	Cape Girardeau Municipal Arpt	1,582	5	Fulton	1,179
6	Lockwood	1,486	6	Sedalia Water Plant	1,191
7	Boonville	1,470	7	Freedom	1,217
8	Springfield Regional Arpt	1,431	8	Canton L and D 20	1,222
9	Advance 1 S	***1,427***	9	Brookfield	1,250
10	Doniphan	1,420	10	Warrenton 1 N	***1,257***
11	Sweet Springs	1,402	11	Lexington 3 NE	1,270
12	Marshfield	1,396	12	Mexico	***1,272***
13	Appleton City	1,390	13	Lees Summit Reed Wlr	1,280
14	Kansas City Int'l Arpt	1,388	14	Columbia Regional Airport	1,293
15	St Charles 7 SSW	1,379	15	Galena 1 SW	1,302
16	Jefferson City Wtr Plant	1,342	16	St Charles	1,305
17	Anderson	1,341	17	Dora	1,309
18	Bolivar 1 NE	1,337	18	Bolivar 1 NE	1,337
19	Dora	1,309	19	Anderson	1,341
20	St Charles	1,305	20	Jefferson City Wtr Plant	1,342
21	Galena 1 SW	1,302	21	St Charles 7 SSW	1,379
22	Columbia Regional Airport	1,293	22	Kansas City Int'l Arpt	1,388
23	Lees Summit Reed Wlr	1,280	23	Appleton City	1,390
24	Mexico	***1,272***	24	Marshfield	1,396
25	Lexington 3 NE	1,270	25	Sweet Springs	1,402

Annual Precipitation

Highest Rank	Station Name	Inches	Lowest Rank	Station Name	Inches
1	Doniphan	49.11	1	Warrenton 1 N	***37.54***
2	Jackson	48.64	2	Amity 4 NE	38.03
3	Lockwood	46.94	3	Bowling Green 2 NE	38.16
4	Bolivar 1 NE	46.77	4	Kansas City Int'l Arpt	38.51
5	Advance 1 S	***46.70***	5	Canton L and D 20	38.88
6	Cape Girardeau Municipal Arpt	46.35	6	Brunswick	38.91
7	Joplin Municipal Arpt	45.95	7	Kansas City Muni Arpt	***39.15***
8	Galena 1 SW	45.28	8	St Louis Lambert Int'l Arpt	40.54
9	Springfield Regional Arpt	44.78	9	St Charles 7 SSW	40.56
10	Dora	44.30	10	Lexington 3 NE	41.25
11	Steelville 2 N	***44.01***	11	Brookfield	41.56
12	Fulton	43.83	12	Columbia Regional Airport	41.84
13	Marshfield	43.52	13	Sweet Springs	42.19
14	Boonville	43.49	14	St Charles	42.30
15	Sedalia Water Plant	43.13	15	Mexico	42.31
16	Freedom	43.08	16	Jefferson City Wtr Plant	42.36
17	Lees Summit Reed Wlr	43.04	17	Appleton City	42.72
18	Anderson	43.00	18	Anderson	43.00
19	Appleton City	42.72	19	Lees Summit Reed Wlr	43.04
20	Jefferson City Wtr Plant	42.36	20	Freedom	43.08
21	Mexico	42.31	21	Sedalia Water Plant	43.13
22	St Charles	42.30	22	Boonville	43.49
23	Sweet Springs	42.19	23	Marshfield	43.52
24	Columbia Regional Airport	41.84	24	Fulton	43.83
25	Brookfield	41.56	25	Steelville 2 N	***44.01***

Rankings include 25 highest/lowest stations. If state has less than 25 stations, all stations are included. The period of record is 1980–2009. See User Guide for detailed explanation of data.

Annual Extreme Maximum Daily Precipitation

Highest

Rank	Station Name	Inches
1	Cape Girardeau Municipal Arpt	11.49
2	Jackson	9.21
3	Appleton City	9.10
4	Lees Summit Reed Wlr	8.02
5	Jefferson City Wtr Plant	7.41
6	Doniphan	7.23
7	Joplin Municipal Arpt	7.12
8	Sweet Springs	7.03
9	Freedom	6.72
10	Amity 4 NE	6.70
11	Canton L and D 20	6.57
12	Sedalia Water Plant	6.50
13	Steelville 2 N	*6.47*
14	Kansas City Muni Arpt	*6.45*
15	Dora	6.40
16	Mexico	*6.28*
17	Springfield Regional Arpt	6.27
18	Lexington 3 NE	*6.17*
18	Marshfield	6.17
20	Lockwood	6.04
21	Boonville	6.00
22	Columbia Regional Airport	5.94
23	St Charles	5.88
24	Brunswick	5.81
25	Advance 1 S	*5.60*

Lowest

Rank	Station Name	Inches
1	St Charles 7 SSW	3.93
2	Bowling Green 2 NE	*4.00*
3	Galena 1 SW	5.05
4	Kansas City Int'l Arpt	5.08
5	Fulton	5.37
6	Brookfield	5.47
7	Anderson	5.48
8	Bolivar 1 NE	5.50
9	St Louis Lambert Int'l Arpt	5.59
10	Advance 1 S	*5.60*
11	Brunswick	5.81
12	St Charles	5.88
13	Columbia Regional Airport	5.94
14	Boonville	6.00
15	Lockwood	6.04
16	Lexington 3 NE	*6.17*
16	Marshfield	6.17
18	Springfield Regional Arpt	6.27
19	Mexico	*6.28*
20	Dora	6.40
21	Kansas City Muni Arpt	*6.45*
22	Steelville 2 N	*6.47*
23	Sedalia Water Plant	6.50
24	Canton L and D 20	6.57
25	Amity 4 NE	6.70

Number of Days Annually With ≥ 0.1 Inches of Precipitation

Highest

Rank	Station Name	Days
1	Cape Girardeau Municipal Arpt	76
2	Jackson	75
3	Advance 1 S	*74*
3	Doniphan	74
5	Mexico	72
5	Springfield Regional Arpt	72
5	St Charles	72
8	Brookfield	71
8	Freedom	71
8	Fulton	71
8	Steelville 2 N	*71*
12	Bolivar 1 NE	70
12	Marshfield	70
14	Columbia Regional Airport	69
14	Jefferson City Wtr Plant	69
14	Joplin Municipal Arpt	69
14	Lockwood	69
14	St Louis Lambert Int'l Arpt	69
19	St Charles 7 SSW	68
19	Sweet Springs	68
21	Appleton City	67
21	Boonville	67
23	Canton L and D 20	66
23	Galena 1 SW	66
23	Lees Summit Reed Wlr	66

Lowest

Rank	Station Name	Days
1	Warrenton 1 N	*52*
2	Bowling Green 2 NE	*60*
3	Brunswick	63
3	Dora	63
5	Amity 4 NE	64
5	Anderson	64
5	Kansas City Muni Arpt	*64*
8	Kansas City Int'l Arpt	65
8	Lexington 3 NE	65
10	Canton L and D 20	66
10	Galena 1 SW	66
10	Lees Summit Reed Wlr	66
10	Sedalia Water Plant	66
14	Appleton City	67
14	Boonville	67
16	St Charles 7 SSW	68
16	Sweet Springs	68
18	Columbia Regional Airport	69
18	Jefferson City Wtr Plant	69
18	Joplin Municipal Arpt	69
18	Lockwood	69
18	St Louis Lambert Int'l Arpt	69
23	Bolivar 1 NE	70
23	Marshfield	70
25	Brookfield	71

Rankings include 25 highest/lowest stations. If state has less than 25 stations, all stations are included. The period of record is 1980–2009. See User Guide for detailed explanation of data.

Number of Days Annually With ≥ 0.5 Inches of Precipitation

Highest Rank	Highest Station Name	Highest Days	Lowest Rank	Lowest Station Name	Lowest Days
1	Jackson	35	1	Amity 4 NE	23
2	Advance 1 S	*32*	2	Bowling Green 2 NE	*25*
2	Bolivar 1 NE	32	2	Brookfield	25
2	Doniphan	32	2	Brunswick	25
2	Lockwood	32	2	Kansas City Muni Arpt	*25*
6	Cape Girardeau Municipal Arpt	31	2	Warrenton 1 N	*25*
6	Dora	31	7	Boonville	26
6	Fulton	31	7	Canton L and D 20	26
6	Steelville 2 N	*31*	9	Columbia Regional Airport	27
10	Anderson	30	9	Kansas City Int'l Arpt	27
10	Appleton City	30	9	Lexington 3 NE	27
10	Freedom	30	9	St Charles 7 SSW	27
10	Galena 1 SW	30	13	Marshfield	28
10	Joplin Municipal Arpt	30	13	St Charles	28
10	Lees Summit Reed Wlr	30	13	St Louis Lambert Int'l Arpt	28
10	Springfield Regional Arpt	30	13	Sweet Springs	28
17	Jefferson City Wtr Plant	29	17	Jefferson City Wtr Plant	29
17	Mexico	29	17	Mexico	29
17	Sedalia Water Plant	29	17	Sedalia Water Plant	29
20	Marshfield	28	20	Anderson	30
20	St Charles	28	20	Appleton City	30
20	St Louis Lambert Int'l Arpt	28	20	Freedom	30
20	Sweet Springs	28	20	Galena 1 SW	30
24	Columbia Regional Airport	27	20	Joplin Municipal Arpt	30
24	Kansas City Int'l Arpt	27	20	Lees Summit Reed Wlr	30

Number of Days Annually With ≥ 1.0 Inches of Precipitation

Highest Rank	Highest Station Name	Highest Days	Lowest Rank	Lowest Station Name	Lowest Days
1	Lockwood	15	1	Canton L and D 20	8
2	Advance 1 S	*14*	1	Kansas City Int'l Arpt	8
2	Bolivar 1 NE	14	3	Brunswick	9
4	Anderson	13	3	Kansas City Muni Arpt	*9*
4	Doniphan	13	5	Columbia Regional Airport	10
4	Joplin Municipal Arpt	13	5	St Charles 7 SSW	10
7	Amity 4 NE	12	7	Appleton City	11
7	Boonville	12	7	Fulton	11
7	Bowling Green 2 NE	*12*	7	Jefferson City Wtr Plant	11
7	Brookfield	12	7	Lees Summit Reed Wlr	11
7	Cape Girardeau Municipal Arpt	12	7	Mexico	11
7	Dora	12	7	Sedalia Water Plant	11
7	Freedom	12	7	St Louis Lambert Int'l Arpt	11
7	Galena 1 SW	12	7	Sweet Springs	11
7	Jackson	12	7	Warrenton 1 N	*11*
7	Lexington 3 NE	12	16	Amity 4 NE	12
7	Marshfield	12	16	Boonville	12
7	Springfield Regional Arpt	12	16	Bowling Green 2 NE	*12*
7	St Charles	12	16	Brookfield	12
7	Steelville 2 N	*12*	16	Cape Girardeau Municipal Arpt	12
21	Appleton City	11	16	Dora	12
21	Fulton	11	16	Freedom	12
21	Jefferson City Wtr Plant	11	16	Galena 1 SW	12
21	Lees Summit Reed Wlr	11	16	Jackson	12
21	Mexico	11	16	Lexington 3 NE	12

Rankings include 25 highest/lowest stations. If state has less than 25 stations, all stations are included. The period of record is 1980–2009. See User Guide for detailed explanation of data.

Annual Snowfall

Highest

Rank	Station Name	Inches
1	Fulton	19.7
2	Columbia Regional Airport	***19.1***
3	Kansas City Int'l Arpt	18.6
4	Mexico	18.5
5	St Louis Lambert Int'l Arpt	18.2
6	Springfield Regional Arpt	17.8
7	Amity 4 NE	17.7
8	Boonville	17.5
9	Sweet Springs	16.5
10	Lockwood	14.6
11	Lexington 3 NE	14.5
12	Kansas City Muni Arpt	***12.7***
13	Brookfield	***12.5***
13	Lees Summit Reed Wlr	12.5
13	Steelville 2 N	***12.5***
16	Appleton City	12.3
16	Jefferson City Wtr Plant	12.3
18	Freedom	***11.5***
19	Anderson	11.3
20	St Charles	***10.9***
21	Warrenton 1 N	***10.7***
22	Brunswick	10.5
23	Bowling Green 2 NE	***10.2***
24	Advance 1 S	***9.5***
24	Sedalia Water Plant	9.5

Lowest

Rank	Station Name	Inches
1	Canton L and D 20	***2.6***
2	Galena 1 SW	***6.7***
3	St Charles 7 SSW	***7.0***
4	Jackson	***7.8***
5	Marshfield	8.8
6	Dora	8.9
7	Doniphan	9.2
8	Advance 1 S	***9.5***
8	Sedalia Water Plant	9.5
10	Bowling Green 2 NE	***10.2***
11	Brunswick	10.5
12	Warrenton 1 N	***10.7***
13	St Charles	***10.9***
14	Anderson	11.3
15	Freedom	***11.5***
16	Appleton City	12.3
16	Jefferson City Wtr Plant	12.3
18	Brookfield	***12.5***
18	Lees Summit Reed Wlr	12.5
18	Steelville 2 N	***12.5***
21	Kansas City Muni Arpt	***12.7***
22	Lexington 3 NE	14.5
23	Lockwood	14.6
24	Sweet Springs	16.5
25	Boonville	17.5

Annual Maximum Snow Depth

Highest

Rank	Station Name	Inches
1	St Louis Lambert Int'l Arpt	20
2	Dora	18
3	Doniphan	17
4	Lockwood	16
4	Sedalia Water Plant	16
4	Springfield Regional Arpt	16
7	Anderson	15
7	Columbia Regional Airport	***15***
9	Brookfield	14
9	Fulton	14
11	Boonville	***13***
11	Lees Summit Reed Wlr	13
11	Lexington 3 NE	***13***
11	Steelville 2 N	***13***
15	Amity 4 NE	***12***
15	Appleton City	12
15	Freedom	***12***
15	Galena 1 SW	12
15	Jackson	***12***
15	Jefferson City Wtr Plant	***12***
21	Kansas City Int'l Arpt	11
21	Sweet Springs	11
23	Brunswick	***10***
23	Marshfield	***10***
23	St Charles	***10***

Lowest

Rank	Station Name	Inches
1	St Charles 7 SSW	***8***
2	Brunswick	***10***
2	Marshfield	***10***
2	St Charles	***10***
5	Kansas City Int'l Arpt	11
5	Sweet Springs	11
7	Amity 4 NE	***12***
7	Appleton City	12
7	Freedom	***12***
7	Galena 1 SW	12
7	Jackson	***12***
7	Jefferson City Wtr Plant	***12***
13	Boonville	***13***
13	Lees Summit Reed Wlr	13
13	Lexington 3 NE	***13***
13	Steelville 2 N	***13***
17	Brookfield	14
17	Fulton	14
19	Anderson	15
19	Columbia Regional Airport	***15***
21	Lockwood	16
21	Sedalia Water Plant	16
21	Springfield Regional Arpt	16
24	Doniphan	17
25	Dora	18

Rankings include 25 highest/lowest stations. If state has less than 25 stations, all stations are included. The period of record is 1980–2009. See User Guide for detailed explanation of data.

Number of Days Annually With ≥ 1.0 Inch Snow Depth

Highest Rank	Highest Station Name	Highest Days	Lowest Rank	Lowest Station Name	Lowest Days
1	Brookfield	30	1	Jackson	***0***
2	Fulton	24	2	St Charles 7 SSW	***2***
3	Kansas City Int'l Arpt	23	3	Freedom	***3***
4	Amity 4 NE	***21***	3	Marshfield	***3***
4	Columbia Regional Airport	***21***	3	St Charles	***3***
6	St Louis Lambert Int'l Arpt	20	6	Galena 1 SW	4
7	Lexington 3 NE	18	7	Jefferson City Wtr Plant	***5***
7	Sweet Springs	18	8	Bowling Green 2 NE	***8***
9	Appleton City	17	8	Sedalia Water Plant	8
9	Boonville	***17***	10	Doniphan	9
9	Springfield Regional Arpt	17	11	Anderson	11
12	Lockwood	15	12	Dora	12
12	Steelville 2 N	***15***	12	Mexico	***12***
14	Brunswick	***14***	14	Lees Summit Reed Wlr	13
15	Lees Summit Reed Wlr	13	15	Brunswick	***14***
16	Dora	12	16	Lockwood	15
16	Mexico	***12***	16	Steelville 2 N	***15***
18	Anderson	11	18	Appleton City	17
19	Doniphan	9	18	Boonville	***17***
20	Bowling Green 2 NE	***8***	18	Springfield Regional Arpt	17
20	Sedalia Water Plant	8	21	Lexington 3 NE	18
22	Jefferson City Wtr Plant	***5***	21	Sweet Springs	18
23	Galena 1 SW	4	23	St Louis Lambert Int'l Arpt	20
24	Freedom	***3***	24	Amity 4 NE	***21***
24	Marshfield	***3***	24	Columbia Regional Airport	***21***

Significant Storm Events in Missouri: 2000 – 2009

Location or County	Date	Type	Mag.	Deaths	Injuries	Property Damage ($mil.)	Crop Damage ($mil.)
Franklin	05/07/00	Flash Flood	na	2	0	100.0	0.0
St. Louis County and St. Louis City	07/02/00	Excessive Heat	na	4	103	0.0	0.0
Eastern Central Missouri	08/28/00	Excessive Heat	na	1	125	0.0	0.0
St. Louis City and Boone, Lincoln, St. Charles, and St. Louis Counties	09/01/00	Excessive Heat	na	1	38	0.0	0.0
St Louis	04/10/01	Hail	2.50 in.	0	0	400.0	0.0
St Louis	04/10/01	Hail	1.50 in.	0	0	300.0	0.0
St Louis	04/10/01	Hail	2.75 in.	0	0	100.0	0.0
St Charles	04/10/01	Hail	2.00 in.	0	0	100.0	0.0
St Charles	04/10/01	Hail	1.00 in.	0	0	50.0	0.0
St Louis	04/10/01	Hail	1.75 in.	0	0	50.0	0.0
St Charles	04/10/01	Hail	1.50 in.	0	0	50.0	0.0
Jasper	04/15/01	Thunderstorm Wind	na	0	10	1.0	0.0
Central and Eastern Missouri	07/07/01	Excessive Heat	na	5	61	0.0	0.0
Eastern Central Missouri	07/21/01	Excessive Heat	na	3	71	0.0	0.0
Eastern Central Missouri	08/07/01	Excessive Heat	na	1	10	0.0	0.0
Northwest, Northern, and Central Missouri	01/30/02	Ice Storm	na	0	0	31.9	0.0
Butler	04/24/02	Tornado	F4	0	14	30.0	0.0
Bollinger	04/27/02	Tornado	F3	1	16	4.0	0.0
Jackson County	07/06/02	Excessive Heat	na	5	0	0.0	0.0
East Central Missouri	07/08/02	Excessive Heat	na	1	26	0.0	0.0
Eastern Central Missouri	08/01/02	Excessive Heat	na	1	59	0.0	0.0
Lawrence	12/17/02	Tornado	F2	2	17	0.5	0.0
Clay	05/04/03	Tornado	F2	0	0	60.0	0.0
Cedar	05/04/03	Tornado	F3	3	37	40.0	3.0
Platte	05/04/03	Tornado	F4	0	0	32.0	0.0
Clay	05/04/03	Tornado	F4	0	13	31.0	0.0
Lawrence	05/04/03	Tornado	F3	5	33	27.5	0.0
Jasper	05/04/03	Tornado	F3	2	15	21.2	0.0
Greene	05/04/03	Tornado	F3	1	12	14.7	0.0
Barton	05/04/03	Tornado	F4	1	10	13.0	1.0
Camden	05/04/03	Tornado	F3	4	27	5.0	1.0
Dallas	05/04/03	Tornado	F3	2	10	3.8	0.0
Eastern Central Missouri	07/03/03	Excessive Heat	na	3	93	0.0	0.0
Eastern Central Missouri	08/15/03	Excessive Heat	na	2	54	0.0	0.0
Benton	07/05/04	Thunderstorm Wind	81 mph	1	48	0.3	0.0
St. Louis City, and Jefferson, St. Charles, and St. Louis Counties	07/09/04	Excessive Heat	na	1	45	0.0	0.0
Central and Eastern Missouri	07/20/05	Excessive Heat	na	4	65	0.0	0.0
Southeastern Missouri	07/21/05	Excessive Heat	na	2	93	0.0	0.0
Perry	03/11/06	Tornado	F3	2	10	1.0	0.0
Christian	03/12/06	Tornado	F3	0	3	50.0	0.0
Randolph	03/12/06	Tornado	F3	4	26	5.0	0.0
Hickory	03/12/06	Tornado	F3	0	19	1.0	0.0
Henry	03/12/06	Tornado	F2	1	13	0.5	0.0
Pemiscot	04/02/06	Tornado	F3	2	130	60.0	0.0
St. Louis City	07/13/06	Excessive Heat	na	4	437	0.0	0.0
Franklin, Jefferson, St. Charles, and St. Louis Co.	07/14/06	Excessive Heat	na	3	306	0.0	0.0
St. Louis City	07/29/06	Excessive Heat	na	1	14	0.0	0.0
St. Charles and and St. Louis Metro Area	08/04/07	Excessive Heat	na	2	519	0.0	0.0
Laclede	01/07/08	Tornado	F3	0	12	8.0	0.0
Newton	05/10/08	Tornado	F4	14	200	35.0	0.0
Jasper	05/10/08	Tornado	F1	1	10	1.0	0.0
Perry	05/08/09	Thunderstorm Wind	85 mph	0	0	50.0	0.0

Note: Deaths, injuries, and damages are date and location specific.

MONTANA

PHYSICAL FEATURES. Montana, with an area of 146,316 square miles, is the fourth largest State of the Union. Climatic variations are large. The half of the State southwest of a line from the southeastern corner to the Canadian Border north of Cut Bank in Glacier County is very mountainous, while the northeastern half is very much like Great Plains country, broken occasionally by wide valleys and isolated groups of hills. The extent of the climatic variations one should expect is indicated by the range in elevation of from 1,800 feet above sea level where the Kootenai River enters Idaho to 12,850 feet at Granite Peak near Yellowstone Park. Half the State lies over 4,000 feet above sea level.

The Continental Divide traverses the western half of the State in roughly a north-south direction. To the west of the Divide, Montana is drained by the Kootenai, Clark Fork, and Flathead Rivers into the Pacific Ocean through the Columbia River. Many of the tributary streams in this region have their origin in the high elevations of the western slopes of the Rockies. Most streams traverse narrow canyons, at least through parts of their length, affording many valuable waterpower sites. A relatively small area located between the Hudson Bay Divide and the Rocky Mountains is drained by the St. Mary River, which finds its way to the Hudson Bay through the Saskatchewan River. The remainder of the State is drained by the Missouri River, which is formed by the confluence of the Gallatin, Madison, and Jefferson Rivers at Three Forks, travels northward through deep canyons in the Big Belt Mountains, and flows through the lower lying northeastern portion of the State. The Yellowstone River, the principal tributary of the Missouri in Montana and which has its source in Wyoming, drains the southeastern section of the State and has its confluence with the Missouri just east of the Montana - North Dakota line.

GENERAL CLIMATE. The Continental Divide exerts a marked influence on the climate of adjacent areas. West of the Divide the climate might be termed a modified north Pacific coast type, while to the east, climatic characteristics are decidedly continental. On the west of the mountain barrier winters are milder, precipitation is more evenly distributed throughout the year, summers are cooler in general, and winds are lighter than on the eastern side. There is more cloudiness in the west in all seasons, humidity runs a bit higher, and the growing season is shorter than in the eastern plains areas.

Cold waves, which cover parts of Montana on the average of six to 12 times a winter, are confined mostly to the sections northeast of a Glacier Park - Miles City line. A few of these cold waves cover the entire area east of the Divide, and one or two a season will cover the State all the way from the Dakotas to Idaho. With temperatures well below 0 and sometimes strong winds with blowing snow, these cold waves can be very inconvenient and even dangerous. In small areas ideally situated for radiation cooling, low temperatures can fall to -50°F. or lower.

During the summer months hot weather occurs fairly often in the eastern parts of the State. Temperatures of over 100 sometimes occur in the lower elevation areas west of the Divide during the summer, but hot spells are less frequent and of shorter duration than in the plains sections. Hot spells nowhere become oppressive, however, because summer nights almost invariably are cool and pleasant. In the areas with elevations above 4,000 feet, extremely hot weather is almost unknown. Summer days, however, are usually warm enough for light summer clothing.

Winters, while usually cold, have few extended cold spells. Between cold waves there are periods, sometimes longer than 10 days, of mild but often windy weather. These warm, windy winter periods occur almost entirely along the eastern slopes of the Divide and are popularly known as "chinook" weather. The so-called "chinook" belt extends from the Browning-Shelby area southeastward to the Yellowstone Valley above Billings. Through this belt, "chinook" winds frequently reach speeds of 25 to 50 m.p.h. or more and can persist, with little interruptions, for several days.

Most Montana lakes freeze over every winter, but Flathead Lake, between Polson and Kalispell, freezes over completely only during the coldest winters, and one year in 10. All rivers carry floating ice during the late winter or early spring. Few streams freeze solid; water generally continues to flow beneath the ice. During coldest winters "anchor" ice, which builds from the bottom of shallow streams, on rare occasions causes some flooding.

PRECIPITATION. Precipitation varies widely and depends largely upon topographic influences. Areas adjacent to mountain ranges in general are the wettest, although there are a few exceptions where the "rain-shadow" effect appears. Generally, nearly half the annual long-term average total falls in the three months, May through July.

SNOWFALL. Annual snowfall varies from quite heavy, 300 inches, in some parts of the mountains in the western half of the State, to around 20 inches at some stations in the two northern Divisions east of the Continental Divide. Most snow falls during the November-March period, but heavy snowstorms can occur as early as mid-September or as late as May 1 in the higher southwestern half of the State. In eastern sections early or late season snows are not very common. Mountain snowpacks in the wetter areas often exceed 100 inches in depth as the annual snow season approaches its end around April 1 to 15.

The greatest volume of flow of Montana's rivers occurs during the spring and early summer months with the melting of the winter snowpack. Heavy rains falling during the spring thaw constitute a serious flood threat. Ice jams, which occur during the spring breakup, usually in March, cause backwater flooding. Flash-floods, although restricted in scope, are probably the most numerous and result from locally heavy rainstorms in the spring and summer.

STORMS. Severe storms of several types can occur, but the most troublesome are hailstorms. Their occurrence is limited mainly to July and August, infrequently in June and September. Tornadoes develop infrequently and occur almost entirely east of the Divide, largely in the eastern third of the State. Severe windstorms of a general nature are rare but can occur locally, mainly east of the Divide, from a few to several times a year. Drought in its most severe form is practically unknown, but dry years do occur in some sections. All parts of the State rarely suffer from dryness at the same time.

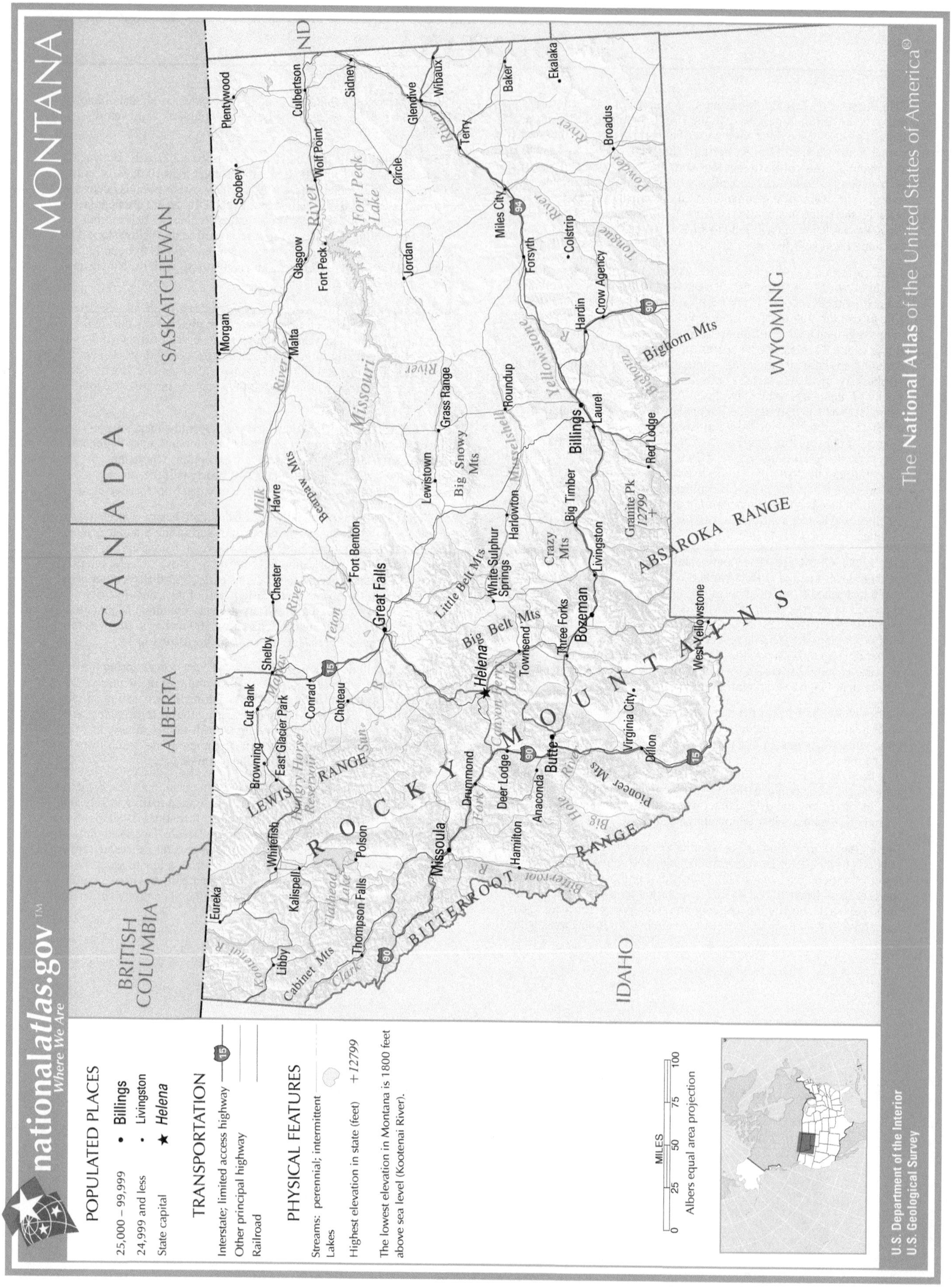
MONTANA
nationalatlas.gov™
Where We Are
POPULATED PLACES
25,000 – 99,999 • Billings
24,999 and less · Livingston
State capital ★ Helena
TRANSPORTATION
Interstate; limited access highway 15
Other principal highway
Railroad
PHYSICAL FEATURES
Streams: perennial; intermittent
Lakes
Highest elevation in state (feet) + 12799
The lowest elevation in Montana is 1800 feet above sea level (Kootenai River).
MILES
0 25 50 75 100
Albers equal area projection
U.S. Department of the Interior
U.S. Geological Survey
The National Atlas of the United States of America®
CANADA
BRITISH COLUMBIA
ALBERTA
SASKATCHEWAN
ND
IDAHO
WYOMING
ROCKY MOUNTAINS
LEWIS RANGE
BITTERROOT RANGE
ABSAROKA RANGE
Bighorn Mts
Pioneer Mts
Big Belt Mts
Little Belt Mts
Big Snowy Mts
Crazy Mts
Bearpaw Mts
Cabinet Mts
Granite Pk 12799
Plentywood
Scobey
Culbertson
Sidney
Wolf Point
Glendive
Wibaux
Baker
Ekalaka
Circle
Terry
Broadus
Miles City
Glasgow
Fort Peck
Fort Peck Lake
Jordan
Forsyth
Colstrip
Crow Agency
Hardin
Morgan
Malta
Grass Range
Roundup
Laurel
Billings
Red Lodge
Lewistown
Havre
Chester
Fort Benton
Great Falls
Harlowton
Big Timber
Livingston
White Sulphur Springs
Bozeman
Three Forks
Townsend
Helena
Canyon Ferry Lake
West Yellowstone
Virginia City
Dillon
Butte
Anaconda
Deer Lodge
Drummond
Hamilton
Missoula
Polson
Choteau
Conrad
Shelby
Cut Bank
Browning
East Glacier Park
Hungry Horse Reservoir
Whitefish
Kalispell
Flathead Lake
Thompson Falls
Eureka
Libby
Missouri River
Milk River
Marias River
Teton R
Sun R
Yellowstone River
Musselshell
Powder River
Tongue River
Bighorn River
Big Hole River
Bitterroot R
Clark Fork
Kootenai R
15
90
94

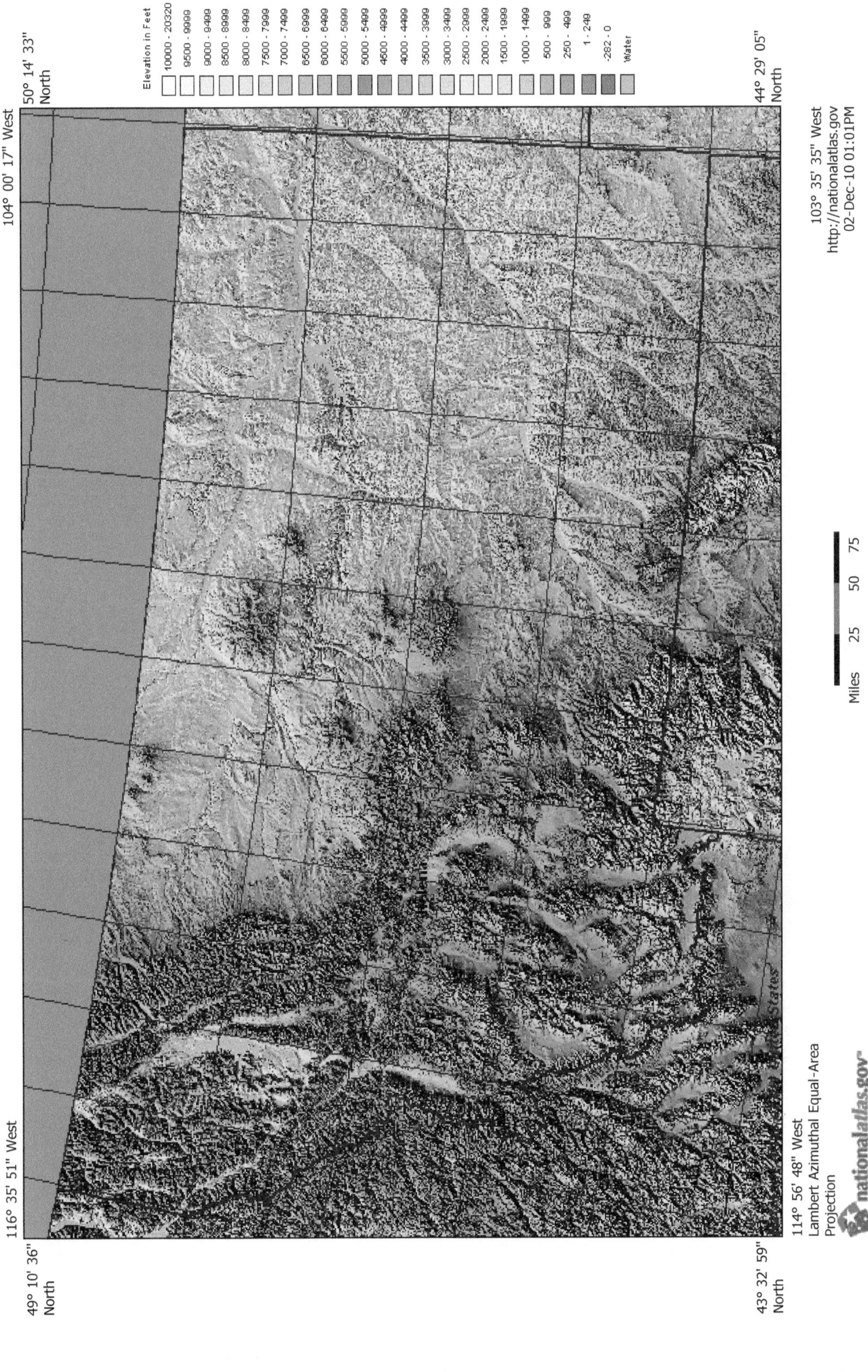
Elevation in Feet
10000 - 20320
9500 - 9999
9000 - 9499
8500 - 8999
8000 - 8499
7500 - 7999
7000 - 7499
6500 - 6999
6000 - 6499
5500 - 5999
5000 - 5499
4500 - 4999
4000 - 4499
3500 - 3999
3000 - 3499
2500 - 2999
2000 - 2499
1500 - 1999
1000 - 1499
500 - 999
250 - 499
1 - 249
-282 - 0
Water
50° 14' 33" North
104° 00' 17" West
44° 29' 05" North
103° 35' 35" West
http://nationalatlas.gov
02-Dec-10 01:01PM
Miles
25
50
75
116° 35' 51" West
49° 10' 36" North
43° 32' 59" North
114° 56' 48" West
Lambert Azimuthal Equal-Area Projection
nationalatlas.gov

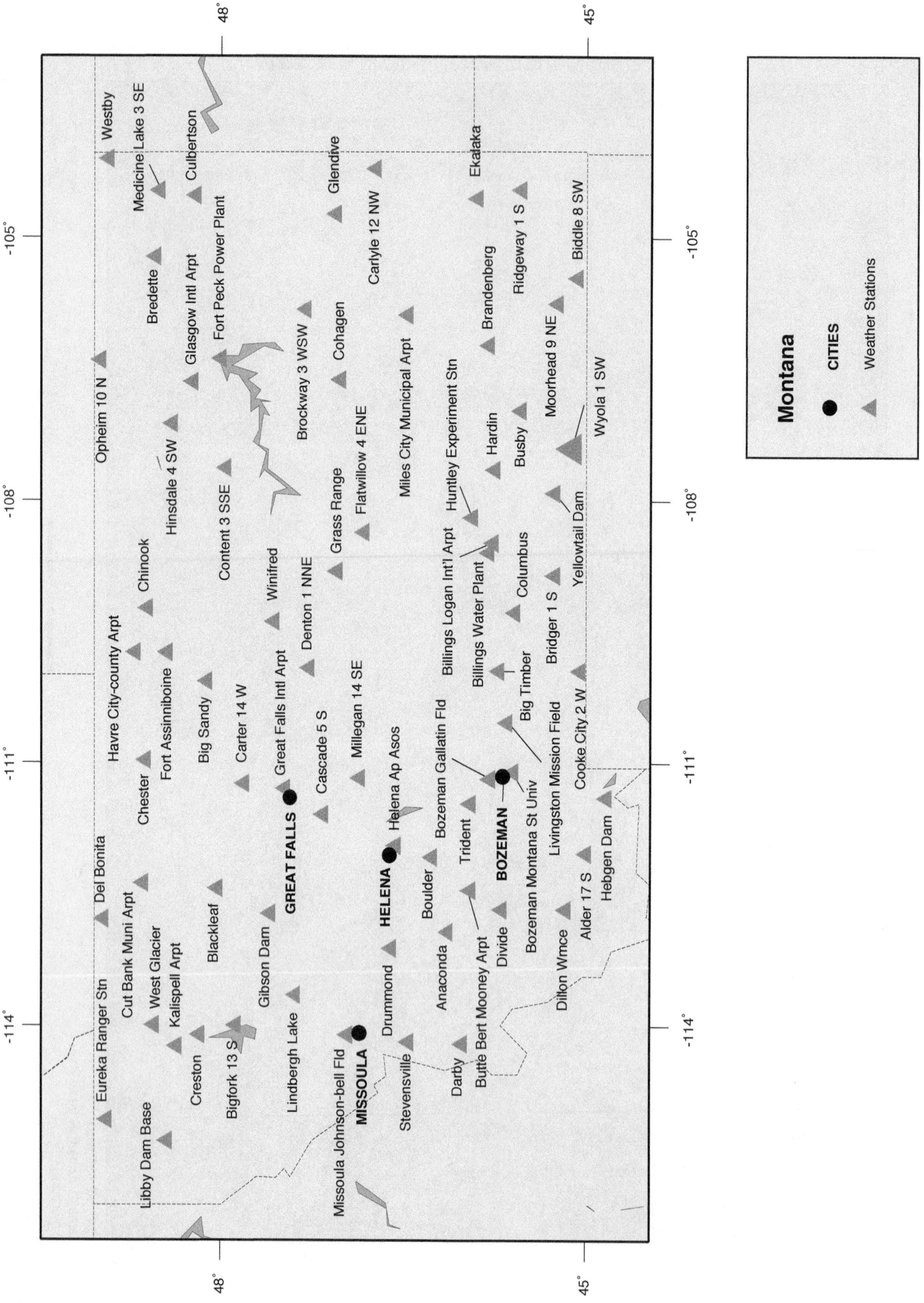
Montana
CITIES
Weather Stations
48°
45°
-105°
-108°
-111°
-114°
Westby
Medicine Lake 3 SE
Culbertson
Glendive
Carlyle 12 NW
Ekalaka
Ridgeway 1 S
Biddle 8 SW
Bredette
Glasgow Intl Arpt
Fort Peck Power Plant
Brockway 3 WSW
Cohagen
Miles City Municipal Arpt
Brandenberg
Moorhead 9 NE
Wyola 1 SW
Opheim 10 N
Hinsdale 4 SW
Content 3 SSE
Grass Range
Flatwillow 4 ENE
Huntley Experiment Stn
Hardin
Busby
Yellowtail Dam
Chinook
Winifred
Denton 1 NNE
Billings Logan Int'l Arpt
Billings Water Plant
Columbus
Bridger 1 S
Havre City-county Arpt
Fort Assinniboine
Big Sandy
Carter 14 W
Great Falls Intl Arpt
Cascade 5 S
Millegan 14 SE
Helena Ap Asos
Bozeman Gallatin Fld
Big Timber
Livingston Mission Field
Cooke City 2 W
Chester
Del Bonita
Cut Bank Muni Arpt
West Glacier
Kalispell Arpt
Blackleaf
Gibson Dam
GREAT FALLS
HELENA
Boulder
Trident
BOZEMAN
Bozeman Montana St Univ
Alder 17 S
Hebgen Dam
Eureka Ranger Stn
Creston
Bigfork 13 S
Lindbergh Lake
Drummond
Anaconda
Butte Bert Mooney Arpt
Divide
Dillon Wmce
Libby Dam Base
Missoula Johnson-bell Fld
MISSOULA
Stevensville
Darby

Montana Weather Stations by County

County	Station Name
Beaverhead	Dillon Wmce
Big Horn	Busby
	Hardin
	Wyola 1 SW
	Yellowtail Dam
Blaine	Chinook
Carbon	Bridger 1 S
Carter	Ekalaka
	Ridgeway 1 S
Cascade	Cascade 5 S
	Great Falls Intl Arpt
Chouteau	Big Sandy
	Carter 14 W
Custer	Miles City Municipal Arpt
Dawson	Glendive
Deer Lodge	Anaconda
Fergus	Denton 1 NNE
	Grass Range
	Winifred
Flathead	Creston
	Kalispell Arpt
	West Glacier
Gallatin	Bozeman Gallatin Fld
	Bozeman Montana St Univ
	Hebgen Dam
	Trident
Garfield	Cohagen
Glacier	Cut Bank Muni Arpt
	Del Bonita
Granite	Drummond
Hill	Fort Assinniboine
	Havre City-County Arpt
Jefferson	Boulder
Lake	Bigfork 13 S
Lewis And Clark	Gibson Dam
	Helena Arpt Asos
Liberty	Chester
Lincoln	Eureka Ranger Stn
	Libby Dam Base
Madison	Alder 17 S
Mccone	Brockway 3 WSW
Mccone *(cont.)*	Fort Peck Power Plant
Meagher	Millegan 14 SE
Missoula	Lindbergh Lake
	Missoula Johnson-Bell Field
Park	Cooke City 2 W
	Livingston Mission Field
Petroleum	Flatwillow 4 ENE
Phillips	Content 3 SSE
Powder River	Biddle 8 SW
	Moorhead 9 NE
Ravalli	Darby
	Stevensville
Roosevelt	Bredette
	Culbertson
Rosebud	Brandenberg
Sheridan	Medicine Lake 3 SE
	Westby
Silver Bow	Butte Bert Mooney Arpt
	Divide
Stillwater	Columbus
Sweet Grass	Big Timber
Teton	Blackleaf
Valley	Glasgow Intl Arpt
	Hinsdale 4 SW
	Opheim 10 N
Wibaux	Carlyle 12 NW
Yellowstone	Billings Logan Int'l Arpt
	Billings Water Plant
	Huntley Experiment Stn

See User Guide for station inclusion criteria.

Montana Weather Stations by City

City	Station Name	Miles
Anaconda-Deer Lodge County	Anaconda	0.4
	Butte Bert Mooney Arpt	24.8
Belgrade	Bozeman Gallatin Fld	0.7
	Bozeman Montana St Univ	10.0
	Trident	18.1
Billings	Billings Water Plant	3.2
	Billings Logan Int'l Arpt	0.9
	Huntley Experiment Stn	17.2
Bozeman	Bozeman Gallatin Fld	9.4
	Bozeman Montana St Univ	0.5
Butte-Silver Bow	Anaconda	22.8
	Butte Bert Mooney Arpt	1.8
	Divide	19.7
Evergreen	Creston	7.0
	Kalispell Arpt	6.3
	West Glacier	23.0
Great Falls	Carter 14 W	20.7
	Great Falls Intl Arpt	5.3
Havre	Chinook	20.6
	Fort Assinniboine	6.3
	Havre City-County Arpt	4.0
Helena	Helena Arpt Asos	3.0
Helena Valley Southeast	Helena Arpt Asos	2.6
Helena Valley W. Central	Helena Arpt Asos	5.0
Kalispell	Creston	8.6
	Kalispell Arpt	8.7
Laurel	Billings Water Plant	15.2
	Billings Logan Int'l Arpt	13.7
	Columbus	24.2
Livingston	Bozeman Montana St Univ	23.5
	Livingston Mission Field	6.1
Miles City	Miles City Municipal Arpt	2.8
Missoula	Missoula Johnson-Bell Field	5.9
	Stevensville	23.8

Note: Miles is the distance between the geographic center of the city and the weather station.

See User Guide for station inclusion criteria.

Montana Weather Stations by Elevation

Feet	Station Name
7,459	Cooke City 2 W
6,488	Hebgen Dam
5,850	Alder 17 S
5,540	Butte Bert Mooney Arpt
5,350	Divide
5,279	Anaconda
5,228	Dillon Wmce
4,970	Millegan 14 SE
4,913	Bozeman Montana St Univ
4,903	Boulder
4,652	Livingston Mission Field
4,589	Gibson Dam
4,426	Bozeman Gallatin Fld
4,336	Del Bonita
4,319	Lindbergh Lake
4,234	Blackleaf
4,100	Big Timber
4,036	Trident
4,000	Drummond
3,879	Darby
3,837	Cut Bank Muni Arpt
3,828	Helena Arpt Asos
3,729	Wyola 1 SW
3,680	Bridger 1 S
3,664	Great Falls Intl Arpt
3,620	Denton 1 NNE
3,597	Biddle 8 SW
3,584	Columbus
3,566	Billings Logan Int'l Arpt
3,490	Grass Range
3,450	Carter 14 W
3,430	Busby
3,424	Ekalaka
3,375	Stevensville
3,359	Cascade 5 S
3,319	Ridgeway 1 S
3,305	Yellowtail Dam
3,243	Winifred
3,220	Moorhead 9 NE
3,191	Missoula Johnson-Bell Field
3,165	Chester
3,153	West Glacier
3,138	Flatwillow 4 ENE
3,097	Billings Water Plant
3,028	Carlyle 12 NW
2,990	Huntley Experiment Stn
2,979	Opheim 10 N
2,971	Kalispell Arpt
2,939	Creston
2,910	Bigfork 13 S
2,904	Hardin
2,771	Brandenberg
2,770	Big Sandy
2,714	Cohagen
2,687	Bredette
2,674	Hinsdale 4 SW
2,629	Brockway 3 WSW
2,627	Miles City Municipal Arpt
2,612	Fort Assinniboine
2,584	Havre City-County Arpt
2,532	Eureka Ranger Stn
2,345	Chinook
2,339	Content 3 SSE
2,293	Glasgow Intl Arpt
2,109	Libby Dam Base
2,103	Westby
2,076	Glendive
2,068	Fort Peck Power Plant
1,952	Medicine Lake 3 SE
1,919	Culbertson

See User Guide for station inclusion criteria.

Billings Logan Int'l Airport

Billings, Montana, at an elevation of 3,100 to 3,600 feet above sea level, is situated in the borderline area between the Great Plains and the Rocky Mountains, and has a semi-arid climate which takes on some of the characteristics of both regions. With irrigation and the favorable distribution of the precipitation a variety of crops successfully grow in the area.

About a third of the annual precipitation falls during May and June, with June being the wettest month. The period of least precipitation is from November through February. These four months normally produce less than 20 percent of the annual precipitation. The heaviest snows occur during the spring and fall months when the temperature and moisture conditions are most favorable. Heavy snows of 6 inches or more also occur during November and December. The occurrence of thawing periods normally prevents the snow from accumulating to great depths on the ground. Thunderstorms are most frequent during the summer months. These storms are frequently accompanied by strong, gusty winds and occasionally by hail. Destructive hailstorms, however, are rather infrequent.

Winter is usually cold, though not extremely so, and generally affords several mild periods of a week to several weeks in length. The winter cold periods are ushered in by moderately strong north to northeast winds and snow. The coldest temperatures occur after the snow ends and the sky clears. True blizzard conditions are not observed very often in town, but in the surrounding rural areas, blizzard conditions may develop several times during the winter. Cold weather improves with the onset of moderate to strong southwest winds. This wind is sometimes a foehn condition (chinook), but is more often a drainage wind moving down the Yellowstone Valley which transports warmer air of Pacific origin to the area.

Spring brings a period of frequent and rapid fluctuations in the weather. It is usually cloudy and cool with frequent periods of rain and/or snow. As the season progresses, snows become less frequent until late May and June when rain is the rule. The last freezing temperatures in spring usually occur before mid-May though they have occurred as late as late June.

The summer season is characterized by warm days with abundant sunshine and low humidities. The nights are cool because of the altitude and the cool air drainage into the valley from the higher terrain. Frequent thunderstorms bring threatening afternoon cloudiness but usually only small amounts of rain.

The first freezing temperatures of the fall season occur in late September, but they have been noted as early as late August. The change to severe winter weather usually arrives after the middle of November. There have been years when the more severe type of winter weather have been delayed until late in December.

Billings Logan Int'l Airport *Yellowstone County* Elevation: 3,566 ft. Latitude: 45° 48' N Longitude: 108° 33' W

	JAN	FEB	MAR	APR	MAY	JUN	JUL	AUG	SEP	OCT	NOV	DEC	YEAR
Mean Maximum Temp. (°F)	36.1	40.3	48.2	57.9	67.9	77.4	87.0	85.6	73.2	59.3	45.7	35.5	59.5
Mean Temp. (°F)	26.9	30.5	37.4	46.5	55.9	64.8	73.0	71.4	60.4	48.2	36.2	26.7	48.1
Mean Minimum Temp. (°F)	17.5	20.6	26.6	34.9	43.9	52.1	58.9	57.2	47.6	37.0	26.6	17.8	36.7
Extreme Maximum Temp. (°F)	67	71	80	90	95	105	108	103	103	90	77	69	108
Extreme Minimum Temp. (°F)	-30	-28	-19	3	22	34	42	35	22	-7	-19	-32	-32
Days Maximum Temp. ≥ 90°F	0	0	0	0	1	4	13	11	2	0	0	0	31
Days Maximum Temp. ≤ 32°F	10	7	4	1	0	0	0	0	0	1	5	11	39
Days Minimum Temp. ≤ 32°F	27	24	22	11	2	0	0	0	1	8	20	28	143
Days Minimum Temp. ≤ 0°F	5	3	1	0	0	0	0	0	0	0	1	4	14
Heating Degree Days (base 65°F)	1,177	969	847	551	293	91	13	19	186	519	858	1,181	6,704
Cooling Degree Days (base 65°F)	0	0	0	2	18	91	268	226	54	4	0	0	663
Mean Precipitation (in.)	0.48	0.49	1.09	1.63	2.26	2.00	1.28	0.69	1.31	1.24	0.58	0.48	13.53
Maximum Precipitation (in.)*	2.3	1.8	2.7	4.4	7.7	5.7	5.1	3.5	4.0	3.8	2.3	2.0	26.8
Minimum Precipitation (in.)*	0.1	0	0.2	0.1	0.4	0.2	trace	0	0.1	trace	trace	0	7.9
Extreme Maximum Daily Precip. (in.)	0.57	0.65	1.13	1.04	2.11	2.91	2.06	1.20	1.13	1.23	0.61	0.43	2.91
Days With ≥ 0.1" Precipitation	1	2	3	5	6	5	3	2	4	3	2	2	38
Days With ≥ 0.5" Precipitation	0	0	0	1	1	1	1	0	1	1	0	0	6
Days With ≥ 1.0" Precipitation	0	0	0	0	0	0	0	0	0	0	0	0	0
Mean Snowfall (in.)	8.6	6.6	10.8	8.3	2.0	trace	trace	trace	1.1	4.7	5.9	7.8	55.8
Maximum Snowfall (in.)*	28	22	27	42	16	2	0	trace	9	23	25	29	127
Maximum 24-hr. Snowfall (in.)*	14	8	11	24	15	2	0	trace	6	10	13	14	24
Maximum Snow Depth (in.)	10	9	14	12	10	trace	trace	trace	7	12	13	13	14
Days With ≥ 1.0" Snow Depth	14	9	8	3	0	0	0	0	0	2	7	14	57
Thunderstorm Days*	< 1	< 1	< 1	1	4	7	7	6	2	< 1	0	< 1	27
Foggy Days*	5	5	6	6	4	2	1	1	3	4	5	5	47
Predominant Sky Cover*	OVR	OVR	OVR	OVR	OVR	BRK	CLR	CLR	CLR	OVR	OVR	OVR	OVR
Mean Relative Humidity 5am (%)*	64	66	69	68	71	72	64	61	64	63	65	64	66
Mean Relative Humidity 5pm (%)*	56	53	48	42	42	41	32	30	37	42	53	56	44
Mean Dewpoint (°F)*	10	15	20	27	37	45	47	45	38	30	20	13	29
Prevailing Wind Direction*	SW	SW	SW	SW	SW	SW	SW	SW	SW	SW	SW	SW	SW
Prevailing Wind Speed (mph)*	15	14	12	10	10	9	9	9	10	12	13	14	12
Maximum Wind Gust (mph)*	63	74	58	69	60	61	69	71	61	61	73	64	74

Note: (*) Period of record is 1948-1995

The period of record for National Weather Service station data is 1980 – 2009 except where noted. See User Guide for detailed explanation of data.

Glasgow Int'l Airport

Founded in the days of national expansion as a railroad shop town, Glasgow is situated in the valley of the Milk River, about 20 miles upstream from where the Milk River joins the Missouri. It lies on the natural route from the plains to Marias Pass in the northern Rockies. The city is located on the valley floor at an average elevation of about 2,100 feet above sea level. Hills rise sharply from the northern edge of the city to flat tableland about 200 feet higher than the valley. The Weather Service Office is located on this flat land about 1 mile north-northeast of the city. A gradual incline commences 3 to 4 miles to the south and southwest of the city and reaches to the rolling hills which separate the Milk River drainage from the Fort Peck Reservoir on the Missouri. The northern shore of Fort Peck Reservoir lies about 15 miles south of Glasgow. The reservoir's average width south of Glasgow is about 10 miles.

The climate in the Glasgow area is continental with a large annual range in temperature and limited precipitation. Fort Peck Reservoir, to the south, seems to have little climatic effect as far north as Glasgow, except for brief periods of morning fog in the late fall which occasionally drift northward from the lake before it freezes. Seventy-eight percent of the annual precipitation falls from April through September, with May and June accounting for about 38 percent of the annual total. This distribution of precipitation helps to make the climate quite favorable for the growing of small grains. Winter precipitation nearly always falls as snow, but as a rule, although snow seldom accumulates to any great depth, it usually is formed into drifts in the open, unprotected areas. Blizzards during the winter months occur occasionally, but usually are of short duration. Glasgow itself is well protected from most strong winds and blizzard conditions by hills to the north of the city, but occasionally the unprotected surrounding areas feel the full brunt of these winter storms.

Glasgow has a wide range of temperature. Winters are quite cold, but mild winter weather occasionally does occur, sometimes caused when the chinook or foehn wind, which descends the eastern slopes of the Rocky Mountains, reaches as far east as Glasgow. Very cold spells also occur, at least once each winter, but as a rule, these last only a few days. Summers are characterized by warm, sunny weather which can last for several weeks at a time. Sunny weather predominates during the warmer season, but interruptions in the form of clouds and showers do occur, usually in the afternoons and evenings. A few days of hot weather in July and August occur at times, but hot days are seldom oppressive because they are usually accompanied by low humidity.

Glasgow Int'l Airport *Valley County* Elevation: 2,293 ft. Latitude: 48° 13' N Longitude: 106° 37' W

	JAN	FEB	MAR	APR	MAY	JUN	JUL	AUG	SEP	OCT	NOV	DEC	YEAR
Mean Maximum Temp. (°F)	23.4	29.3	42.3	58.0	68.3	76.9	85.3	84.2	71.9	56.9	40.1	26.4	55.2
Mean Temp. (°F)	13.7	19.5	31.5	45.1	55.4	64.1	71.3	70.1	58.3	44.7	29.7	16.6	43.3
Mean Minimum Temp. (°F)	4.0	9.6	20.7	32.2	42.5	51.4	57.2	55.9	44.6	32.5	19.3	6.8	31.4
Extreme Maximum Temp. (°F)	61	71	79	91	102	108	106	108	103	90	79	62	108
Extreme Minimum Temp. (°F)	-40	-38	-27	4	20	32	44	37	15	-6	-26	-38	-40
Days Maximum Temp. ≥ 90°F	0	0	0	0	1	3	10	10	2	0	0	0	26
Days Maximum Temp. ≤ 32°F	20	15	7	1	0	0	0	0	0	1	8	18	70
Days Minimum Temp. ≤ 32°F	31	28	28	15	3	0	0	0	2	14	27	31	179
Days Minimum Temp. ≤ 0°F	12	8	2	0	0	0	0	0	0	0	3	10	35
Heating Degree Days (base 65°F)	1,586	1,281	1,031	591	308	100	15	32	234	623	1,052	1,495	8,348
Cooling Degree Days (base 65°F)	0	0	0	1	18	81	216	196	38	1	0	0	551
Mean Precipitation (in.)	0.36	0.25	0.43	0.82	1.80	2.31	1.71	1.18	0.91	0.78	0.40	0.37	11.32
Maximum Precipitation (in.)*	1.4	1.4	1.4	2.6	4.9	6.9	5.9	5.7	4.1	1.8	1.3	1.5	19.0
Minimum Precipitation (in.)*	trace	trace	0	trace	trace	0.1	trace	trace	trace	trace	trace	trace	6.7
Extreme Maximum Daily Precip. (in.)	0.26	0.64	0.68	1.03	1.72	2.55	1.45	2.96	1.12	1.22	0.48	0.36	2.96
Days With ≥ 0.1" Precipitation	1	1	1	3	5	6	4	3	2	2	1	1	30
Days With ≥ 0.5" Precipitation	0	0	0	0	1	1	1	0	0	0	0	0	3
Days With ≥ 1.0" Precipitation	0	0	0	0	0	0	0	0	0	0	0	0	0
Mean Snowfall (in.)	7.6	4.1	4.8	2.0	1.2	trace	trace	trace	0.2	1.4	4.6	7.5	33.4
Maximum Snowfall (in.)*	24	21	15	14	11	1	0	0	2	8	17	15	58
Maximum 24-hr. Snowfall (in.)*	7	8	9	11	10	1	0	0	2	5	10	7	11
Maximum Snow Depth (in.)	24	29	21	12	10	trace	trace	trace	2	11	13	15	29
Days With ≥ 1.0" Snow Depth	24	17	10	1	0	0	0	0	0	1	6	16	75
Thunderstorm Days*	< 1	0	< 1	1	4	7	8	6	2	< 1	< 1	0	28
Foggy Days*	8	6	6	3	3	2	1	1	2	2	5	7	46
Predominant Sky Cover*	OVR	OVR	OVR	OVR	OVR	SCT	SCT	SCT	CLR	OVR	OVR	OVR	OVR
Mean Relative Humidity 5am (%)*	77	80	81	75	73	75	73	68	72	74	79	79	75
Mean Relative Humidity 5pm (%)*	74	71	58	41	39	39	33	31	37	46	65	74	51
Mean Dewpoint (°F)*	4	11	20	27	37	46	49	46	38	30	19	10	28
Prevailing Wind Direction*	ESE	ESE	ESE	ESE	ESE	ESE	ESE	ESE	ESE	ESE	ESE	ESE	ESE
Prevailing Wind Speed (mph)*	13	13	13	13	13	13	12	13	13	12	12	12	13
Maximum Wind Gust (mph)*	61	68	59	63	63	62	86	73	59	61	73	61	86

Note: (*) Period of record is 1948-1995

Great Falls Int'l Airport

The city of Great Falls is located along the main stem of the Missouri River at its confluence with the Sun River. The Weather Service Office is located at the Municipal Airport on a plateau between the Sun and Missouri Rivers. This plateau is about 200 feet higher than most of the immediate valley area, and the airport is about two miles southwest of the Sun and Missouri River Junction. Except to the north and northeast, the valley is encircled by mountain ranges, which lie about 30 miles away from east to south, 40 miles to the southwest, and 60 to 100 miles distant from west to northwest. The combination of valleys and plateaus in the immediate area, contributes to marked temperature differences between the airport and the city proper, either on calm, clear mornings, or when chinook winds reach the airport before they are felt at the lower elevations in town.

Summertime in the area generally is quite pleasant, with cool nights, moderately warm and sunny days, and very little hot, humid weather. Most of the summer rainfall occurs in showers or thunderstorms, and steady rains may occur during late spring or early summer. At the airport, freezing temperatures do not occur in July or August and very rarely in June. Frost occurs frequently in April and October, but more often in the valleys than on the surrounding hills or plateaus.

Winters are not as cold as is usually expected of a continental location at this latitude, largely as a result of the chinook winds for which this area is noted. While sub-zero weather is experienced normally several times during a winter, the coldest weather seldom lasts more than a few days at a time, and is usually terminated by southwest chinook winds which can produce sharp temperature rises of 40 degrees or more in 24 hours.

As a result of recurring chinooks throughout the winter season, snow seldom lies on the ground for more than a few days. In fact, the ground usually is bare, or nearly bare, of snow most of the winter, except in the surrounding mountains and higher foothills. On the other hand, invasions of cold air from the polar regions occur a few times each winter, and sharp temperature falls from above freezing to below zero within 24 hours are observed occasionally.

Precipitation generally falls as snow during late fall, winter, and early spring, although rain can occur in any month. Late spring, summer, and early fall precipitation is almost always rain, but some hail is observed occasionally during summer thunderstorms.

Although average annual precipitation at Great Falls would normally classify the area as semi- arid, it is important to note that about 70 percent of the annual total falls normally during the April to September growing season. The combination of ideal temperatures during the peak of the growing season, long hours of summer sunshine, and adequate precipitation during the six critical months, makes the climate very favorable for dryland farming. Heavy fog occurs about one day per month, but each case lasts only a small part of the day. Although the average windspeed is relatively high, strong winds over 70 mph are seldom observed. Visibility normally is excellent.

Great Falls Int'l Airport *Cascade County* Elevation: 3,664 ft. Latitude: 47° 28' N Longitude: 111° 23' W

	JAN	FEB	MAR	APR	MAY	JUN	JUL	AUG	SEP	OCT	NOV	DEC	YEAR
Mean Maximum Temp. (°F)	35.1	38.4	45.5	56.0	65.2	73.3	83.6	82.1	70.4	57.5	43.7	34.6	57.1
Mean Temp. (°F)	25.2	27.8	34.3	43.8	52.5	60.2	68.0	66.6	56.6	45.5	34.1	25.1	45.0
Mean Minimum Temp. (°F)	15.2	17.2	23.1	31.6	39.7	47.0	52.4	51.1	42.8	33.6	24.5	15.7	32.8
Extreme Maximum Temp. (°F)	67	70	78	89	93	101	104	104	98	91	76	63	104
Extreme Minimum Temp. (°F)	-33	-35	-22	-8	12	31	36	30	16	-11	-25	-42	-42
Days Maximum Temp. ≥ 90°F	0	0	0	0	0	2	8	7	1	0	0	0	18
Days Maximum Temp. ≤ 32°F	10	8	5	1	0	0	0	0	0	1	5	11	41
Days Minimum Temp. ≤ 32°F	27	25	25	17	5	0	0	0	3	14	22	27	165
Days Minimum Temp. ≤ 0°F	7	5	2	0	0	0	0	0	0	0	2	6	22
Heating Degree Days (base 65°F)	1,229	1,045	944	630	390	175	42	63	271	598	920	1,230	7,537
Cooling Degree Days (base 65°F)	0	0	0	1	8	38	141	120	25	2	0	0	335
Mean Precipitation (in.)	0.49	0.49	0.92	1.35	2.50	2.57	1.47	1.52	1.38	0.90	0.54	0.50	14.63
Maximum Precipitation (in.)*	2.0	2.2	2.2	4.6	8.1	5.4	4.7	4.9	3.2	3.4	2.3	1.9	25.2
Minimum Precipitation (in.)*	0	trace	0.1	0	0.7	0.5	trace	trace	0.1	trace	trace	trace	9.0
Extreme Maximum Daily Precip. (in.)	0.53	0.59	0.86	1.22	2.50	2.42	1.61	1.89	1.56	0.84	0.89	0.50	2.50
Days With ≥ 0.1" Precipitation	2	2	3	4	6	6	4	3	4	3	2	2	41
Days With ≥ 0.5" Precipitation	0	0	0	1	1	1	1	1	1	0	0	0	6
Days With ≥ 1.0" Precipitation	0	0	0	0	0	0	0	0	0	0	0	0	0
Mean Snowfall (in.)	8.0	8.3	12.2	8.0	2.7	0.3	trace	0.3	1.2	4.4	7.4	8.0	60.8
Maximum Snowfall (in.)*	23	26	24	35	12	11	0	8	10	17	22	23	117
Maximum 24-hr. Snowfall (in.)*	8	11	12	17	10	8	0	7	6	7	7	7	17
Maximum Snow Depth (in.)	12	10	13	17	12	6	trace	3	5	6	12	12	17
Days With ≥ 1.0" Snow Depth	13	11	9	3	1	0	0	0	0	2	7	12	58
Thunderstorm Days*	< 1	< 1	< 1	1	3	7	7	6	1	< 1	< 1	< 1	25
Foggy Days*	6	6	6	5	4	3	1	1	3	3	5	5	48
Predominant Sky Cover*	OVR	OVR	OVR	OVR	OVR	OVR	SCT	SCT	OVR	OVR	OVR	OVR	OVR
Mean Relative Humidity 5am (%)*	67	67	69	68	70	71	66	64	66	63	64	65	67
Mean Relative Humidity 5pm (%)*	61	55	50	41	40	40	30	30	36	43	55	59	45
Mean Dewpoint (°F)*	10	14	19	25	34	42	44	42	36	29	20	13	27
Prevailing Wind Direction*	SW	SW	SW	SW	SW	SW	SW	SW	SW	SW	SW	SW	SW
Prevailing Wind Speed (mph)*	20	18	16	15	13	13	12	12	13	16	18	20	15
Maximum Wind Gust (mph)*	70	66	66	62	61	75	77	74	61	67	82	68	82

Note: (*) Period of record is 1948-1995

The period of record for National Weather Service station data is 1980 – 2009 except where noted. See User Guide for detailed explanation of data.

Havre City-County Airport

Havre, Montana, is located in a level valley formed by the Milk River, which courses through the city from west to east. Most of the city lies on the south side of the river. On the north side, hills rise abruptly to about 200 feet above the valley floor. The land mass north to the Canadian border is gently rolling and increases slightly in elevation. During winter months, frequent invasions of cold polar continental air move down across these rolling plains, bringing snow and sub-zero temperatures.

The Bearpaw Mountains extend from 15 to 30 miles south of Havre. Most of the peaks are from 4,000 to 5,000 feet above sea level, and several are above 6,000 feet. The highest is Old Baldy, 6,916 feet above sea level.

Winters are cold in the Havre area, but snow cover is seldom more than a few inches, and usually some ground is bare. Spells of mild weather do occur at least a few times each winter, arriving with sometimes fresh to strong southwest to west foehn winds. During winter months, rain rarely falls. Winter precipitation is almost always in the form of snow. The transition from winter to spring conditions is fairly rapid in the usual year, but cold snaps and snow can occur as late as early May or as early as September.

Summers are characterized by warm weather, seldom exceeding 95 degrees. Daytime warmest readings usually run from the 80s to the mid-90s during most of July and August, but summer relative humidities are seldom as high as 50 percent during afternoon hours. Summertime night temperatures are rarely oppressively warm. Most spring and summer precipitation falls as showers, but occasionally steady rains lasting several hours are observed in May and June, and again in September. Fall seasons are characterized by much clear weather, although cold snaps of a day or two, with some snow, can occur as early as mid-September.

Havre City-County Airport *Hill County* Elevation: 2,584 ft. Latitude: 48° 33' N Longitude: 109° 46' W

	JAN	FEB	MAR	APR	MAY	JUN	JUL	AUG	SEP	OCT	NOV	DEC	YEAR
Mean Maximum Temp. (°F)	28.7	34.1	44.5	58.3	67.9	76.0	85.0	83.8	71.7	57.9	42.0	30.5	56.7
Mean Temp. (°F)	17.9	22.7	32.7	44.7	54.3	62.3	69.4	67.9	56.7	44.2	30.7	19.5	43.6
Mean Minimum Temp. (°F)	7.0	11.3	20.9	31.1	40.7	48.6	53.7	52.0	41.7	30.5	19.3	8.4	30.4
Extreme Maximum Temp. (°F)	68	74	79	91	98	105	106	109	101	90	78	64	109
Extreme Minimum Temp. (°F)	-41	-44	-30	-3	14	29	39	33	18	-21	-30	-50	-50
Days Maximum Temp. ≥ 90°F	0	0	0	0	1	3	10	9	2	0	0	0	25
Days Maximum Temp. ≤ 32°F	15	11	6	1	0	0	0	0	0	1	7	14	55
Days Minimum Temp. ≤ 32°F	29	27	28	17	4	0	0	0	4	18	26	30	183
Days Minimum Temp. ≤ 0°F	11	7	2	0	0	0	0	0	0	0	3	9	32
Heating Degree Days (base 65°F)	1,456	1,188	995	602	335	127	27	48	263	638	1,023	1,407	8,109
Cooling Degree Days (base 65°F)	0	0	0	1	11	53	169	145	21	1	0	0	401
Mean Precipitation (in.)	0.33	0.29	0.54	0.81	1.72	2.20	1.53	1.09	1.08	0.64	0.40	0.38	11.01
Maximum Precipitation (in.)*	2.3	1.0	2.0	2.6	5.0	4.7	5.4	3.6	5.8	2.1	1.2	2.0	18.5
Minimum Precipitation (in.)*	trace	0.1	trace	0.1	0.3	0.2	trace	trace	trace	trace	trace	trace	7.0
Extreme Maximum Daily Precip. (in.)	0.30	0.38	0.71	0.98	2.10	1.92	2.15	1.17	1.95	0.77	0.48	0.48	2.15
Days With ≥ 0.1" Precipitation	1	1	2	2	5	5	3	3	3	2	1	1	29
Days With ≥ 0.5" Precipitation	0	0	0	0	1	1	1	1	0	0	0	0	4
Days With ≥ 1.0" Precipitation	0	0	0	0	0	0	0	0	0	0	0	0	0
Mean Snowfall (in.)	***7.2***	***5.9***	6.4	3.0	***1.8***	***trace***	trace	***trace***	0.3	2.3	***4.9***	***7.2***	***39.0***
Maximum Snowfall (in.)*	41	19	30	33	31	trace	0	trace	6	12	19	25	100
Maximum 24-hr. Snowfall (in.)*	11	6	20	16	21	trace	0	trace	6	8	7	5	21
Maximum Snow Depth (in.)	***19***	***18***	10	5	***7***	***trace***	trace	***trace***	trace	9	***9***	13	***19***
Days With ≥ 1.0" Snow Depth	***18***	***12***	8	2	***0***	***0***	0	***0***	0	1	***6***	***14***	***61***
Thunderstorm Days*	0	< 1	0	< 1	3	5	6	5	1	< 1	0	0	20
Foggy Days*	3	4	4	3	2	1	< 1	1	1	2	3	3	27
Predominant Sky Cover*	OVR	OVR	OVR	OVR	OVR	BRK	CLR	CLR	OVR	OVR	OVR	OVR	OVR
Mean Relative Humidity 5am (%)*	74	76	79	75	74	75	72	68	73	73	76	75	74
Mean Relative Humidity 5pm (%)*	68	63	53	40	38	37	31	29	35	44	62	69	48
Mean Dewpoint (°F)*	7	12	21	27	36	44	46	44	37	29	19	10	28
Prevailing Wind Direction*	SW	SW	SW	SW	SW	SW	WSW	WSW	WSW	SW	SW	SW	SW
Prevailing Wind Speed (mph)*	15	14	13	12	10	10	9	9	9	12	13	14	12
Maximum Wind Gust (mph)*	60	53	58	63	58	69	53	70	55	60	78	67	78

Note: (*) Period of record is 1961-1994

Helena Airport ASOS

Helena is located on the south side of an intermountain valley bounded on the west and south by the main chain of the Continental Divide. The valley is approximately 25 miles in width from north to south and 35 miles long from east to west. The average height of the mountains above the valley floor is about 3,000 feet.

The climate of Helena may be described as modified continental. Factors that enter into modifying the continental climate are invasion by Pacific Ocean air masses, drainage of cool air into the valley from the surrounding mountains, and the protecting mountain shield.

The mountains to the north and east sometimes deflect shallow masses of invading cold Arctic air to the east. Following periods of extreme cold, when the return circulation of maritime air has brought warming to most of the eastern part of the state, cold air may remain trapped in the valley for several days before being replaced by warmer air. During these periods of transition from cold-to-warm temperatures, inversions are often quite pronounced.

As may be expected in a northern latitude, cold waves may occur from November through February, with temperatures occasionally dropping to zero or lower.

Summertime temperatures are moderate, with maximum readings generally under 90 degrees and very seldom reaching 100 degrees. Like all mountain stations, there is usually a marked change in temperature from day to night. During the summer this tends to produce an agreeable combination of fairly warm days and cool nights.

Most of the precipitation falls from April through July from frequent showers or thunderstorms, but usually with some steady rains in June, the wettest month of the year. Like summer, fall and winter months are relatively dry. During the April to September growing season, precipitation varies considerably.

Thunderstorms are rather frequent from May through August. Snow can be expected from September through May, but amounts during the spring and fall are usually light, and snow on the ground ordinarily lasts only a day or two. During the winter months snow may remain on the ground for several weeks at a time.

In winter, hours of sunshine are more than would be expected at a mountain location.

Due to the sheltering influence of the mountains, Foehn (Chinook) winds are not as pronounced as might be expected. Strong winds can occur at any time throughout the year, but generally do not last more than a few hours at a time.

Based on the 1951-1980 period, the average first occurrence of 32 degrees Fahrenheit in the fall is September 18 and the average last occurrence in the spring is May 18.

Helena Airport ASOS *Lewis And Clark County* Elevation: 3,828 ft. Latitude: 46° 36' N Longitude: 111° 58' W

	JAN	FEB	MAR	APR	MAY	JUN	JUL	AUG	SEP	OCT	NOV	DEC	YEAR
Mean Maximum Temp. (°F)	32.5	37.8	47.2	57.4	66.8	75.1	85.1	83.7	71.9	57.9	42.7	31.6	57.5
Mean Temp. (°F)	22.5	27.1	35.6	44.7	53.8	61.7	69.6	67.8	57.4	45.1	32.3	21.8	44.9
Mean Minimum Temp. (°F)	12.4	16.3	23.9	32.0	40.8	48.2	54.0	51.8	42.7	32.1	21.9	11.9	32.3
Extreme Maximum Temp. (°F)	62	69	78	86	93	100	105	103	97	87	75	64	105
Extreme Minimum Temp. (°F)	-37	-42	-19	3	20	30	39	28	19	-8	-27	-37	-42
Days Maximum Temp. ≥ 90°F	0	0	0	0	0	3	11	9	2	0	0	0	25
Days Maximum Temp. ≤ 32°F	13	8	3	0	0	0	0	0	0	1	5	15	45
Days Minimum Temp. ≤ 32°F	29	26	27	15	4	0	0	0	3	15	25	30	174
Days Minimum Temp. ≤ 0°F	7	4	1	0	0	0	0	0	0	0	2	6	20
Heating Degree Days (base 65°F)	1,312	1,066	907	603	349	140	28	41	244	612	974	1,334	7,610
Cooling Degree Days (base 65°F)	0	0	0	0	9	48	177	136	22	0	0	0	392
Mean Precipitation (in.)	0.36	0.32	0.61	0.97	1.94	2.07	1.24	1.12	1.16	0.68	0.46	0.38	11.31
Maximum Precipitation (in.)*	2.8	1.2	1.6	3.0	6.1	4.3	4.7	4.2	3.4	2.7	1.5	1.5	20.9
Minimum Precipitation (in.)*	trace	trace	trace	0.1	0.3	0.1	0.1	trace	0.1	trace	trace	trace	6.3
Extreme Maximum Daily Precip. (in.)	0.40	0.31	0.47	0.98	1.93	1.55	1.35	1.82	1.61	0.75	0.55	0.51	1.93
Days With ≥ 0.1" Precipitation	1	1	2	3	5	6	4	3	3	2	2	1	33
Days With ≥ 0.5" Precipitation	0	0	0	0	1	1	0	0	1	0	0	0	3
Days With ≥ 1.0" Precipitation	0	0	0	0	0	0	0	0	0	0	0	0	0
Mean Snowfall (in.)	***6.6***	***5.4***	***6.6***	***3.7***	***0.9***	***trace***	***trace***	***0.3***	***1.3***	***2.6***	***4.4***	***6.8***	***38.6***
Maximum Snowfall (in.)*	36	20	22	21	13	3	trace	6	14	11	33	23	92
Maximum 24-hr. Snowfall (in.)*	9	8	9	13	13	3	trace	3	13	7	19	10	19
Maximum Snow Depth (in.)	***13***	***16***	***13***	***8***	***6***	***trace***	***trace***	***3***	***4***	***7***	***7***	***14***	***16***
Days With ≥ 1.0" Snow Depth	***15***	***10***	***6***	***1***	***0***	***0***	***0***	***0***	***0***	***1***	***5***	***14***	***52***
Thunderstorm Days*	< 1	< 1	< 1	1	4	7	8	8	2	< 1	< 1	< 1	30
Foggy Days*	3	2	2	2	1	1	< 1	1	1	2	3	5	23
Predominant Sky Cover*	OVR	OVR	OVR	OVR	OVR	OVR	CLR	CLR	CLR	OVR	OVR	OVR	OVR
Mean Relative Humidity 5am (%)*	72	73	73	71	73	73	68	68	73	74	73	73	72
Mean Relative Humidity 5pm (%)*	63	56	48	40	39	39	30	30	36	44	58	66	46
Mean Dewpoint (°F)*	10	15	19	26	34	41	44	43	36	29	20	13	28
Prevailing Wind Direction*	W	W	W	W	W	W	W	W	W	W	W	W	W
Prevailing Wind Speed (mph)*	10	10	12	12	12	12	10	9	10	10	10	10	10
Maximum Wind Gust (mph)*	68	63	60	58	69	64	81	61	54	60	61	58	81

Note: (*) Period of record is 1948-1995

The period of record for National Weather Service station data is 1980 – 2009 except where noted. See User Guide for detailed explanation of data.

Kalispell Airport

The climate of the Flathead Valley is influenced by the topography. The high mountains to the east form an effective barrier to many severe winter cold waves that move into areas east of the Rockies from Alberta. The mountains to the east rise abruptly 4,500 feet above the valley floor. The mountain snows and spring rains assure an adequate supply of water for the area.

In addition to Flathead Lake, the valley contains many smaller lakes, three rivers, and numerous streams and sloughs. Until late in the winter when a large portion of the lakes and sloughs become frozen, this water surface tends to limit temperature extremes. This effect is most noticeable in the southern end of the valley, because of the influence of Flathead Lake. Due to its size, Flathead Lake seldom freezes over.

The weather at the airport is considerably different in some respects from the weather in Kalispell. Generally there is more cloudiness at the airport since it is closer to the mountains to the east and north. Moist air moving in from the west and southwest, lifting and cooling as it moves over the mountains, is the major cause. On average there is more precipitation on the east side of the valley than on the west side. Average snowfall during the winter at the airport is 68 inches and in Kalispell it is 49 inches.

The annual prevailing wind direction at Kalispell is from the west. At the airport it is from the south. Wind speeds average considerably stronger at the airport than in Kalispell.

In the winter, when a cold wave moving down the east side of the Continental Divide does come over the mountains, the airport is in direct line of the pass the cold air comes through. During these cold waves the wind is from the northeast and will usually have speeds reaching 30 to 40 mph. The strongest gusts reported during these storms exceed 80 mph. As the cold air moves down the valley it spreads out, decreasing the wind velocity, and mixes with the warmer air of the valley. Unless these cold strong winds persist for three or four days, the wind in the lower part of the valley will be from the northwest, because of the influence of Flathead Lake and the mountains to the west. This wind is always much stronger in the northeast end of the valley where the airport is located than any other place in the valley.

Kalispell Airport *Flathead County* Elevation: 2,971 ft. Latitude: 48° 19' N Longitude: 114° 15' W

	JAN	FEB	MAR	APR	MAY	JUN	JUL	AUG	SEP	OCT	NOV	DEC	YEAR
Mean Maximum Temp. (°F)	30.5	35.4	44.9	55.9	65.0	71.5	81.0	80.8	69.5	54.7	39.5	29.6	54.9
Mean Temp. (°F)	23.3	26.8	35.1	43.7	51.9	58.1	64.6	63.8	54.1	42.1	31.9	22.9	43.2
Mean Minimum Temp. (°F)	16.1	18.2	25.2	31.5	38.9	44.7	48.2	46.7	38.7	29.5	24.3	16.1	31.5
Extreme Maximum Temp. (°F)	51	64	73	82	94	94	102	99	97	86	69	53	102
Extreme Minimum Temp. (°F)	-29	-30	-8	13	21	26	30	30	18	-3	-16	-35	-35
Days Maximum Temp. ≥ 90°F	0	0	0	0	0	1	5	6	1	0	0	0	13
Days Maximum Temp. ≤ 32°F	16	8	2	0	0	0	0	0	0	1	6	18	51
Days Minimum Temp. ≤ 32°F	29	26	27	18	6	1	0	0	5	20	25	30	187
Days Minimum Temp. ≤ 0°F	4	2	0	0	0	0	0	0	0	0	1	3	10
Heating Degree Days (base 65°F)	1,287	1,073	921	631	402	215	75	91	324	702	986	1,299	8,006
Cooling Degree Days (base 65°F)	0	0	0	0	4	15	71	61	5	0	0	0	156
Mean Precipitation (in.)	1.35	1.01	1.09	1.23	2.02	2.52	1.44	0.99	1.35	1.02	1.36	1.60	16.98
Maximum Precipitation (in.)*	3.1	2.0	3.0	2.4	4.8	5.3	6.0	3.8	4.0	3.0	4.4	4.4	23.9
Minimum Precipitation (in.)*	0.2	0.4	0.1	0.3	0.4	0.4	trace	trace	trace	trace	0.3	0.3	11.1
Extreme Maximum Daily Precip. (in.)	1.04	0.77	0.81	1.15	1.34	2.71	2.09	1.27	1.14	0.94	1.06	0.76	2.71
Days With ≥ 0.1" Precipitation	5	4	4	4	6	7	4	3	4	4	5	6	56
Days With ≥ 0.5" Precipitation	0	0	0	0	1	1	1	0	1	0	0	0	4
Days With ≥ 1.0" Precipitation	0	0	0	0	0	0	0	0	0	0	0	0	0
Mean Snowfall (in.)	***14.0***	***9.1***	***6.4***	***2.1***	***0.2***	***0.3***	***trace***	***trace***	***trace***	***1.1***	***9.1***	***17.7***	***60.0***
Maximum Snowfall (in.)*	35	21	19	11	9	6	0	trace	3	11	39	52	115
Maximum 24-hr. Snowfall (in.)*	12	7	7	7	8	6	0	trace	3	5	9	12	12
Maximum Snow Depth (in.)	***52***	46	***50***	***3***	***trace***	***4***	***trace***	***trace***	***trace***	***5***	***35***	***61***	***61***
Days With ≥ 1.0" Snow Depth	***23***	18	***8***	***0***	***0***	***0***	***0***	***0***	***0***	***1***	***6***	***19***	***75***
Thunderstorm Days*	0	< 1	< 1	1	3	5	6	5	2	< 1	< 1	< 1	22
Foggy Days*	12	9	6	3	3	4	3	3	5	9	12	13	82
Predominant Sky Cover*	OVR	OVR	OVR	OVR	OVR	OVR	CLR	CLR	OVR	OVR	OVR	OVR	OVR
Mean Relative Humidity 5am (%)*	81	81	80	77	79	83	83	81	83	85	84	84	82
Mean Relative Humidity 5pm (%)*	75	67	54	43	42	46	37	36	42	54	73	79	54
Mean Dewpoint (°F)*	15	20	23	29	37	44	47	45	39	32	25	19	31
Prevailing Wind Direction*	S	S	S	S	S	S	S	S	S	S	S	S	S
Prevailing Wind Speed (mph)*	9	8	9	9	9	9	8	8	8	8	8	9	9
Maximum Wind Gust (mph)*	66	49	52	51	52	62	51	69	49	54	60	62	69

Note: (*) Period of record is 1948-1995

Miles City Municipal Airport

Miles City is located on the western edge of the northern great plains in a shallow part of the Yellowstone Valley. The Tongue River runs south from its confluence with the Yellowstone just west of the city. To the north the river bluffs are from 200 to 300 feet above the valley floor. There are no nearby mountain ranges to influence climatic conditions. Temperatures range from very cold in winter to quite warm in summer, which is characteristic of continental locations. The climate is classed as semi-arid with less than 10 inches of rainfall in about one year in seven.

The temperature has ranged from less than -65 degrees to more than 110 degrees. Cold waves with temperatures of zero or lower occur frequently during the winter. They are usually accompanied by northerly winds and snow, and last two to four days. Periods of several days with zero or lower can be expected during the winter months. Spring and fall are cool with temperatures of 90 degrees or above rarely occurring. High temperatures of 90 degrees or more do occur frequently in July and August, but humidities are low.

About 70 percent of the precipitation falls during the growing season, April through September, with greatest monthly amounts usually falling during May and June. Precipitation during the spring and summer often falls during periods of shower or thunderstorm activity, however, general rains also are frequent in late spring and early summer. Measurable snowfall can be expected as late as May and as early as September.

Sunny growing seasons, with May and June rainfall being the heaviest of the year, encourage rapid crop development. Crops grown in this area seldom have difficulty in reaching maturity, although hail sometimes causes local damage during the middle of the summer.

Based on the 1951-1980 period, the average first occurrence of 32 degrees Fahrenheit in the fall is September 29 and the average last occurrence in the spring is May 7.

Miles City Municipal Airport *Custer County* Elevation: 2,627 ft. Latitude: 46° 26' N Longitude: 105° 53' W

	JAN	FEB	MAR	APR	MAY	JUN	JUL	AUG	SEP	OCT	NOV	DEC	YEAR
Mean Maximum Temp. (°F)	30.4	36.2	46.7	59.5	69.4	79.2	88.9	87.5	74.7	59.5	43.0	31.8	58.9
Mean Temp. (°F)	20.1	25.5	35.2	47.0	56.9	66.5	74.8	73.2	61.0	47.2	32.4	21.5	46.8
Mean Minimum Temp. (°F)	9.8	14.6	23.6	34.5	44.5	53.7	60.7	58.9	47.2	34.8	21.6	11.1	34.6
Extreme Maximum Temp. (°F)	72	73	83	92	100	106	113	110	106	95	81	66	113
Extreme Minimum Temp. (°F)	-37	-36	-28	5	17	34	44	36	19	-8	-27	-38	-38
Days Maximum Temp. ≥ 90°F	0	0	0	0	1	5	16	14	4	0	0	0	40
Days Maximum Temp. ≤ 32°F	15	10	5	1	0	0	0	0	0	1	6	13	51
Days Minimum Temp. ≤ 32°F	30	27	25	12	3	0	0	0	1	11	25	30	164
Days Minimum Temp. ≤ 0°F	9	5	2	0	0	0	0	0	0	0	2	6	24
Heating Degree Days (base 65°F)	1,386	1,112	918	535	270	74	8	16	180	547	973	1,344	7,363
Cooling Degree Days (base 65°F)	0	0	0	2	26	125	320	277	67	3	0	0	820
Mean Precipitation (in.)	0.33	0.23	0.61	1.33	2.04	2.54	1.54	0.93	1.05	0.97	0.38	0.27	12.22
Maximum Precipitation (in.)*	1.8	1.3	1.8	4.2	6.8	5.2	4.5	4.0	4.0	6.3	2.2	1.8	20.3
Minimum Precipitation (in.)*	0	trace	0.1	trace	0.2	0.7	trace	trace	trace	trace	trace	trace	5.3
Extreme Maximum Daily Precip. (in.)	0.76	0.65	1.20	2.06	1.34	2.45	2.22	1.14	2.04	0.97	0.42	0.37	2.45
Days With ≥ 0.1" Precipitation	1	1	2	3	5	6	4	2	3	3	1	1	32
Days With ≥ 0.5" Precipitation	0	0	0	1	1	2	1	0	1	1	0	0	7
Days With ≥ 1.0" Precipitation	0	0	0	0	0	0	0	0	0	0	0	0	0
Mean Snowfall (in.)	na	*3.7*	na	na	na	na	na	na	na	na	na	na	na
Maximum Snowfall (in.)*	17	19	18	17	12	trace	0	0	7	13	19	18	66
Maximum 24-hr. Snowfall (in.)*	8	10	6	15	8	trace	0	0	7	10	8	7	15
Maximum Snow Depth (in.)	na	*14*	na	na	na	na	na	na	na	na	na	na	na
Days With ≥ 1.0" Snow Depth	na	*12*	na	na	na	na	na	na	na	na	na	na	na
Thunderstorm Days*	0	< 1	< 1	1	4	8	7	6	2	< 1	< 1	0	28
Foggy Days*	6	6	7	4	4	2	1	1	2	3	5	6	47
Predominant Sky Cover*	OVR	OVR	OVR	OVR	OVR	SCT	SCT	CLR	CLR	CLR	OVR	OVR	OVR
Mean Relative Humidity 5am (%)*	75	79	80	75	76	76	68	66	70	73	78	77	74
Mean Relative Humidity 5pm (%)*	70	67	57	43	42	40	31	30	38	46	63	70	50
Mean Dewpoint (°F)*	7	14	21	29	39	48	50	48	40	32	22	13	30
Prevailing Wind Direction*	SSE	SSE	NW	NW	SE	NW	SE	SE	NW	SSE	SSE	SSE	SSE
Prevailing Wind Speed (mph)*	8	8	14	16	12	13	10	10	14	8	8	8	10
Maximum Wind Gust (mph)*	na	na	na	na	na	na	na	na	na	na	na	na	na

Note: (*) Period of record is 1948-1989

The period of record for National Weather Service station data is 1980 – 2009 except where noted. See User Guide for detailed explanation of data.

Missoula Johnson-Bell Field

Missoula is situated in the heart of the Montana Rocky Mountains in the extreme north portion of the Bitterroot Valley, and about five miles east of the confluence of the Bitterroot and Clark Fork Rivers. The Clark Fork Valley begins at Missoula and extends about 20 miles west-northwestward. The Bitterroot Valley extends about 70 miles due southward from Missoula. The Continental Divide is 60 to 80 miles east of Missoula, and the Bitterroot Range is only about 20 miles away to the southwest. These two mountain ranges have a marked effect on the climate of Missoula.

The prevailing flow of air aloft over western Montana is from the west and southwest during spring and summer months, and from the west and northwest during the winter months. Since this air must pass over the Bitterroot Range, it loses much of its moisture on the western slopes of these mountains. As a result, Missoula receives only between 12 inches and 15 inches of precipitation annually. This small amount of precipitation makes for a semi-arid climate. There is sufficient irrigation water, however, from the nearby mountains. The heaviest precipitation, of about two inches, is received in each month of May and June.

Generally the spring months are cool and a little damp, with almost daily shower activity during May and June. There are about 137 growing days each year. The summer months are dry with moderate temperatures and cool nights. Seldom does the temperature reach 100 degrees. Oppressively warm nighttime temperatures are unknown.

In the winter, the Continental Divide shields the Missoula area from much of the severely cold air which moves down the continent from arctic regions. Because of this shielding effect, many of the cold waves which sweep down over eastern Montana miss the Missoula area entirely. Under certain conditions, however, the cold Arctic air does break over the Continental Divide, and moves with force into the Bitterroot and Clark Fork Valleys. When this happens, Missoula experiences severe blizzard conditions. The cold air is funnelled to the city through Hell Gate which is the mouth of the Clark Fork River canyon at Missoula. Locally these blizzards are referred to as Hell Gate Blizzards. After the valleys of western Montana are filled with the cold air, prolonged cold spells may occur. January is the coldest month, although periods of sub-zero weather occur occasionally in December and February. Rarely, there are brief periods of sub-zero weather in November and March. During the winter months the sunshine is limited to about 30 percent of the possible amount.

Missoula Johnson-Bell Field *Missoula County* Elevation: 3,191 ft. Latitude: 46° 55' N Longitude: 114° 06' W

	JAN	FEB	MAR	APR	MAY	JUN	JUL	AUG	SEP	OCT	NOV	DEC	YEAR
Mean Maximum Temp. (°F)	32.2	37.6	48.4	57.8	66.5	74.2	84.7	83.8	72.1	56.8	40.6	30.3	57.1
Mean Temp. (°F)	25.1	29.2	37.9	45.2	53.1	60.3	67.9	66.7	56.8	44.4	32.7	23.6	45.2
Mean Minimum Temp. (°F)	17.9	20.7	27.3	32.6	39.6	46.3	51.1	49.6	41.4	31.9	24.7	16.8	33.3
Extreme Maximum Temp. (°F)	56	66	78	87	95	98	107	100	98	85	73	57	107
Extreme Minimum Temp. (°F)	-24	-27	-9	17	21	30	35	30	20	1	-11	-30	-30
Days Maximum Temp. ≥ 90°F	0	0	0	0	0	2	10	9	1	0	0	0	22
Days Maximum Temp. ≤ 32°F	14	6	1	0	0	0	0	0	0	0	6	17	44
Days Minimum Temp. ≤ 32°F	29	26	25	15	5	0	0	0	3	16	25	30	174
Days Minimum Temp. ≤ 0°F	3	2	0	0	0	0	0	0	0	0	0	3	8
Heating Degree Days (base 65°F)	1,231	1,007	834	587	367	171	43	51	253	632	962	1,279	7,417
Cooling Degree Days (base 65°F)	0	0	0	0	5	35	141	111	13	0	0	0	305
Mean Precipitation (in.)	0.88	0.71	0.99	1.21	2.19	2.00	1.02	1.17	1.14	0.86	0.97	1.04	14.18
Maximum Precipitation (in.)*	2.9	2.2	2.1	3.0	7.4	4.2	2.5	3.3	3.6	3.5	2.5	3.1	19.3
Minimum Precipitation (in.)*	0.2	0.2	0.2	0.1	0.3	0.3	0.1	trace	0	trace	0.2	0.3	8.6
Extreme Maximum Daily Precip. (in.)	0.68	0.43	0.75	1.87	1.83	1.49	1.62	2.03	1.05	0.99	0.87	0.82	2.03
Days With ≥ 0.1" Precipitation	3	2	3	4	6	6	3	3	3	3	3	3	42
Days With ≥ 0.5" Precipitation	0	0	0	0	1	1	0	0	0	0	0	0	2
Days With ≥ 1.0" Precipitation	0	0	0	0	0	0	0	0	0	0	0	0	0
Mean Snowfall (in.)	9.7	6.1	5.8	1.3	0.2	trace	trace	trace	trace	0.6	5.3	10.6	39.6
Maximum Snowfall (in.)*	43	20	16	8	8	trace	0	0	trace	5	16	32	78
Maximum 24-hr. Snowfall (in.)*	11	14	7	7	7	trace	0	0	trace	5	5	10	14
Maximum Snow Depth (in.)	19	17	9	3	trace	trace	trace	trace	trace	3	10	27	27
Days With ≥ 1.0" Snow Depth	21	12	4	0	0	0	0	0	0	0	4	17	58
Thunderstorm Days*	< 1	< 1	< 1	1	3	5	6	6	2	< 1	< 1	0	23
Foggy Days*	12	9	4	2	2	2	1	1	3	6	11	14	67
Predominant Sky Cover*	OVR	OVR	OVR	OVR	OVR	OVR	CLR	CLR	CLR	OVR	OVR	OVR	OVR
Mean Relative Humidity 5am (%)*	85	85	83	79	82	83	77	74	81	85	86	86	82
Mean Relative Humidity 5pm (%)*	76	66	52	41	42	42	31	30	38	50	71	79	51
Mean Dewpoint (°F)*	17	21	25	29	37	44	45	44	39	33	25	19	32
Prevailing Wind Direction*	ESE	WNW	NW	NW	NW	NW	NW	NW	NW	NW	NW	ESE	NW
Prevailing Wind Speed (mph)*	9	7	8	9	9	9	9	9	8	8	7	8	8
Maximum Wind Gust (mph)*	58	46	67	63	56	67	76	67	54	61	55	76	76

Note: (*) Period of record is 1948-1995

Alder 17 S *Madison County* Elevation: 5,850 ft. Latitude: 45° 04' N Longitude: 112° 03' W

	JAN	FEB	MAR	APR	MAY	JUN	JUL	AUG	SEP	OCT	NOV	DEC	YEAR
Mean Maximum Temp. (°F)	33.5	36.5	44.5	53.3	61.7	69.8	79.5	78.7	67.9	56.0	41.1	32.8	54.6
Mean Temp. (°F)	23.9	26.1	33.6	40.9	48.7	56.0	63.5	62.4	53.1	43.0	30.8	23.2	42.1
Mean Minimum Temp. (°F)	14.3	15.7	22.6	28.4	35.7	42.2	47.4	46.0	38.3	29.9	20.4	13.6	29.5
Extreme Maximum Temp. (°F)	58	61	70	80	89	95	96	96	89	83	72	59	96
Extreme Minimum Temp. (°F)	-31	-30	-10	-2	12	25	24	27	8	-9	-18	-41	-41
Days Maximum Temp. ≥ 90°F	0	0	0	0	0	0	2	1	0	0	0	0	3
Days Maximum Temp. ≤ 32°F	13	8	3	0	0	0	0	0	0	1	7	14	46
Days Minimum Temp. ≤ 32°F	29	27	27	21	10	2	0	1	6	19	26	30	198
Days Minimum Temp. ≤ 0°F	4	3	1	0	0	0	0	0	0	0	2	4	14
Heating Degree Days (base 65°F)	1,266	1,092	966	718	498	273	93	110	355	674	1,020	1,288	8,353
Cooling Degree Days (base 65°F)	0	0	0	0	1	10	52	37	4	0	0	0	104
Mean Precipitation (in.)	0.38	0.38	0.75	1.23	2.48	2.60	1.46	1.45	1.23	1.14	0.61	0.40	14.11
Extreme Maximum Daily Precip. (in.)	0.49	0.55	0.90	1.17	2.09	1.53	1.60	0.96	1.22	1.18	0.80	0.44	2.09
Days With ≥ 0.1" Precipitation	1	1	2	4	7	7	4	5	3	4	2	1	41
Days With ≥ 0.5" Precipitation	0	0	0	0	1	2	1	1	1	1	0	0	7
Days With ≥ 1.0" Precipitation	0	0	0	0	0	0	0	0	0	0	0	0	0
Mean Snowfall (in.)	7.6	6.7	9.8	8.7	3.3	0.5	0.0	trace	0.7	3.6	7.4	8.0	56.3
Maximum Snow Depth (in.)	13	***9***	11	9	10	8	0	0	2	7	12	11	***13***
Days With ≥ 1.0" Snow Depth	7	***5***	4	2	0	0	0	0	0	1	5	6	***30***

Anaconda *Deer Lodge County* Elevation: 5,279 ft. Latitude: 46° 08' N Longitude: 112° 57' W

	JAN	FEB	MAR	APR	MAY	JUN	JUL	AUG	SEP	OCT	NOV	DEC	YEAR
Mean Maximum Temp. (°F)	36.3	39.7	47.3	55.5	64.8	73.0	82.2	81.2	70.6	57.6	42.6	33.6	57.0
Mean Temp. (°F)	25.7	28.1	34.8	41.9	50.4	57.8	65.0	63.7	54.6	43.9	31.6	23.2	43.4
Mean Minimum Temp. (°F)	15.0	16.3	22.3	28.2	35.9	42.6	47.8	46.2	38.5	30.2	20.6	12.8	29.7
Extreme Maximum Temp. (°F)	60	65	71	83	89	95	100	98	95	88	71	60	100
Extreme Minimum Temp. (°F)	-28	-35	-12	3	17	27	30	25	12	-9	-22	-38	-38
Days Maximum Temp. ≥ 90°F	0	0	0	0	0	1	5	3	0	0	0	0	9
Days Maximum Temp. ≤ 32°F	10	5	2	0	0	0	0	0	0	1	5	13	36
Days Minimum Temp. ≤ 32°F	30	27	28	22	10	2	0	0	6	19	27	30	201
Days Minimum Temp. ≤ 0°F	4	3	1	0	0	0	0	0	0	0	2	5	15
Heating Degree Days (base 65°F)	1,212	1,037	929	687	450	227	74	88	314	646	994	1,288	7,946
Cooling Degree Days (base 65°F)	0	0	0	0	3	18	80	55	7	0	0	0	163
Mean Precipitation (in.)	0.57	0.58	1.06	1.41	2.01	2.11	1.45	1.48	1.23	0.90	0.94	0.72	14.46
Extreme Maximum Daily Precip. (in.)	0.93	0.74	1.14	1.14	1.38	1.56	1.83	1.09	1.55	0.84	0.82	0.97	1.83
Days With ≥ 0.1" Precipitation	2	2	4	5	6	7	4	4	3	3	3	2	45
Days With ≥ 0.5" Precipitation	0	0	0	0	1	1	1	1	1	0	0	0	5
Days With ≥ 1.0" Precipitation	0	0	0	0	0	0	0	0	0	0	0	0	0
Mean Snowfall (in.)	10.2	10.1	13.5	8.8	2.1	0.4	0.0	0.1	1.2	4.2	11.7	12.4	74.7
Maximum Snow Depth (in.)	15	15	15	10	3	trace	0	3	5	8	15	20	20
Days With ≥ 1.0" Snow Depth	23	16	12	3	0	0	0	0	0	2	13	23	92

Biddle 8 SW *Powder River County* Elevation: 3,597 ft. Latitude: 45° 02' N Longitude: 105° 29' W

	JAN	FEB	MAR	APR	MAY	JUN	JUL	AUG	SEP	OCT	NOV	DEC	YEAR
Mean Maximum Temp. (°F)	36.3	39.9	48.6	59.3	68.7	78.5	88.5	87.3	75.4	60.8	46.5	35.9	60.5
Mean Temp. (°F)	24.3	27.8	35.8	45.4	54.8	64.2	72.5	71.1	59.9	46.9	34.1	24.0	46.7
Mean Minimum Temp. (°F)	12.3	15.7	22.8	31.4	40.9	49.8	56.6	54.8	44.3	33.0	21.7	12.1	32.9
Extreme Maximum Temp. (°F)	69	72	80	90	96	108	109	107	103	90	79	66	109
Extreme Minimum Temp. (°F)	-30	-37	-27	-3	18	31	37	31	13	-17	-24	-43	-43
Days Maximum Temp. ≥ 90°F	0	0	0	0	1	4	15	14	4	0	0	0	38
Days Maximum Temp. ≤ 32°F	10	7	4	1	0	0	0	0	0	1	4	10	37
Days Minimum Temp. ≤ 32°F	30	27	27	16	5	0	0	0	2	14	26	29	176
Days Minimum Temp. ≤ 0°F	7	4	2	0	0	0	0	0	0	0	1	6	20
Heating Degree Days (base 65°F)	1,255	1,045	899	582	321	100	14	20	197	555	919	1,267	7,174
Cooling Degree Days (base 65°F)	0	0	0	1	13	82	254	215	49	1	0	0	615
Mean Precipitation (in.)	0.38	0.41	0.91	1.66	2.44	2.41	1.88	1.09	1.35	1.28	0.50	0.43	14.74
Extreme Maximum Daily Precip. (in.)	0.36	0.63	1.00	1.69	2.72	2.25	2.63	1.00	3.12	1.76	0.69	0.50	3.12
Days With ≥ 0.1" Precipitation	1	2	3	5	6	6	4	3	3	3	2	1	39
Days With ≥ 0.5" Precipitation	0	0	0	1	2	2	1	1	1	1	0	0	9
Days With ≥ 1.0" Precipitation	0	0	0	0	0	0	0	0	0	0	0	0	0
Mean Snowfall (in.)	4.9	4.9	7.6	5.6	1.4	0.0	0.0	0.0	0.5	3.2	3.6	5.8	37.5
Maximum Snow Depth (in.)	14	14	12	36	8	0	0	0	6	7	9	16	36
Days With ≥ 1.0" Snow Depth	20	11	7	2	0	0	0	0	0	1	8	14	63

Big Sandy *Chouteau County* Elevation: 2,770 ft. Latitude: 48° 08' N Longitude: 110° 04' W

	JAN	FEB	MAR	APR	MAY	JUN	JUL	AUG	SEP	OCT	NOV	DEC	YEAR
Mean Maximum Temp. (°F)	32.9	37.3	48.0	61.1	70.6	78.3	87.1	85.8	74.2	60.7	44.8	***32.1***	***59.4***
Mean Temp. (°F)	20.8	24.9	34.8	46.3	55.6	63.3	70.4	68.5	58.0	46.2	32.7	***20.4***	***45.2***
Mean Minimum Temp. (°F)	8.6	12.4	21.6	31.5	40.4	48.1	53.6	51.1	41.8	31.6	20.4	***8.7***	***30.8***
Extreme Maximum Temp. (°F)	64	76	81	91	96	103	108	106	99	90	78	64	108
Extreme Minimum Temp. (°F)	-41	-45	-30	2	17	28	37	25	17	-5	-33	-50	-50
Days Maximum Temp. ≥ 90°F	0	0	0	0	1	4	12	12	3	0	0	0	32
Days Maximum Temp. ≤ 32°F	12	9	4	0	0	0	0	0	0	1	5	11	42
Days Minimum Temp. ≤ 32°F	29	27	27	16	6	0	0	0	3	15	24	27	174
Days Minimum Temp. ≤ 0°F	10	6	2	0	0	0	0	0	0	0	2	8	28
Heating Degree Days (base 65°F)	1,366	1,129	929	555	305	114	26	42	232	575	963	***1,377***	***7,613***
Cooling Degree Days (base 65°F)	0	0	0	1	18	68	200	157	31	1	0	***0***	***476***
Mean Precipitation (in.)	0.44	0.33	0.59	1.00	2.18	2.63	1.58	1.12	1.35	0.85	0.45	0.46	12.98
Extreme Maximum Daily Precip. (in.)	0.68	0.52	0.81	3.32	2.09	2.13	***2.83***	***0.92***	1.30	***1.15***	0.72	***0.80***	***3.32***
Days With ≥ 0.1" Precipitation	2	1	2	3	5	6	4	3	3	2	2	1	34
Days With ≥ 0.5" Precipitation	0	0	0	0	1	1	1	1	1	0	0	0	5
Days With ≥ 1.0" Precipitation	0	0	0	0	0	1	0	0	0	0	0	0	1
Mean Snowfall (in.)	***2.4***	na	na	***trace***	0.2	0.0	0.0	0.0	trace	***0.6***	na	na	na
Maximum Snow Depth (in.)	na	na	na	na	***trace***	***0***	***0***	***0***	***trace***	na	na	na	na
Days With ≥ 1.0" Snow Depth	na	na	na	***0***	0	0	0	0	0	***0***	na	na	na

The period of record for all cooperative weather station data is 1980 – 2009. See User Guide for detailed explanation of data.

Big Timber *Sweet Grass County* Elevation: 4,100 ft. Latitude: 45° 50' N Longitude: 109° 57' W

	JAN	FEB	MAR	APR	MAY	JUN	JUL	AUG	SEP	OCT	NOV	DEC	YEAR
Mean Maximum Temp. (°F)	38.8	42.0	49.5	58.7	68.3	77.0	86.9	85.6	74.2	60.3	46.4	37.5	60.4
Mean Temp. (°F)	28.7	30.8	37.3	45.4	54.2	62.4	70.0	68.4	58.3	47.0	36.2	28.0	47.2
Mean Minimum Temp. (°F)	18.5	19.5	25.0	32.1	40.0	47.6	53.1	51.1	42.3	33.6	25.9	18.4	33.9
Extreme Maximum Temp. (°F)	64	69	77	87	92	104	105	102	98	88	75	65	105
Extreme Minimum Temp. (°F)	-32	-32	-26	-2	20	32	39	29	16	-9	-20	-38	-38
Days Maximum Temp. ≥ 90°F	0	0	0	0	0	3	13	11	2	0	0	0	29
Days Maximum Temp. ≤ 32°F	8	6	3	1	0	0	0	0	0	1	4	8	31
Days Minimum Temp. ≤ 32°F	25	23	24	16	5	0	0	0	3	13	21	26	156
Days Minimum Temp. ≤ 0°F	5	3	1	0	0	0	0	0	0	0	1	4	14
Heating Degree Days (base 65°F)	1,120	961	852	581	335	125	19	30	219	553	858	1,142	6,795
Cooling Degree Days (base 65°F)	0	0	0	0	7	51	182	141	25	1	0	0	407
Mean Precipitation (in.)	0.59	0.53	0.97	1.95	2.74	2.76	1.50	1.02	1.18	1.36	0.62	0.66	15.88
Extreme Maximum Daily Precip. (in.)	0.71	***0.76***	0.95	***1.98***	***2.01***	***3.12***	1.84	***1.32***	1.18	1.70	1.11	1.02	***3.12***
Days With ≥ 0.1" Precipitation	2	2	3	5	6	6	4	3	3	3	2	2	41
Days With ≥ 0.5" Precipitation	0	0	0	1	2	1	1	0	1	1	0	0	7
Days With ≥ 1.0" Precipitation	0	0	0	0	1	1	0	0	0	0	0	0	2
Mean Snowfall (in.)	***4.5***	***5.4***	***4.8***	***2.9***	0.6	0.0	0.0	0.1	0.5	2.6	3.5	***7.5***	***32.4***
Maximum Snow Depth (in.)	13	***15***	***16***	***12***	11	0	0	0	5	11	12	***24***	***24***
Days With ≥ 1.0" Snow Depth	6	***4***	***4***	1	0	0	0	0	0	1	3	***6***	***25***

Bigfork 13 S *Lake County* Elevation: 2,910 ft. Latitude: 47° 53' N Longitude: 114° 02' W

	JAN	FEB	MAR	APR	MAY	JUN	JUL	AUG	SEP	OCT	NOV	DEC	YEAR
Mean Maximum Temp. (°F)	34.3	37.2	45.0	54.7	63.6	70.2	79.4	78.8	68.3	55.4	42.4	34.0	55.3
Mean Temp. (°F)	29.3	31.0	37.3	44.9	53.0	59.6	67.1	66.5	57.3	46.8	36.7	29.3	46.6
Mean Minimum Temp. (°F)	24.2	24.7	29.5	35.3	42.4	48.9	54.8	54.1	46.1	38.1	31.0	24.6	37.8
Extreme Maximum Temp. (°F)	64	62	68	78	86	91	98	95	92	79	68	58	98
Extreme Minimum Temp. (°F)	-17	-21	-8	18	28	31	32	37	26	7	-2	-14	-21
Days Maximum Temp. ≥ 90°F	0	0	0	0	0	0	3	1	0	0	0	0	4
Days Maximum Temp. ≤ 32°F	12	6	2	0	0	0	0	0	0	0	3	12	35
Days Minimum Temp. ≤ 32°F	25	23	21	10	1	0	0	0	0	6	17	26	129
Days Minimum Temp. ≤ 0°F	1	1	0	0	0	0	0	0	0	0	0	1	3
Heating Degree Days (base 65°F)	1,100	954	851	596	367	177	44	44	235	559	842	1,099	6,868
Cooling Degree Days (base 65°F)	0	0	0	0	4	21	122	98	11	0	0	0	256
Mean Precipitation (in.)	1.45	1.06	1.44	1.79	3.07	3.14	1.63	1.41	1.92	1.57	1.65	1.59	21.72
Extreme Maximum Daily Precip. (in.)	1.24	0.88	1.30	1.30	2.07	1.94	3.55	1.05	2.05	1.68	***1.05***	***0.87***	***3.55***
Days With ≥ 0.1" Precipitation	4	4	5	5	7	7	4	3	4	4	5	5	57
Days With ≥ 0.5" Precipitation	1	0	1	1	2	2	1	1	1	1	1	0	12
Days With ≥ 1.0" Precipitation	0	0	0	0	0	0	0	0	0	0	0	0	0
Mean Snowfall (in.)	9.9	5.9	***3.2***	0.1	trace	0.0	0.0	0.0	0.0	0.1	4.5	na	na
Maximum Snow Depth (in.)	26	***18***	***11***	4	trace	0	0	0	0	2	***18***	***28***	***28***
Days With ≥ 1.0" Snow Depth	11	***7***	***3***	0	0	0	0	0	0	0	3	11	***35***

Billings Water Plant *Yellowstone County* Elevation: 3,097 ft. Latitude: 45° 46' N Longitude: 108° 29' W

	JAN	FEB	MAR	APR	MAY	JUN	JUL	AUG	SEP	OCT	NOV	DEC	YEAR
Mean Maximum Temp. (°F)	40.8	45.1	53.6	63.1	72.2	80.6	89.4	88.4	77.7	64.4	49.7	39.5	63.7
Mean Temp. (°F)	28.6	32.1	39.6	48.6	57.6	65.8	73.1	71.5	61.4	49.6	37.2	27.6	49.4
Mean Minimum Temp. (°F)	16.0	19.0	25.6	34.0	43.0	51.0	56.8	54.5	45.1	34.8	24.7	15.7	35.0
Extreme Maximum Temp. (°F)	70	73	82	90	95	103	108	104	100	92	80	69	108
Extreme Minimum Temp. (°F)	-33	-35	-25	-2	22	33	42	33	22	-10	-19	-41	-41
Days Maximum Temp. ≥ 90°F	0	0	0	0	1	6	16	15	4	0	0	0	42
Days Maximum Temp. ≤ 32°F	7	5	2	0	0	0	0	0	0	1	3	7	25
Days Minimum Temp. ≤ 32°F	28	26	24	13	2	0	0	0	1	11	24	29	158
Days Minimum Temp. ≤ 0°F	4	3	1	0	0	0	0	0	0	0	1	4	13
Heating Degree Days (base 65°F)	1,122	923	778	487	242	71	7	14	153	472	827	1,152	6,248
Cooling Degree Days (base 65°F)	0	0	0	1	21	102	267	221	52	2	0	0	666
Mean Precipitation (in.)	0.42	0.48	0.94	1.60	2.28	2.17	1.32	0.78	1.40	1.38	0.54	0.49	13.80
Extreme Maximum Daily Precip. (in.)	0.47	0.74	1.34	1.81	1.75	3.00	2.30	1.43	1.26	1.28	0.79	0.58	3.00
Days With ≥ 0.1" Precipitation	2	2	3	4	5	5	3	2	3	4	2	2	37
Days With ≥ 0.5" Precipitation	0	0	0	1	1	1	1	0	1	1	0	0	6
Days With ≥ 1.0" Precipitation	0	0	0	0	0	0	0	0	0	0	0	0	0
Mean Snowfall (in.)	na	na	na	***2.3***	0.1	0.0	0.0	0.0	0.3	0.7	na	na	na
Maximum Snow Depth (in.)	na	na	na	na	na	na	na	na	na	na	na	na	na
Days With ≥ 1.0" Snow Depth	na	na	na	1	0	0	0	0	0	1	na	na	na

Blackleaf *Teton County* Elevation: 4,234 ft. Latitude: 48° 01' N Longitude: 112° 26' W

	JAN	FEB	MAR	APR	MAY	JUN	JUL	AUG	SEP	OCT	NOV	DEC	YEAR
Mean Maximum Temp. (°F)	***36.4***	38.7	***44.4***	***54.4***	***62.8***	***70.0***	***79.5***	***79.4***	***68.3***	***57.2***	***42.4***	35.9	***55.8***
Mean Temp. (°F)	***23.3***	25.7	***31.9***	***41.2***	***49.3***	***56.6***	***63.8***	***62.7***	***53.1***	***42.7***	***30.1***	23.4	***42.0***
Mean Minimum Temp. (°F)	***10.1***	12.7	19.1	***28.0***	***35.7***	***43.0***	***48.0***	45.8	37.6	***28.2***	***17.8***	10.7	***28.1***
Extreme Maximum Temp. (°F)	***65***	70	***77***	***82***	***88***	94	***102***	101	93	***87***	***76***	68	***102***
Extreme Minimum Temp. (°F)	***-38***	-47	***-32***	***-11***	***15***	26	***28***	25	11	***-20***	***-29***	-41	***-47***
Days Maximum Temp. ≥ 90°F	***0***	0	***0***	***0***	0	0	4	3	0	***0***	0	0	***7***
Days Maximum Temp. ≤ 32°F	***10***	8	***5***	***1***	0	0	0	0	0	***2***	***5***	9	***40***
Days Minimum Temp. ≤ 32°F	***27***	26	28	***20***	10	1	0	1	7	***20***	***25***	28	***193***
Days Minimum Temp. ≤ 0°F	***9***	6	3	***0***	0	0	0	0	0	***1***	4	7	***30***
Heating Degree Days (base 65°F)	***1,291***	1,105	***1,020***	***707***	***483***	***259***	***94***	***117***	***358***	***684***	***1,041***	1,292	***8,451***
Cooling Degree Days (base 65°F)	***0***	0	***0***	***0***	***2***	***11***	***64***	***51***	***7***	***0***	***0***	0	***135***
Mean Precipitation (in.)	***0.34***	0.40	0.68	***0.95***	***2.24***	3.10	***1.42***	1.54	1.28	***0.62***	***0.47***	***0.36***	***13.40***
Extreme Maximum Daily Precip. (in.)	***0.50***	0.75	***0.78***	***1.50***	***1.95***	***2.41***	***1.62***	***2.24***	***1.17***	***1.05***	***0.72***	***0.50***	***2.41***
Days With ≥ 0.1" Precipitation	***2***	2	***2***	***3***	5	5	3	3	3	***3***	2	2	***35***
Days With ≥ 0.5" Precipitation	***0***	0	***0***	***0***	1	2	1	1	1	***0***	0	0	***6***
Days With ≥ 1.0" Precipitation	***0***	0	***0***	***0***	1	1	0	0	0	***0***	0	0	***2***
Mean Snowfall (in.)	na	na	na	na	1.5	0.0	0.0	0.2	1.1	***1.5***	***4.6***	na	na
Maximum Snow Depth (in.)	na	na	na	na	na	na	na	na	na	na	na	na	na
Days With ≥ 1.0" Snow Depth	na	na	na	na	0	0	0	0	0	na	na	na	na

The period of record for all cooperative weather station data is 1980 – 2009. See User Guide for detailed explanation of data.

Boulder *Jefferson County* Elevation: 4,903 ft. Latitude: 46° 14' N Longitude: 112° 07' W

	JAN	FEB	MAR	APR	MAY	JUN	JUL	AUG	SEP	OCT	NOV	DEC	YEAR
Mean Maximum Temp. (°F)	35.4	39.1	46.8	55.9	64.6	73.0	82.7	82.2	71.5	58.3	42.7	33.9	57.2
Mean Temp. (°F)	23.6	26.9	33.9	41.8	50.1	57.9	65.5	64.1	54.4	43.1	30.9	22.4	42.9
Mean Minimum Temp. (°F)	11.7	14.6	21.0	27.6	35.5	42.7	48.2	46.0	37.3	27.8	19.0	10.8	28.5
Extreme Maximum Temp. (°F)	58	65	72	83	89	96	101	97	93	87	71	62	101
Extreme Minimum Temp. (°F)	-35	-39	-22	-6	17	26	31	19	11	-14	-26	-42	-42
Days Maximum Temp. ≥ 90°F	0	0	0	0	0	1	6	4	1	0	0	0	12
Days Maximum Temp. ≤ 32°F	10	6	3	0	0	0	0	0	0	1	5	12	37
Days Minimum Temp. ≤ 32°F	30	27	29	22	10	2	0	1	7	21	27	30	206
Days Minimum Temp. ≤ 0°F	7	4	1	0	0	0	0	0	0	0	3	6	21
Heating Degree Days (base 65°F)	1,276	1,071	955	690	458	225	65	79	319	672	1,018	1,315	8,143
Cooling Degree Days (base 65°F)	0	0	0	0	1	18	86	59	8	0	0	0	172
Mean Precipitation (in.)	0.28	0.27	0.47	0.79	2.07	2.13	1.54	1.24	1.00	0.67	0.49	0.29	11.24
Extreme Maximum Daily Precip. (in.)	0.39	0.60	0.46	0.94	1.70	1.53	1.85	1.46	1.18	0.67	0.59	0.49	1.85
Days With ≥ 0.1" Precipitation	1	1	2	3	6	6	5	4	3	2	2	1	36
Days With ≥ 0.5" Precipitation	0	0	0	0	1	1	1	0	1	0	0	0	4
Days With ≥ 1.0" Precipitation	0	0	0	0	0	0	0	0	0	0	0	0	0
Mean Snowfall (in.)	na	na	na	na	0.3	0.0	0.0	0.0	trace	*0.7*	na	na	na
Maximum Snow Depth (in.)	na	na	na	na	na	na	na	na	na	na	na	na	na
Days With ≥ 1.0" Snow Depth	na	na	na	na	0	0	0	0	0	*1*	na	na	na

Bozeman Gallatin Fld *Gallatin County* Elevation: 4,426 ft. Latitude: 45° 47' N Longitude: 111° 10' W

	JAN	FEB	MAR	APR	MAY	JUN	JUL	AUG	SEP	OCT	NOV	DEC	YEAR
Mean Maximum Temp. (°F)	32.3	36.4	46.5	56.4	65.6	74.4	85.1	83.9	71.7	58.1	41.7	31.1	56.9
Mean Temp. (°F)	20.9	24.6	34.1	42.9	51.6	59.3	67.2	65.7	55.2	43.6	29.7	19.6	42.9
Mean Minimum Temp. (°F)	9.5	12.9	21.7	29.3	37.5	44.2	49.3	47.6	38.7	29.0	17.8	8.0	28.8
Extreme Maximum Temp. (°F)	59	66	76	85	91	100	106	102	99	87	76	63	106
Extreme Minimum Temp. (°F)	-37	-43	-31	0	14	29	34	27	15	-10	-27	-46	-46
Days Maximum Temp. ≥ 90°F	0	0	0	0	0	2	11	8	1	0	0	0	22
Days Maximum Temp. ≤ 32°F	14	9	3	0	0	0	0	0	0	1	7	16	50
Days Minimum Temp. ≤ 32°F	30	27	28	20	7	1	0	0	5	21	27	30	196
Days Minimum Temp. ≤ 0°F	8	5	1	0	0	0	0	0	0	0	3	8	25
Heating Degree Days (base 65°F)	1,357	1,135	951	657	412	188	46	59	298	657	1,051	1,403	8,214
Cooling Degree Days (base 65°F)	0	0	0	0	2	23	122	88	11	0	0	0	246
Mean Precipitation (in.)	0.48	0.49	0.97	1.61	2.52	2.39	1.12	1.05	1.13	1.09	0.72	0.46	14.03
Extreme Maximum Daily Precip. (in.)	0.71	0.62	0.85	0.87	1.91	1.38	1.36	0.90	0.99	1.29	0.70	0.37	1.91
Days With ≥ 0.1" Precipitation	2	2	3	5	7	7	3	4	4	3	2	2	44
Days With ≥ 0.5" Precipitation	0	0	0	1	1	1	0	0	0	0	0	0	3
Days With ≥ 1.0" Precipitation	0	0	0	0	0	0	0	0	0	0	0	0	0
Mean Snowfall (in.)	na	na	na	na	na	na	na	na	na	na	na	na	na
Maximum Snow Depth (in.)	na	na	na	na	na	na	na	na	na	na	na	na	na
Days With ≥ 1.0" Snow Depth	na	na	na	na	na	na	na	na	na	na	na	na	na

Bozeman Montana St Univ *Gallatin County* Elevation: 4,913 ft. Latitude: 45° 40' N Longitude: 111° 03' W

	JAN	FEB	MAR	APR	MAY	JUN	JUL	AUG	SEP	OCT	NOV	DEC	YEAR
Mean Maximum Temp. (°F)	35.4	38.8	47.1	56.6	65.3	73.7	83.1	82.6	71.9	59.0	43.2	34.1	57.6
Mean Temp. (°F)	25.2	28.1	35.7	44.0	52.4	59.8	67.6	66.4	57.0	45.9	33.0	24.1	44.9
Mean Minimum Temp. (°F)	14.9	17.4	24.2	31.3	39.4	46.0	52.0	50.2	42.1	32.7	22.8	14.0	32.2
Extreme Maximum Temp. (°F)	61	64	75	81	88	96	100	99	92	88	73	63	100
Extreme Minimum Temp. (°F)	-26	-31	-14	1	17	27	34	30	16	-5	-18	-32	-32
Days Maximum Temp. ≥ 90°F	0	0	0	0	0	1	6	5	1	0	0	0	13
Days Maximum Temp. ≤ 32°F	10	6	2	0	0	0	0	0	0	1	6	12	37
Days Minimum Temp. ≤ 32°F	29	26	26	18	6	1	0	0	3	15	24	29	177
Days Minimum Temp. ≤ 0°F	5	3	1	0	0	0	0	0	0	0	1	4	14
Heating Degree Days (base 65°F)	1,227	1,037	903	624	389	181	41	49	253	587	953	1,262	7,506
Cooling Degree Days (base 65°F)	0	0	0	0	5	32	127	101	19	1	0	0	285
Mean Precipitation (in.)	0.83	0.80	1.38	2.25	3.25	3.04	1.48	1.40	1.45	1.70	1.13	0.90	19.61
Extreme Maximum Daily Precip. (in.)	0.60	0.75	1.20	1.63	2.68	2.29	2.05	1.06	1.53	1.30	1.62	1.25	2.68
Days With ≥ 0.1" Precipitation	3	3	5	6	8	8	4	4	4	4	3	3	55
Days With ≥ 0.5" Precipitation	0	0	0	1	2	2	1	1	1	1	0	0	9
Days With ≥ 1.0" Precipitation	0	0	0	0	0	0	0	0	0	0	0	0	0
Mean Snowfall (in.)	13.3	11.7	15.8	13.6	4.4	0.7	0.0	0.1	0.9	6.0	12.1	14.2	92.8
Maximum Snow Depth (in.)	23	23	20	15	10	7	0	trace	2	7	24	28	28
Days With ≥ 1.0" Snow Depth	29	23	16	4	1	0	0	0	0	3	14	26	116

Brandenberg *Rosebud County* Elevation: 2,771 ft. Latitude: 45° 49' N Longitude: 106° 13' W

	JAN	FEB	MAR	APR	MAY	JUN	JUL	AUG	SEP	OCT	NOV	DEC	YEAR
Mean Maximum Temp. (°F)	35.5	40.4	49.9	61.7	71.2	80.5	90.5	89.3	76.8	61.4	46.3	35.0	61.5
Mean Temp. (°F)	23.3	27.7	36.5	46.8	56.2	65.1	72.8	71.1	59.8	46.9	34.0	23.1	46.9
Mean Minimum Temp. (°F)	11.0	14.9	23.1	31.8	41.2	49.7	55.1	52.9	42.8	32.4	21.6	11.1	32.3
Extreme Maximum Temp. (°F)	67	72	86	91	101	111	112	109	103	93	81	69	112
Extreme Minimum Temp. (°F)	-36	-39	-28	-2	17	28	37	30	19	-12	-24	-44	-44
Days Maximum Temp. ≥ 90°F	0	0	0	0	1	6	18	17	4	0	0	0	46
Days Maximum Temp. ≤ 32°F	10	7	3	0	0	0	0	0	0	1	4	11	36
Days Minimum Temp. ≤ 32°F	30	27	26	15	5	0	0	0	3	15	26	30	177
Days Minimum Temp. ≤ 0°F	7	5	1	0	0	0	0	0	0	0	2	6	21
Heating Degree Days (base 65°F)	1,288	1,049	876	541	284	85	10	20	193	556	925	1,293	7,120
Cooling Degree Days (base 65°F)	0	0	0	1	18	95	258	217	43	1	0	0	633
Mean Precipitation (in.)	0.51	0.46	0.97	1.49	2.49	2.47	1.30	0.83	1.20	1.33	0.56	0.51	14.12
Extreme Maximum Daily Precip. (in.)	0.61	0.72	1.35	1.75	1.59	1.94	2.45	1.04	1.32	0.99	0.70	1.23	2.45
Days With ≥ 0.1" Precipitation	2	1	3	4	6	6	3	2	3	4	2	2	38
Days With ≥ 0.5" Precipitation	0	0	0	1	2	1	1	0	1	1	0	0	7
Days With ≥ 1.0" Precipitation	0	0	0	0	0	0	0	0	0	0	0	0	0
Mean Snowfall (in.)	7.5	6.4	7.4	4.5	1.0	0.0	0.0	0.0	0.5	2.3	4.7	7.9	42.2
Maximum Snow Depth (in.)	13	15	12	14	7	0	0	0	3	5	10	22	22
Days With ≥ 1.0" Snow Depth	20	14	7	1	0	0	0	0	0	1	7	17	67

The period of record for all cooperative weather station data is 1980 – 2009. See User Guide for detailed explanation of data.

Bredette *Roosevelt County* Elevation: 2,687 ft. Latitude: 48° 33' N Longitude: 105° 16' W

	JAN	FEB	MAR	APR	MAY	JUN	JUL	AUG	SEP	OCT	NOV	DEC	YEAR
Mean Maximum Temp. (°F)	22.4	27.7	39.6	56.6	67.9	76.3	83.7	83.1	70.9	55.3	37.5	24.5	53.8
Mean Temp. (°F)	13.3	18.4	29.5	43.9	54.7	63.2	69.5	68.6	57.5	43.8	28.4	15.6	42.2
Mean Minimum Temp. (°F)	4.2	9.0	19.4	31.1	41.4	50.1	55.3	54.1	44.1	32.2	19.2	6.7	30.6
Extreme Maximum Temp. (°F)	57	65	76	91	100	107	108	108	103	95	76	56	108
Extreme Minimum Temp. (°F)	-36	-36	-30	-1	15	31	40	33	18	-6	-24	-37	-37
Days Maximum Temp. ≥ 90°F	0	0	0	0	1	3	8	8	2	0	0	0	22
Days Maximum Temp. ≤ 32°F	21	16	9	1	0	0	0	0	0	1	10	20	78
Days Minimum Temp. ≤ 32°F	31	27	28	17	5	0	0	0	3	15	26	31	183
Days Minimum Temp. ≤ 0°F	12	8	3	0	0	0	0	0	0	0	3	10	36
Heating Degree Days (base 65°F)	1,599	1,312	1,093	629	330	117	26	46	254	653	1,093	1,526	8,678
Cooling Degree Days (base 65°F)	0	0	0	1	17	70	174	166	36	1	0	0	465
Mean Precipitation (in.)	0.36	0.19	0.47	0.83	1.85	2.77	2.46	1.38	0.98	0.84	0.42	0.33	12.88
Extreme Maximum Daily Precip. (in.)	0.33	0.20	0.46	1.01	1.88	2.84	2.79	1.09	1.14	1.14	0.92	0.25	2.84
Days With ≥ 0.1" Precipitation	1	1	1	3	5	6	5	4	3	2	1	1	33
Days With ≥ 0.5" Precipitation	0	0	0	0	1	2	1	1	0	0	0	0	5
Days With ≥ 1.0" Precipitation	0	0	0	0	0	0	0	0	0	0	0	0	0
Mean Snowfall (in.)	5.9	3.5	4.2	2.3	1.2	trace	0.0	0.0	0.2	2.2	4.6	5.7	29.8
Maximum Snow Depth (in.)	22	21	21	4	7	trace	0	0	2	5	12	15	22
Days With ≥ 1.0" Snow Depth	28	21	13	2	0	0	0	0	0	2	9	23	98

Bridger 1 S *Carbon County* Elevation: 3,680 ft. Latitude: 45° 17' N Longitude: 108° 55' W

	JAN	FEB	MAR	APR	MAY	JUN	JUL	AUG	SEP	OCT	NOV	DEC	YEAR
Mean Maximum Temp. (°F)	36.8	***41.6***	51.2	60.4	70.2	78.3	87.9	86.5	***75.6***	61.4	***47.0***	35.8	***61.0***
Mean Temp. (°F)	25.5	***29.4***	37.6	46.2	55.4	63.0	70.7	68.8	***59.0***	47.0	***35.1***	24.9	***46.9***
Mean Minimum Temp. (°F)	14.1	***17.3***	24.0	31.9	40.5	47.7	53.5	51.0	***42.3***	32.6	22.9	14.0	***32.6***
Extreme Maximum Temp. (°F)	62	70	78	87	94	102	108	***106***	***100***	***90***	76	72	***108***
Extreme Minimum Temp. (°F)	-23	***-32***	-15	-3	20	30	39	***28***	***18***	***-8***	-17	-37	***-37***
Days Maximum Temp. ≥ 90°F	0	0	0	0	1	4	13	***12***	***3***	***0***	0	0	***33***
Days Maximum Temp. ≤ 32°F	9	6	2	0	0	0	0	***0***	***0***	***1***	4	10	***32***
Days Minimum Temp. ≤ 32°F	29	***26***	26	16	4	0	0	***0***	***3***	***15***	***24***	29	***172***
Days Minimum Temp. ≤ 0°F	5	***3***	1	0	0	0	0	***0***	***0***	***0***	1	5	***15***
Heating Degree Days (base 65°F)	1,219	***999***	843	558	306	117	17	29	***210***	552	***892***	1,237	***6,979***
Cooling Degree Days (base 65°F)	0	***0***	0	1	14	65	200	153	***35***	1	***0***	0	***469***
Mean Precipitation (in.)	0.42	0.47	0.82	1.45	2.20	1.82	0.86	***0.56***	***1.12***	***1.25***	0.48	***0.46***	***11.91***
Extreme Maximum Daily Precip. (in.)	0.57	0.50	1.82	1.32	3.08	***2.94***	1.55	***0.92***	***1.60***	***1.07***	0.92	***0.44***	***3.08***
Days With ≥ 0.1" Precipitation	1	2	3	4	5	5	2	***2***	***3***	***3***	2	***2***	***34***
Days With ≥ 0.5" Precipitation	0	0	0	1	1	1	0	***0***	***0***	***1***	0	***0***	***4***
Days With ≥ 1.0" Precipitation	0	0	0	0	0	0	0	***0***	***0***	***0***	0	***0***	***0***
Mean Snowfall (in.)	4.6	***4.5***	7.1	5.6	1.3	0.0	0.0	***0.0***	***0.8***	***2.9***	***3.7***	***5.9***	***36.4***
Maximum Snow Depth (in.)	11	***10***	***18***	30	7	***0***	0	***0***	***4***	***9***	***11***	***13***	***30***
Days With ≥ 1.0" Snow Depth	14	***9***	4	2	0	0	0	***0***	***0***	***1***	***4***	***13***	***47***

Brockway 3 WSW *Mccone County* Elevation: 2,629 ft. Latitude: 47° 17' N Longitude: 105° 49' W

	JAN	FEB	MAR	APR	MAY	JUN	JUL	AUG	SEP	OCT	NOV	DEC	YEAR
Mean Maximum Temp. (°F)	30.0	34.3	45.2	58.9	68.8	77.8	86.3	85.8	73.7	58.8	43.0	30.6	57.8
Mean Temp. (°F)	19.0	23.2	33.2	44.9	54.9	63.8	70.9	69.9	58.4	45.3	31.3	19.4	44.5
Mean Minimum Temp. (°F)	8.0	12.0	21.2	30.9	40.9	49.7	55.4	54.0	43.1	31.7	19.5	8.1	31.2
Extreme Maximum Temp. (°F)	68	71	84	91	101	110	108	108	103	94	78	63	110
Extreme Minimum Temp. (°F)	-38	-38	-36	-9	12	24	38	28	14	-10	-35	-42	-42
Days Maximum Temp. ≥ 90°F	0	0	0	0	1	4	12	12	3	0	0	0	32
Days Maximum Temp. ≤ 32°F	15	11	6	1	0	0	0	0	0	1	6	14	54
Days Minimum Temp. ≤ 32°F	30	27	27	17	5	0	0	0	3	16	26	30	181
Days Minimum Temp. ≤ 0°F	9	6	2	0	0	0	0	0	0	0	2	9	28
Heating Degree Days (base 65°F)	1,421	1,179	979	597	324	110	21	34	233	605	1,005	1,407	7,915
Cooling Degree Days (base 65°F)	0	0	0	1	16	79	210	194	42	1	0	0	543
Mean Precipitation (in.)	0.21	0.16	0.39	1.03	1.79	2.27	1.72	1.08	1.14	0.88	0.19	0.19	11.05
Extreme Maximum Daily Precip. (in.)	0.32	0.21	0.78	2.00	1.92	3.21	1.73	1.15	2.00	1.25	0.34	0.41	3.21
Days With ≥ 0.1" Precipitation	1	1	1	3	4	5	3	3	3	2	1	1	28
Days With ≥ 0.5" Precipitation	0	0	0	0	1	1	1	1	1	0	0	0	5
Days With ≥ 1.0" Precipitation	0	0	0	0	0	0	0	0	0	0	0	0	0
Mean Snowfall (in.)	na	na	na	0.1	0.0	0.0	0.0	0.0	trace	trace	***trace***	***0.3***	na
Maximum Snow Depth (in.)	na	na	na	na	na	na	na	na	na	na	na	na	na
Days With ≥ 1.0" Snow Depth	na	na	***0***	0	0	0	0	0	0	0	***0***	na	na

Busby *Big Horn County* Elevation: 3,430 ft. Latitude: 45° 32' N Longitude: 106° 58' W

	JAN	FEB	MAR	APR	MAY	JUN	JUL	AUG	SEP	OCT	NOV	DEC	YEAR
Mean Maximum Temp. (°F)	34.3	38.6	48.7	60.1	69.3	78.3	88.6	87.9	75.8	60.7	45.9	34.2	60.2
Mean Temp. (°F)	21.3	25.4	35.1	44.9	53.9	62.6	70.4	69.2	58.2	45.3	32.2	21.2	45.0
Mean Minimum Temp. (°F)	8.2	12.2	21.4	29.7	38.4	47.0	52.1	50.4	40.6	29.8	18.5	8.1	29.7
Extreme Maximum Temp. (°F)	69	72	84	87	95	104	109	105	101	90	82	68	109
Extreme Minimum Temp. (°F)	-45	-47	-32	-4	12	29	36	29	12	-21	-31	-52	-52
Days Maximum Temp. ≥ 90°F	0	0	0	0	0	4	16	15	4	0	0	0	39
Days Maximum Temp. ≤ 32°F	11	8	3	1	0	0	0	0	0	1	5	11	40
Days Minimum Temp. ≤ 32°F	31	28	28	19	7	0	0	0	5	19	27	30	194
Days Minimum Temp. ≤ 0°F	8	6	2	0	0	0	0	0	0	0	3	8	27
Heating Degree Days (base 65°F)	1,351	1,113	921	596	345	122	20	28	226	604	977	1,352	7,655
Cooling Degree Days (base 65°F)	0	0	0	0	7	58	194	164	29	0	0	0	452
Mean Precipitation (in.)	0.59	0.52	0.95	1.30	2.21	2.42	1.23	0.76	1.46	1.38	0.76	0.59	14.17
Extreme Maximum Daily Precip. (in.)	0.48	0.71	1.40	1.45	1.70	3.75	3.00	1.26	1.74	1.67	0.75	0.54	3.75
Days With ≥ 0.1" Precipitation	2	2	3	4	6	6	3	3	4	4	3	2	42
Days With ≥ 0.5" Precipitation	0	0	0	1	1	1	1	0	1	1	0	0	6
Days With ≥ 1.0" Precipitation	0	0	0	0	0	0	0	0	0	0	0	0	0
Mean Snowfall (in.)	8.6	7.4	9.3	5.2	1.8	0.0	0.0	0.0	0.8	3.9	6.6	9.4	53.0
Maximum Snow Depth (in.)	19	22	25	12	7	1	0	0	2	6	11	20	25
Days With ≥ 1.0" Snow Depth	25	20	11	2	0	0	0	0	0	2	8	20	88

The period of record for all cooperative weather station data is 1980 – 2009. See User Guide for detailed explanation of data.

Butte Bert Mooney Arpt *Silver Bow County* Elevation: 5,540 ft. Latitude: 45° 58' N Longitude: 112° 30' W

	JAN	FEB	MAR	APR	MAY	JUN	JUL	AUG	SEP	OCT	NOV	DEC	YEAR
Mean Maximum Temp. (°F)	31.4	35.0	43.1	52.1	61.3	70.3	80.6	79.5	68.3	54.9	39.9	29.9	53.9
Mean Temp. (°F)	19.2	22.3	31.1	39.2	47.8	55.7	63.2	61.7	52.0	40.7	27.8	17.9	39.9
Mean Minimum Temp. (°F)	7.1	9.4	19.1	26.3	34.2	41.1	45.8	43.9	35.7	26.5	15.7	5.8	25.9
Extreme Maximum Temp. (°F)	57	61	69	80	88	100	98	99	93	83	70	58	100
Extreme Minimum Temp. (°F)	-38	-44	-25	-16	16	26	30	23	8	-23	-31	-52	-52
Days Maximum Temp. ≥ 90°F	0	0	0	0	0	0	4	3	0	0	0	0	7
Days Maximum Temp. ≤ 32°F	15	9	4	1	0	0	0	0	0	1	7	17	54
Days Minimum Temp. ≤ 32°F	30	28	30	24	12	3	0	1	10	25	28	30	221
Days Minimum Temp. ≤ 0°F	10	7	2	0	0	0	0	0	0	0	4	11	34
Heating Degree Days (base 65°F)	1,410	1,202	1,044	767	526	279	96	122	386	746	1,108	1,455	9,141
Cooling Degree Days (base 65°F)	0	0	0	0	0	8	48	28	2	0	0	0	86
Mean Precipitation (in.)	0.46	0.44	0.77	1.17	2.13	2.28	1.39	1.33	1.04	0.79	0.60	0.49	12.89
Extreme Maximum Daily Precip. (in.)	0.58	0.41	0.60	1.09	1.47	1.40	1.19	1.02	0.86	0.76	0.79	0.74	1.47
Days With ≥ 0.1" Precipitation	2	1	3	4	6	6	4	4	3	3	2	2	40
Days With ≥ 0.5" Precipitation	0	0	0	0	1	1	0	1	0	0	0	0	3
Days With ≥ 1.0" Precipitation	0	0	0	0	0	0	0	0	0	0	0	0	0
Mean Snowfall (in.)	***8.0***	***7.7***	***11.2***	na	na	na	na	na	na	na	na	na	na
Maximum Snow Depth (in.)	***15***	***18***	***17***	na	na	na	na	na	na	na	na	na	na
Days With ≥ 1.0" Snow Depth	***27***	***22***	***14***	na	na	na	na	na	na	na	na	na	na

Carlyle 12 NW *Wibaux County* Elevation: 3,028 ft. Latitude: 46° 45' N Longitude: 104° 17' W

	JAN	FEB	MAR	APR	MAY	JUN	JUL	AUG	SEP	OCT	NOV	DEC	YEAR
Mean Maximum Temp. (°F)	28.3	33.2	43.1	56.5	66.6	75.7	84.5	84.1	72.2	57.3	41.9	29.7	56.1
Mean Temp. (°F)	18.8	23.2	32.0	43.7	53.9	62.9	70.4	69.6	58.5	45.3	31.9	20.4	44.2
Mean Minimum Temp. (°F)	9.3	13.2	20.8	30.8	41.2	50.2	56.3	55.0	44.9	33.2	21.8	11.1	32.3
Extreme Maximum Temp. (°F)	62	69	77	91	99	107	106	104	102	92	78	62	107
Extreme Minimum Temp. (°F)	-38	-35	-25	-8	16	30	40	31	15	-8	-23	-39	-39
Days Maximum Temp. ≥ 90°F	0	0	0	0	0	3	9	10	3	0	0	0	25
Days Maximum Temp. ≤ 32°F	16	12	7	1	0	0	0	0	0	1	7	16	60
Days Minimum Temp. ≤ 32°F	30	27	27	18	5	0	0	0	2	14	25	30	178
Days Minimum Temp. ≤ 0°F	9	6	2	0	0	0	0	0	0	0	2	7	26
Heating Degree Days (base 65°F)	1,426	1,175	1,018	634	349	120	23	36	233	606	989	1,376	7,985
Cooling Degree Days (base 65°F)	0	0	0	1	12	65	198	186	46	2	0	0	510
Mean Precipitation (in.)	0.48	0.44	0.80	1.53	2.22	2.58	1.94	1.57	1.38	1.37	0.63	0.57	15.51
Extreme Maximum Daily Precip. (in.)	0.50	0.33	1.00	2.00	1.42	2.27	2.23	2.94	1.80	1.68	1.75	0.63	2.94
Days With ≥ 0.1" Precipitation	2	1	3	4	6	6	5	4	3	4	2	2	42
Days With ≥ 0.5" Precipitation	0	0	0	1	1	2	1	1	1	1	0	0	8
Days With ≥ 1.0" Precipitation	0	0	0	0	0	0	0	0	0	0	0	0	0
Mean Snowfall (in.)	7.4	7.4	7.4	5.5	1.8	0.0	0.0	0.0	0.4	2.7	5.1	6.8	44.5
Maximum Snow Depth (in.)	na	na	na	na	na	na	na	na	na	na	na	na	na
Days With ≥ 1.0" Snow Depth	na	na	na	0	0	0	0	0	0	0	na	na	na

Carter 14 W *Chouteau County* Elevation: 3,450 ft. Latitude: 47° 48' N Longitude: 111° 13' W

	JAN	FEB	MAR	APR	MAY	JUN	JUL	AUG	SEP	OCT	NOV	DEC	YEAR
Mean Maximum Temp. (°F)	35.7	39.2	46.7	57.9	67.6	75.8	86.0	84.7	72.4	59.0	43.6	34.7	58.6
Mean Temp. (°F)	25.2	27.6	34.5	44.5	53.5	61.4	69.1	68.0	57.7	46.2	33.3	24.7	45.5
Mean Minimum Temp. (°F)	14.6	16.0	22.3	31.0	39.4	46.9	52.1	51.2	43.0	33.3	23.0	14.6	32.3
Extreme Maximum Temp. (°F)	67	75	80	88	94	105	107	107	99	92	76	63	107
Extreme Minimum Temp. (°F)	-35	-32	-27	-4	12	29	31	31	17	-13	-27	-36	-36
Days Maximum Temp. ≥ 90°F	0	0	0	0	0	3	11	10	2	0	0	0	26
Days Maximum Temp. ≤ 32°F	10	8	5	1	0	0	0	0	0	1	5	10	40
Days Minimum Temp. ≤ 32°F	27	25	25	17	6	0	0	0	3	14	23	28	168
Days Minimum Temp. ≤ 0°F	7	5	2	0	0	0	0	0	0	0	2	5	21
Heating Degree Days (base 65°F)	1,229	1,051	938	610	359	147	32	46	245	578	945	1,244	7,424
Cooling Degree Days (base 65°F)	0	0	0	1	10	45	165	145	33	2	0	0	401
Mean Precipitation (in.)	0.35	0.37	0.67	1.26	2.08	2.25	1.39	1.52	1.30	0.83	0.49	0.38	12.89
Extreme Maximum Daily Precip. (in.)	0.63	0.58	0.66	1.11	1.81	2.58	2.00	1.98	1.40	0.85	0.77	0.78	2.58
Days With ≥ 0.1" Precipitation	1	1	2	4	5	6	3	4	3	3	2	1	35
Days With ≥ 0.5" Precipitation	0	0	0	1	1	1	1	1	1	0	0	0	6
Days With ≥ 1.0" Precipitation	0	0	0	0	0	0	0	0	0	0	0	0	0
Mean Snowfall (in.)	6.3	6.7	8.8	5.7	1.7	0.2	0.0	0.2	0.6	2.7	6.3	5.9	45.1
Maximum Snow Depth (in.)	11	14	12	20	12	0	0	0	1	10	13	16	20
Days With ≥ 1.0" Snow Depth	9	7	6	2	0	0	0	0	0	2	6	8	40

Cascade 5 S *Cascade County* Elevation: 3,359 ft. Latitude: 47° 13' N Longitude: 111° 43' W

	JAN	FEB	MAR	APR	MAY	JUN	JUL	AUG	SEP	OCT	NOV	DEC	YEAR
Mean Maximum Temp. (°F)	38.7	41.5	48.6	58.5	67.3	74.8	84.7	83.7	72.8	60.3	46.3	37.7	59.6
Mean Temp. (°F)	28.0	30.2	36.4	45.5	53.6	60.9	67.6	66.3	57.1	47.3	36.5	27.9	46.4
Mean Minimum Temp. (°F)	17.2	18.7	24.1	32.4	39.9	46.8	50.6	48.8	41.4	34.2	26.6	18.1	33.2
Extreme Maximum Temp. (°F)	70	69	80	89	92	101	104	103	99	94	77	66	104
Extreme Minimum Temp. (°F)	-42	-44	-30	-8	8	28	35	29	14	-16	-32	-45	-45
Days Maximum Temp. ≥ 90°F	0	0	0	0	0	2	10	9	2	0	0	0	23
Days Maximum Temp. ≤ 32°F	8	6	4	1	0	0	0	0	0	1	4	8	32
Days Minimum Temp. ≤ 32°F	24	22	23	16	6	0	0	0	4	13	18	23	149
Days Minimum Temp. ≤ 0°F	6	4	2	0	0	0	0	0	0	0	2	5	19
Heating Degree Days (base 65°F)	1,142	979	881	580	352	151	37	57	252	545	849	1,144	6,969
Cooling Degree Days (base 65°F)	0	0	0	1	6	34	125	104	22	3	0	0	295
Mean Precipitation (in.)	0.49	0.52	1.07	1.88	2.95	2.68	1.48	1.54	1.79	1.19	0.64	0.54	16.77
Extreme Maximum Daily Precip. (in.)	0.56	0.53	1.30	2.34	3.35	2.76	2.35	1.72	1.80	2.30	0.76	0.59	3.35
Days With ≥ 0.1" Precipitation	2	2	4	5	6	6	4	4	4	3	2	2	44
Days With ≥ 0.5" Precipitation	0	0	0	1	2	2	1	1	1	1	0	0	9
Days With ≥ 1.0" Precipitation	0	0	0	0	1	0	0	0	0	0	0	0	1
Mean Snowfall (in.)	9.9	10.0	13.9	9.3	1.3	0.0	0.0	0.2	0.9	4.6	9.0	10.1	69.2
Maximum Snow Depth (in.)	11	23	14	17	8	0	0	0	5	8	14	15	23
Days With ≥ 1.0" Snow Depth	8	7	7	2	0	0	0	0	0	2	6	8	40

The period of record for all cooperative weather station data is 1980 – 2009. See User Guide for detailed explanation of data.

Chester *Liberty County* Elevation: 3,165 ft. Latitude: 48° 31' N Longitude: 110° 58' W

	JAN	FEB	MAR	APR	MAY	JUN	JUL	AUG	SEP	OCT	NOV	DEC	YEAR
Mean Maximum Temp. (°F)	30.9	36.2	46.0	58.3	67.8	75.1	83.7	82.8	71.6	58.8	42.7	32.1	57.2
Mean Temp. (°F)	18.2	22.8	32.6	43.7	53.4	61.0	67.6	66.4	55.8	43.8	29.8	19.4	42.9
Mean Minimum Temp. (°F)	5.4	9.4	19.1	29.0	38.9	46.7	51.5	50.0	40.0	28.7	16.9	6.6	28.5
Extreme Maximum Temp. (°F)	66	74	79	88	94	100	104	102	96	89	75	64	104
Extreme Minimum Temp. (°F)	-44	-44	-30	0	14	29	34	28	15	-17	-29	-52	-52
Days Maximum Temp. ≥ 90°F	0	0	0	0	0	2	8	6	1	0	0	0	17
Days Maximum Temp. ≤ 32°F	13	9	5	1	0	0	0	0	0	1	6	12	47
Days Minimum Temp. ≤ 32°F	30	28	29	20	7	0	0	0	5	20	27	30	196
Days Minimum Temp. ≤ 0°F	11	7	2	0	0	0	0	0	0	0	3	9	32
Heating Degree Days (base 65°F)	1,447	1,189	998	634	361	155	43	60	284	652	1,050	1,410	8,283
Cooling Degree Days (base 65°F)	0	0	0	1	9	39	132	111	15	0	0	0	307
Mean Precipitation (in.)	0.35	0.30	0.53	0.74	1.73	2.31	1.46	1.04	0.94	0.57	0.37	0.38	10.72
Extreme Maximum Daily Precip. (in.)	0.72	0.40	1.39	0.85	1.62	3.02	1.92	1.10	1.27	0.84	0.48	0.43	3.02
Days With ≥ 0.1" Precipitation	1	1	2	2	4	6	3	3	3	2	1	1	29
Days With ≥ 0.5" Precipitation	0	0	0	0	1	1	1	0	0	0	0	0	3
Days With ≥ 1.0" Precipitation	0	0	0	0	0	0	0	0	0	0	0	0	0
Mean Snowfall (in.)	na	na	na	***2.3***	0.2	0.1	0.0	0.0	0.0	0.4	***2.4***	na	na
Maximum Snow Depth (in.)	na	na	***9***	***7***	***1***	***1***	***0***	0	0	***5***	na	na	na
Days With ≥ 1.0" Snow Depth	na	na	***5***	***1***	0	0	0	0	0	***0***	***5***	na	na

Chinook *Blaine County* Elevation: 2,345 ft. Latitude: 48° 35' N Longitude: 109° 14' W

	JAN	FEB	MAR	APR	MAY	JUN	JUL	AUG	SEP	OCT	NOV	DEC	YEAR
Mean Maximum Temp. (°F)	30.0	34.9	46.0	60.2	69.2	77.4	85.7	84.3	72.8	58.9	43.1	31.4	57.8
Mean Temp. (°F)	17.2	21.8	32.6	45.2	54.8	63.1	69.3	67.4	56.3	43.9	29.8	18.9	43.3
Mean Minimum Temp. (°F)	4.7	8.7	19.2	30.1	40.3	48.8	52.8	50.4	39.7	28.9	16.5	6.3	28.9
Extreme Maximum Temp. (°F)	67	75	82	92	96	104	103	106	104	90	79	66	106
Extreme Minimum Temp. (°F)	-45	-44	-33	-10	16	30	36	29	13	-24	-38	-50	-50
Days Maximum Temp. ≥ 90°F	0	0	0	0	1	3	10	10	2	0	0	0	26
Days Maximum Temp. ≤ 32°F	15	11	5	0	0	0	0	0	0	1	6	14	52
Days Minimum Temp. ≤ 32°F	30	28	29	18	5	0	0	0	5	20	28	30	193
Days Minimum Temp. ≤ 0°F	11	7	3	0	0	0	0	0	0	0	3	10	34
Heating Degree Days (base 65°F)	1,488	1,215	998	590	322	109	23	50	272	648	1,052	1,425	8,192
Cooling Degree Days (base 65°F)	0	0	0	1	12	60	161	130	17	0	0	0	381
Mean Precipitation (in.)	0.50	0.41	0.62	0.94	2.32	2.49	1.68	1.21	1.36	0.77	0.48	0.45	13.23
Extreme Maximum Daily Precip. (in.)	1.10	0.51	0.67	1.12	1.75	2.29	3.15	1.89	5.50	1.10	0.61	0.94	5.50
Days With ≥ 0.1" Precipitation	2	2	2	3	5	6	4	3	3	2	2	2	36
Days With ≥ 0.5" Precipitation	0	0	0	0	1	1	1	1	1	0	0	0	5
Days With ≥ 1.0" Precipitation	0	0	0	0	0	0	0	0	0	0	0	0	0
Mean Snowfall (in.)	***6.8***	***6.1***	***5.2***	1.3	0.8	0.0	0.0	0.0	0.0	1.0	4.2	6.5	***31.9***
Maximum Snow Depth (in.)	***21***	***15***	***13***	***5***	***7***	***0***	***0***	***0***	***0***	***11***	***9***	na	na
Days With ≥ 1.0" Snow Depth	***10***	***11***	***6***	1	0	0	0	0	0	***0***	***3***	***8***	***39***

Cohagen *Garfield County* Elevation: 2,714 ft. Latitude: 47° 03' N Longitude: 106° 37' W

	JAN	FEB	MAR	APR	MAY	JUN	JUL	AUG	SEP	OCT	NOV	DEC	YEAR
Mean Maximum Temp. (°F)	32.5	37.5	48.2	60.7	69.8	78.7	88.0	86.8	75.4	60.8	45.2	33.3	59.8
Mean Temp. (°F)	20.4	25.0	34.8	45.7	55.1	64.0	71.5	69.9	58.7	46.1	32.5	21.1	45.4
Mean Minimum Temp. (°F)	8.2	12.4	21.3	30.6	40.4	49.2	55.0	53.0	42.0	31.3	19.7	8.9	31.0
Extreme Maximum Temp. (°F)	68	74	83	91	102	109	110	109	104	93	80	66	110
Extreme Minimum Temp. (°F)	-40	-42	-35	-11	14	28	37	28	13	-16	-29	-42	-42
Days Maximum Temp. ≥ 90°F	0	0	0	0	1	5	14	13	4	0	0	0	37
Days Maximum Temp. ≤ 32°F	13	9	4	0	0	0	0	0	0	1	5	12	44
Days Minimum Temp. ≤ 32°F	30	27	27	18	6	0	0	0	4	16	26	30	184
Days Minimum Temp. ≤ 0°F	9	6	2	0	0	0	0	0	0	0	2	8	27
Heating Degree Days (base 65°F)	1,378	1,125	930	574	312	102	15	31	219	582	969	1,355	7,592
Cooling Degree Days (base 65°F)	0	0	0	0	13	77	224	190	37	1	0	0	542
Mean Precipitation (in.)	0.36	0.23	0.48	1.03	1.99	2.12	1.64	0.94	1.09	0.95	0.36	0.38	11.57
Extreme Maximum Daily Precip. (in.)	0.48	0.29	0.53	1.50	2.30	2.22	2.41	0.84	1.95	1.02	0.43	0.61	2.41
Days With ≥ 0.1" Precipitation	1	1	2	3	5	6	3	3	3	3	1	1	32
Days With ≥ 0.5" Precipitation	0	0	0	0	1	1	1	1	0	1	0	0	5
Days With ≥ 1.0" Precipitation	0	0	0	0	0	0	0	0	0	0	0	0	0
Mean Snowfall (in.)	4.9	2.9	4.2	2.2	0.9	0.0	0.0	0.0	0.1	1.1	2.9	4.8	24.0
Maximum Snow Depth (in.)	19	19	17	9	11	0	0	0	1	10	11	14	19
Days With ≥ 1.0" Snow Depth	17	10	6	1	0	0	0	0	0	1	6	13	54

Columbus *Stillwater County* Elevation: 3,584 ft. Latitude: 45° 38' N Longitude: 109° 16' W

	JAN	FEB	MAR	APR	MAY	JUN	JUL	AUG	SEP	OCT	NOV	DEC	YEAR
Mean Maximum Temp. (°F)	38.7	43.0	51.6	61.0	70.0	78.4	87.3	85.8	75.3	62.0	47.4	37.2	61.5
Mean Temp. (°F)	25.5	29.5	37.6	46.1	54.9	62.9	70.0	68.2	58.3	46.9	34.5	24.7	46.6
Mean Minimum Temp. (°F)	12.2	15.8	23.5	31.1	39.8	47.3	52.7	50.5	41.3	31.8	21.6	12.1	31.6
Extreme Maximum Temp. (°F)	66	72	83	87	94	101	106	101	99	92	76	70	106
Extreme Minimum Temp. (°F)	-36	-35	-27	-1	16	28	35	31	18	-9	-22	-42	-42
Days Maximum Temp. ≥ 90°F	0	0	0	0	0	4	13	10	2	0	0	0	29
Days Maximum Temp. ≤ 32°F	8	5	2	0	0	0	0	0	0	1	4	10	30
Days Minimum Temp. ≤ 32°F	30	26	26	17	5	0	0	0	3	16	26	30	179
Days Minimum Temp. ≤ 0°F	7	4	1	0	0	0	0	0	0	0	2	6	20
Heating Degree Days (base 65°F)	1,218	999	843	561	313	110	17	28	215	554	909	1,243	7,010
Cooling Degree Days (base 65°F)	0	0	0	0	8	53	179	134	22	1	0	0	397
Mean Precipitation (in.)	0.59	0.66	1.09	1.90	2.71	2.17	1.19	0.85	1.27	1.34	0.57	0.55	14.89
Extreme Maximum Daily Precip. (in.)	0.70	1.00	0.97	1.90	2.57	2.30	2.18	1.14	1.91	1.18	0.76	0.60	2.57
Days With ≥ 0.1" Precipitation	2	2	4	5	6	5	3	3	3	4	2	2	41
Days With ≥ 0.5" Precipitation	0	0	0	1	2	1	0	0	1	1	0	0	6
Days With ≥ 1.0" Precipitation	0	0	0	0	0	0	0	0	0	0	0	0	0
Mean Snowfall (in.)	***5.2***	***5.8***	***7.0***	2.8	1.5	0.0	0.0	0.0	0.5	3.2	3.4	***6.0***	***35.4***
Maximum Snow Depth (in.)	na	na	na	na	***14***	***0***	***0***	***0***	***11***	***14***	na	***18***	na
Days With ≥ 1.0" Snow Depth	na	***8***	***5***	1	0	0	0	0	0	1	***4***	***11***	na

Content 3 SSE *Phillips County* Elevation: 2,339 ft. Latitude: 47° 59' N Longitude: 107° 33' W

	JAN	FEB	MAR	APR	MAY	JUN	JUL	AUG	SEP	OCT	NOV	DEC	YEAR
Mean Maximum Temp. (°F)	29.5	34.2	45.6	59.2	69.0	77.3	86.2	85.3	72.9	58.8	43.3	31.2	57.7
Mean Temp. (°F)	18.2	22.6	33.4	45.3	55.1	63.3	70.5	69.1	57.6	45.2	31.6	19.7	44.3
Mean Minimum Temp. (°F)	6.9	10.9	21.2	31.4	41.2	49.2	54.7	52.8	42.3	31.6	19.8	8.2	30.8
Extreme Maximum Temp. (°F)	67	73	79	92	100	106	107	107	103	90	79	66	107
Extreme Minimum Temp. (°F)	-42	-45	-39	-5	13	27	38	31	16	-11	-30	-49	-49
Days Maximum Temp. ≥ 90°F	0	0	0	0	1	3	11	11	3	0	0	0	29
Days Maximum Temp. ≤ 32°F	14	11	5	1	0	0	0	0	0	1	6	14	52
Days Minimum Temp. ≤ 32°F	29	27	27	16	5	0	0	0	3	16	25	30	178
Days Minimum Temp. ≤ 0°F	10	7	2	0	0	0	0	0	0	0	3	9	31
Heating Degree Days (base 65°F)	1,445	1,194	972	585	314	114	21	36	247	607	997	1,397	7,929
Cooling Degree Days (base 65°F)	0	0	0	1	15	68	198	169	32	1	0	0	484
Mean Precipitation (in.)	0.34	0.28	0.55	1.05	2.25	2.24	1.55	1.04	1.17	0.92	0.39	0.43	12.21
Extreme Maximum Daily Precip. (in.)	0.60	0.45	0.89	1.90	2.33	1.90	2.50	1.48	5.57	1.50	0.50	0.85	5.57
Days With ≥ 0.1" Precipitation	2	1	3	4	6	6	4	3	3	3	2	2	39
Days With ≥ 0.5" Precipitation	0	0	0	0	1	1	1	1	1	1	0	0	6
Days With ≥ 1.0" Precipitation	0	0	0	0	0	0	0	0	0	0	0	0	0
Mean Snowfall (in.)	na	na	na	trace	0.0	0.0	0.0	0.0	trace	0.2	na	na	na
Maximum Snow Depth (in.)	na	na	na	na	na	na	na	na	na	na	na	na	na
Days With ≥ 1.0" Snow Depth	na	na	na	0	0	0	0	0	0	***0***	na	na	na

Cooke City 2 W *Park County* Elevation: 7,459 ft. Latitude: 45° 01' N Longitude: 109° 58' W

	JAN	FEB	MAR	APR	MAY	JUN	JUL	AUG	SEP	OCT	NOV	DEC	YEAR
Mean Maximum Temp. (°F)	***24.7***	30.0	37.3	44.8	54.8	64.4	74.1	72.6	62.1	48.0	31.9	22.8	***47.3***
Mean Temp. (°F)	***14.6***	17.8	24.9	32.2	41.5	49.4	56.5	54.9	46.2	35.4	22.4	13.4	***34.1***
Mean Minimum Temp. (°F)	***4.5***	5.5	12.4	19.5	28.2	34.3	38.9	37.2	30.3	22.8	12.8	4.0	***20.9***
Extreme Maximum Temp. (°F)	47	68	58	72	80	88	90	88	85	75	58	44	90
Extreme Minimum Temp. (°F)	-39	-43	-26	-18	2	21	23	20	3	-10	-23	-40	-43
Days Maximum Temp. ≥ 90°F	0	0	0	0	0	0	0	0	0	0	0	0	0
Days Maximum Temp. ≤ 32°F	25	15	9	3	0	0	0	0	0	3	15	26	96
Days Minimum Temp. ≤ 32°F	29	27	30	29	25	11	3	5	19	29	28	29	264
Days Minimum Temp. ≤ 0°F	11	9	5	1	0	0	0	0	0	0	5	12	43
Heating Degree Days (base 65°F)	***1,554***	1,329	1,237	978	721	464	257	306	557	910	***1,277***	1,592	***11,182***
Cooling Degree Days (base 65°F)	***0***	0	0	0	0	0	2	1	0	0	0	0	***3***
Mean Precipitation (in.)	1.99	1.62	1.88	1.92	3.02	3.13	2.36	1.92	1.77	1.74	2.00	2.03	25.38
Extreme Maximum Daily Precip. (in.)	***0.86***	***0.58***	***1.10***	***1.80***	***1.26***	***1.37***	***1.90***	***1.12***	na	***1.18***	***1.66***	***1.00***	na
Days With ≥ 0.1" Precipitation	6	5	6	6	9	9	7	6	5	5	6	6	76
Days With ≥ 0.5" Precipitation	0	0	0	1	1	1	1	1	1	1	1	0	8
Days With ≥ 1.0" Precipitation	0	0	0	0	0	0	0	0	0	0	0	0	0
Mean Snowfall (in.)	***34.7***	27.0	26.3	18.3	8.9	2.6	trace	trace	2.1	11.7	25.2	35.3	***192.1***
Maximum Snow Depth (in.)	58	65	72	70	42	15	trace	trace	8	15	23	53	72
Days With ≥ 1.0" Snow Depth	29	27	30	28	11	1	0	0	1	8	25	29	189

Creston *Flathead County* Elevation: 2,939 ft. Latitude: 48° 11' N Longitude: 114° 08' W

	JAN	FEB	MAR	APR	MAY	JUN	JUL	AUG	SEP	OCT	NOV	DEC	YEAR
Mean Maximum Temp. (°F)	31.2	35.7	44.2	54.8	63.8	70.3	79.4	79.6	68.6	54.8	40.1	30.5	54.4
Mean Temp. (°F)	24.2	27.1	34.7	43.3	51.6	57.9	64.5	63.4	53.7	42.6	32.5	24.0	43.3
Mean Minimum Temp. (°F)	17.2	18.4	25.1	31.7	39.5	45.5	49.5	47.2	38.8	30.3	24.9	17.4	32.1
Extreme Maximum Temp. (°F)	52	62	74	82	93	92	97	97	96	80	67	55	97
Extreme Minimum Temp. (°F)	-32	-25	-15	8	24	30	35	31	18	0	-17	-33	-33
Days Maximum Temp. ≥ 90°F	0	0	0	0	0	0	3	3	0	0	0	0	6
Days Maximum Temp. ≤ 32°F	15	8	3	0	0	0	0	0	0	0	5	17	48
Days Minimum Temp. ≤ 32°F	29	27	27	17	4	0	0	0	4	19	24	29	180
Days Minimum Temp. ≤ 0°F	3	3	1	0	0	0	0	0	0	0	1	3	11
Heating Degree Days (base 65°F)	1,258	1,065	934	646	412	222	82	97	335	688	968	1,265	7,972
Cooling Degree Days (base 65°F)	0	0	0	0	4	17	72	55	4	0	0	0	152
Mean Precipitation (in.)	1.37	1.22	1.31	1.78	2.53	3.16	1.69	1.21	1.61	1.28	1.52	1.48	20.16
Extreme Maximum Daily Precip. (in.)	0.88	1.50	1.12	1.10	1.77	2.20	2.85	1.05	1.20	0.92	1.52	0.70	2.85
Days With ≥ 0.1" Precipitation	5	4	5	5	7	8	4	3	5	4	5	5	60
Days With ≥ 0.5" Precipitation	0	0	0	1	1	2	1	1	1	0	0	0	7
Days With ≥ 1.0" Precipitation	0	0	0	0	0	0	0	0	0	0	0	0	0
Mean Snowfall (in.)	11.4	8.7	5.7	1.6	0.1	0.1	0.0	0.0	0.0	0.6	4.9	***14.7***	***47.8***
Maximum Snow Depth (in.)	25	21	19	8	2	3	0	0	0	9	23	32	32
Days With ≥ 1.0" Snow Depth	22	18	9	1	0	0	0	0	0	0	6	20	76

Culbertson *Roosevelt County* Elevation: 1,919 ft. Latitude: 48° 09' N Longitude: 104° 31' W

	JAN	FEB	MAR	APR	MAY	JUN	JUL	AUG	SEP	OCT	NOV	DEC	YEAR
Mean Maximum Temp. (°F)	24.5	31.2	43.8	60.8	71.6	79.5	86.9	86.3	74.4	59.3	40.6	26.8	57.1
Mean Temp. (°F)	12.9	19.5	31.3	45.2	56.1	64.4	70.8	69.5	58.2	44.8	28.8	15.5	43.1
Mean Minimum Temp. (°F)	1.3	7.7	18.6	29.6	40.6	49.2	54.6	52.7	41.8	30.2	16.9	4.2	28.9
Extreme Maximum Temp. (°F)	61	67	81	94	103	109	108	107	104	95	80	57	109
Extreme Minimum Temp. (°F)	-42	-43	-29	-12	11	28	34	30	15	-8	-31	-48	-48
Days Maximum Temp. ≥ 90°F	0	0	0	0	1	4	12	12	3	0	0	0	32
Days Maximum Temp. ≤ 32°F	20	14	6	1	0	0	0	0	0	1	8	18	68
Days Minimum Temp. ≤ 32°F	31	28	29	19	6	0	0	0	4	18	28	31	194
Days Minimum Temp. ≤ 0°F	13	9	3	0	0	0	0	0	0	0	3	11	39
Heating Degree Days (base 65°F)	1,611	1,281	1,038	588	289	93	17	34	233	621	1,081	1,529	8,415
Cooling Degree Days (base 65°F)	0	0	0	1	20	81	202	181	35	1	0	0	521
Mean Precipitation (in.)	0.35	0.20	0.50	0.84	1.87	2.73	2.50	1.34	1.21	0.87	0.43	0.38	13.22
Extreme Maximum Daily Precip. (in.)	0.34	0.90	1.05	2.31	2.00	2.62	2.71	1.72	1.38	1.50	1.21	0.44	2.71
Days With ≥ 0.1" Precipitation	1	1	2	2	5	6	5	4	3	2	1	1	33
Days With ≥ 0.5" Precipitation	0	0	0	0	1	2	1	1	1	0	0	0	6
Days With ≥ 1.0" Precipitation	0	0	0	0	0	1	1	0	0	0	0	0	2
Mean Snowfall (in.)	***4.6***	2.4	***2.5***	0.8	0.4	0.0	0.0	0.0	0.1	1.4	2.8	na	na
Maximum Snow Depth (in.)	19	20	16	8	10	0	0	0	0	6	12	14	20
Days With ≥ 1.0" Snow Depth	26	19	12	1	0	0	0	0	0	1	8	18	85

The period of record for all cooperative weather station data is 1980 – 2009. See User Guide for detailed explanation of data.

Cut Bank Muni Arpt *Glacier County* Elevation: 3,837 ft. Latitude: 48° 36' N Longitude: 112° 22' W

	JAN	FEB	MAR	APR	MAY	JUN	JUL	AUG	SEP	OCT	NOV	DEC	YEAR
Mean Maximum Temp. (°F)	32.3	35.6	42.0	53.4	62.5	70.1	79.2	78.4	67.6	55.2	40.7	32.0	54.1
Mean Temp. (°F)	22.0	24.6	31.1	41.4	50.2	57.8	64.6	63.5	53.9	42.9	30.8	22.2	42.1
Mean Minimum Temp. (°F)	11.6	13.7	20.1	29.3	37.8	45.3	50.0	48.5	40.1	30.6	20.8	12.4	30.0
Extreme Maximum Temp. (°F)	63	71	77	86	91	95	106	103	95	88	72	62	106
Extreme Minimum Temp. (°F)	-37	-44	-34	-2	16	28	32	31	17	-14	-24	-40	-44
Days Maximum Temp. ≥ 90°F	0	0	0	0	0	1	4	3	1	0	0	0	9
Days Maximum Temp. ≤ 32°F	12	9	7	1	0	0	0	0	0	2	6	13	50
Days Minimum Temp. ≤ 32°F	28	26	27	19	8	0	0	0	5	18	25	28	184
Days Minimum Temp. ≤ 0°F	8	6	3	0	0	0	0	0	0	0	3	7	27
Heating Degree Days (base 65°F)	1,325	1,136	1,046	702	455	227	81	103	336	677	1,019	1,320	8,427
Cooling Degree Days (base 65°F)	0	0	0	0	2	17	76	64	9	1	0	0	169
Mean Precipitation (in.)	0.23	0.24	0.49	0.78	2.04	2.58	1.31	1.28	1.24	0.48	0.34	0.22	11.23
Extreme Maximum Daily Precip. (in.)	0.50	0.34	0.81	1.00	2.04	2.43	1.58	1.79	1.45	0.69	0.75	0.49	2.43
Days With ≥ 0.1" Precipitation	1	1	2	3	5	5	3	3	3	2	1	0	29
Days With ≥ 0.5" Precipitation	0	0	0	0	1	2	1	1	1	0	0	0	6
Days With ≥ 1.0" Precipitation	0	0	0	0	0	1	0	0	0	0	0	0	1
Mean Snowfall (in.)	na	na	na	na	na	na	***trace***	na	***0.4***	na	na	na	na
Maximum Snow Depth (in.)	14	9	12	7	6	trace	trace	0	3	8	11	18	18
Days With ≥ 1.0" Snow Depth	14	11	10	2	1	0	0	0	0	2	8	13	61

Darby *Ravalli County* Elevation: 3,879 ft. Latitude: 46° 01' N Longitude: 114° 11' W

	JAN	FEB	MAR	APR	MAY	JUN	JUL	AUG	SEP	OCT	NOV	DEC	YEAR
Mean Maximum Temp. (°F)	37.2	42.2	51.2	59.0	68.0	75.7	85.3	84.4	74.3	61.5	45.5	35.9	60.0
Mean Temp. (°F)	28.4	31.7	39.1	45.4	53.4	60.1	67.1	66.0	57.6	47.1	35.5	27.2	46.5
Mean Minimum Temp. (°F)	19.5	21.2	27.0	31.8	38.7	44.4	48.8	47.5	40.8	32.7	25.5	18.3	33.0
Extreme Maximum Temp. (°F)	61	70	75	84	95	98	105	102	97	88	74	59	105
Extreme Minimum Temp. (°F)	-23	-28	-7	12	19	28	33	27	19	-5	-8	-34	-34
Days Maximum Temp. ≥ 90°F	0	0	0	0	1	2	10	8	1	0	0	0	22
Days Maximum Temp. ≤ 32°F	8	4	1	0	0	0	0	0	0	0	3	10	26
Days Minimum Temp. ≤ 32°F	28	26	24	16	6	0	0	0	3	14	23	28	168
Days Minimum Temp. ≤ 0°F	2	2	0	0	0	0	0	0	0	0	0	2	6
Heating Degree Days (base 65°F)	1,129	935	795	580	360	171	49	56	233	548	879	1,167	6,902
Cooling Degree Days (base 65°F)	0	0	0	0	6	30	120	93	17	0	0	0	266
Mean Precipitation (in.)	1.24	0.96	0.93	1.14	2.01	2.10	1.12	1.20	1.18	***1.13***	1.46	1.32	***15.79***
Extreme Maximum Daily Precip. (in.)	0.88	1.23	1.08	1.70	1.68	1.36	1.25	1.48	1.12	0.95	1.46	1.27	1.70
Days With ≥ 0.1" Precipitation	4	3	3	4	5	6	3	3	3	3	4	4	45
Days With ≥ 0.5" Precipitation	1	0	0	0	1	1	1	0	1	0	1	0	6
Days With ≥ 1.0" Precipitation	0	0	0	0	0	0	0	0	0	0	0	0	0
Mean Snowfall (in.)	na	na	na	***0.1***	trace	0.0	0.0	0.0	0.1	***0.0***	na	na	na
Maximum Snow Depth (in.)	na	na	na	na	na	na	na	na	na	na	na	na	na
Days With ≥ 1.0" Snow Depth	na	na	na	0	0	0	0	0	0	***0***	na	na	na

Del Bonita *Glacier County* Elevation: 4,336 ft. Latitude: 49° 00' N Longitude: 112° 47' W

	JAN	FEB	MAR	APR	MAY	JUN	JUL	AUG	SEP	OCT	NOV	DEC	YEAR
Mean Maximum Temp. (°F)	31.8	34.6	41.5	53.1	63.1	69.7	77.8	77.5	68.1	55.4	39.6	***30.3***	***53.5***
Mean Temp. (°F)	21.2	24.0	30.5	40.5	49.9	56.8	63.0	62.2	53.8	42.8	29.7	***20.8***	***41.3***
Mean Minimum Temp. (°F)	10.7	13.4	19.5	27.9	36.7	43.9	48.2	46.8	39.5	30.2	19.8	***11.0***	***29.0***
Extreme Maximum Temp. (°F)	62	69	75	83	90	91	99	97	93	83	73	60	99
Extreme Minimum Temp. (°F)	-30	-38	-30	-5	12	28	31	24	14	-11	-28	-38	-38
Days Maximum Temp. ≥ 90°F	0	0	0	0	0	0	2	1	0	0	0	0	3
Days Maximum Temp. ≤ 32°F	12	9	6	1	0	0	0	0	0	2	7	13	50
Days Minimum Temp. ≤ 32°F	29	25	28	21	9	1	0	0	5	18	25	27	188
Days Minimum Temp. ≤ 0°F	8	5	3	0	0	0	0	0	0	0	3	7	26
Heating Degree Days (base 65°F)	1,352	1,153	1,061	727	463	250	108	126	339	683	1,051	***1,366***	***8,679***
Cooling Degree Days (base 65°F)	0	0	0	0	3	12	54	46	10	0	0	***0***	***125***
Mean Precipitation (in.)	0.21	0.23	0.61	0.95	2.43	2.96	1.51	1.48	1.42	0.56	0.55	0.39	13.30
Extreme Maximum Daily Precip. (in.)	0.35	0.50	1.03	0.90	3.00	5.00	3.80	1.75	1.80	1.00	0.67	1.00	5.00
Days With ≥ 0.1" Precipitation	1	1	2	3	5	6	4	4	4	2	2	1	35
Days With ≥ 0.5" Precipitation	0	0	0	1	2	2	1	1	1	0	0	0	8
Days With ≥ 1.0" Precipitation	0	0	0	0	1	1	0	0	0	0	0	0	2
Mean Snowfall (in.)	5.9	6.1	9.3	8.6	2.6	0.0	0.0	0.2	1.3	6.6	7.3	8.2	56.1
Maximum Snow Depth (in.)	18	13	14	14	24	3	2	7	4	12	19	23	24
Days With ≥ 1.0" Snow Depth	13	11	9	4	1	0	0	0	0	3	8	13	62

Denton 1 NNE *Fergus County* Elevation: 3,620 ft. Latitude: 47° 20' N Longitude: 109° 57' W

	JAN	FEB	MAR	APR	MAY	JUN	JUL	AUG	SEP	OCT	NOV	DEC	YEAR
Mean Maximum Temp. (°F)	36.7	39.1	46.8	57.1	65.7	73.7	83.3	82.7	71.5	59.3	45.5	35.9	58.1
Mean Temp. (°F)	23.1	25.5	33.0	42.5	51.2	58.9	65.6	64.6	54.5	43.4	31.6	22.6	43.0
Mean Minimum Temp. (°F)	9.4	11.9	19.2	27.8	36.6	44.0	47.8	46.4	37.3	27.5	17.6	9.2	27.9
Extreme Maximum Temp. (°F)	71	72	80	88	93	99	101	104	99	89	77	67	104
Extreme Minimum Temp. (°F)	-47	-45	-35	-14	13	25	28	22	13	-22	-33	-50	-50
Days Maximum Temp. ≥ 90°F	0	0	0	0	0	1	8	7	2	0	0	0	18
Days Maximum Temp. ≤ 32°F	9	8	4	1	0	0	0	0	0	1	5	10	38
Days Minimum Temp. ≤ 32°F	29	27	29	21	10	1	0	1	8	21	27	29	203
Days Minimum Temp. ≤ 0°F	9	6	3	0	0	0	0	0	0	0	3	8	29
Heating Degree Days (base 65°F)	1,294	1,111	985	670	424	199	64	79	320	662	997	1,310	8,115
Cooling Degree Days (base 65°F)	0	0	0	0	3	22	90	74	11	0	0	0	200
Mean Precipitation (in.)	0.41	0.40	0.79	1.38	2.70	2.69	1.63	1.56	1.43	1.07	0.48	0.49	15.03
Extreme Maximum Daily Precip. (in.)	0.38	0.58	1.00	1.39	1.64	2.41	2.08	1.65	1.95	1.29	0.72	1.10	2.41
Days With ≥ 0.1" Precipitation	1	1	3	4	7	7	4	4	4	3	2	2	42
Days With ≥ 0.5" Precipitation	0	0	0	1	2	1	1	1	1	0	0	0	7
Days With ≥ 1.0" Precipitation	0	0	0	0	0	0	0	0	0	0	0	0	0
Mean Snowfall (in.)	7.5	6.2	7.4	2.6	1.4	0.0	0.0	0.0	0.3	1.7	3.4	5.5	36.0
Maximum Snow Depth (in.)	24	17	***15***	12	15	0	0	2	5	***6***	9	20	***24***
Days With ≥ 1.0" Snow Depth	7	6	***4***	2	0	0	0	0	0	***1***	4	6	***30***

The period of record for all cooperative weather station data is 1980 – 2009. See User Guide for detailed explanation of data.

Dillon Wmce *Beaverhead County* Elevation: 5,228 ft. Latitude: 45° 13' N Longitude: 112° 38' W

	JAN	FEB	MAR	APR	MAY	JUN	JUL	AUG	SEP	OCT	NOV	DEC	YEAR
Mean Maximum Temp. (°F)	35.3	40.0	48.4	57.6	66.9	75.0	84.3	82.6	72.4	59.4	43.8	33.8	58.3
Mean Temp. (°F)	25.0	28.3	35.8	43.5	51.9	59.1	66.2	64.3	55.8	45.1	32.8	23.7	44.3
Mean Minimum Temp. (°F)	14.7	16.6	23.1	29.4	36.9	43.2	48.0	45.9	39.1	30.8	21.8	13.5	30.2
Extreme Maximum Temp. (°F)	59	65	73	83	90	94	102	95	94	86	71	63	102
Extreme Minimum Temp. (°F)	-31	-34	-18	-3	19	23	32	25	12	-7	-23	-37	-37
Days Maximum Temp. ≥ 90°F	0	0	0	0	0	1	7	3	0	0	0	0	11
Days Maximum Temp. ≤ 32°F	10	5	2	0	0	0	0	0	0	0	4	12	33
Days Minimum Temp. ≤ 32°F	30	27	27	20	8	1	0	0	5	17	25	30	190
Days Minimum Temp. ≤ 0°F	5	3	1	0	0	0	0	0	0	0	1	4	14
Heating Degree Days (base 65°F)	1,234	1,029	898	637	400	186	44	67	277	609	958	1,275	7,614
Cooling Degree Days (base 65°F)	0	0	0	0	2	16	87	51	7	0	0	0	163
Mean Precipitation (in.)	0.30	0.30	0.63	1.30	2.25	1.91	1.13	1.16	0.92	0.90	0.40	0.32	11.52
Extreme Maximum Daily Precip. (in.)	0.70	0.47	1.15	1.02	1.94	1.65	1.52	1.10	1.30	1.27	0.72	0.55	1.94
Days With ≥ 0.1" Precipitation	1	1	2	4	6	5	3	3	3	3	1	1	33
Days With ≥ 0.5" Precipitation	0	0	0	1	1	1	1	1	0	0	0	0	5
Days With ≥ 1.0" Precipitation	0	0	0	0	0	0	0	0	0	0	0	0	0
Mean Snowfall (in.)	na	na	na	***trace***	0.0	0.0	0.0	0.0	0.1	trace	***0.1***	na	na
Maximum Snow Depth (in.)	na	na	na	na	***trace***	na	***0***	***0***	na	na	na	na	na
Days With ≥ 1.0" Snow Depth	na	na	na	***0***	0	0	0	0	0	***0***	na	na	na

Divide *Silver Bow County* Elevation: 5,350 ft. Latitude: 45° 45' N Longitude: 112° 45' W

	JAN	FEB	MAR	APR	MAY	JUN	JUL	AUG	SEP	OCT	NOV	DEC	YEAR
Mean Maximum Temp. (°F)	32.5	36.7	44.5	52.9	61.8	70.7	80.5	78.8	68.4	56.1	41.0	31.0	54.6
Mean Temp. (°F)	21.1	24.7	33.0	40.1	48.4	56.2	63.5	61.8	52.5	41.8	29.8	20.4	41.1
Mean Minimum Temp. (°F)	9.7	12.3	21.4	27.1	35.0	41.5	46.4	44.7	36.6	27.5	18.5	9.8	27.5
Extreme Maximum Temp. (°F)	58	59	70	80	89	96	101	96	90	82	71	59	101
Extreme Minimum Temp. (°F)	-37	-35	-18	0	16	26	24	26	8	-9	-19	-35	-37
Days Maximum Temp. ≥ 90°F	0	0	0	0	0	0	3	2	0	0	0	0	5
Days Maximum Temp. ≤ 32°F	13	8	3	0	0	0	0	0	0	1	6	15	46
Days Minimum Temp. ≤ 32°F	29	27	28	22	10	2	0	1	8	23	26	29	205
Days Minimum Temp. ≤ 0°F	6	4	1	0	0	0	0	0	0	0	2	6	19
Heating Degree Days (base 65°F)	1,354	1,135	985	742	509	265	95	120	369	712	1,051	***1,382***	***8,719***
Cooling Degree Days (base 65°F)	0	0	0	0	1	9	54	28	2	0	0	***0***	***94***
Mean Precipitation (in.)	0.35	0.37	0.65	0.89	1.93	2.18	1.16	1.19	1.08	0.70	0.55	0.44	11.49
Extreme Maximum Daily Precip. (in.)	0.70	1.25	0.45	0.96	1.60	***1.50***	1.08	0.88	1.63	0.92	0.68	0.90	***1.63***
Days With ≥ 0.1" Precipitation	1	1	2	3	5	6	3	4	3	2	2	1	33
Days With ≥ 0.5" Precipitation	0	0	0	0	1	1	1	1	0	0	0	0	4
Days With ≥ 1.0" Precipitation	0	0	0	0	0	0	0	0	0	0	0	0	0
Mean Snowfall (in.)	3.9	3.1	4.1	1.6	0.1	0.0	0.0	0.1	0.2	0.9	2.6	3.8	20.4
Maximum Snow Depth (in.)	14	13	10	5	5	0	0	0	2	5	8	9	14
Days With ≥ 1.0" Snow Depth	14	7	3	1	0	0	0	0	0	0	5	13	43

Drummond *Granite County* Elevation: 4,000 ft. Latitude: 46° 38' N Longitude: 113° 12' W

	JAN	FEB	MAR	APR	MAY	JUN	JUL	AUG	SEP	OCT	NOV	DEC	YEAR
Mean Maximum Temp. (°F)	32.8	38.3	49.0	58.7	67.3	74.9	84.9	83.9	72.9	58.4	41.2	30.6	57.7
Mean Temp. (°F)	22.9	26.9	35.7	43.3	51.2	58.4	65.0	63.6	54.7	43.4	30.6	21.1	43.1
Mean Minimum Temp. (°F)	13.0	15.5	22.4	27.9	35.0	41.8	45.0	43.3	36.3	28.4	20.1	11.6	28.4
Extreme Maximum Temp. (°F)	57	67	78	83	93	97	104	101	96	83	73	59	104
Extreme Minimum Temp. (°F)	-33	-39	-23	-2	9	20	27	27	14	-7	-22	-43	-43
Days Maximum Temp. ≥ 90°F	0	0	0	0	0	2	10	9	1	0	0	0	22
Days Maximum Temp. ≤ 32°F	13	6	1	0	0	0	0	0	0	0	6	16	42
Days Minimum Temp. ≤ 32°F	30	27	28	22	11	2	0	1	9	21	27	30	208
Days Minimum Temp. ≤ 0°F	6	3	1	0	0	0	0	0	0	0	2	6	18
Heating Degree Days (base 65°F)	1,299	1,070	902	644	423	208	67	86	308	663	1,024	1,354	8,048
Cooling Degree Days (base 65°F)	0	0	0	0	2	17	75	49	4	0	0	0	147
Mean Precipitation (in.)	0.67	0.60	0.74	0.97	1.96	1.89	1.19	1.20	1.09	0.82	0.78	0.73	12.64
Extreme Maximum Daily Precip. (in.)	0.75	0.62	0.50	0.96	1.41	1.42	1.43	1.52	1.33	1.26	0.93	0.95	1.52
Days With ≥ 0.1" Precipitation	2	2	3	3	5	5	3	4	3	3	2	2	37
Days With ≥ 0.5" Precipitation	0	0	0	0	1	1	1	0	0	0	0	0	3
Days With ≥ 1.0" Precipitation	0	0	0	0	0	0	0	0	0	0	0	0	0
Mean Snowfall (in.)	6.5	5.3	5.6	2.4	2.2	0.5	0.0	0.1	0.5	1.0	5.3	6.7	36.1
Maximum Snow Depth (in.)	20	16	11	4	2	trace	0	trace	trace	4	8	31	31
Days With ≥ 1.0" Snow Depth	20	13	6	0	0	0	0	0	0	0	7	17	63

Ekalaka *Carter County* Elevation: 3,424 ft. Latitude: 45° 53' N Longitude: 104° 33' W

	JAN	FEB	MAR	APR	MAY	JUN	JUL	AUG	SEP	OCT	NOV	DEC	YEAR
Mean Maximum Temp. (°F)	32.1	35.6	45.1	57.6	67.7	76.6	85.7	84.1	72.5	58.0	43.1	32.4	57.5
Mean Temp. (°F)	21.5	25.0	33.3	44.4	54.3	63.3	71.2	69.7	58.5	45.4	32.2	21.7	45.1
Mean Minimum Temp. (°F)	10.7	14.4	21.5	31.1	40.9	50.0	56.7	55.3	44.5	32.9	21.3	11.0	32.5
Extreme Maximum Temp. (°F)	65	66	75	87	97	105	105	102	98	87	77	66	105
Extreme Minimum Temp. (°F)	-35	-35	-28	-6	19	31	38	29	15	0	-25	-43	-43
Days Maximum Temp. ≥ 90°F	0	0	0	0	0	3	10	9	2	0	0	0	24
Days Maximum Temp. ≤ 32°F	13	10	5	1	0	0	0	0	0	1	7	13	50
Days Minimum Temp. ≤ 32°F	30	27	27	17	5	0	0	0	3	14	26	30	179
Days Minimum Temp. ≤ 0°F	8	5	2	0	0	0	0	0	0	0	2	7	24
Heating Degree Days (base 65°F)	1,345	1,124	975	612	339	120	22	35	233	601	978	1,336	7,720
Cooling Degree Days (base 65°F)	0	0	0	1	13	78	221	187	45	1	0	0	546
Mean Precipitation (in.)	0.54	0.51	1.02	1.69	2.58	2.73	1.95	1.26	1.41	1.51	0.73	0.56	16.49
Extreme Maximum Daily Precip. (in.)	1.23	0.93	1.23	1.96	2.97	2.88	2.35	2.07	1.94	2.34	2.38	0.55	2.97
Days With ≥ 0.1" Precipitation	2	1	3	4	6	6	4	3	3	4	2	1	39
Days With ≥ 0.5" Precipitation	0	0	0	1	1	2	1	1	1	1	0	0	8
Days With ≥ 1.0" Precipitation	0	0	0	0	0	0	0	0	0	0	0	0	0
Mean Snowfall (in.)	na	na	na	3.1	1.4	0.0	0.0	0.0	0.1	***2.0***	na	na	na
Maximum Snow Depth (in.)	na	na	na	na	na	na	na	na	na	na	na	na	na
Days With ≥ 1.0" Snow Depth	na	na	na	2	0	0	0	0	0	***1***	na	na	na

The period of record for all cooperative weather station data is 1980 – 2009. See User Guide for detailed explanation of data.

Eureka Ranger Stn *Lincoln County* Elevation: 2,532 ft. Latitude: 48° 54' N Longitude: 115° 04' W

	JAN	FEB	MAR	APR	MAY	JUN	JUL	AUG	SEP	OCT	NOV	DEC	YEAR
Mean Maximum Temp. (°F)	31.1	37.9	48.6	59.2	68.9	75.8	85.0	84.5	73.3	57.1	40.4	29.8	57.6
Mean Temp. (°F)	24.4	28.9	37.7	46.1	54.9	61.5	68.1	67.0	57.5	45.0	33.5	24.0	45.7
Mean Minimum Temp. (°F)	17.6	19.9	26.9	33.0	40.9	47.2	51.2	49.4	41.6	32.9	26.5	18.1	33.8
Extreme Maximum Temp. (°F)	55	66	78	89	94	98	105	105	97	86	68	55	105
Extreme Minimum Temp. (°F)	-33	-30	-14	14	22	30	36	32	18	0	-23	-30	-33
Days Maximum Temp. ≥ 90°F	0	0	0	0	1	3	11	10	2	0	0	0	27
Days Maximum Temp. ≤ 32°F	15	6	1	0	0	0	0	0	0	0	5	18	45
Days Minimum Temp. ≤ 32°F	28	25	23	14	4	0	0	0	3	15	21	28	161
Days Minimum Temp. ≤ 0°F	4	3	0	0	0	0	0	0	0	0	1	3	11
Heating Degree Days (base 65°F)	1,254	1,015	839	560	316	140	38	48	239	612	939	1,266	7,266
Cooling Degree Days (base 65°F)	0	0	0	0	10	42	141	117	19	0	0	0	329
Mean Precipitation (in.)	0.97	0.71	0.88	0.95	1.87	2.43	1.52	1.13	1.18	0.99	1.30	1.15	15.08
Extreme Maximum Daily Precip. (in.)	0.69	0.82	0.60	1.03	1.50	1.48	1.29	1.33	1.70	0.76	1.15	0.93	1.70
Days With ≥ 0.1" Precipitation	3	3	3	3	5	6	4	3	4	3	4	4	45
Days With ≥ 0.5" Precipitation	0	0	0	0	1	1	1	1	0	0	0	0	4
Days With ≥ 1.0" Precipitation	0	0	0	0	0	0	0	0	0	0	0	0	0
Mean Snowfall (in.)	8.4	5.3	3.6	0.9	0.2	0.0	0.0	0.0	0.0	0.5	5.0	10.8	34.7
Maximum Snow Depth (in.)	19	19	12	4	1	0	0	0	0	3	21	31	31
Days With ≥ 1.0" Snow Depth	20	12	4	0	0	0	0	0	0	0	5	16	57

Flatwillow 4 ENE *Petroleum County* Elevation: 3,138 ft. Latitude: 46° 51' N Longitude: 108° 19' W

	JAN	FEB	MAR	APR	MAY	JUN	JUL	AUG	SEP	OCT	NOV	DEC	YEAR
Mean Maximum Temp. (°F)	38.0	41.9	50.0	61.1	70.2	78.1	87.4	86.9	75.7	62.2	47.6	37.6	61.4
Mean Temp. (°F)	25.5	28.8	36.6	46.1	55.0	63.2	70.6	69.5	59.3	47.7	34.9	25.0	46.8
Mean Minimum Temp. (°F)	12.9	15.6	23.0	31.0	39.8	48.3	53.6	52.2	42.9	33.2	22.1	12.5	32.2
Extreme Maximum Temp. (°F)	72	76	80	90	96	104	107	105	102	92	79	68	107
Extreme Minimum Temp. (°F)	-42	-37	-25	-7	13	27	38	30	14	-8	-27	-40	-42
Days Maximum Temp. ≥ 90°F	0	0	0	0	1	3	13	13	4	0	0	0	34
Days Maximum Temp. ≤ 32°F	9	7	3	0	0	0	0	0	0	1	4	9	33
Days Minimum Temp. ≤ 32°F	29	26	26	17	6	0	0	0	2	14	24	29	173
Days Minimum Temp. ≤ 0°F	7	5	2	0	0	0	0	0	0	0	2	6	22
Heating Degree Days (base 65°F)	1,219	1,018	875	562	315	109	19	26	204	531	897	1,234	7,009
Cooling Degree Days (base 65°F)	0	0	0	0	11	62	197	174	39	2	0	0	485
Mean Precipitation (in.)	0.42	0.35	0.75	1.20	2.53	2.43	1.33	1.02	0.90	1.00	0.43	0.45	12.81
Extreme Maximum Daily Precip. (in.)	1.04	0.40	0.71	0.98	2.06	2.65	1.50	1.10	1.15	1.15	0.51	0.75	2.65
Days With ≥ 0.1" Precipitation	2	1	3	4	6	6	3	3	3	3	2	1	37
Days With ≥ 0.5" Precipitation	0	0	0	1	1	2	1	0	0	1	0	0	6
Days With ≥ 1.0" Precipitation	0	0	0	0	0	0	0	0	0	0	0	0	0
Mean Snowfall (in.)	5.1	4.4	5.1	2.0	0.7	0.0	0.0	0.0	0.4	1.9	3.5	5.8	28.9
Maximum Snow Depth (in.)	15	***11***	14	9	8	0	0	0	5	12	13	***18***	***18***
Days With ≥ 1.0" Snow Depth	9	6	5	2	0	0	0	0	0	1	4	9	36

Fort Assinniboine *Hill County* Elevation: 2,612 ft. Latitude: 48° 30' N Longitude: 109° 48' W

	JAN	FEB	MAR	APR	MAY	JUN	JUL	AUG	SEP	OCT	NOV	DEC	YEAR
Mean Maximum Temp. (°F)	30.0	35.5	46.1	59.8	69.6	77.6	86.6	85.6	73.7	59.8	43.2	31.7	58.3
Mean Temp. (°F)	19.3	24.0	33.8	45.8	55.4	63.3	70.3	69.0	58.2	45.8	32.1	20.9	44.8
Mean Minimum Temp. (°F)	8.5	12.4	21.4	31.6	41.1	49.0	53.9	52.3	42.6	31.8	20.9	9.9	31.3
Extreme Maximum Temp. (°F)	68	75	82	91	98	108	107	108	101	91	77	64	108
Extreme Minimum Temp. (°F)	-36	-38	-29	2	16	31	39	31	19	-21	-28	-44	-44
Days Maximum Temp. ≥ 90°F	0	0	0	0	1	3	12	12	3	0	0	0	31
Days Maximum Temp. ≤ 32°F	14	10	5	1	0	0	0	0	0	1	6	13	50
Days Minimum Temp. ≤ 32°F	29	26	27	16	4	0	0	0	3	16	25	29	175
Days Minimum Temp. ≤ 0°F	10	6	2	0	0	0	0	0	0	0	2	8	28
Heating Degree Days (base 65°F)	1,415	1,154	961	571	307	111	21	37	229	588	982	1,362	7,738
Cooling Degree Days (base 65°F)	0	0	0	1	16	66	191	167	32	1	0	0	474
Mean Precipitation (in.)	0.42	0.30	0.59	0.94	2.10	2.61	1.70	1.15	1.23	0.81	0.49	0.44	12.78
Extreme Maximum Daily Precip. (in.)	0.45	0.47	0.85	1.08	1.88	1.98	2.97	1.37	2.43	1.68	0.81	0.48	2.97
Days With ≥ 0.1" Precipitation	2	1	2	3	5	6	4	3	3	2	2	2	35
Days With ≥ 0.5" Precipitation	0	0	0	0	1	2	1	1	1	0	0	0	6
Days With ≥ 1.0" Precipitation	0	0	0	0	0	0	0	0	0	0	0	0	0
Mean Snowfall (in.)	6.9	5.0	4.0	1.3	0.5	0.0	0.0	0.0	trace	1.0	4.2	6.7	29.6
Maximum Snow Depth (in.)	18	15	11	6	10	0	0	0	trace	7	8	15	18
Days With ≥ 1.0" Snow Depth	22	16	9	1	0	0	0	0	0	1	7	15	71

Fort Peck Power Plant *Mccone County* Elevation: 2,068 ft. Latitude: 48° 01' N Longitude: 106° 24' W

	JAN	FEB	MAR	APR	MAY	JUN	JUL	AUG	SEP	OCT	NOV	DEC	YEAR
Mean Maximum Temp. (°F)	27.9	34.0	45.8	60.6	71.4	80.2	88.4	87.6	75.6	60.9	43.8	31.1	58.9
Mean Temp. (°F)	17.3	23.4	34.0	47.0	57.5	66.3	73.0	71.9	60.8	48.4	33.5	20.7	46.1
Mean Minimum Temp. (°F)	6.8	12.6	22.1	33.2	43.6	52.4	57.5	56.1	45.9	35.8	23.1	10.3	33.3
Extreme Maximum Temp. (°F)	58	69	79	91	100	107	108	107	103	89	78	63	108
Extreme Minimum Temp. (°F)	-34	-38	-28	5	19	28	41	33	15	-4	-24	-38	-38
Days Maximum Temp. ≥ 90°F	0	0	0	0	1	5	14	14	3	0	0	0	37
Days Maximum Temp. ≤ 32°F	17	11	5	0	0	0	0	0	0	0	6	14	53
Days Minimum Temp. ≤ 32°F	30	27	26	13	3	0	0	0	1	11	23	29	163
Days Minimum Temp. ≤ 0°F	10	6	2	0	0	0	0	0	0	0	2	8	28
Heating Degree Days (base 65°F)	1,473	1,171	954	537	248	65	8	17	173	510	939	1,367	7,462
Cooling Degree Days (base 65°F)	0	0	0	2	24	112	262	237	53	3	0	0	693
Mean Precipitation (in.)	0.27	0.19	0.40	0.88	1.88	2.34	2.08	1.24	0.90	0.89	0.31	0.31	11.69
Extreme Maximum Daily Precip. (in.)	0.38	0.49	1.13	1.19	2.06	2.60	2.64	2.70	1.17	1.76	0.48	0.52	2.70
Days With ≥ 0.1" Precipitation	1	1	1	2	4	6	4	3	3	2	1	1	29
Days With ≥ 0.5" Precipitation	0	0	0	1	1	2	1	1	0	0	0	0	6
Days With ≥ 1.0" Precipitation	0	0	0	0	0	0	0	0	0	0	0	0	0
Mean Snowfall (in.)	na	na	na	***0.0***	0.0	0.0	0.0	0.0	0.0	0.0	na	na	na
Maximum Snow Depth (in.)	na	na	na	na	na	na	na	na	na	na	na	na	na
Days With ≥ 1.0" Snow Depth	na	na	na	***0***	0	0	0	0	0	***0***	na	na	na

The period of record for all cooperative weather station data is 1980 – 2009. See User Guide for detailed explanation of data.

Gibson Dam *Lewis And Clark County* Elevation: 4,589 ft. Latitude: 47° 36' N Longitude: 112° 45' W

	JAN	FEB	MAR	APR	MAY	JUN	JUL	AUG	SEP	OCT	NOV	DEC	YEAR
Mean Maximum Temp. (°F)	35.5	37.5	43.0	51.6	60.7	68.1	78.0	77.2	67.1	55.2	41.9	34.0	54.1
Mean Temp. (°F)	25.4	26.8	32.1	40.1	48.0	54.9	62.1	60.8	52.4	43.1	32.4	24.6	41.9
Mean Minimum Temp. (°F)	15.2	16.0	21.3	28.4	35.3	41.6	46.2	44.4	37.7	31.0	22.9	15.2	29.6
Extreme Maximum Temp. (°F)	62	64	72	81	86	91	100	98	94	88	70	65	100
Extreme Minimum Temp. (°F)	-31	-39	-28	-11	15	28	30	26	9	-10	-21	-39	-39
Days Maximum Temp. ≥ 90°F	0	0	0	0	0	0	2	2	0	0	0	0	4
Days Maximum Temp. ≤ 32°F	10	7	5	1	0	0	0	0	0	1	5	11	40
Days Minimum Temp. ≤ 32°F	28	25	28	22	10	1	0	1	6	18	24	28	191
Days Minimum Temp. ≤ 0°F	6	5	2	0	0	0	0	0	0	0	2	6	21
Heating Degree Days (base 65°F)	1,221	1,074	1,013	743	521	303	121	146	374	670	971	1,246	8,403
Cooling Degree Days (base 65°F)	0	0	0	0	1	6	38	24	2	0	0	0	71
Mean Precipitation (in.)	0.65	0.74	0.90	1.56	2.67	3.03	1.47	1.64	1.52	1.01	0.78	0.69	16.66
Extreme Maximum Daily Precip. (in.)	0.65	0.71	0.72	1.55	2.66	2.23	3.37	2.02	2.05	0.80	0.91	0.55	3.37
Days With ≥ 0.1" Precipitation	2	3	3	4	6	7	4	4	4	3	3	3	46
Days With ≥ 0.5" Precipitation	0	0	0	1	1	2	1	1	1	0	0	0	7
Days With ≥ 1.0" Precipitation	0	0	0	0	1	0	0	0	0	0	0	0	1
Mean Snowfall (in.)	8.4	10.1	11.3	8.2	1.7	0.0	0.0	0.2	0.3	2.6	6.1	7.1	56.0
Maximum Snow Depth (in.)	14	22	***19***	14	10	0	0	0	14	8	9	16	***22***
Days With ≥ 1.0" Snow Depth	9	7	***6***	2	0	0	0	0	0	1	5	7	***37***

Glendive *Dawson County* Elevation: 2,076 ft. Latitude: 47° 06' N Longitude: 104° 43' W

	JAN	FEB	MAR	APR	MAY	JUN	JUL	AUG	SEP	OCT	NOV	DEC	YEAR
Mean Maximum Temp. (°F)	29.7	35.8	46.5	60.9	71.3	80.2	89.1	88.1	76.2	61.0	43.9	31.1	59.5
Mean Temp. (°F)	18.5	24.0	34.2	47.1	57.7	66.8	74.2	72.6	61.1	47.7	33.0	20.5	46.4
Mean Minimum Temp. (°F)	7.3	12.1	21.8	33.3	44.1	53.4	59.3	57.1	45.8	34.2	22.0	9.9	33.4
Extreme Maximum Temp. (°F)	64	71	81	93	102	110	111	109	106	94	80	63	111
Extreme Minimum Temp. (°F)	-41	-41	-28	2	20	35	38	36	22	0	-27	-42	-42
Days Maximum Temp. ≥ 90°F	0	0	0	0	1	6	16	15	5	0	0	0	43
Days Maximum Temp. ≤ 32°F	15	10	5	1	0	0	0	0	0	0	6	14	51
Days Minimum Temp. ≤ 32°F	30	27	27	14	2	0	0	0	2	12	26	30	170
Days Minimum Temp. ≤ 0°F	10	6	2	0	0	0	0	0	0	0	1	7	26
Heating Degree Days (base 65°F)	1,437	1,155	949	532	250	66	10	17	175	533	955	1,374	7,453
Cooling Degree Days (base 65°F)	0	0	0	2	32	126	302	260	63	3	0	0	788
Mean Precipitation (in.)	0.35	0.26	0.60	1.21	1.99	2.32	1.86	1.56	1.21	1.11	0.42	0.38	13.27
Extreme Maximum Daily Precip. (in.)	0.56	0.45	0.88	1.70	1.62	2.36	1.86	2.95	1.77	1.23	1.51	0.68	2.95
Days With ≥ 0.1" Precipitation	1	1	2	3	5	6	4	3	3	3	1	1	33
Days With ≥ 0.5" Precipitation	0	0	0	1	1	1	1	1	1	1	0	0	7
Days With ≥ 1.0" Precipitation	0	0	0	0	0	0	0	0	0	0	0	0	0
Mean Snowfall (in.)	4.6	3.9	3.3	1.5	0.4	0.0	0.0	0.0	trace	1.1	2.9	4.4	22.1
Maximum Snow Depth (in.)	15	13	9	6	9	0	0	0	trace	12	11	11	15
Days With ≥ 1.0" Snow Depth	21	15	7	1	0	0	0	0	0	1	6	16	67

Grass Range *Fergus County* Elevation: 3,490 ft. Latitude: 47° 02' N Longitude: 108° 48' W

	JAN	FEB	MAR	APR	MAY	JUN	JUL	AUG	SEP	OCT	NOV	DEC	YEAR
Mean Maximum Temp. (°F)	39.0	41.6	48.7	59.2	68.4	75.7	84.6	83.7	73.0	60.7	47.5	38.3	60.0
Mean Temp. (°F)	26.4	29.0	35.8	45.2	54.1	61.6	68.6	67.5	57.6	46.8	34.9	26.2	46.1
Mean Minimum Temp. (°F)	13.8	16.3	22.9	31.1	39.7	47.4	52.6	51.1	42.1	32.9	22.3	14.0	32.2
Extreme Maximum Temp. (°F)	74	73	77	94	97	103	104	105	99	90	82	70	105
Extreme Minimum Temp. (°F)	-38	-34	-23	-5	18	29	31	29	15	-9	-23	-39	-39
Days Maximum Temp. ≥ 90°F	0	0	0	0	1	3	9	8	2	0	0	0	23
Days Maximum Temp. ≤ 32°F	8	7	3	1	0	0	0	0	0	1	4	9	33
Days Minimum Temp. ≤ 32°F	28	26	26	17	5	0	0	0	3	14	25	29	173
Days Minimum Temp. ≤ 0°F	7	4	2	0	0	0	0	0	0	0	2	5	20
Heating Degree Days (base 65°F)	1,191	1,014	898	589	340	143	33	42	240	558	896	1,197	7,141
Cooling Degree Days (base 65°F)	0	0	0	1	9	47	151	125	25	1	0	0	359
Mean Precipitation (in.)	0.60	0.39	1.01	1.54	3.19	2.88	1.88	1.48	1.14	1.11	0.59	0.62	16.43
Extreme Maximum Daily Precip. (in.)	0.92	0.45	0.99	1.55	2.62	2.26	2.00	2.29	1.55	1.20	0.87	1.00	2.62
Days With ≥ 0.1" Precipitation	2	2	3	4	6	7	5	4	4	3	2	2	44
Days With ≥ 0.5" Precipitation	0	0	0	1	2	2	1	1	1	1	0	0	9
Days With ≥ 1.0" Precipitation	0	0	0	0	1	0	0	0	0	0	0	0	1
Mean Snowfall (in.)	7.8	6.3	10.5	5.3	0.7	0.0	0.0	trace	0.4	3.7	5.3	8.2	48.2
Maximum Snow Depth (in.)	***15***	na	***11***	***8***	***8***	***0***	***0***	***0***	***2***	***15***	***10***	na	na
Days With ≥ 1.0" Snow Depth	***12***	na	***5***	2	0	0	0	0	0	1	***6***	***12***	na

Hardin *Big Horn County* Elevation: 2,904 ft. Latitude: 45° 44' N Longitude: 107° 37' W

	JAN	FEB	MAR	APR	MAY	JUN	JUL	AUG	SEP	OCT	NOV	DEC	YEAR
Mean Maximum Temp. (°F)	38.0	43.8	53.6	63.8	73.8	83.1	92.0	91.1	79.4	64.9	48.8	37.4	64.1
Mean Temp. (°F)	25.4	30.2	39.2	48.5	58.2	66.9	74.3	72.9	62.0	49.3	35.6	24.8	49.0
Mean Minimum Temp. (°F)	12.7	16.6	24.8	33.2	42.6	50.8	56.6	54.5	44.6	33.6	22.4	12.1	33.7
Extreme Maximum Temp. (°F)	70	74	83	96	97	106	112	108	104	93	81	69	112
Extreme Minimum Temp. (°F)	-39	-32	-17	4	18	32	37	32	15	-13	-25	-47	-47
Days Maximum Temp. ≥ 90°F	0	0	0	0	2	8	20	19	6	0	0	0	55
Days Maximum Temp. ≤ 32°F	9	5	2	0	0	0	0	0	0	0	3	9	28
Days Minimum Temp. ≤ 32°F	29	26	24	13	3	0	0	0	2	13	24	29	163
Days Minimum Temp. ≤ 0°F	6	4	1	0	0	0	0	0	0	0	2	5	18
Heating Degree Days (base 65°F)	1,222	976	792	489	231	59	6	11	147	482	877	1,242	6,534
Cooling Degree Days (base 65°F)	0	0	0	2	25	125	302	265	64	2	0	0	785
Mean Precipitation (in.)	0.40	0.36	0.75	1.32	2.00	1.69	1.20	0.59	1.17	1.25	0.47	0.36	11.56
Extreme Maximum Daily Precip. (in.)	0.88	1.20	1.50	2.00	2.30	***1.92***	3.00	1.18	3.10	1.98	0.60	0.80	***3.10***
Days With ≥ 0.1" Precipitation	2	1	2	4	5	4	3	2	3	3	2	1	32
Days With ≥ 0.5" Precipitation	0	0	0	1	1	1	1	0	1	1	0	0	6
Days With ≥ 1.0" Precipitation	0	0	0	0	0	0	0	0	0	0	0	0	0
Mean Snowfall (in.)	***3.8***	na	na	***0.9***	trace	0.0	0.0	0.0	0.0	0.3	na	na	na
Maximum Snow Depth (in.)	na	na	na	na	na	na	***0***	***0***	na	na	na	na	na
Days With ≥ 1.0" Snow Depth	na	na	***2***	***0***	0	0	0	0	0	***0***	na	na	na

The period of record for all cooperative weather station data is 1980 – 2009. See User Guide for detailed explanation of data.

Hebgen Dam *Gallatin County* Elevation: 6,488 ft. Latitude: 44° 52' N Longitude: 111° 20' W

	JAN	FEB	MAR	APR	MAY	JUN	JUL	AUG	SEP	OCT	NOV	DEC	YEAR
Mean Maximum Temp. (°F)	22.7	27.9	38.4	47.9	59.3	69.1	78.5	77.9	67.4	51.4	33.7	22.1	49.7
Mean Temp. (°F)	13.0	16.4	26.0	35.7	45.9	54.0	61.5	60.5	51.8	39.7	25.9	13.7	37.0
Mean Minimum Temp. (°F)	3.2	4.8	13.5	23.3	32.3	38.9	44.5	43.1	36.1	27.9	18.0	5.2	24.2
Extreme Maximum Temp. (°F)	42	48	60	75	88	92	96	94	87	82	59	45	96
Extreme Minimum Temp. (°F)	-40	-42	-34	-13	13	20	29	28	12	-9	-17	-37	-42
Days Maximum Temp. ≥ 90°F	0	0	0	0	0	0	1	0	0	0	0	0	1
Days Maximum Temp. ≤ 32°F	27	18	7	1	0	0	0	0	0	1	13	27	94
Days Minimum Temp. ≤ 32°F	31	28	30	26	15	3	0	1	7	23	28	30	222
Days Minimum Temp. ≤ 0°F	12	10	5	0	0	0	0	0	0	0	2	11	40
Heating Degree Days (base 65°F)	1,608	1,369	1,205	873	588	324	121	141	391	777	1,168	1,586	10,151
Cooling Degree Days (base 65°F)	0	0	0	0	0	1	19	9	0	0	0	0	29
Mean Precipitation (in.)	2.71	2.31	2.29	1.98	3.03	2.94	2.00	1.56	1.59	1.93	2.49	2.87	27.70
Extreme Maximum Daily Precip. (in.)	1.17	1.03	1.27	2.01	1.38	1.53	1.54	1.20	1.21	2.10	1.12	0.89	2.10
Days With ≥ 0.1" Precipitation	9	7	7	6	8	8	6	4	4	5	8	9	81
Days With ≥ 0.5" Precipitation	1	1	1	1	2	2	1	1	1	1	1	1	14
Days With ≥ 1.0" Precipitation	0	0	0	0	0	0	0	0	0	0	0	0	0
Mean Snowfall (in.)	40.4	31.7	24.6	8.7	1.8	trace	0.0	0.0	0.1	4.2	24.7	44.0	180.2
Maximum Snow Depth (in.)	47	52	56	56	21	trace	0	0	1	10	22	36	56
Days With ≥ 1.0" Snow Depth	30	27	30	18	2	0	0	0	0	2	19	30	158

Hinsdale 4 SW *Valley County* Elevation: 2,674 ft. Latitude: 48° 21' N Longitude: 107° 09' W

	JAN	FEB	MAR	APR	MAY	JUN	JUL	AUG	SEP	OCT	NOV	DEC	YEAR
Mean Maximum Temp. (°F)	25.4	30.5	41.7	57.2	67.8	76.0	83.9	83.2	71.0	56.0	39.3	26.4	54.9
Mean Temp. (°F)	16.8	21.8	31.9	45.2	55.4	63.8	70.5	69.6	58.5	45.2	30.6	17.9	43.9
Mean Minimum Temp. (°F)	8.2	13.2	22.1	33.2	43.0	51.4	57.1	55.9	45.9	34.3	21.9	9.3	32.9
Extreme Maximum Temp. (°F)	58	69	78	90	101	107	105	106	101	87	76	62	107
Extreme Minimum Temp. (°F)	-33	-34	-26	2	22	28	41	37	23	-4	-25	-37	-37
Days Maximum Temp. ≥ 90°F	0	0	0	0	1	3	8	8	2	0	0	0	22
Days Maximum Temp. ≤ 32°F	17	14	7	1	0	0	0	0	0	1	8	17	65
Days Minimum Temp. ≤ 32°F	27	25	25	14	3	0	0	0	2	12	24	27	159
Days Minimum Temp. ≤ 0°F	9	6	2	0	0	0	0	0	0	0	2	8	27
Heating Degree Days (base 65°F)	1,492	1,214	1,019	587	308	107	19	37	232	611	1,027	1,460	8,113
Cooling Degree Days (base 65°F)	0	0	0	1	18	76	199	185	43	2	0	0	524
Mean Precipitation (in.)	0.45	0.29	0.68	1.22	2.78	3.07	1.77	1.40	1.35	1.03	0.56	0.40	15.00
Extreme Maximum Daily Precip. (in.)	0.50	0.43	0.79	1.53	3.27	2.28	2.87	2.85	2.35	1.28	0.81	0.58	3.27
Days With ≥ 0.1" Precipitation	1	1	2	3	5	6	4	3	3	2	2	1	33
Days With ≥ 0.5" Precipitation	0	0	0	1	2	2	1	1	1	0	0	0	8
Days With ≥ 1.0" Precipitation	0	0	0	0	1	1	0	0	0	0	0	0	2
Mean Snowfall (in.)	na	na	na	2.1	1.4	0.0	0.0	0.0	0.1	1.3	na	na	na
Maximum Snow Depth (in.)	na	na	na	na	na	na	na	na	na	na	na	na	na
Days With ≥ 1.0" Snow Depth	na	na	na	0	0	0	0	0	0	0	na	na	na

Huntley Experiment Stn *Yellowstone County* Elevation: 2,990 ft. Latitude: 45° 56' N Longitude: 108° 15' W

	JAN	FEB	MAR	APR	MAY	JUN	JUL	AUG	SEP	OCT	NOV	DEC	YEAR
Mean Maximum Temp. (°F)	37.3	42.0	50.7	61.1	69.8	78.1	87.4	86.6	75.2	61.5	48.0	36.9	61.2
Mean Temp. (°F)	24.4	28.5	36.3	46.2	54.9	63.0	70.3	68.8	58.1	45.8	34.0	23.9	46.2
Mean Minimum Temp. (°F)	11.5	14.9	21.8	31.2	40.0	47.9	53.0	50.9	41.0	30.0	20.0	10.8	31.1
Extreme Maximum Temp. (°F)	67	74	82	89	96	105	109	105	102	93	81	68	109
Extreme Minimum Temp. (°F)	-35	-29	-29	0	15	27	36	32	17	-15	-31	-47	-47
Days Maximum Temp. ≥ 90°F	0	0	0	0	1	4	13	13	3	0	0	0	34
Days Maximum Temp. ≤ 32°F	9	7	3	0	0	0	0	0	0	1	4	9	33
Days Minimum Temp. ≤ 32°F	30	27	27	17	5	0	0	0	4	19	27	29	185
Days Minimum Temp. ≤ 0°F	7	5	2	0	0	0	0	0	0	0	2	6	22
Heating Degree Days (base 65°F)	1,252	1,026	883	559	319	119	23	33	232	589	922	1,269	7,226
Cooling Degree Days (base 65°F)	0	0	0	1	13	66	193	157	31	1	0	0	462
Mean Precipitation (in.)	0.40	0.46	0.97	1.42	2.33	2.05	1.60	0.78	1.31	1.18	0.55	0.49	13.54
Extreme Maximum Daily Precip. (in.)	0.55	1.22	1.21	1.04	1.82	1.68	1.67	1.47	1.57	2.00	0.77	0.41	2.00
Days With ≥ 0.1" Precipitation	2	1	3	4	6	6	4	2	4	3	2	2	39
Days With ≥ 0.5" Precipitation	0	0	0	1	1	1	1	0	1	1	0	0	6
Days With ≥ 1.0" Precipitation	0	0	0	0	0	0	0	0	0	0	0	0	0
Mean Snowfall (in.)	6.2	5.0	7.8	2.3	0.6	0.0	0.0	0.0	0.6	2.1	4.7	6.9	36.2
Maximum Snow Depth (in.)	15	11	15	6	9	0	0	0	7	8	14	18	18
Days With ≥ 1.0" Snow Depth	16	9	7	1	0	0	0	0	0	1	7	14	55

Libby Dam Base *Lincoln County* Elevation: 2,109 ft. Latitude: 48° 25' N Longitude: 115° 19' W

	JAN	FEB	MAR	APR	MAY	JUN	JUL	AUG	SEP	OCT	NOV	DEC	YEAR
Mean Maximum Temp. (°F)	34.3	39.8	48.6	58.8	68.0	75.1	84.8	83.9	74.0	58.0	42.6	34.0	58.5
Mean Temp. (°F)	27.2	30.2	36.8	44.9	53.3	60.1	67.1	65.8	57.4	45.3	34.9	27.6	45.9
Mean Minimum Temp. (°F)	20.1	20.6	25.0	31.0	38.5	45.0	49.3	47.7	40.8	32.5	27.2	21.1	33.2
Extreme Maximum Temp. (°F)	55	67	76	84	97	99	104	106	100	87	69	55	106
Extreme Minimum Temp. (°F)	-17	-15	-6	10	19	31	26	35	22	3	-9	-21	-21
Days Maximum Temp. ≥ 90°F	0	0	0	0	0	2	10	9	1	0	0	0	22
Days Maximum Temp. ≤ 32°F	11	5	1	0	0	0	0	0	0	0	2	11	30
Days Minimum Temp. ≤ 32°F	30	27	28	19	6	0	0	0	2	15	23	29	179
Days Minimum Temp. ≤ 0°F	2	1	0	0	0	0	0	0	0	0	0	1	4
Heating Degree Days (base 65°F)	1,165	977	866	595	361	171	49	60	235	605	897	1,153	7,134
Cooling Degree Days (base 65°F)	0	0	0	0	4	31	119	94	14	0	0	0	262
Mean Precipitation (in.)	1.43	1.06	1.11	1.13	1.82	2.16	1.22	0.87	1.08	1.53	1.88	1.64	16.93
Extreme Maximum Daily Precip. (in.)	0.87	0.92	0.95	1.30	1.80	1.83	1.60	1.05	0.80	0.80	1.75	0.92	1.83
Days With ≥ 0.1" Precipitation	5	4	4	4	6	6	3	3	4	5	6	6	56
Days With ≥ 0.5" Precipitation	0	0	0	0	1	1	1	0	0	1	1	0	5
Days With ≥ 1.0" Precipitation	0	0	0	0	0	0	0	0	0	0	0	0	0
Mean Snowfall (in.)	na	na	na	trace	0.0	0.0	0.0	0.0	0.0	0.1	1.6	na	na
Maximum Snow Depth (in.)	18	14	na	1	trace	0	0	0	0	1	na	na	na
Days With ≥ 1.0" Snow Depth	17	7	na	0	0	0	0	0	0	0	2	na	na

The period of record for all cooperative weather station data is 1980 – 2009. See User Guide for detailed explanation of data.

Lindbergh Lake *Missoula County* Elevation: 4,319 ft. Latitude: 47° 25' N Longitude: 113° 43' W

	JAN	FEB	MAR	APR	MAY	JUN	JUL	AUG	SEP	OCT	NOV	DEC	YEAR
Mean Maximum Temp. (°F)	30.2	34.8	42.1	51.2	60.9	68.4	77.6	77.3	66.9	52.3	36.9	28.6	52.3
Mean Temp. (°F)	22.8	25.9	32.7	40.4	49.3	56.4	63.6	62.8	53.7	42.2	30.4	22.0	41.9
Mean Minimum Temp. (°F)	15.4	17.0	23.5	29.6	37.6	44.3	49.7	48.2	40.4	32.1	23.8	15.3	31.4
Extreme Maximum Temp. (°F)	56	61	71	81	87	91	98	96	91	83	65	53	98
Extreme Minimum Temp. (°F)	-34	-40	-16	4	22	29	35	28	17	-4	-14	-37	-40
Days Maximum Temp. ≥ 90°F	0	0	0	0	0	0	2	1	0	0	0	0	3
Days Maximum Temp. ≤ 32°F	17	9	3	0	0	0	0	0	0	1	9	20	59
Days Minimum Temp. ≤ 32°F	30	28	29	21	7	0	0	0	4	16	27	31	193
Days Minimum Temp. ≤ 0°F	4	3	1	0	0	0	0	0	0	0	1	3	12
Heating Degree Days (base 65°F)	1,300	1,100	994	730	481	262	97	109	339	699	1,031	1,329	8,471
Cooling Degree Days (base 65°F)	0	0	0	0	1	10	62	46	6	0	0	0	125
Mean Precipitation (in.)	2.63	2.00	1.81	1.68	2.22	2.39	1.17	1.26	1.59	1.93	2.82	2.50	24.00
Extreme Maximum Daily Precip. (in.)	2.43	1.11	0.74	1.11	1.53	1.30	1.30	1.13	1.33	2.30	1.31	1.28	2.43
Days With ≥ 0.1" Precipitation	9	6	7	5	7	7	4	4	5	6	8	8	76
Days With ≥ 0.5" Precipitation	1	1	0	1	1	1	1	0	1	1	1	1	10
Days With ≥ 1.0" Precipitation	0	0	0	0	0	0	0	0	0	0	0	0	0
Mean Snowfall (in.)	31.4	21.3	18.1	7.7	1.8	0.4	0.0	trace	0.1	4.0	20.8	27.7	133.3
Maximum Snow Depth (in.)	50	56	65	48	24	2	0	0	trace	10	29	47	65
Days With ≥ 1.0" Snow Depth	31	28	30	17	1	0	0	0	0	2	17	30	156

Livingston Mission Field *Park County* Elevation: 4,652 ft. Latitude: 45° 42' N Longitude: 110° 27' W

	JAN	FEB	MAR	APR	MAY	JUN	JUL	AUG	SEP	OCT	NOV	DEC	YEAR
Mean Maximum Temp. (°F)	37.6	40.8	48.0	56.5	65.7	74.3	85.2	84.5	73.2	59.4	45.0	36.8	58.9
Mean Temp. (°F)	28.3	30.7	36.6	43.8	52.1	59.9	68.1	66.7	57.2	46.4	35.5	27.9	46.1
Mean Minimum Temp. (°F)	19.0	20.5	25.2	31.1	38.4	45.6	50.9	48.9	41.2	33.4	26.1	19.0	33.3
Extreme Maximum Temp. (°F)	67	70	75	83	88	99	104	102	99	88	77	62	104
Extreme Minimum Temp. (°F)	-32	-33	-19	-2	11	27	33	28	10	-11	-21	-41	-41
Days Maximum Temp. ≥ 90°F	0	0	0	0	0	2	10	9	2	0	0	0	23
Days Maximum Temp. ≤ 32°F	9	6	3	1	0	0	0	0	0	1	5	10	35
Days Minimum Temp. ≤ 32°F	26	23	24	17	7	0	0	0	4	14	20	26	161
Days Minimum Temp. ≤ 0°F	5	3	1	0	0	0	0	0	0	0	1	4	14
Heating Degree Days (base 65°F)	1,130	963	873	629	395	174	36	47	249	570	877	1,144	7,087
Cooling Degree Days (base 65°F)	0	0	0	0	3	28	139	107	23	2	0	0	302
Mean Precipitation (in.)	0.58	0.53	0.85	1.72	2.73	2.41	1.48	1.12	1.24	1.24	0.59	0.52	15.01
Extreme Maximum Daily Precip. (in.)	1.60	0.52	1.11	1.19	2.17	2.90	2.04	1.12	1.38	1.74	0.59	1.15	2.90
Days With ≥ 0.1" Precipitation	2	2	3	6	6	6	4	3	3	4	2	2	43
Days With ≥ 0.5" Precipitation	0	0	0	1	2	1	1	0	1	0	0	0	6
Days With ≥ 1.0" Precipitation	0	0	0	0	0	0	0	0	0	0	0	0	0
Mean Snowfall (in.)	na	na	na	na	na	na	***trace***	na	na	na	na	na	na
Maximum Snow Depth (in.)	na	na	na	na	na	na	***trace***	na	na	na	na	na	na
Days With ≥ 1.0" Snow Depth	na	na	na	na	na	na	***0***	na	na	na	na	na	na

Medicine Lake 3 SE *Sheridan County* Elevation: 1,952 ft. Latitude: 48° 29' N Longitude: 104° 27' W

	JAN	FEB	MAR	APR	MAY	JUN	JUL	AUG	SEP	OCT	NOV	DEC	YEAR
Mean Maximum Temp. (°F)	22.6	29.5	41.2	58.0	68.9	77.3	84.3	84.1	72.5	57.8	39.5	25.9	55.1
Mean Temp. (°F)	11.9	18.5	29.6	44.3	55.3	64.0	70.0	69.1	57.6	44.4	28.7	15.3	42.4
Mean Minimum Temp. (°F)	1.1	7.4	18.1	30.5	41.8	50.8	55.7	54.0	42.7	31.0	17.9	4.7	29.6
Extreme Maximum Temp. (°F)	60	68	75	92	101	107	107	104	101	91	74	57	107
Extreme Minimum Temp. (°F)	-40	-40	-32	-4	8	29	37	34	17	-2	-31	-46	-46
Days Maximum Temp. ≥ 90°F	0	0	0	0	1	3	8	9	2	0	0	0	23
Days Maximum Temp. ≤ 32°F	20	14	7	1	0	0	0	0	0	1	8	18	69
Days Minimum Temp. ≤ 32°F	31	27	28	17	5	0	0	0	3	17	28	31	187
Days Minimum Temp. ≤ 0°F	14	9	3	0	0	0	0	0	0	0	3	11	40
Heating Degree Days (base 65°F)	1,645	1,309	1,089	616	312	105	23	39	246	632	1,083	1,536	8,635
Cooling Degree Days (base 65°F)	0	0	0	1	20	83	185	172	31	1	0	0	493
Mean Precipitation (in.)	0.38	0.16	0.46	0.85	1.68	2.61	2.45	1.37	1.10	0.76	0.39	0.35	12.56
Extreme Maximum Daily Precip. (in.)	0.59	0.30	0.82	1.68	1.38	2.60	2.65	***1.17***	1.33	1.40	0.95	0.54	***2.65***
Days With ≥ 0.1" Precipitation	1	1	1	3	5	6	5	3	3	2	1	1	32
Days With ≥ 0.5" Precipitation	0	0	0	0	1	1	1	1	1	0	0	0	5
Days With ≥ 1.0" Precipitation	0	0	0	0	0	0	1	0	0	0	0	0	1
Mean Snowfall (in.)	6.3	2.3	3.2	0.5	0.1	0.0	0.0	0.0	trace	0.9	2.5	***5.1***	***20.9***
Maximum Snow Depth (in.)	29	26	25	6	11	0	0	0	3	10	15	18	29
Days With ≥ 1.0" Snow Depth	***22***	12	7	1	0	0	0	0	0	1	6	16	***65***

Millegan 14 SE *Meagher County* Elevation: 4,970 ft. Latitude: 46° 53' N Longitude: 111° 10' W

	JAN	FEB	MAR	APR	MAY	JUN	JUL	AUG	SEP	OCT	NOV	DEC	YEAR
Mean Maximum Temp. (°F)	***33.2***	***36.4***	***43.9***	***53.4***	***62.5***	***70.8***	***79.7***	79.0	***68.3***	55.1	41.0	***32.6***	***54.7***
Mean Temp. (°F)	***22.2***	***24.3***	***31.6***	***40.1***	***48.6***	***56.1***	***63.1***	61.7	***52.4***	41.4	29.9	***21.6***	***41.1***
Mean Minimum Temp. (°F)	***11.1***	***12.1***	***19.3***	***26.7***	***34.6***	***41.3***	***46.3***	44.4	***36.5***	27.7	18.7	***10.5***	***27.4***
Extreme Maximum Temp. (°F)	***59***	***67***	***70***	***80***	***86***	***95***	***97***	***95***	***92***	***86***	***70***	***60***	***97***
Extreme Minimum Temp. (°F)	***-37***	***-44***	***-21***	***-7***	***15***	***25***	***30***	***22***	***10***	***-19***	***-24***	***-39***	***-44***
Days Maximum Temp. ≥ 90°F	***0***	***0***	***0***	***0***	***0***	***0***	***3***	2	***0***	0	0	***0***	***5***
Days Maximum Temp. ≤ 32°F	***12***	***9***	***4***	***1***	***0***	***0***	***0***	0	***0***	1	6	***13***	***46***
Days Minimum Temp. ≤ 32°F	***31***	***27***	***29***	***24***	***12***	***2***	***0***	1	***8***	22	27	***30***	***213***
Days Minimum Temp. ≤ 0°F	***7***	***5***	***2***	***0***	***0***	***0***	***0***	0	***0***	0	3	***6***	***23***
Heating Degree Days (base 65°F)	***1,321***	***1,144***	***1,029***	***740***	***503***	***271***	***106***	124	***374***	724	1,047	***1,340***	***8,723***
Cooling Degree Days (base 65°F)	***0***	***0***	***0***	***0***	***0***	***9***	***52***	30	***3***	0	0	***0***	***94***
Mean Precipitation (in.)	***0.83***	***0.60***	***1.23***	***1.71***	***2.58***	***3.14***	***2.10***	1.57	***1.46***	1.19	0.88	***0.96***	***18.25***
Extreme Maximum Daily Precip. (in.)	***0.63***	***0.58***	***1.81***	***1.66***	***1.64***	***2.40***	***1.57***	***1.49***	***1.22***	***1.40***	***1.33***	***2.04***	***2.40***
Days With ≥ 0.1" Precipitation	***2***	***2***	***4***	***5***	***7***	***7***	***5***	5	***4***	3	3	***3***	***50***
Days With ≥ 0.5" Precipitation	***0***	***0***	***0***	***1***	***1***	***2***	***1***	1	***1***	1	0	***0***	***8***
Days With ≥ 1.0" Precipitation	***0***	***0***	***0***	***0***	***0***	***0***	***0***	0	***0***	0	0	***0***	***0***
Mean Snowfall (in.)	***19.3***	***17.1***	***23.7***	***16.2***	***4.4***	***1.2***	***0.0***	0.2	***1.2***	9.2	16.8	***19.4***	***128.7***
Maximum Snow Depth (in.)	***30***	***29***	***37***	***18***	***8***	***10***	***0***	***1***	***2***	***28***	***26***	***50***	***50***
Days With ≥ 1.0" Snow Depth	***29***	***24***	***20***	***7***	***1***	***0***	***0***	0	***0***	4	15	***24***	***124***

The period of record for all cooperative weather station data is 1980 – 2009. See User Guide for detailed explanation of data.

Moorhead 9 NE *Powder River County* Elevation: 3,220 ft. Latitude: 45° 11' N Longitude: 105° 45' W

	JAN	FEB	MAR	APR	MAY	JUN	JUL	AUG	SEP	OCT	NOV	DEC	YEAR
Mean Maximum Temp. (°F)	35.7	40.6	50.5	60.7	70.3	79.7	89.4	88.3	76.8	61.7	46.1	35.1	61.3
Mean Temp. (°F)	23.6	28.1	37.1	46.5	55.6	64.8	72.4	70.9	60.0	47.1	33.8	23.2	46.9
Mean Minimum Temp. (°F)	11.3	15.5	23.3	32.2	40.9	49.9	55.4	53.5	43.2	32.5	21.5	11.2	32.5
Extreme Maximum Temp. (°F)	66	73	83	89	96	106	109	107	101	94	77	66	109
Extreme Minimum Temp. (°F)	-37	-40	-27	2	17	32	38	31	9	-13	-23	-48	-48
Days Maximum Temp. ≥ 90°F	0	0	0	0	1	5	16	15	5	0	0	0	42
Days Maximum Temp. ≤ 32°F	10	7	3	1	0	0	0	0	0	0	4	11	36
Days Minimum Temp. ≤ 32°F	30	27	26	14	4	0	0	0	3	15	26	30	175
Days Minimum Temp. ≤ 0°F	7	4	1	0	0	0	0	0	0	0	2	6	20
Heating Degree Days (base 65°F)	1,279	1,037	860	551	298	89	11	18	189	548	929	1,291	7,100
Cooling Degree Days (base 65°F)	0	0	0	1	13	91	248	209	47	1	0	0	610
Mean Precipitation (in.)	0.28	0.30	0.66	1.35	2.25	2.21	1.54	1.03	1.02	1.05	0.40	0.32	12.41
Extreme Maximum Daily Precip. (in.)	0.39	0.40	0.78	2.01	1.94	1.47	3.35	1.33	1.21	1.03	0.46	0.50	3.35
Days With ≥ 0.1" Precipitation	1	1	2	4	5	5	4	3	3	3	1	1	33
Days With ≥ 0.5" Precipitation	0	0	0	1	1	1	1	1	1	0	0	0	6
Days With ≥ 1.0" Precipitation	0	0	0	0	0	0	0	0	0	0	0	0	0
Mean Snowfall (in.)	5.0	3.7	6.0	3.5	0.8	0.0	0.0	0.0	0.3	1.5	3.0	5.0	28.8
Maximum Snow Depth (in.)	12	11	14	24	4	0	0	0	8	9	8	13	24
Days With ≥ 1.0" Snow Depth	16	12	5	2	0	0	0	0	0	1	6	13	55

Opheim 10 N *Valley County* Elevation: 2,979 ft. Latitude: 49° 00' N Longitude: 106° 23' W

	JAN	FEB	MAR	APR	MAY	JUN	JUL	AUG	SEP	OCT	NOV	DEC	YEAR
Mean Maximum Temp. (°F)	22.7	26.8	38.8	55.7	67.0	75.1	81.7	81.9	70.1	55.0	37.5	24.3	53.1
Mean Temp. (°F)	11.7	16.1	27.4	41.2	52.0	60.5	65.9	65.2	54.1	41.3	26.4	13.2	39.6
Mean Minimum Temp. (°F)	0.7	5.3	16.0	26.7	36.9	45.8	50.1	48.5	38.0	27.5	15.4	2.0	26.1
Extreme Maximum Temp. (°F)	56	64	73	91	98	105	102	104	98	89	76	55	105
Extreme Minimum Temp. (°F)	-44	-46	-37	-12	8	20	33	25	2	-19	-33	-47	-47
Days Maximum Temp. ≥ 90°F	0	0	0	0	0	2	5	7	1	0	0	0	15
Days Maximum Temp. ≤ 32°F	21	16	9	1	0	0	0	0	0	2	9	20	78
Days Minimum Temp. ≤ 32°F	31	27	30	22	10	1	0	1	8	22	28	30	210
Days Minimum Temp. ≤ 0°F	14	10	4	0	0	0	0	0	0	0	4	13	45
Heating Degree Days (base 65°F)	1,649	1,376	1,160	707	405	170	62	80	334	728	1,151	1,603	9,425
Cooling Degree Days (base 65°F)	0	0	0	0	8	40	99	94	14	0	0	0	255
Mean Precipitation (in.)	0.25	0.20	0.34	0.66	1.95	3.01	2.28	*1.21*	1.34	0.69	0.25	0.23	*12.41*
Extreme Maximum Daily Precip. (in.)	*0.61*	0.25	1.64	2.10	2.44	2.50	2.96	*1.38*	1.64	0.90	0.80	0.30	*2.96*
Days With ≥ 0.1" Precipitation	1	1	1	2	5	7	5	*4*	3	2	1	1	*33*
Days With ≥ 0.5" Precipitation	0	0	0	0	1	2	1	*1*	1	0	0	0	*6*
Days With ≥ 1.0" Precipitation	0	0	0	0	0	0	0	*0*	0	0	0	0	*0*
Mean Snowfall (in.)	*2.3*	na	*2.6*	*0.9*	0.7	trace	0.0	0.0	trace	*0.4*	*1.7*	*3.4*	na
Maximum Snow Depth (in.)	na	na	na	*7*	*6*	*trace*	*0*	*0*	*1*	na	na	na	na
Days With ≥ 1.0" Snow Depth	na	*8*	*4*	0	0	0	0	0	0	*0*	*3*	na	na

Ridgeway 1 S *Carter County* Elevation: 3,319 ft. Latitude: 45° 30' N Longitude: 104° 27' W

	JAN	FEB	MAR	APR	MAY	JUN	JUL	AUG	SEP	OCT	NOV	DEC	YEAR
Mean Maximum Temp. (°F)	31.4	35.2	44.1	57.2	67.2	76.1	85.2	84.2	72.8	58.5	43.4	32.4	57.3
Mean Temp. (°F)	19.4	23.5	32.1	44.2	54.3	63.2	71.1	69.7	58.1	45.0	31.3	20.2	44.3
Mean Minimum Temp. (°F)	7.3	11.7	20.1	31.1	41.4	50.2	56.9	54.9	43.4	31.4	19.1	8.0	31.3
Extreme Maximum Temp. (°F)	68	69	78	90	97	103	108	106	107	91	80	65	108
Extreme Minimum Temp. (°F)	-37	-39	-36	-6	17	30	35	28	10	-22	-27	-51	-51
Days Maximum Temp. ≥ 90°F	0	0	0	0	0	3	10	9	3	0	0	0	25
Days Maximum Temp. ≤ 32°F	13	10	6	1	0	0	0	0	0	1	6	14	51
Days Minimum Temp. ≤ 32°F	30	27	27	17	5	0	0	0	3	16	27	30	182
Days Minimum Temp. ≤ 0°F	9	6	2	0	0	0	0	0	0	0	2	8	27
Heating Degree Days (base 65°F)	1,410	1,165	1,011	619	335	120	23	33	238	614	1,005	1,382	7,955
Cooling Degree Days (base 65°F)	0	0	0	1	11	72	218	185	39	1	0	0	527
Mean Precipitation (in.)	0.41	0.34	0.78	1.39	2.23	2.36	1.65	1.30	1.26	1.17	0.50	0.43	13.82
Extreme Maximum Daily Precip. (in.)	0.49	*0.51*	*1.50*	*1.12*	2.30	1.85	1.84	3.07	2.32	1.75	2.00	*1.09*	*3.07*
Days With ≥ 0.1" Precipitation	1	1	2	4	5	6	4	3	3	3	2	1	35
Days With ≥ 0.5" Precipitation	0	0	0	1	1	2	1	1	1	1	0	0	8
Days With ≥ 1.0" Precipitation	0	0	0	0	0	0	0	0	0	0	0	0	0
Mean Snowfall (in.)	6.1	6.0	9.4	6.4	1.8	0.0	0.0	0.0	0.6	2.8	5.8	6.7	45.6
Maximum Snow Depth (in.)	na	na	na	na	na	na	na	na	na	na	na	na	na
Days With ≥ 1.0" Snow Depth	na	na	na	1	0	0	0	0	0	0	*2*	na	na

Stevensville *Ravalli County* Elevation: 3,375 ft. Latitude: 46° 31' N Longitude: 114° 05' W

	JAN	FEB	MAR	APR	MAY	JUN	JUL	AUG	SEP	OCT	NOV	DEC	YEAR
Mean Maximum Temp. (°F)	35.7	41.7	51.5	60.8	69.5	76.6	86.6	85.0	74.4	60.2	44.1	33.9	60.0
Mean Temp. (°F)	26.9	30.9	38.7	46.0	54.0	60.9	67.6	65.8	56.8	45.6	34.2	25.5	46.1
Mean Minimum Temp. (°F)	18.0	20.1	25.9	31.1	38.4	45.2	48.6	46.5	39.2	31.0	24.4	17.0	32.1
Extreme Maximum Temp. (°F)	63	70	80	86	97	104	107	101	96	86	74	64	107
Extreme Minimum Temp. (°F)	-30	-33	-14	2	18	29	31	27	16	1	-12	-35	-35
Days Maximum Temp. ≥ 90°F	0	0	0	0	1	3	13	9	1	0	0	0	27
Days Maximum Temp. ≤ 32°F	10	4	1	0	0	0	0	0	0	0	3	13	31
Days Minimum Temp. ≤ 32°F	29	26	26	17	6	0	0	0	5	18	25	29	181
Days Minimum Temp. ≤ 0°F	3	2	0	0	0	0	0	0	0	0	0	3	8
Heating Degree Days (base 65°F)	1,175	957	807	564	341	149	40	52	250	594	917	1,218	7,064
Cooling Degree Days (base 65°F)	0	0	0	0	6	33	128	83	10	0	0	0	260
Mean Precipitation (in.)	0.99	0.81	0.77	0.93	1.62	1.54	0.81	1.11	1.04	0.76	1.07	1.04	12.49
Extreme Maximum Daily Precip. (in.)	1.10	1.08	0.78	0.86	1.70	0.84	1.38	1.72	1.05	1.27	1.02	0.97	1.72
Days With ≥ 0.1" Precipitation	3	3	3	3	5	5	2	3	3	2	3	3	38
Days With ≥ 0.5" Precipitation	0	0	0	0	1	1	0	0	1	0	0	0	3
Days With ≥ 1.0" Precipitation	0	0	0	0	0	0	0	0	0	0	0	0	0
Mean Snowfall (in.)	5.6	3.6	2.3	0.2	0.0	0.0	0.0	0.0	0.0	0.1	2.3	5.4	19.5
Maximum Snow Depth (in.)	17	15	10	trace	0	0	0	0	0	2	7	28	28
Days With ≥ 1.0" Snow Depth	12	7	2	0	0	0	0	0	0	0	2	9	32

The period of record for all cooperative weather station data is 1980 – 2009. See User Guide for detailed explanation of data.

Trident *Gallatin County* Elevation: 4,036 ft. Latitude: 45° 57' N Longitude: 111° 28' W

	JAN	FEB	MAR	APR	MAY	JUN	JUL	AUG	SEP	OCT	NOV	DEC	YEAR
Mean Maximum Temp. (°F)	35.9	40.5	49.6	59.4	69.0	77.1	86.5	86.0	75.0	61.1	44.1	35.1	59.9
Mean Temp. (°F)	24.7	28.8	37.1	45.6	54.6	62.2	69.3	68.1	58.3	46.5	32.8	24.3	46.0
Mean Minimum Temp. (°F)	13.4	17.0	24.6	31.8	40.2	47.3	52.0	50.2	41.6	31.8	21.4	13.4	32.1
Extreme Maximum Temp. (°F)	63	68	75	88	94	102	104	103	97	86	77	65	104
Extreme Minimum Temp. (°F)	-29	-37	-26	4	22	32	32	27	16	-6	-23	-34	-37
Days Maximum Temp. ≥ 90°F	0	0	0	0	1	3	13	12	2	0	0	0	31
Days Maximum Temp. ≤ 32°F	10	6	2	0	0	0	0	0	0	0	5	11	34
Days Minimum Temp. ≤ 32°F	29	25	25	16	4	0	0	0	3	16	25	28	171
Days Minimum Temp. ≤ 0°F	6	3	1	0	0	0	0	0	0	0	2	5	17
Heating Degree Days (base 65°F)	1,245	1,017	856	574	321	125	26	33	221	568	962	1,256	7,204
Cooling Degree Days (base 65°F)	0	0	0	0	7	50	166	135	26	1	0	0	385
Mean Precipitation (in.)	0.46	0.36	0.73	1.39	2.47	2.24	1.59	1.03	1.22	1.03	0.60	0.42	13.54
Extreme Maximum Daily Precip. (in.)	0.71	0.52	0.80	1.37	2.00	1.41	1.56	1.25	1.20	1.13	1.60	***0.80***	***2.00***
Days With ≥ 0.1" Precipitation	1	1	2	4	6	5	4	3	4	3	2	1	36
Days With ≥ 0.5" Precipitation	0	0	0	1	1	1	1	0	1	0	0	0	5
Days With ≥ 1.0" Precipitation	0	0	0	0	0	0	0	0	0	0	0	0	0
Mean Snowfall (in.)	5.1	3.2	6.8	2.7	0.4	0.0	0.0	trace	0.4	1.3	2.9	5.4	28.2
Maximum Snow Depth (in.)	11	8	18	6	1	0	0	0	1	***9***	***7***	14	***18***
Days With ≥ 1.0" Snow Depth	11	6	5	1	0	0	0	0	0	1	5	12	41

West Glacier *Flathead County* Elevation: 3,153 ft. Latitude: 48° 30' N Longitude: 113° 59' W

	JAN	FEB	MAR	APR	MAY	JUN	JUL	AUG	SEP	OCT	NOV	DEC	YEAR
Mean Maximum Temp. (°F)	30.4	34.9	43.0	54.3	65.0	71.9	80.2	79.3	67.9	52.8	37.6	29.1	53.9
Mean Temp. (°F)	24.2	26.8	33.8	42.5	51.6	58.0	64.4	63.2	53.7	42.3	31.7	23.6	43.0
Mean Minimum Temp. (°F)	17.9	18.7	24.6	30.7	38.1	44.2	48.5	47.0	39.3	31.9	25.8	18.0	32.0
Extreme Maximum Temp. (°F)	50	55	66	83	90	93	99	96	95	79	65	48	99
Extreme Minimum Temp. (°F)	-29	-27	-11	10	19	29	33	26	18	-3	-17	-30	-30
Days Maximum Temp. ≥ 90°F	0	0	0	0	0	1	4	2	0	0	0	0	7
Days Maximum Temp. ≤ 32°F	15	8	2	0	0	0	0	0	0	1	6	18	50
Days Minimum Temp. ≤ 32°F	30	27	28	20	6	1	0	0	4	17	24	30	187
Days Minimum Temp. ≤ 0°F	4	3	1	0	0	0	0	0	0	0	1	3	12
Heating Degree Days (base 65°F)	1,259	1,073	960	667	412	217	79	98	337	695	992	1,277	8,066
Cooling Degree Days (base 65°F)	0	0	0	0	2	14	66	49	3	0	0	0	134
Mean Precipitation (in.)	3.24	1.99	2.04	1.82	2.65	3.42	1.71	1.31	2.00	2.41	3.24	3.06	28.89
Extreme Maximum Daily Precip. (in.)	1.60	1.04	0.96	1.17	1.64	1.75	1.48	1.12	1.53	2.09	1.98	1.20	2.09
Days With ≥ 0.1" Precipitation	9	6	7	5	7	8	5	4	6	7	9	9	82
Days With ≥ 0.5" Precipitation	2	1	1	1	1	2	1	1	1	1	2	1	15
Days With ≥ 1.0" Precipitation	0	0	0	0	0	0	0	0	0	0	0	0	0
Mean Snowfall (in.)	32.5	17.6	14.3	2.8	0.3	0.0	0.0	0.0	trace	1.6	17.0	35.3	121.4
Maximum Snow Depth (in.)	46	48	60	41	17	0	0	0	trace	8	26	45	60
Days With ≥ 1.0" Snow Depth	31	28	30	13	1	0	0	0	0	1	13	29	146

Westby *Sheridan County* Elevation: 2,103 ft. Latitude: 48° 52' N Longitude: 104° 03' W

	JAN	FEB	MAR	APR	MAY	JUN	JUL	AUG	SEP	OCT	NOV	DEC	YEAR
Mean Maximum Temp. (°F)	18.9	24.8	36.8	54.8	66.4	74.1	***80.4***	81.0	70.0	54.5	37.0	22.4	***51.8***
Mean Temp. (°F)	8.2	14.2	25.8	41.3	53.1	61.9	***67.4***	66.7	55.3	41.5	26.5	12.2	***39.5***
Mean Minimum Temp. (°F)	-2.4	3.7	14.7	27.8	39.7	49.6	***54.3***	52.3	40.5	28.5	16.1	2.0	***27.2***
Extreme Maximum Temp. (°F)	55	66	75	91	102	103	106	108	103	92	73	53	108
Extreme Minimum Temp. (°F)	-42	-38	-31	-8	13	31	***39***	31	18	-5	-26	-42	***-42***
Days Maximum Temp. ≥ 90°F	0	0	0	0	0	2	5	6	2	0	0	0	15
Days Maximum Temp. ≤ 32°F	24	18	11	1	0	0	0	0	0	1	11	22	88
Days Minimum Temp. ≤ 32°F	31	28	30	21	6	0	0	0	5	21	28	31	201
Days Minimum Temp. ≤ 0°F	16	11	5	0	0	0	0	0	0	0	3	13	48
Heating Degree Days (base 65°F)	1,757	1,432	1,209	705	374	141	***44***	66	305	720	1,148	1,632	***9,533***
Cooling Degree Days (base 65°F)	0	0	0	0	11	54	***125***	124	20	0	0	0	***334***
Mean Precipitation (in.)	0.42	***0.17***	0.50	0.78	1.66	2.98	2.48	1.55	0.97	0.80	0.41	0.30	***13.02***
Extreme Maximum Daily Precip. (in.)	0.53	0.60	0.58	1.10	1.85	***1.67***	***4.50***	1.60	1.75	***1.38***	1.79	0.50	***4.50***
Days With ≥ 0.1" Precipitation	1	1	2	2	4	7	5	3	3	2	1	1	32
Days With ≥ 0.5" Precipitation	0	0	0	0	1	2	1	1	0	0	0	0	5
Days With ≥ 1.0" Precipitation	0	0	0	0	0	1	1	0	0	0	0	0	2
Mean Snowfall (in.)	5.0	2.9	***3.2***	1.4	0.5	0.0	0.0	0.0	trace	1.0	***3.7***	***4.7***	***22.4***
Maximum Snow Depth (in.)	na	na	na	na	***10***	***0***	na	na	na	na	na	na	na
Days With ≥ 1.0" Snow Depth	na	na	***5***	1	0	0	0	0	0	***1***	***2***	na	na

Winifred *Fergus County* Elevation: 3,243 ft. Latitude: 47° 34' N Longitude: 109° 23' W

	JAN	FEB	MAR	APR	MAY	JUN	JUL	AUG	SEP	OCT	NOV	DEC	YEAR
Mean Maximum Temp. (°F)	34.0	38.1	45.6	57.0	66.2	74.5	84.1	83.7	72.0	58.9	45.0	34.5	57.8
Mean Temp. (°F)	22.0	26.1	33.5	43.9	53.1	61.1	68.4	67.4	56.6	44.7	32.9	22.5	44.4
Mean Minimum Temp. (°F)	9.9	14.1	21.4	30.7	39.9	47.7	52.7	51.0	41.1	30.5	20.6	10.4	30.8
Extreme Maximum Temp. (°F)	69	71	79	90	95	102	103	107	100	89	80	65	107
Extreme Minimum Temp. (°F)	-42	-38	-28	-10	13	30	36	29	15	-17	-31	-43	-43
Days Maximum Temp. ≥ 90°F	0	0	0	0	0	2	9	9	2	0	0	0	22
Days Maximum Temp. ≤ 32°F	11	9	5	1	0	0	0	0	0	1	5	11	43
Days Minimum Temp. ≤ 32°F	29	26	27	18	5	0	0	0	4	18	26	30	183
Days Minimum Temp. ≤ 0°F	8	5	2	0	0	0	0	0	0	0	2	7	24
Heating Degree Days (base 65°F)	1,329	1,094	968	627	371	154	37	54	272	623	957	1,312	7,798
Cooling Degree Days (base 65°F)	0	0	0	0	9	45	150	135	26	0	0	0	365
Mean Precipitation (in.)	0.57	0.34	0.80	1.22	2.66	2.90	1.81	1.53	1.29	1.05	0.56	0.59	15.32
Extreme Maximum Daily Precip. (in.)	0.48	0.64	1.05	1.10	2.29	2.14	2.30	2.01	1.76	1.10	0.63	1.24	2.30
Days With ≥ 0.1" Precipitation	2	1	3	3	6	7	4	4	4	3	2	2	41
Days With ≥ 0.5" Precipitation	0	0	0	1	2	2	1	1	1	0	0	0	8
Days With ≥ 1.0" Precipitation	0	0	0	0	0	0	0	0	0	0	0	0	0
Mean Snowfall (in.)	na	na	na	na	0.0	0.0	0.0	0.0	trace	0.2	na	na	na
Maximum Snow Depth (in.)	na	na	na	na	na	na	na	na	na	na	na	na	na
Days With ≥ 1.0" Snow Depth	na	na	na	***0***	0	0	0	0	0	***0***	na	na	na

The period of record for all cooperative weather station data is 1980 – 2009. See User Guide for detailed explanation of data.

Wyola 1 SW *Big Horn County* Elevation: 3,729 ft. Latitude: 45° 07' N Longitude: 107° 24' W

	JAN	FEB	MAR	APR	MAY	JUN	JUL	AUG	SEP	OCT	NOV	DEC	YEAR
Mean Maximum Temp. (°F)	37.7	40.9	50.3	61.4	70.5	***78.8***	87.9	86.7	74.7	***61.9***	***46.3***	***37.5***	***61.2***
Mean Temp. (°F)	24.1	26.8	35.8	45.3	54.0	***62.6***	69.5	***67.5***	57.3	***45.6***	***32.5***	***24.0***	***45.4***
Mean Minimum Temp. (°F)	10.2	12.6	21.3	29.2	37.6	***46.4***	51.1	***48.4***	39.8	***29.3***	***18.6***	***10.4***	***29.6***
Extreme Maximum Temp. (°F)	65	74	79	91	96	107	107	105	96	***92***	77	***70***	***107***
Extreme Minimum Temp. (°F)	-42	***-36***	-25	***-4***	***17***	***28***	33	***27***	15	***-18***	***-25***	***-46***	***-46***
Days Maximum Temp. ≥ 90°F	0	0	0	0	0	4	14	12	2	***0***	0	***0***	***32***
Days Maximum Temp. ≤ 32°F	9	6	2	0	0	0	0	0	0	***1***	4	***9***	***31***
Days Minimum Temp. ≤ 32°F	30	28	28	19	***8***	0	0	0	5	***20***	***27***	***30***	***195***
Days Minimum Temp. ≤ 0°F	7	5	2	0	0	0	0	0	0	***0***	2	***6***	***22***
Heating Degree Days (base 65°F)	1,261	1,074	898	584	337	***118***	24	***38***	250	***594***	***968***	***1,265***	***7,411***
Cooling Degree Days (base 65°F)	0	0	0	0	5	***53***	171	***121***	25	***1***	***0***	***0***	***376***
Mean Precipitation (in.)	0.49	0.62	1.00	1.87	2.66	2.31	1.49	0.73	1.52	***1.47***	0.80	***0.59***	***15.55***
Extreme Maximum Daily Precip. (in.)	0.50	***0.67***	***0.68***	***2.24***	***3.26***	***3.19***	1.71	***1.25***	***0.95***	***1.18***	***1.12***	***0.66***	3.26
Days With ≥ 0.1" Precipitation	***2***	2	3	5	6	5	4	2	4	***4***	3	***2***	***42***
Days With ≥ 0.5" Precipitation	0	0	0	1	2	1	1	0	1	***1***	0	***0***	7
Days With ≥ 1.0" Precipitation	0	0	0	0	0	0	0	0	0	***0***	0	***0***	***0***
Mean Snowfall (in.)	***5.6***	na	***5.2***	***2.2***	0.8	0.0	0.0	0.0	0.9	***1.0***	***3.3***	na	na
Maximum Snow Depth (in.)	na	na	na	na	na	na	na	na	na	na	na	na	na
Days With ≥ 1.0" Snow Depth	na	na	na	na	0	0	0	0	0	na	na	na	na

Yellowtail Dam *Big Horn County* Elevation: 3,305 ft. Latitude: 45° 19' N Longitude: 107° 56' W

	JAN	FEB	MAR	APR	MAY	JUN	JUL	AUG	SEP	OCT	NOV	DEC	YEAR
Mean Maximum Temp. (°F)	41.2	44.5	52.4	62.4	71.7	81.2	91.0	90.2	78.3	63.8	49.6	40.5	63.9
Mean Temp. (°F)	30.9	33.5	40.3	49.7	58.4	67.1	75.0	73.8	63.1	51.4	39.3	30.5	51.1
Mean Minimum Temp. (°F)	20.5	22.6	28.3	36.9	45.1	53.0	59.0	57.3	48.0	38.6	29.0	20.5	38.2
Extreme Maximum Temp. (°F)	68	72	82	89	98	104	109	107	103	93	78	72	109
Extreme Minimum Temp. (°F)	-30	-35	-16	7	22	35	40	35	23	-7	-14	-28	-35
Days Maximum Temp. ≥ 90°F	0	0	0	0	1	6	19	19	5	0	0	0	50
Days Maximum Temp. ≤ 32°F	7	5	2	0	0	0	0	0	0	0	3	7	24
Days Minimum Temp. ≤ 32°F	24	21	20	9	1	0	0	0	1	7	18	24	125
Days Minimum Temp. ≤ 0°F	4	3	1	0	0	0	0	0	0	0	1	3	12
Heating Degree Days (base 65°F)	1,051	883	759	459	227	58	5	10	132	426	765	1,064	5,839
Cooling Degree Days (base 65°F)	0	0	1	5	31	128	323	289	84	9	0	0	870
Mean Precipitation (in.)	0.72	0.76	1.36	1.67	2.73	2.45	1.42	0.74	1.64	1.84	0.81	0.76	16.90
Extreme Maximum Daily Precip. (in.)	0.72	1.25	1.38	1.26	5.00	4.34	4.56	1.75	1.98	2.17	0.82	0.75	5.00
Days With ≥ 0.1" Precipitation	2	2	5	5	6	5	3	2	4	4	3	3	44
Days With ≥ 0.5" Precipitation	0	0	0	1	2	1	1	0	1	1	0	0	7
Days With ≥ 1.0" Precipitation	0	0	0	0	1	0	0	0	0	0	0	0	1
Mean Snowfall (in.)	na	na	na	***1.0***	trace	0.0	0.0	0.0	0.0	1.4	na	na	na
Maximum Snow Depth (in.)	na	na	na	na	na	na	na	na	na	na	na	na	na
Days With ≥ 1.0" Snow Depth	na	na	na	***0***	0	0	0	0	0	0	na	na	na

Montana Weather Station Rankings

Annual Extreme Maximum Temperature

Highest

Rank	Station Name	°F
1	Miles City Municipal Arpt	113
2	Brandenberg	112
2	Hardin	112
4	Glendive	111
5	Brockway 3 WSW	110
5	Cohagen	110
7	Biddle 8 SW	109
7	Busby	109
7	Culbertson	109
7	Havre City-County Arpt	109
7	Huntley Experiment Stn	109
7	Moorhead 9 NE	109
7	Yellowtail Dam	109
14	Big Sandy	108
14	Billings Logan Int'l Arpt	108
14	Billings Water Plant	108
14	Bredette	108
14	Bridger 1 S	***108***
14	Fort Assinniboine	108
14	Fort Peck Power Plant	108
14	Glasgow Intl Arpt	108
14	Ridgeway 1 S	108
14	Westby	108
24	Carlyle 12 NW	107
24	Carter 14 W	107

Lowest

Rank	Station Name	°F
1	Cooke City 2 W	90
2	Alder 17 S	96
2	Hebgen Dam	96
4	Creston	97
4	Millegan 14 SE	***97***
6	Bigfork 13 S	98
6	Lindbergh Lake	98
8	Del Bonita	99
8	West Glacier	99
10	Anaconda	100
10	Bozeman Montana St Univ	100
10	Butte Bert Mooney Arpt	100
10	Gibson Dam	100
14	Boulder	101
14	Divide	101
16	Blackleaf	***102***
16	Dillon Wmce	102
16	Kalispell Arpt	102
19	Cascade 5 S	104
19	Chester	104
19	Denton 1 NNE	104
19	Drummond	104
19	Great Falls Intl Arpt	104
19	Livingston Mission Field	104
19	Trident	104

Annual Mean Maximum Temperature

Highest

Rank	Station Name	°F
1	Hardin	64.1
2	Yellowtail Dam	63.9
3	Billings Water Plant	63.7
4	Brandenberg	61.5
4	Columbus	61.5
6	Flatwillow 4 ENE	61.4
7	Moorhead 9 NE	61.3
8	Huntley Experiment Stn	61.2
8	Wyola 1 SW	***61.2***
10	Bridger 1 S	***61.0***
11	Biddle 8 SW	60.5
12	Big Timber	60.4
13	Busby	60.2
14	Darby	60.0
14	Grass Range	60.0
14	Stevensville	60.0
17	Trident	59.9
18	Cohagen	59.8
19	Cascade 5 S	59.6
20	Billings Logan Int'l Arpt	59.5
20	Glendive	59.5
22	Big Sandy	***59.4***
23	Fort Peck Power Plant	58.9
23	Livingston Mission Field	58.9
23	Miles City Municipal Arpt	58.9

Lowest

Rank	Station Name	°F
1	Cooke City 2 W	***47.3***
2	Hebgen Dam	49.7
3	Westby	***51.8***
4	Lindbergh Lake	52.3
5	Opheim 10 N	53.1
6	Del Bonita	***53.5***
7	Bredette	53.8
8	Butte Bert Mooney Arpt	53.9
8	West Glacier	53.9
10	Cut Bank Muni Arpt	54.1
10	Gibson Dam	54.1
12	Creston	54.4
13	Alder 17 S	54.6
13	Divide	54.6
15	Millegan 14 SE	***54.7***
16	Hinsdale 4 SW	***54.9***
16	Kalispell Arpt	54.9
18	Medicine Lake 3 SE	55.1
19	Glasgow Intl Arpt	55.2
20	Bigfork 13 S	55.3
21	Blackleaf	***55.8***
22	Carlyle 12 NW	56.1
23	Havre City-County Arpt	56.7
24	Bozeman Gallatin Fld	56.9
25	Anaconda	57.0

Rankings include 25 highest/lowest stations. If state has less than 25 stations, all stations are included. The period of record is 1980–2009. See User Guide for detailed explanation of data.

Annual Mean Temperature

Highest			Lowest		
Rank	Station Name	°F	Rank	Station Name	°F
1	Yellowtail Dam	51.1	1	Cooke City 2 W	***34.1***
2	Billings Water Plant	49.4	2	Hebgen Dam	37.0
3	Hardin	49.0	3	Westby	***39.5***
4	Billings Logan Int'l Arpt	48.2	4	Opheim 10 N	39.6
5	Big Timber	47.2	5	Butte Bert Mooney Arpt	39.9
6	Brandenberg	46.9	6	Divide	41.1
6	Bridger 1 S	***46.9***	6	Millegan 14 SE	***41.1***
6	Moorhead 9 NE	46.9	8	Del Bonita	***41.3***
9	Flatwillow 4 ENE	46.8	9	Gibson Dam	41.9
9	Miles City Municipal Arpt	46.8	9	Lindbergh Lake	41.9
11	Biddle 8 SW	46.7	11	Blackleaf	***42.0***
12	Bigfork 13 S	46.6	12	Alder 17 S	42.1
12	Columbus	46.6	12	Cut Bank Muni Arpt	42.1
12	Darby	46.6	14	Bredette	42.2
15	Cascade 5 S	46.4	15	Medicine Lake 3 SE	42.4
15	Glendive	46.4	16	Boulder	42.9
17	Huntley Experiment Stn	46.2	16	Bozeman Gallatin Fld	42.9
18	Fort Peck Power Plant	46.1	16	Chester	42.9
18	Grass Range	46.1	19	Denton 1 NNE	43.0
18	Livingston Mission Field	46.1	19	West Glacier	43.0
18	Stevensville	46.1	21	Culbertson	43.1
22	Trident	46.0	21	Drummond	43.1
23	Libby Dam Base	***45.9***	23	Kalispell Arpt	43.2
24	Eureka Ranger Stn	45.7	24	Creston	43.3
25	Carter 14 W	45.5	25	Anaconda	43.4

Annual Mean Minimum Temperature

Highest			Lowest		
Rank	Station Name	°F	Rank	Station Name	°F
1	Yellowtail Dam	38.2	1	Cooke City 2 W	***20.9***
2	Bigfork 13 S	37.8	2	Hebgen Dam	24.2
3	Billings Logan Int'l Arpt	36.7	3	Butte Bert Mooney Arpt	25.9
4	Billings Water Plant	35.0	4	Opheim 10 N	26.1
5	Miles City Municipal Arpt	34.6	5	Westby	***27.2***
6	Big Timber	33.9	6	Millegan 14 SE	***27.4***
7	Eureka Ranger Stn	33.8	7	Divide	27.6
8	Hardin	33.7	8	Denton 1 NNE	27.9
9	Glendive	33.4	9	Blackleaf	***28.1***
10	Fort Peck Power Plant	33.3	10	Drummond	28.4
10	Livingston Mission Field	33.3	11	Boulder	28.5
10	Missoula Johnson-Bell Field	33.3	11	Chester	28.5
13	Cascade 5 S	33.2	13	Bozeman Gallatin Fld	28.8
13	Libby Dam Base	***33.2***	14	Chinook	28.9
15	Darby	33.0	15	Culbertson	29.0
16	Biddle 8 SW	32.9	15	Del Bonita	***29.0***
16	Hinsdale 4 SW	***32.9***	17	Alder 17 S	29.6
18	Great Falls Intl Arpt	32.8	17	Gibson Dam	29.6
19	Bridger 1 S	***32.7***	17	Medicine Lake 3 SE	29.6
20	Ekalaka	32.5	17	Wyola 1 SW	***29.6***
20	Moorhead 9 NE	32.5	21	Anaconda	29.7
22	Brandenberg	32.3	21	Busby	29.7
22	Carlyle 12 NW	32.3	23	Cut Bank Muni Arpt	30.0
22	Carter 14 W	32.3	24	Dillon Wmce	30.2
22	Helena Arpt Asos	32.3	25	Havre City-County Arpt	30.4

Rankings include 25 highest/lowest stations. If state has less than 25 stations, all stations are included. The period of record is 1980–2009. See User Guide for detailed explanation of data.

Annual Extreme Minimum Temperature

Highest

Rank	Station Name	°F
1	Bigfork 13 S	-21
1	Libby Dam Base	***-21***
3	Missoula Johnson-Bell Field	-30
3	West Glacier	-30
5	Billings Logan Int'l Arpt	-32
5	Bozeman Montana St Univ	-32
7	Creston	-33
7	Eureka Ranger Stn	-33
9	Darby	-34
10	Kalispell Arpt	-35
10	Stevensville	-35
10	Yellowtail Dam	-35
13	Carter 14 W	-36
14	Bredette	-37
14	Bridger 1 S	***-37***
14	Dillon Wmce	-37
14	Divide	-37
14	Hinsdale 4 SW	-37
14	Trident	-37
20	Anaconda	-38
20	Big Timber	-38
20	Del Bonita	-38
20	Fort Peck Power Plant	-38
20	Miles City Municipal Arpt	-38
25	Carlyle 12 NW	-39

Lowest

Rank	Station Name	°F
1	Busby	-52
1	Butte Bert Mooney Arpt	-52
1	Chester	-52
4	Ridgeway 1 S	-51
5	Big Sandy	-50
5	Chinook	-50
5	Denton 1 NNE	-50
5	Havre City-County Arpt	-50
9	Content 3 SSE	-49
10	Culbertson	-48
10	Moorhead 9 NE	-48
12	Blackleaf	***-47***
12	Hardin	-47
12	Huntley Experiment Stn	-47
12	Opheim 10 N	-47
16	Bozeman Gallatin Fld	-46
16	Medicine Lake 3 SE	-46
16	Wyola 1 SW	***-46***
19	Cascade 5 S	-45
20	Brandenberg	-44
20	Cut Bank Muni Arpt	-44
20	Fort Assinniboine	-44
20	Millegan 14 SE	***-44***
24	Biddle 8 SW	-43
24	Cooke City 2 W	-43

July Mean Maximum Temperature

Highest

Rank	Station Name	°F
1	Hardin	92.0
2	Yellowtail Dam	91.0
3	Brandenberg	90.5
4	Billings Water Plant	89.5
5	Moorhead 9 NE	89.4
6	Glendive	89.1
7	Miles City Municipal Arpt	88.9
8	Busby	88.6
9	Biddle 8 SW	88.5
10	Fort Peck Power Plant	88.4
11	Cohagen	88.0
12	Bridger 1 S	87.9
12	Wyola 1 SW	87.9
14	Columbus	87.4
14	Flatwillow 4 ENE	87.4
14	Huntley Experiment Stn	87.4
17	Big Sandy	87.1
18	Billings Logan Int'l Arpt	87.0
19	Big Timber	86.9
19	Culbertson	86.9
21	Fort Assinniboine	86.6
21	Stevensville	86.6
23	Trident	86.5
24	Brockway 3 WSW	86.3
25	Content 3 SSE	86.2

Lowest

Rank	Station Name	°F
1	Cooke City 2 W	74.1
2	Lindbergh Lake	77.6
3	Del Bonita	77.8
4	Gibson Dam	78.0
5	Hebgen Dam	78.5
6	Cut Bank Muni Arpt	79.3
7	Bigfork 13 S	79.4
7	Creston	79.4
9	Alder 17 S	79.5
9	Blackleaf	***79.5***
11	Millegan 14 SE	***79.7***
12	West Glacier	80.2
13	Westby	***80.4***
14	Divide	80.5
15	Butte Bert Mooney Arpt	80.6
16	Kalispell Arpt	81.0
17	Opheim 10 N	81.7
18	Anaconda	82.2
19	Boulder	82.7
20	Bozeman Montana St Univ	83.1
21	Denton 1 NNE	83.4
22	Great Falls Intl Arpt	83.6
23	Bredette	83.7
23	Chester	83.7
25	Hinsdale 4 SW	83.9

Rankings include 25 highest/lowest stations. If state has less than 25 stations, all stations are included. The period of record is 1980–2009. See User Guide for detailed explanation of data.

January Mean Minimum Temperature

Rank	Station Name (Highest)	°F	Rank	Station Name (Lowest)	°F
1	Bigfork 13 S	24.2	1	Westby	-2.4
2	Yellowtail Dam	20.5	2	Opheim 10 N	0.7
3	Libby Dam Base	*20.1*	3	Medicine Lake 3 SE	1.1
4	Darby	19.5	4	Culbertson	1.3
5	Livingston Mission Field	19.0	5	Hebgen Dam	3.2
6	Big Timber	18.5	6	Glasgow Intl Arpt	4.0
7	Stevensville	18.0	7	Bredette	4.2
8	Missoula Johnson-Bell Field	17.9	8	Cooke City 2 W	*4.5*
8	West Glacier	17.9	9	Chinook	4.7
10	Eureka Ranger Stn	17.6	10	Chester	5.4
11	Billings Logan Int'l Arpt	17.5	11	Fort Peck Power Plant	6.8
12	Cascade 5 S	17.2	12	Content 3 SSE	6.9
12	Creston	17.2	13	Havre City-County Arpt	7.0
14	Kalispell Arpt	16.1	14	Butte Bert Mooney Arpt	7.1
15	Billings Water Plant	16.0	15	Glendive	7.3
16	Lindbergh Lake	15.4	15	Ridgeway 1 S	7.3
17	Gibson Dam	15.2	17	Brockway 3 WSW	8.0
17	Great Falls Intl Arpt	15.2	18	Busby	8.2
19	Anaconda	15.0	18	Cohagen	8.2
20	Bozeman Montana St Univ	14.9	18	Hinsdale 4 SW	8.2
21	Dillon Wmce	14.7	21	Fort Assinniboine	8.5
22	Carter 14 W	14.6	22	Big Sandy	8.6
23	Alder 17 S	14.3	23	Carlyle 12 NW	9.3
24	Bridger 1 S	14.1	24	Denton 1 NNE	9.4
25	Grass Range	13.8	25	Bozeman Gallatin Fld	9.5

Number of Days Annually Maximum Temperature ≥ 90°F

Rank	Station Name (Highest)	Days	Rank	Station Name (Lowest)	Days
1	Hardin	55	1	Cooke City 2 W	0
2	Yellowtail Dam	50	2	Hebgen Dam	1
3	Brandenberg	46	3	Alder 17 S	3
4	Glendive	43	3	Del Bonita	3
5	Billings Water Plant	42	3	Lindbergh Lake	3
5	Moorhead 9 NE	42	6	Bigfork 13 S	4
7	Miles City Municipal Arpt	40	6	Gibson Dam	4
8	Busby	39	8	Divide	5
9	Biddle 8 SW	38	8	Millegan 14 SE	*5*
10	Cohagen	37	10	Creston	6
10	Fort Peck Power Plant	37	11	Blackleaf	*7*
12	Flatwillow 4 ENE	34	11	Butte Bert Mooney Arpt	7
12	Huntley Experiment Stn	34	11	West Glacier	7
14	Bridger 1 S	*33*	14	Anaconda	9
15	Big Sandy	32	14	Cut Bank Muni Arpt	9
15	Brockway 3 WSW	32	16	Dillon Wmce	11
15	Culbertson	32	17	Boulder	12
15	Wyola 1 SW	*32*	18	Bozeman Montana St Univ	13
19	Billings Logan Int'l Arpt	31	18	Kalispell Arpt	13
19	Fort Assinniboine	31	20	Opheim 10 N	15
19	Trident	31	20	Westby	15
22	Big Timber	29	22	Chester	17
22	Columbus	29	23	Denton 1 NNE	18
22	Content 3 SSE	29	23	Great Falls Intl Arpt	18
25	Eureka Ranger Stn	27	25	Bozeman Gallatin Fld	22

Rankings include 25 highest/lowest stations. If state has less than 25 stations, all stations are included. The period of record is 1980–2009. See User Guide for detailed explanation of data.

Number of Days Annually Maximum Temperature ≤ 32°F

Highest

Rank	Station Name	Days
1	Cooke City 2 W	96
2	Hebgen Dam	94
3	Westby	88
4	Bredette	78
4	Opheim 10 N	78
6	Glasgow Intl Arpt	70
7	Medicine Lake 3 SE	69
8	Culbertson	68
9	Hinsdale 4 SW	65
10	Carlyle 12 NW	60
11	Lindbergh Lake	59
12	Havre City-County Arpt	55
13	Brockway 3 WSW	54
13	Butte Bert Mooney Arpt	54
15	Fort Peck Power Plant	53
16	Chinook	52
16	Content 3 SSE	52
18	Glendive	51
18	Kalispell Arpt	51
18	Miles City Municipal Arpt	51
18	Ridgeway 1 S	51
22	Bozeman Gallatin Fld	50
22	Cut Bank Muni Arpt	50
22	Del Bonita	50
22	Ekalaka	50

Lowest

Rank	Station Name	Days
1	Yellowtail Dam	24
2	Billings Water Plant	25
3	Darby	26
4	Hardin	28
5	Columbus	30
5	Libby Dam Base	***30***
7	Big Timber	31
7	Stevensville	31
7	Wyola 1 SW	***31***
10	Bridger 1 S	***32***
10	Cascade 5 S	32
12	Dillon Wmce	33
12	Flatwillow 4 ENE	33
12	Grass Range	33
12	Huntley Experiment Stn	33
16	Trident	34
17	Bigfork 13 S	35
17	Livingston Mission Field	35
19	Anaconda	36
19	Brandenberg	36
19	Moorhead 9 NE	36
22	Biddle 8 SW	37
22	Boulder	37
22	Bozeman Montana St Univ	37
25	Denton 1 NNE	38

Number of Days Annually Minimum Temperature ≤ 32°F

Highest

Rank	Station Name	Days
1	Cooke City 2 W	264
2	Hebgen Dam	222
3	Butte Bert Mooney Arpt	221
4	Millegan 14 SE	***213***
5	Opheim 10 N	210
6	Drummond	208
7	Boulder	206
8	Divide	205
9	Denton 1 NNE	203
10	Anaconda	201
10	Westby	201
12	Alder 17 S	198
13	Bozeman Gallatin Fld	196
13	Chester	196
15	Wyola 1 SW	***195***
16	Busby	194
16	Culbertson	194
18	Blackleaf	***193***
18	Chinook	193
18	Lindbergh Lake	193
21	Gibson Dam	191
22	Dillon Wmce	190
23	Del Bonita	188
24	Kalispell Arpt	187
24	Medicine Lake 3 SE	187

Lowest

Rank	Station Name	Days
1	Yellowtail Dam	125
2	Bigfork 13 S	129
3	Billings Logan Int'l Arpt	143
4	Cascade 5 S	149
5	Big Timber	156
6	Billings Water Plant	158
7	Hinsdale 4 SW	159
8	Eureka Ranger Stn	161
8	Livingston Mission Field	161
10	Fort Peck Power Plant	163
10	Hardin	163
12	Miles City Municipal Arpt	164
13	Great Falls Intl Arpt	165
14	Carter 14 W	168
14	Darby	168
16	Glendive	170
17	Trident	171
18	Bridger 1 S	***172***
19	Flatwillow 4 ENE	173
19	Grass Range	173
21	Big Sandy	174
21	Helena Arpt Asos	174
21	Missoula Johnson-Bell Field	174
24	Fort Assinniboine	175
24	Moorhead 9 NE	175

Rankings include 25 highest/lowest stations. If state has less than 25 stations, all stations are included. The period of record is 1980–2009. See User Guide for detailed explanation of data.

Number of Days Annually Minimum Temperature ≤ 0°F

Highest			Lowest		
Rank	Station Name	Days	Rank	Station Name	Days
1	Westby	48	1	Bigfork 13 S	3
2	Opheim 10 N	45	2	Libby Dam Base	***4***
3	Cooke City 2 W	43	3	Darby	6
4	Hebgen Dam	40	4	Missoula Johnson-Bell Field	8
4	Medicine Lake 3 SE	40	4	Stevensville	8
6	Culbertson	39	6	Kalispell Arpt	10
7	Bredette	36	7	Creston	11
8	Glasgow Intl Arpt	35	7	Eureka Ranger Stn	11
9	Butte Bert Mooney Arpt	34	9	Lindbergh Lake	12
9	Chinook	34	9	West Glacier	12
11	Chester	32	9	Yellowtail Dam	12
11	Havre City-County Arpt	32	12	Billings Water Plant	13
13	Content 3 SSE	31	13	Alder 17 S	14
14	Blackleaf	***30***	13	Big Timber	14
15	Denton 1 NNE	29	13	Billings Logan Int'l Arpt	14
16	Big Sandy	28	13	Bozeman Montana St Univ	14
16	Brockway 3 WSW	28	13	Dillon Wmce	14
16	Fort Assinniboine	28	13	Livingston Mission Field	14
16	Fort Peck Power Plant	28	19	Anaconda	15
20	Busby	27	19	Bridger 1 S	***15***
20	Cohagen	27	21	Trident	17
20	Cut Bank Muni Arpt	27	22	Drummond	18
20	Hinsdale 4 SW	27	22	Hardin	18
20	Ridgeway 1 S	27	24	Cascade 5 S	19
25	Carlyle 12 NW	26	24	Divide	19

Number of Annual Heating Degree Days

Highest			Lowest		
Rank	Station Name	Num.	Rank	Station Name	Num.
1	Cooke City 2 W	***11,182***	1	Yellowtail Dam	5,839
2	Hebgen Dam	10,151	2	Billings Water Plant	6,248
3	Westby	***9,533***	3	Hardin	6,534
4	Opheim 10 N	9,425	4	Billings Logan Int'l Arpt	6,704
5	Butte Bert Mooney Arpt	9,141	5	Big Timber	6,795
6	Millegan 14 SE	***8,723***	6	Bigfork 13 S	6,868
7	Divide	***8,719***	7	Darby	6,902
8	Del Bonita	***8,679***	8	Cascade 5 S	6,969
9	Bredette	8,678	9	Bridger 1 S	***6,979***
10	Medicine Lake 3 SE	8,635	10	Flatwillow 4 ENE	7,009
11	Lindbergh Lake	8,471	11	Columbus	7,010
12	Blackleaf	***8,451***	12	Stevensville	7,064
13	Cut Bank Muni Arpt	8,427	13	Livingston Mission Field	7,087
14	Culbertson	8,415	14	Moorhead 9 NE	7,100
15	Gibson Dam	8,403	15	Brandenberg	7,120
16	Alder 17 S	8,353	16	Libby Dam Base	***7,134***
17	Glasgow Intl Arpt	8,348	17	Grass Range	7,141
18	Chester	8,283	18	Biddle 8 SW	7,174
19	Bozeman Gallatin Fld	8,214	19	Trident	7,204
20	Chinook	8,192	20	Huntley Experiment Stn	7,226
21	Boulder	8,143	21	Eureka Ranger Stn	7,266
22	Denton 1 NNE	8,115	22	Miles City Municipal Arpt	7,363
23	Hinsdale 4 SW	***8,113***	23	Wyola 1 SW	***7,411***
24	Havre City-County Arpt	8,109	24	Missoula Johnson-Bell Field	7,417
25	West Glacier	8,066	25	Carter 14 W	7,424

Rankings include 25 highest/lowest stations. If state has less than 25 stations, all stations are included. The period of record is 1980–2009. See User Guide for detailed explanation of data.

Number of Annual Cooling Degree Days

Highest			Lowest		
Rank	Station Name	Num.	Rank	Station Name	Num.
1	Yellowtail Dam	870	1	Cooke City 2 W	***3***
2	Miles City Municipal Arpt	820	2	Hebgen Dam	29
3	Glendive	788	3	Gibson Dam	71
4	Hardin	785	4	Butte Bert Mooney Arpt	86
5	Fort Peck Power Plant	693	5	Divide	***94***
6	Billings Water Plant	666	5	Millegan 14 SE	***94***
7	Billings Logan Int'l Arpt	663	7	Alder 17 S	104
8	Brandenberg	633	8	Del Bonita	***125***
9	Biddle 8 SW	615	8	Lindbergh Lake	125
10	Moorhead 9 NE	610	10	West Glacier	134
11	Glasgow Intl Arpt	551	11	Blackleaf	***135***
12	Ekalaka	546	12	Drummond	147
13	Brockway 3 WSW	543	13	Creston	152
14	Cohagen	542	14	Kalispell Arpt	156
15	Ridgeway 1 S	527	15	Anaconda	163
16	Hinsdale 4 SW	***524***	15	Dillon Wmce	163
17	Culbertson	521	17	Cut Bank Muni Arpt	169
18	Carlyle 12 NW	510	18	Boulder	172
19	Medicine Lake 3 SE	493	19	Denton 1 NNE	200
20	Flatwillow 4 ENE	485	20	Bozeman Gallatin Fld	246
21	Content 3 SSE	484	21	Opheim 10 N	255
22	Big Sandy	***476***	22	Bigfork 13 S	256
23	Fort Assinniboine	474	23	Stevensville	260
24	Bridger 1 S	***469***	24	Libby Dam Base	***262***
25	Bredette	465	25	Darby	266

Annual Precipitation

Highest			Lowest		
Rank	Station Name	Inches	Rank	Station Name	Inches
1	West Glacier	28.89	1	Chester	10.72
2	Hebgen Dam	27.70	2	Havre City-County Arpt	11.01
3	Cooke City 2 W	25.38	3	Brockway 3 WSW	11.05
4	Lindbergh Lake	24.00	4	Cut Bank Muni Arpt	11.23
5	Bigfork 13 S	21.72	5	Boulder	11.24
6	Creston	20.16	6	Helena Arpt Asos	11.31
7	Bozeman Montana St Univ	19.61	7	Glasgow Intl Arpt	11.32
8	Millegan 14 SE	***18.25***	8	Divide	11.49
9	Kalispell Arpt	16.98	9	Dillon Wmce	11.52
10	Libby Dam Base	***16.93***	10	Hardin	11.56
11	Yellowtail Dam	16.90	11	Cohagen	11.57
12	Cascade 5 S	16.77	12	Fort Peck Power Plant	11.69
13	Gibson Dam	16.66	13	Bridger 1 S	***11.91***
14	Ekalaka	16.49	14	Content 3 SSE	12.21
15	Grass Range	16.43	15	Miles City Municipal Arpt	12.22
16	Big Timber	15.88	16	Moorhead 9 NE	12.41
17	Darby	***15.79***	16	Opheim 10 N	***12.41***
18	Wyola 1 SW	***15.55***	18	Stevensville	12.49
19	Carlyle 12 NW	15.51	19	Medicine Lake 3 SE	12.56
20	Winifred	15.32	20	Drummond	12.64
21	Eureka Ranger Stn	15.08	21	Fort Assinniboine	12.78
22	Denton 1 NNE	15.03	22	Flatwillow 4 ENE	12.81
23	Livingston Mission Field	15.01	23	Bredette	12.88
24	Hinsdale 4 SW	15.00	24	Butte Bert Mooney Arpt	12.89
25	Columbus	14.89	24	Carter 14 W	12.89

Rankings include 25 highest/lowest stations. If state has less than 25 stations, all stations are included. The period of record is 1980–2009. See User Guide for detailed explanation of data.

Annual Extreme Maximum Daily Precipitation

Highest

Rank	Station Name	Inches
1	Content 3 SSE	5.57
2	Chinook	5.50
3	Del Bonita	5.00
3	Yellowtail Dam	5.00
5	Westby	***4.50***
6	Busby	3.75
7	Bigfork 13 S	***3.55***
8	Gibson Dam	3.37
9	Cascade 5 S	3.35
9	Moorhead 9 NE	3.35
11	Big Sandy	***3.32***
12	Hinsdale 4 SW	3.27
13	Wyola 1 SW	***3.26***
14	Brockway 3 WSW	3.21
15	Biddle 8 SW	3.12
15	Big Timber	***3.12***
17	Hardin	***3.10***
18	Bridger 1 S	***3.08***
19	Ridgeway 1 S	***3.07***
20	Chester	3.02
21	Billings Water Plant	3.00
22	Ekalaka	2.97
22	Fort Assinniboine	2.97
24	Glasgow Intl Arpt	2.96
24	Opheim 10 N	***2.96***

Lowest

Rank	Station Name	Inches
1	Butte Bert Mooney Arpt	1.47
2	Drummond	1.52
3	Divide	***1.63***
4	Darby	1.70
4	Eureka Ranger Stn	1.70
6	Stevensville	1.72
7	Anaconda	1.83
7	Libby Dam Base	***1.83***
9	Boulder	1.85
10	Bozeman Gallatin Fld	1.91
11	Helena Arpt Asos	1.93
12	Dillon Wmce	1.94
13	Huntley Experiment Stn	***2.00***
13	Trident	***2.00***
15	Missoula Johnson-Bell Field	2.03
16	Alder 17 S	2.09
16	West Glacier	2.09
18	Hebgen Dam	2.10
19	Havre City-County Arpt	2.15
20	Winifred	2.30
21	Millegan 14 SE	***2.40***
22	Blackleaf	***2.41***
22	Cohagen	2.41
22	Denton 1 NNE	2.41
25	Cut Bank Muni Arpt	2.43

Number of Days Annually With ≥ 0.1 Inches of Precipitation

Highest

Rank	Station Name	Days
1	West Glacier	82
2	Hebgen Dam	81
3	Cooke City 2 W	76
3	Lindbergh Lake	76
5	Creston	60
6	Bigfork 13 S	57
7	Kalispell Arpt	56
7	Libby Dam Base	***56***
9	Bozeman Montana St Univ	55
10	Millegan 14 SE	***50***
11	Gibson Dam	46
12	Anaconda	45
12	Darby	45
12	Eureka Ranger Stn	45
15	Bozeman Gallatin Fld	44
15	Cascade 5 S	44
15	Grass Range	44
15	Yellowtail Dam	44
19	Livingston Mission Field	43
20	Busby	42
20	Carlyle 12 NW	42
20	Denton 1 NNE	42
20	Missoula Johnson-Bell Field	42
20	Wyola 1 SW	***42***
25	Alder 17 S	41

Lowest

Rank	Station Name	Days
1	Brockway 3 WSW	28
2	Chester	29
2	Cut Bank Muni Arpt	29
2	Fort Peck Power Plant	29
2	Havre City-County Arpt	29
6	Glasgow Intl Arpt	30
7	Cohagen	32
7	Hardin	32
7	Medicine Lake 3 SE	32
7	Miles City Municipal Arpt	32
7	Westby	32
12	Bredette	33
12	Culbertson	33
12	Dillon Wmce	33
12	Divide	33
12	Glendive	33
12	Helena Arpt Asos	33
12	Hinsdale 4 SW	33
12	Moorhead 9 NE	33
12	Opheim 10 N	***33***
21	Big Sandy	34
21	Bridger 1 S	***34***
23	Blackleaf	***35***
23	Carter 14 W	35
23	Del Bonita	35

Rankings include 25 highest/lowest stations. If state has less than 25 stations, all stations are included. The period of record is 1980–2009. See User Guide for detailed explanation of data.

Number of Days Annually With ≥ 0.5 Inches of Precipitation

Highest

Rank	Station Name	Days
1	West Glacier	15
2	Hebgen Dam	14
3	Bigfork 13 S	12
4	Lindbergh Lake	10
5	Biddle 8 SW	9
5	Bozeman Montana St Univ	9
5	Cascade 5 S	9
5	Grass Range	9
9	Carlyle 12 NW	8
9	Cooke City 2 W	8
9	Del Bonita	8
9	Ekalaka	8
9	Hinsdale 4 SW	8
9	Millegan 14 SE	8
9	Ridgeway 1 S	8
9	Winifred	8
17	Alder 17 S	7
17	Big Timber	7
17	Brandenberg	7
17	Creston	7
17	Denton 1 NNE	7
17	Gibson Dam	7
17	Glendive	7
17	Miles City Municipal Arpt	7
17	Wyola 1 SW	7

Lowest

Rank	Station Name	Days
1	Missoula Johnson-Bell Field	2
2	Bozeman Gallatin Fld	3
2	Butte Bert Mooney Arpt	3
2	Chester	3
2	Drummond	3
2	Glasgow Intl Arpt	3
2	Helena Arpt Asos	3
2	Stevensville	3
9	Boulder	4
9	Bridger 1 S	4
9	Divide	4
9	Eureka Ranger Stn	4
9	Havre City-County Arpt	4
9	Kalispell Arpt	4
15	Anaconda	5
15	Big Sandy	5
15	Bredette	5
15	Brockway 3 WSW	5
15	Chinook	5
15	Cohagen	5
15	Dillon Wmce	5
15	Libby Dam Base	5
15	Medicine Lake 3 SE	5
15	Trident	5
15	Westby	5

Number of Days Annually With ≥ 1.0 Inches of Precipitation

Highest

Rank	Station Name	Days
1	Big Timber	2
1	Blackleaf	2
1	Culbertson	2
1	Del Bonita	2
1	Hinsdale 4 SW	2
1	Westby	2
7	Big Sandy	1
7	Cascade 5 S	1
7	Cut Bank Muni Arpt	1
7	Gibson Dam	1
7	Grass Range	1
7	Medicine Lake 3 SE	1
7	Yellowtail Dam	1
14	Alder 17 S	0
14	Anaconda	0
14	Biddle 8 SW	0
14	Bigfork 13 S	0
14	Billings Logan Int'l Arpt	0
14	Billings Water Plant	0
14	Boulder	0
14	Bozeman Gallatin Fld	0
14	Bozeman Montana St Univ	0
14	Brandenberg	0
14	Bredette	0
14	Bridger 1 S	0

Lowest

Rank	Station Name	Days
1	Alder 17 S	0
1	Anaconda	0
1	Biddle 8 SW	0
1	Bigfork 13 S	0
1	Billings Logan Int'l Arpt	0
1	Billings Water Plant	0
1	Boulder	0
1	Bozeman Gallatin Fld	0
1	Bozeman Montana St Univ	0
1	Brandenberg	0
1	Bredette	0
1	Bridger 1 S	0
1	Brockway 3 WSW	0
1	Busby	0
1	Butte Bert Mooney Arpt	0
1	Carlyle 12 NW	0
1	Carter 14 W	0
1	Chester	0
1	Chinook	0
1	Cohagen	0
1	Columbus	0
1	Content 3 SSE	0
1	Cooke City 2 W	0
1	Creston	0
1	Darby	0

Rankings include 25 highest/lowest stations. If state has less than 25 stations, all stations are included. The period of record is 1980–2009. See User Guide for detailed explanation of data.

Annual Snowfall

Highest

Rank	Station Name	Inches
1	Cooke City 2 W	***192.1***
2	Hebgen Dam	180.2
3	Lindbergh Lake	133.3
4	Millegan 14 SE	***128.7***
5	West Glacier	121.4
6	Bozeman Montana St Univ	92.8
7	Anaconda	74.7
8	Cascade 5 S	69.2
9	Great Falls Intl Arpt	60.8
10	Kalispell Arpt	***60.0***
11	Alder 17 S	56.3
12	Del Bonita	56.1
13	Gibson Dam	56.0
14	Billings Logan Int'l Arpt	55.8
15	Busby	53.0
16	Grass Range	48.2
17	Creston	***47.8***
18	Ridgeway 1 S	45.6
19	Carter 14 W	45.1
20	Carlyle 12 NW	44.5
21	Brandenberg	42.2
22	Missoula Johnson-Bell Field	39.6
23	Havre City-County Arpt	***39.0***
24	Helena Arpt Asos	***38.6***
25	Biddle 8 SW	37.5

Lowest

Rank	Station Name	Inches
1	Stevensville	19.5
2	Divide	20.4
3	Medicine Lake 3 SE	***20.9***
4	Glendive	22.1
5	Westby	***22.4***
6	Cohagen	24.0
7	Trident	28.2
8	Moorhead 9 NE	28.8
9	Flatwillow 4 ENE	28.9
10	Fort Assinniboine	29.6
11	Bredette	29.8
12	Chinook	***31.9***
13	Big Timber	***32.4***
14	Glasgow Intl Arpt	33.4
15	Eureka Ranger Stn	34.7
16	Columbus	***35.4***
17	Denton 1 NNE	36.0
18	Drummond	36.1
19	Huntley Experiment Stn	36.2
20	Bridger 1 S	***36.4***
21	Biddle 8 SW	37.5
22	Helena Arpt Asos	***38.6***
23	Havre City-County Arpt	***39.0***
24	Missoula Johnson-Bell Field	39.6
25	Brandenberg	42.2

Annual Maximum Snow Depth

Highest

Rank	Station Name	Inches
1	Cooke City 2 W	72
2	Lindbergh Lake	65
3	Kalispell Arpt	***61***
4	West Glacier	60
5	Hebgen Dam	56
6	Millegan 14 SE	***50***
7	Biddle 8 SW	36
8	Creston	32
9	Drummond	31
9	Eureka Ranger Stn	31
11	Bridger 1 S	***30***
12	Glasgow Intl Arpt	29
12	Medicine Lake 3 SE	29
14	Bigfork 13 S	***28***
14	Bozeman Montana St Univ	28
14	Stevensville	28
17	Missoula Johnson-Bell Field	27
18	Busby	25
19	Big Timber	***24***
19	Del Bonita	24
19	Denton 1 NNE	***24***
19	Moorhead 9 NE	24
23	Cascade 5 S	23
24	Brandenberg	22
24	Bredette	22

Lowest

Rank	Station Name	Inches
1	Alder 17 S	***13***
2	Billings Logan Int'l Arpt	14
2	Divide	14
4	Glendive	15
5	Helena Arpt Asos	***16***
6	Great Falls Intl Arpt	17
7	Cut Bank Muni Arpt	18
7	Flatwillow 4 ENE	***18***
7	Fort Assinniboine	18
7	Huntley Experiment Stn	***18***
7	Trident	***18***
12	Cohagen	19
12	Havre City-County Arpt	***19***
14	Anaconda	20
14	Carter 14 W	20
14	Culbertson	20
17	Brandenberg	22
17	Bredette	22
17	Gibson Dam	***22***
20	Cascade 5 S	23
21	Big Timber	***24***
21	Del Bonita	24
21	Denton 1 NNE	***24***
21	Moorhead 9 NE	24
25	Busby	25

Rankings include 25 highest/lowest stations. If state has less than 25 stations, all stations are included. The period of record is 1980–2009. See User Guide for detailed explanation of data.

Number of Days Annually With ≥ 1.0 Inch Snow Depth

Highest

Rank	Station Name	Days
1	Cooke City 2 W	189
2	Hebgen Dam	158
3	Lindbergh Lake	156
4	West Glacier	146
5	Millegan 14 SE	***124***
6	Bozeman Montana St Univ	116
7	Bredette	98
8	Anaconda	92
9	Busby	88
10	Culbertson	85
11	Creston	76
12	Glasgow Intl Arpt	75
12	Kalispell Arpt	***75***
14	Fort Assinniboine	71
15	Brandenberg	67
15	Glendive	67
17	Medicine Lake 3 SE	***65***
18	Biddle 8 SW	63
18	Drummond	63
20	Del Bonita	62
21	Cut Bank Muni Arpt	61
21	Havre City-County Arpt	***61***
23	Great Falls Intl Arpt	58
23	Missoula Johnson-Bell Field	58
25	Billings Logan Int'l Arpt	57

Lowest

Rank	Station Name	Days
1	Big Timber	***25***
2	Alder 17 S	***30***
2	Denton 1 NNE	***30***
4	Stevensville	32
5	Bigfork 13 S	***35***
6	Flatwillow 4 ENE	36
7	Gibson Dam	***37***
8	Chinook	***39***
9	Carter 14 W	40
9	Cascade 5 S	40
11	Trident	41
12	Divide	43
13	Bridger 1 S	***47***
14	Helena Arpt Asos	***52***
15	Cohagen	54
16	Huntley Experiment Stn	***55***
16	Moorhead 9 NE	55
18	Billings Logan Int'l Arpt	57
18	Eureka Ranger Stn	57
20	Great Falls Intl Arpt	58
20	Missoula Johnson-Bell Field	58
22	Cut Bank Muni Arpt	61
22	Havre City-County Arpt	***61***
24	Del Bonita	62
25	Biddle 8 SW	63

Rankings include 25 highest/lowest stations. If state has less than 25 stations, all stations are included. The period of record is 1980–2009. See User Guide for detailed explanation of data.

Significant Storm Events in Montana: 2000 – 2009

Location or County	Date	Type	Mag.	Deaths	Injuries	Property Damage ($mil.)	Crop Damage ($mil.)
Lewis and Clark	07/23/00	Wild/Forest Fire	na	0	2	2.5	0.0
Lewis and Clark	08/01/00	Wild/Forest Fire	na	0	2	2.5	0.0
Western Glacier County	09/09/00	Dust Storm	na	1	8	0.0	0.0
Eastern Montana	11/01/00	Winter Storm	na	0	0	3.3	0.0
Southern Big Horn County	04/09/01	Heavy Snow	na	0	0	1.2	0.0
Mccone	07/20/01	Thunderstorm Wind	113 mph	0	0	1.6	0.5
Rocky Mountain Front Region	06/08/02	Winter Storm	na	0	0	3.2	0.0
Ravalli	08/04/02	Hail	1.00 in.	0	0	2.0	0.1
Garfield	07/16/03	Wildfire	na	0	0	2.9	1.0
Northern Sweet Grass County	08/06/03	Wildfire	na	0	0	1.0	0.0
Eastern Roosevelt County, Frazer Montana	02/06/05	Extreme Cold/Wind Chill	na	1	0	0.0	0.0
Roosevelt	07/13/05	Thunderstorm Wind	92 mph	0	0	3.0	0.0
Roosevelt	07/13/05	Thunderstorm Wind	113 mph	0	0	1.2	0.0
Western Glacier County	01/14/06	Avalanche	na	2	0	0.0	0.0
Dawson	06/14/06	Thunderstorm Wind	98 mph	0	0	2.0	0.0
Flathead	11/05/06	Flash Flood	na	0	0	7.0	0.0
Valley	06/16/07	Hail	3.00 in.	0	0	8.0	15.0
Valley	06/16/07	Hail	2.75 in.	0	0	3.0	5.0
Southeast and South Central Montana	05/01/08	Winter Storm	na	0	0	3.0	0.0
Flathead County	12/12/08	Blizzard	na	1	0	0.2	0.0

Note: Deaths, injuries, and damages are date and location specific.

NEBRASKA

PHYSICAL FEATURES. Nebraska, one of the Great Plains States, is located in the north-central portion of the United States. The area of the State is 76,653 square miles, of which about 600 are water. On the eastern boundary, along the Missouri River, the elevation rises from less than 900 feet in the southeast to 1,200 feet in the northeast. The elevation also increases westward to about 3,000 feet in the southwest and 5,000 feet in the northwest. The landscape changes from level or gently rolling prairie in the east, to rounded sandhills in the north-central part, and thence westward to high plains.

All of Nebraska is drained by the Missouri River System. The direction of flow is mostly west to east, but in the southeastern section the flow is from northwest to southeast. The Missouri River forms the eastern boundary of the State and a part of the northern boundary. The major tributary is the Platte River, with its two main branches which rise in the high elevations of Colorado. Other important tributaries are the Niobrara River in the north and the Republican and Big Blue Rivers in the south.

Greatest volume of flow occurs during May, June, and July, the months of heaviest rainfall. Although the heaviest snowfall occurs in February and March, it usually does not accumulate to any considerable depth and so the resultant runoff does not materially affect river stages.

GENERAL CLIMATE. The climate is typical of the interior of large continents in middle latitudes; that is, rather light rainfall, low humidity, hot summers, cold winters, great variations in temperature and rainfall from year to year, and frequent changes in weather from day to day. The rapid changes in weather are brought about by invasion of large masses of air of different characteristics, such as warm, moist air from the Gulf of Mexico; hot, dry air from the Southwest; cool, dry air from the north Pacific Ocean; and cold, dry air from northwestern Canada.

The Rocky Mountains to the west have a profound influence on the climate of Nebraska. Air crossing the mountains from the west loses much of its moisture on the windward side and becomes warmer and drier as it descends on the eastern slopes; therefore, no significant amount of moisture which falls as rain or snow reaches the State from the Pacific Ocean. The moisture supply for precipitation comes from the Gulf of Mexico. The remoteness from the source of supply is one of the reasons for the wide variation in rainfall from year to year. Moist air from the Gulf is often deflected eastward before it reaches Nebraska. Downslope winds from the Rocky Mountains occasionally cause large, rapid changes to higher temperatures, particularly during the winter.

Although hot nights in summer occur rather frequently in the east, they are almost unknown in the higher elevations of the western, less humid, part of the State where rapid cooling after sunset generally occurs.

TEMPERATURE. The mean annual temperature varies from about 53°F. along the eastern half of the southern border to about 45°F. in the northwest corner. Maximum temperatures above 100°F. have occurred throughout the State in the months of June, July, August, and September. Temperatures of 110°F. or higher have been recorded over most of the State, except in parts of the northwest. Minimum temperatures of zero or below occur on an average about 10 days a year in the southeast and 25 days in the northwest. Minima below -40°F. have been recorded a few times at northern and western weather stations. Although the winter climate is classed as cold, there are frequent periods of mild, pleasant weather.

The average date of the last freeze (32°F.) in spring ranges from about April 25 in the extreme southeast to about May 21 in a small area in the northwest portion, while the first in the fall varies from about October 6 in the southeast to about September 20 in the extreme northwest. Hence the average length of the growing season (freeze-free season) ranges from 164 days in the southeast to 122 in the northwest.

PRECIPITATION. The average annual precipitation in the eastern third of the State is about 27 inches; in the central third, about 22 inches; and in the western third, about 18 inches. The amount decreases rather uniformly from 33 inches in the southeast corner to about 14 inches in a small area near the western border. On the average nearly 80 percent of the yearly total falls in the six months from April to September. During July and August, rainfall normally diminishes slowly in the east portion. In the west it decreases more rapidly, so that the August average is only a little over one-half the June average in many localities.

Excessive rates of rainfall for short periods occur frequently in summer thundershowers. In some seasons thundershowers are numerous and well distributed, but sometimes they are scattered and infrequent. The result is great variability in the monthly amounts of rainfall in different years and also in the annual amounts from year to year. In dry years, periods of 15 to 20 days without appreciable rain may occur in June, July, and August; and under such conditions, hot, dry winds often cause serious and extensive damage to crops. The precipitation records show successions of wet and dry epochs.

Floods may be expected once or twice in most years in smaller streams in the eastern third of the State, but less frequently over the west and central portions, and are generally caused by short duration, high intensity rainfall. Severe flooding occurs infrequently on the Missouri and is usually caused by rapid melting of heavy snowpacks in the upper portion of the basin, attended by moderate to heavy rains.

The average seasonal snowfall is approximately 29 inches. Snowfall usually increases during the late winter and reaches a maximum in March over most of the State. The higher regions in the west portion frequently have heavy snows in April, and occasionally in May.

OTHER CLIMATIC ELEMENTS. Sunshine for the year averages about 65 percent of the possible amount, ranging from about 55 percent in December to nearly 80 percent in July.

There are frequent changes in wind direction at all seasons of the year, but the prevailing direction is from the south or southeast from May to September, and from the northwest or north during the remainder of the year, except that westerly winds predominate in the southwest portion during the autumn and winter months. The average is about nine m.p.h.

A few tornadoes occur within the State nearly every year; the average is about 10 per year. Although tornadoes are usually very small, both in width and in length of path, there is almost total destruction where the whirling funnel cloud touches the ground.

The number of hailstorms averages between 20 and 25 per year, occurring mostly in June, July, and August.

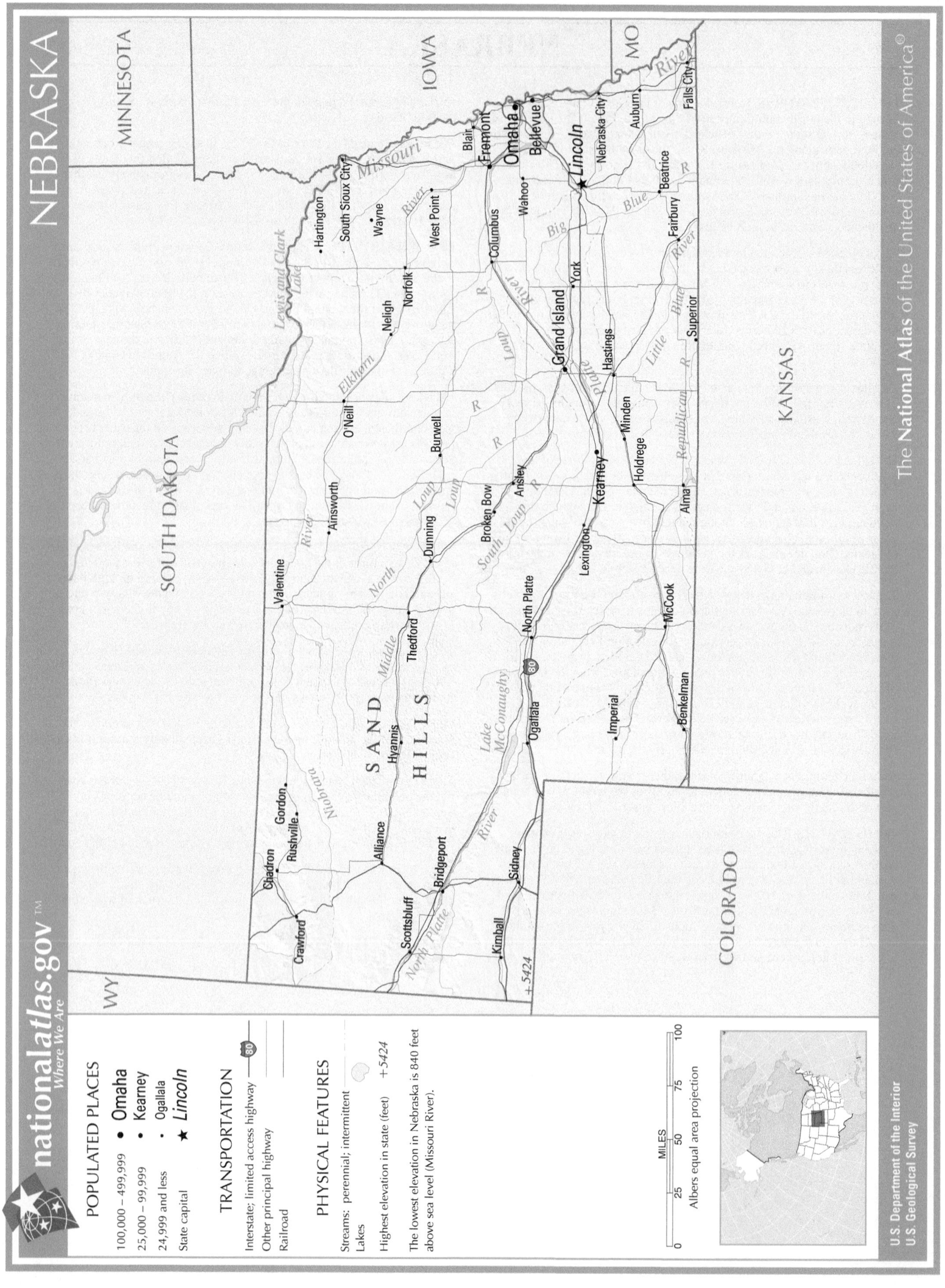
NEBRASKA
nationalatlas.gov™
Where We Are
POPULATED PLACES
100,000 – 499,999 • Omaha
25,000 – 99,999 • Kearney
24,999 and less • Ogallala
State capital ★ Lincoln
TRANSPORTATION
Interstate; limited access highway
Other principal highway
Railroad
PHYSICAL FEATURES
Streams: perennial; intermittent
Lakes
Highest elevation in state (feet) +5424
The lowest elevation in Nebraska is 840 feet above sea level (Missouri River).
MILES
0 25 50 75 100
Albers equal area projection
U.S. Department of the Interior
U.S. Geological Survey
The National Atlas of the United States of America®
MINNESOTA
IOWA
MO
SOUTH DAKOTA
WY
COLORADO
KANSAS
SAND HILLS
Missouri River
Lewis and Clark Lake
Niobrara River
Elkhorn River
North Loup R
Middle Loup R
South Loup R
Loup R
Big Blue R
Little Blue R
Republican R
Platte R
North Platte R
Lake McConaughy
Blair
Fremont
Omaha
Bellevue
Lincoln
Nebraska City
Auburn
Falls City
Beatrice
Fairbury
Wahoo
West Point
Wayne
South Sioux City
Hartington
Norfolk
Neligh
Columbus
York
Grand Island
Hastings
Superior
Minden
Holdrege
Kearney
Alma
Lexington
O'Neill
Burwell
Ainsworth
Ansley
Broken Bow
Dunning
Valentine
Thedford
North Platte
McCook
Imperial
Benkelman
Ogallala
Hyannis
Gordon
Rushville
Chadron
Alliance
Bridgeport
Sidney
Crawford
Scottsbluff
Kimball
80
+5424

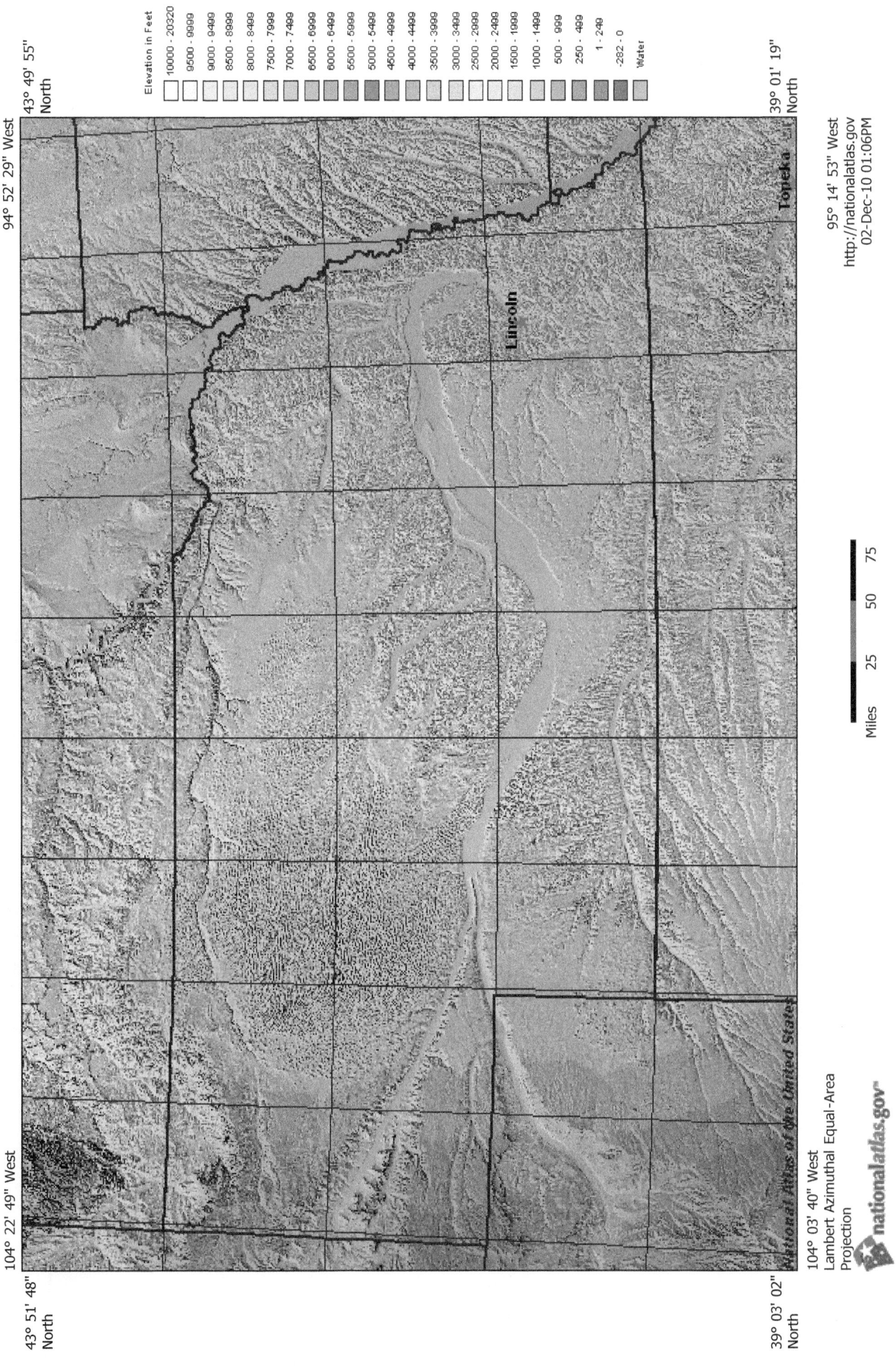

Elevation in Feet
10000 - 20320
9500 - 9999
9000 - 9499
8500 - 8999
8000 - 8499
7500 - 7999
7000 - 7499
6500 - 6999
6000 - 6499
5500 - 5999
5000 - 5499
4500 - 4999
4000 - 4499
3500 - 3999
3000 - 3499
2500 - 2999
2000 - 2499
1500 - 1999
1000 - 1499
500 - 999
250 - 499
1 - 249
-282 - 0
Water
43° 49' 55" North
94° 52' 29" West
39° 01' 19" North
95° 14' 53" West
http://nationalatlas.gov
02-Dec-10 01:06PM
Lincoln
Topeka
Miles
25
50
75
43° 51' 48" North
104° 22' 49" West
39° 03' 02" North
104° 03' 40" West
Lambert Azimuthal Equal-Area Projection
National Atlas of the United States
nationalatlas.gov

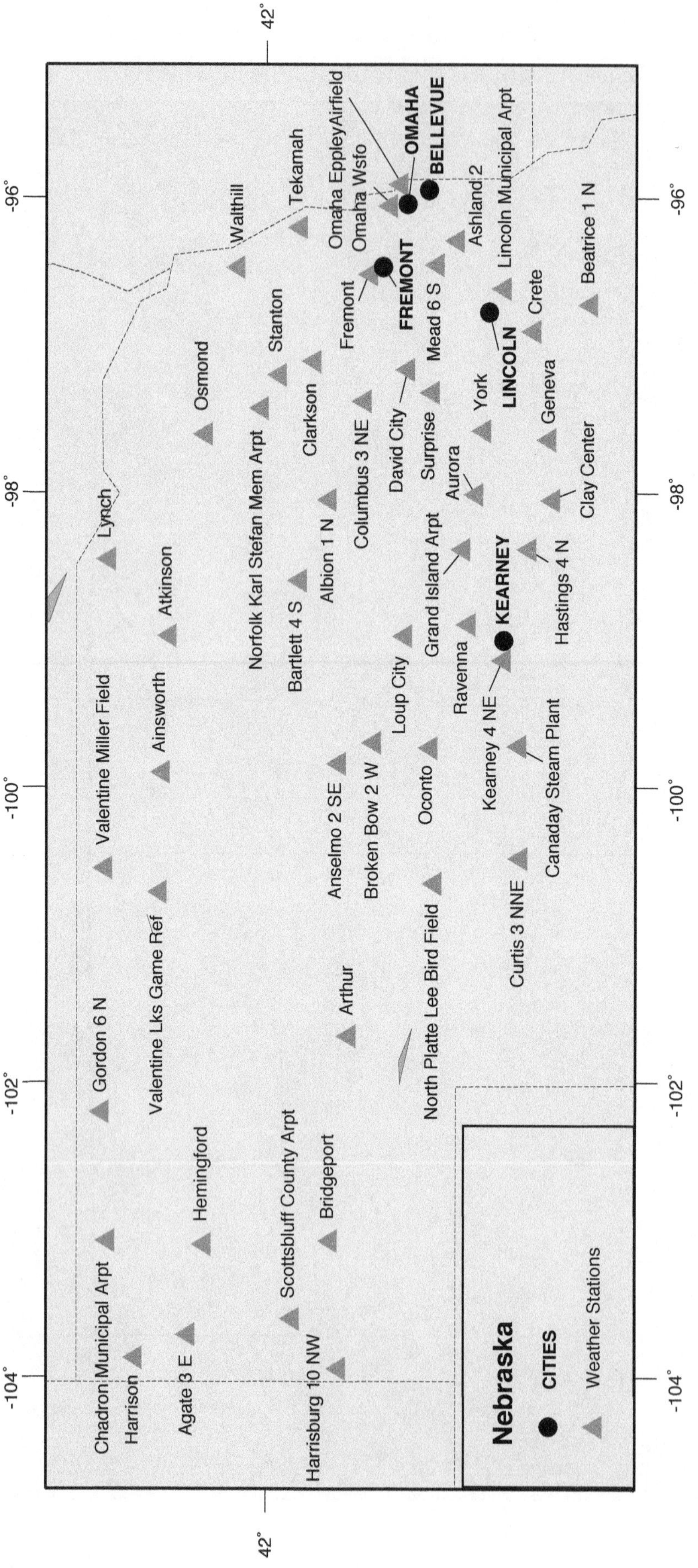
Nebraska
CITIES
Weather Stations
42°
-96°
-98°
-100°
-102°
-104°
OMAHA
BELLEVUE
FREMONT
LINCOLN
KEARNEY
Omaha EppleyAirfield
Omaha Wsfo
Tekamah
Walthill
Ashland 2
Lincoln Municipal Arpt
Beatrice 1 N
Fremont
Mead 6 S
Crete
Stanton
Osmond
Clarkson
Norfolk Karl Stefan Mem Arpt
Columbus 3 NE
David City
Surprise
York
Geneva
Aurora
Clay Center
Lynch
Atkinson
Albion 1 N
Bartlett 4 S
Grand Island Arpt
Hastings 4 N
Loup City
Ravenna
Kearney 4 NE
Canaday Steam Plant
Valentine Miller Field
Ainsworth
Anselmo 2 SE
Broken Bow 2 W
Oconto
Curtis 3 NNE
Valentine Lks Game Ref
Gordon 6 N
Arthur
North Platte Lee Bird Field
Hemingford
Scottsbluff County Arpt
Bridgeport
Chadron Municipal Arpt
Harrison
Agate 3 E
Harrisburg 10 NW

Nebraska Weather Stations by County

County	Station Name
Adams	Hastings 4 N
Arthur	Arthur
Banner	Harrisburg 10 NW
Boone	Albion 1 N
Box Butte	Hemingford
Boyd	Lynch
Brown	Ainsworth
Buffalo	Kearney 4 NE Ravenna
Burt	Tekamah
Butler	David City Surprise
Cherry	Valentine Lakes Game Ref Valentine Miller Field
Clay	Clay Center
Colfax	Clarkson
Custer	Anselmo 2 SE Broken Bow 2 W Oconto
Dawes	Chadron Municipal Arpt
Dodge	Fremont
Douglas	Omaha Eppley Airfield Omaha WSFO
Fillmore	Geneva
Frontier	Curtis 3 NNE
Gage	Beatrice 1 N
Gosper	Canaday Steam Plant
Hall	Grand Island Arpt
Hamilton	Aurora
Holt	Atkinson
Lancaster	Lincoln Municipal Arpt
Lincoln	North Platte Lee Bird Field
Madison	Norfolk Karl Stefan Mem Arpt
Morrill	Bridgeport
Pierce	Osmond

County	Station Name
Platte	Columbus 3 NE
Saline	Crete
Saunders	Ashland 2 Mead 6 S
Scotts Bluff	Scottsbluff County Arpt
Sheridan	Gordon 6 N
Sherman	Loup City
Sioux	Agate 3 E Harrison
Stanton	Stanton
Thurston	Walthill
Wheeler	Bartlett 4 S
York	York

See User Guide for station inclusion criteria.

Nebraska Weather Stations by City

City	Station Name	Miles
Alliance	Hemingford	17.7
Beatrice	Beatrice 1 N	2.2
Bellevue	Glenwood 3 SW, IA	12.9
	Ashland 2	24.1
	Omaha Eppley Airfield	11.3
	Omaha WSFO	15.8
Blair	Fremont	18.7
	Omaha Eppley Airfield	20.2
	Omaha WSFO	14.0
	Tekamah	15.7
Chalco	Glenwood 3 SW, IA	23.0
	Ashland 2	14.5
	Fremont	24.3
	Mead 6 S	18.4
	Omaha Eppley Airfield	15.3
	Omaha WSFO	14.1
Columbus	Clarkson	22.7
	Columbus 3 NE	2.5
	David City	17.4
	Surprise	23.3
Fremont	Fremont	1.3
	Mead 6 S	21.2
Gering	Harrisburg 10 NW	19.7
	Scottsbluff County Arpt	4.5
Grand Island	Aurora	19.2
	Grand Island Arpt	3.7
	Hastings 4 N	19.0
Hastings	Clay Center	18.7
	Hastings 4 N	4.2
Kearney	Kearney 4 NE	4.1
	Ravenna	24.4
La Vista	Glenwood 3 SW, IA	18.9
	Ashland 2	18.8
	Mead 6 S	23.5
	Omaha Eppley Airfield	11.6
	Omaha WSFO	12.7
Lexington	Canaday Steam Plant	6.1
	Oconto	24.3
Lincoln	Ashland 2	23.9
	Crete	19.5
	Lincoln Municipal Arpt	5.2
	Mead 6 S	24.7
Norfolk	Norfolk Karl Stefan Mem Arpt	3.6
	Osmond	23.6
	Stanton	11.3
North Platte	North Platte Lee Bird Field	5.7
Offutt AFB	Glenwood 3 SW, IA	12.7
	Ashland 2	21.5
Offutt AFB *(cont.)*	Omaha Eppley Airfield	13.6
	Omaha WSFO	17.2
Omaha	Glenwood 3 SW, IA	22.4
	Ashland 2	22.1
	Omaha Eppley Airfield	7.8
	Omaha WSFO	7.5
Papillion	Glenwood 3 SW, IA	17.7
	Ashland 2	17.8
	Mead 6 S	23.2
	Omaha Eppley Airfield	13.3
	Omaha WSFO	14.7
Scottsbluff	Harrisburg 10 NW	22.0
	Scottsbluff County Arpt	3.1
South Sioux City	Sioux City Municipal Arpt, IA	6.1
	Walthill	22.3
York	Aurora	21.6
	Geneva	23.2
	Surprise	21.3
	York	0.7

Note: Miles is the distance between the geographic center of the city and the weather station.

See User Guide for station inclusion criteria.

Nebraska Weather Stations by Elevation

Feet	Station Name
4,850	Harrison
4,669	Agate 3 E
4,549	Harrisburg 10 NW
4,270	Hemingford
3,944	Scottsbluff County Arpt
3,700	Gordon 6 N
3,666	Bridgeport
3,500	Arthur
3,299	Chadron Municipal Arpt
2,929	Valentine Lakes Game Ref
2,777	North Platte Lee Bird Field
2,721	Curtis 3 NNE
2,604	Anselmo 2 SE
2,589	Valentine Miller Field
2,580	Oconto
2,509	Ainsworth
2,500	Broken Bow 2 W
2,361	Canaday Steam Plant
2,140	Bartlett 4 S
2,129	Kearney 4 NE
2,109	Atkinson
2,064	Loup City
2,049	Ravenna
1,939	Hastings 4 N
1,839	Grand Island Arpt
1,785	Aurora
1,758	Albion 1 N
1,750	Clay Center
1,649	Osmond
1,629	Geneva
1,609	David City
1,608	York
1,549	Clarkson
1,549	Norfolk Karl Stefan Mem Arpt
1,549	Surprise
1,490	Stanton
1,450	Columbus 3 NE
1,435	Crete
1,390	Lynch
1,309	Omaha WSFO
1,296	Beatrice 1 N
1,220	Walthill
1,189	Lincoln Municipal Arpt
1,180	Fremont
1,154	Mead 6 S
1,069	Ashland 2
1,039	Tekamah
981	Omaha Eppley Airfield

See User Guide for station inclusion criteria.

Grand Island Airport

The Grand Island Weather Service Office is located at the Hall County Regional Airport, three miles northeast of downtown Grand Island. It is situated just west of the mid-point of the north-south runway. The site is less than 50 miles from the geographical center of the contiguous United States and in the shallow Platte River valley. The complex of the Loup River and its tributaries converge approximately 15 miles northwest of the station, then flows eastward across the state. The terrain immediately surrounding the station is flat, sandy, and loam. Just to the north is the southern boundary of the Nebraska sandhills. The terrain slopes gently upward from the Missouri River valley in eastern Nebraska to the Rocky Mountains of Colorado and Wyoming.

The climate is primarily continental in nature with occasional incursions of maritime tropical air from the Gulf of Mexico and modified maritime polar air from the Pacific Ocean. Wintertime outbreaks of cold, dry, Arctic air from Canada are common, usually accompanied by strong biting winds.

The east-west upslope produces periods of fog and low stratus when winds have an easterly component, and the characteristics of a Chinook, with warm dry air, when the component is westerly. Dry-season dust storms occur occasionally with these Chinook winds. These have been reduced in recent years by increased farm irrigation. Growing season humidities have also been increased by the expanding irrigation projects. Summers are usually hot and dry with temperatures often reaching 100 degrees or more. Late spring and early summer is the peak season for severe thunderstorms with frequent hail and tornados occasionally occurring. Winters are punctuated by occasional severe blizzards and have wide variations in temperatures that range from mild to bitterly cold.

Based on the 1951-1980 period, the average first occurrence of 32 degrees Fahrenheit in the fall is October 9 and the average last occurrence in the spring is April 29.

Grand Island Airport *Hall County* Elevation: 1,839 ft. Latitude: 40° 58' N Longitude: 98° 19' W

	JAN	FEB	MAR	APR	MAY	JUN	JUL	AUG	SEP	OCT	NOV	DEC	YEAR
Mean Maximum Temp. (°F)	36.0	39.9	50.9	63.1	72.9	83.2	87.9	85.5	78.0	64.6	49.6	37.2	62.4
Mean Temp. (°F)	25.2	29.1	39.2	50.5	61.3	71.4	76.4	74.1	65.2	52.1	38.3	26.9	50.8
Mean Minimum Temp. (°F)	14.4	18.4	27.4	37.8	49.7	59.4	64.8	62.7	52.3	39.5	26.9	16.6	39.2
Extreme Maximum Temp. (°F)	76	80	90	96	101	107	109	110	104	95	84	71	110
Extreme Minimum Temp. (°F)	-20	-21	-11	10	25	39	47	43	23	9	-8	-26	-26
Days Maximum Temp. ≥ 90°F	0	0	0	1	1	7	13	9	5	0	0	0	36
Days Maximum Temp. ≤ 32°F	12	9	3	0	0	0	0	0	0	0	3	11	38
Days Minimum Temp. ≤ 32°F	31	26	22	8	0	0	0	0	1	7	22	30	147
Days Minimum Temp. ≤ 0°F	5	3	1	0	0	0	0	0	0	0	0	3	12
Heating Degree Days (base 65°F)	1,227	1,007	794	442	166	22	2	7	102	405	795	1,174	6,143
Cooling Degree Days (base 65°F)	0	0	0	14	58	220	362	296	115	12	0	0	1,077
Mean Precipitation (in.)	0.54	0.68	1.79	2.52	4.34	4.12	3.29	3.14	2.20	1.84	1.16	0.61	26.23
Maximum Precipitation (in.)*	1.6	3.4	6.6	7.3	8.9	14.0	10.4	8.7	9.0	3.6	3.8	2.2	38.2
Minimum Precipitation (in.)*	trace	0.1	trace	0.1	0.4	0.5	0.6	0.7	0.2	0	trace	trace	13.6
Extreme Maximum Daily Precip. (in.)	0.75	1.21	1.61	2.67	6.50	4.18	4.23	3.22	3.01	1.68	2.60	0.97	6.50
Days With ≥ 0.1" Precipitation	2	2	4	4	7	6	5	6	4	4	2	2	48
Days With ≥ 0.5" Precipitation	0	0	1	2	3	2	2	2	1	1	1	0	15
Days With ≥ 1.0" Precipitation	0	0	0	1	1	1	1	1	1	0	0	0	6
Mean Snowfall (in.)	6.7	6.1	6.0	1.3	trace	trace	trace	trace	0.2	1.2	3.1	5.1	29.7
Maximum Snowfall (in.)*	18	22	21	9	4	0	0	0	4	10	17	26	58
Maximum 24-hr. Snowfall (in.)*	9	12	12	6	4	0	0	0	4	9	10	11	12
Maximum Snow Depth (in.)	12	15	16	5	trace	trace	trace	trace	1	6	14	18	18
Days With ≥ 1.0" Snow Depth	12	10	4	0	0	0	0	0	0	1	3	10	40
Thunderstorm Days*	< 1	< 1	1	4	7	10	9	8	5	2	< 1	< 1	46
Foggy Days*	7	8	9	8	9	6	7	9	8	7	7	8	93
Predominant Sky Cover*	OVR	OVR	OVR	OVR	OVR	OVR	CLR	CLR	CLR	CLR	OVR	OVR	OVR
Mean Relative Humidity 6am (%)*	78	79	80	78	82	82	83	85	83	79	79	79	81
Mean Relative Humidity 3pm (%)*	59	57	52	45	49	46	47	47	45	42	50	57	50
Mean Dewpoint (°F)*	13	18	25	35	48	57	62	60	50	38	26	17	38
Prevailing Wind Direction*	NNW	NNW	NNW	S	S	S	S	S	S	S	S	NNW	S
Prevailing Wind Speed (mph)*	16	16	17	15	15	14	13	13	13	13	12	15	14
Maximum Wind Gust (mph)*	55	60	64	67	76	78	71	68	66	58	62	58	78

Note: (*) Period of record is 1948-1995

The period of record for National Weather Service station data is 1980 – 2009 except where noted. See User Guide for detailed explanation of data.

Lincoln Municipal Airport

Lincoln is near the center of Lancaster County in southeastern Nebraska. The surrounding area is gently rolling prairie. The western edge of the city is in the flat valley of Salt Creek, which receives a number of tributaries in or near the city and flows northeastward to the lower Platte. The terrain slopes upward to the west and is sufficient to cause instability in moist easterly winds in the Lincoln area. Precipitation with westerly winds is infrequent since they are downslope. The upward slope to the west is a part of the general rise in elevation that begins at the Missouri River 45 miles east of Lincoln and culminates in the Continental Divide about 575 miles to the west. The chinook or foehn effect often produces rapid rises in temperature here during the winter with a shift of the wind to westerly.

The maximum temperature has exceeded 110 degrees. Hot winds, combining unusual wind force and high temperatures, occasionally cause serious injury to crops.

The majority of winter outbreaks of severely cold air from northwestern Canada move over the Lincoln area. The temperature has remained below zero degrees for more than eight consecutive days. The center of some of the cold air masses move southward far enough to the east that their full effect is usually not felt here.

Normally the crop season, April through September, receives over three-fourths of the annual precipitation. Nighttime thunderstorms are predominant in the summer months, so that the needed moisture is received during much of the growing season at a time of least interference with outdoor work.

Annual snowfall is about 25 inches, although the annual snowfall has exceeded 59 inches. Much of the snow is light and melts rapidly. However, at times a considerable amount accumulates on the ground and has exceeded a depth of 21 inches.

In the summer the higher winds are associated with thunderstorms. Lincoln has been relatively free from tornadoes and more than slight hail damage seldom occurs. There is much sunshine, averaging 64 percent of the possible duration. Moderate to low humidities are at comfortable levels except for short periods during the summer when warm, moist, tropical air occasionally reaches this area.

Lincoln Municipal Airport *Lancaster County* Elevation: 1,189 ft. Latitude: 40° 50' N Longitude: 96° 46' W

	JAN	FEB	MAR	APR	MAY	JUN	JUL	AUG	SEP	OCT	NOV	DEC	YEAR
Mean Maximum Temp. (°F)	35.7	40.1	52.1	64.2	74.3	84.2	89.3	86.8	78.8	65.6	50.5	37.3	63.2
Mean Temp. (°F)	24.8	29.0	39.9	51.5	62.4	72.6	77.7	75.3	66.1	53.1	39.1	26.9	51.5
Mean Minimum Temp. (°F)	13.9	17.9	27.7	38.7	50.4	60.9	66.1	63.8	53.3	40.6	27.6	16.5	39.8
Extreme Maximum Temp. (°F)	73	77	89	97	99	107	108	107	106	94	85	70	108
Extreme Minimum Temp. (°F)	-19	-22	-15	12	24	41	45	41	26	8	-4	-27	-27
Days Maximum Temp. ≥ 90°F	0	0	0	1	2	8	15	12	4	0	0	0	42
Days Maximum Temp. ≤ 32°F	12	9	3	0	0	0	0	0	0	0	3	11	38
Days Minimum Temp. ≤ 32°F	30	25	21	8	1	0	0	0	0	6	21	29	141
Days Minimum Temp. ≤ 0°F	5	3	1	0	0	0	0	0	0	0	0	3	12
Heating Degree Days (base 65°F)	1,239	1,011	772	415	141	15	1	4	90	377	772	1,174	6,011
Cooling Degree Days (base 65°F)	0	0	1	15	67	249	402	331	129	16	0	0	1,210
Mean Precipitation (in.)	0.65	0.76	1.93	2.69	4.24	4.12	3.27	3.60	2.91	2.03	1.37	0.97	28.54
Maximum Precipitation (in.)*	3.1	3.5	6.6	7.2	8.0	9.8	12.5	8.6	8.3	5.4	3.8	3.4	42.2
Minimum Precipitation (in.)*	trace	0.1	0.1	0.3	0.9	0.6	0.4	0.1	0.3	trace	trace	trace	17.9
Extreme Maximum Daily Precip. (in.)	0.79	0.87	1.32	2.60	3.35	4.24	5.42	2.94	4.68	2.74	2.34	2.13	5.42
Days With ≥ 0.1" Precipitation	2	2	5	5	7	6	6	6	5	4	3	3	54
Days With ≥ 0.5" Precipitation	0	0	1	2	3	3	2	2	2	1	1	0	17
Days With ≥ 1.0" Precipitation	0	0	0	1	1	1	1	1	1	0	0	0	6
Mean Snowfall (in.)	5.7	5.5	4.9	1.4	trace	trace	trace	trace	trace	0.8	2.1	6.1	26.5
Maximum Snowfall (in.)*	15	14	21	8	trace	0	0	0	1	3	9	20	59
Maximum 24-hr. Snowfall (in.)*	8	7	8	6	trace	0	0	0	1	3	8	10	10
Maximum Snow Depth (in.)	13	18	12	7	trace	trace	trace	trace	trace	10	8	16	18
Days With ≥ 1.0" Snow Depth	12	11	4	1	0	0	0	0	0	0	2	9	39
Thunderstorm Days*	< 1	< 1	2	4	7	9	8	8	5	2	1	< 1	46
Foggy Days*	9	10	11	8	9	7	6	9	8	7	9	11	104
Predominant Sky Cover*	OVR	OVR	OVR	OVR	OVR	OVR	CLR	CLR	CLR	CLR	OVR	OVR	OVR
Mean Relative Humidity 6am (%)*	78	81	81	80	83	83	83	86	84	80	80	80	82
Mean Relative Humidity 3pm (%)*	61	60	55	47	51	49	48	51	49	46	54	60	53
Mean Dewpoint (°F)*	14	19	27	38	50	59	64	63	53	41	28	19	40
Prevailing Wind Direction*	N	N	N	N	S	S	S	S	S	S	S	NNW	S
Prevailing Wind Speed (mph)*	12	13	14	13	13	12	10	10	10	10	9	14	12
Maximum Wind Gust (mph)*	63	55	60	64	55	84	62	79	55	58	59	53	84

Note: (*) Period of record is 1948-1995

Norfolk Karl Stefan Mem. Arpt.

Norfolk is located in northeastern Nebraska, in the valley of the Elkhorn River. The city of Norfolk lies at an average elevation of 1,550 feet above sea level. The surrounding country is moderately rolling in all directions. The terrain becomes more level to the south and southwest. Norfolk is situated near the western limit of the Corn Belt. To the east the climate and soils are favorable for diversified farming and dairying. To the west precipitation becomes lighter, and the farming country gives way to the grazing lands of the Great Plains. There are no local topographic features of sufficient importance to affect the climate of the area.

Northeast Nebraska has a climate typical of the interior of large continents in middle latitudes. The rainfall is moderate. Summers are hot and winters cold, and there are great variations in temperature and precipitation from day to day and from season to season. Most of the moisture which falls over this area is brought in from the Gulf of Mexico. The rapid changes in temperature are caused by the interchange of warm air from the south and southwest with cold air from the north. The rapid day to day changes in weather conditions produce an invigorating and healthful climate in northeast Nebraska.

Daily temperature ranges of 30 to 40 degrees are not uncommon. Summertime precipitation is almost wholly in the form of showers and thunderstorms. Practically all precipitation in the colder months is in the form of snow. As a rule, nearly 85 percent of the snowfall occurs from December to March and the ground is covered by snow during this period.

Norfolk is subject to the strong and persistent winds which prevail over the Great Plains states. Winds of 40 to 50 mph are not uncommon in this area, and gusts up to 100 mph have been recorded at Norfolk. Prevailing winds are from the south and southwest from May through September, with prevailing northwesterly winds during the remainder of the year.

Based on the 1951-1980 period, the average first occurrence of 32 degrees Fahrenheit in the fall is October 5 and the average last occurrence in the spring is May 1.

Norfolk Karl Stefan Mem. Arpt. *Madison County* Elevation: 1,549 ft. Latitude: 41° 59' N Longitude: 97° 26' W

	JAN	FEB	MAR	APR	MAY	JUN	JUL	AUG	SEP	OCT	NOV	DEC	YEAR
Mean Maximum Temp. (°F)	33.5	37.4	48.8	62.0	72.7	82.1	86.8	84.4	76.8	63.5	47.5	34.4	60.8
Mean Temp. (°F)	23.0	27.1	37.5	49.8	60.8	70.5	75.4	73.1	64.1	51.1	36.8	24.7	49.5
Mean Minimum Temp. (°F)	12.5	16.9	26.3	37.5	48.9	58.9	63.9	61.8	51.4	38.7	26.0	14.9	38.1
Extreme Maximum Temp. (°F)	74	76	88	95	99	106	108	107	100	95	83	69	108
Extreme Minimum Temp. (°F)	-23	-26	-14	13	26	38	44	40	26	11	-13	-30	-30
Days Maximum Temp. ≥ 90°F	0	0	0	1	1	6	11	7	3	0	0	0	29
Days Maximum Temp. ≤ 32°F	14	10	4	0	0	0	0	0	0	0	4	13	45
Days Minimum Temp. ≤ 32°F	31	26	23	9	1	0	0	0	1	8	23	30	152
Days Minimum Temp. ≤ 0°F	6	4	1	0	0	0	0	0	0	0	0	4	15
Heating Degree Days (base 65°F)	1,295	1,065	845	465	176	28	3	10	120	433	841	1,244	6,525
Cooling Degree Days (base 65°F)	0	0	0	15	53	201	332	268	100	11	0	0	980
Mean Precipitation (in.)	0.57	0.75	1.77	2.63	3.92	4.03	3.24	3.26	2.62	2.11	1.36	0.75	27.01
Maximum Precipitation (in.)*	2.3	3.2	7.3	7.5	8.6	12.2	9.1	6.0	8.1	4.6	4.0	2.3	36.2
Minimum Precipitation (in.)*	0.1	trace	trace	0.2	1.0	0.5	0.3	0.5	0.3	trace	trace	0.1	15.8
Extreme Maximum Daily Precip. (in.)	1.30	1.67	2.41	2.12	3.23	5.42	3.26	5.06	3.15	2.60	2.03	1.08	5.42
Days With ≥ 0.1" Precipitation	2	2	4	5	7	6	6	6	5	4	3	2	52
Days With ≥ 0.5" Precipitation	0	0	1	2	2	3	2	2	2	1	1	0	16
Days With ≥ 1.0" Precipitation	0	0	0	1	1	1	1	1	1	0	0	0	6
Mean Snowfall (in.)	6.2	5.3	5.2	2.7	trace	trace	trace	trace	trace	0.9	4.1	5.9	30.3
Maximum Snowfall (in.)*	16	23	21	13	trace	0	0	0	1	7	23	19	64
Maximum 24-hr. Snowfall (in.)*	13	19	10	10	trace	0	0	0	1	6	14	9	19
Maximum Snow Depth (in.)	15	18	17	9	trace	trace	trace	trace	trace	3	17	19	19
Days With ≥ 1.0" Snow Depth	14	12	5	1	0	0	0	0	0	0	4	13	49
Thunderstorm Days*	< 1	< 1	1	4	8	10	10	9	5	2	1	< 1	50
Foggy Days*	8	10	11	9	9	7	8	11	9	8	8	9	107
Predominant Sky Cover*	OVR	OVR	OVR	OVR	OVR	OVR	CLR	CLR	CLR	CLR	OVR	OVR	OVR
Mean Relative Humidity 6am (%)*	76	79	81	79	81	82	84	86	84	79	79	78	81
Mean Relative Humidity 3pm (%)*	60	60	55	44	46	46	47	49	46	43	52	61	51
Mean Dewpoint (°F)*	11	16	25	34	46	56	62	61	50	37	25	16	37
Prevailing Wind Direction*	NNW	NNW	NNW	NNW	S	S	S	S	S	NNW	NNW	NNW	NNW
Prevailing Wind Speed (mph)*	17	17	18	18	16	15	14	14	14	16	18	17	16
Maximum Wind Gust (mph)*	64	62	71	74	62	76	78	82	81	61	84	64	84

Note: (*) Period of record is 1948-1995

The period of record for National Weather Service station data is 1980 – 2009 except where noted. See User Guide for detailed explanation of data.

North Platte Lee Bird Field

The climate of North Platte is characterized throughout the year by frequent rapid changes in the weather. During the winter, most North Pacific lows cross the country north of North Platte. The passage usually brings little or no snowfall, and only a moderate drop in temperature. Only when there is a major outbreak of cold air from Canada does the temperature fall to zero or below. The duration of below-zero temperature is hardly more than two mornings, and by the third or fourth day the temperature is ordinarily rising to the 40s or higher. Snowfall at the onset of a cold outbreak is usually less than two inches.

Only when a low moves from the middle Rockies through Nebraska, allowing easterly winds to draw moist air into the low circulation, does snowfall of appreciable amounts occur. Few of these storms move slowly enough, or are intense enough, to deposit much precipitation in the North Platte area. However, during some winters the cold outbreak and intense low from the mid-Rockies combine to produce severe cold and snow several inches in depth, with blizzard conditions following. During and after these snowfalls and blizzards, rail and highway traffic may be stalled until the snow is cleared. Widespread loss of unsheltered livestock and wild life results from such conditions.

The sudden and frequent weather changes of the winter continue through spring with decreasing intensity of temperature changes but increasing precipitation. The summer and fall months bring frequent changes from hot to cool weather. Most summer and fall precipitation is associated with thunderstorms, so the amounts are extremely variable. The surrounding area is occasionally damaged by locally severe winds and hailstorms.

Temperatures may reach into the upper 90s and lower 100s frequently during the summer months, but the elevation and clear skies bring rapid cooling after sunset to lows in the 60s or below by daybreak. Since the humidity is generally low, the extremely hot days of summer are not uncomfortable.

Based on the 1951-1980 period, the average first occurrence of 32 degrees Fahrenheit in the fall is September 24 and the average last occurrence in the spring is May 11.

North Platte Lee Bird Field *Lincoln County* Elevation: 2,777 ft. Latitude: 41° 07' N Longitude: 100° 40' W

	JAN	FEB	MAR	APR	MAY	JUN	JUL	AUG	SEP	OCT	NOV	DEC	YEAR
Mean Maximum Temp. (°F)	39.3	43.1	52.3	62.2	71.9	81.9	88.4	86.1	77.8	64.4	50.4	39.4	63.1
Mean Temp. (°F)	25.6	29.4	38.1	47.9	58.4	68.4	74.7	72.5	62.6	49.2	36.0	25.9	49.1
Mean Minimum Temp. (°F)	11.9	15.6	23.9	33.5	44.9	54.7	60.9	58.8	47.4	33.9	21.6	12.3	35.0
Extreme Maximum Temp. (°F)	73	76	86	98	102	106	108	108	102	94	83	75	108
Extreme Minimum Temp. (°F)	-23	-22	-22	8	18	30	39	38	17	10	-9	-34	-34
Days Maximum Temp. ≥ 90°F	0	0	0	0	1	6	14	11	5	0	0	0	37
Days Maximum Temp. ≤ 32°F	9	7	3	1	0	0	0	0	0	0	3	9	32
Days Minimum Temp. ≤ 32°F	31	27	26	14	2	0	0	0	2	14	27	31	174
Days Minimum Temp. ≤ 0°F	5	3	1	0	0	0	0	0	0	0	1	4	14
Heating Degree Days (base 65°F)	1,215	1,000	827	511	226	45	4	12	144	487	862	1,207	6,540
Cooling Degree Days (base 65°F)	0	0	0	5	29	152	311	251	79	4	0	0	831
Mean Precipitation (in.)	0.35	0.50	1.06	2.19	3.28	3.31	2.96	2.31	1.38	1.54	0.62	0.40	19.90
Maximum Precipitation (in.)*	2.2	2.0	4.4	5.0	8.0	10.5	7.0	7.2	6.0	2.9	2.9	1.2	33.4
Minimum Precipitation (in.)*	trace	trace	0	0.1	0.8	0.3	0.4	0.1	trace	0	trace	trace	10.5
Extreme Maximum Daily Precip. (in.)	0.75	0.89	1.84	1.91	2.95	2.52	2.54	2.13	1.69	1.92	0.99	1.39	2.95
Days With ≥ 0.1" Precipitation	1	1	3	5	7	7	6	4	3	3	2	1	43
Days With ≥ 0.5" Precipitation	0	0	1	1	2	2	2	2	1	1	0	0	12
Days With ≥ 1.0" Precipitation	0	0	0	0	1	1	1	1	0	0	0	0	4
Mean Snowfall (in.)	4.8	5.0	5.0	3.4	trace	trace	trace	trace	0.2	2.2	3.9	4.3	28.8
Maximum Snowfall (in.)*	21	21	22	15	6	trace	0	0	3	16	18	14	49
Maximum 24-hr. Snowfall (in.)*	12	9	12	9	6	trace	0	0	3	9	9	8	12
Maximum Snow Depth (in.)	11	13	18	8	trace	trace	trace	trace	trace	12	10	10	18
Days With ≥ 1.0" Snow Depth	10	7	4	1	0	0	0	0	0	1	4	8	35
Thunderstorm Days*	< 1	< 1	1	3	7	10	11	9	4	1	< 1	0	46
Foggy Days*	6	7	8	7	7	5	5	7	7	6	7	6	78
Predominant Sky Cover*	OVR	OVR	OVR	OVR	OVR	OVR	SCT	SCT	CLR	CLR	OVR	OVR	OVR
Mean Relative Humidity 6am (%)*	79	80	81	80	84	85	84	85	83	81	81	80	82
Mean Relative Humidity 3pm (%)*	54	51	47	41	46	46	44	43	40	38	45	51	45
Mean Dewpoint (°F)*	13	17	23	32	45	55	59	58	47	35	23	16	35
Prevailing Wind Direction*	NW	NW	N	N	SSE	SSE	SSE	SSE	S	NW	NW	NW	NW
Prevailing Wind Speed (mph)*	10	10	15	15	14	13	12	12	12	10	12	10	12
Maximum Wind Gust (mph)*	60	61	76	76	73	73	68	74	58	68	60	63	76

Note: (*) Period of record is 1948-1995

Omaha Eppley Airfield

Omaha, Nebraska, is situated on the west bank of the Missouri River. The river level at Omaha is normally about 965 feet above sea level and the rolling hills in and around Omaha rise to about 1,300 feet above sea level. The climate is typically continental with relatively warm summers and cold, dry winters. It is situated midway between two distinctive climatic zones, the humid east and the dry west. Fluctuations between these two zones produce weather conditions for periods that are characteristic of either zone, or combinations of both. Omaha is also affected by most low pressure systems that cross the country. This causes periodic and rapid changes in weather, especially during the winter months.

Most of the precipitation in Omaha falls during sharp showers or thunderstorms, and these occur mostly during the growing season from April to September. Of the total precipitation, about 75 percent falls during this six-month period. The rain occurs mostly as evening or nighttime showers and thunderstorms. Although winters are relatively cold, precipitation is light, with only 10 percent of the total annual precipitation falling during the winter months.

Sunshine is fairly abundant, ranging around 50 percent of the possible in the winter to 75 percent of the possible in the summer.

Omaha Eppley Airfield *Douglas County* Elevation: 981 ft. Latitude: 41° 19' N Longitude: 95° 54' W

	JAN	FEB	MAR	APR	MAY	JUN	JUL	AUG	SEP	OCT	NOV	DEC	YEAR
Mean Maximum Temp. (°F)	33.6	37.7	50.4	63.2	73.6	82.9	87.2	84.9	77.3	64.2	48.9	35.2	61.6
Mean Temp. (°F)	23.8	28.0	39.1	51.4	62.2	71.9	76.7	74.5	65.6	52.8	38.9	25.9	50.9
Mean Minimum Temp. (°F)	13.9	18.2	27.8	39.5	50.8	60.9	66.2	64.0	53.8	41.3	28.9	16.7	40.2
Extreme Maximum Temp. (°F)	68	77	89	97	98	104	109	107	102	92	83	69	109
Extreme Minimum Temp. (°F)	-23	-21	-11	14	27	38	48	44	25	16	-6	-23	-23
Days Maximum Temp. ≥ 90°F	0	0	0	1	1	6	12	8	3	0	0	0	31
Days Maximum Temp. ≤ 32°F	14	10	3	0	0	0	0	0	0	0	3	12	42
Days Minimum Temp. ≤ 32°F	30	26	22	7	0	0	0	0	0	6	20	30	141
Days Minimum Temp. ≤ 0°F	5	3	1	0	0	0	0	0	0	0	0	4	13
Heating Degree Days (base 65°F)	1,272	1,039	796	419	146	17	1	5	96	387	776	1,204	6,158
Cooling Degree Days (base 65°F)	0	0	1	17	65	231	372	307	121	15	1	0	1,130
Mean Precipitation (in.)	0.70	0.86	1.97	2.91	4.76	4.17	3.74	3.68	2.64	2.26	1.60	1.04	30.33
Maximum Precipitation (in.)*	3.7	3.0	6.0	6.4	10.3	9.9	10.3	10.2	13.8	5.0	4.7	5.4	44.8
Minimum Precipitation (in.)*	trace	0.1	0.1	0.4	0.6	1.0	0.4	0.6	0.4	trace	trace	trace	18.4
Extreme Maximum Daily Precip. (in.)	1.55	1.54	2.44	2.73	4.16	4.07	2.83	6.46	2.71	2.70	1.99	1.52	6.46
Days With ≥ 0.1" Precipitation	2	2	4	6	8	7	6	5	5	4	3	3	55
Days With ≥ 0.5" Precipitation	0	0	1	2	3	3	2	2	2	2	1	0	18
Days With ≥ 1.0" Precipitation	0	0	0	1	1	1	1	1	1	1	0	0	7
Mean Snowfall (in.)	5.8	6.3	4.5	1.0	trace	trace	trace	***trace***	trace	***0.4***	2.4	6.0	***26.4***
Maximum Snowfall (in.)*	23	25	27	10	1	0	0	0	trace	4	12	20	59
Maximum 24-hr. Snowfall (in.)*	12	18	10	9	1	0	0	0	trace	4	8	10	18
Maximum Snow Depth (in.)	17	26	12	8	trace	trace	trace	trace	trace	2	6	17	26
Days With ≥ 1.0" Snow Depth	12	11	4	0	0	0	0	0	0	0	2	10	39
Thunderstorm Days*	< 1	< 1	2	4	7	9	9	8	5	2	1	< 1	47
Foggy Days*	11	11	12	9	10	8	8	12	11	10	10	12	124
Predominant Sky Cover*	OVR	OVR	OVR	OVR	OVR	OVR	SCT	CLR	CLR	CLR	OVR	OVR	OVR
Mean Relative Humidity 6am (%)*	78	80	79	77	80	82	84	87	86	81	80	80	81
Mean Relative Humidity 3pm (%)*	61	59	54	46	49	50	52	54	51	47	55	62	53
Mean Dewpoint (°F)*	13	18	26	37	49	60	65	63	54	41	29	19	40
Prevailing Wind Direction*	NNW	NNW	NNW	SSE	SSE	SSE	SSE	SSE	SSE	SSE	SSE	SSE	SSE
Prevailing Wind Speed (mph)*	15	14	15	12	12	10	9	9	10	9	9	9	12
Maximum Wind Gust (mph)*	58	61	60	70	66	64	64	73	55	53	61	53	73

Note: (*) Period of record is 1948-1995

The period of record for National Weather Service station data is 1980 – 2009 except where noted. See User Guide for detailed explanation of data.

Omaha WSFO

Omaha, Nebraska, is situated on the west bank of the Missouri River. The river level at Omaha is normally about 965 feet above sea level and the rolling hills in and around Omaha rise to about 1,300 feet above sea level. The climate is typically continental with relatively warm summers and cold, dry winters. It is situated midway between two distinctive climatic zones, the humid east and the dry west. Fluctuations between these two zones produce weather conditions for periods that are characteristic of either zone, or combinations of both. Omaha is also affected by most low pressure systems that cross the country. This causes periodic and rapid changes in weather, especially during the winter months.

Most of the precipitation in Omaha falls during sharp showers or thunderstorms, and these occur mostly during the growing season from April to September. Of the total precipitation, about 75 percent falls during this six-month period. The rain occurs mostly as evening or nighttime showers and thunderstorms. Although winters are relatively cold, precipitation is light, with only 10 percent of the total annual precipitation falling during the winter months.

Sunshine is fairly abundant, ranging around 50 percent of the possible in the winter to 75 percent of the possible in the summer.

Omaha WSFO *Douglas County* Elevation: 1,309 ft. Latitude: 41° 22' N Longitude: 96° 01' W

	JAN	FEB	MAR	APR	MAY	JUN	JUL	AUG	SEP	OCT	NOV	DEC	YEAR
Mean Maximum Temp. (°F)	33.4	38.3	48.9	62.6	72.3	81.5	85.6	83.3	75.9	63.5	47.3	na	na
Mean Temp. (°F)	24.4	29.5	38.9	51.7	62.3	71.6	na	na	na	53.2	38.5	na	na
Mean Minimum Temp. (°F)	15.4	20.6	28.7	40.8	52.3	61.6	na	na	na	43.0	29.7	na	na
Extreme Maximum Temp. (°F)	66	74	88	96	98	104	104	na	98	88	81	na	na
Extreme Minimum Temp. (°F)	-22	-25	-9	16	31	40	na	na	na	13	-3	na	na
Days Maximum Temp. ≥ 90°F	0	0	0	1	0	4	9	6	2	0	0	na	na
Days Maximum Temp. ≤ 32°F	14	10	3	0	0	0	0	0	0	0	4	na	na
Days Minimum Temp. ≤ 32°F	29	23	20	6	0	0	na	na	0	4	18	na	na
Days Minimum Temp. ≤ 0°F	4	3	1	0	0	0	na	na	0	0	0	na	na
Heating Degree Days (base 65°F)	1,253	999	805	410	141	18	na	na	na	371	786	na	na
Cooling Degree Days (base 65°F)	0	0	1	18	65	223	na	na	na	13	0	na	na
Mean Precipitation (in.)	0.72	0.82	2.23	na	4.79	4.16	3.87	3.18	2.71	2.40	1.61	0.96	na
Maximum Precipitation (in.)*	1.6	2.4	5.3	7.1	9.0	8.8	9.7	7.9	14.1	5.3	5.1	4.4	41.7
Minimum Precipitation (in.)*	trace	0.1	0.1	0.3	0.5	0.9	1.1	0.6	1.0	0.1	trace	0.1	21.3
Extreme Maximum Daily Precip. (in.)	0.94	na	2.04	na	3.10	2.63	3.96	na	2.64	2.51	na	na	na
Days With ≥ 0.1" Precipitation	2	2	5	6	8	7	6	6	5	5	3	3	58
Days With ≥ 0.5" Precipitation	0	0	2	2	3	3	3	2	2	2	1	0	20
Days With ≥ 1.0" Precipitation	0	0	0	1	1	1	1	1	1	1	0	0	7
Mean Snowfall (in.)	5.1	4.3	4.8	na	0.0	0.0	trace	0.0	trace	1.1	3.0	4.4	na
Maximum Snowfall (in.)*	17	22	18	10	1	0	0	0	trace	6	14	19	74
Maximum 24-hr. Snowfall (in.)*	9	8	9	9	1	0	0	0	trace	6	9	8	9
Maximum Snow Depth (in.)	14	11	na	na	na	na	na	na	na	na	na	na	na
Days With ≥ 1.0" Snow Depth	12	11	5	1	0	0	0	0	0	1	3	9	42
Thunderstorm Days*	< 1	< 1	2	3	7	9	9	8	6	2	1	< 1	47
Foggy Days*	8	10	11	9	10	6	7	10	8	8	10	10	107
Predominant Sky Cover*	OVR	OVR	OVR	OVR	OVR	OVR	CLR	CLR	CLR	CLR	OVR	OVR	OVR
Mean Relative Humidity 6am (%)*	75	77	78	76	79	79	85	87	84	78	78	77	79
Mean Relative Humidity 3pm (%)*	58	58	54	47	51	51	57	57	54	50	61	64	55
Mean Dewpoint (°F)*	16	18	29	37	50	58	64	62	54	39	27	18	39
Prevailing Wind Direction*	NW	NW	SSE	NW	SSE	SSE	SSE	SSE	S	S	NW	NW	SSE
Prevailing Wind Speed (mph)*	14	13	10	14	10	10	9	9	10	10	14	14	12
Maximum Wind Gust (mph)*	59	53	54	55	55	51	73	55	48	48	49	47	73

Note: (*) Period of record is 1984-1993

Scottsbluff County Airport

Scottsbluff is located in the North Platte river valley that extends from central Wyoming southeast across western Nebraska. The valley is approximately 20 miles wide in the vicinity of Scottsbluff with a range of hills both to the north and south, parallel to the river. To the south the hills average 600 to 700 feet above the river with some projections upward to 1,000 feet. To the north, rolling hills range from 300 to 400 feet higher than the river.

Due to the protection of the higher hills to the south, southerly winds in the valley are rare. Prevailing winds are west to northwest during the winter months and east to southeast during the summer months. West to northwest winds are intensified by the funneling action of the valley and velocities of 30 to 50 mph are common during the winter and early spring. Quite often these winds are warmed by the downslope (chinook) effect from the higher elevations to the west and bring rapid warming and melting of the snow. Outbreaks of Arctic air bring cold wave conditions about five times each season. Snow with strong winds causing blowing and drifting snow occur several times each winter with a severe blizzard of extended duration occurring about once every thirty years. Easterly winds during the winter and early spring cause upslope conditions with low cloudiness and precipitation.

The average temperature is in the upper 40s. Summertime highs generally range from the 80s to the 90s with lows around 60. Summer temperatures of 100 degrees are reached or exceeded at least once each summer. In winter, highs average about 40 degrees with lows in the teens. Temperatures of zero or below occur about 15 times each winter.

Most of the precipitation occurs as thunderstorms during the spring and summer months. Severe thunderstorms with destructive hail are quite common during the late spring and summer. Tornadoes are infrequent and usually of short duration.

The Platte River in the vicinity of Scottsbluff is a wide shallow stream and has very little effect on the climate. Water stored in numerous upstream reservoirs is used for extensive irrigation in the valley. Lowland flooding occurs when heavy rains fall upstream and a greater than normal amount of water is being released from the upstream reservoirs.

Based on the 1951-1980 period, the average first occurrence of 32 degrees Fahrenheit in the fall is September 29 and the average last occurrence in the spring is May 7.

Scottsbluff County Airport *Scotts Bluff County* Elevation: 3,944 ft. Latitude: 41° 52' N Longitude: 103° 36' W

	JAN	FEB	MAR	APR	MAY	JUN	JUL	AUG	SEP	OCT	NOV	DEC	YEAR
Mean Maximum Temp. (°F)	40.6	44.4	52.4	61.4	71.7	82.3	89.9	87.6	77.9	64.0	50.2	39.9	63.5
Mean Temp. (°F)	27.3	30.6	38.2	46.8	57.4	67.4	74.3	72.2	61.9	48.5	36.1	26.4	48.9
Mean Minimum Temp. (°F)	13.8	16.7	23.9	32.1	43.1	52.5	58.6	56.6	45.9	33.0	22.0	12.9	34.3
Extreme Maximum Temp. (°F)	74	74	82	93	103	106	109	104	102	91	80	77	109
Extreme Minimum Temp. (°F)	-29	-27	-21	-2	15	32	41	39	19	-6	-13	-42	-42
Days Maximum Temp. ≥ 90°F	0	0	0	0	1	8	17	14	5	0	0	0	45
Days Maximum Temp. ≤ 32°F	7	6	3	1	0	0	0	0	0	1	3	9	30
Days Minimum Temp. ≤ 32°F	30	27	27	15	2	0	0	0	1	13	27	31	173
Days Minimum Temp. ≤ 0°F	4	3	1	0	0	0	0	0	0	0	1	5	14
Heating Degree Days (base 65°F)	1,164	966	824	542	251	57	5	11	150	505	861	1,189	6,525
Cooling Degree Days (base 65°F)	0	0	0	1	23	137	300	240	65	1	0	0	767
Mean Precipitation (in.)	0.44	0.60	1.06	1.76	2.46	2.74	1.82	1.27	1.19	1.14	0.66	0.48	15.62
Maximum Precipitation (in.)*	1.3	1.9	2.6	3.9	7.3	6.6	4.8	3.4	4.2	3.0	2.1	1.5	24.8
Minimum Precipitation (in.)*	trace	trace	0.2	0.3	0.3	0.6	0.2	0.1	trace	trace	trace	trace	7.7
Extreme Maximum Daily Precip. (in.)	0.71	0.86	1.36	1.78	2.30	2.68	2.09	1.77	1.65	1.42	1.43	0.52	2.68
Days With ≥ 0.1" Precipitation	1	2	3	5	6	6	4	3	3	3	2	2	40
Days With ≥ 0.5" Precipitation	0	0	0	1	1	2	1	1	1	1	0	0	8
Days With ≥ 1.0" Precipitation	0	0	0	0	0	1	0	0	0	0	0	0	1
Mean Snowfall (in.)	5.9	6.8	8.0	5.4	0.4	trace	trace	trace	0.5	2.8	5.7	6.8	42.3
Maximum Snowfall (in.)*	24	23	24	18	8	trace	0	0	5	22	19	18	67
Maximum 24-hr. Snowfall (in.)*	9	10	12	8	3	trace	0	0	5	7	8	11	12
Maximum Snow Depth (in.)	13	15	14	7	2	trace	trace	trace	4	12	10	12	15
Days With ≥ 1.0" Snow Depth	11	7	5	2	0	0	0	0	0	1	4	10	40
Thunderstorm Days*	0	0	< 1	2	8	11	11	8	4	1	< 1	< 1	45
Foggy Days*	3	3	5	4	4	3	2	3	4	3	4	3	41
Predominant Sky Cover*	OVR	OVR	OVR	OVR	OVR	CLR	CLR	CLR	CLR	CLR	OVR	OVR	OVR
Mean Relative Humidity 6am (%)*	73	76	77	76	77	76	75	80	78	76	75	75	76
Mean Relative Humidity 3pm (%)*	50	45	43	38	40	37	34	34	32	34	43	51	40
Mean Dewpoint (°F)*	13	17	22	29	41	49	54	53	42	31	21	16	32
Prevailing Wind Direction*	WNW	WNW	WNW	WNW	ESE	ESE	ESE	ESE	ESE	NW	WNW	WNW	WNW
Prevailing Wind Speed (mph)*	14	13	14	15	13	12	10	10	10	12	13	13	13
Maximum Wind Gust (mph)*	74	62	61	63	63	70	68	66	54	54	56	56	74

Note: (*) Period of record is 1948-1995

Valentine Miller Field

Valentine, located near the northern edge of the Sandhills and cattle country of Nebraska, is near the extreme northern border of the state. The city lies in the valley of the Niobrara River, a branch of the Missouri River, about 160 miles above the junction with the Missouri. It is the county seat of Cherry County and had its beginning in the fall of 1882.

The inland location offers a wide variety of weather. The high afternoon temperatures during the two warmest months, July and August, average nearly 90 degrees and the corresponding humidity averages about 40 percent. Uncomfortably warm nights are few with low morning temperatures averaging about 60 degrees. The temperature seldom reaches 100 degrees or more during the summer. The two coldest months are January and February. The minimum temperature generally reaches -20 degrees or colder once each winter.

Valentines location frequently places it in the path of cold Canadian air mass outbreaks during the cold season, alternating with mild, dry air moving across the Rockies from the Pacific. One or two bitterly cold days usually occur each winter when the temperature will stay below zero throughout the day. Blizzards are not frequent, but at least one is likely each winter season. An occasional severe blizzard occurs about once in every three or four winters. Blowing and drifting snow reduce visibility to zero and bring outdoor activities and travel to a complete stop. Lives may be lost for anyone caught away from shelter, and there is usually loss of livestock which varies with the intensity and duration of the storm. Temperatures below 32 degrees have occurred as late as mid-June and as early as early September, and low temperature records in the 30s have occurred during the summer with light frost in low places. However, these are rare occurrences and temperatures below 50 degrees are not common in July and August.

About 65 percent of the annual precipitation falls during the growing season, May through September, and is predominantly the nighttime thunderstorm type with June being the wettest month.

The spring and fall seasons have mostly pleasant days, with the fall season having the most uniform character with lighter winds and gradually falling temperatures as the season progresses. In the spring the weather is windy and extremely variable, with summer-like days mixed with some of cold of winter. The widest extremes of temperature occur in March.

Some of the damaging weather elements other than blizzards, are high winds, which dig blow outs in the sand hills, and an occasional hailstorm. Tornadoes occasionally occur but seldom do much damage.

Valentine Miller Field *Cherry County* Elevation: 2,589 ft. Latitude: 42° 52' N Longitude: 100° 33' W

	JAN	FEB	MAR	APR	MAY	JUN	JUL	AUG	SEP	OCT	NOV	DEC	YEAR
Mean Maximum Temp. (°F)	36.5	40.0	49.0	60.3	71.2	81.2	88.8	86.9	77.4	62.8	47.9	36.9	61.6
Mean Temp. (°F)	23.4	27.1	35.7	46.4	57.6	67.5	74.4	72.5	62.2	48.1	34.5	23.9	47.8
Mean Minimum Temp. (°F)	10.2	14.0	22.4	32.5	44.0	53.7	60.0	58.2	47.0	33.3	21.1	10.9	33.9
Extreme Maximum Temp. (°F)	72	78	85	100	99	110	114	107	104	96	86	74	114
Extreme Minimum Temp. (°F)	-30	-31	-29	3	18	32	41	34	17	-1	-18	-39	-39
Days Maximum Temp. ≥ 90°F	0	0	0	0	1	6	15	13	6	1	0	0	42
Days Maximum Temp. ≤ 32°F	12	9	5	1	0	0	0	0	0	0	5	11	43
Days Minimum Temp. ≤ 32°F	31	28	27	15	3	0	0	0	2	14	27	31	178
Days Minimum Temp. ≤ 0°F	7	5	1	0	0	0	0	0	0	0	1	6	20
Heating Degree Days (base 65°F)	1,285	1,066	902	555	253	60	8	16	161	521	909	1,267	7,003
Cooling Degree Days (base 65°F)	0	0	0	5	31	141	308	257	84	4	0	0	830
Mean Precipitation (in.)	0.26	0.49	1.07	2.13	3.15	3.52	3.14	2.21	1.62	1.28	0.64	0.35	19.86
Maximum Precipitation (in.)*	0.8	1.3	4.2	4.0	6.7	7.1	9.0	6.7	5.9	3.8	2.6	1.8	32.7
Minimum Precipitation (in.)*	trace	0.1	0.2	0.3	0.4	0.4	0.3	0.4	0.3	trace	trace	trace	10.6
Extreme Maximum Daily Precip. (in.)	0.54	0.92	1.03	1.95	2.14	2.96	3.39	2.75	1.80	1.92	1.12	1.23	3.39
Days With ≥ 0.1" Precipitation	1	2	3	4	6	6	5	5	4	3	2	1	42
Days With ≥ 0.5" Precipitation	0	0	1	2	2	2	2	1	1	1	0	0	12
Days With ≥ 1.0" Precipitation	0	0	0	0	1	1	1	1	0	0	0	0	4
Mean Snowfall (in.)	4.1	6.0	7.2	4.8	0.1	trace	0.0	trace	0.7	1.6	5.4	4.9	34.8
Maximum Snowfall (in.)*	15	16	51	30	3	0	0	0	18	12	35	23	84
Maximum 24-hr. Snowfall (in.)*	7	8	17	9	3	0	0	0	18	6	14	18	18
Maximum Snow Depth (in.)	18	12	16	12	trace	trace	0	trace	10	4	19	22	22
Days With ≥ 1.0" Snow Depth	10	10	6	2	0	0	0	0	0	1	5	12	46
Thunderstorm Days*	0	< 1	1	4	10	15	19	17	10	1	< 1	0	77
Foggy Days*	4	7	12	10	9	9	6	9	10	7	9	6	98
Predominant Sky Cover*	OVR	OVR	OVR	OVR	OVR	OVR	SCT	SCT	CLR	CLR	OVR	CLR	OVR
Mean Relative Humidity 6am (%)*	73	74	77	75	76	77	76	78	74	74	74	73	75
Mean Relative Humidity 3pm (%)*	54	51	47	40	41	40	39	40	35	38	47	51	43
Mean Dewpoint (°F)*	10	14	22	30	41	51	55	54	43	31	20	12	32
Prevailing Wind Direction*	NW	NNW	NNW	NNW	SSE	SSE	S	S	S	WNW	WNW	WNW	WNW
Prevailing Wind Speed (mph)*	13	13	13	13	15	13	12	13	13	8	8	8	12
Maximum Wind Gust (mph)*	na	na	na	na	na	na	na	na	na	54	40	51	54

Note: (*) Period of record is 1948-1995

Agate 3 E *Sioux County* Elevation: 4,669 ft. Latitude: 42° 25' N Longitude: 103° 44' W

	JAN	FEB	MAR	APR	MAY	JUN	JUL	AUG	SEP	OCT	NOV	DEC	YEAR
Mean Maximum Temp. (°F)	39.4	42.5	51.3	61.0	70.6	80.6	88.8	87.3	77.7	64.5	48.9	38.7	62.6
Mean Temp. (°F)	24.4	27.6	35.8	44.4	54.4	63.6	70.7	69.0	58.8	46.2	33.0	23.3	45.9
Mean Minimum Temp. (°F)	9.4	12.6	20.3	27.8	38.1	46.6	52.6	50.7	39.9	27.8	17.0	8.0	29.2
Extreme Maximum Temp. (°F)	69	72	80	90	95	106	108	102	98	90	79	69	108
Extreme Minimum Temp. (°F)	-32	-41	-19	-6	12	21	32	27	5	-11	-19	-40	-41
Days Maximum Temp. ≥ 90°F	0	0	0	0	0	5	16	13	3	0	0	0	37
Days Maximum Temp. ≤ 32°F	8	6	3	1	0	0	0	0	0	0	4	9	31
Days Minimum Temp. ≤ 32°F	30	28	29	21	8	2	0	0	7	22	29	31	207
Days Minimum Temp. ≤ 0°F	7	4	1	0	0	0	0	0	0	0	2	8	22
Heating Degree Days (base 65°F)	1,252	1,052	899	611	330	103	15	23	209	578	955	1,285	7,312
Cooling Degree Days (base 65°F)	0	0	0	0	7	69	200	154	30	0	0	0	460
Mean Precipitation (in.)	0.22	0.31	0.58	1.25	2.73	2.19	2.00	1.67	1.42	1.05	0.37	0.23	14.02
Extreme Maximum Daily Precip. (in.)	0.39	1.20	0.98	3.26	2.25	2.22	1.80	2.22	2.17	1.20	0.60	0.42	3.26
Days With ≥ 0.1" Precipitation	1	1	2	3	6	5	5	4	3	3	1	1	35
Days With ≥ 0.5" Precipitation	0	0	0	0	2	1	1	1	1	1	0	0	7
Days With ≥ 1.0" Precipitation	0	0	0	0	1	0	0	0	0	0	0	0	1
Mean Snowfall (in.)	3.5	4.5	6.3	4.2	0.8	0.0	0.0	0.0	0.3	1.6	3.9	4.8	29.9
Maximum Snow Depth (in.)	14	16	10	7	3	0	0	0	4	5	14	17	17
Days With ≥ 1.0" Snow Depth	12	8	6	2	0	0	0	0	0	1	5	11	45

Ainsworth *Brown County* Elevation: 2,509 ft. Latitude: 42° 33' N Longitude: 99° 51' W

	JAN	FEB	MAR	APR	MAY	JUN	JUL	AUG	SEP	OCT	NOV	DEC	YEAR
Mean Maximum Temp. (°F)	36.2	39.8	49.3	60.9	71.1	80.5	87.1	84.9	76.6	63.3	47.5	36.5	61.1
Mean Temp. (°F)	25.7	29.1	37.6	48.4	59.2	68.7	74.9	72.9	63.9	51.1	37.1	26.6	49.6
Mean Minimum Temp. (°F)	15.1	18.4	25.9	35.9	47.2	56.8	62.6	60.9	51.3	39.0	26.6	16.6	38.0
Extreme Maximum Temp. (°F)	70	76	83	97	96	103	107	105	98	92	84	72	107
Extreme Minimum Temp. (°F)	-24	-26	-20	10	24	35	46	42	25	7	-13	-30	-30
Days Maximum Temp. ≥ 90°F	0	0	0	0	1	4	12	8	3	0	0	0	28
Days Maximum Temp. ≤ 32°F	11	9	4	1	0	0	0	0	0	0	5	11	41
Days Minimum Temp. ≤ 32°F	29	25	23	11	1	0	0	0	1	7	21	29	147
Days Minimum Temp. ≤ 0°F	5	3	1	0	0	0	0	0	0	0	1	4	14
Heating Degree Days (base 65°F)	1,212	1,009	844	499	210	40	5	11	122	433	830	1,185	6,400
Cooling Degree Days (base 65°F)	0	0	0	9	38	157	317	263	98	10	0	0	892
Mean Precipitation (in.)	0.34	0.56	1.35	2.36	3.48	3.54	3.04	2.89	2.42	1.70	0.81	0.44	22.93
Extreme Maximum Daily Precip. (in.)	0.95	1.17	1.51	1.81	3.76	2.88	3.55	3.40	3.03	1.58	1.26	1.07	3.76
Days With ≥ 0.1" Precipitation	1	2	3	5	6	6	6	5	4	4	2	1	45
Days With ≥ 0.5" Precipitation	0	0	1	2	2	2	2	2	1	1	0	0	13
Days With ≥ 1.0" Precipitation	0	0	0	0	1	1	1	1	1	0	0	0	5
Mean Snowfall (in.)	5.0	5.9	7.9	5.4	0.2	trace	0.0	0.0	0.2	1.6	5.9	5.5	37.6
Maximum Snow Depth (in.)	30	17	16	12	trace	trace	trace	0	3	6	20	22	30
Days With ≥ 1.0" Snow Depth	13	10	6	2	0	0	0	0	0	1	5	14	51

Albion 1 N *Boone County* Elevation: 1,758 ft. Latitude: 41° 42' N Longitude: 98° 00' W

	JAN	FEB	MAR	APR	MAY	JUN	JUL	AUG	SEP	OCT	NOV	DEC	YEAR
Mean Maximum Temp. (°F)	34.2	38.0	48.4	61.4	71.8	81.8	86.6	84.2	76.9	63.8	47.2	35.8	60.8
Mean Temp. (°F)	22.9	26.7	36.3	48.1	59.3	69.5	74.3	72.1	63.1	50.2	35.6	25.0	48.6
Mean Minimum Temp. (°F)	11.5	15.4	24.1	34.8	46.8	57.1	62.0	60.0	49.2	36.6	24.0	14.2	36.3
Extreme Maximum Temp. (°F)	72	77	90	95	99	105	106	105	99	94	81	69	106
Extreme Minimum Temp. (°F)	-29	-25	-12	7	22	37	42	40	21	8	-13	-27	-29
Days Maximum Temp. ≥ 90°F	0	0	0	1	1	6	11	7	3	0	0	0	29
Days Maximum Temp. ≤ 32°F	14	10	4	0	0	0	0	0	0	0	4	12	44
Days Minimum Temp. ≤ 32°F	31	27	25	12	2	0	0	0	1	10	24	30	162
Days Minimum Temp. ≤ 0°F	6	4	1	0	0	0	0	0	0	0	1	4	16
Heating Degree Days (base 65°F)	1,299	1,076	883	508	209	35	6	13	138	459	874	1,232	6,732
Cooling Degree Days (base 65°F)	0	0	0	8	40	176	302	241	87	7	0	0	861
Mean Precipitation (in.)	0.45	0.69	2.06	2.60	4.22	3.77	3.19	3.29	2.89	1.95	1.44	0.57	27.12
Extreme Maximum Daily Precip. (in.)	0.64	0.92	2.22	2.83	4.05	2.88	2.06	3.15	4.40	1.86	3.00	1.00	4.40
Days With ≥ 0.1" Precipitation	1	2	4	5	7	6	6	5	4	4	3	1	48
Days With ≥ 0.5" Precipitation	0	0	1	2	3	3	2	2	2	1	1	0	17
Days With ≥ 1.0" Precipitation	0	0	1	1	1	1	1	1	1	0	0	0	7
Mean Snowfall (in.)	5.1	6.2	6.1	2.2	0.0	0.0	0.0	0.0	trace	0.7	3.9	4.4	28.6
Maximum Snow Depth (in.)	11	18	24	12	2	0	0	4	trace	*4*	9	15	*24*
Days With ≥ 1.0" Snow Depth	12	12	6	1	0	0	0	0	0	*0*	4	10	*45*

Anselmo 2 SE *Custer County* Elevation: 2,604 ft. Latitude: 41° 36' N Longitude: 99° 50' W

	JAN	FEB	MAR	APR	MAY	JUN	JUL	AUG	SEP	OCT	NOV	DEC	YEAR
Mean Maximum Temp. (°F)	37.6	41.3	50.8	61.6	71.7	81.1	87.4	85.3	76.9	64.2	49.1	37.9	62.1
Mean Temp. (°F)	24.8	28.4	37.1	47.3	58.1	67.8	73.7	71.8	62.3	49.4	36.0	25.6	48.5
Mean Minimum Temp. (°F)	12.0	15.5	23.2	32.8	44.5	54.5	60.0	58.2	47.6	34.5	22.8	13.2	34.9
Extreme Maximum Temp. (°F)	73	78	88	93	99	105	108	109	101	92	84	71	109
Extreme Minimum Temp. (°F)	-32	-28	-22	8	18	32	39	36	16	5	-16	-32	-32
Days Maximum Temp. ≥ 90°F	0	0	0	0	1	5	12	10	4	0	0	0	32
Days Maximum Temp. ≤ 32°F	11	8	4	0	0	0	0	0	0	0	4	10	37
Days Minimum Temp. ≤ 32°F	31	27	26	15	3	0	0	0	2	13	25	31	173
Days Minimum Temp. ≤ 0°F	6	4	1	0	0	0	0	0	0	0	1	5	17
Heating Degree Days (base 65°F)	1,240	1,026	858	531	240	52	7	16	153	482	864	1,216	6,685
Cooling Degree Days (base 65°F)	0	0	0	6	33	143	284	233	78	4	0	0	781
Mean Precipitation (in.)	0.48	0.63	1.50	2.77	3.72	3.72	3.06	2.69	2.16	1.97	1.15	0.50	24.35
Extreme Maximum Daily Precip. (in.)	1.32	1.17	2.65	2.55	2.95	3.83	3.20	3.22	2.25	2.28	2.04	1.22	3.83
Days With ≥ 0.1" Precipitation	1	2	4	5	7	7	5	5	4	4	2	1	47
Days With ≥ 0.5" Precipitation	0	0	1	2	2	3	2	2	1	1	1	0	15
Days With ≥ 1.0" Precipitation	0	0	0	1	1	1	1	1	1	0	0	0	6
Mean Snowfall (in.)	5.7	6.0	7.3	4.1	trace	0.0	0.0	0.0	0.1	2.8	6.0	5.8	37.8
Maximum Snow Depth (in.)	20	15	25	15	0	0	0	0	trace	12	15	18	25
Days With ≥ 1.0" Snow Depth	13	12	6	2	0	0	0	0	0	1	6	12	52

The period of record for all cooperative weather station data is 1980 – 2009. See User Guide for detailed explanation of data.

Arthur *Arthur County* Elevation: 3,500 ft. Latitude: 41° 34' N Longitude: 101° 41' W

	JAN	FEB	MAR	APR	MAY	JUN	JUL	AUG	SEP	OCT	NOV	DEC	YEAR
Mean Maximum Temp. (°F)	37.9	41.8	50.3	60.4	70.6	80.5	87.9	85.8	76.4	62.9	49.0	38.3	61.8
Mean Temp. (°F)	25.4	29.1	37.1	46.7	57.4	66.9	73.7	71.9	61.9	48.3	36.0	25.8	48.4
Mean Minimum Temp. (°F)	13.0	16.3	23.9	33.0	44.1	53.3	59.5	57.9	47.4	33.8	22.9	13.4	34.9
Extreme Maximum Temp. (°F)	71	76	83	93	97	104	107	104	100	91	80	69	107
Extreme Minimum Temp. (°F)	-25	-29	-17	6	17	34	37	36	14	-1	-12	-33	-33
Days Maximum Temp. ≥ 90°F	0	0	0	0	1	5	14	11	4	0	0	0	35
Days Maximum Temp. ≤ 32°F	10	8	4	1	0	0	0	0	0	1	4	10	38
Days Minimum Temp. ≤ 32°F	30	27	26	14	2	0	0	0	1	13	25	30	168
Days Minimum Temp. ≤ 0°F	5	4	1	0	0	0	0	0	0	0	1	4	15
Heating Degree Days (base 65°F)	1,221	1,010	858	550	256	63	8	15	158	512	864	1,208	6,723
Cooling Degree Days (base 65°F)	0	0	0	2	26	128	285	235	73	2	0	0	751
Mean Precipitation (in.)	0.30	0.43	1.12	2.01	3.17	2.88	3.21	2.06	1.87	1.25	0.53	0.32	19.15
Extreme Maximum Daily Precip. (in.)	0.75	1.23	1.90	1.70	2.20	1.65	3.43	1.55	2.55	2.20	1.27	0.85	3.43
Days With ≥ 0.1" Precipitation	1	2	3	5	6	6	6	5	4	3	2	1	44
Days With ≥ 0.5" Precipitation	0	0	0	1	2	2	2	1	1	1	0	0	10
Days With ≥ 1.0" Precipitation	0	0	0	0	1	0	1	0	0	0	0	0	2
Mean Snowfall (in.)	4.5	4.8	7.3	5.5	0.2	trace	trace	trace	0.3	1.8	4.1	4.6	33.1
Maximum Snow Depth (in.)	16	17	25	20	3	trace	trace	trace	4	8	12	15	25
Days With ≥ 1.0" Snow Depth	13	9	6	2	0	0	0	0	0	1	5	11	47

Ashland 2 *Saunders County* Elevation: 1,069 ft. Latitude: 41° 03' N Longitude: 96° 21' W

	JAN	FEB	MAR	APR	MAY	JUN	JUL	AUG	SEP	OCT	NOV	DEC	YEAR
Mean Maximum Temp. (°F)	34.2	38.9	50.5	63.3	73.7	83.4	88.0	85.9	78.5	65.4	49.9	36.2	62.3
Mean Temp. (°F)	23.7	28.0	38.7	50.7	61.7	72.0	76.7	74.4	65.5	52.8	38.8	26.4	50.8
Mean Minimum Temp. (°F)	13.1	16.8	26.8	38.1	49.5	60.5	65.3	62.8	52.5	40.1	27.7	16.5	39.1
Extreme Maximum Temp. (°F)	72	76	90	97	100	104	108	110	108	95	85	69	110
Extreme Minimum Temp. (°F)	-20	-23	-13	15	28	41	47	42	25	11	-6	-26	-26
Days Maximum Temp. ≥ 90°F	0	0	0	1	2	7	13	10	5	0	0	0	38
Days Maximum Temp. ≤ 32°F	13	9	3	0	0	0	0	0	0	0	3	12	40
Days Minimum Temp. ≤ 32°F	31	26	22	9	1	0	0	0	0	7	21	30	147
Days Minimum Temp. ≤ 0°F	6	4	1	0	0	0	0	0	0	0	0	4	15
Heating Degree Days (base 65°F)	1,275	1,039	807	438	160	19	2	7	104	387	778	1,191	6,207
Cooling Degree Days (base 65°F)	0	0	1	16	64	235	370	305	126	16	0	0	1,133
Mean Precipitation (in.)	0.78	0.83	1.86	2.89	4.54	4.16	3.57	4.16	2.58	2.29	1.50	1.06	30.22
Extreme Maximum Daily Precip. (in.)	1.15	1.30	1.32	2.40	3.10	3.09	5.02	3.90	3.00	2.35	2.17	2.48	5.02
Days With ≥ 0.1" Precipitation	2	2	4	6	8	7	5	6	5	5	3	3	56
Days With ≥ 0.5" Precipitation	0	0	1	2	3	3	2	3	2	1	1	1	19
Days With ≥ 1.0" Precipitation	0	0	0	1	1	1	1	1	1	1	0	0	7
Mean Snowfall (in.)	5.2	5.3	3.9	0.9	0.0	0.0	0.0	0.0	0.0	0.7	1.6	5.4	23.0
Maximum Snow Depth (in.)	***14***	na	na	***trace***	***0***	***0***	***0***	***0***	***0***	***3***	***2***	na	na
Days With ≥ 1.0" Snow Depth	***4***	na	***1***	0	0	0	0	0	0	0	0	***5***	na

Atkinson *Holt County* Elevation: 2,109 ft. Latitude: 42° 32' N Longitude: 98° 59' W

	JAN	FEB	MAR	APR	MAY	JUN	JUL	AUG	SEP	OCT	NOV	DEC	YEAR
Mean Maximum Temp. (°F)	35.7	38.7	48.9	61.5	72.0	81.6	87.8	85.9	77.3	63.7	47.3	35.9	61.4
Mean Temp. (°F)	25.0	28.0	37.2	48.9	60.0	69.6	75.4	73.6	64.2	51.1	36.6	25.9	49.6
Mean Minimum Temp. (°F)	13.8	17.1	25.5	36.3	47.9	57.6	62.9	61.3	51.1	38.4	26.0	15.8	37.8
Extreme Maximum Temp. (°F)	72	77	84	94	97	107	109	106	99	93	83	73	109
Extreme Minimum Temp. (°F)	-25	-28	-18	8	24	37	45	41	25	10	-9	-29	-29
Days Maximum Temp. ≥ 90°F	0	0	0	0	1	5	13	10	4	0	0	0	33
Days Maximum Temp. ≤ 32°F	12	10	4	1	0	0	0	0	0	0	5	11	43
Days Minimum Temp. ≤ 32°F	29	26	23	11	1	0	0	0	1	8	22	29	150
Days Minimum Temp. ≤ 0°F	5	4	1	0	0	0	0	0	0	0	1	4	15
Heating Degree Days (base 65°F)	1,233	1,041	853	486	194	32	4	10	121	435	844	1,206	6,459
Cooling Degree Days (base 65°F)	0	0	0	10	46	178	334	284	105	10	0	0	967
Mean Precipitation (in.)	0.45	0.59	1.54	2.76	3.66	3.63	2.67	2.92	2.40	1.98	1.03	0.56	24.19
Extreme Maximum Daily Precip. (in.)	0.70	1.14	2.36	2.22	2.85	2.10	3.45	5.00	4.50	1.70	1.38	1.46	5.00
Days With ≥ 0.1" Precipitation	1	2	3	6	7	7	5	5	4	4	3	2	49
Days With ≥ 0.5" Precipitation	0	0	1	2	3	3	2	2	2	1	1	0	17
Days With ≥ 1.0" Precipitation	0	0	0	1	1	1	1	1	1	1	0	0	7
Mean Snowfall (in.)	5.3	5.4	6.8	4.2	trace	0.0	0.0	0.0	0.1	1.4	5.9	6.0	35.1
Maximum Snow Depth (in.)	***25***	***18***	***26***	13	trace	0	***0***	***0***	trace	***9***	12	***13***	***26***
Days With ≥ 1.0" Snow Depth	***13***	10	6	2	0	0	0	0	0	1	5	***12***	***49***

Aurora *Hamilton County* Elevation: 1,785 ft. Latitude: 40° 52' N Longitude: 98° 00' W

	JAN	FEB	MAR	APR	MAY	JUN	JUL	AUG	SEP	OCT	NOV	DEC	YEAR
Mean Maximum Temp. (°F)	35.0	38.6	49.7	62.4	72.3	82.5	86.8	84.5	77.2	64.9	49.0	36.9	61.7
Mean Temp. (°F)	24.7	28.3	38.5	50.3	61.3	71.2	75.7	73.5	64.7	52.3	38.1	27.0	50.5
Mean Minimum Temp. (°F)	14.2	18.0	27.2	38.1	50.2	59.8	64.6	62.5	52.2	39.7	27.2	17.1	39.2
Extreme Maximum Temp. (°F)	71	79	89	95	98	107	106	108	99	95	84	71	108
Extreme Minimum Temp. (°F)	-21	-20	-9	14	29	39	47	44	24	4	-4	-28	-28
Days Maximum Temp. ≥ 90°F	0	0	0	1	1	7	12	8	3	0	0	0	32
Days Maximum Temp. ≤ 32°F	13	10	3	0	0	0	0	0	0	0	4	11	41
Days Minimum Temp. ≤ 32°F	30	26	23	8	0	0	0	0	1	6	22	30	146
Days Minimum Temp. ≤ 0°F	5	3	1	0	0	0	0	0	0	0	0	3	12
Heating Degree Days (base 65°F)	1,244	1,030	816	446	165	24	3	7	110	397	800	1,171	6,213
Cooling Degree Days (base 65°F)	0	0	1	13	56	216	342	278	108	11	0	0	1,025
Mean Precipitation (in.)	0.60	0.63	2.18	2.82	4.93	4.70	3.57	3.67	3.01	2.32	1.47	0.77	30.67
Extreme Maximum Daily Precip. (in.)	0.80	0.83	2.93	2.82	3.40	6.40	4.14	2.79	3.73	2.59	2.31	1.08	6.40
Days With ≥ 0.1" Precipitation	2	2	5	5	8	7	6	6	5	4	3	2	55
Days With ≥ 0.5" Precipitation	0	0	1	2	4	3	2	3	2	2	1	0	20
Days With ≥ 1.0" Precipitation	0	0	0	1	1	1	1	1	1	1	0	0	7
Mean Snowfall (in.)	5.9	5.4	4.9	1.8	0.0	0.0	0.0	0.0	0.2	0.9	3.4	4.8	27.3
Maximum Snow Depth (in.)	18	16	17	10	0	0	0	0	1	12	14	20	20
Days With ≥ 1.0" Snow Depth	13	11	5	1	0	0	0	0	0	0	3	11	44

The period of record for all cooperative weather station data is 1980 – 2009. See User Guide for detailed explanation of data.

Bartlett 4 S *Wheeler County* Elevation: 2,140 ft. Latitude: 41° 50' N Longitude: 98° 33' W

	JAN	FEB	MAR	APR	MAY	JUN	JUL	AUG	SEP	OCT	NOV	DEC	YEAR
Mean Maximum Temp. (°F)	34.2	37.1	49.5	61.4	72.0	82.3	88.2	85.1	76.9	63.8	48.0	34.9	61.1
Mean Temp. (°F)	23.0	25.9	36.7	47.8	59.1	69.1	74.9	72.4	63.4	50.5	36.4	24.1	48.6
Mean Minimum Temp. (°F)	11.9	14.6	23.9	34.3	45.9	55.9	61.5	59.6	49.9	37.1	24.7	13.3	36.0
Extreme Maximum Temp. (°F)	71	78	87	91	100	105	109	106	101	93	86	70	109
Extreme Minimum Temp. (°F)	-27	-29	-15	7	17	21	35	24	22	6	-7	-29	-29
Days Maximum Temp. ≥ 90°F	0	0	0	0	1	7	14	9	4	0	0	0	35
Days Maximum Temp. ≤ 32°F	13	10	4	1	0	0	0	0	0	0	5	12	45
Days Minimum Temp. ≤ 32°F	29	26	25	13	3	0	0	0	1	9	23	30	159
Days Minimum Temp. ≤ 0°F	6	4	1	0	0	0	0	0	0	0	1	5	17
Heating Degree Days (base 65°F)	1,294	1,100	869	516	216	47	7	19	135	449	853	1,261	6,766
Cooling Degree Days (base 65°F)	0	0	0	8	39	177	320	255	95	7	0	0	901
Mean Precipitation (in.)	0.49	0.65	1.82	2.75	4.29	3.67	2.89	3.22	2.74	2.34	1.24	0.58	26.68
Extreme Maximum Daily Precip. (in.)	1.40	1.07	1.25	4.03	3.01	3.12	3.16	4.03	3.92	1.60	1.50	1.56	4.03
Days With ≥ 0.1" Precipitation	1	2	3	5	7	6	5	5	4	4	2	2	46
Days With ≥ 0.5" Precipitation	0	0	1	2	3	3	2	2	2	2	1	0	18
Days With ≥ 1.0" Precipitation	0	0	1	1	1	1	1	1	1	1	0	0	8
Mean Snowfall (in.)	6.7	5.6	5.7	2.5	0.0	0.0	0.0	0.0	0.0	1.5	4.5	4.3	30.8
Maximum Snow Depth (in.)	11	12	12	8	0	0	0	0	0	5	6	na	na
Days With ≥ 1.0" Snow Depth	2	3	1	0	0	0	0	0	0	0	2	3	11

Beatrice 1 N *Gage County* Elevation: 1,296 ft. Latitude: 40° 18' N Longitude: 96° 45' W

	JAN	FEB	MAR	APR	MAY	JUN	JUL	AUG	SEP	OCT	NOV	DEC	YEAR
Mean Maximum Temp. (°F)	36.2	40.8	52.8	64.2	74.4	84.2	89.0	86.8	79.1	66.4	51.0	38.4	63.6
Mean Temp. (°F)	25.1	29.0	40.1	51.1	62.3	72.4	77.1	74.7	66.0	53.2	39.2	27.6	51.5
Mean Minimum Temp. (°F)	13.9	17.1	27.3	38.0	50.2	60.5	65.2	62.6	52.9	40.0	27.4	16.8	39.3
Extreme Maximum Temp. (°F)	74	79	88	98	100	107	108	106	108	95	85	73	108
Extreme Minimum Temp. (°F)	-17	-19	-14	12	27	38	49	41	27	13	0	-26	-26
Days Maximum Temp. ≥ 90°F	0	0	0	1	1	8	15	11	4	0	0	0	40
Days Maximum Temp. ≤ 32°F	12	9	3	0	0	0	0	0	0	0	3	10	37
Days Minimum Temp. ≤ 32°F	30	26	22	9	1	0	0	0	0	7	22	30	147
Days Minimum Temp. ≤ 0°F	5	3	1	0	0	0	0	0	0	0	0	3	12
Heating Degree Days (base 65°F)	1,231	1,012	766	426	145	17	2	6	94	375	767	1,152	5,993
Cooling Degree Days (base 65°F)	0	0	1	15	67	244	384	314	131	16	1	0	1,173
Mean Precipitation (in.)	0.63	0.87	1.95	2.83	4.86	4.19	4.26	4.04	3.03	2.23	1.26	0.86	31.01
Extreme Maximum Daily Precip. (in.)	0.86	1.10	1.74	2.30	3.20	2.95	4.01	3.19	3.69	2.00	2.02	1.15	4.01
Days With ≥ 0.1" Precipitation	2	3	4	6	7	7	6	6	5	4	3	3	56
Days With ≥ 0.5" Precipitation	0	0	1	2	3	3	3	3	2	2	1	0	20
Days With ≥ 1.0" Precipitation	0	0	0	1	2	1	1	1	1	0	0	0	7
Mean Snowfall (in.)	4.8	4.8	2.5	0.5	0.0	0.0	0.0	0.0	0.0	0.3	1.3	4.9	19.1
Maximum Snow Depth (in.)	9	21	12	7	0	0	0	0	0	2	5	24	24
Days With ≥ 1.0" Snow Depth	9	7	3	0	0	0	0	0	0	0	1	7	27

Bridgeport *Morrill County* Elevation: 3,666 ft. Latitude: 41° 40' N Longitude: 103° 06' W

	JAN	FEB	MAR	APR	MAY	JUN	JUL	AUG	SEP	OCT	NOV	DEC	YEAR
Mean Maximum Temp. (°F)	42.0	45.9	54.7	64.5	74.0	84.5	92.1	89.5	79.9	66.8	51.2	41.2	65.5
Mean Temp. (°F)	28.6	32.0	40.2	49.1	59.5	69.3	76.3	74.0	63.7	50.7	37.2	28.1	50.7
Mean Minimum Temp. (°F)	15.3	18.2	25.6	33.6	44.9	54.0	60.4	58.4	47.4	34.6	23.2	14.8	35.9
Extreme Maximum Temp. (°F)	75	72	82	95	99	106	108	105	102	90	79	73	108
Extreme Minimum Temp. (°F)	-26	-30	-23	3	18	34	43	40	16	-1	-14	-42	-42
Days Maximum Temp. ≥ 90°F	0	0	0	0	2	10	20	18	6	0	0	0	56
Days Maximum Temp. ≤ 32°F	6	4	2	0	0	0	0	0	0	0	2	7	21
Days Minimum Temp. ≤ 32°F	30	27	25	13	1	0	0	0	1	12	26	30	165
Days Minimum Temp. ≤ 0°F	4	3	0	0	0	0	0	0	0	0	1	4	12
Heating Degree Days (base 65°F)	1,121	926	763	474	199	38	3	6	119	438	826	1,138	6,051
Cooling Degree Days (base 65°F)	0	0	0	3	35	173	359	291	85	2	0	0	948
Mean Precipitation (in.)	0.32	0.40	0.91	1.78	2.92	2.88	2.39	2.03	1.54	1.10	0.58	0.39	17.24
Extreme Maximum Daily Precip. (in.)	0.62	0.43	1.20	1.80	1.92	2.10	2.50	2.60	1.35	1.81	1.20	1.00	2.60
Days With ≥ 0.1" Precipitation	1	1	3	4	7	6	5	4	4	3	2	1	41
Days With ≥ 0.5" Precipitation	0	0	1	1	2	2	2	1	1	1	0	0	11
Days With ≥ 1.0" Precipitation	0	0	0	0	1	1	0	1	0	0	0	0	3
Mean Snowfall (in.)	5.9	6.8	6.8	3.4	0.1	0.0	0.0	0.0	0.6	1.2	5.2	7.6	37.6
Maximum Snow Depth (in.)	16	19	19	10	4	0	0	0	9	6	15	19	19
Days With ≥ 1.0" Snow Depth	10	6	3	1	0	0	0	0	0	0	4	9	33

Broken Bow 2 W *Custer County* Elevation: 2,500 ft. Latitude: 41° 25' N Longitude: 99° 41' W

	JAN	FEB	MAR	APR	MAY	JUN	JUL	AUG	SEP	OCT	NOV	DEC	YEAR
Mean Maximum Temp. (°F)	37.2	40.3	50.0	60.7	70.3	79.9	86.0	84.1	76.0	63.5	48.6	37.4	61.2
Mean Temp. (°F)	24.4	27.5	36.4	46.4	57.2	67.2	73.0	71.0	61.6	48.9	35.2	24.9	47.8
Mean Minimum Temp. (°F)	11.5	14.6	22.7	32.1	44.1	54.5	60.0	57.9	47.1	34.2	21.7	12.3	34.4
Extreme Maximum Temp. (°F)	74	79	86	91	100	105	106	104	102	92	84	71	106
Extreme Minimum Temp. (°F)	-33	-27	-20	7	18	33	38	36	16	2	-19	-29	-33
Days Maximum Temp. ≥ 90°F	0	0	0	0	0	5	11	8	3	0	0	0	27
Days Maximum Temp. ≤ 32°F	11	9	4	0	0	0	0	0	0	0	4	11	39
Days Minimum Temp. ≤ 32°F	31	28	27	15	3	0	0	0	2	13	27	31	177
Days Minimum Temp. ≤ 0°F	6	4	1	0	0	0	0	0	0	0	1	5	17
Heating Degree Days (base 65°F)	1,253	1,056	880	556	260	59	10	20	168	497	888	1,238	6,885
Cooling Degree Days (base 65°F)	0	0	0	5	26	133	266	214	73	4	0	0	721
Mean Precipitation (in.)	0.33	0.50	1.43	2.34	3.79	3.90	3.02	2.38	1.99	1.69	0.89	0.34	22.60
Extreme Maximum Daily Precip. (in.)	0.84	0.63	1.85	1.80	3.88	3.78	2.68	2.10	3.17	1.56	1.90	0.94	3.88
Days With ≥ 0.1" Precipitation	1	2	3	5	7	6	5	5	4	4	2	1	45
Days With ≥ 0.5" Precipitation	0	0	1	2	3	3	2	2	1	1	1	0	16
Days With ≥ 1.0" Precipitation	0	0	0	0	1	1	1	1	0	0	0	0	4
Mean Snowfall (in.)	4.7	5.5	5.0	2.2	0.0	0.0	0.0	0.0	0.1	1.7	4.5	5.3	29.0
Maximum Snow Depth (in.)	16	12	25	13	0	0	0	0	2	7	14	20	25
Days With ≥ 1.0" Snow Depth	4	3	2	1	0	0	0	0	0	0	2	3	15

The period of record for all cooperative weather station data is 1980 – 2009. See User Guide for detailed explanation of data.

Canaday Steam Plant *Gosper County* Elevation: 2,361 ft. Latitude: 40° 42' N Longitude: 99° 42' W

	JAN	FEB	MAR	APR	MAY	JUN	JUL	AUG	SEP	OCT	NOV	DEC	YEAR
Mean Maximum Temp. (°F)	37.9	41.2	51.1	62.0	71.7	81.6	86.6	84.6	77.2	64.8	50.4	38.7	62.3
Mean Temp. (°F)	25.9	29.3	38.7	49.1	59.9	69.7	75.0	72.9	64.0	51.2	38.2	27.3	50.1
Mean Minimum Temp. (°F)	13.9	17.4	26.3	36.2	48.0	57.8	63.3	61.2	50.8	37.6	25.9	15.8	37.8
Extreme Maximum Temp. (°F)	75	79	88	93	98	107	106	105	103	93	84	74	107
Extreme Minimum Temp. (°F)	-22	-17	-12	11	23	38	45	42	24	13	-5	-27	-27
Days Maximum Temp. ≥ 90°F	0	0	0	0	1	6	11	8	3	0	0	0	29
Days Maximum Temp. ≤ 32°F	11	8	3	0	0	0	0	0	0	0	3	10	35
Days Minimum Temp. ≤ 32°F	31	27	23	10	1	0	0	0	1	8	23	30	154
Days Minimum Temp. ≤ 0°F	4	3	1	0	0	0	0	0	0	0	0	3	11
Heating Degree Days (base 65°F)	1,205	1,003	808	477	196	34	4	10	119	428	798	1,162	6,244
Cooling Degree Days (base 65°F)	0	0	0	8	44	183	320	262	95	7	0	0	919
Mean Precipitation (in.)	0.40	0.47	1.32	2.00	3.84	3.48	3.33	3.03	1.89	1.82	0.81	0.44	22.83
Extreme Maximum Daily Precip. (in.)	0.90	1.01	1.36	2.14	3.71	5.07	3.70	4.67	2.36	2.00	1.18	1.40	5.07
Days With ≥ 0.1" Precipitation	1	2	3	4	7	6	5	5	4	4	2	1	44
Days With ≥ 0.5" Precipitation	0	0	1	1	2	2	2	2	1	1	1	0	13
Days With ≥ 1.0" Precipitation	0	0	0	0	1	1	1	1	0	0	0	0	4
Mean Snowfall (in.)	4.4	3.9	2.2	1.0	0.0	0.0	0.0	0.0	trace	0.5	2.0	3.4	17.4
Maximum Snow Depth (in.)	14	12	13	8	0	0	0	0	4	3	13	11	14
Days With ≥ 1.0" Snow Depth	6	5	3	1	0	0	0	0	0	0	2	5	22

Chadron Municipal Arpt *Dawes County* Elevation: 3,299 ft. Latitude: 42° 50' N Longitude: 103° 05' W

	JAN	FEB	MAR	APR	MAY	JUN	JUL	AUG	SEP	OCT	NOV	DEC	YEAR
Mean Maximum Temp. (°F)	38.1	41.0	49.9	59.5	69.8	81.0	90.0	88.9	77.6	63.2	47.8	37.9	62.1
Mean Temp. (°F)	26.0	28.7	37.0	46.1	56.7	67.1	75.2	73.8	62.6	48.8	35.5	25.8	48.6
Mean Minimum Temp. (°F)	13.9	16.4	24.0	32.7	43.6	53.1	60.4	58.7	47.5	34.4	23.2	13.7	35.1
Extreme Maximum Temp. (°F)	70	76	83	93	94	107	109	108	102	92	81	72	109
Extreme Minimum Temp. (°F)	-26	-27	-26	7	21	31	37	39	17	-7	-20	-40	-40
Days Maximum Temp. ≥ 90°F	0	0	0	0	1	6	17	16	6	0	0	0	46
Days Maximum Temp. ≤ 32°F	9	8	4	1	0	0	0	0	0	1	5	10	38
Days Minimum Temp. ≤ 32°F	30	26	25	15	3	0	0	0	2	12	23	29	165
Days Minimum Temp. ≤ 0°F	5	4	1	0	0	0	0	0	0	0	1	5	16
Heating Degree Days (base 65°F)	1,202	1,019	863	561	275	64	4	9	157	499	877	1,208	6,738
Cooling Degree Days (base 65°F)	0	0	0	2	25	133	330	288	90	4	0	0	872
Mean Precipitation (in.)	0.43	0.53	1.15	1.79	3.05	2.79	1.93	1.64	1.60	1.30	0.61	0.50	17.32
Extreme Maximum Daily Precip. (in.)	0.88	1.50	1.44	2.45	2.56	2.12	na	na	4.40	1.50	na	0.49	na
Days With ≥ 0.1" Precipitation	1	2	3	5	6	6	4	3	3	3	2	2	40
Days With ≥ 0.5" Precipitation	0	0	1	1	2	2	1	1	1	1	0	0	10
Days With ≥ 1.0" Precipitation	0	0	0	0	0	0	0	0	0	0	0	0	0
Mean Snowfall (in.)	5.1	6.1	9.1	4.1	0.5	0.0	0.0	0.0	0.1	3.2	5.3	7.9	41.4
Maximum Snow Depth (in.)	10	14	32	7	4	0	na	na	2	na	na	12	na
Days With ≥ 1.0" Snow Depth	13	10	7	2	0	0	0	0	0	1	6	12	51

Clarkson *Colfax County* Elevation: 1,549 ft. Latitude: 41° 43' N Longitude: 97° 08' W

	JAN	FEB	MAR	APR	MAY	JUN	JUL	AUG	SEP	OCT	NOV	DEC	YEAR
Mean Maximum Temp. (°F)	32.1	36.9	47.7	62.1	72.5	82.2	86.4	83.8	75.7	62.9	45.7	34.0	60.2
Mean Temp. (°F)	21.8	26.6	36.6	49.4	60.6	70.7	75.2	72.9	63.3	50.5	35.5	24.5	49.0
Mean Minimum Temp. (°F)	11.5	16.3	25.3	36.7	48.7	59.1	64.0	61.9	50.9	38.1	25.3	14.9	37.7
Extreme Maximum Temp. (°F)	75	73	90	97	99	106	106	106	98	89	79	67	106
Extreme Minimum Temp. (°F)	-23	-24	-16	11	27	38	43	40	21	10	-12	-27	-27
Days Maximum Temp. ≥ 90°F	0	0	0	1	1	6	11	7	3	0	0	0	29
Days Maximum Temp. ≤ 32°F	15	11	4	0	0	0	0	0	0	0	5	13	48
Days Minimum Temp. ≤ 32°F	31	26	24	10	1	0	0	0	1	9	24	30	156
Days Minimum Temp. ≤ 0°F	6	4	1	0	0	0	0	0	0	0	0	4	15
Heating Degree Days (base 65°F)	1,332	1,080	875	474	181	30	4	10	137	448	878	1,249	6,698
Cooling Degree Days (base 65°F)	0	0	0	14	52	207	327	261	93	6	0	0	960
Mean Precipitation (in.)	0.58	0.62	1.86	2.43	4.45	4.44	3.36	3.33	2.88	2.03	1.44	0.69	28.11
Extreme Maximum Daily Precip. (in.)	0.98	1.15	2.18	2.63	3.05	4.53	2.67	4.92	4.28	2.17	2.04	1.00	4.92
Days With ≥ 0.1" Precipitation	2	2	4	5	7	6	5	5	4	4	3	2	49
Days With ≥ 0.5" Precipitation	0	0	1	2	3	3	3	2	2	1	1	0	18
Days With ≥ 1.0" Precipitation	0	0	0	1	1	2	1	1	1	0	0	0	7
Mean Snowfall (in.)	4.7	4.6	5.5	2.1	0.0	0.0	0.0	0.0	0.2	0.9	3.2	5.1	26.3
Maximum Snow Depth (in.)	na	na	na	na	na	na	na	na	na	na	na	na	na
Days With ≥ 1.0" Snow Depth	na	5	3	0	0	0	0	0	0	0	2	na	na

Clay Center *Clay County* Elevation: 1,750 ft. Latitude: 40° 31' N Longitude: 98° 03' W

	JAN	FEB	MAR	APR	MAY	JUN	JUL	AUG	SEP	OCT	NOV	DEC	YEAR
Mean Maximum Temp. (°F)	35.9	39.7	50.7	62.8	72.4	82.6	87.3	85.3	77.8	65.1	50.0	37.1	62.2
Mean Temp. (°F)	24.8	28.6	38.4	49.8	60.5	70.7	75.4	73.4	64.7	52.1	38.4	26.7	50.3
Mean Minimum Temp. (°F)	13.6	17.5	26.1	36.5	48.5	58.7	63.5	61.3	51.4	39.0	26.7	16.3	38.3
Extreme Maximum Temp. (°F)	76	80	89	95	99	106	105	107	102	93	84	76	107
Extreme Minimum Temp. (°F)	-30	-24	-7	10	24	35	49	43	21	13	-8	-39	-39
Days Maximum Temp. ≥ 90°F	0	0	0	0	1	7	12	9	4	0	0	0	33
Days Maximum Temp. ≤ 32°F	12	9	3	0	0	0	0	0	0	0	3	11	38
Days Minimum Temp. ≤ 32°F	30	26	23	10	1	0	0	0	1	7	22	30	150
Days Minimum Temp. ≤ 0°F	5	3	1	0	0	0	0	0	0	0	0	3	12
Heating Degree Days (base 65°F)	1,240	1,021	818	460	180	26	3	7	110	403	790	1,181	6,239
Cooling Degree Days (base 65°F)	0	0	0	10	47	202	332	274	106	10	0	0	981
Mean Precipitation (in.)	0.33	0.57	1.50	2.65	4.92	3.92	3.95	3.39	2.44	2.36	1.20	0.67	27.90
Extreme Maximum Daily Precip. (in.)	0.65	1.15	2.15	2.19	3.28	4.03	7.20	3.17	3.40	2.24	2.10	0.76	7.20
Days With ≥ 0.1" Precipitation	1	1	3	4	7	6	5	5	4	3	2	2	43
Days With ≥ 0.5" Precipitation	0	0	1	2	4	3	2	2	1	2	1	0	18
Days With ≥ 1.0" Precipitation	0	0	0	1	2	1	1	1	1	1	0	0	8
Mean Snowfall (in.)	4.5	4.3	2.7	0.7	0.0	0.0	0.0	0.0	trace	0.3	1.7	3.1	17.3
Maximum Snow Depth (in.)	14	11	16	10	0	0	0	0	trace	23	4	15	23
Days With ≥ 1.0" Snow Depth	6	5	2	0	0	0	0	0	0	0	1	5	19

The period of record for all cooperative weather station data is 1980 – 2009. See User Guide for detailed explanation of data.

Columbus 3 NE *Platte County* Elevation: 1,450 ft. Latitude: 41° 28' N Longitude: 97° 20' W

	JAN	FEB	MAR	APR	MAY	JUN	JUL	AUG	SEP	OCT	NOV	DEC	YEAR
Mean Maximum Temp. (°F)	33.4	37.5	49.5	62.9	73.6	83.6	88.1	85.2	77.5	63.4	47.4	34.6	61.4
Mean Temp. (°F)	23.7	27.7	38.5	51.0	62.4	72.4	77.0	74.5	65.7	52.2	37.6	25.4	50.7
Mean Minimum Temp. (°F)	14.0	17.9	27.6	39.1	51.2	61.1	65.8	63.8	53.9	40.9	27.6	16.2	39.9
Extreme Maximum Temp. (°F)	69	76	91	96	99	108	110	105	99	93	80	68	110
Extreme Minimum Temp. (°F)	-21	-20	-7	13	29	40	49	43	24	14	-6	-24	-24
Days Maximum Temp. ≥ 90°F	0	0	0	1	1	8	13	8	4	0	0	0	35
Days Maximum Temp. ≤ 32°F	14	10	4	0	0	0	0	0	0	0	4	13	45
Days Minimum Temp. ≤ 32°F	31	26	22	7	0	0	0	0	0	6	21	30	143
Days Minimum Temp. ≤ 0°F	5	3	0	0	0	0	0	0	0	0	0	3	11
Heating Degree Days (base 65°F)	1,273	1,047	814	429	142	17	1	6	94	402	817	1,220	6,262
Cooling Degree Days (base 65°F)	0	0	1	16	70	245	379	307	122	12	0	0	1,152
Mean Precipitation (in.)	0.54	0.72	1.88	2.69	4.36	4.50	3.46	3.49	2.70	2.22	1.44	0.81	28.81
Extreme Maximum Daily Precip. (in.)	0.67	1.24	1.95	2.87	2.54	3.67	3.53	5.97	3.60	2.67	1.89	1.18	5.97
Days With ≥ 0.1" Precipitation	2	2	4	5	8	7	6	5	5	5	3	2	54
Days With ≥ 0.5" Precipitation	0	0	1	2	3	3	3	2	2	2	1	0	19
Days With ≥ 1.0" Precipitation	0	0	0	1	1	1	1	1	1	0	0	0	6
Mean Snowfall (in.)	5.4	5.6	4.4	1.3	0.0	0.0	0.0	0.0	trace	0.9	3.0	6.0	26.6
Maximum Snow Depth (in.)	23	17	14	6	0	0	0	0	trace	11	17	24	24
Days With ≥ 1.0" Snow Depth	14	11	4	1	0	0	0	0	0	0	3	11	44

Crete *Saline County* Elevation: 1,435 ft. Latitude: 40° 37' N Longitude: 96° 57' W

	JAN	FEB	MAR	APR	MAY	JUN	JUL	AUG	SEP	OCT	NOV	DEC	YEAR
Mean Maximum Temp. (°F)	37.2	42.2	53.1	65.0	74.6	83.9	88.6	86.4	79.4	67.1	51.2	38.3	63.9
Mean Temp. (°F)	26.8	31.2	41.2	52.6	63.0	72.5	77.1	75.1	67.0	54.8	40.5	28.4	52.5
Mean Minimum Temp. (°F)	16.3	20.1	29.2	40.1	51.3	61.1	65.6	63.8	54.7	42.5	29.7	18.5	41.1
Extreme Maximum Temp. (°F)	73	77	88	95	98	105	105	106	105	97	86	71	106
Extreme Minimum Temp. (°F)	-20	-21	-11	15	26	39	46	44	25	8	-3	-25	-25
Days Maximum Temp. ≥ 90°F	0	0	0	1	1	7	13	10	4	0	0	0	36
Days Maximum Temp. ≤ 32°F	11	8	2	0	0	0	0	0	0	0	2	10	33
Days Minimum Temp. ≤ 32°F	30	24	19	7	0	0	0	0	0	5	18	28	131
Days Minimum Temp. ≤ 0°F	4	2	0	0	0	0	0	0	0	0	0	3	9
Heating Degree Days (base 65°F)	1,178	950	732	384	128	14	1	5	77	328	728	1,128	5,653
Cooling Degree Days (base 65°F)	0	0	1	18	72	248	384	324	144	20	0	0	1,211
Mean Precipitation (in.)	0.55	0.62	1.88	2.54	4.71	4.32	3.80	3.38	3.40	2.28	1.19	0.91	29.58
Extreme Maximum Daily Precip. (in.)	0.87	1.14	2.96	2.87	6.05	3.02	3.38	4.01	***4.65***	2.88	2.84	1.80	***6.05***
Days With ≥ 0.1" Precipitation	2	2	4	5	7	6	5	5	5	4	2	2	49
Days With ≥ 0.5" Precipitation	0	0	1	2	3	3	2	2	2	1	1	0	17
Days With ≥ 1.0" Precipitation	0	0	0	1	1	1	1	1	1	0	0	0	6
Mean Snowfall (in.)	4.2	4.4	3.9	0.6	trace	0.0	0.0	0.0	trace	0.5	2.4	5.2	21.2
Maximum Snow Depth (in.)	16	12	13	5	trace	0	0	0	1	12	12	16	16
Days With ≥ 1.0" Snow Depth	12	8	3	0	0	0	0	0	0	0	2	10	35

Curtis 3 NNE *Frontier County* Elevation: 2,721 ft. Latitude: 40° 40' N Longitude: 100° 30' W

	JAN	FEB	MAR	APR	MAY	JUN	JUL	AUG	SEP	OCT	NOV	DEC	YEAR
Mean Maximum Temp. (°F)	***39.6***	43.9	53.2	64.5	***73.3***	83.7	89.9	87.7	***79.8***	66.7	51.3	***41.6***	***64.6***
Mean Temp. (°F)	***25.5***	29.8	38.5	49.0	***59.2***	69.6	75.4	73.3	***63.8***	50.5	36.9	***27.8***	***49.9***
Mean Minimum Temp. (°F)	***11.3***	15.7	23.8	33.5	***45.0***	55.5	60.9	58.9	47.8	34.3	22.3	***13.8***	***35.2***
Extreme Maximum Temp. (°F)	***74***	***77***	88	94	***100***	***107***	110	***107***	***102***	***95***	***85***	***74***	***110***
Extreme Minimum Temp. (°F)	***-26***	***-29***	-14	10	***17***	***33***	41	***39***	***21***	***9***	***-10***	***-31***	***-31***
Days Maximum Temp. ≥ 90°F	***0***	0	0	1	1	8	16	12	6	1	0	***0***	***45***
Days Maximum Temp. ≤ 32°F	***10***	7	3	0	0	0	0	0	0	0	3	***8***	***31***
Days Minimum Temp. ≤ 32°F	***31***	27	26	13	2	0	0	0	2	13	26	***30***	***170***
Days Minimum Temp. ≤ 0°F	***5***	3	1	0	0	0	0	0	0	0	1	***3***	***13***
Heating Degree Days (base 65°F)	***1,218***	988	814	477	***210***	35	4	9	***124***	445	837	***1,150***	***6,311***
Cooling Degree Days (base 65°F)	***0***	0	0	6	***36***	181	333	272	***96***	4	0	***0***	***928***
Mean Precipitation (in.)	***0.38***	***0.52***	1.24	1.92	3.30	3.43	2.86	2.62	1.76	1.58	0.72	***0.44***	***20.77***
Extreme Maximum Daily Precip. (in.)	***1.03***	***1.02***	1.55	***1.47***	***5.80***	***2.41***	3.58	***2.12***	***1.80***	***2.50***	***1.12***	***1.28***	***5.80***
Days With ≥ 0.1" Precipitation	***1***	2	3	4	6	6	5	4	3	3	2	***1***	***40***
Days With ≥ 0.5" Precipitation	***0***	0	1	1	2	3	2	2	1	1	0	***0***	***13***
Days With ≥ 1.0" Precipitation	***0***	0	0	0	1	1	1	1	0	0	0	***0***	***4***
Mean Snowfall (in.)	na	na	na	***2.5***	***0.0***	na	***0.0***	***0.0***	***0.3***	na	***3.0***	na	na
Maximum Snow Depth (in.)	***16***	***10***	10	***6***	na	na	***0***	***0***	na	na	***14***	***12***	na
Days With ≥ 1.0" Snow Depth	***9***	8	4	***1***	***0***	na	***0***	***0***	***0***	na	3	***6***	na

David City *Butler County* Elevation: 1,609 ft. Latitude: 41° 15' N Longitude: 97° 08' W

	JAN	FEB	MAR	APR	MAY	JUN	JUL	AUG	SEP	OCT	NOV	DEC	YEAR
Mean Maximum Temp. (°F)	32.8	37.2	49.0	62.2	72.9	82.3	87.0	84.6	77.2	63.8	47.9	34.4	60.9
Mean Temp. (°F)	23.0	27.1	37.7	49.9	61.0	70.9	75.7	73.5	64.9	52.1	37.6	25.0	49.9
Mean Minimum Temp. (°F)	13.0	16.8	26.4	37.6	49.0	59.5	64.5	62.3	52.5	40.3	27.2	15.6	38.7
Extreme Maximum Temp. (°F)	71	76	89	96	99	106	105	105	102	91	82	68	106
Extreme Minimum Temp. (°F)	-25	-23	-14	12	25	40	46	42	18	6	-7	-27	-27
Days Maximum Temp. ≥ 90°F	0	0	0	1	1	6	12	8	3	0	0	0	31
Days Maximum Temp. ≤ 32°F	15	11	4	0	0	0	0	0	0	0	4	13	47
Days Minimum Temp. ≤ 32°F	31	26	23	9	1	0	0	0	0	7	22	30	149
Days Minimum Temp. ≤ 0°F	6	4	1	0	0	0	0	0	0	0	0	4	15
Heating Degree Days (base 65°F)	1,297	1,066	840	459	173	26	3	9	109	406	815	1,233	6,436
Cooling Degree Days (base 65°F)	0	0	1	13	55	210	343	279	112	12	0	0	1,025
Mean Precipitation (in.)	0.69	0.78	2.14	2.81	4.06	4.73	2.94	3.87	2.86	2.11	1.43	0.99	29.41
Extreme Maximum Daily Precip. (in.)	0.72	0.98	3.15	2.01	3.15	5.47	2.67	4.48	3.23	2.12	1.47	0.98	5.47
Days With ≥ 0.1" Precipitation	2	2	5	5	8	7	5	6	5	4	3	3	55
Days With ≥ 0.5" Precipitation	0	0	1	2	3	3	2	2	2	1	1	1	18
Days With ≥ 1.0" Precipitation	0	0	0	1	1	1	1	1	1	1	0	0	7
Mean Snowfall (in.)	6.4	6.6	5.3	2.2	0.0	0.0	0.0	0.0	0.2	1.1	3.5	6.1	31.4
Maximum Snow Depth (in.)	24	15	14	9	0	0	0	0	1	6	18	24	24
Days With ≥ 1.0" Snow Depth	13	11	5	1	0	0	0	0	0	0	2	11	43

The period of record for all cooperative weather station data is 1980 – 2009. See User Guide for detailed explanation of data.

Fremont *Dodge County* Elevation: 1,180 ft. Latitude: 41° 26' N Longitude: 96° 28' W

	JAN	FEB	MAR	APR	MAY	JUN	JUL	AUG	SEP	OCT	NOV	DEC	YEAR
Mean Maximum Temp. (°F)	34.3	38.8	50.7	64.3	74.8	84.2	87.9	85.6	78.5	65.6	49.6	35.6	62.5
Mean Temp. (°F)	24.3	28.6	39.4	51.8	62.9	72.6	76.7	74.4	66.0	53.3	39.2	26.4	51.3
Mean Minimum Temp. (°F)	14.2	18.4	28.0	39.3	51.0	61.0	65.5	63.1	53.4	41.0	28.7	17.1	40.1
Extreme Maximum Temp. (°F)	72	75	90	95	98	105	108	107	105	93	85	70	108
Extreme Minimum Temp. (°F)	-22	-20	-9	14	27	40	49	42	24	11	-6	-24	-24
Days Maximum Temp. ≥ 90°F	0	0	0	1	2	8	13	9	4	0	0	0	37
Days Maximum Temp. ≤ 32°F	13	9	3	0	0	0	0	0	0	0	3	12	40
Days Minimum Temp. ≤ 32°F	30	25	21	7	0	0	0	0	0	6	20	29	138
Days Minimum Temp. ≤ 0°F	5	3	0	0	0	0	0	0	0	0	0	3	11
Heating Degree Days (base 65°F)	1,255	1,022	788	405	133	14	1	6	90	371	769	1,190	6,044
Cooling Degree Days (base 65°F)	0	0	1	17	75	248	373	305	126	16	0	0	1,161
Mean Precipitation (in.)	0.69	0.78	1.91	2.84	4.20	4.66	3.36	3.40	3.07	2.23	1.32	1.00	29.46
Extreme Maximum Daily Precip. (in.)	1.03	1.07	2.73	2.49	3.43	4.01	4.40	3.69	4.89	3.76	1.42	2.06	4.89
Days With ≥ 0.1" Precipitation	2	2	4	5	8	7	6	5	5	5	3	3	55
Days With ≥ 0.5" Precipitation	0	0	1	2	3	3	2	2	2	1	1	0	17
Days With ≥ 1.0" Precipitation	0	0	0	1	1	2	1	1	1	0	0	0	7
Mean Snowfall (in.)	6.0	6.5	5.7	1.7	trace	0.0	0.0	0.0	0.0	0.8	2.8	6.9	30.4
Maximum Snow Depth (in.)	14	23	15	12	trace	0	0	0	0	4	14	18	23
Days With ≥ 1.0" Snow Depth	14	11	5	1	0	0	0	0	0	0	2	11	44

Geneva *Fillmore County* Elevation: 1,629 ft. Latitude: 40° 32' N Longitude: 97° 36' W

	JAN	FEB	MAR	APR	MAY	JUN	JUL	AUG	SEP	OCT	NOV	DEC	YEAR
Mean Maximum Temp. (°F)	37.2	41.5	52.9	65.0	74.0	83.0	87.4	85.2	78.3	66.0	50.8	38.0	63.3
Mean Temp. (°F)	27.0	31.0	41.1	52.6	62.9	72.1	76.6	74.6	66.5	54.2	40.3	28.5	52.3
Mean Minimum Temp. (°F)	16.7	20.4	29.3	40.1	51.7	61.2	65.8	64.0	54.7	42.5	29.7	19.1	41.3
Extreme Maximum Temp. (°F)	76	79	89	96	99	104	104	106	103	94	85	70	106
Extreme Minimum Temp. (°F)	-20	-18	-7	14	29	41	50	45	25	11	-1	-26	-26
Days Maximum Temp. ≥ 90°F	0	0	0	0	1	6	12	9	4	0	0	0	32
Days Maximum Temp. ≤ 32°F	11	8	2	0	0	0	0	0	0	0	3	10	34
Days Minimum Temp. ≤ 32°F	30	24	20	6	0	0	0	0	0	4	19	29	132
Days Minimum Temp. ≤ 0°F	3	2	0	0	0	0	0	0	0	0	0	2	7
Heating Degree Days (base 65°F)	1,172	956	733	383	129	15	1	5	80	343	736	1,124	5,677
Cooling Degree Days (base 65°F)	0	0	1	18	69	235	369	309	133	17	0	0	1,151
Mean Precipitation (in.)	0.59	0.51	1.90	2.58	4.72	4.37	3.43	3.56	3.27	2.23	1.26	0.71	29.13
Extreme Maximum Daily Precip. (in.)	1.06	0.65	4.22	4.03	4.00	3.89	3.90	5.52	5.75	4.03	1.83	1.16	5.75
Days With ≥ 0.1" Precipitation	2	2	4	5	8	6	5	6	4	4	2	2	50
Days With ≥ 0.5" Precipitation	0	0	1	2	3	3	2	2	2	1	1	0	17
Days With ≥ 1.0" Precipitation	0	0	0	1	2	1	1	1	1	0	0	0	7
Mean Snowfall (in.)	5.1	5.5	4.0	0.7	0.0	0.0	0.0	0.0	0.1	0.2	1.7	3.4	20.7
Maximum Snow Depth (in.)	18	16	15	10	0	0	0	0	4	15	10	16	18
Days With ≥ 1.0" Snow Depth	11	9	3	1	0	0	0	0	0	0	2	8	34

Gordon 6 N *Sheridan County* Elevation: 3,700 ft. Latitude: 42° 54' N Longitude: 102° 12' W

	JAN	FEB	MAR	APR	MAY	JUN	JUL	AUG	SEP	OCT	NOV	DEC	YEAR
Mean Maximum Temp. (°F)	34.6	38.5	47.2	57.7	68.4	78.9	87.5	86.4	75.7	60.7	46.3	35.2	59.8
Mean Temp. (°F)	23.3	26.9	34.7	44.3	54.9	64.9	72.6	71.4	60.7	47.2	34.3	24.1	46.6
Mean Minimum Temp. (°F)	12.0	15.2	22.1	30.8	41.4	50.9	57.6	56.2	45.5	33.5	22.4	13.0	33.4
Extreme Maximum Temp. (°F)	67	72	80	91	94	106	107	104	104	92	81	68	107
Extreme Minimum Temp. (°F)	-29	-32	-18	1	18	32	42	35	16	-4	-14	-40	-40
Days Maximum Temp. ≥ 90°F	0	0	0	0	1	5	14	13	4	0	0	0	37
Days Maximum Temp. ≤ 32°F	12	9	5	1	0	0	0	0	0	1	5	12	45
Days Minimum Temp. ≤ 32°F	30	27	27	17	4	0	0	0	2	13	26	30	176
Days Minimum Temp. ≤ 0°F	6	4	1	0	0	0	0	0	0	0	1	5	17
Heating Degree Days (base 65°F)	1,286	1,071	934	616	323	95	14	20	187	547	912	1,261	7,266
Cooling Degree Days (base 65°F)	0	0	0	2	18	99	257	227	65	2	0	0	670
Mean Precipitation (in.)	0.37	0.46	1.07	1.86	3.04	3.43	2.84	1.63	1.56	1.61	0.64	0.44	18.95
Extreme Maximum Daily Precip. (in.)	***0.78***	***0.82***	2.29	***1.51***	***1.93***	2.46	***2.78***	***1.63***	***1.81***	***2.50***	***1.60***	***0.60***	***2.78***
Days With ≥ 0.1" Precipitation	1	1	3	5	7	7	6	5	4	4	2	2	47
Days With ≥ 0.5" Precipitation	0	0	0	1	2	2	2	1	1	1	0	0	10
Days With ≥ 1.0" Precipitation	0	0	0	0	0	1	1	0	0	0	0	0	2
Mean Snowfall (in.)	5.6	***5.4***	8.1	5.3	0.5	0.0	0.0	0.0	0.2	2.2	4.7	6.0	***38.0***
Maximum Snow Depth (in.)	14	15	15	12	6	0	0	0	1	10	***10***	***15***	***15***
Days With ≥ 1.0" Snow Depth	14	10	8	3	0	0	0	0	0	1	7	15	58

Harrisburg 10 NW *Banner County* Elevation: 4,549 ft. Latitude: 41° 38' N Longitude: 103° 57' W

	JAN	FEB	MAR	APR	MAY	JUN	JUL	AUG	SEP	OCT	NOV	DEC	YEAR
Mean Maximum Temp. (°F)	41.2	43.8	51.0	59.7	69.6	80.0	88.1	86.2	76.6	62.9	50.5	40.8	62.5
Mean Temp. (°F)	27.6	30.0	36.8	44.8	54.9	64.6	71.7	69.8	59.7	46.6	35.7	27.0	47.4
Mean Minimum Temp. (°F)	14.0	16.1	22.5	29.8	40.1	49.1	55.3	53.3	42.8	30.2	20.9	13.1	32.3
Extreme Maximum Temp. (°F)	70	72	81	89	97	104	105	103	100	90	81	74	105
Extreme Minimum Temp. (°F)	-26	-31	-15	-4	13	27	37	34	13	-10	-15	-37	-37
Days Maximum Temp. ≥ 90°F	0	0	0	0	1	5	14	11	3	0	0	0	34
Days Maximum Temp. ≤ 32°F	7	6	3	1	0	0	0	0	0	1	3	8	29
Days Minimum Temp. ≤ 32°F	30	27	27	19	5	0	0	0	4	18	27	30	187
Days Minimum Temp. ≤ 0°F	5	3	1	0	0	0	0	0	0	0	1	5	15
Heating Degree Days (base 65°F)	1,153	984	867	601	319	93	13	22	195	564	872	1,172	6,855
Cooling Degree Days (base 65°F)	0	0	0	0	12	87	228	177	42	1	0	0	547
Mean Precipitation (in.)	0.32	0.48	1.01	1.58	2.38	2.57	2.08	1.84	1.39	1.25	0.62	0.42	15.94
Extreme Maximum Daily Precip. (in.)	0.52	0.66	1.54	1.59	2.30	2.75	2.95	2.21	1.91	1.48	1.13	1.05	2.95
Days With ≥ 0.1" Precipitation	1	2	3	4	6	6	4	4	4	3	2	2	41
Days With ≥ 0.5" Precipitation	0	0	0	1	1	1	1	1	1	1	0	0	7
Days With ≥ 1.0" Precipitation	0	0	0	0	0	1	0	0	0	0	0	0	1
Mean Snowfall (in.)	5.9	7.4	9.1	6.0	0.5	0.0	0.0	0.0	0.7	3.2	5.6	7.9	46.3
Maximum Snow Depth (in.)	13	10	15	14	3	0	0	0	8	16	12	18	18
Days With ≥ 1.0" Snow Depth	12	11	8	3	0	0	0	0	0	2	7	14	57

The period of record for all cooperative weather station data is 1980 – 2009. See User Guide for detailed explanation of data.

Harrison *Sioux County* Elevation: 4,850 ft. Latitude: 42° 41' N Longitude: 103° 53' W

	JAN	FEB	MAR	APR	MAY	JUN	JUL	AUG	SEP	OCT	NOV	DEC	YEAR
Mean Maximum Temp. (°F)	34.8	37.4	45.8	55.0	65.3	76.0	85.3	83.6	72.6	58.5	44.3	34.9	57.8
Mean Temp. (°F)	23.2	26.0	33.7	42.1	52.3	62.3	70.4	68.5	58.0	44.8	32.3	23.3	44.7
Mean Minimum Temp. (°F)	11.7	14.5	21.6	29.2	39.3	48.6	55.4	53.4	43.3	31.1	20.3	11.6	31.7
Extreme Maximum Temp. (°F)	65	67	76	86	93	103	104	100	96	89	76	66	104
Extreme Minimum Temp. (°F)	-22	-31	-17	1	14	26	39	32	13	-8	-16	-39	-39
Days Maximum Temp. ≥ 90°F	0	0	0	0	0	3	11	7	2	0	0	0	23
Days Maximum Temp. ≤ 32°F	12	9	6	1	0	0	0	0	0	1	6	13	48
Days Minimum Temp. ≤ 32°F	30	27	27	20	6	0	0	0	3	16	26	30	185
Days Minimum Temp. ≤ 0°F	6	4	1	0	0	0	0	0	0	0	2	6	19
Heating Degree Days (base 65°F)	1,289	1,098	963	680	392	135	23	34	238	619	973	1,286	7,730
Cooling Degree Days (base 65°F)	0	0	0	0	6	61	197	150	34	0	0	0	448
Mean Precipitation (in.)	0.35	0.40	1.03	2.08	3.31	2.61	1.91	1.46	1.53	1.34	0.57	0.39	16.98
Extreme Maximum Daily Precip. (in.)	0.60	0.50	1.09	2.00	3.47	3.58	1.22	1.96	2.80	1.55	1.23	0.60	3.58
Days With ≥ 0.1" Precipitation	1	1	3	5	7	6	5	3	4	3	2	1	41
Days With ≥ 0.5" Precipitation	0	0	0	1	2	2	1	1	1	1	0	0	9
Days With ≥ 1.0" Precipitation	0	0	0	0	1	0	0	0	0	0	0	0	1
Mean Snowfall (in.)	5.0	6.0	9.5	4.9	0.8	0.0	0.0	0.0	0.5	3.4	5.5	6.1	41.7
Maximum Snow Depth (in.)	11	***18***	***17***	***18***	8	0	0	0	trace	15	***24***	***24***	***24***
Days With ≥ 1.0" Snow Depth	6	5	5	2	0	0	0	0	0	1	2	5	26

Hastings 4 N *Adams County* Elevation: 1,939 ft. Latitude: 40° 39' N Longitude: 98° 23' W

	JAN	FEB	MAR	APR	MAY	JUN	JUL	AUG	SEP	OCT	NOV	DEC	YEAR
Mean Maximum Temp. (°F)	36.3	40.4	51.3	63.3	73.2	83.4	87.9	85.6	78.3	64.8	49.6	37.1	62.6
Mean Temp. (°F)	25.6	29.5	39.3	50.5	61.6	71.5	76.2	73.9	65.3	52.5	38.5	27.0	51.0
Mean Minimum Temp. (°F)	14.9	18.6	27.3	37.7	49.9	59.6	64.5	62.2	52.4	40.1	27.3	16.8	39.3
Extreme Maximum Temp. (°F)	76	80	89	96	99	109	109	109	102	94	84	71	109
Extreme Minimum Temp. (°F)	-22	-18	-15	10	24	40	47	44	26	4	-4	-23	-23
Days Maximum Temp. ≥ 90°F	0	0	0	1	1	8	14	9	4	0	0	0	37
Days Maximum Temp. ≤ 32°F	12	9	3	0	0	0	0	0	0	0	3	11	38
Days Minimum Temp. ≤ 32°F	30	26	22	8	0	0	0	0	0	6	21	30	143
Days Minimum Temp. ≤ 0°F	4	3	1	0	0	0	0	0	0	0	0	3	11
Heating Degree Days (base 65°F)	1,214	997	791	440	158	19	2	7	99	395	788	1,172	6,082
Cooling Degree Days (base 65°F)	0	0	0	13	58	223	357	291	116	13	0	0	1,071
Mean Precipitation (in.)	0.59	0.77	1.88	2.74	4.55	3.51	3.78	3.31	2.65	1.94	1.28	0.76	27.76
Extreme Maximum Daily Precip. (in.)	0.70	1.19	2.29	2.92	2.81	3.74	2.85	5.11	3.94	1.99	3.21	1.46	5.11
Days With ≥ 0.1" Precipitation	2	2	4	5	8	6	6	6	4	4	3	2	52
Days With ≥ 0.5" Precipitation	0	0	1	2	3	2	2	2	2	1	1	0	16
Days With ≥ 1.0" Precipitation	0	0	0	1	1	1	1	1	1	1	0	0	7
Mean Snowfall (in.)	6.4	6.5	5.2	1.2	trace	0.0	0.0	0.0	0.2	1.2	3.0	5.6	29.3
Maximum Snow Depth (in.)	20	15	16	8	trace	0	0	0	4	17	12	20	20
Days With ≥ 1.0" Snow Depth	12	10	4	1	0	0	0	0	0	0	3	9	39

Hemingford *Box Butte County* Elevation: 4,270 ft. Latitude: 42° 19' N Longitude: 103° 04' W

	JAN	FEB	MAR	APR	MAY	JUN	JUL	AUG	SEP	OCT	NOV	DEC	YEAR
Mean Maximum Temp. (°F)	37.6	40.6	47.9	57.3	67.3	78.2	86.9	84.8	74.5	60.7	47.3	37.8	60.1
Mean Temp. (°F)	26.9	29.6	36.4	45.2	55.3	65.4	73.0	71.1	61.1	48.2	36.2	27.1	48.0
Mean Minimum Temp. (°F)	16.1	18.5	24.8	33.0	43.2	52.5	59.2	57.4	47.7	35.7	25.0	16.2	35.8
Extreme Maximum Temp. (°F)	70	71	80	89	94	103	107	102	97	90	79	70	107
Extreme Minimum Temp. (°F)	-18	-25	-13	5	19	33	45	39	20	-3	-12	-35	-35
Days Maximum Temp. ≥ 90°F	0	0	0	0	0	4	13	10	3	0	0	0	30
Days Maximum Temp. ≤ 32°F	10	7	5	1	0	0	0	0	0	1	5	10	39
Days Minimum Temp. ≤ 32°F	29	26	25	14	2	0	0	0	1	10	23	29	159
Days Minimum Temp. ≤ 0°F	4	3	1	0	0	0	0	0	0	0	1	3	12
Heating Degree Days (base 65°F)	1,176	996	881	589	311	85	11	19	174	517	857	1,170	6,786
Cooling Degree Days (base 65°F)	0	0	0	1	17	104	266	216	65	4	0	0	673
Mean Precipitation (in.)	0.27	0.44	1.02	1.65	2.86	2.63	2.30	1.40	1.40	1.16	0.48	0.37	15.98
Extreme Maximum Daily Precip. (in.)	0.50	0.58	1.64	2.10	2.52	2.71	2.35	1.85	1.50	1.18	0.59	0.60	2.71
Days With ≥ 0.1" Precipitation	1	2	3	4	6	6	5	4	4	3	2	1	41
Days With ≥ 0.5" Precipitation	0	0	1	1	2	2	1	1	1	1	0	0	10
Days With ≥ 1.0" Precipitation	0	0	0	0	1	0	0	0	0	0	0	0	1
Mean Snowfall (in.)	5.0	6.8	8.6	6.7	0.3	0.0	0.0	0.0	0.8	3.5	6.0	6.7	44.4
Maximum Snow Depth (in.)	13	16	13	11	2	0	0	0	6	13	11	11	16
Days With ≥ 1.0" Snow Depth	15	12	10	4	0	0	0	0	0	2	8	16	67

Kearney 4 NE *Buffalo County* Elevation: 2,129 ft. Latitude: 40° 44' N Longitude: 99° 01' W

	JAN	FEB	MAR	APR	MAY	JUN	JUL	AUG	SEP	OCT	NOV	DEC	YEAR
Mean Maximum Temp. (°F)	36.5	40.3	50.7	62.6	72.2	82.5	87.5	85.2	77.7	64.7	49.6	37.3	62.2
Mean Temp. (°F)	25.1	28.6	38.0	49.0	60.0	70.2	75.2	73.0	64.0	51.2	37.5	26.4	49.8
Mean Minimum Temp. (°F)	13.6	16.9	25.2	35.4	47.7	57.8	62.9	60.8	50.2	37.6	25.2	15.4	37.4
Extreme Maximum Temp. (°F)	77	78	89	95	100	108	108	105	100	94	83	72	108
Extreme Minimum Temp. (°F)	-20	-21	-17	5	23	36	42	40	19	6	-5	-30	-30
Days Maximum Temp. ≥ 90°F	0	0	0	1	1	7	13	9	4	0	0	0	35
Days Maximum Temp. ≤ 32°F	12	9	3	0	0	0	0	0	0	0	3	11	38
Days Minimum Temp. ≤ 32°F	31	27	25	12	1	0	0	0	1	8	24	31	160
Days Minimum Temp. ≤ 0°F	5	4	1	0	0	0	0	0	0	0	0	3	13
Heating Degree Days (base 65°F)	1,230	1,021	831	482	194	32	4	11	122	428	820	1,191	6,366
Cooling Degree Days (base 65°F)	0	0	0	9	46	192	328	265	99	7	0	0	946
Mean Precipitation (in.)	0.51	0.59	1.83	2.18	4.13	3.83	3.18	3.06	2.09	2.06	0.99	0.57	25.02
Extreme Maximum Daily Precip. (in.)	1.40	0.85	3.20	3.00	3.27	5.95	2.84	2.85	2.73	3.09	1.40	1.21	5.95
Days With ≥ 0.1" Precipitation	2	2	4	4	7	7	5	5	4	4	3	1	48
Days With ≥ 0.5" Precipitation	0	0	1	1	3	2	2	2	1	1	1	0	14
Days With ≥ 1.0" Precipitation	0	0	0	1	1	1	1	1	1	1	0	0	7
Mean Snowfall (in.)	5.3	5.6	5.0	1.9	trace	0.0	0.0	0.0	0.2	0.8	3.2	4.2	26.2
Maximum Snow Depth (in.)	***8***	***9***	***12***	***6***	***trace***	***0***	***0***	***0***	***0***	***4***	***9***	na	na
Days With ≥ 1.0" Snow Depth	***7***	6	***3***	1	0	0	0	0	0	0	1	***6***	***24***

The period of record for all cooperative weather station data is 1980 – 2009. See User Guide for detailed explanation of data.

Loup City *Sherman County* Elevation: 2,064 ft. Latitude: 41° 17' N Longitude: 98° 58' W

	JAN	FEB	MAR	APR	MAY	JUN	JUL	AUG	SEP	OCT	NOV	DEC	YEAR
Mean Maximum Temp. (°F)	36.2	39.8	50.2	62.1	71.7	81.4	87.1	85.1	76.9	64.3	49.4	37.7	61.8
Mean Temp. (°F)	23.7	27.3	37.2	48.4	59.0	68.9	74.6	72.7	63.0	50.1	36.7	25.7	48.9
Mean Minimum Temp. (°F)	11.1	14.8	24.2	34.6	46.2	56.3	62.1	60.1	49.1	35.9	24.0	13.7	36.0
Extreme Maximum Temp. (°F)	75	80	90	93	98	101	105	103	102	94	82	72	105
Extreme Minimum Temp. (°F)	-22	-25	-13	9	24	35	43	39	14	6	-7	-26	-26
Days Maximum Temp. ≥ 90°F	0	0	0	1	1	5	12	9	3	0	0	0	31
Days Maximum Temp. ≤ 32°F	12	10	4	0	0	0	0	0	0	0	3	11	40
Days Minimum Temp. ≤ 32°F	30	27	25	12	1	0	0	0	1	10	25	31	162
Days Minimum Temp. ≤ 0°F	6	4	1	0	0	0	0	0	0	0	0	4	15
Heating Degree Days (base 65°F)	1,275	1,058	855	500	216	41	5	11	137	459	841	1,212	6,610
Cooling Degree Days (base 65°F)	0	0	0	9	36	165	309	256	84	5	0	0	864
Mean Precipitation (in.)	0.54	0.63	1.98	2.91	4.10	4.12	3.09	3.11	2.47	1.86	1.35	0.71	26.87
Extreme Maximum Daily Precip. (in.)	0.95	1.60	3.53	2.40	3.09	4.90	3.19	2.19	5.60	2.05	1.70	1.73	5.60
Days With ≥ 0.1" Precipitation	1	2	4	5	8	7	5	5	4	4	3	2	50
Days With ≥ 0.5" Precipitation	0	0	1	2	3	3	2	2	2	1	1	0	17
Days With ≥ 1.0" Precipitation	0	0	0	1	1	1	1	1	1	0	0	0	6
Mean Snowfall (in.)	7.4	6.1	6.3	1.6	trace	0.0	0.0	0.0	0.1	1.5	4.1	5.9	33.0
Maximum Snow Depth (in.)	15	12	20	8	trace	0	0	0	trace	8	9	10	20
Days With ≥ 1.0" Snow Depth	7	7	3	1	0	0	0	0	0	1	2	7	28

Lynch *Boyd County* Elevation: 1,390 ft. Latitude: 42° 50' N Longitude: 98° 27' W

	JAN	FEB	MAR	APR	MAY	JUN	JUL	AUG	SEP	OCT	NOV	DEC	YEAR
Mean Maximum Temp. (°F)	34.2	37.5	48.5	60.7	72.1	81.6	87.9	86.1	77.2	63.9	47.4	35.5	61.0
Mean Temp. (°F)	21.1	24.5	35.2	46.7	58.8	68.6	74.6	72.6	62.8	48.9	34.3	23.1	47.6
Mean Minimum Temp. (°F)	8.0	11.4	21.9	32.6	45.4	55.6	61.3	59.0	48.4	33.9	21.1	10.6	34.1
Extreme Maximum Temp. (°F)	73	77	86	95	101	108	112	109	101	96	86	75	112
Extreme Minimum Temp. (°F)	-31	-34	-23	7	23	32	41	34	21	9	-16	-36	-36
Days Maximum Temp. ≥ 90°F	0	0	0	0	1	6	13	11	5	1	0	0	37
Days Maximum Temp. ≤ 32°F	14	10	5	1	0	0	0	0	0	0	4	11	45
Days Minimum Temp. ≤ 32°F	31	27	26	15	2	0	0	0	2	13	27	31	174
Days Minimum Temp. ≤ 0°F	9	5	1	0	0	0	0	0	0	0	1	6	22
Heating Degree Days (base 65°F)	1,354	1,141	915	549	227	49	8	16	153	496	916	1,292	7,116
Cooling Degree Days (base 65°F)	0	0	0	6	42	164	313	258	95	5	0	0	883
Mean Precipitation (in.)	0.46	0.60	1.58	3.09	3.66	3.16	2.71	2.84	2.49	2.23	0.94	0.59	24.35
Extreme Maximum Daily Precip. (in.)	0.97	1.02	2.17	2.00	2.83	1.90	2.69	4.10	3.00	2.65	2.18	1.71	4.10
Days With ≥ 0.1" Precipitation	1	2	4	5	6	6	5	5	4	4	2	2	46
Days With ≥ 0.5" Precipitation	0	0	1	2	3	2	2	2	2	2	1	0	17
Days With ≥ 1.0" Precipitation	0	0	0	1	1	1	1	1	1	1	0	0	7
Mean Snowfall (in.)	6.5	6.4	7.9	3.3	0.0	0.0	0.0	0.0	trace	0.6	5.3	6.3	36.3
Maximum Snow Depth (in.)	24	19	22	14	0	0	0	0	trace	4	12	18	24
Days With ≥ 1.0" Snow Depth	11	9	6	1	0	0	0	0	0	0	3	9	39

Mead 6 S *Saunders County* Elevation: 1,154 ft. Latitude: 41° 08' N Longitude: 96° 29' W

	JAN	FEB	MAR	APR	MAY	JUN	JUL	AUG	SEP	OCT	NOV	DEC	YEAR
Mean Maximum Temp. (°F)	34.1	38.4	50.3	63.3	73.5	83.3	87.4	85.2	78.2	65.4	49.6	36.7	62.1
Mean Temp. (°F)	23.3	27.5	38.5	50.6	61.5	71.6	75.7	73.4	65.0	52.4	38.2	26.7	50.4
Mean Minimum Temp. (°F)	12.5	16.5	26.7	37.8	49.5	59.8	63.9	61.5	51.6	39.3	26.9	16.6	38.5
Extreme Maximum Temp. (°F)	71	77	90	97	99	108	107	105	107	93	86	69	108
Extreme Minimum Temp. (°F)	-22	-25	-18	14	27	37	48	38	26	9	-7	-27	-27
Days Maximum Temp. ≥ 90°F	0	0	0	1	1	7	12	9	4	0	0	0	34
Days Maximum Temp. ≤ 32°F	13	10	3	0	0	0	0	0	0	0	3	11	40
Days Minimum Temp. ≤ 32°F	30	26	23	9	1	0	0	0	1	8	22	29	149
Days Minimum Temp. ≤ 0°F	6	4	1	0	0	0	0	0	0	0	0	3	14
Heating Degree Days (base 65°F)	1,284	1,054	817	442	163	20	3	9	106	399	797	1,182	6,276
Cooling Degree Days (base 65°F)	0	0	1	16	61	223	342	275	112	13	0	0	1,043
Mean Precipitation (in.)	0.56	0.65	1.73	2.74	4.14	4.34	3.34	3.84	2.94	2.13	1.46	0.86	28.73
Extreme Maximum Daily Precip. (in.)	1.06	1.35	2.11	2.38	3.62	3.20	5.25	4.05	2.86	2.81	2.38	1.09	5.25
Days With ≥ 0.1" Precipitation	2	2	4	6	8	7	6	6	4	4	3	2	54
Days With ≥ 0.5" Precipitation	0	0	1	2	2	3	2	3	2	1	1	0	17
Days With ≥ 1.0" Precipitation	0	0	0	1	1	1	1	1	1	0	0	0	6
Mean Snowfall (in.)	4.5	4.2	3.1	0.9	0.0	0.0	0.0	0.0	0.0	0.5	2.0	4.8	20.0
Maximum Snow Depth (in.)	11	19	12	6	0	0	0	0	0	8	8	15	19
Days With ≥ 1.0" Snow Depth	11	10	4	1	0	0	0	0	0	0	2	9	37

Oconto *Custer County* Elevation: 2,580 ft. Latitude: 41° 08' N Longitude: 99° 46' W

	JAN	FEB	MAR	APR	MAY	JUN	JUL	AUG	SEP	OCT	NOV	DEC	YEAR
Mean Maximum Temp. (°F)	38.7	42.5	52.5	63.3	72.8	82.4	87.6	85.8	77.8	65.4	49.8	39.7	63.2
Mean Temp. (°F)	25.8	29.7	38.7	48.8	59.5	69.1	74.4	72.6	63.4	50.9	36.6	27.1	49.7
Mean Minimum Temp. (°F)	12.8	16.8	24.8	34.1	46.0	55.8	61.1	59.2	48.8	36.2	23.3	14.6	36.1
Extreme Maximum Temp. (°F)	73	78	87	92	100	106	106	106	102	93	83	74	106
Extreme Minimum Temp. (°F)	-30	-27	-22	7	18	33	42	38	20	4	-15	-29	-30
Days Maximum Temp. ≥ 90°F	0	0	0	0	1	6	12	10	4	0	0	0	33
Days Maximum Temp. ≤ 32°F	10	7	3	0	0	0	0	0	0	0	3	9	32
Days Minimum Temp. ≤ 32°F	31	27	25	13	2	0	0	0	2	11	25	30	166
Days Minimum Temp. ≤ 0°F	5	3	1	0	0	0	0	0	0	0	1	4	14
Heating Degree Days (base 65°F)	1,209	991	809	488	201	34	5	11	127	437	846	1,168	6,326
Cooling Degree Days (base 65°F)	0	0	0	7	36	165	302	251	84	6	0	0	851
Mean Precipitation (in.)	0.36	0.34	1.32	1.88	3.69	3.43	2.79	2.59	2.02	1.63	0.67	0.34	21.06
Extreme Maximum Daily Precip. (in.)	1.02	0.54	2.19	1.71	2.50	4.48	3.52	3.54	3.41	2.08	1.82	1.28	4.48
Days With ≥ 0.1" Precipitation	1	1	3	4	7	6	5	4	4	3	1	1	40
Days With ≥ 0.5" Precipitation	0	0	1	1	3	2	2	2	1	1	0	0	13
Days With ≥ 1.0" Precipitation	0	0	0	0	1	1	1	1	0	0	0	0	4
Mean Snowfall (in.)	4.5	4.9	5.5	2.9	0.0	0.0	0.0	0.0	0.1	1.0	3.9	4.9	27.7
Maximum Snow Depth (in.)	14	9	15	10	0	0	0	0	0	5	15	14	15
Days With ≥ 1.0" Snow Depth	6	5	2	1	0	0	0	0	0	0	2	5	21

The period of record for all cooperative weather station data is 1980 – 2009. See User Guide for detailed explanation of data.

Osmond *Pierce County* Elevation: 1,649 ft. Latitude: 42° 21' N Longitude: 97° 36' W

	JAN	FEB	MAR	APR	MAY	JUN	JUL	AUG	SEP	OCT	NOV	DEC	YEAR
Mean Maximum Temp. (°F)	33.0	37.2	48.6	62.3	73.4	83.1	87.7	85.5	77.5	64.5	46.3	34.1	61.1
Mean Temp. (°F)	22.1	26.5	36.9	49.2	60.8	70.7	75.5	73.2	64.2	51.3	35.5	24.0	49.2
Mean Minimum Temp. (°F)	11.5	15.8	25.1	36.3	48.2	58.3	63.2	61.0	50.8	38.0	24.7	14.1	37.2
Extreme Maximum Temp. (°F)	72	75	87	95	98	105	105	108	98	92	81	68	108
Extreme Minimum Temp. (°F)	-25	-27	-14	9	24	35	43	32	22	12	-13	-28	-28
Days Maximum Temp. ≥ 90°F	0	0	0	1	1	7	13	8	4	0	0	0	34
Days Maximum Temp. ≤ 32°F	14	11	4	0	0	0	0	0	0	0	5	13	47
Days Minimum Temp. ≤ 32°F	30	26	24	11	1	0	0	0	1	9	24	29	155
Days Minimum Temp. ≤ 0°F	7	4	1	0	0	0	0	0	0	0	1	5	18
Heating Degree Days (base 65°F)	1,324	1,082	863	479	176	27	3	10	122	428	879	1,265	6,658
Cooling Degree Days (base 65°F)	0	0	0	12	54	206	335	272	103	8	0	0	990
Mean Precipitation (in.)	0.44	0.63	1.76	2.87	3.78	3.63	3.00	3.23	2.81	1.89	1.31	0.58	25.93
Extreme Maximum Daily Precip. (in.)	0.77	1.56	2.19	2.27	2.74	3.53	3.36	3.25	3.37	2.24	1.96	1.13	3.53
Days With ≥ 0.1" Precipitation	1	2	4	5	7	6	5	5	5	4	3	2	49
Days With ≥ 0.5" Precipitation	0	0	1	2	3	2	2	2	2	1	1	0	16
Days With ≥ 1.0" Precipitation	0	0	0	1	1	1	1	1	1	0	0	0	6
Mean Snowfall (in.)	6.1	5.9	5.6	2.4	0.0	0.0	0.0	0.0	trace	0.9	5.3	5.5	31.7
Maximum Snow Depth (in.)	18	18	15	8	0	0	0	0	trace	2	20	20	20
Days With ≥ 1.0" Snow Depth	13	11	6	1	0	0	0	0	0	0	4	13	48

Ravenna *Buffalo County* Elevation: 2,049 ft. Latitude: 41° 02' N Longitude: 98° 55' W

	JAN	FEB	MAR	APR	MAY	JUN	JUL	AUG	SEP	OCT	NOV	DEC	YEAR
Mean Maximum Temp. (°F)	37.7	41.3	52.2	63.6	73.2	82.3	87.3	85.2	77.4	65.0	50.0	38.1	62.8
Mean Temp. (°F)	25.3	28.9	38.7	49.6	60.5	70.1	75.3	73.3	63.9	51.1	37.4	26.3	50.0
Mean Minimum Temp. (°F)	12.9	16.5	25.2	35.6	47.6	57.7	63.2	61.3	50.4	37.1	24.7	14.4	37.2
Extreme Maximum Temp. (°F)	75	80	90	94	98	106	106	104	99	93	84	72	106
Extreme Minimum Temp. (°F)	-22	-26	-15	8	18	35	43	40	20	4	-7	-31	-31
Days Maximum Temp. ≥ 90°F	0	0	0	1	1	6	12	9	3	0	0	0	32
Days Maximum Temp. ≤ 32°F	11	8	3	0	0	0	0	0	0	0	3	11	36
Days Minimum Temp. ≤ 32°F	31	26	24	11	2	0	0	0	1	10	24	30	159
Days Minimum Temp. ≤ 0°F	5	4	1	0	0	0	0	0	0	0	0	4	14
Heating Degree Days (base 65°F)	1,224	1,013	809	464	182	31	3	9	123	432	823	1,194	6,307
Cooling Degree Days (base 65°F)	0	0	0	10	48	189	329	272	98	8	0	0	954
Mean Precipitation (in.)	0.52	0.56	1.79	2.50	4.07	4.54	3.14	2.95	2.09	1.91	1.18	0.55	25.80
Extreme Maximum Daily Precip. (in.)	1.35	0.66	2.62	3.23	4.35	5.90	3.42	3.22	2.48	2.57	2.12	0.92	5.90
Days With ≥ 0.1" Precipitation	2	2	4	5	8	7	5	5	4	4	3	2	51
Days With ≥ 0.5" Precipitation	0	0	1	2	3	3	2	2	1	1	1	0	16
Days With ≥ 1.0" Precipitation	0	0	0	1	1	1	1	1	1	0	0	0	6
Mean Snowfall (in.)	6.3	5.1	4.5	1.3	0.0	0.0	0.0	0.0	0.1	1.1	3.0	4.6	26.0
Maximum Snow Depth (in.)	11	na	22	10	0	0	0	0	0	6	12	na	na
Days With ≥ 1.0" Snow Depth	4	4	1	0	0	0	0	0	0	0	1	na	na

Stanton *Stanton County* Elevation: 1,490 ft. Latitude: 41° 57' N Longitude: 97° 14' W

	JAN	FEB	MAR	APR	MAY	JUN	JUL	AUG	SEP	OCT	NOV	DEC	YEAR
Mean Maximum Temp. (°F)	33.9	38.5	49.6	63.1	73.2	82.6	86.6	84.4	77.0	64.3	46.7	34.8	61.2
Mean Temp. (°F)	23.3	27.7	37.8	50.2	61.1	70.8	75.2	73.2	64.4	51.8	36.3	24.9	49.7
Mean Minimum Temp. (°F)	12.6	16.9	25.9	37.2	48.9	58.9	63.8	62.0	51.7	39.3	25.8	15.0	38.2
Extreme Maximum Temp. (°F)	74	73	90	95	97	105	104	105	101	91	83	71	105
Extreme Minimum Temp. (°F)	-25	-27	-14	9	26	37	44	39	22	10	-10	-33	-33
Days Maximum Temp. ≥ 90°F	0	0	0	1	1	6	11	8	3	0	0	0	30
Days Maximum Temp. ≤ 32°F	14	10	3	0	0	0	0	0	0	0	4	13	44
Days Minimum Temp. ≤ 32°F	30	26	22	10	1	0	0	0	1	8	23	30	151
Days Minimum Temp. ≤ 0°F	6	4	1	0	0	0	0	0	0	0	0	4	15
Heating Degree Days (base 65°F)	1,288	1,048	836	455	169	27	3	9	118	410	854	1,236	6,453
Cooling Degree Days (base 65°F)	0	0	0	15	55	206	327	271	107	9	0	0	990
Mean Precipitation (in.)	0.52	0.67	2.03	3.02	4.36	4.42	4.04	3.24	2.48	2.06	1.60	0.71	29.15
Extreme Maximum Daily Precip. (in.)	1.25	1.82	2.65	2.40	2.65	3.80	3.72	4.50	2.05	2.08	2.00	1.35	4.50
Days With ≥ 0.1" Precipitation	2	2	4	6	8	7	6	5	5	4	3	2	54
Days With ≥ 0.5" Precipitation	0	0	1	2	3	3	3	2	2	1	1	0	18
Days With ≥ 1.0" Precipitation	0	0	1	1	1	1	1	1	1	1	0	0	8
Mean Snowfall (in.)	na	5.0	4.6	2.3	0.0	0.0	0.0	0.0	trace	0.9	2.9	4.4	na
Maximum Snow Depth (in.)	18	21	17	9	0	0	0	0	trace	5	18	18	21
Days With ≥ 1.0" Snow Depth	12	10	5	0	0	0	0	0	0	0	3	10	40

Surprise *Butler County* Elevation: 1,549 ft. Latitude: 41° 06' N Longitude: 97° 19' W

	JAN	FEB	MAR	APR	MAY	JUN	JUL	AUG	SEP	OCT	NOV	DEC	YEAR
Mean Maximum Temp. (°F)	35.3	40.3	50.2	62.5	73.4	82.8	86.6	85.1	78.5	65.8	50.3	37.3	62.3
Mean Temp. (°F)	24.2	28.9	38.4	49.8	61.6	71.4	75.4	73.5	64.8	52.0	38.5	26.7	50.4
Mean Minimum Temp. (°F)	13.1	17.4	26.6	36.9	49.8	60.0	64.2	61.9	51.0	38.1	26.5	16.0	38.5
Extreme Maximum Temp. (°F)	74	79	84	96	97	106	106	101	103	94	84	71	106
Extreme Minimum Temp. (°F)	-24	-24	-13	7	27	41	44	41	27	6	-11	-27	-27
Days Maximum Temp. ≥ 90°F	0	0	0	1	2	7	12	9	4	1	0	0	36
Days Maximum Temp. ≤ 32°F	13	9	4	0	0	0	0	0	0	0	3	11	40
Days Minimum Temp. ≤ 32°F	30	26	22	10	1	0	0	0	1	9	22	30	151
Days Minimum Temp. ≤ 0°F	5	3	1	0	0	0	0	0	0	0	0	3	12
Heating Degree Days (base 65°F)	1,259	1,016	816	463	164	24	3	7	108	410	789	1,181	6,240
Cooling Degree Days (base 65°F)	0	0	0	12	67	223	333	280	109	13	0	0	1,037
Mean Precipitation (in.)	0.57	0.86	2.05	2.57	4.42	4.22	3.11	3.38	2.78	1.95	1.37	0.84	28.12
Extreme Maximum Daily Precip. (in.)	1.10	2.13	2.55	3.91	4.45	6.10	4.30	4.30	4.40	2.20	1.80	1.40	6.10
Days With ≥ 0.1" Precipitation	2	2	4	5	8	7	5	5	5	4	3	2	52
Days With ≥ 0.5" Precipitation	0	0	1	2	3	3	2	2	2	1	1	1	18
Days With ≥ 1.0" Precipitation	0	0	0	1	1	1	1	1	1	0	0	0	6
Mean Snowfall (in.)	5.4	6.1	4.1	1.2	0.0	0.0	0.0	0.0	0.1	0.7	2.4	4.4	24.4
Maximum Snow Depth (in.)	16	16	15	8	0	0	0	0	0	6	10	17	17
Days With ≥ 1.0" Snow Depth	13	11	5	1	0	0	0	0	0	0	2	9	41

The period of record for all cooperative weather station data is 1980 – 2009. See User Guide for detailed explanation of data.

Tekamah *Burt County* Elevation: 1,039 ft. Latitude: 41° 46' N Longitude: 96° 13' W

	JAN	FEB	MAR	APR	MAY	JUN	JUL	AUG	SEP	OCT	NOV	DEC	YEAR
Mean Maximum Temp. (°F)	31.9	36.3	47.5	61.9	73.0	82.6	86.6	84.3	77.3	64.1	47.8	33.3	60.6
Mean Temp. (°F)	22.1	26.5	36.7	49.9	61.5	71.4	75.5	73.1	64.6	51.8	37.5	24.3	49.6
Mean Minimum Temp. (°F)	12.3	16.5	25.7	37.9	50.1	60.1	64.3	61.8	51.9	39.4	27.2	15.3	38.5
Extreme Maximum Temp. (°F)	69	75	90	96	99	107	110	104	103	94	82	70	110
Extreme Minimum Temp. (°F)	-22	-23	-13	14	30	39	48	42	26	13	-9	-26	-26
Days Maximum Temp. ≥ 90°F	0	0	0	1	1	6	11	7	3	0	0	0	29
Days Maximum Temp. ≤ 32°F	15	11	4	0	0	0	0	0	0	0	4	14	48
Days Minimum Temp. ≤ 32°F	30	26	23	8	0	0	0	0	0	7	22	30	146
Days Minimum Temp. ≤ 0°F	6	4	1	0	0	0	0	0	0	0	0	4	15
Heating Degree Days (base 65°F)	1,323	1,083	872	460	163	21	3	8	110	415	819	1,254	6,531
Cooling Degree Days (base 65°F)	0	0	0	15	64	220	334	266	105	12	0	0	1,016
Mean Precipitation (in.)	0.68	0.74	2.00	3.45	4.40	4.10	3.27	3.63	3.29	2.28	1.54	0.87	30.25
Extreme Maximum Daily Precip. (in.)	0.88	1.22	2.56	3.65	5.06	3.22	2.45	8.25	3.76	2.29	2.02	2.16	8.25
Days With ≥ 0.1" Precipitation	2	2	4	6	8	7	6	5	5	4	3	2	54
Days With ≥ 0.5" Precipitation	0	0	1	2	3	3	2	2	2	2	1	0	18
Days With ≥ 1.0" Precipitation	0	0	0	1	1	1	1	1	1	1	0	0	7
Mean Snowfall (in.)	5.3	5.8	***4.2***	1.6	trace	0.0	0.0	0.0	0.0	0.5	2.2	5.5	***25.1***
Maximum Snow Depth (in.)	***10***	***14***	***11***	***10***	***trace***	***0***	***0***	***0***	***0***	***3***	***6***	***18***	***18***
Days With ≥ 1.0" Snow Depth	***9***	***7***	***3***	1	0	0	0	0	0	0	1	7	***28***

Valentine Lakes Game Ref *Cherry County* Elevation: 2,929 ft. Latitude: 42° 35' N Longitude: 100° 41' W

	JAN	FEB	MAR	APR	MAY	JUN	JUL	AUG	SEP	OCT	NOV	DEC	YEAR
Mean Maximum Temp. (°F)	37.3	40.6	49.5	60.0	70.6	80.2	86.8	85.0	76.4	***62.9***	47.4	***36.4***	***61.1***
Mean Temp. (°F)	26.0	29.0	37.2	47.2	58.2	67.5	73.7	72.1	62.6	***50.0***	36.3	***25.5***	***48.8***
Mean Minimum Temp. (°F)	14.6	17.3	24.9	34.4	45.8	54.8	60.5	59.1	48.8	***37.0***	25.1	***14.5***	***36.4***
Extreme Maximum Temp. (°F)	69	76	81	97	96	105	109	103	98	***92***	83	***73***	***109***
Extreme Minimum Temp. (°F)	-27	-29	-30	6	23	30	41	39	23	***4***	-13	***-29***	***-30***
Days Maximum Temp. ≥ 90°F	0	0	0	0	1	4	12	9	3	***0***	0	***0***	***29***
Days Maximum Temp. ≤ 32°F	10	8	4	1	0	0	0	0	0	***0***	5	***11***	***39***
Days Minimum Temp. ≤ 32°F	29	26	24	13	2	0	0	0	1	***9***	22	***28***	***154***
Days Minimum Temp. ≤ 0°F	5	4	1	0	0	0	0	0	0	***0***	1	***5***	***16***
Heating Degree Days (base 65°F)	1,202	1,012	855	532	235	55	10	13	143	***467***	855	***1,220***	***6,599***
Cooling Degree Days (base 65°F)	0	0	0	6	32	138	285	239	79	***7***	0	***0***	***786***
Mean Precipitation (in.)	0.39	0.56	1.20	2.48	3.72	3.59	3.74	2.68	1.78	***1.52***	0.95	***0.54***	***23.15***
Extreme Maximum Daily Precip. (in.)	***1.66***	1.13	1.31	***2.94***	2.62	2.79	2.95	***3.48***	2.15	***2.42***	2.25	***1.38***	***3.48***
Days With ≥ 0.1" Precipitation	1	2	3	5	7	6	6	4	4	***3***	2	***2***	***45***
Days With ≥ 0.5" Precipitation	0	0	1	2	2	2	2	2	1	***1***	1	***0***	***14***
Days With ≥ 1.0" Precipitation	0	0	0	0	1	1	1	1	0	***0***	0	***0***	***4***
Mean Snowfall (in.)	***5.3***	***6.3***	7.7	5.7	trace	0.0	0.0	***0.0***	0.8	***1.4***	***6.3***	***5.6***	***39.1***
Maximum Snow Depth (in.)	***26***	***15***	***18***	***14***	***trace***	***0***	***0***	***0***	***13***	***9***	***15***	***21***	***26***
Days With ≥ 1.0" Snow Depth	***8***	***8***	***5***	2	0	0	0	0	0	***1***	5	***8***	***37***

Walthill *Thurston County* Elevation: 1,220 ft. Latitude: 42° 09' N Longitude: 96° 29' W

	JAN	FEB	MAR	APR	MAY	JUN	JUL	AUG	SEP	OCT	NOV	DEC	YEAR
Mean Maximum Temp. (°F)	32.3	36.8	49.6	63.5	74.8	84.2	88.0	85.6	78.5	64.9	47.1	32.9	61.5
Mean Temp. (°F)	22.0	26.4	37.7	50.1	61.8	71.6	75.5	73.5	65.0	51.8	36.4	23.4	49.6
Mean Minimum Temp. (°F)	11.6	15.9	25.7	36.7	48.8	58.9	63.1	61.3	51.4	38.7	25.7	13.8	37.6
Extreme Maximum Temp. (°F)	69	72	89	95	96	107	108	103	103	92	82	76	108
Extreme Minimum Temp. (°F)	-23	-28	-19	6	22	35	44	36	20	8	-14	-27	-28
Days Maximum Temp. ≥ 90°F	0	0	0	1	2	8	13	8	4	0	0	0	36
Days Maximum Temp. ≤ 32°F	15	11	3	0	0	0	0	0	0	0	4	13	46
Days Minimum Temp. ≤ 32°F	30	26	23	10	1	0	0	0	1	9	22	30	152
Days Minimum Temp. ≤ 0°F	7	5	1	0	0	0	0	0	0	0	0	5	18
Heating Degree Days (base 65°F)	1,328	1,087	841	455	156	21	2	9	108	414	851	1,284	6,556
Cooling Degree Days (base 65°F)	0	0	0	13	65	224	336	278	115	12	0	0	1,043
Mean Precipitation (in.)	0.62	0.80	2.14	3.26	4.03	4.37	3.57	3.32	2.84	2.27	1.41	0.92	29.55
Extreme Maximum Daily Precip. (in.)	1.25	1.58	2.70	2.37	2.37	5.50	5.48	3.18	2.90	2.36	2.34	1.15	5.50
Days With ≥ 0.1" Precipitation	2	2	4	5	7	7	6	5	5	4	3	3	53
Days With ≥ 0.5" Precipitation	0	0	1	2	3	3	2	2	2	1	1	1	18
Days With ≥ 1.0" Precipitation	0	0	0	1	1	1	1	1	1	1	0	0	7
Mean Snowfall (in.)	5.8	6.4	5.7	2.5	trace	0.0	0.0	0.0	0.0	0.8	4.1	6.6	31.9
Maximum Snow Depth (in.)	14	19	15	10	trace	0	0	0	0	8	18	23	23
Days With ≥ 1.0" Snow Depth	14	12	6	1	0	0	0	0	0	0	3	11	47

York *York County* Elevation: 1,608 ft. Latitude: 40° 52' N Longitude: 97° 36' W

	JAN	FEB	MAR	APR	MAY	JUN	JUL	AUG	SEP	OCT	NOV	DEC	YEAR
Mean Maximum Temp. (°F)	35.3	39.3	50.1	63.1	73.5	84.0	88.6	85.9	78.5	65.7	49.5	37.2	62.6
Mean Temp. (°F)	25.1	28.8	38.9	50.8	62.1	72.6	77.4	74.8	66.1	53.3	38.7	27.6	51.3
Mean Minimum Temp. (°F)	14.9	18.2	27.6	38.4	50.7	61.1	66.2	63.6	53.7	40.8	27.8	17.9	40.1
Extreme Maximum Temp. (°F)	75	81	90	96	100	108	108	108	101	96	87	73	108
Extreme Minimum Temp. (°F)	-20	-18	-8	14	30	40	49	46	26	11	-3	-24	-24
Days Maximum Temp. ≥ 90°F	0	0	0	1	2	8	15	10	5	1	0	0	42
Days Maximum Temp. ≤ 32°F	13	9	3	0	0	0	0	0	0	0	4	11	40
Days Minimum Temp. ≤ 32°F	30	26	21	7	0	0	0	0	0	5	21	29	139
Days Minimum Temp. ≤ 0°F	4	3	0	0	0	0	0	0	0	0	0	3	10
Heating Degree Days (base 65°F)	1,230	1,019	804	433	152	17	2	6	93	371	783	1,153	6,063
Cooling Degree Days (base 65°F)	0	0	1	14	69	251	394	316	134	15	0	0	1,194
Mean Precipitation (in.)	0.74	0.66	2.19	2.65	4.82	4.11	3.74	3.48	2.45	1.84	1.52	0.83	29.03
Extreme Maximum Daily Precip. (in.)	1.02	0.67	2.15	3.31	6.22	6.14	7.20	3.61	3.53	2.16	1.98	1.12	7.20
Days With ≥ 0.1" Precipitation	2	2	4	5	8	6	5	5	4	4	3	2	50
Days With ≥ 0.5" Precipitation	0	0	1	2	4	3	2	3	1	1	1	0	18
Days With ≥ 1.0" Precipitation	0	0	0	1	1	1	1	1	1	0	0	0	6
Mean Snowfall (in.)	6.3	5.9	5.3	0.9	0.0	0.0	0.0	0.0	0.1	0.6	2.6	4.4	26.1
Maximum Snow Depth (in.)	17	18	***14***	7	0	0	0	0	0	8	13	***9***	***18***
Days With ≥ 1.0" Snow Depth	10	7	***3***	0	0	0	0	0	0	0	2	***5***	***27***

The period of record for all cooperative weather station data is 1980 – 2009. See User Guide for detailed explanation of data.

Nebraska Weather Station Rankings

Annual Extreme Maximum Temperature

Highest			Lowest		
Rank	Station Name	°F	Rank	Station Name	°F
1	Valentine Miller Field	114	1	Harrison	104
2	Lynch	***112***	2	Harrisburg 10 NW	105
3	Ashland 2	110	2	Loup City	105
3	Columbus 3 NE	110	2	Stanton	***105***
3	Curtis 3 NNE	***110***	5	Albion 1 N	106
3	Grand Island Arpt	110	5	Broken Bow 2 W	106
3	Tekamah	110	5	Clarkson	***106***
8	Anselmo 2 SE	109	5	Crete	106
8	Atkinson	109	5	David City	106
8	Bartlett 4 S	***109***	5	Geneva	106
8	Chadron Municipal Arpt	***109***	5	Oconto	106
8	Hastings 4 N	109	5	Ravenna	106
8	Omaha Eppley Airfield	109	5	Surprise	***106***
8	Scottsbluff County Arpt	109	14	Ainsworth	107
8	Valentine Lakes Game Ref	***109***	14	Arthur	107
16	Agate 3 E	108	14	Canaday Steam Plant	107
16	Aurora	108	14	Clay Center	107
16	Beatrice 1 N	***108***	14	Gordon 6 N	107
16	Bridgeport	108	14	Hemingford	107
16	Fremont	108	20	Agate 3 E	108
16	Kearney 4 NE	108	20	Aurora	108
16	Lincoln Municipal Arpt	108	20	Beatrice 1 N	***108***
16	Mead 6 S	108	20	Bridgeport	108
16	Norfolk Karl Stefan Mem Arpt	108	20	Fremont	108
16	North Platte Lee Bird Field	108	20	Kearney 4 NE	108

Annual Mean Maximum Temperature

Highest			Lowest		
Rank	Station Name	°F	Rank	Station Name	°F
1	Bridgeport	65.5	1	Harrison	57.8
2	Curtis 3 NNE	***64.6***	2	Gordon 6 N	59.8
3	Crete	63.9	3	Hemingford	60.1
4	Beatrice 1 N	***63.6***	4	Clarkson	***60.2***
5	Scottsbluff County Arpt	63.5	5	Tekamah	60.6
6	Geneva	63.3	6	Albion 1 N	60.8
6	Lincoln Municipal Arpt	63.3	6	Norfolk Karl Stefan Mem Arpt	60.8
8	Oconto	63.2	8	David City	60.9
9	North Platte Lee Bird Field	63.1	9	Ainsworth	61.1
10	Ravenna	62.8	9	Bartlett 4 S	***61.1***
11	Agate 3 E	62.6	9	Lynch	***61.1***
11	Hastings 4 N	62.6	9	Osmond	61.1
11	York	62.6	9	Valentine Lakes Game Ref	***61.1***
14	Fremont	62.5	14	Broken Bow 2 W	61.2
14	Harrisburg 10 NW	62.5	14	Stanton	***61.2***
16	Grand Island Arpt	62.4	16	Atkinson	61.4
16	Surprise	***62.4***	16	Columbus 3 NE	61.4
18	Ashland 2	62.3	18	Walthill	61.5
18	Canaday Steam Plant	62.3	19	Omaha Eppley Airfield	61.6
18	Kearney 4 NE	62.3	19	Valentine Miller Field	61.6
21	Clay Center	62.2	21	Aurora	61.7
22	Anselmo 2 SE	62.1	22	Arthur	61.8
22	Chadron Municipal Arpt	***62.1***	22	Loup City	61.8
22	Mead 6 S	62.1	24	Anselmo 2 SE	62.1
25	Arthur	61.8	24	Chadron Municipal Arpt	***62.1***

 Rankings include 25 highest/lowest stations. If state has less than 25 stations, all stations are included. The period of record is 1980–2009. See User Guide for detailed explanation of data.

Annual Mean Temperature

Highest			Lowest		
Rank	Station Name	°F	Rank	Station Name	°F
1	Crete	52.5	1	Harrison	44.8
2	Geneva	52.3	2	Agate 3 E	45.9
3	Beatrice 1 N	***51.5***	3	Gordon 6 N	46.6
3	Lincoln Municipal Arpt	51.5	4	Harrisburg 10 NW	47.4
5	York	51.4	5	Lynch	***47.6***
6	Fremont	51.3	6	Broken Bow 2 W	47.8
7	Hastings 4 N	51.0	6	Valentine Miller Field	47.8
8	Omaha Eppley Airfield	50.9	8	Hemingford	48.0
9	Ashland 2	50.8	9	Arthur	48.4
9	Grand Island Arpt	50.8	10	Anselmo 2 SE	48.5
11	Bridgeport	50.7	11	Albion 1 N	48.6
11	Columbus 3 NE	50.7	11	Bartlett 4 S	***48.6***
13	Aurora	50.5	11	Chadron Municipal Arpt	***48.6***
14	Mead 6 S	50.4	14	Valentine Lakes Game Ref	***48.8***
14	Surprise	***50.4***	15	Loup City	48.9
16	Clay Center	50.3	15	Scottsbluff County Arpt	48.9
17	Canaday Steam Plant	50.1	17	Clarkson	***49.0***
18	Ravenna	50.0	18	North Platte Lee Bird Field	49.1
19	Curtis 3 NNE	***49.9***	19	Osmond	49.2
19	David City	49.9	20	Norfolk Karl Stefan Mem Arpt	49.5
21	Kearney 4 NE	49.8	21	Ainsworth	49.6
22	Oconto	49.7	21	Atkinson	49.6
22	Stanton	***49.7***	21	Tekamah	49.6
24	Ainsworth	49.6	21	Walthill	49.6
24	Atkinson	49.6	25	Oconto	49.7

Annual Mean Minimum Temperature

Highest			Lowest		
Rank	Station Name	°F	Rank	Station Name	°F
1	Geneva	41.3	1	Agate 3 E	29.2
2	Crete	41.1	2	Harrison	31.7
3	Omaha Eppley Airfield	40.2	3	Harrisburg 10 NW	32.3
4	Fremont	40.1	4	Gordon 6 N	33.4
4	York	40.1	5	Valentine Miller Field	33.9
6	Columbus 3 NE	39.9	6	Lynch	***34.1***
7	Lincoln Municipal Arpt	39.8	7	Scottsbluff County Arpt	34.3
8	Beatrice 1 N	***39.3***	8	Broken Bow 2 W	34.4
8	Hastings 4 N	39.3	9	Anselmo 2 SE	34.9
10	Aurora	39.2	9	Arthur	34.9
10	Grand Island Arpt	39.2	11	North Platte Lee Bird Field	35.0
12	Ashland 2	39.1	12	Chadron Municipal Arpt	***35.1***
13	David City	38.7	13	Curtis 3 NNE	***35.2***
14	Tekamah	38.6	14	Hemingford	35.8
15	Mead 6 S	38.5	15	Bridgeport	35.9
15	Surprise	***38.5***	16	Bartlett 4 S	***36.0***
17	Clay Center	38.3	16	Loup City	36.0
18	Stanton	***38.2***	18	Oconto	36.1
19	Norfolk Karl Stefan Mem Arpt	38.1	19	Albion 1 N	36.3
20	Ainsworth	38.0	20	Valentine Lakes Game Ref	***36.4***
21	Atkinson	37.8	21	Osmond	37.2
21	Canaday Steam Plant	37.8	21	Ravenna	37.2
23	Clarkson	***37.7***	23	Kearney 4 NE	37.4
24	Walthill	37.6	24	Walthill	37.6
25	Kearney 4 NE	37.4	25	Clarkson	***37.7***

Rankings include 25 highest/lowest stations. If state has less than 25 stations, all stations are included. The period of record is 1980–2009. See User Guide for detailed explanation of data.

Annual Extreme Minimum Temperature

Highest

Rank	Station Name	°F
1	Hastings 4 N	-23
1	Omaha Eppley Airfield	-23
3	Columbus 3 NE	-24
3	Fremont	-24
3	York	-24
6	Crete	-25
7	Ashland 2	-26
7	Beatrice 1 N	***-26***
7	Geneva	-26
7	Grand Island Arpt	-26
7	Loup City	-26
7	Tekamah	-26
13	Canaday Steam Plant	-27
13	Clarkson	***-27***
13	David City	-27
13	Lincoln Municipal Arpt	-27
13	Mead 6 S	-27
13	Surprise	***-27***
19	Aurora	-28
19	Osmond	-28
19	Walthill	-28
22	Albion 1 N	-29
22	Atkinson	-29
22	Bartlett 4 S	***-29***
25	Ainsworth	-30

Lowest

Rank	Station Name	°F
1	Bridgeport	-42
1	Scottsbluff County Arpt	-42
3	Agate 3 E	-41
4	Chadron Municipal Arpt	***-40***
4	Gordon 6 N	-40
6	Clay Center	-39
6	Harrison	-39
6	Valentine Miller Field	-39
9	Harrisburg 10 NW	-37
10	Lynch	***-36***
11	Hemingford	-35
12	North Platte Lee Bird Field	-34
13	Arthur	-33
13	Broken Bow 2 W	-33
13	Stanton	***-33***
16	Anselmo 2 SE	-32
17	Curtis 3 NNE	***-31***
17	Ravenna	-31
19	Ainsworth	-30
19	Kearney 4 NE	-30
19	Norfolk Karl Stefan Mem Arpt	-30
19	Oconto	-30
19	Valentine Lakes Game Ref	***-30***
24	Albion 1 N	-29
24	Atkinson	-29

July Mean Maximum Temperature

Highest

Rank	Station Name	°F
1	Bridgeport	92.1
2	Chadron Municipal Arpt	***90.0***
3	Curtis 3 NNE	89.9
3	Scottsbluff County Arpt	89.9
5	Lincoln Municipal Arpt	89.3
6	Beatrice 1 N	***89.0***
7	Agate 3 E	88.8
7	Valentine Miller Field	88.8
9	Crete	88.6
9	York	88.6
11	North Platte Lee Bird Field	88.4
12	Bartlett 4 S	***88.2***
13	Columbus 3 NE	88.1
13	Harrisburg 10 NW	88.1
15	Ashland 2	88.0
15	Walthill	88.0
17	Arthur	87.9
17	Fremont	87.9
17	Grand Island Arpt	87.9
17	Hastings 4 N	87.9
17	Lynch	***87.9***
22	Atkinson	87.8
23	Osmond	87.7
24	Oconto	87.6
25	Gordon 6 N	87.5

Lowest

Rank	Station Name	°F
1	Harrison	85.4
2	Omaha WSFO	***85.6***
3	Broken Bow 2 W	86.0
4	Clarkson	***86.4***
5	Albion 1 N	86.6
5	Canaday Steam Plant	86.6
5	Stanton	***86.6***
5	Surprise	***86.6***
5	Tekamah	86.6
10	Aurora	86.8
10	Norfolk Karl Stefan Mem Arpt	86.8
10	Valentine Lakes Game Ref	86.8
13	Hemingford	86.9
14	David City	87.0
15	Ainsworth	87.1
15	Loup City	87.1
17	Omaha Eppley Airfield	87.2
18	Clay Center	87.3
18	Ravenna	87.3
20	Anselmo 2 SE	87.4
20	Geneva	87.4
22	Gordon 6 N	87.5
22	Kearney 4 NE	87.5
22	Mead 6 S	87.5
25	Oconto	87.6

Rankings include 25 highest/lowest stations. If state has less than 25 stations, all stations are included. The period of record is 1980–2009. See User Guide for detailed explanation of data.

January Mean Minimum Temperature

Highest			Lowest		
Rank	Station Name	°F	Rank	Station Name	°F
1	Geneva	16.7	1	Lynch	***8.0***
2	Crete	16.3	2	Agate 3 E	9.4
3	Hemingford	16.1	3	Valentine Miller Field	10.2
4	Omaha WSFO	***15.4***	4	Loup City	11.1
5	Bridgeport	15.3	5	Curtis 3 NNE	***11.3***
6	Ainsworth	15.1	6	Albion 1 N	11.5
7	Hastings 4 N	14.9	6	Broken Bow 2 W	11.5
7	York	14.9	6	Clarkson	***11.5***
9	Valentine Lakes Game Ref	14.6	6	Osmond	11.5
10	Grand Island Arpt	14.4	10	Walthill	11.6
11	Aurora	14.2	11	Harrison	11.7
11	Fremont	14.2	12	Bartlett 4 S	***11.9***
13	Columbus 3 NE	14.0	12	North Platte Lee Bird Field	11.9
13	Harrisburg 10 NW	14.0	14	Anselmo 2 SE	12.0
15	Beatrice 1 N	***13.9***	14	Gordon 6 N	12.0
15	Canaday Steam Plant	13.9	16	Tekamah	12.3
15	Chadron Municipal Arpt	13.9	17	Mead 6 S	12.5
15	Lincoln Municipal Arpt	13.9	17	Norfolk Karl Stefan Mem Arpt	12.5
15	Omaha Eppley Airfield	13.9	19	Stanton	***12.6***
20	Atkinson	13.8	20	Oconto	12.8
20	Scottsbluff County Arpt	13.8	21	Ravenna	12.9
22	Clay Center	13.6	22	Arthur	13.0
22	Kearney 4 NE	13.6	23	Ashland 2	13.1
24	Ashland 2	13.1	23	David City	13.1
24	David City	13.1	23	Surprise	***13.1***

Number of Days Annually Maximum Temperature ≥ 90°F

Highest			Lowest		
Rank	Station Name	Days	Rank	Station Name	Days
1	Bridgeport	56	1	Harrison	23
2	Chadron Municipal Arpt	***46***	2	Broken Bow 2 W	27
3	Curtis 3 NNE	***45***	3	Ainsworth	28
3	Scottsbluff County Arpt	45	4	Albion 1 N	29
5	Lincoln Municipal Arpt	42	4	Canaday Steam Plant	29
5	Valentine Miller Field	42	4	Clarkson	***29***
5	York	42	4	Norfolk Karl Stefan Mem Arpt	29
8	Beatrice 1 N	***40***	4	Tekamah	29
9	Ashland 2	38	4	Valentine Lakes Game Ref	***29***
10	Agate 3 E	37	10	Hemingford	30
10	Fremont	37	10	Stanton	***30***
10	Gordon 6 N	37	12	David City	31
10	Hastings 4 N	37	12	Loup City	31
10	Lynch	***37***	12	Omaha Eppley Airfield	31
10	North Platte Lee Bird Field	37	15	Anselmo 2 SE	32
16	Crete	36	15	Aurora	32
16	Grand Island Arpt	36	15	Geneva	32
16	Surprise	***36***	15	Ravenna	32
16	Walthill	36	19	Atkinson	33
20	Arthur	35	19	Clay Center	33
20	Bartlett 4 S	***35***	19	Oconto	33
20	Columbus 3 NE	35	22	Harrisburg 10 NW	34
20	Kearney 4 NE	35	22	Mead 6 S	34
24	Harrisburg 10 NW	34	22	Osmond	34
24	Mead 6 S	34	25	Arthur	35

Rankings include 25 highest/lowest stations. If state has less than 25 stations, all stations are included. The period of record is 1980–2009. See User Guide for detailed explanation of data.

Number of Days Annually Maximum Temperature ≤ 32°F

Highest			Lowest		
Rank	Station Name	Days	Rank	Station Name	Days
1	Clarkson	***48***	1	Bridgeport	21
1	Harrison	48	2	Harrisburg 10 NW	29
1	Tekamah	48	3	Scottsbluff County Arpt	30
4	David City	47	4	Agate 3 E	31
4	Osmond	47	4	Curtis 3 NNE	***31***
6	Walthill	46	6	North Platte Lee Bird Field	32
7	Bartlett 4 S	***45***	6	Oconto	32
7	Columbus 3 NE	45	8	Crete	33
7	Gordon 6 N	45	9	Geneva	34
7	Lynch	***45***	10	Canaday Steam Plant	35
7	Norfolk Karl Stefan Mem Arpt	45	11	Ravenna	36
12	Albion 1 N	44	12	Anselmo 2 SE	37
12	Stanton	***44***	12	Beatrice 1 N	***37***
14	Atkinson	43	14	Arthur	38
14	Valentine Miller Field	43	14	Chadron Municipal Arpt	***38***
16	Omaha Eppley Airfield	42	14	Clay Center	38
17	Ainsworth	41	14	Grand Island Arpt	38
17	Aurora	41	14	Hastings 4 N	38
19	Ashland 2	40	14	Kearney 4 NE	38
19	Fremont	40	14	Lincoln Municipal Arpt	38
19	Loup City	40	21	Broken Bow 2 W	39
19	Mead 6 S	40	21	Hemingford	39
19	Surprise	***40***	21	Valentine Lakes Game Ref	***39***
19	York	40	24	Ashland 2	40
25	Broken Bow 2 W	39	24	Fremont	40

Number of Days Annually Minimum Temperature ≤ 32°F

Highest			Lowest		
Rank	Station Name	Days	Rank	Station Name	Days
1	Agate 3 E	207	1	Crete	131
2	Harrisburg 10 NW	187	2	Geneva	132
3	Harrison	185	3	Fremont	138
4	Valentine Miller Field	178	4	York	139
5	Broken Bow 2 W	177	5	Lincoln Municipal Arpt	141
6	Gordon 6 N	176	5	Omaha Eppley Airfield	141
7	Lynch	***174***	7	Columbus 3 NE	143
7	North Platte Lee Bird Field	174	7	Hastings 4 N	143
9	Anselmo 2 SE	173	9	Aurora	146
9	Scottsbluff County Arpt	173	9	Tekamah	146
11	Curtis 3 NNE	***170***	11	Ainsworth	147
12	Arthur	168	11	Ashland 2	147
13	Oconto	166	11	Beatrice 1 N	***147***
14	Bridgeport	165	11	Grand Island Arpt	147
14	Chadron Municipal Arpt	***165***	15	David City	149
16	Albion 1 N	162	15	Mead 6 S	149
16	Loup City	162	17	Atkinson	150
18	Kearney 4 NE	160	17	Clay Center	150
19	Bartlett 4 S	***159***	19	Stanton	***151***
19	Hemingford	159	19	Surprise	***151***
19	Ravenna	159	21	Norfolk Karl Stefan Mem Arpt	152
22	Clarkson	***156***	21	Walthill	152
23	Osmond	155	23	Canaday Steam Plant	154
24	Canaday Steam Plant	154	23	Valentine Lakes Game Ref	***154***
24	Valentine Lakes Game Ref	***154***	25	Osmond	155

 Rankings include 25 highest/lowest stations. If state has less than 25 stations, all stations are included. The period of record is 1980–2009. See User Guide for detailed explanation of data.

Number of Days Annually Minimum Temperature ≤ 0°F

Highest Rank	Highest Station Name	Highest Days	Lowest Rank	Lowest Station Name	Lowest Days
1	Agate 3 E	22	1	Geneva	7
1	Lynch	*22*	2	Crete	9
3	Valentine Miller Field	20	3	York	10
4	Harrison	19	4	Canaday Steam Plant	11
5	Osmond	18	4	Columbus 3 NE	11
5	Walthill	18	4	Fremont	11
7	Anselmo 2 SE	17	4	Hastings 4 N	11
7	Bartlett 4 S	*17*	8	Aurora	12
7	Broken Bow 2 W	17	8	Beatrice 1 N	*12*
7	Gordon 6 N	17	8	Bridgeport	12
11	Albion 1 N	16	8	Clay Center	12
11	Chadron Municipal Arpt	*16*	8	Grand Island Arpt	12
11	Valentine Lakes Game Ref	*16*	8	Hemingford	12
14	Arthur	15	8	Lincoln Municipal Arpt	12
14	Ashland 2	15	8	Surprise	*12*
14	Atkinson	15	16	Curtis 3 NNE	*13*
14	Clarkson	*15*	16	Kearney 4 NE	13
14	David City	15	16	Omaha Eppley Airfield	13
14	Harrisburg 10 NW	15	19	Ainsworth	14
14	Loup City	15	19	Mead 6 S	14
14	Norfolk Karl Stefan Mem Arpt	15	19	North Platte Lee Bird Field	14
14	Stanton	*15*	19	Oconto	14
14	Tekamah	15	19	Ravenna	14
24	Ainsworth	14	19	Scottsbluff County Arpt	14
24	Mead 6 S	14	25	Arthur	15

Number of Annual Heating Degree Days

Highest Rank	Highest Station Name	Highest Num.	Lowest Rank	Lowest Station Name	Lowest Num.
1	Harrison	7,730	1	Crete	5,653
2	Agate 3 E	7,312	2	Geneva	5,677
3	Gordon 6 N	7,266	3	Beatrice 1 N	*5,993*
4	Lynch	*7,116*	4	Lincoln Municipal Arpt	6,011
5	Valentine Miller Field	7,003	5	Fremont	6,044
6	Broken Bow 2 W	6,885	6	Bridgeport	6,051
7	Harrisburg 10 NW	6,855	7	York	6,063
8	Hemingford	6,786	8	Hastings 4 N	6,082
9	Bartlett 4 S	*6,766*	9	Grand Island Arpt	6,143
10	Chadron Municipal Arpt	*6,738*	10	Omaha Eppley Airfield	6,158
11	Albion 1 N	6,732	11	Ashland 2	6,207
12	Arthur	6,723	12	Aurora	6,213
13	Clarkson	*6,698*	13	Clay Center	6,239
14	Anselmo 2 SE	6,685	14	Surprise	*6,240*
15	Osmond	6,658	15	Canaday Steam Plant	6,244
16	Loup City	6,610	16	Columbus 3 NE	6,262
17	Valentine Lakes Game Ref	*6,599*	17	Mead 6 S	6,276
18	Walthill	6,556	18	Ravenna	6,307
19	North Platte Lee Bird Field	6,540	19	Curtis 3 NNE	*6,311*
20	Tekamah	6,531	20	Oconto	6,326
21	Norfolk Karl Stefan Mem Arpt	6,525	21	Kearney 4 NE	6,366
21	Scottsbluff County Arpt	6,525	22	Ainsworth	6,400
23	Atkinson	6,459	23	David City	6,436
24	Stanton	*6,453*	24	Stanton	*6,453*
25	David City	6,436	25	Atkinson	6,459

Rankings include 25 highest/lowest stations. If state has less than 25 stations, all stations are included. The period of record is 1980–2009. See User Guide for detailed explanation of data.

Number of Annual Cooling Degree Days

Highest

Rank	Station Name	Num.
1	Crete	1,211
2	Lincoln Municipal Arpt	1,210
3	York	1,194
4	Beatrice 1 N	***1,173***
5	Fremont	1,161
6	Columbus 3 NE	1,152
7	Geneva	1,151
8	Ashland 2	1,133
9	Omaha Eppley Airfield	1,130
10	Grand Island Arpt	1,077
11	Hastings 4 N	1,071
12	Mead 6 S	1,043
12	Walthill	1,043
14	Surprise	***1,037***
15	Aurora	1,025
15	David City	1,025
17	Tekamah	1,016
18	Osmond	990
18	Stanton	***990***
20	Clay Center	981
21	Norfolk Karl Stefan Mem Arpt	980
22	Atkinson	967
23	Clarkson	***960***
24	Ravenna	954
25	Bridgeport	948

Lowest

Rank	Station Name	Num.
1	Harrison	448
2	Agate 3 E	460
3	Harrisburg 10 NW	547
4	Gordon 6 N	670
5	Hemingford	673
6	Broken Bow 2 W	721
7	Arthur	751
8	Scottsbluff County Arpt	767
9	Anselmo 2 SE	781
10	Valentine Lakes Game Ref	***786***
11	Valentine Miller Field	830
12	North Platte Lee Bird Field	831
13	Oconto	851
14	Albion 1 N	861
15	Loup City	864
16	Chadron Municipal Arpt	***872***
17	Lynch	***883***
18	Ainsworth	892
19	Bartlett 4 S	***901***
20	Canaday Steam Plant	919
21	Curtis 3 NNE	***928***
22	Kearney 4 NE	946
23	Bridgeport	948
24	Ravenna	954
25	Clarkson	***960***

Annual Precipitation

Highest

Rank	Station Name	Inches
1	Beatrice 1 N	***31.01***
2	Aurora	30.67
3	Omaha Eppley Airfield	30.33
4	Tekamah	30.25
5	Ashland 2	30.22
6	Crete	29.58
7	Walthill	29.55
8	Fremont	29.46
9	David City	29.41
10	Stanton	***29.15***
11	Geneva	29.13
12	York	29.03
13	Columbus 3 NE	28.81
14	Mead 6 S	28.73
15	Lincoln Municipal Arpt	28.54
16	Surprise	28.12
17	Clarkson	***28.11***
18	Clay Center	27.90
19	Hastings 4 N	27.76
20	Albion 1 N	27.12
21	Norfolk Karl Stefan Mem Arpt	27.01
22	Loup City	26.87
23	Bartlett 4 S	***26.68***
24	Grand Island Arpt	26.23
25	Osmond	25.93

Lowest

Rank	Station Name	Inches
1	Agate 3 E	14.02
2	Scottsbluff County Arpt	15.62
3	Harrisburg 10 NW	15.94
4	Hemingford	15.98
5	Harrison	16.98
6	Bridgeport	17.24
7	Chadron Municipal Arpt	***17.32***
8	Gordon 6 N	18.95
9	Arthur	19.15
10	Valentine Miller Field	19.86
11	North Platte Lee Bird Field	19.90
12	Curtis 3 NNE	***20.77***
13	Oconto	***21.06***
14	Broken Bow 2 W	22.60
15	Canaday Steam Plant	22.83
16	Ainsworth	22.93
17	Valentine Lakes Game Ref	***23.15***
18	Atkinson	24.19
19	Anselmo 2 SE	24.35
19	Lynch	24.35
21	Kearney 4 NE	25.02
22	Ravenna	25.80
23	Osmond	25.93
24	Grand Island Arpt	26.23
25	Bartlett 4 S	***26.68***

Rankings include 25 highest/lowest stations. If state has less than 25 stations, all stations are included. The period of record is 1980–2009. See User Guide for detailed explanation of data.

Annual Extreme Maximum Daily Precipitation

Highest Rank	Station Name	Inches	Lowest Rank	Station Name	Inches
1	Tekamah	8.25	1	Bridgeport	2.60
2	Clay Center	***7.20***	2	Scottsbluff County Arpt	2.68
2	York	7.20	3	Hemingford	2.71
4	Grand Island Arpt	6.50	4	Gordon 6 N	***2.78***
5	Omaha Eppley Airfield	6.46	5	Harrisburg 10 NW	2.95
6	Aurora	6.40	5	North Platte Lee Bird Field	2.95
7	Surprise	6.10	7	Agate 3 E	3.26
8	Crete	***6.05***	8	Valentine Miller Field	3.39
9	Columbus 3 NE	5.97	9	Arthur	3.43
10	Kearney 4 NE	5.95	10	Valentine Lakes Game Ref	***3.48***
11	Ravenna	5.90	11	Osmond	3.53
12	Curtis 3 NNE	***5.80***	12	Harrison	3.58
13	Geneva	5.75	13	Ainsworth	3.76
14	Loup City	5.60	14	Anselmo 2 SE	3.83
15	Walthill	5.50	15	Broken Bow 2 W	3.88
16	David City	5.47	16	Beatrice 1 N	***4.01***
17	Lincoln Municipal Arpt	5.42	17	Bartlett 4 S	***4.03***
17	Norfolk Karl Stefan Mem Arpt	5.42	18	Lynch	4.10
19	Mead 6 S	5.25	19	Albion 1 N	4.40
20	Hastings 4 N	5.11	20	Oconto	***4.48***
21	Canaday Steam Plant	5.07	21	Stanton	***4.50***
22	Ashland 2	5.02	22	Fremont	4.89
23	Atkinson	5.00	23	Clarkson	***4.92***
24	Clarkson	***4.92***	24	Atkinson	5.00
25	Fremont	4.89	25	Ashland 2	5.02

Number of Days Annually With ≥ 0.1 Inches of Precipitation

Highest Rank	Station Name	Days	Lowest Rank	Station Name	Days
1	Omaha WSFO	***58***	1	Agate 3 E	35
2	Ashland 2	56	2	Chadron Municipal Arpt	***40***
2	Beatrice 1 N	***56***	2	Curtis 3 NNE	***40***
4	Aurora	55	2	Oconto	***40***
4	David City	55	2	Scottsbluff County Arpt	40
4	Fremont	55	6	Bridgeport	41
4	Omaha Eppley Airfield	55	6	Harrisburg 10 NW	41
8	Columbus 3 NE	54	6	Harrison	41
8	Lincoln Municipal Arpt	54	6	Hemingford	41
8	Mead 6 S	54	10	Valentine Miller Field	42
8	Stanton	***54***	11	Clay Center	43
8	Tekamah	54	11	North Platte Lee Bird Field	43
13	Walthill	53	13	Arthur	44
14	Hastings 4 N	52	13	Canaday Steam Plant	44
14	Norfolk Karl Stefan Mem Arpt	52	15	Ainsworth	45
14	Surprise	52	15	Broken Bow 2 W	45
17	Ravenna	51	15	Valentine Lakes Game Ref	***45***
18	Geneva	50	18	Bartlett 4 S	46
18	Loup City	50	18	Lynch	46
18	York	50	20	Anselmo 2 SE	47
21	Atkinson	49	20	Gordon 6 N	47
21	Clarkson	***49***	22	Albion 1 N	48
21	Crete	49	22	Grand Island Arpt	48
21	Osmond	49	22	Kearney 4 NE	48
25	Albion 1 N	48	25	Atkinson	49

Rankings include 25 highest/lowest stations. If state has less than 25 stations, all stations are included. The period of record is 1980–2009. See User Guide for detailed explanation of data.

Number of Days Annually With ≥ 0.5 Inches of Precipitation

Highest Rank	Station Name	Days	Lowest Rank	Station Name	Days
1	Aurora	20	1	Agate 3 E	7
1	Beatrice 1 N	***20***	1	Harrisburg 10 NW	7
1	Omaha WSFO	***20***	3	Scottsbluff County Arpt	8
4	Ashland 2	19	4	Harrison	9
4	Columbus 3 NE	19	5	Arthur	10
6	Bartlett 4 S	18	5	Chadron Municipal Arpt	***10***
6	Clarkson	***18***	5	Gordon 6 N	10
6	Clay Center	18	5	Hemingford	10
6	David City	18	9	Bridgeport	11
6	Omaha Eppley Airfield	18	10	North Platte Lee Bird Field	12
6	Stanton	***18***	10	Valentine Miller Field	12
6	Surprise	18	12	Ainsworth	13
6	Tekamah	18	12	Canaday Steam Plant	13
6	Walthill	18	12	Curtis 3 NNE	***13***
6	York	18	12	Oconto	***13***
16	Albion 1 N	17	16	Kearney 4 NE	14
16	Atkinson	17	16	Valentine Lakes Game Ref	***14***
16	Crete	17	18	Anselmo 2 SE	15
16	Fremont	17	18	Grand Island Arpt	15
16	Geneva	17	20	Broken Bow 2 W	16
16	Lincoln Municipal Arpt	17	20	Hastings 4 N	16
16	Loup City	17	20	Norfolk Karl Stefan Mem Arpt	16
16	Lynch	17	20	Osmond	16
16	Mead 6 S	17	20	Ravenna	16
25	Broken Bow 2 W	16	25	Albion 1 N	17

Number of Days Annually With ≥ 1.0 Inches of Precipitation

Highest Rank	Station Name	Days	Lowest Rank	Station Name	Days
1	Bartlett 4 S	8	1	Chadron Municipal Arpt	***0***
1	Clay Center	8	2	Agate 3 E	1
1	Stanton	***8***	2	Harrisburg 10 NW	1
4	Albion 1 N	7	2	Harrison	1
4	Ashland 2	7	2	Hemingford	1
4	Atkinson	7	2	Scottsbluff County Arpt	1
4	Aurora	7	7	Arthur	2
4	Beatrice 1 N	***7***	7	Gordon 6 N	2
4	Clarkson	***7***	9	Bridgeport	3
4	David City	7	10	Broken Bow 2 W	4
4	Fremont	7	10	Canaday Steam Plant	4
4	Geneva	7	10	Curtis 3 NNE	***4***
4	Hastings 4 N	7	10	North Platte Lee Bird Field	4
4	Kearney 4 NE	7	10	Oconto	***4***
4	Lynch	7	10	Valentine Miller Field	4
4	Omaha Eppley Airfield	7	10	Valentine Lakes Game Ref	***4***
4	Omaha WSFO	***7***	17	Ainsworth	5
4	Tekamah	7	18	Anselmo 2 SE	6
4	Walthill	7	18	Columbus 3 NE	6
20	Anselmo 2 SE	6	18	Crete	6
20	Columbus 3 NE	6	18	Grand Island Arpt	6
20	Crete	6	18	Lincoln Municipal Arpt	6
20	Grand Island Arpt	6	18	Loup City	6
20	Lincoln Municipal Arpt	6	18	Mead 6 S	6
20	Loup City	6	18	Norfolk Karl Stefan Mem Arpt	6

Rankings include 25 highest/lowest stations. If state has less than 25 stations, all stations are included. The period of record is 1980–2009. See User Guide for detailed explanation of data.

Annual Snowfall

Highest Rank	Highest Station Name	Highest Inches	Lowest Rank	Lowest Station Name	Lowest Inches
1	Harrisburg 10 NW	46.3	1	Clay Center	***17.3***
2	Hemingford	44.4	2	Canaday Steam Plant	17.4
3	Scottsbluff County Arpt	42.3	3	Beatrice 1 N	***19.1***
4	Harrison	41.7	4	Mead 6 S	20.0
5	Chadron Municipal Arpt	***41.4***	5	Geneva	20.7
6	Valentine Lakes Game Ref	***39.1***	6	Crete	21.2
7	Gordon 6 N	***38.0***	7	Ashland 2	23.0
8	Anselmo 2 SE	37.8	8	Surprise	24.4
9	Ainsworth	37.6	9	Tekamah	***25.1***
9	Bridgeport	37.6	10	Ravenna	26.0
11	Lynch	36.3	11	York	26.1
12	Atkinson	35.1	12	Kearney 4 NE	26.2
13	Valentine Miller Field	34.8	13	Clarkson	***26.3***
14	Arthur	33.1	14	Omaha Eppley Airfield	***26.4***
15	Loup City	33.0	15	Lincoln Municipal Arpt	26.5
16	Walthill	31.9	16	Columbus 3 NE	26.6
17	Osmond	31.7	17	Aurora	27.3
18	David City	31.4	18	Oconto	***27.7***
19	Bartlett 4 S	***30.8***	19	Albion 1 N	28.6
20	Fremont	30.4	20	North Platte Lee Bird Field	28.8
21	Norfolk Karl Stefan Mem Arpt	30.3	21	Broken Bow 2 W	29.0
22	Agate 3 E	29.9	22	Hastings 4 N	29.3
23	Grand Island Arpt	29.7	23	Grand Island Arpt	29.7
24	Hastings 4 N	29.3	24	Agate 3 E	29.9
25	Broken Bow 2 W	29.0	25	Norfolk Karl Stefan Mem Arpt	30.3

Annual Maximum Snow Depth

Highest Rank	Highest Station Name	Highest Inches	Lowest Rank	Lowest Station Name	Lowest Inches
1	Ainsworth	30	1	Canaday Steam Plant	14
2	Atkinson	***26***	2	Gordon 6 N	***15***
2	Omaha Eppley Airfield	26	2	Oconto	***15***
2	Valentine Lakes Game Ref	***26***	2	Scottsbluff County Arpt	15
5	Anselmo 2 SE	25	5	Crete	16
5	Arthur	25	5	Hemingford	16
5	Broken Bow 2 W	***25***	7	Agate 3 E	17
8	Albion 1 N	***24***	7	Surprise	***17***
8	Beatrice 1 N	***24***	9	Geneva	18
8	Columbus 3 NE	24	9	Grand Island Arpt	18
8	David City	24	9	Harrisburg 10 NW	18
8	Harrison	***24***	9	Lincoln Municipal Arpt	18
8	Lynch	24	9	North Platte Lee Bird Field	18
14	Clay Center	***23***	9	Tekamah	***18***
14	Fremont	23	9	York	***18***
14	Walthill	23	16	Bridgeport	19
17	Valentine Miller Field	22	16	Mead 6 S	19
18	Stanton	***21***	16	Norfolk Karl Stefan Mem Arpt	19
19	Aurora	20	19	Aurora	20
19	Hastings 4 N	20	19	Hastings 4 N	20
19	Loup City	***20***	19	Loup City	***20***
19	Osmond	20	19	Osmond	20
23	Bridgeport	19	23	Stanton	***21***
23	Mead 6 S	19	24	Valentine Miller Field	22
23	Norfolk Karl Stefan Mem Arpt	19	25	Clay Center	***23***

Rankings include 25 highest/lowest stations. If state has less than 25 stations, all stations are included. The period of record is 1980–2009. See User Guide for detailed explanation of data.

Number of Days Annually With ≥ 1.0 Inch Snow Depth

Highest			Lowest		
Rank	**Station Name**	**Days**	**Rank**	**Station Name**	**Days**
1	Hemingford	67	1	Bartlett 4 S	***11***
2	Gordon 6 N	58	2	Broken Bow 2 W	15
3	Harrisburg 10 NW	57	3	Clay Center	***19***
4	Anselmo 2 SE	52	4	Oconto	***21***
5	Ainsworth	51	5	Canaday Steam Plant	22
5	Chadron Municipal Arpt	***51***	6	Kearney 4 NE	***24***
7	Atkinson	***49***	7	Harrison	26
7	Norfolk Karl Stefan Mem Arpt	49	8	Beatrice 1 N	***27***
9	Osmond	48	8	York	***27***
10	Arthur	47	10	Loup City	***28***
10	Walthill	47	10	Tekamah	***28***
12	Valentine Miller Field	46	12	Bridgeport	33
13	Agate 3 E	45	13	Geneva	34
13	Albion 1 N	***45***	14	Crete	35
15	Aurora	44	14	North Platte Lee Bird Field	35
15	Columbus 3 NE	44	16	Mead 6 S	37
15	Fremont	44	16	Valentine Lakes Game Ref	***37***
18	David City	43	18	Hastings 4 N	39
19	Omaha WSFO	***42***	18	Lincoln Municipal Arpt	39
20	Surprise	***41***	18	Lynch	39
21	Grand Island Arpt	40	18	Omaha Eppley Airfield	39
21	Scottsbluff County Arpt	40	22	Grand Island Arpt	40
21	Stanton	***40***	22	Scottsbluff County Arpt	40
24	Hastings 4 N	39	22	Stanton	***40***
24	Lincoln Municipal Arpt	39	25	Surprise	***41***

Rankings include 25 highest/lowest stations. If state has less than 25 stations, all stations are included. The period of record is 1980–2009. See User Guide for detailed explanation of data.

Significant Storm Events in Nebraska: 2000 – 2009

Location or County	Date	Type	Mag.	Deaths	Injuries	Property Damage ($mil.)	Crop Damage ($mil.)
Douglas	04/10/01	Hail	1.75 in.	0	1	300.0	0.0
North Central, Central, and Southwest Nebraska	04/11/01	Winter Storm	na	0	0	10.0	0.0
Douglas	04/30/01	Hail	1.75 in.	0	0	200.0	0.0
Scotts Bluff	07/04/01	Hail	3.00 in.	0	12	50.0	0.0
Buffalo	06/12/02	Hail	5.00 in.	0	15	50.0	2.0
Kearney	06/12/02	Hail	4.50 in.	0	0	20.0	3.0
Buffalo	06/12/02	Hail	5.00 in.	0	0	10.0	3.0
Buffalo	06/12/02	Hail	5.00 in.	0	0	10.0	3.0
Thayer	06/22/03	Tornado	F2	1	7	10.0	1.0
Lancaster	05/22/04	Tornado	F4	1	30	100.0	0.0
Saline	05/22/04	Tornado	F2	0	8	20.0	0.0
Gage	05/22/04	Tornado	F4	0	0	20.0	0.0
Otoe	05/22/04	Tornado	F1	0	0	20.0	0.0
Washington	05/22/04	Hail	2.75 in.	0	0	10.0	0.0
Adams	05/11/05	Hail	2.75 in.	0	0	40.0	2.5
Hall	05/11/05	Flash Flood	na	0	0	10.0	5.0
Adams	05/11/05	Flash Flood	na	0	0	10.0	5.0
South Central Nebraska	12/29/06	Ice Storm	na	0	0	10.0	0.0
Buffalo	05/29/08	Tornado	F2	0	0	11.0	0.5
Douglas	06/27/08	Thunderstorm Wind	115 mph	0	0	53.0	0.0

Note: Deaths, injuries, and damages are date and location specific.

NEVADA

PHYSICAL FEATURES. Nevada is primarily a plateau area. The eastern part has an average elevation of between 5,000 and 6,000 feet above sea level; the western portion between 3,800 and 5,000 feet, the lower limit being in the vicinity of Pyramid Lake and Carson Sink; and the southern part generally between 2,000 and 3,000 feet. From the lower elevations of the west portion there is a fairly rapid rise westward to the summits of the eastern ranges of the Sierra Nevada. The southwestern part slopes down toward Death Valley, California, and the southern portion toward the channel of the Colorado River, the elevation of which is less than 1,000 feet above sea level. The extreme northeastern part slopes northerly, draining into the Snake River and thence into the Columbia.

On the Nevada plateau there are many mountain ranges, most of them 50 to 100 miles long, running generally north and south. The only east-west range is in the northeast. It forms the southern limit of the Columbia River Basin. With the exception of this small drainage area and another limited region in the southeast which drains into the Colorado River, the State lies within the confines of the Great Basin, and the waters of its streams disappear into sinks or flow into lakes with no outlets.

GENERAL CLIMATE. Nevada lies just east and to the leeward of the Sierra Nevada Range, a massive mountain barrier which has a marked influence on the climate of the State. One of the greatest contrasts in precipitation found within a short distance in the United States occurs between the western, or California, slopes of the Sierras and the valleys just to the east of this range. The prevailing winds are from the west, and as moist air associated with storms from the Pacific Ocean ascends the western slopes of the Sierras, a large portion of the original moisture falls as precipitation. As the air descends the eastern slope, it is warmed by compression, so that very little precipitation occurs. The effects of this mountain barrier are felt not only in the extreme western part, but generally throughout the State, with the result that the lowlands of Nevada are largely desert or semidesert.

With its varied and rugged topography—its mountain ranges, narrow valleys and low, sage-covered deserts, ranging in elevation from about 1,500 to more than 10,000 feet—Nevada presents wide local variations of temperature and rainfall. The most striking climatic features are bright sunshine, small annual precipitation in the valleys and deserts, heavy snowfall in the higher mountains, dryness and purity of air, and phenomenally large daily ranges of temperature.

TEMPERATURE. The mean annual temperatures vary from the middle 40s in the northeastern part to around 50°F. in the west, and to the middle 60s in the south. In the northeastern portion summers are short and hot, winters long and cold. In the west, the summers are also short and hot, but the winters are only moderately cold; while in the south the summers are long and hot and the winters short and mild. Prolonged periods of extremely cold weather are rare, due primarily to the mountains east and north of the State which act as a barrier to the intensely cold continental Arctic air masses.

In Nevada there is relatively strong insolation of heat during the day and rapid nighttime cooling, because of the clear air, resulting in wide daily ranges in temperature. Even after the hottest days, the nights are usually cool. At Reno the average range between the highest and the lowest daily temperatures is 29°F. in January, increasing month by month to 45°F. in July. In summer temperatures above 100°F. occur rather frequently in the extreme southern portion and occasionally over the remainder of the State. However, the humidity is normally low so that corresponding temperatures are less disagreeable in Nevada than in more humid climates.

PRECIPITATION. Nevada's precipitation mostly occurs during the winter season and on the average is less than in any other State. Precipitation is lightest over the lower parts of the western plateau, a series of long valleys extending from the State border opposite Death Valley in California northward to the Idaho line. Over the more southerly of those valleys the average annual precipitation is less than 5 inches. From this low average it ranges upward to 18 inches in Lamoille Canyon on the western side of the Ruby Mountains of northeast Nevada, and up to about 28 inches at Marlette Lake high in the most easterly range of the Sierras. Variations in precipitation are due mainly to differences in elevation and exposure to precipitation-bearing winds. The average annual number of days with measurable precipitation varies considerably.

Snowfall is usually heavy in the mountains, particularly in the north. Mountain snowfall forms the main source of water for streamflow. In years when winter and spring snowfall is light, the result is a shortage of water. Melting of the mountain snowpack in the spring usually causes some flooding in northern and extreme western streams during the period April to June, but damaging floods of this type are infrequent. Rain floods in which snowmelt is also a factor usually occur from November to March. Heavy summer thunderstorms cause flooding in local streams, but they usually occur over sparsely settled mountainous areas and, therefore, are seldom destructive.

OTHER CLIMATIC ELEMENTS. The State has a generous supply of sunshine, the average percentage of the possible amount at northern and central locations being generally between 65 and 75 percent and at southern locations above 80 percent.

The low humidity and abundant sunshine produce rapid evaporation. Annual amounts in the extreme southern portion of the State, as measured in evaporation pans, average over 100 inches. In northern and central sections amounts average roughly half as much.

Winds are generally light. Storms with high winds rarely occur, and still more rarely cause appreciable damage, except locally along the east slope of the Sierras. The prevailing wind direction is west, although at a few stations, because of local topography, it is south or southwest.

Dust or sandstorms occur occasionally, particularly over the southern part during the spring months when storms are moving through the region more frequently than at other seasons of the year.

Thunderstorms are infrequent, the average annual number being 12 at Winnemucca, 13 at Reno and Las Vegas, 22 at Elko, and 30 at Ely. Summer thunderstorms develop occasionally into heavy local downpours of rain. These storms, locally termed cloudbursts, may bring to a locality as much rain in a few hours as would normally fall in several months. Tornadoes are extremely rare.

Over the northern and central portions of the State, freezes continue until late in spring and being early in autumn. The shortest freeze-free season is in the extreme northeast, and the longest in the extreme south, the range being from less than 100 days at several weather stations in the northeast to around 140 in the west, and to over 225 in the extreme south.

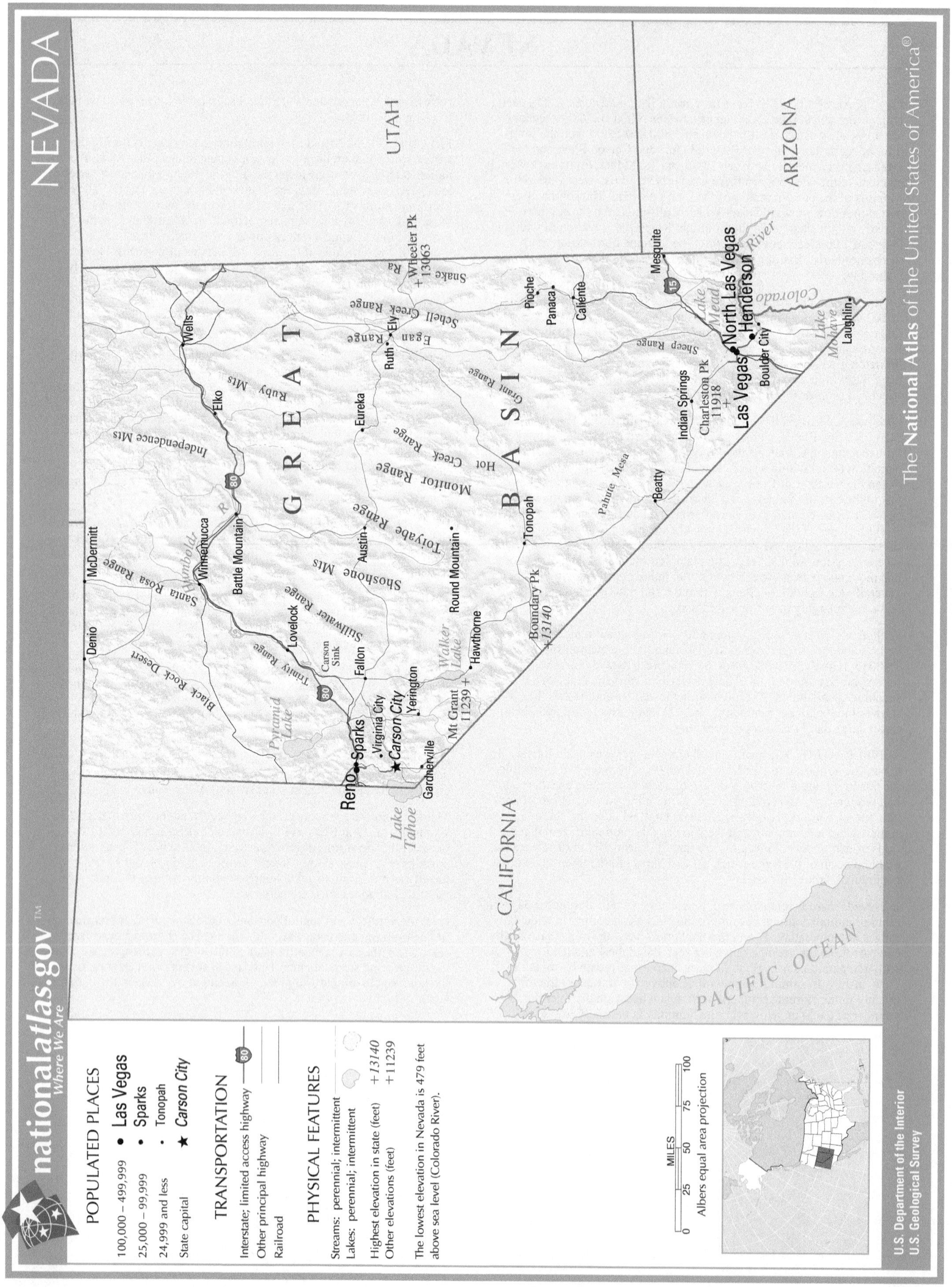
NEVADA
nationalatlas.gov™
Where We Are
POPULATED PLACES
100,000 – 499,999 • Las Vegas
25,000 – 99,999 • Sparks
24,999 and less • Tonopah
State capital ★ Carson City
TRANSPORTATION
Interstate; limited access highway 80
Other principal highway
Railroad
PHYSICAL FEATURES
Streams: perennial; intermittent
Lakes: perennial; intermittent
Highest elevation in state (feet) +13140
Other elevations (feet) +11239
The lowest elevation in Nevada is 479 feet above sea level (Colorado River).
MILES
0 25 50 75 100
Albers equal area projection
U.S. Department of the Interior
U.S. Geological Survey
The National Atlas of the United States of America®
UTAH
ARIZONA
CALIFORNIA
PACIFIC OCEAN
GREAT BASIN
Reno
Sparks
Carson City
Virginia City
Gardnerville
Yerington
Fallon
Lovelock
Winnemucca
Battle Mountain
Elko
Wells
Denio
McDermitt
Austin
Eureka
Ely
Ruth
Tonopah
Hawthorne
Round Mountain
Beatty
Indian Springs
Las Vegas
North Las Vegas
Henderson
Boulder City
Laughlin
Mesquite
Pioche
Panaca
Caliente
Black Rock Desert
Santa Rosa Range
Trinity Range
Stillwater Range
Shoshone Mts
Toiyabe Range
Monitor Range
Hot Creek Range
Independence Mts
Ruby Mts
Egan Range
Schell Creek Range
Snake Ra
Grant Range
Sheep Range
Pahute Mesa
Wheeler Pk 13063
Boundary Pk 13140
Mt Grant 11239
Charleston Pk 11918
Pyramid Lake
Carson Sink
Walker Lake
Lake Tahoe
Lake Mead
Lake Mohave
Humboldt R
Colorado River
80
15

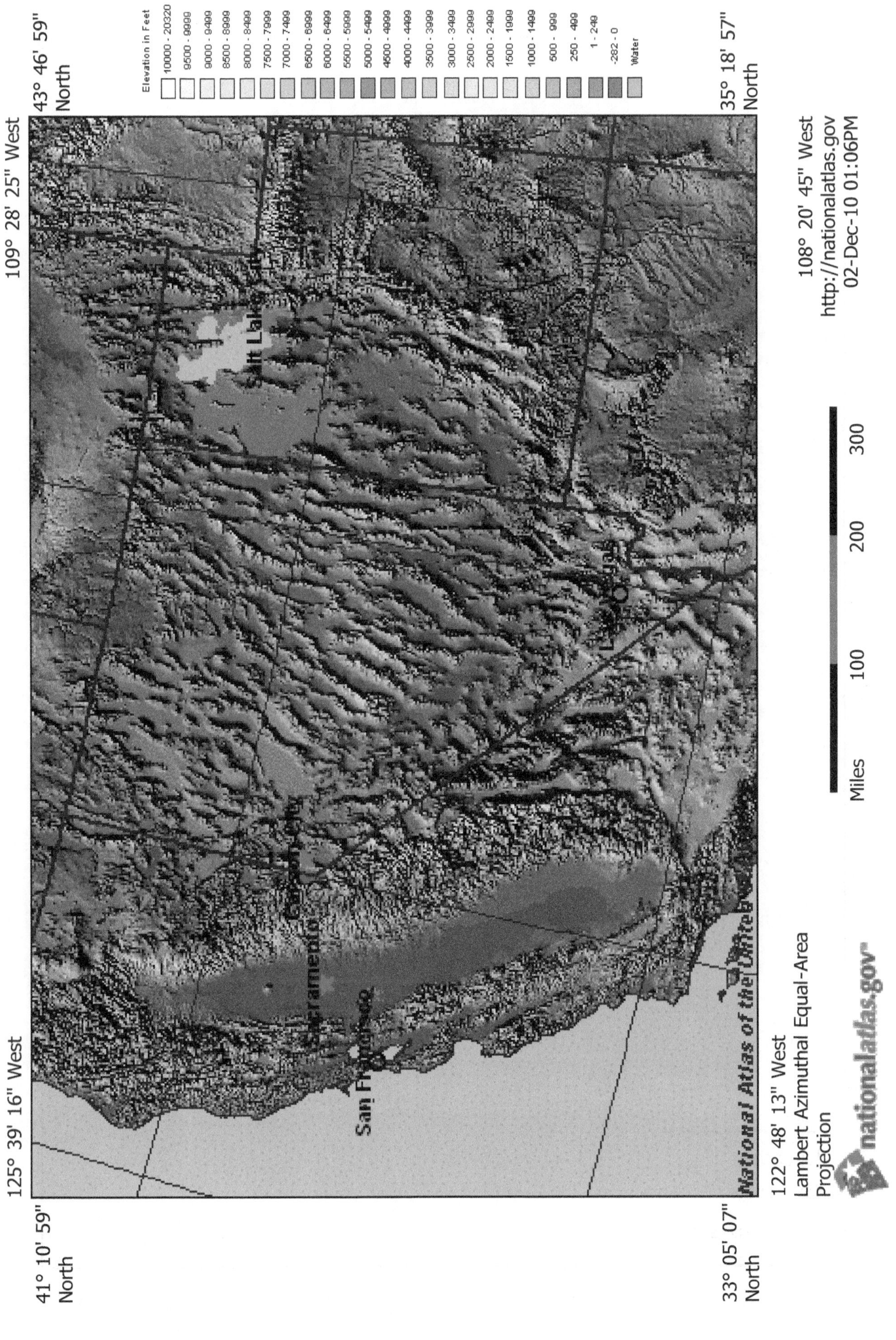
43° 46' 59" North
109° 28' 25" West
41° 10' 59" North
125° 39' 16" West
35° 18' 57" North
108° 20' 45" West
33° 05' 07" North
122° 48' 13" West
Elevation in Feet
10000 - 20320
9500 - 9999
9000 - 9499
8500 - 8999
8000 - 8499
7500 - 7999
7000 - 7499
6500 - 6999
6000 - 6499
5500 - 5999
5000 - 5499
4500 - 4999
4000 - 4499
3500 - 3999
3000 - 3499
2500 - 2999
2000 - 2499
1500 - 1999
1000 - 1499
500 - 999
250 - 499
1 - 249
-282 - 0
Water
Sacramento
San Francisco
Miles
100
200
300
Lambert Azimuthal Equal-Area
Projection
http://nationalatlas.gov
02-Dec-10 01:06PM
nationalatlas.gov

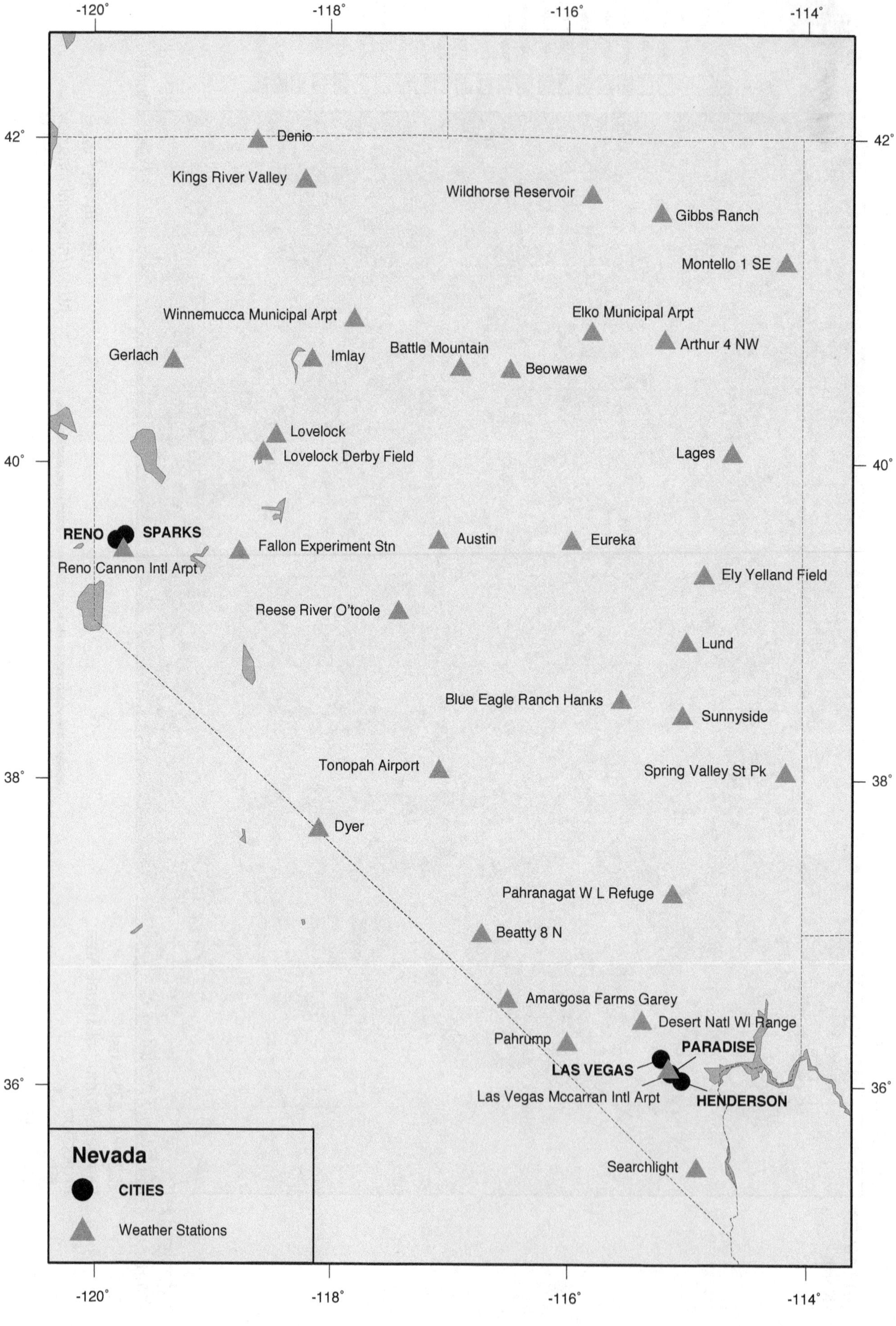
-120°
-118°
-116°
-114°
42°
40°
38°
36°
Denio
Kings River Valley
Wildhorse Reservoir
Gibbs Ranch
Montello 1 SE
Winnemucca Municipal Arpt
Elko Municipal Arpt
Gerlach
Imlay
Battle Mountain
Beowawe
Arthur 4 NW
Lovelock
Lovelock Derby Field
Lages
RENO
SPARKS
Reno Cannon Intl Arpt
Fallon Experiment Stn
Austin
Eureka
Ely Yelland Field
Reese River O'toole
Lund
Blue Eagle Ranch Hanks
Sunnyside
Tonopah Airport
Spring Valley St Pk
Dyer
Pahranagat W L Refuge
Beatty 8 N
Amargosa Farms Garey
Desert Natl Wl Range
Pahrump
PARADISE
LAS VEGAS
Las Vegas Mccarran Intl Arpt
HENDERSON
Searchlight
Nevada
CITIES
Weather Stations

Nevada Weather Stations by County

County	Station Name
Churchill	Fallon Experiment Stn
Clark	Desert Natl Wl Range
	Las Vegas-McCarran Intl Arpt
	Searchlight
Elko	Arthur 4 NW
	Elko Municipal Arpt
	Gibbs Ranch
	Montello 1 SE
	Wildhorse Reservoir
Esmeralda	Dyer
Eureka	Beowawe
	Eureka
Humboldt	Denio
	Kings River Valley
	Winnemucca Municipal Arpt
Lander	Austin
	Battle Mountain
Lincoln	Pahranagat W L Refuge
	Spring Valley State Park
Nye	Amargosa Farms Garey
	Beatty 8 N
	Blue Eagle Ranch Hanks
	Pahrump
	Reese River O'Toole
	Sunnyside
	Tonopah Airport
Pershing	Imlay
	Lovelock
	Lovelock Derby Field
Washoe	Gerlach
	Reno Cannon Intl Arpt
White Pine	Ely Yelland Field
	Lages
	Lund

See User Guide for station inclusion criteria.

Nevada Weather Stations by City

City	Station Name	Miles
Carson City	Boca, CA	23.8
	Reno Cannon Intl Arpt	21.9
Enterprise	Las Vegas-McCarran Intl Arpt	4.1
Henderson	Willow Beach, AZ	23.8
	Las Vegas-McCarran Intl Arpt	7.1
Las Vegas	Desert Natl Wl Range	19.0
	Las Vegas-McCarran Intl Arpt	8.0
North Las Vegas	Desert Natl Wl Range	19.0
	Las Vegas-McCarran Intl Arpt	9.7
Pahrump	Pahrump	6.0
Paradise	Las Vegas-McCarran Intl Arpt	1.3
Reno	Boca, CA	17.8
	Reno Cannon Intl Arpt	3.9
Sparks	Boca, CA	22.6
	Reno Cannon Intl Arpt	5.1
Spring Valley	Desert Natl Wl Range	23.2
	Las Vegas-McCarran Intl Arpt	5.9
Summerlin South	Desert Natl Wl Range	20.7
	Las Vegas-McCarran Intl Arpt	10.4
Sunrise Manor	Desert Natl Wl Range	24.7
	Las Vegas-McCarran Intl Arpt	9.1
Whitney	Las Vegas-McCarran Intl Arpt	5.8
Winchester	Desert Natl Wl Range	24.6
	Las Vegas-McCarran Intl Arpt	4.0

Note: Miles is the distance between the geographic center of the city and the weather station.

See User Guide for station inclusion criteria.

Nevada Weather Stations by Elevation

Feet	Station Name
6,604	Austin
6,549	Reese River O'Toole
6,540	Eureka
6,299	Arthur 4 NW
6,262	Ely Yelland Field
6,226	Wildhorse Reservoir
6,000	Gibbs Ranch
5,959	Lages
5,950	Spring Valley State Park
5,569	Lund
5,430	Tonopah Airport
5,299	Sunnyside
5,080	Elko Municipal Arpt
4,899	Montello 1 SE
4,898	Dyer
4,779	Blue Eagle Ranch Hanks
4,700	Beowawe
4,540	Battle Mountain
4,403	Reno Cannon Intl Arpt
4,296	Winnemucca Municipal Arpt
4,259	Imlay
4,240	Kings River Valley
4,189	Denio
3,975	Lovelock
3,964	Fallon Experiment Stn
3,950	Gerlach
3,899	Lovelock Derby Field
3,549	Beatty 8 N
3,540	Searchlight
3,399	Pahranagat W L Refuge
2,919	Desert Natl Wl Range
2,673	Pahrump
2,450	Amargosa Farms Garey
2,126	Las Vegas-McCarran Intl Arpt

See User Guide for station inclusion criteria.

Elko Municipal Airport

Elko is located in the Humbolt River Valley of northeastern Nevada. Weather observations are taken at the Flight Service Station which is located at the Municipal Airport on the west side of town. The elevation at the airport is just above 5,000 feet.

The Ruby mountain range, with many peaks near or exceeding 10,000 feet in height, dominates the landscape from about 40 miles northeast through 40 miles southeast of Elko. The immediate terrain consists of sagebrush-covered valleys and hills. The highest hills are approximately 2,500 feet above the valley floors. A few areas, mostly in the higher mountains, are covered with sparse stands of juniper, aspen, pinion pine, and spruce. The only heavily forested area in northeastern Nevada is in the Jarbidge Wilderness Area north of Elko near the Idaho border.

Because of the high elevation and proximity of the mountains, there is a wide range between the normal high and low temperatures. High radiative cooling at night makes cool nights the rule, even in mid summer.

Normal precipitation is light, especially during the summer months when the precipitation falls mostly as light showers which do not contribute much toward crop growth. The precipitation that falls between November and June (rain and snow) is critical to agriculture in the area. Not only is the precipitation that falls directly on the fields a benefit to farmers and ranchers, but the runoff from snowfall that accumulates in the mountains is used for irrigation.

The principal crop in northeast Nevada is hay. Cattle ranching is a major industry within the area. The ranges ordinarily furnish excellent summer pasture for cattle. Hay crops are needed for winter feeding.

Mining is another major industry. Many of the mines are located in the mountains at rather high elevations and are affected by daily weather. This is especially true during the winter when snow and rain may cause poor or impassable road conditions, thereby halting mining operations.

Transportation by air, rail, or road is seldom affected by the weather for more than short periods.

Based on the 1951-1980 period, the average first occurrence of 32 degrees Fahrenheit in the fall is September 8 and the average last occurrence in the spring is June 5.

Elko Municipal Airport *Elko County* Elevation: 5,080 ft. Latitude: 40° 50' N Longitude: 115° 48' W

	JAN	FEB	MAR	APR	MAY	JUN	JUL	AUG	SEP	OCT	NOV	DEC	YEAR
Mean Maximum Temp. (°F)	36.8	41.8	51.8	59.9	69.5	80.2	90.6	88.8	78.7	64.8	48.7	37.8	62.4
Mean Temp. (°F)	25.1	29.9	38.7	45.1	53.4	61.9	70.0	68.0	58.5	46.3	34.7	25.8	46.5
Mean Minimum Temp. (°F)	13.4	18.0	25.5	30.3	37.1	43.6	49.4	47.1	38.4	27.8	20.6	13.8	30.4
Extreme Maximum Temp. (°F)	65	70	78	86	97	104	107	105	96	88	78	65	107
Extreme Minimum Temp. (°F)	-21	-29	-2	12	15	26	30	20	12	1	-11	-33	-33
Days Maximum Temp. ≥ 90°F	0	0	0	0	1	6	19	16	3	0	0	0	45
Days Maximum Temp. ≤ 32°F	10	5	1	0	0	0	0	0	0	0	2	8	26
Days Minimum Temp. ≤ 32°F	30	27	26	19	8	1	0	0	7	23	26	29	196
Days Minimum Temp. ≤ 0°F	5	2	0	0	0	0	0	0	0	0	1	3	11
Heating Degree Days (base 65°F)	1,230	985	809	590	360	131	19	30	208	572	903	1,207	7,044
Cooling Degree Days (base 65°F)	0	0	0	0	5	45	180	129	21	0	0	0	380
Mean Precipitation (in.)	1.20	0.88	0.98	0.95	1.04	0.67	0.37	0.37	0.55	0.69	1.08	1.14	9.92
Maximum Precipitation (in.)*	3.3	1.9	2.4	2.2	4.1	2.6	2.3	4.6	3.2	1.9	2.8	4.2	18.3
Minimum Precipitation (in.)*	trace	0.1	trace	trace	trace	trace	0	trace	0	trace	trace	trace	4.8
Extreme Maximum Daily Precip. (in.)	1.16	0.67	0.79	0.86	0.98	0.90	1.28	1.20	0.72	0.91	0.76	1.14	1.28
Days With ≥ 0.1" Precipitation	4	3	3	3	4	2	1	1	2	2	3	4	32
Days With ≥ 0.5" Precipitation	1	0	0	0	0	0	0	0	0	0	0	0	1
Days With ≥ 1.0" Precipitation	0	0	0	0	0	0	0	0	0	0	0	0	0
Mean Snowfall (in.)	10.7	6.3	5.0	2.6	0.5	trace	trace	trace	0.1	0.6	4.4	9.5	39.7
Maximum Snowfall (in.)*	27	25	23	16	11	trace	0	0	2	6	17	33	85
Maximum 24-hr. Snowfall (in.)*	16	9	8	9	8	trace	0	0	2	5	6	9	16
Maximum Snow Depth (in.)	***14***	***19***	na	***4***	na	na	na	***trace***	na	na	na	***9***	na
Days With ≥ 1.0" Snow Depth	***16***	***10***	na	***1***	na	na	***0***	***0***	***0***	***0***	***3***	***11***	na
Thunderstorm Days*	< 1	< 1	< 1	1	3	4	5	4	2	< 1	< 1	< 1	19
Foggy Days*	5	3	3	1	1	< 1	< 1	< 1	< 1	1	2	4	20
Predominant Sky Cover*	OVR	OVR	OVR	OVR	OVR	CLR	CLR	CLR	CLR	CLR	OVR	OVR	CLR
Mean Relative Humidity 7am (%)*	79	80	77	64	58	52	42	45	53	66	77	79	64
Mean Relative Humidity 4pm (%)*	61	54	44	33	31	26	18	18	22	29	48	61	37
Mean Dewpoint (°F)*	16	21	23	25	31	36	37	35	30	25	22	17	26
Prevailing Wind Direction*	SW	WSW	SW	WSW	SW	SW	SW	SW	SW	WSW	SW	SW	SW
Prevailing Wind Speed (mph)*	9	9	9	10	9	9	9	9	9	9	9	9	9
Maximum Wind Gust (mph)*	na	na	na	na	na	na	na	na	na	na	na	na	na

Note: (*) Period of record is 1948-1995

The period of record for National Weather Service station data is 1980 – 2009 except where noted. See User Guide for detailed explanation of data.

Ely Yelland Field

Ely, Nevada, is located within but near the southern rim of the Great Basin. The neighboring terrain consists of alternate mountain ranges and sagebrush covered valleys. Principal cover on the mountains is juniper, pinion, and, at higher elevations, white fir, and white pine. Valley floors in this region are near 6,000 feet above sea level. This high elevation is conducive to sharp nighttime radiation, which produces pleasant summer nights but also reduces the season that is free from freezing temperatures.

The Ely weather station is near the center of Steptoe Valley, which is five miles wide at this point. The mountains of the Egan Range to the west and the Schell Creek Range to the east range up to 4,000 feet above the station elevation and prevent strong surface winds from these directions. A very pronounced drainage wind sweeps down the valley during the morning hours. More precipitation is noted near the mountains than is measured in the center of the valley.

Because of low annual precipitation, farming is limited to areas that can be irrigated from mountain streams or wells. The livestock industry is predominant in agriculture. Cultivated crops consist almost entirely of grains and forage.

The mountain ranges provide fairly good summer pastures for cattle and the lowlands provide food for a good portion of the winter in dry or snow-softened desert plants. All stock, however, has to be finished for market in the feed yards. Sheep share the mountain pastures with cattle in the summer, and as winter approaches move out on the wide flat valleys. These browsers eat snow for water and consume a wide variety of desert plants, including the lowly sagebrush. It is not uncommon for bands of sheep to spend an entire winter without supplemental feed.

Based on the 1951-1980 period, the average first occurrence of 32 degrees Fahrenheit in the fall is September 6 and the average last occurrence in the spring is June 16.

Ely Yelland Field *White Pine County* Elevation: 6,262 ft. Latitude: 39° 18' N Longitude: 114° 51' W

	JAN	FEB	MAR	APR	MAY	JUN	JUL	AUG	SEP	OCT	NOV	DEC	YEAR
Mean Maximum Temp. (°F)	40.2	43.2	50.6	58.5	68.3	79.5	88.0	85.7	76.1	63.0	49.3	40.2	61.9
Mean Temp. (°F)	25.7	29.4	36.4	42.8	51.0	60.1	68.0	66.3	56.9	45.4	34.0	25.5	45.1
Mean Minimum Temp. (°F)	11.3	15.6	22.2	27.1	33.5	40.7	48.0	46.8	37.7	27.6	18.7	10.8	28.3
Extreme Maximum Temp. (°F)	63	67	76	82	92	96	101	97	93	85	74	65	101
Extreme Minimum Temp. (°F)	-25	-30	-9	-5	13	22	28	27	17	-3	-15	-29	-30
Days Maximum Temp. ≥ 90°F	0	0	0	0	0	3	14	8	1	0	0	0	26
Days Maximum Temp. ≤ 32°F	7	4	1	0	0	0	0	0	0	0	2	7	21
Days Minimum Temp. ≤ 32°F	30	27	29	23	14	3	0	0	7	24	28	31	216
Days Minimum Temp. ≤ 0°F	6	4	0	0	0	0	0	0	0	0	1	6	17
Heating Degree Days (base 65°F)	1,210	998	878	659	430	164	20	34	242	602	923	1,217	7,377
Cooling Degree Days (base 65°F)	0	0	0	0	1	23	120	80	8	0	0	0	232
Mean Precipitation (in.)	0.72	0.78	0.95	0.94	1.13	0.68	0.64	0.91	0.88	0.96	0.66	0.52	9.77
Maximum Precipitation (in.)*	2.1	2.2	2.4	3.4	3.3	3.5	2.3	2.5	5.0	3.7	1.8	2.1	15.5
Minimum Precipitation (in.)*	trace	trace	0.1	trace	trace	trace	trace	trace	trace	0	trace	trace	4.2
Extreme Maximum Daily Precip. (in.)	0.80	0.69	1.02	1.31	0.91	1.16	0.95	1.03	2.52	0.94	1.01	0.76	2.52
Days With ≥ 0.1" Precipitation	2	3	4	3	3	2	2	2	2	3	2	2	30
Days With ≥ 0.5" Precipitation	0	0	0	0	1	0	0	0	0	0	0	0	1
Days With ≥ 1.0" Precipitation	0	0	0	0	0	0	0	0	0	0	0	0	0
Mean Snowfall (in.)	***8.8***	na	***8.1***	***5.0***	***2.6***	***0.1***	***trace***	***trace***	***0.5***	***3.1***	***5.7***	***8.1***	na
Maximum Snowfall (in.)*	25	20	25	25	12	2	trace	trace	6	12	17	22	101
Maximum 24-hr. Snowfall (in.)*	12	10	9	6	8	2	trace	trace	4	7	12	9	12
Maximum Snow Depth (in.)	***17***	na	***16***	***9***	***5***	***1***	***trace***	***trace***	***trace***	***9***	***9***	***18***	na
Days With ≥ 1.0" Snow Depth	***16***	na	***4***	***1***	***0***	***0***	***0***	***0***	***0***	***1***	***5***	***12***	na
Thunderstorm Days*	< 1	< 1	1	1	4	5	8	8	3	1	< 1	< 1	31
Foggy Days*	2	1	2	1	1	< 1	< 1	< 1	1	1	1	1	11
Predominant Sky Cover*	OVR	OVR	OVR	OVR	BRK	CLR	CLR	CLR	CLR	CLR	CLR	CLR	CLR
Mean Relative Humidity 7am (%)*	73	74	71	60	53	45	40	46	52	64	71	72	60
Mean Relative Humidity 4pm (%)*	55	50	43	34	31	24	21	23	24	31	46	54	36
Mean Dewpoint (°F)*	13	17	20	22	27	31	35	36	29	24	18	13	24
Prevailing Wind Direction*	S	S	S	S	S	S	S	S	S	S	S	S	S
Prevailing Wind Speed (mph)*	13	13	13	13	12	12	10	12	12	12	12	12	12
Maximum Wind Gust (mph)*	59	52	64	62	63	60	61	60	61	61	59	56	64

Note: (*) Period of record is 1948-1995

Las Vegas McCarran Int'l Arpt.

Las Vegas is situated near the center of a broad desert valley, which is almost surrounded by mountains ranging from 2,000 to 10,000 feet higher than the floor of the valley. This Vegas Valley, comprising about 600 square miles, runs from northwest to southeast, and slopes gradually upward on each side toward the surrounding mountains. Weather observations are taken at McCarran Airport, seven miles south of downtown Las Vegas, and about five miles southwest and 300 feet higher than the lower portions of the valley. Since mountains encircle the valley, drainage winds are usually downslope toward the center, or lowest portion of the valley. This condition also affects minimum temperatures, which in lower portions of the valley can be from 15 to 25 degrees colder than recorded at the airport on clear, calm nights.

The four seasons are well defined. Summers display desert conditions, with maximum temperatures usually in the 100 degree range. The proximity of the mountains contributes to the relatively cool summer nights, with the majority of minimum temperatures in the mid 70s. During about two weeks almost every summer warm, moist air predominates in this area, and causes scattered thunderstorms, occasionally quite severe, together with higher than average humidity. Soil erosion, especially near the mountains and foothills surrounding the valley, is evidence of the intensity of some of the thunderstorm activity. Winters, on the whole, are mild and pleasant. Daytime temperatures average near 60 degrees with mostly clear skies. The spring and fall seasons are generally considered most ideal, although rather sharp temperature changes can occur during these months. There are very few days during the spring and fall months when outdoor activities are affected in any degree by the weather.

The Sierra Nevada Mountains of California and the Spring Mountains immediately west of the Vegas Valley, the latter rising to elevations over 10,000 feet above the valley floor, act as effective barriers to moisture moving eastward from the Pacific Ocean. It is mainly these barriers that result in a minimum of dark overcast and rainy days. Rainy days average less than one in June to three per month in the winter months.

Strong winds, associated with major storms, usually reach this valley from the southwest or through the pass from the northwest. Winds over 50 mph are infrequent but, when they do occur, are probably the most provoking of the elements experienced in the Vegas Valley, because of the blowing dust and sand associated with them.

The average first occurrence of 32 degrees Fahrenheit in the fall is November 21 and the average last occurrence in the spring is March 7.

Las Vegas McCarran Int'l Arpt. *Clark County* Elevation: 2,126 ft. Latitude: 36° 05' N Longitude: 115° 09' W

	JAN	FEB	MAR	APR	MAY	JUN	JUL	AUG	SEP	OCT	NOV	DEC	YEAR
Mean Maximum Temp. (°F)	58.1	62.6	70.2	78.4	88.9	98.7	104.2	102.0	94.0	80.7	66.5	56.8	80.1
Mean Temp. (°F)	47.8	52.1	58.9	66.4	76.4	85.7	91.6	89.8	81.6	68.6	55.6	46.9	68.4
Mean Minimum Temp. (°F)	37.6	41.5	47.5	54.3	64.0	72.7	78.9	77.4	69.2	56.6	44.7	36.8	56.8
Extreme Maximum Temp. (°F)	75	87	92	99	109	115	117	114	108	101	87	77	117
Extreme Minimum Temp. (°F)	21	16	30	36	45	48	60	64	47	36	24	11	11
Days Maximum Temp. ≥ 90°F	0	0	0	4	16	26	30	30	23	5	0	0	134
Days Maximum Temp. ≤ 32°F	0	0	0	0	0	0	0	0	0	0	0	0	0
Days Minimum Temp. ≤ 32°F	6	2	0	0	0	0	0	0	0	0	1	7	16
Days Minimum Temp. ≤ 0°F	0	0	0	0	0	0	0	0	0	0	0	0	0
Heating Degree Days (base 65°F)	525	360	208	69	8	1	0	0	1	44	282	555	2,053
Cooling Degree Days (base 65°F)	0	1	25	117	370	630	830	775	506	164	7	0	3,425
Mean Precipitation (in.)	0.52	0.80	0.46	0.16	0.12	0.07	0.42	0.33	0.25	0.24	0.36	0.44	4.17
Maximum Precipitation (in.)*	3.0	2.5	4.8	2.4	1.0	1.0	2.5	2.6	1.6	1.2	2.2	1.7	9.9
Minimum Precipitation (in.)*	0	0	0	0	0	0	0	0	0	0	0	0	0.6
Extreme Maximum Daily Precip. (in.)	0.81	1.29	1.20	0.63	0.83	0.82	1.36	0.76	0.71	1.05	0.82	1.13	1.36
Days With ≥ 0.1" Precipitation	2	2	1	0	0	0	1	1	1	1	1	1	11
Days With ≥ 0.5" Precipitation	0	1	0	0	0	0	0	0	0	0	0	0	1
Days With ≥ 1.0" Precipitation	0	0	0	0	0	0	0	0	0	0	0	0	0
Mean Snowfall (in.)	na	na	na	na	na	na	na	na	na	na	na	na	na
Maximum Snowfall (in.)*	17	1	trace	trace	0	0	0	0	0	0	4	2	17
Maximum 24-hr. Snowfall (in.)*	7	1	trace	trace	0	0	0	0	0	0	3	2	7
Maximum Snow Depth (in.)	na	na	na	na	na	na	na	na	na	na	na	na	na
Days With ≥ 1.0" Snow Depth	na	na	na	na	na	na	na	na	na	na	na	na	na
Thunderstorm Days*	< 1	< 1	< 1	< 1	1	1	4	4	2	< 1	< 1	< 1	12
Foggy Days*	2	1	< 1	< 1	< 1	0	< 1	< 1	< 1	< 1	1	1	5
Predominant Sky Cover*	CLR	CLR	CLR	CLR	CLR	CLR	CLR	CLR	CLR	CLR	CLR	CLR	CLR
Mean Relative Humidity 7am (%)*	59	53	43	31	27	20	26	31	30	36	47	56	38
Mean Relative Humidity 4pm (%)*	32	26	21	15	13	10	14	16	15	18	26	31	20
Mean Dewpoint (°F)*	23	24	23	24	28	30	40	43	36	29	25	22	29
Prevailing Wind Direction*	WSW	WSW	SW	SW	SW	SW	SW	SW	SW	WSW	WSW	WSW	SW
Prevailing Wind Speed (mph)*	8	8	14	15	15	15	13	13	12	8	8	8	12
Maximum Wind Gust (mph)*	54	73	82	69	73	63	75	90	73	56	70	55	90

Note: (*) Period of record is 1948-1995

The period of record for National Weather Service station data is 1980 – 2009 except where noted. See User Guide for detailed explanation of data.

Reno Cannon Int'l Airport

At an elevation of 4,400 feet above mean sea level, Reno is located at the west edge of Truckee Meadows in a semi-arid plateau lying in the lee of the Sierra Nevada Mountain Range. To the west, the Sierras rise to elevations of 9,000 to 11,000 feet. Hills to the east reach 6,000 to 7,000 feet. The Truckee River, flowing from the Sierras eastward through Reno, drains into Pyramid Lake to the northeast of the city.

The daily temperatures on the whole are mild, but the difference between the high and low often exceeds 45 degrees. While the afternoon high may exceed 90 degrees, a light wrap is often needed shortly after sunset. Nights with low temperatures over 60 degrees are rare. Afternoon temperatures in winter are moderate.

Based on the 1951-1980 period, the average first occurrence of 32 degrees Fahrenheit in the fall is September 16 and the average last occurrence in the spring is June 1.

More than half of the precipitation in Reno occurs mainly as mixed rain and snow, and falls from December to March. Although there is an average of about 25 inches of snow a year, it seldom remains on the ground for more than three or four days at a time. Summer rain comes mainly as brief thunderstorms in the middle and late afternoons. While precipitation is scarce, considerable water is available from the high altitude reservoirs in the Sierra Nevada, where precipitation is heavy.

Humidity is very low during the summer months, and moderately low during the winter. Fogs are rare, and are usually confined to the early morning hours of midwinter. Sunshine is abundant throughout the year.

Reno Cannon Int'l Airport *Washoe County* Elevation: 4,403 ft. Latitude: 39° 29' N Longitude: 119° 46' W

	JAN	FEB	MAR	APR	MAY	JUN	JUL	AUG	SEP	OCT	NOV	DEC	YEAR
Mean Maximum Temp. (°F)	45.7	51.1	57.8	64.1	73.6	83.2	92.1	90.6	81.8	69.3	55.1	45.7	67.5
Mean Temp. (°F)	34.6	38.8	44.4	49.9	58.5	66.5	73.9	72.1	64.0	52.9	41.8	34.4	52.6
Mean Minimum Temp. (°F)	23.4	26.6	31.0	35.6	43.4	49.8	55.5	53.5	46.2	36.4	28.4	23.1	37.7
Extreme Maximum Temp. (°F)	71	75	81	89	97	103	108	105	100	91	77	68	108
Extreme Minimum Temp. (°F)	-3	-16	4	17	26	30	35	35	28	18	3	-13	-16
Days Maximum Temp. ≥ 90°F	0	0	0	0	2	8	22	19	6	0	0	0	57
Days Maximum Temp. ≤ 32°F	2	1	0	0	0	0	0	0	0	0	0	2	5
Days Minimum Temp. ≤ 32°F	27	23	18	10	2	0	0	0	1	9	21	27	138
Days Minimum Temp. ≤ 0°F	0	0	0	0	0	0	0	0	0	0	0	0	0
Heating Degree Days (base 65°F)	936	734	631	448	224	67	6	6	93	372	689	941	5,147
Cooling Degree Days (base 65°F)	0	0	0	1	31	119	287	233	70	2	0	0	743
Mean Precipitation (in.)	1.09	1.00	0.78	0.46	0.50	0.51	0.19	0.25	0.36	0.42	0.81	1.00	7.37
Maximum Precipitation (in.)*	4.1	4.8	2.9	2.0	2.9	1.5	1.1	1.6	2.3	2.1	3.1	5.3	13.2
Minimum Precipitation (in.)*	trace	trace	trace	trace	trace	0	0	0	0	0	0	trace	3.3
Extreme Maximum Daily Precip. (in.)	1.91	1.80	1.21	0.65	1.76	0.64	0.69	0.59	0.59	1.45	1.64	1.74	1.91
Days With ≥ 0.1" Precipitation	3	2	2	2	2	2	1	1	1	1	2	2	21
Days With ≥ 0.5" Precipitation	0	1	0	0	0	0	0	0	0	0	0	1	2
Days With ≥ 1.0" Precipitation	0	0	0	0	0	0	0	0	0	0	0	0	0
Mean Snowfall (in.)	***5.7***	na	na	na	na	na	na	na	na	na	na	***4.3***	na
Maximum Snowfall (in.)*	23	24	29	8	14	trace	0	0	2	5	17	26	64
Maximum 24-hr. Snowfall (in.)*	11	18	14	4	9	trace	0	0	2	4	15	15	18
Maximum Snow Depth (in.)	***20***	***13***	***3***	na	na	***0***	na	na	na	na	na	***16***	na
Days With ≥ 1.0" Snow Depth	***7***	***2***	***1***	na	na	***0***	na	***0***	na	na	na	***4***	na
Thunderstorm Days*	0	< 1	< 1	< 1	2	3	3	3	1	1	0	0	13
Foggy Days*	6	2	1	< 1	1	< 1	< 1	< 1	< 1	< 1	2	5	17
Predominant Sky Cover*	OVR	OVR	OVR	OVR	CLR	CLR	CLR	CLR	CLR	CLR	CLR	OVR	CLR
Mean Relative Humidity 7am (%)*	79	77	71	61	55	50	49	54	63	72	77	80	66
Mean Relative Humidity 4pm (%)*	51	41	34	27	26	22	19	19	21	27	41	51	32
Mean Dewpoint (°F)*	21	23	24	26	32	36	40	39	35	30	25	22	29
Prevailing Wind Direction*	S	S	WNW	WNW	WNW	WNW	WNW	WNW	WNW	S	S	S	WNW
Prevailing Wind Speed (mph)*	9	10	12	13	13	14	14	13	12	7	9	9	12
Maximum Wind Gust (mph)*	90	83	71	64	70	67	67	70	54	81	81	81	90

Note: (*) Period of record is 1945-1995

Winnemucca Municipal Airport

Winnemucca lies at an elevation about 4300 feet above sea level and is effectively cut off by the Sierra Nevada Mountains from the moisture source of the Pacific Ocean. Winnemucca has a climate marked by warm days, cool nights, and light precipitation. Sixty-six percent of the annual rainfall occurs as rain and snow between December and May. The winter snow pack in the surrounding mountains is generally sufficient for essential summertime irrigation. Reservoirs along the streams hold surplus water for less favorable years. As a result of the characteristic dryness of the climate, the neighboring valleys and hills are covered with sagebrush, and trees are found only along streams and in other places where water is sufficient the year round. Though it is heavier in the mountains, snowfall at Winnemucca itself has had measurable amounts fall in every month except July, August and September. During the winter months, snow on the ground permits grazing in many desert regions where there is no other source of stock water. Grazing in the summer months is restricted to mountain range tracts where there is sufficient water. Streams in many areas have been stocked with fish and provide good fishing each year.

Temperatures in this plateau area tend to rise sharply right after sunrise and remain comparatively high during the daylight hours, then drop rapidly about sundown. Daily temperature variations of 50 degrees are not uncommon.

Based on the 1951-1980 period, the average first occurrence of 32 degrees Fahrenheit in the fall is September 10 and the average last occurrence in the spring is June 8.

Winnemucca Municipal Airport *Humboldt County* Elevation: 4,296 ft. Latitude: 40° 54' N Longitude: 117° 48' W

	JAN	FEB	MAR	APR	MAY	JUN	JUL	AUG	SEP	OCT	NOV	DEC	YEAR
Mean Maximum Temp. (°F)	41.5	47.7	55.6	62.7	72.4	82.9	93.2	91.3	80.9	67.1	51.7	41.5	65.7
Mean Temp. (°F)	30.1	35.4	41.1	46.8	55.4	64.1	72.5	70.1	60.3	48.2	37.1	29.3	49.2
Mean Minimum Temp. (°F)	18.5	23.0	26.6	30.8	38.2	45.3	51.8	48.8	39.7	29.2	22.4	17.1	32.6
Extreme Maximum Temp. (°F)	67	74	80	90	98	106	109	108	99	91	77	67	109
Extreme Minimum Temp. (°F)	-12	-28	0	9	10	23	29	28	19	-2	-8	-37	-37
Days Maximum Temp. ≥ 90°F	0	0	0	0	2	10	23	21	6	0	0	0	62
Days Maximum Temp. ≤ 32°F	5	2	0	0	0	0	0	0	0	0	1	5	13
Days Minimum Temp. ≤ 32°F	28	24	24	18	7	1	0	0	5	20	25	28	180
Days Minimum Temp. ≤ 0°F	2	1	0	0	0	0	0	0	0	0	0	2	5
Heating Degree Days (base 65°F)	1,077	830	733	539	305	101	9	17	166	516	831	1,099	6,223
Cooling Degree Days (base 65°F)	0	0	0	0	14	82	249	180	31	0	0	0	556
Mean Precipitation (in.)	0.91	0.66	0.81	0.82	1.13	0.58	0.24	0.19	0.44	0.58	0.85	0.88	8.09
Maximum Precipitation (in.)*	2.7	2.2	1.7	2.9	3.4	2.9	1.7	1.7	1.5	2.2	2.7	3.7	14.5
Minimum Precipitation (in.)*	trace	0	0.1	0.1	trace	0	0	0	0	trace	trace	trace	3.1
Extreme Maximum Daily Precip. (in.)	0.88	0.55	0.65	1.21	1.15	0.71	0.86	0.58	1.04	0.66	0.82	0.94	1.21
Days With ≥ 0.1" Precipitation	3	3	3	2	3	2	1	1	1	2	3	3	27
Days With ≥ 0.5" Precipitation	0	0	0	0	0	0	0	0	0	0	0	0	0
Days With ≥ 1.0" Precipitation	0	0	0	0	0	0	0	0	0	0	0	0	0
Mean Snowfall (in.)	***4.5***	***3.3***	***3.0***	***1.3***	***0.1***	***trace***	***0.0***	***trace***	***0.0***	***0.6***	***2.4***	***5.2***	***20.4***
Maximum Snowfall (in.)*	19	14	23	12	5	trace	0	0	1	7	20	18	51
Maximum 24-hr. Snowfall (in.)*	8	9	8	7	3	trace	0	0	1	4	6	6	9
Maximum Snow Depth (in.)	***15***	***9***	***7***	***2***	***1***	***trace***	***0***	***trace***	***trace***	***3***	***6***	***7***	***15***
Days With ≥ 1.0" Snow Depth	***10***	***5***	***1***	***0***	***0***	***0***	***0***	***0***	***0***	***0***	***2***	***7***	***25***
Thunderstorm Days*	0	< 1	< 1	1	3	3	3	3	2	1	< 1	< 1	16
Foggy Days*	4	2	1	1	< 1	< 1	< 1	< 1	< 1	1	2	3	14
Predominant Sky Cover*	OVR	OVR	OVR	OVR	OVR	CLR	CLR	CLR	CLR	CLR	OVR	OVR	CLR
Mean Relative Humidity 7am (%)*	79	78	72	59	52	45	35	38	47	62	76	80	60
Mean Relative Humidity 4pm (%)*	57	46	38	29	27	22	15	16	20	28	45	58	33
Mean Dewpoint (°F)*	20	23	23	24	30	34	35	33	29	26	24	21	27
Prevailing Wind Direction*	S	S	S	W	W	W	W	W	NE	S	S	S	S
Prevailing Wind Speed (mph)*	9	8	8	10	10	10	10	10	10	7	8	9	9
Maximum Wind Gust (mph)*	59	62	64	58	49	85	56	78	56	43	54	62	85

Note: (*) Period of record is 1949-1995

The period of record for National Weather Service station data is 1980 – 2009 except where noted. See User Guide for detailed explanation of data.

Amargosa Farms Garey *Nye County* Elevation: 2,450 ft. Latitude: 36° 34' N Longitude: 116° 28' W

	JAN	FEB	MAR	APR	MAY	JUN	JUL	AUG	SEP	OCT	NOV	DEC	YEAR
Mean Maximum Temp. (°F)	61.4	65.0	71.2	79.4	88.8	97.9	103.9	102.3	94.9	83.3	69.1	60.3	81.5
Mean Temp. (°F)	46.7	50.3	55.7	62.8	72.0	80.5	86.9	85.4	77.6	66.1	53.3	45.6	65.2
Mean Minimum Temp. (°F)	32.0	35.5	40.2	46.2	55.2	63.1	69.8	68.5	60.1	48.8	37.4	30.8	49.0
Extreme Maximum Temp. (°F)	81	88	93	102	110	115	117	116	110	104	91	80	117
Extreme Minimum Temp. (°F)	14	11	22	27	35	39	53	52	29	28	19	6	6
Days Maximum Temp. ≥ 90°F	0	0	0	4	16	26	30	30	24	9	0	0	139
Days Maximum Temp. ≤ 32°F	0	0	0	0	0	0	0	0	0	0	0	0	0
Days Minimum Temp. ≤ 32°F	17	9	3	0	0	0	0	0	0	0	7	19	55
Days Minimum Temp. ≤ 0°F	0	0	0	0	0	0	0	0	0	0	0	0	0
Heating Degree Days (base 65°F)	560	410	287	117	21	1	0	0	3	73	348	595	2,415
Cooling Degree Days (base 65°F)	0	0	7	58	246	474	685	640	387	114	3	0	2,614
Mean Precipitation (in.)	0.54	0.88	0.64	0.23	0.20	0.09	0.34	0.42	0.28	0.19	0.34	0.40	4.55
Extreme Maximum Daily Precip. (in.)	0.71	1.26	1.82	1.45	0.79	0.54	1.83	1.85	1.10	0.55	0.72	1.05	1.85
Days With ≥ 0.1" Precipitation	2	2	2	1	1	0	1	1	1	1	1	1	14
Days With ≥ 0.5" Precipitation	0	1	0	0	0	0	0	0	0	0	0	0	1
Days With ≥ 1.0" Precipitation	0	0	0	0	0	0	0	0	0	0	0	0	0
Mean Snowfall (in.)	0.0	0.1	0.0	0.0	0.0	0.0	0.0	0.0	0.0	0.0	0.0	trace	0.1
Maximum Snow Depth (in.)	0	1	0	0	0	0	0	0	0	***0***	0	7	***7***
Days With ≥ 1.0" Snow Depth	0	0	0	0	0	0	0	0	0	***0***	0	0	***0***

Arthur 4 NW *Elko County* Elevation: 6,299 ft. Latitude: 40° 47' N Longitude: 115° 11' W

	JAN	FEB	MAR	APR	MAY	JUN	JUL	AUG	SEP	OCT	NOV	DEC	YEAR
Mean Maximum Temp. (°F)	35.3	38.2	45.9	54.6	64.0	***73.0***	82.8	81.6	72.3	60.0	44.9	35.0	***57.3***
Mean Temp. (°F)	25.1	28.1	35.1	42.1	50.4	***57.8***	66.1	65.0	56.5	46.2	33.6	24.7	***44.2***
Mean Minimum Temp. (°F)	14.8	17.8	24.2	29.6	36.7	***42.6***	49.4	48.4	40.7	31.6	22.1	14.5	***31.0***
Extreme Maximum Temp. (°F)	64	63	73	83	89	92	99	98	90	81	70	60	99
Extreme Minimum Temp. (°F)	-17	-19	-1	5	17	25	31	22	21	-4	-8	-26	-26
Days Maximum Temp. ≥ 90°F	0	0	0	0	0	0	4	2	0	0	0	0	6
Days Maximum Temp. ≤ 32°F	11	7	2	0	0	0	0	0	0	0	4	11	35
Days Minimum Temp. ≤ 32°F	30	27	27	19	9	***1***	0	0	4	16	26	30	***189***
Days Minimum Temp. ≤ 0°F	3	2	0	0	0	0	0	0	0	0	1	3	9
Heating Degree Days (base 65°F)	1,231	1,036	921	679	448	***219***	42	55	255	577	938	1,240	***7,641***
Cooling Degree Days (base 65°F)	0	0	0	0	1	***10***	83	63	6	0	0	0	***163***
Mean Precipitation (in.)	1.72	1.47	1.35	1.27	1.50	0.99	0.47	0.62	0.96	1.10	1.61	1.58	14.64
Extreme Maximum Daily Precip. (in.)	2.10	1.53	1.06	1.05	1.26	1.04	0.71	1.20	1.20	1.50	1.46	1.95	2.10
Days With ≥ 0.1" Precipitation	5	5	4	4	5	3	1	2	2	3	5	5	44
Days With ≥ 0.5" Precipitation	1	1	0	0	1	0	0	0	1	1	1	1	7
Days With ≥ 1.0" Precipitation	0	0	0	0	0	0	0	0	0	0	0	0	0
Mean Snowfall (in.)	9.3	5.7	5.1	1.9	0.6	trace	0.0	0.0	0.0	1.3	6.2	8.5	38.6
Maximum Snow Depth (in.)	***45***	47	47	27	8	0	0	0	0	10	25	34	***47***
Days With ≥ 1.0" Snow Depth	***18***	14	10	3	0	0	0	0	0	1	7	12	***65***

Austin *Lander County* Elevation: 6,604 ft. Latitude: 39° 30' N Longitude: 117° 04' W

	JAN	FEB	MAR	APR	MAY	JUN	JUL	AUG	SEP	OCT	NOV	DEC	YEAR
Mean Maximum Temp. (°F)	42.5	44.8	50.0	***57.2***	66.6	***77.6***	***87.3***	85.9	76.2	63.6	49.8	42.3	***62.0***
Mean Temp. (°F)	32.0	33.8	38.5	***44.4***	53.0	***62.2***	***71.3***	69.7	61.0	49.9	38.4	31.8	***48.8***
Mean Minimum Temp. (°F)	21.4	22.7	26.9	***31.5***	39.3	***46.7***	***55.3***	53.5	45.7	36.1	27.0	21.2	***35.6***
Extreme Maximum Temp. (°F)	65	70	76	83	93	95	103	98	93	85	75	63	103
Extreme Minimum Temp. (°F)	-11	-15	4	11	20	***23***	35	23	17	4	-2	-19	***-19***
Days Maximum Temp. ≥ 90°F	0	0	0	0	0	2	11	9	1	0	0	0	23
Days Maximum Temp. ≤ 32°F	4	3	1	0	0	0	0	0	0	0	2	5	15
Days Minimum Temp. ≤ 32°F	27	24	23	15	7	1	0	0	2	10	21	27	157
Days Minimum Temp. ≤ 0°F	0	0	0	0	0	0	0	0	0	0	0	1	1
Heating Degree Days (base 65°F)	1,017	875	814	***612***	***375***	***142***	***11***	20	153	464	790	1,023	***6,296***
Cooling Degree Days (base 65°F)	0	0	0	***0***	***10***	***63***	***215***	171	40	2	0	0	***501***
Mean Precipitation (in.)	***1.38***	0.94	1.56	1.40	1.95	***0.72***	0.44	0.51	0.53	0.75	1.03	1.13	***12.34***
Extreme Maximum Daily Precip. (in.)	***1.64***	***1.13***	***1.76***	***2.01***	***1.34***	***0.97***	***0.77***	0.69	0.92	1.80	0.97	1.19	***2.01***
Days With ≥ 0.1" Precipitation	***4***	3	4	3	4	2	1	1	2	2	3	3	***32***
Days With ≥ 0.5" Precipitation	***1***	0	1	1	1	0	0	0	0	0	0	1	***5***
Days With ≥ 1.0" Precipitation	***0***	0	0	0	0	0	0	0	0	0	0	0	***0***
Mean Snowfall (in.)	***12.9***	10.3	13.7	9.8	4.1	0.5	0.0	0.0	0.4	1.4	7.0	9.8	***69.9***
Maximum Snow Depth (in.)	***27***	***17***	***22***	***20***	13	trace	0	0	6	7	10	***15***	***27***
Days With ≥ 1.0" Snow Depth	***13***	8	***6***	3	1	0	0	0	0	1	4	10	***46***

Battle Mountain *Lander County* Elevation: 4,540 ft. Latitude: 40° 37' N Longitude: 116° 53' W

	JAN	FEB	MAR	APR	MAY	JUN	JUL	AUG	SEP	OCT	NOV	DEC	YEAR
Mean Maximum Temp. (°F)	41.9	48.2	57.1	64.9	74.7	85.4	95.2	93.7	82.9	69.0	52.8	42.2	67.3
Mean Temp. (°F)	29.7	35.2	42.2	48.5	57.3	66.0	73.8	71.6	61.9	49.7	38.1	29.7	50.3
Mean Minimum Temp. (°F)	17.2	22.1	27.2	32.0	39.9	46.5	52.3	49.5	40.8	30.3	23.4	17.3	33.2
Extreme Maximum Temp. (°F)	70	72	84	90	102	104	112	106	103	95	80	70	112
Extreme Minimum Temp. (°F)	-23	-25	-2	8	13	26	31	32	11	3	-8	-39	-39
Days Maximum Temp. ≥ 90°F	0	0	0	0	3	12	26	24	8	0	0	0	73
Days Maximum Temp. ≤ 32°F	5	1	0	0	0	0	0	0	0	0	1	4	11
Days Minimum Temp. ≤ 32°F	28	25	24	16	6	1	0	0	4	19	24	28	175
Days Minimum Temp. ≤ 0°F	3	1	0	0	0	0	0	0	0	0	1	2	7
Heating Degree Days (base 65°F)	1,089	837	700	489	254	72	6	10	135	468	799	1,087	5,946
Cooling Degree Days (base 65°F)	0	0	0	0	23	109	286	223	48	1	0	0	690
Mean Precipitation (in.)	0.95	0.77	0.83	1.06	1.42	0.72	0.26	0.26	0.55	0.60	0.75	0.82	8.99
Extreme Maximum Daily Precip. (in.)	0.71	0.77	1.06	1.10	1.46	1.07	0.90	0.89	0.91	0.76	***0.70***	1.19	***1.46***
Days With ≥ 0.1" Precipitation	3	2	3	3	4	2	1	1	2	2	2	3	28
Days With ≥ 0.5" Precipitation	0	0	0	0	1	0	0	0	0	0	0	0	1
Days With ≥ 1.0" Precipitation	0	0	0	0	0	0	0	0	0	0	0	0	0
Mean Snowfall (in.)	5.7	3.5	2.4	1.1	0.1	trace	0.0	0.0	trace	0.3	1.7	5.0	19.8
Maximum Snow Depth (in.)	18	10	5	5	1	trace	0	0	trace	3	5	14	18
Days With ≥ 1.0" Snow Depth	8	4	1	0	0	0	0	0	0	0	1	5	19

The period of record for all cooperative weather station data is 1980 – 2009. See User Guide for detailed explanation of data.

Beatty 8 N *Nye County* Elevation: 3,549 ft. Latitude: 37° 00' N Longitude: 116° 43' W

	JAN	FEB	MAR	APR	MAY	JUN	JUL	AUG	SEP	OCT	NOV	DEC	YEAR
Mean Maximum Temp. (°F)	54.7	58.4	65.1	72.3	81.9	91.7	97.6	***96.1***	***88.6***	77.4	63.5	54.6	***75.2***
Mean Temp. (°F)	42.0	45.1	50.6	56.7	65.5	73.8	79.8	***78.3***	***71.4***	60.9	48.8	41.5	***59.5***
Mean Minimum Temp. (°F)	29.2	31.9	36.0	41.0	49.0	55.8	62.0	***60.4***	***54.1***	44.4	34.1	28.3	***43.9***
Extreme Maximum Temp. (°F)	76	83	88	94	102	108	112	***109***	104	100	88	75	***112***
Extreme Minimum Temp. (°F)	9	5	16	20	32	35	42	***46***	32	22	8	2	***2***
Days Maximum Temp. ≥ 90°F	0	0	0	0	6	19	28	***28***	15	2	0	0	***98***
Days Maximum Temp. ≤ 32°F	0	0	0	0	0	0	0	***0***	0	0	0	0	***0***
Days Minimum Temp. ≤ 32°F	22	15	9	3	0	0	0	***0***	0	1	12	23	***85***
Days Minimum Temp. ≤ 0°F	0	0	0	0	0	0	0	***0***	0	0	0	0	***0***
Heating Degree Days (base 65°F)	712	555	441	254	79	10	0	***0***	***18***	159	479	723	***3,430***
Cooling Degree Days (base 65°F)	0	0	1	13	102	280	467	***418***	***216***	37	0	0	***1,534***
Mean Precipitation (in.)	0.73	1.00	0.90	0.42	0.28	0.20	0.40	***0.38***	0.42	0.23	0.46	0.50	***5.92***
Extreme Maximum Daily Precip. (in.)	0.90	1.14	1.32	1.49	1.15	0.60	1.60	***1.20***	2.00	0.59	1.16	1.90	***2.00***
Days With ≥ 0.1" Precipitation	2	3	2	1	1	1	1	***1***	1	1	1	1	***16***
Days With ≥ 0.5" Precipitation	0	1	0	0	0	0	0	***0***	0	0	0	0	***1***
Days With ≥ 1.0" Precipitation	0	0	0	0	0	0	0	***0***	0	0	0	0	***0***
Mean Snowfall (in.)	1.0	0.3	0.4	trace	trace	0.0	0.0	***0.0***	0.0	0.0	0.3	0.7	***2.7***
Maximum Snow Depth (in.)	5	4	5	trace	trace	0	0	***0***	0	0	2	9	***9***
Days With ≥ 1.0" Snow Depth	0	1	0	0	0	0	0	***0***	0	0	0	1	***2***

Beowawe *Eureka County* Elevation: 4,700 ft. Latitude: 40° 35' N Longitude: 116° 28' W

	JAN	FEB	MAR	APR	MAY	JUN	JUL	AUG	SEP	OCT	NOV	DEC	YEAR
Mean Maximum Temp. (°F)	38.7	44.9	54.8	62.1	71.9	82.1	91.8	90.3	80.6	66.8	50.4	39.4	64.5
Mean Temp. (°F)	26.4	32.6	40.5	46.4	54.9	63.2	71.2	69.2	60.1	47.8	36.2	27.2	48.0
Mean Minimum Temp. (°F)	14.1	20.2	26.2	30.5	37.7	44.3	50.5	48.1	39.5	28.7	21.9	14.8	31.4
Extreme Maximum Temp. (°F)	67	72	78	90	98	102	108	106	98	90	78	65	108
Extreme Minimum Temp. (°F)	-28	-36	2	7	13	25	33	25	17	1	-9	-43	-43
Days Maximum Temp. ≥ 90°F	0	0	0	0	1	8	20	19	5	0	0	0	53
Days Maximum Temp. ≤ 32°F	8	3	0	0	0	0	0	0	0	0	1	7	19
Days Minimum Temp. ≤ 32°F	30	26	24	16	8	1	0	0	6	21	26	29	187
Days Minimum Temp. ≤ 0°F	6	1	0	0	0	0	0	0	0	0	1	3	11
Heating Degree Days (base 65°F)	1,190	909	752	552	322	113	11	25	173	527	858	1,166	6,598
Cooling Degree Days (base 65°F)	0	0	0	0	14	66	210	162	32	0	0	0	484
Mean Precipitation (in.)	0.95	0.75	0.88	0.96	1.38	0.80	0.25	0.37	0.47	0.64	0.92	0.90	9.27
Extreme Maximum Daily Precip. (in.)	0.78	1.05	0.97	0.95	1.60	1.14	0.68	1.68	1.16	0.80	0.78	0.80	1.68
Days With ≥ 0.1" Precipitation	3	3	3	3	3	2	1	1	2	2	3	3	29
Days With ≥ 0.5" Precipitation	0	0	0	0	1	0	0	0	0	0	0	0	1
Days With ≥ 1.0" Precipitation	0	0	0	0	0	0	0	0	0	0	0	0	0
Mean Snowfall (in.)	***7.9***	3.6	***2.3***	1.8	0.1	0.0	0.0	0.0	0.0	0.4	1.7	5.4	***23.2***
Maximum Snow Depth (in.)	***18***	11	***9***	4	trace	3	0	0	0	***4***	***4***	***9***	***18***
Days With ≥ 1.0" Snow Depth	***13***	6	***0***	0	0	0	0	0	0	0	1	6	***26***

Blue Eagle Ranch Hanks *Nye County* Elevation: 4,779 ft. Latitude: 38° 31' N Longitude: 115° 33' W

	JAN	FEB	MAR	APR	MAY	JUN	JUL	AUG	SEP	OCT	NOV	DEC	YEAR
Mean Maximum Temp. (°F)	40.2	48.3	58.6	67.0	76.8	87.0	94.6	92.2	82.9	69.6	52.7	41.4	67.6
Mean Temp. (°F)	28.6	35.9	44.4	51.5	60.6	69.6	76.3	74.1	65.2	52.8	39.1	29.3	52.3
Mean Minimum Temp. (°F)	17.0	23.1	30.2	35.9	44.3	52.1	58.0	55.9	47.6	36.0	25.4	17.2	36.9
Extreme Maximum Temp. (°F)	63	73	82	92	101	107	109	110	100	93	78	67	110
Extreme Minimum Temp. (°F)	-20	-22	10	13	21	32	40	40	29	14	-9	-16	-22
Days Maximum Temp. ≥ 90°F	0	0	0	0	3	14	26	22	6	0	0	0	71
Days Maximum Temp. ≤ 32°F	6	2	0	0	0	0	0	0	0	0	1	5	14
Days Minimum Temp. ≤ 32°F	30	24	20	10	2	0	0	0	1	9	25	30	151
Days Minimum Temp. ≤ 0°F	3	1	0	0	0	0	0	0	0	0	0	1	5
Heating Degree Days (base 65°F)	1,121	814	631	401	172	35	1	1	69	373	771	1,100	5,489
Cooling Degree Days (base 65°F)	0	0	0	1	42	180	358	289	82	2	0	0	954
Mean Precipitation (in.)	0.70	0.71	0.88	0.89	1.00	0.46	0.51	0.72	0.66	0.89	0.67	0.48	8.57
Extreme Maximum Daily Precip. (in.)	0.76	0.73	0.76	1.11	1.05	0.84	0.73	1.39	1.22	1.11	***0.95***	0.81	***1.39***
Days With ≥ 0.1" Precipitation	2	3	3	3	3	1	2	2	2	2	2	2	27
Days With ≥ 0.5" Precipitation	0	0	0	0	1	0	0	0	0	1	0	0	2
Days With ≥ 1.0" Precipitation	0	0	0	0	0	0	0	0	0	0	0	0	0
Mean Snowfall (in.)	***0.8***	1.8	0.3	0.4	0.0	0.0	0.0	0.0	0.0	0.0	0.5	1.0	***4.8***
Maximum Snow Depth (in.)	12	13	6	9	0	0	0	0	0	0	6	9	13
Days With ≥ 1.0" Snow Depth	10	5	0	0	0	0	0	0	0	0	1	5	21

Denio *Humboldt County* Elevation: 4,189 ft. Latitude: 41° 59' N Longitude: 118° 38' W

	JAN	FEB	MAR	APR	MAY	JUN	JUL	AUG	SEP	OCT	NOV	DEC	YEAR
Mean Maximum Temp. (°F)	41.1	46.1	54.6	62.6	***71.3***	80.8	91.2	89.9	79.9	66.7	50.1	40.5	***64.6***
Mean Temp. (°F)	31.7	35.2	41.7	47.7	***55.2***	63.4	72.0	70.5	61.0	50.3	38.5	30.8	***49.8***
Mean Minimum Temp. (°F)	22.3	24.1	28.7	32.8	***39.0***	46.1	52.8	51.1	42.1	33.8	26.8	21.0	***35.0***
Extreme Maximum Temp. (°F)	67	76	78	90	96	102	107	107	98	92	75	62	107
Extreme Minimum Temp. (°F)	-14	-25	2	11	15	28	29	30	18	-2	-4	-22	-25
Days Maximum Temp. ≥ 90°F	0	0	0	0	1	6	20	18	4	0	0	0	49
Days Maximum Temp. ≤ 32°F	4	2	0	0	0	0	0	0	0	0	1	5	12
Days Minimum Temp. ≤ 32°F	26	23	21	15	6	1	0	0	3	13	21	27	156
Days Minimum Temp. ≤ 0°F	1	0	0	0	0	0	0	0	0	0	0	1	2
Heating Degree Days (base 65°F)	1,025	836	717	513	***310***	113	13	18	153	451	789	1,053	***5,991***
Cooling Degree Days (base 65°F)	0	0	0	0	***14***	73	237	196	41	1	0	0	***562***
Mean Precipitation (in.)	0.81	0.83	1.05	1.04	1.25	0.82	0.25	0.38	0.44	0.67	1.00	0.87	9.41
Extreme Maximum Daily Precip. (in.)	0.92	1.08	1.47	1.30	1.55	1.05	0.65	0.85	0.65	0.81	0.81	0.96	1.55
Days With ≥ 0.1" Precipitation	3	3	3	3	4	3	1	1	2	2	4	3	32
Days With ≥ 0.5" Precipitation	0	0	0	0	0	0	0	0	0	0	0	0	0
Days With ≥ 1.0" Precipitation	0	0	0	0	0	0	0	0	0	0	0	0	0
Mean Snowfall (in.)	4.7	2.7	2.0	***1.0***	0.1	0.0	0.0	0.0	trace	0.6	3.5	5.0	***19.6***
Maximum Snow Depth (in.)	12	12	***2***	trace	trace	0	0	0	0	***5***	8	9	***12***
Days With ≥ 1.0" Snow Depth	3	1	***0***	0	0	0	0	0	0	0	1	3	***8***

The period of record for all cooperative weather station data is 1980 – 2009. See User Guide for detailed explanation of data.

Desert Natl Wl Range *Clark County* Elevation: 2,919 ft. Latitude: 36° 26' N Longitude: 115° 22' W

	JAN	FEB	MAR	APR	MAY	JUN	JUL	AUG	SEP	OCT	NOV	DEC	YEAR
Mean Maximum Temp. (°F)	57.8	61.4	68.9	76.8	87.0	96.7	102.3	100.2	92.3	79.6	65.9	56.7	78.8
Mean Temp. (°F)	44.3	47.6	54.1	60.9	70.3	78.8	84.8	83.2	75.2	63.3	51.3	43.4	63.1
Mean Minimum Temp. (°F)	30.7	33.8	39.2	45.0	53.5	60.9	67.3	66.2	58.2	46.7	36.7	30.0	47.3
Extreme Maximum Temp. (°F)	76	87	96	102	107	112	117	114	107	100	85	78	117
Extreme Minimum Temp. (°F)	10	10	19	25	32	42	47	50	39	24	17	3	3
Days Maximum Temp. ≥ 90°F	0	0	0	3	13	24	30	30	20	4	0	0	124
Days Maximum Temp. ≤ 32°F	0	0	0	0	0	0	0	0	0	0	0	0	0
Days Minimum Temp. ≤ 32°F	20	12	4	1	0	0	0	0	0	0	8	20	65
Days Minimum Temp. ≤ 0°F	0	0	0	0	0	0	0	0	0	0	0	0	0
Heating Degree Days (base 65°F)	635	485	334	154	32	3	0	0	5	107	405	664	2,824
Cooling Degree Days (base 65°F)	0	0	4	38	201	424	621	572	319	60	1	0	2,240
Mean Precipitation (in.)	0.61	0.78	0.60	0.27	0.17	0.12	0.56	0.33	0.35	0.30	0.33	0.44	4.86
Extreme Maximum Daily Precip. (in.)	1.15	1.90	1.80	0.70	1.10	0.51	1.72	1.41	1.01	1.19	1.48	1.40	1.90
Days With ≥ 0.1" Precipitation	2	2	2	1	1	0	1	1	1	1	1	1	14
Days With ≥ 0.5" Precipitation	0	0	0	0	0	0	0	0	0	0	0	0	0
Days With ≥ 1.0" Precipitation	0	0	0	0	0	0	0	0	0	0	0	0	0
Mean Snowfall (in.)	trace	0.1	0.0	0.0	0.0	0.0	0.0	0.0	0.0	0.0	0.0	0.1	0.2
Maximum Snow Depth (in.)	0	2	0	1	0	0	0	0	0	0	0	3	3
Days With ≥ 1.0" Snow Depth	0	0	0	0	0	0	0	0	0	0	0	0	0

Dyer *Esmeralda County* Elevation: 4,898 ft. Latitude: 37° 41' N Longitude: 118° 05' W

	JAN	FEB	MAR	APR	MAY	JUN	JUL	AUG	SEP	OCT	NOV	DEC	YEAR
Mean Maximum Temp. (°F)	47.1	52.9	60.4	67.8	77.1	86.7	93.5	91.3	83.2	71.5	57.3	46.7	69.6
Mean Temp. (°F)	32.5	38.1	44.4	50.7	59.6	68.2	74.5	72.1	64.0	52.6	40.6	31.7	52.4
Mean Minimum Temp. (°F)	17.9	23.3	28.4	33.6	42.1	49.6	55.6	53.0	44.7	33.6	23.9	16.8	35.2
Extreme Maximum Temp. (°F)	68	76	81	90	98	102	107	105	98	93	82	69	107
Extreme Minimum Temp. (°F)	-14	-23	7	10	19	30	37	37	21	13	-3	-15	-23
Days Maximum Temp. ≥ 90°F	0	0	0	0	3	13	25	21	6	0	0	0	68
Days Maximum Temp. ≤ 32°F	2	1	0	0	0	0	0	0	0	0	0	1	4
Days Minimum Temp. ≤ 32°F	29	24	22	13	2	0	0	0	1	14	26	30	161
Days Minimum Temp. ≤ 0°F	1	0	0	0	0	0	0	0	0	0	0	1	2
Heating Degree Days (base 65°F)	1,001	754	631	422	189	37	1	2	83	379	725	1,024	5,248
Cooling Degree Days (base 65°F)	0	0	0	1	29	140	304	231	58	1	0	0	764
Mean Precipitation (in.)	0.55	0.60	0.46	0.47	0.50	0.33	0.37	0.37	0.35	0.30	0.44	0.32	5.06
Extreme Maximum Daily Precip. (in.)	1.98	0.94	0.84	1.24	0.73	0.95	1.07	2.05	1.60	0.82	1.31	0.92	2.05
Days With ≥ 0.1" Precipitation	1	2	1	1	1	1	1	1	1	1	1	1	13
Days With ≥ 0.5" Precipitation	0	0	0	0	0	0	0	0	0	0	0	0	0
Days With ≥ 1.0" Precipitation	0	0	0	0	0	0	0	0	0	0	0	0	0
Mean Snowfall (in.)	3.3	1.7	0.9	1.2	0.2	trace	0.0	0.0	0.1	trace	0.6	1.4	9.4
Maximum Snow Depth (in.)	7	3	5	3	trace	0	0	0	0	trace	8	4	8
Days With ≥ 1.0" Snow Depth	2	0	0	0	0	0	0	0	0	0	0	2	4

Eureka *Eureka County* Elevation: 6,540 ft. Latitude: 39° 31' N Longitude: 115° 58' W

	JAN	FEB	MAR	APR	MAY	JUN	JUL	AUG	SEP	OCT	NOV	DEC	YEAR
Mean Maximum Temp. (°F)	37.5	40.7	47.8	56.0	65.6	76.2	85.3	83.6	74.2	61.5	47.0	38.0	59.4
Mean Temp. (°F)	27.4	30.2	36.3	42.8	51.4	60.5	69.2	68.0	59.1	47.6	35.6	27.7	46.3
Mean Minimum Temp. (°F)	17.2	19.6	24.7	29.5	37.0	44.8	53.1	52.3	44.0	33.7	24.1	17.4	33.1
Extreme Maximum Temp. (°F)	58	64	75	80	91	93	98	96	90	85	72	63	98
Extreme Minimum Temp. (°F)	-17	-18	4	9	18	23	33	35	21	5	-11	-21	-21
Days Maximum Temp. ≥ 90°F	0	0	0	0	0	1	7	3	0	0	0	0	11
Days Maximum Temp. ≤ 32°F	9	6	2	1	0	0	0	0	0	0	3	8	29
Days Minimum Temp. ≤ 32°F	29	26	26	20	10	1	0	0	2	13	24	29	180
Days Minimum Temp. ≤ 0°F	2	1	0	0	0	0	0	0	0	0	0	1	4
Heating Degree Days (base 65°F)	1,159	978	884	662	420	165	18	24	191	532	877	1,150	7,060
Cooling Degree Days (base 65°F)	0	0	0	0	4	36	156	123	22	0	0	0	341
Mean Precipitation (in.)	1.07	1.03	1.37	1.23	1.31	0.63	0.53	0.80	0.88	0.96	0.80	0.83	11.44
Extreme Maximum Daily Precip. (in.)	1.00	1.32	1.85	***1.27***	1.65	1.63	1.06	1.63	1.71	1.40	1.23	1.19	***1.85***
Days With ≥ 0.1" Precipitation	3	3	4	3	3	2	1	2	2	2	2	2	29
Days With ≥ 0.5" Precipitation	0	0	1	1	1	0	0	1	1	1	0	0	6
Days With ≥ 1.0" Precipitation	0	0	0	0	0	0	0	0	0	0	0	0	0
Mean Snowfall (in.)	***4.8***	2.5	4.8	2.9	1.5	0.0	0.0	0.0	0.5	0.6	2.1	***4.6***	***24.3***
Maximum Snow Depth (in.)	na	na	na	na	***7***	***0***	***0***	***0***	***0***	na	na	na	na
Days With ≥ 1.0" Snow Depth	na	na	***0***	0	0	0	0	0	0	0	na	***1***	na

Fallon Experiment Stn *Churchill County* Elevation: 3,964 ft. Latitude: 39° 27' N Longitude: 118° 47' W

	JAN	FEB	MAR	APR	MAY	JUN	JUL	AUG	SEP	OCT	NOV	DEC	YEAR
Mean Maximum Temp. (°F)	44.6	52.1	59.6	65.6	74.3	83.1	92.2	90.3	81.2	69.1	54.9	44.7	67.6
Mean Temp. (°F)	32.5	38.3	44.5	50.3	58.5	66.0	73.5	71.3	62.7	51.7	40.5	32.2	51.8
Mean Minimum Temp. (°F)	20.3	24.4	29.5	34.9	42.6	48.9	54.7	52.3	44.1	34.3	26.0	19.6	36.0
Extreme Maximum Temp. (°F)	71	76	81	90	98	100	108	104	100	89	77	69	108
Extreme Minimum Temp. (°F)	-15	-27	11	16	23	32	36	35	23	12	1	-21	-27
Days Maximum Temp. ≥ 90°F	0	0	0	0	2	9	22	18	5	0	0	0	56
Days Maximum Temp. ≤ 32°F	3	1	0	0	0	0	0	0	0	0	0	3	7
Days Minimum Temp. ≤ 32°F	29	23	20	11	2	0	0	0	1	12	23	27	148
Days Minimum Temp. ≤ 0°F	0	0	0	0	0	0	0	0	0	0	0	1	1
Heating Degree Days (base 65°F)	1,001	749	627	434	223	72	6	9	115	407	730	1,011	5,384
Cooling Degree Days (base 65°F)	0	0	0	1	27	108	275	211	52	2	0	0	676
Mean Precipitation (in.)	0.63	0.47	0.46	0.59	0.67	0.41	0.11	0.18	0.30	0.31	0.45	0.42	5.00
Extreme Maximum Daily Precip. (in.)	1.31	1.00	0.84	1.06	1.55	1.00	0.50	0.65	0.77	0.48	0.79	0.73	1.55
Days With ≥ 0.1" Precipitation	2	2	1	2	2	1	0	1	1	1	1	1	15
Days With ≥ 0.5" Precipitation	0	0	0	0	0	0	0	0	0	0	0	0	0
Days With ≥ 1.0" Precipitation	0	0	0	0	0	0	0	0	0	0	0	0	0
Mean Snowfall (in.)	2.2	1.1	***0.8***	trace	trace	0.0	0.0	0.0	0.0	0.0	0.2	***1.7***	***6.0***
Maximum Snow Depth (in.)	***8***	***11***	***4***	3	***0***	***0***	***0***	***0***	***0***	***0***	***4***	na	na
Days With ≥ 1.0" Snow Depth	***4***	***1***	0	0	0	0	0	0	0	0	***0***	***2***	***7***

Gerlach *Washoe County* Elevation: 3,950 ft. Latitude: 40° 39' N Longitude: 119° 21' W

	JAN	FEB	MAR	APR	MAY	JUN	JUL	AUG	SEP	OCT	NOV	DEC	YEAR
Mean Maximum Temp. (°F)	41.1	47.0	57.0	63.8	72.7	81.8	91.4	90.0	81.0	68.6	51.9	40.4	65.6
Mean Temp. (°F)	31.6	36.4	44.3	50.2	59.0	67.3	75.5	73.6	64.2	52.7	39.3	30.3	52.0
Mean Minimum Temp. (°F)	21.9	25.7	31.6	36.6	45.2	52.8	59.6	57.1	47.4	36.8	26.7	20.2	38.5
Extreme Maximum Temp. (°F)	64	68	81	89	99	102	112	106	101	92	76	64	112
Extreme Minimum Temp. (°F)	-6	-13	2	16	26	34	37	40	29	15	4	-16	-16
Days Maximum Temp. ≥ 90°F	0	0	0	0	2	7	20	18	5	0	0	0	52
Days Maximum Temp. ≤ 32°F	5	2	0	0	0	0	0	0	0	0	1	5	13
Days Minimum Temp. ≤ 32°F	27	23	17	8	1	0	0	0	0	7	23	28	134
Days Minimum Temp. ≤ 0°F	0	0	0	0	0	0	0	0	0	0	0	1	1
Heating Degree Days (base 65°F)	1,030	802	633	438	221	63	4	6	96	377	764	1,069	5,503
Cooling Degree Days (base 65°F)	0	0	0	2	41	139	338	279	80	3	0	0	882
Mean Precipitation (in.)	1.04	0.76	0.73	0.68	1.01	0.63	0.33	0.22	0.32	0.32	0.90	0.84	7.78
Extreme Maximum Daily Precip. (in.)	1.30	0.67	0.83	1.02	2.20	0.97	0.86	0.80	0.75	0.68	0.77	0.96	2.20
Days With ≥ 0.1" Precipitation	3	3	3	2	2	2	1	1	1	1	2	3	24
Days With ≥ 0.5" Precipitation	0	0	0	0	1	0	0	0	0	0	0	0	1
Days With ≥ 1.0" Precipitation	0	0	0	0	0	0	0	0	0	0	0	0	0
Mean Snowfall (in.)	3.5	2.1	1.1	0.3	trace	0.0	0.0	0.0	0.0	trace	1.5	3.2	11.7
Maximum Snow Depth (in.)	na	na	na	na	na	na	na	na	na	na	na	na	na
Days With ≥ 1.0" Snow Depth	na	2	0	0	0	0	0	0	0	0	0	4	na

Gibbs Ranch *Elko County* Elevation: 6,000 ft. Latitude: 41° 33' N Longitude: 115° 13' W

	JAN	FEB	MAR	APR	MAY	JUN	JUL	AUG	SEP	OCT	NOV	DEC	YEAR
Mean Maximum Temp. (°F)	35.2	38.6	46.7	56.2	64.8	74.7	85.3	84.1	75.2	62.4	46.0	36.5	58.8
Mean Temp. (°F)	22.3	25.5	34.0	41.5	49.2	57.3	65.9	64.2	55.9	44.8	32.4	23.7	43.1
Mean Minimum Temp. (°F)	9.3	12.5	21.3	26.9	33.6	39.9	46.3	44.1	36.5	26.9	18.8	10.7	27.2
Extreme Maximum Temp. (°F)	57	62	75	81	90	94	101	99	93	86	72	59	101
Extreme Minimum Temp. (°F)	-28	-33	-9	4	13	22	21	23	15	-3	-16	-38	-38
Days Maximum Temp. ≥ 90°F	0	0	0	0	0	1	8	5	0	0	0	0	14
Days Maximum Temp. ≤ 32°F	10	7	1	0	0	0	0	0	0	0	3	9	30
Days Minimum Temp. ≤ 32°F	30	27	28	23	13	4	0	1	8	23	27	29	213
Days Minimum Temp. ≤ 0°F	7	4	0	0	0	0	0	0	0	0	1	6	18
Heating Degree Days (base 65°F)	1,317	1,107	951	692	484	235	53	72	274	620	970	1,272	8,047
Cooling Degree Days (base 65°F)	0	0	0	0	1	11	88	53	7	0	0	0	160
Mean Precipitation (in.)	1.13	0.80	0.92	0.86	1.44	1.02	0.67	0.47	0.61	0.66	1.15	1.10	10.83
Extreme Maximum Daily Precip. (in.)	0.84	0.94	0.88	1.07	1.65	1.21	0.95	1.17	na	0.73	0.90	0.77	na
Days With ≥ 0.1" Precipitation	3	3	3	3	4	3	2	2	1	2	3	3	32
Days With ≥ 0.5" Precipitation	0	0	0	0	1	0	0	0	0	0	0	0	1
Days With ≥ 1.0" Precipitation	0	0	0	0	0	0	0	0	0	0	0	0	0
Mean Snowfall (in.)	5.6	2.7	3.2	1.0	0.4	0.0	0.0	0.0	0.0	0.2	1.6	3.8	18.5
Maximum Snow Depth (in.)	na	20	14	na	4	0	0	0	0	2	12	na	na
Days With ≥ 1.0" Snow Depth	na	4	1	0	0	0	0	0	0	0	1	5	na

Imlay *Pershing County* Elevation: 4,259 ft. Latitude: 40° 39' N Longitude: 118° 09' W

	JAN	FEB	MAR	APR	MAY	JUN	JUL	AUG	SEP	OCT	NOV	DEC	YEAR
Mean Maximum Temp. (°F)	42.1	48.8	57.3	63.4	72.8	82.1	92.1	90.5	80.8	68.3	52.5	42.1	66.1
Mean Temp. (°F)	30.6	36.3	43.0	48.7	57.6	66.3	74.9	72.3	62.8	50.9	38.4	29.9	51.0
Mean Minimum Temp. (°F)	19.1	23.8	28.6	33.9	42.3	50.5	57.6	54.1	44.8	33.5	24.1	17.6	35.8
Extreme Maximum Temp. (°F)	68	74	82	87	99	101	107	105	100	94	80	66	107
Extreme Minimum Temp. (°F)	-12	-19	9	11	16	30	39	36	24	10	-3	-32	-32
Days Maximum Temp. ≥ 90°F	0	0	0	0	1	8	21	19	6	0	0	0	55
Days Maximum Temp. ≤ 32°F	5	1	0	0	0	0	0	0	0	0	1	5	12
Days Minimum Temp. ≤ 32°F	28	24	21	12	3	0	0	0	2	14	25	28	157
Days Minimum Temp. ≤ 0°F	1	0	0	0	0	0	0	0	0	0	0	1	2
Heating Degree Days (base 65°F)	1,058	803	677	483	250	77	5	10	124	434	793	1,083	5,797
Cooling Degree Days (base 65°F)	0	0	0	1	28	124	318	240	64	4	0	0	779
Mean Precipitation (in.)	0.86	0.76	0.92	0.94	1.11	0.64	0.17	0.21	0.41	0.55	0.75	0.85	8.17
Extreme Maximum Daily Precip. (in.)	0.80	0.83	1.12	0.90	1.17	0.90	0.39	0.62	0.60	0.60	1.05	0.72	1.17
Days With ≥ 0.1" Precipitation	3	3	3	3	3	2	1	1	1	2	2	3	27
Days With ≥ 0.5" Precipitation	0	0	0	0	0	0	0	0	0	0	0	0	0
Days With ≥ 1.0" Precipitation	0	0	0	0	0	0	0	0	0	0	0	0	0
Mean Snowfall (in.)	2.6	0.9	0.8	0.5	0.0	0.0	0.0	0.0	trace	0.3	0.6	3.7	9.4
Maximum Snow Depth (in.)	10	5	trace	2	trace	0	0	0	0	trace	3	10	10
Days With ≥ 1.0" Snow Depth	3	1	0	0	0	0	0	0	0	0	0	3	7

Kings River Valley *Humboldt County* Elevation: 4,240 ft. Latitude: 41° 45' N Longitude: 118° 14' W

	JAN	FEB	MAR	APR	MAY	JUN	JUL	AUG	SEP	OCT	NOV	DEC	YEAR
Mean Maximum Temp. (°F)	39.9	46.0	55.1	63.8	72.7	81.8	91.6	90.4	80.8	67.8	50.9	39.9	65.1
Mean Temp. (°F)	28.3	33.8	41.2	47.7	55.7	63.6	71.9	70.2	61.3	50.0	37.0	28.4	49.1
Mean Minimum Temp. (°F)	16.7	21.5	27.2	31.5	38.9	45.2	52.2	49.9	41.7	32.1	23.2	16.8	33.1
Extreme Maximum Temp. (°F)	64	73	80	89	98	103	109	110	101	93	74	61	110
Extreme Minimum Temp. (°F)	-12	-24	-2	9	16	25	32	29	20	3	-12	-27	-27
Days Maximum Temp. ≥ 90°F	0	0	0	0	2	7	21	17	5	0	0	0	52
Days Maximum Temp. ≤ 32°F	5	2	0	0	0	0	0	0	0	0	1	5	13
Days Minimum Temp. ≤ 32°F	29	25	23	16	6	1	0	0	3	16	24	26	169
Days Minimum Temp. ≤ 0°F	2	1	0	0	0	0	0	0	0	0	0	2	5
Heating Degree Days (base 65°F)	1,132	875	731	514	294	107	12	12	142	458	832	1,130	6,239
Cooling Degree Days (base 65°F)	0	0	0	0	16	72	234	188	37	1	0	0	548
Mean Precipitation (in.)	1.04	0.87	0.71	0.80	0.95	0.59	0.25	0.16	0.41	0.57	0.89	1.22	8.46
Extreme Maximum Daily Precip. (in.)	0.70	0.90	0.71	1.06	0.98	0.85	0.95	0.50	0.99	1.14	0.74	na	na
Days With ≥ 0.1" Precipitation	3	3	2	2	2	1	1	1	1	2	3	3	24
Days With ≥ 0.5" Precipitation	0	0	0	0	0	0	0	0	0	0	0	0	0
Days With ≥ 1.0" Precipitation	0	0	0	0	0	0	0	0	0	0	0	0	0
Mean Snowfall (in.)	6.1	3.7	0.8	0.3	trace	0.0	0.0	0.0	0.0	0.3	2.6	6.5	20.3
Maximum Snow Depth (in.)	17	9	5	2	trace	0	0	0	0	2	9	13	17
Days With ≥ 1.0" Snow Depth	6	3	1	0	0	0	0	0	0	0	1	4	15

The period of record for all cooperative weather station data is 1980 – 2009. See User Guide for detailed explanation of data.

Lages *White Pine County* Elevation: 5,959 ft. Latitude: 40° 04' N Longitude: 114° 37' W

	JAN	FEB	MAR	APR	MAY	JUN	JUL	AUG	SEP	OCT	NOV	DEC	YEAR
Mean Maximum Temp. (°F)	39.3	43.0	52.2	60.0	70.4	80.4	89.4	87.9	77.4	64.3	49.6	39.6	62.8
Mean Temp. (°F)	26.5	30.5	38.4	45.0	54.0	62.7	71.0	69.4	59.1	47.6	35.7	26.5	47.2
Mean Minimum Temp. (°F)	13.6	17.9	24.5	30.0	37.7	45.0	52.6	50.9	40.8	30.7	21.9	13.4	31.6
Extreme Maximum Temp. (°F)	66	76	78	83	94	98	103	100	92	88	78	65	103
Extreme Minimum Temp. (°F)	-23	-26	0	8	14	24	36	34	18	1	-7	-21	-26
Days Maximum Temp. ≥ 90°F	0	0	0	0	0	5	16	13	1	0	0	0	35
Days Maximum Temp. ≤ 32°F	7	4	1	0	0	0	0	0	0	0	2	7	21
Days Minimum Temp. ≤ 32°F	30	26	27	20	7	1	0	0	4	18	26	30	189
Days Minimum Temp. ≤ 0°F	4	2	0	0	0	0	0	0	0	0	1	4	11
Heating Degree Days (base 65°F)	1,188	969	817	593	338	120	8	15	189	533	871	1,186	6,827
Cooling Degree Days (base 65°F)	0	0	0	0	5	59	202	158	20	0	0	0	444
Mean Precipitation (in.)	0.62	0.60	0.77	0.95	0.87	0.70	0.69	0.43	0.63	0.92	0.51	0.40	8.09
Extreme Maximum Daily Precip. (in.)	0.59	0.55	1.71	1.18	1.00	1.20	1.06	0.92	1.28	1.35	0.74	0.75	1.71
Days With ≥ 0.1" Precipitation	2	2	2	3	3	2	2	1	2	2	2	1	24
Days With ≥ 0.5" Precipitation	0	0	0	0	0	0	0	0	0	0	0	0	0
Days With ≥ 1.0" Precipitation	0	0	0	0	0	0	0	0	0	0	0	0	0
Mean Snowfall (in.)	6.6	4.8	2.5	1.1	0.2	0.0	0.0	0.0	0.0	0.5	1.6	4.0	21.3
Maximum Snow Depth (in.)	24	12	na	3	2	0	0	0	0	2	7	10	na
Days With ≥ 1.0" Snow Depth	10	8	2	0	0	0	0	0	0	0	2	6	28

Lovelock *Pershing County* Elevation: 3,975 ft. Latitude: 40° 11' N Longitude: 118° 28' W

	JAN	FEB	MAR	APR	MAY	JUN	JUL	AUG	SEP	OCT	NOV	DEC	YEAR
Mean Maximum Temp. (°F)	41.9	49.7	58.5	65.7	74.7	84.0	92.8	90.9	81.4	68.3	52.9	42.6	67.0
Mean Temp. (°F)	30.7	36.9	43.5	49.8	58.4	66.5	73.9	71.7	63.0	51.4	39.0	30.7	51.3
Mean Minimum Temp. (°F)	19.3	24.1	28.4	33.8	42.1	48.9	54.9	52.6	44.5	34.4	24.9	18.7	35.6
Extreme Maximum Temp. (°F)	65	76	80	91	98	106	108	104	97	92	76	68	108
Extreme Minimum Temp. (°F)	-12	-21	9	11	19	32	38	36	25	12	-1	-23	-23
Days Maximum Temp. ≥ 90°F	0	0	0	0	2	10	23	20	5	0	0	0	60
Days Maximum Temp. ≤ 32°F	5	1	0	0	0	0	0	0	0	0	0	3	9
Days Minimum Temp. ≤ 32°F	29	24	22	13	3	0	0	0	1	12	25	29	158
Days Minimum Temp. ≤ 0°F	1	0	0	0	0	0	0	0	0	0	0	1	2
Heating Degree Days (base 65°F)	1,058	786	660	450	223	62	4	7	106	418	774	1,057	5,605
Cooling Degree Days (base 65°F)	0	0	0	1	27	114	286	223	53	2	0	0	706
Mean Precipitation (in.)	0.68	0.51	0.50	0.61	0.79	0.59	0.15	0.19	0.40	0.48	0.56	0.62	6.08
Extreme Maximum Daily Precip. (in.)	1.16	0.59	0.72	0.86	1.35	1.10	0.46	0.66	1.06	0.75	0.70	0.87	1.35
Days With ≥ 0.1" Precipitation	2	2	2	2	2	2	1	1	1	2	2	2	21
Days With ≥ 0.5" Precipitation	0	0	0	0	0	0	0	0	0	0	0	0	0
Days With ≥ 1.0" Precipitation	0	0	0	0	0	0	0	0	0	0	0	0	0
Mean Snowfall (in.)	4.3	2.4	0.9	0.5	0.0	0.0	0.0	0.0	0.0	0.1	0.9	2.8	11.9
Maximum Snow Depth (in.)	12	6	1	trace	0	0	0	0	0	3	4	7	12
Days With ≥ 1.0" Snow Depth	6	2	0	0	0	0	0	0	0	0	1	3	12

Lovelock Derby Field *Pershing County* Elevation: 3,899 ft. Latitude: 40° 04' N Longitude: 118° 33' W

	JAN	FEB	MAR	APR	MAY	JUN	JUL	AUG	SEP	OCT	NOV	DEC	YEAR
Mean Maximum Temp. (°F)	43.6	50.8	59.5	66.2	76.1	85.6	96.2	93.5	84.0	70.0	54.7	43.9	68.7
Mean Temp. (°F)	31.0	37.0	43.6	50.1	59.5	67.7	76.1	73.1	64.1	51.4	38.8	30.6	51.9
Mean Minimum Temp. (°F)	18.3	23.2	27.7	34.0	42.8	49.8	55.9	52.7	44.1	32.7	22.9	17.4	35.1
Extreme Maximum Temp. (°F)	66	73	83	91	102	106	112	107	102	91	76	72	112
Extreme Minimum Temp. (°F)	-19	-25	4	11	17	30	39	32	24	12	-3	-28	-28
Days Maximum Temp. ≥ 90°F	0	0	0	0	3	13	26	24	10	0	0	0	76
Days Maximum Temp. ≤ 32°F	3	1	0	0	0	0	0	0	0	0	0	3	7
Days Minimum Temp. ≤ 32°F	29	24	22	12	2	0	0	0	2	15	26	29	161
Days Minimum Temp. ≤ 0°F	1	0	0	0	0	0	0	0	0	0	0	1	2
Heating Degree Days (base 65°F)	1,047	784	656	440	206	55	2	5	91	416	779	1,059	5,540
Cooling Degree Days (base 65°F)	0	0	0	1	41	144	351	264	70	2	0	0	873
Mean Precipitation (in.)	0.61	0.48	0.47	0.54	0.64	0.51	0.06	0.27	0.28	0.37	0.46	0.55	5.24
Extreme Maximum Daily Precip. (in.)	0.75	0.48	0.54	1.17	1.13	0.92	0.30	0.87	0.71	0.87	1.07	0.73	1.17
Days With ≥ 0.1" Precipitation	2	2	2	2	2	1	0	1	1	1	1	2	17
Days With ≥ 0.5" Precipitation	0	0	0	0	0	0	0	0	0	0	0	0	0
Days With ≥ 1.0" Precipitation	0	0	0	0	0	0	0	0	0	0	0	0	0
Mean Snowfall (in.)	na	na	na	na	na	na	na	na	na	na	na	na	na
Maximum Snow Depth (in.)	na	na	na	na	na	na	na	na	na	na	na	na	na
Days With ≥ 1.0" Snow Depth	na	na	na	na	na	na	na	na	na	na	na	na	na

Lund *White Pine County* Elevation: 5,569 ft. Latitude: 38° 52' N Longitude: 115° 00' W

	JAN	FEB	MAR	APR	MAY	JUN	JUL	AUG	SEP	OCT	NOV	DEC	YEAR
Mean Maximum Temp. (°F)	43.3	47.1	54.7	62.4	71.6	81.5	89.2	87.4	79.1	67.0	52.8	43.6	65.0
Mean Temp. (°F)	29.4	33.2	39.7	45.9	54.3	62.7	69.7	68.1	60.1	49.2	37.4	29.1	48.2
Mean Minimum Temp. (°F)	15.6	19.3	24.6	29.4	36.9	43.7	50.2	48.8	41.1	31.3	21.9	14.6	31.5
Extreme Maximum Temp. (°F)	64	75	81	83	94	99	102	101	93	88	75	69	102
Extreme Minimum Temp. (°F)	-13	-12	-2	-3	15	23	33	34	19	11	-4	-18	-18
Days Maximum Temp. ≥ 90°F	0	0	0	0	1	5	15	10	1	0	0	0	32
Days Maximum Temp. ≤ 32°F	4	2	0	0	0	0	0	0	0	0	1	4	11
Days Minimum Temp. ≤ 32°F	30	27	27	20	8	1	0	0	3	18	27	30	191
Days Minimum Temp. ≤ 0°F	2	1	0	0	0	0	0	0	0	0	0	2	5
Heating Degree Days (base 65°F)	1,096	891	778	566	331	112	13	18	160	483	823	1,106	6,377
Cooling Degree Days (base 65°F)	0	0	0	0	4	48	166	123	19	0	0	0	360
Mean Precipitation (in.)	0.93	0.93	1.10	0.98	1.01	0.78	0.64	0.96	0.91	1.05	0.77	0.65	10.71
Extreme Maximum Daily Precip. (in.)	1.12	1.05	1.10	1.10	1.30	1.52	1.03	1.20	1.04	1.41	1.15	0.75	1.52
Days With ≥ 0.1" Precipitation	3	3	3	2	3	2	2	3	2	2	2	2	29
Days With ≥ 0.5" Precipitation	0	0	0	1	0	0	0	0	1	1	0	0	3
Days With ≥ 1.0" Precipitation	0	0	0	0	0	0	0	0	0	0	0	0	0
Mean Snowfall (in.)	2.4	3.2	2.0	0.7	0.2	0.0	0.0	0.0	0.0	0.1	1.9	3.2	13.7
Maximum Snow Depth (in.)	8	na	6	11	trace	0	0	0	0	7	8	na	na
Days With ≥ 1.0" Snow Depth	4	3	1	0	0	0	0	0	0	0	1	4	13

The period of record for all cooperative weather station data is 1980 – 2009. See User Guide for detailed explanation of data.

Montello 1 SE *Elko County* Elevation: 4,899 ft. Latitude: 41° 15' N Longitude: 114° 11' W

	JAN	FEB	MAR	APR	MAY	JUN	JUL	AUG	SEP	OCT	NOV	DEC	YEAR
Mean Maximum Temp. (°F)	36.6	41.4	***53.1***	61.7	71.6	82.3	93.0	91.0	80.0	65.8	49.5	38.0	***63.7***
Mean Temp. (°F)	23.2	27.6	***38.0***	44.7	53.6	62.6	71.1	68.8	58.6	46.1	34.0	23.6	***46.0***
Mean Minimum Temp. (°F)	9.8	13.8	***22.9***	27.8	35.6	42.8	49.1	46.7	37.1	26.4	18.4	9.2	***28.3***
Extreme Maximum Temp. (°F)	63	68	79	86	98	103	107	108	98	89	74	69	108
Extreme Minimum Temp. (°F)	-27	-25	***3***	4	12	22	32	25	13	-6	-13	-29	***-29***
Days Maximum Temp. ≥ 90°F	0	0	0	0	1	8	22	20	4	0	0	0	55
Days Maximum Temp. ≤ 32°F	9	5	0	0	0	0	0	0	0	0	1	7	22
Days Minimum Temp. ≤ 32°F	31	26	28	22	10	1	0	0	8	24	27	30	207
Days Minimum Temp. ≤ 0°F	7	4	0	0	0	0	0	0	0	0	1	6	18
Heating Degree Days (base 65°F)	1,288	1,051	***831***	602	352	123	13	21	206	579	924	1,275	***7,265***
Cooling Degree Days (base 65°F)	0	0	***0***	0	6	58	209	147	19	0	0	0	***439***
Mean Precipitation (in.)	0.73	0.52	***0.70***	0.74	1.06	0.86	0.68	0.51	0.72	0.57	0.57	0.46	***8.12***
Extreme Maximum Daily Precip. (in.)	0.98	0.82	***0.72***	***1.01***	***0.98***	***0.88***	***0.80***	0.98	1.15	0.76	***0.73***	***1.02***	***1.15***
Days With ≥ 0.1" Precipitation	2	2	2	2	3	3	2	2	2	2	2	2	26
Days With ≥ 0.5" Precipitation	0	0	0	0	0	0	0	0	0	0	0	0	0
Days With ≥ 1.0" Precipitation	0	0	0	0	0	0	0	0	0	0	0	0	0
Mean Snowfall (in.)	***2.2***	***1.2***	***0.6***	***0.4***	0.0	trace	0.0	0.0	0.0	0.1	***0.2***	na	na
Maximum Snow Depth (in.)	na	na	***6***	na	***0***	***trace***	***0***	***0***	***0***	***2***	na	na	na
Days With ≥ 1.0" Snow Depth	na	na	***0***	***0***	0	0	0	0	0	0	***0***	***4***	na

Pahranagat W L Refuge *Lincoln County* Elevation: 3,399 ft. Latitude: 37° 16' N Longitude: 115° 07' W

	JAN	FEB	MAR	APR	MAY	JUN	JUL	AUG	SEP	OCT	NOV	DEC	YEAR
Mean Maximum Temp. (°F)	***53.6***	***58.5***	***65.7***	***73.6***	83.5	***93.8***	***99.7***	***97.8***	89.9	***77.4***	63.2	***52.9***	***75.8***
Mean Temp. (°F)	***40.8***	***45.1***	***51.1***	***57.9***	67.0	***76.2***	***82.4***	***80.6***	72.5	***60.7***	48.5	***40.0***	***60.2***
Mean Minimum Temp. (°F)	***28.1***	***31.6***	***36.5***	***42.1***	50.4	***58.6***	***65.1***	***63.3***	55.0	***44.0***	33.8	***27.0***	***44.6***
Extreme Maximum Temp. (°F)	71	83	88	95	105	110	113	111	106	102	86	74	113
Extreme Minimum Temp. (°F)	7	4	15	19	31	40	46	49	36	23	11	-1	-1
Days Maximum Temp. ≥ 90°F	0	0	0	1	7	20	28	27	17	2	0	0	102
Days Maximum Temp. ≤ 32°F	0	0	0	0	0	0	0	0	0	0	0	0	0
Days Minimum Temp. ≤ 32°F	23	15	8	2	0	0	0	0	0	1	12	24	85
Days Minimum Temp. ≤ 0°F	0	0	0	0	0	0	0	0	0	0	0	0	0
Heating Degree Days (base 65°F)	***742***	***556***	***424***	***224***	64	***5***	***0***	***0***	13	***164***	488	***768***	***3,448***
Cooling Degree Days (base 65°F)	***0***	***0***	***1***	***17***	132	***349***	***547***	***489***	245	***38***	0	***0***	***1,818***
Mean Precipitation (in.)	0.78	0.76	0.79	0.53	0.38	0.14	0.43	0.68	0.36	0.47	0.54	0.48	6.34
Extreme Maximum Daily Precip. (in.)	1.06	1.15	***0.80***	1.20	***0.72***	0.63	1.66	1.73	0.94	1.00	0.94	***0.92***	***1.73***
Days With ≥ 0.1" Precipitation	2	2	2	1	1	0	1	1	1	1	2	1	15
Days With ≥ 0.5" Precipitation	0	0	0	0	0	0	0	0	0	0	0	0	0
Days With ≥ 1.0" Precipitation	0	0	0	0	0	0	0	0	0	0	0	0	0
Mean Snowfall (in.)	0.5	0.2	trace	0.0	0.0	0.0	0.0	0.0	0.0	0.0	0.3	0.7	1.7
Maximum Snow Depth (in.)	2	trace	0	0	0	0	0	0	0	0	trace	3	3
Days With ≥ 1.0" Snow Depth	0	0	0	0	0	0	0	0	0	0	0	0	0

Pahrump *Nye County* Elevation: 2,673 ft. Latitude: 36° 17' N Longitude: 116° 00' W

	JAN	FEB	MAR	APR	MAY	JUN	JUL	AUG	SEP	OCT	NOV	DEC	YEAR
Mean Maximum Temp. (°F)	58.4	62.1	68.4	75.8	85.3	94.8	100.8	99.4	92.4	80.8	67.4	57.6	78.6
Mean Temp. (°F)	43.5	47.5	53.6	60.1	69.4	78.0	84.3	82.8	74.9	62.9	51.1	42.4	62.5
Mean Minimum Temp. (°F)	28.5	32.8	38.7	44.4	53.4	61.1	67.8	66.1	57.4	45.0	34.6	27.2	46.4
Extreme Maximum Temp. (°F)	76	85	90	97	107	110	113	111	106	101	87	77	113
Extreme Minimum Temp. (°F)	6	6	19	18	30	38	50	46	39	21	11	-2	-2
Days Maximum Temp. ≥ 90°F	0	0	0	2	11	24	30	30	21	5	0	0	123
Days Maximum Temp. ≤ 32°F	0	0	0	0	0	0	0	0	0	0	0	0	0
Days Minimum Temp. ≤ 32°F	23	14	6	1	0	0	0	0	0	1	10	24	79
Days Minimum Temp. ≤ 0°F	0	0	0	0	0	0	0	0	0	0	0	0	0
Heating Degree Days (base 65°F)	660	489	350	174	44	4	0	0	7	116	413	697	2,954
Cooling Degree Days (base 65°F)	0	0	3	35	186	400	607	557	312	58	0	0	2,158
Mean Precipitation (in.)	0.72	0.88	0.66	0.32	0.19	0.07	0.42	0.40	0.32	0.22	0.39	0.47	5.06
Extreme Maximum Daily Precip. (in.)	1.22	1.42	1.03	1.44	0.49	0.44	2.00	1.95	2.70	1.08	1.04	1.12	2.70
Days With ≥ 0.1" Precipitation	2	2	2	1	1	0	1	1	1	1	1	1	14
Days With ≥ 0.5" Precipitation	0	1	0	0	0	0	0	0	0	0	0	0	1
Days With ≥ 1.0" Precipitation	0	0	0	0	0	0	0	0	0	0	0	0	0
Mean Snowfall (in.)	trace	trace	trace	0.0	0.0	0.0	0.0	0.0	0.0	trace	0.0	0.1	0.1
Maximum Snow Depth (in.)	2	trace	trace	0	0	0	0	0	0	trace	0	2	2
Days With ≥ 1.0" Snow Depth	0	0	0	0	0	0	0	0	0	0	0	0	0

Reese River O'Toole *Nye County* Elevation: 6,549 ft. Latitude: 39° 04' N Longitude: 117° 25' W

	JAN	FEB	MAR	APR	MAY	JUN	JUL	AUG	SEP	OCT	NOV	DEC	YEAR
Mean Maximum Temp. (°F)	41.1	43.8	49.7	56.7	66.0	75.9	84.8	83.0	74.5	62.7	50.1	41.4	60.8
Mean Temp. (°F)	26.6	30.0	35.5	40.5	48.5	56.2	63.6	61.7	53.7	43.4	33.9	26.3	43.3
Mean Minimum Temp. (°F)	12.0	16.3	21.3	24.4	31.0	36.5	42.3	40.4	32.9	24.1	17.6	11.2	25.8
Extreme Maximum Temp. (°F)	65	68	78	82	90	100	98	96	91	86	76	67	100
Extreme Minimum Temp. (°F)	-21	-25	-6	3	10	18	23	24	14	-2	-18	-34	-34
Days Maximum Temp. ≥ 90°F	0	0	0	0	0	1	6	2	0	0	0	0	9
Days Maximum Temp. ≤ 32°F	6	3	2	0	0	0	0	0	0	0	2	6	19
Days Minimum Temp. ≤ 32°F	30	27	29	26	18	7	1	3	15	27	27	30	240
Days Minimum Temp. ≤ 0°F	5	2	0	0	0	0	0	0	0	0	2	5	14
Heating Degree Days (base 65°F)	1,184	984	907	728	505	263	78	115	334	661	926	1,192	7,877
Cooling Degree Days (base 65°F)	0	0	0	0	1	6	42	21	1	0	0	0	71
Mean Precipitation (in.)	0.62	0.53	0.67	0.81	1.00	0.66	0.51	0.59	0.45	0.61	0.64	0.48	7.57
Extreme Maximum Daily Precip. (in.)	0.98	0.43	0.58	1.08	0.98	0.88	0.59	1.07	1.18	0.85	0.82	1.02	1.18
Days With ≥ 0.1" Precipitation	2	2	2	3	3	2	2	2	1	2	2	2	25
Days With ≥ 0.5" Precipitation	0	0	0	0	0	0	0	0	0	0	0	0	0
Days With ≥ 1.0" Precipitation	0	0	0	0	0	0	0	0	0	0	0	0	0
Mean Snowfall (in.)	***7.6***	***6.7***	***5.1***	5.8	1.6	0.2	0.0	0.0	trace	***1.8***	***3.9***	5.6	***38.3***
Maximum Snow Depth (in.)	***12***	***10***	***10***	8	***7***	***3***	***0***	***0***	trace	***6***	***12***	***9***	***12***
Days With ≥ 1.0" Snow Depth	***15***	***9***	***4***	2	1	0	0	0	0	1	***4***	***11***	***47***

The period of record for all cooperative weather station data is 1980 – 2009. See User Guide for detailed explanation of data.

Searchlight *Clark County* Elevation: 3,540 ft. Latitude: 35° 28' N Longitude: 114° 55' W

	JAN	FEB	MAR	APR	MAY	JUN	JUL	AUG	SEP	OCT	NOV	DEC	YEAR
Mean Maximum Temp. (°F)	54.6	58.2	65.2	73.3	83.3	92.9	97.8	95.9	88.8	76.8	63.3	53.5	75.3
Mean Temp. (°F)	45.9	48.7	54.2	60.9	70.3	79.3	84.8	83.3	76.6	65.4	53.5	45.1	64.0
Mean Minimum Temp. (°F)	37.1	39.1	43.0	48.5	57.3	65.6	71.8	70.6	64.3	54.0	43.6	36.6	52.6
Extreme Maximum Temp. (°F)	72	81	90	94	102	108	111	107	102	97	83	74	111
Extreme Minimum Temp. (°F)	16	11	23	30	37	40	52	56	41	31	23	8	8
Days Maximum Temp. ≥ 90°F	0	0	0	1	7	21	29	28	15	2	0	0	103
Days Maximum Temp. ≤ 32°F	0	0	0	0	0	0	0	0	0	0	0	0	0
Days Minimum Temp. ≤ 32°F	7	5	2	1	0	0	0	0	0	0	3	9	27
Days Minimum Temp. ≤ 0°F	0	0	0	0	0	0	0	0	0	0	0	0	0
Heating Degree Days (base 65°F)	585	455	336	168	37	3	0	0	5	90	343	611	2,633
Cooling Degree Days (base 65°F)	0	1	7	53	209	439	621	573	359	110	5	0	2,377
Mean Precipitation (in.)	1.05	1.35	0.89	0.36	0.15	0.06	0.84	1.02	0.44	0.54	0.44	0.82	7.96
Extreme Maximum Daily Precip. (in.)	1.21	1.97	1.44	1.06	0.90	0.48	2.04	4.50	1.06	1.53	1.17	2.50	4.50
Days With ≥ 0.1" Precipitation	2	3	2	1	0	0	2	2	1	1	1	2	17
Days With ≥ 0.5" Precipitation	1	1	1	0	0	0	1	1	0	0	0	0	5
Days With ≥ 1.0" Precipitation	0	0	0	0	0	0	0	0	0	0	0	0	0
Mean Snowfall (in.)	0.0	trace	0.0	0.0	0.0	0.0	0.0	0.0	0.0	0.0	0.0	0.7	0.7
Maximum Snow Depth (in.)	0	0	0	0	0	0	0	0	0	0	0	0	0
Days With ≥ 1.0" Snow Depth	0	0	0	0	0	0	0	0	0	0	0	0	0

Spring Valley State Park *Lincoln County* Elevation: 5,950 ft. Latitude: 38° 02' N Longitude: 114° 11' W

	JAN	FEB	MAR	APR	MAY	JUN	JUL	AUG	SEP	OCT	NOV	DEC	YEAR
Mean Maximum Temp. (°F)	42.8	46.4	53.2	61.1	70.6	***82.2***	88.7	85.8	78.1	66.3	53.0	43.3	***64.3***
Mean Temp. (°F)	25.7	***30.7***	36.7	42.5	50.3	***58.6***	65.7	63.6	55.3	44.4	34.5	***25.9***	***44.5***
Mean Minimum Temp. (°F)	8.5	***14.8***	20.2	23.9	30.0	***34.7***	42.8	41.3	32.5	22.5	16.0	***8.5***	***24.6***
Extreme Maximum Temp. (°F)	65	72	80	83	94	97	103	98	96	87	77	64	103
Extreme Minimum Temp. (°F)	-23	-33	-9	-3	10	16	24	21	14	2	-14	-38	-38
Days Maximum Temp. ≥ 90°F	0	0	0	0	0	4	13	8	1	0	0	0	26
Days Maximum Temp. ≤ 32°F	3	2	0	0	0	0	0	0	0	0	1	3	9
Days Minimum Temp. ≤ 32°F	28	24	28	27	20	10	2	3	15	27	26	27	237
Days Minimum Temp. ≤ 0°F	6	3	0	0	0	0	0	0	0	0	1	5	15
Heating Degree Days (base 65°F)	1,214	***966***	870	667	451	***196***	48	78	288	633	907	***1,206***	***7,524***
Cooling Degree Days (base 65°F)	0	***0***	0	0	1	***11***	77	39	4	0	0	***0***	***132***
Mean Precipitation (in.)	1.00	1.28	1.32	0.89	0.97	0.44	0.91	1.13	1.29	1.18	0.61	0.71	11.73
Extreme Maximum Daily Precip. (in.)	***0.85***	***1.29***	***1.02***	***0.92***	***1.06***	***1.10***	***1.53***	***1.20***	***1.22***	***1.29***	***1.41***	na	na
Days With ≥ 0.1" Precipitation	2	3	4	3	2	1	2	3	2	2	2	2	28
Days With ≥ 0.5" Precipitation	0	1	1	0	0	0	0	1	1	1	0	0	5
Days With ≥ 1.0" Precipitation	0	0	0	0	0	0	0	0	0	0	0	0	0
Mean Snowfall (in.)	***5.9***	6.0	***3.9***	1.0	0.2	0.0	0.0	0.0	trace	0.4	2.3	5.1	***24.8***
Maximum Snow Depth (in.)	30	22	19	5	2	2	0	0	trace	4	12	12	30
Days With ≥ 1.0" Snow Depth	13	9	5	1	0	0	0	0	0	0	2	8	38

Sunnyside *Nye County* Elevation: 5,299 ft. Latitude: 38° 25' N Longitude: 115° 01' W

	JAN	FEB	MAR	APR	MAY	JUN	JUL	AUG	SEP	OCT	NOV	DEC	YEAR
Mean Maximum Temp. (°F)	45.4	49.4	56.9	65.0	75.0	84.4	91.5	89.2	***80.4***	***68.8***	***55.0***	***45.1***	***67.2***
Mean Temp. (°F)	31.0	35.0	41.7	48.5	57.5	65.9	72.9	70.6	***61.6***	***50.5***	***38.9***	***30.6***	***50.4***
Mean Minimum Temp. (°F)	16.6	21.1	26.5	31.9	39.8	47.4	54.1	51.8	***42.7***	***32.2***	***22.9***	***16.0***	***33.6***
Extreme Maximum Temp. (°F)	64	74	81	88	97	101	104	101	95	90	77	67	104
Extreme Minimum Temp. (°F)	-11	-17	7	9	17	30	35	31	24	10	-7	-16	-17
Days Maximum Temp. ≥ 90°F	0	0	0	0	1	10	21	15	2	0	0	0	49
Days Maximum Temp. ≤ 32°F	2	1	0	0	0	0	0	0	0	0	1	2	6
Days Minimum Temp. ≤ 32°F	28	25	24	15	4	0	0	0	2	16	23	27	164
Days Minimum Temp. ≤ 0°F	2	1	0	0	0	0	0	0	0	0	0	1	4
Heating Degree Days (base 65°F)	1,046	840	716	488	239	63	2	6	***128***	***442***	***776***	***1,059***	***5,805***
Cooling Degree Days (base 65°F)	0	0	0	0	14	99	253	185	***33***	***0***	***0***	***0***	***584***
Mean Precipitation (in.)	0.85	0.88	1.05	0.99	0.92	0.54	0.70	1.03	0.98	1.12	0.68	0.48	10.22
Extreme Maximum Daily Precip. (in.)	0.83	1.23	0.87	***1.07***	na	1.12	1.28	1.36	1.06	***1.49***	***1.11***	***0.54***	na
Days With ≥ 0.1" Precipitation	3	2	3	2	2	1	2	2	2	2	2	1	24
Days With ≥ 0.5" Precipitation	0	0	0	0	0	0	0	1	1	1	0	0	3
Days With ≥ 1.0" Precipitation	0	0	0	0	0	0	0	0	0	0	0	0	0
Mean Snowfall (in.)	4.5	1.8	1.7	1.2	0.1	0.0	0.0	0.0	trace	0.3	1.4	2.2	13.2
Maximum Snow Depth (in.)	11	12	4	6	trace	0	0	0	trace	2	10	12	12
Days With ≥ 1.0" Snow Depth	7	2	0	0	0	0	0	0	0	0	1	2	12

Tonopah Airport *Nye County* Elevation: 5,430 ft. Latitude: 38° 04' N Longitude: 117° 05' W

	JAN	FEB	MAR	APR	MAY	JUN	JUL	AUG	SEP	OCT	NOV	DEC	YEAR
Mean Maximum Temp. (°F)	44.9	49.4	56.8	64.6	74.5	84.8	92.0	89.7	80.7	68.2	54.0	44.3	67.0
Mean Temp. (°F)	32.7	36.9	42.9	49.7	58.9	68.0	74.7	72.5	64.4	52.8	40.3	31.8	52.1
Mean Minimum Temp. (°F)	20.3	24.4	29.0	34.6	43.3	51.2	57.4	55.3	48.0	37.3	26.5	19.3	37.2
Extreme Maximum Temp. (°F)	65	75	79	88	96	101	103	102	95	90	91	64	103
Extreme Minimum Temp. (°F)	-10	-9	9	15	22	30	40	41	25	13	4	-10	-10
Days Maximum Temp. ≥ 90°F	0	0	0	0	1	11	22	17	2	0	0	0	53
Days Maximum Temp. ≤ 32°F	2	1	0	0	0	0	0	0	0	0	1	3	7
Days Minimum Temp. ≤ 32°F	30	25	22	12	2	0	0	0	0	6	24	30	151
Days Minimum Temp. ≤ 0°F	1	0	0	0	0	0	0	0	0	0	0	1	2
Heating Degree Days (base 65°F)	996	787	678	454	209	48	2	3	81	374	735	1,021	5,388
Cooling Degree Days (base 65°F)	0	0	0	0	27	145	309	244	69	3	0	0	797
Mean Precipitation (in.)	0.49	0.48	0.57	0.43	0.54	0.30	0.45	0.50	0.36	0.32	0.42	0.31	5.17
Extreme Maximum Daily Precip. (in.)	0.67	0.48	0.91	0.84	0.93	0.96	1.30	1.29	0.62	0.55	1.17	0.39	1.30
Days With ≥ 0.1" Precipitation	2	2	2	2	2	1	1	1	1	1	1	1	17
Days With ≥ 0.5" Precipitation	0	0	0	0	0	0	0	0	0	0	0	0	0
Days With ≥ 1.0" Precipitation	0	0	0	0	0	0	0	0	0	0	0	0	0
Mean Snowfall (in.)	***4.7***	***2.7***	***3.3***	***1.4***	***0.6***	na	***0.0***	***trace***	na	na	na	na	na
Maximum Snow Depth (in.)	na	na	na	na	na	na	na	na	na	na	na	na	na
Days With ≥ 1.0" Snow Depth	na	na	na	na	na	na	na	na	na	na	na	na	na

The period of record for all cooperative weather station data is 1980 – 2009. See User Guide for detailed explanation of data.

Wildhorse Reservoir *Elko County* Elevation: 6,226 ft. Latitude: 41° 39' N Longitude: 115° 48' W

	JAN	FEB	MAR	APR	MAY	JUN	JUL	AUG	SEP	OCT	NOV	DEC	YEAR
Mean Maximum Temp. (°F)	31.7	35.0	***43.4***	51.8	62.1	72.1	83.7	82.6	72.7	59.4	43.4	33.3	***55.9***
Mean Temp. (°F)	16.9	19.8	***30.0***	37.7	46.1	53.7	62.0	60.3	51.5	40.8	29.6	19.4	***39.0***
Mean Minimum Temp. (°F)	2.0	4.5	***16.3***	23.5	30.2	35.6	40.2	37.9	30.2	22.2	15.7	5.6	***22.0***
Extreme Maximum Temp. (°F)	52	60	***70***	78	89	93	102	98	91	82	70	58	***102***
Extreme Minimum Temp. (°F)	-32	-38	***-32***	-6	8	17	17	11	5	-3	-18	-42	***-42***
Days Maximum Temp. ≥ 90°F	0	0	***0***	0	0	0	6	3	0	0	0	0	***9***
Days Maximum Temp. ≤ 32°F	16	10	***3***	1	0	0	0	0	0	1	5	15	***51***
Days Minimum Temp. ≤ 32°F	31	28	***30***	28	19	10	4	7	19	28	29	30	***263***
Days Minimum Temp. ≤ 0°F	15	11	***2***	0	0	0	0	0	0	0	3	12	***43***
Heating Degree Days (base 65°F)	1,484	1,274	***1,078***	812	578	334	121	157	401	742	1,056	1,405	***9,442***
Cooling Degree Days (base 65°F)	0	0	***0***	0	0	2	34	17	1	0	0	0	***54***
Mean Precipitation (in.)	1.58	1.25	***1.24***	1.35	1.63	0.97	0.66	0.46	0.57	0.71	1.41	1.75	***13.58***
Extreme Maximum Daily Precip. (in.)	0.66	***0.93***	***0.95***	***0.85***	1.00	1.07	***0.85***	***1.02***	0.71	0.70	0.85	***1.75***	***1.75***
Days With ≥ 0.1" Precipitation	5	4	***4***	5	5	3	2	2	2	2	4	6	***44***
Days With ≥ 0.5" Precipitation	0	0	***0***	0	1	0	0	0	0	0	1	0	***2***
Days With ≥ 1.0" Precipitation	0	0	***0***	0	0	0	0	0	0	0	0	0	***0***
Mean Snowfall (in.)	24.3	19.6	***14.2***	10.5	4.1	0.3	0.0	0.0	0.3	2.5	14.2	25.6	***115.6***
Maximum Snow Depth (in.)	63	***59***	***47***	19	5	1	0	0	1	3	27	55	***63***
Days With ≥ 1.0" Snow Depth	28	26	***20***	6	1	0	0	0	0	1	11	23	***116***

The period of record for all cooperative weather station data is 1980 – 2009. See User Guide for detailed explanation of data.

Nevada Weather Station Rankings

Annual Extreme Maximum Temperature

Highest

Rank	Station Name	°F
1	Amargosa Farms Garey	117
1	Desert Natl Wl Range	117
1	Las Vegas-McCarran Intl Arpt	117
4	Pahranagat W L Refuge	113
4	Pahrump	113
6	Battle Mountain	112
6	Beatty 8 N	***112***
6	Gerlach	***112***
6	Lovelock Derby Field	***112***
10	Searchlight	111
11	Blue Eagle Ranch Hanks	110
11	Kings River Valley	110
13	Winnemucca Municipal Arpt	109
14	Beowawe	108
14	Fallon Experiment Stn	108
14	Lovelock	108
14	Montello 1 SE	108
14	Reno Cannon Intl Arpt	108
19	Denio	107
19	Dyer	107
19	Elko Municipal Arpt	107
19	Imlay	107
23	Sunnyside	104
24	Austin	103
24	Lages	***103***

Lowest

Rank	Station Name	°F
1	Eureka	98
2	Arthur 4 NW	99
3	Reese River O'Toole	100
4	Ely Yelland Field	101
4	Gibbs Ranch	101
6	Lund	102
6	Wildhorse Reservoir	***102***
8	Austin	103
8	Lages	***103***
8	Spring Valley State Park	103
8	Tonopah Airport	103
12	Sunnyside	104
13	Denio	107
13	Dyer	107
13	Elko Municipal Arpt	107
13	Imlay	107
17	Beowawe	108
17	Fallon Experiment Stn	108
17	Lovelock	108
17	Montello 1 SE	108
17	Reno Cannon Intl Arpt	108
22	Winnemucca Municipal Arpt	109
23	Blue Eagle Ranch Hanks	110
23	Kings River Valley	110
25	Searchlight	111

Annual Mean Maximum Temperature

Highest

Rank	Station Name	°F
1	Amargosa Farms Garey	81.5
2	Las Vegas-McCarran Intl Arpt	80.1
3	Desert Natl Wl Range	78.8
4	Pahrump	78.6
5	Pahranagat W L Refuge	***75.8***
6	Searchlight	75.3
7	Beatty 8 N	***75.2***
8	Dyer	69.6
9	Lovelock Derby Field	***68.7***
10	Blue Eagle Ranch Hanks	67.6
10	Fallon Experiment Stn	67.6
12	Reno Cannon Intl Arpt	67.5
13	Battle Mountain	67.3
14	Sunnyside	***67.2***
15	Lovelock	67.0
15	Tonopah Airport	67.0
17	Imlay	66.1
18	Winnemucca Municipal Arpt	65.7
19	Gerlach	***65.6***
20	Kings River Valley	***65.1***
21	Lund	65.0
22	Denio	***64.6***
23	Beowawe	64.5
24	Spring Valley State Park	***64.3***
25	Montello 1 SE	***63.7***

Lowest

Rank	Station Name	°F
1	Wildhorse Reservoir	***56.0***
2	Arthur 4 NW	***57.3***
3	Gibbs Ranch	58.8
4	Eureka	59.5
5	Reese River O'Toole	60.8
6	Ely Yelland Field	61.9
7	Austin	***62.0***
8	Elko Municipal Arpt	62.4
9	Lages	***62.8***
10	Montello 1 SE	***63.7***
11	Spring Valley State Park	***64.3***
12	Beowawe	64.5
13	Denio	***64.6***
14	Lund	65.0
15	Kings River Valley	***65.1***
16	Gerlach	***65.6***
17	Winnemucca Municipal Arpt	65.7
18	Imlay	66.1
19	Lovelock	67.0
19	Tonopah Airport	67.0
21	Sunnyside	***67.2***
22	Battle Mountain	67.3
23	Reno Cannon Intl Arpt	67.5
24	Blue Eagle Ranch Hanks	67.6
24	Fallon Experiment Stn	67.6

Rankings include 25 highest/lowest stations. If state has less than 25 stations, all stations are included. The period of record is 1980–2009. See User Guide for detailed explanation of data.

Annual Mean Temperature

Highest			Lowest		
Rank	Station Name	°F	Rank	Station Name	°F
1	Las Vegas-McCarran Intl Arpt	68.5	1	Wildhorse Reservoir	***39.0***
2	Amargosa Farms Garey	65.2	2	Gibbs Ranch	43.1
3	Searchlight	64.0	3	Reese River O'Toole	43.3
4	Desert Natl Wl Range	63.1	4	Arthur 4 NW	***44.2***
5	Pahrump	62.5	5	Spring Valley State Park	***44.5***
6	Pahranagat W L Refuge	***60.2***	6	Ely Yelland Field	45.1
7	Beatty 8 N	***59.5***	7	Montello 1 SE	***46.0***
8	Reno Cannon Intl Arpt	52.6	8	Eureka	46.3
9	Dyer	52.4	9	Elko Municipal Arpt	46.5
10	Blue Eagle Ranch Hanks	52.3	10	Lages	***47.2***
11	Tonopah Airport	52.1	11	Beowawe	48.0
12	Gerlach	***52.0***	12	Lund	48.2
13	Lovelock Derby Field	***51.9***	13	Austin	***48.8***
14	Fallon Experiment Stn	51.8	14	Kings River Valley	***49.1***
15	Lovelock	51.3	15	Winnemucca Municipal Arpt	49.2
16	Imlay	51.0	16	Denio	***49.8***
17	Sunnyside	***50.4***	17	Battle Mountain	50.3
18	Battle Mountain	50.3	18	Sunnyside	***50.4***
19	Denio	***49.8***	19	Imlay	51.0
20	Winnemucca Municipal Arpt	49.2	20	Lovelock	51.3
21	Kings River Valley	***49.1***	21	Fallon Experiment Stn	51.8
22	Austin	***48.8***	22	Lovelock Derby Field	***51.9***
23	Lund	48.2	23	Gerlach	***52.0***
24	Beowawe	48.0	24	Tonopah Airport	52.1
25	Lages	***47.2***	25	Blue Eagle Ranch Hanks	52.3

Annual Mean Minimum Temperature

Highest			Lowest		
Rank	Station Name	°F	Rank	Station Name	°F
1	Las Vegas-McCarran Intl Arpt	56.8	1	Wildhorse Reservoir	***22.0***
2	Searchlight	52.6	2	Spring Valley State Park	***24.6***
3	Amargosa Farms Garey	49.0	3	Reese River O'Toole	25.8
4	Desert Natl Wl Range	47.3	4	Gibbs Ranch	27.2
5	Pahrump	46.4	5	Ely Yelland Field	28.3
6	Pahranagat W L Refuge	***44.6***	5	Montello 1 SE	***28.3***
7	Beatty 8 N	***43.9***	7	Elko Municipal Arpt	30.4
8	Gerlach	***38.5***	8	Arthur 4 NW	***31.0***
9	Reno Cannon Intl Arpt	37.7	9	Beowawe	31.4
10	Tonopah Airport	37.2	10	Lund	31.5
11	Blue Eagle Ranch Hanks	36.9	11	Lages	***31.6***
12	Fallon Experiment Stn	36.0	12	Winnemucca Municipal Arpt	32.6
13	Imlay	35.8	13	Eureka	33.1
14	Austin	***35.6***	13	Kings River Valley	***33.1***
14	Lovelock	35.6	15	Battle Mountain	33.2
16	Dyer	35.2	16	Sunnyside	***33.6***
17	Lovelock Derby Field	***35.1***	17	Denio	***35.0***
18	Denio	***35.0***	18	Lovelock Derby Field	***35.1***
19	Sunnyside	***33.6***	19	Dyer	35.2
20	Battle Mountain	33.2	20	Austin	***35.6***
21	Eureka	33.1	20	Lovelock	35.6
21	Kings River Valley	***33.1***	22	Imlay	35.8
23	Winnemucca Municipal Arpt	32.6	23	Fallon Experiment Stn	36.0
24	Lages	***31.6***	24	Blue Eagle Ranch Hanks	36.9
25	Lund	31.5	25	Tonopah Airport	37.2

Rankings include 25 highest/lowest stations. If state has less than 25 stations, all stations are included. The period of record is 1980–2009. See User Guide for detailed explanation of data.

Annual Extreme Minimum Temperature

Highest Rank	Highest Station Name	°F	Lowest Rank	Lowest Station Name	°F
1	Las Vegas-McCarran Intl Arpt	11	1	Beowawe	-43
2	Searchlight	8	2	Wildhorse Reservoir	***-42***
3	Amargosa Farms Garey	6	3	Battle Mountain	-39
4	Desert Natl Wl Range	3	4	Gibbs Ranch	-38
5	Beatty 8 N	***2***	4	Spring Valley State Park	-38
6	Pahranagat W L Refuge	-1	6	Winnemucca Municipal Arpt	-37
7	Pahrump	-2	7	Reese River O'Toole	-34
8	Tonopah Airport	-10	8	Elko Municipal Arpt	-33
9	Gerlach	***-16***	9	Imlay	-32
9	Reno Cannon Intl Arpt	-16	10	Ely Yelland Field	-30
11	Sunnyside	-17	11	Montello 1 SE	***-29***
12	Lund	-18	12	Lovelock Derby Field	***-28***
13	Austin	***-19***	13	Fallon Experiment Stn	-27
14	Eureka	-21	13	Kings River Valley	***-27***
15	Blue Eagle Ranch Hanks	-22	15	Arthur 4 NW	-26
16	Dyer	-23	15	Lages	***-26***
16	Lovelock	-23	17	Denio	-25
18	Denio	-25	18	Dyer	-23
19	Arthur 4 NW	-26	18	Lovelock	-23
19	Lages	***-26***	20	Blue Eagle Ranch Hanks	-22
21	Fallon Experiment Stn	-27	21	Eureka	-21
21	Kings River Valley	***-27***	22	Austin	***-19***
23	Lovelock Derby Field	***-28***	23	Lund	-18
24	Montello 1 SE	***-29***	24	Sunnyside	-17
25	Ely Yelland Field	-30	25	Gerlach	***-16***

July Mean Maximum Temperature

Highest Rank	Highest Station Name	°F	Lowest Rank	Lowest Station Name	°F
1	Las Vegas-McCarran Intl Arpt	104.2	1	Arthur 4 NW	82.8
2	Amargosa Farms Garey	103.9	2	Wildhorse Reservoir	83.7
3	Desert Natl Wl Range	102.3	3	Reese River O'Toole	84.8
4	Pahrump	100.8	4	Eureka	85.3
5	Pahranagat W L Refuge	***99.7***	4	Gibbs Ranch	85.3
6	Searchlight	97.8	6	Austin	***87.3***
7	Beatty 8 N	97.7	7	Ely Yelland Field	88.0
8	Lovelock Derby Field	***96.2***	8	Spring Valley State Park	88.7
9	Battle Mountain	95.2	9	Lund	89.2
10	Blue Eagle Ranch Hanks	94.6	10	Lages	***89.4***
11	Dyer	93.5	11	Elko Municipal Arpt	90.6
12	Winnemucca Municipal Arpt	93.2	12	Denio	91.2
13	Montello 1 SE	93.0	13	Gerlach	***91.4***
14	Lovelock	92.8	14	Sunnyside	91.5
15	Fallon Experiment Stn	92.2	15	Kings River Valley	91.6
16	Imlay	92.1	16	Beowawe	91.8
16	Reno Cannon Intl Arpt	92.1	17	Tonopah Airport	92.0
18	Tonopah Airport	92.0	18	Imlay	92.1
19	Beowawe	91.8	18	Reno Cannon Intl Arpt	92.1
20	Kings River Valley	91.6	20	Fallon Experiment Stn	92.2
21	Sunnyside	91.5	21	Lovelock	92.8
22	Gerlach	***91.4***	22	Montello 1 SE	93.0
23	Denio	91.2	23	Winnemucca Municipal Arpt	93.2
24	Elko Municipal Arpt	90.6	24	Dyer	93.5
25	Lages	***89.4***	25	Blue Eagle Ranch Hanks	94.6

Rankings include 25 highest/lowest stations. If state has less than 25 stations, all stations are included. The period of record is 1980–2009. See User Guide for detailed explanation of data.

January Mean Minimum Temperature

Highest			Lowest		
Rank	Station Name	°F	Rank	Station Name	°F
1	Las Vegas-McCarran Intl Arpt	37.6	1	Wildhorse Reservoir	2.0
2	Searchlight	37.1	2	Spring Valley State Park	8.5
3	Amargosa Farms Garey	32.0	3	Gibbs Ranch	9.3
4	Desert Natl Wl Range	30.7	4	Montello 1 SE	9.8
5	Beatty 8 N	29.2	5	Ely Yelland Field	11.3
6	Pahrump	28.5	6	Reese River O'Toole	12.0
7	Pahranagat W L Refuge	***28.1***	7	Elko Municipal Arpt	13.4
8	Reno Cannon Intl Arpt	23.4	8	Lages	***13.6***
9	Denio	22.3	9	Beowawe	14.1
10	Gerlach	***21.9***	10	Arthur 4 NW	14.8
11	Austin	21.4	11	Lund	15.6
12	Fallon Experiment Stn	20.3	12	Sunnyside	16.6
12	Tonopah Airport	20.3	13	Kings River Valley	16.7
14	Lovelock	19.3	14	Blue Eagle Ranch Hanks	17.0
15	Imlay	19.1	15	Battle Mountain	17.2
16	Winnemucca Municipal Arpt	18.5	15	Eureka	17.2
17	Lovelock Derby Field	18.4	17	Dyer	17.9
18	Dyer	17.9	18	Lovelock Derby Field	18.4
19	Battle Mountain	17.2	19	Winnemucca Municipal Arpt	18.5
19	Eureka	17.2	20	Imlay	19.1
21	Blue Eagle Ranch Hanks	17.0	21	Lovelock	19.3
22	Kings River Valley	16.7	22	Fallon Experiment Stn	20.3
23	Sunnyside	16.6	22	Tonopah Airport	20.3
24	Lund	15.6	24	Austin	21.4
25	Arthur 4 NW	14.8	25	Gerlach	***21.9***

Number of Days Annually Maximum Temperature ≥ 90°F

Highest			Lowest		
Rank	Station Name	Days	Rank	Station Name	Days
1	Amargosa Farms Garey	139	1	Arthur 4 NW	6
2	Las Vegas-McCarran Intl Arpt	134	2	Reese River O'Toole	9
3	Desert Natl Wl Range	124	2	Wildhorse Reservoir	***9***
4	Pahrump	123	4	Eureka	11
5	Searchlight	103	5	Gibbs Ranch	14
6	Pahranagat W L Refuge	102	6	Austin	23
7	Beatty 8 N	***98***	7	Ely Yelland Field	26
8	Lovelock Derby Field	***76***	7	Spring Valley State Park	26
9	Battle Mountain	73	9	Lund	32
10	Blue Eagle Ranch Hanks	71	10	Lages	***35***
11	Dyer	68	11	Elko Municipal Arpt	45
12	Winnemucca Municipal Arpt	62	12	Denio	49
13	Lovelock	60	12	Sunnyside	49
14	Reno Cannon Intl Arpt	57	14	Gerlach	***52***
15	Fallon Experiment Stn	56	14	Kings River Valley	***52***
16	Imlay	55	16	Beowawe	53
16	Montello 1 SE	55	16	Tonopah Airport	53
18	Beowawe	53	18	Imlay	55
18	Tonopah Airport	53	18	Montello 1 SE	55
20	Gerlach	***52***	20	Fallon Experiment Stn	56
20	Kings River Valley	***52***	21	Reno Cannon Intl Arpt	57
22	Denio	49	22	Lovelock	60
22	Sunnyside	49	23	Winnemucca Municipal Arpt	62
24	Elko Municipal Arpt	45	24	Dyer	68
25	Lages	***35***	25	Blue Eagle Ranch Hanks	71

Rankings include 25 highest/lowest stations. If state has less than 25 stations, all stations are included. The period of record is 1980–2009. See User Guide for detailed explanation of data.

Number of Days Annually Maximum Temperature ≤ 32°F

Highest Rank	Station Name	Days	Lowest Rank	Station Name	Days
1	Wildhorse Reservoir	*51*	1	Amargosa Farms Garey	0
2	Arthur 4 NW	35	1	Beatty 8 N	*0*
3	Gibbs Ranch	30	1	Desert Natl Wl Range	0
4	Eureka	29	1	Las Vegas-McCarran Intl Arpt	0
5	Elko Municipal Arpt	26	1	Pahranagat W L Refuge	0
6	Montello 1 SE	22	1	Pahrump	0
7	Ely Yelland Field	21	1	Searchlight	0
7	Lages	*21*	8	Dyer	4
9	Beowawe	19	9	Reno Cannon Intl Arpt	5
9	Reese River O'Toole	19	10	Sunnyside	6
11	Austin	15	11	Fallon Experiment Stn	7
12	Blue Eagle Ranch Hanks	14	11	Lovelock Derby Field	*7*
13	Gerlach	*13*	11	Tonopah Airport	7
13	Kings River Valley	13	14	Lovelock	9
13	Winnemucca Municipal Arpt	13	14	Spring Valley State Park	9
16	Denio	12	16	Battle Mountain	11
16	Imlay	12	16	Lund	11
18	Battle Mountain	11	18	Denio	12
18	Lund	11	18	Imlay	12
20	Lovelock	9	20	Gerlach	*13*
20	Spring Valley State Park	9	20	Kings River Valley	13
22	Fallon Experiment Stn	7	20	Winnemucca Municipal Arpt	13
22	Lovelock Derby Field	*7*	23	Blue Eagle Ranch Hanks	14
22	Tonopah Airport	7	24	Austin	15
25	Sunnyside	6	25	Beowawe	19

Number of Days Annually Minimum Temperature ≤ 32°F

Highest Rank	Station Name	Days	Lowest Rank	Station Name	Days
1	Wildhorse Reservoir	*263*	1	Las Vegas-McCarran Intl Arpt	16
2	Reese River O'Toole	240	2	Searchlight	27
3	Spring Valley State Park	237	3	Amargosa Farms Garey	55
4	Ely Yelland Field	216	4	Desert Natl Wl Range	65
5	Gibbs Ranch	*213*	5	Pahrump	79
6	Montello 1 SE	207	6	Beatty 8 N	*85*
7	Elko Municipal Arpt	196	6	Pahranagat W L Refuge	85
8	Lund	191	8	Gerlach	*134*
9	Arthur 4 NW	*189*	9	Reno Cannon Intl Arpt	138
9	Lages	*189*	10	Fallon Experiment Stn	148
11	Beowawe	187	11	Blue Eagle Ranch Hanks	151
12	Eureka	180	11	Tonopah Airport	151
12	Winnemucca Municipal Arpt	180	13	Denio	156
14	Battle Mountain	175	14	Austin	157
15	Kings River Valley	169	14	Imlay	157
16	Sunnyside	164	16	Lovelock	158
17	Dyer	161	17	Dyer	161
17	Lovelock Derby Field	*161*	17	Lovelock Derby Field	*161*
19	Lovelock	158	19	Sunnyside	164
20	Austin	157	20	Kings River Valley	169
20	Imlay	157	21	Battle Mountain	175
22	Denio	156	22	Eureka	180
23	Blue Eagle Ranch Hanks	151	22	Winnemucca Municipal Arpt	180
23	Tonopah Airport	151	24	Beowawe	187
25	Fallon Experiment Stn	148	25	Arthur 4 NW	*189*

Rankings include 25 highest/lowest stations. If state has less than 25 stations, all stations are included. The period of record is 1980–2009. See User Guide for detailed explanation of data.

Number of Days Annually Minimum Temperature ≤ 0°F

Highest

Rank	Station Name	Days
1	Wildhorse Reservoir	***43***
2	Gibbs Ranch	18
2	Montello 1 SE	18
4	Ely Yelland Field	17
5	Spring Valley State Park	15
6	Reese River O'Toole	14
7	Beowawe	11
7	Elko Municipal Arpt	11
7	Lages	***11***
10	Arthur 4 NW	9
11	Battle Mountain	7
12	Blue Eagle Ranch Hanks	5
12	Kings River Valley	5
12	Lund	5
12	Winnemucca Municipal Arpt	5
16	Eureka	4
16	Sunnyside	4
18	Denio	2
18	Dyer	2
18	Imlay	2
18	Lovelock	2
18	Lovelock Derby Field	***2***
18	Tonopah Airport	2
24	Austin	1
24	Fallon Experiment Stn	1

Lowest

Rank	Station Name	Days
1	Amargosa Farms Garey	0
1	Beatty 8 N	***0***
1	Desert Natl Wl Range	0
1	Las Vegas-McCarran Intl Arpt	0
1	Pahranagat W L Refuge	0
1	Pahrump	0
1	Reno Cannon Intl Arpt	0
1	Searchlight	0
9	Austin	1
9	Fallon Experiment Stn	1
9	Gerlach	***1***
12	Denio	2
12	Dyer	2
12	Imlay	2
12	Lovelock	2
12	Lovelock Derby Field	***2***
12	Tonopah Airport	2
18	Eureka	4
18	Sunnyside	4
20	Blue Eagle Ranch Hanks	5
20	Kings River Valley	5
20	Lund	5
20	Winnemucca Municipal Arpt	5
24	Battle Mountain	7
25	Arthur 4 NW	9

Number of Annual Heating Degree Days

Highest

Rank	Station Name	Num.
1	Wildhorse Reservoir	***9,442***
2	Gibbs Ranch	***8,047***
3	Reese River O'Toole	7,877
4	Arthur 4 NW	***7,641***
5	Spring Valley State Park	***7,524***
6	Ely Yelland Field	7,377
7	Montello 1 SE	***7,265***
8	Eureka	7,060
9	Elko Municipal Arpt	7,044
10	Lages	***6,827***
11	Beowawe	6,598
12	Lund	6,377
13	Austin	***6,296***
14	Kings River Valley	***6,239***
15	Winnemucca Municipal Arpt	6,223
16	Denio	***5,991***
17	Battle Mountain	5,946
18	Sunnyside	***5,805***
19	Imlay	5,797
20	Lovelock	5,605
21	Lovelock Derby Field	***5,540***
22	Gerlach	***5,503***
23	Blue Eagle Ranch Hanks	5,489
24	Tonopah Airport	5,388
25	Fallon Experiment Stn	5,384

Lowest

Rank	Station Name	Num.
1	Las Vegas-McCarran Intl Arpt	2,053
2	Amargosa Farms Garey	2,415
3	Searchlight	2,633
4	Desert Natl Wl Range	2,824
5	Pahrump	2,954
6	Beatty 8 N	***3,430***
7	Pahranagat W L Refuge	***3,448***
8	Reno Cannon Intl Arpt	5,147
9	Dyer	5,248
10	Fallon Experiment Stn	5,384
11	Tonopah Airport	5,388
12	Blue Eagle Ranch Hanks	5,489
13	Gerlach	***5,503***
14	Lovelock Derby Field	***5,540***
15	Lovelock	5,605
16	Imlay	5,797
17	Sunnyside	***5,805***
18	Battle Mountain	5,946
19	Denio	***5,991***
20	Winnemucca Municipal Arpt	6,223
21	Kings River Valley	***6,239***
22	Austin	***6,296***
23	Lund	6,377
24	Beowawe	6,598
25	Lages	***6,827***

Rankings include 25 highest/lowest stations. If state has less than 25 stations, all stations are included. The period of record is 1980–2009. See User Guide for detailed explanation of data.

Number of Annual Cooling Degree Days

Highest			Lowest		
Rank	Station Name	Num.	Rank	Station Name	Num.
1	Las Vegas-McCarran Intl Arpt	3,425	1	Wildhorse Reservoir	***54***
2	Amargosa Farms Garey	2,614	2	Reese River O'Toole	71
3	Searchlight	2,377	3	Spring Valley State Park	***132***
4	Desert Natl Wl Range	2,240	4	Gibbs Ranch	***160***
5	Pahrump	2,158	5	Arthur 4 NW	***163***
6	Pahranagat W L Refuge	***1,818***	6	Ely Yelland Field	232
7	Beatty 8 N	***1,534***	7	Eureka	341
8	Blue Eagle Ranch Hanks	954	8	Lund	360
9	Gerlach	***882***	9	Elko Municipal Arpt	380
10	Lovelock Derby Field	***873***	10	Montello 1 SE	***439***
11	Tonopah Airport	797	11	Lages	***444***
12	Imlay	779	12	Beowawe	484
13	Dyer	764	13	Austin	***501***
14	Reno Cannon Intl Arpt	743	14	Kings River Valley	***548***
15	Lovelock	706	15	Winnemucca Municipal Arpt	556
16	Battle Mountain	690	16	Denio	***562***
17	Fallon Experiment Stn	676	17	Sunnyside	***584***
18	Sunnyside	***584***	18	Fallon Experiment Stn	676
19	Denio	***562***	19	Battle Mountain	690
20	Winnemucca Municipal Arpt	556	20	Lovelock	706
21	Kings River Valley	***548***	21	Reno Cannon Intl Arpt	743
22	Austin	***501***	22	Dyer	764
23	Beowawe	484	23	Imlay	779
24	Lages	***444***	24	Tonopah Airport	797
25	Montello 1 SE	***439***	25	Lovelock Derby Field	***873***

Annual Precipitation

Highest			Lowest		
Rank	Station Name	Inches	Rank	Station Name	Inches
1	Arthur 4 NW	14.64	1	Las Vegas-McCarran Intl Arpt	4.17
2	Wildhorse Reservoir	***13.58***	2	Amargosa Farms Garey	4.55
3	Austin	***12.34***	3	Desert Natl Wl Range	4.86
4	Spring Valley State Park	11.73	4	Fallon Experiment Stn	5.00
5	Eureka	11.44	5	Dyer	5.06
6	Gibbs Ranch	10.83	5	Pahrump	5.06
7	Lund	10.71	7	Tonopah Airport	5.17
8	Sunnyside	10.22	8	Lovelock Derby Field	***5.24***
9	Elko Municipal Arpt	9.92	9	Beatty 8 N	***5.92***
10	Ely Yelland Field	9.77	10	Lovelock	6.08
11	Denio	9.41	11	Pahranagat W L Refuge	6.34
12	Beowawe	9.27	12	Reno Cannon Intl Arpt	7.37
13	Battle Mountain	8.99	13	Reese River O'Toole	7.57
14	Blue Eagle Ranch Hanks	8.57	14	Gerlach	***7.78***
15	Kings River Valley	8.46	15	Searchlight	7.96
16	Imlay	8.17	16	Lages	***8.09***
17	Montello 1 SE	***8.12***	16	Winnemucca Municipal Arpt	8.09
18	Lages	***8.09***	18	Montello 1 SE	***8.12***
18	Winnemucca Municipal Arpt	8.09	19	Imlay	8.17
20	Searchlight	7.96	20	Kings River Valley	8.46
21	Gerlach	***7.78***	21	Blue Eagle Ranch Hanks	8.57
22	Reese River O'Toole	7.57	22	Battle Mountain	8.99
23	Reno Cannon Intl Arpt	7.37	23	Beowawe	9.27
24	Pahranagat W L Refuge	6.34	24	Denio	9.41
25	Lovelock	6.08	25	Ely Yelland Field	9.77

Rankings include 25 highest/lowest stations. If state has less than 25 stations, all stations are included. The period of record is 1980–2009. See User Guide for detailed explanation of data.

Annual Extreme Maximum Daily Precipitation

Highest

Rank	Station Name	Inches
1	Searchlight	4.50
2	Pahrump	2.70
3	Ely Yelland Field	2.52
4	Gerlach	***2.20***
5	Arthur 4 NW	2.10
6	Dyer	2.05
7	Austin	***2.01***
8	Beatty 8 N	***2.00***
9	Reno Cannon Intl Arpt	1.91
10	Desert Natl Wl Range	1.90
11	Amargosa Farms Garey	1.85
11	Eureka	***1.85***
13	Wildhorse Reservoir	***1.75***
14	Pahranagat W L Refuge	***1.73***
15	Lages	***1.71***
16	Beowawe	1.68
17	Denio	1.55
17	Fallon Experiment Stn	1.55
19	Lund	***1.52***
20	Battle Mountain	***1.46***
21	Blue Eagle Ranch Hanks	***1.39***
22	Las Vegas-McCarran Intl Arpt	1.36
23	Lovelock	1.35
24	Tonopah Airport	1.30
25	Elko Municipal Arpt	1.28

Lowest

Rank	Station Name	Inches
1	Montello 1 SE	***1.15***
2	Imlay	***1.17***
2	Lovelock Derby Field	***1.17***
4	Reese River O'Toole	1.18
5	Winnemucca Municipal Arpt	1.21
6	Elko Municipal Arpt	1.28
7	Tonopah Airport	1.30
8	Lovelock	1.35
9	Las Vegas-McCarran Intl Arpt	1.36
10	Blue Eagle Ranch Hanks	***1.39***
11	Battle Mountain	***1.46***
12	Lund	***1.52***
13	Denio	1.55
13	Fallon Experiment Stn	1.55
15	Beowawe	1.68
16	Lages	***1.71***
17	Pahranagat W L Refuge	***1.73***
18	Wildhorse Reservoir	***1.75***
19	Amargosa Farms Garey	1.85
19	Eureka	***1.85***
21	Desert Natl Wl Range	1.90
22	Reno Cannon Intl Arpt	1.91
23	Beatty 8 N	***2.00***
24	Austin	***2.01***
25	Dyer	2.05

Number of Days Annually With ≥ 0.1 Inches of Precipitation

Highest

Rank	Station Name	Days
1	Arthur 4 NW	44
1	Wildhorse Reservoir	***44***
3	Austin	***32***
3	Denio	32
3	Elko Municipal Arpt	32
3	Gibbs Ranch	32
7	Ely Yelland Field	30
8	Beowawe	29
8	Eureka	29
8	Lund	29
11	Battle Mountain	28
11	Spring Valley State Park	28
13	Blue Eagle Ranch Hanks	27
13	Imlay	27
13	Winnemucca Municipal Arpt	27
16	Montello 1 SE	26
17	Reese River O'Toole	25
18	Gerlach	***24***
18	Kings River Valley	24
18	Lages	***24***
18	Sunnyside	24
22	Lovelock	21
22	Reno Cannon Intl Arpt	21
24	Lovelock Derby Field	***17***
24	Searchlight	17

Lowest

Rank	Station Name	Days
1	Las Vegas-McCarran Intl Arpt	11
2	Dyer	13
3	Amargosa Farms Garey	14
3	Desert Natl Wl Range	14
3	Pahrump	14
6	Fallon Experiment Stn	15
6	Pahranagat W L Refuge	15
8	Beatty 8 N	***16***
9	Lovelock Derby Field	***17***
9	Searchlight	17
9	Tonopah Airport	17
12	Lovelock	21
12	Reno Cannon Intl Arpt	21
14	Gerlach	***24***
14	Kings River Valley	24
14	Lages	***24***
14	Sunnyside	24
18	Reese River O'Toole	25
19	Montello 1 SE	26
20	Blue Eagle Ranch Hanks	27
20	Imlay	27
20	Winnemucca Municipal Arpt	27
23	Battle Mountain	28
23	Spring Valley State Park	28
25	Beowawe	29

Rankings include 25 highest/lowest stations. If state has less than 25 stations, all stations are included. The period of record is 1980–2009. See User Guide for detailed explanation of data.

Number of Days Annually With ≥ 0.5 Inches of Precipitation					
Highest			Lowest		
Rank	Station Name	Days	Rank	Station Name	Days
1	Arthur 4 NW	7	1	Denio	0
2	Eureka	6	1	Desert Natl Wl Range	0
3	Austin	*5*	1	Dyer	0
3	Searchlight	5	1	Fallon Experiment Stn	0
3	Spring Valley State Park	5	1	Imlay	0
6	Lund	3	1	Kings River Valley	0
6	Sunnyside	3	1	Lages	*0*
8	Blue Eagle Ranch Hanks	2	1	Lovelock	0
8	Reno Cannon Intl Arpt	2	1	Lovelock Derby Field	*0*
8	Wildhorse Reservoir	*2*	1	Montello 1 SE	0
11	Amargosa Farms Garey	1	1	Pahranagat W L Refuge	0
11	Battle Mountain	1	1	Reese River O'Toole	0
11	Beatty 8 N	*1*	1	Tonopah Airport	0
11	Beowawe	1	1	Winnemucca Municipal Arpt	0
11	Elko Municipal Arpt	1	15	Amargosa Farms Garey	1
11	Ely Yelland Field	1	15	Battle Mountain	1
11	Gerlach	*1*	15	Beatty 8 N	*1*
11	Gibbs Ranch	1	15	Beowawe	1
11	Las Vegas-McCarran Intl Arpt	1	15	Elko Municipal Arpt	1
11	Pahrump	1	15	Ely Yelland Field	1
21	Denio	0	15	Gerlach	*1*
21	Desert Natl Wl Range	0	15	Gibbs Ranch	1
21	Dyer	0	15	Las Vegas-McCarran Intl Arpt	1
21	Fallon Experiment Stn	0	15	Pahrump	1
21	Imlay	0	25	Blue Eagle Ranch Hanks	2

Number of Days Annually With ≥ 1.0 Inches of Precipitation					
Highest			Lowest		
Rank	Station Name	Days	Rank	Station Name	Days
1	Amargosa Farms Garey	0	1	Amargosa Farms Garey	0
1	Arthur 4 NW	0	1	Arthur 4 NW	0
1	Austin	*0*	1	Austin	*0*
1	Battle Mountain	0	1	Battle Mountain	0
1	Beatty 8 N	*0*	1	Beatty 8 N	*0*
1	Beowawe	0	1	Beowawe	0
1	Blue Eagle Ranch Hanks	0	1	Blue Eagle Ranch Hanks	0
1	Denio	0	1	Denio	0
1	Desert Natl Wl Range	0	1	Desert Natl Wl Range	0
1	Dyer	0	1	Dyer	0
1	Elko Municipal Arpt	0	1	Elko Municipal Arpt	0
1	Ely Yelland Field	0	1	Ely Yelland Field	0
1	Eureka	0	1	Eureka	0
1	Fallon Experiment Stn	0	1	Fallon Experiment Stn	0
1	Gerlach	*0*	1	Gerlach	*0*
1	Gibbs Ranch	0	1	Gibbs Ranch	0
1	Imlay	0	1	Imlay	0
1	Kings River Valley	0	1	Kings River Valley	0
1	Lages	*0*	1	Lages	*0*
1	Las Vegas-McCarran Intl Arpt	0	1	Las Vegas-McCarran Intl Arpt	0
1	Lovelock	0	1	Lovelock	0
1	Lovelock Derby Field	*0*	1	Lovelock Derby Field	*0*
1	Lund	0	1	Lund	0
1	Montello 1 SE	0	1	Montello 1 SE	0
1	Pahranagat W L Refuge	0	1	Pahranagat W L Refuge	0

Annual Snowfall

Highest			Lowest		
Rank	**Station Name**	**Inches**	**Rank**	**Station Name**	**Inches**
1	Wildhorse Reservoir	***115.6***	1	Amargosa Farms Garey	0.1
2	Austin	***69.9***	1	Pahrump	0.1
3	Elko Municipal Arpt	39.7	3	Desert Natl Wl Range	0.2
4	Arthur 4 NW	38.6	4	Searchlight	0.7
5	Reese River O'Toole	***38.3***	5	Pahranagat W L Refuge	1.7
6	Spring Valley State Park	***24.8***	6	Beatty 8 N	***2.7***
7	Eureka	***24.3***	7	Blue Eagle Ranch Hanks	***4.8***
8	Beowawe	***23.2***	8	Fallon Experiment Stn	***6.0***
9	Lages	***21.3***	9	Dyer	9.4
10	Winnemucca Municipal Arpt	***20.4***	9	Imlay	***9.4***
11	Kings River Valley	20.3	11	Gerlach	***11.7***
12	Battle Mountain	19.8	12	Lovelock	11.9
13	Denio	***19.6***	13	Sunnyside	13.2
14	Gibbs Ranch	***18.5***	14	Lund	***13.7***
15	Lund	***13.7***	15	Gibbs Ranch	***18.5***
16	Sunnyside	13.2	16	Denio	***19.6***
17	Lovelock	11.9	17	Battle Mountain	19.8
18	Gerlach	***11.7***	18	Kings River Valley	20.3
19	Dyer	9.4	19	Winnemucca Municipal Arpt	***20.4***
19	Imlay	***9.4***	20	Lages	***21.3***
21	Fallon Experiment Stn	***6.0***	21	Beowawe	***23.2***
22	Blue Eagle Ranch Hanks	***4.8***	22	Eureka	***24.3***
23	Beatty 8 N	***2.7***	23	Spring Valley State Park	***24.8***
24	Pahranagat W L Refuge	1.7	24	Reese River O'Toole	***38.3***
25	Searchlight	0.7	25	Arthur 4 NW	38.6

Annual Maximum Snow Depth

Highest			Lowest		
Rank	**Station Name**	**Inches**	**Rank**	**Station Name**	**Inches**
1	Wildhorse Reservoir	***63***	1	Searchlight	0
2	Arthur 4 NW	***47***	2	Pahrump	2
3	Spring Valley State Park	30	3	Desert Natl Wl Range	3
4	Austin	***27***	3	Pahranagat W L Refuge	3
5	Battle Mountain	18	5	Amargosa Farms Garey	***7***
5	Beowawe	***18***	6	Dyer	8
7	Kings River Valley	***17***	7	Beatty 8 N	***9***
8	Winnemucca Municipal Arpt	***15***	8	Imlay	***10***
9	Blue Eagle Ranch Hanks	13	9	Denio	***12***
10	Denio	***12***	9	Lovelock	12
10	Lovelock	12	9	Reese River O'Toole	***12***
10	Reese River O'Toole	***12***	9	Sunnyside	12
10	Sunnyside	12	13	Blue Eagle Ranch Hanks	13
14	Imlay	***10***	14	Winnemucca Municipal Arpt	***15***
15	Beatty 8 N	***9***	15	Kings River Valley	***17***
16	Dyer	8	16	Battle Mountain	18
17	Amargosa Farms Garey	***7***	16	Beowawe	***18***
18	Desert Natl Wl Range	3	18	Austin	***27***
18	Pahranagat W L Refuge	3	19	Spring Valley State Park	30
20	Pahrump	2	20	Arthur 4 NW	***47***
21	Searchlight	0	21	Wildhorse Reservoir	***63***

Rankings include 25 highest/lowest stations. If state has less than 25 stations, all stations are included. The period of record is 1980–2009. See User Guide for detailed explanation of data.

Number of Days Annually With ≥ 1.0 Inch Snow Depth

Highest

Rank	Station Name	Days
1	Wildhorse Reservoir	***116***
2	Arthur 4 NW	***65***
3	Reese River O'Toole	***47***
4	Austin	***46***
5	Spring Valley State Park	38
6	Lages	***28***
7	Beowawe	***26***
8	Winnemucca Municipal Arpt	***25***
9	Blue Eagle Ranch Hanks	21
10	Battle Mountain	19
11	Kings River Valley	***15***
12	Lund	***13***
13	Lovelock	12
13	Sunnyside	12
15	Denio	***8***
16	Fallon Experiment Stn	*7*
16	Imlay	*7*
18	Dyer	4
19	Beatty 8 N	***2***
20	Amargosa Farms Garey	***0***
20	Desert Natl Wl Range	0
20	Pahranagat W L Refuge	0
20	Pahrump	0
20	Searchlight	0

Lowest

Rank	Station Name	Days
1	Amargosa Farms Garey	***0***
1	Desert Natl Wl Range	0
1	Pahranagat W L Refuge	0
1	Pahrump	0
1	Searchlight	0
6	Beatty 8 N	***2***
7	Dyer	4
8	Fallon Experiment Stn	*7*
8	Imlay	*7*
10	Denio	***8***
11	Lovelock	12
11	Sunnyside	12
13	Lund	***13***
14	Kings River Valley	***15***
15	Battle Mountain	19
16	Blue Eagle Ranch Hanks	21
17	Winnemucca Municipal Arpt	***25***
18	Beowawe	***26***
19	Lages	***28***
20	Spring Valley State Park	38
21	Austin	***46***
22	Reese River O'Toole	***47***
23	Arthur 4 NW	***65***
24	Wildhorse Reservoir	***116***

Significant Storm Events in Nevada: 2000 – 2009

Location or County	Date	Type	Mag.	Deaths	Injuries	Property Damage ($mil.)	Crop Damage ($mil.)
Las Vegas Valley, Clark County	03/01/02	High Wind	68 mph	1	0	0.1	0.0
Western Nevada Basin-Fernley Area	03/07/02	Winter Storm	na	2	0	0.1	0.0
Washoe	06/21/02	Flash Flood	na	0	0	1.0	0.0
Lyon County	11/07/02	High Wind	70 mph	1	6	0.2	0.0
Clark	11/30/02	Flash Flood	na	1	1	0.0	0.0
Western Nevada	12/14/02	High Wind	93 mph	0	0	5.9	0.0
Greater Lake Tahoe Area	12/15/02	Avalanche	na	1	1	0.0	0.0
Clark	08/19/03	Flash Flood	na	0	0	2.0	0.0
Southern Lincoln and Northeast Clark Counties	01/11/05	Flood	na	0	0	20.0	0.0
Greater Reno and Carson City Area	09/23/05	High Wind	70 mph	1	1	0.0	0.0
Washoe	12/31/05	Flood	na	0	0	5.6	0.0
Carson City	12/31/05	Flood	na	0	0	3.4	0.0
Carson City	01/01/06	Flood	na	0	0	1.2	0.0
Western Nevada Basin and Range, Churchill County	12/21/06	Ice Storm	na	1	0	0.0	0.0
Clark	08/27/07	Flash Flood	na	0	0	5.0	0.0
Clark	08/27/07	Lightning	na	0	0	1.0	0.0
Lyon	01/05/08	Flash Flood	na	0	0	6.6	0.0
Western Nevada Basin and Range	03/15/08	Heavy Snow	na	1	2	0.0	0.0
Lyon	05/27/08	Hail	0.25 in.	1	2	0.0	0.0
Las Vegas Valley, Clark County	07/13/09	Heat	na	1	0	0.0	0.0

Note: Deaths, injuries, and damages are date and location specific.

NEW HAMPSHIRE

PHYSICAL FEATURES. New Hampshire occupies 9,304 square miles. From below the 43d parallel of latitude it extends nearly 200 miles northward to beyond the 45th parallel. At its southern border, New Hampshire extends westward from the Atlantic coastline for nearly 100 miles. It narrows to less than 20 miles in width at its northern tip. The eastern border lies near 71 W. longitude. Its western border is the Connecticut River, except in the extreme north.

The terrain is hilly to mountainous. Elevations of less than 500 feet above sea level are found only in the coastal area of the southeast, the Merrimac River Valley, and the central and southern portions of the Connecticut River Valley. Elsewhere the general elevation is from 500 to 1,500 feet, excepting up to near 2,500 feet in the extreme north. Numerous hills and mountains extend to heights of 2,000 to 4,000 feet above sea level over most of the State except in the southeast. Many White Mountain peaks rise above 4,000 feet; Mt. Washington reaches 6,288 feet above sea level. This is the highest mountain in the northeastern United States.

The glacier of the great Ice Age accounts for much of the topography, including many of the 1,300 lakes and ponds. The largest is Lake Winnepesaukee which covers an area of 71 square miles in the central part of the State. Inland waters cover about 280 square miles. The two principal rivers in the State are the Connecticut and the Merrimack Rivers, both of which flow in a southerly direction.

GENERAL CLIMATE. Characteristics of New Hampshire climate are: (1) changeableness of the weather, (2) large range of temperature, both daily and annual, (3) great differences between the same seasons in different years, (4) equable distribution of precipitation, and (5) considerable diversity from place to place. The regional climatic influences are modified in New Hampshire by varying distances from the ocean, elevations, and types of terrain. The State has been divided into two climatological divisions (Northern and Southern) which take into account the main features of these modifying factors.

New Hampshire lies in the "prevailing westerlies", the belt of generally eastward air movement which encircles the globe in middle latitudes. Embedded in this circulation are extensive masses of air originating in higher or lower latitudes and interacting to produce low-pressure storm systems. Relative to most other sections of the country, a large number of such storms pass over or near New Hampshire. The majority of air masses affecting this State belong to three types: (1) cold, dry air pouring down from subarctic North America, (2) warm, moist air streaming up on a long overland journey from the Gulf of Mexico and eastward, and (3) cool, damp air moving in from the North Atlantic. Because the atmospheric flow is usually offshore, New Hampshire is more influenced by the first two types than it is by the third.

The procession of contrasting air masses and the relatively frequent passage of storms bring about approximately twice-weekly alternation from fair to cloudy or stormy conditions, often attended by abrupt changes in temperature, moisture, sunshine, wind direction and speed. There is no regular or persistent rhythm to this sequence, and it is interrupted by periods during which the weather patterns continue the same for several days, infrequently for several weeks. New Hampshire weather, however, is cited for variety rather than monotony.

The Northern Division is the area least affected by the ocean influences and most affected by higher elevations as well as by its more northerly latitude. In the Southern Division, lower elevation and latitude tend to cause higher temperatures, though this is modified seasonally by ocean influences.

TEMPERATURE. The annual temperature averages near 41°F. in the Northern Division and near 46°F. in the Southern. Summer temperatures are comfortable for the most part. They are reasonably uniform over the State, excepting topographical extremes. Hot days with maxima of 90°F. or higher average from only a few per year in the extreme north to 5 to 15 per year over most of the rest of the State. Average temperatures vary from place to place more in the winter than in summer. Days with subzero readings are relatively few along the immediate coast but are common inland. They average from 25 to 50 in number per year in most of the Northern Division and from 10 to 25 in the Southern Division. The average date of the last freezing temperature in spring ranges from early in June at the colder locations to late in April at a few southern stations. For most of the State the growing season begins in May and usually ends in the latter part of September.

PRECIPITATION. New Hampshire is fortunate in having its precipitation rather evenly distributed through the year. Low pressure, or frontal, storm systems are the principal year-round moisture producers. This activity ebbs somewhat in summer, but thunderstorms are of increased activity at this time, tending to make up the difference. Though brief and often of small extent, the thunderstorms produce the heaviest local rainfall intensities. Rains of one to two inches in one hour can be expected at least once in a 10-year period. Prolonged droughts are infrequent; shorter dry spells in summer are fairly common. Widespread floods are infrequent. Floods occur most often in the spring when they are caused by a combination of rain and melting snow.

Total annual precipitation averages near 44 inches in the Northern Division and 41 inches in the Southern. The distribution is quite uniform over the Southern Division. The mountainous character of much of central and northern New Hampshire, and the generally higher elevations there, account for the greater annual totals and variability from place to place. Considerable rain or wet snow falls along the coast in winter, while farther inland snow is more generally the rule. Occasionally freezing rain occurs, coating exposed surfaces with troublesome ice. This problem is less frequent in northern New Hampshire. Most areas can expect at least one occurrence of glaze in the season. Measurable amounts of precipitation fall on an average of one day in three. Frequency is higher at higher elevations and in extreme northern New Hampshire, up to 140 to 150 days per year.

SNOWFALL. Average annual amounts of snowfall in the Southern Division increase from around 50 inches near the coast to 60 to 80 inches inland. Totals vary greatly in the Northern Division. Along the Connecticut River in the southern portion, totals average near 60 inches but increase to over 100 inches at the higher elevations of the northern and western portions. The summit of Mt. Washington receives nearly 185 inches. Bethlehem, only about 20 miles to the west, receives only about 70 inches per year. The number of days with one inch or more of snowfall varies from near 20 per season over much of the Southern Division up to 30 to 40 in the Northern Division and even to 50 or more at the highest elevations.

Snow cover is continuous through the whole winter season as a rule. Most frequent exceptions are found along the immediate coast and sometimes in extreme southern New Hampshire. Snow cover reaches its maximum depth, on the average, during the latter half of February in the Southern Division. In the Northern Division, the greatest depth comes in early March. Water stored in the snow makes an important contribution to a continuous water supply. The spring melting is usually too gradual to produce serious flooding.

OTHER CLIMATIC ELEMENTS. Sunshine averages over 50 percent of the possible amount in the Southern Division. and the lower elevations of the Northern Division. Higher elevations and peaks are cloudier, especially in winter, reducing the percentage to less than 50 percent generally. Mt. Washington reports an average of only 33 percent. Persistent fogs are sometimes experienced along the coast and on the higher elevations inland. Duration of fogs diminishes inland over flat and valley locations. But the shorter duration heavy ground fogs of early morning occur frequently at susceptible places in these areas. The number of days with fog probably varies from about 20 to 90 per year over the State.

The prevailing wind, on a yearly basis, comes from a westerly direction. It is predominantly from the northwest in winter and from the southwest in summer. Along the coast in spring and summer the sea breeze is important. These onshore winds, from the cool ocean, may come inland for 10 miles or so.

Coastal storms or "northeasters" can be a serious weather hazard in southeastern New Hampshire, decreasing in importance northward. They generate very strong winds and heavy rain or snow. They can produce abnormally high wind-driven tides. Occasionally in summer or fall storms of tropical origin affect New Hampshire. These may be similar (except for snow) to the northeasters. Only a very few retain near or full hurricane force. Tornadoes are not common phenomena, yet many years may have one or more. Most tornadoes are small, affecting a very localized area. About 80 percent of tornadoes occur between May 15 and September 15. Thunder and hailstorms have a similar frequency maximum from mid-spring to early fall. Thunderstorms occur on 15 to 30 days per year. The most severe are attended by hail.

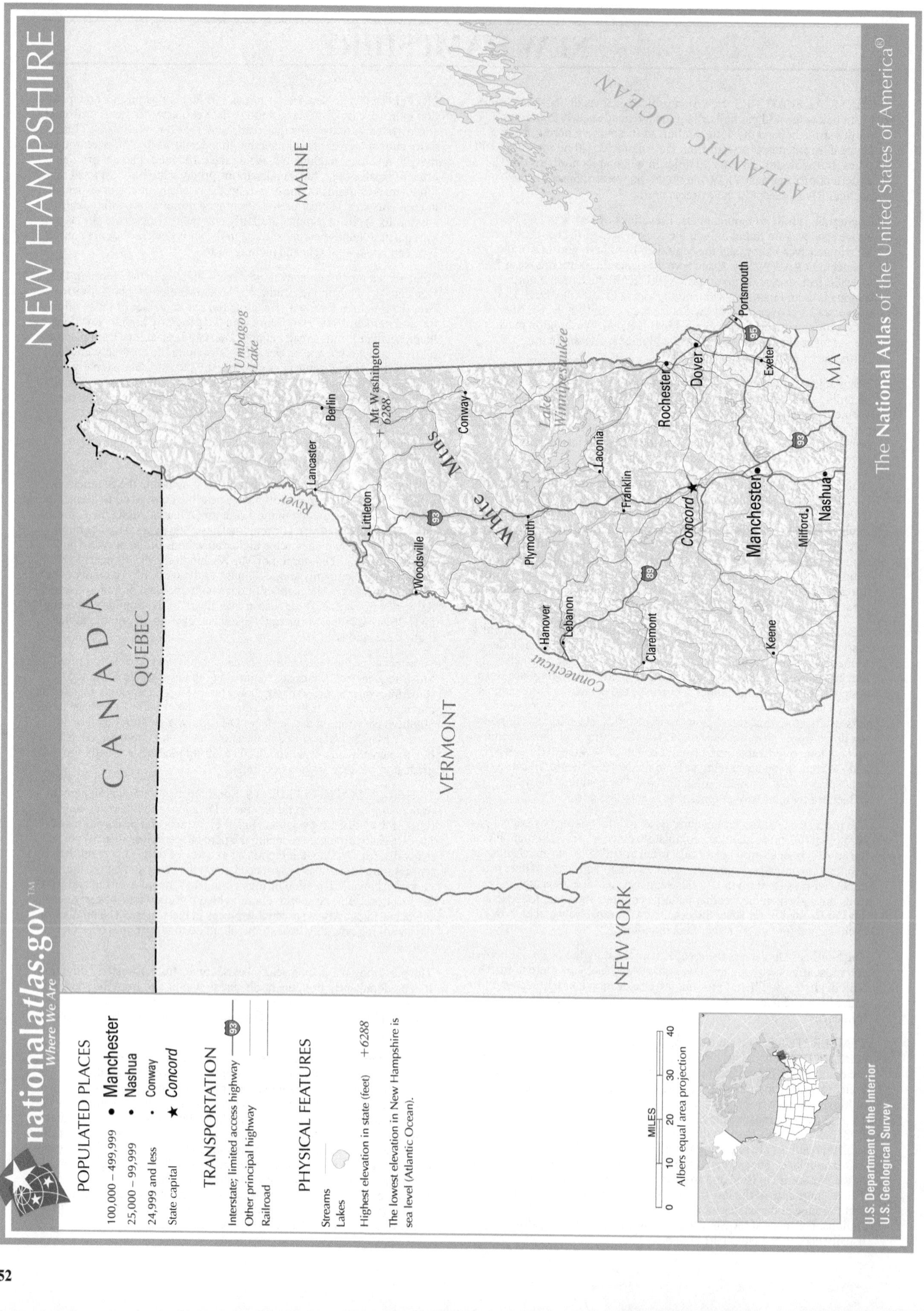
NEW HAMPSHIRE
nationalatlas.gov™
Where We Are
POPULATED PLACES
100,000 – 499,999 • Manchester
25,000 – 99,999 • Nashua
24,999 and less · Conway
State capital ★ Concord
TRANSPORTATION
Interstate; limited access highway 93
Other principal highway
Railroad
PHYSICAL FEATURES
Streams
Lakes
Highest elevation in state (feet) +6288
The lowest elevation in New Hampshire is sea level (Atlantic Ocean).
MILES
0 10 20 30 40
Albers equal area projection
U.S. Department of the Interior
U.S. Geological Survey
The National Atlas of the United States of America®
CANADA
QUÉBEC
MAINE
VERMONT
NEW YORK
MA
ATLANTIC OCEAN
Umbagog Lake
Mt Washington
6288
White Mtns
Lake Winnipesaukee
Connecticut
River
Berlin
Lancaster
Littleton
Woodsville
Conway
Plymouth
Laconia
Franklin
Concord
Hanover
Lebanon
Claremont
Keene
Manchester
Milford
Nashua
Rochester
Dover
Exeter
Portsmouth
93
89
95

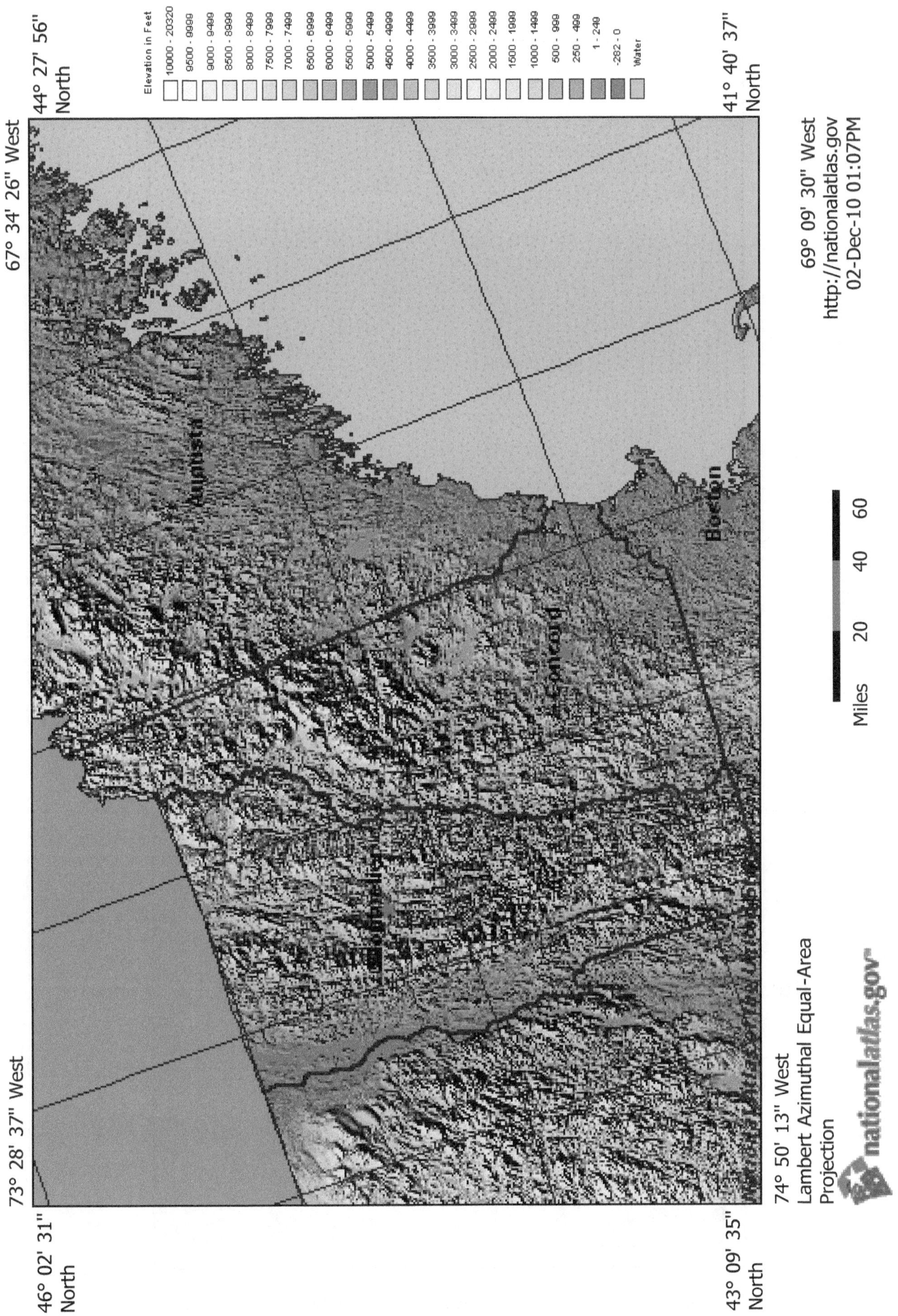
44° 27' 56" North
67° 34' 26" West
46° 02' 31" North
73° 28' 37" West
41° 40' 37" North
69° 09' 30" West
43° 09' 35" North
74° 50' 13" West
Elevation in Feet
10000 - 20320
9500 - 9999
9000 - 9499
8500 - 8999
8000 - 8499
7500 - 7999
7000 - 7499
6500 - 6999
6000 - 6499
5500 - 5999
5000 - 5499
4500 - 4999
4000 - 4499
3500 - 3999
3000 - 3499
2500 - 2999
2000 - 2499
1500 - 1999
1000 - 1499
500 - 999
250 - 499
1 - 249
-282 - 0
Water
Augusta
Concord
Boston
Miles
20
40
60
Lambert Azimuthal Equal-Area
Projection
http://nationalatlas.gov
02-Dec-10 01:07PM
nationalatlas.gov

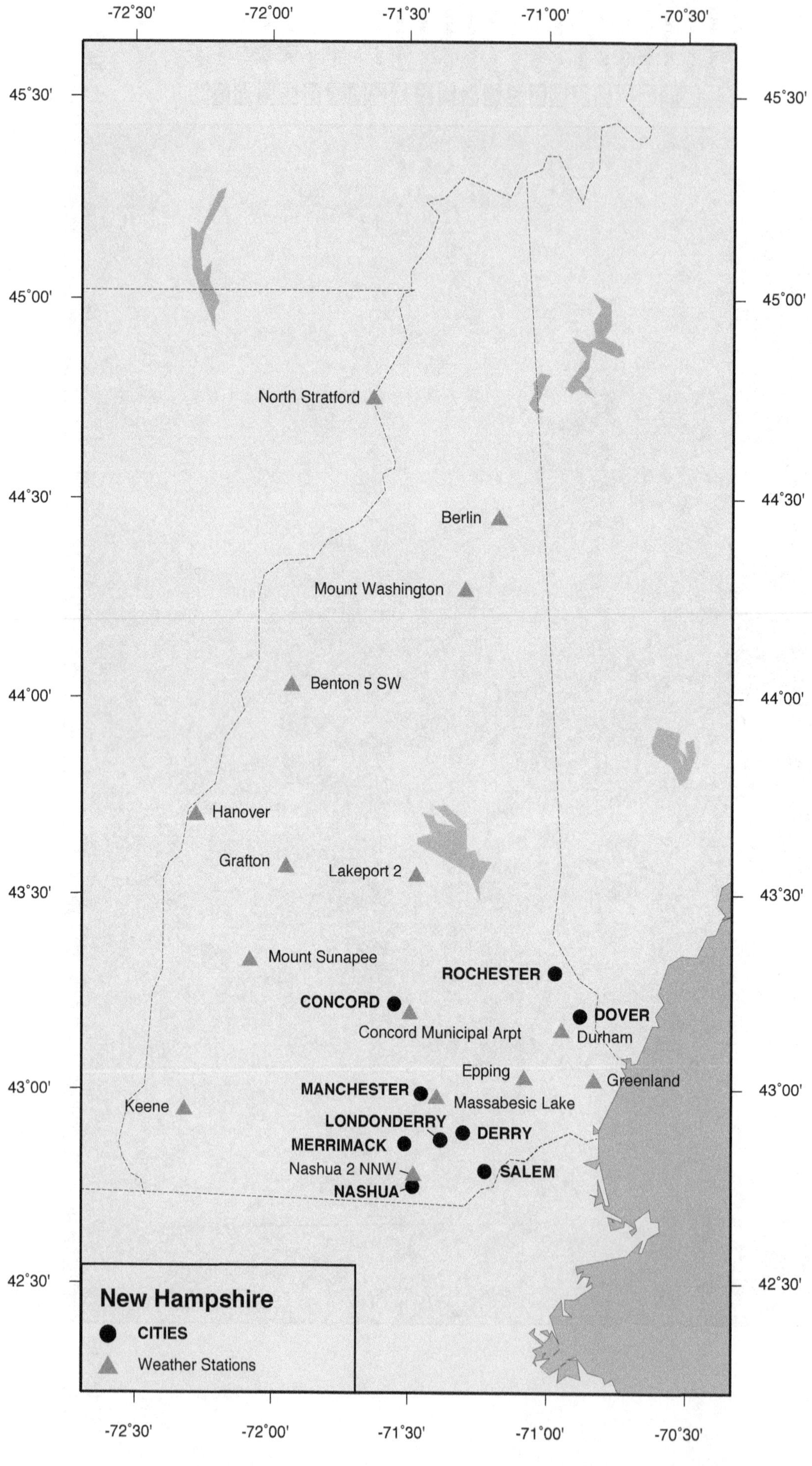
-72°30'
-72°00'
-71°30'
-71°00'
-70°30'
45°30'
45°00'
44°30'
44°00'
43°30'
43°00'
42°30'
North Stratford
Berlin
Mount Washington
Benton 5 SW
Hanover
Grafton
Lakeport 2
Mount Sunapee
ROCHESTER
CONCORD
Concord Municipal Arpt
DOVER
Durham
Epping
Greenland
MANCHESTER
Massabesic Lake
Keene
LONDONDERRY
DERRY
MERRIMACK
Nashua 2 NNW
SALEM
NASHUA
New Hampshire
CITIES
Weather Stations

New Hampshire Weather Stations by County

County	Station Name
Belknap	Lakeport 2
Cheshire	Keene
Coos	Berlin Mount Washington North Stratford
Grafton	Benton 5 SW Grafton Hanover
Hillsborough	Massabesic Lake Nashua 2 NNW
Merrimack	Concord Municipal Arpt Mount Sunapee
Rockingham	Epping Greenland
Strafford	Durham

See User Guide for station inclusion criteria.

New Hampshire Weather Stations by City

City	Station Name	Miles
Bedford	Lawrence, MA	24.6
	Concord Municipal Arpt	17.9
	Epping	23.1
	Massabesic Lake	6.9
	Nashua 2 NNW	11.1
Concord	Concord Municipal Arpt	2.9
	Lakeport 2	22.9
	Massabesic Lake	18.2
Derry	Haverhill, MA	14.4
	Lawrence, MA	14.6
	Middleton, MA	24.5
	Concord Municipal Arpt	23.8
	Epping	14.8
	Massabesic Lake	8.4
	Nashua 2 NNW	11.8
Dover	Sanford 2 NNW, ME	19.7
	Durham	4.5
	Epping	14.9
	Greenland	12.2
Goffstown	Concord Municipal Arpt	13.3
	Epping	23.5
	Massabesic Lake	7.7
	Nashua 2 NNW	16.1
Hampton	Haverhill, MA	17.0
	Lawrence, MA	23.8
	Durham	16.1
	Epping	14.7
	Greenland	5.6
Hudson	Bedford, MA	20.6
	Haverhill, MA	17.7
	Lawrence, MA	13.4
	Middleton, MA	23.2
	Reading, MA	22.3
	Massabesic Lake	15.2
	Nashua 2 NNW	3.7
Keene	Keene	1.5
Laconia	Concord Municipal Arpt	23.7
	Grafton	24.2
	Lakeport 2	0.5
Londonderry	Haverhill, MA	17.2
	Lawrence, MA	15.7
	Concord Municipal Arpt	23.9
	Epping	18.9
	Massabesic Lake	8.2
	Nashua 2 NNW	7.8
Manchester	Haverhill, MA	24.8
	Lawrence, MA	24.6
	Concord Municipal Arpt	14.9
	Epping	19.0
	Massabesic Lake	2.7
	Nashua 2 NNW	14.2
Merrimack	Haverhill, MA	23.6
	Lawrence, MA	20.9
Merrimack *(cont.)*	Concord Municipal Arpt	23.3
	Epping	24.7
	Massabesic Lake	10.0
	Nashua 2 NNW	5.7
Milford	Massabesic Lake	17.0
	Nashua 2 NNW	9.5
Nashua	Bedford, MA	21.0
	Haverhill, MA	21.1
	Lawrence, MA	16.3
	Reading, MA	23.9
	Massabesic Lake	16.7
	Nashua 2 NNW	2.4
Portsmouth	Durham	10.8
	Epping	15.8
	Greenland	4.4
Rochester	Sanford 2 NNW, ME	14.8
	Durham	10.7
	Epping	19.5
	Greenland	21.0
Salem	Bedford, MA	21.2
	Haverhill, MA	7.7
	Lawrence, MA	6.5
	Middleton, MA	16.4
	Reading, MA	19.1
	Epping	18.4
	Massabesic Lake	16.5
	Nashua 2 NNW	13.5

Note: Miles is the distance between the geographic center of the city and the weather station.

See User Guide for station inclusion criteria.

New Hampshire Weather Stations by Elevation

Feet	Station Name
6,261	Mount Washington
1,270	Mount Sunapee
1,200	Benton 5 SW
930	Berlin
910	North Stratford
830	Grafton
603	Hanover
509	Keene
500	Lakeport 2
346	Concord Municipal Arpt
250	Massabesic Lake
160	Epping
129	Nashua 2 NNW
84	Greenland
80	Durham

See User Guide for station inclusion criteria.

Concord Municipal Airport

Concord, the Capital of New Hampshire, is situated near the geographical center of New England at an altitude of approximately 300 feet above sea level on the Merrimack River. Its surroundings are hilly with many lakes and ponds. The countryside is generously wooded, mostly on land reclaimed from fields which were formerly cleared for farming. From the coast about 50 miles to the southeast, the terrain slopes gently upward to the city. West of the city, the land rises some 2,000 feet higher in only half that distance. Mount Washington, at an elevation of 6,288 feet is in the White Mountains 75 miles north of town.

Northwesterly winds are prevalent. They bring cold, dry air during the winter and pleasantly cool, dry air in the summer. Stronger southerly winds occur during July and August, and easterly winds usually accompany summer and winter storms. Winter breezes are somewhat lighter, and winds are frequently calm during the night and early morning hours. Low temperatures, as a rule, do not interrupt normal out-of-doors activity because winds are calm or light, producing a low wind chill factor.

Very hot summer weather is infrequent. During any month, temperatures considerably above the average maxima and much below the normal minima are observed.

The average amount of precipitation for the warmer half of the year differs little from that for the colder half. Precipitation occurrences average approximately one day of three for the year, with a somewhat higher frequency for the April-May period, offsetting the lower frequency of August-October. The more significant rains and heavier snowfalls are associated with easterly winds, especially northeasterly winds. The first snowfall of an inch or more is likely to come between the middle of November and the middle of December. The snow cover normally lasts from mid-December until the last week of March, but bare ground is not rare in the winter, nor is a snowscape rare earlier or later in the season. Rain, sleet, or freezing rain may also occur.

Agriculture is neither intensive nor large-scale in the vicinity of the station. Potatoes and other frost-resistant vegetables, hardy fruits such as apples, forage for the dairy industry, and maple sugar are the principal crops.

Based on the 1951-1980 period, the average first occurrence of 32 degrees Fahrenheit in the fall is September 22 and the average last occurrence in the spring is May 23. Freezing temperatures have occurred as late as June and as early as August.

Concord Municipal Airport *Merrimack County* Elevation: 346 ft. Latitude: 43° 12' N Longitude: 71° 30' W

	JAN	FEB	MAR	APR	MAY	JUN	JUL	AUG	SEP	OCT	NOV	DEC	YEAR
Mean Maximum Temp. (°F)	30.9	34.7	43.6	57.2	68.8	77.3	82.1	80.8	72.5	60.4	48.2	36.2	57.7
Mean Temp. (°F)	20.7	24.0	32.9	44.9	55.7	64.9	69.9	68.5	59.9	48.1	38.2	26.6	46.2
Mean Minimum Temp. (°F)	10.4	13.3	22.2	32.6	42.5	52.4	57.6	56.1	47.2	35.7	28.1	16.9	34.6
Extreme Maximum Temp. (°F)	69	67	89	94	94	98	101	99	95	87	77	73	101
Extreme Minimum Temp. (°F)	-33	-20	-11	8	24	33	40	32	26	17	-5	-21	-33
Days Maximum Temp. ≥ 90°F	0	0	0	0	1	3	4	3	1	0	0	0	12
Days Maximum Temp. ≤ 32°F	18	11	4	0	0	0	0	0	0	0	1	11	45
Days Minimum Temp. ≤ 32°F	30	27	26	16	4	0	0	0	2	13	21	29	168
Days Minimum Temp. ≤ 0°F	7	4	1	0	0	0	0	0	0	0	0	3	15
Heating Degree Days (base 65°F)	1,369	1,152	988	597	299	84	16	33	183	518	798	1,185	7,222
Cooling Degree Days (base 65°F)	0	0	0	2	17	86	176	147	36	2	0	0	466
Mean Precipitation (in.)	2.62	2.53	3.16	3.46	3.64	3.69	3.78	3.22	3.40	3.93	3.72	3.10	40.25
Maximum Precipitation (in.)*	8.1	7.8	7.8	5.9	9.5	7.8	6.5	7.3	7.8	8.8	7.4	7.5	49.3
Minimum Precipitation (in.)*	0.4	trace	0.9	1.0	0.6	0.6	1.0	1.0	0.4	0.9	0.8	0.8	24.2
Extreme Maximum Daily Precip. (in.)	1.98	2.91	2.25	2.40	5.12	2.37	2.57	3.84	3.92	4.37	2.49	1.86	5.12
Days With ≥ 0.1" Precipitation	6	5	7	7	7	8	7	6	6	6	7	6	78
Days With ≥ 0.5" Precipitation	2	2	2	2	2	2	3	2	2	2	3	2	26
Days With ≥ 1.0" Precipitation	0	0	1	1	1	1	1	1	1	1	1	1	10
Mean Snowfall (in.)	17.4	13.4	11.1	2.8	trace	trace	0.0	0.0	trace	0.1	3.0	14.6	62.4
Maximum Snowfall (in.)*	45	50	38	15	1	0	0	0	trace	2	18	38	128
Maximum 24-hr. Snowfall (in.)*	16	14	16	13	1	0	0	0	trace	2	9	12	16
Maximum Snow Depth (in.)	29	42	45	25	trace	trace	0	0	trace	1	8	24	45
Days With ≥ 1.0" Snow Depth	23	22	15	2	0	0	0	0	0	0	3	16	81
Thunderstorm Days*	< 1	< 1	< 1	1	2	4	5	4	2	1	< 1	< 1	19
Foggy Days*	11	10	13	13	15	17	17	20	21	17	15	13	182
Predominant Sky Cover*	OVR	OVR	OVR	OVR	OVR	OVR	OVR	OVR	OVR	OVR	OVR	OVR	OVR
Mean Relative Humidity 7am (%)*	76	76	76	75	76	80	83	87	89	87	83	79	81
Mean Relative Humidity 4pm (%)*	59	54	52	46	47	51	51	53	55	53	61	63	54
Mean Dewpoint (°F)*	12	13	21	31	42	54	59	58	50	39	29	17	35
Prevailing Wind Direction*	NW	NW	NW	NW	NW	NW	NW	NW	NW	NW	NW	NW	NW
Prevailing Wind Speed (mph)*	12	12	12	12	10	10	9	9	9	10	10	12	10
Maximum Wind Gust (mph)*	53	60	56	61	52	59	53	45	52	48	53	58	61

Note: (*) Period of record is 1948-1995

The period of record for National Weather Service station data is 1980 – 2009 except where noted. See User Guide for detailed explanation of data.

Mount Washington

The Mount Washington Observatory is located at the summit of Mount Washington, New Hampshire, highest mountain of the Presidential range. The weather is very severe most of the year, conditions approximating those that would be encountered at a much higher latitude. The upper limits of timberline extend to 4,500 to 5,000 feet.

Prevailing winds are from the west and west-northwest, although the most severe storms are usually from the southeast. Winds are stronger at the summit than at the same elevation at a distance from the mountain, due to the Bernouilli effect. Mount Washington is near the mid-point of a 60-mile-long mountain front trending northeast to southwest. Wind speeds in excess of 100 mph are not uncommon, and the stations highest measured wind, 231 mph, still stands as a world record.

The station is in the clouds approximately 55 percent of the time. This is due partly to the effect of orographic uplift and partly due to the fact that the summit is often above the cloud base when there are low clouds in the area.

Minimum temperatures are not extreme compared to some U. S. valley stations. Annual temperature variations are not as great as they are in the surrounding lowlands, which may actually be colder than the summit when there is a strong inversion. Rime or glaze icing occurs often in winter, when the mountain is frequently in supercooled clouds.

Because of its severe climate, Mount Washington has for many years been used as a natural laboratory for cloud physics research and for the development and testing of instruments, aircraft components, and structures which are required to withstand high winds and icing conditions.

Mount Washington *Coos County* Elevation: 6,261 ft. Latitude: 44° 16' N Longitude: 71° 18' W

	JAN	FEB	MAR	APR	MAY	JUN	JUL	AUG	SEP	OCT	NOV	DEC	YEAR
Mean Maximum Temp. (°F)	13.7	14.8	20.9	30.6	41.5	50.5	54.0	53.3	47.0	36.4	27.9	18.6	34.1
Mean Temp. (°F)	5.2	6.8	13.3	24.0	35.4	44.7	48.8	48.0	41.4	30.5	21.0	10.5	27.5
Mean Minimum Temp. (°F)	-3.3	-1.4	5.6	17.4	29.2	38.8	43.6	42.6	35.7	24.4	14.1	2.4	20.8
Extreme Maximum Temp. (°F)	47	43	55	59	64	72	70	69	69	62	52	47	72
Extreme Minimum Temp. (°F)	-45	-39	-37	-20	2	13	24	20	9	3	-17	-37	-45
Days Maximum Temp. ≥ 90°F	0	0	0	0	0	0	0	0	0	0	0	0	0
Days Maximum Temp. ≤ 32°F	29	26	25	18	6	1	0	0	2	11	19	27	164
Days Minimum Temp. ≤ 32°F	31	28	30	28	19	6	1	2	11	24	28	31	239
Days Minimum Temp. ≤ 0°F	18	15	10	1	0	0	0	0	0	0	3	13	60
Heating Degree Days (base 65°F)	1,850	1,644	1,599	1,223	911	603	494	521	702	1,064	1,312	1,685	13,608
Cooling Degree Days (base 65°F)	0	0	0	0	0	0	0	0	0	0	0	0	0
Mean Precipitation (in.)	6.44	6.23	7.59	7.62	8.15	8.28	8.74	8.37	8.06	9.00	10.11	7.61	96.20
Maximum Precipitation (in.)*	18.2	25.6	16.0	15.2	18.8	16.0	15.5	20.7	15.5	21.3	19.6	17.9	130.
Minimum Precipitation (in.)*	1.3	1.0	2.7	2.2	1.8	2.4	2.7	2.8	2.7	2.2	3.2	1.5	56.2
Extreme Maximum Daily Precip. (in.)	4.56	4.92	6.03	8.19	3.75	5.41	4.95	6.63	5.08	9.71	3.97	4.13	9.71
Days With ≥ 0.1" Precipitation	13	11	14	13	13	13	13	12	11	12	15	15	155
Days With ≥ 0.5" Precipitation	4	4	5	5	6	6	6	6	5	6	7	5	65
Days With ≥ 1.0" Precipitation	1	2	2	2	2	2	3	3	2	2	3	2	26
Mean Snowfall (in.)	42.6	39.6	45.4	34.3	11.8	1.0	trace	0.1	2.2	17.8	38.3	45.3	278.4
Maximum Snowfall (in.)*	95	124	98	111	52	8	1	3	8	34	87	92	449
Maximum 24-hr. Snowfall (in.)*	23	28	27	23	23	5	1	2	8	15	20	26	28
Maximum Snow Depth (in.)	23	24	25	26	15	5	4	trace	3	32	25	25	32
Days With ≥ 1.0" Snow Depth	30	28	31	27	10	0	0	0	1	10	20	29	186
Thunderstorm Days*	< 1	< 1	< 1	1	2	3	4	3	1	1	< 1	< 1	15
Foggy Days*	29	25	28	26	25	26	29	29	27	26	27	29	326
Predominant Sky Cover*	na	na	na	na	na	na	na	na	na	na	na	na	na
Mean Relative Humidity 7am (%)*	na	na	na	na	na	na	na	na	na	na	na	na	na
Mean Relative Humidity 4pm (%)*	na	na	na	na	na	na	na	na	na	na	na	na	na
Mean Dewpoint (°F)*	na	na	na	na	na	na	na	na	na	na	na	na	na
Prevailing Wind Direction*	na	na	na	na	na	na	na	na	na	na	na	na	na
Prevailing Wind Speed (mph)*	na	na	na	na	na	na	na	na	na	na	na	na	na
Maximum Wind Gust (mph)*	153	166	148	229	129	127	119	142	174	150	229	178	229

Note: (*) Period of record is 1948-1995

Benton 5 SW *Grafton County* Elevation: 1,200 ft. Latitude: 44° 02' N Longitude: 71° 56' W

	JAN	FEB	MAR	APR	MAY	JUN	JUL	AUG	SEP	OCT	NOV	DEC	YEAR
Mean Maximum Temp. (°F)	26.5	30.0	38.5	52.4	64.8	73.1	77.3	75.9	67.8	55.5	43.2	31.6	53.0
Mean Temp. (°F)	16.9	19.9	28.7	41.9	53.5	62.1	66.5	64.9	56.8	45.4	35.1	22.9	42.9
Mean Minimum Temp. (°F)	7.3	9.7	18.9	31.3	42.1	51.1	55.6	53.8	45.7	35.3	26.9	14.2	32.7
Extreme Maximum Temp. (°F)	64	63	78	88	87	93	95	94	93	79	71	65	95
Extreme Minimum Temp. (°F)	-29	-26	-17	4	21	27	40	32	23	16	-2	-28	-29
Days Maximum Temp. ≥ 90°F	0	0	0	0	0	0	0	0	0	0	0	0	0
Days Maximum Temp. ≤ 32°F	21	17	9	1	0	0	0	0	0	0	5	17	70
Days Minimum Temp. ≤ 32°F	30	27	28	18	3	0	0	0	2	13	22	29	172
Days Minimum Temp. ≤ 0°F	11	8	3	0	0	0	0	0	0	0	0	5	27
Heating Degree Days (base 65°F)	1,486	1,270	1,117	688	358	131	44	74	256	600	891	1,299	8,214
Cooling Degree Days (base 65°F)	0	0	0	1	8	50	97	77	16	0	0	0	249
Mean Precipitation (in.)	2.22	2.09	2.67	3.04	3.54	3.67	4.12	4.26	3.65	4.00	3.69	2.67	39.62
Extreme Maximum Daily Precip. (in.)	1.61	1.75	2.08	1.95	1.98	2.48	1.75	2.38	3.42	3.06	2.61	2.13	3.42
Days With ≥ 0.1" Precipitation	5	5	7	7	8	8	8	8	7	8	7	7	85
Days With ≥ 0.5" Precipitation	1	1	2	2	2	2	3	3	2	2	3	2	25
Days With ≥ 1.0" Precipitation	0	0	0	1	1	0	1	1	1	1	1	0	7
Mean Snowfall (in.)	15.4	14.9	13.7	4.5	0.2	0.0	0.0	0.0	trace	1.0	4.8	16.9	71.4
Maximum Snow Depth (in.)	25	22	28	16	1	0	0	0	trace	5	10	22	28
Days With ≥ 1.0" Snow Depth	27	25	20	4	0	0	0	0	0	0	6	21	103

Berlin *Coos County* Elevation: 930 ft. Latitude: 44° 27' N Longitude: 71° 11' W

	JAN	FEB	MAR	APR	MAY	JUN	JUL	AUG	SEP	OCT	NOV	DEC	YEAR
Mean Maximum Temp. (°F)	26.4	30.3	38.6	52.5	65.5	74.1	78.3	77.1	69.0	56.4	43.7	31.7	53.6
Mean Temp. (°F)	15.9	18.8	27.8	41.6	53.3	62.5	66.8	65.2	57.1	45.7	35.1	22.4	42.7
Mean Minimum Temp. (°F)	5.3	7.2	17.0	30.7	41.1	50.8	55.2	53.3	45.2	34.9	26.6	13.1	31.7
Extreme Maximum Temp. (°F)	65	65	76	88	91	95	98	94	92	82	73	68	98
Extreme Minimum Temp. (°F)	-26	-29	-21	5	25	32	35	35	25	17	-4	-26	-29
Days Maximum Temp. ≥ 90°F	0	0	0	0	0	1	1	1	0	0	0	0	3
Days Maximum Temp. ≤ 32°F	22	16	9	1	0	0	0	0	0	0	4	16	68
Days Minimum Temp. ≤ 32°F	31	28	28	18	4	0	0	0	2	13	22	30	176
Days Minimum Temp. ≤ 0°F	12	10	4	0	0	0	0	0	0	0	0	6	32
Heating Degree Days (base 65°F)	1,518	1,301	1,147	695	364	125	43	72	248	592	889	1,313	8,307
Cooling Degree Days (base 65°F)	0	0	0	0	8	56	105	86	17	1	0	0	273
Mean Precipitation (in.)	2.44	2.27	2.84	3.39	3.47	4.00	3.83	4.05	3.59	4.34	3.89	3.01	41.12
Extreme Maximum Daily Precip. (in.)	2.60	2.02	2.28	3.41	2.28	4.11	2.56	4.00	6.50	4.46	3.12	2.63	6.50
Days With ≥ 0.1" Precipitation	5	5	7	7	8	9	9	8	7	7	7	7	86
Days With ≥ 0.5" Precipitation	1	2	2	2	2	3	3	2	2	3	3	2	27
Days With ≥ 1.0" Precipitation	0	1	1	1	1	1	1	1	1	1	1	1	11
Mean Snowfall (in.)	17.9	18.5	15.6	4.0	trace	0.0	0.0	0.0	trace	0.4	4.2	19.4	80.0
Maximum Snow Depth (in.)	47	54	61	22	1	0	0	0	trace	4	12	38	61
Days With ≥ 1.0" Snow Depth	29	26	24	5	0	0	0	0	0	0	5	23	112

Durham *Strafford County* Elevation: 80 ft. Latitude: 43° 09' N Longitude: 70° 57' W

	JAN	FEB	MAR	APR	MAY	JUN	JUL	AUG	SEP	OCT	NOV	DEC	YEAR
Mean Maximum Temp. (°F)	33.4	37.4	45.5	58.3	69.2	78.1	83.1	81.6	73.5	61.5	49.5	38.2	59.1
Mean Temp. (°F)	23.4	26.8	34.7	46.1	56.2	65.5	70.7	69.2	61.4	49.7	39.8	28.9	47.7
Mean Minimum Temp. (°F)	13.4	16.1	23.9	33.9	43.1	52.9	58.2	56.8	49.2	37.9	30.1	19.6	36.3
Extreme Maximum Temp. (°F)	68	71	89	93	94	97	99	100	97	85	76	74	100
Extreme Minimum Temp. (°F)	-27	-19	-12	14	22	33	40	32	27	17	-7	-22	-27
Days Maximum Temp. ≥ 90°F	0	0	0	0	1	3	5	3	1	0	0	0	13
Days Maximum Temp. ≤ 32°F	14	8	3	0	0	0	0	0	0	0	1	9	35
Days Minimum Temp. ≤ 32°F	29	26	24	14	3	0	0	0	1	9	18	28	152
Days Minimum Temp. ≤ 0°F	5	3	1	0	0	0	0	0	0	0	0	1	10
Heating Degree Days (base 65°F)	1,282	1,073	932	562	285	72	11	25	148	469	748	1,111	6,718
Cooling Degree Days (base 65°F)	0	0	0	2	17	94	194	162	46	2	0	0	517
Mean Precipitation (in.)	2.66	2.75	3.44	4.27	3.88	3.96	3.84	3.50	3.71	4.33	4.40	3.34	44.08
Extreme Maximum Daily Precip. (in.)	1.95	3.93	2.70	5.46	4.70	4.65	3.85	5.23	4.48	6.30	3.50	2.57	6.30
Days With ≥ 0.1" Precipitation	6	5	7	7	8	7	7	6	6	6	7	6	78
Days With ≥ 0.5" Precipitation	2	2	2	3	3	2	3	2	2	3	3	2	29
Days With ≥ 1.0" Precipitation	0	0	1	1	1	1	1	1	1	1	1	1	10
Mean Snowfall (in.)	11.1	9.5	7.1	1.7	0.0	0.0	0.0	0.0	0.0	trace	1.5	8.9	39.8
Maximum Snow Depth (in.)	30	37	31	11	0	0	0	0	0	trace	10	18	37
Days With ≥ 1.0" Snow Depth	17	16	10	1	0	0	0	0	0	0	1	11	56

Epping *Rockingham County* Elevation: 160 ft. Latitude: 43° 02' N Longitude: 71° 05' W

	JAN	FEB	MAR	APR	MAY	JUN	JUL	AUG	SEP	OCT	NOV	DEC	YEAR
Mean Maximum Temp. (°F)	33.0	36.7	44.9	57.2	68.7	77.4	82.3	80.9	72.9	60.9	49.1	37.4	58.4
Mean Temp. (°F)	23.4	26.5	34.5	45.6	56.1	65.3	70.3	68.9	60.7	49.1	39.5	28.6	47.4
Mean Minimum Temp. (°F)	13.8	16.3	24.1	34.0	43.5	53.1	58.3	56.8	48.5	37.3	29.9	19.7	36.3
Extreme Maximum Temp. (°F)	69	70	82	92	94	96	99	98	95	85	77	71	99
Extreme Minimum Temp. (°F)	-27	-19	-10	12	24	34	40	32	26	15	-5	-22	-27
Days Maximum Temp. ≥ 90°F	0	0	0	0	1	2	3	3	1	0	0	0	10
Days Maximum Temp. ≤ 32°F	15	10	3	0	0	0	0	0	0	0	1	10	39
Days Minimum Temp. ≤ 32°F	30	26	25	14	3	0	0	0	1	10	19	28	156
Days Minimum Temp. ≤ 0°F	5	3	1	0	0	0	0	0	0	0	0	1	10
Heating Degree Days (base 65°F)	1,284	1,081	938	575	287	78	13	28	163	488	758	1,123	6,816
Cooling Degree Days (base 65°F)	0	0	0	2	18	93	185	154	42	2	0	0	496
Mean Precipitation (in.)	3.17	3.11	3.86	4.56	4.02	4.06	3.76	3.42	3.81	4.33	4.25	3.66	46.01
Extreme Maximum Daily Precip. (in.)	1.80	3.33	3.15	4.94	4.34	4.14	3.08	7.40	5.05	5.80	3.00	2.87	7.40
Days With ≥ 0.1" Precipitation	7	6	7	7	8	8	7	6	6	7	7	7	83
Days With ≥ 0.5" Precipitation	2	2	3	3	3	3	3	2	2	3	3	3	32
Days With ≥ 1.0" Precipitation	0	1	1	1	1	1	1	1	1	1	1	1	11
Mean Snowfall (in.)	16.1	11.1	10.9	2.7	0.0	0.0	0.0	0.0	0.0	trace	2.1	11.3	54.2
Maximum Snow Depth (in.)	na	na	na	***10***	***0***	***0***	***0***	***0***	***0***	***trace***	***4***	na	na
Days With ≥ 1.0" Snow Depth	na	na	***13***	1	0	0	0	0	0	0	1	***10***	na

The period of record for all cooperative weather station data is 1980 – 2009. See User Guide for detailed explanation of data.

Grafton *Grafton County* Elevation: 830 ft. Latitude: 43° 34' N Longitude: 71° 57' W

	JAN	FEB	MAR	APR	MAY	JUN	JUL	AUG	SEP	OCT	NOV	DEC	YEAR
Mean Maximum Temp. (°F)	*28.3*	*32.1*	*40.4*	*53.6*	*66.6*	*74.8*	*79.5*	*77.7*	*69.5*	*57.2*	*44.6*	*33.3*	*54.8*
Mean Temp. (°F)	*17.0*	*19.7*	*28.9*	*41.2*	*52.8*	*61.5*	*66.2*	*64.6*	*56.3*	*44.5*	*34.8*	*23.1*	*42.5*
Mean Minimum Temp. (°F)	*5.6*	*7.1*	*17.3*	*28.6*	*38.9*	*48.1*	*52.8*	*51.5*	*43.1*	*31.8*	*25.0*	*12.9*	*30.2*
Extreme Maximum Temp. (°F)	*60*	*63*	*80*	*90*	*90*	*95*	*96*	*97*	*94*	*82*	*74*	*70*	*97*
Extreme Minimum Temp. (°F)	*-40*	*-31*	*-22*	*3*	*19*	*28*	*32*	*29*	*21*	*13*	*-3*	*-29*	*-40*
Days Maximum Temp. ≥ 90°F	*0*	*0*	*0*	*0*	*0*	*1*	*2*	*1*	*0*	*0*	*0*	*0*	*4*
Days Maximum Temp. ≤ 32°F	*20*	*14*	*7*	*0*	*0*	*0*	*0*	*0*	*0*	*0*	*3*	*14*	*58*
Days Minimum Temp. ≤ 32°F	*31*	*27*	*29*	*20*	*9*	*1*	*0*	*0*	*5*	*18*	*24*	*30*	*194*
Days Minimum Temp. ≤ 0°F	*11*	*10*	*3*	*0*	*0*	*0*	*0*	*0*	*0*	*0*	*0*	*5*	*29*
Heating Degree Days (base 65°F)	*1,483*	*1,276*	*1,113*	*709*	*377*	*143*	*54*	*81*	*270*	*629*	*898*	*1,291*	*8,324*
Cooling Degree Days (base 65°F)	*0*	*0*	*0*	*0*	*6*	*45*	*97*	*77*	*16*	*0*	*0*	*0*	*241*
Mean Precipitation (in.)	*2.78*	*2.41*	*3.03*	*3.10*	*3.43*	*3.52*	*3.26*	*3.60*	*3.44*	*3.65*	*3.41*	*2.58*	*38.21*
Extreme Maximum Daily Precip. (in.)	*2.44*	*1.80*	*1.74*	*2.75*	*2.33*	*2.12*	*2.30*	*3.60*	*4.53*	*4.85*	*2.64*	*1.90*	*4.85*
Days With ≥ 0.1" Precipitation	*5*	*5*	*6*	*6*	*7*	*7*	*6*	*6*	*6*	*6*	*7*	*6*	*73*
Days With ≥ 0.5" Precipitation	*2*	*2*	*2*	*2*	*2*	*3*	*3*	*2*	*2*	*3*	*3*	*2*	*28*
Days With ≥ 1.0" Precipitation	*1*	*1*	*1*	*0*	*1*	*1*	*1*	*1*	*1*	*1*	*1*	*0*	*10*
Mean Snowfall (in.)	*20.4*	*16.8*	*15.1*	*4.9*	*trace*	*0.0*	*0.0*	*0.0*	*0.0*	*0.4*	*5.0*	*15.1*	*77.7*
Maximum Snow Depth (in.)	na	na	na	na	na	*0*	na	na	na	na	na	na	na
Days With ≥ 1.0" Snow Depth	na	na	na	*2*	*0*	*0*	*0*	*0*	*0*	*0*	*4*	na	na

Greenland *Rockingham County* Elevation: 84 ft. Latitude: 43° 01' N Longitude: 70° 50' W

	JAN	FEB	MAR	APR	MAY	JUN	JUL	AUG	SEP	OCT	NOV	DEC	YEAR
Mean Maximum Temp. (°F)	34.0	37.7	45.2	56.9	67.5	76.8	82.0	80.7	72.9	61.3	50.0	39.1	58.7
Mean Temp. (°F)	24.6	27.7	35.2	45.8	55.7	65.1	70.4	69.1	61.5	50.2	40.6	30.2	48.0
Mean Minimum Temp. (°F)	15.1	17.8	25.2	34.6	43.8	53.2	58.6	57.4	50.0	39.1	31.3	21.2	37.3
Extreme Maximum Temp. (°F)	62	72	89	94	94	96	101	98	96	86	78	75	101
Extreme Minimum Temp. (°F)	-26	-15	-6	15	15	33	39	33	27	18	-6	-17	-26
Days Maximum Temp. ≥ 90°F	0	0	0	0	1	2	4	3	1	0	0	0	11
Days Maximum Temp. ≤ 32°F	14	8	3	0	0	0	0	0	0	0	1	7	33
Days Minimum Temp. ≤ 32°F	30	26	24	13	3	0	0	0	1	8	18	27	150
Days Minimum Temp. ≤ 0°F	4	2	0	0	0	0	0	0	0	0	0	1	7
Heating Degree Days (base 65°F)	1,247	1,046	916	573	300	82	13	27	147	456	724	1,073	6,604
Cooling Degree Days (base 65°F)	0	0	0	2	17	90	185	160	48	3	0	0	505
Mean Precipitation (in.)	3.52	3.40	4.58	4.81	4.17	4.33	4.03	3.34	4.05	4.55	4.85	4.28	49.91
Extreme Maximum Daily Precip. (in.)	2.44	3.95	4.52	4.12	5.30	5.82	4.17	6.09	4.77	8.41	3.95	3.46	8.41
Days With ≥ 0.1" Precipitation	7	6	8	8	8	8	7	6	6	6	8	7	85
Days With ≥ 0.5" Precipitation	3	2	3	3	3	3	3	2	3	3	3	3	34
Days With ≥ 1.0" Precipitation	1	1	1	1	1	1	1	1	1	1	1	1	12
Mean Snowfall (in.)	17.1	12.6	11.5	2.7	trace	0.0	0.0	0.0	0.0	0.1	2.1	12.8	58.9
Maximum Snow Depth (in.)	32	35	38	22	trace	0	0	0	0	trace	7	26	38
Days With ≥ 1.0" Snow Depth	20	19	12	1	0	0	0	0	0	0	2	12	66

Hanover *Grafton County* Elevation: 603 ft. Latitude: 43° 42' N Longitude: 72° 17' W

	JAN	FEB	MAR	APR	MAY	JUN	JUL	AUG	SEP	OCT	NOV	DEC	YEAR
Mean Maximum Temp. (°F)	29.2	33.9	43.0	57.3	69.8	77.9	82.5	80.9	72.2	58.4	46.0	33.4	57.0
Mean Temp. (°F)	19.5	23.2	32.4	45.4	56.8	65.5	70.5	69.0	60.9	48.2	37.8	25.2	46.2
Mean Minimum Temp. (°F)	9.8	12.4	21.7	33.4	43.8	53.0	58.4	57.0	49.7	37.9	29.5	16.8	35.3
Extreme Maximum Temp. (°F)	64	62	86	93	96	98	101	100	97	83	74	70	101
Extreme Minimum Temp. (°F)	-27	-24	-15	10	24	30	42	36	24	17	3	-27	-27
Days Maximum Temp. ≥ 90°F	0	0	0	0	0	2	4	3	0	0	0	0	9
Days Maximum Temp. ≤ 32°F	19	12	4	0	0	0	0	0	0	0	2	13	50
Days Minimum Temp. ≤ 32°F	30	27	27	15	2	0	0	0	1	9	20	27	158
Days Minimum Temp. ≤ 0°F	8	5	2	0	0	0	0	0	0	0	0	3	18
Heating Degree Days (base 65°F)	1,404	1,176	1,005	584	265	70	12	25	155	516	810	1,230	7,252
Cooling Degree Days (base 65°F)	0	0	0	2	18	91	188	155	39	1	0	0	494
Mean Precipitation (in.)	2.59	2.41	2.97	3.06	3.46	3.45	4.10	3.62	3.40	3.82	3.46	2.85	39.19
Extreme Maximum Daily Precip. (in.)	1.90	3.45	3.20	1.91	2.96	2.10	2.81	3.99	3.22	3.04	1.95	2.41	3.99
Days With ≥ 0.1" Precipitation	6	5	6	7	7	7	7	7	6	6	7	6	77
Days With ≥ 0.5" Precipitation	2	1	2	2	2	2	3	3	2	2	3	2	26
Days With ≥ 1.0" Precipitation	0	0	1	1	1	1	1	1	1	1	1	1	10
Mean Snowfall (in.)	17.1	13.4	10.8	1.9	0.0	0.0	0.0	0.0	trace	0.1	2.6	14.6	60.5
Maximum Snow Depth (in.)	32	35	34	29	0	0	0	0	trace	2	10	23	35
Days With ≥ 1.0" Snow Depth	25	25	18	2	0	0	0	0	0	0	3	19	92

Keene *Cheshire County* Elevation: 509 ft. Latitude: 42° 57' N Longitude: 72° 19' W

	JAN	FEB	MAR	APR	MAY	JUN	JUL	AUG	SEP	OCT	NOV	DEC	YEAR
Mean Maximum Temp. (°F)	31.5	35.9	44.7	58.1	70.1	78.2	82.8	81.5	73.4	61.0	48.4	36.4	58.5
Mean Temp. (°F)	21.2	24.3	32.9	45.2	56.1	65.1	69.8	68.6	60.6	48.5	38.4	26.9	46.5
Mean Minimum Temp. (°F)	10.7	12.7	21.1	32.2	42.2	51.9	56.8	55.7	47.6	36.0	28.3	17.4	34.4
Extreme Maximum Temp. (°F)	65	63	87	93	93	97	99	97	94	86	76	70	99
Extreme Minimum Temp. (°F)	-27	-16	-13	12	25	32	40	30	26	18	3	-23	-27
Days Maximum Temp. ≥ 90°F	0	0	0	0	1	3	4	3	1	0	0	0	12
Days Maximum Temp. ≤ 32°F	16	10	4	0	0	0	0	0	0	0	1	10	41
Days Minimum Temp. ≤ 32°F	30	27	27	16	5	0	0	0	1	13	21	29	169
Days Minimum Temp. ≤ 0°F	8	5	1	0	0	0	0	0	0	0	0	3	17
Heating Degree Days (base 65°F)	1,353	1,145	987	589	285	76	17	31	166	507	793	1,173	7,122
Cooling Degree Days (base 65°F)	0	0	0	2	17	85	174	150	39	3	0	0	470
Mean Precipitation (in.)	2.98	2.61	3.23	3.51	3.93	3.85	4.15	3.83	3.73	4.16	3.80	3.19	42.97
Extreme Maximum Daily Precip. (in.)	2.02	2.13	2.47	2.30	3.80	2.30	2.48	3.06	4.37	8.64	2.23	2.45	8.64
Days With ≥ 0.1" Precipitation	6	6	7	7	8	8	7	6	6	7	7	6	81
Days With ≥ 0.5" Precipitation	2	2	2	2	3	2	3	3	3	3	3	2	30
Days With ≥ 1.0" Precipitation	1	0	1	1	1	1	1	1	1	1	1	0	10
Mean Snowfall (in.)	15.8	11.8	9.9	2.2	trace	0.0	0.0	0.0	0.0	0.1	2.6	11.3	53.7
Maximum Snow Depth (in.)	25	30	33	15	trace	0	0	0	0	1	9	17	33
Days With ≥ 1.0" Snow Depth	24	23	16	2	0	0	0	0	0	0	3	18	86

The period of record for all cooperative weather station data is 1980 – 2009. See User Guide for detailed explanation of data.

Lakeport 2 *Belknap County* Elevation: 500 ft. Latitude: 43° 33' N Longitude: 71° 28' W

	JAN	FEB	MAR	APR	MAY	JUN	JUL	AUG	SEP	OCT	NOV	DEC	YEAR
Mean Maximum Temp. (°F)	29.9	33.7	42.4	55.5	67.4	76.4	81.3	80.5	72.2	59.7	46.9	35.0	56.7
Mean Temp. (°F)	20.6	23.2	31.9	44.5	56.1	65.8	70.9	69.7	61.5	49.5	38.8	27.3	46.7
Mean Minimum Temp. (°F)	11.4	12.6	21.3	33.4	44.7	55.1	60.4	58.9	50.8	39.3	30.6	19.6	36.5
Extreme Maximum Temp. (°F)	64	63	76	92	95	96	98	100	95	83	75	69	100
Extreme Minimum Temp. (°F)	-24	-17	-11	12	28	38	45	40	30	24	7	-13	-24
Days Maximum Temp. ≥ 90°F	0	0	0	0	0	2	3	3	0	0	0	0	8
Days Maximum Temp. ≤ 32°F	18	12	5	0	0	0	0	0	0	0	2	12	49
Days Minimum Temp. ≤ 32°F	30	28	28	15	1	0	0	0	0	6	18	28	154
Days Minimum Temp. ≤ 0°F	6	4	1	0	0	0	0	0	0	0	0	1	12
Heating Degree Days (base 65°F)	1,368	1,177	1,020	610	286	72	10	20	140	476	780	1,161	7,120
Cooling Degree Days (base 65°F)	0	0	0	1	17	101	200	173	43	2	0	0	537
Mean Precipitation (in.)	2.83	2.74	3.21	3.79	3.70	4.30	4.19	3.76	3.47	4.31	3.89	3.21	43.40
Extreme Maximum Daily Precip. (in.)	2.02	1.98	2.51	2.91	3.95	3.06	3.55	3.47	4.04	5.43	3.37	1.85	5.43
Days With ≥ 0.1" Precipitation	6	6	6	7	7	8	7	7	6	7	7	6	80
Days With ≥ 0.5" Precipitation	2	2	2	2	2	3	3	3	2	3	3	2	29
Days With ≥ 1.0" Precipitation	1	1	1	1	1	1	1	1	1	1	1	1	12
Mean Snowfall (in.)	17.0	14.7	11.2	1.8	0.0	0.0	0.0	0.0	0.0	0.0	2.4	13.5	60.6
Maximum Snow Depth (in.)	30	30	29	21	0	0	0	0	0	0	9	17	30
Days With ≥ 1.0" Snow Depth	22	21	15	2	0	0	0	0	0	0	2	14	76

Massabesic Lake *Hillsborough County* Elevation: 250 ft. Latitude: 42° 59' N Longitude: 71° 24' W

	JAN	FEB	MAR	APR	MAY	JUN	JUL	AUG	SEP	OCT	NOV	DEC	YEAR
Mean Maximum Temp. (°F)	32.1	36.4	43.9	56.8	67.7	77.0	82.0	80.7	73.1	60.8	49.8	37.8	58.2
Mean Temp. (°F)	20.6	24.7	32.6	44.9	55.5	65.2	70.0	68.6	60.7	48.6	38.9	27.5	46.5
Mean Minimum Temp. (°F)	9.1	12.8	21.2	32.9	43.4	53.3	58.0	56.5	48.3	36.3	28.0	17.2	34.7
Extreme Maximum Temp. (°F)	62	70	86	94	95	98	100	97	94	85	77	75	100
Extreme Minimum Temp. (°F)	-29	-19	-18	4	19	29	36	37	20	12	-4	-14	-29
Days Maximum Temp. ≥ 90°F	0	0	0	0	0	2	4	3	1	0	0	0	10
Days Maximum Temp. ≤ 32°F	16	10	4	0	0	0	0	0	0	0	1	9	40
Days Minimum Temp. ≤ 32°F	31	27	27	14	2	0	0	0	1	11	21	29	163
Days Minimum Temp. ≤ 0°F	7	4	1	0	0	0	0	0	0	0	0	2	14
Heating Degree Days (base 65°F)	1,370	1,133	998	599	301	80	21	31	163	504	776	1,154	7,130
Cooling Degree Days (base 65°F)	0	0	0	1	15	92	182	149	41	2	0	0	482
Mean Precipitation (in.)	2.54	2.45	2.80	3.67	3.85	4.26	3.74	3.61	3.40	4.00	3.74	3.06	41.12
Extreme Maximum Daily Precip. (in.)	1.76	2.04	2.10	2.50	6.00	3.60	2.80	4.19	5.25	5.70	2.70	2.87	6.00
Days With ≥ 0.1" Precipitation	6	5	6	7	8	8	6	6	6	6	7	5	76
Days With ≥ 0.5" Precipitation	2	2	2	2	2	3	3	2	2	3	2	2	27
Days With ≥ 1.0" Precipitation	0	0	1	1	1	1	1	1	1	1	1	0	9
Mean Snowfall (in.)	14.4	10.1	7.8	1.6	0.0	0.0	0.0	0.0	0.2	trace	1.8	7.9	43.8
Maximum Snow Depth (in.)	na	na	na	16	0	0	0	0	0	1	na	na	na
Days With ≥ 1.0" Snow Depth	na	na	6	0	0	0	0	0	0	0	1	7	na

Mount Sunapee *Merrimack County* Elevation: 1,270 ft. Latitude: 43° 20' N Longitude: 72° 05' W

	JAN	FEB	MAR	APR	MAY	JUN	JUL	AUG	SEP	OCT	NOV	DEC	YEAR
Mean Maximum Temp. (°F)	29.5	32.8	41.2	54.9	67.1	75.0	79.3	77.8	69.7	57.7	45.5	34.1	55.4
Mean Temp. (°F)	21.2	23.8	31.8	44.1	55.7	64.4	69.0	67.7	59.6	48.0	37.5	26.4	45.8
Mean Minimum Temp. (°F)	12.8	14.6	22.4	33.3	44.2	53.6	58.5	57.1	49.4	38.3	29.5	18.7	36.0
Extreme Maximum Temp. (°F)	63	61	82	87	88	93	98	93	89	80	72	67	98
Extreme Minimum Temp. (°F)	-18	-15	-11	10	25	32	39	35	26	18	5	-23	-23
Days Maximum Temp. ≥ 90°F	0	0	0	0	0	1	1	0	0	0	0	0	2
Days Maximum Temp. ≤ 32°F	19	14	6	0	0	0	0	0	0	0	2	14	55
Days Minimum Temp. ≤ 32°F	30	27	26	14	1	0	0	0	0	8	19	28	153
Days Minimum Temp. ≤ 0°F	5	3	1	0	0	0	0	0	0	0	0	2	11
Heating Degree Days (base 65°F)	1,351	1,160	1,022	621	300	91	18	37	185	521	818	1,190	7,314
Cooling Degree Days (base 65°F)	0	0	0	1	16	79	148	127	28	2	0	0	401
Mean Precipitation (in.)	2.77	2.93	3.32	4.03	4.19	4.41	4.04	4.01	4.00	4.79	4.22	3.29	46.00
Extreme Maximum Daily Precip. (in.)	2.00	2.75	1.94	2.96	3.28	2.33	2.94	2.60	4.91	5.85	2.75	2.59	5.85
Days With ≥ 0.1" Precipitation	6	5	6	7	8	8	7	7	7	7	7	6	81
Days With ≥ 0.5" Precipitation	2	2	2	3	2	3	3	3	2	3	3	2	30
Days With ≥ 1.0" Precipitation	1	1	1	1	1	1	1	1	1	1	1	1	12
Mean Snowfall (in.)	18.2	17.0	12.1	3.9	trace	0.0	0.0	0.0	0.0	0.6	2.7	14.3	68.8
Maximum Snow Depth (in.)	na	na	na	na	trace	0	0	0	0	na	8	na	na
Days With ≥ 1.0" Snow Depth	na	na	na	1	0	0	0	0	0	0	1	na	na

Nashua 2 NNW *Hillsborough County* Elevation: 129 ft. Latitude: 42° 47' N Longitude: 71° 29' W

	JAN	FEB	MAR	APR	MAY	JUN	JUL	AUG	SEP	OCT	NOV	DEC	YEAR
Mean Maximum Temp. (°F)	33.3	37.1	45.1	57.3	68.6	77.0	82.2	81.0	73.2	61.2	49.8	38.3	58.7
Mean Temp. (°F)	23.2	26.3	34.4	45.7	56.6	65.6	70.8	69.6	61.5	49.5	39.8	28.9	47.7
Mean Minimum Temp. (°F)	13.0	15.4	23.7	34.1	44.5	54.1	59.5	58.2	49.6	37.8	29.8	19.5	36.6
Extreme Maximum Temp. (°F)	69	70	85	93	93	99	99	99	95	85	77	73	99
Extreme Minimum Temp. (°F)	-24	-17	-8	13	26	34	40	35	27	20	1	-15	-24
Days Maximum Temp. ≥ 90°F	0	0	0	0	0	2	4	3	1	0	0	0	10
Days Maximum Temp. ≤ 32°F	14	9	3	0	0	0	0	0	0	0	1	8	35
Days Minimum Temp. ≤ 32°F	30	26	27	14	1	0	0	0	0	9	20	29	156
Days Minimum Temp. ≤ 0°F	5	2	1	0	0	0	0	0	0	0	0	1	9
Heating Degree Days (base 65°F)	1,289	1,089	943	574	272	71	11	23	145	475	748	1,113	6,753
Cooling Degree Days (base 65°F)	0	0	0	2	19	95	200	172	46	2	0	0	536
Mean Precipitation (in.)	3.40	3.38	4.23	4.54	4.11	4.45	3.98	3.95	3.65	4.36	4.36	3.81	48.22
Extreme Maximum Daily Precip. (in.)	2.17	2.15	2.60	3.70	4.70	3.40	2.48	5.01	4.50	4.80	3.08	2.45	5.01
Days With ≥ 0.1" Precipitation	7	6	7	7	8	8	7	7	6	7	8	7	85
Days With ≥ 0.5" Precipitation	3	2	3	3	3	3	3	3	2	3	3	3	34
Days With ≥ 1.0" Precipitation	1	1	1	1	1	1	1	1	1	1	1	1	12
Mean Snowfall (in.)	16.3	11.8	11.6	1.8	0.0	0.0	0.0	0.0	0.0	trace	2.2	12.5	56.2
Maximum Snow Depth (in.)	na	na	na	na	na	na	na	na	na	na	na	na	na
Days With ≥ 1.0" Snow Depth	na	na	na	0	0	0	0	0	0	0	0	4	na

The period of record for all cooperative weather station data is 1980 – 2009. See User Guide for detailed explanation of data.

North Stratford *Coos County* Elevation: 910 ft. Latitude: 44° 45' N Longitude: 71° 38' W

	JAN	FEB	MAR	APR	MAY	JUN	JUL	AUG	SEP	OCT	NOV	DEC	YEAR
Mean Maximum Temp. (°F)	24.5	29.2	38.5	52.8	66.1	74.8	78.8	77.5	69.0	56.2	42.3	30.8	53.4
Mean Temp. (°F)	13.1	15.9	26.1	40.9	52.6	61.8	66.2	64.9	56.4	44.8	33.6	21.4	41.5
Mean Minimum Temp. (°F)	1.6	2.5	13.7	28.9	39.0	48.8	53.5	52.3	43.7	33.5	24.8	11.9	29.5
Extreme Maximum Temp. (°F)	61	60	na	na	na	95	95	92	90	80	72	62	na
Extreme Minimum Temp. (°F)	-37	-40	na	na	na	28	33	29	20	15	-4	-30	na
Days Maximum Temp. ≥ 90°F	0	0	0	0	0	1	1	1	0	0	0	0	3
Days Maximum Temp. ≤ 32°F	23	17	9	1	0	0	0	0	0	0	5	17	72
Days Minimum Temp. ≤ 32°F	30	28	28	20	8	1	0	0	3	15	23	30	186
Days Minimum Temp. ≤ 0°F	15	14	6	0	0	0	0	0	0	0	0	7	42
Heating Degree Days (base 65°F)	1,606	1,384	1,198	716	385	136	50	77	264	619	936	1,345	8,716
Cooling Degree Days (base 65°F)	0	0	0	0	7	47	95	80	13	0	0	0	242
Mean Precipitation (in.)	2.30	2.16	2.37	3.05	3.70	4.30	4.33	4.48	3.33	4.05	3.36	3.13	40.56
Extreme Maximum Daily Precip. (in.)	2.50	1.45	1.45	1.70	2.05	na	1.82	na	1.99	2.70	1.88	2.50	na
Days With ≥ 0.1" Precipitation	6	6	6	8	9	9	8	9	6	8	8	8	91
Days With ≥ 0.5" Precipitation	1	1	1	2	2	3	3	3	2	3	2	2	25
Days With ≥ 1.0" Precipitation	0	0	0	0	1	1	1	1	1	1	0	0	6
Mean Snowfall (in.)	18.8	19.4	14.3	5.8	0.1	0.0	0.0	0.0	0.0	0.3	5.6	20.0	84.3
Maximum Snow Depth (in.)	43	37	43	26	2	0	0	0	0	3	10	31	43
Days With ≥ 1.0" Snow Depth	28	26	25	5	0	0	0	0	0	0	7	25	116

The period of record for all cooperative weather station data is 1980 – 2009. See User Guide for detailed explanation of data.

New Hampshire Weather Station Rankings

Annual Extreme Maximum Temperature

Highest			Lowest		
Rank	Station Name	°F	Rank	Station Name	°F
1	Concord Municipal Arpt	101	1	Mount Washington	72
1	Greenland	101	2	Benton 5 SW	95
1	Hanover	101	3	Grafton	*97*
4	Durham	100	4	Berlin	98
4	Lakeport 2	100	4	Mount Sunapee	98
4	Massabesic Lake	*100*	6	Epping	99
7	Epping	99	6	Keene	99
7	Keene	99	6	Nashua 2 NNW	*99*
7	Nashua 2 NNW	*99*	9	Durham	100
10	Berlin	98	9	Lakeport 2	100
10	Mount Sunapee	98	9	Massabesic Lake	*100*
12	Grafton	*97*	12	Concord Municipal Arpt	101
13	Benton 5 SW	95	12	Greenland	101
14	Mount Washington	72	12	Hanover	101

Annual Mean Maximum Temperature

Highest			Lowest		
Rank	Station Name	°F	Rank	Station Name	°F
1	Durham	59.1	1	Mount Washington	34.1
2	Greenland	58.7	2	Benton 5 SW	53.0
2	Nashua 2 NNW	58.7	3	North Stratford	*53.4*
4	Keene	58.5	4	Berlin	53.6
5	Epping	58.4	5	Grafton	*54.8*
6	Massabesic Lake	58.2	6	Mount Sunapee	55.4
7	Concord Municipal Arpt	57.7	7	Lakeport 2	56.7
8	Hanover	57.0	8	Hanover	57.0
9	Lakeport 2	56.7	9	Concord Municipal Arpt	57.7
10	Mount Sunapee	55.4	10	Massabesic Lake	58.2
11	Grafton	*54.8*	11	Epping	58.4
12	Berlin	53.6	12	Keene	58.5
13	North Stratford	*53.4*	13	Greenland	58.7
14	Benton 5 SW	53.0	13	Nashua 2 NNW	58.7
15	Mount Washington	34.1	15	Durham	59.1

Rankings include 25 highest/lowest stations. If state has less than 25 stations, all stations are included. The period of record is 1980–2009. See User Guide for detailed explanation of data.

Annual Mean Temperature

Highest Rank	Station Name	°F	Lowest Rank	Station Name	°F
1	Greenland	48.0	1	Mount Washington	27.5
2	Durham	47.7	2	North Stratford	***41.5***
2	Nashua 2 NNW	47.7	3	Grafton	***42.6***
4	Epping	47.4	4	Berlin	42.7
5	Lakeport 2	46.7	5	Benton 5 SW	42.9
6	Keene	46.5	6	Mount Sunapee	45.8
6	Massabesic Lake	46.5	7	Concord Municipal Arpt	46.2
8	Concord Municipal Arpt	46.2	7	Hanover	46.2
8	Hanover	46.2	9	Keene	46.5
10	Mount Sunapee	45.8	9	Massabesic Lake	46.5
11	Benton 5 SW	42.9	11	Lakeport 2	46.7
12	Berlin	42.7	12	Epping	47.4
13	Grafton	***42.6***	13	Durham	47.7
14	North Stratford	***41.5***	13	Nashua 2 NNW	47.7
15	Mount Washington	27.5	15	Greenland	48.0

Annual Mean Minimum Temperature

Highest Rank	Station Name	°F	Lowest Rank	Station Name	°F
1	Greenland	37.3	1	Mount Washington	20.8
2	Nashua 2 NNW	36.6	2	North Stratford	***29.5***
3	Lakeport 2	36.5	3	Grafton	***30.2***
4	Durham	36.3	4	Berlin	31.7
4	Epping	36.3	5	Benton 5 SW	32.7
6	Mount Sunapee	36.0	6	Keene	34.4
7	Hanover	35.3	7	Concord Municipal Arpt	34.6
8	Massabesic Lake	34.8	8	Massabesic Lake	34.8
9	Concord Municipal Arpt	34.6	9	Hanover	35.3
10	Keene	34.4	10	Mount Sunapee	36.0
11	Benton 5 SW	32.7	11	Durham	36.3
12	Berlin	31.7	11	Epping	36.3
13	Grafton	***30.2***	13	Lakeport 2	36.5
14	North Stratford	***29.5***	14	Nashua 2 NNW	36.6
15	Mount Washington	20.8	15	Greenland	37.3

Rankings include 25 highest/lowest stations. If state has less than 25 stations, all stations are included. The period of record is 1980–2009. See User Guide for detailed explanation of data.

Annual Extreme Minimum Temperature

Highest

Rank	Station Name	°F
1	Mount Sunapee	-23
2	Lakeport 2	-24
2	Nashua 2 NNW	***-24***
4	Greenland	-26
5	Durham	-27
5	Epping	-27
5	Hanover	-27
5	Keene	-27
9	Benton 5 SW	-29
9	Berlin	-29
9	Massabesic Lake	***-29***
12	Concord Municipal Arpt	-33
13	Grafton	***-40***
14	Mount Washington	-45

Lowest

Rank	Station Name	°F
1	Mount Washington	-45
2	Grafton	***-40***
3	Concord Municipal Arpt	-33
4	Benton 5 SW	-29
4	Berlin	-29
4	Massabesic Lake	***-29***
7	Durham	-27
7	Epping	-27
7	Hanover	-27
7	Keene	-27
11	Greenland	-26
12	Lakeport 2	-24
12	Nashua 2 NNW	***-24***
14	Mount Sunapee	-23

July Mean Maximum Temperature

Highest

Rank	Station Name	°F
1	Durham	83.1
2	Keene	82.8
3	Hanover	82.5
4	Epping	82.3
5	Nashua 2 NNW	82.2
6	Concord Municipal Arpt	82.1
7	Greenland	82.0
7	Massabesic Lake	82.0
9	Lakeport 2	81.3
10	Grafton	***79.5***
11	Mount Sunapee	79.3
12	North Stratford	***78.9***
13	Berlin	78.3
14	Benton 5 SW	77.3
15	Mount Washington	54.0

Lowest

Rank	Station Name	°F
1	Mount Washington	54.0
2	Benton 5 SW	77.3
3	Berlin	78.3
4	North Stratford	***78.9***
5	Mount Sunapee	79.3
6	Grafton	***79.5***
7	Lakeport 2	81.3
8	Greenland	82.0
8	Massabesic Lake	82.0
10	Concord Municipal Arpt	82.1
11	Nashua 2 NNW	82.2
12	Epping	82.3
13	Hanover	82.5
14	Keene	82.8
15	Durham	83.1

Rankings include 25 highest/lowest stations. If state has less than 25 stations, all stations are included. The period of record is 1980–2009. See User Guide for detailed explanation of data.

January Mean Minimum Temperature

Highest			Lowest		
Rank	Station Name	°F	Rank	Station Name	°F
1	Greenland	15.1	1	Mount Washington	-3.3
2	Epping	13.8	2	North Stratford	***1.6***
3	Durham	13.4	3	Berlin	5.3
4	Nashua 2 NNW	13.0	4	Grafton	***5.6***
5	Mount Sunapee	12.9	5	Benton 5 SW	7.3
6	Lakeport 2	11.4	6	Massabesic Lake	9.1
7	Keene	10.7	7	Hanover	9.8
8	Concord Municipal Arpt	10.4	8	Concord Municipal Arpt	10.4
9	Hanover	9.8	9	Keene	10.7
10	Massabesic Lake	9.1	10	Lakeport 2	11.4
11	Benton 5 SW	7.3	11	Mount Sunapee	12.9
12	Grafton	***5.6***	12	Nashua 2 NNW	13.0
13	Berlin	5.3	13	Durham	13.4
14	North Stratford	***1.6***	14	Epping	13.8
15	Mount Washington	-3.3	15	Greenland	15.1

Number of Days Annually Maximum Temperature ≥ 90°F

Highest			Lowest		
Rank	Station Name	Days	Rank	Station Name	Days
1	Durham	13	1	Benton 5 SW	0
2	Concord Municipal Arpt	12	1	Mount Washington	0
2	Keene	12	3	Mount Sunapee	2
4	Greenland	11	4	Berlin	3
5	Epping	10	4	North Stratford	***3***
5	Massabesic Lake	10	6	Grafton	***4***
5	Nashua 2 NNW	10	7	Lakeport 2	8
8	Hanover	9	8	Hanover	9
9	Lakeport 2	8	9	Epping	10
10	Grafton	***4***	9	Massabesic Lake	10
11	Berlin	3	9	Nashua 2 NNW	10
11	North Stratford	***3***	12	Greenland	11
13	Mount Sunapee	2	13	Concord Municipal Arpt	12
14	Benton 5 SW	0	13	Keene	12
14	Mount Washington	0	15	Durham	13

Rankings include 25 highest/lowest stations. If state has less than 25 stations, all stations are included. The period of record is 1980–2009. See User Guide for detailed explanation of data.

Number of Days Annually Maximum Temperature ≤ 32°F

Highest			Lowest		
Rank	Station Name	Days	Rank	Station Name	Days
1	Mount Washington	164	1	Greenland	33
2	North Stratford	*72*	2	Durham	35
3	Benton 5 SW	70	2	Nashua 2 NNW	35
4	Berlin	68	4	Epping	39
5	Grafton	*58*	5	Massabesic Lake	40
6	Mount Sunapee	55	6	Keene	41
7	Hanover	50	7	Concord Municipal Arpt	45
8	Lakeport 2	49	8	Lakeport 2	49
9	Concord Municipal Arpt	45	9	Hanover	50
10	Keene	41	10	Mount Sunapee	55
11	Massabesic Lake	40	11	Grafton	*58*
12	Epping	39	12	Berlin	68
13	Durham	35	13	Benton 5 SW	70
13	Nashua 2 NNW	35	14	North Stratford	*72*
15	Greenland	33	15	Mount Washington	164

Number of Days Annually Minimum Temperature ≤ 32°F

Highest			Lowest		
Rank	Station Name	Days	Rank	Station Name	Days
1	Mount Washington	239	1	Greenland	150
2	Grafton	*194*	2	Durham	152
3	North Stratford	*186*	3	Mount Sunapee	153
4	Berlin	176	4	Lakeport 2	154
5	Benton 5 SW	172	5	Epping	156
6	Keene	169	5	Nashua 2 NNW	156
7	Concord Municipal Arpt	168	7	Hanover	158
8	Massabesic Lake	163	8	Massabesic Lake	163
9	Hanover	158	9	Concord Municipal Arpt	168
10	Epping	156	10	Keene	169
10	Nashua 2 NNW	156	11	Benton 5 SW	172
12	Lakeport 2	154	12	Berlin	176
13	Mount Sunapee	153	13	North Stratford	*186*
14	Durham	152	14	Grafton	*194*
15	Greenland	150	15	Mount Washington	239

 Rankings include 25 highest/lowest stations. If state has less than 25 stations, all stations are included. The period of record is 1980–2009. See User Guide for detailed explanation of data.

Number of Days Annually Minimum Temperature ≤ 0°F

Highest			Lowest		
Rank	Station Name	Days	Rank	Station Name	Days
1	Mount Washington	60	1	Greenland	7
2	North Stratford	***42***	2	Nashua 2 NNW	9
3	Berlin	32	3	Durham	10
4	Grafton	***29***	3	Epping	10
5	Benton 5 SW	27	5	Mount Sunapee	11
6	Hanover	18	6	Lakeport 2	12
7	Keene	17	7	Massabesic Lake	14
8	Concord Municipal Arpt	15	8	Concord Municipal Arpt	15
9	Massabesic Lake	14	9	Keene	17
10	Lakeport 2	12	10	Hanover	18
11	Mount Sunapee	11	11	Benton 5 SW	27
12	Durham	10	12	Grafton	***29***
12	Epping	10	13	Berlin	32
14	Nashua 2 NNW	9	14	North Stratford	***42***
15	Greenland	7	15	Mount Washington	60

Number of Annual Heating Degree Days

Highest			Lowest		
Rank	Station Name	Num.	Rank	Station Name	Num.
1	Mount Washington	13,608	1	Greenland	6,604
2	North Stratford	***8,716***	2	Durham	6,718
3	Grafton	***8,324***	3	Nashua 2 NNW	6,753
4	Berlin	8,307	4	Epping	6,816
5	Benton 5 SW	8,214	5	Lakeport 2	7,120
6	Mount Sunapee	7,314	6	Keene	7,122
7	Hanover	7,252	7	Massabesic Lake	7,130
8	Concord Municipal Arpt	7,222	8	Concord Municipal Arpt	7,222
9	Massabesic Lake	7,130	9	Hanover	7,252
10	Keene	7,122	10	Mount Sunapee	7,314
11	Lakeport 2	7,120	11	Benton 5 SW	8,214
12	Epping	6,816	12	Berlin	8,307
13	Nashua 2 NNW	6,753	13	Grafton	***8,324***
14	Durham	6,718	14	North Stratford	***8,716***
15	Greenland	6,604	15	Mount Washington	13,608

Rankings include 25 highest/lowest stations. If state has less than 25 stations, all stations are included. The period of record is 1980–2009. See User Guide for detailed explanation of data.

Number of Annual Cooling Degree Days

Highest			Lowest		
Rank	Station Name	Num.	Rank	Station Name	Num.
1	Lakeport 2	537	1	Mount Washington	0
2	Nashua 2 NNW	536	2	Grafton	***241***
3	Durham	517	3	North Stratford	***242***
4	Greenland	505	4	Benton 5 SW	249
5	Epping	496	5	Berlin	273
6	Hanover	494	6	Mount Sunapee	401
7	Massabesic Lake	482	7	Concord Municipal Arpt	466
8	Keene	470	8	Keene	470
9	Concord Municipal Arpt	466	9	Massabesic Lake	482
10	Mount Sunapee	401	10	Hanover	494
11	Berlin	273	11	Epping	496
12	Benton 5 SW	249	12	Greenland	505
13	North Stratford	***242***	13	Durham	517
14	Grafton	***241***	14	Nashua 2 NNW	536
15	Mount Washington	0	15	Lakeport 2	537

Annual Precipitation

Highest			Lowest		
Rank	Station Name	Inches	Rank	Station Name	Inches
1	Mount Washington	96.20	1	Grafton	***38.21***
2	Greenland	49.91	2	Hanover	39.19
3	Nashua 2 NNW	48.22	3	Benton 5 SW	39.62
4	Epping	46.01	4	Concord Municipal Arpt	40.25
5	Mount Sunapee	46.00	5	North Stratford	***40.56***
6	Durham	44.08	6	Berlin	41.12
7	Lakeport 2	43.40	6	Massabesic Lake	41.12
8	Keene	42.97	8	Keene	42.97
9	Berlin	41.12	9	Lakeport 2	43.40
9	Massabesic Lake	41.12	10	Durham	44.08
11	North Stratford	***40.56***	11	Mount Sunapee	46.00
12	Concord Municipal Arpt	40.25	12	Epping	46.01
13	Benton 5 SW	39.62	13	Nashua 2 NNW	48.22
14	Hanover	39.19	14	Greenland	49.91
15	Grafton	***38.21***	15	Mount Washington	96.20

Rankings include 25 highest/lowest stations. If state has less than 25 stations, all stations are included. The period of record is 1980–2009. See User Guide for detailed explanation of data.

Annual Extreme Maximum Daily Precipitation

Highest			Lowest		
Rank	Station Name	Inches	Rank	Station Name	Inches
1	Mount Washington	9.71	1	Benton 5 SW	3.42
2	Keene	8.64	2	Hanover	3.99
3	Greenland	8.41	3	Grafton	***4.85***
4	Epping	7.40	4	Nashua 2 NNW	***5.01***
5	Berlin	6.50	5	Concord Municipal Arpt	5.12
6	Durham	6.30	6	Lakeport 2	5.43
7	Massabesic Lake	***6.00***	7	Mount Sunapee	***5.85***
8	Mount Sunapee	***5.85***	8	Massabesic Lake	***6.00***
9	Lakeport 2	5.43	9	Durham	6.30
10	Concord Municipal Arpt	5.12	10	Berlin	6.50
11	Nashua 2 NNW	***5.01***	11	Epping	7.40
12	Grafton	***4.85***	12	Greenland	8.41
13	Hanover	3.99	13	Keene	8.64
14	Benton 5 SW	3.42	14	Mount Washington	9.71

Number of Days Annually With ≥ 0.1 Inches of Precipitation

Highest			Lowest		
Rank	Station Name	Days	Rank	Station Name	Days
1	Mount Washington	155	1	Grafton	***73***
2	North Stratford	***91***	2	Massabesic Lake	76
3	Berlin	86	3	Hanover	77
4	Benton 5 SW	85	4	Concord Municipal Arpt	78
4	Greenland	85	4	Durham	78
4	Nashua 2 NNW	85	6	Lakeport 2	80
7	Epping	83	7	Keene	81
8	Keene	81	7	Mount Sunapee	81
8	Mount Sunapee	81	9	Epping	83
10	Lakeport 2	80	10	Benton 5 SW	85
11	Concord Municipal Arpt	78	10	Greenland	85
11	Durham	78	10	Nashua 2 NNW	85
13	Hanover	77	13	Berlin	86
14	Massabesic Lake	76	14	North Stratford	***91***
15	Grafton	***73***	15	Mount Washington	155

Number of Days Annually With ≥ 0.5 Inches of Precipitation

Highest Rank	Highest Station Name	Highest Days	Lowest Rank	Lowest Station Name	Lowest Days
1	Mount Washington	65	1	Benton 5 SW	25
2	Greenland	34	1	North Stratford	***25***
2	Nashua 2 NNW	34	3	Concord Municipal Arpt	26
4	Epping	32	3	Hanover	26
5	Keene	30	5	Berlin	27
5	Mount Sunapee	30	5	Massabesic Lake	27
7	Durham	29	7	Grafton	***28***
7	Lakeport 2	29	8	Durham	29
9	Grafton	***28***	8	Lakeport 2	29
10	Berlin	27	10	Keene	30
10	Massabesic Lake	27	10	Mount Sunapee	30
12	Concord Municipal Arpt	26	12	Epping	32
12	Hanover	26	13	Greenland	34
14	Benton 5 SW	25	13	Nashua 2 NNW	34
14	North Stratford	***25***	15	Mount Washington	65

Number of Days Annually With ≥ 1.0 Inches of Precipitation

Highest Rank	Highest Station Name	Highest Days	Lowest Rank	Lowest Station Name	Lowest Days
1	Mount Washington	26	1	North Stratford	***6***
2	Greenland	12	2	Benton 5 SW	7
2	Lakeport 2	12	3	Massabesic Lake	9
2	Mount Sunapee	12	4	Concord Municipal Arpt	10
2	Nashua 2 NNW	12	4	Durham	10
6	Berlin	11	4	Grafton	***10***
6	Epping	11	4	Hanover	10
8	Concord Municipal Arpt	10	4	Keene	10
8	Durham	10	9	Berlin	11
8	Grafton	***10***	9	Epping	11
8	Hanover	10	11	Greenland	12
8	Keene	10	11	Lakeport 2	12
13	Massabesic Lake	9	11	Mount Sunapee	12
14	Benton 5 SW	7	11	Nashua 2 NNW	12
15	North Stratford	***6***	15	Mount Washington	26

Rankings include 25 highest/lowest stations. If state has less than 25 stations, all stations are included. The period of record is 1980–2009. See User Guide for detailed explanation of data.

Annual Snowfall

Highest			Lowest		
Rank	Station Name	Inches	Rank	Station Name	Inches
1	Mount Washington	278.4	1	Durham	39.8
2	North Stratford	***84.3***	2	Massabesic Lake	43.8
3	Berlin	80.0	3	Keene	53.7
4	Grafton	***77.7***	4	Epping	54.2
5	Benton 5 SW	71.4	5	Nashua 2 NNW	56.2
6	Mount Sunapee	***68.8***	6	Greenland	58.9
7	Concord Municipal Arpt	62.4	7	Hanover	60.5
8	Lakeport 2	60.6	8	Lakeport 2	60.6
9	Hanover	60.5	9	Concord Municipal Arpt	62.4
10	Greenland	58.9	10	Mount Sunapee	***68.8***
11	Nashua 2 NNW	56.2	11	Benton 5 SW	71.4
12	Epping	54.2	12	Grafton	***77.7***
13	Keene	53.7	13	Berlin	80.0
14	Massabesic Lake	43.8	14	North Stratford	***84.3***
15	Durham	39.8	15	Mount Washington	278.4

Annual Maximum Snow Depth

Highest			Lowest		
Rank	Station Name	Inches	Rank	Station Name	Inches
1	Berlin	61	1	Benton 5 SW	28
2	Concord Municipal Arpt	45	2	Lakeport 2	***30***
3	North Stratford	***43***	3	Mount Washington	32
4	Greenland	38	4	Keene	33
5	Durham	37	5	Hanover	35
6	Hanover	35	6	Durham	37
7	Keene	33	7	Greenland	38
8	Mount Washington	32	8	North Stratford	***43***
9	Lakeport 2	***30***	9	Concord Municipal Arpt	45
10	Benton 5 SW	28	10	Berlin	61

Rankings include 25 highest/lowest stations. If state has less than 25 stations, all stations are included. The period of record is 1980–2009. See User Guide for detailed explanation of data.

Number of Days Annually With ≥ 1.0 Inch Snow Depth

Highest			Lowest		
Rank	Station Name	Days	Rank	Station Name	Days
1	Mount Washington	186	1	Durham	56
2	North Stratford	***116***	2	Greenland	66
3	Berlin	112	3	Lakeport 2	***76***
4	Benton 5 SW	103	4	Concord Municipal Arpt	81
5	Hanover	92	5	Keene	86
6	Keene	86	6	Hanover	92
7	Concord Municipal Arpt	81	7	Benton 5 SW	103
8	Lakeport 2	***76***	8	Berlin	112
9	Greenland	66	9	North Stratford	***116***
10	Durham	56	10	Mount Washington	186

Rankings include 25 highest/lowest stations. If state has less than 25 stations, all stations are included. The period of record is 1980–2009. See User Guide for detailed explanation of data.

Significant Storm Events in New Hampshire: 2000 – 2009

Location or County	Date	Type	Mag.	Deaths	Injuries	Property Damage ($mil.)	Crop Damage ($mil.)
Cheshire and Hillsborough Counties	03/05/01	Heavy Snow	na	0	0	5.0	0.0
Cheshire	08/06/03	Flash Flood	na	0	0	3.0	0.0
Hillsborough County	11/29/03	High Wind	63 mph	2	2	0.0	0.0
Grafton	06/09/05	Flash Flood	na	0	1	1.0	0.0
Central and Southern New Hampshire	10/08/05	Flood	na	2	0	5.7	0.2
Cheshire	10/09/05	Flash Flood	na	2	0	10.0	0.0
Rockingham	05/13/06	Flood	na	0	0	4.0	0.0
Hillsborough	05/13/06	Flood	na	0	0	2.0	0.0
Strafford	05/13/06	Flood	na	0	0	1.1	0.0
Rockingham County Coast	04/16/07	Coastal Flood	na	0	0	5.0	0.0
Hillsborough	04/16/07	Flood	na	0	0	1.5	0.0
Carroll	04/16/07	Flood	na	0	0	1.2	0.0
Merrimack	04/16/07	Flood	na	0	0	1.0	0.0
Rockingham	04/16/07	Flood	na	0	0	1.0	0.0
Strafford	04/16/07	Flood	na	0	0	1.0	0.0
Belknap	08/07/08	Flash Flood	na	0	0	1.5	0.0
Belknap	08/07/08	Flash Flood	na	1	2	0.7	0.0
Hillsborough County	12/11/08	Ice Storm	na	0	0	15.0	0.0
Western and Central Hillsborough County	12/11/08	Ice Storm	na	0	0	12.0	0.0
Cheshire County	12/11/08	Ice Storm	na	0	0	9.0	0.0

Note: Deaths, injuries, and damages are date and location specific.

NEW JERSEY

PHYSICAL FEATURES. New Jersey, though one of the smaller states, has a varied topography. In the northwestern part a section comprising about one-fifth of the area of the State is known as the Highlands and Kittatinny Valley. This region is traversed by several low mountain ridges extending northeasterly across the State with valleys and rolling hills between. The highest of these ranges is the Kittatinny, which rises from the banks of the Delaware River at the famous Delaware Water Gap. To the eastward the region is studded with numerous lakes, some of the largest of which are Lakes Hopatcong, Mohawk, and Greenwood. Elevations up to 1,800 feet above sea level are found in the Kittatinny Mountains near the New York State line.

South and east of the Highlands is a region of about equal area known as the Red Sandstone Plain, or the Piedmont of New Jersey. It is generally hilly in its northwestern part, becoming rolling and then flat toward the south and southeast. At its northeastern corner are the Palisades, cliffs which rise abruptly from the Hudson River to heights of 200 to 500 feet. The seacoast section extends from Sandy Hook to Cape May, or about 125 miles. This area is characterized by long stretches of sandy beaches. Tidewater marshes become numerous toward the south.

In the southern interior a region known as the Pines is covered with scrubby forests of pine and some oak. The land is low and some of it is swampy. In fact, most of the State that lies south of a line connecting Jersey City and Trenton is low and flat with few elevations higher than 100 feet above mean sea level, these being mainly in Monmouth County.

About 30 percent of the area of New Jersey drains into the Delaware River and Delaware Bay, which form the western boundary. Nearly half of Sussex County, in the northwest, drains northward through the Wallkill River into the Hudson River of New York. The remainder of the State drains directly into the Atlantic Ocean through the Passaic, Hackensack, and Raritan Rivers in the north, and a number of small rivers and streams in the south.

GENERAL CLIMATE. The extreme length of the State is 166 miles and its greatest width only about 65. The difference in climate is quite marked between the southern tip at Cape May and the northern extremity in the Kittatinny Mountains. The former locality is almost surrounded by water and is fairly well removed from the influence of the frequent storms that cross the Great Lakes region and move out the St. Lawrence Valley. The northern extremity is well within the zone of influence of these storms and, in addition, lies at elevations varying from 800 to 1,800 feet. The influence of these high elevations on the temperature is considerable. The differences between these two localities are particularly marked in the winter, Cape May having a normal January temperature about the same as that of southwestern Virginia, while that of Layton, in the extreme northwest, is similar to that of the northern area of Ohio. Since the prevailing winds are mostly offshore, the ocean influence does not have full effect.

TEMPERATURE. Temperature differences between the northern and southern parts of the State are greatest in winter and least in summer. Nearly every weather station has registered readings of 100°F. or higher at some time, and all of them have records of zero or below. In the northern Highland area, the average date of last freeze (32°F.) in spring is about May 2, and that of the first in fall, October 12. On the seacoast corresponding dates are April 6 and November 9, while in the central and southern interior the dates are April 23 and October 19. Freeze-free days in the northern Highlands average 163, with 217 along the seacoast and 179 in the central and southern interior.

PRECIPITATION. Northern New Jersey is near enough to the paths of the storms which cross the Great Lakes region and pass down the St. Lawrence Valley to receive part of its precipitation from that source. However, the heaviest general rains are produced by coastal storms of tropical origin. The centers of these storms usually pass some distance offshore, with heaviest rainfall and strongest wind near the coast. On several occasions tropical storms have moved inland along the south Atlantic coast, and then moved northward either through or to the west of New Jersey. The damage by high tides to coastal installations during the passage of a tropical storm is often severe, whether the storm passes offshore or inland.

The average annual precipitation ranges from about 40 inches along the southeast coast to 51 inches in north-central parts of the State. In other sections the annual averages are mostly between 43 and 47 inches. Rainfall is well distributed during the warm months. Heavy 24-hour falls of seven or eight inches are occasionally recorded. Brief periods of drought during the growing season are not uncommon, but prolonged droughts are relatively rare, occurring on the average once in 15 years. Flooding in New Jersey is usually caused by heavy general rains, at times associated with storms of tropical origin. Local flooding results from ice gorging.

The season during which measurable quantities of snow are likely to fall extends from about October 15 to April 20 in the Highlands, and from about November 15 to March 15 in the vicinity of Cape May. Average seasonal amounts range from about 13 inches at Cape May to nearly 50 inches in the Highlands. Snowfalls of 10 or more inches in a single storm are occasional occurrences.

The number of days a month with measurable precipitation averages eight for each of the fall months (September, October, and November) and nine to 12 for the other months of the year; the average yearly number is 120. Midday relative humidity averages 68 percent along the seacoast and 57 percent or less at inland locations.

Normally, sunshine varies from slightly over one-half of the possible amount in the northern counties to about 60 percent in the south. The prevailing wind is from the northwest from October to April, inclusive, and from the southwest for the other months of the year.

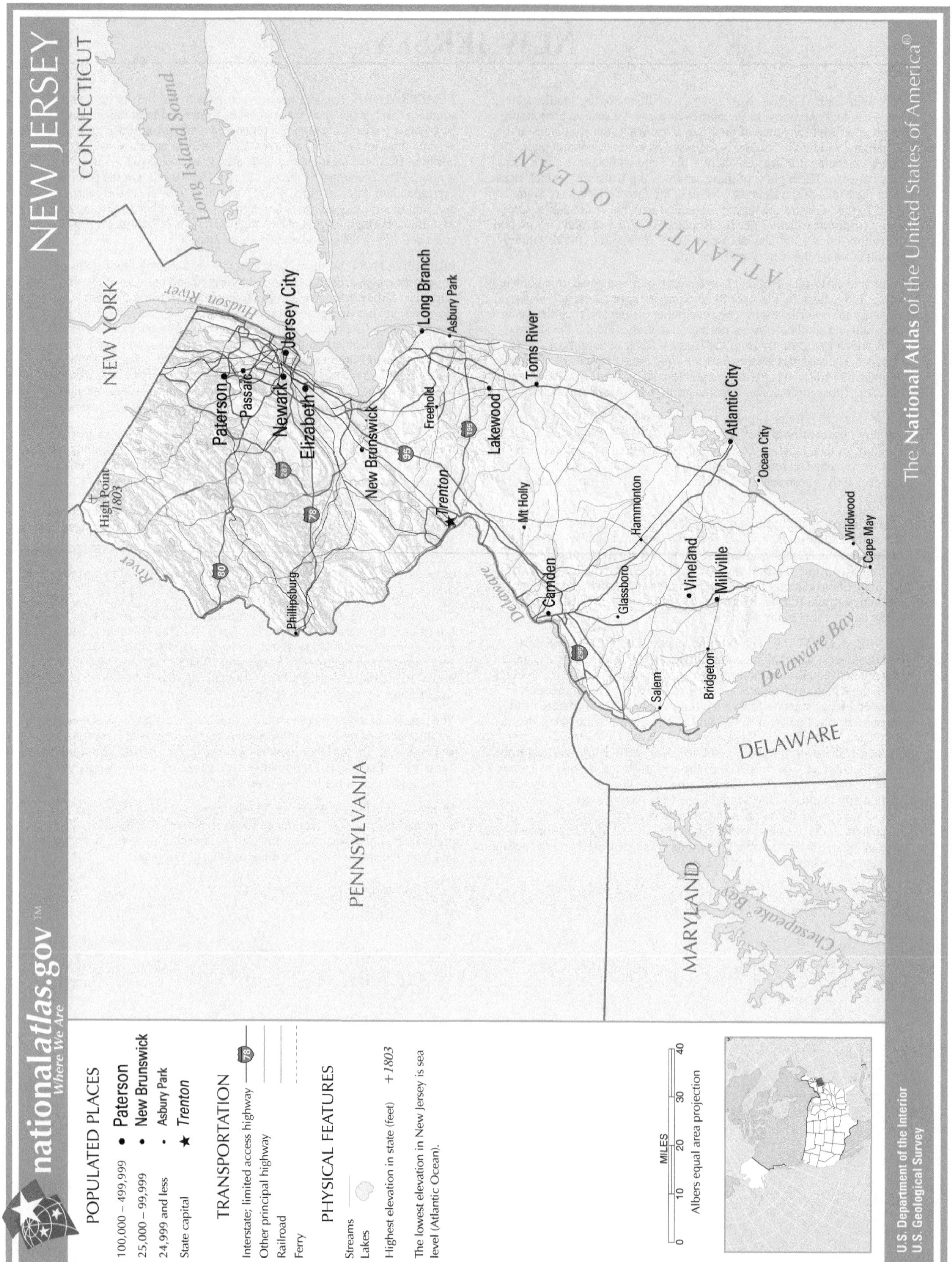
NEW JERSEY
CONNECTICUT
Long Island Sound
NEW YORK
Hudson River
ATLANTIC OCEAN
PENNSYLVANIA
DELAWARE
MARYLAND
Chesapeake Bay
Delaware Bay
Delaware
River
High Point 1803
Paterson
Passaic
Newark
Jersey City
Elizabeth
New Brunswick
Long Branch
Asbury Park
Freehold
Lakewood
Toms River
Trenton
Mt Holly
Hammonton
Atlantic City
Ocean City
Wildwood
Cape May
Camden
Glassboro
Vineland
Millville
Bridgeton
Salem
Phillipsburg
287
78
80
95
195
295
nationalatlas.gov™
Where We Are
POPULATED PLACES
100,000 – 499,999 Paterson
25,000 – 99,999 New Brunswick
24,999 and less Asbury Park
State capital Trenton
TRANSPORTATION
Interstate; limited access highway 78
Other principal highway
Railroad
Ferry
PHYSICAL FEATURES
Streams
Lakes
Highest elevation in state (feet) +1803
The lowest elevation in New Jersey is sea level (Atlantic Ocean).
MILES
0 10 20 30 40
Albers equal area projection
The National Atlas of the United States of America®
U.S. Department of the Interior
U.S. Geological Survey

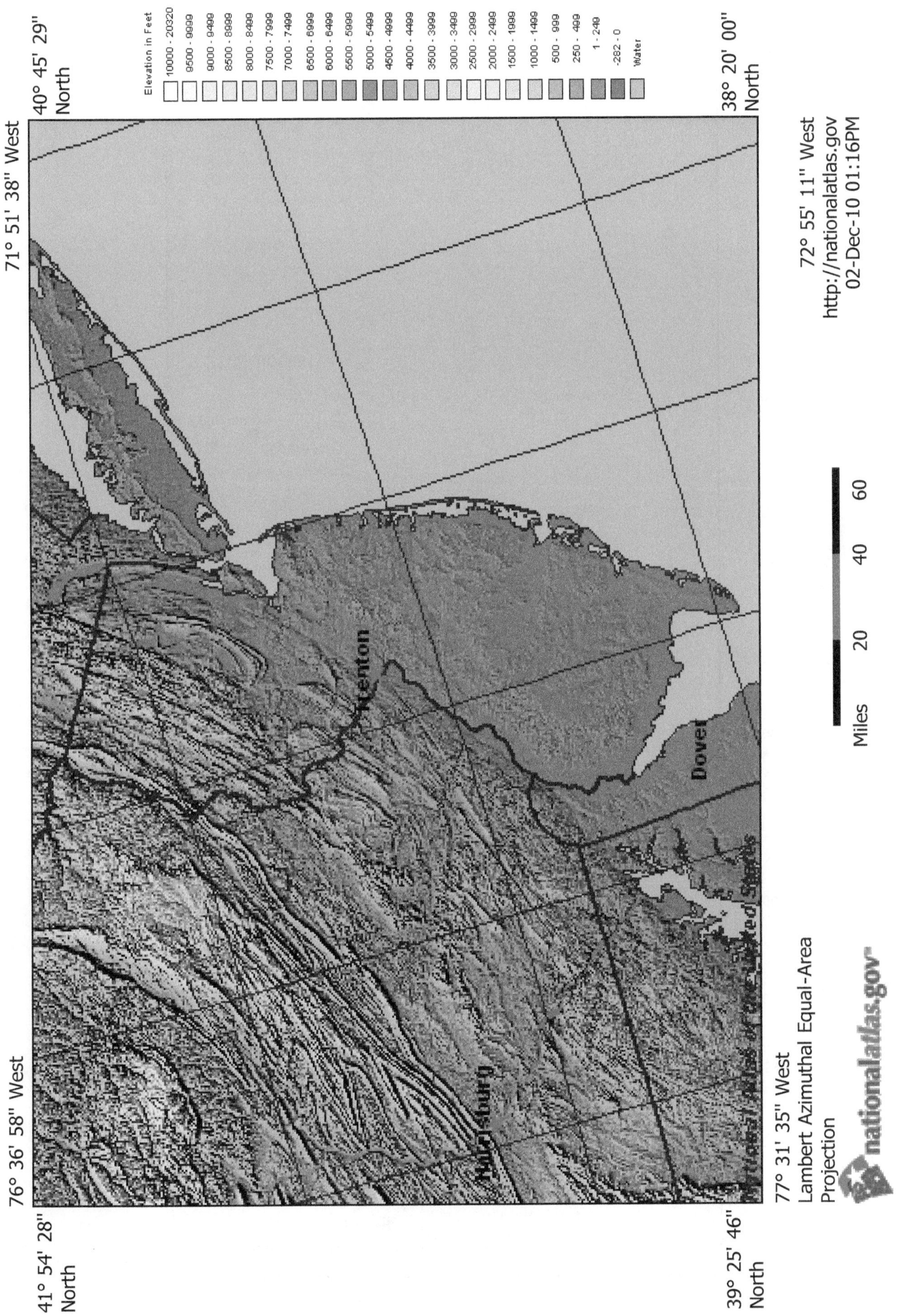
40° 45' 29" North
71° 51' 38" West
Elevation in Feet
10000 - 20320
9500 - 9999
9000 - 9499
8500 - 8999
8000 - 8499
7500 - 7999
7000 - 7499
6500 - 6999
6000 - 6499
5500 - 5999
5000 - 5499
4500 - 4999
4000 - 4499
3500 - 3999
3000 - 3499
2500 - 2999
2000 - 2499
1500 - 1999
1000 - 1499
500 - 999
250 - 499
1 - 249
-282 - 0
Water
38° 20' 00" North
72° 55' 11" West
http://nationalatlas.gov
02-Dec-10 01:16PM
Trenton
Dover
Harrisburg
Miles
20
40
60
76° 36' 58" West
41° 54' 28" North
77° 31' 35" West
Lambert Azimuthal Equal-Area Projection
39° 25' 46" North
nationalatlas.gov

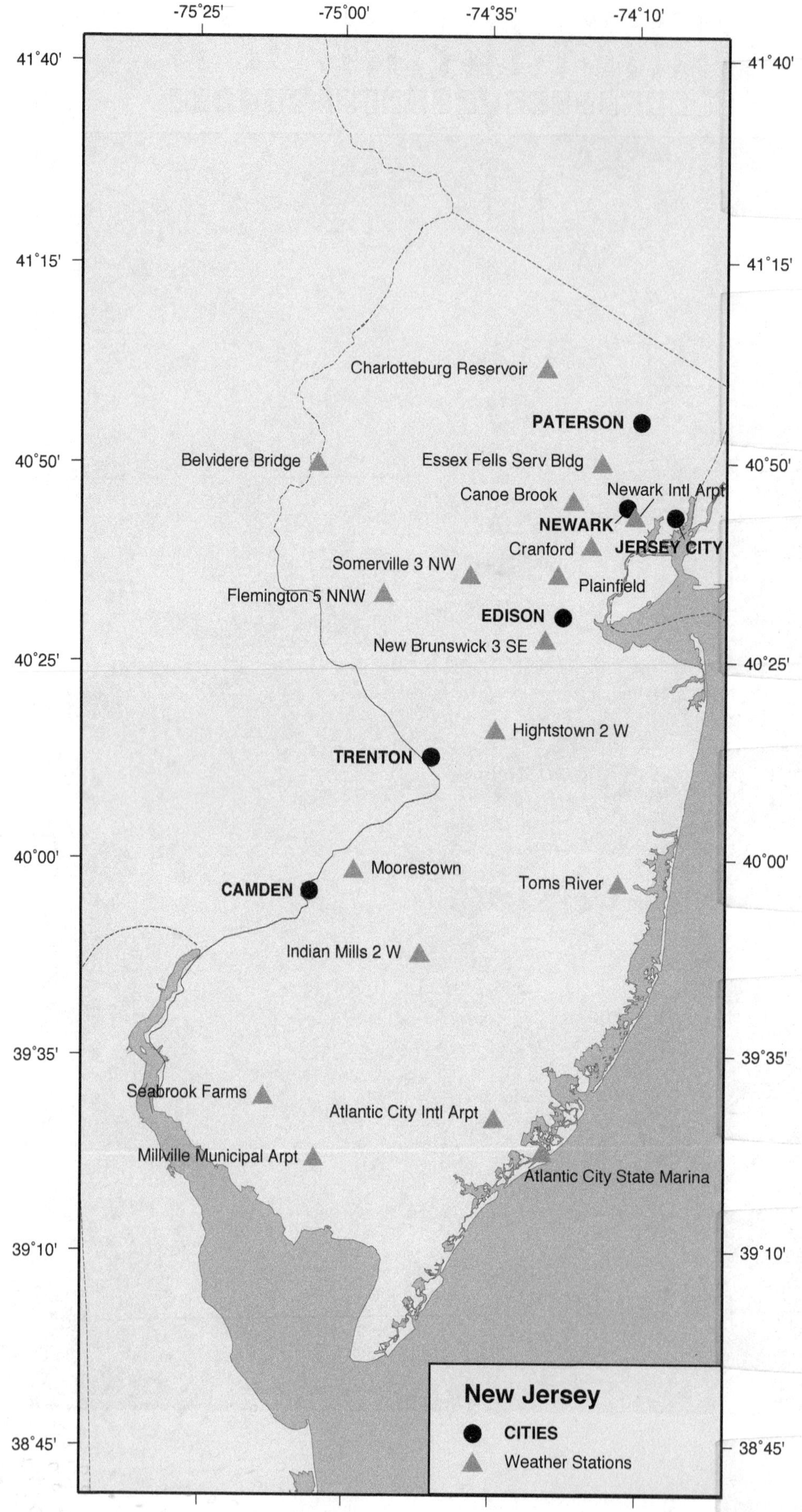
-75°25'
-75°00'
-74°35'
-74°10'
41°40'
41°15'
40°50'
40°25'
40°00'
39°35'
39°10'
38°45'
Charlotteburg Reservoir
PATERSON
Belvidere Bridge
Essex Fells Serv Bldg
Canoe Brook
Newark Intl Arpt
NEWARK
JERSEY CITY
Cranford
Somerville 3 NW
Plainfield
Flemington 5 NNW
EDISON
New Brunswick 3 SE
Hightstown 2 W
TRENTON
Moorestown
CAMDEN
Toms River
Indian Mills 2 W
Seabrook Farms
Atlantic City Intl Arpt
Millville Municipal Arpt
Atlantic City State Marina
New Jersey
CITIES
Weather Stations

New Jersey Weather Stations by County

County	Station Name
Atlantic	Atlantic City Intl Arpt Atlantic City State Marina
Burlington	Indian Mills 2 W Moorestown
Cumberland	Millville Municipal Arpt Seabrook Farms
Essex	Canoe Brook Essex Fells Serv Bldg Newark Intl Arpt
Hunterdon	Flemington 5 NNW
Mercer	Hightstown 2 W
Middlesex	New Brunswick 3 SE
Ocean	Toms River
Passaic	Charlotteburg Reservoir
Somerset	Somerville 3 NW
Union	Cranford Plainfield
Warren	Belvidere Bridge

See User Guide for station inclusion criteria.

New Jersey Weather Stations by City

City	Station Name	Miles
Bayonne	Canoe Brook	13.4
	Cranford	9.6
	Essex Fells Serv Bldg	14.4
	Newark Intl Arpt	4.8
	New Brunswick 3 SE	21.5
	Plainfield	15.4
	New York Ave V Brooklyn, NY	8.5
	New York Central Park Observ, NY	11.3
	New York JFK Int'l Arpt, NY	16.8
	New York Laguardia Arpt, NY	14.7
Brick Twp	Toms River	9.6
Camden	Indian Mills 2 W	19.4
	Moorestown	7.4
	Marcus Hook, PA	18.7
	Neshaminy Falls, PA	16.7
	Philadelphia Int'l Arpt, PA	8.5
	Phoenixville 1 E, PA	24.4
Cherry Hill Twp	Indian Mills 2 W	13.2
	Moorestown	4.6
	Marcus Hook, PA	23.3
	Neshaminy Falls, PA	17.2
	Philadelphia Int'l Arpt, PA	13.0
Clifton	Canoe Brook	13.2
	Charlotteburg Reservoir	18.5
	Cranford	17.0
	Essex Fells Serv Bldg	7.2
	Newark Intl Arpt	10.6
	Plainfield	22.6
	Dobbs Ferry Ardsley, NY	19.0
	New York Ave V Brooklyn, NY	20.6
	New York Central Park Observ, NY	11.4
	New York JFK Int'l Arpt, NY	23.9
	New York Laguardia Arpt, NY	15.3
Dover Twp	Toms River	3.5
East Orange	Canoe Brook	7.3
	Charlotteburg Reservoir	21.9
	Cranford	9.1
	Essex Fells Serv Bldg	6.1
	Newark Intl Arpt	3.6
	New Brunswick 3 SE	23.6
	Plainfield	15.0
	Somerville 3 NW	24.8
	New York Ave V Brooklyn, NY	16.5
	New York Central Park Observ, NY	12.9
	New York JFK Int'l Arpt, NY	23.0
	New York Laguardia Arpt, NY	17.3
Edison	Canoe Brook	16.5
	Cranford	10.4
	Essex Fells Serv Bldg	22.8
	Hightstown 2 W	19.6
	Newark Intl Arpt	17.6
	New Brunswick 3 SE	4.1
	Plainfield	6.1
	Somerville 3 NW	14.4
	New York Ave V Brooklyn, NY	21.9

City	Station Name	Miles
Elizabeth	Canoe Brook	9.3
	Cranford	4.7
	Essex Fells Serv Bldg	12.3
	Newark Intl Arpt	3.9
	New Brunswick 3 SE	17.9
	Plainfield	10.8
	Somerville 3 NW	22.5
	New York Ave V Brooklyn, NY	12.8
	New York Central Park Observ, NY	15.3
	New York JFK Int'l Arpt, NY	21.6
	New York Laguardia Arpt, NY	19.1
Franklin Twp	Canoe Brook	20.2
	Cranford	16.0
	Flemington 5 NNW	20.1
	Hightstown 2 W	15.4
	Newark Intl Arpt	23.6
	New Brunswick 3 SE	4.5
	Plainfield	9.9
	Somerville 3 NW	10.0
Gloucester Twp	Indian Mills 2 W	13.6
	Moorestown	12.3
	Seabrook Farms	23.1
	Marcus Hook, PA	20.1
	Neshaminy Falls, PA	24.8
	Philadelphia Int'l Arpt, PA	11.4
Hamilton Twp	Hightstown 2 W	7.5
	Moorestown	22.4
	New Brunswick 3 SE	22.1
	Neshaminy Falls, PA	14.3
Howell Twp	Hightstown 2 W	20.0
	New Brunswick 3 SE	23.9
	Toms River	14.8
Irvington	Canoe Brook	6.4
	Charlotteburg Reservoir	23.7
	Cranford	6.3
	Essex Fells Serv Bldg	7.9
	Newark Intl Arpt	2.6
	New Brunswick 3 SE	20.8
	Plainfield	12.4
	Somerville 3 NW	22.8
	New York Ave V Brooklyn, NY	15.7
	New York Central Park Observ, NY	14.4
	New York JFK Int'l Arpt, NY	23.2
	New York Laguardia Arpt, NY	18.7
Jackson Twp	Hightstown 2 W	16.9
	New Brunswick 3 SE	24.7
	Toms River	12.9
Jersey City	Canoe Brook	14.9
	Cranford	13.2
	Essex Fells Serv Bldg	13.6
	Newark Intl Arpt	6.1
	Plainfield	19.5
	Dobbs Ferry Ardsley, NY	22.6
	Mineola, NY	23.6
	New York Ave V Brooklyn, NY	9.6
	New York Central Park Observ, NY	6.7
	New York JFK Int'l Arpt, NY	14.9
	New York Laguardia Arpt, NY	10.4

See User Guide for station inclusion criteria.

City	Station Name	Miles
Lakewood Twp	Hightstown 2 W	22.8
	Toms River	9.2
Middletown Twp	Cranford	20.6
	Newark Intl Arpt	22.7
	New Brunswick 3 SE	18.3
	Plainfield	21.3
	New York Ave V Brooklyn, NY	15.4
	New York JFK Int'l Arpt, NY	23.6
New Brunswick	Canoe Brook	18.8
	Cranford	13.6
	Flemington 5 NNW	23.5
	Hightstown 2 W	16.6
	Newark Intl Arpt	21.0
	New Brunswick 3 SE	1.7
	Plainfield	8.1
	Somerville 3 NW	12.4
Newark	Canoe Brook	8.5
	Charlotteburg Reservoir	24.0
	Cranford	8.5
	Essex Fells Serv Bldg	8.2
	Newark Intl Arpt	1.6
	New Brunswick 3 SE	22.8
	Plainfield	14.7
	New York Ave V Brooklyn, NY	14.4
	New York Central Park Observ, NY	12.0
	New York JFK Int'l Arpt, NY	21.3
	New York Laguardia Arpt, NY	16.3
North Bergen Twp	Canoe Brook	17.3
	Cranford	17.5
	Essex Fells Serv Bldg	13.8
	Newark Intl Arpt	9.9
	Plainfield	23.8
	Dobbs Ferry Ardsley, NY	17.4
	Mineola, NY	21.7
	New York Ave V Brooklyn, NY	13.6
	New York Central Park Observ, NY	3.1
	New York JFK Int'l Arpt, NY	15.4
	New York Laguardia Arpt, NY	7.4
Old Bridge Twp	Canoe Brook	23.5
	Cranford	16.4
	Hightstown 2 W	17.1
	Newark Intl Arpt	22.0
	New Brunswick 3 SE	7.8
	Plainfield	13.9
	Somerville 3 NW	21.7
	New York Ave V Brooklyn, NY	21.2
Parsippany-Troy Hills Twp	Canoe Brook	8.8
	Charlotteburg Reservoir	11.6
	Cranford	16.2
	Essex Fells Serv Bldg	7.6
	Newark Intl Arpt	16.2
	Plainfield	18.4
	Somerville 3 NW	21.4
	New York Central Park Observ, NY	24.5
Passaic	Canoe Brook	13.9
	Charlotteburg Reservoir	19.9
	Cranford	17.1
	Essex Fells Serv Bldg	8.3

City	Station Name	Miles
Passaic *(cont.)*	Newark Intl Arpt	10.3
	Plainfield	22.9
	Dobbs Ferry Ardsley, NY	18.2
	New York Ave V Brooklyn, NY	19.5
	New York Central Park Observ, NY	10.0
	New York JFK Int'l Arpt, NY	22.5
	New York Laguardia Arpt, NY	13.9
Paterson	Canoe Brook	15.1
	Charlotteburg Reservoir	16.3
	Cranford	19.7
	Essex Fells Serv Bldg	8.5
	Newark Intl Arpt	13.8
	Dobbs Ferry Ardsley, NY	18.2
	New York Ave V Brooklyn, NY	23.8
	New York Central Park Observ, NY	13.8
	New York Laguardia Arpt, NY	17.3
Piscataway Twp	Canoe Brook	14.7
	Cranford	10.7
	Essex Fells Serv Bldg	21.4
	Flemington 5 NNW	22.3
	Hightstown 2 W	20.6
	Newark Intl Arpt	18.3
	New Brunswick 3 SE	6.1
	Plainfield	4.5
	Somerville 3 NW	9.7
Toms River	Toms River	3.4
Trenton	Flemington 5 NNW	24.7
	Hightstown 2 W	10.6
	Moorestown	20.8
	New Brunswick 3 SE	24.1
	Neshaminy Falls, PA	11.3
Union	Canoe Brook	5.6
	Charlotteburg Reservoir	24.7
	Cranford	3.7
	Essex Fells Serv Bldg	9.4
	Newark Intl Arpt	4.6
	New Brunswick 3 SE	18.2
	Plainfield	9.7
	Somerville 3 NW	20.3
	New York Ave V Brooklyn, NY	16.4
	New York Central Park Observ, NY	16.9
	New York JFK Int'l Arpt, NY	24.8
	New York Laguardia Arpt, NY	21.0
Union City	Canoe Brook	16.7
	Cranford	16.2
	Essex Fells Serv Bldg	13.9
	Newark Intl Arpt	8.7
	Plainfield	22.5
	Dobbs Ferry Ardsley, NY	19.1
	Mineola, NY	21.9
	New York Ave V Brooklyn, NY	11.9
	New York Central Park Observ, NY	3.6
	New York JFK Int'l Arpt, NY	14.6
	New York Laguardia Arpt, NY	7.8
Vineland	Atlantic City Intl Arpt	23.9
	Millville Municipal Arpt	8.4
	Seabrook Farms	11.8

City	Station Name	Miles
Washington Twp	Wilmington Porter Rsvr, DE	24.7
	Indian Mills 2 W	15.7
	Moorestown	16.2
	Seabrook Farms	19.1
	Marcus Hook, PA	19.1
	Philadelphia Int'l Arpt, PA	12.1
Wayne	Canoe Brook	14.8
	Charlotteburg Reservoir	11.5
	Cranford	20.8
	Essex Fells Serv Bldg	8.2
	Newark Intl Arpt	16.3
	Dobbs Ferry Ardsley, NY	21.8
	New York Central Park Observ, NY	18.5
	New York Laguardia Arpt, NY	22.0
Woodbridge Twp	Canoe Brook	12.9
	Cranford	5.7
	Essex Fells Serv Bldg	18.4
	Newark Intl Arpt	12.0
	New Brunswick 3 SE	9.9
	Plainfield	5.8
	Somerville 3 NW	17.8
	New York Ave V Brooklyn, NY	16.7
	New York Central Park Observ, NY	22.9

Note: Miles is the distance between the geographic center of the city and the weather station.

See User Guide for station inclusion criteria.

New Jersey Weather Stations by Elevation

Feet	Station Name
759	Charlotteburg Reservoir
350	Essex Fells Serv Bldg
263	Belvidere Bridge
259	Flemington 5 NNW
180	Canoe Brook
160	Somerville 3 NW
100	Hightstown 2 W
100	Indian Mills 2 W
100	Toms River
89	Plainfield
89	Seabrook Farms
85	New Brunswick 3 SE
75	Cranford
69	Millville Municipal Arpt
60	Atlantic City Intl Arpt
44	Moorestown
9	Atlantic City State Marina
9	Newark Intl Arpt

See User Guide for station inclusion criteria.

Atlantic City Int'l Airport

The Atlantic City National Weather Service Office is located at the National Aviation Facilities Experimental Center, Pomona, which is about 10 miles west-northwest of Atlantic City and the Atlantic Ocean. The surrounding terrain is fairly flat at an elevation of 50 to 60 feet above sea level. Vegetation in the area consists of scrub pine and low underbrush, but clearing for the air facility has been quite extensive. Bays and salt marshes are as near as 6 miles east of the airport. Atlantic City is located on Abescon Island on the southeast coast of New Jersey. Surrounding terrain, composed of tidal marshes and beach sand, is flat and lies slightly above sea level. The climate is principally continental in character. However, the moderating influence of the Atlantic Ocean is apparent throughout the year, being more marked in the city than at the airport. As a result, summers are relatively cooler and winters milder than elsewhere at the same latitude.

Land and sea breezes, local circulations resulting from the differential heating and cooling of the land and sea, often prevail. These winds occur when moderate or intense storms are not present in the area, thus enabling the local circulation to overcome the general wind pattern. During the warm season sea breezes in the late morning and afternoon hours prevent excessive heating. Frequently, the temperature at Atlantic City during the afternoon hours in the summer averages several degrees lower than at the airport and the airport averages several degrees lower than localities farther inland. On occasions, sea breezes have lowered the temperature as much as 15 to 20 degrees within a half hour. However, the major effect of the sea breeze at the airport is preventing the temperature from rising above the 80's. Because the change in ocean temperature lags behind the air temperature from season to season, the weather tends to remain comparatively mild late into the fall, but on the other hand, warming is retarded in the spring. Normal ocean temperatures range from an average near 37 degrees in January to near 72 degrees in August.

Precipitation is moderate and well distributed throughout the year, with June the driest month and August the wettest. Tropical storms or hurricanes occasionally bring excessive rainfall to the area. The bulk of winter precipitation results from storms which move northeastward along or near the east coast of the United States. Snowfall is considerably less than elsewhere at the same latitude and does not remain long on the ground. Precipitation, often beginning as snow, will frequently become mixed with or change to rain while continuing as snow over more interior sections. In addition, ice storms and resultant glaze are relatively infrequent.

Atlantic City Int'l Airport *Atlantic County* Elevation: 60 ft. Latitude: 39° 27' N Longitude: 74° 34' W

	JAN	FEB	MAR	APR	MAY	JUN	JUL	AUG	SEP	OCT	NOV	DEC	YEAR
Mean Maximum Temp. (°F)	42.0	44.7	52.0	62.0	71.7	80.7	85.7	84.0	77.4	66.8	56.6	46.5	64.2
Mean Temp. (°F)	32.7	35.0	41.7	51.3	60.8	70.3	75.8	74.1	66.9	55.7	46.4	37.0	54.0
Mean Minimum Temp. (°F)	23.4	25.2	31.4	40.6	49.9	59.9	65.8	64.2	56.4	44.5	36.2	27.4	43.7
Extreme Maximum Temp. (°F)	72	75	87	94	96	100	101	103	99	90	81	77	103
Extreme Minimum Temp. (°F)	-9	-8	3	20	26	37	42	41	35	20	10	-2	-9
Days Maximum Temp. ≥ 90°F	0	0	0	0	1	4	9	5	1	0	0	0	20
Days Maximum Temp. ≤ 32°F	6	3	1	0	0	0	0	0	0	0	0	3	13
Days Minimum Temp. ≤ 32°F	25	22	17	6	0	0	0	0	0	3	12	22	107
Days Minimum Temp. ≤ 0°F	1	0	0	0	0	0	0	0	0	0	0	0	1
Heating Degree Days (base 65°F)	993	843	715	412	176	27	1	3	56	302	552	861	4,941
Cooling Degree Days (base 65°F)	0	0	1	9	52	194	342	293	121	20	1	0	1,033
Mean Precipitation (in.)	3.22	2.68	4.13	3.76	3.29	3.17	3.70	3.79	3.10	3.38	3.32	3.59	41.13
Maximum Precipitation (in.)*	7.1	5.8	9.3	7.6	6.7	6.4	13.1	12.0	6.3	6.6	9.6	7.3	50.4
Minimum Precipitation (in.)*	0.6	0.8	0.7	0.8	0.5	0.7	0.5	0.4	0.4	0.1	0.7	0.6	25.3
Extreme Maximum Daily Precip. (in.)	2.09	2.37	2.51	2.94	3.07	2.92	3.35	3.29	3.15	2.21	2.40	3.68	3.68
Days With ≥ 0.1" Precipitation	6	6	7	7	6	6	6	6	6	5	6	7	74
Days With ≥ 0.5" Precipitation	2	2	3	2	3	2	2	2	2	3	2	3	28
Days With ≥ 1.0" Precipitation	1	1	1	1	1	1	1	1	1	1	1	1	12
Mean Snowfall (in.)	4.2	*5.3*	1.2	*0.4*	*trace*	*trace*	*trace*	*0.0*	*0.0*	*trace*	*0.3*	*2.5*	*13.9*
Maximum Snowfall (in.)*	20	35	18	4	trace	0	0	0	0	trace	8	9	50
Maximum 24-hr. Snowfall (in.)*	14	17	12	4	trace	0	0	0	0	trace	8	7	17
Maximum Snow Depth (in.)	na	na	na	na	na	na	na	na	na	na	na	na	na
Days With ≥ 1.0" Snow Depth	na	na	na	na	na	na	na	na	na	na	na	na	na
Thunderstorm Days*	< 1	< 1	1	2	4	5	7	5	2	1	1	< 1	28
Foggy Days*	12	11	13	13	15	16	19	19	16	14	12	12	172
Predominant Sky Cover*	OVR	OVR	OVR	OVR	OVR	OVR	OVR	OVR	OVR	OVR	OVR	OVR	OVR
Mean Relative Humidity 7am (%)*	78	78	78	77	79	81	84	87	87	87	83	79	81
Mean Relative Humidity 4pm (%)*	60	57	55	54	57	58	60	62	61	59	61	61	59
Mean Dewpoint (°F)*	22	23	30	38	50	60	65	65	58	47	37	27	44
Prevailing Wind Direction*	WNW	WNW	WNW	S	S	S	S	S	N	NW	WNW	WNW	WNW
Prevailing Wind Speed (mph)*	14	14	15	12	12	10	10	9	8	10	13	14	12
Maximum Wind Gust (mph)*	78	64	68	67	55	64	81	62	83	58	69	71	83

Note: (*) Period of record is 1958-1995

The period of record for National Weather Service station data is 1980 – 2009 except where noted. See User Guide for detailed explanation of data.

Atlantic City State Marina

The Atlantic City State Marina is located on Abescon Island on the southeast coast of New Jersey. Surrounding terrain, composed of tidal marshes and beach sand, is flat and lies slightly above sea level. The climate is principally continental in character. However, the moderating influence of the Atlantic Ocean is apparent throughout the year, being more marked in the city than at the airport. As a result, summers are relatively cooler and winters milder than elsewhere at the same latitude.

Land and sea breezes, local circulations resulting from the differential heating and cooling of the land and sea, often prevail. These winds occur when moderate or intense storms are not present in the area, thus enabling the local circulation to overcome the general wind pattern. During the warm season sea breezes in the late morning and afternoon hours prevent excessive heating. Frequently, the temperature at Atlantic City during the afternoon hours in the summer averages several degrees lower than at the airport and the airport averages several degrees lower than localities farther inland. On occasions, sea breezes have lowered the temperature as much as 15 to 20 degrees within a half hour. However, the major effect of the sea breeze at the airport is preventing the temperature from rising above the 80s. Because the change in ocean temperature lags behind the air temperature from season to season, the weather tends to remain comparatively mild late into the fall, but on the other hand, warming is retarded in the spring. Normal ocean temperatures range from an average near 37 degrees in January to near 72 degrees in August.

Precipitation is moderate and well distributed throughout the year, with June the driest month and August the wettest. Tropical storms or hurricanes occasionally bring excessive rainfall to the area. The bulk of winter precipitation results from storms which move northeastward along or near the east coast of the United States. Snowfall is considerably less than elsewhere at the same latitude and does not remain long on the ground. Precipitation, often beginning as snow, will frequently become mixed with or change to rain while continuing as snow over more interior sections. In addition, ice storms and resultant glaze are relatively infrequent.

Atlantic City State Marina *Atlantic County* Elevation: 9 ft. Latitude: 39° 23' N Longitude: 74° 26' W

	JAN	FEB	MAR	APR	MAY	JUN	JUL	AUG	SEP	OCT	NOV	DEC	YEAR
Mean Maximum Temp. (°F)	41.7	43.7	49.5	57.9	67.0	75.8	81.2	80.5	74.9	65.5	56.0	47.2	61.8
Mean Temp. (°F)	35.2	37.2	43.0	51.6	60.8	69.8	75.3	74.9	69.1	58.9	49.4	40.6	55.5
Mean Minimum Temp. (°F)	28.7	30.7	36.4	45.3	54.4	63.7	69.4	69.3	63.2	52.3	42.8	33.9	49.2
Extreme Maximum Temp. (°F)	72	70	82	90	93	97	101	102	92	90	78	74	102
Extreme Minimum Temp. (°F)	-3	5	4	22	34	47	53	50	44	32	8	4	-3
Days Maximum Temp. ≥ 90°F	0	0	0	0	0	1	3	2	0	0	0	0	6
Days Maximum Temp. ≤ 32°F	5	3	0	0	0	0	0	0	0	0	0	2	10
Days Minimum Temp. ≤ 32°F	20	16	9	1	0	0	0	0	0	0	3	13	62
Days Minimum Temp. ≤ 0°F	0	0	0	0	0	0	0	0	0	0	0	0	0
Heating Degree Days (base 65°F)	916	780	676	398	161	18	0	1	24	207	461	750	4,392
Cooling Degree Days (base 65°F)	0	0	0	4	36	168	327	315	153	26	1	0	1,030
Mean Precipitation (in.)	3.11	2.66	3.95	3.64	2.98	2.61	3.23	3.81	2.98	3.41	3.40	3.73	39.51
Maximum Precipitation (in.)*	8.4	6.9	8.5	6.9	8.8	7.3	11.1	14.8	5.8	5.9	8.9	6.8	62.2
Minimum Precipitation (in.)*	0.3	0.8	0.7	0.8	0.3	0.3	0.3	0.9	0.5	trace	0.8	0.7	27.5
Extreme Maximum Daily Precip. (in.)	2.31	2.91	3.30	3.46	2.47	3.51	6.09	5.42	3.15	3.36	2.82	4.12	6.09
Days With ≥ 0.1" Precipitation	6	5	7	7	6	5	5	5	5	5	6	6	68
Days With ≥ 0.5" Precipitation	2	2	3	2	2	2	2	3	2	2	2	3	27
Days With ≥ 1.0" Precipitation	1	1	1	1	1	1	1	1	1	1	1	1	12
Mean Snowfall (in.)	na	na	na	na	na	na	na	na	na	na	na	na	na
Maximum Snowfall (in.)*	13	13	10	1	0	0	0	0	0	0	3	5	29
Maximum 24-hr. Snowfall (in.)*	11	9	8	1	0	0	0	0	0	0	3	4	11
Maximum Snow Depth (in.)	na	na	na	na	na	na	na	na	na	na	na	na	na
Days With ≥ 1.0" Snow Depth	na	na	na	na	na	na	na	na	na	na	na	na	na
Thunderstorm Days*	0	< 1	2	2	5	5	6	2	1	1	0	0	24
Foggy Days*	7	7	12	9	13	15	12	11	7	13	18	10	134
Predominant Sky Cover*	na	na	na	na	na	na	na	na	na	na	na	na	na
Mean Relative Humidity 7am (%)*	na	na	na	na	na	na	na	na	na	na	na	na	na
Mean Relative Humidity 4pm (%)*	na	na	na	na	na	na	na	na	na	na	na	na	na
Mean Dewpoint (°F)*	na	na	na	na	na	na	na	na	na	na	na	na	na
Prevailing Wind Direction*	na	na	na	na	na	na	na	na	na	na	na	na	na
Prevailing Wind Speed (mph)*	na	na	na	na	na	na	na	na	na	na	na	na	na
Maximum Wind Gust (mph)*	67	69	87	63	53	51	52	71	67	67	67	67	87

Note: (*) Period of record is 1948-1995

Newark Int'l Airport

Terrain in vicinity of the station is flat and rather marshy. To the northwest are ridges oriented roughly in a south-southwest to north-northeast direction. They rise to an elevation of about 200 feet at 4.5 to five miles and to 500 to 600 feet at seven to eight miles. All winds between west-northwest and north-northwest are downslope and therefore are subject to some adiabatic temperature increase. This effect is evident in the rapid improvement which normally occurs with shift of wind to westerly, following a coastal storm or frontal passage. The drying effect of the downslope winds accounts for the relatively few local thunderstorms occurring at the station, compared to areas to the west. Easterly winds, particularly southeasterly, moderate the temperature because of the influence of the Atlantic Ocean.

Temperature falls of five to 15 degrees, depending on the season, are not uncommon when the wind backs from southwesterly to southeasterly. Periods of very hot weather, lasting as long as a week, are associated with a west-southwest air flow which has a long trajectory over land. Extremes of cold are related to rapidly moving outbreaks of cold air traveling southeastward from the Hudson Bay region. Temperatures of zero or below occur in one winter out of four, but are much more common several miles to the west of the station. Average dates of the last occurrence in spring and the first occurrence in autumn of temperatures as low as 32 degrees are in mid-April and the end of October or early November. Areas to the west of the station experience a growing season at least a month shorter than that at the airport.

A considerable amount of precipitation is realized from the Northeasters of the Atlantic coast. These storms, more typical of the fall and winter, generally last for a period of two days and commonly produce between one and two inches of precipitation. Storms producing four inches or more of snow occur from two to five times a winter. Snowstorms producing eight inches or more have occurred in about one-half the winters. As many as three such storms have been experienced in one winter. The frequency and intensity of snow storms and the duration of snow cover increase dramatically within a few miles to the west of the station.

Newark Int'l Airport *Essex County* Elevation: 9 ft. Latitude: 40° 43' N Longitude: 74° 11' W

	JAN	FEB	MAR	APR	MAY	JUN	JUL	AUG	SEP	OCT	NOV	DEC	YEAR
Mean Maximum Temp. (°F)	39.4	42.9	51.0	62.4	72.8	82.0	86.5	84.8	77.3	65.8	55.1	44.1	63.7
Mean Temp. (°F)	32.3	35.1	42.5	53.3	63.4	72.8	77.9	76.4	68.8	57.1	47.3	37.1	55.3
Mean Minimum Temp. (°F)	25.2	27.3	33.9	44.2	53.9	63.6	69.2	68.0	60.3	48.4	39.4	30.0	46.9
Extreme Maximum Temp. (°F)	72	74	86	97	99	102	105	105	100	89	81	76	105
Extreme Minimum Temp. (°F)	-8	3	7	16	37	46	54	45	42	30	18	-1	-8
Days Maximum Temp. ≥ 90°F	0	0	0	0	2	6	10	7	2	0	0	0	27
Days Maximum Temp. ≤ 32°F	8	4	1	0	0	0	0	0	0	0	0	4	17
Days Minimum Temp. ≤ 32°F	23	20	13	1	0	0	0	0	0	0	6	19	82
Days Minimum Temp. ≤ 0°F	0	0	0	0	0	0	0	0	0	0	0	0	0
Heating Degree Days (base 65°F)	1,006	838	693	356	117	12	0	1	35	258	526	859	4,701
Cooling Degree Days (base 65°F)	0	0	2	12	73	253	405	362	155	22	1	0	1,285
Mean Precipitation (in.)	3.54	2.74	4.15	4.34	4.06	4.05	4.79	3.65	3.76	3.59	3.71	3.70	46.08
Maximum Precipitation (in.)*	10.1	5.9	11.1	11.1	10.2	6.4	10.0	11.8	10.3	8.2	11.5	9.5	65.5
Minimum Precipitation (in.)*	0.4	0.8	1.1	0.9	0.5	0.1	0.9	0.4	0.1	0.2	0.5	0.3	26.1
Extreme Maximum Daily Precip. (in.)	2.94	2.06	2.71	6.18	2.39	2.97	3.54	3.12	6.22	4.08	4.34	2.77	6.22
Days With ≥ 0.1" Precipitation	6	6	7	7	7	7	7	6	6	5	6	6	76
Days With ≥ 0.5" Precipitation	3	2	3	3	3	3	3	3	3	3	3	3	35
Days With ≥ 1.0" Precipitation	1	1	1	1	1	1	2	1	1	1	1	1	13
Mean Snowfall (in.)	7.9	8.3	4.8	0.9	trace	trace	trace	trace	trace	trace	0.5	4.7	27.1
Maximum Snowfall (in.)*	27	33	26	14	trace	0	0	0	0	trace	9	29	66
Maximum 24-hr. Snowfall (in.)*	14	18	13	13	trace	0	0	0	0	trace	5	26	26
Maximum Snow Depth (in.)	31	23	13	11	trace	trace	trace	trace	trace	trace	5	14	31
Days With ≥ 1.0" Snow Depth	9	6	3	0	0	0	0	0	0	0	0	3	21
Thunderstorm Days*	< 1	< 1	2	3	6	9	11	8	4	2	1	< 1	46
Foggy Days*	9	9	10	9	11	10	9	10	11	11	9	10	118
Predominant Sky Cover*	OVR	OVR	OVR	OVR	OVR	OVR	OVR	OVR	OVR	OVR	OVR	OVR	OVR
Mean Relative Humidity 7am (%)*	73	71	69	67	70	71	72	76	79	78	76	74	73
Mean Relative Humidity 4pm (%)*	58	54	51	48	51	51	52	54	55	53	57	59	54
Mean Dewpoint (°F)*	21	21	27	36	48	57	63	63	56	45	35	25	42
Prevailing Wind Direction*	WSW	NW	NW	NW	SW	SW	SW	SW	SW	SW	SW	WNW	SW
Prevailing Wind Speed (mph)*	12	16	16	16	10	9	9	9	8	9	9	14	12
Maximum Wind Gust (mph)*	62	60	67	62	58	83	69	68	67	55	63	61	83

Note: (*) Period of record is 1935-1995

The period of record for National Weather Service station data is 1980 – 2009 except where noted. See User Guide for detailed explanation of data.

Belvidere Bridge *Warren County* Elevation: 263 ft. Latitude: 40° 50' N Longitude: 75° 05' W

	JAN	FEB	MAR	APR	MAY	JUN	JUL	AUG	SEP	OCT	NOV	DEC	YEAR
Mean Maximum Temp. (°F)	37.0	40.6	49.0	60.7	71.0	79.5	84.0	82.5	75.7	64.7	53.0	41.2	61.6
Mean Temp. (°F)	28.0	30.6	38.4	49.0	59.0	67.9	72.6	71.3	63.9	52.7	42.6	32.6	50.7
Mean Minimum Temp. (°F)	19.1	20.6	27.7	37.1	46.9	56.3	61.2	60.1	52.1	40.6	32.3	24.0	39.8
Extreme Maximum Temp. (°F)	66	71	85	93	94	96	101	100	98	91	80	73	101
Extreme Minimum Temp. (°F)	-17	-8	1	16	30	39	45	41	34	21	12	-4	-17
Days Maximum Temp. ≥ 90°F	0	0	0	0	0	3	6	4	1	0	0	0	14
Days Maximum Temp. ≤ 32°F	10	5	1	0	0	0	0	0	0	0	0	5	21
Days Minimum Temp. ≤ 32°F	29	26	22	9	1	0	0	0	0	6	17	26	136
Days Minimum Temp. ≤ 0°F	1	1	0	0	0	0	0	0	0	0	0	0	2
Heating Degree Days (base 65°F)	1,139	965	818	479	209	40	4	9	102	382	664	998	5,809
Cooling Degree Days (base 65°F)	0	0	0	5	30	134	246	213	70	7	0	0	705
Mean Precipitation (in.)	3.06	2.34	3.55	3.90	4.21	4.43	4.69	4.03	4.57	4.28	3.57	3.57	46.20
Extreme Maximum Daily Precip. (in.)	1.90	2.07	2.23	2.73	3.00	2.37	2.71	2.45	6.32	6.84	2.40	2.97	6.84
Days With ≥ 0.1" Precipitation	6	5	7	8	8	8	8	7	7	6	6	6	82
Days With ≥ 0.5" Precipitation	2	2	3	3	2	3	3	3	3	2	2	3	31
Days With ≥ 1.0" Precipitation	1	0	1	1	1	1	1	1	1	1	1	1	11
Mean Snowfall (in.)	8.9	6.9	3.1	0.7	0.0	0.0	0.0	0.0	0.0	trace	0.4	4.3	24.3
Maximum Snow Depth (in.)	27	23	11	10	0	0	0	0	0	trace	6	13	27
Days With ≥ 1.0" Snow Depth	11	10	3	0	0	0	0	0	0	0	0	4	28

Canoe Brook *Essex County* Elevation: 180 ft. Latitude: 40° 45' N Longitude: 74° 21' W

	JAN	FEB	MAR	APR	MAY	JUN	JUL	AUG	SEP	OCT	NOV	DEC	YEAR
Mean Maximum Temp. (°F)	38.9	42.1	50.1	61.8	72.2	81.1	85.9	84.6	77.3	65.7	54.6	43.6	63.2
Mean Temp. (°F)	29.2	31.8	39.7	50.4	60.3	69.6	74.5	73.2	65.5	53.5	44.1	34.1	52.2
Mean Minimum Temp. (°F)	19.5	21.4	29.1	39.0	48.4	58.0	63.0	61.8	53.6	41.3	33.6	24.6	41.1
Extreme Maximum Temp. (°F)	72	75	89	96	95	100	103	104	99	90	82	76	104
Extreme Minimum Temp. (°F)	-15	-10	1	18	25	36	44	42	30	23	10	-8	-15
Days Maximum Temp. ≥ 90°F	0	0	0	0	1	4	9	7	2	0	0	0	23
Days Maximum Temp. ≤ 32°F	8	5	1	0	0	0	0	0	0	0	0	4	18
Days Minimum Temp. ≤ 32°F	28	25	20	7	0	0	0	0	0	5	15	26	126
Days Minimum Temp. ≤ 0°F	2	0	0	0	0	0	0	0	0	0	0	0	2
Heating Degree Days (base 65°F)	1,107	936	784	440	184	31	2	7	78	362	624	953	5,508
Cooling Degree Days (base 65°F)	0	0	1	7	43	172	300	266	96	10	0	0	895
Mean Precipitation (in.)	3.53	2.66	4.07	4.44	4.32	4.82	4.74	4.29	4.67	4.61	4.22	3.98	50.35
Extreme Maximum Daily Precip. (in.)	2.25	2.35	2.55	5.34	3.32	5.75	5.06	3.85	7.60	3.70	2.80	2.97	7.60
Days With ≥ 0.1" Precipitation	6	5	7	7	8	7	8	6	6	6	6	6	78
Days With ≥ 0.5" Precipitation	2	2	3	3	3	3	3	3	3	3	3	3	34
Days With ≥ 1.0" Precipitation	1	1	1	1	1	1	1	1	1	1	1	1	12
Mean Snowfall (in.)	7.8	7.4	4.6	0.7	0.0	0.0	0.0	0.0	0.0	0.0	0.6	4.5	25.6
Maximum Snow Depth (in.)	22	19	15	12	0	0	0	0	0	0	5	12	22
Days With ≥ 1.0" Snow Depth	10	8	4	0	0	0	0	0	0	0	0	3	25

Charlotteburg Reservoir *Passaic County* Elevation: 759 ft. Latitude: 41° 02' N Longitude: 74° 26' W

	JAN	FEB	MAR	APR	MAY	JUN	JUL	AUG	SEP	OCT	NOV	DEC	YEAR
Mean Maximum Temp. (°F)	36.3	39.3	47.4	59.1	70.2	78.1	83.0	81.5	74.3	63.5	52.3	40.9	60.5
Mean Temp. (°F)	26.4	28.6	36.5	47.4	57.9	66.1	70.9	69.3	61.7	50.8	41.8	31.6	49.1
Mean Minimum Temp. (°F)	16.6	17.9	25.6	35.8	45.5	53.9	58.8	57.1	49.0	38.0	31.2	22.2	37.6
Extreme Maximum Temp. (°F)	67	74	85	93	94	95	100	99	94	86	79	73	100
Extreme Minimum Temp. (°F)	-24	-12	-10	13	24	34	41	36	27	20	9	-11	-24
Days Maximum Temp. ≥ 90°F	0	0	0	0	0	2	4	3	0	0	0	0	9
Days Maximum Temp. ≤ 32°F	11	7	2	0	0	0	0	0	0	0	0	6	26
Days Minimum Temp. ≤ 32°F	29	26	25	11	1	0	0	0	1	9	18	27	147
Days Minimum Temp. ≤ 0°F	3	1	0	0	0	0	0	0	0	0	0	1	5
Heating Degree Days (base 65°F)	1,189	1,023	877	525	241	65	11	23	140	438	690	1,030	6,252
Cooling Degree Days (base 65°F)	0	0	0	4	27	103	201	163	46	4	0	0	548
Mean Precipitation (in.)	3.76	3.16	4.40	4.62	4.38	4.55	4.51	4.35	4.97	4.21	4.29	4.29	51.49
Extreme Maximum Daily Precip. (in.)	2.40	2.65	4.00	4.60	3.89	3.88	3.10	2.74	6.81	3.52	2.69	3.40	6.81
Days With ≥ 0.1" Precipitation	6	6	7	8	7	7	7	7	6	6	6	6	79
Days With ≥ 0.5" Precipitation	3	2	3	3	3	3	3	3	3	3	3	3	35
Days With ≥ 1.0" Precipitation	1	1	1	1	1	1	1	1	2	1	1	1	13
Mean Snowfall (in.)	9.7	9.7	7.5	1.9	0.0	0.0	0.0	0.0	0.0	trace	0.6	5.0	34.4
Maximum Snow Depth (in.)	35	28	22	13	0	0	0	0	0	trace	4	18	35
Days With ≥ 1.0" Snow Depth	12	11	6	1	0	0	0	0	0	0	1	4	35

Cranford *Union County* Elevation: 75 ft. Latitude: 40° 39' N Longitude: 74° 18' W

	JAN	FEB	MAR	APR	MAY	JUN	JUL	AUG	SEP	OCT	NOV	DEC	YEAR
Mean Maximum Temp. (°F)	40.7	44.3	52.3	63.7	73.6	82.2	86.8	85.0	77.9	66.6	56.1	45.0	64.5
Mean Temp. (°F)	31.3	34.1	41.1	51.5	61.1	70.3	75.2	73.7	66.4	54.7	45.5	35.8	53.4
Mean Minimum Temp. (°F)	21.8	23.8	29.9	39.1	48.5	58.4	63.6	62.4	54.8	42.7	34.8	26.4	42.2
Extreme Maximum Temp. (°F)	73	75	90	97	96	98	102	103	99	88	81	76	103
Extreme Minimum Temp. (°F)	-10	-4	1	12	24	37	44	39	34	22	14	-5	-10
Days Maximum Temp. ≥ 90°F	0	0	0	0	1	5	10	7	2	0	0	0	25
Days Maximum Temp. ≤ 32°F	6	3	1	0	0	0	0	0	0	0	0	3	13
Days Minimum Temp. ≤ 32°F	26	23	19	6	1	0	0	0	0	4	13	23	115
Days Minimum Temp. ≤ 0°F	1	0	0	0	0	0	0	0	0	0	0	0	1
Heating Degree Days (base 65°F)	1,039	867	734	407	162	23	1	4	63	326	579	899	5,104
Cooling Degree Days (base 65°F)	0	0	1	7	48	190	325	282	110	12	0	0	975
Mean Precipitation (in.)	3.69	2.83	4.16	4.48	4.43	4.39	5.21	3.70	4.41	4.35	4.12	4.04	49.81
Extreme Maximum Daily Precip. (in.)	2.76	2.62	2.45	5.28	3.10	2.95	7.05	3.00	9.76	5.60	2.73	2.75	9.76
Days With ≥ 0.1" Precipitation	6	6	7	7	8	7	7	6	6	6	7	7	80
Days With ≥ 0.5" Precipitation	3	2	3	3	3	3	3	3	3	3	3	3	35
Days With ≥ 1.0" Precipitation	1	1	1	1	1	1	1	1	1	1	1	1	12
Mean Snowfall (in.)	6.4	6.5	4.2	0.4	0.0	0.0	0.0	0.0	0.0	trace	0.4	4.2	22.1
Maximum Snow Depth (in.)	23	21	11	6	0	0	0	0	0	trace	6	17	23
Days With ≥ 1.0" Snow Depth	10	9	4	0	0	0	0	0	0	0	0	3	26

The period of record for all cooperative weather station data is 1980 – 2009. See User Guide for detailed explanation of data.

Essex Fells Serv Bldg *Essex County* Elevation: 350 ft. Latitude: 40° 50' N Longitude: 74° 17' W

	JAN	FEB	MAR	APR	MAY	JUN	JUL	AUG	SEP	OCT	NOV	DEC	YEAR
Mean Maximum Temp. (°F)	37.9	***40.8***	48.8	61.0	71.4	***79.7***	***84.6***	83.1	***76.1***	64.5	53.1	42.6	***62.0***
Mean Temp. (°F)	29.0	***31.0***	38.4	49.9	59.8	***68.4***	***73.6***	72.0	***64.5***	52.9	43.4	33.9	***51.4***
Mean Minimum Temp. (°F)	20.0	***21.2***	28.0	38.8	48.2	***57.1***	***62.6***	60.9	***52.9***	41.3	33.6	25.2	***40.8***
Extreme Maximum Temp. (°F)	70	***75***	89	98	93	96	***101***	105	***99***	88	84	74	***105***
Extreme Minimum Temp. (°F)	-14	***-4***	0	15	28	38	***45***	36	***32***	21	14	-6	***-14***
Days Maximum Temp. ≥ 90°F	0	***0***	0	0	1	3	***6***	5	***1***	0	0	0	***16***
Days Maximum Temp. ≤ 32°F	9	***6***	2	0	0	0	***0***	0	***0***	0	0	5	***22***
Days Minimum Temp. ≤ 32°F	27	***25***	22	6	0	0	***0***	0	***0***	5	15	25	***125***
Days Minimum Temp. ≤ 0°F	1	***0***	0	0	0	0	***0***	0	***0***	0	0	0	***1***
Heating Degree Days (base 65°F)	1,110	***954***	817	453	191	***38***	***3***	9	***95***	377	642	958	***5,647***
Cooling Degree Days (base 65°F)	0	***0***	1	7	37	***147***	***277***	233	***88***	9	0	0	***799***
Mean Precipitation (in.)	3.26	***2.62***	3.86	4.82	4.73	4.90	***4.93***	4.46	***4.15***	4.05	4.16	***3.53***	***49.47***
Extreme Maximum Daily Precip. (in.)	3.00	na	***3.11***	***6.60***	***3.42***	***4.65***	***3.98***	***3.14***	***3.50***	***2.80***	***3.03***	***2.75***	na
Days With ≥ 0.1" Precipitation	5	***4***	6	***7***	8	7	***7***	7	***6***	6	6	***5***	***74***
Days With ≥ 0.5" Precipitation	3	***2***	3	***3***	3	3	***4***	3	***3***	3	3	3	***36***
Days With ≥ 1.0" Precipitation	1	***1***	1	2	1	2	***2***	1	***1***	1	1	1	***15***
Mean Snowfall (in.)	***4.7***	***3.0***	***3.4***	0.7	0.0	0.0	***0.0***	0.0	***0.0***	0.0	0.3	***2.7***	***14.8***
Maximum Snow Depth (in.)	na	na	na	na	***0***	na	na	na	na	na	na	na	na
Days With ≥ 1.0" Snow Depth	na	na	***0***	***0***	0	0	***0***	0	***0***	***0***	0	***1***	na

Flemington 5 NNW *Hunterdon County* Elevation: 259 ft. Latitude: 40° 34' N Longitude: 74° 53' W

	JAN	FEB	MAR	APR	MAY	JUN	JUL	AUG	SEP	OCT	NOV	DEC	YEAR
Mean Maximum Temp. (°F)	37.6	41.3	49.7	62.1	72.5	80.8	85.5	83.9	76.6	64.9	53.7	42.3	62.6
Mean Temp. (°F)	28.7	31.5	39.0	50.0	60.0	68.8	73.9	72.4	64.9	52.9	43.3	33.5	51.6
Mean Minimum Temp. (°F)	19.7	21.5	28.2	37.8	47.4	56.8	62.3	60.9	53.2	40.9	32.8	24.6	40.5
Extreme Maximum Temp. (°F)	69	73	88	93	95	96	104	102	100	88	81	75	104
Extreme Minimum Temp. (°F)	-18	-6	-6	18	28	37	45	38	33	21	10	-9	-18
Days Maximum Temp. ≥ 90°F	0	0	0	0	1	3	8	5	1	0	0	0	18
Days Maximum Temp. ≤ 32°F	9	5	1	0	0	0	0	0	0	0	0	5	20
Days Minimum Temp. ≤ 32°F	27	25	21	8	1	0	0	0	0	6	16	25	129
Days Minimum Temp. ≤ 0°F	2	0	0	0	0	0	0	0	0	0	0	0	2
Heating Degree Days (base 65°F)	1,119	942	801	449	187	33	3	9	82	375	643	969	5,612
Cooling Degree Days (base 65°F)	0	0	0	6	39	154	286	246	86	9	0	0	826
Mean Precipitation (in.)	3.75	2.89	4.24	4.34	4.60	4.67	4.89	3.66	4.46	4.43	3.80	4.28	50.01
Extreme Maximum Daily Precip. (in.)	2.58	2.45	2.45	5.72	3.55	3.29	3.64	2.21	8.49	4.23	2.32	2.81	8.49
Days With ≥ 0.1" Precipitation	7	6	7	7	8	7	7	6	6	6	6	6	79
Days With ≥ 0.5" Precipitation	3	2	3	3	3	3	3	2	3	3	3	3	34
Days With ≥ 1.0" Precipitation	1	1	1	1	1	1	2	1	1	2	1	1	14
Mean Snowfall (in.)	8.3	7.9	5.3	1.3	0.0	0.0	0.0	0.0	0.0	trace	0.4	5.1	28.3
Maximum Snow Depth (in.)	27	26	14	9	0	0	0	0	0	trace	4	13	27
Days With ≥ 1.0" Snow Depth	11	8	4	0	0	0	0	0	0	0	0	5	28

Hightstown 2 W *Mercer County* Elevation: 100 ft. Latitude: 40° 16' N Longitude: 74° 34' W

	JAN	FEB	MAR	APR	MAY	JUN	JUL	AUG	SEP	OCT	NOV	DEC	YEAR
Mean Maximum Temp. (°F)	39.4	42.4	50.4	61.8	72.2	81.0	85.6	84.1	77.1	65.7	55.2	44.2	63.3
Mean Temp. (°F)	30.7	33.3	40.7	51.0	60.7	69.8	74.7	73.0	65.8	54.2	45.2	35.5	52.9
Mean Minimum Temp. (°F)	22.0	24.1	30.9	40.1	49.2	58.5	63.6	62.0	54.3	42.6	35.2	26.8	42.5
Extreme Maximum Temp. (°F)	72	75	88	95	95	98	102	102	98	89	80	76	102
Extreme Minimum Temp. (°F)	-12	-8	4	18	30	39	45	40	34	23	11	-5	-12
Days Maximum Temp. ≥ 90°F	0	0	0	0	1	4	9	5	1	0	0	0	20
Days Maximum Temp. ≤ 32°F	8	5	1	0	0	0	0	0	0	0	0	4	18
Days Minimum Temp. ≤ 32°F	26	23	18	5	0	0	0	0	0	4	13	23	112
Days Minimum Temp. ≤ 0°F	1	0	0	0	0	0	0	0	0	0	0	0	1
Heating Degree Days (base 65°F)	1,054	890	748	423	175	30	2	6	74	341	587	907	5,237
Cooling Degree Days (base 65°F)	0	0	1	9	49	180	309	262	103	14	1	0	928
Mean Precipitation (in.)	3.31	2.44	3.99	4.17	4.10	4.36	4.97	4.20	4.12	3.66	3.57	3.70	46.59
Extreme Maximum Daily Precip. (in.)	2.17	1.97	2.21	5.49	2.98	2.89	5.54	4.19	5.60	2.90	1.95	2.81	5.60
Days With ≥ 0.1" Precipitation	6	6	7	7	8	7	7	6	6	6	6	7	79
Days With ≥ 0.5" Precipitation	2	2	3	3	3	3	4	3	3	2	3	3	34
Days With ≥ 1.0" Precipitation	1	0	1	1	1	1	2	1	1	1	1	1	12
Mean Snowfall (in.)	6.2	7.2	3.5	0.9	0.0	0.0	0.0	0.0	0.0	trace	0.4	4.0	22.2
Maximum Snow Depth (in.)	19	20	9	5	0	0	0	0	0	trace	6	15	20
Days With ≥ 1.0" Snow Depth	8	7	3	0	0	0	0	0	0	0	0	3	21

Indian Mills 2 W *Burlington County* Elevation: 100 ft. Latitude: 39° 48' N Longitude: 74° 47' W

	JAN	FEB	MAR	APR	MAY	JUN	JUL	AUG	SEP	OCT	NOV	DEC	YEAR
Mean Maximum Temp. (°F)	42.2	46.1	54.0	65.9	75.6	83.5	87.8	86.1	79.3	68.2	57.7	46.6	66.1
Mean Temp. (°F)	32.5	35.3	42.5	53.0	62.4	71.0	75.6	74.1	67.0	55.7	46.3	36.8	54.4
Mean Minimum Temp. (°F)	22.8	24.6	30.9	40.0	49.0	58.4	63.5	62.0	54.6	43.1	34.9	27.0	42.6
Extreme Maximum Temp. (°F)	73	77	90	97	97	100	103	102	99	90	82	76	103
Extreme Minimum Temp. (°F)	-18	-12	-3	18	28	36	40	37	32	18	12	-4	-18
Days Maximum Temp. ≥ 90°F	0	0	0	1	2	6	12	8	2	0	0	0	31
Days Maximum Temp. ≤ 32°F	6	3	0	0	0	0	0	0	0	0	0	2	11
Days Minimum Temp. ≤ 32°F	26	22	18	7	1	0	0	0	0	5	14	22	115
Days Minimum Temp. ≤ 0°F	1	0	0	0	0	0	0	0	0	0	0	0	1
Heating Degree Days (base 65°F)	1,000	833	693	366	140	19	1	4	59	302	555	866	4,838
Cooling Degree Days (base 65°F)	0	0	2	13	65	205	337	291	125	21	1	0	1,060
Mean Precipitation (in.)	3.56	2.63	4.40	4.17	3.78	4.00	4.44	4.89	3.83	3.75	3.71	4.05	47.21
Extreme Maximum Daily Precip. (in.)	2.96	1.95	2.72	4.10	2.46	2.46	4.94	4.71	4.68	3.04	2.53	3.88	4.94
Days With ≥ 0.1" Precipitation	6	5	7	7	7	6	7	6	5	6	6	7	75
Days With ≥ 0.5" Precipitation	2	2	3	3	3	3	3	3	2	3	3	3	33
Days With ≥ 1.0" Precipitation	1	1	1	1	1	1	1	2	1	1	1	1	13
Mean Snowfall (in.)	6.0	5.2	2.2	0.6	0.0	0.0	0.0	0.0	0.0	0.0	0.2	3.4	17.6
Maximum Snow Depth (in.)	16	25	11	1	0	0	0	0	0	0	trace	24	25
Days With ≥ 1.0" Snow Depth	7	5	2	0	0	0	0	0	0	0	0	3	17

The period of record for all cooperative weather station data is 1980 – 2009. See User Guide for detailed explanation of data.

Millville Municipal Arpt *Cumberland County* Elevation: 69 ft. Latitude: 39° 22' N Longitude: 75° 04' W

	JAN	FEB	MAR	APR	MAY	JUN	JUL	AUG	SEP	OCT	NOV	DEC	YEAR
Mean Maximum Temp. (°F)	41.8	44.6	52.4	63.3	72.9	81.5	86.1	84.4	77.7	66.8	56.6	46.1	64.5
Mean Temp. (°F)	33.0	35.0	42.1	52.2	61.8	71.0	76.3	74.6	67.4	55.8	46.5	36.9	54.4
Mean Minimum Temp. (°F)	24.2	25.3	31.8	41.1	50.5	60.5	66.4	64.9	57.0	44.8	36.2	27.7	44.2
Extreme Maximum Temp. (°F)	71	75	86	93	96	99	101	101	97	90	80	77	101
Extreme Minimum Temp. (°F)	-10	-6	-7	20	29	40	44	44	37	23	12	2	-10
Days Maximum Temp. ≥ 90°F	0	0	0	0	1	4	9	6	1	0	0	0	21
Days Maximum Temp. ≤ 32°F	6	3	1	0	0	0	0	0	0	0	0	3	13
Days Minimum Temp. ≤ 32°F	24	22	17	5	0	0	0	0	0	2	12	22	104
Days Minimum Temp. ≤ 0°F	1	0	0	0	0	0	0	0	0	0	0	0	1
Heating Degree Days (base 65°F)	985	842	703	386	153	19	1	2	49	298	551	863	4,852
Cooling Degree Days (base 65°F)	0	0	1	10	59	206	357	308	128	21	1	0	1,091
Mean Precipitation (in.)	3.09	2.67	4.07	3.86	3.57	3.27	3.69	4.08	3.19	3.37	3.37	3.46	41.69
Extreme Maximum Daily Precip. (in.)	3.07	2.60	2.70	3.74	2.67	2.92	3.61	9.06	2.67	3.06	2.55	2.46	9.06
Days With ≥ 0.1" Precipitation	5	5	7	7	7	6	6	5	5	5	6	6	70
Days With ≥ 0.5" Precipitation	2	2	3	3	2	2	3	3	2	2	2	2	28
Days With ≥ 1.0" Precipitation	1	1	1	1	1	1	1	1	1	1	1	1	12
Mean Snowfall (in.)	na	na	na	na	na	na	na	na	na	na	na	na	na
Maximum Snow Depth (in.)	na	na	na	na	na	na	na	na	na	na	na	na	na
Days With ≥ 1.0" Snow Depth	na	na	na	na	na	na	na	na	na	na	na	na	na

Moorestown *Burlington County* Elevation: 44 ft. Latitude: 39° 58' N Longitude: 74° 58' W

	JAN	FEB	MAR	APR	MAY	JUN	JUL	AUG	SEP	OCT	NOV	DEC	YEAR
Mean Maximum Temp. (°F)	43.0	47.1	55.5	67.2	76.4	84.9	88.7	86.5	79.8	69.0	57.7	46.8	66.9
Mean Temp. (°F)	33.7	36.5	43.9	54.3	63.3	72.5	76.9	74.9	67.9	56.9	47.1	37.5	55.5
Mean Minimum Temp. (°F)	24.3	25.9	32.2	41.3	50.1	60.1	65.1	63.3	56.0	44.7	36.3	28.1	44.0
Extreme Maximum Temp. (°F)	75	76	91	97	96	100	104	104	96	91	82	75	104
Extreme Minimum Temp. (°F)	-10	0	2	22	27	40	48	43	34	22	13	-10	-10
Days Maximum Temp. ≥ 90°F	0	0	0	1	3	9	14	10	3	0	0	0	40
Days Maximum Temp. ≤ 32°F	5	2	0	0	0	0	0	0	0	0	0	3	10
Days Minimum Temp. ≤ 32°F	25	22	17	4	0	0	0	0	0	3	11	22	104
Days Minimum Temp. ≤ 0°F	1	0	0	0	0	0	0	0	0	0	0	0	1
Heating Degree Days (base 65°F)	964	798	651	331	123	14	0	3	45	267	532	845	4,573
Cooling Degree Days (base 65°F)	0	0	2	15	77	245	377	317	139	22	1	0	1,195
Mean Precipitation (in.)	3.49	2.54	4.26	3.98	4.20	4.12	5.03	4.74	4.20	3.70	3.53	3.84	47.63
Extreme Maximum Daily Precip. (in.)	2.04	2.15	2.65	2.80	2.37	2.50	4.82	3.72	5.35	3.11	2.54	3.83	5.35
Days With ≥ 0.1" Precipitation	6	5	7	7	7	7	7	7	6	5	6	7	77
Days With ≥ 0.5" Precipitation	3	2	3	3	3	3	3	3	3	3	3	3	35
Days With ≥ 1.0" Precipitation	1	0	1	1	1	1	1	2	1	1	1	1	12
Mean Snowfall (in.)	na	***1.8***	0.2	0.0	0.0	0.0	0.0	0.0	0.0	0.0	0.0	na	na
Maximum Snow Depth (in.)	na	na	***6***	***0***	***0***	***0***	***0***	***0***	***0***	***0***	***0***	na	na
Days With ≥ 1.0" Snow Depth	na	na	0	0	0	0	0	0	0	0	0	na	na

New Brunswick 3 SE *Middlesex County* Elevation: 85 ft. Latitude: 40° 28' N Longitude: 74° 26' W

	JAN	FEB	MAR	APR	MAY	JUN	JUL	AUG	SEP	OCT	NOV	DEC	YEAR
Mean Maximum Temp. (°F)	39.1	42.4	50.3	61.5	71.7	80.6	85.5	84.0	77.3	65.8	55.2	44.1	63.1
Mean Temp. (°F)	30.4	32.9	40.4	50.7	60.6	69.9	75.0	73.6	66.2	54.4	45.2	35.3	52.9
Mean Minimum Temp. (°F)	21.7	23.4	30.5	39.9	49.4	59.1	64.4	63.1	55.0	42.9	35.2	26.6	42.6
Extreme Maximum Temp. (°F)	72	75	88	95	95	97	103	101	98	91	82	76	103
Extreme Minimum Temp. (°F)	-13	-4	6	16	30	40	45	40	35	25	13	-7	-13
Days Maximum Temp. ≥ 90°F	0	0	0	0	1	4	8	5	1	0	0	0	19
Days Maximum Temp. ≤ 32°F	8	5	1	0	0	0	0	0	0	0	0	4	18
Days Minimum Temp. ≤ 32°F	26	24	19	5	0	0	0	0	0	3	13	24	114
Days Minimum Temp. ≤ 0°F	1	0	0	0	0	0	0	0	0	0	0	0	1
Heating Degree Days (base 65°F)	1,065	900	756	428	175	27	2	4	65	335	587	912	5,256
Cooling Degree Days (base 65°F)	0	0	1	7	44	181	317	277	107	13	0	0	947
Mean Precipitation (in.)	3.60	2.72	4.07	4.37	4.20	4.40	5.11	4.15	4.26	3.78	3.89	3.96	48.51
Extreme Maximum Daily Precip. (in.)	2.23	2.06	2.27	6.43	2.84	2.91	3.64	4.52	5.78	3.99	2.54	3.26	6.43
Days With ≥ 0.1" Precipitation	7	6	7	7	7	7	7	6	6	6	6	7	79
Days With ≥ 0.5" Precipitation	3	2	3	3	3	3	4	3	3	2	3	3	35
Days With ≥ 1.0" Precipitation	1	1	1	1	1	1	2	1	1	1	1	1	13
Mean Snowfall (in.)	8.1	7.9	4.7	1.1	0.0	0.0	0.0	0.0	0.0	0.1	0.5	4.8	27.2
Maximum Snow Depth (in.)	25	20	12	8	0	0	0	0	0	trace	6	15	25
Days With ≥ 1.0" Snow Depth	10	8	3	0	0	0	0	0	0	0	0	4	25

Plainfield *Union County* Elevation: 89 ft. Latitude: 40° 36' N Longitude: 74° 24' W

	JAN	FEB	MAR	APR	MAY	JUN	JUL	AUG	SEP	OCT	NOV	DEC	YEAR
Mean Maximum Temp. (°F)	39.2	43.2	52.4	63.8	74.1	82.4	86.8	85.3	77.9	65.9	54.7	43.4	64.1
Mean Temp. (°F)	31.3	34.3	42.0	52.4	62.1	71.0	75.9	74.4	66.8	55.0	45.3	35.6	53.8
Mean Minimum Temp. (°F)	23.3	25.2	31.6	41.0	50.0	59.5	64.8	63.5	55.7	44.1	35.9	27.8	43.5
Extreme Maximum Temp. (°F)	73	76	91	***97***	99	100	104	104	100	88	81	74	***104***
Extreme Minimum Temp. (°F)	-8	-4	6	18	31	40	48	40	33	23	14	-3	-8
Days Maximum Temp. ≥ 90°F	0	0	0	0	2	6	10	8	2	0	0	0	28
Days Maximum Temp. ≤ 32°F	8	4	1	0	0	0	0	0	0	0	0	4	17
Days Minimum Temp. ≤ 32°F	25	22	17	4	0	0	0	0	0	3	12	22	105
Days Minimum Temp. ≤ 0°F	1	0	0	0	0	0	0	0	0	0	0	0	1
Heating Degree Days (base 65°F)	1,036	863	707	380	142	18	1	3	58	316	584	903	5,011
Cooling Degree Days (base 65°F)	0	0	1	9	58	205	344	302	119	14	0	0	1,052
Mean Precipitation (in.)	3.63	2.85	4.17	3.94	4.25	4.21	5.40	3.55	4.52	4.29	3.98	3.64	48.43
Extreme Maximum Daily Precip. (in.)	2.75	3.04	2.53	2.52	2.82	2.81	3.11	2.97	9.77	5.65	2.82	2.51	9.77
Days With ≥ 0.1" Precipitation	6	5	7	7	7	7	7	6	6	6	6	6	76
Days With ≥ 0.5" Precipitation	3	2	3	3	3	3	3	2	3	3	3	3	34
Days With ≥ 1.0" Precipitation	1	1	1	1	1	1	2	1	1	1	1	1	13
Mean Snowfall (in.)	6.6	6.8	3.9	0.6	0.0	0.0	0.0	0.0	0.0	0.0	0.4	2.8	21.1
Maximum Snow Depth (in.)	22	23	13	10	0	0	0	0	0	***0***	3	***14***	***23***
Days With ≥ 1.0" Snow Depth	7	5	3	0	0	0	0	0	0	0	0	***2***	***17***

The period of record for all cooperative weather station data is 1980 – 2009. See User Guide for detailed explanation of data.

Seabrook Farms *Cumberland County* Elevation: 89 ft. Latitude: 39° 30' N Longitude: 75° 14' W

	JAN	FEB	MAR	APR	MAY	JUN	JUL	AUG	SEP	OCT	NOV	DEC	YEAR
Mean Maximum Temp. (°F)	41.7	43.9	52.2	63.2	72.8	82.0	86.2	84.8	78.3	67.0	56.3	45.6	64.5
Mean Temp. (°F)	33.7	35.4	43.1	53.0	62.6	72.1	76.7	75.3	68.2	56.7	47.3	37.5	55.1
Mean Minimum Temp. (°F)	25.6	27.0	33.9	42.8	52.3	62.1	67.2	65.7	58.1	46.4	38.2	29.4	45.7
Extreme Maximum Temp. (°F)	70	74	86	95	95	100	100	100	96	88	79	74	100
Extreme Minimum Temp. (°F)	-13	0	6	24	35	44	50	44	40	27	17	5	-13
Days Maximum Temp. ≥ 90°F	0	0	0	0	1	5	9	6	2	0	0	0	23
Days Maximum Temp. ≤ 32°F	6	4	1	0	0	0	0	0	0	0	0	3	14
Days Minimum Temp. ≤ 32°F	24	21	14	3	0	0	0	0	0	1	8	20	91
Days Minimum Temp. ≤ 0°F	0	0	0	0	0	0	0	0	0	0	0	0	0
Heating Degree Days (base 65°F)	964	829	674	365	135	15	0	2	41	273	526	845	4,669
Cooling Degree Days (base 65°F)	0	0	2	12	67	233	371	327	145	22	1	0	1,180
Mean Precipitation (in.)	3.71	2.63	4.11	3.71	3.66	3.72	4.06	4.31	3.74	3.52	3.31	3.96	44.44
Extreme Maximum Daily Precip. (in.)	2.22	2.27	4.75	4.46	3.06	4.05	2.82	4.73	3.20	2.51	1.96	3.45	4.75
Days With ≥ 0.1" Precipitation	7	5	7	7	7	7	7	6	6	6	6	6	77
Days With ≥ 0.5" Precipitation	3	2	3	3	3	3	3	3	2	3	3	3	34
Days With ≥ 1.0" Precipitation	1	1	1	1	1	1	1	1	1	1	1	1	12
Mean Snowfall (in.)	4.6	4.6	1.0	0.4	0.0	0.0	0.0	0.0	0.0	0.0	0.3	2.2	13.1
Maximum Snow Depth (in.)	11	16	8	3	0	0	0	0	0	0	6	16	16
Days With ≥ 1.0" Snow Depth	5	6	1	0	0	0	0	0	0	0	0	3	15

Somerville 3 NW *Somerset County* Elevation: 160 ft. Latitude: 40° 36' N Longitude: 74° 38' W

	JAN	FEB	MAR	APR	MAY	JUN	JUL	AUG	SEP	OCT	NOV	DEC	YEAR
Mean Maximum Temp. (°F)	37.1	41.0	49.3	61.3	71.5	80.1	84.6	82.9	75.6	63.9	53.6	41.7	61.9
Mean Temp. (°F)	27.9	31.0	38.5	49.5	59.3	68.3	73.2	71.9	64.1	52.2	43.0	32.7	51.0
Mean Minimum Temp. (°F)	18.7	21.0	27.7	37.5	47.1	56.4	61.8	60.8	52.6	40.4	32.3	23.6	40.0
Extreme Maximum Temp. (°F)	68	75	82	93	94	96	103	99	99	85	79	73	103
Extreme Minimum Temp. (°F)	-16	-6	2	18	29	38	46	41	33	21	10	-7	-16
Days Maximum Temp. ≥ 90°F	0	0	0	0	1	3	7	4	1	0	0	0	16
Days Maximum Temp. ≤ 32°F	10	6	1	0	0	0	0	0	0	0	0	5	22
Days Minimum Temp. ≤ 32°F	28	25	22	9	1	0	0	0	0	6	17	26	134
Days Minimum Temp. ≤ 0°F	2	0	0	0	0	0	0	0	0	0	0	0	2
Heating Degree Days (base 65°F)	1,143	954	814	464	203	36	3	9	97	398	655	995	5,771
Cooling Degree Days (base 65°F)	0	0	0	5	34	142	265	227	77	7	0	0	757
Mean Precipitation (in.)	3.39	2.56	3.82	4.00	4.20	4.22	5.05	3.68	4.09	4.05	3.87	3.59	46.52
Extreme Maximum Daily Precip. (in.)	2.33	1.89	2.32	2.75	2.85	2.58	4.23	4.30	3.81	5.32	2.65	2.12	5.32
Days With ≥ 0.1" Precipitation	6	6	7	7	7	7	8	6	6	5	6	7	78
Days With ≥ 0.5" Precipitation	2	2	3	3	3	3	3	3	3	3	3	3	34
Days With ≥ 1.0" Precipitation	1	1	1	1	1	1	1	1	1	1	1	1	12
Mean Snowfall (in.)	8.3	8.5	5.1	1.7	0.0	0.0	0.0	0.0	0.0	trace	0.7	5.2	29.5
Maximum Snow Depth (in.)	24	23	14	8	0	0	0	0	0	trace	6	18	24
Days With ≥ 1.0" Snow Depth	12	10	4	0	0	0	0	0	0	0	0	5	31

Toms River *Ocean County* Elevation: 100 ft. Latitude: 39° 57' N Longitude: 74° 13' W

	JAN	FEB	MAR	APR	MAY	JUN	JUL	AUG	SEP	OCT	NOV	DEC	YEAR
Mean Maximum Temp. (°F)	42.1	44.7	51.9	62.1	72.5	81.4	86.1	84.5	78.1	67.5	57.4	46.6	64.6
Mean Temp. (°F)	32.0	34.0	40.8	50.5	60.5	69.7	74.8	73.2	66.3	55.0	45.9	36.3	53.2
Mean Minimum Temp. (°F)	21.9	23.2	29.7	38.8	48.6	57.9	63.4	61.9	54.4	42.6	34.4	25.9	41.9
Extreme Maximum Temp. (°F)	72	75	87	97	99	102	105	102	99	91	85	76	105
Extreme Minimum Temp. (°F)	-19	-6	3	12	28	39	46	39	33	21	9	-3	-19
Days Maximum Temp. ≥ 90°F	0	0	0	0	1	5	10	7	2	0	0	0	25
Days Maximum Temp. ≤ 32°F	6	3	1	0	0	0	0	0	0	0	0	3	13
Days Minimum Temp. ≤ 32°F	26	24	19	7	0	0	0	0	0	4	15	24	119
Days Minimum Temp. ≤ 0°F	1	0	0	0	0	0	0	0	0	0	0	0	1
Heating Degree Days (base 65°F)	1,015	871	743	433	180	29	1	4	60	316	566	883	5,101
Cooling Degree Days (base 65°F)	0	0	1	7	49	175	311	264	106	13	1	0	927
Mean Precipitation (in.)	4.05	2.89	4.53	4.26	3.81	3.84	4.74	4.44	4.09	3.71	4.00	4.34	48.70
Extreme Maximum Daily Precip. (in.)	3.36	3.32	3.35	2.80	3.29	3.40	7.07	6.00	6.21	3.50	3.00	5.00	7.07
Days With ≥ 0.1" Precipitation	7	5	7	7	7	7	6	6	6	6	6	7	77
Days With ≥ 0.5" Precipitation	3	2	3	3	3	3	3	3	2	2	3	3	33
Days With ≥ 1.0" Precipitation	1	1	1	1	1	1	2	1	1	1	2	1	14
Mean Snowfall (in.)	na	0.8	0.5	trace	0.0	0.0	0.0	0.0	0.0	0.0	trace	0.9	na
Maximum Snow Depth (in.)	na	na	trace	0	0	0	0	0	0	0	trace	3	na
Days With ≥ 1.0" Snow Depth	na	0	0	0	0	0	0	0	0	0	0	0	na

The period of record for all cooperative weather station data is 1980 – 2009. See User Guide for detailed explanation of data.

New Jersey Weather Station Rankings

Annual Extreme Maximum Temperature

Highest Rank	Station Name	°F	Lowest Rank	Station Name	°F
1	Essex Fells Serv Bldg	***105***	1	Charlotteburg Reservoir	100
1	Newark Intl Arpt	105	1	Seabrook Farms	***100***
1	Toms River	105	3	Belvidere Bridge	***101***
4	Canoe Brook	104	3	Millville Municipal Arpt	101
4	Flemington 5 NNW	104	5	Atlantic City State Marina	102
4	Moorestown	104	5	Hightstown 2 W	102
4	Plainfield	***104***	7	Atlantic City Intl Arpt	103
8	Atlantic City Intl Arpt	103	7	Cranford	103
8	Cranford	103	7	Indian Mills 2 W	103
8	Indian Mills 2 W	103	7	New Brunswick 3 SE	103
8	New Brunswick 3 SE	103	7	Somerville 3 NW	***103***
8	Somerville 3 NW	***103***	12	Canoe Brook	104
13	Atlantic City State Marina	102	12	Flemington 5 NNW	104
13	Hightstown 2 W	102	12	Moorestown	104
15	Belvidere Bridge	***101***	12	Plainfield	***104***
15	Millville Municipal Arpt	101	16	Essex Fells Serv Bldg	***105***
17	Charlotteburg Reservoir	100	16	Newark Intl Arpt	105
17	Seabrook Farms	***100***	16	Toms River	105

Annual Mean Maximum Temperature

Highest Rank	Station Name	°F	Lowest Rank	Station Name	°F
1	Moorestown	66.9	1	Charlotteburg Reservoir	60.5
2	Indian Mills 2 W	66.1	2	Belvidere Bridge	***61.6***
3	Toms River	64.6	3	Atlantic City State Marina	61.8
4	Cranford	64.5	4	Somerville 3 NW	***61.9***
4	Millville Municipal Arpt	64.5	5	Essex Fells Serv Bldg	***62.0***
4	Seabrook Farms	***64.5***	6	Flemington 5 NNW	62.6
7	Atlantic City Intl Arpt	64.2	7	New Brunswick 3 SE	63.1
8	Plainfield	64.1	8	Canoe Brook	63.2
9	Newark Intl Arpt	63.7	9	Hightstown 2 W	63.3
10	Hightstown 2 W	63.3	10	Newark Intl Arpt	63.7
11	Canoe Brook	63.2	11	Plainfield	64.1
12	New Brunswick 3 SE	63.1	12	Atlantic City Intl Arpt	64.2
13	Flemington 5 NNW	62.6	13	Cranford	64.5
14	Essex Fells Serv Bldg	***62.0***	13	Millville Municipal Arpt	64.5
15	Somerville 3 NW	***61.9***	13	Seabrook Farms	***64.5***
16	Atlantic City State Marina	61.8	16	Toms River	64.6
17	Belvidere Bridge	***61.6***	17	Indian Mills 2 W	66.1
18	Charlotteburg Reservoir	60.5	18	Moorestown	66.9

Rankings include 25 highest/lowest stations. If state has less than 25 stations, all stations are included. The period of record is 1980–2009. See User Guide for detailed explanation of data.

Annual Mean Temperature

Highest			Lowest		
Rank	Station Name	°F	Rank	Station Name	°F
1	Atlantic City State Marina	55.5	1	Charlotteburg Reservoir	49.1
1	Moorestown	55.5	2	Belvidere Bridge	***50.7***
3	Newark Intl Arpt	55.3	3	Somerville 3 NW	***51.0***
4	Seabrook Farms	***55.1***	4	Essex Fells Serv Bldg	***51.4***
5	Indian Mills 2 W	54.4	5	Flemington 5 NNW	51.6
5	Millville Municipal Arpt	54.4	6	Canoe Brook	52.2
7	Atlantic City Intl Arpt	54.0	7	Hightstown 2 W	52.9
8	Plainfield	53.8	7	New Brunswick 3 SE	52.9
9	Cranford	53.4	9	Toms River	53.3
10	Toms River	53.3	10	Cranford	53.4
11	Hightstown 2 W	52.9	11	Plainfield	53.8
11	New Brunswick 3 SE	52.9	12	Atlantic City Intl Arpt	54.0
13	Canoe Brook	52.2	13	Indian Mills 2 W	54.4
14	Flemington 5 NNW	51.6	13	Millville Municipal Arpt	54.4
15	Essex Fells Serv Bldg	***51.4***	15	Seabrook Farms	***55.1***
16	Somerville 3 NW	***51.0***	16	Newark Intl Arpt	55.3
17	Belvidere Bridge	***50.7***	17	Atlantic City State Marina	55.5
18	Charlotteburg Reservoir	49.1	17	Moorestown	55.5

Annual Mean Minimum Temperature

Highest			Lowest		
Rank	Station Name	°F	Rank	Station Name	°F
1	Atlantic City State Marina	49.2	1	Charlotteburg Reservoir	37.6
2	Newark Intl Arpt	46.9	2	Belvidere Bridge	***39.8***
3	Seabrook Farms	***45.7***	3	Somerville 3 NW	***40.0***
4	Millville Municipal Arpt	44.2	4	Flemington 5 NNW	40.5
5	Moorestown	44.0	5	Essex Fells Serv Bldg	***40.8***
6	Atlantic City Intl Arpt	43.8	6	Canoe Brook	41.1
7	Plainfield	43.5	7	Toms River	41.9
8	Indian Mills 2 W	42.6	8	Cranford	42.2
8	New Brunswick 3 SE	42.6	9	Hightstown 2 W	42.5
10	Hightstown 2 W	42.5	10	Indian Mills 2 W	42.6
11	Cranford	42.2	10	New Brunswick 3 SE	42.6
12	Toms River	41.9	12	Plainfield	43.5
13	Canoe Brook	41.1	13	Atlantic City Intl Arpt	43.8
14	Essex Fells Serv Bldg	***40.8***	14	Moorestown	44.0
15	Flemington 5 NNW	40.5	15	Millville Municipal Arpt	44.2
16	Somerville 3 NW	***40.0***	16	Seabrook Farms	***45.7***
17	Belvidere Bridge	***39.8***	17	Newark Intl Arpt	46.9
18	Charlotteburg Reservoir	37.6	18	Atlantic City State Marina	49.2

Rankings include 25 highest/lowest stations. If state has less than 25 stations, all stations are included. The period of record is 1980–2009. See User Guide for detailed explanation of data.

Annual Extreme Minimum Temperature

Highest Rank	Station Name	°F	Lowest Rank	Station Name	°F
1	Atlantic City State Marina	-3	1	Charlotteburg Reservoir	-24
2	Newark Intl Arpt	-8	2	Toms River	-19
2	Plainfield	-8	3	Flemington 5 NNW	-18
4	Atlantic City Intl Arpt	-9	3	Indian Mills 2 W	-18
5	Cranford	-10	5	Belvidere Bridge	***-17***
5	Millville Municipal Arpt	-10	6	Somerville 3 NW	***-16***
5	Moorestown	-10	7	Canoe Brook	-15
8	Hightstown 2 W	-12	8	Essex Fells Serv Bldg	***-14***
9	New Brunswick 3 SE	-13	9	New Brunswick 3 SE	-13
9	Seabrook Farms	***-13***	9	Seabrook Farms	***-13***
11	Essex Fells Serv Bldg	***-14***	11	Hightstown 2 W	-12
12	Canoe Brook	-15	12	Cranford	-10
13	Somerville 3 NW	***-16***	12	Millville Municipal Arpt	-10
14	Belvidere Bridge	***-17***	12	Moorestown	-10
15	Flemington 5 NNW	-18	15	Atlantic City Intl Arpt	-9
15	Indian Mills 2 W	-18	16	Newark Intl Arpt	-8
17	Toms River	-19	16	Plainfield	-8
18	Charlotteburg Reservoir	-24	18	Atlantic City State Marina	-3

July Mean Maximum Temperature

Highest Rank	Station Name	°F	Lowest Rank	Station Name	°F
1	Moorestown	88.7	1	Atlantic City State Marina	81.2
2	Indian Mills 2 W	87.8	2	Charlotteburg Reservoir	83.0
3	Cranford	86.8	3	Belvidere Bridge	84.0
3	Plainfield	86.8	4	Essex Fells Serv Bldg	***84.6***
5	Newark Intl Arpt	86.5	4	Somerville 3 NW	***84.6***
6	Seabrook Farms	86.2	6	Flemington 5 NNW	85.5
7	Millville Municipal Arpt	86.1	6	New Brunswick 3 SE	85.5
7	Toms River	86.1	8	Hightstown 2 W	85.6
9	Canoe Brook	85.9	9	Atlantic City Intl Arpt	85.7
10	Atlantic City Intl Arpt	85.7	10	Canoe Brook	85.9
11	Hightstown 2 W	85.6	11	Millville Municipal Arpt	86.1
12	Flemington 5 NNW	85.5	11	Toms River	86.1
12	New Brunswick 3 SE	85.5	13	Seabrook Farms	86.2
14	Essex Fells Serv Bldg	***84.6***	14	Newark Intl Arpt	86.5
14	Somerville 3 NW	***84.6***	15	Cranford	86.8
16	Belvidere Bridge	84.0	15	Plainfield	86.8
17	Charlotteburg Reservoir	83.0	17	Indian Mills 2 W	87.8
18	Atlantic City State Marina	81.2	18	Moorestown	88.7

Rankings include 25 highest/lowest stations. If state has less than 25 stations, all stations are included. The period of record is 1980–2009. See User Guide for detailed explanation of data.

January Mean Minimum Temperature

Highest			Lowest		
Rank	Station Name	°F	Rank	Station Name	°F
1	Atlantic City State Marina	28.7	1	Charlotteburg Reservoir	16.6
2	Seabrook Farms	*25.6*	2	Somerville 3 NW	*18.7*
3	Newark Intl Arpt	25.2	3	Belvidere Bridge	19.1
4	Moorestown	24.3	4	Canoe Brook	19.5
5	Millville Municipal Arpt	24.2	5	Flemington 5 NNW	19.7
6	Atlantic City Intl Arpt	23.4	6	Essex Fells Serv Bldg	20.0
7	Plainfield	23.3	7	New Brunswick 3 SE	21.7
8	Indian Mills 2 W	22.8	8	Cranford	21.8
9	Hightstown 2 W	22.0	9	Toms River	21.9
10	Toms River	21.9	10	Hightstown 2 W	22.0
11	Cranford	21.8	11	Indian Mills 2 W	22.8
12	New Brunswick 3 SE	21.7	12	Plainfield	23.3
13	Essex Fells Serv Bldg	20.0	13	Atlantic City Intl Arpt	23.4
14	Flemington 5 NNW	19.7	14	Millville Municipal Arpt	24.2
15	Canoe Brook	19.5	15	Moorestown	24.3
16	Belvidere Bridge	19.1	16	Newark Intl Arpt	25.2
17	Somerville 3 NW	*18.7*	17	Seabrook Farms	*25.6*
18	Charlotteburg Reservoir	16.6	18	Atlantic City State Marina	28.7

Number of Days Annually Maximum Temperature ≥ 90°F

Highest			Lowest		
Rank	Station Name	Days	Rank	Station Name	Days
1	Moorestown	40	1	Atlantic City State Marina	6
2	Indian Mills 2 W	31	2	Charlotteburg Reservoir	9
3	Plainfield	28	3	Belvidere Bridge	*14*
4	Newark Intl Arpt	27	4	Essex Fells Serv Bldg	*16*
5	Cranford	25	4	Somerville 3 NW	*16*
5	Toms River	25	6	Flemington 5 NNW	18
7	Canoe Brook	23	7	New Brunswick 3 SE	19
7	Seabrook Farms	*23*	8	Atlantic City Intl Arpt	20
9	Millville Municipal Arpt	21	8	Hightstown 2 W	20
10	Atlantic City Intl Arpt	20	10	Millville Municipal Arpt	21
10	Hightstown 2 W	20	11	Canoe Brook	23
12	New Brunswick 3 SE	19	11	Seabrook Farms	*23*
13	Flemington 5 NNW	18	13	Cranford	25
14	Essex Fells Serv Bldg	*16*	13	Toms River	25
14	Somerville 3 NW	*16*	15	Newark Intl Arpt	27
16	Belvidere Bridge	*14*	16	Plainfield	28
17	Charlotteburg Reservoir	9	17	Indian Mills 2 W	31
18	Atlantic City State Marina	6	18	Moorestown	40

Rankings include 25 highest/lowest stations. If state has less than 25 stations, all stations are included. The period of record is 1980–2009. See User Guide for detailed explanation of data.

Number of Days Annually Maximum Temperature ≤ 32°F

Highest

Rank	Station Name	Days
1	Charlotteburg Reservoir	26
2	Essex Fells Serv Bldg	***22***
2	Somerville 3 NW	***22***
4	Belvidere Bridge	***21***
5	Flemington 5 NNW	20
6	Canoe Brook	18
6	Hightstown 2 W	18
6	New Brunswick 3 SE	18
9	Newark Intl Arpt	17
9	Plainfield	17
11	Seabrook Farms	***14***
12	Atlantic City Intl Arpt	13
12	Cranford	13
12	Millville Municipal Arpt	13
12	Toms River	13
16	Indian Mills 2 W	11
17	Atlantic City State Marina	10
17	Moorestown	10

Lowest

Rank	Station Name	Days
1	Atlantic City State Marina	10
1	Moorestown	10
3	Indian Mills 2 W	11
4	Atlantic City Intl Arpt	13
4	Cranford	13
4	Millville Municipal Arpt	13
4	Toms River	13
8	Seabrook Farms	***14***
9	Newark Intl Arpt	17
9	Plainfield	17
11	Canoe Brook	18
11	Hightstown 2 W	18
11	New Brunswick 3 SE	18
14	Flemington 5 NNW	20
15	Belvidere Bridge	***21***
16	Essex Fells Serv Bldg	***22***
16	Somerville 3 NW	***22***
18	Charlotteburg Reservoir	26

Number of Days Annually Minimum Temperature ≤ 32°F

Highest

Rank	Station Name	Days
1	Charlotteburg Reservoir	147
2	Belvidere Bridge	***136***
3	Somerville 3 NW	***134***
4	Flemington 5 NNW	129
5	Canoe Brook	126
6	Essex Fells Serv Bldg	***125***
7	Toms River	119
8	Cranford	115
8	Indian Mills 2 W	115
10	New Brunswick 3 SE	114
11	Hightstown 2 W	112
12	Atlantic City Intl Arpt	107
13	Plainfield	105
14	Millville Municipal Arpt	104
14	Moorestown	104
16	Seabrook Farms	***91***
17	Newark Intl Arpt	82
18	Atlantic City State Marina	62

Lowest

Rank	Station Name	Days
1	Atlantic City State Marina	62
2	Newark Intl Arpt	82
3	Seabrook Farms	***91***
4	Millville Municipal Arpt	104
4	Moorestown	104
6	Plainfield	105
7	Atlantic City Intl Arpt	107
8	Hightstown 2 W	112
9	New Brunswick 3 SE	114
10	Cranford	115
10	Indian Mills 2 W	115
12	Toms River	119
13	Essex Fells Serv Bldg	***125***
14	Canoe Brook	126
15	Flemington 5 NNW	129
16	Somerville 3 NW	***134***
17	Belvidere Bridge	***136***
18	Charlotteburg Reservoir	147

Rankings include 25 highest/lowest stations. If state has less than 25 stations, all stations are included. The period of record is 1980–2009. See User Guide for detailed explanation of data.

Number of Days Annually Minimum Temperature ≤ 0°F

Highest

Rank	Station Name	Days
1	Charlotteburg Reservoir	5
2	Belvidere Bridge	*2*
2	Canoe Brook	2
2	Flemington 5 NNW	2
2	Somerville 3 NW	*2*
6	Atlantic City Intl Arpt	1
6	Cranford	1
6	Essex Fells Serv Bldg	*1*
6	Hightstown 2 W	1
6	Indian Mills 2 W	1
6	Millville Municipal Arpt	1
6	Moorestown	1
6	New Brunswick 3 SE	1
6	Plainfield	1
6	Toms River	1
16	Atlantic City State Marina	0
16	Newark Intl Arpt	0
16	Seabrook Farms	*0*

Lowest

Rank	Station Name	Days
1	Atlantic City State Marina	0
1	Newark Intl Arpt	0
1	Seabrook Farms	*0*
4	Atlantic City Intl Arpt	1
4	Cranford	1
4	Essex Fells Serv Bldg	*1*
4	Hightstown 2 W	1
4	Indian Mills 2 W	1
4	Millville Municipal Arpt	1
4	Moorestown	1
4	New Brunswick 3 SE	1
4	Plainfield	1
4	Toms River	1
14	Belvidere Bridge	*2*
14	Canoe Brook	2
14	Flemington 5 NNW	2
14	Somerville 3 NW	*2*
18	Charlotteburg Reservoir	5

Number of Annual Heating Degree Days

Highest

Rank	Station Name	Num.
1	Charlotteburg Reservoir	6,252
2	Belvidere Bridge	*5,809*
3	Somerville 3 NW	*5,771*
4	Essex Fells Serv Bldg	*5,647*
5	Flemington 5 NNW	5,612
6	Canoe Brook	5,508
7	New Brunswick 3 SE	5,256
8	Hightstown 2 W	5,237
9	Cranford	5,104
10	Toms River	5,101
11	Plainfield	5,011
12	Atlantic City Intl Arpt	4,941
13	Millville Municipal Arpt	4,852
14	Indian Mills 2 W	4,838
15	Newark Intl Arpt	4,701
16	Seabrook Farms	*4,669*
17	Moorestown	4,573
18	Atlantic City State Marina	4,392

Lowest

Rank	Station Name	Num.
1	Atlantic City State Marina	4,392
2	Moorestown	4,573
3	Seabrook Farms	*4,669*
4	Newark Intl Arpt	4,701
5	Indian Mills 2 W	4,838
6	Millville Municipal Arpt	4,852
7	Atlantic City Intl Arpt	4,941
8	Plainfield	5,011
9	Toms River	5,101
10	Cranford	5,104
11	Hightstown 2 W	5,237
12	New Brunswick 3 SE	5,256
13	Canoe Brook	5,508
14	Flemington 5 NNW	5,612
15	Essex Fells Serv Bldg	*5,647*
16	Somerville 3 NW	*5,771*
17	Belvidere Bridge	*5,809*
18	Charlotteburg Reservoir	6,252

Rankings include 25 highest/lowest stations. If state has less than 25 stations, all stations are included. The period of record is 1980–2009. See User Guide for detailed explanation of data.

Number of Annual Cooling Degree Days

Highest

Rank	Station Name	Num.
1	Newark Intl Arpt	1,285
2	Moorestown	1,195
3	Seabrook Farms	***1,180***
4	Millville Municipal Arpt	1,091
5	Indian Mills 2 W	1,060
6	Plainfield	1,052
7	Atlantic City Intl Arpt	1,033
8	Atlantic City State Marina	1,030
9	Cranford	975
10	New Brunswick 3 SE	947
11	Hightstown 2 W	928
12	Toms River	927
13	Canoe Brook	895
14	Flemington 5 NNW	826
15	Essex Fells Serv Bldg	***799***
16	Somerville 3 NW	***757***
17	Belvidere Bridge	***705***
18	Charlotteburg Reservoir	548

Lowest

Rank	Station Name	Num.
1	Charlotteburg Reservoir	548
2	Belvidere Bridge	***705***
3	Somerville 3 NW	***757***
4	Essex Fells Serv Bldg	***799***
5	Flemington 5 NNW	826
6	Canoe Brook	895
7	Toms River	927
8	Hightstown 2 W	928
9	New Brunswick 3 SE	947
10	Cranford	975
11	Atlantic City State Marina	1,030
12	Atlantic City Intl Arpt	1,033
13	Plainfield	1,052
14	Indian Mills 2 W	1,060
15	Millville Municipal Arpt	1,091
16	Seabrook Farms	***1,180***
17	Moorestown	1,195
18	Newark Intl Arpt	1,285

Annual Precipitation

Highest

Rank	Station Name	Inches
1	Charlotteburg Reservoir	51.49
2	Canoe Brook	50.35
3	Flemington 5 NNW	50.01
4	Cranford	49.81
5	Essex Fells Serv Bldg	***49.47***
6	Toms River	48.70
7	New Brunswick 3 SE	48.51
8	Plainfield	48.43
9	Moorestown	47.63
10	Indian Mills 2 W	47.21
11	Hightstown 2 W	46.59
12	Somerville 3 NW	***46.52***
13	Belvidere Bridge	***46.20***
14	Newark Intl Arpt	46.08
15	Seabrook Farms	***44.44***
16	Millville Municipal Arpt	41.69
17	Atlantic City Intl Arpt	41.13
18	Atlantic City State Marina	39.51

Lowest

Rank	Station Name	Inches
1	Atlantic City State Marina	39.51
2	Atlantic City Intl Arpt	41.13
3	Millville Municipal Arpt	41.69
4	Seabrook Farms	***44.44***
5	Newark Intl Arpt	46.08
6	Belvidere Bridge	***46.20***
7	Somerville 3 NW	***46.52***
8	Hightstown 2 W	46.59
9	Indian Mills 2 W	47.21
10	Moorestown	47.63
11	Plainfield	48.43
12	New Brunswick 3 SE	48.51
13	Toms River	48.70
14	Essex Fells Serv Bldg	***49.47***
15	Cranford	49.81
16	Flemington 5 NNW	50.01
17	Canoe Brook	50.35
18	Charlotteburg Reservoir	51.49

Annual Extreme Maximum Daily Precipitation

Highest

Rank	Station Name	Inches
1	Plainfield	9.77
2	Cranford	9.76
3	Millville Municipal Arpt	9.06
4	Flemington 5 NNW	8.49
5	Canoe Brook	7.60
6	Toms River	7.07
7	Belvidere Bridge	*6.84*
8	Charlotteburg Reservoir	6.81
9	New Brunswick 3 SE	6.43
10	Newark Intl Arpt	6.22
11	Atlantic City State Marina	6.09
12	Hightstown 2 W	5.60
13	Moorestown	5.35
14	Somerville 3 NW	*5.32*
15	Indian Mills 2 W	4.94
16	Seabrook Farms	*4.75*
17	Atlantic City Intl Arpt	3.68

Lowest

Rank	Station Name	Inches
1	Atlantic City Intl Arpt	3.68
2	Seabrook Farms	*4.75*
3	Indian Mills 2 W	4.94
4	Somerville 3 NW	*5.32*
5	Moorestown	5.35
6	Hightstown 2 W	5.60
7	Atlantic City State Marina	6.09
8	Newark Intl Arpt	6.22
9	New Brunswick 3 SE	6.43
10	Charlotteburg Reservoir	6.81
11	Belvidere Bridge	*6.84*
12	Toms River	7.07
13	Canoe Brook	7.60
14	Flemington 5 NNW	8.49
15	Millville Municipal Arpt	9.06
16	Cranford	9.76
17	Plainfield	9.77

Number of Days Annually With ≥ 0.1 Inches of Precipitation

Highest

Rank	Station Name	Days
1	Belvidere Bridge	*82*
2	Cranford	80
3	Charlotteburg Reservoir	79
3	Flemington 5 NNW	79
3	Hightstown 2 W	79
3	New Brunswick 3 SE	79
7	Canoe Brook	78
7	Somerville 3 NW	*78*
9	Moorestown	77
9	Seabrook Farms	*77*
9	Toms River	77
12	Newark Intl Arpt	76
12	Plainfield	76
14	Indian Mills 2 W	75
15	Atlantic City Intl Arpt	74
15	Essex Fells Serv Bldg	*74*
17	Millville Municipal Arpt	70
18	Atlantic City State Marina	68

Lowest

Rank	Station Name	Days
1	Atlantic City State Marina	68
2	Millville Municipal Arpt	70
3	Atlantic City Intl Arpt	74
3	Essex Fells Serv Bldg	*74*
5	Indian Mills 2 W	75
6	Newark Intl Arpt	76
6	Plainfield	76
8	Moorestown	77
8	Seabrook Farms	*77*
8	Toms River	77
11	Canoe Brook	78
11	Somerville 3 NW	*78*
13	Charlotteburg Reservoir	79
13	Flemington 5 NNW	79
13	Hightstown 2 W	79
13	New Brunswick 3 SE	79
17	Cranford	80
18	Belvidere Bridge	*82*

Rankings include 25 highest/lowest stations. If state has less than 25 stations, all stations are included. The period of record is 1980–2009. See User Guide for detailed explanation of data.

Number of Days Annually With ≥ 0.5 Inches of Precipitation

Highest			Lowest		
Rank	Station Name	Days	Rank	Station Name	Days
1	Essex Fells Serv Bldg	*36*	1	Atlantic City State Marina	27
2	Charlotteburg Reservoir	35	2	Atlantic City Intl Arpt	28
2	Cranford	35	2	Millville Municipal Arpt	28
2	Moorestown	35	4	Belvidere Bridge	*31*
2	New Brunswick 3 SE	35	5	Indian Mills 2 W	33
2	Newark Intl Arpt	35	5	Toms River	33
7	Canoe Brook	34	7	Canoe Brook	34
7	Flemington 5 NNW	34	7	Flemington 5 NNW	34
7	Hightstown 2 W	34	7	Hightstown 2 W	34
7	Plainfield	34	7	Plainfield	34
7	Seabrook Farms	*34*	7	Seabrook Farms	*34*
7	Somerville 3 NW	*34*	7	Somerville 3 NW	*34*
13	Indian Mills 2 W	33	13	Charlotteburg Reservoir	35
13	Toms River	33	13	Cranford	35
15	Belvidere Bridge	*31*	13	Moorestown	35
16	Atlantic City Intl Arpt	28	13	New Brunswick 3 SE	35
16	Millville Municipal Arpt	28	13	Newark Intl Arpt	35
18	Atlantic City State Marina	27	18	Essex Fells Serv Bldg	*36*

Number of Days Annually With ≥ 1.0 Inches of Precipitation

Highest			Lowest		
Rank	Station Name	Days	Rank	Station Name	Days
1	Essex Fells Serv Bldg	*15*	1	Belvidere Bridge	*11*
2	Flemington 5 NNW	14	2	Atlantic City State Marina	12
2	Toms River	14	2	Atlantic City Intl Arpt	12
4	Charlotteburg Reservoir	13	2	Canoe Brook	12
4	Indian Mills 2 W	13	2	Cranford	12
4	New Brunswick 3 SE	13	2	Hightstown 2 W	12
4	Newark Intl Arpt	13	2	Millville Municipal Arpt	12
4	Plainfield	13	2	Moorestown	12
9	Atlantic City State Marina	12	2	Seabrook Farms	*12*
9	Atlantic City Intl Arpt	12	2	Somerville 3 NW	*12*
9	Canoe Brook	12	11	Charlotteburg Reservoir	13
9	Cranford	12	11	Indian Mills 2 W	13
9	Hightstown 2 W	12	11	New Brunswick 3 SE	13
9	Millville Municipal Arpt	12	11	Newark Intl Arpt	13
9	Moorestown	12	11	Plainfield	13
9	Seabrook Farms	*12*	16	Flemington 5 NNW	14
9	Somerville 3 NW	*12*	16	Toms River	14
18	Belvidere Bridge	*11*	18	Essex Fells Serv Bldg	*15*

Annual Snowfall

Highest			Lowest		
Rank	**Station Name**	**Inches**	**Rank**	**Station Name**	**Inches**
1	Charlotteburg Reservoir	34.4	1	Seabrook Farms	***13.1***
2	Somerville 3 NW	***29.5***	2	Atlantic City Intl Arpt	***13.9***
3	Flemington 5 NNW	28.3	3	Essex Fells Serv Bldg	***14.8***
4	New Brunswick 3 SE	27.2	4	Indian Mills 2 W	17.6
5	Newark Intl Arpt	27.1	5	Plainfield	21.1
6	Canoe Brook	25.6	6	Cranford	22.1
7	Belvidere Bridge	***24.3***	7	Hightstown 2 W	22.2
8	Hightstown 2 W	22.2	8	Belvidere Bridge	***24.3***
9	Cranford	22.1	9	Canoe Brook	25.6
10	Plainfield	21.1	10	Newark Intl Arpt	27.1
11	Indian Mills 2 W	17.6	11	New Brunswick 3 SE	27.2
12	Essex Fells Serv Bldg	***14.8***	12	Flemington 5 NNW	28.3
13	Atlantic City Intl Arpt	***13.9***	13	Somerville 3 NW	***29.5***
14	Seabrook Farms	***13.1***	14	Charlotteburg Reservoir	34.4

Annual Maximum Snow Depth

Highest			Lowest		
Rank	**Station Name**	**Inches**	**Rank**	**Station Name**	**Inches**
1	Charlotteburg Reservoir	35	1	Seabrook Farms	***16***
2	Newark Intl Arpt	31	2	Hightstown 2 W	20
3	Belvidere Bridge	***27***	3	Canoe Brook	22
3	Flemington 5 NNW	27	4	Cranford	23
5	Indian Mills 2 W	25	4	Plainfield	***23***
5	New Brunswick 3 SE	25	6	Somerville 3 NW	***24***
7	Somerville 3 NW	***24***	7	Indian Mills 2 W	25
8	Cranford	23	7	New Brunswick 3 SE	25
8	Plainfield	***23***	9	Belvidere Bridge	***27***
10	Canoe Brook	22	9	Flemington 5 NNW	27
11	Hightstown 2 W	20	11	Newark Intl Arpt	31
12	Seabrook Farms	***16***	12	Charlotteburg Reservoir	35

Rankings include 25 highest/lowest stations. If state has less than 25 stations, all stations are included. The period of record is 1980–2009. See User Guide for detailed explanation of data.

Number of Days Annually With ≥ 1.0 Inch Snow Depth

Highest

Rank	Station Name	Days
1	Charlotteburg Reservoir	35
2	Somerville 3 NW	***31***
3	Belvidere Bridge	***28***
3	Flemington 5 NNW	28
5	Cranford	26
6	Canoe Brook	25
6	New Brunswick 3 SE	25
8	Hightstown 2 W	21
8	Newark Intl Arpt	21
10	Indian Mills 2 W	17
10	Plainfield	***17***
12	Seabrook Farms	***15***

Lowest

Rank	Station Name	Days
1	Seabrook Farms	***15***
2	Indian Mills 2 W	17
2	Plainfield	***17***
4	Hightstown 2 W	21
4	Newark Intl Arpt	21
6	Canoe Brook	25
6	New Brunswick 3 SE	25
8	Cranford	26
9	Belvidere Bridge	***28***
9	Flemington 5 NNW	28
11	Somerville 3 NW	***31***
12	Charlotteburg Reservoir	35

Significant Storm Events in New Jersey: 2000 – 2009

Location or County	Date	Type	Mag.	Deaths	Injuries	Property Damage ($mil.)	Crop Damage ($mil.)
Sussex	08/12/00	Flood	na	0	0	166.5	0.0
Morris	08/12/00	Flood	na	0	0	12.0	0.0
Monmouth	08/02/02	Thunderstorm Wind	83 mph	0	0	10.2	0.0
Bergen, Essex, Hudson, Passaic, and Union Counties	09/11/02	Wind	na	1	12	0.0	0.0
Southern New Jersey	02/16/03	Winter Storm	na	0	2	11.5	0.0
Northern New Jersey	02/16/03	Heavy Snow	na	1	8	8.0	0.0
Burlington	07/12/04	Flash Flood	na	0	0	50.0	0.0
Warren Co.	09/18/04	Flood	na	0	0	28.0	0.0
South and Southwestern New Jersey	01/22/05	Winter Storm	na	0	0	16.2	0.0
Northern and Southwestern New Jersey	01/22/05	Heavy Snow	na	0	0	11.0	0.0
Hunterdon Co.	04/02/05	Flood	na	0	0	30.0	0.0
Bergen, Essex, Hudson, Passaic, and Union Counties	04/02/05	Flood	na	0	0	12.0	0.0
Middlesex	07/17/05	Flash Flood	na	0	0	10.3	0.0
Warren	06/27/06	Flood	na	0	0	15.0	0.0
Mercer	06/28/06	Flood	na	0	0	8.5	0.0
Hunterdon	06/28/06	Flood	na	1	0	7.5	0.0
Somerset	04/15/07	Flood	na	0	0	48.0	0.0
Morris	04/15/07	Flood	na	0	0	26.0	0.0
Burlington	04/15/07	Flood	na	0	0	8.0	0.0
Salem	04/15/07	Flood	na	0	0	7.0	0.0
Bergen	04/15/07	Flood	na	0	0	6.9	0.0

Note: Deaths, injuries, and damages are date and location specific.

NEW MEXICO

PHYSICAL FEATURES. New Mexico, with a total area of 121,666 square miles, is in the southwestern part of the country. The State, approximately 350 miles square, lies mostly between latitudes 32° and 37° N. and longitudes 103° and 109° W. The State's topography consists mainly of high plateaus or mesas, with numerous mountain ranges, canyons, valleys, and normally dry arroyos. Average elevation is about 5,700 feet above sea level. The lowest point is upstream from the Red Bluff Reservoir at 2,817 feet where the Pecos River flows into Texas. The highest point is Wheeler Peak at 13,161 feet above sea level. The principal sources of moisture for the scant rains and snows that fall on the State are the Pacific Ocean, 500 miles to the west, and the Gulf of Mexico, 500 miles to the southeast.

New Mexico is divided into three major areas by mountain ranges and highlands, oriented in a general north-south direction, which merge in the north. The Northern Mountains and Central Highlands, between longitudes 105° and 106° W., are the western boundary of the Northeastern and Southeastern Plains which slope gradually eastward and southeastward. The northern part of these eastern plains lies within the Arkansas River Basin and is drained mostly by the Canadian River and the Cimarron River. West of the mountain ranges that form the Continental Divide, whose height decreases to a markedly lower elevation in southern New Mexico, rivers drain into the Gulf of California through the Colorado River system. Between the Northern Mountains and the Central Highland system and the Continental Divide system is the Rio Grande Valley which widens toward the south.

GENERAL CLIMATE. New Mexico has a mild, arid or semiarid, continental climate characterized by light precipitation totals, abundant sunshine, low relative humidities, and a relatively large annual and diurnal temperature range. The highest mountains have climate characteristics common to the Rocky Mountains.

Location and topography play major roles in determining the climate of New Mexico, particularly true for any specific locality. Both the ruggedness of the terrain and its direction of slope are important. The eastern plains open to the Great Plains of Texas and Oklahoma and to their northward extension into central Canada. At times during winter months, cold continental air masses move southward out of central Canada and invade this area, producing blizzard and cold-wave conditions. These air masses occasionally cross the Central Highlands, which greatly modify and warm the air masses before they reach the Rio Grande Valley.

PRECIPITATION. Average annual precipitation ranges from less than 10 inches over much of the southern desert and the Rio Grande and San Juan Valleys, to more than 20 inches at higher elevations in the State. A wide variation in annual totals is characteristic of arid and semiarid climates.

Summer rains fall almost entirely during brief, but frequently intense, thunderstorms. The general southeasterly circulation from the Gulf of Mexico brings moisture for these storms into the State, and strong surface heating combined with orographic lifting as the air moves over higher terrain causes convective air currents and condensation. July and August are the rainiest months over most of the State, with from 30 to 40 percent of the year's total moisture falling at that time. The San Juan Valley area is least affected by this summer circulation, receiving about 25 percent of its annual rainfall during July and August. During the warmest six months of the year, May through October, total precipitation averages from 60 percent of the annual total in the Northwestern Plateau to 80 percent of the annual total in the eastern plains.

Winter precipitation is caused mainly by frontal activity associated with the general movement of Pacific Ocean storms across the country from west to east. As these storms move inland, much of the moisture is precipitated over the coastal and inland mountain ranges of California, Nevada, Arizona, and Utah. Much of the remaining moisture falls on the western slope of the Continental Divide and over northern and high central mountain ranges. Winter is the driest season in New Mexico except for the portion west of the Continental Divide. This dryness is most noticeable in the Central Valley and on eastern slopes of the mountains.

Much of the winter precipitation falls as snow in the mountain areas, but it may occur as either rain or snow in the valleys. Average annual snowfall ranges from about 3 inches at the Southern Desert and Southeastern Plains stations to well over 100 inches at Northern Mountain stations. It may exceed 300 inches in the highest mountains of the north.

FLOODS. General floods are seldom widespread in New Mexico. Heavy summer thunderstorms may bring several inches of rain to small areas in a short time. Because of the rough terrain and sparse vegetation in many areas, run-offs from these storms frequently cause local flash floods. Normally dry arroyos may overflow their banks for several hours, halting traffic where water crosses highways, and damaging bridges, culverts, and roadways. Snowmelt during April to June, especially in combination with a warm rain, and heavy general rains during August to October may occasionally cause flooding of the larger rivers.

TEMPERATURE. Elevation is a greater factor in determining the temperature of any specific locality than its latitude. During the summer months, individual daytime temperatures quite often exceed 100 at elevations below 5,000 feet; but the average monthly maximum temperatures during July, the warmest month, range from slightly above 90°F. at lower elevations to the upper 70s at high elevations. Warmest days quite often occur in June before the thunderstorm season sets in; during July and August, afternoon convective storms tend to shut off afternoon solar insolation, lowering temperatures before they reach their potential daily high. A preponderance of clear skies and low relative humidity permits rapid cooling by radiation from the earth after sundown; consequently, nights are usually comfortable in summer.

In January, the coldest month, average daytime temperatures range from the middle 50s in the southern and central valleys to the middle 30s in the higher elevations of the north. Minimum temperatures below freezing are common in all sections of the State during the winter, but subzero temperatures are rare except in the mountains. The freeze-free season ranges from more than 200 days in the southern valleys to less than 80 days in the northern mountains where some high mountain valleys have freezes in summer months.

SEVERE STORMS. On rare occasions, a tropical hurricane may cause heavy rain in eastern and central New Mexico as it moves inland from the western part of the Gulf of Mexico. Also on rare occasions, a tropical storm moving inland from the Gulf of California area may cause heavy rain to fall in southwestern New Mexico. Tornadoes are occasionally reported in New Mexico, most frequently during afternoon and early evening hours from May through August.

Thunderstorms are relatively frequent in summer, averaging in numbers from 40 in the south to more than 70 in the northeast, the latter area having the second greatest thunderstorm frequency in the country. Occasionally, these heavy thunderstorms are accompanied by hail, with the greatest hail frequency occurring near and to the east of Los Alamos.

OTHER CLIMATIC ELEMENTS. Plentiful sunshine occurs in New Mexico, with from 75 to 80 percent of the possible sunshine being received. In winter, this prevalence is particularly noticeable with from 70 to 75 percent of the possible sunshine being received. It is not uncommon for as much as 90 percent of the possible sunshine to occur in November and in some of the spring months. The average number of hours of annual sunshine ranges from near 3,700 in the southwest to 2,800 in the north-central portions.

Average relative humidities are lower in the valleys but higher in the mountains because of the lower mountain temperatures. Relative humidity ranges from an average of near 65 percent at about sunrise to near 30 percent in midafternoon; however, afternoon humidities in warmer months are often less than 20 percent and occasionally may go as low as four percent. The prevalent low relative humidities during periods of extreme temperatures ease the effect of summer and winter temperatures on comfort.

Wind speeds over the State are usually moderate, although relatively strong winds often accompany occasional frontal activity during late winter and spring months and sometimes occur just in advance of thunderstorms. Frontal winds may exceed 30 m.p.h. for several hours and reach peak speeds of more than 50 m.p.h. Spring is the windy season. Blowing dust and serious soil erosion of unprotected fields may be a problem during dry spells. Winds are generally stronger in the eastern plains than in other parts of the State. Winds generally predominate from the southeast in summer and from the west in winter, but local surface wind directions will vary greatly because of local topography and mountain and valley breezes.

Potential evaporation in New Mexico is much greater than average annual precipitation.

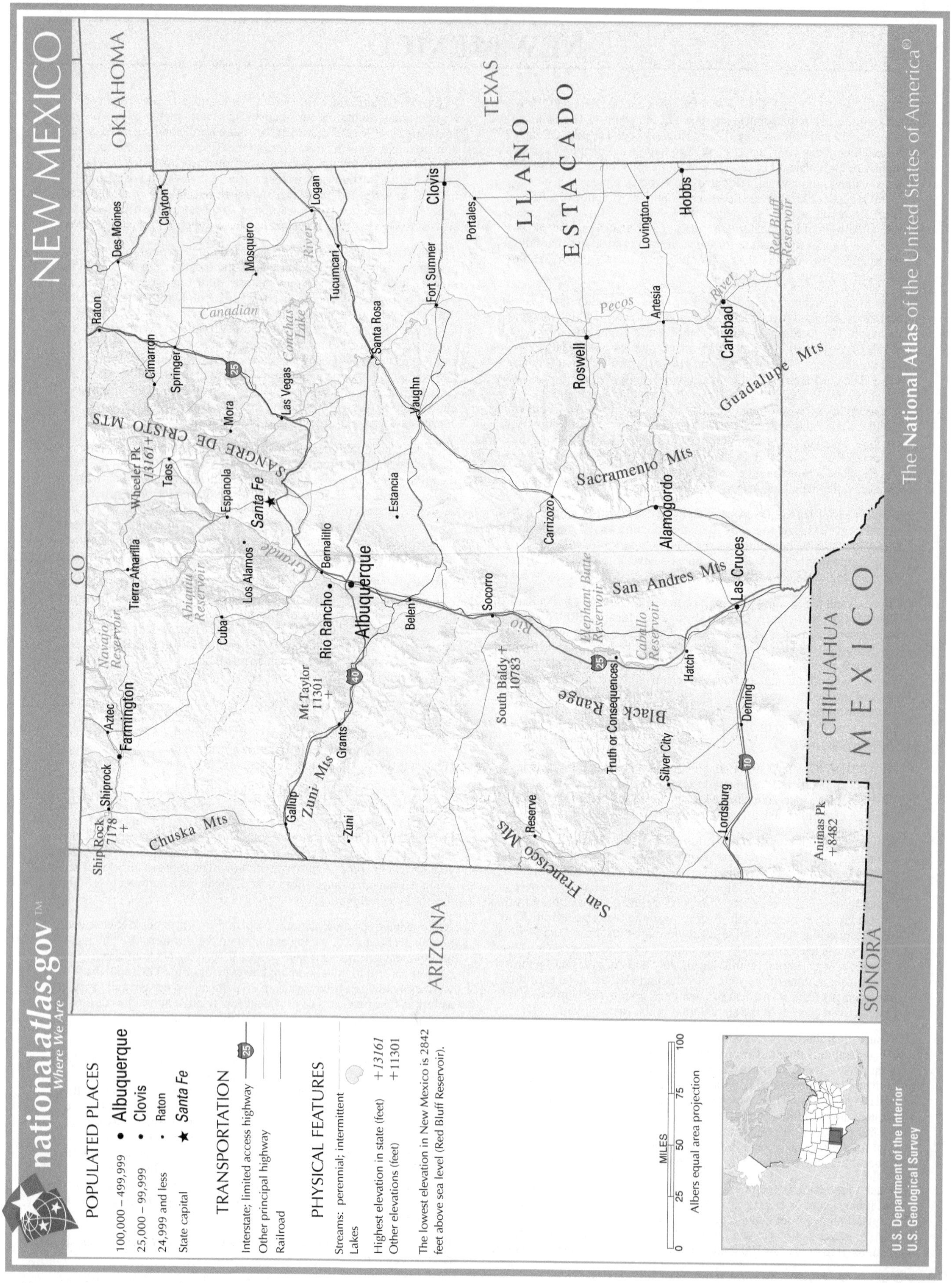
NEW MEXICO
nationalatlas.gov™
Where We Are
POPULATED PLACES
100,000 – 499,999 • Albuquerque
25,000 – 99,999 • Clovis
24,999 and less • Raton
State capital ★ Santa Fe
TRANSPORTATION
Interstate; limited access highway
Other principal highway
Railroad
PHYSICAL FEATURES
Streams: perennial; intermittent
Lakes
Highest elevation in state (feet) +13161
Other elevations (feet) +11301
The lowest elevation in New Mexico is 2842 feet above sea level (Red Bluff Reservoir).
MILES
0 25 50 75 100
Albers equal area projection
U.S. Department of the Interior
U.S. Geological Survey
The National Atlas of the United States of America®
OKLAHOMA
TEXAS
LLANO ESTACADO
CO
ARIZONA
MEXICO
CHIHUAHUA
SONORA
Raton
Des Moines
Clayton
Mosquero
Logan
Tucumcari
Clovis
Portales
Fort Sumner
Lovington
Hobbs
Artesia
Carlsbad
Roswell
Santa Rosa
Vaughn
Cimarron
Springer
Las Vegas
Mora
Taos
Wheeler Pk 13161
SANGRE DE CRISTO MTS
Espanola
Santa Fe
Los Alamos
Tierra Amarilla
Bernalillo
Estancia
Rio Rancho
Albuquerque
Cuba
Belen
Socorro
Carrizozo
Alamogordo
Sacramento Mts
Guadalupe Mts
San Andres Mts
Las Cruces
Elephant Butte Reservoir
Caballo Reservoir
Truth or Consequences
Hatch
Black Range
South Baldy 10783
Mt Taylor 11301
Grants
Zuni Mts
Zuni
Gallup
Chuska Mts
Ship Rock 7178
Shiprock
Farmington
Aztec
Navajo Reservoir
Abiquiu Reservoir
Canadian
Conchas Lake
River
Pecos
River
Rio Grande
Red Bluff Reservoir
Silver City
Deming
Lordsburg
Reserve
San Francisco Mts
Animas Pk 8482
25
40
10

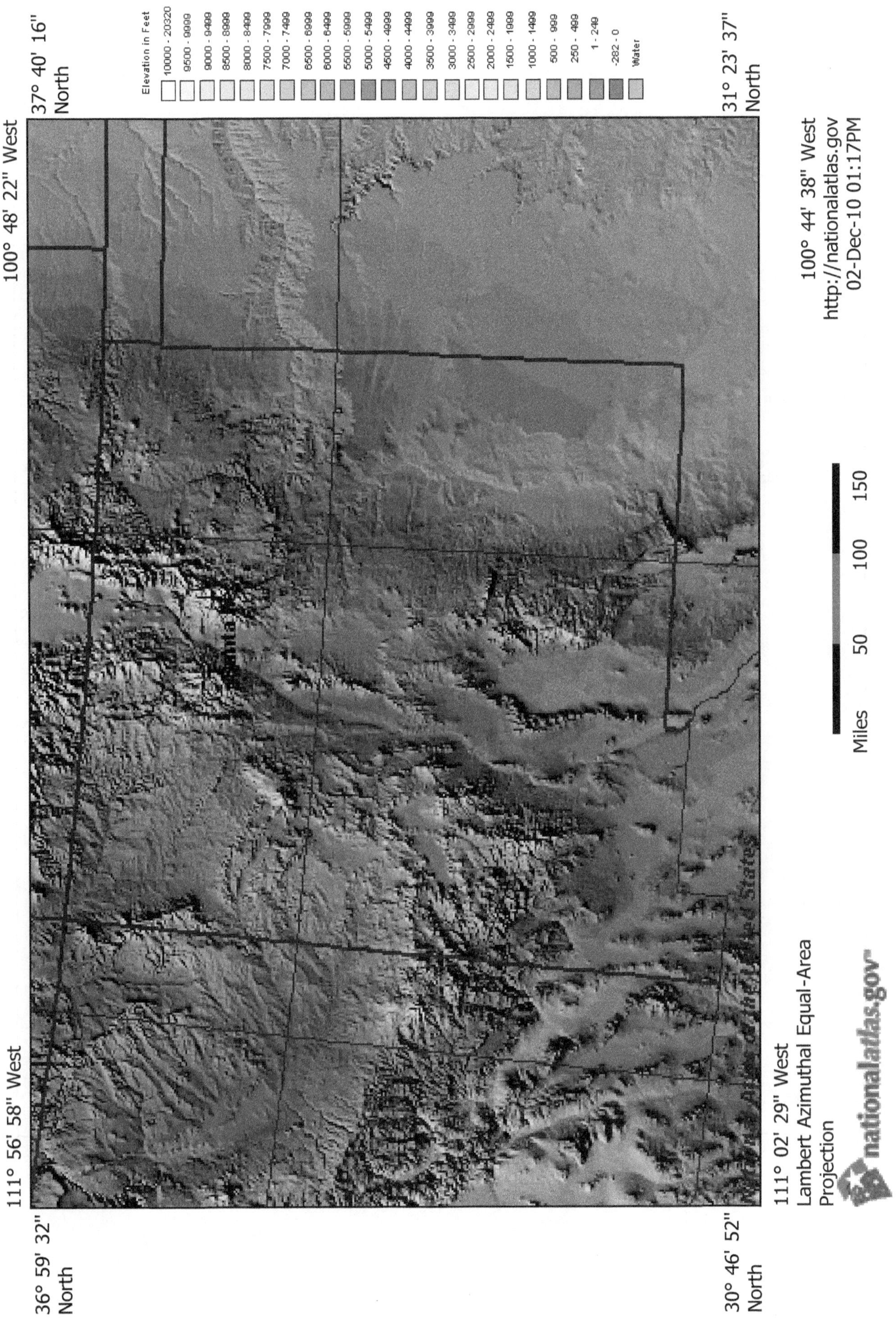
37° 40' 16" North
100° 48' 22" West
31° 23' 37" North
Elevation in Feet
10000 - 20320
9500 - 9999
9000 - 9499
8500 - 8999
8000 - 8499
7500 - 7999
7000 - 7499
6500 - 6999
6000 - 6499
5500 - 5999
5000 - 5499
4500 - 4999
4000 - 4499
3500 - 3999
3000 - 3499
2500 - 2999
2000 - 2499
1500 - 1999
1000 - 1499
500 - 999
250 - 499
1 - 249
-282 - 0
Water
100° 44' 38" West
http://nationalatlas.gov
02-Dec-10 01:17PM
Miles
50
100
150
111° 56' 58" West
36° 59' 32" North
111° 02' 29" West
Lambert Azimuthal Equal-Area Projection
nationalatlas.gov
30° 46' 52" North

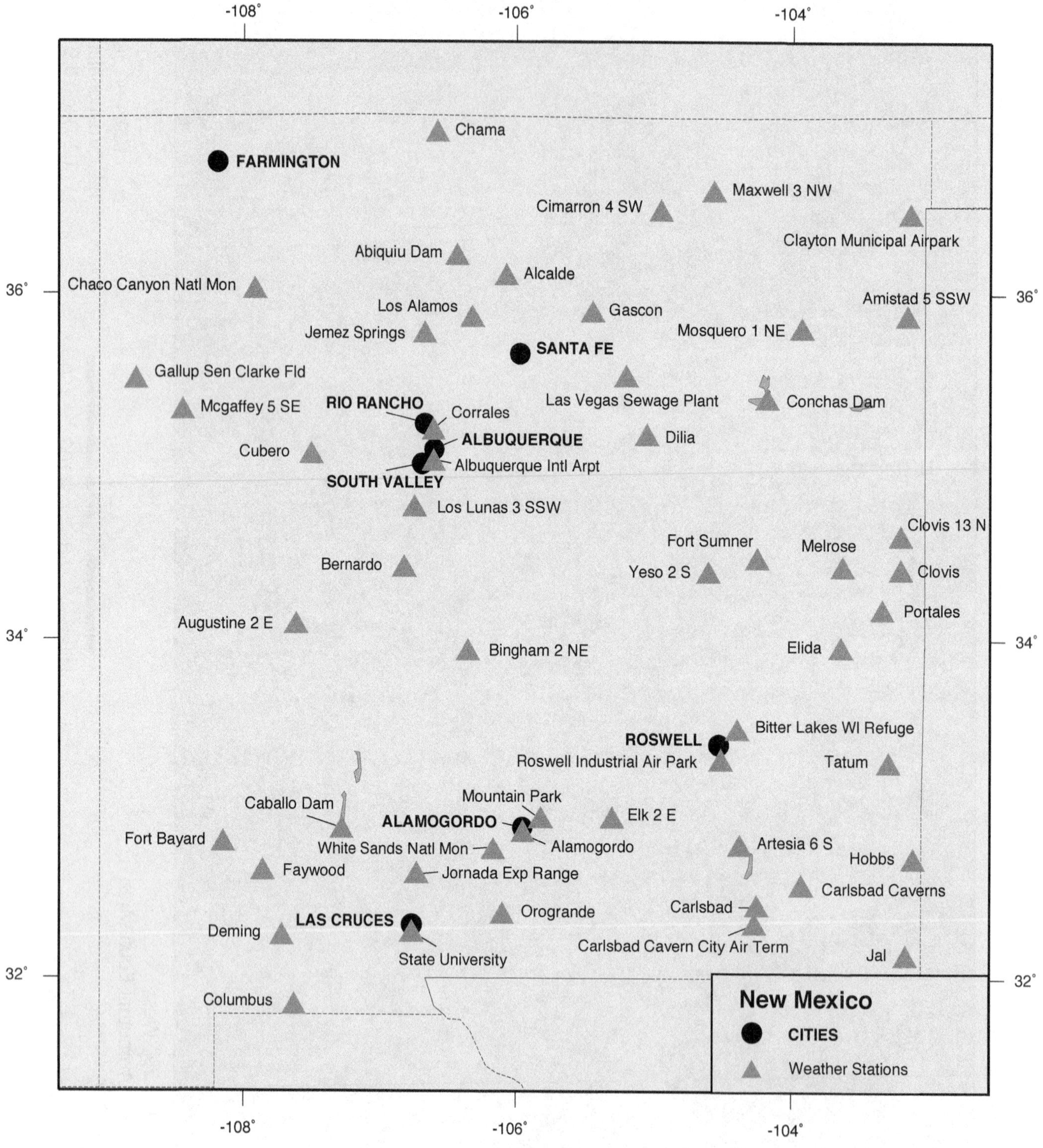
-108°
-106°
-104°
36°
34°
32°
Chama
FARMINGTON
Maxwell 3 NW
Cimarron 4 SW
Clayton Municipal Airpark
Abiquiu Dam
Alcalde
Chaco Canyon Natl Mon
Amistad 5 SSW
Los Alamos
Gascon
Jemez Springs
Mosquero 1 NE
SANTA FE
Gallup Sen Clarke Fld
Las Vegas Sewage Plant
RIO RANCHO
Conchas Dam
Mcgaffey 5 SE
Corrales
ALBUQUERQUE
Dilia
Cubero
Albuquerque Intl Arpt
SOUTH VALLEY
Los Lunas 3 SSW
Clovis 13 N
Fort Sumner
Melrose
Bernardo
Yeso 2 S
Clovis
Portales
Augustine 2 E
Bingham 2 NE
Elida
Bitter Lakes Wl Refuge
ROSWELL
Roswell Industrial Air Park
Tatum
Mountain Park
Caballo Dam
Elk 2 E
ALAMOGORDO
Fort Bayard
White Sands Natl Mon
Alamogordo
Artesia 6 S
Hobbs
Faywood
Jornada Exp Range
Carlsbad Caverns
Carlsbad
Orogrande
LAS CRUCES
Deming
Carlsbad Cavern City Air Term
State University
Jal
Columbus
New Mexico
CITIES
Weather Stations

New Mexico Weather Stations by County

County	Station Name
Bernalillo	Albuquerque Intl Arpt
Chaves	Bitter Lakes Wl Refuge Elk 2 E Roswell Industrial Air Park
Cibola	Cubero
Colfax	Cimarron 4 SW Maxwell 3 NW
Curry	Clovis Clovis 13 N Melrose
Debaca	Fort Sumner Yeso 2 S
Dona Ana	Jornada Exp Range State University
Eddy	Artesia 6 S Carlsbad Carlsbad Cavern City Air Term Carlsbad Caverns
Grant	Faywood Fort Bayard
Guadalupe	Dilia
Harding	Mosquero 1 NE
Lea	Hobbs Jal Tatum
Los Alamos	Los Alamos
Luna	Columbus Deming
Mckinley	Gallup Sen Clarke Fld McGaffey 5 SE
Mora	Gascon
Otero	Alamogordo Mountain Park Orogrande White Sands Natl Mon
Rio Arriba	Abiquiu Dam Alcalde Chama
Roosevelt	Elida Portales
San Juan	Chaco Canyon Natl Mon
San Miguel	Conchas Dam Las Vegas Sewage Plant

County	Station Name
Sandoval	Corrales Jemez Springs
Sierra	Caballo Dam
Socorro	Augustine 2 E Bernardo Bingham 2 NE
Union	Amistad 5 SSW Clayton Municipal Airpark
Valencia	Los Lunas 3 SSW

See User Guide for station inclusion criteria.

New Mexico Weather Stations by City

City	Station Name	Miles
Alamogordo	Alamogordo	0.8
	Mountain Park	8.6
	White Sands Natl Mon	15.7
Albuquerque	Albuquerque Intl Arpt	4.2
	Corrales	8.4
Artesia	Artesia 6 S	5.3
Carlsbad	Carlsbad	1.2
	Carlsbad Cavern City Air Term	6.0
	Carlsbad Caverns	19.6
Clovis	Clovis	0.2
	Clovis 13 N	12.7
	Melrose	23.6
	Portales	19.2
Deming	Deming	1.4
Gallup	Gallup Sen Clarke Fld	2.9
	McGaffey 5 SE	20.5
Hobbs	Hobbs	1.2
Las Cruces	Jornada Exp Range	20.7
	State University	2.4
Las Vegas	Gascon	24.3
	Las Vegas Sewage Plant	4.8
Los Alamos	Abiquiu Dam	24.7
	Alcalde	19.4
	Jemez Springs	23.2
	Los Alamos	2.0
Los Lunas	Albuquerque Intl Arpt	18.6
	Los Lunas 3 SSW	2.8
Lovington	Hobbs	21.5
	Tatum	22.2
North Valley	Albuquerque Intl Arpt	8.6
	Corrales	4.3
Portales	Clovis	18.2
	Elida	23.8
	Melrose	23.5
	Portales	1.1
Rio Rancho	Albuquerque Intl Arpt	15.3
	Corrales	4.5
Roswell	Bitter Lakes Wl Refuge	9.1
	Roswell Industrial Air Park	6.3
Santa Fe	Los Alamos	24.1
Silver City	Fort Bayard	7.3
South Valley	Albuquerque Intl Arpt	5.0
	Corrales	14.7
	Los Lunas 3 SSW	18.7
Sunland Park	El Paso Intl Arpt, TX	11.8
	La Tuna 1 S, TX	11.3

Note: Miles is the distance between the geographic center of the city and the weather station.

See User Guide for station inclusion criteria.

New Mexico Weather Stations by Elevation

Feet	Station Name
8,250	Gascon
8,000	McGaffey 5 SE
7,850	Chama
7,423	Los Alamos
7,000	Augustine 2 E
6,779	Mountain Park
6,540	Cimarron 4 SW
6,465	Gallup Sen Clarke Fld
6,379	Abiquiu Dam
6,349	Las Vegas Sewage Plant
6,263	Jemez Springs
6,194	Cubero
6,173	Chaco Canyon Natl Mon
6,142	Fort Bayard
6,019	Maxwell 3 NW
5,727	Elk 2 E
5,680	Alcalde
5,550	Bingham 2 NE
5,464	Mosquero 1 NE
5,310	Albuquerque Intl Arpt
5,190	Faywood
5,149	Dilia
5,015	Corrales
4,959	Clayton Municipal Airpark
4,850	Yeso 2 S
4,839	Los Lunas 3 SSW
4,734	Bernardo
4,598	Melrose
4,444	Amistad 5 SSW
4,435	Clovis 13 N
4,404	Carlsbad Caverns
4,354	Elida
4,350	Alamogordo
4,299	Deming
4,290	Clovis
4,266	Jornada Exp Range
4,244	Conchas Dam
4,189	Caballo Dam
4,182	Orogrande
4,100	Tatum
4,064	Columbus
4,024	Fort Sumner
4,009	Portales
3,995	White Sands Natl Mon
3,880	State University
3,664	Bitter Lakes Wl Refuge
3,648	Roswell Industrial Air Park
3,615	Hobbs
3,319	Artesia 6 S
3,231	Carlsbad Cavern City Air Term
3,120	Carlsbad
3,060	Jal

See User Guide for station inclusion criteria.

Albuquerque Int'l Airport

The Albuquerque metropolitan area is largely situated in the Rio Grande Valley and on the mesas and piedmont slopes which rise either side of the valley floor. The Rio Grande flows from north to south through the area. The Sandia and Manzano Mountains rise abruptly at the eastern edge of the city with Tijeras Canyon separating the two ranges. The climate of Albuquerque is best described as arid continental with abundant sunshine, low humidity, scant precipitation, and a wide yet tolerable seasonal range of temperatures. Sunny days and low humidity are renowned features of the climate. More than three-fourths of the daylight hours have sunshine, even in the winter months. The air is normally dry and muggy days are rare. The combination of dry air and plentiful solar radiation allows widespread use of energy-efficient devices such as evaporative coolers and solar collectors.

Precipitation within the valley area is adequate only for native desert vegetation and deep-rooted imports. However, irrigation supports successful farming and fruit growing in the Rio Grande Valley.

Meager amounts of precipitation fall in the winter, much of it as snow. Snowfalls of an inch or more occur about four times a year in the Rio Grande Valley, while the mountains receive substantial snowfall on occasion. Snow seldom remains on the ground more than 24 hours in the city proper. However, snow cover on the east slopes of the Sandias is sufficient for skiing during most winters.

Nearly half of the annual precipitation in Albuquerque results from afternoon and evening thunderstorms during the summer. Thunderstorm frequency increases rapidly around July 1st, peaks during August, then tapers off by the end of September. Hailstorms are infrequent and tornadoes rare.

High temperatures during the winter are near 50 degrees with only a few days on which the temperature fails to rise above the freezing mark. In the summer, daytime maxima are about 90 degrees, but with the large daily range, the nights usually are comfortably cool.

The growing season in Albuquerque and adjacent suburbs ranges from around 170 days in the Rio Grande Valley to about 200 days in parts of the northeast section of the city.

Sustained winds of 12 mph or less occur approximately 80 percent of the time at the Albuquerque International Airport. Late winter and spring storms along with occasional east winds out of Tijeras Canyon are the main sources of strong wind conditions. Blowing dust, the least attractive feature of the climate, often accompanies the occasional strong winds of winter and spring.

Albuquerque Int'l Airport *Bernalillo County* Elevation: 5,310 ft. Latitude: 35° 03' N Longitude: 106° 36' W

	JAN	FEB	MAR	APR	MAY	JUN	JUL	AUG	SEP	OCT	NOV	DEC	YEAR
Mean Maximum Temp. (°F)	48.6	54.5	62.0	70.5	80.3	89.9	92.0	88.8	82.1	70.3	57.3	47.6	70.3
Mean Temp. (°F)	37.1	42.0	48.4	56.3	66.0	75.3	78.8	76.5	69.6	57.6	45.3	36.7	57.5
Mean Minimum Temp. (°F)	25.6	29.5	34.8	42.0	51.6	60.6	65.6	64.1	57.0	44.8	33.3	25.6	44.5
Extreme Maximum Temp. (°F)	69	76	84	89	97	107	105	100	99	90	76	68	107
Extreme Minimum Temp. (°F)	0	5	15	19	30	40	52	50	38	21	14	-7	-7
Days Maximum Temp. ≥ 90°F	0	0	0	0	3	17	22	16	3	0	0	0	61
Days Maximum Temp. ≤ 32°F	1	0	0	0	0	0	0	0	0	0	0	1	2
Days Minimum Temp. ≤ 32°F	27	19	11	3	0	0	0	0	0	2	13	27	102
Days Minimum Temp. ≤ 0°F	0	0	0	0	0	0	0	0	0	0	0	0	0
Heating Degree Days (base 65°F)	858	643	506	263	63	3	0	0	21	233	583	871	4,044
Cooling Degree Days (base 65°F)	0	0	0	8	100	318	436	364	164	11	0	0	1,401
Mean Precipitation (in.)	0.39	0.49	0.58	0.61	0.52	0.63	1.42	1.63	1.08	1.02	0.58	0.49	9.44
Maximum Precipitation (in.)*	1.3	1.8	2.2	1.8	2.5	2.6	3.3	3.3	2.6	3.1	1.9	1.8	13.1
Minimum Precipitation (in.)*	0	trace	trace	trace	trace	trace	0.1	trace	trace	0	0	0	4.1
Extreme Maximum Daily Precip. (in.)	0.56	0.90	1.45	1.92	0.97	1.04	1.23	1.75	1.04	1.47	1.41	0.74	1.92
Days With ≥ 0.1" Precipitation	1	2	2	2	2	2	4	4	3	3	2	2	29
Days With ≥ 0.5" Precipitation	0	0	0	0	0	0	1	1	1	1	0	0	4
Days With ≥ 1.0" Precipitation	0	0	0	0	0	0	0	0	0	0	0	0	0
Mean Snowfall (in.)	2.0	1.8	1.2	0.6	trace	trace	trace	trace	trace	0.3	1.1	2.9	9.9
Maximum Snowfall (in.)*	10	10	14	8	trace	0	0	0	trace	3	8	15	34
Maximum 24-hr. Snowfall (in.)*	5	5	9	7	trace	0	0	0	trace	3	4	9	9
Maximum Snow Depth (in.)	7	4	3	9	trace	trace	trace	trace	trace	3	5	10	10
Days With ≥ 1.0" Snow Depth	1	1	0	0	0	0	0	0	0	0	0	1	3
Thunderstorm Days*	< 1	< 1	1	1	4	5	10	10	5	2	1	< 1	39
Foggy Days*	3	2	2	1	< 1	< 1	< 1	< 1	1	2	2	3	16
Predominant Sky Cover*	CLR	CLR	CLR	CLR	CLR	CLR	SCT	SCT	CLR	CLR	CLR	CLR	CLR
Mean Relative Humidity 5am (%)*	68	64	55	48	48	45	59	66	61	59	63	68	59
Mean Relative Humidity 5pm (%)*	41	32	25	19	19	18	27	30	29	29	35	43	29
Mean Dewpoint (°F)*	18	20	20	22	29	36	49	51	43	32	23	19	30
Prevailing Wind Direction*	N	N	N	S	S	S	ESE	SE	SE	N	N	N	N
Prevailing Wind Speed (mph)*	9	9	9	10	10	10	12	8	8	8	8	9	9
Maximum Wind Gust (mph)*	70	63	77	67	70	68	73	67	61	62	63	71	77

Note: (*) Period of record is 1948-1995

The period of record for National Weather Service station data is 1980 – 2009 except where noted. See User Guide for detailed explanation of data.

Clayton Municipal Airpark

Clayton is located on the high plains of northeastern New Mexico some 90 miles southeast of the eastern slope of the Rocky Mountains. The climate is semi-arid. Nearly 80 percent of the rainfall occurs from May through October in sudden thunderstorms which form over the mountains northwest of Clayton and drift southeastward. This makes the growing of small grains and the raising of range cattle profitable. Native grasses in the area remain nutritious even in winter.

The climate of Clayton is characteristic of that found in the higher-altitude sections of the continental southwest. Temperatures are mostly moderate. While daytime temperatures in summer are moderately warm, 90 degrees or slightly higher about half the time in July, hot days recording temperatures of 100 degrees or more, only occur about once a year. Minimum temperatures range from the teens in January to the 60s in July. With clear nocturnal skies and an altitude of about 5,000 feet, summer nights in Clayton are usually comfortable for sleeping. While winter minima are generally below freezing, zero temperatures only occur about three times a year.

From June through August nearly all precipitation is from scattered thunderstorms. As late summer and fall give way to winter, showery precipitation becomes less frequent and copious. Occasional winter snows, caused in part by upslope movement of air from the Gulf of Mexico, supply some winter moisture.

Blizzards are rare but high winds and cold temperatures frequent winter storms and can produce blizzard conditions. These storms may often close highways and, unless proper precautions are taken, they may also cause loss of life and livestock.

Based on the 1951-1980 period, the average first occurrence of 32 degrees Fahrenheit in the fall is October 16 and the average last occurrence in the spring is May 1.

Clayton Municipal Airpark *Union County* Elevation: 4,959 ft. Latitude: 36° 27' N Longitude: 103° 09' W

	JAN	FEB	MAR	APR	MAY	JUN	JUL	AUG	SEP	OCT	NOV	DEC	YEAR
Mean Maximum Temp. (°F)	na	na	na	na	na	na	na	na	na	na	na	na	na
Mean Temp. (°F)	na	na	na	na	na	na	na	na	na	na	na	na	na
Mean Minimum Temp. (°F)	na	na	na	na	na	na	na	na	na	na	na	na	na
Extreme Maximum Temp. (°F)	na	na	na	na	na	na	na	na	na	na	na	na	na
Extreme Minimum Temp. (°F)	na	na	na	na	na	na	na	na	na	na	na	na	na
Days Maximum Temp. ≥ 90°F	na	na	na	na	na	na	na	na	na	na	na	na	na
Days Maximum Temp. ≤ 32°F	na	na	na	na	na	na	na	na	na	na	na	na	na
Days Minimum Temp. ≤ 32°F	na	na	na	na	na	na	na	na	na	na	na	na	na
Days Minimum Temp. ≤ 0°F	na	na	na	na	na	na	na	na	na	na	na	na	na
Heating Degree Days (base 65°F)	na	na	na	na	na	na	na	na	na	na	na	na	na
Cooling Degree Days (base 65°F)	na	na	na	na	na	na	na	na	na	na	na	na	na
Mean Precipitation (in.)	na	na	na	na	na	na	na	na	na	na	na	na	na
Maximum Precipitation (in.)*	1.1	1.6	2.3	3.1	6.8	5.0	7.8	5.8	5.2	4.5	2.1	1.1	25.7
Minimum Precipitation (in.)*	trace	trace	trace	trace	0.3	0.2	0.4	0.3	trace	trace	trace	0	8.8
Extreme Maximum Daily Precip. (in.)	na	na	na	na	na	na	na	na	na	na	na	na	na
Days With ≥ 0.1" Precipitation	na	na	na	na	na	na	na	na	na	na	na	na	na
Days With ≥ 0.5" Precipitation	na	na	na	na	na	na	na	na	na	na	na	na	na
Days With ≥ 1.0" Precipitation	na	na	na	na	na	na	na	na	na	na	na	na	na
Mean Snowfall (in.)	na	na	na	na	na	na	na	na	na	na	na	na	na
Maximum Snowfall (in.)*	12	16	16	11	8	0	0	0	5	8	15	12	49
Maximum 24-hr. Snowfall (in.)*	8	9	9	11	6	0	0	0	3	6	12	8	12
Maximum Snow Depth (in.)	na	na	na	na	na	na	na	na	na	na	na	na	na
Days With ≥ 1.0" Snow Depth	na	na	na	na	na	na	na	na	na	na	na	na	na
Thunderstorm Days*	0	1	1	3	10	14	16	16	5	3	0	< 1	69
Foggy Days*	4	5	7	4	4	3	2	3	5	4	1	3	45
Predominant Sky Cover*	CLR	CLR	OVR	CLR	OVR	CLR	CLR	CLR	CLR	CLR	CLR	CLR	CLR
Mean Relative Humidity 5am (%)*	64	64	64	65	71	71	76	77	73	64	64	62	68
Mean Relative Humidity 5pm (%)*	46	41	35	31	35	34	41	41	40	40	46	51	40
Mean Dewpoint (°F)*	15	17	20	26	38	47	54	54	45	33	23	17	33
Prevailing Wind Direction*	W	W	W	SW	SW	SW	SW	SW	SW	SSW	W	W	SW
Prevailing Wind Speed (mph)*	13	13	14	17	15	15	13	13	14	14	12	13	14
Maximum Wind Gust (mph)*	na	na	na	na	na	na	na	na	na	na	na	na	na

Note: (*) Period of record is 1948-1985

The period of record for National Weather Service station data is 1980 – 2009 except where noted. See User Guide for detailed explanation of data.

Roswell Industrial Airpark

The climate at Roswell conforms to the basic trend of the four seasons, but shows certain deviations related to geography. Higher landmasses almost surround the valley location, with a long, gradual descent from points southwest through west and north. The topography acts to modify air masses, especially the cold outbreaks in wintertime. Downslope warming of air, as well as air interchange within a tempering environment, often prevents sharp cooling. Moreover, the elevation of 3,600 feet is high enough to moderate the heat and humidity compared to locations to the south and east.

Summer moves into a wet phase that delivers the most important rain of the year. Rather frequent showers and thunderstorms from June through September account for over half of the annual precipitation. Storm clouds that build up from the heat of the day, overspread the sky on many afternoons, retarding a further rise in temperature. At the same time, relative humidity shows moderation, ranging from about 70 percent in early morning to 30 percent in the mid-afternoon. Temperatures are quite warm on most summer days with readings of 100 degrees or higher occurring on 10 days in an average year.

Rainfall tapers off markedly in the fall with decline in storm activity. This leaves usually agreeable conditions because of low wind movement and mostly clear skies. Frosty nights alternate with warm days. Relative humidity reaches rather low levels in autumn, but dryness is not as rigorous as in the spring.

In winter, sub-freezing at night is tempered by considerable warming during the day. Zero or lower temperatures occur on only one day in an average winter. Sub-zero cold spells are of short duration. Winter is the season of least precipitation.

Spring ushers in the driest season of the year with respect to relative humidity. Wind movement shows a large increase, especially from the plateau areas of the west. Most of the 60 days a year with winds of 25 mph or more occur from February to May. Destructive storms seldom strike the city, but minor damage results from thundersqualls or hailstorms about once a year. Rain is most erratic in spring, ranging from none of consequence in some years, to excessive amounts in others.

Roswell Industrial Airpark *Chaves County* Elevation: 3,648 ft. Latitude: 33° 18' N Longitude: 104° 32' W

	JAN	FEB	MAR	APR	MAY	JUN	JUL	AUG	SEP	OCT	NOV	DEC	YEAR
Mean Maximum Temp. (°F)	55.6	61.4	68.8	77.3	85.9	93.9	94.5	92.1	85.9	75.9	64.5	55.1	75.9
Mean Temp. (°F)	41.2	46.3	53.2	61.2	70.6	78.8	81.1	79.3	72.5	61.5	49.7	40.8	61.4
Mean Minimum Temp. (°F)	26.6	31.2	37.6	45.1	55.2	63.7	67.7	66.4	59.0	47.1	34.9	26.5	46.7
Extreme Maximum Temp. (°F)	81	87	93	99	107	114	111	107	103	99	88	83	114
Extreme Minimum Temp. (°F)	-3	3	9	25	37	47	56	54	40	14	5	-5	-5
Days Maximum Temp. ≥ 90°F	0	0	0	2	11	22	26	23	11	2	0	0	97
Days Maximum Temp. ≤ 32°F	1	1	0	0	0	0	0	0	0	0	0	2	4
Days Minimum Temp. ≤ 32°F	25	16	7	2	0	0	0	0	0	1	12	24	87
Days Minimum Temp. ≤ 0°F	0	0	0	0	0	0	0	0	0	0	0	0	0
Heating Degree Days (base 65°F)	732	522	362	150	24	0	0	0	14	145	454	743	3,146
Cooling Degree Days (base 65°F)	0	1	4	44	203	421	507	450	245	45	1	0	1,921
Mean Precipitation (in.)	0.40	0.38	0.49	0.63	1.27	1.60	1.96	1.98	1.69	1.20	0.61	0.64	12.85
Maximum Precipitation (in.)*	1.6	2.0	2.0	2.5	4.6	5.0	6.9	6.5	6.6	5.5	1.9	2.7	24.8
Minimum Precipitation (in.)*	trace	0	0	trace	trace	trace	trace	0.3	0	0	0	0	4.5
Extreme Maximum Daily Precip. (in.)	0.55	1.05	2.08	1.48	1.77	3.05	4.34	2.45	2.55	3.46	0.91	1.04	4.34
Days With ≥ 0.1" Precipitation	1	1	1	2	2	3	3	4	3	2	2	2	26
Days With ≥ 0.5" Precipitation	0	0	0	0	1	1	1	1	1	1	0	0	6
Days With ≥ 1.0" Precipitation	0	0	0	0	0	0	0	0	0	0	0	0	0
Mean Snowfall (in.)	3.3	*2.0*	*1.1*	*0.4*	*trace*	*0.0*	*0.0*	*0.0*	*trace*	*0.1*	*1.8*	3.7	*12.4*
Maximum Snowfall (in.)*	17	17	5	5	trace	0	0	0	0	4	12	15	30
Maximum 24-hr. Snowfall (in.)*	8	12	4	3	trace	0	0	0	0	3	7	9	12
Maximum Snow Depth (in.)	10	*9*	*3*	*2*	*trace*	*trace*	*0*	*0*	*0*	*2*	*9*	*16*	*16*
Days With ≥ 1.0" Snow Depth	2	*1*	*0*	*0*	*0*	*0*	*0*	*0*	*0*	*0*	*1*	*2*	*6*
Thunderstorm Days*	< 1	< 1	1	2	5	6	8	8	4	2	1	< 1	37
Foggy Days*	6	5	3	2	2	1	1	2	5	5	4	5	41
Predominant Sky Cover*	CLR	CLR	CLR	CLR	CLR	SCT	SCT	SCT	CLR	CLR	CLR	CLR	CLR
Mean Relative Humidity 5am (%)*	67	64	54	51	57	61	67	70	71	67	65	66	63
Mean Relative Humidity 5pm (%)*	39	33	25	22	24	25	31	34	37	35	37	41	32
Mean Dewpoint (°F)*	21	23	24	29	39	49	56	56	51	39	28	22	37
Prevailing Wind Direction*	S	S	S	S	S	S	S	S	S	S	S	S	S
Prevailing Wind Speed (mph)*	9	9	10	12	12	12	10	9	9	9	9	9	10
Maximum Wind Gust (mph)*	58	62	75	62	66	89	60	68	69	58	55	62	89

Note: (*) Period of record is 1946-1995

The period of record for National Weather Service station data is 1980 – 2009 except where noted. See User Guide for detailed explanation of data.

Abiquiu Dam *Rio Arriba County* Elevation: 6,379 ft. Latitude: 36° 14' N Longitude: 106° 26' W

	JAN	FEB	MAR	APR	MAY	JUN	JUL	AUG	SEP	OCT	NOV	DEC	YEAR
Mean Maximum Temp. (°F)	42.7	47.3	55.2	63.1	73.0	83.4	87.6	84.8	77.9	66.5	54.0	43.5	64.9
Mean Temp. (°F)	30.4	35.0	42.3	49.4	59.0	68.4	73.2	71.2	63.8	52.4	41.1	31.4	51.5
Mean Minimum Temp. (°F)	18.1	22.5	29.4	35.7	45.0	53.4	58.7	57.5	49.7	38.4	28.2	19.4	38.0
Extreme Maximum Temp. (°F)	62	70	85	84	94	100	101	98	94	85	77	67	101
Extreme Minimum Temp. (°F)	-8	-15	5	15	27	31	37	45	20	14	6	-18	-18
Days Maximum Temp. ≥ 90°F	0	0	0	0	0	6	12	6	1	0	0	0	25
Days Maximum Temp. ≤ 32°F	3	1	0	0	0	0	0	0	0	0	0	3	7
Days Minimum Temp. ≤ 32°F	30	26	22	9	1	0	0	0	0	5	22	30	145
Days Minimum Temp. ≤ 0°F	1	0	0	0	0	0	0	0	0	0	0	0	1
Heating Degree Days (base 65°F)	1,064	842	697	460	198	32	2	4	80	382	711	1,035	5,507
Cooling Degree Days (base 65°F)	0	0	0	0	19	140	263	203	52	1	0	0	678
Mean Precipitation (in.)	0.37	0.31	0.51	0.81	0.92	0.81	1.61	1.82	1.22	0.93	0.49	0.41	10.21
Extreme Maximum Daily Precip. (in.)	0.68	0.36	0.82	1.50	1.15	1.17	2.10	1.19	1.19	1.05	0.65	1.04	2.10
Days With ≥ 0.1" Precipitation	1	1	2	2	3	3	5	5	4	3	2	2	33
Days With ≥ 0.5" Precipitation	0	0	0	0	0	0	1	1	0	0	0	0	2
Days With ≥ 1.0" Precipitation	0	0	0	0	0	0	0	0	0	0	0	0	0
Mean Snowfall (in.)	2.4	1.9	0.9	0.4	0.0	0.0	0.0	0.0	0.0	0.1	0.4	***2.8***	***8.9***
Maximum Snow Depth (in.)	12	5	15	5	0	0	0	0	0	2	3	***12***	***15***
Days With ≥ 1.0" Snow Depth	3	2	1	0	0	0	0	0	0	0	0	2	8

Alamogordo *Otero County* Elevation: 4,350 ft. Latitude: 32° 53' N Longitude: 105° 57' W

	JAN	FEB	MAR	APR	MAY	JUN	JUL	AUG	SEP	OCT	NOV	DEC	YEAR
Mean Maximum Temp. (°F)	56.4	61.2	68.1	76.6	85.8	94.0	93.9	90.6	***85.7***	***76.0***	64.7	***55.9***	***75.7***
Mean Temp. (°F)	43.8	48.3	54.2	62.0	71.1	79.3	80.8	78.2	***72.8***	***62.5***	51.4	***43.3***	***62.3***
Mean Minimum Temp. (°F)	31.2	35.3	40.4	47.5	56.4	64.6	67.6	65.8	***59.8***	***49.0***	38.1	***30.5***	***48.8***
Extreme Maximum Temp. (°F)	75	81	87	95	102	110	109	105	101	90	83	75	110
Extreme Minimum Temp. (°F)	8	11	18	26	36	49	56	53	43	24	16	6	6
Days Maximum Temp. ≥ 90°F	0	0	0	1	9	24	24	19	9	0	0	0	86
Days Maximum Temp. ≤ 32°F	0	0	0	0	0	0	0	0	0	0	0	0	0
Days Minimum Temp. ≤ 32°F	18	10	5	1	0	0	0	0	0	1	7	19	61
Days Minimum Temp. ≤ 0°F	0	0	0	0	0	0	0	0	0	0	0	0	0
Heating Degree Days (base 65°F)	650	466	329	125	14	0	0	0	***6***	***117***	402	***667***	***2,776***
Cooling Degree Days (base 65°F)	0	0	3	42	210	437	496	417	***247***	***47***	1	***0***	***1,900***
Mean Precipitation (in.)	0.70	0.63	0.43	0.36	0.51	0.80	1.73	2.40	1.57	1.20	0.67	0.99	11.99
Extreme Maximum Daily Precip. (in.)	0.91	0.81	1.02	0.86	1.13	1.89	1.48	1.80	1.96	1.80	1.34	2.32	2.32
Days With ≥ 0.1" Precipitation	2	2	1	1	1	2	5	6	4	3	2	3	32
Days With ≥ 0.5" Precipitation	0	0	0	0	0	0	1	1	1	1	0	0	4
Days With ≥ 1.0" Precipitation	0	0	0	0	0	0	0	0	0	0	0	0	0
Mean Snowfall (in.)	1.2	0.5	0.3	0.1	0.0	0.0	0.0	0.0	0.0	0.1	0.1	1.3	3.6
Maximum Snow Depth (in.)	4	***1***	trace	0	0	0	0	0	0	***1***	0	4	***4***
Days With ≥ 1.0" Snow Depth	0	***0***	0	0	0	0	0	0	0	***0***	0	0	***0***

Alcalde *Rio Arriba County* Elevation: 5,680 ft. Latitude: 36° 06' N Longitude: 106° 04' W

	JAN	FEB	MAR	APR	MAY	JUN	JUL	AUG	SEP	OCT	NOV	DEC	YEAR
Mean Maximum Temp. (°F)	***47.1***	52.2	60.0	67.7	77.1	86.5	89.3	86.4	80.3	69.9	57.1	***45.7***	***68.3***
Mean Temp. (°F)	***31.9***	36.7	43.2	50.3	59.1	67.7	72.4	70.4	62.7	51.4	40.2	***30.9***	***51.4***
Mean Minimum Temp. (°F)	***16.6***	21.1	26.3	32.9	41.0	48.8	55.4	54.3	45.1	33.0	23.2	***16.1***	***34.5***
Extreme Maximum Temp. (°F)	69	73	84	88	98	101	100	98	95	90	79	68	101
Extreme Minimum Temp. (°F)	-10	-3	1	12	25	32	40	34	27	9	1	-11	-11
Days Maximum Temp. ≥ 90°F	0	0	0	0	1	11	16	9	1	0	0	0	38
Days Maximum Temp. ≤ 32°F	1	0	0	0	0	0	0	0	0	0	0	2	3
Days Minimum Temp. ≤ 32°F	28	26	25	14	3	0	0	0	1	16	26	26	165
Days Minimum Temp. ≤ 0°F	0	0	0	0	0	0	0	0	0	0	0	0	0
Heating Degree Days (base 65°F)	***1,021***	794	669	433	189	27	1	5	95	416	737	***1,050***	***5,437***
Cooling Degree Days (base 65°F)	***0***	0	0	0	12	114	236	179	33	0	0	***0***	***574***
Mean Precipitation (in.)	0.42	0.40	0.64	0.77	0.86	0.83	1.43	1.98	1.35	1.12	0.61	***0.63***	***11.04***
Extreme Maximum Daily Precip. (in.)	0.67	0.56	0.70	***1.28***	0.83	0.89	***1.38***	na	***1.70***	1.30	1.30	1.22	na
Days With ≥ 0.1" Precipitation	1	2	2	2	2	2	4	4	3	3	2	2	29
Days With ≥ 0.5" Precipitation	0	0	0	0	0	1	1	1	1	1	0	0	5
Days With ≥ 1.0" Precipitation	0	0	0	0	0	0	0	0	0	0	0	0	0
Mean Snowfall (in.)	2.1	2.7	1.8	0.3	0.0	0.0	0.0	0.0	0.0	0.3	0.9	***2.5***	***10.6***
Maximum Snow Depth (in.)	13	13	7	4	0	0	0	0	0	4	5	***10***	***13***
Days With ≥ 1.0" Snow Depth	1	1	0	0	0	0	0	0	0	0	0	1	3

Amistad 5 SSW *Union County* Elevation: 4,444 ft. Latitude: 35° 52' N Longitude: 103° 10' W

	JAN	FEB	MAR	APR	MAY	JUN	JUL	AUG	SEP	OCT	NOV	DEC	YEAR
Mean Maximum Temp. (°F)	49.6	53.7	61.0	69.4	78.2	87.4	91.2	88.8	81.8	70.8	59.5	49.0	70.0
Mean Temp. (°F)	35.0	38.3	45.3	53.2	63.0	72.2	76.7	75.0	67.2	55.4	44.3	34.7	55.0
Mean Minimum Temp. (°F)	20.3	22.9	29.6	37.0	47.7	57.0	62.0	61.1	52.5	39.9	29.0	20.3	40.0
Extreme Maximum Temp. (°F)	77	79	90	95	101	106	105	104	102	94	88	80	106
Extreme Minimum Temp. (°F)	-16	-11	2	15	26	39	49	44	29	6	1	-11	-16
Days Maximum Temp. ≥ 90°F	0	0	0	0	4	13	20	16	5	0	0	0	58
Days Maximum Temp. ≤ 32°F	4	2	1	0	0	0	0	0	0	0	0	4	11
Days Minimum Temp. ≤ 32°F	29	24	19	9	1	0	0	0	0	5	20	29	136
Days Minimum Temp. ≤ 0°F	1	1	0	0	0	0	0	0	0	0	0	1	3
Heating Degree Days (base 65°F)	923	747	602	352	120	10	1	2	56	302	614	933	4,662
Cooling Degree Days (base 65°F)	0	0	0	6	64	234	369	317	128	11	0	0	1,129
Mean Precipitation (in.)	0.33	0.38	0.87	0.91	1.97	1.88	2.37	2.87	1.70	1.36	0.53	0.43	15.60
Extreme Maximum Daily Precip. (in.)	0.57	0.77	2.47	1.27	2.80	2.60	2.71	2.10	2.50	4.00	1.40	0.60	4.00
Days With ≥ 0.1" Precipitation	1	1	2	2	4	4	4	5	3	2	1	2	31
Days With ≥ 0.5" Precipitation	0	0	1	1	1	1	2	2	1	1	0	0	10
Days With ≥ 1.0" Precipitation	0	0	0	0	0	0	1	1	0	0	0	0	2
Mean Snowfall (in.)	3.2	3.0	3.1	0.6	0.1	0.0	0.0	0.0	0.0	0.3	1.2	4.6	16.1
Maximum Snow Depth (in.)	8	3	18	4	0	0	0	0	0	1	5	***7***	***18***
Days With ≥ 1.0" Snow Depth	1	1	1	0	0	0	0	0	0	0	0	1	4

The period of record for all cooperative weather station data is 1980 – 2009. See User Guide for detailed explanation of data.

Artesia 6 S *Eddy County* Elevation: 3,319 ft. Latitude: 32° 46' N Longitude: 104° 23' W

	JAN	FEB	MAR	APR	MAY	JUN	JUL	AUG	SEP	OCT	NOV	DEC	YEAR
Mean Maximum Temp. (°F)	57.3	62.4	69.8	78.0	86.5	93.7	94.4	92.5	86.2	77.2	66.1	56.7	76.7
Mean Temp. (°F)	40.1	44.6	51.8	59.5	69.3	77.4	79.5	77.9	70.7	60.2	48.7	39.8	60.0
Mean Minimum Temp. (°F)	22.8	26.8	33.9	41.0	52.1	61.0	64.6	63.1	55.1	43.2	31.2	22.9	43.1
Extreme Maximum Temp. (°F)	81	86	92	100	106	113	108	105	103	98	89	83	113
Extreme Minimum Temp. (°F)	-3	1	8	16	33	44	54	51	35	18	6	-13	-13
Days Maximum Temp. ≥ 90°F	0	0	0	2	12	22	26	24	11	2	0	0	99
Days Maximum Temp. ≤ 32°F	1	1	0	0	0	0	0	0	0	0	0	1	3
Days Minimum Temp. ≤ 32°F	28	22	13	4	0	0	0	0	0	3	18	28	116
Days Minimum Temp. ≤ 0°F	0	0	0	0	0	0	0	0	0	0	0	0	0
Heating Degree Days (base 65°F)	766	569	404	188	32	1	0	0	23	172	484	774	3,413
Cooling Degree Days (base 65°F)	0	0	3	30	172	379	458	406	199	30	1	0	1,678
Mean Precipitation (in.)	0.40	0.41	0.38	0.64	1.31	1.58	1.59	1.93	2.13	1.23	0.75	0.63	12.98
Extreme Maximum Daily Precip. (in.)	0.81	0.78	0.48	3.25	2.11	2.26	2.27	3.39	3.12	2.50	1.61	0.99	3.39
Days With ≥ 0.1" Precipitation	1	1	1	1	3	3	3	4	4	3	2	2	28
Days With ≥ 0.5" Precipitation	0	0	0	0	1	1	1	1	1	1	0	0	6
Days With ≥ 1.0" Precipitation	0	0	0	0	0	0	0	0	0	0	0	0	0
Mean Snowfall (in.)	2.1	0.8	0.3	0.6	trace	0.0	0.0	0.0	0.0	0.1	1.1	2.3	7.3
Maximum Snow Depth (in.)	9	6	2	7	trace	0	0	0	0	2	4	9	9
Days With ≥ 1.0" Snow Depth	2	1	0	0	0	0	0	0	0	0	1	1	5

Augustine 2 E *Socorro County* Elevation: 7,000 ft. Latitude: 34° 05' N Longitude: 107° 37' W

	JAN	FEB	MAR	APR	MAY	JUN	JUL	AUG	SEP	OCT	NOV	DEC	YEAR
Mean Maximum Temp. (°F)	47.9	51.7	57.9	65.5	74.0	83.6	84.3	81.3	76.9	67.4	57.0	48.0	66.3
Mean Temp. (°F)	32.2	35.6	40.3	47.2	56.0	65.0	68.9	66.7	60.5	49.6	39.3	31.5	49.4
Mean Minimum Temp. (°F)	16.4	19.4	22.6	28.9	38.0	46.4	53.4	52.0	44.0	31.7	21.5	14.9	32.4
Extreme Maximum Temp. (°F)	68	73	78	87	93	97	96	95	89	83	75	75	97
Extreme Minimum Temp. (°F)	-16	-10	-5	1	16	22	37	35	20	5	-7	-25	-25
Days Maximum Temp. ≥ 90°F	0	0	0	0	0	4	5	1	0	0	0	0	10
Days Maximum Temp. ≤ 32°F	2	1	0	0	0	0	0	0	0	0	0	2	5
Days Minimum Temp. ≤ 32°F	29	26	27	20	7	1	0	0	2	17	26	29	184
Days Minimum Temp. ≤ 0°F	1	0	0	0	0	0	0	0	0	0	0	2	3
Heating Degree Days (base 65°F)	1,011	826	758	526	277	58	6	19	138	471	764	1,030	5,884
Cooling Degree Days (base 65°F)	0	0	0	0	6	66	133	78	11	0	0	0	294
Mean Precipitation (in.)	0.55	0.57	0.55	0.38	0.72	0.58	2.55	2.87	1.98	1.22	0.62	0.65	13.24
Extreme Maximum Daily Precip. (in.)	1.08	1.25	0.75	2.00	1.12	1.44	1.26	1.67	2.02	2.01	0.93	0.90	2.02
Days With ≥ 0.1" Precipitation	2	2	2	1	2	2	6	7	5	3	2	2	36
Days With ≥ 0.5" Precipitation	0	0	0	0	0	0	2	2	1	1	0	0	6
Days With ≥ 1.0" Precipitation	0	0	0	0	0	0	0	0	0	0	0	0	0
Mean Snowfall (in.)	1.9	2.2	0.6	0.1	trace	0.0	0.0	0.0	0.0	0.4	0.4	2.6	8.2
Maximum Snow Depth (in.)	5	12	5	trace	trace	0	0	0	0	4	2	***11***	***12***
Days With ≥ 1.0" Snow Depth	1	0	0	0	0	0	0	0	0	0	0	0	1

Bernardo *Socorro County* Elevation: 4,734 ft. Latitude: 34° 25' N Longitude: 106° 50' W

	JAN	FEB	MAR	APR	MAY	JUN	JUL	AUG	SEP	OCT	NOV	DEC	YEAR
Mean Maximum Temp. (°F)	54.1	61.1	68.5	77.3	86.4	95.6	96.9	93.5	87.4	76.2	63.2	53.5	76.1
Mean Temp. (°F)	***37.2***	***43.3***	49.9	***57.4***	67.0	***75.2***	***79.1***	***77.0***	***69.7***	57.9	45.8	***37.2***	***58.1***
Mean Minimum Temp. (°F)	***20.5***	***25.3***	30.8	***37.6***	47.6	***54.8***	***61.3***	***60.5***	***51.9***	39.5	28.2	***21.4***	***40.0***
Extreme Maximum Temp. (°F)	76	81	89	96	103	113	111	109	103	96	81	75	113
Extreme Minimum Temp. (°F)	***-10***	***-2***	***3***	7	24	***25***	***44***	***42***	***31***	***10***	***5***	***-2***	***-10***
Days Maximum Temp. ≥ 90°F	0	0	0	1	11	25	27	23	11	1	0	0	99
Days Maximum Temp. ≤ 32°F	0	0	0	0	0	0	0	0	0	0	0	0	0
Days Minimum Temp. ≤ 32°F	***27***	***21***	17	7	1	***0***	0	***0***	0	6	21	26	***126***
Days Minimum Temp. ≤ 0°F	***0***	***0***	0	0	0	***0***	0	***0***	0	0	0	0	***0***
Heating Degree Days (base 65°F)	***854***	***608***	463	***233***	50	***1***	***0***	***0***	***18***	225	570	***854***	***3,876***
Cooling Degree Days (base 65°F)	***0***	***0***	0	***11***	120	***315***	***444***	***378***	***166***	12	0	0	***1,446***
Mean Precipitation (in.)	0.36	0.31	0.46	0.39	0.51	0.56	1.37	1.63	1.24	0.91	0.43	0.56	8.73
Extreme Maximum Daily Precip. (in.)	0.82	0.50	1.39	1.17	0.92	1.30	1.28	1.60	2.07	1.17	1.26	1.15	2.07
Days With ≥ 0.1" Precipitation	1	1	1	1	2	1	3	4	3	3	1	2	23
Days With ≥ 0.5" Precipitation	0	0	0	0	0	0	1	1	1	1	0	0	4
Days With ≥ 1.0" Precipitation	0	0	0	0	0	0	0	0	0	0	0	0	0
Mean Snowfall (in.)	1.5	0.7	0.4	0.2	0.0	0.0	0.0	0.0	0.0	0.3	0.3	2.1	5.5
Maximum Snow Depth (in.)	9	2	trace	0	0	0	0	0	0	2	1	4	9
Days With ≥ 1.0" Snow Depth	0	0	0	0	0	0	0	0	0	0	0	1	1

Bingham 2 NE *Socorro County* Elevation: 5,550 ft. Latitude: 33° 55' N Longitude: 106° 21' W

	JAN	FEB	MAR	APR	MAY	JUN	JUL	AUG	SEP	OCT	NOV	DEC	YEAR
Mean Maximum Temp. (°F)	50.6	56.2	63.3	71.1	***81.2***	89.3	***89.9***	***87.2***	81.6	71.5	59.1	***49.9***	***70.9***
Mean Temp. (°F)	36.4	41.2	47.0	53.9	***63.8***	72.1	***75.0***	***73.2***	66.9	56.2	44.4	***35.9***	***55.5***
Mean Minimum Temp. (°F)	22.1	26.0	30.6	36.6	***46.3***	54.9	***60.0***	***59.2***	52.2	40.9	29.7	21.9	***40.0***
Extreme Maximum Temp. (°F)	69	75	83	88	100	105	102	99	95	89	77	68	105
Extreme Minimum Temp. (°F)	0	-1	2	19	25	35	48	47	34	12	6	-6	-6
Days Maximum Temp. ≥ 90°F	0	0	0	0	3	15	17	11	2	0	0	0	48
Days Maximum Temp. ≤ 32°F	1	0	0	0	0	0	0	0	0	0	0	1	2
Days Minimum Temp. ≤ 32°F	29	23	18	9	1	0	0	0	0	4	20	27	131
Days Minimum Temp. ≤ 0°F	0	0	0	0	0	0	0	0	0	0	0	0	0
Heating Degree Days (base 65°F)	880	665	552	329	***88***	6	***0***	***1***	36	269	611	***896***	***4,333***
Cooling Degree Days (base 65°F)	0	0	0	2	***56***	226	***317***	***262***	101	5	0	***0***	***969***
Mean Precipitation (in.)	0.44	0.46	0.52	0.41	0.53	0.89	2.56	2.40	1.60	1.32	0.58	0.61	12.32
Extreme Maximum Daily Precip. (in.)	0.78	***0.87***	1.02	***1.05***	***1.25***	***1.79***	***3.10***	na	2.01	1.36	***1.67***	***1.02***	na
Days With ≥ 0.1" Precipitation	1	1	1	1	1	2	5	4	4	3	1	2	26
Days With ≥ 0.5" Precipitation	0	0	0	0	0	0	1	1	1	1	0	0	4
Days With ≥ 1.0" Precipitation	0	0	0	0	0	0	0	0	0	0	0	0	0
Mean Snowfall (in.)	2.2	1.4	1.0	0.2	0.0	0.0	0.0	0.0	0.0	0.5	0.3	2.3	7.9
Maximum Snow Depth (in.)	8	3	1	2	0	0	0	0	0	4	3	7	8
Days With ≥ 1.0" Snow Depth	1	0	0	0	0	0	0	0	0	0	0	1	2

The period of record for all cooperative weather station data is 1980 – 2009. See User Guide for detailed explanation of data.

Bitter Lakes Wl Refuge *Chaves County* Elevation: 3,664 ft. Latitude: 33° 28' N Longitude: 104° 24' W

	JAN	FEB	MAR	APR	MAY	JUN	JUL	AUG	SEP	OCT	NOV	DEC	YEAR
Mean Maximum Temp. (°F)	***56.2***	62.2	69.6	78.3	86.7	94.9	96.1	94.0	87.4	77.1	65.8	***55.7***	***77.0***
Mean Temp. (°F)	***38.9***	44.1	51.4	59.7	69.0	77.6	80.2	78.4	71.2	59.6	47.7	***38.6***	***59.7***
Mean Minimum Temp. (°F)	21.5	25.9	33.0	41.0	51.2	60.3	64.3	62.8	55.0	41.9	29.5	21.3	42.3
Extreme Maximum Temp. (°F)	82	89	92	98	110	114	110	110	106	101	89	83	114
Extreme Minimum Temp. (°F)	-8	-1	6	16	28	41	40	40	30	10	2	-9	-9
Days Maximum Temp. ≥ 90°F	0	0	0	3	12	23	26	24	12	3	0	0	103
Days Maximum Temp. ≤ 32°F	1	1	0	0	0	0	0	0	0	0	0	1	3
Days Minimum Temp. ≤ 32°F	26	21	14	5	0	0	0	0	0	4	19	26	115
Days Minimum Temp. ≤ 0°F	0	0	0	0	0	0	0	0	0	0	0	1	1
Heating Degree Days (base 65°F)	***799***	582	419	186	35	2	0	0	22	193	514	***817***	***3,569***
Cooling Degree Days (base 65°F)	***0***	0	3	34	169	387	478	423	215	30	1	***0***	***1,740***
Mean Precipitation (in.)	0.41	0.42	0.55	0.61	1.45	2.01	2.16	2.18	1.77	1.34	0.74	0.62	14.26
Extreme Maximum Daily Precip. (in.)	0.88	1.10	2.04	3.15	3.14	3.98	***3.90***	2.54	1.69	2.55	***1.24***	0.90	***3.98***
Days With ≥ 0.1" Precipitation	1	1	1	1	2	3	3	4	4	3	1	2	26
Days With ≥ 0.5" Precipitation	0	0	0	0	1	1	1	1	1	1	0	0	6
Days With ≥ 1.0" Precipitation	0	0	0	0	0	1	1	1	0	0	0	0	3
Mean Snowfall (in.)	2.6	1.1	0.2	trace	0.0	0.0	0.0	0.0	0.0	0.1	0.9	2.1	7.0
Maximum Snow Depth (in.)	9	16	2	1	0	0	0	0	0	2	9	10	16
Days With ≥ 1.0" Snow Depth	1	1	0	0	0	0	0	0	0	0	0	1	3

Caballo Dam *Sierra County* Elevation: 4,189 ft. Latitude: 32° 54' N Longitude: 107° 18' W

	JAN	FEB	MAR	APR	MAY	JUN	JUL	AUG	SEP	OCT	NOV	DEC	YEAR
Mean Maximum Temp. (°F)	58.1	63.4	69.8	77.8	86.6	95.8	96.3	93.0	88.1	78.2	67.2	57.4	77.7
Mean Temp. (°F)	42.5	46.8	52.9	60.1	69.1	78.1	81.1	78.7	72.5	61.6	50.6	42.0	61.3
Mean Minimum Temp. (°F)	26.7	30.2	36.0	42.4	51.5	60.3	65.7	64.2	56.8	44.9	33.8	26.5	44.9
Extreme Maximum Temp. (°F)	77	85	90	95	104	111	109	106	102	97	87	79	111
Extreme Minimum Temp. (°F)	4	0	12	23	32	41	50	53	41	22	10	3	0
Days Maximum Temp. ≥ 90°F	0	0	0	1	12	25	27	24	14	2	0	0	105
Days Maximum Temp. ≤ 32°F	0	0	0	0	0	0	0	0	0	0	0	0	0
Days Minimum Temp. ≤ 32°F	26	18	9	2	0	0	0	0	0	2	12	26	95
Days Minimum Temp. ≤ 0°F	0	0	0	0	0	0	0	0	0	0	0	0	0
Heating Degree Days (base 65°F)	691	508	369	163	29	1	0	0	6	137	427	708	3,039
Cooling Degree Days (base 65°F)	0	0	1	24	162	401	505	430	237	38	0	0	1,798
Mean Precipitation (in.)	0.51	0.42	0.30	0.26	0.48	0.86	1.80	2.36	1.57	1.07	0.64	0.75	11.02
Extreme Maximum Daily Precip. (in.)	1.05	0.95	1.59	1.25	1.15	2.70	2.20	1.90	3.96	1.90	2.00	1.36	3.96
Days With ≥ 0.1" Precipitation	2	1	1	1	2	2	4	5	3	3	2	2	28
Days With ≥ 0.5" Precipitation	0	0	0	0	0	1	1	1	1	1	0	1	6
Days With ≥ 1.0" Precipitation	0	0	0	0	0	0	0	0	0	0	0	0	0
Mean Snowfall (in.)	0.0	trace	0.0	0.0	0.0	0.0	0.0	0.0	0.0	0.0	0.0	0.6	0.6
Maximum Snow Depth (in.)	trace	1	0	0	0	0	0	0	0	0	0	7	7
Days With ≥ 1.0" Snow Depth	0	0	0	0	0	0	0	0	0	0	0	0	0

Carlsbad *Eddy County* Elevation: 3,120 ft. Latitude: 32° 26' N Longitude: 104° 15' W

	JAN	FEB	MAR	APR	MAY	JUN	JUL	AUG	SEP	OCT	NOV	DEC	YEAR
Mean Maximum Temp. (°F)	58.6	63.6	71.2	79.4	87.7	95.4	96.0	94.1	87.7	79.1	67.7	58.5	78.2
Mean Temp. (°F)	43.6	48.2	55.1	62.9	72.2	80.1	82.1	80.6	73.8	63.5	52.1	43.6	63.2
Mean Minimum Temp. (°F)	28.5	32.7	38.9	46.4	56.5	64.8	68.2	67.0	59.9	48.0	36.6	28.7	48.0
Extreme Maximum Temp. (°F)	86	88	95	99	109	114	111	108	105	100	90	82	114
Extreme Minimum Temp. (°F)	8	10	12	25	40	50	57	54	41	21	11	3	3
Days Maximum Temp. ≥ 90°F	0	0	0	4	14	24	26	25	14	3	0	0	110
Days Maximum Temp. ≤ 32°F	1	1	0	0	0	0	0	0	0	0	0	1	3
Days Minimum Temp. ≤ 32°F	23	14	6	1	0	0	0	0	0	1	9	21	75
Days Minimum Temp. ≤ 0°F	0	0	0	0	0	0	0	0	0	0	0	0	0
Heating Degree Days (base 65°F)	657	469	311	122	14	0	0	0	11	106	383	655	2,728
Cooling Degree Days (base 65°F)	0	1	9	66	244	461	538	490	283	69	3	0	2,164
Mean Precipitation (in.)	0.46	0.53	0.49	0.64	1.24	1.51	1.68	1.92	2.45	1.16	0.75	0.66	13.49
Extreme Maximum Daily Precip. (in.)	0.79	1.25	2.04	2.86	***1.67***	2.73	2.68	2.35	***4.60***	3.00	2.00	***1.18***	***4.60***
Days With ≥ 0.1" Precipitation	1	1	1	1	2	3	3	4	3	3	2	1	25
Days With ≥ 0.5" Precipitation	0	0	0	0	1	1	1	1	2	1	0	0	7
Days With ≥ 1.0" Precipitation	0	0	0	0	0	0	0	0	1	0	0	0	1
Mean Snowfall (in.)	0.7	0.3	0.1	0.0	0.0	0.0	0.0	0.0	0.0	0.0	0.5	1.1	2.7
Maximum Snow Depth (in.)	3	3	2	0	0	0	0	0	0	0	3	5	5
Days With ≥ 1.0" Snow Depth	0	0	0	0	0	0	0	0	0	0	0	0	0

Carlsbad Cavern City Air Term *Eddy County* Elevation: 3,231 ft. Latitude: 32° 20' N Longitude: 104° 16' W

	JAN	FEB	MAR	APR	MAY	JUN	JUL	AUG	SEP	OCT	NOV	DEC	YEAR
Mean Maximum Temp. (°F)	58.3	63.7	71.2	79.7	88.5	95.9	95.8	93.6	87.3	78.1	66.5	57.7	78.0
Mean Temp. (°F)	43.9	48.7	55.4	63.4	72.9	80.5	82.0	80.4	73.7	63.5	51.8	43.5	63.3
Mean Minimum Temp. (°F)	29.4	33.6	39.5	47.1	57.2	65.0	68.2	67.2	60.1	48.9	37.0	29.2	48.5
Extreme Maximum Temp. (°F)	86	90	94	100	110	113	113	108	104	98	90	84	113
Extreme Minimum Temp. (°F)	4	-2	13	20	35	50	58	55	35	22	10	-4	-4
Days Maximum Temp. ≥ 90°F	0	0	0	4	16	25	27	25	13	3	0	0	113
Days Maximum Temp. ≤ 32°F	1	0	0	0	0	0	0	0	0	0	0	1	2
Days Minimum Temp. ≤ 32°F	21	13	6	1	0	0	0	0	0	1	9	21	72
Days Minimum Temp. ≤ 0°F	0	0	0	0	0	0	0	0	0	0	0	0	0
Heating Degree Days (base 65°F)	647	457	303	114	14	0	0	0	10	108	394	660	2,707
Cooling Degree Days (base 65°F)	0	2	11	73	265	472	535	485	280	67	3	0	2,193
Mean Precipitation (in.)	0.37	0.48	0.51	0.58	1.45	1.65	1.70	2.12	2.45	1.02	0.69	0.68	13.70
Extreme Maximum Daily Precip. (in.)	0.40	1.20	2.32	2.16	3.94	3.74	2.90	3.21	3.33	1.43	1.53	1.03	3.94
Days With ≥ 0.1" Precipitation	1	1	1	1	3	3	3	4	4	3	1	2	27
Days With ≥ 0.5" Precipitation	0	0	0	0	1	1	1	1	2	1	0	0	7
Days With ≥ 1.0" Precipitation	0	0	0	0	0	0	0	1	1	0	0	0	2
Mean Snowfall (in.)	na	na	na	na	na	na	na	na	na	na	na	na	na
Maximum Snow Depth (in.)	na	na	na	na	na	na	na	na	na	na	na	na	na
Days With ≥ 1.0" Snow Depth	na	na	na	na	na	na	na	na	na	na	na	na	na

The period of record for all cooperative weather station data is 1980 – 2009. See User Guide for detailed explanation of data.

Carlsbad Caverns *Eddy County* Elevation: 4,404 ft. Latitude: 32° 32' N Longitude: 103° 56' W

	JAN	FEB	MAR	APR	MAY	JUN	JUL	AUG	SEP	OCT	NOV	DEC	YEAR
Mean Maximum Temp. (°F)	56.1	59.7	66.9	74.7	83.6	91.0	91.3	89.4	82.9	74.2	64.3	55.9	74.2
Mean Temp. (°F)	44.9	48.3	54.5	62.0	70.8	77.8	78.9	77.5	***71.1***	62.7	52.9	***44.8***	***62.2***
Mean Minimum Temp. (°F)	33.7	36.9	42.1	49.2	58.1	64.5	66.5	65.6	***59.5***	51.2	41.8	***33.8***	***50.2***
Extreme Maximum Temp. (°F)	80	84	90	95	106	110	106	105	99	97	87	82	110
Extreme Minimum Temp. (°F)	6	4	12	21	38	44	46	52	***34***	15	17	2	***2***
Days Maximum Temp. ≥ 90°F	0	0	0	1	8	18	20	18	6	1	0	0	72
Days Maximum Temp. ≤ 32°F	1	1	0	0	0	0	0	0	0	0	0	1	3
Days Minimum Temp. ≤ 32°F	13	8	5	1	0	0	0	0	***0***	0	5	13	***45***
Days Minimum Temp. ≤ 0°F	0	0	0	0	0	0	0	0	***0***	0	0	0	***0***
Heating Degree Days (base 65°F)	617	467	330	150	28	2	0	1	***25***	132	362	***619***	***2,733***
Cooling Degree Days (base 65°F)	0	2	13	66	214	392	438	396	***216***	69	7	***0***	***1,813***
Mean Precipitation (in.)	0.37	0.51	0.45	0.62	1.52	2.27	2.09	2.43	2.93	1.29	0.68	0.59	15.75
Extreme Maximum Daily Precip. (in.)	0.48	0.79	0.91	1.72	2.18	8.41	3.02	2.35	5.63	1.60	1.09	***0.73***	***8.41***
Days With ≥ 0.1" Precipitation	1	2	1	2	3	4	4	4	4	3	1	1	30
Days With ≥ 0.5" Precipitation	0	0	0	0	1	1	1	2	2	1	0	0	8
Days With ≥ 1.0" Precipitation	0	0	0	0	0	0	1	1	1	0	0	0	3
Mean Snowfall (in.)	1.4	0.7	0.2	0.0	0.0	0.0	0.0	0.0	0.0	trace	0.3	2.2	4.8
Maximum Snow Depth (in.)	***3***	4	4	0	0	0	0	0	***0***	***trace***	3	***7***	***7***
Days With ≥ 1.0" Snow Depth	***0***	0	0	0	0	0	0	0	0	***0***	0	***0***	***0***

Chaco Canyon Natl Mon *San Juan County* Elevation: 6,173 ft. Latitude: 36° 02' N Longitude: 107° 55' W

	JAN	FEB	MAR	APR	MAY	JUN	JUL	AUG	SEP	OCT	NOV	DEC	YEAR
Mean Maximum Temp. (°F)	43.8	49.4	58.3	66.8	76.3	86.5	90.1	87.1	80.2	68.3	54.7	44.0	67.1
Mean Temp. (°F)	28.8	34.2	41.0	48.5	57.6	67.0	72.7	70.5	62.5	50.1	38.0	29.0	50.0
Mean Minimum Temp. (°F)	13.7	19.0	23.7	30.2	38.7	47.5	55.3	54.0	44.8	31.9	21.2	14.0	32.8
Extreme Maximum Temp. (°F)	69	70	85	86	97	103	102	98	94	85	75	67	103
Extreme Minimum Temp. (°F)	-24	-26	-5	1	17	27	34	38	20	7	-11	-37	-37
Days Maximum Temp. ≥ 90°F	0	0	0	0	1	10	18	10	1	0	0	0	40
Days Maximum Temp. ≤ 32°F	3	1	0	0	0	0	0	0	0	0	0	3	7
Days Minimum Temp. ≤ 32°F	30	26	27	18	7	1	0	0	2	16	26	29	182
Days Minimum Temp. ≤ 0°F	4	1	0	0	0	0	0	0	0	0	0	3	8
Heating Degree Days (base 65°F)	1,115	864	736	486	235	42	1	3	103	454	805	1,108	5,952
Cooling Degree Days (base 65°F)	0	0	0	0	11	108	248	183	35	0	0	0	585
Mean Precipitation (in.)	0.56	0.67	0.62	0.65	0.56	0.52	1.26	1.31	1.14	0.79	0.69	0.61	9.38
Extreme Maximum Daily Precip. (in.)	1.02	0.90	1.10	0.87	2.23	0.76	2.26	1.30	2.80	1.22	1.56	0.61	2.80
Days With ≥ 0.1" Precipitation	2	2	2	2	2	1	4	4	3	3	2	2	29
Days With ≥ 0.5" Precipitation	0	0	0	0	0	0	0	1	0	0	0	0	1
Days With ≥ 1.0" Precipitation	0	0	0	0	0	0	0	0	0	0	0	0	0
Mean Snowfall (in.)	3.6	3.2	1.1	0.6	0.0	0.0	0.0	0.0	0.0	0.4	1.2	3.8	13.9
Maximum Snow Depth (in.)	***7***	***10***	5	***1***	0	0	0	0	0	5	8	8	***10***
Days With ≥ 1.0" Snow Depth	***3***	2	0	0	0	0	0	0	0	0	1	3	***9***

Chama *Rio Arriba County* Elevation: 7,850 ft. Latitude: 36° 55' N Longitude: 106° 35' W

	JAN	FEB	MAR	APR	MAY	JUN	JUL	AUG	SEP	OCT	NOV	DEC	YEAR
Mean Maximum Temp. (°F)	38.7	41.6	47.9	56.9	66.2	76.7	81.0	78.3	71.8	61.1	47.9	38.8	58.9
Mean Temp. (°F)	22.7	26.1	32.5	40.5	48.6	57.2	62.9	61.6	54.4	43.9	32.3	23.6	42.2
Mean Minimum Temp. (°F)	6.6	10.5	17.1	24.0	31.1	37.7	44.7	44.9	37.0	26.6	16.7	8.4	25.4
Extreme Maximum Temp. (°F)	57	61	68	76	89	92	93	93	88	80	72	60	93
Extreme Minimum Temp. (°F)	-28	-29	-11	-7	10	18	28	29	16	-2	-13	-30	-30
Days Maximum Temp. ≥ 90°F	0	0	0	0	0	0	1	0	0	0	0	0	1
Days Maximum Temp. ≤ 32°F	7	3	1	0	0	0	0	0	0	0	2	7	20
Days Minimum Temp. ≤ 32°F	31	28	30	27	18	6	1	0	8	25	29	31	234
Days Minimum Temp. ≤ 0°F	9	4	2	0	0	0	0	0	0	0	2	7	24
Heating Degree Days (base 65°F)	1,305	1,094	1,000	729	500	231	79	108	310	647	974	1,276	8,253
Cooling Degree Days (base 65°F)	0	0	0	0	0	3	21	10	1	0	0	0	35
Mean Precipitation (in.)	2.02	2.04	1.98	1.65	1.46	1.09	2.22	3.14	2.38	2.05	1.94	1.87	23.84
Extreme Maximum Daily Precip. (in.)	1.86	1.44	1.98	1.51	1.26	1.18	1.65	2.30	2.15	2.01	1.40	1.15	2.30
Days With ≥ 0.1" Precipitation	5	5	6	5	4	3	6	8	6	5	4	5	62
Days With ≥ 0.5" Precipitation	1	1	1	1	1	1	1	2	1	1	1	1	13
Days With ≥ 1.0" Precipitation	0	0	0	0	0	0	0	0	0	0	0	0	0
Mean Snowfall (in.)	24.3	22.8	15.4	4.9	0.4	trace	0.0	0.0	0.0	3.3	11.6	20.5	103.2
Maximum Snow Depth (in.)	44	56	47	41	2	trace	0	0	trace	16	23	38	56
Days With ≥ 1.0" Snow Depth	26	24	21	4	0	0	0	0	0	2	7	19	103

Cimarron 4 SW *Colfax County* Elevation: 6,540 ft. Latitude: 36° 28' N Longitude: 104° 57' W

	JAN	FEB	MAR	APR	MAY	JUN	JUL	AUG	SEP	OCT	NOV	DEC	YEAR
Mean Maximum Temp. (°F)	46.9	49.9	56.5	64.2	72.1	80.9	83.8	80.8	76.2	67.2	55.3	46.7	65.1
Mean Temp. (°F)	32.1	34.7	40.8	47.9	56.2	64.4	68.0	66.1	60.2	50.5	39.6	31.8	49.4
Mean Minimum Temp. (°F)	17.3	19.4	25.1	31.5	40.2	47.9	52.1	51.4	44.2	33.8	23.9	16.9	33.6
Extreme Maximum Temp. (°F)	75	74	79	83	92	98	97	93	90	85	80	75	98
Extreme Minimum Temp. (°F)	-15	-21	-8	-1	19	31	41	38	22	-5	-7	-22	-22
Days Maximum Temp. ≥ 90°F	0	0	0	0	0	3	4	1	0	0	0	0	8
Days Maximum Temp. ≤ 32°F	3	2	0	0	0	0	0	0	0	0	1	3	9
Days Minimum Temp. ≤ 32°F	30	26	26	17	3	0	0	0	1	13	26	30	172
Days Minimum Temp. ≤ 0°F	1	1	0	0	0	0	0	0	0	0	0	2	4
Heating Degree Days (base 65°F)	1,012	850	743	506	272	63	10	26	147	443	755	1,021	5,848
Cooling Degree Days (base 65°F)	0	0	0	0	6	52	109	67	10	0	0	0	244
Mean Precipitation (in.)	0.58	0.62	0.97	1.42	1.92	2.19	2.58	3.54	1.74	1.16	0.62	0.50	17.84
Extreme Maximum Daily Precip. (in.)	1.61	1.13	1.27	3.89	2.04	2.62	1.84	2.35	1.85	2.31	1.08	0.75	3.89
Days With ≥ 0.1" Precipitation	2	2	3	3	4	5	6	7	4	2	1	2	41
Days With ≥ 0.5" Precipitation	0	0	1	1	1	1	2	2	1	1	0	0	10
Days With ≥ 1.0" Precipitation	0	0	0	0	0	0	0	1	0	0	0	0	1
Mean Snowfall (in.)	8.3	8.8	6.7	5.5	0.6	0.0	0.0	0.0	0.0	1.8	5.5	7.8	45.0
Maximum Snow Depth (in.)	21	18	25	12	4	0	0	0	0	7	10	14	25
Days With ≥ 1.0" Snow Depth	4	3	2	1	0	0	0	0	0	0	2	5	17

The period of record for all cooperative weather station data is 1980 – 2009. See User Guide for detailed explanation of data.

Clovis *Curry County* Elevation: 4,290 ft. Latitude: 34° 25' N Longitude: 103° 12' W

	JAN	FEB	MAR	APR	MAY	JUN	JUL	AUG	SEP	OCT	NOV	DEC	YEAR
Mean Maximum Temp. (°F)	51.4	56.1	63.4	71.8	80.7	88.7	91.3	88.6	82.8	72.5	60.7	51.8	71.6
Mean Temp. (°F)	38.2	42.0	48.5	56.4	66.0	74.4	77.7	75.8	69.2	58.4	47.1	38.7	57.7
Mean Minimum Temp. (°F)	25.0	27.9	33.7	41.1	51.3	60.0	64.1	62.9	55.6	44.3	33.3	25.5	43.7
Extreme Maximum Temp. (°F)	76	83	91	97	103	110	108	106	100	95	85	78	110
Extreme Minimum Temp. (°F)	-4	-4	7	20	31	40	51	52	33	13	-1	-5	-5
Days Maximum Temp. ≥ 90°F	0	0	0	0	5	15	20	16	6	1	0	0	63
Days Maximum Temp. ≤ 32°F	3	2	1	0	0	0	0	0	0	0	1	3	10
Days Minimum Temp. ≤ 32°F	26	20	13	4	0	0	0	0	0	2	13	25	103
Days Minimum Temp. ≤ 0°F	0	0	0	0	0	0	0	0	0	0	0	1	1
Heating Degree Days (base 65°F)	823	643	505	265	74	5	0	1	37	221	532	809	3,915
Cooling Degree Days (base 65°F)	0	0	1	15	112	293	401	344	170	24	0	0	1,360
Mean Precipitation (in.)	0.56	0.42	0.98	0.89	1.89	2.59	2.44	3.39	2.20	1.87	0.80	0.79	18.82
Extreme Maximum Daily Precip. (in.)	0.95	0.88	1.96	1.50	2.75	2.50	3.45	3.24	1.85	3.45	1.79	1.42	3.45
Days With ≥ 0.1" Precipitation	2	1	2	2	4	5	4	6	4	3	2	2	37
Days With ≥ 0.5" Precipitation	0	0	1	1	1	2	2	2	2	1	0	1	13
Days With ≥ 1.0" Precipitation	0	0	0	0	0	1	1	1	0	0	0	0	3
Mean Snowfall (in.)	3.8	2.7	1.4	0.4	0.0	0.0	0.0	0.0	0.0	0.2	1.8	3.9	14.2
Maximum Snow Depth (in.)	14	9	6	2	0	0	0	0	0	2	5	8	14
Days With ≥ 1.0" Snow Depth	4	2	1	0	0	0	0	0	0	0	1	4	12

Clovis 13 N *Curry County* Elevation: 4,435 ft. Latitude: 34° 36' N Longitude: 103° 13' W

	JAN	FEB	MAR	APR	MAY	JUN	JUL	AUG	SEP	OCT	NOV	DEC	YEAR
Mean Maximum Temp. (°F)	52.8	57.7	65.2	73.3	81.6	90.1	91.6	89.0	83.6	73.6	61.8	52.4	72.7
Mean Temp. (°F)	38.5	42.2	48.6	56.2	65.4	73.9	76.8	75.0	68.9	58.4	47.0	38.5	57.4
Mean Minimum Temp. (°F)	24.0	26.6	32.0	38.9	49.0	57.6	61.9	61.0	54.0	43.1	32.1	24.5	42.1
Extreme Maximum Temp. (°F)	79	81	88	95	102	108	105	104	102	93	85	78	108
Extreme Minimum Temp. (°F)	0	-4	4	16	25	41	48	50	28	11	0	-8	-8
Days Maximum Temp. ≥ 90°F	0	0	0	1	6	17	21	17	7	0	0	0	69
Days Maximum Temp. ≤ 32°F	2	1	0	0	0	0	0	0	0	0	0	2	5
Days Minimum Temp. ≤ 32°F	26	21	15	6	0	0	0	0	0	3	14	25	110
Days Minimum Temp. ≤ 0°F	0	0	0	0	0	0	0	0	0	0	0	0	0
Heating Degree Days (base 65°F)	815	639	500	270	76	3	1	1	30	216	534	814	3,899
Cooling Degree Days (base 65°F)	0	0	0	12	94	277	372	316	153	18	0	0	1,242
Mean Precipitation (in.)	0.37	0.35	0.92	0.90	2.17	2.50	2.40	3.42	1.97	2.07	0.56	0.56	18.19
Extreme Maximum Daily Precip. (in.)	1.48	1.36	2.05	2.07	2.57	3.16	2.90	3.05	2.90	3.60	1.07	1.41	3.60
Days With ≥ 0.1" Precipitation	1	1	2	2	4	4	4	5	4	3	1	1	32
Days With ≥ 0.5" Precipitation	0	0	1	1	1	2	1	2	1	1	0	0	10
Days With ≥ 1.0" Precipitation	0	0	0	0	0	1	0	1	1	1	0	0	4
Mean Snowfall (in.)	1.6	1.0	0.9	0.4	0.0	0.0	0.0	0.0	0.0	0.2	0.9	2.4	7.4
Maximum Snow Depth (in.)	10	4	5	3	0	0	0	0	0	2	3	13	13
Days With ≥ 1.0" Snow Depth	1	0	0	0	0	0	0	0	0	0	0	1	2

Columbus *Luna County* Elevation: 4,064 ft. Latitude: 31° 50' N Longitude: 107° 38' W

	JAN	FEB	MAR	APR	MAY	JUN	JUL	AUG	SEP	OCT	NOV	DEC	YEAR
Mean Maximum Temp. (°F)	59.3	64.7	71.4	79.8	88.7	96.7	96.0	92.7	89.0	79.6	67.6	58.2	78.6
Mean Temp. (°F)	45.2	49.9	55.8	63.4	72.6	81.1	82.4	79.9	75.1	64.6	52.9	44.4	63.9
Mean Minimum Temp. (°F)	30.9	35.0	40.1	47.0	56.5	65.5	68.8	67.1	61.1	49.6	38.1	30.7	49.2
Extreme Maximum Temp. (°F)	80	86	91	98	105	111	107	105	101	96	86	80	111
Extreme Minimum Temp. (°F)	5	8	13	26	38	47	60	56	46	27	15	6	5
Days Maximum Temp. ≥ 90°F	0	0	0	1	14	27	28	23	15	2	0	0	110
Days Maximum Temp. ≤ 32°F	0	0	0	0	0	0	0	0	0	0	0	0	0
Days Minimum Temp. ≤ 32°F	18	10	4	1	0	0	0	0	0	0	7	18	58
Days Minimum Temp. ≤ 0°F	0	0	0	0	0	0	0	0	0	0	0	0	0
Heating Degree Days (base 65°F)	608	420	284	97	6	0	0	0	2	80	359	630	2,486
Cooling Degree Days (base 65°F)	0	0	4	57	248	491	548	470	310	76	2	0	2,206
Mean Precipitation (in.)	0.55	0.43	0.33	0.29	0.28	0.61	1.91	2.04	1.19	0.99	0.61	0.78	10.01
Extreme Maximum Daily Precip. (in.)	0.72	0.70	1.15	0.88	0.73	2.90	2.30	1.90	2.20	1.15	1.44	1.22	2.90
Days With ≥ 0.1" Precipitation	2	1	1	1	1	1	4	5	3	2	2	2	25
Days With ≥ 0.5" Precipitation	0	0	0	0	0	0	1	1	1	1	0	1	5
Days With ≥ 1.0" Precipitation	0	0	0	0	0	0	0	0	0	0	0	0	0
Mean Snowfall (in.)	0.4	0.1	trace	0.2	0.0	0.0	0.0	0.0	0.0	0.0	0.2	0.9	1.8
Maximum Snow Depth (in.)	6	1	trace	5	0	0	0	0	0	0	4	3	6
Days With ≥ 1.0" Snow Depth	0	0	0	0	0	0	0	0	0	0	0	0	0

Conchas Dam *San Miguel County* Elevation: 4,244 ft. Latitude: 35° 24' N Longitude: 104° 11' W

	JAN	FEB	MAR	APR	MAY	JUN	JUL	AUG	SEP	OCT	NOV	DEC	YEAR
Mean Maximum Temp. (°F)	53.6	58.0	64.8	72.5	81.7	91.1	94.4	91.9	84.9	74.3	62.8	52.7	73.6
Mean Temp. (°F)	39.1	43.1	50.0	57.8	67.3	76.4	80.4	78.3	71.2	59.9	48.5	39.1	59.3
Mean Minimum Temp. (°F)	24.6	28.2	35.2	43.0	52.8	61.7	66.2	64.7	57.4	45.5	34.1	25.4	44.9
Extreme Maximum Temp. (°F)	80	82	91	97	106	114	107	107	103	97	86	78	114
Extreme Minimum Temp. (°F)	2	-5	9	19	34	41	51	49	35	16	8	-10	-10
Days Maximum Temp. ≥ 90°F	0	0	0	1	6	18	26	22	10	1	0	0	84
Days Maximum Temp. ≤ 32°F	2	1	0	0	0	0	0	0	0	0	0	2	5
Days Minimum Temp. ≤ 32°F	27	20	11	2	0	0	0	0	0	1	13	26	100
Days Minimum Temp. ≤ 0°F	0	0	0	0	0	0	0	0	0	0	0	0	0
Heating Degree Days (base 65°F)	795	610	459	230	59	3	0	0	26	186	490	796	3,654
Cooling Degree Days (base 65°F)	0	0	2	21	137	353	483	420	217	35	1	0	1,669
Mean Precipitation (in.)	0.44	0.40	0.83	0.98	1.71	2.04	2.53	2.86	1.66	1.27	0.65	0.51	15.88
Extreme Maximum Daily Precip. (in.)	1.42	0.88	1.61	1.98	3.32	2.37	2.88	2.80	3.45	2.84	1.48	0.95	3.45
Days With ≥ 0.1" Precipitation	1	1	2	2	3	4	5	6	3	2	1	2	32
Days With ≥ 0.5" Precipitation	0	0	1	1	1	1	2	2	1	1	0	0	10
Days With ≥ 1.0" Precipitation	0	0	0	0	0	0	1	1	0	0	0	0	2
Mean Snowfall (in.)	2.6	2.7	1.2	0.2	0.0	0.0	0.0	0.0	0.0	0.1	1.0	3.2	11.0
Maximum Snow Depth (in.)	15	10	10	2	0	0	0	0	0	3	7	8	15
Days With ≥ 1.0" Snow Depth	1	1	1	0	0	0	0	0	0	0	0	1	4

Corrales *Sandoval County* Elevation: 5,015 ft. Latitude: 35° 14' N Longitude: 106° 36' W

	JAN	FEB	MAR	APR	MAY	JUN	JUL	AUG	SEP	OCT	NOV	DEC	YEAR
Mean Maximum Temp. (°F)	49.3	55.4	63.4	71.7	81.3	89.8	91.7	89.0	82.9	71.5	58.7	48.2	71.1
Mean Temp. (°F)	34.8	39.8	46.3	53.5	62.4	70.5	75.0	73.4	66.0	54.1	42.8	34.0	54.4
Mean Minimum Temp. (°F)	20.2	24.1	29.2	35.2	43.5	51.1	58.2	57.8	49.0	36.5	26.8	19.7	37.6
Extreme Maximum Temp. (°F)	69	77	85	89	102	103	106	101	97	90	78	70	106
Extreme Minimum Temp. (°F)	-5	-2	8	16	27	36	41	39	31	13	7	-6	-6
Days Maximum Temp. ≥ 90°F	0	0	0	0	3	16	21	15	4	0	0	0	59
Days Maximum Temp. ≤ 32°F	1	0	0	0	0	0	0	0	0	0	0	1	2
Days Minimum Temp. ≤ 32°F	29	24	21	10	2	0	0	0	0	9	22	28	145
Days Minimum Temp. ≤ 0°F	0	0	0	0	0	0	0	0	0	0	0	0	0
Heating Degree Days (base 65°F)	930	706	571	340	111	9	0	1	48	334	659	953	4,662
Cooling Degree Days (base 65°F)	0	0	0	1	39	180	316	269	86	1	0	0	892
Mean Precipitation (in.)	0.38	0.46	0.69	0.64	0.57	0.70	1.48	1.87	1.07	0.98	0.65	0.62	10.11
Extreme Maximum Daily Precip. (in.)	0.59	0.78	0.93	1.18	0.54	1.44	1.47	1.25	1.65	1.75	1.21	1.40	1.75
Days With ≥ 0.1" Precipitation	1	1	2	2	2	2	4	5	3	2	2	2	28
Days With ≥ 0.5" Precipitation	0	0	0	0	0	0	1	1	1	1	0	0	4
Days With ≥ 1.0" Precipitation	0	0	0	0	0	0	0	0	0	0	0	0	0
Mean Snowfall (in.)	2.0	1.6	0.8	0.5	0.0	0.0	0.0	0.0	0.0	0.3	0.5	2.3	8.0
Maximum Snow Depth (in.)	10	7	6	trace	0	0	0	0	0	1	1	14	14
Days With ≥ 1.0" Snow Depth	2	1	0	0	0	0	0	0	0	0	0	1	4

Cubero *Cibola County* Elevation: 6,194 ft. Latitude: 35° 05' N Longitude: 107° 31' W

	JAN	FEB	MAR	APR	MAY	JUN	JUL	AUG	SEP	OCT	NOV	DEC	YEAR
Mean Maximum Temp. (°F)	48.0	53.0	59.9	68.1	77.5	87.2	89.6	86.2	80.3	69.4	57.3	47.8	68.7
Mean Temp. (°F)	33.2	37.3	43.2	50.6	59.8	68.8	73.1	70.6	63.5	52.2	41.1	32.6	52.2
Mean Minimum Temp. (°F)	18.3	21.6	26.5	33.1	42.0	50.2	56.5	54.9	46.7	34.9	24.7	17.4	35.6
Extreme Maximum Temp. (°F)	67	75	80	87	97	103	103	100	93	87	78	69	103
Extreme Minimum Temp. (°F)	-13	-7	-1	11	21	31	42	40	26	11	3	-13	-13
Days Maximum Temp. ≥ 90°F	0	0	0	0	1	12	17	9	1	0	0	0	40
Days Maximum Temp. ≤ 32°F	1	0	0	0	0	0	0	0	0	0	0	1	2
Days Minimum Temp. ≤ 32°F	30	26	25	14	3	0	0	0	1	11	25	30	165
Days Minimum Temp. ≤ 0°F	1	0	0	0	0	0	0	0	0	0	0	1	2
Heating Degree Days (base 65°F)	980	775	668	426	175	23	0	3	80	392	711	997	5,230
Cooling Degree Days (base 65°F)	0	0	0	1	21	142	257	182	42	1	0	0	646
Mean Precipitation (in.)	0.60	0.48	0.58	0.63	0.63	0.55	1.86	1.99	1.32	1.04	0.61	0.59	10.88
Extreme Maximum Daily Precip. (in.)	1.13	0.60	1.67	1.15	0.88	0.76	1.95	2.40	2.00	1.77	1.25	0.95	2.40
Days With ≥ 0.1" Precipitation	2	2	1	1	2	2	4	5	3	3	1	2	28
Days With ≥ 0.5" Precipitation	0	0	0	0	0	0	1	1	1	1	0	0	4
Days With ≥ 1.0" Precipitation	0	0	0	0	0	0	0	0	0	0	0	0	0
Mean Snowfall (in.)	5.1	2.0	1.9	0.7	trace	0.0	0.0	0.0	0.0	0.4	1.4	4.8	16.3
Maximum Snow Depth (in.)	23	12	5	7	trace	0	0	0	0	7	5	13	23
Days With ≥ 1.0" Snow Depth	2	1	0	0	0	0	0	0	0	0	0	2	5

Deming *Luna County* Elevation: 4,299 ft. Latitude: 32° 15' N Longitude: 107° 44' W

	JAN	FEB	MAR	APR	MAY	JUN	JUL	AUG	SEP	OCT	NOV	DEC	YEAR
Mean Maximum Temp. (°F)	58.5	63.5	70.6	78.6	87.6	95.3	94.8	92.2	87.8	78.4	66.5	57.0	77.6
Mean Temp. (°F)	42.8	47.0	53.0	60.1	69.0	77.3	79.6	77.8	72.1	61.6	50.0	42.1	61.0
Mean Minimum Temp. (°F)	27.1	30.5	35.2	41.5	50.4	59.2	64.3	63.2	56.3	44.7	33.5	27.1	44.4
Extreme Maximum Temp. (°F)	78	86	90	96	105	109	106	105	100	95	83	75	109
Extreme Minimum Temp. (°F)	7	9	12	21	29	39	49	52	36	22	11	-2	-2
Days Maximum Temp. ≥ 90°F	0	0	0	1	12	24	26	22	12	1	0	0	98
Days Maximum Temp. ≤ 32°F	0	0	0	0	0	0	0	0	0	0	0	0	0
Days Minimum Temp. ≤ 32°F	25	18	10	3	0	0	0	0	0	2	13	25	96
Days Minimum Temp. ≤ 0°F	0	0	0	0	0	0	0	0	0	0	0	0	0
Heating Degree Days (base 65°F)	682	502	367	162	24	0	0	0	5	130	443	704	3,019
Cooling Degree Days (base 65°F)	0	0	1	20	155	375	459	402	224	31	0	0	1,667
Mean Precipitation (in.)	0.55	0.62	0.31	0.28	0.23	0.52	1.93	2.13	1.15	0.96	0.69	0.94	10.31
Extreme Maximum Daily Precip. (in.)	0.80	0.74	0.57	0.81	0.56	1.52	2.00	2.05	1.64	1.37	1.44	1.52	2.05
Days With ≥ 0.1" Precipitation	2	2	1	1	1	1	4	5	3	3	2	3	28
Days With ≥ 0.5" Precipitation	0	0	0	0	0	0	1	1	1	1	0	1	5
Days With ≥ 1.0" Precipitation	0	0	0	0	0	0	0	0	0	0	0	0	0
Mean Snowfall (in.)	0.8	0.5	0.1	0.1	0.0	0.0	0.0	0.0	0.0	trace	0.1	1.1	2.7
Maximum Snow Depth (in.)	1	4	trace	trace	0	0	0	0	0	trace	trace	11	11
Days With ≥ 1.0" Snow Depth	0	0	0	0	0	0	0	0	0	0	0	0	0

Dilia *Guadalupe County* Elevation: 5,149 ft. Latitude: 35° 11' N Longitude: 105° 03' W

	JAN	FEB	MAR	APR	MAY	JUN	JUL	AUG	SEP	OCT	NOV	DEC	YEAR
Mean Maximum Temp. (°F)	53.0	57.2	64.0	72.0	80.0	89.0	91.3	88.8	83.1	73.0	61.6	52.6	72.1
Mean Temp. (°F)	37.6	40.9	47.0	54.4	63.0	71.6	75.2	73.5	66.7	56.2	45.6	37.5	55.8
Mean Minimum Temp. (°F)	22.1	24.5	29.9	36.8	45.9	54.2	59.2	58.1	50.2	39.4	29.5	22.3	39.3
Extreme Maximum Temp. (°F)	76	80	86	92	100	107	105	101	99	92	82	81	107
Extreme Minimum Temp. (°F)	-10	-8	0	10	25	37	47	46	28	10	-2	-28	-28
Days Maximum Temp. ≥ 90°F	0	0	0	0	3	15	21	16	5	0	0	0	60
Days Maximum Temp. ≤ 32°F	1	1	0	0	0	0	0	0	0	0	0	1	3
Days Minimum Temp. ≤ 32°F	28	24	19	8	1	0	0	0	0	5	19	28	132
Days Minimum Temp. ≤ 0°F	0	0	0	0	0	0	0	0	0	0	0	1	1
Heating Degree Days (base 65°F)	842	676	552	315	102	6	0	1	40	269	575	847	4,225
Cooling Degree Days (base 65°F)	0	0	0	3	46	211	325	272	96	4	0	0	957
Mean Precipitation (in.)	0.61	0.55	0.81	0.82	1.26	1.74	2.39	2.63	2.02	1.20	0.79	0.85	15.67
Extreme Maximum Daily Precip. (in.)	1.40	1.26	1.60	3.35	1.45	3.15	1.70	3.51	2.74	2.09	1.20	1.35	3.51
Days With ≥ 0.1" Precipitation	2	1	2	2	3	4	6	6	4	3	2	2	37
Days With ≥ 0.5" Precipitation	0	0	0	0	1	1	1	2	1	1	1	0	8
Days With ≥ 1.0" Precipitation	0	0	0	0	0	0	0	0	1	0	0	0	1
Mean Snowfall (in.)	6.4	4.7	5.8	1.6	trace	0.0	0.0	trace	0.0	0.7	3.7	9.3	32.2
Maximum Snow Depth (in.)	20	10	24	14	trace	0	0	trace	0	4	8	16	24
Days With ≥ 1.0" Snow Depth	2	2	1	0	0	0	0	0	0	0	1	3	9

The period of record for all cooperative weather station data is 1980 – 2009. See User Guide for detailed explanation of data.

Elida *Roosevelt County* Elevation: 4,354 ft. Latitude: 33° 57' N Longitude: 103° 39' W

	JAN	FEB	MAR	APR	MAY	JUN	JUL	AUG	SEP	OCT	NOV	DEC	YEAR
Mean Maximum Temp. (°F)	53.6	58.7	66.4	74.8	83.4	90.7	91.9	89.8	84.0	74.2	62.7	53.3	73.6
Mean Temp. (°F)	38.9	43.1	50.1	57.9	67.3	75.2	77.7	76.2	69.7	59.5	47.9	39.1	58.5
Mean Minimum Temp. (°F)	24.4	27.8	33.6	40.8	51.2	59.7	63.6	62.6	55.3	44.7	32.3	24.9	43.4
Extreme Maximum Temp. (°F)	79	83	90	98	110	112	111	107	104	98	85	78	112
Extreme Minimum Temp. (°F)	-5	-2	4	18	28	40	48	50	30	10	7	-9	-9
Days Maximum Temp. ≥ 90°F	0	0	0	1	8	17	21	17	7	1	0	0	72
Days Maximum Temp. ≤ 32°F	2	1	0	0	0	0	0	0	0	0	0	2	5
Days Minimum Temp. ≤ 32°F	25	20	13	5	0	0	0	0	0	2	15	24	104
Days Minimum Temp. ≤ 0°F	0	0	0	0	0	0	0	0	0	0	0	0	0
Heating Degree Days (base 65°F)	802	612	458	226	53	4	0	0	29	193	508	797	3,682
Cooling Degree Days (base 65°F)	0	0	1	19	131	317	401	354	177	29	0	0	1,429
Mean Precipitation (in.)	0.45	0.38	0.65	0.71	1.51	2.36	3.09	2.64	2.07	1.67	0.74	0.66	16.93
Extreme Maximum Daily Precip. (in.)	0.98	1.24	1.80	1.53	2.32	2.96	2.84	7.26	3.02	2.60	1.48	0.91	7.26
Days With ≥ 0.1" Precipitation	1	1	1	1	3	4	4	4	4	3	2	2	30
Days With ≥ 0.5" Precipitation	0	0	0	0	1	2	2	2	1	1	0	0	9
Days With ≥ 1.0" Precipitation	0	0	0	0	0	1	1	1	1	0	0	0	4
Mean Snowfall (in.)	3.0	1.6	0.9	0.5	0.0	0.0	0.0	0.0	0.0	0.3	1.8	3.6	11.7
Maximum Snow Depth (in.)	12	5	9	3	0	2	0	0	0	4	6	11	12
Days With ≥ 1.0" Snow Depth	2	1	0	0	0	0	0	0	0	0	1	2	6

Elk 2 E *Chaves County* Elevation: 5,727 ft. Latitude: 32° 57' N Longitude: 105° 18' W

	JAN	FEB	MAR	APR	MAY	JUN	JUL	AUG	SEP	OCT	NOV	DEC	YEAR
Mean Maximum Temp. (°F)	54.2	58.0	63.2	70.5	77.9	***84.5***	84.0	***81.6***	77.7	70.7	61.6	***54.4***	***69.9***
Mean Temp. (°F)	37.6	40.9	45.6	52.2	60.2	***67.5***	69.5	***67.9***	62.5	53.9	44.4	***37.4***	***53.3***
Mean Minimum Temp. (°F)	21.0	23.7	27.9	33.9	42.5	***50.5***	54.9	***54.1***	47.3	37.1	27.1	***20.4***	***36.7***
Extreme Maximum Temp. (°F)	76	80	84	89	96	100	102	99	92	88	84	78	102
Extreme Minimum Temp. (°F)	-10	-2	1	11	24	35	43	42	26	-1	5	-15	-15
Days Maximum Temp. ≥ 90°F	0	0	0	0	1	6	4	2	0	0	0	0	13
Days Maximum Temp. ≤ 32°F	1	0	0	0	0	0	0	0	0	0	0	1	2
Days Minimum Temp. ≤ 32°F	27	24	23	12	2	0	0	0	0	8	24	27	147
Days Minimum Temp. ≤ 0°F	0	0	0	0	0	0	0	0	0	0	0	0	0
Heating Degree Days (base 65°F)	845	677	595	379	***162***	***21***	3	***9***	94	339	612	***847***	***4,583***
Cooling Degree Days (base 65°F)	0	0	0	1	***17***	***103***	148	***106***	25	1	0	***0***	***401***
Mean Precipitation (in.)	0.50	0.44	0.45	0.51	1.23	2.21	2.91	3.40	2.54	1.30	0.73	0.72	16.94
Extreme Maximum Daily Precip. (in.)	1.24	***1.02***	***1.00***	1.02	1.90	2.66	***3.05***	***3.45***	2.47	1.95	1.46	***1.35***	***3.45***
Days With ≥ 0.1" Precipitation	1	1	1	1	3	4	6	7	5	3	1	2	35
Days With ≥ 0.5" Precipitation	0	0	0	0	1	1	2	2	2	1	0	0	9
Days With ≥ 1.0" Precipitation	0	0	0	0	0	1	1	1	1	0	0	0	4
Mean Snowfall (in.)	4.7	3.0	2.1	0.5	trace	0.0	0.0	0.0	0.0	1.1	2.6	6.3	20.3
Maximum Snow Depth (in.)	15	13	4	8	trace	0	0	0	0	6	17	24	24
Days With ≥ 1.0" Snow Depth	1	1	0	0	0	0	0	0	0	0	0	1	3

Faywood *Grant County* Elevation: 5,190 ft. Latitude: 32° 38' N Longitude: 107° 52' W

	JAN	FEB	MAR	APR	MAY	JUN	JUL	AUG	SEP	OCT	NOV	DEC	YEAR
Mean Maximum Temp. (°F)	56.3	60.0	66.1	74.2	82.6	91.0	90.7	87.4	83.4	74.3	63.8	55.5	73.8
Mean Temp. (°F)	41.9	45.0	50.1	56.8	65.2	73.5	75.9	73.5	68.6	59.0	48.6	41.4	58.3
Mean Minimum Temp. (°F)	27.6	30.0	34.0	39.4	47.6	55.8	61.2	59.6	53.8	43.6	33.3	27.2	42.8
Extreme Maximum Temp. (°F)	77	80	86	92	100	105	103	101	96	93	82	74	105
Extreme Minimum Temp. (°F)	6	10	9	19	31	35	46	40	30	18	10	2	2
Days Maximum Temp. ≥ 90°F	0	0	0	0	4	18	17	10	4	0	0	0	53
Days Maximum Temp. ≤ 32°F	0	0	0	0	0	0	0	0	0	0	0	0	0
Days Minimum Temp. ≤ 32°F	25	18	12	4	0	0	0	0	0	2	13	24	98
Days Minimum Temp. ≤ 0°F	0	0	0	0	0	0	0	0	0	0	0	0	0
Heating Degree Days (base 65°F)	708	559	456	245	63	3	0	0	16	193	486	725	3,454
Cooling Degree Days (base 65°F)	0	0	0	6	75	263	346	271	131	14	0	0	1,106
Mean Precipitation (in.)	0.79	0.73	0.42	0.29	0.47	0.94	2.44	3.16	1.59	1.31	0.95	1.06	14.15
Extreme Maximum Daily Precip. (in.)	1.50	1.05	0.75	0.76	1.15	2.74	2.00	2.37	2.00	2.05	1.80	1.20	2.74
Days With ≥ 0.1" Precipitation	2	2	1	1	1	2	6	7	4	3	2	3	34
Days With ≥ 0.5" Precipitation	1	0	0	0	0	1	1	2	1	1	1	1	9
Days With ≥ 1.0" Precipitation	0	0	0	0	0	0	0	1	0	0	0	0	1
Mean Snowfall (in.)	0.4	0.3	0.0	0.0	0.0	0.0	0.0	0.0	0.0	0.0	trace	1.0	1.7
Maximum Snow Depth (in.)	2	trace	0	0	0	0	0	0	0	0	trace	trace	2
Days With ≥ 1.0" Snow Depth	0	0	0	0	0	0	0	0	0	0	0	0	0

Fort Bayard *Grant County* Elevation: 6,142 ft. Latitude: 32° 48' N Longitude: 108° 09' W

	JAN	FEB	MAR	APR	MAY	JUN	JUL	AUG	SEP	OCT	NOV	DEC	YEAR
Mean Maximum Temp. (°F)	53.6	57.0	62.6	70.6	78.9	88.0	87.3	84.7	80.9	71.7	61.1	53.2	70.8
Mean Temp. (°F)	40.5	43.2	47.8	54.5	62.8	71.8	73.5	71.7	67.2	57.7	47.2	40.4	56.5
Mean Minimum Temp. (°F)	27.4	29.3	33.0	38.2	46.6	55.6	59.6	58.6	53.3	43.6	33.5	27.6	42.2
Extreme Maximum Temp. (°F)	75	79	84	95	96	106	104	97	94	89	79	73	106
Extreme Minimum Temp. (°F)	6	7	10	17	25	38	46	38	34	20	10	5	5
Days Maximum Temp. ≥ 90°F	0	0	0	0	1	12	12	5	1	0	0	0	31
Days Maximum Temp. ≤ 32°F	0	0	0	0	0	0	0	0	0	0	0	0	0
Days Minimum Temp. ≤ 32°F	24	19	15	6	1	0	0	0	0	2	13	23	103
Days Minimum Temp. ≤ 0°F	0	0	0	0	0	0	0	0	0	0	0	0	0
Heating Degree Days (base 65°F)	752	611	526	312	106	6	1	2	25	226	527	754	3,848
Cooling Degree Days (base 65°F)	0	0	0	3	43	217	270	216	96	7	0	0	852
Mean Precipitation (in.)	0.92	0.89	0.51	0.33	0.68	0.90	3.71	3.26	1.88	1.40	0.96	1.22	16.66
Extreme Maximum Daily Precip. (in.)	1.35	1.22	0.99	0.77	1.77	1.47	3.10	2.50	2.24	2.34	1.70	1.60	3.10
Days With ≥ 0.1" Precipitation	3	3	2	1	2	2	8	8	4	3	2	3	41
Days With ≥ 0.5" Precipitation	0	1	0	0	0	0	3	2	1	1	1	1	10
Days With ≥ 1.0" Precipitation	0	0	0	0	0	0	1	1	0	0	0	0	2
Mean Snowfall (in.)	0.8	0.3	trace	0.0	0.0	0.0	0.0	0.0	0.0	0.0	trace	0.8	1.9
Maximum Snow Depth (in.)	4	3	trace	0	0	0	0	0	0	0	2	6	6
Days With ≥ 1.0" Snow Depth	0	0	0	0	0	0	0	0	0	0	0	0	0

Fort Sumner *Debaca County* Elevation: 4,024 ft. Latitude: 34° 28' N Longitude: 104° 15' W

	JAN	FEB	MAR	APR	MAY	JUN	JUL	AUG	SEP	OCT	NOV	DEC	YEAR
Mean Maximum Temp. (°F)	54.4	59.1	65.9	73.5	81.2	89.2	91.4	89.3	83.0	73.4	63.3	53.9	73.1
Mean Temp. (°F)	38.8	43.0	49.6	57.1	66.0	74.4	77.6	75.9	68.8	58.0	47.3	38.4	57.9
Mean Minimum Temp. (°F)	23.1	26.8	33.1	40.7	50.8	59.6	63.8	62.5	54.6	42.7	31.3	22.8	42.6
Extreme Maximum Temp. (°F)	80	84	92	96	101	108	105	102	99	94	89	81	108
Extreme Minimum Temp. (°F)	-7	-4	4	20	30	44	51	48	32	12	5	-7	-7
Days Maximum Temp. ≥ 90°F	0	0	0	1	5	15	21	17	6	0	0	0	65
Days Maximum Temp. ≤ 32°F	1	1	0	0	0	0	0	0	0	0	0	2	4
Days Minimum Temp. ≤ 32°F	28	21	15	4	0	0	0	0	0	3	17	27	115
Days Minimum Temp. ≤ 0°F	0	0	0	0	0	0	0	0	0	0	0	0	0
Heating Degree Days (base 65°F)	806	616	473	244	63	3	0	0	33	223	525	818	3,804
Cooling Degree Days (base 65°F)	0	0	1	13	102	292	398	345	155	15	0	0	1,321
Mean Precipitation (in.)	0.48	0.49	0.68	0.95	1.32	1.71	2.31	2.80	1.79	1.75	0.62	0.64	15.54
Extreme Maximum Daily Precip. (in.)	0.60	1.05	1.38	3.95	2.86	2.20	3.15	4.10	2.99	4.07	1.20	1.20	4.10
Days With ≥ 0.1" Precipitation	2	1	2	2	3	3	4	5	3	3	2	2	32
Days With ≥ 0.5" Precipitation	0	0	0	1	1	1	1	2	1	1	0	0	8
Days With ≥ 1.0" Precipitation	0	0	0	0	0	0	0	1	0	1	0	0	2
Mean Snowfall (in.)	3.7	2.2	1.1	0.3	0.0	0.0	0.0	0.0	0.0	0.2	1.2	3.9	12.6
Maximum Snow Depth (in.)	16	10	3	3	0	0	0	0	0	4	7	12	16
Days With ≥ 1.0" Snow Depth	3	2	0	0	0	0	0	0	0	0	0	3	8

Gallup Sen Clarke Fld *Mckinley County* Elevation: 6,465 ft. Latitude: 35° 31' N Longitude: 108° 47' W

	JAN	FEB	MAR	APR	MAY	JUN	JUL	AUG	SEP	OCT	NOV	DEC	YEAR
Mean Maximum Temp. (°F)	44.8	49.5	56.3	64.8	***74.7***	***84.8***	***87.8***	***84.8***	***78.9***	67.5	54.2	***45.4***	***66.1***
Mean Temp. (°F)	29.6	34.2	39.7	46.8	***56.0***	***65.0***	***70.7***	***69.0***	***61.4***	49.3	37.6	***29.7***	***49.1***
Mean Minimum Temp. (°F)	14.3	18.9	23.1	28.8	***37.2***	***45.2***	***53.6***	***53.2***	***43.9***	31.1	20.9	***14.0***	***32.0***
Extreme Maximum Temp. (°F)	68	73	79	86	***94***	***98***	***100***	***98***	93	87	78	***66***	***100***
Extreme Minimum Temp. (°F)	-18	-19	-10	6	***20***	***23***	***31***	***37***	20	5	-6	***-34***	***-34***
Days Maximum Temp. ≥ 90°F	0	0	0	0	***0***	***7***	***12***	***5***	1	0	0	***0***	***25***
Days Maximum Temp. ≤ 32°F	2	1	0	0	***0***	***0***	***0***	***0***	0	0	1	***3***	***7***
Days Minimum Temp. ≤ 32°F	30	27	28	21	***8***	***1***	***0***	***0***	2	18	27	***30***	***192***
Days Minimum Temp. ≤ 0°F	3	1	0	0	***0***	***0***	***0***	***0***	0	0	0	***3***	***7***
Heating Degree Days (base 65°F)	1,092	864	776	538	***277***	***67***	***3***	***6***	***125***	480	816	***1,086***	***6,130***
Cooling Degree Days (base 65°F)	0	0	0	0	***5***	***74***	***187***	***138***	***25***	0	0	***0***	***429***
Mean Precipitation (in.)	0.84	0.78	0.88	0.65	***0.54***	***0.50***	***1.54***	***2.27***	***1.17***	1.05	0.87	***0.72***	***11.81***
Extreme Maximum Daily Precip. (in.)	1.22	0.77	0.76	2.36	***0.74***	***1.50***	***2.02***	***1.48***	1.76	1.08	1.25	***0.85***	***2.36***
Days With ≥ 0.1" Precipitation	3	3	3	2	***2***	***1***	***4***	***6***	3	3	3	***3***	***36***
Days With ≥ 0.5" Precipitation	0	0	0	0	***0***	***0***	***1***	***1***	1	0	0	***0***	***3***
Days With ≥ 1.0" Precipitation	0	0	0	0	***0***	***0***	***0***	***0***	0	0	0	***0***	***0***
Mean Snowfall (in.)	***6.5***	***5.9***	***4.9***	***2.6***	***0.4***	***trace***	***trace***	***trace***	***trace***	***0.8***	***4.3***	***6.0***	***31.4***
Maximum Snow Depth (in.)	***10***	***11***	***8***	***4***	***2***	***trace***	***trace***	***trace***	***trace***	***2***	***6***	***13***	***13***
Days With ≥ 1.0" Snow Depth	***7***	***3***	***2***	***1***	***0***	***0***	***0***	***0***	***0***	***0***	***2***	***6***	***21***

Gascon *Mora County* Elevation: 8,250 ft. Latitude: 35° 54' N Longitude: 105° 27' W

	JAN	FEB	MAR	APR	MAY	JUN	JUL	AUG	SEP	OCT	NOV	DEC	YEAR
Mean Maximum Temp. (°F)	43.3	44.7	48.8	55.4	64.0	73.0	75.2	72.7	68.1	59.9	50.5	43.3	58.3
Mean Temp. (°F)	29.9	31.6	35.6	41.4	49.3	57.2	60.3	58.8	53.6	45.1	36.4	30.1	44.1
Mean Minimum Temp. (°F)	16.5	18.5	22.3	27.3	34.5	41.3	45.3	44.8	39.0	30.2	22.3	16.8	29.9
Extreme Maximum Temp. (°F)	71	70	71	77	85	90	90	85	82	79	74	68	90
Extreme Minimum Temp. (°F)	-14	-17	-9	-5	14	23	35	29	20	-1	-6	-13	-17
Days Maximum Temp. ≥ 90°F	0	0	0	0	0	0	0	0	0	0	0	0	0
Days Maximum Temp. ≤ 32°F	4	3	1	1	0	0	0	0	0	0	1	5	15
Days Minimum Temp. ≤ 32°F	30	27	28	23	12	1	0	0	4	20	27	30	202
Days Minimum Temp. ≤ 0°F	2	1	0	0	0	0	0	0	0	0	0	2	5
Heating Degree Days (base 65°F)	1,081	937	904	702	481	233	144	187	335	610	851	1,075	7,540
Cooling Degree Days (base 65°F)	0	0	0	0	1	4	4	1	0	0	0	0	10
Mean Precipitation (in.)	1.13	1.25	2.03	1.99	1.87	2.19	3.85	4.25	2.23	1.72	1.29	1.37	25.17
Extreme Maximum Daily Precip. (in.)	0.98	1.73	3.48	3.83	1.83	1.96	1.68	2.40	1.58	2.31	1.82	1.51	3.83
Days With ≥ 0.1" Precipitation	3	4	4	4	5	5	8	9	5	3	3	3	56
Days With ≥ 0.5" Precipitation	1	1	1	1	1	2	3	3	1	1	1	1	17
Days With ≥ 1.0" Precipitation	0	0	0	0	0	0	1	1	0	0	0	0	2
Mean Snowfall (in.)	19.0	20.3	28.6	17.4	2.6	trace	trace	0.0	0.0	8.3	13.2	22.3	131.7
Maximum Snow Depth (in.)	24	44	31	22	5	1	trace	0	trace	20	20	25	44
Days With ≥ 1.0" Snow Depth	11	8	7	3	0	0	0	0	0	2	5	11	47

Hobbs *Lea County* Elevation: 3,615 ft. Latitude: 32° 42' N Longitude: 103° 08' W

	JAN	FEB	MAR	APR	MAY	JUN	JUL	AUG	SEP	OCT	NOV	DEC	YEAR
Mean Maximum Temp. (°F)	***56.1***	***62.6***	69.6	***78.6***	***86.8***	***94.1***	94.8	***92.5***	***85.7***	77.0	65.2	***56.2***	***76.6***
Mean Temp. (°F)	***42.9***	***48.1***	54.1	***62.8***	***71.5***	***79.0***	81.0	***79.5***	***72.6***	63.0	51.6	***43.0***	***62.4***
Mean Minimum Temp. (°F)	***29.6***	***33.6***	38.6	***46.9***	***56.1***	***63.9***	67.3	***66.4***	***59.5***	49.0	37.9	***29.7***	***48.2***
Extreme Maximum Temp. (°F)	78	***87***	92	98	107	114	108	***104***	103	98	85	80	***114***
Extreme Minimum Temp. (°F)	3	***-2***	10	25	37	46	55	***51***	37	18	9	-1	***-2***
Days Maximum Temp. ≥ 90°F	0	***0***	0	2	11	23	26	***23***	9	1	0	0	***95***
Days Maximum Temp. ≤ 32°F	1	***1***	0	0	0	0	0	***0***	0	0	0	1	***3***
Days Minimum Temp. ≤ 32°F	20	***12***	7	1	0	0	0	***0***	0	0	8	18	***66***
Days Minimum Temp. ≤ 0°F	0	***0***	0	0	0	0	0	***0***	0	0	0	0	***0***
Heating Degree Days (base 65°F)	***679***	***472***	338	***123***	***18***	***1***	0	***1***	***15***	117	398	***674***	***2,836***
Cooling Degree Days (base 65°F)	***0***	***1***	8	***64***	***225***	***428***	504	***457***	***251***	63	2	***0***	***2,003***
Mean Precipitation (in.)	***0.59***	***0.65***	0.71	0.75	2.47	1.92	2.37	***2.26***	3.04	1.33	0.73	0.74	***17.56***
Extreme Maximum Daily Precip. (in.)	***1.90***	***1.39***	2.00	***1.30***	5.20	***2.06***	4.47	***4.45***	***7.50***	5.60	2.00	1.55	***7.50***
Days With ≥ 0.1" Precipitation	***2***	***2***	1	1	3	3	4	***4***	4	2	2	2	***30***
Days With ≥ 0.5" Precipitation	***0***	***0***	1	1	2	2	1	***1***	2	1	1	1	***13***
Days With ≥ 1.0" Precipitation	***0***	***0***	0	0	1	1	1	***1***	1	0	0	0	***5***
Mean Snowfall (in.)	***1.7***	***1.0***	0.2	0.4	0.0	0.0	0.0	***0.0***	0.0	0.1	0.9	1.0	***5.3***
Maximum Snow Depth (in.)	na	***6***	trace	***0***	0	***0***	***0***	***0***	0	0	trace	***5***	na
Days With ≥ 1.0" Snow Depth	na	***0***	0	0	0	0	0	***0***	0	0	0	0	na

The period of record for all cooperative weather station data is 1980 – 2009. See User Guide for detailed explanation of data.

Jal *Lea County* Elevation: 3,060 ft. Latitude: 32° 07' N Longitude: 103° 11' W

	JAN	FEB	MAR	APR	MAY	JUN	JUL	AUG	SEP	OCT	NOV	DEC	YEAR
Mean Maximum Temp. (°F)	60.1	65.5	73.1	81.5	88.7	94.4	95.5	93.6	88.0	79.6	68.3	60.6	79.1
Mean Temp. (°F)	44.7	49.4	56.6	64.4	73.1	80.0	82.0	80.7	74.3	64.7	53.1	44.9	64.0
Mean Minimum Temp. (°F)	29.3	33.4	39.9	47.3	57.5	65.5	68.5	67.7	60.5	49.8	37.9	29.2	48.9
Extreme Maximum Temp. (°F)	82	89	94	99	107	111	110	107	105	100	89	83	111
Extreme Minimum Temp. (°F)	8	-8	10	20	28	50	59	56	37	23	13	3	-8
Days Maximum Temp. ≥ 90°F	0	0	0	5	16	24	26	24	14	3	0	0	112
Days Maximum Temp. ≤ 32°F	1	0	0	0	0	0	0	0	0	0	0	1	2
Days Minimum Temp. ≤ 32°F	21	13	5	1	0	0	0	0	0	1	9	20	70
Days Minimum Temp. ≤ 0°F	0	0	0	0	0	0	0	0	0	0	0	0	0
Heating Degree Days (base 65°F)	621	434	266	92	11	0	0	0	9	85	354	614	2,486
Cooling Degree Days (base 65°F)	0	1	13	81	270	455	535	493	294	84	4	0	2,230
Mean Precipitation (in.)	0.43	0.64	0.50	0.57	1.64	1.52	1.90	1.72	2.39	1.37	0.66	0.55	13.89
Extreme Maximum Daily Precip. (in.)	1.35	1.75	1.75	1.46	3.47	1.80	2.30	2.80	4.40	2.70	2.36	2.26	4.40
Days With ≥ 0.1" Precipitation	1	1	1	1	3	3	3	3	3	2	1	1	23
Days With ≥ 0.5" Precipitation	0	0	0	0	1	1	1	1	2	1	0	0	7
Days With ≥ 1.0" Precipitation	0	0	0	0	1	1	1	1	1	0	0	0	5
Mean Snowfall (in.)	1.1	0.5	0.2	trace	0.0	0.0	0.0	0.0	0.0	0.1	0.5	0.7	3.1
Maximum Snow Depth (in.)	15	2	3	trace	0	0	0	0	0	0	4	5	15
Days With ≥ 1.0" Snow Depth	1	0	0	0	0	0	0	0	0	0	0	0	1

Jemez Springs *Sandoval County* Elevation: 6,263 ft. Latitude: 35° 46' N Longitude: 106° 41' W

	JAN	FEB	MAR	APR	MAY	JUN	JUL	AUG	SEP	OCT	NOV	DEC	YEAR
Mean Maximum Temp. (°F)	47.5	52.1	58.8	67.4	76.5	86.7	89.0	86.0	79.8	68.9	56.1	47.0	68.0
Mean Temp. (°F)	33.8	37.9	43.6	50.7	59.4	68.6	72.4	70.4	63.7	53.1	41.8	33.5	52.4
Mean Minimum Temp. (°F)	20.1	23.7	28.4	33.9	42.2	50.4	55.8	54.7	47.6	37.2	27.5	20.1	36.8
Extreme Maximum Temp. (°F)	66	74	80	83	97	101	102	96	93	90	76	69	102
Extreme Minimum Temp. (°F)	-3	-4	3	10	19	33	41	41	26	15	7	-8	-8
Days Maximum Temp. ≥ 90°F	0	0	0	0	1	11	15	7	1	0	0	0	35
Days Maximum Temp. ≤ 32°F	1	0	0	0	0	0	0	0	0	0	0	1	2
Days Minimum Temp. ≤ 32°F	29	25	24	13	2	0	0	0	0	7	22	28	150
Days Minimum Temp. ≤ 0°F	0	0	0	0	0	0	0	0	0	0	0	0	0
Heating Degree Days (base 65°F)	960	759	656	423	185	21	1	3	75	361	687	968	5,099
Cooling Degree Days (base 65°F)	0	0	0	0	17	135	238	176	44	1	0	0	611
Mean Precipitation (in.)	1.15	0.94	1.26	1.01	0.94	0.94	2.46	2.94	1.94	1.47	1.08	1.04	17.17
Extreme Maximum Daily Precip. (in.)	1.61	1.00	1.91	1.25	1.00	1.76	1.68	2.24	2.14	1.45	1.65	2.00	2.24
Days With ≥ 0.1" Precipitation	3	3	3	2	3	3	6	7	5	3	3	3	44
Days With ≥ 0.5" Precipitation	1	0	1	1	1	0	2	2	1	1	0	1	11
Days With ≥ 1.0" Precipitation	0	0	0	0	0	0	0	1	0	0	0	0	1
Mean Snowfall (in.)	8.8	6.0	4.4	2.2	trace	trace	0.0	0.0	0.0	0.3	2.7	6.5	30.9
Maximum Snow Depth (in.)	20	13	10	8	trace	trace	0	0	0	3	5	14	20
Days With ≥ 1.0" Snow Depth	9	4	1	0	0	0	0	0	0	0	1	6	21

Jornada Exp Range *Dona Ana County* Elevation: 4,266 ft. Latitude: 32° 37' N Longitude: 106° 44' W

	JAN	FEB	MAR	APR	MAY	JUN	JUL	AUG	SEP	OCT	NOV	DEC	YEAR
Mean Maximum Temp. (°F)	***56.8***	***62.4***	68.9	76.9	***85.5***	94.1	***94.7***	91.6	86.4	***77.4***	65.6	***56.4***	***76.4***
Mean Temp. (°F)	***39.0***	***43.8***	50.0	57.2	***66.1***	75.0	***78.9***	***76.7***	70.1	***58.8***	46.8	***39.0***	***58.5***
Mean Minimum Temp. (°F)	***21.0***	***25.3***	30.9	37.5	***46.7***	55.8	***63.0***	61.6	53.7	***40.1***	28.0	***21.6***	***40.4***
Extreme Maximum Temp. (°F)	74	83	89	94	103	110	107	104	100	96	85	76	110
Extreme Minimum Temp. (°F)	-11	6	5	14	28	36	47	50	36	19	8	-12	-12
Days Maximum Temp. ≥ 90°F	0	0	0	1	8	23	23	20	10	1	0	0	86
Days Maximum Temp. ≤ 32°F	0	0	0	0	0	0	0	0	0	0	0	0	0
Days Minimum Temp. ≤ 32°F	26	20	17	8	1	0	0	0	0	5	19	25	121
Days Minimum Temp. ≤ 0°F	0	0	0	0	0	0	0	0	0	0	0	0	0
Heating Degree Days (base 65°F)	***800***	***591***	460	237	***51***	3	***0***	***0***	14	***201***	538	***798***	***3,693***
Cooling Degree Days (base 65°F)	***0***	***0***	0	9	***93***	309	***438***	***369***	174	***17***	0	***0***	***1,409***
Mean Precipitation (in.)	0.55	0.45	0.27	0.30	0.55	0.86	2.15	2.44	1.40	0.99	0.58	0.85	11.39
Extreme Maximum Daily Precip. (in.)	0.59	0.59	***0.63***	0.39	1.15	***1.20***	2.25	2.19	***1.38***	2.00	1.11	1.27	***2.25***
Days With ≥ 0.1" Precipitation	2	1	1	1	1	2	5	5	3	2	1	2	26
Days With ≥ 0.5" Precipitation	0	0	0	0	0	0	1	1	1	0	0	0	3
Days With ≥ 1.0" Precipitation	0	0	0	0	0	0	0	0	0	0	0	0	0
Mean Snowfall (in.)	0.7	0.3	0.1	0.0	0.0	0.0	0.0	0.0	0.0	0.0	0.0	1.0	2.1
Maximum Snow Depth (in.)	6	3	2	0	0	0	0	0	0	0	0	8	8
Days With ≥ 1.0" Snow Depth	0	0	0	0	0	0	0	0	0	0	0	1	1

Las Vegas Sewage Plant *San Miguel County* Elevation: 6,349 ft. Latitude: 35° 32' N Longitude: 105° 12' W

	JAN	FEB	MAR	APR	MAY	JUN	JUL	AUG	SEP	OCT	NOV	DEC	YEAR
Mean Maximum Temp. (°F)	***49.3***	***52.2***	***59.0***	***66.1***	74.9	82.8	85.6	83.2	77.8	68.3	57.4	48.5	***67.1***
Mean Temp. (°F)	***30.5***	***34.0***	***39.8***	***47.0***	***55.5***	63.8	***68.0***	66.5	59.6	48.8	***38.8***	29.8	***48.5***
Mean Minimum Temp. (°F)	***11.4***	***15.7***	***21.0***	27.9	***36.4***	44.7	***50.4***	49.8	41.5	29.3	***19.8***	11.2	***29.9***
Extreme Maximum Temp. (°F)	***72***	***74***	***80***	86	98	98	107	95	98	87	81	74	***107***
Extreme Minimum Temp. (°F)	***-21***	***-29***	***-17***	***10***	***19***	***28***	33	36	20	-2	***-12***	-32	***-32***
Days Maximum Temp. ≥ 90°F	***0***	***0***	***0***	0	1	5	7	3	0	0	0	0	***16***
Days Maximum Temp. ≤ 32°F	***2***	***1***	***0***	0	0	0	0	0	0	0	1	3	***7***
Days Minimum Temp. ≤ 32°F	***30***	***27***	***28***	22	***8***	1	0	0	3	21	***27***	30	***197***
Days Minimum Temp. ≤ 0°F	***3***	***1***	***0***	0	***0***	0	0	0	0	0	***0***	3	***7***
Heating Degree Days (base 65°F)	***1,061***	***870***	***778***	***532***	***289***	74	***8***	21	162	495	***779***	1,082	***6,151***
Cooling Degree Days (base 65°F)	***0***	***0***	***0***	***0***	***3***	45	***107***	75	8	0	***0***	0	***238***
Mean Precipitation (in.)	0.60	***0.48***	0.62	0.86	1.66	2.08	3.15	3.67	2.26	1.50	0.62	0.63	***18.13***
Extreme Maximum Daily Precip. (in.)	1.15	***1.27***	1.33	1.95	1.88	2.00	2.28	2.02	2.76	3.00	1.51	0.80	***3.00***
Days With ≥ 0.1" Precipitation	2	***1***	2	2	4	5	7	8	4	3	2	2	***42***
Days With ≥ 0.5" Precipitation	0	***0***	0	1	1	2	2	2	1	1	0	0	***10***
Days With ≥ 1.0" Precipitation	0	***0***	0	0	0	0	0	1	1	0	0	0	***2***
Mean Snowfall (in.)	***5.8***	***4.3***	2.9	1.3	trace	0.0	0.0	0.0	0.0	1.0	3.0	***4.5***	***22.8***
Maximum Snow Depth (in.)	***20***	na	***21***	***2***	***trace***	***0***	***0***	***0***	***0***	***10***	***8***	***7***	na
Days With ≥ 1.0" Snow Depth	***2***	***1***	1	0	0	0	0	0	0	0	1	***2***	7

The period of record for all cooperative weather station data is 1980 – 2009. See User Guide for detailed explanation of data.

Los Alamos *Los Alamos County* Elevation: 7,423 ft. Latitude: 35° 52' N Longitude: 106° 19' W

	JAN	FEB	MAR	APR	MAY	JUN	JUL	AUG	SEP	OCT	NOV	DEC	YEAR
Mean Maximum Temp. (°F)	40.1	44.1	51.3	59.7	69.1	78.9	81.5	78.1	72.2	61.4	49.1	39.9	60.4
Mean Temp. (°F)	29.6	33.3	39.4	46.7	55.9	65.1	68.3	65.8	59.8	49.1	37.9	29.5	48.4
Mean Minimum Temp. (°F)	19.1	22.3	27.4	33.6	42.6	51.3	55.0	53.5	47.2	36.7	26.7	19.2	36.2
Extreme Maximum Temp. (°F)	60	69	73	79	92	95	94	91	89	84	71	64	95
Extreme Minimum Temp. (°F)	-4	-9	0	8	25	33	40	31	25	6	1	-11	-11
Days Maximum Temp. ≥ 90°F	0	0	0	0	0	1	2	0	0	0	0	0	3
Days Maximum Temp. ≤ 32°F	6	3	1	0	0	0	0	0	0	0	1	6	17
Days Minimum Temp. ≤ 32°F	30	27	24	13	3	0	0	0	0	7	23	30	157
Days Minimum Temp. ≤ 0°F	0	0	0	0	0	0	0	0	0	0	0	1	1
Heating Degree Days (base 65°F)	1,090	891	788	542	285	67	13	32	163	487	805	1,092	6,255
Cooling Degree Days (base 65°F)	0	0	0	0	9	77	122	65	12	0	0	0	285
Mean Precipitation (in.)	0.96	0.85	1.20	1.06	1.40	1.50	2.70	3.55	2.01	1.52	1.00	0.98	18.73
Extreme Maximum Daily Precip. (in.)	1.20	0.97	1.33	1.45	1.05	2.16	1.56	2.04	1.65	1.97	1.39	1.23	2.16
Days With ≥ 0.1" Precipitation	2	3	3	3	4	3	7	9	5	4	2	3	48
Days With ≥ 0.5" Precipitation	1	0	1	1	1	1	2	2	1	1	1	0	12
Days With ≥ 1.0" Precipitation	0	0	0	0	0	0	0	0	0	0	0	0	0
Mean Snowfall (in.)	13.3	10.3	9.8	3.8	0.3	0.0	0.0	0.0	trace	2.4	5.0	11.6	56.5
Maximum Snow Depth (in.)	40	20	15	8	1	0	0	0	trace	12	8	22	40
Days With ≥ 1.0" Snow Depth	20	14	4	1	0	0	0	0	0	1	3	14	57

Los Lunas 3 SSW *Valencia County* Elevation: 4,839 ft. Latitude: 34° 46' N Longitude: 106° 45' W

	JAN	FEB	MAR	APR	MAY	JUN	JUL	AUG	SEP	OCT	NOV	DEC	YEAR
Mean Maximum Temp. (°F)	52.7	59.1	66.3	74.2	82.9	91.9	94.1	91.4	85.5	74.4	61.9	51.8	73.8
Mean Temp. (°F)	35.8	41.1	47.9	55.3	64.4	73.0	77.3	75.4	68.0	56.1	44.0	35.4	56.2
Mean Minimum Temp. (°F)	18.8	23.1	29.6	36.4	45.9	54.0	60.5	59.4	50.6	37.7	26.1	18.9	38.4
Extreme Maximum Temp. (°F)	75	81	87	93	102	107	105	103	100	93	83	74	107
Extreme Minimum Temp. (°F)	-10	3	4	16	28	37	45	44	31	15	3	-5	-10
Days Maximum Temp. ≥ 90°F	0	0	0	0	6	21	26	21	8	0	0	0	82
Days Maximum Temp. ≤ 32°F	0	0	0	0	0	0	0	0	0	0	0	1	1
Days Minimum Temp. ≤ 32°F	30	25	20	9	1	0	0	0	0	7	24	29	145
Days Minimum Temp. ≤ 0°F	0	0	0	0	0	0	0	0	0	0	0	0	0
Heating Degree Days (base 65°F)	900	669	522	286	78	4	0	1	26	274	623	911	4,294
Cooling Degree Days (base 65°F)	0	0	0	3	65	251	389	330	124	5	0	0	1,167
Mean Precipitation (in.)	0.45	0.44	0.62	0.57	0.56	0.59	1.41	1.70	1.32	1.06	0.59	0.55	9.86
Extreme Maximum Daily Precip. (in.)	0.62	0.64	1.64	1.36	0.81	1.05	1.79	2.41	2.20	1.31	1.27	0.89	2.41
Days With ≥ 0.1" Precipitation	2	2	2	2	2	2	4	4	3	3	1	2	29
Days With ≥ 0.5" Precipitation	0	0	0	0	0	0	1	1	1	1	0	0	4
Days With ≥ 1.0" Precipitation	0	0	0	0	0	0	0	0	0	0	0	0	0
Mean Snowfall (in.)	1.7	0.8	0.3	0.3	0.0	0.0	0.0	0.0	0.0	0.3	0.4	2.4	6.2
Maximum Snow Depth (in.)	5	5	2	3	0	0	0	0	0	0	3	6	6
Days With ≥ 1.0" Snow Depth	0	0	0	0	0	0	0	0	0	0	0	1	1

Maxwell 3 NW *Colfax County* Elevation: 6,019 ft. Latitude: 36° 34' N Longitude: 104° 34' W

	JAN	FEB	MAR	APR	MAY	JUN	JUL	AUG	SEP	OCT	NOV	DEC	YEAR
Mean Maximum Temp. (°F)	46.8	51.1	57.9	65.6	73.9	82.1	86.5	84.3	78.3	68.5	56.4	47.2	66.5
Mean Temp. (°F)	29.9	33.4	40.4	47.7	56.7	64.8	69.6	68.2	61.4	50.5	39.3	30.3	49.4
Mean Minimum Temp. (°F)	12.9	15.7	22.9	29.8	39.5	47.5	52.7	52.1	44.4	32.4	22.3	13.4	32.1
Extreme Maximum Temp. (°F)	73	78	84	88	98	100	100	***97***	95	89	86	77	***100***
Extreme Minimum Temp. (°F)	-20	-26	-9	6	19	32	39	40	20	-3	-7	-20	-26
Days Maximum Temp. ≥ 90°F	0	0	0	0	1	6	10	6	1	0	0	0	24
Days Maximum Temp. ≤ 32°F	4	2	1	0	0	0	0	0	0	0	1	4	12
Days Minimum Temp. ≤ 32°F	30	27	28	19	5	0	0	0	1	15	27	31	183
Days Minimum Temp. ≤ 0°F	2	2	0	0	0	0	0	0	0	0	0	3	7
Heating Degree Days (base 65°F)	1,083	883	756	511	257	63	5	12	126	443	761	1,064	5,964
Cooling Degree Days (base 65°F)	0	0	0	0	8	64	156	120	24	0	0	0	372
Mean Precipitation (in.)	0.41	0.29	0.66	0.82	2.09	2.30	2.34	2.98	1.80	0.95	0.45	0.31	15.40
Extreme Maximum Daily Precip. (in.)	0.80	0.69	1.50	1.55	***1.52***	2.18	4.67	***2.63***	1.91	1.94	1.25	1.10	***4.67***
Days With ≥ 0.1" Precipitation	1	1	2	2	4	5	4	6	3	2	1	1	32
Days With ≥ 0.5" Precipitation	0	0	0	0	1	2	1	2	1	1	0	0	8
Days With ≥ 1.0" Precipitation	0	0	0	0	0	0	1	0	0	0	0	0	1
Mean Snowfall (in.)	***5.4***	4.1	3.4	1.4	0.3	0.0	0.0	0.0	trace	1.0	2.5	4.0	***22.1***
Maximum Snow Depth (in.)	***20***	***12***	***13***	***4***	***3***	***0***	***0***	***0***	***0***	***6***	***6***	***10***	***20***
Days With ≥ 1.0" Snow Depth	***3***	3	1	0	0	0	0	0	0	0	1	***2***	***10***

McGaffey 5 SE *Mckinley County* Elevation: 8,000 ft. Latitude: 35° 20' N Longitude: 108° 27' W

	JAN	FEB	MAR	APR	MAY	JUN	JUL	AUG	SEP	OCT	NOV	DEC	YEAR
Mean Maximum Temp. (°F)	40.8	42.8	48.8	56.8	67.2	77.6	81.0	77.7	72.8	63.3	51.0	41.4	60.1
Mean Temp. (°F)	24.5	27.4	33.3	40.4	49.4	58.2	63.7	62.0	55.6	45.3	33.8	25.1	43.2
Mean Minimum Temp. (°F)	8.2	11.9	17.8	24.0	31.5	38.8	46.3	46.2	38.4	27.2	16.6	8.8	26.3
Extreme Maximum Temp. (°F)	69	65	72	80	88	97	98	92	88	83	74	65	98
Extreme Minimum Temp. (°F)	-25	-25	-14	-1	10	15	28	32	18	0	-15	-30	-30
Days Maximum Temp. ≥ 90°F	0	0	0	0	0	1	2	0	0	0	0	0	3
Days Maximum Temp. ≤ 32°F	5	4	1	0	0	0	0	0	0	0	1	5	16
Days Minimum Temp. ≤ 32°F	31	28	30	27	16	4	0	0	6	24	29	31	226
Days Minimum Temp. ≤ 0°F	8	4	1	0	0	0	0	0	0	0	2	7	22
Heating Degree Days (base 65°F)	1,249	1,057	975	731	477	205	65	100	276	606	931	1,231	7,903
Cooling Degree Days (base 65°F)	0	0	0	0	0	8	30	12	1	0	0	0	51
Mean Precipitation (in.)	1.82	1.75	1.97	1.29	0.96	0.72	2.43	3.23	1.82	1.40	1.74	1.68	20.81
Extreme Maximum Daily Precip. (in.)	1.95	1.83	2.20	1.35	2.10	1.12	1.75	2.60	1.42	***2.25***	1.80	1.98	***2.60***
Days With ≥ 0.1" Precipitation	4	4	5	4	3	2	7	8	5	3	4	4	53
Days With ≥ 0.5" Precipitation	1	1	1	1	1	0	1	2	1	1	1	1	12
Days With ≥ 1.0" Precipitation	0	0	0	0	0	0	0	0	0	0	0	0	0
Mean Snowfall (in.)	10.8	***10.0***	8.4	3.0	0.1	trace	0.0	0.0	0.1	2.1	5.9	9.9	***50.3***
Maximum Snow Depth (in.)	***33***	na	***22***	***8***	trace	trace	0	0	0	15	***15***	***13***	na
Days With ≥ 1.0" Snow Depth	***4***	***2***	***2***	1	0	0	0	0	0	0	1	***3***	***13***

The period of record for all cooperative weather station data is 1980 – 2009. See User Guide for detailed explanation of data.

Melrose *Curry County* Elevation: 4,598 ft. Latitude: 34° 26' N Longitude: 103° 37' W

	JAN	FEB	MAR	APR	MAY	JUN	JUL	AUG	SEP	OCT	NOV	DEC	YEAR
Mean Maximum Temp. (°F)	53.3	58.4	65.5	74.2	82.7	90.5	92.1	89.6	83.9	73.8	62.0	52.9	73.2
Mean Temp. (°F)	39.1	43.0	49.4	57.3	66.7	75.0	77.8	76.1	69.5	58.9	47.4	38.9	58.3
Mean Minimum Temp. (°F)	24.9	27.6	33.1	40.4	50.6	59.5	63.5	62.6	55.1	44.0	32.7	25.0	43.2
Extreme Maximum Temp. (°F)	78	81	90	96	103	108	107	105	101	96	86	77	108
Extreme Minimum Temp. (°F)	-4	-8	5	20	30	43	51	51	30	12	8	-6	-8
Days Maximum Temp. ≥ 90°F	0	0	0	0	7	17	22	17	6	1	0	0	70
Days Maximum Temp. ≤ 32°F	2	1	0	0	0	0	0	0	0	0	0	2	5
Days Minimum Temp. ≤ 32°F	26	20	14	4	0	0	0	0	0	2	14	26	106
Days Minimum Temp. ≤ 0°F	0	0	0	0	0	0	0	0	0	0	0	0	0
Heating Degree Days (base 65°F)	796	614	479	237	56	2	0	0	25	203	522	801	3,735
Cooling Degree Days (base 65°F)	0	0	1	13	116	309	404	352	168	21	0	0	1,384
Mean Precipitation (in.)	0.46	0.42	0.83	0.92	1.74	2.19	2.56	3.22	1.83	1.95	0.57	0.62	17.31
Extreme Maximum Daily Precip. (in.)	0.89	0.68	1.55	1.84	2.66	2.36	2.92	4.10	2.68	4.49	1.12	0.85	4.49
Days With ≥ 0.1" Precipitation	1	1	2	2	3	5	5	6	4	3	2	2	36
Days With ≥ 0.5" Precipitation	0	0	1	1	1	1	2	2	1	1	0	0	10
Days With ≥ 1.0" Precipitation	0	0	0	0	0	0	1	0	0	1	0	0	2
Mean Snowfall (in.)	3.4	2.3	1.3	1.0	trace	0.0	0.0	0.0	0.0	0.4	1.6	4.1	14.1
Maximum Snow Depth (in.)	11	8	6	4	trace	0	0	0	0	3	4	14	14
Days With ≥ 1.0" Snow Depth	3	1	0	0	0	0	0	0	0	0	1	2	7

Mosquero 1 NE *Harding County* Elevation: 5,464 ft. Latitude: 35° 48' N Longitude: 103° 56' W

	JAN	FEB	MAR	APR	MAY	JUN	JUL	AUG	SEP	OCT	NOV	DEC	YEAR
Mean Maximum Temp. (°F)	48.6	52.8	60.2	69.0	77.3	85.8	88.7	85.4	79.7	69.7	57.3	47.6	68.5
Mean Temp. (°F)	34.3	37.7	44.3	52.1	61.1	70.0	73.9	71.7	65.3	54.3	42.6	33.9	53.4
Mean Minimum Temp. (°F)	19.9	22.5	28.3	35.1	44.9	54.2	59.1	58.0	50.8	38.8	27.9	20.1	38.3
Extreme Maximum Temp. (°F)	74	82	86	94	100	103	102	104	98	93	82	78	104
Extreme Minimum Temp. (°F)	-14	-12	-1	8	20	36	43	43	22	0	-5	-14	-14
Days Maximum Temp. ≥ 90°F	0	0	0	0	2	11	15	8	2	0	0	0	38
Days Maximum Temp. ≤ 32°F	3	2	0	0	0	0	0	0	0	0	1	3	9
Days Minimum Temp. ≤ 32°F	29	25	21	11	1	0	0	0	0	6	21	29	143
Days Minimum Temp. ≤ 0°F	1	1	0	0	0	0	0	0	0	0	0	1	3
Heating Degree Days (base 65°F)	945	766	636	384	152	18	1	4	65	329	664	958	4,922
Cooling Degree Days (base 65°F)	0	0	0	2	38	176	285	218	79	3	0	0	801
Mean Precipitation (in.)	0.40	0.35	0.88	1.04	1.79	2.27	2.58	3.20	1.94	1.19	0.74	0.53	16.91
Extreme Maximum Daily Precip. (in.)	1.01	0.85	1.17	2.75	2.06	4.06	2.56	2.99	2.94	2.30	1.62	1.04	4.06
Days With ≥ 0.1" Precipitation	1	1	2	2	4	5	5	6	3	2	2	2	35
Days With ≥ 0.5" Precipitation	0	0	1	1	1	1	2	2	1	1	0	0	10
Days With ≥ 1.0" Precipitation	0	0	0	0	0	0	1	1	0	0	0	0	2
Mean Snowfall (in.)	3.7	3.1	4.0	1.7	0.6	0.0	0.0	0.0	trace	1.0	3.4	5.1	22.6
Maximum Snow Depth (in.)	13	9	14	8	2	0	0	0	trace	5	8	12	14
Days With ≥ 1.0" Snow Depth	5	3	1	0	0	0	0	0	0	0	2	6	17

Mountain Park *Otero County* Elevation: 6,779 ft. Latitude: 32° 57' N Longitude: 105° 49' W

	JAN	FEB	MAR	APR	MAY	JUN	JUL	AUG	SEP	OCT	NOV	DEC	YEAR
Mean Maximum Temp. (°F)	49.8	53.2	59.3	67.0	74.7	82.6	81.6	79.3	75.4	67.2	57.1	49.9	66.4
Mean Temp. (°F)	38.5	41.2	45.8	52.6	60.5	68.7	69.5	67.8	63.5	54.7	45.1	38.5	53.8
Mean Minimum Temp. (°F)	27.1	29.1	32.2	38.2	46.2	54.6	57.3	56.3	51.4	42.1	33.0	27.0	41.2
Extreme Maximum Temp. (°F)	70	71	80	85	93	96	96	92	89	85	76	70	96
Extreme Minimum Temp. (°F)	3	2	7	15	24	37	46	47	36	15	9	-3	-3
Days Maximum Temp. ≥ 90°F	0	0	0	0	0	3	2	0	0	0	0	0	5
Days Maximum Temp. ≤ 32°F	1	0	0	0	0	0	0	0	0	0	0	1	2
Days Minimum Temp. ≤ 32°F	24	19	16	7	1	0	0	0	0	3	14	24	108
Days Minimum Temp. ≤ 0°F	0	0	0	0	0	0	0	0	0	0	0	0	0
Heating Degree Days (base 65°F)	815	666	589	366	158	19	5	12	76	315	591	815	4,427
Cooling Degree Days (base 65°F)	0	0	0	1	25	136	150	107	36	2	0	0	457
Mean Precipitation (in.)	1.01	1.22	0.99	0.64	1.07	1.25	3.51	4.11	2.59	1.83	1.20	1.61	21.03
Extreme Maximum Daily Precip. (in.)	1.20	1.27	1.26	0.97	1.55	1.46	2.70	2.62	2.34	2.38	1.76	1.46	2.70
Days With ≥ 0.1" Precipitation	3	4	3	2	3	3	8	9	5	3	3	3	49
Days With ≥ 0.5" Precipitation	1	1	1	1	1	1	2	3	2	1	1	1	16
Days With ≥ 1.0" Precipitation	0	0	0	0	0	0	0	1	1	0	0	0	2
Mean Snowfall (in.)	3.1	4.6	2.8	1.1	trace	0.0	0.0	0.0	0.0	0.9	1.8	5.8	20.1
Maximum Snow Depth (in.)	10	9	9	4	trace	0	0	0	0	1	8	14	14
Days With ≥ 1.0" Snow Depth	2	2	1	0	0	0	0	0	0	0	0	3	8

Orogrande *Otero County* Elevation: 4,182 ft. Latitude: 32° 23' N Longitude: 106° 06' W

	JAN	FEB	MAR	APR	MAY	JUN	JUL	AUG	SEP	OCT	NOV	DEC	YEAR
Mean Maximum Temp. (°F)	***57.5***	62.9	***70.0***	***78.1***	***87.2***	***95.9***	***95.6***	***92.7***	***87.7***	***77.8***	***65.8***	***57.1***	***77.4***
Mean Temp. (°F)	***42.9***	47.8	***53.8***	***61.4***	***70.0***	***79.0***	***80.5***	***78.3***	***73.3***	***62.6***	***50.6***	***42.6***	***61.9***
Mean Minimum Temp. (°F)	***28.3***	32.6	***37.4***	***44.6***	***52.9***	***62.0***	***65.3***	***63.9***	***58.8***	***47.2***	***35.4***	***28.0***	***46.4***
Extreme Maximum Temp. (°F)	***78***	82	***90***	***97***	***103***	***110***	***109***	***106***	***103***	***98***	***85***	***75***	***110***
Extreme Minimum Temp. (°F)	***10***	6	***15***	***22***	***35***	***45***	***40***	***36***	***40***	***21***	***13***	***2***	***2***
Days Maximum Temp. ≥ 90°F	***0***	0	***0***	***1***	***11***	***26***	***27***	***24***	***12***	***1***	***0***	***0***	***102***
Days Maximum Temp. ≤ 32°F	***0***	0	***0***	***0***	***0***	***0***	***0***	***0***	***0***	***0***	***0***	***0***	***0***
Days Minimum Temp. ≤ 32°F	***22***	14	***7***	***2***	***0***	***0***	***0***	***0***	***0***	***1***	***10***	***23***	***79***
Days Minimum Temp. ≤ 0°F	***0***	0	***0***	***0***	***0***	***0***	***0***	***0***	***0***	***0***	***0***	***0***	***0***
Heating Degree Days (base 65°F)	***678***	480	***344***	***142***	***20***	***0***	***0***	***0***	***6***	***114***	***425***	***689***	***2,898***
Cooling Degree Days (base 65°F)	***0***	0	***2***	***41***	***181***	***425***	***486***	***429***	***262***	***44***	***1***	***0***	***1,871***
Mean Precipitation (in.)	***0.46***	0.47	***0.27***	***0.27***	***0.58***	***1.24***	***1.88***	***2.49***	***1.73***	***1.25***	***0.65***	***1.03***	***12.32***
Extreme Maximum Daily Precip. (in.)	***0.75***	***0.77***	***0.60***	***0.63***	***1.75***	***2.90***	***2.50***	***3.08***	***1.72***	***2.70***	***1.90***	***1.20***	***3.08***
Days With ≥ 0.1" Precipitation	***1***	1	***1***	***1***	***1***	***2***	***4***	***5***	***4***	***3***	***2***	***2***	***27***
Days With ≥ 0.5" Precipitation	***0***	0	***0***	***0***	***0***	***1***	***1***	***2***	***1***	***1***	***0***	***1***	***7***
Days With ≥ 1.0" Precipitation	***0***	0	***0***	***0***	***0***	***0***	***0***	***1***	***0***	***0***	***0***	***0***	***1***
Mean Snowfall (in.)	***1.2***	0.3	***trace***	***0.4***	***0.0***	***0.0***	***0.0***	***0.0***	***0.0***	***0.1***	***0.0***	***1.2***	***3.2***
Maximum Snow Depth (in.)	***4***	***7***	***trace***	***0***	***0***	***0***	***0***	***0***	***0***	***trace***	***0***	***3***	***7***
Days With ≥ 1.0" Snow Depth	***0***	***0***	***0***	***0***	***0***	***0***	***0***	***0***	***0***	***0***	***0***	***0***	***0***

The period of record for all cooperative weather station data is 1980 – 2009. See User Guide for detailed explanation of data.

Portales *Roosevelt County* Elevation: 4,009 ft. Latitude: 34° 10' N Longitude: 103° 21' W

	JAN	FEB	MAR	APR	MAY	JUN	JUL	AUG	SEP	OCT	NOV	DEC	YEAR
Mean Maximum Temp. (°F)	54.3	59.5	66.8	75.4	83.8	91.1	92.1	89.6	84.5	74.7	62.8	53.5	74.0
Mean Temp. (°F)	39.2	43.4	49.9	58.2	67.5	75.8	78.2	76.5	70.2	59.4	47.4	38.8	58.7
Mean Minimum Temp. (°F)	24.0	27.2	33.0	40.9	51.2	60.5	64.4	63.3	55.8	43.9	32.0	24.0	43.4
Extreme Maximum Temp. (°F)	76	82	87	93	103	108	105	105	100	95	85	76	108
Extreme Minimum Temp. (°F)	-9	0	6	10	30	43	50	50	29	12	10	-8	-9
Days Maximum Temp. ≥ 90°F	0	0	0	1	8	18	22	18	7	0	0	0	74
Days Maximum Temp. ≤ 32°F	1	1	0	0	0	0	0	0	0	0	0	2	4
Days Minimum Temp. ≤ 32°F	27	21	14	4	0	0	0	0	0	3	16	26	111
Days Minimum Temp. ≤ 0°F	0	0	0	0	0	0	0	0	0	0	0	0	0
Heating Degree Days (base 65°F)	794	603	462	215	46	1	0	1	21	190	521	806	3,660
Cooling Degree Days (base 65°F)	0	0	1	18	131	332	417	364	182	22	0	0	1,467
Mean Precipitation (in.)	0.56	0.39	0.79	0.70	1.59	2.51	2.41	3.18	1.99	1.64	0.68	0.71	17.15
Extreme Maximum Daily Precip. (in.)	1.90	0.55	1.61	1.30	2.00	2.75	2.80	4.40	2.10	2.42	2.02	1.53	4.40
Days With ≥ 0.1" Precipitation	1	1	2	2	3	5	5	6	4	3	2	2	36
Days With ≥ 0.5" Precipitation	0	0	1	0	1	2	2	2	1	1	0	0	10
Days With ≥ 1.0" Precipitation	0	0	0	0	0	1	1	1	0	0	0	0	3
Mean Snowfall (in.)	1.3	1.4	0.7	0.2	0.0	0.0	0.0	0.0	0.0	0.1	0.7	2.6	7.0
Maximum Snow Depth (in.)	8	5	6	2	0	0	0	0	0	2	5	5	8
Days With ≥ 1.0" Snow Depth	1	1	0	0	0	0	0	0	0	0	0	1	3

State University *Dona Ana County* Elevation: 3,880 ft. Latitude: 32° 17' N Longitude: 106° 46' W

	JAN	FEB	MAR	APR	MAY	JUN	JUL	AUG	SEP	OCT	NOV	DEC	YEAR
Mean Maximum Temp. (°F)	58.7	63.6	70.1	77.6	86.7	94.9	95.1	92.1	87.6	78.4	67.2	57.8	77.5
Mean Temp. (°F)	44.1	48.3	54.2	61.3	70.3	78.8	81.6	79.4	73.7	62.9	51.5	43.4	62.4
Mean Minimum Temp. (°F)	29.3	32.9	38.3	44.8	53.8	62.5	68.1	66.7	59.7	47.3	35.8	29.1	47.4
Extreme Maximum Temp. (°F)	77	84	90	96	104	110	107	104	100	95	87	77	110
Extreme Minimum Temp. (°F)	8	12	17	27	36	44	55	58	45	26	17	5	5
Days Maximum Temp. ≥ 90°F	0	0	0	1	10	25	27	23	12	2	0	0	100
Days Maximum Temp. ≤ 32°F	0	0	0	0	0	0	0	0	0	0	0	0	0
Days Minimum Temp. ≤ 32°F	23	14	5	1	0	0	0	0	0	1	9	23	76
Days Minimum Temp. ≤ 0°F	0	0	0	0	0	0	0	0	0	0	0	0	0
Heating Degree Days (base 65°F)	643	466	330	137	17	0	0	0	3	111	399	662	2,768
Cooling Degree Days (base 65°F)	0	0	2	31	187	420	522	454	270	52	1	0	1,939
Mean Precipitation (in.)	0.50	0.42	0.23	0.30	0.42	0.64	1.40	2.22	1.36	0.95	0.46	0.77	9.67
Extreme Maximum Daily Precip. (in.)	0.80	0.95	0.60	0.75	0.93	2.26	3.13	2.09	2.89	1.66	1.17	1.23	3.13
Days With ≥ 0.1" Precipitation	2	1	1	1	1	2	4	5	3	3	1	2	26
Days With ≥ 0.5" Precipitation	0	0	0	0	0	0	1	1	1	1	0	0	4
Days With ≥ 1.0" Precipitation	0	0	0	0	0	0	0	0	0	0	0	0	0
Mean Snowfall (in.)	0.8	0.4	trace	0.2	0.0	0.0	0.0	0.0	0.0	trace	0.1	1.3	2.8
Maximum Snow Depth (in.)	9	4	1	5	0	0	0	0	0	0	2	6	9
Days With ≥ 1.0" Snow Depth	1	0	0	0	0	0	0	0	0	0	0	1	2

Tatum *Lea County* Elevation: 4,100 ft. Latitude: 33° 16' N Longitude: 103° 19' W

	JAN	FEB	MAR	APR	MAY	JUN	JUL	AUG	SEP	OCT	NOV	DEC	YEAR
Mean Maximum Temp. (°F)	54.6	59.3	66.5	74.4	83.0	91.0	91.8	90.4	84.1	74.9	63.5	54.4	74.0
Mean Temp. (°F)	39.1	42.9	49.3	56.9	66.7	75.2	77.4	76.1	69.3	59.1	47.5	39.1	58.2
Mean Minimum Temp. (°F)	23.4	26.5	32.1	39.3	50.3	59.4	62.9	61.8	54.4	43.2	31.4	23.9	42.4
Extreme Maximum Temp. (°F)	81	86	92	97	107	115	109	104	103	98	85	79	115
Extreme Minimum Temp. (°F)	-1	0	5	17	27	42	49	50	32	11	4	-8	-8
Days Maximum Temp. ≥ 90°F	0	0	0	1	8	18	21	19	8	1	0	0	76
Days Maximum Temp. ≤ 32°F	2	1	0	0	0	0	0	0	0	0	0	2	5
Days Minimum Temp. ≤ 32°F	28	22	16	6	0	0	0	0	0	2	16	27	117
Days Minimum Temp. ≤ 0°F	0	0	0	0	0	0	0	0	0	0	0	0	0
Heating Degree Days (base 65°F)	797	617	481	254	63	3	1	1	33	203	520	795	3,768
Cooling Degree Days (base 65°F)	0	0	1	16	121	316	392	353	168	25	1	0	1,393
Mean Precipitation (in.)	0.39	0.37	0.76	0.59	2.17	1.96	2.29	2.34	2.72	1.50	0.80	0.62	16.51
Extreme Maximum Daily Precip. (in.)	0.75	0.80	1.83	2.23	2.96	3.14	3.14	2.40	4.80	***5.55***	1.15	1.32	***5.55***
Days With ≥ 0.1" Precipitation	1	1	1	1	3	4	4	4	4	3	2	2	30
Days With ≥ 0.5" Precipitation	0	0	1	0	1	1	2	1	2	1	0	0	9
Days With ≥ 1.0" Precipitation	0	0	0	0	1	0	1	1	1	0	0	0	4
Mean Snowfall (in.)	1.0	1.0	0.4	0.6	0.0	0.0	0.0	0.0	0.0	0.1	0.8	***1.2***	***5.1***
Maximum Snow Depth (in.)	4	***3***	2	2	0	0	0	0	0	***0***	5	***6***	***6***
Days With ≥ 1.0" Snow Depth	0	***0***	0	0	0	0	0	0	0	0	0	***1***	***1***

White Sands Natl Mon *Otero County* Elevation: 3,995 ft. Latitude: 32° 47' N Longitude: 106° 11' W

	JAN	FEB	MAR	APR	MAY	JUN	JUL	AUG	SEP	OCT	NOV	DEC	YEAR
Mean Maximum Temp. (°F)	57.5	63.1	70.6	79.2	88.3	96.8	97.1	94.1	88.7	78.4	66.1	56.3	78.0
Mean Temp. (°F)	40.1	44.8	51.2	59.4	68.8	77.8	80.5	78.1	71.6	59.8	47.4	38.9	59.9
Mean Minimum Temp. (°F)	22.6	26.6	31.9	39.6	49.3	58.7	64.0	62.0	54.4	41.2	28.6	21.5	41.7
Extreme Maximum Temp. (°F)	78	83	89	96	104	111	110	105	103	97	84	76	111
Extreme Minimum Temp. (°F)	1	4	4	18	28	36	49	50	35	17	4	-5	-5
Days Maximum Temp. ≥ 90°F	0	0	0	2	14	27	28	25	14	2	0	0	112
Days Maximum Temp. ≤ 32°F	0	0	0	0	0	0	0	0	0	0	0	0	0
Days Minimum Temp. ≤ 32°F	28	21	16	7	1	0	0	0	0	5	21	27	126
Days Minimum Temp. ≤ 0°F	0	0	0	0	0	0	0	0	0	0	0	0	0
Heating Degree Days (base 65°F)	766	564	420	186	31	1	0	0	10	179	522	801	3,480
Cooling Degree Days (base 65°F)	0	0	1	26	156	392	488	412	215	26	0	0	1,716
Mean Precipitation (in.)	0.56	0.45	0.29	0.34	0.47	0.93	1.18	2.28	1.51	1.01	0.55	0.87	10.44
Extreme Maximum Daily Precip. (in.)	0.77	1.21	0.51	0.67	0.82	1.64	0.90	2.25	2.20	1.77	1.31	1.25	2.25
Days With ≥ 0.1" Precipitation	2	1	1	1	1	2	3	5	3	3	2	2	26
Days With ≥ 0.5" Precipitation	0	0	0	0	0	0	1	2	1	0	0	1	5
Days With ≥ 1.0" Precipitation	0	0	0	0	0	0	0	1	0	0	0	0	1
Mean Snowfall (in.)	1.0	0.3	trace	0.0	0.0	0.0	0.0	0.0	0.0	0.1	trace	1.4	2.8
Maximum Snow Depth (in.)	4	***2***	trace	0	0	0	0	0	0	1	trace	12	***12***
Days With ≥ 1.0" Snow Depth	0	0	0	0	0	0	0	0	0	0	0	1	1

The period of record for all cooperative weather station data is 1980 – 2009. See User Guide for detailed explanation of data.

Yeso 2 S *Debaca County* Elevation: 4,850 ft. Latitude: 34° 24' N Longitude: 104° 37' W

	JAN	FEB	MAR	APR	MAY	JUN	JUL	AUG	SEP	OCT	NOV	DEC	YEAR
Mean Maximum Temp. (°F)	52.3	57.2	64.6	72.3	80.6	88.6	90.7	88.1	82.1	72.7	61.4	51.4	71.8
Mean Temp. (°F)	***38.1***	42.0	48.4	55.5	64.8	72.8	76.2	74.2	67.6	57.6	46.5	37.7	***56.8***
Mean Minimum Temp. (°F)	***23.9***	26.8	32.1	38.6	48.9	57.0	61.5	60.3	53.0	42.4	31.8	23.9	***41.7***
Extreme Maximum Temp. (°F)	77	81	88	93	100	107	105	102	99	93	89	80	107
Extreme Minimum Temp. (°F)	-13	-9	3	13	26	38	51	46	29	12	7	-11	-13
Days Maximum Temp. ≥ 90°F	0	0	0	0	4	13	19	14	4	0	0	0	54
Days Maximum Temp. ≤ 32°F	2	1	0	0	0	0	0	0	0	0	0	2	5
Days Minimum Temp. ≤ 32°F	26	20	14	6	0	0	0	0	0	3	16	25	110
Days Minimum Temp. ≤ 0°F	0	0	0	0	0	0	0	0	0	0	0	0	0
Heating Degree Days (base 65°F)	***827***	641	509	285	81	4	0	1	35	237	547	840	***4,007***
Cooling Degree Days (base 65°F)	***0***	0	0	7	82	244	355	294	120	12	0	0	***1,114***
Mean Precipitation (in.)	0.56	0.49	0.61	0.97	1.08	1.45	1.49	2.06	1.65	1.45	0.51	0.65	12.97
Extreme Maximum Daily Precip. (in.)	***0.87***	2.00	2.26	2.65	1.80	1.87	***2.51***	***1.90***	2.90	3.70	1.38	***1.01***	***3.70***
Days With ≥ 0.1" Precipitation	2	1	1	2	2	3	3	4	3	2	1	2	26
Days With ≥ 0.5" Precipitation	0	0	0	0	1	1	1	1	1	1	0	0	6
Days With ≥ 1.0" Precipitation	0	0	0	0	0	0	0	0	0	0	0	0	0
Mean Snowfall (in.)	5.1	3.7	1.8	1.5	0.0	0.0	0.0	0.0	0.0	0.4	1.2	5.9	19.6
Maximum Snow Depth (in.)	***10***	17	11	3	0	4	0	0	1	trace	5	12	***17***
Days With ≥ 1.0" Snow Depth	***1***	1	0	0	0	0	0	0	0	0	0	1	***3***

New Mexico Weather Station Rankings

Annual Extreme Maximum Temperature

Highest			Lowest		
Rank	Station Name	°F	Rank	Station Name	°F
1	Tatum	115	1	Gascon	90
2	Bitter Lakes Wl Refuge	114	2	Chama	93
2	Carlsbad	114	3	Los Alamos	95
2	Conchas Dam	114	4	Mountain Park	96
2	Hobbs	***114***	5	Augustine 2 E	97
2	Roswell Industrial Air Park	114	6	Cimarron 4 SW	98
7	Artesia 6 S	113	6	McGaffey 5 SE	98
7	Bernardo	113	8	Gallup Sen Clarke Fld	***100***
7	Carlsbad Cavern City Air Term	113	8	Maxwell 3 NW	***100***
10	Elida	112	10	Abiquiu Dam	101
11	Caballo Dam	111	10	Alcalde	101
11	Columbus	111	12	Elk 2 E	102
11	Jal	111	12	Jemez Springs	102
11	White Sands Natl Mon	111	14	Chaco Canyon Natl Mon	103
15	Alamogordo	110	14	Cubero	103
15	Carlsbad Caverns	110	16	Mosquero 1 NE	104
15	Clovis	110	17	Bingham 2 NE	105
15	Jornada Exp Range	110	17	Faywood	105
15	Orogrande	***110***	19	Amistad 5 SSW	106
15	State University	110	19	Corrales	***106***
21	Deming	109	19	Fort Bayard	106
22	Clovis 13 N	108	22	Albuquerque Intl Arpt	107
22	Fort Sumner	108	22	Dilia	107
22	Melrose	108	22	Las Vegas Sewage Plant	***107***
22	Portales	108	22	Los Lunas 3 SSW	107

Annual Mean Maximum Temperature

Highest			Lowest		
Rank	Station Name	°F	Rank	Station Name	°F
1	Jal	79.1	1	Gascon	58.3
2	Columbus	78.7	2	Chama	58.9
3	Carlsbad	78.3	3	McGaffey 5 SE	60.1
4	Carlsbad Cavern City Air Term	78.0	4	Los Alamos	60.5
4	White Sands Natl Mon	78.0	5	Abiquiu Dam	64.9
6	Caballo Dam	77.7	6	Cimarron 4 SW	65.1
7	Deming	***77.6***	7	Gallup Sen Clarke Fld	***66.1***
8	State University	77.5	8	Augustine 2 E	66.3
9	Orogrande	***77.4***	9	Mountain Park	66.4
10	Bitter Lakes Wl Refuge	***77.0***	10	Maxwell 3 NW	66.6
11	Artesia 6 S	76.7	11	Chaco Canyon Natl Mon	67.1
12	Hobbs	***76.6***	11	Las Vegas Sewage Plant	***67.1***
13	Jornada Exp Range	***76.4***	13	Jemez Springs	68.0
14	Bernardo	76.2	14	Alcalde	***68.3***
15	Roswell Industrial Air Park	75.9	15	Mosquero 1 NE	68.5
16	Alamogordo	***75.7***	16	Cubero	68.7
17	Carlsbad Caverns	74.2	17	Elk 2 E	***69.9***
18	Portales	74.0	18	Amistad 5 SSW	70.0
18	Tatum	74.0	19	Albuquerque Intl Arpt	70.3
20	Los Lunas 3 SSW	73.9	20	Fort Bayard	70.8
21	Faywood	73.8	21	Bingham 2 NE	***70.9***
22	Conchas Dam	73.6	22	Corrales	***71.1***
22	Elida	73.6	23	Clovis	71.6
24	Melrose	73.2	24	Yeso 2 S	71.8
25	Fort Sumner	73.1	25	Dilia	72.1

Rankings include 25 highest/lowest stations. If state has less than 25 stations, all stations are included. The period of record is 1980–2009. See User Guide for detailed explanation of data.

Annual Mean Temperature

Rank	Station Name (Highest)	°F	Rank	Station Name (Lowest)	°F
1	Columbus	64.0	1	Chama	42.2
1	Jal	64.0	2	McGaffey 5 SE	43.2
3	Carlsbad Cavern City Air Term	63.3	3	Gascon	44.1
4	Carlsbad	63.2	4	Los Alamos	48.4
5	Hobbs	***62.4***	5	Las Vegas Sewage Plant	***48.5***
5	State University	62.4	6	Gallup Sen Clarke Fld	***49.1***
7	Alamogordo	***62.3***	7	Augustine 2 E	49.4
8	Carlsbad Caverns	***62.2***	7	Cimarron 4 SW	49.4
9	Orogrande	***61.9***	7	Maxwell 3 NW	49.4
10	Roswell Industrial Air Park	61.4	10	Chaco Canyon Natl Mon	50.0
11	Caballo Dam	61.3	11	Alcalde	***51.4***
12	Deming	***61.0***	12	Abiquiu Dam	51.5
13	Artesia 6 S	60.0	13	Cubero	52.2
14	White Sands Natl Mon	59.9	14	Jemez Springs	52.4
15	Bitter Lakes Wl Refuge	***59.7***	15	Elk 2 E	***53.3***
16	Conchas Dam	59.3	16	Mosquero 1 NE	53.4
17	Portales	58.7	17	Mountain Park	53.9
18	Elida	58.6	18	Corrales	***54.4***
19	Jornada Exp Range	***58.5***	19	Amistad 5 SSW	55.0
20	Faywood	58.3	20	Bingham 2 NE	***55.5***
20	Melrose	58.3	21	Dilia	55.8
22	Tatum	58.2	22	Los Lunas 3 SSW	56.2
23	Bernardo	***58.1***	23	Fort Bayard	56.5
24	Fort Sumner	57.9	24	Yeso 2 S	***56.8***
25	Clovis	57.7	25	Clovis 13 N	57.4

Annual Mean Minimum Temperature

Rank	Station Name (Highest)	°F	Rank	Station Name (Lowest)	°F
1	Carlsbad Caverns	***50.3***	1	Chama	25.4
2	Columbus	49.2	2	McGaffey 5 SE	26.3
3	Alamogordo	***48.9***	3	Gascon	29.9
3	Jal	48.9	3	Las Vegas Sewage Plant	***29.9***
5	Carlsbad Cavern City Air Term	48.5	5	Gallup Sen Clarke Fld	***32.0***
6	Hobbs	***48.2***	6	Maxwell 3 NW	32.1
7	Carlsbad	48.0	7	Augustine 2 E	32.4
8	State University	47.4	8	Chaco Canyon Natl Mon	32.8
9	Roswell Industrial Air Park	46.7	9	Cimarron 4 SW	33.6
10	Orogrande	***46.4***	10	Alcalde	***34.5***
11	Caballo Dam	44.9	11	Cubero	35.6
11	Conchas Dam	44.9	12	Los Alamos	36.2
13	Albuquerque Intl Arpt	44.5	13	Elk 2 E	***36.7***
14	Deming	***44.4***	14	Jemez Springs	36.8
15	Clovis	43.7	15	Corrales	***37.6***
16	Elida	43.4	16	Abiquiu Dam	38.0
16	Portales	43.4	17	Mosquero 1 NE	38.3
18	Melrose	43.3	18	Los Lunas 3 SSW	38.4
19	Artesia 6 S	43.1	19	Dilia	39.3
20	Faywood	42.8	20	Amistad 5 SSW	40.0
21	Fort Sumner	42.7	20	Bernardo	***40.0***
22	Tatum	42.4	20	Bingham 2 NE	***40.0***
23	Bitter Lakes Wl Refuge	42.3	23	Jornada Exp Range	***40.4***
24	Fort Bayard	42.2	24	Mountain Park	41.2
25	Clovis 13 N	42.1	25	White Sands Natl Mon	41.7

Rankings include 25 highest/lowest stations. If state has less than 25 stations, all stations are included. The period of record is 1980–2009. See User Guide for detailed explanation of data.

Annual Extreme Minimum Temperature

Highest

Rank	Station Name	°F
1	Alamogordo	6
2	Columbus	5
2	Fort Bayard	5
2	State University	5
5	Carlsbad	3
6	Carlsbad Caverns	*2*
6	Faywood	2
6	Orogrande	*2*
9	Caballo Dam	0
10	Deming	-2
10	Hobbs	*-2*
12	Mountain Park	-3
13	Carlsbad Cavern City Air Term	-4
14	Clovis	-5
14	Roswell Industrial Air Park	-5
14	White Sands Natl Mon	-5
17	Bingham 2 NE	-6
17	Corrales	*-6*
19	Albuquerque Intl Arpt	-7
19	Fort Sumner	-7
21	Clovis 13 N	-8
21	Jal	-8
21	Jemez Springs	-8
21	Melrose	-8
21	Tatum	-8

Lowest

Rank	Station Name	°F
1	Chaco Canyon Natl Mon	-37
2	Gallup Sen Clarke Fld	*-34*
3	Las Vegas Sewage Plant	*-32*
4	Chama	-30
4	McGaffey 5 SE	-30
6	Dilia	-28
7	Maxwell 3 NW	-26
8	Augustine 2 E	-25
9	Cimarron 4 SW	-22
10	Abiquiu Dam	-18
11	Gascon	-17
12	Amistad 5 SSW	-16
13	Elk 2 E	-15
14	Mosquero 1 NE	-14
15	Artesia 6 S	-13
15	Cubero	-13
15	Yeso 2 S	-13
18	Jornada Exp Range	-12
19	Alcalde	-11
19	Los Alamos	-11
21	Bernardo	*-10*
21	Conchas Dam	-10
21	Los Lunas 3 SSW	-10
24	Bitter Lakes Wl Refuge	-9
24	Elida	-9

July Mean Maximum Temperature

Highest

Rank	Station Name	°F
1	White Sands Natl Mon	97.1
2	Bernardo	96.9
3	Caballo Dam	96.4
4	Bitter Lakes Wl Refuge	96.1
5	Carlsbad	96.0
5	Columbus	96.0
7	Carlsbad Cavern City Air Term	95.8
8	Orogrande	*95.6*
9	Jal	95.5
10	State University	95.1
11	Deming	94.8
11	Hobbs	94.8
13	Jornada Exp Range	*94.7*
14	Roswell Industrial Air Park	94.5
15	Artesia 6 S	94.4
15	Conchas Dam	94.4
17	Los Lunas 3 SSW	94.1
18	Alamogordo	93.9
19	Melrose	92.1
19	Portales	92.1
21	Albuquerque Intl Arpt	92.0
22	Elida	91.9
23	Tatum	91.8
24	Corrales	*91.7*
25	Clovis 13 N	91.6

Lowest

Rank	Station Name	°F
1	Gascon	75.2
2	Chama	81.0
2	McGaffey 5 SE	81.0
4	Los Alamos	81.5
5	Mountain Park	81.6
6	Cimarron 4 SW	83.8
7	Elk 2 E	84.0
8	Augustine 2 E	84.3
9	Las Vegas Sewage Plant	85.6
10	Maxwell 3 NW	86.5
11	Fort Bayard	87.3
12	Abiquiu Dam	87.6
13	Gallup Sen Clarke Fld	*87.8*
14	Mosquero 1 NE	88.7
15	Jemez Springs	89.0
16	Alcalde	89.3
17	Cubero	89.6
18	Bingham 2 NE	*89.9*
19	Chaco Canyon Natl Mon	90.1
20	Faywood	90.7
20	Yeso 2 S	90.7
22	Amistad 5 SSW	91.2
23	Carlsbad Caverns	91.3
23	Clovis	91.3
23	Dilia	91.3

Rankings include 25 highest/lowest stations. If state has less than 25 stations, all stations are included. The period of record is 1980–2009. See User Guide for detailed explanation of data.

January Mean Minimum Temperature

Highest Rank	Highest Station Name	Highest °F	Lowest Rank	Lowest Station Name	Lowest °F
1	Carlsbad Caverns	33.8	1	Chama	6.6
2	Alamogordo	31.2	2	McGaffey 5 SE	8.2
3	Columbus	30.9	3	Las Vegas Sewage Plant	***11.4***
4	Hobbs	***29.6***	4	Maxwell 3 NW	12.9
5	Carlsbad Cavern City Air Term	29.4	5	Chaco Canyon Natl Mon	13.7
6	Jal	29.3	6	Gallup Sen Clarke Fld	14.3
6	State University	29.3	7	Augustine 2 E	16.4
8	Carlsbad	28.5	8	Gascon	16.5
9	Orogrande	***28.3***	9	Alcalde	***16.6***
10	Faywood	27.6	10	Cimarron 4 SW	17.3
11	Fort Bayard	27.4	11	Abiquiu Dam	18.1
12	Deming	27.1	12	Cubero	18.3
12	Mountain Park	27.1	13	Los Lunas 3 SSW	18.8
14	Caballo Dam	26.7	14	Los Alamos	19.1
15	Roswell Industrial Air Park	26.6	15	Mosquero 1 NE	19.9
16	Albuquerque Intl Arpt	25.6	16	Jemez Springs	20.1
17	Clovis	25.0	17	Corrales	20.2
18	Melrose	24.9	18	Amistad 5 SSW	20.3
19	Conchas Dam	24.6	19	Bernardo	***20.5***
20	Elida	24.4	20	Elk 2 E	21.0
21	Clovis 13 N	24.0	20	Jornada Exp Range	***21.0***
21	Portales	24.0	22	Bitter Lakes Wl Refuge	21.6
23	Yeso 2 S	***23.9***	23	Bingham 2 NE	22.1
24	Tatum	23.5	24	Dilia	22.2
25	Fort Sumner	23.1	25	White Sands Natl Mon	22.6

Number of Days Annually Maximum Temperature ≥ 90°F

Highest Rank	Highest Station Name	Highest Days	Lowest Rank	Lowest Station Name	Lowest Days
1	Carlsbad Cavern City Air Term	113	1	Gascon	0
2	Jal	112	2	Chama	1
2	White Sands Natl Mon	112	3	Los Alamos	3
4	Carlsbad	110	3	McGaffey 5 SE	3
4	Columbus	110	5	Mountain Park	5
6	Caballo Dam	105	6	Cimarron 4 SW	8
7	Bitter Lakes Wl Refuge	103	7	Augustine 2 E	10
8	Orogrande	***102***	8	Elk 2 E	13
9	State University	100	9	Las Vegas Sewage Plant	***16***
10	Artesia 6 S	99	10	Maxwell 3 NW	24
10	Bernardo	99	11	Abiquiu Dam	25
12	Deming	98	11	Gallup Sen Clarke Fld	***25***
13	Roswell Industrial Air Park	97	13	Fort Bayard	31
14	Hobbs	***95***	14	Jemez Springs	35
15	Alamogordo	86	15	Alcalde	38
15	Jornada Exp Range	86	15	Mosquero 1 NE	38
17	Conchas Dam	84	17	Chaco Canyon Natl Mon	40
18	Los Lunas 3 SSW	82	17	Cubero	40
19	Tatum	76	19	Bingham 2 NE	48
20	Portales	74	20	Faywood	53
21	Carlsbad Caverns	72	21	Yeso 2 S	54
21	Elida	72	22	Amistad 5 SSW	58
23	Melrose	70	23	Corrales	***59***
24	Clovis 13 N	69	24	Dilia	60
25	Fort Sumner	65	25	Albuquerque Intl Arpt	61

Rankings include 25 highest/lowest stations. If state has less than 25 stations, all stations are included. The period of record is 1980–2009. See User Guide for detailed explanation of data.

Number of Days Annually Maximum Temperature ≤ 32°F

Highest			Lowest		
Rank	Station Name	Days	Rank	Station Name	Days
1	Chama	20	1	Alamogordo	0
2	Los Alamos	17	1	Bernardo	0
3	McGaffey 5 SE	16	1	Caballo Dam	0
4	Gascon	15	1	Columbus	0
5	Maxwell 3 NW	12	1	Deming	0
6	Amistad 5 SSW	11	1	Faywood	0
7	Clovis	10	1	Fort Bayard	0
8	Cimarron 4 SW	9	1	Jornada Exp Range	0
8	Mosquero 1 NE	9	1	Orogrande	***0***
10	Abiquiu Dam	7	1	State University	0
10	Chaco Canyon Natl Mon	7	1	White Sands Natl Mon	0
10	Gallup Sen Clarke Fld	***7***	12	Los Lunas 3 SSW	1
10	Las Vegas Sewage Plant	***7***	13	Albuquerque Intl Arpt	2
14	Augustine 2 E	5	13	Bingham 2 NE	2
14	Clovis 13 N	5	13	Carlsbad Cavern City Air Term	2
14	Conchas Dam	5	13	Corrales	***2***
14	Elida	5	13	Cubero	2
14	Melrose	5	13	Elk 2 E	2
14	Tatum	5	13	Jal	2
14	Yeso 2 S	5	13	Jemez Springs	2
21	Fort Sumner	4	13	Mountain Park	2
21	Portales	4	22	Alcalde	3
21	Roswell Industrial Air Park	4	22	Artesia 6 S	3
24	Alcalde	3	22	Bitter Lakes Wl Refuge	3
24	Artesia 6 S	3	22	Carlsbad	3

Number of Days Annually Minimum Temperature ≤ 32°F

Highest			Lowest		
Rank	Station Name	Days	Rank	Station Name	Days
1	Chama	234	1	Carlsbad Caverns	***45***
2	McGaffey 5 SE	226	2	Columbus	58
3	Gascon	202	3	Alamogordo	61
4	Las Vegas Sewage Plant	***197***	4	Hobbs	***66***
5	Gallup Sen Clarke Fld	***192***	5	Jal	70
6	Augustine 2 E	184	6	Carlsbad Cavern City Air Term	72
7	Maxwell 3 NW	183	7	Carlsbad	75
8	Chaco Canyon Natl Mon	182	8	State University	76
9	Cimarron 4 SW	172	9	Orogrande	***79***
10	Alcalde	165	10	Roswell Industrial Air Park	87
10	Cubero	165	11	Caballo Dam	95
12	Los Alamos	157	12	Deming	96
13	Jemez Springs	150	13	Faywood	98
14	Elk 2 E	147	14	Conchas Dam	100
15	Abiquiu Dam	145	15	Albuquerque Intl Arpt	102
15	Corrales	***145***	16	Clovis	103
15	Los Lunas 3 SSW	145	16	Fort Bayard	103
18	Mosquero 1 NE	143	18	Elida	104
19	Amistad 5 SSW	136	19	Melrose	106
20	Dilia	132	20	Mountain Park	108
21	Bingham 2 NE	131	21	Clovis 13 N	110
22	Bernardo	***126***	21	Yeso 2 S	110
22	White Sands Natl Mon	126	23	Portales	111
24	Jornada Exp Range	121	24	Bitter Lakes Wl Refuge	115
25	Tatum	117	24	Fort Sumner	115

Rankings include 25 highest/lowest stations. If state has less than 25 stations, all stations are included. The period of record is 1980–2009. See User Guide for detailed explanation of data.

Number of Days Annually Minimum Temperature ≤ 0°F

Highest Rank	Station Name	Days	Lowest Rank	Station Name	Days
1	Chama	24	1	Alamogordo	0
2	McGaffey 5 SE	22	1	Albuquerque Intl Arpt	0
3	Chaco Canyon Natl Mon	8	1	Alcalde	0
4	Gallup Sen Clarke Fld	*7*	1	Artesia 6 S	0
4	Las Vegas Sewage Plant	*7*	1	Bernardo	***0***
4	Maxwell 3 NW	7	1	Bingham 2 NE	0
7	Gascon	5	1	Caballo Dam	0
8	Cimarron 4 SW	4	1	Carlsbad	0
9	Amistad 5 SSW	3	1	Carlsbad Cavern City Air Term	0
9	Augustine 2 E	3	1	Carlsbad Caverns	***0***
9	Mosquero 1 NE	3	1	Clovis 13 N	0
12	Cubero	2	1	Columbus	0
13	Abiquiu Dam	1	1	Conchas Dam	0
13	Bitter Lakes Wl Refuge	1	1	Corrales	***0***
13	Clovis	1	1	Deming	0
13	Dilia	1	1	Elida	0
13	Los Alamos	1	1	Elk 2 E	0
18	Alamogordo	0	1	Faywood	0
18	Albuquerque Intl Arpt	0	1	Fort Bayard	0
18	Alcalde	0	1	Fort Sumner	0
18	Artesia 6 S	0	1	Hobbs	***0***
18	Bernardo	***0***	1	Jal	0
18	Bingham 2 NE	0	1	Jemez Springs	0
18	Caballo Dam	0	1	Jornada Exp Range	0
18	Carlsbad	0	1	Los Lunas 3 SSW	0

Number of Annual Heating Degree Days

Highest Rank	Station Name	Num.	Lowest Rank	Station Name	Num.
1	Chama	8,253	1	Columbus	2,486
2	McGaffey 5 SE	7,903	1	Jal	2,486
3	Gascon	7,540	3	Carlsbad Cavern City Air Term	2,707
4	Los Alamos	6,255	4	Carlsbad	2,728
5	Las Vegas Sewage Plant	***6,151***	5	Carlsbad Caverns	***2,733***
6	Gallup Sen Clarke Fld	***6,130***	6	State University	2,768
7	Maxwell 3 NW	5,964	7	Alamogordo	***2,776***
8	Chaco Canyon Natl Mon	5,952	8	Hobbs	***2,836***
9	Augustine 2 E	5,884	9	Orogrande	***2,898***
10	Cimarron 4 SW	5,848	10	Deming	***3,019***
11	Abiquiu Dam	5,507	11	Caballo Dam	3,039
12	Alcalde	***5,437***	12	Roswell Industrial Air Park	3,146
13	Cubero	5,230	13	Artesia 6 S	3,413
14	Jemez Springs	5,099	14	Faywood	3,454
15	Mosquero 1 NE	4,922	15	White Sands Natl Mon	3,480
16	Amistad 5 SSW	4,662	16	Bitter Lakes Wl Refuge	***3,569***
16	Corrales	***4,662***	17	Conchas Dam	3,654
18	Elk 2 E	***4,583***	18	Portales	3,660
19	Mountain Park	4,427	19	Elida	3,682
20	Bingham 2 NE	***4,333***	20	Jornada Exp Range	***3,693***
21	Los Lunas 3 SSW	4,294	21	Melrose	3,735
22	Dilia	4,225	22	Tatum	3,768
23	Albuquerque Intl Arpt	4,044	23	Fort Sumner	3,804
24	Yeso 2 S	***4,007***	24	Fort Bayard	3,848
25	Clovis	3,915	25	Bernardo	***3,876***

Rankings include 25 highest/lowest stations. If state has less than 25 stations, all stations are included. The period of record is 1980–2009. See User Guide for detailed explanation of data.

Number of Annual Cooling Degree Days

Highest Rank	Station Name	Num.	Lowest Rank	Station Name	Num.
1	Jal	2,230	1	Gascon	10
2	Columbus	2,206	2	Chama	35
3	Carlsbad Cavern City Air Term	2,193	3	McGaffey 5 SE	51
4	Carlsbad	2,164	4	Las Vegas Sewage Plant	***238***
5	Hobbs	***2,003***	5	Cimarron 4 SW	244
6	State University	1,939	6	Los Alamos	285
7	Roswell Industrial Air Park	1,921	7	Augustine 2 E	294
8	Alamogordo	***1,900***	8	Maxwell 3 NW	372
9	Orogrande	***1,871***	9	Elk 2 E	***401***
10	Carlsbad Caverns	***1,813***	10	Gallup Sen Clarke Fld	***429***
11	Caballo Dam	1,798	11	Mountain Park	457
12	Bitter Lakes Wl Refuge	***1,740***	12	Alcalde	***574***
13	White Sands Natl Mon	1,716	13	Chaco Canyon Natl Mon	585
14	Artesia 6 S	1,678	14	Jemez Springs	611
15	Conchas Dam	1,669	15	Cubero	646
16	Deming	***1,667***	16	Abiquiu Dam	678
17	Portales	1,467	17	Mosquero 1 NE	801
18	Bernardo	***1,446***	18	Fort Bayard	852
19	Elida	1,429	19	Corrales	***892***
20	Jornada Exp Range	***1,409***	20	Dilia	957
21	Albuquerque Intl Arpt	1,401	21	Bingham 2 NE	***969***
22	Tatum	1,393	22	Faywood	1,106
23	Melrose	1,384	23	Yeso 2 S	***1,114***
24	Clovis	1,360	24	Amistad 5 SSW	1,129
25	Fort Sumner	1,321	25	Los Lunas 3 SSW	1,167

Annual Precipitation

Highest Rank	Station Name	Inches	Lowest Rank	Station Name	Inches
1	Gascon	25.17	1	Bernardo	8.73
2	Chama	23.84	2	Chaco Canyon Natl Mon	9.38
3	Mountain Park	21.03	3	Albuquerque Intl Arpt	9.44
4	McGaffey 5 SE	20.81	4	State University	9.67
5	Clovis	18.82	5	Los Lunas 3 SSW	9.86
6	Los Alamos	18.73	6	Columbus	10.01
7	Clovis 13 N	18.19	7	Corrales	***10.11***
8	Las Vegas Sewage Plant	***18.13***	8	Abiquiu Dam	10.21
9	Cimarron 4 SW	17.84	9	Deming	10.31
10	Hobbs	***17.56***	10	White Sands Natl Mon	10.44
11	Melrose	17.31	11	Cubero	10.88
12	Jemez Springs	17.17	12	Caballo Dam	11.02
13	Portales	17.15	13	Alcalde	***11.04***
14	Elk 2 E	16.94	14	Jornada Exp Range	11.39
15	Elida	16.93	15	Gallup Sen Clarke Fld	***11.81***
16	Mosquero 1 NE	16.91	16	Alamogordo	11.99
17	Fort Bayard	16.66	17	Bingham 2 NE	12.32
18	Tatum	16.51	17	Orogrande	***12.32***
19	Conchas Dam	15.88	19	Roswell Industrial Air Park	12.85
20	Carlsbad Caverns	15.75	20	Yeso 2 S	12.97
21	Dilia	15.67	21	Artesia 6 S	12.98
22	Amistad 5 SSW	15.60	22	Augustine 2 E	13.24
23	Fort Sumner	15.54	23	Carlsbad	13.49
24	Maxwell 3 NW	15.40	24	Carlsbad Cavern City Air Term	13.70
25	Bitter Lakes Wl Refuge	14.26	25	Jal	13.89

Rankings include 25 highest/lowest stations. If state has less than 25 stations, all stations are included. The period of record is 1980–2009. See User Guide for detailed explanation of data.

Annual Extreme Maximum Daily Precipitation

Highest

Rank	Station Name	Inches
1	Carlsbad Caverns	***8.41***
2	Hobbs	***7.50***
3	Elida	7.26
4	Tatum	***5.55***
5	Maxwell 3 NW	***4.67***
6	Carlsbad	***4.60***
7	Melrose	4.49
8	Jal	4.40
8	Portales	4.40
10	Roswell Industrial Air Park	4.34
11	Fort Sumner	4.10
12	Mosquero 1 NE	4.06
13	Amistad 5 SSW	4.00
14	Bitter Lakes Wl Refuge	***3.98***
15	Caballo Dam	3.96
16	Carlsbad Cavern City Air Term	3.94
17	Cimarron 4 SW	3.89
18	Gascon	3.83
19	Yeso 2 S	***3.70***
20	Clovis 13 N	3.60
21	Dilia	3.51
22	Clovis	3.45
22	Conchas Dam	3.45
22	Elk 2 E	***3.45***
25	Artesia 6 S	3.39

Lowest

Rank	Station Name	Inches
1	Corrales	***1.75***
2	Albuquerque Intl Arpt	1.92
3	Augustine 2 E	2.02
4	Deming	2.05
5	Bernardo	2.07
6	Abiquiu Dam	2.10
7	Los Alamos	2.16
8	Jemez Springs	2.24
9	Jornada Exp Range	***2.25***
9	White Sands Natl Mon	2.25
11	Chama	2.30
12	Alamogordo	2.32
13	Gallup Sen Clarke Fld	***2.36***
14	Cubero	2.40
15	Los Lunas 3 SSW	2.41
16	McGaffey 5 SE	***2.60***
17	Mountain Park	2.70
18	Faywood	2.74
19	Chaco Canyon Natl Mon	2.80
20	Columbus	2.90
21	Las Vegas Sewage Plant	***3.00***
22	Orogrande	***3.08***
23	Fort Bayard	3.10
24	State University	3.13
25	Artesia 6 S	3.39

Number of Days Annually With ≥ 0.1 Inches of Precipitation

Highest

Rank	Station Name	Days
1	Chama	62
2	Gascon	56
3	McGaffey 5 SE	53
4	Mountain Park	49
5	Los Alamos	48
6	Jemez Springs	44
7	Las Vegas Sewage Plant	***42***
8	Cimarron 4 SW	41
8	Fort Bayard	41
10	Clovis	37
10	Dilia	37
12	Augustine 2 E	36
12	Gallup Sen Clarke Fld	***36***
12	Melrose	36
12	Portales	36
16	Elk 2 E	35
16	Mosquero 1 NE	35
18	Faywood	34
19	Abiquiu Dam	33
20	Alamogordo	32
20	Clovis 13 N	32
20	Conchas Dam	32
20	Fort Sumner	32
20	Maxwell 3 NW	32
25	Amistad 5 SSW	31

Lowest

Rank	Station Name	Days
1	Bernardo	23
1	Jal	23
3	Carlsbad	25
3	Columbus	25
5	Bingham 2 NE	26
5	Bitter Lakes Wl Refuge	26
5	Jornada Exp Range	26
5	Roswell Industrial Air Park	26
5	State University	26
5	White Sands Natl Mon	26
5	Yeso 2 S	26
12	Carlsbad Cavern City Air Term	27
12	Orogrande	***27***
14	Artesia 6 S	28
14	Caballo Dam	28
14	Corrales	***28***
14	Cubero	28
14	Deming	28
19	Albuquerque Intl Arpt	29
19	Alcalde	29
19	Chaco Canyon Natl Mon	29
19	Los Lunas 3 SSW	29
23	Carlsbad Caverns	30
23	Elida	30
23	Hobbs	***30***

Number of Days Annually With ≥ 0.5 Inches of Precipitation

Highest Rank	Station Name	Days	Lowest Rank	Station Name	Days
1	Gascon	17	1	Chaco Canyon Natl Mon	1
2	Mountain Park	16	2	Abiquiu Dam	2
3	Chama	13	3	Gallup Sen Clarke Fld	*3*
3	Clovis	13	3	Jornada Exp Range	3
3	Hobbs	*13*	5	Alamogordo	4
6	Los Alamos	12	5	Albuquerque Intl Arpt	4
6	McGaffey 5 SE	12	5	Bernardo	4
8	Jemez Springs	11	5	Bingham 2 NE	4
9	Amistad 5 SSW	10	5	Corrales	*4*
9	Cimarron 4 SW	10	5	Cubero	4
9	Clovis 13 N	10	5	Los Lunas 3 SSW	4
9	Conchas Dam	10	5	State University	4
9	Fort Bayard	10	13	Alcalde	5
9	Las Vegas Sewage Plant	*10*	13	Columbus	5
9	Melrose	10	13	Deming	5
9	Mosquero 1 NE	10	13	White Sands Natl Mon	5
9	Portales	10	17	Artesia 6 S	6
18	Elida	9	17	Augustine 2 E	6
18	Elk 2 E	9	17	Bitter Lakes Wl Refuge	6
18	Faywood	9	17	Caballo Dam	6
18	Tatum	9	17	Roswell Industrial Air Park	6
22	Carlsbad Caverns	8	17	Yeso 2 S	6
22	Dilia	8	23	Carlsbad	7
22	Fort Sumner	8	23	Carlsbad Cavern City Air Term	7
22	Maxwell 3 NW	8	23	Jal	7

Number of Days Annually With ≥ 1.0 Inches of Precipitation

Highest Rank	Station Name	Days	Lowest Rank	Station Name	Days
1	Hobbs	*5*	1	Abiquiu Dam	0
1	Jal	5	1	Alamogordo	0
3	Clovis 13 N	4	1	Albuquerque Intl Arpt	0
3	Elida	4	1	Alcalde	0
3	Elk 2 E	4	1	Artesia 6 S	0
3	Tatum	4	1	Augustine 2 E	0
7	Bitter Lakes Wl Refuge	3	1	Bernardo	0
7	Carlsbad Caverns	3	1	Bingham 2 NE	0
7	Clovis	3	1	Caballo Dam	0
7	Portales	3	1	Chaco Canyon Natl Mon	0
11	Amistad 5 SSW	2	1	Chama	0
11	Carlsbad Cavern City Air Term	2	1	Columbus	0
11	Conchas Dam	2	1	Corrales	*0*
11	Fort Bayard	2	1	Cubero	0
11	Fort Sumner	2	1	Deming	0
11	Gascon	2	1	Gallup Sen Clarke Fld	*0*
11	Las Vegas Sewage Plant	*2*	1	Jornada Exp Range	0
11	Melrose	2	1	Los Alamos	0
11	Mosquero 1 NE	2	1	Los Lunas 3 SSW	0
11	Mountain Park	2	1	McGaffey 5 SE	0
21	Carlsbad	1	1	Roswell Industrial Air Park	0
21	Cimarron 4 SW	1	1	State University	0
21	Dilia	1	1	Yeso 2 S	0
21	Faywood	1	24	Carlsbad	1
21	Jemez Springs	1	24	Cimarron 4 SW	1

 Rankings include 25 highest/lowest stations. If state has less than 25 stations, all stations are included. The period of record is 1980–2009. See User Guide for detailed explanation of data.

Annual Snowfall

Highest

Rank	Station Name	Inches
1	Gascon	131.7
2	Chama	103.2
3	Los Alamos	56.5
4	McGaffey 5 SE	***50.3***
5	Cimarron 4 SW	45.0
6	Dilia	32.2
7	Gallup Sen Clarke Fld	***31.4***
8	Jemez Springs	30.9
9	Las Vegas Sewage Plant	***22.8***
10	Mosquero 1 NE	22.6
11	Maxwell 3 NW	***22.1***
12	Elk 2 E	20.3
13	Mountain Park	20.1
14	Yeso 2 S	19.6
15	Cubero	16.3
16	Amistad 5 SSW	16.1
17	Clovis	14.2
18	Melrose	14.1
19	Chaco Canyon Natl Mon	13.9
20	Fort Sumner	12.6
21	Roswell Industrial Air Park	***12.4***
22	Elida	11.7
23	Conchas Dam	11.0
24	Alcalde	***10.6***
25	Albuquerque Intl Arpt	9.9

Lowest

Rank	Station Name	Inches
1	Caballo Dam	0.6
2	Faywood	1.7
3	Columbus	1.8
4	Fort Bayard	1.9
5	Jornada Exp Range	2.1
6	Carlsbad	2.7
6	Deming	2.7
8	State University	2.8
8	White Sands Natl Mon	2.8
10	Jal	3.1
11	Orogrande	***3.2***
12	Alamogordo	3.6
13	Carlsbad Caverns	4.8
14	Tatum	***5.1***
15	Hobbs	***5.3***
16	Bernardo	5.5
17	Los Lunas 3 SSW	6.2
18	Bitter Lakes Wl Refuge	7.0
18	Portales	7.0
20	Artesia 6 S	7.3
21	Clovis 13 N	7.4
22	Bingham 2 NE	7.9
23	Corrales	***8.0***
24	Augustine 2 E	8.2
25	Abiquiu Dam	***8.9***

Annual Maximum Snow Depth

Highest

Rank	Station Name	Inches
1	Chama	56
2	Gascon	44
3	Los Alamos	40
4	Cimarron 4 SW	25
5	Dilia	24
5	Elk 2 E	24
7	Cubero	23
8	Jemez Springs	20
8	Maxwell 3 NW	***20***
10	Amistad 5 SSW	***18***
11	Yeso 2 S	***17***
12	Bitter Lakes Wl Refuge	16
12	Fort Sumner	16
12	Roswell Industrial Air Park	***16***
15	Abiquiu Dam	***15***
15	Conchas Dam	15
15	Jal	15
18	Clovis	14
18	Corrales	***14***
18	Melrose	14
18	Mosquero 1 NE	14
18	Mountain Park	14
23	Alcalde	***13***
23	Clovis 13 N	13
23	Gallup Sen Clarke Fld	***13***

Lowest

Rank	Station Name	Inches
1	Faywood	2
2	Alamogordo	***4***
3	Carlsbad	5
4	Columbus	6
4	Fort Bayard	6
4	Los Lunas 3 SSW	6
4	Tatum	***6***
8	Caballo Dam	7
8	Carlsbad Caverns	***7***
8	Orogrande	***7***
11	Bingham 2 NE	8
11	Jornada Exp Range	8
11	Portales	8
14	Artesia 6 S	9
14	Bernardo	9
14	State University	9
17	Albuquerque Intl Arpt	10
17	Chaco Canyon Natl Mon	***10***
19	Deming	***11***
20	Augustine 2 E	***12***
20	Elida	12
20	White Sands Natl Mon	***12***
23	Alcalde	***13***
23	Clovis 13 N	13
23	Gallup Sen Clarke Fld	***13***

Rankings include 25 highest/lowest stations. If state has less than 25 stations, all stations are included. The period of record is 1980–2009. See User Guide for detailed explanation of data.

Number of Days Annually With ≥ 1.0 Inch Snow Depth

Highest

Rank	Station Name	Days
1	Chama	103
2	Los Alamos	57
3	Gascon	47
4	Gallup Sen Clarke Fld	*21*
4	Jemez Springs	21
6	Cimarron 4 SW	17
6	Mosquero 1 NE	17
8	McGaffey 5 SE	*13*
9	Clovis	12
10	Maxwell 3 NW	*10*
11	Chaco Canyon Natl Mon	*9*
11	Dilia	9
13	Abiquiu Dam	8
13	Fort Sumner	8
13	Mountain Park	8
16	Las Vegas Sewage Plant	*7*
16	Melrose	7
18	Elida	6
18	Roswell Industrial Air Park	*6*
20	Artesia 6 S	5
20	Cubero	5
22	Amistad 5 SSW	4
22	Conchas Dam	4
22	Corrales	*4*
25	Albuquerque Intl Arpt	3

Lowest

Rank	Station Name	Days
1	Alamogordo	*0*
1	Caballo Dam	0
1	Carlsbad	0
1	Carlsbad Caverns	*0*
1	Columbus	0
1	Deming	*0*
1	Faywood	0
1	Fort Bayard	0
1	Orogrande	*0*
10	Augustine 2 E	1
10	Bernardo	1
10	Jal	1
10	Jornada Exp Range	1
10	Los Lunas 3 SSW	1
10	Tatum	*1*
10	White Sands Natl Mon	1
17	Bingham 2 NE	2
17	Clovis 13 N	2
17	State University	2
20	Albuquerque Intl Arpt	3
20	Alcalde	3
20	Bitter Lakes Wl Refuge	3
20	Elk 2 E	3
20	Portales	3
20	Yeso 2 S	*3*

Rankings include 25 highest/lowest stations. If state has less than 25 stations, all stations are included. The period of record is 1980–2009. See User Guide for detailed explanation of data.

Significant Storm Events in New Mexico: 2000 – 2009

Location or County	Date	Type	Mag.	Deaths	Injuries	Property Damage ($mil.)	Crop Damage ($mil.)
Lincoln	05/07/00	Wild/Forest Fire	na	0	0	2.0	0.0
Los Alamos	07/02/01	Flash Flood	na	0	0	3.5	0.0
Lincoln	03/24/02	Wild/Forest Fire	na	0	0	5.0	0.0
Eddy	04/03/04	Flash Flood	na	0	0	2.0	0.1
Dona Ana	04/03/04	Hail	2.00 in.	0	0	2.0	0.0
Bernalillo	10/04/04	Hail	1.75 in.	0	0	4.0	0.0
Socorro	10/05/04	Hail	3.00 in.	0	0	40.0	0.0
Lea	06/06/05	Hail	2.75 in.	0	0	1.2	0.0
Otero	06/22/06	Flash Flood	na	0	0	1.3	0.0
Dona Ana	08/01/06	Flash Flood	na	0	0	3.0	0.0
Dona Ana	08/15/06	Flash Flood	na	0	0	4.0	0.5
Dona Ana	09/13/06	Hail	1.75 in.	0	0	10.0	0.5
Curry	03/23/07	Tornado	F2	2	33	16.5	0.0
Quay	03/23/07	Tornado	F1	0	12	3.5	0.0
Roosevelt	03/23/07	Tornado	F2	0	0	2.5	0.2
Sandia and Manzano Mountains	04/15/08	Wildfire	na	0	0	8.5	0.0
Otero	05/28/08	Hail	2.50 in.	0	0	2.5	0.0
Lincoln	07/26/08	Flood	na	1	0	25.0	0.0
Southern Sacramento Mountains	12/08/09	High Wind	74 mph	0	0	4.0	0.0
Southern New Mexico	12/08/09	High Wind	83 mph	0	2	2.0	0.0

Note: Deaths, injuries, and damages are date and location specific.

NEW YORK

PHYSICAL FEATURES. New York State contains 49,576 square miles, inclusive of 1,637 square miles of inland water, but exclusive of the boundary-water areas of Long Island Sound, New York Harbor, Lake Ontario, and Lake Erie. The major portion of the State lies generally between latitudes 42° and 45° N. and between longitudes 73° 30' and 79° 45' W. However, in the extreme southeast, a triangular portion extends southward to about latitude 40° 30' N., while Long Island lies eastward to about longitude 72° W.

The principal highland regions of the State are the Adirondacks in the northeast and the Appalachian Plateau (Southern Plateau) in the south. A minor highland region occurs in southeastern New York where the Hudson River has cut a valley between the Palisades on the west, near the New Jersey border, and the Taconic Mountains on the east, along the Connecticut and Massachusetts border. Just west of the Adirondacks and the upper Black River Valley in Lewis County is another minor highland known as Tug Hill. Much of the eastern border of the State consists of a long, narrow lowland region which is occupied by Lake Champlain, Lake George, and the middle and lower portions of the Hudson Valley.

Approximately 40 percent of New York State has an elevation of more than 1,000 feet above sea level. In northwestern Essex County are a number of peaks with an elevation of between 4,000 to 5,000 feet. The highest point, Mount Marcy, reaches a height of 5,344 feet above sea level. The Appalachian Plateau merges variously into the Great Lakes Plain of western New York with gradual- to steep-sloping terrain. This Plateau is penetrated by the valleys of the Finger Lakes which extend southward from the Great Lakes Plain. Other prominent lakes plus innumerable smaller lakes and ponds dot the landscape, with more than 1,500 in the Adirondack region alone.

GENERAL CLIMATE. The climate of New York State is broadly representative of the humid continental type which prevails in the Northeastern United States, but its diversity is not usually encountered within an area of comparable size. The geographical position of the State and the usual course of air masses, governed by the large-scale patterns of atmospheric circulation, provide general climatic controls. Differences in latitude, character of the topography, and proximity to large bodies of water have pronounced effects on the climate.

Lengthy periods of either abnormally cold or warm weather result from the movement of great high pressure (anticyclonic) systems into and through the Eastern United States. Cold winter temperatures prevail over New York whenever Arctic air masses, under high barometric pressure, flow southward from central Canada or from Hudson Bay. High pressure systems often move just off the Atlantic coast, become more or less stagnant for several days, and then a persistent air flow from the southwest or south affects the State. This circulation brings the very warm, often humid weather of the summer season and the mild, more pleasant temperatures during the fall, winter, and spring seasons.

TEMPERATURE. Many atmospheric and physiographic controls on the climate result in a considerable variation of temperature conditions over New York State. The average annual mean temperature ranges from about 40°F. in the Adirondacks to near 55°F. in the New York City area. The winters are long and cold in the Plateau Divisions of the State. Winter temperatures are moderated considerably in the Great Lakes Plain of western New York. The moderating influence of Lakes Erie and Ontario is comparable to that produced by the Atlantic Ocean in the southern portion of the Hudson Valley.

The summer climate is cool in the Adirondacks, Catskills, and higher elevations of the Southern Plateau. The New York City area and lower portions of the Hudson Valley have rather warm summers by comparison, with some periods of high, uncomfortable humidity. The remainder of New York State enjoys pleasantly warm summers, marred by only occasional, brief intervals of sultry conditions. Summer daytime temperatures usually range from the upper 70s to mid-80s over much of the State. The moderating effect of Lakes Erie and Ontario on temperatures assumes practical importance during the spring and fall seasons. The lake waters warm slowly in the spring, the effect of which is to reduce the warming of the atmosphere over adjacent land areas. In the fall season, the lake waters cool more slowly than the land areas and thus serve as a heat source.

PRECIPITATION. Moisture for precipitation in New York State is transported primarily from the Gulf of Mexico and Atlantic Ocean through circulation patterns and storm systems of the atmosphere. Distribution of precipitation within the State is greatly influenced by topography and proximity to the Great Lakes or Atlantic Ocean. Average annual amounts in excess of 50 inches occur in the western Adirondacks, Tug Hill area, and the Catskills, while slightly less than that amount is noted in the higher elevations of the Western Plateau southeast of Lake Erie. Areas of least rainfall, with average accumulations of about 30 inches, occur near Lake Ontario in the extreme western counties, in the lower half of the Genesee River Valley, and in the vicinity of Lake Champlain.

New York State has a fairly uniform distribution of precipitation during the year. There are no distinctly dry or wet seasons which are regularly repeated on an annual basis. Minimum precipitation occurs in the winter season. Maximum amounts are noted in the summer season throughout the State except along the Great Lakes where slight peaks of similar magnitude occur in both the spring and fall seasons.

SNOWFALL. The climate of New York State is marked by abundant snowfall. With the exception of the Coastal Division, the State receives an average seasonal amount of 40 inches or more. The average snowfall is greater than 70 inches over some 60 percent of New York's area. The moderating influence of the Atlantic Ocean reduces the snow accumulation to 25 to 35 inches in the New York City area and on Long Island. About one-third of the winter season precipitation in the Coastal Division occurs from storms which also yield at least one inch of snow. The great bulk of the winter precipitation in upstate New York comes as snow.

A durable snow cover generally begins to develop in the Adirondacks and northern lowlands by late November and remains on the ground until various times in April, depending upon late winter snowfall and early spring temperatures. The Southern Plateau, Great Lakes Plain in southern portions of western upstate New York, and the Hudson Valley experience a continuous snow cover from about mid-December to mid-March, with maximum depths usually occurring in February. Bare ground may occur briefly in the lower elevations of these regions during some winters. From late December or early January through February, the Atlantic coastal region of the State experiences alternating periods of measurable snow cover and bare ground.

FLOODS. Although major floods are relatively infrequent, the greatest potential and frequency for floods occur in the early spring when substantial rains combine with rapid snowmelting to produce a heavy runoff. Damaging floods are caused at other times of the year by prolonged periods of heavy rainfall.

WINDS AND STORMS. The prevailing wind is generally from the west in New York State. A southwest component becomes evident in winds during the warmer months while a northwest component is characteristic of the colder one-half of the year. Thunderstorms occur on an average of about 30 days in a year throughout the State. Destructive winds and lightning strikes in local areas are common with the more vigorous warm-season thunderstorms. Locally, hail occurs with more severe thunderstorms. Tornadoes are not common. About 3 or 4 of these storms strike limited, localized areas of New York State in most years. Tornadoes occur generally between late May and late August. Storms of freezing rain occur on one or more occasions during the winter season and often affect a wide area of the State in any one incident. Such storms are usually limited to a thin but dangerous coating of ice on exposed surfaces. Hurricanes and tropical storms periodically cause serious and heavy losses in the vicinity of Long Island and southeastern upstate New York. The greatest storm hazard in terms of area affected is heavy snow. Coastal northeaster storms occur with some frequency in most winters. Blizzard conditions of heavy snow, high winds, and rapidly falling temperature occur occasionally, but are much less characteristic of New York's climate than in the plains of Midwestern United States.

OTHER CLIMATIC ELEMENTS. The climate of the State features much cloudy weather during the months of November, December, and January in upstate New York. From June through September, however, about 60 to 70 percent of the possible sunshine hours is received. In the Atlantic coastal region, the sunshine hours increases from 50 percent of possible in the winter to about 65 percent of possible in the summer. The occurrence of heavy dense fog is variable over the State. The valleys and ridges of the Southern Plateau are most subject to periods of fog, with occurrences averaging about 50 days in a year. In the Great Lakes Plain and northern valleys, the frequency decreases to only 10 to 20 days annually. In those portions of the State with greater maritime influence, the frequency of dense fog in a year ranges from about 35 days on the south shore of Long Island to 25 days in the Hudson Valley.

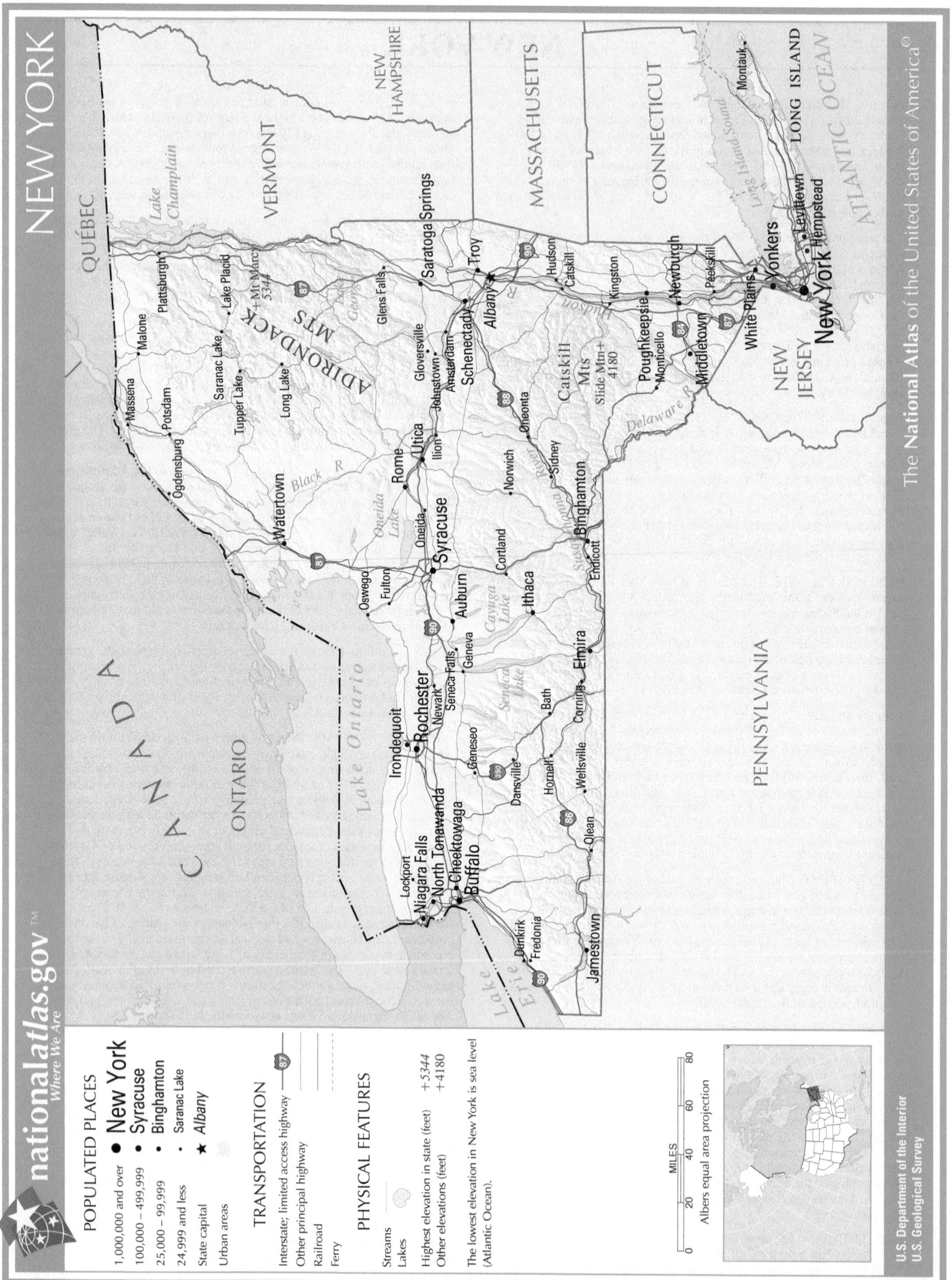
NEW YORK
nationalatlas.gov™
Where We Are
POPULATED PLACES
1,000,000 and over New York
100,000 – 499,999 Syracuse
25,000 – 99,999 Binghamton
24,999 and less Saranac Lake
State capital Albany
Urban areas
TRANSPORTATION
Interstate; limited access highway 87
Other principal highway
Railroad
Ferry
PHYSICAL FEATURES
Streams
Lakes
Highest elevation in state (feet) +5344
Other elevations (feet) +4180
The lowest elevation in New York is sea level (Atlantic Ocean).
MILES
0 20 40 60 80
Albers equal area projection
U.S. Department of the Interior
U.S. Geological Survey
The National Atlas of the United States of America®
QUÉBEC
CANADA
ONTARIO
VERMONT
NEW HAMPSHIRE
MASSACHUSETTS
CONNECTICUT
NEW JERSEY
PENNSYLVANIA
LONG ISLAND
ATLANTIC OCEAN
Long Island Sound
Lake Champlain
Lake Ontario
Lake Erie
Oneida Lake
Cayuga Lake
Seneca Lake
Black R
Hudson R
Delaware R
Susquehanna River
ADIRONDACK MTS
Catskill Mts
Mt Marcy 5344
Slide Mtn 4180
Plattsburgh
Malone
Massena
Potsdam
Ogdensburg
Lake Placid
Saranac Lake
Tupper Lake
Long Lake
Watertown
Glens Falls
Saratoga Springs
Gloversville
Johnstown
Amsterdam
Schenectady
Troy
Albany
Hudson
Catskill
Kingston
Oneonta
Rome
Utica
Ilion
Oneida
Syracuse
Oswego
Fulton
Auburn
Cortland
Norwich
Sidney
Binghamton
Endicott
Ithaca
Geneva
Seneca Falls
Newark
Rochester
Irondequoit
Geneseo
Dansville
Bath
Corning
Elmira
Hornell
Wellsville
Olean
Lockport
Niagara Falls
North Tonawanda
Cheektowaga
Buffalo
Dunkirk
Fredonia
Jamestown
Poughkeepsie
Monticello
Newburgh
Middletown
Peekskill
White Plains
Yonkers
New York
Levittown
Hempstead
Montauk
81
87
88
90
84
86
390

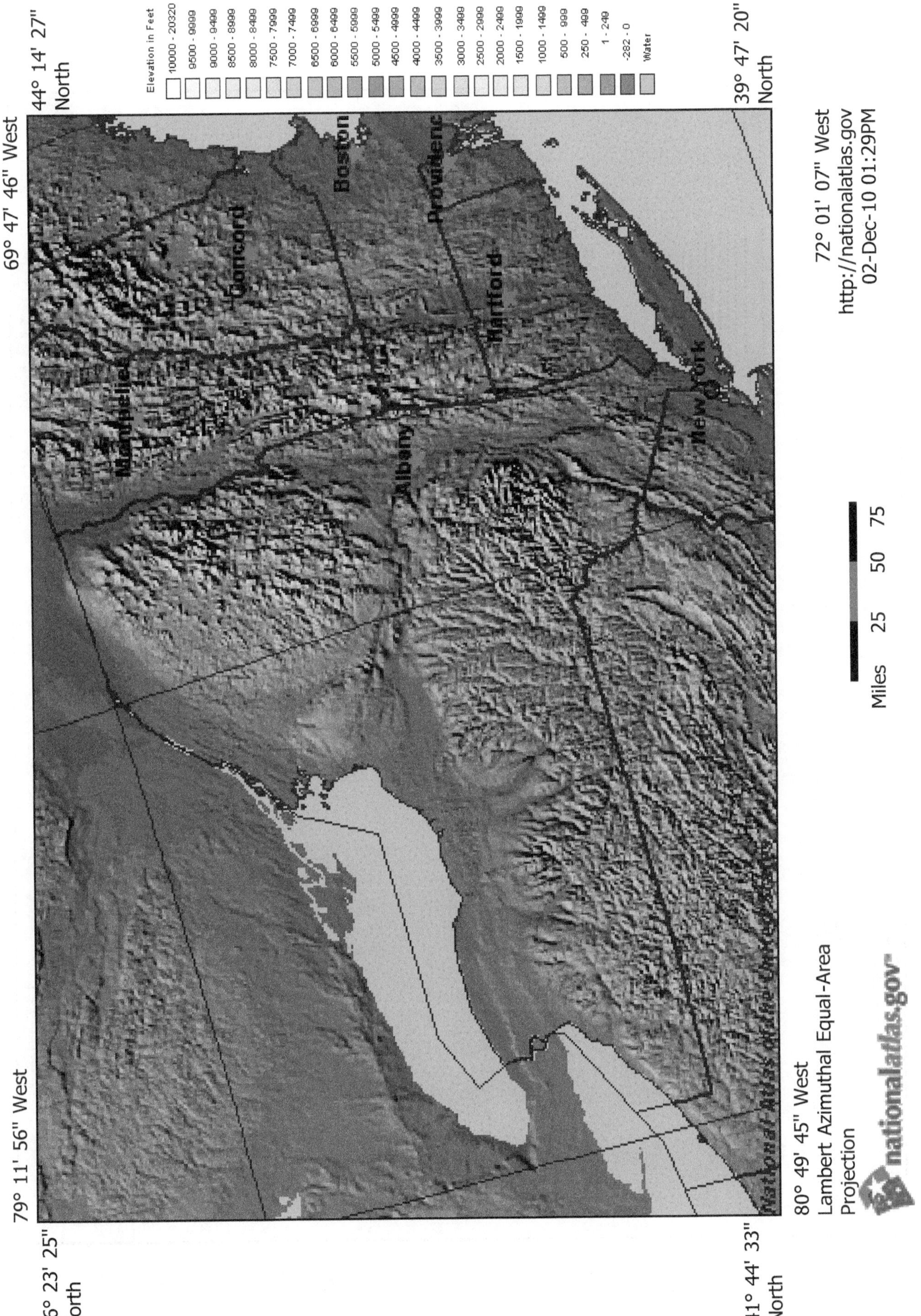
Elevation in Feet
10000 - 20320
9500 - 9999
9000 - 9499
8500 - 8999
8000 - 8499
7500 - 7999
7000 - 7499
6500 - 6999
6000 - 6499
5500 - 5999
5000 - 5499
4500 - 4999
4000 - 4499
3500 - 3999
3000 - 3499
2500 - 2999
2000 - 2499
1500 - 1999
1000 - 1499
500 - 999
250 - 499
1 - 249
-282 - 0
Water
44° 14' 27" North
69° 47' 46" West
39° 47' 20" North
72° 01' 07" West
http://nationalatlas.gov
02-Dec-10 01:29PM
Montpelier
Concord
Boston
Providence
Hartford
Albany
New York
Miles 25 50 75
79° 11' 56" West
46° 23' 25" North
41° 44' 33" North
80° 49' 45" West
Lambert Azimuthal Equal-Area Projection
nationalatlas.gov

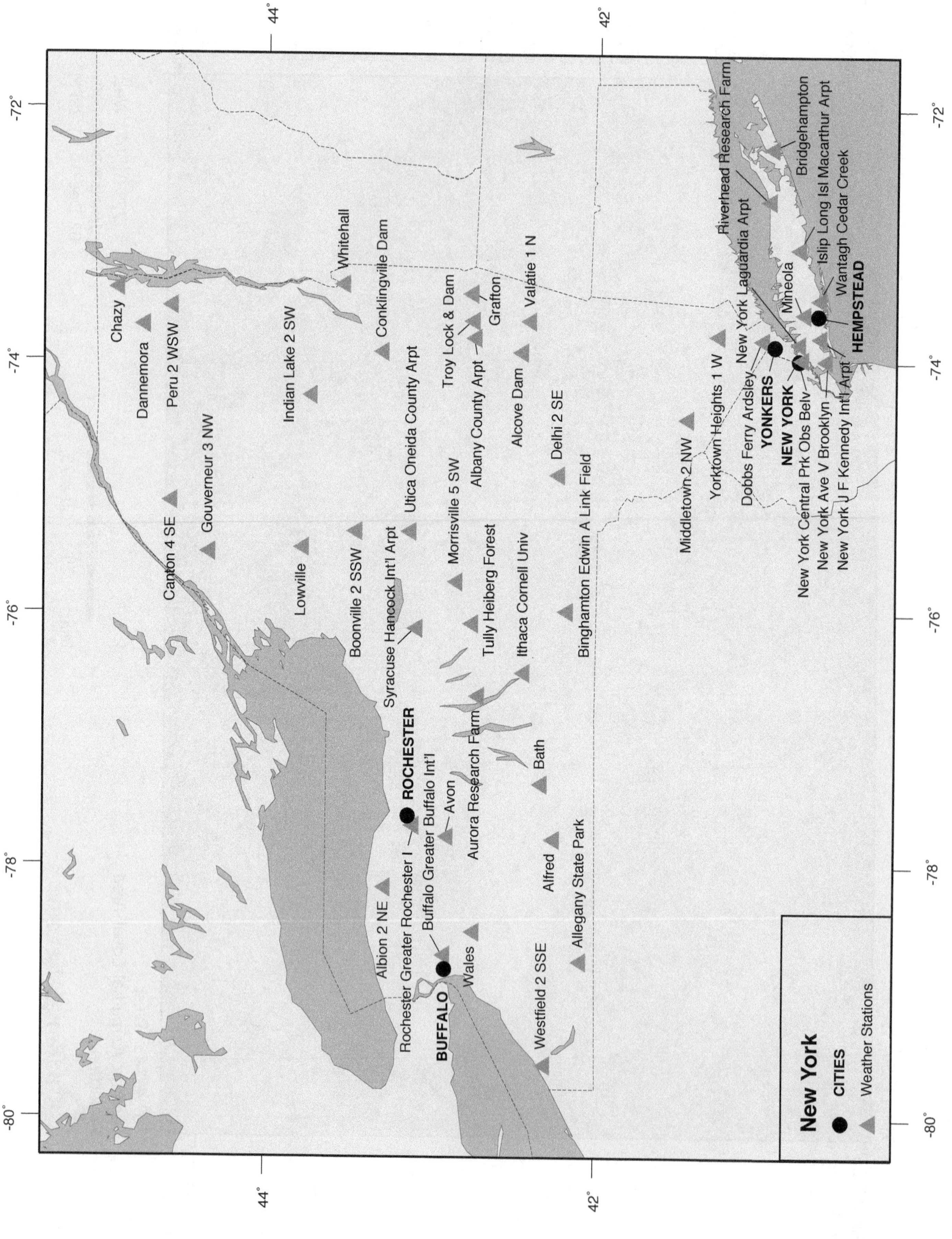
New York
CITIES
Weather Stations
BUFFALO
ROCHESTER
YONKERS
NEW YORK
HEMPSTEAD
Chazy
Dannemora
Peru 2 WSW
Whitehall
Conklingville Dam
Indian Lake 2 SW
Canton 4 SE
Gouverneur 3 NW
Lowville
Boonville 2 SSW
Utica Oneida County Arpt
Syracuse Hancock Int'l Arpt
Troy Lock & Dam
Grafton
Albany County Arpt
Valatie 1 N
Alcove Dam
Delhi 2 SE
Morrisville 5 SW
Tully Heiberg Forest
Ithaca Cornell Univ
Binghamton Edwin A Link Field
Albion 2 NE
Rochester Greater Rochester I
Buffalo Greater Buffalo Int'l
Avon
Aurora Research Farm
Bath
Alfred
Allegany State Park
Wales
Westfield 2 SSE
Middletown 2 NW
Yorktown Heights 1 W
Dobbs Ferry Ardsley
New York Laguardia Arpt
Riverhead Research Farm
Bridgehampton
Islip Long Isl Macarthur Arpt
Wantagh Cedar Creek
Mineola
New York Central Prk Obs Belv
New York Ave V Brooklyn
New York J F Kennedy Int'l Arpt
44°
42°
-72°
-74°
-76°
-78°
-80°

New York Weather Stations by County

County	Station Name
Albany	Albany County Arpt Alcove Dam
Allegany	Alfred
Broome	Binghamton Edwin A Link Field
Cattaraugus	Allegany State Park
Cayuga	Aurora Research Farm
Chautauqua	Westfield 2 SSE
Clinton	Chazy Dannemora Peru 2 WSW
Columbia	Valatie 1 N
Cortland	Tully Heiberg Forest
Delaware	Delhi 2 SE
Erie	Buffalo Greater Buffalo Int'l Wales
Hamilton	Indian Lake 2 SW
Kings	New York Ave V Brooklyn
Lewis	Lowville
Livingston	Avon
Madison	Morrisville 5 SW
Monroe	Rochester Intl Arpt
Nassau	Mineola Wantagh Cedar Creek
New York	New York Central Park Observ
Oneida	Boonville 2 SSW Utica Oneida County Arpt
Onondaga	Syracuse Hancock Int'l Arpt
Orange	Middletown 2 NW
Orleans	Albion 2 NE
Queens	New York J F Kennedy Int'l Arpt New York Laguardia Arpt
Rensselaer	Grafton Troy Lock and Dam
Saratoga	Conklingville Dam
St. Lawrence	Canton 4 SE Gouverneur 3 NW
Steuben	Bath

County	Station Name
Suffolk	Bridgehampton Islip-Macarthur Arpt Riverhead Research Farm
Tompkins	Ithaca Cornell Univ
Washington	Whitehall
Westchester	Dobbs Ferry Ardsley Yorktown Heights 1 W

See User Guide for station inclusion criteria.

New York Weather Stations by City

City	Station Name	Miles
Albany	Albany County Arpt	6.2
	Alcove Dam	15.4
	Grafton	18.3
	Troy Lock and Dam	8.1
	Valatie 1 N	16.5
Amherst	Buffalo Greater Buffalo Int'l	4.5
	Wales	21.1
Babylon	Islip-Macarthur Arpt	14.7
	Mineola	13.2
	New York J F Kennedy Int'l Arpt	23.2
	Wantagh Cedar Creek	8.3
Brentwood	Islip-Macarthur Arpt	7.5
	Mineola	19.8
	Wantagh Cedar Creek	16.2
Bronx	Essex Fells Serv Bldg, NJ	21.0
	Newark Intl Arpt, NJ	18.3
	Dobbs Ferry Ardsley	10.7
	Mineola	16.1
	New York Ave V Brooklyn	18.1
	New York Central Park Observ	6.4
	New York J F Kennedy Int'l Arpt	14.5
	New York Laguardia Arpt	4.6
	Wantagh Cedar Creek	24.3
Brookhaven	Bridgeport Sikorsky Memorial, CT	24.2
	Islip-Macarthur Arpt	7.6
	Riverhead Research Farm	16.3
Brooklyn	Canoe Brook, NJ	21.8
	Cranford, NJ	18.1
	Essex Fells Serv Bldg, NJ	21.4
	Newark Intl Arpt, NJ	12.8
	Plainfield, NJ	23.6
	Mineola	18.6
	New York Ave V Brooklyn	3.8
	New York Central Park Observ	9.2
	New York J F Kennedy Int'l Arpt	8.1
	New York Laguardia Arpt	9.9
	Wantagh Cedar Creek	23.8
Buffalo	Buffalo Greater Buffalo Int'l	6.0
	Wales	20.1
Cheektowaga	Buffalo Greater Buffalo Int'l	2.1
	Wales	16.1
Clarkstown	Stamford 5 N, CT	22.6
	Charlotteburg Reservoir, NJ	24.3
	Dobbs Ferry Ardsley	11.7
	New York Central Park Observ	23.7
	New York Laguardia Arpt	24.3
	Yorktown Heights 1 W	13.6
Clay	Syracuse Hancock Int'l Arpt	5.2
Colonie	Albany County Arpt	1.5
	Alcove Dam	19.7
	Grafton	16.7
	Troy Lock and Dam	5.4
	Valatie 1 N	21.2

City	Station Name	Miles
Greece	Albion 2 NE	24.6
	Avon	22.3
	Rochester Intl Arpt	8.2
Greenburgh	Stamford 5 N, CT	16.0
	Dobbs Ferry Ardsley	2.1
	Mineola	23.5
	New York Central Park Observ	18.4
	New York Laguardia Arpt	17.3
	Yorktown Heights 1 W	16.4
Hamburg	Buffalo Greater Buffalo Int'l	14.0
	Wales	16.8
Hempstead	Dobbs Ferry Ardsley	24.8
	Mineola	3.6
	New York Ave V Brooklyn	19.9
	New York Central Park Observ	19.6
	New York J F Kennedy Int'l Arpt	9.7
	New York Laguardia Arpt	15.6
	Wantagh Cedar Creek	6.6
Huntington	Stamford 5 N, CT	20.7
	Islip-Macarthur Arpt	14.9
	Mineola	15.1
	Wantagh Cedar Creek	15.4
Islip	Islip-Macarthur Arpt	5.2
	Mineola	22.1
	Wantagh Cedar Creek	17.7
Levittown	Islip-Macarthur Arpt	22.0
	Mineola	5.5
	New York Central Park Observ	24.1
	New York J F Kennedy Int'l Arpt	15.9
	New York Laguardia Arpt	19.8
	Wantagh Cedar Creek	5.2
Manhattan	Canoe Brook, NJ	20.3
	Cranford, NJ	19.7
	Essex Fells Serv Bldg, NJ	17.1
	Newark Intl Arpt, NJ	12.2
	Dobbs Ferry Ardsley	16.7
	Mineola	18.5
	New York Ave V Brooklyn	12.5
	New York Central Park Observ	0.2
	New York J F Kennedy Int'l Arpt	12.5
	New York Laguardia Arpt	4.3
Mount Vernon	Stamford 5 N, CT	20.4
	Essex Fells Serv Bldg, NJ	24.2
	Newark Intl Arpt, NJ	22.8
	Dobbs Ferry Ardsley	6.0
	Mineola	16.7
	New York Ave V Brooklyn	23.0
	New York Central Park Observ	11.4
	New York J F Kennedy Int'l Arpt	18.2
	New York Laguardia Arpt	9.3
	Yorktown Heights 1 W	24.5
New Rochelle	Stamford 5 N, CT	18.2
	Dobbs Ferry Ardsley	6.0
	Mineola	15.7

See User Guide for station inclusion criteria.

City	Station Name	Miles
New Rochelle *(cont.)*	New York Ave V Brooklyn	24.5
	New York Central Park Observ	13.5
	New York J F Kennedy Int'l Arpt	18.8
	New York Laguardia Arpt	10.8
	Wantagh Cedar Creek	24.0
	Yorktown Heights 1 W	23.9
New York	Canoe Brook, NJ	22.5
	Cranford, NJ	20.5
	Essex Fells Serv Bldg, NJ	20.4
	Newark Intl Arpt, NJ	13.7
	Dobbs Ferry Ardsley	19.6
	Mineola	15.9
	New York Ave V Brooklyn	9.2
	New York Central Park Observ	4.7
	New York J F Kennedy Int'l Arpt	8.2
	New York Laguardia Arpt	4.5
	Wantagh Cedar Creek	22.7
Niagara Falls	Buffalo Greater Buffalo Int'l	18.2
North Hempstead	Stamford 5 N, CT	24.1
	Dobbs Ferry Ardsley	17.6
	Mineola	4.1
	New York Ave V Brooklyn	20.7
	New York Central Park Observ	15.7
	New York J F Kennedy Int'l Arpt	11.3
	New York Laguardia Arpt	11.4
	Wantagh Cedar Creek	12.5
Oyster Bay	Stamford 5 N, CT	24.8
	Dobbs Ferry Ardsley	24.1
	Islip-Macarthur Arpt	20.8
	Mineola	6.5
	New York Central Park Observ	24.6
	New York J F Kennedy Int'l Arpt	17.6
	New York Laguardia Arpt	20.3
	Wantagh Cedar Creek	7.6
Queens	Cranford, NJ	24.9
	Essex Fells Serv Bldg, NJ	24.8
	Newark Intl Arpt, NJ	18.3
	Dobbs Ferry Ardsley	19.2
	Mineola	11.4
	New York Ave V Brooklyn	11.5
	New York Central Park Observ	8.2
	New York J F Kennedy Int'l Arpt	5.3
	New York Laguardia Arpt	5.0
	Wantagh Cedar Creek	18.2
Ramapo	Charlotteburg Reservoir, NJ	19.7
	Essex Fells Serv Bldg, NJ	22.7
	Dobbs Ferry Ardsley	15.1
	New York Central Park Observ	24.1
	Yorktown Heights 1 W	17.4
Rochester	Avon	18.5
	Rochester Intl Arpt	4.9
Schenectady	Albany County Arpt	7.5
	Alcove Dam	23.3
	Grafton	23.5
	Troy Lock and Dam	13.0
Smithtown	Bridgeport Sikorsky Memorial, CT	22.7

City	Station Name	Miles
Smithtown *(cont.)*	Stamford 5 N, CT	24.9
	Islip-Macarthur Arpt	8.0
	Mineola	22.7
	Wantagh Cedar Creek	20.8
Southampton	Bridgehampton	11.7
	Riverhead Research Farm	12.1
Staten Island	Canoe Brook, NJ	15.8
	Cranford, NJ	9.6
	Essex Fells Serv Bldg, NJ	18.6
	Newark Intl Arpt, NJ	9.2
	New Brunswick 3 SE, NJ	17.7
	Plainfield, NJ	13.8
	New York Ave V Brooklyn	8.1
	New York Central Park Observ	16.1
	New York J F Kennedy Int'l Arpt	18.2
	New York Laguardia Arpt	18.9
Syracuse	Syracuse Hancock Int'l Arpt	5.5
	Tully Heiberg Forest	19.3
Tonawanda	Buffalo Greater Buffalo Int'l	7.0
	Wales	23.4
Union	Binghamton Edwin A Link Field	6.2
	Montrose, PA	19.3
Utica	Utica Oneida County Arpt	8.5
White Plains	Stamford 5 N, CT	12.8
	Dobbs Ferry Ardsley	4.0
	Mineola	21.6
	New York Central Park Observ	19.8
	New York Laguardia Arpt	17.9
	Yorktown Heights 1 W	16.7
Yonkers	Stamford 5 N, CT	20.9
	Essex Fells Serv Bldg, NJ	22.6
	Newark Intl Arpt, NJ	22.2
	Dobbs Ferry Ardsley	4.8
	Mineola	19.5
	New York Ave V Brooklyn	24.0
	New York Central Park Observ	11.7
	New York J F Kennedy Int'l Arpt	20.2
	New York Laguardia Arpt	10.7
	Yorktown Heights 1 W	23.1

Note: Miles is the distance between the geographic center of the city and the weather station.

New York Weather Stations by Elevation

Feet	Station Name
1,898	Tully Heiberg Forest
1,770	Alfred
1,660	Indian Lake 2 SW
1,600	Binghamton Edwin A Link Field
1,580	Boonville 2 SSW
1,560	Grafton
1,500	Allegany State Park
1,439	Delhi 2 SE
1,339	Dannemora
1,299	Morrisville 5 SW
1,120	Bath
1,089	Wales
959	Ithaca Cornell Univ
859	Lowville
830	Aurora Research Farm
808	Conklingville Dam
711	Utica Oneida County Arpt
707	Westfield 2 SSE
705	Buffalo Greater Buffalo Int'l
700	Middletown 2 NW
669	Yorktown Heights 1 W
606	Alcove Dam
600	Rochester Intl Arpt
544	Avon
509	Peru 2 WSW
439	Albion 2 NE
439	Canton 4 SE
419	Gouverneur 3 NW
410	Syracuse Hancock Int'l Arpt
299	Valatie 1 N
274	Albany County Arpt
200	Dobbs Ferry Ardsley
169	Chazy
131	New York Central Park Observ
119	Whitehall
100	Riverhead Research Farm
96	Mineola
83	Islip-Macarthur Arpt
60	Bridgehampton
23	Troy Lock and Dam
20	New York Ave V Brooklyn
16	New York J F Kennedy Int'l Arpt
11	New York Laguardia Arpt
9	Wantagh Cedar Creek

See User Guide for station inclusion criteria.

Albany County Airport

Albany is located on the west bank of the Hudson River some 150 miles north of New York City, and 8 miles south of the confluence of the Mohawk and Hudson Rivers. The river-front portion of the city is only a few feet above sea level, and there is a tidal effect upstream to Troy. Eleven miles west of Albany the Helderberg hill range rises to 1,800 feet. Between it and the Hudson River the valley floor is gently rolling, ranging some 200 to 500 feet above sea level. East of the city there is more rugged terrain 5 or 6 miles wide with elevations of 300 to 600 feet. Farther to the east the terrain rises more sharply. It reaches a north-south range of hills 12 miles east of Albany with elevations ranging to 2,000 feet.

The climate at Albany is primarily continental in character, but is subjected to some modification by the Atlantic Ocean. The moderating effect on temperatures is more pronounced during the warmer months than in winter when outbursts of cold air sweep down from Canada. In the warmer seasons, temperatures rise rapidly in the daytime. However, temperatures also fall rapidly after sunset so that the nights are relatively cool. Occasionally there are extended periods of oppressive heat up to a week or more in duration.

Winters are usually cold and sometimes fairly severe. Maximum temperatures during the colder winters are often below freezing and nighttime lows are frequently below 10 degrees. Sub-zero readings occur about 12 times a year. Snowfall throughout the area is quite variable and snow flurries are quite frequent during the winter. Precipitation is sufficient to serve the economy of the region in most years, and only occasionally do periods of drought exist. Most of the rainfall in the summer is from thunderstorms. Tornadoes are quite rare and hail is not usually of any consequence.

Wind velocities are moderate. The north-south Hudson River Valley has a marked effect on the lighter winds and in the warm months, average wind direction is usually southerly. Destructive winds rarely occur.

The area enjoys one of the highest percentages of sunshine in the entire state. Seldom does the area experience long periods of cloudy days and long periods of smog are rare.

Based on the 1951-1980 period, the average first occurrence of 32 degrees Fahrenheit in the fall is September 29 and the average last occurrence in the spring is May 7.

Albany County Airport *Albany County* Elevation: 274 ft. Latitude: 42° 45' N Longitude: 73° 48' W

	JAN	FEB	MAR	APR	MAY	JUN	JUL	AUG	SEP	OCT	NOV	DEC	YEAR
Mean Maximum Temp. (°F)	31.1	34.9	44.3	58.3	69.6	77.9	82.3	80.5	72.4	60.0	48.2	36.1	58.0
Mean Temp. (°F)	22.8	25.9	34.8	47.6	58.2	67.0	71.6	70.0	61.8	49.8	39.8	28.4	48.2
Mean Minimum Temp. (°F)	14.5	16.8	25.2	36.9	46.8	56.1	60.9	59.5	51.2	39.4	31.3	20.8	38.3
Extreme Maximum Temp. (°F)	71	68	89	92	94	96	99	97	92	86	81	71	99
Extreme Minimum Temp. (°F)	-23	-18	-6	13	28	36	44	34	28	18	6	-20	-23
Days Maximum Temp. ≥ 90°F	0	0	0	0	0	2	4	2	0	0	0	0	8
Days Maximum Temp. ≤ 32°F	17	11	4	0	0	0	0	0	0	0	1	10	43
Days Minimum Temp. ≤ 32°F	29	26	24	9	1	0	0	0	0	7	18	27	141
Days Minimum Temp. ≤ 0°F	5	2	1	0	0	0	0	0	0	0	0	1	9
Heating Degree Days (base 65°F)	1,301	1,099	929	519	231	51	6	19	138	469	749	1,127	6,638
Cooling Degree Days (base 65°F)	0	0	1	4	27	117	217	183	50	4	0	0	603
Mean Precipitation (in.)	2.54	2.09	3.26	3.22	3.58	3.80	4.11	3.62	3.26	3.52	3.27	2.87	39.14
Maximum Precipitation (in.)*	6.4	5.0	5.9	7.9	9.0	7.4	7.0	7.3	7.9	8.8	8.1	6.7	47.2
Minimum Precipitation (in.)*	0.4	0.2	0.3	1.1	1.0	0.6	0.5	0.7	0.4	0.2	0.6	0.6	21.5
Extreme Maximum Daily Precip. (in.)	1.78	1.60	2.02	2.26	2.16	3.30	3.49	2.78	5.60	2.82	2.21	2.79	5.60
Days With ≥ 0.1" Precipitation	6	5	7	7	8	8	7	7	6	6	7	7	81
Days With ≥ 0.5" Precipitation	2	1	2	2	3	3	3	2	2	2	2	2	26
Days With ≥ 1.0" Precipitation	0	0	1	1	0	1	1	1	1	1	1	0	8
Mean Snowfall (in.)	17.7	11.5	11.4	2.3	0.1	trace	trace	0.0	trace	0.3	3.2	13.7	60.2
Maximum Snowfall (in.)*	48	35	35	18	2	0	0	0	0	7	25	58	107
Maximum 24-hr. Snowfall (in.)*	13	17	22	17	2	0	0	0	0	7	22	14	22
Maximum Snow Depth (in.)	24	20	28	13	trace	trace	trace	0	trace	2	10	16	28
Days With ≥ 1.0" Snow Depth	19	16	9	1	0	0	0	0	0	0	2	12	59
Thunderstorm Days*	< 1	< 1	1	1	3	5	6	5	2	1	< 1	< 1	24
Foggy Days*	10	9	11	9	12	13	14	17	17	15	13	12	152
Predominant Sky Cover*	OVR	OVR	OVR	OVR	OVR	OVR	OVR	OVR	OVR	OVR	OVR	OVR	OVR
Mean Relative Humidity 7am (%)*	77	77	76	72	74	77	80	85	88	86	82	80	80
Mean Relative Humidity 4pm (%)*	64	59	54	48	50	53	53	55	57	56	64	67	57
Mean Dewpoint (°F)*	14	15	23	33	45	55	60	59	52	41	31	20	38
Prevailing Wind Direction*	WNW	WNW	WNW	WNW	S	S	S	S	S	S	WNW	WNW	S
Prevailing Wind Speed (mph)*	15	15	15	15	10	9	8	8	9	9	14	14	12
Maximum Wind Gust (mph)*	62	67	61	58	67	59	77	62	64	60	67	63	77

Note: (*) Period of record is 1946-1995

Binghamton Edwin A. Link Field

Binghamton, in south central New York lies in a comparatively narrow valley at the confluence of the Susquehanna and Chenango Rivers. Within a radius of 5 miles, hills rise to elevations of 1,400-1,600 feet above mean sea level. In the spring, melting snow, sometimes supplemented by rainfall, occasionally causes flooding in the city and along the streams.

The climate of Binghamton is representative of the humid area of the north-eastern United States and is primarily continental in type. The area, being adjacent to the so-called St. Lawrence Valley storm track, and also subject to cold air masses approaching from the west and north, has a variable climate, characterized by frequent and rapid changes. Furthermore, diurnal and seasonal changes assist in the production of an invigorating climate. As a rule, the temperature rises rapidly to moderate daytime levels with readings of 90 degrees or above only a few days in any month summer nights provide favorable sleeping conditions.

Winters are usually cold, but not commonly severe. Highest daytime temperatures average in the high 20s to low 30s, while the lowest nighttime readings average from the mid-teens to low 20s. Ordinarily a few sub-zero readings may be expected in January and February, with a lesser number in November, December, and March. The transitional seasons, spring and autumn, are the most variable of the year.

Most of the precipitation in the Binghamton area derives from moisture laden air transported from the Gulf of Mexico and cyclonic systems moving northward along the Atlantic coast. The annual rainfall is rather evenly distributed over the year. However, the greatest average monthly amounts occur during the growing season, April through September. As a rule, rainfall is ample for good crop growth and comes mostly in the form of thunderstorms. Annual snowfall is around 50 inches in Binghamton and above 85 inches at Edwin A. Link Field, some 10 miles to the NNW, and about 700 feet higher in elevation. Most of the snow falls during the normal winter months. However, heavy snows can occur as early as November and as late as April. Being adjacent to the track of storms that move through the St. Lawrence Valley, and being under the influence of winds that sweep across Lakes Erie and Ontario to the interior of the state, the area is subject to much cloudiness and winter snow flurries.

For the most part, the winds at Binghamton have northerly and westerly components. Tornadoes, although rare, have struck in the Binghamton area.

Based on the 1951-1980 period, the growing season averages 150 to 160 days. Usually the last spring frost occurs during early May, and the first frost in autumn during early October.

Binghamton Edwin A. Link Field *Broome County* Elevation: 1,600 ft. Latitude: 42° 12' N Longitude: 75° 59' W

	JAN	FEB	MAR	APR	MAY	JUN	JUL	AUG	SEP	OCT	NOV	DEC	YEAR
Mean Maximum Temp. (°F)	29.4	32.5	41.3	54.6	66.0	74.2	78.3	77.0	69.1	57.2	45.4	33.8	54.9
Mean Temp. (°F)	22.6	25.0	33.0	45.3	56.2	64.7	69.0	67.8	59.9	48.7	38.5	27.5	46.5
Mean Minimum Temp. (°F)	15.8	17.4	24.6	36.0	46.2	55.1	59.7	58.4	50.8	40.2	31.5	21.2	38.1
Extreme Maximum Temp. (°F)	63	63	82	89	89	92	98	95	91	82	77	65	98
Extreme Minimum Temp. (°F)	-15	-10	-7	9	28	33	44	38	27	19	8	-18	-18
Days Maximum Temp. ≥ 90°F	0	0	0	0	0	0	1	1	0	0	0	0	2
Days Maximum Temp. ≤ 32°F	19	15	7	0	0	0	0	0	0	0	3	14	58
Days Minimum Temp. ≤ 32°F	29	26	24	11	1	0	0	0	0	6	18	27	142
Days Minimum Temp. ≤ 0°F	3	1	0	0	0	0	0	0	0	0	0	1	5
Heating Degree Days (base 65°F)	1,307	1,124	987	588	290	85	20	35	180	500	790	1,154	7,060
Cooling Degree Days (base 65°F)	0	0	1	4	22	82	152	128	35	2	0	0	426
Mean Precipitation (in.)	2.38	2.29	3.09	3.53	3.53	4.33	3.67	3.37	3.55	3.30	3.29	2.81	39.14
Maximum Precipitation (in.)*	6.4	4.4	6.0	8.6	6.5	9.5	7.4	7.5	9.7	9.4	7.5	6.1	48.0
Minimum Precipitation (in.)*	0.8	0.4	0.7	1.0	0.8	1.0	0.8	0.6	0.6	0.3	1.0	0.9	29.9
Extreme Maximum Daily Precip. (in.)	1.64	1.80	1.83	2.86	2.91	4.05	1.70	2.73	3.50	2.94	2.35	2.66	4.05
Days With ≥ 0.1" Precipitation	6	6	7	8	8	8	7	7	7	6	7	7	84
Days With ≥ 0.5" Precipitation	1	1	2	2	2	3	3	2	2	2	2	2	24
Days With ≥ 1.0" Precipitation	0	0	0	1	1	1	1	1	1	1	1	0	8
Mean Snowfall (in.)	21.7	15.9	15.5	4.3	0.1	trace	0.0	trace	trace	1.1	7.0	17.2	82.8
Maximum Snowfall (in.)*	44	44	38	23	3	0	0	0	trace	12	29	60	138
Maximum 24-hr. Snowfall (in.)*	18	21	19	12	3	0	0	0	trace	7	11	14	21
Maximum Snow Depth (in.)	32	19	35	9	1	trace	0	trace	trace	3	13	15	35
Days With ≥ 1.0" Snow Depth	23	20	13	2	0	0	0	0	0	0	5	16	79
Thunderstorm Days*	< 1	< 1	1	2	4	6	7	5	3	1	< 1	< 1	29
Foggy Days*	11	10	13	12	14	15	16	19	17	15	14	13	169
Predominant Sky Cover*	OVR	OVR	OVR	OVR	OVR	OVR	OVR	OVR	OVR	OVR	OVR	OVR	OVR
Mean Relative Humidity 7am (%)*	80	79	79	76	78	83	85	89	90	85	82	82	82
Mean Relative Humidity 4pm (%)*	69	65	60	54	54	57	57	59	62	60	68	72	61
Mean Dewpoint (°F)*	15	16	23	32	44	54	59	58	51	40	31	20	37
Prevailing Wind Direction*	WNW	NW	NW	NW	NW	SW	SW	SW	SW	S	SW	WNW	NW
Prevailing Wind Speed (mph)*	14	14	14	13	12	9	8	8	9	9	10	14	12
Maximum Wind Gust (mph)*	61	56	58	64	54	60	74	63	48	51	58	54	74

Note: (*) Period of record is 1948-1995

The period of record for National Weather Service station data is 1980 – 2009 except where noted. See User Guide for detailed explanation of data.

Buffalo Int'l Airport

The country surrounding Buffalo is comparatively low and level to the west. To the east and south the land is gently rolling, rising to pronounced hills within 12 to 18 miles, and to 1,000 feet above the level of Lake Erie about 35 miles south-southeast of the city. A steep slope of 50 to 100 feet lies east-west one and a half miles to the north. The eastern end of Lake Erie is nine miles to the west-southwest, while Lake Ontario lies 25 miles to the north, the two being connected by the Niagara River, which flows north-northwestward from the end of Lake Erie.

Buffalo is located near the mean position of the polar front. Its weather is varied and changeable, characteristic of the latitude. Wide seasonal swings of temperature from hot to cold are tempered appreciably by the proximity of Lakes Erie and Ontario. Lake Erie lies to the southwest, the direction of the prevailing wind. Wind flow throughout the year is somewhat higher due to this exposure. The vigorous interplay of warm and cold air masses during the winter and early spring months causes one or more windstorms. Precipitation is moderate and fairly evenly divided throughout the twelve months.

The spring season is more cloudy and cooler than points not affected by the cold lake. Spring growth of vegetation is retarded, protecting it from late spring frosts. With heavy winter ice accumulations in the lake, typical spring conditions are delayed until late May or early June.

Summer comes suddenly in mid-June. Lake breezes temper the extreme heat of the summer season. Temperatures of 90 degrees and above are infrequent. There is more summer sunshine here than in any other section of the state. Due to the stabilizing effects of Lake Erie, thunderstorms are relatively infrequent. Most of them are caused by frontal action. To the north and south of the city thunderstorms occur more often.

Autumn has long, dry periods and is frost free usually until mid-October. Cloudiness increases in November, continuing mostly cloudy throughout the winter and early spring. Snow flurries off the lake begin in mid-November or early December. Outbreaks of Arctic air in December and throughout the winter months produce locally heavy snowfalls from the lake. At the same time, temperatures of well below zero over Canada and the midwest are raised 10 to 30 degrees in crossing the lakes. Only on rare occasions do polar air masses drop southward from eastern Hudson Bay across Lake Ontario without appreciable warming.

Buffalo Int'l Airport *Erie County* Elevation: 705 ft. Latitude: 42° 56' N Longitude: 78° 44' W

	JAN	FEB	MAR	APR	MAY	JUN	JUL	AUG	SEP	OCT	NOV	DEC	YEAR
Mean Maximum Temp. (°F)	31.8	33.6	42.1	55.2	66.7	75.5	80.1	78.7	71.4	59.3	47.8	36.5	56.6
Mean Temp. (°F)	25.3	26.5	34.0	46.0	57.1	66.4	71.3	69.9	62.5	51.1	41.0	30.3	48.5
Mean Minimum Temp. (°F)	18.8	19.3	25.9	36.9	47.5	57.2	62.4	61.0	53.5	42.9	34.2	24.1	40.3
Extreme Maximum Temp. (°F)	68	71	79	94	91	96	97	96	92	86	73	74	97
Extreme Minimum Temp. (°F)	-16	-6	-7	12	31	38	46	38	32	25	11	-10	-16
Days Maximum Temp. ≥ 90°F	0	0	0	0	0	1	1	1	0	0	0	0	3
Days Maximum Temp. ≤ 32°F	16	14	7	1	0	0	0	0	0	0	2	11	51
Days Minimum Temp. ≤ 32°F	27	25	23	9	0	0	0	0	0	3	13	25	125
Days Minimum Temp. ≤ 0°F	2	1	0	0	0	0	0	0	0	0	0	1	4
Heating Degree Days (base 65°F)	1,223	1,083	953	566	261	61	7	16	126	430	713	1,069	6,508
Cooling Degree Days (base 65°F)	0	0	0	3	25	109	208	175	57	5	0	0	582
Mean Precipitation (in.)	3.13	2.47	2.94	3.03	3.41	3.58	3.24	3.32	3.95	3.57	3.97	3.88	40.49
Maximum Precipitation (in.)*	6.9	5.9	6.0	5.9	7.2	8.4	8.9	10.7	9.0	9.1	9.8	8.7	53.5
Minimum Precipitation (in.)*	1.0	0.8	1.2	1.3	1.2	0.1	0.9	1.1	0.8	0.3	1.5	1.7	28.5
Extreme Maximum Daily Precip. (in.)	1.83	1.74	1.39	1.66	3.41	5.01	2.19	2.41	3.55	2.42	2.31	1.66	5.01
Days With ≥ 0.1" Precipitation	9	7	8	8	8	8	6	7	7	8	9	10	95
Days With ≥ 0.5" Precipitation	1	1	2	2	2	2	2	2	3	3	2	2	24
Days With ≥ 1.0" Precipitation	0	0	0	0	1	1	1	1	1	1	1	0	7
Mean Snowfall (in.)	24.4	17.2	13.4	2.8	0.3	trace	trace	trace	trace	0.9	8.1	26.9	94.0
Maximum Snowfall (in.)*	68	54	29	15	8	0	0	0	trace	3	31	68	176
Maximum 24-hr. Snowfall (in.)*	18	18	15	6	8	0	0	0	trace	3	19	34	34
Maximum Snow Depth (in.)	30	20	20	6	4	trace	trace	trace	trace	22	25	44	44
Days With ≥ 1.0" Snow Depth	21	19	11	1	0	0	0	0	0	0	4	15	71
Thunderstorm Days*	< 1	< 1	1	2	3	5	6	6	4	2	1	< 1	30
Foggy Days*	12	12	14	13	14	13	13	15	13	13	13	13	158
Predominant Sky Cover*	OVR	OVR	OVR	OVR	OVR	OVR	SCT	OVR	OVR	OVR	OVR	OVR	OVR
Mean Relative Humidity 7am (%)*	79	80	80	77	76	77	79	83	83	81	80	80	79
Mean Relative Humidity 4pm (%)*	73	70	65	57	55	54	54	56	59	60	69	73	62
Mean Dewpoint (°F)*	18	18	25	34	44	54	59	59	52	42	33	23	39
Prevailing Wind Direction*	WSW	WSW	SW	SW	SW	SW	SW	SW	SW	SW	W	W	SW
Prevailing Wind Speed (mph)*	18	17	16	15	14	14	13	13	13	15	15	15	15
Maximum Wind Gust (mph)*	71	82	73	74	64	79	59	81	62	63	73	69	82

Note: (*) Period of record is 1946-1995

The period of record for National Weather Service station data is 1980 – 2009 except where noted. See User Guide for detailed explanation of data.

Islip Macarthur Airport

Long Island is the terminal moraine marking the southernmost advance of the ice sheet along the Atlantic Coast during the last ice age. The terrain is generally flat, with only a gradual rise in elevation from Long Island Sound on the northern shore and from the Atlantic Ocean on the southern shore toward the middle of the island. Islip is located about half-way out Long Island on the southern coast. The airport is located about seven miles to the northeast of the city. Islip is protected from flooding during periods of high tides by Fire Island, a natural barrier located about three miles offshore. Most of the air masses affecting Islip are continental in origin, however the ocean has a pronounced influence on the climate of the area.

A cool sea breeze blowing off the ocean during the summer months helps to alleviate the afternoon heat. There are an average of 7 days between June and September when the afternoon temperature exceeds 90 degrees, while farther inland there are 10 to 15 such days.

It is uncommon for the eye of a tropical storm to pass directly over Long Island. Tropical weather systems moving along the Atlantic Coast, however, are capable of producing episodes of heavy rain and strong winds in the late summer or fall.

The winter season is relatively mild. Below zero temperatures are reported on only one or two days in about half the winters. Temperatures of 10 degrees below zero or colder are extremely rare. The seasonal snowfall averages about 29 inches. Almost all of this snow falls between December and March. Coastal low pressure systems, Northeasters, are the principle source of this snow. These weather systems will occasionally produce a heavy snowfall. There are usually extended periods during the winter when the ground is bare of snow.

Based on the 1951-1980 period, the average date of the last spring temperature of 32 degrees is April 27 and the average first fall occurrence is October 21. Inland locations would expect a shorter freeze-free season.

Islip Macarthur Airport *Suffolk County* Elevation: 83 ft. Latitude: 40° 47' N Longitude: 73° 06' W

	JAN	FEB	MAR	APR	MAY	JUN	JUL	AUG	SEP	OCT	NOV	DEC	YEAR
Mean Maximum Temp. (°F)	39.5	41.0	47.8	58.0	67.9	77.2	82.0	81.1	74.2	63.5	53.8	43.9	60.8
Mean Temp. (°F)	31.9	33.0	39.5	49.3	58.8	68.7	74.1	73.3	65.9	54.6	45.5	36.2	52.6
Mean Minimum Temp. (°F)	24.4	24.9	31.2	40.6	49.6	60.2	66.1	65.4	57.6	45.5	37.2	28.5	44.3
Extreme Maximum Temp. (°F)	69	67	82	94	98	96	102	100	92	88	78	77	102
Extreme Minimum Temp. (°F)	-7	2	5	23	32	42	50	50	38	29	11	5	-7
Days Maximum Temp. ≥ 90°F	0	0	0	0	1	2	3	2	0	0	0	0	8
Days Maximum Temp. ≤ 32°F	7	5	1	0	0	0	0	0	0	0	0	4	17
Days Minimum Temp. ≤ 32°F	25	23	18	3	0	0	0	0	0	1	10	21	101
Days Minimum Temp. ≤ 0°F	0	0	0	0	0	0	0	0	0	0	0	0	0
Heating Degree Days (base 65°F)	1,017	898	782	467	211	32	1	2	59	327	579	886	5,261
Cooling Degree Days (base 65°F)	0	0	0	3	24	151	290	266	94	11	0	0	839
Mean Precipitation (in.)	3.79	2.99	4.37	4.25	3.80	4.08	3.29	4.34	3.83	4.01	3.59	4.19	46.53
Maximum Precipitation (in.)*	6.3	5.5	5.5	5.1	10.1	7.9	8.4	13.8	5.1	8.7	8.0	6.1	65.3
Minimum Precipitation (in.)*	1.3	1.1	1.3	1.3	0.7	0.6	1.2	0.5	0.8	0.3	1.3	0.9	34.4
Extreme Maximum Daily Precip. (in.)	3.61	2.32	3.25	4.63	4.01	4.87	3.34	6.74	2.85	5.38	2.63	2.65	6.74
Days With ≥ 0.1" Precipitation	7	6	7	7	7	6	6	6	6	6	6	7	77
Days With ≥ 0.5" Precipitation	3	2	3	3	2	2	2	3	3	3	3	3	32
Days With ≥ 1.0" Precipitation	1	1	1	1	1	1	1	1	1	1	1	1	12
Mean Snowfall (in.)	na	na	na	na	na	na	na	na	na	na	na	na	na
Maximum Snowfall (in.)*	14	20	13	3	0	0	0	0	0	0	8	10	34
Maximum 24-hr. Snowfall (in.)*	6	7	8	3	0	0	0	0	0	0	8	9	9
Maximum Snow Depth (in.)	na	na	na	na	na	na	na	na	na	na	na	na	na
Days With ≥ 1.0" Snow Depth	na	na	na	na	na	na	na	na	na	na	na	na	na
Thunderstorm Days*	< 1	< 1	1	2	3	5	6	4	2	1	1	< 1	25
Foggy Days*	15	14	16	16	18	16	22	19	17	15	14	14	196
Predominant Sky Cover*	OVR	OVR	OVR	OVR	OVR	SCT	OVR	SCT	OVR	CLR	OVR	OVR	OVR
Mean Relative Humidity 7am (%)*	76	76	77	76	76	77	81	84	85	85	80	76	79
Mean Relative Humidity 4pm (%)*	62	59	57	58	59	59	63	63	63	62	62	60	61
Mean Dewpoint (°F)*	22	22	28	38	48	58	65	64	57	46	36	26	43
Prevailing Wind Direction*	WNW	NW	NW	SW	SW	SW	SW	SW	SW	SW	SW	WNW	SW
Prevailing Wind Speed (mph)*	13	13	13	10	10	10	10	9	10	10	10	12	12
Maximum Wind Gust (mph)*	na	na	na	na	na	na	na	na	na	na	na	na	na

Note: (*) Period of record is 1984-1995

The period of record for National Weather Service station data is 1980 – 2009 except where noted. See User Guide for detailed explanation of data.

New York Central Park Observatory

New York City, in area exceeding 300 square miles, is located on the Atlantic coastal plain at the mouth of the Hudson River. The terrain is laced with numerous waterways, all but one of the five boroughs in the city are situated on islands. Elevations range from less than 50 feet over most of Manhattan, Brooklyn, and Queens to almost 300 feet in northern Manhattan and the Bronx, and over 400 feet in Staten Island.

The New York Metropolitan area is close to the path of most storm and frontal systems which move across the North American continent. Therefore, weather conditions affecting the city most often approach from a westerly direction, resulting in higher temperatures in summer and lower ones in winter than would otherwise be expected in a coastal area. However, the frequent passage of weather systems often helps reduce the length of extremes.

Although continental influence predominates, oceanic influence is by no means absent. During the summer local sea breezes, winds blowing onshore from the cool water surface, often moderate the afternoon heat. The effect of the sea breeze diminishes inland. On winter mornings, ocean temperatures which are warm relative to the land reinforce the effect of the city heat island and low temperatures are often 10-20 degrees lower in the inland suburbs than in the central city. The relatively warm water temperatures also delay the advent of winter snows. Conversely, the lag in warming of water temperatures keeps spring temperatures relatively cool.

Precipitation is moderate and distributed fairly evenly throughout the year. Most of the rainfall from May through October comes from thunderstorms, usually of brief duration and sometimes intense. Heavy rains of long duration associated with tropical storms occur infrequently in late summer or fall. For the other seasons precipitation is associated with widespread storm areas, producing day-long rain or snow. Coastal storms, occurring most often in the fall and winter months, produce on occasion considerable amounts of precipitation, record rains, snows, and high winds.

The average annual precipitation is reasonably uniform within the city but higher in the suburbs and less on eastern Long Island. Annual snowfall totals also show a consistent increase to the north and west of the city with lesser amounts along the south shores and the eastern end of Long Island.

Local Climatological Data is published for three locations in New York City, Central Park, La Guardia Airport, and John°F. Kennedy International Airport.

Based on the 1951-1980 period, the average first occurrence of 32 degrees Fahrenheit in the fall is November 11 and the average last occurrence in the spring is April 1.

New York Central Park Observatory *New York County* Elevation: 131 ft. Latitude: 40° 47' N Longitude: 73° 58' W

	JAN	FEB	MAR	APR	MAY	JUN	JUL	AUG	SEP	OCT	NOV	DEC	YEAR
Mean Maximum Temp. (°F)	39.2	42.2	50.3	61.9	71.6	79.9	84.8	83.5	76.0	64.5	54.5	43.8	62.7
Mean Temp. (°F)	33.1	35.5	42.7	53.3	62.8	71.7	76.8	75.8	68.4	57.2	48.0	37.9	55.3
Mean Minimum Temp. (°F)	26.9	28.7	35.0	44.8	54.0	63.5	68.8	68.0	60.8	49.9	41.4	31.9	47.8
Extreme Maximum Temp. (°F)	72	75	86	96	97	98	102	103	99	87	80	75	103
Extreme Minimum Temp. (°F)	-2	4	10	21	40	47	53	50	43	31	18	-1	-2
Days Maximum Temp. ≥ 90°F	0	0	0	0	1	3	7	5	1	0	0	0	17
Days Maximum Temp. ≤ 32°F	8	4	1	0	0	0	0	0	0	0	0	4	17
Days Minimum Temp. ≤ 32°F	21	19	11	1	0	0	0	0	0	0	3	15	70
Days Minimum Temp. ≤ 0°F	0	0	0	0	0	0	0	0	0	0	0	0	0
Heating Degree Days (base 65°F)	983	829	687	355	124	15	0	1	36	254	505	833	4,622
Cooling Degree Days (base 65°F)	0	0	2	12	64	223	374	343	145	20	1	0	1,184
Mean Precipitation (in.)	3.59	2.92	4.13	4.35	4.16	4.51	4.73	4.24	4.21	4.36	4.00	3.88	49.08
Maximum Precipitation (in.)*	10.5	6.0	10.4	8.3	10.2	9.3	11.8	12.4	9.3	7.8	12.4	10.0	67.0
Minimum Precipitation (in.)*	0.6	0.5	0.9	1.3	0.6	1.2	1.3	0.2	1.3	0.1	0.3	0.6	26.1
Extreme Maximum Daily Precip. (in.)	2.73	1.94	3.10	7.56	2.40	3.07	3.75	4.64	5.02	4.35	3.60	2.41	7.56
Days With ≥ 0.1" Precipitation	6	6	7	7	7	7	7	6	6	6	6	7	78
Days With ≥ 0.5" Precipitation	3	2	3	3	3	3	3	3	3	3	3	3	35
Days With ≥ 1.0" Precipitation	1	1	1	1	1	1	1	1	1	1	1	1	12
Mean Snowfall (in.)	7.0	7.6	3.8	0.6	trace	0.0	trace	0.0	0.0	trace	0.3	4.3	23.6
Maximum Snowfall (in.)*	20	26	17	10	trace	0	0	0	0	trace	5	12	53
Maximum 24-hr. Snowfall (in.)*	12	16	10	10	trace	0	0	0	0	trace	4	7	16
Maximum Snow Depth (in.)	***14***	na	***9***	***9***	***trace***	***0***	***trace***	***0***	***0***	***0***	***5***	***10***	na
Days With ≥ 1.0" Snow Depth	***8***	na	***3***	***0***	***0***	***0***	***0***	***0***	***0***	***0***	***0***	***2***	na
Thunderstorm Days*	< 1	< 1	1	1	3	4	5	4	1	1	< 1	< 1	20
Foggy Days*	0	0	0	0	0	0	0	0	0	0	1	< 1	1
Predominant Sky Cover*	OVR	OVR	OVR	OVR	OVR	SCT	SCT	SCT	OVR	CLR	OVR	OVR	OVR
Mean Relative Humidity 7am (%)*	67	67	66	64	72	74	74	76	78	75	72	69	71
Mean Relative Humidity 4pm (%)*	55	53	50	45	52	55	53	54	56	55	58	59	54
Mean Dewpoint (°F)*	18	19	26	34	47	57	62	62	56	44	34	25	40
Prevailing Wind Direction*	NW	NW	NW	NW	NE	SW	SW	SW	SW	W	W	NW	NW
Prevailing Wind Speed (mph)*	12	12	13	12	10	8	8	8	8	9	9	12	10
Maximum Wind Gust (mph)*	52	51	63	46	44	41	46	43	52	46	58	64	64

Note: (*) Period of record is 1965-1995

The period of record for National Weather Service station data is 1980 – 2009 except where noted. See User Guide for detailed explanation of data.

New York JFK Int'l Airport

New York City, in area exceeding 300 square miles, is located on the Atlantic coastal plain at the mouth of the Hudson River. The terrain is laced with numerous waterways, all but one of the five boroughs in the city are situated on islands. Elevations range from less than 50 feet over most of Manhattan, Brooklyn, and Queens to almost 300 feet in northern Manhattan and the Bronx, and over 400 feet in Staten Island.

The New York Metropolitan area is close to the path of most storm and frontal systems which move across the North American continent. Therefore, weather conditions affecting the city most often approach from a westerly direction, resulting in higher temperatures in summer and lower ones in winter than would otherwise be expected in a coastal area. However, the frequent passage of weather systems often helps reduce the length of extremes.

Although continental influence predominates, oceanic influence is by no means absent. During the summer local sea breezes, winds blowing onshore from the cool water surface, often moderate the afternoon heat. The effect of the sea breeze diminishes inland. On winter mornings, ocean temperatures which are warm relative to the land reinforce the effect of the city heat island and low temperatures are often 10-20 degrees lower in the inland suburbs than in the central city. The relatively warm water temperatures also delay the advent of winter snows. Conversely, the lag in warming of water temperatures keeps spring temperatures relatively cool.

Precipitation is moderate and distributed fairly evenly throughout the year. Most of the rainfall from May through October comes from thunderstorms, usually of brief duration and sometimes intense. Heavy rains of long duration associated with tropical storms occur infrequently in late summer or fall. For the other seasons precipitation is associated with widespread storm areas, producing day-long rain or snow. Coastal storms, occurring most often in the fall and winter months, produce on occasion considerable amounts of precipitation, record rains, snows, and high winds.

The average annual precipitation is reasonably uniform within the city but higher in the suburbs and less on eastern Long Island. Annual snowfall totals also show a consistent increase to the north and west of the city with lesser amounts along the south shores and the eastern end of Long Island.

Local Climatological Data is published for three locations in New York City, Central Park, La Guardia Airport, and John°F. Kennedy International Airport.

Based on the 1951-1980 period, the average first occurrence of 32 degrees Fahrenheit in the fall is November 11 and the average last occurrence in the spring is April 1.

New York JFK Int'l Airport *Queens County* Elevation: 16 ft. Latitude: 40° 39' N Longitude: 73° 48' W

	JAN	FEB	MAR	APR	MAY	JUN	JUL	AUG	SEP	OCT	NOV	DEC	YEAR
Mean Maximum Temp. (°F)	39.1	41.7	48.8	58.8	68.4	77.7	82.9	82.0	75.4	64.4	54.3	44.1	61.5
Mean Temp. (°F)	32.8	34.8	41.4	51.2	60.6	70.2	75.7	75.0	68.2	57.1	47.5	37.9	54.4
Mean Minimum Temp. (°F)	26.3	27.9	34.0	43.6	52.8	62.5	68.5	68.0	60.9	49.7	40.8	31.5	47.2
Extreme Maximum Temp. (°F)	71	71	85	90	95	98	102	100	98	90	77	75	102
Extreme Minimum Temp. (°F)	-2	7	8	20	37	48	56	51	43	31	19	2	-2
Days Maximum Temp. ≥ 90°F	0	0	0	0	0	2	4	3	1	0	0	0	10
Days Maximum Temp. ≤ 32°F	7	4	1	0	0	0	0	0	0	0	0	3	15
Days Minimum Temp. ≤ 32°F	22	20	12	1	0	0	0	0	0	0	3	16	74
Days Minimum Temp. ≤ 0°F	0	0	0	0	0	0	0	0	0	0	0	0	0
Heating Degree Days (base 65°F)	993	846	725	410	162	19	0	1	33	255	518	834	4,796
Cooling Degree Days (base 65°F)	0	0	0	3	33	180	341	319	135	15	0	0	1,026
Mean Precipitation (in.)	3.15	2.42	3.77	4.01	3.97	3.93	4.13	3.61	3.39	3.57	3.37	3.32	42.64
Maximum Precipitation (in.)*	8.3	4.9	8.2	9.5	10.7	8.1	8.5	8.3	9.6	6.6	9.5	6.7	59.1
Minimum Precipitation (in.)*	0.5	1.0	0.9	1.4	0.6	trace	0.5	0.2	1.0	0.9	0.3	0.6	25.4
Extreme Maximum Daily Precip. (in.)	3.78	1.62	2.56	3.15	2.70	6.27	3.51	4.10	3.42	4.66	2.45	2.55	6.27
Days With ≥ 0.1" Precipitation	6	5	7	7	7	6	6	6	5	5	6	6	72
Days With ≥ 0.5" Precipitation	2	2	3	3	3	3	3	2	2	3	3	2	31
Days With ≥ 1.0" Precipitation	1	1	1	1	1	1	1	1	1	1	1	1	12
Mean Snowfall (in.)	6.4	7.4	3.6	0.8	trace	0.0	trace	0.0	0.0	trace	0.3	4.2	22.7
Maximum Snowfall (in.)*	20	25	16	8	0	0	0	0	0	trace	4	22	49
Maximum 24-hr. Snowfall (in.)*	13	20	9	8	0	0	0	0	0	trace	3	18	20
Maximum Snow Depth (in.)	22	28	8	8	trace	0	trace	0	0	trace	4	14	28
Days With ≥ 1.0" Snow Depth	7	5	3	0	0	0	0	0	0	0	0	3	18
Thunderstorm Days*	< 1	< 1	1	2	3	4	5	5	2	1	1	< 1	24
Foggy Days*	10	9	11	11	13	12	13	12	11	10	11	10	133
Predominant Sky Cover*	OVR	OVR	OVR	OVR	OVR	OVR	SCT	SCT	OVR	CLR	OVR	OVR	OVR
Mean Relative Humidity 7am (%)*	71	71	71	70	73	74	75	78	79	78	76	73	74
Mean Relative Humidity 4pm (%)*	61	59	57	58	61	63	63	63	62	60	61	62	61
Mean Dewpoint (°F)*	21	22	28	37	48	58	64	63	57	46	36	26	42
Prevailing Wind Direction*	NW	NW	NW	S	S	S	S	S	S	WSW	NW	NW	S
Prevailing Wind Speed (mph)*	16	17	17	13	13	12	12	12	12	10	15	16	14
Maximum Wind Gust (mph)*	59	60	68	61	71	56	54	68	60	62	67	61	71

Note: (*) Period of record is 1948-1995

The period of record for National Weather Service station data is 1980 – 2009 except where noted. See User Guide for detailed explanation of data.

New York Laguardia Airport

New York City, in area exceeding 300 square miles, is located on the Atlantic coastal plain at the mouth of the Hudson River. The terrain is laced with numerous waterways, all but one of the five boroughs in the city are situated on islands. Elevations range from less than 50 feet over most of Manhattan, Brooklyn, and Queens to almost 300 feet in northern Manhattan and the Bronx, and over 400 feet in Staten Island.

The New York Metropolitan area is close to the path of most storm and frontal systems which move across the North American continent. Therefore, weather conditions affecting the city most often approach from a westerly direction, resulting in higher temperatures in summer and lower ones in winter than would otherwise be expected in a coastal area. However, the frequent passage of weather systems often helps reduce the length of extremes.

Although continental influence predominates, oceanic influence is by no means absent. During the summer local sea breezes, winds blowing onshore from the cool water surface, often moderate the afternoon heat. The effect of the sea breeze diminishes inland. On winter mornings, ocean temperatures which are warm relative to the land reinforce the effect of the city heat island and low temperatures are often 10-20 degrees lower in the inland suburbs than in the central city. The relatively warm water temperatures also delay the advent of winter snows. Conversely, the lag in warming of water temperatures keeps spring temperatures relatively cool.

Precipitation is moderate and distributed fairly evenly throughout the year. Most of the rainfall from May through October comes from thunderstorms, usually of brief duration and sometimes intense. Heavy rains of long duration associated with tropical storms occur infrequently in late summer or fall. For the other seasons precipitation is associated with widespread storm areas, producing day-long rain or snow. Coastal storms, occurring most often in the fall and winter months, produce on occasion considerable amounts of precipitation, record rains, snows, and high winds.

The average annual precipitation is reasonably uniform within the city but higher in the suburbs and less on eastern Long Island. Annual snowfall totals also show a consistent increase to the north and west of the city with lesser amounts along the south shores and the eastern end of Long Island.

Local Climatological Data is published for three locations in New York City, Central Park, La Guardia Airport, and John°F. Kennedy International Airport.

Based on the 1951-1980 period, the average first occurrence of 32 degrees Fahrenheit in the fall is November 11 and the average last occurrence in the spring is April 1.

New York Laguardia Airport *Queens County* Elevation: 11 ft. Latitude: 40° 47' N Longitude: 73° 53' W

	JAN	FEB	MAR	APR	MAY	JUN	JUL	AUG	SEP	OCT	NOV	DEC	YEAR
Mean Maximum Temp. (°F)	39.1	42.0	49.4	60.5	71.0	80.1	85.0	83.5	76.1	64.9	54.4	44.2	62.5
Mean Temp. (°F)	33.3	35.6	42.3	52.8	62.8	72.3	77.6	76.6	69.4	58.3	48.4	38.4	55.6
Mean Minimum Temp. (°F)	27.4	29.1	35.1	45.1	54.6	64.4	70.1	69.6	62.6	51.6	42.4	32.6	48.7
Extreme Maximum Temp. (°F)	72	73	83	94	97	100	103	104	96	89	80	75	104
Extreme Minimum Temp. (°F)	-3	4	8	22	38	49	56	51	45	34	20	-1	-3
Days Maximum Temp. ≥ 90°F	0	0	0	0	1	4	7	5	1	0	0	0	18
Days Maximum Temp. ≤ 32°F	8	5	1	0	0	0	0	0	0	0	0	4	18
Days Minimum Temp. ≤ 32°F	21	18	10	1	0	0	0	0	0	0	3	14	67
Days Minimum Temp. ≤ 0°F	0	0	0	0	0	0	0	0	0	0	0	0	0
Heating Degree Days (base 65°F)	976	825	698	366	124	13	0	1	29	227	491	816	4,566
Cooling Degree Days (base 65°F)	0	0	1	8	62	238	395	366	166	25	1	0	1,262
Mean Precipitation (in.)	3.18	2.62	3.94	4.13	3.77	4.00	4.57	4.09	3.67	3.73	3.49	3.47	44.66
Maximum Precipitation (in.)*	8.7	5.7	8.7	11.5	9.3	8.1	12.3	16.0	9.6	7.3	9.9	7.7	60.8
Minimum Precipitation (in.)*	0.5	0.7	0.9	1.0	0.4	trace	0.7	0.1	1.0	0.1	0.3	0.3	22.2
Extreme Maximum Daily Precip. (in.)	2.60	1.63	2.83	6.69	2.57	4.00	3.53	3.54	4.63	4.39	2.91	2.74	6.69
Days With ≥ 0.1" Precipitation	6	5	7	7	7	7	7	6	5	5	6	7	75
Days With ≥ 0.5" Precipitation	2	2	3	2	3	3	3	3	2	3	3	3	32
Days With ≥ 1.0" Precipitation	1	1	1	1	1	1	1	1	1	1	1	1	12
Mean Snowfall (in.)	7.5	8.2	4.5	0.6	trace	0.0	trace	trace	0.0	trace	0.3	4.8	25.9
Maximum Snowfall (in.)*	18	26	19	8	trace	0	0	0	0	1	6	22	60
Maximum 24-hr. Snowfall (in.)*	11	17	14	8	trace	0	0	0	0	1	6	16	17
Maximum Snow Depth (in.)	25	22	9	8	trace	0	trace	trace	0	trace	6	15	25
Days With ≥ 1.0" Snow Depth	7	6	3	0	0	0	0	0	0	0	0	3	19
Thunderstorm Days*	< 1	< 1	1	2	3	4	5	5	2	1	< 1	< 1	23
Foggy Days*	10	9	10	10	11	9	8	8	8	8	9	10	110
Predominant Sky Cover*	OVR	OVR	OVR	OVR	OVR	OVR	SCT	SCT	OVR	OVR	OVR	OVR	OVR
Mean Relative Humidity 7am (%)*	67	67	67	67	71	71	73	75	76	74	71	68	71
Mean Relative Humidity 4pm (%)*	57	55	52	51	53	53	54	56	56	55	57	59	55
Mean Dewpoint (°F)*	20	21	27	36	48	57	63	62	56	45	35	25	41
Prevailing Wind Direction*	NW	WNW	NW	NW	S	S	S	S	S	SW	WNW	WNW	NW
Prevailing Wind Speed (mph)*	17	17	17	16	12	12	12	12	10	12	15	16	14
Maximum Wind Gust (mph)*	61	67	71	63	56	56	59	73	64	71	76	77	77

Note: (*) Period of record is 1947-1995

Rochester Int'l Airport

Rochester is located at the mouth of the Genesee River at about the mid point of the south shore of Lake Ontario. The river flows northward from northwest Pennsylvania and empties into Lake Ontario. The land slopes from a lakeshore elevation of 246 feet to over 1,000 feet some 20 miles south. The airport is located just south of the city.

Lake Ontario plays a major role in the Rochester weather. In the summer its cooling effect inhibits the temperature from rising much above the low to mid 90s. In the winter the modifying temperature effect prevents temperatures from falling below -15 degrees most of the time, although temperatures at locations more than 15 miles inland do drop below -30 degrees.

The lake plays a major role in winter snowfall distribution. Well inland from the lake and toward the airport, the seasonal snowfall is usually less than in the area north of the airport and toward the lakeshore where wide variations occur. This is due to what is called the lake effect. Snowfalls of one to two feet or more in 24 hours are common near the lake in winter due the lake effect alone. The lake rarely freezes over because of its depth. The area is also prone to other heavy snowstorms and blizzards because of its proximity to the paths of low pressure systems coming up the east coast, out of the Ohio Valley.

Precipitation is rather evenly distributed throughout the year. Excessive rains occur infrequently but may be caused by slowly moving thunderstorms, slowly moving or stalled major low pressure systems, or by hurricanes and tropical storms that move inland. Hail occurs occasionally and heavy fog is rare.

The growing season averages 150 to 180 days. The years first frost usually occurs in late September and the last frost typically occurs in mid-May.

Rochester Int'l Airport *Monroe County* Elevation: 600 ft. Latitude: 43° 07' N Longitude: 77° 41' W

	JAN	FEB	MAR	APR	MAY	JUN	JUL	AUG	SEP	OCT	NOV	DEC	YEAR
Mean Maximum Temp. (°F)	32.0	34.2	42.8	56.0	67.8	76.8	81.2	79.4	72.0	59.8	48.2	36.8	57.3
Mean Temp. (°F)	24.9	26.4	34.2	46.4	57.2	66.4	71.0	69.6	62.1	50.8	40.7	30.2	48.3
Mean Minimum Temp. (°F)	17.8	18.6	25.6	36.7	46.5	55.9	60.8	59.7	52.1	41.7	33.2	23.5	39.3
Extreme Maximum Temp. (°F)	68	73	83	93	94	95	98	97	95	85	75	72	98
Extreme Minimum Temp. (°F)	-17	-8	-7	13	30	36	45	38	30	21	9	-12	-17
Days Maximum Temp. ≥ 90°F	0	0	0	0	0	1	3	2	0	0	0	0	6
Days Maximum Temp. ≤ 32°F	16	13	6	0	0	0	0	0	0	0	1	10	46
Days Minimum Temp. ≤ 32°F	28	25	23	10	1	0	0	0	0	4	15	25	131
Days Minimum Temp. ≤ 0°F	3	1	0	0	0	0	0	0	0	0	0	0	4
Heating Degree Days (base 65°F)	1,236	1,084	948	556	265	64	10	20	135	440	723	1,072	6,553
Cooling Degree Days (base 65°F)	0	0	0	5	29	112	204	170	55	6	0	0	581
Mean Precipitation (in.)	2.37	1.90	2.55	2.76	2.83	3.36	3.20	3.49	3.39	2.73	2.92	2.62	34.12
Maximum Precipitation (in.)*	5.8	5.1	5.0	4.1	6.6	6.8	6.0	6.0	6.3	7.8	7.0	4.6	40.5
Minimum Precipitation (in.)*	0.7	0.7	0.5	1.2	0.4	0.2	0.6	0.8	0.3	0.2	0.4	0.6	22.4
Extreme Maximum Daily Precip. (in.)	1.77	1.59	1.44	1.79	2.12	2.19	3.33	2.51	3.08	2.94	1.83	1.46	3.33
Days With ≥ 0.1" Precipitation	7	6	7	7	6	7	6	6	7	6	7	8	80
Days With ≥ 0.5" Precipitation	1	1	1	2	2	2	2	2	2	2	2	1	20
Days With ≥ 1.0" Precipitation	0	0	0	0	0	1	1	1	1	0	0	0	4
Mean Snowfall (in.)	27.0	21.3	17.0	3.9	0.4	trace	trace	0.0	trace	0.1	7.6	22.1	99.4
Maximum Snowfall (in.)*	60	65	40	20	11	0	0	0	trace	3	23	46	152
Maximum 24-hr. Snowfall (in.)*	18	18	18	10	11	0	0	0	trace	3	12	18	18
Maximum Snow Depth (in.)	28	17	34	7	4	trace	trace	0	trace	trace	10	13	34
Days With ≥ 1.0" Snow Depth	21	20	12	1	0	0	0	0	0	0	4	15	73
Thunderstorm Days*	< 1	< 1	1	2	3	5	6	6	3	1	< 1	< 1	27
Foggy Days*	8	9	10	10	10	10	11	13	12	11	11	10	125
Predominant Sky Cover*	OVR	OVR	OVR	OVR	OVR	OVR	SCT	OVR	OVR	OVR	OVR	OVR	OVR
Mean Relative Humidity 7am (%)*	79	80	80	78	77	79	82	86	88	85	82	81	81
Mean Relative Humidity 4pm (%)*	71	69	63	56	53	53	52	55	59	60	69	73	61
Mean Dewpoint (°F)*	18	18	25	35	45	55	60	59	53	42	33	23	39
Prevailing Wind Direction*	WSW	WSW	WSW	WSW	WSW	WSW	SW	SW	SW	WSW	WSW	WSW	WSW
Prevailing Wind Speed (mph)*	16	15	15	14	13	12	8	8	8	12	14	14	13
Maximum Wind Gust (mph)*	63	70	68	71	64	52	56	62	51	60	67	55	71

Note: (*) Period of record is 1948-1995

The period of record for National Weather Service station data is 1980 – 2009 except where noted. See User Guide for detailed explanation of data.

Syracuse Hancock Int'l Airport

Syracuse is located approximately at the geographical center of the state. Gently rolling terrain stretches northward for about 30 miles to the eastern end of Lake Ontario. Oneida Lake is about 8 miles northeast of Syracuse. Approximately five miles south of the city, hills rise to 1,500 feet. Immediately to the west, the terrain is gently rolling with elevations 500 to 800 feet above sea level.

The climate of Syracuse is primarily continental in character and comparatively humid. Nearly all cyclonic systems moving from the interior of the country through the St. Lawrence Valley will affect the Syracuse area. Seasonal and diurnal changes are marked and produce an invigorating climate.

In the summer and in portions of the transitional seasons, temperatures usually rise rapidly during the daytime to moderate levels and as a rule fall rapidly after sunset. The nights are relatively cool and comfortable. There are only a few days in a year when atmospheric humidity causes great personal discomfort.

Winters are usually cold and are sometimes severe in part. Daytime temperatures average in the low 30s with nighttime lows in the teens. Low winter temperatures below -25 degrees have been recorded. The autumn, winter, and spring seasons display marked variability.

Based on the 1951-1980 period, the average first occurrence of 32 degrees Fahrenheit in the fall is October 16 and the average last occurrence in the spring is April 28.

Precipitation in the Syracuse area is derived principally from cyclonic storms which pass from the interior of the country through the St. Lawrence Valley. Lake Ontario provides the source of significant winter precipitation. The lake is quite deep and never freezes so cold air flowing over the lake is quickly saturated and produces the cloudiness and snow squalls which are a well-known feature of winter weather in the Syracuse area.

The precipitation is uncommonly well distributed, averaging about 3 inches per month throughout the year. Snowfall is moderately heavy with an average just over 100 inches. There are about 30 days per year with thunderstorms.

Wind velocities are moderate, but during the winter months there are numerous days with sufficient winds to cause blowing and drifting snow.

During December, January, and February there is much cloudiness. Syracuse receives only about one-third of possible sunshine during winter months. Approximately two-thirds of possible sunshine is received during the warm months.

Syracuse Hancock Int'l Airport *Onondaga County* Elevation: 410 ft. Latitude: 43° 07' N Longitude: 76° 06' W

	JAN	FEB	MAR	APR	MAY	JUN	JUL	AUG	SEP	OCT	NOV	DEC	YEAR
Mean Maximum Temp. (°F)	31.7	34.2	43.0	57.1	68.9	77.5	81.7	80.2	72.3	59.9	48.2	36.5	57.6
Mean Temp. (°F)	23.8	25.7	33.9	46.8	57.6	66.6	71.3	69.9	62.1	50.5	40.5	29.3	48.2
Mean Minimum Temp. (°F)	15.8	17.3	24.8	36.5	46.3	55.7	60.9	59.5	51.8	41.0	32.7	22.0	38.7
Extreme Maximum Temp. (°F)	70	69	87	92	93	97	98	101	95	85	76	72	101
Extreme Minimum Temp. (°F)	-25	-15	-15	12	27	36	46	42	28	22	6	-22	-25
Days Maximum Temp. ≥ 90°F	0	0	0	0	0	2	4	2	0	0	0	0	8
Days Maximum Temp. ≤ 32°F	16	13	6	0	0	0	0	0	0	0	2	11	48
Days Minimum Temp. ≤ 32°F	28	26	24	10	0	0	0	0	0	5	15	26	134
Days Minimum Temp. ≤ 0°F	4	2	1	0	0	0	0	0	0	0	0	1	8
Heating Degree Days (base 65°F)	1,272	1,103	957	543	249	59	7	19	134	446	729	1,100	6,618
Cooling Degree Days (base 65°F)	0	0	1	5	27	114	209	177	53	4	0	0	590
Mean Precipitation (in.)	2.46	2.04	3.00	3.27	3.17	3.24	3.72	3.40	3.62	3.40	3.52	3.06	37.90
Maximum Precipitation (in.)*	5.8	5.4	6.8	8.1	7.4	12.3	9.5	8.4	8.8	8.3	6.8	5.5	57.9
Minimum Precipitation (in.)*	1.0	0.6	1.0	1.2	0.8	1.0	0.9	1.3	0.8	0.2	1.3	0.8	27.1
Extreme Maximum Daily Precip. (in.)	1.41	1.62	1.33	1.60	1.69	2.86	4.29	2.98	2.59	2.98	3.56	1.48	4.29
Days With ≥ 0.1" Precipitation	7	6	8	8	8	7	7	7	7	8	9	8	90
Days With ≥ 0.5" Precipitation	1	1	2	2	2	2	3	2	2	2	2	2	23
Days With ≥ 1.0" Precipitation	0	0	0	0	0	0	1	1	1	1	0	0	4
Mean Snowfall (in.)	34.9	26.2	18.7	3.8	0.1	trace	trace	trace	trace	0.4	9.7	30.7	124.5
Maximum Snowfall (in.)*	72	73	54	16	2	0	0	trace	trace	6	34	65	208
Maximum 24-hr. Snowfall (in.)*	22	21	22	7	2	0	0	trace	trace	3	12	16	22
Maximum Snow Depth (in.)	26	33	35	6	1	trace	trace	trace	trace	trace	10	20	35
Days With ≥ 1.0" Snow Depth	23	21	13	1	0	0	0	0	0	0	4	16	78
Thunderstorm Days*	< 1	< 1	1	2	3	5	6	5	3	1	1	< 1	27
Foggy Days*	10	9	11	10	11	11	12	13	14	12	12	11	136
Predominant Sky Cover*	OVR	OVR	OVR	OVR	OVR	OVR	OVR	OVR	OVR	OVR	OVR	OVR	OVR
Mean Relative Humidity 7am (%)*	77	78	78	76	76	77	79	85	86	84	80	79	80
Mean Relative Humidity 4pm (%)*	69	67	60	52	53	54	54	57	60	60	68	72	60
Mean Dewpoint (°F)*	16	17	24	34	45	55	60	59	53	42	32	22	38
Prevailing Wind Direction*	WSW	WSW	WNW	WNW	WNW	WNW	WSW	WSW	WSW	WSW	WSW	WSW	WSW
Prevailing Wind Speed (mph)*	15	14	14	14	12	12	9	9	9	10	13	14	12
Maximum Wind Gust (mph)*	58	56	61	63	76	67	66	49	48	60	58	63	76

Note: (*) Period of record is 1945-1995

Albion 2 NE *Orleans County* Elevation: 439 ft. Latitude: 43° 17' N Longitude: 78° 10' W

	JAN	FEB	MAR	APR	MAY	JUN	JUL	AUG	SEP	OCT	NOV	DEC	YEAR
Mean Maximum Temp. (°F)	32.3	34.6	43.5	57.1	68.9	78.0	82.1	80.4	73.2	60.7	48.5	37.1	58.0
Mean Temp. (°F)	25.4	26.9	34.8	47.1	57.9	67.4	72.0	70.5	63.5	51.8	41.3	30.6	49.1
Mean Minimum Temp. (°F)	18.4	19.2	26.0	36.9	46.9	56.8	61.8	60.5	53.7	42.9	33.9	24.0	40.1
Extreme Maximum Temp. (°F)	67	74	80	87	91	96	101	98	93	84	74	75	101
Extreme Minimum Temp. (°F)	-15	-6	-5	13	28	35	45	39	32	22	11	-10	-15
Days Maximum Temp. ≥ 90°F	0	0	0	0	0	2	4	2	0	0	0	0	8
Days Maximum Temp. ≤ 32°F	16	13	6	0	0	0	0	0	0	0	1	10	46
Days Minimum Temp. ≤ 32°F	28	25	23	10	1	0	0	0	0	3	14	25	129
Days Minimum Temp. ≤ 0°F	2	1	0	0	0	0	0	0	0	0	0	0	3
Heating Degree Days (base 65°F)	1,222	1,070	931	537	245	53	6	15	110	409	706	1,061	6,365
Cooling Degree Days (base 65°F)	0	0	1	5	32	132	229	192	71	7	0	0	669
Mean Precipitation (in.)	2.68	2.04	2.77	3.01	2.99	3.14	3.01	3.04	3.57	3.13	3.22	2.95	35.55
Extreme Maximum Daily Precip. (in.)	2.00	1.36	1.90	1.85	2.15	3.79	2.31	3.06	3.28	2.28	2.16	1.96	3.79
Days With ≥ 0.1" Precipitation	8	6	7	8	7	7	6	7	7	7	9	8	87
Days With ≥ 0.5" Precipitation	1	1	2	2	2	2	2	2	2	2	2	1	21
Days With ≥ 1.0" Precipitation	0	0	0	0	0	1	1	1	1	1	0	0	5
Mean Snowfall (in.)	19.5	13.6	11.1	2.1	0.3	0.0	0.0	0.0	0.0	0.2	4.5	15.1	66.4
Maximum Snow Depth (in.)	30	25	19	5	6	0	0	0	0	2	9	12	30
Days With ≥ 1.0" Snow Depth	15	11	6	1	0	0	0	0	0	0	3	11	47

Alcove Dam *Albany County* Elevation: 606 ft. Latitude: 42° 28' N Longitude: 73° 56' W

	JAN	FEB	MAR	APR	MAY	JUN	JUL	AUG	SEP	OCT	NOV	DEC	YEAR
Mean Maximum Temp. (°F)	31.3	34.6	42.4	56.3	67.7	75.8	80.0	78.9	71.0	58.9	47.3	35.9	56.7
Mean Temp. (°F)	21.5	24.1	32.0	45.1	55.9	64.6	69.1	67.9	59.8	48.0	38.3	27.2	46.1
Mean Minimum Temp. (°F)	11.6	13.6	21.6	33.9	44.1	53.4	58.1	56.8	48.6	37.1	29.2	18.6	35.5
Extreme Maximum Temp. (°F)	71	70	86	91	90	96	100	96	98	83	81	73	100
Extreme Minimum Temp. (°F)	-29	-16	-13	10	26	32	39	35	28	18	6	-24	-29
Days Maximum Temp. ≥ 90°F	0	0	0	0	0	1	2	2	0	0	0	0	5
Days Maximum Temp. ≤ 32°F	16	12	6	0	0	0	0	0	0	0	2	11	47
Days Minimum Temp. ≤ 32°F	30	27	27	14	2	0	0	0	1	10	21	28	160
Days Minimum Temp. ≤ 0°F	6	3	1	0	0	0	0	0	0	0	0	2	12
Heating Degree Days (base 65°F)	1,343	1,150	1,017	592	291	83	20	36	180	521	794	1,163	7,190
Cooling Degree Days (base 65°F)	0	0	0	2	16	78	153	131	31	1	0	0	412
Mean Precipitation (in.)	2.43	2.05	3.54	3.77	3.48	4.46	3.84	3.54	3.71	3.45	3.48	2.81	40.56
Extreme Maximum Daily Precip. (in.)	2.15	1.80	5.38	3.95	2.25	4.28	3.42	2.84	6.89	3.51	3.38	2.05	6.89
Days With ≥ 0.1" Precipitation	5	5	6	7	7	8	7	7	6	6	6	6	76
Days With ≥ 0.5" Precipitation	2	1	3	3	2	3	3	2	2	2	3	2	28
Days With ≥ 1.0" Precipitation	0	0	1	1	1	1	1	1	1	1	1	1	10
Mean Snowfall (in.)	na	na	na	0.4	trace	0.0	0.0	0.0	0.0	0.1	0.4	na	na
Maximum Snow Depth (in.)	na	na	na	na	na	na	na	na	na	na	na	na	na
Days With ≥ 1.0" Snow Depth	na	na	na	0	0	0	0	0	0	0	0	na	na

Alfred *Allegany County* Elevation: 1,770 ft. Latitude: 42° 16' N Longitude: 77° 47' W

	JAN	FEB	MAR	APR	MAY	JUN	JUL	AUG	SEP	OCT	NOV	DEC	YEAR
Mean Maximum Temp. (°F)	31.4	34.8	43.6	56.7	68.2	76.3	80.1	78.5	70.7	59.1	47.0	36.1	56.9
Mean Temp. (°F)	22.0	24.1	31.9	44.0	54.3	63.0	67.1	65.5	58.2	47.2	37.4	27.3	45.2
Mean Minimum Temp. (°F)	12.6	13.4	20.4	31.3	40.3	49.8	54.1	52.5	45.7	35.3	27.8	18.6	33.5
Extreme Maximum Temp. (°F)	63	65	83	91	93	93	96	98	94	84	77	68	98
Extreme Minimum Temp. (°F)	-25	-15	-16	5	22	28	37	27	20	15	4	-21	-25
Days Maximum Temp. ≥ 90°F	0	0	0	0	0	1	2	1	0	0	0	0	4
Days Maximum Temp. ≤ 32°F	17	13	5	0	0	0	0	0	0	0	2	11	48
Days Minimum Temp. ≤ 32°F	29	27	27	17	7	0	0	0	2	12	21	28	170
Days Minimum Temp. ≤ 0°F	6	5	2	0	0	0	0	0	0	0	0	2	15
Heating Degree Days (base 65°F)	1,325	1,151	1,019	624	339	114	38	60	219	545	821	1,161	7,416
Cooling Degree Days (base 65°F)	0	0	0	2	14	62	110	83	22	1	0	0	294
Mean Precipitation (in.)	2.15	1.71	2.66	2.99	3.32	4.25	3.91	3.63	3.73	3.30	3.29	2.55	37.49
Extreme Maximum Daily Precip. (in.)	1.75	1.29	1.62	1.70	2.23	3.33	2.46	1.96	2.43	2.92	2.10	1.10	3.33
Days With ≥ 0.1" Precipitation	6	6	7	8	8	8	8	7	7	8	8	7	88
Days With ≥ 0.5" Precipitation	1	1	2	2	2	3	3	2	2	2	2	1	23
Days With ≥ 1.0" Precipitation	0	0	0	0	0	1	1	1	1	1	1	0	6
Mean Snowfall (in.)	20.8	16.7	17.1	4.0	0.3	0.0	0.0	0.0	0.0	0.5	8.6	19.6	87.6
Maximum Snow Depth (in.)	na	na	na	***8***	***trace***	***0***	***0***	***0***	***0***	***2***	***8***	na	na
Days With ≥ 1.0" Snow Depth	na	na	na	1	0	0	0	0	0	0	2	na	na

Allegany State Park *Cattaraugus County* Elevation: 1,500 ft. Latitude: 42° 06' N Longitude: 78° 45' W

	JAN	FEB	MAR	APR	MAY	JUN	JUL	AUG	SEP	OCT	NOV	DEC	YEAR
Mean Maximum Temp. (°F)	30.3	32.9	41.8	54.7	66.7	74.6	77.9	76.3	***69.0***	57.2	46.1	34.6	***55.2***
Mean Temp. (°F)	21.8	23.4	31.1	43.2	53.8	62.2	66.0	64.9	***57.9***	46.6	37.6	27.1	***44.6***
Mean Minimum Temp. (°F)	13.3	13.9	20.4	31.5	40.9	49.8	54.0	53.4	***46.7***	36.0	29.1	19.5	***34.0***
Extreme Maximum Temp. (°F)	63	68	80	89	90	92	97	93	***89***	80	75	70	***97***
Extreme Minimum Temp. (°F)	-22	-18	-17	11	21	24	29	31	***26***	14	-1	-16	***-22***
Days Maximum Temp. ≥ 90°F	0	0	0	0	0	0	1	0	0	0	0	0	1
Days Maximum Temp. ≤ 32°F	18	14	7	1	0	0	0	0	0	0	3	13	56
Days Minimum Temp. ≤ 32°F	28	26	26	17	6	1	0	0	1	11	20	27	163
Days Minimum Temp. ≤ 0°F	5	4	2	0	0	0	0	0	0	0	0	2	13
Heating Degree Days (base 65°F)	1,330	1,169	1,045	651	351	127	52	70	***226***	562	816	1,168	***7,567***
Cooling Degree Days (base 65°F)	0	0	0	1	11	50	89	73	***19***	1	0	0	***244***
Mean Precipitation (in.)	3.03	2.34	3.05	3.53	3.78	4.92	4.55	4.08	4.07	3.81	3.88	3.43	44.47
Extreme Maximum Daily Precip. (in.)	2.08	1.64	1.84	2.15	2.30	4.00	2.62	3.38	3.75	2.55	2.05	1.45	4.00
Days With ≥ 0.1" Precipitation	9	7	8	9	8	9	9	7	8	10	9	10	103
Days With ≥ 0.5" Precipitation	1	1	2	2	3	3	3	2	3	2	2	2	26
Days With ≥ 1.0" Precipitation	0	0	0	0	1	1	1	1	1	0	0	0	5
Mean Snowfall (in.)	na	na	***10.5***	2.1	trace	0.0	0.0	0.0	0.0	0.1	***4.3***	na	na
Maximum Snow Depth (in.)	24	21	25	9	trace	0	0	0	0	5	16	24	25
Days With ≥ 1.0" Snow Depth	26	24	18	2	0	0	0	0	0	0	6	19	95

The period of record for all cooperative weather station data is 1980 – 2009. See User Guide for detailed explanation of data.

Aurora Research Farm *Cayuga County* Elevation: 830 ft. Latitude: 42° 44' N Longitude: 76° 39' W

	JAN	FEB	MAR	APR	MAY	JUN	JUL	AUG	SEP	OCT	NOV	DEC	YEAR
Mean Maximum Temp. (°F)	31.9	34.4	42.1	55.8	67.7	76.9	81.3	80.1	72.7	59.9	48.2	36.8	57.3
Mean Temp. (°F)	24.4	26.2	33.5	46.1	57.1	66.6	71.0	69.6	62.5	50.7	40.7	30.0	48.2
Mean Minimum Temp. (°F)	16.9	18.0	24.9	36.4	46.5	56.3	60.6	59.1	52.2	41.5	33.2	23.1	39.0
Extreme Maximum Temp. (°F)	67	67	85	93	94	96	101	97	98	87	81	69	101
Extreme Minimum Temp. (°F)	-21	-15	-11	10	28	34	45	40	27	23	10	-15	-21
Days Maximum Temp. ≥ 90°F	0	0	0	0	0	2	4	2	1	0	0	0	9
Days Maximum Temp. ≤ 32°F	16	12	7	0	0	0	0	0	0	0	1	10	46
Days Minimum Temp. ≤ 32°F	28	25	24	11	1	0	0	0	0	4	14	25	132
Days Minimum Temp. ≤ 0°F	3	1	0	0	0	0	0	0	0	0	0	1	5
Heating Degree Days (base 65°F)	1,252	1,091	970	566	270	70	15	24	132	442	722	1,079	6,633
Cooling Degree Days (base 65°F)	0	0	1	7	32	125	207	174	63	6	0	0	615
Mean Precipitation (in.)	1.85	1.68	2.57	3.26	3.18	3.83	3.53	3.12	4.10	3.36	3.22	2.31	36.01
Extreme Maximum Daily Precip. (in.)	1.75	1.44	1.83	1.91	1.36	***1.91***	2.85	2.98	3.03	1.85	2.73	1.34	***3.03***
Days With ≥ 0.1" Precipitation	5	5	7	8	8	8	8	6	7	7	7	6	82
Days With ≥ 0.5" Precipitation	1	1	1	2	2	2	2	2	3	2	2	1	21
Days With ≥ 1.0" Precipitation	0	0	0	0	0	1	1	1	1	1	0	0	5
Mean Snowfall (in.)	14.5	11.8	12.1	3.9	0.2	0.0	0.0	0.0	0.0	0.2	4.9	11.3	58.9
Maximum Snow Depth (in.)	25	28	43	16	4	0	0	0	0	3	17	17	43
Days With ≥ 1.0" Snow Depth	21	19	12	2	0	0	0	0	0	0	4	13	71

Avon *Livingston County* Elevation: 544 ft. Latitude: 42° 55' N Longitude: 77° 45' W

	JAN	FEB	MAR	APR	MAY	JUN	JUL	AUG	SEP	OCT	NOV	DEC	YEAR
Mean Maximum Temp. (°F)	32.5	34.5	42.6	55.9	68.1	77.3	81.3	79.7	72.5	60.6	48.8	37.0	57.6
Mean Temp. (°F)	24.6	25.8	33.1	45.3	56.5	66.3	70.4	68.7	61.4	50.2	40.4	29.8	47.7
Mean Minimum Temp. (°F)	16.7	17.0	23.5	34.7	44.8	55.2	59.4	57.6	50.2	39.7	31.9	22.6	37.8
Extreme Maximum Temp. (°F)	67	72	84	91	93	95	99	97	93	87	77	71	99
Extreme Minimum Temp. (°F)	-24	-13	-9	11	28	35	45	37	28	21	9	-7	-24
Days Maximum Temp. ≥ 90°F	0	0	0	0	0	2	3	2	0	0	0	0	7
Days Maximum Temp. ≤ 32°F	16	12	7	0	0	0	0	0	0	0	1	10	46
Days Minimum Temp. ≤ 32°F	28	26	25	14	1	0	0	0	0	6	17	26	143
Days Minimum Temp. ≤ 0°F	4	2	1	0	0	0	0	0	0	0	0	1	8
Heating Degree Days (base 65°F)	1,246	1,102	982	587	284	67	13	29	150	456	733	1,083	6,732
Cooling Degree Days (base 65°F)	0	0	0	4	26	113	187	150	48	5	0	0	533
Mean Precipitation (in.)	1.79	1.56	2.42	2.72	2.78	3.25	3.31	3.35	3.35	2.65	2.72	2.09	31.99
Extreme Maximum Daily Precip. (in.)	3.04	1.91	1.95	1.35	1.71	1.85	1.92	5.20	3.12	2.60	1.57	1.23	5.20
Days With ≥ 0.1" Precipitation	5	4	5	6	7	7	7	7	7	7	7	6	75
Days With ≥ 0.5" Precipitation	1	1	1	2	2	2	2	2	2	1	2	1	19
Days With ≥ 1.0" Precipitation	0	0	0	0	0	1	1	1	1	0	0	0	4
Mean Snowfall (in.)	13.3	10.5	10.7	2.1	0.2	0.0	0.0	0.0	0.0	trace	3.7	11.4	51.9
Maximum Snow Depth (in.)	18	14	27	7	4	0	0	0	0	1	10	10	27
Days With ≥ 1.0" Snow Depth	21	19	11	1	0	0	0	0	0	0	3	15	70

Bath *Steuben County* Elevation: 1,120 ft. Latitude: 42° 21' N Longitude: 77° 21' W

	JAN	FEB	MAR	APR	MAY	JUN	JUL	AUG	SEP	OCT	NOV	DEC	YEAR
Mean Maximum Temp. (°F)	31.5	***34.9***	42.7	55.9	68.2	***76.6***	***80.7***	***79.3***	***72.2***	***59.7***	***47.4***	36.4	***57.1***
Mean Temp. (°F)	22.1	***24.6***	31.7	44.0	54.7	***63.5***	***67.8***	***66.5***	***59.2***	***47.6***	***38.0***	27.8	***45.6***
Mean Minimum Temp. (°F)	12.7	***14.2***	20.6	32.0	41.3	***50.5***	***54.9***	***53.7***	***46.1***	***35.3***	***28.6***	19.2	***34.1***
Extreme Maximum Temp. (°F)	***64***	***69***	84	92	94	***93***	***101***	***100***	***94***	***85***	***77***	70	***101***
Extreme Minimum Temp. (°F)	***-24***	***-13***	-18	8	24	***28***	***39***	***28***	***25***	***16***	***1***	-16	***-24***
Days Maximum Temp. ≥ 90°F	0	***0***	0	0	0	***1***	***3***	***2***	***0***	***0***	***0***	0	***6***
Days Maximum Temp. ≤ 32°F	***16***	***12***	6	0	0	***0***	***0***	***0***	***0***	***0***	***2***	10	***46***
Days Minimum Temp. ≤ 32°F	29	***27***	27	17	5	***0***	***0***	***0***	***2***	***13***	***21***	28	***169***
Days Minimum Temp. ≤ 0°F	***5***	***4***	1	0	0	***0***	***0***	***0***	***0***	***0***	***0***	2	***12***
Heating Degree Days (base 65°F)	***1,314***	***1,137***	1,026	626	325	***106***	***33***	***50***	***200***	***534***	***804***	1,146	***7,301***
Cooling Degree Days (base 65°F)	0	***0***	0	3	14	***68***	***127***	***104***	***30***	***1***	***0***	0	***347***
Mean Precipitation (in.)	1.69	***1.48***	2.09	2.79	2.86	***3.75***	***3.19***	***2.84***	3.37	***2.46***	***2.67***	2.05	***31.24***
Extreme Maximum Daily Precip. (in.)	***3.00***	***1.25***	***1.55***	1.73	***2.20***	***4.67***	***2.30***	***2.90***	***2.40***	***2.05***	***2.06***	***1.30***	***4.67***
Days With ≥ 0.1" Precipitation	4	***4***	6	7	7	***7***	***7***	***6***	6	***6***	***6***	5	***71***
Days With ≥ 0.5" Precipitation	1	***1***	1	2	2	***2***	***2***	***2***	2	***1***	***1***	1	***18***
Days With ≥ 1.0" Precipitation	0	***0***	0	0	0	***1***	***0***	***1***	1	***0***	***0***	0	***3***
Mean Snowfall (in.)	***11.1***	***9.1***	***10.3***	1.5	trace	***trace***	***0.0***	***0.0***	0.0	***trace***	***3.6***	9.2	***44.8***
Maximum Snow Depth (in.)	23	***28***	36	9	trace	***trace***	***0***	***0***	0	***trace***	***14***	14	***36***
Days With ≥ 1.0" Snow Depth	***19***	***18***	12	1	0	***0***	***0***	***0***	0	***0***	***4***	13	***67***

Boonville 2 SSW *Oneida County* Elevation: 1,580 ft. Latitude: 43° 27' N Longitude: 75° 21' W

	JAN	FEB	MAR	APR	MAY	JUN	JUL	AUG	SEP	OCT	NOV	DEC	YEAR
Mean Maximum Temp. (°F)	24.7	27.9	36.1	50.5	63.0	71.3	74.9	73.9	65.9	53.9	41.4	29.8	51.1
Mean Temp. (°F)	16.5	19.1	27.5	41.2	53.1	61.6	65.8	64.7	56.9	45.3	34.4	22.6	42.4
Mean Minimum Temp. (°F)	8.3	10.2	18.8	31.9	43.0	52.0	56.7	55.4	47.8	36.6	27.4	15.3	33.6
Extreme Maximum Temp. (°F)	57	55	77	86	88	89	94	90	89	79	68	62	94
Extreme Minimum Temp. (°F)	-31	-22	-18	0	22	29	33	38	25	17	0	-33	-33
Days Maximum Temp. ≥ 90°F	0	0	0	0	0	0	0	0	0	0	0	0	0
Days Maximum Temp. ≤ 32°F	24	19	12	2	0	0	0	0	0	0	6	19	82
Days Minimum Temp. ≤ 32°F	30	27	28	17	3	0	0	0	1	11	22	29	168
Days Minimum Temp. ≤ 0°F	9	7	3	0	0	0	0	0	0	0	0	4	23
Heating Degree Days (base 65°F)	1,498	1,291	1,157	709	373	140	53	74	253	604	910	1,307	8,369
Cooling Degree Days (base 65°F)	0	0	0	1	10	46	86	71	16	0	0	0	230
Mean Precipitation (in.)	4.99	3.95	4.48	4.49	4.52	4.69	4.37	4.69	5.50	5.57	5.37	5.46	58.08
Extreme Maximum Daily Precip. (in.)	3.11	2.65	1.90	3.18	2.66	3.11	3.67	3.01	4.86	3.08	3.15	1.97	4.86
Days With ≥ 0.1" Precipitation	12	10	10	9	9	9	8	8	8	10	11	12	116
Days With ≥ 0.5" Precipitation	3	2	3	3	3	3	3	3	4	4	3	3	37
Days With ≥ 1.0" Precipitation	1	1	1	1	1	1	1	1	2	1	1	1	13
Mean Snowfall (in.)	52.9	39.8	31.4	8.5	0.2	trace	0.0	0.0	trace	2.2	17.8	44.7	197.5
Maximum Snow Depth (in.)	51	48	57	48	2	trace	0	0	trace	9	21	35	57
Days With ≥ 1.0" Snow Depth	29	28	29	10	0	0	0	0	0	1	11	26	134

The period of record for all cooperative weather station data is 1980 – 2009. See User Guide for detailed explanation of data.

Bridgehampton *Suffolk County* Elevation: 60 ft. Latitude: 40° 57' N Longitude: 72° 18' W

	JAN	FEB	MAR	APR	MAY	JUN	JUL	AUG	SEP	OCT	NOV	DEC	YEAR
Mean Maximum Temp. (°F)	38.7	40.4	46.6	56.1	65.9	75.1	80.9	80.2	73.6	63.2	53.5	43.8	59.8
Mean Temp. (°F)	31.0	32.6	38.5	47.6	56.8	66.3	72.1	71.4	64.4	53.8	45.2	35.9	51.3
Mean Minimum Temp. (°F)	23.2	24.8	30.3	39.0	47.6	57.4	63.3	62.7	55.2	44.4	36.8	27.9	42.7
Extreme Maximum Temp. (°F)	67	63	79	92	93	95	102	98	93	83	75	70	102
Extreme Minimum Temp. (°F)	-11	0	6	14	29	39	48	41	35	24	10	-5	-11
Days Maximum Temp. ≥ 90°F	0	0	0	0	0	1	2	2	0	0	0	0	5
Days Maximum Temp. ≤ 32°F	8	5	1	0	0	0	0	0	0	0	0	3	17
Days Minimum Temp. ≤ 32°F	26	23	19	5	0	0	0	0	0	3	11	22	109
Days Minimum Temp. ≤ 0°F	0	0	0	0	0	0	0	0	0	0	0	0	0
Heating Degree Days (base 65°F)	1,047	908	815	518	260	51	4	7	80	347	589	897	5,523
Cooling Degree Days (base 65°F)	0	0	0	1	11	97	232	214	70	7	0	0	632
Mean Precipitation (in.)	3.99	3.52	4.86	4.65	3.73	4.18	3.41	3.95	4.44	4.19	4.41	4.32	49.65
Extreme Maximum Daily Precip. (in.)	2.35	2.49	3.96	3.46	3.25	6.61	3.55	7.04	5.87	5.69	3.19	3.27	7.04
Days With ≥ 0.1" Precipitation	7	6	7	8	7	6	5	5	6	6	7	8	78
Days With ≥ 0.5" Precipitation	3	2	3	3	2	3	2	2	3	3	3	3	32
Days With ≥ 1.0" Precipitation	1	1	1	1	1	1	1	1	1	1	1	1	12
Mean Snowfall (in.)	7.7	7.9	5.3	0.9	0.0	0.0	0.0	0.0	0.0	trace	0.7	4.0	26.5
Maximum Snow Depth (in.)	27	24	13	8	0	0	0	0	0	trace	7	18	27
Days With ≥ 1.0" Snow Depth	8	6	3	0	0	0	0	0	0	0	0	3	20

Canton 4 SE *St. Lawrence County* Elevation: 439 ft. Latitude: 44° 34' N Longitude: 75° 07' W

	JAN	FEB	MAR	APR	MAY	JUN	JUL	AUG	SEP	OCT	NOV	DEC	YEAR
Mean Maximum Temp. (°F)	26.2	29.4	38.7	53.3	65.7	74.4	79.0	77.5	69.4	56.8	44.8	32.3	54.0
Mean Temp. (°F)	15.8	18.6	28.5	43.1	54.9	64.0	68.7	66.8	58.6	46.8	36.4	23.2	43.8
Mean Minimum Temp. (°F)	5.3	7.7	18.4	32.8	44.1	53.6	58.4	56.1	47.7	36.7	27.9	14.1	33.6
Extreme Maximum Temp. (°F)	66	65	92	89	90	93	93	97	93	82	76	69	97
Extreme Minimum Temp. (°F)	-40	-37	-26	6	23	29	35	33	22	15	-5	-37	-40
Days Maximum Temp. ≥ 90°F	0	0	0	0	0	0	1	1	0	0	0	0	2
Days Maximum Temp. ≤ 32°F	20	17	10	1	0	0	0	0	0	0	3	15	66
Days Minimum Temp. ≤ 32°F	30	26	27	15	3	0	0	0	2	11	20	28	162
Days Minimum Temp. ≤ 0°F	12	10	3	0	0	0	0	0	0	0	0	6	31
Heating Degree Days (base 65°F)	1,521	1,308	1,124	653	323	102	30	59	218	559	851	1,287	8,035
Cooling Degree Days (base 65°F)	0	0	0	2	17	80	153	122	33	3	0	0	410
Mean Precipitation (in.)	2.10	1.79	2.13	2.90	3.11	3.26	3.86	3.67	4.03	3.86	3.37	2.56	36.64
Extreme Maximum Daily Precip. (in.)	1.30	1.58	1.17	1.43	1.86	1.75	4.10	2.85	3.20	2.35	2.68	1.46	4.10
Days With ≥ 0.1" Precipitation	6	5	6	7	8	7	7	7	8	8	8	6	83
Days With ≥ 0.5" Precipitation	1	1	1	2	2	2	2	2	3	2	2	1	21
Days With ≥ 1.0" Precipitation	0	0	0	0	0	0	1	1	1	1	0	0	4
Mean Snowfall (in.)	20.1	16.9	12.4	3.6	trace	0.0	0.0	0.0	trace	0.6	5.8	18.5	77.9
Maximum Snow Depth (in.)	30	33	38	11	1	0	0	0	trace	8	8	24	38
Days With ≥ 1.0" Snow Depth	25	23	17	2	0	0	0	0	0	0	6	19	92

Chazy *Clinton County* Elevation: 169 ft. Latitude: 44° 53' N Longitude: 73° 26' W

	JAN	FEB	MAR	APR	MAY	JUN	JUL	AUG	SEP	OCT	NOV	DEC	YEAR
Mean Maximum Temp. (°F)	27.4	30.4	40.1	55.4	67.8	76.3	80.4	78.7	70.1	57.2	44.8	32.9	55.1
Mean Temp. (°F)	17.7	20.2	30.1	44.7	56.3	65.2	69.8	68.0	59.8	48.0	37.0	24.5	45.1
Mean Minimum Temp. (°F)	8.0	10.0	20.2	34.0	44.8	54.1	59.1	57.3	49.5	38.6	29.2	16.1	35.1
Extreme Maximum Temp. (°F)	61	60	79	91	91	97	96	100	95	85	74	66	100
Extreme Minimum Temp. (°F)	-44	-41	-28	6	27	30	38	36	22	17	-2	-26	-44
Days Maximum Temp. ≥ 90°F	0	0	0	0	0	1	1	1	0	0	0	0	3
Days Maximum Temp. ≤ 32°F	20	16	7	0	0	0	0	0	0	0	3	14	60
Days Minimum Temp. ≤ 32°F	29	26	26	14	2	0	0	0	1	9	19	27	153
Days Minimum Temp. ≤ 0°F	10	8	3	0	0	0	0	0	0	0	0	4	25
Heating Degree Days (base 65°F)	1,460	1,260	1,074	604	275	73	16	36	181	523	833	1,249	7,584
Cooling Degree Days (base 65°F)	0	0	0	3	14	84	170	136	32	2	0	0	441
Mean Precipitation (in.)	***0.78***	na	***0.85***	2.25	2.94	3.46	3.53	3.81	3.23	3.05	***2.21***	***0.81***	na
Extreme Maximum Daily Precip. (in.)	***1.30***	na	***1.80***	2.10	1.65	***2.66***	1.76	2.98	2.80	***2.85***	***4.27***	***1.30***	na
Days With ≥ 0.1" Precipitation	***2***	***2***	2	5	7	7	7	7	6	6	***4***	***2***	***57***
Days With ≥ 0.5" Precipitation	***0***	***0***	0	2	2	2	3	3	2	2	***1***	***1***	***18***
Days With ≥ 1.0" Precipitation	***0***	***0***	0	0	0	1	1	1	1	1	0	0	***5***
Mean Snowfall (in.)	13.7	***12.7***	11.1	2.9	0.1	0.0	0.0	0.0	0.0	0.3	***4.6***	11.2	***56.6***
Maximum Snow Depth (in.)	30	31	50	15	0	0	0	0	0	0	***12***	20	***50***
Days With ≥ 1.0" Snow Depth	22	21	16	2	0	0	0	0	0	0	***4***	16	***81***

Conklingville Dam *Saratoga County* Elevation: 808 ft. Latitude: 43° 19' N Longitude: 73° 56' W

	JAN	FEB	MAR	APR	MAY	JUN	JUL	AUG	SEP	OCT	NOV	DEC	YEAR
Mean Maximum Temp. (°F)	29.4	***33.1***	***41.1***	54.3	***66.3***	***74.1***	***78.3***	***76.6***	69.1	57.8	***45.8***	***33.4***	***54.9***
Mean Temp. (°F)	19.4	***22.3***	***31.1***	43.7	***55.4***	***64.0***	***68.4***	***66.9***	59.3	48.1	***37.8***	***25.2***	***45.1***
Mean Minimum Temp. (°F)	9.4	***11.5***	***20.9***	33.1	***44.6***	***53.7***	***58.4***	57.2	49.4	38.3	***29.7***	***17.0***	***35.3***
Extreme Maximum Temp. (°F)	60	61	80	87	89	92	95	91	88	80	75	67	95
Extreme Minimum Temp. (°F)	-29	-22	-13	7	27	30	44	35	28	22	8	-22	-29
Days Maximum Temp. ≥ 90°F	0	0	0	0	0	0	1	0	0	0	0	0	1
Days Maximum Temp. ≤ 32°F	18	12	5	0	0	0	0	0	0	0	1	12	48
Days Minimum Temp. ≤ 32°F	29	25	26	14	1	0	0	0	0	7	18	27	147
Days Minimum Temp. ≤ 0°F	8	5	1	0	0	0	0	0	0	0	0	3	17
Heating Degree Days (base 65°F)	1,408	***1,202***	***1,046***	633	***302***	***89***	***19***	***39***	189	519	***809***	***1,228***	***7,483***
Cooling Degree Days (base 65°F)	0	***0***	***0***	1	***13***	***64***	***131***	***105***	24	1	***0***	***0***	***339***
Mean Precipitation (in.)	3.35	2.77	3.96	3.69	4.06	4.06	4.19	4.02	3.76	3.71	3.84	3.75	45.16
Extreme Maximum Daily Precip. (in.)	2.53	1.71	2.70	2.97	***2.67***	2.25	2.85	2.25	4.01	2.83	2.90	***2.38***	***4.01***
Days With ≥ 0.1" Precipitation	7	6	7	7	8	8	7	6	6	7	7	7	83
Days With ≥ 0.5" Precipitation	2	2	3	2	3	3	3	3	2	2	2	2	29
Days With ≥ 1.0" Precipitation	1	1	1	1	1	1	1	1	1	1	1	1	12
Mean Snowfall (in.)	19.9	13.8	13.8	2.6	trace	0.0	0.0	0.0	0.0	0.1	3.7	16.5	70.4
Maximum Snow Depth (in.)	39	37	45	20	1	0	0	0	0	trace	16	23	45
Days With ≥ 1.0" Snow Depth	24	25	20	3	0	0	0	0	0	0	3	19	94

The period of record for all cooperative weather station data is 1980 – 2009. See User Guide for detailed explanation of data.

Dannemora *Clinton County* Elevation: 1,339 ft. Latitude: 44° 43' N Longitude: 73° 43' W

	JAN	FEB	MAR	APR	MAY	JUN	JUL	AUG	SEP	OCT	NOV	DEC	YEAR
Mean Maximum Temp. (°F)	25.7	29.5	38.4	52.6	65.4	74.0	78.0	76.1	68.5	55.7	42.5	31.0	53.1
Mean Temp. (°F)	16.9	20.4	29.3	43.0	55.0	64.0	68.2	66.4	58.6	46.9	35.1	23.1	43.9
Mean Minimum Temp. (°F)	8.1	11.3	20.2	33.3	44.5	53.9	58.5	56.7	48.8	38.0	27.7	15.1	34.7
Extreme Maximum Temp. (°F)	64	62	77	87	88	94	96	93	93	79	70	65	96
Extreme Minimum Temp. (°F)	-34	-23	-22	2	18	32	42	33	25	17	0	-28	-34
Days Maximum Temp. ≥ 90°F	0	0	0	0	0	1	1	0	0	0	0	0	2
Days Maximum Temp. ≤ 32°F	22	18	10	1	0	0	0	0	0	0	5	17	73
Days Minimum Temp. ≤ 32°F	30	27	27	14	2	0	0	0	1	9	21	29	160
Days Minimum Temp. ≤ 0°F	9	6	2	0	0	0	0	0	0	0	0	4	21
Heating Degree Days (base 65°F)	1,485	1,255	1,098	657	319	97	23	49	210	556	890	1,294	7,933
Cooling Degree Days (base 65°F)	0	0	0	2	15	73	131	100	25	1	0	0	347
Mean Precipitation (in.)	2.45	2.12	2.53	3.32	3.63	3.98	4.18	4.40	3.85	3.94	3.61	2.92	40.93
Extreme Maximum Daily Precip. (in.)	2.79	2.10	1.78	2.30	1.62	1.95	3.01	2.80	4.55	3.09	3.64	2.41	4.55
Days With ≥ 0.1" Precipitation	6	6	8	8	9	9	9	9	8	9	8	8	97
Days With ≥ 0.5" Precipitation	2	1	1	2	2	3	3	3	3	3	2	2	27
Days With ≥ 1.0" Precipitation	0	0	0	0	0	1	1	1	1	1	1	0	6
Mean Snowfall (in.)	na	na	na	*trace*	0.0	0.0	0.0	0.0	0.0	trace	*1.0*	na	na
Maximum Snow Depth (in.)	na	na	na	na	na	na	na	na	na	na	na	na	na
Days With ≥ 1.0" Snow Depth	na	na	na	0	0	0	0	0	0	0	na	na	na

Delhi 2 SE *Delaware County* Elevation: 1,439 ft. Latitude: 42° 15' N Longitude: 74° 54' W

	JAN	FEB	MAR	APR	MAY	JUN	JUL	AUG	SEP	OCT	NOV	DEC	YEAR
Mean Maximum Temp. (°F)	31.1	34.3	42.3	55.4	66.7	75.1	79.2	78.3	70.7	59.4	47.3	35.7	56.3
Mean Temp. (°F)	20.9	23.4	31.4	43.6	53.9	62.7	66.7	65.7	58.3	47.1	37.8	26.7	44.8
Mean Minimum Temp. (°F)	10.6	12.4	20.5	31.8	41.0	50.3	54.2	53.1	45.8	34.7	28.2	17.7	33.3
Extreme Maximum Temp. (°F)	65	64	83	91	91	91	97	96	90	83	77	66	97
Extreme Minimum Temp. (°F)	-32	-24	-18	8	20	26	33	32	23	11	-1	-25	-32
Days Maximum Temp. ≥ 90°F	0	0	0	0	0	1	1	1	0	0	0	0	3
Days Maximum Temp. ≤ 32°F	16	12	6	0	0	0	0	0	0	0	2	12	48
Days Minimum Temp. ≤ 32°F	29	27	26	17	6	0	0	0	2	14	21	28	170
Days Minimum Temp. ≤ 0°F	8	5	2	0	0	0	0	0	0	0	0	3	18
Heating Degree Days (base 65°F)	1,362	1,170	1,035	637	349	121	48	60	218	551	811	1,180	7,542
Cooling Degree Days (base 65°F)	0	0	0	2	11	60	106	89	24	1	0	0	293
Mean Precipitation (in.)	3.23	2.49	3.54	3.94	4.24	4.60	4.55	3.64	4.38	4.02	3.90	3.45	45.98
Extreme Maximum Daily Precip. (in.)	2.05	2.00	2.17	2.46	2.77	4.31	2.91	3.40	4.49	3.15	3.62	2.54	4.49
Days With ≥ 0.1" Precipitation	8	6	8	8	9	9	8	7	7	8	8	8	94
Days With ≥ 0.5" Precipitation	2	1	2	2	3	3	3	3	3	3	3	2	30
Days With ≥ 1.0" Precipitation	0	0	0	1	1	1	1	1	1	1	1	0	8
Mean Snowfall (in.)	18.2	12.4	11.2	3.8	0.1	0.0	0.0	0.0	0.0	0.6	4.3	14.8	65.4
Maximum Snow Depth (in.)	25	23	28	17	3	0	0	0	0	7	9	31	31
Days With ≥ 1.0" Snow Depth	23	20	13	2	0	0	0	0	0	0	4	16	78

Dobbs Ferry Ardsley *Westchester County* Elevation: 200 ft. Latitude: 41° 00' N Longitude: 73° 50' W

	JAN	FEB	MAR	APR	MAY	JUN	JUL	AUG	SEP	OCT	NOV	DEC	YEAR
Mean Maximum Temp. (°F)	38.7	42.3	50.5	62.4	72.4	80.6	85.2	83.6	76.4	65.3	54.3	43.3	62.9
Mean Temp. (°F)	30.9	33.5	40.7	51.4	61.1	69.8	74.8	73.6	66.2	55.1	45.4	35.6	53.2
Mean Minimum Temp. (°F)	23.1	24.6	30.8	40.4	49.6	58.9	64.3	63.5	55.9	44.9	36.4	27.8	43.4
Extreme Maximum Temp. (°F)	72	75	86	96	97	98	104	100	98	88	81	77	104
Extreme Minimum Temp. (°F)	-10	-2	2	17	29	38	49	44	34	27	12	-4	-10
Days Maximum Temp. ≥ 90°F	0	0	0	0	1	4	7	5	1	0	0	0	18
Days Maximum Temp. ≤ 32°F	8	4	1	0	0	0	0	0	0	0	0	4	17
Days Minimum Temp. ≤ 32°F	26	23	18	5	0	0	0	0	0	2	10	22	106
Days Minimum Temp. ≤ 0°F	1	0	0	0	0	0	0	0	0	0	0	0	1
Heating Degree Days (base 65°F)	1,049	884	748	408	160	24	1	3	64	312	582	905	5,140
Cooling Degree Days (base 65°F)	0	0	1	6	45	175	312	277	106	13	0	0	935
Mean Precipitation (in.)	3.78	3.03	4.45	4.74	4.47	4.39	4.64	4.23	4.64	4.48	4.39	4.25	51.49
Extreme Maximum Daily Precip. (in.)	3.11	2.85	2.97	5.34	2.80	4.49	3.22	3.30	7.62	3.27	3.25	3.07	7.62
Days With ≥ 0.1" Precipitation	7	6	7	8	7	7	7	6	6	6	7	7	81
Days With ≥ 0.5" Precipitation	3	2	3	3	3	3	3	3	3	3	3	3	35
Days With ≥ 1.0" Precipitation	1	1	1	1	1	1	2	1	1	1	1	1	13
Mean Snowfall (in.)	9.0	8.4	5.7	0.9	trace	0.0	0.0	0.0	0.0	0.1	0.7	5.8	30.6
Maximum Snow Depth (in.)	26	20	17	10	trace	0	0	0	0	2	4	14	26
Days With ≥ 1.0" Snow Depth	12	11	5	0	0	0	0	0	0	0	0	6	34

Gouverneur 3 NW *St. Lawrence County* Elevation: 419 ft. Latitude: 44° 21' N Longitude: 75° 31' W

	JAN	FEB	MAR	APR	MAY	JUN	JUL	AUG	SEP	OCT	NOV	DEC	YEAR
Mean Maximum Temp. (°F)	27.3	30.6	39.8	54.8	66.9	75.8	80.1	78.8	71.0	57.7	45.4	32.9	55.1
Mean Temp. (°F)	16.5	19.3	28.9	43.6	54.6	64.0	68.3	66.7	58.8	46.9	36.6	23.6	44.0
Mean Minimum Temp. (°F)	5.7	7.9	17.9	32.3	42.1	52.1	56.5	54.6	46.5	36.0	27.7	14.2	32.8
Extreme Maximum Temp. (°F)	65	64	81	87	88	96	95	98	94	81	73	70	98
Extreme Minimum Temp. (°F)	-45	-37	-27	4	23	29	36	32	22	15	-10	-37	-45
Days Maximum Temp. ≥ 90°F	0	0	0	0	0	1	1	1	0	0	0	0	3
Days Maximum Temp. ≤ 32°F	19	16	8	1	0	0	0	0	0	0	3	14	61
Days Minimum Temp. ≤ 32°F	30	27	27	16	4	0	0	0	2	11	20	29	166
Days Minimum Temp. ≤ 0°F	12	10	4	0	0	0	0	0	0	0	0	6	32
Heating Degree Days (base 65°F)	1,498	1,288	1,114	638	327	96	29	51	209	556	846	1,278	7,930
Cooling Degree Days (base 65°F)	0	0	0	2	10	72	138	111	29	2	0	0	364
Mean Precipitation (in.)	2.30	1.97	2.24	3.00	3.09	3.26	3.60	3.44	3.94	4.04	3.72	2.72	37.32
Extreme Maximum Daily Precip. (in.)	1.56	1.45	1.68	1.95	1.72	2.48	4.18	2.50	4.51	2.06	2.70	1.72	4.51
Days With ≥ 0.1" Precipitation	6	5	6	7	7	7	7	7	8	8	9	7	84
Days With ≥ 0.5" Precipitation	1	1	1	2	2	2	3	2	2	3	2	1	22
Days With ≥ 1.0" Precipitation	0	0	0	0	0	1	1	1	1	1	1	0	6
Mean Snowfall (in.)	21.9	18.2	13.6	3.9	trace	trace	0.0	0.0	trace	1.0	6.8	19.2	84.6
Maximum Snow Depth (in.)	30	30	30	8	trace	0	0	0	trace	12	12	19	30
Days With ≥ 1.0" Snow Depth	26	25	19	2	0	0	0	0	0	0	5	20	97

The period of record for all cooperative weather station data is 1980 – 2009. See User Guide for detailed explanation of data.

Grafton *Rensselaer County* Elevation: 1,560 ft. Latitude: 42° 47' N Longitude: 73° 28' W

	JAN	FEB	MAR	APR	MAY	JUN	JUL	AUG	SEP	OCT	NOV	DEC	YEAR
Mean Maximum Temp. (°F)	*28.2*	*32.5*	*41.0*	*54.4*	*66.4*	*73.6*	*77.9*	*75.9*	*68.1*	*56.7*	*44.5*	*33.3*	*54.4*
Mean Temp. (°F)	*20.2*	*23.8*	*31.9*	*44.4*	*55.8*	*63.5*	*68.1*	*66.5*	*58.9*	*47.9*	*36.9*	*25.9*	*45.3*
Mean Minimum Temp. (°F)	*12.1*	*15.0*	*22.7*	*34.3*	*45.2*	*53.4*	*58.2*	*57.1*	*49.8*	*39.1*	*29.3*	*18.5*	*36.2*
Extreme Maximum Temp. (°F)	*61*	*62*	*83*	*88*	*86*	*90*	*93*	*94*	*89*	*79*	*76*	*65*	*94*
Extreme Minimum Temp. (°F)	*-26*	*-21*	*-11*	*5*	*26*	*32*	*40*	*32*	*27*	*18*	*4*	*-23*	*-26*
Days Maximum Temp. ≥ 90°F	*0*	*0*	*0*	*0*	*0*	*0*	*0*	*0*	*0*	*0*	*0*	*0*	*0*
Days Maximum Temp. ≤ 32°F	*21*	*15*	*7*	*0*	*0*	*0*	*0*	*0*	*0*	*0*	*4*	*15*	*62*
Days Minimum Temp. ≤ 32°F	*30*	*26*	*26*	*14*	*1*	*0*	*0*	*0*	*0*	*8*	*20*	*28*	*153*
Days Minimum Temp. ≤ 0°F	*6*	*4*	*1*	*0*	*0*	*0*	*0*	*0*	*0*	*0*	*0*	*2*	*13*
Heating Degree Days (base 65°F)	*1,383*	*1,161*	*1,020*	*613*	*293*	*100*	*24*	*47*	*201*	*524*	*835*	*1,205*	*7,406*
Cooling Degree Days (base 65°F)	*0*	*0*	*0*	*2*	*14*	*62*	*128*	*102*	*26*	*1*	*0*	*0*	*335*
Mean Precipitation (in.)	*2.88*	*2.57*	*3.56*	*3.87*	*4.53*	*4.15*	*4.51*	*4.46*	*4.19*	*3.98*	*4.00*	*3.21*	*45.91*
Extreme Maximum Daily Precip. (in.)	*1.50*	*2.60*	*1.95*	*2.14*	*2.06*	*2.52*	*3.75*	*3.50*	*3.58*	*4.75*	*2.65*	*2.56*	*4.75*
Days With ≥ 0.1" Precipitation	*7*	*6*	*9*	*9*	*9*	*8*	*8*	*8*	*7*	*8*	*9*	*8*	*96*
Days With ≥ 0.5" Precipitation	*2*	*2*	*3*	*3*	*3*	*3*	*3*	*3*	*3*	*3*	*3*	*2*	*33*
Days With ≥ 1.0" Precipitation	*0*	*0*	*1*	*1*	*1*	*1*	*1*	*1*	*1*	*1*	*1*	*1*	*10*
Mean Snowfall (in.)	*20.6*	*14.9*	*15.4*	*5.9*	*0.2*	*0.0*	*0.0*	*0.0*	*trace*	*1.2*	*7.2*	*17.8*	*83.2*
Maximum Snow Depth (in.)	*37*	*31*	*32*	*23*	*trace*	*0*	*0*	*0*	*trace*	*22*	*14*	*23*	*37*
Days With ≥ 1.0" Snow Depth	*24*	*24*	*18*	*3*	*0*	*0*	*0*	*0*	*0*	*0*	*5*	*20*	*94*

Indian Lake 2 SW *Hamilton County* Elevation: 1,660 ft. Latitude: 43° 45' N Longitude: 74° 17' W

	JAN	FEB	MAR	APR	MAY	JUN	JUL	AUG	SEP	OCT	NOV	DEC	YEAR
Mean Maximum Temp. (°F)	25.5	28.7	36.6	49.8	62.5	70.7	74.2	73.1	65.8	53.7	41.6	30.3	51.0
Mean Temp. (°F)	15.3	17.5	25.7	39.1	50.8	59.8	63.8	62.6	55.3	43.7	33.5	21.4	40.7
Mean Minimum Temp. (°F)	5.0	6.3	14.8	28.4	39.0	48.8	53.4	52.1	44.7	33.6	25.4	12.6	30.3
Extreme Maximum Temp. (°F)	55	57	74	85	85	90	91	90	89	78	68	64	91
Extreme Minimum Temp. (°F)	-35	-30	-25	-1	21	29	35	31	23	15	-2	-27	-35
Days Maximum Temp. ≥ 90°F	0	0	0	0	0	0	0	0	0	0	0	0	0
Days Maximum Temp. ≤ 32°F	22	18	11	1	0	0	0	0	0	0	5	18	75
Days Minimum Temp. ≤ 32°F	30	28	29	21	8	0	0	0	2	15	23	30	186
Days Minimum Temp. ≤ 0°F	12	11	5	0	0	0	0	0	0	0	0	6	34
Heating Degree Days (base 65°F)	1,537	1,338	1,211	770	437	178	85	111	295	653	938	1,343	8,896
Cooling Degree Days (base 65°F)	0	0	0	0	4	28	55	44	9	0	0	0	140
Mean Precipitation (in.)	2.83	2.34	2.92	3.20	3.59	3.70	3.85	3.62	3.73	4.22	3.33	2.86	40.19
Extreme Maximum Daily Precip. (in.)	1.70	2.10	2.40	2.09	2.03	3.00	2.42	2.58	3.43	3.34	2.90	1.70	3.43
Days With ≥ 0.1" Precipitation	7	6	7	7	8	8	8	8	7	8	7	7	88
Days With ≥ 0.5" Precipitation	2	1	2	2	2	2	2	3	3	2	2	2	25
Days With ≥ 1.0" Precipitation	0	0	1	1	1	1	1	1	1	1	1	0	9
Mean Snowfall (in.)	na	na	na	3.0	0.1	0.0	0.0	0.0	0.0	0.7	na	na	na
Maximum Snow Depth (in.)	na	na	na	na	na	na	na	na	na	na	na	na	na
Days With ≥ 1.0" Snow Depth	na	na	na	4	0	0	0	0	0	1	na	na	na

Ithaca Cornell Univ *Tompkins County* Elevation: 959 ft. Latitude: 42° 27' N Longitude: 76° 27' W

	JAN	FEB	MAR	APR	MAY	JUN	JUL	AUG	SEP	OCT	NOV	DEC	YEAR
Mean Maximum Temp. (°F)	31.2	33.6	41.4	54.8	67.0	75.5	79.5	78.6	71.2	58.9	47.3	35.8	56.2
Mean Temp. (°F)	23.0	24.7	32.2	44.6	55.4	64.4	68.7	67.7	60.3	48.8	39.3	28.5	46.5
Mean Minimum Temp. (°F)	14.7	15.7	22.9	34.3	43.8	53.4	57.7	56.7	49.3	38.6	31.4	21.1	36.6
Extreme Maximum Temp. (°F)	66	67	83	91	93	94	98	97	92	84	78	69	98
Extreme Minimum Temp. (°F)	-24	-18	-17	11	25	31	40	34	24	18	2	-19	-24
Days Maximum Temp. ≥ 90°F	0	0	0	0	0	1	2	1	0	0	0	0	4
Days Maximum Temp. ≤ 32°F	17	13	7	1	0	0	0	0	0	0	2	12	52
Days Minimum Temp. ≤ 32°F	29	26	25	13	4	0	0	0	1	8	17	27	150
Days Minimum Temp. ≤ 0°F	5	3	1	0	0	0	0	0	0	0	0	2	11
Heating Degree Days (base 65°F)	1,297	1,132	1,011	609	309	96	30	42	175	500	763	1,126	7,090
Cooling Degree Days (base 65°F)	0	0	1	4	20	86	150	133	41	3	0	0	438
Mean Precipitation (in.)	1.99	1.83	2.76	3.27	3.16	3.91	3.86	3.54	3.69	3.29	3.16	2.32	36.78
Extreme Maximum Daily Precip. (in.)	1.87	1.52	2.06	2.13	2.25	2.04	2.08	3.30	3.90	5.08	4.02	1.87	5.08
Days With ≥ 0.1" Precipitation	6	5	6	8	8	9	8	7	7	7	7	6	84
Days With ≥ 0.5" Precipitation	1	1	1	2	2	2	3	2	2	2	2	1	21
Days With ≥ 1.0" Precipitation	0	0	0	0	0	1	1	1	1	1	0	0	5
Mean Snowfall (in.)	17.3	12.7	12.2	3.6	0.0	0.0	0.0	0.0	0.0	0.4	4.8	12.9	63.9
Maximum Snow Depth (in.)	19	20	28	14	0	0	0	0	0	5	12	11	28
Days With ≥ 1.0" Snow Depth	21	20	12	2	0	0	0	0	0	0	4	15	74

Lowville *Lewis County* Elevation: 859 ft. Latitude: 43° 48' N Longitude: 75° 29' W

	JAN	FEB	MAR	APR	MAY	JUN	JUL	AUG	SEP	OCT	NOV	DEC	YEAR
Mean Maximum Temp. (°F)	26.2	29.1	37.5	52.4	65.0	73.6	77.9	76.7	68.7	56.1	43.7	31.6	53.2
Mean Temp. (°F)	16.7	19.1	28.1	42.4	53.9	62.9	67.2	65.8	57.7	46.3	35.7	23.4	43.3
Mean Minimum Temp. (°F)	7.2	9.1	18.6	32.4	42.7	52.2	56.5	54.8	46.7	36.5	27.6	15.0	33.3
Extreme Maximum Temp. (°F)	62	59	80	87	88	97	94	96	92	81	72	67	97
Extreme Minimum Temp. (°F)	-35	-28	-25	5	23	28	39	32	24	18	-1	-29	-35
Days Maximum Temp. ≥ 90°F	0	0	0	0	0	1	1	1	0	0	0	0	3
Days Maximum Temp. ≤ 32°F	21	17	10	1	0	0	0	0	0	0	4	15	68
Days Minimum Temp. ≤ 32°F	30	27	27	17	3	0	0	0	2	11	21	29	167
Days Minimum Temp. ≤ 0°F	10	9	3	0	0	0	0	0	0	0	0	5	27
Heating Degree Days (base 65°F)	1,491	1,292	1,138	673	349	119	40	65	235	573	873	1,285	8,133
Cooling Degree Days (base 65°F)	0	0	0	2	11	63	116	95	23	1	0	0	311
Mean Precipitation (in.)	3.16	2.49	2.73	3.23	3.34	3.35	3.63	3.70	3.96	4.09	3.92	3.64	41.24
Extreme Maximum Daily Precip. (in.)	2.35	2.03	2.12	2.27	2.45	2.10	2.25	3.05	4.78	2.60	3.30	2.02	4.78
Days With ≥ 0.1" Precipitation	8	7	7	7	8	7	7	7	8	9	9	10	94
Days With ≥ 0.5" Precipitation	2	1	2	2	2	2	2	2	3	3	2	2	25
Days With ≥ 1.0" Precipitation	0	0	0	1	1	1	1	1	1	1	1	0	8
Mean Snowfall (in.)	33.0	25.7	14.9	4.7	0.1	0.0	0.0	0.0	trace	0.8	9.3	32.9	121.4
Maximum Snow Depth (in.)	33	26	27	16	1	0	0	0	trace	8	11	28	33
Days With ≥ 1.0" Snow Depth	27	26	20	4	0	0	0	0	0	0	7	23	107

The period of record for all cooperative weather station data is 1980 – 2009. See User Guide for detailed explanation of data.

Middletown 2 NW *Orange County* Elevation: 700 ft. Latitude: 41° 28' N Longitude: 74° 27' W

	JAN	FEB	MAR	APR	MAY	JUN	JUL	AUG	SEP	OCT	NOV	DEC	YEAR
Mean Maximum Temp. (°F)	35.4	39.2	48.1	61.1	71.5	79.4	83.4	82.1	74.9	63.4	51.4	39.7	60.8
Mean Temp. (°F)	27.0	29.8	37.9	50.2	60.4	68.9	73.2	71.9	64.6	53.2	42.9	32.1	51.0
Mean Minimum Temp. (°F)	18.5	20.4	27.7	39.3	49.2	58.3	63.0	61.6	54.3	43.0	34.3	24.5	41.2
Extreme Maximum Temp. (°F)	66	71	85	91	92	93	101	97	94	87	78	71	101
Extreme Minimum Temp. (°F)	-23	-8	-7	17	26	40	47	41	27	19	12	-10	-23
Days Maximum Temp. ≥ 90°F	0	0	0	0	0	2	4	3	1	0	0	0	10
Days Maximum Temp. ≤ 32°F	12	7	2	0	0	0	0	0	0	0	0	7	28
Days Minimum Temp. ≤ 32°F	28	25	21	5	0	0	0	0	0	3	14	25	121
Days Minimum Temp. ≤ 0°F	2	1	0	0	0	0	0	0	0	0	0	0	3
Heating Degree Days (base 65°F)	1,172	990	832	443	177	30	3	7	85	364	658	1,012	5,773
Cooling Degree Days (base 65°F)	0	0	0	6	40	153	265	227	80	7	0	0	778
Mean Precipitation (in.)	2.66	2.34	3.14	4.03	4.13	4.47	3.98	3.98	4.15	3.76	3.58	3.14	43.36
Extreme Maximum Daily Precip. (in.)	2.00	2.52	2.45	3.46	2.51	2.95	2.49	5.00	3.00	4.12	1.94	2.87	5.00
Days With ≥ 0.1" Precipitation	6	5	6	7	8	8	7	6	6	6	6	6	77
Days With ≥ 0.5" Precipitation	2	2	2	3	3	3	3	3	3	3	3	2	32
Days With ≥ 1.0" Precipitation	0	0	1	1	1	1	1	1	1	1	1	1	10
Mean Snowfall (in.)	na	na	na	trace	0.0	0.0	0.0	0.0	0.0	0.0	0.2	na	na
Maximum Snow Depth (in.)	na	na	na	na	na	na	na	na	na	na	na	na	na
Days With ≥ 1.0" Snow Depth	na	na	na	0	0	0	0	0	0	0	0	na	na

Mineola *Nassau County* Elevation: 96 ft. Latitude: 40° 44' N Longitude: 73° 37' W

	JAN	FEB	MAR	APR	MAY	JUN	JUL	AUG	SEP	OCT	NOV	DEC	YEAR
Mean Maximum Temp. (°F)	39.1	42.2	49.4	59.4	69.2	78.8	83.7	82.4	75.1	64.4	55.1	44.3	61.9
Mean Temp. (°F)	32.4	34.7	41.4	50.6	59.7	69.5	74.8	73.7	66.5	56.0	47.5	37.6	53.7
Mean Minimum Temp. (°F)	25.7	27.3	33.2	41.8	50.2	60.2	65.9	64.9	57.8	47.3	39.8	30.8	45.4
Extreme Maximum Temp. (°F)	71	73	85	94	97	101	103	105	95	89	79	76	105
Extreme Minimum Temp. (°F)	-4	3	5	13	34	43	50	46	38	29	18	-1	-4
Days Maximum Temp. ≥ 90°F	0	0	0	0	1	3	6	4	1	0	0	0	15
Days Maximum Temp. ≤ 32°F	8	4	1	0	0	0	0	0	0	0	0	3	16
Days Minimum Temp. ≤ 32°F	23	20	14	2	0	0	0	0	0	0	5	18	82
Days Minimum Temp. ≤ 0°F	0	0	0	0	0	0	0	0	0	0	0	0	0
Heating Degree Days (base 65°F)	1,002	850	725	430	190	23	1	4	56	287	519	844	4,931
Cooling Degree Days (base 65°F)	0	0	0	4	34	167	313	279	107	14	0	0	918
Mean Precipitation (in.)	3.49	2.72	4.28	4.37	3.99	3.90	4.36	3.65	3.81	4.01	3.78	3.72	46.08
Extreme Maximum Daily Precip. (in.)	4.05	2.05	3.11	3.72	2.87	4.30	3.82	4.04	3.52	4.02	2.92	2.95	4.30
Days With ≥ 0.1" Precipitation	6	5	7	7	7	6	6	6	5	6	6	7	74
Days With ≥ 0.5" Precipitation	2	2	3	3	3	3	3	2	3	3	3	3	33
Days With ≥ 1.0" Precipitation	1	1	1	1	1	1	1	1	1	1	1	1	12
Mean Snowfall (in.)	4.9	6.4	3.6	0.6	0.0	0.0	0.0	0.0	0.0	0.0	0.1	4.2	19.8
Maximum Snow Depth (in.)	12	20	8	9	0	0	0	0	0	0	3	14	20
Days With ≥ 1.0" Snow Depth	7	6	2	0	0	0	0	0	0	0	0	3	18

Morrisville 5 SW *Madison County* Elevation: 1,299 ft. Latitude: 42° 50' N Longitude: 75° 44' W

	JAN	FEB	MAR	APR	MAY	JUN	JUL	AUG	SEP	OCT	NOV	DEC	YEAR
Mean Maximum Temp. (°F)	***28.7***	***32.0***	***39.9***	***53.9***	***65.8***	***73.8***	***77.5***	***76.0***	69.1	56.6	***44.8***	***33.6***	***54.3***
Mean Temp. (°F)	***20.0***	***22.6***	***30.2***	***43.5***	***54.6***	***63.0***	***67.0***	***65.6***	58.8	47.0	***37.1***	***26.2***	***44.6***
Mean Minimum Temp. (°F)	***11.4***	***13.1***	***20.4***	***33.1***	***43.4***	***52.2***	***56.3***	***55.3***	48.5	37.3	***29.3***	***18.7***	***34.9***
Extreme Maximum Temp. (°F)	***60***	***60***	***82***	***87***	***87***	***89***	***92***	***90***	***89***	***80***	***75***	***64***	***92***
Extreme Minimum Temp. (°F)	***-27***	***-25***	***-21***	***4***	***24***	***30***	***36***	***35***	***24***	***16***	***1***	***-30***	***-30***
Days Maximum Temp. ≥ 90°F	***0***	***0***	***0***	***0***	***0***	***0***	0	0	0	0	***0***	***0***	***0***
Days Maximum Temp. ≤ 32°F	***19***	***15***	***9***	***1***	***0***	***0***	0	0	0	0	***3***	***15***	***62***
Days Minimum Temp. ≤ 32°F	***29***	***26***	***26***	***15***	***3***	***0***	0	0	1	9	***20***	***28***	***157***
Days Minimum Temp. ≤ 0°F	***7***	***5***	***2***	***0***	***0***	***0***	0	0	0	0	***0***	***2***	***16***
Heating Degree Days (base 65°F)	***1,388***	***1,192***	***1,074***	***641***	***325***	***108***	***36***	***57***	203	551	***830***	***1,196***	***7,601***
Cooling Degree Days (base 65°F)	***0***	***0***	***0***	***2***	***10***	***57***	***104***	***84***	25	1	***0***	***0***	***283***
Mean Precipitation (in.)	3.15	2.99	3.38	3.66	4.09	4.48	4.02	3.57	4.32	4.08	3.94	3.88	45.56
Extreme Maximum Daily Precip. (in.)	1.65	2.39	1.55	2.15	3.39	2.80	2.08	2.36	4.11	2.10	***2.89***	1.67	***4.11***
Days With ≥ 0.1" Precipitation	10	8	9	8	9	8	7	7	8	9	9	11	103
Days With ≥ 0.5" Precipitation	1	2	2	2	3	3	3	2	3	3	2	2	28
Days With ≥ 1.0" Precipitation	0	0	0	0	1	1	1	1	1	1	1	0	7
Mean Snowfall (in.)	30.5	25.7	21.1	5.6	0.2	0.0	0.0	0.0	trace	1.5	12.0	27.5	124.1
Maximum Snow Depth (in.)	45	51	44	29	4	0	0	0	trace	17	16	30	51
Days With ≥ 1.0" Snow Depth	27	27	22	5	0	0	0	0	0	1	9	24	115

New York Ave V Brooklyn *Kings County* Elevation: 20 ft. Latitude: 40° 36' N Longitude: 73° 59' W

	JAN	FEB	MAR	APR	MAY	JUN	JUL	AUG	SEP	OCT	NOV	DEC	YEAR
Mean Maximum Temp. (°F)	39.5	42.3	49.6	60.2	70.4	79.5	84.5	83.3	76.1	64.8	***54.6***	***43.6***	***62.4***
Mean Temp. (°F)	33.4	35.7	42.3	52.4	62.3	71.7	77.1	76.1	68.9	57.6	***48.1***	***37.8***	***55.3***
Mean Minimum Temp. (°F)	27.2	29.0	34.9	44.5	54.2	63.8	69.7	68.9	61.7	50.3	***41.5***	***31.9***	***48.2***
Extreme Maximum Temp. (°F)	70	73	83	91	96	97	***103***	***101***	98	***86***	***79***	***75***	***103***
Extreme Minimum Temp. (°F)	-4	6	10	19	40	48	***57***	***51***	44	***36***	***23***	***-1***	***-4***
Days Maximum Temp. ≥ 90°F	0	0	0	0	1	3	6	4	1	0	***0***	***0***	***15***
Days Maximum Temp. ≤ 32°F	7	4	1	0	0	0	0	0	0	0	***0***	***4***	***16***
Days Minimum Temp. ≤ 32°F	21	18	11	1	0	0	0	0	0	0	***3***	***15***	***69***
Days Minimum Temp. ≤ 0°F	0	0	0	0	0	0	0	0	0	0	***0***	***0***	***0***
Heating Degree Days (base 65°F)	973	822	697	378	130	13	0	1	29	241	***501***	***836***	***4,621***
Cooling Degree Days (base 65°F)	0	0	0	6	54	220	382	353	153	18	***1***	***0***	***1,187***
Mean Precipitation (in.)	3.54	2.66	4.22	4.36	4.19	3.92	4.83	3.68	3.73	3.73	***3.78***	***3.32***	***45.96***
Extreme Maximum Daily Precip. (in.)	3.13	1.68	2.92	5.46	2.36	2.91	***4.62***	***2.85***	4.44	***4.29***	***2.68***	***2.49***	***5.46***
Days With ≥ 0.1" Precipitation	7	6	7	7	7	7	7	6	6	5	***6***	***6***	***77***
Days With ≥ 0.5" Precipitation	3	2	3	2	3	3	3	3	2	2	***3***	***3***	***32***
Days With ≥ 1.0" Precipitation	1	1	1	1	1	1	2	1	1	1	***1***	***1***	***13***
Mean Snowfall (in.)	6.6	7.3	3.9	0.7	0.0	0.0	0.0	0.0	0.0	trace	***0.3***	***3.5***	***22.3***
Maximum Snow Depth (in.)	23	20	10	9	0	0	***0***	***0***	0	***trace***	***4***	***12***	***23***
Days With ≥ 1.0" Snow Depth	7	6	3	0	0	0	0	0	0	0	***0***	***2***	***18***

The period of record for all cooperative weather station data is 1980 – 2009. See User Guide for detailed explanation of data.

Peru 2 WSW *Clinton County* Elevation: 509 ft. Latitude: 44° 34' N Longitude: 73° 34' W

	JAN	FEB	MAR	APR	MAY	JUN	JUL	AUG	SEP	OCT	NOV	DEC	YEAR
Mean Maximum Temp. (°F)	27.9	31.7	41.0	55.7	68.4	77.2	81.4	79.4	71.0	57.9	45.4	33.3	55.8
Mean Temp. (°F)	18.6	21.9	31.1	44.7	56.5	65.7	70.2	68.0	59.9	48.0	37.3	25.1	45.6
Mean Minimum Temp. (°F)	9.2	12.1	21.2	33.8	44.6	54.2	58.9	56.5	48.7	37.9	29.1	16.8	35.3
Extreme Maximum Temp. (°F)	65	63	83	92	93	98	98	98	95	84	75	69	98
Extreme Minimum Temp. (°F)	-34	-30	-17	5	25	29	40	37	24	18	1	-26	-34
Days Maximum Temp. ≥ 90°F	0	0	0	0	0	1	3	2	0	0	0	0	6
Days Maximum Temp. ≤ 32°F	20	15	7	0	0	0	0	0	0	0	3	14	59
Days Minimum Temp. ≤ 32°F	29	26	26	14	2	0	0	0	1	9	19	28	154
Days Minimum Temp. ≤ 0°F	8	6	2	0	0	0	0	0	0	0	0	4	20
Heating Degree Days (base 65°F)	1,434	1,212	1,043	604	276	70	13	37	182	523	825	1,231	7,450
Cooling Degree Days (base 65°F)	0	0	0	3	21	98	180	136	35	2	0	0	475
Mean Precipitation (in.)	1.37	1.29	1.71	2.56	2.73	3.62	3.49	3.51	2.81	3.00	2.67	1.96	30.72
Extreme Maximum Daily Precip. (in.)	1.12	1.26	1.50	1.85	2.40	4.10	3.27	3.11	4.08	2.41	4.80	1.85	4.80
Days With ≥ 0.1" Precipitation	4	3	4	6	7	7	7	7	5	6	6	4	66
Days With ≥ 0.5" Precipitation	1	1	1	2	2	2	3	2	2	2	2	1	21
Days With ≥ 1.0" Precipitation	0	0	0	0	0	1	1	1	1	1	1	0	6
Mean Snowfall (in.)	11.3	10.4	11.1	2.9	0.0	0.0	0.0	0.0	0.0	0.5	3.2	12.6	52.0
Maximum Snow Depth (in.)	na	na	na	na	na	na	na	na	na	na	na	na	na
Days With ≥ 1.0" Snow Depth	na	na	na	0	0	0	0	0	0	0	0	na	na

Riverhead Research Farm *Suffolk County* Elevation: 100 ft. Latitude: 40° 58' N Longitude: 72° 43' W

	JAN	FEB	MAR	APR	MAY	JUN	JUL	AUG	SEP	OCT	NOV	DEC	YEAR
Mean Maximum Temp. (°F)	39.6	41.5	48.6	59.8	70.5	79.3	84.0	82.5	75.7	64.8	54.5	44.5	62.1
Mean Temp. (°F)	32.3	34.0	40.3	50.3	60.3	69.5	74.8	73.7	67.1	56.3	47.1	37.3	53.6
Mean Minimum Temp. (°F)	25.0	26.4	32.0	40.8	50.0	59.7	65.5	64.8	58.4	47.8	39.5	30.1	45.0
Extreme Maximum Temp. (°F)	68	67	80	92	96	97	100	99	97	85	78	76	100
Extreme Minimum Temp. (°F)	-8	4	9	18	32	42	47	45	37	28	17	0	-8
Days Maximum Temp. ≥ 90°F	0	0	0	0	1	2	5	3	0	0	0	0	11
Days Maximum Temp. ≤ 32°F	7	4	1	0	0	0	0	0	0	0	0	3	15
Days Minimum Temp. ≤ 32°F	25	21	17	3	0	0	0	0	0	1	6	19	92
Days Minimum Temp. ≤ 0°F	0	0	0	0	0	0	0	0	0	0	0	0	0
Heating Degree Days (base 65°F)	1,006	870	758	436	172	22	0	2	42	274	532	851	4,965
Cooling Degree Days (base 65°F)	0	0	0	3	33	165	310	280	111	12	0	0	914
Mean Precipitation (in.)	3.71	3.14	4.48	4.49	3.86	4.12	3.21	3.90	3.84	4.22	4.27	4.01	47.25
Extreme Maximum Daily Precip. (in.)	3.10	2.34	3.06	3.18	3.01	5.27	3.38	6.34	3.84	5.58	2.90	3.62	6.34
Days With ≥ 0.1" Precipitation	7	6	7	7	7	7	5	6	6	6	7	7	78
Days With ≥ 0.5" Precipitation	3	2	3	3	3	3	2	3	3	3	3	3	34
Days With ≥ 1.0" Precipitation	1	1	1	1	1	1	1	1	1	1	1	1	12
Mean Snowfall (in.)	8.4	7.6	5.1	0.7	0.0	0.0	0.0	0.0	0.0	0.0	0.5	4.7	27.0
Maximum Snow Depth (in.)	20	16	14	6	0	0	0	0	0	0	7	20	20
Days With ≥ 1.0" Snow Depth	9	6	3	0	0	0	0	0	0	0	0	3	21

Troy Lock and Dam *Rensselaer County* Elevation: 23 ft. Latitude: 42° 45' N Longitude: 73° 41' W

	JAN	FEB	MAR	APR	MAY	JUN	JUL	AUG	SEP	OCT	NOV	DEC	YEAR
Mean Maximum Temp. (°F)	31.7	35.3	44.3	58.6	70.4	78.7	83.5	82.2	74.3	61.6	49.4	37.1	58.9
Mean Temp. (°F)	23.2	25.9	34.7	48.0	59.2	68.2	73.1	71.6	63.5	51.3	40.9	29.6	49.1
Mean Minimum Temp. (°F)	14.6	16.5	25.0	37.4	47.9	57.7	62.6	60.9	52.6	40.9	32.4	22.1	39.2
Extreme Maximum Temp. (°F)	66	67	84	92	92	96	101	99	93	86	81	69	101
Extreme Minimum Temp. (°F)	-23	-14	-7	15	27	39	48	40	31	23	10	-15	-23
Days Maximum Temp. ≥ 90°F	0	0	0	0	0	3	5	4	1	0	0	0	13
Days Maximum Temp. ≤ 32°F	15	11	4	0	0	0	0	0	0	0	1	9	40
Days Minimum Temp. ≤ 32°F	28	26	24	8	0	0	0	0	0	5	16	26	133
Days Minimum Temp. ≤ 0°F	5	2	1	0	0	0	0	0	0	0	0	1	9
Heating Degree Days (base 65°F)	1,290	1,098	933	506	204	40	3	12	107	423	716	1,090	6,422
Cooling Degree Days (base 65°F)	0	0	0	4	30	142	260	224	68	5	0	0	733
Mean Precipitation (in.)	2.23	1.88	2.98	3.26	3.74	4.22	4.42	4.09	3.32	3.65	3.09	2.58	39.46
Extreme Maximum Daily Precip. (in.)	1.80	1.71	3.00	2.20	2.40	2.68	2.70	2.71	3.00	2.22	2.62	2.50	3.00
Days With ≥ 0.1" Precipitation	5	5	6	7	8	7	8	7	6	7	6	6	78
Days With ≥ 0.5" Precipitation	1	1	2	2	3	3	3	3	2	3	2	2	27
Days With ≥ 1.0" Precipitation	0	0	1	1	1	1	1	1	1	1	1	0	9
Mean Snowfall (in.)	12.7	8.0	7.5	1.3	0.0	0.0	0.0	0.0	0.0	0.1	1.8	7.2	38.6
Maximum Snow Depth (in.)	38	39	30	16	0	0	0	0	0	0	10	19	39
Days With ≥ 1.0" Snow Depth	19	16	8	1	0	0	0	0	0	0	1	10	55

Tully Heiberg Forest *Cortland County* Elevation: 1,898 ft. Latitude: 42° 46' N Longitude: 76° 05' W

	JAN	FEB	MAR	APR	MAY	JUN	JUL	AUG	SEP	OCT	NOV	DEC	YEAR
Mean Maximum Temp. (°F)	27.2	29.8	37.5	50.6	63.0	71.6	75.9	74.7	66.9	54.9	***43.1***	31.9	***52.3***
Mean Temp. (°F)	19.5	21.3	28.9	41.5	53.1	61.9	66.4	65.2	57.6	46.1	***35.7***	24.7	***43.5***
Mean Minimum Temp. (°F)	11.6	12.8	20.3	32.2	43.2	52.2	56.9	55.7	48.2	37.2	***28.2***	17.5	***34.7***
Extreme Maximum Temp. (°F)	61	58	80	85	88	89	93	92	89	80	***74***	65	***93***
Extreme Minimum Temp. (°F)	-21	-19	-11	5	24	30	41	33	25	17	***3***	-29	***-29***
Days Maximum Temp. ≥ 90°F	0	0	0	0	0	0	0	0	0	0	***0***	0	***0***
Days Maximum Temp. ≤ 32°F	21	17	11	2	0	0	0	0	0	0	***5***	16	***72***
Days Minimum Temp. ≤ 32°F	30	27	27	16	3	0	0	0	1	10	***21***	29	***164***
Days Minimum Temp. ≤ 0°F	6	5	1	0	0	0	0	0	0	0	***0***	2	***14***
Heating Degree Days (base 65°F)	1,406	1,228	1,113	702	374	141	50	69	238	580	***872***	1,241	***8,014***
Cooling Degree Days (base 65°F)	0	0	0	2	11	53	101	83	21	1	***0***	0	***272***
Mean Precipitation (in.)	2.85	2.67	3.33	3.96	3.99	4.85	4.00	4.04	4.80	3.97	***4.00***	3.28	***45.74***
Extreme Maximum Daily Precip. (in.)	1.91	1.30	2.22	2.23	1.85	3.22	2.30	4.24	4.98	3.56	***3.56***	2.68	***4.98***
Days With ≥ 0.1" Precipitation	9	7	9	9	9	10	8	8	8	9	***9***	8	***103***
Days With ≥ 0.5" Precipitation	1	1	2	2	3	3	2	3	3	2	***3***	2	***27***
Days With ≥ 1.0" Precipitation	0	0	0	1	1	1	1	1	1	1	***1***	0	***8***
Mean Snowfall (in.)	26.3	23.3	21.1	7.6	0.4	trace	0.0	0.0	trace	1.8	***11.9***	23.4	***115.8***
Maximum Snow Depth (in.)	47	43	60	36	5	0	0	0	trace	9	***17***	34	***60***
Days With ≥ 1.0" Snow Depth	28	27	26	8	0	0	0	0	0	1	***10***	24	***124***

The period of record for all cooperative weather station data is 1980 – 2009. See User Guide for detailed explanation of data.

Utica Oneida County Arpt *Oneida County* Elevation: 711 ft. Latitude: 43° 09' N Longitude: 75° 23' W

	JAN	FEB	MAR	APR	MAY	JUN	JUL	AUG	SEP	OCT	NOV	DEC	YEAR
Mean Maximum Temp. (°F)	29.4	32.3	40.9	55.0	67.6	75.9	80.4	78.7	70.6	58.1	46.0	34.0	55.7
Mean Temp. (°F)	21.9	24.1	32.4	45.3	56.8	65.4	70.2	68.6	60.8	49.0	38.8	27.0	46.7
Mean Minimum Temp. (°F)	14.3	15.9	23.9	35.6	46.0	54.9	59.9	58.4	50.9	39.9	31.5	20.1	37.6
Extreme Maximum Temp. (°F)	65	63	85	91	91	94	96	97	92	82	79	69	97
Extreme Minimum Temp. (°F)	-27	-17	-12	9	27	33	45	40	25	21	1	-23	-27
Days Maximum Temp. ≥ 90°F	0	0	0	0	0	1	2	1	0	0	0	0	4
Days Maximum Temp. ≤ 32°F	18	15	7	0	0	0	0	0	0	0	2	13	55
Days Minimum Temp. ≤ 32°F	28	26	24	11	1	0	0	0	0	6	17	27	140
Days Minimum Temp. ≤ 0°F	5	3	1	0	0	0	0	0	0	0	0	2	11
Heating Degree Days (base 65°F)	1,328	1,149	1,005	586	269	77	12	29	162	492	780	1,170	7,059
Cooling Degree Days (base 65°F)	0	0	1	3	22	95	181	148	42	2	0	0	494
Mean Precipitation (in.)	2.94	2.38	3.15	3.47	3.90	4.28	3.86	3.88	4.10	3.66	3.91	3.37	42.90
Extreme Maximum Daily Precip. (in.)	1.64	1.88	2.31	1.96	2.75	2.98	3.24	2.80	4.14	1.88	2.35	2.11	4.14
Days With ≥ 0.1" Precipitation	8	7	8	9	9	8	7	7	7	8	10	9	97
Days With ≥ 0.5" Precipitation	1	1	2	2	2	3	3	3	3	2	2	1	25
Days With ≥ 1.0" Precipitation	0	0	1	0	1	1	1	1	1	1	1	0	8
Mean Snowfall (in.)	na	na	na	na	na	na	na	na	na	na	na	na	na
Maximum Snow Depth (in.)	33	na	na	na	na	na	na	na	na	na	na	na	na
Days With ≥ 1.0" Snow Depth	24	na	na	na	na	na	na	na	na	na	na	na	na

Valatie 1 N *Columbia County* Elevation: 299 ft. Latitude: 42° 26' N Longitude: 73° 41' W

	JAN	FEB	MAR	APR	MAY	JUN	JUL	AUG	SEP	OCT	NOV	DEC	YEAR
Mean Maximum Temp. (°F)	32.2	35.9	44.2	57.7	69.4	77.5	82.2	80.9	73.4	61.1	49.2	37.2	58.4
Mean Temp. (°F)	22.6	26.1	34.2	46.6	57.6	66.2	70.7	69.6	61.7	49.6	39.9	28.3	47.8
Mean Minimum Temp. (°F)	13.0	16.2	24.0	35.3	45.7	54.9	59.2	58.2	49.9	38.1	30.6	19.5	37.1
Extreme Maximum Temp. (°F)	71	69	86	93	92	97	100	97	94	87	81	69	100
Extreme Minimum Temp. (°F)	-25	-13	-9	10	27	34	43	35	28	19	2	-20	-25
Days Maximum Temp. ≥ 90°F	0	0	0	0	0	2	4	3	1	0	0	0	10
Days Maximum Temp. ≤ 32°F	15	11	4	0	0	0	0	0	0	0	1	9	40
Days Minimum Temp. ≤ 32°F	29	26	25	12	2	0	0	0	0	9	18	27	148
Days Minimum Temp. ≤ 0°F	6	2	1	0	0	0	0	0	0	0	0	2	11
Heating Degree Days (base 65°F)	1,308	1,094	950	550	250	65	13	25	142	474	747	1,129	6,747
Cooling Degree Days (base 65°F)	0	0	1	3	27	109	197	173	48	3	0	0	561
Mean Precipitation (in.)	2.05	1.90	2.82	3.74	4.07	4.50	4.06	4.14	3.96	3.91	3.29	2.55	40.99
Extreme Maximum Daily Precip. (in.)	1.28	1.15	3.89	3.65	3.00	2.68	3.87	3.51	5.10	2.94	2.16	2.25	5.10
Days With ≥ 0.1" Precipitation	5	5	6	8	8	8	7	7	7	7	6	6	80
Days With ≥ 0.5" Precipitation	2	1	2	2	3	3	3	3	3	3	2	2	29
Days With ≥ 1.0" Precipitation	0	0	1	1	1	1	1	1	1	1	1	0	9
Mean Snowfall (in.)	10.8	8.2	6.4	2.2	0.0	0.0	0.0	0.0	0.0	0.3	2.4	11.1	41.4
Maximum Snow Depth (in.)	33	24	18	14	0	0	0	0	0	6	9	17	33
Days With ≥ 1.0" Snow Depth	18	15	8	1	0	0	0	0	0	0	1	10	53

Wales *Erie County* Elevation: 1,089 ft. Latitude: 42° 45' N Longitude: 78° 31' W

	JAN	FEB	MAR	APR	MAY	JUN	JUL	AUG	SEP	OCT	NOV	DEC	YEAR
Mean Maximum Temp. (°F)	31.3	32.5	41.2	54.6	65.5	74.0	77.4	76.3	69.5	57.9	46.9	35.2	55.2
Mean Temp. (°F)	23.6	23.6	31.6	44.0	54.4	63.8	67.4	66.1	59.3	48.4	38.9	28.2	45.8
Mean Minimum Temp. (°F)	15.9	14.7	22.0	33.4	43.3	53.7	57.4	55.9	48.9	38.8	30.9	21.1	36.3
Extreme Maximum Temp. (°F)	65	71	82	89	88	92	95	94	90	83	73	68	95
Extreme Minimum Temp. (°F)	-18	-14	-12	12	27	31	40	35	26	21	7	-19	-19
Days Maximum Temp. ≥ 90°F	0	0	0	0	0	0	0	0	0	0	0	0	0
Days Maximum Temp. ≤ 32°F	17	14	9	1	0	0	0	0	0	0	3	12	56
Days Minimum Temp. ≤ 32°F	28	26	26	16	3	0	0	0	1	8	18	27	153
Days Minimum Temp. ≤ 0°F	4	4	1	0	0	0	0	0	0	0	0	1	10
Heating Degree Days (base 65°F)	1,275	1,163	1,027	625	337	103	38	55	195	513	776	1,135	7,242
Cooling Degree Days (base 65°F)	0	0	1	3	17	75	120	96	29	4	0	0	345
Mean Precipitation (in.)	3.49	2.55	3.00	3.35	3.36	4.17	3.90	3.71	4.26	3.72	3.68	3.80	42.99
Extreme Maximum Daily Precip. (in.)	2.47	2.30	1.76	1.64	1.54	5.33	2.97	3.22	3.09	1.89	2.35	1.43	5.33
Days With ≥ 0.1" Precipitation	11	8	8	8	8	8	8	8	8	8	9	11	103
Days With ≥ 0.5" Precipitation	2	1	2	2	2	3	3	3	3	3	3	2	29
Days With ≥ 1.0" Precipitation	0	0	0	0	0	1	1	1	1	1	0	0	5
Mean Snowfall (in.)	32.7	19.0	15.9	4.8	0.3	0.0	0.0	0.0	0.0	0.3	10.1	27.7	110.8
Maximum Snow Depth (in.)	34	28	29	11	6	0	0	0	0	2	20	19	34
Days With ≥ 1.0" Snow Depth	25	23	16	3	0	0	0	0	0	0	6	20	93

Wantagh Cedar Creek *Nassau County* Elevation: 9 ft. Latitude: 40° 39' N Longitude: 73° 30' W

	JAN	FEB	MAR	APR	MAY	JUN	JUL	AUG	SEP	OCT	NOV	DEC	YEAR
Mean Maximum Temp. (°F)	38.3	40.2	47.1	56.4	65.9	76.1	81.4	81.2	74.4	64.0	54.0	43.4	60.2
Mean Temp. (°F)	32.3	33.8	40.3	49.3	58.4	68.7	74.0	73.8	66.7	56.3	47.0	37.4	53.2
Mean Minimum Temp. (°F)	26.2	27.3	33.4	41.9	50.9	61.2	66.7	66.4	59.0	48.5	40.0	31.3	46.1
Extreme Maximum Temp. (°F)	69	67	81	89	95	97	103	103	92	90	78	77	103
Extreme Minimum Temp. (°F)	-3	0	5	19	29	34	45	48	38	28	15	3	-3
Days Maximum Temp. ≥ 90°F	0	0	0	0	0	1	3	2	0	0	0	0	6
Days Maximum Temp. ≤ 32°F	8	5	1	0	0	0	0	0	0	0	0	4	18
Days Minimum Temp. ≤ 32°F	22	21	14	2	0	0	0	0	0	0	6	18	83
Days Minimum Temp. ≤ 0°F	0	0	0	0	0	0	0	0	0	0	0	0	0
Heating Degree Days (base 65°F)	1,008	876	760	466	220	32	7	3	51	279	534	847	5,083
Cooling Degree Days (base 65°F)	0	0	0	2	23	149	295	283	109	16	1	0	878
Mean Precipitation (in.)	3.32	2.62	4.00	4.22	3.60	3.57	3.60	3.29	3.50	3.67	3.46	3.55	42.40
Extreme Maximum Daily Precip. (in.)	4.91	2.19	2.47	4.64	2.44	3.32	3.90	3.89	3.73	5.43	2.21	2.36	5.43
Days With ≥ 0.1" Precipitation	6	5	7	7	6	6	6	5	5	5	6	7	71
Days With ≥ 0.5" Precipitation	2	1	3	3	2	2	3	2	2	2	3	3	28
Days With ≥ 1.0" Precipitation	1	0	1	1	1	1	1	1	1	1	1	1	11
Mean Snowfall (in.)	na	na	na	0.0	0.0	0.0	0.0	0.0	0.0	0.0	0.0	na	na
Maximum Snow Depth (in.)	na	na	na	na	na	na	na	na	na	na	na	na	na
Days With ≥ 1.0" Snow Depth	na	na	na	0	0	0	0	0	0	0	0	na	na

Westfield 2 SSE *Chautauqua County* Elevation: 707 ft. Latitude: 42° 18' N Longitude: 79° 35' W

	JAN	FEB	MAR	APR	MAY	JUN	JUL	AUG	SEP	OCT	NOV	DEC	YEAR
Mean Maximum Temp. (°F)	32.8	35.3	43.1	55.6	67.3	76.1	80.3	78.2	71.0	59.7	48.2	37.4	57.1
Mean Temp. (°F)	26.4	28.0	35.0	46.8	58.3	67.2	71.8	70.1	63.1	52.2	41.8	31.5	49.3
Mean Minimum Temp. (°F)	19.9	20.5	26.9	37.9	49.2	58.1	63.3	62.0	55.2	44.6	35.4	25.6	41.6
Extreme Maximum Temp. (°F)	66	70	82	90	91	97	96	99	92	83	74	72	99
Extreme Minimum Temp. (°F)	-16	-7	-13	14	29	37	49	41	36	27	16	-8	-16
Days Maximum Temp. ≥ 90°F	0	0	0	0	0	2	2	1	0	0	0	0	5
Days Maximum Temp. ≤ 32°F	15	12	6	0	0	0	0	0	0	0	1	10	44
Days Minimum Temp. ≤ 32°F	27	25	23	9	0	0	0	0	0	1	11	24	120
Days Minimum Temp. ≤ 0°F	1	1	0	0	0	0	0	0	0	0	0	0	2
Heating Degree Days (base 65°F)	1,191	1,041	924	546	241	60	7	14	119	398	690	1,032	6,263
Cooling Degree Days (base 65°F)	0	0	1	7	40	131	226	180	70	7	0	0	662
Mean Precipitation (in.)	2.50	2.20	2.90	3.40	3.82	4.14	4.16	3.96	4.89	4.88	4.32	3.42	44.59
Extreme Maximum Daily Precip. (in.)	1.38	2.09	1.11	1.76	2.17	4.29	3.36	2.41	2.85	2.52	3.38	1.65	4.29
Days With ≥ 0.1" Precipitation	7	7	8	8	8	8	7	7	9	10	10	9	98
Days With ≥ 0.5" Precipitation	1	1	2	2	2	2	3	3	4	4	3	2	29
Days With ≥ 1.0" Precipitation	0	0	0	0	1	1	1	1	1	1	1	0	7
Mean Snowfall (in.)	21.2	14.0	12.7	2.7	0.4	0.0	0.0	0.0	trace	0.4	8.7	24.4	84.5
Maximum Snow Depth (in.)	23	22	17	9	na	0	0	0	trace	na	11	25	na
Days With ≥ 1.0" Snow Depth	25	20	12	1	0	0	0	0	0	0	5	17	80

Whitehall *Washington County* Elevation: 119 ft. Latitude: 43° 33' N Longitude: 73° 24' W

	JAN	FEB	MAR	APR	MAY	JUN	JUL	AUG	SEP	OCT	NOV	DEC	YEAR
Mean Maximum Temp. (°F)	30.1	34.4	44.3	58.6	70.8	79.7	84.0	81.8	73.1	60.6	47.5	35.1	58.3
Mean Temp. (°F)	21.0	24.1	34.1	47.5	59.1	68.2	72.6	70.9	62.4	50.6	39.7	27.4	48.1
Mean Minimum Temp. (°F)	11.8	13.7	23.9	36.2	47.0	56.6	61.2	60.1	51.7	40.6	31.8	19.7	37.9
Extreme Maximum Temp. (°F)	64	63	84	94	92	102	100	96	94	83	75	68	102
Extreme Minimum Temp. (°F)	-36	-33	-14	13	23	36	45	37	28	19	4	-25	-36
Days Maximum Temp. ≥ 90°F	0	0	0	0	0	3	4	3	0	0	0	0	10
Days Maximum Temp. ≤ 32°F	17	11	4	0	0	0	0	0	0	0	1	12	45
Days Minimum Temp. ≤ 32°F	29	26	24	11	1	0	0	0	0	6	17	27	141
Days Minimum Temp. ≤ 0°F	7	5	1	0	0	0	0	0	0	0	0	2	15
Heating Degree Days (base 65°F)	1,360	1,150	952	523	204	38	3	13	132	442	755	1,158	6,730
Cooling Degree Days (base 65°F)	0	0	0	5	29	141	246	204	62	3	0	0	690
Mean Precipitation (in.)	3.01	2.52	2.95	3.22	3.67	3.89	4.46	4.16	3.68	3.72	3.55	3.22	42.05
Extreme Maximum Daily Precip. (in.)	1.96	2.40	2.02	2.23	1.85	2.96	3.45	4.01	4.25	2.62	2.59	2.89	4.25
Days With ≥ 0.1" Precipitation	6	5	6	7	8	7	7	7	6	7	7	6	79
Days With ≥ 0.5" Precipitation	2	2	2	2	2	3	3	3	2	2	3	2	28
Days With ≥ 1.0" Precipitation	1	0	1	1	1	1	1	1	1	1	1	1	11
Mean Snowfall (in.)	16.6	12.0	12.5	2.1	0.0	0.0	0.0	0.0	0.0	trace	2.7	13.6	59.5
Maximum Snow Depth (in.)	na	na	na	2	0	0	0	0	0	na	na	na	na
Days With ≥ 1.0" Snow Depth	na	na	na	0	0	0	0	0	0	0	0	na	na

Yorktown Heights 1 W *Westchester County* Elevation: 669 ft. Latitude: 41° 16' N Longitude: 73° 48' W

	JAN	FEB	MAR	APR	MAY	JUN	JUL	AUG	SEP	OCT	NOV	DEC	YEAR
Mean Maximum Temp. (°F)	34.5	38.4	46.8	59.1	69.4	77.5	82.0	80.7	73.5	62.1	51.2	39.6	59.6
Mean Temp. (°F)	26.6	29.7	37.5	49.2	59.2	67.9	72.7	71.4	63.9	52.6	43.1	32.3	50.5
Mean Minimum Temp. (°F)	18.7	21.0	28.2	39.2	48.8	58.2	63.3	62.1	54.4	43.1	35.0	24.9	41.4
Extreme Maximum Temp. (°F)	67	73	85	95	94	95	100	100	95	87	78	73	100
Extreme Minimum Temp. (°F)	-15	-5	0	14	33	39	49	39	32	25	13	-9	-15
Days Maximum Temp. ≥ 90°F	0	0	0	0	0	2	3	2	1	0	0	0	8
Days Maximum Temp. ≤ 32°F	13	8	3	0	0	0	0	0	0	0	1	7	32
Days Minimum Temp. ≤ 32°F	28	25	21	5	0	0	0	0	0	3	12	25	119
Days Minimum Temp. ≤ 0°F	2	0	0	0	0	0	0	0	0	0	0	0	2
Heating Degree Days (base 65°F)	1,183	991	846	474	208	43	4	11	96	385	650	1,008	5,899
Cooling Degree Days (base 65°F)	0	0	1	6	33	136	249	217	71	7	0	0	720
Mean Precipitation (in.)	3.59	2.97	3.96	4.60	4.35	4.76	4.82	4.41	4.53	4.53	4.39	3.88	50.79
Extreme Maximum Daily Precip. (in.)	2.48	2.22	4.60	5.15	3.35	2.82	3.44	4.04	10.95	4.64	2.97	3.00	10.95
Days With ≥ 0.1" Precipitation	7	6	7	8	8	8	7	7	6	6	7	6	83
Days With ≥ 0.5" Precipitation	3	2	3	3	3	3	3	3	3	3	3	3	35
Days With ≥ 1.0" Precipitation	1	1	1	1	1	1	2	1	1	1	1	1	13
Mean Snowfall (in.)	11.0	10.3	7.7	2.1	0.0	0.0	0.0	0.0	0.0	trace	1.3	7.6	40.0
Maximum Snow Depth (in.)	29	29	19	17	0	0	0	0	0	trace	5	15	29
Days With ≥ 1.0" Snow Depth	18	15	9	1	0	0	0	0	0	0	1	10	54

The period of record for all cooperative weather station data is 1980 – 2009. See User Guide for detailed explanation of data.

New York Weather Station Rankings

Annual Extreme Maximum Temperature

Highest			Lowest		
Rank	Station Name	°F	Rank	Station Name	°F
1	Mineola	105	1	Indian Lake 2 SW	91
2	Dobbs Ferry Ardsley	104	2	Morrisville 5 SW	***92***
2	New York Laguardia Arpt	104	3	Tully Heiberg Forest	***93***
4	New York Central Park Observ	103	4	Boonville 2 SSW	94
4	New York Ave V Brooklyn	***103***	4	Grafton	***94***
4	Wantagh Cedar Creek	***103***	6	Conklingville Dam	95
7	Bridgehampton	102	6	Wales	***95***
7	Islip-Macarthur Arpt	***102***	8	Dannemora	96
7	New York J F Kennedy Int'l Arpt	102	9	Allegany State Park	***97***
7	Whitehall	102	9	Buffalo Greater Buffalo Int'l	97
11	Albion 2 NE	101	9	Canton 4 SE	97
11	Aurora Research Farm	101	9	Delhi 2 SE	97
11	Bath	***101***	9	Lowville	97
11	Middletown 2 NW	101	9	Utica Oneida County Arpt	***97***
11	Syracuse Hancock Int'l Arpt	101	15	Alfred	98
11	Troy Lock and Dam	101	15	Binghamton Edwin A Link Field	98
17	Alcove Dam	100	15	Gouverneur 3 NW	98
17	Chazy	100	15	Ithaca Cornell Univ	98
17	Riverhead Research Farm	100	15	Peru 2 WSW	98
17	Valatie 1 N	***100***	15	Rochester Intl Arpt	98
17	Yorktown Heights 1 W	100	21	Albany County Arpt	99
22	Albany County Arpt	99	21	Avon	99
22	Avon	99	21	Westfield 2 SSE	***99***
22	Westfield 2 SSE	***99***	24	Alcove Dam	100
25	Alfred	98	24	Chazy	100

Annual Mean Maximum Temperature

Highest			Lowest		
Rank	Station Name	°F	Rank	Station Name	°F
1	Dobbs Ferry Ardsley	62.9	1	Indian Lake 2 SW	51.0
2	New York Central Park Observ	62.7	2	Boonville 2 SSW	51.1
3	New York Laguardia Arpt	62.5	3	Tully Heiberg Forest	***52.3***
4	New York Ave V Brooklyn	***62.4***	4	Dannemora	53.1
5	Riverhead Research Farm	62.1	5	Lowville	53.2
6	Mineola	61.9	6	Canton 4 SE	54.0
7	New York J F Kennedy Int'l Arpt	61.5	7	Morrisville 5 SW	***54.3***
8	Islip-Macarthur Arpt	***60.8***	8	Grafton	***54.4***
8	Middletown 2 NW	60.8	9	Binghamton Edwin A Link Field	54.9
10	Wantagh Cedar Creek	60.2	9	Conklingville Dam	***54.9***
11	Bridgehampton	59.8	11	Chazy	55.1
12	Yorktown Heights 1 W	59.6	11	Gouverneur 3 NW	55.1
13	Troy Lock and Dam	58.9	13	Allegany State Park	***55.2***
14	Valatie 1 N	***58.4***	13	Wales	***55.2***
15	Whitehall	58.3	15	Utica Oneida County Arpt	***55.7***
16	Albion 2 NE	58.1	16	Peru 2 WSW	55.9
17	Albany County Arpt	58.0	17	Ithaca Cornell Univ	56.2
18	Avon	57.6	18	Delhi 2 SE	56.3
18	Syracuse Hancock Int'l Arpt	57.6	19	Buffalo Greater Buffalo Int'l	56.6
20	Aurora Research Farm	57.3	20	Alcove Dam	56.7
20	Rochester Intl Arpt	57.3	21	Alfred	56.9
22	Bath	***57.1***	22	Bath	***57.1***
22	Westfield 2 SSE	***57.1***	22	Westfield 2 SSE	***57.1***
24	Alfred	56.9	24	Aurora Research Farm	57.3
25	Alcove Dam	56.7	24	Rochester Intl Arpt	57.3

Rankings include 25 highest/lowest stations. If state has less than 25 stations, all stations are included. The period of record is 1980–2009. See User Guide for detailed explanation of data.

Annual Mean Temperature

Highest

Rank	Station Name	°F
1	New York Laguardia Arpt	55.6
2	New York Central Park Observ	55.3
2	New York Ave V Brooklyn	***55.3***
4	New York J F Kennedy Int'l Arpt	54.4
5	Mineola	53.7
6	Riverhead Research Farm	53.6
7	Dobbs Ferry Ardsley	53.2
7	Wantagh Cedar Creek	53.2
9	Islip-Macarthur Arpt	***52.6***
10	Bridgehampton	51.3
11	Middletown 2 NW	51.0
12	Yorktown Heights 1 W	50.5
13	Westfield 2 SSE	***49.4***
14	Albion 2 NE	49.1
14	Troy Lock and Dam	49.1
16	Buffalo Greater Buffalo Int'l	48.5
17	Rochester Intl Arpt	48.3
18	Albany County Arpt	48.2
18	Aurora Research Farm	48.2
18	Syracuse Hancock Int'l Arpt	48.2
21	Whitehall	48.1
22	Valatie 1 N	***47.8***
23	Avon	47.7
24	Utica Oneida County Arpt	***46.7***
25	Binghamton Edwin A Link Field	46.5

Lowest

Rank	Station Name	°F
1	Indian Lake 2 SW	40.7
2	Boonville 2 SSW	42.4
3	Lowville	43.3
4	Tully Heiberg Forest	***43.5***
5	Canton 4 SE	43.8
6	Dannemora	43.9
7	Gouverneur 3 NW	44.0
8	Allegany State Park	***44.6***
8	Morrisville 5 SW	***44.6***
10	Delhi 2 SE	44.8
11	Chazy	45.1
11	Conklingville Dam	***45.1***
13	Alfred	45.2
14	Grafton	***45.3***
15	Bath	***45.6***
15	Peru 2 WSW	45.6
17	Wales	***45.8***
18	Alcove Dam	46.1
19	Binghamton Edwin A Link Field	46.5
19	Ithaca Cornell Univ	46.5
21	Utica Oneida County Arpt	***46.7***
22	Avon	47.7
23	Valatie 1 N	***47.8***
24	Whitehall	48.1
25	Albany County Arpt	48.2

Annual Mean Minimum Temperature

Highest

Rank	Station Name	°F
1	New York Laguardia Arpt	48.7
2	New York Ave V Brooklyn	***48.2***
3	New York Central Park Observ	47.8
4	New York J F Kennedy Int'l Arpt	47.2
5	Wantagh Cedar Creek	46.1
6	Mineola	45.4
7	Riverhead Research Farm	45.0
8	Islip-Macarthur Arpt	***44.3***
9	Dobbs Ferry Ardsley	43.4
10	Bridgehampton	42.7
11	Westfield 2 SSE	***41.6***
12	Yorktown Heights 1 W	41.4
13	Middletown 2 NW	41.2
14	Buffalo Greater Buffalo Int'l	40.3
15	Albion 2 NE	40.1
16	Rochester Intl Arpt	39.3
17	Troy Lock and Dam	39.2
18	Aurora Research Farm	39.1
19	Syracuse Hancock Int'l Arpt	38.7
20	Albany County Arpt	38.3
21	Binghamton Edwin A Link Field	38.1
22	Whitehall	37.9
23	Avon	37.8
24	Utica Oneida County Arpt	***37.6***
25	Valatie 1 N	***37.1***

Lowest

Rank	Station Name	°F
1	Indian Lake 2 SW	30.3
2	Gouverneur 3 NW	32.8
3	Lowville	33.3
4	Delhi 2 SE	33.4
5	Alfred	33.5
6	Boonville 2 SSW	33.6
6	Canton 4 SE	33.6
8	Allegany State Park	***34.0***
9	Bath	***34.1***
10	Dannemora	34.7
10	Tully Heiberg Forest	***34.7***
12	Morrisville 5 SW	***34.9***
13	Chazy	35.1
14	Conklingville Dam	***35.3***
14	Peru 2 WSW	35.3
16	Alcove Dam	35.5
17	Grafton	***36.2***
18	Wales	***36.3***
19	Ithaca Cornell Univ	36.6
20	Valatie 1 N	***37.1***
21	Utica Oneida County Arpt	***37.6***
22	Avon	37.8
23	Whitehall	37.9
24	Binghamton Edwin A Link Field	38.1
25	Albany County Arpt	38.3

Rankings include 25 highest/lowest stations. If state has less than 25 stations, all stations are included. The period of record is 1980–2009. See User Guide for detailed explanation of data.

Annual Extreme Minimum Temperature

Highest			Lowest		
Rank	Station Name	°F	Rank	Station Name	°F
1	New York Central Park Observ	-2	1	Gouverneur 3 NW	-45
1	New York J F Kennedy Int'l Arpt	-2	2	Chazy	-44
3	New York Laguardia Arpt	-3	3	Canton 4 SE	-40
3	Wantagh Cedar Creek	-3	4	Whitehall	-36
5	Mineola	-4	5	Indian Lake 2 SW	-35
5	New York Ave V Brooklyn	***-4***	5	Lowville	-35
7	Islip-Macarthur Arpt	***-7***	7	Dannemora	-34
8	Riverhead Research Farm	-8	7	Peru 2 WSW	-34
9	Dobbs Ferry Ardsley	-10	9	Boonville 2 SSW	-33
10	Bridgehampton	-11	10	Delhi 2 SE	-32
11	Albion 2 NE	-15	11	Morrisville 5 SW	***-30***
11	Yorktown Heights 1 W	-15	12	Alcove Dam	-29
13	Buffalo Greater Buffalo Int'l	-16	12	Conklingville Dam	-29
13	Westfield 2 SSE	***-16***	12	Tully Heiberg Forest	***-29***
15	Rochester Intl Arpt	-17	15	Utica Oneida County Arpt	***-27***
16	Binghamton Edwin A Link Field	-18	16	Grafton	***-26***
17	Wales	***-19***	17	Alfred	-25
18	Aurora Research Farm	-21	17	Syracuse Hancock Int'l Arpt	-25
19	Allegany State Park	***-22***	17	Valatie 1 N	***-25***
20	Albany County Arpt	-23	20	Avon	-24
20	Middletown 2 NW	-23	20	Bath	***-24***
20	Troy Lock and Dam	-23	20	Ithaca Cornell Univ	-24
23	Avon	-24	23	Albany County Arpt	-23
23	Bath	***-24***	23	Middletown 2 NW	-23
23	Ithaca Cornell Univ	-24	23	Troy Lock and Dam	-23

July Mean Maximum Temperature

Highest			Lowest		
Rank	Station Name	°F	Rank	Station Name	°F
1	Dobbs Ferry Ardsley	85.2	1	Indian Lake 2 SW	74.2
2	New York Laguardia Arpt	85.0	2	Boonville 2 SSW	74.9
3	New York Central Park Observ	84.8	3	Tully Heiberg Forest	75.9
4	New York Ave V Brooklyn	84.5	4	Wales	***77.4***
5	Riverhead Research Farm	84.0	5	Morrisville 5 SW	***77.5***
5	Whitehall	84.0	6	Allegany State Park	77.9
7	Mineola	83.7	6	Grafton	***77.9***
8	Troy Lock and Dam	83.5	6	Lowville	77.9
9	Middletown 2 NW	83.4	9	Dannemora	78.0
10	New York J F Kennedy Int'l Arpt	82.9	10	Conklingville Dam	***78.3***
11	Albany County Arpt	82.3	11	Binghamton Edwin A Link Field	78.4
12	Valatie 1 N	***82.2***	12	Canton 4 SE	79.0
13	Albion 2 NE	82.1	13	Delhi 2 SE	79.2
14	Islip-Macarthur Arpt	***82.0***	14	Ithaca Cornell Univ	79.5
14	Yorktown Heights 1 W	82.0	15	Alcove Dam	80.0
16	Syracuse Hancock Int'l Arpt	81.7	16	Alfred	80.1
17	Peru 2 WSW	81.4	16	Buffalo Greater Buffalo Int'l	80.1
17	Wantagh Cedar Creek	81.4	16	Gouverneur 3 NW	80.1
19	Aurora Research Farm	81.3	19	Westfield 2 SSE	***80.3***
19	Avon	81.3	20	Chazy	80.4
21	Rochester Intl Arpt	81.2	20	Utica Oneida County Arpt	80.4
22	Bridgehampton	80.9	22	Bath	***80.7***
23	Bath	***80.7***	23	Bridgehampton	80.9
24	Chazy	80.4	24	Rochester Intl Arpt	81.2
24	Utica Oneida County Arpt	80.4	25	Aurora Research Farm	81.3

Rankings include 25 highest/lowest stations. If state has less than 25 stations, all stations are included. The period of record is 1980–2009. See User Guide for detailed explanation of data.

January Mean Minimum Temperature

Highest

Rank	Station Name	°F
1	New York Laguardia Arpt	27.4
2	New York Ave V Brooklyn	27.2
3	New York Central Park Observ	26.9
4	New York J F Kennedy Int'l Arpt	26.3
5	Wantagh Cedar Creek	26.2
6	Mineola	25.7
7	Riverhead Research Farm	25.0
8	Islip-Macarthur Arpt	***24.4***
9	Bridgehampton	23.2
10	Dobbs Ferry Ardsley	23.1
11	Westfield 2 SSE	***19.9***
12	Buffalo Greater Buffalo Int'l	18.8
13	Yorktown Heights 1 W	18.7
14	Middletown 2 NW	18.5
15	Albion 2 NE	18.4
16	Rochester Intl Arpt	17.8
17	Aurora Research Farm	16.9
18	Avon	16.7
19	Wales	***15.9***
20	Binghamton Edwin A Link Field	15.8
20	Syracuse Hancock Int'l Arpt	15.8
22	Ithaca Cornell Univ	14.7
23	Troy Lock and Dam	14.6
24	Albany County Arpt	14.5
25	Utica Oneida County Arpt	14.3

Lowest

Rank	Station Name	°F
1	Indian Lake 2 SW	5.0
2	Canton 4 SE	5.3
3	Gouverneur 3 NW	5.7
4	Lowville	7.2
5	Chazy	8.0
6	Dannemora	8.1
7	Boonville 2 SSW	8.3
8	Peru 2 WSW	9.2
9	Conklingville Dam	9.4
10	Delhi 2 SE	10.6
11	Morrisville 5 SW	***11.4***
12	Alcove Dam	11.6
13	Tully Heiberg Forest	11.7
14	Whitehall	11.8
15	Grafton	***12.1***
16	Alfred	12.7
16	Bath	12.7
18	Valatie 1 N	***13.0***
19	Allegany State Park	13.4
20	Utica Oneida County Arpt	14.3
21	Albany County Arpt	14.5
22	Troy Lock and Dam	14.6
23	Ithaca Cornell Univ	14.7
24	Binghamton Edwin A Link Field	15.8
24	Syracuse Hancock Int'l Arpt	15.8

Number of Days Annually Maximum Temperature ≥ 90°F

Highest

Rank	Station Name	Days
1	Dobbs Ferry Ardsley	18
1	New York Laguardia Arpt	18
3	New York Central Park Observ	17
4	Mineola	15
4	New York Ave V Brooklyn	***15***
6	Troy Lock and Dam	13
7	Riverhead Research Farm	11
8	Middletown 2 NW	10
8	New York J F Kennedy Int'l Arpt	10
8	Valatie 1 N	***10***
8	Whitehall	10
12	Aurora Research Farm	9
13	Albany County Arpt	8
13	Albion 2 NE	8
13	Islip-Macarthur Arpt	***8***
13	Syracuse Hancock Int'l Arpt	8
13	Yorktown Heights 1 W	8
18	Avon	7
19	Bath	***6***
19	Peru 2 WSW	6
19	Rochester Intl Arpt	6
19	Wantagh Cedar Creek	***6***
23	Alcove Dam	5
23	Bridgehampton	5
23	Westfield 2 SSE	***5***

Lowest

Rank	Station Name	Days
1	Boonville 2 SSW	0
1	Grafton	***0***
1	Indian Lake 2 SW	0
1	Morrisville 5 SW	***0***
1	Tully Heiberg Forest	***0***
1	Wales	***0***
7	Allegany State Park	1
7	Conklingville Dam	1
9	Binghamton Edwin A Link Field	2
9	Canton 4 SE	2
9	Dannemora	2
12	Buffalo Greater Buffalo Int'l	3
12	Chazy	3
12	Delhi 2 SE	3
12	Gouverneur 3 NW	3
12	Lowville	3
17	Alfred	4
17	Ithaca Cornell Univ	4
17	Utica Oneida County Arpt	***4***
20	Alcove Dam	5
20	Bridgehampton	5
20	Westfield 2 SSE	***5***
23	Bath	***6***
23	Peru 2 WSW	6
23	Rochester Intl Arpt	6

Rankings include 25 highest/lowest stations. If state has less than 25 stations, all stations are included. The period of record is 1980–2009. See User Guide for detailed explanation of data.

Number of Days Annually Maximum Temperature ≤ 32°F

Highest Rank	Station Name	Days	Lowest Rank	Station Name	Days
1	Boonville 2 SSW	82	1	New York J F Kennedy Int'l Arpt	15
2	Indian Lake 2 SW	75	1	Riverhead Research Farm	15
3	Dannemora	73	3	Mineola	16
4	Tully Heiberg Forest	***72***	3	New York Ave V Brooklyn	***16***
5	Lowville	68	5	Bridgehampton	17
6	Canton 4 SE	66	5	Dobbs Ferry Ardsley	17
7	Grafton	***62***	5	Islip-Macarthur Arpt	***17***
7	Morrisville 5 SW	***62***	5	New York Central Park Observ	17
9	Gouverneur 3 NW	61	9	New York Laguardia Arpt	18
10	Chazy	60	9	Wantagh Cedar Creek	18
11	Peru 2 WSW	59	11	Middletown 2 NW	28
12	Binghamton Edwin A Link Field	58	12	Yorktown Heights 1 W	32
13	Allegany State Park	56	13	Troy Lock and Dam	40
13	Wales	***56***	13	Valatie 1 N	***40***
15	Utica Oneida County Arpt	***55***	15	Albany County Arpt	43
16	Ithaca Cornell Univ	52	16	Westfield 2 SSE	***44***
17	Buffalo Greater Buffalo Int'l	51	17	Whitehall	45
18	Alfred	48	18	Albion 2 NE	46
18	Conklingville Dam	48	18	Aurora Research Farm	46
18	Delhi 2 SE	48	18	Avon	46
18	Syracuse Hancock Int'l Arpt	48	18	Bath	***46***
22	Alcove Dam	47	18	Rochester Intl Arpt	46
23	Albion 2 NE	46	23	Alcove Dam	47
23	Aurora Research Farm	46	24	Alfred	48
23	Avon	46	24	Conklingville Dam	48

Number of Days Annually Minimum Temperature ≤ 32°F

Highest Rank	Station Name	Days	Lowest Rank	Station Name	Days
1	Indian Lake 2 SW	186	1	New York Laguardia Arpt	67
2	Alfred	170	2	New York Ave V Brooklyn	***69***
2	Delhi 2 SE	170	3	New York Central Park Observ	70
4	Bath	***169***	4	New York J F Kennedy Int'l Arpt	74
5	Boonville 2 SSW	168	5	Mineola	82
6	Lowville	167	6	Wantagh Cedar Creek	83
7	Gouverneur 3 NW	166	7	Riverhead Research Farm	92
8	Tully Heiberg Forest	***164***	8	Islip-Macarthur Arpt	***101***
9	Allegany State Park	163	9	Dobbs Ferry Ardsley	106
10	Canton 4 SE	162	10	Bridgehampton	109
11	Alcove Dam	160	11	Yorktown Heights 1 W	119
11	Dannemora	160	12	Westfield 2 SSE	***120***
13	Morrisville 5 SW	***157***	13	Middletown 2 NW	121
14	Peru 2 WSW	154	14	Buffalo Greater Buffalo Int'l	125
15	Chazy	153	15	Albion 2 NE	129
15	Grafton	***153***	16	Rochester Intl Arpt	131
15	Wales	***153***	17	Aurora Research Farm	132
18	Ithaca Cornell Univ	150	18	Troy Lock and Dam	133
19	Valatie 1 N	***148***	19	Syracuse Hancock Int'l Arpt	134
20	Conklingville Dam	147	20	Utica Oneida County Arpt	***140***
21	Avon	143	21	Albany County Arpt	141
22	Binghamton Edwin A Link Field	142	21	Whitehall	141
23	Albany County Arpt	141	23	Binghamton Edwin A Link Field	142
23	Whitehall	141	24	Avon	143
25	Utica Oneida County Arpt	***140***	25	Conklingville Dam	147

Rankings include 25 highest/lowest stations. If state has less than 25 stations, all stations are included. The period of record is 1980–2009. See User Guide for detailed explanation of data.

Number of Days Annually Minimum Temperature ≤ 0°F

Highest			Lowest		
Rank	**Station Name**	**Days**	**Rank**	**Station Name**	**Days**
1	Indian Lake 2 SW	34	1	Bridgehampton	0
2	Gouverneur 3 NW	32	1	Islip-Macarthur Arpt	***0***
3	Canton 4 SE	31	1	Mineola	0
4	Lowville	27	1	New York Central Park Observ	0
5	Chazy	25	1	New York J F Kennedy Int'l Arpt	0
6	Boonville 2 SSW	23	1	New York Laguardia Arpt	0
7	Dannemora	21	1	New York Ave V Brooklyn	***0***
8	Peru 2 WSW	20	1	Riverhead Research Farm	0
9	Delhi 2 SE	18	1	Wantagh Cedar Creek	0
10	Conklingville Dam	17	10	Dobbs Ferry Ardsley	1
11	Morrisville 5 SW	***16***	11	Westfield 2 SSE	***2***
12	Alfred	15	11	Yorktown Heights 1 W	2
12	Whitehall	15	13	Albion 2 NE	3
14	Tully Heiberg Forest	***14***	13	Middletown 2 NW	3
15	Allegany State Park	13	15	Buffalo Greater Buffalo Int'l	4
15	Grafton	***13***	15	Rochester Intl Arpt	4
17	Alcove Dam	12	17	Aurora Research Farm	5
17	Bath	***12***	17	Binghamton Edwin A Link Field	5
19	Ithaca Cornell Univ	11	19	Avon	8
19	Utica Oneida County Arpt	***11***	19	Syracuse Hancock Int'l Arpt	8
19	Valatie 1 N	***11***	21	Albany County Arpt	9
22	Wales	***10***	21	Troy Lock and Dam	9
23	Albany County Arpt	9	23	Wales	***10***
23	Troy Lock and Dam	9	24	Ithaca Cornell Univ	11
25	Avon	8	24	Utica Oneida County Arpt	***11***

Number of Annual Heating Degree Days

Highest			Lowest		
Rank	**Station Name**	**Num.**	**Rank**	**Station Name**	**Num.**
1	Indian Lake 2 SW	8,896	1	New York Laguardia Arpt	4,566
2	Boonville 2 SSW	8,369	2	New York Ave V Brooklyn	***4,621***
3	Lowville	8,133	3	New York Central Park Observ	4,622
4	Canton 4 SE	8,035	4	New York J F Kennedy Int'l Arpt	4,796
5	Tully Heiberg Forest	***8,014***	5	Mineola	4,931
6	Dannemora	7,933	6	Riverhead Research Farm	4,965
7	Gouverneur 3 NW	7,930	7	Wantagh Cedar Creek	5,083
8	Morrisville 5 SW	***7,601***	8	Dobbs Ferry Ardsley	5,140
9	Chazy	7,584	9	Islip-Macarthur Arpt	***5,261***
10	Allegany State Park	***7,567***	10	Bridgehampton	5,523
11	Delhi 2 SE	7,542	11	Middletown 2 NW	5,773
12	Conklingville Dam	***7,483***	12	Yorktown Heights 1 W	5,899
13	Peru 2 WSW	7,450	13	Westfield 2 SSE	***6,263***
14	Alfred	7,416	14	Albion 2 NE	6,365
15	Grafton	***7,406***	15	Troy Lock and Dam	6,422
16	Bath	***7,301***	16	Buffalo Greater Buffalo Int'l	6,508
17	Wales	***7,242***	17	Rochester Intl Arpt	6,553
18	Alcove Dam	7,190	18	Syracuse Hancock Int'l Arpt	6,618
19	Ithaca Cornell Univ	7,090	19	Aurora Research Farm	6,633
20	Binghamton Edwin A Link Field	7,060	20	Albany County Arpt	6,638
21	Utica Oneida County Arpt	***7,059***	21	Whitehall	6,730
22	Valatie 1 N	***6,747***	22	Avon	6,732
23	Avon	6,732	23	Valatie 1 N	***6,747***
24	Whitehall	6,730	24	Utica Oneida County Arpt	***7,059***
25	Albany County Arpt	6,638	25	Binghamton Edwin A Link Field	7,060

Rankings include 25 highest/lowest stations. If state has less than 25 stations, all stations are included. The period of record is 1980–2009. See User Guide for detailed explanation of data.

Number of Annual Cooling Degree Days

Rank (Highest)	Station Name	Num.	Rank (Lowest)	Station Name	Num.
1	New York Laguardia Arpt	1,262	1	Indian Lake 2 SW	140
2	New York Ave V Brooklyn	***1,187***	2	Boonville 2 SSW	230
3	New York Central Park Observ	1,184	3	Allegany State Park	***244***
4	New York J F Kennedy Int'l Arpt	1,026	4	Tully Heiberg Forest	***272***
5	Dobbs Ferry Ardsley	935	5	Morrisville 5 SW	***283***
6	Mineola	918	6	Delhi 2 SE	293
7	Riverhead Research Farm	914	7	Alfred	294
8	Wantagh Cedar Creek	878	8	Lowville	311
9	Islip-Macarthur Arpt	***839***	9	Grafton	***335***
10	Middletown 2 NW	778	10	Conklingville Dam	***339***
11	Troy Lock and Dam	733	11	Wales	***345***
12	Yorktown Heights 1 W	720	12	Bath	***347***
13	Whitehall	690	12	Dannemora	347
14	Albion 2 NE	669	14	Gouverneur 3 NW	364
15	Westfield 2 SSE	***662***	15	Canton 4 SE	410
16	Bridgehampton	632	16	Alcove Dam	412
17	Aurora Research Farm	615	17	Binghamton Edwin A Link Field	426
18	Albany County Arpt	603	18	Ithaca Cornell Univ	438
19	Syracuse Hancock Int'l Arpt	590	19	Chazy	441
20	Buffalo Greater Buffalo Int'l	582	20	Peru 2 WSW	475
21	Rochester Intl Arpt	581	21	Utica Oneida County Arpt	***494***
22	Valatie 1 N	***561***	22	Avon	533
23	Avon	533	23	Valatie 1 N	***561***
24	Utica Oneida County Arpt	***494***	24	Rochester Intl Arpt	581
25	Peru 2 WSW	475	25	Buffalo Greater Buffalo Int'l	582

Annual Precipitation

Rank (Highest)	Station Name	Inches	Rank (Lowest)	Station Name	Inches
1	Boonville 2 SSW	58.08	1	Peru 2 WSW	30.72
2	Dobbs Ferry Ardsley	51.49	2	Bath	***31.24***
3	Yorktown Heights 1 W	50.79	3	Avon	31.99
4	Bridgehampton	49.65	4	Rochester Intl Arpt	34.12
5	New York Central Park Observ	49.08	5	Albion 2 NE	35.55
6	Riverhead Research Farm	47.25	6	Aurora Research Farm	36.01
7	Islip-Macarthur Arpt	***46.53***	7	Canton 4 SE	36.64
8	Mineola	46.08	8	Ithaca Cornell Univ	36.78
9	Delhi 2 SE	45.98	9	Gouverneur 3 NW	37.32
10	New York Ave V Brooklyn	***45.96***	10	Alfred	37.49
11	Grafton	***45.91***	11	Syracuse Hancock Int'l Arpt	37.90
12	Tully Heiberg Forest	***45.74***	12	Albany County Arpt	39.14
13	Morrisville 5 SW	45.56	12	Binghamton Edwin A Link Field	39.14
14	Conklingville Dam	45.16	14	Troy Lock and Dam	39.46
15	New York Laguardia Arpt	44.66	15	Indian Lake 2 SW	40.19
16	Westfield 2 SSE	***44.59***	16	Buffalo Greater Buffalo Int'l	40.49
17	Allegany State Park	44.47	17	Alcove Dam	40.56
18	Middletown 2 NW	43.36	18	Dannemora	40.93
19	Wales	***42.99***	19	Valatie 1 N	***40.99***
20	Utica Oneida County Arpt	***42.90***	20	Lowville	41.24
21	New York J F Kennedy Int'l Arpt	42.64	21	Whitehall	42.05
22	Wantagh Cedar Creek	42.40	22	Wantagh Cedar Creek	42.40
23	Whitehall	42.05	23	New York J F Kennedy Int'l Arpt	42.64
24	Lowville	41.24	24	Utica Oneida County Arpt	***42.90***
25	Valatie 1 N	***40.99***	25	Wales	***42.99***

Rankings include 25 highest/lowest stations. If state has less than 25 stations, all stations are included. The period of record is 1980–2009. See User Guide for detailed explanation of data.

Annual Extreme Maximum Daily Precipitation

Highest			Lowest		
Rank	Station Name	Inches	Rank	Station Name	Inches
1	Yorktown Heights 1 W	10.95	1	Troy Lock and Dam	3.00
2	Dobbs Ferry Ardsley	7.62	2	Aurora Research Farm	***3.03***
3	New York Central Park Observ	7.56	3	Alfred	3.33
4	Bridgehampton	7.04	3	Rochester Intl Arpt	3.33
5	Alcove Dam	6.89	5	Indian Lake 2 SW	3.43
6	Islip-Macarthur Arpt	***6.74***	6	Albion 2 NE	3.79
7	New York Laguardia Arpt	6.69	7	Allegany State Park	4.00
8	Riverhead Research Farm	6.34	8	Conklingville Dam	***4.01***
9	New York J F Kennedy Int'l Arpt	6.27	9	Binghamton Edwin A Link Field	4.05
10	Albany County Arpt	5.60	10	Canton 4 SE	4.10
11	New York Ave V Brooklyn	***5.46***	11	Morrisville 5 SW	***4.11***
12	Wantagh Cedar Creek	5.43	12	Utica Oneida County Arpt	***4.14***
13	Wales	***5.33***	13	Whitehall	4.25
14	Avon	5.20	14	Syracuse Hancock Int'l Arpt	4.29
15	Valatie 1 N	***5.10***	14	Westfield 2 SSE	***4.29***
16	Ithaca Cornell Univ	5.08	16	Mineola	4.30
17	Buffalo Greater Buffalo Int'l	5.01	17	Delhi 2 SE	4.49
18	Middletown 2 NW	5.00	18	Gouverneur 3 NW	4.51
19	Tully Heiberg Forest	***4.98***	19	Dannemora	4.55
20	Boonville 2 SSW	4.86	20	Bath	***4.67***
21	Peru 2 WSW	4.80	21	Grafton	***4.75***
22	Lowville	4.78	22	Lowville	4.78
23	Grafton	***4.75***	23	Peru 2 WSW	4.80
24	Bath	***4.67***	24	Boonville 2 SSW	4.86
25	Dannemora	4.55	25	Tully Heiberg Forest	***4.98***

Number of Days Annually With ≥ 0.1 Inches of Precipitation

Highest			Lowest		
Rank	Station Name	Days	Rank	Station Name	Days
1	Boonville 2 SSW	116	1	Chazy	***57***
2	Allegany State Park	103	2	Peru 2 WSW	66
2	Morrisville 5 SW	103	3	Bath	***71***
2	Tully Heiberg Forest	***103***	3	Wantagh Cedar Creek	71
2	Wales	***103***	5	New York J F Kennedy Int'l Arpt	72
6	Westfield 2 SSE	***98***	6	Mineola	74
7	Dannemora	97	7	Avon	75
7	Utica Oneida County Arpt	***97***	7	New York Laguardia Arpt	75
9	Grafton	***96***	9	Alcove Dam	76
10	Buffalo Greater Buffalo Int'l	95	10	Islip-Macarthur Arpt	***77***
11	Delhi 2 SE	94	10	Middletown 2 NW	77
11	Lowville	94	10	New York Ave V Brooklyn	***77***
13	Syracuse Hancock Int'l Arpt	90	13	Bridgehampton	78
14	Alfred	88	13	New York Central Park Observ	78
14	Indian Lake 2 SW	88	13	Riverhead Research Farm	78
16	Albion 2 NE	87	13	Troy Lock and Dam	78
17	Binghamton Edwin A Link Field	84	17	Whitehall	79
17	Gouverneur 3 NW	84	18	Rochester Intl Arpt	80
17	Ithaca Cornell Univ	84	18	Valatie 1 N	***80***
20	Canton 4 SE	83	20	Albany County Arpt	81
20	Conklingville Dam	83	20	Dobbs Ferry Ardsley	81
20	Yorktown Heights 1 W	83	22	Aurora Research Farm	82
23	Aurora Research Farm	82	23	Canton 4 SE	83
24	Albany County Arpt	81	23	Conklingville Dam	83
24	Dobbs Ferry Ardsley	81	23	Yorktown Heights 1 W	83

Rankings include 25 highest/lowest stations. If state has less than 25 stations, all stations are included. The period of record is 1980–2009. See User Guide for detailed explanation of data.

Number of Days Annually With ≥ 0.5 Inches of Precipitation

Highest			Lowest		
Rank	Station Name	Days	Rank	Station Name	Days
1	Boonville 2 SSW	37	1	Bath	***18***
2	Dobbs Ferry Ardsley	35	1	Chazy	***18***
2	New York Central Park Observ	35	3	Avon	19
2	Yorktown Heights 1 W	35	4	Rochester Intl Arpt	20
5	Riverhead Research Farm	34	5	Albion 2 NE	21
6	Grafton	***33***	5	Aurora Research Farm	21
6	Mineola	33	5	Canton 4 SE	21
8	Bridgehampton	32	5	Ithaca Cornell Univ	21
8	Islip-Macarthur Arpt	***32***	5	Peru 2 WSW	21
8	Middletown 2 NW	32	10	Gouverneur 3 NW	22
8	New York Laguardia Arpt	32	11	Alfred	23
8	New York Ave V Brooklyn	***32***	11	Syracuse Hancock Int'l Arpt	23
13	New York J F Kennedy Int'l Arpt	31	13	Binghamton Edwin A Link Field	24
14	Delhi 2 SE	30	13	Buffalo Greater Buffalo Int'l	24
15	Conklingville Dam	29	15	Indian Lake 2 SW	25
15	Valatie 1 N	***29***	15	Lowville	25
15	Wales	***29***	15	Utica Oneida County Arpt	***25***
15	Westfield 2 SSE	***29***	18	Albany County Arpt	26
19	Alcove Dam	28	18	Allegany State Park	26
19	Morrisville 5 SW	28	20	Dannemora	27
19	Wantagh Cedar Creek	28	20	Troy Lock and Dam	27
19	Whitehall	28	20	Tully Heiberg Forest	***27***
23	Dannemora	27	23	Alcove Dam	28
23	Troy Lock and Dam	27	23	Morrisville 5 SW	28
23	Tully Heiberg Forest	***27***	23	Wantagh Cedar Creek	28

Number of Days Annually With ≥ 1.0 Inches of Precipitation

Highest			Lowest		
Rank	Station Name	Days	Rank	Station Name	Days
1	Boonville 2 SSW	13	1	Bath	***3***
1	Dobbs Ferry Ardsley	13	2	Avon	4
1	New York Ave V Brooklyn	***13***	2	Canton 4 SE	4
1	Yorktown Heights 1 W	13	2	Rochester Intl Arpt	4
5	Bridgehampton	12	2	Syracuse Hancock Int'l Arpt	4
5	Conklingville Dam	12	6	Albion 2 NE	5
5	Islip-Macarthur Arpt	***12***	6	Allegany State Park	5
5	Mineola	12	6	Aurora Research Farm	5
5	New York Central Park Observ	12	6	Chazy	***5***
5	New York J F Kennedy Int'l Arpt	12	6	Ithaca Cornell Univ	5
5	New York Laguardia Arpt	12	6	Wales	***5***
5	Riverhead Research Farm	12	12	Alfred	6
13	Wantagh Cedar Creek	11	12	Dannemora	6
13	Whitehall	11	12	Gouverneur 3 NW	6
15	Alcove Dam	10	12	Peru 2 WSW	6
15	Grafton	***10***	16	Buffalo Greater Buffalo Int'l	7
15	Middletown 2 NW	10	16	Morrisville 5 SW	7
18	Indian Lake 2 SW	9	16	Westfield 2 SSE	***7***
18	Troy Lock and Dam	9	19	Albany County Arpt	8
18	Valatie 1 N	***9***	19	Binghamton Edwin A Link Field	8
21	Albany County Arpt	8	19	Delhi 2 SE	8
21	Binghamton Edwin A Link Field	8	19	Lowville	8
21	Delhi 2 SE	8	19	Tully Heiberg Forest	***8***
21	Lowville	8	19	Utica Oneida County Arpt	***8***
21	Tully Heiberg Forest	***8***	25	Indian Lake 2 SW	9

Rankings include 25 highest/lowest stations. If state has less than 25 stations, all stations are included. The period of record is 1980–2009. See User Guide for detailed explanation of data.

Annual Snowfall

Highest

Rank	Station Name	Inches
1	Boonville 2 SSW	197.5
2	Syracuse Hancock Int'l Arpt	124.5
3	Morrisville 5 SW	124.1
4	Lowville	121.4
5	Tully Heiberg Forest	***115.8***
6	Wales	***110.8***
7	Rochester Intl Arpt	99.4
8	Buffalo Greater Buffalo Int'l	94.0
9	Alfred	87.6
10	Gouverneur 3 NW	84.6
11	Westfield 2 SSE	***84.5***
12	Grafton	***83.2***
13	Binghamton Edwin A Link Field	82.8
14	Canton 4 SE	77.9
15	Conklingville Dam	70.4
16	Albion 2 NE	66.4
17	Delhi 2 SE	65.4
18	Ithaca Cornell Univ	63.9
19	Albany County Arpt	60.2
20	Whitehall	59.5
21	Aurora Research Farm	58.9
22	Chazy	***56.6***
23	Peru 2 WSW	52.0
24	Avon	51.9
25	Bath	***44.8***

Lowest

Rank	Station Name	Inches
1	Mineola	19.8
2	New York Ave V Brooklyn	***22.3***
3	New York J F Kennedy Int'l Arpt	22.7
4	New York Central Park Observ	23.6
5	New York Laguardia Arpt	25.9
6	Bridgehampton	26.5
7	Riverhead Research Farm	27.0
8	Dobbs Ferry Ardsley	30.6
9	Troy Lock and Dam	38.6
10	Yorktown Heights 1 W	40.0
11	Valatie 1 N	***41.4***
12	Bath	***44.8***
13	Avon	51.9
14	Peru 2 WSW	52.0
15	Chazy	***56.6***
16	Aurora Research Farm	58.9
17	Whitehall	59.5
18	Albany County Arpt	60.2
19	Ithaca Cornell Univ	63.9
20	Delhi 2 SE	65.4
21	Albion 2 NE	66.4
22	Conklingville Dam	70.4
23	Canton 4 SE	77.9
24	Binghamton Edwin A Link Field	82.8
25	Grafton	***83.2***

Annual Maximum Snow Depth

Highest

Rank	Station Name	Inches
1	Tully Heiberg Forest	***60***
2	Boonville 2 SSW	57
3	Morrisville 5 SW	51
4	Chazy	***50***
5	Conklingville Dam	45
6	Buffalo Greater Buffalo Int'l	44
7	Aurora Research Farm	43
8	Troy Lock and Dam	39
9	Canton 4 SE	38
10	Grafton	***37***
11	Bath	***36***
12	Binghamton Edwin A Link Field	35
12	Syracuse Hancock Int'l Arpt	35
14	Rochester Intl Arpt	34
14	Wales	***34***
16	Lowville	33
16	Valatie 1 N	***33***
18	Delhi 2 SE	31
19	Albion 2 NE	30
19	Gouverneur 3 NW	30
21	Yorktown Heights 1 W	29
22	Albany County Arpt	28
22	Ithaca Cornell Univ	28
22	New York J F Kennedy Int'l Arpt	28
25	Avon	27

Lowest

Rank	Station Name	Inches
1	Mineola	20
1	Riverhead Research Farm	20
3	New York Ave V Brooklyn	***23***
4	Allegany State Park	25
4	New York Laguardia Arpt	25
6	Dobbs Ferry Ardsley	26
7	Avon	27
7	Bridgehampton	27
9	Albany County Arpt	28
9	Ithaca Cornell Univ	28
9	New York J F Kennedy Int'l Arpt	28
12	Yorktown Heights 1 W	29
13	Albion 2 NE	30
13	Gouverneur 3 NW	30
15	Delhi 2 SE	31
16	Lowville	33
16	Valatie 1 N	***33***
18	Rochester Intl Arpt	34
18	Wales	***34***
20	Binghamton Edwin A Link Field	35
20	Syracuse Hancock Int'l Arpt	35
22	Bath	***36***
23	Grafton	***37***
24	Canton 4 SE	38
25	Troy Lock and Dam	39

 Rankings include 25 highest/lowest stations. If state has less than 25 stations, all stations are included. The period of record is 1980–2009. See User Guide for detailed explanation of data.

Number of Days Annually With ≥ 1.0 Inch Snow Depth

Highest			Lowest		
Rank	Station Name	Days	Rank	Station Name	Days
1	Boonville 2 SSW	134	1	Mineola	18
2	Tully Heiberg Forest	***124***	1	New York J F Kennedy Int'l Arpt	18
3	Morrisville 5 SW	115	1	New York Ave V Brooklyn	***18***
4	Lowville	107	4	New York Laguardia Arpt	19
5	Gouverneur 3 NW	97	5	Bridgehampton	20
6	Allegany State Park	95	6	Riverhead Research Farm	21
7	Conklingville Dam	94	7	Dobbs Ferry Ardsley	34
7	Grafton	***94***	8	Albion 2 NE	47
9	Wales	***93***	9	Valatie 1 N	***53***
10	Canton 4 SE	92	10	Yorktown Heights 1 W	54
11	Chazy	***81***	11	Troy Lock and Dam	55
12	Westfield 2 SSE	***80***	12	Albany County Arpt	59
13	Binghamton Edwin A Link Field	79	13	Bath	***67***
14	Delhi 2 SE	78	14	Avon	70
14	Syracuse Hancock Int'l Arpt	78	15	Aurora Research Farm	71
16	Ithaca Cornell Univ	74	15	Buffalo Greater Buffalo Int'l	71
17	Rochester Intl Arpt	73	17	Rochester Intl Arpt	73
18	Aurora Research Farm	71	18	Ithaca Cornell Univ	74
18	Buffalo Greater Buffalo Int'l	71	19	Delhi 2 SE	78
20	Avon	70	19	Syracuse Hancock Int'l Arpt	78
21	Bath	***67***	21	Binghamton Edwin A Link Field	79
22	Albany County Arpt	59	22	Westfield 2 SSE	***80***
23	Troy Lock and Dam	55	23	Chazy	***81***
24	Yorktown Heights 1 W	54	24	Canton 4 SE	92
25	Valatie 1 N	***53***	25	Wales	***93***

Rankings include 25 highest/lowest stations. If state has less than 25 stations, all stations are included. The period of record is 1980–2009. See User Guide for detailed explanation of data.

Significant Storm Events in New York: 2000 – 2009

Location or County	Date	Type	Mag.	Deaths	Injuries	Property Damage ($mil.)	Crop Damage ($mil.)
Buffalo Metro Area, Western Southern Tier	11/20/00	Heavy Snow	na	0	0	46.5	0.0
New York City Metro Area	02/17/03	Heavy Snow	na	0	0	20.0	0.0
Northwest New York	04/04/03	Ice Storm	na	1	0	28.5	8.5
Northwestern Central New York	04/04/03	Ice Storm	na	0	0	28.5	0.0
Broome	06/13/03	Flash Flood	na	5	0	0.1	0.0
Sullivan	08/30/04	Flash Flood	na	0	0	20.0	0.0
Delaware	06/27/06	Flash Flood	na	2	0	250.0	0.0
Broome	06/27/06	Flash Flood	na	0	0	200.0	0.0
Tioga	06/27/06	Flash Flood	na	0	0	100.0	0.0
Sullivan	06/27/06	Flash Flood	na	1	0	100.0	0.0
Oneida	06/27/06	Flash Flood	na	0	0	50.0	0.0
Chenango	06/27/06	Flood	na	0	0	50.0	0.0
Otsego	06/27/06	Flash Flood	na	0	0	50.0	0.0
Broome	06/27/06	Flood	na	0	0	50.0	0.0
Chenango	06/27/06	Flash Flood	na	1	0	50.0	0.0
Madison	06/27/06	Flash Flood	na	0	0	25.0	0.0
Southeast New York	08/01/06	Excessive Heat	na	42	0	0.0	0.0
Southwest Suffolk County	04/16/07	Coastal Flood	na	0	0	26.0	0.0
Delaware	06/19/07	Flash Flood	na	4	0	30.0	0.0
Cattaraugus	08/09/09	Flash Flood	na	1	1	45.0	0.0
Chautauqua	08/09/09	Flash Flood	na	0	0	30.0	0.0
Jefferson and Lewis Counties	12/09/09	High Wind	58 mph	0	0	100.0	0.0

Note: Deaths, injuries, and damages are date and location specific.

NORTH CAROLINA

PHYSICAL FEATURES. North Carolina lies between 33.5° and 37° N. latitude and between 75° and 84.5° W. longitude. The span of longitude is greater than that of any other state east of the Mississippi River. The greatest length from east to west is 503 miles. The greatest breadth from north to south is 187 miles. The total area is 52,712 square miles: 49,142 square miles of land and 3,570 square miles of water.

The range of altitude is also the greatest of any eastern state. North Carolina rises from sea level along the Atlantic coast to 6,684 feet at the summit of Mount Mitchell, the highest peak in the eastern United States. Mount Mitchell is in the heart of the Blue Ridge Range. This Range, along with the Great Smokies, lies partly in North Carolina and partly in Tennessee and forms the highest part of the Appalachian Mountains.

The three principal physiographic divisions of the eastern United States are particularly well developed in North Carolina. Beginning in the east, they are: the Coastal Plain, the Piedmont, and the Mountains. The land and water areas of the Coastal Plain Division comprise nearly half the area of the State. The tidewater portion is generally flat and swampy, while the interior is gently sloping and, for the most part, naturally well drained. The Piedmont Division rises gently from about 200 feet at the fall line to near 1,500 feet at the base of the mountains; its area is about one-third of the State. The land is mostly gently rolling. There are several ranges of steeper hills. The Mountain Division is the smallest of the three, little more than one-fifth of the State's area. In elevation it ranges downward from Mount Mitchell's peak to about 1,000 feet above mean sea level in the lowest valleys. There are more than 40 peaks higher than 6,000 feet and about 80 others over 5,000 feet high.

North Carolina rivers fall into two groups: those that flow into the Atlantic Ocean and those that drain westward into the Mississippi River system. The two are separated by a ridge averaging 2,200 feet above mean sea level. A second chain of mountains ranging up to 6,000 feet marks the western boundary of the State. Most of the State, including the Coastal Plain, the Piedmont, and the eastern and southern slopes, drains into the Atlantic Ocean. The principal rivers involved are the Roanoke, Tar, Neuse, Cape Fear, Yadkin, and Catawba. The main stream draining the extreme western part of North Carolina is the French Broad River. The northern mountains are drained by streams flowing into the Ohio River system. All eventually reach the Mississippi.

GENERAL CLIMATE. North Carolina has the most varied climate of any eastern state. This is due mainly to its wide range in elevation and distance from the ocean. In all seasons of the year the average temperature varies more than 20 from the lower coast to the highest mountain elevations. Altitude also has an important effect on rainfall. The rainiest part of the eastern United States, with an annual average of more than 80 inches, is in southwestern North Carolina where moist southerly winds are forced upward in passing over the mountain barrier.

In winter the greater part of North Carolina is partially protected by the mountain ranges from the frequent outbreaks of cold which move southeastward across the Central States. Such outbreaks often spread southward all the way to the Gulf of Mexico without attaining strength and depth to cross the Appalachian Range. When cold waves do break across they are usually modified by the crossing and the descent on the eastern slopes. The temperature drops to around 10 over central North Carolina once or twice during an average winter. Near the coast a comparable figure is some 10 degrees higher, and in the upper mountains 10 degrees lower. Temperatures as low as 0 are rare outside the mountains, but have occurred at one time or another throughout the western part of the State.

Winter temperatures in the eastern Coastal Plain are modified by the proximity of the Atlantic Ocean. This effect raises the average winter temperature and reduces the average day-to-night range. The Gulf Stream, contrary to popular opinion, has little direct effect on North Carolina temperatures, even on the immediate coast. The Stream lies some 50 miles offshore at its nearest point. The southern reaches of the cold Labrador Current pass between the Gulf Stream and the North Carolina coast. This offsets any warming effect the Stream might otherwise have on coastal temperatures. The meeting of the two opposing currents does provide a breeding ground for rough weather. Not infrequently low pressure storms having their origin there develop major proportions, causing rain on the North Carolina coast and over states to the north.

In spring the storm systems that bring cold weather southward reach North Carolina less forcefully than in winter, and temperatures begin to modify. Day-to-day variations in temperature are less pronounced, and warm weather is more likely to occur in conjunction with fair weather. During the summer, when the drying of the air is sufficient to keep cloudiness at a minimum for several days, temperatures may occasionally reach 100°F. or a little higher in interior sections at elevations below 1,500 feet. Ordinarily, however, summer cloudiness develops to limit the sun's heating while temperatures are still in the 90°F. range. Autumn is the season of most rapidly changing temperature, the daily downward trend being greater than the corresponding rise in spring. The dropoff is most rapid in October and continues almost as fast in November.

PRECIPITATION. There are no distinct wet and dry seasons in North Carolina. There is some seasonal variation in average precipitation. Summer rainfall is normally the greatest, and July the wettest month. Since the rain at this time of year comes mostly with thunderstorms and convective showers, it is also more variable than at other seasons. Daily showers are not uncommon, nor are periods of one or two weeks without rain. Autumn is the driest season, and October the driest month. Precipitation in winter and spring occurs mostly with migratory low pressure storms. It appears with greater regularity and more even distribution than summer showers.

Winter precipitation usually occurs with southerly through easterly winds, and is seldom associated with very cold weather. Snow and sleet occur on an average of once or twice a year near the coast, and not much more often over the southeastern half of the State. Over the Mountains and western Piedmont frozen precipitation sometimes occurs with interior low pressure storms. In the extreme west it can happen with a cold front passage from northwest. Average winter snowfall ranges from about one inch per year on the Outer Banks and the lower coast, to about nine inches in the northern Piedmont and southern Mountains. Some of the higher mountain peaks and upper slopes receive an average of nearly 50 inches a year.

OTHER CLIMATIC ELEMENTS. Relative humidity may vary greatly from day to day and even from hour to hour, especially in winter. The average relative humidity, however, does not vary greatly from season to season, there being a slight tendency for highest averages in winter and lowest in spring. The lowest relative humidities are found over the southern Piedmont; the highest are along the immediate coast.

Sunshine is abundant, the average annual percentage of possible ranging from 60 to 65 percent at most recording points. Measurable rain falls on about 120 days. Prevailing winds blow from southwest 10 months of the year, and from northeast during September and October. The average wind speed for interior locations is about eight m.p.h., for coastal points about 12 m.p.h.

STORMS AND FLOODS. Intense rainstorms occur in the precipitous mountain terrain, especially in the southern portion. Streams here rise quickly to flood, and almost as quickly subside when rain ends. Floods occur frequently, affecting some part of North Carolina each year. Floods may occur at any season, but are most frequent in early spring, summer, and early fall. Rains associated with West Indian hurricanes are the main cause of summer and fall floods. The greatest economic loss entailed in North Carolina because of stormy weather is that due to summer thunderstorms. These usually affect only limited areas. In any given locality, 40 to 50 days with thunderstorms may be expected in a year.

North Carolina is outside the principal tornado area of the United States, experiencing an average of less than 4 per year. Tropical hurricanes come close enough to influence North Carolina weather about twice in an average year. Only about once in 10 years, on the average, does this type storm strike the State with sufficient force to do much damage.

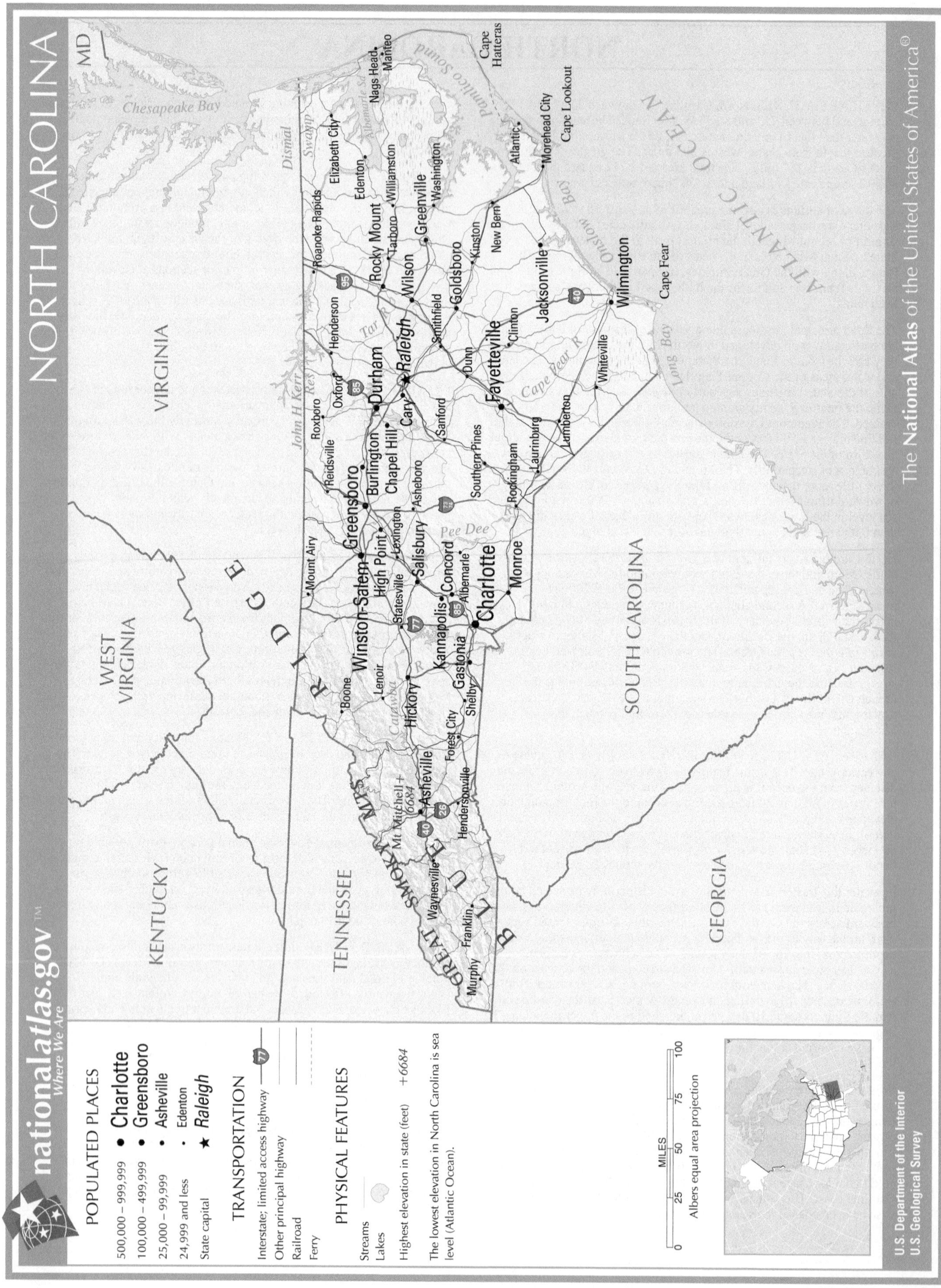
NORTH CAROLINA
nationalatlas.gov™
Where We Are
POPULATED PLACES
500,000 – 999,999 Charlotte
100,000 – 499,999 Greensboro
25,000 – 99,999 Asheville
24,999 and less Edenton
State capital Raleigh
TRANSPORTATION
Interstate; limited access highway 77
Other principal highway
Railroad
Ferry
PHYSICAL FEATURES
Streams
Lakes
Highest elevation in state (feet) +6684
The lowest elevation in North Carolina is sea level (Atlantic Ocean).
MILES
0 25 50 75 100
Albers equal area projection
U.S. Department of the Interior
U.S. Geological Survey
The National Atlas of the United States of America®
VIRGINIA
WEST VIRGINIA
KENTUCKY
TENNESSEE
SOUTH CAROLINA
GEORGIA
MD
Chesapeake Bay
ATLANTIC OCEAN
BLUE RIDGE
GREAT SMOKY MTS
Dismal Swamp
Albemarle Sd
Pamlico Sound
Onslow Bay
Long Bay
Cape Hatteras
Cape Lookout
Cape Fear
John H Kerr Res
Tar R
Cape Fear R
Pee Dee
Catawba R
Mt Mitchell +6684
Charlotte
Raleigh
Greensboro
Winston-Salem
Durham
Fayetteville
Cary
High Point
Wilmington
Asheville
Concord
Gastonia
Jacksonville
Rocky Mount
Chapel Hill
Burlington
Wilson
Greenville
Goldsboro
Hickory
Kannapolis
Salisbury
Monroe
Statesville
Lexington
Asheboro
Sanford
Henderson
Oxford
Roxboro
Reidsville
Mount Airy
Boone
Lenoir
Shelby
Forest City
Hendersonville
Waynesville
Franklin
Murphy
Albemarle
Southern Pines
Rockingham
Laurinburg
Lumberton
Whiteville
Clinton
Dunn
Smithfield
Kinston
New Bern
Washington
Tarboro
Williamston
Edenton
Elizabeth City
Roanoke Rapids
Nags Head
Manteo
Atlantic
Morehead City
95
85
77
40
26

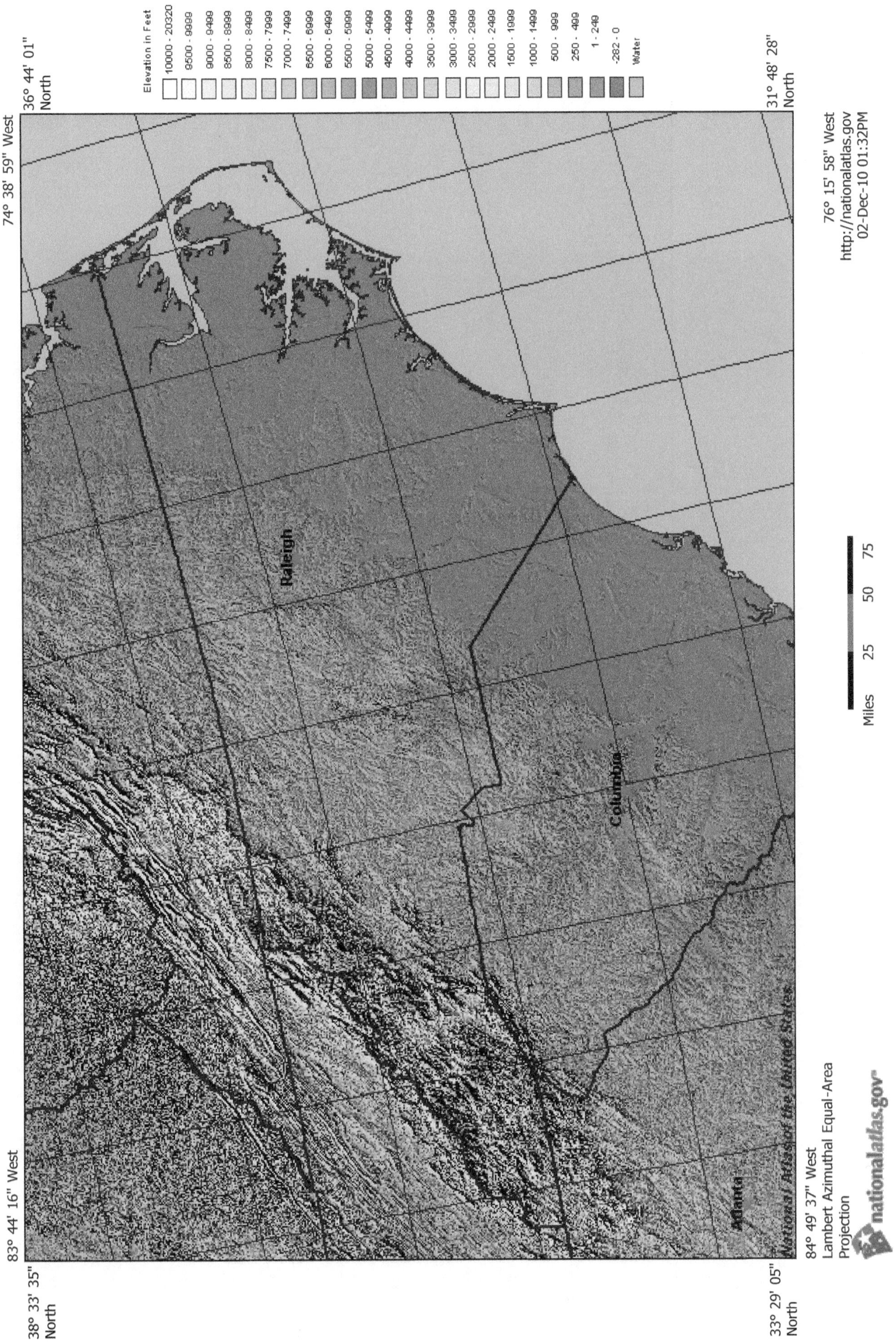
36° 44' 01" North
74° 38' 59" West
Elevation in Feet
10000 - 20320
9500 - 9999
9000 - 9499
8500 - 8999
8000 - 8499
7500 - 7999
7000 - 7499
6500 - 6999
6000 - 6499
5500 - 5999
5000 - 5499
4500 - 4999
4000 - 4499
3500 - 3999
3000 - 3499
2500 - 2999
2000 - 2499
1500 - 1999
1000 - 1499
500 - 999
250 - 499
1 - 249
-282 - 0
Water
31° 48' 28" North
76° 15' 58" West
http://nationalatlas.gov
02-Dec-10 01:32PM
Raleigh
Columbia
Atlanta
Miles
25
50
75
National Atlas of the United States
83° 44' 16" West
38° 33' 35" North
33° 29' 05" North
84° 49' 37" West
Lambert Azimuthal Equal-Area Projection
nationalatlas.gov

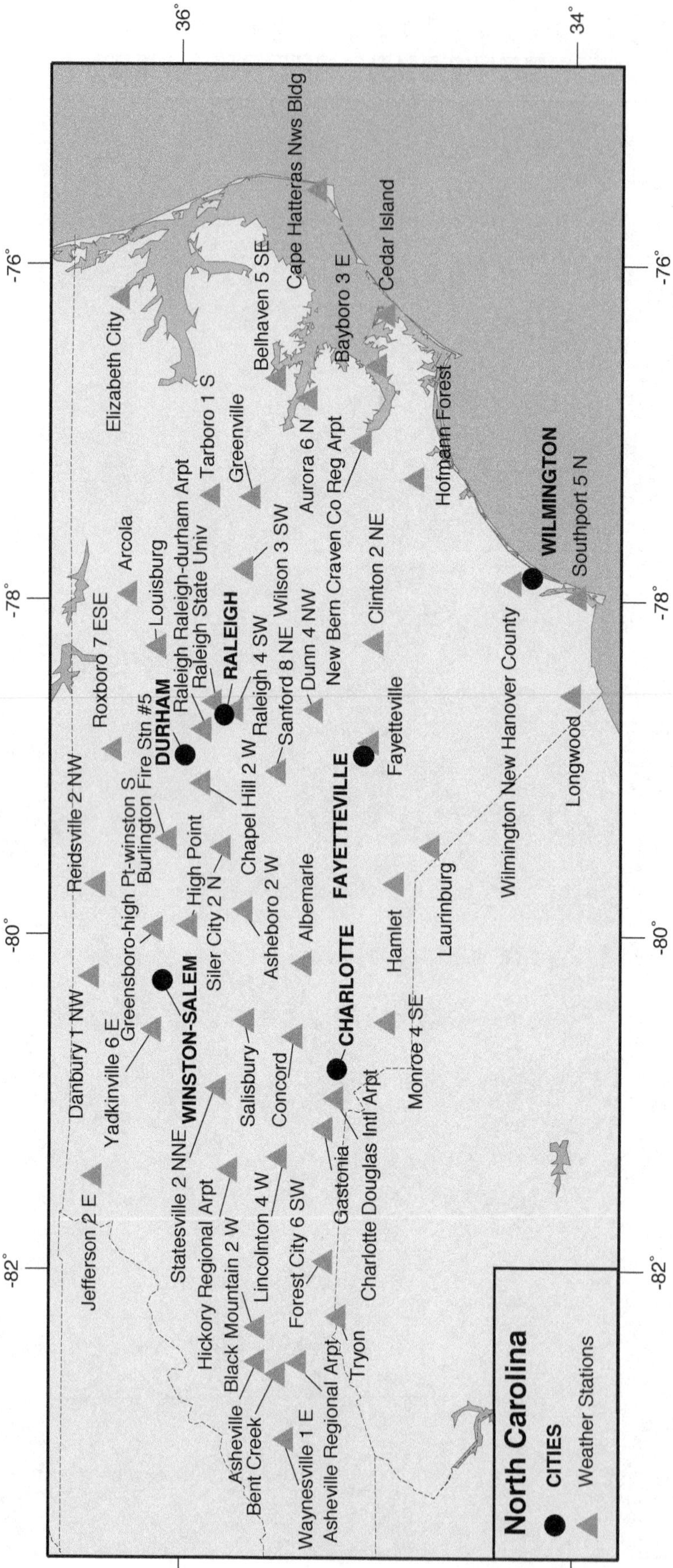
North Carolina
CITIES
Weather Stations
36°
34°
-76°
-78°
-80°
-82°
WINSTON-SALEM
DURHAM
RALEIGH
CHARLOTTE
FAYETTEVILLE
WILMINGTON
Elizabeth City
Cape Hatteras Nws Bldg
Belhaven 5 SE
Bayboro 3 E
Cedar Island
Tarboro 1 S
Greenville
Aurora 6 N
New Bern Craven Co Reg Arpt
Hofmann Forest
Southport 5 N
Arcola
Louisburg
Raleigh Raleigh-durham Arpt
Raleigh State Univ
Wilson 3 SW
Raleigh 4 SW
Sanford 8 NE
Dunn 4 NW
Clinton 2 NE
Roxboro 7 ESE
Fire Stn #5
Chapel Hill 2 W
Fayetteville
Wilmington New Hanover County
Longwood
Reidsville 2 NW
Greensboro-high Pt-winston S
Burlington
High Point
Siler City 2 N
Asheboro 2 W
Albemarle
Hamlet
Laurinburg
Danbury 1 NW
Yadkinville 6 E
Salisbury
Concord
Charlotte Douglas Intl Arpt
Monroe 4 SE
Jefferson 2 E
Statesville 2 NNE
Hickory Regional Arpt
Lincolnton 4 W
Gastonia
Forest City 6 SW
Black Mountain 2 W
Asheville
Bent Creek
Waynesville 1 E
Asheville Regional Arpt
Tryon

North Carolina Weather Stations by County

County	Station Name
Alamance	Burlington Fire Stn #5
Ashe	Jefferson 2 E
Beaufort	Aurora 6 N Belhaven 5 SE
Brunswick	Longwood Southport 5 N
Buncombe	Asheville Asheville Regional Arpt Bent Creek Black Mountain 2 W
Burke	Hickory Regional Arpt
Cabarrus	Concord
Carteret	Cedar Island
Chatham	Siler City 2 N
Craven	New Bern Craven Co Reg Arpt
Cumberland	Fayetteville
Dare	Cape Hatteras NWS Bldg
Edgecombe	Tarboro 1 S
Franklin	Louisburg
Gaston	Gastonia
Guilford	Greensboro-High Pt-Winston Salem High Point
Harnett	Dunn 4 NW
Haywood	Waynesville 1 E
Iredell	Statesville 2 NNE
Lee	Sanford 8 NE
Lincoln	Lincolnton 4 W
Mecklenburg	Charlotte Douglas Intl Arpt
New Hanover	Wilmington New Hanover County
Onslow	Hofmann Forest
Orange	Chapel Hill 2 W
Pamlico	Bayboro 3 E
Pasquotank	Elizabeth City
Person	Roxboro 7 ESE
Pitt	Greenville

County	Station Name
Polk	Tryon
Randolph	Asheboro 2 W
Richmond	Hamlet
Rockingham	Reidsville 2 NW
Rowan	Salisbury
Rutherford	Forest City 6 SW
Sampson	Clinton 2 NE
Scotland	Laurinburg
Stanly	Albemarle
Stokes	Danbury 1 NW
Union	Monroe 4 SE
Wake	Raleigh 4 SW Raleigh State Univ Raleigh-Durham Intl Arpt
Warren	Arcola
Wilson	Wilson 3 SW
Yadkin	Yadkinville 6 E

See User Guide for station inclusion criteria.

North Carolina Weather Stations by City

City	Station Name	Miles
Apex	Chapel Hill 2 W	17.8
	Raleigh-Durham Intl Arpt	9.9
	Raleigh 4 SW	9.8
	Raleigh State Univ	9.9
	Sanford 8 NE	17.7
Asheville	Asheville Regional Arpt	10.3
	Asheville	1.7
	Bent Creek	6.2
	Black Mountain 2 W	11.7
	Waynesville 1 E	24.2
Burlington	Burlington Fire Stn #5	1.6
	Chapel Hill 2 W	23.4
	Reidsville 2 NW	24.8
	Siler City 2 N	22.4
Cary	Chapel Hill 2 W	18.7
	Raleigh-Durham Intl Arpt	6.5
	Raleigh 4 SW	7.2
	Raleigh State Univ	5.9
	Sanford 8 NE	21.7
Chapel Hill	Burlington Fire Stn #5	24.8
	Chapel Hill 2 W	2.4
	Raleigh-Durham Intl Arpt	15.0
	Raleigh 4 SW	24.1
	Raleigh State Univ	21.0
Charlotte	Charlotte Douglas Intl Arpt	7.8
	Concord	19.3
	Gastonia	18.6
	Monroe 4 SE	23.9
	Winthrop University, SC	22.1
Concord	Albemarle	24.3
	Charlotte Douglas Intl Arpt	22.9
	Concord	1.3
	Salisbury	20.8
Durham	Chapel Hill 2 W	10.6
	Raleigh-Durham Intl Arpt	11.0
	Raleigh 4 SW	21.7
	Raleigh State Univ	17.5
	Roxboro 7 ESE	22.9
Fayetteville	Dunn 4 NW	21.9
	Fayetteville	3.8
Fort Bragg	Dunn 4 NW	21.8
	Fayetteville	9.1
Gastonia	Charlotte Douglas Intl Arpt	12.9
	Gastonia	2.6
	Lincolnton 4 W	17.4
	Winthrop University, SC	23.3
Goldsboro	Wilson 3 SW	22.2
Greensboro	Burlington Fire Stn #5	20.9
	Greensboro-High Pt-Winston Salem	7.2
	High Point	11.2
	Reidsville 2 NW	22.1

City	Station Name	Miles
Greenville	Greenville	3.2
	Tarboro 1 S	22.0
Hickory	Hickory Regional Arpt	3.4
	Lincolnton 4 W	19.5
High Point	Asheboro 2 W	21.4
	Greensboro-High Pt-Winston Salem	8.6
	High Point	1.9
Huntersville	Charlotte Douglas Intl Arpt	14.6
	Concord	15.0
	Gastonia	18.3
Jacksonville	Hofmann Forest	8.6
Kannapolis	Concord	5.0
	Salisbury	15.6
Matthews	Charlotte Douglas Intl Arpt	14.9
	Concord	21.7
	Monroe 4 SE	16.0
	Winthrop University, SC	22.0
Monroe	Monroe 4 SE	3.5
	Pageland, SC	17.9
New Bern	Aurora 6 N	25.0
	Bayboro 3 E	20.5
	Hofmann Forest	23.1
	New Bern Craven Co Reg Arpt	3.5
Raleigh	Raleigh-Durham Intl Arpt	8.4
	Raleigh 4 SW	6.6
	Raleigh State Univ	3.6
Rocky Mount	Arcola	24.7
	Tarboro 1 S	16.2
	Wilson 3 SW	19.3
Salisbury	Concord	18.8
	Salisbury	1.0
	Statesville 2 NNE	24.9
Sanford	Sanford 8 NE	8.2
Statesville	Salisbury	23.3
	Statesville 2 NNE	2.0
Wake Forest	Louisburg	14.9
	Raleigh-Durham Intl Arpt	16.7
	Raleigh 4 SW	19.1
	Raleigh State Univ	15.8
Wilmington	Southport 5 N	16.5
	Wilmington New Hanover County	3.3
Wilson	Tarboro 1 S	24.2
	Wilson 3 SW	2.7
Winston-Salem	Danbury 1 NW	21.8
	Greensboro-High Pt-Winston Salem	17.7
	High Point	19.3
	Yadkinville 6 E	15.9

Note: Miles is the distance between the geographic center of the city and the weather station.

See User Guide for station inclusion criteria.

North Carolina Weather Stations by Elevation

Feet	Station Name
2,770	Jefferson 2 E
2,658	Waynesville 1 E
2,290	Black Mountain 2 W
2,240	Asheville
2,140	Asheville Regional Arpt
2,109	Bent Creek
1,143	Hickory Regional Arpt
1,080	Tryon
990	Forest City 6 SW
950	Statesville 2 NNE
899	High Point
899	Lincolnton 4 W
896	Greensboro-High Pt-Winston Salem
890	Reidsville 2 NW
875	Yadkinville 6 E
870	Asheboro 2 W
839	Danbury 1 NW
728	Charlotte Douglas Intl Arpt
709	Roxboro 7 ESE
700	Gastonia
700	Salisbury
689	Concord
660	Burlington Fire Stn #5
609	Albemarle
609	Siler City 2 N
580	Monroe 4 SE
500	Chapel Hill 2 W
419	Raleigh 4 SW
416	Raleigh-Durham Intl Arpt
399	Raleigh State Univ
350	Hamlet
330	Arcola
262	Sanford 8 NE
259	Louisburg
209	Laurinburg
200	Dunn 4 NW
158	Clinton 2 NE
109	Wilson 3 SW
96	Fayetteville
43	Hofmann Forest
40	Longwood
35	Tarboro 1 S
32	Greenville
29	Wilmington New Hanover County
20	Aurora 6 N
20	Southport 5 N
16	New Bern Craven Co Reg Arpt
9	Bayboro 3 E
9	Cape Hatteras NWS Bldg
7	Belhaven 5 SE
7	Cedar Island
7	Elizabeth City

See User Guide for station inclusion criteria.

Asheville Regional Airport

The city of Asheville is located on both banks of the French Broad River, near the center of the French Broad Basin. Upstream from Asheville, the valley runs south for 18 miles and then curves toward the south-southwest. Downstream from the city, the valley is oriented toward the north-northwest. Two miles upstream from the principal section of Asheville, the Swannanoa River joins the French Broad from the east. The entire valley is known as the Asheville Plateau, having an average elevation near 2,200 feet above sea level, and is flanked by mountain ridges to the east and west, whose peaks range from 2,000 to 4,400 feet above the valley floor. At the Carolina-Tennessee border, about 25 miles north-northwest of Asheville, a relatively high ridge of mountains blocks the northern end of the valley. Thirty miles south, the Blue Ridge Mountains form a steep slope, having a general elevation of about 2,700 feet above sea level.

Asheville has a temperate, but invigorating, climate. Considerable variation in temperature often occurs from day to day in summer, as well as during the other seasons.

The growing season in this area is of sufficient length for commercial crops, the average length of freeze-free period being about 195 days. The average last occurrence in spring of a temperature 32 degrees or lower is mid-April and the average first occurrence in fall of 32 degrees is late October.

The orientation of the French Broad Valley appears to have a pronounced influence on the wind direction. Prevailing winds are from the northwest during all months of the year. Also, the shielding effect of the nearby mountain barriers apparently has a direct bearing on the annual amount of precipitation received in this vicinity. In an area northwest of Asheville, the average annual precipitation is the lowest in North Carolina. Precipitation increases sharply in all other directions, especially to the south and southwest.

Destructive events caused directly by meteorological conditions are infrequent. The most frequent, occurring at approximately 12-year intervals, are floods on the French Broad River. These floods are usually associated with heavy rains caused by storms moving out of the Gulf of Mexico. Snowstorms which have seriously disrupted normal life in this community are infrequent. Hailstorms that cause property damage are extremely rare.

Asheville Regional Airport *Buncombe County* Elevation: 2,140 ft. Latitude: 35° 26' N Longitude: 82° 32' W

	JAN	FEB	MAR	APR	MAY	JUN	JUL	AUG	SEP	OCT	NOV	DEC	YEAR
Mean Maximum Temp. (°F)	47.8	51.4	58.8	67.6	74.9	81.3	84.2	83.1	77.0	68.1	58.9	50.1	66.9
Mean Temp. (°F)	37.4	40.5	47.2	55.3	63.1	70.4	73.9	73.0	66.4	56.3	47.4	39.7	55.9
Mean Minimum Temp. (°F)	27.0	29.5	35.5	42.9	51.2	59.5	63.6	62.8	55.8	44.5	35.8	29.3	44.8
Extreme Maximum Temp. (°F)	80	78	83	88	93	95	96	100	92	86	81	75	100
Extreme Minimum Temp. (°F)	-16	-1	2	20	28	37	44	42	35	24	15	-7	-16
Days Maximum Temp. ≥ 90°F	0	0	0	0	0	2	4	3	0	0	0	0	9
Days Maximum Temp. ≤ 32°F	2	1	0	0	0	0	0	0	0	0	0	1	4
Days Minimum Temp. ≤ 32°F	22	18	12	4	0	0	0	0	0	3	13	21	93
Days Minimum Temp. ≤ 0°F	0	0	0	0	0	0	0	0	0	0	0	0	0
Heating Degree Days (base 65°F)	848	687	545	293	105	11	1	2	52	271	523	777	4,115
Cooling Degree Days (base 65°F)	0	0	0	8	52	180	283	256	101	11	1	0	892
Mean Precipitation (in.)	3.55	3.70	3.96	3.42	3.65	4.77	4.31	4.37	3.85	2.89	3.57	3.58	45.62
Maximum Precipitation (in.)*	7.5	7.0	9.9	7.3	8.8	10.7	10.4	11.3	9.1	9.1	9.9	8.5	64.9
Minimum Precipitation (in.)*	0.4	0.2	0.8	0.3	0.5	0.9	0.5	0.5	0.2	0.2	0.8	0.2	26.6
Extreme Maximum Daily Precip. (in.)	4.42	3.36	3.79	2.03	2.93	3.97	2.95	4.32	3.78	3.32	2.41	2.46	4.42
Days With ≥ 0.1" Precipitation	6	6	7	6	7	8	8	7	6	5	6	6	78
Days With ≥ 0.5" Precipitation	2	2	3	3	2	3	3	2	3	2	3	2	30
Days With ≥ 1.0" Precipitation	1	1	1	1	1	1	1	1	1	1	1	1	12
Mean Snowfall (in.)	4.1	2.5	2.1	0.8	trace	trace	trace	trace	0.0	trace	0.1	1.6	11.2
Maximum Snowfall (in.)*	18	26	18	12	trace	0	0	0	0	trace	10	16	50
Maximum 24-hr. Snowfall (in.)*	14	9	14	12	trace	0	0	0	0	trace	5	16	16
Maximum Snow Depth (in.)	14	7	18	12	trace	trace	trace	trace	0	trace	1	10	18
Days With ≥ 1.0" Snow Depth	3	1	1	0	0	0	0	0	0	0	0	1	6
Thunderstorm Days*	< 1	1	2	3	7	9	10	9	3	1	1	< 1	46
Foggy Days*	14	11	12	10	19	23	26	29	26	20	14	14	218
Predominant Sky Cover*	OVR	OVR	OVR	OVR	OVR	OVR	BRK	OVR	OVR	CLR	OVR	OVR	OVR
Mean Relative Humidity 7am (%)*	84	83	83	84	90	92	94	96	96	93	87	85	89
Mean Relative Humidity 4pm (%)*	57	53	50	47	56	60	63	64	62	54	54	56	56
Mean Dewpoint (°F)*	27	28	34	42	53	61	65	64	58	46	36	29	45
Prevailing Wind Direction*	NNW	NNW	NNW	NNW	NNW	NNW	NNW	NNW	NNW	NNW	NNW	NNW	NNW
Prevailing Wind Speed (mph)*	14	14	14	13	10	9	8	8	9	10	13	13	12
Maximum Wind Gust (mph)*	58	54	64	58	49	52	61	43	51	58	55	53	64

Note: (*) Period of record is 1948-1995

Cape Hatteras NWS Bldg

Hatteras Island is the largest and easternmost island in North Carolina. The average elevation of the island is less than 10 feet above mean sea level. It is separated from the mainland by the Pamlico Sound and is part of a chain of islands known as the Outer Banks. The Island is narrow, ranging from a few hundred yards wide to a few miles wide and is about 54 miles long. Much of the island is a National Park and waterfowl reserve.

The Weather Office is located in the village of Buxton about one mile west-northwest of the famous Cape Hatteras Lighthouse. Weather observations have been taken continuously since 1874 from locations all within 10 miles of the present stations location.

With its maritime climate, Cape Hatteras is very humid, with cooler summers and warmer winters than mainland North Carolina. Ninety degree temperatures are rare in summer, as are the teens in winter. The average first occurrence of freezing temperatures is early December, and the average last occurrence is late February.

Average rainfall is greater than any other coastal station in the state. Rainfall is rather evenly distributed throughout the year, with the maximum during July, August, and September. Snowfall is rare and generally light, usually melting as it falls.

Winter storms frequently breed offshore where the warm waters of the Gulf Stream and the southermost penetration of the Labrador Current meet some 20 to 50 miles off the coast. Late summer and fall tracks of tropical cyclones occasionally threaten the island. These storms produce strong winds, heavy rains and tidal flooding from both the ocean and Pamlico Sound. Many ships have been lost near, or wrecked on, the beaches of the island.

More than a million tourists visit the island each year. The proximity of the gulfstream, natural beaches, excellent surf, and offshore fishing make Cape Hatteras a preferred place for vacationers, sportsmen, and campers. The surfing conditions are said to be the best on the east coast.

Cape Hatteras NWS Bldg *Dare County* Elevation: 9 ft. Latitude: 35° 16' N Longitude: 75° 33' W

	JAN	FEB	MAR	APR	MAY	JUN	JUL	AUG	SEP	OCT	NOV	DEC	YEAR
Mean Maximum Temp. (°F)	53.4	54.5	59.6	67.4	74.8	81.9	85.5	85.0	80.8	72.8	64.8	57.1	69.8
Mean Temp. (°F)	46.2	47.2	52.1	60.1	67.7	75.5	79.6	79.0	74.9	66.2	58.0	50.1	63.0
Mean Minimum Temp. (°F)	39.0	39.8	44.5	52.7	60.6	69.0	73.5	72.9	68.9	59.6	51.1	43.0	56.2
Extreme Maximum Temp. (°F)	75	75	81	89	91	92	96	93	91	89	81	78	96
Extreme Minimum Temp. (°F)	6	15	22	32	40	47	55	59	46	36	27	12	6
Days Maximum Temp. ≥ 90°F	0	0	0	0	0	1	3	2	0	0	0	0	6
Days Maximum Temp. ≤ 32°F	1	0	0	0	0	0	0	0	0	0	0	0	1
Days Minimum Temp. ≤ 32°F	8	6	2	0	0	0	0	0	0	0	1	4	21
Days Minimum Temp. ≤ 0°F	0	0	0	0	0	0	0	0	0	0	0	0	0
Heating Degree Days (base 65°F)	577	499	398	172	40	2	0	0	2	65	228	459	2,442
Cooling Degree Days (base 65°F)	1	1	5	31	130	324	459	441	306	110	24	4	1,836
Mean Precipitation (in.)	5.28	3.94	4.83	3.72	3.49	4.13	4.90	6.65	6.02	5.41	5.08	4.28	57.73
Maximum Precipitation (in.)*	12.4	8.4	11.2	9.6	11.4	10.8	10.0	16.1	20.0	15.0	16.2	9.6	90.8
Minimum Precipitation (in.)*	1.8	1.1	1.0	0.4	0.3	0.4	0.4	1.0	0.1	0.5	1.1	0.6	41.5
Extreme Maximum Daily Precip. (in.)	5.95	3.03	4.57	2.73	4.98	4.00	3.75	8.69	5.50	8.30	7.69	2.96	8.69
Days With ≥ 0.1" Precipitation	8	6	7	6	5	7	8	8	7	6	7	6	81
Days With ≥ 0.5" Precipitation	3	3	3	3	2	3	3	4	3	3	3	3	36
Days With ≥ 1.0" Precipitation	2	1	1	1	1	1	1	2	2	2	1	1	16
Mean Snowfall (in.)	na	na	na	na	na	na	na	na	na	na	na	na	na
Maximum Snowfall (in.)*	4	4	9	trace	0	0	0	0	0	0	trace	14	14
Maximum 24-hr. Snowfall (in.)*	4	4	7	trace	0	0	0	0	0	0	trace	8	8
Maximum Snow Depth (in.)	na	na	na	na	na	na	na	na	na	na	na	na	na
Days With ≥ 1.0" Snow Depth	na	na	na	na	na	na	na	na	na	na	na	na	na
Thunderstorm Days*	1	2	2	3	5	5	8	8	3	2	1	1	41
Foggy Days*	13	11	12	8	10	9	8	9	7	10	10	11	118
Predominant Sky Cover*	OVR	OVR	OVR	OVR	OVR	OVR	OVR	OVR	OVR	OVR	OVR	OVR	OVR
Mean Relative Humidity 7am (%)*	80	80	80	78	81	82	85	86	83	82	81	80	82
Mean Relative Humidity 4pm (%)*	69	66	65	62	67	70	72	72	69	68	69	69	68
Mean Dewpoint (°F)*	37	37	43	50	59	67	72	72	67	57	49	41	54
Prevailing Wind Direction*	N	NNE	NNE	SW	SW	SW	SW	SW	NE	NNE	NNE	N	NNE
Prevailing Wind Speed (mph)*	13	14	14	13	12	12	12	12	12	13	13	12	13
Maximum Wind Gust (mph)*	60	69	69	83	55	64	62	98	94	66	78	64	98

Note: (*) Period of record is 1957-1995

Charlotte Douglas Int'l Airport

Charlotte is located in the Piedmont of the Carolinas, a transitional area of rolling country between the mountains to the west and the Coastal Plain to the east. The mountains are to the northwest about 80 miles from Charlotte. The general elevation of the area around Charlotte is about 730 feet. The Atlantic ocean is about 160 miles southeast.

The mountains have a moderating effect on winter temperatures, causing appreciable warming of cold air from the northwest winds. The ocean is too far away to have any immediate effect on summer temperatures but in winter an occasional general and sustained flow of air from the warm ocean waters results in considerable warming.

Charlotte enjoys a moderate climate, characterized by cool winters and quite warm summers. Temperatures fall as low as the freezing point on a little over one-half of the days in the winter months. Winter weather is changeable, with occasional cold periods, but extreme cold is rare. Snow is infrequent, and the first snowfall of the season usually comes in late November or December. Heavy snowfalls have occurred, but any appreciable accumulation of snow on the ground for more than a day or two is rare.

Summers are long and quite warm, with afternoon temperatures frequently in the low 90s. The growing season is also long, the average length of the freeze-free period being 216 days. On the average, the last occurrence in spring with a temperature of 32 degrees is early April. In the fall the average first occurrence of 32 degrees is early November.

Rainfall is generally rather evenly distributed throughout the year, the driest weather usually coming in the fall. Summer rainfall comes principally from thunderstorms with occasional dry spells of one to three weeks duration.

Hurricanes which strike the Carolina coast may produce heavy rain but seldom cause dangerous winds.

Charlotte Douglas Int'l Airport *Mecklenburg County* Elevation: 728 ft. Latitude: 35° 13' N Longitude: 80° 57' W

	JAN	FEB	MAR	APR	MAY	JUN	JUL	AUG	SEP	OCT	NOV	DEC	YEAR
Mean Maximum Temp. (°F)	51.2	55.6	63.4	72.2	79.3	86.3	89.4	88.0	81.6	72.0	62.7	53.6	71.3
Mean Temp. (°F)	41.4	45.0	52.2	60.4	68.4	76.2	79.5	78.4	71.9	61.2	51.8	43.7	60.8
Mean Minimum Temp. (°F)	31.5	34.4	41.0	48.6	57.4	66.1	69.6	68.7	62.1	50.4	40.9	33.8	50.4
Extreme Maximum Temp. (°F)	79	81	87	91	94	100	103	104	96	93	83	80	104
Extreme Minimum Temp. (°F)	-5	7	4	21	35	45	56	50	39	26	13	4	-5
Days Maximum Temp. ≥ 90°F	0	0	0	0	2	10	16	12	3	0	0	0	43
Days Maximum Temp. ≤ 32°F	1	0	0	0	0	0	0	0	0	0	0	0	1
Days Minimum Temp. ≤ 32°F	17	13	6	1	0	0	0	0	0	1	6	15	59
Days Minimum Temp. ≤ 0°F	0	0	0	0	0	0	0	0	0	0	0	0	0
Heating Degree Days (base 65°F)	725	560	399	173	39	2	0	0	16	160	393	655	3,122
Cooling Degree Days (base 65°F)	0	1	8	43	151	345	458	422	229	50	5	1	1,713
Mean Precipitation (in.)	3.40	3.24	4.15	3.07	3.19	3.72	3.69	4.12	3.28	3.41	3.22	3.21	41.70
Maximum Precipitation (in.)*	7.4	7.6	8.8	7.6	12.5	8.3	8.3	10.0	9.7	14.7	8.7	7.5	62.1
Minimum Precipitation (in.)*	0.4	0.2	0.6	0.3	0.3	0.1	0.5	0.6	trace	trace	0.5	0.4	26.9
Extreme Maximum Daily Precip. (in.)	2.35	2.20	2.34	2.07	3.50	2.76	6.88	5.36	3.38	4.21	3.26	2.37	6.88
Days With ≥ 0.1" Precipitation	7	6	7	6	6	6	6	6	5	5	5	6	71
Days With ≥ 0.5" Precipitation	2	2	3	2	2	3	2	3	2	2	3	2	28
Days With ≥ 1.0" Precipitation	1	1	1	1	1	1	1	1	1	1	1	1	12
Mean Snowfall (in.)	2.0	1.4	0.8	trace	trace	trace	0.0	trace	0.0	trace	0.1	0.2	4.5
Maximum Snowfall (in.)*	12	15	19	trace	0	0	0	0	0	0	3	8	23
Maximum 24-hr. Snowfall (in.)*	12	10	10	trace	0	0	0	0	0	0	2	8	12
Maximum Snow Depth (in.)	12	13	9	trace	trace	trace	0	trace	0	trace	trace	2	13
Days With ≥ 1.0" Snow Depth	2	1	0	0	0	0	0	0	0	0	0	0	3
Thunderstorm Days*	1	1	2	3	6	7	9	7	3	1	1	< 1	41
Foggy Days*	13	11	12	9	13	13	16	18	16	13	13	13	160
Predominant Sky Cover*	OVR	OVR	OVR	OVR	OVR	OVR	OVR	OVR	OVR	CLR	CLR	OVR	OVR
Mean Relative Humidity 7am (%)*	78	77	78	78	82	83	86	88	88	86	83	79	82
Mean Relative Humidity 4pm (%)*	53	48	46	43	49	51	54	55	54	50	50	53	51
Mean Dewpoint (°F)*	29	30	36	44	55	63	67	67	61	50	39	32	48
Prevailing Wind Direction*	SW	SW	SW	SW	SW	SW	SW	NE	NE	NNE	NNE	SW	SW
Prevailing Wind Speed (mph)*	10	12	12	12	9	8	8	8	8	9	9	9	9
Maximum Wind Gust (mph)*	64	53	60	56	48	60	55	77	87	40	51	52	87

Note: (*) Period of record is 1948-1995

The period of record for National Weather Service station data is 1980 – 2009 except where noted. See User Guide for detailed explanation of data.

Greensboro Airport

The Greensboro-High Point-Winston-Salem Regional Airport is located in the west-central part of Guilford County, in the northern Piedmont section of North Carolina. The location is near the headwaters of the Haw and Deep Rivers, both branches of the Cape Fear River system. A few miles west is a ridge beyond which lies the Yadkin River Basin. To the north, across a similar ridge, the waters of the Dan River flow northeastward into the Roanoke. West, beyond the Yadkin River Basin, the land gradually rises into the Brushy Mountains. To the northwest, other outcroppings southeast of the Blue Ridge rise into peaks occasionally exceeding 2,500 feet. Winter temperatures and rainfall are both modified by the mountain barrier, but to a lesser extent than in areas closer to the Appalachian Range. Shallow cold air masses from the west tend to be stopped by the mountains, while deeper masses are lifted over the range, losing moisture and warming during the passage. For this reason the lowest temperatures recorded in Forsyth and Guilford Counties usually occur when clear, cold air drifts southward, east of the Appalachian Range. The summer temperatures vary, but are generally mild.

Northwesterly winds seldom bring heavy or prolonged winter rain or snow. Flurries of light snow may fall when cold air blows across the mountains, but the heavier winter precipitation comes with winds blowing from northeast through east and south to southwest. When moist winds blowing from an easterly or southerly direction meet cold air moving out of the north or northwest in the vicinity of North Carolina, snow, sleet, or glaze may occur.

Seasonal snowfall has a wide range and there have been a few winters with only a trace of snow. Snow seldom stays on the ground more than a few days.

Summer precipitation is largely from thunderstorms, mostly local in character. The frequency of these showers and the amount of rain received varies greatly from year to year and from place to place. Sizeable areas are sometimes without significant rain in late spring or early summer for two or more weeks, while other areas in the vicinity may be well watered.

Damaging storms are infrequent in the Northern Piedmont area. The highest winds to occur have been associated with thunderstorms, and were of brief duration. Hail is reported within Guilford and Forsyth Counties each year. The occurrence of tornadoes is rare. Hurricanes have produced heavy rainfall here, but no winds of destructive force.

Based on the 1951-1980 period, the average first occurrence of 32 degrees Fahrenheit in the fall is October 27 and the average last occurrence in the spring is April 11.

Greensboro Airport *Guilford County* Elevation: 896 ft. Latitude: 36° 06' N Longitude: 79° 57' W

	JAN	FEB	MAR	APR	MAY	JUN	JUL	AUG	SEP	OCT	NOV	DEC	YEAR
Mean Maximum Temp. (°F)	48.2	52.4	60.5	69.8	77.2	84.4	87.7	86.1	79.4	69.8	60.5	50.8	68.9
Mean Temp. (°F)	38.6	42.0	49.4	58.2	66.3	74.4	78.1	76.7	69.8	59.0	49.7	41.2	58.6
Mean Minimum Temp. (°F)	29.0	31.6	38.4	46.6	55.2	64.3	68.4	67.2	60.0	48.1	38.9	31.5	48.3
Extreme Maximum Temp. (°F)	78	79	86	91	93	98	101	103	97	92	82	78	103
Extreme Minimum Temp. (°F)	-8	1	8	24	32	45	49	45	37	28	17	1	-8
Days Maximum Temp. ≥ 90°F	0	0	0	0	1	6	12	9	2	0	0	0	30
Days Maximum Temp. ≤ 32°F	2	1	0	0	0	0	0	0	0	0	0	1	4
Days Minimum Temp. ≤ 32°F	21	17	9	1	0	0	0	0	0	1	8	18	75
Days Minimum Temp. ≤ 0°F	0	0	0	0	0	0	0	0	0	0	0	0	0
Heating Degree Days (base 65°F)	811	643	480	227	68	5	0	1	30	212	454	732	3,663
Cooling Degree Days (base 65°F)	0	0	5	31	113	294	412	371	179	32	2	1	1,440
Mean Precipitation (in.)	3.04	2.92	3.73	3.62	3.35	3.79	4.32	3.84	4.06	3.09	3.17	2.93	41.86
Maximum Precipitation (in.)*	7.7	5.8	8.8	8.0	8.3	9.5	12.7	11.7	13.1	12.6	8.3	6.4	56.5
Minimum Precipitation (in.)*	0.7	0.4	0.7	0.4	0.4	trace	1.0	0.7	trace	0.3	0.3	0.3	29.7
Extreme Maximum Daily Precip. (in.)	1.77	2.14	3.60	3.97	3.24	2.63	4.16	4.94	3.94	4.08	2.49	1.90	4.94
Days With ≥ 0.1" Precipitation	6	6	7	7	7	7	8	6	5	5	5	6	75
Days With ≥ 0.5" Precipitation	2	2	3	2	2	3	3	2	3	2	2	2	28
Days With ≥ 1.0" Precipitation	1	1	1	1	1	1	1	1	1	1	1	1	12
Mean Snowfall (in.)	3.3	2.5	1.0	trace	trace	trace	trace	trace	0.0	0.0	0.1	0.7	7.6
Maximum Snowfall (in.)*	23	16	21	trace	0	0	0	0	0	0	6	8	32
Maximum 24-hr. Snowfall (in.)*	10	9	11	trace	0	0	0	0	0	0	3	5	11
Maximum Snow Depth (in.)	9	8	8	trace	trace	trace	trace	trace	0	0	1	5	9
Days With ≥ 1.0" Snow Depth	3	2	0	0	0	0	0	0	0	0	0	1	6
Thunderstorm Days*	< 1	1	2	3	6	8	10	8	3	1	1	< 1	43
Foggy Days*	13	12	12	10	14	16	18	21	18	13	12	12	171
Predominant Sky Cover*	OVR	OVR	OVR	OVR	OVR	OVR	OVR	OVR	OVR	CLR	OVR	OVR	OVR
Mean Relative Humidity 7am (%)*	79	77	78	77	82	84	87	90	90	88	83	79	83
Mean Relative Humidity 4pm (%)*	54	49	46	44	52	54	57	58	56	51	51	53	52
Mean Dewpoint (°F)*	27	28	34	43	54	63	67	66	60	48	37	29	46
Prevailing Wind Direction*	SW	SW	SW	SW	SW	SW	SW	SW	NE	NE	SW	SW	SW
Prevailing Wind Speed (mph)*	9	9	9	9	8	8	7	7	9	9	8	8	8
Maximum Wind Gust (mph)*	63	62	53	55	59	51	98	81	54	60	48	47	98

Note: (*) Period of record is 1948-1995

Raleigh-Durham Airport

The Raleigh-Durham Airport is located in the zone of transition between the Coastal Plain and the Piedmont Plateau. The surrounding terrain is rolling, with an average elevation of around 400 feet, the range over a 10-mile radius is roughly between 200 and 550 feet. Being centrally located between the mountains on the west and the coast on the south and east, the Raleigh-Durham area enjoys a favorable climate. The mountains form a partial barrier to cold air masses moving eastward from the interior of the nation. As a result, there are few days in the heart of the winter season when the temperature falls below 20 degrees. Tropical air is present over the eastern and central sections of North Carolina during much of the summer season, bringing warm temperatures and rather high humidities to the Raleigh-Durham area. Afternoon temperatures reach 90 degrees or higher on about one-fourth of the days in the middle of summer, but reach 100 degrees less than once per year. Even in the hottest weather, early morning temperatures almost always drop into the lower 70s.

Rainfall is well distributed throughout the year as a whole. July and August have the greatest amount of rainfall, and October and November the least. There are times in spring and summer when soil moisture is scanty. This usually results from too many days between rains rather than from a shortage of total rainfall, but occasionally the accumulated total during the growing season falls short of plant needs. Most summer rain is produced by thunderstorms, which may occasionally be accompanied by strong winds, intense rains, and hail. The Raleigh-Durham area is far enough from the coast so that the bad weather effects of coastal storms are reduced.

From September 1887 to December 1950, the office was located in the downtown areas of Raleigh. The various buildings occupied were within an area of three blocks. All thermometers were exposed on the roof, and this, plus the smoke over the city, had an effect on the temperature record of that period. Lowest temperatures at the city office were frequently from two to five degrees higher than those recorded in surrounding rural areas. Maximum temperatures in the city were generally a degree or two lower.

From September 1946 to May 1954, simultaneous records were kept at a surface location on the North Carolina State College campus in Raleigh, and at the Raleigh-Durham Airport 10 and a half air miles to the northwest.

Based on the 1951-1980 period, the average first occurrence of 32 degrees Fahrenheit in the fall is October 27 and the average last occurrence in the spring is April 11.

Raleigh-Durham Airport *Wake County* Elevation: 416 ft. Latitude: 35° 52' N Longitude: 78° 47' W

	JAN	FEB	MAR	APR	MAY	JUN	JUL	AUG	SEP	OCT	NOV	DEC	YEAR
Mean Maximum Temp. (°F)	50.5	54.8	62.7	72.0	79.1	86.5	89.6	88.0	81.5	72.1	63.1	53.5	71.1
Mean Temp. (°F)	40.5	43.9	51.0	59.7	67.5	75.8	79.4	78.0	71.3	60.6	51.6	43.2	60.2
Mean Minimum Temp. (°F)	30.5	33.0	39.2	47.3	55.8	64.9	69.2	67.9	61.1	49.1	40.0	32.9	49.2
Extreme Maximum Temp. (°F)	80	83	90	95	95	101	104	105	101	94	86	81	105
Extreme Minimum Temp. (°F)	-9	0	11	23	36	42	51	49	37	28	18	4	-9
Days Maximum Temp. ≥ 90°F	0	0	0	1	2	11	16	13	4	0	0	0	47
Days Maximum Temp. ≤ 32°F	2	1	0	0	0	0	0	0	0	0	0	1	4
Days Minimum Temp. ≤ 32°F	19	15	8	2	0	0	0	0	0	1	8	17	70
Days Minimum Temp. ≤ 0°F	0	0	0	0	0	0	0	0	0	0	0	0	0
Heating Degree Days (base 65°F)	751	590	439	198	55	4	0	1	20	180	401	671	3,310
Cooling Degree Days (base 65°F)	1	1	10	46	139	333	454	410	216	50	6	2	1,668
Mean Precipitation (in.)	3.52	3.21	4.19	2.93	3.18	3.61	4.70	4.21	4.27	3.24	3.17	3.03	43.26
Maximum Precipitation (in.)*	7.5	6.4	7.8	6.1	7.7	9.4	10.3	12.2	6.8	9.1	8.2	6.6	54.1
Minimum Precipitation (in.)*	0.9	0.3	1.0	0.2	0.9	0.3	0.8	0.8	0.2	0.4	0.6	0.3	33.7
Extreme Maximum Daily Precip. (in.)	3.01	1.88	3.17	2.22	2.46	5.63	4.18	4.18	4.96	5.33	2.97	2.30	5.63
Days With ≥ 0.1" Precipitation	7	6	7	6	6	7	8	6	5	5	5	5	73
Days With ≥ 0.5" Precipitation	2	2	3	2	2	2	3	3	3	2	2	2	28
Days With ≥ 1.0" Precipitation	1	1	1	1	0	1	1	1	1	1	1	1	11
Mean Snowfall (in.)	2.8	1.9	0.8	0.1	trace	trace	trace	0.0	0.0	0.0	0.1	0.4	6.1
Maximum Snowfall (in.)*	14	17	14	2	0	0	0	0	0	0	3	11	21
Maximum 24-hr. Snowfall (in.)*	9	10	9	2	0	0	0	0	0	0	3	9	10
Maximum Snow Depth (in.)	20	6	11	trace	trace	trace	trace	0	0	0	2	3	20
Days With ≥ 1.0" Snow Depth	2	2	0	0	0	0	0	0	0	0	0	0	4
Thunderstorm Days*	< 1	1	2	3	6	7	11	8	3	1	1	< 1	43
Foggy Days*	12	12	12	11	16	18	20	22	19	16	13	13	184
Predominant Sky Cover*	OVR	OVR	OVR	OVR	OVR	OVR	OVR	OVR	OVR	CLR	CLR	OVR	OVR
Mean Relative Humidity 7am (%)*	79	78	80	80	84	86	89	91	92	90	84	80	84
Mean Relative Humidity 4pm (%)*	53	48	46	42	51	54	57	58	57	52	51	53	52
Mean Dewpoint (°F)*	28	29	35	44	56	64	68	68	61	50	39	31	48
Prevailing Wind Direction*	SW	SW	SW	SW	SW	SW	SW	SSW	NE	NNE	SW	SW	SW
Prevailing Wind Speed (mph)*	9	10	10	10	9	8	8	7	8	9	9	9	9
Maximum Wind Gust (mph)*	55	62	60	56	55	51	48	61	46	44	41	55	62

Note: (*) Period of record is 1948-1995

The period of record for National Weather Service station data is 1980 – 2009 except where noted. See User Guide for detailed explanation of data.

Wilmington Airport

Wilmington is located in the tidewater section of southeastern North Carolina, near the Atlantic Ocean. The city proper is built adjacent to the east bank of the Cape Fear River. Because of the curvature of the coastline in this area, the ocean lies about five miles east and about 20 miles south. The surrounding terrain is typical of coastal Carolina. It is low-lying with an average elevation of less than 40 feet, and is characterized by level to gently rolling land with rivers, creeks, and lakes.

The maritime location makes the climate of Wilmington unusually mild for its latitude. All wind directions from the east-northeast through southwest have some moderating effects on temperatures throughout the year, because the ocean is relatively warm in winter and cool in summer. The daily range in temperatures is moderate compared to a continental type of climate. As a rule, summers are quite warm and humid, but excessive heat is rare. Sea breezes, arriving early in the afternoon, tend to alleviate the heat further inland. Long-term averages show afternoon temperatures reach 90 degrees or higher on one-third of the days in midsummer, but several years may pass without 100 degree weather. During the colder part of the year, numerous outbreaks of polar air masses reach the Atlantic Coast, causing sharp drops in temperatures. However, these cold outbreaks are significantly moderated by the long trajectories from the source regions, the effects of passing over the Appalachian Range, and the warming effects of the ocean air. As a result, most winters are short and quite mild.

Rainfall in this area is usually ample and well-distributed throughout the year, the greatest amount occurring in the summer. Summer rainfall comes principally from thunderstorms, and is therefore usually of short duration, but often heavy and unevenly distributed. Thunderstorms occur about one out of three days from June through August. Winter rain is more likely to be of the slow, steady type, lasting one or two days. Generally, the winter rain is evenly distributed and associated with slow-moving, low-pressure systems. Seldom is there a winter without a few flakes of snow, but several years may pass without a measurable amount. Hail occurs less than once a year. Sunshine is abundant, with the area receiving about two-thirds of the sunshine hours possible at its latitude.

Because of these many factors, the growing season is long, averaging 244 days, but records show the range is from 180 days to as long as 302 days.

In common with most Atlantic Coastal localities, the area is subject to the effects of coastal storms and occasional hurricanes which produce high winds, above normal tides, and heavy rains.

Wilmington Airport *New Hanover County* Elevation: 29 ft. Latitude: 34° 16' N Longitude: 77° 54' W

	JAN	FEB	MAR	APR	MAY	JUN	JUL	AUG	SEP	OCT	NOV	DEC	YEAR
Mean Maximum Temp. (°F)	56.4	59.7	66.1	74.0	80.6	86.6	89.7	88.0	83.5	75.4	67.7	59.5	73.9
Mean Temp. (°F)	46.0	48.7	54.8	62.8	70.1	77.5	81.1	79.6	74.6	64.9	56.5	48.7	63.8
Mean Minimum Temp. (°F)	35.6	37.7	43.5	51.5	59.7	68.4	72.4	71.2	65.6	54.4	45.2	37.9	53.6
Extreme Maximum Temp. (°F)	81	82	88	94	96	101	101	103	96	95	86	82	103
Extreme Minimum Temp. (°F)	5	11	9	29	38	48	55	55	44	32	23	0	0
Days Maximum Temp. ≥ 90°F	0	0	0	1	2	9	16	11	4	0	0	0	43
Days Maximum Temp. ≤ 32°F	0	0	0	0	0	0	0	0	0	0	0	0	0
Days Minimum Temp. ≤ 32°F	13	9	4	0	0	0	0	0	0	0	3	10	39
Days Minimum Temp. ≤ 0°F	0	0	0	0	0	0	0	0	0	0	0	0	0
Heating Degree Days (base 65°F)	584	457	325	130	26	1	0	0	4	93	272	503	2,395
Cooling Degree Days (base 65°F)	3	4	16	69	192	384	505	460	298	98	23	5	2,057
Mean Precipitation (in.)	3.81	3.53	4.26	2.74	4.39	4.95	7.64	7.77	6.98	3.85	3.20	3.69	56.81
Maximum Precipitation (in.)*	10.2	8.7	8.3	8.2	9.1	12.9	18.0	14.1	18.9	9.8	7.9	7.1	66.6
Minimum Precipitation (in.)*	0.7	0.6	0.9	0.2	0.9	0.9	1.6	1.7	0.7	0.2	0.5	0.5	36.9
Extreme Maximum Daily Precip. (in.)	3.03	3.37	4.38	2.94	5.02	3.82	6.51	9.55	13.38	6.34	3.83	3.49	13.38
Days With ≥ 0.1" Precipitation	7	6	6	5	6	7	10	9	6	5	5	6	78
Days With ≥ 0.5" Precipitation	3	3	3	2	3	3	5	4	4	2	2	3	37
Days With ≥ 1.0" Precipitation	1	1	1	1	1	2	2	2	2	1	1	1	16
Mean Snowfall (in.)	0.7	0.1	0.4	trace	trace	trace	trace	0.0	0.0	0.0	0.0	0.6	1.8
Maximum Snowfall (in.)*	5	13	7	trace	0	0	0	0	0	0	trace	15	16
Maximum 24-hr. Snowfall (in.)*	5	7	5	trace	0	0	0	0	0	0	trace	10	10
Maximum Snow Depth (in.)	3	trace	7	trace	trace	trace	trace	0	0	0	0	13	13
Days With ≥ 1.0" Snow Depth	0	0	0	0	0	0	0	0	0	0	0	0	0
Thunderstorm Days*	< 1	1	2	3	6	8	12	9	4	1	1	< 1	47
Foggy Days*	15	12	14	12	15	16	14	17	17	16	15	14	177
Predominant Sky Cover*	OVR	OVR	OVR	CLR	OVR	OVR	SCT	OVR	OVR	CLR	CLR	OVR	OVR
Mean Relative Humidity 7am (%)*	82	80	82	81	84	85	87	90	90	89	86	82	85
Mean Relative Humidity 4pm (%)*	58	55	54	51	58	62	66	67	66	60	58	58	59
Mean Dewpoint (°F)*	36	37	43	50	60	68	72	71	66	56	46	38	54
Prevailing Wind Direction*	N	SW	SW	SW	SW	SW	SW	SW	NNE	N	N	N	SW
Prevailing Wind Speed (mph)*	9	12	12	12	10	9	9	8	9	10	10	9	10
Maximum Wind Gust (mph)*	64	63	77	59	55	64	78	64	74	52	54	55	78

Note: (*) Period of record is 1948-1995

Albemarle *Stanly County* Elevation: 609 ft. Latitude: 35° 22' N Longitude: 80° 11' W

	JAN	FEB	MAR	APR	MAY	JUN	JUL	AUG	SEP	OCT	NOV	DEC	YEAR
Mean Maximum Temp. (°F)	51.5	55.8	64.2	72.6	79.6	86.5	89.6	88.1	81.9	72.7	63.7	54.3	71.7
Mean Temp. (°F)	40.9	44.2	51.7	59.5	67.3	75.3	78.9	77.6	71.0	60.4	51.8	43.4	60.2
Mean Minimum Temp. (°F)	30.2	32.6	39.3	46.3	55.1	64.2	68.1	67.0	60.1	48.2	39.8	32.5	48.6
Extreme Maximum Temp. (°F)	79	81	87	92	95	99	103	107	99	94	83	80	107
Extreme Minimum Temp. (°F)	-6	2	5	23	29	42	50	50	35	25	17	2	-6
Days Maximum Temp. ≥ 90°F	0	0	0	0	2	10	16	13	3	0	0	0	44
Days Maximum Temp. ≤ 32°F	1	0	0	0	0	0	0	0	0	0	0	0	1
Days Minimum Temp. ≤ 32°F	19	15	8	2	0	0	0	0	0	1	8	17	70
Days Minimum Temp. ≤ 0°F	0	0	0	0	0	0	0	0	0	0	0	0	0
Heating Degree Days (base 65°F)	742	582	410	196	53	4	0	0	19	177	395	664	3,242
Cooling Degree Days (base 65°F)	0	1	7	37	133	320	438	397	208	43	5	1	1,590
Mean Precipitation (in.)	3.73	3.48	4.85	3.34	3.65	4.57	5.57	4.51	4.12	3.65	3.33	3.35	48.15
Extreme Maximum Daily Precip. (in.)	***2.98***	2.45	***3.02***	4.67	3.22	3.80	***5.25***	4.01	6.25	9.32	2.90	***2.01***	***9.32***
Days With ≥ 0.1" Precipitation	7	6	7	6	7	6	8	6	5	5	5	6	74
Days With ≥ 0.5" Precipitation	2	3	4	2	3	3	4	3	3	2	2	2	33
Days With ≥ 1.0" Precipitation	1	1	2	1	1	1	1	1	1	1	1	1	13
Mean Snowfall (in.)	1.0	0.9	0.8	trace	0.0	0.0	0.0	0.0	0.0	0.0	trace	0.1	2.8
Maximum Snow Depth (in.)	9	6	***7***	trace	0	0	0	0	0	0	trace	1	***9***
Days With ≥ 1.0" Snow Depth	***0***	0	***0***	0	0	0	0	0	0	0	0	0	***0***

Arcola *Warren County* Elevation: 330 ft. Latitude: 36° 17' N Longitude: 77° 59' W

	JAN	FEB	MAR	APR	MAY	JUN	JUL	AUG	SEP	OCT	NOV	DEC	YEAR
Mean Maximum Temp. (°F)	50.7	55.1	***63.1***	72.5	79.4	86.7	90.1	88.3	82.5	73.4	64.5	54.8	***71.8***
Mean Temp. (°F)	***38.4***	42.7	***49.3***	58.0	66.0	74.0	78.0	76.1	69.9	59.4	50.8	42.9	***58.8***
Mean Minimum Temp. (°F)	***26.5***	30.2	***35.5***	43.4	52.6	61.2	65.6	64.0	57.2	45.1	37.1	30.8	***45.8***
Extreme Maximum Temp. (°F)	80	82	***89***	95	96	100	***102***	103	100	94	82	79	***103***
Extreme Minimum Temp. (°F)	-7	-3	***11***	19	30	37	47	43	36	20	17	3	***-7***
Days Maximum Temp. ≥ 90°F	0	0	0	1	2	11	19	14	4	0	0	0	51
Days Maximum Temp. ≤ 32°F	1	0	0	0	0	0	0	0	0	0	0	1	2
Days Minimum Temp. ≤ 32°F	23	18	11	4	0	0	0	0	0	2	11	19	88
Days Minimum Temp. ≤ 0°F	0	0	0	0	0	0	0	0	0	0	0	0	0
Heating Degree Days (base 65°F)	***817***	624	***482***	231	67	5	0	1	25	200	422	680	***3,554***
Cooling Degree Days (base 65°F)	***0***	0	***3***	27	106	281	409	352	178	33	3	1	***1,393***
Mean Precipitation (in.)	3.40	3.26	4.45	3.37	3.47	4.50	5.01	5.09	4.01	3.36	3.36	3.28	46.56
Extreme Maximum Daily Precip. (in.)	2.41	3.72	3.54	5.01	3.98	4.28	5.54	4.02	8.45	4.30	3.40	2.05	8.45
Days With ≥ 0.1" Precipitation	6	6	7	7	6	7	7	7	5	5	5	6	74
Days With ≥ 0.5" Precipitation	2	2	4	2	2	3	3	3	3	2	3	2	31
Days With ≥ 1.0" Precipitation	1	1	1	1	1	1	2	2	1	1	1	1	14
Mean Snowfall (in.)	2.6	2.0	0.6	trace	0.0	0.0	0.0	0.0	0.0	0.0	0.1	0.6	5.9
Maximum Snow Depth (in.)	12	5	11	0	0	0	0	0	0	0	1	3	12
Days With ≥ 1.0" Snow Depth	3	1	0	0	0	0	0	0	0	0	0	0	4

Asheboro 2 W *Randolph County* Elevation: 870 ft. Latitude: 35° 42' N Longitude: 79° 50' W

	JAN	FEB	MAR	APR	MAY	JUN	JUL	AUG	SEP	OCT	NOV	DEC	YEAR
Mean Maximum Temp. (°F)	49.9	54.6	62.9	72.0	78.2	84.9	88.2	86.8	80.6	71.2	62.3	52.9	70.4
Mean Temp. (°F)	40.4	44.1	51.5	59.9	67.1	74.8	78.4	77.1	70.8	60.4	51.5	43.2	59.9
Mean Minimum Temp. (°F)	31.0	33.6	40.1	47.8	55.9	64.6	68.6	67.4	60.9	49.6	40.7	33.4	49.5
Extreme Maximum Temp. (°F)	78	81	90	93	94	97	101	105	100	93	83	79	105
Extreme Minimum Temp. (°F)	-8	2	8	24	33	39	51	49	39	29	16	-1	-8
Days Maximum Temp. ≥ 90°F	0	0	0	0	1	7	13	10	3	0	0	0	34
Days Maximum Temp. ≤ 32°F	2	1	0	0	0	0	0	0	0	0	0	1	4
Days Minimum Temp. ≤ 32°F	18	14	7	1	0	0	0	0	0	1	7	16	64
Days Minimum Temp. ≤ 0°F	0	0	0	0	0	0	0	0	0	0	0	0	0
Heating Degree Days (base 65°F)	756	585	421	189	54	4	0	0	21	180	403	671	3,284
Cooling Degree Days (base 65°F)	0	1	10	43	126	304	424	383	201	44	4	1	1,541
Mean Precipitation (in.)	3.86	3.51	4.11	3.66	3.48	3.90	4.11	4.19	3.93	3.70	3.43	3.24	45.12
Extreme Maximum Daily Precip. (in.)	1.90	2.46	2.66	4.04	2.74	5.17	2.73	3.69	4.69	5.26	2.90	2.23	5.26
Days With ≥ 0.1" Precipitation	7	6	7	6	6	6	7	7	5	5	6	6	74
Days With ≥ 0.5" Precipitation	3	3	3	2	2	3	3	3	3	2	3	2	32
Days With ≥ 1.0" Precipitation	1	1	1	1	1	1	1	1	1	1	1	1	12
Mean Snowfall (in.)	3.0	1.7	0.6	trace	0.0	0.0	0.0	0.0	0.0	0.0	0.2	0.3	5.8
Maximum Snow Depth (in.)	8	3	6	trace	0	0	0	0	0	0	0	2	8
Days With ≥ 1.0" Snow Depth	1	1	0	0	0	0	0	0	0	0	0	0	2

Asheville *Buncombe County* Elevation: 2,240 ft. Latitude: 35° 36' N Longitude: 82° 32' W

	JAN	FEB	MAR	APR	MAY	JUN	JUL	AUG	SEP	OCT	NOV	DEC	YEAR
Mean Maximum Temp. (°F)	46.8	50.4	58.0	67.2	74.9	81.5	84.8	83.7	77.1	67.8	58.3	49.3	66.6
Mean Temp. (°F)	37.4	40.6	47.6	56.1	64.0	71.2	74.7	73.7	67.1	57.0	48.0	40.0	56.4
Mean Minimum Temp. (°F)	28.0	30.8	37.1	45.0	52.9	60.8	64.5	63.7	57.0	46.1	37.6	30.6	46.2
Extreme Maximum Temp. (°F)	78	78	87	89	93	95	98	99	92	86	81	75	99
Extreme Minimum Temp. (°F)	-17	-5	4	19	30	42	51	46	36	26	14	-8	-17
Days Maximum Temp. ≥ 90°F	0	0	0	0	0	2	6	4	0	0	0	0	12
Days Maximum Temp. ≤ 32°F	3	2	1	0	0	0	0	0	0	0	0	2	8
Days Minimum Temp. ≤ 32°F	21	17	11	3	0	0	0	0	0	2	10	19	83
Days Minimum Temp. ≤ 0°F	0	0	0	0	0	0	0	0	0	0	0	0	0
Heating Degree Days (base 65°F)	849	683	534	277	95	10	0	2	48	256	505	769	4,028
Cooling Degree Days (base 65°F)	0	0	2	16	69	203	307	278	116	15	1	0	1,007
Mean Precipitation (in.)	2.83	3.13	3.40	3.11	3.28	3.39	3.32	3.36	3.27	2.18	2.88	2.72	36.87
Extreme Maximum Daily Precip. (in.)	3.34	2.96	2.79	1.83	2.56	3.08	2.08	3.43	3.76	3.07	2.13	2.10	3.76
Days With ≥ 0.1" Precipitation	6	6	7	6	7	7	8	7	6	4	5	6	75
Days With ≥ 0.5" Precipitation	2	2	2	2	2	2	2	2	2	1	2	2	23
Days With ≥ 1.0" Precipitation	0	1	1	1	1	1	1	1	1	0	1	1	10
Mean Snowfall (in.)	4.1	2.7	2.1	1.1	trace	trace	0.0	0.0	0.0	trace	0.4	2.2	12.6
Maximum Snow Depth (in.)	14	4	20	15	trace	trace	0	0	0	trace	2	11	20
Days With ≥ 1.0" Snow Depth	3	2	1	0	0	0	0	0	0	0	0	2	8

The period of record for all cooperative weather station data is 1980 – 2009. See User Guide for detailed explanation of data.

Aurora 6 N *Beaufort County* Elevation: 20 ft. Latitude: 35° 23' N Longitude: 76° 47' W

	JAN	FEB	MAR	APR	MAY	JUN	JUL	AUG	SEP	OCT	NOV	DEC	YEAR
Mean Maximum Temp. (°F)	53.0	55.8	62.4	71.7	79.1	85.9	89.3	87.3	82.5	73.4	64.5	56.1	71.7
Mean Temp. (°F)	43.7	46.2	52.4	61.4	69.3	77.0	80.7	79.0	74.2	64.4	55.4	47.0	62.6
Mean Minimum Temp. (°F)	34.3	36.6	42.3	51.1	59.5	68.1	72.2	70.5	65.8	55.3	46.2	37.8	53.3
Extreme Maximum Temp. (°F)	79	81	90	93	96	101	100	103	100	93	86	82	103
Extreme Minimum Temp. (°F)	-1	8	11	28	44	51	59	55	46	33	21	10	-1
Days Maximum Temp. ≥ 90°F	0	0	0	1	2	9	15	11	3	0	0	0	41
Days Maximum Temp. ≤ 32°F	1	0	0	0	0	0	0	0	0	0	0	0	1
Days Minimum Temp. ≤ 32°F	13	9	3	0	0	0	0	0	0	0	1	8	34
Days Minimum Temp. ≤ 0°F	0	0	0	0	0	0	0	0	0	0	0	0	0
Heating Degree Days (base 65°F)	656	526	393	154	32	2	0	0	3	98	295	555	2,714
Cooling Degree Days (base 65°F)	1	2	10	54	173	368	495	440	285	85	14	3	1,930
Mean Precipitation (in.)	3.90	3.10	4.07	3.31	3.89	4.93	5.63	6.33	4.57	3.41	3.03	3.25	49.42
Extreme Maximum Daily Precip. (in.)	2.94	***2.39***	2.64	3.93	***3.81***	***4.96***	8.82	5.08	***5.87***	***4.02***	6.07	3.45	***8.82***
Days With ≥ 0.1" Precipitation	7	6	6	5	6	7	8	8	6	4	5	6	74
Days With ≥ 0.5" Precipitation	3	2	3	2	2	3	4	4	3	2	2	2	32
Days With ≥ 1.0" Precipitation	1	1	1	1	1	1	2	2	1	1	1	1	14
Mean Snowfall (in.)	0.3	0.0	trace	0.0	0.0	0.0	0.0	0.0	0.0	0.0	0.0	trace	0.3
Maximum Snow Depth (in.)	trace	trace	trace	0	0	0	0	0	0	0	0	0	trace
Days With ≥ 1.0" Snow Depth	0	0	0	0	0	0	0	0	0	0	0	0	0

Bayboro 3 E *Pamlico County* Elevation: 9 ft. Latitude: 35° 09' N Longitude: 76° 43' W

	JAN	FEB	MAR	APR	MAY	JUN	JUL	AUG	SEP	OCT	NOV	DEC	YEAR
Mean Maximum Temp. (°F)	55.9	59.5	65.8	***74.2***	80.4	86.5	89.1	88.0	83.3	75.0	67.3	58.8	***73.6***
Mean Temp. (°F)	44.9	47.8	53.5	***61.7***	69.1	76.5	79.8	78.5	73.5	63.6	55.5	47.7	***62.7***
Mean Minimum Temp. (°F)	33.9	36.0	41.2	***49.2***	57.7	66.4	70.4	68.9	63.6	52.1	43.6	36.4	***51.6***
Extreme Maximum Temp. (°F)	80	83	91	***93***	96	102	100	107	98	96	88	82	***107***
Extreme Minimum Temp. (°F)	-1	5	10	***26***	35	46	52	51	40	27	16	-4	***-4***
Days Maximum Temp. ≥ 90°F	0	0	0	***1***	2	9	15	12	3	0	0	0	***42***
Days Maximum Temp. ≤ 32°F	0	0	0	***0***	0	0	0	0	0	0	0	0	***0***
Days Minimum Temp. ≤ 32°F	14	11	7	***1***	0	0	0	0	0	1	5	12	***51***
Days Minimum Temp. ≤ 0°F	0	0	0	***0***	0	0	0	0	0	0	0	0	***0***
Heating Degree Days (base 65°F)	618	485	363	***150***	34	2	0	0	5	115	296	535	***2,603***
Cooling Degree Days (base 65°F)	2	3	14	***57***	168	353	465	425	266	77	17	4	***1,851***
Mean Precipitation (in.)	3.89	3.18	4.13	***3.41***	4.46	5.29	6.56	7.24	5.82	3.81	3.75	3.66	***55.20***
Extreme Maximum Daily Precip. (in.)	3.15	2.62	3.24	***5.10***	5.05	3.50	4.72	***4.78***	5.48	5.42	5.83	2.77	***5.83***
Days With ≥ 0.1" Precipitation	7	6	6	***5***	6	8	9	8	7	5	5	6	***78***
Days With ≥ 0.5" Precipitation	3	2	3	***2***	3	4	4	4	3	2	2	2	***34***
Days With ≥ 1.0" Precipitation	1	1	1	***1***	1	2	2	2	2	1	1	1	***16***
Mean Snowfall (in.)	0.4	0.2	0.7	***0.0***	0.0	0.0	0.0	0.0	0.0	0.0	0.0	0.5	***1.8***
Maximum Snow Depth (in.)	4	3	0	***0***	0	0	0	0	0	0	0	12	***12***
Days With ≥ 1.0" Snow Depth	0	0	0	***0***	0	0	0	0	0	0	0	0	***0***

Belhaven 5 SE *Beaufort County* Elevation: 7 ft. Latitude: 35° 30' N Longitude: 76° 41' W

	JAN	FEB	MAR	APR	MAY	JUN	JUL	AUG	SEP	OCT	NOV	DEC	YEAR
Mean Maximum Temp. (°F)	52.4	55.7	62.6	71.5	79.0	85.6	***88.3***	86.8	82.1	73.7	64.9	56.0	***71.6***
Mean Temp. (°F)	42.6	45.4	51.8	60.6	68.8	76.4	***79.7***	78.0	72.8	62.9	54.4	46.1	***61.6***
Mean Minimum Temp. (°F)	32.8	35.0	41.0	49.7	58.5	67.1	71.1	69.3	63.5	52.0	43.9	36.1	51.7
Extreme Maximum Temp. (°F)	79	82	89	94	96	101	100	101	97	94	84	81	101
Extreme Minimum Temp. (°F)	-10	4	15	28	40	44	55	51	44	30	23	8	-10
Days Maximum Temp. ≥ 90°F	0	0	0	1	2	8	12	9	2	0	0	0	34
Days Maximum Temp. ≤ 32°F	1	0	0	0	0	0	0	0	0	0	0	0	1
Days Minimum Temp. ≤ 32°F	16	12	6	0	0	0	0	0	0	0	4	12	50
Days Minimum Temp. ≤ 0°F	0	0	0	0	0	0	0	0	0	0	0	0	0
Heating Degree Days (base 65°F)	688	548	411	174	40	2	***0***	0	8	128	322	582	***2,903***
Cooling Degree Days (base 65°F)	1	1	9	49	164	350	***463***	411	249	69	11	2	***1,779***
Mean Precipitation (in.)	3.77	2.93	4.24	3.23	3.78	4.96	6.07	6.31	4.54	2.54	3.20	2.98	48.55
Extreme Maximum Daily Precip. (in.)	2.72	2.05	3.20	3.42	3.37	6.02	4.62	6.00	6.37	3.99	6.90	2.18	6.90
Days With ≥ 0.1" Precipitation	8	6	7	5	7	7	9	8	6	4	5	5	77
Days With ≥ 0.5" Precipitation	3	2	3	2	3	4	4	4	3	2	2	2	34
Days With ≥ 1.0" Precipitation	1	1	1	1	1	2	2	2	1	1	1	1	15
Mean Snowfall (in.)	0.7	0.6	0.9	0.2	0.0	0.0	0.0	0.0	0.0	0.0	0.0	0.6	3.0
Maximum Snow Depth (in.)	4	6	16	4	0	0	0	0	0	0	0	5	16
Days With ≥ 1.0" Snow Depth	0	0	0	0	0	0	0	0	0	0	0	0	0

Bent Creek *Buncombe County* Elevation: 2,109 ft. Latitude: 35° 30' N Longitude: 82° 36' W

	JAN	FEB	MAR	APR	MAY	JUN	JUL	AUG	SEP	OCT	NOV	DEC	YEAR
Mean Maximum Temp. (°F)	48.2	51.9	59.7	68.9	75.8	81.5	84.4	83.4	77.7	68.8	59.4	50.1	67.5
Mean Temp. (°F)	37.1	40.1	46.9	55.1	62.8	69.8	73.2	72.5	66.2	56.3	47.0	39.2	55.5
Mean Minimum Temp. (°F)	26.0	28.2	34.0	41.1	49.7	58.0	62.0	61.4	54.8	43.7	34.6	28.3	43.5
Extreme Maximum Temp. (°F)	81	80	83	90	91	95	97	100	95	88	81	76	100
Extreme Minimum Temp. (°F)	-16	-5	-1	19	26	36	42	41	31	20	11	-5	-16
Days Maximum Temp. ≥ 90°F	0	0	0	0	0	1	5	4	1	0	0	0	11
Days Maximum Temp. ≤ 32°F	2	1	0	0	0	0	0	0	0	0	0	1	4
Days Minimum Temp. ≤ 32°F	23	20	14	5	1	0	0	0	0	5	15	22	105
Days Minimum Temp. ≤ 0°F	0	0	0	0	0	0	0	0	0	0	0	0	0
Heating Degree Days (base 65°F)	858	699	555	299	112	13	1	2	54	274	534	792	4,193
Cooling Degree Days (base 65°F)	0	0	1	8	49	163	262	240	98	10	1	0	832
Mean Precipitation (in.)	3.83	3.79	4.59	3.77	3.75	4.54	4.49	3.98	4.51	2.99	4.09	3.35	47.68
Extreme Maximum Daily Precip. (in.)	3.45	3.44	3.75	2.34	2.68	2.80	3.02	3.95	4.48	3.54	4.34	2.21	4.48
Days With ≥ 0.1" Precipitation	6	6	7	6	6	8	7	7	6	4	5	6	74
Days With ≥ 0.5" Precipitation	2	2	3	2	2	3	3	2	3	2	3	2	29
Days With ≥ 1.0" Precipitation	1	1	1	1	1	1	1	1	1	1	1	1	12
Mean Snowfall (in.)	2.5	1.4	1.1	0.5	0.0	0.0	0.0	0.0	0.0	trace	0.0	***0.4***	***5.9***
Maximum Snow Depth (in.)	12	4	17	13	0	0	0	0	0	trace	2	10	17
Days With ≥ 1.0" Snow Depth	2	1	1	0	0	0	0	0	0	0	0	1	5

The period of record for all cooperative weather station data is 1980 – 2009. See User Guide for detailed explanation of data.

Black Mountain 2 W *Buncombe County* Elevation: 2,290 ft. Latitude: 35° 37' N Longitude: 82° 21' W

	JAN	FEB	MAR	APR	MAY	JUN	JUL	AUG	SEP	OCT	NOV	DEC	YEAR
Mean Maximum Temp. (°F)	49.1	52.1	60.0	68.0	75.2	81.2	84.3	83.2	77.2	69.1	59.9	51.1	67.5
Mean Temp. (°F)	37.5	40.5	47.0	54.6	62.2	69.3	72.8	72.0	65.7	56.3	47.3	39.7	55.4
Mean Minimum Temp. (°F)	26.0	28.8	34.0	41.2	49.2	57.4	61.2	60.7	54.1	43.5	34.6	28.2	43.2
Extreme Maximum Temp. (°F)	77	76	86	90	90	93	99	97	92	85	79	76	99
Extreme Minimum Temp. (°F)	-14	-7	7	18	26	32	44	43	28	19	12	-13	-14
Days Maximum Temp. ≥ 90°F	0	0	0	0	0	2	4	3	0	0	0	0	9
Days Maximum Temp. ≤ 32°F	2	1	0	0	0	0	0	0	0	0	0	1	4
Days Minimum Temp. ≤ 32°F	22	19	14	5	1	0	0	0	0	5	13	21	100
Days Minimum Temp. ≤ 0°F	0	0	0	0	0	0	0	0	0	0	0	0	0
Heating Degree Days (base 65°F)	838	685	550	311	119	17	1	3	60	272	525	779	4,160
Cooling Degree Days (base 65°F)	0	0	1	7	42	152	249	226	87	11	1	0	776
Mean Precipitation (in.)	3.50	3.56	4.09	3.75	4.09	4.58	3.83	3.94	4.43	3.07	3.62	3.42	45.88
Extreme Maximum Daily Precip. (in.)	5.20	3.21	3.30	2.05	4.00	4.22	2.05	6.80	10.00	3.90	2.75	2.00	10.00
Days With ≥ 0.1" Precipitation	6	6	6	7	8	8	8	7	6	5	6	6	79
Days With ≥ 0.5" Precipitation	2	2	3	3	3	3	2	2	3	2	3	3	31
Days With ≥ 1.0" Precipitation	1	1	1	1	1	1	1	1	1	1	1	1	12
Mean Snowfall (in.)	2.6	2.0	1.2	0.6	0.0	0.0	0.0	0.0	0.0	0.0	0.1	1.4	7.9
Maximum Snow Depth (in.)	12	5	5	4	0	0	0	0	0	0	3	5	12
Days With ≥ 1.0" Snow Depth	1	1	0	0	0	0	0	0	0	0	0	0	2

Burlington Fire Stn #5 *Alamance County* Elevation: 660 ft. Latitude: 36° 04' N Longitude: 79° 27' W

	JAN	FEB	MAR	APR	MAY	JUN	JUL	AUG	SEP	OCT	NOV	DEC	YEAR
Mean Maximum Temp. (°F)	50.1	54.0	62.2	71.8	79.1	86.8	90.1	88.7	81.8	72.2	63.1	53.3	71.1
Mean Temp. (°F)	39.4	42.5	49.9	58.7	66.8	75.3	79.0	77.4	70.4	59.4	50.7	42.1	59.3
Mean Minimum Temp. (°F)	28.6	30.9	37.5	45.6	54.3	63.9	67.8	66.3	59.0	46.6	38.2	30.9	47.5
Extreme Maximum Temp. (°F)	84	80	89	95	98	101	102	104	100	93	85	79	104
Extreme Minimum Temp. (°F)	-6	4	8	22	29	43	48	41	36	25	15	-4	-6
Days Maximum Temp. ≥ 90°F	0	0	0	1	2	11	19	14	4	0	0	0	51
Days Maximum Temp. ≤ 32°F	2	1	0	0	0	0	0	0	0	0	0	1	4
Days Minimum Temp. ≤ 32°F	22	17	10	2	0	0	0	0	0	1	9	19	80
Days Minimum Temp. ≤ 0°F	0	0	0	0	0	0	0	0	0	0	0	0	0
Heating Degree Days (base 65°F)	787	630	468	217	65	4	0	1	24	201	427	702	3,526
Cooling Degree Days (base 65°F)	0	0	6	35	126	319	441	393	194	35	3	0	1,552
Mean Precipitation (in.)	3.33	3.05	4.15	3.47	3.44	4.00	4.62	3.95	3.76	3.28	3.19	3.14	43.38
Extreme Maximum Daily Precip. (in.)	2.20	2.81	3.10	3.38	2.40	4.60	4.30	4.67	5.15	2.91	3.20	2.20	5.15
Days With ≥ 0.1" Precipitation	6	5	7	6	6	6	7	6	5	5	6	5	70
Days With ≥ 0.5" Precipitation	3	2	3	2	3	2	3	2	2	2	2	2	28
Days With ≥ 1.0" Precipitation	1	1	1	1	1	1	1	1	1	1	1	1	12
Mean Snowfall (in.)	1.5	1.0	0.2	trace	0.0	0.0	0.0	0.0	0.0	0.0	0.0	trace	2.7
Maximum Snow Depth (in.)	10	*5*	4	trace	0	0	0	0	0	0	0	3	***10***
Days With ≥ 1.0" Snow Depth	0	0	0	0	0	0	0	0	0	0	0	0	0

Cedar Island *Carteret County* Elevation: 7 ft. Latitude: 34° 59' N Longitude: 76° 18' W

	JAN	FEB	MAR	APR	MAY	JUN	JUL	AUG	SEP	OCT	NOV	DEC	YEAR
Mean Maximum Temp. (°F)	54.5	57.0	63.8	72.7	79.8	86.4	89.6	87.8	82.6	74.2	65.6	57.3	72.6
Mean Temp. (°F)	45.5	47.8	54.2	62.7	70.1	77.3	80.7	79.4	74.8	65.6	56.8	48.5	63.6
Mean Minimum Temp. (°F)	36.6	38.6	44.6	52.6	60.4	68.2	71.8	71.0	67.0	57.0	47.8	39.6	54.6
Extreme Maximum Temp. (°F)	79	78	88	93	98	101	102	102	98	98	85	79	102
Extreme Minimum Temp. (°F)	2	13	10	28	38	48	51	57	44	33	22	8	2
Days Maximum Temp. ≥ 90°F	0	0	0	0	2	9	16	12	3	0	0	0	42
Days Maximum Temp. ≤ 32°F	1	0	0	0	0	0	0	0	0	0	0	0	1
Days Minimum Temp. ≤ 32°F	11	8	3	0	0	0	0	0	0	0	2	8	32
Days Minimum Temp. ≤ 0°F	0	0	0	0	0	0	0	0	0	0	0	0	0
Heating Degree Days (base 65°F)	597	481	339	124	21	0	0	0	1	74	258	508	2,403
Cooling Degree Days (base 65°F)	1	1	12	60	186	377	495	454	303	100	17	3	2,009
Mean Precipitation (in.)	4.63	3.41	4.54	3.46	3.93	4.11	6.23	7.33	6.13	4.69	4.03	4.42	56.91
Extreme Maximum Daily Precip. (in.)	2.75	2.12	3.95	2.81	4.68	4.57	5.08	8.90	4.45	4.50	6.35	4.15	8.90
Days With ≥ 0.1" Precipitation	8	7	7	6	6	7	9	9	7	6	6	7	85
Days With ≥ 0.5" Precipitation	3	2	3	2	2	3	4	4	3	3	3	3	35
Days With ≥ 1.0" Precipitation	1	1	1	1	1	1	2	2	2	2	1	1	16
Mean Snowfall (in.)	1.1	0.2	0.6	trace	0.0	0.0	0.0	0.0	0.0	0.0	trace	0.6	2.5
Maximum Snow Depth (in.)	8	1	12	trace	0	0	0	0	0	0	trace	11	12
Days With ≥ 1.0" Snow Depth	0	0	0	0	0	0	0	0	0	0	0	0	0

Chapel Hill 2 W *Orange County* Elevation: 500 ft. Latitude: 35° 55' N Longitude: 79° 05' W

	JAN	FEB	MAR	APR	MAY	JUN	JUL	AUG	SEP	OCT	NOV	DEC	YEAR
Mean Maximum Temp. (°F)	50.1	54.1	61.9	71.4	78.6	85.9	89.3	88.0	81.5	71.7	63.0	53.3	70.7
Mean Temp. (°F)	39.2	42.3	49.5	58.5	66.5	74.6	78.3	77.2	70.4	59.1	50.5	42.1	59.0
Mean Minimum Temp. (°F)	28.3	30.4	37.0	45.5	54.3	63.3	67.2	66.2	59.1	46.4	37.9	30.8	47.2
Extreme Maximum Temp. (°F)	80	83	89	94	95	100	104	106	100	94	87	80	106
Extreme Minimum Temp. (°F)	-8	3	9	23	29	42	48	40	36	24	17	0	-8
Days Maximum Temp. ≥ 90°F	0	0	0	1	2	10	16	13	3	0	0	0	45
Days Maximum Temp. ≤ 32°F	2	1	0	0	0	0	0	0	0	0	0	1	4
Days Minimum Temp. ≤ 32°F	22	18	11	2	0	0	0	0	0	2	10	19	84
Days Minimum Temp. ≤ 0°F	0	0	0	0	0	0	0	0	0	0	0	0	0
Heating Degree Days (base 65°F)	794	636	481	226	69	5	0	1	26	210	434	704	3,586
Cooling Degree Days (base 65°F)	0	1	7	37	122	301	419	385	194	35	4	1	1,506
Mean Precipitation (in.)	3.85	3.44	4.60	3.32	3.82	4.19	4.32	4.58	4.15	3.84	3.76	3.42	47.29
Extreme Maximum Daily Precip. (in.)	3.20	2.42	3.27	2.10	3.27	4.62	5.12	4.80	7.68	4.11	4.42	1.96	7.68
Days With ≥ 0.1" Precipitation	7	6	7	7	7	7	7	7	5	5	6	6	77
Days With ≥ 0.5" Precipitation	3	3	3	2	3	3	3	3	3	2	3	2	33
Days With ≥ 1.0" Precipitation	1	1	1	1	1	1	1	1	1	1	1	1	12
Mean Snowfall (in.)	1.9	1.6	0.6	trace	0.0	0.0	0.0	0.0	0.0	0.0	0.1	0.4	4.6
Maximum Snow Depth (in.)	6	4	0	0	0	0	0	0	0	0	trace	trace	6
Days With ≥ 1.0" Snow Depth	0	0	0	0	0	0	0	0	0	0	0	0	0

The period of record for all cooperative weather station data is 1980 – 2009. See User Guide for detailed explanation of data.

Clinton 2 NE *Sampson County* Elevation: 158 ft. Latitude: 35° 01' N Longitude: 78° 17' W

	JAN	FEB	MAR	APR	MAY	JUN	JUL	AUG	SEP	OCT	NOV	DEC	YEAR
Mean Maximum Temp. (°F)	52.4	56.1	63.4	73.0	80.0	86.9	89.9	88.4	82.9	73.9	65.2	55.7	72.3
Mean Temp. (°F)	41.9	45.1	52.0	60.8	68.6	76.5	80.0	78.5	72.6	61.9	53.5	44.9	61.4
Mean Minimum Temp. (°F)	31.4	34.1	40.5	48.5	57.1	65.9	70.1	68.6	62.3	49.9	41.7	34.0	50.3
Extreme Maximum Temp. (°F)	78	83	89	94	96	101	101	104	100	96	84	81	104
Extreme Minimum Temp. (°F)	-2	3	8	26	35	47	53	52	40	27	20	5	-2
Days Maximum Temp. ≥ 90°F	0	0	0	1	3	11	17	14	5	0	0	0	51
Days Maximum Temp. ≤ 32°F	1	0	0	0	0	0	0	0	0	0	0	0	1
Days Minimum Temp. ≤ 32°F	18	14	7	1	0	0	0	0	0	1	6	15	62
Days Minimum Temp. ≤ 0°F	0	0	0	0	0	0	0	0	0	0	0	0	0
Heating Degree Days (base 65°F)	711	557	408	172	44	3	0	0	12	151	351	620	3,029
Cooling Degree Days (base 65°F)	1	2	10	52	163	353	472	427	247	63	12	2	1,804
Mean Precipitation (in.)	3.68	3.17	4.19	2.98	3.57	4.72	6.15	5.71	4.98	3.25	3.16	3.20	48.76
Extreme Maximum Daily Precip. (in.)	3.01	3.03	3.75	2.08	2.70	4.00	4.45	5.40	10.05	4.45	3.93	2.08	10.05
Days With ≥ 0.1" Precipitation	7	6	7	5	7	7	8	8	6	5	5	6	77
Days With ≥ 0.5" Precipitation	3	2	2	2	2	2	3	4	3	3	2	3	31
Days With ≥ 1.0" Precipitation	1	1	1	1	1	1	2	2	1	1	1	1	14
Mean Snowfall (in.)	0.8	0.6	0.6	trace	0.0	0.0	0.0	0.0	0.0	0.0	trace	0.6	2.6
Maximum Snow Depth (in.)	6	5	10	trace	0	0	0	0	0	0	trace	10	10
Days With ≥ 1.0" Snow Depth	1	0	0	0	0	0	0	0	0	0	0	0	1

Concord *Cabarrus County* Elevation: 689 ft. Latitude: 35° 25' N Longitude: 80° 36' W

	JAN	FEB	MAR	APR	MAY	JUN	JUL	AUG	SEP	OCT	NOV	DEC	YEAR
Mean Maximum Temp. (°F)	51.2	55.5	63.4	72.6	79.9	87.1	90.3	88.9	82.5	72.7	63.5	54.1	71.8
Mean Temp. (°F)	40.0	43.4	50.8	59.5	67.7	76.0	79.7	78.4	71.5	60.3	51.0	42.6	60.1
Mean Minimum Temp. (°F)	28.8	31.2	38.1	46.3	55.5	64.8	68.9	67.8	60.4	47.9	38.5	31.0	48.3
Extreme Maximum Temp. (°F)	79	82	89	95	98	100	105	107	100	96	85	81	107
Extreme Minimum Temp. (°F)	-5	6	1	24	32	43	53	50	40	28	17	4	-5
Days Maximum Temp. ≥ 90°F	0	0	0	1	3	12	19	15	5	0	0	0	55
Days Maximum Temp. ≤ 32°F	1	0	0	0	0	0	0	0	0	0	0	0	1
Days Minimum Temp. ≤ 32°F	21	17	9	1	0	0	0	0	0	1	9	19	77
Days Minimum Temp. ≤ 0°F	0	0	0	0	0	0	0	0	0	0	0	0	0
Heating Degree Days (base 65°F)	768	605	440	201	53	4	0	0	19	182	418	689	3,379
Cooling Degree Days (base 65°F)	0	0	7	42	143	341	461	422	220	45	4	1	1,686
Mean Precipitation (in.)	3.55	3.30	4.34	3.61	3.47	4.27	5.10	3.98	3.88	3.75	3.44	3.15	45.84
Extreme Maximum Daily Precip. (in.)	2.24	2.71	2.77	2.85	3.03	3.87	6.40	8.80	4.62	5.60	3.47	2.10	8.80
Days With ≥ 0.1" Precipitation	7	6	7	6	6	7	7	6	5	5	6	6	74
Days With ≥ 0.5" Precipitation	3	2	3	2	2	3	3	2	2	2	2	2	28
Days With ≥ 1.0" Precipitation	1	1	1	1	1	1	1	1	1	1	1	1	12
Mean Snowfall (in.)	1.7	1.4	0.7	trace	0.0	0.0	0.0	0.0	0.0	0.0	trace	0.1	3.9
Maximum Snow Depth (in.)	9	11	7	trace	0	0	0	0	0	0	1	3	11
Days With ≥ 1.0" Snow Depth	2	1	0	0	0	0	0	0	0	0	0	0	3

Danbury 1 NW *Stokes County* Elevation: 839 ft. Latitude: 36° 25' N Longitude: 80° 13' W

	JAN	FEB	MAR	APR	MAY	JUN	JUL	AUG	SEP	OCT	NOV	DEC	YEAR
Mean Maximum Temp. (°F)	47.7	51.7	59.6	69.7	77.0	84.3	87.4	86.0	79.7	70.3	60.7	50.9	68.8
Mean Temp. (°F)	36.3	39.7	46.5	55.9	63.9	72.3	76.0	74.7	67.8	56.8	47.5	39.4	56.4
Mean Minimum Temp. (°F)	25.0	27.5	33.2	42.0	50.8	60.3	64.7	63.3	55.9	43.1	34.3	27.8	44.0
Extreme Maximum Temp. (°F)	80	79	87	92	99	100	100	103	100	92	86	80	103
Extreme Minimum Temp. (°F)	-10	-8	8	22	28	40	47	42	33	21	12	-1	-10
Days Maximum Temp. ≥ 90°F	0	0	0	0	1	6	12	8	3	0	0	0	30
Days Maximum Temp. ≤ 32°F	2	1	0	0	0	0	0	0	0	0	0	1	4
Days Minimum Temp. ≤ 32°F	25	21	14	4	0	0	0	0	0	4	14	22	104
Days Minimum Temp. ≤ 0°F	0	0	0	0	0	0	0	0	0	0	0	0	0
Heating Degree Days (base 65°F)	881	710	570	287	103	10	1	2	46	265	518	787	4,180
Cooling Degree Days (base 65°F)	0	0	2	19	76	235	350	310	138	17	1	0	1,148
Mean Precipitation (in.)	3.32	3.07	4.41	3.67	4.07	4.07	5.00	4.09	4.43	3.43	3.19	3.52	46.27
Extreme Maximum Daily Precip. (in.)	2.05	2.27	4.00	4.27	4.01	3.62	4.35	5.27	4.60	4.70	2.84	2.20	5.27
Days With ≥ 0.1" Precipitation	6	6	7	6	7	7	8	6	5	5	6	6	75
Days With ≥ 0.5" Precipitation	2	2	3	3	3	3	4	2	3	2	2	3	32
Days With ≥ 1.0" Precipitation	1	1	1	1	1	1	1	1	2	1	1	1	13
Mean Snowfall (in.)	2.1	3.1	1.3	0.1	0.0	0.0	0.0	0.0	0.0	0.0	trace	1.3	7.9
Maximum Snow Depth (in.)	15	*9*	7	0	0	0	0	0	0	0	trace	8	*15*
Days With ≥ 1.0" Snow Depth	3	*1*	0	0	0	0	0	0	0	0	0	1	*5*

Dunn 4 NW *Harnett County* Elevation: 200 ft. Latitude: 35° 19' N Longitude: 78° 41' W

	JAN	FEB	MAR	APR	MAY	JUN	JUL	AUG	SEP	OCT	NOV	DEC	YEAR
Mean Maximum Temp. (°F)	52.0	56.2	63.9	73.1	79.9	86.8	89.6	87.9	82.4	73.1	64.4	55.0	72.0
Mean Temp. (°F)	41.1	44.4	51.4	60.1	67.8	76.0	79.5	78.0	71.9	61.0	52.0	43.8	60.6
Mean Minimum Temp. (°F)	30.1	32.6	38.9	47.0	55.7	65.1	69.3	68.1	61.3	48.8	39.4	32.4	49.1
Extreme Maximum Temp. (°F)	79	82	89	93	97	101	102	108	100	95	85	80	108
Extreme Minimum Temp. (°F)	-4	4	10	25	35	45	52	53	37	24	20	1	-4
Days Maximum Temp. ≥ 90°F	0	0	0	1	2	10	16	12	4	0	0	0	45
Days Maximum Temp. ≤ 32°F	1	0	0	0	0	0	0	0	0	0	0	0	1
Days Minimum Temp. ≤ 32°F	19	15	9	1	0	0	0	0	0	1	9	18	72
Days Minimum Temp. ≤ 0°F	0	0	0	0	0	0	0	0	0	0	0	0	0
Heating Degree Days (base 65°F)	734	575	423	186	49	2	0	0	15	170	392	651	3,197
Cooling Degree Days (base 65°F)	1	1	9	45	143	339	455	411	228	52	7	2	1,693
Mean Precipitation (in.)	3.52	3.30	3.99	3.34	3.49	4.61	6.25	5.36	4.18	3.23	3.10	3.25	47.62
Extreme Maximum Daily Precip. (in.)	2.10	2.95	4.50	3.03	2.42	5.85	4.06	4.85	7.40	4.20	2.83	2.42	7.40
Days With ≥ 0.1" Precipitation	7	6	6	6	6	6	9	7	5	4	5	6	73
Days With ≥ 0.5" Precipitation	3	2	3	2	2	3	4	4	3	2	2	2	32
Days With ≥ 1.0" Precipitation	1	1	1	1	1	2	2	2	1	1	1	1	15
Mean Snowfall (in.)	1.1	0.5	0.4	0.0	0.0	0.0	0.0	0.0	0.0	0.0	0.0	0.3	2.3
Maximum Snow Depth (in.)	5	7	8	0	0	0	0	0	0	0	0	0	8
Days With ≥ 1.0" Snow Depth	0	0	0	0	0	0	0	0	0	0	0	0	0

The period of record for all cooperative weather station data is 1980 – 2009. See User Guide for detailed explanation of data.

Elizabeth City *Pasquotank County* Elevation: 7 ft. Latitude: 36° 19' N Longitude: 76° 12' W

	JAN	FEB	MAR	APR	MAY	JUN	JUL	AUG	SEP	OCT	NOV	DEC	YEAR
Mean Maximum Temp. (°F)	52.5	55.4	63.0	71.9	79.3	86.0	89.3	87.6	82.6	74.0	65.0	55.8	71.9
Mean Temp. (°F)	42.4	44.7	51.5	59.9	67.9	76.0	80.1	78.3	73.1	63.0	54.2	45.5	61.4
Mean Minimum Temp. (°F)	32.1	34.1	40.0	48.2	56.5	66.0	70.8	69.0	63.6	52.1	43.3	35.2	50.9
Extreme Maximum Temp. (°F)	78	82	90	95	98	100	102	103	98	94	85	81	103
Extreme Minimum Temp. (°F)	-2	5	14	26	22	43	54	50	44	30	22	5	-2
Days Maximum Temp. ≥ 90°F	0	0	0	0	2	9	14	11	3	0	0	0	39
Days Maximum Temp. ≤ 32°F	1	0	0	0	0	0	0	0	0	0	0	0	1
Days Minimum Temp. ≤ 32°F	17	13	7	1	0	0	0	0	0	0	5	14	57
Days Minimum Temp. ≤ 0°F	0	0	0	0	0	0	0	0	0	0	0	0	0
Heating Degree Days (base 65°F)	696	568	418	187	50	3	0	0	6	125	327	599	2,979
Cooling Degree Days (base 65°F)	0	1	8	42	146	340	474	420	257	71	10	1	1,770
Mean Precipitation (in.)	3.80	3.25	3.79	3.23	3.74	4.60	5.59	5.55	4.27	3.21	3.33	3.50	47.86
Extreme Maximum Daily Precip. (in.)	2.23	2.26	3.70	4.65	3.52	3.35	4.50	3.14	5.40	4.29	4.29	2.50	5.40
Days With ≥ 0.1" Precipitation	7	6	7	6	6	6	8	7	6	5	5	6	75
Days With ≥ 0.5" Precipitation	3	2	3	2	2	3	3	4	3	2	2	2	31
Days With ≥ 1.0" Precipitation	1	1	1	1	1	1	2	2	1	1	1	1	14
Mean Snowfall (in.)	0.1	0.0	0.0	0.0	0.0	0.0	0.0	0.0	0.0	0.0	0.0	0.0	0.1
Maximum Snow Depth (in.)	2	0	0	0	0	0	0	0	0	0	0	0	2
Days With ≥ 1.0" Snow Depth	0	0	0	0	0	0	0	0	0	0	0	0	0

Fayetteville *Cumberland County* Elevation: 96 ft. Latitude: 35° 04' N Longitude: 78° 52' W

	JAN	FEB	MAR	APR	MAY	JUN	JUL	AUG	SEP	OCT	NOV	DEC	YEAR
Mean Maximum Temp. (°F)	52.6	56.4	64.1	73.4	80.4	87.2	90.3	88.4	82.7	73.4	65.1	55.9	72.5
Mean Temp. (°F)	41.8	44.5	51.6	60.3	68.4	76.6	80.4	78.7	72.5	61.5	52.8	44.5	61.1
Mean Minimum Temp. (°F)	30.9	32.7	39.0	47.3	56.4	65.8	70.4	69.0	62.3	49.7	40.5	33.3	49.8
Extreme Maximum Temp. (°F)	79	83	88	95	97	102	103	105	98	96	86	81	105
Extreme Minimum Temp. (°F)	-1	5	14	20	34	47	53	53	41	29	21	4	-1
Days Maximum Temp. ≥ 90°F	0	0	0	1	3	12	18	13	4	0	0	0	51
Days Maximum Temp. ≤ 32°F	1	0	0	0	0	0	0	0	0	0	0	0	1
Days Minimum Temp. ≤ 32°F	18	15	8	1	0	0	0	0	0	1	8	16	67
Days Minimum Temp. ≤ 0°F	0	0	0	0	0	0	0	0	0	0	0	0	0
Heating Degree Days (base 65°F)	713	573	419	182	45	3	0	0	14	156	367	629	3,101
Cooling Degree Days (base 65°F)	1	1	9	50	158	356	484	432	245	56	9	2	1,803
Mean Precipitation (in.)	3.52	3.09	3.95	3.15	3.17	4.48	5.37	5.33	4.47	3.29	2.99	3.07	45.88
Extreme Maximum Daily Precip. (in.)	2.25	2.70	3.84	2.45	5.10	4.18	3.20	3.30	8.25	3.83	2.77	2.03	8.25
Days With ≥ 0.1" Precipitation	7	6	7	5	6	7	8	8	6	5	5	6	76
Days With ≥ 0.5" Precipitation	3	2	3	2	2	3	4	4	3	2	2	2	32
Days With ≥ 1.0" Precipitation	1	1	1	1	1	1	2	2	1	1	1	1	14
Mean Snowfall (in.)	0.4	trace	0.2	0.0	0.0	0.0	0.0	0.0	0.0	0.0	trace	0.0	0.6
Maximum Snow Depth (in.)	5	6	11	0	0	0	0	0	0	0	trace	2	11
Days With ≥ 1.0" Snow Depth	0	0	0	0	0	0	0	0	0	0	0	0	0

Forest City 6 SW *Rutherford County* Elevation: 990 ft. Latitude: 35° 16' N Longitude: 81° 56' W

	JAN	FEB	MAR	APR	MAY	JUN	JUL	AUG	SEP	OCT	NOV	DEC	YEAR
Mean Maximum Temp. (°F)	*50.4*	*55.0*	*62.4*	*71.2*	*79.1*	*86.0*	*89.7*	*87.6*	*81.3*	*72.0*	*62.6*	*53.1*	*70.9*
Mean Temp. (°F)	*38.5*	*42.4*	*49.1*	*57.3*	*65.7*	*73.4*	*77.3*	*75.6*	*69.1*	*58.8*	*49.7*	*41.0*	*58.2*
Mean Minimum Temp. (°F)	*26.5*	*29.8*	*35.8*	*43.5*	*52.3*	*60.8*	*64.8*	*63.6*	*56.8*	*45.5*	*36.7*	*28.9*	*45.4*
Extreme Maximum Temp. (°F)	*78*	*82*	*87*	*93*	*97*	*101*	*106*	*107*	*97*	*91*	*82*	*78*	*107*
Extreme Minimum Temp. (°F)	*-8*	*2*	*5*	*23*	*27*	*39*	*50*	*45*	*35*	*25*	*18*	*-3*	*-8*
Days Maximum Temp. ≥ 90°F	*0*	*0*	*0*	*0*	*1*	*10*	*16*	*12*	*4*	*0*	*0*	*0*	*43*
Days Maximum Temp. ≤ 32°F	*1*	*0*	*0*	*0*	*0*	*0*	*0*	*0*	*0*	*0*	*0*	*1*	*2*
Days Minimum Temp. ≤ 32°F	*23*	*18*	*11*	*3*	*0*	*0*	*0*	*0*	*0*	*2*	*11*	*21*	*89*
Days Minimum Temp. ≤ 0°F	*0*	*0*	*0*	*0*	*0*	*0*	*0*	*0*	*0*	*0*	*0*	*0*	*0*
Heating Degree Days (base 65°F)	*815*	*633*	*489*	*245*	*71*	*4*	*1*	*1*	*31*	*211*	*455*	*736*	*3,692*
Cooling Degree Days (base 65°F)	*0*	*0*	*3*	*23*	*100*	*265*	*388*	*337*	*160*	*25*	*2*	*0*	*1,303*
Mean Precipitation (in.)	*4.45*	*4.24*	*5.11*	*3.89*	*4.44*	*3.99*	*4.41*	*4.25*	*4.03*	*4.04*	*4.03*	*3.96*	*50.84*
Extreme Maximum Daily Precip. (in.)	*3.12*	*4.00*	*3.71*	*2.32*	*3.40*	*3.50*	*3.30*	*6.50*	*6.65*	*4.35*	*3.05*	*2.95*	*6.65*
Days With ≥ 0.1" Precipitation	*7*	*7*	*7*	*7*	*8*	*7*	*8*	*6*	*6*	*5*	*6*	*7*	*81*
Days With ≥ 0.5" Precipitation	*3*	*3*	*4*	*3*	*3*	*3*	*3*	*3*	*3*	*2*	*3*	*3*	*36*
Days With ≥ 1.0" Precipitation	*2*	*1*	*1*	*1*	*1*	*1*	*1*	*1*	*1*	*1*	*1*	*1*	*13*
Mean Snowfall (in.)	*3.1*	*1.3*	*0.9*	*trace*	*0.0*	*0.0*	*0.0*	*0.0*	*0.0*	*0.0*	*trace*	*0.3*	*5.6*
Maximum Snow Depth (in.)	*13*	*7*	*9*	*trace*	*0*	*0*	*0*	*0*	*0*	*0*	*1*	*2*	*13*
Days With ≥ 1.0" Snow Depth	*2*	*1*	*0*	*0*	*0*	*0*	*0*	*0*	*0*	*0*	*0*	*0*	*3*

Gastonia *Gaston County* Elevation: 700 ft. Latitude: 35° 16' N Longitude: 81° 08' W

	JAN	FEB	MAR	APR	MAY	JUN	JUL	AUG	SEP	OCT	NOV	DEC	YEAR
Mean Maximum Temp. (°F)	52.0	56.1	64.1	72.5	79.8	86.7	89.9	88.5	82.3	72.7	63.6	54.0	71.9
Mean Temp. (°F)	41.5	44.7	52.1	60.3	68.4	76.2	79.6	78.6	72.1	61.4	52.2	43.4	60.9
Mean Minimum Temp. (°F)	30.8	33.3	40.1	48.1	56.9	65.6	69.4	68.7	61.9	50.1	40.8	32.8	49.9
Extreme Maximum Temp. (°F)	79	80	87	91	94	100	102	104	98	94	83	80	104
Extreme Minimum Temp. (°F)	-5	11	-1	25	32	44	54	49	39	28	18	3	-5
Days Maximum Temp. ≥ 90°F	0	0	0	0	2	10	17	14	4	0	0	0	47
Days Maximum Temp. ≤ 32°F	1	0	0	0	0	0	0	0	0	0	0	0	1
Days Minimum Temp. ≤ 32°F	17	14	7	1	0	0	0	0	0	1	7	16	63
Days Minimum Temp. ≤ 0°F	0	0	0	0	0	0	0	0	0	0	0	0	0
Heating Degree Days (base 65°F)	722	568	400	177	38	2	0	0	15	153	383	662	3,120
Cooling Degree Days (base 65°F)	0	1	8	43	150	345	461	429	235	50	5	1	1,728
Mean Precipitation (in.)	3.57	3.36	3.79	2.86	3.13	3.83	3.26	4.47	3.66	3.69	3.04	3.24	41.90
Extreme Maximum Daily Precip. (in.)	2.10	2.35	2.20	2.08	2.65	2.91	3.00	6.10	3.94	4.35	2.88	3.11	6.10
Days With ≥ 0.1" Precipitation	6	6	6	6	6	6	6	6	5	5	5	5	68
Days With ≥ 0.5" Precipitation	3	2	3	2	2	2	2	3	2	2	2	2	27
Days With ≥ 1.0" Precipitation	1	1	1	1	1	1	1	1	1	1	1	1	12
Mean Snowfall (in.)	0.5	0.2	0.0	0.0	0.0	0.0	0.0	0.0	0.0	0.0	0.0	trace	0.7
Maximum Snow Depth (in.)	8	11	0	0	0	0	0	0	0	*0*	0	trace	*11*
Days With ≥ 1.0" Snow Depth	0	0	0	0	0	0	0	0	0	0	0	0	0

The period of record for all cooperative weather station data is 1980 – 2009. See User Guide for detailed explanation of data.

Greenville *Pitt County* Elevation: 32 ft. Latitude: 35° 38' N Longitude: 77° 24' W

	JAN	FEB	MAR	APR	MAY	JUN	JUL	AUG	SEP	OCT	NOV	DEC	YEAR
Mean Maximum Temp. (°F)	52.2	56.2	63.9	73.0	80.2	86.9	90.0	88.4	82.8	73.7	64.9	55.6	72.3
Mean Temp. (°F)	42.0	45.1	52.1	60.9	68.7	76.6	80.2	78.6	72.7	62.0	53.0	44.8	61.4
Mean Minimum Temp. (°F)	31.8	34.0	40.3	48.7	57.3	66.2	70.3	68.8	62.5	50.2	41.1	33.9	50.4
Extreme Maximum Temp. (°F)	80	84	91	96	97	103	103	104	100	95	86	82	104
Extreme Minimum Temp. (°F)	-4	4	15	27	37	45	53	50	40	27	19	1	-4
Days Maximum Temp. ≥ 90°F	0	0	0	1	3	11	18	13	4	0	0	0	50
Days Maximum Temp. ≤ 32°F	1	0	0	0	0	0	0	0	0	0	0	1	2
Days Minimum Temp. ≤ 32°F	17	14	7	1	0	0	0	0	0	1	7	15	62
Days Minimum Temp. ≤ 0°F	0	0	0	0	0	0	0	0	0	0	0	0	0
Heating Degree Days (base 65°F)	707	559	405	173	42	1	0	0	12	151	363	623	3,036
Cooling Degree Days (base 65°F)	2	2	13	57	164	356	478	428	249	64	11	3	1,827
Mean Precipitation (in.)	3.85	3.26	4.05	3.24	3.81	4.44	5.27	6.24	5.46	3.39	3.17	3.28	49.46
Extreme Maximum Daily Precip. (in.)	3.49	3.29	2.24	2.99	3.17	3.63	4.11	7.60	10.75	5.60	3.46	1.94	10.75
Days With ≥ 0.1" Precipitation	8	6	7	6	7	7	8	7	6	5	5	6	78
Days With ≥ 0.5" Precipitation	3	2	3	2	3	3	4	4	3	2	2	2	33
Days With ≥ 1.0" Precipitation	1	1	1	1	1	1	2	2	2	1	1	1	15
Mean Snowfall (in.)	1.6	1.0	0.8	trace	0.0	0.0	0.0	0.0	0.0	0.0	0.0	0.5	3.9
Maximum Snow Depth (in.)	8	7	16	trace	0	0	0	0	0	0	0	6	16
Days With ≥ 1.0" Snow Depth	0	0	0	0	0	0	0	0	0	0	0	0	0

Hamlet *Richmond County* Elevation: 350 ft. Latitude: 34° 53' N Longitude: 79° 42' W

	JAN	FEB	MAR	APR	MAY	JUN	JUL	AUG	SEP	OCT	NOV	DEC	YEAR
Mean Maximum Temp. (°F)	53.1	57.8	65.9	75.0	82.2	88.7	91.5	89.6	83.6	74.2	65.3	56.2	73.6
Mean Temp. (°F)	41.3	44.9	52.1	60.9	68.9	76.6	80.0	78.4	72.0	61.3	52.0	43.7	61.0
Mean Minimum Temp. (°F)	29.5	31.9	38.2	46.7	55.7	64.4	68.3	67.1	60.3	48.3	38.6	31.1	48.4
Extreme Maximum Temp. (°F)	80	84	94	95	99	103	106	108	100	96	85	81	108
Extreme Minimum Temp. (°F)	-6	5	7	17	27	32	49	41	35	24	15	3	-6
Days Maximum Temp. ≥ 90°F	0	0	0	1	5	15	21	16	5	1	0	0	64
Days Maximum Temp. ≤ 32°F	1	0	0	0	0	0	0	0	0	0	0	0	1
Days Minimum Temp. ≤ 32°F	20	16	10	2	0	0	0	0	0	2	10	19	79
Days Minimum Temp. ≤ 0°F	0	0	0	0	0	0	0	0	0	0	0	0	0
Heating Degree Days (base 65°F)	728	563	404	169	36	3	0	0	16	163	391	654	3,127
Cooling Degree Days (base 65°F)	1	1	10	54	165	356	471	423	233	56	7	1	1,778
Mean Precipitation (in.)	3.81	3.41	4.00	2.89	3.17	4.58	6.01	4.74	4.63	4.07	3.37	3.13	47.81
Extreme Maximum Daily Precip. (in.)	3.06	1.90	2.35	1.93	3.09	4.32	6.10	3.72	4.60	5.41	3.61	1.72	6.10
Days With ≥ 0.1" Precipitation	7	6	7	6	6	7	9	7	6	6	6	6	79
Days With ≥ 0.5" Precipitation	3	3	3	2	2	3	4	3	3	2	2	2	32
Days With ≥ 1.0" Precipitation	1	1	1	1	1	1	2	1	1	1	1	1	13
Mean Snowfall (in.)	0.3	0.3	0.5	0.0	0.0	0.0	0.0	0.0	0.0	0.0	0.0	trace	1.1
Maximum Snow Depth (in.)	12	trace	8	0	0	0	0	0	0	0	0	1	12
Days With ≥ 1.0" Snow Depth	0	0	0	0	0	0	0	0	0	0	0	0	0

Hickory Regional Arpt *Burke County* Elevation: 1,143 ft. Latitude: 35° 44' N Longitude: 81° 23' W

	JAN	FEB	MAR	APR	MAY	JUN	JUL	AUG	SEP	OCT	NOV	DEC	YEAR
Mean Maximum Temp. (°F)	49.3	53.4	61.1	70.1	77.5	84.7	87.8	86.4	79.6	70.3	61.0	51.5	69.4
Mean Temp. (°F)	39.4	42.8	50.1	58.5	66.3	74.4	77.9	76.6	69.8	59.3	50.2	41.6	58.9
Mean Minimum Temp. (°F)	29.6	32.2	38.9	46.9	55.1	64.0	67.8	66.9	59.9	48.4	39.4	31.7	48.4
Extreme Maximum Temp. (°F)	77	83	86	92	96	100	102	104	95	91	82	78	104
Extreme Minimum Temp. (°F)	-8	2	9	25	30	46	52	45	40	27	17	2	-8
Days Maximum Temp. ≥ 90°F	0	0	0	0	1	7	13	9	2	0	0	0	32
Days Maximum Temp. ≤ 32°F	2	1	0	0	0	0	0	0	0	0	0	1	4
Days Minimum Temp. ≤ 32°F	19	16	8	1	0	0	0	0	0	1	8	18	71
Days Minimum Temp. ≤ 0°F	0	0	0	0	0	0	0	0	0	0	0	0	0
Heating Degree Days (base 65°F)	785	621	460	217	59	3	0	1	25	200	439	719	3,529
Cooling Degree Days (base 65°F)	0	0	4	30	108	293	406	368	175	32	2	0	1,418
Mean Precipitation (in.)	3.59	3.55	4.39	3.78	3.69	4.16	4.38	4.16	3.80	3.44	3.50	3.72	46.16
Extreme Maximum Daily Precip. (in.)	2.60	3.55	3.86	2.74	2.26	4.56	3.96	4.04	4.01	6.31	2.79	2.73	6.31
Days With ≥ 0.1" Precipitation	6	6	7	7	7	7	7	6	6	5	6	6	76
Days With ≥ 0.5" Precipitation	3	2	3	3	2	3	3	3	2	2	2	3	31
Days With ≥ 1.0" Precipitation	1	1	1	1	1	1	1	1	1	1	1	1	12
Mean Snowfall (in.)	na	na	na	na	na	na	na	na	na	na	na	na	na
Maximum Snow Depth (in.)	na	na	na	na	na	na	na	na	na	na	na	na	na
Days With ≥ 1.0" Snow Depth	na	na	na	na	na	na	na	na	na	na	na	na	na

High Point *Guilford County* Elevation: 899 ft. Latitude: 35° 58' N Longitude: 79° 58' W

	JAN	FEB	MAR	APR	MAY	JUN	JUL	AUG	SEP	OCT	NOV	DEC	YEAR
Mean Maximum Temp. (°F)	50.8	55.4	63.4	72.8	79.7	86.5	89.3	88.1	81.8	72.4	62.5	53.0	71.3
Mean Temp. (°F)	40.2	43.9	51.1	59.9	67.4	75.1	78.4	77.2	70.6	60.3	51.1	42.5	59.8
Mean Minimum Temp. (°F)	29.6	32.3	38.6	46.8	55.1	63.7	67.3	66.3	59.4	48.0	39.7	32.0	48.2
Extreme Maximum Temp. (°F)	80	80	88	94	95	102	101	104	98	94	89	80	104
Extreme Minimum Temp. (°F)	-7	2	7	22	33	39	49	46	35	19	16	0	-7
Days Maximum Temp. ≥ 90°F	0	0	0	0	2	9	16	13	4	0	0	0	44
Days Maximum Temp. ≤ 32°F	1	0	0	0	0	0	0	0	0	0	0	1	2
Days Minimum Temp. ≤ 32°F	20	16	9	2	0	0	0	0	0	1	8	17	73
Days Minimum Temp. ≤ 0°F	0	0	0	0	0	0	0	0	0	0	0	0	0
Heating Degree Days (base 65°F)	762	591	433	190	51	4	0	0	23	181	413	692	3,340
Cooling Degree Days (base 65°F)	0	0	8	43	134	314	421	386	198	40	4	1	1,549
Mean Precipitation (in.)	3.54	3.42	4.18	3.84	3.47	3.87	4.49	4.30	3.91	3.41	3.47	3.37	45.27
Extreme Maximum Daily Precip. (in.)	2.50	2.03	2.80	5.10	2.90	3.78	2.94	5.14	4.50	5.61	2.71	1.92	5.61
Days With ≥ 0.1" Precipitation	7	6	8	7	7	7	8	6	6	5	6	6	79
Days With ≥ 0.5" Precipitation	3	3	3	2	2	3	3	3	3	2	3	2	32
Days With ≥ 1.0" Precipitation	1	1	1	1	1	1	1	1	1	1	1	1	12
Mean Snowfall (in.)	1.4	1.4	0.4	trace	0.0	0.0	0.0	0.0	0.0	0.0	trace	0.3	3.5
Maximum Snow Depth (in.)	15	7	8	trace	0	0	0	0	0	0	trace	2	15
Days With ≥ 1.0" Snow Depth	1	1	0	0	0	0	0	0	0	0	0	0	2

Hofmann Forest *Onslow County* Elevation: 43 ft. Latitude: 34° 50' N Longitude: 77° 18' W

	JAN	FEB	MAR	APR	MAY	JUN	JUL	AUG	SEP	OCT	NOV	DEC	YEAR
Mean Maximum Temp. (°F)	56.8	60.9	67.6	75.4	81.8	87.7	90.5	89.1	84.4	76.7	68.7	59.7	74.9
Mean Temp. (°F)	***45.2***	48.3	54.1	61.8	69.0	76.4	80.0	78.7	73.5	64.1	55.8	47.6	***62.9***
Mean Minimum Temp. (°F)	***33.6***	35.7	40.5	48.2	56.3	65.1	69.5	68.4	62.6	51.4	42.7	35.5	***50.8***
Extreme Maximum Temp. (°F)	81	85	92	97	98	104	102	104	98	93	90	82	104
Extreme Minimum Temp. (°F)	2	10	11	25	32	37	50	50	38	23	14	-2	-2
Days Maximum Temp. ≥ 90°F	0	0	0	1	4	12	19	15	5	1	0	0	57
Days Maximum Temp. ≤ 32°F	0	0	0	0	0	0	0	0	0	0	0	0	0
Days Minimum Temp. ≤ 32°F	14	12	8	2	0	0	0	0	0	1	7	14	58
Days Minimum Temp. ≤ 0°F	0	0	0	0	0	0	0	0	0	0	0	0	0
Heating Degree Days (base 65°F)	***608***	470	346	148	35	2	0	0	7	111	292	537	***2,556***
Cooling Degree Days (base 65°F)	***2***	4	14	61	168	350	471	432	269	89	21	4	***1,885***
Mean Precipitation (in.)	4.35	3.84	4.54	3.30	4.13	5.32	6.89	7.31	6.52	4.10	3.83	3.55	57.68
Extreme Maximum Daily Precip. (in.)	4.19	5.15	5.10	3.05	3.90	3.35	4.85	6.20	7.40	4.55	6.20	2.94	7.40
Days With ≥ 0.1" Precipitation	7	6	7	6	7	8	10	9	7	5	5	6	83
Days With ≥ 0.5" Precipitation	3	2	3	2	3	3	4	5	3	2	2	2	34
Days With ≥ 1.0" Precipitation	1	1	1	1	1	2	2	2	2	1	1	1	16
Mean Snowfall (in.)	0.5	0.1	0.1	trace	0.0	0.0	0.0	0.0	0.0	0.0	trace	0.7	1.4
Maximum Snow Depth (in.)	trace	trace	0	trace	0	0	0	0	0	0	trace	3	3
Days With ≥ 1.0" Snow Depth	0	0	0	0	0	0	0	0	0	0	0	0	0

Jefferson 2 E *Ashe County* Elevation: 2,770 ft. Latitude: 36° 25' N Longitude: 81° 26' W

	JAN	FEB	MAR	APR	MAY	JUN	JUL	AUG	SEP	OCT	NOV	DEC	YEAR
Mean Maximum Temp. (°F)	43.5	46.3	54.1	63.0	71.0	77.9	81.0	80.4	74.2	65.0	56.0	46.5	63.2
Mean Temp. (°F)	32.9	35.3	42.0	50.1	58.2	66.0	69.7	68.7	62.1	51.7	43.2	35.3	51.3
Mean Minimum Temp. (°F)	22.3	24.3	29.8	37.2	45.3	54.0	58.3	57.1	50.0	38.4	30.3	24.0	39.3
Extreme Maximum Temp. (°F)	74	74	81	83	90	93	94	96	94	85	79	74	96
Extreme Minimum Temp. (°F)	-15	-6	2	13	22	28	36	33	26	16	6	-9	-15
Days Maximum Temp. ≥ 90°F	0	0	0	0	0	0	1	1	0	0	0	0	2
Days Maximum Temp. ≤ 32°F	5	3	1	0	0	0	0	0	0	0	0	3	12
Days Minimum Temp. ≤ 32°F	26	23	19	9	3	0	0	0	1	9	19	25	134
Days Minimum Temp. ≤ 0°F	1	0	0	0	0	0	0	0	0	0	0	0	1
Heating Degree Days (base 65°F)	987	832	707	442	218	44	10	15	121	407	647	914	5,344
Cooling Degree Days (base 65°F)	0	0	0	2	14	80	162	138	41	2	0	0	439
Mean Precipitation (in.)	3.65	3.45	4.12	3.91	4.23	3.94	4.60	3.99	3.77	2.93	3.78	3.40	45.77
Extreme Maximum Daily Precip. (in.)	4.12	2.60	3.45	2.53	2.52	4.52	3.30	5.22	4.53	5.36	3.52	2.72	5.36
Days With ≥ 0.1" Precipitation	6	6	7	7	8	7	9	7	6	4	6	6	79
Days With ≥ 0.5" Precipitation	2	2	3	3	3	2	3	3	2	2	2	2	29
Days With ≥ 1.0" Precipitation	1	1	1	1	1	1	1	1	1	1	1	1	12
Mean Snowfall (in.)	4.2	3.9	3.0	0.4	0.0	0.0	0.0	0.0	0.0	trace	0.1	2.8	14.4
Maximum Snow Depth (in.)	20	14	24	3	0	0	0	0	0	trace	2	14	24
Days With ≥ 1.0" Snow Depth	3	3	1	0	0	0	0	0	0	0	0	2	9

Laurinburg *Scotland County* Elevation: 209 ft. Latitude: 34° 45' N Longitude: 79° 27' W

	JAN	FEB	MAR	APR	MAY	JUN	JUL	AUG	SEP	OCT	NOV	DEC	YEAR
Mean Maximum Temp. (°F)	53.9	58.7	66.5	75.7	82.8	89.1	91.7	89.8	84.2	75.4	66.1	56.7	74.2
Mean Temp. (°F)	43.0	46.7	53.8	62.2	70.3	77.7	80.9	79.4	73.4	63.0	54.1	45.5	62.5
Mean Minimum Temp. (°F)	32.1	34.6	41.1	48.6	57.7	66.3	70.1	69.0	62.6	50.7	42.0	34.3	50.8
Extreme Maximum Temp. (°F)	80	84	91	96	98	104	104	107	100	97	87	81	107
Extreme Minimum Temp. (°F)	-3	6	8	24	34	47	55	53	41	28	19	6	-3
Days Maximum Temp. ≥ 90°F	0	0	0	1	5	16	21	16	6	1	0	0	66
Days Maximum Temp. ≤ 32°F	1	0	0	0	0	0	0	0	0	0	0	0	1
Days Minimum Temp. ≤ 32°F	17	12	6	1	0	0	0	0	0	1	6	15	58
Days Minimum Temp. ≤ 0°F	0	0	0	0	0	0	0	0	0	0	0	0	0
Heating Degree Days (base 65°F)	675	514	352	141	27	1	0	0	9	127	333	600	2,779
Cooling Degree Days (base 65°F)	1	2	13	64	198	391	500	454	268	73	13	2	1,979
Mean Precipitation (in.)	3.64	3.40	4.07	2.73	3.06	4.73	4.94	5.13	4.65	3.62	3.11	3.07	46.15
Extreme Maximum Daily Precip. (in.)	2.79	2.50	2.99	1.95	3.02	4.19	4.70	4.75	5.58	4.11	3.27	2.05	5.58
Days With ≥ 0.1" Precipitation	7	6	7	5	6	7	8	7	6	5	5	6	75
Days With ≥ 0.5" Precipitation	3	3	3	2	2	3	3	3	3	2	2	2	31
Days With ≥ 1.0" Precipitation	1	1	1	1	1	1	1	2	1	1	1	1	13
Mean Snowfall (in.)	0.9	0.4	0.5	trace	0.0	0.0	0.0	0.0	0.0	0.0	0.0	trace	1.8
Maximum Snow Depth (in.)	8	4	9	trace	0	0	0	0	0	0	0	1	9
Days With ≥ 1.0" Snow Depth	1	0	0	0	0	0	0	0	0	0	0	0	1

Lincolnton 4 W *Lincoln County* Elevation: 899 ft. Latitude: 35° 28' N Longitude: 81° 20' W

	JAN	FEB	MAR	APR	MAY	JUN	JUL	AUG	SEP	OCT	NOV	DEC	YEAR
Mean Maximum Temp. (°F)	50.7	55.3	63.3	72.0	78.9	85.5	88.5	87.1	80.8	71.6	62.0	52.7	70.7
Mean Temp. (°F)	40.1	43.7	50.9	59.0	66.6	74.3	77.7	76.5	69.9	59.5	50.2	42.0	59.2
Mean Minimum Temp. (°F)	29.4	31.9	38.4	45.9	54.4	63.0	66.7	65.8	59.0	47.4	38.5	31.2	47.6
Extreme Maximum Temp. (°F)	78	80	86	91	94	100	102	105	96	92	83	78	105
Extreme Minimum Temp. (°F)	-6	2	6	22	28	41	50	47	36	23	13	1	-6
Days Maximum Temp. ≥ 90°F	0	0	0	0	1	7	13	9	3	0	0	0	33
Days Maximum Temp. ≤ 32°F	1	0	0	0	0	0	0	0	0	0	0	0	1
Days Minimum Temp. ≤ 32°F	19	16	9	2	0	0	0	0	0	2	9	18	75
Days Minimum Temp. ≤ 0°F	0	0	0	0	0	0	0	0	0	0	0	0	0
Heating Degree Days (base 65°F)	765	597	436	204	55	4	0	1	25	197	438	707	3,429
Cooling Degree Days (base 65°F)	0	0	4	30	112	289	399	364	180	35	2	1	1,416
Mean Precipitation (in.)	3.75	3.56	4.59	3.49	4.04	4.23	4.11	4.40	3.56	4.19	3.63	3.82	47.37
Extreme Maximum Daily Precip. (in.)	2.42	3.48	3.87	3.00	2.71	3.74	4.25	4.95	3.80	5.46	3.09	2.40	5.46
Days With ≥ 0.1" Precipitation	6	6	7	6	7	8	7	6	6	5	6	6	76
Days With ≥ 0.5" Precipitation	3	3	3	3	3	3	3	2	2	3	3	3	34
Days With ≥ 1.0" Precipitation	1	1	1	1	1	1	1	1	1	2	1	1	13
Mean Snowfall (in.)	3.1	1.7	1.0	trace	0.0	0.0	0.0	0.0	0.0	0.0	0.1	0.4	6.3
Maximum Snow Depth (in.)	14	6	9	trace	0	0	0	0	0	0	2	4	14
Days With ≥ 1.0" Snow Depth	2	1	0	0	0	0	0	0	0	0	0	0	3

The period of record for all cooperative weather station data is 1980 – 2009. See User Guide for detailed explanation of data.

Longwood *Brunswick County* Elevation: 40 ft. Latitude: 34° 01' N Longitude: 78° 33' W

	JAN	FEB	MAR	APR	MAY	JUN	JUL	AUG	SEP	OCT	NOV	DEC	YEAR
Mean Maximum Temp. (°F)	56.1	59.6	66.1	73.7	80.6	86.2	89.3	88.1	83.4	75.6	67.9	59.1	73.8
Mean Temp. (°F)	44.4	47.2	53.3	60.8	68.5	75.9	79.6	78.3	72.9	63.2	55.0	46.9	62.2
Mean Minimum Temp. (°F)	32.8	34.8	40.4	47.8	56.2	65.6	69.9	68.5	62.3	50.7	42.1	34.7	50.5
Extreme Maximum Temp. (°F)	80	83	87	94	97	101	101	103	98	95	87	82	103
Extreme Minimum Temp. (°F)	0	11	5	21	32	44	50	51	35	26	19	-4	-4
Days Maximum Temp. ≥ 90°F	0	0	0	1	2	7	14	11	4	0	0	0	39
Days Maximum Temp. ≤ 32°F	0	0	0	0	0	0	0	0	0	0	0	0	0
Days Minimum Temp. ≤ 32°F	17	12	8	1	0	0	0	0	0	1	7	15	61
Days Minimum Temp. ≤ 0°F	0	0	0	0	0	0	0	0	0	0	0	0	0
Heating Degree Days (base 65°F)	631	499	365	162	39	2	0	0	9	123	310	557	2,697
Cooling Degree Days (base 65°F)	1	2	9	43	152	336	461	420	253	73	18	4	1,772
Mean Precipitation (in.)	4.02	3.52	4.06	3.06	3.41	5.01	5.55	7.02	6.75	3.73	3.25	3.76	53.14
Extreme Maximum Daily Precip. (in.)	3.53	4.85	4.38	3.10	3.45	3.23	3.63	6.42	12.85	4.86	2.90	4.65	12.85
Days With ≥ 0.1" Precipitation	7	6	6	5	6	7	9	9	7	5	5	6	78
Days With ≥ 0.5" Precipitation	3	2	3	2	2	3	4	4	3	2	2	2	32
Days With ≥ 1.0" Precipitation	1	1	1	1	1	1	2	2	2	1	1	1	15
Mean Snowfall (in.)	0.2	0.1	0.7	0.0	0.0	0.0	0.0	0.0	0.0	0.0	0.0	0.7	1.7
Maximum Snow Depth (in.)	3	1	11	0	0	0	0	0	0	0	0	trace	11
Days With ≥ 1.0" Snow Depth	0	0	0	0	0	0	0	0	0	0	0	0	0

Louisburg *Franklin County* Elevation: 259 ft. Latitude: 36° 06' N Longitude: 78° 18' W

	JAN	FEB	MAR	APR	MAY	JUN	JUL	AUG	SEP	OCT	NOV	DEC	YEAR
Mean Maximum Temp. (°F)	50.8	54.6	62.7	72.3	79.1	86.8	89.6	88.4	82.1	72.5	63.5	54.0	71.4
Mean Temp. (°F)	38.3	40.9	48.6	57.5	65.2	73.9	77.5	***75.9***	***69.5***	58.5	49.2	41.0	***58.0***
Mean Minimum Temp. (°F)	25.5	27.4	34.4	42.6	51.4	61.0	65.4	63.5	56.8	44.1	35.2	27.8	44.6
Extreme Maximum Temp. (°F)	81	83	91	95	96	101	102	105	100	94	85	80	105
Extreme Minimum Temp. (°F)	-10	-1	8	20	30	36	44	40	33	22	11	3	-10
Days Maximum Temp. ≥ 90°F	0	0	0	1	2	11	17	13	4	0	0	0	48
Days Maximum Temp. ≤ 32°F	2	1	0	0	0	0	0	0	0	0	0	1	4
Days Minimum Temp. ≤ 32°F	23	20	15	4	0	0	0	0	0	4	14	22	102
Days Minimum Temp. ≤ 0°F	0	0	0	0	0	0	0	0	0	0	0	0	0
Heating Degree Days (base 65°F)	821	675	507	249	84	8	1	***2***	***33***	224	469	737	***3,810***
Cooling Degree Days (base 65°F)	0	0	6	31	98	283	394	***346***	***173***	29	3	1	***1,364***
Mean Precipitation (in.)	3.62	3.12	4.25	3.24	3.80	3.90	4.57	5.31	4.18	3.45	3.21	3.07	45.72
Extreme Maximum Daily Precip. (in.)	2.50	2.00	3.37	3.70	4.00	4.90	7.24	6.38	7.55	6.10	2.95	2.10	7.55
Days With ≥ 0.1" Precipitation	7	5	7	6	6	6	7	6	6	5	5	6	72
Days With ≥ 0.5" Precipitation	2	2	3	2	3	3	3	4	3	2	2	2	31
Days With ≥ 1.0" Precipitation	1	1	1	1	1	1	1	2	1	1	1	1	13
Mean Snowfall (in.)	1.4	0.4	0.2	trace	0.0	0.0	0.0	0.0	0.0	0.0	trace	0.2	2.2
Maximum Snow Depth (in.)	10	5	2	trace	0	0	0	0	0	0	trace	1	10
Days With ≥ 1.0" Snow Depth	1	0	0	0	0	0	0	0	0	0	0	0	1

Monroe 4 SE *Union County* Elevation: 580 ft. Latitude: 34° 58' N Longitude: 80° 30' W

	JAN	FEB	MAR	APR	MAY	JUN	JUL	AUG	SEP	OCT	NOV	DEC	YEAR
Mean Maximum Temp. (°F)	52.3	56.6	64.5	73.3	80.3	87.3	90.1	88.5	82.4	73.1	63.8	54.7	72.2
Mean Temp. (°F)	41.7	45.1	52.2	60.4	68.2	76.1	79.3	78.0	71.6	61.0	51.8	43.8	60.8
Mean Minimum Temp. (°F)	31.1	33.5	39.9	47.5	56.1	64.8	68.5	67.4	60.7	48.9	39.7	32.9	49.2
Extreme Maximum Temp. (°F)	79	81	86	92	95	100	103	107	98	93	83	79	107
Extreme Minimum Temp. (°F)	-5	6	5	24	32	44	53	51	38	22	14	5	-5
Days Maximum Temp. ≥ 90°F	0	0	0	0	2	11	17	13	4	0	0	0	47
Days Maximum Temp. ≤ 32°F	1	0	0	0	0	0	0	0	0	0	0	0	1
Days Minimum Temp. ≤ 32°F	18	14	8	2	0	0	0	0	0	2	9	17	70
Days Minimum Temp. ≤ 0°F	0	0	0	0	0	0	0	0	0	0	0	0	0
Heating Degree Days (base 65°F)	715	558	398	175	42	3	0	0	17	165	396	651	3,120
Cooling Degree Days (base 65°F)	0	1	9	45	148	342	450	409	221	49	6	1	1,681
Mean Precipitation (in.)	3.96	3.69	4.53	3.07	2.91	4.27	4.34	5.03	4.22	4.09	3.41	3.66	47.18
Extreme Maximum Daily Precip. (in.)	3.62	2.65	3.93	2.70	3.11	2.70	4.54	5.01	6.74	7.72	3.20	2.40	7.72
Days With ≥ 0.1" Precipitation	7	6	7	6	6	7	7	7	5	5	5	6	74
Days With ≥ 0.5" Precipitation	3	3	3	2	2	3	3	3	3	3	3	2	33
Days With ≥ 1.0" Precipitation	1	1	1	1	1	1	1	2	1	1	1	1	13
Mean Snowfall (in.)	1.9	0.6	0.6	trace	0.0	0.0	0.0	0.0	0.0	0.0	trace	0.2	3.3
Maximum Snow Depth (in.)	12	8	5	trace	0	0	0	0	0	0	trace	1	12
Days With ≥ 1.0" Snow Depth	1	1	0	0	0	0	0	0	0	0	0	0	2

New Bern Craven Co Reg Arpt *Craven County* Elevation: 16 ft. Latitude: 35° 04' N Longitude: 77° 03' W

	JAN	FEB	MAR	APR	MAY	JUN	JUL	AUG	SEP	OCT	NOV	DEC	YEAR
Mean Maximum Temp. (°F)	***54.3***	***58.0***	64.8	73.4	80.3	86.7	89.5	88.0	83.0	***74.6***	***66.8***	***57.8***	***73.1***
Mean Temp. (°F)	***44.0***	***46.9***	53.4	61.9	69.5	77.1	80.6	79.3	74.0	***64.0***	***55.6***	***47.0***	***62.8***
Mean Minimum Temp. (°F)	***33.7***	***35.9***	42.0	50.3	58.7	67.4	71.6	70.6	65.0	***53.5***	***44.3***	***36.1***	***52.4***
Extreme Maximum Temp. (°F)	***80***	***83***	90	95	96	101	102	101	98	***95***	***86***	***81***	***102***
Extreme Minimum Temp. (°F)	***1***	***15***	16	29	38	51	56	56	45	***29***	***23***	***-4***	***-4***
Days Maximum Temp. ≥ 90°F	***0***	***0***	0	1	2	9	16	13	4	***0***	***0***	***0***	***45***
Days Maximum Temp. ≤ 32°F	***0***	***0***	0	0	0	0	0	0	0	***0***	***0***	***0***	***0***
Days Minimum Temp. ≤ 32°F	***14***	***11***	5	0	0	0	0	0	0	***0***	***3***	***13***	***46***
Days Minimum Temp. ≤ 0°F	***0***	***0***	0	0	0	0	0	0	0	***0***	***0***	***0***	***0***
Heating Degree Days (base 65°F)	***645***	***508***	365	147	30	0	0	0	5	***109***	***293***	***556***	***2,658***
Cooling Degree Days (base 65°F)	***2***	***4***	13	60	176	369	490	451	283	***86***	***17***	***4***	***1,955***
Mean Precipitation (in.)	***3.88***	***3.45***	4.59	3.34	4.21	4.41	6.38	6.74	5.21	***3.29***	***3.51***	***3.51***	***52.52***
Extreme Maximum Daily Precip. (in.)	***3.84***	***3.20***	3.28	3.52	3.89	3.65	3.49	8.85	6.79	***6.52***	***3.99***	***2.87***	***8.85***
Days With ≥ 0.1" Precipitation	***7***	***6***	7	6	7	8	10	9	6	***5***	***5***	***6***	***82***
Days With ≥ 0.5" Precipitation	***3***	***3***	3	2	3	3	5	4	3	***2***	***2***	***2***	***35***
Days With ≥ 1.0" Precipitation	***1***	***1***	1	1	1	1	2	2	2	***1***	***1***	***1***	***15***
Mean Snowfall (in.)	na	na	na	na	na	na	na	na	na	na	na	na	na
Maximum Snow Depth (in.)	na	na	na	na	na	na	na	na	na	na	na	na	na
Days With ≥ 1.0" Snow Depth	na	na	na	na	na	na	na	na	na	na	na	na	na

The period of record for all cooperative weather station data is 1980 – 2009. See User Guide for detailed explanation of data.

Raleigh 4 SW *Wake County* Elevation: 419 ft. Latitude: 35° 44' N Longitude: 78° 41' W

	JAN	FEB	MAR	APR	MAY	JUN	JUL	AUG	SEP	OCT	NOV	DEC	YEAR
Mean Maximum Temp. (°F)	52.1	56.4	64.0	72.9	79.8	86.3	89.1	87.9	82.3	72.8	63.7	54.7	71.8
Mean Temp. (°F)	42.1	45.4	52.3	60.6	68.2	75.7	79.0	77.9	71.9	61.5	52.6	44.6	61.0
Mean Minimum Temp. (°F)	31.9	34.3	40.3	48.3	56.5	65.1	68.9	67.8	61.5	50.2	41.5	34.5	50.1
Extreme Maximum Temp. (°F)	78	80	87	92	93	99	103	103	99	92	84	78	103
Extreme Minimum Temp. (°F)	-6	11	12	24	34	46	51	49	37	24	19	5	-6
Days Maximum Temp. ≥ 90°F	0	0	0	0	1	8	15	11	3	0	0	0	38
Days Maximum Temp. ≤ 32°F	1	0	0	0	0	0	0	0	0	0	0	0	1
Days Minimum Temp. ≤ 32°F	17	13	7	1	0	0	0	0	0	1	6	14	59
Days Minimum Temp. ≤ 0°F	0	0	0	0	0	0	0	0	0	0	0	0	0
Heating Degree Days (base 65°F)	705	549	397	174	43	3	0	0	16	156	371	627	3,041
Cooling Degree Days (base 65°F)	1	1	9	50	149	332	442	405	230	55	7	1	1,682
Mean Precipitation (in.)	3.93	3.38	4.39	3.02	3.46	4.88	4.59	4.54	4.18	3.63	3.28	3.14	46.42
Extreme Maximum Daily Precip. (in.)	2.90	2.44	3.76	2.04	3.75	6.72	3.97	3.97	4.85	4.10	3.66	2.65	6.72
Days With ≥ 0.1" Precipitation	6	6	7	6	6	7	7	7	6	5	6	6	75
Days With ≥ 0.5" Precipitation	3	3	3	2	2	3	3	3	3	2	3	2	32
Days With ≥ 1.0" Precipitation	1	1	1	1	1	1	1	1	1	1	1	1	12
Mean Snowfall (in.)	1.8	0.8	0.6	trace	0.0	0.0	0.0	0.0	0.0	0.0	0.0	0.2	3.4
Maximum Snow Depth (in.)	12	5	2	trace	0	0	0	0	0	0	3	2	12
Days With ≥ 1.0" Snow Depth	1	1	0	0	0	0	0	0	0	0	0	0	2

Raleigh State Univ *Wake County* Elevation: 399 ft. Latitude: 35° 48' N Longitude: 78° 42' W

	JAN	FEB	MAR	APR	MAY	JUN	JUL	AUG	SEP	OCT	NOV	DEC	YEAR
Mean Maximum Temp. (°F)	49.6	53.8	61.4	70.9	78.5	85.8	89.0	87.4	81.1	71.0	62.1	52.5	70.2
Mean Temp. (°F)	40.3	43.5	50.6	59.7	67.9	75.9	79.5	78.0	71.6	60.6	52.0	43.1	60.2
Mean Minimum Temp. (°F)	30.9	33.3	39.8	48.5	57.2	65.8	69.9	68.6	62.1	50.1	41.8	33.6	50.1
Extreme Maximum Temp. (°F)	80	81	88	93	94	101	103	104	100	92	83	80	104
Extreme Minimum Temp. (°F)	-6	2	12	26	39	47	55	49	42	30	20	4	-6
Days Maximum Temp. ≥ 90°F	0	0	0	1	2	9	15	12	3	0	0	0	42
Days Maximum Temp. ≤ 32°F	2	1	0	0	0	0	0	0	0	0	0	1	4
Days Minimum Temp. ≤ 32°F	18	14	7	1	0	0	0	0	0	0	5	15	60
Days Minimum Temp. ≤ 0°F	0	0	0	0	0	0	0	0	0	0	0	0	0
Heating Degree Days (base 65°F)	760	601	446	196	50	4	0	0	17	175	389	674	3,312
Cooling Degree Days (base 65°F)	1	1	8	44	146	336	455	411	223	45	5	1	1,676
Mean Precipitation (in.)	3.80	3.30	4.35	2.86	3.51	4.51	4.38	4.47	4.22	3.69	3.40	3.35	45.84
Extreme Maximum Daily Precip. (in.)	2.70	2.16	3.21	2.30	3.60	5.37	3.13	3.80	6.04	5.34	4.67	2.58	6.04
Days With ≥ 0.1" Precipitation	7	6	7	6	6	7	7	7	5	5	5	6	74
Days With ≥ 0.5" Precipitation	2	2	3	2	2	3	3	3	3	2	2	3	30
Days With ≥ 1.0" Precipitation	1	1	1	1	1	1	1	2	1	1	1	1	13
Mean Snowfall (in.)	2.2	0.9	0.6	trace	0.0	0.0	0.0	0.0	0.0	0.0	0.1	0.3	4.1
Maximum Snow Depth (in.)	14	6	8	trace	0	0	0	0	0	0	trace	4	14
Days With ≥ 1.0" Snow Depth	2	1	0	0	0	0	0	0	0	0	0	0	3

Reidsville 2 NW *Rockingham County* Elevation: 890 ft. Latitude: 36° 23' N Longitude: 79° 42' W

	JAN	FEB	MAR	APR	MAY	JUN	JUL	AUG	SEP	OCT	NOV	DEC	YEAR
Mean Maximum Temp. (°F)	47.5	51.5	59.2	68.9	76.6	84.3	87.7	86.4	79.8	69.9	60.4	50.7	68.6
Mean Temp. (°F)	37.8	40.9	48.1	57.5	65.5	73.9	77.4	76.0	69.1	58.3	49.5	40.9	57.9
Mean Minimum Temp. (°F)	28.1	30.4	37.0	46.1	54.3	63.4	67.0	65.5	58.4	46.7	38.6	31.0	47.2
Extreme Maximum Temp. (°F)	79	80	87	92	95	99	100	103	98	93	83	80	103
Extreme Minimum Temp. (°F)	-9	0	10	23	34	44	50	45	35	27	16	-1	-9
Days Maximum Temp. ≥ 90°F	0	0	0	0	1	7	12	10	3	0	0	0	33
Days Maximum Temp. ≤ 32°F	3	1	0	0	0	0	0	0	0	0	0	1	5
Days Minimum Temp. ≤ 32°F	21	17	10	2	0	0	0	0	0	1	8	19	78
Days Minimum Temp. ≤ 0°F	0	0	0	0	0	0	0	0	0	0	0	0	0
Heating Degree Days (base 65°F)	835	674	521	247	83	7	1	2	35	230	460	742	3,837
Cooling Degree Days (base 65°F)	0	0	5	30	104	281	390	348	165	30	2	0	1,355
Mean Precipitation (in.)	3.75	3.29	4.28	3.93	3.71	3.99	4.69	3.87	4.04	3.36	3.48	3.25	45.64
Extreme Maximum Daily Precip. (in.)	2.52	2.65	3.15	5.07	3.60	4.27	3.62	4.45	4.70	4.00	3.00	2.50	5.07
Days With ≥ 0.1" Precipitation	7	6	7	7	7	7	7	6	5	5	5	6	75
Days With ≥ 0.5" Precipitation	3	3	3	3	2	3	3	2	2	2	3	2	31
Days With ≥ 1.0" Precipitation	1	1	1	1	1	1	2	1	1	1	1	1	13
Mean Snowfall (in.)	3.2	3.2	0.9	trace	0.0	0.0	0.0	0.0	0.0	0.0	trace	0.7	8.0
Maximum Snow Depth (in.)	13	10	9	trace	0	0	0	0	0	0	trace	6	13
Days With ≥ 1.0" Snow Depth	3	2	1	0	0	0	0	0	0	0	0	1	7

Roxboro 7 ESE *Person County* Elevation: 709 ft. Latitude: 36° 19' N Longitude: 78° 54' W

	JAN	FEB	MAR	APR	MAY	JUN	JUL	AUG	SEP	OCT	NOV	DEC	YEAR
Mean Maximum Temp. (°F)	48.3	52.6	60.5	70.4	77.2	84.7	88.1	87.1	80.6	70.9	62.1	51.5	69.5
Mean Temp. (°F)	37.1	40.3	47.3	56.7	64.8	72.7	76.6	75.4	68.4	57.4	48.5	39.7	57.1
Mean Minimum Temp. (°F)	25.8	27.9	34.1	43.0	52.3	60.7	65.1	63.7	56.2	43.8	35.1	27.8	44.6
Extreme Maximum Temp. (°F)	79	81	87	96	92	98	102	103	99	93	83	80	103
Extreme Minimum Temp. (°F)	-9	-8	7	20	30	38	45	41	37	22	13	-1	-9
Days Maximum Temp. ≥ 90°F	0	0	0	1	1	7	12	11	3	0	0	0	35
Days Maximum Temp. ≤ 32°F	3	1	0	0	0	0	0	0	0	0	0	1	5
Days Minimum Temp. ≤ 32°F	23	21	14	4	0	0	0	0	0	4	13	21	100
Days Minimum Temp. ≤ 0°F	0	0	0	0	0	0	0	0	0	0	0	0	0
Heating Degree Days (base 65°F)	859	693	546	265	92	10	1	2	42	253	490	778	4,031
Cooling Degree Days (base 65°F)	0	0	4	24	92	249	368	332	151	23	2	0	1,245
Mean Precipitation (in.)	3.63	3.08	4.48	3.43	3.33	3.84	4.65	3.95	3.72	3.90	3.55	3.56	45.12
Extreme Maximum Daily Precip. (in.)	***3.47***	***2.25***	3.70	2.41	***2.92***	***3.21***	3.37	5.21	6.78	4.30	4.71	3.40	***6.78***
Days With ≥ 0.1" Precipitation	6	6	7	6	6	6	7	5	5	5	5	5	69
Days With ≥ 0.5" Precipitation	3	2	3	2	2	2	3	2	2	2	3	2	28
Days With ≥ 1.0" Precipitation	1	1	1	1	1	1	2	1	1	2	1	1	14
Mean Snowfall (in.)	2.3	2.6	1.1	trace	0.0	0.0	0.0	0.0	0.0	trace	0.1	0.8	6.9
Maximum Snow Depth (in.)	10	13	12	trace	0	0	0	0	0	trace	1	6	13
Days With ≥ 1.0" Snow Depth	2	2	0	0	0	0	0	0	0	0	0	1	5

The period of record for all cooperative weather station data is 1980 – 2009. See User Guide for detailed explanation of data.

Salisbury *Rowan County* Elevation: 700 ft. Latitude: 35° 41' N Longitude: 80° 29' W

	JAN	FEB	MAR	APR	MAY	JUN	JUL	AUG	SEP	OCT	NOV	DEC	YEAR
Mean Maximum Temp. (°F)	51.5	56.0	64.0	73.0	79.9	86.5	89.4	88.4	81.7	72.4	63.1	53.3	71.6
Mean Temp. (°F)	40.5	44.2	51.4	60.0	67.7	75.5	78.8	77.9	70.7	60.1	51.2	42.4	60.0
Mean Minimum Temp. (°F)	29.5	32.3	38.7	47.0	55.5	64.4	68.3	67.3	59.7	47.7	39.2	31.4	48.4
Extreme Maximum Temp. (°F)	78	80	89	93	98	98	103	105	99	92	82	79	105
Extreme Minimum Temp. (°F)	-4	4	2	21	32	44	50	48	35	21	18	3	-4
Days Maximum Temp. ≥ 90°F	0	0	0	0	2	10	16	12	4	0	0	0	44
Days Maximum Temp. ≤ 32°F	1	0	0	0	0	0	0	0	0	0	0	0	1
Days Minimum Temp. ≤ 32°F	20	16	8	2	0	0	0	0	0	2	9	18	75
Days Minimum Temp. ≤ 0°F	0	0	0	0	0	0	0	0	0	0	0	0	0
Heating Degree Days (base 65°F)	752	582	422	182	46	3	0	0	22	184	411	696	3,300
Cooling Degree Days (base 65°F)	0	1	6	40	137	324	436	405	201	39	3	1	1,593
Mean Precipitation (in.)	3.03	3.46	4.21	3.56	3.05	3.96	3.84	3.13	3.46	3.31	2.97	3.05	41.03
Extreme Maximum Daily Precip. (in.)	1.80	2.25	2.96	3.32	2.18	3.69	3.30	5.90	4.17	4.48	***2.90***	2.30	***5.90***
Days With ≥ 0.1" Precipitation	6	6	7	6	6	6	6	5	5	5	5	5	68
Days With ≥ 0.5" Precipitation	2	3	3	3	2	2	3	2	2	2	2	2	28
Days With ≥ 1.0" Precipitation	1	1	1	1	1	1	1	1	1	1	1	1	12
Mean Snowfall (in.)	2.1	0.9	0.2	0.0	0.0	0.0	0.0	0.0	0.0	0.0	trace	0.3	3.5
Maximum Snow Depth (in.)	8	10	0	0	0	0	0	0	0	0	***trace***	2	***10***
Days With ≥ 1.0" Snow Depth	***0***	0	0	0	0	0	0	0	0	0	0	0	***0***

Sanford 8 NE *Lee County* Elevation: 262 ft. Latitude: 35° 32' N Longitude: 79° 03' W

	JAN	FEB	MAR	APR	MAY	JUN	JUL	AUG	SEP	OCT	NOV	DEC	YEAR
Mean Maximum Temp. (°F)	52.8	57.4	65.6	74.9	81.4	87.9	90.8	89.0	83.0	73.8	64.3	55.3	73.0
Mean Temp. (°F)	41.0	44.5	51.7	60.2	67.7	75.4	79.0	77.4	71.0	60.4	51.2	43.2	60.2
Mean Minimum Temp. (°F)	29.2	31.5	37.7	45.4	54.0	62.9	67.2	65.8	59.0	46.9	38.1	31.2	47.4
Extreme Maximum Temp. (°F)	80	83	91	93	96	101	104	107	100	93	86	80	107
Extreme Minimum Temp. (°F)	-3	0	11	19	29	35	41	45	34	19	11	2	-3
Days Maximum Temp. ≥ 90°F	0	0	0	1	3	13	19	14	5	0	0	0	55
Days Maximum Temp. ≤ 32°F	1	0	0	0	0	0	0	0	0	0	0	0	1
Days Minimum Temp. ≤ 32°F	20	16	11	4	0	0	0	0	0	3	11	19	84
Days Minimum Temp. ≤ 0°F	0	0	0	0	0	0	0	0	0	0	0	0	0
Heating Degree Days (base 65°F)	737	575	417	187	53	4	0	1	21	184	412	669	3,260
Cooling Degree Days (base 65°F)	1	1	10	49	144	323	441	393	208	47	6	1	1,624
Mean Precipitation (in.)	3.81	3.44	4.07	2.93	3.48	4.71	5.03	4.64	4.18	3.70	3.34	2.96	46.29
Extreme Maximum Daily Precip. (in.)	2.88	2.50	2.60	2.06	3.34	6.10	3.50	4.35	6.14	3.50	3.76	2.16	6.14
Days With ≥ 0.1" Precipitation	6	6	7	5	6	6	8	7	5	5	6	5	72
Days With ≥ 0.5" Precipitation	3	3	3	2	3	3	3	3	3	2	2	2	32
Days With ≥ 1.0" Precipitation	1	1	1	1	1	2	1	1	1	1	1	1	13
Mean Snowfall (in.)	1.3	0.5	0.4	trace	0.0	0.0	0.0	0.0	0.0	0.0	trace	0.2	2.4
Maximum Snow Depth (in.)	17	5	trace	0	0	0	0	0	0	0	1	2	17
Days With ≥ 1.0" Snow Depth	1	0	0	0	0	0	0	0	0	0	0	0	1

Siler City 2 N *Chatham County* Elevation: 609 ft. Latitude: 35° 46' N Longitude: 79° 28' W

	JAN	FEB	MAR	APR	MAY	JUN	JUL	AUG	SEP	OCT	NOV	DEC	YEAR
Mean Maximum Temp. (°F)	49.7	53.7	61.7	70.8	77.8	85.0	88.3	87.1	80.5	70.8	62.0	52.6	70.0
Mean Temp. (°F)	39.4	42.5	49.9	58.5	66.4	74.5	78.1	76.7	69.9	59.1	50.5	42.3	59.0
Mean Minimum Temp. (°F)	29.0	31.2	38.1	46.2	54.9	63.8	67.7	66.3	59.2	47.3	39.1	32.0	47.9
Extreme Maximum Temp. (°F)	79	81	88	92	96	99	101	105	99	92	85	79	105
Extreme Minimum Temp. (°F)	-11	2	0	23	33	44	52	47	34	25	16	1	-11
Days Maximum Temp. ≥ 90°F	0	0	0	0	1	7	13	11	3	0	0	0	35
Days Maximum Temp. ≤ 32°F	2	1	0	0	0	0	0	0	0	0	0	1	4
Days Minimum Temp. ≤ 32°F	21	16	9	2	0	0	0	0	0	1	9	18	76
Days Minimum Temp. ≤ 0°F	0	0	0	0	0	0	0	0	0	0	0	0	0
Heating Degree Days (base 65°F)	788	631	466	226	68	6	0	1	28	211	430	697	3,552
Cooling Degree Days (base 65°F)	0	1	7	37	117	296	412	372	182	33	4	1	1,462
Mean Precipitation (in.)	3.87	3.42	4.61	3.47	3.86	3.89	4.60	4.27	4.09	3.85	3.55	3.22	46.70
Extreme Maximum Daily Precip. (in.)	3.08	2.85	4.65	2.83	3.15	2.79	4.27	6.15	6.00	4.93	2.91	2.04	6.15
Days With ≥ 0.1" Precipitation	7	6	7	6	6	7	7	6	5	5	6	6	74
Days With ≥ 0.5" Precipitation	2	2	3	2	3	3	3	3	2	2	3	2	30
Days With ≥ 1.0" Precipitation	1	1	1	1	1	1	1	1	1	1	1	1	12
Mean Snowfall (in.)	1.2	0.7	0.4	trace	0.0	0.0	0.0	0.0	0.0	0.0	0.0	0.1	2.4
Maximum Snow Depth (in.)	22	3	5	trace	0	0	0	0	0	0	0	trace	22
Days With ≥ 1.0" Snow Depth	0	0	0	0	0	0	0	0	0	0	0	0	0

Southport 5 N *Brunswick County* Elevation: 20 ft. Latitude: 34° 00' N Longitude: 78° 01' W

	JAN	FEB	MAR	APR	MAY	JUN	JUL	AUG	SEP	OCT	NOV	DEC	YEAR
Mean Maximum Temp. (°F)	57.1	59.1	65.6	73.1	79.8	85.9	89.2	***88.3***	83.6	76.0	68.6	59.8	***73.8***
Mean Temp. (°F)	45.3	47.4	54.0	61.3	69.0	76.6	80.4	***79.1***	73.7	64.1	56.1	47.8	***62.9***
Mean Minimum Temp. (°F)	33.3	35.6	42.0	49.6	58.1	67.3	71.6	***69.9***	63.7	52.1	43.6	35.7	***51.9***
Extreme Maximum Temp. (°F)	83	81	88	94	94	101	102	102	96	94	88	83	102
Extreme Minimum Temp. (°F)	0	9	8	25	37	46	52	54	35	25	16	-3	-3
Days Maximum Temp. ≥ 90°F	0	0	0	0	1	7	14	11	3	0	0	0	36
Days Maximum Temp. ≤ 32°F	0	0	0	0	0	0	0	0	0	0	0	0	0
Days Minimum Temp. ≤ 32°F	15	12	6	1	0	0	0	0	0	1	5	13	53
Days Minimum Temp. ≤ 0°F	0	0	0	0	0	0	0	0	0	0	0	0	0
Heating Degree Days (base 65°F)	604	491	344	152	30	2	0	***0***	6	110	280	532	***2,551***
Cooling Degree Days (base 65°F)	1	1	10	48	160	356	483	***444***	273	87	20	5	***1,888***
Mean Precipitation (in.)	4.20	3.73	4.30	2.90	3.58	4.42	5.85	6.94	8.44	4.19	3.63	3.95	56.13
Extreme Maximum Daily Precip. (in.)	2.56	5.00	5.02	***5.10***	5.24	3.86	4.50	***10.00***	18.30	8.60	3.30	2.74	***18.30***
Days With ≥ 0.1" Precipitation	7	6	6	4	6	6	8	9	7	5	5	6	75
Days With ≥ 0.5" Precipitation	3	3	3	2	3	3	4	4	4	2	2	2	35
Days With ≥ 1.0" Precipitation	1	1	1	1	1	1	2	2	3	1	1	1	16
Mean Snowfall (in.)	trace	0.0	0.3	0.0	0.0	0.0	0.0	0.0	0.0	0.0	0.0	0.5	0.8
Maximum Snow Depth (in.)	0	0	8	0	0	0	0	0	0	***0***	0	0	***8***
Days With ≥ 1.0" Snow Depth	0	0	0	0	0	0	0	0	0	0	0	0	0

The period of record for all cooperative weather station data is 1980 – 2009. See User Guide for detailed explanation of data.

Statesville 2 NNE *Iredell County* Elevation: 950 ft. Latitude: 35° 49' N Longitude: 80° 53' W

	JAN	FEB	MAR	APR	MAY	JUN	JUL	AUG	SEP	OCT	NOV	DEC	YEAR
Mean Maximum Temp. (°F)	50.4	54.6	62.8	72.0	79.1	85.8	88.6	87.2	80.8	71.5	61.9	52.1	70.6
Mean Temp. (°F)	38.7	42.0	49.3	57.9	66.1	73.9	77.3	76.1	69.3	58.6	48.9	40.4	58.2
Mean Minimum Temp. (°F)	27.0	29.2	35.8	43.6	52.9	61.9	66.0	65.0	57.8	45.7	35.9	28.9	45.8
Extreme Maximum Temp. (°F)	78	81	88	94	97	101	102	106	99	92	82	79	106
Extreme Minimum Temp. (°F)	-7	2	10	17	29	41	46	44	33	21	13	1	-7
Days Maximum Temp. ≥ 90°F	0	0	0	1	2	9	14	10	3	0	0	0	39
Days Maximum Temp. ≤ 32°F	1	0	0	0	0	0	0	0	0	0	0	1	2
Days Minimum Temp. ≤ 32°F	22	19	12	4	0	0	0	0	0	3	13	21	94
Days Minimum Temp. ≤ 0°F	0	0	0	0	0	0	0	0	0	0	0	0	0
Heating Degree Days (base 65°F)	808	645	482	235	69	5	0	1	30	220	478	756	3,729
Cooling Degree Days (base 65°F)	0	0	3	27	109	277	389	352	166	29	2	1	1,355
Mean Precipitation (in.)	3.40	3.29	4.24	3.59	3.38	4.29	4.06	3.84	3.66	3.38	3.35	3.58	44.06
Extreme Maximum Daily Precip. (in.)	2.29	2.14	4.20	3.73	3.24	6.02	3.24	4.53	4.20	2.80	2.35	2.30	6.02
Days With ≥ 0.1" Precipitation	6	6	7	7	6	7	7	6	5	5	6	6	74
Days With ≥ 0.5" Precipitation	2	2	3	2	2	3	2	2	2	2	3	3	28
Days With ≥ 1.0" Precipitation	1	1	1	1	1	1	1	1	1	1	1	1	12
Mean Snowfall (in.)	2.2	1.2	0.6	0.0	0.0	0.0	0.0	0.0	0.0	0.0	trace	0.4	4.4
Maximum Snow Depth (in.)	8	6	4	0	0	0	0	0	0	0	trace	4	8
Days With ≥ 1.0" Snow Depth	1	1	0	0	0	0	0	0	0	0	0	0	2

Tarboro 1 S *Edgecombe County* Elevation: 35 ft. Latitude: 35° 53' N Longitude: 77° 32' W

	JAN	FEB	MAR	APR	MAY	JUN	JUL	AUG	SEP	OCT	NOV	DEC	YEAR
Mean Maximum Temp. (°F)	51.9	55.4	63.2	72.5	79.9	87.1	90.0	88.5	82.8	73.4	64.1	54.8	72.0
Mean Temp. (°F)	40.8	43.6	50.6	59.4	67.6	75.8	79.4	77.9	71.9	61.2	51.8	43.4	60.3
Mean Minimum Temp. (°F)	29.5	31.6	38.0	46.3	55.3	64.5	68.8	67.3	61.0	48.8	39.5	32.1	48.6
Extreme Maximum Temp. (°F)	79	84	91	96	98	101	103	105	100	94	85	82	105
Extreme Minimum Temp. (°F)	-5	2	8	26	34	44	49	48	37	25	20	0	-5
Days Maximum Temp. ≥ 90°F	0	0	0	1	3	11	17	14	4	0	0	0	50
Days Maximum Temp. ≤ 32°F	1	0	0	0	0	0	0	0	0	0	0	0	1
Days Minimum Temp. ≤ 32°F	20	16	9	2	0	0	0	0	0	1	9	17	74
Days Minimum Temp. ≤ 0°F	0	0	0	0	0	0	0	0	0	0	0	0	0
Heating Degree Days (base 65°F)	745	600	446	202	54	3	0	0	13	165	395	663	3,286
Cooling Degree Days (base 65°F)	1	1	8	42	142	334	454	408	227	53	7	1	1,678
Mean Precipitation (in.)	3.64	3.25	3.90	3.15	3.26	3.93	4.74	5.00	4.28	2.96	2.89	3.02	44.02
Extreme Maximum Daily Precip. (in.)	3.73	2.33	2.18	2.17	3.44	2.80	4.00	3.27	5.80	2.93	5.60	2.50	5.80
Days With ≥ 0.1" Precipitation	7	6	7	6	6	6	7	7	5	4	5	6	72
Days With ≥ 0.5" Precipitation	3	3	3	2	2	3	3	3	2	2	2	2	30
Days With ≥ 1.0" Precipitation	1	1	1	1	1	1	1	2	1	1	1	1	13
Mean Snowfall (in.)	1.8	1.6	1.1	trace	0.0	0.0	0.0	0.0	0.0	0.0	trace	0.8	5.3
Maximum Snow Depth (in.)	8	3	12	trace	0	0	0	0	0	0	trace	12	12
Days With ≥ 1.0" Snow Depth	1	0	0	0	0	0	0	0	0	0	0	0	1

Tryon *Polk County* Elevation: 1,080 ft. Latitude: 35° 12' N Longitude: 82° 14' W

	JAN	FEB	MAR	APR	MAY	JUN	JUL	AUG	SEP	OCT	NOV	DEC	YEAR
Mean Maximum Temp. (°F)	52.2	56.3	64.3	72.8	79.5	85.6	88.5	87.3	81.0	72.1	62.8	54.0	71.4
Mean Temp. (°F)	41.9	45.1	52.2	60.1	67.5	74.6	78.0	76.9	70.6	60.8	52.0	43.9	60.3
Mean Minimum Temp. (°F)	31.6	33.9	40.0	47.3	55.4	63.5	67.5	66.6	60.2	49.3	41.0	33.7	49.2
Extreme Maximum Temp. (°F)	80	82	89	94	97	98	102	103	96	91	83	81	103
Extreme Minimum Temp. (°F)	-8	8	14	26	33	44	51	49	40	26	20	3	-8
Days Maximum Temp. ≥ 90°F	0	0	0	1	1	9	13	11	3	0	0	0	38
Days Maximum Temp. ≤ 32°F	1	0	0	0	0	0	0	0	0	0	0	0	1
Days Minimum Temp. ≤ 32°F	17	13	6	1	0	0	0	0	0	1	6	15	59
Days Minimum Temp. ≤ 0°F	0	0	0	0	0	0	0	0	0	0	0	0	0
Heating Degree Days (base 65°F)	708	556	397	178	44	3	0	0	17	162	387	648	3,100
Cooling Degree Days (base 65°F)	0	0	6	37	127	297	410	378	191	38	3	1	1,488
Mean Precipitation (in.)	4.98	4.75	6.00	4.67	4.73	5.45	5.46	6.02	5.50	4.56	4.81	5.14	62.07
Extreme Maximum Daily Precip. (in.)	4.00	4.69	4.60	2.58	5.50	6.25	6.55	7.15	8.47	5.06	3.83	4.28	8.47
Days With ≥ 0.1" Precipitation	7	7	7	7	8	8	8	7	7	5	6	7	84
Days With ≥ 0.5" Precipitation	3	3	4	3	3	3	3	3	3	3	3	4	38
Days With ≥ 1.0" Precipitation	2	1	2	2	1	2	1	2	2	2	2	2	21
Mean Snowfall (in.)	3.0	1.5	1.0	trace	trace	0.0	0.0	0.0	0.0	0.0	trace	0.4	5.9
Maximum Snow Depth (in.)	16	7	10	trace	trace	0	0	0	0	0	trace	3	16
Days With ≥ 1.0" Snow Depth	2	1	1	0	0	0	0	0	0	0	0	0	4

Waynesville 1 E *Haywood County* Elevation: 2,658 ft. Latitude: 35° 29' N Longitude: 82° 58' W

	JAN	FEB	MAR	APR	MAY	JUN	JUL	AUG	SEP	OCT	NOV	DEC	YEAR
Mean Maximum Temp. (°F)	49.2	52.5	59.7	67.6	74.8	80.9	83.5	82.7	77.0	68.8	60.0	51.5	67.4
Mean Temp. (°F)	36.5	39.3	45.9	53.3	60.9	68.0	71.3	70.6	64.4	54.7	45.9	38.7	54.1
Mean Minimum Temp. (°F)	23.6	26.1	32.0	38.9	47.1	55.1	59.0	58.4	51.7	40.4	31.7	25.7	40.8
Extreme Maximum Temp. (°F)	75	79	84	87	92	92	95	94	92	85	81	72	95
Extreme Minimum Temp. (°F)	-22	-13	-8	15	24	34	40	41	28	17	7	-6	-22
Days Maximum Temp. ≥ 90°F	0	0	0	0	0	1	2	2	0	0	0	0	5
Days Maximum Temp. ≤ 32°F	2	1	0	0	0	0	0	0	0	0	0	1	4
Days Minimum Temp. ≤ 32°F	24	21	17	8	2	0	0	0	0	8	17	23	120
Days Minimum Temp. ≤ 0°F	1	0	0	0	0	0	0	0	0	0	0	0	1
Heating Degree Days (base 65°F)	878	720	587	349	149	23	2	5	76	319	567	810	4,485
Cooling Degree Days (base 65°F)	0	0	1	4	30	120	205	185	64	5	0	0	614
Mean Precipitation (in.)	4.31	4.41	4.63	3.80	4.35	4.03	3.71	4.19	3.95	2.67	3.72	3.95	47.72
Extreme Maximum Daily Precip. (in.)	3.78	3.90	3.45	2.05	3.80	1.78	2.65	3.90	5.25	3.88	3.10	2.37	5.25
Days With ≥ 0.1" Precipitation	8	7	8	8	8	8	9	8	7	5	6	8	90
Days With ≥ 0.5" Precipitation	3	3	3	3	3	3	2	3	2	2	3	3	33
Days With ≥ 1.0" Precipitation	1	1	1	1	1	1	1	1	1	1	1	1	12
Mean Snowfall (in.)	4.4	3.1	2.4	1.2	0.2	0.0	0.0	0.0	0.0	trace	0.4	1.8	13.5
Maximum Snow Depth (in.)	17	5	18	16	5	0	0	0	0	trace	3	13	18
Days With ≥ 1.0" Snow Depth	3	2	1	0	0	0	0	0	0	0	0	1	7

The period of record for all cooperative weather station data is 1980 – 2009. See User Guide for detailed explanation of data.

Wilson 3 SW *Wilson County* Elevation: 109 ft. Latitude: 35° 42' N Longitude: 77° 57' W

	JAN	FEB	MAR	APR	MAY	JUN	JUL	AUG	SEP	OCT	NOV	DEC	YEAR
Mean Maximum Temp. (°F)	51.4	55.2	62.8	72.2	79.8	87.3	90.3	88.8	82.9	73.3	64.5	54.7	71.9
Mean Temp. (°F)	40.9	43.7	50.8	59.6	67.8	76.1	79.6	78.1	71.9	61.1	52.4	43.8	60.5
Mean Minimum Temp. (°F)	30.3	32.3	38.7	47.0	55.8	64.8	68.8	67.4	60.8	48.8	40.2	32.8	49.0
Extreme Maximum Temp. (°F)	81	83	91	96	96	102	104	105	101	94	86	81	105
Extreme Minimum Temp. (°F)	-5	5	7	26	36	43	49	49	38	25	18	3	-5
Days Maximum Temp. ≥ 90°F	0	0	0	1	3	11	18	15	5	0	0	0	53
Days Maximum Temp. ≤ 32°F	1	0	0	0	0	0	0	0	0	0	0	1	2
Days Minimum Temp. ≤ 32°F	19	15	8	1	0	0	0	0	0	1	7	16	67
Days Minimum Temp. ≤ 0°F	0	0	0	0	0	0	0	0	0	0	0	0	0
Heating Degree Days (base 65°F)	741	596	442	197	51	3	0	1	16	167	379	653	3,246
Cooling Degree Days (base 65°F)	1	1	8	43	146	342	459	414	229	51	8	1	1,703
Mean Precipitation (in.)	3.76	3.10	4.29	3.08	3.79	4.08	5.34	4.92	4.79	3.21	2.99	3.26	46.61
Extreme Maximum Daily Precip. (in.)	2.10	2.35	3.66	2.24	4.00	3.77	4.08	5.20	9.53	4.95	2.12	2.28	9.53
Days With ≥ 0.1" Precipitation	7	6	7	6	7	7	8	7	6	5	5	6	77
Days With ≥ 0.5" Precipitation	3	2	3	2	3	3	3	3	3	2	2	2	31
Days With ≥ 1.0" Precipitation	1	1	1	1	1	1	2	2	2	1	1	1	15
Mean Snowfall (in.)	1.0	0.9	0.8	trace	0.0	0.0	0.0	0.0	0.0	0.0	trace	0.3	3.0
Maximum Snow Depth (in.)	8	6	12	trace	0	0	0	0	0	0	trace	4	12
Days With ≥ 1.0" Snow Depth	0	0	0	0	0	0	0	0	0	0	0	0	0

Yadkinville 6 E *Yadkin County* Elevation: 875 ft. Latitude: 36° 08' N Longitude: 80° 33' W

	JAN	FEB	MAR	APR	MAY	JUN	JUL	AUG	SEP	OCT	NOV	DEC	YEAR
Mean Maximum Temp. (°F)	48.9	53.3	61.7	71.2	78.0	85.1	88.0	86.7	80.2	70.7	61.2	51.2	69.7
Mean Temp. (°F)	37.6	40.9	48.3	57.1	64.9	73.0	76.5	75.3	68.6	57.7	48.3	39.8	57.3
Mean Minimum Temp. (°F)	26.3	28.5	34.9	42.9	51.7	60.9	65.0	64.0	57.0	44.7	35.4	28.3	45.0
Extreme Maximum Temp. (°F)	78	82	89	92	96	102	102	104	99	94	83	80	104
Extreme Minimum Temp. (°F)	-8	-1	6	22	30	40	47	44	34	23	12	0	-8
Days Maximum Temp. ≥ 90°F	0	0	0	0	1	8	13	10	3	0	0	0	35
Days Maximum Temp. ≤ 32°F	2	1	0	0	0	0	0	0	0	0	0	1	4
Days Minimum Temp. ≤ 32°F	23	20	13	4	0	0	0	0	0	3	13	22	98
Days Minimum Temp. ≤ 0°F	0	0	0	0	0	0	0	0	0	0	0	0	0
Heating Degree Days (base 65°F)	842	674	514	253	84	7	0	1	36	242	495	776	3,924
Cooling Degree Days (base 65°F)	0	0	3	21	88	255	365	328	151	23	1	0	1,235
Mean Precipitation (in.)	3.45	3.22	4.25	3.67	3.76	4.14	4.65	3.47	3.73	3.29	3.18	3.56	44.37
Extreme Maximum Daily Precip. (in.)	2.42	2.40	4.25	3.25	3.14	3.40	4.00	4.57	3.76	4.50	2.69	2.60	4.57
Days With ≥ 0.1" Precipitation	6	6	7	7	8	8	8	6	5	5	6	6	78
Days With ≥ 0.5" Precipitation	3	2	3	3	2	3	3	2	3	2	2	3	31
Days With ≥ 1.0" Precipitation	1	1	1	1	1	1	1	1	1	1	1	1	12
Mean Snowfall (in.)	4.0	2.7	0.8	trace	0.0	0.0	0.0	0.0	0.0	0.0	trace	1.2	8.7
Maximum Snow Depth (in.)	16	10	6	trace	0	0	0	0	0	0	trace	8	16
Days With ≥ 1.0" Snow Depth	3	2	0	0	0	0	0	0	0	0	0	1	6

The period of record for all cooperative weather station data is 1980 – 2009. See User Guide for detailed explanation of data.

North Carolina Weather Station Rankings

Annual Extreme Maximum Temperature

Highest			Lowest		
Rank	Station Name	°F	Rank	Station Name	°F
1	Dunn 4 NW	108	1	Waynesville 1 E	95
1	Hamlet	108	2	Cape Hatteras NWS Bldg	96
3	Albemarle	107	2	Jefferson 2 E	96
3	Bayboro 3 E	***107***	4	Asheville	99
3	Concord	107	4	Black Mountain 2 W	99
3	Forest City 6 SW	***107***	6	Asheville Regional Arpt	100
3	Laurinburg	107	6	Bent Creek	100
3	Monroe 4 SE	107	8	Belhaven 5 SE	101
3	Sanford 8 NE	107	9	Cedar Island	102
10	Chapel Hill 2 W	106	9	New Bern Craven Co Reg Arpt	***102***
10	Statesville 2 NNE	106	9	Southport 5 N	102
12	Asheboro 2 W	105	12	Arcola	***103***
12	Fayetteville	105	12	Aurora 6 N	103
12	Lincolnton 4 W	105	12	Danbury 1 NW	103
12	Louisburg	105	12	Elizabeth City	103
12	Raleigh-Durham Intl Arpt	105	12	Longwood	103
12	Salisbury	105	12	Greensboro-High Pt-Winston Salem	103
12	Siler City 2 N	105	12	Raleigh 4 SW	103
12	Tarboro 1 S	105	12	Reidsville 2 NW	103
12	Wilson 3 SW	105	12	Roxboro 7 ESE	103
21	Burlington Fire Stn #5	104	12	Tryon	103
21	Charlotte Douglas Intl Arpt	104	12	Wilmington New Hanover County	103
21	Clinton 2 NE	104	23	Burlington Fire Stn #5	104
21	Gastonia	104	23	Charlotte Douglas Intl Arpt	104
21	Greenville	104	23	Clinton 2 NE	104

Annual Mean Maximum Temperature

Highest			Lowest		
Rank	Station Name	°F	Rank	Station Name	°F
1	Hofmann Forest	74.9	1	Jefferson 2 E	63.2
2	Laurinburg	74.2	2	Asheville	66.6
3	Wilmington New Hanover County	73.9	3	Asheville Regional Arpt	66.9
4	Longwood	73.8	4	Waynesville 1 E	67.4
4	Southport 5 N	***73.8***	5	Bent Creek	67.5
6	Bayboro 3 E	***73.7***	5	Black Mountain 2 W	67.5
7	Hamlet	73.6	7	Reidsville 2 NW	68.6
8	New Bern Craven Co Reg Arpt	***73.1***	8	Danbury 1 NW	68.8
9	Sanford 8 NE	73.0	9	Greensboro-High Pt-Winston Salem	68.9
10	Cedar Island	72.6	10	Hickory Regional Arpt	69.4
11	Fayetteville	72.5	11	Roxboro 7 ESE	69.5
12	Clinton 2 NE	72.3	12	Yadkinville 6 E	69.7
12	Greenville	72.3	13	Cape Hatteras NWS Bldg	69.8
14	Monroe 4 SE	72.2	14	Siler City 2 N	70.0
15	Dunn 4 NW	72.0	15	Raleigh State Univ	70.3
15	Tarboro 1 S	72.0	16	Asheboro 2 W	70.4
17	Elizabeth City	71.9	17	Statesville 2 NNE	70.6
17	Gastonia	71.9	18	Chapel Hill 2 W	70.7
17	Raleigh 4 SW	71.9	18	Lincolnton 4 W	70.7
17	Wilson 3 SW	71.9	20	Forest City 6 SW	***70.9***
21	Arcola	***71.8***	21	Burlington Fire Stn #5	71.1
21	Concord	71.8	21	Raleigh-Durham Intl Arpt	71.1
23	Albemarle	71.7	23	Charlotte Douglas Intl Arpt	71.3
23	Aurora 6 N	71.7	23	High Point	71.3
25	Belhaven 5 SE	***71.6***	25	Louisburg	71.4

Rankings include 25 highest/lowest stations. If state has less than 25 stations, all stations are included. The period of record is 1980–2009. See User Guide for detailed explanation of data.

Annual Mean Temperature

Highest

Rank	Station Name	°F
1	Wilmington New Hanover County	63.8
2	Cedar Island	63.6
3	Cape Hatteras NWS Bldg	63.0
4	Hofmann Forest	***62.9***
4	Southport 5 N	***62.9***
6	New Bern Craven Co Reg Arpt	***62.8***
7	Bayboro 3 E	***62.7***
8	Aurora 6 N	62.6
9	Laurinburg	62.5
10	Longwood	62.2
11	Belhaven 5 SE	***61.6***
12	Clinton 2 NE	61.4
12	Elizabeth City	61.4
12	Greenville	61.4
15	Fayetteville	61.2
16	Hamlet	61.0
16	Raleigh 4 SW	61.0
18	Gastonia	60.9
19	Charlotte Douglas Intl Arpt	60.8
19	Monroe 4 SE	60.8
21	Dunn 4 NW	60.6
22	Wilson 3 SW	60.5
23	Tarboro 1 S	60.3
23	Tryon	60.3
25	Albemarle	60.2

Lowest

Rank	Station Name	°F
1	Jefferson 2 E	51.3
2	Waynesville 1 E	54.1
3	Black Mountain 2 W	55.4
4	Bent Creek	55.5
5	Asheville Regional Arpt	55.9
6	Asheville	56.4
6	Danbury 1 NW	56.4
8	Roxboro 7 ESE	57.1
9	Yadkinville 6 E	57.3
10	Reidsville 2 NW	57.9
11	Louisburg	***58.0***
12	Forest City 6 SW	***58.2***
12	Statesville 2 NNE	58.2
14	Greensboro-High Pt-Winston Salem	58.6
15	Arcola	***58.8***
16	Hickory Regional Arpt	58.9
17	Chapel Hill 2 W	59.0
17	Siler City 2 N	59.0
19	Lincolnton 4 W	59.2
20	Burlington Fire Stn #5	59.3
21	High Point	59.8
22	Asheboro 2 W	59.9
23	Salisbury	60.0
24	Concord	60.1
25	Albemarle	60.2

Annual Mean Minimum Temperature

Highest

Rank	Station Name	°F
1	Cape Hatteras NWS Bldg	56.2
2	Cedar Island	54.6
3	Wilmington New Hanover County	53.6
4	Aurora 6 N	53.3
5	New Bern Craven Co Reg Arpt	***52.4***
6	Southport 5 N	***51.9***
7	Belhaven 5 SE	51.7
8	Bayboro 3 E	***51.6***
9	Elizabeth City	50.9
10	Hofmann Forest	***50.8***
10	Laurinburg	50.8
12	Longwood	50.5
13	Charlotte Douglas Intl Arpt	50.4
13	Greenville	50.4
15	Clinton 2 NE	50.3
16	Raleigh 4 SW	50.1
16	Raleigh State Univ	50.1
18	Gastonia	49.9
19	Fayetteville	49.8
20	Asheboro 2 W	49.5
21	Monroe 4 SE	49.2
21	Raleigh-Durham Intl Arpt	49.2
21	Tryon	49.2
24	Dunn 4 NW	49.1
25	Wilson 3 SW	49.0

Lowest

Rank	Station Name	°F
1	Jefferson 2 E	39.3
2	Waynesville 1 E	40.8
3	Black Mountain 2 W	43.2
4	Bent Creek	43.5
5	Danbury 1 NW	44.0
6	Louisburg	44.6
6	Roxboro 7 ESE	44.6
8	Asheville Regional Arpt	44.8
9	Yadkinville 6 E	45.0
10	Forest City 6 SW	***45.4***
11	Arcola	***45.8***
11	Statesville 2 NNE	45.8
13	Asheville	46.2
14	Chapel Hill 2 W	47.2
14	Reidsville 2 NW	47.2
16	Sanford 8 NE	47.4
17	Burlington Fire Stn #5	47.5
18	Lincolnton 4 W	47.6
19	Siler City 2 N	47.9
20	High Point	48.2
21	Concord	48.3
21	Greensboro-High Pt-Winston Salem	48.3
23	Hamlet	48.4
23	Hickory Regional Arpt	48.4
23	Salisbury	48.4

Rankings include 25 highest/lowest stations. If state has less than 25 stations, all stations are included. The period of record is 1980–2009. See User Guide for detailed explanation of data.

Annual Extreme Minimum Temperature

Highest

Rank	Station Name	°F
1	Cape Hatteras NWS Bldg	6
2	Cedar Island	2
3	Wilmington New Hanover County	0
4	Aurora 6 N	-1
4	Fayetteville	-1
6	Clinton 2 NE	-2
6	Elizabeth City	-2
6	Hofmann Forest	-2
9	Laurinburg	-3
9	Sanford 8 NE	-3
9	Southport 5 N	-3
12	Bayboro 3 E	-4
12	Dunn 4 NW	-4
12	Greenville	-4
12	Longwood	-4
12	New Bern Craven Co Reg Arpt	-4
12	Salisbury	-4
18	Charlotte Douglas Intl Arpt	-5
18	Concord	-5
18	Gastonia	-5
18	Monroe 4 SE	-5
18	Tarboro 1 S	-5
18	Wilson 3 SW	-5
24	Albemarle	-6
24	Burlington Fire Stn #5	-6

Lowest

Rank	Station Name	°F
1	Waynesville 1 E	-22
2	Asheville	-17
3	Asheville Regional Arpt	-16
3	Bent Creek	-16
5	Jefferson 2 E	-15
6	Black Mountain 2 W	-14
7	Siler City 2 N	-11
8	Belhaven 5 SE	-10
8	Danbury 1 NW	-10
8	Louisburg	-10
11	Raleigh-Durham Intl Arpt	-9
11	Reidsville 2 NW	-9
11	Roxboro 7 ESE	-9
14	Asheboro 2 W	-8
14	Chapel Hill 2 W	-8
14	Forest City 6 SW	-8
14	Hickory Regional Arpt	-8
14	Greensboro-High Pt-Winston Salem	-8
14	Tryon	-8
14	Yadkinville 6 E	-8
21	Arcola	-7
21	High Point	-7
21	Statesville 2 NNE	-7
24	Albemarle	-6
24	Burlington Fire Stn #5	-6

July Mean Maximum Temperature

Highest

Rank	Station Name	°F
1	Laurinburg	91.7
2	Hamlet	91.5
3	Sanford 8 NE	90.8
4	Hofmann Forest	90.5
5	Concord	90.4
6	Fayetteville	90.3
6	Wilson 3 SW	90.3
8	Arcola	90.2
9	Burlington Fire Stn #5	90.1
9	Monroe 4 SE	90.1
11	Greenville	90.0
11	Tarboro 1 S	90.0
13	Clinton 2 NE	89.9
13	Gastonia	89.9
15	Forest City 6 SW	89.7
15	Wilmington New Hanover County	89.7
17	Albemarle	89.6
17	Cedar Island	89.6
17	Dunn 4 NW	89.6
17	Louisburg	89.6
17	Raleigh-Durham Intl Arpt	89.6
22	New Bern Craven Co Reg Arpt	89.5
23	Charlotte Douglas Intl Arpt	89.4
23	Salisbury	89.4
25	Aurora 6 N	89.3

Lowest

Rank	Station Name	°F
1	Jefferson 2 E	81.0
2	Waynesville 1 E	83.5
3	Asheville Regional Arpt	84.2
4	Black Mountain 2 W	84.3
5	Bent Creek	84.4
6	Asheville	84.8
7	Cape Hatteras NWS Bldg	85.5
8	Danbury 1 NW	87.4
9	Greensboro-High Pt-Winston Salem	87.7
9	Reidsville 2 NW	87.7
11	Hickory Regional Arpt	87.8
12	Yadkinville 6 E	88.0
13	Roxboro 7 ESE	88.1
14	Asheboro 2 W	88.2
15	Belhaven 5 SE	88.3
16	Siler City 2 N	88.4
17	Lincolnton 4 W	88.5
17	Tryon	88.5
19	Statesville 2 NNE	88.6
20	Raleigh State Univ	89.0
21	Bayboro 3 E	89.1
21	Raleigh 4 SW	89.1
23	Southport 5 N	89.2
24	Aurora 6 N	89.3
24	Chapel Hill 2 W	89.3

Rankings include 25 highest/lowest stations. If state has less than 25 stations, all stations are included. The period of record is 1980–2009. See User Guide for detailed explanation of data.

January Mean Minimum Temperature

Highest Rank	Highest Station Name	°F	Lowest Rank	Lowest Station Name	°F
1	Cape Hatteras NWS Bldg	39.0	1	Jefferson 2 E	22.3
2	Cedar Island	36.6	2	Waynesville 1 E	23.6
3	Wilmington New Hanover County	35.6	3	Danbury 1 NW	25.0
4	Aurora 6 N	34.3	4	Louisburg	25.5
5	Bayboro 3 E	33.9	5	Roxboro 7 ESE	25.9
6	New Bern Craven Co Reg Arpt	***33.7***	6	Bent Creek	26.0
7	Hofmann Forest	***33.6***	6	Black Mountain 2 W	26.0
8	Southport 5 N	33.3	8	Yadkinville 6 E	26.3
9	Belhaven 5 SE	32.8	9	Arcola	***26.5***
9	Longwood	32.8	9	Forest City 6 SW	***26.5***
11	Elizabeth City	32.1	11	Asheville Regional Arpt	27.0
11	Laurinburg	32.1	11	Statesville 2 NNE	27.0
13	Raleigh 4 SW	31.9	13	Asheville	28.0
14	Greenville	31.8	14	Reidsville 2 NW	28.1
15	Charlotte Douglas Intl Arpt	31.6	15	Chapel Hill 2 W	28.3
15	Tryon	31.6	16	Burlington Fire Stn #5	28.6
17	Clinton 2 NE	31.4	17	Concord	28.8
18	Monroe 4 SE	31.1	18	Greensboro-High Pt-Winston Salem	29.0
19	Asheboro 2 W	31.0	18	Siler City 2 N	29.0
20	Fayetteville	30.9	20	Sanford 8 NE	29.2
20	Raleigh State Univ	30.9	21	Lincolnton 4 W	29.4
22	Gastonia	30.8	22	Hamlet	29.5
23	Raleigh-Durham Intl Arpt	30.5	22	Salisbury	29.5
24	Wilson 3 SW	30.3	22	Tarboro 1 S	29.5
25	Albemarle	30.2	25	Hickory Regional Arpt	29.6

Number of Days Annually Maximum Temperature ≥ 90°F

Highest Rank	Highest Station Name	Days	Lowest Rank	Lowest Station Name	Days
1	Laurinburg	66	1	Jefferson 2 E	2
2	Hamlet	64	2	Waynesville 1 E	5
3	Hofmann Forest	57	3	Cape Hatteras NWS Bldg	6
4	Concord	55	4	Asheville Regional Arpt	9
4	Sanford 8 NE	55	4	Black Mountain 2 W	9
6	Wilson 3 SW	53	6	Bent Creek	11
7	Arcola	51	7	Asheville	12
7	Burlington Fire Stn #5	51	8	Danbury 1 NW	30
7	Clinton 2 NE	51	8	Greensboro-High Pt-Winston Salem	30
7	Fayetteville	51	10	Hickory Regional Arpt	32
11	Greenville	50	11	Lincolnton 4 W	33
11	Tarboro 1 S	50	11	Reidsville 2 NW	33
13	Louisburg	48	13	Asheboro 2 W	34
14	Gastonia	47	13	Belhaven 5 SE	34
14	Monroe 4 SE	47	15	Roxboro 7 ESE	35
14	Raleigh-Durham Intl Arpt	47	15	Siler City 2 N	35
17	Chapel Hill 2 W	45	15	Yadkinville 6 E	35
17	Dunn 4 NW	45	18	Southport 5 N	36
17	New Bern Craven Co Reg Arpt	***45***	19	Raleigh 4 SW	38
20	Albemarle	44	19	Tryon	38
20	High Point	44	21	Elizabeth City	39
20	Salisbury	44	21	Longwood	39
23	Charlotte Douglas Intl Arpt	43	21	Statesville 2 NNE	39
23	Forest City 6 SW	***43***	24	Aurora 6 N	41
23	Wilmington New Hanover County	43	25	Bayboro 3 E	***42***

Rankings include 25 highest/lowest stations. If state has less than 25 stations, all stations are included. The period of record is 1980–2009. See User Guide for detailed explanation of data.

Number of Days Annually Maximum Temperature ≤ 32°F

Highest Rank	Station Name	Days	Lowest Rank	Station Name	Days
1	Jefferson 2 E	12	1	Bayboro 3 E	*0*
2	Asheville	8	1	Hofmann Forest	0
3	Reidsville 2 NW	5	1	Longwood	0
3	Roxboro 7 ESE	5	1	New Bern Craven Co Reg Arpt	*0*
5	Asheboro 2 W	4	1	Southport 5 N	0
5	Asheville Regional Arpt	4	1	Wilmington New Hanover County	0
5	Bent Creek	4	7	Albemarle	1
5	Black Mountain 2 W	4	7	Aurora 6 N	1
5	Burlington Fire Stn #5	4	7	Belhaven 5 SE	1
5	Chapel Hill 2 W	4	7	Cape Hatteras NWS Bldg	1
5	Danbury 1 NW	4	7	Cedar Island	1
5	Hickory Regional Arpt	4	7	Charlotte Douglas Intl Arpt	1
5	Louisburg	4	7	Clinton 2 NE	1
5	Greensboro-High Pt-Winston Salem	4	7	Concord	1
5	Raleigh-Durham Intl Arpt	4	7	Dunn 4 NW	1
5	Raleigh State Univ	4	7	Elizabeth City	1
5	Siler City 2 N	4	7	Fayetteville	1
5	Waynesville 1 E	4	7	Gastonia	1
5	Yadkinville 6 E	4	7	Hamlet	1
20	Arcola	2	7	Laurinburg	1
20	Forest City 6 SW	*2*	7	Lincolnton 4 W	1
20	Greenville	2	7	Monroe 4 SE	1
20	High Point	2	7	Raleigh 4 SW	1
20	Statesville 2 NNE	2	7	Salisbury	1
20	Wilson 3 SW	2	7	Sanford 8 NE	1

Number of Days Annually Minimum Temperature ≤ 32°F

Highest Rank	Station Name	Days	Lowest Rank	Station Name	Days
1	Jefferson 2 E	134	1	Cape Hatteras NWS Bldg	21
2	Waynesville 1 E	120	2	Cedar Island	32
3	Bent Creek	105	3	Aurora 6 N	34
4	Danbury 1 NW	104	4	Wilmington New Hanover County	39
5	Louisburg	102	5	New Bern Craven Co Reg Arpt	*46*
6	Black Mountain 2 W	100	6	Belhaven 5 SE	50
6	Roxboro 7 ESE	100	7	Bayboro 3 E	*51*
8	Yadkinville 6 E	98	8	Southport 5 N	53
9	Statesville 2 NNE	94	9	Elizabeth City	57
10	Asheville Regional Arpt	93	10	Hofmann Forest	58
11	Forest City 6 SW	*89*	10	Laurinburg	58
12	Arcola	88	12	Charlotte Douglas Intl Arpt	59
13	Chapel Hill 2 W	84	12	Raleigh 4 SW	59
13	Sanford 8 NE	84	12	Tryon	59
15	Asheville	83	15	Raleigh State Univ	60
16	Burlington Fire Stn #5	80	16	Longwood	61
17	Hamlet	79	17	Clinton 2 NE	62
18	Reidsville 2 NW	78	17	Greenville	62
19	Concord	77	19	Gastonia	63
20	Siler City 2 N	76	20	Asheboro 2 W	64
21	Lincolnton 4 W	75	21	Fayetteville	67
21	Greensboro-High Pt-Winston Salem	75	21	Wilson 3 SW	67
21	Salisbury	75	23	Albemarle	70
24	Tarboro 1 S	74	23	Monroe 4 SE	70
25	High Point	73	23	Raleigh-Durham Intl Arpt	70

 Rankings include 25 highest/lowest stations. If state has less than 25 stations, all stations are included. The period of record is 1980–2009. See User Guide for detailed explanation of data.

Number of Days Annually Minimum Temperature ≤ 0°F

Highest Rank	Station Name	Days	Lowest Rank	Station Name	Days
1	Jefferson 2 E	1	1	Albemarle	0
1	Waynesville 1 E	1	1	Arcola	0
3	Albemarle	0	1	Asheboro 2 W	0
3	Arcola	0	1	Asheville	0
3	Asheboro 2 W	0	1	Asheville Regional Arpt	0
3	Asheville	0	1	Aurora 6 N	0
3	Asheville Regional Arpt	0	1	Bayboro 3 E	***0***
3	Aurora 6 N	0	1	Belhaven 5 SE	0
3	Bayboro 3 E	***0***	1	Bent Creek	0
3	Belhaven 5 SE	0	1	Black Mountain 2 W	0
3	Bent Creek	0	1	Burlington Fire Stn #5	0
3	Black Mountain 2 W	0	1	Cape Hatteras NWS Bldg	0
3	Burlington Fire Stn #5	0	1	Cedar Island	0
3	Cape Hatteras NWS Bldg	0	1	Chapel Hill 2 W	0
3	Cedar Island	0	1	Charlotte Douglas Intl Arpt	0
3	Chapel Hill 2 W	0	1	Clinton 2 NE	0
3	Charlotte Douglas Intl Arpt	0	1	Concord	0
3	Clinton 2 NE	0	1	Danbury 1 NW	0
3	Concord	0	1	Dunn 4 NW	0
3	Danbury 1 NW	0	1	Elizabeth City	0
3	Dunn 4 NW	0	1	Fayetteville	0
3	Elizabeth City	0	1	Forest City 6 SW	***0***
3	Fayetteville	0	1	Gastonia	0
3	Forest City 6 SW	***0***	1	Greenville	0
3	Gastonia	0	1	Hamlet	0

Number of Annual Heating Degree Days

Highest Rank	Station Name	Num.	Lowest Rank	Station Name	Num.
1	Jefferson 2 E	5,344	1	Wilmington New Hanover County	2,395
2	Waynesville 1 E	4,485	2	Cedar Island	2,403
3	Bent Creek	4,193	3	Cape Hatteras NWS Bldg	2,442
4	Danbury 1 NW	4,180	4	Southport 5 N	***2,551***
5	Black Mountain 2 W	4,160	5	Hofmann Forest	***2,556***
6	Asheville Regional Arpt	4,115	6	Bayboro 3 E	***2,603***
7	Roxboro 7 ESE	4,031	7	New Bern Craven Co Reg Arpt	***2,658***
8	Asheville	4,028	8	Longwood	2,697
9	Yadkinville 6 E	3,924	9	Aurora 6 N	2,714
10	Reidsville 2 NW	3,837	10	Laurinburg	2,779
11	Louisburg	***3,810***	11	Belhaven 5 SE	***2,903***
12	Statesville 2 NNE	3,729	12	Elizabeth City	2,979
13	Forest City 6 SW	***3,692***	13	Clinton 2 NE	3,029
14	Greensboro-High Pt-Winston Salem	3,663	14	Greenville	3,036
15	Chapel Hill 2 W	3,586	15	Raleigh 4 SW	3,041
16	Arcola	***3,554***	16	Tryon	3,100
17	Siler City 2 N	3,552	17	Fayetteville	3,101
18	Hickory Regional Arpt	3,529	18	Gastonia	3,120
19	Burlington Fire Stn #5	3,526	18	Monroe 4 SE	3,120
20	Lincolnton 4 W	3,429	20	Charlotte Douglas Intl Arpt	3,122
21	Concord	3,379	21	Hamlet	3,127
22	High Point	3,340	22	Dunn 4 NW	3,197
23	Raleigh State Univ	3,312	23	Albemarle	3,242
24	Raleigh-Durham Intl Arpt	3,310	24	Wilson 3 SW	3,246
25	Salisbury	3,300	25	Sanford 8 NE	3,260

Rankings include 25 highest/lowest stations. If state has less than 25 stations, all stations are included. The period of record is 1980–2009. See User Guide for detailed explanation of data.

Number of Annual Cooling Degree Days

Highest

Rank	Station Name	Num.
1	Wilmington New Hanover County	2,057
2	Cedar Island	2,009
3	Laurinburg	1,979
4	New Bern Craven Co Reg Arpt	***1,955***
5	Aurora 6 N	1,930
6	Southport 5 N	***1,888***
7	Hofmann Forest	***1,885***
8	Bayboro 3 E	***1,851***
9	Cape Hatteras NWS Bldg	1,836
10	Greenville	1,827
11	Clinton 2 NE	1,804
12	Fayetteville	1,803
13	Belhaven 5 SE	***1,779***
14	Hamlet	1,778
15	Longwood	1,772
16	Elizabeth City	1,770
17	Gastonia	1,728
18	Charlotte Douglas Intl Arpt	1,713
19	Wilson 3 SW	1,703
20	Dunn 4 NW	1,693
21	Concord	1,686
22	Raleigh 4 SW	1,682
23	Monroe 4 SE	1,681
24	Tarboro 1 S	1,678
25	Raleigh State Univ	1,676

Lowest

Rank	Station Name	Num.
1	Jefferson 2 E	439
2	Waynesville 1 E	614
3	Black Mountain 2 W	776
4	Bent Creek	832
5	Asheville Regional Arpt	892
6	Asheville	1,007
7	Danbury 1 NW	1,148
8	Yadkinville 6 E	1,235
9	Roxboro 7 ESE	1,245
10	Forest City 6 SW	***1,303***
11	Reidsville 2 NW	1,355
11	Statesville 2 NNE	1,355
13	Louisburg	***1,364***
14	Arcola	***1,393***
15	Lincolnton 4 W	1,416
16	Hickory Regional Arpt	1,418
17	Greensboro-High Pt-Winston Salem	1,440
18	Siler City 2 N	1,462
19	Tryon	1,488
20	Chapel Hill 2 W	1,506
21	Asheboro 2 W	1,541
22	High Point	1,549
23	Burlington Fire Stn #5	1,552
24	Albemarle	1,590
25	Salisbury	1,593

Annual Precipitation

Highest

Rank	Station Name	Inches
1	Tryon	62.07
2	Cape Hatteras NWS Bldg	57.73
3	Hofmann Forest	57.68
4	Cedar Island	56.91
5	Wilmington New Hanover County	56.81
6	Southport 5 N	56.13
7	Bayboro 3 E	***55.20***
8	Longwood	53.14
9	New Bern Craven Co Reg Arpt	***52.52***
10	Forest City 6 SW	***50.84***
11	Greenville	49.46
12	Aurora 6 N	49.42
13	Clinton 2 NE	48.76
14	Belhaven 5 SE	48.55
15	Albemarle	48.15
16	Elizabeth City	47.86
17	Hamlet	47.81
18	Waynesville 1 E	47.72
19	Bent Creek	47.68
20	Dunn 4 NW	47.62
21	Lincolnton 4 W	47.37
22	Chapel Hill 2 W	47.29
23	Monroe 4 SE	47.18
24	Siler City 2 N	46.70
25	Wilson 3 SW	46.61

Lowest

Rank	Station Name	Inches
1	Asheville	36.87
2	Salisbury	41.03
3	Charlotte Douglas Intl Arpt	41.70
4	Greensboro-High Pt-Winston Salem	41.86
5	Gastonia	41.90
6	Raleigh-Durham Intl Arpt	43.26
7	Burlington Fire Stn #5	43.38
8	Tarboro 1 S	44.02
9	Statesville 2 NNE	44.06
10	Yadkinville 6 E	44.37
11	Asheboro 2 W	45.12
11	Roxboro 7 ESE	45.12
13	High Point	45.27
14	Asheville Regional Arpt	45.62
15	Reidsville 2 NW	45.64
16	Louisburg	45.72
17	Jefferson 2 E	45.77
18	Concord	45.84
18	Raleigh State Univ	45.84
20	Black Mountain 2 W	45.88
20	Fayetteville	45.88
22	Laurinburg	46.15
23	Hickory Regional Arpt	46.16
24	Danbury 1 NW	46.27
25	Sanford 8 NE	46.29

Rankings include 25 highest/lowest stations. If state has less than 25 stations, all stations are included. The period of record is 1980–2009. See User Guide for detailed explanation of data.

Annual Extreme Maximum Daily Precipitation

Highest Rank	Station Name	Inches	Lowest Rank	Station Name	Inches
1	Southport 5 N	***18.30***	1	Asheville	3.76
2	Wilmington New Hanover County	13.38	2	Asheville Regional Arpt	4.42
3	Longwood	12.85	3	Bent Creek	4.48
4	Greenville	10.75	4	Yadkinville 6 E	4.57
5	Clinton 2 NE	10.05	5	Greensboro-High Pt-Winston Salem	4.94
6	Black Mountain 2 W	10.00	6	Reidsville 2 NW	5.07
7	Wilson 3 SW	9.53	7	Burlington Fire Stn #5	5.15
8	Albemarle	***9.32***	8	Waynesville 1 E	5.25
9	Cedar Island	8.90	9	Asheboro 2 W	5.26
10	New Bern Craven Co Reg Arpt	***8.85***	10	Danbury 1 NW	5.27
11	Aurora 6 N	***8.82***	11	Jefferson 2 E	5.36
12	Concord	8.80	12	Elizabeth City	5.40
13	Cape Hatteras NWS Bldg	8.69	13	Lincolnton 4 W	5.46
14	Tryon	8.47	14	Laurinburg	5.58
15	Arcola	8.45	15	High Point	5.61
16	Fayetteville	8.25	16	Raleigh-Durham Intl Arpt	5.63
17	Monroe 4 SE	7.72	17	Tarboro 1 S	5.80
18	Chapel Hill 2 W	7.68	18	Bayboro 3 E	***5.83***
19	Louisburg	7.55	19	Salisbury	***5.90***
20	Dunn 4 NW	7.40	20	Statesville 2 NNE	6.02
20	Hofmann Forest	7.40	21	Raleigh State Univ	6.04
22	Belhaven 5 SE	6.90	22	Gastonia	6.10
23	Charlotte Douglas Intl Arpt	6.88	22	Hamlet	6.10
24	Roxboro 7 ESE	***6.78***	24	Sanford 8 NE	6.14
25	Raleigh 4 SW	6.72	25	Siler City 2 N	6.15

Number of Days Annually With ≥ 0.1 Inches of Precipitation

Highest Rank	Station Name	Days	Lowest Rank	Station Name	Days
1	Waynesville 1 E	90	1	Gastonia	68
2	Cedar Island	85	1	Salisbury	68
3	Tryon	84	3	Roxboro 7 ESE	69
4	Hofmann Forest	83	4	Burlington Fire Stn #5	70
5	New Bern Craven Co Reg Arpt	***82***	5	Charlotte Douglas Intl Arpt	71
6	Cape Hatteras NWS Bldg	81	6	Louisburg	72
6	Forest City 6 SW	***81***	6	Sanford 8 NE	72
8	Black Mountain 2 W	79	6	Tarboro 1 S	72
8	Hamlet	79	9	Dunn 4 NW	73
8	High Point	79	9	Raleigh-Durham Intl Arpt	73
8	Jefferson 2 E	79	11	Albemarle	74
12	Asheville Regional Arpt	78	11	Arcola	74
12	Bayboro 3 E	***78***	11	Asheboro 2 W	74
12	Greenville	78	11	Aurora 6 N	74
12	Longwood	78	11	Bent Creek	74
12	Wilmington New Hanover County	78	11	Concord	74
12	Yadkinville 6 E	78	11	Monroe 4 SE	74
18	Belhaven 5 SE	77	11	Raleigh State Univ	74
18	Chapel Hill 2 W	77	11	Siler City 2 N	74
18	Clinton 2 NE	77	11	Statesville 2 NNE	74
18	Wilson 3 SW	77	21	Asheville	75
22	Fayetteville	76	21	Danbury 1 NW	75
22	Hickory Regional Arpt	76	21	Elizabeth City	75
22	Lincolnton 4 W	76	21	Laurinburg	75
25	Asheville	75	21	Greensboro-High Pt-Winston Salem	75

Rankings include 25 highest/lowest stations. If state has less than 25 stations, all stations are included. The period of record is 1980–2009. See User Guide for detailed explanation of data.

Number of Days Annually With ≥ 0.5 Inches of Precipitation

Highest Rank	Station Name	Days	Lowest Rank	Station Name	Days
1	Tryon	38	1	Asheville	23
2	Wilmington New Hanover County	37	2	Gastonia	27
3	Cape Hatteras NWS Bldg	36	3	Burlington Fire Stn #5	28
3	Forest City 6 SW	*36*	3	Charlotte Douglas Intl Arpt	28
5	Cedar Island	35	3	Concord	28
5	New Bern Craven Co Reg Arpt	*35*	3	Greensboro-High Pt-Winston Salem	28
5	Southport 5 N	35	3	Raleigh-Durham Intl Arpt	28
8	Bayboro 3 E	*34*	3	Roxboro 7 ESE	28
8	Belhaven 5 SE	34	3	Salisbury	28
8	Hofmann Forest	34	3	Statesville 2 NNE	28
8	Lincolnton 4 W	34	11	Bent Creek	29
12	Albemarle	33	11	Jefferson 2 E	29
12	Chapel Hill 2 W	33	13	Asheville Regional Arpt	30
12	Greenville	33	13	Raleigh State Univ	30
12	Monroe 4 SE	33	13	Siler City 2 N	30
12	Waynesville 1 E	33	13	Tarboro 1 S	30
17	Asheboro 2 W	32	17	Arcola	31
17	Aurora 6 N	32	17	Black Mountain 2 W	31
17	Danbury 1 NW	32	17	Clinton 2 NE	31
17	Dunn 4 NW	32	17	Elizabeth City	31
17	Fayetteville	32	17	Hickory Regional Arpt	31
17	Hamlet	32	17	Laurinburg	31
17	High Point	32	17	Louisburg	31
17	Longwood	32	17	Reidsville 2 NW	31
17	Raleigh 4 SW	32	17	Wilson 3 SW	31

Number of Days Annually With ≥ 1.0 Inches of Precipitation

Highest Rank	Station Name	Days	Lowest Rank	Station Name	Days
1	Tryon	21	1	Asheville	10
2	Bayboro 3 E	*16*	2	Raleigh-Durham Intl Arpt	11
2	Cape Hatteras NWS Bldg	16	3	Asheboro 2 W	12
2	Cedar Island	16	3	Asheville Regional Arpt	12
2	Hofmann Forest	16	3	Bent Creek	12
2	Southport 5 N	16	3	Black Mountain 2 W	12
2	Wilmington New Hanover County	16	3	Burlington Fire Stn #5	12
8	Belhaven 5 SE	15	3	Chapel Hill 2 W	12
8	Dunn 4 NW	15	3	Charlotte Douglas Intl Arpt	12
8	Greenville	15	3	Concord	12
8	Longwood	15	3	Gastonia	12
8	New Bern Craven Co Reg Arpt	*15*	3	Hickory Regional Arpt	12
8	Wilson 3 SW	15	3	High Point	12
14	Arcola	14	3	Jefferson 2 E	12
14	Aurora 6 N	14	3	Greensboro-High Pt-Winston Salem	12
14	Clinton 2 NE	14	3	Raleigh 4 SW	12
14	Elizabeth City	14	3	Salisbury	12
14	Fayetteville	14	3	Siler City 2 N	12
14	Roxboro 7 ESE	14	3	Statesville 2 NNE	12
20	Albemarle	13	3	Waynesville 1 E	12
20	Danbury 1 NW	13	3	Yadkinville 6 E	12
20	Forest City 6 SW	*13*	22	Albemarle	13
20	Hamlet	13	22	Danbury 1 NW	13
20	Laurinburg	13	22	Forest City 6 SW	*13*
20	Lincolnton 4 W	13	22	Hamlet	13

 Rankings include 25 highest/lowest stations. If state has less than 25 stations, all stations are included. The period of record is 1980–2009. See User Guide for detailed explanation of data.

Annual Snowfall

Highest

Rank	Station Name	Inches
1	Jefferson 2 E	14.4
2	Waynesville 1 E	13.5
3	Asheville	12.6
4	Asheville Regional Arpt	11.2
5	Yadkinville 6 E	8.7
6	Reidsville 2 NW	8.0
7	Black Mountain 2 W	7.9
7	Danbury 1 NW	7.9
9	Greensboro-High Pt-Winston Salem	7.6
10	Roxboro 7 ESE	6.9
11	Lincolnton 4 W	6.3
12	Raleigh-Durham Intl Arpt	6.1
13	Arcola	5.9
13	Bent Creek	*5.9*
13	Tryon	5.9
16	Asheboro 2 W	5.8
17	Forest City 6 SW	*5.6*
18	Tarboro 1 S	5.3
19	Chapel Hill 2 W	4.6
20	Charlotte Douglas Intl Arpt	4.5
21	Statesville 2 NNE	4.4
22	Raleigh State Univ	4.1
23	Concord	3.9
23	Greenville	3.9
25	High Point	3.5

Lowest

Rank	Station Name	Inches
1	Elizabeth City	0.1
2	Aurora 6 N	0.3
3	Fayetteville	0.6
4	Gastonia	0.7
5	Southport 5 N	0.8
6	Hamlet	1.1
7	Hofmann Forest	1.4
8	Longwood	1.7
9	Bayboro 3 E	*1.8*
9	Laurinburg	1.8
9	Wilmington New Hanover County	1.8
12	Louisburg	2.2
13	Dunn 4 NW	2.3
14	Sanford 8 NE	2.4
14	Siler City 2 N	2.4
16	Cedar Island	2.5
17	Clinton 2 NE	2.6
18	Burlington Fire Stn #5	2.7
19	Albemarle	2.8
20	Belhaven 5 SE	3.0
20	Wilson 3 SW	3.0
22	Monroe 4 SE	3.3
23	Raleigh 4 SW	3.4
24	High Point	3.5
24	Salisbury	3.5

Annual Maximum Snow Depth

Highest

Rank	Station Name	Inches
1	Jefferson 2 E	24
2	Siler City 2 N	22
3	Asheville	20
3	Raleigh-Durham Intl Arpt	20
5	Asheville Regional Arpt	18
5	Waynesville 1 E	18
7	Bent Creek	17
7	Sanford 8 NE	17
9	Belhaven 5 SE	16
9	Greenville	16
9	Tryon	16
9	Yadkinville 6 E	16
13	Danbury 1 NW	*15*
13	High Point	15
15	Lincolnton 4 W	14
15	Raleigh State Univ	14
17	Charlotte Douglas Intl Arpt	13
17	Forest City 6 SW	*13*
17	Reidsville 2 NW	13
17	Roxboro 7 ESE	13
17	Wilmington New Hanover County	13
22	Arcola	12
22	Bayboro 3 E	*12*
22	Black Mountain 2 W	12
22	Cedar Island	12

Lowest

Rank	Station Name	Inches
1	Aurora 6 N	Trace
2	Elizabeth City	2
3	Hofmann Forest	3
4	Chapel Hill 2 W	6
5	Asheboro 2 W	8
5	Dunn 4 NW	8
5	Southport 5 N	*8*
5	Statesville 2 NNE	8
9	Albemarle	*9*
9	Laurinburg	9
9	Greensboro-High Pt-Winston Salem	9
12	Burlington Fire Stn #5	*10*
12	Clinton 2 NE	10
12	Louisburg	10
12	Salisbury	*10*
16	Concord	11
16	Fayetteville	11
16	Gastonia	*11*
16	Longwood	11
20	Arcola	12
20	Bayboro 3 E	*12*
20	Black Mountain 2 W	12
20	Cedar Island	12
20	Hamlet	12
20	Monroe 4 SE	12

Rankings include 25 highest/lowest stations. If state has less than 25 stations, all stations are included. The period of record is 1980–2009. See User Guide for detailed explanation of data.

Number of Days Annually With ≥ 1.0 Inch Snow Depth

Highest			Lowest		
Rank	Station Name	Days	Rank	Station Name	Days
1	Jefferson 2 E	9	1	Albemarle	*0*
2	Asheville	8	1	Aurora 6 N	0
3	Reidsville 2 NW	7	1	Bayboro 3 E	*0*
3	Waynesville 1 E	7	1	Belhaven 5 SE	0
5	Asheville Regional Arpt	6	1	Burlington Fire Stn #5	0
5	Greensboro-High Pt-Winston Salem	6	1	Cedar Island	0
5	Yadkinville 6 E	6	1	Chapel Hill 2 W	0
8	Bent Creek	5	1	Dunn 4 NW	0
8	Danbury 1 NW	*5*	1	Elizabeth City	0
8	Roxboro 7 ESE	5	1	Fayetteville	0
11	Arcola	4	1	Gastonia	0
11	Raleigh-Durham Intl Arpt	4	1	Greenville	0
11	Tryon	4	1	Hamlet	0
14	Charlotte Douglas Intl Arpt	3	1	Hofmann Forest	0
14	Concord	3	1	Longwood	0
14	Forest City 6 SW	*3*	1	Salisbury	*0*
14	Lincolnton 4 W	3	1	Siler City 2 N	0
14	Raleigh State Univ	3	1	Southport 5 N	0
19	Asheboro 2 W	2	1	Wilmington New Hanover County	0
19	Black Mountain 2 W	2	1	Wilson 3 SW	0
19	High Point	2	21	Clinton 2 NE	1
19	Monroe 4 SE	2	21	Laurinburg	1
19	Raleigh 4 SW	2	21	Louisburg	1
19	Statesville 2 NNE	2	21	Sanford 8 NE	1
25	Clinton 2 NE	1	21	Tarboro 1 S	1

 Rankings include 25 highest/lowest stations. If state has less than 25 stations, all stations are included. The period of record is 1980–2009. See User Guide for detailed explanation of data.

Significant Storm Events in North Carolina: 2000 – 2009

Location or County	Date	Type	Mag.	Deaths	Injuries	Property Damage ($mil.)	Crop Damage ($mil.)
McDowell County	04/13/00	Fog	na	1	14	0.0	0.0
Northwest Piedmont Region	12/04/02	Ice Storm	na	0	0	100.0	0.0
Southwest Piedmont, Charlotte Metro Area	12/04/02	Ice Storm	na	0	0	99.0	0.0
Stanly	06/16/03	Flash Flood	na	5	0	0.0	0.0
Eastern North Carolina	09/17/03	Hurricane Isabel	na	0	0	435.6	14.2
Northeastern North Carolina	09/18/03	Hurricane Isabel	na	1	0	16.9	0.0
Northeast North Carolina	09/18/03	Hurricane Isabel	na	1	0	7.2	0.0
Bladen, Columbus, Pender and Robeson Co.	01/26/04	Ice Storm	na	0	0	13.0	0.0
Coastal Counties, and Outer Banks	08/03/04	Hurricane Alex	na	0	0	7.5	0.0
Pender	08/13/04	Tornado	F2	3	29	1.3	0.0
Bladen, Brunswick, Columbus, New Hanover, and Pender Counties	08/14/04	Hurricane Charley	na	0	3	10.4	2.5
Buncombe Co.	09/07/04	Flood	na	0	0	40.0	1.0
Avery, Burke, Caldwell, McDowell, Mitchell, and Yancey Counties	09/07/04	Flood	na	0	0	25.0	5.5
Haywood, Henderson and Transylvania Co.	09/07/04	Flood	na	0	0	10.5	11.5
Buncombe County	09/08/04	Landslide	na	0	0	10.0	0.0
Buncombe Co.	09/16/04	Flood	na	2	0	40.0	0.0
Haywood Co.	09/16/04	Flood	na	3	0	15.0	0.0
Madison County	09/16/04	Flood	na	0	0	8.0	0.9
Buncombe County	09/17/04	Landslide	na	0	0	10.0	0.0
Avery, Burke, Caldwell, McDowell, and Mitchell Counties	09/17/04	Flood	na	0	0	8.2	4.0
Southeast North Carolina	09/13/05	Hurricane Ophelia	na	0	5	42.1	11.5
Brunswick, New Hanover, and Pender Counties	09/14/05	Hurricane Ophelia	na	0	0	8.3	0.0
Columbus	11/16/06	Tornado	F3	8	20	0.5	0.0
Mecklenburg	08/27/08	Flash Flood	na	0	0	8.5	0.0

Note: Deaths, injuries, and damages are date and location specific.

NORTH DAKOTA

PHYSICAL FEATURES. North Dakota is typically plains country located near the center of the North American Continent. The eastern part of the State is flat, with an elevation in the Red River Valley of 780 feet at Pembina in the north to 962 feet above sea level at Wahpeton in the south. To the westward there is a gradual rise of terrain until an elevation of 3,468 feet is reached at Black Butte in the southwestern part of the State. The Turtle Mountains in the north-central part of the State are only about 500 feet higher than the surrounding area, with the highest elevation about 2,300 feet above sea level.

GENERAL CLIMATE. Summers are usually very pleasant, but hot winds and periods of prolonged high temperatures occur occasionally. However, minimum temperatures are seldom above 70°F., so it is unusual to have uncomfortable nights. Winters are usually cold with occasional mild ones.

TEMPERATURE. The annual mean temperature for North Dakota ranges from about 36°F. in the northeast to 43°F. in the extreme south. Temperatures above 100°F. are occasionally recorded, and zero readings are common in winter. The average number of days a year when the temperature reaches 90°F. or higher is 14, and the average number with zero or lower is 53. The average growing season is about 121 days, ranging from 110 days in the northeast and north-central to 135 in the extreme south. For the State, the average date of the last freeze in spring is May 19, and the first in fall is September 18. Freezing temperatures have occurred, however, as late as the first part of June and as early in the fall as the first few days of September.

PRECIPITATION. Precipitation in the eastern third of the State averages about 19 inches, in the middle third about 16 inches, and in the western third about 15 inches. On an average, about 77 percent of the annual precipitation occurs during the crop-growing freeze-free season, April to September, and almost 50 percent falls during May, June, and July. The normal precipitation for the driest months, November to February, is about one-half inch a month. The greatest amount falls between 5 p.m. and 8 p.m. and again about midnight. In North Dakota, precipitation is considered the most important climatic factor.

Most of the rain in the summer months occurs in storms accompanied by thunder and lightning, often with heavy falls for a short time. The average number of thunderstorm days in 30, mostly in June, July, and August. In most years at least some part of the State is visited by a storm that brings a rainfall of two or three inches in 24 hours, and occasionally five or six inches falls in one day. On an average, rain falls about one day in four during the summer months. The annual number of days with measurable precipitation averages 66, ranging from about 50 in the west to 90 in the east.

The first light snow in autumn occasionally falls in September, but usually very little occurs until after October. The average number of days with 0.1 inch or more of snow is 23. The average annual snowfall is 32 inches with the greatest amount in the northeast and least in the southwest. Occasionally there is heavy snowfall in winter, and the amount of snow on the ground accumulates to a considerable depth.

RIVERS AND FLOODS. The streams of North Dakota fall into two main groups — those in the west and south-central portions draining into the Missouri Basin, and those in the east and north-central portions draining into the Red River of the North.

Some of the important tributaries which drain into the Missouri in North Dakota are: the Cannonball, Grand, Heart, Knife, Little Missouri, and James. Local floods occur occasionally on all the tributaries, mainly associated with ice breakup, notably on the Heart River where serious floods have occurred from ice jams. Floods along the main stem of the Missouri in the past have been caused primarily by snowmelt in the high plains. The resulting flooding has been almost invariably aggravated by ice jams.

The streams draining the east and north-central portions of North Dakota flow into the Red River of the North, which flows in a northerly direction between Minnesota and North Dakota into Canada. The most important tributaries in the eastern portion of North Dakota are the Sheyenne and the Pembina. The latter rises in the province of Manitoba, Canada. In the north-central portion the Souris River originates in the province of Saskatchewan, Canada, flows southeastward into North Dakota, and then curves back into Canada and flows in a northerly direction into the Assiniboine River which empties into the Red River of the North above the International Boundary.

Floods in the Red River of the North Basin occur primarily during the spring season (April and May) and are caused chiefly by melting snow. Ice conditions, particularly on the northward flowing streams, increase flood crests and occasionally cause extremely high flood stages due to jams. Early freeze-up in the fall before snow occurs is also a contributing factor in producing flood conditions in the spring. Considerably higher crests result along the tributaries and the main stem of the river if the snowmelt is accompanied by a period of prolonged heavy rains. Major rainstorms causing more than local flooding (without snowmelt) are extremely rare.

OTHER CLIMATIC ELEMENTS. The prevailing direction of the wind in all months of the year is from the northwest, unless it is influenced by local conditions. More southerly winds are observed during the summer than during the winter. The average annual wind speed is about 11 m.p.h. The highest speeds are in spring and the lowest in late summer. High winds frequently accompany severe thunderstorms. Tornadoes are reported in North Dakota.

The average relative humidity is about 68 percent, slightly higher in the east than in the west. Humidity is frequently low during the afternoon in summer, sometimes below 20 percent. Dense fogs are experienced, on an average, on only eight days of the year.

The average number of clear days is 160, partly cloudy 100, and cloudy 105. On a clear day the sun shines for more than 15 hours from the middle of May to the end of July. The yearly average amount of sunshine is 59 percent of the possible amount, with 74 percent in July and 72 percent in August.

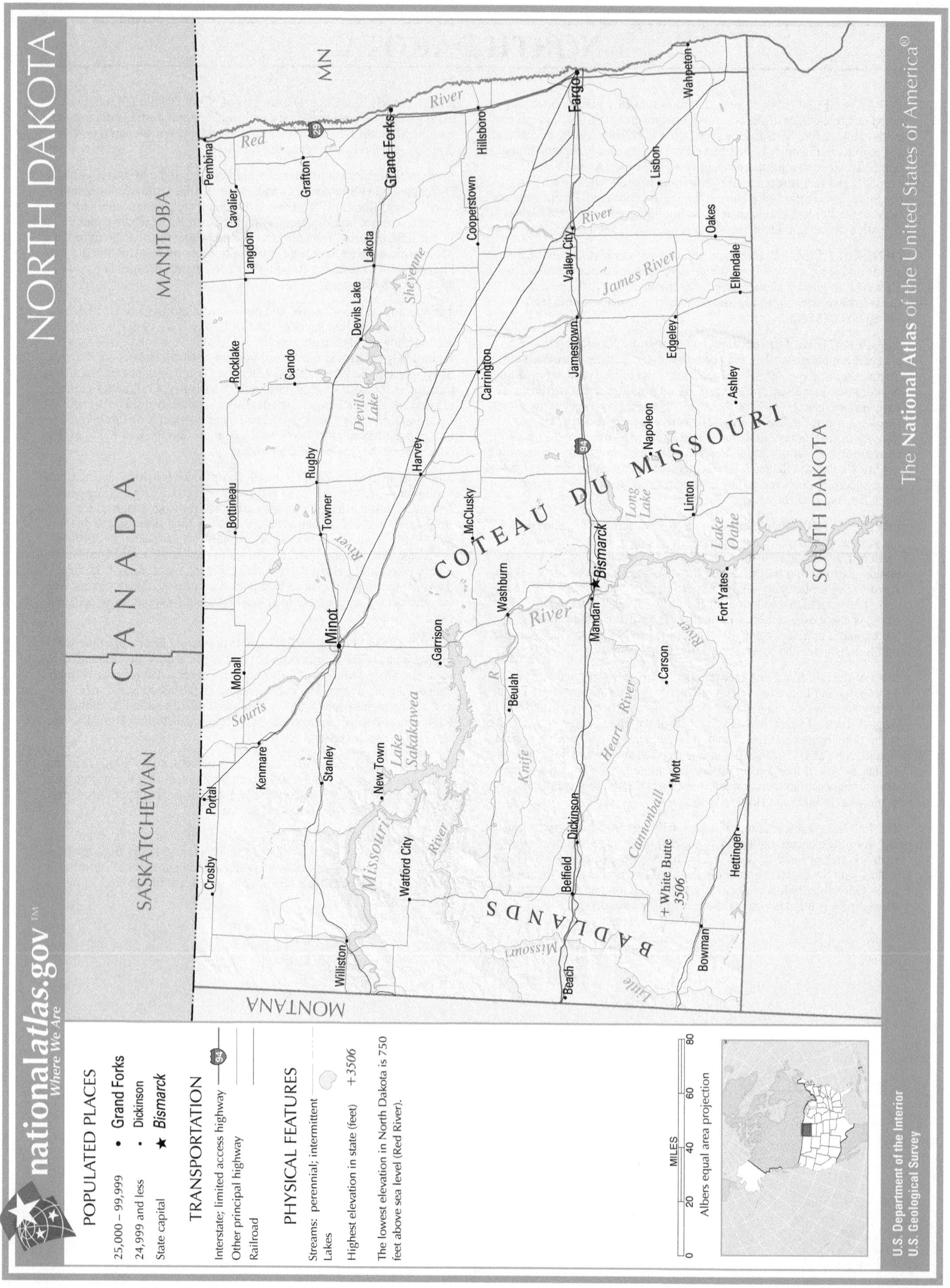
NORTH DAKOTA
nationalatlas.gov™
Where We Are
POPULATED PLACES
25,000 – 99,999 • Grand Forks
24,999 and less • Dickinson
State capital ★ Bismarck
TRANSPORTATION
Interstate; limited access highway
Other principal highway
Railroad
PHYSICAL FEATURES
Streams: perennial; intermittent
Lakes
Highest elevation in state (feet) +3506
The lowest elevation in North Dakota is 750 feet above sea level (Red River).
MILES
0 20 40 60 80
Albers equal area projection
U.S. Department of the Interior
U.S. Geological Survey
The National Atlas of the United States of America®
CANADA
SASKATCHEWAN
MANITOBA
MN
MONTANA
SOUTH DAKOTA
COTEAU DU MISSOURI
BADLANDS
Pembina
Cavalier
Langdon
Rocklake
Bottineau
Mohall
Kenmare
Portal
Crosby
Grafton
Grand Forks
Lakota
Devils Lake
Cando
Rugby
Towner
Minot
Stanley
New Town
Williston
Watford City
Hillsboro
Cooperstown
Carrington
Harvey
McClusky
Washburn
Garrison
Beulah
Fargo
Valley City
Jamestown
Bismarck
Mandan
Dickinson
Belfield
Beach
Wahpeton
Lisbon
Oakes
Ellendale
Edgeley
Napoleon
Ashley
Linton
Fort Yates
Carson
Mott
Hettinger
Bowman
White Butte 3506
Red River
Sheyenne River
James River
Souris River
Devils Lake
Lake Sakakawea
Missouri River
Knife River
Heart River
Cannonball River
Little Missouri River
Long Lake
Lake Oahe
29
94

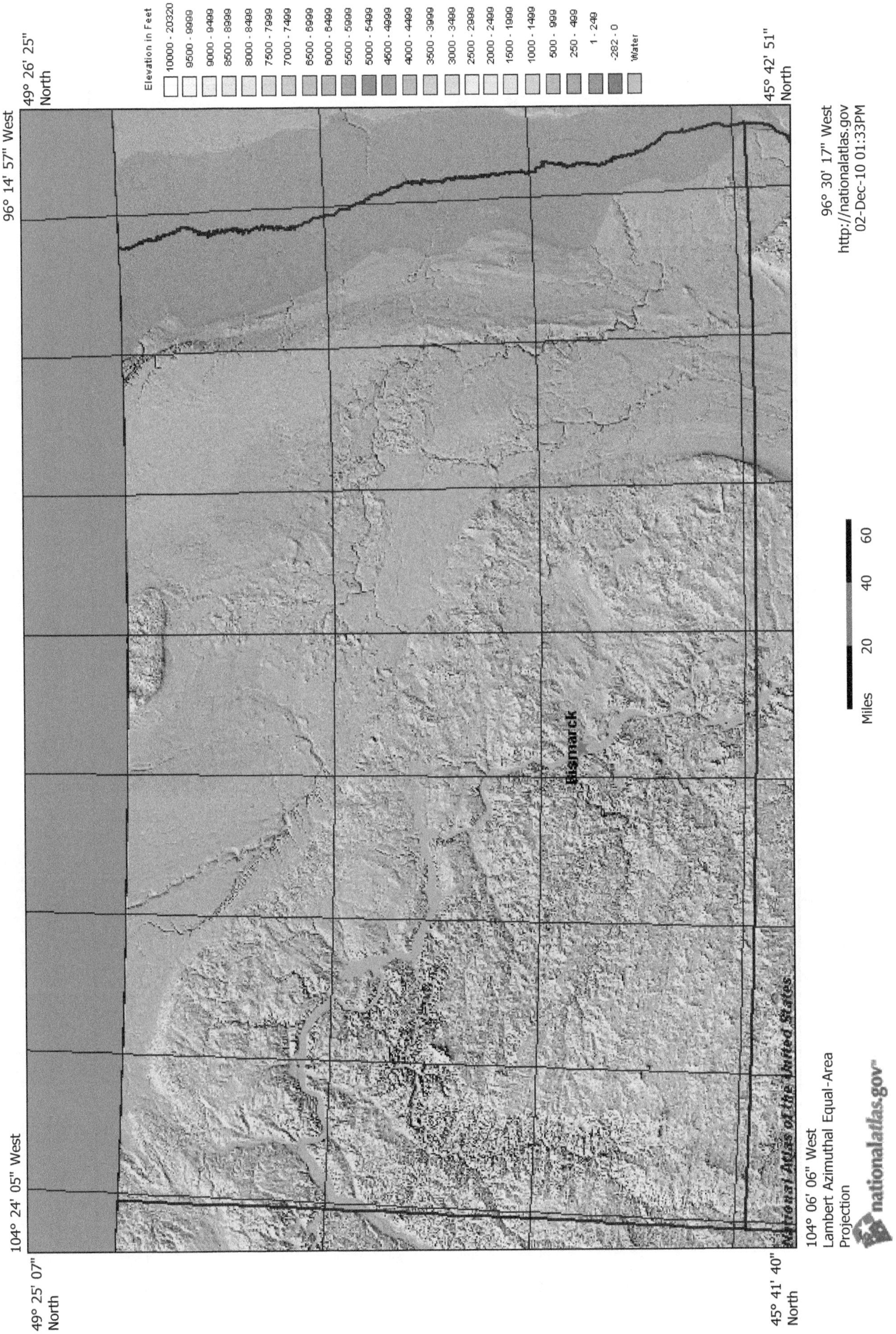
49° 26' 25" North
96° 14' 57" West
49° 25' 07" North
104° 24' 05" West
45° 42' 51" North
96° 30' 17" West
http://nationalatlas.gov
02-Dec-10 01:33PM
45° 41' 40" North
104° 06' 06" West
Lambert Azimuthal Equal-Area Projection
Elevation in Feet
10000 - 20320
9500 - 9999
9000 - 9499
8500 - 8999
8000 - 8499
7500 - 7999
7000 - 7499
6500 - 6999
6000 - 6499
5500 - 5999
5000 - 5499
4500 - 4999
4000 - 4499
3500 - 3999
3000 - 3499
2500 - 2999
2000 - 2499
1500 - 1999
1000 - 1499
500 - 999
250 - 499
1 - 249
-282 - 0
Water
Bismarck
National Atlas of the United States
Miles
20
40
60
nationalatlas.gov

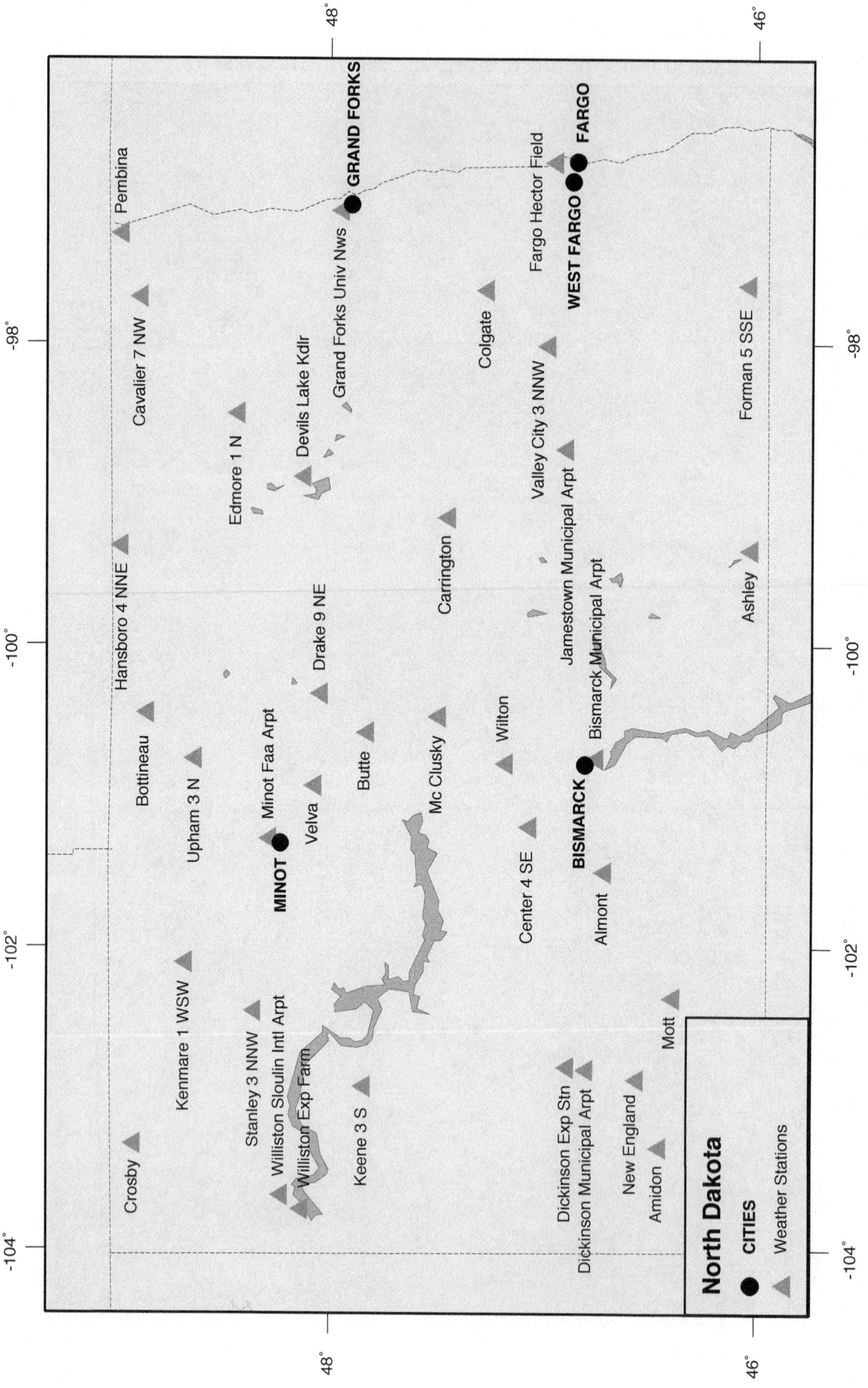
North Dakota
CITIES
Weather Stations
48°
46°
-98°
-100°
-102°
-104°
Pembina
Cavalier 7 NW
Hansboro 4 NNE
Bottineau
Crosby
Kenmare 1 WSW
Upham 3 N
Stanley 3 NNW
Williston Sloulin Intl Arpt
Williston Exp Farm
MINOT
Minot Faa Arpt
Velva
Keene 3 S
Butte
Drake 9 NE
Edmore 1 N
Devils Lake Kdlr
Grand Forks Univ Nws
GRAND FORKS
Mc Clusky
Carrington
Colgate
Wilton
Center 4 SE
Valley City 3 NNW
Fargo Hector Field
WEST FARGO
FARGO
Jamestown Municipal Arpt
Bismarck Municipal Arpt
BISMARCK
Almont
Dickinson Exp Stn
Dickinson Municipal Arpt
New England
Amidon
Mott
Ashley
Forman 5 SSE

North Dakota Weather Stations by County

County	Station Name
Barnes	Valley City 3 NNW
Bottineau	Bottineau
Burleigh	Bismarck Municipal Arpt
Cass	Fargo Hector Field
Divide	Crosby
Foster	Carrington
Grand Forks	Grand Forks Univ Nws
Hettinger	Mott New England
Mchenry	Drake 9 NE Upham 3 N Velva
Mcintosh	Ashley
Mckenzie	Keene 3 S
Mclean	Butte Wilton
Morton	Almont
Mountrail	Stanley 3 NNW
Oliver	Center 4 SE
Pembina	Cavalier 7 NW Pembina
Ramsey	Devils Lake Kdlr Edmore 1 NW
Sargent	Forman 5 SSE
Sheridan	McClusky
Slope	Amidon
Stark	Dickinson Exp Stn Dickinson Municipal Arpt
Steele	Colgate
Stutsman	Jamestown Municipal Arpt
Towner	Hansboro 4 NNE
Ward	Kenmare 1 WSW Minot FAA Arpt
Williams	Williston Exp Farm Williston Sloulin Intl Arpt

See User Guide for station inclusion criteria.

North Dakota Weather Stations by City

City	Station Name	Miles
Bismarck	Bismarck Municipal Arpt	3.6
	Wilton	24.3
Devils Lake	Devils Lake Kdlr	0.6
Dickinson	Dickinson Municipal Arpt	5.9
	Dickinson Exp Stn	0.6
	New England	23.5
Fargo	Georgetown 1 E, MN	15.1
	Fargo Hector Field	4.7
Grand Forks	Crookston NW Exp Stn, MN	22.5
	Grand Forks Univ Nws	2.1
Jamestown	Jamestown Municipal Arpt	1.1
Mandan	Bismarck Municipal Arpt	8.0
	Center 4 SE	21.9
	Wilton	23.8
Minot	Minot FAA Arpt	2.4
	Velva	20.4
Minot AFB	Minot FAA Arpt	11.1
Valley City	Valley City 3 NNW	1.9
Wahpeton	Fergus Falls, MN	23.6
	Rothsay, MN	21.9
West Fargo	Georgetown 1 E, MN	15.8
	Fargo Hector Field	5.8
Williston	Williston Sloulin Intl Arpt	3.0
	Williston Exp Farm	5.1

Note: Miles is the distance between the geographic center of the city and the weather station.

See User Guide for station inclusion criteria.

North Dakota Weather Stations by Elevation

Feet	Station Name
2,910	Amidon
2,639	New England
2,584	Dickinson Municipal Arpt
2,524	Mott
2,470	Keene 3 S
2,459	Dickinson Exp Stn
2,279	Stanley 3 NNW
2,169	Wilton
2,104	Williston Exp Farm
2,000	Ashley
1,990	Center 4 SE
1,952	Crosby
1,924	McClusky
1,915	Almont
1,898	Williston Sloulin Intl Arpt
1,810	Kenmare 1 WSW
1,714	Minot FAA Arpt
1,660	Butte
1,646	Bismarck Municipal Arpt
1,640	Bottineau
1,585	Carrington
1,540	Hansboro 4 NNE
1,535	Edmore 1 NW
1,529	Drake 9 NE
1,509	Velva
1,492	Jamestown Municipal Arpt
1,463	Devils Lake Kdlr
1,424	Upham 3 N
1,250	Forman 5 SSE
1,209	Valley City 3 NNW
1,180	Colgate
899	Fargo Hector Field
890	Cavalier 7 NW
830	Grand Forks Univ Nws
790	Pembina

See User Guide for station inclusion criteria.

Bismarck Municipal Airport

Bismarck, the State Capital and County Seat of Burleigh County, is located in south-central North Dakota, near the center of North America. It is on the east bank of the Missouri River in a shallow basin seven miles wide and 11 miles long.

The Weather Service Forecast Office is located at the Municipal Airport approximately two miles southeast of city center. It is almost entirely surrounded by low-lying hills. The closest hills, three miles to the north, and other hills five miles to the southeast, are about 200 to 300 feet high. West across the Missouri River the land is more hilly and 300 to 600 feet higher.

The climate is semi-arid, typically continental in character, and invigorating. Summers are warm, but there are not many hot days, and very few hot and humid days. Winters tend to be long and quite cold, but there are plenty of mild days to make winter weather pleasant much of the time. Sunshine is abundant, averaging 2,700 hours out of a possible 4,470 hours.

More than 75 percent of annual precipitation falls during the six month period from April through September, and nearly 50 percent during May, June, and July. Snow has been reported in all months except July and August. Three inches or more can be expected on about three days each year.

Most summer precipitation occurs during thunderstorms in the late afternoon and evening. Thunderstorms occur on about 34 days each year, accompanied by hail on two or three of the days. A damaging hailstorm is experienced about once every ten years. Tornadoes are rare, but damaging winds occasionally occur with the heavier thunderstorms.

The winter season usually begins in late November and continues until late March. Winter precipitation is nearly all in the form of snow and is often associated with strong winds and low temperatures. This combination produces winter storms and occasional blizzards that must never be taken lightly. A severe blizzard lasting two or three days may be expected every few years. But several times each winter storms lasting a few hours occur in which drifting snow can make travel difficult and even block roads. A stalled motorist can be in serious trouble if he is not prepared with adequate winter clothing and some kind of emergency provisions.

The temperature range from summer to winter is very large and typical of the Northern Great Plains. The average freeze-free period is 134 days, from mid-May to late September.

Bismarck Municipal Airport *Burleigh County* Elevation: 1,646 ft. Latitude: 46° 46' N Longitude: 100° 45' W

	JAN	FEB	MAR	APR	MAY	JUN	JUL	AUG	SEP	OCT	NOV	DEC	YEAR
Mean Maximum Temp. (°F)	23.5	28.5	40.2	57.1	68.7	77.3	84.8	83.2	72.2	57.3	39.9	26.5	54.9
Mean Temp. (°F)	12.8	18.3	29.6	43.9	55.7	64.7	71.2	69.3	58.6	44.8	29.5	16.4	42.9
Mean Minimum Temp. (°F)	2.1	8.0	19.0	30.7	42.7	52.0	57.4	55.4	45.0	32.1	19.1	6.3	30.8
Extreme Maximum Temp. (°F)	63	69	81	93	96	111	112	106	103	94	79	61	112
Extreme Minimum Temp. (°F)	-44	-43	-28	-1	17	32	39	33	20	-10	-30	-40	-44
Days Maximum Temp. ≥ 90°F	0	0	0	0	1	3	8	8	2	0	0	0	22
Days Maximum Temp. ≤ 32°F	21	16	9	1	0	0	0	0	0	1	9	19	76
Days Minimum Temp. ≤ 32°F	31	28	28	18	4	0	0	0	2	16	28	31	186
Days Minimum Temp. ≤ 0°F	14	9	3	0	0	0	0	0	0	0	2	10	38
Heating Degree Days (base 65°F)	1,614	1,316	1,089	628	298	91	14	35	225	621	1,058	1,501	8,490
Cooling Degree Days (base 65°F)	0	0	0	2	18	87	212	177	40	1	0	0	537
Mean Precipitation (in.)	0.43	0.49	0.84	1.17	2.33	3.14	2.89	2.35	1.51	1.30	0.69	0.45	17.59
Maximum Precipitation (in.)*	1.3	1.6	3.2	5.5	5.2	6.5	13.8	5.0	6.9	4.3	2.1	0.9	27.0
Minimum Precipitation (in.)*	0	trace	0.1	trace	0.3	0.5	0.2	trace	trace	trace	trace	trace	9.3
Extreme Maximum Daily Precip. (in.)	0.58	1.02	0.95	1.96	1.95	3.19	4.32	4.63	4.31	1.29	0.92	0.72	4.63
Days With ≥ 0.1" Precipitation	1	2	2	3	5	6	6	4	3	3	2	1	38
Days With ≥ 0.5" Precipitation	0	0	0	0	1	2	2	2	1	1	0	0	9
Days With ≥ 1.0" Precipitation	0	0	0	0	0	1	1	1	0	0	0	0	3
Mean Snowfall (in.)	8.9	7.8	9.2	4.0	0.4	trace	trace	trace	0.2	2.1	8.4	8.7	49.7
Maximum Snowfall (in.)*	25	26	31	19	10	0	0	0	5	24	30	17	97
Maximum 24-hr. Snowfall (in.)*	8	9	16	12	7	0	0	0	4	9	11	10	16
Maximum Snow Depth (in.)	19	17	17	16	3	trace	trace	trace	2	10	19	15	19
Days With ≥ 1.0" Snow Depth	25	20	12	3	0	0	0	0	0	1	10	19	90
Thunderstorm Days*	0	< 1	< 1	1	4	9	9	8	3	1	< 1	0	35
Foggy Days*	5	6	7	5	4	4	3	4	4	5	5	7	59
Predominant Sky Cover*	OVR	OVR	OVR	OVR	OVR	OVR	SCT	CLR	CLR	OVR	OVR	OVR	OVR
Mean Relative Humidity 6am (%)*	76	78	82	80	79	84	84	84	82	80	81	79	81
Mean Relative Humidity 3pm (%)*	67	66	59	45	43	47	42	40	42	44	58	67	52
Mean Dewpoint (°F)*	2	8	19	29	40	51	55	53	43	32	20	9	30
Prevailing Wind Direction*	WNW	WNW	NW	NNW	SSE	SSE	SSE	SSE	WNW	WNW	WNW	WNW	WNW
Prevailing Wind Speed (mph)*	14	13	16	15	14	13	12	13	13	13	14	14	14
Maximum Wind Gust (mph)*	67	73	64	71	66	59	74	69	84	60	56	63	84

Note: (*) Period of record is 1948-1995

The period of record for National Weather Service station data is 1980 – 2009 except where noted. See User Guide for detailed explanation of data.

Fargo Hector Field

Moorhead, Minnesota, and Fargo are twin cities in the Red River Valley of the north. The Red River of the north flows northward between the two cities and is a part of the Hudson Bay drainage area. The Red River is approximately two miles east of the airport at its nearest point and has no significant effect on the weather. In recent years, spring floods due to melting snow have been common. Summer floods caused by heavy rains are infrequent.

The surrounding terrain is flat and open. Northerly winds blowing up the valley occasionally causing low cloudiness and fog. However, this upslope cloudiness is very infrequent. Aside from this, there are no pronounced climatic differences due to geographical features in the immediate area.

The summers are generally comfortable with very few days of hot and humid weather. Nights, with few exceptions, are comfortably cool. The winter months are cold and dry with temperatures rising above freezing only on an average of six days each month, and nighttime lows dropping below zero approximately half of the time.

Precipitation is the most important climatic factor in the area. The Red River Valley lies in an area where lighter amounts fall to the west and heavier amounts to the east. Seventy-five percent of the precipitation occurs during the growing season (April to September) and is often accompanied by electrical storms and heavy falls in a short time. Winter precipitation is light, indicating that heavy snowfall is the exception rather than the rule. The first light snow in the fall occasionally falls in September, but usually very little, if any, occurs until October or November. The latest fall is generally in April.

With the flat terrain, surface friction has little effect on the wind in the area and this fact has led to the legendary Dakota blizzards. Strong winds with even light snowfall cause much drifting and blowing snow, reducing visibility to near zero. Fortunately, these conditions occur only several times during the winter months.

Fargo Hector Field *Cass County* Elevation: 899 ft. Latitude: 46° 56' N Longitude: 96° 49' W

	JAN	FEB	MAR	APR	MAY	JUN	JUL	AUG	SEP	OCT	NOV	DEC	YEAR
Mean Maximum Temp. (°F)	18.1	23.3	35.6	55.5	69.2	77.1	82.3	80.8	70.6	55.4	37.1	22.2	52.3
Mean Temp. (°F)	9.1	14.4	27.2	44.0	57.0	66.0	70.9	69.0	59.0	45.2	28.8	14.1	42.1
Mean Minimum Temp. (°F)	0.0	5.5	18.9	32.5	44.8	54.9	59.4	57.2	47.4	34.9	20.5	5.9	31.8
Extreme Maximum Temp. (°F)	52	55	76	100	97	100	106	104	97	90	74	56	106
Extreme Minimum Temp. (°F)	-36	-39	-23	5	20	33	39	33	22	9	-24	-31	-39
Days Maximum Temp. ≥ 90°F	0	0	0	0	1	2	4	4	1	0	0	0	12
Days Maximum Temp. ≤ 32°F	26	20	11	1	0	0	0	0	0	1	11	23	93
Days Minimum Temp. ≤ 32°F	31	28	27	16	3	0	0	0	1	13	26	31	176
Days Minimum Temp. ≤ 0°F	16	11	3	0	0	0	0	0	0	0	2	11	43
Heating Degree Days (base 65°F)	1,730	1,426	1,164	627	271	71	15	33	218	610	1,079	1,574	8,818
Cooling Degree Days (base 65°F)	0	0	0	4	31	109	204	164	46	3	0	0	561
Mean Precipitation (in.)	0.68	0.60	1.27	1.31	2.74	3.85	2.67	2.61	2.46	2.19	0.91	0.76	22.05
Maximum Precipitation (in.)*	1.8	1.7	2.6	5.3	7.3	9.4	8.4	6.5	6.1	7.0	4.6	2.2	32.3
Minimum Precipitation (in.)*	0.1	trace	trace	trace	0.5	0.6	0.4	0.2	0.1	0	trace	trace	8.8
Extreme Maximum Daily Precip. (in.)	0.94	0.57	1.12	1.78	2.18	4.64	4.42	3.33	2.50	3.10	1.12	0.76	4.64
Days With ≥ 0.1" Precipitation	2	2	3	4	6	7	5	5	5	4	3	2	48
Days With ≥ 0.5" Precipitation	0	0	1	1	2	2	2	1	2	1	0	0	12
Days With ≥ 1.0" Precipitation	0	0	0	0	1	1	1	1	1	0	0	0	5
Mean Snowfall (in.)	11.1	6.8	9.4	3.1	trace	trace	trace	trace	trace	0.7	7.0	10.1	48.2
Maximum Snowfall (in.)*	32	20	19	13	1	0	0	0	trace	8	24	20	68
Maximum 24-hr. Snowfall (in.)*	16	11	11	9	1	0	0	0	trace	7	12	9	16
Maximum Snow Depth (in.)	na	na	na	na	na	na	na	na	na	na	na	na	na
Days With ≥ 1.0" Snow Depth	na	na	na	na	na	na	na	na	na	na	na	na	na
Thunderstorm Days*	< 1	< 1	< 1	1	4	7	8	7	3	1	< 1	< 1	31
Foggy Days*	7	7	9	6	6	5	4	5	6	6	7	9	77
Predominant Sky Cover*	OVR	OVR	OVR	OVR	OVR	OVR	SCT	SCT	OVR	OVR	OVR	OVR	OVR
Mean Relative Humidity 6am (%)*	75	77	82	79	77	82	86	86	85	80	81	78	81
Mean Relative Humidity 3pm (%)*	70	71	67	51	45	50	50	47	49	51	65	73	57
Mean Dewpoint (°F)*	0	6	19	30	41	53	59	56	46	35	21	7	31
Prevailing Wind Direction*	NNW	N	N	N	SSE	SSE	SSE	SSE	SSE	SSE	SSE	S	SSE
Prevailing Wind Speed (mph)*	16	14	15	16	15	14	13	14	14	15	15	12	14
Maximum Wind Gust (mph)*	60	59	58	63	62	81	71	66	62	58	61	59	81

Note: (*) Period of record is 1948-1995

Williston Sloulin Int'l Airport

Williston lies in a flat valley at the junction of the Missouri River and Little Muddy Creek. The surrounding country is rolling. Hills to the east are highest, ranging from 250 to 300 feet in height at a distance of five to seven miles. Across the Missouri River to the south, the bluffs are about 225 feet high at four miles distance.

Great extremes of temperatures are encountered, winters being cold, while summer days are usually warm. In winter, temperatures below zero are common and lows of -50 degrees have been recorded. When temperatures are lowest, however, the air is generally dry, with little or no wind and the weather is fine and invigorating. At the other extreme, temperatures above 100 degrees have been reached in all months from May to September. The low humidity that generally prevails on the hottest summer days keeps them from becoming oppressive.

The climate of Williston and vicinity is continental, semi-arid, characterized by marked season changes. Winter is the relatively dry season, with only about half an inch of monthly precipitation occurring from November to February. There is considerably less than the average amount of snowfall for similar locations in the United States. Ice crystals, which rarely yield more than a trace of precipitation, are common in the cold months. Summer precipitation is variable from year to year. The amount of rain occurring during the growing period is the most important element of climate for agricultural interests in the vicinity of Williston. Generally, considerably more precipitation occurs in the spring and summer months than in winter.

The growing season averages 131 days. It has ranged from 94 to 172 days during the period of record.

Clear and partly cloudy skies, nearly equally distributed, occur about 70 percent of the time. Heavy fog occurs on the average about ten times a year. Because of the northern latitude of Williston, it enjoys long hours of daylight in the spring and summer. Relatively little cloudiness occurs then, so that the duration of sunshine averages about two-thirds of the possible amount.

Summer storms are generally in the form of thunderstorms or rain showers, occasionally accompanied by hail and squally winds. Tornadoes are rare in this area. In the winter, cold waves and occasionally blizzard conditions occur. Cold waves result when extremely cold air advances southward from northwestern Canada. In blizzard conditions the advancing cold wave is accompanied by winds of gale force and the air is filled with fine, wind-driven snow. In extreme instances in the country, it becomes impossible for persons to ascertain their bearings or to remain alive many hours without shelter in such storms.

Williston Sloulin Int'l Airport *Williams County* Elevation: 1,898 ft. Latitude: 48° 12' N Longitude: 103° 39' W

	JAN	FEB	MAR	APR	MAY	JUN	JUL	AUG	SEP	OCT	NOV	DEC	YEAR
Mean Maximum Temp. (°F)	22.2	28.0	40.5	57.5	68.4	77.2	84.8	83.8	71.7	56.3	38.3	24.9	54.5
Mean Temp. (°F)	11.4	17.6	29.6	44.0	54.8	63.8	70.7	69.2	57.3	43.5	27.8	14.5	42.0
Mean Minimum Temp. (°F)	0.6	7.1	18.5	30.4	41.2	50.4	56.5	54.5	42.8	30.5	17.2	4.2	29.5
Extreme Maximum Temp. (°F)	53	66	78	92	106	106	109	107	104	92	76	56	109
Extreme Minimum Temp. (°F)	-37	-37	-31	-6	10	26	39	34	15	-9	-27	-50	-50
Days Maximum Temp. ≥ 90°F	0	0	0	0	1	3	9	9	2	0	0	0	24
Days Maximum Temp. ≤ 32°F	21	16	8	1	0	0	0	0	0	1	9	20	76
Days Minimum Temp. ≤ 32°F	31	28	29	18	6	0	0	0	3	17	28	31	191
Days Minimum Temp. ≤ 0°F	14	10	3	0	0	0	0	0	0	0	3	12	42
Heating Degree Days (base 65°F)	1,657	1,336	1,092	626	327	105	19	39	255	662	1,110	1,560	8,788
Cooling Degree Days (base 65°F)	0	0	0	1	18	77	201	176	30	1	0	0	504
Mean Precipitation (in.)	0.57	0.39	0.70	0.98	1.79	2.49	2.43	1.43	1.08	0.93	0.62	0.58	13.99
Maximum Precipitation (in.)*	1.4	1.5	2.3	3.3	7.4	6.2	6.3	4.7	3.1	3.6	1.1	1.4	21.8
Minimum Precipitation (in.)*	trace	trace	trace	trace	0.1	0.7	0.3	0.1	0.1	trace	trace	0.1	9.2
Extreme Maximum Daily Precip. (in.)	0.62	0.69	1.39	2.20	1.50	2.21	4.82	3.04	1.26	1.23	1.98	0.92	4.82
Days With ≥ 0.1" Precipitation	2	1	2	3	5	6	5	3	3	3	2	1	36
Days With ≥ 0.5" Precipitation	0	0	0	0	1	2	1	1	0	0	0	0	5
Days With ≥ 1.0" Precipitation	0	0	0	0	0	0	0	0	0	0	0	0	0
Mean Snowfall (in.)	9.7	5.8	6.2	3.8	1.3	trace	trace	trace	0.2	2.5	5.8	8.8	44.1
Maximum Snowfall (in.)*	24	22	31	22	16	0	0	0	4	14	16	16	79
Maximum 24-hr. Snowfall (in.)*	10	7	7	15	12	0	0	0	3	11	7	8	15
Maximum Snow Depth (in.)	24	24	17	15	12	trace	trace	trace	2	5	13	19	24
Days With ≥ 1.0" Snow Depth	25	18	12	2	0	0	0	0	0	1	9	20	87
Thunderstorm Days*	0	< 1	< 1	1	3	8	9	6	2	< 1	0	0	29
Foggy Days*	6	5	6	5	3	3	2	2	3	4	6	7	52
Predominant Sky Cover*	OVR	OVR	OVR	OVR	OVR	OVR	SCT	SCT	CLR	OVR	OVR	OVR	OVR
Mean Relative Humidity 6am (%)*	78	80	83	80	79	81	81	78	80	79	82	80	80
Mean Relative Humidity 3pm (%)*	69	66	57	44	42	44	39	36	42	44	60	68	51
Mean Dewpoint (°F)*	3	10	20	29	39	49	53	50	41	31	19	8	29
Prevailing Wind Direction*	SW	SSW	N	N	N	SE	N	SE	N	SSW	SSW	SSW	N
Prevailing Wind Speed (mph)*	8	8	12	13	13	12	9	12	12	8	8	7	10
Maximum Wind Gust (mph)*	62	53	62	70	76	75	70	55	60	62	64	63	76

Note: (*) Period of record is 1962-1995

The period of record for National Weather Service station data is 1980 – 2009 except where noted. See User Guide for detailed explanation of data.

Almont *Morton County* Elevation: 1,915 ft. Latitude: 46° 44' N Longitude: 101° 30' W

	JAN	FEB	MAR	APR	MAY	JUN	JUL	AUG	SEP	OCT	NOV	DEC	YEAR
Mean Maximum Temp. (°F)	26.2	30.5	42.6	59.2	70.6	78.2	85.2	84.0	74.0	58.8	40.8	28.9	56.6
Mean Temp. (°F)	14.7	19.3	30.7	44.6	56.2	64.7	70.6	68.9	59.0	44.8	29.5	17.7	43.4
Mean Minimum Temp. (°F)	3.3	8.0	18.7	29.9	41.9	51.2	56.0	53.8	43.9	30.7	18.1	6.4	30.2
Extreme Maximum Temp. (°F)	62	70	80	94	96	110	110	105	102	96	83	66	110
Extreme Minimum Temp. (°F)	-47	-45	-30	-8	9	28	39	31	15	-9	-26	-40	-47
Days Maximum Temp. ≥ 90°F	0	0	0	0	1	3	9	8	2	0	0	0	23
Days Maximum Temp. ≤ 32°F	19	15	7	1	0	0	0	0	0	1	8	17	68
Days Minimum Temp. ≤ 32°F	30	28	28	18	5	0	0	0	3	17	27	31	187
Days Minimum Temp. ≤ 0°F	13	8	3	0	0	0	0	0	0	0	2	10	36
Heating Degree Days (base 65°F)	1,555	1,286	1,057	609	282	90	23	37	215	623	1,058	1,462	8,297
Cooling Degree Days (base 65°F)	0	0	0	2	19	88	204	166	41	1	0	0	521
Mean Precipitation (in.)	0.42	0.43	0.73	1.32	2.47	3.13	2.74	1.99	1.32	1.16	0.61	0.40	16.72
Extreme Maximum Daily Precip. (in.)	0.65	0.65	1.35	1.40	2.53	3.10	2.44	4.27	3.26	2.04	0.93	0.92	4.27
Days With ≥ 0.1" Precipitation	2	1	2	3	5	6	5	4	3	3	2	1	37
Days With ≥ 0.5" Precipitation	0	0	0	1	2	2	2	1	1	1	0	0	10
Days With ≥ 1.0" Precipitation	0	0	0	0	0	1	1	0	0	0	0	0	2
Mean Snowfall (in.)	na	4.0	4.2	1.1	trace	0.0	0.0	0.0	trace	0.2	5.4	7.0	na
Maximum Snow Depth (in.)	na	na	na	na	na	na	na	na	na	na	na	na	na
Days With ≥ 1.0" Snow Depth	na	na	4	0	0	0	0	0	0	0	5	6	na

Amidon *Slope County* Elevation: 2,910 ft. Latitude: 46° 29' N Longitude: 103° 19' W

	JAN	FEB	MAR	APR	MAY	JUN	JUL	AUG	SEP	OCT	NOV	DEC	YEAR
Mean Maximum Temp. (°F)	28.8	33.1	42.6	56.3	67.1	76.4	85.0	84.9	72.5	58.1	41.3	30.6	56.4
Mean Temp. (°F)	17.9	22.4	31.2	43.6	54.4	63.3	70.8	69.9	58.3	45.3	30.6	19.9	44.0
Mean Minimum Temp. (°F)	7.5	11.7	19.9	30.8	41.6	50.2	56.6	54.8	44.1	32.3	19.9	9.3	31.5
Extreme Maximum Temp. (°F)	64	68	81	91	98	107	108	108	105	94	81	64	108
Extreme Minimum Temp. (°F)	-34	-35	-21	-5	19	30	40	35	17	-8	-26	-40	-40
Days Maximum Temp. ≥ 90°F	0	0	0	0	1	3	10	11	3	0	0	0	28
Days Maximum Temp. ≤ 32°F	16	11	7	1	0	0	0	0	0	1	8	15	59
Days Minimum Temp. ≤ 32°F	30	27	27	17	4	0	0	0	2	14	25	30	176
Days Minimum Temp. ≤ 0°F	10	6	3	0	0	0	0	0	0	0	2	7	28
Heating Degree Days (base 65°F)	1,455	1,198	1,052	637	338	120	24	36	243	605	1,024	1,393	8,125
Cooling Degree Days (base 65°F)	0	0	0	2	16	77	211	194	49	2	0	0	551
Mean Precipitation (in.)	0.32	0.30	0.61	0.96	2.07	2.85	2.16	1.36	1.28	1.22	0.53	0.38	14.04
Extreme Maximum Daily Precip. (in.)	0.71	0.50	1.94	0.98	2.00	1.64	1.52	1.51	1.68	2.27	1.36	1.05	2.27
Days With ≥ 0.1" Precipitation	1	1	2	3	4	6	5	3	3	2	2	1	33
Days With ≥ 0.5" Precipitation	0	0	0	0	1	2	1	1	1	1	0	0	7
Days With ≥ 1.0" Precipitation	0	0	0	0	0	1	0	0	0	0	0	0	1
Mean Snowfall (in.)	na	4.3	4.0	2.4	0.7	0.0	0.0	0.0	0.0	1.7	na	na	na
Maximum Snow Depth (in.)	na	na	na	14	10	0	0	0	7	4	na	na	na
Days With ≥ 1.0" Snow Depth	na	3	4	1	0	0	0	0	0	0	5	7	na

Ashley *Mcintosh County* Elevation: 2,000 ft. Latitude: 46° 02' N Longitude: 99° 22' W

	JAN	FEB	MAR	APR	MAY	JUN	JUL	AUG	SEP	OCT	NOV	DEC	YEAR
Mean Maximum Temp. (°F)	22.1	27.4	38.4	55.7	67.7	76.2	83.4	81.6	71.4	56.9	39.3	25.5	53.8
Mean Temp. (°F)	12.0	17.2	28.2	43.0	55.4	64.6	70.8	68.5	58.3	44.6	29.2	16.1	42.3
Mean Minimum Temp. (°F)	1.9	7.0	17.9	30.3	43.0	52.8	58.2	55.4	45.2	32.2	19.1	6.7	30.8
Extreme Maximum Temp. (°F)	60	60	76	97	97	107	112	106	102	92	75	59	112
Extreme Minimum Temp. (°F)	-34	-40	-26	2	16	33	39	33	18	-2	-21	-36	-40
Days Maximum Temp. ≥ 90°F	0	0	0	0	1	2	7	6	1	0	0	0	17
Days Maximum Temp. ≤ 32°F	23	17	10	1	0	0	0	0	0	1	9	20	81
Days Minimum Temp. ≤ 32°F	31	28	29	18	4	0	0	0	2	15	28	31	186
Days Minimum Temp. ≤ 0°F	14	9	4	0	0	0	0	0	0	0	2	10	39
Heating Degree Days (base 65°F)	1,639	1,346	1,136	655	311	91	22	42	237	628	1,067	1,510	8,684
Cooling Degree Days (base 65°F)	0	0	0	2	19	85	207	158	43	2	0	0	516
Mean Precipitation (in.)	0.36	0.41	0.86	1.34	2.75	3.48	3.09	2.60	1.81	1.73	0.53	0.30	19.26
Extreme Maximum Daily Precip. (in.)	0.50	0.92	1.38	1.53	2.32	3.06	2.57	2.70	1.87	2.24	0.67	0.83	3.06
Days With ≥ 0.1" Precipitation	1	1	2	4	6	7	6	5	4	4	2	1	43
Days With ≥ 0.5" Precipitation	0	0	0	1	2	2	2	2	1	1	0	0	11
Days With ≥ 1.0" Precipitation	0	0	0	0	1	1	1	1	0	0	0	0	4
Mean Snowfall (in.)	5.8	4.9	6.3	3.0	0.0	0.0	0.0	0.0	trace	0.6	5.0	5.0	30.6
Maximum Snow Depth (in.)	31	34	41	17	0	0	0	0	0	4	15	24	41
Days With ≥ 1.0" Snow Depth	20	18	13	3	0	0	0	0	0	0	9	16	79

Bottineau *Bottineau County* Elevation: 1,640 ft. Latitude: 48° 50' N Longitude: 100° 27' W

	JAN	FEB	MAR	APR	MAY	JUN	JUL	AUG	SEP	OCT	NOV	DEC	YEAR
Mean Maximum Temp. (°F)	15.4	20.9	32.9	53.1	65.9	74.2	79.7	78.9	68.4	52.8	34.3	19.3	49.7
Mean Temp. (°F)	5.4	10.9	23.4	41.0	53.5	62.5	67.5	65.9	55.6	41.1	24.8	10.0	38.5
Mean Minimum Temp. (°F)	-4.6	0.8	13.8	28.9	40.9	50.7	55.3	52.9	42.7	29.3	15.4	0.6	27.2
Extreme Maximum Temp. (°F)	46	63	73	95	98	99	104	102	96	89	73	49	104
Extreme Minimum Temp. (°F)	-40	-39	-31	-6	12	32	39	34	19	-6	-28	-40	-40
Days Maximum Temp. ≥ 90°F	0	0	0	0	1	1	3	3	1	0	0	0	9
Days Maximum Temp. ≤ 32°F	28	22	13	2	0	0	0	0	0	1	13	26	105
Days Minimum Temp. ≤ 32°F	31	28	30	20	6	0	0	0	3	20	29	31	198
Days Minimum Temp. ≤ 0°F	18	14	6	0	0	0	0	0	0	0	4	15	57
Heating Degree Days (base 65°F)	1,845	1,526	1,285	714	366	130	42	69	297	735	1,199	1,703	9,911
Cooling Degree Days (base 65°F)	0	0	0	1	15	62	128	105	21	0	0	0	332
Mean Precipitation (in.)	0.46	0.39	0.80	0.93	2.31	3.53	2.73	2.57	1.55	1.27	0.65	0.50	17.69
Extreme Maximum Daily Precip. (in.)	0.50	1.25	1.63	0.93	2.50	2.94	2.64	4.18	2.50	1.52	0.86	0.79	4.18
Days With ≥ 0.1" Precipitation	2	1	2	3	5	8	5	5	4	3	2	2	42
Days With ≥ 0.5" Precipitation	0	0	0	0	2	2	2	1	1	1	0	0	9
Days With ≥ 1.0" Precipitation	0	0	0	0	0	1	1	1	0	0	0	0	3
Mean Snowfall (in.)	8.4	5.4	6.4	3.4	1.1	trace	0.0	0.0	0.1	2.6	6.7	8.7	42.8
Maximum Snow Depth (in.)	29	30	22	10	6	trace	0	0	1	8	13	21	30
Days With ≥ 1.0" Snow Depth	29	25	21	3	0	0	0	0	0	2	13	27	120

Butte *Mclean County* Elevation: 1,660 ft. Latitude: 47° 49' N Longitude: 100° 35' W

	JAN	FEB	MAR	APR	MAY	JUN	JUL	AUG	SEP	OCT	NOV	DEC	YEAR
Mean Maximum Temp. (°F)	20.5	25.8	37.5	56.6	68.7	77.1	83.1	82.8	71.2	56.5	37.9	24.0	53.5
Mean Temp. (°F)	11.2	16.5	27.6	43.6	55.7	64.7	70.0	69.1	58.6	44.8	28.8	15.2	42.2
Mean Minimum Temp. (°F)	1.8	7.2	17.7	30.6	42.7	52.3	57.0	55.2	45.5	33.0	19.7	6.4	30.7
Extreme Maximum Temp. (°F)	53	64	75	93	98	105	104	103	102	94	76	55	105
Extreme Minimum Temp. (°F)	-34	-38	-26	-8	18	30	41	30	21	-1	-22	-36	-38
Days Maximum Temp. ≥ 90°F	0	0	0	0	1	3	6	8	2	0	0	0	20
Days Maximum Temp. ≤ 32°F	22	18	10	1	0	0	0	0	0	1	10	20	82
Days Minimum Temp. ≤ 32°F	29	27	28	17	4	0	0	0	2	15	26	30	178
Days Minimum Temp. ≤ 0°F	13	9	4	0	0	0	0	0	0	0	2	11	39
Heating Degree Days (base 65°F)	1,667	1,367	1,153	638	305	92	22	41	226	621	1,078	1,537	8,747
Cooling Degree Days (base 65°F)	0	0	0	3	23	90	184	174	41	2	0	0	517
Mean Precipitation (in.)	0.43	0.40	0.73	1.11	2.62	3.34	2.66	1.93	1.36	1.43	0.57	0.33	16.91
Extreme Maximum Daily Precip. (in.)	0.52	1.20	1.38	1.78	2.31	4.00	3.50	2.80	1.21	1.58	0.90	0.80	4.00
Days With ≥ 0.1" Precipitation	1	1	2	3	5	6	5	4	3	3	2	1	36
Days With ≥ 0.5" Precipitation	0	0	0	0	1	2	2	1	1	1	0	0	10
Days With ≥ 1.0" Precipitation	0	0	0	0	1	1	1	0	0	0	0	0	3
Mean Snowfall (in.)	6.2	5.5	4.4	3.4	0.3	0.0	0.0	0.0	trace	2.4	5.4	5.0	32.6
Maximum Snow Depth (in.)	na	14	14	18	6	0	0	0	1	9	16	na	na
Days With ≥ 1.0" Snow Depth	na	4	5	1	0	0	0	0	0	1	4	6	na

Carrington *Foster County* Elevation: 1,585 ft. Latitude: 47° 27' N Longitude: 99° 08' W

	JAN	FEB	MAR	APR	MAY	JUN	JUL	AUG	SEP	OCT	NOV	DEC	YEAR
Mean Maximum Temp. (°F)	18.3	23.7	34.3	52.6	66.8	74.7	79.9	79.5	68.4	54.2	34.4	21.8	50.7
Mean Temp. (°F)	8.8	14.6	25.3	41.2	54.7	63.5	68.6	67.2	56.2	42.9	25.7	13.3	40.2
Mean Minimum Temp. (°F)	-0.7	5.5	16.3	29.7	42.5	52.3	57.2	54.9	43.9	31.6	17.0	4.8	29.6
Extreme Maximum Temp. (°F)	53	59	70	97	95	101	105	102	99	90	73	51	105
Extreme Minimum Temp. (°F)	-32	-36	-26	-1	20	33	42	35	23	0	-22	-34	-36
Days Maximum Temp. ≥ 90°F	0	0	0	0	0	2	3	4	1	0	0	0	10
Days Maximum Temp. ≤ 32°F	25	19	12	2	0	0	0	0	0	1	13	23	95
Days Minimum Temp. ≤ 32°F	31	28	30	20	4	0	0	0	2	16	28	31	190
Days Minimum Temp. ≤ 0°F	16	11	5	0	0	0	0	0	0	0	3	12	47
Heating Degree Days (base 65°F)	1,739	1,421	1,224	711	331	110	30	50	282	679	1,173	1,599	9,349
Cooling Degree Days (base 65°F)	0	0	0	2	17	72	148	125	25	1	0	0	390
Mean Precipitation (in.)	0.70	0.55	0.92	1.18	2.19	3.43	3.77	2.57	1.57	1.52	0.88	0.47	19.75
Extreme Maximum Daily Precip. (in.)	0.90	0.98	1.74	1.67	2.00	2.18	3.45	3.31	1.45	1.61	1.45	0.55	3.45
Days With ≥ 0.1" Precipitation	2	2	3	3	5	7	7	5	4	3	3	1	45
Days With ≥ 0.5" Precipitation	0	0	0	1	1	2	2	2	1	1	0	0	10
Days With ≥ 1.0" Precipitation	0	0	0	0	0	1	1	0	0	0	0	0	2
Mean Snowfall (in.)	9.8	6.5	6.4	3.4	0.4	0.0	0.0	0.0	trace	1.6	8.7	7.3	44.1
Maximum Snow Depth (in.)	na	na	na	na	na	na	na	na	na	na	na	na	na
Days With ≥ 1.0" Snow Depth	na	na	na	0	0	0	0	0	0	0	na	na	na

Cavalier 7 NW *Pembina County* Elevation: 890 ft. Latitude: 48° 52' N Longitude: 97° 42' W

	JAN	FEB	MAR	APR	MAY	JUN	JUL	AUG	SEP	OCT	NOV	DEC	YEAR
Mean Maximum Temp. (°F)	13.9	19.7	30.8	51.4	66.0	73.8	78.4	77.8	67.5	52.2	34.0	18.6	48.7
Mean Temp. (°F)	4.4	9.9	22.1	40.3	53.3	62.6	67.0	65.3	55.2	41.7	25.4	10.0	38.1
Mean Minimum Temp. (°F)	-5.1	0.2	13.4	29.2	40.6	51.4	55.7	52.8	43.0	31.2	16.8	1.3	27.5
Extreme Maximum Temp. (°F)	49	60	69	96	97	98	101	103	102	93	75	51	103
Extreme Minimum Temp. (°F)	-40	-40	-26	-2	18	31	35	30	24	-2	-33	-32	-40
Days Maximum Temp. ≥ 90°F	0	0	0	0	1	1	2	2	0	0	0	0	6
Days Maximum Temp. ≤ 32°F	27	22	16	3	0	0	0	0	0	1	14	25	108
Days Minimum Temp. ≤ 32°F	31	28	30	21	6	0	0	0	3	17	29	31	196
Days Minimum Temp. ≤ 0°F	20	15	6	0	0	0	0	0	0	0	3	14	58
Heating Degree Days (base 65°F)	1,876	1,554	1,323	735	374	125	41	71	303	716	1,180	1,702	10,000
Cooling Degree Days (base 65°F)	0	0	0	1	18	60	111	88	17	1	0	0	296
Mean Precipitation (in.)	0.33	0.35	0.71	1.00	2.44	3.60	3.19	2.57	1.79	1.67	0.78	0.45	18.88
Extreme Maximum Daily Precip. (in.)	0.35	0.87	2.55	1.11	1.77	4.56	2.85	2.30	2.97	2.86	2.56	1.08	4.56
Days With ≥ 0.1" Precipitation	1	1	2	3	5	7	6	5	4	3	2	1	40
Days With ≥ 0.5" Precipitation	0	0	0	1	2	2	2	2	1	1	0	0	11
Days With ≥ 1.0" Precipitation	0	0	0	0	0	1	1	1	0	0	0	0	3
Mean Snowfall (in.)	7.0	4.9	5.4	2.9	0.7	0.0	trace	0.0	trace	2.2	6.4	7.4	36.9
Maximum Snow Depth (in.)	26	28	34	21	5	0	trace	0	trace	7	15	23	34
Days With ≥ 1.0" Snow Depth	31	27	24	4	0	0	0	0	0	2	14	25	127

Center 4 SE *Oliver County* Elevation: 1,990 ft. Latitude: 47° 04' N Longitude: 101° 12' W

	JAN	FEB	MAR	APR	MAY	JUN	JUL	AUG	SEP	OCT	NOV	DEC	YEAR
Mean Maximum Temp. (°F)	24.4	28.6	39.9	56.4	67.6	76.0	83.2	82.4	71.5	56.9	40.0	27.1	54.5
Mean Temp. (°F)	13.1	17.6	28.3	42.9	54.2	63.0	69.2	67.6	57.2	43.9	28.8	16.4	41.9
Mean Minimum Temp. (°F)	1.8	6.8	16.7	29.3	40.8	50.0	55.1	52.9	42.8	30.9	17.6	5.7	29.2
Extreme Maximum Temp. (°F)	60	66	80	94	96	105	107	106	102	93	79	60	107
Extreme Minimum Temp. (°F)	-38	-39	-27	-6	11	26	37	32	18	-3	-20	-37	-39
Days Maximum Temp. ≥ 90°F	0	0	0	0	0	2	7	7	2	0	0	0	18
Days Maximum Temp. ≤ 32°F	20	16	9	1	0	0	0	0	0	1	9	18	74
Days Minimum Temp. ≤ 32°F	30	28	29	19	6	0	0	0	4	17	28	31	192
Days Minimum Temp. ≤ 0°F	14	10	4	0	0	0	0	0	0	0	2	10	40
Heating Degree Days (base 65°F)	1,605	1,334	1,131	660	341	120	29	52	258	648	1,078	1,502	8,758
Cooling Degree Days (base 65°F)	0	0	0	2	14	65	165	141	30	1	0	0	418
Mean Precipitation (in.)	0.42	0.45	0.57	1.36	2.49	3.01	2.73	1.79	1.65	1.48	0.57	0.38	16.90
Extreme Maximum Daily Precip. (in.)	1.05	1.00	1.00	1.70	2.26	2.40	2.50	3.00	3.86	2.15	1.50	0.86	3.86
Days With ≥ 0.1" Precipitation	1	1	2	3	5	7	5	4	3	3	1	1	36
Days With ≥ 0.5" Precipitation	0	0	0	1	2	2	2	1	1	1	0	0	10
Days With ≥ 1.0" Precipitation	0	0	0	0	0	1	0	0	0	0	0	0	1
Mean Snowfall (in.)	5.6	4.5	4.6	1.9	0.1	0.0	0.0	0.0	trace	1.0	4.0	5.2	26.9
Maximum Snow Depth (in.)	30	33	18	14	trace	0	0	0	trace	16	20	24	33
Days With ≥ 1.0" Snow Depth	17	15	8	2	0	0	0	0	0	1	5	14	62

The period of record for all cooperative weather station data is 1980 – 2009. See User Guide for detailed explanation of data.

Colgate *Steele County* Elevation: 1,180 ft. Latitude: 47° 15' N Longitude: 97° 39' W

	JAN	FEB	MAR	APR	MAY	JUN	JUL	AUG	SEP	OCT	NOV	DEC	YEAR
Mean Maximum Temp. (°F)	17.1	23.0	35.0	55.5	69.5	77.2	82.5	81.6	71.1	55.6	36.5	21.9	52.2
Mean Temp. (°F)	7.4	12.9	25.7	42.9	56.0	64.8	***69.7***	68.0	57.9	44.0	27.3	13.0	***40.8***
Mean Minimum Temp. (°F)	-2.1	2.8	16.4	30.2	42.4	52.4	56.7	54.3	44.7	32.3	18.1	3.9	29.3
Extreme Maximum Temp. (°F)	52	56	74	100	100	101	107	105	102	92	73	53	107
Extreme Minimum Temp. (°F)	-37	-40	-31	-3	17	30	37	28	19	5	-31	-34	-40
Days Maximum Temp. ≥ 90°F	0	0	0	0	1	3	5	5	1	0	0	0	15
Days Maximum Temp. ≤ 32°F	25	20	11	2	0	0	0	0	0	1	12	23	94
Days Minimum Temp. ≤ 32°F	31	28	29	19	4	0	0	0	3	15	28	30	187
Days Minimum Temp. ≤ 0°F	17	13	4	0	0	0	0	0	0	0	2	12	48
Heating Degree Days (base 65°F)	1,783	1,457	1,213	660	295	88	***22***	44	240	647	1,125	1,606	***9,180***
Cooling Degree Days (base 65°F)	0	0	0	2	24	88	***174***	143	35	1	0	0	***467***
Mean Precipitation (in.)	0.41	0.37	0.73	0.95	2.63	3.18	2.98	2.50	2.30	1.78	0.70	0.48	19.01
Extreme Maximum Daily Precip. (in.)	0.55	1.59	0.97	1.22	2.31	2.23	2.80	4.36	3.32	2.93	1.46	1.02	4.36
Days With ≥ 0.1" Precipitation	2	1	2	3	6	6	5	5	4	4	2	2	42
Days With ≥ 0.5" Precipitation	0	0	0	0	2	2	2	2	2	1	0	0	11
Days With ≥ 1.0" Precipitation	0	0	0	0	0	1	1	0	1	0	0	0	3
Mean Snowfall (in.)	7.0	4.4	4.7	1.6	0.0	0.0	0.0	0.0	0.0	0.9	5.9	6.4	30.9
Maximum Snow Depth (in.)	30	***28***	27	6	0	0	0	0	0	***8***	19	***20***	***30***
Days With ≥ 1.0" Snow Depth	22	***19***	13	1	0	0	0	0	0	0	7	20	***82***

Crosby *Divide County* Elevation: 1,952 ft. Latitude: 48° 54' N Longitude: 103° 18' W

	JAN	FEB	MAR	APR	MAY	JUN	JUL	AUG	SEP	OCT	NOV	DEC	YEAR
Mean Maximum Temp. (°F)	19.8	25.4	37.7	57.3	69.1	76.8	82.9	81.6	70.0	54.6	36.0	22.3	52.8
Mean Temp. (°F)	10.4	15.9	27.7	43.9	55.4	63.9	69.4	67.8	56.9	43.3	27.0	13.4	41.3
Mean Minimum Temp. (°F)	0.9	6.4	17.6	30.4	41.7	51.1	55.8	54.0	43.7	31.9	17.9	4.5	29.7
Extreme Maximum Temp. (°F)	51	64	75	92	103	105	105	107	98	89	70	52	107
Extreme Minimum Temp. (°F)	-40	-40	-24	-5	16	30	40	33	21	-4	-25	-40	-40
Days Maximum Temp. ≥ 90°F	0	0	0	0	1	3	7	6	1	0	0	0	18
Days Maximum Temp. ≤ 32°F	23	18	10	1	0	0	0	0	0	1	11	22	86
Days Minimum Temp. ≤ 32°F	31	28	29	18	5	0	0	0	2	15	28	31	187
Days Minimum Temp. ≤ 0°F	15	10	4	0	0	0	0	0	0	0	3	11	43
Heating Degree Days (base 65°F)	1,691	1,383	1,151	628	309	102	24	46	261	666	1,134	1,595	8,990
Cooling Degree Days (base 65°F)	0	0	0	2	19	77	167	141	25	0	0	0	431
Mean Precipitation (in.)	0.55	0.31	0.59	0.86	1.91	2.83	2.75	1.60	1.23	1.03	0.53	0.46	14.65
Extreme Maximum Daily Precip. (in.)	0.58	0.89	1.30	1.30	2.00	2.28	2.50	1.53	1.22	1.82	1.06	0.52	2.50
Days With ≥ 0.1" Precipitation	2	1	2	3	5	7	5	4	3	3	2	2	39
Days With ≥ 0.5" Precipitation	0	0	0	0	1	2	2	1	1	0	0	0	7
Days With ≥ 1.0" Precipitation	0	0	0	0	0	0	1	0	0	0	0	0	1
Mean Snowfall (in.)	8.7	5.2	5.5	3.2	0.9	0.0	0.0	0.0	trace	2.7	5.8	7.7	39.7
Maximum Snow Depth (in.)	28	26	24	16	5	0	0	0	trace	7	14	16	28
Days With ≥ 1.0" Snow Depth	24	19	15	2	0	0	0	0	0	2	9	21	92

Devils Lake Kdlr *Ramsey County* Elevation: 1,463 ft. Latitude: 48° 07' N Longitude: 98° 52' W

	JAN	FEB	MAR	APR	MAY	JUN	JUL	AUG	SEP	OCT	NOV	DEC	YEAR
Mean Maximum Temp. (°F)	17.0	22.4	33.6	53.5	66.6	74.4	80.0	79.1	67.9	53.1	34.1	20.9	50.2
Mean Temp. (°F)	8.1	13.6	25.0	42.2	55.1	64.0	69.3	67.8	57.2	43.6	26.4	12.9	40.4
Mean Minimum Temp. (°F)	-0.7	4.7	16.3	31.0	43.5	53.6	58.5	56.4	46.4	34.0	18.6	4.8	30.6
Extreme Maximum Temp. (°F)	53	60	71	97	96	99	100	102	98	93	75	51	102
Extreme Minimum Temp. (°F)	-36	-37	-28	1	20	34	41	***33***	22	-2	-25	-37	***-37***
Days Maximum Temp. ≥ 90°F	0	0	0	0	0	1	3	3	1	0	0	0	8
Days Maximum Temp. ≤ 32°F	25	20	13	2	0	0	0	0	0	1	13	24	98
Days Minimum Temp. ≤ 32°F	31	28	29	18	4	0	0	0	1	13	28	31	183
Days Minimum Temp. ≤ 0°F	***16***	12	5	0	0	0	0	0	0	0	2	12	***47***
Heating Degree Days (base 65°F)	1,764	1,451	1,233	677	321	102	26	44	256	656	1,151	1,614	9,295
Cooling Degree Days (base 65°F)	0	0	0	1	20	79	166	137	28	0	0	0	431
Mean Precipitation (in.)	0.56	0.46	0.87	0.90	2.41	4.03	3.56	2.46	1.72	1.55	0.91	0.61	20.04
Extreme Maximum Daily Precip. (in.)	0.62	0.86	1.95	0.92	2.40	2.92	2.37	1.93	2.18	2.42	1.96	0.68	2.92
Days With ≥ 0.1" Precipitation	2	2	3	3	6	8	7	5	4	4	3	2	49
Days With ≥ 0.5" Precipitation	0	0	0	0	1	3	2	2	1	1	0	0	10
Days With ≥ 1.0" Precipitation	0	0	0	0	0	1	1	1	0	0	0	0	3
Mean Snowfall (in.)	na	***4.0***	na	1.6	0.2	0.0	0.0	0.0	trace	1.7	***6.2***	***8.3***	na
Maximum Snow Depth (in.)	na	na	na	14	6	0	0	0	trace	7	25	na	na
Days With ≥ 1.0" Snow Depth	na	na	na	1	0	0	0	0	0	0	8	na	na

Dickinson Exp Stn *Stark County* Elevation: 2,459 ft. Latitude: 46° 53' N Longitude: 102° 48' W

	JAN	FEB	MAR	APR	MAY	JUN	JUL	AUG	SEP	OCT	NOV	DEC	YEAR
Mean Maximum Temp. (°F)	26.7	31.6	41.2	55.7	66.6	75.5	83.5	83.2	72.0	57.1	41.2	29.2	55.3
Mean Temp. (°F)	14.6	19.3	28.8	41.7	52.9	62.0	68.9	67.7	56.3	42.6	28.8	16.9	41.7
Mean Minimum Temp. (°F)	2.3	6.9	16.4	27.7	39.2	48.5	54.4	52.2	40.5	28.1	16.3	4.6	28.1
Extreme Maximum Temp. (°F)	61	67	77	93	98	105	110	105	102	93	81	64	110
Extreme Minimum Temp. (°F)	-34	-36	-33	-11	14	26	36	30	14	-9	-29	-41	-41
Days Maximum Temp. ≥ 90°F	0	0	0	0	0	2	8	8	3	0	0	0	21
Days Maximum Temp. ≤ 32°F	18	14	8	1	0	0	0	0	0	1	8	16	66
Days Minimum Temp. ≤ 32°F	31	28	30	21	7	0	0	0	5	21	29	31	203
Days Minimum Temp. ≤ 0°F	13	9	4	0	0	0	0	0	0	0	3	11	40
Heating Degree Days (base 65°F)	1,560	1,287	1,116	692	377	143	36	56	285	687	1,081	1,486	8,806
Cooling Degree Days (base 65°F)	0	0	0	1	10	59	165	147	29	1	0	0	412
Mean Precipitation (in.)	0.36	0.39	0.82	1.31	2.18	3.40	2.42	1.63	1.41	1.31	0.58	0.39	16.20
Extreme Maximum Daily Precip. (in.)	0.55	1.15	2.03	1.82	2.45	3.09	3.18	2.95	2.17	1.97	1.15	0.53	3.18
Days With ≥ 0.1" Precipitation	1	1	2	3	5	7	5	4	4	3	2	1	38
Days With ≥ 0.5" Precipitation	0	0	0	1	1	2	2	1	1	1	0	0	9
Days With ≥ 1.0" Precipitation	0	0	0	0	0	1	0	0	0	0	0	0	1
Mean Snowfall (in.)	5.3	5.6	6.6	4.3	0.6	0.0	0.0	0.0	0.3	2.4	3.6	5.9	34.6
Maximum Snow Depth (in.)	16	20	22	19	8	0	0	0	1	17	11	12	22
Days With ≥ 1.0" Snow Depth	12	9	7	2	0	0	0	0	0	1	4	8	43

Dickinson Municipal Arpt *Stark County* Elevation: 2,584 ft. Latitude: 46° 48' N Longitude: 102° 48' W

	JAN	FEB	MAR	APR	MAY	JUN	JUL	AUG	SEP	OCT	NOV	DEC	YEAR
Mean Maximum Temp. (°F)	26.7	31.2	41.3	55.8	66.8	75.7	84.0	83.1	71.5	56.5	40.5	28.6	55.1
Mean Temp. (°F)	16.9	21.2	30.5	43.1	54.1	62.9	70.1	68.8	57.9	44.3	30.3	18.7	43.2
Mean Minimum Temp. (°F)	7.0	11.2	19.6	30.2	41.3	50.2	56.1	54.5	44.1	32.1	20.2	8.8	31.3
Extreme Maximum Temp. (°F)	63	68	78	94	99	103	109	104	102	92	80	66	109
Extreme Minimum Temp. (°F)	-30	-31	-26	-8	15	30	41	34	19	-7	-18	-34	-34
Days Maximum Temp. ≥ 90°F	0	0	0	0	0	3	8	9	2	0	0	0	22
Days Maximum Temp. ≤ 32°F	18	14	8	2	0	0	0	0	0	1	8	17	68
Days Minimum Temp. ≤ 32°F	30	27	28	18	5	0	0	0	2	16	27	31	184
Days Minimum Temp. ≤ 0°F	11	7	3	0	0	0	0	0	0	0	2	9	32
Heating Degree Days (base 65°F)	1,488	1,233	1,063	653	346	120	26	43	246	635	1,034	1,430	8,317
Cooling Degree Days (base 65°F)	0	0	0	1	13	64	190	168	38	2	0	0	476
Mean Precipitation (in.)	0.30	0.33	0.69	1.43	2.24	3.20	2.40	1.59	1.39	1.33	0.54	0.24	15.68
Extreme Maximum Daily Precip. (in.)	0.54	0.92	1.69	2.29	1.98	3.12	3.19	2.95	2.44	2.31	1.82	0.38	3.19
Days With ≥ 0.1" Precipitation	1	1	2	3	5	7	5	3	3	3	1	1	35
Days With ≥ 0.5" Precipitation	0	0	0	1	1	2	2	1	1	1	0	0	9
Days With ≥ 1.0" Precipitation	0	0	0	0	0	1	0	0	0	0	0	0	1
Mean Snowfall (in.)	***5.9***	na	***5.6***	***5.7***	***0.5***	na	na	na	na	na	na	***4.4***	na
Maximum Snow Depth (in.)	***16***	na	***18***	***18***	***7***	na	na	na	na	na	na	***12***	na
Days With ≥ 1.0" Snow Depth	***19***	na	***10***	***4***	***0***	na	na	na	na	na	na	***17***	na

Drake 9 NE *Mchenry County* Elevation: 1,529 ft. Latitude: 48° 03' N Longitude: 100° 19' W

	JAN	FEB	MAR	APR	MAY	JUN	JUL	AUG	SEP	OCT	NOV	DEC	YEAR
Mean Maximum Temp. (°F)	18.7	24.1	35.8	55.3	67.9	76.3	82.5	81.5	70.7	55.4	36.5	22.3	52.3
Mean Temp. (°F)	8.6	13.9	25.8	42.4	55.0	64.2	69.7	68.0	57.4	43.5	27.0	12.8	40.7
Mean Minimum Temp. (°F)	-1.5	3.8	15.8	29.5	42.1	52.0	56.8	54.5	44.1	31.5	17.4	3.3	29.1
Extreme Maximum Temp. (°F)	52	63	77	99	100	105	108	106	101	93	77	55	108
Extreme Minimum Temp. (°F)	-44	-43	-28	-8	14	34	40	28	21	-8	-32	-41	-44
Days Maximum Temp. ≥ 90°F	0	0	0	0	1	2	5	6	1	0	0	0	15
Days Maximum Temp. ≤ 32°F	24	19	11	2	0	0	0	0	0	1	11	22	90
Days Minimum Temp. ≤ 32°F	31	28	29	19	4	0	0	0	2	17	28	31	189
Days Minimum Temp. ≤ 0°F	16	12	5	0	0	0	0	0	0	0	3	13	49
Heating Degree Days (base 65°F)	1,745	1,440	1,208	673	324	96	22	46	252	661	1,135	1,613	9,215
Cooling Degree Days (base 65°F)	0	0	0	2	22	79	173	146	31	1	0	0	454
Mean Precipitation (in.)	0.41	0.44	0.71	1.02	2.39	3.33	2.83	2.13	1.42	1.33	0.77	0.51	17.29
Extreme Maximum Daily Precip. (in.)	0.47	0.76	1.64	2.15	3.70	3.52	1.73	2.10	1.88	2.82	1.26	0.89	3.70
Days With ≥ 0.1" Precipitation	2	1	2	3	5	7	5	5	4	3	2	2	41
Days With ≥ 0.5" Precipitation	0	0	0	0	1	2	2	1	1	1	0	0	8
Days With ≥ 1.0" Precipitation	0	0	0	0	0	1	1	0	0	0	0	0	2
Mean Snowfall (in.)	8.1	5.9	6.7	3.9	0.4	0.0	0.0	0.0	trace	1.8	6.9	7.5	41.2
Maximum Snow Depth (in.)	37	35	24	20	5	0	0	0	1	8	20	26	37
Days With ≥ 1.0" Snow Depth	28	23	22	5	0	0	0	0	0	1	13	24	116

Edmore 1 NW *Ramsey County* Elevation: 1,535 ft. Latitude: 48° 26' N Longitude: 98° 28' W

	JAN	FEB	MAR	APR	MAY	JUN	JUL	AUG	SEP	OCT	NOV	DEC	YEAR
Mean Maximum Temp. (°F)	14.5	20.6	31.3	52.6	66.1	74.3	79.3	78.5	68.2	53.1	33.6	18.5	49.2
Mean Temp. (°F)	4.6	10.6	22.0	40.7	53.2	62.3	67.0	65.4	55.4	41.4	24.4	9.6	38.1
Mean Minimum Temp. (°F)	-5.4	0.5	12.7	28.7	40.3	50.2	54.8	52.3	42.6	29.8	15.3	0.6	26.9
Extreme Maximum Temp. (°F)	48	61	68	97	96	98	107	100	98	91	75	49	107
Extreme Minimum Temp. (°F)	-42	-46	-34	-5	14	28	33	25	18	-4	-30	-38	-46
Days Maximum Temp. ≥ 90°F	0	0	0	0	0	1	3	3	1	0	0	0	8
Days Maximum Temp. ≤ 32°F	27	21	15	2	0	0	0	0	0	2	14	25	106
Days Minimum Temp. ≤ 32°F	30	28	30	20	6	0	0	0	4	19	29	30	196
Days Minimum Temp. ≤ 0°F	19	14	6	0	0	0	0	0	0	0	4	15	58
Heating Degree Days (base 65°F)	1,872	1,537	1,326	726	373	131	45	73	299	723	1,210	1,716	10,031
Cooling Degree Days (base 65°F)	0	0	0	1	14	58	115	94	20	0	0	0	302
Mean Precipitation (in.)	0.52	0.41	0.83	1.08	2.36	3.62	3.23	2.65	1.80	1.52	0.88	0.64	19.54
Extreme Maximum Daily Precip. (in.)	0.68	0.89	1.47	1.09	3.95	2.49	2.42	2.00	1.80	1.33	1.30	0.72	3.95
Days With ≥ 0.1" Precipitation	2	1	2	3	5	7	7	5	4	3	2	2	43
Days With ≥ 0.5" Precipitation	0	0	0	0	1	2	2	2	1	1	0	0	9
Days With ≥ 1.0" Precipitation	0	0	0	0	0	1	0	1	0	0	0	0	2
Mean Snowfall (in.)	5.9	4.1	4.8	2.9	0.4	0.0	0.0	0.0	trace	2.2	6.0	7.0	33.3
Maximum Snow Depth (in.)	20	20	20	8	4	0	0	0	trace	6	12	18	20
Days With ≥ 1.0" Snow Depth	28	24	19	3	0	0	0	0	0	2	12	24	112

Forman 5 SSE *Sargent County* Elevation: 1,250 ft. Latitude: 46° 02' N Longitude: 97° 36' W

	JAN	FEB	MAR	APR	MAY	JUN	JUL	AUG	SEP	OCT	NOV	DEC	YEAR
Mean Maximum Temp. (°F)	19.7	26.1	37.4	55.6	68.8	76.8	83.2	81.7	71.5	56.8	38.3	24.2	53.3
Mean Temp. (°F)	9.7	16.1	27.6	43.8	56.8	65.7	71.3	69.2	58.9	45.2	28.9	15.1	42.4
Mean Minimum Temp. (°F)	-0.5	6.1	17.8	32.0	44.7	54.6	59.5	56.6	46.3	33.5	19.5	5.9	31.3
Extreme Maximum Temp. (°F)	65	60	80	98	97	105	106	106	102	90	78	60	106
Extreme Minimum Temp. (°F)	-36	-40	-27	3	18	35	43	32	20	7	-21	-36	-40
Days Maximum Temp. ≥ 90°F	0	0	0	0	1	3	6	4	1	0	0	0	15
Days Maximum Temp. ≤ 32°F	25	18	10	1	0	0	0	0	0	0	10	21	85
Days Minimum Temp. ≤ 32°F	31	28	28	16	3	0	0	0	2	14	27	31	180
Days Minimum Temp. ≤ 0°F	16	11	4	0	0	0	0	0	0	0	2	11	44
Heating Degree Days (base 65°F)	1,712	1,377	1,153	632	278	76	15	33	221	611	1,077	1,543	8,728
Cooling Degree Days (base 65°F)	0	0	0	3	30	105	219	171	46	2	0	0	576
Mean Precipitation (in.)	0.59	0.53	1.13	1.76	2.70	4.08	3.26	2.26	2.34	2.07	0.90	0.55	22.17
Extreme Maximum Daily Precip. (in.)	0.83	0.77	1.70	2.15	2.30	3.56	2.16	1.50	3.22	2.35	0.95	0.75	3.56
Days With ≥ 0.1" Precipitation	2	2	3	4	5	7	6	5	4	4	2	2	46
Days With ≥ 0.5" Precipitation	0	0	1	1	2	3	2	1	1	1	1	0	13
Days With ≥ 1.0" Precipitation	0	0	0	0	1	1	1	0	0	0	0	0	3
Mean Snowfall (in.)	7.5	5.4	7.0	2.8	trace	0.0	0.0	0.0	trace	0.6	6.1	7.1	36.5
Maximum Snow Depth (in.)	***17***	na	na	***9***	***trace***	***0***	***0***	***0***	***trace***	***4***	***25***	***21***	na
Days With ≥ 1.0" Snow Depth	***10***	na	***6***	1	0	0	0	0	0	0	3	***7***	na

The period of record for all cooperative weather station data is 1980 – 2009. See User Guide for detailed explanation of data.

Grand Forks Univ Nws *Grand Forks County* Elevation: 830 ft. Latitude: 47° 55' N Longitude: 97° 06' W

	JAN	FEB	MAR	APR	MAY	JUN	JUL	AUG	SEP	OCT	NOV	DEC	YEAR
Mean Maximum Temp. (°F)	16.7	23.0	34.7	54.9	68.9	77.2	81.5	80.3	70.0	54.4	35.7	21.2	51.6
Mean Temp. (°F)	8.1	14.2	26.4	43.5	56.4	65.9	70.1	68.5	58.5	44.5	27.8	13.4	41.4
Mean Minimum Temp. (°F)	-0.5	5.4	18.0	32.0	43.8	54.4	58.7	56.5	46.9	34.5	19.9	5.5	31.3
Extreme Maximum Temp. (°F)	54	67	73	98	97	97	105	104	100	93	72	56	105
Extreme Minimum Temp. (°F)	-39	-39	-24	1	21	33	41	34	25	5	-24	-30	-39
Days Maximum Temp. ≥ 90°F	0	0	0	0	1	2	4	3	1	0	0	0	11
Days Maximum Temp. ≤ 32°F	27	20	12	1	0	0	0	0	0	1	12	24	97
Days Minimum Temp. ≤ 32°F	31	28	28	16	4	0	0	0	1	12	27	31	178
Days Minimum Temp. ≤ 0°F	17	11	4	0	0	0	0	0	0	0	2	11	45
Heating Degree Days (base 65°F)	1,760	1,432	1,191	643	291	70	20	37	224	630	1,108	1,597	9,003
Cooling Degree Days (base 65°F)	0	0	0	3	32	102	186	151	36	1	0	0	511
Mean Precipitation (in.)	0.72	0.59	1.00	0.94	2.57	3.45	3.23	3.22	1.95	1.79	0.79	0.63	20.88
Extreme Maximum Daily Precip. (in.)	1.21	0.92	0.93	1.55	2.13	5.07	2.88	2.80	2.28	2.12	1.22	0.72	5.07
Days With ≥ 0.1" Precipitation	2	2	3	3	5	6	6	6	5	4	2	2	46
Days With ≥ 0.5" Precipitation	0	0	1	0	2	2	2	2	1	1	0	0	11
Days With ≥ 1.0" Precipitation	0	0	0	0	0	1	1	1	0	0	0	0	3
Mean Snowfall (in.)	10.4	6.1	7.0	1.2	0.1	0.0	0.0	0.0	trace	1.1	5.0	10.6	41.5
Maximum Snow Depth (in.)	*42*	*20*	*17*	*6*	*1*	*0*	*0*	*0*	*trace*	*11*	*16*	*18*	*42*
Days With ≥ 1.0" Snow Depth	*27*	*21*	*14*	1	0	0	0	0	0	1	7	*21*	*92*

Hansboro 4 NNE *Towner County* Elevation: 1,540 ft. Latitude: 49° 00' N Longitude: 99° 21' W

	JAN	FEB	MAR	APR	MAY	JUN	JUL	AUG	SEP	OCT	NOV	DEC	YEAR
Mean Maximum Temp. (°F)	16.8	22.3	33.3	53.7	66.9	75.1	80.0	79.8	70.1	54.6	35.4	20.1	50.7
Mean Temp. (°F)	6.0	11.6	23.4	41.1	53.4	62.5	66.9	65.6	56.0	42.2	25.2	10.1	38.7
Mean Minimum Temp. (°F)	-4.8	0.8	13.4	28.5	39.8	49.8	53.8	51.4	41.9	29.7	14.7	0.0	26.6
Extreme Maximum Temp. (°F)	54	60	64	96	98	99	99	102	98	93	73	54	102
Extreme Minimum Temp. (°F)	-41	-45	-31	-4	15	28	33	27	20	-10	-31	-39	-45
Days Maximum Temp. ≥ 90°F	0	0	0	0	1	1	3	4	1	0	0	0	10
Days Maximum Temp. ≤ 32°F	26	20	12	2	0	0	0	0	0	1	12	24	97
Days Minimum Temp. ≤ 32°F	31	28	29	20	7	0	0	0	4	19	29	30	197
Days Minimum Temp. ≤ 0°F	19	14	6	0	0	0	0	0	0	0	4	14	57
Heating Degree Days (base 65°F)	1,825	1,509	1,285	712	369	125	43	72	285	702	1,187	1,702	9,816
Cooling Degree Days (base 65°F)	0	0	0	1	15	56	110	98	22	1	0	0	303
Mean Precipitation (in.)	0.58	0.57	0.84	0.83	2.34	3.34	2.73	2.72	1.47	1.27	0.84	0.54	18.07
Extreme Maximum Daily Precip. (in.)	1.97	2.30	1.34	2.00	3.50	3.92	2.56	4.13	2.40	1.68	1.18	0.85	4.13
Days With ≥ 0.1" Precipitation	2	1	2	2	5	7	6	5	4	3	2	2	41
Days With ≥ 0.5" Precipitation	0	0	0	0	1	2	2	2	1	1	1	0	10
Days With ≥ 1.0" Precipitation	0	0	0	0	0	1	1	1	0	0	0	0	3
Mean Snowfall (in.)	7.1	5.4	5.4	2.3	0.5	0.0	0.0	0.0	0.1	2.4	6.1	7.0	36.3
Maximum Snow Depth (in.)	21	18	21	14	4	0	0	0	trace	10	18	19	21
Days With ≥ 1.0" Snow Depth	25	21	19	3	0	0	0	0	0	1	11	21	101

Jamestown Municipal Arpt *Stutsman County* Elevation: 1,492 ft. Latitude: 46° 55' N Longitude: 98° 41' W

	JAN	FEB	MAR	APR	MAY	JUN	JUL	AUG	SEP	OCT	NOV	DEC	YEAR
Mean Maximum Temp. (°F)	20.0	24.9	36.8	55.1	68.3	76.3	82.6	81.2	70.5	55.4	37.4	23.3	52.7
Mean Temp. (°F)	10.6	15.9	27.8	43.2	56.0	65.0	70.5	68.6	58.2	44.5	28.5	14.8	42.0
Mean Minimum Temp. (°F)	1.4	6.8	18.7	31.3	43.6	53.6	58.4	55.9	45.9	33.5	19.6	6.3	31.2
Extreme Maximum Temp. (°F)	54	63	76	97	97	100	108	106	105	94	77	54	108
Extreme Minimum Temp. (°F)	-33	-35	-23	-2	18	34	43	32	23	-1	-19	-37	-37
Days Maximum Temp. ≥ 90°F	0	0	0	0	1	2	6	5	1	0	0	0	15
Days Maximum Temp. ≤ 32°F	24	19	11	1	0	0	0	0	0	1	11	22	89
Days Minimum Temp. ≤ 32°F	30	28	28	17	4	0	0	0	2	14	27	31	181
Days Minimum Temp. ≤ 0°F	14	10	3	0	0	0	0	0	0	0	2	11	40
Heating Degree Days (base 65°F)	1,684	1,384	1,147	649	297	85	17	37	234	630	1,088	1,551	8,803
Cooling Degree Days (base 65°F)	0	0	0	3	24	92	196	155	37	1	0	0	508
Mean Precipitation (in.)	0.47	0.40	0.79	1.17	2.52	3.24	3.26	2.23	1.89	1.58	0.62	0.37	18.54
Extreme Maximum Daily Precip. (in.)	0.80	0.92	1.80	1.35	2.06	2.62	6.35	3.97	2.94	2.59	1.37	0.79	6.35
Days With ≥ 0.1" Precipitation	2	1	2	3	5	7	6	4	4	3	2	1	40
Days With ≥ 0.5" Precipitation	0	0	0	1	2	2	2	1	1	1	0	0	10
Days With ≥ 1.0" Precipitation	0	0	0	0	1	1	1	0	0	0	0	0	3
Mean Snowfall (in.)	na	na	na	na	*0.3*	na	na	na	na	na	na	na	na
Maximum Snow Depth (in.)	na	na	na	na	*4*	na	na	na	na	na	na	na	na
Days With ≥ 1.0" Snow Depth	na	na	na	na	*0*	na	na	na	na	na	na	na	na

Keene 3 S *Mckenzie County* Elevation: 2,470 ft. Latitude: 47° 50' N Longitude: 102° 55' W

	JAN	FEB	MAR	APR	MAY	JUN	JUL	AUG	SEP	OCT	NOV	DEC	YEAR
Mean Maximum Temp. (°F)	23.5	29.4	41.1	58.5	69.5	77.1	84.4	83.9	73.3	57.5	39.1	25.8	55.3
Mean Temp. (°F)	13.3	18.9	29.8	44.3	55.2	63.6	69.8	68.9	58.6	44.6	29.1	15.9	42.7
Mean Minimum Temp. (°F)	3.1	8.3	18.5	30.0	40.8	49.9	55.1	53.9	43.7	31.7	19.0	5.9	30.0
Extreme Maximum Temp. (°F)	55	65	80	96	101	105	108	104	101	92	80	58	108
Extreme Minimum Temp. (°F)	-41	-34	-27	-10	11	28	36	30	16	-7	-24	-43	-43
Days Maximum Temp. ≥ 90°F	0	0	0	0	1	3	8	9	3	0	0	0	24
Days Maximum Temp. ≤ 32°F	20	15	8	1	0	0	0	0	0	1	10	19	74
Days Minimum Temp. ≤ 32°F	31	28	28	18	6	0	0	0	3	16	27	31	188
Days Minimum Temp. ≤ 0°F	13	9	3	0	0	0	0	0	0	0	2	11	38
Heating Degree Days (base 65°F)	1,599	1,299	1,084	616	317	111	27	41	229	626	1,071	1,520	8,540
Cooling Degree Days (base 65°F)	0	0	0	2	19	75	183	170	44	2	0	0	495
Mean Precipitation (in.)	0.46	0.41	0.64	1.09	2.23	3.27	2.84	1.52	1.30	1.30	0.62	0.51	16.19
Extreme Maximum Daily Precip. (in.)	0.52	1.25	1.45	1.65	1.80	2.57	3.10	1.86	1.53	2.02	2.30	0.58	3.10
Days With ≥ 0.1" Precipitation	2	1	2	3	6	7	6	4	4	3	2	2	42
Days With ≥ 0.5" Precipitation	0	0	0	1	1	2	2	1	1	1	0	0	9
Days With ≥ 1.0" Precipitation	0	0	0	0	0	1	1	0	0	0	0	0	2
Mean Snowfall (in.)	*7.9*	na	*4.3*	2.1	0.4	0.0	0.0	0.0	trace	1.9	3.6	*6.7*	na
Maximum Snow Depth (in.)	17	na	*22*	7	7	0	0	0	trace	*10*	*10*	14	na
Days With ≥ 1.0" Snow Depth	8	na	6	1	0	0	0	0	0	1	3	8	na

The period of record for all cooperative weather station data is 1980 – 2009. See User Guide for detailed explanation of data.

Kenmare 1 WSW *Ward County* Elevation: 1,810 ft. Latitude: 48° 40' N Longitude: 102° 06' W

	JAN	FEB	MAR	APR	MAY	JUN	JUL	AUG	SEP	OCT	NOV	DEC	YEAR
Mean Maximum Temp. (°F)	19.5	24.4	35.7	54.0	65.9	74.5	80.6	80.1	69.0	53.9	36.4	22.6	51.4
Mean Temp. (°F)	9.7	14.7	25.8	41.4	53.3	62.6	67.7	66.3	55.6	42.2	26.8	13.4	40.0
Mean Minimum Temp. (°F)	-0.2	5.0	15.8	28.8	40.7	50.6	54.9	52.4	42.2	30.4	17.3	4.2	28.5
Extreme Maximum Temp. (°F)	52	63	73	91	100	103	105	104	99	93	76	56	105
Extreme Minimum Temp. (°F)	-41	-40	-33	-7	14	32	38	28	19	-2	-27	-40	-41
Days Maximum Temp. ≥ 90°F	0	0	0	0	1	2	4	5	1	0	0	0	13
Days Maximum Temp. ≤ 32°F	23	18	11	2	0	0	0	0	0	1	11	21	87
Days Minimum Temp. ≤ 32°F	30	28	30	19	6	0	0	0	3	18	28	29	191
Days Minimum Temp. ≤ 0°F	15	11	5	0	0	0	0	0	0	0	3	12	46
Heating Degree Days (base 65°F)	1,710	1,416	1,209	700	368	127	40	68	297	701	1,139	1,596	9,371
Cooling Degree Days (base 65°F)	0	0	0	1	14	61	131	115	23	1	0	0	346
Mean Precipitation (in.)	0.97	0.67	0.99	1.05	2.16	2.90	2.91	1.89	1.61	1.28	0.73	0.74	17.90
Extreme Maximum Daily Precip. (in.)	1.01	1.91	1.17	1.54	2.84	2.24	3.86	***1.70***	1.58	1.78	1.44	0.96	***3.86***
Days With ≥ 0.1" Precipitation	3	2	3	3	5	7	6	4	4	3	2	2	44
Days With ≥ 0.5" Precipitation	0	0	1	0	1	2	2	1	1	1	0	0	9
Days With ≥ 1.0" Precipitation	0	0	0	0	0	0	1	0	0	0	0	0	1
Mean Snowfall (in.)	11.3	6.4	6.7	3.8	1.0	trace	0.0	0.0	0.1	3.2	5.0	7.5	45.0
Maximum Snow Depth (in.)	na	na	na	na	***10***	***0***	***0***	na	***1***	na	na	na	na
Days With ≥ 1.0" Snow Depth	na	na	***4***	1	0	0	0	0	0	1	***3***	na	na

McClusky *Sheridan County* Elevation: 1,924 ft. Latitude: 47° 29' N Longitude: 100° 27' W

	JAN	FEB	MAR	APR	MAY	JUN	JUL	AUG	SEP	OCT	NOV	DEC	YEAR
Mean Maximum Temp. (°F)	21.0	25.9	37.5	56.3	69.0	77.2	83.1	82.3	71.9	56.5	37.7	24.9	53.6
Mean Temp. (°F)	12.1	16.9	28.0	43.8	56.4	65.3	70.7	69.4	59.3	45.2	28.9	16.4	42.7
Mean Minimum Temp. (°F)	3.0	7.7	18.4	31.3	43.7	53.2	58.3	56.3	46.6	33.8	20.2	7.7	31.7
Extreme Maximum Temp. (°F)	55	61	76	95	97	104	105	105	100	91	75	52	105
Extreme Minimum Temp. (°F)	-33	-33	-23	-1	19	34	41	35	22	-3	-13	-31	-33
Days Maximum Temp. ≥ 90°F	0	0	0	0	1	3	6	6	1	0	0	0	17
Days Maximum Temp. ≤ 32°F	23	18	10	1	0	0	0	0	0	1	10	20	83
Days Minimum Temp. ≤ 32°F	31	28	28	16	3	0	0	0	1	13	27	31	178
Days Minimum Temp. ≤ 0°F	13	9	4	0	0	0	0	0	0	0	2	9	37
Heating Degree Days (base 65°F)	1,637	1,356	1,142	630	283	81	16	33	209	608	1,076	1,502	8,573
Cooling Degree Days (base 65°F)	0	0	0	2	22	94	200	175	44	1	0	0	538
Mean Precipitation (in.)	0.61	0.50	0.69	1.09	2.34	3.39	2.72	2.14	1.48	1.38	0.68	0.51	17.53
Extreme Maximum Daily Precip. (in.)	0.54	1.10	1.03	1.92	1.59	3.13	2.18	4.02	1.72	1.90	0.83	0.68	4.02
Days With ≥ 0.1" Precipitation	2	2	2	3	5	7	6	4	4	3	2	2	42
Days With ≥ 0.5" Precipitation	0	0	0	0	1	2	2	1	1	1	0	0	8
Days With ≥ 1.0" Precipitation	0	0	0	0	0	1	0	0	0	0	0	0	1
Mean Snowfall (in.)	9.2	5.9	5.5	3.7	0.4	0.0	0.0	0.0	trace	2.4	6.6	6.9	40.6
Maximum Snow Depth (in.)	52	23	31	23	4	0	0	0	2	11	17	35	52
Days With ≥ 1.0" Snow Depth	20	15	12	2	0	0	0	0	0	1	10	15	75

Minot FAA Arpt *Ward County* Elevation: 1,714 ft. Latitude: 48° 16' N Longitude: 101° 17' W

	JAN	FEB	MAR	APR	MAY	JUN	JUL	AUG	SEP	OCT	NOV	DEC	YEAR
Mean Maximum Temp. (°F)	20.5	24.9	36.6	55.1	67.2	75.1	81.6	80.8	69.5	54.5	36.8	24.2	52.2
Mean Temp. (°F)	11.7	16.6	27.8	43.5	55.2	64.0	69.8	68.2	57.7	44.2	28.5	16.0	41.9
Mean Minimum Temp. (°F)	3.0	8.3	18.9	31.8	43.2	52.7	58.0	55.6	45.8	33.8	20.2	7.8	31.6
Extreme Maximum Temp. (°F)	56	65	78	94	99	102	105	104	104	92	79	56	105
Extreme Minimum Temp. (°F)	-34	-34	-23	-2	17	34	42	32	25	6	-17	-36	-36
Days Maximum Temp. ≥ 90°F	0	0	0	0	1	2	5	5	1	0	0	0	14
Days Maximum Temp. ≤ 32°F	23	19	11	2	0	0	0	0	0	1	11	21	88
Days Minimum Temp. ≤ 32°F	30	28	28	16	4	0	0	0	1	13	27	30	177
Days Minimum Temp. ≤ 0°F	14	9	3	0	0	0	0	0	0	0	2	10	38
Heating Degree Days (base 65°F)	1,649	1,363	1,148	641	316	101	21	46	245	638	1,088	1,513	8,769
Cooling Degree Days (base 65°F)	0	0	0	2	20	76	177	153	32	1	0	0	461
Mean Precipitation (in.)	0.58	0.41	0.80	1.12	2.33	3.38	2.47	2.12	1.44	1.24	0.79	0.39	17.07
Extreme Maximum Daily Precip. (in.)	0.75	0.67	2.18	3.89	2.08	3.29	2.40	5.73	2.64	1.89	1.71	0.53	5.73
Days With ≥ 0.1" Precipitation	2	1	2	3	5	7	5	4	3	3	2	1	38
Days With ≥ 0.5" Precipitation	0	0	0	1	1	2	2	1	1	1	0	0	9
Days With ≥ 1.0" Precipitation	0	0	0	0	0	1	1	0	0	0	0	0	2
Mean Snowfall (in.)	***10.8***	***5.8***	***6.8***	***4.8***	***0.5***	***trace***	***trace***	***trace***	***0.1***	***2.8***	na	***8.0***	na
Maximum Snow Depth (in.)	***43***	***25***	***25***	***25***	***7***	***trace***	***trace***	***trace***	***1***	***10***	na	***20***	na
Days With ≥ 1.0" Snow Depth	***26***	***21***	***14***	***3***	***0***	***0***	***0***	***0***	***0***	***1***	***12***	***22***	***99***

Mott *Hettinger County* Elevation: 2,524 ft. Latitude: 46° 23' N Longitude: 102° 20' W

	JAN	FEB	MAR	APR	MAY	JUN	JUL	AUG	SEP	OCT	NOV	DEC	YEAR
Mean Maximum Temp. (°F)	27.1	32.0	42.5	56.9	67.9	77.0	85.2	84.6	73.2	58.6	41.3	30.2	56.4
Mean Temp. (°F)	15.4	20.4	30.6	43.2	54.6	63.7	70.7	69.2	57.6	44.3	29.5	18.5	43.1
Mean Minimum Temp. (°F)	3.7	8.7	18.6	29.3	41.2	50.5	56.1	53.7	42.0	29.9	17.8	6.8	29.8
Extreme Maximum Temp. (°F)	67	71	80	95	96	106	110	105	103	95	84	67	110
Extreme Minimum Temp. (°F)	-35	-35	-33	-8	13	29	38	33	19	-8	-25	-39	-39
Days Maximum Temp. ≥ 90°F	0	0	0	0	0	4	10	11	3	0	0	0	28
Days Maximum Temp. ≤ 32°F	17	13	7	2	0	0	0	0	0	1	8	16	64
Days Minimum Temp. ≤ 32°F	31	28	29	19	5	0	0	0	4	18	28	30	192
Days Minimum Temp. ≤ 0°F	12	8	3	0	0	0	0	0	0	0	3	9	35
Heating Degree Days (base 65°F)	1,532	1,258	1,060	650	330	107	23	39	252	636	1,057	1,436	8,380
Cooling Degree Days (base 65°F)	0	0	0	2	15	77	206	175	38	1	0	0	514
Mean Precipitation (in.)	0.35	0.44	0.81	1.53	2.41	2.81	2.17	1.74	1.19	1.24	0.51	0.36	15.56
Extreme Maximum Daily Precip. (in.)	1.00	2.20	1.40	2.30	2.40	2.75	2.90	4.54	1.88	1.72	0.58	0.53	4.54
Days With ≥ 0.1" Precipitation	1	1	3	4	5	6	5	4	3	3	2	1	38
Days With ≥ 0.5" Precipitation	0	0	0	1	2	2	1	1	1	1	0	0	9
Days With ≥ 1.0" Precipitation	0	0	0	0	0	1	0	0	0	0	0	0	1
Mean Snowfall (in.)	5.5	4.6	5.1	3.4	0.6	trace	0.0	0.0	0.3	2.1	4.4	4.9	30.9
Maximum Snow Depth (in.)	***16***	***19***	***13***	***14***	***10***	***trace***	***0***	***0***	***8***	***9***	***13***	na	na
Days With ≥ 1.0" Snow Depth	***8***	***6***	***4***	1	0	0	0	0	0	1	***4***	na	na

The period of record for all cooperative weather station data is 1980 – 2009. See User Guide for detailed explanation of data.

New England *Hettinger County* Elevation: 2,639 ft. Latitude: 46° 33' N Longitude: 102° 52' W

	JAN	FEB	MAR	APR	MAY	JUN	JUL	AUG	SEP	OCT	NOV	DEC	YEAR
Mean Maximum Temp. (°F)	28.1	32.3	42.5	56.8	68.0	76.4	84.5	83.4	72.2	57.5	41.5	30.4	56.1
Mean Temp. (°F)	17.1	21.5	30.9	43.3	54.8	63.5	70.4	69.1	58.1	44.6	30.4	19.6	43.6
Mean Minimum Temp. (°F)	6.1	10.7	19.2	29.9	41.5	50.5	56.2	54.6	43.9	31.7	19.3	8.7	31.0
Extreme Maximum Temp. (°F)	64	71	78	94	97	103	107	103	101	92	80	65	107
Extreme Minimum Temp. (°F)	-36	-35	-31	-9	14	30	40	34	18	-10	-25	-36	-36
Days Maximum Temp. ≥ 90°F	0	0	0	0	1	3	9	8	2	0	0	0	23
Days Maximum Temp. ≤ 32°F	17	13	7	1	0	0	0	0	0	1	8	15	62
Days Minimum Temp. ≤ 32°F	31	28	29	18	5	0	0	0	3	16	28	31	189
Days Minimum Temp. ≤ 0°F	11	7	3	0	0	0	0	0	0	0	2	8	31
Heating Degree Days (base 65°F)	1,478	1,223	1,052	645	324	109	21	33	236	625	1,031	1,402	8,179
Cooling Degree Days (base 65°F)	0	0	0	1	13	71	193	167	35	1	0	0	481
Mean Precipitation (in.)	0.31	0.35	0.89	1.37	2.27	3.19	1.94	1.78	1.30	1.37	0.41	0.27	15.45
Extreme Maximum Daily Precip. (in.)	0.45	0.90	1.48	1.94	1.65	4.07	2.45	2.90	2.67	2.31	0.80	0.46	4.07
Days With ≥ 0.1" Precipitation	1	1	2	3	5	7	5	4	3	3	2	1	37
Days With ≥ 0.5" Precipitation	0	0	0	1	1	2	1	1	1	1	0	0	8
Days With ≥ 1.0" Precipitation	0	0	0	0	0	1	0	0	0	0	0	0	1
Mean Snowfall (in.)	7.1	6.4	7.9	4.6	0.8	0.1	0.0	0.0	trace	2.7	5.1	6.8	41.5
Maximum Snow Depth (in.)	na	na	na	na	na	na	na	na	na	na	na	na	na
Days With ≥ 1.0" Snow Depth	na	na	na	0	0	0	0	0	0	0	*0*	na	na

Pembina *Pembina County* Elevation: 790 ft. Latitude: 48° 58' N Longitude: 97° 14' W

	JAN	FEB	MAR	APR	MAY	JUN	JUL	AUG	SEP	OCT	NOV	DEC	YEAR
Mean Maximum Temp. (°F)	13.2	19.3	31.3	51.8	66.3	74.8	79.2	78.5	68.2	52.2	33.5	18.0	48.9
Mean Temp. (°F)	3.2	8.9	21.7	40.1	53.5	62.9	67.1	65.2	55.1	41.1	24.8	9.1	37.7
Mean Minimum Temp. (°F)	-6.9	-1.5	12.0	28.3	40.7	50.9	54.9	51.9	42.0	30.0	16.0	0.2	26.5
Extreme Maximum Temp. (°F)	48	56	66	96	98	100	99	104	101	93	74	53	104
Extreme Minimum Temp. (°F)	-42	-40	-27	-5	12	27	34	29	18	0	-39	-36	-42
Days Maximum Temp. ≥ 90°F	0	0	0	0	1	2	2	3	0	0	0	0	8
Days Maximum Temp. ≤ 32°F	28	23	15	2	0	0	0	0	0	1	14	26	109
Days Minimum Temp. ≤ 32°F	31	28	30	21	7	0	0	0	4	19	29	31	200
Days Minimum Temp. ≤ 0°F	21	16	7	0	0	0	0	0	0	0	4	15	63
Heating Degree Days (base 65°F)	1,916	1,584	1,336	740	369	122	43	76	308	734	1,201	1,729	10,158
Cooling Degree Days (base 65°F)	0	0	0	1	19	65	114	90	18	0	0	0	307
Mean Precipitation (in.)	0.44	0.39	0.77	0.90	2.59	3.99	3.16	2.64	2.13	1.74	0.92	0.52	20.19
Extreme Maximum Daily Precip. (in.)	0.65	0.80	2.07	1.52	2.27	4.50	3.70	2.90	2.65	2.40	1.35	0.54	4.50
Days With ≥ 0.1" Precipitation	1	1	2	2	6	7	6	5	5	4	2	2	43
Days With ≥ 0.5" Precipitation	0	0	0	1	2	3	2	2	1	1	0	0	12
Days With ≥ 1.0" Precipitation	0	0	0	0	0	1	1	1	0	0	0	0	3
Mean Snowfall (in.)	6.5	4.4	4.6	2.2	0.2	0.0	0.0	0.0	trace	1.6	6.3	7.8	33.6
Maximum Snow Depth (in.)	41	37	31	24	2	0	0	0	trace	10	19	32	41
Days With ≥ 1.0" Snow Depth	27	23	18	3	0	0	0	0	0	1	11	22	105

Stanley 3 NNW *Mountrail County* Elevation: 2,279 ft. Latitude: 48° 21' N Longitude: 102° 25' W

	JAN	FEB	MAR	APR	MAY	JUN	JUL	AUG	SEP	OCT	NOV	DEC	YEAR
Mean Maximum Temp. (°F)	17.9	23.0	34.9	53.1	65.1	73.4	80.1	79.9	68.6	53.1	34.9	21.1	50.4
Mean Temp. (°F)	8.4	13.4	24.6	40.1	51.7	61.0	66.8	65.5	54.7	40.9	25.3	12.0	38.7
Mean Minimum Temp. (°F)	-1.1	3.7	14.3	27.1	38.3	48.6	53.4	51.0	40.8	28.7	15.7	2.8	26.9
Extreme Maximum Temp. (°F)	49	60	75	94	98	102	105	104	100	92	74	52	105
Extreme Minimum Temp. (°F)	-41	-42	-28	-6	16	31	39	31	16	-3	-25	-47	-47
Days Maximum Temp. ≥ 90°F	0	0	0	0	0	2	4	5	1	0	0	0	12
Days Maximum Temp. ≤ 32°F	25	19	12	2	0	0	0	0	0	2	13	23	96
Days Minimum Temp. ≤ 32°F	31	28	30	22	8	0	0	0	4	21	29	31	204
Days Minimum Temp. ≤ 0°F	16	12	5	0	0	0	0	0	0	0	4	13	50
Heating Degree Days (base 65°F)	1,751	1,455	1,245	740	413	158	50	78	320	740	1,183	1,641	9,774
Cooling Degree Days (base 65°F)	0	0	0	0	9	46	111	101	19	0	0	0	286
Mean Precipitation (in.)	0.57	0.44	0.82	1.26	2.49	3.66	2.99	2.12	1.64	1.33	0.72	0.56	18.60
Extreme Maximum Daily Precip. (in.)	0.49	0.68	0.76	1.13	2.08	2.23	2.43	1.75	1.36	1.11	0.78	0.49	2.43
Days With ≥ 0.1" Precipitation	2	1	3	4	6	9	7	5	5	4	3	2	51
Days With ≥ 0.5" Precipitation	0	0	0	1	1	2	2	1	1	1	0	0	9
Days With ≥ 1.0" Precipitation	0	0	0	0	0	0	1	0	0	0	0	0	1
Mean Snowfall (in.)	8.8	5.9	8.0	5.1	1.4	trace	0.0	0.0	0.4	4.0	6.6	7.9	48.1
Maximum Snow Depth (in.)	33	31	28	15	9	0	0	0	2	12	15	25	33
Days With ≥ 1.0" Snow Depth	29	23	19	4	1	0	0	0	0	3	13	27	119

Upham 3 N *Mchenry County* Elevation: 1,424 ft. Latitude: 48° 37' N Longitude: 100° 44' W

	JAN	FEB	MAR	APR	MAY	JUN	JUL	AUG	SEP	OCT	NOV	DEC	YEAR
Mean Maximum Temp. (°F)	16.9	23.2	34.9	55.2	67.7	75.6	81.2	80.6	69.7	54.7	35.7	20.8	51.3
Mean Temp. (°F)	5.7	11.4	24.0	41.6	54.2	63.1	67.9	66.4	55.4	41.1	25.0	10.4	38.8
Mean Minimum Temp. (°F)	-5.6	-0.4	13.0	28.1	40.6	50.4	54.6	52.1	41.0	27.4	14.2	-0.2	26.3
Extreme Maximum Temp. (°F)	49	66	77	98	100	103	103	105	98	93	74	55	105
Extreme Minimum Temp. (°F)	-43	-48	-38	-7	11	32	37	28	17	-10	-29	-42	-48
Days Maximum Temp. ≥ 90°F	0	0	0	0	1	2	4	5	1	0	0	0	13
Days Maximum Temp. ≤ 32°F	26	19	12	2	0	0	0	0	0	1	12	24	96
Days Minimum Temp. ≤ 32°F	31	28	30	21	6	0	0	0	5	23	29	31	204
Days Minimum Temp. ≤ 0°F	18	14	6	0	0	0	0	0	0	0	4	15	57
Heating Degree Days (base 65°F)	1,837	1,512	1,266	695	345	118	36	65	301	735	1,195	1,691	9,796
Cooling Degree Days (base 65°F)	0	0	0	2	17	66	134	115	19	0	0	0	353
Mean Precipitation (in.)	0.58	0.50	0.85	1.04	2.12	3.65	2.68	2.07	1.43	1.30	0.90	0.61	17.73
Extreme Maximum Daily Precip. (in.)	0.51	1.43	1.65	1.58	1.97	3.81	2.81	2.54	1.96	1.97	1.23	0.80	3.81
Days With ≥ 0.1" Precipitation	2	1	2	3	4	7	5	5	4	3	3	2	41
Days With ≥ 0.5" Precipitation	0	0	0	1	1	2	2	1	1	1	0	0	9
Days With ≥ 1.0" Precipitation	0	0	0	0	0	1	1	0	0	0	0	0	2
Mean Snowfall (in.)	9.5	6.3	7.3	4.5	1.0	trace	0.0	0.0	0.1	3.3	8.1	8.7	48.8
Maximum Snow Depth (in.)	27	25	24	16	7	trace	0	0	trace	10	13	17	27
Days With ≥ 1.0" Snow Depth	31	27	22	4	0	0	0	0	0	2	14	27	127

The period of record for all cooperative weather station data is 1980 – 2009. See User Guide for detailed explanation of data.

Valley City 3 NNW *Barnes County* Elevation: 1,209 ft. Latitude: 46° 57' N Longitude: 98° 01' W

	JAN	FEB	MAR	APR	MAY	JUN	JUL	AUG	SEP	OCT	NOV	DEC	YEAR
Mean Maximum Temp. (°F)	18.5	24.4	35.8	54.5	67.8	75.7	81.3	80.2	70.2	55.8	37.5	22.9	52.1
Mean Temp. (°F)	7.9	13.6	25.5	41.5	54.6	63.9	68.9	67.0	57.0	43.5	27.6	13.3	40.4
Mean Minimum Temp. (°F)	-2.8	2.7	15.1	28.5	41.4	52.0	56.5	53.7	43.7	31.2	17.7	3.7	28.6
Extreme Maximum Temp. (°F)	52	58	75	96	95	100	104	102	102	93	75	56	104
Extreme Minimum Temp. (°F)	-42	-44	-32	-6	16	33	40	33	21	3	-25	-37	-44
Days Maximum Temp. ≥ 90°F	0	0	0	0	0	2	4	3	1	0	0	0	10
Days Maximum Temp. ≤ 32°F	25	19	11	1	0	0	0	0	0	1	11	22	90
Days Minimum Temp. ≤ 32°F	31	28	29	20	5	0	0	0	3	18	28	31	193
Days Minimum Temp. ≤ 0°F	17	13	5	0	0	0	0	0	0	0	2	12	49
Heating Degree Days (base 65°F)	1,767	1,450	1,219	698	331	102	27	53	263	660	1,115	1,599	9,284
Cooling Degree Days (base 65°F)	0	0	0	2	17	75	155	121	30	1	0	0	401
Mean Precipitation (in.)	0.49	0.45	0.85	1.12	2.72	3.49	2.76	2.75	2.17	1.80	0.70	0.52	19.82
Extreme Maximum Daily Precip. (in.)	0.67	0.95	1.28	1.40	2.56	2.35	5.46	1.94	3.88	1.50	1.10	0.87	5.46
Days With ≥ 0.1" Precipitation	2	2	3	3	6	7	6	5	4	4	2	2	46
Days With ≥ 0.5" Precipitation	0	0	0	1	2	2	2	2	1	1	0	0	11
Days With ≥ 1.0" Precipitation	0	0	0	0	0	1	0	1	0	0	0	0	2
Mean Snowfall (in.)	8.3	5.2	6.2	2.5	trace	0.0	0.0	0.0	0.0	0.5	5.4	7.3	35.4
Maximum Snow Depth (in.)	na	na	na	***1***	***trace***	***0***	***0***	***0***	***0***	na	na	na	na
Days With ≥ 1.0" Snow Depth	na	na	***6***	0	0	0	0	0	0	0	3	na	na

Velva *Mchenry County* Elevation: 1,509 ft. Latitude: 48° 04' N Longitude: 100° 56' W

	JAN	FEB	MAR	APR	MAY	JUN	JUL	AUG	SEP	OCT	NOV	DEC	YEAR
Mean Maximum Temp. (°F)	20.6	25.9	37.7	56.0	68.4	75.8	81.6	81.0	70.5	56.1	37.9	23.7	52.9
Mean Temp. (°F)	9.8	15.2	27.0	42.3	54.8	63.7	69.0	67.4	56.7	43.5	27.7	13.6	40.9
Mean Minimum Temp. (°F)	-1.0	4.4	16.2	28.6	41.2	51.5	56.2	53.7	43.0	30.7	17.5	3.5	28.8
Extreme Maximum Temp. (°F)	55	60	76	98	100	98	102	103	101	94	78	56	103
Extreme Minimum Temp. (°F)	-50	-37	-36	-8	15	31	37	29	22	-3	-25	-38	-50
Days Maximum Temp. ≥ 90°F	0	0	0	0	1	2	5	6	1	0	0	0	15
Days Maximum Temp. ≤ 32°F	23	18	10	1	0	0	0	0	0	1	10	21	84
Days Minimum Temp. ≤ 32°F	31	28	28	19	6	0	0	0	3	17	28	31	191
Days Minimum Temp. ≤ 0°F	15	12	4	0	0	0	0	0	0	0	3	13	47
Heating Degree Days (base 65°F)	1,706	1,402	1,173	678	328	108	30	53	269	661	1,112	1,588	9,108
Cooling Degree Days (base 65°F)	0	0	0	2	20	75	160	133	27	1	0	0	418
Mean Precipitation (in.)	0.80	0.47	0.72	1.14	2.39	3.77	2.70	2.12	1.52	1.67	1.05	0.60	18.95
Extreme Maximum Daily Precip. (in.)	2.83	***0.70***	1.85	2.26	3.27	***3.57***	1.94	2.38	1.49	2.80	2.65	1.60	***3.57***
Days With ≥ 0.1" Precipitation	3	2	2	3	5	7	6	4	4	3	2	2	43
Days With ≥ 0.5" Precipitation	0	0	0	1	2	2	2	1	1	1	1	0	11
Days With ≥ 1.0" Precipitation	0	0	0	0	0	1	1	1	0	0	0	0	3
Mean Snowfall (in.)	9.6	4.9	5.9	4.2	0.7	0.0	0.0	0.0	trace	2.3	6.4	7.0	41.0
Maximum Snow Depth (in.)	na	na	na	na	na	na	na	na	***trace***	na	na	na	na
Days With ≥ 1.0" Snow Depth	na	na	na	0	0	0	0	0	0	0	***0***	na	na

Williston Exp Farm *Williams County* Elevation: 2,104 ft. Latitude: 48° 08' N Longitude: 103° 44' W

	JAN	FEB	MAR	APR	MAY	JUN	JUL	AUG	SEP	OCT	NOV	DEC	YEAR
Mean Maximum Temp. (°F)	24.0	30.4	42.9	59.7	70.7	78.6	86.0	85.4	74.4	59.0	39.9	26.3	56.4
Mean Temp. (°F)	14.1	20.1	31.6	45.8	56.9	65.3	71.7	70.6	59.8	46.1	30.1	16.9	44.1
Mean Minimum Temp. (°F)	4.1	9.7	20.2	31.9	42.9	52.1	57.4	55.7	45.2	33.2	20.2	7.4	31.7
Extreme Maximum Temp. (°F)	54	65	78	93	102	105	108	106	102	92	76	56	108
Extreme Minimum Temp. (°F)	-37	-36	-23	-1	20	32	43	35	19	-3	-22	-40	-40
Days Maximum Temp. ≥ 90°F	0	0	0	0	1	4	11	11	3	0	0	0	30
Days Maximum Temp. ≤ 32°F	20	14	7	1	0	0	0	0	0	1	8	18	69
Days Minimum Temp. ≤ 32°F	31	27	28	16	4	0	0	0	2	14	26	31	179
Days Minimum Temp. ≤ 0°F	12	8	3	0	0	0	0	0	0	0	2	10	35
Heating Degree Days (base 65°F)	1,574	1,264	1,030	570	271	81	13	28	202	581	1,040	1,485	8,139
Cooling Degree Days (base 65°F)	0	0	0	2	25	98	229	209	53	2	0	0	618
Mean Precipitation (in.)	0.49	0.30	0.59	0.99	1.88	2.76	2.41	1.61	1.22	0.99	0.53	0.40	14.17
Extreme Maximum Daily Precip. (in.)	0.73	0.90	1.28	1.38	1.67	2.81	3.80	3.77	1.70	1.82	1.43	0.58	3.80
Days With ≥ 0.1" Precipitation	1	1	2	3	5	6	5	4	3	3	1	1	35
Days With ≥ 0.5" Precipitation	0	0	0	0	1	2	1	1	1	1	0	0	7
Days With ≥ 1.0" Precipitation	0	0	0	0	0	0	0	0	0	0	0	0	0
Mean Snowfall (in.)	7.2	4.6	4.7	3.2	1.2	0.0	0.0	0.0	0.1	2.4	4.7	6.8	34.9
Maximum Snow Depth (in.)	27	27	20	13	13	0	0	0	trace	9	14	16	27
Days With ≥ 1.0" Snow Depth	21	15	9	1	0	0	0	0	0	1	7	18	72

Wilton *Mclean County* Elevation: 2,169 ft. Latitude: 47° 10' N Longitude: 100° 47' W

	JAN	FEB	MAR	APR	MAY	JUN	JUL	AUG	SEP	OCT	NOV	DEC	YEAR
Mean Maximum Temp. (°F)	20.2	25.1	37.7	54.4	66.3	73.9	***80.7***	79.7	***69.7***	55.1	37.0	22.5	***51.9***
Mean Temp. (°F)	11.1	15.4	28.0	42.5	54.3	62.7	***68.7***	67.0	***57.4***	43.6	27.8	13.7	***41.0***
Mean Minimum Temp. (°F)	2.0	6.0	18.2	30.5	42.2	51.5	***56.5***	54.4	***45.1***	32.0	18.6	4.9	***30.2***
Extreme Maximum Temp. (°F)	57	61	75	93	95	103	106	102	100	92	75	57	106
Extreme Minimum Temp. (°F)	-32	-36	-24	-3	16	32	41	35	22	-6	-24	-36	-36
Days Maximum Temp. ≥ 90°F	0	0	0	0	0	1	4	4	1	0	0	0	10
Days Maximum Temp. ≤ 32°F	23	18	10	2	0	0	0	0	0	1	11	22	87
Days Minimum Temp. ≤ 32°F	30	27	27	17	4	0	0	0	2	15	27	30	179
Days Minimum Temp. ≤ 0°F	13	10	3	0	0	0	0	0	0	0	2	11	39
Heating Degree Days (base 65°F)	1,666	1,398	1,141	671	340	123	***28***	60	***251***	658	1,111	1,585	***9,032***
Cooling Degree Days (base 65°F)	0	0	0	2	15	62	***149***	129	***31***	1	0	0	***389***
Mean Precipitation (in.)	0.49	0.39	0.68	1.32	2.72	3.78	3.22	2.21	1.61	1.41	0.69	0.62	19.14
Extreme Maximum Daily Precip. (in.)	***0.51***	0.33	1.25	***1.53***	***3.40***	***2.51***	4.00	3.06	1.82	1.85	1.50	0.75	***4.00***
Days With ≥ 0.1" Precipitation	2	1	2	3	5	6	5	4	4	3	2	2	39
Days With ≥ 0.5" Precipitation	0	0	0	1	2	2	2	1	1	1	0	0	10
Days With ≥ 1.0" Precipitation	0	0	0	0	1	1	1	0	0	0	0	0	3
Mean Snowfall (in.)	***7.9***	5.1	***5.6***	2.6	0.6	0.0	0.0	0.0	0.1	2.0	5.8	7.4	***37.1***
Maximum Snow Depth (in.)	na	***29***	***28***	27	5	trace	0	0	2	10	***23***	***38***	na
Days With ≥ 1.0" Snow Depth	na	***14***	***8***	2	0	0	0	0	0	1	5	***14***	na

The period of record for all cooperative weather station data is 1980 – 2009. See User Guide for detailed explanation of data.

North Dakota Weather Station Rankings

Annual Extreme Maximum Temperature

Highest

Rank	Station Name	°F
1	Ashley	112
1	Bismarck Municipal Arpt	112
3	Almont	***110***
3	Dickinson Exp Stn	110
3	Mott	110
6	Dickinson Municipal Arpt	109
6	Williston Sloulin Intl Arpt	109
8	Amidon	108
8	Drake 9 NE	108
8	Jamestown Municipal Arpt	108
8	Keene 3 S	108
8	Williston Exp Farm	108
13	Center 4 SE	107
13	Colgate	107
13	Crosby	107
13	Edmore 1 NW	107
13	New England	107
18	Fargo Hector Field	106
18	Forman 5 SSE	106
18	Wilton	106
21	Butte	105
21	Carrington	***105***
21	Grand Forks Univ Nws	105
21	Kenmare 1 WSW	105
21	McClusky	105

Lowest

Rank	Station Name	°F
1	Devils Lake Kdlr	102
1	Hansboro 4 NNE	102
3	Cavalier 7 NW	103
3	Velva	103
5	Bottineau	104
5	Pembina	104
5	Valley City 3 NNW	104
8	Butte	105
8	Carrington	***105***
8	Grand Forks Univ Nws	105
8	Kenmare 1 WSW	105
8	McClusky	105
8	Minot FAA Arpt	105
8	Stanley 3 NNW	105
8	Upham 3 N	105
16	Fargo Hector Field	106
16	Forman 5 SSE	106
16	Wilton	106
19	Center 4 SE	107
19	Colgate	107
19	Crosby	107
19	Edmore 1 NW	107
19	New England	107
24	Amidon	108
24	Drake 9 NE	108

Annual Mean Maximum Temperature

Highest

Rank	Station Name	°F
1	Almont	***56.6***
2	Amidon	***56.4***
2	Mott	56.4
2	Williston Exp Farm	56.4
5	New England	56.1
6	Dickinson Exp Stn	55.3
6	Keene 3 S	55.3
8	Dickinson Municipal Arpt	55.1
9	Bismarck Municipal Arpt	55.0
10	Center 4 SE	54.5
10	Williston Sloulin Intl Arpt	54.5
12	Ashley	53.8
13	McClusky	53.6
14	Butte	53.5
15	Forman 5 SSE	53.4
16	Velva	53.0
17	Crosby	52.8
18	Jamestown Municipal Arpt	52.7
19	Drake 9 NE	52.3
19	Fargo Hector Field	52.3
21	Colgate	52.2
21	Minot FAA Arpt	52.2
23	Valley City 3 NNW	52.1
24	Wilton	***51.9***
25	Grand Forks Univ Nws	51.6

Lowest

Rank	Station Name	°F
1	Cavalier 7 NW	48.7
2	Pembina	48.9
3	Edmore 1 NW	49.2
4	Bottineau	49.7
5	Devils Lake Kdlr	50.2
6	Stanley 3 NNW	50.4
7	Carrington	***50.7***
7	Hansboro 4 NNE	50.7
9	Upham 3 N	51.3
10	Kenmare 1 WSW	51.4
11	Grand Forks Univ Nws	51.6
12	Wilton	***51.9***
13	Valley City 3 NNW	52.1
14	Colgate	52.2
14	Minot FAA Arpt	52.2
16	Drake 9 NE	52.3
16	Fargo Hector Field	52.3
18	Jamestown Municipal Arpt	52.7
19	Crosby	52.8
20	Velva	53.0
21	Forman 5 SSE	53.4
22	Butte	53.5
23	McClusky	53.6
24	Ashley	53.8
25	Center 4 SE	54.5

Rankings include 25 highest/lowest stations. If state has less than 25 stations, all stations are included. The period of record is 1980–2009. See User Guide for detailed explanation of data.

Annual Mean Temperature

Highest Rank	Station Name	°F	Lowest Rank	Station Name	°F
1	Williston Exp Farm	44.1	1	Pembina	37.7
2	Amidon	***44.0***	2	Cavalier 7 NW	38.1
3	New England	43.6	2	Edmore 1 NW	38.1
4	Almont	***43.4***	4	Bottineau	38.5
5	Dickinson Municipal Arpt	43.2	5	Hansboro 4 NNE	38.7
6	Mott	43.1	5	Stanley 3 NNW	38.7
7	Bismarck Municipal Arpt	42.9	7	Upham 3 N	38.8
8	Keene 3 S	42.7	8	Kenmare 1 WSW	40.0
8	McClusky	42.7	9	Carrington	***40.2***
10	Forman 5 SSE	42.4	10	Devils Lake Kdlr	40.4
11	Ashley	42.3	10	Valley City 3 NNW	40.4
12	Butte	42.2	12	Drake 9 NE	40.7
13	Fargo Hector Field	42.1	13	Colgate	***40.8***
14	Jamestown Municipal Arpt	42.0	14	Velva	40.9
14	Williston Sloulin Intl Arpt	42.0	15	Wilton	***41.0***
16	Center 4 SE	41.9	16	Crosby	41.3
16	Minot FAA Arpt	41.9	17	Grand Forks Univ Nws	41.4
18	Dickinson Exp Stn	41.7	18	Dickinson Exp Stn	41.7
19	Grand Forks Univ Nws	41.4	19	Center 4 SE	41.9
20	Crosby	41.3	19	Minot FAA Arpt	41.9
21	Wilton	***41.0***	21	Jamestown Municipal Arpt	42.0
22	Velva	40.9	21	Williston Sloulin Intl Arpt	42.0
23	Colgate	***40.8***	23	Fargo Hector Field	42.1
24	Drake 9 NE	40.7	24	Butte	42.2
25	Devils Lake Kdlr	40.4	25	Ashley	42.3

Annual Mean Minimum Temperature

Highest Rank	Station Name	°F	Lowest Rank	Station Name	°F
1	Fargo Hector Field	31.8	1	Upham 3 N	26.3
2	McClusky	31.7	2	Pembina	26.5
2	Williston Exp Farm	31.7	3	Hansboro 4 NNE	26.6
4	Amidon	***31.6***	4	Edmore 1 NW	26.9
4	Minot FAA Arpt	31.6	4	Stanley 3 NNW	26.9
6	Forman 5 SSE	31.3	6	Bottineau	27.2
6	Grand Forks Univ Nws	31.3	7	Cavalier 7 NW	27.5
6	Dickinson Municipal Arpt	31.3	8	Dickinson Exp Stn	28.1
9	Jamestown Municipal Arpt	31.2	9	Kenmare 1 WSW	28.5
10	New England	31.0	10	Valley City 3 NNW	28.6
11	Ashley	30.8	11	Velva	28.8
11	Bismarck Municipal Arpt	30.8	12	Drake 9 NE	29.1
11	Butte	30.8	13	Center 4 SE	29.2
14	Devils Lake Kdlr	30.6	14	Colgate	29.3
15	Almont	***30.2***	15	Williston Sloulin Intl Arpt	29.5
15	Wilton	***30.2***	16	Carrington	***29.6***
17	Keene 3 S	30.0	17	Crosby	29.7
18	Mott	29.9	18	Mott	29.9
19	Crosby	29.7	19	Keene 3 S	30.0
20	Carrington	***29.6***	20	Almont	***30.2***
21	Williston Sloulin Intl Arpt	29.5	20	Wilton	***30.2***
22	Colgate	29.3	22	Devils Lake Kdlr	30.6
23	Center 4 SE	29.2	23	Ashley	30.8
24	Drake 9 NE	29.1	23	Bismarck Municipal Arpt	30.8
25	Velva	28.8	23	Butte	30.8

Rankings include 25 highest/lowest stations. If state has less than 25 stations, all stations are included. The period of record is 1980–2009. See User Guide for detailed explanation of data.

Annual Extreme Minimum Temperature

Highest Rank	Station Name	°F	Lowest Rank	Station Name	°F
1	McClusky	-33	1	Velva	-50
2	Dickinson Municipal Arpt	-34	1	Williston Sloulin Intl Arpt	-50
3	Carrington	***-36***	3	Upham 3 N	-48
3	Minot FAA Arpt	-36	4	Almont	***-47***
3	New England	-36	4	Stanley 3 NNW	-47
3	Wilton	-36	6	Edmore 1 NW	-46
7	Devils Lake Kdlr	***-37***	7	Hansboro 4 NNE	-45
7	Jamestown Municipal Arpt	-37	8	Bismarck Municipal Arpt	-44
9	Butte	-38	8	Drake 9 NE	-44
10	Center 4 SE	-39	8	Valley City 3 NNW	-44
10	Fargo Hector Field	-39	11	Keene 3 S	-43
10	Grand Forks Univ Nws	-39	12	Pembina	-42
10	Mott	-39	13	Dickinson Exp Stn	-41
14	Amidon	-40	13	Kenmare 1 WSW	-41
14	Ashley	-40	15	Amidon	-40
14	Bottineau	-40	15	Ashley	-40
14	Cavalier 7 NW	-40	15	Bottineau	-40
14	Colgate	-40	15	Cavalier 7 NW	-40
14	Crosby	-40	15	Colgate	-40
14	Forman 5 SSE	-40	15	Crosby	-40
14	Williston Exp Farm	-40	15	Forman 5 SSE	-40
22	Dickinson Exp Stn	-41	15	Williston Exp Farm	-40
22	Kenmare 1 WSW	-41	23	Center 4 SE	-39
24	Pembina	-42	23	Fargo Hector Field	-39
25	Keene 3 S	-43	23	Grand Forks Univ Nws	-39

July Mean Maximum Temperature

Highest Rank	Station Name	°F	Lowest Rank	Station Name	°F
1	Williston Exp Farm	86.0	1	Cavalier 7 NW	78.4
2	Almont	***85.2***	2	Pembina	79.2
2	Mott	85.2	3	Edmore 1 NW	79.3
4	Amidon	85.0	4	Bottineau	79.7
5	Bismarck Municipal Arpt	84.8	5	Carrington	***79.9***
5	Williston Sloulin Intl Arpt	84.8	6	Devils Lake Kdlr	80.0
7	New England	84.5	6	Hansboro 4 NNE	80.0
8	Keene 3 S	84.4	8	Stanley 3 NNW	80.1
9	Dickinson Municipal Arpt	84.0	9	Kenmare 1 WSW	80.6
10	Dickinson Exp Stn	83.5	10	Wilton	***80.7***
11	Ashley	83.4	11	Upham 3 N	81.2
12	Center 4 SE	83.2	12	Valley City 3 NNW	81.3
12	Forman 5 SSE	83.2	13	Grand Forks Univ Nws	81.5
14	Butte	83.1	14	Minot FAA Arpt	81.6
14	McClusky	83.1	14	Velva	81.6
16	Crosby	82.9	16	Fargo Hector Field	82.3
17	Jamestown Municipal Arpt	82.6	17	Colgate	82.5
18	Colgate	82.5	17	Drake 9 NE	82.5
18	Drake 9 NE	82.5	19	Jamestown Municipal Arpt	82.6
20	Fargo Hector Field	82.3	20	Crosby	82.9
21	Minot FAA Arpt	81.6	21	Butte	83.1
21	Velva	81.6	21	McClusky	83.1
23	Grand Forks Univ Nws	81.5	23	Center 4 SE	83.2
24	Valley City 3 NNW	81.3	23	Forman 5 SSE	83.2
25	Upham 3 N	81.2	25	Ashley	83.4

Rankings include 25 highest/lowest stations. If state has less than 25 stations, all stations are included. The period of record is 1980–2009. See User Guide for detailed explanation of data.

January Mean Minimum Temperature

Rank	Station Name (Highest)	°F	Rank	Station Name (Lowest)	°F
1	Amidon	7.5	1	Pembina	-6.9
2	Dickinson Municipal Arpt	7.0	2	Upham 3 N	-5.6
3	New England	6.1	3	Edmore 1 NW	-5.4
4	Williston Exp Farm	4.1	4	Cavalier 7 NW	-5.1
5	Mott	3.7	5	Hansboro 4 NNE	-4.8
6	Almont	***3.3***	6	Bottineau	-4.6
7	Keene 3 S	3.1	7	Valley City 3 NNW	-2.8
7	Minot FAA Arpt	3.1	8	Colgate	-2.1
9	McClusky	3.0	9	Drake 9 NE	-1.5
10	Dickinson Exp Stn	2.4	10	Stanley 3 NNW	-1.1
11	Bismarck Municipal Arpt	2.1	11	Velva	-1.0
12	Wilton	2.0	12	Carrington	***-0.7***
13	Ashley	1.9	12	Devils Lake Kdlr	-0.7
14	Butte	1.8	14	Forman 5 SSE	-0.5
14	Center 4 SE	1.8	14	Grand Forks Univ Nws	-0.5
16	Jamestown Municipal Arpt	1.4	16	Kenmare 1 WSW	-0.2
17	Crosby	0.9	17	Fargo Hector Field	0.0
18	Williston Sloulin Intl Arpt	0.6	18	Williston Sloulin Intl Arpt	0.6
19	Fargo Hector Field	0.0	19	Crosby	0.9
20	Kenmare 1 WSW	-0.2	20	Jamestown Municipal Arpt	1.4
21	Forman 5 SSE	-0.5	21	Butte	1.8
21	Grand Forks Univ Nws	-0.5	21	Center 4 SE	1.8
23	Carrington	***-0.7***	23	Ashley	1.9
23	Devils Lake Kdlr	-0.7	24	Wilton	2.0
25	Velva	-1.0	25	Bismarck Municipal Arpt	2.1

Number of Days Annually Maximum Temperature ≥ 90°F

Rank	Station Name (Highest)	Days	Rank	Station Name (Lowest)	Days
1	Williston Exp Farm	30	1	Cavalier 7 NW	6
2	Amidon	28	2	Devils Lake Kdlr	8
2	Mott	28	2	Edmore 1 NW	8
4	Keene 3 S	24	2	Pembina	8
4	Williston Sloulin Intl Arpt	24	5	Bottineau	9
6	Almont	***23***	6	Carrington	***10***
6	New England	23	6	Hansboro 4 NNE	10
8	Bismarck Municipal Arpt	22	6	Valley City 3 NNW	10
8	Dickinson Municipal Arpt	22	6	Wilton	10
10	Dickinson Exp Stn	21	10	Grand Forks Univ Nws	11
11	Butte	20	11	Fargo Hector Field	12
12	Center 4 SE	18	11	Stanley 3 NNW	12
12	Crosby	18	13	Kenmare 1 WSW	13
14	Ashley	17	13	Upham 3 N	13
14	McClusky	17	15	Minot FAA Arpt	14
16	Colgate	15	16	Colgate	15
16	Drake 9 NE	15	16	Drake 9 NE	15
16	Forman 5 SSE	15	16	Forman 5 SSE	15
16	Jamestown Municipal Arpt	15	16	Jamestown Municipal Arpt	15
16	Velva	15	16	Velva	15
21	Minot FAA Arpt	14	21	Ashley	17
22	Kenmare 1 WSW	13	21	McClusky	17
22	Upham 3 N	13	23	Center 4 SE	18
24	Fargo Hector Field	12	23	Crosby	18
24	Stanley 3 NNW	12	25	Butte	20

 Rankings include 25 highest/lowest stations. If state has less than 25 stations, all stations are included. The period of record is 1980–2009. See User Guide for detailed explanation of data.

Number of Days Annually Maximum Temperature ≤ 32°F

Highest Rank	Station Name	Days	Lowest Rank	Station Name	Days
1	Pembina	109	1	Amidon	***59***
2	Cavalier 7 NW	108	2	New England	62
3	Edmore 1 NW	106	3	Mott	64
4	Bottineau	105	4	Dickinson Exp Stn	66
5	Devils Lake Kdlr	98	5	Almont	***68***
6	Grand Forks Univ Nws	97	5	Dickinson Municipal Arpt	68
6	Hansboro 4 NNE	97	7	Williston Exp Farm	69
8	Stanley 3 NNW	96	8	Center 4 SE	74
8	Upham 3 N	96	8	Keene 3 S	74
10	Carrington	***95***	10	Bismarck Municipal Arpt	76
11	Colgate	94	10	Williston Sloulin Intl Arpt	76
12	Fargo Hector Field	93	12	Ashley	81
13	Drake 9 NE	90	13	Butte	82
13	Valley City 3 NNW	90	14	McClusky	83
15	Jamestown Municipal Arpt	89	15	Velva	84
16	Minot FAA Arpt	88	16	Forman 5 SSE	85
17	Kenmare 1 WSW	87	17	Crosby	86
17	Wilton	87	18	Kenmare 1 WSW	87
19	Crosby	86	18	Wilton	87
20	Forman 5 SSE	85	20	Minot FAA Arpt	88
21	Velva	84	21	Jamestown Municipal Arpt	89
22	McClusky	83	22	Drake 9 NE	90
23	Butte	82	22	Valley City 3 NNW	90
24	Ashley	81	24	Fargo Hector Field	93
25	Bismarck Municipal Arpt	76	25	Colgate	94

Number of Days Annually Minimum Temperature ≤ 32°F

Highest Rank	Station Name	Days	Lowest Rank	Station Name	Days
1	Stanley 3 NNW	204	1	Amidon	***176***
1	Upham 3 N	204	1	Fargo Hector Field	176
3	Dickinson Exp Stn	203	3	Minot FAA Arpt	177
4	Pembina	200	4	Butte	178
5	Bottineau	198	4	Grand Forks Univ Nws	178
6	Hansboro 4 NNE	197	4	McClusky	178
7	Cavalier 7 NW	196	7	Williston Exp Farm	179
7	Edmore 1 NW	196	7	Wilton	179
9	Valley City 3 NNW	193	9	Forman 5 SSE	180
10	Center 4 SE	192	10	Jamestown Municipal Arpt	181
10	Mott	192	11	Devils Lake Kdlr	183
12	Kenmare 1 WSW	191	12	Dickinson Municipal Arpt	184
12	Velva	191	13	Ashley	186
12	Williston Sloulin Intl Arpt	191	13	Bismarck Municipal Arpt	186
15	Carrington	***190***	15	Almont	***187***
16	Drake 9 NE	189	15	Colgate	187
16	New England	189	15	Crosby	187
18	Keene 3 S	188	18	Keene 3 S	188
19	Almont	***187***	19	Drake 9 NE	189
19	Colgate	187	19	New England	189
19	Crosby	187	21	Carrington	***190***
22	Ashley	186	22	Kenmare 1 WSW	191
22	Bismarck Municipal Arpt	186	22	Velva	191
24	Dickinson Municipal Arpt	184	22	Williston Sloulin Intl Arpt	191
25	Devils Lake Kdlr	183	25	Center 4 SE	192

Rankings include 25 highest/lowest stations. If state has less than 25 stations, all stations are included. The period of record is 1980–2009. See User Guide for detailed explanation of data.

Number of Days Annually Minimum Temperature ≤ 0°F

Highest			Lowest		
Rank	Station Name	Days	Rank	Station Name	Days
1	Pembina	63	1	Amidon	28
2	Cavalier 7 NW	58	2	New England	31
2	Edmore 1 NW	58	3	Dickinson Municipal Arpt	32
4	Bottineau	57	4	Mott	35
4	Hansboro 4 NNE	57	4	Williston Exp Farm	35
4	Upham 3 N	57	6	Almont	***36***
7	Stanley 3 NNW	50	7	McClusky	37
8	Drake 9 NE	49	8	Bismarck Municipal Arpt	38
8	Valley City 3 NNW	49	8	Keene 3 S	38
10	Colgate	48	8	Minot FAA Arpt	38
11	Carrington	***47***	11	Ashley	39
11	Devils Lake Kdlr	***47***	11	Butte	39
11	Velva	47	11	Wilton	39
14	Kenmare 1 WSW	46	14	Center 4 SE	40
15	Grand Forks Univ Nws	45	14	Dickinson Exp Stn	40
16	Forman 5 SSE	44	14	Jamestown Municipal Arpt	40
17	Crosby	43	17	Williston Sloulin Intl Arpt	42
17	Fargo Hector Field	43	18	Crosby	43
19	Williston Sloulin Intl Arpt	42	18	Fargo Hector Field	43
20	Center 4 SE	40	20	Forman 5 SSE	44
20	Dickinson Exp Stn	40	21	Grand Forks Univ Nws	45
20	Jamestown Municipal Arpt	40	22	Kenmare 1 WSW	46
23	Ashley	39	23	Carrington	***47***
23	Butte	39	23	Devils Lake Kdlr	***47***
23	Wilton	39	23	Velva	47

Number of Annual Heating Degree Days

Highest			Lowest		
Rank	Station Name	Num.	Rank	Station Name	Num.
1	Pembina	10,158	1	Amidon	***8,125***
2	Edmore 1 NW	10,031	2	Williston Exp Farm	8,139
3	Cavalier 7 NW	10,000	3	New England	8,179
4	Bottineau	9,911	4	Almont	***8,297***
5	Hansboro 4 NNE	9,816	5	Dickinson Municipal Arpt	8,317
6	Upham 3 N	9,796	6	Mott	8,380
7	Stanley 3 NNW	9,774	7	Bismarck Municipal Arpt	8,490
8	Kenmare 1 WSW	9,371	8	Keene 3 S	8,540
9	Carrington	***9,349***	9	McClusky	8,573
10	Devils Lake Kdlr	9,295	10	Ashley	8,684
11	Valley City 3 NNW	9,284	11	Forman 5 SSE	8,728
12	Drake 9 NE	9,215	12	Butte	8,747
13	Colgate	***9,180***	13	Center 4 SE	8,758
14	Velva	9,108	14	Minot FAA Arpt	8,769
15	Wilton	***9,032***	15	Williston Sloulin Intl Arpt	8,788
16	Grand Forks Univ Nws	9,003	16	Jamestown Municipal Arpt	8,803
17	Crosby	8,990	17	Dickinson Exp Stn	8,806
18	Fargo Hector Field	8,818	18	Fargo Hector Field	8,818
19	Dickinson Exp Stn	8,806	19	Crosby	8,990
20	Jamestown Municipal Arpt	8,803	20	Grand Forks Univ Nws	9,003
21	Williston Sloulin Intl Arpt	8,788	21	Wilton	***9,032***
22	Minot FAA Arpt	8,769	22	Velva	9,108
23	Center 4 SE	8,758	23	Colgate	***9,180***
24	Butte	8,747	24	Drake 9 NE	9,215
25	Forman 5 SSE	8,728	25	Valley City 3 NNW	9,284

Rankings include 25 highest/lowest stations. If state has less than 25 stations, all stations are included. The period of record is 1980–2009. See User Guide for detailed explanation of data.

Number of Annual Cooling Degree Days

Highest Rank	Station Name	Num.	Lowest Rank	Station Name	Num.
1	Williston Exp Farm	618	1	Stanley 3 NNW	286
2	Forman 5 SSE	576	2	Cavalier 7 NW	296
3	Fargo Hector Field	561	3	Edmore 1 NW	302
4	Amidon	***551***	4	Hansboro 4 NNE	303
5	McClusky	538	5	Pembina	307
6	Bismarck Municipal Arpt	537	6	Bottineau	332
7	Almont	***521***	7	Kenmare 1 WSW	346
8	Butte	517	8	Upham 3 N	353
9	Ashley	516	9	Wilton	***389***
10	Mott	514	10	Carrington	***390***
11	Grand Forks Univ Nws	511	11	Valley City 3 NNW	401
12	Jamestown Municipal Arpt	508	12	Dickinson Exp Stn	412
13	Williston Sloulin Intl Arpt	504	13	Center 4 SE	418
14	Keene 3 S	495	13	Velva	418
15	New England	481	15	Crosby	431
16	Dickinson Municipal Arpt	476	15	Devils Lake Kdlr	431
17	Colgate	***467***	17	Drake 9 NE	454
18	Minot FAA Arpt	461	18	Minot FAA Arpt	461
19	Drake 9 NE	454	19	Colgate	***467***
20	Crosby	431	20	Dickinson Municipal Arpt	476
20	Devils Lake Kdlr	431	21	New England	481
22	Center 4 SE	418	22	Keene 3 S	495
22	Velva	418	23	Williston Sloulin Intl Arpt	504
24	Dickinson Exp Stn	412	24	Jamestown Municipal Arpt	508
25	Valley City 3 NNW	401	25	Grand Forks Univ Nws	511

Annual Precipitation

Highest Rank	Station Name	Inches	Lowest Rank	Station Name	Inches
1	Forman 5 SSE	22.17	1	Williston Sloulin Intl Arpt	13.99
2	Fargo Hector Field	22.05	2	Amidon	***14.04***
3	Grand Forks Univ Nws	20.88	3	Williston Exp Farm	14.17
4	Pembina	20.19	4	Crosby	14.65
5	Devils Lake Kdlr	20.04	5	New England	15.45
6	Valley City 3 NNW	19.82	6	Mott	15.56
7	Carrington	***19.75***	7	Dickinson Municipal Arpt	15.68
8	Edmore 1 NW	19.54	8	Keene 3 S	16.19
9	Ashley	19.26	9	Dickinson Exp Stn	16.20
10	Wilton	19.14	10	Almont	***16.72***
11	Colgate	19.01	11	Center 4 SE	16.90
12	Velva	18.95	12	Butte	16.91
13	Cavalier 7 NW	18.88	13	Minot FAA Arpt	17.07
14	Stanley 3 NNW	18.60	14	Drake 9 NE	17.29
15	Jamestown Municipal Arpt	18.54	15	McClusky	17.53
16	Hansboro 4 NNE	18.07	16	Bismarck Municipal Arpt	17.59
17	Kenmare 1 WSW	17.90	17	Bottineau	17.69
18	Upham 3 N	17.73	18	Upham 3 N	17.73
19	Bottineau	17.69	19	Kenmare 1 WSW	17.90
20	Bismarck Municipal Arpt	17.59	20	Hansboro 4 NNE	18.07
21	McClusky	17.53	21	Jamestown Municipal Arpt	18.54
22	Drake 9 NE	17.29	22	Stanley 3 NNW	18.60
23	Minot FAA Arpt	17.07	23	Cavalier 7 NW	18.88
24	Butte	16.91	24	Velva	18.95
25	Center 4 SE	16.90	25	Colgate	19.01

Rankings include 25 highest/lowest stations. If state has less than 25 stations, all stations are included. The period of record is 1980–2009. See User Guide for detailed explanation of data.

Annual Extreme Maximum Daily Precipitation

Highest			Lowest		
Rank	Station Name	Inches	Rank	Station Name	Inches
1	Jamestown Municipal Arpt	6.35	1	Amidon	*2.27*
2	Minot FAA Arpt	5.73	2	Stanley 3 NNW	2.43
3	Valley City 3 NNW	5.46	3	Crosby	2.50
4	Grand Forks Univ Nws	5.07	4	Devils Lake Kdlr	2.92
5	Williston Sloulin Intl Arpt	4.82	5	Ashley	3.06
6	Fargo Hector Field	4.64	6	Keene 3 S	3.10
7	Bismarck Municipal Arpt	4.63	7	Dickinson Exp Stn	3.18
8	Cavalier 7 NW	4.56	8	Dickinson Municipal Arpt	3.19
9	Mott	4.54	9	Carrington	*3.45*
10	Pembina	4.50	10	Forman 5 SSE	3.56
11	Colgate	4.36	11	Velva	*3.57*
12	Almont	*4.27*	12	Drake 9 NE	3.70
13	Bottineau	4.18	13	Williston Exp Farm	3.80
14	Hansboro 4 NNE	4.13	14	Upham 3 N	3.81
15	New England	4.07	15	Center 4 SE	3.86
16	McClusky	4.02	15	Kenmare 1 WSW	*3.86*
17	Butte	*4.00*	17	Edmore 1 NW	3.95
17	Wilton	*4.00*	18	Butte	*4.00*
19	Edmore 1 NW	3.95	18	Wilton	*4.00*
20	Center 4 SE	3.86	20	McClusky	4.02
20	Kenmare 1 WSW	*3.86*	21	New England	4.07
22	Upham 3 N	3.81	22	Hansboro 4 NNE	4.13
23	Williston Exp Farm	3.80	23	Bottineau	4.18
24	Drake 9 NE	3.70	24	Almont	*4.27*
25	Velva	*3.57*	25	Colgate	4.36

Number of Days Annually With ≥ 0.1 Inches of Precipitation

Highest			Lowest		
Rank	Station Name	Days	Rank	Station Name	Days
1	Stanley 3 NNW	51	1	Amidon	*33*
2	Devils Lake Kdlr	49	2	Dickinson Municipal Arpt	35
3	Fargo Hector Field	48	2	Williston Exp Farm	35
4	Forman 5 SSE	46	4	Butte	36
4	Grand Forks Univ Nws	46	4	Center 4 SE	36
4	Valley City 3 NNW	46	4	Williston Sloulin Intl Arpt	36
7	Carrington	*45*	7	Almont	*37*
8	Kenmare 1 WSW	44	7	New England	37
9	Ashley	43	9	Bismarck Municipal Arpt	38
9	Edmore 1 NW	43	9	Dickinson Exp Stn	38
9	Pembina	43	9	Minot FAA Arpt	38
9	Velva	43	9	Mott	38
13	Bottineau	42	13	Crosby	39
13	Colgate	42	13	Wilton	39
13	Keene 3 S	42	15	Cavalier 7 NW	40
13	McClusky	42	15	Jamestown Municipal Arpt	40
17	Drake 9 NE	41	17	Drake 9 NE	41
17	Hansboro 4 NNE	41	17	Hansboro 4 NNE	41
17	Upham 3 N	41	17	Upham 3 N	41
20	Cavalier 7 NW	40	20	Bottineau	42
20	Jamestown Municipal Arpt	40	20	Colgate	42
22	Crosby	39	20	Keene 3 S	42
22	Wilton	39	20	McClusky	42
24	Bismarck Municipal Arpt	38	24	Ashley	43
24	Dickinson Exp Stn	38	24	Edmore 1 NW	43

 Rankings include 25 highest/lowest stations. If state has less than 25 stations, all stations are included. The period of record is 1980–2009. See User Guide for detailed explanation of data.

Number of Days Annually With ≥ 0.5 Inches of Precipitation

Highest

Rank	Station Name	Days
1	Forman 5 SSE	13
2	Fargo Hector Field	12
2	Pembina	12
4	Ashley	11
4	Cavalier 7 NW	11
4	Colgate	11
4	Grand Forks Univ Nws	11
4	Valley City 3 NNW	11
4	Velva	11
10	Almont	*10*
10	Butte	10
10	Carrington	*10*
10	Center 4 SE	10
10	Devils Lake Kdlr	10
10	Hansboro 4 NNE	10
10	Jamestown Municipal Arpt	10
10	Wilton	10
18	Bismarck Municipal Arpt	9
18	Bottineau	9
18	Dickinson Exp Stn	9
18	Edmore 1 NW	9
18	Keene 3 S	9
18	Kenmare 1 WSW	9
18	Minot FAA Arpt	9
18	Mott	9

Lowest

Rank	Station Name	Days
1	Williston Sloulin Intl Arpt	5
2	Amidon	*7*
2	Crosby	7
2	Williston Exp Farm	7
5	Drake 9 NE	8
5	McClusky	8
5	New England	8
8	Bismarck Municipal Arpt	9
8	Bottineau	9
8	Dickinson Exp Stn	9
8	Edmore 1 NW	9
8	Keene 3 S	9
8	Kenmare 1 WSW	9
8	Minot FAA Arpt	9
8	Mott	9
8	Stanley 3 NNW	9
8	Dickinson Municipal Arpt	9
8	Upham 3 N	9
19	Almont	*10*
19	Butte	10
19	Carrington	*10*
19	Center 4 SE	10
19	Devils Lake Kdlr	10
19	Hansboro 4 NNE	10
19	Jamestown Municipal Arpt	10

Number of Days Annually With ≥ 1.0 Inches of Precipitation

Highest

Rank	Station Name	Days
1	Fargo Hector Field	5
2	Ashley	4
3	Bismarck Municipal Arpt	3
3	Bottineau	3
3	Butte	3
3	Cavalier 7 NW	3
3	Colgate	3
3	Devils Lake Kdlr	3
3	Forman 5 SSE	3
3	Grand Forks Univ Nws	3
3	Hansboro 4 NNE	3
3	Jamestown Municipal Arpt	3
3	Pembina	3
3	Velva	3
3	Wilton	3
16	Almont	*2*
16	Carrington	*2*
16	Drake 9 NE	2
16	Edmore 1 NW	2
16	Keene 3 S	2
16	Minot FAA Arpt	2
16	Upham 3 N	2
16	Valley City 3 NNW	2
24	Amidon	*1*
24	Center 4 SE	1

Lowest

Rank	Station Name	Days
1	Williston Exp Farm	0
1	Williston Sloulin Intl Arpt	0
3	Amidon	*1*
3	Center 4 SE	1
3	Crosby	1
3	Dickinson Exp Stn	1
3	Kenmare 1 WSW	1
3	McClusky	1
3	Mott	1
3	New England	1
3	Stanley 3 NNW	1
3	Dickinson Municipal Arpt	1
13	Almont	*2*
13	Carrington	*2*
13	Drake 9 NE	2
13	Edmore 1 NW	2
13	Keene 3 S	2
13	Minot FAA Arpt	2
13	Upham 3 N	2
13	Valley City 3 NNW	2
21	Bismarck Municipal Arpt	3
21	Bottineau	3
21	Butte	3
21	Cavalier 7 NW	3
21	Colgate	3

Rankings include 25 highest/lowest stations. If state has less than 25 stations, all stations are included. The period of record is 1980–2009. See User Guide for detailed explanation of data.

Annual Snowfall

Highest			Lowest		
Rank	Station Name	Inches	Rank	Station Name	Inches
1	Bismarck Municipal Arpt	49.7	1	Center 4 SE	26.9
2	Upham 3 N	48.8	2	Ashley	30.6
3	Fargo Hector Field	48.2	3	Colgate	30.9
4	Stanley 3 NNW	48.1	3	Mott	30.9
5	Kenmare 1 WSW	45.0	5	Butte	***32.6***
6	Carrington	***44.1***	6	Edmore 1 NW	33.3
6	Williston Sloulin Intl Arpt	44.1	7	Pembina	33.6
8	Bottineau	42.8	8	Dickinson Exp Stn	34.6
9	Grand Forks Univ Nws	41.5	9	Williston Exp Farm	34.9
9	New England	41.5	10	Valley City 3 NNW	35.4
11	Drake 9 NE	41.2	11	Hansboro 4 NNE	36.3
12	Velva	41.0	12	Forman 5 SSE	36.5
13	McClusky	40.6	13	Cavalier 7 NW	36.9
14	Crosby	39.7	14	Wilton	***37.1***
15	Wilton	***37.1***	15	Crosby	39.7
16	Cavalier 7 NW	36.9	16	McClusky	40.6
17	Forman 5 SSE	36.5	17	Velva	41.0
18	Hansboro 4 NNE	36.3	18	Drake 9 NE	41.2
19	Valley City 3 NNW	35.4	19	Grand Forks Univ Nws	41.5
20	Williston Exp Farm	34.9	19	New England	41.5
21	Dickinson Exp Stn	34.6	21	Bottineau	42.8
22	Pembina	33.6	22	Carrington	***44.1***
23	Edmore 1 NW	33.3	22	Williston Sloulin Intl Arpt	44.1
24	Butte	***32.6***	24	Kenmare 1 WSW	45.0
25	Colgate	30.9	25	Stanley 3 NNW	48.1

Annual Maximum Snow Depth

Highest			Lowest		
Rank	Station Name	Inches	Rank	Station Name	Inches
1	McClusky	52	1	Bismarck Municipal Arpt	19
2	Grand Forks Univ Nws	***42***	2	Edmore 1 NW	20
3	Ashley	41	3	Hansboro 4 NNE	21
3	Pembina	41	4	Dickinson Exp Stn	22
5	Drake 9 NE	37	5	Williston Sloulin Intl Arpt	24
6	Cavalier 7 NW	34	6	Upham 3 N	27
7	Center 4 SE	***33***	6	Williston Exp Farm	27
7	Stanley 3 NNW	33	8	Crosby	28
9	Bottineau	30	9	Bottineau	30
9	Colgate	***30***	9	Colgate	***30***
11	Crosby	28	11	Center 4 SE	***33***
12	Upham 3 N	27	11	Stanley 3 NNW	33
12	Williston Exp Farm	27	13	Cavalier 7 NW	34
14	Williston Sloulin Intl Arpt	24	14	Drake 9 NE	37
15	Dickinson Exp Stn	22	15	Ashley	41
16	Hansboro 4 NNE	21	15	Pembina	41
17	Edmore 1 NW	20	17	Grand Forks Univ Nws	***42***
18	Bismarck Municipal Arpt	19	18	McClusky	52

Rankings include 25 highest/lowest stations. If state has less than 25 stations, all stations are included. The period of record is 1980–2009. See User Guide for detailed explanation of data.

Number of Days Annually With ≥ 1.0 Inch Snow Depth

Highest			Lowest		
Rank	Station Name	Days	Rank	Station Name	Days
1	Cavalier 7 NW	127	1	Dickinson Exp Stn	43
1	Upham 3 N	127	2	Center 4 SE	***62***
3	Bottineau	120	3	Williston Exp Farm	72
4	Stanley 3 NNW	119	4	McClusky	75
5	Drake 9 NE	116	5	Ashley	79
6	Edmore 1 NW	112	6	Colgate	***82***
7	Pembina	105	7	Williston Sloulin Intl Arpt	87
8	Hansboro 4 NNE	101	8	Bismarck Municipal Arpt	90
9	Minot FAA Arpt	***99***	9	Crosby	92
10	Crosby	92	9	Grand Forks Univ Nws	***92***
10	Grand Forks Univ Nws	***92***	11	Minot FAA Arpt	***99***
12	Bismarck Municipal Arpt	90	12	Hansboro 4 NNE	101
13	Williston Sloulin Intl Arpt	87	13	Pembina	105
14	Colgate	***82***	14	Edmore 1 NW	112
15	Ashley	79	15	Drake 9 NE	116
16	McClusky	75	16	Stanley 3 NNW	119
17	Williston Exp Farm	72	17	Bottineau	120
18	Center 4 SE	***62***	18	Cavalier 7 NW	127
19	Dickinson Exp Stn	43	18	Upham 3 N	127

Rankings include 25 highest/lowest stations. If state has less than 25 stations, all stations are included. The period of record is 1980–2009. See User Guide for detailed explanation of data.

Significant Storm Events in North Dakota: 2000 – 2009

Location or County	Date	Type	Mag.	Deaths	Injuries	Property Damage ($mil.)	Crop Damage ($mil.)
Grand Forks	06/12/00	Flash Flood	na	0	0	4.0	0.0
Grand Forks	06/12/00	Flash Flood	na	2	0	4.0	0.0
Grand Forks	06/12/00	Flash Flood	na	0	0	4.0	0.0
Cass	06/19/00	Flash Flood	na	0	0	100.0	0.0
Cass	06/19/00	Flash Flood	na	0	0	5.0	0.0
Cass County	07/31/00	High Wind	na	1	11	3.0	0.0
Ramsey	08/11/00	Thunderstorm Wind	110 mph	0	2	10.0	0.0
Ramsey	08/11/00	Thunderstorm Wind	na	0	0	7.0	0.0
Cass County	04/06/01	Flood	na	0	0	4.0	0.0
Grand Forks	05/15/01	Hail	2.00 in.	0	1	10.0	0.0
Morton	06/09/01	Hail	2.75 in.	0	0	113.0	0.0
Burleigh	06/09/01	Hail	1.75 in.	0	0	113.0	0.0
Benson, Nelson, and Ramsey Co.	08/01/01	Flood	na	0	0	50.0	0.0
Grand Forks	08/08/01	Thunderstorm Wind	101 mph	0	12	18.0	0.0
Benson	06/19/05	Thunderstorm Wind	110 mph	0	0	6.4	0.0
Burleigh	07/21/05	Hail	2.50 in.	0	0	93.0	0.0
Adams	07/21/05	Hail	2.75 in.	0	3	7.0	0.0
Griggs	08/09/06	Thunderstorm Wind	85 mph	0	0	9.0	0.0
Grand Forks	08/26/07	Tornado	F4	1	18	50.0	2.0
Cass	09/21/07	Hail	3.50 in.	0	0	30.0	0.0
Stark	07/08/09	Tornado	F3	0	2	20.0	0.0

Note: Deaths, injuries, and damages are date and location specific.

OHIO

PHYSICAL FEATURES AND GENERAL CLIMATE. The climate of Ohio is remarkably varied. Less than one-half of its area is occupied by typical plains, while most of eastern and much of southern Ohio is hilly. Topography ranges in elevation from 430 feet above sea level at the junction of the Great Miami and Ohio Rivers up to 1,550 feet on a summit near Bellefontaine. In addition to this high point there are innumerable other hills which rise above 1,400 feet (mean sea level). These are located mainly along the dividing line between the Ohio River and Lake Erie drainage basins. Large areas in the State have elevations above 1,000 feet. An extensive area in northwestern Ohio is occupied by a flat lake plain — once the bottom of glacial Lake Maumee which was much larger than the present Lake Erie. The greater part of eastern Ohio is within the Allegheny Plateau, an unglaciated area consisting of picturesque hills, many of which rise above 1,300 feet and comprise many winding rivers and streams.

The Ohio River, which forms the southern and southeastern boundaries of Ohio, and its tributaries drain the greater portion of the State. A number of streams drain northward into Lake Erie. Although this area comprises nearly a third of the State, the divide between the two drainages is only 20 to 40 miles from the lake shore for a distance of more than 100 miles until it dips south of the arrowhead-shaped Maumee Basin. The largest streams in this region are the Maumee, Sandusky, and Cuyahoga Rivers. Principal tributaries flowing southward into the Ohio River include the Muskingum in the east, the Scioto in the central section, and the Great Miami in the west. A small portion in the west-central region drains westward into the Wabash River basin of Indiana.

Located west of the Appalachian Mountains, Ohio has a climate essentially continental in nature, characterized by moderate extremes of heat and cold, and wetness and dryness. Summers are moderately warm and humid, with occasional days when temperatures exceed 100°F.; winters are reasonably cold, with an average of about two days of subzero weather; and autumns are predominately cool, dry, and invigorating. Spring is the wettest season and vegetation is lush and profuse.

PRECIPITATION. Annual precipitation is slightly in excess of the national average and is well distributed, though with peaks in early spring and summer. In spite of the relatively small range in latitude and the compact shape of Ohio, rainfall varies considerably in amount and seasonal distribution. This is accounted for not only by the presence of Lake Erie on the north, but also by its topography and proximity to rain producing storm paths. Annual precipitation averages about 38 inches, being most generous in spring (about four inches in April) and least in the fall (about 2.5 inches in October). Greatest amounts are measured in the southwest where Wilmington has an average of 44.36 inches; the lake shore is driest, with Gilbralter Island having a normal of only 29.06 inches.

The southern half of the State is visited more frequently by productive rainstorms which, together with the general roughness of terrain, accounts for the larger total precipitation. The lifting of moist air masses over the hills tends to increase the yield of rainfall, especially in winter and spring. There is a marked tendency during the cold season for northeastern counties to receive snowfall amounts substantially in excess of those measured elsewhere. Northerly winds have a long fetch across Lake Huron and the widest part of Lake Erie, thus picking up moisture and heat from the lakes. This moisture is then forced to condense as the air is lifted abruptly over the divide a short distance from the lake. Average snowfall ranges from 60 inches in parts of Lake and adjoining counties down to 16 inches or less along the Ohio River.

TEMPERATURE. The normal annual temperature for the State ranges from 49.6°F. at Hiram in Portage County up to 56.9°F. at Portsmouth on the Ohio River. Variations over the State are due mainly to differences in latitude and topography, but the immediate lake shore area experiences a moderating effect due to its proximity to a large body of water. Widest temperature ranges are found generally among the eastern hills. In an average year, 90°F. heat may be expected about 20 times in summer with 100°F. or more once or twice. Readings of zero or lower are generally to be expected on two to four days each winter, and these are just as likely to occur in the south as the north. However, one winter out of six or eight will pass without experiencing zero readings anywhere in the State.

OTHER CLIMATIC ELEMENTS. The growing season, as defined by the period 32°F. or higher, ranges widely because of latitude and proximity to Lake Erie. The longest is about 200 days on the lake shore and the shortest is in the northeastern valleys within the Ohio River drainage. Dates of the average last freezing temperature in spring range from April 15 to May 18 and the mean first freeze date in fall varies from September 30 to November 6, the latter being on the western lake shore.

Damaging windstorms are mostly associated with heavy thunderstorms or line squalls. Three or four tornadoes may be expected to strike in Ohio each year. Most tornadoes, however, are of limited effect having paths that are short and narrow.

Most floods in Ohio are caused by unusual precipitation. The storms causing floods may bring rainfall of unusual intensity or of unusual duration and extent. Some floods may be caused by a series of ordinary storms which follow one another in rapid succession. Others may result from rain falling at relatively high temperatures on snow-covered areas. At times, though infrequent, flood conditions are caused or aggravated by ice gorges, especially in the tributary streams. Severe thunderstorms frequently cause local flash flooding. General flooding occurs most frequently during January to March and rarely occurs during August to October.

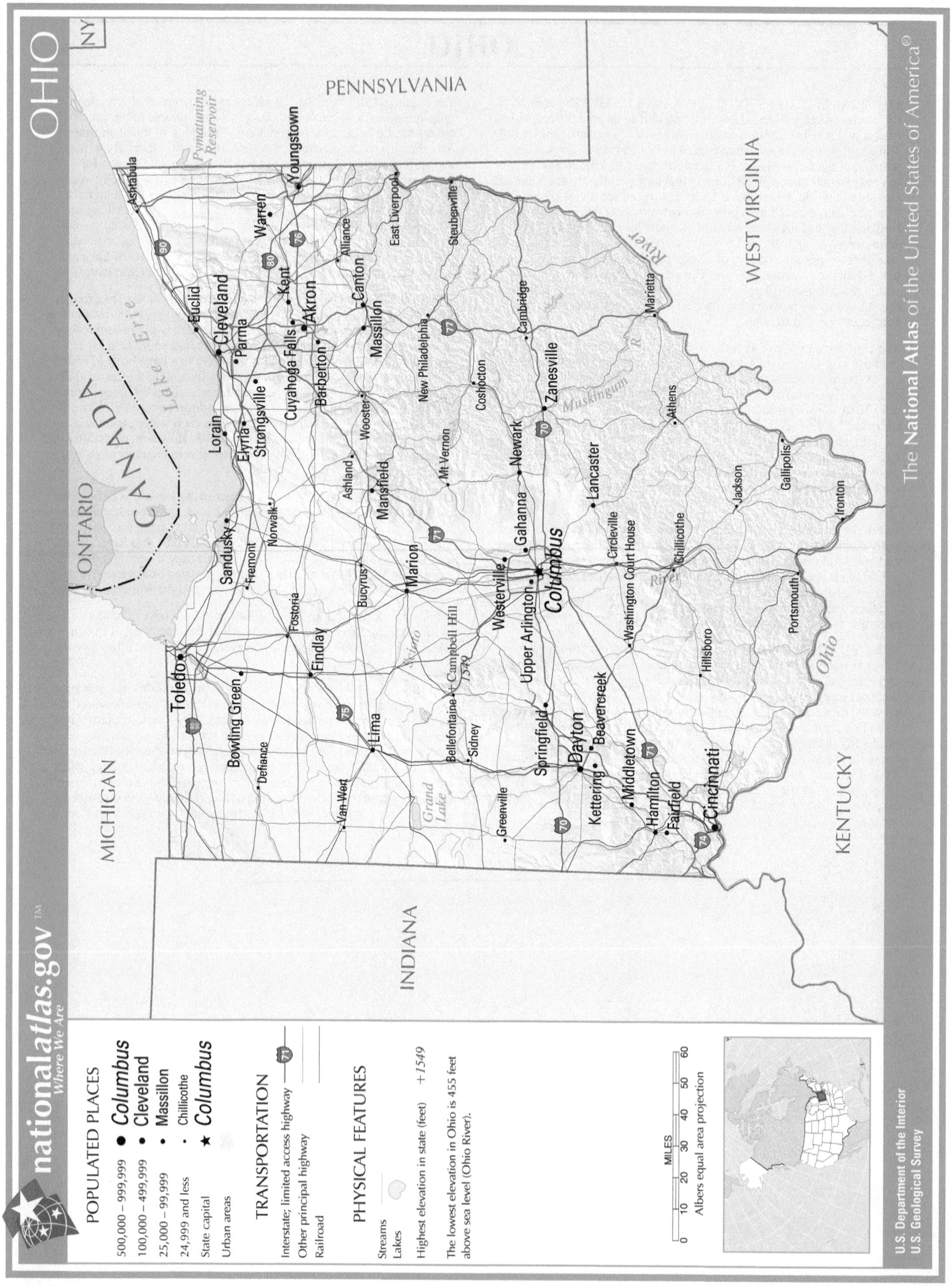
OHIO
The National Atlas of the United States of America®
U.S. Department of the Interior
U.S. Geological Survey
nationalatlas.gov™
Where We Are
POPULATED PLACES
500,000 – 999,999 Columbus
100,000 – 499,999 Cleveland
25,000 – 99,999 Massillon
24,999 and less Chillicothe
State capital Columbus
Urban areas
TRANSPORTATION
Interstate; limited access highway 71
Other principal highway
Railroad
PHYSICAL FEATURES
Streams
Lakes
Highest elevation in state (feet) +1549
The lowest elevation in Ohio is 455 feet above sea level (Ohio River).
MILES
0 10 20 30 40 50 60
Albers equal area projection
MICHIGAN
INDIANA
KENTUCKY
WEST VIRGINIA
PENNSYLVANIA
NY
ONTARIO
CANADA
Lake Erie
Pymatuning Reservoir
Grand Lake
Ohio River
Muskingum R.
Scioto River
Campbell Hill 1549
Toledo
Bowling Green
Defiance
Van Wert
Lima
Findlay
Fostoria
Fremont
Sandusky
Norwalk
Bucyrus
Marion
Bellefontaine
Sidney
Greenville
Dayton
Kettering
Beavercreek
Springfield
Middletown
Hamilton
Fairfield
Cincinnati
Hillsboro
Washington Court House
Circleville
Chillicothe
Portsmouth
Jackson
Gallipolis
Ironton
Athens
Marietta
Lancaster
Columbus
Upper Arlington
Westerville
Gahanna
Newark
Zanesville
Cambridge
Coshocton
Mt Vernon
Mansfield
Ashland
Wooster
New Philadelphia
Massillon
Canton
Alliance
Barberton
Akron
Cuyahoga Falls
Kent
Strongsville
Elyria
Lorain
Parma
Cleveland
Euclid
Ashtabula
Warren
Youngstown
East Liverpool
Steubenville
90
80
76
77
71
70
75
74

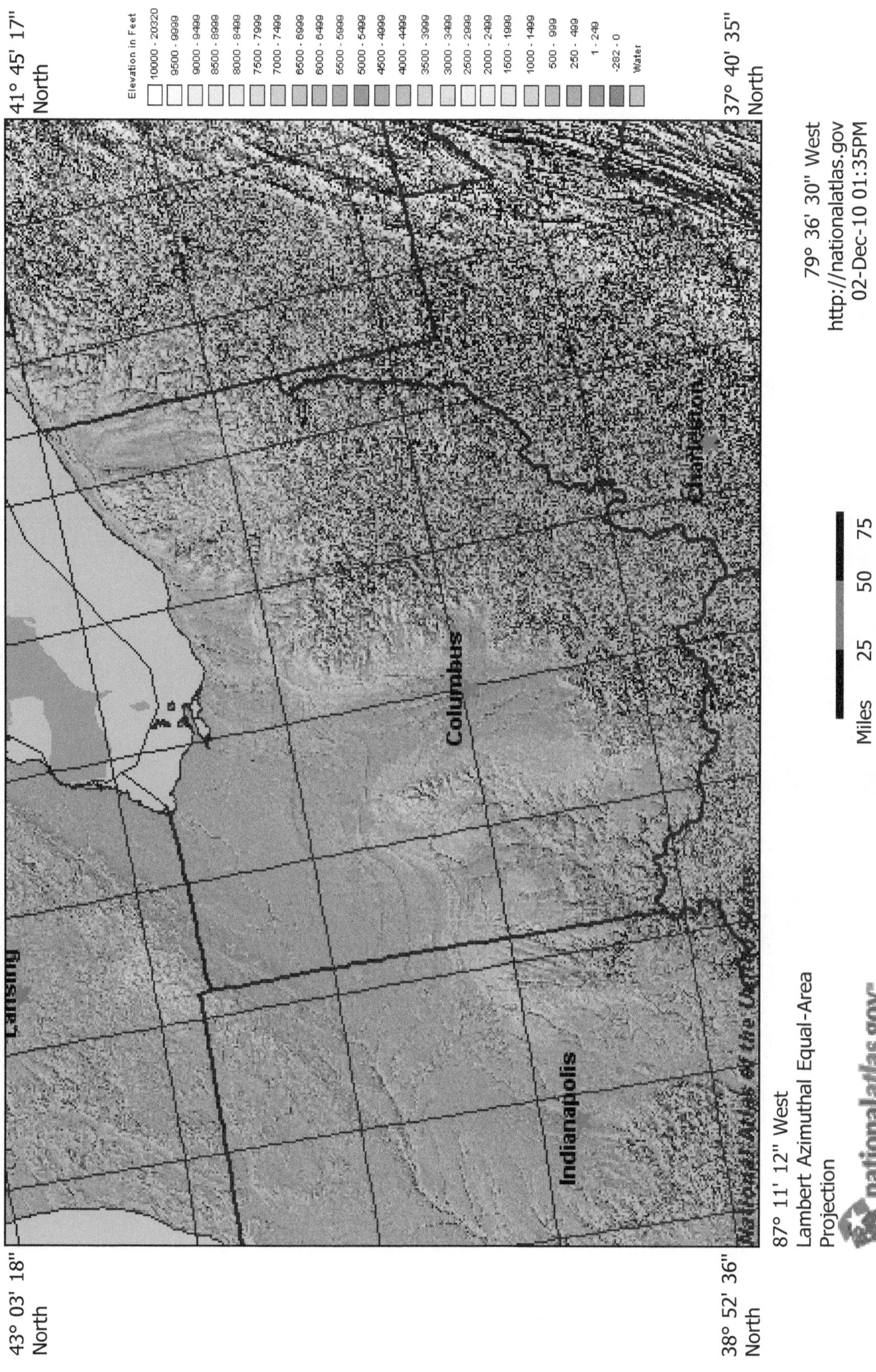
Elevation in Feet
10000 - 20320
9500 - 9999
9000 - 9499
8500 - 8999
8000 - 8499
7500 - 7999
7000 - 7499
6500 - 6999
6000 - 6499
5500 - 5999
5000 - 5499
4500 - 4999
4000 - 4499
3500 - 3999
3000 - 3499
2500 - 2999
2000 - 2499
1500 - 1999
1000 - 1499
500 - 999
250 - 499
1 - 249
-282 - 0
Water
43° 03' 18" North
86° 19' 05" West
78° 16' 49" West
41° 45' 17" North
Lansing
Columbus
Indianapolis
Charleston
38° 52' 36" North
37° 40' 35" North
87° 11' 12" West
Lambert Azimuthal Equal-Area
Projection
79° 36' 30" West
http://nationalatlas.gov
02-Dec-10 01:35PM
Miles 25 50 75
nationalatlas.gov

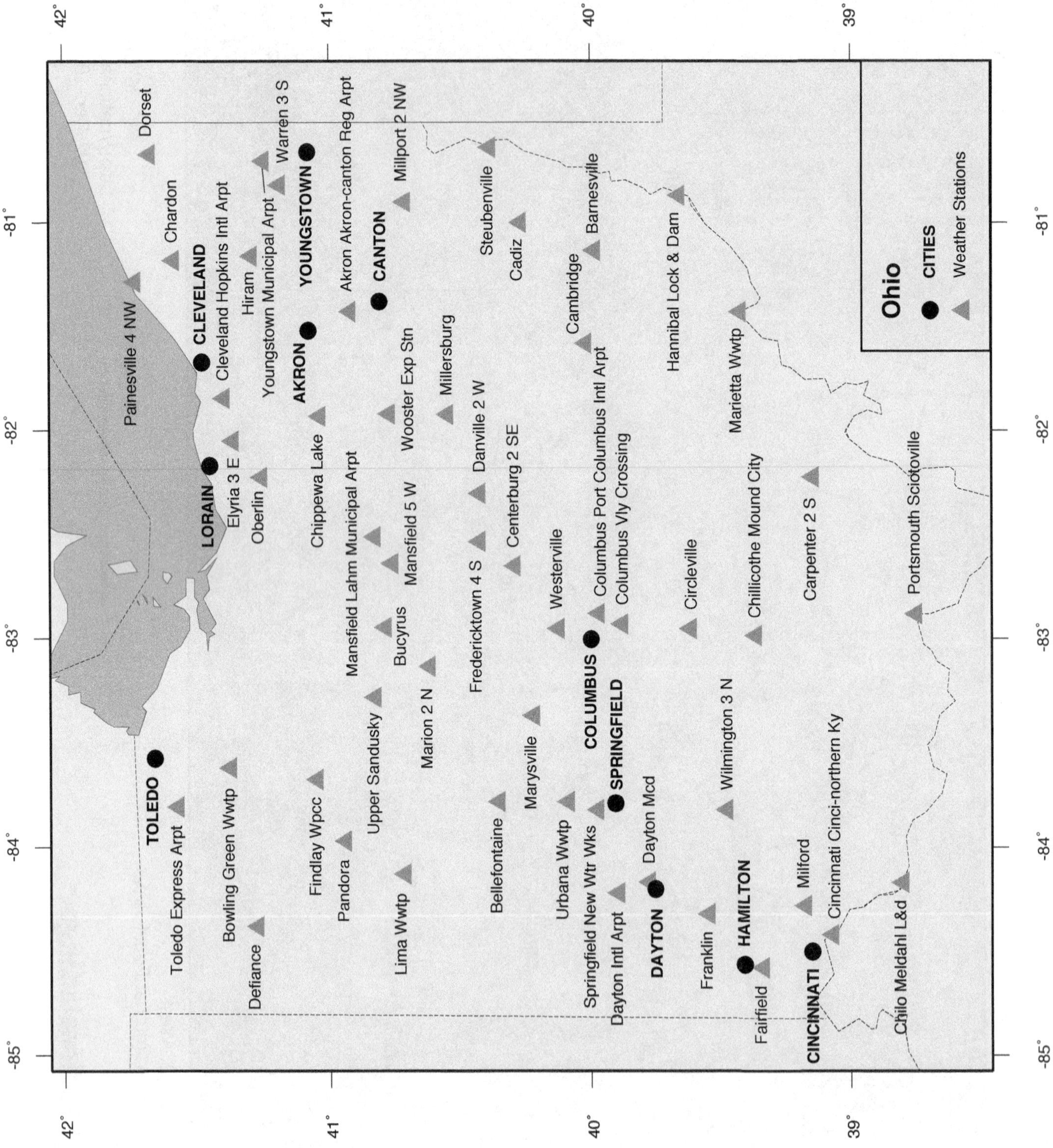
Ohio
CITIES
Weather Stations
TOLEDO
CLEVELAND
LORAIN
AKRON
YOUNGSTOWN
CANTON
COLUMBUS
SPRINGFIELD
DAYTON
HAMILTON
CINCINNATI
Painesville 4 NW
Dorset
Chardon
Cleveland Hopkins Intl Arpt
Hiram
Youngstown Municipal Arpt
Warren 3 S
Akron Akron-canton Reg Arpt
Millport 2 NW
Elyria 3 E
Oberlin
Chippewa Lake
Wooster Exp Stn
Millersburg
Steubenville
Cadiz
Cambridge
Barnesville
Hannibal Lock & Dam
Marietta Wwtp
Mansfield Lahm Municipal Arpt
Mansfield 5 W
Danville 2 W
Centerburg 2 SE
Columbus Port Columbus Intl Arpt
Columbus Vly Crossing
Circleville
Chillicothe Mound City
Carpenter 2 S
Portsmouth Sciotoville
Bucyrus
Fredericktown 4 S
Westerville
Toledo Express Arpt
Bowling Green Wwtp
Defiance
Findlay Wpcc
Pandora
Upper Sandusky
Lima Wwtp
Marion 2 N
Bellefontaine
Marysville
Urbana Wwtp
Springfield New Wtr Wks
Dayton Intl Arpt
Dayton Mcd
Franklin
Wilmington 3 N
Fairfield
Milford
Cincinnati Cinci-northern Ky
Chilo Meldahl L&d
42°
41°
40°
39°
-81°
-82°
-83°
-84°
-85°

Ohio Weather Stations by County

County	Station Name
Allen	Lima WWTP
Ashtabula	Dorset
Belmont	Barnesville
Boone	Cincinnati-Northern Kentucky
Butler	Fairfield
Champaign	Urbana WWTP
Clark	Springfield New Water Works
Clermont	Chilo Meldahl L&D Milford
Clinton	Wilmington 3 N
Columbiana	Millport 2 NW
Crawford	Bucyrus
Cuyahoga	Cleveland Hopkins Intl Arpt
Defiance	Defiance
Franklin	Columbus Valley Crossing Columbus-Port Columbus Intl Westerville
Geauga	Chardon
Guernsey	Cambridge
Hancock	Findlay Wpcc
Harrison	Cadiz
Holmes	Millersburg
Jefferson	Steubenville
Knox	Centerburg 2 SE Danville 2 W Fredericktown 4 S
Lake	Painesville 4 NW
Logan	Bellefontaine
Lorain	Elyria 3 E Oberlin
Lucas	Toledo Express Arpt
Marion	Marion 2 N
Medina	Chippewa Lake
Meigs	Carpenter 2 S
Monroe	Hannibal Lock & Dam

County	Station Name
Montgomery	Dayton Intl Arpt Dayton Mcd
Pickaway	Circleville
Portage	Hiram
Putnam	Pandora
Richland	Mansfield 5 W Mansfield Lahm Municipal Arpt
Ross	Chillicothe Mound City
Scioto	Portsmouth Sciotoville
Summit	Akron Akron-Canton Reg Arpt
Trumbull	Warren 3 S Youngstown Municipal Arpt
Union	Marysville
Warren	Franklin
Washington	Marietta Wwtp
Wayne	Wooster Exp Stn
Wood	Bowling Green WWTP
Wyandot	Upper Sandusky

See User Guide for station inclusion criteria.

Ohio Weather Stations by City

City	Station Name	Miles
Akron	Akron Akron-Canton Reg Arpt	11.9
	Chippewa Lake	21.7
	Hiram	24.6
Beavercreek	Dayton Mcd	6.9
	Dayton Intl Arpt	14.4
	Franklin	18.2
	Springfield New Water Works	21.1
	Wilmington 3 N	21.4
Boardman	Warren 3 S	13.9
	Youngstown Municipal Arpt	14.9
Brunswick	Chippewa Lake	14.8
	Cleveland Hopkins Intl Arpt	10.6
	Elyria 3 E	15.0
	Oberlin	20.5
Canton	Akron Akron-Canton Reg Arpt	7.9
Cincinnati	Cincinnati-Northern Kentucky	10.6
	Fairfield	14.8
	Milford	12.5
Cleveland	Cleveland Hopkins Intl Arpt	11.1
	Elyria 3 E	21.0
Cleveland Heights	Chardon	20.2
	Cleveland Hopkins Intl Arpt	16.8
	Painesville 4 NW	21.3
Columbus	Columbus Valley Crossing	7.6
	Columbus-Port Columbus Intl	6.0
	Westerville	9.5
Cuyahoga Falls	Akron Akron-Canton Reg Arpt	16.0
	Chippewa Lake	24.0
	Hiram	20.7
Dayton	Dayton Mcd	0.6
	Dayton Intl Arpt	9.6
	Franklin	16.1
	Springfield New Water Works	24.5
Delaware	Centerburg 2 SE	22.6
	Columbus-Port Columbus Intl	24.2
	Marion 2 N	22.1
	Marysville	15.9
	Westerville	13.3
Dublin	Columbus Valley Crossing	18.6
	Columbus-Port Columbus Intl	16.4
	Marysville	14.4
	Westerville	10.1
Elyria	Chippewa Lake	23.9
	Cleveland Hopkins Intl Arpt	13.1
	Elyria 3 E	2.7
	Oberlin	9.5
Euclid	Chardon	17.4
	Cleveland Hopkins Intl Arpt	21.8
	Painesville 4 NW	15.6

City	Station Name	Miles
Fairborn	Dayton Mcd	8.9
	Dayton Intl Arpt	12.3
	Franklin	23.5
	Springfield New Water Works	15.7
	Urbana WWTP	24.1
	Wilmington 3 N	24.6
Fairfield	Cincinnati-Northern Kentucky	20.2
	Fairfield	2.7
	Franklin	19.6
	Milford	17.1
Findlay	Bowling Green WWTP	23.4
	Findlay Wpcc	1.4
	Pandora	18.2
	Upper Sandusky	23.7
Gahanna	Centerburg 2 SE	22.1
	Columbus Valley Crossing	9.5
	Columbus-Port Columbus Intl	3.2
	Westerville	8.3
Grove City	Circleville	19.1
	Columbus Valley Crossing	7.8
	Columbus-Port Columbus Intl	12.6
	Westerville	19.0
Hamilton	Brookville, IN	24.0
	Cincinnati-Northern Kentucky	24.6
	Fairfield	3.4
	Franklin	17.0
	Milford	21.2
Huber Heights	Dayton Mcd	6.8
	Dayton Intl Arpt	5.7
	Franklin	23.4
	Springfield New Water Works	18.1
	Urbana WWTP	24.8
Kettering	Dayton Mcd	5.3
	Dayton Intl Arpt	14.7
	Franklin	13.5
	Wilmington 3 N	22.9
Lakewood	Cleveland Hopkins Intl Arpt	6.4
	Elyria 3 E	14.8
Lancaster	Circleville	19.9
	Columbus Valley Crossing	21.5
	Columbus-Port Columbus Intl	23.5
Lima	Lima WWTP	2.1
	Pandora	16.2
Lorain	Cleveland Hopkins Intl Arpt	16.9
	Elyria 3 E	7.6
	Oberlin	12.7
Mansfield	Bucyrus	23.5
	Danville 2 W	25.0
	Fredericktown 4 S	23.1
	Mansfield Lahm Municipal Arpt	4.5
	Mansfield 5 W	4.9

See User Guide for station inclusion criteria.

City	Station Name	Miles
Marion	Bucyrus	17.8
	Marion 2 N	2.0
	Upper Sandusky	18.8
Mason	Fairfield	14.4
	Franklin	13.5
	Milford	12.0
Massillon	Akron Akron-Canton Reg Arpt	9.5
	Wooster Exp Stn	20.6
Mentor	Chardon	10.9
	Painesville 4 NW	4.8
Middletown	Dayton Mcd	20.5
	Fairfield	15.6
	Franklin	4.2
	Milford	22.9
Newark	Centerburg 2 SE	20.3
North Olmsted	Cleveland Hopkins Intl Arpt	3.6
	Elyria 3 E	7.5
	Oberlin	18.9
Parma	Cleveland Hopkins Intl Arpt	6.5
	Elyria 3 E	16.8
Reynoldsburg	Centerburg 2 SE	24.9
	Circleville	24.9
	Columbus Valley Crossing	8.1
	Columbus-Port Columbus Intl	4.6
	Westerville	14.3
Springfield	Dayton Mcd	23.2
	Dayton Intl Arpt	22.2
	Springfield New Water Works	2.8
	Urbana WWTP	11.9
Stow	Akron Akron-Canton Reg Arpt	17.9
	Hiram	16.8
Strongsville	Chippewa Lake	18.9
	Cleveland Hopkins Intl Arpt	6.2
	Elyria 3 E	12.5
	Oberlin	20.3
Toledo	Bowling Green WWTP	19.5
	Toledo Express Arpt	12.5
Upper Arlington	Columbus Valley Crossing	11.1
	Columbus-Port Columbus Intl	10.2
	Marysville	21.4
	Westerville	9.9
Warren	Hiram	17.8
	Warren 3 S	2.7
	Youngstown Municipal Arpt	7.8
Westerville	Centerburg 2 SE	18.8
	Columbus Valley Crossing	15.3
	Columbus-Port Columbus Intl	9.7
	Marysville	25.0
	Westerville	1.9
Westlake	Cleveland Hopkins Intl Arpt	5.3
	Elyria 3 E	8.0
	Oberlin	19.8
Youngstown	Warren 3 S	11.3
	Youngstown Municipal Arpt	11.0
	Mercer, PA	23.6

Note: Miles is the distance between the geographic center of the city and the weather station.

Ohio Weather Stations by Elevation

Feet	Station Name
1,350	Mansfield 5 W
1,294	Mansfield Lahm Municipal Arpt
1,259	Cadiz
1,240	Barnesville
1,229	Hiram
1,208	Akron Akron-Canton Reg Arpt
1,205	Centerburg 2 SE
1,185	Bellefontaine
1,180	Chippewa Lake
1,180	Youngstown Municipal Arpt
1,149	Millport 2 NW
1,129	Chardon
1,049	Fredericktown 4 S
1,029	Wilmington 3 N
1,020	Wooster Exp Stn
1,000	Dayton Intl Arpt
1,000	Marysville
1,000	Urbana WWTP
992	Steubenville
979	Dorset
970	Danville 2 W
964	Marion 2 N
955	Bucyrus
930	Springfield New Water Works
899	Warren 3 S
869	Cincinnati-Northern Kentucky
854	Upper Sandusky
850	Lima WWTP
821	Carpenter 2 S
818	Millersburg
815	Oberlin
810	Columbus-Port Columbus Intl
810	Westerville
799	Cambridge
770	Cleveland Hopkins Intl Arpt
770	Pandora
768	Findlay Wpcc
745	Dayton Mcd
734	Columbus Valley Crossing
729	Elyria 3 E
700	Defiance
674	Bowling Green WWTP
672	Circleville
669	Franklin
668	Toledo Express Arpt
649	Chillicothe Mound City
620	Hannibal Lock & Dam
600	Painesville 4 NW
580	Marietta Wwtp
575	Fairfield
540	Portsmouth Sciotoville
520	Milford
500	Chilo Meldahl L&D

See User Guide for station inclusion criteria.

Akron-Canton Regional Airport

The station at the Akron-Canton Airport is located about midway between Akron and Canton, a few miles south of the crest separating the Lake Erie and Muskingum River drainage areas. Precipitation at the station and southward drains through the Muskingum River into the Ohio, while northward of the crest the Cuyahoga and other streams flow into Lake Erie. The terrain is rolling with highest elevations near 1,300 feet above sea level and many small lakes provide water for local industry as well as recreational facilities for the densely populated region. The area is mainly industrial, agricultural operations having diminished rapidly in recent years.

Lake Erie has considerable influence on the area weather, tempering cold air masses during the late fall and winter, as well as contributing to the formation of brief, but heavy snow squalls until the lake freezes over.

The arrival of spring is late in this area, allowing growing of normally frost-susceptible fruits. Summers are moderately warm, but quite humid, while the months of September, October, and sometimes November are usually pleasant although with considerable morning fog. The average last occurrence of freezing temperatures in spring is the end of April, and the first occurrence in fall is late October. In past years, growing seasons for most vegetation has varied from 120 to 211 days. Temperatures and occurences of frost vary widely over the area because of the hilly terrain. Due to the influence of Lake Erie, snowfall is usually much heavier north of the station.

Akron-Canton Regional Airport *Summit County* Elevation: 1,208 ft. Latitude: 40° 55' N Longitude: 81° 26' W

	JAN	FEB	MAR	APR	MAY	JUN	JUL	AUG	SEP	OCT	NOV	DEC	YEAR
Mean Maximum Temp. (°F)	33.7	37.1	46.9	59.8	69.8	78.3	82.4	80.7	73.4	61.3	49.5	37.7	59.2
Mean Temp. (°F)	26.5	29.2	37.7	49.3	59.2	68.0	72.2	70.8	63.5	51.9	41.8	30.9	50.1
Mean Minimum Temp. (°F)	19.3	21.3	28.4	38.7	48.6	57.6	61.9	60.8	53.4	42.4	34.0	24.1	40.9
Extreme Maximum Temp. (°F)	68	72	81	88	93	100	101	97	93	86	76	76	101
Extreme Minimum Temp. (°F)	-25	-8	-3	15	27	33	43	41	33	22	8	-16	-25
Days Maximum Temp. ≥ 90°F	0	0	0	0	0	2	3	2	0	0	0	0	7
Days Maximum Temp. ≤ 32°F	14	10	4	0	0	0	0	0	0	0	1	10	39
Days Minimum Temp. ≤ 32°F	27	24	21	8	0	0	0	0	0	4	14	25	123
Days Minimum Temp. ≤ 0°F	2	1	0	0	0	0	0	0	0	0	0	1	4
Heating Degree Days (base 65°F)	1,186	1,005	841	472	214	47	5	12	110	407	690	1,050	6,039
Cooling Degree Days (base 65°F)	0	0	1	7	41	142	234	199	70	7	0	0	701
Mean Precipitation (in.)	2.60	2.26	3.03	3.58	4.32	3.76	4.12	3.67	3.38	2.83	3.19	2.84	39.58
Maximum Precipitation (in.)*	8.7	5.2	8.8	6.5	9.6	8.4	11.4	8.2	9.0	8.4	9.4	6.7	65.7
Minimum Precipitation (in.)*	0.7	0.3	1.0	0.9	1.0	0.4	0.7	0.5	0.2	0.4	0.6	0.3	23.8
Extreme Maximum Daily Precip. (in.)	2.04	1.66	1.48	1.99	2.29	2.31	3.98	3.67	3.70	2.07	2.31	1.71	3.98
Days With ≥ 0.1" Precipitation	7	6	8	8	9	8	7	6	6	6	8	8	87
Days With ≥ 0.5" Precipitation	1	1	2	2	3	3	3	2	2	2	2	1	24
Days With ≥ 1.0" Precipitation	0	0	0	1	1	1	1	1	1	0	0	0	6
Mean Snowfall (in.)	12.2	9.6	8.4	2.8	0.1	trace	0.0	trace	trace	0.5	2.9	9.9	46.4
Maximum Snowfall (in.)*	38	20	21	21	3	0	0	0	0	7	22	29	72
Maximum 24-hr. Snowfall (in.)*	9	10	8	20	3	0	0	0	0	4	7	16	20
Maximum Snow Depth (in.)	14	17	17	13	trace	trace	0	trace	trace	2	4	11	17
Days With ≥ 1.0" Snow Depth	15	12	6	1	0	0	0	0	0	0	1	10	45
Thunderstorm Days*	< 1	< 1	2	4	6	7	8	6	3	1	1	< 1	38
Foggy Days*	13	12	13	13	14	15	17	19	17	15	13	14	175
Predominant Sky Cover*	OVR	OVR	OVR	OVR	OVR	OVR	OVR	OVR	OVR	OVR	OVR	OVR	OVR
Mean Relative Humidity 7am (%)*	80	80	79	77	77	80	84	87	88	84	80	81	82
Mean Relative Humidity 4pm (%)*	69	65	59	53	52	54	54	55	56	56	64	70	59
Mean Dewpoint (°F)*	19	20	27	36	47	56	61	60	53	42	32	24	40
Prevailing Wind Direction*	SW	WSW	W	SW	SW	SW	SW	SW	S	S	S	WSW	SW
Prevailing Wind Speed (mph)*	13	12	13	12	10	9	8	8	8	9	12	13	10
Maximum Wind Gust (mph)*	76	58	64	60	56	63	68	62	52	51	58	61	76

Note: (*) Period of record is 1948-1995

Cincinnati Covington Airport

Greater Cincinnati Airport is located on a gently rolling plateau about 12 miles southwest of downtown Cincinnati and two miles south of the Ohio River at its nearest point. The river valley is rather narrow and steep-sided varying from one to three miles in width and the river bed is 500 feet below the level of the airport.

The climate is continental with a rather wide range of temperatures from winter to summer. A precipitation maximum occurs during winter and spring with a late summer and fall minimum. On the average, the maximum snowfall occurs during January, although the heaviest 24-hour amounts have been recorded during late November and February.

The heaviest precipitation, as well as the precipitation of the longest duration, is normally associated with low pressure disturbances moving in a general southwest to northeast direction through the Ohio valley and south of the Cincinnati area.

Summers are warm and rather humid. The temperature will reach 100 degrees or more in one year out of three. However, the temperature will reach 90 degrees or higher on about 19 days each year. Winters are moderately cold with frequent periods of extensive cloudiness.

The freeze free period lasts on the average 187 days from mid-April to the latter part of October.

Cincinnati Covington Airport *Boone County* Elevation: 869 ft. Latitude: 39° 03' N Longitude: 84° 40' W

	JAN	FEB	MAR	APR	MAY	JUN	JUL	AUG	SEP	OCT	NOV	DEC	YEAR
Mean Maximum Temp. (°F)	38.9	42.9	52.9	64.4	73.7	82.0	85.6	84.8	78.0	65.9	53.8	41.9	63.7
Mean Temp. (°F)	30.8	34.2	43.1	53.7	63.2	71.7	75.6	74.6	67.3	55.4	44.8	34.1	54.0
Mean Minimum Temp. (°F)	22.6	25.4	33.2	42.9	52.6	61.4	65.5	64.3	56.6	44.9	35.7	26.3	44.3
Extreme Maximum Temp. (°F)	70	75	84	87	91	102	103	101	97	91	81	75	103
Extreme Minimum Temp. (°F)	-24	-11	-11	15	30	41	47	43	31	20	10	-20	-24
Days Maximum Temp. ≥ 90°F	0	0	0	0	0	4	7	7	2	0	0	0	20
Days Maximum Temp. ≤ 32°F	9	6	1	0	0	0	0	0	0	0	0	7	23
Days Minimum Temp. ≤ 32°F	25	21	16	4	0	0	0	0	0	3	12	22	103
Days Minimum Temp. ≤ 0°F	2	1	0	0	0	0	0	0	0	0	0	1	4
Heating Degree Days (base 65°F)	1,055	866	674	350	125	15	0	2	60	312	602	951	5,012
Cooling Degree Days (base 65°F)	0	0	3	17	75	223	336	306	136	22	1	0	1,119
Mean Precipitation (in.)	3.01	2.77	3.99	3.89	4.90	3.94	3.86	3.51	2.67	3.36	3.28	3.35	42.53
Maximum Precipitation (in.)*	9.4	6.7	12.2	7.2	9.5	7.4	8.4	7.7	8.6	8.6	7.5	7.9	57.6
Minimum Precipitation (in.)*	0.6	0.3	1.1	1.0	1.1	0.9	1.2	0.3	0.2	0.3	0.4	0.5	28.0
Extreme Maximum Daily Precip. (in.)	3.23	2.84	3.25	2.41	2.96	3.04	3.11	3.52	2.55	4.30	1.87	2.47	4.30
Days With ≥ 0.1" Precipitation	6	6	8	8	9	7	7	6	5	6	7	7	82
Days With ≥ 0.5" Precipitation	2	1	2	3	3	3	3	2	2	2	2	2	27
Days With ≥ 1.0" Precipitation	1	1	1	1	1	1	1	1	1	1	1	1	12
Mean Snowfall (in.)	6.6	6.1	3.3	0.5	trace	trace	trace	trace	0.0	0.4	0.4	4.3	21.6
Maximum Snowfall (in.)*	32	20	13	4	trace	0	0	0	0	6	12	13	54
Maximum 24-hr. Snowfall (in.)*	8	9	10	3	trace	0	0	0	0	6	9	8	10
Maximum Snow Depth (in.)	14	14	11	5	trace	trace	trace	trace	0	4	1	9	14
Days With ≥ 1.0" Snow Depth	8	6	2	0	0	0	0	0	0	0	0	4	20
Thunderstorm Days*	1	1	3	4	6	7	8	6	3	1	1	< 1	41
Foggy Days*	13	12	12	9	12	13	16	19	16	14	12	14	162
Predominant Sky Cover*	OVR	OVR	OVR	OVR	OVR	OVR	OVR	OVR	OVR	OVR	OVR	OVR	OVR
Mean Relative Humidity 7am (%)*	80	79	77	76	80	82	85	88	87	83	79	80	81
Mean Relative Humidity 4pm (%)*	65	60	55	50	52	53	54	53	52	51	59	65	56
Mean Dewpoint (°F)*	22	24	31	40	51	60	64	63	56	44	34	26	43
Prevailing Wind Direction*	SSW	SSW	SSW	SSW	SSW	SSW	SW	SSW	SSW	SSW	SSW	SSW	SSW
Prevailing Wind Speed (mph)*	12	12	13	12	9	9	8	7	8	9	12	12	10
Maximum Wind Gust (mph)*	71	55	64	71	59	67	83	62	54	59	56	61	83

Note: (*) Period of record is 1948-1995

The period of record for National Weather Service station data is 1980 – 2009 except where noted. See User Guide for detailed explanation of data.

Cleveland Hopkins Int'l Airport

Cleveland is on the south shore of Lake Erie in northeast Ohio. The metropolitan area has a lake frontage of 31 miles. The surrounding terrain is generally level except for an abrupt ridge on the eastern edge of the city which rises some 500 feet above the shore terrain. The Cuyahoga River, which flows through a rather deep but narrow north-south valley, bisects the city.

Local climate is continental in character but with strong modifying influences by Lake Erie. West to northerly winds blowing off Lake Erie tend to lower daily high temperatures in summer and raise temperatures in winter. Temperatures at Hopkins Airport which is 5 miles south of the lakeshore average from two to four degrees higher than the lakeshore in summer, while overnight low temperatures average from two to four degrees lower than the lakefront during all seasons.

In this area, summers are moderately warm and humid with occasional days when temperatures exceed 90 degrees. Winters are relatively cold and cloudy with an average of five days with sub-zero temperatures. Weather changes occur every few days from the passing of cold fronts.

The daily range in temperature is usually greatest in late summer and least in winter. Annual extremes in temperature normally occur soon after late June and December. Maximum temperatures below freezing occur most often in December, January, and February. Temperatures of 100 degrees or higher are rare. On the average, freezing temperatures in fall are first recorded in October while the last freezing temperature in spring normally occurs in April.

As is characteristic of continental climates, precipitation varies widely from year to year. However, it is normally abundant and well distributed throughout the year with spring being the wettest season. Showers and thunderstorms account for most of the rainfall during the growing season. Thunderstorms are most frequent from April through August. Snowfall may fluctuate widely. Mean annual snowfall increases from west to east in Cuyahoga County ranging from about 45 inches in the west to more than 90 inches in the extreme east.

Damaging winds of 50 mph or greater are usually associated with thunderstorms. Tornadoes, one of the most destructive of all atmospheric storms, occasionally occur in Cuyahoga County.

Cleveland Hopkins Int'l Airport *Cuyahoga County* Elevation: 770 ft. Latitude: 41° 24' N Longitude: 81° 51' W

	JAN	FEB	MAR	APR	MAY	JUN	JUL	AUG	SEP	OCT	NOV	DEC	YEAR
Mean Maximum Temp. (°F)	34.2	37.1	46.0	58.5	69.1	78.2	82.3	80.5	73.7	61.9	50.4	38.2	59.2
Mean Temp. (°F)	27.3	29.6	37.4	48.8	59.0	68.3	72.7	71.3	64.3	53.0	43.1	31.8	50.5
Mean Minimum Temp. (°F)	20.3	22.1	28.7	39.0	48.8	58.4	63.1	62.0	54.8	44.0	35.7	25.3	41.9
Extreme Maximum Temp. (°F)	68	74	82	88	91	104	100	99	93	88	79	77	104
Extreme Minimum Temp. (°F)	-20	-10	-5	11	27	37	45	38	34	19	13	-15	-20
Days Maximum Temp. ≥ 90°F	0	0	0	0	0	2	4	3	0	0	0	0	9
Days Maximum Temp. ≤ 32°F	14	11	4	0	0	0	0	0	0	0	1	9	39
Days Minimum Temp. ≤ 32°F	27	24	21	7	0	0	0	0	0	2	12	24	117
Days Minimum Temp. ≤ 0°F	2	1	0	0	0	0	0	0	0	0	0	1	4
Heating Degree Days (base 65°F)	1,161	994	850	489	223	47	5	10	97	377	652	1,023	5,928
Cooling Degree Days (base 65°F)	0	0	2	9	43	153	250	211	82	11	1	0	762
Mean Precipitation (in.)	2.70	2.28	2.99	3.51	3.62	3.37	3.49	3.53	3.81	3.07	3.51	3.12	39.00
Maximum Precipitation (in.)*	7.0	4.7	6.1	6.6	9.1	9.1	9.1	9.0	7.3	9.5	8.8	8.6	53.8
Minimum Precipitation (in.)*	0.4	0.5	0.8	1.2	1.0	0.6	1.2	0.5	0.7	0.6	0.8	0.7	18.8
Extreme Maximum Daily Precip. (in.)	2.53	1.73	1.87	2.10	2.02	2.57	2.11	3.55	4.59	2.26	2.33	2.39	4.59
Days With ≥ 0.1" Precipitation	7	6	8	8	8	7	7	6	7	7	8	8	87
Days With ≥ 0.5" Precipitation	1	1	2	2	2	2	2	2	3	2	2	2	23
Days With ≥ 1.0" Precipitation	0	0	0	1	1	1	1	1	1	0	1	0	7
Mean Snowfall (in.)	18.4	14.5	12.6	3.3	trace	trace	trace	trace	trace	0.2	4.5	14.1	67.6
Maximum Snowfall (in.)*	43	39	26	13	2	0	0	0	0	8	22	30	97
Maximum 24-hr. Snowfall (in.)*	10	14	11	9	2	0	0	0	0	7	13	12	14
Maximum Snow Depth (in.)	17	22	15	14	trace	trace	trace	trace	trace	trace	9	14	22
Days With ≥ 1.0" Snow Depth	17	13	7	1	0	0	0	0	0	0	2	11	51
Thunderstorm Days*	< 1	< 1	2	3	5	6	6	5	3	2	1	< 1	33
Foggy Days*	13	12	13	12	13	11	12	14	12	11	12	13	148
Predominant Sky Cover*	OVR	OVR	OVR	OVR	OVR	OVR	OVR	OVR	OVR	OVR	OVR	OVR	OVR
Mean Relative Humidity 7am (%)*	79	79	79	76	77	79	81	85	84	81	78	78	80
Mean Relative Humidity 4pm (%)*	70	67	62	56	54	55	55	58	58	58	65	70	61
Mean Dewpoint (°F)*	19	21	27	37	47	57	61	61	54	43	33	24	40
Prevailing Wind Direction*	SW	SW	SW	S	N	SSW	SW	SW	S	SSW	SW	SW	SW
Prevailing Wind Speed (mph)*	13	13	14	13	9	10	9	8	9	10	13	13	12
Maximum Wind Gust (mph)*	82	64	63	78	55	77	67	51	58	54	59	71	82

Note: (*) Period of record is 1948-1995

Columbus-Port Columbus Int'l

Columbus is located in the center of the state and in the drainage area of the Ohio River. The airport is located at the eastern boundary of the city approximately seven miles from the center of the business district.

Four nearly parallel streams run through or adjacent to the city. The Scioto River is the principal stream and flows from the northwest into the center of the city and then flows straight south toward the Ohio River. The Olentangy River runs almost due south and empties into the Scioto just west of the business district. Alum Creek empties into the Big Walnut southeast of the city and the Big Walnut Creek empties into the Scioto a few miles downstream.

The narrow valleys associated with the streams flowing through the city supply the only variation in the micro-climate of the area. The city proper shows the typical metropolitan effect with shrubs and flowers blossoming earlier than in the immediate surroundings and in retarding light frost on clear quiet nights. Many small areas to the southeast and to the north and northeast show marked effects of air drainage as evidenced by the frequent formation of shallow ground fog at daybreak during the summer and fall months and the higher frequency of frost in the spring and fall.

The average occurrence of the last freezing temperature in the spring within the city proper is mid-April, and the first freeze in the fall is very late October, but in the immediate surroundings there is much variation. For example, at Valley Crossing located at the southeastern outskirts of the city, the average occurrence of the last 32 degree temperature in the spring is very early May, while the first 32 degree temperature in the fall is mid-October.

The records show a high frequency of calm or very low wind speeds during the late evening and early morning hours, from June through September. The rolling landscape is conducive to calm winds from the Weather Service location at the airport these are toward the northwest with the wind direction indicated as southeast, at speeds generally 4 mph or less.

Columbus is located in the area of changeable weather. Air masses from central and northwest Canada frequently invade this region. Air from the Gulf of Mexico often reaches central Ohio during the summer and to a much lesser extent in the fall and winter. There are also occasional weather changes brought about by cool outbreaks from the Hudson Bay region of Canada, especially during the spring months. At infrequent intervals the general circulation will bring showers or snow to Columbus from the Atlantic.

Columbus-Port Columbus Int'l *Franklin County* Elevation: 810 ft. Latitude: 39° 59' N Longitude: 82° 53' W

	JAN	FEB	MAR	APR	MAY	JUN	JUL	AUG	SEP	OCT	NOV	DEC	YEAR
Mean Maximum Temp. (°F)	36.7	40.6	50.9	63.2	72.9	81.4	84.8	83.7	77.0	64.9	52.4	40.4	62.4
Mean Temp. (°F)	29.3	32.4	41.3	52.4	62.1	71.0	74.9	73.6	66.5	54.5	43.9	33.3	52.9
Mean Minimum Temp. (°F)	21.9	24.2	31.7	41.6	51.3	60.5	64.8	63.5	55.9	44.1	35.4	26.2	43.4
Extreme Maximum Temp. (°F)	70	75	83	88	93	101	100	101	97	91	80	76	101
Extreme Minimum Temp. (°F)	-22	-10	-6	14	30	39	44	40	33	21	12	-17	-22
Days Maximum Temp. ≥ 90°F	0	0	0	0	0	4	6	5	1	0	0	0	16
Days Maximum Temp. ≤ 32°F	11	8	2	0	0	0	0	0	0	0	1	8	30
Days Minimum Temp. ≤ 32°F	26	22	18	5	0	0	0	0	0	3	12	22	108
Days Minimum Temp. ≤ 0°F	2	1	0	0	0	0	0	0	0	0	0	1	4
Heating Degree Days (base 65°F)	1,100	915	730	383	149	21	1	4	68	334	626	976	5,307
Cooling Degree Days (base 65°F)	0	0	2	12	66	207	313	278	118	16	1	0	1,013
Mean Precipitation (in.)	2.70	2.21	3.05	3.37	4.19	4.00	4.74	3.46	2.85	2.64	3.12	2.99	39.32
Maximum Precipitation (in.)*	8.3	5.1	9.6	6.4	9.1	9.8	12.4	8.6	6.8	5.2	10.7	7.0	53.2
Minimum Precipitation (in.)*	0.6	0.3	1.0	0.7	0.9	0.7	1.0	0.6	0.5	0.1	0.6	0.5	24.5
Extreme Maximum Daily Precip. (in.)	2.41	1.72	1.95	2.23	2.67	2.89	5.13	3.17	2.36	2.31	2.38	2.56	5.13
Days With ≥ 0.1" Precipitation	6	6	7	7	9	7	7	6	5	5	7	7	79
Days With ≥ 0.5" Precipitation	1	1	2	2	3	3	3	2	2	2	2	2	25
Days With ≥ 1.0" Precipitation	0	0	0	0	1	1	1	1	1	1	1	0	7
Mean Snowfall (in.)	9.3	6.3	4.4	1.1	trace	trace	trace	trace	trace	0.2	1.2	5.4	27.9
Maximum Snowfall (in.)*	34	16	14	13	1	0	0	0	trace	5	15	17	48
Maximum 24-hr. Snowfall (in.)*	7	9	9	12	1	0	0	0	trace	4	8	8	12
Maximum Snow Depth (in.)	13	13	18	10	trace	trace	trace	trace	trace	trace	5	7	18
Days With ≥ 1.0" Snow Depth	11	7	3	0	0	0	0	0	0	0	0	5	26
Thunderstorm Days*	< 1	1	2	4	6	8	8	6	3	1	1	< 1	40
Foggy Days*	13	11	12	10	13	14	16	19	15	14	12	14	163
Predominant Sky Cover*	OVR	OVR	OVR	OVR	OVR	OVR	OVR	SCT	OVR	OVR	OVR	OVR	OVR
Mean Relative Humidity 7am (%)*	78	78	76	76	79	81	84	87	87	83	80	80	81
Mean Relative Humidity 4pm (%)*	67	62	55	51	52	53	54	53	53	52	61	67	57
Mean Dewpoint (°F)*	20	22	29	38	49	59	63	62	55	43	34	25	42
Prevailing Wind Direction*	S	S	WNW	S	S	S	S	S	S	S	S	S	S
Prevailing Wind Speed (mph)*	9	9	12	9	8	8	7	7	8	8	9	9	9
Maximum Wind Gust (mph)*	69	58	62	78	76	68	67	66	62	53	53	61	78

Note: (*) Period of record is 1948-1995

The period of record for National Weather Service station data is 1980 – 2009 except where noted. See User Guide for detailed explanation of data.

Dayton Int'l Airport

Dayton is located near the center of the Miami River Valley, which is a nearly flat plain, 50 to 200 feet below the general elevation of the adjacent rolling country. Three Miami River tributaries, the Mad River, the Stillwater River, and Wolf Creek converge, fanwise, from the north to join the master stream within the city limits of Dayton. Heavy rains in March 1913 caused the worst flood disaster in the history of the Miami Valley. During the flood more than 400 people lost their lives and property damage amounted to $100 million. After the 1913 flood, dams were built on the streams north of Dayton, forming retarding basins. No floods have occurred at Dayton since the construction of these dams.

The elevation of the city of Dayton is about 750 feet. Terrain north of the city slopes gradually upward to about 1,100 feet at Indian Lake. Ten miles southeast of Indian Lake, near Bellefontaine, is the highest point in the state, with an elevation of about 1,550 feet. South of the city, the terrain slopes gradually downward to about 450 feet where the Miami River empties into the Ohio River.

Precipitation, which is rather evenly distributed throughout the year, and moderate temperatures help to make the Miami Valley a rich agricultural region. High relative humidities during much of the year cause some discomfort to people with allergies. Temperatures of zero or below will be experienced in about four years out of five, while 100 degrees or higher will be recorded in about one year out of five. Extreme temperatures are usually of short duration. The downward slope of about 700 feet in the 163 miles of the Miami River may have some moderating influence on the winter temperatures in the Miami Valley.

Based on the 1951-1980 period, the average last occurrence in the spring of freezing temperatures is mid-April, and the average first occurrence in the autumn is late October.

Cold, polar air, flowing across the Great Lakes, causes much cloudiness during the winter, and is accompanied by frequent snow flurries. These add little to the total snowfall.

Dayton Int'l Airport *Montgomery County* Elevation: 1,000 ft. Latitude: 39° 54' N Longitude: 84° 13' W

	JAN	FEB	MAR	APR	MAY	JUN	JUL	AUG	SEP	OCT	NOV	DEC	YEAR
Mean Maximum Temp. (°F)	35.3	39.4	49.8	62.1	71.9	80.7	84.4	83.1	76.4	64.0	51.4	38.9	61.4
Mean Temp. (°F)	27.8	31.2	40.4	51.6	61.6	70.7	74.4	73.0	65.6	53.9	43.0	31.7	52.1
Mean Minimum Temp. (°F)	20.3	23.0	31.0	41.1	51.2	60.6	64.4	62.8	54.9	43.8	34.6	24.5	42.7
Extreme Maximum Temp. (°F)	66	73	82	88	92	102	102	102	95	89	77	72	102
Extreme Minimum Temp. (°F)	-25	-12	-7	17	31	40	46	41	33	23	11	-20	-25
Days Maximum Temp. ≥ 90°F	0	0	0	0	0	3	6	5	1	0	0	0	15
Days Maximum Temp. ≤ 32°F	13	9	3	0	0	0	0	0	0	0	1	9	35
Days Minimum Temp. ≤ 32°F	27	23	18	6	0	0	0	0	0	3	14	24	115
Days Minimum Temp. ≤ 0°F	2	1	0	0	0	0	0	0	0	0	0	1	4
Heating Degree Days (base 65°F)	1,146	950	758	407	162	21	2	5	80	352	654	1,026	5,563
Cooling Degree Days (base 65°F)	0	0	2	12	62	197	300	259	106	14	0	0	952
Mean Precipitation (in.)	2.76	2.28	3.41	4.12	4.64	4.28	4.06	3.08	3.11	2.98	3.29	3.12	41.13
Maximum Precipitation (in.)*	9.9	5.8	7.6	6.8	9.0	10.9	8.5	8.0	5.7	6.3	8.1	10.0	59.8
Minimum Precipitation (in.)*	0.3	0.2	1.1	0.6	1.5	0.3	0.5	0.3	0.3	0.2	0.5	0.4	24.2
Extreme Maximum Daily Precip. (in.)	2.58	1.68	1.86	2.53	3.17	3.76	2.82	3.38	3.81	3.54	2.05	2.85	3.81
Days With ≥ 0.1" Precipitation	6	5	8	9	9	7	7	5	5	5	7	7	80
Days With ≥ 0.5" Precipitation	1	1	2	3	3	3	3	2	2	2	2	2	26
Days With ≥ 1.0" Precipitation	0	0	1	1	1	1	1	1	1	1	1	1	10
Mean Snowfall (in.)	8.0	6.3	4.1	0.6	trace	0.0	trace	trace	trace	0.4	0.8	5.1	25.3
Maximum Snowfall (in.)*	40	18	14	5	trace	0	0	0	0	6	13	16	53
Maximum 24-hr. Snowfall (in.)*	12	7	11	5	trace	0	0	0	0	5	8	6	12
Maximum Snow Depth (in.)	16	10	13	6	trace	0	trace	trace	trace	4	5	16	16
Days With ≥ 1.0" Snow Depth	10	8	3	0	0	0	0	0	0	0	0	6	27
Thunderstorm Days*	< 1	1	2	4	6	7	8	6	3	2	1	< 1	40
Foggy Days*	15	12	14	12	13	13	15	18	15	14	14	15	170
Predominant Sky Cover*	OVR	OVR	OVR	OVR	OVR	OVR	OVR	OVR	OVR	OVR	OVR	OVR	OVR
Mean Relative Humidity 7am (%)*	80	79	79	77	78	80	83	86	87	83	81	81	81
Mean Relative Humidity 4pm (%)*	68	64	59	53	52	52	53	53	52	52	63	69	57
Mean Dewpoint (°F)*	20	22	30	39	49	58	63	62	54	43	33	25	42
Prevailing Wind Direction*	W	WNW	WNW	SSW	SSW	SSW	SW	SW	SSW	SSW	SSW	SSW	SSW
Prevailing Wind Speed (mph)*	13	13	13	13	12	10	9	9	9	10	13	13	12
Maximum Wind Gust (mph)*	69	52	67	63	60	60	71	61	48	46	54	62	71

Note: (*) Period of record is 1948-1995

Mansfield Lahm Municipal Airport

Mansfield is in the north central highlands at the geographical and climatological junction of central Ohio, northwest Ohio, and northeast Ohio. The station is on a plateau 3 miles north of the city of Mansfield and surrounded by rolling open farmland. The general elevation ranges from around 1,300 to 1,400 feet above sea level with the 1,000-foot contour east to west some 15 miles to the north. The climate is continental, with the modifying effects of Lake Erie most pronounced in winter. Lake Erie is just 38 miles due north.

The lake influence, plus the elevation, produce cloudy skies and considerable snow shower activity from late November into April with any wind flow from northwest through northeast. Because of this, any windshift with a cold frontal passage in winter does not bring the clearing skies, indeed, more snow is often measured from the flurry activity behind the front than from the pre-frontal conditions. A frozen Lake Erie will allow clearing skies, but an open lake dictates overcast and snow flurries. Usually the lake is open enough to set off the flurries and cloudy conditions. The major snow producer will be an intense storm moving out of the southwest with the Gulf of Mexico moisture available. Snow cover is almost constant from December through March due to almost daily snow flurries, but the depth of cover is rarely more than 8 inches. Daytime winter temperatures are not above the freezing mark too often.

Spring is a short period of rapid transition from hard winter to summer conditions. April usually brings abundant shower activity and the crops and vegetation get a quick start.

Summer is a pleasant season with low humidities and no extremely high temperatures. Rarely does the temperature climb above the 90 degree point. Thunderstorms average about once every three days during the season from June through September. Highest winds are associated with the heavier thunderstorms, and while hail does not occur often, it is of major concern to the applegrowers in the area. Flooding problems are confined to the flash-flood type on the small streams in the area.

The growing season is normally about 153 days. Autumn usually produces many clear warm days and cool invigorating nights. Ground fog is at a maximum incidence during the autumn. Little rainfall occurs to interfere with harvest time and county fair time.

Mansfield Lahm Municipal Airport *Richland County* Elevation: 1,294 ft. Latitude: 40° 49' N Longitude: 82° 31' W

	JAN	FEB	MAR	APR	MAY	JUN	JUL	AUG	SEP	OCT	NOV	DEC	YEAR
Mean Maximum Temp. (°F)	33.2	36.3	46.2	59.2	69.4	78.0	81.7	80.0	73.4	61.5	49.3	37.0	58.8
Mean Temp. (°F)	26.1	28.6	37.3	48.9	58.9	67.8	71.8	70.3	63.3	52.0	41.6	30.3	49.7
Mean Minimum Temp. (°F)	18.9	20.9	28.3	38.6	48.4	57.6	61.8	60.6	53.2	42.4	33.8	23.5	40.7
Extreme Maximum Temp. (°F)	65	71	82	86	90	101	100	97	92	87	76	73	101
Extreme Minimum Temp. (°F)	-22	-11	-6	8	27	37	43	42	33	20	10	-17	-22
Days Maximum Temp. ≥ 90°F	0	0	0	0	0	1	2	2	0	0	0	0	5
Days Maximum Temp. ≤ 32°F	15	11	5	0	0	0	0	0	0	0	2	11	44
Days Minimum Temp. ≤ 32°F	28	24	21	9	0	0	0	0	0	4	15	25	126
Days Minimum Temp. ≤ 0°F	3	1	0	0	0	0	0	0	0	0	0	1	5
Heating Degree Days (base 65°F)	1,200	1,022	854	485	223	51	7	15	114	405	696	1,069	6,141
Cooling Degree Days (base 65°F)	0	0	1	8	42	142	224	187	70	9	0	0	683
Mean Precipitation (in.)	2.85	2.31	3.48	4.19	4.54	4.66	4.46	4.43	3.33	2.94	3.72	3.33	44.24
Maximum Precipitation (in.)*	11.5	5.4	7.0	7.0	8.8	10.0	13.2	8.6	7.8	6.4	12.8	11.2	67.2
Minimum Precipitation (in.)*	0.4	0.3	1.2	0.8	1.1	0.6	0.9	0.6	0.7	0.4	0.7	0.7	21.8
Extreme Maximum Daily Precip. (in.)	1.97	1.63	2.04	2.66	2.62	2.93	3.39	4.34	2.22	3.33	3.11	2.62	4.34
Days With ≥ 0.1" Precipitation	7	6	8	9	10	8	7	7	6	6	7	8	89
Days With ≥ 0.5" Precipitation	2	1	2	3	3	4	3	3	2	2	2	2	29
Days With ≥ 1.0" Precipitation	1	0	1	1	1	1	1	1	1	1	1	1	11
Mean Snowfall (in.)	13.1	10.3	8.0	2.7	trace	trace	0.0	0.0	0.0	0.6	2.5	10.5	47.7
Maximum Snowfall (in.)*	42	18	17	13	1	0	0	0	0	10	12	23	59
Maximum 24-hr. Snowfall (in.)*	10	9	8	12	1	0	0	0	0	8	5	12	12
Maximum Snow Depth (in.)	20	13	15	10	0	trace	0	0	0	2	4	15	20
Days With ≥ 1.0" Snow Depth	15	14	6	1	0	0	0	0	0	0	2	11	49
Thunderstorm Days*	< 1	< 1	2	3	5	6	7	6	3	1	1	< 1	34
Foggy Days*	13	12	14	13	14	13	14	17	15	13	13	15	166
Predominant Sky Cover*	OVR	OVR	OVR	OVR	OVR	OVR	SCT	SCT	OVR	OVR	OVR	OVR	OVR
Mean Relative Humidity 7am (%)*	82	81	81	78	78	81	83	87	87	83	82	83	82
Mean Relative Humidity 4pm (%)*	72	69	64	56	55	56	56	57	58	56	67	74	62
Mean Dewpoint (°F)*	20	21	28	37	47	58	62	61	54	42	33	24	40
Prevailing Wind Direction*	WSW	WSW	WSW	WSW	SSW	SSW	SW	SSW	S	S	SW	WSW	WSW
Prevailing Wind Speed (mph)*	15	14	15	14	13	12	10	10	9	10	14	14	13
Maximum Wind Gust (mph)*	62	59	62	68	60	68	81	69	61	53	69	69	81

Note: (*) Period of record is 1948-1995

The period of record for National Weather Service station data is 1980 – 2009 except where noted. See User Guide for detailed explanation of data.

Toledo Express Airport

Toledo is located on the western end of Lake Erie at the mouth of the Maumee River. Except for a bank up from the river about 30 feet, the terrain is generally level with only a slight slope toward the river and Lake Erie. The city has quite a diversified industrial section and excellent harbor facilities, making it a large transportation center for rail, water, and motor freight. Generally rich agricultural land is found in the surrounding area, especially up the Maumee Valley toward the Indiana state line.

Rainfall is usually sufficient for general agriculture. The terrain is level and drainage rather poor, therefore, a little less than the normal precipitation during the growing season is better than excessive amounts. Snowfall is generally light in this area, distributed throughout the winter from November to March with frequent thaws.

The nearness of Lake Erie and the other Great Lakes has a moderating effect on the temperature, and extremes are seldom recorded. On average, only fifteen days a year experience temperatures of 90 degrees or higher, and only eight days when it drops to zero or lower. The growing season averages 160 days, but has ranged from over 220 to less than 125 days.

Humidity is rather high throughout the year in this area, and there is an excessive amount of cloudiness. In the winter months the sun shines during only about 30 percent of the daylight hours. December and January, the cloudiest months, sometimes have as little as 16 percent of the possible hours of sunshine.

Severe windstorms, causing more than minor damage, occur infrequently. There are on the average twenty-three days per year having a sustained wind velocity of 32 mph or more.

Flooding in the Toledo area is produced by several factors. Heavy rains of one inch or more will cause a sudden rise in creeks and drainage ditches to the point of overflow. The western shores of Lake Erie are subject to flooding when the lake level is high and prolonged periods of east to northeast winds prevail.

Toledo Express Airport *Lucas County* Elevation: 668 ft. Latitude: 41° 35' N Longitude: 83° 48' W

	JAN	FEB	MAR	APR	MAY	JUN	JUL	AUG	SEP	OCT	NOV	DEC	YEAR
Mean Maximum Temp. (°F)	32.5	35.7	46.3	59.6	70.8	80.4	84.3	82.0	75.2	62.4	49.3	36.4	59.6
Mean Temp. (°F)	25.2	27.9	37.1	49.0	59.5	69.1	73.2	71.3	63.9	51.9	41.1	29.6	49.9
Mean Minimum Temp. (°F)	18.0	20.1	27.8	38.3	48.1	57.7	62.1	60.6	52.5	41.3	32.9	22.8	40.2
Extreme Maximum Temp. (°F)	66	71	81	88	94	104	104	99	96	89	80	70	104
Extreme Minimum Temp. (°F)	-20	-14	-6	8	25	37	40	34	30	16	9	-19	-20
Days Maximum Temp. ≥ 90°F	0	0	0	0	1	4	6	4	1	0	0	0	16
Days Maximum Temp. ≤ 32°F	16	11	4	0	0	0	0	0	0	0	1	11	43
Days Minimum Temp. ≤ 32°F	28	25	22	8	1	0	0	0	0	5	15	26	130
Days Minimum Temp. ≤ 0°F	3	2	0	0	0	0	0	0	0	0	0	1	6
Heating Degree Days (base 65°F)	1,226	1,041	859	482	209	37	3	12	108	409	710	1,090	6,186
Cooling Degree Days (base 65°F)	0	0	1	9	45	166	264	215	80	9	0	0	789
Mean Precipitation (in.)	2.05	2.03	2.52	3.13	3.48	3.54	3.21	3.26	2.78	2.62	2.78	2.71	34.11
Maximum Precipitation (in.)*	4.6	5.4	5.7	6.1	5.1	8.5	6.8	8.5	8.1	5.5	6.9	6.8	40.8
Minimum Precipitation (in.)*	0.3	0.3	0.6	0.9	1.0	0.3	0.3	0.4	0.6	0.3	0.5	0.5	22.0
Extreme Maximum Daily Precip. (in.)	1.30	2.59	2.60	2.81	1.85	3.12	3.15	2.21	2.70	2.88	2.71	2.51	3.15
Days With ≥ 0.1" Precipitation	5	5	7	7	7	6	6	6	5	5	6	7	72
Days With ≥ 0.5" Precipitation	1	1	1	2	2	2	2	2	2	2	2	2	21
Days With ≥ 1.0" Precipitation	0	0	0	0	1	1	1	1	1	1	1	0	7
Mean Snowfall (in.)	***11.3***	***8.6***	***5.9***	***1.4***	na	na	na	na	na	na	***1.9***	***7.4***	na
Maximum Snowfall (in.)*	31	17	18	12	1	0	0	0	trace	2	18	24	72
Maximum 24-hr. Snowfall (in.)*	10	8	9	7	1	0	0	0	trace	2	7	14	14
Maximum Snow Depth (in.)	***12***	***16***	***8***	***7***	***1***	na	na	na	na	na	***3***	***7***	na
Days With ≥ 1.0" Snow Depth	***15***	***13***	***6***	***1***	***0***	na	na	***0***	na	na	***1***	***10***	na
Thunderstorm Days*	< 1	1	2	4	5	7	7	6	4	1	1	< 1	38
Foggy Days*	13	11	14	12	12	11	14	18	15	13	14	15	162
Predominant Sky Cover*	OVR	OVR	OVR	OVR	OVR	OVR	SCT	SCT	OVR	OVR	OVR	OVR	OVR
Mean Relative Humidity 7am (%)*	80	80	81	80	80	82	86	91	91	86	83	83	84
Mean Relative Humidity 4pm (%)*	68	65	59	53	51	52	53	56	54	55	65	72	58
Mean Dewpoint (°F)*	17	19	27	36	47	57	62	61	54	42	32	23	40
Prevailing Wind Direction*	WSW	WSW	ENE	WSW	WSW	SW	SW	SW	SW	SW	WSW	WSW	WSW
Prevailing Wind Speed (mph)*	13	13	12	13	12	9	8	8	9	10	13	13	12
Maximum Wind Gust (mph)*	62	52	64	63	58	59	66	75	54	49	55	56	75

Note: (*) Period of record is 1955-1995

Youngstown Municipal Airport

The Youngstown Municipal Airport is located in northeastern Ohio approximately eight miles north of the city of Youngstown in Trumbull County. Airport elevation is 1,178 feet, about 200 feet higher than most communities in the Mahoning and Shenango River Valleys. There are numerous natural and man-made lakes in the region, including Lake Erie, 45 miles to the north. Drainage from the area flows southward through the Mahoning and Shenango Rivers which join to form the Beaver River at New Castle, Pennsylvania. The Beaver empties into the Ohio River at Rochester, Pennsylvania.

This entire area experiences frequent outbreaks of cold Canadian air masses which may be modified by passage over Lake Erie. This effect produces widespread cloudiness especially during the cool months of the year. The winter months are characterized by persistent cloudiness and intermittent snow flurries. The daily temperature range during most winter days is quite small. During most winters, the bulk of the snow falls as flurries of 2 inches or less per occurrence, although several snowstorms per year will produce amounts in the four to 10 inch range.

Destructive storms seldom occur, and tornadoes are not common. During recent years flood control projects have all but eliminated the threat of serious river flooding. Flash flooding of small streams and creeks rarely affects residential areas. Certain communities have well known areas of urban flooding during periods of prolonged heavy thunderstorms.

The climate of the Youngstown district has had an important role in the growth and development of this industrial area. Temperatures seldom reach extreme values especially during the summer months. However, high humidity during most days of the year tends to accentuate the temperature. Rainfall, reasonably well distributed throughout the year, provides a more than adequate supply of water for agriculture, industrial, and residential use.

Based on the 1951-1980 period, the average first occurrence of 32 degrees Fahrenheit in the fall is October 14 and the average last occurrence in the spring is May 6.

Youngstown Municipal Airport *Trumbull County* Elevation: 1,180 ft. Latitude: 41° 15' N Longitude: 80° 40' W

	JAN	FEB	MAR	APR	MAY	JUN	JUL	AUG	SEP	OCT	NOV	DEC	YEAR
Mean Maximum Temp. (°F)	33.2	36.6	46.1	59.3	69.5	77.9	81.9	80.5	73.0	61.0	49.3	37.3	58.8
Mean Temp. (°F)	26.1	28.6	36.7	48.6	58.0	66.6	70.8	69.4	62.2	51.2	41.6	30.6	49.2
Mean Minimum Temp. (°F)	19.0	20.5	27.4	37.7	46.5	55.1	59.6	58.3	51.4	41.3	33.9	23.9	39.6
Extreme Maximum Temp. (°F)	68	73	82	88	90	99	100	97	92	87	78	76	100
Extreme Minimum Temp. (°F)	-22	-8	-10	14	25	34	40	32	29	20	12	-12	-22
Days Maximum Temp. ≥ 90°F	0	0	0	0	0	1	3	2	0	0	0	0	6
Days Maximum Temp. ≤ 32°F	15	11	5	0	0	0	0	0	0	0	2	11	44
Days Minimum Temp. ≤ 32°F	27	24	22	10	1	0	0	0	0	4	15	26	129
Days Minimum Temp. ≤ 0°F	2	1	0	0	0	0	0	0	0	0	0	1	4
Heating Degree Days (base 65°F)	1,199	1,023	871	495	243	65	11	22	133	427	696	1,058	6,243
Cooling Degree Days (base 65°F)	0	0	1	8	34	118	197	166	57	7	0	0	588
Mean Precipitation (in.)	2.51	2.09	3.02	3.36	3.70	3.86	4.41	3.41	3.82	2.74	3.09	2.91	38.92
Maximum Precipitation (in.)*	7.6	5.3	6.2	6.4	6.2	10.7	9.7	7.9	6.1	8.6	9.1	6.5	48.6
Minimum Precipitation (in.)*	0.7	0.5	1.1	1.0	0.8	0.7	1.6	0.5	0.3	0.4	0.9	0.9	23.8
Extreme Maximum Daily Precip. (in.)	1.34	1.63	1.41	1.53	1.95	3.57	4.65	3.47	4.09	2.05	2.73	1.55	4.65
Days With ≥ 0.1" Precipitation	7	6	8	8	9	8	7	6	7	6	7	8	87
Days With ≥ 0.5" Precipitation	1	1	2	2	2	2	3	2	3	2	2	1	23
Days With ≥ 1.0" Precipitation	0	0	0	1	1	1	1	1	1	0	0	0	6
Mean Snowfall (in.)	15.9	11.9	10.8	3.0	trace	trace	trace	trace	trace	0.8	4.0	13.3	59.7
Maximum Snowfall (in.)*	36	23	31	12	5	0	0	0	trace	8	31	30	91
Maximum 24-hr. Snowfall (in.)*	17	9	15	12	5	0	0	0	trace	5	17	12	17
Maximum Snow Depth (in.)	18	14	11	10	trace	trace	trace	trace	trace	1	6	13	18
Days With ≥ 1.0" Snow Depth	17	14	7	1	0	0	0	0	0	0	2	13	54
Thunderstorm Days*	< 1	< 1	2	3	4	7	7	5	3	1	1	< 1	33
Foggy Days*	13	12	14	13	15	16	17	20	17	15	13	14	179
Predominant Sky Cover*	OVR	OVR	OVR	OVR	OVR	OVR	OVR	OVR	OVR	OVR	OVR	OVR	OVR
Mean Relative Humidity 7am (%)*	81	80	80	77	79	82	85	88	89	85	81	82	82
Mean Relative Humidity 4pm (%)*	70	66	60	54	52	54	55	55	57	57	66	72	60
Mean Dewpoint (°F)*	18	19	26	36	46	56	60	60	53	42	32	23	39
Prevailing Wind Direction*	WSW	WSW	W	SW	SW	SW	SW	SW	SW	SW	SW	WSW	SW
Prevailing Wind Speed (mph)*	14	13	13	13	12	9	9	8	9	10	12	14	12
Maximum Wind Gust (mph)*	67	54	78	75	70	58	66	58	62	51	53	62	78

Note: (*) Period of record is 1948-1995

Barnesville *Belmont County* Elevation: 1,240 ft. Latitude: 39° 59' N Longitude: 81° 09' W

	JAN	FEB	MAR	APR	MAY	JUN	JUL	AUG	SEP	OCT	NOV	DEC	YEAR
Mean Maximum Temp. (°F)	*35.5*	*38.8*	*48.6*	*61.1*	*70.2*	*78.7*	*82.5*	*81.3*	*74.3*	*62.8*	*50.9*	*39.4*	*60.4*
Mean Temp. (°F)	*27.6*	*30.1*	*38.5*	*49.8*	*59.4*	*68.1*	*72.3*	*70.6*	*63.4*	*52.2*	*42.0*	*31.9*	*50.5*
Mean Minimum Temp. (°F)	*19.7*	*21.2*	*28.4*	*38.5*	*48.4*	*57.4*	*62.1*	*59.9*	*52.4*	*41.4*	*33.1*	*24.3*	*40.6*
Extreme Maximum Temp. (°F)	*71*	*76*	*82*	*87*	*90*	*96*	*100*	*97*	*93*	*85*	*76*	*75*	*100*
Extreme Minimum Temp. (°F)	*-23*	*-10*	*-5*	*15*	*26*	*33*	*45*	*38*	*30*	*18*	na	*-17*	na
Days Maximum Temp. ≥ 90°F	*0*	*0*	*0*	*0*	*0*	*1*	*2*	*3*	*1*	*0*	*0*	*0*	*7*
Days Maximum Temp. ≤ 32°F	*13*	*9*	*3*	*0*	*0*	*0*	*0*	*0*	*0*	*0*	*2*	*8*	*35*
Days Minimum Temp. ≤ 32°F	*27*	*24*	*21*	*9*	*1*	*0*	*0*	*0*	*0*	*5*	*15*	*24*	*126*
Days Minimum Temp. ≤ 0°F	*2*	*1*	*0*	*0*	*0*	*0*	*0*	*0*	*0*	*0*	*0*	*1*	*4*
Heating Degree Days (base 65°F)	*1,151*	*980*	*815*	*458*	*207*	*44*	*6*	*14*	*115*	*399*	*684*	*1,019*	*5,892*
Cooling Degree Days (base 65°F)	*0*	*0*	*2*	*9*	*40*	*144*	*239*	*196*	*72*	*8*	*0*	*0*	*710*
Mean Precipitation (in.)	*2.97*	*2.62*	*3.54*	*3.91*	*4.50*	*4.63*	*4.39*	*3.74*	*3.23*	*3.09*	*4.01*	*2.97*	*43.60*
Extreme Maximum Daily Precip. (in.)	*2.03*	*2.17*	*1.69*	*1.74*	*2.32*	*2.28*	*3.67*	*5.12*	*2.42*	*1.56*	*2.91*	*1.56*	*5.12*
Days With ≥ 0.1" Precipitation	*7*	*6*	*8*	*9*	*9*	*8*	*7*	*6*	*6*	*6*	*8*	*7*	*87*
Days With ≥ 0.5" Precipitation	*2*	*2*	*2*	*2*	*3*	*3*	*3*	*2*	*2*	*2*	*3*	*2*	*29*
Days With ≥ 1.0" Precipitation	*0*	*0*	*1*	*1*	*1*	*1*	*1*	*1*	*1*	*1*	*1*	*0*	*9*
Mean Snowfall (in.)	*10.1*	*7.7*	*4.9*	*1.2*	*trace*	*0.0*	*0.0*	*trace*	*0.0*	*0.1*	*1.8*	*5.8*	*31.6*
Maximum Snow Depth (in.)	*16*	*20*	*17*	*12*	*trace*	*0*	*0*	*trace*	*0*	*2*	*4*	*8*	*20*
Days With ≥ 1.0" Snow Depth	*12*	*9*	*4*	*0*	*0*	*0*	*0*	*0*	*0*	*0*	*2*	*7*	*34*

Bellefontaine *Logan County* Elevation: 1,185 ft. Latitude: 40° 21' N Longitude: 83° 46' W

	JAN	FEB	MAR	APR	MAY	JUN	JUL	AUG	SEP	OCT	NOV	DEC	YEAR
Mean Maximum Temp. (°F)	33.4	37.5	47.6	60.6	71.1	79.5	82.9	81.8	75.9	63.4	50.4	37.6	60.2
Mean Temp. (°F)	25.7	28.9	38.1	49.8	60.4	69.3	72.8	71.6	64.8	52.8	41.8	30.1	50.5
Mean Minimum Temp. (°F)	17.9	20.2	28.5	38.9	49.6	59.0	62.6	61.4	53.8	42.2	33.0	22.6	40.8
Extreme Maximum Temp. (°F)	66	72	82	87	90	101	99	101	95	89	77	71	101
Extreme Minimum Temp. (°F)	-27	-13	-12	9	28	37	45	39	30	17	8	-22	-27
Days Maximum Temp. ≥ 90°F	0	0	0	0	0	2	4	3	1	0	0	0	10
Days Maximum Temp. ≤ 32°F	14	10	4	0	0	0	0	0	0	0	2	10	40
Days Minimum Temp. ≤ 32°F	28	24	21	8	1	0	0	0	0	5	16	26	129
Days Minimum Temp. ≤ 0°F	3	2	0	0	0	0	0	0	0	0	0	2	7
Heating Degree Days (base 65°F)	1,212	1,014	828	457	188	34	4	10	92	384	691	1,074	5,988
Cooling Degree Days (base 65°F)	0	0	1	8	50	169	253	222	94	13	0	0	810
Mean Precipitation (in.)	2.64	2.13	2.93	3.58	4.13	4.44	4.19	3.57	2.81	2.62	3.17	3.03	39.24
Extreme Maximum Daily Precip. (in.)	3.29	2.30	1.85	2.37	2.47	3.30	4.45	3.02	2.40	2.47	1.78	2.96	4.45
Days With ≥ 0.1" Precipitation	6	5	7	8	9	8	7	6	5	6	7	7	81
Days With ≥ 0.5" Precipitation	1	1	2	3	3	3	3	2	2	1	2	2	25
Days With ≥ 1.0" Precipitation	0	0	0	1	1	1	1	1	1	1	1	1	9
Mean Snowfall (in.)	na	3.2	1.2	0.2	0.0	0.0	0.0	0.0	0.0	0.2	0.4	*2.5*	na
Maximum Snow Depth (in.)	19	14	*10*	1	0	0	0	0	0	*1*	4	*11*	*19*
Days With ≥ 1.0" Snow Depth	7	4	1	0	0	0	0	0	0	0	0	*3*	*15*

Bowling Green WWTP *Wood County* Elevation: 674 ft. Latitude: 41° 23' N Longitude: 83° 37' W

	JAN	FEB	MAR	APR	MAY	JUN	JUL	AUG	SEP	OCT	NOV	DEC	YEAR
Mean Maximum Temp. (°F)	32.2	35.7	46.0	59.4	70.7	80.7	84.1	82.1	75.9	63.0	49.6	36.5	59.7
Mean Temp. (°F)	24.9	27.9	36.6	48.5	59.4	69.7	73.1	71.0	64.1	52.2	41.1	29.6	49.8
Mean Minimum Temp. (°F)	17.6	20.0	27.2	37.5	48.1	58.6	62.0	59.9	52.2	41.4	32.6	22.6	40.0
Extreme Maximum Temp. (°F)	66	72	80	88	92	104	101	98	95	90	78	70	104
Extreme Minimum Temp. (°F)	-20	-13	-5	8	28	39	45	38	30	21	11	-19	-20
Days Maximum Temp. ≥ 90°F	0	0	0	0	1	4	6	4	1	0	0	0	16
Days Maximum Temp. ≤ 32°F	16	11	4	0	0	0	0	0	0	0	1	11	43
Days Minimum Temp. ≤ 32°F	28	25	22	9	0	0	0	0	0	4	16	26	130
Days Minimum Temp. ≤ 0°F	4	2	0	0	0	0	0	0	0	0	0	1	7
Heating Degree Days (base 65°F)	1,238	1,044	873	496	211	32	3	13	103	402	710	1,090	6,215
Cooling Degree Days (base 65°F)	0	0	1	8	46	180	261	206	83	11	0	0	796
Mean Precipitation (in.)	1.91	1.84	2.17	3.14	3.76	3.37	3.66	3.64	2.61	2.82	2.57	2.43	33.92
Extreme Maximum Daily Precip. (in.)	1.47	2.00	1.68	1.90	2.66	4.25	4.08	3.31	2.49	3.37	2.12	2.11	4.25
Days With ≥ 0.1" Precipitation	5	4	6	7	8	7	7	6	5	6	6	6	73
Days With ≥ 0.5" Precipitation	1	1	1	2	2	2	3	2	2	2	2	1	21
Days With ≥ 1.0" Precipitation	0	0	0	1	1	1	1	1	1	1	0	0	7
Mean Snowfall (in.)	7.1	5.4	3.2	0.6	trace	0.0	0.0	0.0	0.0	0.0	0.6	4.7	21.6
Maximum Snow Depth (in.)	14	18	10	7	1	0	0	0	0	0	3	11	18
Days With ≥ 1.0" Snow Depth	14	11	5	0	0	0	0	0	0	0	1	7	38

Bucyrus *Crawford County* Elevation: 955 ft. Latitude: 40° 49' N Longitude: 82° 58' W

	JAN	FEB	MAR	APR	MAY	JUN	JUL	AUG	SEP	OCT	NOV	DEC	YEAR
Mean Maximum Temp. (°F)	32.6	35.7	45.6	59.6	70.2	79.5	83.1	81.4	74.8	61.9	49.2	36.6	59.2
Mean Temp. (°F)	25.2	27.6	36.3	48.5	58.8	68.4	72.3	70.5	63.4	51.4	40.8	29.7	49.4
Mean Minimum Temp. (°F)	17.8	19.5	26.9	37.4	47.4	57.3	61.4	59.6	52.0	40.8	32.4	22.7	39.6
Extreme Maximum Temp. (°F)	64	71	81	88	91	102	100	99	95	87	77	72	102
Extreme Minimum Temp. (°F)	-26	-18	-11	10	27	37	43	39	30	20	12	-18	-26
Days Maximum Temp. ≥ 90°F	0	0	0	0	0	3	4	3	1	0	0	0	11
Days Maximum Temp. ≤ 32°F	16	11	5	0	0	0	0	0	0	0	2	11	45
Days Minimum Temp. ≤ 32°F	27	25	23	10	0	0	0	0	0	5	16	26	132
Days Minimum Temp. ≤ 0°F	3	2	0	0	0	0	0	0	0	0	0	1	6
Heating Degree Days (base 65°F)	1,227	1,052	884	495	225	45	7	16	114	423	721	1,088	6,297
Cooling Degree Days (base 65°F)	0	0	1	7	40	154	240	195	74	9	0	0	720
Mean Precipitation (in.)	2.48	2.02	2.66	3.42	4.26	4.21	4.44	3.84	3.19	2.62	3.07	2.86	39.07
Extreme Maximum Daily Precip. (in.)	2.20	1.45	1.50	1.80	2.18	3.27	3.42	8.68	3.58	2.51	1.57	1.95	8.68
Days With ≥ 0.1" Precipitation	6	5	7	8	9	8	8	6	6	6	7	7	83
Days With ≥ 0.5" Precipitation	1	1	2	2	3	3	3	3	2	1	2	2	25
Days With ≥ 1.0" Precipitation	1	0	0	0	1	1	1	1	1	0	1	0	7
Mean Snowfall (in.)	7.4	4.6	3.4	0.9	0.1	0.0	0.0	0.0	0.0	0.1	0.9	5.1	22.5
Maximum Snow Depth (in.)	14	13	10	8	2	0	0	0	0	1	3	17	17
Days With ≥ 1.0" Snow Depth	12	7	3	0	0	0	0	0	0	0	1	6	29

The period of record for all cooperative weather station data is 1980 – 2009. See User Guide for detailed explanation of data.

Cadiz *Harrison County* Elevation: 1,259 ft. Latitude: 40° 16' N Longitude: 81° 00' W

	JAN	FEB	MAR	APR	MAY	JUN	JUL	AUG	SEP	OCT	NOV	DEC	YEAR
Mean Maximum Temp. (°F)	35.2	38.9	48.5	61.1	70.3	78.5	82.2	81.3	74.7	63.1	50.6	39.0	60.3
Mean Temp. (°F)	27.2	30.3	38.9	50.3	60.0	68.5	72.6	71.1	64.3	52.8	42.0	31.6	50.8
Mean Minimum Temp. (°F)	19.5	21.5	29.1	39.6	49.5	58.3	62.8	61.1	53.9	42.5	33.5	24.1	41.3
Extreme Maximum Temp. (°F)	69	76	81	89	89	95	101	97	94	87	79	75	101
Extreme Minimum Temp. (°F)	-24	-10	-6	14	26	35	47	40	35	22	10	-17	-24
Days Maximum Temp. ≥ 90°F	0	0	0	0	0	1	3	3	1	0	0	0	8
Days Maximum Temp. ≤ 32°F	14	9	4	0	0	0	0	0	0	0	1	9	37
Days Minimum Temp. ≤ 32°F	26	22	18	7	1	0	0	0	0	4	14	24	116
Days Minimum Temp. ≤ 0°F	2	1	0	0	0	0	0	0	0	0	0	1	4
Heating Degree Days (base 65°F)	1,168	978	805	446	196	38	4	11	99	381	683	1,031	5,840
Cooling Degree Days (base 65°F)	0	0	1	12	46	148	246	208	85	11	1	0	758
Mean Precipitation (in.)	3.02	2.37	3.17	3.48	4.39	4.27	4.31	3.80	3.43	2.75	3.37	2.90	41.26
Extreme Maximum Daily Precip. (in.)	2.07	1.75	1.64	2.00	2.32	5.00	3.28	2.70	5.09	1.93	2.90	2.05	5.09
Days With ≥ 0.1" Precipitation	7	6	8	9	9	8	8	6	6	6	7	7	87
Days With ≥ 0.5" Precipitation	2	1	2	2	3	3	3	3	2	2	2	2	27
Days With ≥ 1.0" Precipitation	0	0	0	1	1	1	1	1	1	1	0	0	7
Mean Snowfall (in.)	8.8	6.1	4.9	1.2	0.0	0.0	0.0	0.0	0.0	0.1	1.5	5.6	28.2
Maximum Snow Depth (in.)	10	15	12	2	0	0	0	0	0	trace	3	na	na
Days With ≥ 1.0" Snow Depth	9	6	3	0	0	0	0	0	0	0	1	6	25

Cambridge *Guernsey County* Elevation: 799 ft. Latitude: 40° 01' N Longitude: 81° 35' W

	JAN	FEB	MAR	APR	MAY	JUN	JUL	AUG	SEP	OCT	NOV	DEC	YEAR
Mean Maximum Temp. (°F)	38.0	42.6	52.9	65.7	74.2	82.0	85.2	84.2	77.6	66.0	53.8	41.6	63.6
Mean Temp. (°F)	30.0	33.3	42.0	53.3	62.0	70.2	74.1	73.0	66.0	54.4	44.1	33.7	53.0
Mean Minimum Temp. (°F)	21.8	23.9	31.0	40.8	49.7	58.4	63.0	61.7	54.4	42.7	34.5	25.7	42.3
Extreme Maximum Temp. (°F)	72	76	83	90	92	98	102	99	96	90	80	77	102
Extreme Minimum Temp. (°F)	-32	-12	-3	17	29	38	42	37	32	19	9	-17	-32
Days Maximum Temp. ≥ 90°F	0	0	0	0	0	3	6	5	1	0	0	0	15
Days Maximum Temp. ≤ 32°F	9	6	1	0	0	0	0	0	0	0	1	6	23
Days Minimum Temp. ≤ 32°F	25	22	18	6	1	0	0	0	0	5	13	23	113
Days Minimum Temp. ≤ 0°F	2	1	0	0	0	0	0	0	0	0	0	1	4
Heating Degree Days (base 65°F)	1,080	891	709	359	144	21	2	5	71	335	619	964	5,200
Cooling Degree Days (base 65°F)	0	0	2	14	57	185	292	259	107	13	0	0	929
Mean Precipitation (in.)	2.95	2.19	3.09	3.52	4.18	3.92	4.25	3.62	3.32	2.78	3.26	2.79	39.87
Extreme Maximum Daily Precip. (in.)	2.17	1.83	2.08	2.29	2.01	4.97	2.74	5.45	5.33	2.37	2.32	1.65	5.45
Days With ≥ 0.1" Precipitation	6	6	8	7	9	8	8	6	5	6	7	7	83
Days With ≥ 0.5" Precipitation	2	1	2	2	3	3	3	2	2	2	2	2	26
Days With ≥ 1.0" Precipitation	1	0	0	1	1	1	1	1	1	1	1	0	9
Mean Snowfall (in.)	6.3	4.5	2.8	0.7	trace	0.0	0.0	0.0	0.0	trace	0.7	3.2	18.2
Maximum Snow Depth (in.)	9	19	9	10	trace	0	0	0	0	trace	5	6	19
Days With ≥ 1.0" Snow Depth	11	7	2	0	0	0	0	0	0	0	0	5	25

Carpenter 2 S *Meigs County* Elevation: 821 ft. Latitude: 39° 09' N Longitude: 82° 13' W

	JAN	FEB	MAR	APR	MAY	JUN	JUL	AUG	SEP	OCT	NOV	DEC	YEAR
Mean Maximum Temp. (°F)	39.0	42.8	53.2	64.9	73.3	81.2	84.7	84.0	77.2	66.3	54.6	42.9	63.7
Mean Temp. (°F)	30.2	33.0	41.9	52.6	61.2	69.5	73.3	72.1	64.7	53.4	43.9	33.9	52.5
Mean Minimum Temp. (°F)	21.3	23.1	30.5	40.2	49.1	57.7	61.9	60.2	52.1	40.6	33.2	24.9	41.2
Extreme Maximum Temp. (°F)	75	77	83	89	90	99	101	101	97	87	80	78	101
Extreme Minimum Temp. (°F)	-25	-11	-5	15	27	37	44	35	29	17	8	-4	-25
Days Maximum Temp. ≥ 90°F	0	0	0	0	0	2	5	5	1	0	0	0	13
Days Maximum Temp. ≤ 32°F	9	6	1	0	0	0	0	0	0	0	0	7	23
Days Minimum Temp. ≤ 32°F	26	23	18	7	1	0	0	0	0	7	15	23	120
Days Minimum Temp. ≤ 0°F	2	1	0	0	0	0	0	0	0	0	0	1	4
Heating Degree Days (base 65°F)	1,073	899	714	381	163	25	3	7	93	364	627	958	5,307
Cooling Degree Days (base 65°F)	0	0	3	15	53	167	267	234	90	12	2	0	843
Mean Precipitation (in.)	2.90	2.82	3.67	3.55	4.39	3.76	4.47	3.32	3.22	2.90	3.22	2.82	41.04
Extreme Maximum Daily Precip. (in.)	1.81	3.60	4.87	1.80	2.96	2.23	2.76	3.22	4.34	2.20	2.00	na	na
Days With ≥ 0.1" Precipitation	7	6	7	8	8	7	8	6	6	6	7	6	82
Days With ≥ 0.5" Precipitation	2	2	3	2	3	3	3	2	2	2	2	2	28
Days With ≥ 1.0" Precipitation	0	1	1	1	1	1	1	1	1	1	1	0	10
Mean Snowfall (in.)	6.9	4.4	2.7	0.9	trace	0.0	0.0	0.0	0.0	trace	0.6	3.1	18.6
Maximum Snow Depth (in.)	na	na	na	na	na	na	na	na	na	na	na	na	na
Days With ≥ 1.0" Snow Depth	na	na	1	0	0	0	0	0	0	0	0	na	na

Centerburg 2 SE *Knox County* Elevation: 1,205 ft. Latitude: 40° 18' N Longitude: 82° 39' W

	JAN	FEB	MAR	APR	MAY	JUN	JUL	AUG	SEP	OCT	NOV	DEC	YEAR
Mean Maximum Temp. (°F)	33.7	37.3	47.6	60.9	70.6	79.2	82.6	81.4	74.7	62.6	50.3	37.3	59.8
Mean Temp. (°F)	25.8	28.4	37.8	49.9	59.6	68.6	72.2	70.8	63.5	51.6	41.3	29.7	49.9
Mean Minimum Temp. (°F)	17.4	19.6	28.0	38.6	48.6	57.9	61.6	60.0	52.2	40.6	32.3	22.3	39.9
Extreme Maximum Temp. (°F)	67	73	82	87	89	99	99	97	94	88	78	70	99
Extreme Minimum Temp. (°F)	-29	-16	-6	11	27	37	44	38	32	21	7	-23	-29
Days Maximum Temp. ≥ 90°F	0	0	0	0	0	2	3	3	1	0	0	0	9
Days Maximum Temp. ≤ 32°F	14	10	4	0	0	0	0	0	0	0	2	10	40
Days Minimum Temp. ≤ 32°F	28	25	21	8	1	0	0	0	0	6	16	26	131
Days Minimum Temp. ≤ 0°F	4	2	0	0	0	0	0	0	0	0	0	1	7
Heating Degree Days (base 65°F)	1,210	1,027	836	456	203	39	5	13	108	417	704	1,088	6,106
Cooling Degree Days (base 65°F)	0	0	1	9	42	152	234	201	70	8	0	0	717
Mean Precipitation (in.)	2.85	2.40	3.05	3.76	4.51	4.56	4.43	3.74	3.15	2.90	3.45	3.14	41.94
Extreme Maximum Daily Precip. (in.)	2.82	2.75	2.25	2.11	2.75	3.46	2.95	3.34	2.76	2.81	1.70	2.31	3.46
Days With ≥ 0.1" Precipitation	6	6	7	8	8	8	7	6	5	6	7	7	81
Days With ≥ 0.5" Precipitation	2	2	2	2	3	3	3	3	2	2	3	2	29
Days With ≥ 1.0" Precipitation	0	0	0	1	1	1	1	1	1	1	1	1	9
Mean Snowfall (in.)	4.6	2.1	2.1	0.2	trace	0.0	0.0	0.0	0.0	0.1	0.8	2.5	12.4
Maximum Snow Depth (in.)	23	9	10	7	1	0	0	0	0	1	4	10	23
Days With ≥ 1.0" Snow Depth	9	7	3	1	0	0	0	0	0	0	1	5	26

The period of record for all cooperative weather station data is 1980 – 2009. See User Guide for detailed explanation of data.

Chardon *Geauga County* Elevation: 1,129 ft. Latitude: 41° 35' N Longitude: 81° 11' W

	JAN	FEB	MAR	APR	MAY	JUN	JUL	AUG	SEP	OCT	NOV	DEC	YEAR
Mean Maximum Temp. (°F)	32.3	35.1	43.7	57.1	67.7	76.7	80.4	79.0	72.1	60.2	48.5	36.6	57.5
Mean Temp. (°F)	24.4	25.9	33.9	46.1	56.2	65.3	69.4	68.0	61.0	50.0	40.5	29.5	47.5
Mean Minimum Temp. (°F)	16.3	16.7	24.2	35.0	44.6	53.9	58.3	56.9	49.8	39.7	32.4	22.4	37.5
Extreme Maximum Temp. (°F)	67	73	82	88	90	100	98	96	92	85	79	73	100
Extreme Minimum Temp. (°F)	-23	-17	-17	5	23	33	40	33	29	17	4	-21	-23
Days Maximum Temp. ≥ 90°F	0	0	0	0	0	1	2	2	0	0	0	0	5
Days Maximum Temp. ≤ 32°F	16	13	7	0	0	0	0	0	0	0	2	11	49
Days Minimum Temp. ≤ 32°F	28	26	25	13	2	0	0	0	0	6	16	26	142
Days Minimum Temp. ≤ 0°F	4	3	1	0	0	0	0	0	0	0	0	1	9
Heating Degree Days (base 65°F)	1,253	1,099	956	565	290	86	24	36	160	463	729	1,093	6,754
Cooling Degree Days (base 65°F)	0	0	1	4	23	102	166	136	46	4	0	0	482
Mean Precipitation (in.)	3.59	2.79	3.27	4.03	4.42	4.46	4.38	4.24	4.30	4.06	4.30	4.40	48.24
Extreme Maximum Daily Precip. (in.)	1.78	2.33	2.25	2.30	3.13	3.66	5.50	3.75	2.65	2.00	2.89	2.14	5.50
Days With ≥ 0.1" Precipitation	10	8	9	10	9	8	8	7	8	9	10	12	108
Days With ≥ 0.5" Precipitation	2	1	2	3	3	3	3	3	3	3	3	3	32
Days With ≥ 1.0" Precipitation	0	0	0	1	1	1	1	1	1	1	1	1	9
Mean Snowfall (in.)	28.6	19.2	14.4	4.5	trace	0.0	0.0	0.0	0.0	0.9	9.5	25.7	102.8
Maximum Snow Depth (in.)	23	22	20	14	trace	0	0	0	0	7	47	23	47
Days With ≥ 1.0" Snow Depth	23	20	12	2	0	0	0	0	0	1	5	17	80

Chillicothe Mound City *Ross County* Elevation: 649 ft. Latitude: 39° 22' N Longitude: 83° 00' W

	JAN	FEB	MAR	APR	MAY	JUN	JUL	AUG	SEP	OCT	NOV	DEC	YEAR
Mean Maximum Temp. (°F)	***38.0***	***43.0***	***52.3***	***64.6***	***73.5***	82.5	***85.7***	***85.0***	***78.4***	***67.0***	***54.3***	***42.4***	***63.9***
Mean Temp. (°F)	***29.1***	***33.3***	***41.3***	***52.4***	***61.7***	***70.9***	***74.6***	***73.2***	***65.8***	***54.2***	***44.0***	***33.8***	***52.8***
Mean Minimum Temp. (°F)	***20.1***	***23.4***	***30.2***	***40.1***	***49.8***	***59.2***	***63.4***	***61.4***	***53.0***	***41.4***	***33.6***	***25.0***	***41.7***
Extreme Maximum Temp. (°F)	73	77	88	90	93	103	103	105	100	92	82	80	105
Extreme Minimum Temp. (°F)	-29	-14	-10	16	29	36	41	39	32	17	11	-21	-29
Days Maximum Temp. ≥ 90°F	0	0	0	0	0	4	7	6	2	0	0	0	19
Days Maximum Temp. ≤ 32°F	9	5	1	0	0	0	0	0	0	0	0	6	21
Days Minimum Temp. ≤ 32°F	25	22	18	6	0	0	0	0	0	5	14	22	112
Days Minimum Temp. ≤ 0°F	2	1	0	0	0	0	0	0	0	0	0	1	4
Heating Degree Days (base 65°F)	***1,107***	***891***	***729***	***387***	***157***	***21***	***1***	***6***	***83***	***341***	***625***	***960***	***5,308***
Cooling Degree Days (base 65°F)	***0***	***0***	***3***	***14***	***61***	***205***	***306***	***268***	***112***	***15***	***1***	***0***	***985***
Mean Precipitation (in.)	2.62	2.46	3.49	3.55	4.64	3.26	4.04	3.05	2.67	2.58	2.93	2.82	38.11
Extreme Maximum Daily Precip. (in.)	***1.95***	***2.21***	***1.96***	***3.05***	3.01	4.10	***2.45***	***3.98***	3.06	2.88	***2.04***	***1.72***	***4.10***
Days With ≥ 0.1" Precipitation	5	5	7	7	8	6	7	5	4	5	6	5	70
Days With ≥ 0.5" Precipitation	2	2	2	2	3	2	3	2	2	2	2	2	26
Days With ≥ 1.0" Precipitation	0	1	1	1	1	1	1	1	1	1	0	0	9
Mean Snowfall (in.)	5.2	4.0	2.4	0.4	trace	0.0	0.0	0.0	0.0	0.1	0.4	2.3	14.8
Maximum Snow Depth (in.)	11	10	9	11	trace	0	0	0	0	1	4	8	11
Days With ≥ 1.0" Snow Depth	8	5	2	0	0	0	0	0	0	0	0	3	18

Chilo Meldahl L&D *Clermont County* Elevation: 500 ft. Latitude: 38° 48' N Longitude: 84° 10' W

	JAN	FEB	MAR	APR	MAY	JUN	JUL	AUG	SEP	OCT	NOV	DEC	YEAR
Mean Maximum Temp. (°F)	39.9	43.8	53.8	65.5	73.7	82.3	86.0	85.6	79.5	67.9	55.6	43.7	64.8
Mean Temp. (°F)	31.2	34.2	42.8	53.5	62.4	71.2	75.4	74.8	68.0	56.4	45.6	35.2	54.2
Mean Minimum Temp. (°F)	22.6	24.4	31.7	41.5	51.0	60.1	64.8	63.9	56.3	44.8	35.7	26.6	43.6
Extreme Maximum Temp. (°F)	71	73	83	89	91	98	101	107	98	92	82	73	107
Extreme Minimum Temp. (°F)	-22	-6	-4	22	29	42	48	44	35	23	13	-15	-22
Days Maximum Temp. ≥ 90°F	0	0	0	0	0	3	8	7	2	0	0	0	20
Days Maximum Temp. ≤ 32°F	8	5	1	0	0	0	0	0	0	0	0	5	19
Days Minimum Temp. ≤ 32°F	26	22	18	4	0	0	0	0	0	2	12	23	107
Days Minimum Temp. ≤ 0°F	1	1	0	0	0	0	0	0	0	0	0	1	3
Heating Degree Days (base 65°F)	1,039	865	683	349	134	17	0	2	47	281	575	917	4,909
Cooling Degree Days (base 65°F)	0	0	1	12	59	209	332	313	143	21	0	0	1,090
Mean Precipitation (in.)	2.88	2.82	4.30	3.42	4.64	3.61	3.92	3.21	2.82	3.08	2.90	2.98	40.58
Extreme Maximum Daily Precip. (in.)	2.88	2.00	7.20	2.08	3.80	2.80	3.82	4.45	4.11	5.00	2.46	2.85	7.20
Days With ≥ 0.1" Precipitation	6	6	7	7	8	6	6	5	4	5	6	6	72
Days With ≥ 0.5" Precipitation	2	2	3	2	3	2	3	2	2	2	2	2	27
Days With ≥ 1.0" Precipitation	1	1	1	1	1	1	1	1	1	1	1	1	12
Mean Snowfall (in.)	***0.6***	na	***0.7***	0.0	0.0	0.0	0.0	0.0	0.0	0.0	trace	***1.3***	na
Maximum Snow Depth (in.)	***16***	***5***	***11***	0	0	0	0	***0***	0	***0***	***trace***	***3***	***16***
Days With ≥ 1.0" Snow Depth	***2***	***2***	***0***	0	0	0	0	0	0	0	0	***0***	***4***

Chippewa Lake *Medina County* Elevation: 1,180 ft. Latitude: 41° 03' N Longitude: 81° 56' W

	JAN	FEB	MAR	APR	MAY	JUN	JUL	AUG	SEP	OCT	NOV	DEC	YEAR
Mean Maximum Temp. (°F)	33.3	36.7	46.1	59.4	69.6	78.8	82.5	81.1	74.2	62.2	49.7	37.2	59.2
Mean Temp. (°F)	25.7	28.0	36.4	48.3	58.2	67.6	71.5	70.2	63.1	51.7	41.2	29.9	49.3
Mean Minimum Temp. (°F)	18.0	19.2	26.7	37.2	46.7	56.4	60.4	59.2	52.0	41.1	32.6	22.6	39.3
Extreme Maximum Temp. (°F)	68	74	83	88	90	102	102	99	92	88	78	75	102
Extreme Minimum Temp. (°F)	-26	-17	-14	8	25	34	39	34	31	16	8	-18	-26
Days Maximum Temp. ≥ 90°F	0	0	0	0	0	2	4	2	0	0	0	0	8
Days Maximum Temp. ≤ 32°F	15	11	5	0	0	0	0	0	0	0	2	11	44
Days Minimum Temp. ≤ 32°F	28	25	22	10	1	0	0	0	0	5	16	26	133
Days Minimum Temp. ≤ 0°F	3	2	0	0	0	0	0	0	0	0	0	1	6
Heating Degree Days (base 65°F)	1,213	1,039	880	500	236	51	8	16	118	413	708	1,081	6,263
Cooling Degree Days (base 65°F)	0	0	1	6	33	138	216	185	68	7	0	0	654
Mean Precipitation (in.)	2.54	2.12	2.94	3.46	3.98	3.89	4.21	3.66	3.44	2.79	3.29	3.00	39.32
Extreme Maximum Daily Precip. (in.)	1.93	1.83	1.44	1.63	2.72	2.25	3.91	4.30	3.40	2.29	2.16	2.45	4.30
Days With ≥ 0.1" Precipitation	7	6	8	9	9	7	7	6	6	7	8	7	87
Days With ≥ 0.5" Precipitation	1	1	2	2	2	3	3	3	2	2	2	2	25
Days With ≥ 1.0" Precipitation	0	0	0	1	1	1	1	1	1	0	0	0	6
Mean Snowfall (in.)	9.4	7.1	6.7	1.9	trace	0.0	0.0	0.0	0.0	0.1	2.6	8.1	35.9
Maximum Snow Depth (in.)	16	15	15	6	trace	0	0	0	0	1	7	24	24
Days With ≥ 1.0" Snow Depth	14	12	6	1	0	0	0	0	0	0	2	10	45

Circleville *Pickaway County* Elevation: 672 ft. Latitude: 39° 37' N Longitude: 82° 57' W

	JAN	FEB	MAR	APR	MAY	JUN	JUL	AUG	SEP	OCT	NOV	DEC	YEAR
Mean Maximum Temp. (°F)	37.6	40.9	51.3	63.9	73.2	81.8	85.0	84.1	78.0	66.2	53.6	41.1	63.1
Mean Temp. (°F)	29.8	32.2	41.0	52.2	61.9	70.8	74.2	72.9	66.1	54.6	44.0	33.4	52.8
Mean Minimum Temp. (°F)	21.9	23.5	30.6	40.5	50.5	59.9	63.5	61.7	54.2	42.9	34.4	25.6	42.4
Extreme Maximum Temp. (°F)	70	76	83	90	92	100	100	101	97	91	81	79	101
Extreme Minimum Temp. (°F)	-22	-14	-4	17	31	42	42	40	33	21	12	-19	-22
Days Maximum Temp. ≥ 90°F	0	0	0	0	0	4	7	6	1	0	0	0	18
Days Maximum Temp. ≤ 32°F	10	7	2	0	0	0	0	0	0	0	1	7	27
Days Minimum Temp. ≤ 32°F	25	22	19	6	0	0	0	0	0	4	14	23	113
Days Minimum Temp. ≤ 0°F	2	1	0	0	0	0	0	0	0	0	0	1	4
Heating Degree Days (base 65°F)	1,085	920	739	388	152	20	1	5	70	333	623	974	5,310
Cooling Degree Days (base 65°F)	0	0	2	13	61	201	295	259	112	18	1	0	962
Mean Precipitation (in.)	2.60	2.16	2.97	3.52	4.80	3.65	3.96	3.41	2.92	2.96	3.02	2.83	38.80
Extreme Maximum Daily Precip. (in.)	2.43	1.77	2.07	2.00	3.35	4.12	2.75	2.58	2.70	2.62	1.70	2.73	4.12
Days With ≥ 0.1" Precipitation	6	5	7	8	9	7	7	6	5	6	6	6	78
Days With ≥ 0.5" Precipitation	2	1	2	2	4	2	3	3	2	2	2	2	27
Days With ≥ 1.0" Precipitation	0	0	1	1	1	1	1	1	1	1	1	0	9
Mean Snowfall (in.)	5.5	3.9	1.7	0.4	0.0	0.0	0.0	0.0	0.0	0.0	0.3	2.1	13.9
Maximum Snow Depth (in.)	15	9	7	10	0	0	0	0	0	0	3	*7*	***15***
Days With ≥ 1.0" Snow Depth	7	6	2	0	0	0	0	0	0	0	0	4	19

Columbus Valley Crossing *Franklin County* Elevation: 734 ft. Latitude: 39° 54' N Longitude: 82° 56' W

	JAN	FEB	MAR	APR	MAY	JUN	JUL	AUG	SEP	OCT	NOV	DEC	YEAR
Mean Maximum Temp. (°F)	37.1	41.1	51.5	64.2	73.5	81.9	84.9	83.6	77.8	66.1	53.6	40.6	63.0
Mean Temp. (°F)	29.2	32.3	41.3	52.5	62.1	70.8	74.4	72.8	66.0	54.4	43.9	32.9	52.7
Mean Minimum Temp. (°F)	21.3	23.5	31.0	40.7	50.6	59.8	63.8	61.9	54.1	42.6	34.2	25.2	42.4
Extreme Maximum Temp. (°F)	70	75	83	90	92	100	100	100	96	91	79	76	100
Extreme Minimum Temp. (°F)	-28	-13	-2	17	29	39	45	38	28	20	10	-21	-28
Days Maximum Temp. ≥ 90°F	0	0	0	0	0	3	6	4	1	0	0	0	14
Days Maximum Temp. ≤ 32°F	10	6	2	0	0	0	0	0	0	0	1	7	26
Days Minimum Temp. ≤ 32°F	26	22	18	6	0	0	0	0	0	4	14	24	114
Days Minimum Temp. ≤ 0°F	2	1	0	0	0	0	0	0	0	0	0	1	4
Heating Degree Days (base 65°F)	1,103	917	728	379	144	19	1	4	72	337	627	987	5,318
Cooling Degree Days (base 65°F)	0	0	1	10	61	200	297	251	108	14	1	0	943
Mean Precipitation (in.)	2.93	2.13	3.30	3.74	4.46	4.00	4.45	3.30	3.00	2.85	3.22	3.01	40.39
Extreme Maximum Daily Precip. (in.)	2.34	1.43	2.07	2.76	2.16	3.46	3.77	3.72	2.76	2.36	1.74	2.16	3.77
Days With ≥ 0.1" Precipitation	6	5	7	7	8	6	7	5	5	5	7	6	74
Days With ≥ 0.5" Precipitation	2	1	2	3	3	3	3	2	2	2	2	2	27
Days With ≥ 1.0" Precipitation	1	0	0	1	1	1	1	1	1	1	1	0	9
Mean Snowfall (in.)	5.7	4.0	1.6	0.5	trace	0.0	0.0	0.0	0.0	trace	0.4	2.7	14.9
Maximum Snow Depth (in.)	13	***10***	10	5	trace	0	0	0	0	trace	trace	***6***	***13***
Days With ≥ 1.0" Snow Depth	6	3	1	0	0	0	0	0	0	0	0	3	13

Danville 2 W *Knox County* Elevation: 970 ft. Latitude: 40° 26' N Longitude: 82° 18' W

	JAN	FEB	MAR	APR	MAY	JUN	JUL	AUG	SEP	OCT	NOV	DEC	YEAR
Mean Maximum Temp. (°F)	34.8	38.7	48.9	61.4	71.0	79.8	83.4	82.5	75.7	63.8	51.4	39.0	60.9
Mean Temp. (°F)	25.9	28.7	37.5	48.3	58.0	67.2	71.0	69.7	62.3	50.5	40.8	30.3	49.2
Mean Minimum Temp. (°F)	16.9	18.5	26.2	35.2	44.9	54.6	58.6	56.9	48.9	37.2	30.1	21.5	37.5
Extreme Maximum Temp. (°F)	69	74	83	89	94	102	102	98	96	88	78	74	102
Extreme Minimum Temp. (°F)	-35	-22	-18	9	23	35	35	32	27	15	7	-22	-35
Days Maximum Temp. ≥ 90°F	0	0	0	0	0	2	4	3	1	0	0	0	10
Days Maximum Temp. ≤ 32°F	13	9	3	0	0	0	0	0	0	0	1	9	35
Days Minimum Temp. ≤ 32°F	28	25	23	13	3	0	0	0	1	12	19	26	150
Days Minimum Temp. ≤ 0°F	4	2	0	0	0	0	0	0	0	0	0	2	8
Heating Degree Days (base 65°F)	1,207	1,021	845	496	239	52	10	19	131	448	720	1,070	6,258
Cooling Degree Days (base 65°F)	0	0	0	3	30	125	204	171	58	6	0	0	597
Mean Precipitation (in.)	2.83	2.39	3.20	3.55	4.72	4.58	4.57	3.67	3.14	2.79	3.21	3.22	41.87
Extreme Maximum Daily Precip. (in.)	2.65	2.30	1.45	2.72	2.31	3.20	3.96	5.12	2.30	2.87	2.07	2.30	5.12
Days With ≥ 0.1" Precipitation	6	6	8	8	9	8	8	6	6	6	7	7	85
Days With ≥ 0.5" Precipitation	2	1	2	2	3	3	3	3	2	2	2	2	27
Days With ≥ 1.0" Precipitation	0	0	1	1	1	1	1	1	1	0	1	1	9
Mean Snowfall (in.)	12.2	8.5	6.2	1.8	trace	0.0	0.0	0.0	0.0	trace	2.2	8.2	39.1
Maximum Snow Depth (in.)	22	15	15	5	1	0	0	0	0	1	4	9	22
Days With ≥ 1.0" Snow Depth	15	11	5	1	0	0	0	0	0	0	2	9	43

Dayton Mcd *Montgomery County* Elevation: 745 ft. Latitude: 39° 46' N Longitude: 84° 11' W

	JAN	FEB	MAR	APR	MAY	JUN	JUL	AUG	SEP	OCT	NOV	DEC	YEAR
Mean Maximum Temp. (°F)	36.4	40.9	50.6	63.7	74.3	83.5	87.5	86.2	79.1	66.1	53.0	40.5	63.5
Mean Temp. (°F)	29.3	32.8	41.2	53.3	63.8	73.3	77.3	75.8	68.1	55.7	44.6	33.5	54.0
Mean Minimum Temp. (°F)	22.2	24.6	31.8	42.8	53.3	62.9	67.0	65.2	57.1	45.2	36.1	26.5	44.5
Extreme Maximum Temp. (°F)	69	77	84	90	95	103	104	103	99	92	81	75	104
Extreme Minimum Temp. (°F)	-21	-8	2	19	33	42	51	45	35	26	13	-16	-21
Days Maximum Temp. ≥ 90°F	0	0	0	0	2	8	12	10	3	0	0	0	35
Days Maximum Temp. ≤ 32°F	12	7	2	0	0	0	0	0	0	0	1	8	30
Days Minimum Temp. ≤ 32°F	25	22	17	3	0	0	0	0	0	2	12	22	103
Days Minimum Temp. ≤ 0°F	1	1	0	0	0	0	0	0	0	0	0	1	3
Heating Degree Days (base 65°F)	1,101	906	733	365	122	15	0	2	54	308	606	970	5,182
Cooling Degree Days (base 65°F)	0	0	3	20	92	269	387	342	154	26	1	0	1,294
Mean Precipitation (in.)	2.86	2.31	3.28	4.01	4.94	4.07	4.39	3.01	2.65	2.92	3.21	3.01	40.66
Extreme Maximum Daily Precip. (in.)	2.50	2.28	2.41	2.85	3.90	4.10	2.77	3.15	4.36	2.98	2.20	2.06	4.36
Days With ≥ 0.1" Precipitation	6	5	7	8	9	7	7	5	4	5	6	7	76
Days With ≥ 0.5" Precipitation	2	1	2	3	3	3	3	2	2	2	2	2	27
Days With ≥ 1.0" Precipitation	1	0	0	1	1	1	1	1	1	1	1	1	10
Mean Snowfall (in.)	4.8	2.7	1.6	0.1	0.0	0.0	0.0	0.0	0.0	trace	0.3	2.9	12.4
Maximum Snow Depth (in.)	12	10	7	2	0	0	0	0	0	1	6	7	12
Days With ≥ 1.0" Snow Depth	8	5	2	0	0	0	0	0	0	0	0	4	19

The period of record for all cooperative weather station data is 1980 – 2009. See User Guide for detailed explanation of data.

Defiance *Defiance County* Elevation: 700 ft. Latitude: 41° 17' N Longitude: 84° 23' W

	JAN	FEB	MAR	APR	MAY	JUN	JUL	AUG	SEP	OCT	NOV	DEC	YEAR
Mean Maximum Temp. (°F)	32.3	35.5	46.0	59.7	70.9	80.7	84.4	82.5	75.9	62.7	49.3	36.3	59.7
Mean Temp. (°F)	24.7	27.3	36.5	48.7	59.5	69.5	73.4	71.7	64.4	52.2	40.9	29.3	49.8
Mean Minimum Temp. (°F)	17.0	19.0	27.0	37.6	48.1	58.4	62.3	60.8	52.9	41.5	32.4	22.3	40.0
Extreme Maximum Temp. (°F)	65	73	80	89	93	104	101	99	95	90	78	70	104
Extreme Minimum Temp. (°F)	-22	-19	-5	4	28	39	46	43	32	18	11	-19	-22
Days Maximum Temp. ≥ 90°F	0	0	0	0	1	4	7	4	1	0	0	0	17
Days Maximum Temp. ≤ 32°F	15	12	4	0	0	0	0	0	0	0	1	11	43
Days Minimum Temp. ≤ 32°F	28	25	23	8	0	0	0	0	0	4	16	26	130
Days Minimum Temp. ≤ 0°F	4	3	0	0	0	0	0	0	0	0	0	2	9
Heating Degree Days (base 65°F)	1,243	1,060	877	491	208	35	3	10	99	402	716	1,100	6,244
Cooling Degree Days (base 65°F)	0	0	1	9	46	178	269	223	88	11	0	0	825
Mean Precipitation (in.)	2.01	2.09	2.47	3.36	3.87	3.59	4.10	3.17	3.30	2.98	2.97	2.73	36.64
Extreme Maximum Daily Precip. (in.)	1.93	2.19	1.90	1.87	1.95	2.65	3.37	3.02	2.58	3.89	3.13	2.14	3.89
Days With ≥ 0.1" Precipitation	5	5	6	7	8	7	7	6	6	6	7	7	77
Days With ≥ 0.5" Precipitation	1	1	2	2	3	2	3	2	2	2	2	2	24
Days With ≥ 1.0" Precipitation	0	0	0	1	1	1	1	1	1	1	1	0	8
Mean Snowfall (in.)	6.7	5.6	2.4	0.5	trace	0.0	0.0	0.0	0.0	0.1	0.9	4.5	20.7
Maximum Snow Depth (in.)	12	17	8	4	trace	0	0	0	0	trace	4	10	17
Days With ≥ 1.0" Snow Depth	14	11	4	0	0	0	0	0	0	0	1	8	38

Dorset *Ashtabula County* Elevation: 979 ft. Latitude: 41° 41' N Longitude: 80° 40' W

	JAN	FEB	MAR	APR	MAY	JUN	JUL	AUG	SEP	OCT	NOV	DEC	YEAR
Mean Maximum Temp. (°F)	32.6	35.5	44.6	57.9	68.5	77.3	81.3	79.9	73.5	61.4	49.2	37.0	58.2
Mean Temp. (°F)	24.5	26.2	34.7	46.5	56.5	65.5	69.5	68.2	61.7	50.6	40.9	29.7	47.9
Mean Minimum Temp. (°F)	16.2	16.9	24.7	35.1	44.4	53.6	57.7	56.6	49.9	39.8	32.5	22.3	37.5
Extreme Maximum Temp. (°F)	68	74	83	88	90	99	100	98	95	86	83	74	100
Extreme Minimum Temp. (°F)	-28	-21	-20	-4	22	30	39	30	26	17	4	-22	-28
Days Maximum Temp. ≥ 90°F	0	0	0	0	0	1	3	2	1	0	0	0	7
Days Maximum Temp. ≤ 32°F	16	12	6	0	0	0	0	0	0	0	1	10	45
Days Minimum Temp. ≤ 32°F	28	26	24	13	3	0	0	0	1	6	16	26	143
Days Minimum Temp. ≤ 0°F	4	3	1	0	0	0	0	0	0	0	0	1	9
Heating Degree Days (base 65°F)	1,250	1,091	933	552	284	83	25	34	149	443	716	1,088	6,648
Cooling Degree Days (base 65°F)	0	0	0	5	26	104	172	141	57	5	0	0	510
Mean Precipitation (in.)	2.63	2.15	2.88	3.59	3.94	4.51	4.80	3.82	4.40	3.96	3.72	3.18	43.58
Extreme Maximum Daily Precip. (in.)	1.65	1.85	2.04	1.63	2.50	3.22	3.60	2.80	2.98	2.23	4.29	2.00	4.29
Days With ≥ 0.1" Precipitation	7	6	7	9	8	8	8	7	8	9	9	8	94
Days With ≥ 0.5" Precipitation	1	1	2	2	3	4	3	3	3	3	2	2	29
Days With ≥ 1.0" Precipitation	0	0	0	1	1	1	1	1	1	1	0	0	7
Mean Snowfall (in.)	21.2	13.5	11.6	3.5	trace	0.0	0.0	0.0	0.0	0.5	8.3	20.4	79.0
Maximum Snow Depth (in.)	20	18	20	16	trace	0	0	0	0	4	15	18	20
Days With ≥ 1.0" Snow Depth	21	17	10	2	0	0	0	0	0	0	4	15	69

Elyria 3 E *Lorain County* Elevation: 729 ft. Latitude: 41° 23' N Longitude: 82° 03' W

	JAN	FEB	MAR	APR	MAY	JUN	JUL	AUG	SEP	OCT	NOV	DEC	YEAR
Mean Maximum Temp. (°F)	35.4	38.9	48.3	61.5	71.9	80.9	84.6	82.7	76.1	64.3	52.0	39.3	61.3
Mean Temp. (°F)	28.1	30.6	38.7	50.3	60.5	69.7	73.9	72.3	65.5	54.3	43.8	32.4	51.7
Mean Minimum Temp. (°F)	20.7	22.2	29.1	39.2	49.0	58.6	63.1	61.9	54.9	44.3	35.6	25.5	42.0
Extreme Maximum Temp. (°F)	68	76	84	89	93	104	102	100	94	90	80	76	104
Extreme Minimum Temp. (°F)	-22	-14	-10	11	28	38	44	40	32	18	14	-14	-22
Days Maximum Temp. ≥ 90°F	0	0	0	0	1	4	7	5	1	0	0	0	18
Days Maximum Temp. ≤ 32°F	12	8	3	0	0	0	0	0	0	0	0	8	31
Days Minimum Temp. ≤ 32°F	26	24	21	8	1	0	0	0	0	2	12	24	118
Days Minimum Temp. ≤ 0°F	2	1	0	0	0	0	0	0	0	0	0	1	4
Heating Degree Days (base 65°F)	1,137	967	809	445	186	31	2	7	77	338	629	1,003	5,631
Cooling Degree Days (base 65°F)	0	0	2	12	53	180	284	240	100	14	0	0	885
Mean Precipitation (in.)	2.56	2.25	2.82	3.40	3.72	3.75	3.79	3.82	3.69	3.10	3.27	3.20	39.37
Extreme Maximum Daily Precip. (in.)	1.66	1.92	1.79	2.06	2.45	3.28	2.80	3.25	5.75	3.10	1.80	2.30	5.75
Days With ≥ 0.1" Precipitation	7	7	7	8	9	7	7	7	7	7	8	8	89
Days With ≥ 0.5" Precipitation	1	1	2	2	2	2	3	3	3	2	2	2	25
Days With ≥ 1.0" Precipitation	0	0	0	0	1	1	1	1	1	1	1	0	7
Mean Snowfall (in.)	11.6	9.0	7.2	2.2	trace	trace	0.0	0.0	0.0	trace	2.4	8.6	41.0
Maximum Snow Depth (in.)	13	15	14	6	trace	trace	0	0	0	trace	3	13	15
Days With ≥ 1.0" Snow Depth	15	12	5	1	0	0	0	0	0	0	1	9	43

Fairfield *Butler County* Elevation: 575 ft. Latitude: 39° 21' N Longitude: 84° 35' W

	JAN	FEB	MAR	APR	MAY	JUN	JUL	AUG	SEP	OCT	NOV	DEC	YEAR
Mean Maximum Temp. (°F)	*39.7*	*43.3*	*53.6*	*65.8*	*75.4*	*84.2*	*87.8*	*87.3*	*80.4*	*67.7*	*54.6*	*42.4*	*65.2*
Mean Temp. (°F)	*31.1*	*33.8*	*42.5*	*53.4*	*63.4*	*72.6*	*76.4*	*75.3*	*67.8*	*55.2*	*44.3*	*34.0*	*54.1*
Mean Minimum Temp. (°F)	*22.4*	*24.2*	*31.4*	*40.9*	*51.4*	*60.9*	*65.0*	*63.3*	*55.2*	*42.7*	*34.0*	*25.5*	*43.1*
Extreme Maximum Temp. (°F)	*69*	*76*	*85*	*90*	*93*	*103*	*103*	*104*	*101*	*93*	*82*	*74*	*104*
Extreme Minimum Temp. (°F)	*-23*	*-10*	*4*	*19*	*30*	*40*	*48*	*41*	*33*	*22*	*11*	*-19*	*-23*
Days Maximum Temp. ≥ 90°F	*0*	*0*	*0*	*0*	*1*	*8*	*12*	*11*	*3*	*0*	*0*	*0*	*35*
Days Maximum Temp. ≤ 32°F	*8*	*5*	*1*	*0*	*0*	*0*	*0*	*0*	*0*	*0*	*0*	*6*	*20*
Days Minimum Temp. ≤ 32°F	*25*	*22*	*18*	*5*	*0*	*0*	*0*	*0*	*0*	*4*	*14*	*23*	*111*
Days Minimum Temp. ≤ 0°F	*1*	*1*	*0*	*0*	*0*	*0*	*0*	*0*	*0*	*0*	*0*	*1*	*3*
Heating Degree Days (base 65°F)	*1,045*	*875*	*693*	*356*	*123*	*14*	*0*	*2*	*51*	*317*	*615*	*955*	*5,046*
Cooling Degree Days (base 65°F)	*0*	*0*	*3*	*15*	*81*	*248*	*360*	*329*	*142*	*20*	*1*	*0*	*1,199*
Mean Precipitation (in.)	*3.24*	*2.85*	*3.84*	*4.49*	*5.02*	*4.06*	*4.19*	*3.18*	*3.09*	*3.22*	*2.96*	*3.66*	*43.80*
Extreme Maximum Daily Precip. (in.)	*2.55*	*2.36*	*3.82*	*3.66*	*4.67*	*2.60*	*4.15*	*3.55*	*3.98*	*3.55*	*2.30*	*2.73*	*4.67*
Days With ≥ 0.1" Precipitation	*6*	*6*	*7*	*9*	*9*	*7*	*7*	*5*	*5*	*5*	*6*	*7*	*79*
Days With ≥ 0.5" Precipitation	*2*	*2*	*3*	*3*	*3*	*3*	*3*	*2*	*2*	*2*	*2*	*3*	*30*
Days With ≥ 1.0" Precipitation	*1*	*0*	*1*	*1*	*1*	*1*	*1*	*1*	*1*	*1*	*1*	*1*	*11*
Mean Snowfall (in.)	*3.1*	*2.1*	*0.8*	*0.0*	*0.0*	*0.0*	*0.0*	*0.0*	*0.0*	*0.2*	*0.1*	*1.5*	*7.8*
Maximum Snow Depth (in.)	na	na	na	na	na	na	na	na	na	na	na	na	na
Days With ≥ 1.0" Snow Depth	na	na	*0*	*0*	*0*	*0*	*0*	*0*	*0*	*0*	*0*	na	na

The period of record for all cooperative weather station data is 1980 – 2009. See User Guide for detailed explanation of data.

Findlay Wpcc *Hancock County* Elevation: 768 ft. Latitude: 41° 03' N Longitude: 83° 40' W

	JAN	FEB	MAR	APR	MAY	JUN	JUL	AUG	SEP	OCT	NOV	DEC	YEAR
Mean Maximum Temp. (°F)	33.1	36.5	47.2	60.3	71.3	80.3	83.8	81.9	75.6	62.9	49.7	36.9	60.0
Mean Temp. (°F)	26.3	29.2	38.3	50.1	60.9	70.3	74.0	72.3	65.2	53.2	41.9	30.4	51.0
Mean Minimum Temp. (°F)	19.4	21.7	29.3	39.8	50.4	60.2	64.2	62.7	54.9	43.5	34.1	24.0	42.0
Extreme Maximum Temp. (°F)	66	73	81	86	93	104	101	99	95	90	78	70	104
Extreme Minimum Temp. (°F)	-20	-11	-11	8	29	40	47	42	33	21	9	-18	-20
Days Maximum Temp. ≥ 90°F	0	0	0	0	1	4	5	3	1	0	0	0	14
Days Maximum Temp. ≤ 32°F	15	11	4	0	0	0	0	0	0	0	1	11	42
Days Minimum Temp. ≤ 32°F	27	24	20	6	0	0	0	0	0	3	14	25	119
Days Minimum Temp. ≤ 0°F	2	1	0	0	0	0	0	0	0	0	0	1	4
Heating Degree Days (base 65°F)	1,193	1,007	823	451	178	28	2	7	86	371	685	1,064	5,895
Cooling Degree Days (base 65°F)	0	0	1	10	57	192	288	241	100	13	0	0	902
Mean Precipitation (in.)	2.32	2.08	2.63	3.43	4.06	4.17	3.99	3.77	2.72	2.65	2.85	2.77	37.44
Extreme Maximum Daily Precip. (in.)	2.30	2.04	2.70	1.94	3.80	4.47	2.76	5.62	2.95	2.40	1.54	1.33	5.62
Days With ≥ 0.1" Precipitation	6	5	7	8	8	8	7	6	5	6	6	7	79
Days With ≥ 0.5" Precipitation	1	1	2	2	2	3	3	2	2	2	2	2	24
Days With ≥ 1.0" Precipitation	0	0	0	1	1	1	1	1	1	0	1	0	7
Mean Snowfall (in.)	8.4	5.5	4.4	1.1	0.1	0.0	0.0	0.0	0.0	0.2	1.3	5.9	26.9
Maximum Snow Depth (in.)	14	14	12	4	trace	0	0	0	0	trace	7	12	14
Days With ≥ 1.0" Snow Depth	14	10	3	0	0	0	0	0	0	0	1	8	36

Franklin *Warren County* Elevation: 669 ft. Latitude: 39° 33' N Longitude: 84° 19' W

	JAN	FEB	MAR	APR	MAY	JUN	JUL	AUG	SEP	OCT	NOV	DEC	YEAR
Mean Maximum Temp. (°F)	37.4	41.4	51.5	63.4	73.3	81.8	85.4	84.7	78.1	65.6	53.3	41.0	63.1
Mean Temp. (°F)	28.8	31.9	40.8	51.5	61.5	70.4	74.1	72.9	65.4	53.0	43.3	32.6	52.2
Mean Minimum Temp. (°F)	20.2	22.4	30.0	39.5	49.7	58.9	62.8	61.1	52.6	40.4	33.1	24.2	41.2
Extreme Maximum Temp. (°F)	68	75	86	88	96	100	104	100	96	87	79	74	104
Extreme Minimum Temp. (°F)	-24	-12	-7	18	30	38	42	39	32	19	10	-21	-24
Days Maximum Temp. ≥ 90°F	0	0	0	0	0	4	7	6	2	0	0	0	19
Days Maximum Temp. ≤ 32°F	10	7	2	0	0	0	0	0	0	0	1	7	27
Days Minimum Temp. ≤ 32°F	26	23	19	7	0	0	0	0	0	6	15	24	120
Days Minimum Temp. ≤ 0°F	2	1	0	0	0	0	0	0	0	0	0	1	4
Heating Degree Days (base 65°F)	1,114	927	744	408	158	25	2	6	83	375	646	996	5,484
Cooling Degree Days (base 65°F)	0	0	2	9	57	193	291	258	101	10	0	0	921
Mean Precipitation (in.)	2.49	2.37	3.25	3.70	4.74	3.77	4.06	2.89	2.51	3.05	3.21	3.07	39.11
Extreme Maximum Daily Precip. (in.)	2.49	2.27	3.00	2.79	3.61	2.89	3.66	3.10	3.76	2.83	2.08	2.68	3.76
Days With ≥ 0.1" Precipitation	5	5	7	8	9	7	7	4	4	5	6	6	73
Days With ≥ 0.5" Precipitation	1	1	2	2	3	2	3	2	2	2	2	2	24
Days With ≥ 1.0" Precipitation	0	0	1	1	1	1	1	1	1	1	1	1	10
Mean Snowfall (in.)	***0.9***	***1.4***	***0.4***	trace	0.0	0.0	0.0	0.0	0.0	0.0	0.2	na	na
Maximum Snow Depth (in.)	***4***	na	***6***	3	0	0	0	***0***	0	***0***	***5***	na	na
Days With ≥ 1.0" Snow Depth	***3***	***3***	1	0	0	0	0	0	0	0	0	***1***	***8***

Fredericktown 4 S *Knox County* Elevation: 1,049 ft. Latitude: 40° 25' N Longitude: 82° 32' W

	JAN	FEB	MAR	APR	MAY	JUN	JUL	AUG	SEP	OCT	NOV	DEC	YEAR
Mean Maximum Temp. (°F)	33.2	37.2	46.9	60.1	70.0	78.9	82.3	80.9	74.8	62.7	50.5	38.5	59.7
Mean Temp. (°F)	24.2	27.6	36.3	47.9	57.9	67.0	70.6	68.6	61.7	50.1	40.4	30.3	48.5
Mean Minimum Temp. (°F)	15.2	18.0	25.7	35.7	45.7	55.2	58.8	56.2	48.7	37.4	30.2	22.0	37.4
Extreme Maximum Temp. (°F)	67	72	82	88	91	100	98	98	94	***86***	78	75	***100***
Extreme Minimum Temp. (°F)	-30	-26	-21	12	24	36	38	32	29	***17***	4	-20	***-30***
Days Maximum Temp. ≥ 90°F	0	0	0	0	0	2	3	2	1	0	0	0	8
Days Maximum Temp. ≤ 32°F	15	10	4	0	0	0	0	0	0	0	1	9	39
Days Minimum Temp. ≤ 32°F	28	26	24	12	2	0	0	0	1	10	19	25	147
Days Minimum Temp. ≤ 0°F	5	2	1	0	0	0	0	0	0	0	0	1	9
Heating Degree Days (base 65°F)	1,259	1,051	884	511	244	55	13	28	142	460	732	1,070	6,449
Cooling Degree Days (base 65°F)	0	0	0	5	30	122	192	145	50	4	0	0	548
Mean Precipitation (in.)	2.43	1.87	3.00	3.43	4.32	4.12	4.33	3.35	3.12	2.65	3.02	2.68	38.32
Extreme Maximum Daily Precip. (in.)	2.40	2.10	2.01	3.00	2.70	2.43	2.48	2.30	2.71	2.25	***1.60***	***1.80***	***3.00***
Days With ≥ 0.1" Precipitation	4	4	6	7	8	7	7	5	5	6	6	5	70
Days With ≥ 0.5" Precipitation	1	1	2	3	3	2	3	2	2	2	2	2	25
Days With ≥ 1.0" Precipitation	1	0	0	1	1	1	1	1	1	1	1	1	10
Mean Snowfall (in.)	8.7	5.5	3.5	0.6	trace	0.0	0.0	0.0	0.0	0.0	1.1	5.4	24.8
Maximum Snow Depth (in.)	na	na	na	***trace***	***0***	na	na	***0***	na	na	na	na	na
Days With ≥ 1.0" Snow Depth	na	na	0	0	0	0	0	0	0	0	0	***0***	na

Hannibal Lock & Dam *Monroe County* Elevation: 620 ft. Latitude: 39° 40' N Longitude: 80° 52' W

	JAN	FEB	MAR	APR	MAY	JUN	JUL	AUG	SEP	OCT	NOV	DEC	YEAR
Mean Maximum Temp. (°F)	38.5	42.0	51.1	63.6	72.3	80.5	83.7	83.1	76.6	65.3	53.9	42.1	62.7
Mean Temp. (°F)	29.9	32.5	40.1	51.0	60.2	68.8	73.1	72.6	65.6	54.0	43.8	33.8	52.1
Mean Minimum Temp. (°F)	21.2	22.9	29.0	38.5	48.0	57.0	62.3	61.9	54.6	42.7	33.6	25.6	41.4
Extreme Maximum Temp. (°F)	72	75	83	89	91	96	99	100	95	90	80	74	100
Extreme Minimum Temp. (°F)	-24	-10	-8	18	30	38	44	42	34	22	13	-14	-24
Days Maximum Temp. ≥ 90°F	0	0	0	0	0	2	4	4	1	0	0	0	11
Days Maximum Temp. ≤ 32°F	9	6	2	0	0	0	0	0	0	0	0	6	23
Days Minimum Temp. ≤ 32°F	26	23	21	8	1	0	0	0	0	3	15	23	120
Days Minimum Temp. ≤ 0°F	2	1	0	0	0	0	0	0	0	0	0	0	3
Heating Degree Days (base 65°F)	1,082	914	765	418	178	28	2	5	69	344	631	959	5,395
Cooling Degree Days (base 65°F)	0	0	0	6	37	149	258	246	94	10	0	0	800
Mean Precipitation (in.)	3.06	2.81	3.66	3.41	4.34	3.99	4.41	3.47	3.16	2.57	3.36	3.10	41.34
Extreme Maximum Daily Precip. (in.)	2.84	2.45	3.45	2.43	1.92	2.98	2.49	3.23	4.28	1.93	3.47	3.40	4.28
Days With ≥ 0.1" Precipitation	7	7	7	8	9	7	8	6	5	6	7	7	84
Days With ≥ 0.5" Precipitation	2	2	3	2	3	3	3	2	2	2	2	2	28
Days With ≥ 1.0" Precipitation	1	0	1	0	1	1	1	1	1	0	1	0	8
Mean Snowfall (in.)	na	na	1.9	trace	0.0	0.0	0.0	0.0	0.0	0.0	trace	0.5	na
Maximum Snow Depth (in.)	***15***	***23***	***4***	0	0	0	0	0	0	0	1	6	***23***
Days With ≥ 1.0" Snow Depth	***5***	2	0	0	0	0	0	0	0	0	0	3	***10***

The period of record for all cooperative weather station data is 1980 – 2009. See User Guide for detailed explanation of data.

Hiram *Portage County* Elevation: 1,229 ft. Latitude: 41° 18' N Longitude: 81° 09' W

	JAN	FEB	MAR	APR	MAY	JUN	JUL	AUG	SEP	OCT	NOV	DEC	YEAR
Mean Maximum Temp. (°F)	32.1	35.7	45.0	58.2	68.3	76.9	81.0	79.7	72.5	60.4	48.9	36.3	57.9
Mean Temp. (°F)	24.7	27.3	35.7	47.8	57.8	66.6	70.8	69.6	62.4	51.0	40.8	29.3	48.6
Mean Minimum Temp. (°F)	17.2	18.8	26.3	37.4	47.1	56.2	60.6	59.6	52.3	41.4	32.6	22.2	39.3
Extreme Maximum Temp. (°F)	69	72	81	87	90	100	99	95	91	85	77	73	100
Extreme Minimum Temp. (°F)	-25	-14	-6	12	27	37	41	38	32	22	4	-15	-25
Days Maximum Temp. ≥ 90°F	0	0	0	0	0	1	2	2	0	0	0	0	5
Days Maximum Temp. ≤ 32°F	16	12	5	0	0	0	0	0	0	0	1	12	46
Days Minimum Temp. ≤ 32°F	28	25	23	9	1	0	0	0	0	4	17	27	134
Days Minimum Temp. ≤ 0°F	3	2	0	0	0	0	0	0	0	0	0	1	6
Heating Degree Days (base 65°F)	1,243	1,060	902	515	248	63	11	19	127	434	720	1,100	6,442
Cooling Degree Days (base 65°F)	0	0	1	7	30	116	199	169	55	5	0	0	582
Mean Precipitation (in.)	3.03	2.42	3.32	3.77	4.06	4.00	4.05	3.72	3.82	3.44	3.59	3.45	42.67
Extreme Maximum Daily Precip. (in.)	1.71	1.64	2.93	1.76	2.19	3.22	4.05	3.42	3.30	2.13	2.41	1.98	4.05
Days With ≥ 0.1" Precipitation	8	7	8	9	9	9	7	6	7	8	8	9	95
Days With ≥ 0.5" Precipitation	2	1	2	2	3	2	3	2	3	2	2	2	26
Days With ≥ 1.0" Precipitation	0	0	0	1	1	1	1	1	1	1	0	0	7
Mean Snowfall (in.)	18.2	12.7	10.4	1.9	trace	0.0	0.0	0.0	0.0	0.4	5.3	14.3	63.2
Maximum Snow Depth (in.)	22	15	18	9	trace	0	0	0	0	2	16	16	22
Days With ≥ 1.0" Snow Depth	20	17	9	1	0	0	0	0	0	0	3	14	64

Lima WWTP *Allen County* Elevation: 850 ft. Latitude: 40° 43' N Longitude: 84° 08' W

	JAN	FEB	MAR	APR	MAY	JUN	JUL	AUG	SEP	OCT	NOV	DEC	YEAR
Mean Maximum Temp. (°F)	34.1	37.7	48.0	61.1	71.7	80.5	84.0	82.4	76.5	64.1	50.8	37.8	60.7
Mean Temp. (°F)	26.9	29.7	38.9	50.6	61.1	70.4	74.0	72.6	65.9	54.0	42.8	31.0	51.5
Mean Minimum Temp. (°F)	19.7	21.7	29.7	40.1	50.5	60.3	64.0	62.7	55.3	43.9	34.7	24.1	42.2
Extreme Maximum Temp. (°F)	66	72	81	89	93	97	100	99	95	90	77	70	100
Extreme Minimum Temp. (°F)	-21	-12	-3	8	30	39	46	42	31	19	9	-17	-21
Days Maximum Temp. ≥ 90°F	0	0	0	0	1	3	5	4	1	0	0	0	14
Days Maximum Temp. ≤ 32°F	14	10	3	0	0	0	0	0	0	0	1	10	38
Days Minimum Temp. ≤ 32°F	27	23	20	7	0	0	0	0	0	3	14	25	119
Days Minimum Temp. ≤ 0°F	3	1	0	0	0	0	0	0	0	0	0	1	5
Heating Degree Days (base 65°F)	1,174	989	804	437	174	26	2	7	75	349	657	1,047	5,741
Cooling Degree Days (base 65°F)	0	0	1	12	61	195	289	250	109	16	0	0	933
Mean Precipitation (in.)	2.44	2.18	2.71	3.44	4.16	3.87	4.34	3.50	3.15	2.72	3.26	2.78	38.55
Extreme Maximum Daily Precip. (in.)	2.08	1.98	1.95	2.15	2.50	4.38	2.97	5.08	2.78	3.03	2.10	2.96	5.08
Days With ≥ 0.1" Precipitation	6	5	6	8	9	7	8	6	6	6	7	6	80
Days With ≥ 0.5" Precipitation	1	2	1	2	3	3	3	2	2	2	2	2	25
Days With ≥ 1.0" Precipitation	0	0	0	1	1	1	1	1	1	0	0	0	6
Mean Snowfall (in.)	na	na	na	trace	0.0	0.0	0.0	0.0	0.0	0.0	***0.1***	na	na
Maximum Snow Depth (in.)	na	na	na	***1***	***0***	***0***	***0***	***0***	***0***	na	na	na	na
Days With ≥ 1.0" Snow Depth	na	na	na	0	0	0	0	0	0	0	***0***	na	na

Mansfield 5 W *Richland County* Elevation: 1,350 ft. Latitude: 40° 46' N Longitude: 82° 37' W

	JAN	FEB	MAR	APR	MAY	JUN	JUL	AUG	SEP	OCT	NOV	DEC	YEAR
Mean Maximum Temp. (°F)	32.5	36.2	46.1	59.3	69.7	78.3	81.6	80.2	73.6	61.0	48.8	36.6	58.7
Mean Temp. (°F)	24.5	27.7	36.4	48.4	58.5	67.2	70.9	69.5	62.7	50.8	40.4	29.2	48.8
Mean Minimum Temp. (°F)	16.5	19.2	26.6	37.3	47.2	56.0	60.1	58.8	51.8	40.5	32.0	21.7	39.0
Extreme Maximum Temp. (°F)	66	72	81	87	91	100	99	97	94	84	76	69	100
Extreme Minimum Temp. (°F)	-25	-15	-8	5	24	33	40	37	28	18	9	-19	-25
Days Maximum Temp. ≥ 90°F	0	0	0	0	0	2	2	2	0	0	0	0	6
Days Maximum Temp. ≤ 32°F	16	12	5	0	0	0	0	0	0	0	2	12	47
Days Minimum Temp. ≤ 32°F	28	25	22	11	1	0	0	0	0	7	16	26	136
Days Minimum Temp. ≤ 0°F	4	2	0	0	0	0	0	0	0	0	0	1	7
Heating Degree Days (base 65°F)	1,249	1,047	882	500	231	57	11	20	127	442	731	1,104	6,401
Cooling Degree Days (base 65°F)	0	0	1	8	36	128	200	169	66	7	0	0	615
Mean Precipitation (in.)	2.23	1.81	2.77	3.64	4.55	4.40	4.02	3.80	3.23	2.83	3.08	2.88	39.24
Extreme Maximum Daily Precip. (in.)	2.47	1.87	***2.04***	***1.80***	2.13	4.08	2.55	5.19	2.22	2.02	1.91	2.00	***5.19***
Days With ≥ 0.1" Precipitation	5	5	6	8	10	7	7	7	6	6	7	6	80
Days With ≥ 0.5" Precipitation	1	1	2	2	3	3	3	2	2	2	2	2	25
Days With ≥ 1.0" Precipitation	0	0	0	1	1	1	1	1	1	1	1	0	8
Mean Snowfall (in.)	na	na	na	0.4	0.0	0.0	0.0	0.0	0.0	trace	***0.4***	na	na
Maximum Snow Depth (in.)	na	na	na	***4***	***0***	***0***	***0***	***0***	***0***	na	na	na	na
Days With ≥ 1.0" Snow Depth	na	na	***1***	0	0	0	0	0	0	0	***0***	na	na

Marietta Wwtp *Washington County* Elevation: 580 ft. Latitude: 39° 25' N Longitude: 81° 26' W

	JAN	FEB	MAR	APR	MAY	JUN	JUL	AUG	SEP	OCT	NOV	DEC	YEAR
Mean Maximum Temp. (°F)	39.9	43.7	53.3	65.5	74.0	82.0	85.4	84.7	78.1	66.5	54.9	43.4	64.3
Mean Temp. (°F)	31.4	34.1	42.4	53.3	62.2	70.8	74.7	73.7	66.6	54.8	44.7	35.0	53.6
Mean Minimum Temp. (°F)	22.8	24.6	31.3	41.0	50.3	59.6	64.0	62.6	55.0	43.1	34.4	26.5	42.9
Extreme Maximum Temp. (°F)	74	77	85	91	93	99	102	100	97	91	81	78	102
Extreme Minimum Temp. (°F)	-23	-7	0	19	31	40	44	38	33	23	12	-11	-23
Days Maximum Temp. ≥ 90°F	0	0	0	0	1	4	7	6	1	0	0	0	19
Days Maximum Temp. ≤ 32°F	8	5	1	0	0	0	0	0	0	0	0	6	20
Days Minimum Temp. ≤ 32°F	25	22	18	5	0	0	0	0	0	4	14	22	110
Days Minimum Temp. ≤ 0°F	1	1	0	0	0	0	0	0	0	0	0	0	2
Heating Degree Days (base 65°F)	1,036	866	697	357	141	17	1	3	61	322	603	924	5,028
Cooling Degree Days (base 65°F)	0	0	1	12	59	199	309	278	114	14	1	0	987
Mean Precipitation (in.)	3.12	2.76	3.83	3.41	4.26	4.57	4.54	3.70	3.24	2.91	3.21	3.26	42.81
Extreme Maximum Daily Precip. (in.)	1.60	2.83	3.15	2.12	2.60	4.00	2.70	4.78	4.27	1.93	2.01	2.25	4.78
Days With ≥ 0.1" Precipitation	7	6	8	8	9	8	8	7	6	6	7	7	87
Days With ≥ 0.5" Precipitation	2	2	3	2	3	3	3	3	2	2	2	2	29
Days With ≥ 1.0" Precipitation	0	0	1	1	1	1	1	1	1	1	0	0	8
Mean Snowfall (in.)	7.0	4.6	3.0	0.6	0.0	0.0	0.0	0.0	0.0	trace	0.6	3.0	18.8
Maximum Snow Depth (in.)	19	16	20	10	0	0	0	0	0	trace	2	5	20
Days With ≥ 1.0" Snow Depth	7	4	1	0	0	0	0	0	0	0	0	3	15

Marion 2 N *Marion County* Elevation: 964 ft. Latitude: 40° 37' N Longitude: 83° 08' W

	JAN	FEB	MAR	APR	MAY	JUN	JUL	AUG	SEP	OCT	NOV	DEC	YEAR
Mean Maximum Temp. (°F)	33.2	37.0	46.9	60.4	70.5	80.0	83.4	82.0	75.6	63.3	50.4	37.5	60.0
Mean Temp. (°F)	25.5	28.5	37.3	49.2	59.6	69.3	72.9	71.1	64.0	52.2	41.5	30.1	50.1
Mean Minimum Temp. (°F)	17.7	20.0	27.6	38.0	48.6	58.6	62.3	60.2	52.3	41.1	32.6	22.7	40.1
Extreme Maximum Temp. (°F)	67	73	81	87	91	103	100	99	97	89	79	73	103
Extreme Minimum Temp. (°F)	-23	-20	-5	8	29	39	43	35	24	17	11	-19	-23
Days Maximum Temp. ≥ 90°F	0	0	0	0	0	3	5	4	1	0	0	0	13
Days Maximum Temp. ≤ 32°F	15	10	4	0	0	0	0	0	0	0	1	10	40
Days Minimum Temp. ≤ 32°F	28	25	22	9	0	0	0	0	0	5	16	25	130
Days Minimum Temp. ≤ 0°F	3	2	0	0	0	0	0	0	0	0	0	1	6
Heating Degree Days (base 65°F)	1,219	1,024	853	475	211	37	5	15	106	402	698	1,075	6,120
Cooling Degree Days (base 65°F)	0	0	2	8	49	174	256	212	82	12	0	0	795
Mean Precipitation (in.)	2.45	1.85	2.32	3.56	4.45	4.35	4.31	3.78	3.21	2.90	3.01	2.84	39.03
Extreme Maximum Daily Precip. (in.)	2.00	1.35	1.37	1.80	2.68	3.82	5.33	3.11	2.91	2.25	1.57	1.84	5.33
Days With ≥ 0.1" Precipitation	5	5	6	9	9	7	7	6	6	6	7	6	79
Days With ≥ 0.5" Precipitation	1	1	1	2	3	3	3	3	2	2	2	2	25
Days With ≥ 1.0" Precipitation	1	0	0	1	1	1	1	1	1	1	1	0	9
Mean Snowfall (in.)	7.6	5.2	3.5	0.6	0.0	0.0	0.0	0.0	0.0	trace	0.8	5.3	23.0
Maximum Snow Depth (in.)	15	15	13	2	0	0	0	0	0	trace	3	15	15
Days With ≥ 1.0" Snow Depth	11	9	2	0	0	0	0	0	0	0	0	5	27

Marysville *Union County* Elevation: 1,000 ft. Latitude: 40° 14' N Longitude: 83° 22' W

	JAN	FEB	MAR	APR	MAY	JUN	JUL	AUG	SEP	OCT	NOV	DEC	YEAR
Mean Maximum Temp. (°F)	34.5	38.6	49.2	62.0	72.3	80.8	84.3	82.9	76.3	63.9	50.8	38.3	61.2
Mean Temp. (°F)	27.2	30.4	39.5	51.2	61.4	70.2	74.0	72.4	65.2	53.4	42.4	31.2	51.5
Mean Minimum Temp. (°F)	19.8	22.3	29.8	40.2	50.4	59.5	63.6	61.9	54.0	42.8	34.0	24.1	41.9
Extreme Maximum Temp. (°F)	66	73	82	88	92	101	100	99	96	91	79	74	101
Extreme Minimum Temp. (°F)	-23	-18	-11	12	29	38	44	41	32	18	12	-20	-23
Days Maximum Temp. ≥ 90°F	0	0	0	0	0	3	6	4	1	0	0	0	14
Days Maximum Temp. ≤ 32°F	13	9	3	0	0	0	0	0	0	0	1	9	35
Days Minimum Temp. ≤ 32°F	26	24	20	6	0	0	0	0	0	3	14	24	117
Days Minimum Temp. ≤ 0°F	2	1	0	0	0	0	0	0	0	0	0	1	4
Heating Degree Days (base 65°F)	1,165	971	785	419	165	25	2	7	85	364	671	1,040	5,699
Cooling Degree Days (base 65°F)	0	0	1	11	59	187	287	244	97	11	0	0	897
Mean Precipitation (in.)	2.35	2.00	2.73	3.30	4.43	4.28	4.26	3.25	2.91	2.61	2.99	2.77	37.88
Extreme Maximum Daily Precip. (in.)	2.60	1.18	1.50	2.75	2.37	4.82	3.50	3.28	2.56	2.48	1.66	1.88	4.82
Days With ≥ 0.1" Precipitation	6	5	6	8	9	7	7	6	5	6	6	6	77
Days With ≥ 0.5" Precipitation	1	1	2	2	3	3	3	2	2	2	2	2	25
Days With ≥ 1.0" Precipitation	0	0	0	0	1	1	1	1	1	1	1	0	7
Mean Snowfall (in.)	6.2	4.6	3.8	0.4	0.0	0.0	0.0	0.0	0.0	0.1	0.9	4.5	20.5
Maximum Snow Depth (in.)	16	12	15	4	0	0	0	0	0	3	5	17	17
Days With ≥ 1.0" Snow Depth	12	8	4	0	0	0	0	0	0	0	1	6	31

Milford *Clermont County* Elevation: 520 ft. Latitude: 39° 11' N Longitude: 84° 17' W

	JAN	FEB	MAR	APR	MAY	JUN	JUL	AUG	SEP	OCT	NOV	DEC	YEAR
Mean Maximum Temp. (°F)	38.4	43.1	52.9	64.8	75.1	82.8	87.2	85.9	78.9	67.7	54.8	42.5	64.5
Mean Temp. (°F)	29.3	33.1	41.5	52.2	62.7	71.0	75.4	73.9	66.1	54.5	43.9	33.6	53.1
Mean Minimum Temp. (°F)	20.1	23.1	30.0	39.7	50.1	59.1	63.5	61.9	53.2	41.1	32.7	24.7	41.6
Extreme Maximum Temp. (°F)	72	76	84	89	93	96	104	101	98	87	81	75	104
Extreme Minimum Temp. (°F)	-23	-13	-10	19	31	36	45	41	26	20	12	-22	-23
Days Maximum Temp. ≥ 90°F	0	0	0	0	1	5	11	9	2	0	0	0	28
Days Maximum Temp. ≤ 32°F	9	6	1	0	0	0	0	0	0	0	0	6	22
Days Minimum Temp. ≤ 32°F	26	23	19	7	0	0	0	0	0	5	16	23	119
Days Minimum Temp. ≤ 0°F	2	1	0	0	0	0	0	0	0	0	0	1	4
Heating Degree Days (base 65°F)	1,101	896	724	390	136	19	1	3	75	334	626	966	5,271
Cooling Degree Days (base 65°F)	0	0	2	12	70	206	329	286	115	14	0	0	1,034
Mean Precipitation (in.)	3.06	2.62	3.73	4.14	5.55	4.35	4.27	4.10	3.01	2.96	3.60	3.33	44.72
Extreme Maximum Daily Precip. (in.)	3.10	2.38	2.03	2.50	3.55	2.86	4.45	4.63	3.34	2.53	2.45	2.41	4.63
Days With ≥ 0.1" Precipitation	6	6	7	9	9	8	7	6	5	6	7	6	82
Days With ≥ 0.5" Precipitation	2	2	3	3	4	3	3	3	2	2	3	2	32
Days With ≥ 1.0" Precipitation	1	0	1	1	1	1	1	1	1	1	1	1	11
Mean Snowfall (in.)	na	4.5	1.3	0.3	trace	0.0	0.0	trace	0.0	0.2	0.1	2.6	na
Maximum Snow Depth (in.)	na	na	na	trace	trace	na	0	na	na	na	na	na	na
Days With ≥ 1.0" Snow Depth	na	5	1	0	0	0	0	0	0	0	0	3	na

Millersburg *Holmes County* Elevation: 818 ft. Latitude: 40° 33' N Longitude: 81° 55' W

	JAN	FEB	MAR	APR	MAY	JUN	JUL	AUG	SEP	OCT	NOV	DEC	YEAR
Mean Maximum Temp. (°F)	36.2	38.9	49.1	61.7	71.1	80.4	83.8	82.6	75.9	63.9	51.6	39.3	61.2
Mean Temp. (°F)	27.3	29.1	37.9	48.9	58.3	68.1	71.8	70.4	63.0	51.0	41.2	30.8	49.8
Mean Minimum Temp. (°F)	18.4	19.3	26.7	36.1	45.5	55.7	59.7	58.2	50.1	38.1	30.8	22.2	38.4
Extreme Maximum Temp. (°F)	70	75	82	87	90	95	97	98	95	88	80	76	98
Extreme Minimum Temp. (°F)	-35	-13	-7	14	20	36	43	35	29	19	10	-24	-35
Days Maximum Temp. ≥ 90°F	0	0	0	0	0	3	5	4	1	0	0	0	13
Days Maximum Temp. ≤ 32°F	12	9	3	0	0	0	0	0	0	0	1	8	33
Days Minimum Temp. ≤ 32°F	27	25	23	12	2	0	0	0	0	9	18	26	142
Days Minimum Temp. ≤ 0°F	3	2	0	0	0	0	0	0	0	0	0	1	6
Heating Degree Days (base 65°F)	1,162	1,007	833	480	229	43	6	14	116	434	707	1,055	6,086
Cooling Degree Days (base 65°F)	0	0	0	5	29	142	223	188	61	6	0	0	654
Mean Precipitation (in.)	2.85	1.83	2.89	3.48	4.57	4.81	4.33	3.52	3.14	2.87	2.83	2.67	39.79
Extreme Maximum Daily Precip. (in.)	2.95	1.58	1.63	1.83	1.78	3.42	3.28	3.85	2.86	2.54	1.87	2.38	3.85
Days With ≥ 0.1" Precipitation	6	5	6	7	9	8	8	6	6	6	6	6	79
Days With ≥ 0.5" Precipitation	2	1	2	2	3	3	3	2	2	2	2	2	26
Days With ≥ 1.0" Precipitation	0	0	0	1	1	1	1	1	1	1	0	0	7
Mean Snowfall (in.)	6.3	3.8	2.5	0.3	trace	0.0	0.0	0.0	0.0	trace	0.7	3.9	17.5
Maximum Snow Depth (in.)	11	10	13	6	trace	0	0	0	0	1	4	7	13
Days With ≥ 1.0" Snow Depth	10	8	2	0	0	0	0	0	0	0	1	5	26

The period of record for all cooperative weather station data is 1980 – 2009. See User Guide for detailed explanation of data.

Millport 2 NW *Columbiana County* Elevation: 1,149 ft. Latitude: 40° 43' N Longitude: 80° 54' W

	JAN	FEB	MAR	APR	MAY	JUN	JUL	AUG	SEP	OCT	NOV	DEC	YEAR
Mean Maximum Temp. (°F)	35.7	39.9	49.6	62.1	71.5	79.9	83.6	82.4	75.6	63.9	51.2	39.1	61.2
Mean Temp. (°F)	26.9	29.9	38.2	49.4	58.6	67.3	71.2	69.8	62.8	51.5	41.3	30.7	49.8
Mean Minimum Temp. (°F)	18.1	19.9	26.7	36.7	45.7	54.7	58.9	57.0	49.9	39.1	31.3	22.2	38.4
Extreme Maximum Temp. (°F)	69	77	82	90	91	98	103	99	94	87	79	74	103
Extreme Minimum Temp. (°F)	-34	-19	-17	10	20	33	38	27	26	14	3	-20	-34
Days Maximum Temp. ≥ 90°F	0	0	0	0	0	2	5	4	1	0	0	0	12
Days Maximum Temp. ≤ 32°F	12	8	3	0	0	0	0	0	0	0	1	9	33
Days Minimum Temp. ≤ 32°F	27	25	22	11	3	0	0	0	1	9	17	26	141
Days Minimum Temp. ≤ 0°F	3	2	1	0	0	0	0	0	0	0	0	1	7
Heating Degree Days (base 65°F)	1,175	985	825	467	221	49	8	19	122	419	704	1,057	6,051
Cooling Degree Days (base 65°F)	0	0	0	6	30	125	209	174	61	7	0	0	612
Mean Precipitation (in.)	2.53	2.15	2.83	3.25	3.97	3.78	4.01	3.29	3.28	2.60	3.13	2.81	37.63
Extreme Maximum Daily Precip. (in.)	1.93	1.70	1.61	1.85	3.71	3.70	2.74	3.20	4.80	3.30	2.86	1.93	4.80
Days With ≥ 0.1" Precipitation	7	6	7	8	8	7	7	6	6	6	8	8	84
Days With ≥ 0.5" Precipitation	1	1	2	2	2	3	3	2	2	1	2	2	24
Days With ≥ 1.0" Precipitation	0	0	0	1	1	1	1	1	1	0	0	0	6
Mean Snowfall (in.)	8.0	6.6	5.1	1.5	trace	0.0	0.0	0.0	0.0	trace	1.6	5.9	28.7
Maximum Snow Depth (in.)	***12***	***15***	***6***	10	trace	0	0	0	0	***1***	***5***	***7***	***15***
Days With ≥ 1.0" Snow Depth	***4***	***6***	***1***	0	0	0	0	0	0	0	***1***	***3***	***15***

Oberlin *Lorain County* Elevation: 815 ft. Latitude: 41° 16' N Longitude: 82° 13' W

	JAN	FEB	MAR	APR	MAY	JUN	JUL	AUG	SEP	OCT	NOV	DEC	YEAR
Mean Maximum Temp. (°F)	33.6	36.8	45.9	59.3	70.0	79.2	83.2	81.4	75.0	62.7	50.0	37.6	59.6
Mean Temp. (°F)	25.7	28.2	36.6	48.4	58.8	68.2	72.3	70.4	63.4	51.9	41.6	30.2	49.6
Mean Minimum Temp. (°F)	17.8	19.5	27.3	37.5	47.5	57.1	61.5	59.4	51.7	41.0	33.2	22.8	39.7
Extreme Maximum Temp. (°F)	67	76	82	87	91	104	100	100	94	89	77	75	104
Extreme Minimum Temp. (°F)	-23	-18	-15	11	27	35	41	32	25	16	7	-18	-23
Days Maximum Temp. ≥ 90°F	0	0	0	0	0	3	5	3	1	0	0	0	12
Days Maximum Temp. ≤ 32°F	15	11	5	0	0	0	0	0	0	0	1	10	42
Days Minimum Temp. ≤ 32°F	28	25	22	10	1	0	0	0	0	5	15	25	131
Days Minimum Temp. ≤ 0°F	3	2	0	0	0	0	0	0	0	0	0	1	6
Heating Degree Days (base 65°F)	1,210	1,034	874	500	228	52	8	16	116	408	695	1,071	6,212
Cooling Degree Days (base 65°F)	0	0	1	8	42	153	241	192	74	9	0	0	720
Mean Precipitation (in.)	2.54	2.14	2.74	3.38	3.89	3.69	3.86	3.36	3.31	2.87	3.13	2.84	37.75
Extreme Maximum Daily Precip. (in.)	2.35	2.35	2.06	1.75	2.35	2.72	2.83	2.92	2.64	2.88	1.80	2.00	2.92
Days With ≥ 0.1" Precipitation	6	6	7	8	9	8	7	6	6	7	7	7	84
Days With ≥ 0.5" Precipitation	1	1	2	2	2	2	3	2	2	2	2	2	23
Days With ≥ 1.0" Precipitation	0	0	0	0	1	1	1	1	1	0	1	0	6
Mean Snowfall (in.)	13.3	10.0	8.6	2.2	trace	0.0	0.0	0.0	0.0	trace	2.1	9.6	45.8
Maximum Snow Depth (in.)	17	17	16	7	trace	0	0	0	0	trace	5	15	17
Days With ≥ 1.0" Snow Depth	18	14	7	1	0	0	0	0	0	0	2	11	53

Painesville 4 NW *Lake County* Elevation: 600 ft. Latitude: 41° 45' N Longitude: 81° 18' W

	JAN	FEB	MAR	APR	MAY	JUN	JUL	AUG	SEP	OCT	NOV	DEC	YEAR
Mean Maximum Temp. (°F)	35.2	37.2	45.3	56.8	67.3	76.6	80.9	79.8	74.2	63.0	51.5	39.7	58.9
Mean Temp. (°F)	28.7	30.0	37.2	48.2	58.5	68.1	72.9	71.9	65.8	55.0	44.7	33.6	51.2
Mean Minimum Temp. (°F)	22.2	22.8	29.0	39.5	49.8	59.6	64.8	64.0	57.3	47.0	37.9	27.5	43.4
Extreme Maximum Temp. (°F)	70	76	82	91	92	98	96	93	94	88	77	75	98
Extreme Minimum Temp. (°F)	-19	-4	0	17	30	40	47	39	33	24	16	-11	-19
Days Maximum Temp. ≥ 90°F	0	0	0	0	0	1	2	1	0	0	0	0	4
Days Maximum Temp. ≤ 32°F	13	10	4	0	0	0	0	0	0	0	0	7	34
Days Minimum Temp. ≤ 32°F	26	24	20	6	0	0	0	0	0	1	8	21	106
Days Minimum Temp. ≤ 0°F	1	0	0	0	0	0	0	0	0	0	0	0	1
Heating Degree Days (base 65°F)	1,119	983	857	505	229	42	2	4	67	317	604	966	5,695
Cooling Degree Days (base 65°F)	0	0	1	7	36	143	253	226	97	14	0	0	777
Mean Precipitation (in.)	2.40	1.98	2.80	3.31	3.31	3.66	3.80	3.39	4.03	3.47	3.50	2.98	38.63
Extreme Maximum Daily Precip. (in.)	2.25	2.10	1.97	3.64	2.02	3.10	4.57	2.41	2.51	2.97	2.37	2.70	4.57
Days With ≥ 0.1" Precipitation	7	5	7	8	7	7	7	6	7	8	8	8	85
Days With ≥ 0.5" Precipitation	1	1	2	2	2	2	3	2	3	2	2	1	23
Days With ≥ 1.0" Precipitation	0	0	0	0	1	1	1	1	1	0	1	0	6
Mean Snowfall (in.)	11.5	8.1	6.5	1.2	trace	0.0	0.0	0.0	0.0	trace	2.2	9.7	39.2
Maximum Snow Depth (in.)	24	25	25	7	trace	0	0	0	0	trace	16	15	25
Days With ≥ 1.0" Snow Depth	17	11	5	0	0	0	0	0	0	0	1	9	43

Pandora *Putnam County* Elevation: 770 ft. Latitude: 40° 57' N Longitude: 83° 58' W

	JAN	FEB	MAR	APR	MAY	JUN	JUL	AUG	SEP	OCT	NOV	DEC	YEAR
Mean Maximum Temp. (°F)	32.9	36.6	47.5	60.5	71.5	80.4	83.9	82.0	75.7	62.7	49.7	36.7	60.0
Mean Temp. (°F)	25.7	28.8	38.0	49.7	60.5	69.7	73.2	71.3	64.2	52.5	41.6	29.9	50.4
Mean Minimum Temp. (°F)	18.4	20.9	28.5	38.7	49.5	59.0	62.5	60.5	52.8	42.2	33.4	23.1	40.8
Extreme Maximum Temp. (°F)	67	73	82	89	94	103	101	100	96	90	78	71	103
Extreme Minimum Temp. (°F)	-21	-13	-13	6	26	38	44	40	29	19	8	-19	-21
Days Maximum Temp. ≥ 90°F	0	0	0	0	1	4	6	3	1	0	0	0	15
Days Maximum Temp. ≤ 32°F	15	11	4	0	0	0	0	0	0	0	1	11	42
Days Minimum Temp. ≤ 32°F	28	24	21	8	0	0	0	0	0	4	15	26	126
Days Minimum Temp. ≤ 0°F	4	2	0	0	0	0	0	0	0	0	0	1	7
Heating Degree Days (base 65°F)	1,212	1,018	831	464	189	31	3	12	100	393	696	1,080	6,029
Cooling Degree Days (base 65°F)	0	0	1	10	56	180	265	212	85	12	0	0	821
Mean Precipitation (in.)	2.26	2.01	2.65	3.47	3.94	4.10	3.95	3.43	2.98	2.67	3.07	2.66	37.19
Extreme Maximum Daily Precip. (in.)	1.83	1.76	3.01	1.73	3.41	3.69	2.58	6.19	2.54	2.80	1.91	1.31	6.19
Days With ≥ 0.1" Precipitation	6	5	7	8	8	7	7	6	6	6	7	6	79
Days With ≥ 0.5" Precipitation	1	1	1	2	3	3	3	3	2	2	2	2	25
Days With ≥ 1.0" Precipitation	0	0	0	0	1	1	1	1	1	0	1	0	6
Mean Snowfall (in.)	9.4	6.9	4.4	1.2	trace	0.0	0.0	0.0	trace	0.1	1.9	6.6	30.5
Maximum Snow Depth (in.)	13	16	10	7	trace	0	0	0	trace	trace	5	11	16
Days With ≥ 1.0" Snow Depth	14	11	4	0	0	0	0	0	0	0	1	9	39

Portsmouth Sciotoville *Scioto County* Elevation: 540 ft. Latitude: 38° 45' N Longitude: 82° 53' W

	JAN	FEB	MAR	APR	MAY	JUN	JUL	AUG	SEP	OCT	NOV	DEC	YEAR
Mean Maximum Temp. (°F)	40.6	44.9	54.9	66.5	75.3	83.2	86.6	86.0	79.8	68.4	56.3	44.4	65.6
Mean Temp. (°F)	31.7	35.0	43.8	54.2	63.4	71.7	75.3	73.9	67.0	55.4	45.3	35.4	54.3
Mean Minimum Temp. (°F)	22.7	25.0	32.7	42.1	51.5	60.1	63.9	61.9	54.0	42.5	34.2	26.3	43.1
Extreme Maximum Temp. (°F)	74	76	84	99	93	101	104	104	100	92	82	75	104
Extreme Minimum Temp. (°F)	-29	-8	0	12	28	38	40	35	31	22	10	-18	-29
Days Maximum Temp. ≥ 90°F	0	0	0	0	1	5	10	8	3	0	0	0	27
Days Maximum Temp. ≤ 32°F	7	4	1	0	0	0	0	0	0	0	0	4	16
Days Minimum Temp. ≤ 32°F	25	22	16	5	0	0	0	0	0	4	14	22	108
Days Minimum Temp. ≤ 0°F	1	1	0	0	0	0	0	0	0	0	0	1	3
Heating Degree Days (base 65°F)	1,025	842	652	333	119	14	1	5	61	306	585	912	4,855
Cooling Degree Days (base 65°F)	0	0	2	16	77	221	328	288	126	17	1	0	1,076
Mean Precipitation (in.)	3.06	2.77	3.76	3.61	4.71	3.42	4.39	3.78	2.57	2.62	3.05	3.19	40.93
Extreme Maximum Daily Precip. (in.)	2.52	2.42	3.74	3.95	2.18	2.50	3.69	5.20	2.82	2.17	1.86	2.50	5.20
Days With ≥ 0.1" Precipitation	7	6	8	8	9	7	8	6	5	5	6	7	82
Days With ≥ 0.5" Precipitation	2	2	3	2	3	2	3	2	2	2	2	2	27
Days With ≥ 1.0" Precipitation	1	1	1	1	1	1	1	1	1	0	1	0	10
Mean Snowfall (in.)	3.4	2.1	1.2	0.2	trace	0.0	0.0	0.0	0.0	0.0	0.1	1.0	8.0
Maximum Snow Depth (in.)	21	7	8	5	trace	0	0	0	0	0	1	5	21
Days With ≥ 1.0" Snow Depth	4	2	1	0	0	0	0	0	0	0	0	1	8

Springfield New Water Works *Clark County* Elevation: 930 ft. Latitude: 39° 58' N Longitude: 83° 49' W

	JAN	FEB	MAR	APR	MAY	JUN	JUL	AUG	SEP	OCT	NOV	DEC	YEAR
Mean Maximum Temp. (°F)	35.3	38.9	48.8	61.4	71.6	80.4	83.5	82.8	76.6	64.2	51.5	39.2	61.2
Mean Temp. (°F)	27.0	29.8	38.7	49.9	60.2	69.5	72.8	71.4	64.3	52.5	42.0	31.3	50.8
Mean Minimum Temp. (°F)	18.6	20.5	28.5	38.4	48.7	58.6	62.0	59.9	51.9	40.7	32.4	23.2	40.3
Extreme Maximum Temp. (°F)	68	74	81	87	91	98	98	100	95	89	79	72	100
Extreme Minimum Temp. (°F)	-26	-18	-13	14	29	37	46	39	29	16	10	-26	-26
Days Maximum Temp. ≥ 90°F	0	0	0	0	0	3	4	4	1	0	0	0	12
Days Maximum Temp. ≤ 32°F	12	9	3	0	0	0	0	0	0	0	1	9	34
Days Minimum Temp. ≤ 32°F	27	24	21	8	1	0	0	0	0	6	16	25	128
Days Minimum Temp. ≤ 0°F	3	2	0	0	0	0	0	0	0	0	0	1	6
Heating Degree Days (base 65°F)	1,172	991	810	453	191	33	4	10	100	393	683	1,040	5,880
Cooling Degree Days (base 65°F)	0	0	1	8	49	175	253	215	86	11	0	0	798
Mean Precipitation (in.)	2.40	1.79	2.43	3.41	4.68	4.38	4.60	3.34	3.08	2.82	2.94	2.70	38.57
Extreme Maximum Daily Precip. (in.)	2.51	2.26	1.73	2.80	3.09	3.60	3.78	3.60	3.14	2.65	2.55	2.68	3.78
Days With ≥ 0.1" Precipitation	5	5	6	7	9	8	7	5	5	5	6	6	74
Days With ≥ 0.5" Precipitation	1	1	2	2	4	3	3	2	2	2	2	2	26
Days With ≥ 1.0" Precipitation	0	0	0	1	1	1	1	1	1	1	1	1	9
Mean Snowfall (in.)	na	***2.7***	na	trace	0.0	0.0	0.0	0.0	0.0	trace	trace	***1.4***	na
Maximum Snow Depth (in.)	na	na	na	***trace***	***0***	***0***	***0***	***0***	***0***	***trace***	***trace***	na	na
Days With ≥ 1.0" Snow Depth	na	na	***0***	0	0	0	0	0	0	0	0	na	na

Steubenville *Jefferson County* Elevation: 992 ft. Latitude: 40° 23' N Longitude: 80° 38' W

	JAN	FEB	MAR	APR	MAY	JUN	JUL	AUG	SEP	OCT	NOV	DEC	YEAR
Mean Maximum Temp. (°F)	37.5	41.1	50.3	62.9	71.8	79.9	83.0	82.3	75.6	63.6	52.4	40.7	61.8
Mean Temp. (°F)	29.7	32.3	40.2	51.6	60.7	69.4	73.3	72.4	65.5	53.5	43.7	33.1	52.1
Mean Minimum Temp. (°F)	21.8	23.5	30.2	40.2	49.7	58.9	63.5	62.5	55.4	43.3	34.9	25.4	42.4
Extreme Maximum Temp. (°F)	72	77	83	89	91	97	102	96	93	85	80	77	102
Extreme Minimum Temp. (°F)	-22	-8	-1	16	29	39	46	42	34	22	12	-14	-22
Days Maximum Temp. ≥ 90°F	0	0	0	0	0	2	4	3	1	0	0	0	10
Days Maximum Temp. ≤ 32°F	11	7	2	0	0	0	0	0	0	0	1	8	29
Days Minimum Temp. ≤ 32°F	25	22	19	6	1	0	0	0	0	2	13	24	112
Days Minimum Temp. ≤ 0°F	1	1	0	0	0	0	0	0	0	0	0	0	2
Heating Degree Days (base 65°F)	1,088	917	763	406	174	29	2	6	75	360	634	984	5,438
Cooling Degree Days (base 65°F)	0	0	2	11	49	167	267	244	97	9	1	0	847
Mean Precipitation (in.)	3.00	2.31	3.27	3.41	4.35	4.21	4.38	3.96	3.37	2.81	3.47	2.98	41.52
Extreme Maximum Daily Precip. (in.)	1.75	1.32	1.48	1.56	2.25	3.14	3.42	2.72	5.36	2.37	2.90	1.80	5.36
Days With ≥ 0.1" Precipitation	7	6	8	8	9	8	8	7	6	6	8	7	88
Days With ≥ 0.5" Precipitation	2	1	2	2	3	3	3	3	2	2	2	2	27
Days With ≥ 1.0" Precipitation	1	0	0	0	1	1	1	1	1	0	1	0	7
Mean Snowfall (in.)	na	na	***0.4***	trace	0.0	0.0	0.0	0.0	0.0	0.2	0.2	na	na
Maximum Snow Depth (in.)	na	na	na	na	na	na	na	na	na	na	na	na	na
Days With ≥ 1.0" Snow Depth	na	na	***0***	0	0	0	0	0	0	0	0	na	na

Upper Sandusky *Wyandot County* Elevation: 854 ft. Latitude: 40° 50' N Longitude: 83° 17' W

	JAN	FEB	MAR	APR	MAY	JUN	JUL	AUG	SEP	OCT	NOV	DEC	YEAR
Mean Maximum Temp. (°F)	33.0	37.0	47.1	60.6	70.8	80.2	84.0	82.6	76.6	63.7	50.4	37.1	60.3
Mean Temp. (°F)	25.5	28.7	37.6	49.4	59.6	69.4	73.2	71.6	64.8	52.6	41.6	30.0	50.3
Mean Minimum Temp. (°F)	18.0	20.4	28.0	38.1	48.4	58.6	62.4	60.5	52.8	41.4	32.7	22.8	40.4
Extreme Maximum Temp. (°F)	67	73	82	87	91	104	102	99	97	89	79	72	104
Extreme Minimum Temp. (°F)	-23	-16	-8	9	27	38	43	40	29	18	9	-20	-23
Days Maximum Temp. ≥ 90°F	0	0	0	0	0	4	5	4	1	0	0	0	14
Days Maximum Temp. ≤ 32°F	14	10	4	0	0	0	0	0	0	0	1	10	39
Days Minimum Temp. ≤ 32°F	26	25	21	9	1	0	0	0	0	5	16	25	128
Days Minimum Temp. ≤ 0°F	3	1	0	0	0	0	0	0	0	0	0	1	5
Heating Degree Days (base 65°F)	1,217	1,022	844	472	208	36	4	11	94	393	696	1,078	6,075
Cooling Degree Days (base 65°F)	0	0	1	9	47	176	266	224	94	13	0	0	830
Mean Precipitation (in.)	1.98	1.89	2.50	3.51	4.52	3.92	4.46	3.49	3.13	2.36	3.20	2.56	37.52
Extreme Maximum Daily Precip. (in.)	1.78	1.60	2.05	1.74	2.27	3.21	2.50	9.35	3.74	2.46	2.00	2.05	9.35
Days With ≥ 0.1" Precipitation	5	5	6	8	9	7	7	6	5	6	7	6	77
Days With ≥ 0.5" Precipitation	1	1	1	2	3	3	3	2	2	1	2	1	22
Days With ≥ 1.0" Precipitation	0	0	0	1	1	1	2	1	1	0	1	0	8
Mean Snowfall (in.)	6.4	3.8	2.2	1.1	trace	0.0	0.0	0.0	0.0	trace	0.8	5.1	19.4
Maximum Snow Depth (in.)	12	11	13	9	0	0	0	0	0	trace	4	***19***	***19***
Days With ≥ 1.0" Snow Depth	9	6	2	0	0	0	0	0	0	0	1	4	22

The period of record for all cooperative weather station data is 1980 – 2009. See User Guide for detailed explanation of data.

Urbana WWTP *Champaign County* Elevation: 1,000 ft. Latitude: 40° 06' N Longitude: 83° 47' W

	JAN	FEB	MAR	APR	MAY	JUN	JUL	AUG	SEP	OCT	NOV	DEC	YEAR
Mean Maximum Temp. (°F)	34.5	38.6	47.9	60.8	71.0	80.4	84.1	82.9	76.2	63.5	50.9	38.2	60.7
Mean Temp. (°F)	26.7	30.1	38.3	50.0	60.2	69.5	73.1	71.5	64.3	52.4	42.0	30.8	50.7
Mean Minimum Temp. (°F)	19.0	21.6	28.7	39.1	49.3	58.6	62.0	60.0	52.4	41.2	33.1	23.3	40.7
Extreme Maximum Temp. (°F)	66	71	80	86	91	99	100	101	96	87	76	72	101
Extreme Minimum Temp. (°F)	-26	-18	-6	14	29	36	42	39	28	18	11	-22	-26
Days Maximum Temp. ≥ 90°F	0	0	0	0	0	3	6	4	1	0	0	0	14
Days Maximum Temp. ≤ 32°F	13	9	3	0	0	0	0	0	0	0	1	9	35
Days Minimum Temp. ≤ 32°F	27	24	20	7	0	0	0	0	0	6	15	25	124
Days Minimum Temp. ≤ 0°F	3	1	0	0	0	0	0	0	0	0	0	1	5
Heating Degree Days (base 65°F)	1,179	980	820	452	190	34	4	10	98	394	682	1,054	5,897
Cooling Degree Days (base 65°F)	0	0	0	7	47	175	261	218	84	9	0	0	801
Mean Precipitation (in.)	2.64	2.06	2.81	3.76	4.78	4.50	5.49	3.42	3.08	2.94	3.19	3.04	41.71
Extreme Maximum Daily Precip. (in.)	2.61	1.60	1.82	2.70	2.47	3.50	3.97	3.72	3.60	3.05	1.80	2.30	3.97
Days With ≥ 0.1" Precipitation	6	6	7	8	9	8	7	6	5	6	7	6	81
Days With ≥ 0.5" Precipitation	1	1	2	3	3	3	4	2	2	2	2	2	27
Days With ≥ 1.0" Precipitation	1	0	0	1	1	1	2	1	1	1	1	1	11
Mean Snowfall (in.)	na	na	na	0.1	0.0	0.0	0.0	0.0	0.0	0.0	trace	na	na
Maximum Snow Depth (in.)	na	na	na	***trace***	***0***	***0***	***0***	na	***0***	na	na	na	na
Days With ≥ 1.0" Snow Depth	na	na	na	0	0	0	0	0	0	0	0	na	na

Warren 3 S *Trumbull County* Elevation: 899 ft. Latitude: 41° 12' N Longitude: 80° 49' W

	JAN	FEB	MAR	APR	MAY	JUN	JUL	AUG	SEP	OCT	NOV	DEC	YEAR
Mean Maximum Temp. (°F)	34.7	37.9	47.4	60.6	70.7	79.3	83.1	81.7	74.5	62.6	50.7	38.7	60.2
Mean Temp. (°F)	26.1	28.1	36.4	48.0	57.6	66.6	70.7	69.4	62.1	50.8	41.1	30.5	48.9
Mean Minimum Temp. (°F)	17.3	18.3	25.3	35.3	44.4	53.9	58.2	57.0	49.7	38.9	31.4	22.3	37.7
Extreme Maximum Temp. (°F)	69	75	82	90	91	99	101	99	93	87	79	76	101
Extreme Minimum Temp. (°F)	-26	-13	-11	10	23	32	40	30	28	16	7	-17	-26
Days Maximum Temp. ≥ 90°F	0	0	0	0	0	2	4	3	0	0	0	0	9
Days Maximum Temp. ≤ 32°F	13	10	4	0	0	0	0	0	0	0	1	9	37
Days Minimum Temp. ≤ 32°F	28	25	24	13	3	0	0	0	1	8	18	26	146
Days Minimum Temp. ≤ 0°F	4	2	0	0	0	0	0	0	0	0	0	1	7
Heating Degree Days (base 65°F)	1,200	1,037	881	509	250	61	12	22	136	438	711	1,062	6,319
Cooling Degree Days (base 65°F)	0	0	0	5	28	116	195	164	55	4	0	0	567
Mean Precipitation (in.)	2.60	1.82	3.06	3.51	3.97	3.96	4.80	3.46	3.79	2.92	3.10	2.79	39.78
Extreme Maximum Daily Precip. (in.)	1.81	1.40	1.84	1.80	1.80	2.26	4.41	2.96	3.87	1.74	2.60	1.56	4.41
Days With ≥ 0.1" Precipitation	7	6	8	9	9	8	7	7	7	7	7	7	89
Days With ≥ 0.5" Precipitation	1	1	2	2	3	3	3	2	2	2	2	1	24
Days With ≥ 1.0" Precipitation	0	0	0	1	1	1	1	1	1	0	0	0	6
Mean Snowfall (in.)	11.5	6.9	5.2	0.4	0.0	0.0	0.0	0.0	0.0	trace	0.8	7.0	31.8
Maximum Snow Depth (in.)	16	14	15	6	0	0	0	0	0	trace	3	13	16
Days With ≥ 1.0" Snow Depth	13	9	4	0	0	0	0	0	0	0	1	8	35

Westerville *Franklin County* Elevation: 810 ft. Latitude: 40° 08' N Longitude: 82° 57' W

	JAN	FEB	MAR	APR	MAY	JUN	JUL	AUG	SEP	OCT	NOV	DEC	YEAR
Mean Maximum Temp. (°F)	36.9	41.5	52.1	65.0	74.2	82.4	85.4	84.4	78.2	66.4	53.4	40.7	63.4
Mean Temp. (°F)	28.9	32.3	41.4	52.8	62.2	70.8	74.3	73.2	66.3	54.7	44.2	33.1	52.9
Mean Minimum Temp. (°F)	20.9	23.1	30.7	40.5	50.2	59.2	63.2	61.9	54.3	43.0	34.9	25.5	42.3
Extreme Maximum Temp. (°F)	68	74	82	88	92	100	101	101	97	89	79	76	101
Extreme Minimum Temp. (°F)	-27	-20	-5	14	28	36	41	36	31	18	12	-25	-27
Days Maximum Temp. ≥ 90°F	0	0	0	0	0	4	7	6	2	0	0	0	19
Days Maximum Temp. ≤ 32°F	11	7	2	0	0	0	0	0	0	0	1	7	28
Days Minimum Temp. ≤ 32°F	25	23	18	7	1	0	0	0	0	4	13	23	114
Days Minimum Temp. ≤ 0°F	2	1	0	0	0	0	0	0	0	0	0	1	4
Heating Degree Days (base 65°F)	1,114	918	726	371	146	21	1	5	70	327	619	982	5,300
Cooling Degree Days (base 65°F)	0	0	2	13	67	202	298	265	115	16	0	0	978
Mean Precipitation (in.)	2.66	2.22	2.94	3.49	4.35	4.46	4.27	3.21	2.81	2.78	3.13	2.94	39.26
Extreme Maximum Daily Precip. (in.)	1.95	1.96	1.55	3.84	1.78	3.32	3.19	2.79	2.17	3.06	1.64	1.77	3.84
Days With ≥ 0.1" Precipitation	6	6	7	8	9	8	7	6	5	6	7	7	82
Days With ≥ 0.5" Precipitation	2	1	2	2	3	3	3	2	2	2	2	2	26
Days With ≥ 1.0" Precipitation	1	0	0	0	1	1	1	1	1	0	1	1	8
Mean Snowfall (in.)	6.9	4.6	2.5	0.5	trace	0.0	0.0	0.0	0.0	trace	0.3	3.7	18.5
Maximum Snow Depth (in.)	12	13	11	3	trace	0	0	0	0	trace	1	7	13
Days With ≥ 1.0" Snow Depth	10	6	2	0	0	0	0	0	0	0	0	5	23

Wilmington 3 N *Clinton County* Elevation: 1,029 ft. Latitude: 39° 29' N Longitude: 83° 49' W

	JAN	FEB	MAR	APR	MAY	JUN	JUL	AUG	SEP	OCT	NOV	DEC	YEAR
Mean Maximum Temp. (°F)	35.8	39.5	49.5	61.9	71.6	80.2	83.7	82.8	76.9	65.0	52.3	39.4	61.6
Mean Temp. (°F)	27.9	30.8	39.6	50.8	60.8	69.7	73.1	71.5	64.7	53.4	43.0	31.8	51.4
Mean Minimum Temp. (°F)	19.9	22.1	29.5	39.7	50.0	59.2	62.5	60.1	52.5	41.8	33.5	24.1	41.2
Extreme Maximum Temp. (°F)	69	73	81	87	90	99	99	99	95	91	78	73	99
Extreme Minimum Temp. (°F)	-25	-20	-10	17	29	39	40	37	32	17	11	-24	-25
Days Maximum Temp. ≥ 90°F	0	0	0	0	0	2	4	4	1	0	0	0	11
Days Maximum Temp. ≤ 32°F	12	9	3	0	0	0	0	0	0	0	1	9	34
Days Minimum Temp. ≤ 32°F	27	23	20	6	0	0	0	0	0	5	15	24	120
Days Minimum Temp. ≤ 0°F	3	2	0	0	0	0	0	0	0	0	0	1	6
Heating Degree Days (base 65°F)	1,144	960	783	429	173	29	3	10	90	366	655	1,022	5,664
Cooling Degree Days (base 65°F)	0	0	1	10	50	177	261	218	90	14	1	0	822
Mean Precipitation (in.)	2.81	2.35	3.50	3.92	5.22	3.79	4.19	3.02	2.82	3.10	3.13	2.95	40.80
Extreme Maximum Daily Precip. (in.)	3.42	2.23	1.67	2.85	2.14	2.53	3.03	3.39	2.43	2.83	1.70	2.40	3.42
Days With ≥ 0.1" Precipitation	6	5	7	9	9	8	8	5	5	6	7	7	82
Days With ≥ 0.5" Precipitation	2	1	2	3	4	2	3	2	2	2	2	2	27
Days With ≥ 1.0" Precipitation	1	0	1	1	1	1	1	1	1	1	1	0	10
Mean Snowfall (in.)	6.9	5.8	3.3	0.4	trace	0.0	0.0	0.0	0.0	0.2	0.9	3.5	21.0
Maximum Snow Depth (in.)	16	14	18	5	trace	0	0	0	0	2	5	7	18
Days With ≥ 1.0" Snow Depth	10	8	3	0	0	0	0	0	0	0	0	5	26

The period of record for all cooperative weather station data is 1980 – 2009. See User Guide for detailed explanation of data.

Wooster Exp Stn *Wayne County* Elevation: 1,020 ft. Latitude: 40° 47' N Longitude: 81° 55' W

	JAN	FEB	MAR	APR	MAY	JUN	JUL	AUG	SEP	OCT	NOV	DEC	YEAR
Mean Maximum Temp. (°F)	33.4	36.8	46.7	59.6	69.5	78.2	81.8	80.3	73.3	61.3	49.5	37.4	59.0
Mean Temp. (°F)	26.2	28.8	37.5	49.0	58.7	67.5	71.3	69.8	62.4	51.0	41.2	30.5	49.5
Mean Minimum Temp. (°F)	19.0	20.7	28.2	38.3	47.8	56.8	60.8	59.2	51.6	40.7	32.8	23.5	39.9
Extreme Maximum Temp. (°F)	69	71	80	86	90	100	101	96	94	88	76	74	101
Extreme Minimum Temp. (°F)	-24	-13	-6	14	26	37	41	36	30	17	9	-17	-24
Days Maximum Temp. ≥ 90°F	0	0	0	0	0	1	2	2	0	0	0	0	5
Days Maximum Temp. ≤ 32°F	15	11	4	0	0	0	0	0	0	0	1	11	42
Days Minimum Temp. ≤ 32°F	27	24	21	9	1	0	0	0	0	6	16	26	130
Days Minimum Temp. ≤ 0°F	3	1	0	0	0	0	0	0	0	0	0	1	5
Heating Degree Days (base 65°F)	1,195	1,019	847	480	223	51	8	18	128	432	707	1,064	6,172
Cooling Degree Days (base 65°F)	0	0	1	6	34	133	210	172	57	6	0	0	619
Mean Precipitation (in.)	2.29	1.95	2.83	3.66	4.43	4.34	4.24	4.10	3.36	3.03	3.06	2.70	39.99
Extreme Maximum Daily Precip. (in.)	2.59	1.39	1.63	1.96	2.37	2.47	2.95	3.60	3.25	2.37	2.09	2.08	3.60
Days With ≥ 0.1" Precipitation	6	5	7	8	9	8	7	6	6	6	7	6	81
Days With ≥ 0.5" Precipitation	1	1	2	3	3	3	3	3	2	2	2	2	27
Days With ≥ 1.0" Precipitation	0	0	0	1	1	1	1	1	1	1	0	0	7
Mean Snowfall (in.)	8.4	6.4	5.6	1.1	trace	0.0	0.0	trace	0.0	0.1	1.5	6.2	29.3
Maximum Snow Depth (in.)	13	17	13	8	0	0	0	trace	0	2	4	8	17
Days With ≥ 1.0" Snow Depth	15	12	6	1	0	0	0	0	0	0	1	10	45

The period of record for all cooperative weather station data is 1980 – 2009. See User Guide for detailed explanation of data.

Ohio Weather Station Rankings

Annual Extreme Maximum Temperature

Highest Rank	Station Name	°F	Lowest Rank	Station Name	°F
1	Chilo Meldahl L&D	107	1	Millersburg	***98***
2	Chillicothe Mound City	105	1	Painesville 4 NW	98
3	Bowling Green WWTP	104	3	Centerburg 2 SE	99
3	Cleveland Hopkins Intl Arpt	104	3	Wilmington 3 N	99
3	Dayton Mcd	104	5	Barnesville	***100***
3	Defiance	104	5	Chardon	100
3	Elyria 3 E	104	5	Columbus Valley Crossing	100
3	Fairfield	***104***	5	Dorset	100
3	Findlay Wpcc	104	5	Fredericktown 4 S	***100***
3	Franklin	104	5	Hannibal Lock & Dam	100
3	Milford	***104***	5	Hiram	100
3	Oberlin	104	5	Lima WWTP	100
3	Portsmouth Sciotoville	104	5	Mansfield 5 W	100
3	Toledo Express Arpt	104	5	Springfield New Water Works	100
3	Upper Sandusky	104	5	Youngstown Municipal Arpt	100
16	Cincinnati-Northern Kentucky	103	16	Akron Akron-Canton Reg Arpt	101
16	Marion 2 N	103	16	Bellefontaine	101
16	Millport 2 NW	103	16	Cadiz	101
16	Pandora	103	16	Carpenter 2 S	***101***
20	Bucyrus	102	16	Circleville	101
20	Cambridge	102	16	Columbus-Port Columbus Intl	101
20	Chippewa Lake	102	16	Mansfield Lahm Municipal Arpt	101
20	Danville 2 W	102	16	Marysville	101
20	Dayton Intl Arpt	102	16	Urbana WWTP	101
20	Marietta Wwtp	102	16	Warren 3 S	101

Annual Mean Maximum Temperature

Highest Rank	Station Name	°F	Lowest Rank	Station Name	°F
1	Portsmouth Sciotoville	65.6	1	Chardon	57.5
2	Fairfield	***65.2***	2	Hiram	57.9
3	Chilo Meldahl L&D	64.8	3	Dorset	58.2
4	Milford	***64.5***	4	Mansfield 5 W	58.7
5	Marietta Wwtp	64.3	5	Mansfield Lahm Municipal Arpt	58.8
6	Chillicothe Mound City	***63.9***	5	Youngstown Municipal Arpt	58.8
7	Carpenter 2 S	***63.7***	7	Painesville 4 NW	59.0
7	Cincinnati-Northern Kentucky	63.7	7	Wooster Exp Stn	59.0
9	Cambridge	63.6	9	Akron Akron-Canton Reg Arpt	59.2
10	Dayton Mcd	63.5	9	Bucyrus	59.2
11	Westerville	63.4	9	Chippewa Lake	59.2
12	Circleville	63.1	9	Cleveland Hopkins Intl Arpt	59.2
12	Franklin	63.1	13	Oberlin	59.6
14	Columbus Valley Crossing	63.0	13	Toledo Express Arpt	59.6
15	Hannibal Lock & Dam	62.7	15	Bowling Green WWTP	59.7
16	Columbus-Port Columbus Intl	62.4	15	Defiance	59.7
17	Steubenville	61.8	15	Fredericktown 4 S	59.7
18	Wilmington 3 N	61.6	18	Centerburg 2 SE	59.8
19	Dayton Intl Arpt	61.4	19	Findlay Wpcc	60.0
20	Elyria 3 E	61.3	19	Marion 2 N	60.0
21	Marysville	61.2	19	Pandora	60.0
21	Millersburg	***61.2***	22	Bellefontaine	60.2
21	Millport 2 NW	61.2	22	Warren 3 S	60.2
21	Springfield New Water Works	61.2	24	Cadiz	60.3
25	Danville 2 W	60.9	24	Upper Sandusky	60.3

Rankings include 25 highest/lowest stations. If state has less than 25 stations, all stations are included. The period of record is 1980–2009. See User Guide for detailed explanation of data.

Annual Mean Temperature

Highest			Lowest		
Rank	Station Name	°F	Rank	Station Name	°F
1	Portsmouth Sciotoville	54.4	1	Chardon	47.5
2	Chilo Meldahl L&D	54.2	2	Dorset	47.9
2	Fairfield	***54.2***	3	Fredericktown 4 S	48.5
4	Cincinnati-Northern Kentucky	54.0	4	Hiram	48.6
4	Dayton Mcd	54.0	5	Mansfield 5 W	48.8
6	Marietta Wwtp	53.6	6	Warren 3 S	48.9
7	Milford	***53.1***	7	Danville 2 W	49.2
8	Cambridge	53.0	7	Youngstown Municipal Arpt	49.2
9	Columbus-Port Columbus Intl	52.9	9	Chippewa Lake	49.3
9	Westerville	52.9	10	Bucyrus	49.4
11	Chillicothe Mound City	***52.8***	11	Wooster Exp Stn	49.5
11	Circleville	52.8	12	Oberlin	49.6
13	Columbus Valley Crossing	52.7	13	Mansfield Lahm Municipal Arpt	49.7
14	Carpenter 2 S	***52.5***	14	Bowling Green WWTP	49.8
15	Franklin	52.2	14	Defiance	49.8
16	Dayton Intl Arpt	52.1	14	Millersburg	***49.8***
16	Hannibal Lock & Dam	52.1	14	Millport 2 NW	49.8
16	Steubenville	52.1	18	Centerburg 2 SE	49.9
19	Elyria 3 E	51.7	18	Toledo Express Arpt	49.9
20	Lima WWTP	51.5	20	Akron Akron-Canton Reg Arpt	50.1
20	Marysville	51.5	20	Marion 2 N	50.1
22	Wilmington 3 N	51.4	22	Upper Sandusky	50.3
23	Painesville 4 NW	51.2	23	Pandora	50.4
24	Findlay Wpcc	51.0	24	Barnesville	***50.5***
25	Cadiz	50.8	24	Bellefontaine	50.5

Annual Mean Minimum Temperature

Highest			Lowest		
Rank	Station Name	°F	Rank	Station Name	°F
1	Dayton Mcd	44.6	1	Fredericktown 4 S	37.4
2	Cincinnati-Northern Kentucky	44.3	2	Chardon	37.5
3	Chilo Meldahl L&D	43.6	2	Danville 2 W	37.5
4	Columbus-Port Columbus Intl	43.4	2	Dorset	37.5
4	Painesville 4 NW	43.4	5	Warren 3 S	37.7
6	Fairfield	***43.1***	6	Millersburg	***38.4***
6	Portsmouth Sciotoville	43.1	6	Millport 2 NW	38.4
8	Marietta Wwtp	42.9	8	Mansfield 5 W	39.0
9	Dayton Intl Arpt	42.7	9	Chippewa Lake	39.3
10	Circleville	42.4	9	Hiram	39.3
10	Columbus Valley Crossing	42.4	11	Bucyrus	39.6
10	Steubenville	42.4	11	Youngstown Municipal Arpt	39.6
13	Cambridge	42.3	13	Oberlin	39.7
13	Westerville	42.3	14	Centerburg 2 SE	39.9
15	Lima WWTP	42.2	15	Bowling Green WWTP	40.0
16	Elyria 3 E	42.0	15	Defiance	40.0
16	Findlay Wpcc	42.0	15	Wooster Exp Stn	40.0
18	Cleveland Hopkins Intl Arpt	41.9	18	Marion 2 N	40.1
18	Marysville	41.9	19	Toledo Express Arpt	40.2
20	Chillicothe Mound City	***41.7***	20	Springfield New Water Works	40.3
21	Milford	***41.6***	21	Upper Sandusky	40.4
22	Hannibal Lock & Dam	41.4	22	Barnesville	***40.6***
23	Cadiz	41.3	23	Mansfield Lahm Municipal Arpt	40.7
23	Franklin	41.3	23	Urbana WWTP	40.7
23	Wilmington 3 N	41.3	25	Bellefontaine	40.8

Rankings include 25 highest/lowest stations. If state has less than 25 stations, all stations are included. The period of record is 1980–2009. See User Guide for detailed explanation of data.

Annual Extreme Minimum Temperature

Highest			Lowest		
Rank	Station Name	°F	Rank	Station Name	°F
1	Painesville 4 NW	-19	1	Danville 2 W	-35
2	Bowling Green WWTP	-20	1	Millersburg	***-35***
2	Cleveland Hopkins Intl Arpt	-20	3	Millport 2 NW	-34
2	Findlay Wpcc	-20	4	Cambridge	-32
2	Toledo Express Arpt	-20	5	Fredericktown 4 S	***-30***
6	Dayton Mcd	-21	6	Centerburg 2 SE	-29
6	Lima WWTP	-21	6	Chillicothe Mound City	-29
6	Pandora	-21	6	Portsmouth Sciotoville	-29
9	Chilo Meldahl L&D	-22	9	Columbus Valley Crossing	-28
9	Circleville	-22	9	Dorset	-28
9	Columbus-Port Columbus Intl	-22	11	Bellefontaine	-27
9	Defiance	-22	11	Westerville	-27
9	Elyria 3 E	-22	13	Bucyrus	-26
9	Mansfield Lahm Municipal Arpt	-22	13	Chippewa Lake	-26
9	Steubenville	-22	13	Springfield New Water Works	-26
9	Youngstown Municipal Arpt	-22	13	Urbana WWTP	-26
17	Chardon	-23	13	Warren 3 S	-26
17	Fairfield	***-23***	18	Akron Akron-Canton Reg Arpt	-25
17	Marietta Wwtp	-23	18	Carpenter 2 S	***-25***
17	Marion 2 N	-23	18	Dayton Intl Arpt	-25
17	Marysville	-23	18	Hiram	-25
17	Milford	***-23***	18	Mansfield 5 W	-25
17	Oberlin	-23	18	Wilmington 3 N	-25
17	Upper Sandusky	-23	24	Cadiz	-24
25	Cadiz	-24	24	Cincinnati-Northern Kentucky	-24

July Mean Maximum Temperature

Highest			Lowest		
Rank	Station Name	°F	Rank	Station Name	°F
1	Fairfield	***87.8***	1	Chardon	80.4
2	Dayton Mcd	87.5	2	Painesville 4 NW	80.9
3	Milford	***87.2***	3	Hiram	81.0
4	Portsmouth Sciotoville	86.6	4	Dorset	81.3
5	Chilo Meldahl L&D	86.0	5	Mansfield 5 W	81.6
6	Chillicothe Mound City	***85.7***	6	Mansfield Lahm Municipal Arpt	81.7
7	Cincinnati-Northern Kentucky	85.6	7	Wooster Exp Stn	81.8
8	Franklin	85.4	8	Youngstown Municipal Arpt	81.9
8	Marietta Wwtp	85.4	9	Cadiz	82.2
8	Westerville	85.4	10	Cleveland Hopkins Intl Arpt	82.3
11	Cambridge	85.2	10	Fredericktown 4 S	82.3
12	Circleville	85.0	12	Akron Akron-Canton Reg Arpt	82.4
13	Columbus Valley Crossing	84.9	13	Barnesville	***82.5***
14	Columbus-Port Columbus Intl	84.8	13	Chippewa Lake	82.5
15	Carpenter 2 S	***84.7***	15	Centerburg 2 SE	82.6
16	Elyria 3 E	84.6	16	Bellefontaine	82.9
17	Dayton Intl Arpt	84.4	17	Steubenville	83.0
17	Defiance	84.4	18	Bucyrus	83.1
19	Marysville	84.3	18	Warren 3 S	83.1
19	Toledo Express Arpt	84.3	20	Oberlin	83.2
21	Bowling Green WWTP	84.1	21	Danville 2 W	83.4
21	Urbana WWTP	84.1	21	Marion 2 N	83.4
23	Lima WWTP	84.0	23	Springfield New Water Works	83.5
23	Upper Sandusky	84.0	24	Millport 2 NW	83.6
25	Pandora	83.9	25	Hannibal Lock & Dam	83.7

Rankings include 25 highest/lowest stations. If state has less than 25 stations, all stations are included. The period of record is 1980–2009. See User Guide for detailed explanation of data.

January Mean Minimum Temperature

Highest Rank	Station Name	°F	Lowest Rank	Station Name	°F
1	Marietta Wwtp	22.8	1	Fredericktown 4 S	15.2
2	Portsmouth Sciotoville	22.7	2	Dorset	16.2
3	Chilo Meldahl L&D	22.6	3	Chardon	16.3
3	Cincinnati-Northern Kentucky	22.6	4	Mansfield 5 W	16.5
5	Fairfield	*22.4*	5	Danville 2 W	16.9
6	Dayton Mcd	22.2	6	Defiance	17.0
6	Painesville 4 NW	22.2	7	Hiram	17.2
8	Circleville	21.9	8	Warren 3 S	17.3
8	Columbus-Port Columbus Intl	21.9	9	Centerburg 2 SE	17.4
10	Cambridge	21.8	10	Bowling Green WWTP	17.6
10	Steubenville	21.8	11	Marion 2 N	17.7
12	Carpenter 2 S	*21.3*	12	Bucyrus	17.8
12	Columbus Valley Crossing	21.3	12	Oberlin	17.8
14	Hannibal Lock & Dam	21.2	14	Bellefontaine	17.9
15	Westerville	20.9	15	Chippewa Lake	18.0
16	Elyria 3 E	20.7	15	Toledo Express Arpt	18.0
17	Cleveland Hopkins Intl Arpt	20.3	15	Upper Sandusky	18.0
17	Dayton Intl Arpt	20.3	18	Millport 2 NW	18.1
19	Franklin	20.2	19	Millersburg	*18.4*
20	Chillicothe Mound City	*20.1*	19	Pandora	18.4
20	Milford	*20.1*	21	Springfield New Water Works	18.6
22	Wilmington 3 N	19.9	22	Mansfield Lahm Municipal Arpt	18.9
23	Lima WWTP	19.8	23	Urbana WWTP	19.0
23	Marysville	19.8	23	Wooster Exp Stn	19.0
25	Barnesville	*19.7*	23	Youngstown Municipal Arpt	19.0

Number of Days Annually Maximum Temperature ≥ 90°F

Highest Rank	Station Name	Days	Lowest Rank	Station Name	Days
1	Dayton Mcd	35	1	Painesville 4 NW	4
1	Fairfield	*35*	2	Chardon	5
3	Milford	*28*	2	Hiram	5
4	Portsmouth Sciotoville	27	2	Mansfield Lahm Municipal Arpt	5
5	Chilo Meldahl L&D	20	2	Wooster Exp Stn	5
5	Cincinnati-Northern Kentucky	20	6	Mansfield 5 W	6
7	Chillicothe Mound City	19	6	Youngstown Municipal Arpt	6
7	Franklin	19	8	Akron Akron-Canton Reg Arpt	7
7	Marietta Wwtp	19	8	Barnesville	*7*
7	Westerville	19	8	Dorset	7
11	Circleville	18	11	Cadiz	8
11	Elyria 3 E	18	11	Chippewa Lake	8
13	Defiance	17	11	Fredericktown 4 S	8
14	Bowling Green WWTP	16	14	Centerburg 2 SE	9
14	Columbus-Port Columbus Intl	16	14	Cleveland Hopkins Intl Arpt	9
14	Toledo Express Arpt	16	14	Warren 3 S	9
17	Cambridge	15	17	Bellefontaine	10
17	Dayton Intl Arpt	15	17	Danville 2 W	10
17	Pandora	15	17	Steubenville	10
20	Columbus Valley Crossing	14	20	Bucyrus	11
20	Findlay Wpcc	14	20	Hannibal Lock & Dam	11
20	Lima WWTP	14	20	Wilmington 3 N	11
20	Marysville	14	23	Millport 2 NW	12
20	Upper Sandusky	14	23	Oberlin	12
20	Urbana WWTP	14	23	Springfield New Water Works	12

Rankings include 25 highest/lowest stations. If state has less than 25 stations, all stations are included. The period of record is 1980–2009. See User Guide for detailed explanation of data.

Number of Days Annually Maximum Temperature ≤ 32°F

Highest			Lowest		
Rank	Station Name	Days	Rank	Station Name	Days
1	Chardon	49	1	Portsmouth Sciotoville	16
2	Mansfield 5 W	47	2	Chilo Meldahl L&D	19
3	Hiram	46	3	Fairfield	***20***
4	Bucyrus	45	3	Marietta Wwtp	20
4	Dorset	45	5	Chillicothe Mound City	21
6	Chippewa Lake	44	6	Milford	***22***
6	Mansfield Lahm Municipal Arpt	44	7	Cambridge	23
6	Youngstown Municipal Arpt	44	7	Carpenter 2 S	***23***
9	Bowling Green WWTP	43	7	Cincinnati-Northern Kentucky	23
9	Defiance	43	7	Hannibal Lock & Dam	23
9	Toledo Express Arpt	43	11	Columbus Valley Crossing	26
12	Findlay Wpcc	42	12	Circleville	27
12	Oberlin	42	12	Franklin	27
12	Pandora	42	14	Westerville	28
12	Wooster Exp Stn	42	15	Steubenville	29
16	Bellefontaine	40	16	Columbus-Port Columbus Intl	30
16	Centerburg 2 SE	40	16	Dayton Mcd	30
16	Marion 2 N	40	18	Elyria 3 E	31
19	Akron Akron-Canton Reg Arpt	39	19	Millersburg	***33***
19	Cleveland Hopkins Intl Arpt	39	19	Millport 2 NW	33
19	Fredericktown 4 S	39	21	Painesville 4 NW	34
19	Upper Sandusky	39	21	Springfield New Water Works	34
23	Lima WWTP	38	21	Wilmington 3 N	34
24	Cadiz	37	24	Barnesville	***35***
24	Warren 3 S	37	24	Danville 2 W	35

Number of Days Annually Minimum Temperature ≤ 32°F

Highest			Lowest		
Rank	Station Name	Days	Rank	Station Name	Days
1	Danville 2 W	150	1	Cincinnati-Northern Kentucky	103
2	Fredericktown 4 S	147	1	Dayton Mcd	103
3	Warren 3 S	146	3	Painesville 4 NW	106
4	Dorset	143	4	Chilo Meldahl L&D	107
5	Chardon	142	5	Columbus-Port Columbus Intl	108
5	Millersburg	***142***	5	Portsmouth Sciotoville	108
7	Millport 2 NW	141	7	Marietta Wwtp	110
8	Mansfield 5 W	136	8	Fairfield	***111***
9	Hiram	134	9	Chillicothe Mound City	112
10	Chippewa Lake	133	9	Steubenville	112
11	Bucyrus	132	11	Cambridge	113
12	Centerburg 2 SE	131	11	Circleville	113
12	Oberlin	131	13	Columbus Valley Crossing	114
14	Bowling Green WWTP	130	13	Westerville	114
14	Defiance	130	15	Dayton Intl Arpt	115
14	Marion 2 N	130	16	Cadiz	116
14	Toledo Express Arpt	130	17	Cleveland Hopkins Intl Arpt	117
14	Wooster Exp Stn	130	17	Marysville	117
19	Bellefontaine	129	19	Elyria 3 E	118
19	Youngstown Municipal Arpt	129	20	Findlay Wpcc	119
21	Springfield New Water Works	128	20	Lima WWTP	119
21	Upper Sandusky	128	20	Milford	***119***
23	Barnesville	***126***	23	Carpenter 2 S	***120***
23	Mansfield Lahm Municipal Arpt	126	23	Franklin	120
23	Pandora	126	23	Hannibal Lock & Dam	120

Rankings include 25 highest/lowest stations. If state has less than 25 stations, all stations are included. The period of record is 1980–2009. See User Guide for detailed explanation of data.

Number of Days Annually Minimum Temperature ≤ 0°F

Highest			Lowest		
Rank	Station Name	Days	Rank	Station Name	Days
1	Chardon	9	1	Painesville 4 NW	1
1	Defiance	9	2	Marietta Wwtp	2
1	Dorset	9	2	Steubenville	2
1	Fredericktown 4 S	9	4	Chilo Meldahl L&D	3
5	Danville 2 W	8	4	Dayton Mcd	3
6	Bellefontaine	7	4	Fairfield	*3*
6	Bowling Green WWTP	7	4	Hannibal Lock & Dam	3
6	Centerburg 2 SE	7	4	Portsmouth Sciotoville	3
6	Mansfield 5 W	7	9	Akron Akron-Canton Reg Arpt	4
6	Millport 2 NW	7	9	Barnesville	*4*
6	Pandora	7	9	Cadiz	4
6	Warren 3 S	7	9	Cambridge	4
13	Bucyrus	6	9	Carpenter 2 S	*4*
13	Chippewa Lake	6	9	Chillicothe Mound City	4
13	Hiram	6	9	Cincinnati-Northern Kentucky	4
13	Marion 2 N	6	9	Circleville	4
13	Millersburg	*6*	9	Cleveland Hopkins Intl Arpt	4
13	Oberlin	6	9	Columbus-Port Columbus Intl	4
13	Springfield New Water Works	6	9	Columbus Valley Crossing	4
13	Toledo Express Arpt	6	9	Dayton Intl Arpt	4
13	Wilmington 3 N	6	9	Elyria 3 E	4
22	Lima WWTP	5	9	Findlay Wpcc	4
22	Mansfield Lahm Municipal Arpt	5	9	Franklin	4
22	Upper Sandusky	5	9	Marysville	4
22	Urbana WWTP	5	9	Milford	*4*

Number of Annual Heating Degree Days

Highest			Lowest		
Rank	Station Name	Num.	Rank	Station Name	Num.
1	Chardon	6,754	1	Portsmouth Sciotoville	4,855
2	Dorset	6,648	2	Chilo Meldahl L&D	4,909
3	Fredericktown 4 S	6,449	3	Cincinnati-Northern Kentucky	5,012
4	Hiram	6,442	4	Marietta Wwtp	5,028
5	Mansfield 5 W	6,401	5	Fairfield	*5,046*
6	Warren 3 S	6,319	6	Dayton Mcd	5,182
7	Bucyrus	6,297	7	Cambridge	5,200
8	Chippewa Lake	6,263	8	Milford	*5,271*
9	Danville 2 W	6,258	9	Westerville	5,300
10	Defiance	6,244	10	Carpenter 2 S	*5,307*
11	Youngstown Municipal Arpt	6,243	10	Columbus-Port Columbus Intl	5,307
12	Bowling Green WWTP	6,215	12	Chillicothe Mound City	*5,308*
13	Oberlin	6,212	13	Circleville	5,310
14	Toledo Express Arpt	6,186	14	Columbus Valley Crossing	5,318
15	Wooster Exp Stn	6,172	15	Hannibal Lock & Dam	5,395
16	Mansfield Lahm Municipal Arpt	6,141	16	Steubenville	5,438
17	Marion 2 N	6,120	17	Franklin	5,484
18	Centerburg 2 SE	6,106	18	Dayton Intl Arpt	5,563
19	Millersburg	*6,086*	19	Elyria 3 E	5,631
20	Upper Sandusky	6,075	20	Wilmington 3 N	5,664
21	Millport 2 NW	6,051	21	Painesville 4 NW	5,695
22	Akron Akron-Canton Reg Arpt	6,039	22	Marysville	5,699
23	Pandora	6,029	23	Lima WWTP	5,741
24	Bellefontaine	5,988	24	Cadiz	5,840
25	Cleveland Hopkins Intl Arpt	5,928	25	Springfield New Water Works	5,880

Rankings include 25 highest/lowest stations. If state has less than 25 stations, all stations are included. The period of record is 1980–2009. See User Guide for detailed explanation of data.

Number of Annual Cooling Degree Days

Highest Rank	Station Name	Num.	Lowest Rank	Station Name	Num.
1	Dayton Mcd	1,294	1	Chardon	482
2	Fairfield	***1,199***	2	Dorset	510
3	Cincinnati-Northern Kentucky	1,119	3	Fredericktown 4 S	548
4	Chilo Meldahl L&D	1,090	4	Warren 3 S	567
5	Portsmouth Sciotoville	1,076	5	Hiram	582
6	Milford	***1,034***	6	Youngstown Municipal Arpt	588
7	Columbus-Port Columbus Intl	1,013	7	Danville 2 W	597
8	Marietta Wwtp	987	8	Millport 2 NW	612
9	Chillicothe Mound City	***985***	9	Mansfield 5 W	615
10	Westerville	978	10	Wooster Exp Stn	619
11	Circleville	962	11	Chippewa Lake	654
12	Dayton Intl Arpt	952	11	Millersburg	***654***
13	Columbus Valley Crossing	943	13	Mansfield Lahm Municipal Arpt	683
14	Lima WWTP	933	14	Akron Akron-Canton Reg Arpt	701
15	Cambridge	929	15	Barnesville	***710***
16	Franklin	921	16	Centerburg 2 SE	717
17	Findlay Wpcc	902	17	Bucyrus	720
18	Marysville	897	17	Oberlin	720
19	Elyria 3 E	885	19	Cadiz	758
20	Steubenville	847	20	Cleveland Hopkins Intl Arpt	762
21	Carpenter 2 S	***843***	21	Painesville 4 NW	777
22	Upper Sandusky	830	22	Toledo Express Arpt	789
23	Defiance	825	23	Marion 2 N	795
24	Wilmington 3 N	822	24	Bowling Green WWTP	796
25	Pandora	821	25	Springfield New Water Works	798

Annual Precipitation

Highest Rank	Station Name	Inches	Lowest Rank	Station Name	Inches
1	Chardon	48.24	1	Bowling Green WWTP	33.92
2	Milford	***44.72***	2	Toledo Express Arpt	34.11
3	Mansfield Lahm Municipal Arpt	44.24	3	Defiance	36.64
4	Fairfield	***43.80***	4	Pandora	37.19
5	Barnesville	***43.60***	5	Findlay Wpcc	37.44
6	Dorset	43.58	6	Upper Sandusky	37.52
7	Marietta Wwtp	42.81	7	Millport 2 NW	37.63
8	Hiram	42.67	8	Oberlin	37.75
9	Cincinnati-Northern Kentucky	42.53	9	Marysville	37.88
10	Centerburg 2 SE	41.94	10	Chillicothe Mound City	38.11
11	Danville 2 W	41.87	11	Fredericktown 4 S	38.32
12	Urbana WWTP	41.71	12	Lima WWTP	38.55
13	Steubenville	41.52	13	Springfield New Water Works	38.57
14	Hannibal Lock & Dam	41.34	14	Painesville 4 NW	38.63
15	Cadiz	41.26	15	Circleville	38.80
16	Dayton Intl Arpt	41.13	16	Youngstown Municipal Arpt	38.92
17	Carpenter 2 S	***41.04***	17	Cleveland Hopkins Intl Arpt	39.00
18	Portsmouth Sciotoville	40.93	18	Marion 2 N	39.03
19	Wilmington 3 N	40.80	19	Bucyrus	39.07
20	Dayton Mcd	40.66	20	Franklin	39.11
21	Chilo Meldahl L&D	40.58	21	Bellefontaine	39.24
22	Columbus Valley Crossing	40.39	21	Mansfield 5 W	39.24
23	Wooster Exp Stn	39.99	23	Westerville	39.26
24	Cambridge	39.87	24	Chippewa Lake	39.32
25	Millersburg	***39.79***	24	Columbus-Port Columbus Intl	39.32

Rankings include 25 highest/lowest stations. If state has less than 25 stations, all stations are included. The period of record is 1980–2009. See User Guide for detailed explanation of data.

Annual Extreme Maximum Daily Precipitation

Highest			Lowest		
Rank	Station Name	Inches	Rank	Station Name	Inches
1	Upper Sandusky	9.35	1	Oberlin	2.92
2	Bucyrus	8.68	2	Fredericktown 4 S	***3.00***
3	Chilo Meldahl L&D	7.20	3	Toledo Express Arpt	3.15
4	Pandora	6.19	4	Wilmington 3 N	3.42
5	Elyria 3 E	5.75	5	Centerburg 2 SE	3.46
6	Findlay Wpcc	5.62	6	Wooster Exp Stn	3.60
7	Chardon	5.50	7	Franklin	3.76
8	Cambridge	5.45	8	Columbus Valley Crossing	3.77
9	Steubenville	5.36	9	Springfield New Water Works	3.78
10	Marion 2 N	5.33	10	Dayton Intl Arpt	3.81
11	Portsmouth Sciotoville	5.20	11	Westerville	3.84
12	Mansfield 5 W	***5.19***	12	Millersburg	***3.85***
13	Columbus-Port Columbus Intl	5.13	13	Defiance	3.89
14	Barnesville	***5.12***	14	Urbana WWTP	3.97
14	Danville 2 W	5.12	15	Akron Akron-Canton Reg Arpt	3.98
16	Cadiz	5.09	16	Hiram	4.05
17	Lima WWTP	5.08	17	Chillicothe Mound City	***4.10***
18	Marysville	4.82	18	Circleville	4.12
19	Millport 2 NW	4.80	19	Bowling Green WWTP	4.25
20	Marietta Wwtp	4.78	20	Hannibal Lock & Dam	4.28
21	Fairfield	***4.67***	21	Dorset	4.29
22	Youngstown Municipal Arpt	4.65	22	Chippewa Lake	4.30
23	Milford	***4.63***	22	Cincinnati-Northern Kentucky	4.30
24	Cleveland Hopkins Intl Arpt	4.59	24	Mansfield Lahm Municipal Arpt	4.34
25	Painesville 4 NW	4.57	25	Dayton Mcd	4.36

Number of Days Annually With ≥ 0.1 Inches of Precipitation

Highest			Lowest		
Rank	Station Name	Days	Rank	Station Name	Days
1	Chardon	108	1	Chillicothe Mound City	70
2	Hiram	95	1	Fredericktown 4 S	70
3	Dorset	94	3	Chilo Meldahl L&D	72
4	Elyria 3 E	89	3	Toledo Express Arpt	72
4	Mansfield Lahm Municipal Arpt	89	5	Bowling Green WWTP	73
4	Warren 3 S	89	5	Franklin	73
7	Steubenville	88	7	Columbus Valley Crossing	74
8	Akron Akron-Canton Reg Arpt	87	7	Springfield New Water Works	74
8	Barnesville	***87***	9	Dayton Mcd	76
8	Cadiz	87	10	Defiance	77
8	Chippewa Lake	87	10	Marysville	77
8	Cleveland Hopkins Intl Arpt	87	10	Upper Sandusky	77
8	Marietta Wwtp	87	13	Circleville	78
8	Youngstown Municipal Arpt	87	14	Columbus-Port Columbus Intl	79
15	Danville 2 W	85	14	Fairfield	***79***
15	Painesville 4 NW	85	14	Findlay Wpcc	79
17	Hannibal Lock & Dam	84	14	Marion 2 N	79
17	Millport 2 NW	84	14	Millersburg	***79***
17	Oberlin	84	14	Pandora	79
20	Bucyrus	83	20	Dayton Intl Arpt	80
20	Cambridge	83	20	Lima WWTP	80
22	Carpenter 2 S	***82***	20	Mansfield 5 W	80
22	Cincinnati-Northern Kentucky	82	23	Bellefontaine	81
22	Milford	***82***	23	Centerburg 2 SE	81
22	Portsmouth Sciotoville	82	23	Urbana WWTP	81

Rankings include 25 highest/lowest stations. If state has less than 25 stations, all stations are included. The period of record is 1980–2009. See User Guide for detailed explanation of data.

Number of Days Annually With ≥ 0.5 Inches of Precipitation

Highest

Rank	Station Name	Days
1	Chardon	32
1	Milford	*32*
3	Fairfield	*30*
4	Barnesville	*29*
4	Centerburg 2 SE	29
4	Dorset	29
4	Mansfield Lahm Municipal Arpt	29
4	Marietta Wwtp	29
9	Carpenter 2 S	*28*
9	Hannibal Lock & Dam	28
11	Cadiz	27
11	Chilo Meldahl L&D	27
11	Cincinnati-Northern Kentucky	27
11	Circleville	27
11	Columbus Valley Crossing	27
11	Danville 2 W	27
11	Dayton Mcd	27
11	Portsmouth Sciotoville	27
11	Steubenville	27
11	Urbana WWTP	27
11	Wilmington 3 N	27
11	Wooster Exp Stn	27
23	Cambridge	26
23	Chillicothe Mound City	26
23	Dayton Intl Arpt	26

Lowest

Rank	Station Name	Days
1	Bowling Green WWTP	21
1	Toledo Express Arpt	21
3	Upper Sandusky	22
4	Cleveland Hopkins Intl Arpt	23
4	Oberlin	23
4	Painesville 4 NW	23
4	Youngstown Municipal Arpt	23
8	Akron Akron-Canton Reg Arpt	24
8	Defiance	24
8	Findlay Wpcc	24
8	Franklin	24
8	Millport 2 NW	24
8	Warren 3 S	24
14	Bellefontaine	25
14	Bucyrus	25
14	Chippewa Lake	25
14	Columbus-Port Columbus Intl	25
14	Elyria 3 E	25
14	Fredericktown 4 S	25
14	Lima WWTP	25
14	Mansfield 5 W	25
14	Marion 2 N	25
14	Marysville	25
14	Pandora	25
25	Cambridge	26

Number of Days Annually With ≥ 1.0 Inches of Precipitation

Highest

Rank	Station Name	Days
1	Chilo Meldahl L&D	12
1	Cincinnati-Northern Kentucky	12
3	Fairfield	*11*
3	Mansfield Lahm Municipal Arpt	11
3	Milford	*11*
3	Urbana WWTP	11
7	Carpenter 2 S	*10*
7	Dayton Intl Arpt	10
7	Dayton Mcd	10
7	Franklin	10
7	Fredericktown 4 S	10
7	Portsmouth Sciotoville	10
7	Wilmington 3 N	10
14	Barnesville	*9*
14	Bellefontaine	9
14	Cambridge	9
14	Centerburg 2 SE	9
14	Chardon	9
14	Chillicothe Mound City	9
14	Circleville	9
14	Columbus Valley Crossing	9
14	Danville 2 W	9
14	Marion 2 N	9
14	Springfield New Water Works	9
25	Defiance	8

Lowest

Rank	Station Name	Days
1	Akron Akron-Canton Reg Arpt	6
1	Chippewa Lake	6
1	Lima WWTP	6
1	Millport 2 NW	6
1	Oberlin	6
1	Painesville 4 NW	6
1	Pandora	6
1	Warren 3 S	6
1	Youngstown Municipal Arpt	6
10	Bowling Green WWTP	7
10	Bucyrus	7
10	Cadiz	7
10	Cleveland Hopkins Intl Arpt	7
10	Columbus-Port Columbus Intl	7
10	Dorset	7
10	Elyria 3 E	7
10	Findlay Wpcc	7
10	Hiram	7
10	Marysville	7
10	Millersburg	*7*
10	Steubenville	7
10	Toledo Express Arpt	7
10	Wooster Exp Stn	7
24	Defiance	8
24	Hannibal Lock & Dam	8

Rankings include 25 highest/lowest stations. If state has less than 25 stations, all stations are included. The period of record is 1980–2009. See User Guide for detailed explanation of data.

Annual Snowfall

Highest

Rank	Station Name	Inches
1	Chardon	102.8
2	Dorset	79.0
3	Cleveland Hopkins Intl Arpt	67.6
4	Hiram	63.2
5	Youngstown Municipal Arpt	59.7
6	Mansfield Lahm Municipal Arpt	47.7
7	Akron Akron-Canton Reg Arpt	46.4
8	Oberlin	45.8
9	Elyria 3 E	41.0
10	Painesville 4 NW	39.2
11	Danville 2 W	39.1
12	Chippewa Lake	35.9
13	Warren 3 S	31.8
14	Barnesville	***31.6***
15	Pandora	30.5
16	Wooster Exp Stn	29.3
17	Millport 2 NW	28.7
18	Cadiz	28.2
19	Columbus-Port Columbus Intl	27.9
20	Findlay Wpcc	26.9
21	Dayton Intl Arpt	25.3
22	Fredericktown 4 S	24.8
23	Marion 2 N	23.0
24	Bucyrus	22.5
25	Bowling Green WWTP	21.6

Lowest

Rank	Station Name	Inches
1	Fairfield	***7.8***
2	Portsmouth Sciotoville	8.0
3	Centerburg 2 SE	12.4
3	Dayton Mcd	12.4
5	Circleville	13.9
6	Chillicothe Mound City	14.8
7	Columbus Valley Crossing	14.9
8	Millersburg	***17.5***
9	Cambridge	18.2
10	Westerville	18.5
11	Carpenter 2 S	***18.6***
12	Marietta Wwtp	18.8
13	Upper Sandusky	19.4
14	Marysville	20.5
15	Defiance	20.7
16	Wilmington 3 N	21.0
17	Bowling Green WWTP	21.6
17	Cincinnati-Northern Kentucky	21.6
19	Bucyrus	22.5
20	Marion 2 N	23.0
21	Fredericktown 4 S	24.8
22	Dayton Intl Arpt	25.3
23	Findlay Wpcc	26.9
24	Columbus-Port Columbus Intl	27.9
25	Cadiz	28.2

Annual Maximum Snow Depth

Highest

Rank	Station Name	Inches
1	Chardon	47
2	Painesville 4 NW	25
3	Chippewa Lake	24
4	Centerburg 2 SE	23
4	Hannibal Lock & Dam	***23***
6	Cleveland Hopkins Intl Arpt	22
6	Danville 2 W	22
6	Hiram	22
9	Portsmouth Sciotoville	21
10	Barnesville	***20***
10	Dorset	20
10	Mansfield Lahm Municipal Arpt	20
10	Marietta Wwtp	20
14	Bellefontaine	***19***
14	Cambridge	19
14	Upper Sandusky	***19***
17	Bowling Green WWTP	18
17	Columbus-Port Columbus Intl	18
17	Wilmington 3 N	18
17	Youngstown Municipal Arpt	18
21	Akron Akron-Canton Reg Arpt	17
21	Bucyrus	17
21	Defiance	17
21	Marysville	17
21	Oberlin	17

Lowest

Rank	Station Name	Inches
1	Chillicothe Mound City	11
2	Dayton Mcd	12
3	Columbus Valley Crossing	***13***
3	Millersburg	***13***
3	Westerville	13
6	Cincinnati-Northern Kentucky	14
6	Findlay Wpcc	14
8	Circleville	***15***
8	Elyria 3 E	15
8	Marion 2 N	***15***
8	Millport 2 NW	***15***
12	Chilo Meldahl L&D	***16***
12	Dayton Intl Arpt	16
12	Pandora	16
12	Warren 3 S	16
16	Akron Akron-Canton Reg Arpt	17
16	Bucyrus	17
16	Defiance	17
16	Marysville	17
16	Oberlin	17
16	Wooster Exp Stn	17
22	Bowling Green WWTP	18
22	Columbus-Port Columbus Intl	18
22	Wilmington 3 N	18
22	Youngstown Municipal Arpt	18

Rankings include 25 highest/lowest stations. If state has less than 25 stations, all stations are included. The period of record is 1980–2009. See User Guide for detailed explanation of data.

Number of Days Annually With ≥ 1.0 Inch Snow Depth

Highest Rank	Highest Station Name	Highest Days	Lowest Rank	Lowest Station Name	Lowest Days
1	Chardon	80	1	Chilo Meldahl L&D	***4***
2	Dorset	69	2	Franklin	***8***
3	Hiram	64	2	Portsmouth Sciotoville	8
4	Youngstown Municipal Arpt	54	4	Hannibal Lock & Dam	***10***
5	Oberlin	53	5	Columbus Valley Crossing	13
6	Cleveland Hopkins Intl Arpt	51	6	Bellefontaine	***15***
7	Mansfield Lahm Municipal Arpt	49	6	Marietta Wwtp	15
8	Akron Akron-Canton Reg Arpt	45	6	Millport 2 NW	***15***
8	Chippewa Lake	45	9	Chillicothe Mound City	18
8	Wooster Exp Stn	45	10	Circleville	19
11	Danville 2 W	43	10	Dayton Mcd	19
11	Elyria 3 E	43	12	Cincinnati-Northern Kentucky	20
11	Painesville 4 NW	43	13	Upper Sandusky	22
14	Pandora	39	14	Westerville	23
15	Bowling Green WWTP	38	15	Cadiz	***25***
15	Defiance	38	15	Cambridge	25
17	Findlay Wpcc	36	17	Centerburg 2 SE	26
18	Warren 3 S	35	17	Columbus-Port Columbus Intl	26
19	Barnesville	***34***	17	Millersburg	***26***
20	Marysville	31	17	Wilmington 3 N	26
21	Bucyrus	29	21	Dayton Intl Arpt	27
22	Dayton Intl Arpt	27	21	Marion 2 N	***27***
22	Marion 2 N	***27***	23	Bucyrus	29
24	Centerburg 2 SE	26	24	Marysville	31
24	Columbus-Port Columbus Intl	26	25	Barnesville	***34***

Rankings include 25 highest/lowest stations. If state has less than 25 stations, all stations are included. The period of record is 1980–2009. See User Guide for detailed explanation of data.

Significant Storm Events in Ohio: 2000 – 2009

Location or County	Date	Type	Mag.	Deaths	Injuries	Property Damage ($mil.)	Crop Damage ($mil.)
Preble County	02/07/00	Fog	na	1	14	0.2	0.0
Greene	09/20/00	Tornado	F4	1	100	15.0	0.0
Montgomery	04/09/01	Hail	1.75 in.	0	0	70.0	0.0
Western and Southern Ohio	03/09/02	High Wind	84 mph	1	12	0.9	0.0
Stark	04/28/02	Tornado	F2	0	2	45.5	0.0
Van Wert	11/10/02	Tornado	F4	2	17	30.0	0.0
Franklin	04/20/03	Hail	1.75 in.	0	0	80.0	0.0
Delaware	04/20/03	Hail	1.50 in.	0	0	65.0	0.0
Summit	07/21/03	Flash Flood	na	3	0	100.0	0.0
Stark	07/27/03	Flash Flood	na	0	0	52.0	0.0
Northern Ohio	12/22/04	Winter Storm	na	0	0	54.9	0.0
Northern Ohio	01/05/05	Ice Storm	na	0	0	124.9	0.0
Lake	07/28/06	Flash Flood	na	1	0	320.0	0.0
Licking	10/04/06	Hail	1.75 in.	0	1	100.0	0.0
Franklin	10/04/06	Hail	2.00 in.	0	0	100.0	0.0
Franklin	10/11/06	Tornado	F2	0	0	50.0	0.0
Summit	06/08/07	Hail	4.25 in.	0	0	105.0	0.0
Hancock	08/21/07	Flash Flood	na	0	0	100.0	5.0
Richland	08/21/07	Flash Flood	na	0	0	70.0	5.0
Crawford	08/21/07	Flash Flood	na	0	0	62.0	3.0
Knox, Stark, and Trumbull Counties	03/07/08	Winter Storm	na	0	0	750.0	0.0
Franklin and Logan Counties	09/14/08	High Wind	75 mph	0	0	128.7	0.0
Hamilton County	09/14/08	High Wind	61 mph	1	0	96.6	0.0
Montgomery County	09/14/08	High Wind	69 mph	0	0	63.7	0.0

Note: Deaths, injuries, and damages are date and location specific.

OKLAHOMA

PHYSICAL FEATURES. Oklahoma is located in the southern Great Plains. Of the 50 states, it ranks 18th in size with an area of approximately 70,000 square miles, only 935 of which are covered by lakes and ponds. Its northern boundary is about 465 miles in length and its southern boundary 315 miles in length. Greatest depth is 222 miles.

The terrain is mostly rolling plains, sloping downward from west to east. The plains are broken by scattered hilly areas where most points are 600 feet or less above the adjacent countryside, and by a mountainous area in the southeast where some peaks rise more than 2,000 feet above their base. The hilly areas consist of the Wichita Mountains with some isolated peaks in the southwest the Arbuckle Mountains in the south-central and an extension of the Ozarks in the northeast. The Ouachita Mountains occupy much of the southeast. Elevations in the State range from 4,976 feet above sea level on Black Mesa in the northwestern corner of the Panhandle, to about 305 feet above sea level in the bed of the Red River where it leaves Oklahoma at the southeastern corner of the State.

Oklahoma lies entirely within the drainage basin of the Mississippi River. The two main rivers in the State are the Arkansas which drains the northern two-thirds of Oklahoma and the Red River which drains the southern third and forms the State's southern boundary. Principal tributaries of the Arkansas are the Verdigris, Grand (Neosho), Illinois, Cimarron, North Canadian, and Canadian Rivers. The Red draws largely from the North Fork of the Red, Washita, Boggy, and Little Rivers.

In western Oklahoma, rivers tend to be broad, shallow, sand choked, and dry or nearly dry much of the time. Basins are mostly long and narrow. In the east, rivers are fairly swift and clear and basins more oval in form. Most lakes are manmade and were built for flood control, irrigation, municipal water storage, recreational, and hydroelectric power purposes.

GENERAL CLIMATE. The climate of Oklahoma is mostly continental in type, as in all of the central Great Plains. Warm, moist air moving northward from the Gulf of Mexico exerts much influence at times, particularly over the southern and more eastern sections of the State where, as a result, humidities and cloudiness are generally greater and precipitation considerably heavier than in the western and northern sections. Summers are long and occasionally very hot. Winters are shorter and less rigorous than those of the more northern Plains States. Periods of extreme cold are infrequent.

The mean annual temperature over the State ranges from 64°F. along the southern border to about 60°F. along the northern border. It then decreases westward across the Panhandle to about 57°F. in Cimarron County. Temperatures of 90°F. or higher occur, on an average, about 85 days per year in the western Panhandle and in the northeast corner of the State. In the southwest, the average is about 120 days, and in the southeast from 95 to 100 days. Temperatures of 100°F. or higher are common over the State from May well into September. In the southwest part of the State the average number of 100°F. days is 20 to 25 per year. Other sections of the State will average somewhat less, but very seldom will any location in the State not reach a 100°F. temperature sometime during the summer months.

Low humidities and good southerly breezes usually accompany the high summer temperatures and somewhat lessen their discomforting effect. Occasionally strong, hot winds accompany the high daytime temperatures; this combination produces rapid evaporation and often injures crops. When these conditions persist for long periods of time, droughts develop and occasionally become severe. Nights are generally comfortable because the clear skies and dry air allows for rapid cooling after sunset.

Temperatures of 32°F. or less occur on an average of 55 to 65 days per year along the southern tier of counties and from 90 to 100 days per year along the Kansas border in the north-central and northeastern sections of the State. In the Panhandle, days with 32°F. or less occur, on an average, 125 to 140 days per year.

The average length of the growing season, or freeze-free period, ranges from 168 days in the northwestern corner of the Panhandle, to about 225 days along the Red River in the south-central and southeastern sections of Oklahoma. Freezing temperatures have occurred as late as April 20 along the southern border and as late as May 15 in the extreme northwest and in the Panhandle. Fall freezes have occurred as early as September 20 in the Panhandle and as early as October 9 along the southern border. Frozen soil is not a major problem, nor much of a deterrent to seasonal activities. The average maximum depth that frost penetrates the soil ranges from less than three inches in the southeastern corner of the State to more than 10 inches in the extreme northwestern portion.

PRECIPITATION. The geographical distribution of rainfall decreases sharply from east to west. Average annual precipitation ranges from about 56 inches in the southeastern corner of the State, to 15 inches in the extreme western Panhandle. Frequency of rainfall, as determined from the average number of days with 0.01 inch or more, varies from 95 to 100 days a year in the extreme east to from 70 to 80 days a year over the western third of the State.

Excessively heavy rains occur at times. Amounts of 10 inches or more within a 24-hour period have been recorded. Floods may occur during any season. They occur with greater frequency, however, from May to July and in September and October, representing periods when storms are of greater magnitude and rains of greatest intensities. In general, floods in other seasons are the result of more abnormal and persistent buildup of soil moisture plus a concurrent increase in stream-flow due to prolonged rains.

SNOWFALL. The geographical distribution of annual snowfall is usually almost the reverse of the annual precipitation pattern and ranges, on an average, from approximately two inches in the southeastern corner of the State to approximately 20 inches in the western sections of the Panhandle. Snow rarely remains on the ground more than a few days. At times, strong winds with heavy snowfalls cause bad drifting and occasionally produce blizzard conditions.

OTHER CLIMATIC ELEMENTS. Relative humidity averages about 10 percent higher in the eastern portion of the State because of lower elevations and more frequent inflow of Gulf moisture. Summer afternoon and early evening relative humidities are considerably lower than those of winter.

Oklahoma, along with other states in the southern Great Plains, has at times been subject to droughts of varying degree and duration, although drought years have been far less frequent than dry summers and falls. Average annual lake evaporation varies from about 48 inches in the extreme eastern sections of the State to as high as 65 inches in the southwestern corner. In the western Panhandle approximately 58 inches of water is evaporated each year.

Prevailing winds are southerly although northerly winds predominate during the winter months. Average yearly wind speeds vary from nine m.p.h. in the east to approximately 14 m.p.h. in the west. March and April are the windiest months, and July and August the calmest.

Thunderstorms occur, on an average, on 50 to 60 days per year in the eastern half of the State and from 40 to 50 days per year in the western half. Some of the more severe thunderstorms are accompanied by tornadoes and damaging hail, and approximately 75 percent of these occur during the spring season.

Skies are preponderantly clear in western and central sections and about equally clear and cloudy in eastern sections. Sunshine records show an annual average of 68 percent of the possible amount at Oklahoma City and 63 percent at Tulsa. Summer is the period of greatest possible sunshine and winter the least.

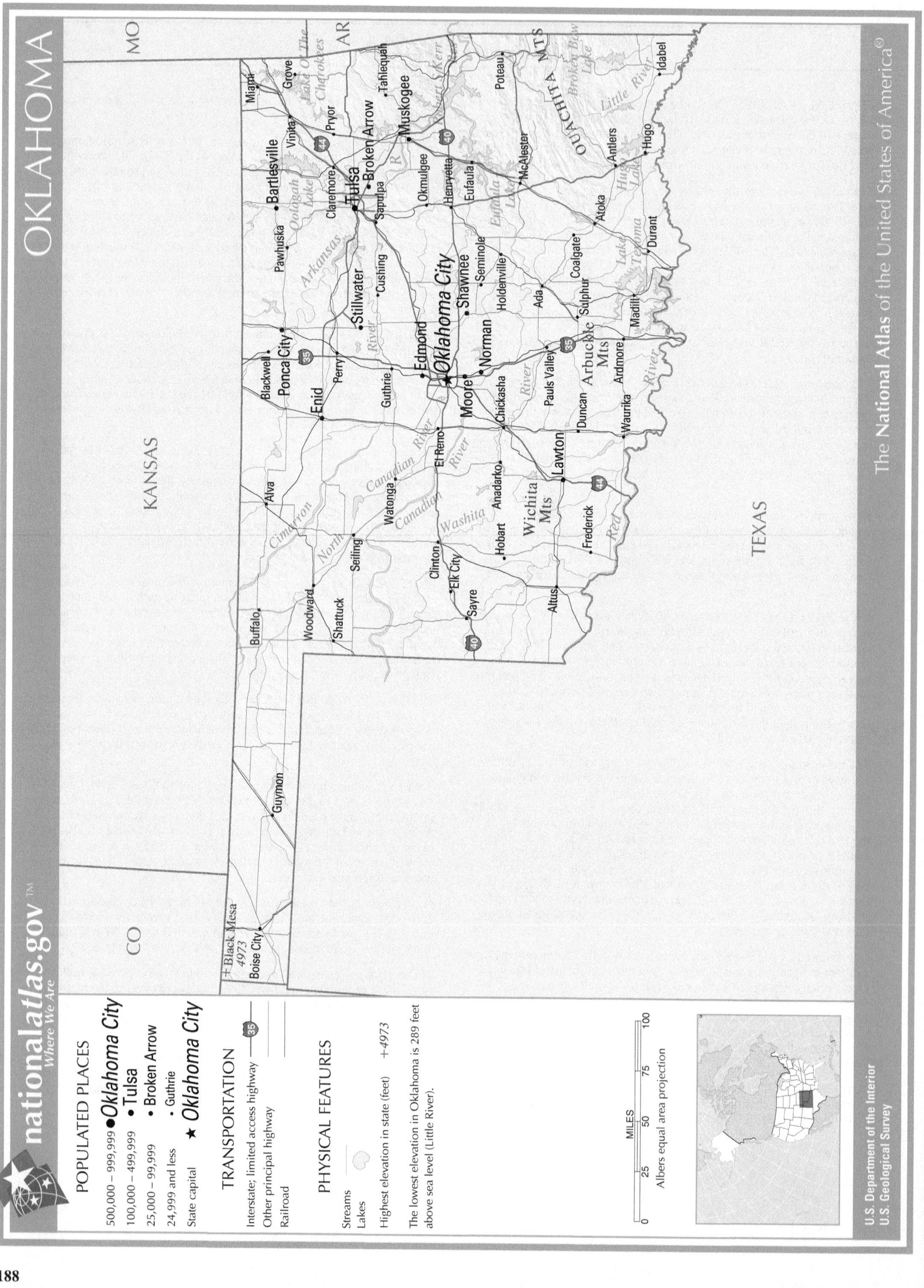
OKLAHOMA
nationalatlas.gov™
Where We Are
POPULATED PLACES
500,000 – 999,999 Oklahoma City
100,000 – 499,999 Tulsa
25,000 – 99,999 Broken Arrow
24,999 and less Guthrie
State capital Oklahoma City
TRANSPORTATION
Interstate; limited access highway
Other principal highway
Railroad
PHYSICAL FEATURES
Streams
Lakes
Highest elevation in state (feet) +4973
The lowest elevation in Oklahoma is 289 feet above sea level (Little River).
MILES
0 25 50 75 100
Albers equal area projection
U.S. Department of the Interior
U.S. Geological Survey
The National Atlas of the United States of America®
KANSAS
TEXAS
CO
MO
AR
Black Mesa 4973
Boise City
Guymon
Buffalo
Woodward
Shattuck
Alva
Seiling
Watonga
Enid
Blackwell
Ponca City
Perry
Guthrie
Stillwater
Cushing
Pawhuska
Bartlesville
Miami
Grove
Vinita
Pryor
Claremore
Tulsa
Broken Arrow
Sapulpa
Okmulgee
Muskogee
Tahlequah
Henryetta
Eufaula
McAlester
Poteau
Edmond
Oklahoma City
Shawnee
Seminole
Holdenville
Norman
Moore
El Reno
Chickasha
Pauls Valley
Ada
Coalgate
Atoka
Antlers
Hugo
Idabel
Durant
Madill
Sulphur
Ardmore
Duncan
Waurika
Lawton
Anadarko
Frederick
Hobart
Clinton
Elk City
Sayre
Altus
Wichita Mts
Arbuckle Mts
OUACHITA MTS
Cimarron
North Canadian River
Canadian
Washita
Red River
Arkansas
Oologah Lake
Lake O' The Cherokees
Eufaula Lake
Broken Bow Lake
Hugo Lake
Lake Texoma
Little River
40
44
35

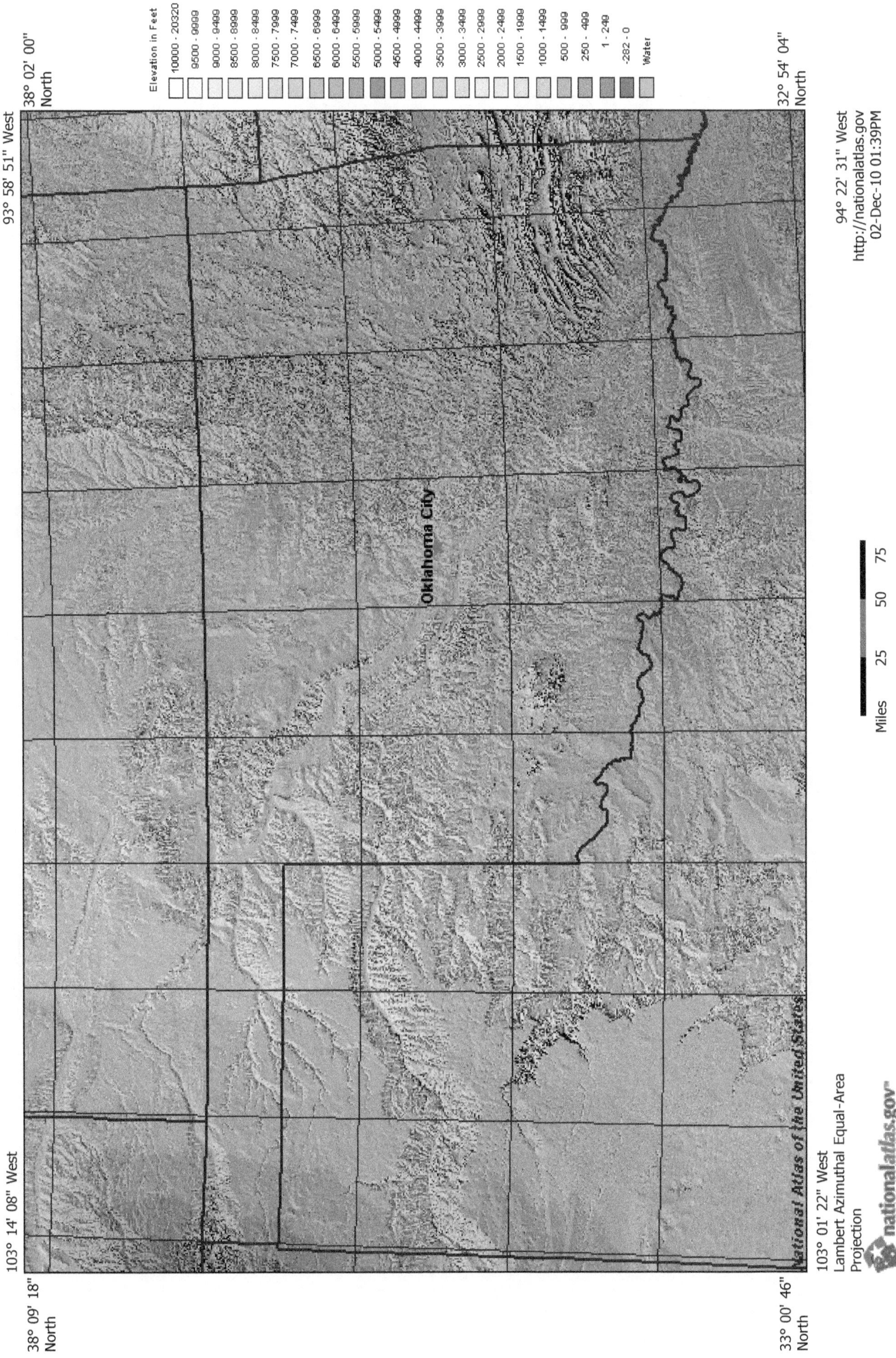
Elevation in Feet
10000 - 20320
9500 - 9999
9000 - 9499
8500 - 8999
8000 - 8499
7500 - 7999
7000 - 7499
6500 - 6999
6000 - 6499
5500 - 5999
5000 - 5499
4500 - 4999
4000 - 4499
3500 - 3999
3000 - 3499
2500 - 2999
2000 - 2499
1500 - 1999
1000 - 1499
500 - 999
250 - 499
1 - 249
-282 - 0
Water
38° 02' 00" North
93° 58' 51" West
32° 54' 04" North
94° 22' 31" West
http://nationalatlas.gov
02-Dec-10 01:39PM
Oklahoma City
Miles 25 50 75
103° 14' 08" West
38° 09' 18" North
33° 00' 46" North
103° 01' 22" West
Lambert Azimuthal Equal-Area Projection
National Atlas of the United States
nationalatlas.gov

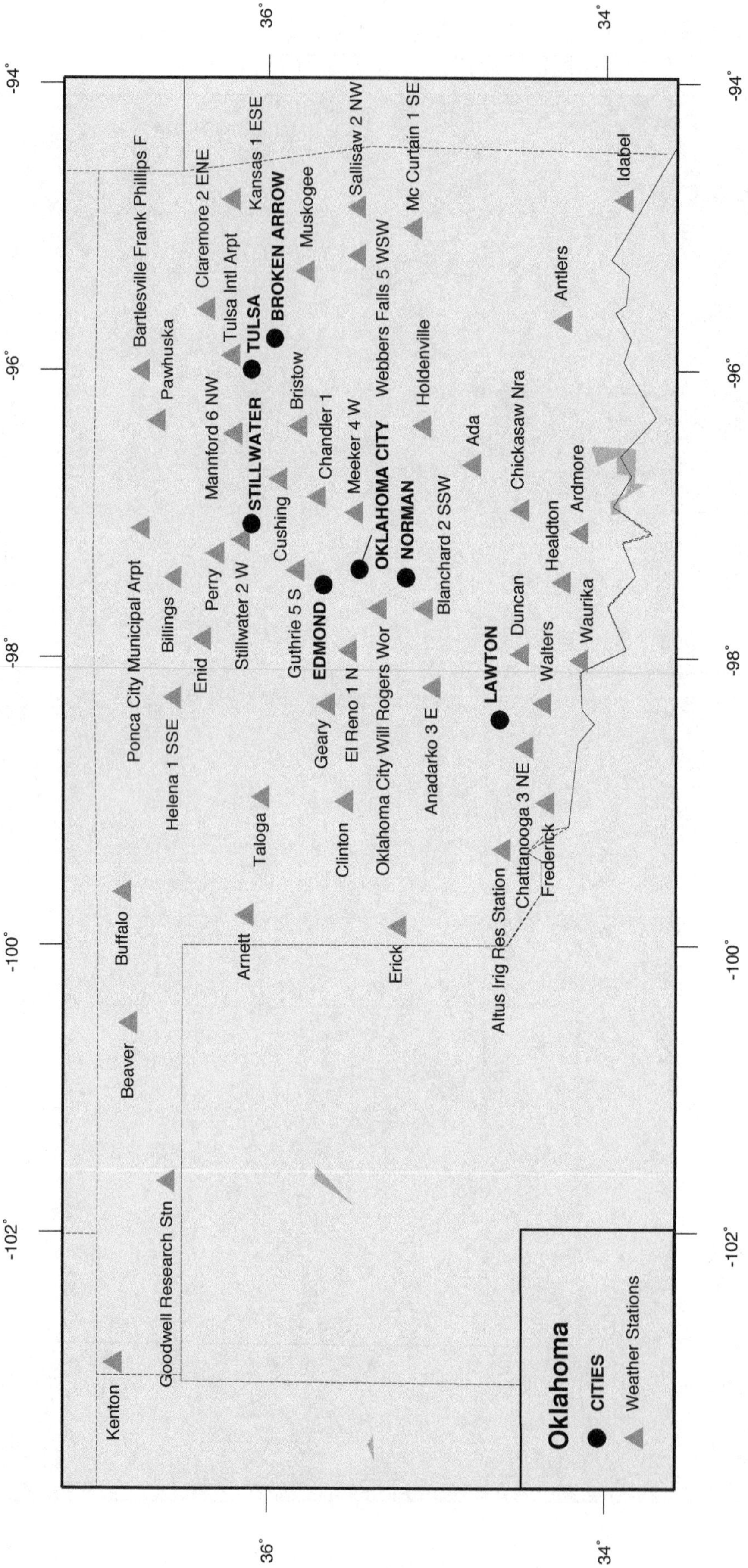
Oklahoma
CITIES
Weather Stations
-94°
-96°
-98°
-100°
-102°
36°
34°
Kenton
Goodwell Research Stn
Beaver
Buffalo
Arnett
Erick
Altus Irig Res Station
Taloga
Clinton
Oklahoma City Will Rogers Wor
Anadarko 3 E
Chattanooga 3 NE
Frederick
Helena 1 SSE
Ponca City Municipal Arpt
Billings
Enid
Perry
Stillwater 2 W
Geary
El Reno 1 N
Guthrie 5 S
EDMOND
LAWTON
Walters
Duncan
Waurika
Healdton
Ardmore
Blanchard 2 SSW
NORMAN
OKLAHOMA CITY
Cushing
STILLWATER
Mannford 6 NW
Chandler 1
Meeker 4 W
Ada
Chickasaw Nra
Bristow
Holdenville
Webbers Falls 5 WSW
Pawhuska
Bartlesville Frank Phillips F
TULSA
Tulsa Intl Arpt
BROKEN ARROW
Claremore 2 ENE
Muskogee
Kansas 1 ESE
Sallisaw 2 NW
Mc Curtain 1 SE
Antlers
Idabel

Oklahoma Weather Stations by County

County	Station Name
Alfalfa	Helena 1 SSE
Beaver	Beaver
Beckham	Erick
Blaine	Geary
Caddo	Anadarko 3 E
Canadian	El Reno 1 N
Carter	Ardmore Healdton
Cimarron	Kenton
Comanche	Chattanooga 3 NE
Cotton	Walters
Creek	Bristow
Custer	Clinton
Delaware	Kansas 1 ESE
Dewey	Taloga
Ellis	Arnett
Garfield	Enid
Harper	Buffalo
Haskell	McCurtain 1 SE
Hughes	Holdenville
Jackson	Altus Irig Res Station
Jefferson	Waurika
Kay	Ponca City Municipal Arpt
Lincoln	Chandler 1 Meeker 4 W
Logan	Guthrie 5 S
Mcclain	Blanchard 2 SSW
Mccurtain	Idabel
Murray	Chickasaw Nra
Muskogee	Muskogee Webbers Falls 5 WSW
Noble	Billings Perry
Oklahoma	Okla City Will Rogers World Arpt

County	Station Name
Osage	Bartlesville Frank Phillips Pawhuska
Pawnee	Mannford 6 NW
Payne	Cushing Stillwater 2 W
Pontotoc	Ada
Pushmataha	Antlers
Rogers	Claremore 2 ENE
Sequoyah	Sallisaw 2 NW
Stephens	Duncan
Texas	Goodwell Research Stn
Tillman	Frederick
Tulsa	Tulsa Intl Arpt

See User Guide for station inclusion criteria.

Oklahoma Weather Stations by City

City	Station Name	Miles
Ardmore	Ardmore	0.7
	Chickasaw Nra	24.2
	Healdton	19.2
Bartlesville	Bartlesville Frank Phillips	2.9
	Pawhuska	22.8
Bixby	Tulsa Intl Arpt	16.0
Broken Arrow	Claremore 2 ENE	23.0
	Tulsa Intl Arpt	12.3
Del City	Okla City Will Rogers World Arpt	9.7
Duncan	Duncan	1.2
	Walters	22.0
	Waurika	24.2
Edmond	Guthrie 5 S	11.9
	Okla City Will Rogers World Arpt	20.0
Enid	Enid	1.8
	Helena 1 SSE	23.6
Lawton	Chattanooga 3 NE	16.1
	Walters	18.8
Midwest City	Guthrie 5 S	24.5
	Meeker 4 W	22.5
	Okla City Will Rogers World Arpt	13.5
Moore	Blanchard 2 SSW	18.4
	Okla City Will Rogers World Arpt	7.0
Muskogee	Muskogee	2.2
	Webbers Falls 5 WSW	20.3
Norman	Blanchard 2 SSW	14.8
	Okla City Will Rogers World Arpt	14.7
Oklahoma City	El Reno 1 N	22.9
	Guthrie 5 S	24.6
	Okla City Will Rogers World Arpt	7.4
Owasso	Claremore 2 ENE	14.7
	Tulsa Intl Arpt	6.1
Ponca City	Billings	24.4
	Ponca City Municipal Arpt	1.8
Sapulpa	Bristow	19.6
	Mannford 6 NW	22.0
	Tulsa Intl Arpt	18.4
Shawnee	Chandler 1	24.6
	Meeker 4 W	11.2
Stillwater	Cushing	19.5
	Perry	16.2
	Stillwater 2 W	1.8
Tulsa	Claremore 2 ENE	23.6
	Tulsa Intl Arpt	6.3
Yukon	El Reno 1 N	12.3
	Okla City Will Rogers World Arpt	11.2

Note: Miles is the distance between the geographic center of the city and the weather station.

See User Guide for station inclusion criteria.

Oklahoma Weather Stations by Elevation

Feet	Station Name
4,350	Kenton
3,310	Goodwell Research Stn
2,464	Arnett
2,464	Beaver
2,060	Erick
1,794	Buffalo
1,705	Taloga
1,609	Clinton
1,595	Geary
1,379	Altus Irig Res Station
1,350	Helena 1 SSE
1,314	El Reno 1 N
1,304	Okla City Will Rogers World Arpt
1,285	Frederick
1,274	Blanchard 2 SSW
1,245	Enid
1,180	Kansas 1 ESE
1,167	Anadarko 3 E
1,153	Chattanooga 3 NE
1,125	Duncan
1,109	Guthrie 5 S
1,024	Perry
1,015	Ada
1,004	Walters
1,000	Billings
1,000	Chickasaw Nra
999	Ponca City Municipal Arpt
950	Cushing
924	Chandler 1
924	Meeker 4 W
895	Stillwater 2 W
879	Ardmore
875	Waurika
859	Holdenville
834	Pawhuska
830	Mannford 6 NW
823	Bristow
733	Healdton
714	Bartlesville Frank Phillips
660	Sallisaw 2 NW
659	McCurtain 1 SE
649	Tulsa Intl Arpt
587	Claremore 2 ENE
583	Muskogee
549	Webbers Falls 5 WSW
520	Antlers
459	Idabel

See User Guide for station inclusion criteria.

Oklahoma City Int'l Airport

Oklahoma City is located along the North Canadian River, a frequently nearly-dry stream, at the geographic center of the state. The surrounding country is gently rolling with the nearest hills or low mountains, the Arbuckles, 80 miles south. The elevation ranges around 1,250 feet above sea level.

Although some influence is exerted at times by warm, moist air currents from the Gulf of Mexico, the climate of Oklahoma City falls mainly under continental controls characteristic of the Great Plains Region. The continental effect produces pronounced daily and seasonal temperature changes and considerable variation in seasonal and annual precipitation. Summers are long and usually hot. Winters are comparatively mild and short.

During the year, temperatures of 100 degrees or more occur on an average of 10 days, but have occurred on as many as 50 days or more. While summers are usually hot, the discomforting effect of extreme heat is considerably mitigated by low humidity and the prevalence of a moderate southerly breeze.

The length of the growing season varies from 180 to 251 days. Average date of last freeze is early April and average date of first freeze is early November. Freezes have occurred in early October.

During an average year, skies are clear approximately 40 percent of the time, partly cloudy 25 percent, and cloudy 35 percent of the time. The city is almost smoke-free as a result of favorable atmospheric conditions and the almost exclusive use of natural gas for heating.

Summer rainfall comes mainly from showers and thunderstorms. Winter precipitation is generally associated with frontal passages. Measurable precipitation has occurred on as many as 122 days and as few as 55 days during the year. The seasonal distribution of precipitation is normally 12 percent in winter, 34 percent in spring, 30 percent in summer, and 24 percent in fall. The The period with the least number of days with precipitation is November through January, and the month with the most rainy days is May. Thunderstorms occur most often in late spring and early summer. Large hail and/or destructive winds on occasion accompany these thunderstorms.

Snowfall averages less than 10 inches per year and seldom remains on the ground very long. Occasional brief periods of freezing rain and sleet storms occur.

Heavy fogs are infrequent. Prevailing winds are southerly except in January and February when northerly breezes predominate.

Oklahoma City Int'l Airport *Oklahoma County* Elevation: 1,304 ft. Latitude: 35° 23' N Longitude: 97° 36' W

	JAN	FEB	MAR	APR	MAY	JUN	JUL	AUG	SEP	OCT	NOV	DEC	YEAR
Mean Maximum Temp. (°F)	49.1	54.1	62.6	71.5	79.4	87.5	93.5	92.9	84.0	72.6	60.8	50.0	71.5
Mean Temp. (°F)	38.5	43.0	51.2	59.9	69.0	77.2	82.3	81.7	73.1	61.6	49.9	39.8	60.6
Mean Minimum Temp. (°F)	27.8	31.8	39.8	48.3	58.6	66.8	71.1	70.4	62.2	50.6	39.0	29.6	49.7
Extreme Maximum Temp. (°F)	80	92	92	98	104	105	110	110	108	95	87	76	110
Extreme Minimum Temp. (°F)	-4	-3	6	22	37	48	58	53	36	16	11	-8	-8
Days Maximum Temp. ≥ 90°F	0	0	0	0	3	11	23	23	9	1	0	0	70
Days Maximum Temp. ≤ 32°F	3	2	0	0	0	0	0	0	0	0	0	3	8
Days Minimum Temp. ≤ 32°F	22	14	7	1	0	0	0	0	0	1	8	19	72
Days Minimum Temp. ≤ 0°F	0	0	0	0	0	0	0	0	0	0	0	0	0
Heating Degree Days (base 65°F)	815	617	429	188	38	1	0	0	22	158	452	774	3,494
Cooling Degree Days (base 65°F)	0	1	9	43	170	373	544	524	273	60	5	0	2,002
Mean Precipitation (in.)	1.35	1.54	3.08	3.04	4.87	4.79	2.75	3.28	4.06	3.79	1.96	1.89	36.40
Maximum Precipitation (in.)*	5.7	4.6	7.8	7.3	12.1	14.7	8.4	6.8	11.8	13.2	5.7	8.1	46.5
Minimum Precipitation (in.)*	0	trace	0.1	0.2	0.9	0.6	trace	0.3	trace	trace	trace	trace	17.8
Extreme Maximum Daily Precip. (in.)	2.13	1.93	3.50	3.79	6.64	4.56	5.60	4.62	6.28	5.45	2.17	2.55	6.64
Days With ≥ 0.1" Precipitation	3	3	5	5	7	6	4	5	5	5	4	3	55
Days With ≥ 0.5" Precipitation	1	1	2	2	3	3	2	2	3	3	1	1	24
Days With ≥ 1.0" Precipitation	0	0	1	1	1	2	1	1	1	1	1	1	11
Mean Snowfall (in.)	2.7	1.4	0.9	trace	trace	trace	trace	trace	trace	trace	0.6	2.4	8.0
Maximum Snowfall (in.)*	17	12	14	1	0	0	0	0	0	trace	8	8	25
Maximum 24-hr. Snowfall (in.)*	8	7	8	1	0	0	0	0	0	trace	6	8	8
Maximum Snow Depth (in.)	12	5	4	trace	trace	trace	trace	trace	trace	trace	3	14	14
Days With ≥ 1.0" Snow Depth	3	1	0	0	0	0	0	0	0	0	0	2	6
Thunderstorm Days*	1	1	3	5	9	9	6	6	5	3	1	1	50
Foggy Days*	11	10	10	8	9	5	4	5	8	7	8	10	95
Predominant Sky Cover*	OVR	OVR	OVR	OVR	OVR	SCT	CLR	CLR	CLR	CLR	CLR	OVR	CLR
Mean Relative Humidity 6am (%)*	79	78	76	78	84	85	82	81	83	79	78	78	80
Mean Relative Humidity 3pm (%)*	53	52	47	46	53	52	45	44	48	46	48	52	49
Mean Dewpoint (°F)*	25	29	35	45	56	64	66	65	59	48	36	28	46
Prevailing Wind Direction*	N	N	SSE	SSE	SSE	SSE	SSE	SSE	SSE	SSE	S	S	SSE
Prevailing Wind Speed (mph)*	15	15	15	15	14	13	10	10	12	13	14	14	14
Maximum Wind Gust (mph)*	55	62	64	92	74	74	93	59	69	55	63	54	93

Note: (*) Period of record is 1945-1995

The period of record for National Weather Service station data is 1980 – 2009 except where noted. See User Guide for detailed explanation of data.

Tulsa Int'l Airport

The city of Tulsa lies along the Arkansas River at an elevation of 700 feet above sea level. The surrounding terrain is gently rolling.

At latitude 36 degrees, Tulsa is far enough north to escape the long periods of heat in summer, yet far enough south to miss the extreme cold of winter. The influence of warm moist air from the Gulf of Mexico is often noted, due to the high humidity, but the climate is essentially continental characterized by rapid changes in temperature. Generally the winter months are mild. Temperatures occasionally fall below zero but only last a very short time. Temperatures of 100 degrees or higher are often experienced from late July to early September, but are usually accompanied by low relative humidity and a good southerly breeze. The fall season is long with a great number of pleasant, sunny days and cool, bracing nights.

Rainfall is ample for most agricultural pursuits and is distributed favorably throughout the year. Spring is the wettest season, having an abundance of rain in the form of showers and thunderstorms. The steady rains of fall are a contrast to the spring and summer showers and provide a good supply of moisture and more ideal conditions for the growth of winter grains and pastures. The greatest amounts of snow are received in January and early March. The snow is usually light and only remains on the ground for brief periods.

The average date of the last 32 degree temperature occurrence is late March and the average date of the first 32 degree occurrence is early November. The average growing season is 216 days.

The Tulsa area is occasionally subjected to large hail and violent windstorms which occur mostly during spring and early summer, although occurrences have been noted throughout the year.

Prevailing surface winds are southerly during most of the year. Heavy fogs are infrequent. Sunshine is abundant. The prevalence of good flying weather throughout the year has contributed to the development of Tulsa as an aviation center.

Tulsa Int'l Airport *Tulsa County* Elevation: 649 ft. Latitude: 36° 12' N Longitude: 95° 53' W

	JAN	FEB	MAR	APR	MAY	JUN	JUL	AUG	SEP	OCT	NOV	DEC	YEAR
Mean Maximum Temp. (°F)	48.2	53.3	62.4	71.8	79.5	87.5	93.4	93.3	84.0	72.8	60.8	49.5	71.4
Mean Temp. (°F)	38.2	42.5	51.5	60.7	69.6	77.9	83.4	82.6	73.4	62.0	50.4	39.9	61.0
Mean Minimum Temp. (°F)	28.1	31.7	40.5	49.6	59.6	68.2	73.2	71.9	62.7	51.1	40.0	30.2	50.6
Extreme Maximum Temp. (°F)	78	90	94	95	97	102	111	109	108	93	86	77	111
Extreme Minimum Temp. (°F)	-5	-11	7	26	35	50	57	50	35	18	13	-8	-11
Days Maximum Temp. ≥ 90°F	0	0	0	1	3	12	24	23	9	1	0	0	73
Days Maximum Temp. ≤ 32°F	4	2	0	0	0	0	0	0	0	0	0	3	9
Days Minimum Temp. ≤ 32°F	21	15	7	1	0	0	0	0	0	1	7	18	70
Days Minimum Temp. ≤ 0°F	0	0	0	0	0	0	0	0	0	0	0	0	0
Heating Degree Days (base 65°F)	825	629	425	177	33	0	0	0	22	156	438	773	3,478
Cooling Degree Days (base 65°F)	0	1	12	56	182	393	577	553	280	69	8	1	2,132
Mean Precipitation (in.)	1.65	1.82	3.30	3.84	5.93	4.67	3.20	2.93	4.28	3.97	2.77	2.42	40.78
Maximum Precipitation (in.)*	6.6	5.7	11.9	8.7	11.3	11.2	11.4	6.7	18.8	9.3	7.3	8.7	69.9
Minimum Precipitation (in.)*	0	0.4	0.1	0.3	1.2	0.5	trace	0.3	trace	trace	trace	0.2	23.2
Extreme Maximum Daily Precip. (in.)	2.13	2.99	3.05	2.76	6.95	3.97	3.78	5.37	5.70	4.90	3.49	3.27	6.95
Days With ≥ 0.1" Precipitation	3	4	6	6	7	7	4	4	6	5	4	4	60
Days With ≥ 0.5" Precipitation	1	1	2	3	4	3	2	2	3	3	2	2	28
Days With ≥ 1.0" Precipitation	0	0	1	1	2	1	1	1	1	1	1	1	11
Mean Snowfall (in.)	2.5	1.9	1.9	trace	trace	trace	trace	0.0	trace	trace	0.7	2.3	9.3
Maximum Snowfall (in.)*	13	10	14	2	0	0	0	0	0	trace	6	10	29
Maximum 24-hr. Snowfall (in.)*	9	4	13	2	0	0	0	0	0	trace	4	8	13
Maximum Snow Depth (in.)	11	5	9	trace	trace	trace	trace	0	trace	trace	2	7	11
Days With ≥ 1.0" Snow Depth	2	2	1	0	0	0	0	0	0	0	0	2	7
Thunderstorm Days*	1	1	3	6	9	8	6	6	5	3	2	1	51
Foggy Days*	11	10	9	7	8	6	5	6	9	8	8	10	97
Predominant Sky Cover*	OVR	OVR	OVR	OVR	OVR	SCT	CLR	CLR	CLR	CLR	CLR	OVR	CLR
Mean Relative Humidity 6am (%)*	79	78	76	78	86	86	82	84	85	82	78	79	81
Mean Relative Humidity 3pm (%)*	54	51	47	47	54	54	48	46	49	46	49	53	50
Mean Dewpoint (°F)*	25	29	35	46	58	66	68	66	60	49	36	29	47
Prevailing Wind Direction*	S	S	S	S	S	S	S	S	S	S	S	S	S
Prevailing Wind Speed (mph)*	12	12	14	14	13	13	10	10	12	12	13	12	12
Maximum Wind Gust (mph)*	52	53	66	73	69	70	58	52	55	66	62	67	73

Note: (*) Period of record is 1948-1995

Ada *Pontotoc County* Elevation: 1,015 ft. Latitude: 34° 47' N Longitude: 96° 41' W

	JAN	FEB	MAR	APR	MAY	JUN	JUL	AUG	SEP	OCT	NOV	DEC	YEAR
Mean Maximum Temp. (°F)	51.9	56.7	65.1	73.5	80.5	87.7	93.5	93.6	85.8	75.0	63.4	52.9	73.3
Mean Temp. (°F)	40.2	44.5	52.6	60.8	69.4	77.0	82.3	81.9	73.6	62.6	51.6	41.5	61.5
Mean Minimum Temp. (°F)	28.4	32.2	40.1	48.0	58.2	66.3	71.1	70.2	61.4	50.2	39.7	30.1	49.7
Extreme Maximum Temp. (°F)	79	91	93	97	98	105	107	106	109	94	84	78	109
Extreme Minimum Temp. (°F)	-3	-1	5	25	38	47	56	51	36	18	14	-8	-8
Days Maximum Temp. ≥ 90°F	0	0	0	0	2	11	25	24	9	1	0	0	72
Days Maximum Temp. ≤ 32°F	2	1	0	0	0	0	0	0	0	0	0	2	5
Days Minimum Temp. ≤ 32°F	21	15	6	1	0	0	0	0	0	1	7	18	69
Days Minimum Temp. ≤ 0°F	0	0	0	0	0	0	0	0	0	0	0	0	0
Heating Degree Days (base 65°F)	762	575	387	160	29	1	0	0	18	134	402	721	3,189
Cooling Degree Days (base 65°F)	0	1	9	42	170	367	543	531	284	67	7	0	2,021
Mean Precipitation (in.)	1.96	2.25	3.60	3.67	5.25	4.85	2.91	2.95	4.38	4.09	2.71	2.62	41.24
Extreme Maximum Daily Precip. (in.)	3.14	3.25	3.44	4.43	5.73	5.16	3.51	6.42	8.16	6.25	2.71	3.37	8.16
Days With ≥ 0.1" Precipitation	4	4	6	5	7	6	4	4	5	5	5	4	59
Days With ≥ 0.5" Precipitation	1	2	3	2	3	3	2	2	3	3	2	2	28
Days With ≥ 1.0" Precipitation	0	1	1	1	2	1	1	1	1	1	1	1	12
Mean Snowfall (in.)	1.5	1.0	0.6	0.0	0.0	0.0	0.0	0.0	0.0	0.0	0.2	0.8	4.1
Maximum Snow Depth (in.)	12	5	trace	0	0	0	0	0	0	0	3	5	12
Days With ≥ 1.0" Snow Depth	0	0	0	0	0	0	0	0	0	0	0	0	0

Altus Irig Res Station *Jackson County* Elevation: 1,379 ft. Latitude: 34° 35' N Longitude: 99° 20' W

	JAN	FEB	MAR	APR	MAY	JUN	JUL	AUG	SEP	OCT	NOV	DEC	YEAR
Mean Maximum Temp. (°F)	54.1	58.5	67.4	76.5	84.6	92.4	97.5	96.2	88.0	77.2	64.9	53.7	75.9
Mean Temp. (°F)	40.5	44.6	53.1	61.7	71.3	79.5	84.1	83.0	74.8	63.4	51.5	41.0	62.4
Mean Minimum Temp. (°F)	26.9	30.6	38.8	46.8	57.9	66.7	70.7	69.8	61.5	49.6	38.1	28.2	48.8
Extreme Maximum Temp. (°F)	88	93	98	101	112	115	112	110	109	104	91	83	115
Extreme Minimum Temp. (°F)	-7	-7	7	23	34	48	55	54	28	17	12	-10	-10
Days Maximum Temp. ≥ 90°F	0	0	1	3	9	20	28	26	14	3	0	0	104
Days Maximum Temp. ≤ 32°F	2	1	0	0	0	0	0	0	0	0	0	2	5
Days Minimum Temp. ≤ 32°F	24	17	8	1	0	0	0	0	0	1	9	22	82
Days Minimum Temp. ≤ 0°F	0	0	0	0	0	0	0	0	0	0	0	0	0
Heating Degree Days (base 65°F)	752	571	376	150	25	0	0	0	16	124	405	737	3,156
Cooling Degree Days (base 65°F)	0	1	13	57	227	443	601	566	316	82	7	0	2,313
Mean Precipitation (in.)	1.06	1.19	2.00	2.33	4.27	4.34	2.00	2.73	2.69	2.77	1.57	1.37	28.32
Extreme Maximum Daily Precip. (in.)	2.12	2.15	3.22	4.06	4.60	5.87	3.18	3.75	5.26	7.10	2.98	1.78	7.10
Days With ≥ 0.1" Precipitation	2	3	4	4	5	6	3	4	4	4	3	3	45
Days With ≥ 0.5" Precipitation	1	1	1	1	3	3	1	2	2	2	1	1	19
Days With ≥ 1.0" Precipitation	0	0	1	1	1	1	0	1	1	1	0	0	7
Mean Snowfall (in.)	0.8	0.7	0.3	0.0	0.0	0.0	0.0	0.0	0.0	0.0	0.3	0.8	2.9
Maximum Snow Depth (in.)	3	4	2	0	0	0	0	0	0	0	6	5	6
Days With ≥ 1.0" Snow Depth	1	0	0	0	0	0	0	0	0	0	0	1	2

Anadarko 3 E *Caddo County* Elevation: 1,167 ft. Latitude: 35° 04' N Longitude: 98° 12' W

	JAN	FEB	MAR	APR	MAY	JUN	JUL	AUG	SEP	OCT	NOV	DEC	YEAR
Mean Maximum Temp. (°F)	50.4	55.0	63.4	72.3	80.6	88.0	93.8	93.3	85.2	73.9	61.9	50.5	72.3
Mean Temp. (°F)	37.6	42.0	50.3	58.8	68.8	76.7	81.8	81.0	72.6	61.0	***49.1***	38.5	***59.8***
Mean Minimum Temp. (°F)	24.8	29.0	37.1	45.2	57.0	65.4	69.8	68.7	59.8	48.1	36.4	26.4	47.3
Extreme Maximum Temp. (°F)	80	89	91	98	104	110	109	107	106	98	86	76	110
Extreme Minimum Temp. (°F)	-13	-3	5	18	33	42	49	45	29	16	11	-17	-17
Days Maximum Temp. ≥ 90°F	0	0	0	0	4	12	24	23	9	1	0	0	73
Days Maximum Temp. ≤ 32°F	3	2	0	0	0	0	0	0	0	0	0	2	7
Days Minimum Temp. ≤ 32°F	25	18	10	3	0	0	0	0	0	2	11	23	92
Days Minimum Temp. ≤ 0°F	0	0	0	0	0	0	0	0	0	0	0	0	0
Heating Degree Days (base 65°F)	840	642	459	216	42	2	0	0	27	175	***471***	816	***3,690***
Cooling Degree Days (base 65°F)	0	0	9	37	167	359	529	504	262	58	***5***	0	***1,930***
Mean Precipitation (in.)	1.11	1.53	2.52	2.64	4.65	4.40	2.25	3.18	2.95	3.46	1.69	1.76	32.14
Extreme Maximum Daily Precip. (in.)	3.68	***1.75***	***2.68***	3.85	3.28	***3.60***	***2.58***	***6.97***	***4.08***	***9.15***	***4.10***	***1.63***	***9.15***
Days With ≥ 0.1" Precipitation	2	3	4	4	6	5	3	4	4	4	3	3	45
Days With ≥ 0.5" Precipitation	1	1	2	2	3	3	2	2	2	2	1	1	22
Days With ≥ 1.0" Precipitation	0	0	1	1	1	1	1	1	1	1	1	0	9
Mean Snowfall (in.)	0.6	0.2	0.1	0.0	0.0	0.0	0.0	0.0	0.0	0.0	trace	0.7	1.6
Maximum Snow Depth (in.)	13	2	trace	0	0	0	0	0	0	0	trace	4	13
Days With ≥ 1.0" Snow Depth	1	0	0	0	0	0	0	0	0	0	0	0	1

Antlers *Pushmataha County* Elevation: 520 ft. Latitude: 34° 15' N Longitude: 95° 39' W

	JAN	FEB	MAR	APR	MAY	JUN	JUL	AUG	SEP	OCT	NOV	DEC	YEAR
Mean Maximum Temp. (°F)	53.6	58.5	66.1	74.9	81.1	88.2	93.2	***93.9***	86.3	75.7	***64.5***	54.7	***74.2***
Mean Temp. (°F)	41.8	46.4	53.8	62.0	69.9	77.4	81.4	***81.4***	73.7	62.8	***53.1***	43.4	***62.3***
Mean Minimum Temp. (°F)	30.0	34.3	41.4	49.0	58.7	66.6	69.6	***68.8***	60.9	49.8	***41.6***	32.0	***50.2***
Extreme Maximum Temp. (°F)	79	90	90	95	97	103	108	108	110	96	86	82	110
Extreme Minimum Temp. (°F)	0	3	11	25	35	47	53	51	37	21	15	-5	-5
Days Maximum Temp. ≥ 90°F	0	0	0	1	2	***12***	24	23	11	1	0	0	***74***
Days Maximum Temp. ≤ 32°F	1	1	0	0	0	0	0	0	0	0	0	1	3
Days Minimum Temp. ≤ 32°F	20	13	6	1	0	0	0	0	0	1	7	17	65
Days Minimum Temp. ≤ 0°F	0	0	0	0	0	0	0	0	0	0	0	0	0
Heating Degree Days (base 65°F)	713	520	352	137	***26***	0	0	***0***	18	132	***363***	665	***2,926***
Cooling Degree Days (base 65°F)	1	2	11	54	***190***	380	516	***514***	284	72	***12***	2	***2,038***
Mean Precipitation (in.)	***2.54***	2.67	4.11	4.14	***5.95***	4.94	3.27	2.33	3.70	5.20	3.96	***3.49***	***46.30***
Extreme Maximum Daily Precip. (in.)	***3.60***	***2.95***	***5.66***	***5.30***	na	***3.20***	***5.50***	***2.70***	***6.62***	***8.58***	na	na	na
Days With ≥ 0.1" Precipitation	***4***	4	5	5	***7***	7	4	3	4	6	4	***5***	***58***
Days With ≥ 0.5" Precipitation	***2***	2	3	2	***4***	3	2	2	2	3	2	***2***	***29***
Days With ≥ 1.0" Precipitation	***1***	1	1	1	***2***	2	1	1	1	2	1	***1***	***15***
Mean Snowfall (in.)	***0.2***	***0.2***	trace	0.0	0.0	0.0	0.0	0.0	0.0	0.0	0.0	trace	***0.4***
Maximum Snow Depth (in.)	***0***	***0***	***0***	0	***0***	***0***	0	***0***	0	***0***	***0***	trace	trace
Days With ≥ 1.0" Snow Depth	***0***	0	0	0	0	0	0	0	0	0	0	0	***0***

The period of record for all cooperative weather station data is 1980 – 2009. See User Guide for detailed explanation of data.

Ardmore *Carter County* Elevation: 879 ft. Latitude: 34° 10' N Longitude: 97° 08' W

	JAN	FEB	MAR	APR	MAY	JUN	JUL	AUG	SEP	OCT	NOV	DEC	YEAR
Mean Maximum Temp. (°F)	53.6	58.1	66.5	74.8	81.8	89.1	94.3	94.8	86.9	76.7	64.4	54.6	74.6
Mean Temp. (°F)	42.8	47.1	55.0	63.4	71.6	79.2	83.8	83.8	76.0	65.4	53.8	44.2	63.8
Mean Minimum Temp. (°F)	32.0	36.1	43.5	51.9	61.4	69.2	73.2	72.7	64.9	54.1	43.1	33.6	53.0
Extreme Maximum Temp. (°F)	83	93	93	99	100	112	110	108	110	98	85	80	112
Extreme Minimum Temp. (°F)	2	-1	12	26	41	50	58	55	39	20	17	-8	-8
Days Maximum Temp. ≥ 90°F	0	0	0	0	4	14	25	25	11	1	0	0	80
Days Maximum Temp. ≤ 32°F	2	1	0	0	0	0	0	0	0	0	0	2	5
Days Minimum Temp. ≤ 32°F	17	9	4	0	0	0	0	0	0	0	4	14	48
Days Minimum Temp. ≤ 0°F	0	0	0	0	0	0	0	0	0	0	0	0	0
Heating Degree Days (base 65°F)	680	501	319	115	17	0	0	0	12	91	344	640	2,719
Cooling Degree Days (base 65°F)	1	2	18	73	231	432	590	589	348	112	14	1	2,411
Mean Precipitation (in.)	1.88	2.18	2.63	3.21	5.42	4.24	2.70	2.15	3.77	4.23	2.39	2.34	37.14
Extreme Maximum Daily Precip. (in.)	3.10	2.59	2.68	5.20	6.18	4.08	3.64	3.00	4.21	6.50	2.79	2.86	6.50
Days With ≥ 0.1" Precipitation	3	4	4	5	7	6	3	4	4	5	4	4	53
Days With ≥ 0.5" Precipitation	1	2	2	2	3	3	2	1	2	3	2	2	25
Days With ≥ 1.0" Precipitation	0	0	1	1	2	1	1	1	1	2	1	1	12
Mean Snowfall (in.)	1.0	0.5	0.3	0.0	0.0	0.0	0.0	0.0	0.0	trace	0.1	0.7	2.6
Maximum Snow Depth (in.)	7	2	2	0	0	0	0	0	0	trace	1	8	8
Days With ≥ 1.0" Snow Depth	0	0	0	0	0	0	0	0	0	0	0	1	1

Arnett *Ellis County* Elevation: 2,464 ft. Latitude: 36° 08' N Longitude: 99° 46' W

	JAN	FEB	MAR	APR	MAY	JUN	JUL	AUG	SEP	OCT	NOV	DEC	YEAR
Mean Maximum Temp. (°F)	46.8	51.0	58.9	69.3	77.5	85.6	92.2	91.5	82.6	71.0	58.0	47.3	69.3
Mean Temp. (°F)	34.3	38.3	45.9	55.7	65.2	73.9	79.7	78.7	69.9	57.9	45.3	35.4	56.7
Mean Minimum Temp. (°F)	21.8	25.5	32.8	42.1	52.8	62.2	67.1	65.9	57.2	44.8	32.5	23.4	44.0
Extreme Maximum Temp. (°F)	85	88	93	98	101	110	109	105	105	97	88	78	110
Extreme Minimum Temp. (°F)	-11	-9	1	18	31	44	52	51	30	14	7	-11	-11
Days Maximum Temp. ≥ 90°F	0	0	0	1	3	10	21	20	8	1	0	0	64
Days Maximum Temp. ≤ 32°F	5	4	1	0	0	0	0	0	0	0	1	5	16
Days Minimum Temp. ≤ 32°F	28	21	15	4	0	0	0	0	0	3	15	27	113
Days Minimum Temp. ≤ 0°F	1	1	0	0	0	0	0	0	0	0	0	1	3
Heating Degree Days (base 65°F)	944	749	589	294	91	10	1	2	51	242	586	912	4,471
Cooling Degree Days (base 65°F)	0	0	3	23	104	284	462	434	206	30	1	0	1,547
Mean Precipitation (in.)	0.75	1.03	2.03	2.22	4.07	3.89	2.17	2.26	2.56	2.42	1.25	1.10	25.75
Extreme Maximum Daily Precip. (in.)	1.00	1.20	2.23	1.91	3.92	4.38	2.50	2.92	2.46	5.55	2.69	1.86	5.55
Days With ≥ 0.1" Precipitation	2	2	4	4	5	6	4	4	4	3	2	2	42
Days With ≥ 0.5" Precipitation	0	1	1	2	3	3	1	1	2	1	1	1	17
Days With ≥ 1.0" Precipitation	0	0	1	1	1	1	1	1	1	1	0	0	8
Mean Snowfall (in.)	1.4	1.7	1.0	trace	0.0	0.0	0.0	0.0	0.0	trace	0.9	na	na
Maximum Snow Depth (in.)	12	7	9	1	0	0	0	0	0	trace	12	10	12
Days With ≥ 1.0" Snow Depth	3	3	1	0	0	0	0	0	0	0	1	4	12

Bartlesville Frank Phillips *Osage County* Elevation: 714 ft. Latitude: 36° 45' N Longitude: 96° 00' W

	JAN	FEB	MAR	APR	MAY	JUN	JUL	AUG	SEP	OCT	NOV	DEC	YEAR
Mean Maximum Temp. (°F)	48.2	53.6	62.7	72.9	80.1	87.8	94.0	94.0	85.3	73.6	60.8	49.2	71.8
Mean Temp. (°F)	36.5	41.2	50.1	60.2	68.7	76.7	82.1	81.2	72.5	60.7	49.0	38.2	59.8
Mean Minimum Temp. (°F)	24.7	28.7	37.5	47.6	57.2	65.6	70.2	68.4	59.7	47.8	37.2	27.2	47.6
Extreme Maximum Temp. (°F)	78	91	92	95	98	104	112	111	109	96	88	78	112
Extreme Minimum Temp. (°F)	-13	-15	4	23	33	44	54	46	29	16	11	-13	-15
Days Maximum Temp. ≥ 90°F	0	0	0	1	3	13	25	24	10	1	0	0	77
Days Maximum Temp. ≤ 32°F	4	2	0	0	0	0	0	0	0	0	0	3	9
Days Minimum Temp. ≤ 32°F	24	18	11	1	0	0	0	0	0	2	11	21	88
Days Minimum Temp. ≤ 0°F	0	0	0	0	0	0	0	0	0	0	0	1	1
Heating Degree Days (base 65°F)	877	667	463	189	42	1	0	0	29	180	479	824	3,751
Cooling Degree Days (base 65°F)	0	1	10	53	162	360	538	510	259	53	6	1	1,953
Mean Precipitation (in.)	1.57	2.06	3.56	4.00	4.99	5.08	3.09	2.86	4.06	3.36	2.76	2.24	39.63
Extreme Maximum Daily Precip. (in.)	2.25	4.44	4.06	3.57	4.85	4.20	5.15	5.50	7.07	3.18	3.12	3.47	7.07
Days With ≥ 0.1" Precipitation	3	4	6	6	7	6	4	4	5	5	4	4	58
Days With ≥ 0.5" Precipitation	1	1	2	3	4	3	2	2	2	2	2	2	26
Days With ≥ 1.0" Precipitation	0	0	1	1	2	2	1	1	1	1	1	1	12
Mean Snowfall (in.)	2.5	2.3	1.5	0.0	0.0	0.0	0.0	0.0	0.0	trace	0.2	2.9	9.4
Maximum Snow Depth (in.)	11	12	5	0	0	0	0	0	0	trace	1	10	12
Days With ≥ 1.0" Snow Depth	3	2	0	0	0	0	0	0	0	0	0	3	8

Beaver *Beaver County* Elevation: 2,464 ft. Latitude: 36° 49' N Longitude: 100° 32' W

	JAN	FEB	MAR	APR	MAY	JUN	JUL	AUG	SEP	OCT	NOV	DEC	YEAR
Mean Maximum Temp. (°F)	47.5	51.8	59.7	70.1	79.0	88.4	94.6	92.9	84.5	72.4	59.7	47.9	70.7
Mean Temp. (°F)	33.2	36.9	44.8	54.7	64.9	74.5	80.4	78.9	70.0	57.1	44.2	33.7	56.1
Mean Minimum Temp. (°F)	18.9	22.0	29.9	39.2	50.7	60.6	66.1	64.9	55.4	41.7	28.6	19.4	41.5
Extreme Maximum Temp. (°F)	80	88	93	102	107	113	109	109	108	98	89	78	113
Extreme Minimum Temp. (°F)	-18	-17	0	16	26	41	47	45	27	13	-6	-13	-18
Days Maximum Temp. ≥ 90°F	0	0	0	1	5	14	24	22	10	2	0	0	78
Days Maximum Temp. ≤ 32°F	5	4	1	0	0	0	0	0	0	0	1	5	16
Days Minimum Temp. ≤ 32°F	30	25	19	7	0	0	0	0	0	5	20	29	135
Days Minimum Temp. ≤ 0°F	1	1	0	0	0	0	0	0	0	0	0	1	3
Heating Degree Days (base 65°F)	978	789	620	325	104	10	1	2	49	271	617	964	4,730
Cooling Degree Days (base 65°F)	0	0	2	21	108	303	486	440	206	33	0	0	1,599
Mean Precipitation (in.)	0.61	0.72	1.84	1.84	2.71	3.69	2.68	2.84	1.68	1.66	0.88	0.98	22.13
Extreme Maximum Daily Precip. (in.)	1.15	1.07	1.88	2.82	4.50	5.07	4.44	4.20	1.76	2.42	2.13	2.57	5.07
Days With ≥ 0.1" Precipitation	2	2	4	4	5	6	4	4	3	3	2	2	41
Days With ≥ 0.5" Precipitation	0	1	1	1	2	2	2	2	1	1	0	0	13
Days With ≥ 1.0" Precipitation	0	0	0	0	0	1	1	1	0	0	0	0	3
Mean Snowfall (in.)	2.3	1.4	1.9	0.3	0.0	0.0	0.0	0.0	0.0	0.1	0.6	1.9	8.5
Maximum Snow Depth (in.)	9	na	21	5	0	0	0	0	0	2	6	18	na
Days With ≥ 1.0" Snow Depth	1	1	0	0	0	0	0	0	0	0	0	1	3

The period of record for all cooperative weather station data is 1980 – 2009. See User Guide for detailed explanation of data.

Billings *Noble County* Elevation: 1,000 ft. Latitude: 36° 32' N Longitude: 97° 27' W

	JAN	FEB	MAR	APR	MAY	JUN	JUL	AUG	SEP	OCT	NOV	DEC	YEAR
Mean Maximum Temp. (°F)	46.1	50.9	59.6	69.4	78.3	87.8	93.9	92.9	84.3	72.4	59.3	47.0	70.2
Mean Temp. (°F)	34.8	39.1	47.8	56.9	67.1	76.6	82.1	81.0	72.1	60.0	47.7	36.4	58.5
Mean Minimum Temp. (°F)	23.5	27.1	35.7	44.4	55.7	65.3	70.3	69.1	59.9	47.5	36.0	25.9	46.7
Extreme Maximum Temp. (°F)	79	90	91	98	104	106	113	110	108	96	87	76	113
Extreme Minimum Temp. (°F)	-15	-12	0	23	31	46	49	45	29	11	11	-13	-15
Days Maximum Temp. ≥ 90°F	0	0	0	0	2	12	24	22	9	1	0	0	70
Days Maximum Temp. ≤ 32°F	5	3	1	0	0	0	0	0	0	0	0	4	13
Days Minimum Temp. ≤ 32°F	26	19	11	3	0	0	0	0	0	2	11	23	95
Days Minimum Temp. ≤ 0°F	0	0	0	0	0	0	0	0	0	0	0	1	1
Heating Degree Days (base 65°F)	929	728	529	264	63	3	0	0	32	198	516	880	4,142
Cooling Degree Days (base 65°F)	0	0	4	28	132	350	537	504	254	47	4	0	1,860
Mean Precipitation (in.)	1.12	1.49	3.22	3.41	4.47	5.00	3.08	3.21	3.33	3.45	2.17	1.58	35.53
Extreme Maximum Daily Precip. (in.)	1.75	3.20	2.75	3.90	3.65	4.80	3.40	4.56	4.33	7.88	3.35	2.12	7.88
Days With ≥ 0.1" Precipitation	2	3	5	5	6	6	4	4	4	4	3	3	49
Days With ≥ 0.5" Precipitation	1	1	2	2	3	3	2	2	2	2	1	1	22
Days With ≥ 1.0" Precipitation	0	0	1	1	2	2	1	1	1	1	1	0	11
Mean Snowfall (in.)	2.0	2.3	1.5	trace	trace	0.0	0.0	0.0	0.0	trace	0.2	2.3	8.3
Maximum Snow Depth (in.)	12	8	12	trace	trace	0	0	0	0	trace	6	9	12
Days With ≥ 1.0" Snow Depth	2	1	1	0	0	0	0	0	0	0	0	2	6

Blanchard 2 SSW *Mcclain County* Elevation: 1,274 ft. Latitude: 35° 07' N Longitude: 97° 40' W

	JAN	FEB	MAR	APR	MAY	JUN	JUL	AUG	SEP	OCT	NOV	DEC	YEAR
Mean Maximum Temp. (°F)	51.1	55.6	63.9	73.0	80.4	87.4	94.0	93.6	85.4	74.3	62.2	51.1	72.7
Mean Temp. (°F)	40.0	43.9	51.9	60.9	69.6	76.8	82.4	81.9	73.7	62.5	51.0	40.5	61.3
Mean Minimum Temp. (°F)	28.9	32.2	39.9	48.7	58.7	66.1	70.8	70.1	61.9	50.6	39.6	29.9	49.8
Extreme Maximum Temp. (°F)	81	91	93	98	102	107	109	107	110	97	86	76	110
Extreme Minimum Temp. (°F)	-6	-2	6	25	35	45	56	52	36	18	10	-11	-11
Days Maximum Temp. ≥ 90°F	0	0	0	0	3	11	24	24	9	1	0	0	72
Days Maximum Temp. ≤ 32°F	3	2	0	0	0	0	0	0	0	0	0	2	7
Days Minimum Temp. ≤ 32°F	20	14	7	1	0	0	0	0	0	1	7	19	69
Days Minimum Temp. ≤ 0°F	0	0	0	0	0	0	0	0	0	0	0	0	0
Heating Degree Days (base 65°F)	769	591	410	172	32	2	0	0	19	140	422	752	3,309
Cooling Degree Days (base 65°F)	0	1	12	51	182	361	548	530	285	70	7	0	2,047
Mean Precipitation (in.)	1.36	1.72	2.93	3.26	5.03	4.45	2.64	3.16	3.83	3.57	2.06	2.04	36.05
Extreme Maximum Daily Precip. (in.)	2.82	2.18	3.13	3.05	7.65	3.30	4.88	5.21	3.50	8.60	2.23	2.72	8.60
Days With ≥ 0.1" Precipitation	2	3	5	4	6	6	4	5	5	5	4	3	52
Days With ≥ 0.5" Precipitation	1	1	2	2	3	3	2	2	3	2	2	1	24
Days With ≥ 1.0" Precipitation	0	0	1	1	2	2	1	1	1	1	0	1	11
Mean Snowfall (in.)	2.2	0.9	0.6	0.0	0.0	0.0	0.0	0.0	0.0	trace	0.5	1.7	5.9
Maximum Snow Depth (in.)	6	***4***	5	0	0	1	0	0	0	0	6	8	***8***
Days With ≥ 1.0" Snow Depth	1	***0***	0	0	0	0	0	0	0	0	0	1	***2***

Bristow *Creek County* Elevation: 823 ft. Latitude: 35° 50' N Longitude: 96° 23' W

	JAN	FEB	MAR	APR	MAY	JUN	JUL	AUG	SEP	OCT	NOV	DEC	YEAR
Mean Maximum Temp. (°F)	51.1	56.4	65.1	74.1	80.7	87.9	93.9	94.1	85.6	74.8	62.6	51.7	73.2
Mean Temp. (°F)	39.5	44.0	52.5	61.2	69.4	76.9	82.0	81.4	73.0	62.0	50.9	40.5	61.1
Mean Minimum Temp. (°F)	27.8	31.4	39.8	48.3	58.0	65.8	70.0	68.7	60.2	49.2	39.1	29.2	49.0
Extreme Maximum Temp. (°F)	78	92	93	98	98	103	111	109	110	95	87	77	111
Extreme Minimum Temp. (°F)	-9	-12	2	24	34	45	54	46	28	16	12	-14	-14
Days Maximum Temp. ≥ 90°F	0	0	0	1	3	12	24	23	10	1	0	0	74
Days Maximum Temp. ≤ 32°F	3	1	0	0	0	0	0	0	0	0	0	2	6
Days Minimum Temp. ≤ 32°F	22	16	8	2	0	0	0	0	0	2	9	19	78
Days Minimum Temp. ≤ 0°F	0	0	0	0	0	0	0	0	0	0	0	0	0
Heating Degree Days (base 65°F)	785	591	396	167	35	1	0	0	24	152	426	753	3,330
Cooling Degree Days (base 65°F)	0	1	14	60	178	363	533	516	269	67	9	1	2,011
Mean Precipitation (in.)	1.64	2.06	3.41	3.54	5.63	4.93	2.65	2.74	4.14	4.28	2.98	2.65	40.65
Extreme Maximum Daily Precip. (in.)	3.05	4.29	2.76	5.73	4.36	3.98	4.10	3.40	4.85	5.60	3.82	3.45	5.73
Days With ≥ 0.1" Precipitation	3	4	5	5	7	6	4	4	5	5	4	4	56
Days With ≥ 0.5" Precipitation	1	1	2	2	4	4	2	2	3	2	2	2	27
Days With ≥ 1.0" Precipitation	1	0	1	1	2	2	1	1	1	1	1	1	13
Mean Snowfall (in.)	2.6	1.6	1.3	0.0	0.0	0.0	0.0	0.0	0.0	trace	0.4	1.9	7.8
Maximum Snow Depth (in.)	11	7	14	0	0	0	0	0	0	1	4	6	14
Days With ≥ 1.0" Snow Depth	2	1	0	0	0	0	0	0	0	0	0	1	4

Buffalo *Harper County* Elevation: 1,794 ft. Latitude: 36° 51' N Longitude: 99° 38' W

	JAN	FEB	MAR	APR	MAY	JUN	JUL	AUG	SEP	OCT	NOV	DEC	YEAR
Mean Maximum Temp. (°F)	50.4	56.0	64.4	73.5	82.3	91.3	97.5	96.0	87.8	75.4	61.9	50.3	73.9
Mean Temp. (°F)	36.3	40.7	49.2	58.0	68.2	77.4	83.2	81.7	73.3	60.7	47.6	37.0	59.5
Mean Minimum Temp. (°F)	22.3	25.9	34.0	42.6	54.1	63.5	68.8	67.5	58.8	45.9	33.4	23.6	45.0
Extreme Maximum Temp. (°F)	87	91	95	105	108	111	115	111	112	100	93	78	115
Extreme Minimum Temp. (°F)	-14	-13	-3	19	30	42	45	45	26	13	6	-10	-14
Days Maximum Temp. ≥ 90°F	0	0	0	2	7	17	26	24	14	3	0	0	93
Days Maximum Temp. ≤ 32°F	3	2	0	0	0	0	0	0	0	0	0	3	8
Days Minimum Temp. ≤ 32°F	27	20	13	4	0	0	0	0	0	2	14	26	106
Days Minimum Temp. ≤ 0°F	0	1	0	0	0	0	0	0	0	0	0	1	2
Heating Degree Days (base 65°F)	882	678	491	244	59	3	0	1	25	191	517	862	3,953
Cooling Degree Days (base 65°F)	0	0	7	41	166	383	571	526	282	63	3	0	2,042
Mean Precipitation (in.)	0.56	0.91	1.90	2.20	3.46	4.06	2.09	2.93	2.01	2.13	1.07	0.94	24.26
Extreme Maximum Daily Precip. (in.)	1.55	1.80	2.65	4.00	3.60	5.45	2.88	4.85	2.92	3.52	2.90	2.55	5.45
Days With ≥ 0.1" Precipitation	2	2	4	4	6	6	4	5	3	4	2	2	44
Days With ≥ 0.5" Precipitation	0	0	1	1	2	3	1	2	1	1	0	0	12
Days With ≥ 1.0" Precipitation	0	0	1	1	1	1	1	1	1	1	0	0	8
Mean Snowfall (in.)	1.8	2.8	1.9	0.2	0.0	0.0	0.0	0.0	0.0	trace	1.6	3.6	11.9
Maximum Snow Depth (in.)	7	6	12	7	0	0	0	0	0	trace	16	***12***	***16***
Days With ≥ 1.0" Snow Depth	1	1	0	0	0	0	0	0	0	0	0	***2***	***4***

The period of record for all cooperative weather station data is 1980 – 2009. See User Guide for detailed explanation of data.

Chandler 1 *Lincoln County* Elevation: 924 ft. Latitude: 35° 42' N Longitude: 96° 53' W

	JAN	FEB	MAR	APR	MAY	JUN	JUL	AUG	SEP	OCT	NOV	DEC	YEAR
Mean Maximum Temp. (°F)	50.2	55.0	64.1	72.8	80.2	87.8	93.5	93.2	84.8	73.9	62.6	51.6	72.5
Mean Temp. (°F)	38.9	42.9	52.0	60.1	69.1	77.1	82.3	81.6	73.1	61.8	51.0	40.4	60.9
Mean Minimum Temp. (°F)	27.6	30.8	39.7	47.3	57.9	66.3	71.0	69.9	61.4	49.7	39.4	29.1	49.2
Extreme Maximum Temp. (°F)	80	92	93	101	100	105	111	108	110	98	86	77	111
Extreme Minimum Temp. (°F)	-6	-7	7	12	31	49	54	52	37	23	11	-13	-13
Days Maximum Temp. ≥ 90°F	0	0	0	1	3	12	23	22	9	1	0	0	71
Days Maximum Temp. ≤ 32°F	3	2	0	0	0	0	0	0	0	0	0	2	7
Days Minimum Temp. ≤ 32°F	22	16	7	2	0	0	0	0	0	1	7	19	74
Days Minimum Temp. ≤ 0°F	0	0	0	0	0	0	0	0	0	0	0	0	0
Heating Degree Days (base 65°F)	801	618	409	190	38	1	0	0	21	155	419	757	3,409
Cooling Degree Days (base 65°F)	0	1	12	50	171	370	542	521	270	61	8	0	2,006
Mean Precipitation (in.)	1.34	1.79	3.16	3.22	4.81	4.55	2.48	3.18	3.90	3.77	2.54	1.81	36.55
Extreme Maximum Daily Precip. (in.)	3.50	***4.15***	***2.63***	***4.10***	***4.42***	***3.35***	***4.50***	4.93	***4.22***	6.41	***3.75***	2.50	***6.41***
Days With ≥ 0.1" Precipitation	2	2	4	4	6	5	3	4	4	4	4	3	45
Days With ≥ 0.5" Precipitation	1	1	2	2	3	3	2	2	3	2	2	1	24
Days With ≥ 1.0" Precipitation	0	1	1	1	2	2	1	1	1	1	1	1	13
Mean Snowfall (in.)	1.8	1.0	0.3	0.0	0.0	0.0	0.0	0.0	0.0	trace	0.3	0.8	4.2
Maximum Snow Depth (in.)	8	4	9	0	0	0	0	0	0	1	6	6	9
Days With ≥ 1.0" Snow Depth	1	0	0	0	0	0	0	0	0	0	0	0	1

Chattanooga 3 NE *Comanche County* Elevation: 1,153 ft. Latitude: 34° 27' N Longitude: 98° 37' W

	JAN	FEB	MAR	APR	MAY	JUN	JUL	AUG	SEP	OCT	NOV	DEC	YEAR
Mean Maximum Temp. (°F)	53.2	57.7	66.0	75.5	83.9	92.4	98.1	97.3	89.0	77.9	64.2	53.4	75.7
Mean Temp. (°F)	40.1	44.2	52.3	61.0	70.9	79.3	84.3	83.6	75.4	64.1	51.2	41.1	62.3
Mean Minimum Temp. (°F)	27.0	30.7	38.6	46.4	57.8	66.2	70.4	69.8	61.7	50.3	38.2	28.6	48.8
Extreme Maximum Temp. (°F)	82	92	94	103	111	116	113	110	113	103	88	81	116
Extreme Minimum Temp. (°F)	-9	-4	5	24	36	47	58	53	34	16	12	-13	-13
Days Maximum Temp. ≥ 90°F	0	0	0	2	8	21	28	27	15	4	0	0	105
Days Maximum Temp. ≤ 32°F	2	1	0	0	0	0	0	0	0	0	0	2	5
Days Minimum Temp. ≤ 32°F	24	16	8	2	0	0	0	0	0	1	9	21	81
Days Minimum Temp. ≤ 0°F	0	0	0	0	0	0	0	0	0	0	0	0	0
Heating Degree Days (base 65°F)	765	582	396	162	25	0	0	0	14	113	413	735	3,205
Cooling Degree Days (base 65°F)	0	0	9	47	216	436	605	583	334	93	6	0	2,329
Mean Precipitation (in.)	1.14	1.51	2.53	2.61	4.75	4.34	1.91	2.69	2.62	3.42	1.70	1.74	30.96
Extreme Maximum Daily Precip. (in.)	1.83	2.09	2.65	4.13	5.15	4.47	3.97	5.00	3.52	4.26	2.62	3.01	5.15
Days With ≥ 0.1" Precipitation	2	3	4	4	6	5	3	4	4	4	3	3	45
Days With ≥ 0.5" Precipitation	1	1	2	2	3	3	1	2	2	2	1	1	21
Days With ≥ 1.0" Precipitation	0	0	1	1	2	1	1	1	1	1	1	0	10
Mean Snowfall (in.)	0.7	0.5	0.1	0.0	0.0	0.0	0.0	0.0	0.0	trace	0.2	0.6	2.1
Maximum Snow Depth (in.)	3	3	trace	0	0	0	0	0	0	trace	4	3	4
Days With ≥ 1.0" Snow Depth	0	0	0	0	0	0	0	0	0	0	0	0	0

Chickasaw Nra *Murray County* Elevation: 1,000 ft. Latitude: 34° 30' N Longitude: 96° 58' W

	JAN	FEB	MAR	APR	MAY	JUN	JUL	AUG	SEP	OCT	NOV	DEC	YEAR
Mean Maximum Temp. (°F)	50.9	55.8	63.8	72.8	79.5	87.2	93.2	93.9	85.7	74.6	62.7	52.6	72.7
Mean Temp. (°F)	39.1	43.7	52.1	60.6	69.0	77.0	82.1	81.9	73.8	62.3	51.1	41.1	61.2
Mean Minimum Temp. (°F)	27.2	31.6	40.4	48.5	58.5	66.8	70.9	69.9	61.8	50.0	39.4	29.6	49.5
Extreme Maximum Temp. (°F)	82	92	94	98	99	108	109	109	111	96	88	78	111
Extreme Minimum Temp. (°F)	-5	-1	5	19	35	44	54	49	33	15	15	-11	-11
Days Maximum Temp. ≥ 90°F	0	0	0	0	2	10	23	24	10	1	0	0	70
Days Maximum Temp. ≤ 32°F	3	2	0	0	0	0	0	0	0	0	0	2	7
Days Minimum Temp. ≤ 32°F	23	15	7	1	0	0	0	0	0	1	8	19	74
Days Minimum Temp. ≤ 0°F	0	0	0	0	0	0	0	0	0	0	0	0	0
Heating Degree Days (base 65°F)	796	596	403	177	39	1	0	0	24	153	421	734	3,344
Cooling Degree Days (base 65°F)	0	1	11	53	172	369	538	531	295	76	9	0	2,055
Mean Precipitation (in.)	1.98	2.17	3.62	3.63	5.64	4.62	3.17	2.45	4.68	4.53	2.67	2.58	41.74
Extreme Maximum Daily Precip. (in.)	3.30	2.42	4.20	5.30	5.27	3.60	4.08	5.10	7.26	5.54	2.11	3.31	7.26
Days With ≥ 0.1" Precipitation	3	4	5	5	7	6	4	4	5	6	4	4	57
Days With ≥ 0.5" Precipitation	1	2	2	2	3	3	2	1	3	3	2	2	26
Days With ≥ 1.0" Precipitation	0	1	1	1	2	1	1	1	2	1	1	1	13
Mean Snowfall (in.)	1.8	0.7	0.4	0.0	0.0	0.0	0.0	0.0	0.0	trace	0.2	0.4	3.5
Maximum Snow Depth (in.)	13	3	1	0	0	0	0	0	0	0	1	3	13
Days With ≥ 1.0" Snow Depth	1	1	0	0	0	0	0	0	0	0	0	1	3

Claremore 2 ENE *Rogers County* Elevation: 587 ft. Latitude: 36° 19' N Longitude: 95° 35' W

	JAN	FEB	MAR	APR	MAY	JUN	JUL	AUG	SEP	OCT	NOV	DEC	YEAR
Mean Maximum Temp. (°F)	46.6	52.0	60.7	70.2	78.1	86.1	92.0	92.4	83.7	72.4	59.7	48.7	70.2
Mean Temp. (°F)	35.3	39.9	48.7	57.9	67.1	75.7	81.0	80.5	71.9	59.9	48.4	37.8	58.7
Mean Minimum Temp. (°F)	24.0	27.7	36.6	45.6	56.2	65.2	69.9	68.5	60.0	47.5	37.0	26.8	47.1
Extreme Maximum Temp. (°F)	77	90	93	95	95	102	108	109	107	92	85	76	109
Extreme Minimum Temp. (°F)	-20	-16	-3	23	33	45	52	51	32	17	13	-12	-20
Days Maximum Temp. ≥ 90°F	0	0	0	0	1	9	22	21	8	1	0	0	62
Days Maximum Temp. ≤ 32°F	4	3	1	0	0	0	0	0	0	0	0	3	11
Days Minimum Temp. ≤ 32°F	25	20	11	2	0	0	0	0	0	2	11	22	93
Days Minimum Temp. ≤ 0°F	0	0	0	0	0	0	0	0	0	0	0	1	1
Heating Degree Days (base 65°F)	913	704	505	240	61	3	0	0	33	199	499	838	3,995
Cooling Degree Days (base 65°F)	0	0	6	35	134	329	502	487	246	48	6	0	1,793
Mean Precipitation (in.)	1.90	2.27	3.65	4.31	5.38	5.02	4.02	3.33	4.63	3.91	3.74	2.78	44.94
Extreme Maximum Daily Precip. (in.)	2.26	4.82	2.88	6.56	4.73	3.50	3.88	4.55	6.41	3.98	4.15	2.80	6.56
Days With ≥ 0.1" Precipitation	4	4	6	6	8	7	5	4	6	5	5	5	65
Days With ≥ 0.5" Precipitation	1	1	3	3	4	3	3	2	3	3	3	2	31
Days With ≥ 1.0" Precipitation	0	1	1	1	2	1	1	1	1	1	1	1	12
Mean Snowfall (in.)	2.2	2.0	1.1	0.0	0.0	0.0	0.0	0.0	0.0	trace	0.3	1.8	7.4
Maximum Snow Depth (in.)	9	7	11	0	0	0	0	0	0	trace	4	10	11
Days With ≥ 1.0" Snow Depth	3	2	1	0	0	0	0	0	0	0	0	3	9

The period of record for all cooperative weather station data is 1980 – 2009. See User Guide for detailed explanation of data.

Clinton *Custer County* Elevation: 1,609 ft. Latitude: 35° 31' N Longitude: 98° 59' W

	JAN	FEB	MAR	APR	MAY	JUN	JUL	AUG	SEP	OCT	NOV	DEC	YEAR
Mean Maximum Temp. (°F)	49.9	54.8	63.4	73.3	81.7	90.2	96.6	95.5	87.0	74.6	61.0	50.8	73.3
Mean Temp. (°F)	37.9	42.3	50.4	59.7	69.4	78.2	83.6	82.5	74.3	61.8	49.1	39.2	60.7
Mean Minimum Temp. (°F)	25.8	29.7	37.4	46.1	56.9	66.1	70.6	69.4	61.5	48.9	37.0	27.6	48.1
Extreme Maximum Temp. (°F)	82	89	92	96	106	112	112	111	109	100	88	79	112
Extreme Minimum Temp. (°F)	-9	-7	4	22	30	47	54	51	33	15	9	-11	-11
Days Maximum Temp. ≥ 90°F	0	0	0	1	5	17	27	25	12	1	0	0	88
Days Maximum Temp. ≤ 32°F	3	2	0	0	0	0	0	0	0	0	0	2	7
Days Minimum Temp. ≤ 32°F	25	17	9	1	0	0	0	0	0	1	9	22	84
Days Minimum Temp. ≤ 0°F	0	0	0	0	0	0	0	0	0	0	0	0	0
Heating Degree Days (base 65°F)	833	637	451	193	39	1	0	0	23	151	474	791	3,593
Cooling Degree Days (base 65°F)	0	0	6	41	181	403	584	550	307	59	3	0	2,134
Mean Precipitation (in.)	1.15	1.26	2.51	2.21	4.86	4.72	1.89	2.96	3.58	3.19	2.02	1.53	31.88
Extreme Maximum Daily Precip. (in.)	1.95	1.95	4.10	2.85	6.95	4.60	2.88	5.01	5.87	8.07	3.41	1.45	8.07
Days With ≥ 0.1" Precipitation	2	3	4	4	6	7	3	5	4	4	3	3	48
Days With ≥ 0.5" Precipitation	1	1	2	2	3	3	1	2	2	2	1	1	21
Days With ≥ 1.0" Precipitation	0	0	1	1	2	1	1	1	1	1	1	0	10
Mean Snowfall (in.)	2.4	2.2	0.8	trace	0.0	0.0	0.0	0.0	0.0	trace	0.5	1.6	7.5
Maximum Snow Depth (in.)	3	na	na	trace	0	0	0	0	0	na	na	na	na
Days With ≥ 1.0" Snow Depth	0	1	0	0	0	0	0	0	0	0	0	na	na

Cushing *Payne County* Elevation: 950 ft. Latitude: 35° 59' N Longitude: 96° 46' W

	JAN	FEB	MAR	APR	MAY	JUN	JUL	AUG	SEP	OCT	NOV	DEC	YEAR
Mean Maximum Temp. (°F)	47.9	52.8	61.1	71.0	78.6	86.5	92.6	92.7	84.1	72.6	60.5	49.0	70.8
Mean Temp. (°F)	37.0	41.4	49.8	59.4	68.3	76.6	81.9	81.4	72.9	61.0	49.7	38.8	59.8
Mean Minimum Temp. (°F)	26.0	29.9	38.3	47.7	57.9	66.7	71.2	70.1	61.6	49.4	38.7	28.5	48.8
Extreme Maximum Temp. (°F)	79	91	93	101	98	103	110	107	107	94	86	76	110
Extreme Minimum Temp. (°F)	-5	-6	6	26	36	49	53	50	35	20	11	-9	-9
Days Maximum Temp. ≥ 90°F	0	0	0	1	2	10	22	22	9	1	0	0	67
Days Maximum Temp. ≤ 32°F	4	3	1	0	0	0	0	0	0	0	0	3	11
Days Minimum Temp. ≤ 32°F	24	17	8	1	0	0	0	0	0	1	8	20	79
Days Minimum Temp. ≤ 0°F	0	0	0	0	0	0	0	0	0	0	0	0	0
Heating Degree Days (base 65°F)	862	662	475	207	45	2	0	0	26	171	461	806	3,717
Cooling Degree Days (base 65°F)	0	0	8	45	155	357	530	516	270	56	6	0	1,943
Mean Precipitation (in.)	1.21	1.73	3.29	3.87	5.68	4.96	2.99	2.78	3.95	3.40	2.60	1.97	38.43
Extreme Maximum Daily Precip. (in.)	2.50	2.10	2.50	4.20	5.23	4.45	3.74	3.50	4.64	5.10	3.45	2.88	5.23
Days With ≥ 0.1" Precipitation	2	3	5	5	7	6	4	4	5	4	3	3	51
Days With ≥ 0.5" Precipitation	1	1	2	3	4	3	2	2	3	2	2	1	26
Days With ≥ 1.0" Precipitation	0	1	1	1	2	2	1	1	1	1	1	1	13
Mean Snowfall (in.)	1.5	1.3	0.5	0.0	0.0	0.0	0.0	0.0	0.0	0.0	0.1	1.9	5.3
Maximum Snow Depth (in.)	9	7	9	0	0	0	0	0	0	0	trace	7	9
Days With ≥ 1.0" Snow Depth	1	0	0	0	0	0	0	0	0	0	0	0	1

Duncan *Stephens County* Elevation: 1,125 ft. Latitude: 34° 30' N Longitude: 97° 58' W

	JAN	FEB	MAR	APR	MAY	JUN	JUL	AUG	SEP	OCT	NOV	DEC	YEAR
Mean Maximum Temp. (°F)	51.6	56.0	64.0	73.1	80.1	88.0	93.9	93.7	85.5	74.9	63.1	52.4	73.0
Mean Temp. (°F)	40.0	44.1	52.4	61.2	69.6	77.7	82.7	82.2	74.1	63.0	51.5	41.1	61.6
Mean Minimum Temp. (°F)	28.3	32.3	40.8	49.2	59.1	67.4	71.5	70.8	62.7	51.1	40.0	29.8	50.2
Extreme Maximum Temp. (°F)	81	90	92	97	104	111	110	106	108	97	87	78	111
Extreme Minimum Temp. (°F)	-4	-2	10	21	41	49	59	55	38	19	14	-7	-7
Days Maximum Temp. ≥ 90°F	0	0	0	0	3	13	25	24	10	1	0	0	76
Days Maximum Temp. ≤ 32°F	2	2	0	0	0	0	0	0	0	0	0	2	6
Days Minimum Temp. ≤ 32°F	22	14	6	1	0	0	0	0	0	1	7	19	70
Days Minimum Temp. ≤ 0°F	0	0	0	0	0	0	0	0	0	0	0	0	0
Heating Degree Days (base 65°F)	769	584	394	159	33	1	0	0	20	132	404	733	3,229
Cooling Degree Days (base 65°F)	0	1	11	51	183	389	556	541	300	78	7	0	2,117
Mean Precipitation (in.)	1.50	1.92	2.82	3.27	5.24	4.91	2.55	2.82	3.40	4.12	2.35	2.19	37.09
Extreme Maximum Daily Precip. (in.)	2.01	2.90	4.50	3.80	6.74	4.10	4.32	6.82	3.72	3.77	2.76	2.80	6.82
Days With ≥ 0.1" Precipitation	3	3	4	4	7	6	3	4	5	5	4	4	52
Days With ≥ 0.5" Precipitation	1	1	2	2	3	4	1	2	2	2	2	1	23
Days With ≥ 1.0" Precipitation	0	0	1	1	2	2	1	1	1	1	1	1	12
Mean Snowfall (in.)	1.3	0.5	0.2	0.0	0.0	0.0	0.0	0.0	0.0	trace	0.3	0.5	2.8
Maximum Snow Depth (in.)	13	trace	7	0	0	0	0	0	0	1	3	8	13
Days With ≥ 1.0" Snow Depth	0	0	0	0	0	0	0	0	0	0	0	0	0

El Reno 1 N *Canadian County* Elevation: 1,314 ft. Latitude: 35° 33' N Longitude: 97° 57' W

	JAN	FEB	MAR	APR	MAY	JUN	JUL	AUG	SEP	OCT	NOV	DEC	YEAR
Mean Maximum Temp. (°F)	49.3	54.1	62.8	72.6	80.4	88.3	94.3	93.7	85.0	73.6	60.3	50.0	72.0
Mean Temp. (°F)	38.1	42.3	50.6	59.9	69.0	76.9	82.5	81.7	72.8	61.7	49.1	39.2	60.3
Mean Minimum Temp. (°F)	26.9	30.4	38.4	47.2	57.5	65.5	70.6	69.6	60.6	49.7	37.8	28.4	48.5
Extreme Maximum Temp. (°F)	80	90	97	97	105	108	109	107	108	98	86	77	109
Extreme Minimum Temp. (°F)	-10	-5	4	25	36	45	53	50	34	17	10	-11	-11
Days Maximum Temp. ≥ 90°F	0	0	0	1	3	13	25	24	10	1	0	0	77
Days Maximum Temp. ≤ 32°F	3	2	0	0	0	0	0	0	0	0	0	3	8
Days Minimum Temp. ≤ 32°F	23	16	8	1	0	0	0	0	0	1	9	20	78
Days Minimum Temp. ≤ 0°F	0	0	0	0	0	0	0	0	0	0	0	0	0
Heating Degree Days (base 65°F)	825	637	450	191	40	2	0	0	27	160	478	793	3,603
Cooling Degree Days (base 65°F)	0	1	9	45	169	364	549	525	265	62	4	0	1,993
Mean Precipitation (in.)	1.15	1.39	2.73	2.72	5.26	5.02	2.17	3.03	3.33	3.18	2.24	1.49	33.71
Extreme Maximum Daily Precip. (in.)	2.58	2.28	3.09	2.76	5.18	4.70	3.00	3.81	4.50	4.25	4.25	2.00	5.18
Days With ≥ 0.1" Precipitation	2	3	5	4	6	6	3	4	5	4	3	3	48
Days With ≥ 0.5" Precipitation	1	1	2	2	3	3	1	2	2	2	1	1	21
Days With ≥ 1.0" Precipitation	0	0	1	1	2	2	1	1	1	1	1	0	11
Mean Snowfall (in.)	1.9	0.8	0.1	0.0	0.0	0.0	0.0	0.0	0.0	0.0	0.3	1.0	4.1
Maximum Snow Depth (in.)	11	3	trace	0	0	0	0	0	0	0	trace	5	11
Days With ≥ 1.0" Snow Depth	0	0	0	0	0	0	0	0	0	0	0	0	0

The period of record for all cooperative weather station data is 1980 – 2009. See User Guide for detailed explanation of data.

Enid *Garfield County* Elevation: 1,245 ft. Latitude: 36° 25' N Longitude: 97° 52' W

	JAN	FEB	MAR	APR	MAY	JUN	JUL	AUG	SEP	OCT	NOV	DEC	YEAR
Mean Maximum Temp. (°F)	47.0	52.4	60.8	70.9	79.9	89.2	95.0	93.8	85.2	72.6	59.3	47.9	71.2
Mean Temp. (°F)	36.5	41.3	49.3	59.1	68.8	77.9	83.4	82.3	73.6	61.2	48.7	38.2	60.0
Mean Minimum Temp. (°F)	26.0	30.1	37.8	47.3	57.8	66.7	71.7	70.6	62.0	49.6	37.9	28.3	48.8
Extreme Maximum Temp. (°F)	79	90	90	99	104	109	111	108	109	97	89	73	111
Extreme Minimum Temp. (°F)	-6	-6	2	25	35	48	53	51	33	17	11	-10	-10
Days Maximum Temp. ≥ 90°F	0	0	0	0	4	16	25	23	11	1	0	0	80
Days Maximum Temp. ≤ 32°F	5	3	1	0	0	0	0	0	0	0	0	3	12
Days Minimum Temp. ≤ 32°F	23	17	9	1	0	0	0	0	0	1	9	20	80
Days Minimum Temp. ≤ 0°F	0	0	0	0	0	0	0	0	0	0	0	0	0
Heating Degree Days (base 65°F)	876	664	485	212	45	2	0	0	25	172	488	826	3,795
Cooling Degree Days (base 65°F)	0	0	6	42	171	396	577	542	290	59	4	0	2,087
Mean Precipitation (in.)	1.06	1.50	2.68	3.08	4.35	5.24	2.73	3.48	2.97	3.40	1.81	1.52	33.82
Extreme Maximum Daily Precip. (in.)	2.00	3.14	2.57	3.10	3.82	5.22	2.64	3.90	5.57	9.06	4.34	1.80	9.06
Days With ≥ 0.1" Precipitation	2	3	4	5	7	7	4	4	4	4	3	3	50
Days With ≥ 0.5" Precipitation	1	1	2	2	3	3	2	2	2	2	1	1	22
Days With ≥ 1.0" Precipitation	0	0	1	1	1	2	1	1	1	1	0	0	9
Mean Snowfall (in.)	2.3	1.7	1.4	trace	0.0	0.0	0.0	0.0	0.0	trace	0.5	2.3	8.2
Maximum Snow Depth (in.)	6	19	13	trace	0	0	0	0	0	trace	1	9	19
Days With ≥ 1.0" Snow Depth	2	2	1	0	0	0	0	0	0	0	0	2	7

Erick *Beckham County* Elevation: 2,060 ft. Latitude: 35° 13' N Longitude: 99° 52' W

	JAN	FEB	MAR	APR	MAY	JUN	JUL	AUG	SEP	OCT	NOV	DEC	YEAR
Mean Maximum Temp. (°F)	51.5	55.6	64.3	73.8	81.3	89.0	95.0	93.8	85.6	74.3	62.2	51.4	73.2
Mean Temp. (°F)	38.1	42.0	50.1	59.1	68.3	76.4	81.6	80.4	72.2	60.6	48.8	38.6	59.7
Mean Minimum Temp. (°F)	24.7	28.3	35.7	44.3	55.2	63.8	68.2	66.9	58.7	47.0	35.2	25.7	46.1
Extreme Maximum Temp. (°F)	85	93	93	100	106	111	110	109	108	102	91	80	111
Extreme Minimum Temp. (°F)	-9	-4	-2	22	32	43	50	50	27	13	8	-9	-9
Days Maximum Temp. ≥ 90°F	0	0	0	2	6	15	25	23	10	2	0	0	83
Days Maximum Temp. ≤ 32°F	3	2	0	0	0	0	0	0	0	0	0	3	8
Days Minimum Temp. ≤ 32°F	26	19	11	2	0	0	0	0	0	2	12	25	97
Days Minimum Temp. ≤ 0°F	0	0	0	0	0	0	0	0	0	0	0	0	0
Heating Degree Days (base 65°F)	827	644	461	207	49	2	0	0	25	176	483	811	3,685
Cooling Degree Days (base 65°F)	0	0	5	36	157	351	523	484	247	48	3	0	1,854
Mean Precipitation (in.)	0.72	0.93	2.09	2.13	4.03	3.95	1.72	2.87	2.77	2.55	1.28	1.11	26.15
Extreme Maximum Daily Precip. (in.)	1.59	1.74	2.72	2.24	4.85	3.57	3.60	3.28	8.61	5.94	2.23	2.20	8.61
Days With ≥ 0.1" Precipitation	2	2	4	4	5	6	3	4	4	4	3	2	43
Days With ≥ 0.5" Precipitation	0	1	1	2	3	3	1	2	2	1	1	1	18
Days With ≥ 1.0" Precipitation	0	0	1	1	1	1	0	1	1	1	0	0	7
Mean Snowfall (in.)	2.7	1.5	1.3	0.1	trace	0.0	0.0	0.0	0.0	0.1	0.9	2.1	8.7
Maximum Snow Depth (in.)	14	8	6	1	trace	0	0	0	0	2	6	8	14
Days With ≥ 1.0" Snow Depth	2	1	1	0	0	0	0	0	0	0	0	2	6

Frederick *Tillman County* Elevation: 1,285 ft. Latitude: 34° 23' N Longitude: 99° 01' W

	JAN	FEB	MAR	APR	MAY	JUN	JUL	AUG	SEP	OCT	NOV	DEC	YEAR
Mean Maximum Temp. (°F)	53.0	56.8	65.3	74.8	82.3	90.8	96.6	95.6	87.1	76.0	63.7	52.8	74.6
Mean Temp. (°F)	40.4	44.3	52.6	61.5	70.0	78.8	84.0	82.8	74.7	63.1	51.2	41.3	62.1
Mean Minimum Temp. (°F)	27.7	31.7	39.9	48.2	57.7	66.8	71.4	70.2	62.1	50.2	38.7	29.1	49.5
Extreme Maximum Temp. (°F)	87	88	94	100	110	115	114	108	109	101	90	82	115
Extreme Minimum Temp. (°F)	1	0	7	24	34	40	55	57	38	21	13	-11	-11
Days Maximum Temp. ≥ 90°F	0	0	0	2	7	18	26	25	13	3	0	0	94
Days Maximum Temp. ≤ 32°F	2	2	0	0	0	0	0	0	0	0	0	2	6
Days Minimum Temp. ≤ 32°F	21	14	6	1	0	0	0	0	0	1	7	19	69
Days Minimum Temp. ≤ 0°F	0	0	0	0	0	0	0	0	0	0	0	0	0
Heating Degree Days (base 65°F)	754	577	389	155	32	1	0	0	16	128	412	727	3,191
Cooling Degree Days (base 65°F)	0	0	12	57	193	422	597	560	313	77	7	0	2,238
Mean Precipitation (in.)	1.12	1.63	2.60	2.75	4.36	4.53	2.11	2.59	2.83	3.34	1.88	1.52	31.26
Extreme Maximum Daily Precip. (in.)	1.62	2.10	2.77	4.15	3.00	3.25	2.30	2.50	4.00	4.35	2.30	4.20	4.35
Days With ≥ 0.1" Precipitation	2	3	4	4	5	5	3	4	4	4	3	2	43
Days With ≥ 0.5" Precipitation	1	1	2	2	3	3	1	2	2	2	1	1	21
Days With ≥ 1.0" Precipitation	0	0	1	1	1	2	1	1	1	1	1	0	10
Mean Snowfall (in.)	0.5	0.8	trace	0.0	0.0	0.0	0.0	0.0	0.0	0.0	0.7	0.4	2.4
Maximum Snow Depth (in.)	9	4	trace	0	0	0	0	0	0	0	5	1	9
Days With ≥ 1.0" Snow Depth	0	0	0	0	0	0	0	0	0	0	0	0	0

Geary *Blaine County* Elevation: 1,595 ft. Latitude: 35° 38' N Longitude: 98° 19' W

	JAN	FEB	MAR	APR	MAY	JUN	JUL	AUG	SEP	OCT	NOV	DEC	YEAR
Mean Maximum Temp. (°F)	48.9	53.4	62.0	71.3	79.6	87.4	93.1	92.7	84.3	72.8	60.1	49.5	71.3
Mean Temp. (°F)	38.1	41.9	50.0	59.1	68.5	76.6	81.7	81.2	72.7	61.4	48.8	39.1	59.9
Mean Minimum Temp. (°F)	27.2	30.4	38.0	46.8	57.2	65.7	70.3	69.6	61.1	49.8	37.4	28.7	48.5
Extreme Maximum Temp. (°F)	79	90	90	98	103	109	107	107	107	97	89	79	109
Extreme Minimum Temp. (°F)	-10	-3	-1	23	34	47	53	51	33	21	9	-12	-12
Days Maximum Temp. ≥ 90°F	0	0	0	0	3	11	23	22	8	0	0	0	67
Days Maximum Temp. ≤ 32°F	3	2	0	0	0	0	0	0	0	0	0	3	8
Days Minimum Temp. ≤ 32°F	22	16	8	1	0	0	0	0	0	1	8	20	76
Days Minimum Temp. ≤ 0°F	0	0	0	0	0	0	0	0	0	0	0	0	0
Heating Degree Days (base 65°F)	827	646	463	208	43	1	0	0	24	160	481	795	3,648
Cooling Degree Days (base 65°F)	0	0	6	37	158	355	526	509	261	54	2	0	1,908
Mean Precipitation (in.)	0.98	1.24	2.59	2.72	4.57	4.53	1.75	3.18	3.08	3.07	1.68	1.32	30.71
Extreme Maximum Daily Precip. (in.)	2.10	2.40	5.24	3.00	5.79	3.13	2.40	10.41	5.90	3.93	5.30	1.95	10.41
Days With ≥ 0.1" Precipitation	2	3	4	4	5	6	3	4	3	4	2	2	42
Days With ≥ 0.5" Precipitation	1	1	2	2	3	3	1	2	2	2	1	1	21
Days With ≥ 1.0" Precipitation	0	0	1	1	1	2	1	1	1	1	0	0	9
Mean Snowfall (in.)	1.9	1.2	0.2	trace	0.0	0.0	0.0	0.0	0.0	trace	0.6	0.9	4.8
Maximum Snow Depth (in.)	6	6	3	trace	0	0	0	0	0	1	3	8	8
Days With ≥ 1.0" Snow Depth	1	1	0	0	0	0	0	0	0	0	0	1	3

The period of record for all cooperative weather station data is 1980 – 2009. See User Guide for detailed explanation of data.

Goodwell Research Stn *Texas County* Elevation: 3,310 ft. Latitude: 36° 36' N Longitude: 101° 37' W

	JAN	FEB	MAR	APR	MAY	JUN	JUL	AUG	SEP	OCT	NOV	DEC	YEAR
Mean Maximum Temp. (°F)	48.8	52.4	60.5	69.4	78.2	88.5	94.1	92.0	84.3	72.1	59.5	48.8	70.7
Mean Temp. (°F)	34.6	37.8	45.4	54.0	63.8	73.9	79.2	77.5	69.3	56.8	44.7	34.8	56.0
Mean Minimum Temp. (°F)	20.3	23.1	30.2	38.6	49.2	59.2	64.2	63.0	54.2	41.5	29.8	20.9	41.2
Extreme Maximum Temp. (°F)	82	85	94	100	103	111	110	106	109	98	89	80	111
Extreme Minimum Temp. (°F)	-14	-11	-2	16	29	40	47	49	28	11	0	-13	-14
Days Maximum Temp. ≥ 90°F	0	0	0	1	4	15	24	21	11	2	0	0	78
Days Maximum Temp. ≤ 32°F	4	3	1	0	0	0	0	0	0	0	1	4	13
Days Minimum Temp. ≤ 32°F	29	24	19	7	0	0	0	0	0	5	18	29	131
Days Minimum Temp. ≤ 0°F	1	1	0	0	0	0	0	0	0	0	0	1	3
Heating Degree Days (base 65°F)	935	763	602	337	116	11	1	2	52	274	604	927	4,624
Cooling Degree Days (base 65°F)	0	0	1	14	84	285	447	396	187	27	0	0	1,441
Mean Precipitation (in.)	0.33	0.39	1.11	1.34	2.46	2.49	2.36	2.27	1.46	1.43	0.47	0.48	16.59
Extreme Maximum Daily Precip. (in.)	1.10	0.64	1.57	1.98	2.95	1.96	2.92	2.24	2.94	2.50	0.94	2.90	2.95
Days With ≥ 0.1" Precipitation	1	1	3	3	5	5	4	4	2	3	1	1	33
Days With ≥ 0.5" Precipitation	0	0	1	1	2	2	2	2	1	1	0	0	12
Days With ≥ 1.0" Precipitation	0	0	0	0	1	1	1	1	0	0	0	0	4
Mean Snowfall (in.)	2.6	1.6	2.2	1.0	trace	0.0	0.0	0.0	0.1	trace	0.9	2.1	10.5
Maximum Snow Depth (in.)	14	12	4	11	trace	0	0	0	2	trace	5	8	14
Days With ≥ 1.0" Snow Depth	2	2	1	0	0	0	0	0	0	0	0	1	6

Guthrie 5 S *Logan County* Elevation: 1,109 ft. Latitude: 35° 49' N Longitude: 97° 24' W

	JAN	FEB	MAR	APR	MAY	JUN	JUL	AUG	SEP	OCT	NOV	DEC	YEAR
Mean Maximum Temp. (°F)	50.2	55.2	64.0	73.7	81.0	88.4	94.7	94.7	85.9	74.4	62.0	50.9	72.9
Mean Temp. (°F)	38.4	42.9	51.2	60.6	69.4	77.3	82.9	82.4	73.7	62.0	50.2	39.9	60.9
Mean Minimum Temp. (°F)	26.5	30.5	38.4	47.5	57.7	66.3	71.0	70.2	61.3	49.7	38.3	28.9	48.8
Extreme Maximum Temp. (°F)	82	93	93	99	104	107	113	111	112	98	89	77	113
Extreme Minimum Temp. (°F)	-12	-14	3	20	33	43	53	53	32	17	11	-13	-14
Days Maximum Temp. ≥ 90°F	0	0	0	1	4	13	25	24	11	1	0	0	79
Days Maximum Temp. ≤ 32°F	3	2	0	0	0	0	0	0	0	0	0	2	7
Days Minimum Temp. ≤ 32°F	23	16	9	2	0	0	0	0	0	1	9	19	79
Days Minimum Temp. ≤ 0°F	0	0	0	0	0	0	0	0	0	0	0	0	0
Heating Degree Days (base 65°F)	819	619	434	184	41	2	0	0	23	157	446	771	3,496
Cooling Degree Days (base 65°F)	0	1	14	60	183	379	561	548	287	72	8	0	2,113
Mean Precipitation (in.)	1.44	1.77	3.55	3.24	4.88	5.21	2.56	3.28	3.65	3.62	2.55	2.09	37.84
Extreme Maximum Daily Precip. (in.)	2.15	2.30	4.90	3.87	6.55	4.25	3.52	4.45	5.00	3.50	3.16	2.50	6.55
Days With ≥ 0.1" Precipitation	3	3	5	5	6	7	4	4	5	4	4	4	54
Days With ≥ 0.5" Precipitation	1	1	3	2	3	4	2	2	2	2	2	2	26
Days With ≥ 1.0" Precipitation	0	0	1	1	2	2	1	1	1	1	1	0	11
Mean Snowfall (in.)	3.0	1.4	0.6	0.0	0.0	0.0	0.0	0.0	0.0	trace	0.2	2.2	7.4
Maximum Snow Depth (in.)	10	***6***	7	0	0	0	0	0	0	0	3	6	***10***
Days With ≥ 1.0" Snow Depth	2	***1***	0	0	0	0	0	0	0	0	0	2	***5***

Healdton *Carter County* Elevation: 733 ft. Latitude: 34° 13' N Longitude: 97° 28' W

	JAN	FEB	MAR	APR	MAY	JUN	JUL	AUG	SEP	OCT	NOV	DEC	YEAR
Mean Maximum Temp. (°F)	53.1	57.9	65.9	74.8	81.5	89.1	95.3	***95.9***	86.8	76.1	64.4	53.9	***74.5***
Mean Temp. (°F)	40.9	45.3	53.3	61.7	70.1	77.9	82.8	***82.8***	74.1	63.3	52.2	42.1	***62.2***
Mean Minimum Temp. (°F)	28.7	32.8	40.7	48.6	58.6	66.5	70.3	***69.6***	61.4	50.5	39.9	30.4	***49.8***
Extreme Maximum Temp. (°F)	83	91	95	98	101	114	112	108	111	98	86	81	114
Extreme Minimum Temp. (°F)	-3	1	1	19	35	43	56	51	35	18	14	-10	-10
Days Maximum Temp. ≥ 90°F	0	0	0	1	4	15	25	24	12	2	0	0	83
Days Maximum Temp. ≤ 32°F	2	1	0	0	0	0	0	0	0	0	0	2	5
Days Minimum Temp. ≤ 32°F	21	13	7	1	0	0	0	0	0	1	8	19	70
Days Minimum Temp. ≤ 0°F	0	0	0	0	0	0	0	0	0	0	0	0	0
Heating Degree Days (base 65°F)	740	552	371	151	29	0	0	***0***	18	130	388	702	***3,081***
Cooling Degree Days (base 65°F)	0	1	15	58	194	394	559	***559***	299	85	10	1	***2,175***
Mean Precipitation (in.)	1.72	2.12	3.11	3.02	5.56	4.33	2.46	2.42	4.04	4.07	2.42	2.37	37.64
Extreme Maximum Daily Precip. (in.)	2.24	2.38	2.96	5.81	4.63	4.10	3.73	3.37	4.88	4.52	2.69	3.04	5.81
Days With ≥ 0.1" Precipitation	4	4	5	4	6	6	4	3	5	5	4	3	53
Days With ≥ 0.5" Precipitation	1	2	2	2	3	3	2	1	3	3	2	2	26
Days With ≥ 1.0" Precipitation	0	0	1	1	2	2	1	1	1	1	1	1	12
Mean Snowfall (in.)	0.9	0.6	0.5	0.0	0.0	0.0	0.0	0.0	0.0	0.0	0.1	0.7	2.8
Maximum Snow Depth (in.)	9	***2***	11	0	0	0	0	0	0	0	3	9	***11***
Days With ≥ 1.0" Snow Depth	1	0	0	0	0	0	0	0	0	0	0	0	1

Helena 1 SSE *Alfalfa County* Elevation: 1,350 ft. Latitude: 36° 32' N Longitude: 98° 17' W

	JAN	FEB	MAR	APR	MAY	JUN	JUL	AUG	SEP	OCT	NOV	DEC	YEAR
Mean Maximum Temp. (°F)	46.3	50.9	59.9	69.7	79.3	88.9	95.0	93.8	84.9	72.0	58.7	46.8	70.5
Mean Temp. (°F)	34.5	38.5	47.3	56.7	67.0	76.7	82.2	81.0	72.2	59.3	46.5	35.7	58.1
Mean Minimum Temp. (°F)	22.7	26.2	34.7	43.6	54.8	64.4	69.3	68.2	59.4	46.7	34.2	24.5	45.7
Extreme Maximum Temp. (°F)	79	90	90	99	105	112	113	108	108	97	91	77	113
Extreme Minimum Temp. (°F)	-14	-15	0	19	33	47	50	48	31	12	8	-15	-15
Days Maximum Temp. ≥ 90°F	0	0	0	1	4	15	25	23	11	1	0	0	80
Days Maximum Temp. ≤ 32°F	5	3	1	0	0	0	0	0	0	0	1	5	15
Days Minimum Temp. ≤ 32°F	28	21	12	3	0	0	0	0	0	2	14	26	106
Days Minimum Temp. ≤ 0°F	0	1	0	0	0	0	0	0	0	0	0	1	2
Heating Degree Days (base 65°F)	937	742	545	270	68	3	0	1	32	212	551	902	4,263
Cooling Degree Days (base 65°F)	0	0	3	28	138	359	539	505	255	45	2	0	1,874
Mean Precipitation (in.)	1.06	1.32	2.79	2.93	4.10	4.52	2.65	3.31	2.80	3.06	1.67	1.39	31.60
Extreme Maximum Daily Precip. (in.)	2.69	2.55	4.90	7.12	3.65	3.27	2.31	3.34	8.74	5.00	3.35	1.60	8.74
Days With ≥ 0.1" Precipitation	2	3	5	5	6	6	4	5	4	4	3	3	50
Days With ≥ 0.5" Precipitation	1	1	2	2	3	3	2	2	1	2	1	1	21
Days With ≥ 1.0" Precipitation	0	0	1	1	1	1	1	1	1	1	0	0	8
Mean Snowfall (in.)	3.1	3.3	3.1	trace	0.0	0.0	0.0	0.0	0.0	0.1	0.7	4.4	14.7
Maximum Snow Depth (in.)	14	18	13	trace	0	0	0	0	0	2	5	16	18
Days With ≥ 1.0" Snow Depth	5	4	2	0	0	0	0	0	0	0	1	5	17

The period of record for all cooperative weather station data is 1980 – 2009. See User Guide for detailed explanation of data.

Holdenville *Hughes County* Elevation: 859 ft. Latitude: 35° 05' N Longitude: 96° 24' W

	JAN	FEB	MAR	APR	MAY	JUN	JUL	AUG	SEP	OCT	NOV	DEC	YEAR
Mean Maximum Temp. (°F)	51.1	55.4	65.0	73.7	80.6	88.4	94.2	94.4	85.9	74.6	62.7	51.7	73.1
Mean Temp. (°F)	39.6	43.4	52.6	61.1	69.6	77.3	82.1	81.8	73.4	62.3	51.2	40.8	61.3
Mean Minimum Temp. (°F)	28.1	31.4	40.2	48.4	58.5	66.1	69.9	69.2	60.8	50.0	39.6	29.8	49.3
Extreme Maximum Temp. (°F)	78	93	93	100	100	103	110	108	111	95	85	76	111
Extreme Minimum Temp. (°F)	-13	-6	5	27	35	45	54	46	35	18	14	-8	-13
Days Maximum Temp. ≥ 90°F	0	0	0	0	3	13	25	24	10	1	0	0	76
Days Maximum Temp. ≤ 32°F	2	2	0	0	0	0	0	0	0	0	0	2	6
Days Minimum Temp. ≤ 32°F	22	16	7	1	0	0	0	0	0	1	8	19	74
Days Minimum Temp. ≤ 0°F	0	0	0	0	0	0	0	0	0	0	0	0	0
Heating Degree Days (base 65°F)	781	604	387	164	31	0	0	0	20	146	416	743	3,292
Cooling Degree Days (base 65°F)	0	1	11	53	180	376	536	529	279	70	8	0	2,043
Mean Precipitation (in.)	1.71	2.24	3.26	3.83	5.17	4.52	2.99	3.32	4.29	4.41	3.04	2.56	41.34
Extreme Maximum Daily Precip. (in.)	3.00	3.18	2.50	3.80	4.74	3.91	3.76	4.41	6.76	4.25	2.75	3.16	6.76
Days With ≥ 0.1" Precipitation	3	4	5	5	7	6	4	4	6	6	5	4	59
Days With ≥ 0.5" Precipitation	1	2	3	2	3	3	2	2	3	3	2	2	28
Days With ≥ 1.0" Precipitation	0	1	1	1	2	2	1	1	1	1	1	1	13
Mean Snowfall (in.)	0.9	1.1	0.3	0.0	0.0	0.0	0.0	0.0	0.0	0.0	0.2	0.2	2.7
Maximum Snow Depth (in.)	11	3	1	0	0	0	0	0	0	0	0	4	11
Days With ≥ 1.0" Snow Depth	0	0	0	0	0	0	0	0	0	0	0	0	0

Idabel *Mccurtain County* Elevation: 459 ft. Latitude: 33° 53' N Longitude: 94° 49' W

	JAN	FEB	MAR	APR	MAY	JUN	JUL	AUG	SEP	OCT	NOV	DEC	YEAR
Mean Maximum Temp. (°F)	53.5	59.1	66.4	73.9	81.1	88.5	92.9	94.0	86.3	75.9	64.5	55.2	74.3
Mean Temp. (°F)	41.6	46.4	53.7	60.9	69.7	77.5	81.5	81.8	74.0	63.1	52.2	43.6	62.2
Mean Minimum Temp. (°F)	29.5	33.6	40.9	47.7	58.2	66.4	70.1	69.6	61.6	50.2	39.8	32.0	50.0
Extreme Maximum Temp. (°F)	79	89	90	93	98	101	108	110	109	98	86	81	110
Extreme Minimum Temp. (°F)	2	2	10	21	34	49	57	53	36	23	19	-2	-2
Days Maximum Temp. ≥ 90°F	0	0	0	0	2	14	24	24	10	1	0	0	75
Days Maximum Temp. ≤ 32°F	1	1	0	0	0	0	0	0	0	0	0	1	3
Days Minimum Temp. ≤ 32°F	21	14	6	1	0	0	0	0	0	1	8	17	68
Days Minimum Temp. ≤ 0°F	0	0	0	0	0	0	0	0	0	0	0	0	0
Heating Degree Days (base 65°F)	721	522	359	165	26	1	0	0	15	126	386	658	2,979
Cooling Degree Days (base 65°F)	1	2	14	48	178	382	519	529	291	74	8	2	2,048
Mean Precipitation (in.)	2.94	3.81	4.78	4.22	6.30	4.33	3.57	2.51	4.16	5.53	5.00	4.78	51.93
Extreme Maximum Daily Precip. (in.)	3.17	3.27	4.43	3.53	5.35	4.80	5.09	2.99	4.93	4.98	5.62	4.33	5.62
Days With ≥ 0.1" Precipitation	5	5	6	5	8	6	4	4	5	6	5	6	65
Days With ≥ 0.5" Precipitation	2	3	3	3	4	3	2	2	3	3	3	3	34
Days With ≥ 1.0" Precipitation	1	1	2	2	2	1	1	1	1	2	2	1	17
Mean Snowfall (in.)	0.6	0.9	0.1	0.0	0.0	0.0	0.0	0.0	0.0	0.0	trace	0.4	2.0
Maximum Snow Depth (in.)	trace	na	2	0	0	0	0	0	0	0	trace	1	na
Days With ≥ 1.0" Snow Depth	0	0	0	0	0	0	0	0	0	0	0	0	0

Kansas 1 ESE *Delaware County* Elevation: 1,180 ft. Latitude: 36° 12' N Longitude: 94° 47' W

	JAN	FEB	MAR	APR	MAY	JUN	JUL	AUG	SEP	OCT	NOV	DEC	YEAR
Mean Maximum Temp. (°F)	48.2	53.5	62.6	71.3	77.7	84.7	90.6	91.0	82.9	72.0	60.3	49.5	70.4
Mean Temp. (°F)	38.2	42.8	51.2	59.8	67.4	74.9	79.9	79.7	71.7	60.9	50.1	39.9	59.7
Mean Minimum Temp. (°F)	28.1	32.0	39.9	48.1	56.9	65.0	69.1	68.4	60.6	49.8	39.9	30.3	49.0
Extreme Maximum Temp. (°F)	75	88	89	94	92	100	108	105	105	90	83	76	108
Extreme Minimum Temp. (°F)	-11	-8	1	23	35	45	54	49	33	16	9	-13	-13
Days Maximum Temp. ≥ 90°F	0	0	0	0	0	4	17	18	6	0	0	0	45
Days Maximum Temp. ≤ 32°F	3	2	0	0	0	0	0	0	0	0	0	2	7
Days Minimum Temp. ≤ 32°F	21	15	8	1	0	0	0	0	0	1	8	18	72
Days Minimum Temp. ≤ 0°F	0	0	0	0	0	0	0	0	0	0	0	0	0
Heating Degree Days (base 65°F)	825	622	429	194	47	2	0	0	28	171	443	770	3,531
Cooling Degree Days (base 65°F)	0	1	9	43	127	305	469	463	237	51	4	0	1,709
Mean Precipitation (in.)	2.62	2.72	4.11	4.43	5.24	5.07	3.21	3.67	4.89	4.31	3.98	3.71	47.96
Extreme Maximum Daily Precip. (in.)	4.87	2.96	3.99	3.06	4.41	4.00	3.80	4.45	9.42	6.40	5.25	3.00	9.42
Days With ≥ 0.1" Precipitation	4	5	6	7	7	7	5	5	6	6	5	5	68
Days With ≥ 0.5" Precipitation	2	2	3	3	4	4	2	2	3	3	3	2	33
Days With ≥ 1.0" Precipitation	1	1	1	1	2	2	1	1	1	1	1	1	14
Mean Snowfall (in.)	2.8	1.8	1.9	trace	0.0	0.0	0.0	0.0	0.0	0.1	0.4	1.8	8.8
Maximum Snow Depth (in.)	9	8	15	trace	0	0	0	0	0	2	3	6	15
Days With ≥ 1.0" Snow Depth	2	2	1	0	0	0	0	0	0	0	0	1	6

Kenton *Cimarron County* Elevation: 4,350 ft. Latitude: 36° 54' N Longitude: 102° 58' W

	JAN	FEB	MAR	APR	MAY	JUN	JUL	AUG	SEP	OCT	NOV	DEC	YEAR
Mean Maximum Temp. (°F)	50.4	53.6	60.3	68.7	77.7	87.2	92.3	89.0	82.9	71.6	na	50.0	na
Mean Temp. (°F)	34.8	37.8	45.0	53.4	63.1	72.6	77.7	75.4	68.2	55.7	na	35.0	na
Mean Minimum Temp. (°F)	19.2	22.0	29.7	38.1	48.4	57.8	63.1	61.8	53.5	39.7	na	19.8	na
Extreme Maximum Temp. (°F)	80	82	88	94	102	107	107	103	104	94	na	82	na
Extreme Minimum Temp. (°F)	-22	-19	-4	13	27	40	48	44	27	6	na	-17	na
Days Maximum Temp. ≥ 90°F	0	0	0	0	4	12	22	16	8	0	na	0	na
Days Maximum Temp. ≤ 32°F	3	2	1	0	0	0	0	0	0	0	na	4	na
Days Minimum Temp. ≤ 32°F	28	24	20	7	0	0	0	0	0	6	na	29	na
Days Minimum Temp. ≤ 0°F	1	1	0	0	0	0	0	0	0	0	na	1	na
Heating Degree Days (base 65°F)	930	760	613	351	121	15	1	3	55	295	na	923	na
Cooling Degree Days (base 65°F)	0	0	1	10	69	248	403	335	160	12	na	0	na
Mean Precipitation (in.)	0.54	0.46	0.89	1.25	2.25	2.06	3.10	2.93	1.48	1.04	na	na	na
Extreme Maximum Daily Precip. (in.)	1.95	na	na	3.02	3.18	2.08	2.60	2.76	2.90	na	na	na	na
Days With ≥ 0.1" Precipitation	1	1	2	3	4	4	5	5	3	2	na	na	na
Days With ≥ 0.5" Precipitation	0	0	0	1	2	2	2	2	1	1	na	na	na
Days With ≥ 1.0" Precipitation	0	0	0	0	0	0	1	1	0	0	na	na	na
Mean Snowfall (in.)	5.1	3.5	5.0	1.5	0.2	0.0	0.0	0.0	0.1	1.2	na	na	na
Maximum Snow Depth (in.)	16	11	na	6	3	trace	0	0	1	15	na	na	na
Days With ≥ 1.0" Snow Depth	4	2	1	0	0	0	0	0	0	0	na	na	na

The period of record for all cooperative weather station data is 1980 – 2009. See User Guide for detailed explanation of data.

Mannford 6 NW *Pawnee County* Elevation: 830 ft. Latitude: 36° 10' N Longitude: 96° 26' W

	JAN	FEB	MAR	APR	MAY	JUN	JUL	AUG	SEP	OCT	NOV	DEC	YEAR
Mean Maximum Temp. (°F)	49.9	55.1	64.2	74.0	79.6	87.0	93.6	93.9	84.8	73.7	61.9	50.5	72.4
Mean Temp. (°F)	38.6	43.2	52.2	61.4	68.8	76.6	82.0	81.2	72.7	61.8	50.6	39.8	60.7
Mean Minimum Temp. (°F)	27.2	31.1	40.1	48.8	58.0	66.2	70.3	68.7	60.6	49.9	39.3	29.0	49.1
Extreme Maximum Temp. (°F)	80	92	95	100	96	103	113	112	112	95	88	79	113
Extreme Minimum Temp. (°F)	-10	-14	3	22	33	45	53	49	31	13	10	-16	-16
Days Maximum Temp. ≥ 90°F	0	0	0	1	2	10	23	22	9	1	0	0	68
Days Maximum Temp. ≤ 32°F	3	2	0	0	0	0	0	0	0	0	0	2	7
Days Minimum Temp. ≤ 32°F	22	16	8	1	0	0	0	0	0	1	9	20	77
Days Minimum Temp. ≤ 0°F	0	0	0	0	0	0	0	0	0	0	0	0	0
Heating Degree Days (base 65°F)	813	613	407	167	38	1	0	0	26	158	434	776	3,433
Cooling Degree Days (base 65°F)	0	1	17	67	163	358	533	509	264	66	10	1	1,989
Mean Precipitation (in.)	1.70	2.10	3.60	4.00	5.78	5.06	3.21	3.16	3.83	3.62	2.94	2.33	41.33
Extreme Maximum Daily Precip. (in.)	2.72	3.88	2.72	4.46	4.60	4.58	3.27	3.62	5.42	4.14	3.41	1.80	5.42
Days With ≥ 0.1" Precipitation	3	4	5	5	7	7	4	5	6	5	5	4	60
Days With ≥ 0.5" Precipitation	1	1	2	3	4	3	2	2	3	2	2	2	27
Days With ≥ 1.0" Precipitation	0	0	1	1	2	2	1	1	1	1	1	1	12
Mean Snowfall (in.)	2.3	2.0	1.6	0.0	0.0	0.0	0.0	0.0	0.0	trace	0.2	2.7	8.8
Maximum Snow Depth (in.)	10	5	3	0	0	0	0	0	0	trace	2	***5***	***10***
Days With ≥ 1.0" Snow Depth	0	0	0	0	0	0	0	0	0	0	0	0	0

McCurtain 1 SE *Haskell County* Elevation: 659 ft. Latitude: 35° 09' N Longitude: 94° 58' W

	JAN	FEB	MAR	APR	MAY	JUN	JUL	AUG	SEP	OCT	NOV	DEC	YEAR
Mean Maximum Temp. (°F)	52.3	57.0	65.9	74.7	81.0	87.8	94.3	94.5	86.3	75.9	63.8	53.5	73.9
Mean Temp. (°F)	41.7	45.8	54.3	62.8	70.3	77.5	83.0	82.5	74.3	63.8	52.8	43.0	62.6
Mean Minimum Temp. (°F)	31.0	34.6	42.7	50.9	59.6	67.2	71.7	70.5	62.2	51.6	41.7	32.5	51.3
Extreme Maximum Temp. (°F)	79	93	92	96	97	103	110	109	111	95	86	79	111
Extreme Minimum Temp. (°F)	-7	-4	5	22	36	47	52	50	33	20	11	-9	-9
Days Maximum Temp. ≥ 90°F	0	0	0	0	2	12	25	25	11	2	0	0	77
Days Maximum Temp. ≤ 32°F	2	1	0	0	0	0	0	0	0	0	0	2	5
Days Minimum Temp. ≤ 32°F	18	12	6	1	0	0	0	0	0	1	7	16	61
Days Minimum Temp. ≤ 0°F	0	0	0	0	0	0	0	0	0	0	0	0	0
Heating Degree Days (base 65°F)	717	539	349	134	25	1	0	0	18	121	373	675	2,952
Cooling Degree Days (base 65°F)	1	4	22	74	197	383	564	551	303	90	14	2	2,205
Mean Precipitation (in.)	2.86	2.95	4.26	4.68	5.82	4.88	3.00	2.89	4.50	3.75	4.79	3.43	47.81
Extreme Maximum Daily Precip. (in.)	3.75	2.85	4.04	5.22	4.25	8.35	3.50	3.05	3.65	3.60	4.78	3.00	8.35
Days With ≥ 0.1" Precipitation	5	5	6	6	8	7	4	4	5	5	5	5	65
Days With ≥ 0.5" Precipitation	2	2	3	3	4	3	2	2	3	2	3	2	31
Days With ≥ 1.0" Precipitation	1	1	1	1	2	2	1	1	2	1	2	1	16
Mean Snowfall (in.)	2.3	1.7	1.0	0.0	0.0	0.0	0.0	0.0	0.0	trace	trace	0.5	5.5
Maximum Snow Depth (in.)	10	10	9	0	0	0	0	0	0	trace	trace	3	10
Days With ≥ 1.0" Snow Depth	2	1	1	0	0	0	0	0	0	0	0	1	5

Meeker 4 W *Lincoln County* Elevation: 924 ft. Latitude: 35° 30' N Longitude: 96° 59' W

	JAN	FEB	MAR	APR	MAY	JUN	JUL	AUG	SEP	OCT	NOV	DEC	YEAR
Mean Maximum Temp. (°F)	49.7	54.7	63.0	72.3	78.8	86.3	92.2	92.3	83.8	73.2	61.8	50.8	71.6
Mean Temp. (°F)	38.5	42.7	50.8	59.9	68.2	76.1	81.2	80.7	72.1	61.4	50.3	39.9	60.1
Mean Minimum Temp. (°F)	27.1	30.6	38.6	47.4	57.6	65.8	70.1	69.0	60.4	49.5	38.7	28.9	48.6
Extreme Maximum Temp. (°F)	80	91	92	98	99	104	110	110	107	95	87	77	110
Extreme Minimum Temp. (°F)	-6	-4	5	25	33	46	53	50	33	18	12	-15	-15
Days Maximum Temp. ≥ 90°F	0	0	0	0	1	9	21	21	7	1	0	0	60
Days Maximum Temp. ≤ 32°F	3	2	0	0	0	0	0	0	0	0	0	2	7
Days Minimum Temp. ≤ 32°F	22	16	9	2	0	0	0	0	0	1	9	19	78
Days Minimum Temp. ≤ 0°F	0	0	0	0	0	0	0	0	0	0	0	0	0
Heating Degree Days (base 65°F)	816	626	443	193	47	2	0	0	28	163	443	773	3,534
Cooling Degree Days (base 65°F)	0	1	11	47	153	340	509	493	248	58	7	1	1,868
Mean Precipitation (in.)	1.43	2.06	3.17	3.16	5.12	5.23	2.68	2.85	4.47	4.64	2.63	2.10	39.54
Extreme Maximum Daily Precip. (in.)	1.55	6.93	2.65	2.77	4.36	4.78	3.10	3.94	5.60	7.55	4.01	2.33	7.55
Days With ≥ 0.1" Precipitation	3	3	5	5	7	6	4	4	5	5	4	3	54
Days With ≥ 0.5" Precipitation	1	1	2	2	3	3	2	2	3	2	2	1	24
Days With ≥ 1.0" Precipitation	0	1	1	1	2	2	1	1	1	1	1	1	13
Mean Snowfall (in.)	1.3	0.3	0.3	0.0	0.0	0.0	0.0	0.0	0.0	trace	0.3	1.0	3.2
Maximum Snow Depth (in.)	8	***4***	trace	0	0	0	0	0	0	0	5	6	***8***
Days With ≥ 1.0" Snow Depth	0	0	0	0	0	0	0	0	0	0	0	0	0

Muskogee *Muskogee County* Elevation: 583 ft. Latitude: 35° 46' N Longitude: 95° 20' W

	JAN	FEB	MAR	APR	MAY	JUN	JUL	AUG	SEP	OCT	NOV	DEC	YEAR
Mean Maximum Temp. (°F)	49.5	54.1	***63.9***	73.0	80.0	87.1	93.1	93.5	85.1	74.3	61.8	50.4	***72.1***
Mean Temp. (°F)	38.7	42.9	***52.1***	61.3	69.6	77.0	82.2	81.9	73.5	62.5	51.0	40.2	***61.1***
Mean Minimum Temp. (°F)	28.0	31.7	***40.3***	49.5	59.2	66.9	71.1	70.2	61.8	50.7	40.1	30.2	***50.0***
Extreme Maximum Temp. (°F)	77	90	***93***	97	96	101	112	108	109	93	88	78	***112***
Extreme Minimum Temp. (°F)	-5	-4	***3***	21	31	47	37	52	34	26	13	-7	***-7***
Days Maximum Temp. ≥ 90°F	0	0	***0***	0	2	11	24	23	9	1	0	0	***70***
Days Maximum Temp. ≤ 32°F	2	2	***0***	0	0	0	0	0	0	0	0	2	***6***
Days Minimum Temp. ≤ 32°F	22	15	***7***	1	0	0	0	0	0	1	8	18	***72***
Days Minimum Temp. ≤ 0°F	0	0	***0***	0	0	0	0	0	0	0	0	0	***0***
Heating Degree Days (base 65°F)	807	616	***406***	165	32	1	0	0	20	141	421	762	***3,371***
Cooling Degree Days (base 65°F)	0	0	***14***	61	182	368	539	530	281	70	8	1	***2,054***
Mean Precipitation (in.)	2.20	2.41	***3.65***	3.78	5.73	5.01	3.00	2.84	4.86	4.33	3.73	2.92	***44.46***
Extreme Maximum Daily Precip. (in.)	2.81	2.92	***2.95***	3.23	3.96	3.75	***3.55***	3.96	6.07	7.70	3.25	3.34	***7.70***
Days With ≥ 0.1" Precipitation	3	5	***5***	6	7	6	4	4	5	5	5	4	***59***
Days With ≥ 0.5" Precipitation	1	2	***3***	3	4	4	2	2	3	2	3	2	***31***
Days With ≥ 1.0" Precipitation	1	1	***1***	1	2	2	1	1	2	1	1	1	***15***
Mean Snowfall (in.)	***1.4***	***1.0***	***1.0***	0.0	0.0	0.0	0.0	0.0	0.0	trace	trace	1.5	***4.9***
Maximum Snow Depth (in.)	***6***	***4***	***0***	0	0	0	0	0	0	***0***	1	4	***6***
Days With ≥ 1.0" Snow Depth	***0***	***0***	***0***	0	0	0	0	0	0	0	0	0	***0***

The period of record for all cooperative weather station data is 1980 – 2009. See User Guide for detailed explanation of data.

Pawhuska *Osage County* Elevation: 834 ft. Latitude: 36° 40' N Longitude: 96° 21' W

	JAN	FEB	MAR	APR	MAY	JUN	JUL	AUG	SEP	OCT	NOV	DEC	YEAR
Mean Maximum Temp. (°F)	48.1	53.6	63.1	72.5	79.2	86.6	92.6	92.9	84.5	73.1	60.5	48.9	71.3
Mean Temp. (°F)	36.5	41.3	50.6	59.9	68.2	76.2	81.5	81.0	72.3	60.8	49.1	38.0	59.6
Mean Minimum Temp. (°F)	24.9	28.9	38.0	47.3	57.1	65.7	70.4	69.0	60.1	48.5	37.6	27.1	47.9
Extreme Maximum Temp. (°F)	78	90	90	95	95	104	111	109	108	94	88	77	111
Extreme Minimum Temp. (°F)	-12	-15	4	23	34	44	53	46	29	15	9	-14	-15
Days Maximum Temp. ≥ 90°F	0	0	0	1	1	9	23	22	8	0	0	0	64
Days Maximum Temp. ≤ 32°F	3	2	0	0	0	0	0	0	0	0	0	3	8
Days Minimum Temp. ≤ 32°F	24	18	10	2	0	0	0	0	0	2	10	22	88
Days Minimum Temp. ≤ 0°F	0	0	0	0	0	0	0	0	0	0	0	1	1
Heating Degree Days (base 65°F)	877	665	450	199	46	2	0	0	28	178	477	829	3,751
Cooling Degree Days (base 65°F)	0	1	11	53	151	344	519	502	255	57	6	1	1,900
Mean Precipitation (in.)	1.52	2.20	3.82	4.87	5.84	6.16	3.82	3.30	4.58	3.97	3.05	2.22	45.35
Extreme Maximum Daily Precip. (in.)	2.44	3.25	4.32	7.92	4.40	6.01	5.21	3.90	7.14	6.21	3.19	2.58	7.92
Days With ≥ 0.1" Precipitation	3	4	6	6	8	7	5	4	5	5	4	4	61
Days With ≥ 0.5" Precipitation	1	1	3	3	4	4	2	2	3	3	2	2	30
Days With ≥ 1.0" Precipitation	0	1	1	2	2	2	1	1	1	1	1	1	14
Mean Snowfall (in.)	2.0	2.4	1.0	trace	0.0	0.0	0.0	0.0	0.0	0.0	0.2	3.0	8.6
Maximum Snow Depth (in.)	11	12	6	trace	0	0	0	0	0	0	trace	8	12
Days With ≥ 1.0" Snow Depth	2	2	0	0	0	0	0	0	0	0	0	1	5

Perry *Noble County* Elevation: 1,024 ft. Latitude: 36° 17' N Longitude: 97° 17' W

	JAN	FEB	MAR	APR	MAY	JUN	JUL	AUG	SEP	OCT	NOV	DEC	YEAR
Mean Maximum Temp. (°F)	48.8	53.8	62.7	73.0	81.0	89.0	94.7	94.4	85.9	74.3	61.3	49.5	72.4
Mean Temp. (°F)	37.3	41.7	50.4	60.2	69.6	77.9	83.1	82.5	73.8	61.8	49.8	38.6	60.5
Mean Minimum Temp. (°F)	25.7	29.6	38.0	47.4	58.2	66.7	71.3	70.5	61.6	49.4	38.2	27.7	48.7
Extreme Maximum Temp. (°F)	81	91	91	100	103	109	114	110	109	98	88	76	114
Extreme Minimum Temp. (°F)	-8	-12	5	18	35	46	54	48	30	17	12	-18	-18
Days Maximum Temp. ≥ 90°F	0	0	0	1	4	15	25	24	11	1	0	0	81
Days Maximum Temp. ≤ 32°F	4	3	0	0	0	0	0	0	0	0	0	3	10
Days Minimum Temp. ≤ 32°F	24	17	9	1	0	0	0	0	0	1	9	21	82
Days Minimum Temp. ≤ 0°F	0	0	0	0	0	0	0	0	0	0	0	1	1
Heating Degree Days (base 65°F)	852	651	459	192	38	2	0	0	23	158	457	811	3,643
Cooling Degree Days (base 65°F)	0	1	11	56	187	396	567	550	293	66	6	0	2,133
Mean Precipitation (in.)	1.16	1.71	2.92	3.53	5.09	4.73	3.06	3.33	3.92	3.14	2.05	1.60	36.24
Extreme Maximum Daily Precip. (in.)	2.20	2.60	4.18	4.64	3.92	3.00	2.75	5.17	7.03	4.01	4.02	2.27	7.03
Days With ≥ 0.1" Precipitation	2	3	5	5	7	6	4	4	5	5	3	3	52
Days With ≥ 0.5" Precipitation	1	1	2	3	3	3	2	2	2	2	1	1	23
Days With ≥ 1.0" Precipitation	0	0	1	1	2	2	1	1	1	1	1	1	12
Mean Snowfall (in.)	1.8	1.6	1.1	0.0	0.0	0.0	0.0	0.0	0.0	0.0	0.2	1.9	6.6
Maximum Snow Depth (in.)	6	2	2	0	0	0	0	0	0	0	3	9	9
Days With ≥ 1.0" Snow Depth	0	0	0	0	0	0	0	0	0	0	0	1	1

Ponca City Municipal Arpt *Kay County* Elevation: 999 ft. Latitude: 36° 44' N Longitude: 97° 06' W

	JAN	FEB	MAR	APR	MAY	JUN	JUL	AUG	SEP	OCT	NOV	DEC	YEAR
Mean Maximum Temp. (°F)	46.5	52.1	61.3	71.1	79.4	88.0	93.9	93.4	84.5	72.3	59.6	47.7	70.8
Mean Temp. (°F)	36.0	40.7	49.6	59.1	68.6	77.5	82.9	82.2	73.1	61.0	48.7	37.5	59.7
Mean Minimum Temp. (°F)	25.5	29.2	37.9	47.1	57.8	67.0	71.9	71.0	61.7	49.6	37.7	27.4	48.6
Extreme Maximum Temp. (°F)	79	92	90	99	100	106	116	108	110	96	88	76	116
Extreme Minimum Temp. (°F)	-12	-8	0	22	33	45	51	49	28	15	11	-10	-12
Days Maximum Temp. ≥ 90°F	0	0	0	1	3	13	23	22	9	1	0	0	72
Days Maximum Temp. ≤ 32°F	5	3	0	0	0	0	0	0	0	0	0	3	11
Days Minimum Temp. ≤ 32°F	25	17	10	2	0	0	0	0	0	1	10	21	86
Days Minimum Temp. ≤ 0°F	0	0	0	0	0	0	0	0	0	0	0	1	1
Heating Degree Days (base 65°F)	892	681	479	217	49	1	0	0	27	179	489	844	3,858
Cooling Degree Days (base 65°F)	0	1	9	48	167	383	563	541	278	61	6	0	2,057
Mean Precipitation (in.)	1.02	1.36	2.78	3.34	4.78	5.09	3.25	3.18	3.28	3.40	1.80	1.44	34.72
Extreme Maximum Daily Precip. (in.)	3.67	2.85	2.77	3.42	4.32	5.40	4.63	4.30	5.76	6.58	2.97	2.13	6.58
Days With ≥ 0.1" Precipitation	2	3	5	5	7	7	5	4	4	4	3	3	52
Days With ≥ 0.5" Precipitation	1	1	2	2	3	4	2	2	2	2	1	1	24
Days With ≥ 1.0" Precipitation	0	0	1	1	2	2	1	1	1	1	0	0	10
Mean Snowfall (in.)	na	na	na	na	na	na	na	na	na	na	na	na	na
Maximum Snow Depth (in.)	na	na	na	na	na	na	na	na	na	na	na	na	na
Days With ≥ 1.0" Snow Depth	na	na	na	na	na	na	na	na	na	na	na	na	na

Sallisaw 2 NW *Sequoyah County* Elevation: 660 ft. Latitude: 35° 27' N Longitude: 94° 48' W

	JAN	FEB	MAR	APR	MAY	JUN	JUL	AUG	SEP	OCT	NOV	DEC	YEAR
Mean Maximum Temp. (°F)	49.7	54.6	63.3	72.3	79.2	86.9	92.6	92.7	85.0	73.8	61.8	50.7	71.9
Mean Temp. (°F)	39.1	43.4	51.9	60.5	68.9	76.6	81.5	81.3	73.5	62.2	51.0	40.6	60.9
Mean Minimum Temp. (°F)	28.2	32.1	40.4	48.7	58.5	66.3	70.3	69.9	62.0	50.5	40.2	30.3	49.8
Extreme Maximum Temp. (°F)	78	84	87	92	94	102	108	107	107	93	86	79	108
Extreme Minimum Temp. (°F)	-9	-8	7	24	36	45	50	50	33	18	14	-9	-9
Days Maximum Temp. ≥ 90°F	0	0	0	0	1	10	22	22	9	1	0	0	65
Days Maximum Temp. ≤ 32°F	2	1	0	0	0	0	0	0	0	0	0	2	5
Days Minimum Temp. ≤ 32°F	22	14	7	1	0	0	0	0	0	1	7	18	70
Days Minimum Temp. ≤ 0°F	0	0	0	0	0	0	0	0	0	0	0	0	0
Heating Degree Days (base 65°F)	795	606	410	174	34	1	0	0	20	146	420	752	3,358
Cooling Degree Days (base 65°F)	0	1	10	46	161	356	518	513	281	66	6	1	1,959
Mean Precipitation (in.)	2.66	2.94	3.94	4.50	5.86	4.49	3.16	3.18	4.55	4.39	4.36	3.14	47.17
Extreme Maximum Daily Precip. (in.)	3.64	3.27	4.24	4.20	4.39	2.96	6.40	3.29	3.40	3.90	3.55	2.25	6.40
Days With ≥ 0.1" Precipitation	3	5	6	6	8	7	4	4	6	5	5	4	63
Days With ≥ 0.5" Precipitation	2	2	3	3	4	3	2	2	3	2	3	2	31
Days With ≥ 1.0" Precipitation	1	1	1	2	2	1	1	1	2	1	2	1	16
Mean Snowfall (in.)	1.3	0.8	0.5	0.0	0.0	0.0	0.0	0.0	0.0	trace	0.1	0.5	3.2
Maximum Snow Depth (in.)	9	9	9	0	0	0	0	0	0	trace	1	4	9
Days With ≥ 1.0" Snow Depth	1	1	0	0	0	0	0	0	0	0	0	1	3

The period of record for all cooperative weather station data is 1980 – 2009. See User Guide for detailed explanation of data.

Stillwater 2 W *Payne County* Elevation: 895 ft. Latitude: 36° 07' N Longitude: 97° 06' W

	JAN	FEB	MAR	APR	MAY	JUN	JUL	AUG	SEP	OCT	NOV	DEC	YEAR
Mean Maximum Temp. (°F)	48.5	53.1	61.5	71.5	79.2	87.2	93.1	93.2	84.6	73.4	61.0	49.4	71.3
Mean Temp. (°F)	36.5	40.9	49.5	58.9	68.3	76.7	81.9	81.4	72.4	60.5	49.0	38.2	59.5
Mean Minimum Temp. (°F)	24.5	28.6	37.4	46.2	57.2	66.0	70.6	69.4	60.1	47.6	37.1	27.0	47.6
Extreme Maximum Temp. (°F)	81	92	93	100	101	105	112	109	111	95	87	78	112
Extreme Minimum Temp. (°F)	-11	-18	0	24	33	46	53	50	31	15	12	-15	-18
Days Maximum Temp. ≥ 90°F	0	0	0	1	3	12	23	23	10	1	0	0	73
Days Maximum Temp. ≤ 32°F	4	3	0	0	0	0	0	0	0	0	0	3	10
Days Minimum Temp. ≤ 32°F	26	19	10	2	0	0	0	0	0	2	11	23	93
Days Minimum Temp. ≤ 0°F	0	0	0	0	0	0	0	0	0	0	0	1	1
Heating Degree Days (base 65°F)	876	677	482	223	49	2	0	0	31	186	478	823	3,827
Cooling Degree Days (base 65°F)	0	1	8	46	157	358	530	514	260	54	6	0	1,934
Mean Precipitation (in.)	1.35	1.59	3.20	3.52	5.28	4.96	2.91	3.21	3.74	3.30	2.30	1.77	37.13
Extreme Maximum Daily Precip. (in.)	2.05	2.50	3.34	5.50	4.75	3.00	4.27	5.31	4.95	3.41	3.23	2.46	5.50
Days With ≥ 0.1" Precipitation	3	3	5	5	7	7	4	4	5	4	4	3	54
Days With ≥ 0.5" Precipitation	1	1	2	2	3	4	2	2	3	2	2	1	25
Days With ≥ 1.0" Precipitation	0	0	1	1	1	2	1	1	1	1	1	0	10
Mean Snowfall (in.)	2.5	1.5	1.3	0.0	0.0	0.0	0.0	0.0	0.0	0.0	0.1	2.8	8.2
Maximum Snow Depth (in.)	9	8	9	0	0	0	0	0	0	0	1	12	12
Days With ≥ 1.0" Snow Depth	2	1	0	0	0	0	0	0	0	0	0	1	4

Taloga *Dewey County* Elevation: 1,705 ft. Latitude: 36° 02' N Longitude: 98° 58' W

	JAN	FEB	MAR	APR	MAY	JUN	JUL	AUG	SEP	OCT	NOV	DEC	YEAR
Mean Maximum Temp. (°F)	49.7	53.9	61.9	71.8	80.4	89.0	95.3	94.0	85.2	73.4	60.9	49.4	72.1
Mean Temp. (°F)	36.4	40.2	48.3	57.8	67.3	76.6	81.9	80.8	71.9	59.7	47.2	36.9	58.8
Mean Minimum Temp. (°F)	23.0	26.5	34.6	43.8	54.3	64.2	68.5	67.5	58.6	46.0	33.5	24.3	45.4
Extreme Maximum Temp. (°F)	82	91	93	97	103	110	113	108	109	99	91	79	113
Extreme Minimum Temp. (°F)	-15	-17	2	20	30	44	49	47	29	9	4	-16	-17
Days Maximum Temp. ≥ 90°F	0	0	0	1	5	16	26	24	11	1	0	0	84
Days Maximum Temp. ≤ 32°F	3	2	0	0	0	0	0	0	0	0	0	3	8
Days Minimum Temp. ≤ 32°F	27	21	12	3	0	0	0	0	0	3	15	26	107
Days Minimum Temp. ≤ 0°F	0	0	0	0	0	0	0	0	0	0	0	1	1
Heating Degree Days (base 65°F)	879	694	515	239	61	3	0	0	32	202	527	865	4,017
Cooling Degree Days (base 65°F)	0	0	4	31	139	358	532	498	246	44	2	0	1,854
Mean Precipitation (in.)	0.87	1.04	2.24	2.78	4.47	4.27	2.18	2.63	2.71	2.92	1.60	1.21	28.92
Extreme Maximum Daily Precip. (in.)	1.87	1.70	3.42	3.08	4.16	5.80	2.40	3.05	7.02	5.42	3.19	3.30	7.02
Days With ≥ 0.1" Precipitation	2	2	4	4	6	6	4	5	4	4	3	3	47
Days With ≥ 0.5" Precipitation	1	1	2	2	3	3	2	2	2	2	1	1	22
Days With ≥ 1.0" Precipitation	0	0	1	1	1	1	1	1	1	1	0	0	8
Mean Snowfall (in.)	3.6	3.0	1.9	0.1	0.0	0.0	0.0	0.0	0.0	0.1	1.0	4.0	13.7
Maximum Snow Depth (in.)	12	8	10	2	0	0	0	0	0	2	6	11	12
Days With ≥ 1.0" Snow Depth	3	2	1	0	0	0	0	0	0	0	0	3	9

Walters *Cotton County* Elevation: 1,004 ft. Latitude: 34° 22' N Longitude: 98° 18' W

	JAN	FEB	MAR	APR	MAY	JUN	JUL	AUG	SEP	OCT	NOV	DEC	YEAR
Mean Maximum Temp. (°F)	53.6	58.3	66.8	75.8	83.1	90.9	96.8	96.9	88.1	76.7	64.4	***53.0***	***75.4***
Mean Temp. (°F)	41.0	45.3	53.4	62.0	70.8	78.8	83.8	83.5	75.1	63.9	51.9	***41.1***	***62.5***
Mean Minimum Temp. (°F)	28.3	32.2	39.9	48.1	58.4	66.6	70.6	70.1	62.0	51.0	39.4	29.2	49.7
Extreme Maximum Temp. (°F)	83	91	93	101	109	114	111	111	111	99	90	79	114
Extreme Minimum Temp. (°F)	-3	-1	8	24	34	48	56	54	36	21	15	-9	-9
Days Maximum Temp. ≥ 90°F	0	0	0	1	7	18	27	27	13	2	0	0	95
Days Maximum Temp. ≤ 32°F	2	1	0	0	0	0	0	0	0	0	0	2	5
Days Minimum Temp. ≤ 32°F	21	14	7	1	0	0	0	0	0	1	8	19	71
Days Minimum Temp. ≤ 0°F	0	0	0	0	0	0	0	0	0	0	0	0	0
Heating Degree Days (base 65°F)	739	549	367	141	24	0	0	0	15	117	398	***732***	***3,082***
Cooling Degree Days (base 65°F)	0	1	13	57	210	420	588	581	323	90	7	***0***	***2,290***
Mean Precipitation (in.)	1.40	1.89	2.79	2.83	4.59	4.44	1.97	2.69	3.37	3.76	2.15	1.73	33.61
Extreme Maximum Daily Precip. (in.)	2.25	2.90	3.35	4.60	11.64	5.40	4.55	8.50	***3.25***	***3.80***	2.20	***2.80***	***11.64***
Days With ≥ 0.1" Precipitation	2	4	4	4	6	5	3	4	4	4	3	3	46
Days With ≥ 0.5" Precipitation	1	1	2	2	3	3	1	2	2	2	2	1	22
Days With ≥ 1.0" Precipitation	0	0	1	1	1	2	1	1	1	1	1	1	11
Mean Snowfall (in.)	0.3	0.3	0.2	0.0	0.0	0.0	0.0	0.0	0.0	0.0	0.2	0.5	1.5
Maximum Snow Depth (in.)	5	4	trace	0	0	0	0	0	0	0	trace	4	5
Days With ≥ 1.0" Snow Depth	0	0	0	0	0	0	0	0	0	0	0	0	0

Waurika *Jefferson County* Elevation: 875 ft. Latitude: 34° 10' N Longitude: 98° 00' W

	JAN	FEB	MAR	APR	MAY	JUN	JUL	AUG	SEP	OCT	NOV	DEC	YEAR
Mean Maximum Temp. (°F)	55.3	59.6	68.3	76.5	83.9	90.8	96.6	96.4	88.7	78.0	65.4	56.2	76.3
Mean Temp. (°F)	43.1	47.2	55.5	63.7	72.3	79.5	84.4	83.9	76.2	65.5	53.5	44.5	64.1
Mean Minimum Temp. (°F)	30.8	34.7	42.6	50.7	60.6	68.1	72.1	71.5	63.8	53.0	41.5	32.7	51.8
Extreme Maximum Temp. (°F)	83	93	94	99	108	115	112	109	114	100	87	81	115
Extreme Minimum Temp. (°F)	0	-8	5	28	38	50	57	53	36	19	16	-10	-10
Days Maximum Temp. ≥ 90°F	0	0	0	1	7	19	28	27	15	3	0	0	100
Days Maximum Temp. ≤ 32°F	1	1	0	0	0	0	0	0	0	0	0	1	3
Days Minimum Temp. ≤ 32°F	18	12	5	0	0	0	0	0	0	1	6	16	58
Days Minimum Temp. ≤ 0°F	0	0	0	0	0	0	0	0	0	0	0	0	0
Heating Degree Days (base 65°F)	673	499	311	113	16	0	0	0	11	91	352	630	2,696
Cooling Degree Days (base 65°F)	1	2	21	79	249	441	608	594	355	113	13	1	2,477
Mean Precipitation (in.)	1.37	1.88	2.59	2.59	4.58	4.03	2.11	2.25	2.99	3.22	2.03	1.87	31.51
Extreme Maximum Daily Precip. (in.)	2.50	2.98	4.01	3.03	4.48	4.02	2.60	3.61	2.95	4.02	2.25	2.80	4.48
Days With ≥ 0.1" Precipitation	3	3	4	4	6	5	3	3	4	4	3	3	45
Days With ≥ 0.5" Precipitation	1	1	2	2	3	3	1	2	2	2	1	1	21
Days With ≥ 1.0" Precipitation	0	0	1	1	1	1	1	1	1	1	1	1	10
Mean Snowfall (in.)	1.2	0.6	0.5	0.0	0.0	0.0	0.0	0.0	0.0	trace	0.2	0.4	2.9
Maximum Snow Depth (in.)	3	***5***	trace	0	0	0	0	0	0	trace	trace	trace	***5***
Days With ≥ 1.0" Snow Depth	0	0	0	0	0	0	0	0	0	0	0	0	0

The period of record for all cooperative weather station data is 1980 – 2009. See User Guide for detailed explanation of data.

Webbers Falls 5 WSW *Muskogee County* Elevation: 549 ft. Latitude: 35° 29' N Longitude: 95° 12' W

	JAN	FEB	MAR	APR	MAY	JUN	JUL	AUG	SEP	OCT	NOV	DEC	YEAR
Mean Maximum Temp. (°F)	49.3	54.1	62.6	72.3	79.5	87.4	94.0	93.9	86.1	74.6	61.7	51.6	72.2
Mean Temp. (°F)	37.8	42.1	50.5	59.5	68.3	76.4	81.8	81.2	73.3	61.6	50.0	40.4	60.2
Mean Minimum Temp. (°F)	26.2	30.1	38.4	46.7	57.0	65.3	69.5	68.4	60.5	48.6	38.3	29.1	48.2
Extreme Maximum Temp. (°F)	77	92	91	96	98	104	112	111	112	96	85	80	112
Extreme Minimum Temp. (°F)	-4	-4	2	21	34	45	54	50	35	19	15	-11	-11
Days Maximum Temp. ≥ 90°F	0	0	0	0	2	12	23	22	10	1	0	0	70
Days Maximum Temp. ≤ 32°F	3	2	0	0	0	0	0	0	0	0	0	2	7
Days Minimum Temp. ≤ 32°F	24	16	8	2	0	0	0	0	0	1	10	20	81
Days Minimum Temp. ≤ 0°F	0	0	0	0	0	0	0	0	0	0	0	0	0
Heating Degree Days (base 65°F)	836	643	447	198	45	1	0	0	26	158	450	756	3,560
Cooling Degree Days (base 65°F)	0	0	9	40	153	349	527	509	281	60	7	0	1,935
Mean Precipitation (in.)	2.65	2.65	3.94	4.01	5.77	4.49	2.99	2.92	5.04	4.36	4.42	3.52	46.76
Extreme Maximum Daily Precip. (in.)	3.32	3.04	2.40	3.10	4.05	2.75	4.56	3.94	5.60	9.46	3.85	3.25	9.46
Days With ≥ 0.1" Precipitation	4	4	6	6	7	6	4	4	6	5	6	5	63
Days With ≥ 0.5" Precipitation	2	2	3	3	4	3	2	2	3	2	3	3	32
Days With ≥ 1.0" Precipitation	1	1	1	1	2	2	1	1	2	1	2	1	16
Mean Snowfall (in.)	2.2	1.3	1.3	0.0	0.0	0.0	0.0	0.0	0.0	trace	0.3	0.6	5.7
Maximum Snow Depth (in.)	9	3	7	1	0	0	0	0	0	0	4	3	9
Days With ≥ 1.0" Snow Depth	1	1	0	0	0	0	0	0	0	0	0	0	2

Oklahoma Weather Station Rankings

Annual Extreme Maximum Temperature

Highest

Rank	Station Name	°F
1	Chattanooga 3 NE	116
1	Ponca City Municipal Arpt	116
3	Altus Irig Res Station	115
3	Buffalo	115
3	Frederick	115
3	Waurika	115
7	Healdton	114
7	Perry	114
7	Walters	114
10	Beaver	113
10	Billings	113
10	Guthrie 5 S	113
10	Helena 1 SSE	113
10	Mannford 6 NW	113
10	Taloga	113
16	Ardmore	112
16	Bartlesville Frank Phillips	112
16	Clinton	*112*
16	Muskogee	*112*
16	Stillwater 2 W	112
16	Webbers Falls 5 WSW	*112*
22	Bristow	111
22	Chandler 1	111
22	Chickasaw Nra	111
22	Duncan	111

Lowest

Rank	Station Name	°F
1	Kansas 1 ESE	108
1	Sallisaw 2 NW	108
3	Ada	109
3	Claremore 2 ENE	109
3	El Reno 1 N	109
3	Geary	109
7	Anadarko 3 E	110
7	Antlers	110
7	Arnett	*110*
7	Blanchard 2 SSW	110
7	Cushing	110
7	Idabel	*110*
7	Meeker 4 W	110
7	Okla City Will Rogers World Arpt	110
15	Bristow	111
15	Chandler 1	111
15	Chickasaw Nra	111
15	Duncan	111
15	Enid	111
15	Erick	111
15	Goodwell Research Stn	111
15	Holdenville	111
15	McCurtain 1 SE	111
15	Pawhuska	111
15	Tulsa Intl Arpt	111

Annual Mean Maximum Temperature

Highest

Rank	Station Name	°F
1	Waurika	76.3
2	Altus Irig Res Station	75.9
3	Chattanooga 3 NE	75.7
4	Walters	*75.4*
5	Ardmore	74.6
5	Frederick	*74.6*
5	Healdton	*74.6*
8	Idabel	*74.3*
9	Antlers	*74.2*
10	Buffalo	73.9
10	McCurtain 1 SE	73.9
12	Ada	73.3
12	Clinton	*73.3*
14	Bristow	73.2
14	Erick	73.2
16	Holdenville	*73.1*
17	Duncan	73.0
18	Guthrie 5 S	72.9
19	Blanchard 2 SSW	72.7
19	Chickasaw Nra	72.7
21	Chandler 1	72.5
22	Anadarko 3 E	72.4
22	Mannford 6 NW	72.4
22	Perry	72.4
25	Webbers Falls 5 WSW	*72.2*

Lowest

Rank	Station Name	°F
1	Arnett	*69.3*
2	Billings	70.2
2	Claremore 2 ENE	70.2
4	Kansas 1 ESE	70.4
5	Helena 1 SSE	70.5
6	Beaver	70.7
6	Goodwell Research Stn	70.7
8	Cushing	70.8
8	Ponca City Municipal Arpt	70.8
10	Enid	71.2
11	Geary	71.3
11	Pawhuska	71.3
11	Stillwater 2 W	71.3
14	Tulsa Intl Arpt	71.4
15	Okla City Will Rogers World Arpt	71.5
16	Meeker 4 W	71.6
17	Bartlesville Frank Phillips	71.8
18	Sallisaw 2 NW	71.9
19	El Reno 1 N	72.0
20	Muskogee	*72.1*
20	Taloga	72.1
22	Webbers Falls 5 WSW	*72.2*
23	Anadarko 3 E	72.4
23	Mannford 6 NW	72.4
23	Perry	72.4

Rankings include 25 highest/lowest stations. If state has less than 25 stations, all stations are included. The period of record is 1980–2009. See User Guide for detailed explanation of data.

Annual Mean Temperature

Highest Rank	Station Name	°F	Lowest Rank	Station Name	°F
1	Waurika	64.1	1	Goodwell Research Stn	56.0
2	Ardmore	63.8	2	Beaver	56.1
3	McCurtain 1 SE	62.7	3	Arnett	***56.7***
4	Walters	***62.5***	4	Helena 1 SSE	58.1
5	Altus Irig Res Station	62.4	5	Billings	58.5
6	Antlers	***62.3***	6	Claremore 2 ENE	58.7
6	Chattanooga 3 NE	62.3	7	Taloga	58.8
8	Healdton	***62.2***	8	Buffalo	59.5
8	Idabel	***62.2***	8	Stillwater 2 W	59.5
10	Frederick	***62.1***	10	Pawhuska	59.6
11	Duncan	61.7	11	Erick	59.7
12	Ada	61.5	11	Kansas 1 ESE	59.7
13	Blanchard 2 SSW	61.3	13	Bartlesville Frank Phillips	59.8
13	Holdenville	***61.3***	13	Cushing	59.8
15	Chickasaw Nra	61.2	13	Ponca City Municipal Arpt	59.8
16	Bristow	61.1	16	Anadarko 3 E	***59.9***
16	Muskogee	***61.1***	16	Geary	59.9
18	Tulsa Intl Arpt	61.0	18	Enid	60.0
19	Chandler 1	60.9	19	Meeker 4 W	60.1
19	Guthrie 5 S	60.9	20	Webbers Falls 5 WSW	***60.2***
19	Sallisaw 2 NW	60.9	21	El Reno 1 N	***60.3***
22	Mannford 6 NW	60.8	22	Okla City Will Rogers World Arpt	60.6
23	Clinton	***60.7***	22	Perry	60.6
24	Okla City Will Rogers World Arpt	60.6	24	Clinton	***60.7***
24	Perry	60.6	25	Mannford 6 NW	60.8

Annual Mean Minimum Temperature

Highest Rank	Station Name	°F	Lowest Rank	Station Name	°F
1	Ardmore	53.0	1	Goodwell Research Stn	41.2
2	Waurika	51.8	2	Beaver	41.5
3	McCurtain 1 SE	51.3	3	Arnett	***44.0***
4	Tulsa Intl Arpt	50.6	4	Buffalo	45.0
5	Antlers	***50.2***	5	Taloga	45.4
5	Duncan	50.2	6	Helena 1 SSE	45.7
7	Idabel	***50.0***	7	Erick	46.1
7	Muskogee	***50.0***	8	Billings	46.7
9	Blanchard 2 SSW	49.8	9	Claremore 2 ENE	47.1
9	Healdton	***49.8***	10	Anadarko 3 E	47.3
9	Sallisaw 2 NW	49.8	11	Bartlesville Frank Phillips	47.6
12	Ada	49.7	11	Stillwater 2 W	47.6
12	Okla City Will Rogers World Arpt	49.7	13	Pawhuska	47.9
12	Walters	49.7	14	Clinton	***48.1***
15	Chickasaw Nra	49.5	15	Webbers Falls 5 WSW	***48.2***
15	Frederick	49.5	16	Geary	48.5
17	Holdenville	***49.3***	17	El Reno 1 N	***48.6***
18	Chandler 1	49.2	17	Meeker 4 W	48.6
19	Mannford 6 NW	49.1	19	Perry	48.7
20	Bristow	49.0	19	Ponca City Municipal Arpt	48.7
20	Kansas 1 ESE	49.0	21	Altus Irig Res Station	48.8
22	Guthrie 5 S	48.9	21	Chattanooga 3 NE	48.8
23	Altus Irig Res Station	48.8	21	Cushing	48.8
23	Chattanooga 3 NE	48.8	21	Enid	48.8
23	Cushing	48.8	25	Guthrie 5 S	48.9

Rankings include 25 highest/lowest stations. If state has less than 25 stations, all stations are included. The period of record is 1980–2009. See User Guide for detailed explanation of data.

Annual Extreme Minimum Temperature

Highest

Rank	Station Name	°F
1	Idabel	***-2***
2	Antlers	-5
3	Duncan	-7
3	Muskogee	***-7***
5	Ada	-8
5	Ardmore	-8
5	Okla City Will Rogers World Arpt	-8
8	Cushing	-9
8	Erick	-9
8	McCurtain 1 SE	-9
8	Sallisaw 2 NW	-9
8	Walters	-9
13	Altus Irig Res Station	-10
13	Enid	-10
13	Healdton	-10
13	Waurika	-10
17	Arnett	***-11***
17	Blanchard 2 SSW	-11
17	Chickasaw Nra	-11
17	Clinton	***-11***
17	El Reno 1 N	***-11***
17	Frederick	-11
17	Tulsa Intl Arpt	-11
17	Webbers Falls 5 WSW	***-11***
25	Geary	-12

Lowest

Rank	Station Name	°F
1	Claremore 2 ENE	-20
2	Beaver	-18
2	Perry	-18
2	Stillwater 2 W	-18
5	Anadarko 3 E	-17
5	Taloga	-17
7	Mannford 6 NW	-16
8	Bartlesville Frank Phillips	-15
8	Billings	-15
8	Helena 1 SSE	-15
8	Meeker 4 W	-15
8	Pawhuska	-15
13	Bristow	-14
13	Buffalo	-14
13	Goodwell Research Stn	-14
13	Guthrie 5 S	-14
17	Chandler 1	-13
17	Chattanooga 3 NE	-13
17	Holdenville	-13
17	Kansas 1 ESE	-13
21	Geary	-12
21	Ponca City Municipal Arpt	-12
23	Arnett	***-11***
23	Blanchard 2 SSW	-11
23	Chickasaw Nra	-11

July Mean Maximum Temperature

Highest

Rank	Station Name	°F
1	Chattanooga 3 NE	98.1
2	Altus Irig Res Station	97.5
2	Buffalo	97.5
4	Walters	96.8
5	Waurika	96.7
6	Clinton	96.6
6	Frederick	96.6
8	Taloga	95.4
9	Healdton	95.3
10	Enid	95.0
10	Erick	95.0
10	Helena 1 SSE	95.0
13	Guthrie 5 S	94.7
13	Perry	94.7
15	Beaver	94.6
16	Ardmore	94.3
16	El Reno 1 N	94.3
16	McCurtain 1 SE	94.3
19	Holdenville	94.2
20	Goodwell Research Stn	94.1
21	Bartlesville Frank Phillips	94.0
21	Blanchard 2 SSW	94.0
21	Webbers Falls 5 WSW	***94.0***
24	Billings	93.9
24	Bristow	93.9

Lowest

Rank	Station Name	°F
1	Kansas 1 ESE	90.6
2	Claremore 2 ENE	92.0
3	Arnett	***92.2***
3	Meeker 4 W	92.2
5	Kenton	92.3
6	Cushing	92.6
6	Pawhuska	92.6
6	Sallisaw 2 NW	92.6
9	Idabel	92.9
10	Geary	93.1
10	Muskogee	93.1
10	Stillwater 2 W	93.1
13	Antlers	93.2
13	Chickasaw Nra	93.2
15	Tulsa Intl Arpt	93.4
16	Ada	93.5
16	Chandler 1	93.5
16	Okla City Will Rogers World Arpt	93.5
19	Mannford 6 NW	93.6
20	Anadarko 3 E	93.8
21	Billings	93.9
21	Bristow	93.9
21	Duncan	93.9
21	Ponca City Municipal Arpt	93.9
25	Bartlesville Frank Phillips	94.0

Rankings include 25 highest/lowest stations. If state has less than 25 stations, all stations are included. The period of record is 1980–2009. See User Guide for detailed explanation of data.

January Mean Minimum Temperature

Highest Rank	Highest Station Name	Highest °F	Lowest Rank	Lowest Station Name	Lowest °F
1	Ardmore	32.0	1	Beaver	18.9
2	McCurtain 1 SE	31.0	2	Kenton	*19.2*
3	Waurika	30.8	3	Goodwell Research Stn	20.3
4	Antlers	30.0	4	Arnett	*21.8*
5	Idabel	*29.5*	5	Buffalo	22.3
6	Blanchard 2 SSW	28.9	6	Helena 1 SSE	22.7
7	Healdton	28.7	7	Taloga	23.0
8	Ada	28.4	8	Billings	23.5
8	Walters	28.4	9	Claremore 2 ENE	24.0
10	Duncan	28.3	10	Stillwater 2 W	24.5
11	Sallisaw 2 NW	28.2	11	Bartlesville Frank Phillips	24.7
12	Holdenville	28.1	11	Erick	24.7
12	Kansas 1 ESE	28.1	13	Anadarko 3 E	24.8
12	Tulsa Intl Arpt	28.1	14	Pawhuska	24.9
15	Muskogee	28.0	15	Ponca City Municipal Arpt	25.5
16	Bristow	27.8	16	Perry	25.7
16	Frederick	27.8	17	Clinton	25.8
16	Okla City Will Rogers World Arpt	27.8	18	Cushing	26.0
19	Chandler 1	27.6	18	Enid	26.0
20	Chickasaw Nra	27.2	20	Webbers Falls 5 WSW	26.2
20	Geary	27.2	21	Guthrie 5 S	26.5
20	Mannford 6 NW	27.2	22	Altus Irig Res Station	26.9
23	Meeker 4 W	27.1	22	El Reno 1 N	26.9
24	Chattanooga 3 NE	27.0	24	Chattanooga 3 NE	27.0
25	Altus Irig Res Station	26.9	25	Meeker 4 W	27.1

Number of Days Annually Maximum Temperature ≥ 90°F

Highest Rank	Highest Station Name	Highest Days	Lowest Rank	Lowest Station Name	Lowest Days
1	Chattanooga 3 NE	105	1	Kansas 1 ESE	45
2	Altus Irig Res Station	104	2	Meeker 4 W	60
3	Waurika	100	3	Claremore 2 ENE	62
4	Walters	95	4	Arnett	*64*
5	Frederick	94	4	Pawhuska	64
6	Buffalo	93	6	Sallisaw 2 NW	65
7	Clinton	*88*	7	Cushing	67
8	Taloga	84	7	Geary	67
9	Erick	83	9	Mannford 6 NW	68
9	Healdton	83	10	Billings	70
11	Perry	81	10	Chickasaw Nra	70
12	Ardmore	80	10	Muskogee	*70*
12	Enid	80	10	Okla City Will Rogers World Arpt	70
12	Helena 1 SSE	80	10	Webbers Falls 5 WSW	*70*
15	Guthrie 5 S	79	15	Chandler 1	71
16	Beaver	78	16	Ada	72
16	Goodwell Research Stn	78	16	Blanchard 2 SSW	72
18	Bartlesville Frank Phillips	77	16	Ponca City Municipal Arpt	72
18	El Reno 1 N	77	19	Anadarko 3 E	73
18	McCurtain 1 SE	77	19	Stillwater 2 W	73
21	Duncan	76	19	Tulsa Intl Arpt	73
21	Holdenville	*76*	22	Antlers	*74*
23	Idabel	*75*	22	Bristow	74
24	Antlers	*74*	24	Idabel	*75*
24	Bristow	74	25	Duncan	76

Rankings include 25 highest/lowest stations. If state has less than 25 stations, all stations are included. The period of record is 1980–2009. See User Guide for detailed explanation of data.

Number of Days Annually Maximum Temperature ≤ 32°F

Highest			Lowest		
Rank	Station Name	Days	Rank	Station Name	Days
1	Arnett	***16***	1	Antlers	3
1	Beaver	16	1	Idabel	***3***
3	Helena 1 SSE	15	1	Waurika	3
4	Billings	13	4	Ada	5
4	Goodwell Research Stn	13	4	Altus Irig Res Station	5
6	Enid	12	4	Ardmore	5
7	Claremore 2 ENE	11	4	Chattanooga 3 NE	5
7	Cushing	11	4	Healdton	5
7	Ponca City Municipal Arpt	11	4	McCurtain 1 SE	5
10	Perry	10	4	Sallisaw 2 NW	5
10	Stillwater 2 W	10	4	Walters	5
12	Bartlesville Frank Phillips	9	12	Bristow	6
12	Tulsa Intl Arpt	9	12	Duncan	6
14	Buffalo	8	12	Frederick	6
14	El Reno 1 N	8	12	Holdenville	6
14	Erick	8	12	Muskogee	***6***
14	Geary	8	17	Anadarko 3 E	7
14	Okla City Will Rogers World Arpt	8	17	Blanchard 2 SSW	7
14	Pawhuska	8	17	Chandler 1	7
14	Taloga	8	17	Chickasaw Nra	7
21	Anadarko 3 E	7	17	Clinton	***7***
21	Blanchard 2 SSW	7	17	Guthrie 5 S	7
21	Chandler 1	7	17	Kansas 1 ESE	7
21	Chickasaw Nra	7	17	Mannford 6 NW	7
21	Clinton	***7***	17	Meeker 4 W	7

Number of Days Annually Minimum Temperature ≤ 32°F

Highest			Lowest		
Rank	Station Name	Days	Rank	Station Name	Days
1	Beaver	135	1	Ardmore	48
2	Goodwell Research Stn	131	2	Waurika	58
3	Arnett	***113***	3	McCurtain 1 SE	61
4	Taloga	107	4	Antlers	65
5	Buffalo	106	5	Idabel	***68***
5	Helena 1 SSE	106	6	Ada	69
7	Erick	97	6	Blanchard 2 SSW	69
8	Billings	95	6	Frederick	69
9	Claremore 2 ENE	93	9	Duncan	70
9	Stillwater 2 W	93	9	Healdton	70
11	Anadarko 3 E	92	9	Sallisaw 2 NW	70
12	Bartlesville Frank Phillips	88	9	Tulsa Intl Arpt	70
12	Pawhuska	88	13	Walters	71
14	Ponca City Municipal Arpt	86	14	Kansas 1 ESE	72
15	Clinton	***84***	14	Muskogee	***72***
16	Altus Irig Res Station	82	14	Okla City Will Rogers World Arpt	72
16	Perry	82	17	Chandler 1	74
18	Chattanooga 3 NE	81	17	Chickasaw Nra	74
18	Webbers Falls 5 WSW	***81***	17	Holdenville	74
20	Enid	80	20	Geary	76
21	Cushing	79	21	Mannford 6 NW	77
21	Guthrie 5 S	79	22	Bristow	78
23	Bristow	78	22	El Reno 1 N	***78***
23	El Reno 1 N	***78***	22	Meeker 4 W	78
23	Meeker 4 W	78	25	Cushing	79

 Rankings include 25 highest/lowest stations. If state has less than 25 stations, all stations are included. The period of record is 1980–2009. See User Guide for detailed explanation of data.

Number of Days Annually Minimum Temperature ≤ 0°F

Highest Rank	Station Name	Days	Lowest Rank	Station Name	Days
1	Arnett	***3***	1	Ada	0
1	Beaver	3	1	Altus Irig Res Station	0
1	Goodwell Research Stn	3	1	Anadarko 3 E	0
4	Buffalo	2	1	Antlers	0
4	Helena 1 SSE	2	1	Ardmore	0
6	Bartlesville Frank Phillips	1	1	Blanchard 2 SSW	0
6	Billings	1	1	Bristow	0
6	Claremore 2 ENE	1	1	Chandler 1	0
6	Pawhuska	1	1	Chattanooga 3 NE	0
6	Perry	1	1	Chickasaw Nra	0
6	Ponca City Municipal Arpt	1	1	Clinton	***0***
6	Stillwater 2 W	1	1	Cushing	0
6	Taloga	1	1	Duncan	0
14	Ada	0	1	El Reno 1 N	***0***
14	Altus Irig Res Station	0	1	Enid	0
14	Anadarko 3 E	0	1	Erick	0
14	Antlers	0	1	Frederick	0
14	Ardmore	0	1	Geary	0
14	Blanchard 2 SSW	0	1	Guthrie 5 S	0
14	Bristow	0	1	Healdton	0
14	Chandler 1	0	1	Holdenville	0
14	Chattanooga 3 NE	0	1	Idabel	***0***
14	Chickasaw Nra	0	1	Kansas 1 ESE	0
14	Clinton	***0***	1	Mannford 6 NW	0
14	Cushing	0	1	McCurtain 1 SE	0

Number of Annual Heating Degree Days

Highest Rank	Station Name	Num.	Lowest Rank	Station Name	Num.
1	Beaver	4,730	1	Waurika	2,696
2	Goodwell Research Stn	4,624	2	Ardmore	2,719
3	Arnett	***4,471***	3	Antlers	***2,926***
4	Helena 1 SSE	4,263	4	McCurtain 1 SE	2,952
5	Billings	4,142	5	Idabel	***2,979***
6	Taloga	4,017	6	Healdton	***3,081***
7	Claremore 2 ENE	3,995	7	Walters	***3,082***
8	Buffalo	3,953	8	Altus Irig Res Station	3,156
9	Ponca City Municipal Arpt	3,858	9	Ada	3,189
10	Stillwater 2 W	3,827	10	Frederick	***3,191***
11	Enid	3,795	11	Chattanooga 3 NE	3,205
12	Bartlesville Frank Phillips	3,751	12	Duncan	3,229
12	Pawhuska	3,751	13	Holdenville	***3,292***
14	Cushing	3,717	14	Blanchard 2 SSW	3,309
15	Anadarko 3 E	***3,690***	15	Bristow	3,330
16	Erick	3,685	16	Chickasaw Nra	3,344
17	Geary	3,648	17	Sallisaw 2 NW	3,358
18	Perry	3,643	18	Muskogee	***3,371***
19	El Reno 1 N	***3,603***	19	Chandler 1	3,409
20	Clinton	***3,593***	20	Mannford 6 NW	3,433
21	Webbers Falls 5 WSW	***3,560***	21	Tulsa Intl Arpt	3,478
22	Meeker 4 W	3,534	22	Okla City Will Rogers World Arpt	3,494
23	Kansas 1 ESE	3,531	23	Guthrie 5 S	3,496
24	Guthrie 5 S	3,496	24	Kansas 1 ESE	3,531
25	Okla City Will Rogers World Arpt	3,494	25	Meeker 4 W	3,534

Rankings include 25 highest/lowest stations. If state has less than 25 stations, all stations are included. The period of record is 1980–2009. See User Guide for detailed explanation of data.

Number of Annual Cooling Degree Days

Highest Rank	Station Name	Num.	Lowest Rank	Station Name	Num.
1	Waurika	2,477	1	Goodwell Research Stn	1,441
2	Ardmore	2,411	2	Arnett	*1,547*
3	Chattanooga 3 NE	2,329	3	Beaver	1,599
4	Altus Irig Res Station	2,313	4	Kansas 1 ESE	1,709
5	Walters	*2,290*	5	Claremore 2 ENE	1,793
6	Frederick	*2,238*	6	Erick	1,854
7	McCurtain 1 SE	2,205	6	Taloga	1,854
8	Healdton	*2,175*	8	Billings	1,860
9	Clinton	*2,134*	9	Meeker 4 W	1,868
10	Perry	2,133	10	Helena 1 SSE	1,874
11	Tulsa Intl Arpt	2,132	11	Pawhuska	1,900
12	Duncan	2,117	12	Geary	1,908
13	Guthrie 5 S	2,113	13	Anadarko 3 E	*1,930*
14	Enid	2,087	14	Stillwater 2 W	1,934
15	Ponca City Municipal Arpt	2,057	15	Webbers Falls 5 WSW	*1,935*
16	Chickasaw Nra	2,055	16	Cushing	1,943
17	Muskogee	*2,054*	17	Bartlesville Frank Phillips	1,953
18	Idabel	*2,048*	18	Sallisaw 2 NW	1,959
19	Blanchard 2 SSW	2,047	19	Mannford 6 NW	1,989
20	Holdenville	*2,043*	20	El Reno 1 N	*1,993*
21	Buffalo	2,042	21	Okla City Will Rogers World Arpt	2,002
22	Antlers	*2,038*	22	Chandler 1	2,006
23	Ada	2,021	23	Bristow	2,011
24	Bristow	2,011	24	Ada	2,021
25	Chandler 1	2,006	25	Antlers	*2,038*

Annual Precipitation

Highest Rank	Station Name	Inches	Lowest Rank	Station Name	Inches
1	Idabel	*51.93*	1	Goodwell Research Stn	16.59
2	Kansas 1 ESE	47.96	2	Beaver	22.13
3	McCurtain 1 SE	47.81	3	Buffalo	24.26
4	Sallisaw 2 NW	47.17	4	Arnett	*25.75*
5	Webbers Falls 5 WSW	*46.76*	5	Erick	26.15
6	Antlers	*46.30*	6	Altus Irig Res Station	28.32
7	Pawhuska	45.35	7	Taloga	28.92
8	Claremore 2 ENE	44.94	8	Geary	30.71
9	Muskogee	*44.46*	9	Chattanooga 3 NE	30.96
10	Chickasaw Nra	41.74	10	Frederick	31.26
11	Holdenville	41.34	11	Waurika	31.51
12	Mannford 6 NW	41.33	12	Helena 1 SSE	31.60
13	Ada	41.24	13	Clinton	*31.88*
14	Tulsa Intl Arpt	40.78	14	Anadarko 3 E	32.14
15	Bristow	40.65	15	Walters	33.61
16	Bartlesville Frank Phillips	39.63	16	El Reno 1 N	33.71
17	Meeker 4 W	39.54	17	Enid	33.82
18	Cushing	38.43	18	Ponca City Municipal Arpt	34.72
19	Guthrie 5 S	37.84	19	Billings	35.53
20	Healdton	37.64	20	Blanchard 2 SSW	36.05
21	Ardmore	37.14	21	Perry	36.24
22	Stillwater 2 W	37.13	22	Okla City Will Rogers World Arpt	36.40
23	Duncan	37.09	23	Chandler 1	36.55
24	Chandler 1	36.55	24	Duncan	37.09
25	Okla City Will Rogers World Arpt	36.40	25	Stillwater 2 W	37.13

 Rankings include 25 highest/lowest stations. If state has less than 25 stations, all stations are included. The period of record is 1980–2009. See User Guide for detailed explanation of data.

Annual Extreme Maximum Daily Precipitation

Highest Rank	Station Name	Inches	Lowest Rank	Station Name	Inches
1	Walters	***11.64***	1	Goodwell Research Stn	2.95
2	Geary	***10.41***	2	Frederick	***4.35***
3	Webbers Falls 5 WSW	***9.46***	3	Waurika	4.48
4	Kansas 1 ESE	9.42	4	Beaver	5.07
5	Anadarko 3 E	***9.15***	5	Chattanooga 3 NE	5.15
6	Enid	9.06	6	El Reno 1 N	***5.18***
7	Helena 1 SSE	8.74	7	Cushing	5.23
8	Erick	8.61	8	Mannford 6 NW	5.42
9	Blanchard 2 SSW	8.60	9	Buffalo	5.45
10	McCurtain 1 SE	8.35	10	Stillwater 2 W	5.50
11	Ada	8.16	11	Arnett	***5.55***
12	Clinton	***8.07***	12	Idabel	***5.62***
13	Pawhuska	7.92	13	Bristow	5.73
14	Billings	7.88	14	Healdton	5.81
15	Muskogee	***7.70***	15	Sallisaw 2 NW	6.40
16	Meeker 4 W	7.55	16	Chandler 1	***6.41***
17	Chickasaw Nra	7.26	17	Ardmore	6.50
18	Altus Irig Res Station	7.10	18	Guthrie 5 S	6.55
19	Bartlesville Frank Phillips	7.07	19	Claremore 2 ENE	6.56
20	Perry	7.03	20	Ponca City Municipal Arpt	6.58
21	Taloga	7.02	21	Okla City Will Rogers World Arpt	6.64
22	Tulsa Intl Arpt	6.95	22	Holdenville	***6.76***
23	Duncan	***6.82***	23	Duncan	***6.82***
24	Holdenville	***6.76***	24	Tulsa Intl Arpt	6.95
25	Okla City Will Rogers World Arpt	6.64	25	Taloga	7.02

Number of Days Annually With ≥ 0.1 Inches of Precipitation

Highest Rank	Station Name	Days	Lowest Rank	Station Name	Days
1	Kansas 1 ESE	68	1	Goodwell Research Stn	33
2	Claremore 2 ENE	65	2	Beaver	41
2	Idabel	***65***	3	Arnett	***42***
2	McCurtain 1 SE	65	3	Geary	42
5	Sallisaw 2 NW	63	5	Erick	43
5	Webbers Falls 5 WSW	***63***	5	Frederick	43
7	Pawhuska	61	7	Buffalo	44
8	Mannford 6 NW	60	8	Altus Irig Res Station	45
8	Tulsa Intl Arpt	60	8	Anadarko 3 E	45
10	Ada	59	8	Chandler 1	45
10	Holdenville	***59***	8	Chattanooga 3 NE	45
10	Muskogee	***59***	8	Waurika	45
13	Antlers	***58***	13	Walters	46
13	Bartlesville Frank Phillips	58	14	Taloga	47
15	Chickasaw Nra	57	15	Clinton	***48***
16	Bristow	56	15	El Reno 1 N	48
17	Okla City Will Rogers World Arpt	55	17	Billings	49
18	Guthrie 5 S	54	18	Enid	50
18	Meeker 4 W	54	18	Helena 1 SSE	50
18	Stillwater 2 W	54	20	Cushing	51
21	Ardmore	53	21	Blanchard 2 SSW	52
21	Healdton	53	21	Duncan	52
23	Blanchard 2 SSW	52	21	Perry	52
23	Duncan	52	21	Ponca City Municipal Arpt	52
23	Perry	52	25	Ardmore	53

Rankings include 25 highest/lowest stations. If state has less than 25 stations, all stations are included. The period of record is 1980–2009. See User Guide for detailed explanation of data.

Number of Days Annually With ≥ 0.5 Inches of Precipitation

Highest Rank	Station Name	Days	Lowest Rank	Station Name	Days
1	Idabel	*34*	1	Buffalo	12
2	Kansas 1 ESE	33	1	Goodwell Research Stn	12
3	Webbers Falls 5 WSW	*32*	3	Beaver	13
4	Claremore 2 ENE	31	4	Arnett	*17*
4	McCurtain 1 SE	31	5	Erick	18
4	Muskogee	*31*	6	Altus Irig Res Station	19
4	Sallisaw 2 NW	31	7	Chattanooga 3 NE	21
8	Pawhuska	30	7	Clinton	*21*
9	Antlers	*29*	7	El Reno 1 N	21
10	Ada	28	7	Frederick	21
10	Holdenville	*28*	7	Geary	21
10	Tulsa Intl Arpt	28	7	Helena 1 SSE	21
13	Bristow	27	7	Waurika	21
13	Mannford 6 NW	27	14	Anadarko 3 E	22
15	Bartlesville Frank Phillips	26	14	Billings	22
15	Chickasaw Nra	26	14	Enid	22
15	Cushing	26	14	Taloga	22
15	Guthrie 5 S	26	14	Walters	22
15	Healdton	26	19	Duncan	23
20	Ardmore	25	19	Perry	23
20	Stillwater 2 W	25	21	Blanchard 2 SSW	24
22	Blanchard 2 SSW	24	21	Chandler 1	24
22	Chandler 1	24	21	Meeker 4 W	24
22	Meeker 4 W	24	21	Okla City Will Rogers World Arpt	24
22	Okla City Will Rogers World Arpt	24	21	Ponca City Municipal Arpt	24

Number of Days Annually With ≥ 1.0 Inches of Precipitation

Highest Rank	Station Name	Days	Lowest Rank	Station Name	Days
1	Idabel	*17*	1	Beaver	3
2	McCurtain 1 SE	16	2	Goodwell Research Stn	4
2	Sallisaw 2 NW	16	3	Altus Irig Res Station	7
2	Webbers Falls 5 WSW	*16*	3	Erick	7
5	Antlers	*15*	5	Arnett	*8*
5	Muskogee	*15*	5	Buffalo	8
7	Kansas 1 ESE	14	5	Helena 1 SSE	8
7	Pawhuska	14	5	Taloga	8
9	Bristow	13	9	Anadarko 3 E	9
9	Chandler 1	13	9	Enid	9
9	Chickasaw Nra	13	9	Geary	9
9	Cushing	13	12	Chattanooga 3 NE	10
9	Holdenville	*13*	12	Clinton	*10*
9	Meeker 4 W	13	12	Frederick	10
15	Ada	12	12	Ponca City Municipal Arpt	10
15	Ardmore	12	12	Stillwater 2 W	10
15	Bartlesville Frank Phillips	12	12	Waurika	10
15	Claremore 2 ENE	12	18	Billings	11
15	Duncan	12	18	Blanchard 2 SSW	11
15	Healdton	12	18	El Reno 1 N	11
15	Mannford 6 NW	12	18	Guthrie 5 S	11
15	Perry	12	18	Okla City Will Rogers World Arpt	11
23	Billings	11	18	Tulsa Intl Arpt	11
23	Blanchard 2 SSW	11	18	Walters	11
23	El Reno 1 N	11	25	Ada	12

 Rankings include 25 highest/lowest stations. If state has less than 25 stations, all stations are included. The period of record is 1980–2009. See User Guide for detailed explanation of data.

Annual Snowfall

Highest Rank	Station Name	Inches	Lowest Rank	Station Name	Inches
1	Helena 1 SSE	14.7	1	Antlers	***0.4***
2	Taloga	13.7	2	Walters	1.5
3	Buffalo	11.9	3	Anadarko 3 E	1.6
4	Goodwell Research Stn	10.5	4	Idabel	***2.0***
5	Bartlesville Frank Phillips	9.4	5	Chattanooga 3 NE	2.1
6	Tulsa Intl Arpt	9.3	6	Frederick	2.4
7	Kansas 1 ESE	8.8	7	Ardmore	2.6
7	Mannford 6 NW	8.8	8	Holdenville	***2.7***
9	Erick	8.7	9	Duncan	2.8
10	Pawhuska	8.6	9	Healdton	2.8
11	Beaver	***8.5***	11	Altus Irig Res Station	2.9
12	Billings	8.3	11	Waurika	2.9
13	Enid	***8.2***	13	Meeker 4 W	3.2
13	Stillwater 2 W	8.2	13	Sallisaw 2 NW	3.2
15	Okla City Will Rogers World Arpt	8.0	15	Chickasaw Nra	3.5
16	Bristow	7.8	16	Ada	4.1
17	Clinton	***7.5***	16	El Reno 1 N	***4.1***
18	Claremore 2 ENE	7.4	18	Chandler 1	4.2
18	Guthrie 5 S	7.4	19	Geary	4.8
20	Perry	6.6	20	Muskogee	***4.9***
21	Blanchard 2 SSW	5.9	21	Cushing	5.3
22	Webbers Falls 5 WSW	***5.7***	22	McCurtain 1 SE	5.5
23	McCurtain 1 SE	5.5	23	Webbers Falls 5 WSW	***5.7***
24	Cushing	5.3	24	Blanchard 2 SSW	5.9
25	Muskogee	***4.9***	25	Perry	6.6

Annual Maximum Snow Depth

Highest Rank	Station Name	Inches	Lowest Rank	Station Name	Inches
1	Enid	19	1	Antlers	Trace
2	Helena 1 SSE	18	2	Chattanooga 3 NE	4
3	Buffalo	***16***	3	Walters	5
4	Kansas 1 ESE	15	3	Waurika	***5***
5	Bristow	14	5	Altus Irig Res Station	6
5	Erick	14	5	Muskogee	***6***
5	Goodwell Research Stn	14	7	Ardmore	8
5	Okla City Will Rogers World Arpt	14	7	Blanchard 2 SSW	***8***
9	Anadarko 3 E	13	7	Geary	8
9	Chickasaw Nra	13	7	Meeker 4 W	***8***
9	Duncan	***13***	11	Chandler 1	9
12	Ada	12	11	Cushing	9
12	Arnett	***12***	11	Frederick	***9***
12	Bartlesville Frank Phillips	***12***	11	Perry	9
12	Billings	12	11	Sallisaw 2 NW	9
12	Pawhuska	12	11	Webbers Falls 5 WSW	***9***
12	Stillwater 2 W	12	17	Guthrie 5 S	***10***
12	Taloga	12	17	Mannford 6 NW	***10***
19	Claremore 2 ENE	11	17	McCurtain 1 SE	10
19	El Reno 1 N	***11***	20	Claremore 2 ENE	11
19	Healdton	***11***	20	El Reno 1 N	***11***
19	Holdenville	***11***	20	Healdton	***11***
19	Tulsa Intl Arpt	11	20	Holdenville	***11***
24	Guthrie 5 S	***10***	20	Tulsa Intl Arpt	11
24	Mannford 6 NW	***10***	25	Ada	12

Rankings include 25 highest/lowest stations. If state has less than 25 stations, all stations are included. The period of record is 1980–2009. See User Guide for detailed explanation of data.

Number of Days Annually With ≥ 1.0 Inch Snow Depth

Highest Rank	Highest Station Name	Highest Days	Lowest Rank	Lowest Station Name	Lowest Days
1	Helena 1 SSE	17	1	Ada	0
2	Arnett	*12*	1	Antlers	*0*
3	Claremore 2 ENE	9	1	Chattanooga 3 NE	0
3	Taloga	9	1	Duncan	0
5	Bartlesville Frank Phillips	*8*	1	El Reno 1 N	*0*
6	Enid	7	1	Frederick	0
6	Tulsa Intl Arpt	7	1	Holdenville	*0*
8	Billings	6	1	Idabel	*0*
8	Erick	6	1	Mannford 6 NW	0
8	Goodwell Research Stn	6	1	Meeker 4 W	0
8	Kansas 1 ESE	6	1	Muskogee	*0*
8	Okla City Will Rogers World Arpt	6	1	Walters	0
13	Guthrie 5 S	*5*	1	Waurika	0
13	McCurtain 1 SE	5	14	Anadarko 3 E	1
13	Pawhuska	5	14	Ardmore	1
16	Bristow	4	14	Chandler 1	1
16	Buffalo	*4*	14	Cushing	1
16	Stillwater 2 W	4	14	Healdton	1
19	Beaver	*3*	14	Perry	1
19	Chickasaw Nra	3	20	Altus Irig Res Station	2
19	Geary	3	20	Blanchard 2 SSW	*2*
19	Sallisaw 2 NW	3	20	Webbers Falls 5 WSW	*2*
23	Altus Irig Res Station	2	23	Beaver	*3*
23	Blanchard 2 SSW	*2*	23	Chickasaw Nra	3
23	Webbers Falls 5 WSW	*2*	23	Geary	3

Rankings include 25 highest/lowest stations. If state has less than 25 stations, all stations are included. The period of record is 1980–2009. See User Guide for detailed explanation of data.

Significant Storm Events in Oklahoma: 2000 – 2009

Location or County	Date	Type	Mag.	Deaths	Injuries	Property Damage ($mil.)	Crop Damage ($mil.)
Central, Southeastern, and Western Oklahoma	12/26/00	Ice Storm	na	0	0	74.2	0.0
Comanche	05/27/01	Thunderstorm Wind	na	1	0	11.0	0.0
Western and Central Oklahoma	07/04/01	Excessive Heat	na	8	0	0.0	0.0
Washita	10/09/01	Tornado	F3	0	9	100.0	0.0
Northwestern Oklahoma	01/30/02	Ice Storm	na	0	0	300.0	0.0
Cleveland	05/08/03	Tornado	F3	0	45	210.0	0.0
Oklahoma	05/08/03	Tornado	F4	0	89	160.0	0.0
Tulsa	11/18/03	Hail	2.75 in.	0	0	20.0	0.0
Tulsa	04/05/05	Hail	3.00 in.	0	0	65.0	0.0
Northeastern Oklahoma	11/27/05	Wildfire	na	1	11	1.5	0.0
Statewide	01/01/06	Drought	na	0	0	15.0	0.7
Lincoln and Stephens Counties	03/01/06	Wildfire	na	1	7	15.0	0.2
Statewide	07/16/06	Heat	na	10	100	0.0	0.0
Statewide	08/01/06	Heat	na	8	0	0.0	0.0
Ottawa	07/01/07	Flood	na	0	0	20.0	0.0
Craig County	12/08/07	Ice Storm	na	0	0	50.0	0.0
Northeastern Oklahoma	12/08/07	Ice Storm	na	0	0	50.0	0.0
Blaine, Canadian, Kay, Logan, Major, and Payne Counties	12/09/07	Ice Storm	na	0	0	150.0	0.0
Delaware and Wagoner Counties	12/09/07	Ice Storm	na	0	0	35.0	0.0
Cherokee and McIntosh Counties	12/09/07	Ice Storm	na	0	0	15.0	0.0
Ottawa	05/10/08	Tornado	F4	6	150	15.0	0.0
Jackson	06/05/08	Thunderstorm Wind	87 mph	0	0	750.0	0.0
Pittsburg and Tulsa Counties	08/01/08	Excessive Heat	na	2	46	0.0	0.0
Cleveland	11/05/08	Hail	1.75 in.	0	0	40.0	0.0
Carter	02/10/09	Tornado	F4	8	0	3.0	0.0
Caddo	05/13/09	Tornado	F2	0	0	50.0	0.0

Note: Deaths, injuries, and damages are date and location specific.

OREGON

PHYSICAL FEATURES AND GENERAL CLIMATE. Oregon enjoys a mild though varied climate with only a rare occurrence of devastating weather elements. The single most important geographic feature of the climate of Oregon is the Pacific Ocean whose coastline makes up the western border. Because of the normal movement of air masses from west to east, most of the systems moving across Oregon have been modified extensively in traveling over the Pacific. As a result, winter minimum and summer maximum temperatures in the west, and to a lesser extent in the eastern portion, are greatly moderated. The occurrence of extreme low or high temperatures is generally associated with the occasional invasion of the continental air masses. The unlimited supply of moisture available to those air masses that move across the Pacific is largely responsible for the abundant rainfall over western Oregon and the higher elevations of the eastern portion.

Beginning near and following the coast the full length of the State, the Coast Range is the farthest west of the three mountain ranges that exert an important influence on Oregon's climate. This range, disrupts the path of the moisture laden marine air moving in from the Pacific, forcing it to rise as it moves eastward. The resultant cooling and condensation produces some of the heaviest annual rainfalls in the United States along the higher western slopes, and materially reduces the available moisture in the air.

The Cascade Mountains parallel the Coast Range about 75 miles to the east. The Cascades rise from the broad valley of the Willamette eastward to an average height of about 5,000 feet, with a few peaks over 10,000 feet. One of these, Mount Hood, at an elevation of 11,245 feet, is the highest point in the State. Once again, the air masses from the west are forced to ascend causing them to give up additional moisture. The rain potential of the marine air, however, was greatly reduced by passage over the Coast Range; therefore, the rainfall on the west slopes of the Cascades at a corresponding elevation is only about one-half to two-thirds as great as on the Coast Range. Precipitation amounts decrease rapidly once the crest is crossed and descent down the eastward side begins.

Cutting through both the Cascade and the Coast Ranges, the Columbia River Gorge offers ready passage of marine air from the Pacific. Temperatures are moderated to the east in both summer and winter. Continental air occasionally passes in reverse and produces the more extreme low temperatures in the western valleys. Winding through the rugged terrain that makes up much of Oregon are the Columbia and Snake River Basins, the valleys of the many streams that head in the mountains and several very wide plateau regions. The Columbia Plateau covers about two-thirds of the State's total area and extends from the eastern border westward to the eastern slopes of the Cascade Mountains and from the southern border north to the Columbia River. Its elevation ranges from 4,000 to 6,000 feet and because of its arid nature and scant vegetation, summer heating and winter cooling often become extreme.

TEMPERATURE. Few states have greater temperature extremes than Oregon. The most extreme temperatures generally occur east of the Cascades. In the coastal sections they never drop as low as zero and on very few occasions pass the 100°F. mark. Here the mean of the coldest month, January, is 45°F., only 15 less than that of July, the warmest month. In the Willamette Valley, mean temperatures average 38°F. in January and 66°F. in July. In the inland valleys of the southwest the average summer temperatures are about 5 higher than in the northwest and maximums of 90°F. or more occur 40 to 50 days a year. In south-central Oregon the median annual maximum temperatures over a period of years have been between 95 and 100°F.; in most other areas east of the Cascades this variance is between 100 and 105°F. Median annual minimum temperatures for eastern Oregon vary from near zero in the more protected areas of the Columbia Basin to -26°F. in the high mountain and plateau regions.

PRECIPITATION. The average annual rainfall in Oregon varies from less than 8 inches in drier Plateau Regions to as much as 200 inches at points along the upper west slopes of the Coast Range. The State as a whole has a very definite winter rainfall climate. West of the Cascades about one-half of the annual total precipitation falls from December through February, about one-fourth in the spring and fall, and very little during the summer months. East of the Cascades the differences are not as pronounced, with slightly more precipitation in winter than in spring and fall, while only about 10 percent falls during the summer. Along the coast the normal annual total is from 75 to 90 inches, and increases up the west slopes of the Coast Range to almost 200 inches near the crest. Amounts decrease on the eastern slopes and in the Willamette Valley. On the western slopes of the Cascades there is again a marked increase in precipitation with elevation as annual averages range up to 75 inches. Amounts decrease rapidly on the east side. The annual average precipitation for the great plateau of the State is often less than 8 inches. In the Columbia River Basin and the Blue Mountains, totals are about 15 to 20 inches; however, some of the mountain regions receive as much as 35 inches.

SNOWFALL. In the high Cascades, where the State's heaviest snowfalls occur, it appears that annual average totals can range from 300 to 550 inches. Winter precipitation along the Coast Range, due to its lower elevations, occurs largely in the form of rain, although it too is occasionally subject to very heavy snows. In the Blue Mountains, seasonal totals range between 150 to 300 inches and depths on the ground may occasionally exceed 120 inches. The periods of continuous snow cover vary with elevation. On the peaks of the Cascades higher than 7,000 feet above sea level, it persists in glacial form the year around. In most mountain areas above 4,500 feet, snow cover lasts from early December until the latter part of April. Along the coast the average annual snowfall is only one to three inches, with many years in which there is no measurable amount.

STORMS. Hailstorms occur each year, but are generally light and cover very small areas. Practically all of these storms occur east of the Cascades. In the western part of the State thunderstorms occur in the valleys an average of 4 or 5 days a year and are not usually severe. In the eastern part, they occur on 12 to 15 days with heavier precipitation and greater wind damage. It is in the mountain areas that these storms occur most frequently and each year many forest fires are started by the accompanying lightning.

Several times each year winds of hurricane force (74 m.p.h. and over) strike the Oregon coast. They sometimes move inland to the western valleys and up the Columbia Gorge. The few tornadoes reported have been short lived. The prevailing wind direction is influenced by the surrounding terrain. In the Columbia Gorge the prevailing direction of the wind follows the orientation of the gorge at that point. Similarly, in the Willamette Valley prevailing directions are aligned north-south with the valley. The very strong winds, of course, are determined by the direction of the major storm movements.

FLOODS. Most of the State is drained into the Pacific Ocean through the Columbia River. The Snake River makes up more than half of Oregon's eastern border and drains practically all of the State east of the Blue Mountains. The west slope of the Coast Range and all areas south of the Willamette Basin and west of the summit of the Cascades are drained directly into the Pacific Ocean by three large river systems — the Umpqua, Rogue and Smith Rivers. The only major river draining south central Oregon is the Klamath. The remainder of the area lying south of the Deschutes and John Day Basins and between the Cascades and the Blue Mountains has only internal drainage into brackish lakes. Many of these lakes become dry during the summer months.

Major flooding in the Willamette Basin and the coastal streams may result from several days of moderate to heavy rain extending over the entire Basin. When combined with sharply rising air temperatures and a warm southerly wind, the melting of a heavy snowpack on the middle and upper slopes of the Coast Range and/or the Cascades greatly increases the flood potential. Flooding in the main channel of the Columbia River usually occurs during late spring and early summer when snow melt in the mountains is most rapid. Simultaneous occurrences of heavy, warm rain over large parts of the Columbia Basin have, on occasion, produced some very damaging floods.

During the early morning hours the relative humidity is greatest and there is little variation at this time between winter and summer readings in eastern and western Oregon. In contrast, the afternoon averages, when the relative humidities are least, show a very marked difference between summer and winter and also between the areas east and west of the Cascades.

SUNSHINE. The north coastal area has the least sunshine, while the southeast corner of the State has the most. The sun shines about 20 percent of the time possible in the coastal area and 45 percent of the time possible in the southeast. These values increase in April to values of 50 to 70 percent in July to 55 percent in the northwest and 90 percent in the southeast. By October they have declined to 40 and 65 percent respectively.

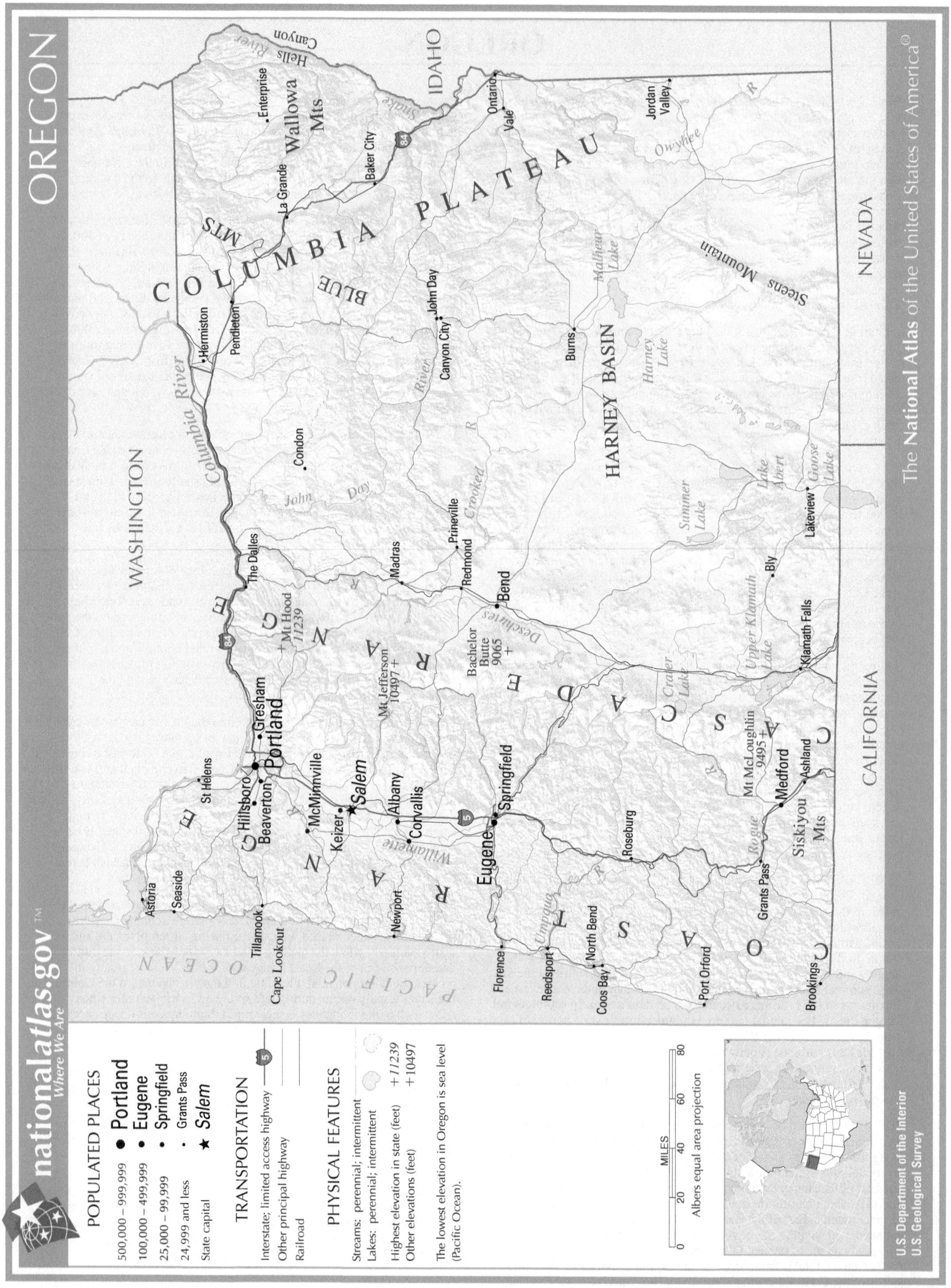
OREGON
nationalatlas.gov™
Where We Are
POPULATED PLACES
500,000 – 999,999 ● Portland
100,000 – 499,999 ● Eugene
25,000 – 99,999 • Springfield
24,999 and less · Grants Pass
State capital ★ Salem
TRANSPORTATION
Interstate; limited access highway 5
Other principal highway
Railroad
PHYSICAL FEATURES
Streams: perennial; intermittent
Lakes: perennial; intermittent
Highest elevation in state (feet) +11239
Other elevations (feet) +10497
The lowest elevation in Oregon is sea level (Pacific Ocean).
MILES
0 20 40 60 80
Albers equal area projection
U.S. Department of the Interior
U.S. Geological Survey
The National Atlas of the United States of America®
WASHINGTON
IDAHO
NEVADA
CALIFORNIA
PACIFIC OCEAN
COLUMBIA PLATEAU
BLUE MTS
Wallowa Mts
HARNEY BASIN
CASCADE RANGE
COAST RANGE
Siskiyou Mts
Steens Mountain
Columbia River
Hells Canyon
Snake River
John Day River
Crooked R
Deschutes R
Willamette R
Umpqua R
Rogue R
Owyhee R
Malheur Lake
Harney Lake
Summer Lake
Lake Abert
Goose Lake
Upper Klamath Lake
Crater Lake
Mt Hood 11239
Mt Jefferson 10497
Bachelor Butte 9065
Mt McLoughlin 9495
Astoria
Seaside
St Helens
Tillamook
Cape Lookout
Hillsboro
Beaverton
Portland
Gresham
McMinnville
Salem
Keizer
Newport
Albany
Corvallis
Eugene
Springfield
Florence
Reedsport
North Bend
Coos Bay
Roseburg
Port Orford
Grants Pass
Medford
Ashland
Brookings
The Dalles
Hermiston
Pendleton
La Grande
Enterprise
Baker City
Ontario
Vale
Jordan Valley
Condon
Madras
Prineville
Redmond
Bend
John Day
Canyon City
Burns
Bly
Lakeview
Klamath Falls
84
5

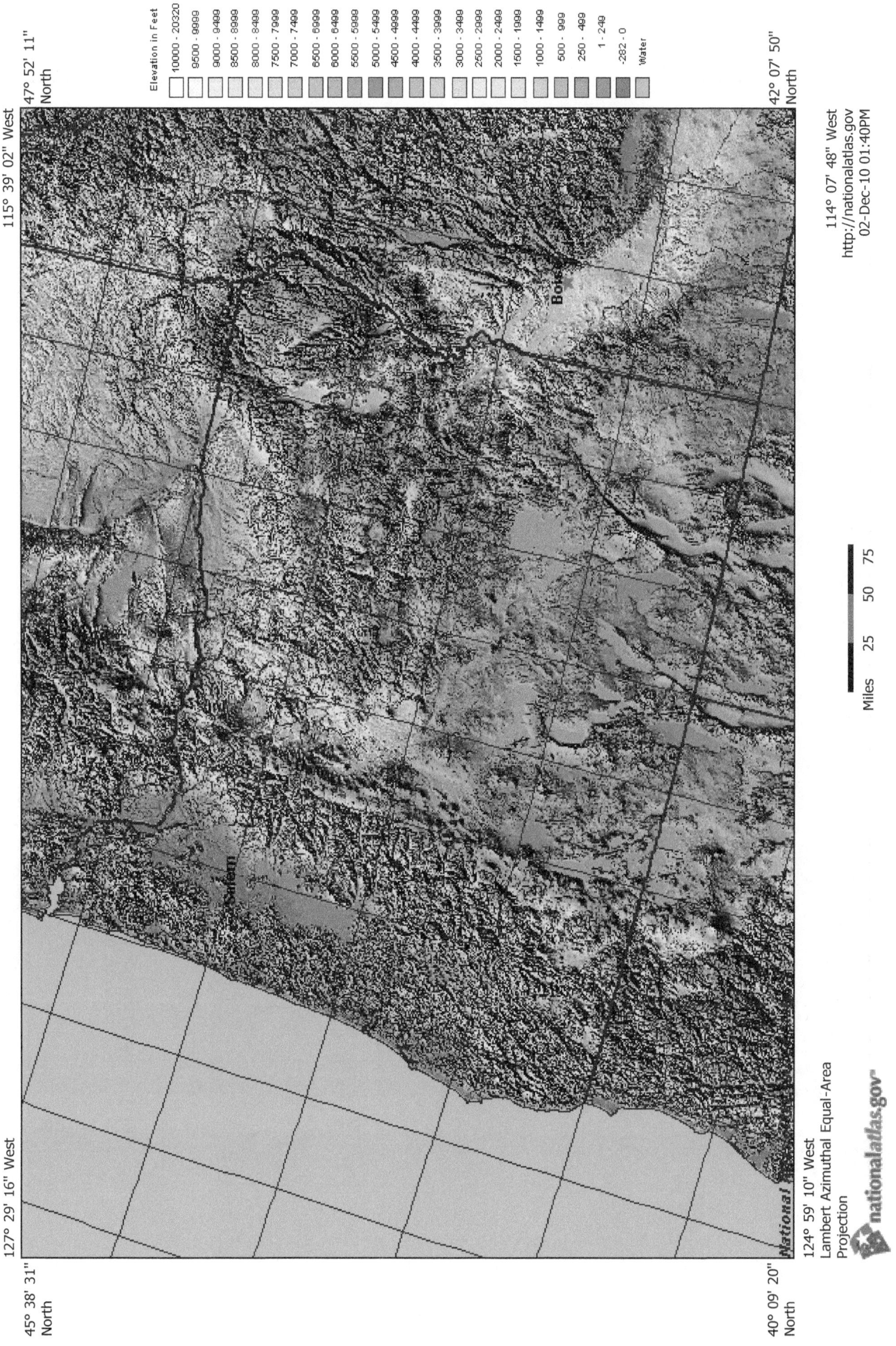
115° 39' 02" West
47° 52' 11" North
Elevation in Feet
10000 - 20320
9500 - 9999
9000 - 9499
8500 - 8999
8000 - 8499
7500 - 7999
7000 - 7499
6500 - 6999
6000 - 6499
5500 - 5999
5000 - 5499
4500 - 4999
4000 - 4499
3500 - 3999
3000 - 3499
2500 - 2999
2000 - 2499
1500 - 1999
1000 - 1499
500 - 999
250 - 499
1 - 249
-282 - 0
Water
42° 07' 50" North
114° 07' 48" West
http://nationalatlas.gov
02-Dec-10 01:40PM
Miles
25
50
75
Salem
127° 29' 16" West
45° 38' 31" North
40° 09' 20" North
124° 59' 10" West
Lambert Azimuthal Equal-Area
Projection
nationalatlas.gov

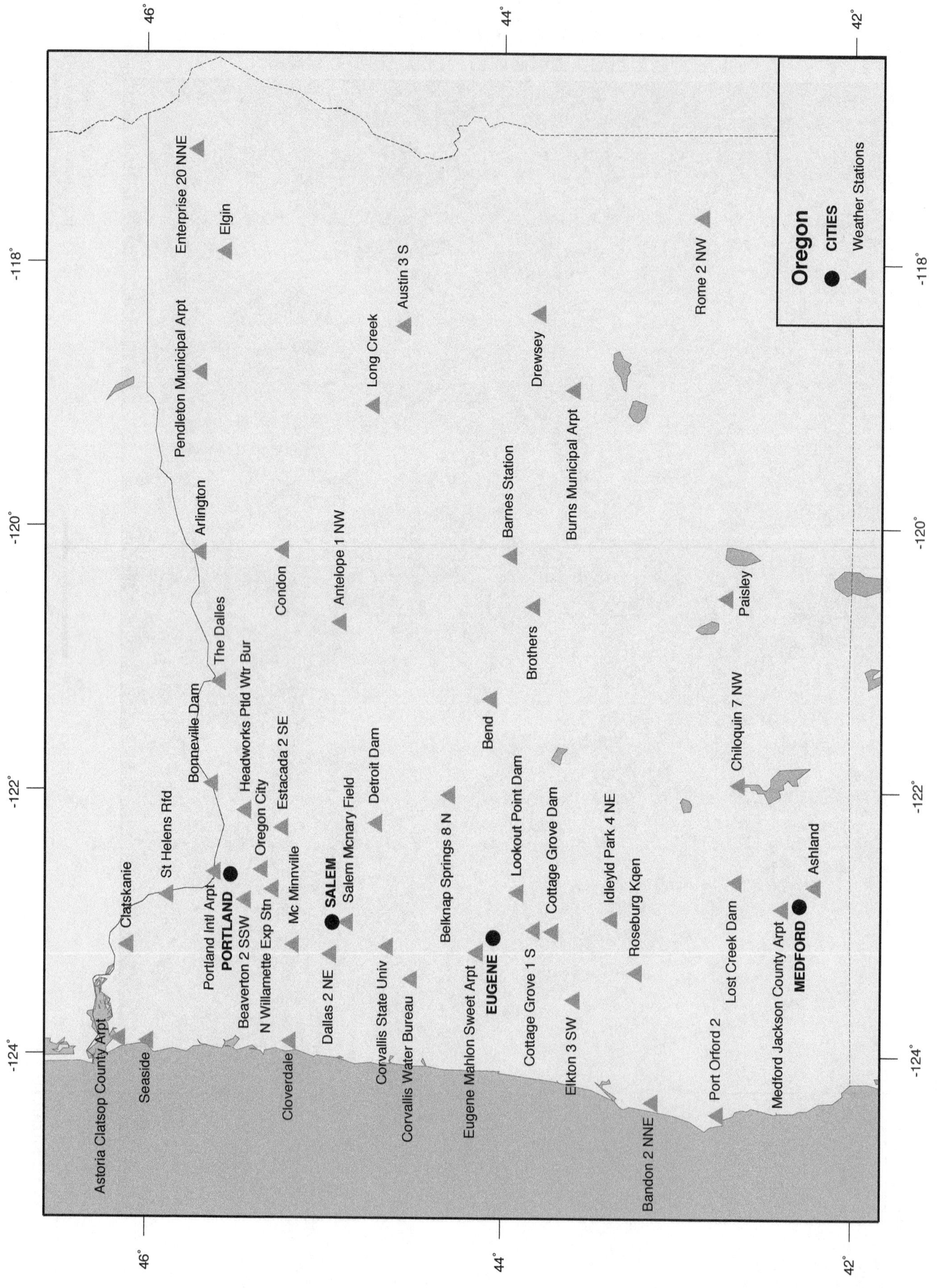
Oregon
CITIES
Weather Stations
46°
44°
42°
-124°
-122°
-120°
-118°
Astoria Clatsop County Arpt
Seaside
Clatskanie
St Helens Rfd
Portland Intl Arpt
PORTLAND
Beaverton 2 SSW
N Willamette Exp Stn
Headworks Ptld Wtr Bur
Oregon City
Estacada 2 SE
Bonneville Dam
The Dalles
Arlington
Condon
Pendleton Municipal Arpt
Enterprise 20 NNE
Elgin
Cloverdale
Mc Minnville
Dallas 2 NE
SALEM
Salem Mcnary Field
Antelope 1 NW
Long Creek
Austin 3 S
Corvallis State Univ
Corvallis Water Bureau
Detroit Dam
Eugene Mahlon Sweet Arpt
EUGENE
Belknap Springs 8 N
Bend
Barnes Station
Brothers
Drewsey
Burns Municipal Arpt
Lookout Point Dam
Cottage Grove 1 S
Cottage Grove Dam
Elkton 3 SW
Idleyld Park 4 NE
Roseburg Kqen
Bandon 2 NNE
Port Orford 2
Lost Creek Dam
Chiloquin 7 NW
Paisley
Rome 2 NW
Medford Jackson County Arpt
MEDFORD
Ashland

Oregon Weather Stations by County

County	Station Name
Benton	Corvallis State Univ
	Corvallis Water Bureau
Clackamas	Estacada 2 SE
	Headworks Ptld Wtr Bur
	N Willamette Exp Stn
	Oregon City
Clatsop	Astoria Clatsop County Arpt
	Seaside
Columbia	Clatskanie
	St Helens Rfd
Coos	Bandon 2 NNE
Crook	Barnes Station
Curry	Port Orford 2
Deschutes	Bend
	Brothers
Douglas	Elkton 3 SW
	Idleyld Park 4 NE
	Roseburg KQEN
Gilliam	Arlington
	Condon
Grant	Austin 3 S
	Long Creek
Harney	Burns Municipal Arpt
	Drewsey
Jackson	Ashland
	Lost Creek Dam
	Medford Jackson County Arpt
Klamath	Chiloquin 7 NW
Lake	Paisley
Lane	Cottage Grove 1 S
	Cottage Grove Dam
	Eugene Mahlon Sweet Arpt
	Lookout Point Dam
Linn	Belknap Springs 8 N
Malheur	Rome 2 NW
Marion	Detroit Dam
	Salem McNary Field
Multnomah	Bonneville Dam
	Portland Intl Arpt
Polk	Dallas 2 NE
Tillamook	Cloverdale
Umatilla	Pendleton Municipal Arpt

County	Station Name
Union	Elgin
Wallowa	Enterprise 20 NNE
Wasco	Antelope 1 NW
	The Dalles
Washington	Beaverton 2 SSW
Yamhill	McMinnville

See User Guide for station inclusion criteria.

Oregon Weather Stations by City

City	Station Name	Miles
Albany	Corvallis State Univ	4.5
	Corvallis Water Bureau	19.1
	Dallas 2 NE	24.3
	Salem McNary Field	19.5
Aloha	Beaverton 2 SSW	4.0
	McMinnville	23.8
	N Willamette Exp Stn	15.6
	Oregon City	16.5
	Portland Intl Arpt	14.5
	Vancouver 4 NNE, WA	17.1
Ashland	Ashland	2.0
	Medford Jackson County Arpt	15.8
Beaverton	Beaverton 2 SSW	1.6
	McMinnville	24.5
	N Willamette Exp Stn	13.6
	Oregon City	13.6
	Portland Intl Arpt	13.1
	Vancouver 4 NNE, WA	16.6
Bend	Bend	0.8
Corvallis	Corvallis State Univ	6.1
	Corvallis Water Bureau	9.4
Eugene	Cottage Grove 1 S	17.9
	Cottage Grove Dam	23.6
	Eugene Mahlon Sweet Arpt	6.8
	Lookout Point Dam	19.6
Forest Grove	Beaverton 2 SSW	14.9
	McMinnville	21.4
	N Willamette Exp Stn	23.9
	Portland Intl Arpt	24.3
	Vancouver 4 NNE, WA	24.7
Grants Pass	Medford Jackson County Arpt	23.8
Gresham	Beaverton 2 SSW	18.5
	Estacada 2 SE	17.5
	Headworks Ptld Wtr Bur	14.7
	N Willamette Exp Stn	21.4
	Oregon City	13.1
	Portland Intl Arpt	10.7
	Vancouver 4 NNE, WA	15.9
Hayesville	Dallas 2 NE	15.3
	McMinnville	18.9
	N Willamette Exp Stn	23.6
	Salem McNary Field	5.7
Hillsboro	Beaverton 2 SSW	8.0
	McMinnville	23.8
	N Willamette Exp Stn	19.1
	Oregon City	20.6
	Portland Intl Arpt	16.8
	St Helens Rfd	24.5
	Vancouver 4 NNE, WA	18.1
Keizer	Dallas 2 NE	13.2
	McMinnville	16.4
	N Willamette Exp Stn	23.6

City	Station Name	Miles
Keizer *(cont.)*	Salem McNary Field	7.1
Klamath Falls	Tulelake, CA	24.8
Lake Oswego	Beaverton 2 SSW	6.0
	Estacada 2 SE	21.4
	N Willamette Exp Stn	9.4
	Oregon City	6.8
	Portland Intl Arpt	13.5
	Vancouver 4 NNE, WA	18.7
McMinnville	Beaverton 2 SSW	24.9
	Dallas 2 NE	18.5
	McMinnville	1.7
	N Willamette Exp Stn	22.5
	Salem McNary Field	23.6
Medford	Ashland	10.9
	Lost Creek Dam	24.7
	Medford Jackson County Arpt	3.5
Milwaukie	Beaverton 2 SSW	9.6
	Estacada 2 SE	19.2
	Headworks Ptld Wtr Bur	22.8
	N Willamette Exp Stn	12.9
	Oregon City	6.7
	Portland Intl Arpt	10.7
	Vancouver 4 NNE, WA	16.5
Newberg	Beaverton 2 SSW	12.3
	McMinnville	11.5
	N Willamette Exp Stn	10.6
	Oregon City	18.1
Oregon City	Beaverton 2 SSW	13.1
	Estacada 2 SE	14.6
	Headworks Ptld Wtr Bur	23.0
	N Willamette Exp Stn	8.4
	Oregon City	0.7
	Portland Intl Arpt	17.9
	Vancouver 4 NNE, WA	23.8
Portland	Beaverton 2 SSW	10.4
	Estacada 2 SE	23.1
	Headworks Ptld Wtr Bur	23.6
	N Willamette Exp Stn	17.4
	Oregon City	11.8
	Portland Intl Arpt	5.5
	Vancouver 4 NNE, WA	11.3
Roseburg	Idleyld Park 4 NE	22.2
	Roseburg KQEN	0.4
Salem	Corvallis State Univ	21.8
	Dallas 2 NE	12.7
	McMinnville	21.1
	Salem McNary Field	2.3
Springfield	Cottage Grove 1 S	17.8
	Cottage Grove Dam	23.5
	Eugene Mahlon Sweet Arpt	12.4
	Lookout Point Dam	14.3
Tigard	Beaverton 2 SSW	2.3

See User Guide for station inclusion criteria.

City	Station Name	Miles
Tigard *(cont.)*	McMinnville	23.5
	N Willamette Exp Stn	9.9
	Oregon City	10.4
	Portland Intl Arpt	14.6
	Vancouver 4 NNE, WA	19.0
Tualatin	Beaverton 2 SSW	5.7
	Estacada 2 SE	23.1
	McMinnville	22.4
	N Willamette Exp Stn	6.5
	Oregon City	8.3
	Portland Intl Arpt	17.1
	Vancouver 4 NNE, WA	22.0
West Linn	Beaverton 2 SSW	10.5
	Estacada 2 SE	16.9
	Headworks Ptld Wtr Bur	23.9
	N Willamette Exp Stn	8.5
	Oregon City	2.2
	Portland Intl Arpt	15.7
	Vancouver 4 NNE, WA	21.5
Woodburn	Beaverton 2 SSW	21.1
	Dallas 2 NE	24.9
	McMinnville	15.9
	N Willamette Exp Stn	10.8
	Oregon City	18.8
	Salem McNary Field	18.4

Note: Miles is the distance between the geographic center of the city and the weather station.

Oregon Weather Stations by Elevation

Feet	Station Name
4,640	Brothers
4,359	Paisley
4,212	Austin 3 S
4,154	Chiloquin 7 NW
4,140	Burns Municipal Arpt
3,970	Barnes Station
3,720	Long Creek
3,660	Bend
3,515	Drewsey
3,404	Rome 2 NW
3,279	Enterprise 20 NNE
2,839	Antelope 1 NW
2,839	Condon
2,654	Elgin
2,151	Belknap Springs 8 N
1,724	Ashland
1,580	Lost Creek Dam
1,481	Pendleton Municipal Arpt
1,299	Medford Jackson County Arpt
1,220	Detroit Dam
1,080	Idleyld Park 4 NE
831	Cottage Grove Dam
748	Headworks Ptld Wtr Bur
711	Lookout Point Dam
595	Cottage Grove 1 S
591	Corvallis Water Bureau
450	Estacada 2 SE
424	Roseburg KQEN
354	Eugene Mahlon Sweet Arpt
290	Dallas 2 NE
276	Arlington
270	Beaverton 2 SSW
225	Corvallis State Univ
195	Salem McNary Field
167	Oregon City
154	McMinnville
149	N Willamette Exp Stn
149	The Dalles
120	Elkton 3 SW
100	St Helens Rfd
62	Bonneville Dam
42	Port Orford 2
21	Clatskanie
20	Bandon 2 NNE
19	Portland Intl Arpt
12	Cloverdale
9	Seaside
8	Astoria Clatsop County Arpt

See User Guide for station inclusion criteria.

Astoria Clatsop County Airport

Astoria is ringed by low mountains on the north, east, and south. On the west, the area is open to the Pacific Ocean at the mouth of the Columbia River. North of the station, eight to 12 miles distant, the Washington hills rise to 1,000 to 1,200 feet. Maximum visibility is 19 miles north-northeastward to the Willapa Hills. East-northeastward two to four miles, the Astoria hills rise to 600 feet. East-southeastward four to 14 miles, consecutively, rise other ridges of the Coast Ranges, and southeastward is the most prominent landmark, Saddle Mountain, 3,283 feet high. Forests cover most of the uplands. From Seaside northward to the south bank of the Columbia are 18 miles of sandy beaches, and a two to three mile wide stretch of dune lands.

The airport sits by the south bank of the Columbia estuary, west of Youngs Bay, on the flood plain or tidal flats. Low dikes prevent flooding and increase the bog-like characteristics of the area. When air temperature falls below water temperature, fog forms easily, or rolls in from the ocean, river, or bay. This usually begins from late afternoon to early morning, and may persist well into the following day. During the summer months, sea breezes commonly blow up the river by noon and stop the diurnal rise in temperature. In winter, cold air may funnel down the Columbia from the interior.

Weather hazards occasionally occur. Flying hazards, the greatest are fog and gales. Even with moderate surface velocities, wind and turbulence at 800 feet may be severe enough to upset a heavy plane. Heavy rains inundate lowlands, and high tides aggravated by gales may push seawater across highways or up beaches. Rains may cause earthslides, mostly in highway cuts. Lightning strikes are rare. Showers of ice pellets may briefly whiten the ground during many of the months. Occasionally in winter there may be rather brief periods of freezing temperatures, with snow or ice.

The climate is generally healthful, except for dampness and a lack of sunshine in winter. Heat waves are uncommon and usually brief. Soil leaching necessitates supplementary mineral diets for both animals and plants.

Astoria Clatsop County Airport *Clatsop County* Elevation: 8 ft. Latitude: 46° 09' N Longitude: 123° 53' W

	JAN	FEB	MAR	APR	MAY	JUN	JUL	AUG	SEP	OCT	NOV	DEC	YEAR
Mean Maximum Temp. (°F)	49.5	51.6	53.7	56.6	60.6	64.3	67.6	68.6	67.6	61.0	53.9	48.8	58.7
Mean Temp. (°F)	43.5	44.5	46.4	48.9	53.3	57.3	60.5	61.0	58.5	52.8	47.3	42.9	51.4
Mean Minimum Temp. (°F)	37.5	37.4	39.0	41.1	45.9	50.2	53.4	53.3	49.5	44.5	40.6	37.0	44.1
Extreme Maximum Temp. (°F)	67	72	73	83	93	92	96	96	92	85	71	64	96
Extreme Minimum Temp. (°F)	11	9	24	29	31	37	43	41	33	29	19	6	6
Days Maximum Temp. ≥ 90°F	0	0	0	0	0	0	0	0	0	0	0	0	0
Days Maximum Temp. ≤ 32°F	0	0	0	0	0	0	0	0	0	0	0	1	1
Days Minimum Temp. ≤ 32°F	7	7	4	1	0	0	0	0	0	1	4	8	32
Days Minimum Temp. ≤ 0°F	0	0	0	0	0	0	0	0	0	0	0	0	0
Heating Degree Days (base 65°F)	658	572	571	478	358	228	137	124	193	373	524	677	4,893
Cooling Degree Days (base 65°F)	0	0	0	0	2	3	5	6	6	1	0	0	23
Mean Precipitation (in.)	10.07	7.26	7.42	5.10	3.21	2.47	1.03	1.16	2.07	5.81	11.14	9.92	66.66
Maximum Precipitation (in.)*	18.9	21.9	13.5	9.5	6.6	5.5	4.4	5.2	6.9	12.6	17.5	16.6	87.4
Minimum Precipitation (in.)*	0.7	1.3	0.9	1.3	0.4	0.5	trace	0.1	trace	0.5	1.4	2.7	41.6
Extreme Maximum Daily Precip. (in.)	4.53	3.71	2.61	2.73	1.32	1.60	1.25	1.92	2.67	3.52	5.56	3.15	5.56
Days With ≥ 0.1" Precipitation	16	13	15	12	9	7	3	3	5	11	17	16	127
Days With ≥ 0.5" Precipitation	8	5	5	3	2	1	0	1	1	4	8	7	45
Days With ≥ 1.0" Precipitation	2	2	2	1	0	0	0	0	0	1	3	3	14
Mean Snowfall (in.)	na	na	na	na	na	na	na	na	na	na	na	na	na
Maximum Snowfall (in.)*	26	4	7	1	trace	0	0	0	0	trace	5	19	27
Maximum 24-hr. Snowfall (in.)*	11	4	5	1	trace	0	0	0	0	trace	4	6	11
Maximum Snow Depth (in.)	na	na	na	na	na	na	na	na	na	na	na	na	na
Days With ≥ 1.0" Snow Depth	na	na	na	na	na	na	na	na	na	na	na	na	na
Thunderstorm Days*	1	< 1	< 1	1	< 1	< 1	< 1	< 1	1	1	1	1	6
Foggy Days*	18	16	15	14	12	13	13	17	18	20	17	18	191
Predominant Sky Cover*	OVR	OVR	OVR	OVR	OVR	OVR	OVR	OVR	OVR	OVR	OVR	OVR	OVR
Mean Relative Humidity 7am (%)*	87	88	89	88	86	86	87	90	90	91	88	87	88
Mean Relative Humidity 4pm (%)*	78	75	71	70	70	71	70	71	70	73	78	81	73
Mean Dewpoint (°F)*	37	39	39	42	46	50	53	54	52	47	42	38	45
Prevailing Wind Direction*	E	E	SE	SW	NW	NW	NW	NW	SW	ESE	E	E	ESE
Prevailing Wind Speed (mph)*	8	8	6	10	13	13	12	12	9	6	7	8	9
Maximum Wind Gust (mph)*	79	76	70	63	61	45	45	46	56	67	68	79	79

Note: (*) Period of record is 1953-1995

Eugene Mahlon Sweet Airport

Eugene is located at the upper or southern end of the fertile Willamette Valley. Mahlon Sweet Field, location of the National Weather Service Office, is nine miles northwest of the city center. The Cascade Mountains to the east and the Coast Range to the west bound the valley, and low hills to the south nearly close it, but northward the level valley floor broadens rapidly. Hills of the rolling, wooded Coast Range begin about five miles west of the airport and rise to elevations of 1,500 to 2,500 feet midway between Eugene and the Pacific Ocean lying 50 miles to the west. About 10 miles east, the Coburg Hills, rising to an elevation of 2,500 feet, obscure the snow-covered peaks of the Cascade Range, which reach elevations of 10,000 feet about 75 miles away.

The Willamette River passes about five miles east of the airport. The Fern Ridge flood control reservoir, with a normal area of 9,360 acres, begins about two miles southwest. These two water areas are the main sources of local fog, but numerous small creeks and low places, which fill with water in the wet season, also produce considerable fog. The Coast Range acts as a barrier to coastal fog, but active storms cross these ridges with little hindrance. The Cascade Range blocks westward passage of all but the strongest continental air masses, but when air does flow into the valley from the east, dry, hot weather develops in summer causing an extreme fire hazard. In winter this situation causes clear, sunny days and cool, frosty nights.

The centers of low barometric pressure, result in southwest winds with speeds of 10 to 20 mph that usually accompany rainfall. Heavier storms bring winds of 30 to 40 mph. Fair weather in both summer and winter is most often accompanied by calm nights and daytime northerly winds increasing to speeds of five to 15 mph in the afternoon.

The first fall rains usually arrive during the second or third week of September, July and August are normally very dry. When snow occurs, it frequently melts on contact with the ground or within a few hours, but occasionally an accumulation of a few inches will persist as a ground covering for several days. Snowfall for a winter season exceeds five inches in about one-third of the years.

Temperatures are so largely controlled by maritime air from the Pacific that long periods of extremely hot or severely cold weather never occur. Temperatures of 95 degrees or higher have occurred only in the months of June, July, August, and September, and average three days a year.

Based on the 1951-1980 period, the average first occurrence of 32 degrees Fahrenheit in the fall is October 25 and the average last occurrence in the spring is April 24.

Eugene Mahlon Sweet Airport *Lane County* Elevation: 354 ft. Latitude: 44° 07' N Longitude: 123° 13' W

	JAN	FEB	MAR	APR	MAY	JUN	JUL	AUG	SEP	OCT	NOV	DEC	YEAR
Mean Maximum Temp. (°F)	47.0	51.0	56.2	60.9	67.1	73.2	82.2	82.7	77.0	64.3	52.3	45.6	63.3
Mean Temp. (°F)	40.6	43.0	46.8	50.4	55.4	60.5	67.0	67.0	62.1	52.9	45.1	39.8	52.6
Mean Minimum Temp. (°F)	34.1	35.0	37.4	39.8	43.7	47.8	51.7	51.3	47.2	41.5	37.9	34.0	41.8
Extreme Maximum Temp. (°F)	67	72	78	84	95	102	106	108	103	94	71	66	108
Extreme Minimum Temp. (°F)	8	4	24	27	29	33	39	38	31	17	15	4	4
Days Maximum Temp. ≥ 90°F	0	0	0	0	0	1	6	6	2	0	0	0	15
Days Maximum Temp. ≤ 32°F	1	0	0	0	0	0	0	0	0	0	0	1	2
Days Minimum Temp. ≤ 32°F	13	10	6	2	1	0	0	0	0	2	7	13	54
Days Minimum Temp. ≤ 0°F	0	0	0	0	0	0	0	0	0	0	0	0	0
Heating Degree Days (base 65°F)	751	615	557	432	296	149	32	27	111	370	589	773	4,702
Cooling Degree Days (base 65°F)	0	0	0	0	6	22	100	96	32	2	0	0	258
Mean Precipitation (in.)	6.97	5.43	4.98	3.33	2.66	1.48	0.56	0.59	1.26	3.14	7.81	8.09	46.30
Maximum Precipitation (in.)*	15.4	14.2	12.5	7.8	6.9	4.8	3.0	5.8	4.6	12.7	20.5	21.0	65.6
Minimum Precipitation (in.)*	0.3	0.7	0.8	0.5	0.1	trace	0	0	trace	0.1	1.2	1.2	29.3
Extreme Maximum Daily Precip. (in.)	4.15	3.69	2.13	2.05	1.30	1.67	2.41	1.52	1.34	3.70	4.03	4.89	4.89
Days With ≥ 0.1" Precipitation	12	10	12	9	7	4	1	1	3	7	13	13	92
Days With ≥ 0.5" Precipitation	5	4	3	2	1	1	0	0	1	2	6	5	30
Days With ≥ 1.0" Precipitation	2	1	1	0	0	0	0	0	0	1	2	2	9
Mean Snowfall (in.)	na	na	na	na	na	na	na	na	na	na	na	na	na
Maximum Snowfall (in.)*	47	9	11	trace	trace	0	0	0	0	trace	6	10	47
Maximum 24-hr. Snowfall (in.)*	14	6	5	trace	trace	0	0	0	0	trace	4	5	14
Maximum Snow Depth (in.)	na	na	na	na	na	na	na	na	na	na	na	na	na
Days With ≥ 1.0" Snow Depth	na	na	na	na	na	na	na	na	na	na	na	na	na
Thunderstorm Days*	< 1	< 1	< 1	< 1	1	1	1	1	< 1	< 1	< 1	< 1	4
Foggy Days*	18	15	11	7	6	4	2	5	10	20	20	20	138
Predominant Sky Cover*	OVR	OVR	OVR	OVR	OVR	OVR	CLR	CLR	CLR	OVR	OVR	OVR	OVR
Mean Relative Humidity 7am (%)*	91	92	91	88	84	81	78	82	89	94	93	92	88
Mean Relative Humidity 4pm (%)*	80	72	64	58	54	49	38	39	44	61	79	84	60
Mean Dewpoint (°F)*	36	38	39	42	46	50	52	52	49	46	41	37	44
Prevailing Wind Direction*	S	S	S	S	N	N	N	N	N	S	S	S	N
Prevailing Wind Speed (mph)*	10	10	10	9	9	10	10	10	10	8	10	10	10
Maximum Wind Gust (mph)*	66	53	60	58	51	41	51	39	36	43	58	61	66

Note: (*) Period of record is 1948-1995

The period of record for National Weather Service station data is 1980 – 2009 except where noted. See User Guide for detailed explanation of data.

Medford Jackson County Airport

Medford is located in a mountain valley formed by the famous Rogue River and one of its tributaries, Bear Creek. The major portion of the valley ranges in elevation from 1,300 to 1,400 feet above sea level. Mountains surround the valley on all sides, to the east the Cascades, ranging up to 9,500 feet, to the south the Siskiyous, ranging up to 7,600 feet, and to the west and north, the Coast Range and Umpqua Divide, ranging up to 5,500 feet above sea level. The valley exits to the ocean 80 miles westward through the narrow canyon of the Rogue River.

Medford has a moderate climate of marked seasonal characteristics. Late fall, winter, and early spring months are damp, cloudy, and cool under the influence of marine air. Late spring, summer, and early fall are warm, dry, and sunny.

Most of the light annual rainfall falls during the winter season. Summertime rainfall is brought by thunderstorm activity. Snowfall is quite heavy in the surrounding mountains during the winter. The mountains provide irrigation water storage which is necessary for production of most commercial crops during the dry summer. Snowfall is light.

High temperatures in the summer months average slightly below 90 degrees, and are always accompanied by low humidity. Hot days give way to cool nights as cool air drains down the mountain slopes into the valley. The length of the growing season is 170 days, from late April to mid-October. The last date of 32 degrees in the spring normally occurs in mid-June and the first date of 32 degrees in the fall occurs in mid- September.

Valley winds are usually very light, prevailing from the north or northwest much of the year. Winds exceeding 10 mph during the winter months nearly always come from the southerly quadrant. Summer thunderstorms produce gusty winds to 40 or 50 mph which may come from any direction.

Fog often fills the lower portion of the valley during the winter and early spring months. Duration of the fog is seldom more than three days. Geographical and meteorological conditions contribute to a smoke problem, which occasionally reduces visibility to one to three miles.

Medford Jackson County Airport *Jackson County* Elevation: 1,299 ft. Latitude: 42° 23' N Longitude: 122° 52' W

	JAN	FEB	MAR	APR	MAY	JUN	JUL	AUG	SEP	OCT	NOV	DEC	YEAR
Mean Maximum Temp. (°F)	47.8	54.4	59.3	65.2	73.5	81.5	90.9	90.6	83.8	70.0	53.1	45.7	68.0
Mean Temp. (°F)	39.7	43.9	47.8	52.6	59.5	66.3	73.9	73.3	66.5	55.5	44.3	38.7	55.2
Mean Minimum Temp. (°F)	31.7	33.3	36.3	39.9	45.4	51.1	56.8	55.9	49.2	40.9	35.5	31.7	42.3
Extreme Maximum Temp. (°F)	71	79	83	93	103	111	110	114	110	99	77	69	114
Extreme Minimum Temp. (°F)	10	9	22	25	28	35	41	41	34	19	16	-4	-4
Days Maximum Temp. ≥ 90°F	0	0	0	0	3	7	18	18	10	1	0	0	57
Days Maximum Temp. ≤ 32°F	0	0	0	0	0	0	0	0	0	0	0	1	1
Days Minimum Temp. ≤ 32°F	17	13	8	3	1	0	0	0	0	3	10	17	72
Days Minimum Temp. ≤ 0°F	0	0	0	0	0	0	0	0	0	0	0	0	0
Heating Degree Days (base 65°F)	776	591	526	369	200	58	6	3	58	297	614	808	4,306
Cooling Degree Days (base 65°F)	0	0	0	3	35	105	288	267	110	8	0	0	816
Mean Precipitation (in.)	2.42	2.03	1.68	1.34	1.28	0.62	0.28	0.37	0.55	1.11	3.03	3.43	18.14
Maximum Precipitation (in.)*	6.2	5.7	5.5	3.1	4.2	2.9	1.6	2.8	4.2	9.2	7.0	12.7	30.1
Minimum Precipitation (in.)*	0.2	0.2	0.3	0.2	trace	0	0	0	0	trace	0.2	0.4	10.4
Extreme Maximum Daily Precip. (in.)	1.77	1.73	0.92	0.98	0.90	0.98	0.56	1.15	1.93	0.91	2.68	2.68	2.68
Days With ≥ 0.1" Precipitation	7	5	5	5	4	2	1	1	2	3	8	8	51
Days With ≥ 0.5" Precipitation	1	1	0	0	1	0	0	0	0	0	2	2	7
Days With ≥ 1.0" Precipitation	0	0	0	0	0	0	0	0	0	0	0	1	1
Mean Snowfall (in.)	***1.4***	***0.6***	***0.5***	***trace***	***trace***	***trace***	***trace***	na	***0.0***	***trace***	***0.1***	***1.5***	na
Maximum Snowfall (in.)*	20	12	8	4	trace	0	0	0	0	1	11	12	23
Maximum 24-hr. Snowfall (in.)*	7	4	5	4	trace	0	0	0	0	1	7	4	7
Maximum Snow Depth (in.)	***3***	***3***	***1***	***trace***	***trace***	***trace***	***trace***	na	***0***	***trace***	***1***	***3***	na
Days With ≥ 1.0" Snow Depth	***0***	***0***	***0***	***0***	***0***	***0***	***0***	na	***0***	***0***	***0***	***1***	na
Thunderstorm Days*	0	< 1	< 1	1	2	2	2	1	1	< 1	< 1	< 1	9
Foggy Days*	20	13	6	2	2	1	< 1	1	2	11	20	22	100
Predominant Sky Cover*	OVR	OVR	OVR	OVR	OVR	CLR	CLR	CLR	CLR	OVR	OVR	OVR	OVR
Mean Relative Humidity 7am (%)*	91	90	88	83	76	70	64	69	78	89	92	92	82
Mean Relative Humidity 4pm (%)*	71	59	50	44	39	34	26	27	31	45	67	77	47
Mean Dewpoint (°F)*	32	35	35	38	42	46	49	49	45	42	37	34	40
Prevailing Wind Direction*	N	N	NW	NW	NW	NW	WNW	WNW	WNW	S	N	N	NW
Prevailing Wind Speed (mph)*	5	6	7	8	8	8	9	8	8	6	6	6	7
Maximum Wind Gust (mph)*	56	47	53	47	39	53	46	46	55	40	62	59	62

Note: (*) Period of record is 1948-1995

Pendleton Municipal Airport

Pendleton is located in the southeastern part of the Columbia Basin, that low country of northern Oregon and central and eastern Washington which is almost entirely surrounded by mountains; these have important influences on the general climate of Pendleton and the surrounding territory.

The Weather Service Office at Pendleton Airport is located in rolling country which slopes generally upward toward the Blue Mountains about 15 miles to the east and southeast. The Columbia River approaches the area from the northwest to its junction with the Walla Walla River at an elevation of 351 feet and some 25 miles north of Pendleton, then turns southwestward to be joined a few miles below by the Umatilla River. The observation station is at an elevation of nearly 1,500 feet, about three miles northwest of downtown Pendleton.

Precipitation in the Pendleton area is definitely seasonal in occurrence with an average of only 10 percent of the annual total occurring in the three-month period, July-September. Most precipitation reaching this area accompanies cyclonic storms moving in from the Pacific Ocean. These storms reach their greatest intensity and frequency from October through April. This influence is felt, particularly, in the desert area of the central part of the Basin. A gradual rise in elevation from the Columbia River to the foothills of the Blue Mountains again results in increased precipitation.

The lighter summertime precipitation usually accompanies thunderstorms which often move into the area from the south or southwest. These storms can bee quite intense, causing flash flooding.

The last occurrence in spring of temperatures as low as 32 degrees is mid-April, and the average last occurrence in the fall of 32 degrees is late October. At the city station, where cool air settles in the valley on still nights, temperatures of 32 degrees have been recorded later in the spring and earlier in the fall. Under usual atmospheric conditions, air from the Pacific, with moderate temperature characteristics, moves across the Cascades or through the Columbia Gorge resulting in mild temperatures in the Pendleton area. When this flow of air from the west is impeded by slow-moving high pressure systems over the interior of the continent, temperature conditions sometimes become rather severe, hot in summer and cold in winter. During winter, coldest temperatures occur when air from a cold high pressure system in central Canada moves southwestward across the Rockies and flows down into the Columbia Basin. Extreme winter temperatures are not particularly common in the Pendleton area. Below zero readings are recorded in approximately 60 percent of winters. Maximum temperatures usually reach 100 degrees or slightly higher on a few days during the summer.

Pendleton Municipal Airport *Umatilla County* Elevation: 1,481 ft. Latitude: 45° 42' N Longitude: 118° 50' W

	JAN	FEB	MAR	APR	MAY	JUN	JUL	AUG	SEP	OCT	NOV	DEC	YEAR
Mean Maximum Temp. (°F)	40.9	46.1	54.5	61.8	69.7	77.8	87.6	86.3	77.1	63.3	49.0	39.3	62.8
Mean Temp. (°F)	34.7	38.1	44.8	50.6	57.7	64.6	72.5	71.5	63.3	51.7	41.3	33.3	52.0
Mean Minimum Temp. (°F)	28.4	30.1	35.0	39.3	45.7	51.5	57.3	56.7	49.4	40.1	33.6	27.2	41.2
Extreme Maximum Temp. (°F)	70	75	80	87	100	102	109	110	100	92	80	67	110
Extreme Minimum Temp. (°F)	-11	-13	1	22	27	35	42	40	30	14	-12	-19	-19
Days Maximum Temp. ≥ 90°F	0	0	0	0	1	4	15	11	3	0	0	0	34
Days Maximum Temp. ≤ 32°F	7	3	0	0	0	0	0	0	0	0	2	9	21
Days Minimum Temp. ≤ 32°F	21	17	10	3	1	0	0	0	0	4	12	23	91
Days Minimum Temp. ≤ 0°F	0	0	0	0	0	0	0	0	0	0	0	1	1
Heating Degree Days (base 65°F)	934	752	618	427	243	84	11	10	109	407	704	977	5,276
Cooling Degree Days (base 65°F)	0	0	0	1	24	80	249	220	63	3	0	0	640
Mean Precipitation (in.)	1.45	1.13	1.34	1.14	1.32	0.95	0.34	0.37	0.56	1.00	1.49	1.41	12.50
Maximum Precipitation (in.)*	3.9	2.6	2.8	2.8	3.2	2.3	1.4	2.6	2.1	2.7	3.8	4.7	17.8
Minimum Precipitation (in.)*	0.2	0.1	0.3	trace	trace	trace	trace	0	0	trace	0.2	0.2	6.8
Extreme Maximum Daily Precip. (in.)	0.83	1.12	1.00	1.24	1.27	1.08	1.04	2.19	1.10	1.40	1.07	0.93	2.19
Days With ≥ 0.1" Precipitation	5	4	5	4	4	3	1	1	2	3	4	5	41
Days With ≥ 0.5" Precipitation	0	0	0	0	0	0	0	0	0	0	0	0	0
Days With ≥ 1.0" Precipitation	0	0	0	0	0	0	0	0	0	0	0	0	0
Mean Snowfall (in.)	4.3	3.4	0.8	trace	trace	trace	trace	0.0	0.0	0.1	1.2	5.6	15.4
Maximum Snowfall (in.)*	42	17	5	2	trace	0	0	0	0	3	15	27	53
Maximum 24-hr. Snowfall (in.)*	11	16	4	2	trace	0	0	0	0	3	8	10	16
Maximum Snow Depth (in.)	12	12	6	trace	trace	trace	trace	0	0	1	6	15	15
Days With ≥ 1.0" Snow Depth	5	3	1	0	0	0	0	0	0	0	1	5	15
Thunderstorm Days*	0	< 1	< 1	1	2	2	2	2	1	< 1	< 1	< 1	10
Foggy Days*	14	9	4	1	1	1	< 1	< 1	1	2	11	15	59
Predominant Sky Cover*	OVR	OVR	OVR	OVR	OVR	CLR	CLR	CLR	CLR	OVR	OVR	OVR	OVR
Mean Relative Humidity 7am (%)*	80	78	74	68	62	56	47	50	60	72	80	81	67
Mean Relative Humidity 4pm (%)*	74	65	50	42	37	32	23	26	32	46	69	77	48
Mean Dewpoint (°F)*	26	30	31	34	39	43	43	43	40	37	32	28	36
Prevailing Wind Direction*	SSE	SSE	W	W	W	W	W	W	SE	SE	SSE	SSE	W
Prevailing Wind Speed (mph)*	7	7	16	16	15	15	13	14	7	6	6	7	10
Maximum Wind Gust (mph)*	76	69	74	64	60	62	62	55	56	51	58	63	76

Note: (*) Period of record is 1948-1995

The period of record for National Weather Service station data is 1980 – 2009 except where noted. See User Guide for detailed explanation of data.

Portland Int'l Airport

The Portland Weather Service Office is located 6 miles north-northeast of downtown Portland. Portland is situated about 65 miles inland from the Pacific Coast and midway between the northerly oriented low coast range on the west and the higher Cascade range on the east, each about 30 miles distant. The airport lies on the south bank of the Columbia River. The coast range provides limited shielding from the Pacific Ocean. The Cascade range provides a steep slope for orographic lift of moisture-laden westerly winds and consequent moderate rainfall, and also forms a barrier from continental air masses originating over the interior Columbia Basin. Airflow is usually northwesterly in Portland in spring and summer and southeasterly in fall and winter. The Portland Airport location is drier than most surrounding localities.

Portland has a very definite winter rainfall climate. Approximately 88 percent of the annual total occurs in the months of October through May, nine percent in June and September, while only three percent comes in July and August. Precipitation is mostly rain, as on the average there are only five days each year with measurable snow. Snowfalls are seldom more than a couple of inches, and generally last only a few days.

The winter season is marked by relatively mild temperatures, cloudy skies and rain with southeasterly surface winds predominating. Summer produces pleasantly mild temperatures, northwesterly winds and very little precipitation. Fall and spring are transitional in nature. Fall and early winter are times with most frequent fog.

At all times, incursions of marine air are a frequent moderating influence. Outbreaks of continental high pressure from east of the Cascade Mountains produce strong easterly flow through the Columbia Gorge into the Portland area. In winter this brings the coldest weather with the extremes of low temperature registered in the cold air mass. Freezing rain and ice glaze are sometimes transitional effects. Temperatures below zero are very infrequent. In summer, hot, dry continental air brings the highest temperatures. Temperatures above 100 degrees are infrequent, but 90 degrees or higher are reached every year, but seldom persist for more than two or three days.

Destructive storms are infrequent in the Portland area. Surface winds seldom exceed gale force and rarely in the period of record have winds reached higher than 75 mph. Thunderstorms occur about once a month through the spring and summer months. Heavy downpours are infrequent but gentle rains occur almost daily during winter months.

Based on the 1951-1980 period, the average first occurrence of 32 degrees Fahrenheit in the fall is November 7 and the average last occurrence in the spring is April 3.

Portland Int'l Airport *Multnomah County* Elevation: 19 ft. Latitude: 45° 36' N Longitude: 122° 37' W

	JAN	FEB	MAR	APR	MAY	JUN	JUL	AUG	SEP	OCT	NOV	DEC	YEAR
Mean Maximum Temp. (°F)	46.7	51.1	56.5	61.6	68.0	73.5	80.5	81.0	75.9	63.9	52.9	45.6	63.1
Mean Temp. (°F)	41.1	43.7	48.1	52.4	58.4	63.7	69.3	69.5	64.5	55.0	46.8	40.5	54.4
Mean Minimum Temp. (°F)	35.4	36.2	39.6	43.2	48.8	53.7	57.9	58.0	53.1	46.0	40.6	35.2	45.7
Extreme Maximum Temp. (°F)	66	71	77	90	100	102	106	107	105	92	71	65	107
Extreme Minimum Temp. (°F)	13	9	19	31	37	42	45	44	37	27	13	11	9
Days Maximum Temp. ≥ 90°F	0	0	0	0	1	1	5	5	2	0	0	0	14
Days Maximum Temp. ≤ 32°F	1	0	0	0	0	0	0	0	0	0	0	1	2
Days Minimum Temp. ≤ 32°F	10	8	2	0	0	0	0	0	0	0	4	10	34
Days Minimum Temp. ≤ 0°F	0	0	0	0	0	0	0	0	0	0	0	0	0
Heating Degree Days (base 65°F)	734	597	517	372	215	85	15	9	69	305	541	754	4,213
Cooling Degree Days (base 65°F)	0	0	0	1	19	52	154	156	61	2	0	0	445
Mean Precipitation (in.)	5.00	3.70	3.66	2.72	2.39	1.64	0.63	0.67	1.41	2.91	5.62	5.53	35.88
Maximum Precipitation (in.)*	12.8	11.4	8.1	6.2	4.4	4.1	2.7	4.5	5.5	8.4	14.4	17.4	55.5
Minimum Precipitation (in.)*	0.1	0.6	0.8	0.5	0.1	trace	0	trace	trace	0.2	0.4	1.4	22.5
Extreme Maximum Daily Precip. (in.)	2.49	2.16	1.54	1.25	1.45	1.46	1.06	1.13	2.03	2.44	2.69	2.08	2.69
Days With ≥ 0.1" Precipitation	12	9	11	8	7	5	2	2	3	7	13	12	91
Days With ≥ 0.5" Precipitation	3	2	2	1	1	1	0	0	1	2	3	3	19
Days With ≥ 1.0" Precipitation	1	0	0	0	0	0	0	0	0	0	1	1	3
Mean Snowfall (in.)	na	na	na	na	na	na	na	na	na	na	na	na	na
Maximum Snowfall (in.)*	41	13	13	trace	trace	0	0	0	0	0	8	16	44
Maximum 24-hr. Snowfall (in.)*	9	6	8	trace	trace	0	0	0	0	0	7	8	9
Maximum Snow Depth (in.)	na	na	na	na	na	na	na	na	na	na	na	na	na
Days With ≥ 1.0" Snow Depth	na	na	na	na	na	na	na	na	na	na	na	na	na
Thunderstorm Days*	< 1	< 1	1	1	1	1	1	1	1	< 1	< 1	< 1	7
Foggy Days*	15	12	9	7	5	4	3	5	12	18	17	16	123
Predominant Sky Cover*	OVR	OVR	OVR	OVR	OVR	OVR	CLR	CLR	CLR	OVR	OVR	OVR	OVR
Mean Relative Humidity 7am (%)*	85	86	86	84	80	78	77	81	87	90	88	87	84
Mean Relative Humidity 4pm (%)*	75	67	60	55	53	51	45	45	48	61	74	78	59
Mean Dewpoint (°F)*	33	36	38	41	46	50	53	54	51	47	40	36	44
Prevailing Wind Direction*	ESE	ESE	ESE	NW	NW	NW	NW	NW	NW	ESE	ESE	ESE	ESE
Prevailing Wind Speed (mph)*	13	12	10	8	8	8	9	8	8	9	12	13	10
Maximum Wind Gust (mph)*	63	68	71	63	48	40	35	38	51	78	71	61	78

Note: (*) Period of record is 1926-1995

Salem McNary Field

Salem is located in the middle Willamette Valley some 60 airline miles east of the Pacific Ocean. The valley here is approximately 50 miles wide with the city about equidistant from the valley walls formed by the Coast Range on the west and the Cascade Range on the east.

The usual movement of very moist maritime air masses from the Pacific Ocean inland over the Coast Range produces, near its crest, some of the heaviest yearly rainfall in the United States. Annual totals of nearly 170 inches have been recorded in the mountains. From the ridge crest of the Coast Range, approximately 3,000 feet above sea level, there is a gradual decrease of rainfall downslope to the valley floor where annual totals are between 35 and 45 inches. As these marine conditioned air masses continue to move farther inland they are forced to ascend the west slopes of the Cascades to approximately 5,000 feet above sea level and again rainfall amounts substantially increase with elevation.

Most of this precipitation in both the valley and its bordering mountain ranges occurs during the winter. At Salem, 70 percent of the annual total occurs during the five months of November through March while only 6 percent occurs during the three summer months, with practically all of it falling in the form of rain. In the immediate area, there are only three or four days a year with measurable amounts of snow.

The seasonal difference in temperatures is much less marked than that of precipitation. There is a range of about 28 degrees between the temperature for January, the coldest month, and July, the warmest. Highs of 100 degrees or more seldom occur, and only in a few years since records began in 1892, have 0 degree or lower temperatures been observed. There is an average growing season of six and a half months.

The mild temperatures, long growing season, and plentiful supply of moisture are ideal for a wide variety of crops. In dollar value of agricultural returns, this is the most productive area in Oregon. Large orchards of sweet cherries are grown and processed here for maraschino cherries. Hops, filberts, walnuts, cane, and strawberries each contribute many millions of dollars to the annual farm income. A wide variety of vegetables is raised for both the fresh market and to support a large number of processing plants located in Salem. This climate is also suitable for the production of a number of specialty crops including mint, several seed crops, and nursery stock, particularly roses and ornamental shrubs.

Based on the 1951-1980 period, the average first occurrence of 32 degrees Fahrenheit in the fall is October 22 and the average last occurrence in the spring is May 5.

Salem McNary Field *Marion County* Elevation: 195 ft. Latitude: 44° 54' N Longitude: 123° 00' W

	JAN	FEB	MAR	APR	MAY	JUN	JUL	AUG	SEP	OCT	NOV	DEC	YEAR
Mean Maximum Temp. (°F)	47.6	51.6	56.4	61.3	67.8	73.9	81.9	82.2	76.9	64.3	52.7	46.3	63.6
Mean Temp. (°F)	41.1	43.0	46.8	50.5	56.2	61.5	67.5	67.5	62.6	53.2	45.6	40.1	53.0
Mean Minimum Temp. (°F)	34.6	34.5	37.1	39.6	44.6	49.2	53.0	52.6	48.2	42.1	38.4	33.9	42.3
Extreme Maximum Temp. (°F)	65	71	77	85	100	105	107	108	104	92	70	68	108
Extreme Minimum Temp. (°F)	8	-1	23	26	29	33	38	36	32	20	17	7	-1
Days Maximum Temp. ≥ 90°F	0	0	0	0	1	2	6	6	2	0	0	0	17
Days Maximum Temp. ≤ 32°F	0	0	0	0	0	0	0	0	0	0	0	1	1
Days Minimum Temp. ≤ 32°F	12	11	7	3	0	0	0	0	0	2	7	13	55
Days Minimum Temp. ≤ 0°F	0	0	0	0	0	0	0	0	0	0	0	0	0
Heating Degree Days (base 65°F)	733	614	558	430	275	128	29	24	103	360	576	765	4,595
Cooling Degree Days (base 65°F)	0	0	0	0	11	31	113	108	37	1	0	0	301
Mean Precipitation (in.)	6.18	4.56	3.93	2.78	2.15	1.52	0.47	0.44	1.25	2.90	6.46	6.87	39.51
Maximum Precipitation (in.)*	15.4	12.3	8.6	5.6	4.5	4.2	2.6	4.2	4.0	10.7	15.3	12.4	56.5
Minimum Precipitation (in.)*	0.2	0.5	0.9	0.6	0	trace	0	0	0	0.1	1.0	1.3	23.7
Extreme Maximum Daily Precip. (in.)	2.22	2.64	1.31	1.22	1.76	1.28	1.80	0.98	1.35	2.71	2.85	2.55	2.85
Days With ≥ 0.1" Precipitation	13	10	11	8	6	4	1	1	3	6	13	13	89
Days With ≥ 0.5" Precipitation	4	3	2	1	1	1	0	0	1	2	4	5	24
Days With ≥ 1.0" Precipitation	1	1	0	0	0	0	0	0	0	0	1	2	5
Mean Snowfall (in.)	na	na	na	na	na	na	na	na	na	na	na	na	na
Maximum Snowfall (in.)*	33	14	11	trace	trace	0	0	0	0	trace	6	15	34
Maximum 24-hr. Snowfall (in.)*	6	12	7	trace	trace	0	0	0	0	trace	6	8	12
Maximum Snow Depth (in.)	na	na	na	na	na	na	na	na	na	na	na	na	na
Days With ≥ 1.0" Snow Depth	na	na	na	na	na	na	na	na	na	na	na	na	na
Thunderstorm Days*	< 1	< 1	< 1	< 1	1	1	1	1	1	< 1	< 1	< 1	5
Foggy Days*	16	11	8	5	3	2	1	3	8	16	17	17	107
Predominant Sky Cover*	OVR	OVR	OVR	OVR	OVR	OVR	CLR	CLR	CLR	OVR	OVR	OVR	OVR
Mean Relative Humidity 7am (%)*	87	89	88	85	80	77	75	79	87	91	90	89	85
Mean Relative Humidity 4pm (%)*	76	69	62	56	53	49	40	40	45	61	76	81	59
Mean Dewpoint (°F)*	34	37	38	40	45	49	52	52	49	45	40	36	43
Prevailing Wind Direction*	S	S	S	S	S	S	N	N	S	S	S	S	S
Prevailing Wind Speed (mph)*	13	12	12	9	8	7	8	8	8	9	12	13	10
Maximum Wind Gust (mph)*	61	53	61	60	46	38	36	37	39	47	71	59	71

Note: (*) Period of record is 1948-1995

The period of record for National Weather Service station data is 1980 – 2009 except where noted. See User Guide for detailed explanation of data.

Antelope 1 NW *Wasco County* Elevation: 2,839 ft. Latitude: 44° 55' N Longitude: 120° 44' W

	JAN	FEB	MAR	APR	MAY	JUN	JUL	AUG	SEP	OCT	NOV	DEC	YEAR
Mean Maximum Temp. (°F)	40.4	44.5	51.9	58.1	66.1	74.1	84.4	84.1	75.2	62.2	47.3	39.1	60.6
Mean Temp. (°F)	32.8	35.4	41.0	45.6	52.4	59.3	67.3	66.7	59.3	48.9	38.3	31.4	48.2
Mean Minimum Temp. (°F)	25.2	26.2	30.1	33.1	38.8	44.4	50.2	49.3	43.2	35.6	29.1	23.7	35.7
Extreme Maximum Temp. (°F)	61	68	74	87	98	100	105	105	101	89	73	63	105
Extreme Minimum Temp. (°F)	-10	-13	12	16	21	27	33	31	25	9	-7	-17	-17
Days Maximum Temp. ≥ 90°F	0	0	0	0	0	2	10	9	2	0	0	0	23
Days Maximum Temp. ≤ 32°F	6	3	0	0	0	0	0	0	0	0	1	7	17
Days Minimum Temp. ≤ 32°F	25	22	20	14	6	1	0	0	2	10	20	26	146
Days Minimum Temp. ≤ 0°F	0	1	0	0	0	0	0	0	0	0	0	1	2
Heating Degree Days (base 65°F)	990	831	737	574	391	199	60	58	198	492	796	1,034	6,360
Cooling Degree Days (base 65°F)	0	0	0	0	8	34	139	119	34	1	0	0	335
Mean Precipitation (in.)	1.67	1.29	1.25	1.30	1.54	1.13	0.37	0.40	0.67	1.13	1.89	1.71	14.35
Extreme Maximum Daily Precip. (in.)	1.28	0.98	0.56	1.90	1.25	1.22	0.55	0.62	1.75	0.96	2.37	1.91	2.37
Days With ≥ 0.1" Precipitation	5	4	5	4	4	3	1	1	2	3	6	5	43
Days With ≥ 0.5" Precipitation	1	0	0	0	1	1	0	0	0	0	1	1	5
Days With ≥ 1.0" Precipitation	0	0	0	0	0	0	0	0	0	0	0	0	0
Mean Snowfall (in.)	3.4	2.3	0.8	0.7	0.0	0.0	0.0	0.0	0.0	0.1	1.5	4.0	12.8
Maximum Snow Depth (in.)	14	na	2	1	0	1	0	0	0	na	2	9	na
Days With ≥ 1.0" Snow Depth	1	1	0	0	0	0	0	0	0	0	0	1	3

Arlington *Gilliam County* Elevation: 276 ft. Latitude: 45° 43' N Longitude: 120° 12' W

	JAN	FEB	MAR	APR	MAY	JUN	JUL	AUG	SEP	OCT	NOV	DEC	YEAR
Mean Maximum Temp. (°F)	42.0	47.0	57.1	65.6	74.3	81.8	90.9	89.7	80.7	65.6	50.5	40.4	65.5
Mean Temp. (°F)	36.5	39.2	47.1	54.1	62.2	69.1	76.6	75.5	66.7	54.1	43.2	35.1	55.0
Mean Minimum Temp. (°F)	30.9	31.4	37.1	42.6	50.0	56.4	62.4	61.3	52.7	42.5	35.8	29.8	44.4
Extreme Maximum Temp. (°F)	65	70	78	88	107	110	111	106	102	89	71	65	111
Extreme Minimum Temp. (°F)	-9	-9	19	23	32	38	42	41	31	11	-3	-7	-9
Days Maximum Temp. ≥ 90°F	0	0	0	0	2	7	18	16	4	0	0	0	47
Days Maximum Temp. ≤ 32°F	4	2	0	0	0	0	0	0	0	0	1	5	12
Days Minimum Temp. ≤ 32°F	16	15	7	2	0	0	0	0	0	3	10	17	70
Days Minimum Temp. ≤ 0°F	0	0	0	0	0	0	0	0	0	0	0	0	0
Heating Degree Days (base 65°F)	876	722	547	323	138	28	2	2	56	336	648	919	4,597
Cooling Degree Days (base 65°F)	0	0	0	5	58	158	370	336	114	5	0	0	1,046
Mean Precipitation (in.)	1.39	1.01	0.77	0.63	0.71	0.43	0.11	0.23	0.33	0.68	1.19	1.59	9.07
Extreme Maximum Daily Precip. (in.)	0.91	1.01	0.62	1.49	0.85	1.09	0.40	1.69	0.83	1.00	2.33	1.40	2.33
Days With ≥ 0.1" Precipitation	5	3	3	2	2	1	0	1	1	2	4	5	29
Days With ≥ 0.5" Precipitation	0	0	0	0	0	0	0	0	0	0	0	1	1
Days With ≥ 1.0" Precipitation	0	0	0	0	0	0	0	0	0	0	0	0	0
Mean Snowfall (in.)	2.3	1.6	0.2	0.0	0.0	0.0	0.0	0.0	0.0	0.1	0.3	2.2	6.7
Maximum Snow Depth (in.)	15	7	1	0	0	0	0	0	0	trace	4	8	15
Days With ≥ 1.0" Snow Depth	2	1	0	0	0	0	0	0	0	0	0	3	6

Ashland *Jackson County* Elevation: 1,724 ft. Latitude: 42° 13' N Longitude: 122° 43' W

	JAN	FEB	MAR	APR	MAY	JUN	JUL	AUG	SEP	OCT	NOV	DEC	YEAR
Mean Maximum Temp. (°F)	48.8	53.9	58.0	63.5	71.0	78.7	87.6	87.0	80.4	68.3	53.6	47.4	66.5
Mean Temp. (°F)	39.3	42.5	45.5	49.9	56.4	62.8	69.5	68.6	62.1	52.7	43.2	38.3	52.6
Mean Minimum Temp. (°F)	29.8	31.1	33.1	36.3	41.7	46.9	51.4	50.1	43.8	37.0	32.6	29.3	38.6
Extreme Maximum Temp. (°F)	70	78	82	88	101	105	106	108	103	97	77	70	108
Extreme Minimum Temp. (°F)	9	8	18	21	27	33	39	37	30	13	13	0	0
Days Maximum Temp. ≥ 90°F	0	0	0	0	1	4	13	12	5	0	0	0	35
Days Maximum Temp. ≤ 32°F	0	0	0	0	0	0	0	0	0	0	0	0	0
Days Minimum Temp. ≤ 32°F	20	17	15	8	2	0	0	0	1	7	16	21	107
Days Minimum Temp. ≤ 0°F	0	0	0	0	0	0	0	0	0	0	0	0	0
Heating Degree Days (base 65°F)	790	629	596	447	276	113	22	23	122	378	648	820	4,864
Cooling Degree Days (base 65°F)	0	0	0	1	16	54	167	141	42	3	0	0	424
Mean Precipitation (in.)	2.40	1.92	1.98	1.69	1.68	0.82	0.52	0.53	0.66	1.37	3.00	3.22	19.79
Extreme Maximum Daily Precip. (in.)	2.86	1.62	1.39	1.46	1.59	1.14	1.35	0.99	1.18	1.47	1.94	2.48	2.86
Days With ≥ 0.1" Precipitation	6	5	6	6	5	3	1	1	2	4	8	8	55
Days With ≥ 0.5" Precipitation	1	1	1	0	1	0	0	0	0	1	2	2	9
Days With ≥ 1.0" Precipitation	0	0	0	0	0	0	0	0	0	0	0	1	1
Mean Snowfall (in.)	0.4	0.4	0.2	trace	0.0	0.0	0.0	0.0	0.0	0.0	trace	0.5	1.5
Maximum Snow Depth (in.)	3	2	1	trace	0	0	0	0	0	0	0	4	4
Days With ≥ 1.0" Snow Depth	0	0	0	0	0	0	0	0	0	0	0	0	0

Austin 3 S *Grant County* Elevation: 4,212 ft. Latitude: 44° 34' N Longitude: 118° 29' W

	JAN	FEB	MAR	APR	MAY	JUN	JUL	AUG	SEP	OCT	NOV	DEC	YEAR
Mean Maximum Temp. (°F)	35.7	40.4	47.6	55.3	63.8	72.3	82.6	82.9	73.3	60.2	43.6	34.7	57.7
Mean Temp. (°F)	24.2	27.6	34.5	40.6	47.9	54.5	61.5	60.8	52.6	43.0	32.4	23.7	41.9
Mean Minimum Temp. (°F)	12.6	14.6	21.4	25.8	31.9	36.7	40.4	38.7	31.9	25.7	21.3	12.7	26.2
Extreme Maximum Temp. (°F)	55	65	72	85	92	97	107	99	99	89	72	57	107
Extreme Minimum Temp. (°F)	-24	-35	-10	7	15	21	26	22	15	-5	-23	-37	-37
Days Maximum Temp. ≥ 90°F	0	0	0	0	0	1	7	7	1	0	0	0	16
Days Maximum Temp. ≤ 32°F	10	4	1	0	0	0	0	0	0	0	3	11	29
Days Minimum Temp. ≤ 32°F	31	28	30	25	16	8	3	5	16	25	27	31	245
Days Minimum Temp. ≤ 0°F	5	3	0	0	0	0	0	0	0	0	1	5	14
Heating Degree Days (base 65°F)	1,258	1,052	937	726	526	314	136	150	369	676	972	1,274	8,390
Cooling Degree Days (base 65°F)	0	0	0	0	1	5	36	27	3	0	0	0	72
Mean Precipitation (in.)	2.67	1.79	1.97	1.46	1.70	1.55	0.81	0.90	0.83	1.14	2.61	3.24	20.67
Extreme Maximum Daily Precip. (in.)	1.78	0.73	0.91	1.23	1.18	0.93	1.43	2.04	0.89	0.88	1.98	1.66	2.04
Days With ≥ 0.1" Precipitation	8	6	7	5	6	4	2	2	2	4	8	10	64
Days With ≥ 0.5" Precipitation	1	1	1	0	0	1	0	0	0	0	1	1	6
Days With ≥ 1.0" Precipitation	0	0	0	0	0	0	0	0	0	0	0	0	0
Mean Snowfall (in.)	17.7	10.6	7.3	3.1	0.4	trace	0.0	0.0	0.1	0.8	10.2	21.5	71.7
Maximum Snow Depth (in.)	36	36	34	12	3	0	0	0	trace	4	18	31	36
Days With ≥ 1.0" Snow Depth	23	21	14	3	0	0	0	0	0	1	9	23	94

The period of record for all cooperative weather station data is 1980 – 2009. See User Guide for detailed explanation of data.

Bandon 2 NNE *Coos County* Elevation: 20 ft. Latitude: 43° 09' N Longitude: 124° 24' W

	JAN	FEB	MAR	APR	MAY	JUN	JUL	AUG	SEP	OCT	NOV	DEC	YEAR
Mean Maximum Temp. (°F)	54.8	56.0	56.8	58.6	61.8	64.8	67.5	68.2	67.4	63.7	57.6	54.2	61.0
Mean Temp. (°F)	46.9	47.5	48.5	50.1	53.5	56.9	59.4	59.6	57.7	54.1	49.8	46.4	52.5
Mean Minimum Temp. (°F)	38.9	39.0	40.1	41.6	45.1	48.8	51.3	50.9	47.9	44.4	41.8	38.5	44.0
Extreme Maximum Temp. (°F)	73	79	78	89	87	83	85	85	100	97	78	77	100
Extreme Minimum Temp. (°F)	16	14	26	27	32	35	38	40	31	27	22	8	8
Days Maximum Temp. ≥ 90°F	0	0	0	0	0	0	0	0	0	0	0	0	0
Days Maximum Temp. ≤ 32°F	0	0	0	0	0	0	0	0	0	0	0	0	0
Days Minimum Temp. ≤ 32°F	6	5	3	1	0	0	0	0	0	0	2	6	23
Days Minimum Temp. ≤ 0°F	0	0	0	0	0	0	0	0	0	0	0	0	0
Heating Degree Days (base 65°F)	555	489	505	439	351	237	166	162	214	332	451	570	4,471
Cooling Degree Days (base 65°F)	0	0	0	0	1	0	1	1	1	1	0	0	5
Mean Precipitation (in.)	9.37	7.25	6.95	4.51	3.09	1.76	0.39	0.63	1.28	3.94	8.77	10.27	58.21
Extreme Maximum Daily Precip. (in.)	3.22	2.63	1.98	2.20	2.62	1.59	1.14	1.95	1.91	3.18	6.25	5.61	6.25
Days With ≥ 0.1" Precipitation	15	12	14	11	7	5	1	1	3	8	15	14	106
Days With ≥ 0.5" Precipitation	7	5	5	3	2	1	0	0	1	2	6	7	39
Days With ≥ 1.0" Precipitation	3	2	1	1	1	0	0	0	0	1	2	3	14
Mean Snowfall (in.)	0.0	0.2	trace	0.0	0.0	0.0	0.0	0.0	0.0	0.0	0.0	0.1	0.3
Maximum Snow Depth (in.)	0	trace	0	0	0	0	0	0	0	0	0	2	2
Days With ≥ 1.0" Snow Depth	0	0	0	0	0	0	0	0	0	0	0	0	0

Barnes Station *Crook County* Elevation: 3,970 ft. Latitude: 43° 57' N Longitude: 120° 13' W

	JAN	FEB	MAR	APR	MAY	JUN	JUL	AUG	SEP	OCT	NOV	DEC	YEAR
Mean Maximum Temp. (°F)	40.2	44.4	51.8	58.8	67.3	75.6	85.8	85.4	77.2	64.2	47.3	39.3	61.4
Mean Temp. (°F)	30.2	33.6	39.4	44.3	51.6	58.4	66.3	65.1	57.4	47.4	36.4	29.3	46.6
Mean Minimum Temp. (°F)	20.1	22.6	27.1	29.8	35.8	41.1	46.7	44.8	37.5	30.5	25.5	19.3	31.7
Extreme Maximum Temp. (°F)	60	70	76	86	94	99	107	102	100	91	72	62	107
Extreme Minimum Temp. (°F)	-19	-26	0	10	15	23	27	26	18	-6	-18	-29	-29
Days Maximum Temp. ≥ 90°F	0	0	0	0	1	2	12	10	3	0	0	0	28
Days Maximum Temp. ≤ 32°F	4	2	0	0	0	0	0	0	0	0	1	5	12
Days Minimum Temp. ≤ 32°F	28	25	24	19	10	3	1	1	7	19	23	28	188
Days Minimum Temp. ≤ 0°F	2	1	0	0	0	0	0	0	0	0	0	2	5
Heating Degree Days (base 65°F)	1,074	881	785	613	414	214	63	70	236	539	851	1,100	6,840
Cooling Degree Days (base 65°F)	0	0	0	0	5	23	110	80	15	0	0	0	233
Mean Precipitation (in.)	1.47	1.14	1.16	1.15	1.44	1.13	0.68	0.65	0.60	0.86	1.61	1.78	13.67
Extreme Maximum Daily Precip. (in.)	1.02	1.04	0.56	0.70	1.08	1.38	1.91	2.20	0.64	1.14	1.07	1.11	2.20
Days With ≥ 0.1" Precipitation	6	5	4	4	5	4	2	2	2	3	6	6	49
Days With ≥ 0.5" Precipitation	0	0	0	0	1	0	0	0	0	0	0	1	2
Days With ≥ 1.0" Precipitation	0	0	0	0	0	0	0	0	0	0	0	0	0
Mean Snowfall (in.)	10.0	7.7	3.2	1.6	0.2	trace	trace	0.0	trace	0.9	6.6	11.5	41.7
Maximum Snow Depth (in.)	19	15	17	1	trace	trace	trace	0	trace	5	10	15	19
Days With ≥ 1.0" Snow Depth	17	10	1	0	0	0	0	0	0	0	4	13	45

Beaverton 2 SSW *Washington County* Elevation: 270 ft. Latitude: 45° 27' N Longitude: 122° 49' W

	JAN	FEB	MAR	APR	MAY	JUN	JUL	AUG	SEP	OCT	NOV	DEC	YEAR
Mean Maximum Temp. (°F)	47.6	51.4	57.2	62.4	68.1	73.4	***79.5***	***80.7***	***75.8***	***64.1***	52.5	46.2	***63.2***
Mean Temp. (°F)	41.1	43.3	47.5	51.6	56.9	62.0	***66.8***	***67.0***	***62.5***	***53.6***	45.4	40.0	***53.1***
Mean Minimum Temp. (°F)	34.5	35.1	37.7	40.8	45.7	50.5	***54.0***	***53.4***	***49.1***	***43.2***	38.3	33.8	***43.0***
Extreme Maximum Temp. (°F)	66	73	79	***94***	***100***	***103***	***106***	105	***101***	91	***72***	64	***106***
Extreme Minimum Temp. (°F)	11	8	19	***28***	***32***	***33***	***41***	40	***30***	27	***9***	0	***0***
Days Maximum Temp. ≥ 90°F	0	0	0	0	1	2	5	4	***2***	0	0	0	***14***
Days Maximum Temp. ≤ 32°F	1	0	0	0	0	0	0	0	***0***	0	0	1	***2***
Days Minimum Temp. ≤ 32°F	12	9	5	2	0	0	0	0	***0***	1	6	12	***47***
Days Minimum Temp. ≤ 0°F	0	0	0	0	0	0	0	0	***0***	0	0	0	***0***
Heating Degree Days (base 65°F)	***736***	606	541	398	***264***	***128***	***40***	***36***	***114***	***353***	***578***	***770***	***4,564***
Cooling Degree Days (base 65°F)	***0***	0	0	2	***17***	***40***	***102***	***104***	***40***	***2***	***0***	***0***	***307***
Mean Precipitation (in.)	5.93	4.63	3.97	2.96	2.27	1.72	0.57	0.62	1.31	3.02	6.49	6.60	40.09
Extreme Maximum Daily Precip. (in.)	1.95	2.72	1.80	***1.59***	***0.90***	***1.49***	***0.92***	***1.20***	***1.81***	4.39	***2.65***	***2.54***	***4.39***
Days With ≥ 0.1" Precipitation	12	11	11	9	7	5	2	1	4	8	13	12	95
Days With ≥ 0.5" Precipitation	4	3	2	1	1	1	0	0	1	2	4	5	24
Days With ≥ 1.0" Precipitation	1	1	0	0	0	0	0	0	0	0	1	1	4
Mean Snowfall (in.)	0.5	0.6	0.1	0.0	0.0	0.0	0.0	0.0	0.0	0.0	0.3	0.1	1.6
Maximum Snow Depth (in.)	2	2	2	***0***	***0***	***0***	***0***	***0***	***0***	***0***	***0***	***2***	***2***
Days With ≥ 1.0" Snow Depth	0	0	0	0	0	0	0	0	0	0	***0***	0	***0***

Belknap Springs 8 N *Linn County* Elevation: 2,151 ft. Latitude: 44° 17' N Longitude: 122° 02' W

	JAN	FEB	MAR	APR	MAY	JUN	JUL	AUG	SEP	OCT	NOV	DEC	YEAR
Mean Maximum Temp. (°F)	39.2	44.5	51.3	57.4	65.8	72.8	82.4	82.6	76.4	62.0	46.5	37.8	59.9
Mean Temp. (°F)	33.8	36.6	41.3	46.0	52.9	58.9	65.9	65.6	60.1	50.0	39.7	33.0	48.7
Mean Minimum Temp. (°F)	28.3	28.7	31.2	34.5	39.9	44.8	49.4	48.6	43.8	38.0	32.9	28.2	37.4
Extreme Maximum Temp. (°F)	69	72	78	93	100	102	105	105	105	92	69	58	105
Extreme Minimum Temp. (°F)	6	-2	18	18	26	32	36	35	28	22	8	-1	-2
Days Maximum Temp. ≥ 90°F	0	0	0	0	1	2	8	8	4	0	0	0	23
Days Maximum Temp. ≤ 32°F	2	1	0	0	0	0	0	0	0	0	0	3	6
Days Minimum Temp. ≤ 32°F	24	21	20	11	2	0	0	0	1	5	14	25	123
Days Minimum Temp. ≤ 0°F	0	0	0	0	0	0	0	0	0	0	0	0	0
Heating Degree Days (base 65°F)	960	796	729	563	379	202	65	61	170	458	751	985	6,119
Cooling Degree Days (base 65°F)	0	0	0	0	10	26	101	87	31	1	0	0	256
Mean Precipitation (in.)	11.20	8.42	7.55	5.71	4.35	2.74	0.95	1.00	1.87	5.49	11.73	13.00	74.01
Extreme Maximum Daily Precip. (in.)	3.69	***4.68***	3.21	3.45	2.60	2.80	1.48	2.02	1.95	3.91	5.83	5.28	***5.83***
Days With ≥ 0.1" Precipitation	13	12	14	12	9	7	2	2	4	9	15	15	114
Days With ≥ 0.5" Precipitation	7	5	5	4	3	2	1	1	1	3	8	8	48
Days With ≥ 1.0" Precipitation	3	2	1	1	0	0	0	0	0	1	3	4	15
Mean Snowfall (in.)	18.6	10.9	6.2	1.2	trace	0.0	0.0	0.0	0.0	trace	4.8	17.3	59.0
Maximum Snow Depth (in.)	58	69	34	17	trace	0	0	0	0	1	16	37	69
Days With ≥ 1.0" Snow Depth	16	14	9	1	0	0	0	0	0	0	3	16	59

The period of record for all cooperative weather station data is 1980 – 2009. See User Guide for detailed explanation of data.

Bend *Deschutes County* Elevation: 3,660 ft. Latitude: 44° 03' N Longitude: 121° 17' W

	JAN	FEB	MAR	APR	MAY	JUN	JUL	AUG	SEP	OCT	NOV	DEC	YEAR
Mean Maximum Temp. (°F)	41.5	44.8	51.4	57.4	65.1	72.6	81.9	81.7	73.8	62.2	47.8	39.9	60.0
Mean Temp. (°F)	32.8	34.6	39.5	44.0	50.8	57.2	64.7	64.1	56.7	47.5	38.0	31.3	46.8
Mean Minimum Temp. (°F)	24.1	24.4	27.6	30.5	36.5	41.8	47.5	46.4	39.5	32.7	28.1	22.7	33.5
Extreme Maximum Temp. (°F)	65	73	77	86	93	95	100	101	100	89	74	66	101
Extreme Minimum Temp. (°F)	-15	-17	7	14	19	26	29	30	19	0	-7	-18	-18
Days Maximum Temp. ≥ 90°F	0	0	0	0	0	1	6	5	1	0	0	0	13
Days Maximum Temp. ≤ 32°F	4	3	0	0	0	0	0	0	0	0	1	5	13
Days Minimum Temp. ≤ 32°F	25	24	24	19	10	2	0	0	5	15	21	27	172
Days Minimum Temp. ≤ 0°F	0	1	0	0	0	0	0	0	0	0	0	1	2
Heating Degree Days (base 65°F)	990	853	783	623	439	247	87	93	259	536	804	1,036	6,750
Cooling Degree Days (base 65°F)	0	0	0	0	6	21	87	71	16	0	0	0	201
Mean Precipitation (in.)	1.58	1.13	0.72	0.71	0.92	0.82	0.55	0.47	0.40	0.57	1.41	2.09	11.37
Extreme Maximum Daily Precip. (in.)	1.87	1.04	0.91	0.85	1.02	1.61	1.28	0.89	1.17	1.56	2.60	2.50	2.60
Days With ≥ 0.1" Precipitation	5	4	2	2	3	2	2	2	1	2	3	5	33
Days With ≥ 0.5" Precipitation	1	0	0	0	1	0	0	0	0	0	1	1	4
Days With ≥ 1.0" Precipitation	0	0	0	0	0	0	0	0	0	0	0	0	0
Mean Snowfall (in.)	7.0	5.5	1.2	0.5	trace	0.0	0.0	0.0	0.0	0.2	2.5	8.2	25.1
Maximum Snow Depth (in.)	23	13	8	8	trace	0	0	0	0	1	10	17	23
Days With ≥ 1.0" Snow Depth	8	5	1	0	0	0	0	0	0	0	2	9	25

Bonneville Dam *Multnomah County* Elevation: 62 ft. Latitude: 45° 38' N Longitude: 121° 57' W

	JAN	FEB	MAR	APR	MAY	JUN	JUL	AUG	SEP	OCT	NOV	DEC	YEAR
Mean Maximum Temp. (°F)	43.9	47.9	54.9	60.6	67.3	72.6	79.6	80.1	75.0	63.6	51.4	43.1	61.7
Mean Temp. (°F)	39.3	41.8	46.9	51.6	57.6	62.8	68.5	68.6	64.0	55.3	46.1	38.8	53.4
Mean Minimum Temp. (°F)	34.7	35.6	39.0	42.6	47.8	53.0	57.4	57.1	52.9	46.9	40.7	34.5	45.2
Extreme Maximum Temp. (°F)	64	68	75	88	98	104	107	105	100	86	69	65	107
Extreme Minimum Temp. (°F)	9	7	20	26	33	40	43	46	38	31	9	6	6
Days Maximum Temp. ≥ 90°F	0	0	0	0	0	1	4	4	1	0	0	0	10
Days Maximum Temp. ≤ 32°F	2	1	0	0	0	0	0	0	0	0	0	2	5
Days Minimum Temp. ≤ 32°F	9	7	2	0	0	0	0	0	0	0	2	9	29
Days Minimum Temp. ≤ 0°F	0	0	0	0	0	0	0	0	0	0	0	0	0
Heating Degree Days (base 65°F)	790	650	552	395	240	106	22	16	82	300	561	804	4,518
Cooling Degree Days (base 65°F)	0	0	0	1	17	48	137	136	59	4	0	0	402
Mean Precipitation (in.)	11.13	8.88	7.83	6.04	3.98	3.17	0.91	1.16	2.62	6.05	12.60	12.52	76.89
Extreme Maximum Daily Precip. (in.)	4.07	3.75	3.75	4.85	2.35	2.74	1.60	1.70	2.16	4.47	5.08	3.82	5.08
Days With ≥ 0.1" Precipitation	16	13	15	13	10	7	2	2	5	10	17	16	126
Days With ≥ 0.5" Precipitation	8	6	6	4	2	2	0	1	2	4	9	9	53
Days With ≥ 1.0" Precipitation	3	3	2	1	1	0	0	0	1	2	4	4	21
Mean Snowfall (in.)	5.2	2.8	0.8	0.0	0.0	0.0	0.0	0.0	0.0	0.0	0.4	3.1	12.3
Maximum Snow Depth (in.)	63	11	9	0	0	0	0	0	0	0	12	11	63
Days With ≥ 1.0" Snow Depth	2	1	0	0	0	0	0	0	0	0	0	1	4

Brothers *Deschutes County* Elevation: 4,640 ft. Latitude: 43° 49' N Longitude: 120° 36' W

	JAN	FEB	MAR	APR	MAY	JUN	JUL	AUG	SEP	OCT	NOV	DEC	YEAR
Mean Maximum Temp. (°F)	37.9	41.3	48.3	56.1	64.0	71.7	82.1	81.5	73.1	61.0	45.2	37.3	58.3
Mean Temp. (°F)	27.8	30.5	35.8	41.2	48.0	54.9	62.9	62.0	54.0	44.7	33.8	27.0	43.6
Mean Minimum Temp. (°F)	17.7	19.6	23.3	26.2	32.1	38.1	43.8	42.4	34.8	28.3	22.4	16.6	28.8
Extreme Maximum Temp. (°F)	61	67	73	85	92	95	102	98	97	87	72	59	102
Extreme Minimum Temp. (°F)	-19	-19	-1	8	8	17	22	22	11	1	-16	-30	-30
Days Maximum Temp. ≥ 90°F	0	0	0	0	0	1	6	5	1	0	0	0	13
Days Maximum Temp. ≤ 32°F	7	4	1	0	0	0	0	0	0	0	2	8	22
Days Minimum Temp. ≤ 32°F	29	26	27	22	16	7	2	3	11	22	26	29	220
Days Minimum Temp. ≤ 0°F	2	1	0	0	0	0	0	0	0	0	1	2	6
Heating Degree Days (base 65°F)	1,146	970	897	709	522	307	121	131	331	623	927	1,171	7,855
Cooling Degree Days (base 65°F)	0	0	0	0	3	13	63	46	7	0	0	0	132
Mean Precipitation (in.)	0.62	0.43	0.58	0.57	1.05	0.87	0.56	0.39	0.55	0.63	0.91	0.95	8.11
Extreme Maximum Daily Precip. (in.)	1.30	0.50	0.50	***0.60***	1.70	0.95	1.96	1.30	1.25	0.64	1.10	2.00	***2.00***
Days With ≥ 0.1" Precipitation	2	2	2	2	3	3	1	1	2	2	3	3	26
Days With ≥ 0.5" Precipitation	0	0	0	0	0	0	0	0	0	0	0	0	0
Days With ≥ 1.0" Precipitation	0	0	0	0	0	0	0	0	0	0	0	0	0
Mean Snowfall (in.)	6.4	2.8	1.8	0.6	0.4	trace	0.0	0.0	trace	0.4	2.7	4.9	20.0
Maximum Snow Depth (in.)	10	10	5	3	1	trace	0	0	0	3	6	10	10
Days With ≥ 1.0" Snow Depth	9	5	1	0	0	0	0	0	0	0	2	8	25

Burns Municipal Arpt *Harney County* Elevation: 4,140 ft. Latitude: 43° 36' N Longitude: 118° 57' W

	JAN	FEB	MAR	APR	MAY	JUN	JUL	AUG	SEP	OCT	NOV	DEC	YEAR
Mean Maximum Temp. (°F)	34.8	39.0	49.4	56.9	66.3	75.0	85.9	84.7	75.4	61.5	45.1	34.5	59.0
Mean Temp. (°F)	24.7	28.4	37.4	43.1	51.4	58.3	66.7	64.8	55.9	44.5	33.4	24.4	44.4
Mean Minimum Temp. (°F)	14.5	17.7	25.4	29.2	36.6	41.7	47.5	44.8	36.4	27.4	21.6	14.1	29.7
Extreme Maximum Temp. (°F)	57	64	74	84	94	100	107	102	97	89	70	57	107
Extreme Minimum Temp. (°F)	-27	-28	-14	10	13	21	25	22	17	-7	-15	-28	-28
Days Maximum Temp. ≥ 90°F	0	0	0	0	0	2	12	9	2	0	0	0	25
Days Maximum Temp. ≤ 32°F	11	5	0	0	0	0	0	0	0	0	3	11	30
Days Minimum Temp. ≤ 32°F	30	27	27	20	9	3	0	1	8	23	27	30	205
Days Minimum Temp. ≤ 0°F	4	2	0	0	0	0	0	0	0	0	1	4	11
Heating Degree Days (base 65°F)	1,243	1,028	848	651	419	215	56	75	274	628	942	1,253	7,632
Cooling Degree Days (base 65°F)	0	0	0	0	5	22	116	75	9	0	0	0	227
Mean Precipitation (in.)	1.08	1.04	1.11	0.91	1.23	0.75	0.41	0.34	0.45	0.77	1.14	1.47	10.70
Extreme Maximum Daily Precip. (in.)	0.73	0.81	0.71	0.55	1.00	1.07	0.82	0.99	0.92	0.75	0.62	0.82	1.07
Days With ≥ 0.1" Precipitation	4	4	4	3	4	2	1	1	1	3	4	5	36
Days With ≥ 0.5" Precipitation	0	0	0	0	0	0	0	0	0	0	0	0	0
Days With ≥ 1.0" Precipitation	0	0	0	0	0	0	0	0	0	0	0	0	0
Mean Snowfall (in.)	na	na	na	na	na	na	na	na	na	na	na	na	na
Maximum Snow Depth (in.)	***23***	***26***	***26***	***4***	trace	trace	***0***	***0***	***trace***	***5***	***8***	***18***	***26***
Days With ≥ 1.0" Snow Depth	***14***	***12***	3	0	0	0	0	0	0	0	4	13	***46***

The period of record for all cooperative weather station data is 1980 – 2009. See User Guide for detailed explanation of data.

Chiloquin 7 NW *Klamath County* Elevation: 4,154 ft. Latitude: 42° 39' N Longitude: 121° 57' W

	JAN	FEB	MAR	APR	MAY	JUN	JUL	AUG	SEP	OCT	NOV	DEC	YEAR
Mean Maximum Temp. (°F)	37.4	42.2	49.5	56.7	65.6	73.5	82.2	81.9	74.9	62.9	46.1	37.3	59.2
Mean Temp. (°F)	28.2	31.7	37.6	42.8	49.5	55.9	62.6	62.0	55.1	45.8	35.3	28.5	44.6
Mean Minimum Temp. (°F)	19.0	21.1	25.7	28.8	33.4	38.2	42.9	42.0	35.3	28.6	24.4	19.5	29.9
Extreme Maximum Temp. (°F)	56	64	72	84	93	98	102	104	99	85	69	56	104
Extreme Minimum Temp. (°F)	-11	-19	-1	12	18	25	30	27	15	0	-7	-18	-19
Days Maximum Temp. ≥ 90°F	0	0	0	0	0	1	6	4	1	0	0	0	12
Days Maximum Temp. ≤ 32°F	7	2	0	0	0	0	0	0	0	0	2	6	17
Days Minimum Temp. ≤ 32°F	29	26	27	22	15	5	1	1	9	23	26	29	213
Days Minimum Temp. ≤ 0°F	1	1	0	0	0	0	0	0	0	0	0	1	3
Heating Degree Days (base 65°F)	1,132	933	841	660	475	275	113	119	293	589	885	1,126	7,441
Cooling Degree Days (base 65°F)	0	0	0	0	2	9	44	31	4	0	0	0	90
Mean Precipitation (in.)	3.06	2.34	1.90	1.39	1.36	0.63	0.47	0.48	0.54	1.07	2.83	3.90	19.97
Extreme Maximum Daily Precip. (in.)	1.83	1.90	1.69	1.60	1.05	0.74	1.20	1.15	0.85	1.23	1.34	2.50	2.50
Days With ≥ 0.1" Precipitation	8	7	5	4	4	2	1	1	2	3	7	9	53
Days With ≥ 0.5" Precipitation	2	1	1	1	1	0	0	0	0	0	2	2	10
Days With ≥ 1.0" Precipitation	0	0	0	0	0	0	0	0	0	0	0	1	1
Mean Snowfall (in.)	18.1	10.3	5.8	2.1	0.2	0.0	0.0	0.0	trace	0.4	7.1	19.4	63.4
Maximum Snow Depth (in.)	42	45	36	15	2	0	0	0	trace	3	18	30	45
Days With ≥ 1.0" Snow Depth	23	17	9	1	0	0	0	0	0	0	6	17	73

Clatskanie *Columbia County* Elevation: 21 ft. Latitude: 46° 06' N Longitude: 123° 12' W

	JAN	FEB	MAR	APR	MAY	JUN	JUL	AUG	SEP	OCT	NOV	DEC	YEAR
Mean Maximum Temp. (°F)	46.3	50.5	54.8	59.1	64.5	68.9	74.4	75.4	71.9	61.8	51.4	45.0	60.3
Mean Temp. (°F)	39.9	42.0	45.7	49.1	54.4	58.8	63.4	63.9	59.7	51.7	44.2	38.9	51.0
Mean Minimum Temp. (°F)	33.5	33.4	36.6	39.0	44.2	48.8	52.4	52.3	47.5	41.5	36.9	32.8	41.6
Extreme Maximum Temp. (°F)	60	72	78	86	94	99	101	103	100	88	66	64	103
Extreme Minimum Temp. (°F)	9	1	21	25	29	35	40	40	30	17	9	1	1
Days Maximum Temp. ≥ 90°F	0	0	0	0	0	1	2	1	0	0	0	0	4
Days Maximum Temp. ≤ 32°F	0	0	0	0	0	0	0	0	0	0	0	1	1
Days Minimum Temp. ≤ 32°F	14	13	8	4	0	0	0	0	0	3	8	15	65
Days Minimum Temp. ≤ 0°F	0	0	0	0	0	0	0	0	0	0	0	0	0
Heating Degree Days (base 65°F)	771	644	591	471	326	191	85	71	164	406	617	801	5,138
Cooling Degree Days (base 65°F)	0	0	0	0	4	13	43	42	12	1	0	0	115
Mean Precipitation (in.)	8.03	5.85	5.59	4.04	2.63	1.82	0.71	0.78	1.70	4.11	9.10	8.96	53.32
Extreme Maximum Daily Precip. (in.)	3.15	4.20	3.21	4.17	1.24	1.29	1.05	1.69	1.76	3.32	3.45	6.68	6.68
Days With ≥ 0.1" Precipitation	14	12	14	11	8	6	2	2	5	9	16	15	114
Days With ≥ 0.5" Precipitation	5	4	3	2	1	1	0	0	1	2	6	6	31
Days With ≥ 1.0" Precipitation	2	1	1	0	0	0	0	0	0	1	2	2	9
Mean Snowfall (in.)	1.6	1.0	0.2	0.0	0.0	0.0	0.0	0.0	0.0	0.0	0.2	1.2	4.2
Maximum Snow Depth (in.)	8	15	1	0	0	0	0	0	0	0	3	10	15
Days With ≥ 1.0" Snow Depth	1	1	0	0	0	0	0	0	0	0	0	1	3

Cloverdale *Tillamook County* Elevation: 12 ft. Latitude: 45° 12' N Longitude: 123° 54' W

	JAN	FEB	MAR	APR	MAY	JUN	JUL	AUG	SEP	OCT	NOV	DEC	YEAR
Mean Maximum Temp. (°F)	51.6	53.8	55.2	58.1	62.1	65.6	69.8	70.9	69.5	63.5	55.5	50.9	60.5
Mean Temp. (°F)	45.1	46.2	47.3	49.5	53.4	56.8	60.0	60.6	58.8	54.0	48.4	44.4	52.0
Mean Minimum Temp. (°F)	38.5	38.4	39.4	40.9	44.5	48.0	50.1	50.3	48.0	44.3	41.3	37.7	43.5
Extreme Maximum Temp. (°F)	67	76	76	85	99	98	99	106	96	94	74	71	106
Extreme Minimum Temp. (°F)	14	11	26	31	30	35	36	37	33	26	17	9	9
Days Maximum Temp. ≥ 90°F	0	0	0	0	0	0	0	0	0	0	0	0	0
Days Maximum Temp. ≤ 32°F	0	0	0	0	0	0	0	0	0	0	0	0	0
Days Minimum Temp. ≤ 32°F	5	5	3	1	0	0	0	0	0	0	3	6	23
Days Minimum Temp. ≤ 0°F	0	0	0	0	0	0	0	0	0	0	0	0	0
Heating Degree Days (base 65°F)	611	526	541	459	357	242	153	134	186	337	491	634	4,671
Cooling Degree Days (base 65°F)	0	0	0	0	3	4	4	5	7	2	0	0	25
Mean Precipitation (in.)	11.59	8.52	8.75	6.09	4.48	3.29	1.16	1.22	2.98	6.16	12.62	11.98	78.84
Extreme Maximum Daily Precip. (in.)	4.30	3.20	2.50	2.25	2.10	3.19	2.18	1.30	2.65	4.80	5.20	4.10	5.20
Days With ≥ 0.1" Precipitation	17	14	17	13	10	7	3	3	6	11	17	16	134
Days With ≥ 0.5" Precipitation	10	6	7	5	4	2	1	1	2	5	10	9	62
Days With ≥ 1.0" Precipitation	3	2	2	1	1	1	0	0	1	2	3	4	20
Mean Snowfall (in.)	0.4	0.1	0.4	0.1	0.0	0.0	0.0	0.0	0.0	0.0	0.1	0.2	1.3
Maximum Snow Depth (in.)	trace	trace	trace	trace	0	0	0	0	0	0	0	1	1
Days With ≥ 1.0" Snow Depth	0	0	0	0	0	0	0	0	0	0	0	0	0

Condon *Gilliam County* Elevation: 2,839 ft. Latitude: 45° 14' N Longitude: 120° 11' W

	JAN	FEB	MAR	APR	MAY	JUN	JUL	AUG	SEP	OCT	NOV	DEC	YEAR
Mean Maximum Temp. (°F)	38.7	43.0	50.9	57.5	65.6	72.7	82.5	81.9	73.3	60.8	46.4	37.6	59.2
Mean Temp. (°F)	31.7	34.7	40.7	45.7	52.8	59.0	66.6	66.2	58.5	48.3	38.0	30.4	47.7
Mean Minimum Temp. (°F)	24.6	26.3	30.4	33.9	40.0	45.2	50.6	50.3	43.7	35.7	29.5	23.2	36.1
Extreme Maximum Temp. (°F)	63	71	74	83	96	98	102	102	99	88	74	63	102
Extreme Minimum Temp. (°F)	-7	-19	11	18	24	28	35	33	22	6	-14	-22	-22
Days Maximum Temp. ≥ 90°F	0	0	0	0	0	1	6	5	1	0	0	0	13
Days Maximum Temp. ≤ 32°F	8	4	0	0	0	0	0	0	0	0	2	9	23
Days Minimum Temp. ≤ 32°F	26	22	21	13	5	0	0	0	1	10	19	27	144
Days Minimum Temp. ≤ 0°F	1	1	0	0	0	0	0	0	0	0	0	1	3
Heating Degree Days (base 65°F)	1,026	851	748	571	379	202	61	60	212	512	804	1,064	6,490
Cooling Degree Days (base 65°F)	0	0	0	0	9	27	117	105	24	1	0	0	283
Mean Precipitation (in.)	1.62	1.27	1.28	1.36	1.57	1.07	0.46	0.43	0.51	1.07	1.70	1.76	14.10
Extreme Maximum Daily Precip. (in.)	1.25	0.69	0.88	1.23	1.09	1.27	2.21	1.12	1.04	1.09	2.25	1.40	2.25
Days With ≥ 0.1" Precipitation	5	4	5	5	5	3	1	2	2	3	6	6	47
Days With ≥ 0.5" Precipitation	0	0	0	0	1	0	0	0	0	0	0	1	2
Days With ≥ 1.0" Precipitation	0	0	0	0	0	0	0	0	0	0	0	0	0
Mean Snowfall (in.)	6.1	4.3	2.1	0.7	trace	0.0	0.0	0.0	0.0	0.4	2.6	7.0	23.2
Maximum Snow Depth (in.)	22	12	5	6	trace	0	0	0	0	2	18	17	22
Days With ≥ 1.0" Snow Depth	9	4	1	0	0	0	0	0	0	0	3	8	25

The period of record for all cooperative weather station data is 1980 – 2009. See User Guide for detailed explanation of data.

Corvallis State Univ *Benton County* Elevation: 225 ft. Latitude: 44° 38' N Longitude: 123° 11' W

	JAN	FEB	MAR	APR	MAY	JUN	JUL	AUG	SEP	OCT	NOV	DEC	YEAR
Mean Maximum Temp. (°F)	47.0	50.8	55.9	60.7	67.2	73.1	81.6	82.5	77.1	64.8	52.6	45.7	63.3
Mean Temp. (°F)	40.6	42.9	46.8	50.4	55.8	60.9	66.9	66.9	62.5	53.4	45.4	39.7	52.7
Mean Minimum Temp. (°F)	34.2	34.9	37.6	39.9	44.3	48.7	52.1	51.3	47.8	41.9	38.2	33.7	42.1
Extreme Maximum Temp. (°F)	66	68	76	83	96	102	105	108	103	92	72	66	108
Extreme Minimum Temp. (°F)	10	7	26	28	28	35	38	38	27	22	15	7	7
Days Maximum Temp. ≥ 90°F	0	0	0	0	0	1	6	6	2	0	0	0	15
Days Maximum Temp. ≤ 32°F	0	0	0	0	0	0	0	0	0	0	0	1	1
Days Minimum Temp. ≤ 32°F	13	11	6	3	0	0	0	0	0	2	6	13	54
Days Minimum Temp. ≤ 0°F	0	0	0	0	0	0	0	0	0	0	0	0	0
Heating Degree Days (base 65°F)	749	619	558	433	287	144	37	31	107	356	580	777	4,678
Cooling Degree Days (base 65°F)	0	0	0	0	9	29	102	97	38	1	0	0	276
Mean Precipitation (in.)	6.37	5.09	4.44	2.92	2.25	1.48	0.49	0.52	1.19	2.99	6.96	7.74	42.44
Extreme Maximum Daily Precip. (in.)	2.16	3.26	2.07	1.30	1.11	1.33	1.26	1.48	1.82	2.00	4.45	3.43	4.45
Days With ≥ 0.1" Precipitation	13	10	12	9	6	4	1	1	3	7	14	14	94
Days With ≥ 0.5" Precipitation	5	4	3	1	1	1	0	0	1	2	5	6	29
Days With ≥ 1.0" Precipitation	1	1	0	0	0	0	0	0	0	0	1	2	5
Mean Snowfall (in.)	0.6	1.7	0.1	trace	0.0	0.0	0.0	0.0	0.0	trace	trace	1.1	3.5
Maximum Snow Depth (in.)	4	10	1	0	0	0	0	0	0	trace	trace	8	10
Days With ≥ 1.0" Snow Depth	1	1	0	0	0	0	0	0	0	0	0	1	3

Corvallis Water Bureau *Benton County* Elevation: 591 ft. Latitude: 44° 31' N Longitude: 123° 27' W

	JAN	FEB	MAR	APR	MAY	JUN	JUL	AUG	SEP	OCT	NOV	DEC	YEAR
Mean Maximum Temp. (°F)	45.5	49.3	54.5	59.7	66.2	71.3	79.2	79.5	74.6	62.9	50.9	44.1	61.5
Mean Temp. (°F)	39.2	41.4	45.1	49.0	54.7	59.4	65.1	65.0	60.8	51.8	43.6	38.1	51.1
Mean Minimum Temp. (°F)	32.9	33.5	35.8	38.2	43.1	47.5	51.0	50.5	47.0	40.7	36.2	32.1	40.7
Extreme Maximum Temp. (°F)	63	66	78	84	95	102	105	103	96	88	69	61	105
Extreme Minimum Temp. (°F)	9	2	23	24	28	33	39	38	33	22	11	2	2
Days Maximum Temp. ≥ 90°F	0	0	0	0	0	1	4	3	1	0	0	0	9
Days Maximum Temp. ≤ 32°F	0	0	0	0	0	0	0	0	0	0	0	1	1
Days Minimum Temp. ≤ 32°F	16	14	9	4	1	0	0	0	0	2	10	16	72
Days Minimum Temp. ≤ 0°F	0	0	0	0	0	0	0	0	0	0	0	0	0
Heating Degree Days (base 65°F)	794	661	609	473	322	182	63	56	143	404	636	826	5,169
Cooling Degree Days (base 65°F)	0	0	0	0	7	22	72	65	24	1	0	0	191
Mean Precipitation (in.)	11.31	8.54	7.24	4.52	2.74	1.71	0.41	0.53	1.48	4.19	10.97	13.13	66.77
Extreme Maximum Daily Precip. (in.)	3.53	5.23	3.15	2.07	1.82	2.65	0.98	0.83	2.25	2.89	6.29	5.51	6.29
Days With ≥ 0.1" Precipitation	15	13	14	10	7	5	1	1	4	8	15	16	109
Days With ≥ 0.5" Precipitation	8	6	5	3	2	1	0	0	1	3	8	9	46
Days With ≥ 1.0" Precipitation	4	3	2	1	0	0	0	0	0	1	4	4	19
Mean Snowfall (in.)	1.6	3.5	0.5	0.1	0.0	0.0	0.0	0.0	0.0	0.0	0.2	1.9	7.8
Maximum Snow Depth (in.)	14	26	3	1	0	0	0	0	0	0	4	10	26
Days With ≥ 1.0" Snow Depth	2	2	0	0	0	0	0	0	0	0	0	1	5

Cottage Grove 1 S *Lane County* Elevation: 595 ft. Latitude: 43° 48' N Longitude: 123° 03' W

	JAN	FEB	MAR	APR	MAY	JUN	JUL	AUG	SEP	OCT	NOV	DEC	YEAR
Mean Maximum Temp. (°F)	48.3	52.9	57.7	62.3	68.7	74.3	82.4	83.0	77.7	65.5	53.4	47.0	64.4
Mean Temp. (°F)	41.0	43.5	46.9	50.3	55.7	60.8	66.3	66.1	61.2	53.1	45.5	40.3	52.6
Mean Minimum Temp. (°F)	33.7	34.0	36.1	38.3	42.7	47.2	50.1	49.1	44.8	40.7	37.6	33.6	40.6
Extreme Maximum Temp. (°F)	67	75	81	87	98	101	104	105	104	96	76	68	105
Extreme Minimum Temp. (°F)	0	0	22	24	25	32	35	32	26	17	9	1	0
Days Maximum Temp. ≥ 90°F	0	0	0	0	0	2	6	6	2	0	0	0	16
Days Maximum Temp. ≤ 32°F	0	0	0	0	0	0	0	0	0	0	0	1	1
Days Minimum Temp. ≤ 32°F	14	12	9	5	1	0	0	0	1	3	7	14	66
Days Minimum Temp. ≤ 0°F	0	0	0	0	0	0	0	0	0	0	0	0	0
Heating Degree Days (base 65°F)	737	603	555	434	289	148	45	43	132	362	577	759	4,684
Cooling Degree Days (base 65°F)	0	0	0	0	8	27	90	84	25	1	0	0	235
Mean Precipitation (in.)	6.47	4.95	4.76	3.89	2.87	1.62	0.56	0.60	1.22	3.28	7.37	7.39	44.98
Extreme Maximum Daily Precip. (in.)	3.00	2.67	1.50	2.21	2.01	1.01	1.84	1.38	1.55	2.12	3.13	3.36	3.36
Days With ≥ 0.1" Precipitation	13	11	12	10	8	4	2	1	4	7	14	14	100
Days With ≥ 0.5" Precipitation	4	3	3	2	2	1	0	0	1	2	5	5	28
Days With ≥ 1.0" Precipitation	1	1	0	0	0	0	0	0	0	1	1	2	6
Mean Snowfall (in.)	0.9	1.0	0.1	trace	0.0	0.0	0.0	0.0	0.0	0.0	trace	0.7	2.7
Maximum Snow Depth (in.)	4	7	0	2	0	0	0	0	0	0	2	5	7
Days With ≥ 1.0" Snow Depth	0	1	0	0	0	0	0	0	0	0	0	1	2

Cottage Grove Dam *Lane County* Elevation: 831 ft. Latitude: 43° 43' N Longitude: 123° 03' W

	JAN	FEB	MAR	APR	MAY	JUN	JUL	AUG	SEP	OCT	NOV	DEC	YEAR
Mean Maximum Temp. (°F)	47.5	51.4	56.1	60.1	66.1	71.2	79.5	80.5	75.6	64.2	52.2	45.8	62.5
Mean Temp. (°F)	40.2	42.4	46.0	49.3	54.6	59.3	65.3	65.6	61.1	52.7	44.4	39.1	51.7
Mean Minimum Temp. (°F)	32.9	33.4	35.8	38.4	43.0	47.2	51.0	50.6	46.6	41.2	36.5	32.4	40.8
Extreme Maximum Temp. (°F)	71	74	78	88	100	99	103	105	100	94	76	67	105
Extreme Minimum Temp. (°F)	7	1	24	28	29	36	41	41	33	19	16	1	1
Days Maximum Temp. ≥ 90°F	0	0	0	0	0	1	3	3	2	0	0	0	9
Days Maximum Temp. ≤ 32°F	0	0	0	0	0	0	0	0	0	0	0	1	1
Days Minimum Temp. ≤ 32°F	15	12	9	2	0	0	0	0	0	1	8	16	63
Days Minimum Temp. ≤ 0°F	0	0	0	0	0	0	0	0	0	0	0	0	0
Heating Degree Days (base 65°F)	762	632	582	465	323	182	58	49	136	374	613	795	4,971
Cooling Degree Days (base 65°F)	0	0	0	0	8	16	73	73	27	2	0	0	199
Mean Precipitation (in.)	6.79	5.35	5.09	4.23	3.18	1.69	0.63	0.67	1.33	3.69	7.49	7.48	47.62
Extreme Maximum Daily Precip. (in.)	2.58	***3.67***	1.80	2.49	2.46	1.38	2.11	0.89	2.25	2.70	5.72	***4.76***	***5.72***
Days With ≥ 0.1" Precipitation	11	10	12	10	8	5	2	2	3	7	13	12	95
Days With ≥ 0.5" Precipitation	4	4	3	2	2	1	0	0	1	2	5	4	28
Days With ≥ 1.0" Precipitation	1	1	0	0	0	0	0	0	0	1	2	2	7
Mean Snowfall (in.)	0.1	1.3	0.1	trace	0.0	0.0	0.0	0.0	0.0	0.0	trace	0.1	1.6
Maximum Snow Depth (in.)	2	4	2	trace	0	0	0	0	0	0	trace	2	4
Days With ≥ 1.0" Snow Depth	0	0	0	0	0	0	0	0	0	0	0	0	0

The period of record for all cooperative weather station data is 1980 – 2009. See User Guide for detailed explanation of data.

Dallas 2 NE *Polk County* Elevation: 290 ft. Latitude: 44° 57' N Longitude: 123° 17' W

	JAN	FEB	MAR	APR	MAY	JUN	JUL	AUG	SEP	OCT	NOV	DEC	YEAR
Mean Maximum Temp. (°F)	46.4	50.8	56.1	61.5	68.0	73.8	82.2	82.7	77.7	65.0	51.6	44.8	63.4
Mean Temp. (°F)	40.6	43.1	46.9	50.7	56.4	61.1	66.8	66.8	62.8	54.0	45.1	39.5	52.8
Mean Minimum Temp. (°F)	34.7	35.3	37.6	39.9	44.5	48.4	51.3	50.8	47.9	42.8	38.5	34.1	42.1
Extreme Maximum Temp. (°F)	65	67	76	85	98	102	104	103	103	91	68	65	104
Extreme Minimum Temp. (°F)	9	7	22	26	30	36	39	34	32	27	12	5	5
Days Maximum Temp. ≥ 90°F	0	0	0	0	0	2	6	6	3	0	0	0	17
Days Maximum Temp. ≤ 32°F	1	0	0	0	0	0	0	0	0	0	0	1	2
Days Minimum Temp. ≤ 32°F	12	10	6	3	0	0	0	0	0	2	6	13	52
Days Minimum Temp. ≤ 0°F	0	0	0	0	0	0	0	0	0	0	0	0	0
Heating Degree Days (base 65°F)	750	613	556	422	271	142	34	31	103	338	591	786	4,637
Cooling Degree Days (base 65°F)	0	0	0	0	12	31	97	93	44	3	0	0	280
Mean Precipitation (in.)	7.69	5.71	4.85	3.07	2.15	1.52	0.41	0.53	1.10	3.09	7.76	9.04	46.92
Extreme Maximum Daily Precip. (in.)	*2.90*	na	na	na	*1.57*	1.60	1.75	0.90	0.98	3.92	*2.67*	na	na
Days With ≥ 0.1" Precipitation	11	9	10	6	6	3	1	1	3	6	12	11	79
Days With ≥ 0.5" Precipitation	5	3	2	2	1	1	0	0	1	2	5	5	27
Days With ≥ 1.0" Precipitation	2	1	1	0	0	0	0	0	0	1	2	2	9
Mean Snowfall (in.)	0.6	1.9	0.1	trace	0.0	0.0	0.0	0.0	0.0	0.0	trace	1.2	3.8
Maximum Snow Depth (in.)	3	12	trace	trace	0	0	0	0	0	0	trace	4	12
Days With ≥ 1.0" Snow Depth	0	1	0	0	0	0	0	0	0	0	0	0	1

Detroit Dam *Marion County* Elevation: 1,220 ft. Latitude: 44° 43' N Longitude: 122° 15' W

	JAN	FEB	MAR	APR	MAY	JUN	JUL	AUG	SEP	OCT	NOV	DEC	YEAR
Mean Maximum Temp. (°F)	43.9	47.3	52.8	58.2	65.0	70.9	79.3	79.9	74.1	61.8	49.6	43.3	60.5
Mean Temp. (°F)	38.9	40.8	44.6	48.6	54.5	59.8	66.1	66.7	62.1	53.1	44.0	38.6	51.5
Mean Minimum Temp. (°F)	33.9	34.2	36.4	39.0	44.0	48.8	53.0	53.4	50.0	44.4	38.4	33.9	42.4
Extreme Maximum Temp. (°F)	63	71	75	87	104	101	104	104	107	92	66	64	107
Extreme Minimum Temp. (°F)	12	5	20	26	27	36	40	40	35	25	15	7	5
Days Maximum Temp. ≥ 90°F	0	0	0	0	0	1	4	4	1	0	0	0	10
Days Maximum Temp. ≤ 32°F	0	0	0	0	0	0	0	0	0	0	0	1	1
Days Minimum Temp. ≤ 32°F	11	9	4	1	0	0	0	0	0	0	4	10	39
Days Minimum Temp. ≤ 0°F	0	0	0	0	0	0	0	0	0	0	0	0	0
Heating Degree Days (base 65°F)	801	679	626	485	329	179	58	46	126	364	623	811	5,127
Cooling Degree Days (base 65°F)	0	0	0	1	11	30	101	105	45	2	0	0	295
Mean Precipitation (in.)	12.80	10.17	9.66	7.62	5.77	3.91	0.94	1.10	2.73	6.76	14.45	14.53	90.44
Extreme Maximum Daily Precip. (in.)	4.24	4.35	3.60	5.56	2.50	2.68	1.40	1.39	2.21	3.74	4.80	5.05	5.56
Days With ≥ 0.1" Precipitation	16	14	16	14	12	8	2	3	5	10	17	17	134
Days With ≥ 0.5" Precipitation	9	7	8	6	4	3	1	1	2	5	10	10	66
Days With ≥ 1.0" Precipitation	4	3	2	1	1	1	0	0	1	2	5	5	25
Mean Snowfall (in.)	4.2	3.2	0.7	0.1	0.0	0.0	0.0	0.0	0.0	0.0	0.4	1.5	10.1
Maximum Snow Depth (in.)	14	14	5	1	0	0	0	0	0	0	8	8	14
Days With ≥ 1.0" Snow Depth	3	3	0	0	0	0	0	0	0	0	0	2	8

Drewsey *Harney County* Elevation: 3,515 ft. Latitude: 43° 48' N Longitude: 118° 23' W

	JAN	FEB	MAR	APR	MAY	JUN	JUL	AUG	SEP	OCT	NOV	DEC	YEAR
Mean Maximum Temp. (°F)	35.2	41.8	53.0	61.4	70.5	78.9	89.6	88.0	78.8	64.5	46.5	35.1	61.9
Mean Temp. (°F)	25.6	30.7	39.3	45.7	54.2	61.4	69.4	66.8	57.4	45.9	34.3	25.2	46.3
Mean Minimum Temp. (°F)	15.9	19.6	25.6	29.9	37.8	43.8	49.1	45.7	36.1	27.2	22.0	15.3	30.7
Extreme Maximum Temp. (°F)	64	67	76	86	100	100	107	104	100	89	75	60	107
Extreme Minimum Temp. (°F)	-25	-33	-19	9	14	25	29	26	15	-5	-17	-35	-35
Days Maximum Temp. ≥ 90°F	0	0	0	0	1	4	18	14	4	0	0	0	41
Days Maximum Temp. ≤ 32°F	10	4	0	0	0	0	0	0	0	0	2	10	26
Days Minimum Temp. ≤ 32°F	29	26	25	18	7	2	0	1	10	22	26	29	195
Days Minimum Temp. ≤ 0°F	4	1	0	0	0	0	0	0	0	0	1	3	9
Heating Degree Days (base 65°F)	1,215	962	789	573	338	145	25	45	233	586	916	1,227	7,054
Cooling Degree Days (base 65°F)	0	0	0	0	9	43	168	109	13	0	0	0	342
Mean Precipitation (in.)	1.22	1.03	1.06	0.86	1.14	0.94	0.38	0.40	0.42	0.75	1.33	1.59	11.12
Extreme Maximum Daily Precip. (in.)	1.20	0.95	0.99	0.61	1.42	1.53	1.05	1.11	0.95	2.32	1.75	1.00	2.32
Days With ≥ 0.1" Precipitation	5	4	4	3	4	2	1	1	1	2	5	5	37
Days With ≥ 0.5" Precipitation	0	0	0	0	0	0	0	0	0	0	0	1	1
Days With ≥ 1.0" Precipitation	0	0	0	0	0	0	0	0	0	0	0	0	0
Mean Snowfall (in.)	9.0	5.9	1.7	0.4	trace	0.0	0.0	0.0	0.0	0.1	3.1	10.0	30.2
Maximum Snow Depth (in.)	25	28	28	1	0	0	0	0	0	0	8	14	28
Days With ≥ 1.0" Snow Depth	15	10	2	0	0	0	0	0	0	0	2	13	42

Elgin *Union County* Elevation: 2,654 ft. Latitude: 45° 34' N Longitude: 117° 55' W

	JAN	FEB	MAR	APR	MAY	JUN	JUL	AUG	SEP	OCT	NOV	DEC	YEAR
Mean Maximum Temp. (°F)	38.9	44.4	53.1	61.1	*69.2*	76.7	*86.0*	87.0	78.0	*64.6*	*47.1*	*38.5*	*62.0*
Mean Temp. (°F)	30.9	34.1	41.1	47.0	*54.0*	60.3	*66.4*	66.1	58.1	*47.7*	*37.5*	*30.2*	*47.8*
Mean Minimum Temp. (°F)	22.9	23.8	29.0	33.0	*38.7*	43.9	*46.6*	45.1	38.0	*30.8*	*27.9*	*21.9*	*33.5*
Extreme Maximum Temp. (°F)	60	68	75	91	98	100	*107*	103	*102*	*92*	*73*	*61*	*107*
Extreme Minimum Temp. (°F)	-22	-22	0	16	20	28	*29*	25	19	*8*	*-23*	*-31*	*-31*
Days Maximum Temp. ≥ 90°F	0	0	0	0	1	3	*12*	14	4	*0*	*0*	*0*	*34*
Days Maximum Temp. ≤ 32°F	5	2	0	0	0	0	*0*	0	0	*0*	*1*	*6*	*14*
Days Minimum Temp. ≤ 32°F	26	22	21	14	6	1	*0*	1	7	*18*	*20*	*26*	*162*
Days Minimum Temp. ≤ 0°F	1	1	0	0	0	0	*0*	0	0	*0*	*0*	*2*	*4*
Heating Degree Days (base 65°F)	1,049	867	734	532	*341*	166	*51*	57	218	*530*	*819*	*1,071*	*6,435*
Cooling Degree Days (base 65°F)	0	0	0	0	*7*	30	*100*	97	16	*0*	*0*	*0*	*250*
Mean Precipitation (in.)	3.26	2.40	2.13	*2.04*	*2.14*	1.66	*0.83*	0.68	0.89	*1.67*	*3.12*	*3.11*	*23.93*
Extreme Maximum Daily Precip. (in.)	1.72	1.75	1.38	*1.28*	1.54	1.02	*1.05*	1.40	1.20	*1.21*	*2.55*	*1.68*	*2.55*
Days With ≥ 0.1" Precipitation	8	6	6	*6*	6	5	*2*	2	3	*5*	*9*	*8*	*66*
Days With ≥ 0.5" Precipitation	2	1	1	*1*	1	1	*0*	0	0	*1*	*1*	*2*	*11*
Days With ≥ 1.0" Precipitation	1	0	0	*0*	0	0	*0*	0	0	*0*	*0*	*0*	*1*
Mean Snowfall (in.)	17.3	7.7	1.9	0.5	0.0	0.0	*0.0*	0.0	0.0	*trace*	*4.8*	*15.0*	*47.2*
Maximum Snow Depth (in.)	*25*	*23*	*20*	*trace*	*0*	*0*	*0*	*0*	*0*	na	na	na	na
Days With ≥ 1.0" Snow Depth	*13*	*6*	1	0	0	0	*0*	0	0	*0*	*2*	*7*	*29*

The period of record for all cooperative weather station data is 1980 – 2009. See User Guide for detailed explanation of data.

Elkton 3 SW *Douglas County* Elevation: 120 ft. Latitude: 43° 36' N Longitude: 123° 35' W

	JAN	FEB	MAR	APR	MAY	JUN	JUL	AUG	SEP	OCT	NOV	DEC	YEAR
Mean Maximum Temp. (°F)	49.4	54.4	59.4	64.4	70.8	76.2	83.8	84.5	80.0	67.7	54.2	48.0	66.1
Mean Temp. (°F)	43.4	46.2	49.7	53.1	58.3	62.8	68.2	68.2	64.3	56.3	47.9	42.6	55.1
Mean Minimum Temp. (°F)	37.3	38.0	40.0	41.7	45.7	49.4	52.6	52.0	48.6	44.8	41.5	37.2	44.1
Extreme Maximum Temp. (°F)	70	76	79	93	102	103	106	104	101	96	73	68	106
Extreme Minimum Temp. (°F)	10	4	26	28	34	37	41	40	32	25	18	4	4
Days Maximum Temp. ≥ 90°F	0	0	0	0	1	3	8	8	4	0	0	0	24
Days Maximum Temp. ≤ 32°F	0	0	0	0	0	0	0	0	0	0	0	0	0
Days Minimum Temp. ≤ 32°F	6	5	2	1	0	0	0	0	0	1	2	6	23
Days Minimum Temp. ≤ 0°F	0	0	0	0	0	0	0	0	0	0	0	0	0
Heating Degree Days (base 65°F)	663	524	468	352	219	99	18	12	68	267	508	686	3,884
Cooling Degree Days (base 65°F)	0	0	0	2	17	41	125	119	54	5	0	0	363
Mean Precipitation (in.)	7.88	6.09	5.53	4.03	2.49	1.22	0.35	0.40	1.16	2.98	8.89	10.08	51.10
Extreme Maximum Daily Precip. (in.)	3.74	4.49	1.80	***2.07***	1.44	1.36	0.95	1.03	1.03	***2.05***	***5.35***	6.88	***6.88***
Days With ≥ 0.1" Precipitation	13	11	12	9	6	3	1	1	3	6	13	14	92
Days With ≥ 0.5" Precipitation	5	4	4	2	2	1	0	0	1	2	6	6	33
Days With ≥ 1.0" Precipitation	2	2	1	0	0	0	0	0	0	1	2	3	11
Mean Snowfall (in.)	0.2	0.1	trace	trace	0.0	0.0	0.0	0.0	0.0	0.0	0.0	trace	0.3
Maximum Snow Depth (in.)	2	0	trace	trace	0	0	0	0	0	0	0	4	4
Days With ≥ 1.0" Snow Depth	0	0	0	0	0	0	0	0	0	0	0	0	0

Enterprise 20 NNE *Wallowa County* Elevation: 3,279 ft. Latitude: 45° 43' N Longitude: 117° 09' W

	JAN	FEB	MAR	APR	MAY	JUN	JUL	AUG	SEP	OCT	NOV	DEC	YEAR
Mean Maximum Temp. (°F)	37.7	43.9	***53.0***	60.6	68.1	***75.7***	86.2	86.5	77.2	63.4	45.1	36.3	***61.1***
Mean Temp. (°F)	27.7	31.9	***39.3***	45.4	52.1	***58.3***	65.4	64.4	56.4	46.1	34.7	26.6	***45.7***
Mean Minimum Temp. (°F)	17.6	19.8	***25.4***	30.2	35.6	***40.9***	44.5	42.4	35.7	28.7	24.2	16.9	***30.1***
Extreme Maximum Temp. (°F)	56	71	***81***	92	98	***100***	108	107	105	97	74	61	***108***
Extreme Minimum Temp. (°F)	-28	-30	***-6***	11	15	***23***	28	24	16	-1	-21	-33	***-33***
Days Maximum Temp. ≥ 90°F	0	0	***0***	0	1	***3***	13	12	5	0	0	0	***34***
Days Maximum Temp. ≤ 32°F	6	2	***0***	0	0	***0***	0	0	0	0	2	7	***17***
Days Minimum Temp. ≤ 32°F	30	27	***27***	19	10	***3***	1	1	10	22	26	30	***206***
Days Minimum Temp. ≤ 0°F	3	2	***0***	0	0	***0***	0	0	0	0	0	3	***8***
Heating Degree Days (base 65°F)	1,149	930	***791***	582	398	***212***	72	76	262	581	904	1,184	***7,141***
Cooling Degree Days (base 65°F)	0	0	***0***	0	5	***18***	91	66	11	0	0	0	***191***
Mean Precipitation (in.)	1.67	1.32	1.75	1.89	2.14	***2.16***	1.28	1.07	1.01	1.13	2.06	1.80	***19.28***
Extreme Maximum Daily Precip. (in.)	0.87	***1.00***	***1.25***	1.27	1.45	***1.55***	2.00	***2.40***	***1.00***	1.45	***1.15***	***1.35***	2.40
Days With ≥ 0.1" Precipitation	6	5	6	6	6	***6***	3	3	3	4	7	6	***61***
Days With ≥ 0.5" Precipitation	1	0	0	1	1	***1***	1	1	1	0	1	1	***9***
Days With ≥ 1.0" Precipitation	0	0	0	0	0	***0***	0	0	0	0	0	0	***0***
Mean Snowfall (in.)	***6.4***	4.5	2.0	trace	trace	***0.0***	0.0	0.0	0.0	0.0	***1.8***	***5.2***	***19.9***
Maximum Snow Depth (in.)	***22***	***30***	***15***	***trace***	***trace***	***0***	0	***0***	***0***	***2***	***12***	***26***	***30***
Days With ≥ 1.0" Snow Depth	***8***	4	2	0	0	***0***	0	0	0	0	2	***6***	***22***

Estacada 2 SE *Clackamas County* Elevation: 450 ft. Latitude: 45° 16' N Longitude: 122° 19' W

	JAN	FEB	MAR	APR	MAY	JUN	JUL	AUG	SEP	OCT	NOV	DEC	YEAR
Mean Maximum Temp. (°F)	47.0	50.9	55.7	60.5	66.6	71.8	79.1	79.5	74.1	62.0	51.9	45.8	62.1
Mean Temp. (°F)	41.1	43.4	47.0	50.7	56.1	60.9	66.3	66.4	61.8	53.0	45.5	40.1	52.7
Mean Minimum Temp. (°F)	35.2	35.8	38.2	40.8	45.6	50.0	53.5	53.3	49.3	43.9	39.1	34.3	43.3
Extreme Maximum Temp. (°F)	67	71	83	90	105	103	109	105	105	90	72	68	109
Extreme Minimum Temp. (°F)	14	8	26	28	32	37	42	42	33	26	13	6	6
Days Maximum Temp. ≥ 90°F	0	0	0	0	0	1	4	3	2	0	0	0	10
Days Maximum Temp. ≤ 32°F	0	0	0	0	0	0	0	0	0	0	0	1	1
Days Minimum Temp. ≤ 32°F	10	8	4	1	0	0	0	0	0	0	5	11	39
Days Minimum Temp. ≤ 0°F	0	0	0	0	0	0	0	0	0	0	0	0	0
Heating Degree Days (base 65°F)	733	605	552	423	280	144	42	35	122	369	577	765	4,647
Cooling Degree Days (base 65°F)	0	0	0	1	12	28	89	87	32	2	0	0	251
Mean Precipitation (in.)	8.02	6.30	6.27	5.17	3.94	2.82	0.92	0.93	2.08	4.78	8.57	8.24	58.04
Extreme Maximum Daily Precip. (in.)	5.28	3.20	2.60	2.95	1.77	1.73	1.42	1.53	1.47	5.27	3.96	3.10	5.28
Days With ≥ 0.1" Precipitation	14	12	14	13	10	6	3	2	5	9	15	15	118
Days With ≥ 0.5" Precipitation	6	4	4	3	3	2	0	1	1	3	6	6	39
Days With ≥ 1.0" Precipitation	2	1	1	1	0	1	0	0	0	1	2	2	11
Mean Snowfall (in.)	0.6	0.6	0.1	0.0	0.0	0.0	0.0	0.0	0.0	0.0	trace	0.3	1.6
Maximum Snow Depth (in.)	4	5	2	0	0	0	0	0	0	0	1	9	9
Days With ≥ 1.0" Snow Depth	0	0	0	0	0	0	0	0	0	0	0	0	0

Headworks Ptld Wtr Bur *Clackamas County* Elevation: 748 ft. Latitude: 45° 27' N Longitude: 122° 09' W

	JAN	FEB	MAR	APR	MAY	JUN	JUL	AUG	SEP	OCT	NOV	DEC	YEAR
Mean Maximum Temp. (°F)	46.1	50.0	54.5	60.2	66.6	71.8	79.2	79.7	74.3	63.0	51.2	45.1	61.8
Mean Temp. (°F)	40.7	43.0	46.2	50.4	55.9	60.7	66.3	66.7	62.3	54.0	45.5	40.0	52.7
Mean Minimum Temp. (°F)	35.3	35.9	37.9	40.6	45.2	49.6	53.4	53.7	50.3	45.0	39.7	34.8	43.4
Extreme Maximum Temp. (°F)	63	72	82	88	99	102	105	103	104	94	73	63	105
Extreme Minimum Temp. (°F)	11	5	24	30	32	38	43	40	36	28	16	5	5
Days Maximum Temp. ≥ 90°F	0	0	0	0	1	1	4	4	2	0	0	0	12
Days Maximum Temp. ≤ 32°F	0	0	0	0	0	0	0	0	0	0	0	1	1
Days Minimum Temp. ≤ 32°F	10	8	4	1	0	0	0	0	0	0	3	9	35
Days Minimum Temp. ≤ 0°F	0	0	0	0	0	0	0	0	0	0	0	0	0
Heating Degree Days (base 65°F)	746	616	575	431	287	149	43	33	112	338	580	769	4,679
Cooling Degree Days (base 65°F)	0	0	0	1	12	28	91	94	38	5	0	0	269
Mean Precipitation (in.)	10.40	8.14	8.10	6.92	5.47	4.06	1.32	1.41	3.61	6.40	11.05	11.04	77.92
Extreme Maximum Daily Precip. (in.)	4.20	4.04	2.05	3.45	2.74	2.43	1.83	1.81	2.68	6.80	4.25	3.63	6.80
Days With ≥ 0.1" Precipitation	17	14	16	14	11	8	3	3	6	11	17	17	137
Days With ≥ 0.5" Precipitation	8	6	6	5	4	3	1	1	3	5	8	8	58
Days With ≥ 1.0" Precipitation	3	2	2	1	1	1	0	0	1	1	3	3	18
Mean Snowfall (in.)	1.5	0.7	0.4	trace	0.0	0.0	0.0	0.0	0.0	0.0	0.5	1.7	4.8
Maximum Snow Depth (in.)	18	9	4	trace	0	0	0	0	0	0	8	27	27
Days With ≥ 1.0" Snow Depth	1	1	0	0	0	0	0	0	0	0	0	1	3

The period of record for all cooperative weather station data is 1980 – 2009. See User Guide for detailed explanation of data.

Idleyld Park 4 NE *Douglas County* Elevation: 1,080 ft. Latitude: 43° 22' N Longitude: 122° 58' W

	JAN	FEB	MAR	APR	MAY	JUN	JUL	AUG	SEP	OCT	NOV	DEC	YEAR
Mean Maximum Temp. (°F)	46.1	51.5	56.9	62.6	69.6	75.5	83.5	83.6	77.9	64.7	50.8	44.4	63.9
Mean Temp. (°F)	39.7	42.8	46.5	50.5	56.1	61.1	66.7	66.2	61.2	52.5	44.0	38.7	52.2
Mean Minimum Temp. (°F)	33.3	34.0	36.1	38.4	42.6	46.7	49.8	48.7	44.5	40.3	37.1	32.9	40.4
Extreme Maximum Temp. (°F)	70	75	79	90	102	101	103	103	102	96	71	63	103
Extreme Minimum Temp. (°F)	11	6	24	25	26	31	35	32	29	19	17	3	3
Days Maximum Temp. ≥ 90°F	0	0	0	0	1	2	7	7	3	0	0	0	20
Days Maximum Temp. ≤ 32°F	0	0	0	0	0	0	0	0	0	0	0	1	1
Days Minimum Temp. ≤ 32°F	16	13	10	4	2	0	0	0	1	4	9	16	75
Days Minimum Temp. ≤ 0°F	0	0	0	0	0	0	0	0	0	0	0	0	0
Heating Degree Days (base 65°F)	777	623	566	430	278	135	34	36	131	382	624	808	4,824
Cooling Degree Days (base 65°F)	0	0	0	0	10	25	94	79	25	1	0	0	234
Mean Precipitation (in.)	8.83	6.56	6.52	5.35	3.63	1.95	0.74	0.69	1.70	4.55	9.98	10.82	61.32
Extreme Maximum Daily Precip. (in.)	3.35	3.42	2.20	2.59	1.59	1.90	2.26	1.35	2.40	2.22	6.12	3.86	6.12
Days With ≥ 0.1" Precipitation	14	12	14	13	8	5	1	1	3	8	15	15	109
Days With ≥ 0.5" Precipitation	7	5	4	4	2	1	0	0	1	4	8	8	44
Days With ≥ 1.0" Precipitation	2	1	1	1	1	0	0	0	0	1	3	3	13
Mean Snowfall (in.)	4.0	3.7	1.6	0.4	trace	0.0	0.0	0.0	0.0	trace	0.6	3.6	13.9
Maximum Snow Depth (in.)	13	12	8	3	trace	0	0	0	0	trace	3	16	16
Days With ≥ 1.0" Snow Depth	4	2	0	0	0	0	0	0	0	0	0	3	9

Long Creek *Grant County* Elevation: 3,720 ft. Latitude: 44° 43' N Longitude: 119° 06' W

	JAN	FEB	MAR	APR	MAY	JUN	JUL	AUG	SEP	OCT	NOV	DEC	YEAR
Mean Maximum Temp. (°F)	40.1	44.5	50.3	56.3	***64.7***	***72.8***	82.4	82.8	***73.8***	***61.4***	47.6	39.2	***59.7***
Mean Temp. (°F)	31.7	34.5	39.3	43.9	***51.1***	***57.5***	64.5	64.5	***57.0***	***47.7***	38.0	30.6	***46.7***
Mean Minimum Temp. (°F)	23.2	24.5	28.2	31.5	***37.4***	***42.1***	46.6	46.2	***40.1***	***33.9***	28.1	21.9	***33.6***
Extreme Maximum Temp. (°F)	63	69	74	85	94	96	106	101	97	88	75	65	106
Extreme Minimum Temp. (°F)	-14	-21	2	13	21	27	31	29	21	-1	-10	-25	-25
Days Maximum Temp. ≥ 90°F	0	0	0	0	0	1	7	6	1	0	0	0	15
Days Maximum Temp. ≤ 32°F	6	2	0	0	0	0	0	0	0	0	1	6	15
Days Minimum Temp. ≤ 32°F	26	22	21	17	7	1	0	0	4	12	20	26	156
Days Minimum Temp. ≤ 0°F	1	1	0	0	0	0	0	0	0	0	0	1	3
Heating Degree Days (base 65°F)	1,027	855	791	624	***429***	***235***	86	83	***247***	***530***	804	1,059	***6,770***
Cooling Degree Days (base 65°F)	0	0	0	0	***5***	***15***	78	74	***15***	***1***	0	0	***188***
Mean Precipitation (in.)	1.77	1.36	1.89	1.87	2.13	1.49	0.75	0.77	0.73	1.42	1.95	1.87	18.00
Extreme Maximum Daily Precip. (in.)	0.95	***0.70***	***1.40***	***1.45***	***0.99***	***1.19***	1.30	1.60	***0.88***	1.00	***2.05***	***1.50***	***2.05***
Days With ≥ 0.1" Precipitation	7	4	6	6	6	4	2	2	2	4	6	6	55
Days With ≥ 0.5" Precipitation	1	0	1	0	1	1	0	0	0	1	0	0	5
Days With ≥ 1.0" Precipitation	0	0	0	0	0	0	0	0	0	0	0	0	0
Mean Snowfall (in.)	8.1	5.3	5.6	2.0	0.2	0.1	trace	0.0	0.0	0.5	4.4	8.8	35.0
Maximum Snow Depth (in.)	16	9	9	9	trace	trace	trace	0	0	2	9	13	16
Days With ≥ 1.0" Snow Depth	7	3	1	0	0	0	0	0	0	0	2	7	20

Lookout Point Dam *Lane County* Elevation: 711 ft. Latitude: 43° 55' N Longitude: 122° 46' W

	JAN	FEB	MAR	APR	MAY	JUN	JUL	AUG	SEP	OCT	NOV	DEC	YEAR
Mean Maximum Temp. (°F)	47.9	51.8	56.0	60.1	66.1	71.8	80.3	80.7	75.3	64.2	53.1	46.7	62.8
Mean Temp. (°F)	41.7	44.1	47.5	50.9	55.8	60.8	67.1	67.0	62.9	54.9	46.8	41.1	53.4
Mean Minimum Temp. (°F)	35.5	36.4	39.0	41.6	45.4	49.8	53.8	53.2	50.4	45.6	40.4	35.4	43.9
Extreme Maximum Temp. (°F)	68	73	79	84	93	101	102	106	101	89	73	68	106
Extreme Minimum Temp. (°F)	10	7	27	31	30	37	44	43	33	27	19	3	3
Days Maximum Temp. ≥ 90°F	0	0	0	0	0	1	4	3	1	0	0	0	9
Days Maximum Temp. ≤ 32°F	0	0	0	0	0	0	0	0	0	0	0	1	1
Days Minimum Temp. ≤ 32°F	10	7	2	0	0	0	0	0	0	0	3	9	31
Days Minimum Temp. ≤ 0°F	0	0	0	0	0	0	0	0	0	0	0	0	0
Heating Degree Days (base 65°F)	715	583	536	418	289	146	35	29	98	309	541	734	4,433
Cooling Degree Days (base 65°F)	0	0	0	1	10	27	106	97	42	4	0	0	287
Mean Precipitation (in.)	6.02	4.78	4.83	4.23	3.57	2.15	0.75	0.76	1.52	3.27	7.03	7.04	45.95
Extreme Maximum Daily Precip. (in.)	2.51	3.32	1.55	2.54	2.04	1.34	1.49	2.07	2.32	1.83	5.50	4.62	5.50
Days With ≥ 0.1" Precipitation	13	10	13	12	9	6	2	2	4	8	14	14	107
Days With ≥ 0.5" Precipitation	4	3	3	2	2	1	0	1	1	2	5	5	29
Days With ≥ 1.0" Precipitation	1	1	0	0	0	0	0	0	0	0	2	1	5
Mean Snowfall (in.)	0.4	0.5	0.0	0.0	0.0	0.0	0.0	0.0	0.0	0.0	trace	0.5	1.4
Maximum Snow Depth (in.)	4	6	1	0	0	0	0	0	0	0	trace	5	6
Days With ≥ 1.0" Snow Depth	0	1	0	0	0	0	0	0	0	0	0	1	2

Lost Creek Dam *Jackson County* Elevation: 1,580 ft. Latitude: 42° 40' N Longitude: 122° 41' W

	JAN	FEB	MAR	APR	MAY	JUN	JUL	AUG	SEP	OCT	NOV	DEC	YEAR
Mean Maximum Temp. (°F)	48.4	53.7	58.4	63.9	71.7	79.3	89.1	89.4	83.3	70.5	53.7	46.9	67.4
Mean Temp. (°F)	38.9	41.8	45.5	50.1	56.6	62.6	69.8	69.5	63.4	53.6	43.3	38.1	52.8
Mean Minimum Temp. (°F)	29.3	29.9	32.7	36.3	41.4	45.9	50.4	49.6	43.5	36.6	32.8	29.3	38.1
Extreme Maximum Temp. (°F)	70	78	83	94	101	104	109	112	108	104	78	63	112
Extreme Minimum Temp. (°F)	7	2	17	19	27	31	39	35	28	15	13	-6	-6
Days Maximum Temp. ≥ 90°F	0	0	0	0	2	5	16	17	10	2	0	0	52
Days Maximum Temp. ≤ 32°F	0	0	0	0	0	0	0	0	0	0	0	0	0
Days Minimum Temp. ≤ 32°F	22	18	17	9	2	0	0	0	1	8	15	21	113
Days Minimum Temp. ≤ 0°F	0	0	0	0	0	0	0	0	0	0	0	0	0
Heating Degree Days (base 65°F)	803	648	597	442	273	120	23	18	105	351	645	827	4,852
Cooling Degree Days (base 65°F)	0	0	0	2	19	55	177	167	64	4	0	0	488
Mean Precipitation (in.)	4.74	3.69	3.42	2.49	2.11	1.01	0.54	0.48	0.83	2.21	5.30	6.14	32.96
Extreme Maximum Daily Precip. (in.)	2.46	2.57	2.70	1.56	1.16	1.08	1.25	1.12	2.10	2.02	3.03	2.79	3.03
Days With ≥ 0.1" Precipitation	11	9	10	8	6	3	1	1	2	5	12	12	80
Days With ≥ 0.5" Precipitation	3	2	2	1	1	0	0	0	0	1	3	4	17
Days With ≥ 1.0" Precipitation	1	1	0	0	0	0	0	0	0	0	1	2	5
Mean Snowfall (in.)	0.4	0.3	0.1	trace	0.0	0.0	0.0	0.0	0.0	0.0	trace	0.9	1.7
Maximum Snow Depth (in.)	7	5	4	trace	0	0	0	0	0	0	trace	7	7
Days With ≥ 1.0" Snow Depth	1	0	0	0	0	0	0	0	0	0	0	1	2

The period of record for all cooperative weather station data is 1980 – 2009. See User Guide for detailed explanation of data.

McMinnville *Yamhill County* Elevation: 154 ft. Latitude: 45° 13' N Longitude: 123° 10' W

	JAN	FEB	MAR	APR	MAY	JUN	JUL	AUG	SEP	OCT	NOV	DEC	YEAR
Mean Maximum Temp. (°F)	47.2	51.4	56.6	62.4	69.2	75.2	82.9	83.0	77.4	64.7	52.9	45.9	64.1
Mean Temp. (°F)	41.0	43.4	47.1	51.3	57.0	62.2	67.6	67.5	62.7	53.8	45.9	40.1	53.3
Mean Minimum Temp. (°F)	34.8	35.3	37.6	40.1	44.9	49.2	52.3	51.9	48.0	42.9	38.9	34.2	42.5
Extreme Maximum Temp. (°F)	64	69	75	85	100	103	107	105	105	95	68	64	107
Extreme Minimum Temp. (°F)	9	8	22	27	29	33	39	37	32	28	15	11	8
Days Maximum Temp. ≥ 90°F	0	0	0	0	1	2	6	6	3	0	0	0	18
Days Maximum Temp. ≤ 32°F	1	0	0	0	0	0	0	0	0	0	0	1	2
Days Minimum Temp. ≤ 32°F	11	10	6	3	0	0	0	0	0	1	6	11	48
Days Minimum Temp. ≤ 0°F	0	0	0	0	0	0	0	0	0	0	0	0	0
Heating Degree Days (base 65°F)	736	604	547	405	257	118	28	28	103	343	565	766	4,500
Cooling Degree Days (base 65°F)	0	0	0	0	15	41	116	110	42	2	0	0	326
Mean Precipitation (in.)	6.34	4.72	4.30	2.78	1.84	1.18	0.39	0.39	1.26	2.88	6.64	7.05	39.77
Extreme Maximum Daily Precip. (in.)	2.14	***3.50***	***1.61***	***1.97***	***1.28***	***1.07***	***1.05***	0.63	***3.10***	1.34	2.50	***2.20***	***3.50***
Days With ≥ 0.1" Precipitation	10	8	10	7	5	3	1	1	3	6	11	11	76
Days With ≥ 0.5" Precipitation	4	3	2	1	1	1	0	0	1	2	4	5	24
Days With ≥ 1.0" Precipitation	1	1	1	0	0	0	0	0	0	0	1	2	6
Mean Snowfall (in.)	0.6	0.4	0.0	trace	0.0	0.0	0.0	0.0	0.0	0.0	0.1	0.6	1.7
Maximum Snow Depth (in.)	3	7	2	trace	0	0	0	0	0	0	trace	4	7
Days With ≥ 1.0" Snow Depth	0	0	0	0	0	0	0	0	0	0	0	0	0

N Willamette Exp Stn *Clackamas County* Elevation: 149 ft. Latitude: 45° 17' N Longitude: 122° 45' W

	JAN	FEB	MAR	APR	MAY	JUN	JUL	AUG	SEP	OCT	NOV	DEC	YEAR
Mean Maximum Temp. (°F)	47.8	51.6	56.7	61.3	67.6	73.6	80.9	81.6	76.4	64.5	52.8	45.6	63.4
Mean Temp. (°F)	41.3	43.5	47.5	51.1	56.8	62.2	67.5	67.6	62.8	53.7	45.6	39.3	53.2
Mean Minimum Temp. (°F)	34.7	35.2	38.1	40.7	46.0	50.7	54.1	53.5	49.2	42.8	38.3	32.9	43.0
Extreme Maximum Temp. (°F)	65	71	78	87	101	104	104	105	105	95	70	67	105
Extreme Minimum Temp. (°F)	11	8	22	19	29	39	42	42	36	29	14	-15	-15
Days Maximum Temp. ≥ 90°F	0	0	0	0	1	2	5	6	2	0	0	0	16
Days Maximum Temp. ≤ 32°F	1	0	0	0	0	0	0	0	0	0	0	1	2
Days Minimum Temp. ≤ 32°F	12	9	5	2	0	0	0	0	0	1	7	14	50
Days Minimum Temp. ≤ 0°F	0	0	0	0	0	0	0	0	0	0	0	0	0
Heating Degree Days (base 65°F)	728	602	537	413	263	120	30	28	103	346	575	791	4,536
Cooling Degree Days (base 65°F)	0	0	0	1	15	44	115	115	45	2	0	0	337
Mean Precipitation (in.)	6.10	4.77	4.49	3.24	2.40	1.82	0.61	0.63	1.53	3.53	6.60	6.65	42.37
Extreme Maximum Daily Precip. (in.)	2.02	2.70	2.00	1.32	1.78	1.59	1.76	1.40	2.04	4.80	3.71	2.09	4.80
Days With ≥ 0.1" Precipitation	13	11	12	10	7	5	1	2	4	8	***14***	13	***100***
Days With ≥ 0.5" Precipitation	4	3	2	1	1	1	0	0	1	2	4	5	24
Days With ≥ 1.0" Precipitation	1	1	1	0	0	0	0	0	0	1	1	2	7
Mean Snowfall (in.)	0.1	***0.2***	0.0	0.0	0.0	0.0	0.0	0.0	***0.0***	***0.0***	trace	***0.2***	***0.5***
Maximum Snow Depth (in.)	***1***	***trace***	***0***	0	0	0	***0***	***0***	***0***	***0***	***trace***	***trace***	***1***
Days With ≥ 1.0" Snow Depth	***0***	***0***	0	0	0	0	0	0	***0***	***0***	0	***0***	***0***

Oregon City *Clackamas County* Elevation: 167 ft. Latitude: 45° 21' N Longitude: 122° 36' W

	JAN	FEB	MAR	APR	MAY	JUN	JUL	AUG	SEP	OCT	NOV	DEC	YEAR
Mean Maximum Temp. (°F)	48.3	52.9	57.8	63.7	***70.0***	75.8	82.8	83.1	78.3	65.4	53.2	46.7	***64.8***
Mean Temp. (°F)	42.3	45.0	48.8	53.3	***59.0***	64.2	69.6	69.6	65.2	55.7	46.8	41.1	***55.0***
Mean Minimum Temp. (°F)	36.2	37.1	39.7	42.8	***47.9***	52.5	56.4	56.0	52.2	45.9	40.3	35.5	***45.2***
Extreme Maximum Temp. (°F)	66	75	81	92	104	103	108	107	105	96	73	68	108
Extreme Minimum Temp. (°F)	15	10	24	29	33	39	44	41	37	28	15	6	6
Days Maximum Temp. ≥ 90°F	0	0	0	0	1	2	7	6	3	0	0	0	19
Days Maximum Temp. ≤ 32°F	0	0	0	0	0	0	0	0	0	0	0	1	1
Days Minimum Temp. ≤ 32°F	9	7	3	1	0	0	0	0	0	0	4	9	33
Days Minimum Temp. ≤ 0°F	0	0	0	0	0	0	0	0	0	0	0	0	0
Heating Degree Days (base 65°F)	696	558	496	347	***205***	80	14	9	61	288	540	733	***4,027***
Cooling Degree Days (base 65°F)	0	0	0	3	***26***	63	164	159	75	6	0	0	***496***
Mean Precipitation (in.)	6.42	4.65	4.74	3.32	2.44	1.75	0.66	0.77	1.40	3.50	6.70	7.05	43.40
Extreme Maximum Daily Precip. (in.)	2.50	2.63	1.95	1.92	***1.90***	***1.70***	***1.06***	1.37	***1.50***	***3.35***	3.30	***2.35***	***3.35***
Days With ≥ 0.1" Precipitation	12	9	11	9	6	4	1	2	3	7	12	12	88
Days With ≥ 0.5" Precipitation	4	3	3	2	1	1	0	0	1	2	5	5	27
Days With ≥ 1.0" Precipitation	1	1	0	0	0	0	0	0	0	0	1	2	5
Mean Snowfall (in.)	0.4	0.7	0.1	trace	0.0	0.0	0.0	0.0	0.0	0.0	trace	0.9	2.1
Maximum Snow Depth (in.)	2	3	trace	0	0	0	0	0	0	0	0	4	4
Days With ≥ 1.0" Snow Depth	0	0	0	0	0	0	0	0	0	0	0	0	0

Paisley *Lake County* Elevation: 4,359 ft. Latitude: 42° 42' N Longitude: 120° 32' W

	JAN	FEB	MAR	APR	MAY	JUN	JUL	AUG	SEP	OCT	NOV	DEC	YEAR
Mean Maximum Temp. (°F)	43.0	46.4	53.2	59.9	***68.4***	76.0	85.8	85.0	***76.5***	***65.3***	***48.9***	***41.2***	***62.5***
Mean Temp. (°F)	33.1	35.3	41.1	46.3	***53.8***	60.2	67.1	***66.1***	***58.5***	***48.9***	***37.5***	***31.5***	***48.3***
Mean Minimum Temp. (°F)	23.2	24.2	28.8	32.5	***39.3***	44.3	48.8	***47.5***	***40.3***	***32.5***	***26.0***	***21.8***	***34.1***
Extreme Maximum Temp. (°F)	65	72	76	85	92	96	104	100	98	90	75	65	104
Extreme Minimum Temp. (°F)	-9	-25	7	13	10	26	29	27	19	0	-7	-16	-25
Days Maximum Temp. ≥ 90°F	0	0	0	0	0	1	10	9	1	0	0	0	21
Days Maximum Temp. ≤ 32°F	3	2	0	0	0	0	0	0	0	0	1	3	9
Days Minimum Temp. ≤ 32°F	24	21	20	14	6	1	0	0	4	14	20	23	147
Days Minimum Temp. ≤ 0°F	0	0	0	0	0	0	0	0	0	0	0	1	1
Heating Degree Days (base 65°F)	981	832	734	557	***349***	171	46	***53***	***206***	***492***	***820***	***1,029***	***6,270***
Cooling Degree Days (base 65°F)	0	0	0	0	***9***	33	118	***97***	***21***	***1***	***0***	***0***	***279***
Mean Precipitation (in.)	1.34	0.95	0.96	1.00	1.02	0.90	0.46	0.55	0.59	0.61	1.20	1.26	10.84
Extreme Maximum Daily Precip. (in.)	***2.38***	***0.98***	0.94	1.26	***1.06***	***1.87***	1.37	1.85	1.27	0.81	***1.90***	***1.90***	***2.38***
Days With ≥ 0.1" Precipitation	3	3	3	3	3	3	1	1	1	2	3	3	29
Days With ≥ 0.5" Precipitation	0	0	0	0	0	0	0	0	0	0	0	1	1
Days With ≥ 1.0" Precipitation	0	0	0	0	0	0	0	0	0	0	0	0	0
Mean Snowfall (in.)	***1.2***	1.8	1.1	0.2	trace	0.0	0.0	0.0	trace	trace	1.5	2.5	***8.3***
Maximum Snow Depth (in.)	14	12	6	4	trace	0	0	0	0	1	5	10	14
Days With ≥ 1.0" Snow Depth	3	2	0	0	0	0	0	0	0	0	1	3	9

The period of record for all cooperative weather station data is 1980 – 2009. See User Guide for detailed explanation of data.

Port Orford 2 *Curry County* Elevation: 42 ft. Latitude: 42° 45' N Longitude: 124° 30' W

	JAN	FEB	MAR	APR	MAY	JUN	JUL	AUG	SEP	OCT	NOV	DEC	YEAR
Mean Maximum Temp. (°F)	54.8	55.2	55.8	57.5	60.8	63.9	67.3	68.3	67.6	63.5	57.2	54.5	60.5
Mean Temp. (°F)	47.8	48.0	48.8	50.4	53.8	57.1	60.2	60.6	59.0	55.2	50.4	47.4	53.2
Mean Minimum Temp. (°F)	40.8	40.8	41.8	43.3	46.8	50.3	53.0	52.8	50.5	46.9	43.4	40.3	45.9
Extreme Maximum Temp. (°F)	74	78	78	84	85	84	97	86	93	89	76	80	97
Extreme Minimum Temp. (°F)	21	19	29	32	31	38	43	39	37	28	27	13	13
Days Maximum Temp. ≥ 90°F	0	0	0	0	0	0	0	0	0	0	0	0	0
Days Maximum Temp. ≤ 32°F	0	0	0	0	0	0	0	0	0	0	0	0	0
Days Minimum Temp. ≤ 32°F	3	3	1	0	0	0	0	0	0	0	1	4	12
Days Minimum Temp. ≤ 0°F	0	0	0	0	0	0	0	0	0	0	0	0	0
Heating Degree Days (base 65°F)	525	474	496	430	340	231	145	133	176	298	433	538	4,219
Cooling Degree Days (base 65°F)	0	0	0	0	1	0	2	2	3	2	0	0	10
Mean Precipitation (in.)	11.35	8.67	9.03	5.82	3.68	2.15	0.56	0.73	1.52	4.93	10.57	12.93	71.94
Extreme Maximum Daily Precip. (in.)	3.53	3.55	3.65	3.44	2.22	2.05	1.96	1.95	2.06	3.26	5.65	7.53	7.53
Days With ≥ 0.1" Precipitation	15	13	15	12	7	5	1	1	3	7	15	16	110
Days With ≥ 0.5" Precipitation	9	6	7	4	2	2	0	0	1	3	8	9	51
Days With ≥ 1.0" Precipitation	4	3	3	1	1	0	0	0	0	2	3	4	21
Mean Snowfall (in.)	0.0	0.1	0.0	0.0	0.0	0.0	0.0	0.0	0.0	0.0	0.0	0.1	0.2
Maximum Snow Depth (in.)	2	trace	0	0	0	0	0	0	0	0	0	2	2
Days With ≥ 1.0" Snow Depth	0	0	0	0	0	0	0	0	0	0	0	0	0

Rome 2 NW *Malheur County* Elevation: 3,404 ft. Latitude: 42° 52' N Longitude: 117° 39' W

	JAN	FEB	MAR	APR	MAY	JUN	JUL	AUG	SEP	OCT	NOV	DEC	YEAR
Mean Maximum Temp. (°F)	40.1	46.9	56.5	64.0	73.1	82.1	92.1	90.9	81.2	67.4	50.6	39.3	65.4
Mean Temp. (°F)	29.8	35.2	42.1	48.2	56.7	64.2	72.1	69.9	60.5	49.0	37.5	28.9	49.5
Mean Minimum Temp. (°F)	19.5	23.3	27.6	32.2	40.2	46.2	52.0	48.8	39.9	30.5	24.4	18.4	33.6
Extreme Maximum Temp. (°F)	64	70	80	91	100	104	110	107	102	92	78	65	110
Extreme Minimum Temp. (°F)	-27	-17	0	10	16	27	28	30	19	-2	-9	-26	-27
Days Maximum Temp. ≥ 90°F	0	0	0	0	2	8	21	20	6	0	0	0	57
Days Maximum Temp. ≤ 32°F	6	2	0	0	0	0	0	0	0	0	1	6	15
Days Minimum Temp. ≤ 32°F	28	24	22	15	5	1	0	0	5	18	24	28	170
Days Minimum Temp. ≤ 0°F	1	1	0	0	0	0	0	0	0	0	0	2	4
Heating Degree Days (base 65°F)	1,084	837	703	500	270	96	12	18	160	490	818	1,112	6,100
Cooling Degree Days (base 65°F)	0	0	0	1	19	79	239	176	33	0	0	0	547
Mean Precipitation (in.)	0.69	0.57	0.78	0.95	1.38	0.92	0.38	0.18	0.44	0.62	0.72	0.88	8.51
Extreme Maximum Daily Precip. (in.)	1.45	0.67	1.10	0.95	1.56	0.91	1.30	0.48	2.21	0.98	0.55	0.73	2.21
Days With ≥ 0.1" Precipitation	2	2	3	4	4	3	1	1	1	2	3	3	29
Days With ≥ 0.5" Precipitation	0	0	0	0	1	0	0	0	0	0	0	0	1
Days With ≥ 1.0" Precipitation	0	0	0	0	0	0	0	0	0	0	0	0	0
Mean Snowfall (in.)	1.8	0.2	0.6	0.1	0.2	0.0	0.0	0.0	0.0	trace	0.8	2.2	5.9
Maximum Snow Depth (in.)	12	7	2	1	trace	0	0	0	0	trace	8	13	13
Days With ≥ 1.0" Snow Depth	6	2	0	0	0	0	0	0	0	0	1	6	15

Roseburg KQEN *Douglas County* Elevation: 424 ft. Latitude: 43° 13' N Longitude: 123° 22' W

	JAN	FEB	MAR	APR	MAY	JUN	JUL	AUG	SEP	OCT	NOV	DEC	YEAR
Mean Maximum Temp. (°F)	50.0	54.4	59.7	64.5	71.5	77.6	85.9	86.4	80.9	68.3	55.1	48.4	66.9
Mean Temp. (°F)	43.0	45.4	49.1	52.9	59.0	64.4	70.8	70.6	65.2	56.1	47.7	42.2	55.5
Mean Minimum Temp. (°F)	36.0	36.4	38.5	41.2	46.4	51.2	55.6	54.8	49.5	43.9	40.2	35.9	44.1
Extreme Maximum Temp. (°F)	72	78	85	95	107	106	111	110	105	101	78	73	111
Extreme Minimum Temp. (°F)	9	3	24	28	32	38	43	44	35	21	20	3	3
Days Maximum Temp. ≥ 90°F	0	0	0	0	2	3	11	11	6	1	0	0	34
Days Maximum Temp. ≤ 32°F	0	0	0	0	0	0	0	0	0	0	0	1	1
Days Minimum Temp. ≤ 32°F	8	7	4	1	0	0	0	0	0	1	3	8	32
Days Minimum Temp. ≤ 0°F	0	0	0	0	0	0	0	0	0	0	0	0	0
Heating Degree Days (base 65°F)	675	546	486	360	208	81	13	8	67	276	513	701	3,934
Cooling Degree Days (base 65°F)	0	0	0	3	28	70	199	189	81	8	0	0	578
Mean Precipitation (in.)	5.02	3.70	3.52	2.62	2.02	0.97	0.40	0.42	0.88	2.15	5.28	6.17	33.15
Extreme Maximum Daily Precip. (in.)	2.10	2.51	1.80	2.43	1.30	1.11	1.60	0.92	1.27	2.02	4.35	3.53	4.35
Days With ≥ 0.1" Precipitation	11	9	10	8	6	3	1	1	2	6	12	13	82
Days With ≥ 0.5" Precipitation	3	2	2	1	1	0	0	0	0	1	3	4	17
Days With ≥ 1.0" Precipitation	1	0	0	0	0	0	0	0	0	0	1	1	3
Mean Snowfall (in.)	trace	0.3	trace	0.0	0.0	0.0	0.0	0.0	0.0	0.0	trace	0.1	0.4
Maximum Snow Depth (in.)	trace	6	trace	0	0	0	0	0	0	0	trace	trace	6
Days With ≥ 1.0" Snow Depth	0	0	0	0	0	0	0	0	0	0	0	0	0

Seaside *Clatsop County* Elevation: 9 ft. Latitude: 45° 59' N Longitude: 123° 55' W

	JAN	FEB	MAR	APR	MAY	JUN	JUL	AUG	SEP	OCT	NOV	DEC	YEAR
Mean Maximum Temp. (°F)	52.3	53.7	55.2	57.4	61.0	63.6	66.9	67.8	67.7	62.2	55.0	51.3	59.5
Mean Temp. (°F)	45.3	45.8	47.2	49.3	53.3	56.6	59.6	60.2	58.3	53.5	48.1	44.3	51.8
Mean Minimum Temp. (°F)	38.2	37.8	39.3	41.2	45.5	49.5	52.3	52.6	48.9	44.8	41.2	37.2	44.0
Extreme Maximum Temp. (°F)	71	77	77	85	98	95	101	98	96	92	70	68	101
Extreme Minimum Temp. (°F)	11	9	25	26	32	38	39	41	31	27	15	7	7
Days Maximum Temp. ≥ 90°F	0	0	0	0	0	0	0	0	0	0	0	0	0
Days Maximum Temp. ≤ 32°F	0	0	0	0	0	0	0	0	0	0	0	0	0
Days Minimum Temp. ≤ 32°F	7	7	4	2	0	0	0	0	0	1	4	7	32
Days Minimum Temp. ≤ 0°F	0	0	0	0	0	0	0	0	0	0	0	0	0
Heating Degree Days (base 65°F)	605	537	543	463	358	248	163	146	201	350	500	636	4,750
Cooling Degree Days (base 65°F)	0	0	0	0	2	3	3	5	7	1	0	0	21
Mean Precipitation (in.)	10.65	8.40	8.37	5.89	4.02	2.99	1.46	1.25	2.49	6.06	11.65	10.50	73.73
Extreme Maximum Daily Precip. (in.)	***3.69***	4.18	3.53	3.07	3.01	2.50	2.00	3.10	3.02	2.62	6.00	3.85	***6.00***
Days With ≥ 0.1" Precipitation	15	12	15	11	9	6	3	3	5	9	16	15	119
Days With ≥ 0.5" Precipitation	8	6	5	4	2	2	1	1	1	4	8	7	49
Days With ≥ 1.0" Precipitation	3	2	2	1	1	0	0	0	1	2	3	3	18
Mean Snowfall (in.)	0.0	trace	0.0	0.0	0.0	0.0	0.0	0.0	0.0	0.0	0.0	0.0	trace
Maximum Snow Depth (in.)	0	0	0	0	0	0	0	0	0	0	0	trace	trace
Days With ≥ 1.0" Snow Depth	0	0	0	0	0	0	0	0	0	0	0	0	0

The period of record for all cooperative weather station data is 1980 – 2009. See User Guide for detailed explanation of data.

St Helens Rfd *Columbia County* Elevation: 100 ft. Latitude: 45° 52' N Longitude: 122° 49' W

	JAN	FEB	MAR	APR	MAY	JUN	JUL	AUG	SEP	OCT	NOV	DEC	YEAR
Mean Maximum Temp. (°F)	47.1	51.7	57.7	63.5	70.2	75.5	82.3	83.1	77.9	65.2	52.6	45.9	64.4
Mean Temp. (°F)	40.5	43.1	47.9	52.1	58.0	63.3	68.8	69.2	***64.7***	54.8	45.6	39.8	***54.0***
Mean Minimum Temp. (°F)	34.0	34.4	38.1	40.6	45.8	51.0	55.2	55.3	***51.5***	44.3	38.5	33.7	***43.5***
Extreme Maximum Temp. (°F)	63	71	82	90	102	104	106	107	106	94	71	62	107
Extreme Minimum Temp. (°F)	9	4	1	20	21	34	38	30	34	20	10	1	1
Days Maximum Temp. ≥ 90°F	0	0	0	0	1	2	7	7	3	0	0	0	20
Days Maximum Temp. ≤ 32°F	1	0	0	0	0	0	0	0	0	0	0	1	2
Days Minimum Temp. ≤ 32°F	12	10	6	2	1	0	0	0	0	1	5	12	49
Days Minimum Temp. ≤ 0°F	0	0	0	0	0	0	0	0	0	0	0	0	0
Heating Degree Days (base 65°F)	753	613	522	383	233	101	25	16	***73***	313	575	775	***4,382***
Cooling Degree Days (base 65°F)	0	0	0	2	24	55	148	155	***71***	4	0	0	***459***
Mean Precipitation (in.)	6.36	4.83	4.61	3.55	2.66	1.99	0.69	0.91	1.56	3.32	6.95	6.97	44.40
Extreme Maximum Daily Precip. (in.)	2.30	***2.00***	2.75	1.85	1.07	2.00	1.10	***1.39***	***1.80***	***1.99***	2.50	3.90	***3.90***
Days With ≥ 0.1" Precipitation	12	9	11	10	7	5	2	2	3	7	12	12	92
Days With ≥ 0.5" Precipitation	4	3	2	2	1	1	0	0	1	2	4	5	25
Days With ≥ 1.0" Precipitation	1	1	0	0	0	0	0	0	0	1	1	1	5
Mean Snowfall (in.)	1.3	0.4	trace	0.0	0.0	0.0	0.0	0.0	0.0	0.0	0.2	0.9	2.8
Maximum Snow Depth (in.)	18	3	trace	0	0	0	0	0	0	0	0	2	18
Days With ≥ 1.0" Snow Depth	0	0	0	0	0	0	0	0	0	0	0	0	0

The Dalles *Wasco County* Elevation: 149 ft. Latitude: 45° 36' N Longitude: 121° 12' W

	JAN	FEB	MAR	APR	MAY	JUN	JUL	AUG	SEP	OCT	NOV	DEC	YEAR
Mean Maximum Temp. (°F)	43.4	49.1	58.3	65.5	73.6	***80.1***	87.8	88.3	81.5	67.6	52.3	***42.1***	***65.8***
Mean Temp. (°F)	37.2	40.1	47.4	53.2	61.0	***67.4***	73.6	73.5	66.2	54.5	44.1	***36.3***	***54.5***
Mean Minimum Temp. (°F)	30.9	31.2	36.4	40.9	48.3	***54.6***	59.4	58.5	50.8	41.4	35.9	***30.5***	***43.2***
Extreme Maximum Temp. (°F)	65	71	79	92	107	***107***	109	***109***	***104***	92	***75***	***66***	***109***
Extreme Minimum Temp. (°F)	-3	-3	14	26	30	***38***	41	***41***	***27***	18	***0***	***-6***	***-6***
Days Maximum Temp. ≥ 90°F	0	0	0	0	2	***6***	13	14	7	0	0	***0***	***42***
Days Maximum Temp. ≤ 32°F	3	1	0	0	0	***0***	0	0	0	0	1	***4***	***9***
Days Minimum Temp. ≤ 32°F	17	16	7	3	0	***0***	0	0	0	3	9	***18***	***73***
Days Minimum Temp. ≤ 0°F	0	0	0	0	0	***0***	0	0	0	0	0	***0***	***0***
Heating Degree Days (base 65°F)	855	697	540	350	161	***49***	7	4	62	325	620	***883***	***4,553***
Cooling Degree Days (base 65°F)	0	0	0	4	45	***127***	280	274	104	6	0	***0***	***840***
Mean Precipitation (in.)	2.60	1.88	1.25	0.81	0.65	***0.46***	0.16	0.28	0.40	0.95	2.21	***2.75***	***14.40***
Extreme Maximum Daily Precip. (in.)	1.90	1.22	0.91	1.03	0.62	***0.87***	1.04	***0.82***	***0.88***	1.63	***1.31***	***2.00***	***2.00***
Days With ≥ 0.1" Precipitation	***7***	5	4	3	2	***2***	0	1	1	3	6	***7***	***41***
Days With ≥ 0.5" Precipitation	***1***	1	0	0	0	***0***	0	0	0	0	1	***2***	***5***
Days With ≥ 1.0" Precipitation	0	0	0	0	0	***0***	0	0	0	0	0	***0***	***0***
Mean Snowfall (in.)	***3.8***	0.8	0.2	0.0	0.0	***0.0***	0.0	0.0	0.0	trace	0.9	***2.2***	***7.9***
Maximum Snow Depth (in.)	***26***	na	***1***	0	***0***	***0***	***0***	***0***	***0***	***trace***	***trace***	na	na
Days With ≥ 1.0" Snow Depth	***1***	***0***	0	0	0	***0***	0	0	0	0	***0***	***1***	2

Oregon Weather Station Rankings

Annual Extreme Maximum Temperature

Highest Rank	Station Name	°F	Lowest Rank	Station Name	°F
1	Medford Jackson County Arpt	114	1	Astoria Clatsop County Arpt	96
2	Lost Creek Dam	112	2	Port Orford 2	97
3	Arlington	111	3	Bandon 2 NNE	100
3	Roseburg KQEN	111	4	Bend	101
5	Pendleton Municipal Arpt	110	4	Seaside	101
5	Rome 2 NW	110	6	Brothers	102
7	Estacada 2 SE	109	6	Condon	102
7	The Dalles	***109***	8	Clatskanie	103
9	Ashland	108	8	Idleyld Park 4 NE	103
9	Corvallis State Univ	108	10	Chiloquin 7 NW	104
9	Enterprise 20 NNE	***108***	10	Dallas 2 NE	104
9	Eugene Mahlon Sweet Arpt	108	10	Paisley	104
9	Oregon City	108	13	Antelope 1 NW	105
9	Salem McNary Field	108	13	Belknap Springs 8 N	105
15	Austin 3 S	107	13	Corvallis Water Bureau	105
15	Barnes Station	107	13	Cottage Grove 1 S	105
15	Bonneville Dam	107	13	Cottage Grove Dam	105
15	Burns Municipal Arpt	107	13	Headworks Ptld Wtr Bur	105
15	Detroit Dam	107	13	N Willamette Exp Stn	105
15	Drewsey	107	20	Beaverton 2 SSW	***106***
15	Elgin	***107***	20	Cloverdale	106
15	McMinnville	107	20	Elkton 3 SW	106
15	Portland Intl Arpt	107	20	Long Creek	106
15	St Helens Rfd	107	20	Lookout Point Dam	106
25	Beaverton 2 SSW	***106***	25	Austin 3 S	107

Annual Mean Maximum Temperature

Highest Rank	Station Name	°F	Lowest Rank	Station Name	°F
1	Medford Jackson County Arpt	68.0	1	Austin 3 S	57.7
2	Lost Creek Dam	67.4	2	Brothers	58.3
3	Roseburg KQEN	66.9	3	Astoria Clatsop County Arpt	58.7
4	Ashland	66.5	4	Burns Municipal Arpt	59.0
5	Elkton 3 SW	66.1	5	Chiloquin 7 NW	59.2
6	The Dalles	***65.8***	5	Condon	59.2
7	Arlington	65.5	7	Seaside	59.5
8	Rome 2 NW	65.4	8	Long Creek	***59.7***
9	Oregon City	***64.8***	9	Belknap Springs 8 N	59.9
10	Cottage Grove 1 S	64.4	10	Bend	60.0
10	St Helens Rfd	64.4	11	Clatskanie	60.4
12	McMinnville	64.1	12	Detroit Dam	60.5
13	Idleyld Park 4 NE	63.9	12	Port Orford 2	60.5
14	Salem McNary Field	63.6	14	Antelope 1 NW	***60.6***
15	Dallas 2 NE	63.4	14	Cloverdale	60.6
15	N Willamette Exp Stn	63.4	16	Bandon 2 NNE	61.0
17	Corvallis State Univ	63.3	17	Enterprise 20 NNE	***61.1***
17	Eugene Mahlon Sweet Arpt	63.3	18	Barnes Station	61.5
19	Beaverton 2 SSW	***63.2***	18	Corvallis Water Bureau	61.5
20	Portland Intl Arpt	63.1	20	Bonneville Dam	61.7
21	Lookout Point Dam	62.8	21	Headworks Ptld Wtr Bur	61.8
21	Pendleton Municipal Arpt	62.8	22	Drewsey	61.9
23	Cottage Grove Dam	62.5	23	Elgin	***62.0***
23	Paisley	***62.5***	24	Estacada 2 SE	62.1
25	Estacada 2 SE	62.1	25	Cottage Grove Dam	62.5

Rankings include 25 highest/lowest stations. If state has less than 25 stations, all stations are included. The period of record is 1980–2009. See User Guide for detailed explanation of data.

Annual Mean Temperature

Highest Rank	Station Name	°F	Lowest Rank	Station Name	°F
1	Roseburg KQEN	55.5	1	Austin 3 S	41.9
2	Medford Jackson County Arpt	55.2	2	Brothers	43.6
3	Elkton 3 SW	55.1	3	Burns Municipal Arpt	44.4
3	Oregon City	***55.1***	4	Chiloquin 7 NW	44.6
5	Arlington	55.0	5	Enterprise 20 NNE	***45.7***
6	The Dalles	***54.5***	6	Drewsey	46.3
7	Portland Intl Arpt	54.4	7	Barnes Station	46.6
8	St Helens Rfd	***54.0***	8	Long Creek	***46.7***
9	Bonneville Dam	53.5	9	Bend	46.8
10	Lookout Point Dam	53.4	10	Condon	47.7
11	McMinnville	53.3	11	Elgin	***47.8***
12	N Willamette Exp Stn	53.2	12	Antelope 1 NW	***48.2***
12	Port Orford 2	53.2	13	Paisley	***48.3***
14	Beaverton 2 SSW	***53.1***	14	Belknap Springs 8 N	48.7
15	Salem McNary Field	53.0	15	Rome 2 NW	49.5
16	Dallas 2 NE	52.8	16	Clatskanie	51.0
16	Lost Creek Dam	52.8	17	Corvallis Water Bureau	51.1
18	Corvallis State Univ	52.7	18	Astoria Clatsop County Arpt	51.4
18	Estacada 2 SE	52.7	19	Detroit Dam	51.5
18	Headworks Ptld Wtr Bur	52.7	20	Cottage Grove Dam	51.7
21	Ashland	52.6	21	Seaside	51.8
21	Cottage Grove 1 S	52.6	22	Cloverdale	52.0
21	Eugene Mahlon Sweet Arpt	52.6	22	Pendleton Municipal Arpt	52.0
24	Bandon 2 NNE	52.5	24	Idleyld Park 4 NE	52.2
25	Idleyld Park 4 NE	52.2	25	Bandon 2 NNE	52.5

Annual Mean Minimum Temperature

Highest Rank	Station Name	°F	Lowest Rank	Station Name	°F
1	Port Orford 2	45.9	1	Austin 3 S	26.2
2	Portland Intl Arpt	45.7	2	Brothers	28.8
3	Bonneville Dam	45.2	3	Burns Municipal Arpt	29.7
3	Oregon City	***45.2***	4	Chiloquin 7 NW	29.9
5	Arlington	44.4	5	Enterprise 20 NNE	***30.2***
6	Astoria Clatsop County Arpt	44.1	6	Drewsey	30.7
6	Elkton 3 SW	44.1	7	Barnes Station	31.7
6	Roseburg KQEN	44.1	8	Bend	33.5
6	Seaside	44.1	8	Elgin	***33.5***
10	Bandon 2 NNE	44.0	10	Rome 2 NW	33.6
11	Lookout Point Dam	43.9	11	Long Creek	***33.7***
12	Cloverdale	43.5	12	Paisley	***34.1***
12	St Helens Rfd	***43.5***	13	Antelope 1 NW	***35.8***
14	Headworks Ptld Wtr Bur	43.4	14	Condon	36.1
15	Estacada 2 SE	43.3	15	Belknap Springs 8 N	37.4
16	The Dalles	***43.2***	16	Lost Creek Dam	38.1
17	Beaverton 2 SSW	***43.0***	17	Ashland	38.6
17	N Willamette Exp Stn	43.0	18	Idleyld Park 4 NE	40.4
19	McMinnville	42.5	19	Cottage Grove 1 S	40.6
20	Detroit Dam	42.4	20	Corvallis Water Bureau	40.7
21	Medford Jackson County Arpt	42.3	21	Cottage Grove Dam	40.8
21	Salem McNary Field	42.3	22	Pendleton Municipal Arpt	41.2
23	Corvallis State Univ	42.1	23	Clatskanie	41.6
23	Dallas 2 NE	42.1	24	Eugene Mahlon Sweet Arpt	41.8
25	Eugene Mahlon Sweet Arpt	41.8	25	Corvallis State Univ	42.1

Rankings include 25 highest/lowest stations. If state has less than 25 stations, all stations are included. The period of record is 1980–2009. See User Guide for detailed explanation of data.

Annual Extreme Minimum Temperature

Rank	Station Name (Highest)	°F	Rank	Station Name (Lowest)	°F
1	Port Orford 2	13	1	Austin 3 S	-37
2	Cloverdale	9	2	Drewsey	-35
2	Portland Intl Arpt	9	3	Enterprise 20 NNE	***-33***
4	Bandon 2 NNE	8	4	Elgin	***-31***
4	McMinnville	8	5	Brothers	-30
6	Corvallis State Univ	7	6	Barnes Station	-29
6	Seaside	7	7	Burns Municipal Arpt	-28
8	Astoria Clatsop County Arpt	6	8	Rome 2 NW	-27
8	Bonneville Dam	6	9	Long Creek	-25
8	Estacada 2 SE	6	9	Paisley	-25
8	Oregon City	6	11	Condon	-22
12	Dallas 2 NE	5	12	Chiloquin 7 NW	-19
12	Detroit Dam	5	12	Pendleton Municipal Arpt	-19
12	Headworks Ptld Wtr Bur	5	14	Bend	-18
15	Elkton 3 SW	4	15	Antelope 1 NW	-17
15	Eugene Mahlon Sweet Arpt	4	16	N Willamette Exp Stn	-15
17	Idleyld Park 4 NE	3	17	Arlington	-9
17	Lookout Point Dam	3	18	Lost Creek Dam	-6
17	Roseburg KQEN	3	18	The Dalles	***-6***
20	Corvallis Water Bureau	2	20	Medford Jackson County Arpt	-4
21	Clatskanie	1	21	Belknap Springs 8 N	-2
21	Cottage Grove Dam	1	22	Salem McNary Field	-1
21	St Helens Rfd	1	23	Ashland	0
24	Ashland	0	23	Beaverton 2 SSW	***0***
24	Beaverton 2 SSW	***0***	23	Cottage Grove 1 S	0

July Mean Maximum Temperature

Rank	Station Name (Highest)	°F	Rank	Station Name (Lowest)	°F
1	Rome 2 NW	92.1	1	Seaside	66.9
2	Arlington	90.9	2	Port Orford 2	67.3
2	Medford Jackson County Arpt	90.9	3	Bandon 2 NNE	67.5
4	Drewsey	89.6	4	Astoria Clatsop County Arpt	67.6
5	Lost Creek Dam	89.1	5	Cloverdale	69.8
6	The Dalles	87.8	6	Clatskanie	74.4
7	Ashland	87.6	7	Estacada 2 SE	79.1
7	Pendleton Municipal Arpt	87.6	8	Corvallis Water Bureau	79.2
9	Enterprise 20 NNE	86.2	8	Headworks Ptld Wtr Bur	79.2
10	Elgin	***86.1***	10	Detroit Dam	79.3
11	Barnes Station	85.9	11	Beaverton 2 SSW	***79.5***
11	Burns Municipal Arpt	85.9	11	Cottage Grove Dam	79.5
11	Roseburg KQEN	85.9	13	Bonneville Dam	79.6
14	Paisley	85.8	14	Lookout Point Dam	80.3
15	Antelope 1 NW	84.4	15	Portland Intl Arpt	80.5
16	Elkton 3 SW	83.8	16	N Willamette Exp Stn	80.9
17	Idleyld Park 4 NE	83.5	17	Corvallis State Univ	81.6
18	McMinnville	82.9	18	Bend	81.9
19	Oregon City	82.8	18	Salem McNary Field	81.9
20	Austin 3 S	82.6	20	Brothers	82.1
21	Condon	82.5	21	Chiloquin 7 NW	82.2
22	Belknap Springs 8 N	82.4	21	Dallas 2 NE	82.2
22	Cottage Grove 1 S	82.4	21	Eugene Mahlon Sweet Arpt	82.2
22	Long Creek	82.4	24	St Helens Rfd	82.3
25	St Helens Rfd	82.3	25	Belknap Springs 8 N	82.4

Rankings include 25 highest/lowest stations. If state has less than 25 stations, all stations are included. The period of record is 1980–2009. See User Guide for detailed explanation of data.

January Mean Minimum Temperature

Highest			Lowest		
Rank	Station Name	°F	Rank	Station Name	°F
1	Port Orford 2	40.8	1	Austin 3 S	12.6
2	Bandon 2 NNE	38.9	2	Burns Municipal Arpt	14.5
3	Cloverdale	38.5	3	Drewsey	15.9
4	Seaside	38.2	4	Enterprise 20 NNE	17.6
5	Astoria Clatsop County Arpt	37.5	5	Brothers	17.7
6	Elkton 3 SW	37.3	6	Chiloquin 7 NW	19.0
7	Oregon City	36.2	7	Rome 2 NW	19.5
8	Roseburg KQEN	36.0	8	Barnes Station	20.1
9	Lookout Point Dam	35.5	9	Elgin	22.9
10	Portland Intl Arpt	35.4	10	Long Creek	23.2
11	Headworks Ptld Wtr Bur	35.3	10	Paisley	23.2
12	Estacada 2 SE	35.2	12	Bend	24.1
13	McMinnville	34.8	13	Condon	24.6
14	Bonneville Dam	34.7	14	Antelope 1 NW	25.2
14	Dallas 2 NE	34.7	15	Belknap Springs 8 N	28.3
14	N Willamette Exp Stn	34.7	16	Pendleton Municipal Arpt	28.4
17	Salem McNary Field	34.6	17	Lost Creek Dam	29.3
18	Beaverton 2 SSW	34.5	18	Ashland	29.8
19	Corvallis State Univ	34.2	19	Arlington	30.9
20	Eugene Mahlon Sweet Arpt	34.1	19	The Dalles	30.9
21	St Helens Rfd	34.0	21	Medford Jackson County Arpt	31.7
22	Detroit Dam	33.9	22	Corvallis Water Bureau	32.9
23	Cottage Grove 1 S	33.7	22	Cottage Grove Dam	32.9
24	Clatskanie	33.5	24	Idleyld Park 4 NE	33.3
25	Idleyld Park 4 NE	33.3	25	Clatskanie	33.5

Number of Days Annually Maximum Temperature ≥ 90°F

Highest			Lowest		
Rank	Station Name	Days	Rank	Station Name	Days
1	Medford Jackson County Arpt	57	1	Astoria Clatsop County Arpt	0
1	Rome 2 NW	57	1	Bandon 2 NNE	0
3	Lost Creek Dam	52	1	Cloverdale	0
4	Arlington	47	1	Port Orford 2	0
5	The Dalles	***42***	1	Seaside	0
6	Drewsey	41	6	Clatskanie	4
7	Ashland	35	7	Corvallis Water Bureau	9
8	Elgin	***34***	7	Cottage Grove Dam	9
8	Enterprise 20 NNE	***34***	7	Lookout Point Dam	9
8	Pendleton Municipal Arpt	34	10	Bonneville Dam	10
8	Roseburg KQEN	34	10	Detroit Dam	10
12	Barnes Station	28	10	Estacada 2 SE	10
13	Burns Municipal Arpt	25	13	Chiloquin 7 NW	12
14	Elkton 3 SW	24	13	Headworks Ptld Wtr Bur	12
15	Antelope 1 NW	23	15	Bend	13
15	Belknap Springs 8 N	23	15	Brothers	13
17	Paisley	21	15	Condon	13
18	Idleyld Park 4 NE	20	18	Beaverton 2 SSW	***14***
18	St Helens Rfd	20	18	Portland Intl Arpt	14
20	Oregon City	19	20	Corvallis State Univ	15
21	McMinnville	18	20	Eugene Mahlon Sweet Arpt	15
22	Dallas 2 NE	17	20	Long Creek	15
22	Salem McNary Field	17	23	Austin 3 S	16
24	Austin 3 S	16	23	Cottage Grove 1 S	16
24	Cottage Grove 1 S	16	23	N Willamette Exp Stn	16

Rankings include 25 highest/lowest stations. If state has less than 25 stations, all stations are included. The period of record is 1980–2009. See User Guide for detailed explanation of data.

Number of Days Annually Maximum Temperature ≤ 32°F

Highest Rank	Highest Station Name	Highest Days	Lowest Rank	Lowest Station Name	Lowest Days
1	Burns Municipal Arpt	30	1	Ashland	0
2	Austin 3 S	29	1	Bandon 2 NNE	0
3	Drewsey	26	1	Cloverdale	0
4	Condon	23	1	Elkton 3 SW	0
5	Brothers	22	1	Lost Creek Dam	0
6	Pendleton Municipal Arpt	21	1	Port Orford 2	0
7	Antelope 1 NW	17	1	Seaside	0
7	Chiloquin 7 NW	17	8	Astoria Clatsop County Arpt	1
7	Enterprise 20 NNE	*17*	8	Clatskanie	1
10	Long Creek	15	8	Corvallis State Univ	1
10	Rome 2 NW	15	8	Corvallis Water Bureau	1
12	Elgin	*14*	8	Cottage Grove 1 S	1
13	Bend	13	8	Cottage Grove Dam	1
14	Arlington	12	8	Detroit Dam	1
14	Barnes Station	12	8	Estacada 2 SE	1
16	Paisley	9	8	Headworks Ptld Wtr Bur	1
16	The Dalles	*9*	8	Idleyld Park 4 NE	1
18	Belknap Springs 8 N	6	8	Lookout Point Dam	1
19	Bonneville Dam	5	8	Medford Jackson County Arpt	1
20	Beaverton 2 SSW	*2*	8	Oregon City	1
20	Dallas 2 NE	2	8	Roseburg KQEN	1
20	Eugene Mahlon Sweet Arpt	2	8	Salem McNary Field	1
20	McMinnville	2	23	Beaverton 2 SSW	*2*
20	N Willamette Exp Stn	2	23	Dallas 2 NE	2
20	Portland Intl Arpt	2	23	Eugene Mahlon Sweet Arpt	2

Number of Days Annually Minimum Temperature ≤ 32°F

Highest Rank	Highest Station Name	Highest Days	Lowest Rank	Lowest Station Name	Lowest Days
1	Austin 3 S	245	1	Port Orford 2	12
2	Brothers	220	2	Bandon 2 NNE	23
3	Chiloquin 7 NW	213	2	Cloverdale	23
4	Enterprise 20 NNE	*206*	2	Elkton 3 SW	23
5	Burns Municipal Arpt	205	5	Bonneville Dam	29
6	Drewsey	195	6	Lookout Point Dam	31
7	Barnes Station	188	7	Astoria Clatsop County Arpt	32
8	Bend	172	7	Roseburg KQEN	32
9	Rome 2 NW	170	7	Seaside	32
10	Elgin	*162*	10	Oregon City	33
11	Long Creek	156	11	Portland Intl Arpt	34
12	Paisley	147	12	Headworks Ptld Wtr Bur	35
13	Antelope 1 NW	146	13	Detroit Dam	39
14	Condon	144	13	Estacada 2 SE	39
15	Belknap Springs 8 N	123	15	Beaverton 2 SSW	*47*
16	Lost Creek Dam	113	16	McMinnville	48
17	Ashland	107	17	St Helens Rfd	49
18	Pendleton Municipal Arpt	91	18	N Willamette Exp Stn	50
19	Idleyld Park 4 NE	75	19	Dallas 2 NE	52
20	The Dalles	*73*	20	Corvallis State Univ	54
21	Corvallis Water Bureau	72	20	Eugene Mahlon Sweet Arpt	54
21	Medford Jackson County Arpt	72	22	Salem McNary Field	55
23	Arlington	70	23	Cottage Grove Dam	63
24	Cottage Grove 1 S	66	24	Clatskanie	65
25	Clatskanie	65	25	Cottage Grove 1 S	66

 Rankings include 25 highest/lowest stations. If state has less than 25 stations, all stations are included. The period of record is 1980–2009. See User Guide for detailed explanation of data.

Number of Days Annually Minimum Temperature ≤ 0°F

Highest

Rank	Station Name	Days
1	Austin 3 S	14
2	Burns Municipal Arpt	11
3	Drewsey	9
4	Enterprise 20 NNE	*8*
5	Brothers	6
6	Barnes Station	5
7	Elgin	*4*
7	Rome 2 NW	4
9	Chiloquin 7 NW	3
9	Condon	3
9	Long Creek	3
12	Antelope 1 NW	2
12	Bend	2
14	Paisley	1
14	Pendleton Municipal Arpt	1
16	Arlington	0
16	Ashland	0
16	Astoria Clatsop County Arpt	0
16	Bandon 2 NNE	0
16	Beaverton 2 SSW	*0*
16	Belknap Springs 8 N	0
16	Bonneville Dam	0
16	Clatskanie	0
16	Cloverdale	0
16	Corvallis State Univ	0

Lowest

Rank	Station Name	Days
1	Arlington	0
1	Ashland	0
1	Astoria Clatsop County Arpt	0
1	Bandon 2 NNE	0
1	Beaverton 2 SSW	*0*
1	Belknap Springs 8 N	0
1	Bonneville Dam	0
1	Clatskanie	0
1	Cloverdale	0
1	Corvallis State Univ	0
1	Corvallis Water Bureau	0
1	Cottage Grove 1 S	0
1	Cottage Grove Dam	0
1	Dallas 2 NE	0
1	Detroit Dam	0
1	Elkton 3 SW	0
1	Estacada 2 SE	0
1	Eugene Mahlon Sweet Arpt	0
1	Headworks Ptld Wtr Bur	0
1	Idleyld Park 4 NE	0
1	Lookout Point Dam	0
1	Lost Creek Dam	0
1	McMinnville	0
1	Medford Jackson County Arpt	0
1	N Willamette Exp Stn	0

Number of Annual Heating Degree Days

Highest

Rank	Station Name	Num.
1	Austin 3 S	8,390
2	Brothers	7,855
3	Burns Municipal Arpt	7,632
4	Chiloquin 7 NW	7,441
5	Enterprise 20 NNE	*7,141*
6	Drewsey	7,054
7	Barnes Station	6,840
8	Long Creek	*6,770*
9	Bend	6,750
10	Condon	6,490
11	Elgin	*6,435*
12	Antelope 1 NW	*6,360*
13	Paisley	*6,270*
14	Belknap Springs 8 N	6,119
15	Rome 2 NW	6,100
16	Pendleton Municipal Arpt	5,276
17	Corvallis Water Bureau	5,169
18	Clatskanie	5,138
19	Detroit Dam	5,127
20	Cottage Grove Dam	4,971
21	Astoria Clatsop County Arpt	4,893
22	Ashland	4,864
23	Lost Creek Dam	4,852
24	Idleyld Park 4 NE	4,824
25	Seaside	4,750

Lowest

Rank	Station Name	Num.
1	Elkton 3 SW	3,884
2	Roseburg KQEN	3,934
3	Oregon City	*4,027*
4	Portland Intl Arpt	4,213
5	Port Orford 2	4,219
6	Medford Jackson County Arpt	4,306
7	St Helens Rfd	*4,382*
8	Lookout Point Dam	4,433
9	Bandon 2 NNE	4,471
10	McMinnville	4,500
11	Bonneville Dam	4,518
12	N Willamette Exp Stn	4,536
13	The Dalles	*4,553*
14	Beaverton 2 SSW	*4,564*
15	Salem McNary Field	4,595
16	Arlington	4,597
17	Dallas 2 NE	4,637
18	Estacada 2 SE	4,647
19	Cloverdale	4,671
20	Corvallis State Univ	4,678
21	Headworks Ptld Wtr Bur	4,679
22	Cottage Grove 1 S	4,684
23	Eugene Mahlon Sweet Arpt	4,702
24	Seaside	4,750
25	Idleyld Park 4 NE	4,824

Number of Annual Cooling Degree Days

Highest			Lowest		
Rank	Station Name	Num.	Rank	Station Name	Num.
1	Arlington	1,046	1	Bandon 2 NNE	5
2	The Dalles	***840***	2	Port Orford 2	10
3	Medford Jackson County Arpt	816	3	Seaside	21
4	Pendleton Municipal Arpt	640	4	Astoria Clatsop County Arpt	23
5	Roseburg KQEN	578	5	Cloverdale	25
6	Rome 2 NW	547	6	Austin 3 S	72
7	Oregon City	***496***	7	Chiloquin 7 NW	90
8	Lost Creek Dam	488	8	Clatskanie	115
9	St Helens Rfd	***459***	9	Brothers	132
10	Portland Intl Arpt	445	10	Long Creek	***188***
11	Ashland	424	11	Corvallis Water Bureau	191
12	Bonneville Dam	402	11	Enterprise 20 NNE	***191***
13	Elkton 3 SW	363	13	Cottage Grove Dam	199
14	Drewsey	342	14	Bend	201
15	N Willamette Exp Stn	337	15	Burns Municipal Arpt	227
16	Antelope 1 NW	***335***	16	Barnes Station	233
17	McMinnville	326	17	Idleyld Park 4 NE	234
18	Beaverton 2 SSW	***307***	18	Cottage Grove 1 S	235
19	Salem McNary Field	301	19	Elgin	***250***
20	Detroit Dam	295	20	Estacada 2 SE	251
21	Lookout Point Dam	287	21	Belknap Springs 8 N	256
22	Condon	283	22	Eugene Mahlon Sweet Arpt	258
23	Dallas 2 NE	280	23	Headworks Ptld Wtr Bur	269
24	Paisley	***279***	24	Corvallis State Univ	276
25	Corvallis State Univ	276	25	Paisley	***279***

Annual Precipitation

Highest			Lowest		
Rank	Station Name	Inches	Rank	Station Name	Inches
1	Detroit Dam	90.44	1	Brothers	8.11
2	Cloverdale	78.84	2	Rome 2 NW	8.51
3	Headworks Ptld Wtr Bur	77.92	3	Arlington	9.07
4	Bonneville Dam	76.89	4	Burns Municipal Arpt	10.70
5	Belknap Springs 8 N	74.01	5	Paisley	10.84
6	Seaside	73.73	6	Drewsey	11.12
7	Port Orford 2	71.94	7	Bend	11.37
8	Corvallis Water Bureau	66.77	8	Pendleton Municipal Arpt	12.50
9	Astoria Clatsop County Arpt	66.66	9	Barnes Station	13.67
10	Idleyld Park 4 NE	61.32	10	Condon	14.10
11	Bandon 2 NNE	58.21	11	Antelope 1 NW	14.35
12	Estacada 2 SE	58.04	12	The Dalles	***14.40***
13	Clatskanie	53.32	13	Long Creek	18.00
14	Elkton 3 SW	51.10	14	Medford Jackson County Arpt	18.14
15	Cottage Grove Dam	47.62	15	Enterprise 20 NNE	***19.28***
16	Dallas 2 NE	46.92	16	Ashland	19.79
17	Eugene Mahlon Sweet Arpt	46.30	17	Chiloquin 7 NW	19.97
18	Lookout Point Dam	45.95	18	Austin 3 S	20.67
19	Cottage Grove 1 S	44.98	19	Elgin	***23.93***
20	St Helens Rfd	44.40	20	Lost Creek Dam	32.96
21	Oregon City	43.40	21	Roseburg KQEN	33.15
22	Corvallis State Univ	42.44	22	Portland Intl Arpt	35.88
23	N Willamette Exp Stn	42.37	23	Salem McNary Field	39.51
24	Beaverton 2 SSW	40.09	24	McMinnville	39.77
25	McMinnville	39.77	25	Beaverton 2 SSW	40.09

Rankings include 25 highest/lowest stations. If state has less than 25 stations, all stations are included. The period of record is 1980–2009. See User Guide for detailed explanation of data.

Annual Extreme Maximum Daily Precipitation

Highest Rank	Station Name	Inches	Lowest Rank	Station Name	Inches
1	Port Orford 2	7.53	1	Burns Municipal Arpt	1.07
2	Elkton 3 SW	***6.88***	2	Brothers	***2.00***
3	Headworks Ptld Wtr Bur	6.80	2	The Dalles	***2.00***
4	Clatskanie	6.68	4	Austin 3 S	2.04
5	Corvallis Water Bureau	6.29	5	Long Creek	***2.05***
6	Bandon 2 NNE	6.25	6	Pendleton Municipal Arpt	2.19
7	Idleyld Park 4 NE	6.12	7	Barnes Station	2.20
8	Seaside	***6.00***	8	Rome 2 NW	2.21
9	Belknap Springs 8 N	***5.83***	9	Condon	2.25
10	Cottage Grove Dam	***5.72***	10	Drewsey	2.32
11	Astoria Clatsop County Arpt	5.56	11	Arlington	2.33
11	Detroit Dam	5.56	12	Antelope 1 NW	***2.37***
13	Lookout Point Dam	5.50	13	Paisley	***2.38***
14	Estacada 2 SE	5.28	14	Enterprise 20 NNE	***2.40***
15	Cloverdale	5.20	15	Chiloquin 7 NW	2.50
16	Bonneville Dam	5.08	16	Elgin	***2.55***
17	Eugene Mahlon Sweet Arpt	4.89	17	Bend	2.60
18	N Willamette Exp Stn	4.80	18	Medford Jackson County Arpt	2.68
19	Corvallis State Univ	4.45	19	Portland Intl Arpt	2.69
20	Beaverton 2 SSW	***4.39***	20	Salem McNary Field	2.85
21	Roseburg KQEN	4.35	21	Ashland	2.86
22	St Helens Rfd	***3.90***	22	Lost Creek Dam	3.03
23	McMinnville	***3.50***	23	Oregon City	***3.35***
24	Cottage Grove 1 S	3.36	24	Cottage Grove 1 S	3.36
25	Oregon City	***3.35***	25	McMinnville	***3.50***

Number of Days Annually With ≥ 0.1 Inches of Precipitation

Highest Rank	Station Name	Days	Lowest Rank	Station Name	Days
1	Headworks Ptld Wtr Bur	137	1	Brothers	26
2	Cloverdale	134	2	Arlington	29
2	Detroit Dam	134	2	Paisley	29
4	Astoria Clatsop County Arpt	127	2	Rome 2 NW	29
5	Bonneville Dam	126	5	Bend	33
6	Seaside	119	6	Burns Municipal Arpt	36
7	Estacada 2 SE	118	7	Drewsey	37
8	Belknap Springs 8 N	114	8	Pendleton Municipal Arpt	41
8	Clatskanie	114	8	The Dalles	***41***
10	Port Orford 2	110	10	Antelope 1 NW	43
11	Corvallis Water Bureau	109	11	Condon	47
11	Idleyld Park 4 NE	109	12	Barnes Station	49
13	Lookout Point Dam	107	13	Medford Jackson County Arpt	51
14	Bandon 2 NNE	106	14	Chiloquin 7 NW	53
15	Cottage Grove 1 S	100	15	Ashland	55
15	N Willamette Exp Stn	***100***	15	Long Creek	55
17	Beaverton 2 SSW	95	17	Enterprise 20 NNE	***61***
17	Cottage Grove Dam	95	18	Austin 3 S	64
19	Corvallis State Univ	94	19	Elgin	***66***
20	Elkton 3 SW	92	20	McMinnville	76
20	Eugene Mahlon Sweet Arpt	92	21	Dallas 2 NE	79
20	St Helens Rfd	92	22	Lost Creek Dam	80
23	Portland Intl Arpt	91	23	Roseburg KQEN	82
24	Salem McNary Field	89	24	Oregon City	88
25	Oregon City	88	25	Salem McNary Field	89

Rankings include 25 highest/lowest stations. If state has less than 25 stations, all stations are included. The period of record is 1980–2009. See User Guide for detailed explanation of data.

Number of Days Annually With ≥ 0.5 Inches of Precipitation

Highest Rank	Station Name	Days	Lowest Rank	Station Name	Days
1	Detroit Dam	66	1	Brothers	0
2	Cloverdale	62	1	Burns Municipal Arpt	0
3	Headworks Ptld Wtr Bur	58	1	Pendleton Municipal Arpt	0
4	Bonneville Dam	53	4	Arlington	1
5	Port Orford 2	51	4	Drewsey	1
6	Seaside	49	4	Paisley	1
7	Belknap Springs 8 N	48	4	Rome 2 NW	1
8	Corvallis Water Bureau	46	8	Barnes Station	2
9	Astoria Clatsop County Arpt	45	8	Condon	2
10	Idleyld Park 4 NE	44	10	Bend	4
11	Bandon 2 NNE	39	11	Antelope 1 NW	5
11	Estacada 2 SE	39	11	Long Creek	5
13	Elkton 3 SW	33	11	The Dalles	*5*
14	Clatskanie	31	14	Austin 3 S	6
15	Eugene Mahlon Sweet Arpt	30	15	Medford Jackson County Arpt	7
16	Corvallis State Univ	29	16	Ashland	9
16	Lookout Point Dam	29	16	Enterprise 20 NNE	*9*
18	Cottage Grove 1 S	28	18	Chiloquin 7 NW	10
18	Cottage Grove Dam	28	19	Elgin	*11*
20	Dallas 2 NE	27	20	Lost Creek Dam	17
20	Oregon City	27	20	Roseburg KQEN	17
22	St Helens Rfd	25	22	Portland Intl Arpt	19
23	Beaverton 2 SSW	24	23	Beaverton 2 SSW	24
23	McMinnville	24	23	McMinnville	24
23	N Willamette Exp Stn	24	23	N Willamette Exp Stn	24

Number of Days Annually With ≥ 1.0 Inches of Precipitation

Highest Rank	Station Name	Days	Lowest Rank	Station Name	Days
1	Detroit Dam	25	1	Antelope 1 NW	0
2	Bonneville Dam	21	1	Arlington	0
2	Port Orford 2	21	1	Austin 3 S	0
4	Cloverdale	20	1	Barnes Station	0
5	Corvallis Water Bureau	19	1	Bend	0
6	Headworks Ptld Wtr Bur	18	1	Brothers	0
6	Seaside	18	1	Burns Municipal Arpt	0
8	Belknap Springs 8 N	15	1	Condon	0
9	Astoria Clatsop County Arpt	14	1	Drewsey	0
9	Bandon 2 NNE	14	1	Enterprise 20 NNE	*0*
11	Idleyld Park 4 NE	13	1	Long Creek	0
12	Elkton 3 SW	11	1	Paisley	0
12	Estacada 2 SE	11	1	Pendleton Municipal Arpt	0
14	Clatskanie	9	1	Rome 2 NW	0
14	Dallas 2 NE	9	1	The Dalles	*0*
14	Eugene Mahlon Sweet Arpt	9	16	Ashland	1
17	Cottage Grove Dam	7	16	Chiloquin 7 NW	1
17	N Willamette Exp Stn	7	16	Elgin	*1*
19	Cottage Grove 1 S	6	16	Medford Jackson County Arpt	1
19	McMinnville	6	20	Portland Intl Arpt	3
21	Corvallis State Univ	5	20	Roseburg KQEN	3
21	Lookout Point Dam	5	22	Beaverton 2 SSW	4
21	Lost Creek Dam	5	23	Corvallis State Univ	5
21	Oregon City	5	23	Lookout Point Dam	5
21	St Helens Rfd	5	23	Lost Creek Dam	5

 Rankings include 25 highest/lowest stations. If state has less than 25 stations, all stations are included. The period of record is 1980–2009. See User Guide for detailed explanation of data.

Annual Snowfall

Highest			Lowest		
Rank	Station Name	Inches	Rank	Station Name	Inches
1	Austin 3 S	71.7	1	Seaside	Trace
2	Chiloquin 7 NW	63.4	2	Port Orford 2	0.2
3	Belknap Springs 8 N	59.0	3	Bandon 2 NNE	0.3
4	Elgin	*47.2*	3	Elkton 3 SW	0.3
5	Barnes Station	41.7	5	Roseburg KQEN	0.4
6	Long Creek	35.0	6	N Willamette Exp Stn	*0.5*
7	Drewsey	30.2	7	Cloverdale	1.3
8	Bend	25.1	8	Lookout Point Dam	1.4
9	Condon	23.2	9	Ashland	1.5
10	Brothers	20.0	10	Beaverton 2 SSW	1.6
11	Enterprise 20 NNE	*19.9*	10	Cottage Grove Dam	1.6
12	Pendleton Municipal Arpt	15.4	10	Estacada 2 SE	1.6
13	Idleyld Park 4 NE	13.9	13	Lost Creek Dam	1.7
14	Antelope 1 NW	12.8	13	McMinnville	1.7
15	Bonneville Dam	12.3	15	Oregon City	2.1
16	Detroit Dam	10.1	16	Cottage Grove 1 S	2.7
17	Paisley	*8.3*	17	St Helens Rfd	2.8
18	The Dalles	*7.9*	18	Corvallis State Univ	3.5
19	Corvallis Water Bureau	7.8	19	Dallas 2 NE	3.8
20	Arlington	6.7	20	Clatskanie	4.2
21	Rome 2 NW	5.9	21	Headworks Ptld Wtr Bur	4.8
22	Headworks Ptld Wtr Bur	4.8	22	Rome 2 NW	5.9
23	Clatskanie	4.2	23	Arlington	6.7
24	Dallas 2 NE	3.8	24	Corvallis Water Bureau	7.8
25	Corvallis State Univ	3.5	25	The Dalles	*7.9*

Annual Maximum Snow Depth

Highest			Lowest		
Rank	Station Name	Inches	Rank	Station Name	Inches
1	Belknap Springs 8 N	69	1	Seaside	Trace
2	Bonneville Dam	63	2	Cloverdale	1
3	Chiloquin 7 NW	45	2	N Willamette Exp Stn	*1*
4	Austin 3 S	36	4	Bandon 2 NNE	2
5	Enterprise 20 NNE	*30*	4	Beaverton 2 SSW	*2*
6	Drewsey	28	4	Port Orford 2	2
7	Headworks Ptld Wtr Bur	27	7	Ashland	4
8	Burns Municipal Arpt	*26*	7	Cottage Grove Dam	4
8	Corvallis Water Bureau	26	7	Elkton 3 SW	4
10	Bend	23	7	Oregon City	4
11	Condon	22	11	Lookout Point Dam	6
12	Barnes Station	19	11	Roseburg KQEN	6
13	St Helens Rfd	18	13	Cottage Grove 1 S	7
14	Idleyld Park 4 NE	16	13	Lost Creek Dam	7
14	Long Creek	16	13	McMinnville	7
16	Arlington	15	16	Estacada 2 SE	9
16	Clatskanie	15	17	Brothers	10
16	Pendleton Municipal Arpt	15	17	Corvallis State Univ	10
19	Detroit Dam	14	19	Dallas 2 NE	12
19	Paisley	14	20	Rome 2 NW	13
21	Rome 2 NW	13	21	Detroit Dam	14
22	Dallas 2 NE	12	21	Paisley	14
23	Brothers	10	23	Arlington	15
23	Corvallis State Univ	10	23	Clatskanie	15
25	Estacada 2 SE	9	23	Pendleton Municipal Arpt	15

Rankings include 25 highest/lowest stations. If state has less than 25 stations, all stations are included. The period of record is 1980–2009. See User Guide for detailed explanation of data.

Number of Days Annually With ≥ 1.0 Inch Snow Depth

Highest

Rank	Station Name	Days
1	Austin 3 S	94
2	Chiloquin 7 NW	73
3	Belknap Springs 8 N	59
4	Burns Municipal Arpt	*46*
5	Barnes Station	45
6	Drewsey	42
7	Elgin	*29*
8	Bend	25
8	Brothers	25
8	Condon	25
11	Enterprise 20 NNE	*22*
12	Long Creek	20
13	Pendleton Municipal Arpt	15
13	Rome 2 NW	15
15	Idleyld Park 4 NE	9
15	Paisley	9
17	Detroit Dam	8
18	Arlington	6
19	Corvallis Water Bureau	5
20	Bonneville Dam	4
21	Antelope 1 NW	*3*
21	Clatskanie	3
21	Corvallis State Univ	3
21	Headworks Ptld Wtr Bur	3
25	Cottage Grove 1 S	2

Lowest

Rank	Station Name	Days
1	Ashland	0
1	Bandon 2 NNE	0
1	Beaverton 2 SSW	*0*
1	Cloverdale	0
1	Cottage Grove Dam	0
1	Elkton 3 SW	0
1	Estacada 2 SE	0
1	McMinnville	0
1	N Willamette Exp Stn	*0*
1	Oregon City	0
1	Port Orford 2	0
1	Roseburg KQEN	0
1	St Helens Rfd	0
1	Seaside	0
15	Dallas 2 NE	1
16	Cottage Grove 1 S	2
16	Lookout Point Dam	2
16	Lost Creek Dam	2
16	The Dalles	*2*
20	Antelope 1 NW	*3*
20	Clatskanie	3
20	Corvallis State Univ	3
20	Headworks Ptld Wtr Bur	3
24	Bonneville Dam	4
25	Corvallis Water Bureau	5

Rankings include 25 highest/lowest stations. If state has less than 25 stations, all stations are included. The period of record is 1980–2009. See User Guide for detailed explanation of data.

Significant Storm Events in Oregon: 2000 – 2009

Location or County	Date	Type	Mag.	Deaths	Injuries	Property Damage ($mil.)	Crop Damage ($mil.)
Marion	08/12/01	Wild/Forest Fire	na	0	0	4.3	0.0
Lane and Linn Counties	02/07/02	High Wind	70 mph	0	4	6.0	0.0
Jefferson	07/09/02	Wild/Forest Fire	na	0	0	5.5	0.0
Douglas, Coos, Curry, Jackson, and Josephine Counties	12/26/05	Flood	na	0	0	14.2	0.0
Crook	06/12/06	Hail	1.50 in.	0	0	20.0	0.0
Deschutes	06/12/06	Hail	2.00 in.	0	0	7.0	0.0
Tillamook	11/06/06	Flood	na	0	0	15.0	0.0
Hood River	11/07/06	Flood	na	0	0	30.0	0.0
Clackamas	11/07/06	Flood	na	0	0	3.0	0.0
Tillamook	12/02/07	Flood	na	0	0	26.5	0.0
Northern Oregon Coast	12/03/07	High Wind	129 mph	0	0	62.6	0.0
Columbia	12/03/07	Flood	na	0	0	36.0	0.0
Clatsop, Columbia, and Tillamook Counties	12/03/07	High Wind	74 mph	0	0	20.4	0.0
Northern and Central Oregon Coasts	12/03/07	Coastal Flood	na	0	0	18.3	0.0
Washington	12/03/07	Flood	na	1	0	2.3	0.0
Yamhill	12/04/07	Flood	na	0	0	9.6	0.0
Northern Oregon Coast Range	12/11/07	Landslide	na	0	0	1.5	0.0
Jackson County	01/03/08	High Wind	81 mph	1	0	1.0	0.0
Umatilla County	01/04/08	High Wind	73 mph	0	0	1.7	0.0
Tillamook	11/13/08	Flood	na	0	0	3.8	0.0

Note: Deaths, injuries, and damages are date and location specific.

PENNSYLVANIA

PHYSICAL FEATURES. The erratic course of the Delaware River is the only natural boundary of Pennsylvania. All others are arbitrary boundaries that do not conform to physical features. Notable contrasts in topography, climate, and soils exist. Within this 45,126-square-mile area lies a great variety of physical land forms of which the most notable is the Appalachian Mountain system composed of two ranges, the Blue Ridge and the Allegheny. These mountains divide the Commonwealth into three major topographical sections. In addition, two plain areas of relatively small size also exist, one in the southeast and the other in the northwest.

In the extreme southeast is the Coastal Plain situated along the Delaware River and covering an area 50 miles long and 10 miles wide. The land is low, flat, and poorly drained. Bordering the Coastal Plain and extending 60 to 80 miles northwest to the Blue Ridge is the Piedmont Plateau, with elevations ranging from 100 to 500 feet and including rolling or undulating uplands, low hills, fertile valleys, and well-drained soils. Just northwest of the Piedmont and between the Blue Ridge and Allegheny Mountains is the Ridge and Valley Region, 80 to 100 miles wide and characterized by parallel ridges and valleys oriented northeast-southwest. The mountain ridges vary from 1,300 to 1,600 feet above sea level. North and west of the Ridge and Valley Region and extending to the New York and Ohio borders is the area known as the Allegheny Plateau. This is the largest natural division of the State and occupies more than half its area. It is crossed by many deep narrow valleys and drained by the Delaware, Susquehanna, Allegheny, and Monongahela River systems. Elevations are generally 1,000 to 2,000 feet above sea level. Bordering Lake Erie is a narrow 40-mile strip of flat, rich land three to four miles wide called the Lake Erie Plain.

GENERAL CLIMATE. Pennsylvania is generally considered to have a humid continental type of climate, but the varied physiographic features have a marked effect on the weather and climate of the various sections within the State. The prevailing westerly winds carry most of the weather disturbances that affect Pennsylvania from the interior of the continent, so that the Atlantic Ocean has only limited influence upon the climate of the State.

TEMPERATURE. Throughout the State temperatures generally remain between 0 and 100°F. and average from near 47°F. annually in the north-central mountains to 57°F. annually in the extreme southeast. Summers are generally warm, averaging about 68°F. along Lake Erie to 74°F. in southeastern counties. High temperatures, 90°F. or above, occur on the average of 10 to 20 days per year in most sections. During the coldest months temperatures average near the freezing point with daily minimum readings sometimes near 0°F. or below. Freezing temperatures occur on the average of 100 or more days annually with the greatest number of occurrences in mountainous regions.

PRECIPITATION. Precipitation is fairly evenly distributed throughout the year. Annual amounts generally range between 34 to 52 inches, while the majority of places receive 38 to 46 inches. Greatest amounts usually occur in spring and summer months, while February is the driest month. Precipitation tends to be somewhat greater in eastern sections due primarily to coastal storms which occasionally frequent the area. During the warm season these storms bring heavy rain, while in winter heavy snow or a mixture of rain and snow may be produced. Thunderstorms, which average between 30 and 35 per year, are concentrated in the warm months and are responsible for most of the summertime rainfall. Winter precipitation is usually three to four inches less than summer rainfall and is produced most frequently from northeastward-moving storms. When temperatures are low enough these storms sometimes cause heavy snow which may accumulate to 20 inches or more. Annual snowfall ranges between wide limits from year to year and place to place. Some years are quite lean as snowfall may total less than 10 inches while other years may produce upwards to 100 inches mostly in northern and mountainous areas. Measurable snow generally occurs between November 20 and March 15 although snow has been observed as early as the beginning of October and as late as May, especially in northern counties. Greatest monthly amounts usually fall in December and January, however, greatest amounts from individual storms generally occur in March as the moisture supply increases with the annual march of temperature.

STORMS. Hurricanes or low pressure systems with a tropical origin seldom affect the State. However, tornadoes do occur in Pennsylvania. At least one tornado has been noted in almost all counties. On the average, five or six tornadoes are observed annually in Pennsylvania, and the State ranks 27th nationally. June is the month of highest frequency, followed closely by July and August. Principal areas of tornado concentration are in the extreme northwest, the Southwest Plateau, and the Southeastern Piedmont.

CLIMATIC AREAS. The topographic features of Pennsylvania divide the State into four rather distinct climatic areas: (1) the Southeastern Coastal Plain and Piedmont Plateau; (2) the Ridge and Valley Province; (3) the Allegheny Plateau; and (4) the Lake Erie Plain.

In the Southeastern Coastal Plain and Piedmont Plateau summers are long and at times uncomfortably hot. Daily temperatures reach 90°F. or above on the average of 25 days during the summer season. From about July 1 to the middle of September this area occasionally experiences uncomfortably warm periods, four to five days to a week in length, during which light wind movement and high relative humidity make conditions oppressive. In general, the winters are comparatively mild, with an average of less than 100 days with minimum temperatures below the freezing point. Average annual precipitation in the area ranges from about 30 inches in the lower Susquehanna Valley to about 46 in Chester County. Under the influence of an occasional severe coastal storm, a normal month's rainfall, or more, may occur within a period of 48 hours. The average seasonal snowfall is about 30 inches, and fields are ordinarily snow covered about one-third of the time during the winter season.

The Ridge and Valley Province is not rugged enough for a true mountain type of climate, but it does have many of the characteristics of such a climate. The mountain-and-valley influence on the air movements causes somewhat greater temperature extremes than are experienced in the southeastern part of the State where the modifying coastal and Chesapeake Bay influence hold them relatively constant, and the daily range of temperature increases somewhat under the valley influences. The effects of nocturnal radiation in the valleys and the tendency for cool airmasses to flow down them at night result in a shortening of the growing season by causing freezes later in spring and earlier in fall than would otherwise occur. The annual precipitation in this area has a mean value of three or four inches more than in the southeastern part of the State, but its geographic distribution is less uniform. The mountain ridges are high enough to have some deflecting influence on general storm winds, while summer showers and thunderstorms are often shunted up the valleys. Seasonal snowfall of the Ridge and Valley Province varies considerably within short distances.

The Allegheny Plateau is fairly typical of a continental type of climate, with changeable temperatures and more frequent precipitation than other parts of the State. In the more northerly sections the influence of latitude, together with higher elevation and radiation conditions, serve to make this the coldest area in the State. Occasionally, winter minimum temperatures are severe. The daily temperature range is fairly large. Annual precipitation has a mean of about 41 inches, ranging from less than 35 inches to more than 45 inches. The seasonal snowfall averages 54 inches in northern areas, while southern sections receive several inches less. Fields are normally snow covered three-fourths of the time during the winter season. Although average annual precipitation is about equal to that for the State as a whole, it usually occurs in smaller amounts at more frequent intervals.

Although the Lake Erie Plain is of relatively small size, it has a unique and agriculturally advantageous climate typical of the coastal areas surrounding much of the Great Lakes. Both in spring and autumn the lake water exerts a retarding influence on the temperature regime and the freeze-free season is extended about 45 days. In the autumn this prevents early freezing temperatures. Annual precipitation totals about 34.5 inches, which is fairly evenly distributed throughout the year. Snowfall exceeds 54 inches per year, with heavy snows sometimes experienced late in April.

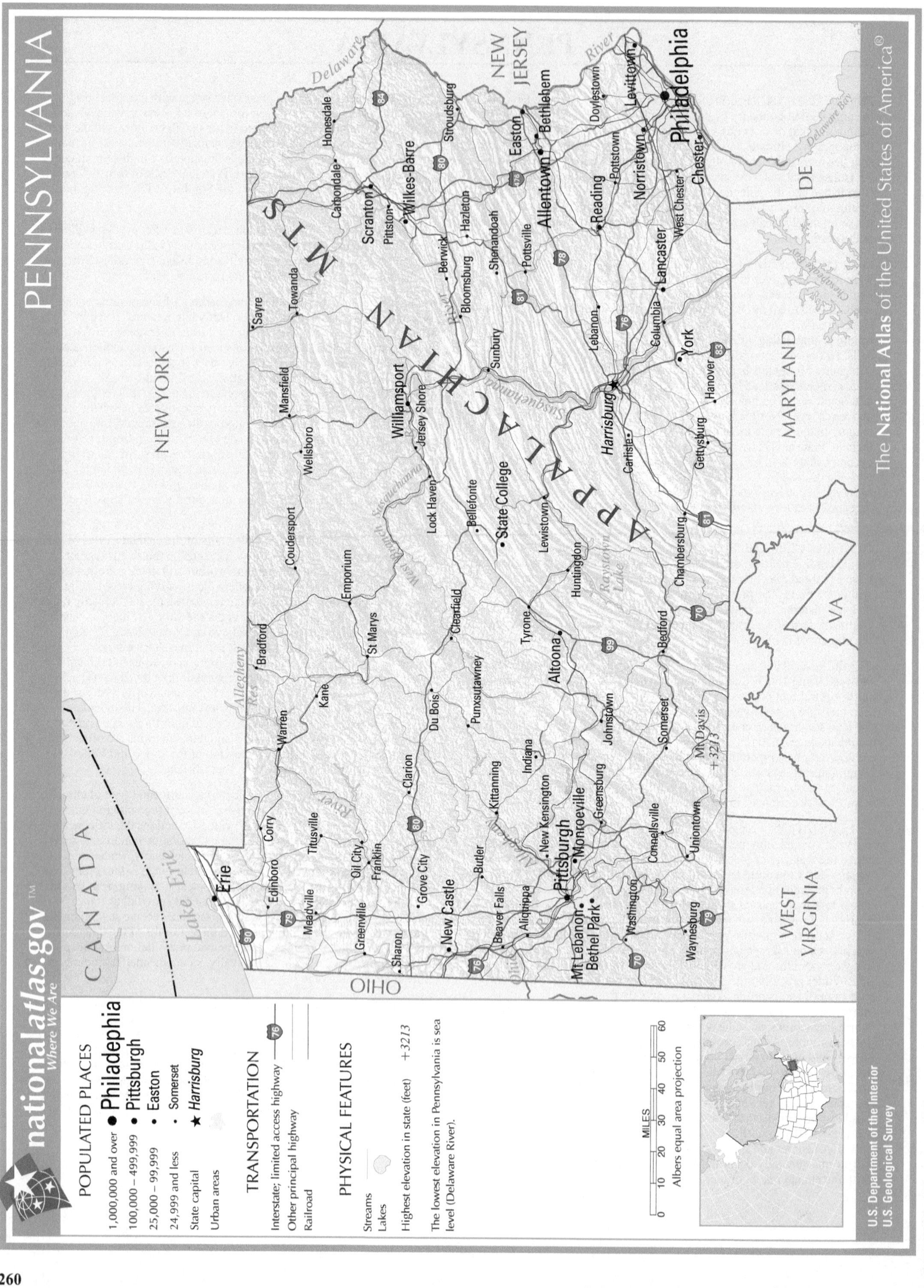
PENNSYLVANIA
nationalatlas.gov™
Where We Are
POPULATED PLACES
1,000,000 and over ● Philadephia
100,000 – 499,999 ● Pittsburgh
25,000 – 99,999 • Easton
24,999 and less · Somerset
State capital ★ Harrisburg
Urban areas
TRANSPORTATION
Interstate; limited access highway 76
Other principal highway
Railroad
PHYSICAL FEATURES
Streams
Lakes
Highest elevation in state (feet) +3213
The lowest elevation in Pennsylvania is sea level (Delaware River).
MILES
0 10 20 30 40 50 60
Albers equal area projection
U.S. Department of the Interior
U.S. Geological Survey
The National Atlas of the United States of America®
CANADA
NEW YORK
NEW JERSEY
OHIO
WEST VIRGINIA
MARYLAND
DE
VA
Lake Erie
APPALACHIAN MTS
Delaware River
Delaware Bay
Chesapeake Bay
Susquehanna
West Branch Susquehanna
Allegheny Res
Allegheny River
Raystown Lake
Mt Davis +3213
Philadelphia
Pittsburgh
Erie
Harrisburg
Allentown
Reading
Scranton
Wilkes-Barre
Lancaster
York
Altoona
Bethlehem
Easton
Chester
Norristown
Levittown
Williamsport
State College
Johnstown
New Castle
Monroeville
Mt Lebanon
Bethel Park
Sayre
Towanda
Mansfield
Wellsboro
Coudersport
Emporium
Bradford
Warren
Kane
St Marys
Corry
Edinboro
Titusville
Meadville
Oil City
Franklin
Greenville
Sharon
Grove City
Clarion
Butler
Beaver Falls
Aliquippa
New Kensington
Kittanning
Indiana
Punxsutawney
Du Bois
Clearfield
Tyrone
Huntingdon
Lewistown
Bellefonte
Lock Haven
Jersey Shore
Sunbury
Bloomsburg
Berwick
Hazleton
Shenandoah
Pottsville
Lebanon
Columbia
Hanover
Gettysburg
Carlisle
Chambersburg
Bedford
Somerset
Greensburg
Connellsville
Uniontown
Washington
Waynesburg
Pittston
Carbondale
Honesdale
Stroudsburg
Pottstown
West Chester
Doylestown

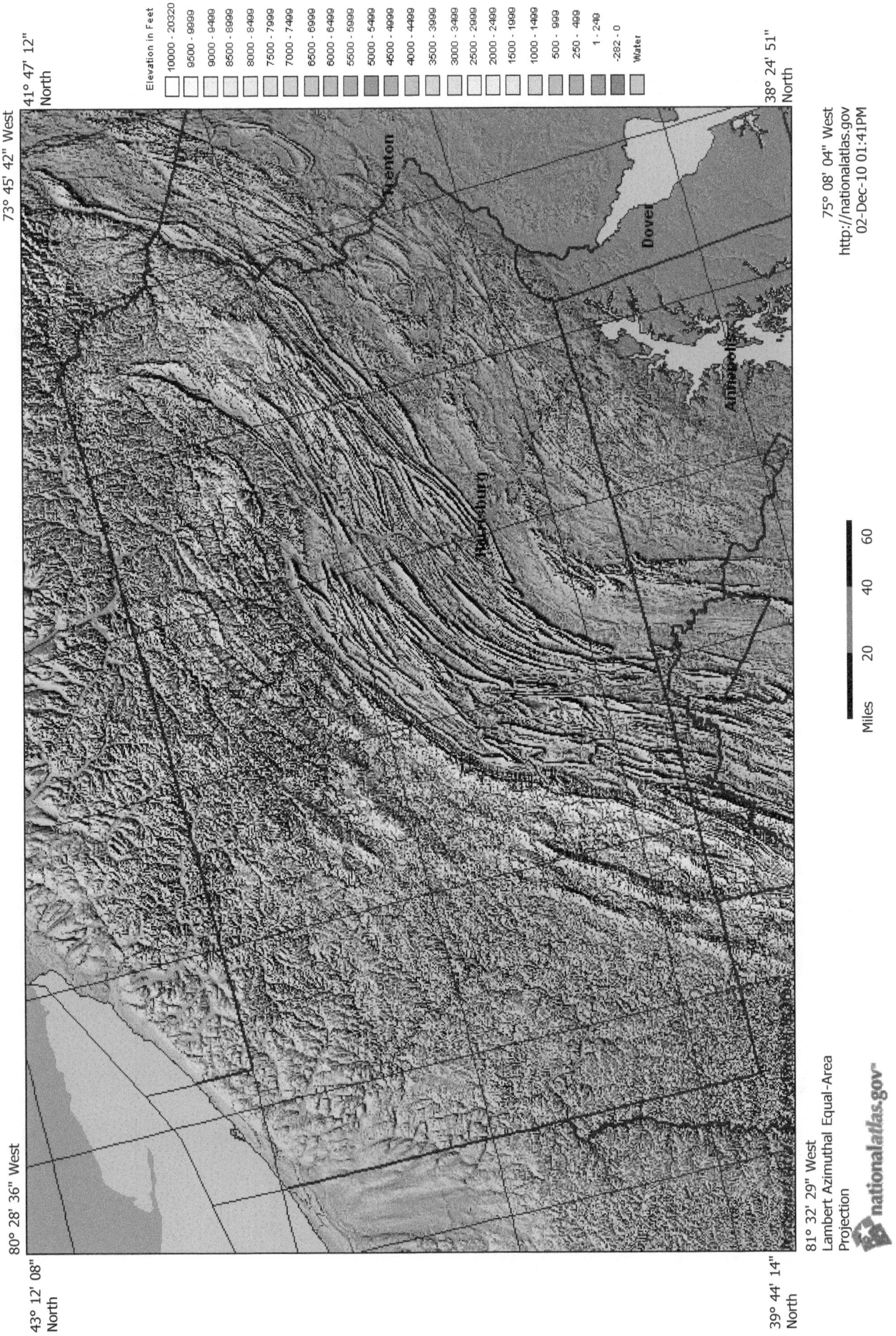
Elevation in Feet
10000 - 20320
9500 - 9999
9000 - 9499
8500 - 8999
8000 - 8499
7500 - 7999
7000 - 7499
6500 - 6999
6000 - 6499
5500 - 5999
5000 - 5499
4500 - 4999
4000 - 4499
3500 - 3999
3000 - 3499
2500 - 2999
2000 - 2499
1500 - 1999
1000 - 1499
500 - 999
250 - 499
1 - 249
-282 - 0
Water
41° 47' 12" North
73° 45' 42" West
38° 24' 51" North
75° 08' 04" West
http://nationalatlas.gov
02-Dec-10 01:41PM
Trenton
Dover
Annapolis
Harrisburg
Miles
0
20
40
60
80° 28' 36" West
43° 12' 08" North
39° 44' 14" North
81° 32' 29" West
Lambert Azimuthal Equal-Area
Projection
nationalatlas.gov

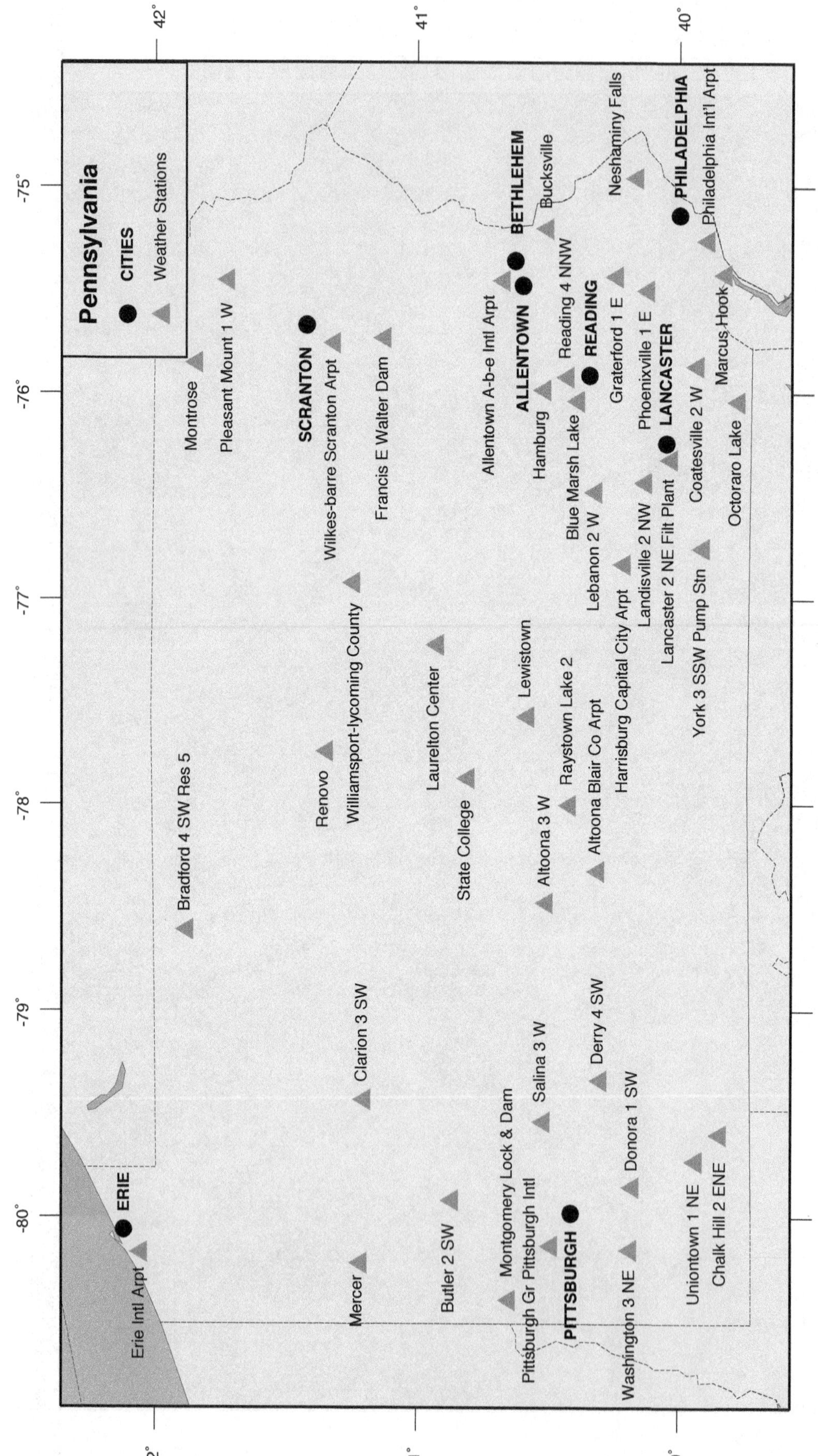
Pennsylvania
CITIES
Weather Stations
42°
41°
40°
-75°
-76°
-77°
-78°
-79°
-80°
ERIE
Erie Intl Arpt
Bradford 4 SW Res 5
Montrose
Pleasant Mount 1 W
Mercer
Clarion 3 SW
Renovo
Williamsport-lycoming County
SCRANTON
Wilkes-barre Scranton Arpt
Francis E Walter Dam
Butler 2 SW
State College
Laurelton Center
Montgomery Lock & Dam
Pittsburgh Gr Pittsburgh Intl
PITTSBURGH
Salina 3 W
Altoona 3 W
Raystown Lake 2
Lewistown
Allentown A-b-e Intl Arpt
ALLENTOWN
BETHLEHEM
Hamburg
Bucksville
Reading 4 NNW
READING
Blue Marsh Lake
Washington 3 NE
Donora 1 SW
Derry 4 SW
Altoona Blair Co Arpt
Lebanon 2 W
Harrisburg Capital City Arpt
Graterford 1 E
Neshaminy Falls
Landisville 2 NW
Phoenixville 1 E
LANCASTER
Lancaster 2 NE Filt Plant
PHILADELPHIA
Uniontown 1 NE
Chalk Hill 2 ENE
York 3 SSW Pump Stn
Coatesville 2 W
Philadelphia Int'l Arpt
Octoraro Lake
Marcus Hook

Pennsylvania Weather Stations by County

County	Station Name
Allegheny	Pittsburgh Intl Arpt
Beaver	Montgomery Lock & Dam
Berks	Blue Marsh Lake Hamburg Reading 4 NNW
Blair	Altoona 3 W Altoona Blair Co Arpt
Bucks	Bucksville Neshaminy Falls
Butler	Butler 2 SW
Centre	State College
Chester	Coatesville 2 W Phoenixville 1 E
Clarion	Clarion 3 SW
Clinton	Renovo
Delaware	Marcus Hook
Erie	Erie Intl Arpt
Fayette	Chalk Hill 2 ENE Uniontown 1 NE
Huntingdon	Raystown Lake 2
Lancaster	Lancaster 2 NE Filt Plant Landisville 2 NW Octoraro Lake
Lebanon	Lebanon 2 W
Lehigh	Allentown A-B-E Intl Arpt
Luzerne	Francis E Walter Dam Wilkes-Barre Scranton Arpt
Lycoming	Williamsport-Lycoming County
Mckean	Bradford 4 SW Res 5
Mercer	Mercer
Mifflin	Lewistown
Montgomery	Graterford 1 E
Philadelphia	Philadelphia Int'l Arpt
Susquehanna	Montrose
Union	Laurelton Center
Washington	Donora 1 SW Washington 3 NE

County	Station Name
Wayne	Pleasant Mount 1 W
Westmoreland	Derry 4 SW Salina 3 W
York	Harrisburg Capital City Arpt York 3 SSW Pump Stn

See User Guide for station inclusion criteria.

Pennsylvania Weather Stations by City

City	Station Name	Miles
Abington Twp	Moorestown, NJ	13.2
	Graterford 1 E	18.2
	Neshaminy Falls	9.6
	Philadelphia Int'l Arpt	18.0
	Phoenixville 1 E	19.8
Allentown	Allentown A-B-E Intl Arpt	3.7
	Bucksville	16.0
Altoona	Altoona Blair Co Arpt	15.3
	Altoona 3 W	3.6
	Raystown Lake 2	21.7
Bensalem Twp	Hightstown 2 W, NJ	22.4
	Indian Mills 2 W, NJ	23.2
	Moorestown, NJ	10.2
	Neshaminy Falls	2.6
	Philadelphia Int'l Arpt	23.0
Bethel Park	Donora 1 SW	14.1
	Pittsburgh Intl Arpt	15.9
	Washington 3 NE	12.3
Bethlehem	Belvidere Bridge, NJ	20.9
	Allentown A-B-E Intl Arpt	4.2
	Bucksville	12.8
Bristol Twp	Hightstown 2 W, NJ	18.3
	Indian Mills 2 W, NJ	23.2
	Moorestown, NJ	12.5
	Neshaminy Falls	4.7
Cheltenham Twp	Moorestown, NJ	11.8
	Graterford 1 E	19.0
	Marcus Hook	23.3
	Neshaminy Falls	11.1
	Philadelphia Int'l Arpt	15.4
	Phoenixville 1 E	19.4
Chester	Newark University Farm, DE	23.0
	Wilm. New Castle Co. Arpt, DE	17.6
	Wilmington Porter Rsvr, DE	10.4
	Moorestown, NJ	22.9
	Marcus Hook	3.4
	Philadelphia Int'l Arpt	7.4
	Phoenixville 1 E	19.5
Erie	Erie Intl Arpt	6.0
Falls Twp	Hightstown 2 W, NJ	15.0
	Moorestown, NJ	16.4
	Neshaminy Falls	6.8
Harrisburg	Harrisburg Capital City Arpt	3.8
	Lebanon 2 W	21.9
Haverford Twp	Wilmington Porter Rsvr, DE	19.0
	Moorestown, NJ	18.3
	Graterford 1 E	18.5
	Marcus Hook	12.8
	Neshaminy Falls	22.3
	Philadelphia Int'l Arpt	9.0
	Phoenixville 1 E	13.6

City	Station Name	Miles
Hempfield Twp	Derry 4 SW	12.7
	Donora 1 SW	17.7
	Salina 3 W	15.6
Lancaster	Coatesville 2 W	23.5
	Lancaster 2 NE Filt Plant	1.4
	Landisville 2 NW	8.7
	Lebanon 2 W	22.1
	Octoraro Lake	21.3
Levittown	Hightstown 2 W, NJ	16.9
	Indian Mills 2 W, NJ	24.7
	Moorestown, NJ	14.3
	Neshaminy Falls	5.2
Lower Macungie Twp	Allentown A-B-E Intl Arpt	9.4
	Bucksville	19.2
	Graterford 1 E	22.5
	Hamburg	22.2
	Reading 4 NNW	21.4
Lower Makefield Twp	Flemington 5 NNW, NJ	23.7
	Hightstown 2 W, NJ	15.3
	Moorestown, NJ	18.8
	Neshaminy Falls	7.4
Lower Merion Twp	Wilmington Porter Rsvr, DE	21.9
	Moorestown, NJ	16.8
	Graterford 1 E	17.2
	Marcus Hook	15.6
	Neshaminy Falls	19.6
	Philadelphia Int'l Arpt	10.5
	Phoenixville 1 E	13.7
Lower Paxton Twp	Harrisburg Capital City Arpt	7.0
	Landisville 2 NW	23.6
	Lebanon 2 W	17.7
Manheim Twp	Blue Marsh Lake	25.0
	Coatesville 2 W	24.0
	Lancaster 2 NE Filt Plant	2.6
	Landisville 2 NW	7.4
	Lebanon 2 W	19.3
	Octoraro Lake	23.7
Middletown Twp	Hightstown 2 W, NJ	18.9
	Moorestown, NJ	14.5
	Neshaminy Falls	2.9
Millcreek Twp	Erie Intl Arpt	3.1
Mount Lebanon	Donora 1 SW	17.4
	Pittsburgh Intl Arpt	12.9
	Washington 3 NE	15.1
Norristown	Moorestown, NJ	22.5
	Graterford 1 E	9.1
	Marcus Hook	21.4
	Neshaminy Falls	20.8
	Philadelphia Int'l Arpt	18.5
	Phoenixville 1 E	8.4
Northampton Twp	Hightstown 2 W, NJ	22.8
	Moorestown, NJ	16.5
	Bucksville	23.2

See User Guide for station inclusion criteria.

City	Station Name	Miles
Northampton Twp *(cont.)*	Graterford 1 E	23.4
	Neshaminy Falls	4.4
Penn Hills	Donora 1 SW	21.3
	Pittsburgh Intl Arpt	21.4
	Salina 3 W	14.9
Philadelphia	Indian Mills 2 W, NJ	23.7
	Moorestown, NJ	9.6
	Graterford 1 E	22.1
	Marcus Hook	19.6
	Neshaminy Falls	14.2
	Philadelphia Int'l Arpt	10.7
	Phoenixville 1 E	20.5
Pittsburgh	Donora 1 SW	19.8
	Pittsburgh Intl Arpt	14.3
	Salina 3 W	22.7
	Washington 3 NE	21.1
Radnor Twp	Wilmington Porter Rsvr, DE	20.5
	Moorestown, NJ	21.5
	Graterford 1 E	14.4
	Marcus Hook	15.2
	Neshaminy Falls	23.3
	Philadelphia Int'l Arpt	13.4
	Phoenixville 1 E	9.3
Reading	Blue Marsh Lake	6.4
	Coatesville 2 W	24.9
	Hamburg	14.7
	Reading 4 NNW	5.2
Ross Twp	Butler 2 SW	22.9
	Montgomery Lock & Dam	20.7
	Pittsburgh Intl Arpt	11.2
	Salina 3 W	24.9
Scranton	Francis E Walter Dam	20.8
	Pleasant Mount 1 W	24.8
	Wilkes-Barre Scranton Arpt	6.6
State College	Lewistown	21.1
	State College	0.6
Upper Darby Twp	Wilmington Porter Rsvr, DE	18.3
	Moorestown, NJ	16.9
	Graterford 1 E	21.1
	Marcus Hook	11.6
	Neshaminy Falls	22.4
	Philadelphia Int'l Arpt	6.4
	Phoenixville 1 E	16.2
Warminster Twp	Moorestown, NJ	17.7
	Bucksville	21.2
	Graterford 1 E	18.1
	Neshaminy Falls	8.4
	Philadelphia Int'l Arpt	24.4
	Phoenixville 1 E	22.3
Wilkes-Barre	Francis E Walter Dam	11.6
	Wilkes-Barre Scranton Arpt	9.9
York	Harrisburg Capital City Arpt	18.7
York *(cont.)*	Lancaster 2 NE Filt Plant	24.4
	Landisville 2 NW	19.0
	York 3 SSW Pump Stn	3.3

Note: Miles is the distance between the geographic center of the city and the weather station.

Pennsylvania Weather Stations by Elevation

Feet	Station Name
1,979	Chalk Hill 2 ENE
1,798	Pleasant Mount 1 W
1,691	Bradford 4 SW Res 5
1,507	Francis E Walter Dam
1,479	Altoona Blair Co Arpt
1,419	Montrose
1,319	Altoona 3 W
1,299	Washington 3 NE
1,220	Mercer
1,169	State College
1,149	Pittsburgh Intl Arpt
1,108	Salina 3 W
1,060	Derry 4 SW
1,040	Clarion 3 SW
1,000	Butler 2 SW
956	Uniontown 1 NE
930	Wilkes-Barre Scranton Arpt
839	Raystown Lake 2
799	Laurelton Center
762	Donora 1 SW
729	Erie Intl Arpt
689	Montgomery Lock & Dam
660	Renovo
640	Coatesville 2 W
520	Williamsport-Lycoming County
459	Bucksville
459	Lewistown
450	Lebanon 2 W
390	Allentown A-B-E Intl Arpt
390	York 3 SSW Pump Stn
359	Landisville 2 NW
359	Reading 4 NNW
350	Blue Marsh Lake
350	Hamburg
339	Harrisburg Capital City Arpt
270	Lancaster 2 NE Filt Plant
259	Octoraro Lake
240	Graterford 1 E
104	Phoenixville 1 E
60	Neshaminy Falls
9	Marcus Hook
4	Philadelphia Int'l Arpt

See User Guide for station inclusion criteria.

Allentown A-B-E Int'l Airport

Allentown is located in the east central section of the state and in the Lehigh River valley. Twelve miles to the north is Blue Mountain, a ridge from 1,000 to 1,800 feet in height. The South Mountain, 500 to 1,000 feet high, fringes the southern edge of the city. Otherwise the country is generally rolling with numerous small streams. A modified climate prevails. Temperatures are usually moderate and precipitation generally ample with the largest amounts occurring during the summer months when precipitation is generally showery. General climatological features of the area are slightly modified by the mountain ranges so that at times during the winter there is a temperature difference of 10 to 15 degrees between Allentown and Philadelphia, only 50 miles to the south.

The growing season averages 177 days, and generally ranges from 170 to 185 days. It begins late in April and ends late in October. The average occurrence of the last temperature of 32 degrees in the spring is late April, and the average first fall minimum of 32 degrees is mid-October.

Maximum temperatures during most years are not excessively high and temperatures above 100 degrees are seldom recorded. However, the average humidity in the valley is quite high, and combined with the normal summer temperatures, causes periods of discomfort.

Winters in the valley are comparatively mild. Minimum temperatures during December, January, and February are usually below freezing, but below zero temperatures are seldom recorded.

Seasonal snowfall is quite variable. Freezing rain is a common problem throughout the Lehigh Valley. Snowstorms producing 10 inches or more occur an average of once in two years. The accumulation of snowfall over the drainage area of the Lehigh River to the north of Allentown, combined with spring rains, frequently presents a flood threat to the city and surrounding area. The valley is also subject to torrential rains that cause quick rises in the river and feeder creeks.

The area is seldom subject to destructive storms of large extent. Heavy thunderstorms and tornadoes occasionally cause damage over limited areas. An exception to the usual weather was the storm that battered the east coast on November 25, 1950, when gusts of 88 mph were observed at the station.

Allentown A-B-E Int'l Airport *Lehigh County* Elevation: 390 ft. Latitude: 40° 39' N Longitude: 75° 27' W

	JAN	FEB	MAR	APR	MAY	JUN	JUL	AUG	SEP	OCT	NOV	DEC	YEAR
Mean Maximum Temp. (°F)	36.4	40.1	49.4	61.5	71.8	80.3	84.5	82.9	75.4	63.9	52.6	40.9	61.6
Mean Temp. (°F)	28.6	31.4	39.6	50.6	60.6	69.7	74.2	72.5	64.7	53.2	43.3	32.9	51.8
Mean Minimum Temp. (°F)	20.7	22.6	29.7	39.6	49.4	59.1	63.7	62.1	54.0	42.5	34.0	24.9	41.8
Extreme Maximum Temp. (°F)	70	76	87	92	94	97	101	99	99	90	79	72	101
Extreme Minimum Temp. (°F)	-15	-8	4	16	29	40	46	41	32	21	15	-5	-15
Days Maximum Temp. ≥ 90°F	0	0	0	0	1	3	7	4	1	0	0	0	16
Days Maximum Temp. ≤ 32°F	11	6	1	0	0	0	0	0	0	0	0	6	24
Days Minimum Temp. ≤ 32°F	27	24	19	6	0	0	0	0	0	4	14	25	119
Days Minimum Temp. ≤ 0°F	1	0	0	0	0	0	0	0	0	0	0	0	1
Heating Degree Days (base 65°F)	1,122	944	781	432	175	24	2	7	87	368	644	987	5,573
Cooling Degree Days (base 65°F)	0	0	1	6	46	171	293	247	85	9	0	0	858
Mean Precipitation (in.)	2.97	2.59	3.38	3.59	4.12	4.36	4.71	3.66	4.43	3.82	3.50	3.51	44.64
Maximum Precipitation (in.)*	8.4	5.4	7.2	10.1	10.6	8.6	10.4	12.1	8.9	7.5	9.7	7.9	67.7
Minimum Precipitation (in.)*	0.7	0.9	1.0	0.6	0.1	0.3	0.4	0.8	0.9	0.1	0.7	0.4	29.8
Extreme Maximum Daily Precip. (in.)	1.93	2.94	2.72	3.46	2.90	2.66	3.37	4.19	6.37	8.71	2.66	2.16	8.71
Days With ≥ 0.1" Precipitation	6	5	7	7	8	8	7	6	6	6	6	6	78
Days With ≥ 0.5" Precipitation	2	2	2	2	3	3	3	2	3	2	2	3	29
Days With ≥ 1.0" Precipitation	1	0	1	1	1	1	1	1	1	1	1	1	11
Mean Snowfall (in.)	10.0	10.0	5.5	***1.0***	trace	***trace***	0.0	0.0	0.0	trace	0.8	5.4	***32.7***
Maximum Snowfall (in.)*	34	30	31	13	trace	0	0	0	0	1	8	28	74
Maximum 24-hr. Snowfall (in.)*	12	24	17	11	trace	0	0	0	0	1	6	13	24
Maximum Snow Depth (in.)	na	na	na	na	na	na	na	na	na	na	na	na	na
Days With ≥ 1.0" Snow Depth	na	na	na	na	na	na	na	na	na	na	na	na	na
Thunderstorm Days*	< 1	< 1	1	2	4	6	7	6	3	1	1	< 1	31
Foggy Days*	14	12	13	12	16	16	18	20	19	17	15	14	186
Predominant Sky Cover*	OVR	OVR	OVR	OVR	OVR	OVR	OVR	OVR	OVR	OVR	OVR	OVR	OVR
Mean Relative Humidity 7am (%)*	77	76	76	75	78	79	82	86	88	87	82	79	80
Mean Relative Humidity 4pm (%)*	62	57	52	48	51	52	52	55	57	55	60	64	55
Mean Dewpoint (°F)*	19	20	26	36	48	57	62	62	55	44	33	23	41
Prevailing Wind Direction*	W	W	WNW	WSW	WSW	WSW	WSW	WSW	WSW	WSW	W	W	WSW
Prevailing Wind Speed (mph)*	14	15	16	10	9	9	8	8	8	9	13	13	12
Maximum Wind Gust (mph)*	68	64	60	68	54	77	66	92	60	63	78	62	92

Note: (*) Period of record is 1948-1995

The period of record for National Weather Service station data is 1980 – 2009 except where noted. See User Guide for detailed explanation of data.

Erie Int'l Airport

Erie is located on the southeast shore of Lake Erie and observations are made at Erie International Airport, which is six miles southwest of the center of the city and about one mile from the lake shore. The terrain rises gradually in a series of ridges paralleling the shoreline to 500 feet above the lake level three to four miles inland and to 1,000 feet about 15 miles inland. Snowfall from instability showers moving southward off the lake usually increases due to the upslope terrain. Snowfall is somewhat higher south of the city than along the lake shore.

During the winter months, the many cold air masses moving south from Canada are modified by the relatively warm waters of Lake Erie. However, the temperature difference between air and water produces an excess of cloudiness and frequent snow from November through March.

Spring weather is quite variable in Erie, but generally cloudy and cool. Proximity to the lake frequently prevents killing frosts that occur inland. This has led to the establishment of numerous vineyards and orchards in a narrow belt along the shore. Summer heat waves are tempered by cool lake breezes that may reach several miles inland, and days with temperatures above 90 degrees are infrequent. Summer thunderstorms are usually less destructive in Erie than inland areas because of the stabilizing effects of Lake Erie.

Autumn, with long dry periods and an abundance of sunshine, is usually the most pleasant period of the year in Erie. The growing season is extended by the influence of the warmer waters of the lake. Precipitation is well distributed throughout the year, although the number of days with measurable amounts varies considerably from a low average of about one day in three for the period June through September to about one-half of the days from November through March, when snow flurries and squalls move in from the lake.

Erie Int'l Airport *Erie County* Elevation: 729 ft. Latitude: 42° 05' N Longitude: 80° 11' W

	JAN	FEB	MAR	APR	MAY	JUN	JUL	AUG	SEP	OCT	NOV	DEC	YEAR
Mean Maximum Temp. (°F)	33.8	35.5	43.5	55.7	66.5	75.6	79.8	78.6	72.0	60.6	49.7	38.3	57.5
Mean Temp. (°F)	27.4	28.4	35.5	46.9	57.4	67.0	71.7	70.7	64.0	53.0	43.3	32.6	49.8
Mean Minimum Temp. (°F)	21.1	21.2	27.5	38.1	48.2	58.3	63.5	62.7	55.9	45.3	36.8	26.7	42.1
Extreme Maximum Temp. (°F)	70	75	82	89	90	100	99	94	93	87	78	75	100
Extreme Minimum Temp. (°F)	-18	-11	-9	12	30	38	48	37	37	25	17	-6	-18
Days Maximum Temp. ≥ 90°F	0	0	0	0	0	1	1	1	0	0	0	0	3
Days Maximum Temp. ≤ 32°F	15	12	6	0	0	0	0	0	0	0	1	9	43
Days Minimum Temp. ≤ 32°F	26	24	22	9	0	0	0	0	0	1	9	23	114
Days Minimum Temp. ≤ 0°F	2	1	0	0	0	0	0	0	0	0	0	0	3
Heating Degree Days (base 65°F)	1,157	1,029	908	543	264	60	6	10	99	375	646	999	6,096
Cooling Degree Days (base 65°F)	0	0	2	7	34	126	220	193	75	10	0	0	667
Mean Precipitation (in.)	2.90	2.35	3.04	3.37	3.38	3.79	3.54	3.63	4.65	4.07	3.89	3.84	42.45
Maximum Precipitation (in.)*	5.5	5.7	6.8	7.1	7.8	7.7	7.7	11.1	10.6	9.9	10.4	6.9	61.7
Minimum Precipitation (in.)*	0.9	0.6	0.6	1.6	1.0	0.8	0.6	1.0	1.3	0.4	1.5	1.4	28.1
Extreme Maximum Daily Precip. (in.)	1.51	2.11	1.56	1.54	1.86	4.61	2.01	3.29	3.91	2.76	2.47	1.48	4.61
Days With ≥ 0.1" Precipitation	8	7	8	9	8	7	7	6	8	9	9	11	97
Days With ≥ 0.5" Precipitation	1	1	1	2	2	2	2	2	3	3	2	2	23
Days With ≥ 1.0" Precipitation	0	0	0	0	0	1	1	1	1	1	0	0	5
Mean Snowfall (in.)	29.0	17.3	14.0	3.3	trace	trace	trace	trace	trace	0.2	7.9	27.9	99.6
Maximum Snowfall (in.)*	62	32	27	10	trace	0	0	0	0	4	36	67	147
Maximum 24-hr. Snowfall (in.)*	13	12	12	7	trace	0	0	0	0	3	17	14	17
Maximum Snow Depth (in.)	na	na	na	na	na	na	na	na	na	na	na	na	na
Days With ≥ 1.0" Snow Depth	na	*17*	na	*1*	na	na	na	na	na	na	na	*13*	na
Thunderstorm Days*	< 1	< 1	2	3	4	6	7	7	4	2	1	< 1	36
Foggy Days*	12	12	14	12	12	11	10	11	11	10	12	13	140
Predominant Sky Cover*	OVR	OVR	OVR	OVR	OVR	OVR	SCT	OVR	OVR	OVR	OVR	OVR	OVR
Mean Relative Humidity 7am (%)*	78	79	78	75	75	78	79	82	81	77	76	77	78
Mean Relative Humidity 4pm (%)*	73	72	67	60	58	60	61	62	63	64	69	73	65
Mean Dewpoint (°F)*	19	20	26	35	45	56	61	60	54	43	33	24	40
Prevailing Wind Direction*	SSW	WSW	WSW	WSW	S	S	S	S	S	S	S	SSW	S
Prevailing Wind Speed (mph)*	14	14	14	14	9	9	8	8	9	10	13	14	12
Maximum Wind Gust (mph)*	78	74	67	71	54	62	69	54	69	62	69	60	78

Note: (*) Period of record is 1948-1995

The period of record for National Weather Service station data is 1980 – 2009 except where noted. See User Guide for detailed explanation of data.

Harrisburg Capital City Airport

Harrisburg, the capital of Pennsylvania, is situated on the east bank of the Susquehanna River. It is in the Great Valley formed by the eastern foothills of the Appalachian Chain, and about 60 miles southeast of the Commonwealths geographic center. It is nestled in a saucer-like bowl, 10 miles south of Blue Mountain, which serves as a barrier to the severe winter climate experienced 50 to 100 miles to the north and west. Although the severity of the winter climate is lessened, the city lies a little too far inland to derive the full benefits of the coastal climate.

Air masses change with some regularity, and any one condition does not persist for many days in succession. The mountain barrier occasionally prevents cold waves from reaching the Great Valley. The city is favorably located to receive precipitation produced when warm, maritime air from the Atlantic Ocean is forced upslope to cross the Blue Ridge Mountains.

The growing season in the Harrisburg area is about 192 days. Prolonged dry spells occur on occasion. Flood stage on the Susquehanna River occurs on the average of about every three years in Harrisburg, but serious flooding is much less frequent. About one-third of all floods have occurred during the month of March. Tropical hurricanes rarely reach Harrisburg with destructive winds, but have produced rainfalls in excess of 15 inches.

Harrisburg Capital City Airport *York County* Elevation: 339 ft. Latitude: 40° 13' N Longitude: 76° 51' W

	JAN	FEB	MAR	APR	MAY	JUN	JUL	AUG	SEP	OCT	NOV	DEC	YEAR
Mean Maximum Temp. (°F)	na	na	na	na	na	na	na	na	na	na	na	na	na
Mean Temp. (°F)	na	na	na	na	na	na	na	na	na	na	na	na	na
Mean Minimum Temp. (°F)	na	na	na	na	na	na	na	na	na	na	na	na	na
Extreme Maximum Temp. (°F)	na	na	na	na	na	na	na	na	na	na	na	na	na
Extreme Minimum Temp. (°F)	na	na	na	na	na	na	na	na	na	na	na	na	na
Days Maximum Temp. ≥ 90°F	na	na	na	na	na	na	na	na	na	na	na	na	na
Days Maximum Temp. ≤ 32°F	na	na	na	na	na	na	na	na	na	na	na	na	na
Days Minimum Temp. ≤ 32°F	na	na	na	na	na	na	na	na	na	na	na	na	na
Days Minimum Temp. ≤ 0°F	na	na	na	na	na	na	na	na	na	na	na	na	na
Heating Degree Days (base 65°F)	na	na	na	na	na	na	na	na	na	na	na	na	na
Cooling Degree Days (base 65°F)	na	na	na	na	na	na	na	na	na	na	na	na	na
Mean Precipitation (in.)	na	na	na	na	na	na	na	na	na	na	na	na	na
Maximum Precipitation (in.)*	8.0	5.9	6.1	8.0	9.7	18.5	9.7	9.1	15.0	9.9	7.2	7.6	59.3
Minimum Precipitation (in.)*	0.4	0.2	1.0	0.4	0.5	0.1	0.8	0.9	0.6	trace	0.8	0.2	29.0
Extreme Maximum Daily Precip. (in.)	na	na	na	na	na	na	na	na	na	na	na	na	na
Days With ≥ 0.1" Precipitation	na	na	na	na	na	na	na	na	na	na	na	na	na
Days With ≥ 0.5" Precipitation	na	na	na	na	na	na	na	na	na	na	na	na	na
Days With ≥ 1.0" Precipitation	na	na	na	na	na	na	na	na	na	na	na	na	na
Mean Snowfall (in.)	na	na	na	na	na	na	na	na	na	na	na	na	na
Maximum Snowfall (in.)*	34	30	23	10	trace	0	0	0	0	1	15	28	82
Maximum 24-hr. Snowfall (in.)*	14	24	11	6	trace	0	0	0	0	1	9	10	24
Maximum Snow Depth (in.)	na	na	na	na	na	na	na	na	na	na	na	na	na
Days With ≥ 1.0" Snow Depth	na	na	na	na	na	na	na	na	na	na	na	na	na
Thunderstorm Days*	< 1	< 1	1	2	5	6	7	5	3	1	1	< 1	31
Foggy Days*	12	11	11	10	13	12	13	16	15	15	13	12	153
Predominant Sky Cover*	OVR	OVR	OVR	OVR	OVR	OVR	OVR	OVR	OVR	OVR	OVR	OVR	OVR
Mean Relative Humidity 7am (%)*	71	71	70	71	75	77	79	83	85	82	77	72	76
Mean Relative Humidity 4pm (%)*	56	53	49	47	51	51	52	54	55	53	56	58	53
Mean Dewpoint (°F)*	18	20	26	36	48	58	63	62	56	44	33	23	41
Prevailing Wind Direction*	WNW	WNW	WNW	WNW	W	W	W	W	W	W	WNW	WNW	WNW
Prevailing Wind Speed (mph)*	13	14	14	13	8	8	7	7	7	8	13	13	10
Maximum Wind Gust (mph)*	na	na	na	na	na	na	na	na	na	30	na	na	30

Note: (*) Period of record is 1948-1991

The period of record for National Weather Service station data is 1980 – 2009 except where noted. See User Guide for detailed explanation of data.

Philadelphia Int'l Airport

The Appalachian Mountains to the west and the Atlantic Ocean to the east have a moderating effect on climate. Periods of very high or very low temperatures seldom last for more than three or four days. Temperatures below zero or above 100 degrees are a rarity. On occasion, the area becomes engulfed with maritime air during the summer months, and high humidity adds to the discomfort of seasonably warm temperatures.

Precipitation is fairly evenly distributed throughout the year with maximum amounts during the late summer months. Much of the summer rainfall is from local thunderstorms and amounts vary in different areas of the city. This is due, in part, to the higher elevations to the west and north. Snowfall amounts are often considerably larger in the northern suburbs than in the central and southern parts of the city. In many cases, the precipitation will change from snow to rain within the city. Single storms of 10 inches or more occur about every five years.

The prevailing wind direction for the summer months is from the southwest, while northwesterly winds prevail during the winter. The annual prevailing direction is from the west-southwest. Destructive velocities are comparatively rare and occur mostly in gustiness during summer thunderstorms. High winds occurring in the winter months, as a rule, come with the advance of cold air after the passage of a deep low pressure system. Only rarely have hurricanes in the vicinity caused widespread damage, primarily because of flooding.

Flood stages in the Schuylkill River normally occur about twice a year. Flood stages seldom last over 12 hours and usually occur after excessive thunderstorms. Flooding rarely occurs on the Delaware River.

Philadelphia Int'l Airport *Philadelphia County* Elevation: 4 ft. Latitude: 39° 52' N Longitude: 75° 14' W

	JAN	FEB	MAR	APR	MAY	JUN	JUL	AUG	SEP	OCT	NOV	DEC	YEAR
Mean Maximum Temp. (°F)	40.2	43.7	52.3	63.8	73.8	82.5	87.0	85.3	78.0	66.5	55.8	44.8	64.5
Mean Temp. (°F)	32.9	35.6	43.2	53.9	63.8	73.0	78.0	76.6	69.1	57.4	47.5	37.4	55.7
Mean Minimum Temp. (°F)	25.5	27.4	34.1	43.9	53.8	63.4	68.9	67.9	60.2	48.3	39.0	30.0	46.9
Extreme Maximum Temp. (°F)	73	74	86	95	97	100	103	101	98	89	81	73	103
Extreme Minimum Temp. (°F)	-7	3	7	19	35	44	52	44	40	28	19	1	-7
Days Maximum Temp. ≥ 90°F	0	0	0	0	1	5	11	7	2	0	0	0	26
Days Maximum Temp. ≤ 32°F	7	4	1	0	0	0	0	0	0	0	0	3	15
Days Minimum Temp. ≤ 32°F	24	21	13	1	0	0	0	0	0	0	6	19	84
Days Minimum Temp. ≤ 0°F	0	0	0	0	0	0	0	0	0	0	0	0	0
Heating Degree Days (base 65°F)	989	824	668	339	107	9	0	1	33	253	520	848	4,591
Cooling Degree Days (base 65°F)	0	0	1	12	77	255	409	368	163	25	1	0	1,311
Mean Precipitation (in.)	3.03	2.48	3.77	3.63	3.73	3.42	4.36	3.45	3.75	3.18	3.02	3.47	41.29
Maximum Precipitation (in.)*	8.9	6.4	7.0	8.1	7.4	7.9	10.4	9.7	8.8	6.0	9.1	7.4	54.4
Minimum Precipitation (in.)*	0.4	0.7	0.7	0.5	0.5	0.1	0.6	0.5	0.4	0.1	0.3	0.3	29.3
Extreme Maximum Daily Precip. (in.)	2.32	1.90	2.24	4.19	2.49	2.48	4.68	4.40	6.63	5.53	2.07	2.72	6.63
Days With ≥ 0.1" Precipitation	6	5	7	7	7	6	6	5	5	5	6	6	71
Days With ≥ 0.5" Precipitation	2	2	3	2	3	2	3	2	2	2	2	2	27
Days With ≥ 1.0" Precipitation	1	0	1	1	1	1	1	1	1	1	1	1	11
Mean Snowfall (in.)	5.4	6.6	3.0	0.5	trace	trace	trace	0.0	0.0	trace	0.3	3.0	18.8
Maximum Snowfall (in.)*	23	28	13	4	trace	0	0	0	0	2	9	19	57
Maximum 24-hr. Snowfall (in.)*	9	21	12	4	trace	0	0	0	0	2	5	12	21
Maximum Snow Depth (in.)	12	23	12	3	trace	trace	trace	0	0	trace	5	21	23
Days With ≥ 1.0" Snow Depth	6	5	2	0	0	0	0	0	0	0	0	2	15
Thunderstorm Days*	< 1	< 1	1	2	4	5	6	5	2	1	1	< 1	27
Foggy Days*	13	11	12	11	14	15	16	16	15	15	13	13	164
Predominant Sky Cover*	OVR	OVR	OVR	OVR	OVR	OVR	OVR	OVR	OVR	OVR	OVR	OVR	OVR
Mean Relative Humidity 7am (%)*	74	73	73	72	75	77	79	82	83	83	79	75	77
Mean Relative Humidity 4pm (%)*	59	55	51	48	51	52	54	55	55	54	57	60	54
Mean Dewpoint (°F)*	22	22	29	38	50	59	65	64	57	46	36	26	43
Prevailing Wind Direction*	WNW	WNW	WNW	WNW	SW	SW	SW	SW	SW	WSW	WNW	WNW	SW
Prevailing Wind Speed (mph)*	13	14	14	13	10	9	9	8	9	8	12	13	12
Maximum Wind Gust (mph)*	59	60	69	64	67	54	61	56	53	63	61	63	69

Note: (*) Period of record is 1948-1995

The period of record for National Weather Service station data is 1980 – 2009 except where noted. See User Guide for detailed explanation of data.

Pittsburgh Int'l Airport

Pittsburgh lies at the foothills of the Allegheny Mountains at the confluence of the Allegheny and Monongahela Rivers which form the Ohio. The city is a little over 100 miles southeast of Lake Erie. It has a humid continental type of climate modified only slightly by its nearness to the Atlantic Seaboard and the Great Lakes.

The predominant winter air masses influencing the climate of Pittsburgh have a polar continental source in Canada and move in from the Hudson Bay region or the Canadian Rockies. During the summer, frequent invasions of air from the Gulf of Mexico bring warm humid weather. Occasionally, Gulf air reaches as far north as Pittsburgh during the winter and produces intermittent periods of thawing. The last spring temperature of 32 degrees usually occurs in late April and the first in late October. The average growing season is about 180 days. There is a wide variation in the time of the first and last frosts over a radius of 25 miles from the center of Pittsburgh due to terrain differences.

Precipitation is distributed well throughout the year. During the winter months about a fourth of the precipitation occurs as snow and there is about a 50 percent chance of measurable precipitation on any day. Thunderstorms occur normally during all months, except midwinter, and have a maximum frequency in midsummer. The first appreciable snowfall generally occurs in late November and usually the last occurs early in April. Snow lies on the ground in the suburbs on an average of about 33 days during the year.

Seven months of the year, April through October, have sunshine more than 50 percent of the possible time. During the remaining five months cloudiness is heavier because the track of migratory storms from west to east is closer to the area and because of the frequent periods of cloudy, showery weather associated with northwest winds from across the Great Lakes. Cold air drainage induced by the many hills leads to the frequent formation of early morning fog which may be quite persistent in the river valleys during the colder months.

The Allegheny River flowing south and the Monongahela River flowing north meet to form the Ohio River at Pittsburgh. Heavier rainfall and steeper topography cause the Monongahela River to flood more frequently than the Allegheny River.

Both rivers combine to cause the Ohio River at Pittsburgh to reach the 25 foot flood stage approximately once every four years. The serious flood level of 30 feet is reached much less frequently.

Pittsburgh Int'l Airport *Allegheny County* Elevation: 1,149 ft. Latitude: 40° 30' N Longitude: 80° 14' W

	JAN	FEB	MAR	APR	MAY	JUN	JUL	AUG	SEP	OCT	NOV	DEC	YEAR
Mean Maximum Temp. (°F)	36.1	39.6	49.2	61.7	71.0	79.3	82.8	81.7	74.6	62.7	51.3	39.9	60.8
Mean Temp. (°F)	28.6	31.3	39.5	50.9	60.2	68.7	72.8	71.6	64.4	52.8	43.0	32.6	51.4
Mean Minimum Temp. (°F)	21.1	22.9	29.8	40.0	49.2	58.1	62.8	61.6	54.0	42.8	34.7	25.3	41.9
Extreme Maximum Temp. (°F)	72	76	82	89	91	98	103	100	93	87	79	74	103
Extreme Minimum Temp. (°F)	-22	-7	-1	14	28	36	45	39	34	23	10	-12	-22
Days Maximum Temp. ≥ 90°F	0	0	0	0	0	2	4	3	0	0	0	0	9
Days Maximum Temp. ≤ 32°F	12	9	3	0	0	0	0	0	0	0	1	9	34
Days Minimum Temp. ≤ 32°F	26	23	20	7	1	0	0	0	0	4	13	24	118
Days Minimum Temp. ≤ 0°F	1	1	0	0	0	0	0	0	0	0	0	1	3
Heating Degree Days (base 65°F)	1,121	947	784	427	188	35	4	8	94	381	655	997	5,641
Cooling Degree Days (base 65°F)	0	0	2	10	45	154	252	221	81	9	0	0	774
Mean Precipitation (in.)	2.65	2.33	3.06	3.15	3.91	4.27	3.96	3.59	3.04	2.30	3.11	2.84	38.21
Maximum Precipitation (in.)*	6.3	6.0	6.1	7.6	6.6	10.3	8.7	7.9	6.0	8.2	11.0	8.5	52.2
Minimum Precipitation (in.)*	0.8	0.5	1.1	0.5	1.2	0.6	1.6	0.5	0.3	0.2	0.9	0.4	26.8
Extreme Maximum Daily Precip. (in.)	1.82	1.19	1.61	1.50	2.48	3.11	3.48	2.30	5.95	1.66	1.86	2.76	5.95
Days With ≥ 0.1" Precipitation	7	6	8	8	8	8	7	6	6	6	7	7	84
Days With ≥ 0.5" Precipitation	1	2	2	2	3	3	3	3	2	1	2	2	26
Days With ≥ 1.0" Precipitation	0	0	0	0	1	1	1	1	0	0	0	0	4
Mean Snowfall (in.)	11.4	8.8	7.8	1.5	trace	trace	trace	trace	trace	0.4	2.4	8.1	40.4
Maximum Snowfall (in.)*	40	24	34	8	3	0	0	0	0	9	30	21	77
Maximum 24-hr. Snowfall (in.)*	12	10	24	5	3	0	0	0	0	7	12	9	24
Maximum Snow Depth (in.)	15	12	25	7	trace	trace	trace	trace	trace	1	7	8	25
Days With ≥ 1.0" Snow Depth	13	10	5	1	0	0	0	0	0	0	1	8	38
Thunderstorm Days*	< 1	< 1	2	3	5	7	7	6	3	1	1	< 1	35
Foggy Days*	14	12	13	11	15	16	18	21	18	15	13	14	180
Predominant Sky Cover*	OVR	OVR	OVR	OVR	OVR	OVR	OVR	OVR	OVR	OVR	OVR	OVR	OVR
Mean Relative Humidity 7am (%)*	76	75	76	73	76	79	82	85	85	81	78	77	79
Mean Relative Humidity 4pm (%)*	64	60	54	49	50	51	53	54	54	53	60	65	55
Mean Dewpoint (°F)*	18	20	27	36	46	56	60	60	53	41	32	23	40
Prevailing Wind Direction*	WSW	WSW	WSW	WSW	WSW	WSW	WSW	WSW	WSW	WSW	WSW	WSW	WSW
Prevailing Wind Speed (mph)*	14	13	14	14	12	10	9	9	10	12	13	14	12
Maximum Wind Gust (mph)*	68	78	76	74	61	71	83	89	62	77	71	62	89

Note: (*) Period of record is 1948-1995

Wilkes-Barre Scranton Airport

The Wilkes-Barre Scranton National Weather Service Office is located about midway between the two cities, at the southwest end of the crescent-shaped Lackawanna River Valley. The river flows through this valley and empties into the Susquehanna River and the Wyoming Valley a few miles west of the airport. The surrounding mountains protect both cities and the airport from high winds. They influence the temperature and precipitation during both summer and winter, causing wide departures in both within a few miles of the station. Because of the proximity of the mountains, the climate is relatively cool in summer with frequent shower and thunderstorm activity, usually of brief duration. The winter temperatures in the valley are not severe.

Although severe snowstorms are infrequent, when they do occur they approach blizzard conditions.

While the incidence of tornadoes is very low, Wilkes-Barre has occasionally been hit with these storms which caused loss of life and great property damage.

The area has felt the effects of tropical storms. Considerable wind damage has occasionally occurred, but the most devastating damage has come from flooding caused by the large amounts of precipitation deposited by the storms.

Wilkes-Barre Scranton Airport *Luzerne County* Elevation: 930 ft. Latitude: 41° 20' N Longitude: 75° 44' W

	JAN	FEB	MAR	APR	MAY	JUN	JUL	AUG	SEP	OCT	NOV	DEC	YEAR
Mean Maximum Temp. (°F)	33.7	37.1	46.3	59.2	70.1	77.9	82.1	80.5	72.6	61.0	49.6	37.9	59.0
Mean Temp. (°F)	26.4	29.2	37.2	49.0	59.1	67.5	71.9	70.4	62.7	51.4	41.7	31.1	49.8
Mean Minimum Temp. (°F)	19.2	21.2	28.1	38.7	48.2	56.9	61.5	60.3	52.7	41.7	33.8	24.3	40.5
Extreme Maximum Temp. (°F)	67	71	85	93	93	95	101	98	95	87	80	71	101
Extreme Minimum Temp. (°F)	-21	-6	-3	14	29	35	44	38	29	22	9	-9	-21
Days Maximum Temp. ≥ 90°F	0	0	0	0	0	2	4	3	1	0	0	0	10
Days Maximum Temp. ≤ 32°F	14	10	3	0	0	0	0	0	0	0	1	9	37
Days Minimum Temp. ≤ 32°F	27	24	21	7	1	0	0	0	0	4	14	25	123
Days Minimum Temp. ≤ 0°F	2	0	0	0	0	0	0	0	0	0	0	1	3
Heating Degree Days (base 65°F)	1,188	1,007	855	481	210	47	7	15	123	420	692	1,044	6,089
Cooling Degree Days (base 65°F)	0	0	1	6	35	127	226	189	60	6	0	0	650
Mean Precipitation (in.)	2.33	2.05	2.56	3.32	3.53	4.06	3.83	3.41	3.97	3.25	3.15	2.59	38.05
Maximum Precipitation (in.)*	6.5	8.1	4.8	9.6	8.0	7.6	7.3	11.8	8.1	8.1	7.7	6.6	50.8
Minimum Precipitation (in.)*	0.4	0.2	0.5	1.0	0.8	0.3	1.0	0.7	0.8	trace	0.8	0.3	26.2
Extreme Maximum Daily Precip. (in.)	2.06	2.86	2.22	2.83	1.92	2.85	2.82	3.69	5.98	4.01	3.37	2.16	5.98
Days With ≥ 0.1" Precipitation	5	5	7	7	8	8	7	7	6	5	6	6	77
Days With ≥ 0.5" Precipitation	1	1	2	2	2	2	3	2	2	2	2	2	23
Days With ≥ 1.0" Precipitation	0	0	0	1	1	1	1	1	1	1	1	0	8
Mean Snowfall (in.)	na	na	na	na	na	na	na	na	na	na	na	na	na
Maximum Snowfall (in.)*	42	22	32	27	2	0	0	0	trace	4	23	34	82
Maximum 24-hr. Snowfall (in.)*	18	13	19	9	2	0	0	0	trace	4	19	12	19
Maximum Snow Depth (in.)	na	na	na	na	na	na	na	na	na	na	na	na	na
Days With ≥ 1.0" Snow Depth	na	na	na	na	na	na	na	na	na	na	na	na	na
Thunderstorm Days*	< 1	< 1	1	2	4	6	7	5	3	1	< 1	< 1	29
Foggy Days*	12	9	11	9	11	12	14	15	15	12	11	12	143
Predominant Sky Cover*	OVR	OVR	OVR	OVR	OVR	OVR	OVR	OVR	OVR	OVR	OVR	OVR	OVR
Mean Relative Humidity 7am (%)*	76	75	74	72	76	81	83	86	87	84	79	78	79
Mean Relative Humidity 4pm (%)*	64	60	55	50	50	53	54	56	58	56	63	66	57
Mean Dewpoint (°F)*	17	18	25	34	45	56	60	60	53	42	32	22	39
Prevailing Wind Direction*	SW	SW	NW	SW	SW	SW	SW	SW	SW	SW	SW	SW	SW
Prevailing Wind Speed (mph)*	10	10	12	10	10	9	9	8	9	9	9	9	9
Maximum Wind Gust (mph)*	74	59	56	64	64	58	58	51	52	58	61	64	74

Note: (*) Period of record is 1949-1995

The period of record for National Weather Service station data is 1980 – 2009 except where noted. See User Guide for detailed explanation of data.

Williamsport Airport

The climate of the Lycoming valley is favorably influenced by the lower elevation of the area compared to the surrounding terrain. Since the prevailing winds reach the area from the southwest to the north, there is a slight moderating effect on winter extremes of cold. Radiation cooling on clear nights is somewhat more frequent than in adjacent areas. Deep valley fogs occasionally persist until nearly midday. Cold air drainage from the surrounding hills is experienced during several nights but the cool temperatures are often modified by the proximity of the river and adjacent damp areas. The winters are milder than those experienced to the west and cold spells are frequently interrupted by incursions of warmer coastal weather. In summer the air frequently becomes trapped in the valley and higher temperatures and humidities result, generally benefitting the local agriculture.

The long irregular range south of the river forms an effective barrier to free air movement. Moderate or strong south to southwest winds are deflected to southeast or south winds in crossing the range and the air becomes quite turbulent with distinct wave effects. Banner clouds with one to three rolls are frequently observed with low overcasts.

An average growing season of 168 days extends from April 29 to October 14. Snowfall in the valley is generally uniform but varies considerably with the rise in terrain. Snow depth on the ridge two miles south of the observation point is frequently double the amount at the station.

Williamsport Airport *Lycoming County* Elevation: 520 ft. Latitude: 41° 15' N Longitude: 76° 55' W

	JAN	FEB	MAR	APR	MAY	JUN	JUL	AUG	SEP	OCT	NOV	DEC	YEAR
Mean Maximum Temp. (°F)	34.7	38.6	48.2	61.3	72.1	80.1	84.2	82.4	74.1	62.4	50.3	38.7	60.6
Mean Temp. (°F)	27.0	30.0	38.3	50.1	60.0	68.8	73.0	71.6	63.7	52.0	41.8	31.4	50.6
Mean Minimum Temp. (°F)	19.3	21.2	28.3	38.9	47.8	57.3	61.9	60.7	53.1	41.5	33.2	24.1	40.6
Extreme Maximum Temp. (°F)	65	71	87	94	96	97	103	99	96	90	81	70	103
Extreme Minimum Temp. (°F)	-20	-8	-2	15	28	36	46	39	32	21	13	-13	-20
Days Maximum Temp. ≥ 90°F	0	0	0	0	1	3	6	4	1	0	0	0	15
Days Maximum Temp. ≤ 32°F	12	7	2	0	0	0	0	0	0	0	0	8	29
Days Minimum Temp. ≤ 32°F	28	24	21	7	1	0	0	0	0	4	14	25	124
Days Minimum Temp. ≤ 0°F	2	1	0	0	0	0	0	0	0	0	0	1	4
Heating Degree Days (base 65°F)	1,170	985	821	445	190	33	3	10	102	402	690	1,034	5,885
Cooling Degree Days (base 65°F)	0	0	0	6	42	152	259	221	69	6	0	0	755
Mean Precipitation (in.)	2.58	2.32	3.08	3.39	3.62	3.92	4.26	3.79	4.03	3.40	3.68	2.84	40.91
Maximum Precipitation (in.)*	8.3	8.4	6.0	7.5	7.3	16.8	9.6	7.7	10.0	9.6	8.1	7.4	61.3
Minimum Precipitation (in.)*	0.5	0.3	0.8	0.7	0.8	0.7	1.0	0.9	0.5	0.2	0.8	0.7	31.1
Extreme Maximum Daily Precip. (in.)	2.62	2.21	1.93	2.36	1.81	2.75	3.29	4.32	6.29	2.95	3.68	3.29	6.29
Days With ≥ 0.1" Precipitation	5	5	7	7	8	8	7	6	6	6	6	6	77
Days With ≥ 0.5" Precipitation	2	2	2	2	3	3	3	3	2	2	2	2	28
Days With ≥ 1.0" Precipitation	0	0	1	1	1	1	1	1	1	1	1	1	10
Mean Snowfall (in.)	11.1	8.1	7.1	1.1	trace	trace	trace	trace	0.0	0.1	2.1	7.0	36.6
Maximum Snowfall (in.)*	40	34	30	14	trace	0	0	0	0	1	14	36	77
Maximum 24-hr. Snowfall (in.)*	20	20	15	9	trace	0	0	0	0	1	11	15	20
Maximum Snow Depth (in.)	***26***	***16***	na	na	na	na	na	***trace***	na	na	na	na	na
Days With ≥ 1.0" Snow Depth	***13***	***11***	na	na	na	na	na	***0***	na	na	na	na	na
Thunderstorm Days*	< 1	< 1	1	2	5	7	8	6	3	1	1	< 1	34
Foggy Days*	14	12	14	13	16	19	21	24	23	20	16	15	207
Predominant Sky Cover*	OVR	OVR	OVR	OVR	OVR	OVR	OVR	OVR	OVR	OVR	OVR	OVR	OVR
Mean Relative Humidity 7am (%)*	76	76	76	75	80	84	87	90	92	88	81	78	82
Mean Relative Humidity 4pm (%)*	60	56	51	47	49	52	53	55	57	55	61	63	55
Mean Dewpoint (°F)*	18	19	25	35	47	57	62	61	55	43	33	22	40
Prevailing Wind Direction*	W	WNW	WNW	W	W	W	W	W	W	W	W	W	W
Prevailing Wind Speed (mph)*	13	13	13	12	9	9	8	8	8	9	12	12	10
Maximum Wind Gust (mph)*	59	55	60	60	55	79	58	61	54	47	63	64	79

Note: (*) Period of record is 1948-1995

Altoona 3 W *Blair County* Elevation: 1,319 ft. Latitude: 40° 30' N Longitude: 78° 28' W

	JAN	FEB	MAR	APR	MAY	JUN	JUL	AUG	SEP	OCT	NOV	DEC	YEAR
Mean Maximum Temp. (°F)	33.0	36.4	45.2	58.4	68.3	76.8	80.7	79.6	72.0	60.6	49.0	37.2	58.1
Mean Temp. (°F)	25.6	28.2	36.1	48.3	57.9	66.5	70.6	69.4	62.2	50.7	41.0	30.2	48.9
Mean Minimum Temp. (°F)	18.1	19.9	27.1	38.1	47.4	56.1	60.5	59.2	52.3	40.8	32.9	23.0	39.6
Extreme Maximum Temp. (°F)	67	71	83	89	90	92	99	98	92	85	80	72	99
Extreme Minimum Temp. (°F)	-20	-8	-3	11	30	34	44	34	33	20	11	-11	-20
Days Maximum Temp. ≥ 90°F	0	0	0	0	0	1	2	2	0	0	0	0	5
Days Maximum Temp. ≤ 32°F	15	10	4	0	0	0	0	0	0	0	1	10	40
Days Minimum Temp. ≤ 32°F	28	25	22	8	1	0	0	0	0	5	15	27	131
Days Minimum Temp. ≤ 0°F	2	1	0	0	0	0	0	0	0	0	0	1	4
Heating Degree Days (base 65°F)	1,215	1,033	888	500	242	56	10	20	127	440	714	1,073	6,318
Cooling Degree Days (base 65°F)	0	0	1	6	28	107	191	166	50	5	0	0	554
Mean Precipitation (in.)	2.61	2.47	3.56	3.60	4.46	4.04	3.86	3.58	3.79	3.49	4.01	3.06	42.53
Extreme Maximum Daily Precip. (in.)	2.35	1.58	2.46	1.61	2.78	3.27	3.00	2.80	3.83	3.32	4.49	2.04	4.49
Days With ≥ 0.1" Precipitation	6	6	8	8	9	8	7	6	6	6	7	7	84
Days With ≥ 0.5" Precipitation	2	2	2	3	3	3	3	3	2	2	2	2	29
Days With ≥ 1.0" Precipitation	0	0	1	1	1	1	1	1	1	1	1	0	9
Mean Snowfall (in.)	10.6	8.3	6.9	0.9	trace	0.0	0.0	0.0	0.0	trace	1.4	6.9	35.0
Maximum Snow Depth (in.)	22	16	30	6	trace	0	0	0	0	1	14	13	30
Days With ≥ 1.0" Snow Depth	13	11	7	1	0	0	0	0	0	0	1	8	41

Altoona Blair Co Arpt *Blair County* Elevation: 1,479 ft. Latitude: 40° 18' N Longitude: 78° 19' W

	JAN	FEB	MAR	APR	MAY	JUN	JUL	AUG	SEP	OCT	NOV	DEC	YEAR
Mean Maximum Temp. (°F)	34.3	38.2	46.5	59.7	69.3	77.7	81.8	80.2	72.8	61.4	49.9	38.1	59.2
Mean Temp. (°F)	27.5	30.4	37.7	49.4	58.7	67.4	71.5	69.9	62.6	51.7	42.0	31.3	50.0
Mean Minimum Temp. (°F)	20.6	22.6	28.8	39.0	48.2	57.2	61.2	59.5	52.3	41.9	34.0	24.4	40.8
Extreme Maximum Temp. (°F)	68	74	85	88	92	94	100	96	94	82	77	74	100
Extreme Minimum Temp. (°F)	-25	-9	1	12	27	35	44	36	31	21	11	-11	-25
Days Maximum Temp. ≥ 90°F	0	0	0	0	0	1	4	2	0	0	0	0	7
Days Maximum Temp. ≤ 32°F	14	9	4	0	0	0	0	0	0	0	1	10	38
Days Minimum Temp. ≤ 32°F	27	24	20	7	1	0	0	0	0	4	13	25	121
Days Minimum Temp. ≤ 0°F	1	0	0	0	0	0	0	0	0	0	0	0	1
Heating Degree Days (base 65°F)	1,154	972	843	467	220	49	6	19	127	412	683	1,039	5,991
Cooling Degree Days (base 65°F)	0	0	2	6	32	129	216	178	61	7	0	0	631
Mean Precipitation (in.)	2.19	2.09	3.11	3.28	3.67	3.35	3.33	2.91	3.42	2.49	3.31	2.16	35.31
Extreme Maximum Daily Precip. (in.)	1.94	2.34	1.64	2.56	2.37	2.10	2.66	2.19	5.55	2.08	5.03	1.65	5.55
Days With ≥ 0.1" Precipitation	5	5	7	7	8	7	7	6	6	5	6	5	74
Days With ≥ 0.5" Precipitation	1	1	2	2	2	2	2	2	2	2	2	1	21
Days With ≥ 1.0" Precipitation	0	0	1	1	1	1	1	1	1	1	1	0	9
Mean Snowfall (in.)	na	na	na	na	na	na	na	na	na	na	na	na	na
Maximum Snow Depth (in.)	na	na	na	na	na	na	na	na	na	na	na	na	na
Days With ≥ 1.0" Snow Depth	na	na	na	na	na	na	na	na	na	na	na	na	na

Blue Marsh Lake *Berks County* Elevation: 350 ft. Latitude: 40° 23' N Longitude: 76° 02' W

	JAN	FEB	MAR	APR	MAY	JUN	JUL	AUG	SEP	OCT	NOV	DEC	YEAR
Mean Maximum Temp. (°F)	***36.0***	39.4	47.7	60.4	70.6	79.8	84.4	82.9	75.4	63.8	***52.0***	***40.9***	***61.1***
Mean Temp. (°F)	***27.8***	30.1	38.2	49.5	59.5	68.8	73.7	72.2	64.2	***52.4***	***42.7***	***32.9***	***51.0***
Mean Minimum Temp. (°F)	***19.4***	20.7	28.6	38.4	48.4	57.7	62.8	61.5	53.0	***41.3***	***33.3***	24.7	***40.8***
Extreme Maximum Temp. (°F)	70	74	85	90	95	97	102	101	97	91	79	73	102
Extreme Minimum Temp. (°F)	-17	-12	0	15	29	35	46	40	30	21	14	-2	-17
Days Maximum Temp. ≥ 90°F	0	0	0	0	0	3	6	4	1	0	0	0	14
Days Maximum Temp. ≤ 32°F	11	7	2	0	0	0	0	0	0	0	0	6	26
Days Minimum Temp. ≤ 32°F	26	23	20	7	1	0	0	0	0	5	14	24	120
Days Minimum Temp. ≤ 0°F	1	0	0	0	0	0	0	0	0	0	0	0	1
Heating Degree Days (base 65°F)	***1,147***	981	829	463	201	36	4	9	99	***392***	***664***	***987***	***5,812***
Cooling Degree Days (base 65°F)	***0***	0	0	5	39	157	279	241	82	***8***	***0***	***0***	***811***
Mean Precipitation (in.)	3.03	2.50	3.62	3.91	4.09	4.52	4.45	3.79	4.39	3.66	3.73	3.68	45.37
Extreme Maximum Daily Precip. (in.)	na	na	na	na	na	***3.63***	na	***4.00***	***4.69***	na	na	na	na
Days With ≥ 0.1" Precipitation	4	4	5	5	6	6	6	5	5	4	4	5	59
Days With ≥ 0.5" Precipitation	2	1	2	2	2	3	3	2	2	1	2	2	24
Days With ≥ 1.0" Precipitation	0	0	1	1	1	1	1	1	1	1	1	1	10
Mean Snowfall (in.)	7.0	6.2	3.6	0.5	0.0	0.0	0.0	0.0	0.0	0.0	0.5	3.3	21.1
Maximum Snow Depth (in.)	38	25	17	5	0	0	0	0	0	0	4	11	38
Days With ≥ 1.0" Snow Depth	8	7	3	0	0	0	0	0	0	0	0	3	21

Bradford 4 SW Res 5 *Mckean County* Elevation: 1,691 ft. Latitude: 41° 54' N Longitude: 78° 43' W

	JAN	FEB	MAR	APR	MAY	JUN	JUL	AUG	SEP	OCT	NOV	DEC	YEAR
Mean Maximum Temp. (°F)	30.3	33.1	41.9	55.6	67.0	75.0	78.6	77.1	70.1	58.2	46.2	34.3	55.6
Mean Temp. (°F)	21.2	23.0	31.2	43.8	54.0	62.6	66.4	65.1	58.1	46.8	37.3	26.2	44.6
Mean Minimum Temp. (°F)	12.1	12.8	20.5	32.0	41.0	50.2	54.1	53.1	46.0	35.3	28.3	18.0	33.6
Extreme Maximum Temp. (°F)	64	66	83	87	90	91	98	93	91	83	75	68	98
Extreme Minimum Temp. (°F)	-26	-18	-22	8	21	28	35	28	28	14	1	-22	-26
Days Maximum Temp. ≥ 90°F	0	0	0	0	0	0	1	0	0	0	0	0	1
Days Maximum Temp. ≤ 32°F	18	14	8	1	0	0	0	0	0	0	3	14	58
Days Minimum Temp. ≤ 32°F	29	27	27	17	6	0	0	0	2	13	22	29	172
Days Minimum Temp. ≤ 0°F	6	5	2	0	0	0	0	0	0	0	0	3	16
Heating Degree Days (base 65°F)	1,352	1,182	1,040	631	346	121	48	65	220	559	825	1,197	7,586
Cooling Degree Days (base 65°F)	0	0	0	2	12	56	97	75	19	1	0	0	262
Mean Precipitation (in.)	3.14	2.51	3.42	3.76	4.32	5.29	4.94	4.58	4.38	4.04	4.04	3.71	48.13
Extreme Maximum Daily Precip. (in.)	1.66	1.78	2.00	1.63	2.60	3.20	3.12	4.18	4.02	2.50	2.20	1.56	4.18
Days With ≥ 0.1" Precipitation	9	7	8	9	9	9	9	8	8	9	10	11	106
Days With ≥ 0.5" Precipitation	2	1	2	3	3	4	4	3	3	3	2	2	32
Days With ≥ 1.0" Precipitation	0	0	0	0	1	1	1	1	1	1	1	0	7
Mean Snowfall (in.)	18.0	13.5	10.8	2.2	0.1	0.0	0.0	0.0	0.0	0.5	7.5	19.5	72.1
Maximum Snow Depth (in.)	23	31	25	6	1	0	0	0	0	4	20	35	35
Days With ≥ 1.0" Snow Depth	25	23	16	2	0	0	0	0	0	0	5	19	90

The period of record for all cooperative weather station data is 1980 – 2009. See User Guide for detailed explanation of data.

Bucksville *Bucks County* Elevation: 459 ft. Latitude: 40° 30' N Longitude: 75° 12' W

	JAN	FEB	MAR	APR	MAY	JUN	JUL	AUG	SEP	OCT	NOV	DEC	YEAR
Mean Maximum Temp. (°F)	37.5	40.9	49.5	62.4	72.0	80.0	84.2	***82.1***	***75.2***	***64.3***	***53.5***	42.3	***62.0***
Mean Temp. (°F)	28.3	30.9	38.6	50.2	59.9	68.7	73.2	***71.5***	***64.1***	***52.6***	***43.0***	33.2	***51.2***
Mean Minimum Temp. (°F)	19.0	20.9	27.6	38.0	47.8	57.4	62.1	***60.7***	***52.9***	***41.0***	***32.5***	24.0	***40.3***
Extreme Maximum Temp. (°F)	69	74	88	94	94	96	100	100	***98***	87	***80***	***75***	***100***
Extreme Minimum Temp. (°F)	-23	-19	-3	15	27	36	44	39	***31***	21	***11***	***-9***	***-23***
Days Maximum Temp. ≥ 90°F	0	0	0	0	1	3	6	4	***1***	0	***0***	0	***15***
Days Maximum Temp. ≤ 32°F	10	6	1	0	0	0	0	0	***0***	0	***0***	4	***21***
Days Minimum Temp. ≤ 32°F	28	24	22	8	1	0	0	0	***0***	6	***16***	25	***130***
Days Minimum Temp. ≤ 0°F	2	1	0	0	0	0	0	0	***0***	0	***0***	0	***3***
Heating Degree Days (base 65°F)	1,131	958	814	442	193	34	3	***10***	***96***	***383***	***653***	980	***5,697***
Cooling Degree Days (base 65°F)	0	0	0	6	42	151	262	***217***	***76***	***8***	***0***	0	***762***
Mean Precipitation (in.)	3.52	2.86	3.96	4.42	4.19	4.34	5.27	4.04	***4.65***	4.35	***3.83***	4.29	***49.72***
Extreme Maximum Daily Precip. (in.)	2.63	***3.15***	***2.30***	***4.73***	***3.21***	3.88	***3.44***	***4.63***	***5.55***	na	***3.61***	***4.38***	na
Days With ≥ 0.1" Precipitation	6	5	6	6	7	7	7	5	***5***	5	***5***	6	***70***
Days With ≥ 0.5" Precipitation	3	2	3	3	3	3	4	3	***3***	2	***3***	3	***35***
Days With ≥ 1.0" Precipitation	1	1	1	1	1	1	2	1	***1***	1	***1***	1	***13***
Mean Snowfall (in.)	7.7	7.1	4.8	1.5	0.0	trace	0.0	0.0	***0.0***	trace	***0.6***	3.3	***25.0***
Maximum Snow Depth (in.)	26	24	18	10	0	trace	0	0	***0***	***trace***	***5***	***14***	***26***
Days With ≥ 1.0" Snow Depth	10	10	4	0	0	0	0	0	***0***	***0***	***0***	5	***29***

Butler 2 SW *Butler County* Elevation: 1,000 ft. Latitude: 40° 51' N Longitude: 79° 55' W

	JAN	FEB	MAR	APR	MAY	JUN	JUL	AUG	SEP	OCT	NOV	DEC	YEAR
Mean Maximum Temp. (°F)	35.3	38.4	47.2	60.6	70.4	78.8	82.5	81.7	74.6	62.5	50.9	39.2	60.2
Mean Temp. (°F)	26.8	29.0	36.6	48.1	57.5	66.4	70.5	69.6	62.3	50.8	41.3	31.1	49.2
Mean Minimum Temp. (°F)	18.4	19.4	26.0	35.5	44.7	54.0	58.4	57.5	50.0	39.0	31.7	23.0	38.1
Extreme Maximum Temp. (°F)	69	75	84	90	91	97	102	100	94	87	79	74	102
Extreme Minimum Temp. (°F)	-20	-14	-7	9	25	33	39	32	31	17	10	-14	-20
Days Maximum Temp. ≥ 90°F	0	0	0	0	0	2	4	3	1	0	0	0	10
Days Maximum Temp. ≤ 32°F	13	9	4	0	0	0	0	0	0	0	1	8	35
Days Minimum Temp. ≤ 32°F	27	25	23	12	2	0	0	0	0	7	17	26	139
Days Minimum Temp. ≤ 0°F	3	2	0	0	0	0	0	0	0	0	0	1	6
Heating Degree Days (base 65°F)	1,176	1,013	873	505	249	61	12	19	128	438	704	1,044	6,222
Cooling Degree Days (base 65°F)	0	0	0	4	25	111	188	170	54	4	0	0	556
Mean Precipitation (in.)	2.83	2.44	3.25	3.41	4.11	3.96	4.41	3.84	3.74	2.77	3.50	3.11	41.37
Extreme Maximum Daily Precip. (in.)	1.83	1.67	1.98	1.80	3.32	2.30	2.94	3.95	4.72	2.73	2.02	1.93	4.72
Days With ≥ 0.1" Precipitation	7	6	8	8	9	8	8	7	7	7	8	7	90
Days With ≥ 0.5" Precipitation	1	1	2	2	3	3	3	3	2	2	2	2	26
Days With ≥ 1.0" Precipitation	0	0	0	1	1	1	1	1	1	0	1	0	7
Mean Snowfall (in.)	11.7	8.0	5.4	0.8	trace	0.0	0.0	0.0	0.0	0.1	1.1	7.0	34.1
Maximum Snow Depth (in.)	22	17	15	5	trace	0	0	0	0	1	5	12	22
Days With ≥ 1.0" Snow Depth	16	13	6	1	0	0	0	0	0	0	2	10	48

Chalk Hill 2 ENE *Fayette County* Elevation: 1,979 ft. Latitude: 39° 51' N Longitude: 79° 35' W

	JAN	FEB	MAR	APR	MAY	JUN	JUL	AUG	SEP	OCT	NOV	DEC	YEAR
Mean Maximum Temp. (°F)	34.8	38.7	47.8	60.7	68.8	75.1	78.0	76.7	70.2	60.4	49.5	38.5	58.3
Mean Temp. (°F)	27.0	29.7	37.7	48.9	57.4	65.0	68.6	67.4	60.7	50.2	40.7	30.8	48.7
Mean Minimum Temp. (°F)	19.2	20.7	27.6	37.1	45.9	54.8	59.2	58.1	51.1	40.0	31.8	23.1	39.1
Extreme Maximum Temp. (°F)	70	72	83	87	89	88	94	91	87	80	77	73	94
Extreme Minimum Temp. (°F)	-27	-15	-12	7	25	31	37	32	29	18	2	-17	-27
Days Maximum Temp. ≥ 90°F	0	0	0	0	0	0	0	0	0	0	0	0	0
Days Maximum Temp. ≤ 32°F	14	9	4	0	0	0	0	0	0	0	2	10	39
Days Minimum Temp. ≤ 32°F	27	24	21	11	2	0	0	0	0	7	16	25	133
Days Minimum Temp. ≤ 0°F	3	2	0	0	0	0	0	0	0	0	0	1	6
Heating Degree Days (base 65°F)	1,170	991	840	480	246	69	20	32	155	453	723	1,052	6,231
Cooling Degree Days (base 65°F)	0	0	1	3	16	74	139	113	32	2	0	0	380
Mean Precipitation (in.)	4.21	3.66	4.75	4.95	5.36	5.06	5.35	4.30	4.38	3.60	4.44	4.18	54.24
Extreme Maximum Daily Precip. (in.)	2.24	2.08	2.19	2.10	2.08	2.36	3.19	4.64	2.88	2.35	2.90	2.08	4.64
Days With ≥ 0.1" Precipitation	10	9	10	11	11	10	9	8	8	7	9	10	112
Days With ≥ 0.5" Precipitation	3	2	3	3	4	3	4	3	3	3	3	3	37
Days With ≥ 1.0" Precipitation	1	1	1	1	1	1	1	1	1	1	1	1	12
Mean Snowfall (in.)	26.0	18.1	14.8	5.0	0.1	0.0	0.0	0.0	0.0	0.7	6.4	16.6	87.7
Maximum Snow Depth (in.)	28	38	29	12	trace	0	0	0	0	5	22	24	38
Days With ≥ 1.0" Snow Depth	22	20	11	2	0	0	0	0	0	0	5	16	76

Clarion 3 SW *Clarion County* Elevation: 1,040 ft. Latitude: 41° 12' N Longitude: 79° 26' W

	JAN	FEB	MAR	APR	MAY	JUN	JUL	AUG	SEP	OCT	NOV	DEC	YEAR
Mean Maximum Temp. (°F)	33.7	37.0	47.0	60.7	71.5	79.4	82.9	81.7	74.2	61.8	48.9	36.9	59.6
Mean Temp. (°F)	25.3	27.2	35.5	47.4	57.7	66.1	70.1	69.1	61.9	50.1	39.8	29.3	48.3
Mean Minimum Temp. (°F)	16.9	17.4	23.9	34.1	43.8	52.7	57.2	56.4	49.5	38.4	30.6	21.6	36.9
Extreme Maximum Temp. (°F)	69	72	84	90	93	99	100	98	93	86	78	70	100
Extreme Minimum Temp. (°F)	-23	-16	-12	10	21	27	37	31	26	19	9	-14	-23
Days Maximum Temp. ≥ 90°F	0	0	0	0	1	2	4	3	0	0	0	0	10
Days Maximum Temp. ≤ 32°F	14	10	4	0	0	0	0	0	0	0	2	10	40
Days Minimum Temp. ≤ 32°F	28	26	25	14	3	0	0	0	1	9	18	27	151
Days Minimum Temp. ≤ 0°F	3	2	1	0	0	0	0	0	0	0	0	1	7
Heating Degree Days (base 65°F)	1,225	1,062	910	524	247	66	15	21	135	459	750	1,100	6,514
Cooling Degree Days (base 65°F)	0	0	0	2	26	104	178	153	48	3	0	0	514
Mean Precipitation (in.)	3.02	2.50	3.16	3.69	4.16	4.99	5.01	4.53	4.54	3.29	4.04	3.38	46.31
Extreme Maximum Daily Precip. (in.)	1.60	1.60	2.26	2.60	2.15	2.52	4.95	2.39	4.10	2.18	2.17	1.69	4.95
Days With ≥ 0.1" Precipitation	8	7	8	9	9	9	8	8	7	8	8	8	97
Days With ≥ 0.5" Precipitation	2	1	2	2	3	4	4	3	3	2	3	2	31
Days With ≥ 1.0" Precipitation	0	0	0	1	1	1	2	1	1	0	1	0	8
Mean Snowfall (in.)	10.2	7.5	5.1	0.8	0.0	0.0	0.0	0.0	0.0	trace	1.5	7.3	32.4
Maximum Snow Depth (in.)	21	15	12	4	0	0	0	0	0	1	6	16	21
Days With ≥ 1.0" Snow Depth	18	16	8	1	0	0	0	0	0	0	2	11	56

The period of record for all cooperative weather station data is 1980 – 2009. See User Guide for detailed explanation of data.

Coatesville 2 W *Chester County* Elevation: 640 ft. Latitude: 39° 59' N Longitude: 75° 52' W

	JAN	FEB	MAR	APR	MAY	JUN	JUL	AUG	SEP	OCT	NOV	DEC	YEAR
Mean Maximum Temp. (°F)	38.2	41.0	50.2	61.8	71.9	80.6	84.7	83.2	75.3	64.6	53.5	42.1	62.2
Mean Temp. (°F)	29.9	31.9	40.0	50.5	60.4	69.4	74.0	72.7	64.5	53.7	43.6	33.7	52.0
Mean Minimum Temp. (°F)	21.5	22.7	29.7	39.2	48.9	58.2	63.3	62.1	53.7	42.6	33.7	25.2	41.7
Extreme Maximum Temp. (°F)	71	74	88	92	94	96	100	100	96	89	80	75	100
Extreme Minimum Temp. (°F)	-14	-5	-4	21	29	36	45	39	34	21	10	-3	-14
Days Maximum Temp. ≥ 90°F	0	0	0	0	1	3	7	4	1	0	0	0	16
Days Maximum Temp. ≤ 32°F	9	6	1	0	0	0	0	0	0	0	0	5	21
Days Minimum Temp. ≤ 32°F	27	24	20	6	0	0	0	0	0	4	15	25	121
Days Minimum Temp. ≤ 0°F	1	0	0	0	0	0	0	0	0	0	0	0	1
Heating Degree Days (base 65°F)	1,083	930	770	434	182	27	2	7	92	357	635	963	5,482
Cooling Degree Days (base 65°F)	0	0	1	7	46	168	288	252	84	12	0	0	858
Mean Precipitation (in.)	4.12	3.19	4.71	4.14	4.44	3.93	4.75	4.00	5.07	4.24	4.21	4.07	50.87
Extreme Maximum Daily Precip. (in.)	2.41	1.82	3.60	3.19	3.05	3.12	2.77	3.58	7.85	6.62	2.84	3.27	7.85
Days With ≥ 0.1" Precipitation	7	6	7	7	8	7	7	6	6	6	7	7	81
Days With ≥ 0.5" Precipitation	3	2	3	3	3	3	3	3	3	3	3	3	35
Days With ≥ 1.0" Precipitation	1	1	1	1	1	1	1	1	2	1	1	1	13
Mean Snowfall (in.)	10.8	10.2	5.2	1.4	0.0	trace	0.0	0.0	0.0	trace	1.0	4.3	32.9
Maximum Snow Depth (in.)	29	21	15	5	0	trace	0	0	0	trace	4	12	29
Days With ≥ 1.0" Snow Depth	12	11	4	0	0	0	0	0	0	0	1	6	34

Derry 4 SW *Westmoreland County* Elevation: 1,060 ft. Latitude: 40° 18' N Longitude: 79° 20' W

	JAN	FEB	MAR	APR	MAY	JUN	JUL	AUG	SEP	OCT	NOV	DEC	YEAR
Mean Maximum Temp. (°F)	37.2	40.1	49.1	61.6	71.4	79.5	83.4	82.1	75.4	64.0	52.2	40.6	61.4
Mean Temp. (°F)	28.5	30.7	38.2	49.2	58.9	67.6	71.8	70.6	63.6	52.3	42.4	32.4	50.5
Mean Minimum Temp. (°F)	19.8	21.3	27.2	36.7	46.4	55.7	60.1	59.1	51.8	40.5	32.6	24.1	39.6
Extreme Maximum Temp. (°F)	72	76	84	90	93	96	102	98	93	88	83	76	102
Extreme Minimum Temp. (°F)	-29	-18	-10	6	21	32	36	32	24	17	7	-14	-29
Days Maximum Temp. ≥ 90°F	0	0	0	0	0	2	5	3	1	0	0	0	11
Days Maximum Temp. ≤ 32°F	11	7	3	0	0	0	0	0	0	0	1	8	30
Days Minimum Temp. ≤ 32°F	26	24	21	11	2	0	0	0	1	6	15	24	130
Days Minimum Temp. ≤ 0°F	3	1	0	0	0	0	0	0	0	0	0	1	5
Heating Degree Days (base 65°F)	1,124	965	827	474	220	49	7	15	109	396	671	1,005	5,862
Cooling Degree Days (base 65°F)	0	0	2	6	36	135	230	197	74	8	0	0	688
Mean Precipitation (in.)	3.62	3.05	4.09	4.32	4.83	4.76	4.99	4.29	4.39	3.06	4.36	3.57	49.33
Extreme Maximum Daily Precip. (in.)	2.34	2.10	2.10	2.04	2.00	2.30	4.15	3.58	5.51	2.07	2.15	2.10	5.51
Days With ≥ 0.1" Precipitation	10	9	11	11	11	10	9	8	8	8	10	10	115
Days With ≥ 0.5" Precipitation	2	1	3	3	4	3	3	3	3	2	3	2	32
Days With ≥ 1.0" Precipitation	0	0	1	1	1	1	1	1	1	0	1	0	8
Mean Snowfall (in.)	14.4	9.7	7.9	1.2	trace	0.0	0.0	0.0	0.0	0.2	2.1	9.3	44.8
Maximum Snow Depth (in.)	21	20	19	3	trace	0	0	0	0	2	12	26	26
Days With ≥ 1.0" Snow Depth	14	11	5	1	0	0	0	0	0	0	2	9	42

Donora 1 SW *Washington County* Elevation: 762 ft. Latitude: 40° 10' N Longitude: 79° 52' W

	JAN	FEB	MAR	APR	MAY	JUN	JUL	AUG	SEP	OCT	NOV	DEC	YEAR
Mean Maximum Temp. (°F)	39.6	43.2	52.4	64.7	74.0	81.8	85.1	84.3	78.0	66.7	54.9	43.3	64.0
Mean Temp. (°F)	30.9	33.5	41.3	52.3	61.5	70.0	74.0	73.1	66.4	54.8	44.8	34.6	53.1
Mean Minimum Temp. (°F)	22.1	23.6	30.2	39.6	49.0	58.1	62.8	61.8	54.7	42.9	34.6	25.8	42.1
Extreme Maximum Temp. (°F)	74	78	85	92	93	99	102	98	95	89	82	77	102
Extreme Minimum Temp. (°F)	-19	-5	0	12	26	37	40	41	34	21	12	-11	-19
Days Maximum Temp. ≥ 90°F	0	0	0	0	1	3	6	5	1	0	0	0	16
Days Maximum Temp. ≤ 32°F	9	5	1	0	0	0	0	0	0	0	0	6	21
Days Minimum Temp. ≤ 32°F	26	23	19	7	1	0	0	0	0	3	13	24	116
Days Minimum Temp. ≤ 0°F	1	0	0	0	0	0	0	0	0	0	0	0	1
Heating Degree Days (base 65°F)	1,051	886	728	384	157	24	1	4	63	323	601	936	5,158
Cooling Degree Days (base 65°F)	0	0	1	10	55	180	287	261	112	14	0	0	920
Mean Precipitation (in.)	2.52	2.16	3.21	3.20	4.06	3.89	3.89	3.45	2.91	2.50	3.14	2.65	37.58
Extreme Maximum Daily Precip. (in.)	2.00	1.55	1.80	1.94	2.10	1.92	3.45	3.72	4.36	1.52	1.95	2.00	4.36
Days With ≥ 0.1" Precipitation	6	5	8	8	9	8	8	6	6	6	7	7	84
Days With ≥ 0.5" Precipitation	1	1	2	2	3	3	3	2	2	2	2	1	24
Days With ≥ 1.0" Precipitation	0	0	1	0	1	1	1	1	1	0	1	0	7
Mean Snowfall (in.)	6.1	3.1	3.4	0.2	0.0	0.0	0.0	0.0	0.0	trace	0.6	3.6	17.0
Maximum Snow Depth (in.)	24	14	20	1	0	0	0	0	0	0	3	10	24
Days With ≥ 1.0" Snow Depth	8	4	2	0	0	0	0	0	0	0	1	5	20

Francis E Walter Dam *Luzerne County* Elevation: 1,507 ft. Latitude: 41° 07' N Longitude: 75° 44' W

	JAN	FEB	MAR	APR	MAY	JUN	JUL	AUG	SEP	OCT	NOV	DEC	YEAR
Mean Maximum Temp. (°F)	na	35.2	43.5	56.4	67.7	75.5	79.3	78.7	70.3	59.1	na	na	na
Mean Temp. (°F)	na	24.8	32.6	44.3	55.1	63.3	67.3	66.3	58.1	47.0	na	na	na
Mean Minimum Temp. (°F)	na	14.5	21.7	32.2	42.5	51.0	55.1	54.0	45.8	34.9	na	na	na
Extreme Maximum Temp. (°F)	67	69	84	90	91	95	95	98	91	86	77	66	98
Extreme Minimum Temp. (°F)	-26	-15	-8	5	24	29	35	32	23	12	4	-22	-26
Days Maximum Temp. ≥ 90°F	0	0	0	0	0	1	1	1	0	0	0	0	3
Days Maximum Temp. ≤ 32°F	13	10	5	0	0	0	0	0	0	0	2	10	40
Days Minimum Temp. ≤ 32°F	25	23	24	15	4	0	0	0	2	13	18	24	148
Days Minimum Temp. ≤ 0°F	4	3	1	0	0	0	0	0	0	0	0	2	10
Heating Degree Days (base 65°F)	na	1,130	995	617	312	110	39	54	222	550	na	na	na
Cooling Degree Days (base 65°F)	na	0	0	2	13	65	116	99	21	0	na	na	na
Mean Precipitation (in.)	2.89	2.44	3.14	4.02	4.34	5.02	4.68	4.37	4.67	4.08	3.88	3.32	46.85
Extreme Maximum Daily Precip. (in.)	na	2.16	na	na	3.16	3.35	2.89	3.00	5.44	2.55	na	na	na
Days With ≥ 0.1" Precipitation	4	5	6	7	7	8	7	7	6	6	5	5	73
Days With ≥ 0.5" Precipitation	1	1	2	2	3	3	3	3	3	2	2	2	27
Days With ≥ 1.0" Precipitation	0	0	0	1	1	1	1	1	1	1	1	1	9
Mean Snowfall (in.)	12.9	9.3	8.9	3.6	0.0	0.0	0.0	0.0	0.0	0.4	2.1	7.9	45.1
Maximum Snow Depth (in.)	33	28	50	15	0	0	0	0	0	5	7	14	50
Days With ≥ 1.0" Snow Depth	18	16	10	2	0	0	0	0	0	0	2	10	58

The period of record for all cooperative weather station data is 1980 – 2009. See User Guide for detailed explanation of data.

Graterford 1 E *Montgomery County* Elevation: 240 ft. Latitude: 40° 14' N Longitude: 75° 26' W

	JAN	FEB	MAR	APR	MAY	JUN	JUL	AUG	SEP	OCT	NOV	DEC	YEAR
Mean Maximum Temp. (°F)	38.2	41.3	49.5	61.4	71.2	80.5	85.2	***83.5***	76.7	65.8	54.7	43.3	***62.6***
Mean Temp. (°F)	28.5	31.2	38.6	49.5	59.2	68.8	73.6	***71.3***	63.8	***52.2***	***43.7***	32.9	***51.1***
Mean Minimum Temp. (°F)	19.0	21.1	28.2	37.6	47.1	57.1	61.8	***59.0***	50.8	***38.7***	***32.3***	22.6	***39.6***
Extreme Maximum Temp. (°F)	72	71	87	93	94	99	103	***101***	99	91	82	75	***103***
Extreme Minimum Temp. (°F)	-17	-9	2	13	21	28	41	***28***	22	***10***	8	-3	***-17***
Days Maximum Temp. ≥ 90°F	0	0	0	0	1	4	8	***5***	1	0	0	0	***19***
Days Maximum Temp. ≤ 32°F	9	5	1	0	0	0	0	0	0	0	0	4	19
Days Minimum Temp. ≤ 32°F	29	24	22	8	1	0	0	***0***	1	***9***	***16***	26	***136***
Days Minimum Temp. ≤ 0°F	1	0	0	0	0	0	0	***0***	0	***0***	0	0	***1***
Heating Degree Days (base 65°F)	1,123	947	812	465	210	42	4	***17***	108	***401***	***633***	987	***5,749***
Cooling Degree Days (base 65°F)	0	0	1	6	37	163	276	***217***	77	***11***	***1***	0	***789***
Mean Precipitation (in.)	3.01	2.13	3.49	3.97	4.08	3.93	4.38	4.19	4.52	3.81	3.72	3.55	44.78
Extreme Maximum Daily Precip. (in.)	2.14	2.29	3.23	4.00	3.64	3.59	3.19	***4.09***	5.90	3.40	2.50	3.05	***5.90***
Days With ≥ 0.1" Precipitation	5	4	6	7	7	7	7	***7***	5	6	6	6	***73***
Days With ≥ 0.5" Precipitation	2	1	2	3	3	3	3	***3***	3	3	3	3	***32***
Days With ≥ 1.0" Precipitation	1	0	1	1	1	1	1	***1***	1	1	1	1	***11***
Mean Snowfall (in.)	***2.9***	4.3	0.9	0.3	0.0	0.0	0.0	0.0	0.0	0.0	0.2	1.9	***10.5***
Maximum Snow Depth (in.)	***9***	***25***	***8***	3	***0***	***0***	***0***	***0***	***0***	***0***	***5***	***8***	***25***
Days With ≥ 1.0" Snow Depth	***1***	***0***	0	0	0	0	0	0	0	0	0	0	***1***

Hamburg *Berks County* Elevation: 350 ft. Latitude: 40° 33' N Longitude: 75° 59' W

	JAN	FEB	MAR	APR	MAY	JUN	JUL	AUG	SEP	OCT	NOV	DEC	YEAR
Mean Maximum Temp. (°F)	36.7	40.4	49.3	61.8	72.1	80.6	84.7	83.1	75.3	64.0	52.5	40.6	61.8
Mean Temp. (°F)	28.1	31.1	39.5	50.7	60.8	69.7	74.1	72.6	64.6	52.6	43.1	32.3	51.6
Mean Minimum Temp. (°F)	19.5	21.8	29.6	39.6	49.3	58.8	63.4	62.0	53.8	41.1	33.6	23.9	41.4
Extreme Maximum Temp. (°F)	69	75	88	95	96	97	103	100	96	89	80	75	103
Extreme Minimum Temp. (°F)	-19	-4	3	15	31	39	41	41	34	22	14	-6	-19
Days Maximum Temp. ≥ 90°F	0	0	0	0	1	3	7	5	1	0	0	0	17
Days Maximum Temp. ≤ 32°F	10	6	1	0	0	0	0	0	0	0	0	6	23
Days Minimum Temp. ≤ 32°F	28	25	19	5	0	0	0	0	0	4	15	27	123
Days Minimum Temp. ≤ 0°F	1	0	0	0	0	0	0	0	0	0	0	0	1
Heating Degree Days (base 65°F)	1,136	952	785	428	172	26	2	6	87	385	651	1,006	5,636
Cooling Degree Days (base 65°F)	0	0	1	7	47	174	290	249	81	8	0	0	857
Mean Precipitation (in.)	2.97	2.61	3.47	3.66	4.38	4.84	4.51	3.95	4.50	3.76	3.83	3.60	46.08
Extreme Maximum Daily Precip. (in.)	1.80	1.92	2.88	3.87	4.21	3.69	3.02	4.00	3.73	3.11	3.67	3.14	4.21
Days With ≥ 0.1" Precipitation	6	5	7	7	8	8	7	7	6	6	6	6	79
Days With ≥ 0.5" Precipitation	2	2	2	2	3	3	3	2	3	2	3	2	29
Days With ≥ 1.0" Precipitation	1	1	1	1	1	1	1	1	1	1	1	1	12
Mean Snowfall (in.)	6.6	5.7	3.1	0.5	0.0	0.0	0.0	0.0	0.0	0.0	0.4	3.0	19.3
Maximum Snow Depth (in.)	24	19	16	4	0	0	0	0	0	0	2	9	24
Days With ≥ 1.0" Snow Depth	10	7	3	0	0	0	0	0	0	0	0	5	25

Lancaster 2 NE Filt Plant *Lancaster County* Elevation: 270 ft. Latitude: 40° 03' N Longitude: 76° 17' W

	JAN	FEB	MAR	APR	MAY	JUN	JUL	AUG	SEP	OCT	NOV	DEC	YEAR
Mean Maximum Temp. (°F)	38.4	41.8	50.8	62.9	72.9	81.2	85.3	83.9	76.5	65.1	53.9	42.6	63.0
Mean Temp. (°F)	30.4	33.0	40.9	51.9	61.5	70.4	74.9	73.4	65.9	54.3	44.4	34.6	53.0
Mean Minimum Temp. (°F)	22.3	24.1	31.0	40.7	50.1	59.6	64.3	62.9	55.2	43.4	34.8	26.5	42.9
Extreme Maximum Temp. (°F)	70	76	88	93	94	96	102	101	99	91	82	76	102
Extreme Minimum Temp. (°F)	-16	-7	-2	16	32	36	46	37	34	23	12	-3	-16
Days Maximum Temp. ≥ 90°F	0	0	0	0	1	4	7	5	1	0	0	0	18
Days Maximum Temp. ≤ 32°F	9	5	1	0	0	0	0	0	0	0	0	5	20
Days Minimum Temp. ≤ 32°F	27	23	18	5	0	0	0	0	0	3	13	24	113
Days Minimum Temp. ≤ 0°F	1	0	0	0	0	0	0	0	0	0	0	0	1
Heating Degree Days (base 65°F)	1,067	899	740	395	153	21	1	5	69	339	612	936	5,237
Cooling Degree Days (base 65°F)	0	0	1	8	53	190	314	272	102	12	0	0	952
Mean Precipitation (in.)	2.87	2.40	3.38	3.42	3.93	4.09	4.35	3.20	4.42	3.90	3.55	3.20	42.71
Extreme Maximum Daily Precip. (in.)	1.80	1.88	3.24	2.45	2.80	2.74	4.54	2.24	6.11	5.60	2.75	2.60	6.11
Days With ≥ 0.1" Precipitation	6	6	7	7	8	7	7	6	6	6	6	6	78
Days With ≥ 0.5" Precipitation	2	1	2	2	3	3	3	2	3	2	3	2	28
Days With ≥ 1.0" Precipitation	0	0	1	1	1	1	1	1	1	1	1	1	10
Mean Snowfall (in.)	6.5	6.1	2.1	0.4	0.0	0.0	0.0	0.0	0.0	0.0	0.4	2.9	18.4
Maximum Snow Depth (in.)	26	24	13	2	0	0	0	0	0	0	3	14	26
Days With ≥ 1.0" Snow Depth	6	6	2	0	0	0	0	0	0	0	0	3	17

Landisville 2 NW *Lancaster County* Elevation: 359 ft. Latitude: 40° 07' N Longitude: 76° 26' W

	JAN	FEB	MAR	APR	MAY	JUN	JUL	AUG	SEP	OCT	NOV	DEC	YEAR
Mean Maximum Temp. (°F)	38.6	42.4	51.8	64.3	74.3	82.5	86.1	84.9	77.8	66.4	54.5	42.6	63.9
Mean Temp. (°F)	29.9	32.7	40.8	51.8	61.9	70.6	74.3	72.9	65.4	54.2	44.3	34.0	52.7
Mean Minimum Temp. (°F)	21.1	22.9	29.8	39.3	49.4	58.8	62.3	60.8	53.1	41.8	34.1	25.4	41.6
Extreme Maximum Temp. (°F)	69	77	86	91	94	98	102	102	97	91	81	76	102
Extreme Minimum Temp. (°F)	-24	-16	-4	18	30	34	42	35	31	21	11	-8	-24
Days Maximum Temp. ≥ 90°F	0	0	0	0	1	4	8	6	2	0	0	0	21
Days Maximum Temp. ≤ 32°F	8	4	1	0	0	0	0	0	0	0	0	5	18
Days Minimum Temp. ≤ 32°F	26	23	19	7	0	0	0	0	0	6	14	24	119
Days Minimum Temp. ≤ 0°F	1	1	0	0	0	0	0	0	0	0	0	0	2
Heating Degree Days (base 65°F)	1,082	907	742	397	147	18	2	7	77	343	613	953	5,288
Cooling Degree Days (base 65°F)	0	0	1	8	56	194	296	258	97	14	0	0	924
Mean Precipitation (in.)	2.77	2.38	3.36	3.52	4.08	4.10	4.55	3.59	4.17	3.60	3.68	3.06	42.86
Extreme Maximum Daily Precip. (in.)	1.80	2.60	1.75	2.15	3.10	3.04	4.37	3.38	4.64	4.10	3.00	1.86	4.64
Days With ≥ 0.1" Precipitation	6	5	7	7	8	7	7	6	6	6	6	6	77
Days With ≥ 0.5" Precipitation	2	2	3	3	3	3	3	2	3	2	3	2	31
Days With ≥ 1.0" Precipitation	1	0	1	1	1	1	1	1	1	1	1	1	11
Mean Snowfall (in.)	8.0	7.5	3.8	0.5	0.0	0.0	0.0	0.0	0.0	0.0	0.6	3.9	24.3
Maximum Snow Depth (in.)	27	21	16	4	0	0	0	0	0	0	4	9	27
Days With ≥ 1.0" Snow Depth	9	8	3	0	0	0	0	0	0	0	0	5	25

The period of record for all cooperative weather station data is 1980 – 2009. See User Guide for detailed explanation of data.

Laurelton Center *Union County* Elevation: 799 ft. Latitude: 40° 54' N Longitude: 77° 13' W

	JAN	FEB	MAR	APR	MAY	JUN	JUL	AUG	SEP	OCT	NOV	DEC	YEAR
Mean Maximum Temp. (°F)	36.9	41.8	51.2	65.4	75.5	82.7	86.5	84.8	76.5	65.4	52.7	40.1	63.3
Mean Temp. (°F)	27.7	31.3	39.0	51.2	61.1	69.1	73.4	71.9	64.1	52.7	42.3	31.4	51.3
Mean Minimum Temp. (°F)	18.4	20.8	26.7	36.9	46.6	55.4	60.2	58.9	51.6	40.1	31.7	22.6	39.2
Extreme Maximum Temp. (°F)	67	76	89	94	98	100	105	99	97	87	81	74	105
Extreme Minimum Temp. (°F)	-22	-6	-8	15	26	33	42	33	30	20	12	-11	-22
Days Maximum Temp. ≥ 90°F	0	0	0	0	2	5	10	6	1	0	0	0	24
Days Maximum Temp. ≤ 32°F	10	4	1	0	0	0	0	0	0	0	0	6	21
Days Minimum Temp. ≤ 32°F	29	25	23	10	2	0	0	0	0	7	17	26	139
Days Minimum Temp. ≤ 0°F	2	1	0	0	0	0	0	0	0	0	0	1	4
Heating Degree Days (base 65°F)	1,150	947	801	416	166	28	3	8	97	380	676	1,035	5,707
Cooling Degree Days (base 65°F)	0	0	1	8	51	157	268	229	75	7	0	0	796
Mean Precipitation (in.)	2.81	2.46	3.43	3.85	3.98	4.39	4.14	3.99	4.49	3.41	3.90	2.72	43.57
Extreme Maximum Daily Precip. (in.)	2.82	3.39	2.10	2.15	2.53	2.75	4.40	4.30	5.11	4.13	3.26	1.76	5.11
Days With ≥ 0.1" Precipitation	6	5	7	8	8	8	7	7	7	6	7	6	82
Days With ≥ 0.5" Precipitation	2	2	2	3	3	3	3	3	3	2	3	2	31
Days With ≥ 1.0" Precipitation	1	0	1	1	1	1	1	1	1	1	1	1	11
Mean Snowfall (in.)	9.4	na	4.2	0.9	0.0	0.0	0.0	0.0	0.0	0.1	0.8	na	na
Maximum Snow Depth (in.)	52	24	26	5	0	0	0	0	0	2	6	11	52
Days With ≥ 1.0" Snow Depth	10	7	4	0	0	0	0	0	0	0	1	7	29

Lebanon 2 W *Lebanon County* Elevation: 450 ft. Latitude: 40° 20' N Longitude: 76° 28' W

	JAN	FEB	MAR	APR	MAY	JUN	JUL	AUG	SEP	OCT	NOV	DEC	YEAR
Mean Maximum Temp. (°F)	37.0	40.6	49.6	61.8	71.8	80.2	84.2	82.7	75.3	64.2	52.9	41.3	61.8
Mean Temp. (°F)	28.9	31.7	39.5	50.5	60.2	69.0	73.3	71.7	64.3	53.1	43.2	33.2	51.6
Mean Minimum Temp. (°F)	20.8	22.8	29.4	39.0	48.5	57.8	62.4	60.9	53.3	41.9	33.4	25.0	41.3
Extreme Maximum Temp. (°F)	67	75	84	91	93	96	102	98	98	89	82	75	102
Extreme Minimum Temp. (°F)	-22	-10	-4	18	30	37	44	38	33	21	12	-2	-22
Days Maximum Temp. ≥ 90°F	0	0	0	0	0	3	6	4	1	0	0	0	14
Days Maximum Temp. ≤ 32°F	10	6	1	0	0	0	0	0	0	0	0	6	23
Days Minimum Temp. ≤ 32°F	27	24	20	7	0	0	0	0	0	4	14	25	121
Days Minimum Temp. ≤ 0°F	1	0	0	0	0	0	0	0	0	0	0	0	1
Heating Degree Days (base 65°F)	1,110	935	783	434	183	29	2	9	92	371	647	979	5,574
Cooling Degree Days (base 65°F)	0	0	0	5	40	157	267	225	77	9	0	0	780
Mean Precipitation (in.)	2.73	2.42	3.18	3.74	4.10	4.19	4.51	3.59	3.80	3.45	3.49	3.23	42.43
Extreme Maximum Daily Precip. (in.)	2.00	2.04	2.70	2.10	2.60	4.27	3.33	2.70	5.16	3.68	2.75	2.56	5.16
Days With ≥ 0.1" Precipitation	6	5	6	7	8	7	7	6	6	6	6	6	76
Days With ≥ 0.5" Precipitation	2	2	2	3	3	3	3	2	3	2	2	2	29
Days With ≥ 1.0" Precipitation	1	0	1	1	1	1	1	1	1	1	1	1	11
Mean Snowfall (in.)	7.6	6.3	3.2	0.2	0.0	0.0	0.0	0.0	0.0	trace	0.6	4.0	21.9
Maximum Snow Depth (in.)	30	na	14	3	0	0	0	0	0	trace	1	na	na
Days With ≥ 1.0" Snow Depth	7	6	2	0	0	0	0	0	0	0	0	4	19

Lewistown *Mifflin County* Elevation: 459 ft. Latitude: 40° 35' N Longitude: 77° 34' W

	JAN	FEB	MAR	APR	MAY	JUN	JUL	AUG	SEP	OCT	NOV	DEC	YEAR
Mean Maximum Temp. (°F)	36.5	40.0	49.0	61.9	72.2	80.2	84.4	83.4	75.5	63.9	52.1	40.3	61.6
Mean Temp. (°F)	28.3	30.9	38.7	50.2	60.0	68.6	72.9	71.8	64.2	52.3	42.6	32.4	51.1
Mean Minimum Temp. (°F)	20.1	21.8	28.3	38.5	47.7	56.8	61.4	60.2	52.5	40.7	33.1	24.6	40.5
Extreme Maximum Temp. (°F)	71	76	87	94	96	95	102	98	98	89	80	75	102
Extreme Minimum Temp. (°F)	-17	-6	3	15	28	38	41	35	30	21	11	-6	-17
Days Maximum Temp. ≥ 90°F	0	0	0	0	1	3	6	5	1	0	0	0	16
Days Maximum Temp. ≤ 32°F	10	6	2	0	0	0	0	0	0	0	0	6	24
Days Minimum Temp. ≤ 32°F	28	25	21	7	1	0	0	0	0	5	15	25	127
Days Minimum Temp. ≤ 0°F	1	0	0	0	0	0	0	0	0	0	0	0	1
Heating Degree Days (base 65°F)	1,130	957	810	443	189	33	3	8	92	393	665	1,002	5,725
Cooling Degree Days (base 65°F)	0	0	1	6	40	147	256	227	74	8	0	0	759
Mean Precipitation (in.)	2.59	2.29	3.44	3.44	4.20	4.18	3.96	3.43	3.84	3.29	3.53	2.90	41.09
Extreme Maximum Daily Precip. (in.)	1.60	2.85	3.27	2.35	2.74	2.53	2.65	2.71	5.40	3.70	3.54	1.99	5.40
Days With ≥ 0.1" Precipitation	6	5	7	8	9	8	7	6	6	6	7	6	81
Days With ≥ 0.5" Precipitation	2	2	2	3	3	3	3	2	2	2	2	2	28
Days With ≥ 1.0" Precipitation	0	0	1	0	1	1	1	1	1	1	1	0	8
Mean Snowfall (in.)	9.0	6.3	5.4	0.3	0.0	0.0	0.0	0.0	0.0	trace	0.5	4.6	26.1
Maximum Snow Depth (in.)	33	19	22	2	0	0	0	0	0	1	4	12	33
Days With ≥ 1.0" Snow Depth	11	8	4	0	0	0	0	0	0	0	1	6	30

Marcus Hook *Delaware County* Elevation: 9 ft. Latitude: 39° 49' N Longitude: 75° 25' W

	JAN	FEB	MAR	APR	MAY	JUN	JUL	AUG	SEP	OCT	NOV	DEC	YEAR
Mean Maximum Temp. (°F)	39.9	44.0	51.5	63.7	73.5	82.5	87.1	85.1	77.5	65.4	55.0	44.3	64.1
Mean Temp. (°F)	34.1	37.2	43.9	55.0	64.6	73.8	78.7	77.0	69.6	57.8	48.3	38.4	56.5
Mean Minimum Temp. (°F)	28.2	30.4	36.3	46.3	55.5	65.0	70.2	68.8	61.8	50.2	41.5	32.5	48.9
Extreme Maximum Temp. (°F)	67	71	83	95	97	100	103	100	100	87	77	74	103
Extreme Minimum Temp. (°F)	-4	6	10	20	40	50	58	50	43	34	20	3	-4
Days Maximum Temp. ≥ 90°F	0	0	0	0	1	5	12	7	2	0	0	0	27
Days Maximum Temp. ≤ 32°F	7	3	1	0	0	0	0	0	0	0	0	3	14
Days Minimum Temp. ≤ 32°F	20	17	9	1	0	0	0	0	0	0	4	15	66
Days Minimum Temp. ≤ 0°F	0	0	0	0	0	0	0	0	0	0	0	0	0
Heating Degree Days (base 65°F)	953	779	648	308	97	8	0	1	30	239	496	818	4,377
Cooling Degree Days (base 65°F)	0	0	1	14	90	276	431	379	175	23	1	0	1,390
Mean Precipitation (in.)	2.42	2.26	3.24	3.22	3.66	2.95	4.14	2.81	4.25	3.01	3.09	2.86	37.91
Extreme Maximum Daily Precip. (in.)	1.95	2.63	2.40	2.00	2.50	3.41	7.50	2.78	11.68	4.64	2.68	1.97	11.68
Days With ≥ 0.1" Precipitation	5	4	5	6	6	6	5	4	5	5	6	5	62
Days With ≥ 0.5" Precipitation	2	2	2	2	3	2	2	2	3	2	2	2	26
Days With ≥ 1.0" Precipitation	1	1	1	1	1	1	1	1	1	1	1	1	12
Mean Snowfall (in.)	na	2.7	na	trace	0.0	0.0	0.0	0.0	0.0	0.0	trace	na	na
Maximum Snow Depth (in.)	na	na	na	na	na	na	na	na	na	na	na	na	na
Days With ≥ 1.0" Snow Depth	na	0	na	0	0	0	0	0	0	0	0	0	na

The period of record for all cooperative weather station data is 1980 – 2009. See User Guide for detailed explanation of data.

Mercer *Mercer County* Elevation: 1,220 ft. Latitude: 41° 13' N Longitude: 80° 14' W

	JAN	FEB	MAR	APR	MAY	JUN	JUL	AUG	SEP	OCT	NOV	DEC	YEAR
Mean Maximum Temp. (°F)	34.7	38.4	47.9	60.8	70.3	77.7	81.6	80.5	74.1	62.4	49.9	39.1	59.8
Mean Temp. (°F)	25.6	28.3	36.4	47.9	57.5	65.4	69.4	***67.9***	61.5	50.3	40.4	30.5	***48.4***
Mean Minimum Temp. (°F)	16.4	18.0	24.9	34.9	44.6	53.0	57.1	***55.6***	48.8	38.1	30.7	21.5	***37.0***
Extreme Maximum Temp. (°F)	68	74	82	88	90	94	99	96	93	88	78	73	99
Extreme Minimum Temp. (°F)	-32	-16	-13	11	21	29	36	31	25	17	7	-18	-32
Days Maximum Temp. ≥ 90°F	0	0	0	0	0	1	3	2	0	0	0	0	6
Days Maximum Temp. ≤ 32°F	13	9	3	0	0	0	0	0	0	0	1	8	34
Days Minimum Temp. ≤ 32°F	28	25	24	13	3	0	0	0	1	9	18	25	146
Days Minimum Temp. ≤ 0°F	4	2	1	0	0	0	0	0	0	0	0	1	8
Heating Degree Days (base 65°F)	1,215	1,032	881	511	249	75	21	***32***	147	452	731	1,062	***6,408***
Cooling Degree Days (base 65°F)	0	0	1	4	24	93	165	***129***	48	4	0	0	***468***
Mean Precipitation (in.)	2.89	2.46	3.18	3.63	3.82	4.51	4.67	3.86	4.01	2.92	3.53	3.27	42.75
Extreme Maximum Daily Precip. (in.)	1.90	1.44	1.98	1.58	***2.12***	3.29	***3.42***	***2.84***	4.47	2.03	***2.77***	1.77	***4.47***
Days With ≥ 0.1" Precipitation	7	6	8	8	8	8	7	6	7	6	7	8	86
Days With ≥ 0.5" Precipitation	1	1	2	2	2	3	3	3	2	2	2	2	26
Days With ≥ 1.0" Precipitation	0	0	1	1	1	1	1	1	1	0	0	0	7
Mean Snowfall (in.)	13.3	9.6	7.9	2.3	trace	0.0	0.0	0.0	0.0	0.2	3.6	9.8	46.7
Maximum Snow Depth (in.)	15	12	9	6	trace	0	0	0	0	2	6	14	15
Days With ≥ 1.0" Snow Depth	19	15	8	1	0	0	0	0	0	0	3	11	57

Montgomery Lock & Dam *Beaver County* Elevation: 689 ft. Latitude: 40° 39' N Longitude: 80° 23' W

	JAN	FEB	MAR	APR	MAY	JUN	JUL	AUG	SEP	OCT	NOV	DEC	YEAR
Mean Maximum Temp. (°F)	37.1	40.9	50.2	63.6	72.5	80.4	83.6	82.3	75.8	64.2	52.5	40.8	62.0
Mean Temp. (°F)	29.8	32.3	40.1	51.6	60.8	69.3	73.3	72.1	65.5	54.2	44.0	33.7	52.2
Mean Minimum Temp. (°F)	22.5	23.8	30.0	39.6	49.1	58.0	62.9	61.8	55.2	44.2	35.5	26.5	42.4
Extreme Maximum Temp. (°F)	71	76	82	89	89	98	105	100	93	86	82	74	105
Extreme Minimum Temp. (°F)	-18	-4	-4	14	26	37	45	39	35	25	8	-9	-18
Days Maximum Temp. ≥ 90°F	0	0	0	0	0	2	4	3	0	0	0	0	9
Days Maximum Temp. ≤ 32°F	11	7	2	0	0	0	0	0	0	0	0	6	26
Days Minimum Temp. ≤ 32°F	25	22	19	7	1	0	0	0	0	2	11	22	109
Days Minimum Temp. ≤ 0°F	1	0	0	0	0	0	0	0	0	0	0	0	1
Heating Degree Days (base 65°F)	1,084	917	766	402	165	28	2	6	74	336	623	964	5,367
Cooling Degree Days (base 65°F)	0	0	0	7	43	162	266	232	96	10	0	0	816
Mean Precipitation (in.)	2.53	2.10	2.93	3.24	3.84	3.72	4.38	3.37	3.62	2.36	3.06	2.71	37.86
Extreme Maximum Daily Precip. (in.)	1.96	1.34	1.60	1.78	1.94	2.40	4.99	3.27	8.74	2.00	1.93	2.72	8.74
Days With ≥ 0.1" Precipitation	6	6	7	8	8	8	8	6	6	6	7	7	83
Days With ≥ 0.5" Precipitation	1	1	2	2	3	3	3	2	2	1	2	1	23
Days With ≥ 1.0" Precipitation	0	0	0	0	1	1	1	1	1	0	0	0	5
Mean Snowfall (in.)	***4.0***	2.9	2.4	0.2	0.0	0.0	0.0	0.0	0.0	trace	0.2	2.4	***12.1***
Maximum Snow Depth (in.)	13	12	19	4	0	0	0	0	0	0	5	7	19
Days With ≥ 1.0" Snow Depth	9	7	3	0	0	0	0	0	0	0	0	5	24

Montrose *Susquehanna County* Elevation: 1,419 ft. Latitude: 41° 52' N Longitude: 75° 51' W

	JAN	FEB	MAR	APR	MAY	JUN	JUL	AUG	SEP	OCT	NOV	DEC	YEAR
Mean Maximum Temp. (°F)	30.4	33.6	41.9	54.8	66.4	74.9	79.2	77.8	70.4	58.5	46.1	34.7	55.7
Mean Temp. (°F)	21.5	23.8	31.8	43.8	54.6	63.7	67.9	66.4	58.9	47.4	37.3	26.6	45.3
Mean Minimum Temp. (°F)	12.6	14.0	21.7	32.8	42.8	52.4	56.5	55.0	47.3	36.3	28.4	18.5	34.9
Extreme Maximum Temp. (°F)	62	65	83	90	89	95	97	94	92	83	78	66	97
Extreme Minimum Temp. (°F)	-22	-18	-17	7	20	30	38	35	23	17	3	-17	-22
Days Maximum Temp. ≥ 90°F	0	0	0	0	0	0	1	1	0	0	0	0	2
Days Maximum Temp. ≤ 32°F	18	13	6	1	0	0	0	0	0	0	2	13	53
Days Minimum Temp. ≤ 32°F	29	27	26	15	4	0	0	0	1	11	21	29	163
Days Minimum Temp. ≤ 0°F	6	4	1	0	0	0	0	0	0	0	0	2	13
Heating Degree Days (base 65°F)	1,344	1,160	1,025	634	331	103	32	50	206	541	828	1,186	7,440
Cooling Degree Days (base 65°F)	0	0	0	3	13	68	126	99	27	1	0	0	337
Mean Precipitation (in.)	3.10	2.73	3.44	4.11	3.99	4.52	4.27	3.49	3.95	3.92	3.76	3.30	44.58
Extreme Maximum Daily Precip. (in.)	1.69	1.67	2.38	3.85	3.18	6.63	2.10	2.57	5.40	3.58	2.77	2.52	6.63
Days With ≥ 0.1" Precipitation	8	7	8	8	8	9	8	7	6	7	8	8	92
Days With ≥ 0.5" Precipitation	2	2	2	3	3	3	3	2	2	3	2	2	29
Days With ≥ 1.0" Precipitation	0	0	1	1	1	1	1	1	1	1	1	1	10
Mean Snowfall (in.)	21.5	15.5	15.9	5.6	0.1	0.0	0.0	0.0	trace	0.7	7.0	15.5	81.8
Maximum Snow Depth (in.)	40	31	28	13	2	0	0	0	trace	5	21	18	40
Days With ≥ 1.0" Snow Depth	23	22	15	2	0	0	0	0	0	0	4	16	82

Neshaminy Falls *Bucks County* Elevation: 60 ft. Latitude: 40° 09' N Longitude: 74° 57' W

	JAN	FEB	MAR	APR	MAY	JUN	JUL	AUG	SEP	OCT	NOV	DEC	YEAR
Mean Maximum Temp. (°F)	42.0	45.0	52.8	64.2	74.1	83.0	87.2	85.9	79.0	67.4	56.8	45.4	65.2
Mean Temp. (°F)	31.7	33.8	41.0	51.5	61.3	70.8	75.4	74.0	66.8	54.7	45.2	35.1	53.4
Mean Minimum Temp. (°F)	21.2	22.6	29.4	38.9	48.5	58.4	63.5	62.0	54.3	42.0	33.4	24.9	41.6
Extreme Maximum Temp. (°F)	73	73	88	95	96	100	102	102	98	88	82	76	102
Extreme Minimum Temp. (°F)	-11	-3	-1	16	32	34	45	37	30	20	11	-10	-11
Days Maximum Temp. ≥ 90°F	0	0	0	0	2	6	11	9	2	0	0	0	30
Days Maximum Temp. ≤ 32°F	6	3	1	0	0	0	0	0	0	0	0	3	13
Days Minimum Temp. ≤ 32°F	27	24	20	7	0	0	0	0	0	4	15	25	122
Days Minimum Temp. ≤ 0°F	1	0	0	0	0	0	0	0	0	0	0	0	1
Heating Degree Days (base 65°F)	1,026	877	736	407	160	20	1	3	57	324	589	921	5,121
Cooling Degree Days (base 65°F)	0	0	0	8	51	201	330	290	117	12	1	0	1,010
Mean Precipitation (in.)	3.48	2.68	4.27	4.20	4.32	4.51	5.16	4.14	4.53	3.75	3.73	3.87	48.64
Extreme Maximum Daily Precip. (in.)	2.55	1.96	2.27	4.95	2.72	3.94	4.18	3.85	5.83	5.63	2.96	4.20	5.83
Days With ≥ 0.1" Precipitation	7	6	8	7	7	7	7	6	6	6	6	7	80
Days With ≥ 0.5" Precipitation	2	2	3	3	3	3	3	3	3	3	3	3	34
Days With ≥ 1.0" Precipitation	1	1	1	1	1	1	2	1	1	1	1	1	13
Mean Snowfall (in.)	***3.7***	***3.4***	2.1	0.3	0.0	0.0	0.0	0.0	0.0	trace	trace	***2.4***	***11.9***
Maximum Snow Depth (in.)	23	17	9	9	0	0	0	0	0	0	4	***14***	***23***
Days With ≥ 1.0" Snow Depth	***6***	5	2	0	0	0	0	0	0	0	0	***2***	***15***

Octoraro Lake *Lancaster County* Elevation: 259 ft. Latitude: 39° 48' N Longitude: 76° 03' W

	JAN	FEB	MAR	APR	MAY	JUN	JUL	AUG	SEP	OCT	NOV	DEC	YEAR
Mean Maximum Temp. (°F)	40.1	44.1	52.8	65.3	75.1	83.3	87.1	85.6	78.1	66.9	55.2	44.1	64.8
Mean Temp. (°F)	30.2	33.1	41.1	51.6	61.6	70.3	74.6	73.1	65.5	54.2	43.9	34.2	52.8
Mean Minimum Temp. (°F)	20.4	22.1	29.2	38.0	47.9	57.1	61.9	60.5	52.8	41.2	32.5	24.3	40.7
Extreme Maximum Temp. (°F)	72	75	91	95	95	99	103	104	97	88	80	75	104
Extreme Minimum Temp. (°F)	-19	-17	-4	18	24	34	42	36	31	12	11	-4	-19
Days Maximum Temp. ≥ 90°F	0	0	0	0	2	6	11	8	2	0	0	0	29
Days Maximum Temp. ≤ 32°F	7	3	1	0	0	0	0	0	0	0	0	4	15
Days Minimum Temp. ≤ 32°F	27	25	20	9	1	0	0	0	0	6	16	25	129
Days Minimum Temp. ≤ 0°F	1	0	0	0	0	0	0	0	0	0	0	0	1
Heating Degree Days (base 65°F)	1,072	893	734	403	149	21	1	5	74	339	625	946	5,262
Cooling Degree Days (base 65°F)	0	0	0	7	52	187	304	263	96	12	0	0	921
Mean Precipitation (in.)	3.34	2.74	3.94	3.78	4.09	3.87	4.12	3.93	4.76	3.71	3.67	3.65	45.60
Extreme Maximum Daily Precip. (in.)	2.20	2.70	3.95	2.52	2.50	3.80	2.55	3.70	6.82	5.24	3.16	3.49	6.82
Days With ≥ 0.1" Precipitation	7	5	7	7	8	6	7	6	6	5	6	7	77
Days With ≥ 0.5" Precipitation	2	2	3	3	3	3	3	3	3	2	3	3	33
Days With ≥ 1.0" Precipitation	1	1	1	1	1	1	1	1	1	1	1	1	12
Mean Snowfall (in.)	***4.1***	***6.2***	***1.2***	0.2	0.0	0.0	0.0	0.0	0.0	0.0	0.3	2.5	***14.5***
Maximum Snow Depth (in.)	na	na	na	***5***	***0***	***0***	***0***	***0***	***0***	***0***	***1***	na	na
Days With ≥ 1.0" Snow Depth	na	na	***1***	0	0	0	0	0	0	0	0	***2***	na

Phoenixville 1 E *Chester County* Elevation: 104 ft. Latitude: 40° 07' N Longitude: 75° 30' W

	JAN	FEB	MAR	APR	MAY	JUN	JUL	AUG	SEP	OCT	NOV	DEC	YEAR
Mean Maximum Temp. (°F)	***40.7***	***43.5***	***51.9***	63.9	***74.0***	***82.4***	86.1	84.8	77.8	66.5	55.4	43.7	***64.2***
Mean Temp. (°F)	***31.2***	***33.4***	***40.9***	51.9	***61.6***	***70.5***	74.8	73.4	65.9	54.4	44.3	34.2	***53.1***
Mean Minimum Temp. (°F)	***21.7***	***23.2***	***29.9***	39.9	49.2	***58.6***	63.5	61.9	54.0	42.3	33.1	24.7	***41.8***
Extreme Maximum Temp. (°F)	***71***	***75***	***84***	***94***	***96***	***100***	103	***103***	***98***	91	***83***	77	***103***
Extreme Minimum Temp. (°F)	***-13***	***1***	***5***	***19***	***30***	***33***	42	***34***	***32***	21	***8***	-4	***-13***
Days Maximum Temp. ≥ 90°F	***0***	***0***	***0***	0	1	***5***	9	6	2	0	0	0	***23***
Days Maximum Temp. ≤ 32°F	***6***	***3***	***1***	0	0	***0***	0	0	0	0	0	4	***14***
Days Minimum Temp. ≤ 32°F	***27***	***24***	***19***	6	0	***0***	0	0	0	5	15	26	***122***
Days Minimum Temp. ≤ 0°F	***1***	***0***	***0***	0	0	***0***	0	0	0	0	0	0	***1***
Heating Degree Days (base 65°F)	***1,039***	***886***	***739***	396	***156***	***19***	1	6	71	336	616	949	***5,214***
Cooling Degree Days (base 65°F)	***0***	***0***	***0***	10	***57***	***192***	314	275	106	15	1	0	***970***
Mean Precipitation (in.)	***2.97***	***2.46***	3.47	3.66	3.54	***3.67***	4.08	3.38	4.09	3.39	3.60	3.71	***42.02***
Extreme Maximum Daily Precip. (in.)	***1.80***	***2.63***	***2.63***	***3.98***	***3.25***	***2.57***	2.91	***2.33***	***5.13***	4.20	***2.05***	2.47	***5.13***
Days With ≥ 0.1" Precipitation	***6***	***6***	7	6	7	***6***	7	6	5	6	6	6	***74***
Days With ≥ 0.5" Precipitation	***2***	***2***	3	3	2	***2***	3	2	3	2	3	3	***30***
Days With ≥ 1.0" Precipitation	***1***	***0***	1	1	1	***1***	1	1	1	1	1	1	***11***
Mean Snowfall (in.)	na	na	na	0.0	0.0	***0.0***	0.0	0.0	0.0	0.0	***0.0***	***trace***	na
Maximum Snow Depth (in.)	na	na	na	***0***	***0***	na	***0***	***0***	***0***	***0***	na	na	na
Days With ≥ 1.0" Snow Depth	na	na	na	0	0	***0***	0	0	0	0	***0***	***0***	na

Pleasant Mount 1 W *Wayne County* Elevation: 1,798 ft. Latitude: 41° 44' N Longitude: 75° 27' W

	JAN	FEB	MAR	APR	MAY	JUN	JUL	AUG	SEP	OCT	NOV	DEC	YEAR
Mean Maximum Temp. (°F)	28.8	32.1	39.7	52.9	64.3	72.3	76.6	75.5	68.0	56.6	44.8	33.2	53.7
Mean Temp. (°F)	20.2	22.5	29.9	42.4	53.2	61.9	66.1	65.0	57.3	46.1	36.3	25.4	43.9
Mean Minimum Temp. (°F)	11.5	12.9	20.1	31.8	42.1	51.5	55.6	54.4	46.7	35.6	27.8	17.5	34.0
Extreme Maximum Temp. (°F)	61	67	79	86	89	90	95	92	88	82	75	65	95
Extreme Minimum Temp. (°F)	-25	-16	-14	4	19	30	39	33	25	15	3	-24	-25
Days Maximum Temp. ≥ 90°F	0	0	0	0	0	0	0	0	0	0	0	0	0
Days Maximum Temp. ≤ 32°F	20	15	9	1	0	0	0	0	0	0	3	15	63
Days Minimum Temp. ≤ 32°F	30	27	28	17	4	0	0	0	1	13	22	29	171
Days Minimum Temp. ≤ 0°F	6	4	1	0	0	0	0	0	0	0	0	3	14
Heating Degree Days (base 65°F)	1,384	1,194	1,081	672	366	132	48	67	240	579	854	1,223	7,840
Cooling Degree Days (base 65°F)	0	0	0	1	8	47	89	74	17	1	0	0	237
Mean Precipitation (in.)	3.20	2.66	3.35	4.21	4.66	4.98	4.55	4.05	4.77	4.54	4.11	3.62	48.70
Extreme Maximum Daily Precip. (in.)	2.01	1.82	1.88	3.72	2.73	5.22	2.98	2.50	4.75	3.31	3.20	3.53	5.22
Days With ≥ 0.1" Precipitation	7	6	7	9	9	9	8	8	7	7	7	7	91
Days With ≥ 0.5" Precipitation	2	2	2	3	3	3	3	3	3	3	3	2	32
Days With ≥ 1.0" Precipitation	0	0	1	1	1	1	1	1	1	1	1	1	10
Mean Snowfall (in.)	18.9	13.6	11.7	3.3	trace	0.0	0.0	0.0	0.0	0.3	4.5	13.4	65.7
Maximum Snow Depth (in.)	51	39	40	12	trace	0	0	0	0	6	18	24	51
Days With ≥ 1.0" Snow Depth	25	24	18	3	0	0	0	0	0	0	4	17	91

Raystown Lake 2 *Huntingdon County* Elevation: 839 ft. Latitude: 40° 26' N Longitude: 78° 00' W

	JAN	FEB	MAR	APR	MAY	JUN	JUL	AUG	SEP	OCT	NOV	DEC	YEAR
Mean Maximum Temp. (°F)	36.3	39.5	48.0	60.8	70.8	79.5	83.8	82.7	75.2	63.4	51.7	40.5	61.0
Mean Temp. (°F)	28.1	30.2	37.6	49.4	59.0	67.9	72.5	71.3	63.9	52.4	42.5	32.7	50.6
Mean Minimum Temp. (°F)	19.9	20.9	27.3	38.0	47.2	56.2	61.2	59.8	52.6	41.3	33.2	24.9	40.2
Extreme Maximum Temp. (°F)	70	79	84	91	93	97	104	99	96	89	82	74	104
Extreme Minimum Temp. (°F)	-15	-3	1	15	29	36	42	37	29	20	14	-7	-15
Days Maximum Temp. ≥ 90°F	0	0	0	0	0	2	6	4	1	0	0	0	13
Days Maximum Temp. ≤ 32°F	11	7	3	0	0	0	0	0	0	0	1	7	29
Days Minimum Temp. ≤ 32°F	27	24	22	8	1	0	0	0	0	5	14	25	126
Days Minimum Temp. ≤ 0°F	1	0	0	0	0	0	0	0	0	0	0	0	1
Heating Degree Days (base 65°F)	1,137	978	842	468	212	43	4	10	99	392	669	994	5,848
Cooling Degree Days (base 65°F)	0	0	1	6	33	134	242	212	73	9	0	0	710
Mean Precipitation (in.)	2.46	2.10	3.11	3.48	3.99	3.72	3.38	3.34	3.31	3.13	3.35	2.66	38.03
Extreme Maximum Daily Precip. (in.)	2.73	1.96	2.06	1.76	3.02	2.27	2.58	3.17	4.55	3.72	3.42	2.62	4.55
Days With ≥ 0.1" Precipitation	5	5	6	7	8	8	6	6	6	5	6	5	73
Days With ≥ 0.5" Precipitation	1	1	2	2	3	2	2	2	2	2	2	2	23
Days With ≥ 1.0" Precipitation	0	0	0	0	1	1	1	1	1	1	1	0	7
Mean Snowfall (in.)	***6.3***	***6.7***	3.5	0.6	0.0	0.0	0.0	0.0	0.0	trace	0.9	3.7	***21.7***
Maximum Snow Depth (in.)	***20***	na	***15***	***2***	***0***	***0***	***0***	***0***	***0***	***0***	***5***	na	na
Days With ≥ 1.0" Snow Depth	***6***	na	2	0	0	0	0	0	0	0	0	***4***	na

The period of record for all cooperative weather station data is 1980 – 2009. See User Guide for detailed explanation of data.

Reading 4 NNW *Berks County* Elevation: 359 ft. Latitude: 40° 25' N Longitude: 75° 56' W

	JAN	FEB	MAR	APR	MAY	JUN	JUL	AUG	SEP	OCT	NOV	DEC	YEAR
Mean Maximum Temp. (°F)	37.8	41.2	50.0	62.0	72.8	81.0	85.4	84.0	76.7	65.5	53.9	42.2	62.7
Mean Temp. (°F)	29.4	32.2	40.2	51.1	61.6	70.3	75.0	73.5	65.8	54.3	44.6	34.1	52.7
Mean Minimum Temp. (°F)	21.1	23.1	30.3	40.1	50.4	59.6	64.5	63.0	54.8	43.0	35.1	25.9	42.6
Extreme Maximum Temp. (°F)	71	77	88	93	96	97	102	102	100	92	82	77	102
Extreme Minimum Temp. (°F)	-20	-5	-2	16	30	39	46	42	34	23	16	-4	-20
Days Maximum Temp. ≥ 90°F	0	0	0	0	1	4	9	6	1	0	0	0	21
Days Maximum Temp. ≤ 32°F	9	5	1	0	0	0	0	0	0	0	0	5	20
Days Minimum Temp. ≤ 32°F	26	23	19	5	0	0	0	0	0	3	12	23	111
Days Minimum Temp. ≤ 0°F	1	0	0	0	0	0	0	0	0	0	0	0	1
Heating Degree Days (base 65°F)	1,096	923	764	418	156	25	2	7	76	342	607	951	5,367
Cooling Degree Days (base 65°F)	0	0	1	8	59	192	318	277	105	16	1	0	977
Mean Precipitation (in.)	2.95	2.66	3.44	3.65	4.04	4.29	4.53	3.54	4.36	3.64	3.52	3.14	43.76
Extreme Maximum Daily Precip. (in.)	3.00	2.55	2.79	2.25	3.77	3.68	4.35	4.08	6.25	4.65	2.85	3.22	6.25
Days With ≥ 0.1" Precipitation	6	5	7	7	8	8	7	6	6	5	6	6	77
Days With ≥ 0.5" Precipitation	2	2	2	2	2	3	3	2	3	3	3	2	29
Days With ≥ 1.0" Precipitation	1	1	1	1	1	1	1	1	1	1	1	1	12
Mean Snowfall (in.)	na	***6.8***	3.6	0.2	0.0	0.0	0.0	0.0	0.0	0.0	0.6	***3.8***	na
Maximum Snow Depth (in.)	na	na	***18***	***trace***	***0***	***0***	***0***	***0***	***0***	***0***	***3***	na	na
Days With ≥ 1.0" Snow Depth	na	***3***	1	0	0	0	0	0	0	0	0	***2***	na

Renovo *Clinton County* Elevation: 660 ft. Latitude: 41° 20' N Longitude: 77° 44' W

	JAN	FEB	MAR	APR	MAY	JUN	JUL	AUG	SEP	OCT	NOV	DEC	YEAR
Mean Maximum Temp. (°F)	34.7	38.5	47.4	60.9	72.0	79.8	83.6	82.4	74.4	62.7	50.3	38.6	60.4
Mean Temp. (°F)	26.5	28.9	36.7	48.5	58.4	67.1	71.3	70.3	62.7	51.2	41.1	31.0	49.5
Mean Minimum Temp. (°F)	18.2	19.3	25.9	36.0	44.8	54.4	59.0	58.2	51.0	39.7	31.7	23.4	38.5
Extreme Maximum Temp. (°F)	68	72	86	92	96	96	103	98	96	88	81	73	103
Extreme Minimum Temp. (°F)	-16	-5	-2	15	25	36	42	40	32	20	11	-9	-16
Days Maximum Temp. ≥ 90°F	0	0	0	0	1	3	6	4	1	0	0	0	15
Days Maximum Temp. ≤ 32°F	12	7	2	0	0	0	0	0	0	0	1	7	29
Days Minimum Temp. ≤ 32°F	28	25	23	11	2	0	0	0	0	6	17	26	138
Days Minimum Temp. ≤ 0°F	3	1	0	0	0	0	0	0	0	0	0	1	5
Heating Degree Days (base 65°F)	1,188	1,014	870	493	226	50	7	12	118	424	712	1,046	6,160
Cooling Degree Days (base 65°F)	0	0	0	5	28	120	210	183	57	5	0	0	608
Mean Precipitation (in.)	2.37	2.25	3.11	3.34	3.42	4.30	3.74	3.76	3.80	3.05	3.49	2.72	39.35
Extreme Maximum Daily Precip. (in.)	1.73	2.42	2.12	1.84	2.25	3.30	2.30	3.48	4.57	2.85	3.28	1.87	4.57
Days With ≥ 0.1" Precipitation	6	6	7	8	9	9	7	7	7	6	7	6	85
Days With ≥ 0.5" Precipitation	1	1	2	2	2	3	3	3	3	2	2	2	26
Days With ≥ 1.0" Precipitation	0	0	1	0	0	1	1	1	1	1	1	0	7
Mean Snowfall (in.)	9.7	7.2	5.7	0.5	0.0	0.0	0.0	0.0	0.0	0.1	1.2	6.1	30.5
Maximum Snow Depth (in.)	18	17	24	4	0	0	0	0	0	trace	6	13	24
Days With ≥ 1.0" Snow Depth	16	12	6	0	0	0	0	0	0	0	1	8	43

Salina 3 W *Westmoreland County* Elevation: 1,108 ft. Latitude: 40° 31' N Longitude: 79° 33' W

	JAN	FEB	MAR	APR	MAY	JUN	JUL	AUG	SEP	OCT	NOV	DEC	YEAR
Mean Maximum Temp. (°F)	36.9	40.1	49.1	62.0	71.4	79.7	83.2	82.3	75.7	63.8	52.3	40.8	61.5
Mean Temp. (°F)	27.2	29.5	37.2	48.7	57.8	66.4	70.3	69.1	62.4	51.1	41.7	31.4	49.4
Mean Minimum Temp. (°F)	17.5	18.8	25.4	35.3	44.4	53.0	57.5	56.1	49.3	38.4	31.1	21.9	37.4
Extreme Maximum Temp. (°F)	71	76	83	90	92	96	101	100	95	88	80	74	101
Extreme Minimum Temp. (°F)	-30	-16	-9	12	21	29	36	32	29	17	8	-20	-30
Days Maximum Temp. ≥ 90°F	0	0	0	0	0	2	4	4	1	0	0	0	11
Days Maximum Temp. ≤ 32°F	12	8	3	0	0	0	0	0	0	0	1	7	31
Days Minimum Temp. ≤ 32°F	28	25	24	13	3	0	0	0	1	9	17	26	146
Days Minimum Temp. ≤ 0°F	3	2	0	0	0	0	0	0	0	0	0	1	6
Heating Degree Days (base 65°F)	1,164	999	856	486	243	62	13	22	128	431	691	1,035	6,130
Cooling Degree Days (base 65°F)	0	0	0	5	27	110	184	155	57	6	0	0	544
Mean Precipitation (in.)	2.88	2.41	3.34	3.53	4.16	4.28	4.66	4.04	3.54	2.64	3.67	3.06	42.21
Extreme Maximum Daily Precip. (in.)	2.51	2.22	1.80	1.80	2.02	1.95	4.09	2.25	5.99	2.00	2.07	2.43	5.99
Days With ≥ 0.1" Precipitation	8	6	8	9	9	8	8	7	7	6	8	8	92
Days With ≥ 0.5" Precipitation	1	1	2	2	3	3	3	3	2	2	2	2	26
Days With ≥ 1.0" Precipitation	0	0	1	1	1	1	1	1	1	0	1	0	8
Mean Snowfall (in.)	9.8	6.6	4.6	0.6	0.0	0.0	0.0	0.0	0.0	trace	1.4	5.2	28.2
Maximum Snow Depth (in.)	27	18	16	3	0	0	0	0	0	trace	7	23	27
Days With ≥ 1.0" Snow Depth	13	11	5	0	0	0	0	0	0	0	1	7	37

State College *Centre County* Elevation: 1,169 ft. Latitude: 40° 48' N Longitude: 77° 52' W

	JAN	FEB	MAR	APR	MAY	JUN	JUL	AUG	SEP	OCT	NOV	DEC	YEAR
Mean Maximum Temp. (°F)	34.2	37.5	46.1	59.5	69.7	77.8	81.5	80.2	72.4	60.9	49.7	38.2	59.0
Mean Temp. (°F)	26.7	29.1	36.5	48.9	58.9	67.6	71.5	70.1	62.4	50.9	41.2	31.0	49.6
Mean Minimum Temp. (°F)	19.1	20.6	26.8	38.1	48.0	57.3	61.4	60.0	52.4	40.9	32.8	23.8	40.1
Extreme Maximum Temp. (°F)	67	73	84	90	93	94	102	97	93	86	80	71	102
Extreme Minimum Temp. (°F)	-18	-4	-1	11	29	35	44	36	33	16	10	-11	-18
Days Maximum Temp. ≥ 90°F	0	0	0	0	0	1	3	2	0	0	0	0	6
Days Maximum Temp. ≤ 32°F	13	9	3	0	0	0	0	0	0	0	1	9	35
Days Minimum Temp. ≤ 32°F	27	25	22	8	0	0	0	0	0	5	16	26	129
Days Minimum Temp. ≤ 0°F	2	1	0	0	0	0	0	0	0	0	0	0	3
Heating Degree Days (base 65°F)	1,181	1,008	878	484	219	48	7	17	127	436	706	1,047	6,158
Cooling Degree Days (base 65°F)	0	0	1	7	37	132	216	182	56	6	0	0	637
Mean Precipitation (in.)	2.68	2.49	3.42	3.32	3.42	4.09	3.46	3.84	3.61	3.03	3.37	2.79	39.52
Extreme Maximum Daily Precip. (in.)	1.78	2.38	2.90	2.07	1.64	2.59	1.63	3.66	5.05	3.65	3.25	2.05	5.05
Days With ≥ 0.1" Precipitation	6	6	7	8	8	8	8	6	6	6	6	6	81
Days With ≥ 0.5" Precipitation	1	2	2	2	2	3	2	3	2	2	2	2	25
Days With ≥ 1.0" Precipitation	0	0	1	0	1	1	1	1	1	1	1	0	8
Mean Snowfall (in.)	12.5	10.4	10.2	1.4	trace	0.0	0.0	0.0	0.0	0.4	2.6	7.8	45.3
Maximum Snow Depth (in.)	22	20	31	4	trace	0	0	0	0	3	13	12	31
Days With ≥ 1.0" Snow Depth	15	13	7	0	0	0	0	0	0	0	2	9	46

The period of record for all cooperative weather station data is 1980 – 2009. See User Guide for detailed explanation of data.

Uniontown 1 NE *Fayette County* Elevation: 956 ft. Latitude: 39° 55' N Longitude: 79° 43' W

	JAN	FEB	MAR	APR	MAY	JUN	JUL	AUG	SEP	OCT	NOV	DEC	YEAR
Mean Maximum Temp. (°F)	39.4	42.3	51.1	63.0	72.4	80.4	83.9	82.9	76.6	64.9	53.9	42.8	62.8
Mean Temp. (°F)	30.2	32.1	39.3	49.9	59.4	67.9	72.0	70.9	63.9	52.3	42.9	33.6	51.2
Mean Minimum Temp. (°F)	21.0	21.9	27.4	36.8	46.4	55.4	60.2	58.8	51.3	39.6	31.8	24.3	39.6
Extreme Maximum Temp. (°F)	73	77	84	93	92	96	102	99	94	88	81	77	102
Extreme Minimum Temp. (°F)	-22	-15	-3	15	26	34	37	34	29	16	9	-14	-22
Days Maximum Temp. ≥ 90°F	0	0	0	0	0	2	5	4	1	0	0	0	12
Days Maximum Temp. ≤ 32°F	10	6	2	0	0	0	0	0	0	0	1	7	26
Days Minimum Temp. ≤ 32°F	26	24	21	11	2	0	0	0	0	8	17	24	133
Days Minimum Temp. ≤ 0°F	2	1	0	0	0	0	0	0	0	0	0	1	4
Heating Degree Days (base 65°F)	1,071	924	792	453	204	44	6	13	102	396	658	967	5,630
Cooling Degree Days (base 65°F)	0	0	1	7	38	138	232	203	76	8	0	0	703
Mean Precipitation (in.)	3.04	2.73	3.74	3.65	4.50	4.34	4.68	3.73	3.42	2.95	3.67	3.05	43.50
Extreme Maximum Daily Precip. (in.)	1.77	1.68	2.75	2.04	2.65	2.75	3.82	2.70	2.38	1.82	3.23	1.64	3.82
Days With ≥ 0.1" Precipitation	8	7	8	9	10	9	8	7	7	7	8	8	96
Days With ≥ 0.5" Precipitation	2	2	2	2	3	3	3	3	2	2	2	2	28
Days With ≥ 1.0" Precipitation	0	0	1	0	1	1	1	1	1	1	1	0	8
Mean Snowfall (in.)	***8.9***	***5.3***	4.7	0.4	trace	0.0	0.0	0.0	0.0	trace	0.9	4.3	***24.5***
Maximum Snow Depth (in.)	***20***	***15***	***19***	***1***	trace	***0***	0	0	***0***	***1***	***6***	***16***	***20***
Days With ≥ 1.0" Snow Depth	***9***	5	***3***	0	0	0	0	0	0	0	1	***6***	***24***

Washington 3 NE *Washington County* Elevation: 1,299 ft. Latitude: 40° 11' N Longitude: 80° 11' W

	JAN	FEB	MAR	APR	MAY	JUN	JUL	AUG	SEP	OCT	NOV	DEC	YEAR
Mean Maximum Temp. (°F)	36.3	39.1	48.7	60.8	69.8	78.1	81.8	81.1	74.1	62.4	51.3	39.6	60.3
Mean Temp. (°F)	28.2	30.3	38.5	49.8	58.8	67.3	71.3	70.3	63.2	51.9	42.6	31.9	50.3
Mean Minimum Temp. (°F)	20.1	21.6	28.5	38.7	47.8	56.5	60.9	59.4	52.2	41.3	33.8	24.2	40.4
Extreme Maximum Temp. (°F)	70	75	82	87	90	***93***	100	***99***	95	87	80	82	***100***
Extreme Minimum Temp. (°F)	-25	-8	0	10	20	***34***	40	***29***	30	20	10	-16	***-25***
Days Maximum Temp. ≥ 90°F	0	0	0	0	0	1	3	3	0	0	0	0	7
Days Maximum Temp. ≤ 32°F	13	9	4	0	0	0	0	0	0	0	2	9	37
Days Minimum Temp. ≤ 32°F	27	24	20	9	1	0	0	0	0	5	15	25	126
Days Minimum Temp. ≤ 0°F	2	1	0	0	0	0	0	0	0	0	0	1	4
Heating Degree Days (base 65°F)	1,133	973	817	461	223	52	8	16	113	410	668	1,019	5,893
Cooling Degree Days (base 65°F)	0	0	2	10	38	129	213	186	65	10	0	0	653
Mean Precipitation (in.)	3.00	2.31	3.31	3.03	4.25	3.94	3.89	3.18	3.35	2.40	3.49	2.95	39.10
Extreme Maximum Daily Precip. (in.)	1.92	1.86	1.60	1.35	2.14	***2.20***	3.93	***2.60***	5.18	***1.24***	2.11	2.30	***5.18***
Days With ≥ 0.1" Precipitation	7	6	7	8	9	8	7	6	6	6	8	7	85
Days With ≥ 0.5" Precipitation	2	1	2	2	3	2	3	2	2	1	2	2	24
Days With ≥ 1.0" Precipitation	1	0	1	0	1	1	1	1	1	0	1	0	8
Mean Snowfall (in.)	8.5	5.4	4.8	0.9	trace	0.0	0.0	0.0	0.0	trace	1.4	5.1	26.1
Maximum Snow Depth (in.)	20	***16***	26	9	trace	0	0	***0***	0	***trace***	7	10	***26***
Days With ≥ 1.0" Snow Depth	12	10	5	1	0	0	0	0	0	0	1	8	37

York 3 SSW Pump Stn *York County* Elevation: 390 ft. Latitude: 39° 55' N Longitude: 76° 45' W

	JAN	FEB	MAR	APR	MAY	JUN	JUL	AUG	SEP	OCT	NOV	DEC	YEAR
Mean Maximum Temp. (°F)	40.5	44.7	54.1	66.2	75.8	83.6	87.3	85.7	78.7	67.8	55.6	44.0	65.3
Mean Temp. (°F)	31.1	34.2	42.2	52.9	62.4	71.0	75.2	73.6	66.5	55.2	44.9	34.9	53.7
Mean Minimum Temp. (°F)	21.7	23.7	30.4	39.6	49.0	58.4	62.9	61.5	54.2	42.5	34.1	25.8	42.0
Extreme Maximum Temp. (°F)	73	78	88	93	98	98	102	101	98	92	85	77	102
Extreme Minimum Temp. (°F)	-21	-14	-3	17	29	35	43	35	33	19	12	-3	-21
Days Maximum Temp. ≥ 90°F	0	0	0	0	2	6	11	7	2	0	0	0	28
Days Maximum Temp. ≤ 32°F	7	3	1	0	0	0	0	0	0	0	0	4	15
Days Minimum Temp. ≤ 32°F	27	23	19	7	1	0	0	0	0	5	15	24	121
Days Minimum Temp. ≤ 0°F	1	0	0	0	0	0	0	0	0	0	0	0	1
Heating Degree Days (base 65°F)	1,043	864	700	365	137	18	1	5	66	316	598	926	5,039
Cooling Degree Days (base 65°F)	0	0	1	10	63	206	323	279	117	19	0	0	1,018
Mean Precipitation (in.)	3.01	2.84	3.77	3.59	4.23	3.73	3.91	3.41	4.14	3.26	3.60	3.22	42.71
Extreme Maximum Daily Precip. (in.)	2.52	3.39	2.03	2.17	3.04	3.00	3.68	2.20	5.19	2.82	3.58	3.14	5.19
Days With ≥ 0.1" Precipitation	6	6	7	7	8	7	7	6	6	5	6	6	77
Days With ≥ 0.5" Precipitation	2	2	3	3	3	2	3	2	2	2	2	2	28
Days With ≥ 1.0" Precipitation	1	1	1	1	1	1	1	1	1	1	1	1	12
Mean Snowfall (in.)	8.5	7.7	3.5	0.5	0.0	0.0	0.0	0.0	0.0	0.0	0.7	3.2	24.1
Maximum Snow Depth (in.)	33	***24***	***8***	***1***	0	0	0	0	***0***	***0***	***3***	9	***33***
Days With ≥ 1.0" Snow Depth	8	***7***	1	0	0	0	0	0	0	0	0	4	***20***

The period of record for all cooperative weather station data is 1980 – 2009. See User Guide for detailed explanation of data.

Pennsylvania Weather Station Rankings

Annual Extreme Maximum Temperature

Highest			Lowest		
Rank	**Station Name**	**°F**	**Rank**	**Station Name**	**°F**
1	Laurelton Center	***105***	1	Chalk Hill 2 ENE	94
1	Montgomery Lock & Dam	105	2	Pleasant Mount 1 W	95
3	Octoraro Lake	104	3	Montrose	97
3	Raystown Lake 2	104	4	Bradford 4 SW Res 5	98
5	Graterford 1 E	***103***	4	Francis E Walter Dam	98
5	Hamburg	103	6	Altoona 3 W	99
5	Marcus Hook	***103***	6	Mercer	99
5	Philadelphia Int'l Arpt	103	8	Altoona Blair Co Arpt	100
5	Phoenixville 1 E	***103***	8	Bucksville	***100***
5	Pittsburgh Intl Arpt	103	8	Clarion 3 SW	100
5	Renovo	103	8	Coatesville 2 W	***100***
5	Williamsport-Lycoming County	103	8	Erie Intl Arpt	100
13	Blue Marsh Lake	102	8	Washington 3 NE	***100***
13	Butler 2 SW	102	14	Allentown A-B-E Intl Arpt	101
13	Derry 4 SW	102	14	Salina 3 W	101
13	Donora 1 SW	102	14	Wilkes-Barre Scranton Arpt	101
13	Lancaster 2 NE Filt Plant	102	17	Blue Marsh Lake	102
13	Landisville 2 NW	102	17	Butler 2 SW	102
13	Lebanon 2 W	102	17	Derry 4 SW	102
13	Lewistown	102	17	Donora 1 SW	102
13	Neshaminy Falls	102	17	Lancaster 2 NE Filt Plant	102
13	Reading 4 NNW	102	17	Landisville 2 NW	102
13	State College	102	17	Lebanon 2 W	102
13	Uniontown 1 NE	102	17	Lewistown	102
13	York 3 SSW Pump Stn	102	17	Neshaminy Falls	102

Annual Mean Maximum Temperature

Highest			Lowest		
Rank	**Station Name**	**°F**	**Rank**	**Station Name**	**°F**
1	York 3 SSW Pump Stn	65.3	1	Pleasant Mount 1 W	53.7
2	Neshaminy Falls	65.2	2	Bradford 4 SW Res 5	55.6
3	Octoraro Lake	64.8	3	Montrose	55.7
4	Philadelphia Int'l Arpt	64.5	4	Erie Intl Arpt	57.5
5	Phoenixville 1 E	***64.2***	5	Altoona 3 W	58.1
6	Marcus Hook	***64.1***	6	Chalk Hill 2 ENE	58.3
7	Donora 1 SW	64.0	7	State College	59.0
8	Landisville 2 NW	63.9	7	Wilkes-Barre Scranton Arpt	59.0
9	Laurelton Center	***63.3***	9	Altoona Blair Co Arpt	59.2
10	Lancaster 2 NE Filt Plant	63.0	10	Clarion 3 SW	59.6
11	Uniontown 1 NE	62.8	11	Mercer	59.8
12	Reading 4 NNW	62.7	12	Butler 2 SW	60.2
13	Graterford 1 E	***62.6***	13	Washington 3 NE	60.3
14	Coatesville 2 W	***62.3***	14	Renovo	60.4
15	Bucksville	***62.0***	15	Williamsport-Lycoming County	60.6
15	Montgomery Lock & Dam	62.0	16	Pittsburgh Intl Arpt	60.8
17	Hamburg	61.8	17	Raystown Lake 2	61.0
17	Lebanon 2 W	61.8	18	Blue Marsh Lake	***61.1***
19	Allentown A-B-E Intl Arpt	61.6	19	Derry 4 SW	61.4
19	Lewistown	61.6	20	Salina 3 W	61.5
21	Salina 3 W	61.5	21	Allentown A-B-E Intl Arpt	61.6
22	Derry 4 SW	61.4	21	Lewistown	61.6
23	Blue Marsh Lake	***61.1***	23	Hamburg	61.8
24	Raystown Lake 2	61.0	23	Lebanon 2 W	61.8
25	Pittsburgh Intl Arpt	60.8	25	Bucksville	***62.0***

Rankings include 25 highest/lowest stations. If state has less than 25 stations, all stations are included. The period of record is 1980–2009. See User Guide for detailed explanation of data.

Annual Mean Temperature

Highest			Lowest		
Rank	**Station Name**	**°F**	**Rank**	**Station Name**	**°F**
1	Marcus Hook	***56.5***	1	Pleasant Mount 1 W	43.9
2	Philadelphia Int'l Arpt	55.7	2	Bradford 4 SW Res 5	44.6
3	York 3 SSW Pump Stn	53.7	3	Montrose	45.3
4	Neshaminy Falls	53.4	4	Clarion 3 SW	48.3
5	Donora 1 SW	53.1	5	Mercer	***48.4***
5	Phoenixville 1 E	***53.1***	6	Chalk Hill 2 ENE	48.7
7	Lancaster 2 NE Filt Plant	53.0	7	Altoona 3 W	48.9
8	Octoraro Lake	52.8	8	Butler 2 SW	49.2
9	Landisville 2 NW	52.7	9	Salina 3 W	49.4
9	Reading 4 NNW	52.7	10	Renovo	49.5
11	Montgomery Lock & Dam	52.2	11	State College	49.6
12	Coatesville 2 W	***52.0***	12	Erie Intl Arpt	49.8
13	Allentown A-B-E Intl Arpt	51.8	12	Wilkes-Barre Scranton Arpt	49.8
14	Hamburg	51.6	14	Altoona Blair Co Arpt	50.0
14	Lebanon 2 W	51.6	15	Washington 3 NE	50.4
16	Pittsburgh Intl Arpt	51.4	16	Derry 4 SW	50.5
17	Laurelton Center	***51.3***	17	Raystown Lake 2	50.6
18	Bucksville	***51.2***	17	Williamsport-Lycoming County	50.6
18	Uniontown 1 NE	51.2	19	Blue Marsh Lake	***51.0***
20	Graterford 1 E	***51.1***	20	Graterford 1 E	***51.1***
20	Lewistown	51.1	20	Lewistown	51.1
22	Blue Marsh Lake	***51.0***	22	Bucksville	***51.2***
23	Raystown Lake 2	50.6	22	Uniontown 1 NE	51.2
23	Williamsport-Lycoming County	50.6	24	Laurelton Center	***51.3***
25	Derry 4 SW	50.5	25	Pittsburgh Intl Arpt	51.4

Annual Mean Minimum Temperature

Highest			Lowest		
Rank	**Station Name**	**°F**	**Rank**	**Station Name**	**°F**
1	Marcus Hook	***48.9***	1	Bradford 4 SW Res 5	33.6
2	Philadelphia Int'l Arpt	46.9	2	Pleasant Mount 1 W	34.0
3	Lancaster 2 NE Filt Plant	42.9	3	Montrose	34.9
4	Reading 4 NNW	42.6	4	Clarion 3 SW	36.9
5	Montgomery Lock & Dam	42.4	5	Mercer	***37.0***
6	Donora 1 SW	42.1	6	Salina 3 W	37.4
6	Erie Intl Arpt	42.1	7	Butler 2 SW	38.1
8	York 3 SSW Pump Stn	42.0	8	Renovo	38.5
9	Allentown A-B-E Intl Arpt	41.9	9	Chalk Hill 2 ENE	39.1
9	Pittsburgh Intl Arpt	41.9	10	Laurelton Center	***39.2***
11	Phoenixville 1 E	***41.8***	11	Altoona 3 W	39.6
12	Coatesville 2 W	***41.7***	11	Derry 4 SW	39.6
13	Landisville 2 NW	41.6	11	Graterford 1 E	***39.6***
13	Neshaminy Falls	41.6	11	Uniontown 1 NE	39.6
15	Hamburg	41.4	15	State College	40.1
16	Lebanon 2 W	41.3	16	Raystown Lake 2	40.2
17	Altoona Blair Co Arpt	40.8	17	Bucksville	***40.3***
17	Blue Marsh Lake	***40.8***	18	Washington 3 NE	40.4
19	Octoraro Lake	40.7	19	Lewistown	40.5
20	Wilkes-Barre Scranton Arpt	40.6	20	Wilkes-Barre Scranton Arpt	40.6
20	Williamsport-Lycoming County	40.6	20	Williamsport-Lycoming County	40.6
22	Lewistown	40.5	22	Octoraro Lake	40.7
23	Washington 3 NE	40.4	23	Altoona Blair Co Arpt	40.8
24	Bucksville	***40.3***	23	Blue Marsh Lake	***40.8***
25	Raystown Lake 2	40.2	25	Lebanon 2 W	41.3

Rankings include 25 highest/lowest stations. If state has less than 25 stations, all stations are included. The period of record is 1980–2009. See User Guide for detailed explanation of data.

Annual Extreme Minimum Temperature

Highest Rank	Station Name	°F	Lowest Rank	Station Name	°F
1	Marcus Hook	*-4*	1	Mercer	-32
2	Philadelphia Int'l Arpt	-7	2	Salina 3 W	-30
3	Neshaminy Falls	-11	3	Derry 4 SW	-29
4	Phoenixville 1 E	*-13*	4	Chalk Hill 2 ENE	-27
5	Coatesville 2 W	*-14*	5	Bradford 4 SW Res 5	-26
6	Allentown A-B-E Intl Arpt	-15	5	Francis E Walter Dam	-26
6	Raystown Lake 2	-15	7	Altoona Blair Co Arpt	-25
8	Lancaster 2 NE Filt Plant	-16	7	Pleasant Mount 1 W	-25
8	Renovo	-16	7	Washington 3 NE	*-25*
10	Blue Marsh Lake	-17	10	Landisville 2 NW	-24
10	Graterford 1 E	*-17*	11	Bucksville	*-23*
10	Lewistown	-17	11	Clarion 3 SW	-23
13	Erie Intl Arpt	-18	13	Laurelton Center	*-22*
13	Montgomery Lock & Dam	-18	13	Lebanon 2 W	-22
13	State College	-18	13	Montrose	-22
16	Donora 1 SW	-19	13	Pittsburgh Intl Arpt	-22
16	Hamburg	-19	13	Uniontown 1 NE	-22
16	Octoraro Lake	-19	18	Wilkes-Barre Scranton Arpt	-21
19	Altoona 3 W	-20	18	York 3 SSW Pump Stn	-21
19	Butler 2 SW	-20	20	Altoona 3 W	-20
19	Reading 4 NNW	-20	20	Butler 2 SW	-20
19	Williamsport-Lycoming County	-20	20	Reading 4 NNW	-20
23	Wilkes-Barre Scranton Arpt	-21	20	Williamsport-Lycoming County	-20
23	York 3 SSW Pump Stn	-21	24	Donora 1 SW	-19
25	Laurelton Center	*-22*	24	Hamburg	-19

July Mean Maximum Temperature

Highest Rank	Station Name	°F	Lowest Rank	Station Name	°F
1	York 3 SSW Pump Stn	87.3	1	Pleasant Mount 1 W	76.6
2	Neshaminy Falls	87.2	2	Chalk Hill 2 ENE	78.0
3	Marcus Hook	*87.1*	3	Bradford 4 SW Res 5	78.6
3	Octoraro Lake	87.1	4	Montrose	79.2
5	Philadelphia Int'l Arpt	87.0	5	Francis E Walter Dam	79.3
6	Laurelton Center	*86.5*	6	Erie Intl Arpt	79.8
7	Landisville 2 NW	86.1	7	Altoona 3 W	80.7
7	Phoenixville 1 E	86.1	8	State College	81.5
9	Reading 4 NNW	85.4	9	Mercer	81.6
10	Lancaster 2 NE Filt Plant	85.3	10	Altoona Blair Co Arpt	81.8
11	Graterford 1 E	85.2	10	Washington 3 NE	81.8
12	Donora 1 SW	85.1	12	Wilkes-Barre Scranton Arpt	82.1
13	Coatesville 2 W	*84.7*	13	Butler 2 SW	82.5
13	Hamburg	84.7	14	Pittsburgh Intl Arpt	82.8
15	Allentown A-B-E Intl Arpt	84.6	15	Clarion 3 SW	82.9
16	Blue Marsh Lake	84.4	16	Salina 3 W	83.2
16	Lewistown	84.4	17	Derry 4 SW	83.4
18	Bucksville	84.2	18	Renovo	83.6
18	Lebanon 2 W	84.2	19	Montgomery Lock & Dam	83.7
18	Williamsport-Lycoming County	84.2	20	Raystown Lake 2	83.8
21	Uniontown 1 NE	83.9	21	Uniontown 1 NE	83.9
22	Raystown Lake 2	83.8	22	Bucksville	84.2
23	Montgomery Lock & Dam	83.7	22	Lebanon 2 W	84.2
24	Renovo	83.6	22	Williamsport-Lycoming County	84.2
25	Derry 4 SW	83.4	25	Blue Marsh Lake	84.4

January Mean Minimum Temperature

Highest Rank	Highest Station Name	°F	Lowest Rank	Lowest Station Name	°F
1	Marcus Hook	28.2	1	Pleasant Mount 1 W	11.5
2	Philadelphia Int'l Arpt	25.5	2	Bradford 4 SW Res 5	12.1
3	Montgomery Lock & Dam	22.5	3	Montrose	12.6
4	Lancaster 2 NE Filt Plant	22.3	4	Mercer	16.4
5	Donora 1 SW	22.1	5	Clarion 3 SW	16.9
6	Phoenixville 1 E	*21.8*	6	Salina 3 W	17.5
7	York 3 SSW Pump Stn	21.7	7	Altoona 3 W	18.1
8	Coatesville 2 W	*21.5*	8	Renovo	18.2
9	Neshaminy Falls	21.2	9	Butler 2 SW	18.4
10	Erie Intl Arpt	21.1	9	Laurelton Center	18.4
10	Landisville 2 NW	21.1	11	Bucksville	19.0
10	Pittsburgh Intl Arpt	21.1	11	Graterford 1 E	19.0
10	Reading 4 NNW	21.1	13	State College	19.1
14	Uniontown 1 NE	21.0	14	Wilkes-Barre Scranton Arpt	19.2
15	Lebanon 2 W	20.8	15	Chalk Hill 2 ENE	19.3
16	Allentown A-B-E Intl Arpt	20.7	15	Williamsport-Lycoming County	19.3
17	Altoona Blair Co Arpt	20.6	17	Blue Marsh Lake	*19.5*
18	Octoraro Lake	20.4	17	Hamburg	19.5
19	Lewistown	20.1	19	Derry 4 SW	19.8
19	Washington 3 NE	20.1	20	Raystown Lake 2	19.9
21	Raystown Lake 2	19.9	21	Lewistown	20.1
22	Derry 4 SW	19.8	21	Washington 3 NE	20.1
23	Blue Marsh Lake	*19.5*	23	Octoraro Lake	20.4
23	Hamburg	19.5	24	Altoona Blair Co Arpt	20.6
25	Chalk Hill 2 ENE	19.3	25	Allentown A-B-E Intl Arpt	20.7

Number of Days Annually Maximum Temperature ≥ 90°F

Highest Rank	Highest Station Name	Days	Lowest Rank	Lowest Station Name	Days
1	Neshaminy Falls	30	1	Chalk Hill 2 ENE	0
2	Octoraro Lake	29	1	Pleasant Mount 1 W	0
3	York 3 SSW Pump Stn	28	3	Bradford 4 SW Res 5	1
4	Marcus Hook	*27*	4	Montrose	2
5	Philadelphia Int'l Arpt	26	5	Erie Intl Arpt	3
6	Laurelton Center	*24*	5	Francis E Walter Dam	3
7	Phoenixville 1 E	*23*	7	Altoona 3 W	5
8	Landisville 2 NW	21	8	Mercer	6
8	Reading 4 NNW	21	8	State College	6
10	Graterford 1 E	*19*	10	Altoona Blair Co Arpt	7
11	Lancaster 2 NE Filt Plant	18	10	Washington 3 NE	7
12	Hamburg	17	12	Montgomery Lock & Dam	9
13	Allentown A-B-E Intl Arpt	16	12	Pittsburgh Intl Arpt	9
13	Coatesville 2 W	*16*	14	Butler 2 SW	10
13	Donora 1 SW	16	14	Clarion 3 SW	10
13	Lewistown	16	14	Wilkes-Barre Scranton Arpt	10
17	Bucksville	*15*	17	Derry 4 SW	11
17	Renovo	15	17	Salina 3 W	11
17	Williamsport-Lycoming County	15	19	Uniontown 1 NE	12
20	Blue Marsh Lake	14	20	Raystown Lake 2	13
20	Lebanon 2 W	14	21	Blue Marsh Lake	14
22	Raystown Lake 2	13	21	Lebanon 2 W	14
23	Uniontown 1 NE	12	23	Bucksville	*15*
24	Derry 4 SW	11	23	Renovo	15
24	Salina 3 W	11	23	Williamsport-Lycoming County	15

 Rankings include 25 highest/lowest stations. If state has less than 25 stations, all stations are included. The period of record is 1980–2009. See User Guide for detailed explanation of data.

Number of Days Annually Maximum Temperature ≤ 32°F

Highest			Lowest		
Rank	**Station Name**	**Days**	**Rank**	**Station Name**	**Days**
1	Pleasant Mount 1 W	63	1	Neshaminy Falls	13
2	Bradford 4 SW Res 5	58	2	Marcus Hook	***14***
3	Montrose	53	2	Phoenixville 1 E	***14***
4	Erie Intl Arpt	43	4	Octoraro Lake	15
5	Altoona 3 W	40	4	Philadelphia Int'l Arpt	15
5	Clarion 3 SW	40	4	York 3 SSW Pump Stn	15
5	Francis E Walter Dam	40	7	Landisville 2 NW	18
8	Chalk Hill 2 ENE	39	8	Graterford 1 E	19
9	Altoona Blair Co Arpt	38	9	Lancaster 2 NE Filt Plant	20
10	Washington 3 NE	37	9	Reading 4 NNW	20
10	Wilkes-Barre Scranton Arpt	37	11	Bucksville	***21***
12	Butler 2 SW	35	11	Coatesville 2 W	***21***
12	State College	35	11	Donora 1 SW	21
14	Mercer	34	11	Laurelton Center	***21***
14	Pittsburgh Intl Arpt	34	15	Hamburg	23
16	Salina 3 W	31	15	Lebanon 2 W	23
17	Derry 4 SW	30	17	Allentown A-B-E Intl Arpt	24
18	Raystown Lake 2	29	17	Lewistown	24
18	Renovo	29	19	Blue Marsh Lake	26
18	Williamsport-Lycoming County	29	19	Montgomery Lock & Dam	26
21	Blue Marsh Lake	26	19	Uniontown 1 NE	26
21	Montgomery Lock & Dam	26	22	Raystown Lake 2	29
21	Uniontown 1 NE	26	22	Renovo	29
24	Allentown A-B-E Intl Arpt	24	22	Williamsport-Lycoming County	29
24	Lewistown	24	25	Derry 4 SW	30

Number of Days Annually Minimum Temperature ≤ 32°F

Highest			Lowest		
Rank	**Station Name**	**Days**	**Rank**	**Station Name**	**Days**
1	Bradford 4 SW Res 5	172	1	Marcus Hook	***66***
2	Pleasant Mount 1 W	171	2	Philadelphia Int'l Arpt	84
3	Montrose	163	3	Montgomery Lock & Dam	109
4	Clarion 3 SW	151	4	Reading 4 NNW	111
5	Francis E Walter Dam	148	5	Lancaster 2 NE Filt Plant	113
6	Mercer	146	6	Erie Intl Arpt	114
6	Salina 3 W	146	7	Donora 1 SW	116
8	Butler 2 SW	139	8	Pittsburgh Intl Arpt	118
8	Laurelton Center	***139***	9	Allentown A-B-E Intl Arpt	119
10	Renovo	138	9	Landisville 2 NW	119
11	Graterford 1 E	***136***	11	Blue Marsh Lake	120
12	Chalk Hill 2 ENE	133	12	Altoona Blair Co Arpt	121
12	Uniontown 1 NE	133	12	Coatesville 2 W	***121***
14	Altoona 3 W	131	12	Lebanon 2 W	121
15	Bucksville	***130***	12	York 3 SSW Pump Stn	121
15	Derry 4 SW	130	16	Neshaminy Falls	122
17	Octoraro Lake	129	16	Phoenixville 1 E	***122***
17	State College	129	18	Hamburg	123
19	Lewistown	127	18	Wilkes-Barre Scranton Arpt	123
20	Raystown Lake 2	126	20	Williamsport-Lycoming County	124
20	Washington 3 NE	126	21	Raystown Lake 2	126
22	Williamsport-Lycoming County	124	21	Washington 3 NE	126
23	Hamburg	123	23	Lewistown	127
23	Wilkes-Barre Scranton Arpt	123	24	Octoraro Lake	129
25	Neshaminy Falls	122	24	State College	129

Rankings include 25 highest/lowest stations. If state has less than 25 stations, all stations are included. The period of record is 1980–2009. See User Guide for detailed explanation of data.

Number of Days Annually Minimum Temperature ≤ 0°F

Highest			Lowest		
Rank	**Station Name**	**Days**	**Rank**	**Station Name**	**Days**
1	Bradford 4 SW Res 5	16	1	Marcus Hook	***0***
2	Pleasant Mount 1 W	14	1	Philadelphia Int'l Arpt	0
3	Montrose	13	3	Allentown A-B-E Intl Arpt	1
4	Francis E Walter Dam	10	3	Altoona Blair Co Arpt	1
5	Mercer	8	3	Blue Marsh Lake	1
6	Clarion 3 SW	7	3	Coatesville 2 W	***1***
7	Butler 2 SW	6	3	Donora 1 SW	1
7	Chalk Hill 2 ENE	6	3	Graterford 1 E	***1***
7	Salina 3 W	6	3	Hamburg	1
10	Derry 4 SW	5	3	Lancaster 2 NE Filt Plant	1
10	Renovo	5	3	Lebanon 2 W	1
12	Altoona 3 W	4	3	Lewistown	1
12	Laurelton Center	***4***	3	Montgomery Lock & Dam	1
12	Uniontown 1 NE	4	3	Neshaminy Falls	1
12	Washington 3 NE	4	3	Octoraro Lake	1
12	Williamsport-Lycoming County	4	3	Phoenixville 1 E	***1***
17	Bucksville	***3***	3	Raystown Lake 2	1
17	Erie Intl Arpt	3	3	Reading 4 NNW	1
17	Pittsburgh Intl Arpt	3	3	York 3 SSW Pump Stn	1
17	State College	3	20	Landisville 2 NW	2
17	Wilkes-Barre Scranton Arpt	3	21	Bucksville	***3***
22	Landisville 2 NW	2	21	Erie Intl Arpt	3
23	Allentown A-B-E Intl Arpt	1	21	Pittsburgh Intl Arpt	3
23	Altoona Blair Co Arpt	1	21	State College	3
23	Blue Marsh Lake	1	21	Wilkes-Barre Scranton Arpt	3

Number of Annual Heating Degree Days

Highest			Lowest		
Rank	**Station Name**	**Num.**	**Rank**	**Station Name**	**Num.**
1	Pleasant Mount 1 W	7,840	1	Marcus Hook	***4,377***
2	Bradford 4 SW Res 5	7,586	2	Philadelphia Int'l Arpt	4,591
3	Montrose	7,440	3	York 3 SSW Pump Stn	5,039
4	Clarion 3 SW	6,514	4	Neshaminy Falls	5,121
5	Mercer	***6,408***	5	Donora 1 SW	5,158
6	Altoona 3 W	6,318	6	Phoenixville 1 E	***5,214***
7	Chalk Hill 2 ENE	6,231	7	Lancaster 2 NE Filt Plant	5,237
8	Butler 2 SW	6,222	8	Octoraro Lake	5,262
9	Renovo	6,160	9	Landisville 2 NW	5,288
10	State College	6,158	10	Montgomery Lock & Dam	5,367
11	Salina 3 W	6,130	10	Reading 4 NNW	5,367
12	Erie Intl Arpt	6,096	12	Coatesville 2 W	***5,482***
13	Wilkes-Barre Scranton Arpt	6,089	13	Allentown A-B-E Intl Arpt	5,573
14	Altoona Blair Co Arpt	5,991	14	Lebanon 2 W	5,574
15	Washington 3 NE	5,893	15	Uniontown 1 NE	5,630
16	Williamsport-Lycoming County	5,885	16	Hamburg	5,636
17	Derry 4 SW	***5,862***	17	Pittsburgh Intl Arpt	5,641
18	Raystown Lake 2	5,848	18	Bucksville	***5,697***
19	Blue Marsh Lake	***5,812***	19	Laurelton Center	***5,707***
20	Graterford 1 E	***5,749***	20	Lewistown	5,725
21	Lewistown	5,725	21	Graterford 1 E	***5,749***
22	Laurelton Center	***5,707***	22	Blue Marsh Lake	***5,812***
23	Bucksville	***5,697***	23	Raystown Lake 2	5,848
24	Pittsburgh Intl Arpt	5,641	24	Derry 4 SW	***5,862***
25	Hamburg	5,636	25	Williamsport-Lycoming County	5,885

 Rankings include 25 highest/lowest stations. If state has less than 25 stations, all stations are included. The period of record is 1980–2009. See User Guide for detailed explanation of data.

Number of Annual Cooling Degree Days

Highest Rank	Highest Station Name	Highest Num.	Lowest Rank	Lowest Station Name	Lowest Num.
1	Marcus Hook	***1,390***	1	Pleasant Mount 1 W	237
2	Philadelphia Int'l Arpt	1,311	2	Bradford 4 SW Res 5	262
3	York 3 SSW Pump Stn	1,018	3	Montrose	337
4	Neshaminy Falls	1,010	4	Chalk Hill 2 ENE	380
5	Reading 4 NNW	977	5	Mercer	***468***
6	Phoenixville 1 E	***970***	6	Clarion 3 SW	514
7	Lancaster 2 NE Filt Plant	952	7	Salina 3 W	544
8	Landisville 2 NW	924	8	Altoona 3 W	554
9	Octoraro Lake	921	9	Butler 2 SW	556
10	Donora 1 SW	920	10	Renovo	608
11	Allentown A-B-E Intl Arpt	858	11	Altoona Blair Co Arpt	631
11	Coatesville 2 W	***858***	12	State College	637
13	Hamburg	857	13	Wilkes-Barre Scranton Arpt	650
14	Montgomery Lock & Dam	816	14	Washington 3 NE	653
15	Blue Marsh Lake	***811***	15	Erie Intl Arpt	667
16	Laurelton Center	***796***	16	Derry 4 SW	***688***
17	Graterford 1 E	***789***	17	Uniontown 1 NE	703
18	Lebanon 2 W	780	18	Raystown Lake 2	710
19	Pittsburgh Intl Arpt	774	19	Williamsport-Lycoming County	755
20	Bucksville	***762***	20	Lewistown	759
21	Lewistown	759	21	Bucksville	***762***
22	Williamsport-Lycoming County	755	22	Pittsburgh Intl Arpt	774
23	Raystown Lake 2	710	23	Lebanon 2 W	780
24	Uniontown 1 NE	703	24	Graterford 1 E	***789***
25	Derry 4 SW	***688***	25	Laurelton Center	***796***

Annual Precipitation

Highest Rank	Highest Station Name	Highest Inches	Lowest Rank	Lowest Station Name	Lowest Inches
1	Chalk Hill 2 ENE	54.24	1	Altoona Blair Co Arpt	35.31
2	Coatesville 2 W	***50.87***	2	Donora 1 SW	37.58
3	Bucksville	***49.72***	3	Montgomery Lock & Dam	37.86
4	Derry 4 SW	49.33	4	Marcus Hook	***37.91***
5	Pleasant Mount 1 W	48.70	5	Raystown Lake 2	38.03
6	Neshaminy Falls	48.64	6	Wilkes-Barre Scranton Arpt	38.05
7	Bradford 4 SW Res 5	48.13	7	Pittsburgh Intl Arpt	38.21
8	Francis E Walter Dam	46.85	8	Washington 3 NE	39.10
9	Clarion 3 SW	46.31	9	Renovo	39.35
10	Hamburg	46.08	10	State College	39.52
11	Octoraro Lake	45.60	11	Williamsport-Lycoming County	40.91
12	Blue Marsh Lake	45.37	12	Lewistown	41.09
13	Graterford 1 E	44.78	13	Philadelphia Int'l Arpt	41.29
14	Allentown A-B-E Intl Arpt	44.64	14	Butler 2 SW	41.37
15	Montrose	44.58	15	Phoenixville 1 E	***42.02***
16	Reading 4 NNW	43.76	16	Salina 3 W	42.21
17	Laurelton Center	***43.57***	17	Lebanon 2 W	42.43
18	Uniontown 1 NE	43.50	18	Erie Intl Arpt	42.45
19	Landisville 2 NW	42.86	19	Altoona 3 W	42.53
20	Mercer	42.75	20	Lancaster 2 NE Filt Plant	42.71
21	Lancaster 2 NE Filt Plant	42.71	20	York 3 SSW Pump Stn	42.71
21	York 3 SSW Pump Stn	42.71	22	Mercer	42.75
23	Altoona 3 W	42.53	23	Landisville 2 NW	42.86
24	Erie Intl Arpt	42.45	24	Uniontown 1 NE	43.50
25	Lebanon 2 W	42.43	25	Laurelton Center	***43.57***

Rankings include 25 highest/lowest stations. If state has less than 25 stations, all stations are included. The period of record is 1980–2009. See User Guide for detailed explanation of data.

Annual Extreme Maximum Daily Precipitation

Highest

Rank	Station Name	Inches
1	Marcus Hook	***11.68***
2	Montgomery Lock & Dam	8.74
3	Allentown A-B-E Intl Arpt	8.71
4	Coatesville 2 W	***7.85***
5	Octoraro Lake	6.82
6	Montrose	6.63
6	Philadelphia Int'l Arpt	6.63
8	Williamsport-Lycoming County	6.29
9	Reading 4 NNW	6.25
10	Lancaster 2 NE Filt Plant	6.11
11	Salina 3 W	5.99
12	Wilkes-Barre Scranton Arpt	5.98
13	Pittsburgh Intl Arpt	5.95
14	Graterford 1 E	***5.90***
15	Neshaminy Falls	5.83
16	Altoona Blair Co Arpt	5.55
17	Derry 4 SW	5.51
18	Lewistown	5.40
19	Pleasant Mount 1 W	5.22
20	York 3 SSW Pump Stn	5.19
21	Washington 3 NE	***5.18***
22	Lebanon 2 W	5.16
23	Phoenixville 1 E	***5.13***
24	Laurelton Center	***5.11***
25	State College	5.05

Lowest

Rank	Station Name	Inches
1	Uniontown 1 NE	3.82
2	Bradford 4 SW Res 5	4.18
3	Hamburg	4.21
4	Donora 1 SW	4.36
5	Mercer	***4.47***
6	Altoona 3 W	4.49
7	Raystown Lake 2	4.55
8	Renovo	4.57
9	Erie Intl Arpt	4.61
10	Chalk Hill 2 ENE	4.64
10	Landisville 2 NW	4.64
12	Butler 2 SW	4.72
13	Clarion 3 SW	4.95
14	State College	5.05
15	Laurelton Center	***5.11***
16	Phoenixville 1 E	***5.13***
17	Lebanon 2 W	5.16
18	Washington 3 NE	***5.18***
19	York 3 SSW Pump Stn	5.19
20	Pleasant Mount 1 W	5.22
21	Lewistown	5.40
22	Derry 4 SW	5.51
23	Altoona Blair Co Arpt	5.55
24	Neshaminy Falls	5.83
25	Graterford 1 E	***5.90***

Number of Days Annually With ≥ 0.1 Inches of Precipitation

Highest

Rank	Station Name	Days
1	Derry 4 SW	115
2	Chalk Hill 2 ENE	112
3	Bradford 4 SW Res 5	106
4	Clarion 3 SW	97
4	Erie Intl Arpt	97
6	Uniontown 1 NE	96
7	Montrose	92
7	Salina 3 W	92
9	Pleasant Mount 1 W	91
10	Butler 2 SW	90
11	Mercer	86
12	Renovo	85
12	Washington 3 NE	85
14	Altoona 3 W	84
14	Donora 1 SW	84
14	Pittsburgh Intl Arpt	84
17	Montgomery Lock & Dam	83
18	Laurelton Center	***82***
19	Coatesville 2 W	***81***
19	Lewistown	81
19	State College	81
22	Neshaminy Falls	80
23	Hamburg	79
24	Allentown A-B-E Intl Arpt	78
24	Lancaster 2 NE Filt Plant	78

Lowest

Rank	Station Name	Days
1	Blue Marsh Lake	59
2	Marcus Hook	***62***
3	Bucksville	***70***
4	Philadelphia Int'l Arpt	71
5	Francis E Walter Dam	73
5	Graterford 1 E	***73***
5	Raystown Lake 2	73
8	Altoona Blair Co Arpt	74
8	Phoenixville 1 E	***74***
10	Lebanon 2 W	76
11	Landisville 2 NW	77
11	Octoraro Lake	77
11	Reading 4 NNW	77
11	Wilkes-Barre Scranton Arpt	77
11	Williamsport-Lycoming County	77
11	York 3 SSW Pump Stn	77
17	Allentown A-B-E Intl Arpt	78
17	Lancaster 2 NE Filt Plant	78
19	Hamburg	79
20	Neshaminy Falls	80
21	Coatesville 2 W	***81***
21	Lewistown	81
21	State College	81
24	Laurelton Center	***82***
25	Montgomery Lock & Dam	83

 Rankings include 25 highest/lowest stations. If state has less than 25 stations, all stations are included. The period of record is 1980–2009. See User Guide for detailed explanation of data.

Number of Days Annually With ≥ 0.5 Inches of Precipitation

Highest Rank	Station Name	Days	Lowest Rank	Station Name	Days
1	Chalk Hill 2 ENE	37	1	Altoona Blair Co Arpt	21
2	Bucksville	*35*	2	Erie Intl Arpt	23
2	Coatesville 2 W	*35*	2	Montgomery Lock & Dam	23
4	Neshaminy Falls	34	2	Raystown Lake 2	23
5	Octoraro Lake	33	2	Wilkes-Barre Scranton Arpt	23
6	Bradford 4 SW Res 5	32	6	Blue Marsh Lake	24
6	Derry 4 SW	32	6	Donora 1 SW	24
6	Graterford 1 E	*32*	6	Washington 3 NE	24
6	Pleasant Mount 1 W	32	9	State College	25
10	Clarion 3 SW	31	10	Butler 2 SW	26
10	Landisville 2 NW	31	10	Marcus Hook	*26*
10	Laurelton Center	*31*	10	Mercer	26
13	Phoenixville 1 E	*30*	10	Pittsburgh Intl Arpt	26
14	Allentown A-B-E Intl Arpt	29	10	Renovo	26
14	Altoona 3 W	29	10	Salina 3 W	26
14	Hamburg	29	16	Francis E Walter Dam	27
14	Lebanon 2 W	29	16	Philadelphia Int'l Arpt	27
14	Montrose	29	18	Lancaster 2 NE Filt Plant	28
14	Reading 4 NNW	29	18	Lewistown	28
20	Lancaster 2 NE Filt Plant	28	18	Uniontown 1 NE	28
20	Lewistown	28	18	Williamsport-Lycoming County	28
20	Uniontown 1 NE	28	18	York 3 SSW Pump Stn	28
20	Williamsport-Lycoming County	28	23	Allentown A-B-E Intl Arpt	29
20	York 3 SSW Pump Stn	28	23	Altoona 3 W	29
25	Francis E Walter Dam	27	23	Hamburg	29

Number of Days Annually With ≥ 1.0 Inches of Precipitation

Highest Rank	Station Name	Days	Lowest Rank	Station Name	Days
1	Bucksville	*13*	1	Pittsburgh Intl Arpt	4
1	Coatesville 2 W	*13*	2	Erie Intl Arpt	5
1	Neshaminy Falls	13	2	Montgomery Lock & Dam	5
4	Chalk Hill 2 ENE	12	4	Bradford 4 SW Res 5	7
4	Hamburg	12	4	Butler 2 SW	7
4	Marcus Hook	*12*	4	Donora 1 SW	7
4	Octoraro Lake	12	4	Mercer	7
4	Reading 4 NNW	12	4	Raystown Lake 2	7
4	York 3 SSW Pump Stn	12	4	Renovo	7
10	Allentown A-B-E Intl Arpt	11	10	Clarion 3 SW	8
10	Graterford 1 E	*11*	10	Derry 4 SW	8
10	Landisville 2 NW	11	10	Lewistown	8
10	Laurelton Center	*11*	10	Salina 3 W	8
10	Lebanon 2 W	11	10	State College	8
10	Philadelphia Int'l Arpt	11	10	Uniontown 1 NE	8
10	Phoenixville 1 E	*11*	10	Washington 3 NE	8
17	Blue Marsh Lake	10	10	Wilkes-Barre Scranton Arpt	8
17	Lancaster 2 NE Filt Plant	10	18	Altoona 3 W	9
17	Montrose	10	18	Altoona Blair Co Arpt	9
17	Pleasant Mount 1 W	10	18	Francis E Walter Dam	9
17	Williamsport-Lycoming County	10	21	Blue Marsh Lake	10
22	Altoona 3 W	9	21	Lancaster 2 NE Filt Plant	10
22	Altoona Blair Co Arpt	9	21	Montrose	10
22	Francis E Walter Dam	9	21	Pleasant Mount 1 W	10
25	Clarion 3 SW	8	21	Williamsport-Lycoming County	10

Rankings include 25 highest/lowest stations. If state has less than 25 stations, all stations are included. The period of record is 1980–2009. See User Guide for detailed explanation of data.

Annual Snowfall

Highest Rank	Station Name	Inches	Lowest Rank	Station Name	Inches
1	Erie Intl Arpt	99.6	1	Graterford 1 E	*10.5*
2	Chalk Hill 2 ENE	87.7	2	Neshaminy Falls	*11.9*
3	Montrose	81.8	3	Montgomery Lock & Dam	*12.1*
4	Bradford 4 SW Res 5	72.1	4	Octoraro Lake	*14.5*
5	Pleasant Mount 1 W	65.7	5	Donora 1 SW	17.0
6	Mercer	46.7	6	Lancaster 2 NE Filt Plant	18.4
7	State College	45.3	7	Philadelphia Int'l Arpt	18.8
8	Francis E Walter Dam	45.1	8	Hamburg	19.3
9	Derry 4 SW	44.8	9	Blue Marsh Lake	21.1
10	Pittsburgh Intl Arpt	40.4	10	Raystown Lake 2	*21.7*
11	Williamsport-Lycoming County	36.6	11	Lebanon 2 W	*21.9*
12	Altoona 3 W	35.0	12	York 3 SSW Pump Stn	24.1
13	Butler 2 SW	34.1	13	Landisville 2 NW	24.3
14	Coatesville 2 W	*32.9*	14	Uniontown 1 NE	*24.5*
15	Allentown A-B-E Intl Arpt	*32.7*	15	Bucksville	*25.0*
16	Clarion 3 SW	32.4	16	Lewistown	26.1
17	Renovo	30.5	16	Washington 3 NE	26.1
18	Salina 3 W	28.2	18	Salina 3 W	28.2
19	Lewistown	26.1	19	Renovo	30.5
19	Washington 3 NE	26.1	20	Clarion 3 SW	32.4
21	Bucksville	*25.0*	21	Allentown A-B-E Intl Arpt	*32.7*
22	Uniontown 1 NE	*24.5*	22	Coatesville 2 W	*32.9*
23	Landisville 2 NW	24.3	23	Butler 2 SW	34.1
24	York 3 SSW Pump Stn	24.1	24	Altoona 3 W	35.0
25	Lebanon 2 W	*21.9*	25	Williamsport-Lycoming County	36.6

Annual Maximum Snow Depth

Highest Rank	Station Name	Inches	Lowest Rank	Station Name	Inches
1	Laurelton Center	*52*	1	Mercer	15
2	Pleasant Mount 1 W	51	2	Montgomery Lock & Dam	19
3	Francis E Walter Dam	50	3	Uniontown 1 NE	*20*
4	Montrose	40	4	Clarion 3 SW	21
5	Blue Marsh Lake	38	5	Butler 2 SW	22
5	Chalk Hill 2 ENE	38	6	Neshaminy Falls	*23*
7	Bradford 4 SW Res 5	35	6	Philadelphia Int'l Arpt	23
8	Lewistown	33	8	Donora 1 SW	24
8	York 3 SSW Pump Stn	*33*	8	Hamburg	24
10	State College	31	8	Renovo	24
11	Altoona 3 W	30	11	Graterford 1 E	*25*
12	Coatesville 2 W	*29*	11	Pittsburgh Intl Arpt	25
13	Landisville 2 NW	27	13	Bucksville	*26*
13	Salina 3 W	27	13	Derry 4 SW	*26*
15	Bucksville	*26*	13	Lancaster 2 NE Filt Plant	26
15	Derry 4 SW	*26*	13	Washington 3 NE	*26*
15	Lancaster 2 NE Filt Plant	26	17	Landisville 2 NW	27
15	Washington 3 NE	*26*	17	Salina 3 W	27
19	Graterford 1 E	*25*	19	Coatesville 2 W	*29*
19	Pittsburgh Intl Arpt	25	20	Altoona 3 W	30
21	Donora 1 SW	24	21	State College	31
21	Hamburg	24	22	Lewistown	33
21	Renovo	24	22	York 3 SSW Pump Stn	*33*
24	Neshaminy Falls	*23*	24	Bradford 4 SW Res 5	35
24	Philadelphia Int'l Arpt	23	25	Blue Marsh Lake	38

 Rankings include 25 highest/lowest stations. If state has less than 25 stations, all stations are included. The period of record is 1980–2009. See User Guide for detailed explanation of data.

Number of Days Annually With ≥ 1.0 Inch Snow Depth

Highest			Lowest		
Rank	**Station Name**	**Days**	**Rank**	**Station Name**	**Days**
1	Pleasant Mount 1 W	91	1	Graterford 1 E	***1***
2	Bradford 4 SW Res 5	90	2	Neshaminy Falls	***15***
3	Montrose	82	2	Philadelphia Int'l Arpt	15
4	Chalk Hill 2 ENE	76	4	Lancaster 2 NE Filt Plant	17
5	Francis E Walter Dam	58	5	Lebanon 2 W	***19***
6	Mercer	57	6	Donora 1 SW	20
7	Clarion 3 SW	56	6	York 3 SSW Pump Stn	***20***
8	Butler 2 SW	48	8	Blue Marsh Lake	21
9	State College	46	9	Montgomery Lock & Dam	24
10	Renovo	43	9	Uniontown 1 NE	***24***
11	Derry 4 SW	42	11	Hamburg	25
12	Altoona 3 W	41	11	Landisville 2 NW	25
13	Pittsburgh Intl Arpt	38	13	Bucksville	***29***
14	Salina 3 W	37	13	Laurelton Center	***29***
14	Washington 3 NE	37	15	Lewistown	30
16	Coatesville 2 W	***34***	16	Coatesville 2 W	***34***
17	Lewistown	30	17	Salina 3 W	37
18	Bucksville	***29***	17	Washington 3 NE	37
18	Laurelton Center	***29***	19	Pittsburgh Intl Arpt	38
20	Hamburg	25	20	Altoona 3 W	41
20	Landisville 2 NW	25	21	Derry 4 SW	42
22	Montgomery Lock & Dam	24	22	Renovo	43
22	Uniontown 1 NE	***24***	23	State College	46
24	Blue Marsh Lake	21	24	Butler 2 SW	48
25	Donora 1 SW	20	25	Clarion 3 SW	56

Significant Storm Events in Pennsylvania: 2000 – 2009

Location or County	Date	Type	Mag.	Deaths	Injuries	Property Damage ($mil.)	Crop Damage ($mil.)
Chester and Philadelphia Counties	05/06/00	Excessive Heat	na	7	0	0.0	0.0
Philadelphia County	08/07/00	Excessive Heat	na	5	0	0.0	0.0
Montgomery	06/16/01	Flood	na	1	0	33.5	0.0
Southeast Pennsylvania	08/06/01	Excessive Heat	na	22	0	0.0	0.0
Allegheny	05/31/02	Thunderstorm Wind	105 mph	1	54	10.0	0.0
Southeast Pennsylvania	07/01/02	Excessive Heat	na	15	0	0.0	0.0
Southeast Pennsylvania	08/01/02	Excessive Heat	na	9	0	0.0	0.0
Southeast Pennsylvania	08/11/02	Excessive Heat	na	8	0	0.0	0.0
Mercer	11/10/02	Tornado	F2	1	19	1.0	0.0
Mckean	07/21/03	Tornado	F1	0	0	45.7	0.0
Crawford	07/21/03	Flash Flood	na	1	0	30.0	0.0
Southeast Pennsylvania	09/18/03	High Wind	60 mph	0	0	32.2	0.0
Centre and Clinton Counties	01/06/04	Winter Weather/Mix	na	6	12	1.5	0.0
Central Pennsylvania	09/17/04	Flood	na	2	0	50.0	0.0
Allegheny Co.	09/17/04	Flood	na	1	92	26.0	0.0
Bradford	09/17/04	Flash Flood	na	0	0	20.0	0.0
Luzerne	09/18/04	Flash Flood	na	0	0	100.0	0.0
Bucks County	09/18/04	Flood	na	0	0	24.0	0.0
Northhampton Co.	04/02/05	Flood	na	0	0	40.0	0.0
Monroe Co.	04/02/05	Flood	na	0	0	40.0	0.0
Bucks Co.	04/03/05	Flood	na	0	0	40.0	0.0
Bucks, Chester, Delaware, Montgomery, and Philadelphia Counties	07/18/05	Excessive Heat	na	6	0	0.0	0.0
Southeast Pennsylvania	07/25/05	Excessive Heat	na	7	0	0.0	0.0
Southeast Pennsylvania	08/02/05	Excessive Heat	na	5	0	0.0	0.0
Luzerne	06/27/06	Flash Flood	na	3	0	100.0	0.0
Susquehanna	06/27/06	Flash Flood	na	1	0	100.0	0.0
Wyoming	06/27/06	Flash Flood	na	0	0	60.0	0.0
Wayne	06/27/06	Flash Flood	na	1	0	50.0	0.0
Lackawanna	06/27/06	Flash Flood	na	0	0	50.0	0.0
Bradford	06/27/06	Flash Flood	na	0	0	25.0	0.0
Montgomery	06/27/06	Flood	na	0	0	22.0	0.0
Bucks	06/28/06	Flood	na	0	0	30.0	0.0
Southeast Pennsylvania	08/01/06	Excessive Heat	na	24	40	0.0	0.0

Note: Deaths, injuries, and damages are date and location specific.

RHODE ISLAND

PHYSICAL FEATURES. Rhode Island, the smallest of the states, shares the southeastern corner of New England with a portion of Massachusetts. The State extends for 50 miles in a north-south direction and has an average width of about 30 miles. The total area, including Block Island some 10 miles offshore, is 1,497 square miles of which Narragansett Bay occupies about 25 percent. There are three topographical divisions of the State. A narrow coastal plain with an elevation of less than 100 feet occurs along the south shore and around Narragansett Bay. A second division with gently rolling uplands of up to 200 feet elevation lies to the north and east of the Bay. The western two-thirds of Rhode Island consists of predominantly hilly uplands of mostly 200 to 600 feet elevation, rising to a maximum of 800 feet above sea level in the northwest corner of the State.

Narragansett Bay has a very irregular shoreline, indented by numerous small bays or coves and the mouths of the Taunton and Blackstone Rivers. The Bay contains several islands of which the one known as Aquidneck, or Rhode Island, is the largest. The shore line facing Long Island Sound is about 20 miles long. No point in the State is more than 25 miles from the ocean. The Blackstone River in northeastern Rhode Island is the principal river. A number of smaller rivers or brooks originating in the western uplands of the State or in southeastern Massachusetts empty into Narragansett Bay or Long Island Sound.

GENERAL CLIMATE. The chief characteristics of Rhode Island's climate may be summarized as follows: (1) equable distribution of precipitation among the four seasons; (2) large ranges of temperature both daily and annual; (3) great differences in the same season of different years; and (4) considerable diversity of the weather over short periods of time. These characteristics are modified by nearness to the Bay or ocean, elevation, and nature of the terrain.

Rhode Island lies in the "prevailing westerlies," the belt of generally eastward air movement which encircles the globe in middle latitudes. Embedded in this circulation are extensive masses of air originating in higher and lower latitudes and interacting to produce storm systems. A large number of these systems and air-mass fronts pass near or over Rhode Island in a year.

Air masses affecting the State belong to three types: (1) cold, dry air pouring down from subarctic North America; (2) warm, moist air streaming up on a long overland journey from the Gulf of Mexico and adjacent waters; and (3) cool, damp air moving from the North Atlantic. Because the atmospheric flow is usually from continental areas, Rhode Island is more influenced by the first two types than it is by the third. The ocean constitutes an important modifying factor, particularly in southeast sections of the State, but does not dominate the climate as it would if the prevailing circulation was onshore.

The procession of contrasting air masses and the relatively frequent passage of low-pressure systems bring about a roughly twice-weekly alternation from fair to cloudy or stormy weather, usually attended by abrupt changes in temperature, moisture, sunshine, wind direction, and speed. There is no regular or persistent rhythm to this sequence, and it is sometimes interrupted by periods of several days, or infrequently of a few weeks, with the same weather pattern.

TEMPERATURE. The mean annual temperature ranges from 48 to 49°F., except near the south shore, Narragansett Bay, and in the area around Providence, where it is 50 to 51°F. Southwestern Rhode Island, from four to 10 miles inland, exhibits a coolness not suggested by the nearness to the ocean or the general elevation of 50 to 150 feet. Here the annual mean temperature is not more than 48°F., making the section as cool as the cooler areas of the northwest interior.

The average daily minimum temperature in January and February is 19 to 20°F. over about two-thirds of the State, increasing to near 25°F. in immediate coastal sections. The number of days with minimum temperatures of zero or below averages one or less per year in the Bay and coastal areas, increasing to about five per year in most of the interior. A maximum temperature of 32°F. or lower occurs on an average of 20 to 25 days per year along the shoreline and 30 to 40 days in the remainder of the State. Summer temperatures are considerably influenced by proximity to the coastal waters and the frequent onshore flow of air during the warmer months. The average July maximum temperature is about 80°F., except in the northwestern interior where it is a few degrees higher. The greatest number of hot days occurs in the metropolitan areas and in parts of the northern interior. Here, about eight to 10 days of temperatures 90°F. or higher may be expected per year. Near the immediate coast the occurrence of 90°F. temperatures is limited to one day in the average summer, if it occurs at all. The length of the freeze-free season, as limited by the occurrence of temperatures of 32°F. or lower, averages from 155 to 180 days in most of the State. Climatic differences of temperature in this small State are very striking in the fall season. Autumnal coloration of foliage will be past its peak of brilliance in the northwestern interior before leaves have begun to noticeably turn color in the Newport area of the southeast.

PRECIPITATION. The climate of Rhode Island is characterized by the rather even distribution of precipitation throughout the year. Storm centers and their accompanying fronts are the principal year-round producers of precipitation. Storms moving up the Atlantic coast generally yield the heaviest amounts of rain and snow. Bands and patches of thunderstorms or convective showers contribute considerable precipitation in the summer and make up the difference resulting from decreased activity of the storm centers. In comparison with the general storms, these are of brief duration, but they yield the heaviest local rainfall.

Annual precipitation averages 42 to 46 inches over most of the State, with a tendency for decreasing amounts from west to east. It varies from about 40 inches in the immediate southeastern Bay area and on Block Island to 48 inches in the western uplands. Total precipitation in the freeze-free season of April through October shows similar differences over the State with an average of 22 to 24 inches near the Bay and 26 to 29 inches in the western interior. While there are no pronounced wet and dry months as in other climates, the months of May through July are relatively dry in proximity of the Bay. Measurable precipitation falls on an average of one day in three or on approximately 120 days per year. Periods of five days or more of successive daily precipitation occur a few times during most years. Extended periods of little or no precipitation are observed nearly every summer or early fall. Such a period may last from 10 to 20 days.

SNOWFALL. The average annual snowfall in Rhode Island increases from about 20 inches on Block Island and along the southeast shores of Narragansett Bay to from 40 to 55 inches in the western third of the State. Most of the snow falls in January and February; however, there are occasional winters when in coastal sections particularly, heavier monthly amounts will occur in December or March. In the western and northern portions of the State the first snowfall of one inch or more usually occurs in mid or late November. The southeastern Bay area does not observe measurable snow before December in the great majority of years. The last measurable snowfall usually occurs by late March in the populous areas of the State, although an April snowstorm is by no means rare. The average number of days with one inch or more of snow on the ground also increases from the shore areas to the western interior. In the latter, a snowcover prevails most of the time from mid or late December to about mid-March. Near the Bay a snow cover does not last more than a few days unless a heavy snowstorm is followed by prolonged cold temperatures.

WINDS AND STORMS. The prevailing wind in Rhode Island is northwesterly from December through March, and southwesterly in the remaining months. An important feature of the climate is the sea breeze which affects a considerable portion of the State's area. From approximately late spring to mid autumn this cool onshore wind blows during the afternoon hours and penetrates from five to 10 miles inland. The fact that much of Rhode Island is within 10 miles of the Sound or Bay, accounts for the relatively cool summer maximum temperatures. Aside from hurricanes, coastal storms or "northeasters" are the most serious weather hazard in Rhode Island. They generate very strong winds and heavy rains, and produce the greatest snowfalls in the winter. Hurricanes or storms of tropical origin occasionally affect the State during the summer or fall months. Localized thunderstorms with heavy and intense rainfall on occasions cause damaging flash floods in the small as well as the larger streams of the State.

OTHER CLIMATIC ELEMENTS. The percentage of possible sunshine averages 55 to 60 percent, ranging from about 50 percent in the winter months to a little over 60 percent during the summer. The average number of clear and cloudy days per year are about equal. The highest number of clear days per month usually occurs in September or October, while the maximum number of cloudy days are noted in December and January. Heavy fog is observed on an average of about 50 days per year in the southeastern areas of the Bay. This number decreases to 30 or 35 along the western and northern shores of the Bay, and to about 25 days in the western interior.

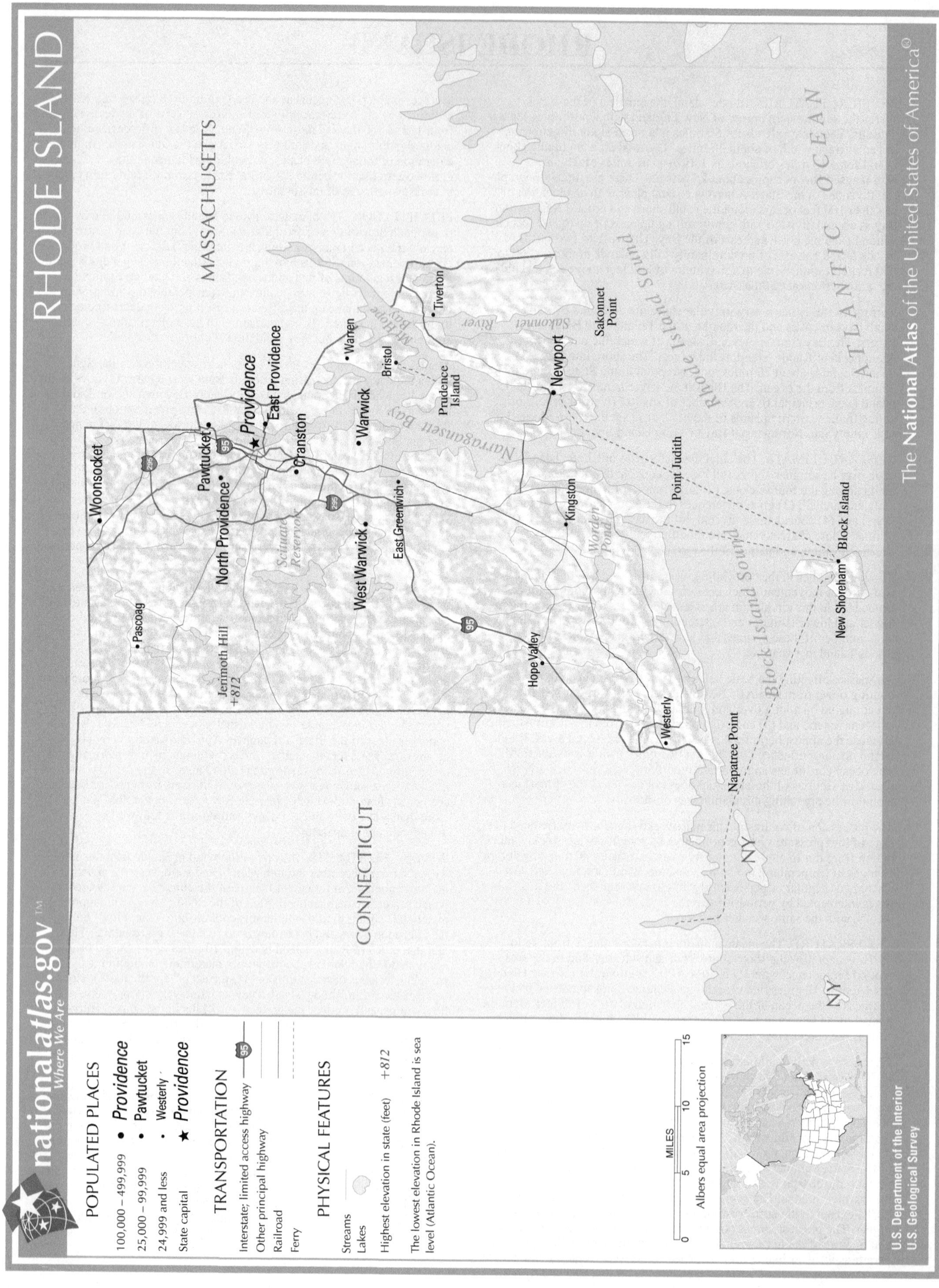
RHODE ISLAND
nationalatlas.gov™
Where We Are
POPULATED PLACES
100,000 – 499,999 • Providence
25,000 – 99,999 • Pawtucket
24,999 and less · Westerly
State capital ★ Providence
TRANSPORTATION
Interstate; limited access highway 95
Other principal highway
Railroad
Ferry
PHYSICAL FEATURES
Streams
Lakes
Highest elevation in state (feet) +812
The lowest elevation in Rhode Island is sea level (Atlantic Ocean).
MILES
0 5 10 15
Albers equal area projection
U.S. Department of the Interior
U.S. Geological Survey
The National Atlas of the United States of America®
MASSACHUSETTS
CONNECTICUT
NY
NY
ATLANTIC OCEAN
Rhode Island Sound
Block Island Sound
Narragansett Bay
Mt Hope Bay
Sakonnet River
Scituate Reservoir
Worden Pond
Woonsocket
Pawtucket
North Providence
Providence
East Providence
Cranston
Warwick
West Warwick
East Greenwich
Warren
Bristol
Tiverton
Prudence Island
Newport
Sakonnet Point
Point Judith
Kingston
Block Island
New Shoreham
Pascoag
Jerimoth Hill +812
Hope Valley
Westerly
Napatree Point
95
295

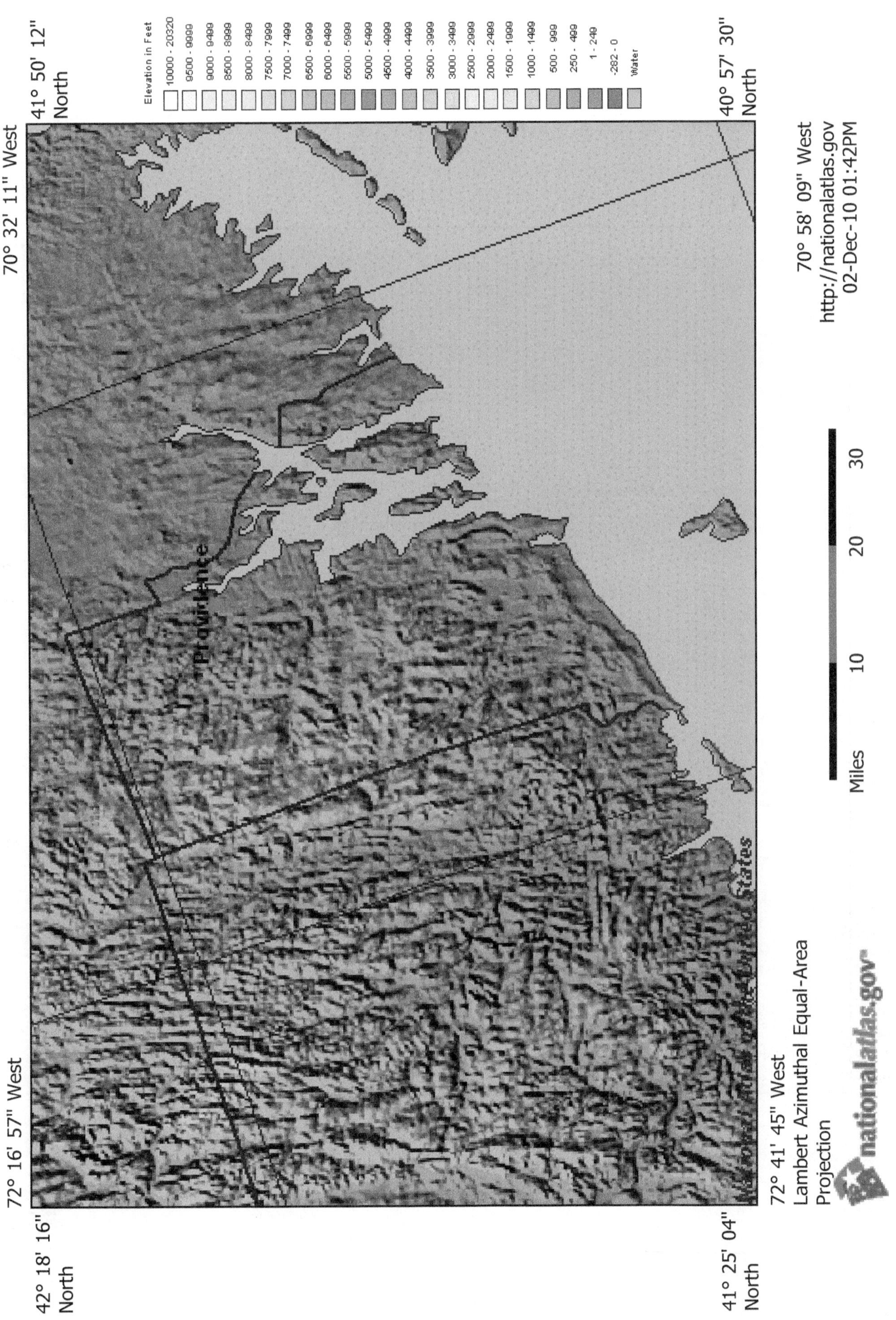
42° 18' 16" North
72° 16' 57" West
70° 32' 11" West
41° 50' 12" North
Elevation in Feet
10000 - 20320
9500 - 9999
9000 - 9499
8500 - 8999
8000 - 8499
7500 - 7999
7000 - 7499
6500 - 6999
6000 - 6499
5500 - 5999
5000 - 5499
4500 - 4999
4000 - 4499
3500 - 3999
3000 - 3499
2500 - 2999
2000 - 2499
1500 - 1999
1000 - 1499
500 - 999
250 - 499
1 - 249
-282 - 0
Water
40° 57' 30" North
Providence
70° 58' 09" West
http://nationalatlas.gov
02-Dec-10 01:42PM
Miles
10
20
30
41° 25' 04" North
72° 41' 45" West
Lambert Azimuthal Equal-Area Projection
nationalatlas.gov

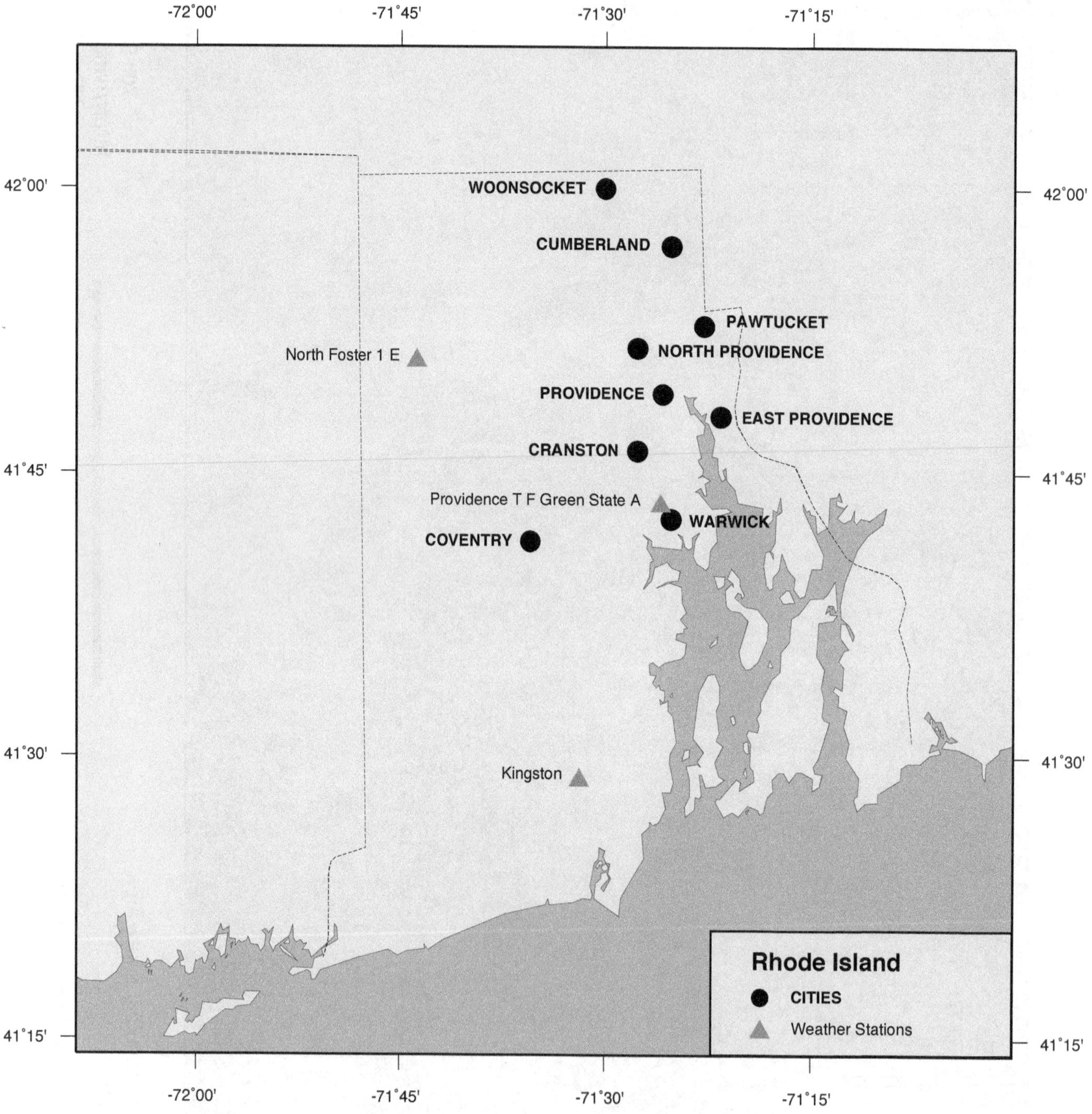
-72°00'
-71°45'
-71°30'
-71°15'
42°00'
41°45'
41°30'
41°15'
WOONSOCKET
CUMBERLAND
PAWTUCKET
North Foster 1 E
NORTH PROVIDENCE
PROVIDENCE
EAST PROVIDENCE
CRANSTON
Providence T F Green State A
WARWICK
COVENTRY
Kingston
Rhode Island
CITIES
Weather Stations

Rhode Island Weather Stations by County

County	Station Name
Kent	Providence T F Green State Arpt
Providence	North Foster 1 E
Washington	Kingston

See User Guide for station inclusion criteria.

Rhode Island Weather Stations by City

City	Station Name	Miles
Bristol	New Bedford, MA	17.6
	Rochester, MA	19.4
	Taunton, MA	18.3
	Kingston	19.4
	Providence T F Green State Arpt	8.9
Coventry	Kingston	14.8
	North Foster 1 E	13.2
	Providence T F Green State Arpt	8.0
Cranston	Taunton, MA	21.9
	West Medway, MA	25.0
	Kingston	20.4
	North Foster 1 E	15.3
	Providence T F Green State Arpt	4.0
Cumberland	Milton Blue Hill Observatory, MA	24.0
	Brockton, MA	22.5
	Taunton, MA	18.3
	Walpole 2, MA	17.2
	West Medway, MA	12.7
	North Foster 1 E	17.7
	Providence T F Green State Arpt	16.2
East Providence	New Bedford, MA	25.0
	Rochester, MA	22.9
	Taunton, MA	16.5
	West Medway, MA	23.1
	Kingston	23.8
	North Foster 1 E	19.5
	Providence T F Green State Arpt	7.1
Johnston	Taunton, MA	22.8
	West Medway, MA	21.4
	Kingston	23.8
	North Foster 1 E	12.2
	Providence T F Green State Arpt	8.3
Lincoln	Brockton, MA	24.4
	Taunton, MA	19.4
	Walpole 2, MA	19.7
	West Medway, MA	14.8
	North Foster 1 E	15.7
	Providence T F Green State Arpt	14.0
Newport	New Bedford, MA	21.9
	Kingston	11.5
	Providence T F Green State Arpt	16.8
North Kingstown	Kingston	7.7
	North Foster 1 E	23.2
	Providence T F Green State Arpt	9.4
North Providence	Taunton, MA	20.3
	Walpole 2, MA	23.7
	West Medway, MA	18.9
	North Foster 1 E	14.2
	Providence T F Green State Arpt	10.0
Pawtucket	Brockton, MA	22.8
	Rochester, MA	24.6
	Taunton, MA	16.1
	Walpole 2, MA	21.1
	West Medway, MA	18.0

City	Station Name	Miles
Pawtucket *(cont.)*	North Foster 1 E	18.4
	Providence T F Green State Arpt	11.4
Providence	Taunton, MA	19.2
	West Medway, MA	21.4
	Kingston	24.1
	North Foster 1 E	16.0
	Providence T F Green State Arpt	7.4
Smithfield	Taunton, MA	24.0
	Walpole 2, MA	24.1
	West Medway, MA	17.7
	North Foster 1 E	10.6
	Providence T F Green State Arpt	13.0
South Kingstown	Kingston	2.3
	Providence T F Green State Arpt	19.0
Warwick	Taunton, MA	22.4
	Kingston	17.0
	North Foster 1 E	18.5
	Providence T F Green State Arpt	0.6
West Warwick	Kingston	15.0
	North Foster 1 E	15.2
	Providence T F Green State Arpt	4.5
Westerly	Groton, CT	12.7
	Norwich Public Util Plant, CT	17.6
	Kingston	16.2
Woonsocket	Milton Blue Hill Observatory, MA	24.8
	Taunton, MA	23.6
	Walpole 2, MA	17.3
	West Medway, MA	9.7
	North Foster 1 E	15.8
	Providence T F Green State Arpt	20.1

Note: Miles is the distance between the geographic center of the city and the weather station.

See User Guide for station inclusion criteria.

Rhode Island Weather Stations by Elevation

Feet	Station Name
629	North Foster 1 E
100	Kingston
50	Providence T F Green State Arpt

See User Guide for station inclusion criteria.

Providence T F Green State Arpt.

The proximity to Narragansett Bay and the Atlantic Ocean plays an important part in determining the climate for Providence and vicinity. In winter, the temperatures are modified considerably, and many major snowstorms change to rain before reaching the area. In summer, many days that could be uncomfortably warm are cooled by refreshing sea breezes. At other times of the year, sea fog may be advected in over land by onshore winds. In fact, most cases of dense fog are produced this way, but the number of such days is few, averaging two or three days per month. In early fall, severe coastal storms of tropical origin sometimes bring destructive winds to this area. Even at other times of the year, it is usually coastal storms which produce the severest weather.

The temperature for the entire year averages around 50 degrees with 70 degree temperatures common from near the end of May to the latter part of September. During this period, there may be several days reaching 90 degrees or more. Temperatures of 100 degrees and more are rare.

Freezing temperatures occur on the average about 125 days per year. They become a common daily occurrence in the latter part of November, and become less frequent near the end of March. The average date for the last freeze in spring is mid-April, while the average date for the first freeze in fall is late October, making the growing season about 195 days in length. Sub-zero weather in winter seldom occurs, averaging less than one day for December and one or two days each for January and February.

Measurable precipitation occurs on about one day out of every three, and is fairly evenly distributed throughout the year. There is usually no definite dry season, but occasionally droughts do occur.

Thunderstorms are responsible for much of the rainfall from May through August. They usually produce heavy, and sometimes even excessive amounts of rainfall. However, since their duration is relatively short, damage is ordinarily light. The thunderstorms of summer are frequently accompanied by extremely gusty winds.

The first measurable snowfall of winter usually comes toward the end of November, and the last in spring is about the middle of March. Winters with over 50 inches of snow are not common. The area normally receives less than 25 inches. The month of greatest snowfall is usually February, but January and March are close seconds. It is unusual for the ground to remain well covered with snow for any long period of time.

Providence T F Green State Arpt. *Kent County* Elevation: 50 ft. Latitude: 41° 43' N Longitude: 71° 26' W

	JAN	FEB	MAR	APR	MAY	JUN	JUL	AUG	SEP	OCT	NOV	DEC	YEAR
Mean Maximum Temp. (°F)	37.4	40.2	47.6	58.4	68.3	77.4	82.8	81.4	74.2	63.2	53.1	42.4	60.5
Mean Temp. (°F)	29.3	31.9	38.7	49.0	58.5	67.8	73.5	72.4	64.7	53.5	44.4	34.3	51.5
Mean Minimum Temp. (°F)	21.1	23.5	29.8	39.6	48.6	58.3	64.2	63.3	55.3	43.7	35.7	26.2	42.4
Extreme Maximum Temp. (°F)	69	72	80	93	95	97	102	100	100	85	78	72	102
Extreme Minimum Temp. (°F)	-12	-2	4	18	31	41	48	41	33	22	6	-10	-12
Days Maximum Temp. ≥ 90°F	0	0	0	0	1	2	4	3	1	0	0	0	11
Days Maximum Temp. ≤ 32°F	9	6	2	0	0	0	0	0	0	0	0	5	22
Days Minimum Temp. ≤ 32°F	27	24	19	4	0	0	0	0	0	2	12	24	112
Days Minimum Temp. ≤ 0°F	1	0	0	0	0	0	0	0	0	0	0	0	1
Heating Degree Days (base 65°F)	1,101	930	809	475	220	42	2	6	82	359	611	945	5,582
Cooling Degree Days (base 65°F)	0	0	0	2	25	134	274	242	80	8	0	0	765
Mean Precipitation (in.)	3.69	3.23	4.73	4.49	3.52	3.63	3.23	3.58	3.87	3.90	4.50	4.13	46.50
Maximum Precipitation (in.)*	11.7	7.2	8.8	12.7	10.6	11.1	8.1	11.1	7.9	11.9	11.0	10.8	67.5
Minimum Precipitation (in.)*	0.5	0.4	0.6	1.5	0.7	0	0.3	0.7	0.8	0.4	0.8	0.6	25.4
Extreme Maximum Daily Precip. (in.)	2.90	2.74	3.40	4.30	5.15	3.29	3.57	3.37	3.95	4.38	3.52	3.28	5.15
Days With ≥ 0.1" Precipitation	7	6	8	7	7	6	6	6	6	6	7	7	79
Days With ≥ 0.5" Precipitation	3	2	3	3	2	2	2	3	2	2	3	3	30
Days With ≥ 1.0" Precipitation	1	1	1	1	1	1	1	1	1	1	1	1	12
Mean Snowfall (in.)	9.8	8.6	5.7	0.6	***trace***	***trace***	***0.0***	***0.0***	***0.0***	***trace***	1.6	***8.2***	***34.5***
Maximum Snowfall (in.)*	32	31	32	8	trace	0	0	0	0	3	8	20	71
Maximum 24-hr. Snowfall (in.)*	10	18	15	7	trace	0	0	0	0	3	8	11	18
Maximum Snow Depth (in.)	20	15	8	5	trace	***trace***	0	0	***0***	***trace***	7	14	***20***
Days With ≥ 1.0" Snow Depth	10	7	3	0	0	***0***	0	0	***0***	***0***	1	5	***26***
Thunderstorm Days*	< 1	< 1	1	1	3	4	4	4	2	1	1	< 1	21
Foggy Days*	11	10	13	13	15	16	17	17	15	14	13	12	166
Predominant Sky Cover*	OVR	OVR	OVR	OVR	OVR	OVR	OVR	OVR	OVR	OVR	OVR	OVR	OVR
Mean Relative Humidity 7am (%)*	71	71	71	70	73	76	78	81	83	81	78	74	76
Mean Relative Humidity 4pm (%)*	58	55	54	51	55	58	58	60	60	58	60	60	57
Mean Dewpoint (°F)*	18	18	25	34	45	56	62	61	54	43	34	23	39
Prevailing Wind Direction*	NW	NW	NW	NW	S	S	SW	SW	SW	N	NW	NW	WNW
Prevailing Wind Speed (mph)*	13	13	13	13	10	9	10	9	10	10	12	13	12
Maximum Wind Gust (mph)*	73	68	71	61	54	54	54	105	81	59	71	68	105

Note: (*) Period of record is 1948-1995

Kingston *Washington County* Elevation: 100 ft. Latitude: 41° 29' N Longitude: 71° 32' W

	JAN	FEB	MAR	APR	MAY	JUN	JUL	AUG	SEP	OCT	NOV	DEC	YEAR
Mean Maximum Temp. (°F)	39.1	41.9	48.5	58.7	68.6	77.3	82.3	81.3	74.6	64.1	54.1	43.8	61.2
Mean Temp. (°F)	29.3	31.8	38.0	47.6	57.0	66.1	71.4	70.5	63.3	52.4	43.8	34.2	50.4
Mean Minimum Temp. (°F)	19.4	21.6	27.6	36.5	45.3	54.9	60.5	59.6	51.9	40.6	33.5	24.6	39.7
Extreme Maximum Temp. (°F)	65	67	79	89	95	95	98	97	92	85	78	73	98
Extreme Minimum Temp. (°F)	-21	-15	-2	17	25	35	41	34	28	16	-4	-12	-21
Days Maximum Temp. ≥ 90°F	0	0	0	0	0	1	3	2	0	0	0	0	6
Days Maximum Temp. ≤ 32°F	7	4	1	0	0	0	0	0	0	0	0	3	15
Days Minimum Temp. ≤ 32°F	27	24	22	10	2	0	0	0	0	8	16	25	134
Days Minimum Temp. ≤ 0°F	2	1	0	0	0	0	0	0	0	0	0	0	3
Heating Degree Days (base 65°F)	1,101	933	829	515	256	57	6	14	108	391	630	948	5,788
Cooling Degree Days (base 65°F)	0	0	0	1	14	97	212	192	63	6	0	0	585
Mean Precipitation (in.)	4.07	3.56	5.23	5.16	3.94	4.22	3.61	4.31	4.06	4.27	5.04	4.62	52.09
Extreme Maximum Daily Precip. (in.)	2.85	3.12	3.82	3.08	4.24	4.95	4.61	4.20	2.91	6.42	4.43	4.28	6.42
Days With ≥ 0.1" Precipitation	7	6	7	7	8	7	6	6	6	6	7	7	80
Days With ≥ 0.5" Precipitation	3	2	3	4	2	2	2	3	3	3	3	3	33
Days With ≥ 1.0" Precipitation	1	1	2	2	1	1	1	1	1	1	2	1	15
Mean Snowfall (in.)	8.8	7.7	4.8	1.1	trace	0.0	0.0	0.0	0.0	0.0	0.9	6.8	30.1
Maximum Snow Depth (in.)	22	18	9	7	trace	0	0	0	0	0	7	17	22
Days With ≥ 1.0" Snow Depth	11	8	4	0	0	0	0	0	0	0	0	5	28

North Foster 1 E *Providence County* Elevation: 629 ft. Latitude: 41° 51' N Longitude: 71° 44' W

	JAN	FEB	MAR	APR	MAY	JUN	JUL	AUG	SEP	OCT	NOV	DEC	YEAR
Mean Maximum Temp. (°F)	34.7	38.2	46.3	57.9	68.2	75.9	80.5	79.1	71.9	61.1	50.4	39.2	58.6
Mean Temp. (°F)	26.0	28.9	36.3	47.1	56.9	65.4	70.5	69.3	61.8	50.9	41.4	30.9	48.8
Mean Minimum Temp. (°F)	17.2	19.6	26.2	36.2	45.6	54.8	60.4	59.4	51.6	40.6	32.3	22.5	38.8
Extreme Maximum Temp. (°F)	67	68	88	94	93	94	97	96	94	82	78	75	97
Extreme Minimum Temp. (°F)	-13	-10	-1	14	27	36	42	40	31	21	4	-15	-15
Days Maximum Temp. ≥ 90°F	0	0	0	0	0	1	2	1	0	0	0	0	4
Days Maximum Temp. ≤ 32°F	13	8	3	0	0	0	0	0	0	0	1	8	33
Days Minimum Temp. ≤ 32°F	29	26	24	10	1	0	0	0	0	5	17	27	139
Days Minimum Temp. ≤ 0°F	3	1	0	0	0	0	0	0	0	0	0	1	5
Heating Degree Days (base 65°F)	1,203	1,014	884	535	264	72	10	21	135	436	703	1,052	6,329
Cooling Degree Days (base 65°F)	0	0	0	3	19	90	186	160	46	4	0	0	508
Mean Precipitation (in.)	4.20	3.81	5.20	4.82	3.85	4.57	3.87	4.27	3.96	4.78	4.99	4.70	53.02
Extreme Maximum Daily Precip. (in.)	2.74	2.33	4.38	3.84	3.09	5.25	4.68	7.01	4.29	4.66	2.87	3.58	7.01
Days With ≥ 0.1" Precipitation	8	6	8	8	8	7	6	6	6	7	7	8	85
Days With ≥ 0.5" Precipitation	3	3	3	3	3	3	3	3	3	3	4	3	37
Days With ≥ 1.0" Precipitation	1	1	1	1	1	1	1	1	1	2	1	1	13
Mean Snowfall (in.)	14.4	12.0	11.6	3.0	trace	0.0	0.0	0.0	0.0	0.1	2.7	13.3	57.1
Maximum Snow Depth (in.)	30	27	24	23	trace	0	0	0	0	trace	14	22	30
Days With ≥ 1.0" Snow Depth	19	16	10	1	0	0	0	0	0	0	2	12	60

Rhode Island Weather Station Rankings

Annual Extreme Maximum Temperature

Highest Rank	Station Name	°F	Lowest Rank	Station Name	°F
1	Providence T F Green State Arpt	102	1	North Foster 1 E	97
2	Kingston	98	2	Kingston	98
3	North Foster 1 E	97	3	Providence T F Green State Arpt	102

Annual Mean Maximum Temperature

Highest Rank	Station Name	°F	Lowest Rank	Station Name	°F
1	Kingston	61.2	1	North Foster 1 E	58.6
2	Providence T F Green State Arpt	60.5	2	Providence T F Green State Arpt	60.5
3	North Foster 1 E	58.6	3	Kingston	61.2

 Rankings include 25 highest/lowest stations. If state has less than 25 stations, all stations are included. The period of record is 1980–2009. See User Guide for detailed explanation of data.

Annual Mean Temperature

Highest			Lowest		
Rank	**Station Name**	**°F**	**Rank**	**Station Name**	**°F**
1	Providence T F Green State Arpt	51.5	1	North Foster 1 E	48.8
2	Kingston	50.4	2	Kingston	50.4
3	North Foster 1 E	48.8	3	Providence T F Green State Arpt	51.5

Annual Mean Minimum Temperature

Highest			Lowest		
Rank	**Station Name**	**°F**	**Rank**	**Station Name**	**°F**
1	Providence T F Green State Arpt	42.4	1	North Foster 1 E	38.9
2	Kingston	39.7	2	Kingston	39.7
3	North Foster 1 E	38.9	3	Providence T F Green State Arpt	42.4

Rankings include 25 highest/lowest stations. If state has less than 25 stations, all stations are included. The period of record is 1980–2009. See User Guide for detailed explanation of data.

Annual Extreme Minimum Temperature

Highest

Rank	Station Name	°F
1	Providence T F Green State Arpt	-12
2	North Foster 1 E	-15
3	Kingston	-21

Lowest

Rank	Station Name	°F
1	Kingston	-21
2	North Foster 1 E	-15
3	Providence T F Green State Arpt	-12

July Mean Maximum Temperature

Highest

Rank	Station Name	°F
1	Providence T F Green State Arpt	82.8
2	Kingston	82.3
3	North Foster 1 E	80.5

Lowest

Rank	Station Name	°F
1	North Foster 1 E	80.5
2	Kingston	82.3
3	Providence T F Green State Arpt	82.8

 Rankings include 25 highest/lowest stations. If state has less than 25 stations, all stations are included. The period of record is 1980–2009. See User Guide for detailed explanation of data.

January Mean Minimum Temperature

Highest			Lowest		
Rank	Station Name	°F	Rank	Station Name	°F
1	Providence T F Green State Arpt	21.1	1	North Foster 1 E	17.2
2	Kingston	19.4	2	Kingston	19.4
3	North Foster 1 E	17.2	3	Providence T F Green State Arpt	21.1

Number of Days Annually Maximum Temperature ≥ 90°F

Highest			Lowest		
Rank	Station Name	Days	Rank	Station Name	Days
1	Providence T F Green State Arpt	11	1	North Foster 1 E	4
2	Kingston	6	2	Kingston	6
3	North Foster 1 E	4	3	Providence T F Green State Arpt	11

Number of Days Annually Maximum Temperature ≤ 32°F

Highest			Lowest		
Rank	Station Name	Days	Rank	Station Name	Days
1	North Foster 1 E	33	1	Kingston	15
2	Providence T F Green State Arpt	22	2	Providence T F Green State Arpt	22
3	Kingston	15	3	North Foster 1 E	33

Number of Days Annually Minimum Temperature ≤ 32°F

Highest			Lowest		
Rank	Station Name	Days	Rank	Station Name	Days
1	North Foster 1 E	139	1	Providence T F Green State Arpt	112
2	Kingston	134	2	Kingston	134
3	Providence T F Green State Arpt	112	3	North Foster 1 E	139

Rankings include 25 highest/lowest stations. If state has less than 25 stations, all stations are included. The period of record is 1980–2009. See User Guide for detailed explanation of data.

Number of Days Annually Minimum Temperature ≤ 0°F					
Highest			Lowest		
Rank	Station Name	Days	Rank	Station Name	Days
1	North Foster 1 E	5	1	Providence T F Green State Arpt	1
2	Kingston	3	2	Kingston	3
3	Providence T F Green State Arpt	1	3	North Foster 1 E	5

Number of Annual Heating Degree Days					
Highest			Lowest		
Rank	Station Name	Num.	Rank	Station Name	Num.
1	North Foster 1 E	6,329	1	Providence T F Green State Arpt	5,582
2	Kingston	5,788	2	Kingston	5,788
3	Providence T F Green State Arpt	5,582	3	North Foster 1 E	6,329

Number of Annual Cooling Degree Days

Highest			Lowest		
Rank	Station Name	Num.	Rank	Station Name	Num.
1	Providence T F Green State Arpt	765	1	North Foster 1 E	508
2	Kingston	585	2	Kingston	585
3	North Foster 1 E	508	3	Providence T F Green State Arpt	765

Annual Precipitation

Highest			Lowest		
Rank	Station Name	Inches	Rank	Station Name	Inches
1	North Foster 1 E	53.02	1	Providence T F Green State Arpt	46.50
2	Kingston	52.09	2	Kingston	52.09
3	Providence T F Green State Arpt	46.50	3	North Foster 1 E	53.02

Rankings include 25 highest/lowest stations. If state has less than 25 stations, all stations are included. The period of record is 1980–2009. See User Guide for detailed explanation of data.

Annual Extreme Maximum Daily Precipitation

Highest

Rank	Station Name	Inches
1	North Foster 1 E	7.01
2	Kingston	6.42
3	Providence T F Green State Arpt	5.15

Lowest

Rank	Station Name	Inches
1	Providence T F Green State Arpt	5.15
2	Kingston	6.42
3	North Foster 1 E	7.01

Number of Days Annually With ≥ 0.1 Inches of Precipitation

Highest

Rank	Station Name	Days
1	North Foster 1 E	85
2	Kingston	80
3	Providence T F Green State Arpt	79

Lowest

Rank	Station Name	Days
1	Providence T F Green State Arpt	79
2	Kingston	80
3	North Foster 1 E	85

Number of Days Annually With ≥ 0.5 Inches of Precipitation

Highest			Lowest		
Rank	Station Name	Days	Rank	Station Name	Days
1	North Foster 1 E	37	1	Providence T F Green State Arpt	30
2	Kingston	33	2	Kingston	33
3	Providence T F Green State Arpt	30	3	North Foster 1 E	37

Number of Days Annually With ≥ 1.0 Inches of Precipitation

Highest			Lowest		
Rank	Station Name	Days	Rank	Station Name	Days
1	Kingston	15	1	Providence T F Green State Arpt	12
2	North Foster 1 E	13	2	North Foster 1 E	13
3	Providence T F Green State Arpt	12	3	Kingston	15

 Rankings include 25 highest/lowest stations. If state has less than 25 stations, all stations are included. The period of record is 1980–2009. See User Guide for detailed explanation of data.

Annual Snowfall

Highest			Lowest		
Rank	Station Name	Inches	Rank	Station Name	Inches
1	North Foster 1 E	57.1	1	Kingston	30.1
2	Providence T F Green State Arpt	***34.5***	2	Providence T F Green State Arpt	***34.5***
3	Kingston	30.1	3	North Foster 1 E	57.1

Annual Maximum Snow Depth

Highest			Lowest		
Rank	Station Name	Inches	Rank	Station Name	Inches
1	North Foster 1 E	30	1	Providence T F Green State Arpt	***20***
2	Kingston	22	2	Kingston	22
3	Providence T F Green State Arpt	***20***	3	North Foster 1 E	30

Number of Days Annually With ≥ 1.0 Inch Snow Depth

Highest

Rank	Station Name	Days
1	North Foster 1 E	60
2	Kingston	28
3	Providence T F Green State Arpt	***26***

Lowest

Rank	Station Name	Days
1	Providence T F Green State Arpt	***26***
2	Kingston	28
3	North Foster 1 E	60

Significant Storm Events in Rhode Island: 2000 – 2009

Location or County	Date	Type	Mag.	Deaths	Injuries	Property Damage ($mil.)	Crop Damage ($mil.)
Kent and Providence Counties	03/05/01	Heavy Snow	na	0	0	10.0	0.0
Northwest Providence	03/22/01	Flood	na	0	0	3.0	0.0
Washington County	09/18/03	Heavy Surf/High Surf	na	1	0	0.0	0.0
Washington	08/11/04	Lightning	na	1	1	0.0	0.0
Kent, Providence and Washington Counties	10/15/05	Flood	na	0	0	1.6	0.0
Southeast Providence County	06/09/08	Heat	na	2	0	0.0	0.0
Washington County	09/28/08	High Surf	na	2	0	0.0	0.0

Note: Deaths, injuries, and damages are date and location specific.

SOUTH CAROLINA

PHYSICAL FEATURES. South Carolina is located on the southeastern coast of the United States between the southern part of the Appalachian Mountains and the Atlantic Ocean. Its north-south extent is 220 miles, from 32° to 35.2° N. latitude. The mountains in the extreme northwestern part of the State are 240 miles from the coastline. The coastline is 185 miles long and oriented southwest to northeast.

South Carolina shares some common topographic features with several eastern seaboard states. All of these features have a southwest to northeast orientation and extend across the whole State. The Blue Ridge Range of the Appalachian Mountains lies in the extreme northwestern part of the State. Elevations range from 1,000 to 2,000 feet with several peaks going over 3,000 feet. Sassafras Mountain, at 3,554 feet elevation, is the highest point in the State. The Mountain Region covers less than 10 percent of the State's area and to its southeast lies the Piedmont Plateau. The Plateau extends nearly to the center of the State with elevations decreasing northwest to southeast from 1,000 to 500 feet. There is a narrow hilly region where the Plateau descends to the Coastal Plain. In South Carolina this "fall line" region is known as the "Sand Hills;" where elevations range from 500 to 200 feet. The width of the Sand Hills area is about 30 to 40 miles. Between the Sand Hills and the Atlantic Ocean lies the Coastal Plain. The Plain is broad and nearly level with elevations mostly between 50 and 200 feet. About 40 percent of the area of the State lies in the Coastal Plain.

All of the State's rivers drain southeast from the Mountain Region or Piedmont Plateau toward the ocean. There are three major and one minor river-basin systems. The Santee is the largest and drains the entire center portion of the State. The Savannah drains the western part of the State. The third major system is the Pee Dee, located in the northeastern section. The Edisto is a lesser river system lying between the Santee and Savannah.

There are many low sea islands separated from the mainland by shallow straits, sounds, and coastal streams. The Intracoastal Waterway can be found along much of the coastline.

GENERAL CLIMATE. Several major factors combine to give South Carolina a pleasant, mild, and humid climate. It is located at a relatively low latitude (32 to 35° N.) and most of the State is under 1,000 feet in elevation. It has a long coastline along which moves the warm Gulf Stream current. The mountains to the north and west block or delay many cold air masses approaching from those directions. Even the deep cold air masses which cross the mountains rapidly are warmed somewhat as the air is heated by compression when it descends on the southeastern side. This effect can be seen on the maps of minimum temperature in January and to a lesser degree in July, where a fairly large area of relatively higher temperature appears just southeast of the mountains.

It is convenient for climatic discussion to divide the State into areas coinciding closely with the topographic features already discussed. Six areas can be defined: (1) the Outer Coastal Plain; (2) the Inner Coastal Plain; (3) the Sand Hills; (4) the Lower Piedmont Plateau; (5) the Upper Piedmont Plateau; and (6) the Mountain Region.

TEMPERATURE. Lower temperatures can be expected in the Upper Piedmont and Mountain Region, where latitude, elevation and distance inland all have large values. Higher temperatures will result from smaller values of the three factors, as are found along the southern coast. There is a gradual decrease in annual average temperature northwestward from 68°F. at the coast to 58°F. at the edge of the mountains. Within the Mountain Region, variations in temperature are due almost entirely to elevation differences. The ocean waters have very small daily and annual changes in temperature when compared with the land surface. The air over the coastal water is cooler than the air over the land in summer and warmer than the air over land in winter, and this has a controlling effect on the temperatures of locations on and very near the coast. The highest temperatures are found in the central part of the State with the coast being four to five degrees cooler. Clouds and rainfall have a minor effect on temperature. Maximum temperatures in summer are reduced slightly in areas where afternoon cloudiness and rain are persistent. Such an area is found along the Outer Coastal Plain where sea breezes produce clouds and rain nearly every summer day and dissipate at night. Summers are rather hot and air conditioning is desirable at elevations below 500 feet. Fall and spring are mild and winters are rather cool at elevations above 500 feet.

PRECIPITATION. Rainfall is adequate in all parts of the State. Annual rainfall averages up to 80 inches in the highest part of the Mountain Region and less than 42 inches in parts of the Inner Coastal Plain and the Sand Hills. The Mountain Region is wet with amounts of 56 inches or more, the Upper Piedmont is relatively wet with amounts of 48 to 55 inches, the Lower Piedmont is relatively dry with amounts of 43 to 47 inches, the Outer Coastal Plain is relatively wet with amounts of 48 to 53 inches, and the Inner Coastal Plain is relatively dry with amounts of 38 to 47 inches. The Sand Hills area is less clear cut but is in general a relatively wet strip with a small dry area imbedded in it a few miles south of Columbia. The immediate south coast is also on the dry side. The driest period is in October and November when there is little cyclonic storm activity. Rainfall increases gradually and reaches a peak in March when cyclone and cold front activity are at a maximum. There is a general decrease again to a dry period from late April through early June. From the latter part of June through early September is a wet period primarily due to thunderstorm and shower activity which reaches its peak in July, the wettest summer month. The summer maximum stretches a little into the fall along the coast due to occasional tropical storm activity.

Solid forms of precipitation include snow, sleet, and hail. Hail is not frequent but does occur with spring thunderstorms from March through early May. Snow and sleet may occur separately, combined or mixed with rain during the winter months of December through February. Snow may occur from one to three times in winter. Seldom do accumulations remain very long on the ground except in the mountains. Statewide snows of notable amounts can occur when a cyclonic storm moves northeastward along or just off the coast. Freezing rain also occurs from one to three times per winter in the northern half of the State. Severe drought occurs about once in 15 years with less severe and less widespread droughts about once in seven or eight years.

OTHER CLIMATIC ELEMENTS. The percent of possible sunshine received varies over the State, similar to the variation in cloudiness and precipitation. Values in winter range from 50 to 60 percent, in summer from 60 to 70, with the dry periods in spring and fall receiving 70 to 75 percent. The variation in relative humidity with time of day is considerably greater than day to day and month to month variations. Highest values of 80 to 90 percent or more are reached at about sunrise and the lowest values of 45 to 50 percent occur an hour or two after local noon. There is about a 10 percent difference between winter and summer, with summer being the higher of the two seasons. The prevailing surface winds tend to be either from northeast or southwest due to the presence and orientation of the Appalachian Mountains. Winds of all directions occur throughout the State during the year, but the prevailing directions by seasons are: spring—southwest; summer—south and southwest; autumn—northeast; and winter—northeast and southwest.

STORMS. Severe weather comes to South Carolina occasionally in the form of violent thunderstorms, tornadoes and hurricanes. Although thunderstorms are common in the summer months, the more violent ones generally accompany the squall lines and active cold fronts of spring. Generally, they bring high winds, hail, and considerable lightning, and sometimes spawn a tornado (average of seven or eight a year). Sixty percent of the tornadoes occur from March through June with April being the peak month with 25 percent. Tropical storms or hurricanes affect the State about one year out of two. Most of the occurrences are tropical storms which do little damage, frequently bringing rains at a time when they are needed. Most of the hurricanes affect only the Outer Coastal Plain. If they do come far inland, they decrease in intensity quite rapidly. Considerable flooding accompanies hurricanes which come very far inland and high tides occur along the coast to the north and east of the storm centers.

There is minor flooding somewhere in the State every year. It can occur on any of the many streams and rivers. There is a major flood about once every seven or eight years.

There have been many earth tremors in South Carolina over the years. The southern part of the Coastal Plain is indicated as earthquake prone.

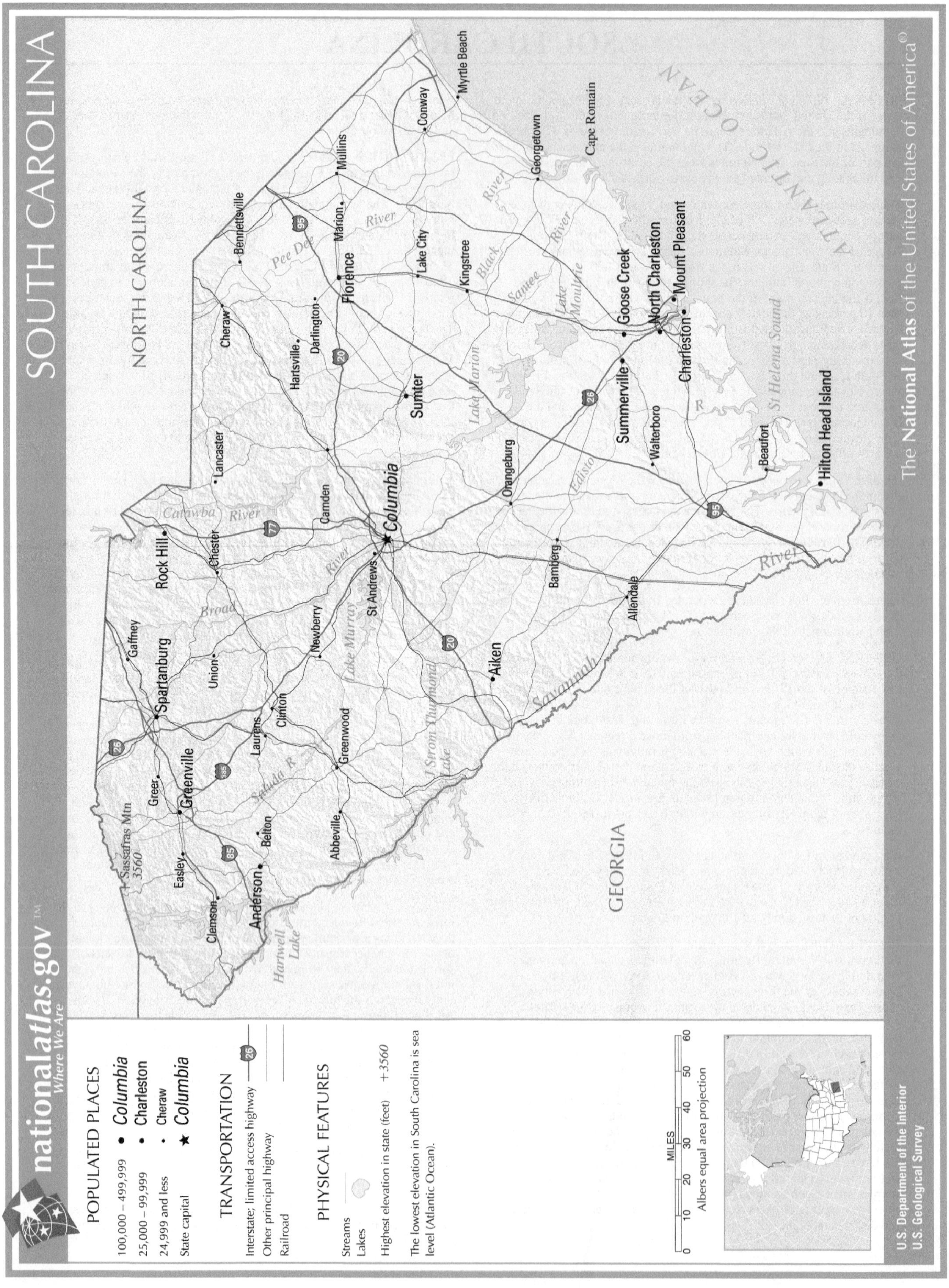
SOUTH CAROLINA
nationalatlas.gov™
Where We Are
POPULATED PLACES
100,000 – 499,999 • Columbia
25,000 – 99,999 • Charleston
24,999 and less · Cheraw
State capital ★ Columbia
TRANSPORTATION
Interstate; limited access highway 26
Other principal highway
Railroad
PHYSICAL FEATURES
Streams
Lakes
Highest elevation in state (feet) +3560
The lowest elevation in South Carolina is sea level (Atlantic Ocean).
MILES
0 10 20 30 40 50 60
Albers equal area projection
U.S. Department of the Interior
U.S. Geological Survey
The National Atlas of the United States of America®
NORTH CAROLINA
GEORGIA
ATLANTIC OCEAN
Sassafras Mtn 3560
Clemson
Easley
Anderson
Belton
Greer
Greenville
Spartanburg
Gaffney
Laurens
Clinton
Union
Rock Hill
Chester
Lancaster
Greenwood
Abbeville
Newberry
St Andrews
Columbia
Camden
Aiken
Allendale
Bamberg
Orangeburg
Sumter
Hartsville
Darlington
Cheraw
Bennettsville
Florence
Marion
Mullins
Lake City
Kingstree
Conway
Myrtle Beach
Georgetown
Cape Romain
Goose Creek
North Charleston
Mount Pleasant
Charleston
Summerville
Walterboro
Beaufort
Hilton Head Island
St Helena Sound
Hartwell Lake
J Strom Thurmond Lake
Lake Murray
Lake Marion
Lake Moultrie
Catawba River
Broad River
Saluda R
Savannah River
Edisto
Santee River
Black River
Pee Dee River
26
20
77
95
85
385

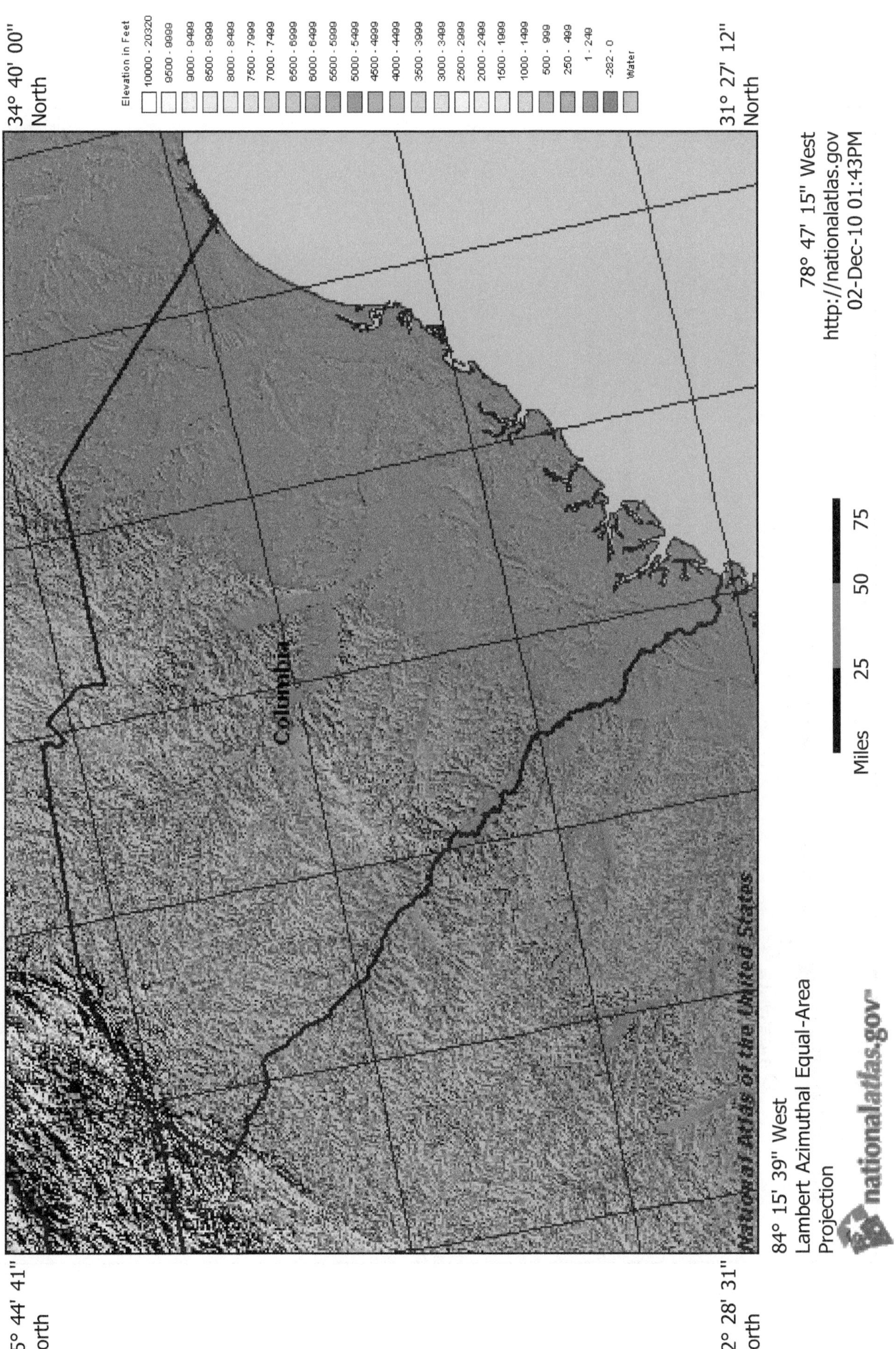
34° 40' 00" North
77° 53' 58" West
35° 44' 41" North
83° 34' 53" West
32° 28' 31" North
31° 27' 12" North
Elevation in Feet
10000 - 20320
9500 - 9999
9000 - 9499
8500 - 8999
8000 - 8499
7500 - 7999
7000 - 7499
6500 - 6999
6000 - 6499
5500 - 5999
5000 - 5499
4500 - 4999
4000 - 4499
3500 - 3999
3000 - 3499
2500 - 2999
2000 - 2499
1500 - 1999
1000 - 1499
500 - 999
250 - 499
1 - 249
-282 - 0
Water
Columbia
National Atlas of the United States
84° 15' 39" West
Lambert Azimuthal Equal-Area
Projection
nationalatlas.gov
78° 47' 15" West
http://nationalatlas.gov
02-Dec-10 01:43PM
Miles
25
50
75

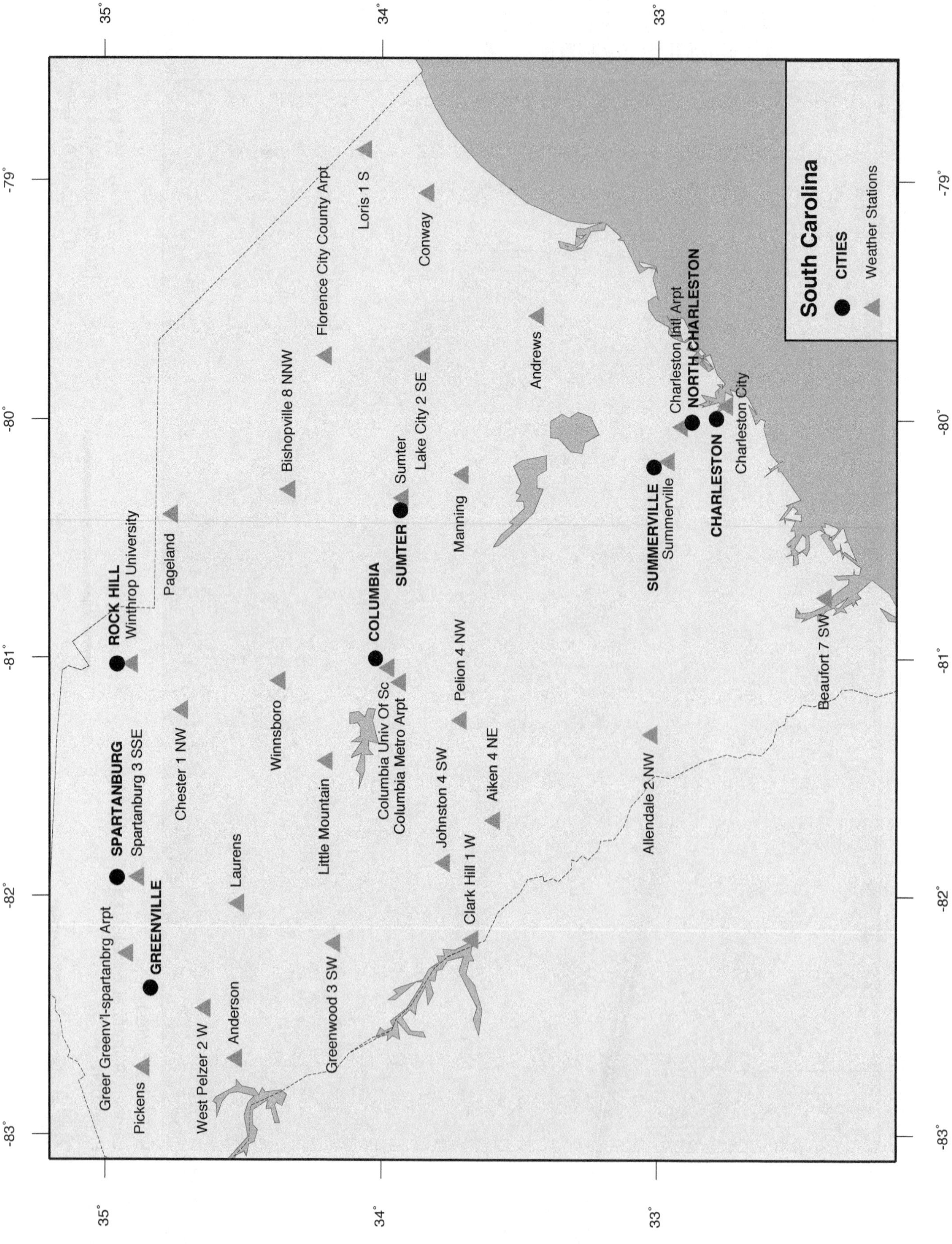
South Carolina
CITIES
Weather Stations
SPARTANBURG
GREENVILLE
ROCK HILL
COLUMBIA
SUMTER
SUMMERVILLE
NORTH CHARLESTON
CHARLESTON
Greer Greenv'l-spartanbrg Arpt
Pickens
Spartanburg 3 SSE
Winthrop University
West Pelzer 2 W
Anderson
Laurens
Chester 1 NW
Pageland
Winnsboro
Bishopville 8 NNW
Greenwood 3 SW
Little Mountain
Florence City County Arpt
Loris 1 S
Columbia Univ Of Sc
Columbia Metro Arpt
Sumter
Conway
Lake City 2 SE
Johnston 4 SW
Clark Hill 1 W
Pelion 4 NW
Manning
Aiken 4 NE
Andrews
Allendale 2 NW
Summerville
Charleston Intl Arpt
Charleston City
Beaufort 7 SW
35°
34°
33°
-79°
-80°
-81°
-82°
-83°

South Carolina Weather Stations by County

County	Station Name
Aiken	Aiken 4 NE
Allendale	Allendale 2 NW
Anderson	Anderson West Pelzer 2 W
Beaufort	Beaufort 7 SW
Charleston	Charleston City Charleston Intl Arpt
Chester	Chester 1 NW
Chesterfield	Pageland
Clarendon	Manning
Dorchester	Summerville
Edgefield	Johnston 4 SW
Fairfield	Winnsboro
Florence	Florence City County Arpt Lake City 2 SE
Georgetown	Andrews
Greenwood	Greenwood 3 SW
Horry	Conway Loris 1 S
Laurens	Laurens
Lee	Bishopville 8 NNW
Lexington	Columbia Metro Arpt Pelion 4 NW
Mccormick	Clark Hill 1 W
Newberry	Little Mountain
Pickens	Pickens
Richland	Columbia Univ of SC
Spartanburg	Greer Greenville-Spartanbrg Arpt Spartanburg 3 SSE
Sumter	Sumter
York	Winthrop University

See User Guide for station inclusion criteria.

South Carolina Weather Stations by City

City	Station Name	Miles
Aiken	Augusta Bush Field, GA	18.4
	Aiken 4 NE	4.7
	Johnston 4 SW	18.2
Anderson	Hartwell, GA	20.0
	Anderson	1.6
	West Pelzer 2 W	13.1
Charleston	Charleston Intl Arpt	7.9
	Charleston City	3.1
	Summerville	17.5
Columbia	Columbia Metro Arpt	7.7
	Columbia Univ of SC	2.4
	Winnsboro	24.6
Easley	Anderson	20.6
	Greer Greenville-Spartanbrg Arpt	21.8
	Pickens	8.2
	West Pelzer 2 W	13.5
Florence	Florence City County Arpt	2.7
	Lake City 2 SE	23.1
Goose Creek	Charleston Intl Arpt	6.1
	Charleston City	14.1
	Summerville	11.1
Greenville	Greer Greenville-Spartanbrg Arpt	9.9
	Pickens	19.4
	West Pelzer 2 W	14.7
Greenwood	Greenwood 3 SW	3.2
	Laurens	23.4
Greer	Tryon, NC	18.5
	Greer Greenville-Spartanbrg Arpt	2.4
	Spartanburg 3 SSE	18.0
	West Pelzer 2 W	24.2
Hilton Head Island	Beaufort 7 SW	13.1
Mauldin	Greer Greenville-Spartanbrg Arpt	9.4
	Laurens	24.0
	Pickens	24.4
	Spartanburg 3 SSE	23.3
	West Pelzer 2 W	13.8
Mount Pleasant	Charleston Intl Arpt	11.9
	Charleston City	5.9
	Summerville	22.3
Myrtle Beach	Conway	13.3
	Loris 1 S	23.5
North Augusta	Appling 2 NW, GA	21.4
	Augusta Bush Field, GA	10.2
	Aiken 4 NE	17.3
	Clark Hill 1 W	16.3
	Johnston 4 SW	19.8
North Charleston	Charleston Intl Arpt	0.5
	Charleston City	9.4
	Summerville	10.8

City	Station Name	Miles
Rock Hill	Charlotte Douglas Intl Arpt, NC	19.6
	Gastonia, NC	23.3
	Chester 1 NW	18.9
	Winthrop University	0.7
Spartanburg	Forest City 6 SW, NC	22.3
	Tryon, NC	24.6
	Greer Greenville-Spartanbrg Arpt	16.5
	Spartanburg 3 SSE	3.2
St. Andrews	Columbia Metro Arpt	7.0
	Columbia Univ of SC	6.9
	Little Mountain	20.5
	Pelion 4 NW	24.9
	Winnsboro	21.8
Summerville	Charleston Intl Arpt	11.3
	Charleston City	21.0
	Summerville	1.2
Sumter	Manning	18.3
	Sumter	1.7
Taylors	Tryon, NC	20.4
	Greer Greenville-Spartanbrg Arpt	5.5
	Pickens	23.0
	Spartanburg 3 SSE	22.5
	West Pelzer 2 W	20.6
Wade Hampton	Tryon, NC	22.7
	Greer Greenville-Spartanbrg Arpt	6.7
	Pickens	21.7
	Spartanburg 3 SSE	23.6
	West Pelzer 2 W	18.1

Note: Miles is the distance between the geographic center of the city and the weather station.

See User Guide for station inclusion criteria.

South Carolina Weather Stations by Elevation

Feet	Station Name
1,162	Pickens
957	Greer Greenville-Spartanbrg Arpt
861	West Pelzer 2 W
799	Anderson
710	Little Mountain
689	Winthrop University
620	Johnston 4 SW
620	Pageland
615	Greenwood 3 SW
609	Spartanburg 3 SSE
588	Laurens
560	Winnsboro
520	Chester 1 NW
450	Pelion 4 NW
399	Aiken 4 NE
379	Clark Hill 1 W
249	Bishopville 8 NNW
242	Columbia Univ of SC
212	Columbia Metro Arpt
180	Allendale 2 NW
176	Sumter
146	Florence City County Arpt
100	Manning
89	Loris 1 S
75	Lake City 2 SE
40	Charleston Intl Arpt
35	Andrews
35	Summerville
20	Beaufort 7 SW
20	Conway
9	Charleston City

See User Guide for station inclusion criteria.

Charleston Int'l Airport

Charleston is a peninsula city bounded on the west and south by the Ashley River, on the east by the Cooper River, and on the southeast by a spacious harbor. Weather records for the airport are from a site some 10 miles inland. The terrain is generally level, ranging in elevation from sea level to 20 feet on the peninsula, with gradual increases in elevation toward inland areas.

The climate is temperate, modified considerably by the nearness to the ocean. The marine influence is noticeable during winter when the low temperatures are sometimes 10-15 degrees higher on the peninsula than at the airport. By the same token, high temperatures are generally a few degrees lower on the peninsula. The prevailing winds are northerly in the fall and winter, southerly in the spring and summer.

Summer is warm and humid. Temperatures of 100 degrees or more are infrequent. High temperatures are generally several degrees lower along the coast than inland due to the cooling effect of the sea breeze. Summer is the rainiest season with 41 percent of the annual total. The rain, except during occasional tropical storms, generally occurs as showers or thunderstorms.

The fall season passes through the warm Indian Summer period to the pre-winter cold spells which begin late in November. From late September to early November the weather is mostly sunny and temperature extremes are rare. Late summer and early fall is the period of maximum threat to the South Carolina coast from hurricanes.

The winter months, December through February, are mild with periods of rain. However, the winter rainfall is generally of a more uniform type. There is some chance of a snow flurry, with the best probability of its occurrence in January, but a significant amount is rarely measured. An average winter would experience less than one cold wave and severe freeze. Temperatures of 20 degrees or less on the peninsula and along the coast are very unusual.

The most spectacular time of the year, weatherwise, is spring with its rapid changes from windy and cold in March to warm and pleasant in May. Severe local storms are more likely to occur in spring than in summer.

The average occurrence of the first freeze in the fall is early December, and the average last freeze is late February, giving an average growing season of about 294 days.

Charleston Int'l Airport *Charleston County* Elevation: 40 ft. Latitude: 32° 54' N Longitude: 80° 02' W

	JAN	FEB	MAR	APR	MAY	JUN	JUL	AUG	SEP	OCT	NOV	DEC	YEAR
Mean Maximum Temp. (°F)	59.1	62.8	69.5	76.4	83.1	88.3	91.2	89.6	84.9	77.0	69.7	61.7	76.1
Mean Temp. (°F)	48.7	52.0	58.4	65.1	72.7	79.2	82.4	81.2	76.4	67.1	58.8	51.3	66.1
Mean Minimum Temp. (°F)	38.3	41.2	47.2	53.8	62.2	70.0	73.6	72.8	67.9	57.2	48.0	40.8	56.1
Extreme Maximum Temp. (°F)	81	87	89	95	98	101	104	105	98	94	87	82	105
Extreme Minimum Temp. (°F)	6	16	15	30	42	53	62	57	46	34	24	11	6
Days Maximum Temp. ≥ 90°F	0	0	0	1	4	13	21	16	5	1	0	0	61
Days Maximum Temp. ≤ 32°F	0	0	0	0	0	0	0	0	0	0	0	0	0
Days Minimum Temp. ≤ 32°F	9	5	2	0	0	0	0	0	0	0	1	7	24
Days Minimum Temp. ≤ 0°F	0	0	0	0	0	0	0	0	0	0	0	0	0
Heating Degree Days (base 65°F)	501	368	228	83	9	0	0	0	2	62	212	426	1,891
Cooling Degree Days (base 65°F)	3	7	30	93	254	432	548	511	351	135	35	8	2,407
Mean Precipitation (in.)	3.63	2.92	3.83	3.00	3.09	5.48	6.43	6.84	5.56	3.77	2.49	3.07	50.11
Maximum Precipitation (in.)*	8.9	6.3	11.1	9.5	9.3	27.2	18.5	17.0	17.3	12.1	7.3	7.1	73.0
Minimum Precipitation (in.)*	0.6	0.3	0.7	trace	0.7	1.0	1.8	0.7	0.2	0.2	0.5	0.7	30.3
Extreme Maximum Daily Precip. (in.)	3.90	3.02	4.13	3.73	2.45	4.91	5.39	4.53	6.00	6.57	3.50	3.18	6.57
Days With ≥ 0.1" Precipitation	6	5	5	5	5	8	9	9	7	5	4	6	74
Days With ≥ 0.5" Precipitation	3	2	2	2	2	4	4	5	3	2	2	2	33
Days With ≥ 1.0" Precipitation	1	1	1	1	1	2	2	2	2	1	1	1	16
Mean Snowfall (in.)	0.0	***trace***	***0.1***	trace	trace	trace	trace	0.0	0.0	0.0	trace	0.5	***0.6***
Maximum Snowfall (in.)*	1	7	2	0	0	0	0	0	0	0	trace	8	9
Maximum 24-hr. Snowfall (in.)*	1	5	2	0	0	0	0	0	0	0	trace	6	6
Maximum Snow Depth (in.)	trace	***1***	***1***	trace	trace	trace	trace	0	0	0	trace	8	***8***
Days With ≥ 1.0" Snow Depth	0	***0***	0	0	0	0	0	0	0	0	0	0	***0***
Thunderstorm Days*	1	1	2	3	7	10	14	12	5	2	1	1	59
Foggy Days*	14	11	13	12	14	13	11	14	16	14	14	14	160
Predominant Sky Cover*	OVR	OVR	OVR	CLR	OVR	BRK	BRK	BRK	OVR	CLR	CLR	OVR	OVR
Mean Relative Humidity 7am (%)*	83	81	83	84	85	86	88	90	91	89	86	83	86
Mean Relative Humidity 4pm (%)*	55	52	51	51	56	62	66	66	65	58	56	55	58
Mean Dewpoint (°F)*	38	39	45	52	61	68	72	72	67	57	47	40	55
Prevailing Wind Direction*	NNE	SSW	SSW	SSW	S	S	SSW	S	NNE	NNE	NNE	NNE	NNE
Prevailing Wind Speed (mph)*	9	12	12	12	9	8	9	8	9	9	9	9	9
Maximum Wind Gust (mph)*	67	62	69	71	60	64	61	69	98	54	55	55	98

Note: (*) Period of record is 1945-1995

The period of record for National Weather Service station data is 1980 – 2009 except where noted. See User Guide for detailed explanation of data.

Columbia Metro Airport

Columbia is centrally located within the state of South Carolina and lies on the Congaree River near the confluence of the Broad and Saluda Rivers. The surrounding terrain is rolling, sloping from about 350 feet above sea level in northern Columbia to about 200 feet in the southeastern part of the city.

The climate in the Columbia area is relatively temperate. The Appalachian Mountain chain, some 150 miles to the northwest, frequently retards the approach of unseasonable cold weather in the winter. The terrain offers little moderating effect on the summer heat.

Long summers are prevalent with warm weather usually lasting from sometime in May into September. In summer the Bermuda high is the greatest single weather factor influencing the area. This permanent high more or less blocks the entry of cold fronts so that many stall before reaching central South Carolina. Also, the southwestern flow around the offshore Bermuda high pressure supplies moisture for the many summer thunderstorms. There are relatively few breaks in the heat during midsummer. The typical summer has about six days with 100 degrees or more. Thunderstorm activity usually shows a decided increase during June, decreasing about the first of September. About once or twice a year, passing tropical storms produce strong winds and heavy rains. The incidence of these storms is greatest in September, although they represent a possible threat from midsummer to late fall. Damage from tropical storms is usually minor in the Columbia area.

Fall is the most pleasant time of the year. Rainfall during the late fall is at an annual minimum, while the sunshine is at a relative maximum. Winters are mild with the cold weather usually lasting from late November to mid-March. The winter weather at Columbia is largely made up of polar air outbreaks that reach this area in a much modified form. On rare occasions in winter, Arctic air masses push southward as far as central South Carolina and cause some of the coldest temperatures. Disruption of activities from snowfall is unusual, in fact, more than three days of sustained snow cover is rare.

Spring is the most changeable season of the year. The temperature varies from an occasional cold snap in March to generally warm and pleasant in May. While tornadoes are infrequent, they occur most often in the spring. Hailstorms are not frequent, with the annual incidence at a maximum in spring and early summer. The average occurrence of the last spring freeze is very late March, and the first fall freeze is early November, for a growing period of about 218 days.

Columbia Metro Airport *Lexington County* Elevation: 212 ft. Latitude: 33° 57' N Longitude: 81° 07' W

	JAN	FEB	MAR	APR	MAY	JUN	JUL	AUG	SEP	OCT	NOV	DEC	YEAR
Mean Maximum Temp. (°F)	56.0	60.4	68.1	76.1	83.7	89.7	92.6	90.8	85.1	75.9	67.2	58.4	75.3
Mean Temp. (°F)	44.8	48.5	55.4	63.1	71.4	78.7	82.0	80.7	74.6	63.8	54.6	46.8	63.7
Mean Minimum Temp. (°F)	33.6	36.5	42.6	50.0	59.0	67.7	71.3	70.5	64.0	51.7	42.0	35.2	52.0
Extreme Maximum Temp. (°F)	80	84	90	94	101	106	106	107	99	95	86	82	107
Extreme Minimum Temp. (°F)	-1	13	4	26	35	44	55	56	41	27	19	6	-1
Days Maximum Temp. ≥ 90°F	0	0	0	1	6	17	23	19	8	1	0	0	75
Days Maximum Temp. ≤ 32°F	0	0	0	0	0	0	0	0	0	0	0	0	0
Days Minimum Temp. ≤ 32°F	15	11	5	1	0	0	0	0	0	1	7	14	54
Days Minimum Temp. ≤ 0°F	0	0	0	0	0	0	0	0	0	0	0	0	0
Heating Degree Days (base 65°F)	619	464	309	123	18	1	0	0	8	114	319	560	2,535
Cooling Degree Days (base 65°F)	1	3	18	73	222	418	534	493	300	85	14	3	2,164
Mean Precipitation (in.)	3.62	3.57	4.00	2.65	3.05	4.63	5.25	5.18	3.71	3.16	2.75	3.21	44.78
Maximum Precipitation (in.)*	9.3	8.7	10.9	6.8	8.8	14.8	17.5	16.7	8.8	12.1	7.2	8.5	70.5
Minimum Precipitation (in.)*	0.8	0.3	0.6	0.3	0.3	0.7	0.6	1.0	0.1	trace	0.4	0.3	27.4
Extreme Maximum Daily Precip. (in.)	2.27	2.68	3.22	2.35	4.47	4.84	4.00	4.72	5.17	3.83	2.60	3.06	5.17
Days With ≥ 0.1" Precipitation	7	6	6	5	5	7	8	7	5	4	5	5	70
Days With ≥ 0.5" Precipitation	3	3	3	2	2	3	3	3	2	2	2	2	30
Days With ≥ 1.0" Precipitation	1	1	1	1	1	1	2	2	1	1	1	1	14
Mean Snowfall (in.)	0.6	0.4	0.2	trace	trace	trace	0.0	trace	0.0	0.0	trace	0.1	1.3
Maximum Snowfall (in.)*	4	16	4	0	0	0	0	0	0	0	trace	9	18
Maximum 24-hr. Snowfall (in.)*	4	12	4	0	0	0	0	0	0	0	trace	9	12
Maximum Snow Depth (in.)	4	4	4	trace	trace	trace	0	trace	0	0	trace	1	4
Days With ≥ 1.0" Snow Depth	0	0	0	0	0	0	0	0	0	0	0	0	0
Thunderstorm Days*	1	2	3	4	6	9	13	10	4	1	1	< 1	54
Foggy Days*	13	12	13	10	14	15	15	20	18	15	13	13	171
Predominant Sky Cover*	OVR	OVR	OVR	CLR	OVR	SCT	SCT	SCT	OVR	CLR	CLR	OVR	OVR
Mean Relative Humidity 7am (%)*	83	83	84	83	84	85	88	91	91	90	88	84	86
Mean Relative Humidity 4pm (%)*	51	47	44	41	46	50	54	56	54	49	48	51	49
Mean Dewpoint (°F)*	34	35	41	48	58	65	69	69	64	52	43	36	51
Prevailing Wind Direction*	WSW	WSW	SW	SW	SW	SW	SW	SW	NE	NE	SW	WSW	SW
Prevailing Wind Speed (mph)*	8	9	9	9	8	8	7	7	9	9	8	8	8
Maximum Wind Gust (mph)*	54	69	69	61	61	78	64	56	70	54	51	49	78

Note: (*) Period of record is 1948-1995

Greenville-Spartanbrg Airport

This station, three miles south of Greer, South Carolina, is located in the Piedmont section, on the eastern slope of the Southern Appalachian Mountains. It is rolling country with the first ridge of the mountains about 20 miles to the northwest and the main ridge about 55 miles to the northwest. These mountains usually protect this area from the full force of the cold air masses which move southeastward from central Canada during the winter months.

At present, the National Weather Service Office is located at the Greenville-Spartanburg Jet Age Airport, on a level with, or slightly higher than, most of the surrounding countryside. No bodies of water are nearby. Temperatures are quite consistent with those in Greer, Greenville, and Spartanburg.

The elevation of the area, ranging from 800 to 1,100 feet is conducive to cool nights, especially during the summer months. Winters are quite pleasant, with the temperature remaining below freezing throughout the daylight hours only a few times during a normal year. There are usually two freezing rainstorms each winter and two or three small snowstorms.

Rainfall in this section is usually abundant and spread quite evenly through the months. Droughts have been experienced, but are usually of short duration.

The mountain ridges, which lie in a northeast-southwest direction, appear to have a definite overall influence on the direction of the wind. The prevailing directions are northeast and southwest, divided almost evenly, with fall and winter favoring northeast and spring and summer favoring southwest. Destructive winds occur occasionally, while tornadoes are infrequent in this vicinity.

In the southern two-thirds of Greenville and Spartanburg Counties, including the cities of the same names, the average occurrence of the last temperature of 32 degrees in spring is late March and the average occurrence of the first in fall is early November, giving an average growing season of 225 days. In a normal year some flowering shrubs bloom through the winter. In the higher elevations in the northern thirds of these counties, the growing season begins about one month later and ends about one month earlier.

Greenville-Spartanbrg Airport *Spartanburg County* Elevation: 957 ft. Latitude: 34° 54' N Longitude: 82° 13' W

	JAN	FEB	MAR	APR	MAY	JUN	JUL	AUG	SEP	OCT	NOV	DEC	YEAR
Mean Maximum Temp. (°F)	51.7	55.8	63.5	71.8	79.4	86.5	89.5	87.8	81.3	71.8	62.6	53.6	71.3
Mean Temp. (°F)	41.8	45.2	52.2	59.9	68.1	75.9	79.3	78.1	71.4	60.9	51.8	43.8	60.7
Mean Minimum Temp. (°F)	31.8	34.5	40.7	47.8	56.7	65.3	69.0	68.2	61.5	50.0	40.9	34.0	50.0
Extreme Maximum Temp. (°F)	78	81	89	93	94	100	104	105	96	92	83	79	105
Extreme Minimum Temp. (°F)	-4	8	11	24	31	47	56	53	39	26	19	5	-4
Days Maximum Temp. ≥ 90°F	0	0	0	0	2	10	16	12	3	0	0	0	43
Days Maximum Temp. ≤ 32°F	1	0	0	0	0	0	0	0	0	0	0	0	1
Days Minimum Temp. ≤ 32°F	17	12	6	1	0	0	0	0	0	1	6	15	58
Days Minimum Temp. ≤ 0°F	0	0	0	0	0	0	0	0	0	0	0	0	0
Heating Degree Days (base 65°F)	714	554	398	183	39	2	0	0	17	165	394	652	3,118
Cooling Degree Days (base 65°F)	0	0	7	36	141	336	450	412	216	45	4	1	1,648
Mean Precipitation (in.)	3.77	3.87	4.81	3.41	3.76	3.97	4.62	4.39	3.55	3.49	3.71	4.09	47.44
Maximum Precipitation (in.)*	7.2	7.4	11.4	11.3	8.9	10.1	13.6	17.4	11.6	10.2	7.8	8.4	70.4
Minimum Precipitation (in.)*	0.3	0.3	1.1	0.7	1.1	0.2	0.8	0.9	0.3	0.2	1.3	0.4	35.5
Extreme Maximum Daily Precip. (in.)	3.05	3.42	2.83	2.63	3.25	3.58	4.68	9.32	4.00	4.48	2.42	3.29	9.32
Days With ≥ 0.1" Precipitation	7	6	7	6	6	7	7	6	5	5	6	6	74
Days With ≥ 0.5" Precipitation	3	3	3	3	3	3	3	3	2	2	3	3	34
Days With ≥ 1.0" Precipitation	1	1	2	1	1	1	1	1	1	1	1	1	13
Mean Snowfall (in.)	2.4	1.2	1.0	trace	trace	trace	trace	trace	0.0	0.0	0.1	0.3	5.0
Maximum Snowfall (in.)*	12	12	10	trace	0	0	0	0	0	0	2	11	19
Maximum 24-hr. Snowfall (in.)*	12	8	9	trace	0	0	0	0	0	0	2	11	12
Maximum Snow Depth (in.)	12	6	5	trace	trace	trace	trace	trace	0	0	1	2	12
Days With ≥ 1.0" Snow Depth	2	0	0	0	0	0	0	0	0	0	0	0	2
Thunderstorm Days*	1	1	2	3	6	7	10	7	3	1	1	< 1	42
Foggy Days*	13	11	11	9	12	14	16	19	15	11	11	12	154
Predominant Sky Cover*	OVR	OVR	OVR	CLR	OVR	OVR	OVR	OVR	OVR	CLR	CLR	OVR	OVR
Mean Relative Humidity 7am (%)*	77	75	77	78	83	85	88	90	90	85	81	78	82
Mean Relative Humidity 4pm (%)*	52	47	46	44	51	54	57	58	57	51	51	53	52
Mean Dewpoint (°F)*	28	29	37	44	55	63	68	67	61	49	39	32	48
Prevailing Wind Direction*	SW	NE	SW	SW	SW	SW	SW	NNE	NE	NNE	NNE	SW	NE
Prevailing Wind Speed (mph)*	9	9	10	10	9	8	8	7	8	8	8	9	9
Maximum Wind Gust (mph)*	63	66	61	71	53	60	66	58	45	48	53	51	71

Note: (*) Period of record is 1962-1995

The period of record for National Weather Service station data is 1980 – 2009 except where noted. See User Guide for detailed explanation of data.

Aiken 4 NE *Aiken County* Elevation: 399 ft. Latitude: 33° 36' N Longitude: 81° 41' W

	JAN	FEB	MAR	APR	MAY	JUN	JUL	AUG	SEP	OCT	NOV	DEC	YEAR
Mean Maximum Temp. (°F)	57.7	62.6	70.3	78.7	85.9	91.4	94.2	92.0	86.8	77.6	69.2	60.1	77.2
Mean Temp. (°F)	45.4	49.4	56.5	63.9	71.8	78.9	82.0	80.4	74.4	64.2	55.4	47.2	64.1
Mean Minimum Temp. (°F)	33.0	36.2	42.4	49.2	57.6	66.3	69.9	68.8	62.0	50.8	41.6	34.3	51.0
Extreme Maximum Temp. (°F)	82	88	89	99	101	107	108	109	100	97	85	82	109
Extreme Minimum Temp. (°F)	-4	9	13	21	34	42	51	52	37	25	16	4	-4
Days Maximum Temp. ≥ 90°F	0	0	0	2	9	20	26	21	10	1	0	0	89
Days Maximum Temp. ≤ 32°F	0	0	0	0	0	0	0	0	0	0	0	0	0
Days Minimum Temp. ≤ 32°F	16	11	6	2	0	0	0	0	0	1	7	14	57
Days Minimum Temp. ≤ 0°F	0	0	0	0	0	0	0	0	0	0	0	0	0
Heating Degree Days (base 65°F)	602	438	279	109	18	0	0	0	6	106	295	541	2,394
Cooling Degree Days (base 65°F)	1	4	22	82	235	422	535	485	295	89	15	2	2,187
Mean Precipitation (in.)	4.90	4.31	5.13	3.08	3.26	5.48	4.89	5.23	3.95	3.41	3.29	3.56	50.49
Extreme Maximum Daily Precip. (in.)	3.50	3.85	3.42	3.20	4.10	4.10	3.62	3.60	4.79	***4.00***	3.52	2.70	***4.79***
Days With ≥ 0.1" Precipitation	8	6	6	6	5	8	8	8	5	4	5	6	75
Days With ≥ 0.5" Precipitation	4	3	4	2	2	4	4	3	2	2	2	2	34
Days With ≥ 1.0" Precipitation	1	1	2	1	1	2	1	1	1	1	1	1	14
Mean Snowfall (in.)	0.4	trace	trace	0.0	0.0	0.0	0.0	0.0	0.0	0.0	trace	0.0	0.4
Maximum Snow Depth (in.)	3	trace	1	***0***	0	0	0	0	0	***0***	***trace***	3	***3***
Days With ≥ 1.0" Snow Depth	0	0	0	0	0	0	0	0	0	0	0	0	0

Allendale 2 NW *Allendale County* Elevation: 180 ft. Latitude: 33° 01' N Longitude: 81° 19' W

	JAN	FEB	MAR	APR	MAY	JUN	JUL	AUG	SEP	OCT	NOV	DEC	YEAR
Mean Maximum Temp. (°F)	58.3	62.6	69.9	77.3	84.7	90.3	93.1	91.0	***86.2***	77.9	69.6	60.6	***76.8***
Mean Temp. (°F)	46.0	49.7	56.5	63.4	71.4	78.5	81.6	80.1	***74.7***	65.0	56.1	48.1	***64.2***
Mean Minimum Temp. (°F)	33.5	36.8	43.0	49.5	58.0	66.7	70.0	69.0	***63.1***	52.0	42.6	35.6	***51.7***
Extreme Maximum Temp. (°F)	82	87	88	97	100	106	106	106	***103***	96	88	83	***106***
Extreme Minimum Temp. (°F)	-2	13	16	25	38	46	56	53	***41***	28	17	5	***-2***
Days Maximum Temp. ≥ 90°F	0	0	0	2	8	18	24	20	***10***	1	0	0	***83***
Days Maximum Temp. ≤ 32°F	0	0	0	0	0	0	0	0	***0***	0	0	0	***0***
Days Minimum Temp. ≤ 32°F	15	10	5	1	0	0	0	0	***0***	1	6	13	***51***
Days Minimum Temp. ≤ 0°F	0	0	0	0	0	0	0	0	***0***	0	0	0	***0***
Heating Degree Days (base 65°F)	586	430	278	115	18	0	0	0	***5***	95	279	522	***2,328***
Cooling Degree Days (base 65°F)	2	5	22	74	222	413	520	474	***302***	100	19	5	***2,158***
Mean Precipitation (in.)	4.08	3.48	4.04	2.86	3.01	5.57	4.90	5.33	***3.56***	3.09	3.00	3.62	***46.54***
Extreme Maximum Daily Precip. (in.)	2.40	2.30	3.54	2.90	3.21	8.00	3.20	5.77	***4.35***	7.16	***4.20***	5.28	***8.00***
Days With ≥ 0.1" Precipitation	7	6	6	5	5	7	8	8	***5***	4	5	6	***72***
Days With ≥ 0.5" Precipitation	3	2	3	2	2	3	4	4	***2***	2	2	3	***32***
Days With ≥ 1.0" Precipitation	1	1	1	1	1	2	1	2	***1***	1	1	1	***14***
Mean Snowfall (in.)	trace	0.1	trace	0.0	0.0	0.0	0.0	0.0	***0.0***	0.0	trace	0.0	***0.1***
Maximum Snow Depth (in.)	trace	0	trace	0	0	0	0	0	***0***	0	***0***	0	trace
Days With ≥ 1.0" Snow Depth	0	0	0	0	0	0	0	0	***0***	0	0	0	***0***

Anderson *Anderson County* Elevation: 799 ft. Latitude: 34° 32' N Longitude: 82° 40' W

	JAN	FEB	MAR	APR	MAY	JUN	JUL	AUG	SEP	OCT	NOV	DEC	YEAR
Mean Maximum Temp. (°F)	54.3	58.6	66.5	74.9	81.8	89.0	91.5	90.1	84.1	74.5	65.1	56.1	73.9
Mean Temp. (°F)	42.6	46.2	53.1	61.0	68.9	76.7	79.9	78.8	72.6	62.0	52.7	44.5	61.6
Mean Minimum Temp. (°F)	30.8	33.7	39.6	46.9	55.9	64.4	68.3	67.5	60.9	49.5	40.2	32.9	49.2
Extreme Maximum Temp. (°F)	80	80	88	94	100	102	106	104	100	91	85	80	106
Extreme Minimum Temp. (°F)	-5	10	5	24	33	42	53	52	40	28	14	4	-5
Days Maximum Temp. ≥ 90°F	0	0	0	0	2	14	21	18	6	0	0	0	61
Days Maximum Temp. ≤ 32°F	0	0	0	0	0	0	0	0	0	0	0	0	0
Days Minimum Temp. ≤ 32°F	18	13	7	1	0	0	0	0	0	1	7	16	63
Days Minimum Temp. ≤ 0°F	0	0	0	0	0	0	0	0	0	0	0	0	0
Heating Degree Days (base 65°F)	687	526	369	157	30	1	0	0	11	137	366	629	2,913
Cooling Degree Days (base 65°F)	0	0	6	43	157	360	469	435	245	53	5	1	1,774
Mean Precipitation (in.)	4.37	4.26	4.87	3.28	3.15	3.30	4.07	3.97	4.00	3.64	4.10	4.53	47.54
Extreme Maximum Daily Precip. (in.)	3.30	3.00	***3.20***	4.60	***4.05***	***2.70***	3.62	5.00	4.85	4.90	2.55	2.86	***5.00***
Days With ≥ 0.1" Precipitation	6	6	6	6	5	5	7	6	5	4	6	7	69
Days With ≥ 0.5" Precipitation	3	3	3	3	2	2	3	3	3	2	3	3	33
Days With ≥ 1.0" Precipitation	1	1	2	1	1	1	1	1	2	1	1	1	14
Mean Snowfall (in.)	0.6	0.7	0.4	0.0	0.0	0.0	0.0	0.0	0.0	0.0	0.0	0.1	1.8
Maximum Snow Depth (in.)	7	3	4	0	0	0	0	0	0	0	0	trace	7
Days With ≥ 1.0" Snow Depth	0	0	0	0	0	0	0	0	0	0	0	0	0

Andrews *Georgetown County* Elevation: 35 ft. Latitude: 33° 26' N Longitude: 79° 34' W

	JAN	FEB	MAR	APR	MAY	JUN	JUL	AUG	SEP	OCT	NOV	DEC	YEAR
Mean Maximum Temp. (°F)	58.4	62.1	69.3	76.8	83.3	88.1	91.1	89.3	84.4	76.8	69.2	61.0	75.8
Mean Temp. (°F)	47.3	50.2	56.7	63.8	71.2	77.8	81.2	80.0	74.7	65.4	57.1	49.4	64.6
Mean Minimum Temp. (°F)	36.0	38.3	44.1	50.8	59.1	67.5	71.2	70.5	65.0	54.0	44.9	37.7	53.3
Extreme Maximum Temp. (°F)	82	85	90	95	99	105	103	105	97	95	89	85	105
Extreme Minimum Temp. (°F)	2	14	15	28	36	46	54	56	40	30	22	9	2
Days Maximum Temp. ≥ 90°F	0	0	0	1	5	13	20	15	5	1	0	0	60
Days Maximum Temp. ≤ 32°F	0	0	0	0	0	0	0	0	0	0	0	0	0
Days Minimum Temp. ≤ 32°F	12	8	4	0	0	0	0	0	0	0	4	11	39
Days Minimum Temp. ≤ 0°F	0	0	0	0	0	0	0	0	0	0	0	0	0
Heating Degree Days (base 65°F)	543	416	271	103	16	1	0	0	4	81	255	482	2,172
Cooling Degree Days (base 65°F)	2	5	21	74	215	392	509	471	302	102	24	6	2,123
Mean Precipitation (in.)	4.10	3.31	3.60	3.05	3.67	4.97	5.69	6.08	5.24	3.88	3.02	3.23	49.84
Extreme Maximum Daily Precip. (in.)	3.80	2.60	3.35	4.15	2.75	2.85	3.30	***5.30***	***6.20***	5.30	4.30	2.50	***6.20***
Days With ≥ 0.1" Precipitation	7	6	5	4	5	7	8	8	5	4	4	5	68
Days With ≥ 0.5" Precipitation	3	3	3	2	3	4	4	4	3	2	2	2	35
Days With ≥ 1.0" Precipitation	1	1	1	1	1	2	2	2	2	1	1	1	16
Mean Snowfall (in.)	0.2	trace	0.1	0.0	0.0	0.0	0.0	0.0	0.0	0.0	0.0	0.4	0.7
Maximum Snow Depth (in.)	0	0	0	0	0	0	0	0	0	0	0	8	8
Days With ≥ 1.0" Snow Depth	0	0	0	0	0	0	0	0	0	0	0	0	0

The period of record for all cooperative weather station data is 1980 – 2009. See User Guide for detailed explanation of data.

Beaufort 7 SW *Beaufort County* Elevation: 20 ft. Latitude: 32° 23' N Longitude: 80° 46' W

	JAN	FEB	MAR	APR	MAY	JUN	JUL	AUG	SEP	OCT	NOV	DEC	YEAR
Mean Maximum Temp. (°F)	59.6	62.8	69.5	76.4	82.9	87.9	90.8	89.2	84.8	77.1	69.5	61.3	76.0
Mean Temp. (°F)	50.1	53.0	59.3	66.1	73.5	79.6	82.7	81.5	77.0	68.5	60.3	52.1	67.0
Mean Minimum Temp. (°F)	40.5	43.2	49.0	55.8	64.0	71.3	74.6	73.7	69.1	59.8	51.1	42.9	57.9
Extreme Maximum Temp. (°F)	80	83	87	90	96	101	103	104	99	92	86	85	104
Extreme Minimum Temp. (°F)	5	19	21	33	46	53	66	56	52	39	31	10	5
Days Maximum Temp. ≥ 90°F	0	0	0	0	3	11	21	15	6	0	0	0	56
Days Maximum Temp. ≤ 32°F	0	0	0	0	0	0	0	0	0	0	0	0	0
Days Minimum Temp. ≤ 32°F	6	4	1	0	0	0	0	0	0	0	0	4	15
Days Minimum Temp. ≤ 0°F	0	0	0	0	0	0	0	0	0	0	0	0	0
Heating Degree Days (base 65°F)	458	338	199	62	6	0	0	0	1	44	175	401	1,684
Cooling Degree Days (base 65°F)	3	6	29	102	274	445	557	519	367	158	41	9	2,510
Mean Precipitation (in.)	4.00	3.31	3.80	3.16	2.66	6.11	5.41	6.89	4.86	3.85	2.84	2.84	49.73
Extreme Maximum Daily Precip. (in.)	3.08	5.10	3.12	4.06	1.98	7.65	5.55	5.69	na	6.59	3.40	2.45	na
Days With ≥ 0.1" Precipitation	7	6	6	5	5	8	7	9	6	5	5	5	74
Days With ≥ 0.5" Precipitation	3	2	2	2	2	4	3	4	3	2	2	2	31
Days With ≥ 1.0" Precipitation	1	1	1	1	1	2	1	2	1	1	1	1	14
Mean Snowfall (in.)	trace	trace	trace	0.0	0.0	0.0	0.0	0.0	0.0	0.0	0.0	0.2	0.2
Maximum Snow Depth (in.)	trace	trace	trace	0	0	na	0	0	na	na	0	5	na
Days With ≥ 1.0" Snow Depth	0	0	0	0	0	0	0	0	0	na	0	0	na

Bishopville 8 NNW *Lee County* Elevation: 249 ft. Latitude: 34° 20' N Longitude: 80° 18' W

	JAN	FEB	MAR	APR	MAY	JUN	JUL	AUG	SEP	OCT	NOV	DEC	YEAR
Mean Maximum Temp. (°F)	54.0	58.7	66.4	74.8	82.2	88.6	91.1	89.7	83.8	75.0	66.5	57.8	74.1
Mean Temp. (°F)	42.7	46.5	53.4	61.5	69.7	77.4	80.2	79.0	73.0	62.9	53.6	46.0	62.2
Mean Minimum Temp. (°F)	31.4	34.2	40.5	48.1	57.2	66.1	69.2	68.3	62.1	50.6	40.7	34.1	50.2
Extreme Maximum Temp. (°F)	82	85	88	93	100	104	105	106	98	96	87	83	106
Extreme Minimum Temp. (°F)	-2	11	8	24	31	48	54	55	41	28	18	5	-2
Days Maximum Temp. ≥ 90°F	0	0	0	1	4	14	20	16	6	0	0	0	61
Days Maximum Temp. ≤ 32°F	1	0	0	0	0	0	0	0	0	0	0	0	1
Days Minimum Temp. ≤ 32°F	18	13	7	1	0	0	0	0	0	1	7	15	62
Days Minimum Temp. ≤ 0°F	0	0	0	0	0	0	0	0	0	0	0	0	0
Heating Degree Days (base 65°F)	685	520	363	153	31	1	0	0	10	129	346	586	2,824
Cooling Degree Days (base 65°F)	1	2	12	55	185	379	479	442	257	71	11	2	1,896
Mean Precipitation (in.)	3.71	3.36	3.85	2.80	3.17	4.19	4.41	5.02	3.78	3.29	3.01	3.15	43.74
Extreme Maximum Daily Precip. (in.)	2.50	3.01	3.15	2.70	2.70	2.73	2.70	6.05	3.48	7.10	2.90	6.07	7.10
Days With ≥ 0.1" Precipitation	7	6	6	5	5	7	7	7	5	5	5	5	70
Days With ≥ 0.5" Precipitation	2	2	3	2	2	3	3	3	2	2	2	2	28
Days With ≥ 1.0" Precipitation	1	1	1	1	1	1	1	1	1	1	1	1	12
Mean Snowfall (in.)	0.2	0.2	0.2	0.0	0.0	0.0	0.0	0.0	0.0	0.0	0.0	0.1	0.7
Maximum Snow Depth (in.)	3	2	3	0	0	0	0	0	0	0	0	0	3
Days With ≥ 1.0" Snow Depth	0	0	0	0	0	0	0	0	0	0	0	0	0

Charleston City *Charleston County* Elevation: 9 ft. Latitude: 32° 47' N Longitude: 79° 56' W

	JAN	FEB	MAR	APR	MAY	JUN	JUL	AUG	SEP	OCT	NOV	DEC	YEAR
Mean Maximum Temp. (°F)	57.3	60.1	65.6	72.5	79.3	84.8	88.1	86.8	82.6	75.1	67.6	60.2	73.3
Mean Temp. (°F)	50.1	52.8	58.6	65.6	73.1	79.3	82.5	81.4	77.1	68.7	60.6	53.0	66.9
Mean Minimum Temp. (°F)	42.8	45.5	51.5	58.6	67.0	73.8	76.8	76.0	71.7	62.3	53.4	45.7	60.4
Extreme Maximum Temp. (°F)	78	82	87	94	96	104	101	103	98	93	84	81	104
Extreme Minimum Temp. (°F)	10	19	22	36	49	58	65	59	55	40	32	18	10
Days Maximum Temp. ≥ 90°F	0	0	0	0	1	5	11	8	3	0	0	0	28
Days Maximum Temp. ≤ 32°F	0	0	0	0	0	0	0	0	0	0	0	0	0
Days Minimum Temp. ≤ 32°F	3	1	0	0	0	0	0	0	0	0	0	2	6
Days Minimum Temp. ≤ 0°F	0	0	0	0	0	0	0	0	0	0	0	0	0
Heating Degree Days (base 65°F)	457	342	212	66	6	0	0	0	1	37	163	373	1,657
Cooling Degree Days (base 65°F)	1	4	21	90	266	437	549	516	371	160	38	8	2,461
Mean Precipitation (in.)	2.94	2.44	3.44	2.64	2.26	4.62	5.40	6.31	5.66	3.68	2.10	2.60	44.09
Extreme Maximum Daily Precip. (in.)	2.40	2.56	3.45	3.67	2.23	7.38	4.05	5.39	8.50	5.46	3.57	3.82	8.50
Days With ≥ 0.1" Precipitation	6	5	5	5	4	6	7	8	6	5	4	5	66
Days With ≥ 0.5" Precipitation	2	2	2	2	1	3	4	4	3	2	1	2	28
Days With ≥ 1.0" Precipitation	1	1	1	1	1	1	2	2	1	1	1	1	14
Mean Snowfall (in.)	na	na	na	na	na	na	na	na	na	na	na	na	na
Maximum Snow Depth (in.)	na	na	na	na	na	na	na	na	na	na	na	na	na
Days With ≥ 1.0" Snow Depth	na	na	na	na	na	na	na	na	na	na	na	na	na

Chester 1 NW *Chester County* Elevation: 520 ft. Latitude: 34° 43' N Longitude: 81° 13' W

	JAN	FEB	MAR	APR	MAY	JUN	JUL	AUG	SEP	OCT	NOV	DEC	YEAR
Mean Maximum Temp. (°F)	52.5	56.9	65.0	73.6	80.6	87.6	90.7	89.1	83.0	73.3	64.3	55.0	72.6
Mean Temp. (°F)	40.7	44.2	51.5	59.4	67.5	75.8	79.3	78.1	71.6	60.4	51.1	42.9	60.2
Mean Minimum Temp. (°F)	28.9	31.4	38.0	45.2	54.4	64.1	67.9	67.1	60.1	47.4	37.9	30.8	47.8
Extreme Maximum Temp. (°F)	80	83	88	92	96	101	105	106	98	93	84	79	106
Extreme Minimum Temp. (°F)	-3	5	4	21	31	43	53	50	37	22	14	4	-3
Days Maximum Temp. ≥ 90°F	0	0	0	1	2	12	19	15	5	0	0	0	54
Days Maximum Temp. ≤ 32°F	1	0	0	0	0	0	0	0	0	0	0	0	1
Days Minimum Temp. ≤ 32°F	20	17	10	3	0	0	0	0	0	3	11	19	83
Days Minimum Temp. ≤ 0°F	0	0	0	0	0	0	0	0	0	0	0	0	0
Heating Degree Days (base 65°F)	747	583	419	197	50	3	0	0	17	183	415	679	3,293
Cooling Degree Days (base 65°F)	0	0	7	37	136	335	451	414	221	46	6	1	1,654
Mean Precipitation (in.)	4.08	3.67	4.44	3.34	2.87	4.20	3.90	4.66	3.72	3.43	3.57	3.52	45.40
Extreme Maximum Daily Precip. (in.)	3.51	2.84	3.12	2.50	3.55	3.37	3.73	7.13	5.72	4.00	3.32	3.70	7.13
Days With ≥ 0.1" Precipitation	7	6	6	5	5	7	7	6	4	4	5	6	68
Days With ≥ 0.5" Precipitation	3	3	3	2	2	3	3	3	2	2	3	3	32
Days With ≥ 1.0" Precipitation	1	1	1	1	1	1	1	1	1	1	1	1	12
Mean Snowfall (in.)	1.0	0.5	0.5	0.0	0.0	0.0	0.0	0.0	0.0	0.0	0.0	0.1	2.1
Maximum Snow Depth (in.)	8	12	8	0	0	0	0	0	0	0	0	3	12
Days With ≥ 1.0" Snow Depth	1	0	0	0	0	0	0	0	0	0	0	0	1

The period of record for all cooperative weather station data is 1980 – 2009. See User Guide for detailed explanation of data.

Clark Hill 1 W *Mccormick County* Elevation: 379 ft. Latitude: 33° 40' N Longitude: 82° 11' W

	JAN	FEB	MAR	APR	MAY	JUN	JUL	AUG	SEP	OCT	NOV	DEC	YEAR
Mean Maximum Temp. (°F)	55.5	60.1	68.1	76.4	84.2	90.3	93.6	92.3	86.6	76.9	67.6	57.6	75.8
Mean Temp. (°F)	42.9	46.7	53.8	61.5	69.7	77.0	80.7	79.4	73.4	62.7	53.7	45.1	62.2
Mean Minimum Temp. (°F)	30.3	33.4	39.5	46.5	55.1	63.7	67.7	66.5	60.2	48.5	39.8	32.7	48.7
Extreme Maximum Temp. (°F)	83	84	91	94	98	104	109	108	103	94	87	81	109
Extreme Minimum Temp. (°F)	-2	5	12	23	32	45	56	49	38	25	19	9	-2
Days Maximum Temp. ≥ 90°F	0	0	0	1	7	18	25	22	11	1	0	0	85
Days Maximum Temp. ≤ 32°F	0	0	0	0	0	0	0	0	0	0	0	0	0
Days Minimum Temp. ≤ 32°F	19	14	7	2	0	0	0	0	0	2	8	15	67
Days Minimum Temp. ≤ 0°F	0	0	0	0	0	0	0	0	0	0	0	0	0
Heating Degree Days (base 65°F)	677	511	349	151	28	1	0	0	10	132	340	608	2,807
Cooling Degree Days (base 65°F)	0	1	11	52	180	369	492	454	269	68	10	1	1,907
Mean Precipitation (in.)	4.16	4.10	4.69	2.75	2.79	4.40	4.17	4.16	3.45	3.84	3.13	3.43	45.07
Extreme Maximum Daily Precip. (in.)	***2.25***	3.10	3.90	3.22	2.90	3.90	5.27	3.41	7.10	9.40	5.55	***2.13***	***9.40***
Days With ≥ 0.1" Precipitation	6	6	7	5	5	7	7	6	5	4	5	5	68
Days With ≥ 0.5" Precipitation	3	3	3	2	2	3	3	2	2	2	2	2	29
Days With ≥ 1.0" Precipitation	1	1	2	1	1	1	1	1	1	1	1	1	13
Mean Snowfall (in.)	0.0	0.3	0.0	0.0	0.0	0.0	0.0	0.0	0.0	0.0	0.0	0.0	0.3
Maximum Snow Depth (in.)	0	8	0	0	0	0	0	0	0	0	0	0	8
Days With ≥ 1.0" Snow Depth	0	0	0	0	0	0	0	0	0	0	0	0	0

Columbia Univ of SC *Richland County* Elevation: 242 ft. Latitude: 33° 59' N Longitude: 81° 01' W

	JAN	FEB	MAR	APR	MAY	JUN	JUL	AUG	SEP	OCT	NOV	DEC	YEAR
Mean Maximum Temp. (°F)	58.2	63.1	71.0	79.2	86.5	92.2	94.9	93.2	87.9	78.4	68.9	60.3	77.8
Mean Temp. (°F)	47.5	51.5	58.5	66.2	73.9	80.5	83.5	82.2	76.6	66.4	57.2	49.4	66.1
Mean Minimum Temp. (°F)	36.7	39.9	46.0	53.2	61.3	68.8	72.1	71.3	65.3	54.3	45.4	38.5	54.4
Extreme Maximum Temp. (°F)	83	86	92	97	102	109	109	109	102	96	88	84	109
Extreme Minimum Temp. (°F)	1	12	12	29	39	50	58	58	44	32	23	7	1
Days Maximum Temp. ≥ 90°F	0	0	0	3	10	21	27	24	13	1	0	0	99
Days Maximum Temp. ≤ 32°F	0	0	0	0	0	0	0	0	0	0	0	0	0
Days Minimum Temp. ≤ 32°F	12	7	3	0	0	0	0	0	0	0	3	10	35
Days Minimum Temp. ≤ 0°F	0	0	0	0	0	0	0	0	0	0	0	0	0
Heating Degree Days (base 65°F)	539	381	228	73	8	0	0	0	3	72	250	480	2,034
Cooling Degree Days (base 65°F)	2	6	35	117	290	472	580	542	359	122	23	5	2,553
Mean Precipitation (in.)	3.91	3.65	4.56	2.75	2.91	5.32	5.41	4.58	3.53	3.24	3.11	3.40	46.37
Extreme Maximum Daily Precip. (in.)	3.11	2.19	3.17	2.48	4.19	4.22	4.83	4.29	4.26	4.02	2.88	3.93	4.83
Days With ≥ 0.1" Precipitation	7	6	7	6	5	8	8	7	5	5	5	5	74
Days With ≥ 0.5" Precipitation	3	3	3	2	2	3	4	3	2	2	2	2	31
Days With ≥ 1.0" Precipitation	1	1	2	1	1	2	2	1	1	1	1	1	15
Mean Snowfall (in.)	0.4	0.3	0.1	0.0	0.0	0.0	0.0	0.0	0.0	0.0	0.0	trace	0.8
Maximum Snow Depth (in.)	4	2	trace	0	0	0	0	0	0	0	0	trace	4
Days With ≥ 1.0" Snow Depth	1	0	0	0	0	0	0	0	0	0	0	0	1

Conway *Horry County* Elevation: 20 ft. Latitude: 33° 50' N Longitude: 79° 03' W

	JAN	FEB	MAR	APR	MAY	JUN	JUL	AUG	SEP	OCT	NOV	DEC	YEAR
Mean Maximum Temp. (°F)	57.6	61.0	67.8	75.5	82.5	88.1	91.2	89.6	84.8	76.8	69.2	60.3	75.4
Mean Temp. (°F)	46.0	49.1	55.7	63.3	71.2	78.2	81.6	80.4	75.0	65.4	57.0	48.7	64.3
Mean Minimum Temp. (°F)	34.6	37.1	43.5	51.1	59.7	68.3	72.0	71.0	65.2	54.0	44.8	37.2	53.2
Extreme Maximum Temp. (°F)	82	84	90	96	98	103	104	105	100	96	88	82	105
Extreme Minimum Temp. (°F)	4	12	12	22	41	42	56	55	45	30	24	8	4
Days Maximum Temp. ≥ 90°F	0	0	0	1	4	12	20	16	6	1	0	0	60
Days Maximum Temp. ≤ 32°F	0	0	0	0	0	0	0	0	0	0	0	0	0
Days Minimum Temp. ≤ 32°F	13	8	3	0	0	0	0	0	0	0	3	11	38
Days Minimum Temp. ≤ 0°F	0	0	0	0	0	0	0	0	0	0	0	0	0
Heating Degree Days (base 65°F)	583	448	300	115	18	1	0	0	3	86	255	506	2,315
Cooling Degree Days (base 65°F)	2	4	17	71	217	405	522	483	310	106	23	6	2,166
Mean Precipitation (in.)	4.07	3.42	4.08	3.08	3.55	4.94	6.92	7.32	5.35	3.30	2.77	3.45	52.25
Extreme Maximum Daily Precip. (in.)	3.45	4.00	4.07	3.10	2.90	3.08	6.55	5.07	11.35	4.82	3.20	6.60	11.35
Days With ≥ 0.1" Precipitation	7	6	6	5	5	7	9	8	6	5	4	6	74
Days With ≥ 0.5" Precipitation	3	2	3	2	2	3	4	5	3	2	2	2	33
Days With ≥ 1.0" Precipitation	1	1	2	1	1	1	2	2	2	1	1	1	16
Mean Snowfall (in.)	0.2	trace	0.0	0.0	0.0	0.0	0.0	0.0	0.0	0.0	0.0	0.5	0.7
Maximum Snow Depth (in.)	0	trace	6	0	0	0	0	0	0	0	0	13	13
Days With ≥ 1.0" Snow Depth	0	0	0	0	0	0	0	0	0	0	0	0	0

Florence City County Arpt *Florence County* Elevation: 146 ft. Latitude: 34° 12' N Longitude: 79° 44' W

	JAN	FEB	MAR	APR	MAY	JUN	JUL	AUG	SEP	OCT	NOV	DEC	YEAR
Mean Maximum Temp. (°F)	55.7	59.9	67.8	76.0	82.9	88.6	91.4	89.8	84.5	75.7	67.3	58.3	74.8
Mean Temp. (°F)	45.4	48.8	55.8	63.4	71.2	78.3	81.5	80.2	74.5	64.5	55.6	47.6	63.9
Mean Minimum Temp. (°F)	34.9	37.7	43.8	50.8	59.4	67.9	71.5	70.5	64.5	53.2	43.8	36.8	52.9
Extreme Maximum Temp. (°F)	81	85	89	97	97	105	104	106	100	97	89	86	106
Extreme Minimum Temp. (°F)	0	11	11	26	36	49	57	55	43	30	20	8	0
Days Maximum Temp. ≥ 90°F	0	0	0	2	5	14	21	17	7	0	0	0	66
Days Maximum Temp. ≤ 32°F	0	0	0	0	0	0	0	0	0	0	0	0	0
Days Minimum Temp. ≤ 32°F	13	9	4	0	0	0	0	0	0	0	4	11	41
Days Minimum Temp. ≤ 0°F	0	0	0	0	0	0	0	0	0	0	0	0	0
Heating Degree Days (base 65°F)	605	456	297	118	20	1	0	0	7	103	293	538	2,438
Cooling Degree Days (base 65°F)	2	5	20	77	218	406	517	478	298	93	18	5	2,137
Mean Precipitation (in.)	3.25	2.81	3.53	2.66	3.24	4.37	5.12	5.25	3.51	3.08	2.66	3.03	42.51
Extreme Maximum Daily Precip. (in.)	2.10	2.07	3.81	2.62	2.42	3.67	3.47	4.22	3.72	4.35	2.35	4.09	4.35
Days With ≥ 0.1" Precipitation	6	6	6	5	6	7	8	7	6	4	5	6	72
Days With ≥ 0.5" Precipitation	2	2	2	2	2	3	4	3	2	2	2	2	28
Days With ≥ 1.0" Precipitation	1	1	1	1	1	1	1	2	1	1	1	1	13
Mean Snowfall (in.)	na	na	na	na	na	na	na	na	na	na	na	na	na
Maximum Snow Depth (in.)	na	na	na	na	na	na	na	na	na	na	na	na	na
Days With ≥ 1.0" Snow Depth	na	na	na	na	na	na	na	na	na	na	na	na	na

The period of record for all cooperative weather station data is 1980 – 2009. See User Guide for detailed explanation of data.

Greenwood 3 SW *Greenwood County* Elevation: 615 ft. Latitude: 34° 10' N Longitude: 82° 12' W

	JAN	FEB	MAR	APR	MAY	JUN	JUL	AUG	SEP	OCT	NOV	DEC	YEAR
Mean Maximum Temp. (°F)	52.8	57.6	65.4	73.7	81.0	87.7	91.0	89.4	83.3	73.2	64.1	54.8	72.8
Mean Temp. (°F)	41.6	45.4	52.0	60.0	68.2	76.1	79.6	78.6	71.9	61.0	51.7	43.5	60.8
Mean Minimum Temp. (°F)	30.4	33.0	38.6	46.2	55.2	64.5	68.2	67.7	60.4	48.8	39.2	32.1	48.7
Extreme Maximum Temp. (°F)	77	80	89	92	95	102	106	105	97	92	82	78	106
Extreme Minimum Temp. (°F)	-2	8	3	24	32	41	53	52	36	25	17	5	-2
Days Maximum Temp. ≥ 90°F	0	0	0	0	2	12	19	15	5	0	0	0	53
Days Maximum Temp. ≤ 32°F	1	0	0	0	0	0	0	0	0	0	0	0	1
Days Minimum Temp. ≤ 32°F	19	14	9	2	0	0	0	0	0	1	8	16	69
Days Minimum Temp. ≤ 0°F	0	0	0	0	0	0	0	0	0	0	0	0	0
Heating Degree Days (base 65°F)	719	548	401	185	42	2	0	0	15	167	397	661	3,137
Cooling Degree Days (base 65°F)	0	0	6	40	148	343	461	428	228	50	5	1	1,710
Mean Precipitation (in.)	4.15	4.13	4.73	2.93	2.93	3.78	3.60	3.62	3.20	3.43	3.67	3.70	43.87
Extreme Maximum Daily Precip. (in.)	2.61	3.07	2.63	2.50	na	3.20	2.79	6.08	3.47	3.83	2.70	2.32	na
Days With ≥ 0.1" Precipitation	7	6	6	5	4	6	6	5	5	4	5	5	64
Days With ≥ 0.5" Precipitation	3	3	3	2	2	2	2	2	2	2	3	2	28
Days With ≥ 1.0" Precipitation	1	1	2	1	1	1	1	1	1	1	1	1	13
Mean Snowfall (in.)	1.1	0.5	0.4	0.0	0.0	0.0	0.0	0.0	0.0	0.0	0.0	0.2	2.2
Maximum Snow Depth (in.)	6	3	4	0	0	0	0	0	0	0	0	0	6
Days With ≥ 1.0" Snow Depth	0	0	0	0	0	0	0	0	0	0	0	0	0

Johnston 4 SW *Edgefield County* Elevation: 620 ft. Latitude: 33° 47' N Longitude: 81° 51' W

	JAN	FEB	MAR	APR	MAY	JUN	JUL	AUG	SEP	OCT	NOV	DEC	YEAR
Mean Maximum Temp. (°F)	54.4	58.9	66.3	74.7	83.1	89.6	92.8	90.9	84.8	74.8	66.1	56.9	74.4
Mean Temp. (°F)	42.8	46.3	53.2	60.7	69.3	76.8	80.1	78.6	72.7	61.8	53.2	45.0	61.7
Mean Minimum Temp. (°F)	31.1	33.5	39.9	46.6	55.4	63.9	67.4	66.3	60.5	48.8	40.2	33.0	48.9
Extreme Maximum Temp. (°F)	81	83	89	94	100	105	107	110	105	93	88	81	110
Extreme Minimum Temp. (°F)	-2	9	1	19	34	46	52	47	41	24	18	5	-2
Days Maximum Temp. ≥ 90°F	0	0	0	1	6	17	24	19	9	0	0	0	76
Days Maximum Temp. ≤ 32°F	0	0	0	0	0	0	0	0	0	0	0	0	0
Days Minimum Temp. ≤ 32°F	18	14	7	2	0	0	0	0	0	1	7	17	66
Days Minimum Temp. ≤ 0°F	0	0	0	0	0	0	0	0	0	0	0	0	0
Heating Degree Days (base 65°F)	682	526	369	169	34	2	0	0	12	148	357	616	2,915
Cooling Degree Days (base 65°F)	0	2	8	46	172	361	476	430	250	56	9	1	1,811
Mean Precipitation (in.)	4.24	4.15	4.86	3.02	3.05	4.57	4.07	4.78	3.85	3.44	3.41	3.54	46.98
Extreme Maximum Daily Precip. (in.)	2.48	3.35	3.91	2.60	2.92	5.13	3.44	4.33	5.36	5.03	3.95	2.68	5.36
Days With ≥ 0.1" Precipitation	7	6	7	6	5	6	7	7	5	4	5	6	71
Days With ≥ 0.5" Precipitation	3	3	3	2	2	3	3	3	2	2	2	2	30
Days With ≥ 1.0" Precipitation	1	1	2	1	1	1	1	1	1	1	1	1	13
Mean Snowfall (in.)	0.8	0.5	0.2	0.0	0.0	0.0	0.0	0.0	0.0	0.0	0.0	0.1	1.6
Maximum Snow Depth (in.)	6	1	2	0	0	0	0	0	0	0	0	trace	6
Days With ≥ 1.0" Snow Depth	0	0	0	0	0	0	0	0	0	0	0	0	0

Lake City 2 SE *Florence County* Elevation: 75 ft. Latitude: 33° 51' N Longitude: 79° 44' W

	JAN	FEB	MAR	APR	MAY	JUN	JUL	AUG	SEP	OCT	NOV	DEC	YEAR
Mean Maximum Temp. (°F)	56.6	60.3	67.8	75.8	***82.9***	88.7	91.7	90.2	84.9	76.4	68.5	59.2	***75.3***
Mean Temp. (°F)	44.9	48.0	54.8	62.2	***70.0***	***77.6***	81.0	79.8	73.9	63.8	55.1	46.9	***63.2***
Mean Minimum Temp. (°F)	33.1	35.5	41.7	48.4	***57.0***	***66.2***	70.2	69.4	62.8	51.2	41.6	34.7	***51.0***
Extreme Maximum Temp. (°F)	81	84	90	94	98	104	105	104	99	97	87	82	105
Extreme Minimum Temp. (°F)	2	14	10	26	35	46	53	55	42	27	20	6	2
Days Maximum Temp. ≥ 90°F	0	0	0	1	4	14	21	18	7	1	0	0	66
Days Maximum Temp. ≤ 32°F	0	0	0	0	0	0	0	0	0	0	0	0	0
Days Minimum Temp. ≤ 32°F	16	11	6	1	0	0	0	0	0	1	6	13	54
Days Minimum Temp. ≤ 0°F	0	0	0	0	0	0	0	0	0	0	0	0	0
Heating Degree Days (base 65°F)	617	473	326	137	***28***	***1***	0	0	6	112	309	555	***2,564***
Cooling Degree Days (base 65°F)	1	3	14	61	***190***	***385***	503	466	279	83	20	3	***2,008***
Mean Precipitation (in.)	3.76	3.27	4.27	2.84	2.92	4.36	5.15	5.93	4.41	3.11	2.70	3.40	46.12
Extreme Maximum Daily Precip. (in.)	3.60	3.68	***6.50***	***2.52***	2.43	***3.32***	3.02	5.38	4.20	7.30	***2.35***	***6.44***	***7.30***
Days With ≥ 0.1" Precipitation	6	5	5	4	4	6	6	7	5	4	4	5	61
Days With ≥ 0.5" Precipitation	2	2	3	2	2	3	3	4	3	2	2	2	30
Days With ≥ 1.0" Precipitation	1	1	1	1	1	1	2	2	2	1	1	1	15
Mean Snowfall (in.)	0.4	0.3	0.3	0.0	0.0	0.0	0.0	0.0	0.0	0.0	0.0	0.3	1.3
Maximum Snow Depth (in.)	7	5	2	0	0	0	0	0	0	***0***	0	8	***8***
Days With ≥ 1.0" Snow Depth	0	0	0	0	0	0	0	0	0	0	0	0	0

Laurens *Laurens County* Elevation: 588 ft. Latitude: 34° 31' N Longitude: 82° 02' W

	JAN	FEB	MAR	APR	MAY	JUN	JUL	AUG	SEP	OCT	NOV	DEC	YEAR
Mean Maximum Temp. (°F)	53.4	57.5	65.5	73.9	81.7	88.6	91.6	90.3	84.0	74.2	65.1	55.9	73.5
Mean Temp. (°F)	40.8	44.1	51.6	59.5	68.2	76.1	79.5	78.2	71.5	60.2	51.0	43.0	60.3
Mean Minimum Temp. (°F)	28.2	30.6	37.6	45.1	54.6	63.6	67.4	66.1	58.8	46.2	36.9	30.1	47.1
Extreme Maximum Temp. (°F)	80	82	89	93	97	107	107	105	99	93	85	80	107
Extreme Minimum Temp. (°F)	-2	5	6	23	31	45	54	49	33	21	13	5	-2
Days Maximum Temp. ≥ 90°F	0	0	0	0	4	15	21	18	7	0	0	0	65
Days Maximum Temp. ≤ 32°F	1	0	0	0	0	0	0	0	0	0	0	0	1
Days Minimum Temp. ≤ 32°F	21	18	9	3	0	0	0	0	0	3	11	20	85
Days Minimum Temp. ≤ 0°F	0	0	0	0	0	0	0	0	0	0	0	0	0
Heating Degree Days (base 65°F)	744	586	415	194	42	2	0	0	18	181	418	676	3,276
Cooling Degree Days (base 65°F)	0	0	5	36	147	342	456	418	219	38	4	1	1,666
Mean Precipitation (in.)	4.16	3.98	4.91	3.28	3.12	4.02	3.55	3.65	3.50	3.64	3.63	3.94	45.38
Extreme Maximum Daily Precip. (in.)	2.68	2.27	3.00	3.05	2.95	4.18	4.68	5.11	4.27	5.35	4.25	2.85	5.35
Days With ≥ 0.1" Precipitation	7	7	7	6	5	7	6	5	5	4	5	6	70
Days With ≥ 0.5" Precipitation	3	3	3	2	2	3	2	2	2	2	3	3	30
Days With ≥ 1.0" Precipitation	1	1	1	1	1	1	1	1	1	1	1	1	12
Mean Snowfall (in.)	0.7	0.4	0.3	0.0	0.0	0.0	0.0	0.0	0.0	0.0	trace	0.1	1.5
Maximum Snow Depth (in.)	1	4	4	0	0	0	0	0	0	0	trace	3	4
Days With ≥ 1.0" Snow Depth	0	0	0	0	0	0	0	0	0	0	0	0	0

Little Mountain *Newberry County* Elevation: 710 ft. Latitude: 34° 12' N Longitude: 81° 25' W

	JAN	FEB	MAR	APR	MAY	JUN	JUL	AUG	SEP	OCT	NOV	DEC	YEAR
Mean Maximum Temp. (°F)	53.6	58.3	65.8	73.7	80.7	87.0	89.9	88.2	82.6	73.3	64.5	55.8	72.8
Mean Temp. (°F)	44.1	47.7	54.5	62.0	69.6	76.6	79.7	78.4	72.5	62.6	54.1	46.1	62.3
Mean Minimum Temp. (°F)	34.5	37.2	43.2	50.3	58.5	66.2	69.3	68.5	62.4	52.0	43.6	36.3	51.8
Extreme Maximum Temp. (°F)	78	80	87	92	95	101	106	105	98	96	87	78	106
Extreme Minimum Temp. (°F)	-2	7	9	24	38	49	57	52	41	27	19	4	-2
Days Maximum Temp. ≥ 90°F	0	0	0	0	2	10	17	12	4	0	0	0	45
Days Maximum Temp. ≤ 32°F	1	0	0	0	0	0	0	0	0	0	0	0	1
Days Minimum Temp. ≤ 32°F	13	9	4	1	0	0	0	0	0	0	4	12	43
Days Minimum Temp. ≤ 0°F	0	0	0	0	0	0	0	0	0	0	0	0	0
Heating Degree Days (base 65°F)	642	483	331	139	29	1	0	0	13	132	331	582	2,683
Cooling Degree Days (base 65°F)	0	1	13	56	179	356	461	422	245	66	10	2	1,811
Mean Precipitation (in.)	4.14	3.93	4.54	2.97	2.78	4.16	4.59	4.59	3.85	3.50	3.32	3.62	45.99
Extreme Maximum Daily Precip. (in.)	2.18	2.60	2.92	2.23	2.53	4.18	5.22	6.46	3.99	3.41	3.84	2.89	6.46
Days With ≥ 0.1" Precipitation	7	6	7	6	5	6	7	7	5	5	5	6	72
Days With ≥ 0.5" Precipitation	3	3	3	2	2	3	3	3	2	2	3	2	31
Days With ≥ 1.0" Precipitation	1	1	2	1	1	1	1	2	1	1	1	1	14
Mean Snowfall (in.)	1.1	0.5	0.5	0.0	0.0	0.0	0.0	0.0	0.0	0.0	trace	0.2	2.3
Maximum Snow Depth (in.)	9	2	6	0	0	0	0	0	0	0	trace	1	9
Days With ≥ 1.0" Snow Depth	1	0	0	0	0	0	0	0	0	0	0	0	1

Loris 1 S *Horry County* Elevation: 89 ft. Latitude: 34° 03' N Longitude: 78° 52' W

	JAN	FEB	MAR	APR	MAY	JUN	JUL	AUG	SEP	OCT	NOV	DEC	YEAR
Mean Maximum Temp. (°F)	56.0	60.0	66.8	74.5	81.7	86.9	90.4	89.0	84.2	76.1	68.0	58.4	74.3
Mean Temp. (°F)	44.3	47.5	53.4	61.2	69.0	76.0	80.1	78.8	73.3	63.4	54.7	46.1	62.3
Mean Minimum Temp. (°F)	32.7	35.0	40.1	47.6	56.2	65.1	69.6	68.5	62.4	50.6	41.4	33.9	50.3
Extreme Maximum Temp. (°F)	80	85	89	95	99	103	101	104	96	93	85	82	104
Extreme Minimum Temp. (°F)	2	11	12	21	35	47	53	50	43	27	20	9	2
Days Maximum Temp. ≥ 90°F	0	0	0	1	3	10	19	15	6	1	0	0	55
Days Maximum Temp. ≤ 32°F	0	0	0	0	0	0	0	0	0	0	0	0	0
Days Minimum Temp. ≤ 32°F	16	13	7	1	0	0	0	0	0	1	7	15	60
Days Minimum Temp. ≤ 0°F	0	0	0	0	0	0	0	0	0	0	0	0	0
Heating Degree Days (base 65°F)	635	492	364	159	36	2	0	0	9	123	316	582	2,718
Cooling Degree Days (base 65°F)	1	3	12	49	166	340	473	434	263	80	16	4	1,841
Mean Precipitation (in.)	4.01	3.58	4.09	3.06	3.73	5.31	6.12	6.88	5.84	3.03	2.71	2.93	51.29
Extreme Maximum Daily Precip. (in.)	2.50	3.99	4.52	2.99	3.08	3.32	3.40	5.78	10.02	4.11	2.26	2.43	10.02
Days With ≥ 0.1" Precipitation	7	6	6	5	6	7	8	9	6	4	4	5	73
Days With ≥ 0.5" Precipitation	3	2	3	2	2	4	4	4	3	1	2	2	32
Days With ≥ 1.0" Precipitation	1	1	1	1	1	2	2	2	2	1	1	1	16
Mean Snowfall (in.)	0.2	0.3	0.6	0.0	0.0	0.0	0.0	0.0	0.0	0.0	0.0	0.6	1.7
Maximum Snow Depth (in.)	3	3	7	0	0	0	0	0	0	0	0	14	14
Days With ≥ 1.0" Snow Depth	0	0	0	0	0	0	0	0	0	0	0	0	0

Manning *Clarendon County* Elevation: 100 ft. Latitude: 33° 42' N Longitude: 80° 14' W

	JAN	FEB	MAR	APR	MAY	JUN	JUL	AUG	SEP	OCT	NOV	DEC	YEAR
Mean Maximum Temp. (°F)	56.9	61.3	69.2	77.8	85.2	90.8	93.4	92.2	86.1	76.9	68.7	59.6	76.5
Mean Temp. (°F)	45.3	48.7	55.7	63.5	71.4	78.4	81.4	80.4	74.3	64.2	55.7	47.6	63.9
Mean Minimum Temp. (°F)	33.7	36.0	42.1	49.3	57.5	65.9	69.3	68.7	62.5	51.4	42.7	35.5	51.2
Extreme Maximum Temp. (°F)	88	84	92	98	105	104	108	108	101	99	89	82	108
Extreme Minimum Temp. (°F)	0	12	7	24	34	40	48	49	37	24	20	7	0
Days Maximum Temp. ≥ 90°F	0	0	0	2	9	19	25	22	10	1	0	0	88
Days Maximum Temp. ≤ 32°F	0	0	0	0	0	0	0	0	0	0	0	0	0
Days Minimum Temp. ≤ 32°F	16	11	6	1	0	0	0	0	0	1	6	13	54
Days Minimum Temp. ≤ 0°F	0	0	0	0	0	0	0	0	0	0	0	0	0
Heating Degree Days (base 65°F)	605	459	301	114	20	1	0	0	7	108	290	538	2,443
Cooling Degree Days (base 65°F)	2	3	19	77	224	408	514	485	292	90	19	4	2,137
Mean Precipitation (in.)	4.16	3.69	4.03	3.32	3.78	5.25	5.47	5.78	4.37	3.45	2.91	3.57	49.78
Extreme Maximum Daily Precip. (in.)	3.50	2.72	3.08	2.50	2.33	2.80	3.62	3.80	2.80	2.80	2.80	2.49	3.80
Days With ≥ 0.1" Precipitation	8	7	6	6	7	9	8	8	6	6	5	6	82
Days With ≥ 0.5" Precipitation	3	2	3	2	2	4	4	4	3	2	2	2	33
Days With ≥ 1.0" Precipitation	1	1	1	1	1	1	1	2	1	1	1	1	13
Mean Snowfall (in.)	0.6	0.1	0.2	0.0	0.0	0.0	0.0	0.0	0.0	0.0	0.0	0.1	1.0
Maximum Snow Depth (in.)	5	6	4	0	0	0	0	0	0	0	0	1	6
Days With ≥ 1.0" Snow Depth	0	0	0	0	0	0	0	0	0	0	0	0	0

Pageland *Chesterfield County* Elevation: 620 ft. Latitude: 34° 46' N Longitude: 80° 24' W

	JAN	FEB	MAR	APR	MAY	JUN	JUL	AUG	SEP	OCT	NOV	DEC	YEAR
Mean Maximum Temp. (°F)	54.7	59.4	66.9	75.1	81.9	88.4	91.1	89.6	83.9	74.7	66.0	57.3	74.1
Mean Temp. (°F)	44.0	47.7	54.2	62.3	69.7	77.1	80.4	79.1	73.2	62.9	54.2	46.6	62.6
Mean Minimum Temp. (°F)	33.2	35.9	41.5	49.4	57.6	65.7	69.6	68.5	62.5	51.0	42.3	35.9	51.1
Extreme Maximum Temp. (°F)	79	82	87	96	98	102	103	106	104	93	85	80	106
Extreme Minimum Temp. (°F)	3	5	6	23	32	46	54	54	40	28	19	4	3
Days Maximum Temp. ≥ 90°F	0	0	0	1	3	14	20	15	6	0	0	0	59
Days Maximum Temp. ≤ 32°F	0	0	0	0	0	0	0	0	0	0	0	0	0
Days Minimum Temp. ≤ 32°F	15	11	6	1	0	0	0	0	0	0	6	12	51
Days Minimum Temp. ≤ 0°F	0	0	0	0	0	0	0	0	0	0	0	0	0
Heating Degree Days (base 65°F)	646	486	341	141	29	2	0	0	10	129	328	566	2,678
Cooling Degree Days (base 65°F)	1	2	14	66	183	371	484	443	263	71	10	2	1,910
Mean Precipitation (in.)	4.12	3.58	4.21	3.09	2.73	3.94	4.88	4.74	3.58	3.88	3.43	3.44	45.62
Extreme Maximum Daily Precip. (in.)	3.70	2.32	2.83	2.60	2.50	4.70	4.90	4.76	4.30	11.00	5.40	2.03	11.00
Days With ≥ 0.1" Precipitation	7	6	7	6	6	6	7	7	5	5	5	6	73
Days With ≥ 0.5" Precipitation	3	3	3	2	2	3	3	3	2	2	2	2	30
Days With ≥ 1.0" Precipitation	1	1	1	1	1	1	2	2	1	1	1	1	14
Mean Snowfall (in.)	0.9	0.3	0.4	0.0	0.0	0.0	0.0	0.0	0.0	0.0	0.0	0.1	1.7
Maximum Snow Depth (in.)	9	3	trace	0	0	0	0	0	0	0	0	trace	9
Days With ≥ 1.0" Snow Depth	0	0	0	0	0	0	0	0	0	0	0	0	0

The period of record for all cooperative weather station data is 1980 – 2009. See User Guide for detailed explanation of data.

Pelion 4 NW *Lexington County* Elevation: 450 ft. Latitude: 33° 43' N Longitude: 81° 16' W

	JAN	FEB	MAR	APR	MAY	JUN	JUL	AUG	SEP	OCT	NOV	DEC	YEAR
Mean Maximum Temp. (°F)	56.5	61.1	68.8	76.6	83.7	89.2	91.6	90.2	85.1	76.3	67.5	58.8	75.4
Mean Temp. (°F)	44.6	48.2	55.0	62.5	70.6	77.5	80.7	79.4	73.6	63.2	54.2	46.4	63.0
Mean Minimum Temp. (°F)	32.7	35.2	41.3	48.3	57.4	65.9	69.6	68.6	62.1	50.1	40.8	34.0	50.5
Extreme Maximum Temp. (°F)	83	84	89	94	98	103	107	107	99	98	85	83	107
Extreme Minimum Temp. (°F)	-2	10	-1	17	32	42	51	50	38	22	14	5	-2
Days Maximum Temp. ≥ 90°F	0	0	0	1	5	15	21	17	7	0	0	0	66
Days Maximum Temp. ≤ 32°F	0	0	0	0	0	0	0	0	0	0	0	0	0
Days Minimum Temp. ≤ 32°F	16	12	7	2	0	0	0	0	0	2	8	15	62
Days Minimum Temp. ≤ 0°F	0	0	0	0	0	0	0	0	0	0	0	0	0
Heating Degree Days (base 65°F)	625	472	317	132	21	1	0	0	8	122	331	572	2,601
Cooling Degree Days (base 65°F)	1	3	16	63	202	384	492	453	273	74	12	2	1,975
Mean Precipitation (in.)	4.36	4.13	4.58	3.03	3.00	5.29	5.60	5.37	4.17	3.47	3.35	3.75	50.10
Extreme Maximum Daily Precip. (in.)	3.65	3.20	3.23	3.05	2.65	5.11	4.36	5.30	7.10	3.82	3.02	2.80	7.10
Days With ≥ 0.1" Precipitation	8	7	7	6	5	8	9	8	6	5	5	6	80
Days With ≥ 0.5" Precipitation	3	3	3	2	2	3	4	4	3	2	2	2	33
Days With ≥ 1.0" Precipitation	1	1	2	1	1	2	2	2	1	1	1	1	16
Mean Snowfall (in.)	0.5	0.1	trace	0.0	0.0	0.0	0.0	0.0	0.0	0.0	0.0	trace	0.6
Maximum Snow Depth (in.)	3	trace	4	0	0	0	0	0	0	0	0	trace	4
Days With ≥ 1.0" Snow Depth	0	0	0	0	0	0	0	0	0	0	0	0	0

Pickens *Pickens County* Elevation: 1,162 ft. Latitude: 34° 53' N Longitude: 82° 43' W

	JAN	FEB	MAR	APR	MAY	JUN	JUL	AUG	SEP	OCT	NOV	DEC	YEAR
Mean Maximum Temp. (°F)	52.1	56.3	64.7	73.0	79.9	86.6	89.3	88.2	82.0	72.5	63.2	53.8	71.8
Mean Temp. (°F)	41.2	44.8	52.3	60.0	67.7	75.2	78.4	77.6	71.3	61.0	51.4	43.2	60.3
Mean Minimum Temp. (°F)	30.3	33.3	39.9	47.1	55.6	63.7	67.5	66.9	60.5	49.4	39.6	32.5	48.8
Extreme Maximum Temp. (°F)	79	81	89	93	98	99	104	105	100	89	85	77	105
Extreme Minimum Temp. (°F)	-6	1	8	24	35	46	52	52	39	26	15	2	-6
Days Maximum Temp. ≥ 90°F	0	0	0	1	2	10	16	13	4	0	0	0	46
Days Maximum Temp. ≤ 32°F	1	0	0	0	0	0	0	0	0	0	0	0	1
Days Minimum Temp. ≤ 32°F	19	13	7	2	0	0	0	0	0	1	8	17	67
Days Minimum Temp. ≤ 0°F	0	0	0	0	0	0	0	0	0	0	0	0	0
Heating Degree Days (base 65°F)	730	565	391	180	42	2	0	0	14	163	403	670	3,160
Cooling Degree Days (base 65°F)	0	0	5	38	135	314	424	396	209	45	3	0	1,569
Mean Precipitation (in.)	4.85	4.49	5.05	3.76	4.00	4.30	4.80	5.03	4.41	3.97	4.18	4.93	53.77
Extreme Maximum Daily Precip. (in.)	5.25	3.69	4.85	2.40	2.92	5.56	3.40	5.18	8.02	3.16	3.58	3.60	8.02
Days With ≥ 0.1" Precipitation	7	7	7	7	6	7	7	7	6	5	6	7	79
Days With ≥ 0.5" Precipitation	3	3	3	3	3	3	3	3	3	2	3	4	36
Days With ≥ 1.0" Precipitation	1	1	2	1	1	1	1	2	1	1	1	2	15
Mean Snowfall (in.)	0.8	0.6	trace	trace	0.0	0.0	0.0	0.0	0.0	0.0	trace	0.1	1.5
Maximum Snow Depth (in.)	12	***3***	6	trace	0	0	0	0	0	0	trace	1	***12***
Days With ≥ 1.0" Snow Depth	0	***0***	0	0	0	0	0	0	0	0	0	0	***0***

Spartanburg 3 SSE *Spartanburg County* Elevation: 609 ft. Latitude: 34° 54' N Longitude: 81° 55' W

	JAN	FEB	MAR	APR	MAY	JUN	JUL	AUG	SEP	OCT	NOV	DEC	YEAR
Mean Maximum Temp. (°F)	55.0	59.4	67.2	75.6	81.8	88.2	90.9	89.8	83.9	75.0	65.2	56.4	74.0
Mean Temp. (°F)	42.5	45.9	52.7	60.3	67.9	75.4	78.9	78.0	71.7	61.1	51.5	43.9	60.8
Mean Minimum Temp. (°F)	29.9	32.4	38.1	44.9	53.9	62.6	66.8	66.3	59.4	47.2	37.6	31.4	47.6
Extreme Maximum Temp. (°F)	79	82	90	94	96	101	106	106	98	94	84	80	106
Extreme Minimum Temp. (°F)	-5	6	12	22	29	37	51	46	35	23	13	0	-5
Days Maximum Temp. ≥ 90°F	0	0	0	1	3	13	19	15	5	0	0	0	56
Days Maximum Temp. ≤ 32°F	0	0	0	0	0	0	0	0	0	0	0	0	0
Days Minimum Temp. ≤ 32°F	19	15	10	3	0	0	0	0	0	3	11	18	79
Days Minimum Temp. ≤ 0°F	0	0	0	0	0	0	0	0	0	0	0	0	0
Heating Degree Days (base 65°F)	692	534	381	170	39	2	0	1	15	160	402	646	3,042
Cooling Degree Days (base 65°F)	0	0	6	36	136	322	438	411	222	48	2	0	1,621
Mean Precipitation (in.)	4.19	3.93	4.88	3.58	3.50	4.69	3.92	4.20	3.58	4.24	3.73	4.29	48.73
Extreme Maximum Daily Precip. (in.)	3.25	2.50	3.25	2.55	4.15	***3.47***	3.30	6.50	3.18	8.40	3.20	2.60	***8.40***
Days With ≥ 0.1" Precipitation	7	6	7	6	6	6	7	6	5	5	6	6	73
Days With ≥ 0.5" Precipitation	3	3	4	3	2	3	3	2	3	2	3	3	34
Days With ≥ 1.0" Precipitation	1	1	2	1	1	2	1	1	1	1	1	1	14
Mean Snowfall (in.)	0.9	0.1	0.2	0.0	0.0	0.0	0.0	0.0	0.0	0.0	0.0	0.1	1.3
Maximum Snow Depth (in.)	***12***	***1***	***0***	***0***	***0***	***0***	0	0	0	***0***	0	1	***12***
Days With ≥ 1.0" Snow Depth	***1***	0	0	0	0	0	0	0	0	0	0	0	***1***

Summerville *Dorchester County* Elevation: 35 ft. Latitude: 32° 59' N Longitude: 80° 11' W

	JAN	FEB	MAR	APR	MAY	JUN	JUL	AUG	SEP	OCT	NOV	DEC	YEAR
Mean Maximum Temp. (°F)	58.6	62.3	***69.6***	***76.0***	83.5	***88.4***	***91.4***	***89.9***	***85.3***	***76.7***	***69.0***	***61.4***	***76.0***
Mean Temp. (°F)	46.8	49.8	***56.5***	***62.4***	71.2	***77.9***	***81.2***	***80.1***	***75.0***	***65.1***	***56.3***	***49.1***	***64.3***
Mean Minimum Temp. (°F)	34.9	37.3	***43.3***	***48.9***	58.9	***67.3***	***71.0***	***70.4***	***64.7***	***53.4***	***43.6***	***36.8***	***52.5***
Extreme Maximum Temp. (°F)	80	87	90	***96***	97	***103***	***104***	***104***	***97***	***94***	***85***	***87***	***104***
Extreme Minimum Temp. (°F)	5	15	19	***27***	38	***49***	***56***	***55***	***43***	***31***	***23***	***9***	***5***
Days Maximum Temp. ≥ 90°F	0	0	0	***1***	5	***14***	***21***	***17***	***7***	***1***	***0***	***0***	***66***
Days Maximum Temp. ≤ 32°F	0	0	0	***0***	0	***0***	***0***	***0***	***0***	***0***	***0***	***0***	***0***
Days Minimum Temp. ≤ 32°F	15	9	4	***0***	0	***0***	***0***	***0***	***0***	***0***	***4***	***12***	***44***
Days Minimum Temp. ≤ 0°F	0	0	0	***0***	0	***0***	***0***	***0***	***0***	***0***	***0***	***0***	***0***
Heating Degree Days (base 65°F)	562	428	***277***	***129***	17	***1***	***0***	***0***	***4***	***94***	***274***	***490***	***2,276***
Cooling Degree Days (base 65°F)	2	4	***19***	***59***	215	***394***	***510***	***477***	***312***	***104***	***21***	***5***	***2,122***
Mean Precipitation (in.)	4.34	3.23	4.03	***3.43***	3.37	***5.72***	***5.96***	***6.60***	***5.52***	***3.92***	***3.29***	***3.29***	***52.70***
Extreme Maximum Daily Precip. (in.)	***3.60***	***3.30***	***4.45***	***3.33***	***3.56***	***4.30***	***3.92***	***4.20***	na	***5.52***	***3.37***	na	na
Days With ≥ 0.1" Precipitation	7	5	***5***	***5***	5	***7***	***8***	***9***	***6***	***5***	***6***	***6***	***74***
Days With ≥ 0.5" Precipitation	3	2	3	***2***	2	***3***	***4***	***4***	***3***	***2***	***2***	***2***	***32***
Days With ≥ 1.0" Precipitation	1	1	1	***1***	1	***2***	***2***	***2***	***2***	***1***	***1***	***1***	***16***
Mean Snowfall (in.)	***0.1***	0.1	***0.0***	***0.0***	0.0	***0.0***	***0.0***	***0.0***	***0.0***	***0.0***	***0.0***	***0.3***	***0.5***
Maximum Snow Depth (in.)	***1***	***2***	***1***	***0***	0	***0***	***0***	***0***	***0***	***0***	***0***	***5***	***5***
Days With ≥ 1.0" Snow Depth	***0***	0	0	***0***	0	***0***	***0***	***0***	***0***	***0***	***0***	***0***	***0***

The period of record for all cooperative weather station data is 1980 – 2009. See User Guide for detailed explanation of data.

Sumter *Sumter County* Elevation: 176 ft. Latitude: 33° 56' N Longitude: 80° 21' W

	JAN	FEB	MAR	APR	MAY	JUN	JUL	AUG	SEP	OCT	NOV	DEC	YEAR
Mean Maximum Temp. (°F)	55.7	59.8	67.4	75.6	82.8	88.7	91.6	89.9	84.6	75.3	67.1	58.2	74.7
Mean Temp. (°F)	44.3	47.7	54.4	62.3	70.1	77.4	80.8	79.3	73.7	63.2	54.4	46.5	62.8
Mean Minimum Temp. (°F)	32.9	35.5	41.3	49.0	57.3	65.9	69.9	68.6	62.6	51.0	41.6	34.8	50.9
Extreme Maximum Temp. (°F)	81	85	90	93	100	103	105	105	99	96	86	83	105
Extreme Minimum Temp. (°F)	2	13	11	26	37	46	56	53	40	27	19	9	2
Days Maximum Temp. ≥ 90°F	0	0	0	1	5	14	22	17	6	0	0	0	65
Days Maximum Temp. ≤ 32°F	0	0	0	0	0	0	0	0	0	0	0	0	0
Days Minimum Temp. ≤ 32°F	16	12	6	1	0	0	0	0	0	1	6	14	56
Days Minimum Temp. ≤ 0°F	0	0	0	0	0	0	0	0	0	0	0	0	0
Heating Degree Days (base 65°F)	635	487	336	135	26	1	0	0	8	122	324	569	2,643
Cooling Degree Days (base 65°F)	1	3	14	62	190	380	496	449	275	73	13	3	1,959
Mean Precipitation (in.)	3.98	3.45	4.00	3.06	3.33	5.05	5.07	4.84	3.92	3.41	3.03	3.32	46.46
Extreme Maximum Daily Precip. (in.)	2.40	2.70	3.36	3.12	3.56	4.40	5.50	4.62	4.61	8.21	2.75	3.87	8.21
Days With ≥ 0.1" Precipitation	7	6	7	5	6	7	8	7	5	5	5	6	74
Days With ≥ 0.5" Precipitation	3	2	3	2	2	3	3	3	2	2	2	2	29
Days With ≥ 1.0" Precipitation	1	1	1	1	1	1	2	1	1	1	1	1	13
Mean Snowfall (in.)	0.1	0.2	trace	0.0	0.0	0.0	0.0	0.0	0.0	0.0	0.0	trace	0.3
Maximum Snow Depth (in.)	4	0	0	0	0	0	0	0	0	0	0	1	4
Days With ≥ 1.0" Snow Depth	0	0	0	0	0	0	0	0	0	0	0	0	0

West Pelzer 2 W *Anderson County* Elevation: 861 ft. Latitude: 34° 39' N Longitude: 82° 29' W

	JAN	FEB	MAR	APR	MAY	JUN	JUL	AUG	SEP	OCT	NOV	DEC	YEAR
Mean Maximum Temp. (°F)	52.4	56.5	64.5	72.9	80.2	86.9	90.6	88.8	82.3	72.7	63.9	54.6	72.2
Mean Temp. (°F)	41.4	44.9	52.1	60.1	68.1	75.8	79.5	78.3	71.6	60.8	51.9	43.6	60.7
Mean Minimum Temp. (°F)	30.5	33.2	39.6	47.2	55.9	64.6	68.5	67.7	60.7	48.8	39.8	32.5	49.1
Extreme Maximum Temp. (°F)	78	81	89	93	94	100	104	104	97	92	84	79	104
Extreme Minimum Temp. (°F)	-4	7	7	23	32	45	56	54	39	27	19	1	-4
Days Maximum Temp. ≥ 90°F	0	0	0	0	2	10	17	13	4	0	0	0	46
Days Maximum Temp. ≤ 32°F	1	0	0	0	0	0	0	0	0	0	0	0	1
Days Minimum Temp. ≤ 32°F	18	14	7	1	0	0	0	0	0	1	8	16	65
Days Minimum Temp. ≤ 0°F	0	0	0	0	0	0	0	0	0	0	0	0	0
Heating Degree Days (base 65°F)	724	562	400	179	40	2	0	0	16	166	391	659	3,139
Cooling Degree Days (base 65°F)	0	0	6	39	141	333	459	420	221	42	4	1	1,666
Mean Precipitation (in.)	4.20	4.01	4.51	2.95	3.01	3.23	3.32	3.49	3.60	3.34	3.71	4.00	43.37
Extreme Maximum Daily Precip. (in.)	3.24	3.35	2.44	***4.33***	2.75	2.49	3.95	12.81	4.06	2.43	3.84	3.97	***12.81***
Days With ≥ 0.1" Precipitation	6	6	6	5	5	5	5	5	4	4	5	6	62
Days With ≥ 0.5" Precipitation	3	3	3	2	2	2	2	2	2	2	3	3	29
Days With ≥ 1.0" Precipitation	1	1	2	1	1	1	1	1	1	1	1	1	13
Mean Snowfall (in.)	1.2	0.8	0.7	0.0	0.0	0.0	0.0	0.0	0.0	0.0	0.1	0.1	2.9
Maximum Snow Depth (in.)	11	3	5	0	0	0	0	0	0	0	1	trace	11
Days With ≥ 1.0" Snow Depth	1	0	0	0	0	0	0	0	0	0	0	0	1

Winnsboro *Fairfield County* Elevation: 560 ft. Latitude: 34° 22' N Longitude: 81° 06' W

	JAN	FEB	MAR	APR	MAY	JUN	JUL	AUG	SEP	OCT	NOV	DEC	YEAR
Mean Maximum Temp. (°F)	53.2	57.8	65.7	74.2	81.5	88.2	91.4	89.4	83.2	73.8	64.8	55.4	73.2
Mean Temp. (°F)	42.5	46.1	53.3	61.5	69.6	77.2	80.8	79.3	72.8	62.3	52.9	44.7	61.9
Mean Minimum Temp. (°F)	31.7	34.3	40.8	48.8	57.6	66.1	70.1	69.2	62.2	50.6	40.9	33.8	50.5
Extreme Maximum Temp. (°F)	79	82	87	92	97	102	106	106	98	93	84	79	106
Extreme Minimum Temp. (°F)	-1	8	5	26	36	42	58	56	41	30	19	7	-1
Days Maximum Temp. ≥ 90°F	0	0	0	1	3	14	21	16	6	0	0	0	61
Days Maximum Temp. ≤ 32°F	1	0	0	0	0	0	0	0	0	0	0	0	1
Days Minimum Temp. ≤ 32°F	17	13	7	1	0	0	0	0	0	0	6	15	59
Days Minimum Temp. ≤ 0°F	0	0	0	0	0	0	0	0	0	0	0	0	0
Heating Degree Days (base 65°F)	691	530	369	156	32	2	0	0	12	140	365	625	2,922
Cooling Degree Days (base 65°F)	0	2	12	57	181	375	497	451	252	62	9	1	1,899
Mean Precipitation (in.)	4.07	3.76	4.35	3.04	2.84	4.20	3.85	4.41	3.40	3.38	3.22	3.34	43.86
Extreme Maximum Daily Precip. (in.)	2.21	2.90	3.62	2.25	2.70	4.20	5.25	4.50	6.65	3.97	2.50	3.80	6.65
Days With ≥ 0.1" Precipitation	7	6	6	6	5	6	6	7	5	4	5	6	69
Days With ≥ 0.5" Precipitation	3	2	3	2	2	3	2	3	2	2	2	2	28
Days With ≥ 1.0" Precipitation	1	1	2	1	1	1	1	1	1	1	1	1	13
Mean Snowfall (in.)	0.4	0.1	0.1	0.0	0.0	0.0	0.0	0.0	0.0	0.0	0.0	0.0	0.6
Maximum Snow Depth (in.)	8	0	4	0	0	0	0	0	0	0	0	0	8
Days With ≥ 1.0" Snow Depth	0	0	0	0	0	0	0	0	0	0	0	0	0

Winthrop University *York County* Elevation: 689 ft. Latitude: 34° 56' N Longitude: 81° 02' W

	JAN	FEB	MAR	APR	MAY	JUN	JUL	AUG	SEP	OCT	NOV	DEC	YEAR
Mean Maximum Temp. (°F)	52.4	57.0	64.9	73.6	80.5	87.4	90.5	88.9	82.5	72.9	63.9	54.7	72.4
Mean Temp. (°F)	42.6	46.2	53.3	61.6	69.4	77.1	80.4	79.2	72.6	62.3	53.0	44.8	61.9
Mean Minimum Temp. (°F)	32.8	35.4	41.7	49.6	58.3	66.7	70.3	69.4	62.8	51.6	42.1	34.9	51.3
Extreme Maximum Temp. (°F)	80	83	87	93	95	101	104	106	96	92	84	80	106
Extreme Minimum Temp. (°F)	-4	7	4	22	37	46	56	54	41	26	17	3	-4
Days Maximum Temp. ≥ 90°F	0	0	0	0	2	12	18	14	4	0	0	0	50
Days Maximum Temp. ≤ 32°F	1	0	0	0	0	0	0	0	0	0	0	0	1
Days Minimum Temp. ≤ 32°F	15	11	6	1	0	0	0	0	0	0	6	13	52
Days Minimum Temp. ≤ 0°F	0	0	0	0	0	0	0	0	0	0	0	0	0
Heating Degree Days (base 65°F)	687	526	364	146	29	1	0	0	11	137	358	619	2,878
Cooling Degree Days (base 65°F)	1	1	9	50	172	370	485	445	248	59	6	1	1,847
Mean Precipitation (in.)	3.72	3.65	4.40	3.17	2.82	4.15	3.81	3.98	3.60	3.51	3.49	3.41	43.71
Extreme Maximum Daily Precip. (in.)	2.82	2.91	2.87	2.45	2.55	2.90	4.51	5.34	3.90	3.83	2.90	2.89	5.34
Days With ≥ 0.1" Precipitation	7	6	7	6	6	7	6	6	4	5	6	6	72
Days With ≥ 0.5" Precipitation	3	3	3	3	2	3	3	2	2	2	3	3	32
Days With ≥ 1.0" Precipitation	1	1	1	1	1	1	1	1	1	1	1	1	12
Mean Snowfall (in.)	1.8	1.4	0.5	trace	0.0	0.0	0.0	0.0	0.0	0.0	0.1	0.1	3.9
Maximum Snow Depth (in.)	12	17	10	trace	0	0	0	0	0	0	trace	3	17
Days With ≥ 1.0" Snow Depth	2	1	0	0	0	0	0	0	0	0	0	0	3

The period of record for all cooperative weather station data is 1980 – 2009. See User Guide for detailed explanation of data.

South Carolina Weather Station Rankings

Annual Extreme Maximum Temperature

Highest Rank	Station Name	°F	Lowest Rank	Station Name	°F
1	Johnston 4 SW	110	1	Beaufort 7 SW	***104***
2	Aiken 4 NE	109	1	Charleston City	104
2	Clark Hill 1 W	109	1	Loris 1 S	***104***
2	Columbia Univ of SC	109	1	Summerville	***104***
5	Manning	108	1	West Pelzer 2 W	104
6	Columbia Metro Arpt	107	6	Andrews	105
6	Laurens	107	6	Charleston Intl Arpt	105
6	Pelion 4 NW	107	6	Conway	105
9	Allendale 2 NW	***106***	6	Greer Greenville-Spartanbrg Arpt	105
9	Anderson	106	6	Lake City 2 SE	105
9	Bishopville 8 NNW	106	6	Pickens	105
9	Chester 1 NW	106	6	Sumter	105
9	Florence City County Arpt	106	13	Allendale 2 NW	***106***
9	Greenwood 3 SW	106	13	Anderson	106
9	Little Mountain	106	13	Bishopville 8 NNW	106
9	Pageland	106	13	Chester 1 NW	106
9	Spartanburg 3 SSE	106	13	Florence City County Arpt	106
9	Winnsboro	106	13	Greenwood 3 SW	106
9	Winthrop University	106	13	Little Mountain	106
20	Andrews	105	13	Pageland	106
20	Charleston Intl Arpt	105	13	Spartanburg 3 SSE	106
20	Conway	105	13	Winnsboro	106
20	Greer Greenville-Spartanbrg Arpt	105	13	Winthrop University	106
20	Lake City 2 SE	105	24	Columbia Metro Arpt	107
20	Pickens	105	24	Laurens	107

Annual Mean Maximum Temperature

Highest Rank	Station Name	°F	Lowest Rank	Station Name	°F
1	Columbia Univ of SC	77.8	1	Greer Greenville-Spartanbrg Arpt	71.3
2	Aiken 4 NE	77.2	2	Pickens	71.8
3	Allendale 2 NW	***76.8***	3	West Pelzer 2 W	72.2
4	Manning	76.5	4	Winthrop University	72.4
5	Charleston Intl Arpt	76.1	5	Chester 1 NW	72.6
6	Beaufort 7 SW	***76.0***	6	Greenwood 3 SW	72.8
6	Summerville	***76.0***	6	Little Mountain	72.8
8	Andrews	75.8	8	Winnsboro	73.2
8	Clark Hill 1 W	75.8	9	Charleston City	73.3
10	Conway	75.4	10	Laurens	73.5
10	Pelion 4 NW	75.4	11	Anderson	73.9
12	Columbia Metro Arpt	75.3	12	Spartanburg 3 SSE	74.0
12	Lake City 2 SE	***75.3***	13	Bishopville 8 NNW	74.1
14	Florence City County Arpt	74.8	13	Pageland	74.1
15	Sumter	74.7	15	Loris 1 S	***74.3***
16	Johnston 4 SW	74.5	16	Johnston 4 SW	74.5
17	Loris 1 S	***74.3***	17	Sumter	74.7
18	Bishopville 8 NNW	74.1	18	Florence City County Arpt	74.8
18	Pageland	74.1	19	Columbia Metro Arpt	75.3
20	Spartanburg 3 SSE	74.0	19	Lake City 2 SE	***75.3***
21	Anderson	73.9	21	Conway	75.4
22	Laurens	73.5	21	Pelion 4 NW	75.4
23	Charleston City	73.3	23	Andrews	75.8
24	Winnsboro	73.2	23	Clark Hill 1 W	75.8
25	Greenwood 3 SW	72.8	25	Beaufort 7 SW	***76.0***

 Rankings include 25 highest/lowest stations. If state has less than 25 stations, all stations are included. The period of record is 1980–2009. See User Guide for detailed explanation of data.

Annual Mean Temperature

Highest Rank	Station Name	°F	Lowest Rank	Station Name	°F
1	Beaufort 7 SW	***67.0***	1	Chester 1 NW	60.2
2	Charleston City	66.9	2	Laurens	60.3
3	Charleston Intl Arpt	66.1	3	Pickens	60.4
3	Columbia Univ of SC	66.1	4	Greer Greenville-Spartanbrg Arpt	60.7
5	Andrews	64.6	4	West Pelzer 2 W	60.7
6	Allendale 2 NW	***64.3***	6	Greenwood 3 SW	60.8
6	Conway	64.3	6	Spartanburg 3 SSE	60.8
6	Summerville	***64.3***	8	Anderson	61.6
9	Aiken 4 NE	64.1	9	Johnston 4 SW	61.7
10	Florence City County Arpt	63.9	10	Winnsboro	61.9
10	Manning	63.9	10	Winthrop University	61.9
12	Columbia Metro Arpt	63.7	12	Bishopville 8 NNW	62.2
13	Lake City 2 SE	***63.2***	12	Clark Hill 1 W	62.2
14	Pelion 4 NW	63.0	14	Little Mountain	62.3
15	Sumter	62.8	14	Loris 1 S	***62.3***
16	Pageland	62.6	16	Pageland	62.6
17	Little Mountain	62.3	17	Sumter	62.8
17	Loris 1 S	***62.3***	18	Pelion 4 NW	63.0
19	Bishopville 8 NNW	62.2	19	Lake City 2 SE	***63.2***
19	Clark Hill 1 W	62.2	20	Columbia Metro Arpt	63.7
21	Winnsboro	61.9	21	Florence City County Arpt	63.9
21	Winthrop University	61.9	21	Manning	63.9
23	Johnston 4 SW	61.7	23	Aiken 4 NE	64.1
24	Anderson	61.6	24	Allendale 2 NW	***64.3***
25	Greenwood 3 SW	60.8	24	Conway	64.3

Annual Mean Minimum Temperature

Highest Rank	Station Name	°F	Lowest Rank	Station Name	°F
1	Charleston City	60.4	1	Laurens	47.1
2	Beaufort 7 SW	***57.9***	2	Spartanburg 3 SSE	47.6
3	Charleston Intl Arpt	56.1	3	Chester 1 NW	47.8
4	Columbia Univ of SC	54.4	4	Clark Hill 1 W	48.7
5	Andrews	53.3	4	Greenwood 3 SW	48.7
6	Conway	53.2	6	Johnston 4 SW	48.9
7	Florence City County Arpt	52.9	6	Pickens	48.9
8	Summerville	***52.5***	8	West Pelzer 2 W	49.1
9	Columbia Metro Arpt	52.0	9	Anderson	49.2
10	Little Mountain	51.8	10	Greer Greenville-Spartanbrg Arpt	50.0
11	Allendale 2 NW	***51.7***	11	Bishopville 8 NNW	50.2
12	Winthrop University	51.3	12	Loris 1 S	***50.3***
13	Manning	51.2	13	Pelion 4 NW	50.5
14	Pageland	51.1	13	Winnsboro	50.5
15	Aiken 4 NE	51.0	15	Sumter	50.9
15	Lake City 2 SE	***51.0***	16	Aiken 4 NE	51.0
17	Sumter	50.9	16	Lake City 2 SE	***51.0***
18	Pelion 4 NW	50.5	18	Pageland	51.1
18	Winnsboro	50.5	19	Manning	51.2
20	Loris 1 S	***50.3***	20	Winthrop University	51.3
21	Bishopville 8 NNW	50.2	21	Allendale 2 NW	***51.7***
22	Greer Greenville-Spartanbrg Arpt	50.0	22	Little Mountain	51.8
23	Anderson	49.2	23	Columbia Metro Arpt	52.0
24	West Pelzer 2 W	49.1	24	Summerville	***52.5***
25	Johnston 4 SW	48.9	25	Florence City County Arpt	52.9

Rankings include 25 highest/lowest stations. If state has less than 25 stations, all stations are included. The period of record is 1980–2009. See User Guide for detailed explanation of data.

Annual Extreme Minimum Temperature

Highest Rank	Station Name	°F	Lowest Rank	Station Name	°F
1	Charleston City	10	1	Pickens	-6
2	Charleston Intl Arpt	6	2	Anderson	-5
3	Beaufort 7 SW	*5*	2	Spartanburg 3 SSE	-5
3	Summerville	*5*	4	Aiken 4 NE	-4
5	Conway	4	4	Greer Greenville-Spartanbrg Arpt	-4
6	Pageland	3	4	West Pelzer 2 W	-4
7	Andrews	2	4	Winthrop University	-4
7	Lake City 2 SE	2	8	Chester 1 NW	-3
7	Loris 1 S	*2*	9	Allendale 2 NW	*-2*
7	Sumter	2	9	Bishopville 8 NNW	-2
11	Columbia Univ of SC	1	9	Clark Hill 1 W	-2
12	Florence City County Arpt	0	9	Greenwood 3 SW	-2
12	Manning	0	9	Johnston 4 SW	-2
14	Columbia Metro Arpt	-1	9	Laurens	-2
14	Winnsboro	-1	9	Little Mountain	-2
16	Allendale 2 NW	*-2*	9	Pelion 4 NW	-2
16	Bishopville 8 NNW	-2	17	Columbia Metro Arpt	-1
16	Clark Hill 1 W	-2	17	Winnsboro	-1
16	Greenwood 3 SW	-2	19	Florence City County Arpt	0
16	Johnston 4 SW	-2	19	Manning	0
16	Laurens	-2	21	Columbia Univ of SC	1
16	Little Mountain	-2	22	Andrews	2
16	Pelion 4 NW	-2	22	Lake City 2 SE	2
24	Chester 1 NW	-3	22	Loris 1 S	*2*
25	Aiken 4 NE	-4	22	Sumter	2

July Mean Maximum Temperature

Highest Rank	Station Name	°F	Lowest Rank	Station Name	°F
1	Columbia Univ of SC	94.9	1	Charleston City	88.1
2	Aiken 4 NE	94.2	2	Pickens	89.3
3	Clark Hill 1 W	93.6	3	Greer Greenville-Spartanbrg Arpt	89.5
4	Manning	93.4	4	Little Mountain	89.9
5	Allendale 2 NW	93.1	5	Loris 1 S	*90.4*
6	Johnston 4 SW	92.8	6	Winthrop University	90.5
7	Columbia Metro Arpt	92.6	7	West Pelzer 2 W	90.6
8	Lake City 2 SE	91.7	8	Chester 1 NW	90.7
9	Laurens	91.6	9	Beaufort 7 SW	*90.8*
9	Pelion 4 NW	91.6	10	Spartanburg 3 SSE	90.9
9	Sumter	91.6	11	Greenwood 3 SW	91.0
12	Anderson	91.5	12	Andrews	91.1
13	Florence City County Arpt	91.4	12	Bishopville 8 NNW	91.1
13	Summerville	*91.4*	12	Pageland	91.1
13	Winnsboro	91.4	15	Charleston Intl Arpt	91.2
16	Charleston Intl Arpt	91.2	15	Conway	91.2
16	Conway	91.2	17	Florence City County Arpt	91.4
18	Andrews	91.1	17	Summerville	*91.4*
18	Bishopville 8 NNW	91.1	17	Winnsboro	91.4
18	Pageland	91.1	20	Anderson	91.5
21	Greenwood 3 SW	91.0	21	Laurens	91.6
22	Spartanburg 3 SSE	90.9	21	Pelion 4 NW	91.6
23	Beaufort 7 SW	*90.8*	21	Sumter	91.6
24	Chester 1 NW	90.7	24	Lake City 2 SE	91.7
25	West Pelzer 2 W	90.6	25	Columbia Metro Arpt	92.6

 Rankings include 25 highest/lowest stations. If state has less than 25 stations, all stations are included. The period of record is 1980–2009. See User Guide for detailed explanation of data.

January Mean Minimum Temperature

Highest			Lowest		
Rank	**Station Name**	**°F**	**Rank**	**Station Name**	**°F**
1	Charleston City	42.8	1	Laurens	28.2
2	Beaufort 7 SW	***40.5***	2	Chester 1 NW	28.9
3	Charleston Intl Arpt	38.3	3	Spartanburg 3 SSE	29.9
4	Columbia Univ of SC	36.7	4	Clark Hill 1 W	30.3
5	Andrews	36.0	4	Pickens	30.3
6	Florence City County Arpt	34.9	6	Greenwood 3 SW	30.4
6	Summerville	34.9	7	West Pelzer 2 W	30.5
8	Conway	34.6	8	Anderson	30.8
9	Little Mountain	34.5	9	Johnston 4 SW	31.1
10	Manning	33.7	10	Bishopville 8 NNW	31.4
11	Columbia Metro Arpt	33.6	11	Winnsboro	31.7
12	Allendale 2 NW	33.5	12	Greer Greenville-Spartanbrg Arpt	31.8
13	Pageland	33.2	13	Loris 1 S	***32.7***
14	Lake City 2 SE	33.1	13	Pelion 4 NW	32.7
15	Aiken 4 NE	33.0	15	Winthrop University	32.8
16	Sumter	32.9	16	Sumter	32.9
17	Winthrop University	32.8	17	Aiken 4 NE	33.0
18	Loris 1 S	***32.7***	18	Lake City 2 SE	33.1
18	Pelion 4 NW	32.7	19	Pageland	33.2
20	Greer Greenville-Spartanbrg Arpt	31.8	20	Allendale 2 NW	33.5
21	Winnsboro	31.7	21	Columbia Metro Arpt	33.6
22	Bishopville 8 NNW	31.4	22	Manning	33.7
23	Johnston 4 SW	31.1	23	Little Mountain	34.5
24	Anderson	30.8	24	Conway	34.6
25	West Pelzer 2 W	30.5	25	Florence City County Arpt	34.9

Number of Days Annually Maximum Temperature ≥ 90°F

Highest			Lowest		
Rank	**Station Name**	**Days**	**Rank**	**Station Name**	**Days**
1	Columbia Univ of SC	99	1	Charleston City	28
2	Aiken 4 NE	89	2	Greer Greenville-Spartanbrg Arpt	43
3	Manning	88	3	Little Mountain	45
4	Clark Hill 1 W	85	4	Pickens	46
5	Allendale 2 NW	***83***	4	West Pelzer 2 W	46
6	Johnston 4 SW	76	6	Winthrop University	50
7	Columbia Metro Arpt	75	7	Greenwood 3 SW	53
8	Florence City County Arpt	66	8	Chester 1 NW	54
8	Lake City 2 SE	66	9	Loris 1 S	***55***
8	Pelion 4 NW	66	10	Beaufort 7 SW	***56***
8	Summerville	***66***	10	Spartanburg 3 SSE	56
12	Laurens	65	12	Pageland	59
12	Sumter	65	13	Andrews	60
14	Anderson	61	13	Conway	60
14	Bishopville 8 NNW	61	15	Anderson	61
14	Charleston Intl Arpt	61	15	Bishopville 8 NNW	61
14	Winnsboro	61	15	Charleston Intl Arpt	61
18	Andrews	60	15	Winnsboro	61
18	Conway	60	19	Laurens	65
20	Pageland	59	19	Sumter	65
21	Beaufort 7 SW	***56***	21	Florence City County Arpt	66
21	Spartanburg 3 SSE	56	21	Lake City 2 SE	66
23	Loris 1 S	***55***	21	Pelion 4 NW	66
24	Chester 1 NW	54	21	Summerville	***66***
25	Greenwood 3 SW	53	25	Columbia Metro Arpt	75

Rankings include 25 highest/lowest stations. If state has less than 25 stations, all stations are included. The period of record is 1980–2009. See User Guide for detailed explanation of data.

Number of Days Annually Maximum Temperature ≤ 32°F

Highest			Lowest		
Rank	Station Name	Days	Rank	Station Name	Days
1	Bishopville 8 NNW	1	1	Aiken 4 NE	0
1	Chester 1 NW	1	1	Allendale 2 NW	*0*
1	Greenwood 3 SW	1	1	Anderson	0
1	Greer Greenville-Spartanbrg Arpt	1	1	Andrews	0
1	Laurens	1	1	Beaufort 7 SW	*0*
1	Little Mountain	1	1	Charleston City	0
1	Pickens	1	1	Charleston Intl Arpt	0
1	West Pelzer 2 W	1	1	Clark Hill 1 W	0
1	Winnsboro	1	1	Columbia Metro Arpt	0
1	Winthrop University	1	1	Columbia Univ of SC	0
11	Aiken 4 NE	0	1	Conway	0
11	Allendale 2 NW	*0*	1	Florence City County Arpt	0
11	Anderson	0	1	Johnston 4 SW	0
11	Andrews	0	1	Lake City 2 SE	0
11	Beaufort 7 SW	*0*	1	Loris 1 S	*0*
11	Charleston City	0	1	Manning	0
11	Charleston Intl Arpt	0	1	Pageland	0
11	Clark Hill 1 W	0	1	Pelion 4 NW	0
11	Columbia Metro Arpt	0	1	Spartanburg 3 SSE	0
11	Columbia Univ of SC	0	1	Summerville	*0*
11	Conway	0	1	Sumter	0
11	Florence City County Arpt	0	22	Bishopville 8 NNW	1
11	Johnston 4 SW	0	22	Chester 1 NW	1
11	Lake City 2 SE	0	22	Greenwood 3 SW	1
11	Loris 1 S	*0*	22	Greer Greenville-Spartanbrg Arpt	1

Number of Days Annually Minimum Temperature ≤ 32°F

Highest			Lowest		
Rank	Station Name	Days	Rank	Station Name	Days
1	Laurens	85	1	Charleston City	6
2	Chester 1 NW	83	2	Beaufort 7 SW	*15*
3	Spartanburg 3 SSE	79	3	Charleston Intl Arpt	24
4	Greenwood 3 SW	69	4	Columbia Univ of SC	35
5	Clark Hill 1 W	67	5	Conway	38
5	Pickens	67	6	Andrews	39
7	Johnston 4 SW	66	7	Florence City County Arpt	41
8	West Pelzer 2 W	65	8	Little Mountain	43
9	Anderson	63	9	Summerville	*44*
10	Bishopville 8 NNW	62	10	Allendale 2 NW	*51*
10	Pelion 4 NW	62	10	Pageland	51
12	Loris 1 S	*60*	12	Winthrop University	52
13	Winnsboro	59	13	Columbia Metro Arpt	54
14	Greer Greenville-Spartanbrg Arpt	58	13	Lake City 2 SE	54
15	Aiken 4 NE	57	13	Manning	54
16	Sumter	56	16	Sumter	56
17	Columbia Metro Arpt	54	17	Aiken 4 NE	57
17	Lake City 2 SE	54	18	Greer Greenville-Spartanbrg Arpt	58
17	Manning	54	19	Winnsboro	59
20	Winthrop University	52	20	Loris 1 S	*60*
21	Allendale 2 NW	*51*	21	Bishopville 8 NNW	62
21	Pageland	51	21	Pelion 4 NW	62
23	Summerville	*44*	23	Anderson	63
24	Little Mountain	43	24	West Pelzer 2 W	65
25	Florence City County Arpt	41	25	Johnston 4 SW	66

Rankings include 25 highest/lowest stations. If state has less than 25 stations, all stations are included. The period of record is 1980–2009. See User Guide for detailed explanation of data.

Number of Days Annually Minimum Temperature ≤ 0°F

Highest

Rank	Station Name	Days
1	Aiken 4 NE	0
1	Allendale 2 NW	***0***
1	Anderson	0
1	Andrews	0
1	Beaufort 7 SW	***0***
1	Bishopville 8 NNW	0
1	Charleston City	0
1	Charleston Intl Arpt	0
1	Chester 1 NW	0
1	Clark Hill 1 W	0
1	Columbia Metro Arpt	0
1	Columbia Univ of SC	0
1	Conway	0
1	Florence City County Arpt	0
1	Greenwood 3 SW	0
1	Greer Greenville-Spartanbrg Arpt	0
1	Johnston 4 SW	0
1	Lake City 2 SE	0
1	Laurens	0
1	Little Mountain	0
1	Loris 1 S	***0***
1	Manning	0
1	Pageland	0
1	Pelion 4 NW	0
1	Pickens	0

Lowest

Rank	Station Name	Days
1	Aiken 4 NE	0
1	Allendale 2 NW	***0***
1	Anderson	0
1	Andrews	0
1	Beaufort 7 SW	***0***
1	Bishopville 8 NNW	0
1	Charleston City	0
1	Charleston Intl Arpt	0
1	Chester 1 NW	0
1	Clark Hill 1 W	0
1	Columbia Metro Arpt	0
1	Columbia Univ of SC	0
1	Conway	0
1	Florence City County Arpt	0
1	Greenwood 3 SW	0
1	Greer Greenville-Spartanbrg Arpt	0
1	Johnston 4 SW	0
1	Lake City 2 SE	0
1	Laurens	0
1	Little Mountain	0
1	Loris 1 S	***0***
1	Manning	0
1	Pageland	0
1	Pelion 4 NW	0
1	Pickens	0

Number of Annual Heating Degree Days

Highest

Rank	Station Name	Num.
1	Chester 1 NW	3,293
2	Laurens	3,276
3	Pickens	3,160
4	West Pelzer 2 W	3,139
5	Greenwood 3 SW	3,137
6	Greer Greenville-Spartanbrg Arpt	3,118
7	Spartanburg 3 SSE	3,042
8	Winnsboro	2,922
9	Johnston 4 SW	2,915
10	Anderson	2,913
11	Winthrop University	2,878
12	Bishopville 8 NNW	2,824
13	Clark Hill 1 W	2,807
14	Loris 1 S	***2,718***
15	Little Mountain	2,683
16	Pageland	2,678
17	Sumter	2,643
18	Pelion 4 NW	2,601
19	Lake City 2 SE	***2,564***
20	Columbia Metro Arpt	2,535
21	Manning	2,443
22	Florence City County Arpt	2,438
23	Aiken 4 NE	2,394
24	Allendale 2 NW	***2,328***
25	Conway	2,315

Lowest

Rank	Station Name	Num.
1	Charleston City	1,657
2	Beaufort 7 SW	***1,684***
3	Charleston Intl Arpt	1,891
4	Columbia Univ of SC	2,034
5	Andrews	2,172
6	Summerville	***2,276***
7	Conway	2,315
8	Allendale 2 NW	***2,328***
9	Aiken 4 NE	2,394
10	Florence City County Arpt	2,438
11	Manning	2,443
12	Columbia Metro Arpt	2,535
13	Lake City 2 SE	***2,564***
14	Pelion 4 NW	2,601
15	Sumter	2,643
16	Pageland	2,678
17	Little Mountain	2,683
18	Loris 1 S	***2,718***
19	Clark Hill 1 W	2,807
20	Bishopville 8 NNW	2,824
21	Winthrop University	2,878
22	Anderson	2,913
23	Johnston 4 SW	2,915
24	Winnsboro	2,922
25	Spartanburg 3 SSE	3,042

Rankings include 25 highest/lowest stations. If state has less than 25 stations, all stations are included. The period of record is 1980–2009. See User Guide for detailed explanation of data.

Number of Annual Cooling Degree Days

Highest

Rank	Station Name	Num.
1	Columbia Univ of SC	2,553
2	Beaufort 7 SW	***2,510***
3	Charleston City	2,461
4	Charleston Intl Arpt	2,407
5	Aiken 4 NE	2,187
6	Conway	2,166
7	Columbia Metro Arpt	2,164
8	Allendale 2 NW	***2,158***
9	Florence City County Arpt	2,137
9	Manning	2,137
11	Andrews	2,123
12	Summerville	***2,122***
13	Lake City 2 SE	***2,008***
14	Pelion 4 NW	1,975
15	Sumter	1,959
16	Pageland	1,910
17	Clark Hill 1 W	1,907
18	Winnsboro	1,899
19	Bishopville 8 NNW	1,896
20	Winthrop University	1,847
21	Loris 1 S	***1,841***
22	Johnston 4 SW	1,811
22	Little Mountain	1,811
24	Anderson	1,774
25	Greenwood 3 SW	1,710

Lowest

Rank	Station Name	Num.
1	Pickens	1,569
2	Spartanburg 3 SSE	1,621
3	Greer Greenville-Spartanbrg Arpt	1,648
4	Chester 1 NW	1,654
5	Laurens	1,666
5	West Pelzer 2 W	1,666
7	Greenwood 3 SW	1,710
8	Anderson	1,774
9	Johnston 4 SW	1,811
9	Little Mountain	1,811
11	Loris 1 S	***1,841***
12	Winthrop University	1,847
13	Bishopville 8 NNW	1,896
14	Winnsboro	1,899
15	Clark Hill 1 W	1,907
16	Pageland	1,910
17	Sumter	1,959
18	Pelion 4 NW	1,975
19	Lake City 2 SE	***2,008***
20	Summerville	***2,122***
21	Andrews	2,123
22	Florence City County Arpt	2,137
22	Manning	2,137
24	Allendale 2 NW	***2,158***
25	Columbia Metro Arpt	2,164

Annual Precipitation

Highest

Rank	Station Name	Inches
1	Pickens	53.77
2	Summerville	***52.70***
3	Conway	52.25
4	Loris 1 S	***51.29***
5	Aiken 4 NE	50.49
6	Charleston Intl Arpt	50.11
7	Pelion 4 NW	50.10
8	Andrews	49.84
9	Manning	49.78
10	Beaufort 7 SW	***49.73***
11	Spartanburg 3 SSE	48.73
12	Anderson	47.54
13	Greer Greenville-Spartanbrg Arpt	47.44
14	Johnston 4 SW	46.98
15	Allendale 2 NW	***46.54***
16	Sumter	46.46
17	Columbia Univ of SC	46.37
18	Lake City 2 SE	46.12
19	Little Mountain	45.99
20	Pageland	45.62
21	Chester 1 NW	45.40
22	Laurens	45.38
23	Clark Hill 1 W	45.07
24	Columbia Metro Arpt	44.78
25	Charleston City	44.09

Lowest

Rank	Station Name	Inches
1	Florence City County Arpt	42.51
2	West Pelzer 2 W	43.37
3	Winthrop University	43.71
4	Bishopville 8 NNW	43.74
5	Winnsboro	43.86
6	Greenwood 3 SW	43.87
7	Charleston City	44.09
8	Columbia Metro Arpt	44.78
9	Clark Hill 1 W	45.07
10	Laurens	45.38
11	Chester 1 NW	45.40
12	Pageland	45.62
13	Little Mountain	45.99
14	Lake City 2 SE	46.12
15	Columbia Univ of SC	46.37
16	Sumter	46.46
17	Allendale 2 NW	***46.54***
18	Johnston 4 SW	46.98
19	Greer Greenville-Spartanbrg Arpt	47.44
20	Anderson	47.54
21	Spartanburg 3 SSE	48.73
22	Beaufort 7 SW	***49.73***
23	Manning	49.78
24	Andrews	49.84
25	Pelion 4 NW	50.10

 Rankings include 25 highest/lowest stations. If state has less than 25 stations, all stations are included. The period of record is 1980–2009. See User Guide for detailed explanation of data.

Annual Extreme Maximum Daily Precipitation

Highest Rank	Station Name	Inches	Lowest Rank	Station Name	Inches
1	West Pelzer 2 W	***12.81***	1	Manning	***3.80***
2	Conway	11.35	2	Florence City County Arpt	4.35
3	Pageland	11.00	3	Aiken 4 NE	***4.79***
4	Loris 1 S	***10.02***	4	Columbia Univ of SC	4.83
5	Clark Hill 1 W	***9.40***	5	Anderson	***5.00***
6	Greer Greenville-Spartanbrg Arpt	9.32	6	Columbia Metro Arpt	5.17
7	Charleston City	8.50	7	Winthrop University	5.34
8	Spartanburg 3 SSE	***8.40***	8	Laurens	5.35
9	Sumter	8.21	9	Johnston 4 SW	5.36
10	Pickens	8.02	10	Andrews	***6.20***
11	Allendale 2 NW	***8.00***	11	Little Mountain	6.46
12	Lake City 2 SE	***7.30***	12	Charleston Intl Arpt	6.57
13	Chester 1 NW	7.13	13	Winnsboro	6.65
14	Bishopville 8 NNW	7.10	14	Bishopville 8 NNW	7.10
14	Pelion 4 NW	7.10	14	Pelion 4 NW	7.10
16	Winnsboro	6.65	16	Chester 1 NW	7.13
17	Charleston Intl Arpt	6.57	17	Lake City 2 SE	***7.30***
18	Little Mountain	6.46	18	Allendale 2 NW	***8.00***
19	Andrews	***6.20***	19	Pickens	8.02
20	Johnston 4 SW	5.36	20	Sumter	8.21
21	Laurens	5.35	21	Spartanburg 3 SSE	***8.40***
22	Winthrop University	5.34	22	Charleston City	8.50
23	Columbia Metro Arpt	5.17	23	Greer Greenville-Spartanbrg Arpt	9.32
24	Anderson	***5.00***	24	Clark Hill 1 W	***9.40***
25	Columbia Univ of SC	4.83	25	Loris 1 S	***10.02***

Number of Days Annually With ≥ 0.1 Inches of Precipitation

Highest Rank	Station Name	Days	Lowest Rank	Station Name	Days
1	Manning	82	1	Lake City 2 SE	61
2	Pelion 4 NW	80	2	West Pelzer 2 W	62
3	Pickens	79	3	Greenwood 3 SW	64
4	Aiken 4 NE	75	4	Charleston City	66
5	Beaufort 7 SW	***74***	5	Andrews	68
5	Charleston Intl Arpt	74	5	Chester 1 NW	68
5	Columbia Univ of SC	74	5	Clark Hill 1 W	68
5	Conway	74	8	Anderson	69
5	Greer Greenville-Spartanbrg Arpt	74	8	Winnsboro	69
5	Summerville	***74***	10	Bishopville 8 NNW	70
5	Sumter	74	10	Columbia Metro Arpt	70
12	Loris 1 S	***73***	10	Laurens	70
12	Pageland	73	13	Johnston 4 SW	71
12	Spartanburg 3 SSE	73	14	Allendale 2 NW	***72***
15	Allendale 2 NW	***72***	14	Florence City County Arpt	72
15	Florence City County Arpt	72	14	Little Mountain	72
15	Little Mountain	72	14	Winthrop University	72
15	Winthrop University	72	18	Loris 1 S	***73***
19	Johnston 4 SW	71	18	Pageland	73
20	Bishopville 8 NNW	70	18	Spartanburg 3 SSE	73
20	Columbia Metro Arpt	70	21	Beaufort 7 SW	***74***
20	Laurens	70	21	Charleston Intl Arpt	74
23	Anderson	69	21	Columbia Univ of SC	74
23	Winnsboro	69	21	Conway	74
25	Andrews	68	21	Greer Greenville-Spartanbrg Arpt	74

Rankings include 25 highest/lowest stations. If state has less than 25 stations, all stations are included. The period of record is 1980–2009. See User Guide for detailed explanation of data.

Number of Days Annually With ≥ 0.5 Inches of Precipitation

Highest			Lowest		
Rank	Station Name	Days	Rank	Station Name	Days
1	Pickens	36	1	Bishopville 8 NNW	28
2	Andrews	35	1	Charleston City	28
3	Aiken 4 NE	34	1	Florence City County Arpt	28
3	Greer Greenville-Spartanbrg Arpt	34	1	Greenwood 3 SW	28
3	Spartanburg 3 SSE	34	1	Winnsboro	28
6	Anderson	33	6	Clark Hill 1 W	29
6	Charleston Intl Arpt	33	6	Sumter	29
6	Conway	33	6	West Pelzer 2 W	29
6	Manning	33	9	Columbia Metro Arpt	30
6	Pelion 4 NW	33	9	Johnston 4 SW	30
11	Allendale 2 NW	***32***	9	Lake City 2 SE	30
11	Chester 1 NW	32	9	Laurens	30
11	Loris 1 S	***32***	9	Pageland	30
11	Summerville	***32***	14	Beaufort 7 SW	***31***
11	Winthrop University	32	14	Columbia Univ of SC	31
16	Beaufort 7 SW	***31***	14	Little Mountain	31
16	Columbia Univ of SC	31	17	Allendale 2 NW	***32***
16	Little Mountain	31	17	Chester 1 NW	32
19	Columbia Metro Arpt	30	17	Loris 1 S	***32***
19	Johnston 4 SW	30	17	Summerville	***32***
19	Lake City 2 SE	30	17	Winthrop University	32
19	Laurens	30	22	Anderson	33
19	Pageland	30	22	Charleston Intl Arpt	33
24	Clark Hill 1 W	29	22	Conway	33
24	Sumter	29	22	Manning	33

Number of Days Annually With ≥ 1.0 Inches of Precipitation

Highest			Lowest		
Rank	Station Name	Days	Rank	Station Name	Days
1	Andrews	16	1	Bishopville 8 NNW	12
1	Charleston Intl Arpt	16	1	Chester 1 NW	12
1	Conway	16	1	Laurens	12
1	Loris 1 S	***16***	1	Winthrop University	12
1	Pelion 4 NW	16	5	Clark Hill 1 W	13
1	Summerville	***16***	5	Florence City County Arpt	13
7	Columbia Univ of SC	15	5	Greenwood 3 SW	13
7	Lake City 2 SE	15	5	Greer Greenville-Spartanbrg Arpt	13
7	Pickens	15	5	Johnston 4 SW	13
10	Aiken 4 NE	14	5	Manning	13
10	Allendale 2 NW	***14***	5	Sumter	13
10	Anderson	14	5	West Pelzer 2 W	13
10	Beaufort 7 SW	***14***	5	Winnsboro	13
10	Charleston City	14	14	Aiken 4 NE	14
10	Columbia Metro Arpt	14	14	Allendale 2 NW	***14***
10	Little Mountain	14	14	Anderson	14
10	Pageland	14	14	Beaufort 7 SW	***14***
10	Spartanburg 3 SSE	14	14	Charleston City	14
19	Clark Hill 1 W	13	14	Columbia Metro Arpt	14
19	Florence City County Arpt	13	14	Little Mountain	14
19	Greenwood 3 SW	13	14	Pageland	14
19	Greer Greenville-Spartanbrg Arpt	13	14	Spartanburg 3 SSE	14
19	Johnston 4 SW	13	23	Columbia Univ of SC	15
19	Manning	13	23	Lake City 2 SE	15
19	Sumter	13	23	Pickens	15

Rankings include 25 highest/lowest stations. If state has less than 25 stations, all stations are included. The period of record is 1980–2009. See User Guide for detailed explanation of data.

Annual Snowfall

Highest

Rank	Station Name	Inches
1	Greer Greenville-Spartanbrg Arpt	5.0
2	Winthrop University	3.9
3	West Pelzer 2 W	2.9
4	Little Mountain	2.3
5	Greenwood 3 SW	2.2
6	Chester 1 NW	2.1
7	Anderson	1.8
8	Loris 1 S	***1.7***
8	Pageland	1.7
10	Johnston 4 SW	1.6
11	Laurens	1.5
11	Pickens	1.5
13	Columbia Metro Arpt	1.3
13	Lake City 2 SE	1.3
13	Spartanburg 3 SSE	1.3
16	Manning	1.0
17	Columbia Univ of SC	0.8
18	Andrews	0.7
18	Bishopville 8 NNW	0.7
18	Conway	0.7
21	Charleston Intl Arpt	***0.6***
21	Pelion 4 NW	0.6
21	Winnsboro	0.6
24	Summerville	***0.5***
25	Aiken 4 NE	0.4

Lowest

Rank	Station Name	Inches
1	Allendale 2 NW	***0.1***
2	Beaufort 7 SW	***0.2***
3	Clark Hill 1 W	0.3
3	Sumter	0.3
5	Aiken 4 NE	0.4
6	Summerville	***0.5***
7	Charleston Intl Arpt	***0.6***
7	Pelion 4 NW	0.6
7	Winnsboro	0.6
10	Andrews	0.7
10	Bishopville 8 NNW	0.7
10	Conway	0.7
13	Columbia Univ of SC	0.8
14	Manning	1.0
15	Columbia Metro Arpt	1.3
15	Lake City 2 SE	1.3
15	Spartanburg 3 SSE	1.3
18	Laurens	1.5
18	Pickens	1.5
20	Johnston 4 SW	1.6
21	Loris 1 S	***1.7***
21	Pageland	1.7
23	Anderson	1.8
24	Chester 1 NW	2.1
25	Greenwood 3 SW	2.2

Annual Maximum Snow Depth

Highest

Rank	Station Name	Inches
1	Winthrop University	17
2	Loris 1 S	***14***
3	Conway	13
4	Chester 1 NW	12
4	Greer Greenville-Spartanbrg Arpt	12
4	Pickens	***12***
4	Spartanburg 3 SSE	***12***
8	West Pelzer 2 W	11
9	Little Mountain	9
9	Pageland	9
11	Andrews	8
11	Charleston Intl Arpt	***8***
11	Clark Hill 1 W	8
11	Lake City 2 SE	***8***
11	Winnsboro	8
16	Anderson	7
17	Greenwood 3 SW	6
17	Johnston 4 SW	6
17	Manning	6
20	Summerville	***5***
21	Columbia Metro Arpt	4
21	Columbia Univ of SC	4
21	Laurens	4
21	Pelion 4 NW	4
21	Sumter	4

Lowest

Rank	Station Name	Inches
1	Allendale 2 NW	Trace
2	Aiken 4 NE	***3***
2	Bishopville 8 NNW	3
4	Columbia Metro Arpt	4
4	Columbia Univ of SC	4
4	Laurens	4
4	Pelion 4 NW	4
4	Sumter	4
9	Summerville	***5***
10	Greenwood 3 SW	6
10	Johnston 4 SW	6
10	Manning	6
13	Anderson	7
14	Andrews	8
14	Charleston Intl Arpt	***8***
14	Clark Hill 1 W	8
14	Lake City 2 SE	***8***
14	Winnsboro	8
19	Little Mountain	9
19	Pageland	9
21	West Pelzer 2 W	11
22	Chester 1 NW	12
22	Greer Greenville-Spartanbrg Arpt	12
22	Pickens	***12***
22	Spartanburg 3 SSE	***12***

Rankings include 25 highest/lowest stations. If state has less than 25 stations, all stations are included. The period of record is 1980–2009. See User Guide for detailed explanation of data.

Number of Days Annually With ≥ 1.0 Inch Snow Depth

Highest

Rank	Station Name	Days
1	Winthrop University	3
2	Greer Greenville-Spartanbrg Arpt	2
3	Chester 1 NW	1
3	Columbia Univ of SC	1
3	Little Mountain	1
3	Spartanburg 3 SSE	*1*
3	West Pelzer 2 W	1
8	Aiken 4 NE	0
8	Allendale 2 NW	*0*
8	Anderson	0
8	Andrews	0
8	Bishopville 8 NNW	0
8	Charleston Intl Arpt	*0*
8	Clark Hill 1 W	0
8	Columbia Metro Arpt	0
8	Conway	0
8	Greenwood 3 SW	0
8	Johnston 4 SW	0
8	Lake City 2 SE	0
8	Laurens	0
8	Loris 1 S	*0*
8	Manning	0
8	Pageland	0
8	Pelion 4 NW	0
8	Pickens	*0*

Lowest

Rank	Station Name	Days
1	Aiken 4 NE	0
1	Allendale 2 NW	*0*
1	Anderson	0
1	Andrews	0
1	Bishopville 8 NNW	0
1	Charleston Intl Arpt	*0*
1	Clark Hill 1 W	0
1	Columbia Metro Arpt	0
1	Conway	0
1	Greenwood 3 SW	0
1	Johnston 4 SW	0
1	Lake City 2 SE	0
1	Laurens	0
1	Loris 1 S	*0*
1	Manning	0
1	Pageland	0
1	Pelion 4 NW	0
1	Pickens	*0*
1	Summerville	*0*
1	Sumter	0
1	Winnsboro	0
22	Chester 1 NW	1
22	Columbia Univ of SC	1
22	Little Mountain	1
22	Spartanburg 3 SSE	*1*

 Rankings include 25 highest/lowest stations. If state has less than 25 stations, all stations are included. The period of record is 1980–2009. See User Guide for detailed explanation of data.

Significant Storm Events in South Carolina: 2000 – 2009

Location or County	Date	Type	Mag.	Deaths	Injuries	Property Damage ($mil.)	Crop Damage ($mil.)
Florence	05/25/00	Hail	4.50 in.	0	2	30.0	0.0
Horry	07/13/00	Flood	na	0	0	2.0	0.0
Anderson	07/04/01	Thunderstorm Wind	58 mph	0	0	1.5	0.0
Horry	07/06/01	Tornado	F2	0	39	8.0	0.0
Horry County	11/27/01	Fog	na	1	10	0.0	0.0
Northwest South Carolina	12/04/02	Ice Storm	na	0	0	100.0	0.0
Darlington, Dillon, and Marlboro Counties	01/25/04	Ice Storm	na	0	0	3.0	0.0
Northeast South Carolina	01/26/04	Ice Storm	na	0	0	23.2	0.0
Northwest South Carolina	02/26/04	Heavy Snow	na	0	0	1.8	0.0
Greenville	07/29/04	Flash Flood	na	0	0	3.5	0.0
Georgetown and Horry Counties	08/14/04	Hurricane Charley	na	0	3	6.5	0.0
Berkeley, Charleston, and Dorchester Counties	08/29/04	Tropical Storm	na	0	0	16.6	0.0
Sumter	09/07/04	Tornado	F2	0	3	1.7	0.0
Fairfield	09/27/04	Tornado	F2	1	13	0.0	0.0
Laurens	01/13/05	Tornado	F2	0	1	2.0	0.0
Spartanburg	08/10/05	Flash Flood	na	0	0	1.5	0.0
Georgetown	10/06/05	Heavy Rain	na	0	0	1.5	0.0
Richland	06/12/06	Lightning	na	0	0	1.5	0.0
Spartanburg	06/14/07	Thunderstorm Wind	69 mph	0	0	8.0	0.0
Greenwood	03/15/08	Hail	1.75 in.	0	0	2.8	0.0
Aiken	04/10/09	Tornado	F3	0	14	5.0	0.0
Horry County	04/22/09	Wildfire	na	0	0	40.0	0.0

Note: Deaths, injuries, and damages are date and location specific.

SOUTH DAKOTA

PHYSICAL FEATURES. Rolling plains are the main feature of South Dakota, varying from nearly level land to hilly ridges, and increasing in elevation from the eastern border to the western edge of the State. The general elevation above sea level in the extreme eastern portion is about 1,500 feet, and in the extreme west is about 3,000 feet, except in the Black Hills area. The Black Hills, an isolated group of forest-covered mountains, have a climate of their own.

The soil covering the State was laid down in past ages by glaciers, water, and wind. There are occasional outcroppings of bedrock. The Missouri River and its tributaries drain all of South Dakota except for a small portion of the northeastern part of the State. Some of this small drainage area is in the headwaters of the Red River of the North in the Hudson Bay Drainage, and the remainder is in the headwater area of the Minnesota River which forms a part of the upper Mississippi River Basin.

South Dakota is bisected by the Missouri River which flows in a southerly direction to Pierre and then turns to the south-southeast where it forms the South Dakota-Nebraska State line. West of the Missouri lies a country of canyons, broad upland flats, and buttes. The principal tributaries which drain this region are the Grand, the Moreau and Cheyenne which drain the Black Hills, and the White. To the east of the Missouri is mostly prairie land with numerous small ponds and lakes, some of which dry up in periods of droughts. The principal rivers in this area are the James and the Big Sioux. The larger of the two, the James River, has an extremely low slope and consequently is sluggish and meanders. Water falling on much of the eastern area does not reach the stream valleys at all, but lies in depressions until it evaporates or soaks into the ground.

GENERAL CLIMATE. Since South Dakota is situated in the heart of the North American Continent, it is near the paths of many cyclones and anticyclones, and has the extremes of summer heat and winter cold that are characteristic of continental climates. Rapid fluctuations in temperature are common. Partly because of the great distance from any large body of water, the ranges of daily, monthly, and annual temperatures are very large. Temperatures of 100°F. or higher are experienced in some part of the State each summer, and on rare occasions such readings have been noted as early as April and as late as October. These high temperatures are usually attended by low humidity, which greatly reduces the oppressiveness of the heat. Below-zero temperatures occur frequently on midwinter mornings, but it is not often that the temperature stays below zero during the entire day. In the north, subzero temperatures can occur in October and April.

Warm "chinook" winds and frequent sunny skies make the Black Hills area the warmest part of the State in winter. Also, because of the tendency for very cold air masses to stay at low elevations, some of the Arctic air outbreaks that blanket the eastern counties do not reach the higher counties in the west. During summer, the higher elevation of the Black Hills results in that section having cooler temperatures than the rest of the State. At this season, the central and southeastern counties are warmest. The freeze-free season is shortest high in the Black Hills where brief freezing has been known to occur at any time of summer. Elsewhere, the first autumn freeze generally occurs in mid-September in the northwest, in late September in the central and east, and in the first week of October in the extreme southeastern corner. The average time of the last freeze in spring ranges from early May in the southeast to late May in the northwest.

PRECIPITATION. The annual precipitation decreases northwestward from about 25 inches in the extreme southeast to less than 13 inches in part of the northwest. The Black Hills are again an exception, varying from 16 inches in their southern portion to almost 25 inches in the northern, where rain and snow are often formed when the prevailing winds are abruptly forced up the mountainsides. Most of the State's precipitation occurs from April through September. On the average, it reaches a maximum during June, and decreases sharply in early July. The least precipitation is received during winter.

SNOWFALL. Occasionally there is heavy snowfall in winter and the amount of snow on the ground accumulates to a considerable depth, but as a rule the snow cover is not great. Wind usually accompanies the snow, causing a large proportion of it to collect in gullies and behind windbreaks. In the worst storms, isolated drifts many feet deep may block roads, while windswept fields nearby are nearly bare of snow. Snow that falls early in the season seldom stays on the ground very long. Snow that falls after the ground has frozen deeply and the days become very short remains longer. Once a snow cover is present, there is a tendency for it to continue, since the temperature falls to much lower levels over snow than over bare ground. Snowfall reaches a maximum in February and early March, and decreases markedly near the end of March. Violent, cold winds carrying snow picked up from the ground, commonly called "blizzards," are occasional occurances.

STORMS. Rainstorms occur most frequently in early summer, hailstorms are most frequent in midsummer, and lightning does its worst damage in late summer. In dry seasons, and particularly in the west in late summer, thunderstorm bases may be as high as two miles above the ground; consequently, the rain showers may evaporate before reaching ground. When the thundershowers do reach the ground during summer, there is a high incidence of hail. Tornadoes are not as frequent as in states farther south and east. Much more damage is caused by straight-line thunderstorm winds. Such winds are not impeded by trees or other obstacles on the open prairie, and speeds near the ground become very high.

The most serious flooding has been caused by rapid melting of a heavy snow pack and aggravated by ice jams. Heavy rainfall alone causes severe floods on tributary streams, especially in the eastern part of the State. Intense local storms result in flash flooding along minor tributaries.

OTHER CLIMATIC ELEMENTS. South Dakota has considerable fair weather. The air is generally clear with excellent visibility, since much of it arrives by way of the Rocky Mountains and Canada. The wind is most frequently from the south and southeast during the summer, and from the north and northwest during the winter. Wind speeds are often moderate to brisk at midday and almost calm at night, averaging 11 or 12 m.p.h. on a year-round basis.

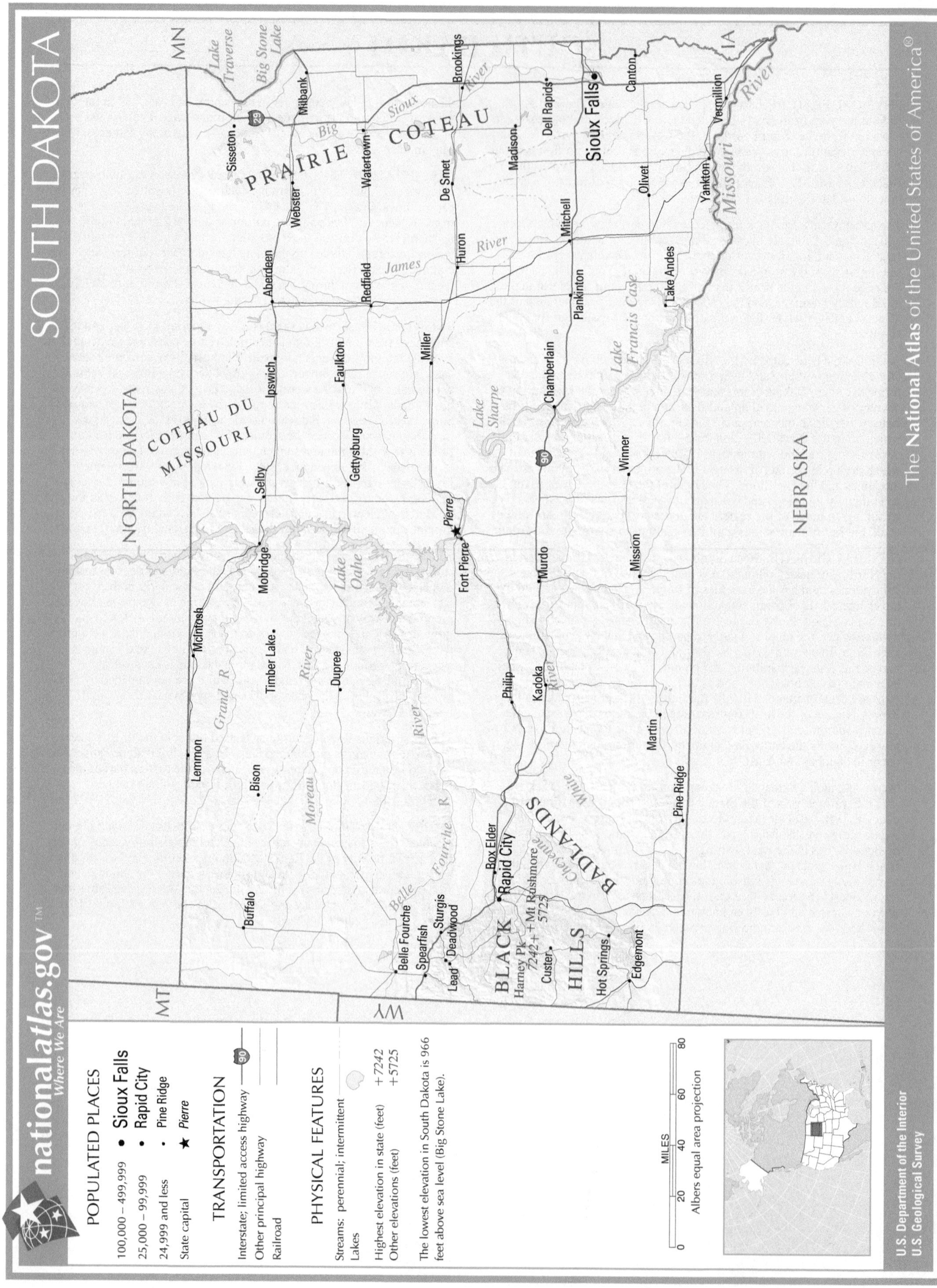
SOUTH DAKOTA
nationalatlas.gov™
Where We Are
POPULATED PLACES
100,000 – 499,999 • Sioux Falls
25,000 – 99,999 • Rapid City
24,999 and less • Pine Ridge
State capital ★ Pierre
TRANSPORTATION
Interstate; limited access highway
Other principal highway
Railroad
PHYSICAL FEATURES
Streams: perennial; intermittent
Lakes
Highest elevation in state (feet) +7242
Other elevations (feet) +5725
The lowest elevation in South Dakota is 966 feet above sea level (Big Stone Lake).
MILES
0 20 40 60 80
Albers equal area projection
U.S. Department of the Interior
U.S. Geological Survey
The National Atlas of the United States of America®
NORTH DAKOTA
NEBRASKA
MN
IA
MT
WY
COTEAU DU MISSOURI
PRAIRIE COTEAU
BLACK HILLS
BADLANDS
Lake Traverse
Big Stone Lake
Big Sioux River
James River
Missouri River
Lake Francis Case
Lake Sharpe
Lake Oahe
Grand R
Moreau River
Belle Fourche R
Cheyenne River
White River
Sisseton
Milbank
Watertown
Brookings
Webster
Aberdeen
Redfield
Huron
De Smet
Madison
Dell Rapids
Sioux Falls
Canton
Vermillion
Yankton
Olivet
Mitchell
Plankinton
Lake Andes
Chamberlain
Miller
Faulkton
Ipswich
Gettysburg
Selby
Mobridge
Pierre
Fort Pierre
Murdo
Winner
Mission
McIntosh
Timber Lake
Dupree
Lemmon
Bison
Philip
Kadoka
Martin
Pine Ridge
Box Elder
Rapid City
Mt Rushmore 5725
Harney Pk 7242
Custer
Hot Springs
Edgemont
Buffalo
Belle Fourche
Spearfish
Sturgis
Deadwood
Lead
29
90

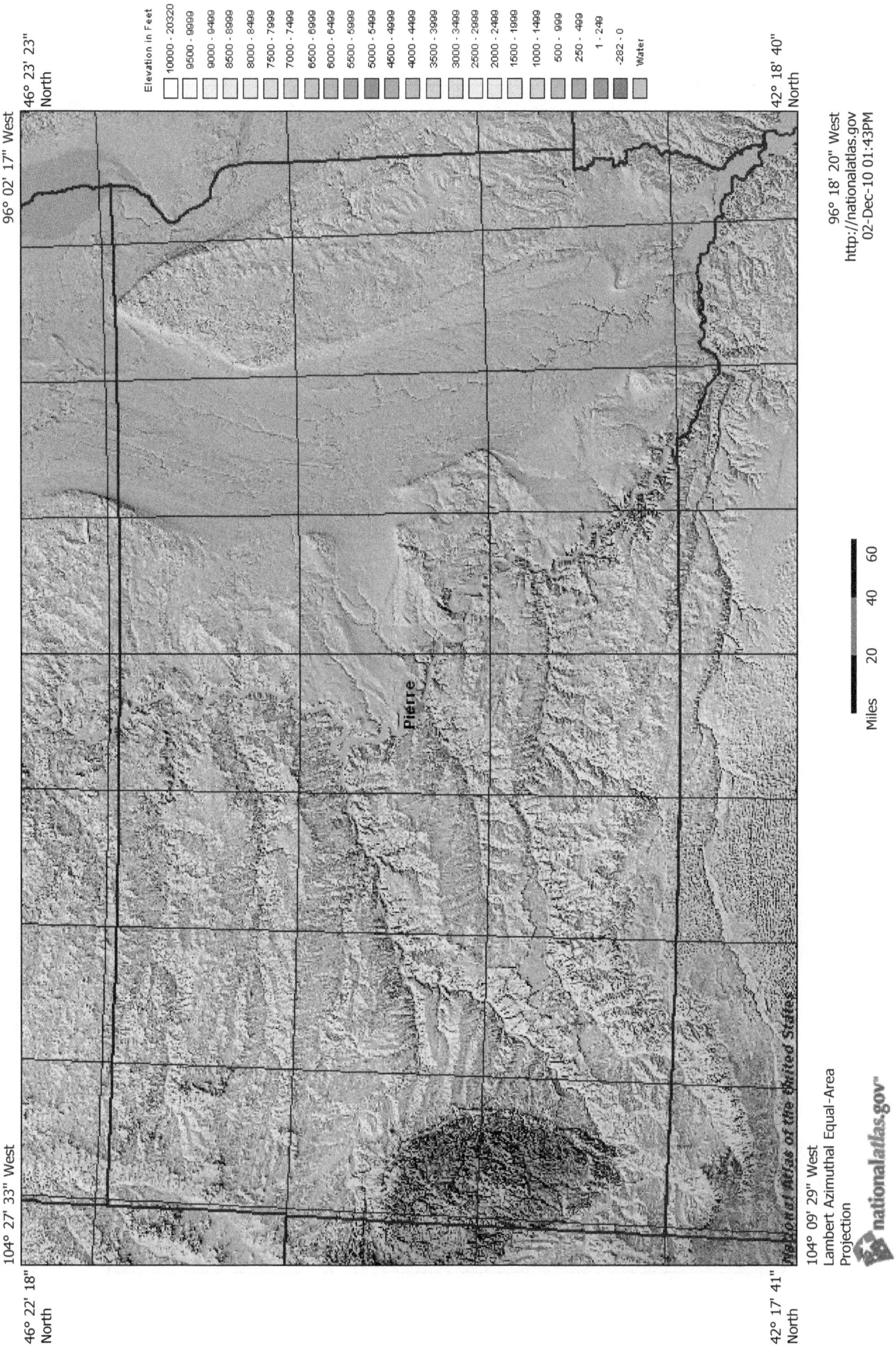
Elevation in Feet
10000 - 20320
9500 - 9999
9000 - 9499
8500 - 8999
8000 - 8499
7500 - 7999
7000 - 7499
6500 - 6999
6000 - 6499
5500 - 5999
5000 - 5499
4500 - 4999
4000 - 4499
3500 - 3999
3000 - 3499
2500 - 2999
2000 - 2499
1500 - 1999
1000 - 1499
500 - 999
250 - 499
1 - 249
-282 - 0
Water
46° 23' 23" North
96° 02' 17" West
42° 18' 40" North
96° 18' 20" West
http://nationalatlas.gov
02-Dec-10 01:43PM
Pierre
Miles 20 40 60
104° 27' 33" West
46° 22' 18" North
42° 17' 41" North
104° 09' 29" West
Lambert Azimuthal Equal-Area Projection
National Atlas of the United States
nationalatlas.gov

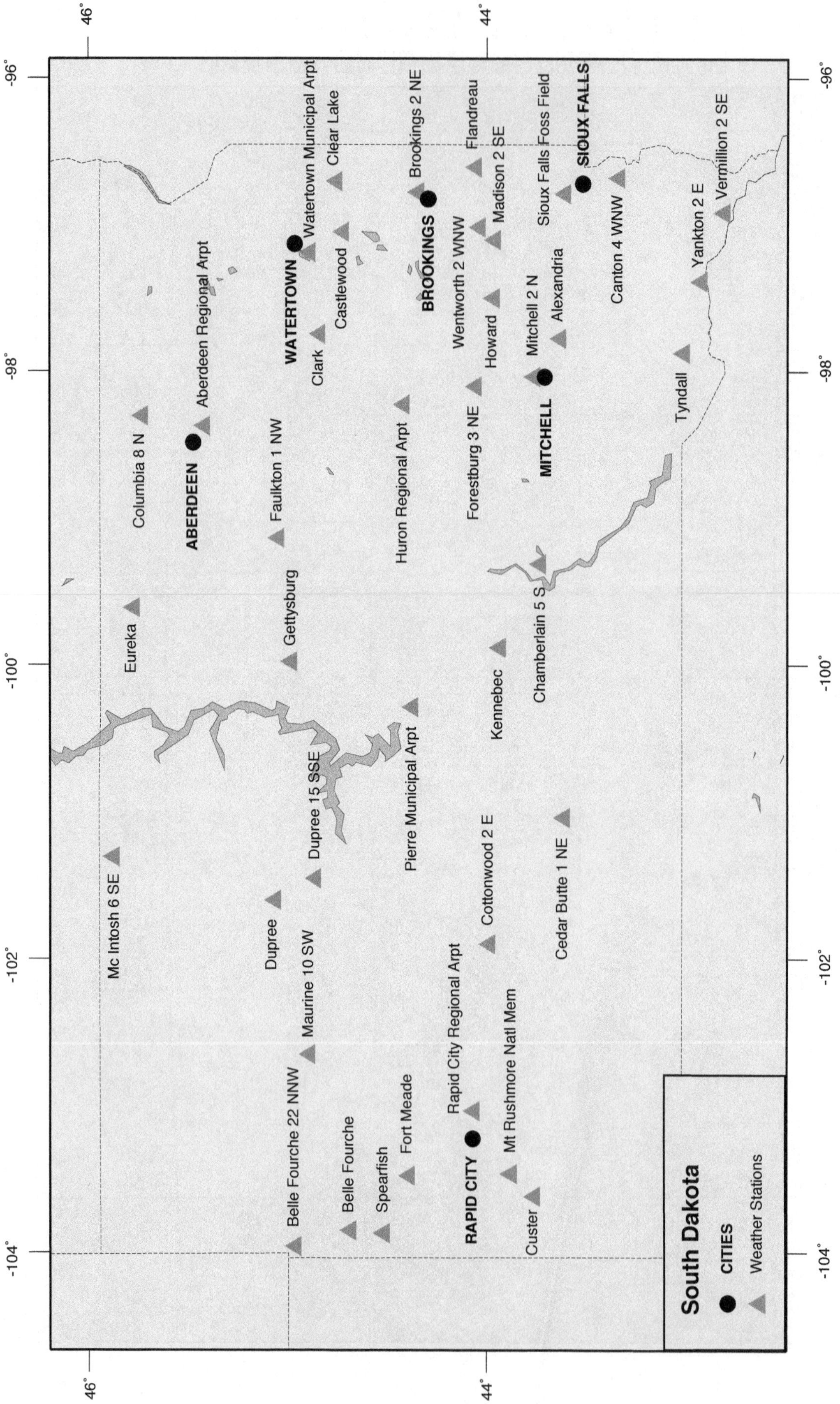
South Dakota
CITIES
Weather Stations
ABERDEEN
WATERTOWN
BROOKINGS
MITCHELL
SIOUX FALLS
RAPID CITY
Columbia 8 N
Aberdeen Regional Arpt
Eureka
Mc Intosh 6 SE
Faulkton 1 NW
Gettysburg
Dupree
Dupree 15 SSE
Maurine 10 SW
Belle Fourche 22 NNW
Belle Fourche
Spearfish
Fort Meade
Rapid City Regional Arpt
Mt Rushmore Natl Mem
Custer
Cottonwood 2 E
Cedar Butte 1 NE
Pierre Municipal Arpt
Kennebec
Chamberlain 5 S
Huron Regional Arpt
Forestburg 3 NE
Clark
Watertown Municipal Arpt
Clear Lake
Castlewood
Brookings 2 NE
Wentworth 2 WNW
Flandreau
Howard
Madison 2 SE
Mitchell 2 N
Alexandria
Sioux Falls Foss Field
Canton 4 WNW
Tyndall
Yankton 2 E
Vermillion 2 SE
46°
44°
-96°
-98°
-100°
-102°
-104°

South Dakota Weather Stations by County

County	Station Name
Beadle	Huron Regional Arpt
Bon Homme	Tyndall
Brookings	Brookings 2 NE
Brown	Aberdeen Regional Arpt Columbia 8 N
Brule	Chamberlain 5 S
Butte	Belle Fourche Belle Fourche 22 NNW
Clark	Clark
Clay	Vermillion 2 SE
Codington	Watertown Municipal Arpt
Corson	McIntosh 6 SE
Custer	Custer
Davison	Mitchell 2 N
Deuel	Clear Lake
Faulk	Faulkton 1 NW
Hamlin	Castlewood
Hanson	Alexandria
Hughes	Pierre Municipal Arpt
Jackson	Cottonwood 2 E
Lake	Madison 2 SE Wentworth 2 WNW
Lawrence	Spearfish
Lincoln	Canton 4 WNW
Lyman	Kennebec
Mcpherson	Eureka
Meade	Fort Meade Maurine 10 SW
Mellette	Cedar Butte 1 NE
Miner	Howard
Minnehaha	Sioux Falls Foss Field
Moody	Flandreau
Pennington	Mt Rushmore Natl Mem Rapid City Regional Arpt
Potter	Gettysburg

County	Station Name
Sanborn	Forestburg 3 NE
Yankton	Yankton 2 E
Ziebach	Dupree Dupree 15 SSE

See User Guide for station inclusion criteria.

South Dakota Weather Stations by City

City	Station Name	Miles
Aberdeen	Aberdeen Regional Arpt	3.2
	Columbia 8 N	20.6
Brandon	Canton 4 WNW	19.3
	Sioux Falls Foss Field	8.5
Brookings	Brookings 2 NE	1.3
	Flandreau	20.0
	Wentworth 2 WNW	22.6
Huron	Forestburg 3 NE	22.4
	Huron Regional Arpt	3.1
Madison	Howard	20.9
	Madison 2 SE	1.8
	Wentworth 2 WNW	5.6
Mitchell	Alexandria	12.9
	Forestburg 3 NE	23.4
	Mitchell 2 N	1.5
Pierre	Pierre Municipal Arpt	2.8
Rapid City	Mt Rushmore Natl Mem	16.9
	Rapid City Regional Arpt	9.4
Rapid Valley	Mt Rushmore Natl Mem	19.8
	Rapid City Regional Arpt	4.7
Sioux Falls	Canton 4 WNW	15.4
	Sioux Falls Foss Field	3.7
Spearfish	Belle Fourche	12.3
	Fort Meade	18.9
	Spearfish	2.0
Sturgis	Belle Fourche	24.3
	Fort Meade	1.7
	Spearfish	18.9
Vermillion	Vermillion 2 SE	1.2
	Yankton 2 E	23.4
Watertown	Castlewood	13.6
	Clear Lake	23.9
	Watertown Municipal Arpt	1.7
Yankton	Tyndall	25.0
	Yankton 2 E	1.3

Note: Miles is the distance between the geographic center of the city and the weather station.

See User Guide for station inclusion criteria.

South Dakota Weather Stations by Elevation

Feet	Station Name
5,479	Custer
5,250	Mt Rushmore Natl Mem
3,640	Spearfish
3,299	Fort Meade
3,200	Belle Fourche 22 NNW
3,160	Rapid City Regional Arpt
3,020	Belle Fourche
2,709	Maurine 10 SW
2,414	Cottonwood 2 E
2,375	Dupree
2,250	Cedar Butte 1 NE
2,174	McIntosh 6 SE
2,100	Dupree 15 SSE
2,069	Gettysburg
1,859	Eureka
1,799	Clear Lake
1,779	Clark
1,750	Watertown Municipal Arpt
1,726	Pierre Municipal Arpt
1,700	Kennebec
1,689	Wentworth 2 WNW
1,685	Castlewood
1,660	Chamberlain 5 S
1,660	Madison 2 SE
1,640	Brookings 2 NE
1,569	Faulkton 1 NW
1,560	Flandreau
1,560	Howard
1,428	Sioux Falls Foss Field
1,419	Tyndall
1,353	Alexandria
1,345	Canton 4 WNW
1,299	Columbia 8 N
1,295	Aberdeen Regional Arpt
1,279	Huron Regional Arpt
1,250	Mitchell 2 N
1,229	Forestburg 3 NE
1,189	Vermillion 2 SE
1,180	Yankton 2 E

See User Guide for station inclusion criteria.

Aberdeen Regional Airport

Aberdeen is located in the northeast quarter of South Dakota, approximately 200 miles south of the geographical center of the North American continent. The surrounding area, extensively cultivated, is the bed of glacial Lake Dakota, which is by far the largest flat area in South Dakota. The lake bed slopes gently to the south. The elevation of Aberdeen at the northern end of the lake bed is 1,300 feet. The elevation at the southern end, some 30 miles distant is 1,280 feet. Low hills rim the area on the east and west. These hills effect ceilings, visibility, and precipitation. Located near the center of the North American land mass, the climate is continental with distinct seasons. Frequent and rapid weather changes occur during all seasons of the year as migratory storms sweep through the area. The winters are cold and dry. Sub-zero minimum temperatures may set in as early as late November, although temperatures of zero and below are generally not recorded until mid-December. Lowest temperatures of the winter generally occur in the period from mid-January to mid-February. During the coldest periods the days are generally sunny with light winds, and these conditions partially moderate the discomfort experienced at such low temperatures. Some days of the winter will be extremely unpleasant with temperatures near or below zero and brisk winds. Heavy snowfalls rarely occur during the first two-thirds of the winter season, with heaviest snowfalls developing during late February and early March as temperatures moderate. Blizzards are infrequent, and many winters will pass without a single occurrence of this type of weather phenomenon. However, difficult driving conditions occur several times during most winters during periods of weather termed ground blizzards by state residents.

Spring is a very short and transitional period, the shortest season of the four distinct seasons, and one marked by very rapid weather changes. Cool to quite cold nights prevail into mid-May, although afternoon temperatures may be quite warm, as high as the mid-80s. By mid-May temperatures below the freezing point rarely occur and frost is rarely experienced after the end of May.

Summers are pleasant with a maximum of sunshine, warm days, and generally cool and comfortable nights. Temperatures of 100 degrees or above may occur several times during the summer season, but low humidities, brisk winds during the heat of the day, and rapid cooling during the evening hours, which generally occur during the periods of elevated temperatures, markedly moderate the physical discomfort normally experienced at these high temperatures. Thunderstorms occur frequently.

Autumn is most pleasant with mild days, cool nights, ample sunshine, and declining occurrences and amounts of precipitation. The first frost may be expected by late September, although it may occur as early as late August.

Aberdeen Regional Airport *Brown County* Elevation: 1,295 ft. Latitude: 45° 27' N Longitude: 98° 25' W

	JAN	FEB	MAR	APR	MAY	JUN	JUL	AUG	SEP	OCT	NOV	DEC	YEAR
Mean Maximum Temp. (°F)	23.4	28.7	40.4	57.7	69.6	78.0	84.3	82.3	72.8	58.2	40.5	26.4	55.2
Mean Temp. (°F)	13.0	18.6	30.4	45.1	57.3	66.4	72.1	69.7	59.8	46.0	30.3	16.8	43.8
Mean Minimum Temp. (°F)	2.6	8.5	20.5	32.5	44.9	54.7	59.8	57.0	46.7	33.8	20.1	7.1	32.3
Extreme Maximum Temp. (°F)	60	62	80	98	96	108	109	107	101	91	77	59	109
Extreme Minimum Temp. (°F)	-42	-45	-32	6	13	36	41	32	20	8	-24	-34	-45
Days Maximum Temp. ≥ 90°F	0	0	0	0	1	3	7	5	2	0	0	0	18
Days Maximum Temp. ≤ 32°F	22	16	8	1	0	0	0	0	0	0	8	20	75
Days Minimum Temp. ≤ 32°F	31	27	27	15	3	0	0	0	2	14	27	31	177
Days Minimum Temp. ≤ 0°F	14	9	2	0	0	0	0	0	0	0	2	10	37
Heating Degree Days (base 65°F)	1,609	1,306	1,065	592	260	62	10	28	200	584	1,034	1,489	8,239
Cooling Degree Days (base 65°F)	0	0	0	3	27	111	237	180	52	2	0	0	612
Mean Precipitation (in.)	0.44	0.53	1.20	1.78	3.01	3.60	2.94	2.59	2.08	2.00	0.72	0.46	21.35
Maximum Precipitation (in.)*	1.6	2.1	3.4	7.9	7.4	8.4	7.7	5.9	5.3	5.1	2.4	1.6	28.1
Minimum Precipitation (in.)*	0	0.1	trace	0.1	0.3	0.4	0.3	0.3	0	trace	trace	trace	7.9
Extreme Maximum Daily Precip. (in.)	0.66	0.56	3.05	1.84	7.62	2.54	2.81	3.25	3.02	3.75	0.68	0.86	7.62
Days With ≥ 0.1" Precipitation	1	2	3	4	5	7	6	5	4	4	2	1	44
Days With ≥ 0.5" Precipitation	0	0	1	1	2	2	2	2	1	1	0	0	12
Days With ≥ 1.0" Precipitation	0	0	0	0	1	1	1	1	0	1	0	0	5
Mean Snowfall (in.)	6.1	6.8	7.6	3.2	trace	trace	trace	trace	trace	0.7	6.9	6.1	37.4
Maximum Snowfall (in.)*	16	25	28	24	2	0	0	0	trace	6	30	16	63
Maximum 24-hr. Snowfall (in.)*	8	14	12	13	2	0	0	0	trace	3	12	9	14
Maximum Snow Depth (in.)	30	25	24	12	7	trace	trace	trace	trace	3	23	21	30
Days With ≥ 1.0" Snow Depth	20	16	11	1	0	0	0	0	0	0	6	15	69
Thunderstorm Days*	0	0	< 1	2	5	10	10	8	3	1	0	0	39
Foggy Days*	8	8	11	9	7	6	6	7	8	7	8	10	95
Predominant Sky Cover*	OVR	OVR	OVR	OVR	OVR	OVR	SCT	CLR	CLR	OVR	OVR	OVR	OVR
Mean Relative Humidity 6am (%)*	76	79	83	81	81	85	86	87	85	81	82	80	82
Mean Relative Humidity 3pm (%)*	69	68	63	48	46	52	47	45	46	47	60	69	55
Mean Dewpoint (°F)*	3	11	21	32	43	55	59	57	46	35	22	10	33
Prevailing Wind Direction*	S	S	N	N	SSE	S	SSE	SSE	S	S	S	S	S
Prevailing Wind Speed (mph)*	10	10	16	15	15	12	12	13	13	12	10	10	13
Maximum Wind Gust (mph)*	63	56	56	66	62	61	68	69	58	52	58	59	69

Note: (*) Period of record is 1948-1995

The period of record for National Weather Service station data is 1980 – 2009 except where noted. See User Guide for detailed explanation of data.

Huron Regional Airport

Located on the west bank of the James River at about the middle of the river valley, Huron has a climate that can be classified as continental with frequent daily temperature fluctuations and distinct seasons. The seasons have varied quite markedly from year to year.

Winter is characteristically cold and dry with storms of short duration. Normal temperatures for the season are in the middle teens and precipitation is mainly in the form of snow. Seasonal snowfall has varied from under nine inches to over 75 inches. Wintertime storms of blizzard proportions are infrequent, but they do occur. These blizzards are characterized by strong winds, low temperatures, snow, and very poor visibility. Many mild days can be expected during the winter since about 39 percent of the daily maximum temperatures are above the freezing mark.

Spring is characterized by marked upward trends in both precipitation and temperature with the moisture amounts increasing some three to four fold over winter. Nearly one-third, over five inches, of the annual total precipitation usually falls during the spring months. In early spring some of the precipitation falls as snow. As a consequence, the month of March has a slightly higher snowfall average than any of the winter months.

Based on the 1951-1980 period, the average first occurrence of 32 degrees Fahrenheit in the fall is September 29 and the average last occurrence in the spring is May 11.

Summers are hot but not extreme. Temperatures of 100 degrees or higher usually occur three or four times a year, but nights are normally cool and comfortable. Summertime precipitation is mainly in the form of showers and thunderstorms. Hail occurs about three times a year in the summertime thunderstorms. Sunshine also reaches its maximum during the summer months, when the sun shines during more than 70 percent of the daylight hours.

Autumn, with a relatively slow drop in temperature and steadily lessening amounts of rainfall, is a delightful season with mildly warm days, cool nights, and plentiful sunshine.

The terrain around Huron is exceptionally level and flat. Even the James River has a slope of only 4 to 6 inches per mile. Heavy rains from summertime thunderstorms may, at times, cause some local flooding problems in the city. Moderate to fresh winds occur quite frequently during the daytime in all seasons of the year. Winds are normally from the north in the winter and from the south in the summer. The unusually level terrain helps to accentuate this tendency toward windy days.

Huron Regional Airport *Beadle County* Elevation: 1,279 ft. Latitude: 44° 24' N Longitude: 98° 13' W

	JAN	FEB	MAR	APR	MAY	JUN	JUL	AUG	SEP	OCT	NOV	DEC	YEAR
Mean Maximum Temp. (°F)	27.2	32.0	43.5	59.1	70.5	79.7	86.1	83.9	74.9	60.2	43.2	29.2	57.5
Mean Temp. (°F)	17.0	21.9	33.0	46.6	58.3	67.9	73.8	71.6	61.9	47.9	32.9	19.6	46.0
Mean Minimum Temp. (°F)	6.9	11.8	22.5	34.1	46.1	56.0	61.5	59.3	48.9	35.5	22.5	9.9	34.6
Extreme Maximum Temp. (°F)	62	70	81	97	98	109	110	107	104	94	86	66	110
Extreme Minimum Temp. (°F)	-37	-41	-20	7	17	34	44	37	23	8	-19	-30	-41
Days Maximum Temp. ≥ 90°F	0	0	0	0	1	4	11	7	3	0	0	0	26
Days Maximum Temp. ≤ 32°F	19	14	6	1	0	0	0	0	0	0	7	17	64
Days Minimum Temp. ≤ 32°F	31	27	26	13	2	0	0	0	1	12	25	31	168
Days Minimum Temp. ≤ 0°F	10	7	2	0	0	0	0	0	0	0	1	7	27
Heating Degree Days (base 65°F)	1,482	1,212	984	550	232	48	7	19	162	527	957	1,403	7,583
Cooling Degree Days (base 65°F)	0	0	0	5	32	141	287	231	77	4	0	0	777
Mean Precipitation (in.)	0.48	0.59	1.49	2.25	3.05	3.86	2.81	2.51	2.38	1.79	0.92	0.47	22.60
Maximum Precipitation (in.)*	2.2	3.9	5.9	5.8	7.7	11.6	6.7	6.7	6.8	6.4	3.0	2.1	31.7
Minimum Precipitation (in.)*	trace	trace	0.1	trace	0.3	0.7	0.1	0.1	0.1	trace	trace	trace	9.7
Extreme Maximum Daily Precip. (in.)	1.03	0.81	2.82	1.82	3.39	3.68	4.25	2.88	2.43	1.88	2.37	0.78	4.25
Days With ≥ 0.1" Precipitation	1	2	3	5	6	7	6	5	5	4	2	1	47
Days With ≥ 0.5" Precipitation	0	0	1	1	2	3	1	2	2	1	0	0	13
Days With ≥ 1.0" Precipitation	0	0	0	1	1	1	1	1	1	0	0	0	6
Mean Snowfall (in.)	6.9	7.2	9.2	4.0	trace	trace	trace	trace	trace	1.1	7.2	7.1	42.7
Maximum Snowfall (in.)*	28	40	34	26	4	0	0	0	1	11	33	26	81
Maximum 24-hr. Snowfall (in.)*	12	16	18	12	3	0	0	0	1	9	10	10	18
Maximum Snow Depth (in.)	35	36	36	16	trace	trace	trace	trace	trace	6	16	20	36
Days With ≥ 1.0" Snow Depth	18	16	9	2	0	0	0	0	0	0	5	17	67
Thunderstorm Days*	< 1	< 1	< 1	2	5	9	9	8	4	1	< 1	< 1	38
Foggy Days*	5	6	6	5	4	4	4	5	5	5	5	6	60
Predominant Sky Cover*	OVR	OVR	OVR	OVR	OVR	OVR	SCT	CLR	CLR	CLR	OVR	OVR	OVR
Mean Relative Humidity 6am (%)*	77	81	84	83	84	86	87	88	86	82	82	81	83
Mean Relative Humidity 3pm (%)*	66	66	61	49	49	51	46	46	46	46	58	66	54
Mean Dewpoint (°F)*	6	13	23	33	45	56	60	59	48	36	23	13	35
Prevailing Wind Direction*	NW	NNW	NNW	SSE	SSE	SSE	SSE	SSE	SSE	SSE	NW	SSE	SSE
Prevailing Wind Speed (mph)*	14	14	15	16	15	14	14	14	14	14	15	13	14
Maximum Wind Gust (mph)*	61	52	62	68	60	71	82	76	75	58	58	60	82

Note: (*) Period of record is 1900-1995

Rapid City Regional Airport

Rapid City, which is not far from the geographical center of North America, experiences the large temperature ranges, both daily and seasonal, that are typical of semi-arid continental climates.

The city is surrounded by contrasting landforms, with the forested Black Hills rising immediately west of the city, and rolling prairie extending out in the other directions. From 40 to 70 miles southeast lie the eroded Badlands. The Black Hills, many of which are more than 5,000 feet above sea level, with a number of peaks above 7,000 feet, exert a pronounced influence on the climate of this area. The rolling land to the east of the city is cut by the valleys of the Box Elder and Rapid Creeks, which flow generally east-southeastward. The station is located on the north slope of the irrigated Rapid Valley. An east-west ridge 200 to 300 feet higher than the airport separates the station from the Box Elder Creek Valley.

Although the annual precipitation is light at lower elevations, the distribution is beneficial to agriculture with the greatest amounts occurring during the growing season. The heaviest snows are expected in the spring, which helps to furnish moisture for the early maturing crops such as wheat, while heavy winter snows at the higher elevations provide irrigation water for the fertile valleys.

Summer days are normally warm with cool, comfortable nights. Nearly all of the summer precipitation occurs as thunderstorms. Hail is often associated with the more severe thunderstorms, with resultant damage to vegetation as well as other fragile material in the path of the storms. Autumn, which begins soon after the first of September, is characterized by mild, balmy days, and cool, invigorating mornings and evenings. Autumn weather usually extends into November and often into December.

Temperatures for the winter months of December, January, and February are among the warmest in South Dakota due to the protection of the Black Hills, the frequent occurrence of Chinook winds, and the fact that the winter tracks of arctic air masses usually pass east of Rapid City.

Snowfall is normally light with the greatest monthly average of about eight inches occurring in March. Cold waves can be expected occasionally, and one or more blizzards may occur each winter.

Spring is characterized by unsettled conditions. Wide variations usually occur in temperatures, and snows may fall as late as May.

Based on the 1951-1980 period, the average first occurrence of 32 degrees Fahrenheit in the fall is September 29 and the average last occurrence in the spring is May 7.

Rapid City Regional Airport *Pennington County* Elevation: 3,160 ft. Latitude: 44° 03' N Longitude: 103° 03' W

	JAN	FEB	MAR	APR	MAY	JUN	JUL	AUG	SEP	OCT	NOV	DEC	YEAR
Mean Maximum Temp. (°F)	37.2	39.9	47.7	58.7	68.0	78.1	87.5	86.4	75.5	61.7	46.9	37.4	60.4
Mean Temp. (°F)	25.2	27.8	35.4	45.5	55.4	65.0	73.1	71.8	61.0	48.1	34.8	25.6	47.4
Mean Minimum Temp. (°F)	13.2	15.7	23.0	32.2	42.8	51.7	58.7	57.1	46.3	34.5	22.6	13.7	34.3
Extreme Maximum Temp. (°F)	76	75	83	93	94	109	111	107	103	94	83	70	111
Extreme Minimum Temp. (°F)	-24	-31	-21	6	20	32	39	38	18	-2	-14	-30	-31
Days Maximum Temp. ≥ 90°F	0	0	0	0	1	4	13	12	4	0	0	0	34
Days Maximum Temp. ≤ 32°F	11	9	5	1	0	0	0	0	0	0	5	10	41
Days Minimum Temp. ≤ 32°F	30	27	26	16	3	0	0	0	2	12	25	30	171
Days Minimum Temp. ≤ 0°F	6	4	1	0	0	0	0	0	0	0	1	5	17
Heating Degree Days (base 65°F)	1,227	1,045	912	581	306	89	11	16	182	519	900	1,216	7,004
Cooling Degree Days (base 65°F)	0	0	0	3	16	94	271	234	67	3	0	0	688
Mean Precipitation (in.)	0.29	0.45	0.95	1.76	3.17	2.52	1.86	1.62	1.23	1.36	0.55	0.34	16.10
Maximum Precipitation (in.)*	1.7	2.5	2.7	5.2	7.0	7.0	6.1	4.8	3.1	3.8	2.2	1.6	26.0
Minimum Precipitation (in.)*	trace	0.1	0.1	trace	0.3	0.6	0.4	0.3	trace	trace	0.1	trace	9.1
Extreme Maximum Daily Precip. (in.)	0.41	0.75	1.25	3.19	2.80	2.51	2.00	2.60	1.76	2.49	0.62	0.92	3.19
Days With ≥ 0.1" Precipitation	1	2	3	4	6	6	4	4	3	3	2	1	39
Days With ≥ 0.5" Precipitation	0	0	0	1	2	1	1	1	1	1	0	0	8
Days With ≥ 1.0" Precipitation	0	0	0	0	1	0	0	0	0	0	0	0	1
Mean Snowfall (in.)	*4.3*	*5.9*	*8.9*	na	*1.0*	*trace*	*trace*	*trace*	*0.2*	*1.6*	*6.2*	*5.4*	na
Maximum Snowfall (in.)*	24	24	31	31	12	4	0	0	2	10	34	18	79
Maximum 24-hr. Snowfall (in.)*	9	9	15	16	7	4	0	0	2	7	9	10	16
Maximum Snow Depth (in.)	*16*	*14*	*14*	*12*	*8*	*trace*	*trace*	*trace*	*trace*	*5*	*15*	*11*	*16*
Days With ≥ 1.0" Snow Depth	*10*	*9*	*7*	*3*	*0*	*0*	*0*	*0*	*0*	*1*	*5*	*12*	*47*
Thunderstorm Days*	0	0	< 1	1	6	10	12	8	3	< 1	< 1	< 1	40
Foggy Days*	3	5	5	5	4	3	2	2	2	2	4	4	41
Predominant Sky Cover*	OVR	OVR	OVR	OVR	OVR	SCT	SCT	SCT	CLR	CLR	OVR	OVR	OVR
Mean Relative Humidity 6am (%)*	69	73	76	72	73	74	70	69	69	68	71	70	71
Mean Relative Humidity 3pm (%)*	54	53	49	42	45	47	38	33	35	38	49	56	45
Mean Dewpoint (°F)*	13	15	22	29	41	51	53	50	40	31	21	14	32
Prevailing Wind Direction*	NNW	NNW	NNW	NNW	NNW	NNW	NNW	NNW	NNW	NNW	NNW	NNW	NNW
Prevailing Wind Speed (mph)*	18	18	20	20	17	15	14	14	16	17	18	18	17
Maximum Wind Gust (mph)*	68	69	73	69	83	68	73	69	75	73	75	66	83

Note: (*) Period of record is 1949-1995

Sioux Falls Foss Field

Sioux Falls is located in the Big Sioux River Valley in southeast South Dakota. The surrounding terrain is gently rolling. The land slopes upward for about 100 miles north and northwest to an elevation about 400 feet higher than the city. To the southeast, the land slopes downward 200 to 300 feet over the same distance. The climate is of the continental type. There are frequent weather changes from day to day or week to week as the locality is visited by differing air masses. Cold air masses arrive from the interior of Canada, cool, dry air from the northern Pacific, warm, moist air from the Gulf of Mexico, or hot, dry air from the southwest.

Temperatures fluctuate frequently as cold air masses move in very rapidly. During the late fall and winter, cold fronts accompanied by strong, gusty winds drop temperatures by 20 to 30 degrees in a 24-hour period. Severe cold spells usually last only a few days. The winter months of December through February have experienced cold spells with average temperatures under 8 degrees and more than 60 consecutive days below 32 degrees.

Temperatures of 100 degrees and above occur about one in every three years. Summer nights are usually comfortable with temperatures below 70 degrees.

Rainfall is heavier during the spring and summer with lighter amounts in winter. Nearly 64 percent of the normal yearly precipitation falls during the growing season of April through August.

One or two very heavy snows usually fall each winter. Eight to 12 inches of snow may fall in 24 hours. There have been a few snows in excess of 15 inches and almost 30 inches have fallen during a severe winter storm. Strong winds often cause drifting snow, and blizzard conditions may block highways for a day or so.

Southerly winds prevail from late spring to early fall with northwest winds the remainder of the year. Strong winds of 70 mph with gusts to 90 mph have occurred.

Thunderstorms are frequent during the late spring and summer with June and July the most active months. The thunderstorms usually occur during the late afternoon and evening with a secondary peak of activity between 2 and 5 in the morning.

There is occasional flooding in the lower areas of Sioux Falls along the Big Sioux River and Skunk Creek. A diversion canal around Sioux Falls has reduced the threat of damaging floods.

Based on the 1951-1980 period, the average first occurrence of 32 degrees Fahrenheit in the fall is October 1 and the average last occurrence in the spring is May 10.

Sioux Falls Foss Field *Minnehaha County* Elevation: 1,428 ft. Latitude: 43° 35' N Longitude: 96° 45' W

	JAN	FEB	MAR	APR	MAY	JUN	JUL	AUG	SEP	OCT	NOV	DEC	YEAR
Mean Maximum Temp. (°F)	27.1	31.8	43.4	59.0	70.4	79.8	84.7	82.1	73.9	59.9	43.2	29.1	57.0
Mean Temp. (°F)	17.4	22.2	33.3	46.9	58.6	68.4	73.6	71.0	61.8	48.2	33.3	19.9	46.2
Mean Minimum Temp. (°F)	7.7	12.5	23.1	34.7	46.8	56.9	62.3	59.9	49.8	36.5	23.3	10.6	35.3
Extreme Maximum Temp. (°F)	66	70	81	93	95	110	108	105	98	90	81	63	110
Extreme Minimum Temp. (°F)	-29	-29	-15	5	20	37	43	39	23	12	-13	-28	-29
Days Maximum Temp. ≥ 90°F	0	0	0	0	1	3	8	5	2	0	0	0	19
Days Maximum Temp. ≤ 32°F	20	14	6	1	0	0	0	0	0	0	7	17	65
Days Minimum Temp. ≤ 32°F	31	27	25	13	1	0	0	0	1	11	25	31	165
Days Minimum Temp. ≤ 0°F	10	6	1	0	0	0	0	0	0	0	1	7	25
Heating Degree Days (base 65°F)	1,471	1,205	976	545	228	44	6	18	160	520	945	1,393	7,511
Cooling Degree Days (base 65°F)	0	0	0	8	38	152	278	212	72	6	0	0	766
Mean Precipitation (in.)	0.52	0.57	1.74	2.95	3.41	3.73	2.85	2.93	2.65	2.18	1.35	0.65	25.53
Maximum Precipitation (in.)*	1.8	4.0	4.1	6.0	9.0	8.4	8.4	9.3	9.3	5.7	2.9	3.0	36.1
Minimum Precipitation (in.)*	trace	trace	0.1	0.2	0.1	0.9	0.3	0.5	0.3	trace	trace	trace	11.4
Extreme Maximum Daily Precip. (in.)	1.04	0.90	3.27	3.72	4.22	3.58	3.35	3.99	2.73	2.36	1.92	0.88	4.22
Days With ≥ 0.1" Precipitation	1	2	4	6	6	7	5	5	5	4	3	2	50
Days With ≥ 0.5" Precipitation	0	0	1	2	2	2	2	2	2	1	1	0	15
Days With ≥ 1.0" Precipitation	0	0	0	1	1	1	1	1	1	0	0	0	6
Mean Snowfall (in.)	7.3	6.5	8.4	4.6	trace	trace	trace	trace	trace	1.3	7.3	7.7	43.1
Maximum Snowfall (in.)*	21	48	32	18	3	0	0	0	1	10	22	41	78
Maximum 24-hr. Snowfall (in.)*	11	18	18	11	3	0	0	0	1	9	10	12	18
Maximum Snow Depth (in.)	18	22	14	9	trace	trace	trace	trace	trace	3	13	19	22
Days With ≥ 1.0" Snow Depth	20	16	10	2	0	0	0	0	0	0	6	16	70
Thunderstorm Days*	< 1	< 1	1	3	5	8	8	7	5	2	< 1	< 1	39
Foggy Days*	8	8	9	7	6	5	5	7	6	6	8	10	85
Predominant Sky Cover*	OVR	OVR	OVR	OVR	OVR	OVR	SCT	CLR	CLR	CLR	OVR	OVR	OVR
Mean Relative Humidity 6am (%)*	75	78	81	79	80	82	84	86	84	80	80	79	81
Mean Relative Humidity 3pm (%)*	65	64	60	47	47	50	48	49	49	47	58	66	54
Mean Dewpoint (°F)*	6	13	23	33	45	55	60	59	49	36	24	13	35
Prevailing Wind Direction*	NW	NW	NNW	N	S	S	S	S	S	S	NW	NW	S
Prevailing Wind Speed (mph)*	15	15	15	14	14	13	13	13	13	13	16	15	14
Maximum Wind Gust (mph)*	69	67	61	66	69	73	82	74	53	62	74	55	82

Note: (*) Period of record is 1932-1995

Alexandria *Hanson County* Elevation: 1,353 ft. Latitude: 43° 39' N Longitude: 97° 47' W

	JAN	FEB	MAR	APR	MAY	JUN	JUL	AUG	SEP	OCT	NOV	DEC	YEAR
Mean Maximum Temp. (°F)	29.4	34.7	46.3	61.7	72.9	81.9	87.2	84.9	77.2	62.9	45.0	30.8	59.6
Mean Temp. (°F)	19.9	24.8	35.6	49.2	60.8	70.2	75.3	73.1	64.5	50.9	35.3	21.9	48.5
Mean Minimum Temp. (°F)	10.2	14.8	24.9	36.6	48.7	58.4	63.5	61.3	51.8	38.9	25.5	13.0	37.3
Extreme Maximum Temp. (°F)	66	73	81	96	98	107	108	105	100	94	80	67	108
Extreme Minimum Temp. (°F)	-26	-34	-17	6	23	36	43	41	24	10	-10	-31	-34
Days Maximum Temp. ≥ 90°F	0	0	0	0	1	5	12	7	3	0	0	0	28
Days Maximum Temp. ≤ 32°F	17	12	5	0	0	0	0	0	0	0	5	16	55
Days Minimum Temp. ≤ 32°F	31	26	23	11	1	0	0	0	1	8	23	30	154
Days Minimum Temp. ≤ 0°F	8	5	1	0	0	0	0	0	0	0	1	6	21
Heating Degree Days (base 65°F)	1,394	1,131	904	478	175	27	3	10	114	441	884	1,330	6,891
Cooling Degree Days (base 65°F)	0	0	0	11	52	190	331	269	107	10	0	0	970
Mean Precipitation (in.)	0.47	0.57	1.38	2.83	3.19	3.80	2.86	2.81	2.45	2.02	1.16	0.50	24.04
Extreme Maximum Daily Precip. (in.)	1.10	1.25	1.65	3.18	4.85	3.26	2.70	2.57	4.15	2.33	1.40	1.05	4.85
Days With ≥ 0.1" Precipitation	1	2	4	6	7	6	5	5	4	4	3	2	49
Days With ≥ 0.5" Precipitation	0	0	1	2	2	3	2	2	2	1	1	0	16
Days With ≥ 1.0" Precipitation	0	0	0	1	1	1	1	1	1	1	0	0	7
Mean Snowfall (in.)	5.5	5.4	5.7	3.9	trace	trace	trace	trace	trace	0.9	4.2	6.2	31.8
Maximum Snow Depth (in.)	15	11	11	10	trace	trace	trace	trace	trace	5	12	***13***	***15***
Days With ≥ 1.0" Snow Depth	11	9	4	1	0	0	0	0	0	0	4	9	38

Belle Fourche *Butte County* Elevation: 3,020 ft. Latitude: 44° 40' N Longitude: 103° 51' W

	JAN	FEB	MAR	APR	MAY	JUN	JUL	AUG	SEP	OCT	NOV	DEC	YEAR
Mean Maximum Temp. (°F)	37.1	***42.0***	48.6	***61.8***	70.7	80.4	88.7	88.2	76.9	***62.6***	***48.3***	37.3	***61.9***
Mean Temp. (°F)	24.6	***28.8***	35.3	***47.2***	56.7	66.2	73.5	72.2	60.8	***47.9***	***35.7***	25.1	***47.8***
Mean Minimum Temp. (°F)	12.0	***15.5***	21.9	***32.5***	42.7	51.9	58.2	56.1	44.7	***33.1***	***23.1***	12.8	***33.7***
Extreme Maximum Temp. (°F)	***72***	***73***	80	***93***	97	***103***	110	106	101	***91***	***83***	***69***	***110***
Extreme Minimum Temp. (°F)	-25	***-32***	-29	***4***	21	***33***	38	36	18	***-12***	***-12***	***-44***	***-44***
Days Maximum Temp. ≥ 90°F	0	***0***	0	***0***	1	5	15	14	5	***0***	***0***	0	***40***
Days Maximum Temp. ≤ 32°F	10	***6***	4	***1***	0	0	0	0	0	***0***	***4***	10	***35***
Days Minimum Temp. ≤ 32°F	29	***26***	26	***15***	3	0	0	0	2	***14***	***25***	29	***169***
Days Minimum Temp. ≤ 0°F	6	***4***	2	***0***	0	0	0	0	0	***0***	***1***	6	***19***
Heating Degree Days (base 65°F)	1,247	***1,019***	914	***530***	268	64	9	11	173	***525***	***871***	1,232	***6,863***
Cooling Degree Days (base 65°F)	0	***0***	0	***2***	18	105	279	240	54	***2***	***0***	0	***700***
Mean Precipitation (in.)	0.35	***0.48***	0.98	***1.90***	2.94	2.75	2.00	1.28	1.51	***1.71***	***0.61***	0.66	***17.17***
Extreme Maximum Daily Precip. (in.)	0.54	***0.72***	2.30	***1.93***	4.25	***2.75***	2.30	1.14	2.50	***2.49***	***0.80***	***0.80***	***4.25***
Days With ≥ 0.1" Precipitation	1	***1***	3	***4***	6	6	5	4	3	***4***	***2***	2	***41***
Days With ≥ 0.5" Precipitation	0	***0***	1	***1***	2	2	1	1	1	***1***	***0***	0	***10***
Days With ≥ 1.0" Precipitation	0	***0***	0	***0***	1	0	0	0	0	***0***	***0***	0	***1***
Mean Snowfall (in.)	***5.1***	***3.3***	8.5	***4.1***	0.8	0.0	0.0	0.0	0.1	***1.3***	***3.6***	***6.0***	***32.8***
Maximum Snow Depth (in.)	na	na	na	na	na	na	na	na	***trace***	na	na	na	na
Days With ≥ 1.0" Snow Depth	na	na	***2***	***1***	0	0	0	0	0	***0***	***2***	na	na

Belle Fourche 22 NNW *Butte County* Elevation: 3,200 ft. Latitude: 44° 59' N Longitude: 103° 56' W

	JAN	FEB	MAR	APR	MAY	JUN	JUL	AUG	SEP	OCT	NOV	DEC	YEAR
Mean Maximum Temp. (°F)	32.8	36.1	44.2	***56.6***	***67.0***	77.0	86.5	86.1	***74.2***	59.3	44.5	33.6	***58.2***
Mean Temp. (°F)	21.2	24.3	32.1	***43.3***	***54.2***	63.7	71.6	70.4	***58.8***	45.1	32.2	21.4	***44.8***
Mean Minimum Temp. (°F)	9.6	12.4	20.0	***29.9***	***41.3***	50.3	56.6	54.6	***43.3***	30.8	19.8	9.1	***31.5***
Extreme Maximum Temp. (°F)	67	74	82	***89***	96	109	110	107	101	92	83	67	***110***
Extreme Minimum Temp. (°F)	-30	-39	-32	***0***	16	31	34	35	16	-12	-25	-40	***-40***
Days Maximum Temp. ≥ 90°F	0	0	0	***0***	0	3	12	11	3	0	0	0	***29***
Days Maximum Temp. ≤ 32°F	13	10	7	***2***	0	0	0	0	0	1	6	12	***51***
Days Minimum Temp. ≤ 32°F	30	27	27	***18***	4	0	0	0	3	17	27	30	***183***
Days Minimum Temp. ≤ 0°F	8	5	2	***0***	0	0	0	0	0	0	2	7	***24***
Heating Degree Days (base 65°F)	1,353	1,141	1,013	***648***	***339***	111	21	27	***225***	612	979	1,347	***7,816***
Cooling Degree Days (base 65°F)	0	0	0	***1***	***12***	80	232	204	***46***	1	0	0	***576***
Mean Precipitation (in.)	0.22	***0.31***	***0.79***	***1.50***	2.55	2.36	1.93	1.25	1.03	1.25	0.40	0.28	***13.87***
Extreme Maximum Daily Precip. (in.)	0.40	***0.50***	***1.50***	***1.42***	***2.62***	***2.40***	***2.30***	1.69	2.18	1.74	2.15	0.33	***2.62***
Days With ≥ 0.1" Precipitation	1	***1***	***2***	***4***	6	5	5	3	3	3	1	1	***35***
Days With ≥ 0.5" Precipitation	0	***0***	***0***	***1***	1	1	1	1	1	1	0	0	***7***
Days With ≥ 1.0" Precipitation	0	***0***	***0***	***0***	1	0	0	0	0	0	0	0	***1***
Mean Snowfall (in.)	***3.1***	***3.0***	na	***2.0***	0.7	0.0	0.0	0.0	trace	***0.7***	***2.1***	***3.8***	na
Maximum Snow Depth (in.)	13	***11***	***15***	***20***	4	0	0	0	4	***10***	12	***12***	***20***
Days With ≥ 1.0" Snow Depth	6	***6***	***6***	***2***	0	0	0	0	0	***1***	3	***8***	***32***

Brookings 2 NE *Brookings County* Elevation: 1,640 ft. Latitude: 44° 19' N Longitude: 96° 46' W

	JAN	FEB	MAR	APR	MAY	JUN	JUL	AUG	SEP	OCT	NOV	DEC	YEAR
Mean Maximum Temp. (°F)	23.1	27.9	39.0	55.2	67.6	76.7	81.7	79.3	71.2	57.4	40.4	26.3	53.8
Mean Temp. (°F)	13.1	17.9	29.5	43.7	56.0	65.7	70.3	67.9	59.0	45.5	30.7	17.0	43.0
Mean Minimum Temp. (°F)	3.1	7.9	19.9	32.1	44.4	54.7	58.9	56.3	46.7	33.5	21.0	7.6	32.2
Extreme Maximum Temp. (°F)	65	69	75	93	95	103	102	102	94	90	77	63	103
Extreme Minimum Temp. (°F)	-36	-37	-19	4	17	35	41	33	23	9	-17	-28	-37
Days Maximum Temp. ≥ 90°F	0	0	0	0	0	2	4	2	1	0	0	0	9
Days Maximum Temp. ≤ 32°F	23	17	10	1	0	0	0	0	0	0	9	20	80
Days Minimum Temp. ≤ 32°F	31	28	27	16	3	0	0	0	2	15	27	31	180
Days Minimum Temp. ≤ 0°F	13	9	3	0	0	0	0	0	0	0	1	9	35
Heating Degree Days (base 65°F)	1,604	1,326	1,095	636	294	75	19	42	218	601	1,023	1,484	8,417
Cooling Degree Days (base 65°F)	0	0	0	2	23	104	192	137	45	2	0	0	505
Mean Precipitation (in.)	0.33	0.37	1.20	2.14	2.91	4.29	3.10	3.10	2.90	2.04	0.90	0.36	23.64
Extreme Maximum Daily Precip. (in.)	0.63	0.66	1.33	2.45	2.23	5.54	2.75	3.15	4.11	2.20	1.73	0.85	5.54
Days With ≥ 0.1" Precipitation	1	1	3	5	6	7	6	5	5	4	2	1	46
Days With ≥ 0.5" Precipitation	0	0	1	1	2	3	2	2	2	1	0	0	14
Days With ≥ 1.0" Precipitation	0	0	0	0	0	1	1	1	1	1	0	0	5
Mean Snowfall (in.)	5.2	5.4	7.8	3.4	trace	0.0	0.0	0.0	trace	0.7	5.4	6.5	34.4
Maximum Snow Depth (in.)	20	19	25	11	trace	0	0	0	trace	4	13	20	25
Days With ≥ 1.0" Snow Depth	19	16	10	3	0	0	0	0	0	0	6	16	70

The period of record for all cooperative weather station data is 1980 – 2009. See User Guide for detailed explanation of data.

Canton 4 WNW *Lincoln County* Elevation: 1,345 ft. Latitude: 43° 19' N Longitude: 96° 39' W

	JAN	FEB	MAR	APR	MAY	JUN	JUL	AUG	SEP	OCT	NOV	DEC	YEAR
Mean Maximum Temp. (°F)	27.8	33.2	45.1	61.0	73.0	81.7	84.7	82.2	75.2	61.8	43.9	29.2	58.2
Mean Temp. (°F)	17.6	23.1	34.4	48.1	60.6	69.7	73.3	70.9	62.7	49.6	34.1	19.9	47.0
Mean Minimum Temp. (°F)	7.3	13.0	23.5	35.1	48.1	57.7	61.9	59.5	50.1	37.3	24.2	10.5	35.7
Extreme Maximum Temp. (°F)	67	69	82	95	97	105	107	104	96	92	82	65	107
Extreme Minimum Temp. (°F)	-33	-35	-17	5	20	35	44	37	21	11	-15	-30	-35
Days Maximum Temp. ≥ 90°F	0	0	0	1	1	5	7	4	2	0	0	0	20
Days Maximum Temp. ≤ 32°F	19	13	5	1	0	0	0	0	0	0	6	17	61
Days Minimum Temp. ≤ 32°F	31	27	25	13	1	0	0	0	1	10	23	30	161
Days Minimum Temp. ≤ 0°F	10	6	2	0	0	0	0	0	0	0	1	7	26
Heating Degree Days (base 65°F)	1,466	1,178	942	512	184	30	6	17	139	478	921	1,394	7,267
Cooling Degree Days (base 65°F)	0	0	0	11	53	178	270	205	78	7	0	0	802
Mean Precipitation (in.)	0.41	0.44	1.43	2.70	3.22	3.77	3.37	3.23	2.21	2.29	1.15	0.60	24.82
Extreme Maximum Daily Precip. (in.)	0.86	0.75	1.51	2.45	1.97	4.13	3.59	2.79	1.95	2.52	2.58	0.95	4.13
Days With ≥ 0.1" Precipitation	1	2	3	5	7	6	6	5	4	4	3	2	48
Days With ≥ 0.5" Precipitation	0	0	1	2	2	3	2	2	1	1	1	0	15
Days With ≥ 1.0" Precipitation	0	0	0	1	0	1	1	1	0	1	0	0	5
Mean Snowfall (in.)	6.2	4.7	5.0	2.1	trace	0.0	0.0	0.0	0.0	0.7	5.0	7.3	31.0
Maximum Snow Depth (in.)	20	20	14	9	trace	0	0	0	0	5	18	23	23
Days With ≥ 1.0" Snow Depth	20	15	9	1	0	0	0	0	0	1	6	17	69

Castlewood *Hamlin County* Elevation: 1,685 ft. Latitude: 44° 43' N Longitude: 97° 02' W

	JAN	FEB	MAR	APR	MAY	JUN	JUL	AUG	SEP	OCT	NOV	DEC	YEAR
Mean Maximum Temp. (°F)	23.1	28.2	39.4	56.1	68.5	77.3	82.7	80.5	71.8	58.1	40.3	26.2	54.3
Mean Temp. (°F)	12.5	17.7	29.0	43.6	56.1	65.6	70.6	68.2	58.9	45.3	30.0	16.6	42.8
Mean Minimum Temp. (°F)	1.9	7.1	18.6	31.0	43.6	53.8	58.5	55.8	45.9	32.5	19.6	6.9	31.3
Extreme Maximum Temp. (°F)	66	67	76	97	94	104	101	104	97	90	79	58	104
Extreme Minimum Temp. (°F)	-37	-44	-22	4	15	32	39	31	17	8	-22	-33	-44
Days Maximum Temp. ≥ 90°F	0	0	0	0	0	2	6	3	1	0	0	0	12
Days Maximum Temp. ≤ 32°F	23	17	9	1	0	0	0	0	0	0	8	20	78
Days Minimum Temp. ≤ 32°F	31	27	28	18	4	0	0	0	2	16	26	30	182
Days Minimum Temp. ≤ 0°F	14	9	3	0	0	0	0	0	0	0	2	9	37
Heating Degree Days (base 65°F)	1,622	1,333	1,108	638	291	76	21	38	220	604	1,043	1,496	8,490
Cooling Degree Days (base 65°F)	0	0	0	3	21	100	202	143	43	2	0	0	514
Mean Precipitation (in.)	0.52	0.50	1.30	2.17	2.96	4.24	3.48	3.09	2.92	2.07	0.73	0.47	24.45
Extreme Maximum Daily Precip. (in.)	0.94	0.80	4.30	3.24	2.48	4.44	3.92	3.12	3.22	2.20	1.18	0.80	4.44
Days With ≥ 0.1" Precipitation	2	2	3	4	6	7	6	5	5	4	2	2	48
Days With ≥ 0.5" Precipitation	0	0	1	1	2	3	2	2	2	1	0	0	14
Days With ≥ 1.0" Precipitation	0	0	0	0	1	1	1	1	1	1	0	0	6
Mean Snowfall (in.)	6.0	5.1	5.0	2.3	trace	0.0	0.0	0.0	trace	trace	4.6	5.1	28.1
Maximum Snow Depth (in.)	20	19	20	15	trace	0	0	0	trace	trace	14	18	20
Days With ≥ 1.0" Snow Depth	19	18	9	1	0	0	0	0	0	0	5	14	66

Cedar Butte 1 NE *Mellette County* Elevation: 2,250 ft. Latitude: 43° 36' N Longitude: 101° 01' W

	JAN	FEB	MAR	APR	MAY	JUN	JUL	AUG	SEP	OCT	NOV	DEC	YEAR
Mean Maximum Temp. (°F)	36.6	40.0	50.2	61.0	71.8	82.0	90.5	89.4	79.2	64.1	48.4	37.0	62.5
Mean Temp. (°F)	24.5	28.0	37.3	47.1	58.7	68.3	75.9	74.5	64.4	50.5	36.5	25.8	49.3
Mean Minimum Temp. (°F)	12.5	15.9	24.3	33.6	45.4	54.5	61.2	59.6	49.5	36.9	24.5	14.4	36.0
Extreme Maximum Temp. (°F)	73	77	86	96	100	112	116	110	106	97	87	73	116
Extreme Minimum Temp. (°F)	-26	-29	-15	4	22	35	40	38	22	1	-12	-30	-30
Days Maximum Temp. ≥ 90°F	0	0	0	0	2	6	17	17	7	1	0	0	50
Days Maximum Temp. ≤ 32°F	11	9	4	1	0	0	0	0	0	0	5	10	40
Days Minimum Temp. ≤ 32°F	28	26	24	14	2	0	0	0	1	9	23	29	156
Days Minimum Temp. ≤ 0°F	6	4	1	0	0	0	0	0	0	0	1	5	17
Heating Degree Days (base 65°F)	1,249	1,041	847	538	230	48	6	10	129	451	849	1,210	6,608
Cooling Degree Days (base 65°F)	0	0	0	8	40	154	349	311	116	10	0	0	988
Mean Precipitation (in.)	0.38	0.49	1.28	2.09	3.14	3.48	2.77	1.78	1.57	1.70	0.64	0.37	19.69
Extreme Maximum Daily Precip. (in.)	0.74	0.97	1.98	2.04	2.83	4.08	1.91	1.79	1.50	2.26	1.30	0.50	4.08
Days With ≥ 0.1" Precipitation	1	1	3	5	6	6	5	3	3	4	2	1	40
Days With ≥ 0.5" Precipitation	0	0	1	1	2	2	2	1	1	1	0	0	11
Days With ≥ 1.0" Precipitation	0	0	0	0	1	1	1	0	0	0	0	0	3
Mean Snowfall (in.)	5.1	6.1	8.0	5.3	trace	0.0	0.0	0.0	0.1	1.2	6.2	6.1	38.1
Maximum Snow Depth (in.)	12	15	18	18	trace	0	0	0	1	4	20	16	20
Days With ≥ 1.0" Snow Depth	12	11	7	2	0	0	0	0	0	1	6	14	53

Chamberlain 5 S *Brule County* Elevation: 1,660 ft. Latitude: 43° 44' N Longitude: 99° 19' W

	JAN	FEB	MAR	APR	MAY	JUN	JUL	AUG	SEP	OCT	NOV	DEC	YEAR
Mean Maximum Temp. (°F)	30.5	35.6	45.8	59.3	70.5	80.2	88.5	86.9	77.2	62.0	45.4	32.1	59.5
Mean Temp. (°F)	19.9	24.5	34.0	46.3	57.7	67.6	74.7	72.9	63.2	49.0	34.4	22.0	47.2
Mean Minimum Temp. (°F)	9.2	13.3	22.1	33.4	44.8	54.9	60.7	58.9	49.0	35.9	23.4	11.8	34.8
Extreme Maximum Temp. (°F)	68	75	84	93	100	111	113	112	104	98	86	73	113
Extreme Minimum Temp. (°F)	-28	-34	-19	8	24	32	46	39	24	8	-13	-30	-34
Days Maximum Temp. ≥ 90°F	0	0	0	0	1	5	15	12	5	1	0	0	39
Days Maximum Temp. ≤ 32°F	16	12	6	1	0	0	0	0	0	0	6	15	56
Days Minimum Temp. ≤ 32°F	31	27	27	14	2	0	0	0	1	10	25	31	168
Days Minimum Temp. ≤ 0°F	9	6	1	0	0	0	0	0	0	0	1	7	24
Heating Degree Days (base 65°F)	1,394	1,137	955	558	248	54	8	13	146	496	911	1,328	7,248
Cooling Degree Days (base 65°F)	0	0	0	5	29	138	315	265	98	7	0	0	857
Mean Precipitation (in.)	0.49	0.54	1.45	2.56	3.55	3.93	2.51	2.56	2.27	1.98	0.90	0.56	23.30
Extreme Maximum Daily Precip. (in.)	1.15	0.99	1.65	2.47	3.80	2.80	2.02	6.01	3.52	2.20	1.30	1.29	6.01
Days With ≥ 0.1" Precipitation	1	2	3	6	7	7	5	4	4	4	3	2	48
Days With ≥ 0.5" Precipitation	0	0	1	1	2	3	1	2	2	1	0	0	13
Days With ≥ 1.0" Precipitation	0	0	0	0	1	1	1	1	1	0	0	0	5
Mean Snowfall (in.)	5.6	6.0	8.8	5.1	trace	trace	0.0	0.0	0.0	1.0	6.2	6.7	39.4
Maximum Snow Depth (in.)	18	20	20	20	trace	1	0	0	0	8	12	14	20
Days With ≥ 1.0" Snow Depth	15	12	10	2	0	0	0	0	0	1	6	14	60

Clark *Clark County* Elevation: 1,779 ft. Latitude: 44° 53' N Longitude: 97° 44' W

	JAN	FEB	MAR	APR	MAY	JUN	JUL	AUG	SEP	OCT	NOV	DEC	YEAR
Mean Maximum Temp. (°F)	22.6	27.6	38.9	55.5	67.8	76.6	82.7	80.7	71.3	56.8	39.3	25.6	53.8
Mean Temp. (°F)	13.2	18.0	29.2	44.0	56.5	65.9	71.6	69.4	59.8	45.9	30.4	16.8	43.4
Mean Minimum Temp. (°F)	3.7	8.4	19.4	32.4	45.2	55.1	60.5	58.0	48.2	34.9	21.4	8.0	32.9
Extreme Maximum Temp. (°F)	66	63	74	95	95	106	106	105	97	88	78	61	106
Extreme Minimum Temp. (°F)	-32	-36	-17	2	16	36	44	41	25	5	-16	-33	-36
Days Maximum Temp. ≥ 90°F	0	0	0	0	0	1	5	4	1	0	0	0	11
Days Maximum Temp. ≤ 32°F	23	17	9	1	0	0	0	0	0	0	10	20	80
Days Minimum Temp. ≤ 32°F	31	28	28	16	2	0	0	0	1	12	26	31	175
Days Minimum Temp. ≤ 0°F	13	9	3	0	0	0	0	0	0	0	1	9	35
Heating Degree Days (base 65°F)	1,602	1,324	1,105	629	279	71	14	29	202	588	1,032	1,488	8,363
Cooling Degree Days (base 65°F)	0	0	0	3	23	103	227	172	52	2	0	0	582
Mean Precipitation (in.)	0.53	0.56	1.23	1.95	2.90	3.80	3.41	2.92	2.66	2.09	0.92	0.49	23.46
Extreme Maximum Daily Precip. (in.)	1.01	0.78	2.05	2.62	4.47	2.81	4.42	2.72	3.31	2.90	1.13	0.72	4.47
Days With ≥ 0.1" Precipitation	2	2	4	4	6	7	6	5	5	4	3	2	50
Days With ≥ 0.5" Precipitation	0	0	1	1	2	3	2	2	2	1	1	0	15
Days With ≥ 1.0" Precipitation	0	0	0	0	1	1	1	1	1	1	0	0	6
Mean Snowfall (in.)	5.9	5.9	5.5	2.2	trace	0.0	0.0	0.0	trace	0.8	5.4	5.3	31.0
Maximum Snow Depth (in.)	24	28	28	12	trace	0	0	0	trace	7	15	17	28
Days With ≥ 1.0" Snow Depth	24	17	13	2	0	0	0	0	0	1	6	15	78

Clear Lake *Deuel County* Elevation: 1,799 ft. Latitude: 44° 45' N Longitude: 96° 41' W

	JAN	FEB	MAR	APR	MAY	JUN	JUL	AUG	SEP	OCT	NOV	DEC	YEAR
Mean Maximum Temp. (°F)	23.0	27.5	38.9	56.0	68.3	76.8	81.7	79.4	70.9	57.2	39.9	25.7	53.8
Mean Temp. (°F)	13.9	18.4	29.5	44.5	57.0	66.2	71.2	68.9	60.0	46.6	31.2	17.4	43.7
Mean Minimum Temp. (°F)	4.9	9.2	20.1	33.1	45.6	55.5	60.6	58.4	49.0	36.1	22.4	9.0	33.7
Extreme Maximum Temp. (°F)	66	62	75	94	96	102	102	101	96	87	78	60	102
Extreme Minimum Temp. (°F)	-31	-33	-17	3	21	34	43	36	19	9	-12	-30	-33
Days Maximum Temp. ≥ 90°F	0	0	0	0	0	1	4	2	1	0	0	0	8
Days Maximum Temp. ≤ 32°F	22	17	9	1	0	0	0	0	0	0	9	21	79
Days Minimum Temp. ≤ 32°F	31	27	26	15	2	0	0	0	1	11	25	31	169
Days Minimum Temp. ≤ 0°F	12	8	3	0	0	0	0	0	0	0	1	9	33
Heating Degree Days (base 65°F)	1,578	1,313	1,093	610	269	66	14	31	196	565	1,008	1,471	8,214
Cooling Degree Days (base 65°F)	0	0	0	4	27	108	213	160	52	3	0	0	567
Mean Precipitation (in.)	0.71	0.69	1.65	2.42	3.03	4.45	3.49	3.01	2.95	2.33	1.25	0.66	26.64
Extreme Maximum Daily Precip. (in.)	1.64	0.98	3.10	2.13	2.22	4.55	2.88	2.95	4.40	2.58	1.87	0.78	4.55
Days With ≥ 0.1" Precipitation	2	3	4	5	7	7	7	5	6	5	3	2	56
Days With ≥ 0.5" Precipitation	0	0	1	1	2	3	3	2	2	2	1	0	17
Days With ≥ 1.0" Precipitation	0	0	0	1	1	1	1	1	1	1	0	0	7
Mean Snowfall (in.)	9.1	8.6	10.8	4.9	trace	0.0	0.0	trace	0.1	1.1	8.4	8.4	51.4
Maximum Snow Depth (in.)	26	43	28	17	trace	0	0	trace	0	9	19	18	43
Days With ≥ 1.0" Snow Depth	23	20	15	3	0	0	0	0	0	1	8	18	88

Columbia 8 N *Brown County* Elevation: 1,299 ft. Latitude: 45° 44' N Longitude: 98° 18' W

	JAN	FEB	MAR	APR	MAY	JUN	JUL	AUG	SEP	OCT	NOV	DEC	YEAR
Mean Maximum Temp. (°F)	21.3	26.9	38.4	55.9	68.3	76.8	83.0	81.2	71.4	57.0	39.0	25.3	53.7
Mean Temp. (°F)	10.9	16.5	28.5	44.0	56.7	65.9	71.3	69.0	58.9	45.1	29.3	15.6	42.6
Mean Minimum Temp. (°F)	0.4	6.2	18.5	32.0	45.1	55.0	59.7	56.8	46.2	33.1	19.5	5.9	31.5
Extreme Maximum Temp. (°F)	60	63	79	94	93	105	104	103	99	88	79	60	105
Extreme Minimum Temp. (°F)	-39	-45	-28	2	18	35	43	37	20	5	-26	-37	-45
Days Maximum Temp. ≥ 90°F	0	0	0	0	0	2	5	3	1	0	0	0	11
Days Maximum Temp. ≤ 32°F	23	17	9	1	0	0	0	0	0	0	9	21	80
Days Minimum Temp. ≤ 32°F	31	28	29	16	3	0	0	0	2	15	28	31	183
Days Minimum Temp. ≤ 0°F	15	10	3	0	0	0	0	0	0	0	2	11	41
Heating Degree Days (base 65°F)	1,673	1,365	1,126	626	272	69	15	31	218	610	1,066	1,527	8,598
Cooling Degree Days (base 65°F)	0	0	0	2	22	103	218	163	41	1	0	0	550
Mean Precipitation (in.)	0.46	0.41	1.26	1.78	3.15	3.36	3.45	2.74	2.29	1.99	0.70	0.40	21.99
Extreme Maximum Daily Precip. (in.)	0.75	0.65	3.68	1.84	7.62	3.34	3.52	2.88	5.32	2.85	1.06	0.73	7.62
Days With ≥ 0.1" Precipitation	1	1	3	4	6	6	6	5	4	4	2	1	43
Days With ≥ 0.5" Precipitation	0	0	1	1	2	2	2	2	1	1	0	0	12
Days With ≥ 1.0" Precipitation	0	0	0	0	1	1	1	1	0	1	0	0	5
Mean Snowfall (in.)	7.0	6.1	7.6	3.4	trace	0.0	0.0	0.0	trace	0.7	6.9	6.3	38.0
Maximum Snow Depth (in.)	49	49	44	11	trace	0	0	0	trace	4	27	31	49
Days With ≥ 1.0" Snow Depth	26	21	15	2	0	0	0	0	0	0	9	20	93

Cottonwood 2 E *Jackson County* Elevation: 2,414 ft. Latitude: 43° 58' N Longitude: 101° 52' W

	JAN	FEB	MAR	APR	MAY	JUN	JUL	AUG	SEP	OCT	NOV	DEC	YEAR
Mean Maximum Temp. (°F)	35.2	39.2	47.8	60.2	70.6	80.5	89.8	89.1	78.5	63.2	47.7	36.2	61.5
Mean Temp. (°F)	21.8	25.6	34.1	45.3	56.4	66.4	74.3	72.5	61.4	47.2	33.5	22.6	46.8
Mean Minimum Temp. (°F)	8.3	11.9	20.3	30.4	42.3	52.2	58.8	55.9	44.3	31.2	19.3	8.9	32.0
Extreme Maximum Temp. (°F)	72	75	85	95	99	111	117	111	108	96	85	71	117
Extreme Minimum Temp. (°F)	-33	-34	-33	4	16	31	42	32	16	-7	-24	-33	-34
Days Maximum Temp. ≥ 90°F	0	0	0	0	1	6	17	16	7	1	0	0	48
Days Maximum Temp. ≤ 32°F	12	9	5	1	0	0	0	0	0	0	5	12	44
Days Minimum Temp. ≤ 32°F	31	28	28	18	4	0	0	0	3	17	28	31	188
Days Minimum Temp. ≤ 0°F	8	5	2	0	0	0	0	0	0	0	2	7	24
Heating Degree Days (base 65°F)	1,333	1,109	952	588	285	75	10	18	178	546	939	1,308	7,341
Cooling Degree Days (base 65°F)	0	0	0	3	26	122	305	256	73	3	0	0	788
Mean Precipitation (in.)	0.36	0.56	1.16	1.65	2.75	2.94	2.15	1.47	1.30	1.38	0.64	0.40	16.76
Extreme Maximum Daily Precip. (in.)	0.86	1.18	1.19	1.76	2.24	2.86	1.86	2.33	2.15	1.57	1.36	0.46	2.86
Days With ≥ 0.1" Precipitation	1	2	3	4	6	7	4	3	3	3	2	1	39
Days With ≥ 0.5" Precipitation	0	0	1	1	2	2	1	1	1	1	0	0	10
Days With ≥ 1.0" Precipitation	0	0	0	0	1	1	0	0	0	0	0	0	2
Mean Snowfall (in.)	5.1	6.2	7.9	5.2	0.1	0.0	0.0	0.0	trace	1.1	5.4	5.6	36.6
Maximum Snow Depth (in.)	15	21	20	11	2	0	0	0	0	4	21	21	21
Days With ≥ 1.0" Snow Depth	15	10	9	2	0	0	0	0	0	1	7	14	58

The period of record for all cooperative weather station data is 1980 – 2009. See User Guide for detailed explanation of data.

Custer *Custer County* Elevation: 5,479 ft. Latitude: 43° 46' N Longitude: 103° 37' W

	JAN	FEB	MAR	APR	MAY	JUN	JUL	AUG	SEP	OCT	NOV	DEC	YEAR
Mean Maximum Temp. (°F)	36.7	38.3	45.1	53.2	62.7	***72.4***	80.0	78.9	70.3	56.8	***44.3***	36.1	***56.2***
Mean Temp. (°F)	25.4	27.0	33.2	41.1	50.6	***59.8***	66.9	65.5	56.5	44.2	***33.2***	25.3	***44.1***
Mean Minimum Temp. (°F)	14.0	15.6	21.4	28.9	38.6	46.9	53.8	52.0	42.8	31.6	***22.1***	14.4	***31.8***
Extreme Maximum Temp. (°F)	68	66	71	84	88	96	99	96	97	85	72	64	99
Extreme Minimum Temp. (°F)	-24	-31	-18	-2	16	27	37	34	11	-5	-15	-34	-34
Days Maximum Temp. ≥ 90°F	0	0	0	0	0	1	4	1	0	0	0	0	6
Days Maximum Temp. ≤ 32°F	10	8	5	2	0	0	0	0	0	1	5	10	41
Days Minimum Temp. ≤ 32°F	29	27	27	20	8	1	0	0	4	16	24	29	185
Days Minimum Temp. ≤ 0°F	5	4	1	0	0	0	0	0	0	0	1	4	15
Heating Degree Days (base 65°F)	1,222	1,068	977	711	440	***186***	53	64	271	637	***946***	1,225	***7,800***
Cooling Degree Days (base 65°F)	0	0	0	0	2	***35***	119	86	24	0	***0***	0	***266***
Mean Precipitation (in.)	0.32	0.64	1.09	1.97	3.37	2.92	2.88	2.49	1.63	1.49	***0.65***	0.44	***19.89***
Extreme Maximum Daily Precip. (in.)	0.50	0.73	1.04	2.56	2.56	***1.94***	2.02	3.20	1.45	1.48	***0.80***	0.55	***3.20***
Days With ≥ 0.1" Precipitation	1	2	3	5	7	7	7	5	4	4	***2***	2	***49***
Days With ≥ 0.5" Precipitation	0	0	0	1	2	2	2	1	1	1	***0***	0	***10***
Days With ≥ 1.0" Precipitation	0	0	0	0	1	0	1	0	0	0	***0***	0	***2***
Mean Snowfall (in.)	6.1	***10.1***	12.7	11.8	1.5	0.2	0.0	0.0	0.7	4.3	***7.4***	7.2	***62.0***
Maximum Snow Depth (in.)	na	na	na	na	na	na	na	na	na	na	na	na	na
Days With ≥ 1.0" Snow Depth	na	na	na	***1***	0	0	0	0	0	1	***1***	na	na

Dupree *Ziebach County* Elevation: 2,375 ft. Latitude: 45° 03' N Longitude: 101° 36' W

	JAN	FEB	MAR	APR	MAY	JUN	JUL	AUG	SEP	OCT	NOV	DEC	YEAR
Mean Maximum Temp. (°F)	30.6	34.5	44.0	59.4	70.5	79.6	87.9	87.2	76.3	60.3	43.2	31.2	58.7
Mean Temp. (°F)	20.1	24.0	32.7	45.9	57.2	66.2	73.5	72.3	61.6	47.4	32.5	21.0	46.2
Mean Minimum Temp. (°F)	9.5	13.4	21.3	32.4	43.9	52.8	59.1	57.2	46.9	34.4	21.7	10.9	33.6
Extreme Maximum Temp. (°F)	68	71	81	96	99	109	113	109	103	94	78	67	113
Extreme Minimum Temp. (°F)	-29	-34	-31	1	19	35	42	37	20	-6	-22	-34	-34
Days Maximum Temp. ≥ 90°F	0	0	0	0	1	4	13	12	4	0	0	0	34
Days Maximum Temp. ≤ 32°F	15	12	6	1	0	0	0	0	0	1	7	14	56
Days Minimum Temp. ≤ 32°F	30	27	27	15	3	0	0	0	2	12	26	30	172
Days Minimum Temp. ≤ 0°F	8	6	2	0	0	0	0	0	0	0	1	7	24
Heating Degree Days (base 65°F)	1,387	1,154	996	571	262	67	10	16	169	542	968	1,358	7,500
Cooling Degree Days (base 65°F)	0	0	0	4	28	111	280	247	75	3	0	0	748
Mean Precipitation (in.)	0.33	0.52	1.10	1.71	2.83	3.26	2.39	1.66	1.25	1.61	0.50	0.34	17.50
Extreme Maximum Daily Precip. (in.)	0.70	1.20	2.02	1.73	1.75	3.38	3.33	3.33	2.34	2.26	0.77	0.66	3.38
Days With ≥ 0.1" Precipitation	1	2	3	4	6	6	5	4	3	3	2	1	40
Days With ≥ 0.5" Precipitation	0	0	1	1	2	2	1	1	1	1	0	0	10
Days With ≥ 1.0" Precipitation	0	0	0	0	0	1	1	0	0	0	0	0	2
Mean Snowfall (in.)	4.7	6.2	8.0	4.4	0.2	0.0	0.0	0.0	trace	1.1	4.5	5.4	34.5
Maximum Snow Depth (in.)	26	20	20	12	0	0	0	0	trace	4	20	26	26
Days With ≥ 1.0" Snow Depth	16	12	9	2	0	0	0	0	0	1	7	13	60

Dupree 15 SSE *Ziebach County* Elevation: 2,100 ft. Latitude: 44° 52' N Longitude: 101° 28' W

	JAN	FEB	MAR	APR	MAY	JUN	JUL	AUG	SEP	OCT	NOV	DEC	YEAR
Mean Maximum Temp. (°F)	29.8	34.1	43.2	57.8	68.9	79.0	87.4	86.8	75.8	60.3	43.6	31.3	58.2
Mean Temp. (°F)	19.5	23.7	32.5	45.4	56.6	66.6	73.9	72.6	61.6	47.5	32.7	21.3	46.2
Mean Minimum Temp. (°F)	9.1	13.1	21.7	32.9	44.3	54.2	60.4	58.3	47.5	34.6	21.8	11.3	34.1
Extreme Maximum Temp. (°F)	67	73	82	97	101	111	114	111	106	95	83	69	114
Extreme Minimum Temp. (°F)	-27	-32	-30	1	19	33	44	37	13	-5	-12	-31	-32
Days Maximum Temp. ≥ 90°F	0	0	0	0	1	4	13	13	4	0	0	0	35
Days Maximum Temp. ≤ 32°F	16	13	7	1	0	0	0	0	0	1	7	15	60
Days Minimum Temp. ≤ 32°F	30	27	26	15	3	0	0	0	2	12	26	30	171
Days Minimum Temp. ≤ 0°F	9	5	2	0	0	0	0	0	0	0	1	6	23
Heating Degree Days (base 65°F)	1,406	1,163	1,001	586	280	67	11	17	172	541	962	1,348	7,554
Cooling Degree Days (base 65°F)	0	0	0	4	26	121	293	260	78	5	0	0	787
Mean Precipitation (in.)	0.30	0.48	1.04	1.61	2.95	3.05	2.69	1.83	1.43	1.70	0.57	0.39	18.04
Extreme Maximum Daily Precip. (in.)	0.65	0.96	2.05	2.71	2.28	3.52	2.43	2.72	3.80	2.36	1.26	0.75	3.80
Days With ≥ 0.1" Precipitation	1	2	3	4	6	7	5	4	3	3	2	1	41
Days With ≥ 0.5" Precipitation	0	0	1	1	2	2	2	1	1	1	0	0	11
Days With ≥ 1.0" Precipitation	0	0	0	0	1	1	1	0	0	0	0	0	3
Mean Snowfall (in.)	5.3	6.1	7.1	6.3	0.2	trace	0.0	0.0	trace	1.5	5.4	5.9	37.8
Maximum Snow Depth (in.)	32	27	18	30	5	trace	0	0	0	8	16	30	32
Days With ≥ 1.0" Snow Depth	14	11	10	3	0	0	0	0	0	1	8	14	61

Eureka *Mcpherson County* Elevation: 1,859 ft. Latitude: 45° 47' N Longitude: 99° 38' W

	JAN	FEB	MAR	APR	MAY	JUN	JUL	AUG	SEP	OCT	NOV	DEC	YEAR
Mean Maximum Temp. (°F)	22.6	28.1	39.8	57.6	69.5	77.6	84.6	83.0	72.9	57.7	39.1	25.3	54.8
Mean Temp. (°F)	13.0	18.4	29.4	44.5	56.6	65.4	71.6	69.8	59.6	45.7	29.5	16.3	43.3
Mean Minimum Temp. (°F)	3.3	8.6	19.0	31.4	43.6	53.3	58.6	56.5	46.3	33.6	19.8	7.3	31.8
Extreme Maximum Temp. (°F)	59	64	77	96	98	107	109	109	103	90	74	57	109
Extreme Minimum Temp. (°F)	-38	-41	-24	2	16	35	39	32	18	0	-20	-39	-41
Days Maximum Temp. ≥ 90°F	0	0	0	0	1	2	8	6	2	0	0	0	19
Days Maximum Temp. ≤ 32°F	22	16	9	1	0	0	0	0	0	1	10	20	79
Days Minimum Temp. ≤ 32°F	31	28	28	17	3	0	0	0	2	14	27	31	181
Days Minimum Temp. ≤ 0°F	13	9	3	0	0	0	0	0	0	0	1	9	35
Heating Degree Days (base 65°F)	1,609	1,313	1,098	610	277	75	15	30	205	595	1,059	1,504	8,390
Cooling Degree Days (base 65°F)	0	0	0	3	22	95	226	185	51	2	0	0	584
Mean Precipitation (in.)	0.32	0.45	0.86	1.59	2.75	3.67	2.99	2.42	1.61	1.81	0.66	0.32	19.45
Extreme Maximum Daily Precip. (in.)	0.84	1.89	1.48	2.44	2.16	4.25	3.05	2.31	1.76	2.92	1.12	0.78	4.25
Days With ≥ 0.1" Precipitation	1	1	2	4	6	7	6	4	4	4	2	1	42
Days With ≥ 0.5" Precipitation	0	0	0	1	2	2	2	2	1	1	0	0	11
Days With ≥ 1.0" Precipitation	0	0	0	0	1	1	1	1	0	1	0	0	5
Mean Snowfall (in.)	7.1	6.7	7.5	3.8	0.0	0.0	0.0	0.0	0.0	0.9	7.6	6.6	40.2
Maximum Snow Depth (in.)	***53***	***50***	30	20	2	0	0	0	0	6	32	44	***53***
Days With ≥ 1.0" Snow Depth	***20***	***18***	12	3	0	0	0	0	0	0	8	12	***73***

The period of record for all cooperative weather station data is 1980 – 2009. See User Guide for detailed explanation of data.

Faulkton 1 NW *Faulk County* Elevation: 1,569 ft. Latitude: 45° 02' N Longitude: 99° 08' W

	JAN	FEB	MAR	APR	MAY	JUN	JUL	AUG	SEP	OCT	NOV	DEC	YEAR
Mean Maximum Temp. (°F)	25.6	31.0	41.8	58.4	70.0	78.9	86.1	84.7	74.9	59.8	42.2	28.3	56.8
Mean Temp. (°F)	15.8	20.9	31.3	45.6	57.5	66.7	72.9	71.1	61.2	47.4	32.0	18.9	45.1
Mean Minimum Temp. (°F)	5.9	10.7	20.8	32.7	44.9	54.5	59.7	57.4	47.5	35.0	21.8	9.4	33.4
Extreme Maximum Temp. (°F)	66	69	78	98	98	111	114	109	106	93	82	66	114
Extreme Minimum Temp. (°F)	-30	-35	-21	7	14	34	42	35	20	2	-17	-35	-35
Days Maximum Temp. ≥ 90°F	0	0	0	0	1	4	11	9	3	0	0	0	28
Days Maximum Temp. ≤ 32°F	20	15	8	1	0	0	0	0	0	0	8	18	70
Days Minimum Temp. ≤ 32°F	30	27	27	15	3	0	0	0	2	12	26	30	172
Days Minimum Temp. ≤ 0°F	12	8	2	0	0	0	0	0	0	0	1	8	31
Heating Degree Days (base 65°F)	1,521	1,242	1,036	580	256	61	12	23	177	542	982	1,425	7,857
Cooling Degree Days (base 65°F)	0	0	0	4	29	120	263	218	71	4	0	0	709
Mean Precipitation (in.)	0.49	0.68	1.31	1.97	2.88	3.31	2.92	2.62	2.09	1.84	0.85	0.47	21.43
Extreme Maximum Daily Precip. (in.)	1.35	0.96	2.31	2.10	2.58	2.94	6.70	5.55	3.67	3.00	1.13	0.89	6.70
Days With ≥ 0.1" Precipitation	2	2	3	4	6	7	5	4	4	4	2	2	45
Days With ≥ 0.5" Precipitation	0	0	1	1	2	2	2	2	1	1	0	0	12
Days With ≥ 1.0" Precipitation	0	0	0	0	1	1	1	1	0	0	0	0	4
Mean Snowfall (in.)	5.4	6.3	5.7	3.5	0.0	0.0	0.0	0.0	0.0	0.7	5.0	5.3	31.9
Maximum Snow Depth (in.)	na	na	na	na	na	na	na	na	na	na	na	na	na
Days With ≥ 1.0" Snow Depth	na	na	*4*	1	0	0	0	0	0	0	2	na	na

Flandreau *Moody County* Elevation: 1,560 ft. Latitude: 44° 03' N Longitude: 96° 36' W

	JAN	FEB	MAR	APR	MAY	JUN	JUL	AUG	SEP	OCT	NOV	DEC	YEAR
Mean Maximum Temp. (°F)	24.1	28.8	39.9	56.0	68.2	77.1	82.1	79.8	71.9	58.4	41.3	26.9	54.5
Mean Temp. (°F)	13.7	18.4	29.9	44.3	56.7	66.3	71.1	68.4	59.5	46.2	31.4	17.4	43.6
Mean Minimum Temp. (°F)	3.3	8.0	19.9	32.6	45.1	55.5	60.0	57.0	47.0	34.0	21.4	7.9	32.6
Extreme Maximum Temp. (°F)	64	68	78	93	94	105	102	103	96	91	78	63	105
Extreme Minimum Temp. (°F)	-36	-36	-22	0	19	35	43	35	22	10	-16	-28	-36
Days Maximum Temp. ≥ 90°F	0	0	0	0	1	2	5	3	1	0	0	0	12
Days Maximum Temp. ≤ 32°F	22	16	9	1	0	0	0	0	0	0	8	19	75
Days Minimum Temp. ≤ 32°F	31	28	27	15	2	0	0	0	2	14	26	31	176
Days Minimum Temp. ≤ 0°F	13	9	3	0	0	0	0	0	0	0	1	9	35
Heating Degree Days (base 65°F)	1,586	1,311	1,082	616	276	66	16	36	205	578	1,003	1,470	8,245
Cooling Degree Days (base 65°F)	0	0	0	4	25	113	211	149	47	3	0	0	552
Mean Precipitation (in.)	0.45	0.51	1.43	2.59	3.03	4.19	3.29	3.42	2.85	2.28	1.12	0.57	25.73
Extreme Maximum Daily Precip. (in.)	1.17	0.81	1.82	3.80	2.62	2.52	2.72	2.72	2.75	2.79	1.35	0.90	3.80
Days With ≥ 0.1" Precipitation	2	2	4	5	6	7	5	5	5	4	3	2	50
Days With ≥ 0.5" Precipitation	0	0	1	2	2	3	2	2	2	1	1	0	16
Days With ≥ 1.0" Precipitation	0	0	0	0	1	1	1	1	1	1	0	0	6
Mean Snowfall (in.)	6.1	5.1	7.0	3.6	0.0	0.0	0.0	0.0	0.0	1.1	6.2	7.0	36.1
Maximum Snow Depth (in.)	na	na	*25*	5	*0*	0	*0*	0	0	*trace*	16	na	na
Days With ≥ 1.0" Snow Depth	na	*11*	5	1	0	0	0	0	0	0	1	*7*	na

Forestburg 3 NE *Sanborn County* Elevation: 1,229 ft. Latitude: 44° 03' N Longitude: 98° 04' W

	JAN	FEB	MAR	APR	MAY	JUN	JUL	AUG	SEP	OCT	NOV	DEC	YEAR
Mean Maximum Temp. (°F)	28.2	33.6	45.3	61.4	72.4	81.2	87.1	85.1	76.8	61.9	44.2	30.3	59.0
Mean Temp. (°F)	17.6	22.7	34.0	47.9	59.5	68.8	74.2	72.1	63.1	49.1	33.6	20.3	46.9
Mean Minimum Temp. (°F)	7.0	11.7	22.5	34.3	46.5	56.3	61.3	59.1	49.4	36.4	23.0	10.3	34.8
Extreme Maximum Temp. (°F)	65	73	82	99	99	112	109	109	104	95	83	69	112
Extreme Minimum Temp. (°F)	-36	-40	-19	6	17	36	40	38	20	9	-18	-33	-40
Days Maximum Temp. ≥ 90°F	0	0	0	0	1	5	11	8	4	0	0	0	29
Days Maximum Temp. ≤ 32°F	18	12	5	1	0	0	0	0	0	0	6	16	58
Days Minimum Temp. ≤ 32°F	31	27	26	13	2	0	0	0	1	11	25	31	167
Days Minimum Temp. ≤ 0°F	10	6	2	0	0	0	0	0	0	0	1	7	26
Heating Degree Days (base 65°F)	1,464	1,190	955	513	201	37	5	15	139	491	934	1,379	7,323
Cooling Degree Days (base 65°F)	0	0	0	7	37	157	299	242	90	6	0	0	838
Mean Precipitation (in.)	0.46	0.56	1.31	2.80	3.42	3.55	2.62	2.45	2.20	1.91	1.07	0.46	22.81
Extreme Maximum Daily Precip. (in.)	1.00	1.28	2.70	2.28	3.78	2.87	2.25	2.59	2.74	2.02	2.16	0.70	3.78
Days With ≥ 0.1" Precipitation	2	2	3	6	6	7	6	5	5	4	3	2	51
Days With ≥ 0.5" Precipitation	0	0	1	2	2	2	2	2	2	1	0	0	14
Days With ≥ 1.0" Precipitation	0	0	0	1	1	1	1	1	0	0	0	0	5
Mean Snowfall (in.)	5.7	5.2	5.9	3.6	trace	0.0	0.0	0.0	trace	0.7	5.4	5.7	32.2
Maximum Snow Depth (in.)	32	27	26	15	trace	0	0	0	0	6	15	24	32
Days With ≥ 1.0" Snow Depth	19	15	8	2	0	0	0	0	0	1	5	17	67

Fort Meade *Meade County* Elevation: 3,299 ft. Latitude: 44° 25' N Longitude: 103° 29' W

	JAN	FEB	MAR	APR	MAY	JUN	JUL	AUG	SEP	OCT	NOV	DEC	YEAR
Mean Maximum Temp. (°F)	38.1	40.4	47.6	58.9	68.4	78.2	87.0	86.0	75.7	61.3	47.1	38.3	60.6
Mean Temp. (°F)	26.8	29.0	35.8	46.3	56.2	65.5	73.4	72.0	62.0	48.7	36.0	27.1	48.2
Mean Minimum Temp. (°F)	15.4	17.5	24.0	33.8	43.9	52.7	59.7	57.9	48.3	36.1	24.9	15.8	35.8
Extreme Maximum Temp. (°F)	72	75	82	90	93	106	109	105	101	92	83	73	109
Extreme Minimum Temp. (°F)	-24	-26	-20	2	21	34	43	39	24	-1	-16	-30	-30
Days Maximum Temp. ≥ 90°F	0	0	0	0	0	4	12	11	4	0	0	0	31
Days Maximum Temp. ≤ 32°F	10	7	5	1	0	0	0	0	0	1	5	9	38
Days Minimum Temp. ≤ 32°F	28	26	25	14	3	0	0	0	1	10	23	29	159
Days Minimum Temp. ≤ 0°F	5	4	1	0	0	0	0	0	0	0	1	4	15
Heating Degree Days (base 65°F)	1,180	1,011	900	558	288	80	9	15	159	502	864	1,170	6,736
Cooling Degree Days (base 65°F)	0	0	0	5	21	102	276	238	77	4	0	0	723
Mean Precipitation (in.)	0.45	0.64	1.50	2.52	3.92	3.27	2.24	1.58	1.41	1.87	0.98	0.55	20.93
Extreme Maximum Daily Precip. (in.)	0.68	0.77	2.53	2.17	3.83	3.38	2.46	2.17	2.29	3.21	3.26	0.62	3.83
Days With ≥ 0.1" Precipitation	2	2	4	5	6	7	5	4	3	4	3	2	47
Days With ≥ 0.5" Precipitation	0	0	1	2	3	2	1	1	1	1	0	0	12
Days With ≥ 1.0" Precipitation	0	0	0	0	1	1	0	0	0	0	0	0	2
Mean Snowfall (in.)	*2.9*	*3.3*	*5.1*	5.1	0.9	0.0	0.0	0.0	trace	0.6	2.8	na	na
Maximum Snow Depth (in.)	11	18	24	48	9	0	0	0	2	12	20	18	48
Days With ≥ 1.0" Snow Depth	7	8	8	3	0	0	0	0	0	1	4	9	40

The period of record for all cooperative weather station data is 1980 – 2009. See User Guide for detailed explanation of data.

Gettysburg *Potter County* Elevation: 2,069 ft. Latitude: 45° 01' N Longitude: 99° 58' W

	JAN	FEB	MAR	APR	MAY	JUN	JUL	AUG	SEP	OCT	NOV	DEC	YEAR
Mean Maximum Temp. (°F)	25.4	29.7	40.9	56.3	68.3	77.1	84.7	83.4	73.5	58.0	41.6	27.8	55.6
Mean Temp. (°F)	15.4	19.8	30.4	44.2	56.3	65.5	72.0	70.4	60.1	46.2	31.4	18.4	44.2
Mean Minimum Temp. (°F)	5.3	9.7	19.8	32.0	44.1	53.8	59.2	57.3	46.7	34.3	21.2	8.8	32.7
Extreme Maximum Temp. (°F)	63	66	85	97	100	108	113	107	102	92	80	65	113
Extreme Minimum Temp. (°F)	-30	-34	-23	3	20	35	42	39	20	1	-13	-31	-34
Days Maximum Temp. ≥ 90°F	0	0	0	0	1	3	9	8	3	0	0	0	24
Days Maximum Temp. ≤ 32°F	20	15	9	1	0	0	0	0	0	1	8	18	72
Days Minimum Temp. ≤ 32°F	31	27	27	16	3	0	0	0	2	13	26	31	176
Days Minimum Temp. ≤ 0°F	11	8	3	0	0	0	0	0	0	0	1	8	31
Heating Degree Days (base 65°F)	1,535	1,272	1,067	622	284	79	15	26	198	580	1,002	1,440	8,120
Cooling Degree Days (base 65°F)	0	0	0	3	22	100	239	201	59	3	0	0	627
Mean Precipitation (in.)	0.34	0.56	1.09	1.77	2.78	3.40	2.85	2.36	1.71	1.73	0.57	0.39	19.55
Extreme Maximum Daily Precip. (in.)	0.75	0.80	2.05	2.15	3.02	4.68	4.50	3.48	2.27	3.37	0.90	0.63	4.68
Days With ≥ 0.1" Precipitation	1	2	3	4	6	7	5	4	4	3	2	1	42
Days With ≥ 0.5" Precipitation	0	0	1	1	2	2	2	1	1	1	0	0	11
Days With ≥ 1.0" Precipitation	0	0	0	0	1	1	1	1	0	0	0	0	4
Mean Snowfall (in.)	***5.5***	***8.6***	***6.6***	3.0	trace	0.0	0.0	0.0	trace	0.5	4.4	***6.2***	***34.8***
Maximum Snow Depth (in.)	na	na	na	na	***trace***	***0***	***0***	***0***	***trace***	***2***	***13***	na	na
Days With ≥ 1.0" Snow Depth	na	na	***7***	1	0	0	0	0	0	0	3	***12***	na

Howard *Miner County* Elevation: 1,560 ft. Latitude: 44° 01' N Longitude: 97° 32' W

	JAN	FEB	MAR	APR	MAY	JUN	JUL	AUG	SEP	OCT	NOV	DEC	YEAR
Mean Maximum Temp. (°F)	25.5	30.7	42.6	58.4	70.2	79.1	84.8	82.3	73.5	59.3	42.1	27.8	56.4
Mean Temp. (°F)	15.8	20.9	32.1	46.4	58.4	67.7	73.1	70.6	61.4	47.6	32.4	18.5	45.4
Mean Minimum Temp. (°F)	6.0	11.1	21.6	34.3	46.5	56.4	61.3	58.9	49.3	35.9	22.6	9.2	34.4
Extreme Maximum Temp. (°F)	61	69	79	96	95	108	107	102	100	90	78	65	108
Extreme Minimum Temp. (°F)	-34	-36	-18	6	19	37	44	39	20	8	-15	-31	-36
Days Maximum Temp. ≥ 90°F	0	0	0	0	1	3	8	5	2	0	0	0	19
Days Maximum Temp. ≤ 32°F	20	15	7	1	0	0	0	0	0	0	8	19	70
Days Minimum Temp. ≤ 32°F	31	27	26	13	2	0	0	0	1	11	25	30	166
Days Minimum Temp. ≤ 0°F	10	7	2	0	0	0	0	0	0	0	1	8	28
Heating Degree Days (base 65°F)	1,521	1,241	1,013	558	232	50	9	20	168	536	973	1,437	7,758
Cooling Degree Days (base 65°F)	0	0	0	6	34	139	266	200	68	4	0	0	717
Mean Precipitation (in.)	0.53	0.58	1.47	2.75	3.02	4.02	3.18	3.12	2.62	2.23	1.16	0.59	25.27
Extreme Maximum Daily Precip. (in.)	0.95	0.75	1.92	2.40	3.02	3.00	2.45	2.61	3.87	3.35	1.78	1.08	3.87
Days With ≥ 0.1" Precipitation	2	2	4	6	7	7	6	5	5	4	3	2	53
Days With ≥ 0.5" Precipitation	0	0	1	2	2	3	3	2	2	2	1	0	18
Days With ≥ 1.0" Precipitation	0	0	0	1	1	1	1	1	1	1	0	0	7
Mean Snowfall (in.)	6.0	6.0	7.0	3.5	0.0	0.0	0.0	0.0	0.1	0.9	5.4	6.4	35.3
Maximum Snow Depth (in.)	na	na	na	na	na	na	na	na	na	na	na	na	na
Days With ≥ 1.0" Snow Depth	na	na	***1***	0	0	0	0	0	0	0	1	na	na

Kennebec *Lyman County* Elevation: 1,700 ft. Latitude: 43° 55' N Longitude: 99° 52' W

	JAN	FEB	MAR	APR	MAY	JUN	JUL	AUG	SEP	OCT	NOV	DEC	YEAR
Mean Maximum Temp. (°F)	33.1	38.0	48.5	62.8	73.5	82.7	90.6	88.9	79.7	64.2	46.4	33.7	61.8
Mean Temp. (°F)	21.6	26.1	35.9	48.3	59.7	69.3	76.3	74.5	64.5	50.2	34.7	22.6	48.6
Mean Minimum Temp. (°F)	10.1	14.2	23.1	33.8	45.9	55.8	61.9	60.0	49.3	36.1	22.9	11.5	35.4
Extreme Maximum Temp. (°F)	69	75	89	99	100	111	112	112	108	96	89	74	112
Extreme Minimum Temp. (°F)	-37	-38	-25	6	15	33	41	36	20	5	-18	-31	-38
Days Maximum Temp. ≥ 90°F	0	0	0	1	2	7	17	15	6	1	0	0	49
Days Maximum Temp. ≤ 32°F	14	10	5	1	0	0	0	0	0	0	5	13	48
Days Minimum Temp. ≤ 32°F	30	27	26	14	2	0	0	0	2	11	25	31	168
Days Minimum Temp. ≤ 0°F	8	5	1	0	0	0	0	0	0	0	1	6	21
Heating Degree Days (base 65°F)	1,340	1,092	897	502	205	38	4	10	123	461	903	1,308	6,883
Cooling Degree Days (base 65°F)	0	0	0	8	47	173	360	311	115	8	0	0	1,022
Mean Precipitation (in.)	0.37	0.46	1.24	2.09	3.10	3.32	2.38	2.03	1.73	1.69	0.76	0.37	19.54
Extreme Maximum Daily Precip. (in.)	0.90	0.68	1.80	2.30	4.00	3.22	2.58	3.73	2.00	2.18	2.05	0.50	4.00
Days With ≥ 0.1" Precipitation	1	2	3	5	6	6	5	4	4	3	2	1	42
Days With ≥ 0.5" Precipitation	0	0	1	1	2	2	2	1	1	1	0	0	11
Days With ≥ 1.0" Precipitation	0	0	0	0	1	1	1	0	0	0	0	0	3
Mean Snowfall (in.)	5.0	6.3	8.2	4.4	0.0	trace	0.0	0.0	0.1	0.9	6.2	6.5	37.6
Maximum Snow Depth (in.)	19	15	22	18	0	trace	0	0	0	4	25	29	29
Days With ≥ 1.0" Snow Depth	10	8	6	1	0	0	0	0	0	0	5	11	41

Madison 2 SE *Lake County* Elevation: 1,660 ft. Latitude: 43° 59' N Longitude: 97° 06' W

	JAN	FEB	MAR	APR	MAY	JUN	JUL	AUG	SEP	OCT	NOV	DEC	YEAR
Mean Maximum Temp. (°F)	24.5	28.8	40.4	56.6	68.6	77.9	83.0	80.9	72.2	58.7	40.9	27.5	55.0
Mean Temp. (°F)	15.0	19.4	30.8	45.3	57.3	66.9	71.9	69.5	60.4	46.9	31.4	18.5	44.5
Mean Minimum Temp. (°F)	5.3	10.0	21.2	34.0	46.1	55.8	60.7	58.1	48.4	35.2	21.9	9.4	33.9
Extreme Maximum Temp. (°F)	66	68	77	94	94	105	104	104	97	89	78	64	105
Extreme Minimum Temp. (°F)	-28	-31	-15	6	18	35	42	35	25	10	-14	-28	-31
Days Maximum Temp. ≥ 90°F	0	0	0	0	1	2	6	4	1	0	0	0	14
Days Maximum Temp. ≤ 32°F	22	16	8	1	0	0	0	0	0	0	9	18	74
Days Minimum Temp. ≤ 32°F	31	28	26	13	1	0	0	0	2	12	26	31	170
Days Minimum Temp. ≤ 0°F	11	8	2	0	0	0	0	0	0	0	1	8	30
Heating Degree Days (base 65°F)	1,546	1,284	1,052	587	258	60	13	28	189	556	1,000	1,436	8,009
Cooling Degree Days (base 65°F)	0	0	0	5	29	124	233	175	57	3	0	0	626
Mean Precipitation (in.)	0.42	0.52	1.39	2.86	3.24	4.01	2.97	3.12	3.03	1.92	1.19	0.54	25.21
Extreme Maximum Daily Precip. (in.)	0.95	***0.80***	1.14	2.36	3.44	4.22	2.71	2.68	3.20	3.00	1.62	0.90	***4.22***
Days With ≥ 0.1" Precipitation	1	2	4	6	7	7	5	5	5	4	3	2	51
Days With ≥ 0.5" Precipitation	0	0	1	2	2	3	2	2	2	1	1	0	16
Days With ≥ 1.0" Precipitation	0	0	0	1	1	1	1	1	1	1	0	0	7
Mean Snowfall (in.)	5.4	6.4	6.6	3.1	trace	0.0	0.0	0.0	0.1	0.8	5.9	6.4	34.7
Maximum Snow Depth (in.)	na	na	na	na	na	na	na	na	na	na	na	na	na
Days With ≥ 1.0" Snow Depth	na	na	***8***	1	0	0	0	0	0	0	4	***12***	na

The period of record for all cooperative weather station data is 1980 – 2009. See User Guide for detailed explanation of data.

Maurine 10 SW *Meade County* Elevation: 2,709 ft. Latitude: 44° 54' N Longitude: 102° 39' W

	JAN	FEB	MAR	APR	MAY	JUN	JUL	AUG	SEP	OCT	NOV	DEC	YEAR
Mean Maximum Temp. (°F)	31.1	35.3	44.6	58.5	68.9	78.7	87.6	86.7	76.0	60.8	44.3	32.6	58.8
Mean Temp. (°F)	19.7	23.5	32.4	44.4	55.5	65.2	72.9	71.3	60.3	46.4	32.0	20.8	45.4
Mean Minimum Temp. (°F)	8.1	11.8	20.2	30.3	42.2	51.6	58.1	55.8	44.6	32.0	19.6	8.9	31.9
Extreme Maximum Temp. (°F)	69	72	83	93	101	110	113	110	107	98	82	69	113
Extreme Minimum Temp. (°F)	-32	-36	-26	-2	18	31	39	35	20	-10	-24	-36	-36
Days Maximum Temp. ≥ 90°F	0	0	0	0	1	4	13	13	5	0	0	0	36
Days Maximum Temp. ≤ 32°F	15	11	6	1	0	0	0	0	0	1	7	14	55
Days Minimum Temp. ≤ 32°F	30	27	28	18	4	0	0	0	3	15	27	30	182
Days Minimum Temp. ≤ 0°F	9	6	2	0	0	0	0	0	0	0	2	7	26
Heating Degree Days (base 65°F)	1,398	1,168	1,003	610	305	86	15	22	197	572	986	1,366	7,728
Cooling Degree Days (base 65°F)	0	0	0	2	19	99	266	226	64	2	0	0	678
Mean Precipitation (in.)	0.59	0.61	1.52	1.93	2.98	2.88	2.39	1.69	1.09	1.42	0.75	0.72	18.57
Extreme Maximum Daily Precip. (in.)	0.83	1.00	2.35	2.00	2.55	3.08	2.58	2.51	1.83	1.95	2.07	0.92	3.08
Days With ≥ 0.1" Precipitation	3	2	4	5	6	7	5	4	3	3	2	3	47
Days With ≥ 0.5" Precipitation	0	0	1	1	2	2	2	1	1	1	0	0	11
Days With ≥ 1.0" Precipitation	0	0	0	0	1	0	0	0	0	0	0	0	1
Mean Snowfall (in.)	5.2	6.0	9.9	5.8	0.7	0.0	0.0	0.0	trace	1.4	4.4	6.2	39.6
Maximum Snow Depth (in.)	30	32	24	14	6	0	0	0	trace	15	27	33	33
Days With ≥ 1.0" Snow Depth	19	12	10	3	0	0	0	0	0	1	8	15	68

McIntosh 6 SE *Corson County* Elevation: 2,174 ft. Latitude: 45° 53' N Longitude: 101° 18' W

	JAN	FEB	MAR	APR	MAY	JUN	JUL	AUG	SEP	OCT	NOV	DEC	YEAR
Mean Maximum Temp. (°F)	26.8	31.4	42.1	58.2	69.8	78.7	86.5	85.2	74.3	58.8	40.9	28.7	56.8
Mean Temp. (°F)	16.6	21.4	31.3	45.2	56.7	65.8	72.5	70.8	60.2	46.3	30.7	18.8	44.7
Mean Minimum Temp. (°F)	6.1	11.2	20.4	32.2	43.6	52.8	58.4	56.3	46.1	33.9	20.4	8.9	32.5
Extreme Maximum Temp. (°F)	68	71	80	96	99	111	112	104	101	94	80	65	112
Extreme Minimum Temp. (°F)	-32	-35	-25	-1	21	31	42	37	20	-8	-19	-34	-35
Days Maximum Temp. ≥ 90°F	0	0	0	0	1	4	11	10	3	0	0	0	29
Days Maximum Temp. ≤ 32°F	18	14	8	1	0	0	0	0	0	1	9	17	68
Days Minimum Temp. ≤ 32°F	31	28	28	16	3	0	0	0	2	13	27	31	179
Days Minimum Temp. ≤ 0°F	11	7	2	0	0	0	0	0	0	0	2	8	30
Heating Degree Days (base 65°F)	1,495	1,227	1,039	589	272	75	11	21	195	574	1,024	1,427	7,949
Cooling Degree Days (base 65°F)	0	0	0	3	22	105	250	207	58	2	0	0	647
Mean Precipitation (in.)	0.32	0.42	0.78	1.27	2.29	3.21	2.36	1.94	1.23	1.43	0.48	0.32	16.05
Extreme Maximum Daily Precip. (in.)	0.87	0.73	1.47	2.07	1.52	3.28	2.46	2.83	2.92	1.62	0.89	0.62	3.28
Days With ≥ 0.1" Precipitation	1	1	2	4	5	6	5	4	3	3	2	1	37
Days With ≥ 0.5" Precipitation	0	0	0	1	1	2	1	1	1	1	0	0	8
Days With ≥ 1.0" Precipitation	0	0	0	0	0	1	0	1	0	0	0	0	2
Mean Snowfall (in.)	6.3	6.2	8.3	4.8	0.3	0.0	0.0	0.0	0.2	1.4	5.2	5.7	38.4
Maximum Snow Depth (in.)	33	41	39	14	1	0	0	0	2	8	16	32	41
Days With ≥ 1.0" Snow Depth	22	17	13	3	0	0	0	0	0	1	10	16	82

Mitchell 2 N *Davison County* Elevation: 1,250 ft. Latitude: 43° 44' N Longitude: 98° 01' W

	JAN	FEB	MAR	APR	MAY	JUN	JUL	AUG	SEP	OCT	NOV	DEC	YEAR
Mean Maximum Temp. (°F)	*28.2*	*33.6*	*44.1*	*58.7*	*70.6*	*80.4*	*86.0*	*84.4*	*75.4*	*61.0*	*43.5*	*30.9*	*58.1*
Mean Temp. (°F)	*17.8*	*23.1*	*33.3*	*47.0*	*59.2*	*69.2*	*74.5*	*72.5*	*62.5*	*48.5*	*33.3*	*20.8*	*46.8*
Mean Minimum Temp. (°F)	*7.4*	*12.5*	*22.4*	*35.2*	*47.8*	*57.9*	*63.0*	*60.6*	*49.5*	*36.0*	*23.1*	*10.7*	*35.5*
Extreme Maximum Temp. (°F)	*67*	*73*	*82*	*97*	*97*	*107*	*108*	*109*	*101*	*96*	*81*	*70*	*109*
Extreme Minimum Temp. (°F)	*-32*	*-40*	*-16*	*10*	*25*	*35*	*45*	*39*	*25*	*12*	*-12*	*-30*	*-40*
Days Maximum Temp. ≥ 90°F	*0*	*0*	*0*	*0*	*1*	*5*	*10*	*8*	*3*	*0*	*0*	*0*	*27*
Days Maximum Temp. ≤ 32°F	*19*	*13*	*7*	*1*	*0*	*0*	*0*	*0*	*0*	*0*	*7*	*15*	*62*
Days Minimum Temp. ≤ 32°F	*31*	*27*	*25*	*12*	*1*	*0*	*0*	*0*	*1*	*11*	*25*	*31*	*164*
Days Minimum Temp. ≤ 0°F	*10*	*7*	*2*	*0*	*0*	*0*	*0*	*0*	*0*	*0*	*1*	*7*	*27*
Heating Degree Days (base 65°F)	*1,458*	*1,179*	*976*	*542*	*213*	*41*	*8*	*14*	*153*	*509*	*944*	*1,364*	*7,401*
Cooling Degree Days (base 65°F)	*0*	*0*	*0*	*8*	*42*	*173*	*310*	*253*	*83*	*4*	*0*	*0*	*873*
Mean Precipitation (in.)	*0.57*	*0.75*	*1.60*	*3.02*	*3.21*	*3.70*	*2.59*	*2.47*	*2.32*	*1.61*	*1.26*	*0.56*	*23.66*
Extreme Maximum Daily Precip. (in.)	*2.10*	*1.56*	*2.21*	*2.00*	*3.05*	*2.96*	*3.10*	*4.35*	*3.00*	*1.85*	*2.27*	*1.50*	*4.35*
Days With ≥ 0.1" Precipitation	*1*	*2*	*4*	*6*	*6*	*6*	*5*	*4*	*4*	*3*	*2*	*2*	*45*
Days With ≥ 0.5" Precipitation	*0*	*0*	*1*	*2*	*2*	*2*	*2*	*2*	*2*	*1*	*1*	*0*	*15*
Days With ≥ 1.0" Precipitation	*0*	*0*	*0*	*1*	*1*	*1*	*0*	*1*	*1*	*0*	*0*	*0*	*5*
Mean Snowfall (in.)	*5.7*	*5.6*	*4.8*	*2.3*	*0.0*	*0.0*	*0.0*	*0.0*	*0.0*	*0.4*	*5.1*	na	na
Maximum Snow Depth (in.)	na	na	na	na	na	na	na	na	na	na	na	na	na
Days With ≥ 1.0" Snow Depth	na	na	*4*	*1*	*0*	*0*	*0*	*0*	*0*	*0*	*2*	na	na

Mt Rushmore Natl Mem *Pennington County* Elevation: 5,250 ft. Latitude: 43° 53' N Longitude: 103° 27' W

	JAN	FEB	MAR	APR	MAY	JUN	JUL	AUG	SEP	OCT	NOV	DEC	YEAR
Mean Maximum Temp. (°F)	36.8	37.7	43.6	51.9	61.7	71.8	80.0	78.8	68.7	55.7	44.1	36.1	55.6
Mean Temp. (°F)	27.9	28.6	34.2	42.2	51.9	61.8	69.6	68.4	58.6	46.4	35.4	27.4	46.0
Mean Minimum Temp. (°F)	18.8	19.5	24.7	32.5	42.0	51.7	59.2	57.8	48.5	37.0	26.8	18.7	36.4
Extreme Maximum Temp. (°F)	68	68	74	85	89	98	100	98	95	83	74	67	100
Extreme Minimum Temp. (°F)	-19	-29	-11	4	18	27	35	37	19	1	-12	-31	-31
Days Maximum Temp. ≥ 90°F	0	0	0	0	0	1	4	3	1	0	0	0	9
Days Maximum Temp. ≤ 32°F	10	9	6	2	0	0	0	0	0	1	6	11	45
Days Minimum Temp. ≤ 32°F	26	24	24	15	4	0	0	0	2	10	21	27	153
Days Minimum Temp. ≤ 0°F	4	3	1	0	0	0	0	0	0	0	1	3	12
Heating Degree Days (base 65°F)	1,145	1,022	950	678	411	157	36	43	238	573	880	1,158	7,291
Cooling Degree Days (base 65°F)	0	0	0	1	11	66	186	154	53	3	0	0	474
Mean Precipitation (in.)	0.37	0.57	1.23	2.17	3.89	3.36	2.88	2.07	1.78	1.73	0.62	0.41	21.08
Extreme Maximum Daily Precip. (in.)	0.56	0.95	1.08	2.30	3.38	1.88	1.77	2.26	1.61	1.83	1.11	0.58	3.38
Days With ≥ 0.1" Precipitation	1	2	4	5	8	8	7	5	4	4	2	2	52
Days With ≥ 0.5" Precipitation	0	0	1	1	3	2	2	1	1	1	0	0	12
Days With ≥ 1.0" Precipitation	0	0	0	0	1	1	1	0	0	0	0	0	3
Mean Snowfall (in.)	5.8	7.3	10.3	10.9	1.4	0.1	0.0	0.0	0.7	3.7	6.4	6.0	52.6
Maximum Snow Depth (in.)	19	14	29	30	6	3	0	0	5	13	16	20	30
Days With ≥ 1.0" Snow Depth	10	10	10	5	1	0	0	0	0	2	7	12	57

The period of record for all cooperative weather station data is 1980 – 2009. See User Guide for detailed explanation of data.

Pierre Municipal Arpt *Hughes County* Elevation: 1,726 ft. Latitude: 44° 23' N Longitude: 100° 17' W

	JAN	FEB	MAR	APR	MAY	JUN	JUL	AUG	SEP	OCT	NOV	DEC	YEAR
Mean Maximum Temp. (°F)	30.7	35.8	45.9	60.4	71.2	80.8	89.6	87.7	77.5	61.5	44.9	32.2	59.8
Mean Temp. (°F)	20.6	25.1	34.7	47.5	58.6	68.3	75.9	74.0	63.6	49.1	34.4	22.4	47.8
Mean Minimum Temp. (°F)	10.4	14.4	23.4	34.5	46.0	55.7	62.2	60.2	49.6	36.7	23.9	12.6	35.8
Extreme Maximum Temp. (°F)	68	75	87	98	102	112	117	114	108	98	87	77	117
Extreme Minimum Temp. (°F)	-27	-35	-19	7	24	34	46	41	21	4	-11	-31	-35
Days Maximum Temp. ≥ 90°F	0	0	0	0	1	5	16	14	6	1	0	0	43
Days Maximum Temp. ≤ 32°F	16	11	5	1	0	0	0	0	0	0	6	14	53
Days Minimum Temp. ≤ 32°F	30	27	25	12	2	0	0	0	1	9	25	30	161
Days Minimum Temp. ≤ 0°F	8	5	1	0	0	0	0	0	0	0	1	6	21
Heating Degree Days (base 65°F)	1,369	1,122	934	524	225	45	5	11	137	491	911	1,315	7,089
Cooling Degree Days (base 65°F)	0	0	0	5	34	150	350	297	101	5	0	0	942
Mean Precipitation (in.)	0.43	0.54	1.18	1.75	3.07	3.52	2.56	1.87	1.78	1.76	0.70	0.48	19.64
Extreme Maximum Daily Precip. (in.)	0.91	0.88	1.74	1.47	2.72	3.32	4.00	2.59	2.74	2.54	0.82	0.71	4.00
Days With ≥ 0.1" Precipitation	1	2	3	4	6	6	5	4	3	4	2	2	42
Days With ≥ 0.5" Precipitation	0	0	1	1	2	2	1	1	1	1	0	0	10
Days With ≥ 1.0" Precipitation	0	0	0	0	1	1	1	0	0	0	0	0	3
Mean Snowfall (in.)	***5.7***	***6.6***	***6.0***	***3.6***	na	***trace***	na	na	***trace***	na	na	na	na
Maximum Snow Depth (in.)	***22***	***14***	***16***	***12***	na	***trace***	na	na	***trace***	na	na	na	na
Days With ≥ 1.0" Snow Depth	***16***	***12***	***9***	***1***	na	***0***	na	na	***0***	na	na	na	na

Spearfish *Lawrence County* Elevation: 3,640 ft. Latitude: 44° 31' N Longitude: 103° 52' W

	JAN	FEB	MAR	APR	MAY	JUN	JUL	AUG	SEP	OCT	NOV	DEC	YEAR
Mean Maximum Temp. (°F)	38.2	39.1	46.6	57.5	67.1	76.7	85.9	84.4	73.9	59.8	***46.5***	38.3	***59.5***
Mean Temp. (°F)	27.5	28.5	35.7	45.7	55.5	64.6	72.9	71.0	60.9	48.4	***36.2***	27.9	***47.9***
Mean Minimum Temp. (°F)	16.7	17.8	24.8	33.9	43.9	52.6	59.9	57.6	47.9	36.8	***25.8***	17.4	***36.2***
Extreme Maximum Temp. (°F)	69	75	78	91	96	103	109	104	100	***90***	***78***	***70***	***109***
Extreme Minimum Temp. (°F)	-30	-25	-16	4	23	33	40	32	22	***9***	***-17***	***-31***	***-31***
Days Maximum Temp. ≥ 90°F	0	0	0	0	0	3	11	8	3	0	0	0	25
Days Maximum Temp. ≤ 32°F	10	8	5	1	0	0	0	0	0	1	5	9	39
Days Minimum Temp. ≤ 32°F	27	24	23	13	2	0	0	0	1	9	20	26	145
Days Minimum Temp. ≤ 0°F	5	4	1	0	0	0	0	0	0	0	1	4	15
Heating Degree Days (base 65°F)	1,157	1,026	903	576	307	95	12	21	181	513	***857***	1,145	***6,793***
Cooling Degree Days (base 65°F)	0	0	0	3	19	91	265	215	65	4	***0***	0	***662***
Mean Precipitation (in.)	0.51	0.69	1.31	2.15	3.41	3.64	2.05	1.55	1.76	1.98	0.86	0.75	20.66
Extreme Maximum Daily Precip. (in.)	0.70	0.93	1.69	1.98	3.51	4.00	2.18	1.51	2.20	2.37	***2.84***	***1.45***	***4.00***
Days With ≥ 0.1" Precipitation	2	2	3	4	7	7	5	4	4	4	2	2	46
Days With ≥ 0.5" Precipitation	0	0	1	1	2	2	1	1	1	1	0	0	10
Days With ≥ 1.0" Precipitation	0	0	0	1	1	1	0	0	0	0	0	0	3
Mean Snowfall (in.)	***6.8***	7.2	***10.3***	6.4	0.5	0.0	0.0	0.0	trace	***2.2***	***3.6***	***8.8***	***45.8***
Maximum Snow Depth (in.)	***12***	***10***	***30***	***33***	***8***	***0***	0	***0***	***1***	na	na	na	na
Days With ≥ 1.0" Snow Depth	***11***	***7***	***6***	3	0	0	0	0	0	***1***	***6***	***11***	***45***

Tyndall *Bon Homme County* Elevation: 1,419 ft. Latitude: 42° 59' N Longitude: 97° 52' W

	JAN	FEB	MAR	APR	MAY	JUN	JUL	AUG	SEP	OCT	NOV	DEC	YEAR
Mean Maximum Temp. (°F)	30.8	35.6	46.5	60.6	71.7	81.6	87.0	84.9	76.7	62.5	45.6	32.3	59.6
Mean Temp. (°F)	20.7	25.3	35.6	48.5	60.2	70.1	75.4	73.3	64.1	50.4	35.4	22.9	48.5
Mean Minimum Temp. (°F)	10.5	14.8	24.6	36.4	48.6	58.6	63.7	61.6	51.4	38.2	25.3	13.3	37.2
Extreme Maximum Temp. (°F)	70	74	84	96	100	108	109	108	101	94	84	68	109
Extreme Minimum Temp. (°F)	-26	-29	-12	9	25	38	46	40	24	12	-10	-31	-31
Days Maximum Temp. ≥ 90°F	0	0	0	0	1	6	11	8	4	0	0	0	30
Days Maximum Temp. ≤ 32°F	16	11	6	1	0	0	0	0	0	0	6	15	55
Days Minimum Temp. ≤ 32°F	31	27	24	11	1	0	0	0	1	8	23	30	156
Days Minimum Temp. ≤ 0°F	8	5	1	0	0	0	0	0	0	0	1	5	20
Heating Degree Days (base 65°F)	1,368	1,120	905	498	194	32	4	9	126	455	881	1,300	6,892
Cooling Degree Days (base 65°F)	0	0	0	11	51	192	333	272	105	8	0	0	972
Mean Precipitation (in.)	0.50	0.70	1.52	2.70	3.61	3.24	3.12	3.14	2.32	1.93	1.20	0.66	24.64
Extreme Maximum Daily Precip. (in.)	1.01	1.11	2.22	2.22	2.52	3.15	3.51	3.07	3.51	1.70	1.40	1.20	3.51
Days With ≥ 0.1" Precipitation	1	2	4	6	7	6	5	5	4	4	3	2	49
Days With ≥ 0.5" Precipitation	0	0	1	2	3	2	2	2	1	2	1	0	16
Days With ≥ 1.0" Precipitation	0	0	0	1	1	1	1	1	1	0	0	0	6
Mean Snowfall (in.)	6.1	5.8	6.0	3.4	0.0	0.0	0.0	0.0	trace	0.7	5.4	7.0	34.4
Maximum Snow Depth (in.)	***22***	***13***	***15***	15	0	0	0	0	trace	***2***	20	***19***	***22***
Days With ≥ 1.0" Snow Depth	***14***	***11***	5	1	0	0	0	0	0	0	3	12	***46***

Vermillion 2 SE *Clay County* Elevation: 1,189 ft. Latitude: 42° 46' N Longitude: 96° 55' W

	JAN	FEB	MAR	APR	MAY	JUN	JUL	AUG	SEP	OCT	NOV	DEC	YEAR
Mean Maximum Temp. (°F)	32.8	37.8	49.5	64.2	74.7	83.9	87.6	85.7	78.8	65.6	48.1	34.0	61.9
Mean Temp. (°F)	21.9	26.5	37.5	50.4	61.7	71.6	75.8	73.7	65.3	52.2	36.9	23.7	49.8
Mean Minimum Temp. (°F)	10.9	15.1	25.4	36.7	48.7	59.2	64.0	61.7	51.7	38.8	25.7	13.4	37.6
Extreme Maximum Temp. (°F)	71	74	86	96	100	108	108	105	101	93	83	68	108
Extreme Minimum Temp. (°F)	-27	-33	-17	9	24	38	42	40	23	11	-18	-30	-33
Days Maximum Temp. ≥ 90°F	0	0	0	1	2	7	12	8	4	1	0	0	35
Days Maximum Temp. ≤ 32°F	14	10	4	0	0	0	0	0	0	0	4	13	45
Days Minimum Temp. ≤ 32°F	30	26	24	11	1	0	0	0	1	8	22	30	153
Days Minimum Temp. ≤ 0°F	7	5	1	0	0	0	0	0	0	0	1	6	20
Heating Degree Days (base 65°F)	1,332	1,082	847	447	163	20	3	8	102	403	836	1,274	6,517
Cooling Degree Days (base 65°F)	0	0	0	17	67	225	345	286	117	14	0	0	1,071
Mean Precipitation (in.)	0.45	0.58	1.71	3.12	3.85	3.76	3.34	2.81	2.79	2.35	1.45	0.59	26.80
Extreme Maximum Daily Precip. (in.)	0.81	1.10	2.25	2.55	3.00	2.50	4.45	2.29	4.82	2.70	2.30	1.30	4.82
Days With ≥ 0.1" Precipitation	1	2	4	6	7	7	5	5	4	5	3	2	51
Days With ≥ 0.5" Precipitation	0	0	1	2	3	3	2	2	2	1	1	0	17
Days With ≥ 1.0" Precipitation	0	0	0	1	1	1	1	1	1	1	0	0	7
Mean Snowfall (in.)	6.5	6.2	5.2	2.6	trace	0.0	0.0	trace	trace	1.1	5.5	6.7	33.8
Maximum Snow Depth (in.)	26	29	13	6	trace	trace	0	trace	trace	4	15	24	29
Days With ≥ 1.0" Snow Depth	12	9	4	1	0	0	0	0	0	0	4	11	41

The period of record for all cooperative weather station data is 1980 – 2009. See User Guide for detailed explanation of data.

Watertown Municipal Arpt *Codington County* Elevation: 1,750 ft. Latitude: 44° 55' N Longitude: 97° 09' W

	JAN	FEB	MAR	APR	MAY	JUN	JUL	AUG	SEP	OCT	NOV	DEC	YEAR
Mean Maximum Temp. (°F)	23.5	27.2	39.7	56.4	68.6	77.3	83.3	80.7	71.2	56.6	40.2	25.6	54.2
Mean Temp. (°F)	13.7	17.5	30.0	44.4	56.9	66.1	71.7	69.1	59.5	45.8	30.9	16.8	43.5
Mean Minimum Temp. (°F)	3.8	7.8	20.2	32.4	45.0	54.8	60.0	57.5	47.8	34.8	21.6	7.8	32.8
Extreme Maximum Temp. (°F)	65	65	74	95	94	105	104	101	97	89	77	57	105
Extreme Minimum Temp. (°F)	-34	-35	-19	7	20	32	42	38	23	8	-17	-30	-35
Days Maximum Temp. ≥ 90°F	0	0	0	0	0	2	6	4	1	0	0	0	13
Days Maximum Temp. ≤ 32°F	22	17	9	1	0	0	0	0	0	0	9	21	79
Days Minimum Temp. ≤ 32°F	31	28	27	16	2	0	0	0	2	13	26	31	176
Days Minimum Temp. ≤ 0°F	12	9	3	0	0	0	0	0	0	0	1	10	35
Heating Degree Days (base 65°F)	1,587	1,338	1,079	613	272	70	14	33	205	591	1,015	1,490	8,307
Cooling Degree Days (base 65°F)	0	0	0	3	26	108	228	169	46	2	0	0	582
Mean Precipitation (in.)	0.43	0.51	1.12	1.94	2.53	3.82	2.89	2.82	2.40	1.77	0.75	0.47	21.45
Extreme Maximum Daily Precip. (in.)	0.50	0.89	1.15	2.32	1.53	2.66	2.33	4.32	2.87	2.08	1.00	0.89	4.32
Days With ≥ 0.1" Precipitation	2	2	3	4	6	7	6	5	5	4	2	1	47
Days With ≥ 0.5" Precipitation	0	0	0	0	1	2	3	2	2	1	0	0	13
Days With ≥ 1.0" Precipitation	0	0	0	0	0	1	1	1	0	0	0	0	3
Mean Snowfall (in.)	5.5	***6.8***	***6.4***	3.2	***trace***	***trace***	***trace***	***0.0***	***trace***	1.2	***4.9***	***5.9***	***33.9***
Maximum Snow Depth (in.)	17	***22***	***29***	19	***trace***	trace	***trace***	***0***	***trace***	5	***14***	***19***	***29***
Days With ≥ 1.0" Snow Depth	23	***21***	***12***	2	***0***	0	***0***	***0***	***0***	1	***6***	***18***	***83***

Wentworth 2 WNW *Lake County* Elevation: 1,689 ft. Latitude: 44° 01' N Longitude: 97° 00' W

	JAN	FEB	MAR	APR	MAY	JUN	JUL	AUG	SEP	OCT	NOV	DEC	YEAR
Mean Maximum Temp. (°F)	26.6	31.9	42.8	59.6	70.7	79.2	83.8	81.1	73.4	60.1	41.9	28.6	56.6
Mean Temp. (°F)	17.0	22.2	32.6	47.3	59.0	68.1	72.7	70.3	61.7	48.6	32.7	19.8	46.0
Mean Minimum Temp. (°F)	7.3	12.3	22.3	34.9	47.2	57.0	61.5	59.3	49.9	37.1	23.5	10.9	35.3
Extreme Maximum Temp. (°F)	66	68	82	95	96	104	103	101	97	92	79	64	104
Extreme Minimum Temp. (°F)	-29	-34	-17	5	23	38	44	39	25	10	-14	-29	-34
Days Maximum Temp. ≥ 90°F	0	0	0	0	1	3	6	3	1	0	0	0	14
Days Maximum Temp. ≤ 32°F	20	14	6	1	0	0	0	0	0	0	8	18	67
Days Minimum Temp. ≤ 32°F	31	27	25	12	2	0	0	0	1	10	24	31	163
Days Minimum Temp. ≤ 0°F	10	6	2	0	0	0	0	0	0	0	1	7	26
Heating Degree Days (base 65°F)	1,485	1,205	998	531	217	44	8	23	157	504	961	1,396	7,529
Cooling Degree Days (base 65°F)	0	0	0	7	37	143	253	193	65	4	0	0	702
Mean Precipitation (in.)	0.48	0.63	1.37	2.49	3.11	4.35	3.33	2.95	3.03	1.75	1.38	0.50	25.37
Extreme Maximum Daily Precip. (in.)	0.80	1.00	1.20	2.32	2.13	4.25	3.80	2.82	2.49	2.12	1.70	0.98	4.25
Days With ≥ 0.1" Precipitation	1	2	4	6	7	7	6	5	5	4	4	2	53
Days With ≥ 0.5" Precipitation	0	0	1	2	2	3	2	2	2	1	1	0	16
Days With ≥ 1.0" Precipitation	0	0	0	0	1	1	1	1	1	0	0	0	5
Mean Snowfall (in.)	6.4	6.6	7.6	4.0	0.0	0.0	0.0	0.0	trace	1.4	8.2	6.3	40.5
Maximum Snow Depth (in.)	25	31	24	10	0	0	0	0	trace	***6***	14	20	***31***
Days With ≥ 1.0" Snow Depth	21	17	11	2	0	0	0	0	0	***1***	9	17	***78***

Yankton 2 E *Yankton County* Elevation: 1,180 ft. Latitude: 42° 53' N Longitude: 97° 22' W

	JAN	FEB	MAR	APR	MAY	JUN	JUL	AUG	SEP	OCT	NOV	DEC	YEAR
Mean Maximum Temp. (°F)	31.1	35.6	46.6	61.0	72.5	82.4	87.4	85.3	77.1	63.3	46.4	33.6	60.2
Mean Temp. (°F)	20.4	24.7	35.0	48.1	59.9	70.2	75.2	72.9	63.8	50.4	35.5	23.3	48.3
Mean Minimum Temp. (°F)	9.6	13.7	23.4	35.2	47.3	57.9	62.8	60.5	50.5	37.5	24.5	12.9	36.3
Extreme Maximum Temp. (°F)	74	78	86	95	100	110	108	107	100	96	83	70	110
Extreme Minimum Temp. (°F)	-26	-25	-10	11	24	41	46	39	23	14	-13	-31	-31
Days Maximum Temp. ≥ 90°F	0	0	0	1	2	7	12	9	4	0	0	0	35
Days Maximum Temp. ≤ 32°F	16	12	5	0	0	0	0	0	0	0	5	13	51
Days Minimum Temp. ≤ 32°F	30	27	25	12	1	0	0	0	1	9	24	31	160
Days Minimum Temp. ≤ 0°F	8	5	1	0	0	0	0	0	0	0	1	5	20
Heating Degree Days (base 65°F)	1,378	1,135	922	511	199	31	4	11	129	453	880	1,288	6,941
Cooling Degree Days (base 65°F)	0	0	0	11	49	194	328	265	100	9	0	0	956
Mean Precipitation (in.)	0.52	0.69	1.72	2.99	3.71	3.78	2.76	2.93	2.52	2.34	1.37	0.78	26.11
Extreme Maximum Daily Precip. (in.)	0.99	1.80	1.70	2.15	3.50	4.20	2.60	2.20	3.25	2.73	1.88	1.25	4.20
Days With ≥ 0.1" Precipitation	1	2	4	6	7	7	5	5	5	4	3	2	51
Days With ≥ 0.5" Precipitation	0	0	1	2	3	2	2	2	2	1	1	0	16
Days With ≥ 1.0" Precipitation	0	0	0	1	1	1	1	1	1	1	0	0	7
Mean Snowfall (in.)	6.1	5.9	6.0	2.9	trace	0.0	0.0	0.0	trace	0.8	5.8	7.3	34.8
Maximum Snow Depth (in.)	18	22	15	7	trace	0	0	0	trace	5	15	23	23
Days With ≥ 1.0" Snow Depth	15	12	7	1	0	0	0	0	0	0	5	13	53

The period of record for all cooperative weather station data is 1980 – 2009. See User Guide for detailed explanation of data.

South Dakota Weather Station Rankings

Annual Extreme Maximum Temperature

Highest			Lowest		
Rank	Station Name	°F	Rank	Station Name	°F
1	Cottonwood 2 E	117	1	Custer	99
1	Pierre Municipal Arpt	117	2	Mt Rushmore Natl Mem	100
3	Cedar Butte 1 NE	116	3	Clear Lake	102
4	Dupree 15 SSE	114	4	Brookings 2 NE	103
4	Faulkton 1 NW	114	5	Castlewood	104
6	Chamberlain 5 S	113	5	Wentworth 2 WNW	104
6	Dupree	113	7	Columbia 8 N	105
6	Gettysburg	113	7	Flandreau	105
6	Maurine 10 SW	113	7	Madison 2 SE	105
10	Forestburg 3 NE	112	7	Watertown Municipal Arpt	105
10	Kennebec	112	11	Clark	106
10	McIntosh 6 SE	112	12	Canton 4 WNW	***107***
13	Rapid City Regional Arpt	111	13	Alexandria	108
14	Belle Fourche	***110***	13	Howard	108
14	Belle Fourche 22 NNW	***110***	13	Vermillion 2 SE	108
14	Huron Regional Arpt	110	16	Aberdeen Regional Arpt	109
14	Sioux Falls Foss Field	110	16	Eureka	109
14	Yankton 2 E	110	16	Fort Meade	109
19	Aberdeen Regional Arpt	109	16	Mitchell 2 N	***109***
19	Eureka	109	16	Spearfish	***109***
19	Fort Meade	109	16	Tyndall	109
19	Mitchell 2 N	***109***	22	Belle Fourche	***110***
19	Spearfish	***109***	22	Belle Fourche 22 NNW	***110***
19	Tyndall	109	22	Huron Regional Arpt	110
25	Alexandria	108	22	Sioux Falls Foss Field	110

Annual Mean Maximum Temperature

Highest			Lowest		
Rank	Station Name	°F	Rank	Station Name	°F
1	Cedar Butte 1 NE	62.5	1	Columbia 8 N	53.7
2	Belle Fourche	***61.9***	2	Brookings 2 NE	53.8
2	Vermillion 2 SE	61.9	2	Clark	53.8
4	Kennebec	61.8	2	Clear Lake	53.8
5	Cottonwood 2 E	61.5	5	Watertown Municipal Arpt	54.2
6	Fort Meade	60.6	6	Castlewood	54.3
7	Rapid City Regional Arpt	60.4	7	Flandreau	54.5
8	Yankton 2 E	60.2	8	Eureka	54.8
9	Pierre Municipal Arpt	59.8	9	Madison 2 SE	55.0
10	Tyndall	59.7	10	Aberdeen Regional Arpt	55.2
11	Alexandria	59.6	11	Gettysburg	55.6
12	Chamberlain 5 S	59.5	11	Mt Rushmore Natl Mem	55.6
12	Spearfish	***59.5***	13	Custer	***56.2***
14	Forestburg 3 NE	59.0	14	Howard	56.4
15	Maurine 10 SW	58.8	15	Wentworth 2 WNW	56.6
16	Dupree	58.7	16	Faulkton 1 NW	56.8
17	Belle Fourche 22 NNW	***58.2***	16	McIntosh 6 SE	56.8
17	Canton 4 WNW	***58.2***	18	Sioux Falls Foss Field	57.0
17	Dupree 15 SSE	58.2	19	Huron Regional Arpt	57.5
20	Mitchell 2 N	***58.1***	20	Mitchell 2 N	***58.1***
21	Huron Regional Arpt	57.5	21	Belle Fourche 22 NNW	***58.2***
22	Sioux Falls Foss Field	57.0	21	Canton 4 WNW	***58.2***
23	Faulkton 1 NW	56.8	21	Dupree 15 SSE	58.2
23	McIntosh 6 SE	56.8	24	Dupree	58.7
25	Wentworth 2 WNW	56.6	25	Maurine 10 SW	58.8

Rankings include 25 highest/lowest stations. If state has less than 25 stations, all stations are included. The period of record is 1980–2009. See User Guide for detailed explanation of data.

Annual Mean Temperature

Highest

Rank	Station Name	°F
1	Vermillion 2 SE	49.8
2	Cedar Butte 1 NE	49.3
3	Kennebec	48.6
4	Alexandria	48.5
4	Tyndall	48.5
6	Yankton 2 E	48.3
7	Fort Meade	48.2
8	Spearfish	***47.9***
9	Belle Fourche	***47.8***
9	Pierre Municipal Arpt	47.8
11	Rapid City Regional Arpt	47.4
12	Chamberlain 5 S	47.2
13	Canton 4 WNW	***47.0***
14	Forestburg 3 NE	46.9
15	Cottonwood 2 E	46.8
15	Mitchell 2 N	***46.8***
17	Dupree	46.2
17	Dupree 15 SSE	46.2
17	Sioux Falls Foss Field	46.2
20	Huron Regional Arpt	46.1
21	Mt Rushmore Natl Mem	46.0
21	Wentworth 2 WNW	46.0
23	Howard	45.4
23	Maurine 10 SW	45.4
25	Faulkton 1 NW	45.1

Lowest

Rank	Station Name	°F
1	Columbia 8 N	42.6
2	Castlewood	42.8
3	Brookings 2 NE	43.0
4	Eureka	43.3
5	Clark	43.4
6	Watertown Municipal Arpt	43.5
7	Flandreau	43.6
8	Clear Lake	43.7
9	Aberdeen Regional Arpt	43.8
10	Custer	***44.1***
11	Gettysburg	44.2
12	Madison 2 SE	44.5
13	McIntosh 6 SE	44.7
14	Belle Fourche 22 NNW	***44.9***
15	Faulkton 1 NW	45.1
16	Howard	45.4
16	Maurine 10 SW	45.4
18	Mt Rushmore Natl Mem	46.0
18	Wentworth 2 WNW	46.0
20	Huron Regional Arpt	46.1
21	Dupree	46.2
21	Dupree 15 SSE	46.2
21	Sioux Falls Foss Field	46.2
24	Cottonwood 2 E	46.8
24	Mitchell 2 N	***46.8***

Annual Mean Minimum Temperature

Highest

Rank	Station Name	°F
1	Vermillion 2 SE	37.6
2	Alexandria	37.3
3	Tyndall	37.2
4	Mt Rushmore Natl Mem	36.4
5	Spearfish	***36.3***
5	Yankton 2 E	36.3
7	Cedar Butte 1 NE	36.0
8	Fort Meade	35.8
8	Pierre Municipal Arpt	35.8
10	Canton 4 WNW	***35.7***
11	Mitchell 2 N	***35.5***
12	Kennebec	35.4
13	Sioux Falls Foss Field	35.3
13	Wentworth 2 WNW	35.3
15	Chamberlain 5 S	34.8
15	Forestburg 3 NE	34.8
17	Huron Regional Arpt	34.6
18	Howard	34.4
19	Rapid City Regional Arpt	34.3
20	Dupree 15 SSE	34.1
21	Madison 2 SE	33.9
22	Belle Fourche	***33.7***
22	Clear Lake	33.7
24	Dupree	33.6
25	Faulkton 1 NW	33.4

Lowest

Rank	Station Name	°F
1	Castlewood	31.3
2	Belle Fourche 22 NNW	***31.5***
2	Columbia 8 N	31.5
4	Custer	***31.8***
4	Eureka	31.8
6	Maurine 10 SW	31.9
7	Cottonwood 2 E	32.0
8	Brookings 2 NE	32.2
9	Aberdeen Regional Arpt	32.3
10	McIntosh 6 SE	32.5
11	Flandreau	32.6
12	Gettysburg	32.7
13	Watertown Municipal Arpt	32.8
14	Clark	32.9
15	Faulkton 1 NW	33.4
16	Dupree	33.6
17	Belle Fourche	***33.7***
17	Clear Lake	33.7
19	Madison 2 SE	33.9
20	Dupree 15 SSE	34.1
21	Rapid City Regional Arpt	34.3
22	Howard	34.4
23	Huron Regional Arpt	34.6
24	Chamberlain 5 S	34.8
24	Forestburg 3 NE	34.8

Rankings include 25 highest/lowest stations. If state has less than 25 stations, all stations are included. The period of record is 1980–2009. See User Guide for detailed explanation of data.

Annual Extreme Minimum Temperature

Highest Rank	Highest Station Name	°F	Lowest Rank	Lowest Station Name	°F
1	Sioux Falls Foss Field	-29	1	Aberdeen Regional Arpt	-45
2	Cedar Butte 1 NE	-30	1	Columbia 8 N	-45
2	Fort Meade	-30	3	Belle Fourche	***-44***
4	Madison 2 SE	-31	3	Castlewood	-44
4	Mt Rushmore Natl Mem	-31	5	Eureka	-41
4	Rapid City Regional Arpt	-31	5	Huron Regional Arpt	-41
4	Spearfish	***-31***	7	Belle Fourche 22 NNW	***-40***
4	Tyndall	-31	7	Forestburg 3 NE	-40
4	Yankton 2 E	-31	7	Mitchell 2 N	***-40***
10	Dupree 15 SSE	-32	10	Kennebec	-38
11	Clear Lake	-33	11	Brookings 2 NE	-37
11	Vermillion 2 SE	-33	12	Clark	-36
13	Alexandria	-34	12	Flandreau	-36
13	Chamberlain 5 S	-34	12	Howard	-36
13	Cottonwood 2 E	-34	12	Maurine 10 SW	-36
13	Custer	-34	16	Canton 4 WNW	***-35***
13	Dupree	-34	16	Faulkton 1 NW	-35
13	Gettysburg	-34	16	McIntosh 6 SE	-35
13	Wentworth 2 WNW	-34	16	Pierre Municipal Arpt	-35
20	Canton 4 WNW	***-35***	16	Watertown Municipal Arpt	-35
20	Faulkton 1 NW	-35	21	Alexandria	-34
20	McIntosh 6 SE	-35	21	Chamberlain 5 S	-34
20	Pierre Municipal Arpt	-35	21	Cottonwood 2 E	-34
20	Watertown Municipal Arpt	-35	21	Custer	-34
25	Clark	-36	21	Dupree	-34

July Mean Maximum Temperature

Highest Rank	Highest Station Name	°F	Lowest Rank	Lowest Station Name	°F
1	Kennebec	90.6	1	Custer	80.0
2	Cedar Butte 1 NE	90.5	1	Mt Rushmore Natl Mem	80.0
3	Cottonwood 2 E	89.8	3	Brookings 2 NE	81.7
4	Pierre Municipal Arpt	89.6	3	Clear Lake	81.7
5	Belle Fourche	88.7	5	Flandreau	82.1
6	Chamberlain 5 S	88.5	6	Castlewood	82.7
7	Dupree	87.9	6	Clark	82.7
8	Maurine 10 SW	87.6	8	Columbia 8 N	83.0
8	Vermillion 2 SE	87.6	8	Madison 2 SE	83.0
10	Rapid City Regional Arpt	87.5	10	Watertown Municipal Arpt	83.4
11	Dupree 15 SSE	87.4	11	Wentworth 2 WNW	83.8
11	Yankton 2 E	87.4	12	Aberdeen Regional Arpt	84.3
13	Alexandria	87.2	13	Eureka	84.6
14	Forestburg 3 NE	87.1	14	Canton 4 WNW	84.7
15	Fort Meade	87.0	14	Gettysburg	84.7
15	Tyndall	87.0	14	Sioux Falls Foss Field	84.7
17	Belle Fourche 22 NNW	86.5	17	Howard	84.8
17	McIntosh 6 SE	86.5	18	Spearfish	85.9
19	Faulkton 1 NW	86.1	19	Mitchell 2 N	***86.0***
19	Huron Regional Arpt	86.1	20	Faulkton 1 NW	86.1
21	Mitchell 2 N	***86.0***	20	Huron Regional Arpt	86.1
22	Spearfish	85.9	22	Belle Fourche 22 NNW	86.5
23	Howard	84.8	22	McIntosh 6 SE	86.5
24	Canton 4 WNW	84.7	24	Fort Meade	87.0
24	Gettysburg	84.7	24	Tyndall	87.0

Rankings include 25 highest/lowest stations. If state has less than 25 stations, all stations are included. The period of record is 1980–2009. See User Guide for detailed explanation of data.

January Mean Minimum Temperature

Rank	Station Name (Highest)	°F	Rank	Station Name (Lowest)	°F
1	Mt Rushmore Natl Mem	18.9	1	Columbia 8 N	0.4
2	Spearfish	16.7	2	Castlewood	1.9
3	Fort Meade	15.4	3	Aberdeen Regional Arpt	2.6
4	Custer	14.0	4	Brookings 2 NE	3.2
5	Rapid City Regional Arpt	13.3	5	Eureka	3.3
6	Cedar Butte 1 NE	12.5	5	Flandreau	3.3
7	Belle Fourche	12.0	7	Clark	3.7
8	Vermillion 2 SE	10.9	8	Watertown Municipal Arpt	3.8
9	Tyndall	10.5	9	Clear Lake	4.9
10	Pierre Municipal Arpt	10.4	10	Gettysburg	5.3
11	Alexandria	10.2	10	Madison 2 SE	5.3
12	Kennebec	10.1	12	Faulkton 1 NW	5.9
13	Belle Fourche 22 NNW	9.6	13	Howard	6.0
13	Yankton 2 E	9.6	14	McIntosh 6 SE	6.1
15	Dupree	9.5	15	Huron Regional Arpt	6.9
16	Chamberlain 5 S	9.2	16	Forestburg 3 NE	7.0
17	Dupree 15 SSE	9.1	17	Canton 4 WNW	7.3
18	Cottonwood 2 E	8.3	17	Wentworth 2 WNW	7.3
19	Maurine 10 SW	8.1	19	Mitchell 2 N	*7.4*
20	Sioux Falls Foss Field	7.7	20	Sioux Falls Foss Field	7.7
21	Mitchell 2 N	*7.4*	21	Maurine 10 SW	8.1
22	Canton 4 WNW	7.3	22	Cottonwood 2 E	8.3
22	Wentworth 2 WNW	7.3	23	Dupree 15 SSE	9.1
24	Forestburg 3 NE	7.0	24	Chamberlain 5 S	9.2
25	Huron Regional Arpt	6.9	25	Dupree	9.5

Number of Days Annually Maximum Temperature ≥ 90°F

Rank	Station Name (Highest)	Days	Rank	Station Name (Lowest)	Days
1	Cedar Butte 1 NE	50	1	Custer	6
2	Kennebec	49	2	Clear Lake	8
3	Cottonwood 2 E	48	3	Brookings 2 NE	9
4	Pierre Municipal Arpt	43	3	Mt Rushmore Natl Mem	9
5	Belle Fourche	*40*	5	Clark	11
6	Chamberlain 5 S	39	5	Columbia 8 N	11
7	Maurine 10 SW	36	7	Castlewood	12
8	Dupree 15 SSE	35	7	Flandreau	12
8	Vermillion 2 SE	35	9	Watertown Municipal Arpt	13
8	Yankton 2 E	35	10	Madison 2 SE	14
11	Dupree	34	10	Wentworth 2 WNW	14
11	Rapid City Regional Arpt	34	12	Aberdeen Regional Arpt	18
13	Fort Meade	31	13	Eureka	19
14	Tyndall	30	13	Howard	19
15	Belle Fourche 22 NNW	*29*	13	Sioux Falls Foss Field	19
15	Forestburg 3 NE	29	16	Canton 4 WNW	*20*
15	McIntosh 6 SE	29	17	Gettysburg	24
18	Alexandria	28	18	Spearfish	25
18	Faulkton 1 NW	28	19	Huron Regional Arpt	26
20	Mitchell 2 N	*27*	20	Mitchell 2 N	*27*
21	Huron Regional Arpt	26	21	Alexandria	28
22	Spearfish	25	21	Faulkton 1 NW	28
23	Gettysburg	24	23	Belle Fourche 22 NNW	*29*
24	Canton 4 WNW	*20*	23	Forestburg 3 NE	29
25	Eureka	19	23	McIntosh 6 SE	29

Rankings include 25 highest/lowest stations. If state has less than 25 stations, all stations are included. The period of record is 1980–2009. See User Guide for detailed explanation of data.

Number of Days Annually Maximum Temperature ≤ 32°F

Highest			Lowest		
Rank	Station Name	Days	Rank	Station Name	Days
1	Brookings 2 NE	80	1	Belle Fourche	***35***
1	Clark	80	2	Fort Meade	38
1	Columbia 8 N	80	3	Spearfish	39
4	Clear Lake	79	4	Cedar Butte 1 NE	40
4	Eureka	79	5	Custer	41
4	Watertown Municipal Arpt	79	5	Rapid City Regional Arpt	41
7	Castlewood	78	7	Cottonwood 2 E	44
8	Aberdeen Regional Arpt	75	8	Mt Rushmore Natl Mem	45
8	Flandreau	75	8	Vermillion 2 SE	45
10	Madison 2 SE	74	10	Kennebec	48
11	Gettysburg	72	11	Belle Fourche 22 NNW	***51***
12	Faulkton 1 NW	70	11	Yankton 2 E	51
12	Howard	70	13	Pierre Municipal Arpt	53
14	McIntosh 6 SE	68	14	Alexandria	55
15	Wentworth 2 WNW	67	14	Maurine 10 SW	55
16	Sioux Falls Foss Field	65	14	Tyndall	55
17	Huron Regional Arpt	64	17	Chamberlain 5 S	56
18	Mitchell 2 N	***62***	17	Dupree	56
19	Canton 4 WNW	***61***	19	Forestburg 3 NE	58
20	Dupree 15 SSE	60	20	Dupree 15 SSE	60
21	Forestburg 3 NE	58	21	Canton 4 WNW	***61***
22	Chamberlain 5 S	56	22	Mitchell 2 N	***62***
22	Dupree	56	23	Huron Regional Arpt	64
24	Alexandria	55	24	Sioux Falls Foss Field	65
24	Maurine 10 SW	55	25	Wentworth 2 WNW	67

Number of Days Annually Minimum Temperature ≤ 32°F

Highest			Lowest		
Rank	Station Name	Days	Rank	Station Name	Days
1	Cottonwood 2 E	188	1	Spearfish	145
2	Custer	185	2	Mt Rushmore Natl Mem	153
3	Belle Fourche 22 NNW	***183***	2	Vermillion 2 SE	153
3	Columbia 8 N	183	4	Alexandria	154
5	Castlewood	182	5	Cedar Butte 1 NE	156
5	Maurine 10 SW	182	5	Tyndall	156
7	Eureka	181	7	Fort Meade	159
8	Brookings 2 NE	180	8	Yankton 2 E	160
9	McIntosh 6 SE	179	9	Canton 4 WNW	***161***
10	Aberdeen Regional Arpt	177	9	Pierre Municipal Arpt	161
11	Flandreau	176	11	Wentworth 2 WNW	163
11	Gettysburg	176	12	Mitchell 2 N	***164***
11	Watertown Municipal Arpt	176	13	Sioux Falls Foss Field	165
14	Clark	175	14	Howard	166
15	Dupree	172	15	Forestburg 3 NE	167
15	Faulkton 1 NW	172	16	Chamberlain 5 S	168
17	Dupree 15 SSE	171	16	Huron Regional Arpt	168
17	Rapid City Regional Arpt	171	16	Kennebec	168
19	Madison 2 SE	170	19	Belle Fourche	***169***
20	Belle Fourche	***169***	19	Clear Lake	169
20	Clear Lake	169	21	Madison 2 SE	170
22	Chamberlain 5 S	168	22	Dupree 15 SSE	171
22	Huron Regional Arpt	168	22	Rapid City Regional Arpt	171
22	Kennebec	168	24	Dupree	172
25	Forestburg 3 NE	167	24	Faulkton 1 NW	172

Number of Days Annually Minimum Temperature ≤ 0°F

Highest Rank	Station Name	Days	Lowest Rank	Station Name	Days
1	Columbia 8 N	41	1	Mt Rushmore Natl Mem	12
2	Aberdeen Regional Arpt	37	2	Custer	15
2	Castlewood	37	2	Fort Meade	15
4	Brookings 2 NE	35	2	Spearfish	15
4	Clark	35	5	Cedar Butte 1 NE	17
4	Eureka	35	5	Rapid City Regional Arpt	17
4	Flandreau	35	7	Belle Fourche	*19*
4	Watertown Municipal Arpt	35	8	Tyndall	20
9	Clear Lake	33	8	Vermillion 2 SE	20
10	Faulkton 1 NW	31	8	Yankton 2 E	20
10	Gettysburg	31	11	Alexandria	21
12	Madison 2 SE	30	11	Kennebec	21
12	McIntosh 6 SE	30	11	Pierre Municipal Arpt	21
14	Howard	28	14	Dupree 15 SSE	23
15	Huron Regional Arpt	27	15	Belle Fourche 22 NNW	*24*
15	Mitchell 2 N	*27*	15	Chamberlain 5 S	24
17	Canton 4 WNW	*26*	15	Cottonwood 2 E	24
17	Forestburg 3 NE	26	15	Dupree	24
17	Maurine 10 SW	26	19	Sioux Falls Foss Field	25
17	Wentworth 2 WNW	26	20	Canton 4 WNW	*26*
21	Sioux Falls Foss Field	25	20	Forestburg 3 NE	26
22	Belle Fourche 22 NNW	*24*	20	Maurine 10 SW	26
22	Chamberlain 5 S	24	20	Wentworth 2 WNW	26
22	Cottonwood 2 E	24	24	Huron Regional Arpt	27
22	Dupree	24	24	Mitchell 2 N	*27*

Number of Annual Heating Degree Days

Highest Rank	Station Name	Num.	Lowest Rank	Station Name	Num.
1	Columbia 8 N	8,598	1	Vermillion 2 SE	6,517
2	Castlewood	8,490	2	Cedar Butte 1 NE	6,608
3	Brookings 2 NE	8,417	3	Fort Meade	6,736
4	Eureka	8,390	4	Spearfish	*6,793*
5	Clark	8,363	5	Belle Fourche	*6,863*
6	Watertown Municipal Arpt	8,307	6	Kennebec	6,883
7	Flandreau	8,245	7	Alexandria	6,891
8	Aberdeen Regional Arpt	8,239	8	Tyndall	6,892
9	Clear Lake	8,214	9	Yankton 2 E	6,941
10	Gettysburg	8,120	10	Rapid City Regional Arpt	7,004
11	Madison 2 SE	8,009	11	Pierre Municipal Arpt	7,089
12	McIntosh 6 SE	7,949	12	Chamberlain 5 S	7,248
13	Faulkton 1 NW	7,857	13	Canton 4 WNW	*7,267*
14	Belle Fourche 22 NNW	*7,816*	14	Mt Rushmore Natl Mem	7,291
15	Custer	*7,800*	15	Forestburg 3 NE	7,323
16	Howard	7,758	16	Cottonwood 2 E	7,341
17	Maurine 10 SW	7,728	17	Mitchell 2 N	*7,401*
18	Huron Regional Arpt	7,583	18	Dupree	7,500
19	Dupree 15 SSE	7,554	19	Sioux Falls Foss Field	7,511
20	Wentworth 2 WNW	7,529	20	Wentworth 2 WNW	7,529
21	Sioux Falls Foss Field	7,511	21	Dupree 15 SSE	7,554
22	Dupree	7,500	22	Huron Regional Arpt	7,583
23	Mitchell 2 N	*7,401*	23	Maurine 10 SW	7,728
24	Cottonwood 2 E	7,341	24	Howard	7,758
25	Forestburg 3 NE	7,323	25	Custer	*7,800*

Rankings include 25 highest/lowest stations. If state has less than 25 stations, all stations are included. The period of record is 1980–2009. See User Guide for detailed explanation of data.

Number of Annual Cooling Degree Days

Highest Rank	Station Name	Num.	Lowest Rank	Station Name	Num.
1	Vermillion 2 SE	1,071	1	Custer	***266***
2	Kennebec	1,022	2	Mt Rushmore Natl Mem	474
3	Cedar Butte 1 NE	988	3	Brookings 2 NE	505
4	Tyndall	972	4	Castlewood	514
5	Alexandria	970	5	Columbia 8 N	550
6	Yankton 2 E	956	6	Flandreau	552
7	Pierre Municipal Arpt	942	7	Clear Lake	567
8	Mitchell 2 N	***873***	8	Belle Fourche 22 NNW	***576***
9	Chamberlain 5 S	857	9	Clark	582
10	Forestburg 3 NE	838	9	Watertown Municipal Arpt	582
11	Canton 4 WNW	***802***	11	Eureka	584
12	Cottonwood 2 E	788	12	Aberdeen Regional Arpt	612
13	Dupree 15 SSE	787	13	Madison 2 SE	626
14	Huron Regional Arpt	777	14	Gettysburg	627
15	Sioux Falls Foss Field	766	15	McIntosh 6 SE	647
16	Dupree	748	16	Spearfish	***662***
17	Fort Meade	723	17	Maurine 10 SW	678
18	Howard	717	18	Rapid City Regional Arpt	688
19	Faulkton 1 NW	709	19	Belle Fourche	***700***
20	Wentworth 2 WNW	702	20	Wentworth 2 WNW	702
21	Belle Fourche	***700***	21	Faulkton 1 NW	709
22	Rapid City Regional Arpt	688	22	Howard	717
23	Maurine 10 SW	678	23	Fort Meade	723
24	Spearfish	***662***	24	Dupree	748
25	McIntosh 6 SE	647	25	Sioux Falls Foss Field	766

Annual Precipitation

Highest Rank	Station Name	Inches	Lowest Rank	Station Name	Inches
1	Vermillion 2 SE	26.80	1	Belle Fourche 22 NNW	***13.87***
2	Clear Lake	26.64	2	McIntosh 6 SE	16.05
3	Yankton 2 E	26.11	3	Rapid City Regional Arpt	16.10
4	Flandreau	25.73	4	Cottonwood 2 E	16.76
5	Sioux Falls Foss Field	25.53	5	Belle Fourche	***17.17***
6	Wentworth 2 WNW	25.37	6	Dupree	17.50
7	Howard	25.27	7	Dupree 15 SSE	18.04
8	Madison 2 SE	25.21	8	Maurine 10 SW	18.57
9	Canton 4 WNW	***24.82***	9	Eureka	19.45
10	Tyndall	24.64	10	Kennebec	19.54
11	Castlewood	24.45	11	Gettysburg	19.55
12	Alexandria	24.04	12	Pierre Municipal Arpt	19.64
13	Mitchell 2 N	***23.66***	13	Cedar Butte 1 NE	19.69
14	Brookings 2 NE	23.64	14	Custer	***19.89***
15	Clark	23.46	15	Spearfish	20.66
16	Chamberlain 5 S	23.30	16	Fort Meade	20.93
17	Forestburg 3 NE	22.81	17	Mt Rushmore Natl Mem	21.08
18	Huron Regional Arpt	22.60	18	Aberdeen Regional Arpt	21.35
19	Columbia 8 N	21.99	19	Faulkton 1 NW	21.43
20	Watertown Municipal Arpt	21.45	20	Watertown Municipal Arpt	21.45
21	Faulkton 1 NW	21.43	21	Columbia 8 N	21.99
22	Aberdeen Regional Arpt	21.35	22	Huron Regional Arpt	22.60
23	Mt Rushmore Natl Mem	21.08	23	Forestburg 3 NE	22.81
24	Fort Meade	20.93	24	Chamberlain 5 S	23.30
25	Spearfish	20.66	25	Clark	23.46

Rankings include 25 highest/lowest stations. If state has less than 25 stations, all stations are included. The period of record is 1980–2009. See User Guide for detailed explanation of data.

Annual Extreme Maximum Daily Precipitation

Highest Rank	Station Name	Inches	Lowest Rank	Station Name	Inches
1	Aberdeen Regional Arpt	7.62	1	Belle Fourche 22 NNW	***2.62***
1	Columbia 8 N	7.62	2	Cottonwood 2 E	2.86
3	Faulkton 1 NW	6.70	3	Maurine 10 SW	3.08
4	Chamberlain 5 S	6.01	4	Rapid City Regional Arpt	3.19
5	Brookings 2 NE	5.54	5	Custer	***3.20***
6	Alexandria	4.85	6	McIntosh 6 SE	3.28
7	Vermillion 2 SE	4.82	7	Dupree	3.38
8	Gettysburg	4.68	7	Mt Rushmore Natl Mem	3.38
9	Clear Lake	4.55	9	Tyndall	3.51
10	Clark	4.47	10	Forestburg 3 NE	3.78
11	Castlewood	4.44	11	Dupree 15 SSE	3.80
12	Mitchell 2 N	***4.35***	11	Flandreau	3.80
13	Watertown Municipal Arpt	4.32	13	Fort Meade	3.83
14	Belle Fourche	***4.25***	14	Howard	3.87
14	Eureka	4.25	15	Kennebec	4.00
14	Huron Regional Arpt	4.25	15	Pierre Municipal Arpt	4.00
14	Wentworth 2 WNW	4.25	15	Spearfish	***4.00***
18	Madison 2 SE	***4.22***	18	Cedar Butte 1 NE	4.08
18	Sioux Falls Foss Field	4.22	19	Canton 4 WNW	***4.13***
20	Yankton 2 E	4.20	20	Yankton 2 E	4.20
21	Canton 4 WNW	***4.13***	21	Madison 2 SE	***4.22***
22	Cedar Butte 1 NE	4.08	21	Sioux Falls Foss Field	4.22
23	Kennebec	4.00	23	Belle Fourche	***4.25***
23	Pierre Municipal Arpt	4.00	23	Eureka	4.25
23	Spearfish	***4.00***	23	Huron Regional Arpt	4.25

Number of Days Annually With ≥ 0.1 Inches of Precipitation

Highest Rank	Station Name	Days	Lowest Rank	Station Name	Days
1	Clear Lake	56	1	Belle Fourche 22 NNW	***35***
2	Howard	53	2	McIntosh 6 SE	37
2	Wentworth 2 WNW	53	3	Cottonwood 2 E	39
4	Mt Rushmore Natl Mem	52	3	Rapid City Regional Arpt	39
5	Forestburg 3 NE	51	5	Cedar Butte 1 NE	40
5	Madison 2 SE	51	5	Dupree	40
5	Vermillion 2 SE	51	7	Belle Fourche	***41***
5	Yankton 2 E	51	7	Dupree 15 SSE	41
9	Clark	50	9	Eureka	42
9	Flandreau	50	9	Gettysburg	42
9	Sioux Falls Foss Field	50	9	Kennebec	42
12	Alexandria	49	9	Pierre Municipal Arpt	42
12	Custer	***49***	13	Columbia 8 N	43
12	Tyndall	49	14	Aberdeen Regional Arpt	44
15	Canton 4 WNW	***48***	15	Faulkton 1 NW	45
15	Castlewood	48	15	Mitchell 2 N	***45***
15	Chamberlain 5 S	48	17	Brookings 2 NE	46
18	Fort Meade	47	17	Spearfish	46
18	Huron Regional Arpt	47	19	Fort Meade	47
18	Maurine 10 SW	47	19	Huron Regional Arpt	47
18	Watertown Municipal Arpt	47	19	Maurine 10 SW	47
22	Brookings 2 NE	46	19	Watertown Municipal Arpt	47
22	Spearfish	46	23	Canton 4 WNW	***48***
24	Faulkton 1 NW	45	23	Castlewood	48
24	Mitchell 2 N	***45***	23	Chamberlain 5 S	48

Rankings include 25 highest/lowest stations. If state has less than 25 stations, all stations are included. The period of record is 1980–2009. See User Guide for detailed explanation of data.

Number of Days Annually With ≥ 0.5 Inches of Precipitation

Highest			Lowest		
Rank	Station Name	Days	Rank	Station Name	Days
1	Howard	18	1	Belle Fourche 22 NNW	*7*
2	Clear Lake	17	2	McIntosh 6 SE	8
2	Vermillion 2 SE	17	2	Rapid City Regional Arpt	8
4	Alexandria	16	4	Belle Fourche	***10***
4	Flandreau	16	4	Cottonwood 2 E	10
4	Madison 2 SE	16	4	Custer	***10***
4	Tyndall	16	4	Dupree	10
4	Wentworth 2 WNW	16	4	Pierre Municipal Arpt	10
4	Yankton 2 E	16	4	Spearfish	10
10	Canton 4 WNW	***15***	10	Cedar Butte 1 NE	11
10	Clark	15	10	Dupree 15 SSE	11
10	Mitchell 2 N	***15***	10	Eureka	11
10	Sioux Falls Foss Field	15	10	Gettysburg	11
14	Brookings 2 NE	14	10	Kennebec	11
14	Castlewood	14	10	Maurine 10 SW	11
14	Forestburg 3 NE	14	16	Aberdeen Regional Arpt	12
17	Chamberlain 5 S	13	16	Columbia 8 N	12
17	Huron Regional Arpt	13	16	Faulkton 1 NW	12
17	Watertown Municipal Arpt	13	16	Fort Meade	12
20	Aberdeen Regional Arpt	12	16	Mt Rushmore Natl Mem	12
20	Columbia 8 N	12	21	Chamberlain 5 S	13
20	Faulkton 1 NW	12	21	Huron Regional Arpt	13
20	Fort Meade	12	21	Watertown Municipal Arpt	13
20	Mt Rushmore Natl Mem	12	24	Brookings 2 NE	14
25	Cedar Butte 1 NE	11	24	Castlewood	14

Number of Days Annually With ≥ 1.0 Inches of Precipitation

Highest			Lowest		
Rank	Station Name	Days	Rank	Station Name	Days
1	Alexandria	7	1	Belle Fourche	***1***
1	Clear Lake	7	1	Belle Fourche 22 NNW	***1***
1	Howard	7	1	Maurine 10 SW	1
1	Madison 2 SE	7	1	Rapid City Regional Arpt	1
1	Vermillion 2 SE	7	5	Cottonwood 2 E	2
1	Yankton 2 E	7	5	Custer	***2***
7	Castlewood	6	5	Dupree	2
7	Clark	6	5	Fort Meade	2
7	Flandreau	6	5	McIntosh 6 SE	2
7	Huron Regional Arpt	6	10	Cedar Butte 1 NE	3
7	Sioux Falls Foss Field	6	10	Dupree 15 SSE	3
7	Tyndall	6	10	Kennebec	3
13	Aberdeen Regional Arpt	5	10	Mt Rushmore Natl Mem	3
13	Brookings 2 NE	5	10	Pierre Municipal Arpt	3
13	Canton 4 WNW	***5***	10	Spearfish	3
13	Chamberlain 5 S	5	10	Watertown Municipal Arpt	3
13	Columbia 8 N	5	17	Faulkton 1 NW	4
13	Eureka	5	17	Gettysburg	4
13	Forestburg 3 NE	5	19	Aberdeen Regional Arpt	5
13	Mitchell 2 N	***5***	19	Brookings 2 NE	5
13	Wentworth 2 WNW	5	19	Canton 4 WNW	***5***
22	Faulkton 1 NW	4	19	Chamberlain 5 S	5
22	Gettysburg	4	19	Columbia 8 N	5
24	Cedar Butte 1 NE	3	19	Eureka	5
24	Dupree 15 SSE	3	19	Forestburg 3 NE	5

Rankings include 25 highest/lowest stations. If state has less than 25 stations, all stations are included. The period of record is 1980–2009. See User Guide for detailed explanation of data.

Annual Snowfall

Highest

Rank	Station Name	Inches
1	Custer	***62.0***
2	Mt Rushmore Natl Mem	52.6
3	Clear Lake	51.4
4	Spearfish	***45.8***
5	Sioux Falls Foss Field	43.1
6	Huron Regional Arpt	42.7
7	Wentworth 2 WNW	40.5
8	Eureka	40.2
9	Maurine 10 SW	39.6
10	Chamberlain 5 S	39.4
11	McIntosh 6 SE	38.4
12	Cedar Butte 1 NE	38.1
13	Columbia 8 N	38.0
14	Dupree 15 SSE	37.8
15	Kennebec	37.6
16	Aberdeen Regional Arpt	37.4
17	Cottonwood 2 E	36.6
18	Flandreau	36.1
19	Howard	35.3
20	Gettysburg	***34.8***
20	Yankton 2 E	34.8
22	Madison 2 SE	34.7
23	Dupree	34.5
24	Brookings 2 NE	34.4
24	Tyndall	34.4

Lowest

Rank	Station Name	Inches
1	Castlewood	28.1
2	Canton 4 WNW	***31.0***
2	Clark	31.0
4	Alexandria	31.8
5	Faulkton 1 NW	31.9
6	Forestburg 3 NE	32.2
7	Belle Fourche	***32.8***
8	Vermillion 2 SE	33.8
9	Watertown Municipal Arpt	***33.9***
10	Brookings 2 NE	34.4
10	Tyndall	34.4
12	Dupree	34.5
13	Madison 2 SE	34.7
14	Gettysburg	***34.8***
14	Yankton 2 E	34.8
16	Howard	35.3
17	Flandreau	36.1
18	Cottonwood 2 E	36.6
19	Aberdeen Regional Arpt	37.4
20	Kennebec	37.6
21	Dupree 15 SSE	37.8
22	Columbia 8 N	38.0
23	Cedar Butte 1 NE	38.1
24	McIntosh 6 SE	38.4
25	Chamberlain 5 S	39.4

Annual Maximum Snow Depth

Highest

Rank	Station Name	Inches
1	Eureka	***53***
2	Columbia 8 N	49
3	Fort Meade	48
4	Clear Lake	43
5	McIntosh 6 SE	41
6	Huron Regional Arpt	36
7	Maurine 10 SW	33
8	Dupree 15 SSE	32
8	Forestburg 3 NE	32
10	Wentworth 2 WNW	***31***
11	Aberdeen Regional Arpt	30
11	Mt Rushmore Natl Mem	30
13	Kennebec	29
13	Vermillion 2 SE	29
13	Watertown Municipal Arpt	***29***
16	Clark	28
17	Dupree	26
18	Brookings 2 NE	25
19	Canton 4 WNW	***23***
19	Yankton 2 E	23
21	Sioux Falls Foss Field	22
21	Tyndall	***22***
23	Cottonwood 2 E	21
24	Belle Fourche 22 NNW	***20***
24	Castlewood	***20***

Lowest

Rank	Station Name	Inches
1	Alexandria	***15***
2	Rapid City Regional Arpt	***16***
3	Belle Fourche 22 NNW	***20***
3	Castlewood	***20***
3	Cedar Butte 1 NE	20
3	Chamberlain 5 S	20
7	Cottonwood 2 E	21
8	Sioux Falls Foss Field	22
8	Tyndall	***22***
10	Canton 4 WNW	***23***
10	Yankton 2 E	23
12	Brookings 2 NE	25
13	Dupree	26
14	Clark	28
15	Kennebec	29
15	Vermillion 2 SE	29
15	Watertown Municipal Arpt	***29***
18	Aberdeen Regional Arpt	30
18	Mt Rushmore Natl Mem	30
20	Wentworth 2 WNW	***31***
21	Dupree 15 SSE	32
21	Forestburg 3 NE	32
23	Maurine 10 SW	33
24	Huron Regional Arpt	36
25	McIntosh 6 SE	41

Rankings include 25 highest/lowest stations. If state has less than 25 stations, all stations are included. The period of record is 1980–2009. See User Guide for detailed explanation of data.

Number of Days Annually With ≥ 1.0 Inch Snow Depth

Highest			Lowest		
Rank	Station Name	Days	Rank	Station Name	Days
1	Columbia 8 N	93	1	Belle Fourche 22 NNW	***32***
2	Clear Lake	88	2	Alexandria	38
3	Watertown Municipal Arpt	***83***	3	Fort Meade	40
4	McIntosh 6 SE	82	4	Kennebec	41
5	Clark	78	4	Vermillion 2 SE	41
5	Wentworth 2 WNW	***78***	6	Spearfish	***45***
7	Eureka	***73***	7	Tyndall	***46***
8	Brookings 2 NE	70	8	Rapid City Regional Arpt	***47***
8	Sioux Falls Foss Field	70	9	Cedar Butte 1 NE	53
10	Aberdeen Regional Arpt	69	9	Yankton 2 E	53
10	Canton 4 WNW	***69***	11	Mt Rushmore Natl Mem	57
12	Maurine 10 SW	68	12	Cottonwood 2 E	58
13	Forestburg 3 NE	67	13	Chamberlain 5 S	60
13	Huron Regional Arpt	67	13	Dupree	60
15	Castlewood	66	15	Dupree 15 SSE	61
16	Dupree 15 SSE	61	16	Castlewood	66
17	Chamberlain 5 S	60	17	Forestburg 3 NE	67
17	Dupree	60	17	Huron Regional Arpt	67
19	Cottonwood 2 E	58	19	Maurine 10 SW	68
20	Mt Rushmore Natl Mem	57	20	Aberdeen Regional Arpt	69
21	Cedar Butte 1 NE	53	20	Canton 4 WNW	***69***
21	Yankton 2 E	53	22	Brookings 2 NE	70
23	Rapid City Regional Arpt	***47***	22	Sioux Falls Foss Field	70
24	Tyndall	***46***	24	Eureka	***73***
25	Spearfish	***45***	25	Clark	78

Rankings include 25 highest/lowest stations. If state has less than 25 stations, all stations are included. The period of record is 1980–2009. See User Guide for detailed explanation of data.

Significant Storm Events in South Dakota: 2000 – 2009

Location or County	Date	Type	Mag.	Deaths	Injuries	Property Damage ($mil.)	Crop Damage ($mil.)
Lawrence	08/01/00	Thunderstorm Wind	109 mph	0	6	9.5	0.0
Davison	08/05/00	Thunderstorm Wind	120 mph	0	10	8.0	0.0
Haakon	06/09/01	Thunderstorm Wind	81 mph	0	0	3.0	0.0
Minnehaha	06/12/01	Flash Flood	na	0	0	5.0	0.0
Davison	07/24/02	Hail	2.50 in.	0	0	3.0	0.0
Brookings	07/28/02	Thunderstorm Wind	90 mph	0	0	3.0	0.0
Turner	06/24/03	Tornado	F2	0	0	3.0	0.0
Kingsbury	06/24/03	Tornado	F4	0	4	3.0	0.0
Minnehaha	06/24/03	Tornado	F1	0	0	2.5	0.0
Minnehaha	06/16/04	Flash Flood	na	0	0	10.0	0.0
Southeast Central South Dakota	11/27/05	Ice Storm	na	0	0	15.0	0.0
Northwest South Dakota	04/18/06	Winter Storm	na	0	0	8.0	0.0
Beadle	08/24/06	Tornado	F3	0	2	15.0	0.0
Brown	05/05/07	Flash Flood	na	0	0	5.0	0.0
Custer	08/17/07	Flash Flood	na	0	0	3.0	0.0
Northwest South Dakota	03/23/09	Blizzard	na	0	0	6.5	0.0
Northwest South Dakota	03/23/09	Blizzard	na	0	0	4.2	0.0
Yankton	07/09/09	Hail	2.50 in.	0	0	5.0	7.0
Hutchinson	07/09/09	Hail	1.75 in.	0	0	3.0	3.0
Yankton	07/09/09	Hail	1.75 in.	0	0	3.0	0.0

Note: Deaths, injuries, and damages are date and location specific.

TENNESSEE

PHYSICAL FEATURES. The topography of Tennessee is quite varied, stretching from the lowlands of the Mississippi Valley to the mountain peaks in the east. The westernmost part of the State, between the bluffs overlooking the Mississippi River and the western valley of the Tennessee River, is a region of gently rolling plains sloping gradually from 200 to 250 feet in the west to about 600 feet above sea level in the hills overlooking the Tennessee River. The hilly Highland Rim, in a wide circle touching the Tennessee River Valley on the west and the Cumberland Plateau on the east, together with the enclosed Central Basin makes up the whole of Middle Tennessee. The Highland Rim ranges from about 600 feet in elevation along the Tennessee River to 1,000 feet in the east and rises 300 to 400 feet above the Central Basin. The Cumberland Plateau, with an average elevation of 2,000 feet above sea level, extends roughly northeast-southwest across the State in a belt 30 to 50 miles wide, being bounded on the west by the Highland Rim and overlooking the Great Valley of East Tennessee on the east. The Great Valley, paralleling the Plateau to the west and the Great Smoky Mountains to the east, is a funnel-shaped valley varying in width from about 30 miles in the south to about 90 miles in the north. Within the valley, which slopes from 1,500 feet in the north to 700 feet above sea level in the south, are a series of northeast-southwest ridges. Along the Tennessee-North Carolina border lie the Great Smoky Mountains, the most rugged and elevated portion of Tennessee, with numerous peaks from 4,000 to 6,000 feet above sea level.

Tennessee, except for a small area east of Chattanooga, lies entirely within the drainage of the Mississippi River system. The extreme western section of the State is drained through several relatively small rivers directly into the Mississippi River. Otherwise drainage is into either the Cumberland or Tennessee Rivers, both of which flow northward near the end of their courses to join the Ohio River along the Kentucky-Illinois border.

TEMPERATURE. Most aspects of the State's climate are related to the widely varying topography within its borders. The decrease of temperature with elevation is quite apparent, averaging 3°F. per 1,000 feet increase in elevation. Thus higher portions of the State, such as the Cumberland Plateau and the mountains of the east, have lower average temperatures than the Great Valley of East Tennessee, which they flank, and other lower parts of the State. In the Great Valley temperature increases from north to south. Across the State, the average annual temperature varies from over 62°F. in the extreme southwest to near 45°F. atop the highest peaks of the east. While most of the State can be described as having a warm, humid summer and a mild winter, this must be qualified to include variations with elevation. Thus with increasing elevations, summers become cooler and more pleasant while winters become colder and more blustery.

Length of growing season (freeze-free period) is linked to topography in a way similar to temperature, varying from 237 days at low-lying Memphis to near 130 days on the highest mountains in the east. Most of the State is included in the range.

PRECIPITATION. Since the principal source of moist air for this area is the Gulf region, there exists a gradual decrease of average precipitation from south to north. This effect is largely obscured, however, by the overruling influence of topography. Air forced to ascend cools and condenses out a portion of its moisture charge; thus average precipitation is generally greater at higher elevations. This is apparent in all parts of the State. In West Tennessee average annual precipitation ranges from 46 to 54 inches, increasing from Mississippi bottomlands to the slight hills farther east. In Middle Tennessee the variation is from a minimum of 45 inches in the Central Basin to 50 to 55 inches in the surrounding hilly Highland Rim. Over the elevated Cumberland Plateau average annual precipitation is generally from 50 to 55 inches. In contrast, average annual precipitation in the Great Valley of East Tennessee increases from near 40 inches in northern portions to over 50 inches in the south. The northern minimum, lowest for the entire State, results from the shielding influence of the Great Smoky Mountains to the southeast and the Cumberland Plateau to the northwest. The mountainous eastern border of the State is its wettest part, having average annual precipitation ranging up to about 80 inches on the higher, well-exposed peaks of the Smokies.

Over most of the State greatest precipitation occurs during the winter and early spring due to the more frequent passage of large scale storms over and near the State during those months. A secondary maximum of precipitation occurs in midsummer in response to shower and thundershower activity. This is especially pronounced in the mountains of the east where July rainfall exceeds the precipitation of any other month. Lightest precipitation, observed in the fall, is brought about by the maximum occurrence of slow moving, rain suppressing high pressure areas during that season. Although all parts of Tennessee are generally well supplied with precipitation, there occurs on the average one or more prolonged dry spells each year during summer and fall.

The most important flood season is during the winter and early spring (December through March) when the frequent migratory storms bring general rains of high intensity. During this period both widespread flooding and local flash floods can occur. During summer, heavy thunderstorm rains frequently result in local flash flooding. In the fall, while flood producing rains are rare, hurricanes on occasion cause serious floods in the east.

Average snowfall varies from four to six inches in southern and western parts of the State and in most of the Great Valley of East Tennessee, to more than 10 inches over the northern Cumberland Plateau and the mountains of the east. Over most of the State, due to relatively mild winter temperatures, a snow cover rarely persists for more than a few days.

STORMS. Severe storms are relatively infrequent in Tennessee, being east of the center of tornado activity, south of most blizzard conditions, and too far inland to be often affected by hurricanes. On the average four or five tornadoes are observed in the State each year, with greatest frequency in March, when one or two usually occur. Tornado occurrence is not evenly distributed throughout the State, being largely confined to areas west of the Cumberland Plateau. Damage from tropical storms is rare, occurring only about once every 18 years. Hailstorms are observed two or three times a year and damaging glaze storms occur in the State every five or six years. Thunderstorms are frequent and severe thunderstorms with damaging winds are experienced at scattered locations throughout the State each year during the warm season.

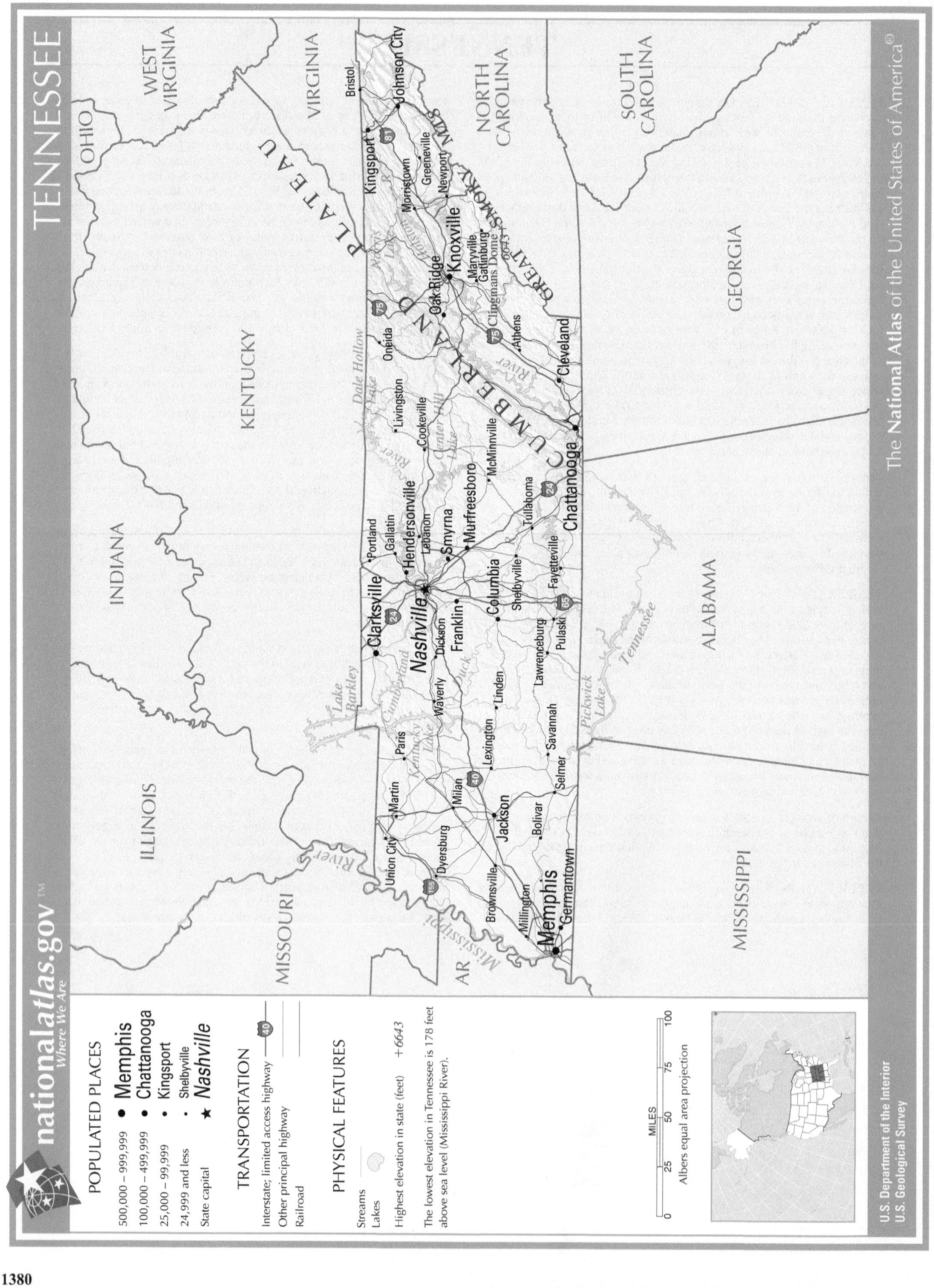
TENNESSEE
nationalatlas.gov™
Where We Are
POPULATED PLACES
500,000 – 999,999 Memphis
100,000 – 499,999 Chattanooga
25,000 – 99,999 Kingsport
24,999 and less Shelbyville
State capital Nashville
TRANSPORTATION
Interstate; limited access highway
Other principal highway
Railroad
PHYSICAL FEATURES
Streams
Lakes
Highest elevation in state (feet) +6643
The lowest elevation in Tennessee is 178 feet above sea level (Mississippi River).
MILES
0 25 50 75 100
Albers equal area projection
U.S. Department of the Interior
U.S. Geological Survey
The National Atlas of the United States of America®
OHIO
WEST VIRGINIA
VIRGINIA
KENTUCKY
INDIANA
ILLINOIS
MISSOURI
AR
NORTH CAROLINA
SOUTH CAROLINA
GEORGIA
ALABAMA
MISSISSIPPI
CUMBERLAND PLATEAU
GREAT SMOKY MTS
Clingmans Dome +6643
Bristol
Kingsport
Johnson City
Greeneville
Morristown
Newport
Knoxville
Maryville
Gatlinburg
Oak Ridge
Oneida
Athens
Cleveland
Chattanooga
Livingston
Cookeville
McMinnville
Tullahoma
Murfreesboro
Smyrna
Lebanon
Hendersonville
Gallatin
Portland
Clarksville
Nashville
Dickson
Franklin
Columbia
Shelbyville
Fayetteville
Lawrenceburg
Pulaski
Linden
Waverly
Paris
Lexington
Savannah
Selmer
Milan
Martin
Union City
Dyersburg
Jackson
Bolivar
Brownsville
Millington
Memphis
Germantown
Dale Hollow Lake
Center Hill Lake
Norris Lake
Lake Barkley
Kentucky Lake
Pickwick Lake
Mississippi River
Tennessee River
Cumberland River
Duck River

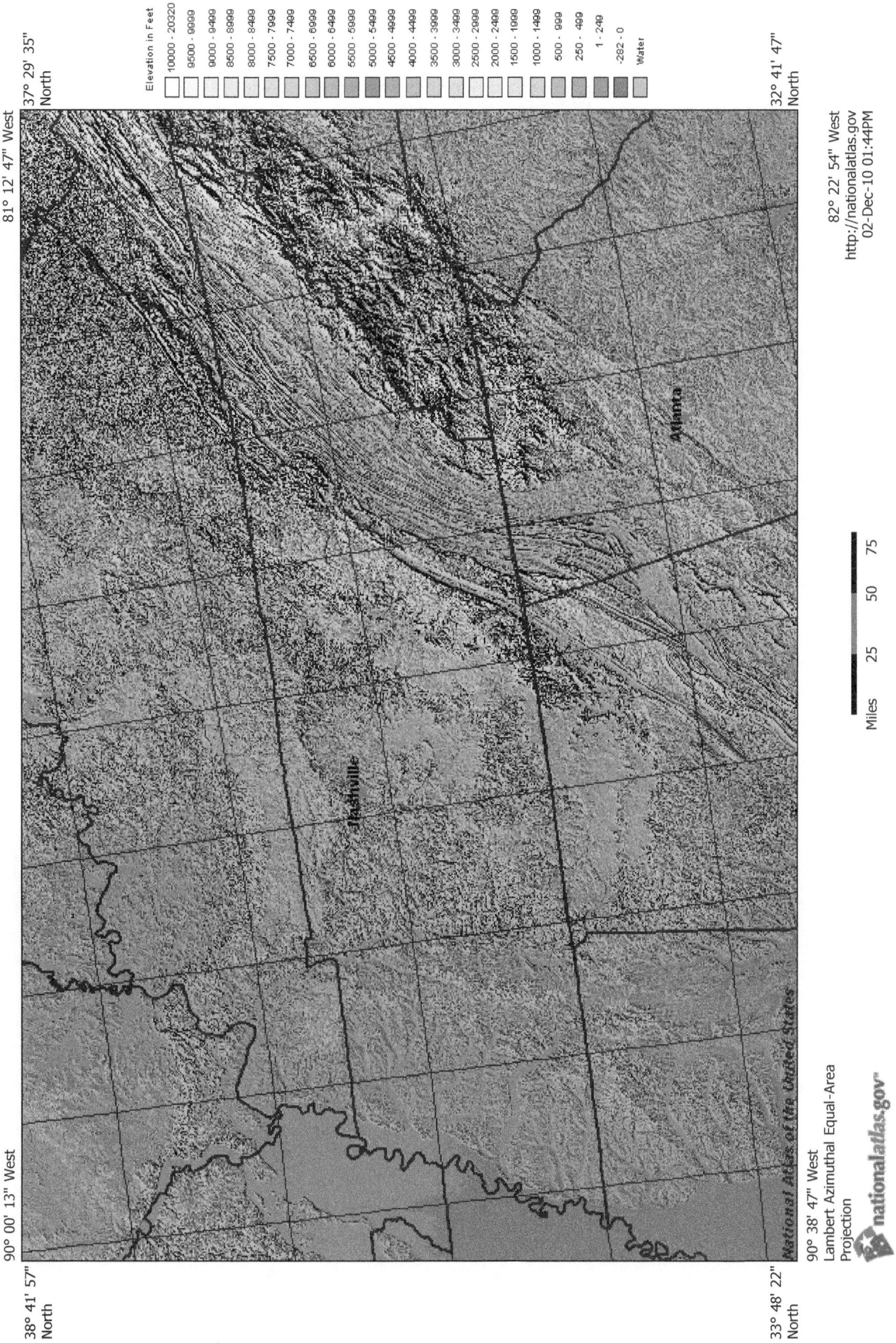
81° 12' 47" West
37° 29' 35" North
90° 00' 13" West
38° 41' 57" North
32° 41' 47" North
33° 48' 22" North
82° 22' 54" West
http://nationalatlas.gov
02-Dec-10 01:44PM
90° 38' 47" West
Lambert Azimuthal Equal-Area
Projection
nationalatlas.gov
National Atlas of the United States
Elevation in Feet
10000 - 20320
9500 - 9999
9000 - 9499
8500 - 8999
8000 - 8499
7500 - 7999
7000 - 7499
6500 - 6999
6000 - 6499
5500 - 5999
5000 - 5499
4500 - 4999
4000 - 4499
3500 - 3999
3000 - 3499
2500 - 2999
2000 - 2499
1500 - 1999
1000 - 1499
500 - 999
250 - 499
1 - 249
-282 - 0
Water
Miles
25
50
75
Nashville
Atlanta

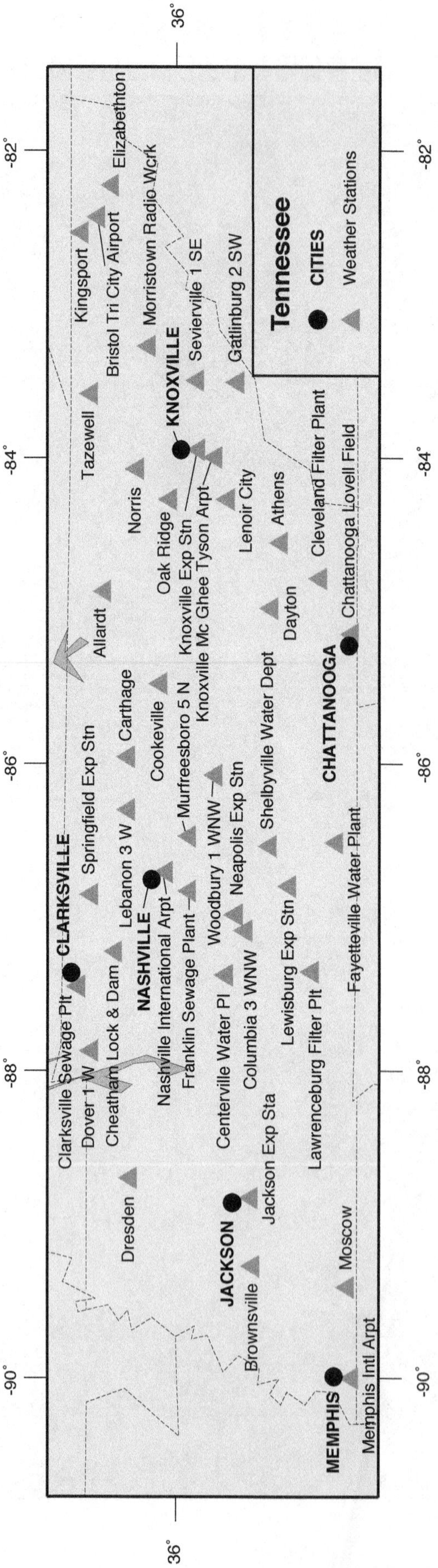
Tennessee
CITIES
Weather Stations
36°
-82°
-84°
-86°
-88°
-90°
MEMPHIS
Memphis Intl Arpt
Brownsville
JACKSON
Moscow
Dresden
Jackson Exp Sta
Lawrenceburg Filter Plt
Clarksville Sewage Plt
Dover 1 W
Cheatham Lock & Dam
Nashville International Arpt
Franklin Sewage Plant
Centerville Water Pl
Columbia 3 WNW
Lewisburg Exp Stn
Fayetteville Water Plant
NASHVILLE
CLARKSVILLE
Woodbury 1 WNW
Neapolis Exp Stn
Lebanon 3 W
Springfield Exp Stn
Murfreesboro 5 N
Shelbyville Water Dept
CHATTANOOGA
Cookeville
Carthage
Knoxville Mc Ghee Tyson Arpt
Knoxville Exp Stn
Allardt
Oak Ridge
Dayton
Chattanooga Lovell Field
Cleveland Filter Plant
Athens
Lenoir City
Norris
Tazewell
KNOXVILLE
Sevierville 1 SE
Gatlinburg 2 SW
Morristown Radio Wcrk
Bristol Tri City Airport
Kingsport
Elizabethton

Tennessee Weather Stations by County

County	Station Name
Anderson	Norris Oak Ridge
Bedford	Shelbyville Water Dept
Blount	Knoxville McGhee Tyson Arpt
Bradley	Cleveland Filter Plant
Cannon	Woodbury 1 WNW
Carter	Elizabethton
Cheatham	Cheatham Lock and Dam
Claiborne	Tazewell
Davidson	Nashville International Arpt
Fayette	Moscow
Fentress	Allardt
Hamblen	Morristown Radio WCRK
Hamilton	Chattanooga Lovell Field
Haywood	Brownsville
Hickman	Centerville Water Pl
Knox	Knoxville Exp Stn
Lawrence	Lawrenceburg Filter Plant
Lincoln	Fayetteville Water Plant
Loudon	Lenoir City
Madison	Jackson Exp Station
Marshall	Lewisburg Exp Stn
Maury	Columbia 3 WNW Neapolis Exp Stn
Mcminn	Athens
Montgomery	Clarksville Sewage Plant
Putnam	Cookeville
Rhea	Dayton
Robertson	Springfield Exp Stn
Rutherford	Murfreesboro 5 N
Sevier	Gatlinburg 2 SW Sevierville 1 SE
Shelby	Memphis Intl Arpt
Smith	Carthage

County	Station Name
Stewart	Dover 1 W
Sullivan	Bristol Tri City Airport Kingsport
Weakley	Dresden
Williamson	Franklin Sewage Plant
Wilson	Lebanon 3 W

See User Guide for station inclusion criteria.

Tennessee Weather Stations by City

City	Station Name	Miles
Bartlett	West Memphis, AR	20.5
	Memphis Intl Arpt	14.8
Brentwood	Franklin Sewage Plant	5.4
	Murfreesboro 5 N	23.4
	Nashville International Arpt	10.2
	Neapolis Exp Stn	22.2
Bristol	Bristol Tri City Airport	14.0
	Elizabethton	14.6
	Kingsport	19.6
	Abingdon 3 S, VA	13.8
Chattanooga	Chattanooga Lovell Field	3.2
Clarksville	Hopkinsville, KY	21.5
	Cheatham Lock and Dam	19.0
	Clarksville Sewage Plant	1.3
Cleveland	Athens	23.9
	Chattanooga Lovell Field	21.2
	Cleveland Filter Plant	4.8
	Dayton	21.2
Collierville	Memphis Intl Arpt	18.1
	Moscow	14.9
Columbia	Centerville Water Pl	23.3
	Columbia 3 WNW	3.0
	Lewisburg Exp Stn	19.7
	Neapolis Exp Stn	8.1
Cookeville	Cookeville	4.6
Farragut	Knoxville Exp Stn	12.9
	Knoxville McGhee Tyson Arpt	11.8
	Lenoir City	8.0
	Norris	24.4
	Oak Ridge	9.4
Franklin	Columbia 3 WNW	23.0
	Franklin Sewage Plant	1.5
	Nashville International Arpt	16.3
	Neapolis Exp Stn	16.3
Gallatin	Lebanon 3 W	11.3
	Nashville International Arpt	22.4
	Springfield Exp Stn	22.9
Germantown	West Memphis, AR	22.3
	Memphis Intl Arpt	12.2
	Moscow	21.2
Hendersonville	Lebanon 3 W	14.3
	Nashville International Arpt	13.2
	Springfield Exp Stn	17.7
Jackson	Brownsville	24.2
	Jackson Exp Station	2.1
Johnson City	Bristol Tri City Airport	9.8
	Elizabethton	8.2
	Kingsport	15.9

City	Station Name	Miles
Kingsport	Bristol Tri City Airport	9.9
	Elizabethton	21.4
	Kingsport	2.1
Knoxville	Knoxville Exp Stn	6.3
	Knoxville McGhee Tyson Arpt	11.1
	Lenoir City	22.1
	Norris	17.9
	Oak Ridge	16.9
	Sevierville 1 SE	23.6
La Vergne	Franklin Sewage Plant	17.7
	Lebanon 3 W	18.5
	Murfreesboro 5 N	12.1
	Nashville International Arpt	9.7
Lebanon	Carthage	20.4
	Lebanon 3 W	3.4
	Murfreesboro 5 N	20.7
	Nashville International Arpt	21.7
Maryville	Gatlinburg 2 SW	24.7
	Knoxville Exp Stn	9.3
	Knoxville McGhee Tyson Arpt	4.7
	Lenoir City	17.0
	Oak Ridge	23.5
	Sevierville 1 SE	24.7
Memphis	West Memphis, AR	12.9
	Memphis Intl Arpt	5.1
Morristown	Morristown Radio WCRK	1.4
	Tazewell	22.9
Murfreesboro	Murfreesboro 5 N	4.3
	Nashville International Arpt	24.5
	Woodbury 1 WNW	17.1
Nashville	Franklin Sewage Plant	15.0
	Lebanon 3 W	22.2
	Nashville International Arpt	4.2
	Springfield Exp Stn	22.9
Oak Ridge	Knoxville Exp Stn	19.6
	Knoxville McGhee Tyson Arpt	20.7
	Lenoir City	16.1
	Norris	17.5
	Oak Ridge	1.3
Shelbyville	Fayetteville Water Plant	23.7
	Lewisburg Exp Stn	20.1
	Shelbyville Water Dept	1.9
Smyrna	Franklin Sewage Plant	19.5
	Lebanon 3 W	19.6
	Murfreesboro 5 N	8.7
	Nashville International Arpt	13.3
Spring Hill	Columbia 3 WNW	12.5
	Franklin Sewage Plant	13.2
	Lewisburg Exp Stn	24.7
	Neapolis Exp Stn	5.2

Note: Miles is the distance between the geographic center of the city and the weather station.

See User Guide for station inclusion criteria.

Tennessee Weather Stations by Elevation

Feet	Station Name
1,753	Elizabethton
1,674	Allardt
1,500	Bristol Tri City Airport
1,454	Gatlinburg 2 SW
1,365	Tazewell
1,359	Morristown Radio WCRK
1,284	Kingsport
1,109	Norris
1,089	Cookeville
961	Knoxville McGhee Tyson Arpt
939	Athens
930	Sevierville 1 SE
904	Oak Ridge
870	Lawrenceburg Filter Plant
865	Dayton
830	Knoxville Exp Stn
799	Cleveland Filter Plant
787	Lewisburg Exp Stn
785	Lenoir City
759	Shelbyville Water Dept
750	Woodbury 1 WNW
745	Springfield Exp Stn
725	Fayetteville Water Plant
700	Neapolis Exp Stn
670	Chattanooga Lovell Field
660	Centerville Water Pl
654	Franklin Sewage Plant
649	Columbia 3 WNW
580	Nashville International Arpt
549	Murfreesboro 5 N
535	Lebanon 3 W
515	Carthage
475	Dover 1 W
450	Dresden
399	Jackson Exp Station
392	Cheatham Lock and Dam
381	Clarksville Sewage Plant
334	Moscow
330	Brownsville
265	Memphis Intl Arpt

See User Guide for station inclusion criteria.

Bristol Tri-City Airport

The Weather Service Office is located an almost equal distance of 15 miles in the middle of a geographical triangle between the cities of Bristol, Tennessee-Virginia, Kingsport and Johnson City, Tennessee, and is more commonly known as the Tri-City Area. This location is situated in the extreme upper East Tennessee Valley. The terrain immediately surrounding the station ranges from gently rolling on the east and south to very hilly on the west and north. Mountain ranges begin about 10 miles to the southeast and about 15 miles to the west and north, with many peaks and ridges rising to 4,000 feet, and some to 6,000 feet toward the southeast.

This section does not lie directly within any of the principal storm tracks that cross the country, but comes under the influence of storm centers that pass along the Gulf Coast and then up the Atlantic Coast toward the northeast. Being quite varied, the topography has considerable influence on the weather. Moist air from the east is forced up the slopes of the mountains causing much of the moisture to be precipitated before the air mass reaches the Bristol area. The same process occurs to a lesser extent when air masses move over the smaller mountain ranges to the west and north. The maximum monthly precipitation occurs in July, usually from afternoon and early evening thunderstorms. A second maximum of precipitation occurs in the late winter months, due mainly to moist air associated with storm centers to the south or northeast. Annual precipitation amounts recorded in mountainous sections to the east and southeast are almost double what they are in the immediate vicinity.

Lowest temperatures normally occur during the early morning hours, but rise rapidly during the morning hours. Periods of cold weather are generally associated with air flow from winter storm centers near the northeast coast. Periods of unusually high temperatures occur most frequently when Gulf air associated with the Bermuda high pressure system dominates the area.

Snowfall seldom occurs before November and rarely remains on the ground for more than a few days. However, mountains to the east and south of the station are frequently well blanketed with snow for much longer periods of time.

Agricultural activies within this area include such staple crops as tobacco, beans, and hay. The last freezing temperature in spring normally occurs in late April, and the first in autumn around mid-October. The growing season of 180 days, usually coupled with ample sunshine and rainfall, permits a second planting and harvesting of some staple crops.

Bristol Tri-City Airport *Sullivan County* Elevation: 1,500 ft. Latitude: 36° 28' N Longitude: 82° 24' W

	JAN	FEB	MAR	APR	MAY	JUN	JUL	AUG	SEP	OCT	NOV	DEC	YEAR
Mean Maximum Temp. (°F)	45.5	50.0	59.0	67.8	75.8	82.8	85.4	85.1	79.3	69.1	58.6	48.4	67.2
Mean Temp. (°F)	35.8	39.3	47.0	55.5	63.8	71.7	74.9	74.1	67.6	56.6	46.9	38.4	56.0
Mean Minimum Temp. (°F)	26.0	28.6	35.0	43.1	51.7	60.5	64.5	63.2	55.9	44.0	35.2	28.3	44.7
Extreme Maximum Temp. (°F)	76	79	83	89	91	96	100	101	97	89	81	76	101
Extreme Minimum Temp. (°F)	-21	-15	-2	21	30	40	48	43	34	24	11	-6	-21
Days Maximum Temp. ≥ 90°F	0	0	0	0	0	3	6	6	2	0	0	0	17
Days Maximum Temp. ≤ 32°F	4	2	0	0	0	0	0	0	0	0	0	2	8
Days Minimum Temp. ≤ 32°F	23	19	13	4	0	0	0	0	0	3	14	21	97
Days Minimum Temp. ≤ 0°F	0	0	0	0	0	0	0	0	0	0	0	0	0
Heating Degree Days (base 65°F)	899	720	551	292	100	8	0	1	45	269	536	819	4,240
Cooling Degree Days (base 65°F)	0	0	1	12	68	216	315	292	130	15	1	0	1,050
Mean Precipitation (in.)	3.38	3.42	3.56	3.37	3.80	3.84	4.77	3.34	2.96	2.09	3.01	3.32	40.86
Maximum Precipitation (in.)*	9.2	7.8	9.6	5.8	9.7	7.0	9.7	7.1	7.1	5.6	5.9	6.8	54.5
Minimum Precipitation (in.)*	1.4	0.3	1.3	0.2	1.3	0.8	0.7	0.5	0.5	0.1	1.1	0.2	30.7
Extreme Maximum Daily Precip. (in.)	2.29	2.48	2.95	2.23	2.86	2.22	2.85	3.50	3.15	2.22	2.27	2.66	3.50
Days With ≥ 0.1" Precipitation	7	7	8	8	8	8	9	7	6	5	6	7	86
Days With ≥ 0.5" Precipitation	2	2	2	2	3	3	4	2	2	1	2	2	27
Days With ≥ 1.0" Precipitation	1	1	1	0	1	1	1	1	1	0	1	0	9
Mean Snowfall (in.)	***4.6***	***3.3***	***1.5***	***1.1***	***trace***	***trace***	***0.0***	***0.0***	***trace***	***0.1***	***0.2***	***2.1***	***12.9***
Maximum Snowfall (in.)*	22	20	28	15	trace	0	0	0	0	1	18	13	48
Maximum 24-hr. Snowfall (in.)*	9	10	13	10	trace	0	0	0	0	1	16	9	16
Maximum Snow Depth (in.)	***10***	***17***	***9***	***11***	***trace***	***trace***	***0***	***0***	***trace***	***1***	***1***	***6***	***17***
Days With ≥ 1.0" Snow Depth	***4***	***3***	***1***	***0***	***0***	***0***	***0***	***0***	***0***	***0***	***0***	***1***	***9***
Thunderstorm Days*	< 1	1	2	4	7	8	9	7	3	1	< 1	< 1	42
Foggy Days*	13	10	9	8	15	17	20	22	18	15	13	12	172
Predominant Sky Cover*	OVR	OVR	OVR	OVR	OVR	OVR	OVR	SCT	OVR	CLR	OVR	OVR	OVR
Mean Relative Humidity 7am (%)*	82	81	80	80	87	89	91	93	92	89	84	82	86
Mean Relative Humidity 4pm (%)*	59	54	49	46	52	54	57	57	54	50	53	59	54
Mean Dewpoint (°F)*	27	28	34	41	53	61	65	64	58	46	36	29	45
Prevailing Wind Direction*	WSW	WSW	WSW	WSW	WSW	WSW	WSW	NE	NE	NE	WSW	WSW	WSW
Prevailing Wind Speed (mph)*	10	12	12	12	9	8	8	5	5	5	10	10	9
Maximum Wind Gust (mph)*	60	53	58	68	60	59	87	54	54	43	53	52	87

Note: (*) Period of record is 1948-1995

The period of record for National Weather Service station data is 1980 – 2009 except where noted. See User Guide for detailed explanation of data.

Chattanooga Lovell Field

Chattanooga is located in the southern portion of the Great Valley of Tennessee, an area of the Tennessee River between the Cumberland Mountains to the west and the Appalachian Mountains to the east. The Tennessee River approaches Chattanooga from the northeast and forms a loop southwest to west to northwest of the city at an elevation of about 630 feet above mean sea level. Most of the city lies on the south side of the river. On the north and southwest sides, the terrain rises abruptly to about 1,200 feet above the river. This complex topography results in marked variations in air drainage, wind, and minimum temperatures within short distances. In winter the Cumberland Mountains have a moderating influence on the local climate by retarding the flow of cold air from the north and west.

Chattanooga enjoys a moderate climate, characterized by cool winters and quite warm summers. Because of the sheltering effect of the mountains, winter temperatures average about 3.0 degrees warmer than at stations on the southern Cumberland Plateau section of the state. Winter weather is changeable and alternates between cool spells with an occasional cold period, but extreme cold is rare. Temperatures fall as low as the freezing point on a little over one-half of the winter days, but temperatures below zero rarely occur. Snowfall from year to year is highly variable with some winters having little or none. Heavy snowfalls have occurred, but any accumulation of snow seldom remains on the ground more than a few days. Ice storms of freezing rain or glaze are not uncommon, occasionally midwinter icing becomes severe enough to do some damage in the area.

Summer temperatures are either in the high 80s or low 90s and temperatures over 100 degrees are unusual. Most afternoon temperatures are modified by thunderstorms. Temperatures frequently plunge 10 to 15 degrees in a matter of minutes during one of these showers.

Precipitation in the Chattanooga area is well distributed throughout the year with the greater amounts in wintertime when cyclonic storms from the Gulf of Mexico reach the area with greater intensity and frequency. A second peak rainfall period generally occurs in July, principally from thunderstorms that move into the area from the south and southwest. During any year there are usually a few of these storms that can be classified as severe, with hail and damaging winds.

Based on the 1951-1980 period, the growing season averages 228 days. The average occurrence of last freezing temperature in spring is early April and the average first freezing temperature in the fall is early November.

Chattanooga Lovell Field *Hamilton County* Elevation: 670 ft. Latitude: 35° 02' N Longitude: 85° 12' W

	JAN	FEB	MAR	APR	MAY	JUN	JUL	AUG	SEP	OCT	NOV	DEC	YEAR
Mean Maximum Temp. (°F)	50.3	54.9	63.6	72.4	79.7	86.9	90.2	89.6	83.0	72.7	62.1	52.5	71.5
Mean Temp. (°F)	40.6	44.4	52.1	60.3	68.4	76.2	80.0	79.3	72.4	61.2	51.1	42.9	60.7
Mean Minimum Temp. (°F)	30.9	33.8	40.6	48.1	57.1	65.5	69.7	69.0	61.8	49.7	40.1	33.2	50.0
Extreme Maximum Temp. (°F)	77	79	88	92	94	101	105	105	101	91	84	77	105
Extreme Minimum Temp. (°F)	-10	2	9	25	38	46	57	53	40	28	19	-2	-10
Days Maximum Temp. ≥ 90°F	0	0	0	0	2	11	18	17	5	0	0	0	53
Days Maximum Temp. ≤ 32°F	2	1	0	0	0	0	0	0	0	0	0	1	4
Days Minimum Temp. ≤ 32°F	18	13	6	1	0	0	0	0	0	0	8	16	62
Days Minimum Temp. ≤ 0°F	0	0	0	0	0	0	0	0	0	0	0	0	0
Heating Degree Days (base 65°F)	749	577	400	174	36	1	0	0	14	158	412	681	3,202
Cooling Degree Days (base 65°F)	0	0	7	39	150	345	471	451	242	48	3	1	1,757
Mean Precipitation (in.)	4.87	4.79	5.40	4.07	4.06	4.07	4.86	3.41	4.16	3.25	4.88	4.88	52.70
Maximum Precipitation (in.)*	11.0	9.7	16.3	11.9	9.2	9.4	11.9	7.5	14.2	9.9	13.6	13.7	73.7
Minimum Precipitation (in.)*	0.9	0.7	1.2	1.0	1.1	0.6	0.2	0.6	0.5	0.2	0.9	0.9	34.9
Extreme Maximum Daily Precip. (in.)	3.79	3.11	6.19	3.36	3.28	3.72	3.33	3.28	5.24	2.79	2.72	3.69	6.19
Days With ≥ 0.1" Precipitation	7	7	8	7	7	7	8	6	6	5	7	8	83
Days With ≥ 0.5" Precipitation	3	4	4	3	3	3	3	3	3	2	3	3	37
Days With ≥ 1.0" Precipitation	1	1	2	1	1	1	1	1	1	1	2	2	15
Mean Snowfall (in.)	***1.5***	***0.9***	***1.1***	***0.1***	***trace***	***trace***	***0.0***	***0.0***	***trace***	***trace***	***trace***	***0.2***	***3.8***
Maximum Snowfall (in.)*	10	10	20	3	0	0	0	0	0	trace	3	9	23
Maximum 24-hr. Snowfall (in.)*	10	9	19	3	0	0	0	0	0	trace	3	6	19
Maximum Snow Depth (in.)	***8***	***4***	***19***	***2***	***trace***	***trace***	***0***	***0***	***trace***	***trace***	***trace***	***2***	***19***
Days With ≥ 1.0" Snow Depth	***1***	***1***	***0***	***0***	***0***	***0***	***0***	***0***	***0***	***0***	***0***	***0***	***2***
Thunderstorm Days*	1	2	4	5	7	9	11	9	4	1	1	1	55
Foggy Days*	13	11	11	8	13	14	16	19	17	16	14	13	165
Predominant Sky Cover*	OVR	OVR	OVR	OVR	OVR	SCT	SCT	SCT	OVR	CLR	OVR	OVR	OVR
Mean Relative Humidity 7am (%)*	82	82	82	83	89	89	90	92	92	91	86	83	87
Mean Relative Humidity 4pm (%)*	58	52	48	44	51	53	55	55	55	50	52	57	53
Mean Dewpoint (°F)*	30	32	38	46	57	65	68	68	62	50	39	33	49
Prevailing Wind Direction*	S	S	S	S	S	S	S	S	S	S	S	S	S
Prevailing Wind Speed (mph)*	8	9	9	9	8	7	6	6	7	7	8	8	8
Maximum Wind Gust (mph)*	60	53	60	53	54	68	67	75	52	39	47	45	75

Note: (*) Period of record is 1948-1995

Knoxville McGhee Tyson Airport

Knoxville is located in a broad valley between the Cumberland Mountains, which lie northwest of the city, and the Great Smoky Mountains, which lie southeast of the city. These two mountain ranges exercise a marked influence upon the climate of the valley. The Cumberland Mountains, to the northwest, serve to retard and weaken the force of the cold winter air which frequently penetrates far south of the latitude of Knoxville over the plains areas to the west of the mountains.

The mountains also serve to modify the hot summer winds which are common to the plains to the west. In addition, they serve as a fixed incline plane which lifts the warm, moist air flowing northward from the Gulf of Mexico and thereby increases the frequency of afternoon thunderstorms. Relief from extremely high temperatures which such thunderstorms produce serves to reduce the number of extremely warm days in the valley.

July is usually the warmest month of the year. The coldest weather usually occurs during the month of January. Sudden great temperature changes occur infrequently. This again is due mainly to the retarding effect of the mountains. Summer nights are nearly always comfortable.

Rainfall is ample for agricultural purposes and is favorably distributed during the year for most crops. Precipitation is greatest in the wintertime. Another peak period occurs during the late spring and summer months. The period of lowest rainfall occurs during the fall. A cumulative total of approximately 12 inches of snow falls annually. However, this usually comes in amounts of less than 4 inches at one time. It is unusual for snow to remain on the ground in measurable amounts longer than one week.

The topography also has a pronounced effect upon the prevailing wind direction. Daytime winds usually have a southwesterly component, while nighttime winds usually move from the northeast. The winds are relatively light and tornadoes are extremely rare.

Knoxville McGhee Tyson Airport *Blount County* Elevation: 961 ft. Latitude: 35° 49' N Longitude: 83° 59' W

	JAN	FEB	MAR	APR	MAY	JUN	JUL	AUG	SEP	OCT	NOV	DEC	YEAR
Mean Maximum Temp. (°F)	47.5	52.5	61.4	70.2	78.0	85.2	88.2	87.8	81.7	71.0	60.2	50.2	69.5
Mean Temp. (°F)	38.4	42.4	50.2	58.6	66.9	74.7	78.3	77.7	71.1	59.6	49.4	40.9	59.0
Mean Minimum Temp. (°F)	29.3	32.2	38.9	46.9	55.7	64.2	68.3	67.5	60.3	48.2	38.6	31.5	48.5
Extreme Maximum Temp. (°F)	75	83	85	91	93	102	102	102	97	89	83	80	102
Extreme Minimum Temp. (°F)	-24	-8	1	22	32	44	49	53	37	25	15	-6	-24
Days Maximum Temp. ≥ 90°F	0	0	0	0	0	6	13	12	4	0	0	0	35
Days Maximum Temp. ≤ 32°F	2	1	0	0	0	0	0	0	0	0	0	1	4
Days Minimum Temp. ≤ 32°F	19	15	9	2	0	0	0	0	0	1	9	18	73
Days Minimum Temp. ≤ 0°F	0	0	0	0	0	0	0	0	0	0	0	0	0
Heating Degree Days (base 65°F)	816	633	457	217	58	2	0	0	22	197	463	741	3,606
Cooling Degree Days (base 65°F)	0	0	5	30	123	301	420	401	210	37	3	0	1,530
Mean Precipitation (in.)	4.30	4.19	4.54	4.03	4.50	3.83	5.00	3.25	3.18	2.43	3.92	4.48	47.65
Maximum Precipitation (in.)*	11.7	8.8	11.8	7.9	11.0	8.2	10.1	6.7	9.2	6.7	10.4	11.6	63.3
Minimum Precipitation (in.)*	0.9	0.3	1.7	0.4	0.7	0.5	0.3	0.8	0.4	trace	1.2	0.4	32.5
Extreme Maximum Daily Precip. (in.)	3.40	2.70	5.75	3.61	3.04	2.86	3.27	3.00	3.31	1.52	2.26	4.00	5.75
Days With ≥ 0.1" Precipitation	8	7	8	7	8	7	8	6	5	5	7	8	84
Days With ≥ 0.5" Precipitation	3	3	3	3	3	3	3	2	2	2	3	3	33
Days With ≥ 1.0" Precipitation	1	1	1	1	1	1	2	1	1	1	1	1	13
Mean Snowfall (in.)	2.7	***2.1***	***1.1***	***0.5***	***trace***	***trace***	***0.0***	***trace***	***trace***	***trace***	***trace***	***0.6***	***7.0***
Maximum Snowfall (in.)*	15	23	20	11	0	0	0	0	0	trace	18	13	54
Maximum 24-hr. Snowfall (in.)*	10	18	11	11	0	0	0	0	0	trace	16	7	18
Maximum Snow Depth (in.)	7	8	15	7	trace	trace	***0***	***trace***	***trace***	***trace***	***trace***	***3***	***15***
Days With ≥ 1.0" Snow Depth	2	1	0	0	0	0	***0***	***0***	***0***	***0***	***0***	***0***	***3***
Thunderstorm Days*	1	1	3	4	7	8	10	7	3	1	1	1	47
Foggy Days*	14	12	11	9	14	15	17	20	18	17	14	14	175
Predominant Sky Cover*	OVR	OVR	OVR	OVR	OVR	OVR	SCT	SCT	OVR	CLR	OVR	OVR	OVR
Mean Relative Humidity 7am (%)*	81	80	80	80	85	87	89	91	91	89	84	83	85
Mean Relative Humidity 4pm (%)*	60	54	50	47	52	55	56	56	54	51	54	60	54
Mean Dewpoint (°F)*	29	31	37	45	56	64	67	67	61	49	38	32	48
Prevailing Wind Direction*	NE	NE	SW	SW	SW	SW	SW	NE	NE	NE	NE	NE	NE
Prevailing Wind Speed (mph)*	7	8	12	12	9	9	8	7	7	7	7	7	8
Maximum Wind Gust (mph)*	60	60	56	59	53	58	69	86	43	51	64	59	86

Note: (*) Period of record is 1948-1995

The period of record for National Weather Service station data is 1980 – 2009 except where noted. See User Guide for detailed explanation of data.

Memphis Int'l Airport

Topography varies from the level alluvial area in east-central Arkansas to the slightly rolling area in northwestern Mississippi and southwestern Tennessee.

Agricultural interests are varied, with major crops being cotton, corn, hay, soybeans, peaches, apples, and a considerable number of vegetables. The climate is quite favorable for dairy interests, and for the raising of cattle and hogs.

The growing season is about 230 days in length. The average date for the last occurrence of temperatures as low as 32 degrees is late March. The average date of the first temperature of 32 degrees or below is early November.

Precipitation of nearly 50 inches per year is fairly well distributed. Crops and pastures receive, on the average, an adequate supply of moisture during the growing season, with lesser amounts during the fall harvesting period.

Sunshine averages slightly over 70 percent of the possible amount during the growing season. Relative humidity averages about 70 percent for the year.

Memphis, although not in the normal paths of storms coming from the Gulf or from western Canada, is affected by both, and thereby has comparatively frequent changes in weather. Extremely high or low temperatures, however, are relatively rare.

Memphis Int'l Airport *Shelby County* Elevation: 265 ft. Latitude: 35° 03' N Longitude: 90° 00' W

	JAN	FEB	MAR	APR	MAY	JUN	JUL	AUG	SEP	OCT	NOV	DEC	YEAR
Mean Maximum Temp. (°F)	50.0	54.8	63.7	72.8	81.1	88.8	91.7	91.3	85.1	74.3	62.6	52.3	72.4
Mean Temp. (°F)	41.5	45.6	53.9	62.8	71.7	79.5	82.9	82.1	75.3	64.0	53.2	43.9	63.0
Mean Minimum Temp. (°F)	32.9	36.4	44.1	52.8	62.2	70.2	74.0	72.8	65.4	53.8	43.8	35.3	53.6
Extreme Maximum Temp. (°F)	79	80	86	94	96	101	108	107	102	95	86	81	108
Extreme Minimum Temp. (°F)	-4	4	16	28	42	50	60	53	42	30	20	-4	-4
Days Maximum Temp. ≥ 90°F	0	0	0	0	3	15	22	20	9	1	0	0	70
Days Maximum Temp. ≤ 32°F	2	1	0	0	0	0	0	0	0	0	0	2	5
Days Minimum Temp. ≤ 32°F	15	10	4	0	0	0	0	0	0	0	4	13	46
Days Minimum Temp. ≤ 0°F	0	0	0	0	0	0	0	0	0	0	0	0	0
Heating Degree Days (base 65°F)	722	543	355	136	17	0	0	0	10	118	359	651	2,911
Cooling Degree Days (base 65°F)	1	2	18	78	231	443	561	536	325	94	12	3	2,304
Mean Precipitation (in.)	3.96	4.29	5.40	5.52	5.08	3.81	4.54	2.84	3.26	4.01	5.44	5.72	53.87
Maximum Precipitation (in.)*	15.9	10.5	12.1	17.1	11.6	7.5	8.8	9.6	7.6	7.8	10.5	13.8	76.8
Minimum Precipitation (in.)*	0.6	1.1	1.5	1.4	0.8	trace	0.4	0.4	0.2	trace	0.5	1.0	38.5
Extreme Maximum Daily Precip. (in.)	3.85	4.10	4.26	4.25	3.18	4.12	4.14	3.08	3.82	3.40	5.88	4.24	5.88
Days With ≥ 0.1" Precipitation	7	6	7	7	7	6	6	4	5	5	6	7	73
Days With ≥ 0.5" Precipitation	3	3	4	4	4	3	3	2	2	3	3	4	38
Days With ≥ 1.0" Precipitation	1	1	2	2	2	1	2	1	1	1	2	2	18
Mean Snowfall (in.)	***1.9***	***1.1***	***0.5***	***trace***	***trace***	***trace***	***0.0***	***0.0***	***0.0***	***trace***	***trace***	***0.2***	***3.7***
Maximum Snowfall (in.)*	12	8	17	trace	0	0	0	0	0	trace	2	14	22
Maximum 24-hr. Snowfall (in.)*	8	5	9	trace	0	0	0	0	0	trace	1	14	14
Maximum Snow Depth (in.)	***8***	***6***	***5***	***trace***	***trace***	***trace***	***0***	***0***	***0***	***trace***	***1***	***2***	***8***
Days With ≥ 1.0" Snow Depth	***1***	***1***	***0***	***0***	***0***	***0***	***0***	***0***	***0***	***0***	***0***	***0***	***2***
Thunderstorm Days*	2	2	4	6	7	8	8	6	3	2	2	2	52
Foggy Days*	13	10	9	7	8	6	7	9	10	9	10	11	109
Predominant Sky Cover*	OVR	OVR	OVR	OVR	OVR	SCT	SCT	SCT	CLR	CLR	OVR	OVR	OVR
Mean Relative Humidity 7am (%)*	79	78	75	74	77	77	80	81	82	81	79	78	78
Mean Relative Humidity 4pm (%)*	60	56	52	49	53	53	55	54	53	49	54	60	54
Mean Dewpoint (°F)*	30	34	40	48	59	66	70	69	62	50	40	33	50
Prevailing Wind Direction*	S	S	S	S	S	S	S	S	NNE	S	S	S	S
Prevailing Wind Speed (mph)*	12	10	12	12	9	8	8	7	9	8	10	10	9
Maximum Wind Gust (mph)*	58	53	61	81	66	71	60	55	43	59	55	64	81

Note: (*) Period of record is 1948-1995

The period of record for National Weather Service station data is 1980 – 2009 except where noted. See User Guide for detailed explanation of data.

Nashville Int'l Airport

The city of Nashville is located on the Cumberland River, in the northwestern corner of the Central Basin of middle Tennessee near the escarpment of the Highland Rim. The Rim, as it is called, rises to the height of 300 to 400 feet above the mean elevation of the basin, forming an amphitheater about the city from the southwest to the southeast, with the south being more or less open but undulating.

Temperatures are moderate, with great extremes of either heat or cold rarely occurring, yet there are changes of sufficient amplitude and frequency to give variety.

Based on the 1951-1980 period, the average first occurrence of 32 degrees Fahrenheit in the fall is October 29 and the average last occurrence in the spring is April 5.

The average relative humidity is moderate as compared with the general conditions east of the Mississippi River and south of the Ohio.

Nashville is in the zone of moderate frequency of thunderstorms. The thunderstorm season usually begins in the latter part of March and continues through September.

Nashville Int'l Airport *Davidson County* Elevation: 580 ft. Latitude: 36° 07' N Longitude: 86° 41' W

	JAN	FEB	MAR	APR	MAY	JUN	JUL	AUG	SEP	OCT	NOV	DEC	YEAR
Mean Maximum Temp. (°F)	47.6	52.2	61.5	70.8	78.6	86.3	89.8	89.4	82.9	71.9	60.6	50.3	70.2
Mean Temp. (°F)	38.4	42.2	50.5	59.3	67.9	76.0	79.9	79.2	72.1	60.7	50.3	41.1	59.8
Mean Minimum Temp. (°F)	29.1	32.1	39.4	47.9	57.2	65.7	70.0	68.9	61.3	49.3	39.9	31.9	49.4
Extreme Maximum Temp. (°F)	75	83	86	91	93	103	105	106	102	91	84	79	106
Extreme Minimum Temp. (°F)	-17	-3	2	23	35	47	57	49	36	26	18	-10	-17
Days Maximum Temp. ≥ 90°F	0	0	0	0	1	9	17	15	6	0	0	0	48
Days Maximum Temp. ≤ 32°F	3	2	0	0	0	0	0	0	0	0	0	2	7
Days Minimum Temp. ≤ 32°F	20	15	9	2	0	0	0	0	0	1	8	17	72
Days Minimum Temp. ≤ 0°F	0	0	0	0	0	0	0	0	0	0	0	0	0
Heating Degree Days (base 65°F)	819	639	454	206	49	1	0	0	20	179	440	735	3,542
Cooling Degree Days (base 65°F)	0	1	10	43	146	339	471	447	241	52	5	1	1,756
Mean Precipitation (in.)	3.70	3.84	4.24	4.01	5.16	4.07	3.56	2.97	3.41	3.00	4.21	4.22	46.39
Maximum Precipitation (in.)*	13.9	10.3	12.3	8.4	11.0	9.4	7.8	8.0	11.4	6.1	7.8	13.6	70.1
Minimum Precipitation (in.)*	0.2	0.6	1.2	0.5	0.8	0.4	0.7	0.7	0.3	trace	0.5	1.0	30.2
Extreme Maximum Daily Precip. (in.)	2.77	4.73	3.35	2.61	4.63	3.41	3.20	3.22	3.71	2.32	4.20	3.07	4.73
Days With ≥ 0.1" Precipitation	6	7	8	7	8	7	7	5	5	5	6	7	78
Days With ≥ 0.5" Precipitation	3	2	3	3	3	3	2	2	2	2	3	3	31
Days With ≥ 1.0" Precipitation	1	1	1	1	2	1	1	1	1	1	1	1	13
Mean Snowfall (in.)	***2.3***	na	***1.0***	na	na	na	na	na	na	na	na	na	na
Maximum Snowfall (in.)*	19	19	16	1	0	0	0	0	0	trace	9	13	39
Maximum 24-hr. Snowfall (in.)*	8	7	8	1	0	0	0	0	0	trace	7	6	8
Maximum Snow Depth (in.)	***7***	na	***3***	***trace***	na	na	na	na	na	na	na	***2***	na
Days With ≥ 1.0" Snow Depth	***2***	na	***0***	***0***	na	na	na	na	na	na	na	***0***	na
Thunderstorm Days*	1	2	4	5	7	8	10	8	4	2	2	1	54
Foggy Days*	14	13	11	9	12	11	14	16	15	14	12	13	154
Predominant Sky Cover*	OVR	OVR	OVR	OVR	OVR	SCT	SCT	SCT	CLR	CLR	OVR	OVR	OVR
Mean Relative Humidity 6am (%)*	81	81	80	81	86	86	88	90	90	87	82	82	85
Mean Relative Humidity 3pm (%)*	61	56	51	48	52	53	54	53	52	49	55	60	54
Mean Dewpoint (°F)*	29	31	37	46	57	64	68	67	61	49	39	32	48
Prevailing Wind Direction*	S	S	S	S	S	S	S	S	S	S	S	S	S
Prevailing Wind Speed (mph)*	10	9	10	9	8	7	7	7	7	8	9	9	8
Maximum Wind Gust (mph)*	66	53	56	94	55	59	58	70	51	48	60	54	94

Note: (*) Period of record is 1948-1995

The period of record for National Weather Service station data is 1980 – 2009 except where noted. See User Guide for detailed explanation of data.

Oak Ridge

Oak Ridge is located in a broad valley between the Cumberland Mountains, which lie to the northwest of the area, and the Great Smoky Mountains, to the southeast. These mountain ranges are oriented northeast-southwest and the valley between is corrugated by broken ridges 300 to 500 feet high and oriented parallel to the main valley. During periods of light winds, daytime winds are usually southwesterly, nighttime winds northeasterly. Wind velocities are somewhat decreased by the ridges. Tornadoes rarely occur in the valley between the Cumberlands and the Great Smokies. In winter the Cumberland Mountains have a moderating influence on the local climate by retarding the flow of cold air from the north and west.

Temperatures of 100 degrees or more have occurred during less than one-half of the years of the period of record, and temperatures of zero or below are rare. Summer nights are seldom oppressively hot and humid.

Precipitation is more than adequate for agriculture and is normally well distributed through the year for agricultural purposes.

Occasionally there is sufficient dry weather in late summer or early fall to cause small damage to crops and pastures and to create conditions favorable for destructive forest fires. Winter and early spring are the seasons of heaviest precipitation. A few of the larger monthly precipitation amounts recorded have occurred in the normally drier fall months.

Light snow usually occurs in all of the months from November through March, but the total monthly snowfall is often only a trace. Snowfalls sufficiently heavy to interfere with traffic and outdoor activities occur infrequently.

Based on the 1951-1980 period, the average first occurrence of 32 degrees Fahrenheit in the fall is October 27 and the average last occurrence in the spring is April 11.

Oak Ridge *Anderson County* Elevation: 904 ft. Latitude: 36° 00' N Longitude: 84° 15' W

	JAN	FEB	MAR	APR	MAY	JUN	JUL	AUG	SEP	OCT	NOV	DEC	YEAR
Mean Maximum Temp. (°F)	47.1	52.3	62.0	70.9	78.5	85.4	88.6	88.1	82.0	71.8	60.1	49.3	69.7
Mean Temp. (°F)	37.4	41.4	49.6	57.8	66.4	74.1	77.9	77.2	70.6	59.5	48.6	39.7	58.3
Mean Minimum Temp. (°F)	27.7	30.4	37.1	44.8	54.2	62.8	67.1	66.1	59.3	47.1	37.0	30.0	47.0
Extreme Maximum Temp. (°F)	74	77	87	92	93	101	103	103	101	90	85	78	103
Extreme Minimum Temp. (°F)	-17	-13	1	20	32	41	49	50	36	26	16	-7	-17
Days Maximum Temp. ≥ 90°F	0	0	0	0	1	7	15	13	4	0	0	0	40
Days Maximum Temp. ≤ 32°F	3	1	0	0	0	0	0	0	0	0	0	2	6
Days Minimum Temp. ≤ 32°F	22	17	11	3	0	0	0	0	0	2	11	20	86
Days Minimum Temp. ≤ 0°F	0	0	0	0	0	0	0	0	0	0	0	0	0
Heating Degree Days (base 65°F)	849	661	476	235	66	3	0	0	25	199	488	778	3,780
Cooling Degree Days (base 65°F)	0	0	4	27	115	283	405	384	200	34	2	0	1,454
Mean Precipitation (in.)	4.73	4.99	5.16	4.69	4.71	4.35	5.37	3.39	3.89	3.01	4.78	5.30	54.37
Maximum Precipitation (in.)*	9.6	9.8	12.2	9.8	10.7	11.1	19.3	9.1	8.9	6.9	10.8	12.6	76.3
Minimum Precipitation (in.)*	0.9	0.7	2.2	0.9	0.8	0.5	1.2	1.3	1.4	trace	1.8	0.7	38.8
Extreme Maximum Daily Precip. (in.)	3.70	3.57	3.71	3.55	3.15	3.10	4.76	2.52	3.40	2.21	2.72	4.89	4.89
Days With ≥ 0.1" Precipitation	8	8	8	8	8	8	8	6	5	5	7	8	87
Days With ≥ 0.5" Precipitation	3	3	4	3	3	3	4	2	2	2	4	4	37
Days With ≥ 1.0" Precipitation	1	1	1	1	1	1	1	1	1	1	1	2	13
Mean Snowfall (in.)	2.5	2.5	0.7	0.2	trace	trace	trace	trace	0.0	trace	trace	1.0	6.9
Maximum Snowfall (in.)*	10	17	12	6	0	0	0	0	0	trace	1	15	25
Maximum 24-hr. Snowfall (in.)*	7	5	7	3	0	0	0	0	0	trace	1	8	8
Maximum Snow Depth (in.)	7	12	3	3	trace	trace	trace	trace	0	trace	1	5	12
Days With ≥ 1.0" Snow Depth	2	2	0	0	0	0	0	0	0	0	0	0	4
Thunderstorm Days*	0	1	0	0	0	0	0	0	0	0	0	0	1
Foggy Days*	1	2	0	0	0	0	0	0	0	0	2	0	5
Predominant Sky Cover*	na	na	na	na	na	na	na	na	na	na	na	na	na
Mean Relative Humidity 7am (%)*	na	na	na	na	na	na	na	na	na	na	na	na	na
Mean Relative Humidity 4pm (%)*	na	na	na	na	na	na	na	na	na	na	na	na	na
Mean Dewpoint (°F)*	na	na	na	na	na	na	na	na	na	na	na	na	na
Prevailing Wind Direction*	na	na	na	na	na	na	na	na	na	na	na	na	na
Prevailing Wind Speed (mph)*	na	na	na	na	na	na	na	na	na	na	na	na	na
Maximum Wind Gust (mph)*	na	na	na	na	na	na	na	na	na	na	na	na	na

Note: (*) Period of record is 1962-1995

Allardt *Fentress County* Elevation: 1,674 ft. Latitude: 36° 23' N Longitude: 84° 53' W

	JAN	FEB	MAR	APR	MAY	JUN	JUL	AUG	SEP	OCT	NOV	DEC	YEAR
Mean Maximum Temp. (°F)	45.0	49.2	57.9	67.1	73.9	80.7	83.5	83.3	77.7	68.0	57.4	47.4	65.9
Mean Temp. (°F)	35.9	39.4	47.1	55.7	63.0	70.5	73.8	73.0	67.1	56.7	47.2	38.3	55.6
Mean Minimum Temp. (°F)	26.7	29.5	36.3	44.3	52.0	60.2	64.0	62.8	56.3	45.4	37.0	29.2	45.3
Extreme Maximum Temp. (°F)	74	74	84	88	88	98	103	100	94	86	81	75	103
Extreme Minimum Temp. (°F)	-27	-11	-4	17	31	41	47	42	33	19	11	-12	-27
Days Maximum Temp. ≥ 90°F	0	0	0	0	0	1	3	3	1	0	0	0	8
Days Maximum Temp. ≤ 32°F	4	3	1	0	0	0	0	0	0	0	0	3	11
Days Minimum Temp. ≤ 32°F	22	18	12	4	0	0	0	0	0	3	11	20	90
Days Minimum Temp. ≤ 0°F	1	0	0	0	0	0	0	0	0	0	0	0	1
Heating Degree Days (base 65°F)	897	718	549	288	113	13	1	3	52	266	527	821	4,248
Cooling Degree Days (base 65°F)	0	0	2	16	57	184	280	258	121	16	1	0	935
Mean Precipitation (in.)	4.63	4.29	4.96	4.48	5.49	5.08	4.77	4.26	3.76	3.13	4.55	5.08	54.48
Extreme Maximum Daily Precip. (in.)	2.80	3.04	3.85	1.91	4.43	2.82	2.92	3.64	4.60	3.36	4.24	3.94	4.60
Days With ≥ 0.1" Precipitation	8	8	8	8	9	9	8	6	6	6	7	9	92
Days With ≥ 0.5" Precipitation	3	3	4	3	4	3	3	3	2	2	3	3	36
Days With ≥ 1.0" Precipitation	1	1	1	1	1	2	1	1	1	1	1	1	13
Mean Snowfall (in.)	4.2	3.8	2.1	0.4	0.0	0.0	0.0	0.0	0.0	0.1	0.1	2.2	12.9
Maximum Snow Depth (in.)	9	17	16	3	0	0	0	0	0	1	1	8	17
Days With ≥ 1.0" Snow Depth	4	3	1	0	0	0	0	0	0	0	0	2	10

Athens *Mcminn County* Elevation: 939 ft. Latitude: 35° 26' N Longitude: 84° 35' W

	JAN	FEB	MAR	APR	MAY	JUN	JUL	AUG	SEP	OCT	NOV	DEC	YEAR
Mean Maximum Temp. (°F)	48.0	52.5	61.3	70.3	77.9	85.1	88.2	87.8	81.9	71.5	60.8	50.6	69.7
Mean Temp. (°F)	37.7	41.2	49.1	57.3	65.7	73.7	77.3	76.6	70.3	58.8	48.8	40.2	58.1
Mean Minimum Temp. (°F)	27.3	29.9	36.8	44.3	53.5	62.2	66.3	65.4	58.6	46.0	36.6	29.7	46.4
Extreme Maximum Temp. (°F)	74	77	85	90	92	101	105	103	97	90	83	76	105
Extreme Minimum Temp. (°F)	-16	-4	2	22	33	42	53	52	37	25	12	-3	-16
Days Maximum Temp. ≥ 90°F	0	0	0	0	0	6	13	11	4	0	0	0	34
Days Maximum Temp. ≤ 32°F	2	1	0	0	0	0	0	0	0	0	0	1	4
Days Minimum Temp. ≤ 32°F	22	18	11	3	0	0	0	0	0	2	12	20	88
Days Minimum Temp. ≤ 0°F	0	0	0	0	0	0	0	0	0	0	0	0	0
Heating Degree Days (base 65°F)	840	667	490	247	73	4	0	0	27	215	482	763	3,808
Cooling Degree Days (base 65°F)	0	0	4	24	101	272	388	368	191	30	2	1	1,381
Mean Precipitation (in.)	5.29	4.91	5.05	4.72	4.66	4.21	4.83	3.86	4.72	3.30	4.82	5.17	55.54
Extreme Maximum Daily Precip. (in.)	3.92	3.05	4.67	4.93	8.10	3.58	3.90	4.40	5.56	2.87	3.05	3.22	8.10
Days With ≥ 0.1" Precipitation	8	8	8	8	8	7	9	7	6	5	7	8	89
Days With ≥ 0.5" Precipitation	4	4	4	3	3	3	3	3	3	2	3	4	39
Days With ≥ 1.0" Precipitation	2	2	2	1	1	1	1	1	2	1	2	1	17
Mean Snowfall (in.)	1.8	1.4	0.9	0.4	0.0	0.0	0.0	0.0	0.0	0.0	0.1	0.5	5.1
Maximum Snow Depth (in.)	10	7	14	5	0	0	0	0	0	0	trace	1	14
Days With ≥ 1.0" Snow Depth	1	1	0	0	0	0	0	0	0	0	0	0	2

Brownsville *Haywood County* Elevation: 330 ft. Latitude: 35° 35' N Longitude: 89° 15' W

	JAN	FEB	MAR	APR	MAY	JUN	JUL	AUG	SEP	OCT	NOV	DEC	YEAR
Mean Maximum Temp. (°F)	47.2	52.0	61.0	71.0	79.2	86.8	90.3	89.9	83.5	72.8	61.2	50.1	70.4
Mean Temp. (°F)	38.4	42.5	51.0	60.5	69.4	77.1	80.7	79.7	72.4	61.1	51.0	41.1	60.4
Mean Minimum Temp. (°F)	29.5	32.9	40.9	49.8	59.6	67.4	71.0	69.4	61.2	49.4	40.8	32.1	50.3
Extreme Maximum Temp. (°F)	76	81	87	92	93	100	105	107	100	92	86	80	107
Extreme Minimum Temp. (°F)	-10	3	12	25	38	50	57	49	38	27	18	-8	-10
Days Maximum Temp. ≥ 90°F	0	0	0	0	1	11	19	17	6	0	0	0	54
Days Maximum Temp. ≤ 32°F	3	2	0	0	0	0	0	0	0	0	0	2	7
Days Minimum Temp. ≤ 32°F	20	14	7	1	0	0	0	0	0	1	7	17	67
Days Minimum Temp. ≤ 0°F	0	0	0	0	0	0	0	0	0	0	0	0	0
Heating Degree Days (base 65°F)	819	633	440	188	36	1	0	0	22	174	420	734	3,467
Cooling Degree Days (base 65°F)	1	1	12	59	180	371	493	462	250	60	8	1	1,898
Mean Precipitation (in.)	4.06	4.35	4.97	4.82	5.47	4.28	4.19	2.67	3.54	4.05	5.02	6.09	53.51
Extreme Maximum Daily Precip. (in.)	2.40	3.62	3.19	2.68	5.85	2.69	4.86	4.30	4.63	3.50	6.00	7.30	7.30
Days With ≥ 0.1" Precipitation	7	7	7	7	8	6	6	4	5	6	7	8	78
Days With ≥ 0.5" Precipitation	3	3	3	3	4	3	3	2	2	3	3	4	36
Days With ≥ 1.0" Precipitation	1	1	2	2	2	1	1	1	1	1	1	2	16
Mean Snowfall (in.)	1.4	1.6	0.4	0.1	0.0	0.0	0.0	0.0	0.0	trace	trace	0.3	3.8
Maximum Snow Depth (in.)	8	8	2	1	0	0	0	0	0	trace	trace	2	8
Days With ≥ 1.0" Snow Depth	2	1	0	0	0	0	0	0	0	0	0	0	3

Carthage *Smith County* Elevation: 515 ft. Latitude: 36° 15' N Longitude: 85° 57' W

	JAN	FEB	MAR	APR	MAY	JUN	JUL	AUG	SEP	OCT	NOV	DEC	YEAR
Mean Maximum Temp. (°F)	46.8	51.7	60.4	69.5	77.4	85.0	88.5	88.5	82.4	71.5	60.4	50.0	69.3
Mean Temp. (°F)	37.1	40.9	48.7	57.2	65.8	73.9	77.9	77.4	70.8	59.2	49.1	40.2	58.2
Mean Minimum Temp. (°F)	27.3	30.0	36.9	44.9	54.1	62.9	67.3	66.2	59.2	46.8	37.8	30.3	47.0
Extreme Maximum Temp. (°F)	74	82	88	90	93	101	106	105	100	92	85	77	106
Extreme Minimum Temp. (°F)	-17	-8	10	21	32	45	53	49	37	25	13	-9	-17
Days Maximum Temp. ≥ 90°F	0	0	0	0	1	7	14	14	4	0	0	0	40
Days Maximum Temp. ≤ 32°F	3	2	0	0	0	0	0	0	0	0	0	2	7
Days Minimum Temp. ≤ 32°F	21	17	12	3	0	0	0	0	0	2	10	20	85
Days Minimum Temp. ≤ 0°F	1	0	0	0	0	0	0	0	0	0	0	0	1
Heating Degree Days (base 65°F)	858	675	505	251	76	5	0	1	25	212	473	763	3,844
Cooling Degree Days (base 65°F)	0	0	6	25	108	280	407	392	206	38	3	1	1,466
Mean Precipitation (in.)	4.20	4.29	4.71	3.96	5.22	4.39	4.90	3.55	3.56	3.14	4.08	4.98	50.98
Extreme Maximum Daily Precip. (in.)	2.68	6.10	3.26	2.47	3.80	4.20	3.34	5.80	3.33	2.28	3.95	3.25	6.10
Days With ≥ 0.1" Precipitation	6	7	8	7	8	6	7	5	5	5	5	7	76
Days With ≥ 0.5" Precipitation	3	3	3	3	3	3	3	2	2	2	3	3	33
Days With ≥ 1.0" Precipitation	1	1	1	1	2	1	2	1	1	1	1	2	15
Mean Snowfall (in.)	2.0	*0.6*	0.3	0.0	0.0	0.0	0.0	0.0	0.0	0.0	trace	0.3	*3.2*
Maximum Snow Depth (in.)	7	*5*	3	0	0	0	0	*0*	0	*0*	trace	*2*	7
Days With ≥ 1.0" Snow Depth	1	*0*	0	0	0	0	0	0	0	0	0	0	*1*

The period of record for all cooperative weather station data is 1980 – 2009. See User Guide for detailed explanation of data.

Centerville Water Pl *Hickman County* Elevation: 660 ft. Latitude: 35° 45' N Longitude: 87° 26' W

	JAN	FEB	MAR	APR	MAY	JUN	JUL	AUG	SEP	OCT	NOV	DEC	YEAR
Mean Maximum Temp. (°F)	49.5	55.3	64.3	74.7	80.2	86.0	89.6	89.2	83.4	73.3	62.3	51.3	71.6
Mean Temp. (°F)	38.2	42.5	50.1	59.4	66.7	73.7	77.7	76.6	***70.1***	59.2	49.5	40.1	***58.7***
Mean Minimum Temp. (°F)	26.8	29.5	35.9	44.2	53.2	61.3	65.8	64.0	***56.7***	45.0	36.7	28.8	***45.7***
Extreme Maximum Temp. (°F)	73	84	87	91	93	100	103	101	101	90	89	76	103
Extreme Minimum Temp. (°F)	-26	-6	0	20	29	40	51	42	***27***	20	10	-10	***-26***
Days Maximum Temp. ≥ 90°F	0	0	0	1	1	8	16	15	5	0	0	0	46
Days Maximum Temp. ≤ 32°F	2	1	0	0	0	0	0	0	0	0	0	2	5
Days Minimum Temp. ≤ 32°F	22	18	13	5	0	0	0	0	0	4	11	20	93
Days Minimum Temp. ≤ 0°F	1	0	0	0	0	0	0	0	0	0	0	0	1
Heating Degree Days (base 65°F)	824	628	461	197	60	4	0	1	***33***	208	462	766	***3,644***
Cooling Degree Days (base 65°F)	0	0	6	37	119	270	401	369	***192***	33	4	1	***1,432***
Mean Precipitation (in.)	3.88	4.52	5.00	4.78	5.58	4.25	4.31	2.87	3.65	3.22	4.97	5.23	52.26
Extreme Maximum Daily Precip. (in.)	2.25	3.95	3.35	4.00	6.20	3.80	4.38	3.60	6.35	***2.40***	3.45	4.57	***6.35***
Days With ≥ 0.1" Precipitation	7	7	8	8	8	7	7	5	5	5	7	***8***	***82***
Days With ≥ 0.5" Precipitation	3	3	3	4	4	3	3	2	2	2	4	***4***	***37***
Days With ≥ 1.0" Precipitation	1	1	2	1	2	1	1	1	1	1	2	2	16
Mean Snowfall (in.)	0.6	0.7	0.1	0.0	0.0	0.0	0.0	0.0	0.0	0.0	trace	0.2	1.6
Maximum Snow Depth (in.)	7	***3***	2	0	0	0	0	0	0	***0***	trace	2	***7***
Days With ≥ 1.0" Snow Depth	0	***0***	0	0	0	0	0	0	0	***0***	0	0	***0***

Cheatham Lock and Dam *Cheatham County* Elevation: 392 ft. Latitude: 36° 19' N Longitude: 87° 13' W

	JAN	FEB	MAR	APR	MAY	JUN	JUL	AUG	SEP	OCT	NOV	DEC	YEAR
Mean Maximum Temp. (°F)	48.9	53.7	63.1	70.9	78.3	86.3	90.3	90.4	83.4	72.1	61.2	51.2	70.8
Mean Temp. (°F)	37.6	41.1	49.3	56.5	65.0	73.5	77.9	77.1	70.0	58.0	48.1	39.4	57.8
Mean Minimum Temp. (°F)	26.2	28.5	35.4	41.9	51.7	60.4	65.4	63.7	56.4	43.8	34.8	27.8	44.7
Extreme Maximum Temp. (°F)	75	83	88	90	94	103	105	105	102	93	85	78	105
Extreme Minimum Temp. (°F)	-18	-3	0	19	29	38	46	42	33	19	6	-13	-18
Days Maximum Temp. ≥ 90°F	0	0	0	0	1	9	18	18	7	0	0	0	53
Days Maximum Temp. ≤ 32°F	3	1	0	0	0	0	0	0	0	0	0	2	6
Days Minimum Temp. ≤ 32°F	22	19	13	6	0	0	0	0	0	4	13	20	97
Days Minimum Temp. ≤ 0°F	1	0	0	0	0	0	0	0	0	0	0	0	1
Heating Degree Days (base 65°F)	842	670	486	274	91	7	0	1	37	242	504	790	3,944
Cooling Degree Days (base 65°F)	0	0	6	27	98	267	407	383	192	30	2	1	1,413
Mean Precipitation (in.)	3.40	4.38	4.52	4.34	5.59	4.51	3.72	2.58	3.65	3.45	3.96	4.77	48.87
Extreme Maximum Daily Precip. (in.)	3.21	4.20	3.30	4.55	5.85	5.80	2.20	2.70	6.70	4.02	3.39	3.47	6.70
Days With ≥ 0.1" Precipitation	6	6	7	7	8	7	7	5	6	5	7	7	78
Days With ≥ 0.5" Precipitation	2	3	3	3	4	3	3	2	3	2	3	3	34
Days With ≥ 1.0" Precipitation	1	1	1	1	2	1	1	1	1	1	1	2	14
Mean Snowfall (in.)	0.9	0.9	0.2	0.0	0.0	0.0	0.0	0.0	0.0	0.0	0.0	0.1	2.1
Maximum Snow Depth (in.)	7	7	4	0	0	0	0	0	0	0	1	2	7
Days With ≥ 1.0" Snow Depth	1	1	0	0	0	0	0	0	0	0	0	0	2

Clarksville Sewage Plant *Montgomery County* Elevation: 381 ft. Latitude: 36° 33' N Longitude: 87° 21' W

	JAN	FEB	MAR	APR	MAY	JUN	JUL	AUG	SEP	OCT	NOV	DEC	YEAR
Mean Maximum Temp. (°F)	46.5	51.3	61.2	71.1	78.7	86.5	90.2	89.9	83.1	71.9	60.4	49.2	70.0
Mean Temp. (°F)	36.6	40.6	49.1	58.6	67.1	75.4	79.5	78.5	71.1	59.4	48.9	39.2	58.7
Mean Minimum Temp. (°F)	26.7	29.9	37.0	46.1	55.4	64.2	68.8	67.0	59.0	46.7	37.4	29.3	47.3
Extreme Maximum Temp. (°F)	77	82	87	92	94	103	105	107	101	93	85	78	107
Extreme Minimum Temp. (°F)	-15	-3	0	22	32	43	53	44	32	20	15	-12	-15
Days Maximum Temp. ≥ 90°F	0	0	0	0	1	11	18	16	6	0	0	0	52
Days Maximum Temp. ≤ 32°F	4	2	0	0	0	0	0	0	0	0	0	3	9
Days Minimum Temp. ≤ 32°F	22	18	11	3	0	0	0	0	0	2	10	20	86
Days Minimum Temp. ≤ 0°F	0	0	0	0	0	0	0	0	0	0	0	0	0
Heating Degree Days (base 65°F)	875	683	493	225	59	3	0	0	28	208	479	793	3,846
Cooling Degree Days (base 65°F)	0	0	7	40	131	320	457	424	217	40	4	0	1,640
Mean Precipitation (in.)	3.83	4.15	4.47	4.44	5.52	4.16	4.21	2.98	3.60	3.87	4.44	5.25	50.92
Extreme Maximum Daily Precip. (in.)	3.71	3.24	4.94	2.31	4.85	3.15	3.05	3.50	6.90	4.02	3.38	3.44	6.90
Days With ≥ 0.1" Precipitation	7	6	8	8	8	7	7	5	5	6	7	7	81
Days With ≥ 0.5" Precipitation	3	3	3	3	3	4	3	2	3	3	3	3	36
Days With ≥ 1.0" Precipitation	1	1	1	1	2	1	1	1	1	1	2	2	15
Mean Snowfall (in.)	1.1	1.2	0.2	0.0	0.0	0.0	0.0	0.0	0.0	0.0	0.0	0.3	2.8
Maximum Snow Depth (in.)	1	3	3	0	0	0	0	0	0	0	0	0	3
Days With ≥ 1.0" Snow Depth	0	0	0	0	0	0	0	0	0	0	0	0	0

Cleveland Filter Plant *Bradley County* Elevation: 799 ft. Latitude: 35° 13' N Longitude: 84° 48' W

	JAN	FEB	MAR	APR	MAY	JUN	JUL	AUG	SEP	OCT	NOV	DEC	YEAR
Mean Maximum Temp. (°F)	49.2	53.7	62.2	70.9	78.2	85.1	88.5	87.9	81.7	71.7	61.0	51.1	70.1
Mean Temp. (°F)	38.8	42.5	49.9	58.0	66.0	74.0	77.6	76.9	70.2	59.2	48.9	40.8	58.6
Mean Minimum Temp. (°F)	28.4	31.4	37.5	45.0	53.9	62.7	66.7	65.8	58.7	46.7	36.8	30.4	47.0
Extreme Maximum Temp. (°F)	74	78	86	91	92	96	105	104	98	89	82	76	105
Extreme Minimum Temp. (°F)	-16	-2	0	20	33	43	51	51	36	24	11	-4	-16
Days Maximum Temp. ≥ 90°F	0	0	0	0	0	6	13	11	3	0	0	0	33
Days Maximum Temp. ≤ 32°F	2	1	0	0	0	0	0	0	0	0	0	1	4
Days Minimum Temp. ≤ 32°F	20	16	10	3	0	0	0	0	0	2	11	19	81
Days Minimum Temp. ≤ 0°F	0	0	0	0	0	0	0	0	0	0	0	0	0
Heating Degree Days (base 65°F)	804	628	466	228	64	3	0	0	25	203	478	743	3,642
Cooling Degree Days (base 65°F)	0	0	5	24	103	278	398	376	189	31	2	0	1,406
Mean Precipitation (in.)	4.89	4.57	5.28	4.29	4.85	4.57	4.59	3.52	4.32	3.24	4.93	4.96	54.01
Extreme Maximum Daily Precip. (in.)	3.86	3.50	6.76	4.30	4.54	4.76	5.10	3.03	5.32	2.58	3.18	3.95	6.76
Days With ≥ 0.1" Precipitation	8	8	8	7	8	8	7	6	6	5	8	8	87
Days With ≥ 0.5" Precipitation	3	3	4	3	4	3	3	3	3	2	4	3	38
Days With ≥ 1.0" Precipitation	1	1	1	1	1	1	1	1	2	1	2	1	14
Mean Snowfall (in.)	0.2	0.3	0.1	0.1	0.0	0.0	0.0	0.0	0.0	0.0	trace	0.2	0.9
Maximum Snow Depth (in.)	6	5	1	0	0	0	0	0	0	0	trace	1	6
Days With ≥ 1.0" Snow Depth	0	0	0	0	0	0	0	0	0	0	0	0	0

The period of record for all cooperative weather station data is 1980 – 2009. See User Guide for detailed explanation of data.

Columbia 3 WNW *Maury County* Elevation: 649 ft. Latitude: 35° 39' N Longitude: 87° 05' W

	JAN	FEB	MAR	APR	MAY	JUN	JUL	AUG	SEP	OCT	NOV	DEC	YEAR
Mean Maximum Temp. (°F)	47.5	52.0	61.1	70.3	78.0	85.3	88.8	88.6	82.4	71.3	60.7	50.1	69.7
Mean Temp. (°F)	37.0	40.6	48.5	56.8	65.6	73.5	77.6	76.8	69.8	57.8	48.3	39.5	57.7
Mean Minimum Temp. (°F)	26.4	29.2	35.7	43.6	53.2	61.7	66.4	65.0	57.2	44.4	35.9	28.9	45.6
Extreme Maximum Temp. (°F)	75	81	87	90	93	100	105	105	100	90	85	76	105
Extreme Minimum Temp. (°F)	-20	-7	4	20	31	40	54	48	34	23	15	-10	-20
Days Maximum Temp. ≥ 90°F	0	0	0	0	1	8	15	13	5	0	0	0	42
Days Maximum Temp. ≤ 32°F	3	1	0	0	0	0	0	0	0	0	0	2	6
Days Minimum Temp. ≤ 32°F	22	18	13	4	0	0	0	0	0	4	13	21	95
Days Minimum Temp. ≤ 0°F	0	0	0	0	0	0	0	0	0	0	0	0	0
Heating Degree Days (base 65°F)	861	683	511	264	77	6	0	1	34	242	497	783	3,959
Cooling Degree Days (base 65°F)	0	0	5	24	103	267	399	375	184	28	3	0	1,388
Mean Precipitation (in.)	4.18	4.56	5.42	4.87	5.60	4.28	5.05	3.59	3.82	3.35	4.49	5.38	54.59
Extreme Maximum Daily Precip. (in.)	4.27	3.70	3.30	4.27	5.62	2.80	4.30	4.40	4.90	3.30	3.78	3.94	5.62
Days With ≥ 0.1" Precipitation	7	7	8	8	8	7	8	5	6	5	7	8	84
Days With ≥ 0.5" Precipitation	3	3	4	3	4	3	4	2	2	2	3	4	37
Days With ≥ 1.0" Precipitation	1	1	2	1	2	1	1	1	1	1	1	2	15
Mean Snowfall (in.)	0.5	0.5	0.2	0.0	0.0	0.0	0.0	0.0	0.0	0.0	0.0	0.1	1.3
Maximum Snow Depth (in.)	2	4	2	0	0	0	0	0	0	0	0	2	4
Days With ≥ 1.0" Snow Depth	0	0	0	0	0	0	0	0	0	0	0	0	0

Cookeville *Putnam County* Elevation: 1,089 ft. Latitude: 36° 06' N Longitude: 85° 30' W

	JAN	FEB	MAR	APR	MAY	JUN	JUL	AUG	SEP	OCT	NOV	DEC	YEAR
Mean Maximum Temp. (°F)	46.6	50.8	59.6	68.8	76.8	84.1	87.4	87.1	81.3	71.0	60.3	49.7	68.6
Mean Temp. (°F)	36.3	39.4	47.3	55.7	64.4	72.6	76.4	75.4	68.8	57.6	48.0	39.1	56.8
Mean Minimum Temp. (°F)	25.9	27.9	34.9	42.6	52.1	61.0	65.3	63.7	56.3	44.2	35.6	28.6	44.8
Extreme Maximum Temp. (°F)	76	80	85	90	92	98	104	104	97	92	85	77	104
Extreme Minimum Temp. (°F)	-22	-13	-1	20	33	41	46	46	36	23	14	-8	-22
Days Maximum Temp. ≥ 90°F	0	0	0	0	0	5	10	11	4	0	0	0	30
Days Maximum Temp. ≤ 32°F	4	2	0	0	0	0	0	0	0	0	0	2	8
Days Minimum Temp. ≤ 32°F	23	20	14	5	0	0	0	0	0	4	13	21	100
Days Minimum Temp. ≤ 0°F	1	0	0	0	0	0	0	0	0	0	0	0	1
Heating Degree Days (base 65°F)	884	718	545	288	96	9	0	2	40	250	506	795	4,133
Cooling Degree Days (base 65°F)	0	0	4	17	87	243	361	332	161	27	3	0	1,235
Mean Precipitation (in.)	5.05	4.81	5.03	4.60	5.30	4.57	4.98	3.52	4.09	3.18	4.57	5.62	55.32
Extreme Maximum Daily Precip. (in.)	4.15	4.65	3.68	2.98	5.27	4.24	3.93	3.09	4.36	3.20	4.10	4.43	5.27
Days With ≥ 0.1" Precipitation	8	8	8	8	9	7	8	6	6	6	7	9	90
Days With ≥ 0.5" Precipitation	4	3	3	3	4	3	3	2	3	2	3	4	37
Days With ≥ 1.0" Precipitation	1	1	1	1	2	1	2	1	1	1	1	2	15
Mean Snowfall (in.)	2.1	2.1	0.7	trace	0.0	0.0	0.0	0.0	0.0	0.0	0.1	0.7	5.7
Maximum Snow Depth (in.)	7	8	8	1	0	0	0	0	0	0	0	4	8
Days With ≥ 1.0" Snow Depth	2	2	1	0	0	0	0	0	0	0	0	0	5

Dayton *Rhea County* Elevation: 865 ft. Latitude: 35° 28' N Longitude: 85° 00' W

	JAN	FEB	MAR	APR	MAY	JUN	JUL	AUG	SEP	OCT	NOV	DEC	YEAR
Mean Maximum Temp. (°F)	47.5	52.4	61.8	71.3	78.2	85.4	88.0	87.7	81.1	70.6	59.8	49.7	69.5
Mean Temp. (°F)	38.3	42.0	50.2	58.8	66.5	74.1	77.4	76.9	70.3	59.1	49.4	40.6	58.6
Mean Minimum Temp. (°F)	29.1	31.5	38.5	46.3	54.8	62.8	66.8	66.2	59.4	47.6	38.8	31.3	47.8
Extreme Maximum Temp. (°F)	74	78	85	92	94	100	107	104	97	90	82	76	107
Extreme Minimum Temp. (°F)	-15	-4	3	22	34	44	53	52	36	25	17	-5	-15
Days Maximum Temp. ≥ 90°F	0	0	0	0	0	6	12	11	3	0	0	0	32
Days Maximum Temp. ≤ 32°F	2	1	0	0	0	0	0	0	0	0	0	1	4
Days Minimum Temp. ≤ 32°F	20	15	9	2	0	0	0	0	0	2	9	18	75
Days Minimum Temp. ≤ 0°F	0	0	0	0	0	0	0	0	0	0	0	0	0
Heating Degree Days (base 65°F)	820	645	456	208	54	2	0	0	23	205	463	751	3,627
Cooling Degree Days (base 65°F)	0	0	3	29	109	282	392	377	188	29	1	0	1,410
Mean Precipitation (in.)	4.89	4.81	5.09	4.29	5.04	3.83	4.84	4.23	4.46	3.22	5.04	5.40	55.14
Extreme Maximum Daily Precip. (in.)	2.55	4.30	3.75	3.86	7.21	3.18	3.09	4.42	7.57	4.09	2.78	4.33	7.57
Days With ≥ 0.1" Precipitation	7	7	8	7	8	7	8	6	6	5	7	8	84
Days With ≥ 0.5" Precipitation	3	3	3	3	3	3	3	3	3	2	4	4	37
Days With ≥ 1.0" Precipitation	1	1	1	1	1	1	1	1	1	1	2	2	14
Mean Snowfall (in.)	1.0	1.0	0.4	0.1	0.0	0.0	0.0	0.0	0.0	0.0	trace	0.3	2.8
Maximum Snow Depth (in.)	7	4	8	trace	0	0	0	0	0	0	trace	3	8
Days With ≥ 1.0" Snow Depth	1	1	0	0	0	0	0	0	0	0	0	0	2

Dover 1 W *Stewart County* Elevation: 475 ft. Latitude: 36° 29' N Longitude: 87° 52' W

	JAN	FEB	MAR	APR	MAY	JUN	JUL	AUG	SEP	OCT	NOV	DEC	YEAR
Mean Maximum Temp. (°F)	44.8	49.9	59.9	69.9	76.9	84.3	88.4	87.6	81.4	70.2	59.2	47.9	68.4
Mean Temp. (°F)	35.7	39.8	48.8	58.3	66.2	74.1	78.2	76.7	69.9	58.4	48.8	38.7	57.8
Mean Minimum Temp. (°F)	26.5	29.6	37.7	46.6	55.4	63.9	68.0	66.1	58.4	46.5	38.4	29.5	47.2
Extreme Maximum Temp. (°F)	73	82	88	91	92	101	104	105	100	92	84	77	105
Extreme Minimum Temp. (°F)	-15	-3	0	22	30	42	52	46	29	23	15	-13	-15
Days Maximum Temp. ≥ 90°F	0	0	0	0	0	5	13	12	4	0	0	0	34
Days Maximum Temp. ≤ 32°F	5	3	0	0	0	0	0	0	0	0	0	3	11
Days Minimum Temp. ≤ 32°F	23	18	11	2	0	0	0	0	0	2	9	18	83
Days Minimum Temp. ≤ 0°F	1	0	0	0	0	0	0	0	0	0	0	0	1
Heating Degree Days (base 65°F)	902	709	504	236	71	5	0	1	37	235	482	808	3,990
Cooling Degree Days (base 65°F)	0	1	9	40	115	285	417	371	191	36	4	1	1,470
Mean Precipitation (in.)	3.79	4.44	4.47	4.74	5.26	4.27	4.03	3.30	3.66	4.02	4.54	5.04	51.56
Extreme Maximum Daily Precip. (in.)	4.09	3.29	5.68	4.06	4.28	5.44	3.56	7.60	4.15	3.60	4.02	4.90	7.60
Days With ≥ 0.1" Precipitation	6	6	7	8	8	7	6	5	5	6	7	7	78
Days With ≥ 0.5" Precipitation	3	3	3	3	4	3	3	2	2	3	3	3	35
Days With ≥ 1.0" Precipitation	1	1	1	1	2	1	1	1	1	2	1	1	14
Mean Snowfall (in.)	1.8	2.1	0.6	trace	0.0	0.0	0.0	0.0	0.0	trace	0.1	0.4	5.0
Maximum Snow Depth (in.)	7	11	6	1	0	0	0	0	0	trace	2	4	11
Days With ≥ 1.0" Snow Depth	2	2	0	0	0	0	0	0	0	0	0	0	4

The period of record for all cooperative weather station data is 1980 – 2009. See User Guide for detailed explanation of data.

Dresden *Weakley County* Elevation: 450 ft. Latitude: 36° 17' N Longitude: 88° 42' W

	JAN	FEB	MAR	APR	MAY	JUN	JUL	AUG	SEP	OCT	NOV	DEC	YEAR
Mean Maximum Temp. (°F)	45.0	49.6	59.6	69.5	77.8	85.5	88.7	88.5	82.4	71.3	59.7	48.0	68.8
Mean Temp. (°F)	35.7	39.5	48.7	58.2	67.2	75.2	78.8	77.9	71.0	59.4	49.2	38.7	58.3
Mean Minimum Temp. (°F)	26.4	29.6	37.8	46.8	56.4	64.8	68.8	67.2	59.5	47.6	38.8	29.5	47.7
Extreme Maximum Temp. (°F)	75	80	87	90	93	100	102	104	99	90	87	78	104
Extreme Minimum Temp. (°F)	-17	-3	7	22	35	46	54	47	36	23	15	-11	-17
Days Maximum Temp. ≥ 90°F	0	0	0	0	0	8	15	14	5	0	0	0	42
Days Maximum Temp. ≤ 32°F	4	3	0	0	0	0	0	0	0	0	0	3	10
Days Minimum Temp. ≤ 32°F	23	18	10	2	0	0	0	0	0	2	8	20	83
Days Minimum Temp. ≤ 0°F	0	0	0	0	0	0	0	0	0	0	0	0	0
Heating Degree Days (base 65°F)	902	715	507	237	58	3	0	1	28	209	470	807	3,937
Cooling Degree Days (base 65°F)	0	0	8	38	131	315	434	406	214	43	4	1	1,594
Mean Precipitation (in.)	3.65	4.40	4.70	4.89	5.36	4.77	4.55	2.90	3.68	3.90	4.60	5.43	52.83
Extreme Maximum Daily Precip. (in.)	4.20	4.07	6.95	3.49	4.80	4.69	3.78	3.79	3.72	2.80	4.53	3.40	6.95
Days With ≥ 0.1" Precipitation	6	6	8	8	8	7	6	4	5	5	7	7	77
Days With ≥ 0.5" Precipitation	3	3	3	4	3	3	3	2	2	3	3	3	35
Days With ≥ 1.0" Precipitation	1	1	1	1	2	1	1	1	1	1	2	2	15
Mean Snowfall (in.)	1.0	*0.6*	0.2	0.0	0.0	0.0	0.0	0.0	0.0	0.0	0.0	0.1	*1.9*
Maximum Snow Depth (in.)	5	5	3	0	0	0	0	0	0	0	0	1	5
Days With ≥ 1.0" Snow Depth	0	0	0	0	0	0	0	0	0	0	0	0	0

Elizabethton *Carter County* Elevation: 1,753 ft. Latitude: 36° 22' N Longitude: 82° 14' W

	JAN	FEB	MAR	APR	MAY	JUN	JUL	AUG	SEP	OCT	NOV	DEC	YEAR
Mean Maximum Temp. (°F)	46.6	50.4	*58.9*	68.0	76.0	82.7	85.3	85.1	79.7	69.6	59.4	49.1	*67.6*
Mean Temp. (°F)	36.6	39.8	*47.1*	55.4	64.1	71.5	74.7	74.2	68.1	57.5	47.8	39.2	*56.3*
Mean Minimum Temp. (°F)	26.6	29.2	*35.3*	42.8	52.1	60.3	64.1	63.2	56.5	45.2	36.2	29.2	*45.0*
Extreme Maximum Temp. (°F)	78	80	*83*	89	94	96	99	99	97	90	84	76	*99*
Extreme Minimum Temp. (°F)	-21	-12	*-1*	20	28	39	46	43	34	22	11	-9	*-21*
Days Maximum Temp. ≥ 90°F	0	0	*0*	0	0	2	6	6	2	0	0	0	*16*
Days Maximum Temp. ≤ 32°F	3	2	*1*	0	0	0	0	0	0	0	0	2	*8*
Days Minimum Temp. ≤ 32°F	22	18	*12*	5	0	0	0	0	0	3	12	20	*92*
Days Minimum Temp. ≤ 0°F	0	0	*0*	0	0	0	0	0	0	0	0	0	*0*
Heating Degree Days (base 65°F)	873	705	*548*	296	100	10	0	2	39	249	509	795	*4,126*
Cooling Degree Days (base 65°F)	0	0	*1*	15	79	212	308	294	140	22	2	0	*1,073*
Mean Precipitation (in.)	3.35	3.70	*3.76*	3.58	4.45	4.73	5.23	3.91	2.88	2.32	3.27	3.43	*44.61*
Extreme Maximum Daily Precip. (in.)	2.00	2.10	*2.70*	2.55	3.05	*3.06*	2.31	3.30	2.60	1.82	3.09	2.75	*3.30*
Days With ≥ 0.1" Precipitation	8	7	*8*	8	9	8	9	8	6	5	6	8	*90*
Days With ≥ 0.5" Precipitation	2	2	*2*	3	3	3	4	2	2	2	2	2	*29*
Days With ≥ 1.0" Precipitation	1	1	*1*	1	1	1	1	1	1	0	1	1	*11*
Mean Snowfall (in.)	2.9	2.9	*0.3*	0.9	trace	0.0	0.0	0.0	0.0	trace	0.1	1.0	*8.1*
Maximum Snow Depth (in.)	18	10	*21*	14	trace	0	0	0	0	trace	2	5	*21*
Days With ≥ 1.0" Snow Depth	3	2	*0*	0	0	0	0	0	0	0	0	1	*6*

Fayetteville Water Plant *Lincoln County* Elevation: 725 ft. Latitude: 35° 09' N Longitude: 86° 32' W

	JAN	FEB	MAR	APR	MAY	JUN	JUL	AUG	SEP	OCT	NOV	DEC	YEAR
Mean Maximum Temp. (°F)	49.5	54.1	62.7	71.5	79.4	86.4	89.6	89.8	83.9	73.3	62.4	51.9	71.2
Mean Temp. (°F)	39.1	42.8	50.5	58.6	67.1	74.4	78.2	77.6	71.2	59.9	50.2	41.4	59.3
Mean Minimum Temp. (°F)	28.5	31.4	38.2	45.6	54.9	62.4	66.6	65.5	58.4	46.5	38.0	30.8	47.2
Extreme Maximum Temp. (°F)	76	82	86	90	93	100	103	105	100	92	86	77	105
Extreme Minimum Temp. (°F)	-20	3	1	19	30	39	52	48	33	20	13	-8	-20
Days Maximum Temp. ≥ 90°F	0	0	0	0	1	10	17	17	6	0	0	0	51
Days Maximum Temp. ≤ 32°F	2	1	0	0	0	0	0	0	0	0	0	1	4
Days Minimum Temp. ≤ 32°F	20	16	10	4	0	0	0	0	0	4	10	19	83
Days Minimum Temp. ≤ 0°F	0	0	0	0	0	0	0	0	0	0	0	0	0
Heating Degree Days (base 65°F)	798	622	450	219	56	4	0	1	28	195	442	726	3,541
Cooling Degree Days (base 65°F)	1	0	7	34	130	293	415	400	219	45	5	1	1,550
Mean Precipitation (in.)	4.65	4.69	5.38	4.45	4.91	4.35	4.23	3.32	3.96	3.57	5.18	5.93	54.62
Extreme Maximum Daily Precip. (in.)	3.60	4.00	3.30	3.70	2.80	3.37	3.10	3.62	3.85	3.05	3.00	4.65	4.65
Days With ≥ 0.1" Precipitation	7	7	8	7	8	7	8	6	5	5	7	8	83
Days With ≥ 0.5" Precipitation	3	3	4	3	3	3	3	2	3	2	4	4	37
Days With ≥ 1.0" Precipitation	1	1	2	1	1	1	1	1	1	1	2	2	15
Mean Snowfall (in.)	0.6	0.6	0.4	trace	0.0	0.0	0.0	0.0	0.0	0.0	trace	0.2	1.8
Maximum Snow Depth (in.)	8	4	6	0	0	0	0	0	0	0	trace	3	8
Days With ≥ 1.0" Snow Depth	1	1	0	0	0	0	0	0	0	0	0	0	2

Franklin Sewage Plant *Williamson County* Elevation: 654 ft. Latitude: 35° 57' N Longitude: 86° 52' W

	JAN	FEB	MAR	APR	MAY	JUN	JUL	AUG	SEP	OCT	NOV	DEC	YEAR
Mean Maximum Temp. (°F)	47.5	52.1	60.8	70.0	77.9	85.5	89.3	88.8	82.8	71.9	60.8	50.4	69.8
Mean Temp. (°F)	37.4	41.0	48.9	57.5	66.0	74.2	78.2	77.2	70.5	58.8	49.1	40.3	58.3
Mean Minimum Temp. (°F)	27.4	30.0	36.9	44.9	54.1	62.9	67.1	65.5	58.2	45.7	37.4	30.1	46.7
Extreme Maximum Temp. (°F)	75	81	87	90	92	100	105	106	99	91	84	76	106
Extreme Minimum Temp. (°F)	-21	-5	0	22	30	39	53	47	32	21	15	-11	-21
Days Maximum Temp. ≥ 90°F	0	0	0	0	0	8	16	14	5	0	0	0	43
Days Maximum Temp. ≤ 32°F	3	2	0	0	0	0	0	0	0	0	0	2	7
Days Minimum Temp. ≤ 32°F	21	18	12	4	0	0	0	0	0	4	10	19	88
Days Minimum Temp. ≤ 0°F	1	0	0	0	0	0	0	0	0	0	0	0	1
Heating Degree Days (base 65°F)	847	672	498	249	72	5	0	1	31	224	473	760	3,832
Cooling Degree Days (base 65°F)	0	0	7	30	109	288	417	386	203	40	3	1	1,484
Mean Precipitation (in.)	4.03	4.52	5.06	4.54	5.64	3.96	4.35	3.51	3.88	3.19	4.62	5.29	52.59
Extreme Maximum Daily Precip. (in.)	3.50	3.73	3.25	3.50	6.53	5.21	4.81	3.10	3.84	4.00	4.57	3.35	6.53
Days With ≥ 0.1" Precipitation	7	7	8	7	8	7	7	6	6	5	7	7	82
Days With ≥ 0.5" Precipitation	3	3	4	3	3	3	3	2	3	2	3	3	35
Days With ≥ 1.0" Precipitation	1	1	2	1	2	1	1	1	1	1	1	2	15
Mean Snowfall (in.)	1.0	0.5	0.4	0.0	0.0	0.0	0.0	0.0	0.0	trace	trace	0.1	2.0
Maximum Snow Depth (in.)	6	3	4	0	0	0	0	0	0	trace	1	1	6
Days With ≥ 1.0" Snow Depth	0	0	0	0	0	0	0	0	0	0	0	0	0

The period of record for all cooperative weather station data is 1980 – 2009. See User Guide for detailed explanation of data.

Gatlinburg 2 SW *Sevier County* Elevation: 1,454 ft. Latitude: 35° 41' N Longitude: 83° 32' W

	JAN	FEB	MAR	APR	MAY	JUN	JUL	AUG	SEP	OCT	NOV	DEC	YEAR
Mean Maximum Temp. (°F)	48.4	52.3	61.0	69.7	76.5	82.5	84.9	84.1	79.0	69.9	60.7	50.8	68.3
Mean Temp. (°F)	37.3	40.2	47.3	55.4	63.0	70.4	73.5	72.7	67.0	56.4	47.4	39.5	55.8
Mean Minimum Temp. (°F)	26.1	28.0	33.7	41.0	49.5	58.2	62.2	61.3	55.0	42.8	34.1	28.0	43.3
Extreme Maximum Temp. (°F)	76	85	86	90	91	93	97	99	95	87	83	78	99
Extreme Minimum Temp. (°F)	-18	-10	-6	19	30	41	48	41	34	23	13	-4	-18
Days Maximum Temp. ≥ 90°F	0	0	0	0	0	2	5	4	1	0	0	0	12
Days Maximum Temp. ≤ 32°F	3	2	0	0	0	0	0	0	0	0	0	2	7
Days Minimum Temp. ≤ 32°F	23	20	16	6	1	0	0	0	0	5	15	22	108
Days Minimum Temp. ≤ 0°F	0	0	0	0	0	0	0	0	0	0	0	0	0
Heating Degree Days (base 65°F)	852	695	544	298	113	12	1	1	46	276	522	784	4,144
Cooling Degree Days (base 65°F)	0	0	2	15	59	180	271	247	113	15	2	0	904
Mean Precipitation (in.)	4.51	4.30	4.84	4.35	5.66	5.45	6.11	4.50	4.41	2.63	4.15	4.27	55.18
Extreme Maximum Daily Precip. (in.)	3.50	2.30	4.12	2.95	3.50	3.20	3.80	2.53	2.75	2.13	3.32	3.10	4.12
Days With ≥ 0.1" Precipitation	9	8	9	9	10	9	10	9	7	5	7	8	100
Days With ≥ 0.5" Precipitation	3	3	4	3	4	4	4	3	3	2	3	3	39
Days With ≥ 1.0" Precipitation	1	1	1	1	1	2	2	1	1	0	1	1	13
Mean Snowfall (in.)	3.1	2.1	2.1	0.7	0.0	0.0	0.0	0.0	0.0	trace	0.1	1.2	9.3
Maximum Snow Depth (in.)	***8***	***14***	***2***	trace	0	0	0	0	0	***trace***	1	***6***	***14***
Days With ≥ 1.0" Snow Depth	***2***	2	0	0	0	0	0	0	0	0	0	1	***5***

Jackson Exp Station *Madison County* Elevation: 399 ft. Latitude: 35° 37' N Longitude: 88° 50' W

	JAN	FEB	MAR	APR	MAY	JUN	JUL	AUG	SEP	OCT	NOV	DEC	YEAR
Mean Maximum Temp. (°F)	47.3	52.0	61.3	70.8	78.6	85.9	89.4	89.3	83.2	72.6	61.2	50.2	70.2
Mean Temp. (°F)	38.3	42.2	50.8	59.8	68.5	76.1	79.8	79.0	72.0	60.7	50.7	41.0	59.9
Mean Minimum Temp. (°F)	29.2	32.4	40.3	48.6	58.2	66.3	70.1	68.5	60.6	48.7	40.1	31.7	49.6
Extreme Maximum Temp. (°F)	75	81	87	91	92	100	101	105	100	92	85	78	105
Extreme Minimum Temp. (°F)	-10	1	11	23	35	46	56	48	35	26	17	-7	-10
Days Maximum Temp. ≥ 90°F	0	0	0	0	1	9	17	16	6	0	0	0	49
Days Maximum Temp. ≤ 32°F	3	2	0	0	0	0	0	0	0	0	0	2	7
Days Minimum Temp. ≤ 32°F	20	15	8	2	0	0	0	0	0	2	8	17	72
Days Minimum Temp. ≤ 0°F	0	0	0	0	0	0	0	0	0	0	0	0	0
Heating Degree Days (base 65°F)	821	639	445	205	48	2	0	1	25	184	430	739	3,539
Cooling Degree Days (base 65°F)	0	1	12	54	161	342	465	440	240	58	7	1	1,781
Mean Precipitation (in.)	4.12	4.20	5.06	4.77	4.92	4.96	4.70	2.92	3.56	3.91	4.84	5.40	53.36
Extreme Maximum Daily Precip. (in.)	2.61	3.67	3.70	3.08	5.24	3.80	3.99	2.91	7.15	2.84	4.70	7.86	7.86
Days With ≥ 0.1" Precipitation	7	7	8	7	7	7	6	4	5	5	6	7	76
Days With ≥ 0.5" Precipitation	3	3	3	3	4	3	3	2	2	3	3	4	36
Days With ≥ 1.0" Precipitation	1	1	1	2	1	1	2	1	1	1	2	2	16
Mean Snowfall (in.)	1.3	1.5	0.4	0.1	0.0	0.0	0.0	0.0	0.0	trace	trace	0.3	3.6
Maximum Snow Depth (in.)	6	6	6	3	0	0	0	0	0	trace	trace	3	6
Days With ≥ 1.0" Snow Depth	1	1	0	0	0	0	0	0	0	0	0	0	2

Kingsport *Sullivan County* Elevation: 1,284 ft. Latitude: 36° 31' N Longitude: 82° 32' W

	JAN	FEB	MAR	APR	MAY	JUN	JUL	AUG	SEP	OCT	NOV	DEC	YEAR
Mean Maximum Temp. (°F)	46.6	51.3	61.0	70.4	78.0	84.6	87.2	86.7	80.9	70.9	60.0	49.2	68.9
Mean Temp. (°F)	37.2	40.7	48.8	57.5	65.6	73.1	76.4	75.7	69.4	58.5	48.6	39.7	57.6
Mean Minimum Temp. (°F)	27.7	30.1	36.6	44.6	53.2	61.5	65.5	64.6	57.8	46.1	37.2	30.2	46.3
Extreme Maximum Temp. (°F)	74	81	86	91	92	97	98	101	97	89	83	77	101
Extreme Minimum Temp. (°F)	-18	-11	-2	24	31	42	49	45	36	25	14	-3	-18
Days Maximum Temp. ≥ 90°F	0	0	0	0	0	5	10	8	3	0	0	0	26
Days Maximum Temp. ≤ 32°F	3	1	0	0	0	0	0	0	0	0	0	2	6
Days Minimum Temp. ≤ 32°F	21	17	11	3	0	0	0	0	0	2	11	19	84
Days Minimum Temp. ≤ 0°F	0	0	0	0	0	0	0	0	0	0	0	0	0
Heating Degree Days (base 65°F)	856	680	497	241	71	5	0	1	29	219	487	776	3,862
Cooling Degree Days (base 65°F)	0	0	3	24	97	255	360	340	167	26	1	0	1,273
Mean Precipitation (in.)	3.63	3.64	3.78	3.53	4.04	3.46	5.03	3.66	3.05	2.33	3.12	3.64	42.91
Extreme Maximum Daily Precip. (in.)	2.65	2.26	3.44	2.55	3.00	1.84	2.60	3.02	2.65	1.90	2.27	4.50	4.50
Days With ≥ 0.1" Precipitation	8	7	8	8	8	7	9	7	6	5	7	7	87
Days With ≥ 0.5" Precipitation	2	3	2	2	3	3	4	3	2	1	2	2	29
Days With ≥ 1.0" Precipitation	1	1	1	1	1	1	1	1	1	0	0	1	10
Mean Snowfall (in.)	3.4	2.3	0.8	0.4	trace	0.0	0.0	0.0	0.0	trace	0.1	1.3	8.3
Maximum Snow Depth (in.)	11	14	14	10	trace	0	0	0	0	trace	1	5	14
Days With ≥ 1.0" Snow Depth	3	2	0	0	0	0	0	0	0	0	0	1	6

Knoxville Exp Stn *Knox County* Elevation: 830 ft. Latitude: 35° 53' N Longitude: 83° 57' W

	JAN	FEB	MAR	APR	MAY	JUN	JUL	AUG	SEP	OCT	NOV	DEC	YEAR
Mean Maximum Temp. (°F)	47.2	51.9	61.4	69.5	77.4	84.7	***87.6***	87.3	***81.8***	71.3	60.4	49.8	***69.2***
Mean Temp. (°F)	36.8	40.8	48.8	56.7	65.5	73.4	***77.0***	76.2	***69.9***	58.7	48.4	39.5	***57.6***
Mean Minimum Temp. (°F)	26.4	29.6	36.1	43.8	53.5	61.9	***66.4***	65.1	***57.9***	45.9	36.2	29.1	***46.0***
Extreme Maximum Temp. (°F)	75	81	86	90	92	100	***100***	102	***96***	90	82	78	***102***
Extreme Minimum Temp. (°F)	-20	-12	2	21	32	42	***48***	50	***37***	26	15	-5	***-20***
Days Maximum Temp. ≥ 90°F	0	0	0	0	0	6	***11***	10	***4***	0	0	0	***31***
Days Maximum Temp. ≤ 32°F	3	1	0	0	0	0	***0***	0	***0***	0	0	1	***5***
Days Minimum Temp. ≤ 32°F	22	18	12	4	0	0	***0***	0	***0***	3	11	21	***91***
Days Minimum Temp. ≤ 0°F	0	0	0	0	0	0	***0***	0	***0***	0	0	0	***0***
Heating Degree Days (base 65°F)	867	677	499	261	78	5	***0***	1	***30***	218	494	785	***3,915***
Cooling Degree Days (base 65°F)	0	0	3	20	101	262	***381***	355	***183***	29	1	0	***1,335***
Mean Precipitation (in.)	4.84	4.59	4.90	4.34	4.87	3.89	5.57	3.47	3.57	2.81	4.29	5.04	52.18
Extreme Maximum Daily Precip. (in.)	3.05	2.98	3.48	3.20	4.92	2.97	3.34	3.00	5.15	1.80	3.07	3.07	5.15
Days With ≥ 0.1" Precipitation	8	8	9	8	8	7	8	6	5	5	7	8	87
Days With ≥ 0.5" Precipitation	4	3	3	3	3	3	4	2	3	2	3	3	36
Days With ≥ 1.0" Precipitation	1	1	1	1	1	1	2	1	1	1	1	1	13
Mean Snowfall (in.)	***0.0***	***trace***	trace	0.0	0.0	0.0	0.0	0.0	0.0	0.0	trace	0.1	***0.1***
Maximum Snow Depth (in.)	***0***	***trace***	0	0	0	0	***0***	0	***0***	0	trace	0	trace
Days With ≥ 1.0" Snow Depth	***0***	***0***	0	0	0	0	0	0	0	0	0	0	***0***

The period of record for all cooperative weather station data is 1980 – 2009. See User Guide for detailed explanation of data.

Lawrenceburg Filter Plant *Lawrence County* Elevation: 870 ft. Latitude: 35° 16' N Longitude: 87° 21' W

	JAN	FEB	MAR	APR	MAY	JUN	JUL	AUG	SEP	OCT	NOV	DEC	YEAR
Mean Maximum Temp. (°F)	48.9	53.3	62.3	71.1	77.9	84.8	88.1	87.9	82.2	71.8	61.3	50.7	70.0
Mean Temp. (°F)	38.5	42.2	50.4	58.5	66.4	73.8	77.3	76.6	70.3	59.3	49.7	40.8	58.7
Mean Minimum Temp. (°F)	28.2	31.1	38.4	45.9	54.9	62.7	66.5	65.3	58.3	46.7	38.1	30.7	47.2
Extreme Maximum Temp. (°F)	74	81	84	89	94	99	103	104	99	89	83	75	104
Extreme Minimum Temp. (°F)	-14	-4	4	22	33	43	51	47	36	24	16	-10	-14
Days Maximum Temp. ≥ 90°F	0	0	0	0	0	6	12	12	4	0	0	0	34
Days Maximum Temp. ≤ 32°F	2	1	0	0	0	0	0	0	0	0	0	2	5
Days Minimum Temp. ≤ 32°F	21	16	10	3	0	0	0	0	0	3	10	18	81
Days Minimum Temp. ≤ 0°F	0	0	0	0	0	0	0	0	0	0	0	0	0
Heating Degree Days (base 65°F)	815	637	452	217	61	3	0	1	29	206	454	746	3,621
Cooling Degree Days (base 65°F)	0	0	6	30	113	273	389	368	193	35	3	1	1,411
Mean Precipitation (in.)	5.15	5.17	5.71	4.93	5.80	4.34	5.38	3.71	4.43	3.83	5.26	6.18	59.89
Extreme Maximum Daily Precip. (in.)	5.65	4.41	5.22	3.32	4.68	5.38	8.76	4.46	4.31	4.92	3.74	4.61	8.76
Days With ≥ 0.1" Precipitation	7	7	8	8	7	7	8	6	5	5	7	8	83
Days With ≥ 0.5" Precipitation	3	3	4	3	4	3	3	2	3	3	4	4	39
Days With ≥ 1.0" Precipitation	2	2	2	2	2	1	2	1	1	1	2	2	20
Mean Snowfall (in.)	1.4	1.7	0.3	trace	0.0	0.0	0.0	0.0	0.0	trace	trace	0.6	4.0
Maximum Snow Depth (in.)	10	7	trace	1	0	0	0	0	0	trace	trace	3	10
Days With ≥ 1.0" Snow Depth	1	1	0	0	0	0	0	0	0	0	0	0	2

Lebanon 3 W *Wilson County* Elevation: 535 ft. Latitude: 36° 14' N Longitude: 86° 22' W

	JAN	FEB	MAR	APR	MAY	JUN	JUL	AUG	SEP	OCT	NOV	DEC	YEAR
Mean Maximum Temp. (°F)	46.7	51.3	60.4	69.9	78.4	86.3	90.1	89.8	83.2	72.1	60.7	49.8	69.9
Mean Temp. (°F)	36.2	39.8	48.1	57.0	66.1	74.5	78.7	77.6	70.2	58.4	48.5	39.1	57.8
Mean Minimum Temp. (°F)	25.6	28.2	35.8	44.2	53.7	62.7	67.2	65.3	57.2	44.6	36.2	28.3	45.8
Extreme Maximum Temp. (°F)	75	80	87	90	94	102	105	107	102	94	85	79	107
Extreme Minimum Temp. (°F)	-20	-6	-2	20	29	42	51	43	33	21	11	-11	-20
Days Maximum Temp. ≥ 90°F	0	0	0	0	1	11	18	17	6	0	0	0	53
Days Maximum Temp. ≤ 32°F	4	2	0	0	0	0	0	0	0	0	0	2	8
Days Minimum Temp. ≤ 32°F	22	19	13	4	0	0	0	0	0	5	12	20	95
Days Minimum Temp. ≤ 0°F	1	0	0	0	0	0	0	0	0	0	0	0	1
Heating Degree Days (base 65°F)	885	707	523	266	80	5	0	1	37	235	493	796	4,028
Cooling Degree Days (base 65°F)	0	0	7	33	121	298	431	399	198	37	4	1	1,529
Mean Precipitation (in.)	4.20	4.35	4.78	4.20	5.45	4.48	4.59	3.37	3.74	3.21	4.41	4.97	51.75
Extreme Maximum Daily Precip. (in.)	3.92	5.22	3.26	3.65	3.85	4.46	3.76	3.54	5.75	3.46	3.28	3.24	5.75
Days With ≥ 0.1" Precipitation	7	7	8	7	8	7	7	5	5	5	6	7	79
Days With ≥ 0.5" Precipitation	3	3	3	3	4	3	3	2	2	2	3	3	34
Days With ≥ 1.0" Precipitation	1	1	1	1	2	1	1	1	1	1	1	1	13
Mean Snowfall (in.)	0.1	1.0	0.3	trace	0.0	0.0	0.0	0.0	0.0	0.0	trace	0.1	1.5
Maximum Snow Depth (in.)	8	6	5	trace	0	0	0	0	0	0	1	3	8
Days With ≥ 1.0" Snow Depth	2	1	0	0	0	0	0	0	0	0	0	1	4

Lenoir City *Loudon County* Elevation: 785 ft. Latitude: 35° 47' N Longitude: 84° 16' W

	JAN	FEB	MAR	APR	MAY	JUN	JUL	AUG	SEP	OCT	NOV	DEC	YEAR
Mean Maximum Temp. (°F)	47.8	52.5	61.7	70.6	78.5	85.7	88.8	88.5	82.7	72.1	61.2	51.1	70.1
Mean Temp. (°F)	37.8	41.5	49.6	57.9	66.7	74.9	78.6	77.9	71.4	59.7	49.6	40.9	58.9
Mean Minimum Temp. (°F)	27.7	30.3	37.5	45.2	54.9	64.1	68.3	67.3	60.0	47.3	37.8	30.6	47.6
Extreme Maximum Temp. (°F)	75	80	85	91	92	101	104	104	98	90	82	77	104
Extreme Minimum Temp. (°F)	-14	-7	1	23	36	43	51	53	37	28	17	-5	-14
Days Maximum Temp. ≥ 90°F	0	0	0	0	0	7	14	13	5	0	0	0	39
Days Maximum Temp. ≤ 32°F	2	1	0	0	0	0	0	0	0	0	0	1	4
Days Minimum Temp. ≤ 32°F	21	17	10	2	0	0	0	0	0	1	10	18	79
Days Minimum Temp. ≤ 0°F	0	0	0	0	0	0	0	0	0	0	0	0	0
Heating Degree Days (base 65°F)	837	660	474	233	62	3	0	0	21	194	459	741	3,684
Cooling Degree Days (base 65°F)	0	0	4	27	121	308	428	407	219	36	2	0	1,552
Mean Precipitation (in.)	4.59	4.83	4.77	4.41	4.60	3.78	5.06	3.64	3.70	2.80	4.08	4.88	51.14
Extreme Maximum Daily Precip. (in.)	2.41	4.00	4.03	3.96	3.21	2.21	4.00	3.07	5.85	2.15	2.35	3.76	5.85
Days With ≥ 0.1" Precipitation	8	8	8	7	8	7	8	6	5	5	7	8	85
Days With ≥ 0.5" Precipitation	3	3	3	3	3	3	3	2	2	2	3	3	33
Days With ≥ 1.0" Precipitation	1	1	1	1	1	1	1	1	1	1	1	1	12
Mean Snowfall (in.)	1.8	1.6	0.7	0.3	0.0	0.0	0.0	0.0	0.0	trace	trace	0.4	4.8
Maximum Snow Depth (in.)	5	8	11	3	0	0	0	0	0	trace	trace	2	11
Days With ≥ 1.0" Snow Depth	1	1	0	0	0	0	0	0	0	0	0	0	2

Lewisburg Exp Stn *Marshall County* Elevation: 787 ft. Latitude: 35° 25' N Longitude: 86° 48' W

	JAN	FEB	MAR	APR	MAY	JUN	JUL	AUG	SEP	OCT	NOV	DEC	YEAR
Mean Maximum Temp. (°F)	47.7	52.1	60.8	70.1	78.5	86.1	89.5	89.7	83.4	72.4	61.2	50.3	70.2
Mean Temp. (°F)	37.0	40.4	48.1	56.6	65.6	73.8	77.6	76.7	69.8	58.4	48.6	39.3	57.6
Mean Minimum Temp. (°F)	26.2	28.5	35.3	43.1	52.7	61.4	65.6	63.7	56.1	44.3	36.0	28.3	45.1
Extreme Maximum Temp. (°F)	75	81	85	91	96	102	102	106	102	94	86	76	106
Extreme Minimum Temp. (°F)	-20	-5	2	18	29	39	51	44	32	20	12	-12	-20
Days Maximum Temp. ≥ 90°F	0	0	0	0	1	10	17	17	7	0	0	0	52
Days Maximum Temp. ≤ 32°F	3	2	0	0	0	0	0	0	0	0	0	2	7
Days Minimum Temp. ≤ 32°F	22	19	13	5	0	0	0	0	0	5	13	20	97
Days Minimum Temp. ≤ 0°F	1	0	0	0	0	0	0	0	0	0	0	0	1
Heating Degree Days (base 65°F)	861	691	522	270	82	6	0	2	37	234	488	791	3,984
Cooling Degree Days (base 65°F)	0	0	4	25	108	276	398	372	188	35	3	0	1,409
Mean Precipitation (in.)	4.48	4.35	5.57	4.60	5.19	4.46	4.53	3.59	4.33	3.47	4.68	5.35	54.60
Extreme Maximum Daily Precip. (in.)	6.05	4.34	5.73	3.32	4.20	3.69	5.23	3.41	4.22	3.95	4.98	3.56	6.05
Days With ≥ 0.1" Precipitation	7	7	8	7	7	7	8	5	5	5	7	7	80
Days With ≥ 0.5" Precipitation	3	3	4	3	3	3	3	2	3	2	3	4	36
Days With ≥ 1.0" Precipitation	1	1	1	1	1	1	1	1	2	1	1	2	14
Mean Snowfall (in.)	1.1	0.6	0.4	trace	0.0	0.0	0.0	0.0	0.0	0.0	trace	0.3	2.4
Maximum Snow Depth (in.)	8	11	6	trace	0	0	0	0	0	0	trace	3	11
Days With ≥ 1.0" Snow Depth	1	1	0	0	0	0	0	0	0	0	0	0	2

Morristown Radio WCRK *Hamblen County* Elevation: 1,359 ft. Latitude: 36° 12' N Longitude: 83° 17' W

	JAN	FEB	MAR	APR	MAY	JUN	JUL	AUG	SEP	OCT	NOV	DEC	YEAR
Mean Maximum Temp. (°F)	46.6	51.4	60.8	69.2	76.8	83.8	86.5	86.1	80.2	70.5	59.5	49.1	68.4
Mean Temp. (°F)	37.0	40.8	48.7	56.8	65.0	72.8	76.2	75.6	69.0	58.4	48.3	39.6	57.3
Mean Minimum Temp. (°F)	27.4	30.1	36.6	44.4	53.0	61.8	65.8	65.0	57.8	46.2	37.0	30.0	46.3
Extreme Maximum Temp. (°F)	76	79	84	90	90	98	98	100	95	87	81	78	100
Extreme Minimum Temp. (°F)	-19	-13	0	21	31	41	49	46	35	24	14	-4	-19
Days Maximum Temp. ≥ 90°F	0	0	0	0	0	3	8	7	2	0	0	0	20
Days Maximum Temp. ≤ 32°F	3	1	0	0	0	0	0	0	0	0	0	2	6
Days Minimum Temp. ≤ 32°F	21	17	11	3	0	0	0	0	0	3	11	19	85
Days Minimum Temp. ≤ 0°F	0	0	0	0	0	0	0	0	0	0	0	0	0
Heating Degree Days (base 65°F)	861	677	500	261	83	6	0	1	33	224	498	781	3,925
Cooling Degree Days (base 65°F)	0	0	3	21	89	247	354	334	160	26	1	0	1,235
Mean Precipitation (in.)	3.95	4.04	4.05	3.97	4.15	3.92	4.68	3.50	2.95	2.22	3.48	4.10	45.01
Extreme Maximum Daily Precip. (in.)	2.68	2.50	3.08	2.80	3.47	2.36	3.50	3.57	3.58	1.56	2.44	2.94	3.58
Days With ≥ 0.1" Precipitation	7	7	8	7	8	7	8	6	5	5	7	8	83
Days With ≥ 0.5" Precipitation	3	3	3	3	3	3	3	2	2	1	2	3	31
Days With ≥ 1.0" Precipitation	1	1	1	1	1	1	1	1	1	0	1	1	11
Mean Snowfall (in.)	3.7	3.2	1.5	0.7	0.0	0.0	0.0	0.0	0.0	trace	0.1	1.5	10.7
Maximum Snow Depth (in.)	***6***	***5***	***4***	***trace***	***0***	***0***	***0***	***0***	***0***	***trace***	***trace***	***trace***	***6***
Days With ≥ 1.0" Snow Depth	***1***	0	0	0	0	0	0	0	0	0	0	0	***1***

Moscow *Fayette County* Elevation: 334 ft. Latitude: 35° 04' N Longitude: 89° 25' W

	JAN	FEB	MAR	APR	MAY	JUN	JUL	AUG	SEP	OCT	NOV	DEC	YEAR
Mean Maximum Temp. (°F)	50.3	55.4	64.3	73.3	80.1	86.9	90.3	90.0	84.2	73.9	64.0	52.9	72.1
Mean Temp. (°F)	40.6	44.8	52.9	61.5	69.6	76.7	80.2	79.4	72.7	61.5	52.7	43.0	61.3
Mean Minimum Temp. (°F)	30.7	34.1	41.5	49.7	59.2	66.4	70.1	68.7	61.1	49.1	41.3	33.1	50.4
Extreme Maximum Temp. (°F)	78	82	86	94	94	101	102	105	100	92	85	80	105
Extreme Minimum Temp. (°F)	-9	1	13	25	39	46	54	48	36	25	18	-6	-9
Days Maximum Temp. ≥ 90°F	0	0	0	0	1	11	19	17	6	0	0	0	54
Days Maximum Temp. ≤ 32°F	2	1	0	0	0	0	0	0	0	0	0	1	4
Days Minimum Temp. ≤ 32°F	18	13	7	1	0	0	0	0	0	2	7	16	64
Days Minimum Temp. ≤ 0°F	0	0	0	0	0	0	0	0	0	0	0	0	0
Heating Degree Days (base 65°F)	746	568	381	156	27	1	0	0	16	158	373	675	3,101
Cooling Degree Days (base 65°F)	1	1	14	57	178	358	479	453	253	56	9	1	1,860
Mean Precipitation (in.)	3.45	4.17	5.09	5.18	5.11	3.85	4.66	3.56	3.73	4.14	4.45	5.30	52.69
Extreme Maximum Daily Precip. (in.)	2.93	3.24	4.00	***3.39***	4.32	4.05	6.53	4.40	8.04	***4.20***	***3.79***	3.48	***8.04***
Days With ≥ 0.1" Precipitation	5	6	6	6	6	5	5	4	5	5	5	5	63
Days With ≥ 0.5" Precipitation	3	3	3	3	3	3	3	2	2	3	3	4	35
Days With ≥ 1.0" Precipitation	1	1	2	2	2	1	2	1	1	1	2	2	18
Mean Snowfall (in.)	0.4	0.6	0.2	0.1	0.0	0.0	0.0	0.0	0.0	trace	trace	0.1	1.4
Maximum Snow Depth (in.)	8	6	4	2	0	0	0	0	0	trace	trace	1	8
Days With ≥ 1.0" Snow Depth	1	1	0	0	0	0	0	0	0	0	0	0	2

Murfreesboro 5 N *Rutherford County* Elevation: 549 ft. Latitude: 35° 55' N Longitude: 86° 23' W

	JAN	FEB	MAR	APR	MAY	JUN	JUL	AUG	SEP	OCT	NOV	DEC	YEAR
Mean Maximum Temp. (°F)	47.3	51.9	60.7	70.2	78.0	85.8	89.2	89.3	83.1	72.2	61.1	50.2	69.9
Mean Temp. (°F)	37.0	40.5	48.6	57.4	66.2	74.5	78.3	77.6	70.5	58.9	49.2	39.8	58.2
Mean Minimum Temp. (°F)	26.5	29.0	36.4	44.7	54.1	63.0	67.4	65.8	57.9	45.5	37.3	29.4	46.4
Extreme Maximum Temp. (°F)	75	81	86	90	93	102	106	106	101	91	86	76	106
Extreme Minimum Temp. (°F)	-13	-10	2	19	33	43	53	44	35	23	14	-9	-13
Days Maximum Temp. ≥ 90°F	0	0	0	0	1	9	16	15	6	0	0	0	47
Days Maximum Temp. ≤ 32°F	3	2	0	0	0	0	0	0	0	0	0	2	7
Days Minimum Temp. ≤ 32°F	22	18	12	3	0	0	0	0	0	3	11	20	89
Days Minimum Temp. ≤ 0°F	1	0	0	0	0	0	0	0	0	0	0	0	1
Heating Degree Days (base 65°F)	862	688	507	251	73	5	0	1	31	220	471	774	3,883
Cooling Degree Days (base 65°F)	0	0	6	31	117	295	420	397	203	38	4	0	1,511
Mean Precipitation (in.)	4.29	4.26	5.08	4.11	5.08	4.67	4.80	3.49	4.16	3.25	4.46	5.26	52.91
Extreme Maximum Daily Precip. (in.)	2.95	3.66	3.59	2.37	3.68	3.67	4.85	2.96	8.13	2.59	4.51	3.25	8.13
Days With ≥ 0.1" Precipitation	7	7	8	7	8	7	7	6	5	5	6	8	81
Days With ≥ 0.5" Precipitation	3	3	4	3	3	3	3	3	3	3	3	4	38
Days With ≥ 1.0" Precipitation	1	1	1	1	1	1	1	1	1	1	2	2	14
Mean Snowfall (in.)	0.9	0.7	0.4	0.0	0.0	0.0	0.0	0.0	0.0	trace	trace	0.2	2.2
Maximum Snow Depth (in.)	7	5	7	0	0	0	0	0	0	trace	trace	1	7
Days With ≥ 1.0" Snow Depth	1	1	0	0	0	0	0	0	0	0	0	0	2

Neapolis Exp Stn *Maury County* Elevation: 700 ft. Latitude: 35° 43' N Longitude: 86° 59' W

	JAN	FEB	MAR	APR	MAY	JUN	JUL	AUG	SEP	OCT	NOV	DEC	YEAR
Mean Maximum Temp. (°F)	48.0	52.4	61.5	70.6	78.8	86.1	89.8	89.9	83.4	72.8	61.9	50.9	70.5
Mean Temp. (°F)	37.3	40.8	49.1	57.5	66.3	74.3	78.1	77.3	70.2	58.9	49.3	40.0	58.3
Mean Minimum Temp. (°F)	26.4	29.2	36.6	44.4	53.8	62.4	66.3	64.8	57.0	44.8	36.8	29.0	46.0
Extreme Maximum Temp. (°F)	80	82	90	92	94	103	104	109	104	94	87	80	109
Extreme Minimum Temp. (°F)	-23	-8	3	19	31	40	53	46	34	21	12	-12	-23
Days Maximum Temp. ≥ 90°F	0	0	0	0	1	10	18	17	6	0	0	0	52
Days Maximum Temp. ≤ 32°F	3	2	0	0	0	0	0	0	0	0	0	2	7
Days Minimum Temp. ≤ 32°F	22	18	12	4	0	0	0	0	0	4	12	20	92
Days Minimum Temp. ≤ 0°F	1	0	0	0	0	0	0	0	0	0	0	0	1
Heating Degree Days (base 65°F)	854	677	494	248	72	5	0	1	35	223	467	769	3,845
Cooling Degree Days (base 65°F)	0	0	7	31	120	290	412	390	198	39	4	1	1,492
Mean Precipitation (in.)	4.48	4.85	5.21	4.70	5.46	3.95	4.55	3.38	4.03	3.76	4.97	5.89	55.23
Extreme Maximum Daily Precip. (in.)	3.78	3.90	3.41	4.87	4.50	4.04	8.14	3.18	6.00	3.45	4.65	4.08	8.14
Days With ≥ 0.1" Precipitation	8	7	8	8	8	8	8	5	6	5	7	8	86
Days With ≥ 0.5" Precipitation	3	3	4	3	4	3	3	2	3	3	3	4	38
Days With ≥ 1.0" Precipitation	1	1	1	2	2	1	1	1	1	1	2	2	16
Mean Snowfall (in.)	1.2	1.5	0.6	trace	0.0	0.0	0.0	0.0	0.0	0.0	trace	0.3	3.6
Maximum Snow Depth (in.)	***5***	***1***	***2***	trace	0	0	0	0	0	0	trace	1	***5***
Days With ≥ 1.0" Snow Depth	***0***	0	0	0	0	0	0	0	0	0	0	0	***0***

The period of record for all cooperative weather station data is 1980 – 2009. See User Guide for detailed explanation of data.

Norris *Anderson County* Elevation: 1,109 ft. Latitude: 36° 13' N Longitude: 84° 04' W

	JAN	FEB	MAR	APR	MAY	JUN	JUL	AUG	SEP	OCT	NOV	DEC	YEAR
Mean Maximum Temp. (°F)	45.3	50.6	60.6	70.1	77.3	83.4	86.3	85.7	80.2	70.0	58.9	47.6	68.0
Mean Temp. (°F)	35.5	39.4	47.4	55.7	64.2	71.6	75.2	74.9	68.5	57.3	47.2	37.9	56.2
Mean Minimum Temp. (°F)	25.8	28.2	34.2	41.3	51.0	59.8	64.1	63.7	56.8	44.6	35.4	28.3	44.4
Extreme Maximum Temp. (°F)	76	77	86	92	90	100	102	99	95	88	88	72	102
Extreme Minimum Temp. (°F)	-19	-17	-3	20	26	39	45	44	36	25	14	-3	-19
Days Maximum Temp. ≥ 90°F	0	0	0	0	0	3	7	6	3	0	0	0	19
Days Maximum Temp. ≤ 32°F	3	2	0	0	0	0	0	0	0	0	0	2	7
Days Minimum Temp. ≤ 32°F	23	20	14	6	0	0	0	0	0	3	12	21	99
Days Minimum Temp. ≤ 0°F	0	0	0	0	0	0	0	0	0	0	0	0	0
Heating Degree Days (base 65°F)	906	717	541	285	94	9	0	1	35	248	529	833	4,198
Cooling Degree Days (base 65°F)	0	0	1	13	75	214	324	313	148	17	1	0	1,106
Mean Precipitation (in.)	4.70	4.46	4.92	4.80	4.56	4.76	4.84	3.93	3.78	2.83	4.36	5.09	53.03
Extreme Maximum Daily Precip. (in.)	2.69	4.72	3.51	6.06	4.65	3.63	4.53	2.71	3.21	2.00	2.82	5.13	6.06
Days With ≥ 0.1" Precipitation	8	7	8	7	8	8	9	6	6	5	7	8	87
Days With ≥ 0.5" Precipitation	4	3	3	3	3	3	3	3	3	2	3	3	36
Days With ≥ 1.0" Precipitation	1	1	1	1	1	1	1	1	1	1	1	1	12
Mean Snowfall (in.)	1.5	1.6	0.6	0.3	0.0	0.0	0.0	0.0	0.0	trace	trace	0.2	4.2
Maximum Snow Depth (in.)	5	*12*	10	trace	0	0	0	0	0	trace	trace	*3*	*12*
Days With ≥ 1.0" Snow Depth	1	1	0	0	0	0	0	0	0	0	0	0	2

Sevierville 1 SE *Sevier County* Elevation: 930 ft. Latitude: 35° 52' N Longitude: 83° 33' W

	JAN	FEB	MAR	APR	MAY	JUN	JUL	AUG	SEP	OCT	NOV	DEC	YEAR
Mean Maximum Temp. (°F)	48.5	53.3	62.8	71.1	79.0	85.9	88.6	88.4	82.6	72.5	61.3	51.2	70.4
Mean Temp. (°F)	37.8	41.5	49.3	57.5	65.7	73.7	77.0	76.6	70.2	58.9	48.6	40.3	58.1
Mean Minimum Temp. (°F)	27.1	29.7	35.7	43.8	52.3	61.4	65.3	64.6	57.6	45.3	35.9	29.4	45.7
Extreme Maximum Temp. (°F)	80	85	87	90	92	98	101	104	101	91	83	79	104
Extreme Minimum Temp. (°F)	-24	-16	-4	18	28	39	46	49	33	22	14	-7	-24
Days Maximum Temp. ≥ 90°F	0	0	0	0	1	8	14	13	5	0	0	0	41
Days Maximum Temp. ≤ 32°F	2	1	0	0	0	0	0	0	0	0	0	1	4
Days Minimum Temp. ≤ 32°F	21	18	12	3	0	0	0	0	0	3	12	20	89
Days Minimum Temp. ≤ 0°F	0	0	0	0	0	0	0	0	0	0	0	0	0
Heating Degree Days (base 65°F)	837	659	483	239	69	4	0	0	26	210	487	759	3,773
Cooling Degree Days (base 65°F)	0	0	4	21	96	272	379	365	187	29	2	0	1,355
Mean Precipitation (in.)	3.58	3.67	4.00	3.61	4.43	3.83	4.35	3.25	3.23	2.32	3.34	3.69	43.30
Extreme Maximum Daily Precip. (in.)	3.40	4.03	3.91	3.24	3.10	2.00	3.51	2.30	2.52	2.10	3.30	2.15	4.03
Days With ≥ 0.1" Precipitation	6	7	8	7	8	7	8	6	5	5	6	7	80
Days With ≥ 0.5" Precipitation	3	2	3	3	3	3	3	2	2	2	3	3	32
Days With ≥ 1.0" Precipitation	1	1	1	1	1	1	1	1	1	0	1	1	11
Mean Snowfall (in.)	2.2	1.2	0.9	0.6	0.0	0.0	0.0	0.0	0.0	0.0	0.1	0.2	5.2
Maximum Snow Depth (in.)	6	4	1	2	0	0	0	0	0	*0*	trace	4	*6*
Days With ≥ 1.0" Snow Depth	1	0	0	0	0	0	0	0	0	0	0	0	1

Shelbyville Water Dept *Bedford County* Elevation: 759 ft. Latitude: 35° 30' N Longitude: 86° 29' W

	JAN	FEB	MAR	APR	MAY	JUN	JUL	AUG	SEP	OCT	NOV	DEC	YEAR
Mean Maximum Temp. (°F)	49.3	53.7	62.6	71.4	79.3	86.4	89.6	89.4	83.4	72.9	61.5	51.5	70.9
Mean Temp. (°F)	39.2	42.9	50.8	59.0	67.6	75.0	78.7	78.0	71.4	60.3	50.2	41.4	59.5
Mean Minimum Temp. (°F)	29.1	32.0	38.9	46.5	55.8	63.6	67.8	66.5	59.3	47.7	38.8	31.3	48.1
Extreme Maximum Temp. (°F)	74	79	85	92	95	101	104	104	101	92	85	77	104
Extreme Minimum Temp. (°F)	-20	-6	3	21	33	43	53	49	35	24	15	-9	-20
Days Maximum Temp. ≥ 90°F	0	0	0	0	1	9	16	16	6	0	0	0	48
Days Maximum Temp. ≤ 32°F	2	1	0	0	0	0	0	0	0	0	0	2	5
Days Minimum Temp. ≤ 32°F	19	16	9	3	0	0	0	0	0	3	10	18	78
Days Minimum Temp. ≤ 0°F	0	0	0	0	0	0	0	0	0	0	0	0	0
Heating Degree Days (base 65°F)	795	620	439	210	50	2	0	0	23	186	441	726	3,492
Cooling Degree Days (base 65°F)	0	0	8	36	137	310	432	410	222	47	4	1	1,607
Mean Precipitation (in.)	4.74	4.74	5.51	4.30	5.45	4.66	4.82	3.59	3.91	3.45	4.99	5.46	55.62
Extreme Maximum Daily Precip. (in.)	4.55	4.70	3.99	4.00	4.90	3.58	2.81	2.70	5.19	3.53	4.33	4.07	5.19
Days With ≥ 0.1" Precipitation	7	8	8	7	8	8	8	5	6	5	7	8	85
Days With ≥ 0.5" Precipitation	3	3	4	3	3	3	3	2	3	2	3	4	36
Days With ≥ 1.0" Precipitation	1	1	2	1	2	1	1	1	1	1	2	2	16
Mean Snowfall (in.)	0.9	0.9	0.6	trace	0.0	0.0	0.0	0.0	0.0	trace	trace	0.2	2.6
Maximum Snow Depth (in.)	7	4	7	trace	0	0	0	0	0	trace	trace	1	7
Days With ≥ 1.0" Snow Depth	1	1	0	0	0	0	0	0	0	0	0	0	2

Springfield Exp Stn *Robertson County* Elevation: 745 ft. Latitude: 36° 28' N Longitude: 86° 51' W

	JAN	FEB	MAR	APR	MAY	JUN	JUL	AUG	SEP	OCT	NOV	DEC	YEAR
Mean Maximum Temp. (°F)	44.8	49.3	58.7	68.3	76.6	84.7	88.5	88.5	81.9	70.5	58.9	47.9	68.2
Mean Temp. (°F)	34.9	38.5	47.0	56.3	65.1	73.5	77.3	76.3	69.3	57.9	47.9	37.9	56.8
Mean Minimum Temp. (°F)	25.0	27.7	35.3	44.2	53.5	62.2	66.0	64.1	56.7	45.3	36.9	27.9	45.4
Extreme Maximum Temp. (°F)	74	82	87	89	92	101	103	106	101	94	85	76	106
Extreme Minimum Temp. (°F)	-17	-6	1	16	31	42	50	44	31	22	10	-16	-17
Days Maximum Temp. ≥ 90°F	0	0	0	0	0	7	15	14	5	0	0	0	41
Days Maximum Temp. ≤ 32°F	5	3	0	0	0	0	0	0	0	0	0	3	11
Days Minimum Temp. ≤ 32°F	24	19	14	4	0	0	0	0	0	4	12	21	98
Days Minimum Temp. ≤ 0°F	1	0	0	0	0	0	0	0	0	0	0	0	1
Heating Degree Days (base 65°F)	926	742	558	284	95	8	0	2	44	249	509	832	4,249
Cooling Degree Days (base 65°F)	0	0	6	30	105	269	387	360	181	35	4	0	1,377
Mean Precipitation (in.)	3.63	4.07	4.40	4.54	5.39	4.26	3.97	2.96	3.56	3.71	4.08	4.72	49.29
Extreme Maximum Daily Precip. (in.)	4.37	2.92	2.74	3.35	4.17	3.54	3.18	3.94	5.20	3.67	3.40	3.28	5.20
Days With ≥ 0.1" Precipitation	7	6	7	8	8	7	7	5	5	5	7	7	79
Days With ≥ 0.5" Precipitation	2	3	3	3	4	3	3	2	2	2	3	3	33
Days With ≥ 1.0" Precipitation	1	1	1	1	2	1	1	1	1	1	1	2	14
Mean Snowfall (in.)	2.2	2.8	0.9	0.1	0.0	0.0	0.0	0.0	0.0	trace	trace	0.7	6.7
Maximum Snow Depth (in.)	6	8	11	1	0	0	0	0	0	0	trace	2	11
Days With ≥ 1.0" Snow Depth	2	2	0	0	0	0	0	0	0	0	0	0	4

The period of record for all cooperative weather station data is 1980 – 2009. See User Guide for detailed explanation of data.

Tazewell *Claiborne County* Elevation: 1,365 ft. Latitude: 36° 28' N Longitude: 83° 34' W

	JAN	FEB	MAR	APR	MAY	JUN	JUL	AUG	SEP	OCT	NOV	DEC	YEAR
Mean Maximum Temp. (°F)	45.2	49.6	58.7	68.0	76.0	83.3	86.4	86.0	80.4	69.8	58.9	48.1	67.5
Mean Temp. (°F)	34.1	37.5	45.2	53.9	62.8	71.0	74.9	74.1	67.4	55.6	45.5	36.8	54.9
Mean Minimum Temp. (°F)	22.9	25.4	31.6	39.8	49.7	58.6	63.4	62.2	54.4	41.3	32.2	25.4	42.2
Extreme Maximum Temp. (°F)	75	78	84	90	90	97	99	102	95	90	82	78	102
Extreme Minimum Temp. (°F)	-24	-22	-10	18	28	28	41	43	29	20	10	-8	-24
Days Maximum Temp. ≥ 90°F	0	0	0	0	0	3	8	7	3	0	0	0	21
Days Maximum Temp. ≤ 32°F	4	2	1	0	0	0	0	0	0	0	0	2	9
Days Minimum Temp. ≤ 32°F	25	22	17	7	1	0	0	0	0	7	17	24	120
Days Minimum Temp. ≤ 0°F	1	1	0	0	0	0	0	0	0	0	0	0	2
Heating Degree Days (base 65°F)	952	770	607	335	124	13	1	2	53	299	578	868	4,602
Cooling Degree Days (base 65°F)	0	0	1	8	64	199	315	292	131	14	0	0	1,024
Mean Precipitation (in.)	4.47	4.56	4.55	4.64	4.68	4.13	4.83	3.76	3.35	2.67	4.06	4.59	50.29
Extreme Maximum Daily Precip. (in.)	2.43	4.27	3.00	6.32	3.82	2.86	2.59	3.13	3.30	1.95	3.29	3.41	6.32
Days With ≥ 0.1" Precipitation	8	8	9	8	8	8	8	6	6	5	7	8	89
Days With ≥ 0.5" Precipitation	4	3	3	3	3	3	4	3	2	2	3	3	36
Days With ≥ 1.0" Precipitation	1	1	1	1	1	1	1	1	1	1	1	1	12
Mean Snowfall (in.)	4.3	3.8	1.7	0.3	0.0	0.0	0.0	0.0	0.0	0.1	trace	1.9	12.1
Maximum Snow Depth (in.)	8	13	18	8	0	0	0	0	0	0	2	6	18
Days With ≥ 1.0" Snow Depth	3	3	1	0	0	0	0	0	0	0	0	1	8

Woodbury 1 WNW *Cannon County* Elevation: 750 ft. Latitude: 35° 50' N Longitude: 86° 05' W

	JAN	FEB	MAR	APR	MAY	JUN	JUL	AUG	SEP	OCT	NOV	DEC	YEAR
Mean Maximum Temp. (°F)	49.4	54.0	62.8	71.8	79.6	87.0	89.9	90.0	84.0	73.6	62.6	51.9	71.4
Mean Temp. (°F)	38.1	41.7	49.4	57.6	66.0	74.0	77.6	76.9	70.0	58.8	49.1	40.5	58.3
Mean Minimum Temp. (°F)	26.8	29.3	36.1	43.4	52.4	60.9	65.1	63.8	56.0	44.0	35.6	28.9	45.2
Extreme Maximum Temp. (°F)	76	83	87	91	94	103	106	109	102	92	85	79	109
Extreme Minimum Temp. (°F)	-28	-14	0	18	29	38	51	44	31	20	10	-9	-28
Days Maximum Temp. ≥ 90°F	0	0	0	0	1	11	17	17	6	0	0	0	52
Days Maximum Temp. ≤ 32°F	3	1	0	0	0	0	0	0	0	0	0	2	6
Days Minimum Temp. ≤ 32°F	21	18	13	5	0	0	0	0	0	5	13	20	95
Days Minimum Temp. ≤ 0°F	1	0	0	0	0	0	0	0	0	0	0	0	1
Heating Degree Days (base 65°F)	826	653	482	241	70	4	0	1	32	219	471	755	3,754
Cooling Degree Days (base 65°F)	0	0	6	26	108	280	397	376	188	34	3	1	1,419
Mean Precipitation (in.)	4.74	4.59	5.36	4.28	5.32	4.50	5.27	3.59	4.07	3.16	4.45	5.51	54.84
Extreme Maximum Daily Precip. (in.)	4.35	3.96	4.60	2.81	4.10	3.26	4.38	2.75	4.44	3.29	4.31	4.08	4.60
Days With ≥ 0.1" Precipitation	8	7	8	7	8	7	8	6	5	6	7	8	85
Days With ≥ 0.5" Precipitation	3	3	4	3	3	3	4	2	2	2	3	4	36
Days With ≥ 1.0" Precipitation	1	1	1	1	2	1	2	1	1	1	1	1	14
Mean Snowfall (in.)	***0.3***	0.2	0.5	trace	0.0	0.0	0.0	0.0	0.0	trace	trace	trace	***1.0***
Maximum Snow Depth (in.)	***6***	*7*	*7*	***trace***	***0***	***0***	***0***	***0***	***0***	***0***	***1***	***5***	*7*
Days With ≥ 1.0" Snow Depth	***0***	1	0	0	0	0	0	0	0	0	0	0	***1***

The period of record for all cooperative weather station data is 1980 – 2009. See User Guide for detailed explanation of data.

Tennessee Weather Station Rankings

Annual Extreme Maximum Temperature

Highest Rank	Highest Station Name	Highest °F	Lowest Rank	Lowest Station Name	Lowest °F
1	Neapolis Exp Stn	109	1	Elizabethton	***99***
1	Woodbury 1 WNW	109	1	Gatlinburg 2 SW	99
3	Memphis Intl Arpt	108	3	Morristown Radio WCRK	100
4	Brownsville	107	4	Bristol Tri City Airport	101
4	Clarksville Sewage Plant	107	4	Kingsport	101
4	Dayton	107	6	Knoxville Exp Stn	***102***
4	Lebanon 3 W	107	6	Knoxville McGhee Tyson Arpt	102
8	Carthage	106	6	Norris	102
8	Franklin Sewage Plant	106	6	Tazewell	102
8	Lewisburg Exp Stn	106	10	Allardt	103
8	Murfreesboro 5 N	106	10	Centerville Water Pl	103
8	Nashville International Arpt	106	10	Oak Ridge	103
8	Springfield Exp Stn	106	13	Cookeville	104
14	Athens	105	13	Dresden	104
14	Chattanooga Lovell Field	105	13	Lawrenceburg Filter Plant	104
14	Cheatham Lock and Dam	105	13	Lenoir City	104
14	Cleveland Filter Plant	105	13	Sevierville 1 SE	104
14	Columbia 3 WNW	105	13	Shelbyville Water Dept	104
14	Dover 1 W	105	19	Athens	105
14	Fayetteville Water Plant	105	19	Chattanooga Lovell Field	105
14	Jackson Exp Station	105	19	Cheatham Lock and Dam	105
14	Moscow	105	19	Cleveland Filter Plant	105
23	Cookeville	104	19	Columbia 3 WNW	105
23	Dresden	104	19	Dover 1 W	105
23	Lawrenceburg Filter Plant	104	19	Fayetteville Water Plant	105

Annual Mean Maximum Temperature

Highest Rank	Highest Station Name	Highest °F	Lowest Rank	Lowest Station Name	Lowest °F
1	Memphis Intl Arpt	72.4	1	Allardt	65.9
2	Moscow	72.1	2	Bristol Tri City Airport	67.2
3	Centerville Water Pl	71.6	3	Tazewell	67.5
4	Chattanooga Lovell Field	71.5	4	Elizabethton	***67.6***
5	Woodbury 1 WNW	71.4	5	Norris	68.0
6	Fayetteville Water Plant	71.2	6	Springfield Exp Stn	68.2
7	Shelbyville Water Dept	70.9	7	Gatlinburg 2 SW	68.3
8	Cheatham Lock and Dam	70.8	8	Dover 1 W	68.4
9	Neapolis Exp Stn	70.5	8	Morristown Radio WCRK	68.4
10	Brownsville	70.4	10	Cookeville	68.6
10	Sevierville 1 SE	70.4	11	Dresden	68.8
12	Jackson Exp Station	70.2	12	Kingsport	68.9
12	Lewisburg Exp Stn	70.2	13	Knoxville Exp Stn	***69.2***
12	Nashville International Arpt	70.2	14	Carthage	69.3
15	Cleveland Filter Plant	70.1	15	Dayton	69.5
15	Lenoir City	70.1	15	Knoxville McGhee Tyson Arpt	69.5
17	Clarksville Sewage Plant	70.0	17	Athens	69.7
17	Lawrenceburg Filter Plant	70.0	17	Columbia 3 WNW	69.7
19	Lebanon 3 W	69.9	17	Oak Ridge	69.7
19	Murfreesboro 5 N	69.9	20	Franklin Sewage Plant	69.8
21	Franklin Sewage Plant	69.8	21	Lebanon 3 W	69.9
22	Athens	69.7	21	Murfreesboro 5 N	69.9
22	Columbia 3 WNW	69.7	23	Clarksville Sewage Plant	70.0
22	Oak Ridge	69.7	23	Lawrenceburg Filter Plant	70.0
25	Dayton	69.5	25	Cleveland Filter Plant	70.1

Rankings include 25 highest/lowest stations. If state has less than 25 stations, all stations are included. The period of record is 1980–2009. See User Guide for detailed explanation of data.

Annual Mean Temperature

Highest

Rank	Station Name	°F
1	Memphis Intl Arpt	63.0
2	Moscow	61.3
3	Chattanooga Lovell Field	60.8
4	Brownsville	60.4
5	Jackson Exp Station	59.9
6	Nashville International Arpt	59.8
7	Shelbyville Water Dept	59.5
8	Fayetteville Water Plant	59.3
9	Knoxville McGhee Tyson Arpt	59.0
10	Lenoir City	58.9
11	Centerville Water Pl	***58.7***
11	Clarksville Sewage Plant	58.7
11	Lawrenceburg Filter Plant	58.7
14	Cleveland Filter Plant	58.6
14	Dayton	58.6
16	Dresden	58.3
16	Franklin Sewage Plant	58.3
16	Neapolis Exp Stn	58.3
16	Oak Ridge	58.3
16	Woodbury 1 WNW	58.3
21	Carthage	58.2
21	Murfreesboro 5 N	58.2
23	Athens	58.1
23	Sevierville 1 SE	58.1
25	Cheatham Lock and Dam	57.8

Lowest

Rank	Station Name	°F
1	Tazewell	54.9
2	Allardt	55.6
3	Gatlinburg 2 SW	55.8
4	Bristol Tri City Airport	56.0
5	Norris	56.2
6	Elizabethton	***56.3***
7	Cookeville	56.8
7	Springfield Exp Stn	56.8
9	Morristown Radio WCRK	57.3
10	Kingsport	57.6
10	Knoxville Exp Stn	***57.6***
12	Columbia 3 WNW	57.7
12	Lewisburg Exp Stn	57.7
14	Cheatham Lock and Dam	57.8
14	Dover 1 W	57.8
14	Lebanon 3 W	57.8
17	Athens	58.1
17	Sevierville 1 SE	58.1
19	Carthage	58.2
19	Murfreesboro 5 N	58.2
21	Dresden	58.3
21	Franklin Sewage Plant	58.3
21	Neapolis Exp Stn	58.3
21	Oak Ridge	58.3
21	Woodbury 1 WNW	58.3

Annual Mean Minimum Temperature

Highest

Rank	Station Name	°F
1	Memphis Intl Arpt	53.6
2	Moscow	50.4
3	Brownsville	50.3
4	Chattanooga Lovell Field	50.0
5	Jackson Exp Station	49.6
6	Nashville International Arpt	49.4
7	Knoxville McGhee Tyson Arpt	48.5
8	Shelbyville Water Dept	48.1
9	Dayton	47.8
9	Dresden	47.8
11	Lenoir City	47.6
12	Clarksville Sewage Plant	47.3
12	Fayetteville Water Plant	47.3
14	Dover 1 W	47.2
14	Lawrenceburg Filter Plant	47.2
16	Carthage	47.0
16	Cleveland Filter Plant	47.0
16	Oak Ridge	47.0
19	Franklin Sewage Plant	46.7
20	Athens	46.4
20	Murfreesboro 5 N	46.4
22	Kingsport	46.3
22	Morristown Radio WCRK	46.3
24	Knoxville Exp Stn	***46.0***
24	Neapolis Exp Stn	46.0

Lowest

Rank	Station Name	°F
1	Tazewell	42.2
2	Gatlinburg 2 SW	43.3
3	Norris	44.4
4	Bristol Tri City Airport	44.7
4	Cheatham Lock and Dam	44.7
6	Cookeville	44.8
7	Elizabethton	***45.1***
7	Lewisburg Exp Stn	45.1
9	Woodbury 1 WNW	45.2
10	Allardt	45.3
11	Springfield Exp Stn	45.4
12	Columbia 3 WNW	45.6
13	Centerville Water Pl	***45.7***
13	Sevierville 1 SE	45.7
15	Lebanon 3 W	45.8
16	Knoxville Exp Stn	***46.0***
16	Neapolis Exp Stn	46.0
18	Kingsport	46.3
18	Morristown Radio WCRK	46.3
20	Athens	46.4
20	Murfreesboro 5 N	46.4
22	Franklin Sewage Plant	46.7
23	Carthage	47.0
23	Cleveland Filter Plant	47.0
23	Oak Ridge	47.0

Rankings include 25 highest/lowest stations. If state has less than 25 stations, all stations are included. The period of record is 1980–2009. See User Guide for detailed explanation of data.

Annual Extreme Minimum Temperature

Highest Rank	Station Name	°F	Lowest Rank	Station Name	°F
1	Memphis Intl Arpt	-4	1	Woodbury 1 WNW	-28
2	Moscow	-9	2	Allardt	-27
3	Brownsville	-10	3	Centerville Water Pl	***-26***
3	Chattanooga Lovell Field	-10	4	Knoxville McGhee Tyson Arpt	-24
3	Jackson Exp Station	-10	4	Sevierville 1 SE	-24
6	Murfreesboro 5 N	-13	4	Tazewell	-24
7	Lawrenceburg Filter Plant	-14	7	Neapolis Exp Stn	-23
7	Lenoir City	-14	8	Cookeville	-22
9	Clarksville Sewage Plant	-15	9	Bristol Tri City Airport	-21
9	Dayton	-15	9	Elizabethton	***-21***
9	Dover 1 W	-15	9	Franklin Sewage Plant	-21
12	Athens	-16	12	Columbia 3 WNW	-20
12	Cleveland Filter Plant	-16	12	Fayetteville Water Plant	-20
14	Carthage	-17	12	Knoxville Exp Stn	***-20***
14	Dresden	-17	12	Lebanon 3 W	-20
14	Nashville International Arpt	-17	12	Lewisburg Exp Stn	-20
14	Oak Ridge	-17	12	Shelbyville Water Dept	-20
14	Springfield Exp Stn	-17	18	Morristown Radio WCRK	-19
19	Cheatham Lock and Dam	-18	18	Norris	-19
19	Gatlinburg 2 SW	-18	20	Cheatham Lock and Dam	-18
19	Kingsport	-18	20	Gatlinburg 2 SW	-18
22	Morristown Radio WCRK	-19	20	Kingsport	-18
22	Norris	-19	23	Carthage	-17
24	Columbia 3 WNW	-20	23	Dresden	-17
24	Fayetteville Water Plant	-20	23	Nashville International Arpt	-17

July Mean Maximum Temperature

Highest Rank	Station Name	°F	Lowest Rank	Station Name	°F
1	Memphis Intl Arpt	91.7	1	Allardt	83.5
2	Brownsville	90.3	2	Gatlinburg 2 SW	84.9
2	Cheatham Lock and Dam	90.3	3	Elizabethton	85.3
2	Moscow	90.3	4	Bristol Tri City Airport	85.4
5	Chattanooga Lovell Field	90.2	5	Norris	86.3
5	Clarksville Sewage Plant	90.2	6	Tazewell	86.4
7	Lebanon 3 W	90.1	7	Morristown Radio WCRK	86.5
8	Woodbury 1 WNW	90.0	8	Kingsport	87.2
9	Nashville International Arpt	89.8	9	Cookeville	87.4
9	Neapolis Exp Stn	89.8	10	Knoxville Exp Stn	***87.6***
11	Centerville Water Pl	89.6	11	Dayton	88.0
11	Fayetteville Water Plant	89.6	12	Lawrenceburg Filter Plant	88.1
11	Shelbyville Water Dept	89.6	13	Athens	88.2
14	Lewisburg Exp Stn	89.5	13	Knoxville McGhee Tyson Arpt	88.2
15	Jackson Exp Station	89.4	15	Dover 1 W	88.4
16	Franklin Sewage Plant	89.3	16	Carthage	88.5
17	Murfreesboro 5 N	89.2	16	Cleveland Filter Plant	88.5
18	Columbia 3 WNW	88.8	16	Springfield Exp Stn	88.5
18	Lenoir City	88.8	19	Oak Ridge	88.6
20	Dresden	88.7	19	Sevierville 1 SE	88.6
21	Oak Ridge	88.6	21	Dresden	88.7
21	Sevierville 1 SE	88.6	22	Columbia 3 WNW	88.8
23	Carthage	88.5	22	Lenoir City	88.8
23	Cleveland Filter Plant	88.5	24	Murfreesboro 5 N	89.2
23	Springfield Exp Stn	88.5	25	Franklin Sewage Plant	89.3

Rankings include 25 highest/lowest stations. If state has less than 25 stations, all stations are included. The period of record is 1980–2009. See User Guide for detailed explanation of data.

January Mean Minimum Temperature

Highest Rank	Station Name	°F	Lowest Rank	Station Name	°F
1	Memphis Intl Arpt	33.0	1	Tazewell	22.9
2	Chattanooga Lovell Field	30.9	2	Springfield Exp Stn	25.0
3	Moscow	30.7	3	Lebanon 3 W	25.6
4	Brownsville	29.5	4	Norris	25.8
5	Knoxville McGhee Tyson Arpt	29.3	5	Cookeville	25.9
6	Jackson Exp Station	29.2	6	Bristol Tri City Airport	26.0
7	Dayton	29.1	7	Gatlinburg 2 SW	26.1
7	Nashville International Arpt	29.1	8	Cheatham Lock and Dam	26.2
7	Shelbyville Water Dept	29.1	8	Lewisburg Exp Stn	26.2
10	Fayetteville Water Plant	28.5	10	Columbia 3 WNW	26.4
11	Cleveland Filter Plant	28.4	10	Dresden	26.4
12	Lawrenceburg Filter Plant	28.2	10	Knoxville Exp Stn	26.4
13	Kingsport	27.8	10	Neapolis Exp Stn	26.4
14	Lenoir City	27.7	14	Dover 1 W	26.5
14	Oak Ridge	27.7	14	Murfreesboro 5 N	26.5
16	Franklin Sewage Plant	27.4	16	Elizabethton	26.6
16	Morristown Radio WCRK	27.4	17	Allardt	26.7
18	Athens	27.3	17	Clarksville Sewage Plant	26.7
18	Carthage	27.3	19	Woodbury 1 WNW	26.8
20	Sevierville 1 SE	27.1	20	Centerville Water Pl	26.9
21	Centerville Water Pl	26.9	21	Sevierville 1 SE	27.1
22	Woodbury 1 WNW	26.8	22	Athens	27.3
23	Allardt	26.7	22	Carthage	27.3
23	Clarksville Sewage Plant	26.7	24	Franklin Sewage Plant	27.4
25	Elizabethton	26.6	24	Morristown Radio WCRK	27.4

Number of Days Annually Maximum Temperature ≥ 90°F

Highest Rank	Station Name	Days	Lowest Rank	Station Name	Days
1	Memphis Intl Arpt	70	1	Allardt	8
2	Brownsville	54	2	Gatlinburg 2 SW	12
2	Moscow	54	3	Elizabethton	*16*
4	Chattanooga Lovell Field	53	4	Bristol Tri City Airport	17
4	Cheatham Lock and Dam	53	5	Norris	19
4	Lebanon 3 W	53	6	Morristown Radio WCRK	20
7	Clarksville Sewage Plant	52	7	Tazewell	21
7	Lewisburg Exp Stn	52	8	Kingsport	26
7	Neapolis Exp Stn	52	9	Cookeville	30
7	Woodbury 1 WNW	52	10	Knoxville Exp Stn	*31*
11	Fayetteville Water Plant	51	11	Dayton	32
12	Jackson Exp Station	49	12	Cleveland Filter Plant	33
13	Nashville International Arpt	48	13	Athens	34
13	Shelbyville Water Dept	48	13	Dover 1 W	34
15	Murfreesboro 5 N	47	13	Lawrenceburg Filter Plant	34
16	Centerville Water Pl	46	16	Knoxville McGhee Tyson Arpt	35
17	Franklin Sewage Plant	43	17	Lenoir City	39
18	Columbia 3 WNW	42	18	Carthage	40
18	Dresden	42	18	Oak Ridge	40
20	Sevierville 1 SE	41	20	Sevierville 1 SE	41
20	Springfield Exp Stn	41	20	Springfield Exp Stn	41
22	Carthage	40	22	Columbia 3 WNW	42
22	Oak Ridge	40	22	Dresden	42
24	Lenoir City	39	24	Franklin Sewage Plant	43
25	Knoxville McGhee Tyson Arpt	35	25	Centerville Water Pl	46

 Rankings include 25 highest/lowest stations. If state has less than 25 stations, all stations are included. The period of record is 1980–2009. See User Guide for detailed explanation of data.

Number of Days Annually Maximum Temperature ≤ 32°F

Highest			Lowest		
Rank	Station Name	Days	Rank	Station Name	Days
1	Allardt	11	1	Athens	4
1	Dover 1 W	11	1	Chattanooga Lovell Field	4
1	Springfield Exp Stn	11	1	Cleveland Filter Plant	4
4	Dresden	10	1	Dayton	4
5	Clarksville Sewage Plant	9	1	Fayetteville Water Plant	4
5	Tazewell	9	1	Knoxville McGhee Tyson Arpt	4
7	Bristol Tri City Airport	8	1	Lenoir City	4
7	Cookeville	8	1	Moscow	4
7	Elizabethton	***8***	1	Sevierville 1 SE	4
7	Lebanon 3 W	8	10	Centerville Water Pl	5
11	Brownsville	7	10	Knoxville Exp Stn	***5***
11	Carthage	7	10	Lawrenceburg Filter Plant	5
11	Franklin Sewage Plant	7	10	Memphis Intl Arpt	5
11	Gatlinburg 2 SW	7	10	Shelbyville Water Dept	5
11	Jackson Exp Station	7	15	Cheatham Lock and Dam	6
11	Lewisburg Exp Stn	7	15	Columbia 3 WNW	6
11	Murfreesboro 5 N	7	15	Kingsport	6
11	Nashville International Arpt	7	15	Morristown Radio WCRK	6
11	Neapolis Exp Stn	7	15	Oak Ridge	6
11	Norris	7	15	Woodbury 1 WNW	6
21	Cheatham Lock and Dam	6	21	Brownsville	7
21	Columbia 3 WNW	6	21	Carthage	7
21	Kingsport	6	21	Franklin Sewage Plant	7
21	Morristown Radio WCRK	6	21	Gatlinburg 2 SW	7
21	Oak Ridge	6	21	Jackson Exp Station	7

Number of Days Annually Minimum Temperature ≤ 32°F

Highest			Lowest		
Rank	Station Name	Days	Rank	Station Name	Days
1	Tazewell	120	1	Memphis Intl Arpt	46
2	Gatlinburg 2 SW	108	2	Chattanooga Lovell Field	62
3	Cookeville	100	3	Moscow	64
4	Norris	99	4	Brownsville	67
5	Springfield Exp Stn	98	5	Jackson Exp Station	72
6	Bristol Tri City Airport	97	5	Nashville International Arpt	72
6	Cheatham Lock and Dam	97	7	Knoxville McGhee Tyson Arpt	73
6	Lewisburg Exp Stn	97	8	Dayton	75
9	Columbia 3 WNW	95	9	Shelbyville Water Dept	78
9	Lebanon 3 W	95	10	Lenoir City	79
9	Woodbury 1 WNW	95	11	Cleveland Filter Plant	81
12	Centerville Water Pl	93	11	Lawrenceburg Filter Plant	81
13	Elizabethton	***92***	13	Dover 1 W	83
13	Neapolis Exp Stn	92	13	Dresden	83
15	Knoxville Exp Stn	***91***	13	Fayetteville Water Plant	83
16	Allardt	90	16	Kingsport	84
17	Murfreesboro 5 N	89	17	Carthage	85
17	Sevierville 1 SE	89	17	Morristown Radio WCRK	85
19	Athens	88	19	Clarksville Sewage Plant	86
19	Franklin Sewage Plant	88	19	Oak Ridge	86
21	Clarksville Sewage Plant	86	21	Athens	88
21	Oak Ridge	86	21	Franklin Sewage Plant	88
23	Carthage	85	23	Murfreesboro 5 N	89
23	Morristown Radio WCRK	85	23	Sevierville 1 SE	89
25	Kingsport	84	25	Allardt	90

Rankings include 25 highest/lowest stations. If state has less than 25 stations, all stations are included. The period of record is 1980–2009. See User Guide for detailed explanation of data.

Number of Days Annually Minimum Temperature ≤ 0°F

Highest Rank	Highest Station Name	Highest Days	Lowest Rank	Lowest Station Name	Lowest Days
1	Tazewell	2	1	Athens	0
2	Allardt	1	1	Bristol Tri City Airport	0
2	Carthage	1	1	Brownsville	0
2	Centerville Water Pl	1	1	Chattanooga Lovell Field	0
2	Cheatham Lock and Dam	1	1	Clarksville Sewage Plant	0
2	Cookeville	1	1	Cleveland Filter Plant	0
2	Dover 1 W	1	1	Columbia 3 WNW	0
2	Franklin Sewage Plant	1	1	Dayton	0
2	Lebanon 3 W	1	1	Dresden	0
2	Lewisburg Exp Stn	1	1	Elizabethton	***0***
2	Murfreesboro 5 N	1	1	Fayetteville Water Plant	0
2	Neapolis Exp Stn	1	1	Gatlinburg 2 SW	0
2	Springfield Exp Stn	1	1	Jackson Exp Station	0
2	Woodbury 1 WNW	1	1	Kingsport	0
15	Athens	0	1	Knoxville Exp Stn	***0***
15	Bristol Tri City Airport	0	1	Knoxville McGhee Tyson Arpt	0
15	Brownsville	0	1	Lawrenceburg Filter Plant	0
15	Chattanooga Lovell Field	0	1	Lenoir City	0
15	Clarksville Sewage Plant	0	1	Memphis Intl Arpt	0
15	Cleveland Filter Plant	0	1	Morristown Radio WCRK	0
15	Columbia 3 WNW	0	1	Moscow	0
15	Dayton	0	1	Nashville International Arpt	0
15	Dresden	0	1	Norris	0
15	Elizabethton	***0***	1	Oak Ridge	0
15	Fayetteville Water Plant	0	1	Sevierville 1 SE	0

Number of Annual Heating Degree Days

Highest Rank	Highest Station Name	Highest Num.	Lowest Rank	Lowest Station Name	Lowest Num.
1	Tazewell	4,602	1	Memphis Intl Arpt	2,911
2	Springfield Exp Stn	4,249	2	Moscow	3,101
3	Allardt	4,248	3	Chattanooga Lovell Field	3,202
4	Bristol Tri City Airport	4,240	4	Brownsville	3,467
5	Norris	4,198	5	Shelbyville Water Dept	3,492
6	Gatlinburg 2 SW	4,144	6	Jackson Exp Station	3,539
7	Cookeville	4,133	7	Fayetteville Water Plant	3,541
8	Elizabethton	***4,126***	8	Nashville International Arpt	3,542
9	Lebanon 3 W	4,028	9	Knoxville McGhee Tyson Arpt	3,606
10	Dover 1 W	3,990	10	Lawrenceburg Filter Plant	3,621
11	Lewisburg Exp Stn	3,984	11	Dayton	3,627
12	Columbia 3 WNW	3,959	12	Cleveland Filter Plant	3,642
13	Cheatham Lock and Dam	3,944	13	Centerville Water Pl	***3,644***
14	Dresden	3,937	14	Lenoir City	3,684
15	Morristown Radio WCRK	3,925	15	Woodbury 1 WNW	3,754
16	Knoxville Exp Stn	***3,915***	16	Sevierville 1 SE	3,773
17	Murfreesboro 5 N	3,883	17	Oak Ridge	3,780
18	Kingsport	3,862	18	Athens	3,808
19	Clarksville Sewage Plant	3,846	19	Franklin Sewage Plant	3,832
20	Neapolis Exp Stn	3,845	20	Carthage	3,844
21	Carthage	3,844	21	Neapolis Exp Stn	3,845
22	Franklin Sewage Plant	3,832	22	Clarksville Sewage Plant	3,846
23	Athens	3,808	23	Kingsport	3,862
24	Oak Ridge	3,780	24	Murfreesboro 5 N	3,883
25	Sevierville 1 SE	3,773	25	Knoxville Exp Stn	***3,915***

Rankings include 25 highest/lowest stations. If state has less than 25 stations, all stations are included. The period of record is 1980–2009. See User Guide for detailed explanation of data.

Number of Annual Cooling Degree Days

Highest Rank	Station Name	Num.	Lowest Rank	Station Name	Num.
1	Memphis Intl Arpt	2,304	1	Gatlinburg 2 SW	904
2	Brownsville	1,898	2	Allardt	935
3	Moscow	1,860	3	Tazewell	1,024
4	Jackson Exp Station	1,781	4	Bristol Tri City Airport	1,050
5	Chattanooga Lovell Field	1,757	5	Elizabethton	***1,073***
6	Nashville International Arpt	1,756	6	Norris	1,106
7	Clarksville Sewage Plant	1,640	7	Cookeville	1,235
8	Shelbyville Water Dept	1,607	7	Morristown Radio WCRK	1,235
9	Dresden	1,594	9	Kingsport	1,273
10	Lenoir City	1,552	10	Knoxville Exp Stn	***1,335***
11	Fayetteville Water Plant	1,550	11	Sevierville 1 SE	1,355
12	Knoxville McGhee Tyson Arpt	1,530	12	Springfield Exp Stn	1,377
13	Lebanon 3 W	1,529	13	Athens	1,381
14	Murfreesboro 5 N	1,511	14	Columbia 3 WNW	1,388
15	Neapolis Exp Stn	1,492	15	Cleveland Filter Plant	1,406
16	Franklin Sewage Plant	1,484	16	Lewisburg Exp Stn	1,409
17	Dover 1 W	1,470	17	Dayton	1,410
18	Carthage	1,466	18	Lawrenceburg Filter Plant	1,411
19	Oak Ridge	1,454	19	Cheatham Lock and Dam	1,413
20	Centerville Water Pl	***1,432***	20	Woodbury 1 WNW	1,419
21	Woodbury 1 WNW	1,419	21	Centerville Water Pl	***1,432***
22	Cheatham Lock and Dam	1,413	22	Oak Ridge	1,454
23	Lawrenceburg Filter Plant	1,411	23	Carthage	1,466
24	Dayton	1,410	24	Dover 1 W	1,470
25	Lewisburg Exp Stn	1,409	25	Franklin Sewage Plant	1,484

Annual Precipitation

Highest Rank	Station Name	Inches	Lowest Rank	Station Name	Inches
1	Lawrenceburg Filter Plant	59.89	1	Bristol Tri City Airport	40.86
2	Shelbyville Water Dept	55.62	2	Kingsport	42.91
3	Athens	55.54	3	Sevierville 1 SE	43.30
4	Cookeville	55.32	4	Elizabethton	***44.61***
5	Neapolis Exp Stn	55.23	5	Morristown Radio WCRK	45.01
6	Gatlinburg 2 SW	55.18	6	Nashville International Arpt	46.39
7	Dayton	55.14	7	Knoxville McGhee Tyson Arpt	47.65
8	Woodbury 1 WNW	54.84	8	Cheatham Lock and Dam	48.87
9	Fayetteville Water Plant	54.62	9	Springfield Exp Stn	49.29
10	Lewisburg Exp Stn	54.60	10	Tazewell	50.29
11	Columbia 3 WNW	54.59	11	Clarksville Sewage Plant	50.92
12	Allardt	54.48	12	Carthage	50.98
13	Oak Ridge	54.37	13	Lenoir City	51.14
14	Cleveland Filter Plant	54.01	14	Dover 1 W	51.56
15	Memphis Intl Arpt	53.87	15	Lebanon 3 W	51.75
16	Brownsville	53.51	16	Knoxville Exp Stn	52.18
17	Jackson Exp Station	53.36	17	Centerville Water Pl	52.26
18	Norris	53.03	18	Franklin Sewage Plant	52.59
19	Murfreesboro 5 N	52.91	19	Moscow	52.69
20	Dresden	52.83	20	Chattanooga Lovell Field	52.70
21	Chattanooga Lovell Field	52.70	21	Dresden	52.83
22	Moscow	52.69	22	Murfreesboro 5 N	52.91
23	Franklin Sewage Plant	52.59	23	Norris	53.03
24	Centerville Water Pl	52.26	24	Jackson Exp Station	53.36
25	Knoxville Exp Stn	52.18	25	Brownsville	53.51

Rankings include 25 highest/lowest stations. If state has less than 25 stations, all stations are included. The period of record is 1980–2009. See User Guide for detailed explanation of data.

Annual Extreme Maximum Daily Precipitation

Highest

Rank	Station Name	Inches
1	Lawrenceburg Filter Plant	8.76
2	Neapolis Exp Stn	8.14
3	Murfreesboro 5 N	8.13
4	Athens	8.10
5	Moscow	***8.04***
6	Jackson Exp Station	7.86
7	Dover 1 W	7.60
8	Dayton	7.57
9	Brownsville	7.30
10	Dresden	6.95
11	Clarksville Sewage Plant	6.90
12	Cleveland Filter Plant	6.76
13	Cheatham Lock and Dam	6.70
14	Franklin Sewage Plant	6.53
15	Centerville Water Pl	***6.35***
16	Tazewell	6.32
17	Chattanooga Lovell Field	6.19
18	Carthage	6.10
19	Norris	6.06
20	Lewisburg Exp Stn	6.05
21	Memphis Intl Arpt	5.88
22	Lenoir City	5.85
23	Knoxville McGhee Tyson Arpt	5.75
23	Lebanon 3 W	5.75
25	Columbia 3 WNW	5.62

Lowest

Rank	Station Name	Inches
1	Elizabethton	***3.30***
2	Bristol Tri City Airport	3.50
3	Morristown Radio WCRK	3.58
4	Sevierville 1 SE	4.03
5	Gatlinburg 2 SW	4.12
6	Kingsport	4.50
7	Allardt	4.60
7	Woodbury 1 WNW	4.60
9	Fayetteville Water Plant	4.65
10	Nashville International Arpt	4.73
11	Oak Ridge	4.89
12	Knoxville Exp Stn	5.15
13	Shelbyville Water Dept	5.19
14	Springfield Exp Stn	5.20
15	Cookeville	5.27
16	Columbia 3 WNW	5.62
17	Knoxville McGhee Tyson Arpt	5.75
17	Lebanon 3 W	5.75
19	Lenoir City	5.85
20	Memphis Intl Arpt	5.88
21	Lewisburg Exp Stn	6.05
22	Norris	6.06
23	Carthage	6.10
24	Chattanooga Lovell Field	6.19
25	Tazewell	6.32

Number of Days Annually With ≥ 0.1 Inches of Precipitation

Highest

Rank	Station Name	Days
1	Gatlinburg 2 SW	100
2	Allardt	92
3	Cookeville	90
3	Elizabethton	***90***
5	Athens	89
5	Tazewell	89
7	Cleveland Filter Plant	87
7	Kingsport	87
7	Knoxville Exp Stn	87
7	Norris	87
7	Oak Ridge	87
12	Bristol Tri City Airport	86
12	Neapolis Exp Stn	86
14	Lenoir City	85
14	Shelbyville Water Dept	85
14	Woodbury 1 WNW	85
17	Columbia 3 WNW	84
17	Dayton	84
17	Knoxville McGhee Tyson Arpt	84
20	Chattanooga Lovell Field	83
20	Fayetteville Water Plant	83
20	Lawrenceburg Filter Plant	83
20	Morristown Radio WCRK	83
24	Centerville Water Pl	***82***
24	Franklin Sewage Plant	82

Lowest

Rank	Station Name	Days
1	Moscow	63
2	Memphis Intl Arpt	73
3	Carthage	76
3	Jackson Exp Station	76
5	Dresden	77
6	Brownsville	78
6	Cheatham Lock and Dam	78
6	Dover 1 W	78
6	Nashville International Arpt	78
10	Lebanon 3 W	79
10	Springfield Exp Stn	79
12	Lewisburg Exp Stn	80
12	Sevierville 1 SE	80
14	Clarksville Sewage Plant	81
14	Murfreesboro 5 N	81
16	Centerville Water Pl	***82***
16	Franklin Sewage Plant	82
18	Chattanooga Lovell Field	83
18	Fayetteville Water Plant	83
18	Lawrenceburg Filter Plant	83
18	Morristown Radio WCRK	83
22	Columbia 3 WNW	84
22	Dayton	84
22	Knoxville McGhee Tyson Arpt	84
25	Lenoir City	85

Rankings include 25 highest/lowest stations. If state has less than 25 stations, all stations are included. The period of record is 1980–2009. See User Guide for detailed explanation of data.

Number of Days Annually With ≥ 0.5 Inches of Precipitation

Highest			Lowest		
Rank	Station Name	Days	Rank	Station Name	Days
1	Athens	39	1	Bristol Tri City Airport	27
1	Gatlinburg 2 SW	39	2	Elizabethton	***29***
1	Lawrenceburg Filter Plant	39	2	Kingsport	29
4	Cleveland Filter Plant	38	4	Morristown Radio WCRK	31
4	Memphis Intl Arpt	38	4	Nashville International Arpt	31
4	Murfreesboro 5 N	38	6	Sevierville 1 SE	32
4	Neapolis Exp Stn	38	7	Carthage	33
8	Centerville Water Pl	***37***	7	Knoxville McGhee Tyson Arpt	33
8	Chattanooga Lovell Field	37	7	Lenoir City	33
8	Columbia 3 WNW	37	7	Springfield Exp Stn	33
8	Cookeville	37	11	Cheatham Lock and Dam	34
8	Dayton	37	11	Lebanon 3 W	34
8	Fayetteville Water Plant	37	13	Dover 1 W	35
8	Oak Ridge	37	13	Dresden	35
15	Allardt	36	13	Franklin Sewage Plant	35
15	Brownsville	36	13	Moscow	35
15	Clarksville Sewage Plant	36	17	Allardt	36
15	Jackson Exp Station	36	17	Brownsville	36
15	Knoxville Exp Stn	36	17	Clarksville Sewage Plant	36
15	Lewisburg Exp Stn	36	17	Jackson Exp Station	36
15	Norris	36	17	Knoxville Exp Stn	36
15	Shelbyville Water Dept	36	17	Lewisburg Exp Stn	36
15	Tazewell	36	17	Norris	36
15	Woodbury 1 WNW	36	17	Shelbyville Water Dept	36
25	Dover 1 W	35	17	Tazewell	36

Number of Days Annually With ≥ 1.0 Inches of Precipitation

Highest			Lowest		
Rank	Station Name	Days	Rank	Station Name	Days
1	Lawrenceburg Filter Plant	20	1	Bristol Tri City Airport	9
2	Memphis Intl Arpt	18	2	Kingsport	10
2	Moscow	18	3	Elizabethton	***11***
4	Athens	17	3	Morristown Radio WCRK	11
5	Brownsville	16	3	Sevierville 1 SE	11
5	Centerville Water Pl	16	6	Lenoir City	12
5	Jackson Exp Station	16	6	Norris	12
5	Neapolis Exp Stn	16	6	Tazewell	12
5	Shelbyville Water Dept	16	9	Allardt	13
10	Carthage	15	9	Gatlinburg 2 SW	13
10	Chattanooga Lovell Field	15	9	Knoxville Exp Stn	13
10	Clarksville Sewage Plant	15	9	Knoxville McGhee Tyson Arpt	13
10	Columbia 3 WNW	15	9	Lebanon 3 W	13
10	Cookeville	15	9	Nashville International Arpt	13
10	Dresden	15	9	Oak Ridge	13
10	Fayetteville Water Plant	15	16	Cheatham Lock and Dam	14
10	Franklin Sewage Plant	15	16	Cleveland Filter Plant	14
18	Cheatham Lock and Dam	14	16	Dayton	14
18	Cleveland Filter Plant	14	16	Dover 1 W	14
18	Dayton	14	16	Lewisburg Exp Stn	14
18	Dover 1 W	14	16	Murfreesboro 5 N	14
18	Lewisburg Exp Stn	14	16	Springfield Exp Stn	14
18	Murfreesboro 5 N	14	16	Woodbury 1 WNW	14
18	Springfield Exp Stn	14	24	Carthage	15
18	Woodbury 1 WNW	14	24	Chattanooga Lovell Field	15

Rankings include 25 highest/lowest stations. If state has less than 25 stations, all stations are included. The period of record is 1980–2009. See User Guide for detailed explanation of data.

Annual Snowfall

Highest			Lowest		
Rank	Station Name	Inches	Rank	Station Name	Inches
1	Allardt	12.9	1	Knoxville Exp Stn	***0.1***
1	Bristol Tri City Airport	***12.9***	2	Cleveland Filter Plant	0.9
3	Tazewell	12.1	3	Woodbury 1 WNW	***1.0***
4	Morristown Radio WCRK	10.7	4	Columbia 3 WNW	1.3
5	Gatlinburg 2 SW	9.3	5	Moscow	1.4
6	Kingsport	8.3	6	Lebanon 3 W	1.5
7	Elizabethton	***8.1***	7	Centerville Water Pl	1.6
8	Knoxville McGhee Tyson Arpt	***7.0***	8	Fayetteville Water Plant	1.8
9	Oak Ridge	6.9	9	Dresden	***1.9***
10	Springfield Exp Stn	6.7	10	Franklin Sewage Plant	2.0
11	Cookeville	5.7	11	Cheatham Lock and Dam	2.1
12	Sevierville 1 SE	5.2	12	Murfreesboro 5 N	2.2
13	Athens	5.1	13	Lewisburg Exp Stn	2.4
14	Dover 1 W	5.0	14	Shelbyville Water Dept	2.6
15	Lenoir City	4.8	15	Clarksville Sewage Plant	2.8
16	Norris	4.2	15	Dayton	2.8
17	Lawrenceburg Filter Plant	4.0	17	Carthage	***3.2***
18	Brownsville	3.8	18	Jackson Exp Station	3.6
18	Chattanooga Lovell Field	***3.8***	18	Neapolis Exp Stn	3.6
20	Memphis Intl Arpt	***3.7***	20	Memphis Intl Arpt	***3.7***
21	Jackson Exp Station	3.6	21	Brownsville	3.8
21	Neapolis Exp Stn	3.6	21	Chattanooga Lovell Field	***3.8***
23	Carthage	***3.2***	23	Lawrenceburg Filter Plant	4.0
24	Clarksville Sewage Plant	2.8	24	Norris	4.2
24	Dayton	2.8	25	Lenoir City	4.8

Annual Maximum Snow Depth

Highest			Lowest		
Rank	Station Name	Inches	Rank	Station Name	Inches
1	Elizabethton	***21***	1	Knoxville Exp Stn	Trace
2	Chattanooga Lovell Field	***19***	2	Clarksville Sewage Plant	3
3	Tazewell	18	3	Columbia 3 WNW	4
4	Allardt	17	4	Dresden	5
4	Bristol Tri City Airport	***17***	4	Neapolis Exp Stn	***5***
6	Knoxville McGhee Tyson Arpt	***15***	6	Cleveland Filter Plant	6
7	Athens	14	6	Franklin Sewage Plant	6
7	Gatlinburg 2 SW	***14***	6	Jackson Exp Station	6
7	Kingsport	14	6	Morristown Radio WCRK	***6***
10	Norris	***12***	6	Sevierville 1 SE	***6***
10	Oak Ridge	12	11	Carthage	***7***
12	Dover 1 W	11	11	Centerville Water Pl	***7***
12	Lenoir City	11	11	Cheatham Lock and Dam	7
12	Lewisburg Exp Stn	11	11	Murfreesboro 5 N	7
12	Springfield Exp Stn	11	11	Shelbyville Water Dept	7
16	Lawrenceburg Filter Plant	10	11	Woodbury 1 WNW	***7***
17	Brownsville	8	17	Brownsville	8
17	Cookeville	8	17	Cookeville	8
17	Dayton	8	17	Dayton	8
17	Fayetteville Water Plant	8	17	Fayetteville Water Plant	8
17	Lebanon 3 W	8	17	Lebanon 3 W	8
17	Memphis Intl Arpt	***8***	17	Memphis Intl Arpt	***8***
17	Moscow	8	17	Moscow	8
24	Carthage	***7***	24	Lawrenceburg Filter Plant	10
24	Centerville Water Pl	***7***	25	Dover 1 W	11

Rankings include 25 highest/lowest stations. If state has less than 25 stations, all stations are included. The period of record is 1980–2009. See User Guide for detailed explanation of data.

Number of Days Annually With ≥ 1.0 Inch Snow Depth

Highest

Rank	Station Name	Days
1	Allardt	10
2	Bristol Tri City Airport	***9***
3	Tazewell	8
4	Elizabethton	***6***
4	Kingsport	6
6	Cookeville	5
6	Gatlinburg 2 SW	***5***
8	Dover 1 W	4
8	Lebanon 3 W	4
8	Oak Ridge	4
8	Springfield Exp Stn	4
12	Brownsville	3
12	Knoxville McGhee Tyson Arpt	***3***
14	Athens	2
14	Chattanooga Lovell Field	***2***
14	Cheatham Lock and Dam	2
14	Dayton	2
14	Fayetteville Water Plant	2
14	Jackson Exp Station	2
14	Lawrenceburg Filter Plant	2
14	Lenoir City	2
14	Lewisburg Exp Stn	2
14	Memphis Intl Arpt	***2***
14	Moscow	2
14	Murfreesboro 5 N	2

Lowest

Rank	Station Name	Days
1	Centerville Water Pl	***0***
1	Clarksville Sewage Plant	0
1	Cleveland Filter Plant	0
1	Columbia 3 WNW	0
1	Dresden	0
1	Franklin Sewage Plant	0
1	Knoxville Exp Stn	***0***
1	Neapolis Exp Stn	***0***
9	Carthage	***1***
9	Morristown Radio WCRK	***1***
9	Sevierville 1 SE	1
9	Woodbury 1 WNW	***1***
13	Athens	2
13	Chattanooga Lovell Field	***2***
13	Cheatham Lock and Dam	2
13	Dayton	2
13	Fayetteville Water Plant	2
13	Jackson Exp Station	2
13	Lawrenceburg Filter Plant	2
13	Lenoir City	2
13	Lewisburg Exp Stn	2
13	Memphis Intl Arpt	***2***
13	Moscow	2
13	Murfreesboro 5 N	2
13	Norris	2

Rankings include 25 highest/lowest stations. If state has less than 25 stations, all stations are included. The period of record is 1980–2009. See User Guide for detailed explanation of data.

Significant Storm Events in Tennessee: 2000 – 2009

Location or County	Date	Type	Mag.	Deaths	Injuries	Property Damage ($mil.)	Crop Damage ($mil.)
Henry	11/26/01	Tornado	F3	2	12	1.5	0.0
Rutherford	04/28/02	Tornado	F3	0	31	2.3	0.0
Morgan	11/10/02	Tornado	F3	7	28	0.9	0.0
Cumberland	11/10/02	Tornado	F3	4	18	0.5	0.0
Coffee	11/10/02	Tornado	F2	2	24	0.2	0.0
East Tennessee	02/14/03	Flood	na	0	0	18.0	0.0
Dyer	05/04/03	Tornado	F2	0	10	50.0	0.0
Madison	05/04/03	Tornado	F4	11	66	30.0	0.0
Henderson	05/04/03	Tornado	F4	0	20	10.0	0.0
Marion	05/05/03	Flash Flood	na	0	0	11.6	0.0
Hamilton	05/06/03	Flash Flood	na	0	0	23.2	0.0
Mcminn	05/06/03	Flash Flood	na	0	0	16.7	0.0
Bradley	05/06/03	Flash Flood	na	0	0	13.9	0.0
Monroe	05/06/03	Flash Flood	na	0	0	11.1	0.0
Hamilton	05/08/03	Flash Flood	na	0	0	23.2	0.0
Marion	05/08/03	Flash Flood	na	0	0	11.6	0.0
Shelby	07/22/03	Thunderstorm Wind	109 mph	1	3	40.0	0.0
Henry	11/15/05	Tornado	F2	0	13	6.5	0.0
Gibson	04/02/06	Tornado	F3	6	42	25.0	0.0
Dyer	04/02/06	Tornado	F3	16	70	20.0	0.0
Gibson	04/02/06	Tornado	F3	2	6	15.0	0.0
Sumner	04/07/06	Tornado	F3	7	121	69.0	0.0
Shelby	02/05/08	Tornado	F2	3	13	100.0	0.0
Madison	02/05/08	Tornado	F4	0	51	100.0	0.0
Hardin	02/05/08	Tornado	F4	3	5	17.6	0.0
Macon	02/05/08	Tornado	F3	13	44	14.1	1.0
Madison	02/05/08	Tornado	F3	2	14	10.0	0.0
Sumner	02/05/08	Tornado	F3	7	14	10.0	0.0
Rutherford	04/10/09	Tornado	F4	2	58	100.0	0.0
Carroll and Shelby Counties	06/17/09	Heat	na	7	0	0.0	0.0

Note: Deaths, injuries, and damages are date and location specific.

TEXAS

PHYSICAL FEATURES. Texas has been called "the crossroads of North American geology." Within the State's boundaries four great physiographic subdivisions of the North American Continent come together. These are: the Gulf Coastal Forested Plain; Great Western Lower Plains; Great Western High Plains; and the Rocky Mountain Region. Texas may be described as a vast amphitheater, sloping upward from sea level along the coast of the Gulf of Mexico to more than 4,000 feet general elevation along the Texas-New Mexico line. While much of the State is relatively flat, there are 90 mountains a mile or more high, all of them in the Trans-Pecos region. Guadalupe Peak, at 8,751 feet, is the State's highest.

Texas contains 267,339 square miles or 7.4 percent of the Nation's total area. In straight-line distance, Texas extends 801 miles from north to south and 773 miles from east to west. The boundary of Texas extends 4,137 miles. The Rio Grande forms the longest segment of the boundary, 1,569 miles. The second longest segment, 726 miles, is formed by the Red River. The tidewater coastline extends 624 miles. Texas ranks second only to Alaska among the 50 states in volume of inland water with nearly 6,000 square miles of lakes and streams. Most Texas rivers parallel each other and flow directly into the Gulf, but the Canadian, Red, and Sulphur Rivers are part of the Mississippi River system. The Brazos is the largest river between the Rio Grande and the Red and third in size of all rivers flowing either partly or wholly in Texas. Other principal rivers are the Colorado, Trinity, Sabine, Nueces, Neches, and Guadalupe.

GENERAL CLIMATE. Wedged between the warm waters of the Gulf of Mexico and the high plateaus and mountain ranges of the North American Continent, Texas has diverse meteorological and climatological conditions. Continental, marine, and mountain types of climates are all found in Texas, the marine climate modified by surges of continental air. The High Plains, separated from the Lower Plains by the Cap Rock Escarpment, lies in a cool-temperature climatic zone. Most of the remainder of the State lies in a warm-temperature subtropical zone.

The proximity to the Gulf of Mexico, the persistent southerly and southeasterly flow of warm tropical maritime air into Texas from around the westward extension of the Azores High, and adequate rainfall combine to produce a humid subtropical climate with hot summers across the eastern third of the State. The Gulf moisture supply gradually decreases westward and is cut off more frequently during the colder months by intrusions of drier polar air from the north and west; as a result, most of Central Texas, as far north as the High Plains, has a subtropical climate with dry winters and humid summers. This region is semi-arid. As the distance from the Gulf increases westward, the summer moisture supply continues to decrease gradually, producing a subtropical steppe climate across a broad section along the middle Rio Grande Valley that extends as far west as the Pecos Valley. The area west of the Pecos is mostly arid subtropical. The mountain climates in the Trans-Pecos are cooler throughout the year than those of the adjacent lowlands.

Stretching over the largest level plain of its kind in the United States, the High Plains rise gradually from about 2,700 feet on the east to more than 4,000 feet in spots along the New Mexico border. The combination of high elevation, remoteness from moisture source regions, and frequent intrusions of dry polar airmasses, results in a dry steppe climate with relatively mild winters.

While the changes in climate across Texas are considerable, they are nevertheless gradual; no natural boundary separates the moist East from the dry West or the cool North from the warm South.

PRECIPITATION. Rainfall in Texas is not evenly distributed over the State and varies greatly from year to year. Average annual rainfall along the Louisiana border exceeds 56 inches, and in the western extremity of the State, is less than 8 inches. Except along the upper Texas coast, it is possible for one or two thunderstorms to account for the entire month's rainfall. Torrential rains of 10 to 20 inches or more may accompany a tropical storm as it moves inland across the Texas coast. Rains occur most frequently in late spring as a result of squall-line thunderstorms; consequently, most areas of the State show a peak in May. Rainfall in the Pecos Valley, most of southern Texas, the lower Rio Grande Valley, and in the coastal section, shows a peak in September, with a secondary peak in May. On the High Plains a significant percentage of the total annual precipitation occurs during the summer months (following the May peak). Throughout the central part of the State, July and August are relatively dry months. In the mountainous Trans-Pecos area of West Texas, afternoon thundershowers during July, August, and September account for most of the annual rainfall. Throughout most of East Texas, rainfall is fairly evenly distributed throughout the year. East of about 96° W. longitude, annual rainfall exceeds average potential evapotranspiration. West of this meridian, average potential evapotranspiration exceeds annual average rainfall.

FLOOD AND DROUGHT. In most of Texas a large portion of the annual rainfall occurs within short periods of time, resulting in excessive run-off and frequently producing damaging floods. Flood stage is reached on some Texas streams nearly every year. From the early days of Texas history recorded by Spaniards exploring the Southwest, drought has been a re-occurring problem. A drought in Central Texas dried up the San Gabriel River in 1756, forcing the abandonment of a settlement of missionaries and Indians. Stephen F. Austin's first colonists also were hurt by drought. Their initial corn crop was snuffed out in 1822, forcing the once ambitious farmers into desperate hunters. In most years, some sections of the State receive less than normal rainfall, while other sections receive a greater than normal supply. Severe drought or excessively wet conditions rarely exist over the entire State at the same time.

TEMPERATURE. The vast land area of Texas experiences a wide range of temperatures. The High Plains experiences rather low temperatures in winter, while there are several separate areas within the State that experience very high temperatures in summer. Extended periods of subfreezing temperatures are rare, even on the High Plains. In South Texas, subfreezing temperatures associated with Arctic airmasses ordinarily are confined to several hours prior to sunrise, and seasons may pass with no subfreezing temperatures at all. In summer, the temperature contrast is much less pronounced from north to south with daily highs generally in the 90s. August is the hottest month.

OTHER CLIMATIC ELEMENTS. Relative humidity is highest in the coastal region, and decreases gradually inland, as the distance from the Gulf of Mexico increases. Mean annual relative humidity at noon varies from slightly more than 60 percent near the coast to around 35 percent in the El Paso area. As temperatures increase, relative humidities generally decrease.

Sunshine is abundant in the extreme southwestern section of the State, decreasing gradually eastward. On an average, the western Trans-Pecos receives 80 percent of the total possible sunshine annually, while the Upper Coast receives only 60 percent.

Significant amounts of snowfall are confined almost entirely to the mountainous Trans-Pecos region and the High Plains. Measurable snow falls south of the High Plains but usually melts almost as fast as it falls. Blizzards, characterized by subfreezing temperatures, very strong winds, and considerable blowing or drifting of snow, may occur in extreme West Texas or Northwest Texas during the winter or early spring months, but are rare.

STORMS. Tropical cyclones are a threat to all sections of the Texas coast during the summer and fall. Those tropical cyclones with sustained wind speeds of 64 knots (74 m.p.h.) or greater are known as hurricanes. Virtually all tropical cyclones which have affected the Texas coast originated in the Gulf of Mexico, the Caribbean Sea, or the southern part of the North Atlantic Ocean. The season extends from June to October; storms are most frequent in August and September, and rarely affect the Texas coast after the first days of October. The average storm frequency for the entire Texas coast is approximately one per year.

Tornadoes have occurred in Texas during all seasons; however, they have occurred with greatest frequency during April, May, and June. Approximately one-fourth of the total annual number of tornadoes occur in the month of May alone. Hailstorms occur in all parts of the State. The most frequent and most damaging of these occur in spring and early summer. Thunderstorms, from which most damaging local weather develops (tornadoes, hail, windstorms, and high intensity showers) occur on about 60 days each year in the extreme eastern section of the State. The mean annual number of thunderstorm days decreases to about 40 in extreme West Texas, and to 30 in the lower Rio Grande Valley.

Blowing dust and sand may occur occasionally in West Texas where strong winds are more frequent and vegetation is sparse.

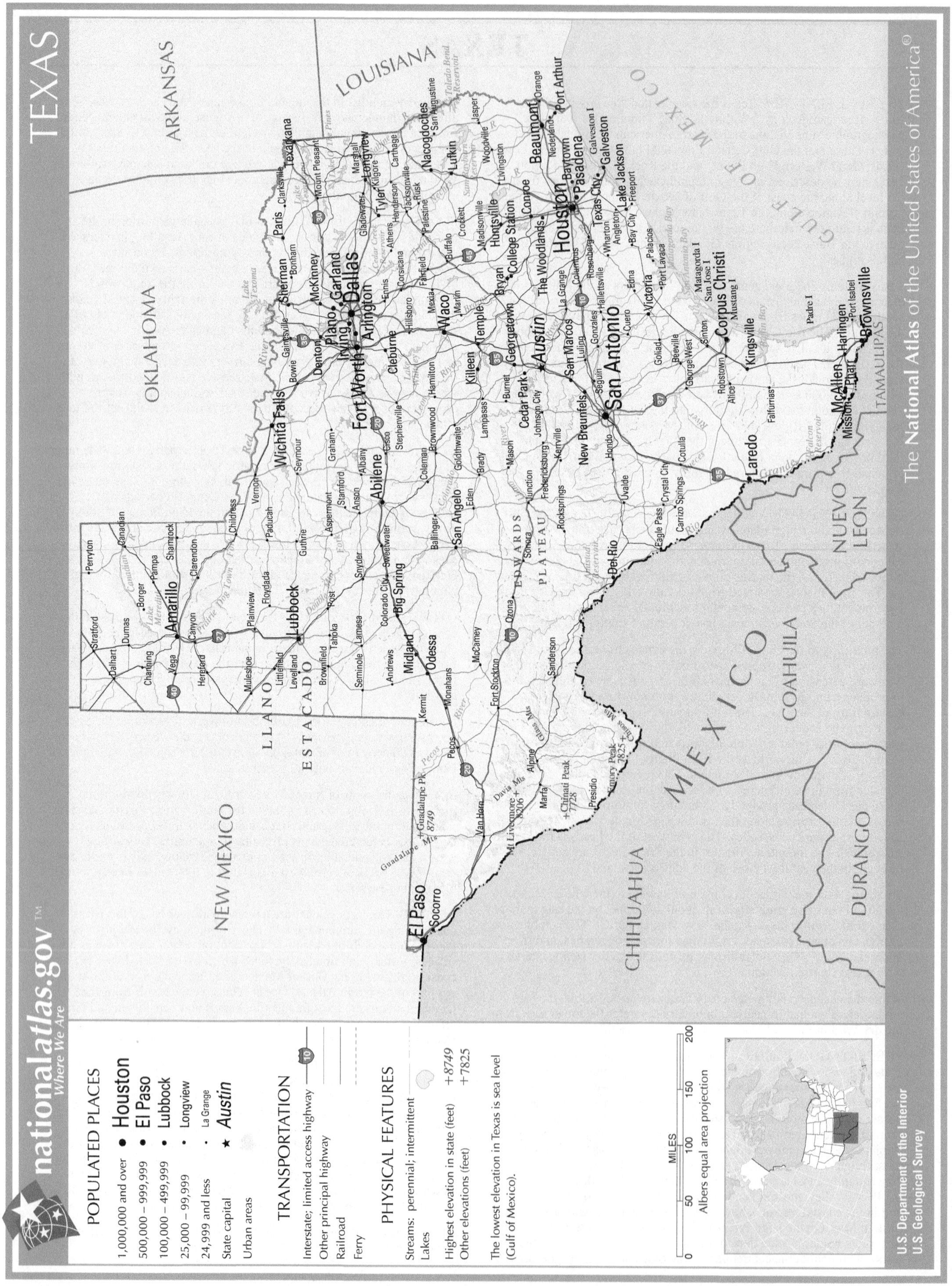
TEXAS
nationalatlas.gov™
Where We Are
POPULATED PLACES
1,000,000 and over • Houston
500,000 – 999,999 • El Paso
100,000 – 499,999 • Lubbock
25,000 – 99,999 • Longview
24,999 and less • La Grange
State capital ★ Austin
Urban areas
TRANSPORTATION
Interstate; limited access highway
Other principal highway
Railroad
Ferry
PHYSICAL FEATURES
Streams: perennial; intermittent
Lakes
Highest elevation in state (feet) +8749
Other elevations (feet) +7825
The lowest elevation in Texas is sea level (Gulf of Mexico).
MILES
0 50 100 150 200
Albers equal area projection
U.S. Department of the Interior
U.S. Geological Survey
The National Atlas of the United States of America®
ARKANSAS
LOUISIANA
OKLAHOMA
NEW MEXICO
MEXICO
CHIHUAHUA
COAHUILA
NUEVO LEON
TAMAULIPAS
DURANGO
GULF OF MEXICO
LLANO ESTACADO
EDWARDS PLATEAU
Houston
Dallas
San Antonio
Austin
El Paso
Fort Worth
Arlington
Corpus Christi
Plano
Garland
Irving
Lubbock
Laredo
Amarillo
Brownsville
Pasadena
Beaumont
Waco
Abilene
Wichita Falls
Midland
Odessa
San Angelo
Tyler
Killeen
McAllen
Guadalupe Pk 8749
Emory Peak 7825
Mt Livermore 8206
Chinati Peak 7728

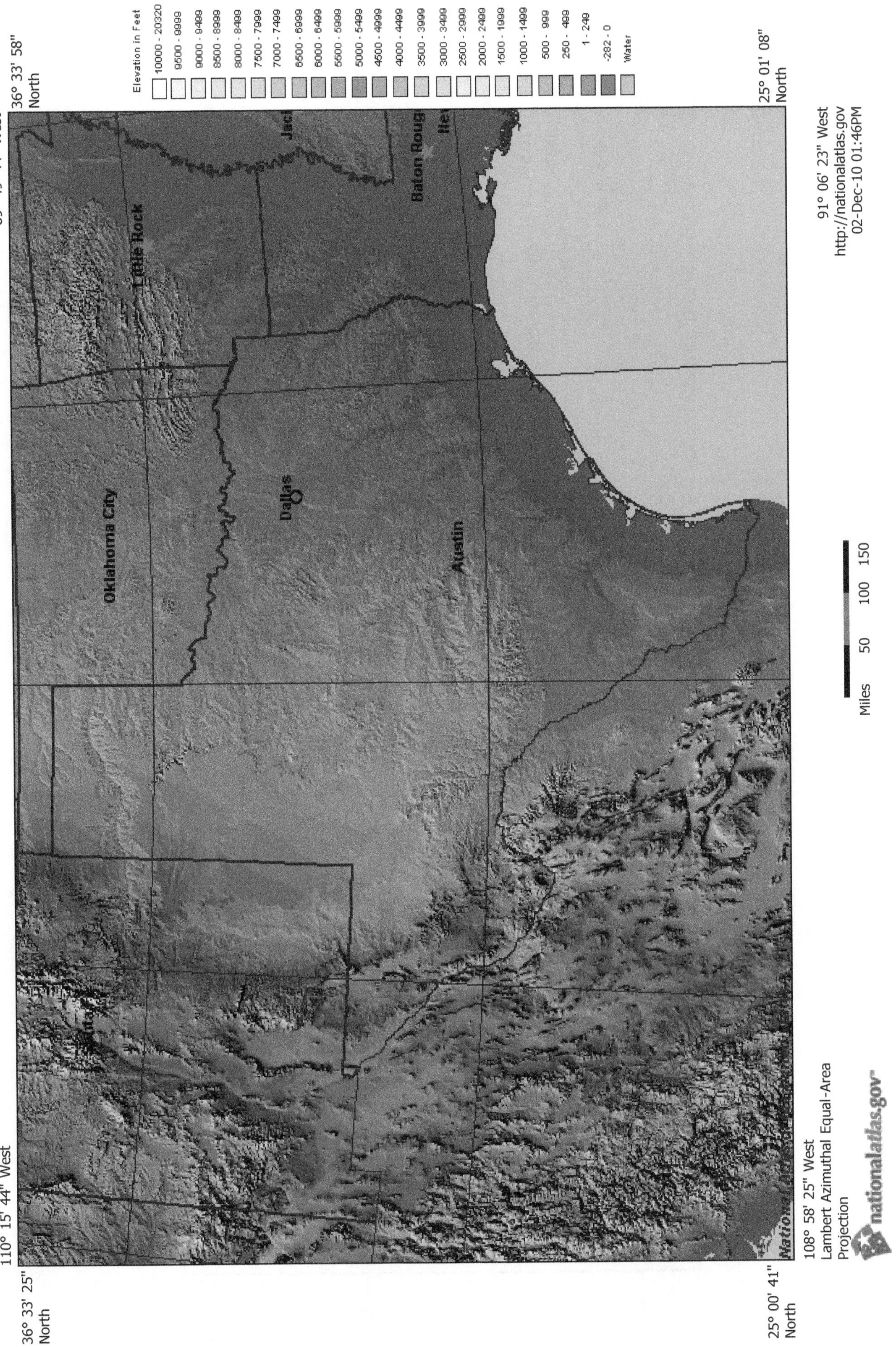
Elevation in Feet
10000 - 20320
9500 - 9999
9000 - 9499
8500 - 8999
8000 - 8499
7500 - 7999
7000 - 7499
6500 - 6999
6000 - 6499
5500 - 5999
5000 - 5499
4500 - 4999
4000 - 4499
3500 - 3999
3000 - 3499
2500 - 2999
2000 - 2499
1500 - 1999
1000 - 1499
500 - 999
250 - 499
1 - 249
-282 - 0
Water
36° 33' 58" North
89° 49' 44" West
25° 01' 08" North
91° 06' 23" West
http://nationalatlas.gov
02-Dec-10 01:46PM
Little Rock
Baton Roug
Oklahoma City
Dallas
Austin
Miles 50 100 150
110° 15' 44" West
36° 33' 25" North
25° 00' 41" North
108° 58' 25" West
Lambert Azimuthal Equal-Area Projection
nationalatlas.gov

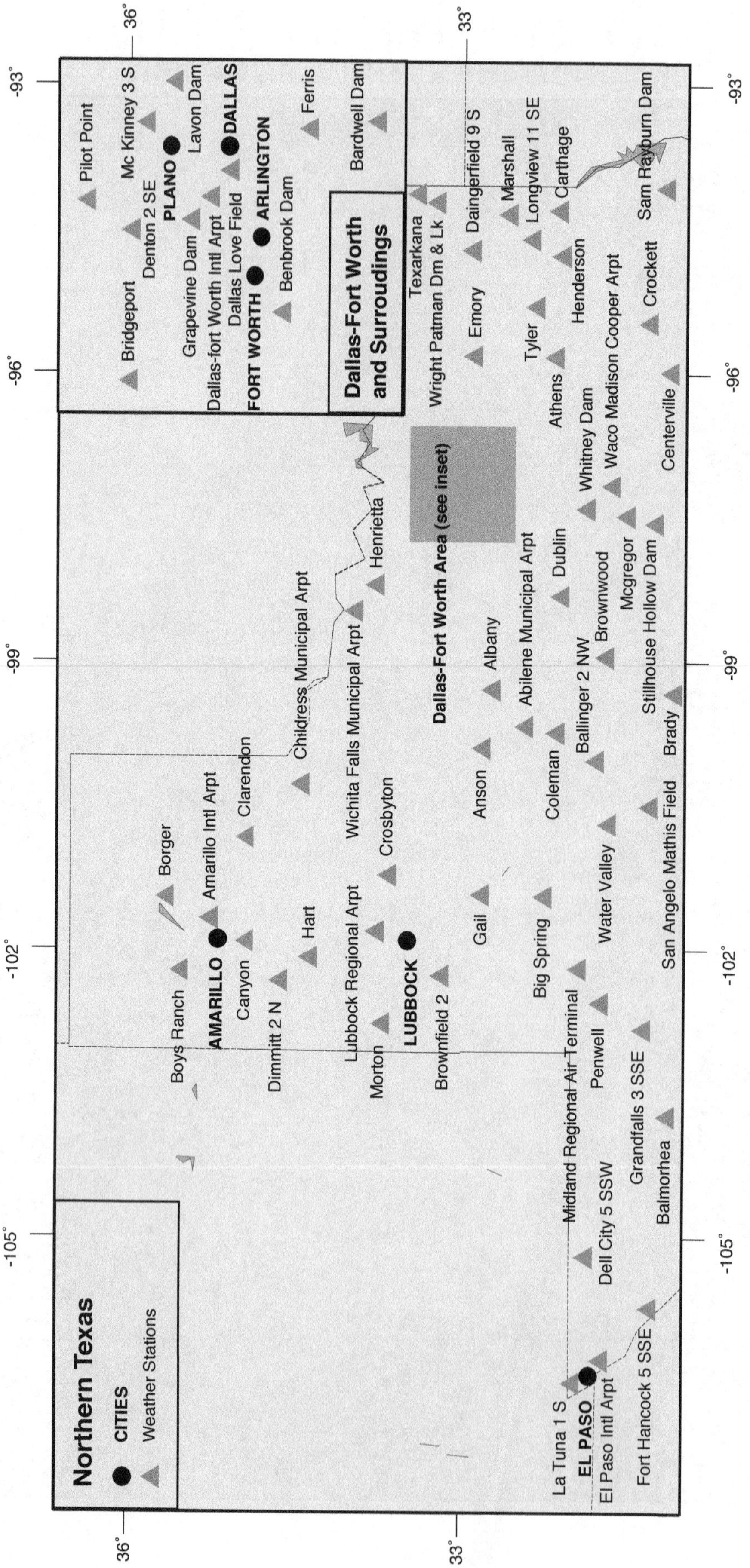
Northern Texas
CITIES
Weather Stations
Dallas-Fort Worth and Surroudings
Dallas-Fort Worth Area (see inset)
-93°
-96°
-99°
-102°
-105°
36°
33°
Pilot Point
Mc Kinney 3 S
Lavon Dam
PLANO
DALLAS
Denton 2 SE
Bridgeport
Grapevine Dam
Dallas-fort Worth Intl Arpt
Dallas Love Field
FORT WORTH
ARLINGTON
Benbrook Dam
Ferris
Bardwell Dam
Texarkana
Wright Patman Dm & Lk
Daingerfield 9 S
Emory
Marshall
Longview 11 SE
Carthage
Tyler
Henderson
Athens
Whitney Dam
Waco Madison Cooper Arpt
Sam Rayburn Dam
Crockett
Centerville
Henrietta
Childress Municipal Arpt
Wichita Falls Municipal Arpt
Crosbyton
Albany
Abilene Municipal Arpt
Dublin
Brownwood
Mcgregor
Stillhouse Hollow Dam
Anson
Coleman
Ballinger 2 NW
Brady
San Angelo Mathis Field
Water Valley
Big Spring
Gail
Borger
Amarillo Intl Arpt
Clarendon
Boys Ranch
AMARILLO
Canyon
Dimmitt 2 N
Hart
Lubbock Regional Arpt
LUBBOCK
Morton
Brownfield 2
Midland Regional Air Terminal
Penwell
Grandfalls 3 SSE
Balmorhea
Dell City 5 SSW
La Tuna 1 S
EL PASO
El Paso Intl Arpt
Fort Hancock 5 SSE

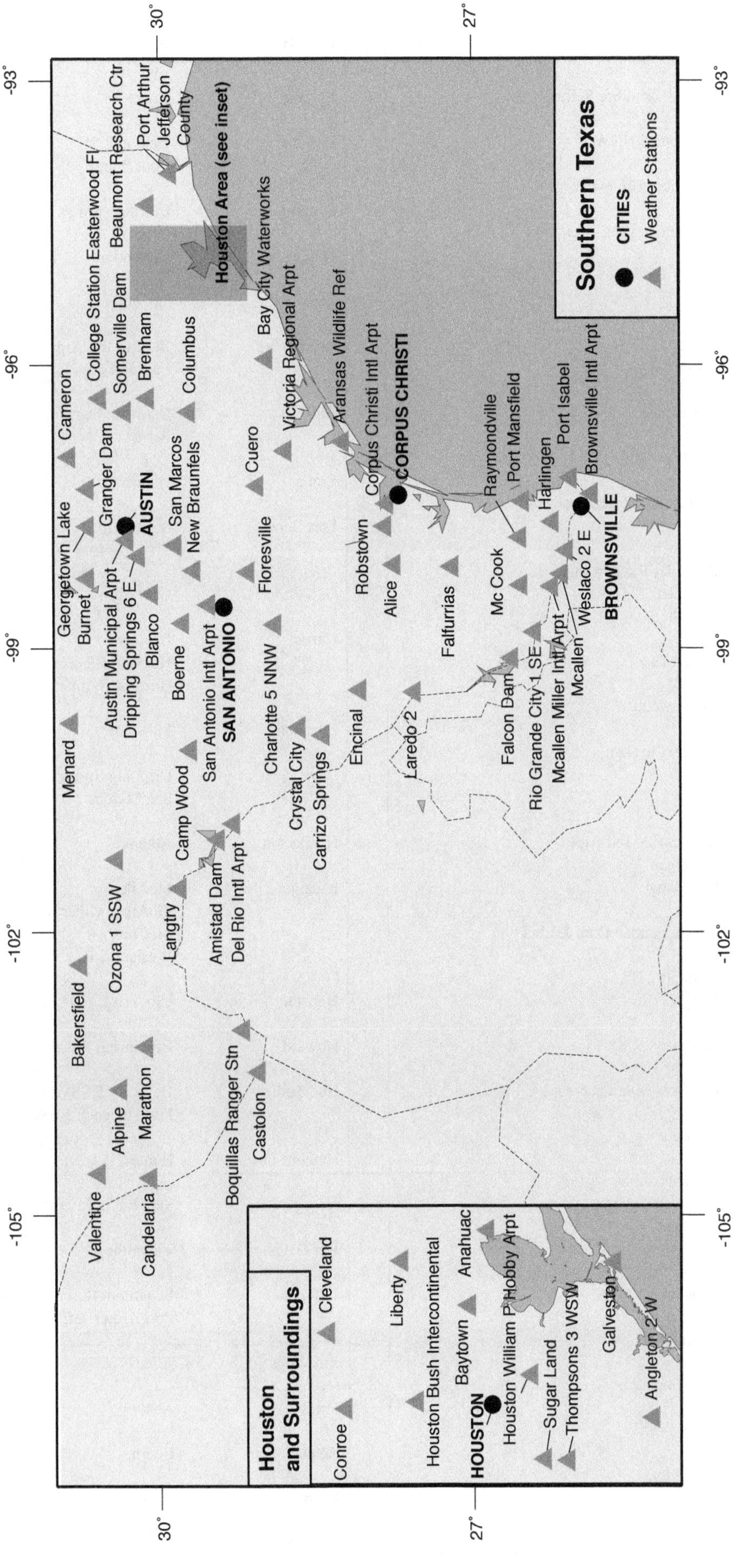
Southern Texas
CITIES
Weather Stations
Houston Area (see inset)
Houston and Surroundings
AUSTIN
SAN ANTONIO
CORPUS CHRISTI
BROWNSVILLE
HOUSTON
Valentine
Candelaria
Alpine
Marathon
Bakersfield
Boquillas Ranger Stn
Castolon
Ozona 1 SSW
Langtry
Amistad Dam
Del Rio Intl Arpt
Camp Wood
Menard
San Antonio Intl Arpt
Charlotte 5 NNW
Crystal City
Carrizo Springs
Encinal
Laredo 2
Boerne
Blanco
Dripping Springs 6 E
Austin Municipal Arpt
Burnet
Georgetown Lake
Granger Dam
Cameron
College Station Easterwood Fl
Somerville Dam
Brenham
Columbus
San Marcos
New Braunfels
Floresville
Cuero
Bay City Waterworks
Victoria Regional Arpt
Aransas Wildlife Ref
Corpus Christi Intl Arpt
Robstown
Alice
Falfurrias
Falcon Dam
Rio Grande City 1 SE
Mcallen Miller Intl Arpt
Mcallen
Weslaco 2 E
Mc Cook
Raymondville
Port Mansfield
Harlingen
Port Isabel
Brownsville Intl Arpt
Beaumont Research Ctr
Port Arthur Jefferson County
Conroe
Cleveland
Liberty
Houston Bush Intercontinental
Baytown
Anahuac
Houston William P. Hobby Arpt
Sugar Land
Thompsons 3 WSW
Galveston
Angleton 2 W
30°
27°
-93°
-96°
-99°
-102°
-105°

Texas Weather Stations by County

County	Station Name
Aransas	Aransas Wildlife Refuge
Atascosa	Charlotte 5 NNW
Bell	Stillhouse Hollow Dam
Bexar	San Antonio Intl Arpt
Blanco	Blanco
Borden	Gail
Bosque	Whitney Dam
Bowie	Texarkana
Brazoria	Angleton 2 W
Brazos	College Station Easterwood
Brewster	Alpine Boquillas Ranger Stn Castolon Marathon
Brooks	Falfurrias
Brown	Brownwood
Burleson	Somerville Dam
Burnet	Burnet
Cameron	Brownsville Intl Arpt Harlingen Port Isabel
Cass	Wright Patman Dam & Lock
Castro	Dimmitt 2 N Hart
Chambers	Anahuac
Childress	Childress Municipal Arpt
Clay	Henrietta
Cochran	Morton
Coleman	Coleman
Collin	Lavon Dam McKinney 3 S
Colorado	Columbus
Comal	New Braunfels
Crockett	Ozona 1 SSW
Crosby	Crosbyton
Dallas	Dallas Love Field

County	Station Name
De Witt	Cuero
Denton	Denton 2 SE Pilot Point
Dimmit	Carrizo Springs
Donley	Clarendon
Ector	Penwell
El Paso	El Paso Intl Arpt La Tuna 1 S
Ellis	Bardwell Dam Ferris
Erath	Dublin
Fort Bend	Sugar Land Thompsons 3 WSW
Galveston	Galveston
Harris	Baytown Houston Bush Intercontinental Houston William P Hobby Arpt
Harrison	Marshall
Hays	Dripping Springs 6 E San Marcos
Henderson	Athens
Hidalgo	McAllen McAllen Miller Intl Arpt McCook Weslaco 2 E
Houston	Crockett
Howard	Big Spring
Hudspeth	Dell City 5 SSW Fort Hancock 5 SSE
Hutchinson	Borger
Jasper	Sam Rayburn Dam
Jeff Davis	Valentine
Jefferson	Beaumont Research Ctr Port Arthur Jefferson County
Jim Wells	Alice
Jones	Anson
Kendall	Boerne
Leon	Centerville

See User Guide for station inclusion criteria.

County	Station Name
Liberty	Cleveland Liberty
Lubbock	Lubbock Regional Arpt
Matagorda	Bay City Waterworks
Mcculloch	Brady
Mclennan	McGregor Waco Madison Cooper Arpt
Menard	Menard
Midland	Midland Regional Air Terminal
Milam	Cameron
Montgomery	Conroe
Morris	Daingerfield 9 S
Nueces	Corpus Christi Intl Arpt Robstown
Oldham	Boys Ranch
Panola	Carthage
Pecos	Bakersfield
Potter	Amarillo Intl Arpt
Presidio	Candelaria
Rains	Emory
Randall	Canyon
Real	Camp Wood
Reeves	Balmorhea
Runnels	Ballinger 2 NW
Rusk	Henderson Longview 11 SE
Shackelford	Albany
Smith	Tyler
Starr	Falcon Dam Rio Grande City 1 SE
Tarrant	Benbrook Dam Dallas-Fort Worth Intl Arpt Grapevine Dam
Taylor	Abilene Municipal Arpt
Terry	Brownfield 2
Tom Green	San Angelo Mathis Field Water Valley

County	Station Name
Travis	Austin Municipal Arpt
Val Verde	Amistad Dam Del Rio Intl Arpt Langtry
Victoria	Victoria Regional Arpt
Ward	Grandfalls 3 SSE
Washington	Brenham
Webb	Encinal Laredo 2
Wichita	Wichita Falls Municipal Arpt
Willacy	Port Mansfield Raymondville
Williamson	Georgetown Lake Granger Dam
Wilson	Floresville
Wise	Bridgeport
Zavala	Crystal City

Texas Weather Stations by City

City	Station Name	Miles
Abilene	Abilene Municipal Arpt	4.4
	Anson	24.0
	Coleman	21.4
Allen	Dallas-Fort Worth Intl Arpt	24.5
	Dallas Love Field	20.1
	Grapevine Dam	24.5
	Lavon Dam	11.4
	McKinney 3 S	5.6
Amarillo	Amarillo Intl Arpt	9.0
	Canyon	15.0
Arlington	Benbrook Dam	19.5
	Dallas-Fort Worth Intl Arpt	14.8
	Dallas Love Field	18.7
	Grapevine Dam	17.5
Atascocita	Baytown	15.5
	Houston Bush Intercontinental	10.9
	Houston William P Hobby Arpt	24.3
	Liberty	23.6
Austin	Austin Municipal Arpt	2.8
	Dripping Springs 6 E	15.2
Baytown	Anahuac	18.4
	Baytown	5.9
	Houston William P Hobby Arpt	20.0
	Liberty	24.0
Beaumont	Beaumont Research Ctr	8.8
	Port Arthur Jefferson County	11.9
Brownsville	Brownsville Intl Arpt	3.3
	Harlingen	22.3
	Port Isabel	19.0
Bryan	College Station Easterwood	5.5
	Somerville Dam	25.0
Carrollton	Dallas-Fort Worth Intl Arpt	9.6
	Dallas Love Field	10.0
	Denton 2 SE	18.9
	Grapevine Dam	9.7
	Lavon Dam	23.8
	McKinney 3 S	20.0
Cedar Park	Austin Municipal Arpt	16.3
	Dripping Springs 6 E	21.8
	Georgetown Lake	14.2
College Station	College Station Easterwood	3.4
	Somerville Dam	22.8
Conroe	Cleveland	21.9
	Conroe	1.8
	Houston Bush Intercontinental	22.5
Corpus Christi	Corpus Christi Intl Arpt	7.1
	Robstown	16.2
Dallas	Dallas-Fort Worth Intl Arpt	14.8
	Dallas Love Field	4.6

City	Station Name	Miles
Dallas *(cont.)*	Ferris	21.8
	Grapevine Dam	18.1
	Lavon Dam	22.9
Denton	Dallas-Fort Worth Intl Arpt	22.6
	Denton 2 SE	1.8
	Grapevine Dam	18.7
	Pilot Point	15.0
Edinburg	McAllen	8.9
	McAllen Miller Intl Arpt	9.4
	McCook	18.3
	Raymondville	24.8
	Weslaco 2 E	16.3
El Paso	El Paso Intl Arpt	3.8
	La Tuna 1 S	12.6
Euless	Benbrook Dam	24.8
	Dallas-Fort Worth Intl Arpt	5.8
	Dallas Love Field	14.1
	Denton 2 SE	24.4
	Grapevine Dam	7.6
Flower Mound	Dallas-Fort Worth Intl Arpt	9.6
	Dallas Love Field	17.9
	Denton 2 SE	11.8
	Grapevine Dam	5.8
Fort Worth	Benbrook Dam	8.9
	Dallas-Fort Worth Intl Arpt	21.7
	Grapevine Dam	22.2
Frisco	Dallas-Fort Worth Intl Arpt	20.5
	Dallas Love Field	19.9
	Denton 2 SE	17.8
	Grapevine Dam	19.2
	Lavon Dam	19.7
	McKinney 3 S	10.9
	Pilot Point	19.6
Galveston	Galveston	1.6
Garland	Dallas-Fort Worth Intl Arpt	22.1
	Dallas Love Field	13.0
	Grapevine Dam	24.2
	Lavon Dam	12.5
	McKinney 3 S	18.1
Grand Prairie	Dallas-Fort Worth Intl Arpt	12.6
	Dallas Love Field	13.3
	Ferris	24.6
	Grapevine Dam	16.2
Grapevine	Dallas-Fort Worth Intl Arpt	5.1
	Dallas Love Field	15.4
	Denton 2 SE	18.8
	Grapevine Dam	3.2
Harlingen	Harlingen	1.7
	Raymondville	21.5
	Weslaco 2 E	17.2
Houston	Houston Bush Intercontinental	17.7

See User Guide for station inclusion criteria.

City	Station Name	Miles
Houston *(cont.)*	Houston William P Hobby Arpt	10.4
	Sugar Land	16.0
	Thompsons 3 WSW	22.5
Irving	Dallas-Fort Worth Intl Arpt	4.8
	Dallas Love Field	6.8
	Grapevine Dam	8.7
Killeen	Stillhouse Hollow Dam	12.2
Laredo	Laredo 2	3.1
League City	Baytown	23.1
	Galveston	22.5
	Houston William P Hobby Arpt	15.3
Lewisville	Dallas-Fort Worth Intl Arpt	9.2
	Dallas Love Field	15.7
	Denton 2 SE	12.6
	Grapevine Dam	6.2
	McKinney 3 S	24.6
	Pilot Point	24.3
Longview	Henderson	22.9
	Longview 11 SE	13.0
	Marshall	23.9
Lubbock	Lubbock Regional Arpt	8.6
Mansfield	Benbrook Dam	19.3
	Dallas-Fort Worth Intl Arpt	22.9
	Dallas Love Field	24.6
McAllen	McAllen	1.7
	McAllen Miller Intl Arpt	2.7
	McCook	20.1
	Weslaco 2 E	17.6
McKinney	Lavon Dam	14.5
	McKinney 3 S	2.5
	Pilot Point	22.6
Mesquite	Dallas-Fort Worth Intl Arpt	24.8
	Dallas Love Field	14.6
	Ferris	18.8
	Lavon Dam	18.7
Midland	Midland Regional Air Terminal	5.8
Mission	McAllen	4.5
	McAllen Miller Intl Arpt	5.9
	McCook	18.8
	Weslaco 2 E	22.4
Missouri City	Houston William P Hobby Arpt	16.0
	Sugar Land	6.0
	Thompsons 3 WSW	9.1
New Braunfels	New Braunfels	2.4
	San Antonio Intl Arpt	23.6
	San Marcos	14.7
North Richland Hills	Benbrook Dam	19.6
	Dallas-Fort Worth Intl Arpt	12.2
	Dallas Love Field	21.5

City	Station Name	Miles
North Richland Hills *(cont.)*	Denton 2 SE	24.7
	Grapevine Dam	11.8
Odessa	Midland Regional Air Terminal	12.0
	Penwell	15.9
Pasadena	Baytown	15.2
	Houston William P Hobby Arpt	6.6
Pearland	Houston William P Hobby Arpt	6.6
	Sugar Land	21.8
	Thompsons 3 WSW	21.9
Pharr	McAllen	4.2
	McAllen Miller Intl Arpt	2.9
	McCook	24.4
	Weslaco 2 E	13.8
Plano	Dallas-Fort Worth Intl Arpt	18.8
	Dallas Love Field	15.1
	Denton 2 SE	23.0
	Grapevine Dam	19.0
	Lavon Dam	15.2
	McKinney 3 S	11.0
Port Arthur	Beaumont Research Ctr	23.3
	Port Arthur Jefferson County	5.4
Richardson	Dallas-Fort Worth Intl Arpt	17.9
	Dallas Love Field	11.0
	Grapevine Dam	19.3
	Lavon Dam	14.4
	McKinney 3 S	15.2
Round Rock	Austin Municipal Arpt	14.8
	Georgetown Lake	12.1
	Granger Dam	23.9
Rowlett	Dallas Love Field	18.1
	Lavon Dam	9.4
	McKinney 3 S	18.4
San Angelo	San Angelo Mathis Field	7.3
	Water Valley	22.2
San Antonio	San Antonio Intl Arpt	5.7
Sugar Land	Houston William P Hobby Arpt	20.0
	Sugar Land	1.7
	Thompsons 3 WSW	8.2
Temple	McGregor	23.8
	Stillhouse Hollow Dam	10.5
The Woodlands	Conroe	11.1
	Houston Bush Intercontinental	14.5
Tyler	Tyler	1.7
Victoria	Victoria Regional Arpt	4.3
Waco	McGregor	16.2
	Waco Madison Cooper Arpt	6.4
	Whitney Dam	24.2

City	Station Name	Miles
Wichita Falls	Henrietta	19.6
	Wichita Falls Municipal Arpt	5.8

Note: Miles is the distance between the geographic center of the city and the weather station.

Texas Weather Stations by Elevation

Feet	Station Name
4,529	Alpine
4,430	Valentine
4,089	Marathon
3,917	El Paso Intl Arpt
3,904	Fort Hancock 5 SSE
3,850	Dimmitt 2 N
3,799	La Tuna 1 S
3,770	Dell City 5 SSW
3,759	Morton
3,640	Hart
3,589	Canyon
3,585	Amarillo Intl Arpt
3,299	Brownfield 2
3,253	Lubbock Regional Arpt
3,219	Balmorhea
3,190	Boys Ranch
3,140	Borger
3,009	Crosbyton
2,939	Penwell
2,875	Candelaria
2,861	Midland Regional Air Terminal
2,703	Clarendon
2,540	Bakersfield
2,528	Gail
2,500	Big Spring
2,439	Grandfalls 3 SSE
2,339	Ozona 1 SSW
2,167	Castolon
2,120	Water Valley
1,951	Childress Municipal Arpt
1,951	Menard
1,916	San Angelo Mathis Field
1,879	Boquillas Ranger Stn
1,790	Abilene Municipal Arpt
1,754	Ballinger 2 NW
1,727	Coleman
1,720	Brady
1,709	Anson
1,501	Dublin
1,470	Camp Wood
1,443	Boerne
1,419	Albany
1,384	Brownwood
1,370	Blanco
1,290	Langtry
1,274	Burnet
1,157	Amistad Dam
1,120	Dripping Springs 6 E
1,029	Wichita Falls Municipal Arpt
999	Del Rio Intl Arpt
930	Henrietta
839	Georgetown Lake
809	San Antonio Intl Arpt
790	Benbrook Dam
745	Bridgeport

Feet	Station Name
723	McGregor
709	New Braunfels
706	Stillhouse Hollow Dam
689	Pilot Point
629	Denton 2 SE
621	Austin Municipal Arpt
612	Carrizo Springs
611	San Marcos
595	McKinney 3 S
589	Encinal
584	Grapevine Dam
580	Crystal City
574	Whitney Dam
564	Granger Dam
560	Dallas-Fort Worth Intl Arpt
549	Tyler
509	Lavon Dam
500	Waco Madison Cooper Arpt
470	Ferris
460	Bardwell Dam
448	Athens
440	Charlotte 5 NNW
439	Dallas Love Field
435	Emory
430	Laredo 2
419	Henderson
407	Longview 11 SE
399	Floresville
390	Texarkana
363	Cameron
352	Marshall
347	Crockett
339	Carthage
319	Centerville
319	Falcon Dam
313	College Station Easterwood
312	Brenham
299	Daingerfield 9 S
282	Wright Patman Dam & Lock
263	Somerville Dam
245	Conroe
220	McCook
201	Alice
199	Columbus
195	Cleveland
188	Sam Rayburn Dam
178	Cuero
171	Rio Grande City 1 SE
120	Falfurrias
115	Victoria Regional Arpt
100	McAllen
100	McAllen Miller Intl Arpt
95	Houston Bush Intercontinental
84	Robstown
82	Sugar Land

See User Guide for station inclusion criteria.

Feet	Station Name
75	Weslaco 2 E
71	Thompsons 3 WSW
51	Bay City Waterworks
49	Houston William P Hobby Arpt
43	Corpus Christi Intl Arpt
38	Harlingen
35	Liberty
34	Baytown
30	Raymondville
26	Angleton 2 W
26	Beaumont Research Ctr
23	Anahuac
19	Brownsville Intl Arpt
17	Port Isabel
16	Port Arthur Jefferson County
15	Aransas Wildlife Refuge
15	Galveston
8	Port Mansfield

See User Guide for station inclusion criteria.

Abilene Municipal Airport

Abilene is located in north central Texas. The station elevation is 1,750 feet above sea level. Topography of the area includes rolling plains, treeless except for mesquite, broken by low hills to the south and west. The land rises gently to the east and southeast. Regional agricultural products are mainly cattle, dry-land cotton, and feed crops.

Abilene is on the boundary between the humid east Texas climate and the semi-arid west and north Texas climate. The rainfall pattern is typical of the Great Plains. Most precipitation occurs from April to October and is usually associated with thunderstorms. Severe storms are infrequent, occurring mostly in the spring.

The large range of high and low temperatures, characteristic of the Great Plains, extends south to the Abilene area. High daytime temperatures prevail in the summer, but are normally broken by thunderstorms about five times a month. Rapid cooling after sunset results in pleasant nights with low summertime temperatures in the upper 60s and low 70s. High summer temperatures are usually associated with fair skies, southwesterly winds, and low humidities.

Rapid wintertime temperature changes occur when cold, dry, arctic air replaces warm moist tropical air. Drops in temperature of 20 to 30 degrees in one hour are not unusual. However, cold weather periods are short lived. Fair, mild weather is typical.

South is the prevailing wind direction, and southerly winds are frequently high and persist for several days. Strong northerly winds often occur during the passage of cold fronts. Dusty conditions are infrequent, occurring mostly with westerly winds. Dust storm frequency and intensity depend on soil conditions in eastern New Mexico, west Texas, and the Texas Panhandle.

Based on the 1951-1980 period, the average first occurrence of 32 degrees Fahrenheit in the fall is November 13 and the average last occurrence in the spring is March 25.

Abilene Municipal Airport *Taylor County* Elevation: 1,790 ft. Latitude: 32° 25' N Longitude: 99° 41' W

	JAN	FEB	MAR	APR	MAY	JUN	JUL	AUG	SEP	OCT	NOV	DEC	YEAR
Mean Maximum Temp. (°F)	56.8	60.8	68.7	77.4	84.6	90.6	94.5	94.0	86.7	77.2	66.0	56.9	76.2
Mean Temp. (°F)	45.1	48.9	56.5	64.7	73.0	79.6	83.4	82.9	75.5	65.8	54.5	45.4	64.6
Mean Minimum Temp. (°F)	33.3	36.9	44.2	51.9	61.4	68.6	72.3	71.7	64.3	54.4	43.0	33.9	53.0
Extreme Maximum Temp. (°F)	87	93	95	98	109	109	107	107	107	99	92	87	109
Extreme Minimum Temp. (°F)	5	-7	10	27	39	51	57	50	38	23	16	-7	-7
Days Maximum Temp. ≥ 90°F	0	0	1	3	9	19	26	25	12	2	0	0	97
Days Maximum Temp. ≤ 32°F	1	1	0	0	0	0	0	0	0	0	0	1	3
Days Minimum Temp. ≤ 32°F	15	9	4	0	0	0	0	0	0	0	5	14	47
Days Minimum Temp. ≤ 0°F	0	0	0	0	0	0	0	0	0	0	0	0	0
Heating Degree Days (base 65°F)	612	455	288	107	17	0	0	0	12	90	326	602	2,509
Cooling Degree Days (base 65°F)	1	6	31	104	272	445	577	561	334	122	19	1	2,473
Mean Precipitation (in.)	0.94	1.31	1.70	1.58	3.23	3.48	1.67	2.63	2.37	2.96	1.46	1.24	24.57
Maximum Precipitation (in.)*	4.3	3.6	5.2	6.8	13.2	9.6	7.1	8.2	11.0	10.7	4.6	6.3	36.8
Minimum Precipitation (in.)*	trace	trace	trace	trace	0.1	trace	trace	trace	trace	0	0	trace	9.8
Extreme Maximum Daily Precip. (in.)	1.82	1.77	1.71	2.40	4.72	3.62	5.67	4.79	2.85	3.83	1.55	2.17	5.67
Days With ≥ 0.1" Precipitation	2	3	3	3	5	5	3	4	4	4	3	3	42
Days With ≥ 0.5" Precipitation	1	1	1	1	2	3	1	2	2	2	1	1	18
Days With ≥ 1.0" Precipitation	0	0	0	0	1	1	0	1	1	1	0	0	5
Mean Snowfall (in.)	1.8	0.7	0.4	0.4	trace	trace	trace	trace	0.0	trace	0.7	1.2	5.2
Maximum Snowfall (in.)*	14	8	7	0	0	0	0	0	0	trace	8	8	19
Maximum 24-hr. Snowfall (in.)*	7	5	6	0	0	0	0	0	0	trace	4	4	7
Maximum Snow Depth (in.)	5	5	5	6	trace	trace	trace	trace	0	trace	3	3	6
Days With ≥ 1.0" Snow Depth	1	1	0	0	0	0	0	0	0	0	0	1	3
Thunderstorm Days*	1	1	3	5	8	6	5	5	4	3	1	1	43
Foggy Days*	7	7	4	4	4	2	1	1	5	5	5	7	52
Predominant Sky Cover*	OVR	OVR	CLR	CLR	CLR	CLR	CLR	CLR	CLR	CLR	CLR	CLR	CLR
Mean Relative Humidity 6am (%)*	73	73	69	72	80	79	73	73	78	76	74	72	74
Mean Relative Humidity 3pm (%)*	45	44	37	38	43	41	38	38	44	42	42	44	41
Mean Dewpoint (°F)*	28	32	36	45	56	62	63	62	59	49	38	30	47
Prevailing Wind Direction*	S	S	S	SSE	SSE	S	SSE	SSE	SSE	S	S	S	S
Prevailing Wind Speed (mph)*	13	13	15	15	14	14	12	10	10	12	13	13	13
Maximum Wind Gust (mph)*	51	56	74	61	71	73	78	55	59	58	62	59	78

Note: (*) Period of record is 1948-1995

Amarillo Int'l Airport

The station is located 7 statute miles east northeast of the downtown post office in a region of rather flat topography. The Canadian River flows eastward 18 miles north of the station, with its bed about 800 feet below the plains. The Prairie Dog Town Fork of the Red River flows southeastward about 15 miles south of the station where it enters the Palo Duro Canyon, which is about 1,000 feet deep. There are numerous shallow Playa lakes, often dry, over the area, and the nearly treeless grasslands slope downward to the east. The terrain gradually rises to the west and northwest.

Three-fourths of the total annual precipitation falls from April through September, occurring from thunderstorm activity. Snow usually melts within a few days after it falls. Heavier snowfalls of 10 inches or more, usually with near blizzard conditions, average once every five years and last two to three days.

The Amarillo area is subject to rapid and large temperature changes, especially during the winter months when cold fronts from the northern Rocky Mountain and Plains states sweep across the area. Temperature drops of 50 to 60 degrees within a 12-hour period are not uncommon. Temperature drops of 40 degrees have occurred within a few minutes.

Humidity averages are low, occasionally dropping below 20 percent in the spring. Low humidity moderates the effect of high summer afternoon temperatures, permits evaporative cooling systems to be very effective, and provides many pleasant evenings and nights.

Severe local storms are infrequent, although a few thunderstorms with damaging hail, lightning, and wind in a very localized area occur most years, usually in spring and summer. These storms are often accompanied by very heavy rain, which produces local flooding, particularly of roads and streets. Tornadoes are rare.

Based on the 1951-1980 period, the average first occurrence of 32 degrees Fahrenheit in the fall is October 29 and the average last occurrence in the spring is April 14.

Amarillo Int'l Airport *Potter County* Elevation: 3,585 ft. Latitude: 35° 13' N Longitude: 101° 42' W

	JAN	FEB	MAR	APR	MAY	JUN	JUL	AUG	SEP	OCT	NOV	DEC	YEAR
Mean Maximum Temp. (°F)	50.3	54.5	62.4	70.9	79.3	87.7	91.6	89.2	82.1	71.6	59.8	49.9	70.8
Mean Temp. (°F)	36.9	40.5	47.8	56.1	65.5	74.4	78.5	76.7	69.3	58.1	46.1	37.0	57.2
Mean Minimum Temp. (°F)	23.5	26.5	33.1	41.3	51.7	61.0	65.3	64.2	56.3	44.5	32.5	24.0	43.7
Extreme Maximum Temp. (°F)	80	84	92	98	103	108	106	105	103	99	87	80	108
Extreme Minimum Temp. (°F)	-11	-12	4	17	31	41	51	52	30	12	3	-8	-12
Days Maximum Temp. ≥ 90°F	0	0	0	1	5	13	21	17	6	1	0	0	64
Days Maximum Temp. ≤ 32°F	3	2	1	0	0	0	0	0	0	0	1	4	11
Days Minimum Temp. ≤ 32°F	27	21	14	4	0	0	0	0	0	2	15	27	110
Days Minimum Temp. ≤ 0°F	0	0	0	0	0	0	0	0	0	0	0	1	1
Heating Degree Days (base 65°F)	863	687	529	278	84	6	0	1	43	237	560	862	4,150
Cooling Degree Days (base 65°F)	0	0	2	19	108	293	425	372	177	29	1	0	1,426
Mean Precipitation (in.)	0.71	0.53	1.38	1.31	2.31	3.17	2.59	2.89	1.91	1.64	0.73	0.72	19.89
Maximum Precipitation (in.)*	2.3	1.8	4.0	2.8	9.8	10.7	7.6	7.5	5.0	4.8	2.3	4.5	36.6
Minimum Precipitation (in.)*	0	trace	trace	trace	trace	trace	0.1	0.3	trace	0	0	trace	9.6
Extreme Maximum Daily Precip. (in.)	1.57	1.20	1.84	2.65	3.40	4.92	3.47	2.30	2.33	2.38	0.88	1.16	4.92
Days With ≥ 0.1" Precipitation	2	1	3	3	4	5	4	5	4	3	2	2	38
Days With ≥ 0.5" Precipitation	1	0	1	1	2	2	2	2	1	1	0	0	13
Days With ≥ 1.0" Precipitation	0	0	0	0	0	1	1	1	0	0	0	0	3
Mean Snowfall (in.)	4.8	2.6	2.7	0.7	0.2	trace	trace	trace	trace	0.2	2.6	4.0	17.8
Maximum Snowfall (in.)*	15	17	15	6	1	0	0	0	trace	4	14	15	47
Maximum 24-hr. Snowfall (in.)*	9	11	8	4	1	0	0	0	trace	3	8	8	11
Maximum Snow Depth (in.)	10	14	12	3	2	trace	trace	trace	trace	3	7	15	15
Days With ≥ 1.0" Snow Depth	4	3	1	0	0	0	0	0	0	0	1	3	12
Thunderstorm Days*	< 1	< 1	2	3	8	10	9	9	4	2	1	< 1	48
Foggy Days*	7	8	8	6	8	4	3	4	6	6	6	7	73
Predominant Sky Cover*	CLR	CLR	CLR	CLR	CLR	CLR	SCT	SCT	CLR	CLR	CLR	CLR	CLR
Mean Relative Humidity 6am (%)*	71	72	68	69	76	77	75	78	78	73	71	70	73
Mean Relative Humidity 3pm (%)*	42	41	34	31	37	37	36	39	40	36	38	40	38
Mean Dewpoint (°F)*	19	22	25	33	45	55	58	58	51	39	28	21	38
Prevailing Wind Direction*	SW	SW	SW	S	S	S	S	S	S	SSW	SW	SW	S
Prevailing Wind Speed (mph)*	14	14	15	16	16	16	14	13	14	14	14	13	14
Maximum Wind Gust (mph)*	64	67	76	81	70	69	69	66	60	74	73	63	81

Note: (*) Period of record is 1948-1995

 The period of record for National Weather Service station data is 1980 – 2009 except where noted. See User Guide for detailed explanation of data.

Austin Municipal Airport

Austin, capital of Texas, is located on the Colorado River where the stream crosses the Balcones steep slope separating the Texas Hill Country from the Blackland Prairies to the east. Elevations within the city vary from 400 feet to nearly 1,000 feet above sea level. Native trees include cedar, oak, walnut, mesquite, and pecan.

The climate of Austin is humid subtropical with hot summers. Winters are mild, with below freezing temperatures occurring on an average of about 25 days each year. Rather strong northerly winds, accompanied by sharp drops in temperature, frequently occur during the winter months in connection with cold fronts, but cold spells are usually of short duration, seldom lasting more than two days. Daytime temperatures in summer are hot, but summer nights are usually pleasant.

Precipitation is fairly evenly distributed throughout the year, with heaviest amounts occurring in late spring. A secondary rainfall peak occurs in September, primarily because of tropical cyclones that migrate out of the Gulf of Mexico. Precipitation from April through September usually results from thunderstorms, with fairly large amounts of rain falling within short periods of time. While thunderstorms and heavy rains may occur in all months of the year, most of the winter precipitation consists of light rain. Snow is insignificant as a source of moisture, and usually melts as rapidly as it falls. The city may experience several seasons in succession with no measurable snowfall.

Prevailing winds are southerly, however in winter, northerly winds are about as frequent as those from the south. Destructive winds and damaging hailstorms are infrequent. On rare occasions dissipating tropical storms produce strong winds and heavy rains in the area. Blowing dust occurs occasionally in spring, but visibility rarely drops substantially, and then only for a few hours.

The average length of the warm season (freeze-free period) is 273 days. The average occurrence of the last temperature of 32 degrees in spring is early March and the average occurrence of the first temperature of 32 degrees is late November.

Austin Municipal Airport *Travis County* Elevation: 621 ft. Latitude: 30° 18' N Longitude: 97° 42' W

	JAN	FEB	MAR	APR	MAY	JUN	JUL	AUG	SEP	OCT	NOV	DEC	YEAR
Mean Maximum Temp. (°F)	61.6	65.4	72.2	79.7	86.2	92.1	95.6	96.7	90.5	81.6	71.2	62.6	79.6
Mean Temp. (°F)	51.6	55.2	61.8	69.1	76.4	82.2	85.0	85.7	80.0	71.1	60.9	52.5	69.3
Mean Minimum Temp. (°F)	41.6	44.9	51.4	58.4	66.6	72.3	74.4	74.6	69.5	60.6	50.5	42.4	58.9
Extreme Maximum Temp. (°F)	87	99	96	99	102	108	107	110	112	98	91	86	112
Extreme Minimum Temp. (°F)	11	14	19	34	46	57	67	62	48	30	26	4	4
Days Maximum Temp. ≥ 90°F	0	0	0	2	10	22	28	29	19	6	0	0	116
Days Maximum Temp. ≤ 32°F	0	0	0	0	0	0	0	0	0	0	0	0	0
Days Minimum Temp. ≤ 32°F	5	3	1	0	0	0	0	0	0	0	1	5	15
Days Minimum Temp. ≤ 0°F	0	0	0	0	0	0	0	0	0	0	0	0	0
Heating Degree Days (base 65°F)	419	292	157	38	1	0	0	0	2	29	177	395	1,510
Cooling Degree Days (base 65°F)	11	21	65	168	363	523	627	648	460	226	60	15	3,187
Mean Precipitation (in.)	2.14	1.99	2.76	2.09	4.44	4.14	1.83	2.39	2.74	3.92	3.05	2.41	33.90
Maximum Precipitation (in.)*	9.2	6.6	6.0	9.9	10.0	15.0	10.5	8.9	7.4	12.3	7.3	14.2	52.2
Minimum Precipitation (in.)*	trace	0.3	trace	0.1	0.8	trace	0	0	0.1	trace	trace	trace	11.4
Extreme Maximum Daily Precip. (in.)	4.41	2.56	3.26	2.23	3.88	5.66	2.17	5.68	3.17	6.24	7.55	4.21	7.55
Days With ≥ 0.1" Precipitation	4	4	5	4	5	5	3	3	4	5	4	4	50
Days With ≥ 0.5" Precipitation	1	1	2	1	3	3	1	1	2	2	2	1	20
Days With ≥ 1.0" Precipitation	1	0	1	1	2	1	0	1	1	1	1	1	11
Mean Snowfall (in.)	***0.4***	***0.2***	***trace***	***trace***	***trace***	***trace***	***0.0***	***0.0***	***0.0***	***0.0***	***0.1***	trace	***0.7***
Maximum Snowfall (in.)*	8	6	2	0	0	0	0	0	0	0	2	trace	9
Maximum 24-hr. Snowfall (in.)*	7	5	2	0	0	0	0	0	0	0	1	trace	7
Maximum Snow Depth (in.)	4	1	trace	trace	***trace***	***trace***	***0***	0	***0***	0	trace	trace	***4***
Days With ≥ 1.0" Snow Depth	0	0	0	0	***0***	***0***	***0***	0	***0***	0	0	0	***0***
Thunderstorm Days*	1	2	3	5	7	5	4	5	4	3	2	1	42
Foggy Days*	13	11	12	12	12	7	4	4	9	11	11	12	118
Predominant Sky Cover*	OVR	OVR	OVR	OVR	OVR	SCT	SCT	SCT	CLR	CLR	OVR	OVR	OVR
Mean Relative Humidity 6am (%)*	80	80	80	83	89	89	89	87	86	84	81	80	84
Mean Relative Humidity 3pm (%)*	53	51	47	50	54	50	43	42	47	47	49	52	49
Mean Dewpoint (°F)*	38	41	46	55	64	69	69	68	65	56	47	40	55
Prevailing Wind Direction*	N	S	S	S	SSE	S	S	S	S	S	S	S	S
Prevailing Wind Speed (mph)*	14	9	12	10	10	10	9	8	8	8	9	9	10
Maximum Wind Gust (mph)*	54	55	56	58	63	54	69	47	81	46	58	63	81

Note: (*) Period of record is 1948-1995

Brownsville Int'l Airport

Brownsville is located at the southern tip of Texas. It is the largest city in the four county area referred to as the Lower Rio Grande Valley or just the Valley.

The Gulf of Mexico, located about 18 miles east, is the dominant influence on local weather. Prevailing southeast breezes off the Gulf provide a humid but generally mild climate. Winds are frequently strong and gusty in the spring.

Brownsville weather is generally favorable for outdoor activities and the Valley is a popular tourist area, especially for Winter Texans who come to enjoy the mild winters. High temperatures range mostly in the 70s and 80s from October through April, with lows in the 50s and 60s during the same period. For the remainder of the year highs are frequently in the 90s with lows in the 70s.

Temperature extremes are rare but do occur. Temperatures in the 90s have occurred in every month of the year, with 100 degree readings noted as early as March and as late as September. Very hot temperatures are often moderated by a cooling sea breeze from the Gulf during the afternoon hours.

Located about 150 miles north of the tropics, cold weather in Brownsville is infrequent and of short duration. Some winters pass without a single day with freezing temperatures. This climate permits year around gardening and cultivation of citrus and other cold sensitive tropical and sub-tropical plants. Damaging cold comes from frigid air masses, called northers or arctic outbreaks, plunging south from Canada or the Arctic. The worst of these can drop temperatures well below freezing for several hours, and a few have produced readings in the teens. Fortunately such events are very rare since they are disasterous to the local economy.

Rainfall is not well distributed. Heaviest rains occur in May through June and mid August through mid October. Extended periods of cool rainy weather, called overrunning, can occur in winter. Torrential rains of 10 to 20 inches or more may accompany tropical storms or hurricanes that occasionally move over the area in summer or fall. Rainy spells may be followed by long dry periods. Irrigation is required to ensure production of corps such as cotton, grains, and vegetables. Snow and freezing rain or drizzle are so rare that years may pass between occurrences.

Damaging hail or winds from heavy thunderstorms are generally limited to the spring and many years elapse between occurrences. Tornadoes are even more rare. Tropical storms and hurricanes from the Gulf are a threat each summer and fall, but damaging storms are quite rare.

Brownsville Int'l Airport *Cameron County* Elevation: 19 ft. Latitude: 25° 54' N Longitude: 97° 26' W

	JAN	FEB	MAR	APR	MAY	JUN	JUL	AUG	SEP	OCT	NOV	DEC	YEAR
Mean Maximum Temp. (°F)	70.9	73.9	79.1	83.9	88.5	92.4	93.9	94.4	90.8	85.6	79.0	71.8	83.7
Mean Temp. (°F)	61.3	64.4	69.5	74.8	80.4	84.1	85.1	85.3	82.0	76.2	69.2	62.3	74.5
Mean Minimum Temp. (°F)	51.7	54.7	59.8	65.7	72.3	75.8	76.3	76.2	73.1	66.8	59.4	52.6	65.4
Extreme Maximum Temp. (°F)	91	94	106	102	102	102	104	104	105	96	97	91	106
Extreme Minimum Temp. (°F)	25	28	32	38	52	61	68	69	55	35	31	16	16
Days Maximum Temp. ≥ 90°F	0	0	1	4	14	26	29	29	21	8	1	0	133
Days Maximum Temp. ≤ 32°F	0	0	0	0	0	0	0	0	0	0	0	0	0
Days Minimum Temp. ≤ 32°F	1	0	0	0	0	0	0	0	0	0	0	1	2
Days Minimum Temp. ≤ 0°F	0	0	0	0	0	0	0	0	0	0	0	0	0
Heating Degree Days (base 65°F)	173	104	41	8	0	0	0	0	0	7	51	163	547
Cooling Degree Days (base 65°F)	66	92	186	310	485	580	631	637	515	361	184	84	4,131
Mean Precipitation (in.)	1.28	1.00	1.20	1.48	2.60	2.31	1.92	2.65	5.54	3.82	1.89	1.21	26.90
Maximum Precipitation (in.)*	4.8	10.3	3.5	10.3	9.1	8.5	9.4	9.6	20.2	17.1	7.7	4.0	47.5
Minimum Precipitation (in.)*	trace	trace	trace	trace	trace	trace	trace	trace	0.1	0.3	trace	trace	11.6
Extreme Maximum Daily Precip. (in.)	2.28	2.32	4.79	9.17	4.56	4.42	6.68	5.46	7.90	9.09	4.08	2.86	9.17
Days With ≥ 0.1" Precipitation	3	2	2	2	3	3	3	4	6	5	3	3	39
Days With ≥ 0.5" Precipitation	1	1	1	1	2	1	1	2	3	2	1	1	17
Days With ≥ 1.0" Precipitation	0	0	0	0	1	1	1	1	2	1	1	0	8
Mean Snowfall (in.)	*trace*	*0.0*	*trace*	*0.0*	*0.0*	*0.0*	*0.0*	*trace*	*0.0*	*0.0*	*trace*	*trace*	*trace*
Maximum Snowfall (in.)*	trace	trace	0	0	0	0	0	0	0	0	trace	trace	trace
Maximum 24-hr. Snowfall (in.)*	trace	trace	0	0	0	0	0	0	0	0	trace	trace	trace
Maximum Snow Depth (in.)	*trace*	*0*	*trace*	*0*	*0*	*0*	*0*	*trace*	*0*	*0*	*trace*	*trace*	trace
Days With ≥ 1.0" Snow Depth	*0*	*0*	*0*	*0*	*0*	*0*	*0*	*0*	*0*	*0*	*0*	*0*	*0*
Thunderstorm Days*	< 1	1	1	2	3	3	3	5	5	2	1	< 1	26
Foggy Days*	17	14	13	12	9	4	3	3	5	7	11	15	113
Predominant Sky Cover*	OVR	OVR	OVR	OVR	BRK	SCT	SCT	SCT	SCT	SCT	OVR	OVR	OVR
Mean Relative Humidity 6am (%)*	88	89	88	89	90	91	92	92	91	89	87	87	90
Mean Relative Humidity 3pm (%)*	63	60	57	58	60	59	54	55	60	58	59	62	59
Mean Dewpoint (°F)*	52	55	59	65	70	73	73	73	72	66	59	54	64
Prevailing Wind Direction*	NNW	SSE	SSE	SSE	SE	SE	SSE	SE	SE	SE	SSE	NNW	SSE
Prevailing Wind Speed (mph)*	13	15	16	17	14	13	13	12	10	10	13	12	13
Maximum Wind Gust (mph)*	53	68	59	66	81	62	51	78	109	55	53	53	109

Note: (*) Period of record is 1948-1995

The period of record for National Weather Service station data is 1980 – 2009 except where noted. See User Guide for detailed explanation of data.

Corpus Christi Int'l Airport

Corpus Christi is located on Corpus Christi Bay, an inlet of the Gulf of Mexico, in south Texas. The climatic conditions vary between the humid subtropical region to the northeast along the Texas coast and the semi-arid region to the west and southwest. Temperatures at the International Airport, which is about 7 miles west of downtown Corpus Christi, may be substantially different than those in the city during calm winter mornings and during summer afternoon sea breezes.

Peak rainfall months are May and September. Winter months have the least amounts of rainfall. The hurricane season from June to November can greatly effect the rainfall totals. Dry periods frequently occur. Several months during the years of record have had no rainfall, or only a trace. Snow falls on an average of about one day every two years.

There is little change in the day-to-day weather of the summer months, except for an occasional rainshower or a tropical storm in the area. High temperatures range in the high 80s to mid 90s, except for brief periods in the high 90s. The sea breeze during the afternoon and evening hours moderates the summer heat. Low temperatures are usually in the mid 70s. Summertime temperatures rarely reach 100 degrees near the bay, but occasionally do in most other parts of the city. In the summer season the region receives nearly 80 percent of the possible sunshine.

September and October are an extension of summer. November is a transition to the conditions of the coming winter months, with greater temperature extremes, stronger winds, and the first occurrences of northers. The winter months are relatively mild, but with temperatures sufficiently low to be stimulating. January is the coldest month with a prevailing northerly wind. Daytime highs that do not exceed 32 degrees, do not occur more than once every three or four years. The earliest occurrence of a temperature below 32 degrees is in early November and the latest occurrence in the spring is mid to late March.

Relative humidity, because of the nearness of the Gulf of Mexico, is high throughout the year. However, during the afternoons the humidity usually drops to between 50 and 60 percent.

Severe tropical storms average about one every ten years. Lesser strength storms average about one every five years. The city of Corpus Christi has a bluff that rises 30 to 40 feet above the level of the lowlands area near the bay. This serves as a natural protection from high water.

Chief hurricane months are August and September, although tropical storms have occurred as early as June and as late as October. The majority of the storms pass either to the south or east of the city.

Corpus Christi Int'l Airport *Nueces County* Elevation: 43 ft. Latitude: 27° 46' N Longitude: 97° 31' W

	JAN	FEB	MAR	APR	MAY	JUN	JUL	AUG	SEP	OCT	NOV	DEC	YEAR
Mean Maximum Temp. (°F)	67.2	70.7	76.0	81.8	86.5	91.0	93.3	94.2	90.2	84.2	75.8	68.2	81.6
Mean Temp. (°F)	57.3	60.6	66.3	72.3	78.3	82.5	84.0	84.6	81.1	74.5	66.0	58.4	72.2
Mean Minimum Temp. (°F)	47.4	50.6	56.5	62.8	70.0	73.9	74.7	75.0	72.0	64.8	56.1	48.6	62.7
Extreme Maximum Temp. (°F)	90	97	102	102	103	106	103	104	109	97	98	90	109
Extreme Minimum Temp. (°F)	19	23	24	33	52	59	67	64	52	28	28	13	13
Days Maximum Temp. ≥ 90°F	0	1	1	3	7	22	27	28	19	6	0	0	114
Days Maximum Temp. ≤ 32°F	0	0	0	0	0	0	0	0	0	0	0	0	0
Days Minimum Temp. ≤ 32°F	2	1	0	0	0	0	0	0	0	0	0	2	5
Days Minimum Temp. ≤ 0°F	0	0	0	0	0	0	0	0	0	0	0	0	0
Heating Degree Days (base 65°F)	265	170	77	17	0	0	0	0	0	12	90	247	878
Cooling Degree Days (base 65°F)	34	54	124	242	419	530	596	615	490	313	126	50	3,593
Mean Precipitation (in.)	1.49	1.81	1.86	1.79	3.15	3.13	2.58	3.38	4.65	3.67	2.04	1.81	31.36
Maximum Precipitation (in.)*	10.8	8.1	4.9	8.0	9.4	13.3	11.9	14.8	20.3	11.0	5.2	9.8	48.1
Minimum Precipitation (in.)*	trace	trace	trace	trace	trace	trace	0	0.1	0.5	0	trace	trace	14.7
Extreme Maximum Daily Precip. (in.)	2.89	4.70	3.66	6.18	4.00	8.62	9.85	6.93	5.30	7.92	4.55	6.77	9.85
Days With ≥ 0.1" Precipitation	3	2	3	2	4	4	3	4	6	4	3	3	41
Days With ≥ 0.5" Precipitation	1	1	1	1	2	2	2	2	3	2	1	1	19
Days With ≥ 1.0" Precipitation	0	1	1	0	1	1	1	1	1	1	1	0	9
Mean Snowfall (in.)	***trace***	na	na	na	na	na	na	na	na	na	na	***0.2***	na
Maximum Snowfall (in.)*	1	1	trace	0	0	0	0	0	0	0	trace	trace	1
Maximum 24-hr. Snowfall (in.)*	1	1	trace	0	0	0	0	0	0	0	trace	trace	1
Maximum Snow Depth (in.)	***trace***	***trace***	na	***trace***	na	na	na	na	na	na	na	***4***	na
Days With ≥ 1.0" Snow Depth	***0***	***0***	***0***	***0***	na	na	na	***0***	na	na	na	***0***	na
Thunderstorm Days*	1	1	1	2	4	3	2	4	5	2	1	1	27
Foggy Days*	16	14	14	12	9	4	2	3	5	7	10	14	110
Predominant Sky Cover*	OVR	OVR	OVR	OVR	BRK	SCT	SCT	SCT	SCT	CLR	OVR	OVR	OVR
Mean Relative Humidity 6am (%)*	87	88	87	89	92	92	93	92	90	89	86	86	89
Mean Relative Humidity 3pm (%)*	62	60	58	61	64	62	56	56	60	57	58	60	59
Mean Dewpoint (°F)*	48	51	56	63	70	73	74	74	71	64	56	50	62
Prevailing Wind Direction*	SSE	SSE	SSE	SE	SE	SE	SE	SE	SE	SE	SSE	SSE	SE
Prevailing Wind Speed (mph)*	15	16	17	15	14	13	13	13	12	12	15	15	14
Maximum Wind Gust (mph)*	53	61	54	67	62	61	58	161	70	53	60	54	161

Note: (*) Period of record is 1948-1995

Dallas-Fort Worth Int'l Airport

The Dallas-Fort Worth Metroplex is located in North Central Texas, approximately 250 miles north of the Gulf of Mexico. It is near the headwaters of the Trinity River, which lie in the upper margins of the Coastal Plain. The rolling hills in the area range from 500 to 800 feet in elevation.

The Dallas-Fort Worth climate is humid subtropical with hot summers. It is also continental, characterized by a wide annual temperature range. Precipitation also varies considerably, ranging from less than 20 to more than 50 inches.

Winters are mild, but northers occur about three times each month, and often are accompanied by sudden drops in temperature. Periods of extreme cold that occasionally occur are short-lived, so that even in January mild weather occurs frequently.

The highest temperatures of summer are associated with fair skies, westerly winds and low humidities. Characteristically, hot spells in summer are broken into three-to-five day periods by thunderstorm activity. There are only a few nights each summer when the low temperature exceeds 80 degrees. Summer daytime temperatures frequently exceed 100 degrees. Air conditioners are recommended for maximum comfort indoors and while traveling via automobile.

Throughout the year, rainfall occurs more frequently during the night. Usually, periods of rainy weather last for only a day or two, and are followed by several days with fair skies. A large part of the annual precipitation results from thunderstorm activity, with occasional heavy rainfall over brief periods of time. Thunderstorms occur throughout the year, but are most frequent in the spring. Hail falls on about two or three days a year, ordinarily with only slight and scattered damage. Windstorms occurring during thunderstorm activity are sometimes destructive. Snowfall is rare.

The average length of the warm season (freeze-free period) in the Dallas-Fort Worth Metroplex is about 249 days. The average last occurrence of 32 degrees or below is mid March and the average first occurrence of 32 degrees or below is in late November.

Dallas-Fort Worth Int'l Airport *Tarrant County* Elevation: 560 ft. Latitude: 32° 54' N Longitude: 97° 01' W

	JAN	FEB	MAR	APR	MAY	JUN	JUL	AUG	SEP	OCT	NOV	DEC	YEAR
Mean Maximum Temp. (°F)	56.4	60.8	68.3	76.2	83.7	91.5	96.1	96.2	88.6	78.2	66.8	57.2	76.7
Mean Temp. (°F)	46.0	50.1	57.6	65.4	73.9	81.4	85.7	85.6	78.1	67.5	56.5	47.2	66.3
Mean Minimum Temp. (°F)	35.6	39.4	46.9	54.5	64.1	71.3	75.2	75.1	67.5	56.7	46.1	37.1	55.8
Extreme Maximum Temp. (°F)	84	95	96	101	103	113	110	109	111	97	89	89	113
Extreme Minimum Temp. (°F)	7	7	15	29	44	54	62	59	43	29	23	-1	-1
Days Maximum Temp. ≥ 90°F	0	0	0	1	6	21	28	27	16	3	0	0	102
Days Maximum Temp. ≤ 32°F	1	1	0	0	0	0	0	0	0	0	0	1	3
Days Minimum Temp. ≤ 32°F	12	7	2	0	0	0	0	0	0	0	2	10	33
Days Minimum Temp. ≤ 0°F	0	0	0	0	0	0	0	0	0	0	0	0	0
Heating Degree Days (base 65°F)	585	421	255	81	8	0	0	0	6	66	276	550	2,248
Cooling Degree Days (base 65°F)	3	6	33	100	291	499	648	647	406	150	28	5	2,816
Mean Precipitation (in.)	2.12	2.60	3.39	3.03	4.97	3.82	2.08	1.90	2.46	4.21	2.70	2.55	35.83
Maximum Precipitation (in.)*	5.4	6.2	6.7	12.2	13.7	8.8	11.1	6.8	9.5	14.2	6.2	8.8	53.5
Minimum Precipitation (in.)*	trace	0.1	0.1	0.1	1.0	trace	0	trace	0.1	trace	trace	trace	18.5
Extreme Maximum Daily Precip. (in.)	3.15	2.90	4.39	3.18	3.50	3.08	3.83	3.90	3.90	3.81	2.23	4.22	4.39
Days With ≥ 0.1" Precipitation	4	4	5	4	6	6	3	3	4	5	4	4	52
Days With ≥ 0.5" Precipitation	1	2	2	2	4	3	1	1	2	3	2	2	25
Days With ≥ 1.0" Precipitation	0	1	1	1	2	1	1	0	1	1	1	1	11
Mean Snowfall (in.)	na	***0.6***	na	***trace***	na	na	na	na	na	na	na	***0.3***	na
Maximum Snowfall (in.)*	12	14	3	0	0	0	0	0	0	trace	5	3	18
Maximum 24-hr. Snowfall (in.)*	8	8	3	0	0	0	0	0	0	trace	5	2	8
Maximum Snow Depth (in.)	***2***	***3***	na	na	na	***trace***	na	na	na	na	na	***2***	na
Days With ≥ 1.0" Snow Depth	***0***	***1***	na	na	na	***0***	na	na	na	na	na	***0***	na
Thunderstorm Days*	1	2	4	6	8	6	5	5	4	3	2	1	47
Foggy Days*	11	9	9	8	8	3	2	2	5	7	8	10	82
Predominant Sky Cover*	OVR	OVR	OVR	OVR	OVR	SCT	CLR	CLR	CLR	CLR	CLR	OVR	CLR
Mean Relative Humidity 6am (%)*	80	79	79	82	87	85	80	80	84	82	81	80	82
Mean Relative Humidity 3pm (%)*	53	51	48	50	53	48	42	41	47	47	49	52	48
Mean Dewpoint (°F)*	32	36	42	52	61	67	68	67	63	53	43	35	52
Prevailing Wind Direction*	S	S	S	S	S	S	S	S	S	S	S	S	S
Prevailing Wind Speed (mph)*	13	13	15	15	14	13	12	10	12	12	13	12	13
Maximum Wind Gust (mph)*	69	64	79	76	71	69	71	83	64	63	68	60	83

Note: (*) Period of record is 1948-1995

Del Rio Int'l Airport

Del Rio is located on the Rio Grande River, on the western tip of the Balcones escarpment, in southwest Texas. Elevation is near 1,000 feet and varies little within the city but rises to 2,300 feet in the northern part of the county. Regional agriculture is chiefly wool and mohair production to the north and west of Del Rio and garden crops to the southeast. Lake Amistad, a reservoir of 65,000 surface acres, lies 10 miles west of Del Rio.

The climate of Del Rio is semi-arid continental. Annual precipitation is insufficient for dry farming. However, San Felipe Springs and the Rio Grande provide adequate water for irrigation farming. Over 80 percent of the average annual precipitation occurs from April through October. During this period, rainfall is chiefly in the form of showers and thunderstorms, often as heavy downpours, resulting in flash flooding. The small amount of precipitation for November through March usually falls as steady light rain.

Hail occurs in the vicinity of Del Rio about once per year and reaches severe proportions about once every five years. Sleet or snow falls on an average of once a year, but frequently melts as it falls. A snowfall heavy enough to blanket the ground only occurs about once every four or five years, and seldom remains more than 24 hours.

Temperature averages indicate mild winters and quite warm summers. Cold periods in winter are ushered in by strong, dry, dusty north, and northwest winds known as northers, and temperature drops of as much as 25 degrees in a few hours are not uncommon. Cold weather periods usually do not last more than two or three days. Temperatures as low as 32 degrees have occurred as early as October and as late as March. Normal occurrences of the earliest freezing temperature in autumn and the latest in spring are early December and mid February, which results in an average growing season of 300 days. Hot weather is rather persistent from late May to mid September and temperatures above 100 degrees have been recorded as early as March and as late as October. Low humidity and fresh breezes tend to alleviate uncomfortable conditions usually associated with high temperatures. The mean early morning humidity is about 79 percent, and the mean afternoon humidity is near 44 percent.

Clear to partly cloudy skies predominate, and even in the more cloudy winter months, the mean number of cloudy days are less than the number of clear days.

Del Rio Int'l Airport *Val Verde County* Elevation: 999 ft. Latitude: 29° 23' N Longitude: 100° 56' W

	JAN	FEB	MAR	APR	MAY	JUN	JUL	AUG	SEP	OCT	NOV	DEC	YEAR
Mean Maximum Temp. (°F)	64.1	69.0	76.3	83.7	89.9	94.8	96.9	96.9	90.9	82.2	71.9	63.9	81.7
Mean Temp. (°F)	52.4	57.1	64.3	71.6	78.9	84.1	86.1	86.1	80.4	71.6	60.7	52.5	70.5
Mean Minimum Temp. (°F)	40.8	45.1	52.2	59.5	68.0	73.4	75.2	75.1	69.8	61.0	49.6	41.0	59.2
Extreme Maximum Temp. (°F)	90	99	99	106	109	112	108	108	110	99	96	89	112
Extreme Minimum Temp. (°F)	15	14	21	33	49	60	65	66	43	28	25	10	10
Days Maximum Temp. ≥ 90°F	0	0	2	7	16	25	28	29	20	5	0	0	132
Days Maximum Temp. ≤ 32°F	0	0	0	0	0	0	0	0	0	0	0	0	0
Days Minimum Temp. ≤ 32°F	5	2	1	0	0	0	0	0	0	0	1	5	14
Days Minimum Temp. ≤ 0°F	0	0	0	0	0	0	0	0	0	0	0	0	0
Heating Degree Days (base 65°F)	386	238	108	25	0	0	0	0	2	23	168	385	1,335
Cooling Degree Days (base 65°F)	3	20	92	231	440	581	660	660	470	235	47	4	3,443
Mean Precipitation (in.)	0.65	0.84	1.11	1.47	2.63	2.33	1.63	1.63	2.19	2.23	0.99	0.68	18.38
Maximum Precipitation (in.)*	1.9	3.8	3.2	7.5	10.2	5.7	13.2	6.1	15.8	11.3	3.4	3.1	33.2
Minimum Precipitation (in.)*	trace	0	trace	trace	trace	trace	trace	0	trace	0	trace	trace	4.3
Extreme Maximum Daily Precip. (in.)	1.81	2.57	1.64	2.90	6.53	2.90	3.86	6.09	2.65	7.59	2.02	1.70	7.59
Days With ≥ 0.1" Precipitation	2	2	2	2	4	3	2	2	3	3	2	2	29
Days With ≥ 0.5" Precipitation	0	0	1	1	2	1	1	1	1	1	1	0	10
Days With ≥ 1.0" Precipitation	0	0	0	0	1	1	1	0	1	1	0	0	5
Mean Snowfall (in.)	na	na	na	na	na	na	na	na	na	na	na	na	na
Maximum Snowfall (in.)*	10	3	3	0	0	0	0	0	0	1	trace	trace	10
Maximum 24-hr. Snowfall (in.)*	8	3	3	0	0	0	0	0	0	1	trace	trace	8
Maximum Snow Depth (in.)	na	na	na	na	na	na	na	na	na	na	na	na	na
Days With ≥ 1.0" Snow Depth	na	na	na	na	na	na	na	na	na	na	na	na	na
Thunderstorm Days*	< 1	1	2	4	8	4	3	4	3	2	1	< 1	32
Foggy Days*	10	7	6	6	6	2	1	1	3	5	8	9	64
Predominant Sky Cover*	OVR	CLR	CLR	OVR	OVR	CLR	CLR	CLR	CLR	CLR	CLR	CLR	CLR
Mean Relative Humidity 6am (%)*	76	73	70	76	82	82	78	78	81	80	78	75	77
Mean Relative Humidity 3pm (%)*	44	40	35	40	45	42	37	38	43	43	43	42	41
Mean Dewpoint (°F)*	35	36	42	52	61	65	65	65	63	55	44	36	52
Prevailing Wind Direction*	SE	SE	SE	SE	SE	SE	SE	ESE	SE	SE	SE	SE	SE
Prevailing Wind Speed (mph)*	9	10	13	13	13	13	12	10	10	10	10	9	12
Maximum Wind Gust (mph)*	59	54	56	59	71	52	46	52	54	53	44	56	71

Note: (*) Period of record is 1951-1979

El Paso Int'l Airport

The city of El Paso is located in the extreme west point of Texas at an elevation of about 3,700 feet . The National Weather Service station is located on a mesa about 200 feet higher than the city. The climate of the region is characterized by an abundance of sunshine throughout the year, high daytime summer temperatures, very low humidity, scanty rainfall, and a relatively mild winter season. The Franklin Mountains begin within the city limits and extend northward for about 16 miles. Peaks of these mountains range from 4,687 to 7,152 feet above sea level.

Rainfall throughout the year is light, insufficient for any growth except desert vegetation. Irrigation is necessary for crops, gardens, and lawns. Dry periods lasting several months are not unusual. Almost half of the precipitation occurs in the three-month period, July through September, from brief but often heavy thunderstorms. Small amounts of snow fall nearly every winter, but snow cover rarely amounts to more than an inch and seldom remains on the ground for more than a few hours.

Daytime summer temperatures are high, frequently above 90 degrees and occasionally above 100 degrees. Summer nights are usually comfortable, with temperatures in the 60s. When temperatures are high the relative humidity is generally quite low. With temperatures above 90 degrees in April, May, and June the humidity averaged from 10 to 14 percent, while in July, August, and September it averaged 22 to 24 percent.

Winter daytime temperatures are mild. At night they drop below freezing about half the time in December and January. The flat, irrigated land of the Rio Grande Valley in the vicinity of El Paso is noticeably cooler, particularly at night, than the airport or the city proper, both in summer and winter. This results in more comfortable temperatures in summer but increases the severity of freezes in winter. The cooler air in the Valley also causes marked short-period fluctuations of temperature and dewpoint at the airport with changes in wind direction, especially during the early morning hours.

Dust and sandstorms are the most unpleasant features of the weather in El Paso. While wind velocities are not excessively high, the soil surface is dry and loose and natural vegetation is sparse, so moderately strong winds raise considerable dust and sand. Duststorms are most frequent in March and April, and comparatively rare in the period July through December. prevailing winds are from the north in winter and the south in summer.

El Paso Int'l Airport *El Paso County* Elevation: 3,917 ft. Latitude: 31° 49' N Longitude: 106° 23' W

	JAN	FEB	MAR	APR	MAY	JUN	JUL	AUG	SEP	OCT	NOV	DEC	YEAR
Mean Maximum Temp. (°F)	58.4	64.0	71.0	79.2	88.4	96.3	95.6	93.0	88.1	78.6	66.7	57.7	78.1
Mean Temp. (°F)	45.3	50.3	56.7	64.6	73.9	81.9	83.0	81.1	75.4	64.9	53.0	44.9	64.6
Mean Minimum Temp. (°F)	32.1	36.6	42.3	49.9	59.3	67.3	70.3	69.0	62.6	51.1	39.3	32.0	51.0
Extreme Maximum Temp. (°F)	77	83	89	98	105	114	111	108	104	96	87	79	114
Extreme Minimum Temp. (°F)	9	8	16	23	35	46	57	57	43	26	17	6	6
Days Maximum Temp. ≥ 90°F	0	0	0	2	14	26	27	24	14	2	0	0	109
Days Maximum Temp. ≤ 32°F	0	0	0	0	0	0	0	0	0	0	0	0	0
Days Minimum Temp. ≤ 32°F	16	9	3	1	0	0	0	0	0	0	7	17	53
Days Minimum Temp. ≤ 0°F	0	0	0	0	0	0	0	0	0	0	0	0	0
Heating Degree Days (base 65°F)	604	411	262	90	7	0	0	0	3	83	356	616	2,432
Cooling Degree Days (base 65°F)	0	1	10	85	289	512	565	505	320	86	3	0	2,376
Mean Precipitation (in.)	0.39	0.43	0.27	0.24	0.47	0.90	1.52	2.06	1.52	0.64	0.51	0.77	9.72
Maximum Precipitation (in.)*	1.8	1.7	2.3	1.4	4.2	3.2	5.5	5.6	6.7	3.1	1.6	3.3	17.2
Minimum Precipitation (in.)*	0	0	0	0	0	trace	trace	trace	trace	0	0	0	4.3
Extreme Maximum Daily Precip. (in.)	0.76	0.99	0.62	0.63	1.26	1.85	1.77	2.84	2.20	1.13	0.85	1.46	2.84
Days With ≥ 0.1" Precipitation	2	1	1	1	1	2	4	4	3	2	2	2	25
Days With ≥ 0.5" Precipitation	0	0	0	0	0	1	1	1	1	0	0	0	4
Days With ≥ 1.0" Precipitation	0	0	0	0	0	0	0	0	0	0	0	0	0
Mean Snowfall (in.)	na	na	na	na	na	na	na	na	na	na	na	na	na
Maximum Snowfall (in.)*	8	9	7	17	0	0	0	0	0	1	13	26	33
Maximum 24-hr. Snowfall (in.)*	5	7	6	7	0	0	0	0	0	1	7	15	15
Maximum Snow Depth (in.)	na	na	na	na	na	na	na	na	na	na	na	na	na
Days With ≥ 1.0" Snow Depth	na	na	na	na	na	na	na	na	na	na	na	na	na
Thunderstorm Days*	< 1	< 1	1	1	3	4	10	10	4	2	< 1	< 1	35
Foggy Days*	2	1	1	< 1	< 1	< 1	< 1	< 1	1	1	1	2	9
Predominant Sky Cover*	CLR	CLR	CLR	CLR	CLR	CLR	SCT	SCT	CLR	CLR	CLR	CLR	CLR
Mean Relative Humidity 6am (%)*	68	60	50	43	44	46	63	69	72	66	63	68	59
Mean Relative Humidity 3pm (%)*	34	27	21	17	17	17	28	30	32	29	30	36	26
Mean Dewpoint (°F)*	24	24	24	26	34	42	54	56	52	40	29	26	36
Prevailing Wind Direction*	NNE	WSW	W	WSW	WSW	SE	SE	SE	SE	N	NNE	N	WSW
Prevailing Wind Speed (mph)*	7	12	15	14	13	8	8	7	7	7	7	7	9
Maximum Wind Gust (mph)*	61	73	84	74	55	69	73	67	63	59	59	74	84

Note: (*) Period of record is 1948-1995

The period of record for National Weather Service station data is 1980 – 2009 except where noted. See User Guide for detailed explanation of data.

Galveston

The city of Galveston is located on Galveston Island off the southeast coast of Texas. The island is about two and three fourths miles across at the widest point and 29 miles long. It is bounded on the southeast by the Gulf of Mexico and on the northwest by Galveston Bay, which is about three miles wide at this point. The climate of the Galveston area is predominantly marine, with periods of modified continental influence during the colder months, when cold fronts from the northwest sometimes reach the coast.

Because of its coastal location and relatively low latitude, cold fronts which do reach the area are very seldom severe and temperatures below 32 degrees are recorded on an average only four times a year. Normal monthly high temperatures range from about 60 degrees in January to nearly 88 degrees in August. Lows range from about 48 degrees in January to the upper 70s during the summer season.

High humidities prevail throughout the year. Annual precipitation averages about 42 inches. Rainfall during the summer months may vary greatly on different parts of the island, as most of the rain in this season is from local thunderstorm activity. Hail is rare because the necessary strong vertical lifting is usually absent. There have been several instances when a monthly rainfall total amounted to only a trace, but these have been offset in the means by many monthly totals in excess of 15 inches. Winter precipitation comes mainly from frontal activity and from low stratus clouds, which produce slow, steady rains.

The island has been subject at infrequent intervals to major tropical storms of hurricane force.

Galveston *Galveston County* Elevation: 15 ft. Latitude: 29° 18' N Longitude: 94° 48' W

	JAN	FEB	MAR	APR	MAY	JUN	JUL	AUG	SEP	OCT	NOV	DEC	YEAR
Mean Maximum Temp. (°F)	na	63.4	68.2	74.7	81.1	86.6	89.0	89.5	86.4	79.1	na	62.8	na
Mean Temp. (°F)	na	57.2	62.6	69.6	76.6	na	84.5	84.5	80.8	73.4	na	56.5	na
Mean Minimum Temp. (°F)	na	50.9	56.9	64.4	72.1	na	79.9	79.5	75.1	67.7	na	49.9	na
Extreme Maximum Temp. (°F)	78	80	86	90	94	99	100	102	100	92	na	81	na
Extreme Minimum Temp. (°F)	20	24	26	42	56	64	69	69	54	39	na	14	na
Days Maximum Temp. ≥ 90°F	0	0	0	0	0	4	12	14	7	0	na	0	na
Days Maximum Temp. ≤ 32°F	0	0	0	0	0	0	0	0	0	0	na	0	na
Days Minimum Temp. ≤ 32°F	1	1	0	0	0	0	0	0	0	0	na	1	na
Days Minimum Temp. ≤ 0°F	0	0	0	0	0	0	0	0	0	0	na	0	na
Heating Degree Days (base 65°F)	na	223	109	20	0	na	0	0	0	13	na	278	na
Cooling Degree Days (base 65°F)	na	8	42	164	366	na	612	611	479	283	na	20	na
Mean Precipitation (in.)	4.39	2.88	3.00	2.02	3.29	5.04	2.87	3.48	5.05	3.72	na	3.65	na
Maximum Precipitation (in.)*	10.8	8.3	9.5	10.4	11.0	13.0	17.5	13.4	14.3	9.0	9.5	9.0	60.5
Minimum Precipitation (in.)*	0.2	0.2	0.1	trace	trace	0.4	0.1	0.2	0.3	0	0.6	0.5	29.3
Extreme Maximum Daily Precip. (in.)	4.10	4.51	3.60	5.00	4.04	6.90	2.86	10.86	6.59	3.81	na	na	na
Days With ≥ 0.1" Precipitation	6	4	4	3	4	5	4	4	6	5	na	5	na
Days With ≥ 0.5" Precipitation	3	2	2	1	2	3	2	2	3	2	na	2	na
Days With ≥ 1.0" Precipitation	1	1	1	1	1	2	1	1	2	1	na	1	na
Mean Snowfall (in.)	trace	trace	trace	trace	trace	0.0	0.0	0.0	0.0	0.0	na	0.0	na
Maximum Snowfall (in.)*	3	2	trace	0	0	0	0	0	0	0	0	1	4
Maximum 24-hr. Snowfall (in.)*	3	2	trace	0	0	0	0	0	0	0	0	1	3
Maximum Snow Depth (in.)	trace	trace	trace	trace	trace	0	0	0	0	0	na	1	na
Days With ≥ 1.0" Snow Depth	0	0	0	0	0	0	0	0	0	0	na	0	na
Thunderstorm Days*	1	< 1	1	3	4	2	2	4	3	2	1	< 1	23
Foggy Days*	9	6	10	10	3	3	1	2	2	6	5	8	65
Predominant Sky Cover*	na	na	na	na	na	na	na	na	na	na	na	na	na
Mean Relative Humidity 7am (%)*	na	na	na	na	na	na	na	na	na	na	na	na	na
Mean Relative Humidity 4pm (%)*	na	na	na	na	na	na	na	na	na	na	na	na	na
Mean Dewpoint (°F)*	na	na	na	na	na	na	na	na	na	na	na	na	na
Prevailing Wind Direction*	na	na	na	na	na	na	na	na	na	na	na	na	na
Prevailing Wind Speed (mph)*	na	na	na	na	na	na	na	na	na	na	na	na	na
Maximum Wind Gust (mph)*	na	na	na	na	na	na	na	na	na	na	na	na	na

Note: (*) Period of record is 1963-1995

Houston Bush Intercontinental

Houston, the largest city in Texas, is located in the flat Coastal Plains, about 50 miles from the Gulf of Mexico and about 25 miles from Galveston Bay. The climate is predominantly marine. The terrain includes numerous small streams and bayous which, together with the nearness to Galveston Bay, favor the development of both ground and advective fogs. Prevailing winds are from the southeast and south, except in January, when frequent passages of high pressure areas bring invasions of polar air and prevailing northerly winds.

Temperatures are moderated by the influence of winds from the Gulf, which result in mild winters. Another effect of the nearness of the Gulf is abundant rainfall, except for rare extended dry periods. Polar air penetrates the area frequently enough to provide variability in the weather.

Records of sky cover for daylight hours indicate about one-fourth of the days per year as clear, with a high number of clear days in October and November. Cloudy days are relatively frequent from December to May and partly cloudy days are the more frequent for June through September. Sunshine averages nearly 60 percent of the possible amount for the year ranging from 42 percent in January to 67 percent in June.

Heavy fog occurs on an average of 16 days a year and light fog occurs about 62 days a year in the city. The frequency of heavy fog is considerably higher at William P. Hobby Airport and at Intercontinental Airport.

Destructive windstorms are fairly infrequent, but both thundersqualls and tropical storms occasionally pass through the area.

Houston Bush Intercontinental *Harris County* Elevation: 95 ft. Latitude: 30° 00' N Longitude: 95° 22' W

	JAN	FEB	MAR	APR	MAY	JUN	JUL	AUG	SEP	OCT	NOV	DEC	YEAR
Mean Maximum Temp. (°F)	63.0	66.4	73.0	79.5	86.1	91.4	93.9	94.3	89.7	81.6	72.3	64.2	79.6
Mean Temp. (°F)	52.9	56.2	62.4	69.1	76.6	82.0	84.2	84.2	79.5	70.9	61.7	54.1	69.5
Mean Minimum Temp. (°F)	42.7	45.9	51.9	58.6	67.0	72.5	74.4	74.0	69.2	60.1	51.2	43.9	59.3
Extreme Maximum Temp. (°F)	83	91	91	95	99	104	104	107	109	96	89	85	109
Extreme Minimum Temp. (°F)	12	20	22	31	46	53	62	60	49	29	27	7	7
Days Maximum Temp. ≥ 90°F	0	0	0	1	8	21	27	27	18	4	0	0	106
Days Maximum Temp. ≤ 32°F	0	0	0	0	0	0	0	0	0	0	0	0	0
Days Minimum Temp. ≤ 32°F	4	2	1	0	0	0	0	0	0	0	1	4	12
Days Minimum Temp. ≤ 0°F	0	0	0	0	0	0	0	0	0	0	0	0	0
Heating Degree Days (base 65°F)	384	268	143	39	0	0	0	0	1	31	161	358	1,385
Cooling Degree Days (base 65°F)	15	26	71	168	365	516	601	601	441	221	70	27	3,122
Mean Precipitation (in.)	3.50	3.16	3.53	3.28	5.15	5.84	3.41	3.78	4.16	5.83	4.32	3.68	49.64
Maximum Precipitation (in.)*	9.8	6.0	8.5	10.9	14.4	16.3	8.1	9.4	11.3	16.0	8.9	9.3	70.2
Minimum Precipitation (in.)*	0.4	0.4	0.9	0.4	0.8	0.3	0.5	0.3	0.8	0	0.4	0.6	22.9
Extreme Maximum Daily Precip. (in.)	2.58	2.22	4.56	3.52	6.87	10.34	5.40	6.69	7.73	9.25	5.19	5.64	10.34
Days With ≥ 0.1" Precipitation	5	5	5	4	5	7	5	6	5	5	5	6	63
Days With ≥ 0.5" Precipitation	2	2	2	2	3	4	2	2	2	3	3	2	29
Days With ≥ 1.0" Precipitation	1	1	1	1	2	2	1	1	1	2	1	1	15
Mean Snowfall (in.)	0.0	0.1	trace	trace	trace	trace	0.0	0.0	0.0	0.0	0.0	0.1	0.2
Maximum Snowfall (in.)*	2	3	0	0	0	0	0	0	0	0	trace	2	5
Maximum 24-hr. Snowfall (in.)*	2	1	0	0	0	0	0	0	0	0	trace	2	2
Maximum Snow Depth (in.)	trace	trace	trace	trace	trace	trace	0	0	0	0	0	trace	trace
Days With ≥ 1.0" Snow Depth	0	0	0	0	0	0	0	0	0	0	0	0	0
Thunderstorm Days*	2	2	4	4	7	8	10	11	8	4	3	2	65
Foggy Days*	18	15	18	17	19	13	11	14	16	16	15	17	189
Predominant Sky Cover*	OVR	OVR	OVR	OVR	OVR	SCT	SCT	SCT	SCT	CLR	OVR	OVR	OVR
Mean Relative Humidity 6am (%)*	86	87	88	89	92	92	93	93	93	91	89	87	90
Mean Relative Humidity 3pm (%)*	58	55	54	55	57	57	54	55	56	52	55	57	55
Mean Dewpoint (°F)*	42	45	51	58	66	71	72	72	68	60	51	46	59
Prevailing Wind Direction*	N	N	SE	SE	SE	SE	S	S	ENE	SE	N	N	SE
Prevailing Wind Speed (mph)*	9	9	12	12	10	10	8	8	7	9	8	9	9
Maximum Wind Gust (mph)*	44	61	54	59	69	68	68	98	56	58	49	56	98

Note: (*) Period of record is 1969-1995

The period of record for National Weather Service station data is 1980 – 2009 except where noted. See User Guide for detailed explanation of data.

Lubbock Regional Airport

Lubbock is located on a plateau area of Northwestern Texas that is referred to locally as the South Plains Region. The general elevation of the area is about 3,250 feet. The Region is a major part of the Llano Estacado (staked plains). The latter, which includes a large portion of Northwest Texas, is bounded on the east and southeast by an erosional escarpment that is usually referred to as the Cap Rock. The Llano Estacado extends southwestward into the upper Pecos Valley and westward into eastern New Mexico.

The South Plains are predominately flat, but contain numerous small playas (or clay lined depressions) and small stream valleys. During the rainy months the playas collect run-off water and form small lakes or ponds. The stream valleys drain into the major rivers of West Texas, but throughout most of the year these streams carry only very light flows.

Cap Rock causes a noticeable distortion of the smooth wind flow patterns across the South Plains, the most noticeable on southeasterly winds as they are deflected upward along its face.

The Lubbock area is the heart of the largest cotton-producing section of Texas. Irrigation from underground sources is often used as a supplement to natural rainfall to improve crop yields. The soils of the region are sandy clay loams.

The area is semi-arid, transitional between the desert conditions on the west and the humid climates to the east and southeast. The greatest monthly rainfall totals occur from May through September when warm moist tropical air may be carried into the area from the Gulf of Mexico. This air mass often brings moderate to heavy afternoon and evening thunderstorms, accompanied by hail. Precipitation across the area is characterized by its variability. The monthly precipitation extremes range from trace amounts in several isolated months to 14 inches.

Snow may occur from late October until April. Each snowfall is generally light and seldom remains on the ground for more than two or three days at any one period.

High winds are associated primarily with intense thunderstorms and at times may cause significant damage to structures. Winds in excess of 25 mph occasionally occur for periods of 12 hours or longer. These prolonged winds are generally associated with late winter and springtime low-pressure centers. Spring winds often bring widespread dust.

The summer heat is moderated by a variable, but usually gentle, wind. Dry air from the west often reduce any discomfort from the summer heat and lower temperatures into the 60s.

The average first occurrence of temperatures below 32 degrees Fahrenheit in the fall is the first of November and the average last occurrence in the spring is in mid April.

Lubbock Regional Airport *Lubbock County* Elevation: 3,253 ft. Latitude: 33° 40' N Longitude: 101° 49' W

	JAN	FEB	MAR	APR	MAY	JUN	JUL	AUG	SEP	OCT	NOV	DEC	YEAR
Mean Maximum Temp. (°F)	54.0	59.1	66.8	75.5	83.8	90.8	93.3	91.3	84.4	75.0	63.4	54.1	74.3
Mean Temp. (°F)	40.6	44.9	52.1	60.8	70.1	77.7	80.8	79.2	71.8	61.6	49.9	40.8	60.9
Mean Minimum Temp. (°F)	27.0	30.7	37.4	46.0	56.3	64.7	68.3	67.1	59.2	48.2	36.3	27.6	47.4
Extreme Maximum Temp. (°F)	83	89	95	100	109	114	108	105	103	100	90	81	114
Extreme Minimum Temp. (°F)	0	3	8	22	37	46	54	54	33	18	7	-2	-2
Days Maximum Temp. ≥ 90°F	0	0	0	2	10	18	24	21	9	2	0	0	86
Days Maximum Temp. ≤ 32°F	2	1	0	0	0	0	0	0	0	0	0	2	5
Days Minimum Temp. ≤ 32°F	24	16	9	1	0	0	0	0	0	1	10	23	84
Days Minimum Temp. ≤ 0°F	0	0	0	0	0	0	0	0	0	0	0	0	0
Heating Degree Days (base 65°F)	751	562	400	172	37	1	0	0	21	154	449	742	3,289
Cooling Degree Days (base 65°F)	0	0	8	53	201	389	498	448	232	56	2	0	1,887
Mean Precipitation (in.)	0.62	0.70	1.01	1.30	2.37	3.01	1.67	1.92	2.60	1.85	0.92	0.77	18.74
Maximum Precipitation (in.)*	4.0	2.5	3.2	3.5	7.8	7.9	7.2	8.8	8.2	10.8	2.7	2.2	29.4
Minimum Precipitation (in.)*	0	trace	trace	trace	0.1	trace	trace	0	trace	0	0	trace	10.8
Extreme Maximum Daily Precip. (in.)	1.39	1.17	1.90	2.18	2.67	3.51	2.65	2.45	7.46	5.43	1.59	1.22	7.46
Days With ≥ 0.1" Precipitation	2	2	2	3	4	5	3	4	4	3	2	2	36
Days With ≥ 0.5" Precipitation	0	0	1	1	2	2	1	1	1	1	1	0	11
Days With ≥ 1.0" Precipitation	0	0	0	0	1	1	0	0	1	0	0	0	3
Mean Snowfall (in.)	2.6	1.5	0.5	0.3	trace	trace	trace	0.0	trace	trace	1.6	2.2	8.7
Maximum Snowfall (in.)*	25	17	14	5	0	0	0	0	0	8	21	10	36
Maximum 24-hr. Snowfall (in.)*	11	12	8	4	0	0	0	0	0	4	11	6	12
Maximum Snow Depth (in.)	17	7	3	3	trace	trace	trace	0	trace	trace	11	8	17
Days With ≥ 1.0" Snow Depth	2	1	0	0	0	0	0	0	0	0	1	2	6
Thunderstorm Days*	< 1	1	2	4	8	9	8	7	5	3	1	< 1	48
Foggy Days*	7	7	5	4	6	3	2	3	6	6	6	6	61
Predominant Sky Cover*	CLR	CLR	CLR	CLR	CLR	CLR	SCT	SCT	CLR	CLR	CLR	CLR	CLR
Mean Relative Humidity 6am (%)*	73	72	68	68	76	78	73	78	82	77	74	73	74
Mean Relative Humidity 3pm (%)*	41	39	32	29	34	36	38	42	45	38	38	41	38
Mean Dewpoint (°F)*	22	25	29	36	47	57	60	60	56	43	32	24	41
Prevailing Wind Direction*	WSW	WSW	S	S	S	S	S	S	S	S	SW	WSW	S
Prevailing Wind Speed (mph)*	12	13	14	15	15	14	13	12	12	12	12	10	13
Maximum Wind Gust (mph)*	59	66	77	71	70	85	85	59	58	64	66	64	85

Note: (*) Period of record is 1948-1995

Midland Regional Air Terminal

The Midland-Odessa region is on the southern extension of the South Plains of Texas. The terrain is level with only slight occasional undulations.

The climate is typical of a semi-arid region. The vegetation of the area consists mostly of native grasses and a few trees, mostly of the mesquite variety.

Most of the annual precipitation in the area comes as a result of very violent spring and early summer thunderstorms. These are usually accompanied by excessive rainfall, over limited areas, and sometimes hail. Due to the flat nature of the countryside, local flooding occurs, but is of short duration. Tornadoes are occasionally sighted.

During the late winter and early spring months, blowing dust occurs frequently. The flat plains of the area with only grass as vegetation offer little resistance to the strong winds. The sky is occasionally obscured by dust but in most storms visibilities range from one to three miles.

Daytime temperatures are quite hot in the summer, but there is a large diurnal range of temperature and most nights are comfortable. The temperature drops below 32 degrees in the fall about mid- November and the last temperature below 32 degrees in spring comes early in April.

Winters are characterized by frequent cold periods followed by rapid warming. Cold frontal passages are followed by chilly weather for two or three days. Cloudiness is at a minimum. Summers are hot and dry with numerous small convective showers.

The prevailing wind direction in this area is from the southeast. This, together with the upslope of the terrain from the same direction, causes occasional low cloudiness and drizzle during winter and spring months. Snow is infrequent. Maximum temperatures during the summer months frequently are from two to six degrees cooler than those at places 100 miles southeast, due to the cooling effect of the upslope winds.

Very low humidities are conducive to personal comfort, because even though summer afternoon temperatures are frequently above 90 degrees, the low humidity with resultant rapid evaporation, has a cooling effect. The climate of the area is generally quite pleasant with the most disagreeable weather concentrated in the late winter and spring months.

Midland Regional Air Terminal *Midland County* Elevation: 2,861 ft. Latitude: 31° 57' N Longitude: 102° 11' W

	JAN	FEB	MAR	APR	MAY	JUN	JUL	AUG	SEP	OCT	NOV	DEC	YEAR
Mean Maximum Temp. (°F)	57.5	62.6	70.1	79.1	87.4	93.3	94.9	93.4	86.7	77.6	66.3	57.9	77.2
Mean Temp. (°F)	44.0	48.6	55.5	64.1	73.5	80.3	82.3	81.1	74.4	64.7	52.7	44.4	63.8
Mean Minimum Temp. (°F)	30.4	34.5	40.9	49.0	59.5	67.2	69.7	68.7	62.0	51.7	39.1	30.8	50.3
Extreme Maximum Temp. (°F)	83	90	95	101	108	116	112	106	104	101	90	84	116
Extreme Minimum Temp. (°F)	5	-11	9	25	39	47	58	54	36	24	11	-1	-11
Days Maximum Temp. ≥ 90°F	0	0	0	4	14	22	27	25	12	3	0	0	107
Days Maximum Temp. ≤ 32°F	1	1	0	0	0	0	0	0	0	0	0	1	3
Days Minimum Temp. ≤ 32°F	19	12	5	1	0	0	0	0	0	0	7	18	62
Days Minimum Temp. ≤ 0°F	0	0	0	0	0	0	0	0	0	0	0	0	0
Heating Degree Days (base 65°F)	645	460	302	111	15	0	0	0	12	97	367	632	2,641
Cooling Degree Days (base 65°F)	0	2	16	90	285	465	544	507	299	94	6	0	2,308
Mean Precipitation (in.)	0.52	0.66	0.58	0.61	1.75	1.72	1.76	1.86	2.11	1.73	0.72	0.64	14.66
Maximum Precipitation (in.)*	3.7	2.5	2.9	2.8	7.6	4.0	8.5	4.4	9.7	7.4	2.3	3.3	32.1
Minimum Precipitation (in.)*	0	trace	trace	0	0.1	trace	trace	0.2	0.1	0	0	0	4.6
Extreme Maximum Daily Precip. (in.)	0.96	1.13	0.72	1.33	2.72	3.07	3.59	2.72	3.29	3.59	1.55	1.05	3.59
Days With ≥ 0.1" Precipitation	1	2	2	2	3	3	3	3	3	3	2	2	29
Days With ≥ 0.5" Precipitation	0	0	0	0	1	1	1	1	2	1	0	0	7
Days With ≥ 1.0" Precipitation	0	0	0	0	0	1	0	1	1	1	0	0	4
Mean Snowfall (in.)	2.0	0.5	0.2	0.1	trace	trace	trace	trace	trace	trace	0.8	1.6	5.2
Maximum Snowfall (in.)*	9	4	6	1	0	0	0	0	0	1	7	9	12
Maximum 24-hr. Snowfall (in.)*	6	3	5	1	0	0	0	0	0	1	6	4	6
Maximum Snow Depth (in.)	6	5	3	trace	trace	trace	trace	trace	trace	1	8	5	8
Days With ≥ 1.0" Snow Depth	1	0	0	0	0	0	0	0	0	0	0	0	1
Thunderstorm Days*	< 1	1	1	3	7	6	6	6	4	3	1	< 1	38
Foggy Days*	7	7	4	3	3	1	1	1	4	5	6	7	49
Predominant Sky Cover*	CLR	CLR	CLR	CLR	CLR	CLR	CLR	CLR	CLR	CLR	CLR	CLR	CLR
Mean Relative Humidity 6am (%)*	72	72	65	67	75	76	73	74	79	78	74	71	73
Mean Relative Humidity 3pm (%)*	38	35	27	27	31	32	34	34	40	37	35	37	34
Mean Dewpoint (°F)*	25	28	30	38	48	57	59	59	56	46	34	27	43
Prevailing Wind Direction*	S	S	S	S	SSE	SSE	SSE	SSE	SSE	S	S	S	S
Prevailing Wind Speed (mph)*	9	10	13	13	14	13	12	10	10	12	10	10	12
Maximum Wind Gust (mph)*	59	63	74	76	83	71	82	66	82	69	60	69	83

Note: (*) Period of record is 1948-1995

Port Arthur Jefferson County

Port Arthur is located on the flat Coastal Plain in the extreme southeast corner of Texas. The climate is a mixture of tropical and temperate zone conditions.

Sea breezes prevent extremely high temperatures in the summer, except on rare occasions. The area lies far enough south so that cold air masses modify in severity but still provide freezing temperatures up to six times a year.

High humidity is the result of fairly evenly distributed high normal rainfall and prevailing southerly winds from the Gulf of Mexico.

Cloudy, rainy weather is most common in the winter. Only slightly more than half the winters record even a trace of sleet or snow. Heavy rainfall in summer occurs in short duration thunderstorms and in infrequent tropical storms.

Slow moving systems in the spring and fall often result in three to five days of stormy weather and heavy rain. The lightest precipitation usually occurs in March and October. Funnel clouds and waterspouts are common near the coast. The area enjoys approximately 60 percent of possible sunshine.

Fog, most frequent in midwinter and early spring, is rare in summer. It usually dissipates before noon, but occasionally under stagnant conditions lasts a day or two. Along the immediate coast, fog usually does not form until daybreak, but inland it may form before midnight.

The average wind movement is near ll mph. Except for severe storms and tropical disturbances, wind seldom exceeds 45 mph. It exceeds 30 mph on only about 40 days in any one year.

The climate is favorable for outdoor activities throughout the year. The abundant rainfall, moderate temperatures, and the short period of temperatures below freezing are particularly favorable for farming and livestock production. Heaviest rain usually falls in the summer when needed for rice. The comparatively dry harvest season simplifies the gathering of rice and feed crops. Cattle on the open range of the coastal marshes need little supplemental feeding or protection. Improved pastures are easily provided because of the moderate temperatures and abundant rainfall.

Port Arthur Jefferson County *Jefferson County* Elevation: 16 ft. Latitude: 29° 57' N Longitude: 94° 01' W

	JAN	FEB	MAR	APR	MAY	JUN	JUL	AUG	SEP	OCT	NOV	DEC	YEAR
Mean Maximum Temp. (°F)	62.3	65.6	72.0	78.2	84.6	89.7	91.8	92.1	88.3	80.5	71.6	63.8	78.4
Mean Temp. (°F)	53.0	56.2	62.4	68.7	75.9	81.3	83.1	83.2	79.2	70.6	61.7	54.4	69.1
Mean Minimum Temp. (°F)	43.7	46.9	52.7	59.1	67.2	72.8	74.4	74.1	70.0	60.6	51.8	45.0	59.9
Extreme Maximum Temp. (°F)	82	85	89	94	98	102	103	108	105	94	88	82	108
Extreme Minimum Temp. (°F)	15	20	23	32	47	56	61	60	49	30	28	12	12
Days Maximum Temp. ≥ 90°F	0	0	0	0	3	18	25	25	14	2	0	0	87
Days Maximum Temp. ≤ 32°F	0	0	0	0	0	0	0	0	0	0	0	0	0
Days Minimum Temp. ≤ 32°F	4	2	1	0	0	0	0	0	0	0	0	3	10
Days Minimum Temp. ≤ 0°F	0	0	0	0	0	0	0	0	0	0	0	0	0
Heating Degree Days (base 65°F)	376	261	137	37	1	0	0	0	1	32	157	345	1,347
Cooling Degree Days (base 65°F)	12	19	62	154	347	495	569	570	432	212	66	24	2,962
Mean Precipitation (in.)	5.32	3.46	3.66	3.23	5.46	7.01	5.57	5.28	6.53	5.78	4.43	5.19	60.92
Maximum Precipitation (in.)*	14.9	13.1	10.2	8.7	13.2	18.9	18.7	17.3	22.0	15.1	10.8	18.0	81.5
Minimum Precipitation (in.)*	0.6	0.2	0.1	0.3	0.1	0.8	0.6	1.0	0.5	0	0.1	1.3	33.1
Extreme Maximum Daily Precip. (in.)	4.30	2.97	3.84	5.75	9.89	4.87	4.99	5.79	11.80	6.58	6.32	8.04	11.80
Days With ≥ 0.1" Precipitation	7	5	5	4	5	7	7	7	7	5	6	6	71
Days With ≥ 0.5" Precipitation	3	2	2	2	3	4	4	3	3	3	3	3	35
Days With ≥ 1.0" Precipitation	1	1	1	1	2	2	2	2	2	2	1	2	19
Mean Snowfall (in.)	na	na	na	na	na	na	na	na	na	na	na	na	na
Maximum Snowfall (in.)*	3	4	1	0	0	0	0	0	0	0	trace	1	4
Maximum 24-hr. Snowfall (in.)*	3	4	1	0	0	0	0	0	0	0	trace	1	4
Maximum Snow Depth (in.)	na	na	na	na	na	na	na	na	na	na	na	na	na
Days With ≥ 1.0" Snow Depth	na	na	na	na	na	na	na	na	na	na	na	na	na
Thunderstorm Days*	3	3	4	4	6	8	14	12	7	3	3	2	69
Foggy Days*	18	16	17	15	14	10	8	11	14	16	15	17	171
Predominant Sky Cover*	OVR	OVR	OVR	OVR	SCT	SCT	SCT	SCT	SCT	CLR	OVR	OVR	OVR
Mean Relative Humidity 6am (%)*	88	88	88	90	92	93	94	94	92	91	89	89	91
Mean Relative Humidity 3pm (%)*	64	61	59	61	62	62	64	62	60	55	59	64	61
Mean Dewpoint (°F)*	45	47	52	60	67	72	74	74	70	61	52	47	60
Prevailing Wind Direction*	N	S	S	SSE	S	S	S	S	NE	N	N	N	S
Prevailing Wind Speed (mph)*	12	12	13	14	12	10	8	8	9	9	10	12	10
Maximum Wind Gust (mph)*	56	54	60	59	62	76	69	59	58	48	61	61	76

Note: (*) Period of record is 1948-1995

San Angelo Mathis Field

San Angelo is located near the center of Texas at the northern edge of the Edwards Plateau. Ground elevation ranges from about 1,700 to 2,700 feet above sea level. Topography varies from level and slightly rolling to broken. The climate is generally classified as semi-arid or steppe, but has some humid temperate characteristics. Warm, dry weather predominates, although changes may be rapid and frequent with the passage of cold fronts or northers.

High temperatures of summer are associated with fair skies, south to southwest winds and dry air. Low humidities, however, are conducive to personal comfort because of rapid evaporation. Rapid temperature drops occur after sunset, and most nights are pleasant with lows in the upper 60s and lower 70s. Rapid temperature drops occur in the winter as cold polar air invades the region. Temperature drops of 20 to 30 degrees in a short time are not uncommon. Cold polar outbreaks have produced record low temperatures of zero or below throughout the area.

The rainfall is typical of the Great Plains. Much of the rainfall occurs from thunderstorm activity, and wide variations in annual precipitation occur from year to year. Heavy rainfall occurs in April, May, June, September and October. Also, in the late summer months, heavy precipitation may occur when tropical disturbances move inland over south Texas and pass near the San Angelo area.

The prevailing wind direction is from the south, and winds are frequently high and persistent for several days. Dusty conditions are infrequent and occur in early spring when west or northwest winds predominate. The frequency and intensity of the dust storms are dependent on soil conditions in the Texas Panhandle and in New Mexico.

Agriculture in the region consists of cattle, sheep, and goat raising. Cotton, from dry-land and irrigated fields, maize, corn, melons, truck farming, and pecan production are also important crops.

San Angelo Mathis Field *Tom Green County* Elevation: 1,916 ft. Latitude: 31° 21' N Longitude: 100° 30' W

	JAN	FEB	MAR	APR	MAY	JUN	JUL	AUG	SEP	OCT	NOV	DEC	YEAR
Mean Maximum Temp. (°F)	59.5	63.8	71.1	80.1	87.1	92.1	95.3	94.6	87.6	78.7	68.1	59.9	78.2
Mean Temp. (°F)	46.4	50.4	57.7	65.8	74.3	80.3	83.2	82.5	75.5	66.0	55.1	46.7	65.3
Mean Minimum Temp. (°F)	33.2	36.9	44.1	51.5	61.5	68.5	70.9	70.3	63.3	53.3	42.1	33.6	52.4
Extreme Maximum Temp. (°F)	87	97	95	101	109	110	109	109	107	99	93	88	110
Extreme Minimum Temp. (°F)	5	-1	8	26	37	49	56	54	37	26	18	-4	-4
Days Maximum Temp. ≥ 90°F	0	0	1	5	13	21	27	26	13	3	0	0	109
Days Maximum Temp. ≤ 32°F	1	1	0	0	0	0	0	0	0	0	0	1	3
Days Minimum Temp. ≤ 32°F	16	9	4	1	0	0	0	0	0	0	6	15	51
Days Minimum Temp. ≤ 0°F	0	0	0	0	0	0	0	0	0	0	0	0	0
Heating Degree Days (base 65°F)	571	413	254	89	10	0	0	0	9	81	308	560	2,295
Cooling Degree Days (base 65°F)	1	5	33	120	306	466	570	550	330	120	18	1	2,520
Mean Precipitation (in.)	0.88	1.29	1.48	1.35	2.93	2.63	1.15	2.33	2.77	2.64	1.23	0.89	21.57
Maximum Precipitation (in.)*	3.6	4.4	5.0	5.1	11.2	6.0	7.2	8.1	11.0	8.7	3.5	4.0	33.9
Minimum Precipitation (in.)*	0	trace	trace	0.1	0.3	0	trace	trace	trace	0	0	trace	7.4
Extreme Maximum Daily Precip. (in.)	1.64	3.16	2.05	2.28	2.26	2.82	2.31	4.00	6.24	3.24	2.19	1.52	6.24
Days With ≥ 0.1" Precipitation	2	3	3	2	5	4	2	3	3	4	2	2	35
Days With ≥ 0.5" Precipitation	1	1	1	1	2	2	1	1	2	2	1	0	15
Days With ≥ 1.0" Precipitation	0	0	0	0	1	1	0	1	1	1	0	0	5
Mean Snowfall (in.)	***1.4***	***0.3***	***0.1***	***0.0***	***trace***	***trace***	***trace***	***0.0***	***trace***	***trace***	***0.3***	***0.3***	***2.4***
Maximum Snowfall (in.)*	9	6	3	trace	0	0	0	0	0	trace	9	4	14
Maximum 24-hr. Snowfall (in.)*	7	3	3	trace	0	0	0	0	0	trace	6	3	7
Maximum Snow Depth (in.)	***6***	***2***	***2***	***trace***	***trace***	***trace***	***trace***	***0***	***trace***	***trace***	***3***	***3***	***6***
Days With ≥ 1.0" Snow Depth	***1***	***0***	***0***	***0***	***0***	***0***	***0***	***0***	***0***	***0***	***0***	***0***	***1***
Thunderstorm Days*	1	1	2	4	7	5	4	5	4	3	1	1	38
Foggy Days*	7	6	4	3	4	1	1	1	4	4	5	6	46
Predominant Sky Cover*	OVR	CLR	CLR	CLR	CLR	CLR	CLR	CLR	CLR	CLR	CLR	CLR	CLR
Mean Relative Humidity 6am (%)*	76	76	71	74	81	80	77	77	82	81	78	76	77
Mean Relative Humidity 3pm (%)*	44	41	35	35	40	40	36	36	44	43	41	43	40
Mean Dewpoint (°F)*	30	33	37	46	56	62	62	62	60	51	40	32	48
Prevailing Wind Direction*	SSW	SSW	S	S	S	S	S	S	S	S	SSW	SSW	S
Prevailing Wind Speed (mph)*	13	13	14	14	13	13	12	10	10	12	12	13	13
Maximum Wind Gust (mph)*	61	59	63	76	93	71	68	67	76	68	74	60	93

Note: (*) Period of record is 1948-1995

San Antonio Int'l Airport

The city of San Antonio is located in the south-central portion of Texas on the Balcones escarpment. Northwest of the city, the terrain slopes upward to the Edwards Plateau and to the southeast it slopes downward to the Gulf Coastal Plains. Soils are blackland clay and silty loam on the Plains and thin limestone soils on the Edwards Plateau.

The location of San Antonio on the edge of the Gulf Coastal Plains is influenced by a modified subtropical climate, predominantly continental during the winter months and marine during the summer months. Temperatures range from 50 degrees in January to the middle 80s in July and August. While the summer is hot, with daily temperatures above 90 degrees over 80 percent of the time, extremely high temperatures are rare. Mild weather prevails during much of the winter months, with below-freezing temperatures occurring on an average of about 20 days each year.

San Antonio is situated between a semi-arid area to the west and the coastal area of heavy precipitation to the east. Precipitation is fairly well distributed throughout the year with the heaviest amounts occurring during May and September. The precipitation from April through September usually occurs from thunderstorms. Most of the winter precipitation occurs as light rain or drizzle. Thunderstorms and heavy rains have occurred in all months of the year. Hail of damaging intensity seldom occurs but light hail is frequent with the springtime thunderstorms. Measurable snow occurs only once in three or four years.

Northerly winds prevail during most of the winter, and strong northerly winds occasionally occur during storms called northers. Southeasterly winds from the Gulf of Mexico also occur frequently during winter and are predominant in summer.

Since San Antonio is located only 140 miles from the Gulf of Mexico, tropical storms occasionally affect the city with strong winds and heavy rains. One of the fastest winds recorded, 74 mph, occurred as a tropical storm moved inland east of the city in August 1942.

Relative humidity is above 80 percent during the early morning hours most of the year, dropping to near 50 percent in the late afternoon.

San Antonio has about 50 percent of the possible amount of sunshine during the winter months and more than 70 percent during the summer months. Skies are clear to partly cloudy more than 60 percent of the time and cloudy less than 40 percent.

The first occurrence of 32 degrees Fahrenheit is in late November and the average last occurrence is in early March.

San Antonio Int'l Airport *Bexar County* Elevation: 809 ft. Latitude: 29° 32' N Longitude: 98° 28' W

	JAN	FEB	MAR	APR	MAY	JUN	JUL	AUG	SEP	OCT	NOV	DEC	YEAR
Mean Maximum Temp. (°F)	63.1	67.3	73.7	80.8	87.1	92.5	95.0	96.0	90.5	82.3	72.2	64.1	80.4
Mean Temp. (°F)	51.9	55.8	62.3	69.5	77.0	82.6	84.9	85.4	79.9	71.3	61.1	53.0	69.5
Mean Minimum Temp. (°F)	40.7	44.3	50.9	58.0	66.8	72.6	74.7	74.7	69.3	60.2	49.9	41.8	58.7
Extreme Maximum Temp. (°F)	86	100	100	101	104	107	106	108	111	99	94	88	111
Extreme Minimum Temp. (°F)	13	14	19	31	43	57	64	61	46	27	23	6	6
Days Maximum Temp. ≥ 90°F	0	0	1	3	10	23	28	29	19	5	0	0	118
Days Maximum Temp. ≤ 32°F	0	0	0	0	0	0	0	0	0	0	0	0	0
Days Minimum Temp. ≤ 32°F	6	4	1	0	0	0	0	0	0	0	1	6	18
Days Minimum Temp. ≤ 0°F	0	0	0	0	0	0	0	0	0	0	0	0	0
Heating Degree Days (base 65°F)	407	276	147	38	1	0	0	0	2	31	174	382	1,458
Cooling Degree Days (base 65°F)	9	23	71	178	379	533	623	639	456	232	63	16	3,222
Mean Precipitation (in.)	1.63	1.67	2.27	2.04	4.07	4.01	2.63	2.17	2.89	4.14	2.39	1.91	31.82
Maximum Precipitation (in.)*	8.5	6.4	6.1	9.3	12.8	11.9	8.3	11.1	13.1	9.8	6.0	14.0	52.3
Minimum Precipitation (in.)*	trace	trace	trace	0.1	0.2	trace	trace	0	0.5	trace	trace	trace	13.7
Extreme Maximum Daily Precip. (in.)	2.50	2.44	2.50	3.60	6.26	5.13	9.52	5.73	3.21	11.26	3.47	5.97	11.26
Days With ≥ 0.1" Precipitation	4	3	4	3	5	5	3	3	4	5	4	3	46
Days With ≥ 0.5" Precipitation	1	1	1	1	3	3	1	1	2	2	2	1	19
Days With ≥ 1.0" Precipitation	0	0	1	1	1	1	1	1	1	1	1	0	9
Mean Snowfall (in.)	0.7	0.1	trace	trace	trace	trace	0.0	0.0	0.0	trace	trace	trace	0.8
Maximum Snowfall (in.)*	16	4	trace	0	0	0	0	0	0	trace	trace	trace	16
Maximum 24-hr. Snowfall (in.)*	13	3	trace	0	0	0	0	0	0	trace	trace	trace	13
Maximum Snow Depth (in.)	9	trace	trace	trace	trace	trace	0	0	0	trace	trace	trace	9
Days With ≥ 1.0" Snow Depth	0	0	0	0	0	0	0	0	0	0	0	0	0
Thunderstorm Days*	1	1	3	4	6	5	3	4	4	3	2	1	37
Foggy Days*	14	12	13	13	12	6	4	4	7	10	12	13	120
Predominant Sky Cover*	OVR	OVR	OVR	OVR	OVR	SCT	SCT	SCT	SCT	CLR	OVR	OVR	OVR
Mean Relative Humidity 6am (%)*	80	80	79	82	87	88	87	86	85	83	81	80	83
Mean Relative Humidity 3pm (%)*	51	48	45	48	52	49	43	42	46	46	48	50	47
Mean Dewpoint (°F)*	38	41	46	55	64	68	69	68	65	57	47	41	55
Prevailing Wind Direction*	N	N	SSE	SE	SE	SSE	SSE	SSE	SE	SSE	N	N	SSE
Prevailing Wind Speed (mph)*	10	12	12	12	12	12	10	9	9	9	10	10	10
Maximum Wind Gust (mph)*	54	56	64	74	63	58	77	49	61	54	54	48	77

Note: (*) Period of record is 1948-1995

Victoria Regional Airport

The city of Victoria is located in the south-central Texas Coastal Plain. The climate is classified as humid subtropical. Summers are hot with about 100 days with temperatures of 90 degrees or above. However, pleasant sea breezes from the nearby Gulf of Mexico make the high temperatures bearable.

Spring is characterized by mild days, brisk winds, and occasional showers and thunderstorms. Strong southeast winds begin in March, diminish in April and May, and become pleasant sea breezes in the first half of June. Thunderstorm activity increases through March and April, reaching a peak in May. Considerable cloudiness is the rule, with almost 50 percent of the days in the spring having overcast or nearly overcast skies.

The sea breeze diminishes during the summer, and at times fails altogether, and some hot nights are experienced in late June, July, and early August. High summer humidity gives way to clear, drier air in late August. Nighttime temperatures drop to pleasant levels. Thunderstorms continue, and lawns and fields remain green.

The first norther usually arrives near the beginning of fall, in late September. October and November are ideal fall months with long periods of clear days with mild temperatures and cool nights. The amount of rainfall decreases.

The winter season weather conditions alternate between clear, cold, dry periods and cloudy, mild, drizzly days as fronts move down from the north. The temperature drops below 32 degrees on an average of about a dozen mornings per year.

The normal rainfall of about 36 inches is well distributed throughout the year, with the heaviest falls coming during the growing season. Some of the smaller streams dry up in the late summer, and during occasional periods of general drought some of the larger streams may reach pool stage.

The area is subject to occasional tropical disturbances during summer and fall. Destructive winds and torrential rains may occur in these storms. Approximately 50 days per year have thunderstorms, but hail is infrequent. Destructive storms with tornados are rare.

Victoria Regional Airport *Victoria County* Elevation: 115 ft. Latitude: 28° 52' N Longitude: 96° 56' W

	JAN	FEB	MAR	APR	MAY	JUN	JUL	AUG	SEP	OCT	NOV	DEC	YEAR
Mean Maximum Temp. (°F)	64.8	68.3	74.1	80.5	86.5	91.6	94.1	94.8	90.4	83.2	74.0	66.0	80.7
Mean Temp. (°F)	54.4	57.7	63.7	70.2	77.3	82.4	84.4	84.6	80.2	72.4	63.3	55.5	70.5
Mean Minimum Temp. (°F)	44.0	47.2	53.3	59.9	68.1	73.1	74.7	74.4	70.0	61.6	52.4	45.0	60.3
Extreme Maximum Temp. (°F)	85	95	97	95	99	106	103	105	111	99	93	85	111
Extreme Minimum Temp. (°F)	14	19	21	33	45	59	67	62	48	31	26	9	9
Days Maximum Temp. ≥ 90°F	0	0	0	1	8	22	28	29	20	6	0	0	114
Days Maximum Temp. ≤ 32°F	0	0	0	0	0	0	0	0	0	0	0	0	0
Days Minimum Temp. ≤ 32°F	3	2	1	0	0	0	0	0	0	0	0	3	9
Days Minimum Temp. ≤ 0°F	0	0	0	0	0	0	0	0	0	0	0	0	0
Heating Degree Days (base 65°F)	340	230	116	27	0	0	0	0	1	22	130	318	1,184
Cooling Degree Days (base 65°F)	18	32	84	191	388	528	608	616	464	259	84	31	3,303
Mean Precipitation (in.)	2.56	2.03	2.78	2.77	5.23	4.36	3.76	3.03	3.87	4.67	3.24	2.29	40.59
Maximum Precipitation (in.)*	7.8	9.1	6.9	11.1	14.7	12.7	13.6	7.7	19.0	10.5	8.7	7.0	56.7
Minimum Precipitation (in.)*	trace	0.2	trace	trace	0.7	trace	0.1	0.3	0.8	0.3	trace	0.4	14.3
Extreme Maximum Daily Precip. (in.)	3.14	2.69	4.35	9.87	7.65	3.94	7.58	4.07	3.65	6.46	6.94	3.55	9.87
Days With ≥ 0.1" Precipitation	4	4	4	3	5	5	5	5	6	5	4	4	54
Days With ≥ 0.5" Precipitation	2	1	2	1	3	3	2	2	3	3	2	1	25
Days With ≥ 1.0" Precipitation	1	1	1	1	2	2	1	1	1	2	1	1	15
Mean Snowfall (in.)	na	na	na	na	na	na	na	na	na	na	na	na	na
Maximum Snowfall (in.)*	2	3	trace	0	0	0	0	0	0	0	trace	trace	3
Maximum 24-hr. Snowfall (in.)*	2	3	trace	0	0	0	0	0	0	0	trace	trace	3
Maximum Snow Depth (in.)	na	na	na	na	na	na	na	na	na	na	na	na	na
Days With ≥ 1.0" Snow Depth	na	na	na	na	na	na	na	na	na	na	na	na	na
Thunderstorm Days*	1	2	3	4	6	6	7	9	8	4	2	1	53
Foggy Days*	18	17	19	18	19	12	10	12	15	16	16	17	189
Predominant Sky Cover*	OVR	OVR	OVR	OVR	OVR	SCT	SCT	SCT	SCT	CLR	OVR	OVR	OVR
Mean Relative Humidity 6am (%)*	87	87	86	88	91	92	92	92	91	89	87	86	89
Mean Relative Humidity 3pm (%)*	59	56	54	56	59	58	53	53	56	52	54	58	56
Mean Dewpoint (°F)*	44	47	53	61	67	72	73	73	70	61	53	47	60
Prevailing Wind Direction*	N	N	SSE	SSE	SSE	SSE	S	S	SE	N	N	N	SSE
Prevailing Wind Speed (mph)*	14	14	13	14	13	12	10	10	9	10	13	13	12
Maximum Wind Gust (mph)*	59	63	59	62	68	81	99	67	54	75	55	54	99

Note: (*) Period of record is 1953-1995

The period of record for National Weather Service station data is 1980 – 2009 except where noted. See User Guide for detailed explanation of data.

Waco Madison Cooper Airport

One of the major cities of Texas, Waco is located in the rich agricultural region of the Brazos River Valley in North Central Texas. The city lies on the edge of the gently rolling Blackland Prairies. To the west lies the rolling to hilly Grand Prairie. Waco is a commercial hub with an economy based on industry, education and agriculture. Baylor University, founded in 1845, is located here. Regional agriculture includes chiefly cattle, poultry, sorghum, cotton and corn. Soils are black waxy, loam and sandy types. Lake Waco, a reservoir of 7,260 surface acres, lies within the Waco city limits, with the north shoreline approximately 0.8 mile south of the Municipal Airport.

The climate of Waco is humid subtropical with hot summers. It is a continental type climate characterized by extreme variations in temperature. Tropical maritime air masses predominate throughout the late spring, summer and early fall months, while Polar air masses frequent the area in winter. In an average year, April and May are the wettest months, while the July-August period is the driest. Most warm season rainfall occurs from thunderstorm activity. Consequently, considerable spatial variation in amounts occur.

Winters are mild. Cold fronts moving down from the High Plains often are accompanied by strong, gusty, northerly winds and sharp drops in temperature. Cold spells are of short duration, rarely lasting longer than two or three days before a rapid warming occurs. Winter precipitation is closely associated with frontal activity, and may fall as rain, freezing rain, sleet or snow. During most years, snowfall is of little or no consequence.

Daytime temperatures are hot in summer, particularly in July and August. The highest temperatures are associated with fair skies, light winds, and comparatively low humidities. There is little variety in the day-to-day weather during July and August. Air conditioning is recommended for maximum comfort indoors or while traveling.

The spring and fall seasons are very pleasant at Waco. Temperatures are comfortable. Cloudiness and showers are more frequent in the spring than in the fall. The average first occurrence of 32 degrees Fahrenheit is late November and the average last occurrence is in mid March.

Waco Madison Cooper Airport *Mclennan County* Elevation: 500 ft. Latitude: 31° 37' N Longitude: 97° 14' W

	JAN	FEB	MAR	APR	MAY	JUN	JUL	AUG	SEP	OCT	NOV	DEC	YEAR
Mean Maximum Temp. (°F)	58.7	62.4	69.8	78.0	85.3	92.3	97.0	97.4	90.3	80.2	68.9	59.5	78.3
Mean Temp. (°F)	47.7	51.3	58.6	66.4	74.7	81.7	85.7	85.8	78.6	68.6	57.8	48.7	67.1
Mean Minimum Temp. (°F)	36.6	40.1	47.4	54.7	64.0	71.0	74.4	74.1	66.8	56.8	46.7	37.8	55.9
Extreme Maximum Temp. (°F)	86	96	97	98	102	109	109	109	111	101	92	87	111
Extreme Minimum Temp. (°F)	6	4	16	26	37	54	60	53	40	25	22	-4	-4
Days Maximum Temp. ≥ 90°F	0	0	0	2	8	22	29	29	18	5	0	0	113
Days Maximum Temp. ≤ 32°F	0	0	0	0	0	0	0	0	0	0	0	1	1
Days Minimum Temp. ≤ 32°F	11	6	2	0	0	0	0	0	0	0	3	10	32
Days Minimum Temp. ≤ 0°F	0	0	0	0	0	0	0	0	0	0	0	0	0
Heating Degree Days (base 65°F)	534	391	230	73	5	0	0	0	5	56	247	506	2,047
Cooling Degree Days (base 65°F)	4	9	39	122	313	507	648	650	419	174	38	7	2,930
Mean Precipitation (in.)	2.02	2.58	3.07	2.69	4.41	3.25	1.68	1.89	2.81	3.89	2.86	2.81	33.96
Maximum Precipitation (in.)*	5.8	6.3	5.6	13.4	15.0	12.1	8.6	8.9	7.3	10.5	6.2	8.4	48.9
Minimum Precipitation (in.)*	trace	0.2	trace	0.1	0.6	0.3	0	trace	0	0	0.1	trace	14.9
Extreme Maximum Daily Precip. (in.)	3.21	3.97	3.15	5.07	4.23	3.37	4.93	3.76	3.51	3.60	2.99	7.98	7.98
Days With ≥ 0.1" Precipitation	4	4	5	4	5	5	3	3	4	5	5	4	51
Days With ≥ 0.5" Precipitation	1	2	2	2	3	2	1	1	2	3	2	2	23
Days With ≥ 1.0" Precipitation	0	1	1	1	1	1	0	1	1	1	1	1	10
Mean Snowfall (in.)	***0.3***	na	***0.1***	***0.2***	***trace***	***0.0***	***0.0***	***trace***	***0.0***	***trace***	***0.2***	***trace***	na
Maximum Snowfall (in.)*	7	5	1	0	0	0	0	0	0	trace	2	1	7
Maximum 24-hr. Snowfall (in.)*	7	4	1	0	0	0	0	0	0	trace	2	1	7
Maximum Snow Depth (in.)	***4***	na	***1***	***1***	***trace***	***0***	***0***	***trace***	***0***	***trace***	***2***	***trace***	na
Days With ≥ 1.0" Snow Depth	***0***	na	***0***	***0***	***0***	***0***	***0***	***0***	***0***	***0***	***0***	***0***	na
Thunderstorm Days*	1	2	4	6	8	6	4	4	4	3	2	1	45
Foggy Days*	12	11	11	11	11	5	3	4	8	10	11	12	109
Predominant Sky Cover*	OVR	OVR	OVR	OVR	OVR	CLR	CLR	SCT	CLR	CLR	CLR	OVR	CLR
Mean Relative Humidity 6am (%)*	83	83	81	84	88	86	83	82	85	84	83	82	83
Mean Relative Humidity 3pm (%)*	56	53	49	52	54	49	42	40	46	47	50	54	49
Mean Dewpoint (°F)*	36	39	45	54	63	68	69	68	64	55	45	38	54
Prevailing Wind Direction*	S	S	S	S	S	S	S	S	S	S	S	S	S
Prevailing Wind Speed (mph)*	13	13	15	15	14	14	13	12	13	12	13	13	13
Maximum Wind Gust (mph)*	54	60	75	87	61	61	49	54	60	64	58	66	87

Note: (*) Period of record is 1948-1995

Wichita Falls Municipal Airport

Wichita Falls is located in the West Cross Timbers subdivision of the North Central Plains of Texas, about 10 miles south of the Red River and 400 miles northwest of the nearest portion of the Gulf of Mexico. The topography is gently rolling mesquite plain, and the elevation of the area is about 1,000 feet.

This region lies between the humid subtropical climate of east Texas and a continental climate to the north and west. The climate of Wichita Falls is classified as continental. It is characterized by rapid changes in temperature, large daily and annual temperature extremes, and by rather erratic rainfall.

The area lies in the path of polar air masses which move down from the north during the winter season. With the passage of cold fronts or northers in the fall and winter, abrupt drops in temperature of as much as 20 to 30 degrees within an hour sometimes occur. January, the coldest month, has an average temperature around 40 degrees.

The summers in Wichita Falls are generally of the continental climate type, characterized by low humidity and windy conditions. Temperatures over 100 degrees are frequent during the common periods of hot weather. July and August, the hottest months, have average temperatures in the middle 80s.

The normal rainfall is nearly 27 inches per year, but the distribution is erratic. Several lakes in the area provide water for domestic, industrial, and irrigation purposes. The greater part of the rainfall comes in the form of showers rather than general rains. Over 75 percent of the annual moisture occurs during the period from late March to mid November, but dry periods of three to four weeks are to be expected during this time almost every year. Moderate flooding along Holliday Creek and the Wichita River, which run through the city, occur about once in each ten-year period. Snowfall, measuring an inch or more, occurs on average only two days a year.

Wind speeds average over 11 mph, and southerly winds prevail. Rather strong winds are observed in all months.

Wichita Falls Municipal Airport *Wichita County* Elevation: 1,029 ft. Latitude: 33° 59' N Longitude: 98° 30' W

	JAN	FEB	MAR	APR	MAY	JUN	JUL	AUG	SEP	OCT	NOV	DEC	YEAR
Mean Maximum Temp. (°F)	54.4	58.6	67.1	75.9	83.7	91.5	97.4	96.7	88.2	77.0	65.0	54.7	75.8
Mean Temp. (°F)	42.5	46.4	54.4	62.9	72.0	80.0	85.1	84.5	76.1	64.8	53.0	43.2	63.7
Mean Minimum Temp. (°F)	30.6	34.2	41.7	49.9	60.3	68.3	72.7	72.2	64.0	52.6	41.0	31.6	51.6
Extreme Maximum Temp. (°F)	85	93	98	102	110	117	114	110	111	102	89	83	117
Extreme Minimum Temp. (°F)	2	-8	8	27	39	51	58	53	38	21	15	-7	-8
Days Maximum Temp. ≥ 90°F	0	0	1	2	8	20	28	27	15	3	0	0	104
Days Maximum Temp. ≤ 32°F	2	1	0	0	0	0	0	0	0	0	0	2	5
Days Minimum Temp. ≤ 32°F	19	12	5	1	0	0	0	0	0	0	6	17	60
Days Minimum Temp. ≤ 0°F	0	0	0	0	0	0	0	0	0	0	0	0	0
Heating Degree Days (base 65°F)	691	522	343	132	20	0	0	0	12	104	366	670	2,860
Cooling Degree Days (base 65°F)	1	2	22	75	244	456	630	610	352	106	13	1	2,512
Mean Precipitation (in.)	1.13	1.69	2.19	2.48	3.87	4.04	1.49	2.46	2.88	3.11	1.69	1.68	28.71
Maximum Precipitation (in.)*	4.5	4.5	5.4	8.5	13.2	8.6	11.9	7.6	10.2	7.9	5.7	6.9	41.6
Minimum Precipitation (in.)*	0	trace	trace	0.3	trace	0.3	trace	trace	trace	trace	0	trace	16.1
Extreme Maximum Daily Precip. (in.)	2.11	1.88	3.60	5.20	4.54	5.36	2.01	3.65	6.19	4.34	2.06	2.25	6.19
Days With ≥ 0.1" Precipitation	2	3	4	4	5	5	3	4	4	4	3	3	44
Days With ≥ 0.5" Precipitation	1	1	1	2	3	3	1	2	2	2	1	1	20
Days With ≥ 1.0" Precipitation	0	0	1	1	1	1	0	1	1	1	1	0	8
Mean Snowfall (in.)	***1.7***	***0.8***	***0.5***	***trace***	***trace***	***trace***	***trace***	***0.0***	***0.0***	***0.0***	***0.2***	***1.0***	***4.2***
Maximum Snowfall (in.)*	12	12	11	1	0	0	0	0	0	1	4	7	17
Maximum 24-hr. Snowfall (in.)*	8	4	10	1	0	0	0	0	0	1	4	6	10
Maximum Snow Depth (in.)	5	***8***	***10***	***trace***	***trace***	***trace***	***trace***	***0***	***0***	***1***	***2***	***8***	***10***
Days With ≥ 1.0" Snow Depth	1	***1***	***0***	***0***	***0***	***0***	***0***	***0***	***0***	***0***	***0***	***0***	***2***
Thunderstorm Days*	1	1	3	5	9	7	5	5	4	3	2	1	46
Foggy Days*	9	9	8	7	7	4	2	3	6	6	7	9	77
Predominant Sky Cover*	OVR	OVR	CLR	CLR	OVR	CLR	CLR	CLR	CLR	CLR	CLR	CLR	CLR
Mean Relative Humidity 6am (%)*	79	78	76	78	85	83	78	78	83	81	79	78	80
Mean Relative Humidity 3pm (%)*	48	47	42	42	47	44	38	38	44	43	44	47	44
Mean Dewpoint (°F)*	28	32	37	47	58	64	65	64	60	50	38	30	48
Prevailing Wind Direction*	N	N	S	S	SSE	SSE	S	S	SSE	S	S	S	S
Prevailing Wind Speed (mph)*	14	14	15	15	14	14	13	12	12	13	13	12	13
Maximum Wind Gust (mph)*	62	75	69	69	90	79	74	81	69	68	62	61	90

Note: (*) Period of record is 1948-1995

The period of record for National Weather Service station data is 1980 – 2009 except where noted. See User Guide for detailed explanation of data.

Albany *Shackelford County* Elevation: 1,419 ft. Latitude: 32° 44' N Longitude: 99° 18' W

	JAN	FEB	MAR	APR	MAY	JUN	JUL	AUG	SEP	OCT	NOV	DEC	YEAR
Mean Maximum Temp. (°F)	58.2	61.6	69.7	78.1	84.7	91.0	95.3	95.4	88.0	78.9	67.9	58.6	77.3
Mean Temp. (°F)	45.4	48.6	56.2	64.1	72.3	79.2	83.0	82.7	75.1	65.5	54.9	46.0	64.4
Mean Minimum Temp. (°F)	32.5	35.6	42.6	50.1	59.7	67.3	70.8	69.9	62.2	52.0	41.9	33.4	51.5
Extreme Maximum Temp. (°F)	89	96	97	102	113	111	108	109	111	102	94	86	113
Extreme Minimum Temp. (°F)	7	3	8	27	35	49	57	55	37	19	14	-6	-6
Days Maximum Temp. ≥ 90°F	0	0	1	3	9	19	27	26	14	3	0	0	102
Days Maximum Temp. ≤ 32°F	1	1	0	0	0	0	0	0	0	0	0	1	3
Days Minimum Temp. ≤ 32°F	16	11	5	1	0	0	0	0	0	1	6	15	55
Days Minimum Temp. ≤ 0°F	0	0	0	0	0	0	0	0	0	0	0	0	0
Heating Degree Days (base 65°F)	601	462	295	111	19	1	0	0	13	92	317	584	2,495
Cooling Degree Days (base 65°F)	1	6	29	92	251	433	566	555	324	113	20	2	2,392
Mean Precipitation (in.)	1.01	1.89	2.28	2.44	3.81	4.00	1.99	2.04	2.56	2.87	1.93	1.55	28.37
Extreme Maximum Daily Precip. (in.)	1.38	1.92	2.49	5.85	4.39	3.97	2.60	3.95	2.60	3.87	2.40	2.39	5.85
Days With ≥ 0.1" Precipitation	3	3	4	3	5	5	3	3	3	4	3	2	41
Days With ≥ 0.5" Precipitation	1	1	2	2	3	3	2	1	2	2	1	1	21
Days With ≥ 1.0" Precipitation	0	1	1	1	1	1	1	1	1	1	1	0	10
Mean Snowfall (in.)	0.6	0.6	0.3	0.1	0.0	0.0	0.0	0.0	0.0	0.0	0.4	0.8	2.8
Maximum Snow Depth (in.)	1	2	7	3	0	0	0	0	0	0	3	5	7
Days With ≥ 1.0" Snow Depth	0	0	0	0	0	0	0	0	0	0	0	0	0

Alice *Jim Wells County* Elevation: 201 ft. Latitude: 27° 44' N Longitude: 98° 04' W

	JAN	FEB	MAR	APR	MAY	JUN	JUL	AUG	SEP	OCT	NOV	DEC	YEAR
Mean Maximum Temp. (°F)	68.0	72.0	78.2	84.7	89.3	94.4	96.3	96.8	92.2	85.5	77.4	69.4	83.7
Mean Temp. (°F)	56.8	60.7	66.8	73.1	79.2	83.8	85.3	85.7	81.6	74.3	66.2	58.2	72.6
Mean Minimum Temp. (°F)	45.6	49.3	55.3	61.6	69.0	73.3	74.2	74.5	70.9	63.0	55.0	46.9	61.5
Extreme Maximum Temp. (°F)	91	100	102	107	108	111	106	105	110	98	97	90	111
Extreme Minimum Temp. (°F)	19	25	23	37	52	57	65	65	52	28	28	12	12
Days Maximum Temp. ≥ 90°F	0	1	2	8	16	26	29	29	22	10	1	0	144
Days Maximum Temp. ≤ 32°F	0	0	0	0	0	0	0	0	0	0	0	0	0
Days Minimum Temp. ≤ 32°F	2	1	0	0	0	0	0	0	0	0	0	2	5
Days Minimum Temp. ≤ 0°F	0	0	0	0	0	0	0	0	0	0	0	0	0
Heating Degree Days (base 65°F)	275	177	78	16	1	0	0	0	0	14	96	253	910
Cooling Degree Days (base 65°F)	28	59	139	267	448	572	635	650	505	309	138	50	3,800
Mean Precipitation (in.)	1.17	1.47	1.46	1.27	3.05	2.74	2.92	2.67	4.05	3.03	1.68	1.13	26.64
Extreme Maximum Daily Precip. (in.)	1.60	2.35	3.00	4.37	6.64	4.96	4.92	7.30	5.23	6.80	5.50	3.45	7.30
Days With ≥ 0.1" Precipitation	2	3	3	2	4	4	3	3	4	3	2	2	35
Days With ≥ 0.5" Precipitation	1	1	1	1	2	2	2	2	2	2	1	1	18
Days With ≥ 1.0" Precipitation	0	1	0	0	1	1	1	1	1	1	0	0	7
Mean Snowfall (in.)	0.0	0.0	0.0	0.0	0.0	0.0	0.0	0.0	0.0	0.0	0.0	0.3	0.3
Maximum Snow Depth (in.)	0	0	0	0	0	0	0	0	0	0	0	0	0
Days With ≥ 1.0" Snow Depth	0	0	0	0	0	0	0	0	0	0	0	0	0

Alpine *Brewster County* Elevation: 4,529 ft. Latitude: 30° 22' N Longitude: 103° 40' W

	JAN	FEB	MAR	APR	MAY	JUN	JUL	AUG	SEP	OCT	NOV	DEC	YEAR
Mean Maximum Temp. (°F)	61.6	65.4	71.6	79.0	86.3	90.6	89.3	87.6	83.8	77.8	68.7	61.6	76.9
Mean Temp. (°F)	47.0	50.2	55.5	62.7	71.0	76.5	76.7	75.2	70.6	63.3	54.0	47.1	62.5
Mean Minimum Temp. (°F)	32.4	35.0	39.4	46.4	55.7	62.3	63.9	62.7	57.4	48.8	39.2	32.6	48.0
Extreme Maximum Temp. (°F)	80	84	89	96	101	106	103	100	100	97	86	79	106
Extreme Minimum Temp. (°F)	2	-1	10	20	34	45	53	51	36	21	14	-3	-3
Days Maximum Temp. ≥ 90°F	0	0	0	1	10	18	16	13	6	1	0	0	65
Days Maximum Temp. ≤ 32°F	0	0	0	0	0	0	0	0	0	0	0	0	0
Days Minimum Temp. ≤ 32°F	16	11	7	2	0	0	0	0	0	1	7	15	59
Days Minimum Temp. ≤ 0°F	0	0	0	0	0	0	0	0	0	0	0	0	0
Heating Degree Days (base 65°F)	549	412	296	121	na	0	0	0	17	105	326	546	na
Cooling Degree Days (base 65°F)	0	1	7	59	na	352	369	323	192	57	4	0	na
Mean Precipitation (in.)	0.46	0.64	0.45	0.62	1.28	2.67	2.65	3.06	2.77	1.55	0.51	0.63	17.29
Extreme Maximum Daily Precip. (in.)	0.96	2.71	1.35	1.40	1.00	3.77	2.31	3.92	2.61	1.81	1.32	1.02	3.92
Days With ≥ 0.1" Precipitation	1	1	1	1	3	5	5	6	5	3	1	1	33
Days With ≥ 0.5" Precipitation	0	0	0	0	1	2	2	2	2	1	0	0	10
Days With ≥ 1.0" Precipitation	0	0	0	0	0	1	1	1	1	0	0	0	4
Mean Snowfall (in.)	0.4	0.1	trace	trace	0.0	0.0	0.0	0.0	0.0	trace	0.4	0.3	1.2
Maximum Snow Depth (in.)	2	na	trace	trace	0	0	0	0	0	na	na	3	na
Days With ≥ 1.0" Snow Depth	0	0	0	0	0	0	0	0	0	0	0	0	0

Amistad Dam *Val Verde County* Elevation: 1,157 ft. Latitude: 29° 28' N Longitude: 101° 02' W

	JAN	FEB	MAR	APR	MAY	JUN	JUL	AUG	SEP	OCT	NOV	DEC	YEAR
Mean Maximum Temp. (°F)	63.5	68.2	75.8	83.6	90.1	95.2	97.6	97.7	91.5	82.3	72.1	63.4	81.7
Mean Temp. (°F)	51.9	56.1	63.5	71.0	78.4	84.0	86.0	86.0	80.3	71.1	60.8	52.2	70.1
Mean Minimum Temp. (°F)	40.2	44.1	51.2	58.3	66.7	72.6	74.4	74.3	69.0	59.9	49.5	41.0	58.4
Extreme Maximum Temp. (°F)	88	98	99	105	109	113	114	110	110	98	95	90	114
Extreme Minimum Temp. (°F)	17	17	24	34	48	60	63	65	47	30	29	9	9
Days Maximum Temp. ≥ 90°F	0	0	2	8	18	26	29	29	21	6	0	0	139
Days Maximum Temp. ≤ 32°F	0	0	0	0	0	0	0	0	0	0	0	0	0
Days Minimum Temp. ≤ 32°F	5	2	1	0	0	0	0	0	0	0	0	4	12
Days Minimum Temp. ≤ 0°F	0	0	0	0	0	0	0	0	0	0	0	0	0
Heating Degree Days (base 65°F)	402	258	120	29	1	0	0	0	2	27	165	393	1,397
Cooling Degree Days (base 65°F)	2	14	81	215	425	575	658	658	466	224	46	3	3,367
Mean Precipitation (in.)	0.67	0.75	1.17	1.12	2.47	1.94	1.81	2.02	2.69	1.87	1.12	0.70	18.33
Extreme Maximum Daily Precip. (in.)	1.04	1.53	2.53	2.10	2.49	3.45	5.58	7.10	4.10	4.38	1.50	2.16	7.10
Days With ≥ 0.1" Precipitation	2	2	2	2	4	3	3	3	3	3	2	2	31
Days With ≥ 0.5" Precipitation	1	0	1	1	2	1	1	1	2	1	1	0	12
Days With ≥ 1.0" Precipitation	0	0	0	0	1	1	1	1	1	0	0	0	5
Mean Snowfall (in.)	0.2	0.0	0.0	0.0	0.0	0.0	0.0	0.0	0.0	0.0	0.0	0.0	0.2
Maximum Snow Depth (in.)	3	0	0	0	0	0	0	0	0	0	0	0	3
Days With ≥ 1.0" Snow Depth	0	0	0	0	0	0	0	0	0	0	0	0	0

The period of record for all cooperative weather station data is 1980 – 2009. See User Guide for detailed explanation of data.

Anahuac *Chambers County* Elevation: 23 ft. Latitude: 29° 47' N Longitude: 94° 40' W

	JAN	FEB	MAR	APR	MAY	JUN	JUL	AUG	SEP	OCT	NOV	DEC	YEAR
Mean Maximum Temp. (°F)	61.8	64.7	71.0	77.2	84.0	89.3	91.5	92.1	88.4	80.7	71.8	63.4	78.0
Mean Temp. (°F)	52.2	55.3	61.4	67.9	75.3	81.0	83.1	83.1	78.7	70.1	61.6	53.7	68.6
Mean Minimum Temp. (°F)	42.6	45.8	51.7	58.5	66.6	72.6	74.7	74.0	68.9	59.4	51.4	43.9	59.2
Extreme Maximum Temp. (°F)	82	82	85	93	97	102	103	103	105	100	89	81	105
Extreme Minimum Temp. (°F)	16	21	24	36	48	56	64	60	50	33	28	8	8
Days Maximum Temp. ≥ 90°F	0	0	0	0	3	15	23	24	14	2	0	0	81
Days Maximum Temp. ≤ 32°F	0	0	0	0	0	0	0	0	0	0	0	0	0
Days Minimum Temp. ≤ 32°F	4	2	1	0	0	0	0	0	0	0	1	3	11
Days Minimum Temp. ≤ 0°F	0	0	0	0	0	0	0	0	0	0	0	0	0
Heating Degree Days (base 65°F)	397	282	152	41	1	0	0	0	1	34	157	363	1,428
Cooling Degree Days (base 65°F)	9	13	47	133	329	487	569	568	418	199	62	18	2,852
Mean Precipitation (in.)	4.65	3.00	3.56	3.63	5.28	6.45	5.18	5.12	6.38	5.13	4.10	4.46	56.94
Extreme Maximum Daily Precip. (in.)	6.26	3.50	7.55	8.06	7.20	13.20	9.80	6.10	6.00	8.20	5.50	6.55	13.20
Days With ≥ 0.1" Precipitation	6	5	5	4	5	7	7	7	7	5	5	6	69
Days With ≥ 0.5" Precipitation	3	2	2	2	3	3	3	3	3	3	3	3	33
Days With ≥ 1.0" Precipitation	1	1	1	1	2	2	2	2	2	2	1	1	18
Mean Snowfall (in.)	0.0	trace	0.0	0.0	0.0	0.0	0.0	0.0	0.0	0.0	0.0	trace	trace
Maximum Snow Depth (in.)	0	trace	0	0	0	0	0	0	0	0	0	trace	trace
Days With ≥ 1.0" Snow Depth	0	0	0	0	0	0	0	0	0	0	0	0	0

Angleton 2 W *Brazoria County* Elevation: 26 ft. Latitude: 29° 09' N Longitude: 95° 27' W

	JAN	FEB	MAR	APR	MAY	JUN	JUL	AUG	SEP	OCT	NOV	DEC	YEAR
Mean Maximum Temp. (°F)	63.7	66.4	71.9	77.6	83.8	89.1	91.4	92.0	88.3	81.2	73.0	65.5	78.7
Mean Temp. (°F)	53.9	57.0	62.7	68.4	75.4	80.6	82.6	82.8	78.9	71.1	62.9	55.6	69.3
Mean Minimum Temp. (°F)	44.1	47.5	53.4	59.0	66.9	72.0	73.6	73.5	69.5	60.9	52.8	45.8	59.9
Extreme Maximum Temp. (°F)	81	86	88	93	98	98	100	101	107	95	90	88	107
Extreme Minimum Temp. (°F)	15	20	22	31	44	55	62	60	49	30	27	7	7
Days Maximum Temp. ≥ 90°F	0	0	0	0	2	14	23	25	13	2	0	0	79
Days Maximum Temp. ≤ 32°F	0	0	0	0	0	0	0	0	0	0	0	0	0
Days Minimum Temp. ≤ 32°F	3	2	1	0	0	0	0	0	0	0	1	3	10
Days Minimum Temp. ≤ 0°F	0	0	0	0	0	0	0	0	0	0	0	0	0
Heating Degree Days (base 65°F)	352	246	130	38	1	0	0	0	1	28	134	313	1,243
Cooling Degree Days (base 65°F)	14	26	66	145	330	475	551	558	426	225	79	30	2,925
Mean Precipitation (in.)	4.74	3.26	3.82	3.45	4.60	6.06	4.43	5.16	6.93	5.40	4.73	4.43	57.01
Extreme Maximum Daily Precip. (in.)	4.86	3.49	4.75	8.62	8.30	12.36	4.40	10.30	11.42	10.65	5.25	11.00	12.36
Days With ≥ 0.1" Precipitation	6	6	5	4	5	6	6	6	7	6	5	6	68
Days With ≥ 0.5" Precipitation	3	2	2	2	3	3	3	3	4	3	3	3	34
Days With ≥ 1.0" Precipitation	1	1	1	1	2	2	2	1	2	2	1	1	17
Mean Snowfall (in.)	0.0	trace	0.0	0.0	0.0	0.0	0.0	0.0	0.0	0.0	0.0	trace	trace
Maximum Snow Depth (in.)	0	trace	0	0	0	0	0	0	0	0	0	trace	trace
Days With ≥ 1.0" Snow Depth	0	0	0	0	0	0	0	0	0	0	0	0	0

Anson *Jones County* Elevation: 1,709 ft. Latitude: 32° 46' N Longitude: 99° 54' W

	JAN	FEB	MAR	APR	MAY	JUN	JUL	AUG	SEP	OCT	NOV	DEC	YEAR
Mean Maximum Temp. (°F)	57.8	***61.0***	69.4	***78.8***	86.1	92.3	95.9	95.4	87.9	***78.3***	***66.5***	***57.4***	***77.2***
Mean Temp. (°F)	45.4	***48.6***	56.1	***65.1***	73.7	80.5	83.9	83.5	75.8	***65.9***	***54.3***	***45.5***	***64.9***
Mean Minimum Temp. (°F)	32.7	***36.3***	42.9	***51.3***	61.2	68.6	71.9	71.5	63.8	***53.5***	***42.1***	***33.5***	***52.4***
Extreme Maximum Temp. (°F)	88	95	98	***101***	113	114	109	109	109	***104***	***92***	***85***	***114***
Extreme Minimum Temp. (°F)	6	-4	9	***26***	38	52	58	50	32	***24***	***16***	***-12***	***-12***
Days Maximum Temp. ≥ 90°F	0	0	1	***4***	12	20	26	26	14	3	0	0	***106***
Days Maximum Temp. ≤ 32°F	1	1	0	***0***	0	0	0	0	0	0	***0***	1	***3***
Days Minimum Temp. ≤ 32°F	15	10	4	***1***	0	0	0	0	0	0	***5***	***13***	***48***
Days Minimum Temp. ≤ 0°F	0	0	0	***0***	0	0	0	0	0	0	0	0	***0***
Heating Degree Days (base 65°F)	604	***460***	296	***99***	16	0	0	0	13	***88***	***331***	***599***	***2,506***
Cooling Degree Days (base 65°F)	1	***5***	28	***109***	294	471	592	579	345	***123***	***17***	***1***	***2,565***
Mean Precipitation (in.)	1.04	1.70	1.64	***1.85***	3.34	3.80	2.02	2.68	2.82	2.53	***1.69***	1.47	***26.58***
Extreme Maximum Daily Precip. (in.)	1.87	***2.70***	2.00	***2.30***	3.10	4.63	3.50	2.73	5.60	***2.51***	***2.10***	***2.67***	***5.60***
Days With ≥ 0.1" Precipitation	2	3	3	***3***	5	5	3	4	4	4	***3***	***3***	***42***
Days With ≥ 0.5" Precipitation	1	1	1	***1***	2	3	1	2	2	2	1	***1***	***18***
Days With ≥ 1.0" Precipitation	0	0	0	***1***	1	1	1	1	1	1	0	***0***	7
Mean Snowfall (in.)	1.1	***0.5***	0.3	0.5	0.0	0.0	0.0	0.0	0.0	0.0	***1.0***	***1.2***	***4.6***
Maximum Snow Depth (in.)	4	***4***	4	***8***	0	0	0	0	0	***0***	***8***	***4***	***8***
Days With ≥ 1.0" Snow Depth	0	1	0	0	0	0	0	0	0	***0***	***0***	1	***2***

Aransas Wildlife Refuge *Aransas County* Elevation: 15 ft. Latitude: 28° 16' N Longitude: 96° 48' W

	JAN	FEB	MAR	APR	MAY	JUN	JUL	AUG	SEP	OCT	NOV	DEC	YEAR
Mean Maximum Temp. (°F)	64.3	66.9	72.5	77.8	83.2	88.1	89.8	90.5	87.7	81.7	73.8	65.4	78.5
Mean Temp. (°F)	55.4	58.3	64.3	70.5	77.2	82.0	83.4	83.7	80.3	73.5	65.3	56.5	70.9
Mean Minimum Temp. (°F)	46.4	49.7	56.1	63.2	71.2	75.8	76.9	76.8	72.7	65.1	56.6	47.5	63.2
Extreme Maximum Temp. (°F)	80	86	91	94	102	97	98	99	102	99	96	82	102
Extreme Minimum Temp. (°F)	17	20	22	30	47	60	67	65	51	28	28	9	9
Days Maximum Temp. ≥ 90°F	0	0	0	0	1	8	18	22	10	1	0	0	60
Days Maximum Temp. ≤ 32°F	0	0	0	0	0	0	0	0	0	0	0	0	0
Days Minimum Temp. ≤ 32°F	2	1	1	0	0	0	0	0	0	0	0	2	6
Days Minimum Temp. ≤ 0°F	0	0	0	0	0	0	0	0	0	0	0	0	0
Heating Degree Days (base 65°F)	303	206	95	21	0	0	0	0	0	15	94	286	1,020
Cooling Degree Days (base 65°F)	14	24	81	193	387	518	578	586	464	286	111	28	3,270
Mean Precipitation (in.)	3.10	2.61	2.71	1.76	4.34	3.78	3.82	3.40	4.23	4.46	3.54	2.13	39.88
Extreme Maximum Daily Precip. (in.)	3.34	10.73	4.74	4.20	8.80	7.31	7.02	3.50	7.45	7.00	7.40	3.98	10.73
Days With ≥ 0.1" Precipitation	4	4	3	3	4	4	3	4	5	4	4	4	46
Days With ≥ 0.5" Precipitation	2	1	1	1	2	2	2	2	2	2	2	1	20
Days With ≥ 1.0" Precipitation	1	1	1	1	1	1	1	1	1	1	1	0	11
Mean Snowfall (in.)	trace	trace	trace	0.0	0.0	0.0	0.0	0.0	0.0	0.0	0.0	0.2	0.2
Maximum Snow Depth (in.)	trace	trace	trace	0	0	0	0	0	0	0	0	0	trace
Days With ≥ 1.0" Snow Depth	0	0	0	0	0	0	0	0	0	0	0	0	0

The period of record for all cooperative weather station data is 1980 – 2009. See User Guide for detailed explanation of data.

Athens *Henderson County* Elevation: 448 ft. Latitude: 32° 10' N Longitude: 95° 50' W

	JAN	FEB	MAR	APR	MAY	JUN	JUL	AUG	SEP	OCT	NOV	DEC	YEAR
Mean Maximum Temp. (°F)	57.7	62.3	69.5	76.6	83.0	89.3	93.4	94.9	88.6	78.5	67.6	58.7	76.7
Mean Temp. (°F)	46.7	50.7	57.7	64.7	72.6	79.2	82.5	83.0	76.7	66.6	56.3	47.7	65.4
Mean Minimum Temp. (°F)	35.6	39.0	45.8	52.8	62.1	69.1	71.5	71.1	64.8	54.6	44.9	36.6	54.0
Extreme Maximum Temp. (°F)	84	93	90	93	97	101	106	108	109	97	88	84	109
Extreme Minimum Temp. (°F)	-5	-6	15	25	39	41	54	55	38	26	18	-2	-6
Days Maximum Temp. ≥ 90°F	0	0	0	0	3	16	26	26	15	2	0	0	88
Days Maximum Temp. ≤ 32°F	0	0	0	0	0	0	0	0	0	0	0	1	1
Days Minimum Temp. ≤ 32°F	13	8	3	0	0	0	0	0	0	0	4	12	40
Days Minimum Temp. ≤ 0°F	0	0	0	0	0	0	0	0	0	0	0	0	0
Heating Degree Days (base 65°F)	565	408	249	86	9	0	0	0	5	73	277	537	2,209
Cooling Degree Days (base 65°F)	4	8	30	85	251	433	549	565	364	130	23	7	2,449
Mean Precipitation (in.)	3.09	3.88	4.01	3.23	4.91	4.27	2.01	2.35	2.49	4.96	3.81	3.78	42.79
Extreme Maximum Daily Precip. (in.)	5.23	4.08	3.72	7.19	6.28	3.90	3.81	4.63	***3.06***	4.96	3.65	3.58	***7.19***
Days With ≥ 0.1" Precipitation	5	5	5	4	5	5	3	3	3	5	5	5	53
Days With ≥ 0.5" Precipitation	2	2	3	2	3	3	1	1	2	3	2	3	27
Days With ≥ 1.0" Precipitation	1	1	2	1	2	2	1	1	1	2	2	1	17
Mean Snowfall (in.)	0.3	0.3	trace	0.0	0.0	0.0	0.0	0.0	0.0	0.0	0.0	0.2	0.8
Maximum Snow Depth (in.)	2	2	1	0	0	0	0	0	0	0	0	3	3
Days With ≥ 1.0" Snow Depth	0	0	0	0	0	0	0	0	0	0	0	0	0

Bakersfield *Pecos County* Elevation: 2,540 ft. Latitude: 30° 53' N Longitude: 102° 19' W

	JAN	FEB	MAR	APR	MAY	JUN	JUL	AUG	SEP	OCT	NOV	DEC	YEAR
Mean Maximum Temp. (°F)	60.8	65.4	73.2	81.8	89.4	94.2	95.8	94.8	89.1	79.7	69.5	61.1	79.6
Mean Temp. (°F)	47.2	51.7	59.0	67.3	75.9	81.9	83.9	83.0	76.9	67.3	56.3	47.6	66.5
Mean Minimum Temp. (°F)	33.6	37.9	44.8	52.7	62.3	69.5	71.9	71.1	64.7	54.9	43.0	34.0	53.4
Extreme Maximum Temp. (°F)	86	91	97	101	111	114	110	107	108	102	91	86	114
Extreme Minimum Temp. (°F)	10	3	12	26	40	51	60	57	39	24	14	5	3
Days Maximum Temp. ≥ 90°F	0	0	1	7	16	23	28	27	16	4	0	0	122
Days Maximum Temp. ≤ 32°F	1	0	0	0	0	0	0	0	0	0	0	1	2
Days Minimum Temp. ≤ 32°F	14	8	3	0	0	0	0	0	0	0	5	14	44
Days Minimum Temp. ≤ 0°F	0	0	0	0	0	0	0	0	0	0	0	0	0
Heating Degree Days (base 65°F)	544	374	216	71	7	0	0	0	7	65	274	533	2,091
Cooling Degree Days (base 65°F)	0	4	38	145	352	513	592	564	371	144	18	0	2,741
Mean Precipitation (in.)	0.61	0.68	0.62	1.12	1.61	1.69	1.18	1.57	2.32	2.09	0.72	0.63	14.84
Extreme Maximum Daily Precip. (in.)	1.90	2.51	1.40	7.10	2.24	2.44	2.77	1.93	4.28	4.46	2.76	1.35	7.10
Days With ≥ 0.1" Precipitation	2	2	2	2	3	3	2	3	3	3	2	2	29
Days With ≥ 0.5" Precipitation	0	0	0	1	1	1	1	1	2	1	1	0	9
Days With ≥ 1.0" Precipitation	0	0	0	0	1	0	0	0	1	1	0	0	3
Mean Snowfall (in.)	0.7	trace	trace	0.0	0.0	0.0	0.0	0.0	0.0	trace	0.6	0.3	1.6
Maximum Snow Depth (in.)	5	1	trace	0	0	0	0	0	0	1	5	5	5
Days With ≥ 1.0" Snow Depth	0	0	0	0	0	0	0	0	0	0	0	0	0

Ballinger 2 NW *Runnels County* Elevation: 1,754 ft. Latitude: 31° 44' N Longitude: 99° 59' W

	JAN	FEB	MAR	APR	MAY	JUN	JUL	AUG	SEP	OCT	NOV	DEC	YEAR
Mean Maximum Temp. (°F)	60.0	64.7	72.1	80.9	87.3	92.3	95.3	94.8	88.3	79.8	68.9	60.1	78.7
Mean Temp. (°F)	46.2	50.5	58.0	66.3	74.4	80.4	83.2	82.8	75.9	66.7	55.7	46.7	65.6
Mean Minimum Temp. (°F)	32.4	36.3	43.9	51.5	61.5	68.5	71.0	70.7	63.5	53.4	42.5	33.1	52.4
Extreme Maximum Temp. (°F)	90	98	97	101	110	110	110	107	107	100	92	88	110
Extreme Minimum Temp. (°F)	3	-3	8	26	40	48	56	51	38	22	16	-3	-3
Days Maximum Temp. ≥ 90°F	0	0	1	6	13	21	27	26	14	4	0	0	112
Days Maximum Temp. ≤ 32°F	1	0	0	0	0	0	0	0	0	0	0	1	2
Days Minimum Temp. ≤ 32°F	16	10	4	1	0	0	0	0	0	0	5	15	51
Days Minimum Temp. ≤ 0°F	0	0	0	0	0	0	0	0	0	0	0	0	0
Heating Degree Days (base 65°F)	577	407	244	80	9	0	0	0	8	73	293	562	2,253
Cooling Degree Days (base 65°F)	1	5	34	124	308	469	570	559	342	131	20	1	2,564
Mean Precipitation (in.)	0.94	1.51	1.94	1.36	3.38	3.37	1.46	2.37	2.73	2.48	1.44	1.14	24.12
Extreme Maximum Daily Precip. (in.)	1.02	2.15	2.98	2.47	3.52	6.78	2.76	3.36	6.19	4.04	2.94	2.90	6.78
Days With ≥ 0.1" Precipitation	2	3	4	3	4	5	3	3	4	4	3	2	40
Days With ≥ 0.5" Precipitation	1	1	1	1	2	2	1	2	2	2	1	1	17
Days With ≥ 1.0" Precipitation	0	0	0	0	1	1	0	1	1	1	0	0	5
Mean Snowfall (in.)	***0.2***	0.1	trace	0.0	0.0	0.0	0.0	0.0	0.0	0.0	0.1	0.1	***0.5***
Maximum Snow Depth (in.)	4	2	trace	0	0	0	0	0	0	0	trace	2	4
Days With ≥ 1.0" Snow Depth	0	0	0	0	0	0	0	0	0	0	0	0	0

Balmorhea *Reeves County* Elevation: 3,219 ft. Latitude: 30° 59' N Longitude: 103° 44' W

	JAN	FEB	MAR	APR	MAY	JUN	JUL	AUG	SEP	OCT	NOV	DEC	YEAR
Mean Maximum Temp. (°F)	61.2	66.2	73.2	81.1	89.2	94.9	95.1	93.3	87.2	79.6	69.9	60.9	79.3
Mean Temp. (°F)	46.0	50.1	56.3	64.2	73.0	79.7	81.0	79.6	73.3	64.5	54.1	45.4	63.9
Mean Minimum Temp. (°F)	30.7	33.9	39.4	47.3	56.8	64.4	66.8	65.8	59.3	49.4	38.3	30.0	48.5
Extreme Maximum Temp. (°F)	86	90	96	99	106	111	108	106	105	101	90	87	111
Extreme Minimum Temp. (°F)	8	2	13	27	38	45	59	55	40	26	15	2	2
Days Maximum Temp. ≥ 90°F	0	0	1	6	17	24	26	25	13	4	0	0	116
Days Maximum Temp. ≤ 32°F	1	0	0	0	0	0	0	0	0	0	0	1	2
Days Minimum Temp. ≤ 32°F	19	12	6	1	0	0	0	0	0	0	7	20	65
Days Minimum Temp. ≤ 0°F	0	0	0	0	0	0	0	0	0	0	0	0	0
Heating Degree Days (base 65°F)	583	417	279	105	14	1	0	0	13	94	328	600	2,434
Cooling Degree Days (base 65°F)	0	3	17	90	269	449	502	459	268	85	8	0	2,150
Mean Precipitation (in.)	0.59	0.70	0.26	0.68	1.20	1.25	1.56	2.14	2.64	1.25	0.59	0.59	13.45
Extreme Maximum Daily Precip. (in.)	0.75	1.71	0.73	2.34	2.40	2.20	1.46	***2.24***	3.23	2.00	1.48	***2.00***	***3.23***
Days With ≥ 0.1" Precipitation	2	1	1	1	3	3	4	4	4	3	1	1	28
Days With ≥ 0.5" Precipitation	0	0	0	0	1	1	1	1	2	1	0	1	8
Days With ≥ 1.0" Precipitation	0	0	0	0	0	0	0	1	1	0	0	0	2
Mean Snowfall (in.)	1.2	0.2	trace	trace	0.0	0.0	0.0	0.0	0.0	0.0	trace	0.3	1.7
Maximum Snow Depth (in.)	8	***2***	trace	1	0	0	0	***0***	0	0	trace	***4***	***8***
Days With ≥ 1.0" Snow Depth	0	***0***	0	0	0	0	0	0	0	0	0	0	***0***

The period of record for all cooperative weather station data is 1980 – 2009. See User Guide for detailed explanation of data.

Bardwell Dam *Ellis County* Elevation: 460 ft. Latitude: 32° 16' N Longitude: 96° 38' W

	JAN	FEB	MAR	APR	MAY	JUN	JUL	AUG	SEP	OCT	NOV	DEC	YEAR
Mean Maximum Temp. (°F)	57.3	61.3	68.2	75.9	83.4	90.5	95.3	96.0	89.3	79.4	67.8	58.4	76.9
Mean Temp. (°F)	45.0	49.2	56.4	64.1	72.7	79.6	83.6	83.7	76.6	66.1	55.5	46.4	64.9
Mean Minimum Temp. (°F)	32.7	37.0	44.6	52.5	62.0	68.8	72.0	71.5	64.0	52.7	43.1	34.3	52.9
Extreme Maximum Temp. (°F)	84	95	90	97	100	108	108	108	110	99	89	83	110
Extreme Minimum Temp. (°F)	2	8	11	25	43	49	57	53	37	26	21	-7	-7
Days Maximum Temp. ≥ 90°F	0	0	0	1	5	19	27	27	16	4	0	0	99
Days Maximum Temp. ≤ 32°F	1	1	0	0	0	0	0	0	0	0	0	1	3
Days Minimum Temp. ≤ 32°F	16	8	3	0	0	0	0	0	0	0	4	13	44
Days Minimum Temp. ≤ 0°F	0	0	0	0	0	0	0	0	0	0	0	0	0
Heating Degree Days (base 65°F)	614	447	281	98	11	0	0	0	10	81	301	574	2,417
Cooling Degree Days (base 65°F)	1	5	22	79	257	447	585	589	364	123	22	3	2,497
Mean Precipitation (in.)	2.65	2.91	3.60	2.98	4.50	4.04	1.82	2.19	2.93	4.23	3.23	3.23	38.31
Extreme Maximum Daily Precip. (in.)	4.51	2.53	3.95	3.53	3.15	4.90	1.40	3.10	3.74	7.87	5.27	6.40	7.87
Days With ≥ 0.1" Precipitation	4	5	5	4	6	5	3	4	4	5	5	4	54
Days With ≥ 0.5" Precipitation	2	2	2	2	3	3	1	1	2	2	2	2	24
Days With ≥ 1.0" Precipitation	1	1	1	1	2	1	1	0	1	1	1	1	12
Mean Snowfall (in.)	0.1	trace	0.0	0.0	0.0	0.0	0.0	0.0	0.0	0.0	0.0	0.1	0.2
Maximum Snow Depth (in.)	0	0	0	0	0	0	0	0	0	0	0	trace	trace
Days With ≥ 1.0" Snow Depth	0	0	0	0	0	0	0	0	0	0	0	0	0

Bay City Waterworks *Matagorda County* Elevation: 51 ft. Latitude: 28° 59' N Longitude: 95° 59' W

	JAN	FEB	MAR	APR	MAY	JUN	JUL	AUG	SEP	OCT	NOV	DEC	YEAR
Mean Maximum Temp. (°F)	64.0	67.0	72.6	78.6	84.3	89.6	91.9	92.5	89.2	82.1	73.5	65.7	79.2
Mean Temp. (°F)	54.5	57.7	63.5	69.8	76.2	81.6	83.4	83.6	79.8	72.3	63.7	56.0	70.2
Mean Minimum Temp. (°F)	45.0	48.2	54.4	60.9	68.0	73.5	74.9	74.6	70.4	62.5	53.9	46.4	61.1
Extreme Maximum Temp. (°F)	86	84	90	93	97	100	107	103	109	96	88	83	109
Extreme Minimum Temp. (°F)	14	20	22	36	43	58	65	61	50	29	28	7	7
Days Maximum Temp. ≥ 90°F	0	0	0	0	2	16	25	26	16	3	0	0	88
Days Maximum Temp. ≤ 32°F	0	0	0	0	0	0	0	0	0	0	0	0	0
Days Minimum Temp. ≤ 32°F	3	1	1	0	0	0	0	0	0	0	0	2	7
Days Minimum Temp. ≤ 0°F	0	0	0	0	0	0	0	0	0	0	0	0	0
Heating Degree Days (base 65°F)	335	226	115	27	2	0	0	0	1	22	122	302	1,152
Cooling Degree Days (base 65°F)	17	25	75	177	355	503	577	582	453	255	90	31	3,140
Mean Precipitation (in.)	4.00	2.90	3.17	3.09	4.94	4.72	4.47	3.78	4.84	6.70	4.14	3.54	50.29
Extreme Maximum Daily Precip. (in.)	6.24	3.86	2.60	6.31	7.18	5.76	4.24	3.79	7.48	20.85	3.84	6.20	20.85
Days With ≥ 0.1" Precipitation	6	5	4	3	5	6	5	6	6	6	5	5	62
Days With ≥ 0.5" Precipitation	2	2	2	2	3	3	3	2	2	3	2	2	28
Days With ≥ 1.0" Precipitation	1	1	1	1	2	1	2	1	1	2	1	1	15
Mean Snowfall (in.)	0.0	0.0	0.0	0.0	0.0	0.0	0.0	0.0	0.0	0.0	0.0	0.0	0.0
Maximum Snow Depth (in.)	0	0	0	0	0	0	0	0	0	0	0	8	8
Days With ≥ 1.0" Snow Depth	0	0	0	0	0	0	0	0	0	0	0	0	0

Baytown *Harris County* Elevation: 34 ft. Latitude: 29° 50' N Longitude: 95° 00' W

	JAN	FEB	MAR	APR	MAY	JUN	JUL	AUG	SEP	OCT	NOV	DEC	YEAR
Mean Maximum Temp. (°F)	62.5	66.1	71.7	77.7	84.0	89.3	91.7	92.5	88.5	81.1	72.0	63.8	78.4
Mean Temp. (°F)	52.8	56.5	62.5	68.8	76.2	81.6	83.9	84.0	79.1	70.9	62.2	54.1	69.4
Mean Minimum Temp. (°F)	43.1	46.8	53.3	59.9	68.3	73.9	76.0	75.4	69.8	60.6	52.3	44.4	60.3
Extreme Maximum Temp. (°F)	82	86	90	93	96	100	102	103	109	96	88	84	109
Extreme Minimum Temp. (°F)	17	20	25	35	47	59	64	61	48	30	27	7	7
Days Maximum Temp. ≥ 90°F	0	0	0	0	3	16	24	25	14	2	0	0	84
Days Maximum Temp. ≤ 32°F	0	0	0	0	0	0	0	0	0	0	0	0	0
Days Minimum Temp. ≤ 32°F	4	2	1	0	0	0	0	0	0	0	1	3	11
Days Minimum Temp. ≤ 0°F	0	0	0	0	0	0	0	0	0	0	0	0	0
Heating Degree Days (base 65°F)	383	254	133	36	1	0	0	0	1	28	149	350	1,335
Cooling Degree Days (base 65°F)	13	20	64	158	354	506	593	595	432	217	71	21	3,044
Mean Precipitation (in.)	4.68	3.85	3.70	3.68	5.52	7.07	4.81	4.94	5.68	6.11	5.24	4.73	60.01
Extreme Maximum Daily Precip. (in.)	8.29	3.97	6.23	6.33	4.53	9.50	5.98	5.55	6.19	15.74	4.81	4.68	15.74
Days With ≥ 0.1" Precipitation	6	5	5	4	5	7	7	7	7	6	6	7	72
Days With ≥ 0.5" Precipitation	3	2	2	2	4	4	3	3	3	3	3	3	35
Days With ≥ 1.0" Precipitation	1	1	1	1	2	2	2	1	2	1	2	1	17
Mean Snowfall (in.)	0.0	0.0	0.0	0.0	0.0	0.0	0.0	0.0	0.0	0.0	0.0	0.0	0.0
Maximum Snow Depth (in.)	0	0	0	0	0	0	0	0	0	0	0	0	0
Days With ≥ 1.0" Snow Depth	0	0	0	0	0	0	0	0	0	0	0	0	0

Beaumont Research Ctr *Jefferson County* Elevation: 26 ft. Latitude: 30° 04' N Longitude: 94° 17' W

	JAN	FEB	MAR	APR	MAY	JUN	JUL	AUG	SEP	OCT	NOV	DEC	YEAR
Mean Maximum Temp. (°F)	61.9	65.1	71.7	78.2	85.0	90.0	92.2	92.7	88.5	80.8	71.8	63.6	78.5
Mean Temp. (°F)	51.8	55.0	61.4	68.0	75.5	80.8	82.8	82.7	78.2	69.7	61.1	53.4	68.4
Mean Minimum Temp. (°F)	41.6	44.8	51.1	57.8	65.9	71.6	73.4	72.7	67.9	58.6	50.3	43.1	58.2
Extreme Maximum Temp. (°F)	82	86	87	94	98	99	103	104	107	96	88	83	107
Extreme Minimum Temp. (°F)	13	19	23	30	46	52	61	58	48	27	26	8	8
Days Maximum Temp. ≥ 90°F	0	0	0	0	5	20	26	26	15	2	0	0	94
Days Maximum Temp. ≤ 32°F	0	0	0	0	0	0	0	0	0	0	0	0	0
Days Minimum Temp. ≤ 32°F	6	3	1	0	0	0	0	0	0	0	1	5	16
Days Minimum Temp. ≤ 0°F	0	0	0	0	0	0	0	0	0	0	0	0	0
Heating Degree Days (base 65°F)	414	294	160	47	2	0	0	0	2	40	171	373	1,503
Cooling Degree Days (base 65°F)	10	16	56	145	334	482	560	557	406	194	59	20	2,839
Mean Precipitation (in.)	4.56	3.93	3.64	2.96	5.51	8.05	4.80	4.92	5.64	5.93	4.60	4.78	59.32
Extreme Maximum Daily Precip. (in.)	3.55	6.56	3.34	4.32	6.02	15.21	4.09	4.80	10.28	9.15	6.57	6.14	15.21
Days With ≥ 0.1" Precipitation	6	6	5	4	5	8	7	7	7	5	5	6	71
Days With ≥ 0.5" Precipitation	3	2	2	2	3	4	3	3	3	3	3	3	34
Days With ≥ 1.0" Precipitation	2	1	1	1	2	2	1	2	2	2	2	1	19
Mean Snowfall (in.)	trace	0.0	0.0	0.0	0.0	0.0	0.0	0.0	0.0	0.0	0.0	0.0	trace
Maximum Snow Depth (in.)	trace	0	0	0	0	0	0	0	0	0	0	3	3
Days With ≥ 1.0" Snow Depth	0	0	0	0	0	0	0	0	0	0	0	0	0

The period of record for all cooperative weather station data is 1980 – 2009. See User Guide for detailed explanation of data.

Benbrook Dam *Tarrant County* Elevation: 790 ft. Latitude: 32° 39' N Longitude: 97° 27' W

	JAN	FEB	MAR	APR	MAY	JUN	JUL	AUG	SEP	OCT	NOV	DEC	YEAR
Mean Maximum Temp. (°F)	57.0	60.8	67.8	76.0	83.3	90.8	95.9	96.2	88.4	78.6	67.4	57.6	76.6
Mean Temp. (°F)	45.0	48.9	56.0	64.2	72.4	80.0	84.2	84.3	76.6	66.5	55.9	46.1	65.0
Mean Minimum Temp. (°F)	32.9	36.9	44.2	52.4	61.5	69.2	72.5	72.3	64.8	54.3	44.4	34.6	53.3
Extreme Maximum Temp. (°F)	88	94	94	99	99	110	110	107	110	98	89	87	110
Extreme Minimum Temp. (°F)	4	5	12	29	38	53	59	54	40	22	20	-6	-6
Days Maximum Temp. ≥ 90°F	0	0	0	1	6	19	28	27	15	3	0	0	99
Days Maximum Temp. ≤ 32°F	1	1	0	0	0	0	0	0	0	0	0	1	3
Days Minimum Temp. ≤ 32°F	15	9	3	0	0	0	0	0	0	0	4	12	43
Days Minimum Temp. ≤ 0°F	0	0	0	0	0	0	0	0	0	0	0	0	0
Heating Degree Days (base 65°F)	615	453	295	102	13	0	0	0	9	79	291	580	2,437
Cooling Degree Days (base 65°F)	1	5	23	84	250	457	602	605	363	131	25	2	2,548
Mean Precipitation (in.)	1.85	2.40	3.25	2.84	4.59	3.88	1.81	2.09	3.15	3.97	2.57	2.35	34.75
Extreme Maximum Daily Precip. (in.)	3.02	3.65	3.83	2.80	4.38	5.35	2.20	3.50	2.88	6.36	3.20	4.00	6.36
Days With ≥ 0.1" Precipitation	4	4	5	4	6	6	4	3	4	5	4	4	53
Days With ≥ 0.5" Precipitation	1	1	2	2	3	3	1	1	2	2	2	2	22
Days With ≥ 1.0" Precipitation	0	1	1	1	2	1	0	1	1	1	1	0	10
Mean Snowfall (in.)	trace	0.1	trace	0.0	0.0	0.0	0.0	0.0	0.0	0.0	trace	0.1	0.2
Maximum Snow Depth (in.)	1	2	trace	0	0	0	0	0	0	0	0	trace	2
Days With ≥ 1.0" Snow Depth	0	0	0	0	0	0	0	0	0	0	0	0	0

Big Spring *Howard County* Elevation: 2,500 ft. Latitude: 32° 15' N Longitude: 101° 27' W

	JAN	FEB	MAR	APR	MAY	JUN	JUL	AUG	SEP	OCT	NOV	DEC	YEAR
Mean Maximum Temp. (°F)	57.0	61.1	69.2	78.5	86.7	92.0	94.9	93.4	87.3	77.9	66.9	57.3	76.9
Mean Temp. (°F)	44.5	48.1	55.6	64.3	73.4	79.8	83.1	82.0	75.6	65.5	53.9	44.8	64.2
Mean Minimum Temp. (°F)	31.6	35.2	41.8	50.2	60.1	67.5	71.3	70.6	63.7	53.0	40.9	32.2	51.5
Extreme Maximum Temp. (°F)	85	90	95	100	109	114	108	***106***	***108***	101	***92***	82	***114***
Extreme Minimum Temp. (°F)	4	-5	13	27	40	49	51	***50***	***39***	27	***16***	1	***-5***
Days Maximum Temp. ≥ 90°F	0	0	0	4	13	20	26	24	13	3	0	0	103
Days Maximum Temp. ≤ 32°F	1	1	0	0	0	0	0	0	0	0	0	2	4
Days Minimum Temp. ≤ 32°F	18	10	4	0	0	0	0	0	0	0	6	16	54
Days Minimum Temp. ≤ 0°F	0	0	0	0	0	0	0	0	0	0	0	0	0
Heating Degree Days (base 65°F)	630	472	306	112	17	1	0	0	12	91	336	620	2,597
Cooling Degree Days (base 65°F)	0	2	21	98	286	451	568	535	337	113	11	0	2,422
Mean Precipitation (in.)	0.67	0.85	0.98	1.21	2.49	2.69	1.42	2.74	2.98	1.86	0.92	0.65	19.46
Extreme Maximum Daily Precip. (in.)	1.10	2.30	4.20	***2.90***	***4.84***	2.10	2.20	***5.09***	***3.79***	2.90	***2.10***	1.60	***5.09***
Days With ≥ 0.1" Precipitation	1	2	2	2	4	4	2	4	3	3	2	2	31
Days With ≥ 0.5" Precipitation	1	1	1	1	1	2	1	2	2	1	1	0	14
Days With ≥ 1.0" Precipitation	0	0	0	0	1	1	0	1	1	1	0	0	5
Mean Snowfall (in.)	0.4	***0.3***	0.1	trace	0.0	0.0	0.0	0.0	0.0	0.0	0.6	0.7	***2.1***
Maximum Snow Depth (in.)	4	***4***	trace	trace	0	0	0	***0***	***0***	0	***6***	7	***7***
Days With ≥ 1.0" Snow Depth	0	***0***	0	0	0	0	0	0	0	0	0	0	***0***

Blanco *Blanco County* Elevation: 1,370 ft. Latitude: 30° 06' N Longitude: 98° 25' W

	JAN	FEB	MAR	APR	MAY	JUN	JUL	AUG	SEP	OCT	NOV	DEC	YEAR
Mean Maximum Temp. (°F)	59.9	63.7	70.2	77.8	84.1	89.9	93.4	94.6	88.6	79.3	69.1	60.8	77.6
Mean Temp. (°F)	47.3	50.8	57.8	65.0	72.9	78.9	81.7	82.1	76.1	66.9	56.9	48.6	65.4
Mean Minimum Temp. (°F)	34.7	37.9	45.3	52.1	61.6	67.8	70.0	69.5	63.6	54.5	44.7	36.4	53.2
Extreme Maximum Temp. (°F)	87	98	93	100	101	106	105	106	110	96	89	87	110
Extreme Minimum Temp. (°F)	6	2	14	27	34	46	58	53	38	22	18	0	0
Days Maximum Temp. ≥ 90°F	0	0	0	1	6	17	25	27	14	2	0	0	92
Days Maximum Temp. ≤ 32°F	0	0	0	0	0	0	0	0	0	0	0	0	0
Days Minimum Temp. ≤ 32°F	14	9	4	1	0	0	0	0	0	0	5	12	45
Days Minimum Temp. ≤ 0°F	0	0	0	0	0	0	0	0	0	0	0	0	0
Heating Degree Days (base 65°F)	542	401	249	92	9	0	0	0	7	74	265	507	2,146
Cooling Degree Days (base 65°F)	2	7	33	98	259	422	525	537	348	141	30	5	2,407
Mean Precipitation (in.)	1.94	1.96	2.93	2.32	4.18	4.20	2.29	2.00	3.11	4.39	2.93	2.32	34.57
Extreme Maximum Daily Precip. (in.)	2.65	2.95	3.14	2.90	3.34	5.10	4.50	3.14	6.75	5.53	6.33	3.60	6.75
Days With ≥ 0.1" Precipitation	4	4	5	4	6	5	3	3	4	5	4	4	51
Days With ≥ 0.5" Precipitation	1	1	2	2	3	3	1	1	2	3	2	1	22
Days With ≥ 1.0" Precipitation	0	1	1	1	2	1	1	1	1	1	1	1	12
Mean Snowfall (in.)	0.3	0.1	trace	0.0	0.0	0.0	0.0	0.0	0.0	0.0	trace	trace	0.4
Maximum Snow Depth (in.)	10	0	trace	0	0	0	0	0	0	0	trace	trace	10
Days With ≥ 1.0" Snow Depth	0	0	0	0	0	0	0	0	0	0	0	0	0

Boerne *Kendall County* Elevation: 1,443 ft. Latitude: 29° 48' N Longitude: 98° 44' W

	JAN	FEB	MAR	APR	MAY	JUN	JUL	AUG	SEP	OCT	NOV	DEC	YEAR
Mean Maximum Temp. (°F)	61.0	64.9	71.3	78.5	84.2	89.7	92.8	93.9	88.6	80.0	70.1	61.7	78.0
Mean Temp. (°F)	48.4	51.8	58.4	65.6	73.0	78.8	81.3	81.6	76.2	67.4	57.5	49.2	65.8
Mean Minimum Temp. (°F)	35.6	38.7	45.5	52.6	61.8	67.8	69.7	69.2	63.8	54.7	44.9	36.6	53.4
Extreme Maximum Temp. (°F)	86	98	95	100	99	105	103	105	109	97	90	85	109
Extreme Minimum Temp. (°F)	8	5	14	27	34	45	56	55	37	21	17	2	2
Days Maximum Temp. ≥ 90°F	0	0	0	2	6	16	24	27	14	2	0	0	91
Days Maximum Temp. ≤ 32°F	0	0	0	0	0	0	0	0	0	0	0	0	0
Days Minimum Temp. ≤ 32°F	13	8	4	1	0	0	0	0	0	0	5	12	43
Days Minimum Temp. ≤ 0°F	0	0	0	0	0	0	0	0	0	0	0	0	0
Heating Degree Days (base 65°F)	512	374	233	82	7	0	0	0	6	67	249	488	2,018
Cooling Degree Days (base 65°F)	3	8	36	106	264	420	512	520	348	148	32	5	2,402
Mean Precipitation (in.)	1.97	2.23	2.98	2.24	4.64	4.57	3.02	2.80	3.34	4.27	3.23	2.21	37.50
Extreme Maximum Daily Precip. (in.)	1.74	3.39	4.48	2.89	4.95	8.93	6.76	7.33	4.38	5.80	4.75	5.68	8.93
Days With ≥ 0.1" Precipitation	5	4	5	4	6	5	3	3	5	5	4	4	53
Days With ≥ 0.5" Precipitation	1	1	2	1	3	3	1	1	2	2	2	1	20
Days With ≥ 1.0" Precipitation	0	1	1	1	2	2	1	1	1	2	1	1	14
Mean Snowfall (in.)	0.3	trace	0.0	0.0	0.0	0.0	0.0	0.0	0.0	0.0	trace	trace	0.3
Maximum Snow Depth (in.)	11	2	0	0	0	0	0	0	0	0	trace	trace	11
Days With ≥ 1.0" Snow Depth	0	0	0	0	0	0	0	0	0	0	0	0	0

The period of record for all cooperative weather station data is 1980 – 2009. See User Guide for detailed explanation of data.

Boquillas Ranger Stn *Brewster County* Elevation: 1,879 ft. Latitude: 29° 11' N Longitude: 102° 58' W

	JAN	FEB	MAR	APR	MAY	JUN	JUL	AUG	SEP	OCT	NOV	DEC	YEAR
Mean Maximum Temp. (°F)	69.6	74.6	82.7	91.7	99.5	103.6	103.0	101.3	97.0	88.4	77.7	68.6	88.1
Mean Temp. (°F)	50.5	55.3	63.2	71.9	81.6	87.3	87.5	86.1	81.3	71.3	59.2	50.1	70.4
Mean Minimum Temp. (°F)	31.3	36.1	43.6	52.1	63.6	71.0	72.0	70.9	65.6	54.0	40.7	31.6	52.7
Extreme Maximum Temp. (°F)	92	99	103	112	116	117	116	112	110	105	97	90	117
Extreme Minimum Temp. (°F)	13	13	14	29	44	59	59	61	40	24	16	4	4
Days Maximum Temp. ≥ 90°F	0	2	9	20	28	28	30	30	26	16	3	0	192
Days Maximum Temp. ≤ 32°F	0	0	0	0	0	0	0	0	0	0	0	0	0
Days Minimum Temp. ≤ 32°F	18	9	3	0	0	0	0	0	0	0	5	18	53
Days Minimum Temp. ≤ 0°F	0	0	0	0	0	0	0	0	0	0	0	0	0
Heating Degree Days (base 65°F)	444	275	121	27	0	0	0	0	2	27	197	455	1,548
Cooling Degree Days (base 65°F)	0	8	71	241	521	676	705	661	499	228	30	1	3,641
Mean Precipitation (in.)	0.41	0.42	0.25	0.44	1.20	1.32	1.07	1.22	0.99	1.37	0.60	0.39	9.68
Extreme Maximum Daily Precip. (in.)	1.02	1.01	0.55	1.76	1.83	1.75	1.84	2.06	1.53	2.14	1.75	1.16	2.14
Days With ≥ 0.1" Precipitation	1	1	1	1	3	3	2	3	2	3	2	1	23
Days With ≥ 0.5" Precipitation	0	0	0	0	1	1	1	1	1	1	0	0	6
Days With ≥ 1.0" Precipitation	0	0	0	0	0	0	0	0	0	0	0	0	0
Mean Snowfall (in.)	trace	0.0	0.0	0.0	0.0	0.0	0.0	0.0	0.0	0.0	0.0	trace	trace
Maximum Snow Depth (in.)	3	0	0	0	0	0	0	0	0	0	0	trace	3
Days With ≥ 1.0" Snow Depth	0	0	0	0	0	0	0	0	0	0	0	0	0

Borger *Hutchinson County* Elevation: 3,140 ft. Latitude: 35° 39' N Longitude: 101° 27' W

	JAN	FEB	MAR	APR	MAY	JUN	JUL	AUG	SEP	OCT	NOV	DEC	YEAR
Mean Maximum Temp. (°F)	50.9	55.6	63.7	72.2	80.6	88.6	93.1	91.1	84.0	73.4	60.7	50.3	72.0
Mean Temp. (°F)	38.1	41.9	49.4	57.7	66.9	75.2	79.9	78.3	70.9	59.7	47.6	38.1	58.6
Mean Minimum Temp. (°F)	25.3	28.2	35.0	43.1	53.1	61.8	66.6	65.5	57.7	46.0	34.5	25.8	45.2
Extreme Maximum Temp. (°F)	81	84	92	97	103	108	107	107	105	99	88	79	108
Extreme Minimum Temp. (°F)	-4	-5	4	16	29	45	51	51	29	13	7	-7	-7
Days Maximum Temp. ≥ 90°F	0	0	0	1	6	14	23	20	8	1	0	0	73
Days Maximum Temp. ≤ 32°F	3	2	0	0	0	0	0	0	0	0	1	3	9
Days Minimum Temp. ≤ 32°F	25	18	12	3	0	0	0	0	0	2	12	24	96
Days Minimum Temp. ≤ 0°F	0	0	0	0	0	0	0	0	0	0	0	1	1
Heating Degree Days (base 65°F)	826	646	481	241	67	5	1	1	30	196	518	828	3,840
Cooling Degree Days (base 65°F)	0	0	4	27	131	319	468	420	214	40	2	0	1,625
Mean Precipitation (in.)	0.75	0.70	1.68	1.80	2.84	3.28	2.65	3.59	2.13	1.89	0.99	0.84	23.14
Extreme Maximum Daily Precip. (in.)	1.67	1.12	3.32	2.50	3.82	2.87	3.66	2.51	6.27	2.87	1.77	1.40	6.27
Days With ≥ 0.1" Precipitation	2	2	3	3	5	5	5	6	3	3	2	2	41
Days With ≥ 0.5" Precipitation	1	0	1	1	2	3	2	2	1	1	1	1	16
Days With ≥ 1.0" Precipitation	0	0	0	0	1	1	1	1	0	0	0	0	4
Mean Snowfall (in.)	5.3	4.0	3.5	0.9	trace	trace	0.0	trace	trace	0.2	2.4	5.3	21.6
Maximum Snow Depth (in.)	13	15	13	3	trace	trace	0	trace	0	4	8	17	17
Days With ≥ 1.0" Snow Depth	3	2	1	0	0	0	0	0	0	0	1	3	10

Boys Ranch *Oldham County* Elevation: 3,190 ft. Latitude: 35° 32' N Longitude: 102° 15' W

	JAN	FEB	MAR	APR	MAY	JUN	JUL	AUG	SEP	OCT	NOV	DEC	YEAR
Mean Maximum Temp. (°F)	52.6	56.8	64.5	72.9	81.0	89.0	92.7	90.4	83.8	73.5	62.2	52.2	72.6
Mean Temp. (°F)	36.9	41.0	48.3	56.9	66.4	75.2	79.3	77.4	69.8	57.9	46.0	36.8	57.7
Mean Minimum Temp. (°F)	21.1	25.2	32.1	40.9	51.8	61.4	65.8	64.4	55.8	42.4	29.7	21.2	42.7
Extreme Maximum Temp. (°F)	80	85	95	96	103	109	110	104	104	96	89	80	110
Extreme Minimum Temp. (°F)	-8	-7	3	19	29	44	49	51	28	13	-2	-11	-11
Days Maximum Temp. ≥ 90°F	0	0	0	1	6	15	23	20	8	1	0	0	74
Days Maximum Temp. ≤ 32°F	2	2	0	0	0	0	0	0	0	0	1	3	8
Days Minimum Temp. ≤ 32°F	29	23	16	5	0	0	0	0	0	4	19	28	124
Days Minimum Temp. ≤ 0°F	0	0	0	0	0	0	0	0	0	0	0	1	1
Heating Degree Days (base 65°F)	863	672	511	261	70	5	0	1	37	238	564	875	4,097
Cooling Degree Days (base 65°F)	0	0	2	20	122	317	450	393	188	26	0	0	1,518
Mean Precipitation (in.)	0.52	0.36	1.12	1.33	2.11	2.55	2.69	3.46	1.96	1.59	0.69	0.62	19.00
Extreme Maximum Daily Precip. (in.)	1.61	0.67	1.54	2.10	4.20	2.78	3.00	3.13	4.50	2.99	1.29	1.06	4.50
Days With ≥ 0.1" Precipitation	1	1	3	2	4	5	5	5	3	2	2	2	35
Days With ≥ 0.5" Precipitation	0	0	1	1	2	2	2	2	1	1	0	0	12
Days With ≥ 1.0" Precipitation	0	0	0	0	0	1	1	1	1	1	0	0	5
Mean Snowfall (in.)	3.3	1.4	1.1	0.3	0.1	0.0	0.0	0.0	0.0	0.0	1.6	2.7	10.5
Maximum Snow Depth (in.)	10	2	5	3	0	0	0	0	0	3	8	14	14
Days With ≥ 1.0" Snow Depth	1	0	0	0	0	0	0	0	0	0	0	1	2

Brady *Mcculloch County* Elevation: 1,720 ft. Latitude: 31° 07' N Longitude: 99° 20' W

	JAN	FEB	MAR	APR	MAY	JUN	JUL	AUG	SEP	OCT	NOV	DEC	YEAR
Mean Maximum Temp. (°F)	59.5	63.3	70.3	78.9	85.4	91.1	94.7	95.1	88.6	79.5	68.9	60.0	77.9
Mean Temp. (°F)	46.7	50.5	57.4	65.2	73.2	79.3	82.4	82.5	76.0	66.6	56.3	47.4	65.3
Mean Minimum Temp. (°F)	33.9	37.6	44.5	51.4	60.9	67.5	70.1	69.9	63.4	53.6	43.6	34.8	52.6
Extreme Maximum Temp. (°F)	89	99	95	101	107	110	109	108	109	98	92	88	110
Extreme Minimum Temp. (°F)	5	3	11	27	38	51	59	51	40	24	19	-2	-2
Days Maximum Temp. ≥ 90°F	0	0	1	3	9	20	27	27	15	3	0	0	105
Days Maximum Temp. ≤ 32°F	1	1	0	0	0	0	0	0	0	0	0	1	3
Days Minimum Temp. ≤ 32°F	15	8	4	1	0	0	0	0	0	0	4	13	45
Days Minimum Temp. ≤ 0°F	0	0	0	0	0	0	0	0	0	0	0	0	0
Heating Degree Days (base 65°F)	561	411	259	90	11	1	0	0	8	75	279	540	2,235
Cooling Degree Days (base 65°F)	2	6	31	103	270	437	547	551	345	130	23	3	2,448
Mean Precipitation (in.)	1.14	1.74	2.18	1.87	3.68	3.34	2.14	2.10	3.02	2.74	1.92	1.56	27.43
Extreme Maximum Daily Precip. (in.)	2.12	2.15	2.77	4.55	5.94	3.78	3.74	3.32	5.03	2.28	4.25	4.42	5.94
Days With ≥ 0.1" Precipitation	3	4	4	3	5	5	3	3	4	4	3	3	44
Days With ≥ 0.5" Precipitation	1	1	2	1	3	2	1	2	2	2	1	1	19
Days With ≥ 1.0" Precipitation	0	0	0	0	1	1	1	1	1	1	1	0	7
Mean Snowfall (in.)	0.0	0.0	0.0	0.0	0.0	0.0	0.0	0.0	0.0	0.0	trace	0.1	0.1
Maximum Snow Depth (in.)	0	0	0	0	0	0	0	0	0	0	0	1	1
Days With ≥ 1.0" Snow Depth	0	0	0	0	0	0	0	0	0	0	0	0	0

The period of record for all cooperative weather station data is 1980 – 2009. See User Guide for detailed explanation of data.

Brenham *Washington County* Elevation: 312 ft. Latitude: 30° 10' N Longitude: 96° 24' W

	JAN	FEB	MAR	APR	MAY	JUN	JUL	AUG	SEP	OCT	NOV	DEC	YEAR
Mean Maximum Temp. (°F)	61.8	65.5	72.4	79.6	86.2	92.0	95.3	96.5	91.2	82.0	71.5	62.7	79.7
Mean Temp. (°F)	51.3	54.6	61.2	68.5	75.9	81.8	84.7	85.1	79.7	70.5	60.6	52.2	68.8
Mean Minimum Temp. (°F)	40.7	43.7	50.0	57.2	65.5	71.6	73.7	73.6	68.1	58.8	49.6	41.5	57.8
Extreme Maximum Temp. (°F)	83	94	92	94	101	105	106	107	113	97	89	85	113
Extreme Minimum Temp. (°F)	7	15	19	33	44	53	64	61	46	29	24	4	4
Days Maximum Temp. ≥ 90°F	0	0	0	1	9	22	28	29	20	6	0	0	115
Days Maximum Temp. ≤ 32°F	0	0	0	0	0	0	0	0	0	0	0	0	0
Days Minimum Temp. ≤ 32°F	6	3	1	0	0	0	0	0	0	0	1	6	17
Days Minimum Temp. ≤ 0°F	0	0	0	0	0	0	0	0	0	0	0	0	0
Heating Degree Days (base 65°F)	429	305	172	44	2	0	0	0	1	37	185	408	1,583
Cooling Degree Days (base 65°F)	11	18	61	154	346	511	616	628	448	213	60	17	3,083
Mean Precipitation (in.)	3.53	2.94	3.40	2.90	4.66	4.80	2.54	2.87	4.49	5.20	4.34	3.41	45.08
Extreme Maximum Daily Precip. (in.)	5.65	3.03	3.64	4.12	3.43	5.37	5.44	5.81	5.87	10.38	5.39	3.34	10.38
Days With ≥ 0.1" Precipitation	6	5	5	4	6	6	4	4	5	6	5	6	62
Days With ≥ 0.5" Precipitation	2	2	2	2	3	3	2	2	3	3	3	2	29
Days With ≥ 1.0" Precipitation	1	1	1	1	2	2	1	1	1	2	1	1	15
Mean Snowfall (in.)	0.1	trace	trace	0.0	0.0	0.0	0.0	0.0	0.0	0.0	0.0	trace	0.1
Maximum Snow Depth (in.)	1	1	trace	0	0	0	0	0	0	0	0	trace	1
Days With ≥ 1.0" Snow Depth	0	0	0	0	0	0	0	0	0	0	0	0	0

Bridgeport *Wise County* Elevation: 745 ft. Latitude: 33° 12' N Longitude: 97° 46' W

	JAN	FEB	MAR	APR	MAY	JUN	JUL	AUG	SEP	OCT	NOV	DEC	YEAR
Mean Maximum Temp. (°F)	***57.1***	***60.8***	68.2	77.2	83.8	90.8	96.7	96.7	88.9	78.6	67.0	57.7	***77.0***
Mean Temp. (°F)	***44.3***	***48.0***	55.2	63.7	71.9	79.1	83.7	83.1	75.5	65.0	54.4	45.1	***64.1***
Mean Minimum Temp. (°F)	***31.5***	***35.2***	42.1	50.2	60.0	67.5	70.7	69.5	62.1	51.4	41.7	32.4	***51.2***
Extreme Maximum Temp. (°F)	***85***	***96***	94	97	***102***	***115***	***113***	***110***	***111***	98	92	86	***115***
Extreme Minimum Temp. (°F)	***2***	***3***	9	24	***35***	***48***	***56***	***52***	***33***	21	19	-8	***-8***
Days Maximum Temp. ≥ 90°F	***0***	***0***	0	1	6	18	28	27	15	3	0	0	***98***
Days Maximum Temp. ≤ 32°F	***1***	***0***	0	0	0	0	0	0	0	0	0	1	***2***
Days Minimum Temp. ≤ 32°F	***18***	***11***	6	1	0	0	0	0	0	0	7	16	***59***
Days Minimum Temp. ≤ 0°F	***0***	***0***	0	0	0	0	0	0	0	0	0	0	***0***
Heating Degree Days (base 65°F)	***636***	***478***	319	113	19	1	0	0	13	98	329	612	***2,618***
Cooling Degree Days (base 65°F)	***1***	***3***	23	81	240	431	587	570	336	106	17	2	***2,397***
Mean Precipitation (in.)	1.55	2.40	2.85	2.74	5.21	4.12	1.95	1.90	3.07	4.57	2.34	2.13	34.83
Extreme Maximum Daily Precip. (in.)	1.70	***2.44***	2.85	3.38	6.00	3.74	4.75	2.90	4.43	8.09	2.72	3.08	***8.09***
Days With ≥ 0.1" Precipitation	3	4	4	4	6	5	3	3	4	5	4	4	49
Days With ≥ 0.5" Precipitation	1	2	2	2	3	3	1	1	2	3	2	1	23
Days With ≥ 1.0" Precipitation	0	1	1	1	2	2	1	1	1	1	1	1	13
Mean Snowfall (in.)	0.3	0.8	0.1	0.1	0.0	0.0	0.0	0.0	0.0	0.0	0.2	0.3	1.8
Maximum Snow Depth (in.)	2	5	6	2	0	0	0	0	0	0	1	1	6
Days With ≥ 1.0" Snow Depth	0	0	0	0	0	0	0	0	0	0	0	0	0

Brownfield 2 *Terry County* Elevation: 3,299 ft. Latitude: 33° 11' N Longitude: 102° 16' W

	JAN	FEB	MAR	APR	MAY	JUN	JUL	AUG	SEP	OCT	NOV	DEC	YEAR
Mean Maximum Temp. (°F)	55.0	59.9	67.3	76.0	84.2	90.9	92.8	91.3	84.9	76.2	64.5	55.2	74.8
Mean Temp. (°F)	41.1	45.0	51.7	60.0	69.4	77.0	79.6	78.3	71.4	61.7	50.1	41.5	60.6
Mean Minimum Temp. (°F)	27.1	30.1	36.1	43.9	54.5	63.0	66.3	65.2	57.8	47.1	35.7	27.7	46.2
Extreme Maximum Temp. (°F)	81	86	95	98	110	111	108	106	103	101	88	82	111
Extreme Minimum Temp. (°F)	5	2	9	23	36	45	56	52	36	19	9	-1	-1
Days Maximum Temp. ≥ 90°F	0	0	0	2	10	19	24	21	9	2	0	0	87
Days Maximum Temp. ≤ 32°F	2	1	0	0	0	0	0	0	0	0	0	2	5
Days Minimum Temp. ≤ 32°F	25	17	10	2	0	0	0	0	0	1	10	23	88
Days Minimum Temp. ≤ 0°F	0	0	0	0	0	0	0	0	0	0	0	0	0
Heating Degree Days (base 65°F)	734	559	409	184	40	2	0	0	22	150	442	721	3,263
Cooling Degree Days (base 65°F)	0	1	5	40	183	367	460	418	221	54	2	0	1,751
Mean Precipitation (in.)	0.64	0.68	0.96	1.08	2.81	2.98	2.09	1.89	2.54	1.60	0.94	0.79	19.00
Extreme Maximum Daily Precip. (in.)	1.90	1.21	2.04	2.09	4.37	2.62	2.63	3.38	4.53	5.05	2.57	1.24	5.05
Days With ≥ 0.1" Precipitation	2	2	2	2	4	4	4	4	4	3	2	2	35
Days With ≥ 0.5" Precipitation	0	0	1	1	2	2	1	1	2	1	1	1	13
Days With ≥ 1.0" Precipitation	0	0	0	0	1	1	1	1	1	0	0	0	5
Mean Snowfall (in.)	2.1	1.5	0.2	0.2	0.0	0.0	0.0	0.0	0.0	trace	0.6	1.6	6.2
Maximum Snow Depth (in.)	***12***	3	4	trace	0	0	0	0	0	trace	4	6	***12***
Days With ≥ 1.0" Snow Depth	1	0	0	0	0	0	0	0	0	0	0	1	2

Brownwood *Brown County* Elevation: 1,384 ft. Latitude: 31° 41' N Longitude: 98° 58' W

	JAN	FEB	MAR	APR	MAY	JUN	JUL	AUG	SEP	OCT	NOV	DEC	YEAR
Mean Maximum Temp. (°F)	60.3	64.0	71.2	79.5	85.9	91.7	96.0	96.6	89.6	80.4	69.4	60.9	78.8
Mean Temp. (°F)	46.1	50.0	57.3	65.1	73.2	79.5	83.1	83.4	76.2	66.2	55.8	46.7	65.2
Mean Minimum Temp. (°F)	31.9	35.9	43.1	50.7	60.5	67.3	70.2	70.1	62.7	51.9	42.1	32.5	51.6
Extreme Maximum Temp. (°F)	90	98	95	102	105	106	109	110	109	100	91	89	110
Extreme Minimum Temp. (°F)	2	6	10	26	39	51	53	51	37	21	16	-6	-6
Days Maximum Temp. ≥ 90°F	0	0	1	4	10	21	28	27	17	4	0	0	112
Days Maximum Temp. ≤ 32°F	0	0	0	0	0	0	0	0	0	0	0	1	1
Days Minimum Temp. ≤ 32°F	18	10	5	1	0	0	0	0	0	1	6	16	57
Days Minimum Temp. ≤ 0°F	0	0	0	0	0	0	0	0	0	0	0	0	0
Heating Degree Days (base 65°F)	579	423	259	92	10	1	0	0	6	81	291	561	2,303
Cooling Degree Days (base 65°F)	1	4	27	103	273	444	570	576	348	124	21	1	2,492
Mean Precipitation (in.)	1.32	2.36	2.62	2.24	3.97	4.66	1.84	2.36	2.97	2.96	1.79	1.61	30.70
Extreme Maximum Daily Precip. (in.)	1.85	3.49	3.62	2.26	2.88	***6.60***	2.57	5.73	***3.32***	***3.20***	2.07	2.80	***6.60***
Days With ≥ 0.1" Precipitation	3	3	4	3	5	5	3	3	4	4	3	3	43
Days With ≥ 0.5" Precipitation	1	2	2	1	3	3	1	2	2	2	1	1	21
Days With ≥ 1.0" Precipitation	0	1	1	0	1	2	1	1	1	1	1	0	10
Mean Snowfall (in.)	0.4	trace	trace	0.1	0.0	0.0	0.0	0.0	0.0	0.0	0.1	0.3	0.9
Maximum Snow Depth (in.)	6	trace	0	3	0	0	0	0	***0***	***0***	trace	3	***6***
Days With ≥ 1.0" Snow Depth	0	0	0	0	0	0	0	0	0	0	0	0	0

The period of record for all cooperative weather station data is 1980 – 2009. See User Guide for detailed explanation of data.

Burnet *Burnet County* Elevation: 1,274 ft. Latitude: 30° 44' N Longitude: 98° 14' W

	JAN	FEB	MAR	APR	MAY	JUN	JUL	AUG	SEP	OCT	NOV	DEC	YEAR
Mean Maximum Temp. (°F)	59.6	62.7	69.5	77.6	83.6	89.5	93.3	94.2	87.9	79.0	68.6	59.6	77.1
Mean Temp. (°F)	47.3	50.4	57.4	65.4	72.9	78.7	82.2	82.4	76.3	66.8	56.8	47.8	65.4
Mean Minimum Temp. (°F)	35.0	38.1	45.3	53.2	62.2	68.2	71.1	70.6	64.5	55.0	45.0	35.9	53.7
Extreme Maximum Temp. (°F)	87	97	95	100	101	106	103	105	108	96	92	84	108
Extreme Minimum Temp. (°F)	5	-1	12	27	38	50	58	50	38	22	17	-4	-4
Days Maximum Temp. ≥ 90°F	0	0	0	1	6	16	25	26	13	2	0	0	89
Days Maximum Temp. ≤ 32°F	0	0	0	0	0	0	0	0	0	0	0	1	1
Days Minimum Temp. ≤ 32°F	13	8	3	0	0	0	0	0	0	0	4	11	39
Days Minimum Temp. ≤ 0°F	0	0	0	0	0	0	0	0	0	0	0	0	0
Heating Degree Days (base 65°F)	542	411	253	82	9	0	0	0	7	71	263	529	2,167
Cooling Degree Days (base 65°F)	2	6	26	103	261	419	541	547	352	134	25	3	2,419
Mean Precipitation (in.)	1.65	2.05	2.76	2.14	4.25	4.58	2.00	1.75	3.38	3.71	2.75	2.06	33.08
Extreme Maximum Daily Precip. (in.)	1.95	1.98	2.80	3.30	4.02	5.65	3.00	3.01	6.10	6.10	3.85	4.52	6.10
Days With ≥ 0.1" Precipitation	4	4	5	3	5	5	3	3	4	5	4	4	49
Days With ≥ 0.5" Precipitation	1	2	2	2	3	3	1	1	2	2	2	1	22
Days With ≥ 1.0" Precipitation	0	1	1	1	1	2	1	1	1	1	1	1	12
Mean Snowfall (in.)	trace	trace	0.0	0.0	0.0	0.0	0.0	0.0	0.0	0.0	0.1	0.0	0.1
Maximum Snow Depth (in.)	0	0	0	0	0	0	0	0	0	0	0	0	0
Days With ≥ 1.0" Snow Depth	0	0	0	0	0	0	0	0	0	0	0	0	0

Cameron *Milam County* Elevation: 363 ft. Latitude: 30° 51' N Longitude: 96° 58' W

	JAN	FEB	MAR	APR	MAY	JUN	JUL	AUG	SEP	OCT	NOV	DEC	YEAR
Mean Maximum Temp. (°F)	61.3	64.8	71.6	78.8	84.6	90.0	93.9	94.9	89.5	80.7	70.7	62.4	78.6
Mean Temp. (°F)	50.2	53.7	60.6	67.7	74.8	80.4	83.4	83.8	78.4	69.4	59.8	51.2	67.8
Mean Minimum Temp. (°F)	39.1	42.5	49.4	56.5	65.0	70.8	72.9	72.7	67.2	58.1	48.8	40.0	56.9
Extreme Maximum Temp. (°F)	85	98	96	95	100	105	104	107	110	96	89	85	110
Extreme Minimum Temp. (°F)	8	10	17	28	40	56	61	58	44	27	17	2	2
Days Maximum Temp. ≥ 90°F	0	0	0	1	6	18	25	26	16	3	0	0	95
Days Maximum Temp. ≤ 32°F	0	0	0	0	0	0	0	0	0	0	0	0	0
Days Minimum Temp. ≤ 32°F	9	5	2	0	0	0	0	0	0	0	2	8	26
Days Minimum Temp. ≤ 0°F	0	0	0	0	0	0	0	0	0	0	0	0	0
Heating Degree Days (base 65°F)	460	331	186	55	4	0	0	0	3	45	204	437	1,725
Cooling Degree Days (base 65°F)	9	18	56	143	316	469	578	591	410	189	54	15	2,848
Mean Precipitation (in.)	2.31	2.64	2.69	2.39	5.26	3.65	1.95	2.14	2.92	4.00	3.33	2.88	36.16
Extreme Maximum Daily Precip. (in.)	2.66	3.03	2.73	6.90	6.00	3.40	4.67	2.86	4.00	7.00	3.34	6.08	7.00
Days With ≥ 0.1" Precipitation	5	4	5	4	6	6	3	3	4	5	5	5	55
Days With ≥ 0.5" Precipitation	1	2	2	2	3	2	1	1	2	2	2	2	22
Days With ≥ 1.0" Precipitation	1	1	1	1	2	1	1	1	1	1	1	1	13
Mean Snowfall (in.)	trace	trace	trace	0.0	0.0	0.0	0.0	0.0	0.0	0.0	0.0	0.0	trace
Maximum Snow Depth (in.)	0	trace	trace	0	0	0	0	0	0	0	0	0	trace
Days With ≥ 1.0" Snow Depth	0	0	0	0	0	0	0	0	0	0	0	0	0

Camp Wood *Real County* Elevation: 1,470 ft. Latitude: 29° 41' N Longitude: 100° 01' W

	JAN	FEB	MAR	APR	MAY	JUN	JUL	AUG	SEP	OCT	NOV	DEC	YEAR
Mean Maximum Temp. (°F)	62.1	65.7	72.5	79.7	86.0	90.8	93.7	94.1	***89.4***	***80.3***	70.6	62.6	***79.0***
Mean Temp. (°F)	48.1	51.6	58.8	66.2	74.2	79.5	81.8	81.8	***76.8***	***67.7***	57.1	48.7	***66.0***
Mean Minimum Temp. (°F)	34.0	37.3	45.0	52.6	62.3	68.1	69.9	69.4	***64.2***	***55.0***	43.6	34.8	***53.0***
Extreme Maximum Temp. (°F)	89	96	96	101	105	108	106	109	109	***96***	93	87	***109***
Extreme Minimum Temp. (°F)	11	5	12	26	40	49	55	59	42	***26***	20	5	***5***
Days Maximum Temp. ≥ 90°F	0	0	1	3	9	19	25	26	16	***3***	0	0	***102***
Days Maximum Temp. ≤ 32°F	0	0	0	0	0	0	0	0	0	0	0	0	0
Days Minimum Temp. ≤ 32°F	15	9	4	1	0	0	0	0	0	0	5	14	48
Days Minimum Temp. ≤ 0°F	0	0	0	0	0	0	0	0	0	0	0	0	0
Heating Degree Days (base 65°F)	518	376	217	73	4	0	0	0	***5***	***53***	255	500	***2,001***
Cooling Degree Days (base 65°F)	1	3	32	115	296	442	528	527	***365***	***143***	24	2	***2,478***
Mean Precipitation (in.)	1.22	1.40	2.05	1.96	3.10	3.73	2.30	2.45	3.35	3.35	2.49	1.45	28.85
Extreme Maximum Daily Precip. (in.)	1.89	3.10	4.08	5.57	3.02	5.10	4.46	4.75	***3.95***	4.50	8.37	3.76	***8.37***
Days With ≥ 0.1" Precipitation	3	3	3	3	5	5	4	3	4	4	3	3	43
Days With ≥ 0.5" Precipitation	1	1	1	1	2	2	1	1	2	2	1	1	16
Days With ≥ 1.0" Precipitation	0	0	1	0	1	1	1	1	1	1	1	0	8
Mean Snowfall (in.)	0.1	0.1	0.0	0.0	0.0	0.0	0.0	0.0	0.0	0.0	0.1	0.0	0.3
Maximum Snow Depth (in.)	10	4	0	0	0	0	0	0	0	***0***	0	1	***10***
Days With ≥ 1.0" Snow Depth	0	0	0	0	0	0	0	0	0	***0***	0	0	***0***

Candelaria *Presidio County* Elevation: 2,875 ft. Latitude: 30° 08' N Longitude: 104° 41' W

	JAN	FEB	MAR	APR	MAY	JUN	JUL	AUG	SEP	OCT	NOV	DEC	YEAR
Mean Maximum Temp. (°F)	66.7	72.8	80.6	88.9	96.4	101.4	99.9	97.7	93.4	85.8	74.4	66.6	85.4
Mean Temp. (°F)	49.1	54.3	60.7	68.6	76.8	83.7	84.4	82.6	77.8	68.5	56.3	49.1	67.6
Mean Minimum Temp. (°F)	31.5	35.7	40.8	48.3	57.2	65.9	68.8	67.4	62.2	51.2	38.2	31.5	49.9
Extreme Maximum Temp. (°F)	85	92	99	103	109	115	114	110	109	103	93	86	115
Extreme Minimum Temp. (°F)	9	14	16	21	35	49	56	50	37	22	15	6	6
Days Maximum Temp. ≥ 90°F	0	0	3	16	27	29	30	27	23	10	0	0	165
Days Maximum Temp. ≤ 32°F	0	0	0	0	0	0	0	0	0	0	0	0	0
Days Minimum Temp. ≤ 32°F	17	10	5	1	0	0	0	0	0	0	7	17	57
Days Minimum Temp. ≤ 0°F	0	0	0	0	0	0	0	0	0	0	0	0	0
Heating Degree Days (base 65°F)	486	299	154	33	1	0	0	0	1	34	261	487	1,756
Cooling Degree Days (base 65°F)	0	4	29	147	373	566	607	551	391	151	6	0	2,825
Mean Precipitation (in.)	0.51	0.47	0.36	0.53	0.72	1.95	2.12	2.56	2.02	1.47	0.46	0.58	13.75
Extreme Maximum Daily Precip. (in.)	0.90	1.12	1.25	1.42	1.83	2.50	1.80	2.62	2.21	3.43	2.05	1.27	3.43
Days With ≥ 0.1" Precipitation	1	1	1	1	2	4	5	5	4	3	1	1	29
Days With ≥ 0.5" Precipitation	0	0	0	0	0	1	2	2	1	1	0	0	7
Days With ≥ 1.0" Precipitation	0	0	0	0	0	0	0	0	0	0	0	0	0
Mean Snowfall (in.)	0.1	0.0	0.0	trace	0.0	0.0	0.0	0.0	0.0	0.0	trace	0.0	0.1
Maximum Snow Depth (in.)	0	0	0	trace	0	0	0	0	0	0	0	0	trace
Days With ≥ 1.0" Snow Depth	0	0	0	0	0	0	0	0	0	0	0	0	0

Canyon *Randall County* Elevation: 3,589 ft. Latitude: 34° 59' N Longitude: 101° 56' W

	JAN	FEB	MAR	APR	MAY	JUN	JUL	AUG	SEP	OCT	NOV	DEC	YEAR
Mean Maximum Temp. (°F)	52.8	57.3	65.2	73.8	82.2	90.0	92.7	90.5	84.5	74.6	62.2	52.6	73.2
Mean Temp. (°F)	38.7	42.4	49.8	58.2	67.6	75.9	79.6	77.8	70.7	60.1	47.9	38.8	59.0
Mean Minimum Temp. (°F)	24.6	27.4	34.3	42.5	52.9	61.8	66.3	65.0	57.0	45.5	33.6	25.2	44.7
Extreme Maximum Temp. (°F)	79	82	93	97	103	109	106	104	103	98	87	82	109
Extreme Minimum Temp. (°F)	-3	-11	5	19	27	44	51	51	29	15	5	-6	-11
Days Maximum Temp. ≥ 90°F	0	0	0	1	7	17	23	20	9	1	0	0	78
Days Maximum Temp. ≤ 32°F	2	2	0	0	0	0	0	0	0	0	0	2	6
Days Minimum Temp. ≤ 32°F	26	19	12	3	0	0	0	0	0	2	13	24	99
Days Minimum Temp. ≤ 0°F	0	0	0	0	0	0	0	0	0	0	0	0	0
Heating Degree Days (base 65°F)	808	633	469	226	57	2	0	0	30	184	506	805	3,720
Cooling Degree Days (base 65°F)	0	0	4	28	145	337	458	403	209	38	1	0	1,623
Mean Precipitation (in.)	0.56	0.48	1.10	1.05	2.50	3.33	2.11	3.13	2.23	1.88	0.72	0.65	19.74
Extreme Maximum Daily Precip. (in.)	1.15	1.22	2.10	2.11	3.80	4.57	2.50	3.20	7.18	2.58	1.10	1.28	7.18
Days With ≥ 0.1" Precipitation	1	1	2	2	4	5	4	5	3	3	2	2	34
Days With ≥ 0.5" Precipitation	0	0	1	1	2	2	1	2	1	1	0	0	11
Days With ≥ 1.0" Precipitation	0	0	0	0	1	1	1	1	1	1	0	0	6
Mean Snowfall (in.)	2.6	1.9	1.1	0.4	0.1	0.0	0.0	0.0	0.0	trace	1.4	3.0	10.5
Maximum Snow Depth (in.)	11	16	4	1	0	0	0	0	0	trace	6	14	16
Days With ≥ 1.0" Snow Depth	1	1	0	0	0	0	0	0	0	0	0	1	3

Carrizo Springs *Dimmit County* Elevation: 612 ft. Latitude: 28° 29' N Longitude: 99° 52' W

	JAN	FEB	MAR	APR	MAY	JUN	JUL	AUG	SEP	OCT	NOV	DEC	YEAR
Mean Maximum Temp. (°F)	66.6	71.0	78.1	85.7	91.6	96.6	98.6	98.9	93.2	85.0	75.1	66.1	83.9
Mean Temp. (°F)	53.7	57.7	65.0	72.7	79.7	84.8	86.5	86.7	81.4	72.8	62.4	53.3	71.4
Mean Minimum Temp. (°F)	40.7	44.6	51.8	59.6	67.7	73.1	74.5	74.6	69.5	60.5	49.7	40.6	58.9
Extreme Maximum Temp. (°F)	90	101	105	111	109	111	110	109	111	103	96	92	111
Extreme Minimum Temp. (°F)	18	16	21	34	47	61	66	62	49	31	***25***	***10***	***10***
Days Maximum Temp. ≥ 90°F	0	1	3	11	19	26	27	29	23	10	1	0	150
Days Maximum Temp. ≤ 32°F	0	0	0	0	0	0	0	0	0	0	0	0	0
Days Minimum Temp. ≤ 32°F	6	3	1	0	0	0	0	0	0	0	1	8	19
Days Minimum Temp. ≤ 0°F	0	0	0	0	0	0	0	0	0	0	0	0	0
Heating Degree Days (base 65°F)	355	230	104	22	1	0	0	0	1	24	141	367	1,245
Cooling Degree Days (base 65°F)	11	30	111	259	463	602	674	681	499	273	73	12	3,688
Mean Precipitation (in.)	1.06	0.98	1.15	1.36	2.89	2.12	1.86	1.68	2.26	2.13	1.27	0.77	19.53
Extreme Maximum Daily Precip. (in.)	1.30	3.40	2.18	1.96	***5.17***	3.40	8.78	***4.38***	3.59	4.35	***1.94***	0.92	***8.78***
Days With ≥ 0.1" Precipitation	2	2	2	2	3	3	3	2	4	3	2	2	30
Days With ≥ 0.5" Precipitation	1	0	1	1	2	1	1	1	1	1	1	0	11
Days With ≥ 1.0" Precipitation	0	0	0	0	1	1	0	0	1	1	0	0	4
Mean Snowfall (in.)	0.0	0.0	0.0	0.0	0.0	0.0	0.0	0.0	0.0	0.0	0.0	0.0	0.0
Maximum Snow Depth (in.)	0	0	0	0	0	0	0	0	0	0	trace	0	trace
Days With ≥ 1.0" Snow Depth	0	0	0	0	0	0	0	0	0	0	0	0	0

Carthage *Panola County* Elevation: 339 ft. Latitude: 32° 08' N Longitude: 94° 21' W

	JAN	FEB	MAR	APR	MAY	JUN	JUL	AUG	SEP	OCT	NOV	DEC	YEAR
Mean Maximum Temp. (°F)	56.8	61.8	69.5	76.1	83.0	***89.6***	***93.6***	***94.0***	87.9	78.0	67.4	58.5	***76.4***
Mean Temp. (°F)	45.9	50.0	57.4	63.8	72.0	***78.9***	***82.4***	***82.2***	75.6	65.3	55.5	47.2	***64.7***
Mean Minimum Temp. (°F)	34.9	38.2	45.2	51.5	60.9	***68.2***	***71.2***	***70.3***	63.3	52.5	43.6	36.0	***53.0***
Extreme Maximum Temp. (°F)	81	90	89	93	98	101	106	108	109	95	86	82	109
Extreme Minimum Temp. (°F)	5	10	18	28	40	45	56	50	38	26	19	1	1
Days Maximum Temp. ≥ 90°F	0	0	0	0	4	17	26	26	13	2	0	0	88
Days Maximum Temp. ≤ 32°F	1	0	0	0	0	0	0	0	0	0	0	1	2
Days Minimum Temp. ≤ 32°F	14	9	3	0	0	0	0	0	0	0	4	13	43
Days Minimum Temp. ≤ 0°F	0	0	0	0	0	0	0	0	0	0	0	0	0
Heating Degree Days (base 65°F)	589	425	260	110	12	***0***	***0***	***0***	9	93	297	549	***2,344***
Cooling Degree Days (base 65°F)	3	7	31	82	236	***426***	***547***	***539***	334	109	20	6	***2,340***
Mean Precipitation (in.)	4.28	4.44	4.16	3.97	4.77	4.91	3.12	3.09	3.61	5.09	4.79	5.13	51.36
Extreme Maximum Daily Precip. (in.)	6.31	3.45	5.54	9.25	3.73	6.72	4.78	5.87	4.10	6.82	7.14	4.65	9.25
Days With ≥ 0.1" Precipitation	6	6	6	4	6	5	4	4	5	5	6	6	63
Days With ≥ 0.5" Precipitation	3	3	3	2	3	3	2	2	2	3	3	3	32
Days With ≥ 1.0" Precipitation	1	2	1	1	2	1	1	1	1	2	2	2	17
Mean Snowfall (in.)	0.4	0.2	0.1	trace	0.0	0.0	0.0	0.0	0.0	0.0	trace	0.2	0.9
Maximum Snow Depth (in.)	3	3	2	trace	0	0	0	0	0	0	0	trace	3
Days With ≥ 1.0" Snow Depth	0	0	0	0	0	0	0	0	0	0	0	0	0

Castolon *Brewster County* Elevation: 2,167 ft. Latitude: 29° 08' N Longitude: 103° 30' W

	JAN	FEB	MAR	APR	MAY	JUN	JUL	AUG	SEP	OCT	NOV	DEC	YEAR
Mean Maximum Temp. (°F)	68.1	74.4	82.8	91.4	99.6	103.6	102.3	100.6	96.2	88.0	77.3	68.1	87.7
Mean Temp. (°F)	51.4	57.4	65.3	73.7	83.0	88.4	88.3	86.9	82.1	72.8	60.8	51.8	71.8
Mean Minimum Temp. (°F)	34.6	40.4	47.8	56.2	66.4	73.1	74.3	73.2	68.2	57.5	44.3	35.4	55.9
Extreme Maximum Temp. (°F)	90	97	105	109	114	117	115	114	110	105	99	90	117
Extreme Minimum Temp. (°F)	15	15	23	29	44	58	60	64	47	29	21	7	7
Days Maximum Temp. ≥ 90°F	0	1	8	19	28	29	30	29	25	15	2	0	186
Days Maximum Temp. ≤ 32°F	0	0	0	0	0	0	0	0	0	0	0	0	0
Days Minimum Temp. ≤ 32°F	12	3	1	0	0	0	0	0	0	0	2	11	29
Days Minimum Temp. ≤ 0°F	0	0	0	0	0	0	0	0	0	0	0	0	0
Heating Degree Days (base 65°F)	414	224	88	18	0	0	0	0	1	20	161	405	1,331
Cooling Degree Days (base 65°F)	0	17	105	287	566	708	730	687	522	268	42	1	3,933
Mean Precipitation (in.)	0.42	0.32	0.27	0.42	0.97	1.46	1.67	1.73	1.44	1.24	0.42	0.32	10.68
Extreme Maximum Daily Precip. (in.)	0.68	1.14	0.64	1.61	1.66	1.92	1.49	1.90	1.65	3.95	1.33	0.63	3.95
Days With ≥ 0.1" Precipitation	1	1	1	1	2	3	3	4	3	2	1	1	23
Days With ≥ 0.5" Precipitation	0	0	0	0	1	1	1	1	1	1	0	0	6
Days With ≥ 1.0" Precipitation	0	0	0	0	0	0	0	0	0	0	0	0	0
Mean Snowfall (in.)	0.1	trace	trace	0.0	0.0	0.0	0.0	0.0	0.0	0.0	trace	trace	0.1
Maximum Snow Depth (in.)	3	trace	trace	0	0	0	0	0	0	0	trace	trace	3
Days With ≥ 1.0" Snow Depth	0	0	0	0	0	0	0	0	0	0	0	0	0

The period of record for all cooperative weather station data is 1980 – 2009. See User Guide for detailed explanation of data.

Centerville *Leon County* Elevation: 319 ft. Latitude: 31° 15' N Longitude: 95° 58' W

	JAN	FEB	MAR	APR	MAY	JUN	JUL	AUG	SEP	OCT	NOV	DEC	YEAR
Mean Maximum Temp. (°F)	59.0	62.8	70.0	77.3	84.0	90.3	94.1	95.0	89.1	79.4	69.2	60.2	77.5
Mean Temp. (°F)	47.3	50.9	57.9	65.1	73.1	79.5	82.8	82.9	76.7	66.5	57.1	48.5	65.7
Mean Minimum Temp. (°F)	35.6	39.0	45.7	52.8	62.1	68.7	71.4	70.8	64.3	53.5	45.0	36.7	53.8
Extreme Maximum Temp. (°F)	83	94	91	94	98	106	105	107	110	96	88	84	110
Extreme Minimum Temp. (°F)	5	12	15	26	39	49	56	52	42	27	18	1	1
Days Maximum Temp. ≥ 90°F	0	0	0	1	5	18	27	27	16	3	0	0	97
Days Maximum Temp. ≤ 32°F	0	0	0	0	0	0	0	0	0	0	0	1	1
Days Minimum Temp. ≤ 32°F	13	8	3	1	0	0	0	0	0	0	4	13	42
Days Minimum Temp. ≤ 0°F	0	0	0	0	0	0	0	0	0	0	0	0	0
Heating Degree Days (base 65°F)	546	401	248	93	10	0	0	0	6	78	264	515	2,161
Cooling Degree Days (base 65°F)	5	8	34	101	267	442	559	562	365	130	33	9	2,515
Mean Precipitation (in.)	3.27	3.44	3.77	2.83	4.84	4.06	2.50	2.65	2.82	4.98	3.85	3.66	42.67
Extreme Maximum Daily Precip. (in.)	3.77	3.00	2.87	3.01	5.21	4.14	3.75	7.25	3.60	6.00	3.40	3.55	7.25
Days With ≥ 0.1" Precipitation	5	5	5	4	5	6	4	4	5	5	5	5	58
Days With ≥ 0.5" Precipitation	2	2	3	2	3	2	2	2	2	3	3	3	29
Days With ≥ 1.0" Precipitation	1	1	1	1	2	1	1	1	1	2	1	1	14
Mean Snowfall (in.)	0.2	0.2	trace	0.1	0.0	0.0	0.0	0.0	0.0	0.0	0.0	0.0	0.5
Maximum Snow Depth (in.)	0	trace	0	0	0	0	0	0	0	0	0	0	trace
Days With ≥ 1.0" Snow Depth	0	0	0	0	0	0	0	0	0	0	0	0	0

Charlotte 5 NNW *Atascosa County* Elevation: 440 ft. Latitude: 28° 56' N Longitude: 98° 45' W

	JAN	FEB	MAR	APR	MAY	JUN	JUL	AUG	SEP	OCT	NOV	DEC	YEAR
Mean Maximum Temp. (°F)	67.7	71.7	77.9	84.7	89.9	94.5	96.8	97.5	92.5	85.3	76.1	68.0	83.6
Mean Temp. (°F)	54.9	58.7	65.0	71.8	78.5	83.1	84.9	85.1	80.7	73.1	63.8	55.7	71.3
Mean Minimum Temp. (°F)	42.1	45.6	52.0	58.7	67.1	71.7	72.9	72.7	68.9	60.8	51.4	43.5	58.9
Extreme Maximum Temp. (°F)	88	100	99	107	104	109	106	105	110	99	97	89	110
Extreme Minimum Temp. (°F)	15	14	17	28	44	54	59	60	46	27	23	6	6
Days Maximum Temp. ≥ 90°F	0	1	2	7	17	25	29	30	22	10	1	0	144
Days Maximum Temp. ≤ 32°F	0	0	0	0	0	0	0	0	0	0	0	0	0
Days Minimum Temp. ≤ 32°F	6	3	1	0	0	0	0	0	0	0	1	6	17
Days Minimum Temp. ≤ 0°F	0	0	0	0	0	0	0	0	0	0	0	0	0
Heating Degree Days (base 65°F)	325	212	103	24	1	0	0	0	1	19	125	308	1,118
Cooling Degree Days (base 65°F)	18	40	109	233	427	551	624	631	478	277	96	29	3,513
Mean Precipitation (in.)	1.32	1.63	1.96	1.86	3.03	3.28	2.20	2.18	2.82	3.13	1.88	1.52	26.81
Extreme Maximum Daily Precip. (in.)	2.25	4.48	3.27	3.52	6.70	4.15	5.50	4.60	5.04	4.31	5.35	4.27	6.70
Days With ≥ 0.1" Precipitation	3	3	3	3	4	4	3	3	4	4	3	3	40
Days With ≥ 0.5" Precipitation	1	1	1	1	2	2	1	1	2	2	1	1	16
Days With ≥ 1.0" Precipitation	0	0	1	1	1	1	1	1	1	1	1	0	9
Mean Snowfall (in.)	0.0	0.0	0.0	0.0	0.0	0.0	0.0	0.0	0.0	trace	0.0	trace	trace
Maximum Snow Depth (in.)	7	0	0	0	0	0	0	0	0	trace	0	trace	7
Days With ≥ 1.0" Snow Depth	0	0	0	0	0	0	0	0	0	0	0	0	0

Childress Municipal Arpt *Childress County* Elevation: 1,951 ft. Latitude: 34° 26' N Longitude: 100° 17' W

	JAN	FEB	MAR	APR	MAY	JUN	JUL	AUG	SEP	OCT	NOV	DEC	YEAR
Mean Maximum Temp. (°F)	53.7	57.6	66.4	76.1	83.2	90.5	95.1	94.3	86.1	75.6	64.0	53.6	74.7
Mean Temp. (°F)	40.8	44.4	52.8	62.1	70.7	78.4	82.8	81.9	73.6	62.6	51.1	41.3	61.9
Mean Minimum Temp. (°F)	27.8	31.3	39.2	48.0	58.1	66.2	70.5	69.4	61.0	49.5	38.2	29.0	49.0
Extreme Maximum Temp. (°F)	87	93	100	100	111	117	110	107	107	103	93	84	117
Extreme Minimum Temp. (°F)	3	-5	10	25	37	50	55	55	34	21	9	-5	-5
Days Maximum Temp. ≥ 90°F	0	0	1	4	8	18	26	24	12	2	0	0	95
Days Maximum Temp. ≤ 32°F	2	2	0	0	0	0	0	0	0	0	0	2	6
Days Minimum Temp. ≤ 32°F	23	16	7	1	0	0	0	0	0	1	8	20	76
Days Minimum Temp. ≤ 0°F	0	0	0	0	0	0	0	0	0	0	0	0	0
Heating Degree Days (base 65°F)	744	576	385	150	32	1	0	0	19	140	417	728	3,192
Cooling Degree Days (base 65°F)	0	1	16	69	214	409	560	534	284	71	7	0	2,165
Mean Precipitation (in.)	0.66	0.89	1.56	1.78	3.17	4.08	1.90	2.47	2.41	2.14	1.30	0.93	23.29
Extreme Maximum Daily Precip. (in.)	1.41	1.07	2.92	1.64	2.79	4.46	2.97	4.53	5.16	5.32	2.28	2.03	5.32
Days With ≥ 0.1" Precipitation	2	2	3	4	5	6	4	4	4	3	3	2	42
Days With ≥ 0.5" Precipitation	0	1	1	1	2	3	1	2	1	1	1	0	14
Days With ≥ 1.0" Precipitation	0	0	0	0	1	1	0	1	1	1	0	0	5
Mean Snowfall (in.)	na	na	na	na	na	na	na	na	na	na	na	na	na
Maximum Snow Depth (in.)	na	na	na	na	na	na	na	na	na	na	na	na	na
Days With ≥ 1.0" Snow Depth	na	na	na	na	na	na	na	na	na	na	na	na	na

Clarendon *Donley County* Elevation: 2,703 ft. Latitude: 34° 56' N Longitude: 100° 53' W

	JAN	FEB	MAR	APR	MAY	JUN	JUL	AUG	SEP	OCT	NOV	DEC	YEAR
Mean Maximum Temp. (°F)	52.8	56.6	64.4	73.3	81.3	89.1	94.7	93.0	85.2	74.5	62.8	52.7	73.4
Mean Temp. (°F)	38.4	41.9	49.4	58.1	67.3	75.6	80.5	79.1	71.0	59.7	48.2	38.7	59.0
Mean Minimum Temp. (°F)	24.0	27.2	34.3	42.8	53.2	62.2	66.3	65.1	56.9	44.9	33.5	24.8	44.6
Extreme Maximum Temp. (°F)	84	89	98	100	109	112	110	107	108	104	92	83	112
Extreme Minimum Temp. (°F)	-3	-7	2	21	31	42	48	48	30	17	10	-11	-11
Days Maximum Temp. ≥ 90°F	0	0	0	2	7	15	25	23	10	2	0	0	84
Days Maximum Temp. ≤ 32°F	3	2	1	0	0	0	0	0	0	0	1	3	10
Days Minimum Temp. ≤ 32°F	27	20	13	3	0	0	0	0	0	2	14	26	105
Days Minimum Temp. ≤ 0°F	0	0	0	0	0	0	0	0	0	0	0	0	0
Heating Degree Days (base 65°F)	818	645	482	235	63	4	0	0	33	200	502	807	3,789
Cooling Degree Days (base 65°F)	0	0	5	33	141	330	487	444	221	42	4	0	1,707
Mean Precipitation (in.)	0.72	0.77	1.48	2.17	3.30	3.56	2.02	3.06	2.46	2.12	1.05	1.01	23.72
Extreme Maximum Daily Precip. (in.)	1.29	1.28	2.14	8.71	9.25	4.46	3.08	3.23	2.28	3.47	2.58	1.72	9.25
Days With ≥ 0.1" Precipitation	2	2	3	3	5	5	3	5	4	3	2	2	39
Days With ≥ 0.5" Precipitation	0	0	1	1	2	2	1	2	2	1	1	1	14
Days With ≥ 1.0" Precipitation	0	0	0	1	1	1	1	1	1	1	0	0	7
Mean Snowfall (in.)	1.7	0.6	0.7	0.3	0.0	0.0	0.0	0.0	0.0	0.0	0.7	2.3	6.3
Maximum Snow Depth (in.)	6	14	9	0	0	0	0	0	0	0	0	12	14
Days With ≥ 1.0" Snow Depth	1	1	0	0	0	0	0	0	0	0	0	1	3

The period of record for all cooperative weather station data is 1980 – 2009. See User Guide for detailed explanation of data.

Cleveland *Liberty County* Elevation: 195 ft. Latitude: 30° 22' N Longitude: 95° 06' W

	JAN	FEB	MAR	APR	MAY	JUN	JUL	AUG	SEP	OCT	NOV	DEC	YEAR
Mean Maximum Temp. (°F)	60.8	64.6	71.6	77.6	84.0	89.3	92.2	93.2	88.3	79.5	69.6	61.8	77.7
Mean Temp. (°F)	49.8	53.2	60.0	66.3	73.9	79.5	82.1	82.3	77.3	68.1	58.6	50.8	66.8
Mean Minimum Temp. (°F)	38.8	41.7	48.4	54.9	63.8	69.6	71.9	71.3	66.1	56.6	47.5	39.9	55.9
Extreme Maximum Temp. (°F)	83	90	91	92	98	101	105	107	110	95	87	84	110
Extreme Minimum Temp. (°F)	11	16	20	29	44	51	59	54	46	28	25	5	5
Days Maximum Temp. ≥ 90°F	0	0	0	0	4	16	24	26	14	2	0	0	86
Days Maximum Temp. ≤ 32°F	0	0	0	0	0	0	0	0	0	0	0	0	0
Days Minimum Temp. ≤ 32°F	10	5	2	0	0	0	0	0	0	0	3	10	30
Days Minimum Temp. ≤ 0°F	0	0	0	0	0	0	0	0	0	0	0	0	0
Heating Degree Days (base 65°F)	472	343	195	67	4	0	0	0	3	58	226	446	1,814
Cooling Degree Days (base 65°F)	8	15	47	112	288	441	537	542	377	160	41	14	2,582
Mean Precipitation (in.)	4.12	4.11	3.92	3.43	5.53	5.57	3.27	3.45	4.48	6.28	5.55	4.57	54.28
Extreme Maximum Daily Precip. (in.)	3.65	6.74	2.74	3.26	9.06	5.58	5.55	4.99	6.90	13.17	9.00	5.08	13.17
Days With ≥ 0.1" Precipitation	6	6	6	4	5	8	6	5	6	6	6	7	71
Days With ≥ 0.5" Precipitation	3	3	3	3	3	3	2	2	2	3	3	3	33
Days With ≥ 1.0" Precipitation	1	1	1	1	2	2	1	1	1	2	2	1	16
Mean Snowfall (in.)	0.1	0.2	0.0	0.0	0.0	0.0	0.0	0.0	0.0	0.0	0.0	trace	0.3
Maximum Snow Depth (in.)	1	2	0	0	0	0	0	0	0	0	0	2	2
Days With ≥ 1.0" Snow Depth	0	0	0	0	0	0	0	0	0	0	0	0	0

Coleman *Coleman County* Elevation: 1,727 ft. Latitude: 32° 08' N Longitude: 99° 45' W

	JAN	FEB	MAR	APR	MAY	JUN	JUL	AUG	SEP	OCT	NOV	DEC	YEAR
Mean Maximum Temp. (°F)	59.4	62.9	70.6	79.2	85.6	91.1	95.1	95.2	88.3	79.2	68.2	59.3	77.9
Mean Temp. (°F)	46.9	50.3	57.6	65.4	73.2	79.2	82.6	82.5	75.7	66.4	55.9	47.1	65.2
Mean Minimum Temp. (°F)	34.3	37.6	44.5	51.6	60.8	67.3	70.1	69.8	63.1	53.6	43.4	34.9	52.6
Extreme Maximum Temp. (°F)	89	99	97	100	110	107	108	110	109	99	91	88	110
Extreme Minimum Temp. (°F)	3	8	9	25	40	52	58	55	36	25	19	-4	-4
Days Maximum Temp. ≥ 90°F	0	0	1	3	10	19	27	26	15	4	0	0	105
Days Maximum Temp. ≤ 32°F	1	1	0	0	0	0	0	0	0	0	0	1	3
Days Minimum Temp. ≤ 32°F	14	8	3	0	0	0	0	0	0	0	4	12	41
Days Minimum Temp. ≤ 0°F	0	0	0	0	0	0	0	0	0	0	0	0	0
Heating Degree Days (base 65°F)	556	415	255	86	11	0	0	0	8	74	287	549	2,241
Cooling Degree Days (base 65°F)	1	6	32	106	273	434	553	549	338	126	19	1	2,438
Mean Precipitation (in.)	1.10	2.02	2.44	1.86	3.84	4.46	1.81	2.48	2.91	2.95	1.92	1.38	29.17
Extreme Maximum Daily Precip. (in.)	1.70	3.25	2.85	4.30	2.95	4.04	4.72	3.08	5.35	4.00	2.43	5.25	5.35
Days With ≥ 0.1" Precipitation	3	3	4	3	6	5	2	4	4	4	3	3	44
Days With ≥ 0.5" Precipitation	1	1	2	1	3	3	1	1	2	2	1	1	19
Days With ≥ 1.0" Precipitation	0	1	1	1	1	2	1	1	1	1	1	0	11
Mean Snowfall (in.)	0.6	0.5	0.2	0.1	0.0	0.0	0.0	0.0	0.0	trace	0.2	0.5	2.1
Maximum Snow Depth (in.)	2	3	trace	3	0	0	0	0	0	0	1	4	4
Days With ≥ 1.0" Snow Depth	0	0	0	0	0	0	0	0	0	0	0	0	0

College Station Easterwood *Brazos County* Elevation: 313 ft. Latitude: 30° 35' N Longitude: 96° 22' W

	JAN	FEB	MAR	APR	MAY	JUN	JUL	AUG	SEP	OCT	NOV	DEC	YEAR
Mean Maximum Temp. (°F)	60.9	***64.8***	71.8	79.1	85.5	91.7	94.9	96.1	90.5	81.4	71.2	62.3	***79.2***
Mean Temp. (°F)	50.7	***54.2***	61.2	68.4	75.8	81.9	84.4	85.0	79.6	70.5	60.5	52.0	***68.7***
Mean Minimum Temp. (°F)	40.5	***43.6***	50.5	57.6	66.0	72.0	73.9	73.9	68.6	59.5	49.8	41.6	***58.1***
Extreme Maximum Temp. (°F)	83	***99***	91	94	100	106	105	109	112	96	89	86	***112***
Extreme Minimum Temp. (°F)	9	***14***	17	30	45	57	63	60	44	29	20	2	***2***
Days Maximum Temp. ≥ 90°F	0	***0***	0	1	8	22	28	29	19	4	0	0	***111***
Days Maximum Temp. ≤ 32°F	0	***0***	0	0	0	0	0	0	0	0	0	0	***0***
Days Minimum Temp. ≤ 32°F	6	***4***	1	0	0	0	0	0	0	0	1	6	***18***
Days Minimum Temp. ≤ 0°F	0	***0***	0	0	0	0	0	0	0	0	0	0	***0***
Heating Degree Days (base 65°F)	446	***319***	171	48	2	0	0	0	2	37	187	414	***1,626***
Cooling Degree Days (base 65°F)	11	***20***	60	156	343	513	609	627	447	213	60	17	***3,076***
Mean Precipitation (in.)	3.18	***2.77***	3.31	2.45	4.64	4.25	2.18	2.65	3.27	4.48	3.21	3.23	***39.62***
Extreme Maximum Daily Precip. (in.)	5.63	***4.76***	4.20	3.62	6.23	3.58	3.18	3.47	4.86	5.28	4.56	5.79	***6.23***
Days With ≥ 0.1" Precipitation	5	***4***	5	4	6	6	4	4	4	5	5	5	***57***
Days With ≥ 0.5" Precipitation	2	***2***	2	2	3	3	2	2	2	3	2	2	***27***
Days With ≥ 1.0" Precipitation	1	***1***	1	1	1	1	1	1	1	1	1	1	***12***
Mean Snowfall (in.)	na	na	na	na	na	na	na	na	na	na	na	na	na
Maximum Snow Depth (in.)	na	na	na	na	na	na	na	na	na	na	na	na	na
Days With ≥ 1.0" Snow Depth	na	na	na	na	na	na	na	na	na	na	na	na	na

Columbus *Colorado County* Elevation: 199 ft. Latitude: 29° 43' N Longitude: 96° 32' W

	JAN	FEB	MAR	APR	MAY	JUN	JUL	AUG	SEP	OCT	NOV	DEC	YEAR
Mean Maximum Temp. (°F)	64.6	67.7	74.5	80.9	87.1	92.7	95.6	97.6	93.1	84.6	74.4	65.6	81.5
Mean Temp. (°F)	51.1	54.3	61.1	67.8	75.2	80.6	82.5	83.2	78.4	69.5	60.4	52.0	68.0
Mean Minimum Temp. (°F)	37.6	40.9	47.7	54.6	63.3	68.4	69.4	68.8	63.6	54.5	46.4	38.5	54.5
Extreme Maximum Temp. (°F)	88	97	93	95	102	106	108	109	116	102	93	88	116
Extreme Minimum Temp. (°F)	10	8	8	28	40	49	59	46	40	25	18	4	4
Days Maximum Temp. ≥ 90°F	0	0	0	2	11	24	29	29	23	9	0	0	127
Days Maximum Temp. ≤ 32°F	0	0	0	0	0	0	0	0	0	0	0	0	0
Days Minimum Temp. ≤ 32°F	10	6	3	0	0	0	0	0	0	0	4	10	33
Days Minimum Temp. ≤ 0°F	0	0	0	0	0	0	0	0	0	0	0	0	0
Heating Degree Days (base 65°F)	435	315	176	53	3	0	0	0	3	45	191	413	1,634
Cooling Degree Days (base 65°F)	11	19	63	143	327	473	551	571	411	192	61	18	2,840
Mean Precipitation (in.)	3.63	2.81	3.17	3.12	4.83	4.92	3.05	2.89	3.07	4.78	4.51	3.23	44.01
Extreme Maximum Daily Precip. (in.)	3.35	2.90	2.80	5.10	3.80	5.90	2.50	3.31	3.30	8.50	5.33	3.15	8.50
Days With ≥ 0.1" Precipitation	6	5	5	4	6	6	4	5	5	6	6	6	64
Days With ≥ 0.5" Precipitation	2	2	2	2	3	3	2	2	2	3	3	2	28
Days With ≥ 1.0" Precipitation	1	1	1	1	2	2	1	1	1	2	1	1	15
Mean Snowfall (in.)	0.0	0.0	trace	0.0	0.0	0.0	0.0	0.0	0.0	0.0	0.0	trace	trace
Maximum Snow Depth (in.)	0	0	trace	0	0	0	0	0	0	0	0	trace	trace
Days With ≥ 1.0" Snow Depth	0	0	0	0	0	0	0	0	0	0	0	0	0

The period of record for all cooperative weather station data is 1980 – 2009. See User Guide for detailed explanation of data.

Conroe *Montgomery County* Elevation: 245 ft. Latitude: 30° 20' N Longitude: 95° 29' W

	JAN	FEB	MAR	APR	MAY	JUN	JUL	AUG	SEP	OCT	NOV	DEC	YEAR
Mean Maximum Temp. (°F)	61.6	64.8	72.1	78.6	85.3	91.0	94.1	94.5	89.3	80.7	71.1	62.2	78.8
Mean Temp. (°F)	51.0	54.1	61.1	67.8	75.2	81.1	83.6	83.7	78.5	69.5	60.4	51.7	68.1
Mean Minimum Temp. (°F)	40.4	43.4	50.1	57.0	65.1	71.0	73.1	72.8	67.7	58.2	49.6	41.2	57.5
Extreme Maximum Temp. (°F)	82	91	89	93	100	104	105	106	109	96	89	83	109
Extreme Minimum Temp. (°F)	11	13	18	33	46	52	60	58	44	26	24	3	3
Days Maximum Temp. ≥ 90°F	0	0	0	1	7	20	27	27	17	3	0	0	102
Days Maximum Temp. ≤ 32°F	0	0	0	0	0	0	0	0	0	0	0	0	0
Days Minimum Temp. ≤ 32°F	7	3	1	0	0	0	0	0	0	0	1	6	18
Days Minimum Temp. ≤ 0°F	0	0	0	0	0	0	0	0	0	0	0	0	0
Heating Degree Days (base 65°F)	439	317	171	51	3	0	0	0	2	44	185	420	1,632
Cooling Degree Days (base 65°F)	10	16	57	144	327	489	584	586	415	190	53	14	2,885
Mean Precipitation (in.)	3.90	3.38	3.24	2.91	5.15	5.15	2.87	3.70	3.63	5.84	5.02	3.84	48.63
Extreme Maximum Daily Precip. (in.)	4.20	2.77	2.50	2.90	6.20	***3.53***	2.68	4.16	3.50	7.95	6.01	3.50	***7.95***
Days With ≥ 0.1" Precipitation	6	5	5	4	5	6	5	5	5	5	5	6	62
Days With ≥ 0.5" Precipitation	2	2	2	2	3	3	2	2	2	3	3	3	29
Days With ≥ 1.0" Precipitation	1	1	1	1	2	1	1	1	1	2	2	1	15
Mean Snowfall (in.)	trace	trace	0.0	0.0	0.0	0.0	0.0	0.0	0.0	0.0	0.0	trace	trace
Maximum Snow Depth (in.)	1	trace	0	0	0	0	0	0	0	0	0	trace	1
Days With ≥ 1.0" Snow Depth	0	0	0	0	0	0	0	0	0	0	0	0	0

Crockett *Houston County* Elevation: 347 ft. Latitude: 31° 18' N Longitude: 95° 27' W

	JAN	FEB	MAR	APR	MAY	JUN	JUL	AUG	SEP	OCT	NOV	DEC	YEAR
Mean Maximum Temp. (°F)	58.9	63.2	70.0	77.3	84.0	90.3	93.9	94.8	89.2	***80.0***	69.0	60.2	***77.6***
Mean Temp. (°F)	48.0	51.7	58.4	65.4	73.6	80.2	83.2	83.5	77.7	***67.8***	57.6	49.1	***66.3***
Mean Minimum Temp. (°F)	37.1	40.2	46.8	53.5	63.1	69.9	72.4	72.1	66.2	***55.5***	46.1	38.0	***55.1***
Extreme Maximum Temp. (°F)	83	95	90	95	100	106	109	107	110	99	90	84	110
Extreme Minimum Temp. (°F)	6	13	18	28	40	50	59	55	41	27	21	0	0
Days Maximum Temp. ≥ 90°F	0	0	0	1	4	17	25	26	15	4	0	0	92
Days Maximum Temp. ≤ 32°F	0	0	0	0	0	0	0	0	0	0	0	0	0
Days Minimum Temp. ≤ 32°F	11	6	2	0	0	0	0	0	0	0	3	10	32
Days Minimum Temp. ≤ 0°F	0	0	0	0	0	0	0	0	0	0	0	0	0
Heating Degree Days (base 65°F)	525	378	235	81	6	0	0	0	4	***61***	252	494	***2,036***
Cooling Degree Days (base 65°F)	6	9	37	101	279	461	570	580	393	***156***	36	9	***2,637***
Mean Precipitation (in.)	3.94	3.49	3.65	3.19	4.70	4.63	2.98	2.99	3.31	4.69	3.88	3.86	45.31
Extreme Maximum Daily Precip. (in.)	5.83	3.56	6.27	3.67	3.22	9.11	4.49	3.21	6.83	5.14	3.20	4.40	9.11
Days With ≥ 0.1" Precipitation	6	5	6	4	5	6	4	4	5	5	5	6	61
Days With ≥ 0.5" Precipitation	2	2	3	2	3	2	2	2	2	3	3	3	29
Days With ≥ 1.0" Precipitation	1	1	1	1	2	1	1	1	1	2	1	1	14
Mean Snowfall (in.)	0.2	trace	0.0	0.0	0.0	0.0	0.0	0.0	0.0	0.0	trace	trace	0.2
Maximum Snow Depth (in.)	trace	trace	0	0	0	0	0	0	0	0	trace	trace	trace
Days With ≥ 1.0" Snow Depth	0	0	0	0	0	0	0	0	0	0	0	0	0

Crosbyton *Crosby County* Elevation: 3,009 ft. Latitude: 33° 39' N Longitude: 101° 15' W

	JAN	FEB	MAR	APR	MAY	JUN	JUL	AUG	SEP	OCT	NOV	DEC	YEAR
Mean Maximum Temp. (°F)	53.9	58.4	66.2	75.2	82.5	89.1	92.8	91.4	84.3	75.1	63.7	53.9	73.9
Mean Temp. (°F)	40.1	43.8	51.1	59.8	68.7	76.3	79.8	78.7	71.4	61.4	49.9	40.6	60.1
Mean Minimum Temp. (°F)	26.3	29.3	36.0	44.4	54.9	63.5	66.7	65.9	58.4	47.7	36.0	27.3	46.4
Extreme Maximum Temp. (°F)	85	89	96	99	111	113	108	106	104	101	92	81	113
Extreme Minimum Temp. (°F)	3	-3	10	21	36	45	53	55	32	19	10	-6	-6
Days Maximum Temp. ≥ 90°F	0	0	0	2	8	15	23	22	9	2	0	0	81
Days Maximum Temp. ≤ 32°F	2	2	0	0	0	0	0	0	0	0	0	2	6
Days Minimum Temp. ≤ 32°F	25	18	10	2	0	0	0	0	0	1	10	23	89
Days Minimum Temp. ≤ 0°F	0	0	0	0	0	0	0	0	0	0	0	0	0
Heating Degree Days (base 65°F)	764	592	430	194	47	2	0	0	26	159	450	749	3,413
Cooling Degree Days (base 65°F)	0	0	6	45	169	348	465	432	224	55	3	0	1,747
Mean Precipitation (in.)	0.81	0.91	1.34	1.86	2.83	3.11	2.05	2.57	3.03	2.12	1.14	0.99	22.76
Extreme Maximum Daily Precip. (in.)	1.98	1.25	2.35	3.25	2.95	2.66	3.27	5.02	5.75	4.98	2.05	1.49	5.75
Days With ≥ 0.1" Precipitation	2	2	3	3	5	5	3	4	4	3	2	2	38
Days With ≥ 0.5" Precipitation	0	1	1	1	2	2	1	2	2	1	1	1	15
Days With ≥ 1.0" Precipitation	0	0	0	1	1	1	1	1	1	1	0	0	7
Mean Snowfall (in.)	2.2	1.3	0.6	0.1	0.0	0.0	0.0	0.0	0.0	trace	1.2	1.6	7.0
Maximum Snow Depth (in.)	trace	3	trace	trace	0	0	0	0	0	trace	trace	3	3
Days With ≥ 1.0" Snow Depth	0	0	0	0	0	0	0	0	0	0	0	0	0

Crystal City *Zavala County* Elevation: 580 ft. Latitude: 28° 41' N Longitude: 99° 50' W

	JAN	FEB	MAR	APR	MAY	JUN	JUL	AUG	SEP	OCT	NOV	DEC	YEAR
Mean Maximum Temp. (°F)	67.4	72.1	79.0	85.5	90.9	95.6	97.3	97.8	92.9	85.0	75.0	67.7	83.9
Mean Temp. (°F)	55.8	60.1	66.8	73.7	80.3	85.1	86.5	86.8	82.2	74.2	64.2	56.3	72.7
Mean Minimum Temp. (°F)	44.1	48.0	54.6	61.8	69.7	74.5	75.6	75.8	71.5	63.4	53.2	44.9	61.4
Extreme Maximum Temp. (°F)	89	100	102	107	106	109	109	108	115	100	95	90	115
Extreme Minimum Temp. (°F)	19	17	22	36	50	62	67	65	47	29	26	11	11
Days Maximum Temp. ≥ 90°F	0	1	3	9	18	27	29	30	23	9	0	0	149
Days Maximum Temp. ≤ 32°F	0	0	0	0	0	0	0	0	0	0	0	0	0
Days Minimum Temp. ≤ 32°F	3	1	1	0	0	0	0	0	0	0	0	3	8
Days Minimum Temp. ≤ 0°F	0	0	0	0	0	0	0	0	0	0	0	0	0
Heating Degree Days (base 65°F)	297	178	75	15	0	0	0	0	0	15	113	284	977
Cooling Degree Days (base 65°F)	17	46	138	282	481	608	673	684	523	307	94	22	3,875
Mean Precipitation (in.)	1.04	1.01	1.40	1.46	2.27	2.62	2.15	1.67	1.91	2.09	1.22	0.75	19.59
Extreme Maximum Daily Precip. (in.)	1.44	2.15	2.97	2.15	2.37	3.81	4.44	3.54	2.70	2.23	2.28	1.52	4.44
Days With ≥ 0.1" Precipitation	2	2	2	2	4	4	3	3	3	3	2	2	32
Days With ≥ 0.5" Precipitation	1	1	1	1	2	2	1	1	1	1	1	0	13
Days With ≥ 1.0" Precipitation	0	0	0	0	1	1	1	0	0	1	0	0	4
Mean Snowfall (in.)	0.2	trace	0.0	0.0	0.0	0.0	0.0	0.0	0.0	trace	0.0	0.0	0.2
Maximum Snow Depth (in.)	3	trace	0	0	0	0	0	0	0	trace	0	0	3
Days With ≥ 1.0" Snow Depth	0	0	0	0	0	0	0	0	0	0	0	0	0

The period of record for all cooperative weather station data is 1980 – 2009. See User Guide for detailed explanation of data.

Cuero *De Witt County* Elevation: 178 ft. Latitude: 29° 05' N Longitude: 97° 19' W

	JAN	FEB	MAR	APR	MAY	JUN	JUL	AUG	SEP	OCT	NOV	DEC	YEAR
Mean Maximum Temp. (°F)	66.5	69.7	75.4	81.5	87.8	92.9	95.4	96.6	92.3	84.8	75.6	67.2	82.1
Mean Temp. (°F)	54.3	57.5	63.4	69.5	76.9	81.9	83.9	84.4	79.9	71.8	62.8	54.9	70.1
Mean Minimum Temp. (°F)	42.1	45.3	51.4	57.5	66.0	70.9	72.3	72.2	67.5	58.7	49.9	42.8	58.0
Extreme Maximum Temp. (°F)	89	98	96	98	100	108	106	106	113	99	98	87	113
Extreme Minimum Temp. (°F)	13	17	18	31	41	50	61	54	44	24	21	7	7
Days Maximum Temp. ≥ 90°F	0	0	1	2	11	24	29	30	22	9	1	0	129
Days Maximum Temp. ≤ 32°F	0	0	0	0	0	0	0	0	0	0	0	0	0
Days Minimum Temp. ≤ 32°F	7	4	2	0	0	0	0	0	0	0	2	6	21
Days Minimum Temp. ≤ 0°F	0	0	0	0	0	0	0	0	0	0	0	0	0
Heating Degree Days (base 65°F)	345	239	126	36	1	0	0	0	0	27	145	336	1,255
Cooling Degree Days (base 65°F)	20	33	83	179	377	514	591	609	454	244	83	29	3,216
Mean Precipitation (in.)	2.18	1.83	2.61	2.84	3.54	4.32	2.66	2.39	3.37	3.39	2.77	2.21	34.11
Extreme Maximum Daily Precip. (in.)	3.20	2.30	3.57	7.50	4.20	7.50	3.60	3.80	7.00	5.00	5.30	4.38	7.50
Days With ≥ 0.1" Precipitation	3	3	4	3	4	5	3	3	4	4	3	4	43
Days With ≥ 0.5" Precipitation	2	1	2	1	2	3	2	2	2	2	2	2	23
Days With ≥ 1.0" Precipitation	1	1	1	1	1	1	1	1	1	1	1	1	12
Mean Snowfall (in.)	0.0	trace	0.0	0.0	0.0	0.0	0.0	0.0	0.0	0.0	0.0	0.1	0.1
Maximum Snow Depth (in.)	6	trace	0	0	0	0	0	0	0	0	0	0	6
Days With ≥ 1.0" Snow Depth	0	0	0	0	0	0	0	0	0	0	0	0	0

Daingerfield 9 S *Morris County* Elevation: 299 ft. Latitude: 32° 55' N Longitude: 94° 43' W

	JAN	FEB	MAR	APR	MAY	JUN	JUL	AUG	SEP	OCT	NOV	DEC	YEAR
Mean Maximum Temp. (°F)	57.3	61.7	69.4	77.0	83.9	90.6	94.5	95.5	88.6	78.4	68.0	58.5	77.0
Mean Temp. (°F)	46.8	50.6	58.1	65.7	73.8	80.7	84.3	84.6	77.7	67.2	57.2	48.1	66.2
Mean Minimum Temp. (°F)	36.2	39.5	46.7	54.4	63.6	70.7	74.1	73.7	66.8	55.9	46.5	37.7	55.5
Extreme Maximum Temp. (°F)	81	91	92	96	100	104	107	112	111	97	95	83	112
Extreme Minimum Temp. (°F)	10	9	17	33	43	55	60	56	44	26	22	5	5
Days Maximum Temp. ≥ 90°F	0	0	0	1	6	19	27	27	15	2	0	0	97
Days Maximum Temp. ≤ 32°F	0	0	0	0	0	0	0	0	0	0	0	1	1
Days Minimum Temp. ≤ 32°F	12	7	2	0	0	0	0	0	0	0	2	10	33
Days Minimum Temp. ≤ 0°F	0	0	0	0	0	0	0	0	0	0	0	0	0
Heating Degree Days (base 65°F)	561	407	242	81	6	0	0	0	6	67	256	521	2,147
Cooling Degree Days (base 65°F)	4	8	34	109	286	477	606	615	394	141	30	6	2,710
Mean Precipitation (in.)	3.22	3.82	4.58	3.62	4.82	4.14	3.07	2.66	3.38	4.59	4.31	4.38	46.59
Extreme Maximum Daily Precip. (in.)	2.43	4.83	3.20	2.84	5.42	5.98	7.50	2.94	5.19	3.85	3.42	3.89	7.50
Days With ≥ 0.1" Precipitation	5	6	6	5	6	6	4	4	4	5	5	6	62
Days With ≥ 0.5" Precipitation	2	3	3	2	3	3	2	2	2	3	3	3	31
Days With ≥ 1.0" Precipitation	1	1	1	1	1	1	1	1	1	2	2	2	15
Mean Snowfall (in.)	0.3	0.1	trace	0.0	trace	0.0	0.0	0.0	0.0	0.0	trace	0.2	0.6
Maximum Snow Depth (in.)	4	trace	trace	0	trace	0	0	0	0	0	trace	trace	4
Days With ≥ 1.0" Snow Depth	0	0	0	0	0	0	0	0	0	0	0	0	0

Dallas Love Field *Dallas County* Elevation: 439 ft. Latitude: 32° 51' N Longitude: 96° 51' W

	JAN	FEB	MAR	APR	MAY	JUN	JUL	AUG	SEP	OCT	NOV	DEC	YEAR
Mean Maximum Temp. (°F)	56.7	60.9	69.0	76.8	83.9	91.5	96.0	96.3	88.7	78.4	67.3	57.5	76.9
Mean Temp. (°F)	46.9	51.0	58.8	66.5	74.6	82.1	86.3	86.5	78.8	68.2	57.4	48.0	67.1
Mean Minimum Temp. (°F)	37.1	40.9	48.5	56.1	65.1	72.6	76.6	76.7	68.8	58.0	47.4	38.4	57.2
Extreme Maximum Temp. (°F)	83	95	95	100	103	112	108	109	110	97	89	88	112
Extreme Minimum Temp. (°F)	7	10	16	33	45	53	60	60	43	27	23	1	1
Days Maximum Temp. ≥ 90°F	0	0	0	1	7	21	28	27	15	3	0	0	102
Days Maximum Temp. ≤ 32°F	1	1	0	0	0	0	0	0	0	0	0	1	3
Days Minimum Temp. ≤ 32°F	10	6	2	0	0	0	0	0	0	0	2	8	28
Days Minimum Temp. ≤ 0°F	0	0	0	0	0	0	0	0	0	0	0	0	0
Heating Degree Days (base 65°F)	557	400	228	71	6	0	0	0	5	59	256	525	2,107
Cooling Degree Days (base 65°F)	4	10	41	122	310	518	668	674	426	166	35	5	2,979
Mean Precipitation (in.)	1.99	2.60	3.43	3.14	5.06	4.14	2.21	1.90	2.68	4.72	2.80	2.49	37.16
Extreme Maximum Daily Precip. (in.)	3.23	3.35	6.89	2.84	3.37	5.28	4.12	3.41	4.68	3.91	3.06	3.98	6.89
Days With ≥ 0.1" Precipitation	3	4	4	4	6	5	3	3	4	5	4	4	49
Days With ≥ 0.5" Precipitation	1	2	2	2	3	3	1	1	2	3	2	2	24
Days With ≥ 1.0" Precipitation	0	1	1	1	2	1	1	1	1	2	1	1	13
Mean Snowfall (in.)	*0.5*	*0.3*	*trace*	*trace*	*trace*	*trace*	*0.0*	*0.0*	*0.0*	*trace*	*0.1*	*0.3*	*1.2*
Maximum Snow Depth (in.)	*3*	*2*	*1*	*trace*	*trace*	*trace*	*0*	*0*	*0*	*trace*	*1*	*2*	*3*
Days With ≥ 1.0" Snow Depth	*0*	*0*	*0*	*0*	*0*	*0*	*0*	*0*	*0*	*0*	*0*	*0*	*0*

Dell City 5 SSW *Hudspeth County* Elevation: 3,770 ft. Latitude: 31° 54' N Longitude: 105° 13' W

	JAN	FEB	MAR	APR	MAY	JUN	JUL	AUG	SEP	OCT	NOV	DEC	YEAR
Mean Maximum Temp. (°F)	59.7	64.7	72.2	80.2	89.2	97.1	97.1	94.3	88.8	79.9	67.9	59.2	79.2
Mean Temp. (°F)	42.7	47.7	54.0	61.5	71.0	79.0	80.9	78.9	72.6	62.2	50.2	42.5	61.9
Mean Minimum Temp. (°F)	25.7	30.6	35.8	42.7	52.8	60.8	64.8	63.4	56.3	44.5	32.5	25.8	44.6
Extreme Maximum Temp. (°F)	81	87	92	100	108	115	112	108	105	101	90	79	115
Extreme Minimum Temp. (°F)	6	6	11	20	32	44	53	50	34	21	9	-5	-5
Days Maximum Temp. ≥ 90°F	0	0	0	4	16	27	28	26	16	4	0	0	121
Days Maximum Temp. ≤ 32°F	0	0	0	0	0	0	0	0	0	0	0	0	0
Days Minimum Temp. ≤ 32°F	26	17	10	3	0	0	0	0	0	2	15	26	99
Days Minimum Temp. ≤ 0°F	0	0	0	0	0	0	0	0	0	0	0	0	0
Heating Degree Days (base 65°F)	684	484	338	144	16	0	0	0	11	127	440	691	2,935
Cooling Degree Days (base 65°F)	0	0	4	45	209	427	502	437	246	49	1	0	1,920
Mean Precipitation (in.)	0.42	0.46	0.30	0.24	0.96	0.97	1.48	1.91	1.75	1.05	0.54	0.54	10.62
Extreme Maximum Daily Precip. (in.)	0.90	0.95	0.76	0.90	2.44	1.76	2.00	1.62	1.80	1.49	2.00	1.15	2.44
Days With ≥ 0.1" Precipitation	1	1	1	1	2	2	3	4	3	3	1	1	23
Days With ≥ 0.5" Precipitation	0	0	0	0	0	0	1	1	1	1	0	0	4
Days With ≥ 1.0" Precipitation	0	0	0	0	0	0	0	0	0	0	0	0	0
Mean Snowfall (in.)	0.3	0.1	0.0	0.0	0.0	0.0	0.0	0.0	0.0	0.0	0.1	0.1	0.6
Maximum Snow Depth (in.)	0	0	0	0	0	0	0	0	0	0	0	0	0
Days With ≥ 1.0" Snow Depth	0	0	0	0	0	0	0	0	0	0	0	0	0

The period of record for all cooperative weather station data is 1980 – 2009. See User Guide for detailed explanation of data.

Denton 2 SE *Denton County* Elevation: 629 ft. Latitude: 33° 12' N Longitude: 97° 06' W

	JAN	FEB	MAR	APR	MAY	JUN	JUL	AUG	SEP	OCT	NOV	DEC	YEAR
Mean Maximum Temp. (°F)	55.8	59.7	67.8	75.7	82.6	90.1	95.1	95.2	87.4	77.2	65.8	56.2	75.7
Mean Temp. (°F)	45.3	48.7	56.7	64.4	72.6	80.0	84.5	84.2	76.6	66.2	55.3	46.4	65.1
Mean Minimum Temp. (°F)	34.6	37.9	45.5	53.1	62.4	69.9	73.8	73.2	65.7	55.1	44.7	36.1	54.3
Extreme Maximum Temp. (°F)	83	92	94	100	104	108	108	109	111	95	88	86	111
Extreme Minimum Temp. (°F)	4	6	13	30	40	51	59	58	40	24	20	0	0
Days Maximum Temp. ≥ 90°F	0	0	0	1	4	18	27	26	13	2	0	0	91
Days Maximum Temp. ≤ 32°F	1	1	0	0	0	0	0	0	0	0	0	1	3
Days Minimum Temp. ≤ 32°F	14	8	3	0	0	0	0	0	0	0	3	11	39
Days Minimum Temp. ≤ 0°F	0	0	0	0	0	0	0	0	0	0	0	0	0
Heating Degree Days (base 65°F)	606	458	276	98	13	0	0	0	9	80	303	573	2,416
Cooling Degree Days (base 65°F)	2	5	26	86	255	457	611	602	363	123	19	3	2,552
Mean Precipitation (in.)	2.08	2.81	3.16	3.20	5.37	3.66	2.29	2.14	3.07	4.79	2.94	2.51	38.02
Extreme Maximum Daily Precip. (in.)	2.31	7.11	5.00	8.08	7.30	3.75	4.20	4.04	4.88	6.25	4.54	2.38	8.08
Days With ≥ 0.1" Precipitation	4	4	4	4	6	5	3	3	4	5	4	4	50
Days With ≥ 0.5" Precipitation	1	2	2	2	3	3	2	1	2	3	2	2	25
Days With ≥ 1.0" Precipitation	1	1	1	1	2	1	1	1	1	1	1	1	13
Mean Snowfall (in.)	0.1	0.2	0.1	0.0	0.0	0.0	0.0	0.0	0.0	0.0	trace	0.2	0.6
Maximum Snow Depth (in.)	5	2	0	0	0	0	0	0	0	0	trace	4	5
Days With ≥ 1.0" Snow Depth	0	0	0	0	0	0	0	0	0	0	0	0	0

Dimmitt 2 N *Castro County* Elevation: 3,850 ft. Latitude: 34° 36' N Longitude: 102° 19' W

	JAN	FEB	MAR	APR	MAY	JUN	JUL	AUG	SEP	OCT	NOV	DEC	YEAR
Mean Maximum Temp. (°F)	50.8	55.4	63.0	71.5	80.5	88.1	91.3	89.1	82.6	72.2	60.2	50.3	71.2
Mean Temp. (°F)	36.1	39.7	46.6	54.7	64.5	73.1	76.5	75.0	67.8	56.8	44.9	36.0	56.0
Mean Minimum Temp. (°F)	21.4	23.9	30.1	37.8	48.5	58.0	61.8	60.8	53.0	41.5	29.5	21.7	40.7
Extreme Maximum Temp. (°F)	78	83	92	98	104	108	111	105	102	97	87	78	111
Extreme Minimum Temp. (°F)	-7	-9	0	18	28	40	47	49	29	14	-2	-8	-9
Days Maximum Temp. ≥ 90°F	0	0	0	1	6	14	20	16	7	1	0	0	65
Days Maximum Temp. ≤ 32°F	4	2	1	0	0	0	0	0	0	0	1	3	11
Days Minimum Temp. ≤ 32°F	29	24	19	8	0	0	0	0	0	4	19	28	131
Days Minimum Temp. ≤ 0°F	0	0	0	0	0	0	0	0	0	0	0	1	1
Heating Degree Days (base 65°F)	888	709	565	314	100	8	1	2	50	264	596	892	4,389
Cooling Degree Days (base 65°F)	0	0	0	11	91	258	364	318	142	17	0	0	1,201
Mean Precipitation (in.)	0.59	0.53	1.03	1.01	2.84	3.80	2.13	3.32	2.58	1.79	0.74	0.78	21.14
Extreme Maximum Daily Precip. (in.)	1.40	1.11	1.59	1.57	3.90	2.67	2.67	3.16	4.15	4.38	1.23	1.33	4.38
Days With ≥ 0.1" Precipitation	1	2	3	3	4	6	4	5	4	3	2	2	39
Days With ≥ 0.5" Precipitation	0	0	1	1	2	3	1	2	2	1	0	0	13
Days With ≥ 1.0" Precipitation	0	0	0	0	1	1	0	1	1	1	0	0	5
Mean Snowfall (in.)	3.2	1.5	1.0	0.4	0.0	0.0	0.0	0.0	0.0	0.1	1.3	3.4	10.9
Maximum Snow Depth (in.)	17	3	7	3	0	0	0	0	0	2	6	5	17
Days With ≥ 1.0" Snow Depth	2	1	1	0	0	0	0	0	0	0	1	2	7

Dripping Springs 6 E *Hays County* Elevation: 1,120 ft. Latitude: 30° 13' N Longitude: 97° 59' W

	JAN	FEB	MAR	APR	MAY	JUN	JUL	AUG	SEP	OCT	NOV	DEC	YEAR
Mean Maximum Temp. (°F)	*61.2*	*65.2*	*72.1*	*79.6*	*85.6*	*91.1*	*94.4*	*95.8*	*89.6*	*80.5*	*69.8*	61.8	*78.9*
Mean Temp. (°F)	*50.0*	*53.9*	*60.2*	*67.6*	*74.8*	*80.2*	*83.0*	*83.5*	*77.5*	*68.8*	*58.7*	50.8	*67.4*
Mean Minimum Temp. (°F)	*38.7*	*42.5*	*48.3*	*55.6*	*63.9*	*69.3*	*71.5*	*71.2*	*65.4*	*57.1*	*47.6*	39.8	*55.9*
Extreme Maximum Temp. (°F)	*86*	*99*	*95*	*100*	*101*	*106*	*106*	*109*	*111*	*98*	*89*	*84*	*111*
Extreme Minimum Temp. (°F)	*10*	*4*	*16*	*25*	*38*	*51*	*59*	*52*	*38*	*22*	*18*	*-2*	*-2*
Days Maximum Temp. ≥ 90°F	*0*	*0*	*0*	*2*	*8*	*20*	*26*	*28*	*17*	*3*	*0*	0	*104*
Days Maximum Temp. ≤ 32°F	*0*	*0*	*0*	*0*	*0*	*0*	*0*	*0*	*0*	*0*	*0*	0	*0*
Days Minimum Temp. ≤ 32°F	*10*	*5*	*3*	*0*	*0*	*0*	*0*	*0*	*0*	*0*	*3*	9	*30*
Days Minimum Temp. ≤ 0°F	*0*	*0*	*0*	*0*	*0*	*0*	*0*	*0*	*0*	*0*	*0*	0	*0*
Heating Degree Days (base 65°F)	*465*	*326*	*192*	*55*	*4*	*0*	*0*	*0*	*4*	*53*	*223*	443	*1,765*
Cooling Degree Days (base 65°F)	*5*	*18*	*51*	*141*	*314*	*463*	*564*	*581*	*387*	*178*	*40*	10	*2,752*
Mean Precipitation (in.)	*2.42*	*2.30*	*2.90*	*2.36*	*4.04*	*4.70*	*2.24*	*1.80*	*2.78*	*3.99*	*3.39*	2.82	*35.74*
Extreme Maximum Daily Precip. (in.)	*4.36*	*3.66*	*3.09*	*2.52*	*3.13*	*6.59*	*4.46*	*3.20*	*4.06*	*6.66*	*4.26*	*5.65*	*6.66*
Days With ≥ 0.1" Precipitation	*4*	*4*	*5*	*4*	*5*	*5*	*4*	*3*	*4*	*5*	*4*	4	*51*
Days With ≥ 0.5" Precipitation	*1*	*2*	*2*	*2*	*2*	*2*	*3*	*1*	*2*	*3*	*2*	2	*23*
Days With ≥ 1.0" Precipitation	*1*	*1*	*1*	*1*	*2*	*2*	*1*	*1*	*1*	*1*	*1*	1	*14*
Mean Snowfall (in.)	*0.5*	*0.2*	*trace*	*trace*	*0.0*	*0.0*	*0.0*	*0.0*	*0.0*	*0.0*	*trace*	0.1	*0.8*
Maximum Snow Depth (in.)	*8*	*2*	*trace*	*trace*	*0*	*0*	*0*	*0*	*0*	*0*	*trace*	*1*	*8*
Days With ≥ 1.0" Snow Depth	*0*	*0*	*0*	*0*	*0*	*0*	*0*	*0*	*0*	*0*	*0*	0	*0*

Dublin *Erath County* Elevation: 1,501 ft. Latitude: 32° 06' N Longitude: 98° 20' W

	JAN	FEB	MAR	APR	MAY	JUN	JUL	AUG	SEP	OCT	NOV	DEC	YEAR
Mean Maximum Temp. (°F)	55.4	59.6	67.0	75.6	82.3	88.7	93.5	94.2	86.6	76.6	65.3	56.1	75.1
Mean Temp. (°F)	44.1	47.9	55.0	63.1	71.3	77.9	81.9	82.2	74.9	65.2	54.4	45.2	63.6
Mean Minimum Temp. (°F)	32.7	36.3	43.0	50.6	60.2	67.0	70.3	70.2	63.1	53.8	43.5	34.2	52.1
Extreme Maximum Temp. (°F)	84	96	93	99	104	107	106	107	109	96	92	82	109
Extreme Minimum Temp. (°F)	3	2	9	12	41	51	57	56	39	25	18	-7	-7
Days Maximum Temp. ≥ 90°F	0	0	0	1	5	14	24	24	12	2	0	0	82
Days Maximum Temp. ≤ 32°F	1	1	0	0	0	0	0	0	0	0	0	1	3
Days Minimum Temp. ≤ 32°F	16	9	4	1	0	0	0	0	0	0	4	13	47
Days Minimum Temp. ≤ 0°F	0	0	0	0	0	0	0	0	0	0	0	0	0
Heating Degree Days (base 65°F)	643	480	323	122	18	1	0	0	12	92	327	608	2,626
Cooling Degree Days (base 65°F)	1	4	20	73	219	394	532	540	316	105	15	1	2,220
Mean Precipitation (in.)	1.61	2.65	2.97	2.81	5.08	5.10	1.91	2.88	3.47	3.63	2.59	2.22	36.92
Extreme Maximum Daily Precip. (in.)	1.50	4.00	3.80	6.09	6.50	4.72	2.52	4.50	3.01	3.24	4.00	3.75	6.50
Days With ≥ 0.1" Precipitation	3	4	5	4	6	6	3	4	4	5	4	4	52
Days With ≥ 0.5" Precipitation	1	2	2	2	3	3	1	2	2	3	2	1	24
Days With ≥ 1.0" Precipitation	0	1	1	1	2	2	1	1	1	1	1	1	13
Mean Snowfall (in.)	0.3	0.2	trace	0.1	0.0	0.0	0.0	0.0	0.0	trace	0.1	0.4	1.1
Maximum Snow Depth (in.)	6	4	2	2	0	0	0	0	0	trace	0	3	6
Days With ≥ 1.0" Snow Depth	0	0	0	0	0	0	0	0	0	0	0	0	0

The period of record for all cooperative weather station data is 1980 – 2009. See User Guide for detailed explanation of data.

Emory *Rains County* Elevation: 435 ft. Latitude: 32° 52' N Longitude: 95° 46' W

	JAN	FEB	MAR	APR	MAY	JUN	JUL	AUG	SEP	OCT	NOV	DEC	YEAR
Mean Maximum Temp. (°F)	55.2	59.2	66.9	74.4	81.2	87.9	92.5	93.4	86.7	76.7	66.0	56.5	74.7
Mean Temp. (°F)	44.0	47.6	55.4	62.9	70.9	78.3	81.9	81.9	75.1	64.7	54.5	45.3	63.5
Mean Minimum Temp. (°F)	32.8	35.9	43.9	51.1	60.6	68.6	71.3	70.4	63.4	52.2	42.9	34.0	52.3
Extreme Maximum Temp. (°F)	80	91	88	93	96	101	105	107	108	96	85	82	108
Extreme Minimum Temp. (°F)	3	4	15	28	39	50	57	53	39	23	18	-5	-5
Days Maximum Temp. ≥ 90°F	0	0	0	0	1	11	23	25	12	2	0	0	74
Days Maximum Temp. ≤ 32°F	1	1	0	0	0	0	0	0	0	0	0	1	3
Days Minimum Temp. ≤ 32°F	17	11	4	0	0	0	0	0	0	0	5	15	52
Days Minimum Temp. ≤ 0°F	0	0	0	0	0	0	0	0	0	0	0	0	0
Heating Degree Days (base 65°F)	647	489	307	122	19	1	0	0	13	100	326	608	2,632
Cooling Degree Days (base 65°F)	2	3	18	65	208	405	532	532	323	97	17	3	2,205
Mean Precipitation (in.)	2.98	3.52	4.37	3.28	5.17	4.09	2.73	2.21	3.12	5.15	3.78	3.80	44.20
Extreme Maximum Daily Precip. (in.)	4.55	4.25	4.85	3.05	5.41	5.65	4.00	2.60	3.94	5.60	4.10	4.55	5.65
Days With ≥ 0.1" Precipitation	5	5	6	5	6	5	3	3	4	5	4	5	56
Days With ≥ 0.5" Precipitation	2	2	3	2	3	3	2	2	2	3	3	3	30
Days With ≥ 1.0" Precipitation	1	1	1	1	2	1	1	1	1	2	2	1	15
Mean Snowfall (in.)	0.2	0.3	trace	0.0	0.0	0.0	0.0	0.0	0.0	0.0	0.0	0.3	0.8
Maximum Snow Depth (in.)	2	1	trace	0	0	0	0	0	0	0	0	trace	2
Days With ≥ 1.0" Snow Depth	0	0	0	0	0	0	0	0	0	0	0	0	0

Encinal *Webb County* Elevation: 589 ft. Latitude: 28° 03' N Longitude: 99° 26' W

	JAN	FEB	MAR	APR	MAY	JUN	JUL	AUG	SEP	OCT	NOV	DEC	YEAR
Mean Maximum Temp. (°F)	67.1	71.5	79.7	87.2	92.5	97.9	98.9	99.5	93.7	85.9	76.3	67.8	84.8
Mean Temp. (°F)	54.5	58.7	65.7	73.3	79.7	85.1	86.1	86.5	81.6	73.2	63.7	55.6	72.0
Mean Minimum Temp. (°F)	42.0	45.8	51.6	59.4	66.9	72.4	73.2	73.5	69.4	60.5	51.0	43.4	59.1
Extreme Maximum Temp. (°F)	93	101	103	109	110	116	109	109	111	102	98	93	116
Extreme Minimum Temp. (°F)	20	19	24	36	45	57	64	60	50	31	30	12	12
Days Maximum Temp. ≥ 90°F	0	1	5	13	21	26	28	30	24	11	2	0	161
Days Maximum Temp. ≤ 32°F	0	0	0	0	0	0	0	0	0	0	0	0	0
Days Minimum Temp. ≤ 32°F	4	2	1	0	0	0	0	0	0	0	0	3	10
Days Minimum Temp. ≤ 0°F	0	0	0	0	0	0	0	0	0	0	0	0	0
Heating Degree Days (base 65°F)	330	214	96	16	1	0	0	0	1	21	124	309	1,112
Cooling Degree Days (base 65°F)	13	41	123	271	464	611	660	675	504	284	90	23	3,759
Mean Precipitation (in.)	0.89	0.74	1.33	1.15	2.92	2.35	2.02	2.06	2.63	2.05	1.15	0.84	20.13
Extreme Maximum Daily Precip. (in.)	1.80	2.00	4.10	2.15	4.20	na	2.66	5.50	2.98	3.35	na	na	na
Days With ≥ 0.1" Precipitation	1	1	2	2	4	2	2	2	3	2	2	1	24
Days With ≥ 0.5" Precipitation	1	0	1	1	2	1	1	1	2	1	1	0	12
Days With ≥ 1.0" Precipitation	0	0	1	0	1	1	1	1	1	1	0	0	7
Mean Snowfall (in.)	trace	0.0	0.0	0.0	0.0	0.0	0.0	0.0	0.0	0.0	0.0	0.2	0.2
Maximum Snow Depth (in.)	trace	0	0	0	0	0	0	0	0	0	na	5	na
Days With ≥ 1.0" Snow Depth	0	0	0	0	0	0	0	0	0	0	0	0	0

Falcon Dam *Starr County* Elevation: 319 ft. Latitude: 26° 33' N Longitude: 99° 08' W

	JAN	FEB	MAR	APR	MAY	JUN	JUL	AUG	SEP	OCT	NOV	DEC	YEAR
Mean Maximum Temp. (°F)	69.1	74.2	82.1	88.6	94.4	98.9	100.3	100.3	94.4	87.6	78.5	69.6	86.5
Mean Temp. (°F)	57.9	62.4	69.4	75.7	82.3	86.6	87.6	87.5	83.0	76.0	67.2	58.7	74.5
Mean Minimum Temp. (°F)	46.6	50.5	56.7	62.7	70.2	74.3	74.8	74.8	71.5	64.5	55.8	47.6	62.5
Extreme Maximum Temp. (°F)	97	102	105	109	114	116	110	109	112	101	97	94	116
Extreme Minimum Temp. (°F)	23	24	27	30	49	59	63	64	51	31	32	15	15
Days Maximum Temp. ≥ 90°F	0	2	7	15	24	28	30	30	24	14	4	0	178
Days Maximum Temp. ≤ 32°F	0	0	0	0	0	0	0	0	0	0	0	0	0
Days Minimum Temp. ≤ 32°F	1	1	0	0	0	0	0	0	0	0	0	1	3
Days Minimum Temp. ≤ 0°F	0	0	0	0	0	0	0	0	0	0	0	0	0
Heating Degree Days (base 65°F)	249	146	55	13	1	0	0	0	1	12	82	237	796
Cooling Degree Days (base 65°F)	36	78	200	341	545	656	707	705	547	362	154	47	4,378
Mean Precipitation (in.)	0.91	0.98	0.64	1.42	2.35	1.95	1.83	2.19	3.88	1.83	1.24	0.94	20.16
Extreme Maximum Daily Precip. (in.)	1.32	2.75	1.66	2.61	4.42	2.99	5.25	3.41	7.70	3.40	3.20	2.00	7.70
Days With ≥ 0.1" Precipitation	3	2	1	2	3	3	3	3	5	3	2	2	32
Days With ≥ 0.5" Precipitation	0	0	0	1	1	1	1	1	2	1	1	0	9
Days With ≥ 1.0" Precipitation	0	0	0	0	1	1	1	1	1	0	0	0	5
Mean Snowfall (in.)	0.0	0.0	0.0	0.0	0.0	0.0	0.0	0.0	0.0	0.0	0.0	0.0	0.0
Maximum Snow Depth (in.)	0	0	0	0	0	0	0	0	0	0	0	0	0
Days With ≥ 1.0" Snow Depth	0	0	0	0	0	0	0	0	0	0	0	0	0

Falfurrias *Brooks County* Elevation: 120 ft. Latitude: 27° 13' N Longitude: 98° 08' W

	JAN	FEB	MAR	APR	MAY	JUN	JUL	AUG	SEP	OCT	NOV	DEC	YEAR
Mean Maximum Temp. (°F)	68.5	72.3	78.7	85.5	90.9	95.5	97.3	97.5	92.2	85.9	77.3	69.4	84.3
Mean Temp. (°F)	56.7	60.2	66.4	73.4	79.9	84.4	85.7	85.6	81.3	74.1	65.5	57.9	72.6
Mean Minimum Temp. (°F)	44.8	48.0	54.0	61.2	68.8	73.2	74.0	73.7	70.3	62.3	53.6	46.4	60.9
Extreme Maximum Temp. (°F)	95	99	104	108	109	115	107	107	111	100	96	93	115
Extreme Minimum Temp. (°F)	21	25	23	34	48	55	66	65	50	28	25	13	13
Days Maximum Temp. ≥ 90°F	0	1	3	10	19	25	26	27	20	11	2	0	144
Days Maximum Temp. ≤ 32°F	0	0	0	0	0	0	0	0	0	0	0	0	0
Days Minimum Temp. ≤ 32°F	3	2	1	0	0	0	0	0	0	0	1	3	10
Days Minimum Temp. ≤ 0°F	0	0	0	0	0	0	0	0	0	0	0	0	0
Heating Degree Days (base 65°F)	285	185	90	21	0	0	0	0	0	18	105	267	971
Cooling Degree Days (base 65°F)	34	56	140	279	468	587	649	647	497	308	125	54	3,844
Mean Precipitation (in.)	1.05	1.45	1.15	1.12	2.74	2.73	2.40	2.74	3.66	3.38	1.36	1.26	25.04
Extreme Maximum Daily Precip. (in.)	1.30	3.78	1.72	1.78	5.01	3.67	6.90	7.36	4.35	4.60	2.20	3.21	7.36
Days With ≥ 0.1" Precipitation	3	3	2	2	4	4	3	3	5	3	2	2	36
Days With ≥ 0.5" Precipitation	1	1	1	1	2	2	1	1	2	2	1	1	16
Days With ≥ 1.0" Precipitation	0	0	0	0	1	1	1	1	1	1	0	0	6
Mean Snowfall (in.)	0.0	0.0	0.0	0.0	0.0	0.0	0.0	0.0	0.0	0.0	0.0	0.0	0.0
Maximum Snow Depth (in.)	0	0	0	0	0	0	0	0	0	0	0	0	0
Days With ≥ 1.0" Snow Depth	0	0	0	0	0	0	0	0	0	0	0	0	0

The period of record for all cooperative weather station data is 1980 – 2009. See User Guide for detailed explanation of data.

Ferris *Ellis County* Elevation: 470 ft. Latitude: 32° 31' N Longitude: 96° 40' W

	JAN	FEB	MAR	APR	MAY	JUN	JUL	AUG	SEP	OCT	NOV	DEC	YEAR
Mean Maximum Temp. (°F)	57.3	61.9	68.6	76.8	83.6	90.8	96.2	96.6	89.7	79.2	68.0	57.8	77.2
Mean Temp. (°F)	46.0	50.3	57.0	64.7	73.0	80.1	84.3	84.4	77.5	67.1	56.6	46.8	65.6
Mean Minimum Temp. (°F)	34.7	38.6	45.3	52.5	62.3	69.3	72.5	72.2	65.4	54.9	45.1	35.8	54.0
Extreme Maximum Temp. (°F)	84	96	93	99	102	110	109	111	111	97	91	87	111
Extreme Minimum Temp. (°F)	7	7	14	29	42	53	57	56	42	26	23	-1	-1
Days Maximum Temp. ≥ 90°F	0	0	0	1	5	20	28	27	17	3	0	0	101
Days Maximum Temp. ≤ 32°F	0	1	0	0	0	0	0	0	0	0	0	1	2
Days Minimum Temp. ≤ 32°F	14	8	3	0	0	0	0	0	0	0	3	12	40
Days Minimum Temp. ≤ 0°F	0	0	0	0	0	0	0	0	0	0	0	0	0
Heating Degree Days (base 65°F)	585	415	267	93	9	0	0	0	6	68	273	561	2,277
Cooling Degree Days (base 65°F)	3	6	26	90	264	459	606	609	389	139	27	5	2,623
Mean Precipitation (in.)	2.86	2.95	3.90	3.13	4.60	3.97	1.86	2.44	2.58	4.59	3.00	3.38	39.26
Extreme Maximum Daily Precip. (in.)	6.15	2.50	5.21	2.26	4.70	3.86	3.50	3.23	3.68	4.88	2.73	5.20	6.15
Days With ≥ 0.1" Precipitation	4	4	5	4	6	5	3	3	4	5	4	4	51
Days With ≥ 0.5" Precipitation	2	2	3	2	3	3	1	2	2	3	2	2	27
Days With ≥ 1.0" Precipitation	1	1	1	1	2	1	1	1	1	1	1	1	13
Mean Snowfall (in.)	0.1	0.3	trace	0.0	0.0	0.0	0.0	0.0	0.0	0.0	trace	0.3	0.7
Maximum Snow Depth (in.)	3	2	3	0	0	0	0	0	0	0	trace	3	3
Days With ≥ 1.0" Snow Depth	0	0	0	0	0	0	0	0	0	0	0	0	0

Floresville *Wilson County* Elevation: 399 ft. Latitude: 29° 08' N Longitude: 98° 10' W

	JAN	FEB	MAR	APR	MAY	JUN	JUL	AUG	SEP	OCT	NOV	DEC	YEAR
Mean Maximum Temp. (°F)	64.8	68.9	75.0	82.1	88.2	93.5	96.3	97.2	91.9	83.9	74.5	66.0	81.9
Mean Temp. (°F)	51.7	55.7	62.5	69.4	77.2	82.5	84.9	85.1	79.7	71.1	61.6	52.8	69.5
Mean Minimum Temp. (°F)	38.6	42.3	49.9	56.7	66.1	71.3	73.4	73.0	67.5	58.2	48.6	39.5	57.1
Extreme Maximum Temp. (°F)	87	99	97	100	109	109	107	110	111	99	95	89	111
Extreme Minimum Temp. (°F)	5	10	16	30	37	46	62	58	43	26	20	7	5
Days Maximum Temp. ≥ 90°F	0	0	1	4	14	25	28	29	21	8	0	0	130
Days Maximum Temp. ≤ 32°F	0	0	0	0	0	0	0	0	0	0	0	0	0
Days Minimum Temp. ≤ 32°F	10	5	2	0	0	0	0	0	0	0	2	9	28
Days Minimum Temp. ≤ 0°F	0	0	0	0	0	0	0	0	0	0	0	0	0
Heating Degree Days (base 65°F)	416	280	144	41	2	0	0	0	2	36	167	388	1,476
Cooling Degree Days (base 65°F)	11	22	75	180	385	530	622	632	449	233	71	18	3,228
Mean Precipitation (in.)	1.42	1.66	2.06	2.03	3.22	2.92	2.31	2.39	2.85	2.89	2.27	1.46	27.48
Extreme Maximum Daily Precip. (in.)	2.14	3.45	***4.50***	4.04	4.00	3.15	3.05	***5.07***	6.36	3.75	8.82	***3.01***	***8.82***
Days With ≥ 0.1" Precipitation	3	3	3	3	4	4	3	3	4	4	3	3	40
Days With ≥ 0.5" Precipitation	1	1	1	1	2	2	1	1	2	2	1	1	16
Days With ≥ 1.0" Precipitation	0	0	1	1	1	1	1	1	1	1	1	0	9
Mean Snowfall (in.)	0.4	0.0	0.0	0.0	0.0	0.0	0.0	0.0	0.0	trace	0.0	0.0	0.4
Maximum Snow Depth (in.)	0	0	0	0	0	0	0	0	0	trace	0	0	trace
Days With ≥ 1.0" Snow Depth	0	0	0	0	0	0	0	0	0	0	0	0	0

Fort Hancock 5 SSE *Hudspeth County* Elevation: 3,904 ft. Latitude: 31° 13' N Longitude: 105° 47' W

	JAN	FEB	MAR	APR	MAY	JUN	JUL	AUG	SEP	OCT	NOV	DEC	YEAR
Mean Maximum Temp. (°F)	61.2	66.8	73.8	82.0	91.3	97.8	96.2	93.1	89.1	81.0	70.0	60.4	80.2
Mean Temp. (°F)	43.5	48.5	***55.3***	62.8	72.3	80.4	81.3	79.0	73.6	63.5	51.9	43.1	***62.9***
Mean Minimum Temp. (°F)	25.6	30.2	***36.6***	43.4	53.3	62.8	66.4	64.9	57.9	45.7	33.4	26.0	***45.5***
Extreme Maximum Temp. (°F)	83	87	92	98	107	113	111	106	104	100	89	81	113
Extreme Minimum Temp. (°F)	7	9	15	23	34	42	53	53	40	***24***	12	-1	***-1***
Days Maximum Temp. ≥ 90°F	0	0	0	4	20	27	27	24	16	4	0	0	122
Days Maximum Temp. ≤ 32°F	0	0	0	0	0	0	0	0	0	0	0	0	0
Days Minimum Temp. ≤ 32°F	26	17	9	2	0	0	0	0	0	2	14	26	96
Days Minimum Temp. ≤ 0°F	0	0	0	0	0	0	0	0	0	0	0	0	0
Heating Degree Days (base 65°F)	660	460	***296***	110	7	0	0	0	5	101	388	671	***2,698***
Cooling Degree Days (base 65°F)	0	0	***3***	49	243	466	512	441	268	61	2	0	***2,045***
Mean Precipitation (in.)	0.49	0.33	0.24	0.28	0.45	0.89	1.56	1.52	1.55	0.95	0.40	0.59	9.25
Extreme Maximum Daily Precip. (in.)	2.01	0.78	0.70	1.65	1.27	1.27	2.60	1.12	3.70	2.70	0.97	1.06	3.70
Days With ≥ 0.1" Precipitation	1	1	1	1	1	2	4	5	3	2	1	2	24
Days With ≥ 0.5" Precipitation	0	0	0	0	0	0	1	1	1	0	0	0	3
Days With ≥ 1.0" Precipitation	0	0	0	0	0	0	0	0	0	0	0	0	0
Mean Snowfall (in.)	0.1	trace	0.0	0.0	0.0	0.0	0.0	0.0	0.0	0.0	trace	0.3	0.4
Maximum Snow Depth (in.)	trace	0	0	0	0	0	0	0	0	***0***	***trace***	3	***3***
Days With ≥ 1.0" Snow Depth	0	0	0	0	0	0	0	0	0	0	0	0	0

Gail *Borden County* Elevation: 2,528 ft. Latitude: 32° 46' N Longitude: 101° 27' W

	JAN	FEB	MAR	APR	MAY	JUN	JUL	AUG	SEP	OCT	NOV	DEC	YEAR
Mean Maximum Temp. (°F)	58.0	62.6	70.7	79.7	86.8	***92.2***	94.9	***93.6***	86.5	77.7	66.5	57.9	***77.3***
Mean Temp. (°F)	45.0	49.0	56.3	64.8	73.0	***79.3***	82.3	***81.2***	74.2	64.9	53.3	45.1	***64.0***
Mean Minimum Temp. (°F)	32.1	35.3	41.9	49.8	59.2	***66.3***	69.6	***68.8***	61.8	52.0	40.1	32.3	***50.8***
Extreme Maximum Temp. (°F)	87	91	96	101	111	116	113	107	106	103	91	84	116
Extreme Minimum Temp. (°F)	4	0	9	25	38	45	57	55	36	21	8	-1	-1
Days Maximum Temp. ≥ 90°F	0	0	1	4	13	18	25	23	12	3	0	0	99
Days Maximum Temp. ≤ 32°F	1	1	0	0	0	0	0	0	0	0	0	1	3
Days Minimum Temp. ≤ 32°F	15	11	5	1	0	0	0	0	0	0	6	15	53
Days Minimum Temp. ≤ 0°F	0	0	0	0	0	0	0	0	0	0	0	0	0
Heating Degree Days (base 65°F)	613	451	287	100	17	***0***	0	***0***	13	98	354	610	***2,543***
Cooling Degree Days (base 65°F)	0	3	24	102	272	***435***	542	***511***	296	101	8	0	***2,294***
Mean Precipitation (in.)	0.63	0.72	0.95	1.29	2.77	2.67	1.78	2.25	2.71	1.96	0.90	0.80	19.43
Extreme Maximum Daily Precip. (in.)	1.30	1.56	1.70	2.85	3.52	3.35	2.93	4.25	4.52	2.95	2.40	1.56	4.52
Days With ≥ 0.1" Precipitation	2	2	2	2	4	4	3	3	4	3	2	2	33
Days With ≥ 0.5" Precipitation	0	0	1	1	2	2	1	1	2	1	1	1	13
Days With ≥ 1.0" Precipitation	0	0	0	0	1	1	1	1	1	1	0	0	6
Mean Snowfall (in.)	0.1	0.2	trace	trace	0.0	0.0	0.0	0.0	0.0	0.0	0.1	0.3	0.7
Maximum Snow Depth (in.)	trace	trace	trace	0	0	0	0	0	0	0	trace	3	3
Days With ≥ 1.0" Snow Depth	0	0	0	0	0	0	0	0	0	0	0	0	0

The period of record for all cooperative weather station data is 1980 – 2009. See User Guide for detailed explanation of data.

Georgetown Lake *Williamson County* Elevation: 839 ft. Latitude: 30° 41' N Longitude: 97° 43' W

	JAN	FEB	MAR	APR	MAY	JUN	JUL	AUG	SEP	OCT	NOV	DEC	YEAR
Mean Maximum Temp. (°F)	59.9	63.7	70.5	78.3	***85.4***	90.8	95.1	96.1	89.5	80.5	69.7	60.5	***78.3***
Mean Temp. (°F)	48.0	51.8	59.1	66.4	***74.7***	80.0	83.5	83.9	77.6	68.5	58.3	49.2	***66.8***
Mean Minimum Temp. (°F)	36.0	39.9	47.6	54.5	***63.9***	69.2	71.8	71.7	65.7	56.5	47.0	37.8	***55.1***
Extreme Maximum Temp. (°F)	88	98	97	99	100	105	108	109	111	98	93	84	111
Extreme Minimum Temp. (°F)	6	6	20	31	42	50	59	57	34	28	23	-2	-2
Days Maximum Temp. ≥ 90°F	0	0	0	2	8	19	27	28	17	4	0	0	105
Days Maximum Temp. ≤ 32°F	0	1	0	0	0	0	0	0	0	0	0	1	2
Days Minimum Temp. ≤ 32°F	10	6	2	0	0	0	0	0	0	0	2	9	29
Days Minimum Temp. ≤ 0°F	0	0	0	0	0	0	0	0	0	0	0	0	0
Heating Degree Days (base 65°F)	523	376	220	70	***5***	0	0	0	5	53	227	489	***1,968***
Cooling Degree Days (base 65°F)	3	9	44	120	***312***	459	580	593	390	171	34	5	***2,720***
Mean Precipitation (in.)	2.14	2.51	3.06	2.74	4.48	4.33	2.02	2.25	3.26	4.37	3.21	2.58	36.95
Extreme Maximum Daily Precip. (in.)	2.50	4.19	2.85	5.50	3.30	3.56	3.40	3.98	4.79	3.50	3.72	4.17	5.50
Days With ≥ 0.1" Precipitation	5	4	5	4	6	5	3	3	4	5	4	4	52
Days With ≥ 0.5" Precipitation	1	2	2	2	3	3	1	1	2	3	2	2	24
Days With ≥ 1.0" Precipitation	1	0	1	1	2	2	1	1	1	2	1	1	14
Mean Snowfall (in.)	0.0	0.0	0.0	0.0	0.0	0.0	0.0	0.0	0.0	0.0	0.0	trace	trace
Maximum Snow Depth (in.)	7	0	0	0	0	0	0	0	0	0	0	trace	7
Days With ≥ 1.0" Snow Depth	0	0	0	0	0	0	0	0	0	0	0	0	0

Grandfalls 3 SSE *Ward County* Elevation: 2,439 ft. Latitude: 31° 18' N Longitude: 102° 50' W

	JAN	FEB	MAR	APR	MAY	JUN	JUL	AUG	SEP	OCT	NOV	DEC	YEAR
Mean Maximum Temp. (°F)	***61.8***	***66.9***	***75.1***	83.3	***91.3***	97.8	98.4	***97.0***	***90.6***	82.2	70.9	***61.1***	***81.4***
Mean Temp. (°F)	***44.7***	***49.4***	***57.3***	65.3	***74.4***	***82.7***	83.9	***82.5***	***75.9***	66.2	53.8	***44.7***	***65.1***
Mean Minimum Temp. (°F)	***27.7***	***32.0***	***39.4***	47.1	***57.5***	***67.3***	69.3	***68.0***	***61.0***	50.0	36.6	***28.2***	***48.7***
Extreme Maximum Temp. (°F)	***86***	***94***	97	104	***110***	117	116	***112***	***107***	100	94	***85***	***117***
Extreme Minimum Temp. (°F)	***8***	***-9***	12	24	***37***	51	55	***52***	***36***	22	7	***0***	***-9***
Days Maximum Temp. ≥ 90°F	***0***	***0***	2	10	***18***	25	29	***28***	na	7	0	***0***	na
Days Maximum Temp. ≤ 32°F	***1***	***0***	0	0	***0***	0	0	***0***	***0***	0	0	***1***	***2***
Days Minimum Temp. ≤ 32°F	***23***	***15***	6	1	***0***	0	0	***0***	***0***	1	***10***	***22***	***78***
Days Minimum Temp. ≤ 0°F	***0***	***0***	0	0	***0***	0	0	***0***	***0***	0	0	***0***	***0***
Heating Degree Days (base 65°F)	***622***	***436***	***258***	95	***12***	***0***	0	***0***	***10***	77	339	***622***	***2,471***
Cooling Degree Days (base 65°F)	***0***	***2***	***24***	109	***312***	***537***	591	***551***	***343***	120	9	***0***	***2,598***
Mean Precipitation (in.)	***0.48***	***0.69***	0.48	0.90	***1.70***	1.50	1.42	***1.74***	***2.50***	1.55	0.59	***0.83***	***14.38***
Extreme Maximum Daily Precip. (in.)	***1.31***	***1.35***	***1.30***	***3.00***	***2.30***	2.34	2.20	***2.82***	na	***2.45***	***1.63***	na	na
Days With ≥ 0.1" Precipitation	***2***	***2***	1	2	3	3	3	***3***	***3***	3	2	***2***	***29***
Days With ≥ 0.5" Precipitation	***0***	***0***	0	1	1	1	1	***1***	***1***	1	0	***1***	***8***
Days With ≥ 1.0" Precipitation	***0***	***0***	0	0	0	1	0	***0***	***1***	1	0	***0***	***3***
Mean Snowfall (in.)	***1.0***	***0.1***	0.1	0.0	0.0	0.0	0.0	***0.0***	***0.0***	0.0	0.3	***0.4***	***1.9***
Maximum Snow Depth (in.)	***5***	***4***	2	1	***0***	0	0	***0***	na	***0***	***0***	***4***	na
Days With ≥ 1.0" Snow Depth	***0***	***0***	0	0	0	0	0	***0***	***0***	0	***0***	***0***	***0***

Granger Dam *Williamson County* Elevation: 564 ft. Latitude: 30° 42' N Longitude: 97° 20' W

	JAN	FEB	MAR	APR	MAY	JUN	JUL	AUG	SEP	OCT	NOV	DEC	YEAR
Mean Maximum Temp. (°F)	59.7	63.9	70.0	78.0	84.5	90.7	94.6	95.5	89.8	80.0	69.8	60.4	78.1
Mean Temp. (°F)	48.3	52.5	59.3	66.8	74.3	80.4	83.5	84.0	78.3	68.6	58.7	49.7	67.0
Mean Minimum Temp. (°F)	36.8	41.0	48.5	55.6	64.0	70.1	72.3	72.5	66.7	57.2	47.5	39.0	55.9
Extreme Maximum Temp. (°F)	86	98	94	97	100	105	104	107	110	98	89	84	110
Extreme Minimum Temp. (°F)	7	3	19	31	42	51	58	57	44	27	21	2	2
Days Maximum Temp. ≥ 90°F	0	0	0	1	7	20	27	28	17	4	0	0	104
Days Maximum Temp. ≤ 32°F	0	0	0	0	0	0	0	0	0	0	0	1	1
Days Minimum Temp. ≤ 32°F	10	5	2	0	0	0	0	0	0	0	2	8	27
Days Minimum Temp. ≤ 0°F	0	0	0	0	0	0	0	0	0	0	0	0	0
Heating Degree Days (base 65°F)	516	358	214	64	6	0	0	0	4	53	222	474	1,911
Cooling Degree Days (base 65°F)	4	12	44	126	300	468	581	596	410	174	41	8	2,764
Mean Precipitation (in.)	2.20	2.22	2.71	2.00	5.01	4.24	1.62	2.02	3.00	3.68	2.69	2.89	34.28
Extreme Maximum Daily Precip. (in.)	2.88	2.07	2.80	2.80	3.80	5.40	3.53	3.33	4.12	6.05	3.50	7.84	7.84
Days With ≥ 0.1" Precipitation	4	4	5	4	6	5	3	3	4	5	4	4	51
Days With ≥ 0.5" Precipitation	1	2	2	1	3	3	1	1	2	2	2	2	22
Days With ≥ 1.0" Precipitation	1	0	1	0	2	2	0	1	1	1	1	1	11
Mean Snowfall (in.)	0.0	0.0	0.0	0.0	0.0	0.0	0.0	0.0	0.0	0.0	0.0	trace	trace
Maximum Snow Depth (in.)	0	0	0	0	0	0	0	0	0	0	0	trace	trace
Days With ≥ 1.0" Snow Depth	0	0	0	0	0	0	0	0	0	0	0	0	0

Grapevine Dam *Tarrant County* Elevation: 584 ft. Latitude: 32° 57' N Longitude: 97° 03' W

	JAN	FEB	MAR	APR	MAY	JUN	JUL	AUG	SEP	OCT	NOV	DEC	YEAR
Mean Maximum Temp. (°F)	56.3	60.5	67.5	75.8	83.3	91.0	96.0	96.4	88.7	78.6	66.9	56.9	76.5
Mean Temp. (°F)	44.3	48.6	55.8	63.7	72.4	80.0	84.4	84.4	76.6	65.9	55.2	45.3	64.7
Mean Minimum Temp. (°F)	32.1	36.4	43.9	51.6	61.4	68.9	72.7	72.4	64.4	53.2	43.3	33.8	52.8
Extreme Maximum Temp. (°F)	85	95	96	101	101	109	110	108	109	100	89	83	110
Extreme Minimum Temp. (°F)	6	4	13	29	41	50	57	55	38	22	19	-1	-1
Days Maximum Temp. ≥ 90°F	0	0	0	1	6	20	27	27	15	4	0	0	100
Days Maximum Temp. ≤ 32°F	1	1	0	0	0	0	0	0	0	0	0	1	3
Days Minimum Temp. ≤ 32°F	17	9	3	0	0	0	0	0	0	0	4	13	46
Days Minimum Temp. ≤ 0°F	0	0	0	0	0	0	0	0	0	0	0	0	0
Heating Degree Days (base 65°F)	637	461	303	108	14	1	0	0	10	88	308	603	2,533
Cooling Degree Days (base 65°F)	1	5	24	77	250	456	607	609	363	123	20	2	2,537
Mean Precipitation (in.)	2.17	2.77	3.48	3.13	4.81	3.89	2.26	1.82	3.12	4.00	2.94	2.69	37.08
Extreme Maximum Daily Precip. (in.)	3.93	3.92	3.78	2.80	6.47	8.30	7.50	1.94	4.67	5.01	3.40	3.67	8.30
Days With ≥ 0.1" Precipitation	4	4	5	4	6	5	3	3	4	5	4	5	52
Days With ≥ 0.5" Precipitation	1	2	2	2	3	3	1	1	2	3	2	2	24
Days With ≥ 1.0" Precipitation	0	1	1	1	2	1	1	0	1	1	1	1	11
Mean Snowfall (in.)	0.0	0.2	0.0	0.0	0.0	0.0	0.0	0.0	0.0	0.0	0.0	0.1	0.3
Maximum Snow Depth (in.)	trace	2	0	0	0	0	0	0	0	0	0	3	3
Days With ≥ 1.0" Snow Depth	0	0	0	0	0	0	0	0	0	0	0	0	0

The period of record for all cooperative weather station data is 1980 – 2009. See User Guide for detailed explanation of data.

Harlingen *Cameron County* Elevation: 38 ft. Latitude: 26° 12' N Longitude: 97° 40' W

	JAN	FEB	MAR	APR	MAY	JUN	JUL	AUG	SEP	OCT	NOV	DEC	YEAR
Mean Maximum Temp. (°F)	69.8	73.6	79.4	84.4	89.2	93.7	95.1	95.6	91.6	85.7	78.6	70.6	83.9
Mean Temp. (°F)	59.9	63.2	68.8	74.3	80.0	84.1	85.2	85.4	82.0	75.6	68.3	60.7	74.0
Mean Minimum Temp. (°F)	49.8	52.7	58.1	64.2	70.7	74.6	75.3	75.3	72.3	65.6	57.9	50.8	63.9
Extreme Maximum Temp. (°F)	93	95	104	103	102	104	102	104	106	97	97	89	106
Extreme Minimum Temp. (°F)	26	28	29	37	49	57	67	67	56	33	33	15	15
Days Maximum Temp. ≥ 90°F	0	1	2	7	17	26	29	29	22	8	1	0	142
Days Maximum Temp. ≤ 32°F	0	0	0	0	0	0	0	0	0	0	0	0	0
Days Minimum Temp. ≤ 32°F	1	0	0	0	0	0	0	0	0	0	0	1	2
Days Minimum Temp. ≤ 0°F	0	0	0	0	0	0	0	0	0	0	0	0	0
Heating Degree Days (base 65°F)	208	129	53	12	0	0	0	0	0	9	64	198	673
Cooling Degree Days (base 65°F)	56	83	177	298	471	580	633	641	517	345	169	72	4,042
Mean Precipitation (in.)	1.26	1.62	1.44	1.92	3.11	2.25	2.08	2.49	5.06	3.25	1.49	1.62	27.59
Extreme Maximum Daily Precip. (in.)	1.73	7.95	2.32	9.79	6.09	3.46	5.77	5.77	5.05	4.66	2.88	3.19	9.79
Days With ≥ 0.1" Precipitation	3	2	3	2	3	3	3	4	6	4	3	3	39
Days With ≥ 0.5" Precipitation	1	1	1	1	2	1	1	2	3	2	1	1	17
Days With ≥ 1.0" Precipitation	0	0	1	0	1	1	1	1	1	1	0	0	7
Mean Snowfall (in.)	0.0	0.0	0.0	0.0	0.0	0.0	0.0	0.0	0.0	0.0	0.0	0.1	0.1
Maximum Snow Depth (in.)	0	0	0	0	0	0	0	0	0	0	0	2	2
Days With ≥ 1.0" Snow Depth	0	0	0	0	0	0	0	0	0	0	0	0	0

Hart *Castro County* Elevation: 3,640 ft. Latitude: 34° 22' N Longitude: 102° 05' W

	JAN	FEB	MAR	APR	MAY	JUN	JUL	AUG	SEP	OCT	NOV	DEC	YEAR
Mean Maximum Temp. (°F)	51.6	56.7	63.5	72.2	80.7	88.0	90.0	88.2	82.0	73.4	61.2	51.4	71.6
Mean Temp. (°F)	37.0	41.0	47.6	56.1	66.0	73.9	76.5	75.1	68.1	58.0	46.1	37.0	56.9
Mean Minimum Temp. (°F)	22.3	25.3	31.7	39.9	51.2	59.9	63.0	62.0	54.1	42.7	30.8	22.6	42.1
Extreme Maximum Temp. (°F)	81	85	91	98	108	110	103	104	107	98	91	80	110
Extreme Minimum Temp. (°F)	2	-1	3	20	32	44	52	50	34	16	-2	-11	-11
Days Maximum Temp. ≥ 90°F	0	0	0	1	6	14	18	15	5	1	0	0	60
Days Maximum Temp. ≤ 32°F	3	1	1	0	0	0	0	0	0	0	1	3	9
Days Minimum Temp. ≤ 32°F	29	23	16	5	0	0	0	0	0	3	18	28	122
Days Minimum Temp. ≤ 0°F	0	0	0	0	0	0	0	0	0	0	0	1	1
Heating Degree Days (base 65°F)	861	671	533	277	78	4	1	2	43	229	562	861	4,122
Cooling Degree Days (base 65°F)	0	0	1	16	115	279	366	322	142	20	0	0	1,261
Mean Precipitation (in.)	0.54	0.56	1.03	1.16	2.61	2.85	1.77	2.74	1.95	1.34	0.84	0.70	18.09
Extreme Maximum Daily Precip. (in.)	1.02	1.14	1.18	2.10	3.66	3.75	1.91	2.41	2.73	2.62	1.10	1.10	3.75
Days With ≥ 0.1" Precipitation	1	1	3	3	4	5	4	5	3	3	2	2	36
Days With ≥ 0.5" Precipitation	0	0	1	1	2	2	1	2	1	1	1	0	12
Days With ≥ 1.0" Precipitation	0	0	0	0	1	1	0	1	1	0	0	0	4
Mean Snowfall (in.)	0.5	0.8	0.5	trace	0.0	0.0	0.0	0.0	0.0	0.0	0.9	1.0	3.7
Maximum Snow Depth (in.)	7	na	na	trace	0	0	0	0	0	na	na	na	na
Days With ≥ 1.0" Snow Depth	0	0	0	0	0	0	0	0	0	0	0	0	0

Henderson *Rusk County* Elevation: 419 ft. Latitude: 32° 11' N Longitude: 94° 48' W

	JAN	FEB	MAR	APR	MAY	JUN	JUL	AUG	SEP	OCT	NOV	DEC	YEAR
Mean Maximum Temp. (°F)	57.0	61.3	68.4	75.8	82.6	89.2	93.0	93.9	87.7	77.8	67.4	58.6	76.0
Mean Temp. (°F)	46.0	49.7	56.5	63.8	71.9	78.7	82.2	82.4	75.9	65.6	55.9	47.4	64.7
Mean Minimum Temp. (°F)	35.0	38.2	44.6	51.7	61.2	68.2	71.4	70.8	64.1	53.4	44.4	36.2	53.2
Extreme Maximum Temp. (°F)	83	93	88	93	101	104	108	110	111	96	86	82	111
Extreme Minimum Temp. (°F)	4	11	16	25	38	51	55	54	40	24	20	-1	-1
Days Maximum Temp. ≥ 90°F	0	0	0	0	3	16	25	25	14	2	0	0	85
Days Maximum Temp. ≤ 32°F	1	1	0	0	0	0	0	0	0	0	0	1	3
Days Minimum Temp. ≤ 32°F	14	9	4	0	0	0	0	0	0	0	4	12	43
Days Minimum Temp. ≤ 0°F	0	0	0	0	0	0	0	0	0	0	0	0	0
Heating Degree Days (base 65°F)	586	432	282	111	13	0	0	0	9	90	291	545	2,359
Cooling Degree Days (base 65°F)	4	7	25	80	234	418	540	545	342	116	24	6	2,341
Mean Precipitation (in.)	3.78	4.17	4.26	3.74	4.80	5.05	2.96	2.76	3.57	4.80	4.74	4.44	49.07
Extreme Maximum Daily Precip. (in.)	3.00	2.71	11.05	4.26	4.73	6.33	4.57	3.72	6.25	4.27	5.50	3.30	11.05
Days With ≥ 0.1" Precipitation	6	6	6	5	6	6	5	4	5	5	6	6	66
Days With ≥ 0.5" Precipitation	2	3	3	3	3	3	2	2	2	3	3	3	32
Days With ≥ 1.0" Precipitation	1	1	1	1	2	1	1	1	1	2	2	2	16
Mean Snowfall (in.)	0.4	0.3	trace	trace	0.0	0.0	0.0	0.0	0.0	0.0	trace	0.2	0.9
Maximum Snow Depth (in.)	2	2	trace	0	0	0	0	0	0	0	trace	trace	2
Days With ≥ 1.0" Snow Depth	0	0	0	0	0	0	0	0	0	0	0	0	0

Henrietta *Clay County* Elevation: 930 ft. Latitude: 33° 49' N Longitude: 98° 12' W

	JAN	FEB	MAR	APR	MAY	JUN	JUL	AUG	SEP	OCT	NOV	DEC	YEAR
Mean Maximum Temp. (°F)	54.3	58.2	66.2	75.5	83.0	90.2	96.6	96.6	88.6	77.4	65.1	55.3	75.6
Mean Temp. (°F)	41.3	45.2	53.0	61.9	70.8	78.3	83.7	83.2	75.3	64.0	52.1	42.7	62.6
Mean Minimum Temp. (°F)	28.4	32.1	39.6	48.2	58.5	66.4	70.6	69.8	62.0	50.5	39.1	30.1	49.6
Extreme Maximum Temp. (°F)	86	95	98	100	103	115	113	111	107	100	90	84	115
Extreme Minimum Temp. (°F)	3	-7	6	27	38	48	57	51	37	20	16	-8	-8
Days Maximum Temp. ≥ 90°F	0	0	0	1	7	17	27	27	15	3	0	0	97
Days Maximum Temp. ≤ 32°F	2	1	0	0	0	0	0	0	0	0	0	2	5
Days Minimum Temp. ≤ 32°F	22	14	7	1	0	0	0	0	0	1	8	19	72
Days Minimum Temp. ≤ 0°F	0	0	0	0	0	0	0	0	0	0	0	0	0
Heating Degree Days (base 65°F)	727	554	380	152	25	1	0	0	17	117	390	684	3,047
Cooling Degree Days (base 65°F)	0	1	13	65	212	408	585	571	334	91	10	1	2,291
Mean Precipitation (in.)	1.56	2.20	2.60	2.70	4.31	3.95	1.73	2.51	2.82	3.50	2.00	2.29	32.17
Extreme Maximum Daily Precip. (in.)	2.04	4.56	2.12	3.76	3.75	3.12	4.17	3.93	4.46	4.56	2.47	5.39	5.39
Days With ≥ 0.1" Precipitation	3	4	5	4	5	5	3	4	4	5	3	4	49
Days With ≥ 0.5" Precipitation	1	1	2	2	3	3	1	2	2	2	1	2	22
Days With ≥ 1.0" Precipitation	0	1	1	1	1	2	0	1	1	1	1	1	11
Mean Snowfall (in.)	0.2	0.1	trace	0.0	0.0	0.0	0.0	0.0	0.0	trace	0.1	0.2	0.6
Maximum Snow Depth (in.)	2	1	7	0	0	0	0	0	0	0	trace	1	7
Days With ≥ 1.0" Snow Depth	0	0	0	0	0	0	0	0	0	0	0	0	0

The period of record for all cooperative weather station data is 1980 – 2009. See User Guide for detailed explanation of data.

Houston William P Hobby Arpt *Harris County* Elevation: 49 ft. Latitude: 29° 39' N Longitude: 95° 17' W

	JAN	FEB	MAR	APR	MAY	JUN	JUL	AUG	SEP	OCT	NOV	DEC	YEAR
Mean Maximum Temp. (°F)	62.8	65.9	72.4	78.8	85.3	90.2	92.3	92.6	88.4	81.0	72.3	64.5	78.9
Mean Temp. (°F)	53.9	57.2	63.4	69.7	77.0	82.0	83.9	84.1	80.1	71.9	63.0	55.6	70.2
Mean Minimum Temp. (°F)	45.1	48.4	54.4	60.6	68.7	73.8	75.5	75.6	71.6	62.8	53.6	46.6	61.4
Extreme Maximum Temp. (°F)	82	87	90	92	100	102	103	104	108	94	88	84	108
Extreme Minimum Temp. (°F)	15	20	24	22	49	56	45	65	53	33	28	9	9
Days Maximum Temp. ≥ 90°F	0	0	0	1	5	18	25	25	14	2	0	0	90
Days Maximum Temp. ≤ 32°F	0	0	0	0	0	0	0	0	0	0	0	0	0
Days Minimum Temp. ≤ 32°F	2	1	1	0	0	0	0	0	0	0	0	2	6
Days Minimum Temp. ≤ 0°F	0	0	0	0	0	0	0	0	0	0	0	0	0
Heating Degree Days (base 65°F)	351	242	117	28	0	0	0	0	0	22	134	316	1,210
Cooling Degree Days (base 65°F)	16	27	75	177	379	517	593	600	459	245	80	30	3,198
Mean Precipitation (in.)	4.01	3.24	3.28	3.28	4.94	6.99	4.31	4.81	4.93	5.79	4.24	3.84	53.66
Extreme Maximum Daily Precip. (in.)	4.10	3.54	3.09	5.38	9.48	9.28	3.47	8.58	8.08	7.86	4.28	4.18	9.48
Days With ≥ 0.1" Precipitation	6	5	5	4	5	7	6	6	6	6	5	5	66
Days With ≥ 0.5" Precipitation	3	2	2	2	3	4	3	3	3	3	3	2	33
Days With ≥ 1.0" Precipitation	1	1	1	1	2	2	1	1	2	2	1	1	16
Mean Snowfall (in.)	na	na	na	na	na	na	na	na	na	na	na	na	na
Maximum Snow Depth (in.)	na	na	na	na	na	na	na	na	na	na	na	na	na
Days With ≥ 1.0" Snow Depth	na	na	na	na	na	na	na	na	na	na	na	na	na

La Tuna 1 S *El Paso County* Elevation: 3,799 ft. Latitude: 31° 58' N Longitude: 106° 36' W

	JAN	FEB	MAR	APR	MAY	JUN	JUL	AUG	SEP	OCT	NOV	DEC	YEAR
Mean Maximum Temp. (°F)	58.7	64.8	71.9	80.4	89.0	96.6	96.3	93.5	89.0	79.9	67.5	57.7	78.8
Mean Temp. (°F)	44.4	49.8	56.1	64.1	73.0	81.0	82.6	80.4	75.1	64.6	52.5	43.9	63.9
Mean Minimum Temp. (°F)	30.1	34.7	40.3	47.6	57.0	65.4	69.0	67.3	61.2	49.2	37.4	30.0	49.1
Extreme Maximum Temp. (°F)	77	83	***91***	98	105	112	109	106	102	95	86	75	***112***
Extreme Minimum Temp. (°F)	6	12	18	27	36	48	53	51	40	24	17	9	6
Days Maximum Temp. ≥ 90°F	0	0	0	2	14	26	28	25	15	2	0	0	112
Days Maximum Temp. ≤ 32°F	0	0	0	0	0	0	0	0	0	0	0	0	0
Days Minimum Temp. ≤ 32°F	20	11	4	0	0	0	0	0	0	1	8	21	65
Days Minimum Temp. ≤ 0°F	0	0	0	0	0	0	0	0	0	0	0	0	0
Heating Degree Days (base 65°F)	631	424	275	86	6	0	0	0	3	81	370	649	2,525
Cooling Degree Days (base 65°F)	0	0	7	64	261	487	552	486	312	75	1	0	2,245
Mean Precipitation (in.)	0.54	0.35	0.19	0.08	0.38	0.93	1.67	2.05	1.20	0.70	0.42	0.69	9.20
Extreme Maximum Daily Precip. (in.)	2.08	0.93	0.48	0.36	1.83	4.25	2.00	2.65	***2.00***	***1.08***	0.90	1.80	***4.25***
Days With ≥ 0.1" Precipitation	1	1	1	0	1	1	3	4	3	2	1	2	20
Days With ≥ 0.5" Precipitation	0	0	0	0	0	1	1	1	1	1	0	0	5
Days With ≥ 1.0" Precipitation	0	0	0	0	0	0	0	0	0	0	0	0	0
Mean Snowfall (in.)	0.0	trace	0.0	0.0	0.0	0.0	0.0	0.0	0.0	0.0	trace	0.0	trace
Maximum Snow Depth (in.)	0	trace	***0***	0	0	0	0	***0***	0	***0***	***trace***	***0***	trace
Days With ≥ 1.0" Snow Depth	0	0	0	0	0	0	0	0	0	0	0	***0***	***0***

Langtry *Val Verde County* Elevation: 1,290 ft. Latitude: 29° 48' N Longitude: 101° 34' W

	JAN	FEB	MAR	APR	MAY	JUN	JUL	AUG	SEP	OCT	NOV	DEC	YEAR
Mean Maximum Temp. (°F)	63.6	68.5	76.2	84.9	91.6	96.2	98.3	98.2	92.5	82.9	72.2	63.6	82.4
Mean Temp. (°F)	49.6	54.5	62.7	71.1	79.6	85.0	87.2	86.9	80.9	70.8	59.3	49.9	69.8
Mean Minimum Temp. (°F)	35.6	40.3	49.1	57.3	67.4	73.8	76.0	75.7	69.3	58.7	46.3	36.2	57.1
Extreme Maximum Temp. (°F)	93	100	98	110	110	113	111	112	112	100	97	89	113
Extreme Minimum Temp. (°F)	16	11	21	31	47	58	57	62	46	26	21	9	9
Days Maximum Temp. ≥ 90°F	0	1	2	9	20	26	29	29	22	7	1	0	146
Days Maximum Temp. ≤ 32°F	0	0	0	0	0	0	0	0	0	0	0	0	0
Days Minimum Temp. ≤ 32°F	12	5	2	0	0	0	0	0	0	0	2	11	32
Days Minimum Temp. ≤ 0°F	0	0	0	0	0	0	0	0	0	0	0	0	0
Heating Degree Days (base 65°F)	470	300	138	32	1	0	0	0	2	33	201	461	1,638
Cooling Degree Days (base 65°F)	0	9	72	222	459	608	694	687	485	220	37	1	3,494
Mean Precipitation (in.)	0.61	0.69	0.88	0.98	1.87	1.62	1.12	1.80	1.90	1.86	0.77	0.46	14.56
Extreme Maximum Daily Precip. (in.)	1.01	1.95	2.92	4.32	2.11	2.10	2.12	6.04	4.19	3.20	1.50	1.78	6.04
Days With ≥ 0.1" Precipitation	2	2	2	2	3	3	2	2	3	3	2	1	27
Days With ≥ 0.5" Precipitation	0	0	1	1	1	1	1	1	1	1	1	0	9
Days With ≥ 1.0" Precipitation	0	0	0	0	1	0	0	1	1	1	0	0	4
Mean Snowfall (in.)	0.3	0.0	0.0	0.0	0.0	0.0	0.0	0.0	0.0	0.0	0.0	0.0	0.3
Maximum Snow Depth (in.)	trace	0	0	0	0	0	0	0	0	0	0	0	trace
Days With ≥ 1.0" Snow Depth	0	0	0	0	0	0	0	0	0	0	0	0	0

Laredo 2 *Webb County* Elevation: 430 ft. Latitude: 27° 34' N Longitude: 99° 30' W

	JAN	FEB	MAR	APR	MAY	JUN	JUL	AUG	SEP	OCT	NOV	DEC	YEAR
Mean Maximum Temp. (°F)	68.1	73.1	80.7	88.5	94.4	99.1	100.4	100.6	94.4	86.8	76.9	68.4	85.9
Mean Temp. (°F)	56.8	61.4	68.5	76.0	82.6	87.2	88.3	88.4	83.2	75.7	65.7	57.3	74.3
Mean Minimum Temp. (°F)	45.5	49.8	56.4	63.5	70.8	75.2	76.1	76.2	72.0	64.5	54.4	46.1	62.5
Extreme Maximum Temp. (°F)	93	103	105	110	114	114	113	111	110	103	99	92	114
Extreme Minimum Temp. (°F)	21	21	27	32	45	61	66	67	50	28	27	11	11
Days Maximum Temp. ≥ 90°F	0	2	6	15	24	29	30	30	24	13	2	0	175
Days Maximum Temp. ≤ 32°F	0	0	0	0	0	0	0	0	0	0	0	0	0
Days Minimum Temp. ≤ 32°F	3	1	0	0	0	0	0	0	0	0	0	3	7
Days Minimum Temp. ≤ 0°F	0	0	0	0	0	0	0	0	0	0	0	0	0
Heating Degree Days (base 65°F)	278	163	65	13	0	0	0	0	1	14	102	270	906
Cooling Degree Days (base 65°F)	30	69	181	349	554	672	729	733	554	352	129	37	4,389
Mean Precipitation (in.)	0.84	0.91	1.13	1.31	2.45	2.15	2.06	2.01	2.79	2.24	1.20	0.89	19.98
Extreme Maximum Daily Precip. (in.)	1.20	2.25	2.71	2.12	4.43	4.29	6.65	3.92	4.60	4.75	2.84	2.41	6.65
Days With ≥ 0.1" Precipitation	2	2	2	2	3	3	3	3	4	3	2	2	31
Days With ≥ 0.5" Precipitation	0	1	1	1	2	1	1	1	2	1	1	1	13
Days With ≥ 1.0" Precipitation	0	0	0	0	1	1	1	1	1	1	0	0	6
Mean Snowfall (in.)	trace	trace	0.0	0.0	0.0	0.0	0.0	0.0	0.0	trace	0.0	trace	trace
Maximum Snow Depth (in.)	trace	trace	0	0	0	0	0	0	0	trace	0	1	1
Days With ≥ 1.0" Snow Depth	0	0	0	0	0	0	0	0	0	0	0	0	0

Lavon Dam *Collin County* Elevation: 509 ft. Latitude: 33° 02' N Longitude: 96° 29' W

	JAN	FEB	MAR	APR	MAY	JUN	JUL	AUG	SEP	OCT	NOV	DEC	YEAR
Mean Maximum Temp. (°F)	55.5	59.8	66.6	75.0	82.4	90.0	94.5	95.5	88.6	78.5	67.0	56.8	75.9
Mean Temp. (°F)	***43.7***	48.4	55.5	63.8	72.1	79.5	83.3	83.6	76.4	65.8	55.5	45.6	***64.4***
Mean Minimum Temp. (°F)	32.4	36.8	44.3	52.5	61.7	68.8	72.1	71.5	64.2	53.0	43.8	34.6	53.0
Extreme Maximum Temp. (°F)	82	96	93	97	99	107	109	107	111	100	88	85	111
Extreme Minimum Temp. (°F)	5	7	12	28	39	49	58	54	36	26	19	-3	-3
Days Maximum Temp. ≥ 90°F	0	0	0	0	4	18	27	27	15	3	0	0	94
Days Maximum Temp. ≤ 32°F	1	1	0	0	0	0	0	0	0	0	0	1	3
Days Minimum Temp. ≤ 32°F	16	9	3	0	0	0	0	0	0	0	4	12	44
Days Minimum Temp. ≤ 0°F	0	0	0	0	0	0	0	0	0	0	0	0	0
Heating Degree Days (base 65°F)	***653***	465	307	105	12	0	0	0	8	82	302	596	***2,530***
Cooling Degree Days (base 65°F)	***1***	3	18	74	238	440	574	582	358	112	21	2	***2,423***
Mean Precipitation (in.)	2.55	2.91	3.63	3.46	5.19	4.53	2.02	1.84	3.19	4.41	3.61	3.21	40.55
Extreme Maximum Daily Precip. (in.)	3.11	3.45	4.79	3.90	6.08	4.00	3.10	2.68	3.91	4.76	2.92	4.03	6.08
Days With ≥ 0.1" Precipitation	4	5	5	5	6	6	3	3	5	5	5	5	57
Days With ≥ 0.5" Precipitation	2	2	3	2	3	3	1	1	2	2	3	2	26
Days With ≥ 1.0" Precipitation	1	1	1	1	2	1	1	1	1	1	1	1	13
Mean Snowfall (in.)	0.0	0.1	0.0	0.0	0.0	0.0	0.0	0.0	0.0	0.0	0.0	0.1	0.2
Maximum Snow Depth (in.)	0	3	0	0	0	0	0	0	0	***0***	0	3	***3***
Days With ≥ 1.0" Snow Depth	0	0	0	0	0	0	0	0	0	0	0	0	0

Liberty *Liberty County* Elevation: 35 ft. Latitude: 30° 04' N Longitude: 94° 48' W

	JAN	FEB	MAR	APR	MAY	JUN	JUL	AUG	SEP	OCT	NOV	DEC	YEAR
Mean Maximum Temp. (°F)	62.7	65.8	72.6	78.4	85.0	90.4	92.9	93.4	88.9	81.2	71.9	63.8	78.9
Mean Temp. (°F)	52.3	55.5	62.0	68.1	75.6	81.2	83.5	83.6	78.8	70.4	61.0	53.5	68.8
Mean Minimum Temp. (°F)	41.7	45.1	51.3	57.8	66.1	71.9	74.1	73.8	68.6	59.4	50.1	43.2	58.6
Extreme Maximum Temp. (°F)	82	87	93	93	97	102	103	107	107	95	90	86	107
Extreme Minimum Temp. (°F)	14	19	22	31	45	54	62	60	48	31	26	7	7
Days Maximum Temp. ≥ 90°F	0	0	0	1	4	20	26	26	15	3	0	0	95
Days Maximum Temp. ≤ 32°F	0	0	0	0	0	0	0	0	0	0	0	0	0
Days Minimum Temp. ≤ 32°F	5	2	1	0	0	0	0	0	0	0	1	5	14
Days Minimum Temp. ≤ 0°F	0	0	0	0	0	0	0	0	0	0	0	0	0
Heating Degree Days (base 65°F)	399	282	149	45	1	0	0	0	1	34	174	369	1,454
Cooling Degree Days (base 65°F)	11	19	63	145	336	491	581	583	420	208	62	22	2,941
Mean Precipitation (in.)	4.47	4.05	4.00	3.80	5.51	7.11	4.84	4.59	6.00	7.18	5.32	4.95	61.82
Extreme Maximum Daily Precip. (in.)	7.02	3.60	4.90	4.20	10.60	11.79	6.50	5.40	7.40	18.50	7.00	4.20	18.50
Days With ≥ 0.1" Precipitation	6	6	5	4	5	8	7	6	7	6	5	6	71
Days With ≥ 0.5" Precipitation	3	2	3	2	3	4	3	3	3	3	3	3	35
Days With ≥ 1.0" Precipitation	1	1	1	1	2	2	1	1	2	2	2	2	18
Mean Snowfall (in.)	0.1	trace	0.0	0.0	0.0	0.0	0.0	0.0	0.0	0.0	0.0	0.1	0.2
Maximum Snow Depth (in.)	trace	trace	0	0	0	0	0	0	0	0	0	0	trace
Days With ≥ 1.0" Snow Depth	0	0	0	0	0	0	0	0	0	0	0	0	0

Longview 11 SE *Rusk County* Elevation: 407 ft. Latitude: 32° 21' N Longitude: 94° 39' W

	JAN	FEB	MAR	APR	MAY	JUN	JUL	AUG	SEP	OCT	NOV	DEC	YEAR
Mean Maximum Temp. (°F)	57.7	61.6	69.0	76.2	83.1	89.5	93.5	94.2	87.7	77.8	67.5	58.8	76.4
Mean Temp. (°F)	47.7	51.4	58.3	65.3	73.3	79.6	83.2	83.3	76.9	66.9	57.3	48.8	66.0
Mean Minimum Temp. (°F)	37.7	41.0	47.6	54.4	63.4	69.7	73.0	72.4	66.0	55.8	47.0	38.7	55.6
Extreme Maximum Temp. (°F)	83	90	88	93	98	102	106	109	111	96	86	83	111
Extreme Minimum Temp. (°F)	4	10	17	30	45	54	62	56	41	27	23	2	2
Days Maximum Temp. ≥ 90°F	0	0	0	0	4	17	25	26	13	2	0	0	87
Days Maximum Temp. ≤ 32°F	0	0	0	0	0	0	0	0	0	0	0	1	1
Days Minimum Temp. ≤ 32°F	10	6	2	0	0	0	0	0	0	0	2	9	29
Days Minimum Temp. ≤ 0°F	0	0	0	0	0	0	0	0	0	0	0	0	0
Heating Degree Days (base 65°F)	533	388	235	81	6	0	0	0	5	72	257	503	2,080
Cooling Degree Days (base 65°F)	5	10	34	98	270	446	573	575	369	137	30	8	2,555
Mean Precipitation (in.)	3.76	4.19	4.43	3.67	5.18	5.21	2.99	2.87	3.44	4.65	4.69	4.80	49.88
Extreme Maximum Daily Precip. (in.)	3.70	2.80	7.80	5.06	3.86	8.69	4.30	3.80	3.46	5.15	4.26	4.87	8.69
Days With ≥ 0.1" Precipitation	6	6	6	5	6	6	4	4	5	6	6	6	66
Days With ≥ 0.5" Precipitation	3	3	3	2	3	3	2	2	2	3	3	3	32
Days With ≥ 1.0" Precipitation	1	1	2	1	2	2	1	1	1	2	2	2	18
Mean Snowfall (in.)	0.5	0.4	trace	trace	0.0	0.0	0.0	0.0	0.0	0.0	trace	0.2	1.1
Maximum Snow Depth (in.)	8	6	1	trace	0	0	0	0	0	0	trace	3	8
Days With ≥ 1.0" Snow Depth	1	0	0	0	0	0	0	0	0	0	0	0	1

Marathon *Brewster County* Elevation: 4,089 ft. Latitude: 30° 13' N Longitude: 103° 14' W

	JAN	FEB	MAR	APR	MAY	JUN	JUL	AUG	SEP	OCT	NOV	DEC	YEAR
Mean Maximum Temp. (°F)	62.4	66.1	***73.1***	80.5	87.7	***91.4***	90.7	89.7	85.0	***78.9***	69.9	63.7	***78.2***
Mean Temp. (°F)	46.3	49.6	***55.9***	63.1	71.2	***76.4***	76.9	76.1	71.3	***63.4***	53.5	47.4	***62.6***
Mean Minimum Temp. (°F)	30.0	33.1	***38.7***	45.6	54.8	***61.4***	63.0	62.4	57.6	***47.9***	37.2	31.1	***46.9***
Extreme Maximum Temp. (°F)	82	88	90	100	105	108	105	103	100	96	89	81	108
Extreme Minimum Temp. (°F)	9	7	11	19	35	48	50	51	36	17	9	0	0
Days Maximum Temp. ≥ 90°F	0	0	0	3	14	18	19	17	8	2	0	0	81
Days Maximum Temp. ≤ 32°F	0	0	0	0	0	0	0	0	0	0	0	0	0
Days Minimum Temp. ≤ 32°F	19	13	6	2	0	0	0	0	0	1	9	18	68
Days Minimum Temp. ≤ 0°F	0	0	0	0	0	0	0	0	0	0	0	0	0
Heating Degree Days (base 65°F)	574	431	***282***	105	10	***0***	0	0	14	***97***	340	540	***2,393***
Cooling Degree Days (base 65°F)	0	1	***8***	53	211	***350***	375	350	210	***55***	3	0	***1,616***
Mean Precipitation (in.)	0.48	0.35	0.35	0.65	1.54	2.08	2.36	2.19	1.99	1.81	0.39	0.47	14.66
Extreme Maximum Daily Precip. (in.)	1.20	1.37	1.30	1.53	2.96	1.91	2.15	2.60	2.00	2.96	1.60	1.57	2.96
Days With ≥ 0.1" Precipitation	1	1	1	1	3	4	4	4	4	3	1	1	28
Days With ≥ 0.5" Precipitation	0	0	0	0	1	1	2	1	1	1	0	0	7
Days With ≥ 1.0" Precipitation	0	0	0	0	0	0	1	1	1	1	0	0	4
Mean Snowfall (in.)	0.6	trace	trace	trace	0.0	0.0	0.0	0.0	0.0	trace	0.2	0.1	0.9
Maximum Snow Depth (in.)	***trace***	***trace***	***0***	***0***	***0***	***0***	0	0	***0***	***trace***	trace	2	***2***
Days With ≥ 1.0" Snow Depth	***0***	0	0	0	0	0	0	0	0	0	0	0	***0***

The period of record for all cooperative weather station data is 1980 – 2009. See User Guide for detailed explanation of data.

Marshall *Harrison County* Elevation: 352 ft. Latitude: 32° 32' N Longitude: 94° 21' W

	JAN	FEB	MAR	APR	MAY	JUN	JUL	AUG	SEP	OCT	NOV	DEC	YEAR
Mean Maximum Temp. (°F)	55.8	60.1	67.4	75.1	82.1	88.7	92.7	93.1	86.9	76.6	66.6	57.3	75.2
Mean Temp. (°F)	45.4	49.4	56.7	64.0	72.0	78.9	82.5	82.5	75.9	65.1	55.9	47.0	64.6
Mean Minimum Temp. (°F)	34.9	38.6	45.9	52.8	61.9	69.1	72.3	71.9	64.8	53.4	45.1	36.7	54.0
Extreme Maximum Temp. (°F)	81	90	87	94	97	104	105	107	105	96	88	82	107
Extreme Minimum Temp. (°F)	0	10	16	30	42	48	52	55	35	27	22	3	0
Days Maximum Temp. ≥ 90°F	0	0	0	0	3	14	24	24	12	1	0	0	78
Days Maximum Temp. ≤ 32°F	1	0	0	0	0	0	0	0	0	0	0	1	2
Days Minimum Temp. ≤ 32°F	14	8	3	0	0	0	0	0	0	0	3	11	39
Days Minimum Temp. ≤ 0°F	0	0	0	0	0	0	0	0	0	0	0	0	0
Heating Degree Days (base 65°F)	605	442	280	105	13	0	0	0	9	93	288	554	2,389
Cooling Degree Days (base 65°F)	4	6	29	82	238	423	550	550	342	106	23	5	2,358
Mean Precipitation (in.)	3.77	4.28	4.50	3.83	5.01	5.11	3.24	2.63	3.39	4.88	4.60	5.04	50.28
Extreme Maximum Daily Precip. (in.)	4.15	2.60	8.58	4.23	5.10	6.84	5.55	2.90	4.08	4.35	3.40	6.95	8.58
Days With ≥ 0.1" Precipitation	6	6	6	5	6	6	5	4	5	6	6	6	67
Days With ≥ 0.5" Precipitation	3	3	3	3	3	3	2	2	2	3	3	3	33
Days With ≥ 1.0" Precipitation	1	2	1	1	2	2	1	1	1	2	2	2	18
Mean Snowfall (in.)	0.3	0.1	0.0	0.0	0.0	0.0	0.0	0.0	0.0	0.0	0.0	trace	0.4
Maximum Snow Depth (in.)	4	2	1	0	0	0	0	0	0	0	0	0	4
Days With ≥ 1.0" Snow Depth	0	0	0	0	0	0	0	0	0	0	0	0	0

McAllen *Hidalgo County* Elevation: 100 ft. Latitude: 26° 12' N Longitude: 98° 15' W

	JAN	FEB	MAR	APR	MAY	JUN	JUL	AUG	SEP	OCT	NOV	DEC	YEAR
Mean Maximum Temp. (°F)	69.8	73.9	80.4	85.7	90.3	95.1	96.3	97.1	92.8	***87.0***	78.8	70.7	***84.8***
Mean Temp. (°F)	59.6	63.4	69.5	75.3	80.8	85.2	86.2	86.8	82.8	***76.4***	68.2	60.4	***74.5***
Mean Minimum Temp. (°F)	49.3	52.8	58.4	64.8	71.3	75.3	76.1	76.5	72.8	***65.8***	57.6	50.0	***64.2***
Extreme Maximum Temp. (°F)	92	100	104	105	109	108	107	106	108	***99***	97	92	***109***
Extreme Minimum Temp. (°F)	24	29	31	39	40	59	68	66	54	***44***	33	18	***18***
Days Maximum Temp. ≥ 90°F	0	1	4	9	19	27	29	29	23	***12***	2	0	***155***
Days Maximum Temp. ≤ 32°F	0	0	0	0	0	0	0	0	0	***0***	0	0	***0***
Days Minimum Temp. ≤ 32°F	1	0	0	0	0	0	0	0	0	***0***	0	1	***2***
Days Minimum Temp. ≤ 0°F	0	0	0	0	0	0	0	0	0	***0***	0	0	***0***
Heating Degree Days (base 65°F)	214	129	50	10	0	0	0	0	0	***4***	65	201	***673***
Cooling Degree Days (base 65°F)	52	89	195	325	498	613	664	684	542	***367***	170	65	***4,264***
Mean Precipitation (in.)	0.96	1.15	0.87	1.29	2.22	2.10	1.92	2.02	3.72	***2.18***	0.97	0.95	***20.35***
Extreme Maximum Daily Precip. (in.)	2.36	5.25	2.41	2.97	4.48	3.50	7.78	7.81	3.20	***2.50***	2.03	1.84	***7.81***
Days With ≥ 0.1" Precipitation	2	2	2	2	3	3	2	3	5	***4***	2	2	***32***
Days With ≥ 0.5" Precipitation	0	1	0	1	1	1	1	1	2	***2***	1	1	***12***
Days With ≥ 1.0" Precipitation	0	0	0	0	1	1	1	1	1	***1***	0	0	***6***
Mean Snowfall (in.)	trace	0.0	0.0	0.0	0.0	0.0	0.0	0.0	0.0	***0.0***	0.0	0.1	***0.1***
Maximum Snow Depth (in.)	trace	0	0	0	0	0	0	0	0	***0***	0	2	***2***
Days With ≥ 1.0" Snow Depth	0	0	0	0	0	0	0	0	0	***0***	0	0	***0***

McAllen Miller Intl Arpt *Hidalgo County* Elevation: 100 ft. Latitude: 26° 11' N Longitude: 98° 14' W

	JAN	FEB	MAR	APR	MAY	JUN	JUL	AUG	SEP	OCT	NOV	DEC	YEAR
Mean Maximum Temp. (°F)	***70.7***	***74.9***	82.0	87.5	91.7	95.9	97.4	97.9	93.2	***87.7***	***79.9***	71.8	***85.9***
Mean Temp. (°F)	***60.7***	***64.5***	71.1	76.9	82.0	85.8	86.9	87.3	83.4	***77.3***	***69.3***	61.9	***75.6***
Mean Minimum Temp. (°F)	***50.6***	***54.1***	60.1	66.2	72.3	75.6	76.4	76.6	73.5	***66.9***	***58.6***	51.9	***65.2***
Extreme Maximum Temp. (°F)	***93***	***101***	105	107	110	107	109	108	***107***	***103***	***102***	***92***	***110***
Extreme Minimum Temp. (°F)	***26***	***24***	31	40	51	61	69	57	***37***	***44***	***32***	***18***	***18***
Days Maximum Temp. ≥ 90°F	***0***	***2***	5	13	22	28	29	30	24	***14***	***3***	1	***171***
Days Maximum Temp. ≤ 32°F	***0***	***0***	0	0	0	0	0	0	0	***0***	***0***	0	***0***
Days Minimum Temp. ≤ 32°F	***0***	***0***	0	0	0	0	0	0	0	***0***	***0***	1	***1***
Days Minimum Temp. ≤ 0°F	***0***	***0***	0	0	0	0	0	0	0	***0***	***0***	0	***0***
Heating Degree Days (base 65°F)	***189***	***114***	36	7	0	0	0	0	0	***7***	***56***	175	***584***
Cooling Degree Days (base 65°F)	***63***	***107***	230	370	534	631	686	698	559	***396***	***190***	85	***4,549***
Mean Precipitation (in.)	***1.05***	***1.11***	0.77	1.14	2.40	2.25	2.09	2.46	4.15	***2.03***	***0.98***	1.29	***21.72***
Extreme Maximum Daily Precip. (in.)	***1.51***	***4.00***	2.92	3.24	4.30	3.89	4.25	9.42	***6.89***	***2.74***	***4.08***	***2.93***	***9.42***
Days With ≥ 0.1" Precipitation	***3***	***2***	1	2	3	3	3	3	5	***4***	***2***	3	***34***
Days With ≥ 0.5" Precipitation	***1***	***1***	0	1	1	1	1	1	2	***1***	***1***	1	***12***
Days With ≥ 1.0" Precipitation	***0***	***0***	0	0	1	1	1	1	1	***1***	***0***	0	***6***
Mean Snowfall (in.)	na	na	na	na	na	na	na	na	na	na	na	na	na
Maximum Snow Depth (in.)	na	na	na	na	na	na	na	na	na	na	na	na	na
Days With ≥ 1.0" Snow Depth	na	na	na	na	na	na	na	na	na	na	na	na	na

McCook *Hidalgo County* Elevation: 220 ft. Latitude: 26° 29' N Longitude: 98° 23' W

	JAN	FEB	MAR	APR	MAY	JUN	JUL	AUG	SEP	OCT	NOV	DEC	YEAR
Mean Maximum Temp. (°F)	69.7	74.1	80.9	86.8	91.1	96.1	97.8	98.6	93.4	87.0	78.7	70.4	85.4
Mean Temp. (°F)	58.9	62.9	69.2	75.1	80.7	84.9	86.2	86.4	82.1	75.6	67.8	59.8	74.1
Mean Minimum Temp. (°F)	48.1	51.6	57.4	63.4	70.2	73.7	74.5	74.2	70.8	64.1	56.7	49.2	62.8
Extreme Maximum Temp. (°F)	95	100	105	108	110	113	110	109	110	101	97	92	113
Extreme Minimum Temp. (°F)	22	25	28	36	49	56	65	65	53	39	33	14	14
Days Maximum Temp. ≥ 90°F	0	1	5	12	20	27	29	30	23	13	3	0	163
Days Maximum Temp. ≤ 32°F	0	0	0	0	0	0	0	0	0	0	0	0	0
Days Minimum Temp. ≤ 32°F	1	1	0	0	0	0	0	0	0	0	0	1	3
Days Minimum Temp. ≤ 0°F	0	0	0	0	0	0	0	0	0	0	0	0	0
Heating Degree Days (base 65°F)	232	143	55	13	0	0	0	0	1	13	78	222	757
Cooling Degree Days (base 65°F)	51	87	192	323	493	605	663	672	521	349	169	68	4,193
Mean Precipitation (in.)	0.94	1.07	0.80	1.06	2.50	2.36	2.13	1.48	3.59	2.69	1.04	1.12	20.78
Extreme Maximum Daily Precip. (in.)	1.55	2.98	3.20	***3.49***	5.65	4.04	8.28	***2.98***	4.55	***7.44***	***3.78***	2.17	***8.28***
Days With ≥ 0.1" Precipitation	2	2	2	2	3	3	3	2	5	3	2	3	32
Days With ≥ 0.5" Precipitation	0	1	0	1	2	1	1	1	2	1	0	1	11
Days With ≥ 1.0" Precipitation	0	0	0	0	1	1	0	0	1	1	0	0	4
Mean Snowfall (in.)	0.0	0.0	trace	0.0	0.0	0.0	0.0	0.0	0.0	0.0	0.0	0.1	0.1
Maximum Snow Depth (in.)	0	0	trace	0	0	0	0	0	0	0	0	2	2
Days With ≥ 1.0" Snow Depth	0	0	0	0	0	0	0	0	0	0	0	0	0

The period of record for all cooperative weather station data is 1980 – 2009. See User Guide for detailed explanation of data.

McGregor *Mclennan County* Elevation: 723 ft. Latitude: 31° 26' N Longitude: 97° 24' W

	JAN	FEB	MAR	APR	MAY	JUN	JUL	AUG	SEP	OCT	NOV	DEC	YEAR
Mean Maximum Temp. (°F)	57.4	61.1	68.1	76.3	83.3	89.9	95.0	95.4	88.8	78.5	67.3	58.4	76.6
Mean Temp. (°F)	46.2	49.9	57.0	64.8	72.9	79.6	83.7	84.0	77.3	67.1	56.7	47.7	65.6
Mean Minimum Temp. (°F)	35.0	38.7	45.8	53.3	62.5	69.3	72.4	72.4	65.7	55.7	46.0	37.0	54.5
Extreme Maximum Temp. (°F)	90	95	95	96	100	109	106	107	108	98	89	82	109
Extreme Minimum Temp. (°F)	5	10	14	29	37	52	58	53	40	27	21	-1	-1
Days Maximum Temp. ≥ 90°F	0	0	0	1	4	17	27	27	15	3	0	0	94
Days Maximum Temp. ≤ 32°F	1	1	0	0	0	0	0	0	0	0	0	1	3
Days Minimum Temp. ≤ 32°F	13	7	3	0	0	0	0	0	0	0	2	9	34
Days Minimum Temp. ≤ 0°F	0	0	0	0	0	0	0	0	0	0	0	0	0
Heating Degree Days (base 65°F)	577	426	270	90	10	0	0	0	6	67	268	537	2,251
Cooling Degree Days (base 65°F)	2	6	29	92	262	446	587	594	381	141	25	5	2,570
Mean Precipitation (in.)	2.20	2.63	3.31	2.79	4.58	3.74	1.72	2.33	2.59	4.26	2.98	2.86	35.99
Extreme Maximum Daily Precip. (in.)	3.20	2.95	3.50	3.07	3.80	3.45	2.90	4.78	3.30	6.00	2.62	6.45	6.45
Days With ≥ 0.1" Precipitation	4	4	5	4	6	5	3	3	4	5	5	4	52
Days With ≥ 0.5" Precipitation	1	2	2	2	3	2	1	2	2	3	2	2	24
Days With ≥ 1.0" Precipitation	1	1	1	1	1	1	0	1	1	2	1	1	12
Mean Snowfall (in.)	0.2	trace	0.0	0.0	0.0	0.0	0.0	0.0	0.0	0.0	trace	0.0	0.2
Maximum Snow Depth (in.)	0	0	0	0	0	0	0	0	0	0	0	0	0
Days With ≥ 1.0" Snow Depth	0	0	0	0	0	0	0	0	0	0	0	0	0

McKinney 3 S *Collin County* Elevation: 595 ft. Latitude: 33° 10' N Longitude: 96° 37' W

	JAN	FEB	MAR	APR	MAY	JUN	JUL	AUG	SEP	OCT	NOV	DEC	YEAR
Mean Maximum Temp. (°F)	56.0	59.9	68.0	76.3	83.0	89.7	94.8	95.6	88.3	78.0	66.3	56.7	76.1
Mean Temp. (°F)	45.1	48.5	56.4	64.3	72.4	79.3	83.8	83.9	76.3	65.9	55.3	46.2	64.8
Mean Minimum Temp. (°F)	34.1	37.1	44.8	52.3	61.7	68.9	72.6	71.7	64.3	53.8	44.3	35.7	53.4
Extreme Maximum Temp. (°F)	81	86	92	100	99	108	109	107	109	96	89	88	109
Extreme Minimum Temp. (°F)	5	6	13	28	40	52	58	54	39	24	21	-4	-4
Days Maximum Temp. ≥ 90°F	0	0	0	1	4	16	27	27	14	2	0	0	91
Days Maximum Temp. ≤ 32°F	1	1	0	0	0	0	0	0	0	0	0	1	3
Days Minimum Temp. ≤ 32°F	14	9	3	0	0	0	0	0	0	0	5	12	43
Days Minimum Temp. ≤ 0°F	0	0	0	0	0	0	0	0	0	0	0	0	0
Heating Degree Days (base 65°F)	612	462	282	99	10	0	0	0	11	83	305	577	2,441
Cooling Degree Days (base 65°F)	1	3	24	84	247	437	590	593	358	116	22	3	2,478
Mean Precipitation (in.)	2.76	3.15	3.72	3.54	5.85	4.27	2.25	1.94	2.90	4.20	3.78	3.35	41.71
Extreme Maximum Daily Precip. (in.)	4.14	3.93	4.70	4.25	7.75	4.30	4.65	3.95	3.09	4.70	4.01	3.39	7.75
Days With ≥ 0.1" Precipitation	4	4	5	5	6	6	3	3	4	4	4	4	52
Days With ≥ 0.5" Precipitation	2	2	2	3	3	3	1	1	2	2	2	2	25
Days With ≥ 1.0" Precipitation	1	1	1	1	2	1	1	1	1	1	1	1	13
Mean Snowfall (in.)	0.3	0.5	0.2	0.0	0.0	0.0	0.0	0.0	0.0	0.0	0.1	0.2	1.3
Maximum Snow Depth (in.)	3	4	3	0	0	0	0	0	0	0	1	4	4
Days With ≥ 1.0" Snow Depth	0	1	0	0	0	0	0	0	0	0	0	1	2

Menard *Menard County* Elevation: 1,951 ft. Latitude: 30° 55' N Longitude: 99° 47' W

	JAN	FEB	MAR	APR	MAY	JUN	JUL	AUG	SEP	OCT	NOV	DEC	YEAR
Mean Maximum Temp. (°F)	60.6	64.7	71.9	80.6	86.4	91.2	94.8	94.3	88.2	79.4	68.8	60.7	78.5
Mean Temp. (°F)	46.1	50.1	57.5	65.2	73.2	78.8	81.6	81.1	74.7	65.5	54.8	46.5	64.6
Mean Minimum Temp. (°F)	31.6	35.5	43.0	49.9	60.0	66.3	68.5	67.7	61.1	51.6	40.8	32.3	50.7
Extreme Maximum Temp. (°F)	89	97	95	102	108	108	107	109	108	98	91	87	109
Extreme Minimum Temp. (°F)	3	-1	7	21	34	48	53	50	33	21	12	-2	-2
Days Maximum Temp. ≥ 90°F	0	0	1	4	11	20	25	25	13	2	0	0	101
Days Maximum Temp. ≤ 32°F	1	1	0	0	0	0	0	0	0	0	0	1	3
Days Minimum Temp. ≤ 32°F	18	11	6	2	0	0	0	0	0	1	8	16	62
Days Minimum Temp. ≤ 0°F	0	0	0	0	0	0	0	0	0	0	0	0	0
Heating Degree Days (base 65°F)	579	420	255	94	11	0	0	0	10	90	315	567	2,341
Cooling Degree Days (base 65°F)	1	5	29	107	274	421	523	505	306	114	16	1	2,302
Mean Precipitation (in.)	1.04	1.52	1.88	1.49	3.25	3.26	1.94	1.99	2.31	2.45	1.65	1.18	23.96
Extreme Maximum Daily Precip. (in.)	1.78	2.39	3.03	2.20	4.35	2.96	3.65	4.00	4.12	3.92	3.12	3.22	4.35
Days With ≥ 0.1" Precipitation	2	3	4	2	5	5	3	3	3	4	3	2	39
Days With ≥ 0.5" Precipitation	1	1	1	1	2	2	1	1	2	2	1	1	16
Days With ≥ 1.0" Precipitation	0	0	0	0	1	1	1	1	1	1	1	0	7
Mean Snowfall (in.)	0.8	0.2	trace	0.0	0.0	0.0	0.0	0.0	0.0	0.0	trace	0.2	1.2
Maximum Snow Depth (in.)	2	trace	trace	0	0	0	0	0	0	0	4	6	6
Days With ≥ 1.0" Snow Depth	0	0	0	0	0	0	0	0	0	0	0	0	0

Morton *Cochran County* Elevation: 3,759 ft. Latitude: 33° 43' N Longitude: 102° 46' W

	JAN	FEB	MAR	APR	MAY	JUN	JUL	AUG	SEP	OCT	NOV	DEC	YEAR
Mean Maximum Temp. (°F)	53.8	58.6	65.6	74.3	82.9	90.4	92.0	90.0	83.5	74.3	63.1	53.7	73.5
Mean Temp. (°F)	39.1	43.1	49.5	57.8	67.5	75.8	78.3	76.6	69.6	59.6	48.3	39.5	58.7
Mean Minimum Temp. (°F)	24.5	27.4	33.3	41.2	52.1	61.0	64.5	63.1	55.7	44.7	33.4	25.2	43.8
Extreme Maximum Temp. (°F)	80	85	92	98	107	110	107	105	102	99	87	80	110
Extreme Minimum Temp. (°F)	-4	0	7	21	34	43	52	53	32	16	7	-6	-6
Days Maximum Temp. ≥ 90°F	0	0	0	1	8	18	22	18	8	1	0	0	76
Days Maximum Temp. ≤ 32°F	2	1	0	0	0	0	0	0	0	0	1	2	6
Days Minimum Temp. ≤ 32°F	27	21	14	4	0	0	0	0	0	2	14	25	107
Days Minimum Temp. ≤ 0°F	0	0	0	0	0	0	0	0	0	0	0	0	0
Heating Degree Days (base 65°F)	794	614	477	233	56	3	0	1	32	194	495	784	3,683
Cooling Degree Days (base 65°F)	0	0	2	22	141	333	419	367	178	33	1	0	1,496
Mean Precipitation (in.)	0.63	0.64	1.06	0.86	2.20	2.53	2.57	2.67	2.50	1.77	0.89	0.79	19.11
Extreme Maximum Daily Precip. (in.)	1.77	1.60	1.93	2.10	2.65	3.85	3.30	4.10	3.59	3.00	1.31	1.22	4.10
Days With ≥ 0.1" Precipitation	2	2	2	2	4	5	4	5	4	3	2	2	37
Days With ≥ 0.5" Precipitation	0	0	1	0	1	2	2	1	2	1	1	0	11
Days With ≥ 1.0" Precipitation	0	0	0	0	0	1	1	1	1	1	0	0	5
Mean Snowfall (in.)	2.2	1.3	0.4	0.3	0.0	0.0	0.0	0.0	0.0	0.1	1.4	2.9	8.6
Maximum Snow Depth (in.)	5	2	5	1	0	0	0	0	0	trace	7	4	7
Days With ≥ 1.0" Snow Depth	0	0	0	0	0	0	0	0	0	0	0	0	0

The period of record for all cooperative weather station data is 1980 – 2009. See User Guide for detailed explanation of data.

New Braunfels *Comal County* Elevation: 709 ft. Latitude: 29° 44' N Longitude: 98° 07' W

	JAN	FEB	MAR	APR	MAY	JUN	JUL	AUG	SEP	OCT	NOV	DEC	YEAR
Mean Maximum Temp. (°F)	62.6	65.8	73.0	80.1	86.3	91.6	94.7	95.9	90.2	81.6	72.0	62.9	79.7
Mean Temp. (°F)	50.3	53.2	60.4	67.5	75.3	80.8	83.6	83.9	78.3	69.3	60.0	50.9	67.8
Mean Minimum Temp. (°F)	38.0	40.5	47.8	55.0	64.2	69.9	72.4	71.9	66.3	56.8	47.9	38.8	55.8
Extreme Maximum Temp. (°F)	84	98	97	100	100	110	105	107	112	97	94	84	112
Extreme Minimum Temp. (°F)	9	11	17	29	37	46	61	58	43	24	24	2	2
Days Maximum Temp. ≥ 90°F	0	0	0	2	10	22	27	29	19	5	0	0	114
Days Maximum Temp. ≤ 32°F	0	0	0	0	0	0	0	0	0	0	0	0	0
Days Minimum Temp. ≤ 32°F	10	6	3	0	0	0	0	0	0	0	2	9	30
Days Minimum Temp. ≤ 0°F	0	0	0	0	0	0	0	0	0	0	0	0	0
Heating Degree Days (base 65°F)	456	337	188	56	3	0	0	0	3	48	195	440	1,726
Cooling Degree Days (base 65°F)	7	11	53	139	329	479	583	592	410	187	51	10	2,851
Mean Precipitation (in.)	1.93	1.89	2.40	2.10	4.00	4.74	2.47	2.25	2.98	4.35	2.52	2.43	34.06
Extreme Maximum Daily Precip. (in.)	2.25	2.24	3.36	2.49	4.51	4.25	5.89	4.50	4.00	18.35	3.91	4.81	18.35
Days With ≥ 0.1" Precipitation	4	4	4	3	5	5	3	3	4	4	4	3	46
Days With ≥ 0.5" Precipitation	1	1	1	1	3	3	1	1	2	2	2	1	19
Days With ≥ 1.0" Precipitation	0	0	1	1	1	2	1	1	1	1	1	1	11
Mean Snowfall (in.)	0.3	0.0	0.0	0.0	0.0	0.0	0.0	0.0	0.0	0.0	0.0	0.0	0.3
Maximum Snow Depth (in.)	trace	0	0	0	0	0	0	0	0	0	0	0	trace
Days With ≥ 1.0" Snow Depth	0	0	0	0	0	0	0	0	0	0	0	0	0

Ozona 1 SSW *Crockett County* Elevation: 2,339 ft. Latitude: 30° 41' N Longitude: 101° 12' W

	JAN	FEB	MAR	APR	MAY	JUN	JUL	AUG	SEP	OCT	NOV	DEC	YEAR
Mean Maximum Temp. (°F)	59.2	63.5	71.1	79.2	86.7	91.1	93.2	93.1	87.2	78.4	67.6	59.5	77.5
Mean Temp. (°F)	44.7	48.9	56.4	64.4	73.5	79.1	81.0	80.7	74.3	64.9	53.7	45.1	63.9
Mean Minimum Temp. (°F)	30.2	34.2	41.7	49.5	60.3	67.0	68.8	68.2	61.4	51.4	39.7	30.6	50.3
Extreme Maximum Temp. (°F)	86	93	94	102	106	107	107	107	107	96	89	85	107
Extreme Minimum Temp. (°F)	0	9	8	22	36	49	50	51	34	20	13	-2	-2
Days Maximum Temp. ≥ 90°F	0	0	0	3	11	18	24	24	12	1	0	0	93
Days Maximum Temp. ≤ 32°F	1	0	0	0	0	0	0	0	0	0	0	1	2
Days Minimum Temp. ≤ 32°F	19	13	6	1	0	0	0	0	0	1	8	18	66
Days Minimum Temp. ≤ 0°F	0	0	0	0	0	0	0	0	0	0	0	0	0
Heating Degree Days (base 65°F)	622	450	277	100	9	0	0	0	12	94	340	609	2,513
Cooling Degree Days (base 65°F)	0	1	17	88	280	429	503	492	299	96	9	0	2,214
Mean Precipitation (in.)	0.91	0.95	1.58	1.29	2.33	2.11	0.98	2.10	2.21	2.32	1.06	0.71	18.55
Extreme Maximum Daily Precip. (in.)	1.50	2.10	3.50	2.55	3.50	2.38	2.82	3.10	4.72	4.00	2.60	1.51	4.72
Days With ≥ 0.1" Precipitation	2	2	3	3	3	4	2	3	3	3	2	2	32
Days With ≥ 0.5" Precipitation	1	1	1	1	2	1	1	1	2	1	1	0	13
Days With ≥ 1.0" Precipitation	0	0	0	0	1	1	0	1	1	1	0	0	5
Mean Snowfall (in.)	0.1	0.0	trace	0.0	0.0	0.0	0.0	0.0	0.0	0.1	0.3	trace	0.5
Maximum Snow Depth (in.)	0	0	trace	0	0	0	0	0	0	0	3	trace	3
Days With ≥ 1.0" Snow Depth	0	0	0	0	0	0	0	0	0	0	0	0	0

Penwell *Ector County* Elevation: 2,939 ft. Latitude: 31° 44' N Longitude: 102° 35' W

	JAN	FEB	MAR	APR	MAY	JUN	JUL	AUG	SEP	OCT	NOV	DEC	YEAR
Mean Maximum Temp. (°F)	58.9	63.4	70.9	79.4	88.2	94.3	95.5	94.5	88.1	79.0	68.0	58.5	78.2
Mean Temp. (°F)	44.4	48.9	56.0	64.1	73.6	80.8	82.6	81.6	75.1	65.2	53.7	44.4	64.2
Mean Minimum Temp. (°F)	29.8	34.3	41.0	48.7	59.0	67.2	69.6	68.6	62.1	51.3	39.4	30.3	50.1
Extreme Maximum Temp. (°F)	83	90	94	101	110	116	111	108	105	102	91	82	116
Extreme Minimum Temp. (°F)	6	-12	8	24	39	49	56	57	38	22	10	1	-12
Days Maximum Temp. ≥ 90°F	0	0	0	5	15	23	27	26	14	4	0	0	114
Days Maximum Temp. ≤ 32°F	1	1	0	0	0	0	0	0	0	0	0	1	3
Days Minimum Temp. ≤ 32°F	20	11	5	1	0	0	0	0	0	1	7	18	63
Days Minimum Temp. ≤ 0°F	0	0	0	0	0	0	0	0	0	0	0	0	0
Heating Degree Days (base 65°F)	633	450	290	109	14	1	0	0	12	90	339	632	2,570
Cooling Degree Days (base 65°F)	0	1	16	88	289	480	553	521	321	103	8	0	2,380
Mean Precipitation (in.)	0.57	0.69	0.60	0.62	2.20	1.57	1.18	1.52	2.12	1.41	0.74	0.61	13.83
Extreme Maximum Daily Precip. (in.)	2.00	1.78	1.04	2.23	2.97	2.10	2.00	3.00	3.63	2.50	3.40	1.38	3.63
Days With ≥ 0.1" Precipitation	1	2	1	1	3	3	2	2	3	2	1	1	22
Days With ≥ 0.5" Precipitation	0	0	0	0	1	1	1	1	1	1	0	0	6
Days With ≥ 1.0" Precipitation	0	0	0	0	1	0	0	0	1	0	0	0	2
Mean Snowfall (in.)	0.6	0.3	0.1	0.0	0.0	0.0	0.0	0.0	0.0	0.0	trace	0.5	1.5
Maximum Snow Depth (in.)	0	0	0	0	0	0	0	0	0	0	0	6	6
Days With ≥ 1.0" Snow Depth	0	0	0	0	0	0	0	0	0	0	0	0	0

Pilot Point *Denton County* Elevation: 689 ft. Latitude: 33° 23' N Longitude: 96° 58' W

	JAN	FEB	MAR	APR	MAY	JUN	JUL	AUG	SEP	OCT	NOV	DEC	YEAR
Mean Maximum Temp. (°F)	54.2	58.9	66.6	75.5	83.3	90.3	96.6	96.5	89.3	77.7	65.3	55.8	75.8
Mean Temp. (°F)	42.7	47.0	54.1	62.9	71.9	79.6	85.2	84.9	77.4	66.0	53.6	44.7	64.2
Mean Minimum Temp. (°F)	31.2	35.0	41.6	50.2	60.3	68.9	74.0	73.2	65.5	54.2	41.8	33.5	52.5
Extreme Maximum Temp. (°F)	81	93	94	98	103	102	111	109	112	97	89	82	112
Extreme Minimum Temp. (°F)	1	1	10	28	39	49	50	57	40	24	17	-2	-2
Days Maximum Temp. ≥ 90°F	0	0	0	1	6	19	28	27	16	3	0	0	100
Days Maximum Temp. ≤ 32°F	1	1	0	0	0	0	0	0	0	0	0	1	3
Days Minimum Temp. ≤ 32°F	17	10	4	1	0	0	0	0	0	0	5	13	50
Days Minimum Temp. ≤ 0°F	0	0	0	0	0	0	0	0	0	0	0	0	0
Heating Degree Days (base 65°F)	683	504	343	124	16	1	0	0	11	86	350	624	2,742
Cooling Degree Days (base 65°F)	0	3	14	67	236	446	634	625	391	121	13	1	2,551
Mean Precipitation (in.)	2.45	3.57	3.89	3.19	6.71	4.28	2.32	2.69	3.64	5.21	3.74	3.57	45.26
Extreme Maximum Daily Precip. (in.)	2.20	5.60	4.10	2.50	13.00	5.10	5.40	3.20	na	na	4.46	3.60	na
Days With ≥ 0.1" Precipitation	5	5	6	6	8	6	4	4	5	6	5	5	65
Days With ≥ 0.5" Precipitation	2	2	3	3	4	3	1	2	2	3	3	2	30
Days With ≥ 1.0" Precipitation	1	1	1	1	3	1	1	1	1	2	1	1	15
Mean Snowfall (in.)	0.1	0.5	trace	0.0	0.0	0.0	0.0	0.0	0.0	0.0	trace	0.1	0.7
Maximum Snow Depth (in.)	trace	2	trace	0	0	0	0	0	0	na	0	trace	na
Days With ≥ 1.0" Snow Depth	0	0	0	0	0	0	0	0	0	na	0	0	na

The period of record for all cooperative weather station data is 1980 – 2009. See User Guide for detailed explanation of data.

Port Isabel *Cameron County* Elevation: 17 ft. Latitude: 26° 04' N Longitude: 97° 13' W

	JAN	FEB	MAR	APR	MAY	JUN	JUL	AUG	SEP	OCT	NOV	DEC	YEAR
Mean Maximum Temp. (°F)	68.5	71.0	75.6	80.2	85.2	89.3	90.5	91.2	88.6	84.1	77.4	70.0	81.0
Mean Temp. (°F)	60.9	63.6	68.5	73.8	79.4	83.3	84.1	84.5	81.9	77.1	70.0	62.2	74.1
Mean Minimum Temp. (°F)	53.2	56.2	61.3	67.4	73.6	77.2	77.6	77.8	75.1	70.1	62.5	54.4	67.2
Extreme Maximum Temp. (°F)	87	91	98	96	98	96	99	99	103	95	95	87	103
Extreme Minimum Temp. (°F)	28	28	34	42	52	68	69	70	55	37	37	17	17
Days Maximum Temp. ≥ 90°F	0	0	0	1	3	15	21	25	14	4	0	0	83
Days Maximum Temp. ≤ 32°F	0	0	0	0	0	0	0	0	0	0	0	0	0
Days Minimum Temp. ≤ 32°F	0	0	0	0	0	0	0	0	0	0	0	0	0
Days Minimum Temp. ≤ 0°F	0	0	0	0	0	0	0	0	0	0	0	0	0
Heating Degree Days (base 65°F)	171	107	44	8	0	0	0	0	0	6	45	158	539
Cooling Degree Days (base 65°F)	53	75	159	280	454	556	598	612	513	389	201	79	3,969
Mean Precipitation (in.)	1.82	1.48	1.43	1.44	2.21	2.14	1.70	1.87	5.78	4.11	2.55	1.53	28.06
Extreme Maximum Daily Precip. (in.)	3.70	2.65	5.00	6.37	3.45	4.30	4.87	3.35	4.89	5.62	7.80	2.86	7.80
Days With ≥ 0.1" Precipitation	4	3	2	2	3	3	3	3	6	5	4	3	41
Days With ≥ 0.5" Precipitation	1	1	1	1	2	1	1	1	3	2	1	1	16
Days With ≥ 1.0" Precipitation	0	0	0	0	1	1	0	1	2	1	1	0	7
Mean Snowfall (in.)	0.0	0.0	0.0	0.0	0.0	0.0	0.0	0.0	0.0	0.0	0.0	0.1	0.1
Maximum Snow Depth (in.)	0	0	0	0	0	0	0	0	0	0	0	3	3
Days With ≥ 1.0" Snow Depth	0	0	0	0	0	0	0	0	0	0	0	0	0

Port Mansfield *Willacy County* Elevation: 8 ft. Latitude: 26° 33' N Longitude: 97° 26' W

	JAN	FEB	MAR	APR	MAY	JUN	JUL	AUG	SEP	OCT	NOV	DEC	YEAR
Mean Maximum Temp. (°F)	65.6	68.7	73.6	78.4	83.0	87.5	88.8	***89.2***	86.6	81.6	74.9	67.5	***78.8***
Mean Temp. (°F)	57.8	61.2	66.9	72.3	78.0	82.2	***83.2***	***83.2***	80.0	74.7	67.5	59.6	***72.2***
Mean Minimum Temp. (°F)	49.9	53.7	60.1	66.2	73.0	76.8	77.5	77.2	73.4	67.8	60.0	51.7	65.6
Extreme Maximum Temp. (°F)	86	90	101	98	104	101	113	99	102	96	98	88	113
Extreme Minimum Temp. (°F)	23	26	29	41	37	60	65	67	55	32	34	15	15
Days Maximum Temp. ≥ 90°F	0	0	0	1	1	7	11	13	6	2	0	0	41
Days Maximum Temp. ≤ 32°F	0	0	0	0	0	0	0	0	0	0	0	0	0
Days Minimum Temp. ≤ 32°F	1	1	0	0	0	0	0	0	0	0	0	1	3
Days Minimum Temp. ≤ 0°F	0	0	0	0	0	0	0	0	0	0	0	0	0
Heating Degree Days (base 65°F)	251	157	65	14	0	0	***0***	***0***	0	12	71	215	***785***
Cooling Degree Days (base 65°F)	33	55	131	241	411	523	***569***	***571***	457	321	152	57	***3,521***
Mean Precipitation (in.)	1.32	1.72	1.36	1.26	2.55	2.15	1.94	1.62	4.99	3.22	1.79	1.33	25.25
Extreme Maximum Daily Precip. (in.)	2.50	4.50	4.00	2.05	2.68	4.40	8.48	***2.08***	6.11	3.50	6.73	2.80	***8.48***
Days With ≥ 0.1" Precipitation	3	3	2	2	3	3	2	3	6	4	3	3	37
Days With ≥ 0.5" Precipitation	1	1	1	1	2	1	1	1	3	2	1	1	16
Days With ≥ 1.0" Precipitation	0	0	0	1	1	1	0	0	2	1	1	0	7
Mean Snowfall (in.)	trace	0.0	0.0	0.0	0.0	0.0	0.0	0.0	0.0	0.0	0.0	0.1	0.1
Maximum Snow Depth (in.)	trace	0	0	0	0	0	0	0	0	0	0	2	2
Days With ≥ 1.0" Snow Depth	0	0	0	0	0	0	0	0	0	0	0	0	0

Raymondville *Willacy County* Elevation: 30 ft. Latitude: 26° 29' N Longitude: 97° 49' W

	JAN	FEB	MAR	APR	MAY	JUN	JUL	AUG	SEP	OCT	NOV	DEC	YEAR
Mean Maximum Temp. (°F)	70.6	74.3	80.4	86.0	90.2	94.6	97.0	97.2	92.7	87.1	79.4	71.5	85.1
Mean Temp. (°F)	59.4	62.8	68.5	74.5	79.9	84.1	85.7	85.7	81.9	75.7	67.7	60.2	73.8
Mean Minimum Temp. (°F)	48.1	51.2	56.6	62.9	69.7	73.5	74.3	74.3	71.0	64.3	56.1	48.8	62.5
Extreme Maximum Temp. (°F)	91	97	104	106	107	108	107	107	107	100	99	92	108
Extreme Minimum Temp. (°F)	22	24	28	33	46	57	63	65	45	33	31	15	15
Days Maximum Temp. ≥ 90°F	0	1	4	10	18	27	28	28	23	13	3	0	155
Days Maximum Temp. ≤ 32°F	0	0	0	0	0	0	0	0	0	0	0	0	0
Days Minimum Temp. ≤ 32°F	1	1	0	0	0	0	0	0	0	0	0	2	4
Days Minimum Temp. ≤ 0°F	0	0	0	0	0	0	0	0	0	0	0	0	0
Heating Degree Days (base 65°F)	220	139	63	13	0	0	0	0	1	11	76	213	736
Cooling Degree Days (base 65°F)	52	82	178	303	470	578	647	650	514	350	164	70	4,058
Mean Precipitation (in.)	1.16	1.44	1.48	1.28	3.00	2.26	2.17	2.47	5.08	3.38	1.30	1.17	26.19
Extreme Maximum Daily Precip. (in.)	1.72	2.84	3.70	4.00	4.65	6.23	5.74	3.07	4.53	4.36	1.66	2.37	6.23
Days With ≥ 0.1" Precipitation	3	3	2	2	3	3	3	4	6	4	2	2	37
Days With ≥ 0.5" Precipitation	1	1	1	1	2	1	1	1	3	2	1	1	16
Days With ≥ 1.0" Precipitation	0	0	0	0	1	1	1	1	2	1	0	0	7
Mean Snowfall (in.)	0.0	0.0	0.0	0.0	0.0	0.0	0.0	0.0	0.0	0.0	0.0	0.1	0.1
Maximum Snow Depth (in.)	0	0	0	0	0	0	0	0	0	0	0	4	4
Days With ≥ 1.0" Snow Depth	0	0	0	0	0	0	0	0	0	0	0	0	0

Rio Grande City 1 SE *Starr County* Elevation: 171 ft. Latitude: 26° 23' N Longitude: 98° 49' W

	JAN	FEB	MAR	APR	MAY	JUN	JUL	AUG	SEP	OCT	NOV	DEC	YEAR
Mean Maximum Temp. (°F)	70.3	75.0	82.1	88.6	93.3	97.7	99.4	99.6	94.3	87.6	79.0	70.4	86.4
Mean Temp. (°F)	58.1	62.3	69.0	75.6	81.8	86.1	87.3	87.4	82.8	75.7	67.0	58.5	74.3
Mean Minimum Temp. (°F)	45.9	49.5	55.9	62.6	70.3	74.5	75.1	75.1	71.2	63.7	55.0	46.5	62.1
Extreme Maximum Temp. (°F)	97	100	105	108	111	116	111	110	111	101	97	93	116
Extreme Minimum Temp. (°F)	22	24	25	34	50	55	59	66	51	29	26	16	16
Days Maximum Temp. ≥ 90°F	1	3	7	15	23	29	30	30	24	14	3	0	179
Days Maximum Temp. ≤ 32°F	0	0	0	0	0	0	0	0	0	0	0	0	0
Days Minimum Temp. ≤ 32°F	2	1	0	0	0	0	0	0	0	0	1	3	7
Days Minimum Temp. ≤ 0°F	0	0	0	0	0	0	0	0	0	0	0	0	0
Heating Degree Days (base 65°F)	249	150	61	12	0	0	0	0	1	13	88	247	821
Cooling Degree Days (base 65°F)	42	79	192	338	529	640	698	701	542	350	155	52	4,318
Mean Precipitation (in.)	0.98	1.09	0.80	1.15	2.35	2.86	1.84	1.94	4.12	2.55	1.18	0.97	21.83
Extreme Maximum Daily Precip. (in.)	2.23	3.17	2.66	2.30	4.97	6.13	3.80	4.97	5.50	5.00	2.21	2.09	6.13
Days With ≥ 0.1" Precipitation	3	2	2	2	3	3	3	3	5	3	2	2	33
Days With ≥ 0.5" Precipitation	0	1	0	1	2	1	1	1	3	1	1	0	12
Days With ≥ 1.0" Precipitation	0	0	0	0	1	1	1	1	2	1	0	0	7
Mean Snowfall (in.)	trace	0.0	0.0	0.0	0.0	0.0	0.0	0.0	0.0	0.0	0.0	0.1	0.1
Maximum Snow Depth (in.)	trace	0	0	0	0	0	0	0	0	0	0	3	3
Days With ≥ 1.0" Snow Depth	0	0	0	0	0	0	0	0	0	0	0	0	0

The period of record for all cooperative weather station data is 1980 – 2009. See User Guide for detailed explanation of data.

Robstown *Nueces County* Elevation: 84 ft. Latitude: 27° 47' N Longitude: 97° 40' W

	JAN	FEB	MAR	APR	MAY	JUN	JUL	AUG	SEP	OCT	NOV	DEC	YEAR
Mean Maximum Temp. (°F)	66.8	70.1	76.0	82.4	87.3	92.4	94.4	95.4	91.2	84.5	76.1	68.0	82.1
Mean Temp. (°F)	56.6	59.8	66.0	72.5	78.6	83.2	84.9	85.5	81.5	74.4	66.0	57.9	72.2
Mean Minimum Temp. (°F)	46.4	49.5	56.0	62.5	69.9	74.0	75.2	75.5	71.8	64.3	55.8	47.7	62.4
Extreme Maximum Temp. (°F)	90	95	104	104	104	108	103	113	109	98	98	91	113
Extreme Minimum Temp. (°F)	19	20	23	37	52	60	63	66	53	32	29	12	12
Days Maximum Temp. ≥ 90°F	0	0	1	4	11	25	28	29	20	7	1	0	126
Days Maximum Temp. ≤ 32°F	0	0	0	0	0	0	0	0	0	0	0	0	0
Days Minimum Temp. ≤ 32°F	2	1	0	0	0	0	0	0	0	0	0	2	5
Days Minimum Temp. ≤ 0°F	0	0	0	0	0	0	0	0	0	0	0	0	0
Heating Degree Days (base 65°F)	282	185	84	16	0	0	0	0	0	13	90	259	929
Cooling Degree Days (base 65°F)	29	45	122	246	429	554	622	641	503	312	128	44	3,675
Mean Precipitation (in.)	1.74	1.94	1.94	1.56	3.07	2.76	3.24	3.33	4.28	3.59	2.26	1.62	31.33
Extreme Maximum Daily Precip. (in.)	5.00	3.63	3.15	4.35	4.52	3.05	5.24	5.36	6.08	5.15	6.80	5.10	6.80
Days With ≥ 0.1" Precipitation	4	3	3	2	4	4	4	4	5	4	3	3	43
Days With ≥ 0.5" Precipitation	1	1	1	1	2	2	2	2	2	2	1	1	18
Days With ≥ 1.0" Precipitation	0	1	1	0	1	1	1	1	1	1	1	0	9
Mean Snowfall (in.)	0.0	trace	0.0	0.0	0.0	0.0	0.0	0.0	0.0	0.0	0.0	0.2	0.2
Maximum Snow Depth (in.)	0	trace	0	0	0	0	0	0	0	0	0	5	5
Days With ≥ 1.0" Snow Depth	0	0	0	0	0	0	0	0	0	0	0	0	0

Sam Rayburn Dam *Jasper County* Elevation: 188 ft. Latitude: 31° 04' N Longitude: 94° 06' W

	JAN	FEB	MAR	APR	MAY	JUN	JUL	AUG	SEP	OCT	NOV	DEC	YEAR
Mean Maximum Temp. (°F)	58.4	62.2	69.6	76.9	84.3	90.3	93.2	93.7	88.6	79.0	68.8	60.3	77.1
Mean Temp. (°F)	47.6	51.1	58.3	65.2	73.4	79.5	81.9	81.9	76.9	66.8	57.6	49.4	65.8
Mean Minimum Temp. (°F)	36.8	39.9	47.0	53.4	62.5	68.6	70.6	70.0	65.1	54.6	46.4	38.5	54.5
Extreme Maximum Temp. (°F)	83	88	91	93	101	103	107	107	109	95	87	84	109
Extreme Minimum Temp. (°F)	11	14	19	24	38	50	59	52	39	20	18	7	7
Days Maximum Temp. ≥ 90°F	0	0	0	1	6	19	25	26	14	2	0	0	93
Days Maximum Temp. ≤ 32°F	0	0	0	0	0	0	0	0	0	0	0	0	0
Days Minimum Temp. ≤ 32°F	12	7	3	0	0	0	0	0	0	0	3	10	35
Days Minimum Temp. ≤ 0°F	0	0	0	0	0	0	0	0	0	0	0	0	0
Heating Degree Days (base 65°F)	538	396	238	89	8	0	0	0	4	74	249	484	2,080
Cooling Degree Days (base 65°F)	6	10	38	102	276	440	532	530	367	136	35	9	2,481
Mean Precipitation (in.)	5.30	4.69	5.18	4.09	4.86	6.16	3.97	4.00	4.30	5.63	6.23	6.11	60.52
Extreme Maximum Daily Precip. (in.)	4.32	7.85	9.04	4.26	3.45	6.38	3.95	3.75	14.00	10.10	7.36	5.66	14.00
Days With ≥ 0.1" Precipitation	7	6	6	5	6	7	6	6	6	5	6	7	73
Days With ≥ 0.5" Precipitation	4	3	3	3	3	4	3	3	2	3	4	4	39
Days With ≥ 1.0" Precipitation	2	1	2	1	2	2	1	1	1	2	2	2	19
Mean Snowfall (in.)	trace	0.0	0.0	0.0	0.0	0.0	0.0	0.0	0.0	0.0	0.0	trace	trace
Maximum Snow Depth (in.)	1	0	0	0	0	0	0	0	0	0	0	trace	1
Days With ≥ 1.0" Snow Depth	0	0	0	0	0	0	0	0	0	0	0	0	0

San Marcos *Hays County* Elevation: 611 ft. Latitude: 29° 51' N Longitude: 97° 57' W

	JAN	FEB	MAR	APR	MAY	JUN	JUL	AUG	SEP	OCT	NOV	DEC	YEAR
Mean Maximum Temp. (°F)	62.9	66.3	72.9	80.1	86.2	92.2	95.2	96.3	90.8	82.4	72.1	63.3	80.1
Mean Temp. (°F)	51.4	54.3	61.1	68.2	75.8	81.9	84.3	84.9	79.4	70.4	60.5	51.7	68.7
Mean Minimum Temp. (°F)	39.7	42.3	49.2	56.3	65.4	71.4	73.4	73.5	67.9	58.3	48.9	40.1	57.2
Extreme Maximum Temp. (°F)	85	99	97	98	100	109	104	107	111	97	91	85	111
Extreme Minimum Temp. (°F)	11	17	17	32	44	52	62	60	42	28	24	4	4
Days Maximum Temp. ≥ 90°F	0	0	0	2	10	23	28	29	20	5	0	0	117
Days Maximum Temp. ≤ 32°F	0	0	0	0	0	0	0	0	0	0	0	0	0
Days Minimum Temp. ≤ 32°F	7	4	1	0	0	0	0	0	0	0	1	7	20
Days Minimum Temp. ≤ 0°F	0	0	0	0	0	0	0	0	0	0	0	0	0
Heating Degree Days (base 65°F)	422	311	170	46	2	0	0	0	2	35	178	416	1,582
Cooling Degree Days (base 65°F)	8	15	55	149	345	512	605	624	439	208	51	11	3,022
Mean Precipitation (in.)	2.08	1.93	2.40	2.40	4.62	4.87	2.34	2.19	3.41	4.22	3.05	2.29	35.80
Extreme Maximum Daily Precip. (in.)	2.27	2.65	2.50	2.48	3.30	13.98	4.53	4.41	4.70	15.78	3.48	5.98	15.78
Days With ≥ 0.1" Precipitation	4	4	5	4	6	6	3	3	4	5	4	3	51
Days With ≥ 0.5" Precipitation	1	1	2	2	3	3	1	1	2	2	2	1	21
Days With ≥ 1.0" Precipitation	1	0	1	1	2	1	1	1	1	1	1	1	12
Mean Snowfall (in.)	trace	0.1	0.0	0.0	0.0	0.0	0.0	0.0	0.0	0.0	trace	trace	0.1
Maximum Snow Depth (in.)	trace	trace	0	0	0	0	0	0	0	0	0	trace	trace
Days With ≥ 1.0" Snow Depth	0	0	0	0	0	0	0	0	0	0	0	0	0

Somerville Dam *Burleson County* Elevation: 263 ft. Latitude: 30° 20' N Longitude: 96° 32' W

	JAN	FEB	MAR	APR	MAY	JUN	JUL	AUG	SEP	OCT	NOV	DEC	YEAR
Mean Maximum Temp. (°F)	61.0	64.4	71.1	78.4	85.2	91.9	95.4	96.4	91.1	81.6	71.3	62.5	79.2
Mean Temp. (°F)	49.1	52.8	59.8	66.9	74.7	81.2	84.2	84.4	78.5	68.9	59.3	50.4	67.5
Mean Minimum Temp. (°F)	37.2	41.1	48.4	55.4	64.2	70.6	72.9	72.3	65.9	56.1	47.3	38.3	55.8
Extreme Maximum Temp. (°F)	83	96	90	96	100	109	107	108	114	98	90	84	114
Extreme Minimum Temp. (°F)	8	13	16	29	44	54	57	59	42	28	18	3	3
Days Maximum Temp. ≥ 90°F	0	0	0	1	7	22	29	29	20	5	0	0	113
Days Maximum Temp. ≤ 32°F	0	0	0	0	0	0	0	0	0	0	0	0	0
Days Minimum Temp. ≤ 32°F	10	5	2	0	0	0	0	0	0	0	2	10	29
Days Minimum Temp. ≤ 0°F	0	0	0	0	0	0	0	0	0	0	0	0	0
Heating Degree Days (base 65°F)	489	348	200	61	4	0	0	0	4	52	210	455	1,823
Cooling Degree Days (base 65°F)	4	9	46	126	312	494	601	608	415	180	47	10	2,852
Mean Precipitation (in.)	2.92	2.86	3.10	2.80	4.24	4.31	1.81	2.48	3.23	4.64	3.61	3.09	39.09
Extreme Maximum Daily Precip. (in.)	2.50	3.78	2.11	2.65	2.90	4.75	2.43	3.32	3.85	15.25	3.82	3.16	15.25
Days With ≥ 0.1" Precipitation	5	5	5	4	6	6	4	4	4	6	5	5	59
Days With ≥ 0.5" Precipitation	2	2	2	2	3	2	1	2	2	3	2	2	25
Days With ≥ 1.0" Precipitation	1	1	1	1	1	1	0	1	1	2	1	1	12
Mean Snowfall (in.)	0.0	trace	0.0	0.0	0.0	0.0	0.0	0.0	0.0	0.0	0.0	0.0	trace
Maximum Snow Depth (in.)	0	trace	0	0	0	0	0	0	0	0	0	0	trace
Days With ≥ 1.0" Snow Depth	0	0	0	0	0	0	0	0	0	0	0	0	0

The period of record for all cooperative weather station data is 1980 – 2009. See User Guide for detailed explanation of data.

Stillhouse Hollow Dam *Bell County* Elevation: 706 ft. Latitude: 31° 02' N Longitude: 97° 32' W

	JAN	FEB	MAR	APR	MAY	JUN	JUL	AUG	SEP	OCT	NOV	DEC	YEAR
Mean Maximum Temp. (°F)	59.7	64.7	70.7	78.5	85.0	91.4	95.6	96.4	90.2	80.7	70.3	***60.8***	***78.7***
Mean Temp. (°F)	47.4	52.0	58.4	66.2	74.0	80.4	83.8	84.1	78.0	68.2	58.2	***49.0***	***66.7***
Mean Minimum Temp. (°F)	35.1	39.3	46.1	53.8	63.0	69.3	72.0	71.8	65.6	55.7	46.0	***37.2***	***54.6***
Extreme Maximum Temp. (°F)	88	98	93	99	100	106	108	109	110	99	92	86	110
Extreme Minimum Temp. (°F)	6	12	15	31	41	52	57	57	39	22	19	-5	-5
Days Maximum Temp. ≥ 90°F	0	0	0	2	7	20	28	28	18	5	0	0	108
Days Maximum Temp. ≤ 32°F	0	0	0	0	0	0	0	0	0	0	0	1	1
Days Minimum Temp. ≤ 32°F	12	6	2	0	0	0	0	0	0	0	2	9	31
Days Minimum Temp. ≤ 0°F	0	0	0	0	0	0	0	0	0	0	0	0	0
Heating Degree Days (base 65°F)	540	372	232	70	5	0	0	0	5	57	233	***496***	***2,010***
Cooling Degree Days (base 65°F)	3	11	35	112	293	469	590	600	402	163	36	***8***	***2,722***
Mean Precipitation (in.)	2.22	2.54	3.06	2.62	4.88	4.03	1.79	2.27	3.49	3.82	3.02	2.59	36.33
Extreme Maximum Daily Precip. (in.)	2.10	4.17	3.63	3.30	3.97	6.51	2.70	6.04	5.38	4.82	3.05	5.68	6.51
Days With ≥ 0.1" Precipitation	4	4	5	4	6	5	3	3	5	5	5	4	53
Days With ≥ 0.5" Precipitation	1	2	2	2	3	3	1	1	2	2	2	1	22
Days With ≥ 1.0" Precipitation	1	1	1	1	2	1	1	1	1	1	1	1	13
Mean Snowfall (in.)	0.0	0.0	trace	0.0	0.0	0.0	0.0	0.0	0.0	0.0	trace	trace	trace
Maximum Snow Depth (in.)	0	0	trace	0	0	0	0	0	0	0	trace	trace	trace
Days With ≥ 1.0" Snow Depth	0	0	0	0	0	0	0	0	0	0	0	0	0

Sugar Land *Fort Bend County* Elevation: 82 ft. Latitude: 29° 37' N Longitude: 95° 38' W

	JAN	FEB	MAR	APR	MAY	JUN	JUL	AUG	SEP	OCT	NOV	DEC	YEAR
Mean Maximum Temp. (°F)	***62.5***	66.5	72.7	79.5	***86.0***	***91.1***	***93.8***	***94.1***	***89.8***	***82.0***	***72.3***	***64.5***	***79.6***
Mean Temp. (°F)	***52.7***	56.3	62.6	69.1	***76.7***	***82.1***	***84.4***	***84.4***	***79.8***	***71.3***	***61.8***	***54.3***	***69.6***
Mean Minimum Temp. (°F)	***42.9***	46.1	52.3	58.8	***67.4***	73.0	***75.1***	***74.6***	***69.8***	***60.5***	***51.3***	***44.0***	***59.6***
Extreme Maximum Temp. (°F)	84	89	92	94	99	104	103	104	108	95	90	85	108
Extreme Minimum Temp. (°F)	12	19	21	32	47	59	63	64	47	30	26	6	6
Days Maximum Temp. ≥ 90°F	0	0	0	1	7	20	26	25	17	4	0	0	100
Days Maximum Temp. ≤ 32°F	0	0	0	0	0	0	0	0	0	0	0	0	0
Days Minimum Temp. ≤ 32°F	3	2	1	0	0	0	0	0	0	0	1	3	10
Days Minimum Temp. ≤ 0°F	0	0	0	0	0	0	0	0	0	0	0	0	0
Heating Degree Days (base 65°F)	***387***	263	142	36	***1***	***0***	***0***	***0***	***1***	***28***	***160***	***347***	***1,365***
Cooling Degree Days (base 65°F)	***15***	24	72	167	***371***	***520***	***609***	***609***	***451***	***230***	***70***	***22***	***3,160***
Mean Precipitation (in.)	3.75	2.97	3.55	3.37	4.50	5.62	3.68	4.33	4.82	5.02	4.35	3.21	49.17
Extreme Maximum Daily Precip. (in.)	***3.00***	***2.92***	3.55	***4.46***	3.27	10.60	4.04	***8.29***	***7.02***	7.10	***7.69***	3.85	***10.60***
Days With ≥ 0.1" Precipitation	5	4	5	3	5	6	5	5	5	5	4	5	57
Days With ≥ 0.5" Precipitation	2	2	2	2	3	4	2	2	2	3	2	2	28
Days With ≥ 1.0" Precipitation	1	1	1	1	2	2	1	1	1	2	1	1	15
Mean Snowfall (in.)	trace	trace	trace	0.0	0.0	0.0	0.0	0.0	0.0	0.0	0.0	trace	trace
Maximum Snow Depth (in.)	1	trace	trace	0	0	0	0	0	0	0	0	trace	1
Days With ≥ 1.0" Snow Depth	0	0	0	0	0	0	0	0	0	0	0	0	0

Texarkana *Bowie County* Elevation: 390 ft. Latitude: 33° 25' N Longitude: 94° 05' W

	JAN	FEB	MAR	APR	MAY	JUN	JUL	AUG	SEP	OCT	NOV	DEC	YEAR
Mean Maximum Temp. (°F)	54.4	58.8	66.8	75.0	81.7	88.9	93.1	93.6	86.6	76.3	65.2	56.0	74.7
Mean Temp. (°F)	43.9	47.6	55.4	63.3	71.7	79.1	83.0	82.8	75.6	64.7	54.3	45.7	63.9
Mean Minimum Temp. (°F)	33.4	36.4	43.9	51.6	61.6	69.3	72.8	72.0	64.5	53.2	43.4	35.4	53.1
Extreme Maximum Temp. (°F)	81	90	89	95	98	101	105	106	108	95	85	83	108
Extreme Minimum Temp. (°F)	3	8	15	29	42	53	59	55	38	27	23	-6	-6
Days Maximum Temp. ≥ 90°F	0	0	0	0	3	15	24	24	12	1	0	0	79
Days Maximum Temp. ≤ 32°F	1	1	0	0	0	0	0	0	0	0	0	1	3
Days Minimum Temp. ≤ 32°F	17	10	3	0	0	0	0	0	0	0	4	13	47
Days Minimum Temp. ≤ 0°F	0	0	0	0	0	0	0	0	0	0	0	0	0
Heating Degree Days (base 65°F)	650	491	312	118	15	0	0	0	10	102	329	594	2,621
Cooling Degree Days (base 65°F)	2	3	21	74	229	431	565	560	336	101	16	4	2,342
Mean Precipitation (in.)	4.02	4.20	4.81	4.27	5.21	4.81	3.60	2.20	3.74	5.24	5.00	5.07	52.17
Extreme Maximum Daily Precip. (in.)	2.98	4.02	5.45	3.86	3.96	6.35	4.57	2.73	3.63	4.95	5.30	5.15	6.35
Days With ≥ 0.1" Precipitation	6	6	7	6	7	6	4	4	4	6	6	6	68
Days With ≥ 0.5" Precipitation	3	3	3	3	3	4	3	2	2	3	3	3	35
Days With ≥ 1.0" Precipitation	1	1	1	1	2	2	1	1	1	2	2	2	17
Mean Snowfall (in.)	0.5	0.5	trace	0.0	0.0	0.0	0.0	0.0	0.0	0.0	0.0	0.1	1.1
Maximum Snow Depth (in.)	8	5	trace	0	0	0	0	0	0	0	0	2	8
Days With ≥ 1.0" Snow Depth	1	0	0	0	0	0	0	0	0	0	0	0	1

Thompsons 3 WSW *Fort Bend County* Elevation: 71 ft. Latitude: 29° 29' N Longitude: 95° 38' W

	JAN	FEB	MAR	APR	MAY	JUN	JUL	AUG	SEP	OCT	NOV	DEC	YEAR
Mean Maximum Temp. (°F)	63.7	66.7	73.0	79.9	86.6	91.9	93.7	94.7	90.4	82.9	73.5	65.3	80.2
Mean Temp. (°F)	53.7	56.6	62.8	69.3	76.7	82.0	83.9	84.3	79.9	71.6	63.1	55.1	69.9
Mean Minimum Temp. (°F)	43.9	46.5	52.7	58.7	66.5	72.1	74.0	74.0	69.3	60.4	52.7	45.0	59.7
Extreme Maximum Temp. (°F)	85	88	92	94	99	105	106	106	106	97	***91***	87	***106***
Extreme Minimum Temp. (°F)	14	20	21	35	46	45	64	60	51	32	27	8	8
Days Maximum Temp. ≥ 90°F	0	0	0	1	9	23	26	28	19	5	0	0	111
Days Maximum Temp. ≤ 32°F	0	0	0	0	0	0	0	0	0	0	0	0	0
Days Minimum Temp. ≤ 32°F	3	2	1	0	0	0	0	0	0	0	0	3	9
Days Minimum Temp. ≤ 0°F	0	0	0	0	0	0	0	0	0	0	0	0	0
Heating Degree Days (base 65°F)	360	257	133	33	1	0	0	0	1	26	140	327	1,278
Cooling Degree Days (base 65°F)	17	25	73	168	369	516	592	607	454	239	90	28	3,178
Mean Precipitation (in.)	3.99	2.82	3.37	3.38	3.95	4.77	3.92	4.36	4.48	4.80	4.30	3.57	47.71
Extreme Maximum Daily Precip. (in.)	***3.37***	***3.04***	***2.79***	***8.65***	***3.75***	4.00	***5.70***	8.80	***9.53***	5.40	***7.81***	3.20	***9.53***
Days With ≥ 0.1" Precipitation	6	4	4	3	4	6	6	6	6	5	5	5	60
Days With ≥ 0.5" Precipitation	3	2	2	2	2	3	2	3	2	3	2	2	28
Days With ≥ 1.0" Precipitation	1	1	1	1	1	2	1	1	1	2	1	1	14
Mean Snowfall (in.)	***trace***	***trace***	***0.0***	***0.0***	***0.0***	***0.0***	0.0	***0.0***	***0.0***	***0.0***	***0.0***	***0.1***	***0.1***
Maximum Snow Depth (in.)	***trace***	***0***	***0***	***0***	***0***	***0***	***0***	***0***	***0***	***0***	***0***	***0***	trace
Days With ≥ 1.0" Snow Depth	***0***	***0***	***0***	***0***	***0***	0	0	***0***	***0***	***0***	***0***	***0***	***0***

The period of record for all cooperative weather station data is 1980 – 2009. See User Guide for detailed explanation of data.

Tyler *Smith County* Elevation: 549 ft. Latitude: 32° 18' N Longitude: 95° 18' W

	JAN	FEB	MAR	APR	MAY	JUN	JUL	AUG	SEP	OCT	NOV	DEC	YEAR
Mean Maximum Temp. (°F)	58.5	63.1	70.7	77.8	84.1	90.0	93.4	94.1	87.9	78.5	67.5	58.9	77.0
Mean Temp. (°F)	48.0	52.2	59.3	66.4	73.9	80.0	83.3	83.3	77.1	67.4	57.3	48.9	66.4
Mean Minimum Temp. (°F)	37.6	41.3	47.8	55.0	63.6	69.9	73.1	72.5	66.2	56.3	47.1	38.9	55.8
Extreme Maximum Temp. (°F)	83	90	92	94	101	102	105	107	107	97	86	83	107
Extreme Minimum Temp. (°F)	9	11	19	30	43	52	61	55	43	27	23	0	0
Days Maximum Temp. ≥ 90°F	0	0	0	1	5	19	26	26	14	2	0	0	93
Days Maximum Temp. ≤ 32°F	0	0	0	0	0	0	0	0	0	0	0	1	1
Days Minimum Temp. ≤ 32°F	10	6	2	0	0	0	0	0	0	0	2	9	29
Days Minimum Temp. ≤ 0°F	0	0	0	0	0	0	0	0	0	0	0	0	0
Heating Degree Days (base 65°F)	524	367	215	67	6	0	0	0	5	60	254	500	1,998
Cooling Degree Days (base 65°F)	6	12	44	117	288	456	574	575	374	142	29	8	2,625
Mean Precipitation (in.)	3.66	4.22	4.27	3.44	4.45	4.76	2.66	2.83	3.20	5.02	4.45	4.70	47.66
Extreme Maximum Daily Precip. (in.)	3.71	5.48	3.67	3.99	3.06	4.19	4.68	6.47	3.24	8.02	4.54	3.36	8.02
Days With ≥ 0.1" Precipitation	6	6	6	5	6	7	4	4	4	5	6	6	65
Days With ≥ 0.5" Precipitation	2	2	3	2	3	3	2	2	2	3	3	3	30
Days With ≥ 1.0" Precipitation	1	1	2	1	1	1	1	1	1	2	1	2	15
Mean Snowfall (in.)	0.2	0.6	0.1	trace	0.0	0.0	0.0	0.0	0.0	0.0	trace	trace	0.9
Maximum Snow Depth (in.)	3	5	1	trace	0	0	0	0	0	0	trace	trace	5
Days With ≥ 1.0" Snow Depth	0	0	0	0	0	0	0	0	0	0	0	0	0

Valentine *Jeff Davis County* Elevation: 4,430 ft. Latitude: 30° 35' N Longitude: 104° 30' W

	JAN	FEB	MAR	APR	MAY	JUN	JUL	AUG	SEP	OCT	NOV	DEC	YEAR
Mean Maximum Temp. (°F)	60.0	65.0	71.6	79.7	87.7	93.6	92.2	90.2	86.1	78.7	68.4	60.3	77.8
Mean Temp. (°F)	43.7	48.0	53.9	61.6	70.2	77.2	77.6	76.0	71.3	62.8	51.9	44.0	61.5
Mean Minimum Temp. (°F)	27.2	30.9	36.0	43.4	52.6	60.8	63.0	61.7	56.4	46.9	35.3	27.6	45.2
Extreme Maximum Temp. (°F)	83	84	89	97	101	108	106	103	100	96	86	77	108
Extreme Minimum Temp. (°F)	3	7	12	21	32	46	51	50	39	17	8	0	0
Days Maximum Temp. ≥ 90°F	0	0	0	2	12	24	21	18	9	1	0	0	87
Days Maximum Temp. ≤ 32°F	0	0	0	0	0	0	0	0	0	0	0	0	0
Days Minimum Temp. ≤ 32°F	23	16	10	3	0	0	0	0	0	1	10	23	86
Days Minimum Temp. ≤ 0°F	0	0	0	0	0	0	0	0	0	0	0	0	0
Heating Degree Days (base 65°F)	651	475	341	132	15	0	0	0	10	111	388	642	2,765
Cooling Degree Days (base 65°F)	0	0	2	37	183	373	398	347	206	51	2	0	1,599
Mean Precipitation (in.)	0.42	0.48	0.27	0.41	0.76	2.14	2.30	2.17	2.11	1.44	0.47	0.51	13.48
Extreme Maximum Daily Precip. (in.)	0.86	1.60	1.12	1.30	1.40	3.06	2.80	2.40	2.22	2.93	2.10	1.10	3.06
Days With ≥ 0.1" Precipitation	1	1	1	1	2	4	5	5	4	3	1	1	29
Days With ≥ 0.5" Precipitation	0	0	0	0	0	1	1	1	2	1	0	0	6
Days With ≥ 1.0" Precipitation	0	0	0	0	0	1	1	0	0	0	0	0	2
Mean Snowfall (in.)	0.7	trace	trace	0.1	0.0	0.0	0.0	0.0	0.0	trace	0.1	0.8	1.7
Maximum Snow Depth (in.)	trace	1	trace	0	0	0	0	0	0	trace	trace	8	8
Days With ≥ 1.0" Snow Depth	0	0	0	0	0	0	0	0	0	0	0	0	0

Water Valley *Tom Green County* Elevation: 2,120 ft. Latitude: 31° 40' N Longitude: 100° 44' W

	JAN	FEB	MAR	APR	MAY	JUN	JUL	AUG	SEP	OCT	NOV	DEC	YEAR
Mean Maximum Temp. (°F)	59.6	63.3	70.7	79.6	87.0	92.0	95.2	94.4	87.7	79.0	68.3	59.1	78.0
Mean Temp. (°F)	44.6	48.1	55.7	63.9	73.0	79.4	82.3	81.4	74.4	64.7	53.4	44.4	63.8
Mean Minimum Temp. (°F)	29.5	32.8	40.8	48.1	59.0	66.6	69.3	68.4	61.0	50.4	38.6	29.7	49.5
Extreme Maximum Temp. (°F)	88	97	96	102	112	112	109	107	108	103	93	86	112
Extreme Minimum Temp. (°F)	3	5	5	23	38	48	54	51	33	23	12	-4	-4
Days Maximum Temp. ≥ 90°F	0	0	1	5	13	19	26	26	13	4	0	0	107
Days Maximum Temp. ≤ 32°F	1	1	0	0	0	0	0	0	0	0	0	1	3
Days Minimum Temp. ≤ 32°F	21	14	6	2	0	0	0	0	0	1	9	20	73
Days Minimum Temp. ≤ 0°F	0	0	0	0	0	0	0	0	0	0	0	0	0
Heating Degree Days (base 65°F)	627	475	301	119	17	0	0	0	14	101	351	632	2,637
Cooling Degree Days (base 65°F)	0	3	20	91	272	438	544	516	302	99	10	0	2,295
Mean Precipitation (in.)	0.75	1.23	1.50	1.45	2.86	3.06	1.67	2.80	2.63	2.81	1.10	0.98	22.84
Extreme Maximum Daily Precip. (in.)	1.65	3.13	3.30	2.61	2.35	3.06	3.30	5.35	5.32	4.43	2.60	2.15	5.35
Days With ≥ 0.1" Precipitation	2	2	3	2	5	4	3	4	3	3	2	2	35
Days With ≥ 0.5" Precipitation	0	1	1	1	2	2	1	2	1	2	1	1	15
Days With ≥ 1.0" Precipitation	0	0	0	0	1	1	1	1	1	1	0	0	6
Mean Snowfall (in.)	0.7	0.1	0.0	0.2	0.0	0.0	0.0	0.0	0.0	0.0	0.6	0.2	1.8
Maximum Snow Depth (in.)	5	trace	trace	3	0	0	0	0	0	0	4	2	5
Days With ≥ 1.0" Snow Depth	0	0	0	0	0	0	0	0	0	0	0	0	0

Weslaco 2 E *Hidalgo County* Elevation: 75 ft. Latitude: 26° 09' N Longitude: 97° 58' W

	JAN	FEB	MAR	APR	MAY	JUN	JUL	AUG	SEP	OCT	NOV	DEC	YEAR
Mean Maximum Temp. (°F)	70.5	74.7	80.6	85.6	90.1	94.2	96.1	96.5	92.1	86.9	79.4	71.9	84.9
Mean Temp. (°F)	60.1	64.0	69.7	75.1	80.6	84.5	85.7	85.9	82.1	76.1	68.9	61.3	74.5
Mean Minimum Temp. (°F)	49.6	53.2	58.8	64.4	71.0	74.7	75.3	75.3	72.1	65.4	58.3	50.8	64.1
Extreme Maximum Temp. (°F)	91	98	104	102	105	105	104	104	107	100	99	91	107
Extreme Minimum Temp. (°F)	25	28	30	36	50	61	66	64	56	33	34	16	16
Days Maximum Temp. ≥ 90°F	0	1	3	8	18	27	28	29	22	12	2	0	150
Days Maximum Temp. ≤ 32°F	0	0	0	0	0	0	0	0	0	0	0	0	0
Days Minimum Temp. ≤ 32°F	0	0	0	0	0	0	0	0	0	0	0	1	1
Days Minimum Temp. ≤ 0°F	0	0	0	0	0	0	0	0	0	0	0	0	0
Heating Degree Days (base 65°F)	198	114	45	10	0	0	0	0	0	8	59	185	619
Cooling Degree Days (base 65°F)	54	91	198	319	490	591	649	656	521	360	183	81	4,193
Mean Precipitation (in.)	1.13	1.31	1.11	1.36	2.71	2.49	2.15	2.33	4.95	2.43	1.42	1.25	24.64
Extreme Maximum Daily Precip. (in.)	1.56	2.65	2.93	2.80	3.64	4.35	7.20	4.81	8.50	4.26	3.80	2.38	8.50
Days With ≥ 0.1" Precipitation	3	3	2	2	3	3	3	3	6	4	3	3	38
Days With ≥ 0.5" Precipitation	1	1	1	1	1	1	1	1	3	2	1	1	15
Days With ≥ 1.0" Precipitation	0	0	0	0	1	1	0	1	2	1	0	0	6
Mean Snowfall (in.)	0.0	0.0	0.0	0.0	0.0	0.0	0.0	0.0	0.0	0.0	0.0	0.0	0.0
Maximum Snow Depth (in.)	0	0	0	0	0	0	0	0	0	0	0	0	0
Days With ≥ 1.0" Snow Depth	0	0	0	0	0	0	0	0	0	0	0	0	0

The period of record for all cooperative weather station data is 1980 – 2009. See User Guide for detailed explanation of data.

Whitney Dam *Bosque County* Elevation: 574 ft. Latitude: 31° 51' N Longitude: 97° 22' W

	JAN	FEB	MAR	APR	MAY	JUN	JUL	AUG	SEP	OCT	NOV	DEC	YEAR
Mean Maximum Temp. (°F)	58.7	62.1	69.3	77.3	84.9	91.6	96.7	97.1	90.3	79.9	68.7	59.0	78.0
Mean Temp. (°F)	46.7	49.8	57.4	65.1	73.8	80.3	84.2	84.2	77.7	67.2	56.8	47.3	65.9
Mean Minimum Temp. (°F)	34.7	37.5	45.5	52.9	62.6	69.0	71.6	71.3	65.0	54.4	44.8	35.5	53.7
Extreme Maximum Temp. (°F)	87	97	97	103	101	110	109	111	113	99	90	91	113
Extreme Minimum Temp. (°F)	4	7	15	28	42	52	59	56	38	26	21	-3	-3
Days Maximum Temp. ≥ 90°F	0	0	0	1	8	21	29	28	18	5	0	0	110
Days Maximum Temp. ≤ 32°F	0	1	0	0	0	0	0	0	0	0	0	1	2
Days Minimum Temp. ≤ 32°F	14	8	3	0	0	0	0	0	0	0	4	12	41
Days Minimum Temp. ≤ 0°F	0	0	0	0	0	0	0	0	0	0	0	0	0
Heating Degree Days (base 65°F)	565	427	256	90	7	0	0	0	6	67	267	547	2,232
Cooling Degree Days (base 65°F)	3	6	30	100	285	466	602	602	393	141	28	4	2,660
Mean Precipitation (in.)	2.03	2.38	3.52	2.82	4.20	4.52	1.63	2.06	2.67	4.00	2.78	2.77	35.38
Extreme Maximum Daily Precip. (in.)	3.58	2.70	6.87	5.75	6.50	5.76	2.71	3.55	5.66	3.18	3.38	5.15	6.87
Days With ≥ 0.1" Precipitation	4	4	5	4	6	6	3	3	4	5	4	4	52
Days With ≥ 0.5" Precipitation	1	2	2	2	3	3	1	1	2	3	2	2	24
Days With ≥ 1.0" Precipitation	0	1	1	1	1	1	1	1	1	1	1	1	11
Mean Snowfall (in.)	0.0	trace	0.0	0.0	0.0	0.0	0.0	0.0	0.0	0.0	0.0	0.1	0.1
Maximum Snow Depth (in.)	12	trace	0	0	0	0	0	0	0	0	0	2	12
Days With ≥ 1.0" Snow Depth	0	0	0	0	0	0	0	0	0	0	0	0	0

Wright Patman Dam & Lock *Cass County* Elevation: 282 ft. Latitude: 33° 18' N Longitude: 94° 10' W

	JAN	FEB	MAR	APR	MAY	JUN	JUL	AUG	SEP	OCT	NOV	DEC	YEAR
Mean Maximum Temp. (°F)	54.3	58.9	66.8	74.5	82.0	88.9	92.9	93.4	86.4	76.0	65.3	55.6	74.6
Mean Temp. (°F)	43.6	47.8	55.8	63.0	71.6	78.5	82.3	81.9	74.7	63.8	54.2	45.2	63.5
Mean Minimum Temp. (°F)	32.8	36.7	44.7	51.5	61.1	68.1	71.6	70.4	62.9	51.5	43.0	34.8	52.4
Extreme Maximum Temp. (°F)	82	88	90	93	95	103	107	108	109	93	86	84	109
Extreme Minimum Temp. (°F)	4	5	14	28	40	52	56	51	39	27	19	-1	-1
Days Maximum Temp. ≥ 90°F	0	0	0	0	3	16	24	24	11	1	0	0	79
Days Maximum Temp. ≤ 32°F	1	1	0	0	0	0	0	0	0	0	0	1	3
Days Minimum Temp. ≤ 32°F	17	9	3	0	0	0	0	0	0	0	5	13	47
Days Minimum Temp. ≤ 0°F	0	0	0	0	0	0	0	0	0	0	0	0	0
Heating Degree Days (base 65°F)	660	482	302	121	14	0	0	0	12	115	332	608	2,646
Cooling Degree Days (base 65°F)	3	3	23	69	225	413	542	532	309	84	14	4	2,221
Mean Precipitation (in.)	3.74	3.97	4.52	3.91	4.66	4.56	3.23	2.50	3.18	5.09	4.56	4.59	48.51
Extreme Maximum Daily Precip. (in.)	3.43	4.35	5.25	3.75	4.00	4.15	3.94	2.73	3.56	5.42	3.67	5.85	5.85
Days With ≥ 0.1" Precipitation	5	6	6	6	6	6	5	4	5	6	6	6	67
Days With ≥ 0.5" Precipitation	2	3	3	3	4	3	2	2	2	3	3	3	33
Days With ≥ 1.0" Precipitation	1	1	1	1	1	2	1	1	1	2	2	1	15
Mean Snowfall (in.)	0.1	0.4	0.0	0.0	0.0	0.0	0.0	0.0	0.0	0.0	trace	0.1	0.6
Maximum Snow Depth (in.)	4	3	0	0	0	0	0	0	0	0	trace	1	4
Days With ≥ 1.0" Snow Depth	0	0	0	0	0	0	0	0	0	0	0	0	0

The period of record for all cooperative weather station data is 1980 – 2009. See User Guide for detailed explanation of data.

Texas Weather Station Rankings

Annual Extreme Maximum Temperature

Highest			Lowest		
Rank	Station Name	°F	Rank	Station Name	°F
1	Boquillas Ranger Stn	***117***	1	Aransas Wildlife Refuge	102
1	Castolon	117	2	Port Isabel	103
1	Childress Municipal Arpt	117	3	Anahuac	105
1	Grandfalls 3 SSE	***117***	4	Alpine	***106***
1	Wichita Falls Municipal Arpt	117	4	Brownsville Intl Arpt	106
6	Columbus	116	4	Harlingen	106
6	Encinal	***116***	4	Thompsons 3 WSW	***106***
6	Falcon Dam	116	8	Angleton 2 W	107
6	Gail	116	8	Beaumont Research Ctr	107
6	Midland Regional Air Terminal	116	8	Liberty	107
6	Penwell	116	8	Marshall	107
6	Rio Grande City 1 SE	116	8	Ozona 1 SSW	107
13	Bridgeport	***115***	8	Tyler	***107***
13	Candelaria	115	8	Weslaco 2 E	107
13	Crystal City	115	15	Amarillo Intl Arpt	108
13	Dell City 5 SSW	115	15	Borger	108
13	Falfurrias	115	15	Burnet	108
13	Henrietta	***115***	15	Emory	***108***
19	Amistad Dam	114	15	Houston William P Hobby Arpt	108
19	Anson	***114***	15	Marathon	108
19	Bakersfield	114	15	Port Arthur Jefferson County	108
19	Big Spring	***114***	15	Raymondville	108
19	El Paso Intl Arpt	114	15	Sugar Land	108
19	Laredo 2	114	15	Texarkana	108
19	Lubbock Regional Arpt	114	15	Valentine	108

Annual Mean Maximum Temperature

Highest			Lowest		
Rank	Station Name	°F	Rank	Station Name	°F
1	Boquillas Ranger Stn	***88.1***	1	Amarillo Intl Arpt	70.8
2	Castolon	87.7	2	Dimmitt 2 N	71.3
3	Falcon Dam	86.5	3	Hart	***71.6***
4	Rio Grande City 1 SE	86.4	4	Borger	72.0
5	Laredo 2	85.9	5	Boys Ranch	72.6
5	McAllen Miller Intl Arpt	***85.9***	6	Canyon	73.2
7	Candelaria	85.4	7	Clarendon	73.4
7	McCook	85.4	8	Morton	73.5
9	Raymondville	85.1	9	Crosbyton	73.9
10	Weslaco 2 E	84.9	10	Lubbock Regional Arpt	74.3
11	Encinal	***84.8***	11	Wright Patman Dam & Lock	74.6
11	McAllen	***84.8***	12	Childress Municipal Arpt	74.7
13	Falfurrias	84.3	12	Emory	***74.7***
14	Carrizo Springs	83.9	12	Texarkana	74.7
14	Crystal City	83.9	15	Brownfield 2	74.9
14	Harlingen	83.9	16	Dublin	75.1
17	Alice	***83.7***	17	Marshall	75.2
17	Brownsville Intl Arpt	83.7	18	Henrietta	***75.6***
19	Charlotte 5 NNW	83.6	19	Denton 2 SE	75.7
20	Langtry	82.4	20	Pilot Point	***75.8***
21	Cuero	82.1	20	Wichita Falls Municipal Arpt	75.8
21	Robstown	82.1	22	Lavon Dam	75.9
23	Floresville	81.9	23	Henderson	76.0
24	Amistad Dam	81.8	24	McKinney 3 S	***76.1***
25	Del Rio Intl Arpt	81.7	25	Abilene Municipal Arpt	76.2

Rankings include 25 highest/lowest stations. If state has less than 25 stations, all stations are included. The period of record is 1980–2009. See User Guide for detailed explanation of data.

Annual Mean Temperature

Highest

Rank	Station Name	°F
1	McAllen Miller Intl Arpt	***75.6***
2	Brownsville Intl Arpt	74.6
2	McAllen	***74.6***
4	Falcon Dam	74.5
4	Weslaco 2 E	74.5
6	Laredo 2	74.3
6	Rio Grande City 1 SE	74.3
8	McCook	74.1
8	Port Isabel	74.1
10	Harlingen	74.0
11	Raymondville	73.8
12	Crystal City	72.7
13	Alice	***72.6***
13	Falfurrias	72.6
15	Robstown	72.3
16	Corpus Christi Intl Arpt	72.2
16	Port Mansfield	***72.2***
18	Encinal	***72.0***
19	Castolon	71.8
20	Carrizo Springs	71.4
21	Charlotte 5 NNW	71.3
22	Aransas Wildlife Refuge	70.9
23	Del Rio Intl Arpt	70.5
23	Victoria Regional Arpt	70.5
25	Boquillas Ranger Stn	***70.4***

Lowest

Rank	Station Name	°F
1	Dimmitt 2 N	56.0
2	Hart	***56.9***
3	Amarillo Intl Arpt	57.2
4	Boys Ranch	57.7
5	Borger	58.6
6	Morton	58.7
7	Canyon	59.0
7	Clarendon	59.0
9	Crosbyton	60.1
10	Brownfield 2	60.6
11	Lubbock Regional Arpt	60.9
12	Valentine	61.5
13	Childress Municipal Arpt	61.9
13	Dell City 5 SSW	61.9
15	Alpine	***62.5***
16	Henrietta	***62.6***
16	Marathon	***62.6***
18	Fort Hancock 5 SSE	***62.9***
19	Emory	***63.5***
19	Wright Patman Dam & Lock	63.5
21	Dublin	63.6
22	Wichita Falls Municipal Arpt	63.7
23	Midland Regional Air Terminal	63.8
23	Water Valley	63.8
25	Balmorhea	63.9

Annual Mean Minimum Temperature

Highest

Rank	Station Name	°F
1	Port Isabel	67.2
2	Port Mansfield	65.6
3	Brownsville Intl Arpt	65.4
4	McAllen Miller Intl Arpt	***65.2***
5	McAllen	***64.2***
6	Weslaco 2 E	64.1
7	Harlingen	63.9
8	Aransas Wildlife Refuge	63.2
9	McCook	62.8
10	Corpus Christi Intl Arpt	62.7
11	Raymondville	62.6
12	Falcon Dam	62.5
12	Laredo 2	62.5
14	Robstown	62.4
15	Rio Grande City 1 SE	62.1
16	Alice	***61.5***
17	Crystal City	61.4
17	Houston William P Hobby Arpt	61.4
19	Bay City Waterworks	61.1
20	Falfurrias	60.9
21	Baytown	60.3
21	Victoria Regional Arpt	60.3
23	Angleton 2 W	59.9
23	Port Arthur Jefferson County	59.9
25	Sugar Land	***59.7***

Lowest

Rank	Station Name	°F
1	Dimmitt 2 N	40.7
2	Hart	***42.1***
3	Boys Ranch	42.7
4	Amarillo Intl Arpt	43.7
5	Morton	43.8
6	Clarendon	44.6
6	Dell City 5 SSW	44.6
8	Canyon	44.7
9	Borger	45.2
9	Valentine	45.2
11	Fort Hancock 5 SSE	***45.5***
12	Brownfield 2	46.2
13	Crosbyton	46.4
14	Marathon	***46.9***
15	Lubbock Regional Arpt	47.4
16	Alpine	***48.0***
17	Balmorhea	48.5
18	Grandfalls 3 SSE	***48.7***
19	Childress Municipal Arpt	49.0
20	La Tuna 1 S	49.1
21	Water Valley	49.5
22	Henrietta	***49.6***
23	Candelaria	49.9
24	Penwell	50.1
25	Midland Regional Air Terminal	50.3

Rankings include 25 highest/lowest stations. If state has less than 25 stations, all stations are included. The period of record is 1980–2009. See User Guide for detailed explanation of data.

Annual Extreme Minimum Temperature

Highest Rank	Station Name	°F	Lowest Rank	Station Name	°F
1	McAllen	***18***	1	Amarillo Intl Arpt	-12
1	McAllen Miller Intl Arpt	***18***	1	Anson	***-12***
3	Port Isabel	17	1	Penwell	-12
4	Brownsville Intl Arpt	16	4	Boys Ranch	-11
4	Rio Grande City 1 SE	16	4	Canyon	-11
4	Weslaco 2 E	16	4	Clarendon	-11
7	Falcon Dam	15	4	Hart	***-11***
7	Harlingen	15	4	Midland Regional Air Terminal	-11
7	Port Mansfield	15	9	Dimmitt 2 N	-9
7	Raymondville	15	9	Grandfalls 3 SSE	***-9***
11	McCook	14	11	Bridgeport	***-8***
12	Corpus Christi Intl Arpt	13	11	Henrietta	***-8***
12	Falfurrias	13	11	Wichita Falls Municipal Arpt	-8
14	Alice	***12***	14	Abilene Municipal Arpt	-7
14	Encinal	***12***	14	Bardwell Dam	-7
14	Port Arthur Jefferson County	12	14	Borger	-7
14	Robstown	12	14	Dublin	-7
18	Crystal City	11	18	Albany	***-6***
18	Laredo 2	11	18	Athens	-6
20	Carrizo Springs	***10***	18	Benbrook Dam	-6
20	Del Rio Intl Arpt	10	18	Brownwood	-6
22	Amistad Dam	9	18	Crosbyton	-6
22	Aransas Wildlife Refuge	9	18	Morton	-6
22	Houston William P Hobby Arpt	9	18	Texarkana	-6
22	Langtry	9	25	Big Spring	***-5***

July Mean Maximum Temperature

Highest Rank	Station Name	°F	Lowest Rank	Station Name	°F
1	Boquillas Ranger Stn	***103.0***	1	Port Mansfield	88.8
2	Castolon	102.3	2	Galveston	***89.0***
3	Laredo 2	100.4	3	Alpine	89.3
4	Falcon Dam	100.3	4	Aransas Wildlife Refuge	89.8
5	Candelaria	99.9	5	Hart	***90.0***
6	Rio Grande City 1 SE	99.4	6	Port Isabel	90.5
7	Encinal	***98.9***	7	Marathon	90.7
8	Carrizo Springs	98.6	8	Dimmitt 2 N	91.3
9	Grandfalls 3 SSE	98.4	9	Angleton 2 W	91.4
10	Langtry	98.3	10	Anahuac	91.5
11	McCook	97.8	11	Amarillo Intl Arpt	91.6
12	Amistad Dam	97.6	12	Baytown	91.7
13	McAllen Miller Intl Arpt	97.4	13	Port Arthur Jefferson County	91.8
13	Wichita Falls Municipal Arpt	97.4	14	Bay City Waterworks	91.9
15	Crystal City	97.3	15	Morton	92.0
15	Falfurrias	97.3	16	Beaumont Research Ctr	92.2
17	Dell City 5 SSW	97.1	16	Cleveland	92.2
18	Raymondville	97.0	16	Valentine	92.2
18	Waco Madison Cooper Arpt	97.0	19	Houston William P Hobby Arpt	92.3
20	Del Rio Intl Arpt	96.9	20	Emory	***92.5***
21	Charlotte 5 NNW	96.8	21	Boys Ranch	92.7
22	Bridgeport	96.7	21	Canyon	92.7
22	Whitney Dam	96.7	21	Marshall	92.7
24	Henrietta	***96.6***	24	Boerne	92.8
24	Pilot Point	***96.6***	24	Brownfield 2	92.8

Rankings include 25 highest/lowest stations. If state has less than 25 stations, all stations are included. The period of record is 1980–2009. See User Guide for detailed explanation of data.

January Mean Minimum Temperature

Highest			Lowest		
Rank	Station Name	°F	Rank	Station Name	°F
1	Port Isabel	53.2	1	Boys Ranch	21.1
2	Brownsville Intl Arpt	51.7	2	Dimmitt 2 N	21.4
3	McAllen Miller Intl Arpt	***50.6***	3	Hart	***22.3***
4	Port Mansfield	49.9	4	Amarillo Intl Arpt	23.5
5	Harlingen	49.8	5	Clarendon	24.0
6	Weslaco 2 E	49.6	6	Morton	24.5
7	McAllen	49.3	7	Canyon	24.6
8	McCook	48.1	8	Borger	25.3
8	Raymondville	48.1	9	Fort Hancock 5 SSE	25.6
10	Corpus Christi Intl Arpt	47.4	10	Dell City 5 SSW	25.7
11	Falcon Dam	46.7	11	Crosbyton	26.3
12	Aransas Wildlife Refuge	46.4	12	Lubbock Regional Arpt	27.0
12	Robstown	46.4	13	Brownfield 2	27.1
14	Rio Grande City 1 SE	45.9	14	Valentine	27.2
15	Alice	***45.6***	15	Grandfalls 3 SSE	***27.7***
16	Laredo 2	45.5	16	Childress Municipal Arpt	27.8
17	Houston William P Hobby Arpt	45.1	17	Henrietta	***28.4***
18	Bay City Waterworks	45.0	18	Water Valley	29.5
19	Falfurrias	44.8	19	Penwell	29.8
20	Angleton 2 W	44.1	20	Marathon	30.0
20	Crystal City	44.1	21	La Tuna 1 S	30.1
22	Victoria Regional Arpt	44.0	22	Ozona 1 SSW	30.2
23	Thompsons 3 WSW	43.9	23	Midland Regional Air Terminal	30.4
24	Port Arthur Jefferson County	43.7	24	Wichita Falls Municipal Arpt	30.6
25	Baytown	43.1	25	Balmorhea	30.7

Number of Days Annually Maximum Temperature ≥ 90°F

Highest			Lowest		
Rank	Station Name	Days	Rank	Station Name	Days
1	Boquillas Ranger Stn	***192***	1	Port Mansfield	41
2	Castolon	186	2	Aransas Wildlife Refuge	60
3	Rio Grande City 1 SE	179	2	Hart	***60***
4	Falcon Dam	178	4	Amarillo Intl Arpt	64
5	Laredo 2	175	5	Alpine	***65***
6	McAllen Miller Intl Arpt	***171***	5	Dimmitt 2 N	65
7	Candelaria	165	7	Borger	73
8	McCook	163	8	Boys Ranch	74
9	Encinal	***161***	8	Emory	***74***
10	McAllen	***155***	10	Morton	76
10	Raymondville	155	11	Canyon	78
12	Carrizo Springs	150	11	Marshall	78
12	Weslaco 2 E	150	13	Angleton 2 W	79
14	Crystal City	149	13	Texarkana	79
15	Langtry	146	13	Wright Patman Dam & Lock	79
16	Alice	144	16	Anahuac	81
16	Charlotte 5 NNW	144	16	Crosbyton	81
16	Falfurrias	144	16	Marathon	81
19	Harlingen	142	19	Dublin	82
20	Amistad Dam	139	20	Port Isabel	83
21	Brownsville Intl Arpt	133	21	Baytown	84
22	Del Rio Intl Arpt	132	21	Clarendon	84
23	Floresville	130	23	Henderson	85
24	Cuero	129	24	Cleveland	86
25	Columbus	127	24	Lubbock Regional Arpt	86

Rankings include 25 highest/lowest stations. If state has less than 25 stations, all stations are included. The period of record is 1980–2009. See User Guide for detailed explanation of data.

Number of Days Annually Maximum Temperature ≤ 32°F

Highest

Rank	Station Name	Days
1	Amarillo Intl Arpt	11
1	Dimmitt 2 N	11
3	Clarendon	10
4	Borger	9
4	Hart	*9*
6	Boys Ranch	8
7	Canyon	6
7	Childress Municipal Arpt	6
7	Crosbyton	6
7	Morton	6
11	Brownfield 2	5
11	Henrietta	*5*
11	Lubbock Regional Arpt	5
11	Wichita Falls Municipal Arpt	5
15	Big Spring	4
16	Abilene Municipal Arpt	3
16	Albany	*3*
16	Anson	*3*
16	Bardwell Dam	3
16	Benbrook Dam	3
16	Brady	3
16	Coleman	3
16	Dallas-Fort Worth Intl Arpt	3
16	Dallas Love Field	3
16	Denton 2 SE	3

Lowest

Rank	Station Name	Days
1	Alice	0
1	Alpine	*0*
1	Amistad Dam	0
1	Anahuac	0
1	Angleton 2 W	0
1	Aransas Wildlife Refuge	0
1	Austin Municipal Arpt	0
1	Bay City Waterworks	0
1	Baytown	0
1	Beaumont Research Ctr	0
1	Blanco	0
1	Boerne	0
1	Boquillas Ranger Stn	*0*
1	Brenham	0
1	Brownsville Intl Arpt	0
1	Cameron	0
1	Camp Wood	0
1	Candelaria	0
1	Carrizo Springs	0
1	Castolon	0
1	Charlotte 5 NNW	0
1	Cleveland	0
1	College Station Easterwood	*0*
1	Columbus	0
1	Conroe	0

Number of Days Annually Minimum Temperature ≤ 32°F

Highest

Rank	Station Name	Days
1	Dimmitt 2 N	131
2	Boys Ranch	124
3	Hart	*122*
4	Amarillo Intl Arpt	110
5	Morton	107
6	Clarendon	105
7	Canyon	99
7	Dell City 5 SSW	99
9	Borger	96
9	Fort Hancock 5 SSE	96
11	Crosbyton	89
12	Brownfield 2	88
13	Valentine	86
14	Lubbock Regional Arpt	84
15	Grandfalls 3 SSE	*78*
16	Childress Municipal Arpt	76
17	Water Valley	73
18	Henrietta	*72*
19	Marathon	68
20	Ozona 1 SSW	66
21	Balmorhea	65
21	La Tuna 1 S	65
23	Penwell	63
24	Menard	62
24	Midland Regional Air Terminal	62

Lowest

Rank	Station Name	Days
1	Port Isabel	0
2	McAllen Miller Intl Arpt	*1*
2	Weslaco 2 E	1
4	Brownsville Intl Arpt	2
4	Harlingen	2
4	McAllen	*2*
7	Falcon Dam	3
7	McCook	3
7	Port Mansfield	3
10	Raymondville	4
11	Alice	5
11	Corpus Christi Intl Arpt	5
11	Robstown	5
14	Aransas Wildlife Refuge	6
14	Houston William P Hobby Arpt	6
16	Bay City Waterworks	7
16	Laredo 2	7
16	Rio Grande City 1 SE	7
19	Crystal City	8
20	Thompsons 3 WSW	9
20	Victoria Regional Arpt	9
22	Angleton 2 W	10
22	Encinal	*10*
22	Falfurrias	10
22	Port Arthur Jefferson County	10

Rankings include 25 highest/lowest stations. If state has less than 25 stations, all stations are included. The period of record is 1980–2009. See User Guide for detailed explanation of data.

Number of Days Annually Minimum Temperature ≤ 0°F

Highest Rank	Highest Station Name	Highest Days	Lowest Rank	Lowest Station Name	Lowest Days
1	Amarillo Intl Arpt	1	1	Abilene Municipal Arpt	0
1	Borger	1	1	Albany	*0*
1	Boys Ranch	1	1	Alice	0
1	Dimmitt 2 N	1	1	Alpine	*0*
1	Hart	*1*	1	Amistad Dam	0
6	Abilene Municipal Arpt	0	1	Anahuac	0
6	Albany	*0*	1	Angleton 2 W	0
6	Alice	0	1	Anson	*0*
6	Alpine	*0*	1	Aransas Wildlife Refuge	0
6	Amistad Dam	0	1	Athens	0
6	Anahuac	0	1	Austin Municipal Arpt	0
6	Angleton 2 W	0	1	Bakersfield	0
6	Anson	*0*	1	Ballinger 2 NW	0
6	Aransas Wildlife Refuge	0	1	Balmorhea	0
6	Athens	0	1	Bardwell Dam	0
6	Austin Municipal Arpt	0	1	Bay City Waterworks	0
6	Bakersfield	0	1	Baytown	0
6	Ballinger 2 NW	0	1	Beaumont Research Ctr	0
6	Balmorhea	0	1	Benbrook Dam	0
6	Bardwell Dam	0	1	Big Spring	0
6	Bay City Waterworks	0	1	Blanco	0
6	Baytown	0	1	Boerne	0
6	Beaumont Research Ctr	0	1	Boquillas Ranger Stn	*0*
6	Benbrook Dam	0	1	Brady	0
6	Big Spring	0	1	Brenham	0

Number of Annual Heating Degree Days

Highest Rank	Highest Station Name	Highest Num.	Lowest Rank	Lowest Station Name	Lowest Num.
1	Dimmitt 2 N	4,389	1	Port Isabel	539
2	Amarillo Intl Arpt	4,150	2	Brownsville Intl Arpt	547
3	Hart	*4,122*	3	McAllen Miller Intl Arpt	*584*
4	Boys Ranch	4,097	4	Weslaco 2 E	619
5	Borger	3,840	5	Harlingen	673
6	Clarendon	3,789	5	McAllen	*673*
7	Canyon	3,720	7	Raymondville	736
8	Morton	3,683	8	McCook	757
9	Crosbyton	3,413	9	Port Mansfield	*785*
10	Lubbock Regional Arpt	3,289	10	Falcon Dam	796
11	Brownfield 2	3,263	11	Rio Grande City 1 SE	821
12	Childress Municipal Arpt	3,192	12	Corpus Christi Intl Arpt	878
13	Henrietta	*3,047*	13	Laredo 2	906
14	Dell City 5 SSW	2,935	14	Alice	*910*
15	Wichita Falls Municipal Arpt	2,860	15	Robstown	929
16	Valentine	2,765	16	Falfurrias	971
17	Pilot Point	*2,742*	17	Crystal City	977
18	Fort Hancock 5 SSE	*2,698*	18	Aransas Wildlife Refuge	1,020
19	Wright Patman Dam & Lock	2,646	19	Encinal	*1,112*
20	Midland Regional Air Terminal	2,641	20	Charlotte 5 NNW	1,118
21	Water Valley	2,637	21	Bay City Waterworks	1,152
22	Emory	*2,632*	22	Victoria Regional Arpt	1,184
23	Dublin	2,626	23	Houston William P Hobby Arpt	1,210
24	Texarkana	2,621	24	Angleton 2 W	1,243
25	Bridgeport	*2,618*	25	Carrizo Springs	1,245

Rankings include 25 highest/lowest stations. If state has less than 25 stations, all stations are included. The period of record is 1980–2009. See User Guide for detailed explanation of data.

Number of Annual Cooling Degree Days

Highest Rank	Highest Station Name	Highest Num.	Lowest Rank	Lowest Station Name	Lowest Num.
1	McAllen Miller Intl Arpt	***4,549***	1	Dimmitt 2 N	1,201
2	Laredo 2	4,389	2	Hart	***1,261***
3	Falcon Dam	4,378	3	Amarillo Intl Arpt	1,426
4	Rio Grande City 1 SE	4,318	4	Morton	1,496
5	McAllen	***4,264***	5	Boys Ranch	1,518
6	McCook	4,193	6	Valentine	1,599
6	Weslaco 2 E	4,193	7	Marathon	***1,616***
8	Brownsville Intl Arpt	4,131	8	Canyon	1,623
9	Raymondville	4,058	9	Borger	1,625
10	Harlingen	4,042	10	Clarendon	1,707
11	Port Isabel	3,969	11	Crosbyton	1,747
12	Castolon	3,933	12	Brownfield 2	1,751
13	Crystal City	3,875	13	Lubbock Regional Arpt	1,887
14	Falfurrias	3,844	14	Dell City 5 SSW	1,920
15	Alice	***3,800***	15	Fort Hancock 5 SSE	***2,045***
16	Encinal	***3,759***	16	Balmorhea	2,150
17	Carrizo Springs	3,688	17	Childress Municipal Arpt	2,165
18	Robstown	3,675	18	Emory	***2,205***
19	Boquillas Ranger Stn	***3,641***	19	Ozona 1 SSW	2,214
20	Corpus Christi Intl Arpt	3,593	20	Dublin	2,220
21	Port Mansfield	***3,521***	21	Wright Patman Dam & Lock	2,221
22	Charlotte 5 NNW	3,513	22	La Tuna 1 S	2,245
23	Langtry	3,494	23	Henrietta	***2,291***
24	Del Rio Intl Arpt	3,443	24	Gail	***2,294***
25	Amistad Dam	3,367	25	Water Valley	2,295

Annual Precipitation

Highest Rank	Highest Station Name	Highest Inches	Lowest Rank	Lowest Station Name	Lowest Inches
1	Liberty	61.82	1	La Tuna 1 S	9.20
2	Port Arthur Jefferson County	60.92	2	Fort Hancock 5 SSE	9.25
3	Sam Rayburn Dam	60.52	3	Boquillas Ranger Stn	***9.68***
4	Baytown	60.01	4	El Paso Intl Arpt	9.72
5	Beaumont Research Ctr	59.32	5	Dell City 5 SSW	10.62
6	Angleton 2 W	57.01	6	Castolon	10.68
7	Anahuac	56.94	7	Balmorhea	13.45
8	Cleveland	54.28	8	Valentine	13.48
9	Houston William P Hobby Arpt	53.66	9	Candelaria	13.75
10	Texarkana	52.17	10	Penwell	13.83
11	Carthage	51.36	11	Grandfalls 3 SSE	***14.38***
12	Bay City Waterworks	50.29	12	Langtry	14.56
13	Marshall	50.28	13	Marathon	14.66
14	Longview 11 SE	49.88	13	Midland Regional Air Terminal	14.66
15	Houston Bush Intercontinental	49.64	15	Bakersfield	14.84
16	Sugar Land	49.17	16	Alpine	***17.29***
17	Henderson	49.07	17	Hart	***18.09***
18	Conroe	48.63	18	Amistad Dam	18.33
19	Wright Patman Dam & Lock	48.51	19	Del Rio Intl Arpt	18.38
20	Thompsons 3 WSW	47.71	20	Ozona 1 SSW	18.55
21	Tyler	***47.66***	21	Lubbock Regional Arpt	18.74
22	Daingerfield 9 S	46.59	22	Boys Ranch	19.00
23	Crockett	45.31	22	Brownfield 2	19.00
24	Pilot Point	***45.26***	24	Morton	19.11
25	Brenham	45.08	25	Gail	19.43

Rankings include 25 highest/lowest stations. If state has less than 25 stations, all stations are included. The period of record is 1980–2009. See User Guide for detailed explanation of data.

Annual Extreme Maximum Daily Precipitation

Highest

Rank	Station Name	Inches
1	Bay City Waterworks	20.85
2	Liberty	18.50
3	New Braunfels	***18.35***
4	San Marcos	15.78
5	Baytown	15.74
6	Somerville Dam	15.25
7	Beaumont Research Ctr	15.21
8	Sam Rayburn Dam	14.00
9	Anahuac	13.20
10	Cleveland	13.17
11	Angleton 2 W	12.36
12	Port Arthur Jefferson County	11.80
13	San Antonio Intl Arpt	11.26
14	Henderson	11.05
15	Aransas Wildlife Refuge	10.73
16	Sugar Land	***10.60***
17	Brenham	10.38
18	Houston Bush Intercontinental	10.34
19	Victoria Regional Arpt	9.87
20	Corpus Christi Intl Arpt	9.85
21	Harlingen	9.79
22	Thompsons 3 WSW	***9.53***
23	Houston William P Hobby Arpt	9.48
24	McAllen Miller Intl Arpt	***9.42***
25	Carthage	9.25

Lowest

Rank	Station Name	Inches
1	Boquillas Ranger Stn	***2.14***
2	Dell City 5 SSW	2.44
3	El Paso Intl Arpt	2.84
4	Marathon	2.96
5	Valentine	3.06
6	Balmorhea	***3.23***
7	Candelaria	3.43
8	Midland Regional Air Terminal	3.59
9	Penwell	***3.63***
10	Fort Hancock 5 SSE	3.70
11	Hart	***3.75***
12	Alpine	***3.92***
13	Castolon	3.95
14	Morton	4.10
15	La Tuna 1 S	***4.25***
16	Menard	4.35
17	Dimmitt 2 N	4.38
18	Dallas-Fort Worth Intl Arpt	4.39
19	Crystal City	4.44
20	Boys Ranch	4.50
21	Gail	4.52
22	Ozona 1 SSW	4.72
23	Amarillo Intl Arpt	4.92
24	Brownfield 2	5.05
25	Big Spring	***5.09***

Number of Days Annually With ≥ 0.1 Inches of Precipitation

Highest

Rank	Station Name	Days
1	Sam Rayburn Dam	73
2	Baytown	72
3	Beaumont Research Ctr	71
3	Cleveland	71
3	Liberty	71
3	Port Arthur Jefferson County	71
7	Anahuac	69
8	Angleton 2 W	68
8	Texarkana	68
10	Marshall	67
10	Wright Patman Dam & Lock	67
12	Henderson	66
12	Houston William P Hobby Arpt	66
12	Longview 11 SE	66
15	Pilot Point	***65***
15	Tyler	***65***
17	Columbus	64
18	Carthage	63
18	Houston Bush Intercontinental	63
20	Bay City Waterworks	62
20	Brenham	62
20	Conroe	62
20	Daingerfield 9 S	62
24	Crockett	61
25	Thompsons 3 WSW	60

Lowest

Rank	Station Name	Days
1	La Tuna 1 S	20
2	Penwell	22
3	Boquillas Ranger Stn	***23***
3	Castolon	23
3	Dell City 5 SSW	23
6	Encinal	***24***
6	Fort Hancock 5 SSE	24
8	El Paso Intl Arpt	25
9	Langtry	27
10	Balmorhea	28
10	Marathon	28
12	Bakersfield	29
12	Candelaria	29
12	Del Rio Intl Arpt	29
12	Grandfalls 3 SSE	***29***
12	Midland Regional Air Terminal	29
12	Valentine	29
18	Carrizo Springs	30
19	Amistad Dam	31
19	Big Spring	31
19	Laredo 2	31
22	Crystal City	32
22	Falcon Dam	32
22	McAllen	***32***
22	McCook	32

 Rankings include 25 highest/lowest stations. If state has less than 25 stations, all stations are included. The period of record is 1980–2009. See User Guide for detailed explanation of data.

Number of Days Annually With ≥ 0.5 Inches of Precipitation

Highest			Lowest		
Rank	Station Name	Days	Rank	Station Name	Days
1	Sam Rayburn Dam	39	1	Fort Hancock 5 SSE	3
2	Baytown	35	2	Dell City 5 SSW	4
2	Liberty	35	2	El Paso Intl Arpt	4
2	Port Arthur Jefferson County	35	4	La Tuna 1 S	5
2	Texarkana	35	5	Boquillas Ranger Stn	***6***
6	Angleton 2 W	34	5	Castolon	6
6	Beaumont Research Ctr	34	5	Penwell	6
8	Anahuac	33	5	Valentine	6
8	Cleveland	33	9	Candelaria	7
8	Houston William P Hobby Arpt	33	9	Marathon	7
8	Marshall	33	9	Midland Regional Air Terminal	7
8	Wright Patman Dam & Lock	33	12	Balmorhea	8
13	Carthage	32	12	Grandfalls 3 SSE	***8***
13	Henderson	32	14	Bakersfield	9
13	Longview 11 SE	32	14	Falcon Dam	9
16	Daingerfield 9 S	31	14	Langtry	9
17	Emory	***30***	17	Alpine	***10***
17	Pilot Point	***30***	17	Del Rio Intl Arpt	10
17	Tyler	***30***	19	Canyon	11
20	Brenham	29	19	Carrizo Springs	11
20	Centerville	29	19	Lubbock Regional Arpt	11
20	Conroe	29	19	McCook	11
20	Crockett	29	19	Morton	11
20	Houston Bush Intercontinental	29	24	Amistad Dam	12
25	Bay City Waterworks	28	24	Boys Ranch	12

Number of Days Annually With ≥ 1.0 Inches of Precipitation

Highest			Lowest		
Rank	Station Name	Days	Rank	Station Name	Days
1	Beaumont Research Ctr	19	1	Boquillas Ranger Stn	***0***
1	Port Arthur Jefferson County	19	1	Candelaria	0
1	Sam Rayburn Dam	19	1	Castolon	0
4	Anahuac	18	1	Dell City 5 SSW	0
4	Liberty	18	1	El Paso Intl Arpt	0
4	Longview 11 SE	18	1	Fort Hancock 5 SSE	0
4	Marshall	18	1	La Tuna 1 S	0
8	Angleton 2 W	17	8	Balmorhea	2
8	Athens	17	8	Penwell	2
8	Baytown	17	8	Valentine	2
8	Carthage	17	11	Amarillo Intl Arpt	3
8	Texarkana	17	11	Bakersfield	3
13	Cleveland	16	11	Grandfalls 3 SSE	***3***
13	Henderson	16	11	Lubbock Regional Arpt	3
13	Houston William P Hobby Arpt	16	15	Alpine	***4***
16	Bay City Waterworks	15	15	Borger	4
16	Brenham	15	15	Carrizo Springs	4
16	Columbus	15	15	Crystal City	4
16	Conroe	15	15	Hart	***4***
16	Daingerfield 9 S	15	15	Langtry	4
16	Emory	***15***	15	Marathon	4
16	Houston Bush Intercontinental	15	15	McCook	4
16	Pilot Point	***15***	15	Midland Regional Air Terminal	4
16	Sugar Land	15	24	Abilene Municipal Arpt	5
16	Tyler	***15***	24	Amistad Dam	5

Rankings include 25 highest/lowest stations. If state has less than 25 stations, all stations are included. The period of record is 1980–2009. See User Guide for detailed explanation of data.

Annual Snowfall

Highest

Rank	Station Name	Inches
1	Borger	21.6
2	Amarillo Intl Arpt	17.8
3	Dimmitt 2 N	10.9
4	Boys Ranch	10.5
4	Canyon	10.5
6	Lubbock Regional Arpt	8.7
7	Morton	8.6
8	Crosbyton	7.0
9	Clarendon	6.3
10	Brownfield 2	6.2
11	Abilene Municipal Arpt	***5.2***
11	Midland Regional Air Terminal	5.2
13	Anson	***4.6***
14	Wichita Falls Municipal Arpt	***4.2***
15	Hart	***3.7***
16	Albany	***2.8***
17	San Angelo Mathis Field	***2.4***
18	Big Spring	***2.1***
18	Coleman	2.1
20	Grandfalls 3 SSE	***1.9***
21	Bridgeport	1.8
21	Water Valley	1.8
23	Balmorhea	1.7
23	Valentine	1.7
25	Bakersfield	1.6

Lowest

Rank	Station Name	Inches
1	Bay City Waterworks	0.0
1	Baytown	0.0
1	Carrizo Springs	0.0
1	Falcon Dam	0.0
1	Falfurrias	0.0
1	Weslaco 2 E	0.0
7	Anahuac	Trace
7	Angleton 2 W	Trace
7	Beaumont Research Ctr	Trace
7	Boquillas Ranger Stn	***Trace***
7	Brownsville Intl Arpt	***Trace***
7	Cameron	Trace
7	Charlotte 5 NNW	Trace
7	Columbus	Trace
7	Conroe	Trace
7	Georgetown Lake	Trace
7	Granger Dam	Trace
7	La Tuna 1 S	Trace
7	Laredo 2	Trace
7	Sam Rayburn Dam	Trace
7	Somerville Dam	Trace
7	Stillhouse Hollow Dam	Trace
7	Sugar Land	Trace
24	Brady	0.1
24	Brenham	0.1

Annual Maximum Snow Depth

Highest

Rank	Station Name	Inches
1	Borger	17
1	Dimmitt 2 N	17
1	Lubbock Regional Arpt	17
4	Canyon	16
5	Amarillo Intl Arpt	15
6	Boys Ranch	14
6	Clarendon	14
8	Brownfield 2	***12***
8	Whitney Dam	12
10	Boerne	11
11	Blanco	10
11	Camp Wood	***10***
11	Wichita Falls Municipal Arpt	***10***
14	San Antonio Intl Arpt	9
15	Anson	***8***
15	Balmorhea	***8***
15	Bay City Waterworks	8
15	Dripping Springs 6 E	***8***
15	Longview 11 SE	8
15	Midland Regional Air Terminal	8
15	Texarkana	8
15	Valentine	8
23	Albany	***7***
23	Big Spring	***7***
23	Charlotte 5 NNW	7

Lowest

Rank	Station Name	Inches
1	Alice	***0***
1	Baytown	0
1	Burnet	0
1	Dell City 5 SSW	0
1	Falcon Dam	0
1	Falfurrias	0
1	McGregor	0
1	Weslaco 2 E	0
9	Anahuac	Trace
9	Angleton 2 W	Trace
9	Aransas Wildlife Refuge	Trace
9	Bardwell Dam	Trace
9	Brownsville Intl Arpt	Trace
9	Cameron	Trace
9	Candelaria	Trace
9	Carrizo Springs	Trace
9	Centerville	Trace
9	Columbus	Trace
9	Crockett	Trace
9	Floresville	Trace
9	Granger Dam	Trace
9	Houston Bush Intercontinental	Trace
9	La Tuna 1 S	Trace
9	Langtry	Trace
9	Liberty	Trace

Rankings include 25 highest/lowest stations. If state has less than 25 stations, all stations are included. The period of record is 1980–2009. See User Guide for detailed explanation of data.

Number of Days Annually With ≥ 1.0 Inch Snow Depth

Highest

Rank	Station Name	Days
1	Amarillo Intl Arpt	12
2	Borger	10
3	Dimmitt 2 N	7
4	Lubbock Regional Arpt	6
5	Abilene Municipal Arpt	*3*
5	Canyon	3
5	Clarendon	3
8	Anson	*2*
8	Boys Ranch	2
8	Brownfield 2	2
8	McKinney 3 S	*2*
8	Wichita Falls Municipal Arpt	*2*
13	Longview 11 SE	1
13	Midland Regional Air Terminal	1
13	San Angelo Mathis Field	*1*
13	Texarkana	1
17	Albany	*0*
17	Alice	0
17	Alpine	*0*
17	Amistad Dam	0
17	Anahuac	0
17	Angleton 2 W	0
17	Aransas Wildlife Refuge	0
17	Athens	0
17	Austin Municipal Arpt	*0*

Lowest

Rank	Station Name	Days
1	Albany	*0*
1	Alice	0
1	Alpine	*0*
1	Amistad Dam	0
1	Anahuac	0
1	Angleton 2 W	0
1	Aransas Wildlife Refuge	0
1	Athens	0
1	Austin Municipal Arpt	*0*
1	Bakersfield	0
1	Ballinger 2 NW	0
1	Balmorhea	*0*
1	Bardwell Dam	0
1	Bay City Waterworks	0
1	Baytown	0
1	Beaumont Research Ctr	0
1	Benbrook Dam	0
1	Big Spring	*0*
1	Blanco	0
1	Boerne	0
1	Boquillas Ranger Stn	*0*
1	Brady	0
1	Brenham	0
1	Bridgeport	0
1	Brownsville Intl Arpt	*0*

Rankings include 25 highest/lowest stations. If state has less than 25 stations, all stations are included. The period of record is 1980–2009. See User Guide for detailed explanation of data.

Significant Storm Events in Texas: 2000 – 2009

Location or County	Date	Type	Mag.	Deaths	Injuries	Property Damage ($mil.)	Crop Damage ($mil.)
Tarrant	03/28/00	Tornado	F3	2	80	0.0	0.0
North Texas	07/01/00	Excessive Heat	na	8	0	0.0	0.0
Southeast Texas	07/06/00	Excessive Heat	na	19	0	0.0	0.0
North Texas	08/01/00	Excessive Heat	na	5	0	0.0	0.0
North Texas	09/01/00	Excessive Heat	na	5	0	0.0	0.0
Southeast Texas	09/01/00	Excessive Heat	na	5	0	0.0	0.0
Northeast Texas	12/12/00	Ice Storm	na	0	0	123.0	0.0
Bexar	05/06/01	Hail	4.00 in.	0	0	120.0	30.0
Travis	05/20/01	Thunderstorm Wind	na	0	10	2.0	0.1
Galveston Island	06/05/01	Tropical Storm	na	22	0	5,150.0	0.0
Medina	10/12/01	Tornado	F2	0	25	20.0	0.0
Travis	11/15/01	Flash Flood	na	2	50	0.5	0.0
Williamson	11/15/01	Flash Flood	na	2	10	0.5	0.0
Blanco	11/15/01	Flash Flood	na	1	10	0.1	0.0
Llano	11/15/01	Flash Flood	na	1	20	0.1	0.0
Bexar	03/19/02	Tornado	F2	0	30	2.0	0.0
Bexar	03/19/02	Thunderstorm Wind	na	0	10	2.0	0.1
Nueces	10/24/02	Tornado	F2	1	20	75.0	0.0
Cameron	04/08/03	Hail	2.75 in.	0	5	50.0	0.0
Hidalgo	04/30/03	Tornado	F1	0	11	1.5	0.0
Houston	09/14/04	Lightning	na	1	40	0.0	0.0
Travis	03/25/05	Hail	2.00 in.	0	0	100.0	0.0
Chambers, Harris, Houston, and Montgomery Counties	09/21/05	Excessive Heat	na	49	0	0.0	0.0
Southeast Texas	09/23/05	Hurricane Rita	na	1	0	2,090.0	0.0
Extreme Southeast Texas	09/23/05	Hurricane Rita	na	3	3	159.5	0.0
Central Texas	12/01/05	Drought	na	0	0	50.0	0.0
Texas Panhandle Region	12/17/05	Winter Weather/Mix	na	5	15	0.1	0.0
Cross Plains	12/27/05	Wildfire	na	2	16	11.0	0.0
Cooke, Hood and Tarrant Counties	12/27/05	Wildfire	na	1	10	5.8	0.0
Carson and Gray County	03/12/06	Wildfire	na	12	8	49.9	45.4
Northwest Texas	04/01/06	Drought	na	0	0	100.0	0.0
Hays	04/20/06	Hail	4.25 in.	0	1	100.0	0.0
El Paso	08/01/06	Flash Flood	na	0	0	180.0	0.0
Johnson	12/29/06	Tornado	F2	0	12	2.0	0.0
Limestone	12/29/06	Tornado	F2	1	20	1.0	0.0
Moore	04/21/07	Tornado	F2	0	14	1.3	0.0
Maverick	04/24/07	Tornado	F3	7	0	80.0	0.0
Burnet	06/26/07	Flash Flood	na	2	0	137.0	0.0
Southwestern Jefferson County	09/13/07	Hurricane Humberto	na	0	12	25.0	0.0
Potter County	12/22/07	Winter Weather	na	1	137	1.2	0.0
Gray County	12/22/07	Winter Weather	na	1	13	0.4	0.0
Bowie	03/31/08	Hail	2.75 in.	0	0	120.0	0.0
Travis	05/14/08	Thunderstorm Wind	81 mph	0	0	50.0	0.0
Texas Gulf Coast near Galveston	09/12/08	Storm Surge/Tide	na	11	0	4,000.0	0.0
Harris and Matagorda Co.	09/12/08	Hurricane Ike	na	0	0	1,000.0	0.0
Southeast Texas	09/12/08	Hurricane Ike	na	0	0	500.0	0.0
Jefferson and Orange County	09/12/08	Storm Surge/Tide	na	0	0	500.0	0.0
Jefferson and Newton Co.	09/12/08	Hurricane Ike	na	0	0	100.0	0.0
Orange County	09/12/08	Hurricane Ike	na	0	0	75.0	0.0
Hardin County	09/12/08	Hurricane Ike	na	0	0	70.0	0.0
Southern Jasper County	09/12/08	Hurricane Ike	na	0	0	53.0	0.0
Travis	03/25/09	Hail	3.00 in.	0	0	160.0	0.0
Midland	04/11/09	Hail	2.00 in.	0	1	161.2	0.0
Harris	04/18/09	Flash Flood	na	5	0	3.5	0.0

Location or County	Date	Type	Mag.	Deaths	Injuries	Property Damage ($mil.)	Crop Damage ($mil.)
Dallas	05/02/09	Thunderstorm Wind	70 mph	0	12	5.0	0.0
Jefferson	08/18/09	Tornado	F1	0	10	20.0	0.0
El Paso	09/16/09	Hail	1.75 in.	0	10	100.0	0.0

Note: Deaths, injuries, and damages are date and location specific.

UTAH

PHYSICAL FEATURES. The topography of Utah is extremely varied, with most of the State being mountainous. A series of mountains (including the Wasatch Range), which runs generally north and south through the middle of Utah, and the Uinta Mountains, which extend east and west through the northeast portion, are the principal ranges. Crest lines of these mountains are mostly above 10,000 feet. Less extensive ranges are scattered over the remainder of the State. The lowest area is the Virgin River Valley in the southwestern part with elevations between 2,500 and 3,500 feet, while the highest point is Kings Peak in the Uinta Mountains (13,498 feet).

Practically all of eastern Utah is drained by the Colorado River and its principal tributary within the State, the Green River, although neither rises within its borders. Western Utah is almost entirely within the Great Basin, with no outlet to the sea. The largest rivers in this area are the Bear, Weber, Jordan, Provo, and Sevier, the first three of which empty into Great Salt Lake. The Sevier River drains the west-central area and empties into Sevier Lake, a brackish saline basin in southwest Utah. The main streams in the eastern portion of the State flow through canyons or very narrow, confined mountain valleys and finally into desert canyons. Highest flow occurs in this region in May and June during spring runoff from melting snow.

Great Salt Lake, in northwestern Utah, lies in the Great Basin, the largest closed basin in North America. Part of this drainage area is below 4,500 feet in elevation, with the Lake being about 4,200 feet. Great Salt Lake is the largest lake at the highest elevation in the world. In glacial times it was a fresh water lake occupying an area 346 miles long and 145 miles wide; due to increased evaporation and/or reduced precipitation, it gradually shrank in size and the salinity increased. Since this large body of water now has no drainage outlet, the salt content is high, averaging about 25 percent. Thus the Lake, which never freezes over, provides a moderating effect throughout the year on temperatures in the immediate vicinity.

GENERAL CLIMATE. Utah's climate is determined by its distance from the equator, its elevation above sea level, the location of the State with respect to the average storm paths over the Intermountain Region, and its distance from the principal moisture sources of the area, namely, the Pacific Ocean and the Gulf of Mexico. Also, the mountain ranges over the western United States, particularly the Sierra Nevada and Cascade Ranges and the Rocky Mountains, have a marked influence on the climate of the State. Pacific storms, before reaching Utah, must first cross the Sierras or Cascades. As the moist air is forced to rise over these high mountains, a large portion of the original moisture falls as precipitation. Thus, the prevailing westerly air currents reaching Utah are comparatively dry, resulting in light precipitation over most of the State.

TEMPERATURE. There are definite variations in temperature with altitude and with latitude. Naturally, the mountains and the elevated valleys have the cooler climates, with the lower areas of the State having the higher temperatures. There is about a 3°F. decrease in mean annual temperature for each 1,000-foot increase in altitude, and approximately 1.5 to 2°F. decrease in average yearly temperature for each one degree increase in latitude.

Temperatures over 100°F. occur occasionally in summer in nearly all parts of the State. However, low humidity makes these high temperatures more bearable than in more humid regions. Temperatures below zero during winter and early spring are uncommon in most areas of the State, and prolonged periods of extremely cold weather are rare. This is primarily due to the mountains east and north of the State, which act as a barrier to intensely cold continental Arctic air masses. Utah experiences relatively strong insolation during the day and rapid nocturnal cooling, resulting in wide daily ranges in temperature. Even after the hottest days, nights are usually cool over the State. On clear nights the colder air accumulates, by drainage, on the valley bottoms, while the foothills and bench areas remain relatively warm.

PRECIPITATION. Precipitation varies greatly, from an average of less than five inches annually over the Great Salt Lake Desert (west of Great Salt Lake), to more than 40 inches in some parts of the Wasatch Mountains. In the mountains, winter snows form the chief reservoirs of moisture. The areas of the State below an elevation of 4,000 feet, all in the southern part, generally receive less than 10 inches of moisture annually.

Northwestern Utah, over and along the mountains, receives appreciably more precipitation in a year than is received at similar elevations over the rest of the State, primarily due to terrain and the direction of normal storm tracks. The bulk of the moisture falling over that area can be attributed to the movement of Pacific storms through the region during the winter and spring months. In summer northwestern Utah is comparatively dry. The eastern portion receives appreciable rain from summer thunderstorms, which are usually associated with moisture-laden air masses from the Gulf of Mexico.

Snowfall is moderately heavy in the mountains, especially over the northern part. A deep snow cover seldom remains long on the ground. Runoff from melting mountain snow usually reaches a peak in April, May or early June, and sometimes causes flooding along the lower streams. However, damaging floods of this kind are infrequent. Flash floods from summer thunderstorms are more frequent, but they affect only small, local areas.

OTHER CLIMATIC ELEMENTS. Sunny skies prevail most of the year in Utah. There is an average of about 65 to 75 percent of the possible amount of sunshine at Salt Lake City during spring, summer, and fall. In winter Salt Lake City has about 50 percent of the possible sunshine.

During the late fall and winter months, anticyclones tend to settle over the Great Basin for as long as several weeks at a time. Under these conditions, smoke and haze accumulate in the lower levels of the stagnant air over the valleys of northwestern Utah, frequently becoming an obstruction to visibility. This is also true of fog which may persist for several weeks at a time.

Wind speeds are usually light to moderate, ranging below 20 miles per hour. There are only a few tornadoes in Utah as a rule, and those reported usually cause only slight damage. However, strong winds occur occasionally, each year sometimes attaining damaging proportions in local areas, particularly in the vicinity of the canyon mouths along the western slopes of the Wasatch Mountains. Duststorms occur occasionally, principally over western Utah. These storms are associated with the movement of low pressure disturbances through the area during the spring months.

Hailstorms may occur in limited areas during spring and summer, although the hail is usually small.

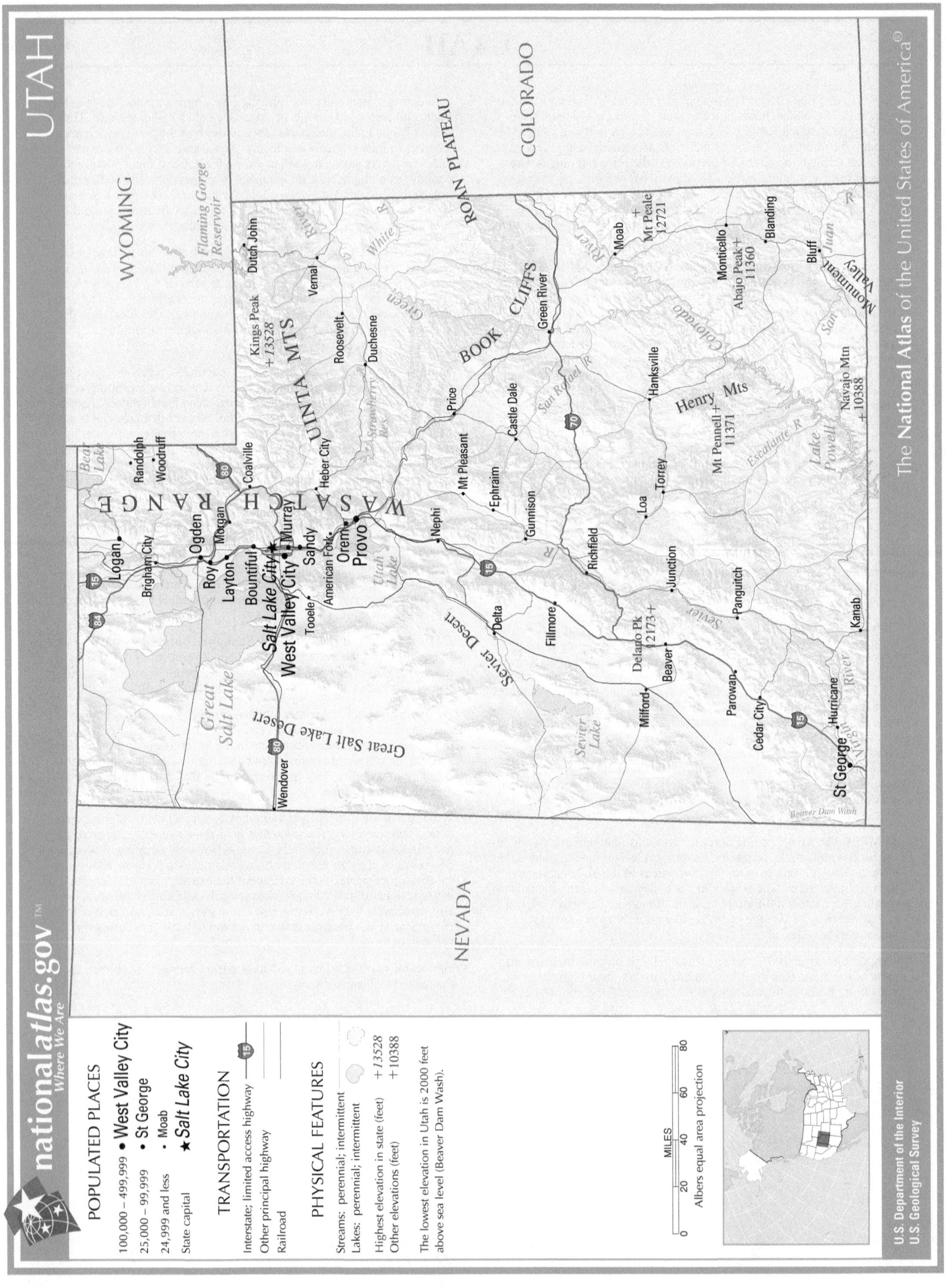
UTAH
nationalatlas.gov™
Where We Are
POPULATED PLACES
100,000 – 499,999 • West Valley City
25,000 – 99,999 • St George
24,999 and less · Moab
State capital ★ Salt Lake City
TRANSPORTATION
Interstate; limited access highway
Other principal highway
Railroad
PHYSICAL FEATURES
Streams: perennial; intermittent
Lakes: perennial; intermittent
Highest elevation in state (feet) +13528
Other elevations (feet) +10388
The lowest elevation in Utah is 2000 feet above sea level (Beaver Dam Wash).
MILES
0 20 40 60 80
Albers equal area projection
U.S. Department of the Interior
U.S. Geological Survey
The National Atlas of the United States of America®
WYOMING
COLORADO
NEVADA
Flaming Gorge Reservoir
Dutch John
Kings Peak +13528
UINTA MTS
Vernal
Roosevelt
Duchesne
ROAN PLATEAU
BOOK CLIFFS
Green River
Price
Castle Dale
Mt Pleasant
Ephraim
Heber City
Coalville
Randolph
Woodruff
Bear Lake
WASATCH RANGE
Logan
Brigham City
Ogden
Morgan
Roy
Layton
Bountiful
Salt Lake City
West Valley City
Murray
Sandy
American Fork
Orem
Provo
Utah Lake
Tooele
Great Salt Lake
Great Salt Lake Desert
Wendover
Nephi
Gunnison
Richfield
Delta
Sevier Desert
Fillmore
Delano Pk 12173 +
Beaver
Milford
Sevier Lake
Junction
Panguitch
Parowan
Cedar City
Hurricane
St George
Beaver Dam Wash
Kanab
Loa
Torrey
Hanksville
Henry Mts
Mt Pennell + 11371
Moab
Mt Peale + 12721
Monticello
Abajo Peak + 11360
Blanding
Bluff
Monument Valley
Navajo Mtn + 10388
Lake Powell
Escalante R
San Rafael R
Colorado
Green
White R
San Juan R
Virgin River
Sevier
Strawberry Res

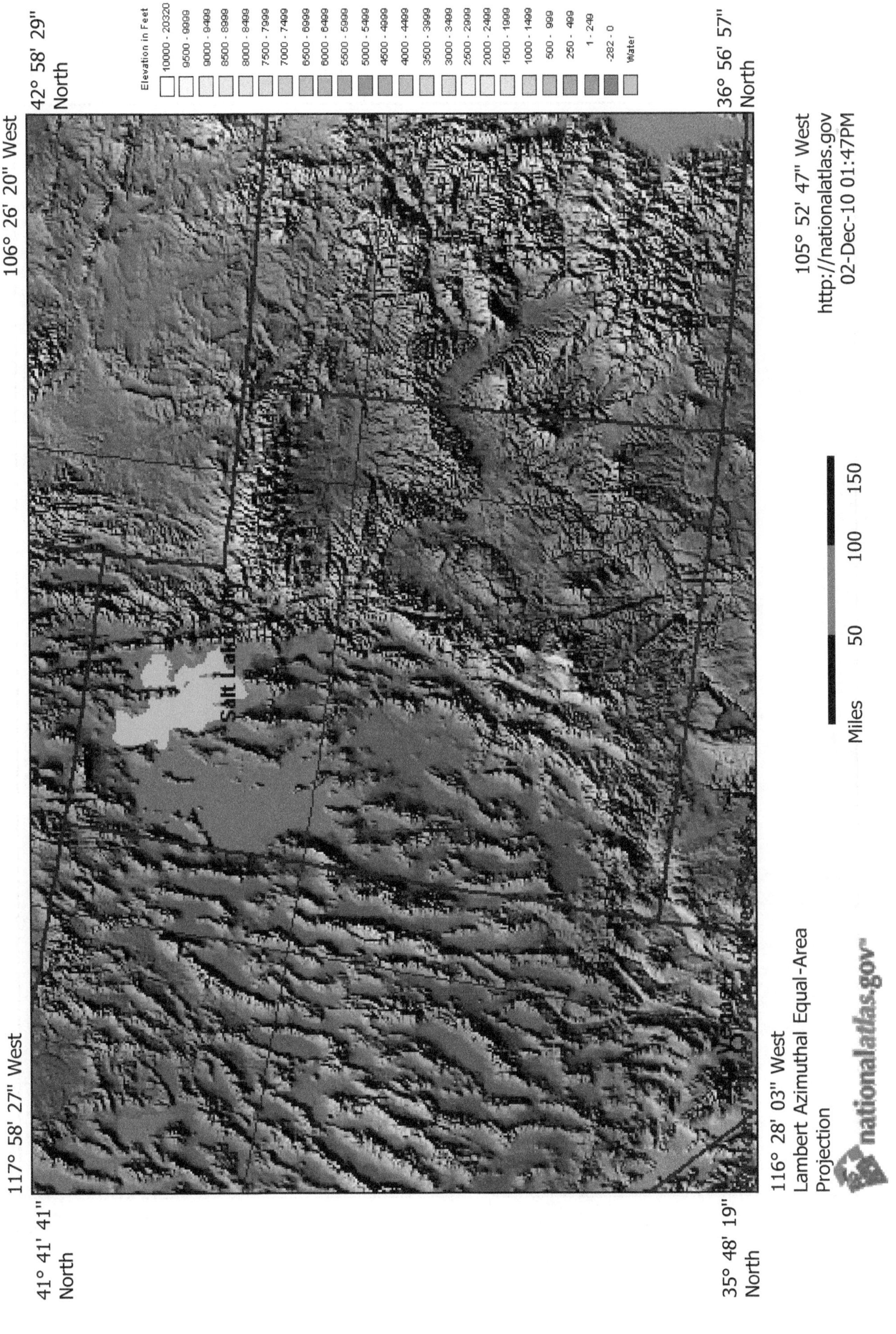
42° 58' 29" North
106° 26' 20" West
36° 56' 57" North
105° 52' 47" West
http://nationalatlas.gov
02-Dec-10 01:47PM
41° 41' 41" North
117° 58' 27" West
35° 48' 19" North
116° 28' 03" West
Lambert Azimuthal Equal-Area Projection
Salt Lake
Miles
50
100
150
Elevation in Feet
10000 - 20320
9500 - 9999
9000 - 9499
8500 - 8999
8000 - 8499
7500 - 7999
7000 - 7499
6500 - 6999
6000 - 6499
5500 - 5999
5000 - 5499
4500 - 4999
4000 - 4499
3500 - 3999
3000 - 3499
2500 - 2999
2000 - 2499
1500 - 1999
1000 - 1499
500 - 999
250 - 499
1 - 249
-282 - 0
Water
nationalatlas.gov

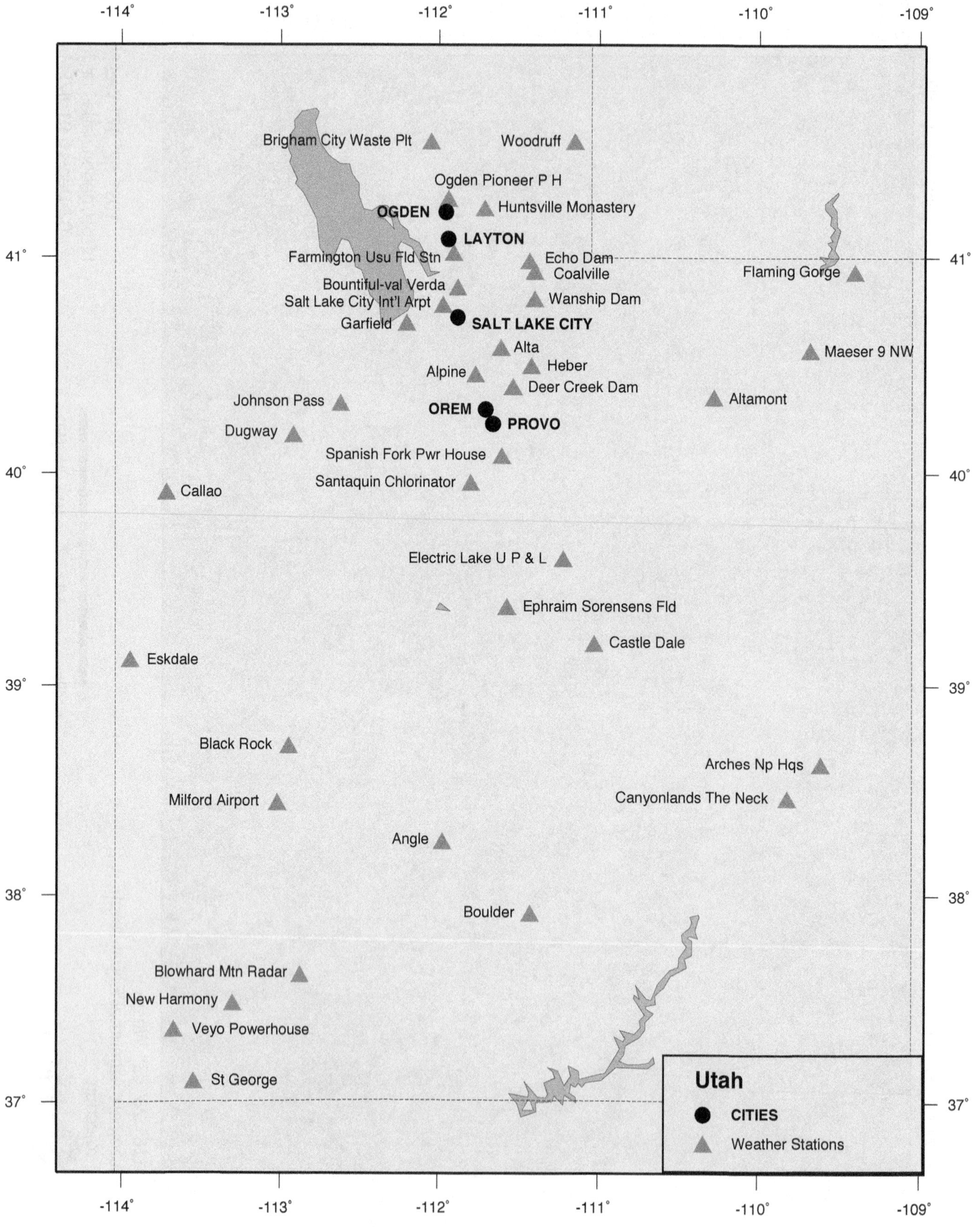
-114°
-113°
-112°
-111°
-110°
-109°
41°
40°
39°
38°
37°
Brigham City Waste Plt
Woodruff
Ogden Pioneer P H
OGDEN
Huntsville Monastery
LAYTON
Farmington Usu Fld Stn
Echo Dam
Coalville
Flaming Gorge
Bountiful-val Verda
Salt Lake City Int'l Arpt
Wanship Dam
Garfield
SALT LAKE CITY
Alta
Maeser 9 NW
Heber
Alpine
Deer Creek Dam
Johnson Pass
Altamont
OREM
PROVO
Dugway
Spanish Fork Pwr House
Santaquin Chlorinator
Callao
Electric Lake U P & L
Ephraim Sorensens Fld
Castle Dale
Eskdale
Black Rock
Arches Np Hqs
Milford Airport
Canyonlands The Neck
Angle
Boulder
Blowhard Mtn Radar
New Harmony
Veyo Powerhouse
St George
Utah
CITIES
Weather Stations

Utah Weather Stations by County

County	Station Name
Beaver	Milford Airport
Box Elder	Brigham City Waste Plt
Daggett	Flaming Gorge
Davis	Bountiful-Val Verda Farmington Usu Fld Stn
Duchesne	Altamont
Emery	Castle Dale Electric Lake U P & L
Garfield	Boulder
Grand	Arches Np Hqs
Iron	Blowhard Mtn Radar
Juab	Callao
Millard	Black Rock Eskdale
Piute	Angle
Rich	Woodruff
Salt Lake	Alta Garfield Salt Lake City Int'l Arpt
San Juan	Canyonlands The Neck
Sanpete	Ephraim Sorensens Fld
Summit	Coalville Echo Dam Wanship Dam
Tooele	Dugway Johnson Pass
Uintah	Maeser 9 NW
Utah	Alpine Santaquin Chlorinator Spanish Fork Pwr House
Wasatch	Deer Creek Dam Heber
Washington	New Harmony St George Veyo Powerhouse
Weber	Huntsville Monastery Ogden Pioneer P H

See User Guide for station inclusion criteria.

Utah Weather Stations by City

City	Station Name	Miles
American Fork	Alpine	4.7
	Alta	17.1
	Deer Creek Dam	13.8
	Heber	21.4
	Spanish Fork Pwr House	23.2
Bountiful	Alta	22.9
	Bountiful-Val Verda	2.0
	Coalville	24.8
	Echo Dam	23.8
	Farmington Usu Fld Stn	9.9
	Garfield	20.4
	Salt Lake City Int'l Arpt	8.2
Cedar City	Blowhard Mtn Radar	12.5
	New Harmony	19.2
Clearfield	Bountiful-Val Verda	19.1
	Farmington Usu Fld Stn	8.3
	Huntsville Monastery	18.2
	Ogden Pioneer P H	10.7
	Salt Lake City Int'l Arpt	22.5
Cottonwood Heights	Alpine	11.8
	Alta	9.9
	Bountiful-Val Verda	16.5
	Deer Creek Dam	21.2
	Garfield	21.1
	Heber	22.7
	Salt Lake City Int'l Arpt	13.9
	Wanship Dam	24.8
Draper	Alpine	7.2
	Alta	14.1
	Bountiful-Val Verda	23.4
	Deer Creek Dam	19.6
	Garfield	22.1
	Heber	24.2
	Salt Lake City Int'l Arpt	19.3
Kaysville	Bountiful-Val Verda	12.8
	Farmington Usu Fld Stn	1.4
	Huntsville Monastery	18.0
	Ogden Pioneer P H	15.1
	Salt Lake City Int'l Arpt	17.2
Kearns	Alpine	18.9
	Alta	20.0
	Bountiful-Val Verda	15.2
	Garfield	11.0
	Salt Lake City Int'l Arpt	9.4
Layton	Bountiful-Val Verda	16.3
	Farmington Usu Fld Stn	4.8
	Huntsville Monastery	16.5
	Ogden Pioneer P H	11.8
	Salt Lake City Int'l Arpt	20.4
Lehi	Alpine	5.7
	Alta	17.9
	Deer Creek Dam	16.9
	Heber	24.0
Logan	Preston, ID	23.8

City	Station Name	Miles
Logan *(cont.)*	Brigham City Waste Plt	19.3
Magna	Alpine	24.0
	Alta	24.6
	Bountiful-Val Verda	14.8
	Farmington Usu Fld Stn	23.6
	Garfield	6.2
	Salt Lake City Int'l Arpt	8.5
Midvale	Alpine	13.0
	Alta	13.4
	Bountiful-Val Verda	16.2
	Deer Creek Dam	23.8
	Garfield	17.8
	Salt Lake City Int'l Arpt	12.4
Millcreek	Alpine	17.0
	Alta	13.5
	Bountiful-Val Verda	11.5
	Farmington Usu Fld Stn	23.2
	Garfield	17.6
	Salt Lake City Int'l Arpt	8.7
Murray	Alpine	15.3
	Alta	14.0
	Bountiful-Val Verda	13.8
	Garfield	16.7
	Salt Lake City Int'l Arpt	10.0
Ogden	Brigham City Waste Plt	20.4
	Farmington Usu Fld Stn	14.8
	Huntsville Monastery	12.5
	Ogden Pioneer P H	1.5
Orem	Alpine	11.0
	Alta	21.0
	Deer Creek Dam	11.1
	Heber	20.2
	Santaquin Chlorinator	24.6
	Spanish Fork Pwr House	15.8
Pleasant Grove	Alpine	5.8
	Alta	16.8
	Deer Creek Dam	10.8
	Heber	19.0
	Spanish Fork Pwr House	21.0
Provo	Alpine	15.2
	Alta	24.5
	Deer Creek Dam	12.5
	Heber	21.7
	Santaquin Chlorinator	21.5
	Spanish Fork Pwr House	11.7
Riverton	Alpine	11.0
	Alta	17.7
	Bountiful-Val Verda	23.1
	Deer Creek Dam	23.6
	Garfield	18.7
	Salt Lake City Int'l Arpt	18.2
Roy	Bountiful-Val Verda	23.8
	Brigham City Waste Plt	23.8
	Farmington Usu Fld Stn	12.7

See User Guide for station inclusion criteria.

City	Station Name	Miles
Roy *(cont.)*	Huntsville Monastery	17.7
	Ogden Pioneer P H	7.4
Salt Lake City	Alpine	21.8
	Alta	16.8
	Bountiful-Val Verda	6.6
	Farmington Usu Fld Stn	18.2
	Garfield	16.9
	Salt Lake City Int'l Arpt	4.9
Sandy	Alpine	9.6
	Alta	11.7
	Bountiful-Val Verda	19.2
	Deer Creek Dam	20.6
	Garfield	20.7
	Heber	23.5
	Salt Lake City Int'l Arpt	15.7
South Jordan	Alpine	12.8
	Alta	17.1
	Bountiful-Val Verda	20.0
	Garfield	16.5
	Salt Lake City Int'l Arpt	15.1
Spanish Fork	Alpine	24.6
	Deer Creek Dam	21.0
	Santaquin Chlorinator	13.2
	Spanish Fork Pwr House	2.7
Springville	Alpine	21.7
	Deer Creek Dam	16.7
	Santaquin Chlorinator	17.7
	Spanish Fork Pwr House	5.5
St. George	Beaver Dam, AZ	24.5
	St George	0.9
	Veyo Powerhouse	17.9
Taylorsville	Alpine	17.2
	Alta	17.0
	Bountiful-Val Verda	13.7
	Farmington Usu Fld Stn	24.9
	Garfield	13.8
	Salt Lake City Int'l Arpt	8.7
Tooele	Garfield	13.6
	Johnson Pass	21.8
	Salt Lake City Int'l Arpt	24.4
West Jordan	Alpine	15.1
	Alta	17.5
	Bountiful-Val Verda	17.4
	Garfield	14.4
	Salt Lake City Int'l Arpt	12.3
West Valley City	Alpine	20.3
	Alta	19.8
	Bountiful-Val Verda	12.4
	Farmington Usu Fld Stn	22.9
	Garfield	11.1
	Salt Lake City Int'l Arpt	6.6

Note: Miles is the distance between the geographic center of the city and the weather station.

Utah Weather Stations by Elevation

Feet	Station Name
10,693	Blowhard Mtn Radar
8,729	Alta
8,379	Electric Lake U P & L
6,680	Boulder
6,439	Maeser 9 NW
6,399	Angle
6,370	Altamont
6,314	Woodruff
6,270	Flaming Gorge
5,939	Wanship Dam
5,930	Canyonlands The Neck
5,629	Heber
5,629	Johnson Pass
5,620	Castle Dale
5,549	Coalville
5,509	Ephraim Sorensens Fld
5,470	Echo Dam
5,270	Deer Creek Dam
5,265	New Harmony
5,164	Santaquin Chlorinator
5,140	Huntsville Monastery
5,069	Alpine
5,029	Milford Airport
4,979	Eskdale
4,895	Black Rock
4,720	Spanish Fork Pwr House
4,600	Veyo Powerhouse
4,540	Bountiful-Val Verda
4,350	Ogden Pioneer P H
4,339	Dugway
4,339	Farmington Usu Fld Stn
4,330	Callao
4,330	Garfield
4,229	Brigham City Waste Plt
4,222	Salt Lake City Int'l Arpt
4,129	Arches Np Hqs
2,770	St George

See User Guide for station inclusion criteria.

Milford Airport

Milford is located in Beaver County in the west-central portion of the state. The city is situated in a flat to gently sloping valley 15 to 20 miles in width. The Mineral Mountains, 10 miles to the east of the station, and the San Francisco Range, 15 miles to the northwest, rise about 5,000 feet above the valley floor.

The station is in the Sevier River Basin, and drainage is toward the north. The Beaver River just to the east extends north-south through the valley, but no significant body of water is reached by it. The river is dry most of the time due to the low annual rainfall in the area, and to the Minersville Reservoir 6 miles east of Minersville, which regulates the flow of water in the stream. Water for the irrigation of agricultural land in the valley is obtained from the diversion of surface water from this reservoir and from numerous deep wells.

The climate is temperate and dry. Irrigation water is necessary for the economic production of most crops.

Snowfall is rather evenly distributed during the season. The snow is usually light and powdery with below average moisture content. January, the coldest month of the year, has the greatest average monthly total.

Relative humidity is rather low during the summer months. It increases considerably in the change from summer to winter, and winters are cold and uncomfortable. In four out of five years the temperature can be expected to drop to -10 degrees or lower.

Summers are characterized by warm days and cool nights. Temperatures of 100 degrees or more occur about once in every two years.

Diurnal heating is a factor in producing strong southerly winds during the spring and summer months. Winter winds may cause considerable drifting snow, with resultant hazards to stock and transportation in the area.

Low pressure storm systems are rare during the summer months. Precipitation during this period occurs as showers or thundershowers and rainfall amounts from these storms are quite variable. As winter approaches, the number of atmospheric disturbances increases.

Based on the 1951-1980 period, the average first occurrence of 32 degrees Fahrenheit in the fall is September 22 and the average last occurrence in the spring is May 25.

Milford Airport *Beaver County* Elevation: 5,029 ft. Latitude: 38° 26' N Longitude: 113° 01' W

	JAN	FEB	MAR	APR	MAY	JUN	JUL	AUG	SEP	OCT	NOV	DEC	YEAR
Mean Maximum Temp. (°F)	na	47.3	57.5	65.6	75.0	85.8	92.3	na	na	68.7	53.8	42.7	na
Mean Temp. (°F)	na	33.7	41.9	48.9	57.3	66.8	74.1	na	na	51.1	38.7	29.1	na
Mean Minimum Temp. (°F)	na	20.0	26.3	32.1	39.5	47.7	55.9	na	na	33.3	23.6	15.3	na
Extreme Maximum Temp. (°F)	69	75	88	86	na	102	107	na	na	90	na	na	na
Extreme Minimum Temp. (°F)	-21	-29	-2	13	na	26	34	na	na	10	na	na	na
Days Maximum Temp. ≥ 90°F	0	0	0	0	1	11	22	na	na	0	0	0	na
Days Maximum Temp. ≤ 32°F	6	2	0	0	0	0	0	na	na	0	1	6	na
Days Minimum Temp. ≤ 32°F	29	25	25	15	5	0	0	na	na	14	25	29	na
Days Minimum Temp. ≤ 0°F	4	2	0	0	0	0	0	na	na	0	0	3	na
Heating Degree Days (base 65°F)	na	880	709	478	246	53	2	na	na	427	783	1,108	na
Cooling Degree Days (base 65°F)	na	0	0	0	14	112	291	na	na	1	0	0	na
Mean Precipitation (in.)	0.71	0.84	1.14	0.98	0.80	0.53	0.75	0.89	1.02	1.21	0.69	0.80	10.36
Maximum Precipitation (in.)*	1.9	1.7	2.0	2.3	1.9	2.4	1.4	2.5	2.6	2.6	2.2	2.4	13.1
Minimum Precipitation (in.)*	0	trace	0	trace	trace	trace	trace	trace	trace	0	0	0	4.5
Extreme Maximum Daily Precip. (in.)	0.94	0.75	0.95	1.00	1.35	1.18	1.22	1.42	1.42	3.00	1.28	1.48	3.00
Days With ≥ 0.1" Precipitation	2	3	4	4	2	2	2	2	3	3	2	2	31
Days With ≥ 0.5" Precipitation	0	0	0	0	0	0	0	0	0	1	0	0	1
Days With ≥ 1.0" Precipitation	0	0	0	0	0	0	0	0	0	0	0	0	0
Mean Snowfall (in.)	4.3	4.0	5.9	2.0	0.6	0.0	0.0	0.0	0.1	1.3	2.3	5.2	25.7
Maximum Snowfall (in.)*	30	19	20	24	11	trace	0	0	8	17	14	31	78
Maximum 24-hr. Snowfall (in.)*	12	9	9	7	8	trace	0	0	6	6	8	13	13
Maximum Snow Depth (in.)	16	11	17	9	3	2	0	0	2	3	9	15	17
Days With ≥ 1.0" Snow Depth	10	7	3	2	0	0	0	0	0	0	2	8	32
Thunderstorm Days*	< 1	< 1	< 1	3	3	4	9	6	3	< 1	< 1	< 1	28
Foggy Days*	6	6	3	1	1	0	0	0	< 1	1	2	9	29
Predominant Sky Cover*	OVR	OVR	OVR	OVR	SCT	CLR	SCT	CLR	CLR	CLR	CLR	OVR	CLR
Mean Relative Humidity 5am (%)*	83	83	73	68	65	54	56	57	55	67	78	82	66
Mean Relative Humidity 5pm (%)*	60	53	37	27	23	18	20	22	20	28	46	61	35
Mean Dewpoint (°F)*	18	20	22	23	29	31	40	40	33	28	23	19	27
Prevailing Wind Direction*	SSW	SSW	SSW	SSW	SSW	SSW	SSW	SSW	SSW	SSW	SSW	SSW	SSW
Prevailing Wind Speed (mph)*	16	15	17	17	17	16	15	15	15	14	15	15	16
Maximum Wind Gust (mph)*	53	59	69	67	68	75	64	77	56	63	60	56	77

Note: (*) Period of record is 1948-1989

Salt Lake City Int'l Airport

Salt Lake City is located in a northern Utah valley surrounded by mountains on three sides and the Great Salt Lake to the northwest. The city varies in altitude from near 4,200 to 5,000 feet above sea level.

The Wasatch Mountains to the east have peaks to nearly 12,000 feet above sea level. Their orographic effects cause more precipitation in the eastern part of the city than over the western part.

The Oquirrh Mountains to the southwest of the city have several peaks to above 10,000 feet above sea level. The Traverse Mountain Range at the south end of the Salt Lake Valley rises to above 6,000 feet above sea level. These mountain ranges help to shelter the valleys from storms from the southwest in the winter, but are instrumental in developing thunderstorms which can drift over the valley in the summer.

Besides the mountain ranges, the most influential natural condition affecting the climate of Salt Lake City is the Great Salt Lake. This large inland body of water, which never freezes over due to its high salt content, can moderate the temperatures of cold winter winds blowing from the northwest and helps drive a lake/valley wind system. The warmer lake water during the winter and spring also contributes to increased precipitation in the valley downwind from the lake.

Salt Lake City normally has a semi-arid continental climate with four well-defined seasons. Summers are characterized by hot, dry weather, but the high temperatures are usually not oppressive since the relative humidity is generally low and the nights usually cool. July is the hottest month with temperature readings in the 90s.

The mean diurnal temperature range is about 30 degrees in the summer and 18 degrees during the winter. Temperatures above 102 degrees in the summer or colder than -10 degrees in the winter are likely to occur one season out of four.

Winters are cold, but usually not severe. Mountains to the north and east act as a barrier to frequent invasions of cold continental air. The average annual snowfall is under 60 inches at the airport but much higher amounts fall in higher bench locations. Heavy fog can develop under temperature inversions in the winter and persist for several days.

Precipitation, generally light during the summer and early fall, is heavy in the spring.

The growing season is over five months in length. The last freezing temperature in the spring averages late April and the first freeze of the fall is mid-October.

Salt Lake City Int'l Airport *Salt Lake County* Elevation: 4,222 ft. Latitude: 40° 47' N Longitude: 111° 58' W

	JAN	FEB	MAR	APR	MAY	JUN	JUL	AUG	SEP	OCT	NOV	DEC	YEAR
Mean Maximum Temp. (°F)	37.8	43.4	53.8	62.0	72.2	83.3	92.8	90.7	79.2	64.8	49.9	38.2	64.0
Mean Temp. (°F)	29.8	34.3	43.8	50.9	60.1	69.9	78.9	77.2	66.3	53.0	40.3	30.5	52.9
Mean Minimum Temp. (°F)	21.8	25.2	33.7	39.7	47.9	56.4	64.9	63.6	53.3	41.2	30.7	22.7	41.8
Extreme Maximum Temp. (°F)	63	68	78	89	99	103	107	106	99	88	75	69	107
Extreme Minimum Temp. (°F)	-6	-14	12	19	26	36	47	42	33	20	3	-11	-14
Days Maximum Temp. ≥ 90°F	0	0	0	0	1	9	23	20	4	0	0	0	57
Days Maximum Temp. ≤ 32°F	9	4	0	0	0	0	0	0	0	0	1	9	23
Days Minimum Temp. ≤ 32°F	28	22	13	5	0	0	0	0	0	3	18	27	116
Days Minimum Temp. ≤ 0°F	1	0	0	0	0	0	0	0	0	0	0	0	1
Heating Degree Days (base 65°F)	1,084	861	651	422	196	45	2	2	78	371	734	1,063	5,509
Cooling Degree Days (base 65°F)	0	0	0	5	50	198	438	388	123	7	0	0	1,209
Mean Precipitation (in.)	1.33	1.31	1.81	1.94	1.94	0.96	0.65	0.64	1.23	1.51	1.40	1.32	16.04
Maximum Precipitation (in.)*	3.2	2.8	4.0	4.6	4.8	2.8	2.6	3.7	7.0	3.9	3.0	4.4	24.3
Minimum Precipitation (in.)*	0.1	0.1	0.1	0.4	0.1	trace	trace	trace	trace	0	trace	0.1	8.7
Extreme Maximum Daily Precip. (in.)	0.92	1.23	0.93	1.57	1.20	1.48	1.25	1.31	2.27	1.53	1.27	1.14	2.27
Days With ≥ 0.1" Precipitation	4	4	6	6	5	3	2	2	3	4	4	4	47
Days With ≥ 0.5" Precipitation	0	0	1	1	1	0	0	0	1	1	0	0	5
Days With ≥ 1.0" Precipitation	0	0	0	0	0	0	0	0	0	0	0	0	0
Mean Snowfall (in.)	13.3	10.7	7.0	3.9	0.3	trace	trace	trace	trace	1.3	7.0	12.9	56.4
Maximum Snowfall (in.)*	50	28	42	26	8	trace	0	0	4	20	33	35	100
Maximum 24-hr. Snowfall (in.)*	10	11	12	12	5	trace	0	0	4	14	10	13	14
Maximum Snow Depth (in.)	25	17	14	7	trace	trace	trace	trace	trace	9	11	14	25
Days With ≥ 1.0" Snow Depth	17	11	3	1	0	0	0	0	0	0	4	14	50
Thunderstorm Days*	< 1	1	2	2	6	5	7	7	4	2	1	< 1	37
Foggy Days*	13	8	3	1	1	< 1	< 1	< 1	< 1	1	5	13	45
Predominant Sky Cover*	OVR	OVR	OVR	OVR	OVR	CLR	CLR	CLR	CLR	CLR	OVR	OVR	OVR
Mean Relative Humidity 5am (%)*	79	78	71	67	66	60	53	54	60	68	75	80	68
Mean Relative Humidity 5pm (%)*	69	59	47	39	33	26	22	23	28	41	59	71	43
Mean Dewpoint (°F)*	20	24	27	31	37	41	45	45	40	34	28	22	33
Prevailing Wind Direction*	SSE	SSE	SSE	SSE	SSE	SSE	SSE	SSE	SSE	SSE	SSE	SSE	SSE
Prevailing Wind Speed (mph)*	9	10	10	10	10	10	10	12	10	9	9	9	10
Maximum Wind Gust (mph)*	69	54	62	69	69	94	74	74	71	71	59	60	94

Note: (*) Period of record is 1948-1995

The period of record for National Weather Service station data is 1980 – 2009 except where noted. See User Guide for detailed explanation of data.

Alpine *Utah County* Elevation: 5,069 ft. Latitude: 40° 27' N Longitude: 111° 46' W

	JAN	FEB	MAR	APR	MAY	JUN	JUL	AUG	SEP	OCT	NOV	DEC	YEAR
Mean Maximum Temp. (°F)	38.8	43.7	53.7	62.2	71.9	82.1	90.1	88.0	78.0	***64.6***	50.1	38.9	***63.5***
Mean Temp. (°F)	29.6	33.2	41.8	49.0	57.4	65.9	73.4	72.1	62.6	***50.8***	39.3	29.9	***50.4***
Mean Minimum Temp. (°F)	20.3	22.6	29.9	35.7	42.9	49.7	56.8	56.1	47.2	***37.0***	28.5	20.9	***37.3***
Extreme Maximum Temp. (°F)	61	70	79	87	93	100	104	101	95	***87***	74	66	***104***
Extreme Minimum Temp. (°F)	-14	-20	5	12	24	31	39	38	25	***19***	4	-7	***-20***
Days Maximum Temp. ≥ 90°F	0	0	0	0	0	6	17	12	1	***0***	0	0	***36***
Days Maximum Temp. ≤ 32°F	7	3	0	0	0	0	0	0	0	***0***	1	8	***19***
Days Minimum Temp. ≤ 32°F	28	24	20	10	2	0	0	0	1	***8***	20	28	***141***
Days Minimum Temp. ≤ 0°F	1	1	0	0	0	0	0	0	0	***0***	0	1	***3***
Heating Degree Days (base 65°F)	1,092	893	712	476	247	71	4	5	115	***432***	764	1,081	***5,892***
Cooling Degree Days (base 65°F)	0	0	0	1	19	106	273	230	50	***1***	0	0	***680***
Mean Precipitation (in.)	2.00	1.96	2.05	2.10	2.32	1.08	0.72	1.01	1.47	***2.04***	1.69	2.11	***20.55***
Extreme Maximum Daily Precip. (in.)	1.56	1.20	0.97	1.87	1.78	1.85	1.20	1.02	1.54	***1.46***	1.26	***1.70***	***1.87***
Days With ≥ 0.1" Precipitation	5	5	6	6	6	3	2	3	4	***5***	5	5	***55***
Days With ≥ 0.5" Precipitation	1	1	1	1	1	1	0	0	1	***1***	1	1	***10***
Days With ≥ 1.0" Precipitation	0	0	0	0	0	0	0	0	0	***0***	0	0	***0***
Mean Snowfall (in.)	***14.8***	***12.5***	***7.7***	4.4	0.3	trace	0.0	0.0	trace	***1.3***	8.1	***15.6***	***64.7***
Maximum Snow Depth (in.)	***20***	***27***	***15***	***8***	trace	0	0	0	trace	***6***	***14***	***15***	***27***
Days With ≥ 1.0" Snow Depth	***20***	***18***	***5***	0	0	0	0	0	0	***0***	5	***19***	***67***

Alta *Salt Lake County* Elevation: 8,729 ft. Latitude: 40° 36' N Longitude: 111° 38' W

	JAN	FEB	MAR	APR	MAY	JUN	JUL	AUG	SEP	OCT	NOV	DEC	YEAR
Mean Maximum Temp. (°F)	30.5	31.0	35.3	42.1	52.1	63.5	72.0	70.6	61.4	49.0	36.7	30.1	47.9
Mean Temp. (°F)	22.3	22.8	27.1	33.4	42.5	52.6	60.8	59.6	50.9	39.7	28.3	22.0	38.5
Mean Minimum Temp. (°F)	14.0	14.7	18.8	24.7	32.9	41.6	49.6	48.5	40.4	30.4	19.9	13.9	29.1
Extreme Maximum Temp. (°F)	57	55	65	69	76	81	86	84	79	71	62	58	86
Extreme Minimum Temp. (°F)	-19	-19	-8	1	10	20	31	30	16	3	-12	-25	-25
Days Maximum Temp. ≥ 90°F	0	0	0	0	0	0	0	0	0	0	0	0	0
Days Maximum Temp. ≤ 32°F	19	16	12	6	1	0	0	0	0	3	11	18	86
Days Minimum Temp. ≤ 32°F	31	28	30	24	14	4	0	0	5	18	27	30	211
Days Minimum Temp. ≤ 0°F	2	2	0	0	0	0	0	0	0	0	1	3	8
Heating Degree Days (base 65°F)	1,317	1,185	1,169	940	689	367	138	167	415	776	1,094	1,325	9,582
Cooling Degree Days (base 65°F)	0	0	0	0	0	1	15	6	0	0	0	0	22
Mean Precipitation (in.)	5.95	5.53	6.23	5.00	4.01	2.18	1.71	1.85	3.06	4.01	5.20	5.81	50.54
Extreme Maximum Daily Precip. (in.)	3.08	2.88	2.90	2.61	2.74	2.54	1.87	1.73	3.43	2.81	3.50	3.18	3.50
Days With ≥ 0.1" Precipitation	10	10	11	9	8	4	4	5	6	7	10	10	94
Days With ≥ 0.5" Precipitation	4	4	4	3	3	2	1	1	2	3	4	4	35
Days With ≥ 1.0" Precipitation	2	1	2	1	1	0	0	0	1	1	1	1	11
Mean Snowfall (in.)	85.3	77.3	83.7	60.2	27.9	5.6	0.1	0.0	5.0	30.5	67.6	84.0	527.2
Maximum Snow Depth (in.)	120	141	144	***150***	141	111	12	0	28	46	72	125	***150***
Days With ≥ 1.0" Snow Depth	30	27	30	***29***	22	7	0	0	1	8	23	29	***206***

Altamont *Duchesne County* Elevation: 6,370 ft. Latitude: 40° 21' N Longitude: 110° 17' W

	JAN	FEB	MAR	APR	MAY	JUN	JUL	AUG	SEP	OCT	NOV	DEC	YEAR
Mean Maximum Temp. (°F)	32.0	36.6	48.2	57.4	66.7	76.3	83.9	81.8	72.2	59.3	44.7	32.4	57.6
Mean Temp. (°F)	19.9	24.3	35.2	43.2	52.2	60.9	68.3	66.4	57.4	45.5	32.5	21.0	43.9
Mean Minimum Temp. (°F)	7.9	12.0	22.1	29.0	37.7	45.4	52.7	51.0	42.4	31.6	20.2	9.6	30.1
Extreme Maximum Temp. (°F)	59	69	76	86	90	93	97	94	90	80	68	57	97
Extreme Minimum Temp. (°F)	-23	-29	-6	7	17	25	34	28	19	10	-8	-32	-32
Days Maximum Temp. ≥ 90°F	0	0	0	0	0	1	5	1	0	0	0	0	7
Days Maximum Temp. ≤ 32°F	15	8	2	0	0	0	0	0	0	0	3	15	43
Days Minimum Temp. ≤ 32°F	31	28	29	20	8	1	0	0	3	17	29	31	197
Days Minimum Temp. ≤ 0°F	7	4	0	0	0	0	0	0	0	0	1	5	17
Heating Degree Days (base 65°F)	1,390	1,144	918	648	393	150	22	30	232	599	970	1,357	7,853
Cooling Degree Days (base 65°F)	0	0	0	0	3	33	132	82	9	0	0	0	259
Mean Precipitation (in.)	0.69	0.72	0.58	0.71	0.99	0.74	0.81	0.85	1.30	1.09	0.64	0.60	9.72
Extreme Maximum Daily Precip. (in.)	0.52	0.75	0.85	0.87	1.14	1.44	1.00	1.37	1.05	1.00	1.30	0.90	1.44
Days With ≥ 0.1" Precipitation	3	3	2	2	3	2	3	3	3	3	2	2	31
Days With ≥ 0.5" Precipitation	0	0	0	0	0	0	0	0	1	1	0	0	2
Days With ≥ 1.0" Precipitation	0	0	0	0	0	0	0	0	0	0	0	0	0
Mean Snowfall (in.)	9.8	8.3	3.6	2.3	0.1	trace	0.0	0.0	0.0	0.9	4.5	8.4	37.9
Maximum Snow Depth (in.)	18	25	20	5	2	1	0	0	0	5	9	14	25
Days With ≥ 1.0" Snow Depth	20	16	6	1	0	0	0	0	0	1	3	16	63

Angle *Piute County* Elevation: 6,399 ft. Latitude: 38° 15' N Longitude: 111° 58' W

	JAN	FEB	MAR	APR	MAY	JUN	JUL	AUG	SEP	OCT	NOV	DEC	YEAR
Mean Maximum Temp. (°F)	40.9	45.7	53.1	60.2	70.1	80.0	86.3	83.9	76.5	65.2	52.2	42.1	63.0
Mean Temp. (°F)	23.7	29.6	36.7	42.9	51.8	59.6	66.2	64.6	56.2	45.3	34.3	25.0	44.6
Mean Minimum Temp. (°F)	6.4	13.5	20.2	25.6	33.4	39.1	46.0	45.2	35.8	25.3	16.3	7.8	26.2
Extreme Maximum Temp. (°F)	66	70	80	82	94	96	102	97	92	90	75	68	102
Extreme Minimum Temp. (°F)	-29	-31	-2	8	13	22	28	26	16	4	-18	-32	-32
Days Maximum Temp. ≥ 90°F	0	0	0	0	0	2	8	4	0	0	0	0	14
Days Maximum Temp. ≤ 32°F	5	2	1	0	0	0	0	0	0	0	1	5	14
Days Minimum Temp. ≤ 32°F	31	28	29	25	13	3	0	0	10	27	29	31	226
Days Minimum Temp. ≤ 0°F	9	3	0	0	0	0	0	0	0	0	1	7	20
Heating Degree Days (base 65°F)	1,274	992	872	656	404	169	31	50	262	606	917	1,233	7,466
Cooling Degree Days (base 65°F)	0	0	0	0	1	12	75	43	3	0	0	0	134
Mean Precipitation (in.)	***0.42***	0.36	0.67	0.69	0.77	0.65	1.01	1.47	1.10	1.00	0.46	0.33	***8.93***
Extreme Maximum Daily Precip. (in.)	***0.67***	0.57	***1.27***	0.74	0.91	1.64	1.17	1.12	1.36	1.12	0.85	0.92	***1.64***
Days With ≥ 0.1" Precipitation	***1***	1	2	3	3	2	3	4	3	3	2	1	***28***
Days With ≥ 0.5" Precipitation	***0***	0	0	0	0	0	0	1	1	1	0	0	***3***
Days With ≥ 1.0" Precipitation	***0***	0	0	0	0	0	0	0	0	0	0	0	***0***
Mean Snowfall (in.)	***5.1***	3.6	***3.6***	1.8	0.4	trace	0.0	0.0	trace	0.5	2.1	4.2	***21.3***
Maximum Snow Depth (in.)	***10***	***4***	***9***	***2***	1	***trace***	0	0	0	***2***	3	***5***	***10***
Days With ≥ 1.0" Snow Depth	***6***	***3***	***2***	***1***	0	0	0	0	0	0	1	***2***	***15***

Arches Np Hqs *Grand County* Elevation: 4,129 ft. Latitude: 38° 37' N Longitude: 109° 37' W

	JAN	FEB	MAR	APR	MAY	JUN	JUL	AUG	SEP	OCT	NOV	DEC	YEAR
Mean Maximum Temp. (°F)	43.1	50.9	62.2	70.6	81.6	92.9	99.2	96.4	86.9	72.7	56.4	43.5	71.4
Mean Temp. (°F)	31.8	38.9	48.8	56.4	66.3	76.7	83.3	81.0	71.1	57.4	43.7	32.7	57.3
Mean Minimum Temp. (°F)	20.4	26.8	35.3	42.1	51.0	60.4	67.3	65.5	55.2	42.0	30.9	21.9	43.2
Extreme Maximum Temp. (°F)	63	74	87	93	105	110	116	109	105	95	79	69	116
Extreme Minimum Temp. (°F)	-3	-8	10	21	28	42	50	47	26	20	10	-4	-8
Days Maximum Temp. ≥ 90°F	0	0	0	0	7	21	29	27	13	1	0	0	98
Days Maximum Temp. ≤ 32°F	4	1	0	0	0	0	0	0	0	0	0	2	7
Days Minimum Temp. ≤ 32°F	29	22	11	3	0	0	0	0	0	3	18	29	115
Days Minimum Temp. ≤ 0°F	0	0	0	0	0	0	0	0	0	0	0	0	0
Heating Degree Days (base 65°F)	1,023	732	497	269	82	6	0	0	27	247	633	993	4,509
Cooling Degree Days (base 65°F)	0	0	1	17	129	364	573	501	216	17	0	0	1,818
Mean Precipitation (in.)	0.56	0.47	0.77	0.75	0.66	0.41	0.86	0.94	0.85	1.24	0.62	0.52	8.65
Extreme Maximum Daily Precip. (in.)	0.73	0.62	1.20	0.91	1.30	0.64	1.59	1.45	1.62	1.28	0.77	0.70	1.62
Days With ≥ 0.1" Precipitation	2	2	2	2	2	1	2	3	3	3	2	2	26
Days With ≥ 0.5" Precipitation	0	0	0	0	0	0	0	0	0	1	0	0	1
Days With ≥ 1.0" Precipitation	0	0	0	0	0	0	0	0	0	0	0	0	0
Mean Snowfall (in.)	1.8	0.8	0.7	trace	0.0	0.0	0.0	0.0	0.0	trace	0.6	2.4	6.3
Maximum Snow Depth (in.)	10	6	4	trace	0	0	0	0	0	trace	3	6	10
Days With ≥ 1.0" Snow Depth	7	3	0	0	0	0	0	0	0	0	0	3	13

Black Rock *Millard County* Elevation: 4,895 ft. Latitude: 38° 43' N Longitude: 112° 57' W

	JAN	FEB	MAR	APR	MAY	JUN	JUL	AUG	SEP	OCT	NOV	DEC	YEAR
Mean Maximum Temp. (°F)	41.2	48.0	58.7	67.0	76.3	86.2	93.0	90.4	80.8	67.9	53.4	41.1	67.0
Mean Temp. (°F)	28.4	33.9	42.4	49.2	57.5	66.1	73.6	71.7	61.9	49.9	38.1	27.9	50.0
Mean Minimum Temp. (°F)	15.5	19.8	26.1	31.4	38.7	46.0	54.1	52.9	42.9	31.8	22.7	14.6	33.0
Extreme Maximum Temp. (°F)	68	75	83	90	98	103	104	101	97	89	80	67	104
Extreme Minimum Temp. (°F)	-23	-28	1	11	17	26	32	29	22	8	-16	-37	-37
Days Maximum Temp. ≥ 90°F	0	0	0	0	2	12	24	18	4	0	0	0	60
Days Maximum Temp. ≤ 32°F	7	2	0	0	0	0	0	0	0	0	1	6	16
Days Minimum Temp. ≤ 32°F	29	26	25	17	6	1	0	0	3	18	25	29	179
Days Minimum Temp. ≤ 0°F	4	2	0	0	0	0	0	0	0	0	1	4	11
Heating Degree Days (base 65°F)	1,129	874	693	467	238	60	3	4	130	462	801	1,145	6,006
Cooling Degree Days (base 65°F)	0	0	0	0	14	101	277	218	42	1	0	0	653
Mean Precipitation (in.)	0.59	0.71	1.01	0.91	0.84	0.50	0.65	0.86	0.82	1.00	0.71	0.59	9.19
Extreme Maximum Daily Precip. (in.)	1.07	1.00	1.75	0.92	0.84	1.51	1.87	1.16	1.23	1.57	1.04	1.50	1.87
Days With ≥ 0.1" Precipitation	2	3	3	3	3	2	2	2	2	3	2	2	29
Days With ≥ 0.5" Precipitation	0	0	0	0	0	0	0	0	0	1	0	0	1
Days With ≥ 1.0" Precipitation	0	0	0	0	0	0	0	0	0	0	0	0	0
Mean Snowfall (in.)	4.9	4.8	5.0	1.6	0.2	trace	0.0	0.0	0.1	0.2	3.3	4.5	24.6
Maximum Snow Depth (in.)	24	10	16	4	0	0	0	0	trace	3	12	10	24
Days With ≥ 1.0" Snow Depth	10	7	2	0	0	0	0	0	0	0	2	8	29

Blowhard Mtn Radar *Iron County* Elevation: 10,693 ft. Latitude: 37° 36' N Longitude: 112° 52' W

	JAN	FEB	MAR	APR	MAY	JUN	JUL	AUG	SEP	OCT	NOV	DEC	YEAR
Mean Maximum Temp. (°F)	29.3	28.9	32.4	39.3	47.4	58.1	64.8	62.7	55.7	45.9	35.0	29.8	44.1
Mean Temp. (°F)	22.0	21.8	25.1	31.2	39.2	49.8	56.6	54.9	48.0	38.1	27.6	22.2	36.4
Mean Minimum Temp. (°F)	14.6	14.7	17.7	23.1	31.1	41.5	48.3	47.1	40.3	30.3	20.1	14.6	28.6
Extreme Maximum Temp. (°F)	52	54	55	75	79	80	90	82	75	74	63	57	90
Extreme Minimum Temp. (°F)	-18	-18	-7	-4	4	18	29	33	19	1	-9	-20	-20
Days Maximum Temp. ≥ 90°F	0	0	0	0	0	0	0	0	0	0	0	0	0
Days Maximum Temp. ≤ 32°F	19	17	14	7	1	0	0	0	0	3	11	19	91
Days Minimum Temp. ≤ 32°F	30	26	28	24	15	4	0	0	4	17	26	29	203
Days Minimum Temp. ≤ 0°F	2	2	1	0	0	0	0	0	0	0	1	2	8
Heating Degree Days (base 65°F)	1,327	1,214	1,231	1,005	792	449	260	308	503	826	1,118	1,321	10,354
Cooling Degree Days (base 65°F)	0	0	0	0	0	0	6	2	0	0	0	0	8
Mean Precipitation (in.)	3.12	3.36	4.31	2.60	1.50	0.78	1.97	2.94	1.87	1.90	2.39	2.50	29.24
Extreme Maximum Daily Precip. (in.)	1.90	1.78	2.97	1.93	na	1.63	2.05	1.71	1.75	1.44	2.25	2.21	na
Days With ≥ 0.1" Precipitation	6	7	7	6	3	2	5	7	4	4	5	5	61
Days With ≥ 0.5" Precipitation	2	2	3	2	1	0	1	2	1	1	1	1	17
Days With ≥ 1.0" Precipitation	1	1	1	0	0	0	0	1	0	0	0	1	5
Mean Snowfall (in.)	38.5	40.6	47.9	28.6	12.0	3.1	0.0	trace	1.8	15.7	28.6	31.3	248.1
Maximum Snow Depth (in.)	120	130	148	141	136	80	12	1	20	30	68	80	148
Days With ≥ 1.0" Snow Depth	31	28	31	29	24	7	0	0	1	9	23	30	213

Boulder *Garfield County* Elevation: 6,680 ft. Latitude: 37° 54' N Longitude: 111° 25' W

	JAN	FEB	MAR	APR	MAY	JUN	JUL	AUG	SEP	OCT	NOV	DEC	YEAR
Mean Maximum Temp. (°F)	40.6	44.5	52.6	60.4	69.4	79.2	84.7	82.0	74.4	62.9	49.8	40.8	61.8
Mean Temp. (°F)	29.9	33.5	40.6	47.4	56.2	65.6	72.0	69.8	62.1	50.9	38.7	30.2	49.7
Mean Minimum Temp. (°F)	19.2	22.4	28.6	34.4	42.9	51.9	59.3	57.5	49.7	38.8	27.5	19.5	37.6
Extreme Maximum Temp. (°F)	61	69	73	82	89	94	96	95	90	83	70	64	96
Extreme Minimum Temp. (°F)	-8	-17	6	11	24	30	39	40	26	15	4	-11	-17
Days Maximum Temp. ≥ 90°F	0	0	0	0	0	2	5	2	0	0	0	0	9
Days Maximum Temp. ≤ 32°F	4	2	0	0	0	0	0	0	0	0	1	5	12
Days Minimum Temp. ≤ 32°F	30	26	22	13	3	0	0	0	1	7	21	30	153
Days Minimum Temp. ≤ 0°F	0	0	0	0	0	0	0	0	0	0	0	0	0
Heating Degree Days (base 65°F)	1,080	886	749	522	279	67	5	10	121	431	782	1,073	6,005
Cooling Degree Days (base 65°F)	0	0	0	0	12	92	229	164	39	1	0	0	537
Mean Precipitation (in.)	1.00	1.01	0.97	0.47	0.66	0.38	0.89	1.67	1.49	1.26	0.60	0.70	11.10
Extreme Maximum Daily Precip. (in.)	1.51	1.21	1.01	0.97	1.20	0.97	1.55	1.62	1.65	2.88	1.50	1.25	2.88
Days With ≥ 0.1" Precipitation	3	3	3	1	2	1	3	5	4	3	2	2	32
Days With ≥ 0.5" Precipitation	1	1	1	0	0	0	0	1	1	1	0	0	6
Days With ≥ 1.0" Precipitation	0	0	0	0	0	0	0	0	0	0	0	0	0
Mean Snowfall (in.)	14.5	9.0	5.0	1.3	trace	trace	0.0	0.0	trace	0.4	3.3	8.6	42.1
Maximum Snow Depth (in.)	27	34	8	4	3	trace	0	0	trace	2	8	25	34
Days With ≥ 1.0" Snow Depth	15	8	2	0	0	0	0	0	0	0	1	7	33

The period of record for all cooperative weather station data is 1980 – 2009. See User Guide for detailed explanation of data.

Bountiful-Val Verda *Davis County* Elevation: 4,540 ft. Latitude: 40° 51' N Longitude: 111° 53' W

	JAN	FEB	MAR	APR	MAY	JUN	JUL	AUG	SEP	OCT	NOV	DEC	YEAR
Mean Maximum Temp. (°F)	36.8	41.4	51.7	59.6	69.7	80.0	89.6	87.7	76.7	63.2	48.5	37.7	61.9
Mean Temp. (°F)	29.5	33.5	42.6	49.8	58.9	68.1	76.8	75.0	64.6	52.4	40.0	30.5	51.8
Mean Minimum Temp. (°F)	22.2	25.6	33.5	39.8	48.0	56.1	64.0	62.2	52.4	41.5	31.4	23.2	41.6
Extreme Maximum Temp. (°F)	59	65	76	86	97	100	104	101	95	85	74	68	104
Extreme Minimum Temp. (°F)	-3	-5	11	22	29	34	47	40	33	19	5	-9	-9
Days Maximum Temp. ≥ 90°F	0	0	0	0	0	5	17	13	1	0	0	0	36
Days Maximum Temp. ≤ 32°F	11	5	0	0	0	0	0	0	0	0	2	9	27
Days Minimum Temp. ≤ 32°F	28	23	14	5	0	0	0	0	0	4	17	27	118
Days Minimum Temp. ≤ 0°F	0	0	0	0	0	0	0	0	0	0	0	0	0
Heating Degree Days (base 65°F)	1,092	884	688	455	226	61	4	4	101	390	744	1,063	5,712
Cooling Degree Days (base 65°F)	0	0	0	4	43	161	378	322	95	5	0	0	1,008
Mean Precipitation (in.)	1.91	1.98	2.52	3.01	2.74	1.44	0.89	0.86	1.73	2.28	2.05	2.01	23.42
Extreme Maximum Daily Precip. (in.)	1.40	1.42	2.15	1.45	1.96	1.39	1.25	2.39	2.09	1.67	1.60	1.63	2.39
Days With ≥ 0.1" Precipitation	5	5	6	7	6	3	2	2	4	5	5	5	55
Days With ≥ 0.5" Precipitation	1	1	2	2	2	1	1	0	1	2	1	1	15
Days With ≥ 1.0" Precipitation	0	0	0	1	1	0	0	0	0	0	0	0	2
Mean Snowfall (in.)	13.5	13.3	8.3	3.8	0.2	trace	0.0	0.0	0.0	0.9	6.5	14.0	60.5
Maximum Snow Depth (in.)	28	24	14	6	1	trace	0	0	0	8	16	20	28
Days With ≥ 1.0" Snow Depth	21	15	7	2	0	0	0	0	0	1	5	18	69

Brigham City Waste Plt *Box Elder County* Elevation: 4,229 ft. Latitude: 41° 31' N Longitude: 112° 03' W

	JAN	FEB	MAR	APR	MAY	JUN	JUL	AUG	SEP	OCT	NOV	DEC	YEAR
Mean Maximum Temp. (°F)	35.7	41.8	53.0	62.0	71.6	82.1	90.9	89.3	78.9	65.0	48.9	37.1	63.0
Mean Temp. (°F)	26.7	31.4	41.6	49.0	57.5	66.2	73.7	72.1	62.5	50.4	38.0	28.3	49.8
Mean Minimum Temp. (°F)	17.7	21.0	30.2	36.0	43.4	50.3	56.4	54.8	46.0	35.8	27.1	19.5	36.5
Extreme Maximum Temp. (°F)	60	66	76	85	94	101	104	102	96	87	73	66	104
Extreme Minimum Temp. (°F)	-25	-23	3	17	23	30	35	34	27	17	0	-25	-25
Days Maximum Temp. ≥ 90°F	0	0	0	0	0	6	20	17	2	0	0	0	45
Days Maximum Temp. ≤ 32°F	11	4	0	0	0	0	0	0	0	0	1	9	25
Days Minimum Temp. ≤ 32°F	29	25	20	9	2	0	0	0	1	11	23	29	149
Days Minimum Temp. ≤ 0°F	3	2	0	0	0	0	0	0	0	0	0	1	6
Heating Degree Days (base 65°F)	1,179	943	718	477	246	65	5	7	121	447	803	1,130	6,141
Cooling Degree Days (base 65°F)	0	0	0	1	21	108	281	233	53	1	0	0	698
Mean Precipitation (in.)	1.64	1.42	1.62	1.77	2.20	1.11	0.75	0.67	1.55	1.80	1.41	1.28	17.22
Extreme Maximum Daily Precip. (in.)	1.84	1.30	1.24	1.21	1.67	1.68	1.73	1.35	2.93	1.43	1.12	1.41	2.93
Days With ≥ 0.1" Precipitation	5	4	5	5	5	2	2	2	3	4	4	4	45
Days With ≥ 0.5" Precipitation	1	0	1	1	1	1	0	0	1	1	1	1	9
Days With ≥ 1.0" Precipitation	0	0	0	0	0	0	0	0	0	0	0	0	0
Mean Snowfall (in.)	10.0	7.3	4.1	0.9	trace	0.0	0.0	0.0	0.0	0.4	3.0	10.1	35.8
Maximum Snow Depth (in.)	***23***	17	14	3	trace	0	0	0	0	2	***7***	***25***	***25***
Days With ≥ 1.0" Snow Depth	***16***	11	2	0	0	0	0	0	0	0	1	***9***	***39***

Callao *Juab County* Elevation: 4,330 ft. Latitude: 39° 54' N Longitude: 113° 43' W

	JAN	FEB	MAR	APR	MAY	JUN	JUL	AUG	SEP	OCT	NOV	DEC	YEAR
Mean Maximum Temp. (°F)	39.2	45.6	56.8	64.8	73.5	83.1	91.4	89.7	79.4	65.8	51.2	40.3	65.1
Mean Temp. (°F)	27.2	32.8	42.5	49.8	58.1	66.8	74.4	72.8	62.2	49.6	37.4	27.9	50.1
Mean Minimum Temp. (°F)	15.1	20.0	28.2	34.7	42.5	50.5	57.3	55.8	45.0	33.4	23.5	15.4	35.1
Extreme Maximum Temp. (°F)	68	72	81	89	96	100	104	106	97	87	76	72	106
Extreme Minimum Temp. (°F)	-17	-23	6	12	21	30	38	28	25	14	0	-23	-23
Days Maximum Temp. ≥ 90°F	0	0	0	0	1	8	22	18	3	0	0	0	52
Days Maximum Temp. ≤ 32°F	9	3	0	0	0	0	0	0	0	0	0	6	18
Days Minimum Temp. ≤ 32°F	30	26	23	11	2	0	0	0	2	14	26	29	163
Days Minimum Temp. ≤ 0°F	3	1	0	0	0	0	0	0	0	0	0	2	6
Heating Degree Days (base 65°F)	1,166	904	690	452	236	64	4	7	132	471	822	1,145	6,093
Cooling Degree Days (base 65°F)	0	0	0	2	27	125	302	254	56	1	0	0	767
Mean Precipitation (in.)	0.43	0.39	0.47	0.63	0.90	0.62	0.47	0.66	0.59	0.76	0.35	0.29	6.56
Extreme Maximum Daily Precip. (in.)	0.73	0.68	0.91	0.75	1.51	1.67	0.86	1.41	2.12	1.21	1.13	0.64	2.12
Days With ≥ 0.1" Precipitation	2	2	1	2	3	2	1	2	1	2	1	1	20
Days With ≥ 0.5" Precipitation	0	0	0	0	0	0	0	0	0	0	0	0	0
Days With ≥ 1.0" Precipitation	0	0	0	0	0	0	0	0	0	0	0	0	0
Mean Snowfall (in.)	3.3	1.3	0.7	0.1	0.0	trace	0.0	0.0	0.0	trace	0.7	1.9	8.0
Maximum Snow Depth (in.)	18	14	9	2	0	trace	0	0	0	***1***	9	***8***	***18***
Days With ≥ 1.0" Snow Depth	5	3	1	0	0	0	0	0	0	0	0	1	10

Canyonlands The Neck *San Juan County* Elevation: 5,930 ft. Latitude: 38° 27' N Longitude: 109° 49' W

	JAN	FEB	MAR	APR	MAY	JUN	JUL	AUG	SEP	OCT	NOV	DEC	YEAR
Mean Maximum Temp. (°F)	37.6	43.5	53.2	62.0	72.7	84.2	90.5	87.5	78.2	64.3	48.7	37.4	63.3
Mean Temp. (°F)	29.6	34.9	43.2	50.8	61.0	72.2	78.5	75.9	66.7	53.6	40.2	29.6	53.0
Mean Minimum Temp. (°F)	21.5	26.2	33.1	39.7	49.3	60.2	66.4	64.2	55.3	42.8	31.5	21.8	42.7
Extreme Maximum Temp. (°F)	58	67	78	84	97	102	105	101	96	89	72	62	105
Extreme Minimum Temp. (°F)	-1	-13	9	19	22	26	45	47	25	13	8	-10	-13
Days Maximum Temp. ≥ 90°F	0	0	0	0	0	8	19	12	1	0	0	0	40
Days Maximum Temp. ≤ 32°F	8	2	0	0	0	0	0	0	0	0	1	8	19
Days Minimum Temp. ≤ 32°F	29	22	15	7	1	0	0	0	0	4	16	28	122
Days Minimum Temp. ≤ 0°F	0	0	0	0	0	0	0	0	0	0	0	0	0
Heating Degree Days (base 65°F)	1,091	845	669	422	175	28	1	1	67	356	739	1,090	5,484
Cooling Degree Days (base 65°F)	0	0	0	4	59	251	426	346	125	9	0	0	1,220
Mean Precipitation (in.)	0.51	0.49	0.87	0.74	0.78	0.43	0.89	1.07	1.06	1.26	0.65	0.55	9.30
Extreme Maximum Daily Precip. (in.)	0.64	0.75	0.74	0.95	0.83	0.82	1.12	1.13	1.37	1.45	0.84	0.71	1.45
Days With ≥ 0.1" Precipitation	2	2	3	2	2	1	3	3	3	3	2	2	28
Days With ≥ 0.5" Precipitation	0	0	0	0	0	0	0	1	1	1	0	0	3
Days With ≥ 1.0" Precipitation	0	0	0	0	0	0	0	0	0	0	0	0	0
Mean Snowfall (in.)	5.6	2.9	3.6	1.4	0.1	0.0	0.0	0.0	0.0	0.7	2.6	4.9	21.8
Maximum Snow Depth (in.)	10	7	7	4	1	0	0	0	0	5	6	8	10
Days With ≥ 1.0" Snow Depth	17	9	2	1	0	0	0	0	0	0	3	11	43

The period of record for all cooperative weather station data is 1980 – 2009. See User Guide for detailed explanation of data.

Castle Dale *Emery County* Elevation: 5,620 ft. Latitude: 39° 12' N Longitude: 111° 01' W

	JAN	FEB	MAR	APR	MAY	JUN	JUL	AUG	SEP	OCT	NOV	DEC	YEAR
Mean Maximum Temp. (°F)	38.4	44.9	55.7	64.2	73.4	83.4	89.8	86.9	78.8	66.3	51.4	39.7	64.4
Mean Temp. (°F)	23.8	30.4	40.1	47.5	56.4	65.0	71.7	69.3	60.8	49.1	36.1	25.5	48.0
Mean Minimum Temp. (°F)	9.2	15.9	24.5	30.8	39.4	46.6	53.5	51.7	42.7	31.7	20.7	11.2	31.5
Extreme Maximum Temp. (°F)	67	70	83	86	97	103	107	106	97	87	75	67	107
Extreme Minimum Temp. (°F)	-23	-21	0	10	18	25	35	33	23	10	-10	-28	-28
Days Maximum Temp. ≥ 90°F	0	0	0	0	1	7	17	11	2	0	0	0	38
Days Maximum Temp. ≤ 32°F	8	2	0	0	0	0	0	0	0	0	0	6	16
Days Minimum Temp. ≤ 32°F	31	28	27	18	5	0	0	0	3	18	28	31	189
Days Minimum Temp. ≤ 0°F	7	2	0	0	0	0	0	0	0	0	0	3	12
Heating Degree Days (base 65°F)	1,269	972	764	518	267	69	4	9	144	488	860	1,218	6,582
Cooling Degree Days (base 65°F)	0	0	0	0	8	77	218	150	24	0	0	0	477
Mean Precipitation (in.)	0.63	0.62	0.64	0.52	0.60	0.47	0.67	1.07	1.06	0.99	0.48	0.44	8.19
Extreme Maximum Daily Precip. (in.)	0.73	0.90	1.10	0.92	1.65	1.24	1.29	2.15	1.39	1.51	0.66	0.63	2.15
Days With ≥ 0.1" Precipitation	2	2	2	2	2	2	2	3	3	3	2	2	27
Days With ≥ 0.5" Precipitation	0	0	0	0	0	0	0	0	1	0	0	0	1
Days With ≥ 1.0" Precipitation	0	0	0	0	0	0	0	0	0	0	0	0	0
Mean Snowfall (in.)	6.1	3.9	1.8	0.5	0.1	0.0	0.0	0.0	0.0	0.3	1.3	4.5	18.5
Maximum Snow Depth (in.)	17	13	9	1	0	0	0	0	0	1	7	8	17
Days With ≥ 1.0" Snow Depth	15	7	1	0	0	0	0	0	0	0	1	6	30

Coalville *Summit County* Elevation: 5,549 ft. Latitude: 40° 55' N Longitude: 111° 24' W

	JAN	FEB	MAR	APR	MAY	JUN	JUL	AUG	SEP	OCT	NOV	DEC	YEAR
Mean Maximum Temp. (°F)	36.7	41.7	52.0	61.0	70.3	79.9	87.9	85.9	76.7	64.5	48.3	36.4	61.8
Mean Temp. (°F)	24.6	28.6	37.8	45.0	52.9	60.6	67.6	66.0	57.2	46.6	34.7	24.8	45.5
Mean Minimum Temp. (°F)	12.3	15.4	23.6	29.0	35.5	41.3	47.3	46.1	37.7	28.7	21.0	13.1	29.3
Extreme Maximum Temp. (°F)	60	68	77	85	95	98	102	100	93	86	74	64	102
Extreme Minimum Temp. (°F)	-26	-33	-13	5	17	23	31	24	14	5	-14	-26	-33
Days Maximum Temp. ≥ 90°F	0	0	0	0	0	4	13	9	1	0	0	0	27
Days Maximum Temp. ≤ 32°F	10	4	0	0	0	0	0	0	0	0	3	10	27
Days Minimum Temp. ≤ 32°F	30	27	28	21	10	2	0	0	8	22	26	30	204
Days Minimum Temp. ≤ 0°F	6	4	0	0	0	0	0	0	0	0	1	5	16
Heating Degree Days (base 65°F)	1,247	1,023	835	593	370	147	22	35	234	564	904	1,239	7,213
Cooling Degree Days (base 65°F)	0	0	0	0	3	22	110	74	7	0	0	0	216
Mean Precipitation (in.)	1.36	1.21	1.63	1.58	1.98	1.32	1.02	1.05	1.37	1.59	1.59	1.30	17.00
Extreme Maximum Daily Precip. (in.)	1.00	0.81	1.02	1.03	1.72	1.17	1.10	2.60	1.59	1.37	1.28	0.85	2.60
Days With ≥ 0.1" Precipitation	5	4	6	6	6	4	3	3	4	5	5	4	55
Days With ≥ 0.5" Precipitation	1	0	1	1	1	1	0	0	1	1	1	0	8
Days With ≥ 1.0" Precipitation	0	0	0	0	0	0	0	0	0	0	0	0	0
Mean Snowfall (in.)	16.5	14.5	11.1	4.6	1.1	0.1	0.0	0.0	0.3	1.7	11.8	16.5	78.2
Maximum Snow Depth (in.)	29	28	16	5	2	trace	0	0	4	10	14	14	29
Days With ≥ 1.0" Snow Depth	17	13	5	0	0	0	0	0	0	0	6	15	56

Deer Creek Dam *Wasatch County* Elevation: 5,270 ft. Latitude: 40° 24' N Longitude: 111° 32' W

	JAN	FEB	MAR	APR	MAY	JUN	JUL	AUG	SEP	OCT	NOV	DEC	YEAR
Mean Maximum Temp. (°F)	33.8	38.0	48.4	58.2	67.1	76.9	85.7	84.3	74.8	62.4	47.5	35.4	59.4
Mean Temp. (°F)	22.2	25.3	35.2	43.7	51.5	59.3	66.7	65.5	56.8	46.1	34.8	24.7	44.3
Mean Minimum Temp. (°F)	10.5	12.6	22.0	29.1	35.7	41.6	47.7	46.7	38.8	29.6	22.0	14.1	29.2
Extreme Maximum Temp. (°F)	58	65	74	80	90	96	100	96	91	83	72	64	100
Extreme Minimum Temp. (°F)	-28	-39	-16	12	18	26	33	29	19	15	-8	-30	-39
Days Maximum Temp. ≥ 90°F	0	0	0	0	0	1	8	4	0	0	0	0	13
Days Maximum Temp. ≤ 32°F	13	7	1	0	0	0	0	0	0	0	3	11	35
Days Minimum Temp. ≤ 32°F	30	27	29	21	9	1	0	0	5	21	27	30	200
Days Minimum Temp. ≤ 0°F	6	4	1	0	0	0	0	0	0	0	0	2	13
Heating Degree Days (base 65°F)	1,320	1,115	916	633	414	178	27	37	243	579	899	1,241	7,602
Cooling Degree Days (base 65°F)	0	0	0	0	0	14	88	61	5	0	0	0	168
Mean Precipitation (in.)	3.14	2.76	2.23	1.73	2.01	1.26	0.85	1.03	1.73	2.14	2.40	2.60	23.88
Extreme Maximum Daily Precip. (in.)	4.52	3.73	2.88	1.17	1.26	1.81	1.19	0.98	1.86	2.07	2.27	2.00	4.52
Days With ≥ 0.1" Precipitation	6	6	5	5	6	3	2	3	4	4	5	6	55
Days With ≥ 0.5" Precipitation	2	2	1	1	1	1	0	0	1	1	1	2	13
Days With ≥ 1.0" Precipitation	1	1	0	0	0	0	0	0	0	0	0	0	2
Mean Snowfall (in.)	21.8	13.2	5.3	1.0	0.0	0.0	0.0	0.0	0.0	0.6	7.4	19.5	68.8
Maximum Snow Depth (in.)	37	33	27	4	0	0	0	0	0	9	18	28	37
Days With ≥ 1.0" Snow Depth	22	19	11	1	0	0	0	0	0	0	6	17	76

Dugway *Tooele County* Elevation: 4,339 ft. Latitude: 40° 11' N Longitude: 112° 55' W

	JAN	FEB	MAR	APR	MAY	JUN	JUL	AUG	SEP	OCT	NOV	DEC	YEAR
Mean Maximum Temp. (°F)	38.8	45.5	55.8	64.3	74.9	86.2	95.5	93.2	81.9	66.8	51.3	39.5	66.1
Mean Temp. (°F)	27.0	33.5	42.3	49.6	59.1	69.3	77.8	75.7	64.6	50.6	38.0	27.6	51.3
Mean Minimum Temp. (°F)	15.2	21.5	28.8	34.8	43.3	52.2	60.1	58.2	47.2	34.3	24.6	15.6	36.3
Extreme Maximum Temp. (°F)	64	71	81	91	100	106	109	106	102	91	77	69	109
Extreme Minimum Temp. (°F)	-25	-29	4	11	19	28	42	33	23	12	-2	-27	-29
Days Maximum Temp. ≥ 90°F	0	0	0	0	3	13	26	24	7	0	0	0	73
Days Maximum Temp. ≤ 32°F	8	3	0	0	0	0	0	0	0	0	1	8	20
Days Minimum Temp. ≤ 32°F	30	25	22	12	2	0	0	0	1	13	25	30	160
Days Minimum Temp. ≤ 0°F	4	1	0	0	0	0	0	0	0	0	0	3	8
Heating Degree Days (base 65°F)	1,171	884	696	459	211	46	2	3	98	441	805	1,153	5,969
Cooling Degree Days (base 65°F)	0	0	0	3	37	180	407	342	92	2	0	0	1,063
Mean Precipitation (in.)	0.66	0.68	0.87	0.93	1.17	0.58	0.49	0.63	0.67	0.85	0.55	0.57	8.65
Extreme Maximum Daily Precip. (in.)	1.00	0.63	1.34	0.89	1.24	0.95	1.11	1.46	1.07	1.04	0.66	0.71	1.46
Days With ≥ 0.1" Precipitation	2	2	3	3	3	2	2	2	2	3	2	2	28
Days With ≥ 0.5" Precipitation	0	0	0	0	1	0	0	0	0	0	0	0	1
Days With ≥ 1.0" Precipitation	0	0	0	0	0	0	0	0	0	0	0	0	0
Mean Snowfall (in.)	4.0	3.4	1.6	0.7	trace	trace	0.0	0.0	0.0	0.1	1.1	3.6	14.5
Maximum Snow Depth (in.)	na	10	6	3	trace	trace	0	0	0	trace	2	na	na
Days With ≥ 1.0" Snow Depth	na	4	1	0	0	0	0	0	0	0	0	3	na

The period of record for all cooperative weather station data is 1980 – 2009. See User Guide for detailed explanation of data.

Echo Dam *Summit County* Elevation: 5,470 ft. Latitude: 40° 58' N Longitude: 111° 26' W

	JAN	FEB	MAR	APR	MAY	JUN	JUL	AUG	SEP	OCT	NOV	DEC	YEAR
Mean Maximum Temp. (°F)	34.2	38.8	49.6	58.8	68.1	78.4	86.9	85.7	76.1	63.1	46.7	34.8	60.1
Mean Temp. (°F)	22.9	26.6	36.8	44.7	52.8	60.9	68.5	67.2	58.0	46.8	34.4	24.2	45.3
Mean Minimum Temp. (°F)	11.6	14.3	23.9	30.5	37.5	43.4	50.0	48.6	39.8	30.4	22.1	13.6	30.5
Extreme Maximum Temp. (°F)	58	65	76	81	91	95	100	98	93	85	73	65	100
Extreme Minimum Temp. (°F)	-28	-34	-15	2	17	22	33	29	16	9	-8	-32	-34
Days Maximum Temp. ≥ 90°F	0	0	0	0	0	2	10	6	0	0	0	0	18
Days Maximum Temp. ≤ 32°F	13	7	1	0	0	0	0	0	0	0	4	12	37
Days Minimum Temp. ≤ 32°F	30	27	28	19	6	1	0	0	5	20	26	30	192
Days Minimum Temp. ≤ 0°F	6	4	0	0	0	0	0	0	0	0	1	4	15
Heating Degree Days (base 65°F)	1,299	1,079	869	604	371	143	17	23	215	558	911	1,258	7,347
Cooling Degree Days (base 65°F)	0	0	0	0	2	27	132	99	12	0	0	0	272
Mean Precipitation (in.)	1.13	1.00	1.31	1.36	1.90	1.24	0.85	0.87	1.37	1.54	1.50	1.04	15.11
Extreme Maximum Daily Precip. (in.)	0.85	0.86	1.18	1.26	1.41	1.11	1.20	1.21	1.55	1.50	1.11	0.98	1.55
Days With ≥ 0.1" Precipitation	4	4	4	4	6	3	3	2	4	4	5	3	46
Days With ≥ 0.5" Precipitation	0	0	0	1	1	1	0	0	1	1	1	0	6
Days With ≥ 1.0" Precipitation	0	0	0	0	0	0	0	0	0	0	0	0	0
Mean Snowfall (in.)	15.8	14.1	10.8	5.2	1.2	0.2	0.0	0.0	0.5	2.4	12.4	14.9	77.5
Maximum Snow Depth (in.)	22	24	19	5	3	trace	0	0	6	8	14	15	24
Days With ≥ 1.0" Snow Depth	25	20	7	1	0	0	0	0	0	1	8	22	84

Electric Lake U P & L *Emery County* Elevation: 8,379 ft. Latitude: 39° 36' N Longitude: 111° 13' W

	JAN	FEB	MAR	APR	MAY	JUN	JUL	AUG	SEP	OCT	NOV	DEC	YEAR
Mean Maximum Temp. (°F)	26.5	30.5	36.6	43.9	54.5	65.4	73.3	70.8	***61.3***	***48.5***	34.9	25.9	***47.7***
Mean Temp. (°F)	13.9	16.3	23.1	31.3	41.5	50.2	57.3	55.5	***47.2***	***36.4***	24.6	14.7	***34.3***
Mean Minimum Temp. (°F)	1.4	2.1	9.6	18.6	28.5	34.9	41.2	40.2	***33.0***	***24.3***	14.3	3.5	***21.0***
Extreme Maximum Temp. (°F)	49	53	61	73	78	83	89	92	81	***73***	60	49	***92***
Extreme Minimum Temp. (°F)	-31	-48	-21	-17	5	16	29	23	14	***3***	-22	-34	***-48***
Days Maximum Temp. ≥ 90°F	0	0	0	0	0	0	0	0	0	***0***	0	0	***0***
Days Maximum Temp. ≤ 32°F	***24***	16	11	4	1	0	0	0	0	***3***	12	24	***95***
Days Minimum Temp. ≤ 32°F	31	28	31	29	23	9	1	1	14	***28***	30	30	***255***
Days Minimum Temp. ≤ 0°F	14	13	6	1	0	0	0	0	0	***0***	3	11	***48***
Heating Degree Days (base 65°F)	1,577	1,368	1,291	1,005	721	436	235	286	***529***	***879***	1,205	1,554	***11,086***
Cooling Degree Days (base 65°F)	0	0	0	0	0	0	2	1	***0***	***0***	0	0	***3***
Mean Precipitation (in.)	2.47	2.64	2.72	2.21	1.87	1.15	1.18	1.57	1.79	***2.11***	2.33	2.46	***24.50***
Extreme Maximum Daily Precip. (in.)	***1.80***	***1.68***	***1.20***	***1.15***	***1.55***	1.69	***1.15***	***1.60***	***1.17***	***1.40***	***1.12***	***1.43***	***1.80***
Days With ≥ 0.1" Precipitation	6	7	8	7	6	4	4	5	5	***6***	6	6	***70***
Days With ≥ 0.5" Precipitation	1	1	1	1	1	0	0	1	1	***1***	1	1	***10***
Days With ≥ 1.0" Precipitation	0	0	0	0	0	0	0	0	0	***0***	0	0	***0***
Mean Snowfall (in.)	na	na	na	na	***0.0***	0.0	0.0	0.0	0.0	***0.0***	na	na	na
Maximum Snow Depth (in.)	na	na	na	na	na	na	na	na	na	na	na	na	na
Days With ≥ 1.0" Snow Depth	na	na	na	na	***0***	0	0	0	0	na	na	na	na

Ephraim Sorensens Fld *Sanpete County* Elevation: 5,509 ft. Latitude: 39° 22' N Longitude: 111° 35' W

	JAN	FEB	MAR	APR	MAY	JUN	JUL	AUG	SEP	OCT	NOV	DEC	YEAR
Mean Maximum Temp. (°F)	36.9	42.7	52.4	61.2	71.4	82.5	90.9	88.4	78.5	65.3	50.1	37.4	63.1
Mean Temp. (°F)	25.1	30.9	39.4	46.6	55.2	64.3	72.1	70.1	60.7	48.9	36.7	25.5	48.0
Mean Minimum Temp. (°F)	13.2	19.0	26.3	31.9	39.1	46.1	53.2	51.7	42.9	32.4	23.2	13.6	32.7
Extreme Maximum Temp. (°F)	59	69	85	88	99	102	108	104	97	90	76	66	108
Extreme Minimum Temp. (°F)	-28	-22	-9	14	15	28	34	29	18	12	-19	-34	-34
Days Maximum Temp. ≥ 90°F	0	0	0	0	1	7	20	14	2	0	0	0	44
Days Maximum Temp. ≤ 32°F	9	3	1	0	0	0	0	0	0	0	2	9	24
Days Minimum Temp. ≤ 32°F	30	27	25	16	5	0	0	0	3	15	26	30	177
Days Minimum Temp. ≤ 0°F	5	2	0	0	0	0	0	0	0	0	0	4	11
Heating Degree Days (base 65°F)	1,230	958	787	547	303	87	5	8	152	493	843	1,217	6,630
Cooling Degree Days (base 65°F)	0	0	0	0	7	74	232	173	31	0	0	0	517
Mean Precipitation (in.)	0.98	1.12	1.38	1.20	1.31	0.76	0.71	0.88	1.24	1.45	1.06	1.04	13.13
Extreme Maximum Daily Precip. (in.)	1.10	1.45	0.95	0.68	1.17	0.98	0.90	1.00	1.10	1.00	1.05	0.72	1.45
Days With ≥ 0.1" Precipitation	3	4	5	5	4	2	2	3	4	4	3	4	43
Days With ≥ 0.5" Precipitation	0	0	1	0	1	0	0	0	1	1	1	1	6
Days With ≥ 1.0" Precipitation	0	0	0	0	0	0	0	0	0	0	0	0	0
Mean Snowfall (in.)	na	na	na	0.6	0.1	0.0	0.0	0.0	0.0	0.0	na	na	na
Maximum Snow Depth (in.)	na	na	na	na	na	na	na	na	na	na	na	na	na
Days With ≥ 1.0" Snow Depth	na	na	***1***	0	0	0	0	0	0	0	***0***	na	na

Eskdale *Millard County* Elevation: 4,979 ft. Latitude: 39° 07' N Longitude: 113° 57' W

	JAN	FEB	MAR	APR	MAY	JUN	JUL	AUG	SEP	OCT	NOV	DEC	YEAR
Mean Maximum Temp. (°F)	41.6	47.1	57.4	65.7	75.2	85.5	93.0	91.2	81.3	68.3	53.1	42.0	66.8
Mean Temp. (°F)	28.2	33.6	42.9	50.1	58.7	68.0	75.5	73.8	63.6	51.2	38.3	28.5	51.1
Mean Minimum Temp. (°F)	14.9	20.1	28.2	34.5	42.2	50.5	58.0	56.4	45.9	34.1	23.6	14.9	35.3
Extreme Maximum Temp. (°F)	69	75	81	87	97	101	105	102	98	89	79	67	105
Extreme Minimum Temp. (°F)	-20	-31	5	12	20	30	39	34	24	8	-4	-20	-31
Days Maximum Temp. ≥ 90°F	0	0	0	0	1	12	25	21	4	0	0	0	63
Days Maximum Temp. ≤ 32°F	7	3	0	0	0	0	0	0	0	0	1	6	17
Days Minimum Temp. ≤ 32°F	29	25	21	12	3	0	0	0	2	14	25	29	160
Days Minimum Temp. ≤ 0°F	3	1	0	0	0	0	0	0	0	0	0	2	6
Heating Degree Days (base 65°F)	1,133	881	677	442	214	51	2	3	105	421	793	1,125	5,847
Cooling Degree Days (base 65°F)	0	0	0	2	27	148	336	283	70	2	0	0	868
Mean Precipitation (in.)	0.33	0.43	0.69	0.71	0.74	0.63	0.55	0.62	0.75	0.70	0.38	0.25	6.78
Extreme Maximum Daily Precip. (in.)	1.60	***1.27***	1.10	1.18	0.81	1.32	2.30	1.32	0.92	1.17	0.77	***0.67***	***2.30***
Days With ≥ 0.1" Precipitation	1	2	2	2	2	2	1	2	2	2	1	1	20
Days With ≥ 0.5" Precipitation	0	0	0	0	0	0	0	0	0	0	0	0	0
Days With ≥ 1.0" Precipitation	0	0	0	0	0	0	0	0	0	0	0	0	0
Mean Snowfall (in.)	3.1	2.9	2.0	1.0	0.0	0.0	0.0	0.0	0.0	0.4	0.8	***2.8***	***13.0***
Maximum Snow Depth (in.)	***8***	***13***	***11***	3	0	0	***0***	***0***	1	***4***	***8***	***12***	***13***
Days With ≥ 1.0" Snow Depth	***3***	2	1	0	0	0	0	0	0	0	1	***3***	***10***

Farmington Usu Fld Stn *Davis County* Elevation: 4,339 ft. Latitude: 41° 01' N Longitude: 111° 55' W

	JAN	FEB	MAR	APR	MAY	JUN	JUL	AUG	SEP	OCT	NOV	DEC	YEAR
Mean Maximum Temp. (°F)	38.2	43.8	54.4	63.3	73.0	83.6	92.5	90.6	79.9	66.0	50.4	39.3	64.6
Mean Temp. (°F)	29.9	34.3	43.4	51.3	59.9	69.1	77.3	75.4	65.5	52.9	40.5	31.0	52.5
Mean Minimum Temp. (°F)	21.5	24.7	32.3	39.3	46.6	54.5	61.9	60.2	51.0	39.8	30.5	22.6	40.4
Extreme Maximum Temp. (°F)	58	69	78	87	97	102	105	104	99	93	77	68	105
Extreme Minimum Temp. (°F)	-8	-9	11	22	29	35	46	40	30	18	3	-12	-12
Days Maximum Temp. ≥ 90°F	0	0	0	0	1	9	23	19	3	0	0	0	55
Days Maximum Temp. ≤ 32°F	8	3	0	0	0	0	0	0	0	0	1	6	18
Days Minimum Temp. ≤ 32°F	29	23	16	6	0	0	0	0	0	4	18	28	124
Days Minimum Temp. ≤ 0°F	0	0	0	0	0	0	0	0	0	0	0	0	0
Heating Degree Days (base 65°F)	1,082	862	664	407	197	46	2	2	82	372	729	1,047	5,492
Cooling Degree Days (base 65°F)	0	0	0	5	44	175	388	332	102	4	0	0	1,050
Mean Precipitation (in.)	2.05	2.11	2.58	2.40	2.75	1.45	0.84	0.68	1.57	2.11	2.06	1.89	22.49
Extreme Maximum Daily Precip. (in.)	1.52	1.25	1.65	1.68	1.72	2.40	1.68	3.14	2.16	1.64	1.56	1.91	3.14
Days With ≥ 0.1" Precipitation	6	5	6	6	6	3	2	2	3	4	5	5	53
Days With ≥ 0.5" Precipitation	1	1	2	2	2	1	1	0	1	1	1	1	14
Days With ≥ 1.0" Precipitation	0	0	0	0	1	0	0	0	0	0	0	0	1
Mean Snowfall (in.)	14.5	10.3	***3.8***	***1.1***	trace	0.0	0.0	0.0	0.0	0.2	5.0	12.8	***47.7***
Maximum Snow Depth (in.)	31	19	15	7	1	0	0	0	0	4	10	23	31
Days With ≥ 1.0" Snow Depth	19	13	4	1	0	0	0	0	0	0	4	13	54

Flaming Gorge *Daggett County* Elevation: 6,270 ft. Latitude: 40° 56' N Longitude: 109° 25' W

	JAN	FEB	MAR	APR	MAY	JUN	JUL	AUG	SEP	OCT	NOV	DEC	YEAR
Mean Maximum Temp. (°F)	36.8	40.2	49.0	58.0	68.4	78.7	86.7	84.3	74.7	61.7	46.2	36.7	60.1
Mean Temp. (°F)	23.6	26.5	35.4	43.1	52.2	60.9	68.4	66.6	57.4	45.9	33.2	24.2	44.8
Mean Minimum Temp. (°F)	10.3	12.7	21.8	28.1	36.0	43.0	50.1	48.8	40.0	30.0	20.2	11.6	29.4
Extreme Maximum Temp. (°F)	60	66	76	82	93	100	102	99	91	83	71	64	102
Extreme Minimum Temp. (°F)	-29	-31	-10	-1	15	22	30	26	15	-2	-13	-36	-36
Days Maximum Temp. ≥ 90°F	0	0	0	0	0	2	11	6	0	0	0	0	19
Days Maximum Temp. ≤ 32°F	9	6	1	0	0	0	0	0	0	0	3	10	29
Days Minimum Temp. ≤ 32°F	30	28	28	22	10	2	0	0	5	19	27	30	201
Days Minimum Temp. ≤ 0°F	7	5	1	0	0	0	0	0	0	0	1	5	19
Heating Degree Days (base 65°F)	1,277	1,082	911	650	390	146	21	33	231	586	948	1,259	7,534
Cooling Degree Days (base 65°F)	0	0	0	0	2	29	132	89	10	0	0	0	262
Mean Precipitation (in.)	0.47	0.62	1.09	1.31	1.45	1.15	0.92	1.37	1.28	1.34	0.66	0.49	12.15
Extreme Maximum Daily Precip. (in.)	0.62	0.80	0.85	***0.88***	1.60	1.32	1.26	2.50	1.72	***1.77***	0.52	1.70	***2.50***
Days With ≥ 0.1" Precipitation	2	2	4	4	4	3	3	4	3	3	2	1	35
Days With ≥ 0.5" Precipitation	0	0	0	1	1	1	0	1	1	1	0	0	6
Days With ≥ 1.0" Precipitation	0	0	0	0	0	0	0	0	0	0	0	0	0
Mean Snowfall (in.)	7.9	8.2	8.8	4.8	1.2	0.2	0.0	0.0	0.2	2.2	6.9	7.4	47.8
Maximum Snow Depth (in.)	19	21	20	8	10	4	0	0	3	8	12	21	21
Days With ≥ 1.0" Snow Depth	19	16	7	2	0	0	0	0	0	1	6	16	67

Garfield *Salt Lake County* Elevation: 4,330 ft. Latitude: 40° 43' N Longitude: 112° 12' W

	JAN	FEB	MAR	APR	MAY	JUN	JUL	AUG	SEP	OCT	NOV	DEC	YEAR
Mean Maximum Temp. (°F)	37.9	42.5	53.3	62.0	72.1	82.9	92.3	90.3	78.3	63.7	***49.4***	39.1	***63.7***
Mean Temp. (°F)	31.1	35.1	44.6	52.5	61.9	71.9	81.1	79.2	67.7	54.4	***41.8***	32.1	***54.5***
Mean Minimum Temp. (°F)	24.2	27.6	35.8	43.0	51.7	60.9	69.9	67.9	57.1	45.1	***34.1***	25.1	***45.2***
Extreme Maximum Temp. (°F)	65	67	81	89	99	105	108	105	98	89	76	72	108
Extreme Minimum Temp. (°F)	-2	-4	15	24	30	33	50	42	33	18	3	-6	-6
Days Maximum Temp. ≥ 90°F	0	0	0	0	1	9	22	18	3	0	0	0	53
Days Maximum Temp. ≤ 32°F	9	3	0	0	0	0	0	0	0	0	1	7	20
Days Minimum Temp. ≤ 32°F	26	21	10	2	0	0	0	0	0	1	13	25	98
Days Minimum Temp. ≤ 0°F	0	0	0	0	0	0	0	0	0	0	0	0	0
Heating Degree Days (base 65°F)	1,045	839	626	378	166	36	1	1	63	330	***689***	1,012	***5,186***
Cooling Degree Days (base 65°F)	0	0	0	10	77	250	508	446	151	11	***0***	0	***1,453***
Mean Precipitation (in.)	1.33	1.35	1.76	2.12	2.50	1.14	0.97	0.90	1.62	1.99	1.75	1.40	18.83
Extreme Maximum Daily Precip. (in.)	***1.00***	1.40	1.20	1.32	***1.81***	1.48	***1.70***	2.74	3.17	2.01	***1.30***	***2.00***	***3.17***
Days With ≥ 0.1" Precipitation	4	4	5	5	5	3	2	2	3	4	5	4	46
Days With ≥ 0.5" Precipitation	0	1	1	1	2	1	1	0	1	1	1	1	11
Days With ≥ 1.0" Precipitation	0	0	0	0	0	0	0	0	0	0	0	0	0
Mean Snowfall (in.)	***7.1***	***4.2***	***1.1***	0.1	0.0	0.0	0.0	0.0	0.0	trace	3.2	6.4	***22.1***
Maximum Snow Depth (in.)	***23***	***16***	***4***	trace	0	0	0	0	0	trace	***8***	***11***	23
Days With ≥ 1.0" Snow Depth	***11***	6	***1***	0	0	0	0	0	0	0	3	***9***	***30***

Heber *Wasatch County* Elevation: 5,629 ft. Latitude: 40° 30' N Longitude: 111° 25' W

	JAN	FEB	MAR	APR	MAY	JUN	JUL	AUG	SEP	OCT	NOV	DEC	YEAR
Mean Maximum Temp. (°F)	36.1	40.6	51.3	61.1	70.8	80.8	88.5	87.1	78.0	65.5	49.4	36.9	62.2
Mean Temp. (°F)	24.3	28.1	38.0	46.1	54.4	62.1	69.4	68.1	59.5	48.6	36.3	25.6	46.7
Mean Minimum Temp. (°F)	12.4	15.6	24.7	31.1	37.8	43.4	50.1	49.0	40.9	31.6	23.2	14.2	31.2
Extreme Maximum Temp. (°F)	58	68	79	85	92	100	102	102	98	88	78	68	102
Extreme Minimum Temp. (°F)	-29	-36	-8	10	20	18	33	30	17	8	-10	-34	-36
Days Maximum Temp. ≥ 90°F	0	0	0	0	0	4	15	10	1	0	0	0	30
Days Maximum Temp. ≤ 32°F	10	5	1	0	0	0	0	0	0	0	2	9	27
Days Minimum Temp. ≤ 32°F	30	27	27	17	6	1	0	0	4	17	26	30	185
Days Minimum Temp. ≤ 0°F	5	4	0	0	0	0	0	0	0	0	0	4	13
Heating Degree Days (base 65°F)	1,256	1,036	829	559	327	116	12	17	177	503	854	1,215	6,901
Cooling Degree Days (base 65°F)	0	0	0	0	4	36	155	118	18	0	0	0	331
Mean Precipitation (in.)	1.90	1.69	1.37	1.18	1.42	0.87	0.77	0.85	1.33	1.58	1.43	1.36	15.75
Extreme Maximum Daily Precip. (in.)	1.71	1.32	1.02	1.02	1.28	1.05	1.50	0.80	1.10	1.30	1.17	0.81	1.71
Days With ≥ 0.1" Precipitation	5	4	4	4	5	3	2	3	4	4	4	5	47
Days With ≥ 0.5" Precipitation	1	1	1	0	0	0	0	0	1	1	1	1	7
Days With ≥ 1.0" Precipitation	0	0	0	0	0	0	0	0	0	0	0	0	0
Mean Snowfall (in.)	19.1	15.7	7.0	3.3	0.8	trace	0.0	0.0	0.1	1.6	8.9	15.5	72.0
Maximum Snow Depth (in.)	39	27	17	2	2	trace	0	0	2	7	11	30	39
Days With ≥ 1.0" Snow Depth	25	20	7	0	0	0	0	0	0	0	5	18	75

The period of record for all cooperative weather station data is 1980 – 2009. See User Guide for detailed explanation of data.

Huntsville Monastery *Weber County* Elevation: 5,140 ft. Latitude: 41° 14' N Longitude: 111° 43' W

	JAN	FEB	MAR	APR	MAY	JUN	JUL	AUG	SEP	OCT	NOV	DEC	YEAR
Mean Maximum Temp. (°F)	34.5	39.9	50.1	60.4	70.0	80.1	88.5	87.5	77.1	63.7	47.1	34.9	61.1
Mean Temp. (°F)	22.3	26.6	36.5	45.2	53.0	60.8	68.1	67.2	57.8	46.5	34.2	23.3	45.1
Mean Minimum Temp. (°F)	10.0	13.3	22.8	30.0	35.9	41.4	47.7	46.8	38.4	29.2	21.3	11.6	29.0
Extreme Maximum Temp. (°F)	57	62	73	84	93	99	102	102	95	88	73	64	102
Extreme Minimum Temp. (°F)	-26	-34	-17	0	19	24	31	23	18	6	-15	-37	-37
Days Maximum Temp. ≥ 90°F	0	0	0	0	0	4	14	12	1	0	0	0	31
Days Maximum Temp. ≤ 32°F	12	5	0	0	0	0	0	0	0	0	2	11	30
Days Minimum Temp. ≤ 32°F	31	27	28	20	10	2	0	0	7	21	27	30	203
Days Minimum Temp. ≤ 0°F	8	5	0	0	0	0	0	0	0	0	1	6	20
Heating Degree Days (base 65°F)	1,319	1,078	877	587	368	146	21	25	223	568	918	1,286	7,416
Cooling Degree Days (base 65°F)	0	0	0	0	2	27	124	100	12	0	0	0	265
Mean Precipitation (in.)	2.62	2.29	2.12	1.94	2.13	1.38	0.84	0.79	1.64	1.90	2.30	2.38	22.33
Extreme Maximum Daily Precip. (in.)	1.52	1.97	1.40	1.72	1.30	1.32	1.66	2.80	2.38	2.15	1.63	2.20	2.80
Days With ≥ 0.1" Precipitation	7	6	6	5	6	4	2	2	3	4	6	6	57
Days With ≥ 0.5" Precipitation	2	1	1	1	1	1	0	0	1	1	1	1	11
Days With ≥ 1.0" Precipitation	0	0	0	0	0	0	0	0	0	0	0	0	0
Mean Snowfall (in.)	18.6	14.7	6.7	1.6	0.2	0.0	0.0	0.0	trace	0.8	9.3	21.2	73.1
Maximum Snow Depth (in.)	40	48	40	11	2	2	0	0	trace	7	14	36	48
Days With ≥ 1.0" Snow Depth	25	24	14	1	0	0	0	0	0	0	7	21	92

Johnson Pass *Tooele County* Elevation: 5,629 ft. Latitude: 40° 20' N Longitude: 112° 37' W

	JAN	FEB	MAR	APR	MAY	JUN	JUL	AUG	SEP	OCT	NOV	DEC	YEAR
Mean Maximum Temp. (°F)	39.4	43.5	51.9	60.1	70.7	82.2	91.3	89.0	77.9	63.4	49.0	39.3	63.2
Mean Temp. (°F)	28.7	32.6	40.0	47.3	56.6	66.3	75.1	73.4	63.2	50.5	37.8	28.8	50.0
Mean Minimum Temp. (°F)	18.0	21.6	28.1	34.4	42.4	50.3	58.8	57.7	48.5	37.6	26.5	18.3	36.9
Extreme Maximum Temp. (°F)	62	67	78	86	99	101	107	104	95	87	74	66	107
Extreme Minimum Temp. (°F)	-9	-14	3	11	19	23	38	36	23	13	-1	-19	-19
Days Maximum Temp. ≥ 90°F	0	0	0	0	1	8	21	16	3	0	0	0	49
Days Maximum Temp. ≤ 32°F	7	3	0	0	0	0	0	0	0	0	2	7	19
Days Minimum Temp. ≤ 32°F	30	24	21	13	4	0	0	0	1	8	22	29	152
Days Minimum Temp. ≤ 0°F	1	1	0	0	0	0	0	0	0	0	0	1	3
Heating Degree Days (base 65°F)	1,118	910	767	526	280	83	6	6	122	445	809	1,115	6,187
Cooling Degree Days (base 65°F)	0	0	0	1	25	128	327	274	75	4	0	0	834
Mean Precipitation (in.)	1.50	1.69	1.61	1.64	2.03	1.08	1.10	1.00	1.23	1.49	1.29	1.41	17.07
Extreme Maximum Daily Precip. (in.)	1.23	1.15	0.98	1.20	1.73	1.73	1.53	1.70	1.48	1.80	1.20	1.73	1.80
Days With ≥ 0.1" Precipitation	4	4	5	5	5	3	3	3	3	4	4	4	47
Days With ≥ 0.5" Precipitation	0	1	1	1	1	1	0	1	1	1	1	1	10
Days With ≥ 1.0" Precipitation	0	0	0	0	0	0	0	0	0	0	0	0	0
Mean Snowfall (in.)	14.4	14.5	11.1	6.5	0.8	0.1	0.0	0.0	0.2	1.9	7.6	13.7	70.8
Maximum Snow Depth (in.)	28	34	28	20	2	trace	0	0	trace	4	17	28	34
Days With ≥ 1.0" Snow Depth	26	20	7	1	0	0	0	0	0	1	5	20	80

Maeser 9 NW *Uintah County* Elevation: 6,439 ft. Latitude: 40° 34' N Longitude: 109° 40' W

	JAN	FEB	MAR	APR	MAY	JUN	JUL	AUG	SEP	OCT	NOV	DEC	YEAR
Mean Maximum Temp. (°F)	33.2	37.8	49.0	58.5	67.9	77.7	85.3	83.1	73.1	60.0	44.1	33.1	58.6
Mean Temp. (°F)	21.2	26.0	36.7	45.1	53.9	62.8	70.5	68.4	59.1	47.3	32.9	21.9	45.5
Mean Minimum Temp. (°F)	9.2	14.1	24.2	31.7	39.8	47.8	55.4	53.7	45.0	34.4	21.7	10.7	32.3
Extreme Maximum Temp. (°F)	57	60	74	80	94	95	100	96	90	80	67	57	100
Extreme Minimum Temp. (°F)	-21	-26	-4	7	21	26	39	35	21	11	-4	-33	-33
Days Maximum Temp. ≥ 90°F	0	0	0	0	0	2	8	3	0	0	0	0	13
Days Maximum Temp. ≤ 32°F	14	6	1	0	0	0	0	0	0	0	3	14	38
Days Minimum Temp. ≤ 32°F	31	28	27	16	5	0	0	0	2	11	27	31	178
Days Minimum Temp. ≤ 0°F	6	2	0	0	0	0	0	0	0	0	1	4	13
Heating Degree Days (base 65°F)	1,350	1,098	872	591	341	113	11	16	190	543	955	1,329	7,409
Cooling Degree Days (base 65°F)	0	0	0	0	4	53	189	129	21	0	0	0	396
Mean Precipitation (in.)	0.82	1.00	1.07	1.25	1.43	1.21	1.04	1.06	1.72	1.65	0.96	0.81	14.02
Extreme Maximum Daily Precip. (in.)	0.70	0.83	1.02	0.85	1.05	1.85	1.34	1.12	1.23	2.05	0.91	***1.07***	***2.05***
Days With ≥ 0.1" Precipitation	3	3	3	4	4	4	3	3	4	4	3	3	41
Days With ≥ 0.5" Precipitation	0	0	0	1	1	0	0	0	1	1	0	0	4
Days With ≥ 1.0" Precipitation	0	0	0	0	0	0	0	0	0	0	0	0	0
Mean Snowfall (in.)	12.5	13.1	7.7	***4.3***	0.7	0.1	0.0	0.0	0.1	2.3	7.9	12.6	***61.3***
Maximum Snow Depth (in.)	***28***	***35***	***28***	***9***	2	0	0	0	1	***6***	15	***19***	***35***
Days With ≥ 1.0" Snow Depth	***25***	***24***	***12***	***1***	0	0	0	0	0	1	7	19	***89***

New Harmony *Washington County* Elevation: 5,265 ft. Latitude: 37° 29' N Longitude: 113° 19' W

	JAN	FEB	MAR	APR	MAY	JUN	JUL	AUG	SEP	OCT	NOV	DEC	YEAR
Mean Maximum Temp. (°F)	44.5	48.0	55.3	62.9	73.4	83.5	89.3	87.1	79.7	67.6	54.6	44.6	65.9
Mean Temp. (°F)	33.0	36.1	42.5	48.9	58.0	67.2	73.9	72.1	64.2	52.9	41.4	33.0	51.9
Mean Minimum Temp. (°F)	21.4	24.3	29.6	34.8	42.5	50.9	58.4	57.0	48.7	38.1	28.3	21.3	37.9
Extreme Maximum Temp. (°F)	67	76	80	85	95	98	104	101	94	88	77	69	104
Extreme Minimum Temp. (°F)	-7	-20	9	12	26	29	40	40	23	17	5	-19	-20
Days Maximum Temp. ≥ 90°F	0	0	0	0	1	6	16	10	1	0	0	0	34
Days Maximum Temp. ≤ 32°F	2	1	0	0	0	0	0	0	0	0	1	3	7
Days Minimum Temp. ≤ 32°F	29	25	20	12	2	0	0	0	1	7	21	29	146
Days Minimum Temp. ≤ 0°F	0	0	0	0	0	0	0	0	0	0	0	1	1
Heating Degree Days (base 65°F)	986	809	692	477	230	49	1	2	82	372	700	986	5,386
Cooling Degree Days (base 65°F)	0	0	0	0	19	123	283	229	65	3	0	0	722
Mean Precipitation (in.)	2.13	2.34	2.09	1.12	0.75	0.51	1.19	1.73	1.37	1.66	1.31	1.46	17.66
Extreme Maximum Daily Precip. (in.)	2.46	3.09	2.66	1.02	1.21	1.55	1.33	2.61	2.19	4.14	2.58	2.20	4.14
Days With ≥ 0.1" Precipitation	4	4	4	3	2	1	3	4	3	3	3	3	37
Days With ≥ 0.5" Precipitation	2	2	1	0	0	0	1	1	1	1	1	1	11
Days With ≥ 1.0" Precipitation	1	0	0	0	0	0	0	0	0	0	0	0	1
Mean Snowfall (in.)	***9.7***	11.5	7.2	1.5	trace	trace	0.0	0.0	0.0	0.3	3.5	8.7	***42.4***
Maximum Snow Depth (in.)	28	***22***	***12***	9	trace	trace	0	***0***	***0***	***2***	***13***	***23***	***28***
Days With ≥ 1.0" Snow Depth	***6***	4	2	1	0	0	0	0	0	0	1	4	***18***

The period of record for all cooperative weather station data is 1980 – 2009. See User Guide for detailed explanation of data.

Ogden Pioneer P H *Weber County* Elevation: 4,350 ft. Latitude: 41° 15' N Longitude: 111° 57' W

	JAN	FEB	MAR	APR	MAY	JUN	JUL	AUG	SEP	OCT	NOV	DEC	YEAR
Mean Maximum Temp. (°F)	37.0	43.0	53.6	62.4	72.1	82.0	91.1	89.4	78.6	65.0	49.3	38.1	63.5
Mean Temp. (°F)	29.3	33.8	43.3	51.0	60.0	69.0	77.5	76.0	65.8	53.2	40.2	30.4	52.4
Mean Minimum Temp. (°F)	21.5	24.5	33.0	39.7	47.8	55.9	63.8	62.5	52.9	41.4	31.0	22.7	41.4
Extreme Maximum Temp. (°F)	60	68	76	87	97	101	106	102	97	93	75	66	106
Extreme Minimum Temp. (°F)	-7	-11	9	19	21	33	45	44	33	21	9	-12	-12
Days Maximum Temp. ≥ 90°F	0	0	0	0	0	7	21	18	3	0	0	0	49
Days Maximum Temp. ≤ 32°F	9	4	0	0	0	0	0	0	0	0	1	8	22
Days Minimum Temp. ≤ 32°F	28	23	15	5	1	0	0	0	0	3	17	27	119
Days Minimum Temp. ≤ 0°F	0	0	0	0	0	0	0	0	0	0	0	0	0
Heating Degree Days (base 65°F)	1,100	875	665	418	199	52	2	3	81	364	739	1,065	5,563
Cooling Degree Days (base 65°F)	0	0	0	6	51	178	396	350	111	6	0	0	1,098
Mean Precipitation (in.)	2.26	2.06	2.22	2.26	2.82	1.56	0.91	0.91	1.70	2.26	2.01	1.91	22.88
Extreme Maximum Daily Precip. (in.)	1.29	1.24	1.57	2.30	2.29	1.70	1.96	2.70	3.19	2.30	1.20	2.05	3.19
Days With ≥ 0.1" Precipitation	6	5	6	5	6	3	2	2	3	4	5	5	52
Days With ≥ 0.5" Precipitation	1	1	1	1	2	1	1	1	1	1	1	1	13
Days With ≥ 1.0" Precipitation	0	0	0	0	0	0	0	0	0	1	0	0	1
Mean Snowfall (in.)	***7.8***	***6.3***	na	0.7	0.0	0.0	0.0	0.0	0.0	0.1	2.8	na	na
Maximum Snow Depth (in.)	23	***23***	12	2	0	0	0	0	0	4	13	24	***24***
Days With ≥ 1.0" Snow Depth	16	***11***	3	0	0	0	0	0	0	0	3	8	***41***

Santaquin Chlorinator *Utah County* Elevation: 5,164 ft. Latitude: 39° 57' N Longitude: 111° 47' W

	JAN	FEB	MAR	APR	MAY	JUN	JUL	AUG	SEP	OCT	NOV	DEC	YEAR
Mean Maximum Temp. (°F)	39.2	43.3	53.2	61.1	71.1	81.6	91.1	89.6	79.0	65.1	49.9	38.7	63.6
Mean Temp. (°F)	28.9	32.5	41.4	48.5	57.6	66.8	76.0	74.4	63.9	51.1	38.5	28.7	50.7
Mean Minimum Temp. (°F)	18.6	21.7	29.5	35.8	44.0	52.0	60.8	59.2	48.7	37.1	27.1	18.7	37.8
Extreme Maximum Temp. (°F)	61	71	82	86	96	100	108	104	98	88	78	69	108
Extreme Minimum Temp. (°F)	-10	-19	7	15	24	29	37	35	24	15	-2	-20	-20
Days Maximum Temp. ≥ 90°F	0	0	0	0	1	7	21	17	3	0	0	0	49
Days Maximum Temp. ≤ 32°F	7	3	0	0	0	0	0	0	0	0	1	8	19
Days Minimum Temp. ≤ 32°F	28	25	21	11	2	0	0	0	1	8	22	29	147
Days Minimum Temp. ≤ 0°F	1	0	0	0	0	0	0	0	0	0	0	1	2
Heating Degree Days (base 65°F)	1,113	913	726	492	253	76	6	4	113	426	788	1,118	6,028
Cooling Degree Days (base 65°F)	0	0	0	3	31	138	353	304	85	4	0	0	918
Mean Precipitation (in.)	1.62	1.79	2.04	2.04	2.16	1.04	0.65	0.88	1.47	2.13	1.69	1.52	19.03
Extreme Maximum Daily Precip. (in.)	1.64	1.98	1.91	1.33	1.66	1.63	1.20	1.17	1.94	1.52	1.60	1.47	1.98
Days With ≥ 0.1" Precipitation	4	4	5	6	4	3	2	2	3	4	4	4	45
Days With ≥ 0.5" Precipitation	1	1	1	1	1	0	0	0	1	1	1	1	9
Days With ≥ 1.0" Precipitation	0	0	0	0	0	0	0	0	0	0	0	0	0
Mean Snowfall (in.)	12.5	12.5	7.1	3.5	0.4	trace	0.0	0.0	0.1	1.0	7.4	12.0	56.5
Maximum Snow Depth (in.)	***22***	***30***	14	15	5	1	0	0	0	4	12	***17***	***30***
Days With ≥ 1.0" Snow Depth	***19***	***16***	5	1	0	0	0	0	0	0	5	13	***59***

Spanish Fork Pwr House *Utah County* Elevation: 4,720 ft. Latitude: 40° 05' N Longitude: 111° 36' W

	JAN	FEB	MAR	APR	MAY	JUN	JUL	AUG	SEP	OCT	NOV	DEC	YEAR
Mean Maximum Temp. (°F)	37.4	43.6	55.1	64.5	74.4	85.0	92.7	90.3	80.0	66.0	49.8	37.7	64.7
Mean Temp. (°F)	29.3	34.0	43.5	51.3	60.1	68.8	76.4	74.6	65.1	53.2	40.2	29.9	52.2
Mean Minimum Temp. (°F)	21.2	24.5	31.9	38.1	45.6	52.6	60.2	58.9	50.2	40.3	30.6	22.1	39.7
Extreme Maximum Temp. (°F)	60	72	81	87	97	101	106	103	95	87	75	65	106
Extreme Minimum Temp. (°F)	-10	-20	5	15	28	33	41	40	28	18	0	-14	-20
Days Maximum Temp. ≥ 90°F	0	0	0	0	1	11	24	18	3	0	0	0	57
Days Maximum Temp. ≤ 32°F	9	4	0	0	0	0	0	0	0	0	2	9	24
Days Minimum Temp. ≤ 32°F	28	23	16	6	1	0	0	0	0	4	17	27	122
Days Minimum Temp. ≤ 0°F	1	0	0	0	0	0	0	0	0	0	0	0	1
Heating Degree Days (base 65°F)	1,100	869	659	406	187	44	2	2	78	364	737	1,082	5,530
Cooling Degree Days (base 65°F)	0	0	0	3	40	165	363	308	89	4	0	0	972
Mean Precipitation (in.)	2.01	2.26	2.35	2.27	2.29	1.20	0.70	0.86	1.64	2.22	2.11	1.99	21.90
Extreme Maximum Daily Precip. (in.)	1.97	1.49	2.03	1.49	1.68	1.55	1.22	1.67	1.58	1.68	1.22	2.08	2.08
Days With ≥ 0.1" Precipitation	6	6	6	6	5	3	2	2	4	5	5	5	55
Days With ≥ 0.5" Precipitation	1	1	2	1	2	1	0	0	1	1	1	1	12
Days With ≥ 1.0" Precipitation	0	0	0	0	0	0	0	0	0	0	0	0	0
Mean Snowfall (in.)	17.2	14.3	7.0	3.8	trace	0.0	0.0	0.0	trace	0.8	8.0	15.9	67.0
Maximum Snow Depth (in.)	20	27	9	4	trace	2	0	0	0	3	10	24	27
Days With ≥ 1.0" Snow Depth	20	15	3	1	0	0	0	0	0	0	6	17	62

St George *Washington County* Elevation: 2,770 ft. Latitude: 37° 06' N Longitude: 113° 34' W

	JAN	FEB	MAR	APR	MAY	JUN	JUL	AUG	SEP	OCT	NOV	DEC	YEAR
Mean Maximum Temp. (°F)	55.5	60.5	69.3	77.4	***87.8***	97.7	***102.7***	100.5	92.9	***80.1***	64.5	54.1	***78.6***
Mean Temp. (°F)	***42.9***	47.4	54.8	62.3	***72.4***	81.3	***87.5***	85.6	77.1	***64.0***	50.8	41.8	***64.0***
Mean Minimum Temp. (°F)	***30.4***	34.2	40.3	47.1	***56.9***	64.8	***72.2***	70.7	61.3	47.8	36.9	29.5	***49.3***
Extreme Maximum Temp. (°F)	71	84	91	97	108	114	117	112	109	99	83	71	117
Extreme Minimum Temp. (°F)	12	8	22	29	37	43	53	53	42	26	17	3	3
Days Maximum Temp. ≥ 90°F	0	0	0	3	14	25	29	29	22	3	0	0	125
Days Maximum Temp. ≤ 32°F	0	0	0	0	0	0	0	0	0	0	0	0	0
Days Minimum Temp. ≤ 32°F	20	11	3	0	0	0	0	0	0	0	7	21	62
Days Minimum Temp. ≤ 0°F	0	0	0	0	0	0	0	0	0	0	0	0	0
Heating Degree Days (base 65°F)	***679***	491	313	130	***21***	1	***0***	0	3	***95***	421	718	***2,872***
Cooling Degree Days (base 65°F)	0	0	4	55	***257***	496	***703***	647	373	68	0	0	***2,603***
Mean Precipitation (in.)	1.20	1.25	1.03	0.61	0.22	0.20	0.55	0.65	0.57	0.71	0.70	0.71	8.40
Extreme Maximum Daily Precip. (in.)	***2.08***	1.10	1.33	1.00	***0.59***	***0.75***	***0.99***	1.11	1.32	0.90	1.01	1.85	***2.08***
Days With ≥ 0.1" Precipitation	***3***	3	3	2	1	1	2	2	2	2	2	2	***25***
Days With ≥ 0.5" Precipitation	1	1	0	0	0	0	0	0	0	0	0	0	2
Days With ≥ 1.0" Precipitation	0	0	0	0	0	0	0	0	0	0	0	0	0
Mean Snowfall (in.)	0.4	0.3	0.2	trace	0.0	0.0	0.0	0.0	0.0	0.0	0.1	0.1	1.1
Maximum Snow Depth (in.)	5	2	1	0	0	0	0	0	0	0	trace	trace	5
Days With ≥ 1.0" Snow Depth	0	0	0	0	0	0	0	0	0	0	0	0	0

The period of record for all cooperative weather station data is 1980 – 2009. See User Guide for detailed explanation of data.

Veyo Powerhouse *Washington County* Elevation: 4,600 ft. Latitude: 37° 21' N Longitude: 113° 40' W

	JAN	FEB	MAR	APR	MAY	JUN	JUL	AUG	SEP	OCT	NOV	DEC	YEAR
Mean Maximum Temp. (°F)	48.4	51.9	58.3	66.3	76.5	86.7	92.6	90.3	83.2	70.9	57.4	47.8	69.2
Mean Temp. (°F)	37.7	40.8	46.3	53.1	62.2	71.1	77.2	75.2	68.4	57.0	45.1	37.1	55.9
Mean Minimum Temp. (°F)	26.9	29.7	34.3	39.9	47.9	55.4	61.8	60.1	53.5	43.2	32.8	26.3	42.7
Extreme Maximum Temp. (°F)	69	75	83	85	101	101	107	102	98	90	78	66	107
Extreme Minimum Temp. (°F)	2	3	17	19	30	32	44	45	25	24	9	-3	-3
Days Maximum Temp. ≥ 90°F	0	0	0	0	2	13	23	18	4	0	0	0	60
Days Maximum Temp. ≤ 32°F	1	1	0	0	0	0	0	0	0	0	0	1	3
Days Minimum Temp. ≤ 32°F	26	19	13	4	0	0	0	0	0	2	15	25	104
Days Minimum Temp. ≤ 0°F	0	0	0	0	0	0	0	0	0	0	0	0	0
Heating Degree Days (base 65°F)	840	677	572	353	135	21	1	0	31	256	589	859	4,334
Cooling Degree Days (base 65°F)	0	0	0	3	56	210	387	325	139	16	0	0	1,136
Mean Precipitation (in.)	1.51	1.90	2.22	1.14	0.57	0.43	0.95	1.12	1.17	1.23	1.07	1.24	14.55
Extreme Maximum Daily Precip. (in.)	1.70	1.93	1.67	1.09	0.88	0.87	1.58	1.70	2.40	1.45	1.53	2.15	2.40
Days With ≥ 0.1" Precipitation	3	4	5	3	2	1	2	3	2	3	3	3	34
Days With ≥ 0.5" Precipitation	1	1	2	1	0	0	1	1	1	1	1	1	11
Days With ≥ 1.0" Precipitation	0	0	0	0	0	0	0	0	0	0	0	0	0
Mean Snowfall (in.)	***0.7***	***2.7***	1.6	0.3	0.0	0.0	0.0	0.0	0.0	0.0	0.8	2.7	***8.8***
Maximum Snow Depth (in.)	***12***	***8***	***12***	4	0	0	0	***0***	0	0	8	***10***	***12***
Days With ≥ 1.0" Snow Depth	***0***	1	1	0	0	0	0	0	0	0	0	1	***3***

Wanship Dam *Summit County* Elevation: 5,939 ft. Latitude: 40° 47' N Longitude: 111° 24' W

	JAN	FEB	MAR	APR	MAY	JUN	JUL	AUG	SEP	OCT	NOV	DEC	YEAR
Mean Maximum Temp. (°F)	36.9	40.7	49.5	59.4	69.3	79.6	88.0	86.8	76.6	63.5	48.0	37.1	61.3
Mean Temp. (°F)	24.5	27.9	36.3	44.3	52.7	60.6	68.0	66.7	57.5	46.4	34.4	25.2	45.4
Mean Minimum Temp. (°F)	12.0	15.0	23.1	29.2	36.0	41.6	47.9	46.5	38.5	29.4	20.9	13.2	29.4
Extreme Maximum Temp. (°F)	58	65	78	83	94	97	101	99	93	85	72	65	101
Extreme Minimum Temp. (°F)	-25	-37	-15	4	16	22	26	23	12	2	-21	-28	-37
Days Maximum Temp. ≥ 90°F	0	0	0	0	0	3	13	10	1	0	0	0	27
Days Maximum Temp. ≤ 32°F	9	4	0	0	0	0	0	0	0	0	2	9	24
Days Minimum Temp. ≤ 32°F	30	27	27	20	9	3	0	0	7	20	26	29	198
Days Minimum Temp. ≤ 0°F	6	3	0	0	0	0	0	0	0	0	1	4	14
Heating Degree Days (base 65°F)	1,250	1,042	883	613	378	152	25	30	228	570	909	1,229	7,309
Cooling Degree Days (base 65°F)	0	0	0	0	3	28	123	89	11	0	0	0	254
Mean Precipitation (in.)	1.23	1.04	1.48	1.74	2.05	1.19	1.00	1.04	1.58	1.74	1.64	1.06	16.79
Extreme Maximum Daily Precip. (in.)	0.88	0.75	0.87	1.06	1.47	1.09	1.76	1.43	1.76	1.47	1.30	0.69	1.76
Days With ≥ 0.1" Precipitation	4	4	5	5	6	4	3	3	4	5	5	4	52
Days With ≥ 0.5" Precipitation	0	0	0	1	1	1	1	0	1	1	1	0	7
Days With ≥ 1.0" Precipitation	0	0	0	0	0	0	0	0	0	0	0	0	0
Mean Snowfall (in.)	***17.7***	***13.9***	***10.0***	5.2	0.8	0.1	0.0	0.0	0.3	2.0	***13.0***	***14.7***	***77.7***
Maximum Snow Depth (in.)	***33***	***20***	***14***	***5***	4	trace	0	0	4	***5***	***14***	na	na
Days With ≥ 1.0" Snow Depth	na	***21***	***6***	1	0	0	0	0	0	0	***8***	***22***	na

Woodruff *Rich County* Elevation: 6,314 ft. Latitude: 41° 32' N Longitude: 111° 09' W

	JAN	FEB	MAR	APR	MAY	JUN	JUL	AUG	SEP	OCT	NOV	DEC	YEAR
Mean Maximum Temp. (°F)	28.3	31.5	43.7	55.5	64.8	74.3	82.7	81.5	71.9	59.1	42.2	29.3	55.4
Mean Temp. (°F)	15.7	18.5	30.6	40.1	48.6	56.6	63.5	61.8	52.6	41.5	28.6	17.0	39.6
Mean Minimum Temp. (°F)	3.0	5.5	17.5	24.6	32.3	38.9	44.2	42.1	33.3	24.0	15.0	4.7	23.8
Extreme Maximum Temp. (°F)	55	58	71	80	89	93	97	94	90	82	69	60	97
Extreme Minimum Temp. (°F)	-40	-46	-29	-1	9	21	28	20	8	-5	-26	-44	-46
Days Maximum Temp. ≥ 90°F	0	0	0	0	0	0	4	2	0	0	0	0	6
Days Maximum Temp. ≤ 32°F	19	13	4	0	0	0	0	0	0	0	6	18	60
Days Minimum Temp. ≤ 32°F	31	28	30	27	15	4	0	2	14	27	29	31	238
Days Minimum Temp. ≤ 0°F	13	10	2	0	0	0	0	0	0	0	3	12	40
Heating Degree Days (base 65°F)	1,523	1,309	1,059	741	503	248	73	109	365	721	1,085	1,481	9,217
Cooling Degree Days (base 65°F)	0	0	0	0	0	3	34	17	1	0	0	0	55
Mean Precipitation (in.)	0.52	0.53	0.60	0.89	1.32	1.05	0.70	0.90	1.24	1.08	0.68	0.48	9.99
Extreme Maximum Daily Precip. (in.)	0.67	0.87	1.02	1.13	0.86	1.74	1.20	1.30	1.65	1.16	0.66	0.56	1.74
Days With ≥ 0.1" Precipitation	2	2	2	3	4	3	2	3	3	3	2	2	31
Days With ≥ 0.5" Precipitation	0	0	0	0	0	1	0	0	1	1	0	0	3
Days With ≥ 1.0" Precipitation	0	0	0	0	0	0	0	0	0	0	0	0	0
Mean Snowfall (in.)	8.5	9.0	6.4	4.4	1.0	0.1	0.0	0.0	0.9	2.9	6.6	8.2	48.0
Maximum Snow Depth (in.)	27	25	22	7	7	trace	0	0	11	10	13	18	27
Days With ≥ 1.0" Snow Depth	14	14	9	2	0	0	0	0	0	1	5	13	58

The period of record for all cooperative weather station data is 1980 – 2009. See User Guide for detailed explanation of data.

Utah Weather Station Rankings

Annual Extreme Maximum Temperature

Highest

Rank	Station Name	°F
1	St George	117
2	Arches Np Hqs	116
3	Dugway	109
4	Ephraim Sorensens Fld	108
4	Garfield	108
4	Santaquin Chlorinator	108
7	Castle Dale	107
7	Johnson Pass	107
7	Salt Lake City Int'l Arpt	107
7	Veyo Powerhouse	107
11	Callao	106
11	Ogden Pioneer P H	106
11	Spanish Fork Pwr House	106
14	Canyonlands The Neck	105
14	Eskdale	105
14	Farmington Usu Fld Stn	105
17	Alpine	***104***
17	Black Rock	104
17	Bountiful-Val Verda	104
17	Brigham City Waste Plt	104
17	New Harmony	104
22	Angle	102
22	Coalville	102
22	Flaming Gorge	102
22	Heber	102

Lowest

Rank	Station Name	°F
1	Alta	86
2	Blowhard Mtn Radar	***90***
3	Electric Lake U P & L	***92***
4	Boulder	96
5	Altamont	97
5	Woodruff	97
7	Deer Creek Dam	100
7	Echo Dam	100
7	Maeser 9 NW	100
10	Wanship Dam	101
11	Angle	102
11	Coalville	102
11	Flaming Gorge	102
11	Heber	102
11	Huntsville Monastery	102
16	Alpine	***104***
16	Black Rock	104
16	Bountiful-Val Verda	104
16	Brigham City Waste Plt	104
16	New Harmony	104
21	Canyonlands The Neck	105
21	Eskdale	105
21	Farmington Usu Fld Stn	105
24	Callao	106
24	Ogden Pioneer P H	106

Annual Mean Maximum Temperature

Highest

Rank	Station Name	°F
1	St George	***78.6***
2	Arches Np Hqs	71.4
3	Veyo Powerhouse	69.2
4	Black Rock	67.0
5	Eskdale	66.8
6	Dugway	66.1
7	New Harmony	65.9
8	Callao	65.1
9	Spanish Fork Pwr House	64.7
10	Farmington Usu Fld Stn	64.6
11	Castle Dale	64.4
12	Salt Lake City Int'l Arpt	64.0
13	Garfield	***63.7***
14	Santaquin Chlorinator	63.6
15	Alpine	***63.5***
15	Ogden Pioneer P H	63.5
17	Canyonlands The Neck	63.3
18	Johnson Pass	63.2
19	Ephraim Sorensens Fld	63.1
20	Angle	63.0
20	Brigham City Waste Plt	63.0
22	Heber	62.2
23	Bountiful-Val Verda	61.9
24	Boulder	61.8
24	Coalville	61.8

Lowest

Rank	Station Name	°F
1	Blowhard Mtn Radar	***44.1***
2	Electric Lake U P & L	***47.7***
3	Alta	47.9
4	Woodruff	55.4
5	Altamont	57.6
6	Maeser 9 NW	58.6
7	Deer Creek Dam	59.4
8	Echo Dam	60.1
8	Flaming Gorge	60.1
10	Huntsville Monastery	61.2
11	Wanship Dam	61.3
12	Boulder	61.8
12	Coalville	61.8
14	Bountiful-Val Verda	61.9
15	Heber	62.2
16	Angle	63.0
16	Brigham City Waste Plt	63.0
18	Ephraim Sorensens Fld	63.1
19	Johnson Pass	63.2
20	Canyonlands The Neck	63.3
21	Alpine	***63.5***
21	Ogden Pioneer P H	63.5
23	Santaquin Chlorinator	63.6
24	Garfield	***63.7***
25	Salt Lake City Int'l Arpt	64.0

Rankings include 25 highest/lowest stations. If state has less than 25 stations, all stations are included. The period of record is 1980–2009. See User Guide for detailed explanation of data.

Annual Mean Temperature

Highest Rank	Station Name	°F	Lowest Rank	Station Name	°F
1	St George	***64.0***	1	Electric Lake U P & L	***34.3***
2	Arches Np Hqs	57.3	2	Blowhard Mtn Radar	***36.4***
3	Veyo Powerhouse	55.9	3	Alta	38.5
4	Garfield	***54.5***	4	Woodruff	39.6
5	Canyonlands The Neck	53.0	5	Altamont	43.9
6	Salt Lake City Int'l Arpt	52.9	6	Deer Creek Dam	44.3
7	Farmington Usu Fld Stn	52.5	7	Angle	44.6
7	Ogden Pioneer P H	52.5	8	Flaming Gorge	44.8
9	Spanish Fork Pwr House	52.2	9	Huntsville Monastery	45.1
10	New Harmony	51.9	10	Echo Dam	45.3
11	Bountiful-Val Verda	51.8	11	Wanship Dam	45.4
12	Dugway	51.3	12	Coalville	45.5
13	Eskdale	51.1	12	Maeser 9 NW	45.5
14	Santaquin Chlorinator	50.7	14	Heber	46.7
15	Alpine	***50.4***	15	Castle Dale	48.0
16	Black Rock	50.1	15	Ephraim Sorensens Fld	48.0
16	Callao	50.1	17	Boulder	49.7
18	Johnson Pass	50.0	18	Brigham City Waste Plt	49.8
19	Brigham City Waste Plt	49.8	19	Johnson Pass	50.0
20	Boulder	49.7	20	Black Rock	50.1
21	Castle Dale	48.0	20	Callao	50.1
21	Ephraim Sorensens Fld	48.0	22	Alpine	***50.4***
23	Heber	46.7	23	Santaquin Chlorinator	50.7
24	Coalville	45.5	24	Eskdale	51.1
24	Maeser 9 NW	45.5	25	Dugway	51.3

Annual Mean Minimum Temperature

Highest Rank	Station Name	°F	Lowest Rank	Station Name	°F
1	St George	***49.3***	1	Electric Lake U P & L	***21.0***
2	Garfield	***45.2***	2	Woodruff	23.8
3	Arches Np Hqs	43.2	3	Angle	26.2
4	Canyonlands The Neck	42.7	4	Blowhard Mtn Radar	***28.6***
4	Veyo Powerhouse	42.7	5	Huntsville Monastery	29.0
6	Salt Lake City Int'l Arpt	41.8	6	Alta	29.1
7	Bountiful-Val Verda	41.7	7	Deer Creek Dam	29.2
8	Ogden Pioneer P H	41.4	8	Coalville	29.3
9	Farmington Usu Fld Stn	40.4	9	Flaming Gorge	29.4
10	Spanish Fork Pwr House	39.7	9	Wanship Dam	29.4
11	New Harmony	37.9	11	Altamont	30.1
12	Santaquin Chlorinator	37.8	12	Echo Dam	30.5
13	Boulder	37.6	13	Heber	31.2
14	Alpine	***37.3***	14	Castle Dale	31.5
15	Johnson Pass	36.9	15	Maeser 9 NW	32.3
16	Brigham City Waste Plt	36.5	16	Ephraim Sorensens Fld	32.7
17	Dugway	36.3	17	Black Rock	33.1
18	Eskdale	35.3	18	Callao	35.1
19	Callao	35.1	19	Eskdale	35.3
20	Black Rock	33.1	20	Dugway	36.3
21	Ephraim Sorensens Fld	32.7	21	Brigham City Waste Plt	36.5
22	Maeser 9 NW	32.3	22	Johnson Pass	36.9
23	Castle Dale	31.5	23	Alpine	***37.3***
24	Heber	31.2	24	Boulder	37.6
25	Echo Dam	30.5	25	Santaquin Chlorinator	37.8

Rankings include 25 highest/lowest stations. If state has less than 25 stations, all stations are included. The period of record is 1980–2009. See User Guide for detailed explanation of data.

Annual Extreme Minimum Temperature

Highest			Lowest		
Rank	Station Name	°F	Rank	Station Name	°F
1	St George	3	1	Electric Lake U P & L	***-48***
2	Veyo Powerhouse	-3	2	Woodruff	-46
3	Garfield	-6	3	Deer Creek Dam	-39
4	Arches Np Hqs	-8	4	Black Rock	-37
5	Bountiful-Val Verda	-9	4	Huntsville Monastery	-37
6	Farmington Usu Fld Stn	-12	4	Wanship Dam	-37
6	Ogden Pioneer P H	-12	7	Flaming Gorge	-36
8	Canyonlands The Neck	-13	7	Heber	-36
9	Salt Lake City Int'l Arpt	-14	9	Echo Dam	-34
10	Boulder	-17	9	Ephraim Sorensens Fld	-34
11	Johnson Pass	-19	11	Coalville	-33
12	Alpine	***-20***	11	Maeser 9 NW	-33
12	Blowhard Mtn Radar	***-20***	13	Altamont	-32
12	New Harmony	-20	13	Angle	-32
12	Santaquin Chlorinator	-20	15	Eskdale	-31
12	Spanish Fork Pwr House	-20	16	Dugway	-29
17	Callao	-23	17	Castle Dale	-28
18	Alta	-25	18	Alta	-25
18	Brigham City Waste Plt	-25	18	Brigham City Waste Plt	-25
20	Castle Dale	-28	20	Callao	-23
21	Dugway	-29	21	Alpine	***-20***
22	Eskdale	-31	21	Blowhard Mtn Radar	***-20***
23	Altamont	-32	21	New Harmony	-20
23	Angle	-32	21	Santaquin Chlorinator	-20
25	Coalville	-33	21	Spanish Fork Pwr House	-20

July Mean Maximum Temperature

Highest			Lowest		
Rank	Station Name	°F	Rank	Station Name	°F
1	St George	***102.7***	1	Blowhard Mtn Radar	***64.8***
2	Arches Np Hqs	99.2	2	Alta	72.0
3	Dugway	95.5	3	Electric Lake U P & L	73.3
4	Black Rock	93.0	4	Woodruff	82.7
4	Eskdale	93.0	5	Altamont	83.9
6	Salt Lake City Int'l Arpt	92.8	6	Boulder	84.7
7	Spanish Fork Pwr House	92.7	7	Maeser 9 NW	85.4
8	Veyo Powerhouse	92.6	8	Deer Creek Dam	85.7
9	Farmington Usu Fld Stn	92.5	9	Angle	86.3
10	Garfield	92.3	10	Flaming Gorge	86.7
10	Milford Airport	***92.3***	11	Echo Dam	86.9
12	Callao	91.4	12	Coalville	87.9
13	Johnson Pass	91.3	13	Wanship Dam	88.0
14	Ogden Pioneer P H	91.1	14	Heber	88.5
14	Santaquin Chlorinator	91.1	14	Huntsville Monastery	88.5
16	Brigham City Waste Plt	90.9	16	New Harmony	89.3
16	Ephraim Sorensens Fld	90.9	17	Bountiful-Val Verda	89.6
18	Canyonlands The Neck	90.5	18	Castle Dale	89.8
19	Alpine	90.1	19	Alpine	90.1
20	Castle Dale	89.8	20	Canyonlands The Neck	90.5
21	Bountiful-Val Verda	89.6	21	Brigham City Waste Plt	90.9
22	New Harmony	89.3	21	Ephraim Sorensens Fld	90.9
23	Heber	88.5	23	Ogden Pioneer P H	91.1
23	Huntsville Monastery	88.5	23	Santaquin Chlorinator	91.1
25	Wanship Dam	88.0	25	Johnson Pass	91.3

 Rankings include 25 highest/lowest stations. If state has less than 25 stations, all stations are included. The period of record is 1980–2009. See User Guide for detailed explanation of data.

January Mean Minimum Temperature

Highest Rank	Station Name	°F	Lowest Rank	Station Name	°F
1	St George	***30.4***	1	Electric Lake U P & L	1.4
2	Veyo Powerhouse	27.0	2	Woodruff	3.0
3	Garfield	24.2	3	Angle	6.4
4	Bountiful-Val Verda	22.2	4	Altamont	7.9
5	Salt Lake City Int'l Arpt	21.8	5	Castle Dale	9.2
6	Canyonlands The Neck	21.5	5	Maeser 9 NW	9.2
6	Farmington Usu Fld Stn	21.5	7	Huntsville Monastery	10.0
6	Ogden Pioneer P H	21.5	8	Flaming Gorge	10.3
9	New Harmony	21.4	9	Deer Creek Dam	10.5
10	Spanish Fork Pwr House	21.2	10	Echo Dam	11.6
11	Arches Np Hqs	20.4	11	Wanship Dam	12.0
12	Alpine	20.3	12	Coalville	12.3
13	Boulder	19.2	13	Heber	12.4
14	Santaquin Chlorinator	18.6	14	Ephraim Sorensens Fld	13.2
15	Johnson Pass	18.0	15	Alta	14.0
16	Brigham City Waste Plt	17.8	16	Blowhard Mtn Radar	14.6
17	Black Rock	15.5	17	Eskdale	14.9
18	Dugway	15.2	18	Callao	15.1
19	Callao	15.1	19	Dugway	15.2
20	Eskdale	14.9	20	Black Rock	15.5
21	Blowhard Mtn Radar	14.6	21	Brigham City Waste Plt	17.8
22	Alta	14.0	22	Johnson Pass	18.0
23	Ephraim Sorensens Fld	13.2	23	Santaquin Chlorinator	18.6
24	Heber	12.4	24	Boulder	19.2
25	Coalville	12.3	25	Alpine	20.3

Number of Days Annually Maximum Temperature ≥ 90°F

Highest Rank	Station Name	Days	Lowest Rank	Station Name	Days
1	St George	125	1	Alta	0
2	Arches Np Hqs	98	1	Blowhard Mtn Radar	***0***
3	Dugway	73	1	Electric Lake U P & L	***0***
4	Eskdale	63	4	Woodruff	6
5	Black Rock	60	5	Altamont	7
5	Veyo Powerhouse	60	6	Boulder	9
7	Salt Lake City Int'l Arpt	57	7	Deer Creek Dam	13
7	Spanish Fork Pwr House	57	7	Maeser 9 NW	13
9	Farmington Usu Fld Stn	55	9	Angle	14
10	Garfield	53	10	Echo Dam	18
11	Callao	52	11	Flaming Gorge	19
12	Johnson Pass	49	12	Coalville	27
12	Ogden Pioneer P H	49	12	Wanship Dam	27
12	Santaquin Chlorinator	49	14	Heber	30
15	Brigham City Waste Plt	45	15	Huntsville Monastery	31
16	Ephraim Sorensens Fld	44	16	New Harmony	34
17	Canyonlands The Neck	40	17	Alpine	***36***
18	Castle Dale	38	17	Bountiful-Val Verda	36
19	Alpine	***36***	19	Castle Dale	38
19	Bountiful-Val Verda	36	20	Canyonlands The Neck	40
21	New Harmony	34	21	Ephraim Sorensens Fld	44
22	Huntsville Monastery	31	22	Brigham City Waste Plt	45
23	Heber	30	23	Johnson Pass	49
24	Coalville	27	23	Ogden Pioneer P H	49
24	Wanship Dam	27	23	Santaquin Chlorinator	49

Number of Days Annually Maximum Temperature ≤ 32°F

Highest			Lowest		
Rank	Station Name	Days	Rank	Station Name	Days
1	Electric Lake U P & L	*95*	1	St George	0
2	Blowhard Mtn Radar	*91*	2	Veyo Powerhouse	3
3	Alta	86	3	Arches Np Hqs	7
4	Woodruff	60	3	New Harmony	7
5	Altamont	43	5	Boulder	12
6	Maeser 9 NW	38	6	Angle	14
7	Echo Dam	37	7	Black Rock	16
8	Deer Creek Dam	35	7	Castle Dale	16
9	Huntsville Monastery	30	9	Eskdale	17
10	Flaming Gorge	29	10	Callao	18
11	Bountiful-Val Verda	27	10	Farmington Usu Fld Stn	18
11	Coalville	27	12	Alpine	*19*
11	Heber	27	12	Canyonlands The Neck	19
14	Brigham City Waste Plt	25	12	Johnson Pass	19
15	Ephraim Sorensens Fld	24	12	Santaquin Chlorinator	19
15	Spanish Fork Pwr House	24	16	Dugway	20
15	Wanship Dam	24	16	Garfield	20
18	Salt Lake City Int'l Arpt	23	18	Ogden Pioneer P H	22
19	Ogden Pioneer P H	22	19	Salt Lake City Int'l Arpt	23
20	Dugway	20	20	Ephraim Sorensens Fld	24
20	Garfield	20	20	Spanish Fork Pwr House	24
22	Alpine	*19*	20	Wanship Dam	24
22	Canyonlands The Neck	19	23	Brigham City Waste Plt	25
22	Johnson Pass	19	24	Bountiful-Val Verda	27
22	Santaquin Chlorinator	19	24	Coalville	27

Number of Days Annually Minimum Temperature ≤ 32°F

Highest			Lowest		
Rank	Station Name	Days	Rank	Station Name	Days
1	Electric Lake U P & L	*255*	1	St George	62
2	Woodruff	238	2	Garfield	98
3	Angle	226	3	Veyo Powerhouse	104
4	Alta	211	4	Arches Np Hqs	115
5	Coalville	204	5	Salt Lake City Int'l Arpt	116
6	Blowhard Mtn Radar	*203*	6	Bountiful-Val Verda	118
6	Huntsville Monastery	203	7	Ogden Pioneer P H	119
8	Flaming Gorge	201	8	Canyonlands The Neck	122
9	Deer Creek Dam	200	8	Spanish Fork Pwr House	122
10	Wanship Dam	198	10	Farmington Usu Fld Stn	124
11	Altamont	197	11	Alpine	*141*
12	Echo Dam	192	12	New Harmony	146
13	Castle Dale	189	13	Santaquin Chlorinator	147
14	Heber	185	14	Brigham City Waste Plt	149
15	Black Rock	179	15	Johnson Pass	152
16	Maeser 9 NW	178	16	Boulder	153
17	Ephraim Sorensens Fld	177	17	Dugway	160
18	Callao	163	17	Eskdale	160
19	Dugway	160	19	Callao	163
19	Eskdale	160	20	Ephraim Sorensens Fld	177
21	Boulder	153	21	Maeser 9 NW	178
22	Johnson Pass	152	22	Black Rock	179
23	Brigham City Waste Plt	149	23	Heber	185
24	Santaquin Chlorinator	147	24	Castle Dale	189
25	New Harmony	146	25	Echo Dam	192

 Rankings include 25 highest/lowest stations. If state has less than 25 stations, all stations are included. The period of record is 1980–2009. See User Guide for detailed explanation of data.

Number of Days Annually Minimum Temperature ≤ 0°F

Highest Rank	Station Name	Days	Lowest Rank	Station Name	Days
1	Electric Lake U P & L	***48***	1	Arches Np Hqs	0
2	Woodruff	40	1	Boulder	0
3	Angle	20	1	Bountiful-Val Verda	0
3	Huntsville Monastery	20	1	Canyonlands The Neck	0
5	Flaming Gorge	19	1	Farmington Usu Fld Stn	0
6	Altamont	17	1	Garfield	0
7	Coalville	16	1	Ogden Pioneer P H	0
8	Echo Dam	15	1	St George	0
9	Wanship Dam	14	1	Veyo Powerhouse	0
10	Deer Creek Dam	13	10	New Harmony	1
10	Heber	13	10	Salt Lake City Int'l Arpt	1
10	Maeser 9 NW	13	10	Spanish Fork Pwr House	1
13	Castle Dale	12	13	Santaquin Chlorinator	2
14	Black Rock	11	14	Alpine	***3***
14	Ephraim Sorensens Fld	11	14	Johnson Pass	3
16	Alta	8	16	Brigham City Waste Plt	6
16	Blowhard Mtn Radar	***8***	16	Callao	6
16	Dugway	8	16	Eskdale	6
19	Brigham City Waste Plt	6	19	Alta	8
19	Callao	6	19	Blowhard Mtn Radar	***8***
19	Eskdale	6	19	Dugway	8
22	Alpine	***3***	22	Black Rock	11
22	Johnson Pass	3	22	Ephraim Sorensens Fld	11
24	Santaquin Chlorinator	2	24	Castle Dale	12
25	New Harmony	1	25	Deer Creek Dam	13

Number of Annual Heating Degree Days

Highest Rank	Station Name	Num.	Lowest Rank	Station Name	Num.
1	Electric Lake U P & L	***11,086***	1	St George	***2,872***
2	Blowhard Mtn Radar	***10,354***	2	Veyo Powerhouse	4,334
3	Alta	9,582	3	Arches Np Hqs	4,509
4	Woodruff	9,217	4	Garfield	***5,186***
5	Altamont	7,853	5	New Harmony	5,386
6	Deer Creek Dam	7,602	6	Canyonlands The Neck	5,484
7	Flaming Gorge	7,534	7	Farmington Usu Fld Stn	5,492
8	Angle	7,466	8	Salt Lake City Int'l Arpt	5,509
9	Huntsville Monastery	7,416	9	Spanish Fork Pwr House	5,530
10	Maeser 9 NW	7,409	10	Ogden Pioneer P H	5,563
11	Echo Dam	7,347	11	Bountiful-Val Verda	5,712
12	Wanship Dam	7,309	12	Eskdale	5,847
13	Coalville	7,213	13	Alpine	***5,892***
14	Heber	6,901	14	Dugway	5,969
15	Ephraim Sorensens Fld	6,630	15	Boulder	6,005
16	Castle Dale	6,582	16	Black Rock	6,006
17	Johnson Pass	6,187	17	Santaquin Chlorinator	6,028
18	Brigham City Waste Plt	6,141	18	Callao	6,093
19	Callao	6,093	19	Brigham City Waste Plt	6,141
20	Santaquin Chlorinator	6,028	20	Johnson Pass	6,187
21	Black Rock	6,006	21	Castle Dale	6,582
22	Boulder	6,005	22	Ephraim Sorensens Fld	6,630
23	Dugway	5,969	23	Heber	6,901
24	Alpine	***5,892***	24	Coalville	7,213
25	Eskdale	5,847	25	Wanship Dam	7,309

Rankings include 25 highest/lowest stations. If state has less than 25 stations, all stations are included. The period of record is 1980–2009. See User Guide for detailed explanation of data.

Number of Annual Cooling Degree Days

Highest			Lowest		
Rank	Station Name	Num.	Rank	Station Name	Num.
1	St George	***2,603***	1	Electric Lake U P & L	***3***
2	Arches Np Hqs	1,818	2	Blowhard Mtn Radar	***8***
3	Garfield	***1,453***	3	Alta	22
4	Canyonlands The Neck	1,220	4	Woodruff	55
5	Salt Lake City Int'l Arpt	1,209	5	Angle	134
6	Veyo Powerhouse	1,136	6	Deer Creek Dam	168
7	Ogden Pioneer P H	1,098	7	Coalville	216
8	Dugway	1,063	8	Wanship Dam	254
9	Farmington Usu Fld Stn	1,050	9	Altamont	259
10	Bountiful-Val Verda	1,008	10	Flaming Gorge	262
11	Spanish Fork Pwr House	972	11	Huntsville Monastery	265
12	Santaquin Chlorinator	918	12	Echo Dam	272
13	Eskdale	868	13	Heber	331
14	Johnson Pass	834	14	Maeser 9 NW	396
15	Callao	767	15	Castle Dale	477
16	New Harmony	722	16	Ephraim Sorensens Fld	517
17	Brigham City Waste Plt	698	17	Boulder	537
18	Alpine	***680***	18	Black Rock	653
19	Black Rock	653	19	Alpine	***680***
20	Boulder	537	20	Brigham City Waste Plt	698
21	Ephraim Sorensens Fld	517	21	New Harmony	722
22	Castle Dale	477	22	Callao	767
23	Maeser 9 NW	396	23	Johnson Pass	834
24	Heber	331	24	Eskdale	868
25	Echo Dam	272	25	Santaquin Chlorinator	918

Annual Precipitation

Highest			Lowest		
Rank	Station Name	Inches	Rank	Station Name	Inches
1	Alta	50.54	1	Callao	6.56
2	Blowhard Mtn Radar	***29.24***	2	Eskdale	6.78
3	Electric Lake U P & L	***24.50***	3	Castle Dale	8.19
4	Deer Creek Dam	23.88	4	St George	8.40
5	Bountiful-Val Verda	23.42	5	Arches Np Hqs	8.65
6	Ogden Pioneer P H	22.88	5	Dugway	8.65
7	Farmington Usu Fld Stn	22.49	7	Angle	***8.93***
8	Huntsville Monastery	22.33	8	Black Rock	9.19
9	Spanish Fork Pwr House	21.90	9	Canyonlands The Neck	9.30
10	Alpine	***20.55***	10	Altamont	9.72
11	Santaquin Chlorinator	19.03	11	Woodruff	9.99
12	Garfield	18.83	12	Milford Airport	***10.36***
13	New Harmony	17.66	13	Boulder	11.10
14	Brigham City Waste Plt	17.22	14	Flaming Gorge	12.15
15	Johnson Pass	17.07	15	Ephraim Sorensens Fld	13.13
16	Coalville	17.00	16	Maeser 9 NW	14.02
17	Wanship Dam	16.79	17	Veyo Powerhouse	14.55
18	Salt Lake City Int'l Arpt	16.04	18	Echo Dam	15.11
19	Heber	15.75	19	Heber	15.75
20	Echo Dam	15.11	20	Salt Lake City Int'l Arpt	16.04
21	Veyo Powerhouse	14.55	21	Wanship Dam	16.79
22	Maeser 9 NW	14.02	22	Coalville	17.00
23	Ephraim Sorensens Fld	13.13	23	Johnson Pass	17.07
24	Flaming Gorge	12.15	24	Brigham City Waste Plt	17.22
25	Boulder	11.10	25	New Harmony	17.66

Rankings include 25 highest/lowest stations. If state has less than 25 stations, all stations are included. The period of record is 1980–2009. See User Guide for detailed explanation of data.

Annual Extreme Maximum Daily Precipitation

Highest			Lowest		
Rank	Station Name	Inches	Rank	Station Name	Inches
1	Deer Creek Dam	4.52	1	Altamont	1.44
2	New Harmony	4.14	2	Canyonlands The Neck	1.45
3	Alta	3.50	2	Ephraim Sorensens Fld	1.45
4	Ogden Pioneer P H	3.19	4	Dugway	1.46
5	Garfield	***3.17***	5	Echo Dam	1.55
6	Farmington Usu Fld Stn	3.14	6	Arches Np Hqs	1.62
7	Milford Airport	***3.00***	7	Angle	***1.64***
8	Brigham City Waste Plt	2.93	8	Heber	1.71
9	Boulder	2.88	9	Woodruff	1.74
10	Huntsville Monastery	2.80	10	Wanship Dam	1.76
11	Coalville	2.60	11	Electric Lake U P & L	***1.80***
12	Flaming Gorge	***2.50***	11	Johnson Pass	1.80
13	Veyo Powerhouse	2.40	13	Alpine	***1.87***
14	Bountiful-Val Verda	2.39	13	Black Rock	1.87
15	Eskdale	***2.30***	15	Santaquin Chlorinator	1.98
16	Salt Lake City Int'l Arpt	2.27	16	Maeser 9 NW	***2.05***
17	Castle Dale	2.15	17	Spanish Fork Pwr House	2.08
18	Callao	2.12	17	St George	***2.08***
19	Spanish Fork Pwr House	2.08	19	Callao	2.12
19	St George	***2.08***	20	Castle Dale	2.15
21	Maeser 9 NW	***2.05***	21	Salt Lake City Int'l Arpt	2.27
22	Santaquin Chlorinator	1.98	22	Eskdale	***2.30***
23	Alpine	***1.87***	23	Bountiful-Val Verda	2.39
23	Black Rock	1.87	24	Veyo Powerhouse	2.40
25	Electric Lake U P & L	***1.80***	25	Flaming Gorge	***2.50***

Number of Days Annually With ≥ 0.1 Inches of Precipitation

Highest			Lowest		
Rank	Station Name	Days	Rank	Station Name	Days
1	Alta	94	1	Callao	20
2	Electric Lake U P & L	***70***	1	Eskdale	20
3	Blowhard Mtn Radar	***61***	3	St George	***25***
4	Huntsville Monastery	57	4	Arches Np Hqs	26
5	Alpine	***55***	5	Castle Dale	27
5	Bountiful-Val Verda	55	6	Angle	***28***
5	Coalville	55	6	Canyonlands The Neck	28
5	Deer Creek Dam	55	6	Dugway	28
5	Spanish Fork Pwr House	55	9	Black Rock	29
10	Farmington Usu Fld Stn	53	10	Altamont	31
11	Ogden Pioneer P H	52	10	Milford Airport	***31***
11	Wanship Dam	52	10	Woodruff	31
13	Heber	47	13	Boulder	32
13	Johnson Pass	47	14	Veyo Powerhouse	34
13	Salt Lake City Int'l Arpt	47	15	Flaming Gorge	35
16	Echo Dam	46	16	New Harmony	37
16	Garfield	46	17	Maeser 9 NW	41
18	Brigham City Waste Plt	45	18	Ephraim Sorensens Fld	43
18	Santaquin Chlorinator	45	19	Brigham City Waste Plt	45
20	Ephraim Sorensens Fld	43	19	Santaquin Chlorinator	45
21	Maeser 9 NW	41	21	Echo Dam	46
22	New Harmony	37	21	Garfield	46
23	Flaming Gorge	35	23	Heber	47
24	Veyo Powerhouse	34	23	Johnson Pass	47
25	Boulder	32	23	Salt Lake City Int'l Arpt	47

Rankings include 25 highest/lowest stations. If state has less than 25 stations, all stations are included. The period of record is 1980–2009. See User Guide for detailed explanation of data.

Number of Days Annually With ≥ 0.5 Inches of Precipitation

Highest Rank	Highest Station Name	Highest Days	Lowest Rank	Lowest Station Name	Lowest Days
1	Alta	35	1	Callao	0
2	Blowhard Mtn Radar	*17*	1	Eskdale	0
3	Bountiful-Val Verda	15	3	Arches Np Hqs	1
4	Farmington Usu Fld Stn	14	3	Black Rock	1
5	Deer Creek Dam	13	3	Castle Dale	1
5	Ogden Pioneer P H	13	3	Dugway	1
7	Spanish Fork Pwr House	12	3	Milford Airport	*1*
8	Garfield	11	8	Altamont	2
8	Huntsville Monastery	11	8	St George	2
8	New Harmony	11	10	Angle	*3*
8	Veyo Powerhouse	11	10	Canyonlands The Neck	3
12	Alpine	*10*	10	Woodruff	3
12	Electric Lake U P & L	*10*	13	Maeser 9 NW	4
12	Johnson Pass	10	14	Salt Lake City Int'l Arpt	5
15	Brigham City Waste Plt	9	15	Boulder	6
15	Santaquin Chlorinator	9	15	Echo Dam	6
17	Coalville	8	15	Ephraim Sorensens Fld	6
18	Heber	7	15	Flaming Gorge	6
18	Wanship Dam	7	19	Heber	7
20	Boulder	6	19	Wanship Dam	7
20	Echo Dam	6	21	Coalville	8
20	Ephraim Sorensens Fld	6	22	Brigham City Waste Plt	9
20	Flaming Gorge	6	22	Santaquin Chlorinator	9
24	Salt Lake City Int'l Arpt	5	24	Alpine	*10*
25	Maeser 9 NW	4	24	Electric Lake U P & L	*10*

Number of Days Annually With ≥ 1.0 Inches of Precipitation

Highest Rank	Highest Station Name	Highest Days	Lowest Rank	Lowest Station Name	Lowest Days
1	Alta	11	1	Alpine	*0*
2	Blowhard Mtn Radar	*5*	1	Altamont	0
3	Bountiful-Val Verda	2	1	Angle	*0*
3	Deer Creek Dam	2	1	Arches Np Hqs	0
5	Farmington Usu Fld Stn	1	1	Black Rock	0
5	New Harmony	1	1	Boulder	0
5	Ogden Pioneer P H	1	1	Brigham City Waste Plt	0
8	Alpine	*0*	1	Callao	0
8	Altamont	0	1	Canyonlands The Neck	0
8	Angle	*0*	1	Castle Dale	0
8	Arches Np Hqs	0	1	Coalville	0
8	Black Rock	0	1	Dugway	0
8	Boulder	0	1	Echo Dam	0
8	Brigham City Waste Plt	0	1	Electric Lake U P & L	*0*
8	Callao	0	1	Ephraim Sorensens Fld	0
8	Canyonlands The Neck	0	1	Eskdale	0
8	Castle Dale	0	1	Flaming Gorge	0
8	Coalville	0	1	Garfield	0
8	Dugway	0	1	Heber	0
8	Echo Dam	0	1	Huntsville Monastery	0
8	Electric Lake U P & L	*0*	1	Johnson Pass	0
8	Ephraim Sorensens Fld	0	1	Maeser 9 NW	0
8	Eskdale	0	1	Milford Airport	*0*
8	Flaming Gorge	0	1	Salt Lake City Int'l Arpt	0
8	Garfield	0	1	Santaquin Chlorinator	0

Rankings include 25 highest/lowest stations. If state has less than 25 stations, all stations are included. The period of record is 1980–2009. See User Guide for detailed explanation of data.

Annual Snowfall

Highest Rank	Station Name	Inches	Lowest Rank	Station Name	Inches
1	Alta	527.2	1	St George	1.1
2	Blowhard Mtn Radar	***248.1***	2	Arches Np Hqs	6.3
3	Coalville	78.2	3	Callao	8.0
4	Wanship Dam	***77.7***	4	Veyo Powerhouse	***8.8***
5	Echo Dam	77.5	5	Eskdale	***13.0***
6	Huntsville Monastery	73.1	6	Dugway	14.5
7	Heber	72.0	7	Castle Dale	18.5
8	Johnson Pass	70.8	8	Angle	***21.3***
9	Deer Creek Dam	***68.8***	9	Canyonlands The Neck	21.8
10	Spanish Fork Pwr House	67.0	10	Garfield	***22.1***
11	Alpine	***64.7***	11	Black Rock	24.6
12	Maeser 9 NW	***61.3***	12	Milford Airport	***25.7***
13	Bountiful-Val Verda	60.5	13	Brigham City Waste Plt	35.8
14	Santaquin Chlorinator	56.5	14	Altamont	37.9
15	Salt Lake City Int'l Arpt	56.4	15	Boulder	42.1
16	Woodruff	48.0	16	New Harmony	***42.4***
17	Flaming Gorge	47.8	17	Farmington Usu Fld Stn	***47.7***
18	Farmington Usu Fld Stn	***47.7***	18	Flaming Gorge	47.8
19	New Harmony	***42.4***	19	Woodruff	48.0
20	Boulder	42.1	20	Salt Lake City Int'l Arpt	56.4
21	Altamont	37.9	21	Santaquin Chlorinator	56.5
22	Brigham City Waste Plt	35.8	22	Bountiful-Val Verda	60.5
23	Milford Airport	***25.7***	23	Maeser 9 NW	***61.3***
24	Black Rock	24.6	24	Alpine	***64.7***
25	Garfield	***22.1***	25	Spanish Fork Pwr House	67.0

Annual Maximum Snow Depth

Highest Rank	Station Name	Inches	Lowest Rank	Station Name	Inches
1	Alta	***150***	1	St George	5
2	Blowhard Mtn Radar	***148***	2	Angle	***10***
3	Huntsville Monastery	48	2	Arches Np Hqs	10
4	Heber	39	2	Canyonlands The Neck	10
5	Deer Creek Dam	37	5	Veyo Powerhouse	***12***
6	Maeser 9 NW	***35***	6	Eskdale	***13***
7	Boulder	34	7	Castle Dale	17
7	Johnson Pass	34	7	Milford Airport	***17***
9	Farmington Usu Fld Stn	31	9	Callao	***18***
10	Santaquin Chlorinator	***30***	10	Flaming Gorge	21
11	Coalville	***29***	11	Garfield	***23***
12	Bountiful-Val Verda	28	12	Black Rock	24
12	New Harmony	***28***	12	Echo Dam	24
14	Alpine	***27***	12	Ogden Pioneer P H	***24***
14	Spanish Fork Pwr House	27	15	Altamont	25
14	Woodruff	27	15	Brigham City Waste Plt	***25***
17	Altamont	25	15	Salt Lake City Int'l Arpt	25
17	Brigham City Waste Plt	***25***	18	Alpine	***27***
17	Salt Lake City Int'l Arpt	25	18	Spanish Fork Pwr House	27
20	Black Rock	24	18	Woodruff	27
20	Echo Dam	24	21	Bountiful-Val Verda	28
20	Ogden Pioneer P H	***24***	21	New Harmony	***28***
23	Garfield	***23***	23	Coalville	***29***
24	Flaming Gorge	21	24	Santaquin Chlorinator	***30***
25	Callao	***18***	25	Farmington Usu Fld Stn	31

Rankings include 25 highest/lowest stations. If state has less than 25 stations, all stations are included. The period of record is 1980–2009. See User Guide for detailed explanation of data.

Number of Days Annually With ≥ 1.0 Inch Snow Depth

Highest

Rank	Station Name	Days
1	Blowhard Mtn Radar	***213***
2	Alta	***206***
3	Huntsville Monastery	92
4	Maeser 9 NW	***89***
5	Echo Dam	84
6	Johnson Pass	80
7	Deer Creek Dam	76
8	Heber	75
9	Bountiful-Val Verda	69
10	Alpine	***67***
10	Flaming Gorge	67
12	Altamont	63
13	Spanish Fork Pwr House	62
14	Santaquin Chlorinator	***59***
15	Woodruff	58
16	Coalville	***56***
17	Farmington Usu Fld Stn	54
18	Salt Lake City Int'l Arpt	50
19	Canyonlands The Neck	43
20	Ogden Pioneer P H	***41***
21	Brigham City Waste Plt	***39***
22	Boulder	33
23	Milford Airport	***32***
24	Castle Dale	30
24	Garfield	***30***

Lowest

Rank	Station Name	Days
1	St George	0
2	Veyo Powerhouse	***3***
3	Callao	10
3	Eskdale	***10***
5	Arches Np Hqs	13
6	Angle	***15***
7	New Harmony	***18***
8	Black Rock	29
9	Castle Dale	30
9	Garfield	***30***
11	Milford Airport	***32***
12	Boulder	33
13	Brigham City Waste Plt	***39***
14	Ogden Pioneer P H	***41***
15	Canyonlands The Neck	43
16	Salt Lake City Int'l Arpt	50
17	Farmington Usu Fld Stn	54
18	Coalville	***56***
19	Woodruff	58
20	Santaquin Chlorinator	***59***
21	Spanish Fork Pwr House	62
22	Altamont	63
23	Alpine	***67***
23	Flaming Gorge	67
25	Bountiful-Val Verda	69

 Rankings include 25 highest/lowest stations. If state has less than 25 stations, all stations are included. The period of record is 1980–2009. See User Guide for detailed explanation of data.

Significant Storm Events in Utah: 2000 – 2009

Location or County	Date	Type	Mag.	Deaths	Injuries	Property Damage ($mil.)	Crop Damage ($mil.)
East Carbon, Salt Lake, and Weber Counties, and Tooele Valley	03/20/00	High Wind	115 mph	0	1	2.5	0.1
Northern Utah	04/07/01	Heavy Snow	na	1	10	0.1	0.0
Davis and Salt Lake Counties, Tooele Valley	05/02/01	High Wind	77 mph	0	0	3.0	0.4
Northern Utah	11/29/01	Winter Storm	na	3	13	0.1	0.0
Great Salt Lake Desert and Mountains	02/03/02	Fog	na	3	3	0.5	0.0
Northern Utah	03/07/02	Winter Storm	na	2	50	0.2	0.0
Statewide	04/15/02	High Wind	86 mph	0	10	2.0	0.1
Sanpete	09/08/02	Tornado	F2	0	0	2.0	0.1
Utah	09/12/02	Flash Flood	na	0	0	3.0	0.1
Salt alke and Tooele Valleys	01/10/03	Dense Fog	na	2	1	0.2	0.0
San Juan	09/09/03	Flash Flood	na	0	0	1.0	0.0
Northern Utah	12/20/03	Heavy Snow	na	1	0	0.1	0.0
Tooele Valley, Wasatch Mountains, and Davis and Salt Lake Counties	12/25/03	Winter Storm	na	0	0	1.4	0.0
Statewide	12/28/03	Winter Storm	na	2	0	0.3	0.0
West and Central Utah	01/10/05	Flood	na	1	6	300.0	0.0
Utah	08/01/06	Thunderstorm Wind	92 mph	0	0	4.0	0.0
Utah	08/01/06	Thunderstorm Wind	106 mph	0	0	3.0	0.0
Salt Lake	08/01/06	Thunderstorm Wind	86 mph	0	0	2.0	0.0
Wayne	10/06/06	Flash Flood	na	0	0	8.0	0.0
Duchesne and Uintah Counties	06/29/07	Wildfire	na	3	0	0.5	0.0
Duchesne and Uintah Counties	07/01/07	Wildfire	na	3	0	0.2	0.0
Washington	08/01/07	Flash Flood	na	0	0	1.9	0.0

Note: Deaths, injuries, and damages are date and location specific.

VERMONT

PHYSICAL FEATURES. The Green Mountain State occupies 9,609 square miles. Though Vermont is the only New England state without a coastline on the Atlantic Ocean, most of its boundary is water. The Connecticut River forms the entire eastern border. Lake Champlain marks over 100 miles of the western boundary. Vermont extends southward from near the 45 parallel of latitude almost 160 miles to about 20 miles south of the 43rd parallel. Vermont widens northward from about 40 to 90 miles across.

The terrain is hilly to mountainous. The Green Mountains extend the length of the State. They rise to their highest elevation at Mt. Mansfield, 4,393 feet above sea level. Many peaks in this range rise to over 3,000 feet, as do several others in eastern Vermont. Elevations of less than 500 feet above sea level are mostly confined to the lowlands paralleling Lake Champlain in the west and to the central and southern portions of the Connecticut Valley in the east. Much of the State ranges from 500 to 2,000 feet in elevation. The glacier of the great Ice Age accounts for many topographical features, lakes, and soils. Inland waters cover more than 300 square miles.

GENERAL CLIMATE. Vermont shares with the other New England states in the chief climatic characteristics. These include: (1) changeableness of the weather; (2) large range of temperature, both daily and annual; (3) great differences between the same seasons in different years; (4) equable distribution of precipitation; and (5) considerable diversity from place to place. The regional climatic influences are modified in Vermont by varying elevations, types of terrain, and distances from the Atlantic Ocean and from Lake Champlain. The State has been divided into three climatological divisions- (Western, Northeastern, and Southeastern).

Vermont lies in the "prevailing westerlies," the belt of generally eastward air movement which encircles the globe in middle latitudes. Embedded in this circulation are extensive masses of air originating in higher or lower latitudes and interacting to produce low-pressure storm systems. Relative to most other sections of the country, a large number of such storms pass over or near Vermont. The majority of air masses affecting this State belong to three types: (1) cold, dry air pouring down from subarctic North America; (2) warm, moist air streaming up on a long overland journey from the Gulf of Mexico and other subtropical waters; and (3) cool, damp air moving in from the North Atlantic. Because the atmospheric flow is usually from a westerly direction, Vermont is more influenced by the first two types than it is by the third.

The procession of contrasting air masses and the relatively frequent passage of low pressure systems resulting an average of a twice-weekly alternation from fair to cloudy or stormy conditions, attended by often abrupt changes in temperature, moisture, sunshine, wind direction and speed. There is no regular or persistent rhythm to this sequence, and it is interrupted by periods during which the weather patterns continue the same for several days, infrequently for several weeks.

TEMPERATURE. The annual mean temperature is near 43°F. in the Northeastern Division, 44°F. in the Southeastern, and 46°F. in the Western. Summer temperatures are comfortable as a rule. They are also reasonably uniform over the State, excepting topographical extremes. Long-period means for July average near 70°F. in the western division and near 68°F. in the other Divisions. Average daily minima in July are in the 50s over nearly the entire State. The average daily maxima reach only near 80°F. Hot days with maxima of 90°F. or higher average less than 10 per year at most weather stations. Even after one of these hot days the temperature is likely to fall to 60°F. or lower during the night.

Temperatures from place to place vary more in winter than in summer. The Northeastern Division average in January is near 17°F. The Southeastern Division average is nearly 19°F. and the Western Division, 21°F. Days with subzero readings are common at most stations in winter. They number from 10 to 40 per year in the southern portion and from 20 to 50 in the north. The growing season for vegetation subject to injury from freezing temperature averages 130 to 150 days in much of the Western Division and along the Connecticut River in the Southeastern Division. Elsewhere, and including the extreme southern portion of the Western Division, the season varies from 100 to 130 days.

PRECIPITATION. Vermont's precipitation, fortunately, is well distributed through the year. Winter precipitation is noticeably less than summer rainfall in the northern and western portions of the State. This difference is greater in those areas than in any other part of New England. New England as a whole is noted for the even distribution of its precipitation throughout the year, an effect due to the influence of the Atlantic Ocean. This ocean influence is still strongly felt in southeastern Vermont, but it becomes weaker with increasing distance from the ocean. Low-pressure, or frontal, storm systems are the principal year-round moisture producers. When this activity ebbs somewhat in summer, bands or patches of thunderstorms increase in activity, more than making up the difference. Though brief and often of small extent, the thunderstorms produce the heaviest local rainfall intensities.

Floods occur most often in the spring when they are caused by rainfall and melting snow. Stages of spring over-bank flooding are frequently increased by ice jams. Local flash floods result on occasions from short period summer storms between May and November. The Connecticut River and its tributaries drain the major portion of Vermont. In the northwest portion, rivers drain into Lake Champlain or directly to the St. Lawrence. A small area in southwest Vermont drains to the Hudson River.

Occasionally freezing rain occurs, coating exposed surfaces with troublesome ice. Most areas can expect at least one such occurrence in a winter. Frequency of days with measurable precipitation is between 120 and 160 days per year.

SNOWFALL. Average annual total snowfall is from 55 to 65 inches in much of the Western Division and also in parts of the Connecticut River Valley. Elsewhere the annual averages vary greatly. They range upward to as much as 100 inches. Topographical differences cause large variations in a short distance. The average number of days with 1 inch or more of snowfall in a season varies from 20 to 40. The frequency increases with elevation. Most winters have several snowstorms of five inches or more per year. Snow cover is continuous throughout the winter season as a rule. Depth of snow on the ground reaches its maximum for much of the State in the latter part of February. At the highest elevations, however, the date falls in the middle of March. Water stored in the snow is an important contribution to the water supply. Spring melting is usually too gradual to produce serious flooding.

OTHER CLIMATIC ELEMENTS. Sunshine averages near 50 percent of possible on a year-round basis, but varies with topography. Higher elevations and peaks are much more cloudy, especially in winter. Sunshine is most abundant during the summer season. Persistent fogs are sometimes experienced on the higher elevations. The duration of fog diminishes over flatland valley locations; short duration, heavy ground fogs of early morning do occur frequently at susceptible places in these areas. The number of days with fog varies from 10 to 60 per year over the State.

WINDS AND STORMS. Vermont lies in the region of prevailing westerlies — wind from the northwest in winter, and from the southwest in the warmer part of the year. But because the rugged topography has a strong influence on the direction of the wind, many areas have prevailing winds paralleling a valley. The major valleys tend to lie in a north-south direction. Thus prevailing winds may be from the north in winter and from the south in the warmer seasons in those areas.

Coastal storms, or "northeasters," are well known to New England. Their influence on Vermont is minimized by its inland location. They remain a factor, however, especially in the Southeastern Division. They generate very strong winds and heavy rain or snow. Storms of tropical origin may occasionally affect Vermont in summer or fall, but only rarely contain destructive winds. Vermont is far enough inland so that, usually, winds are considerably weakened by the time tropical storms reach the State. Rainfall associated with these storms may, however, remain heavy.

Tornadoes are not common phenomena, yet one or more of these most violent storms may occur in a year. The peak months are June and July. Thunder and hailstorms have a frequency maximum from midspring to early fall. Thunderstorms occur on 20 to 30 days per year. The most severe are attended by hail. The size of an area struck by a hailstorm, however, is usually small.

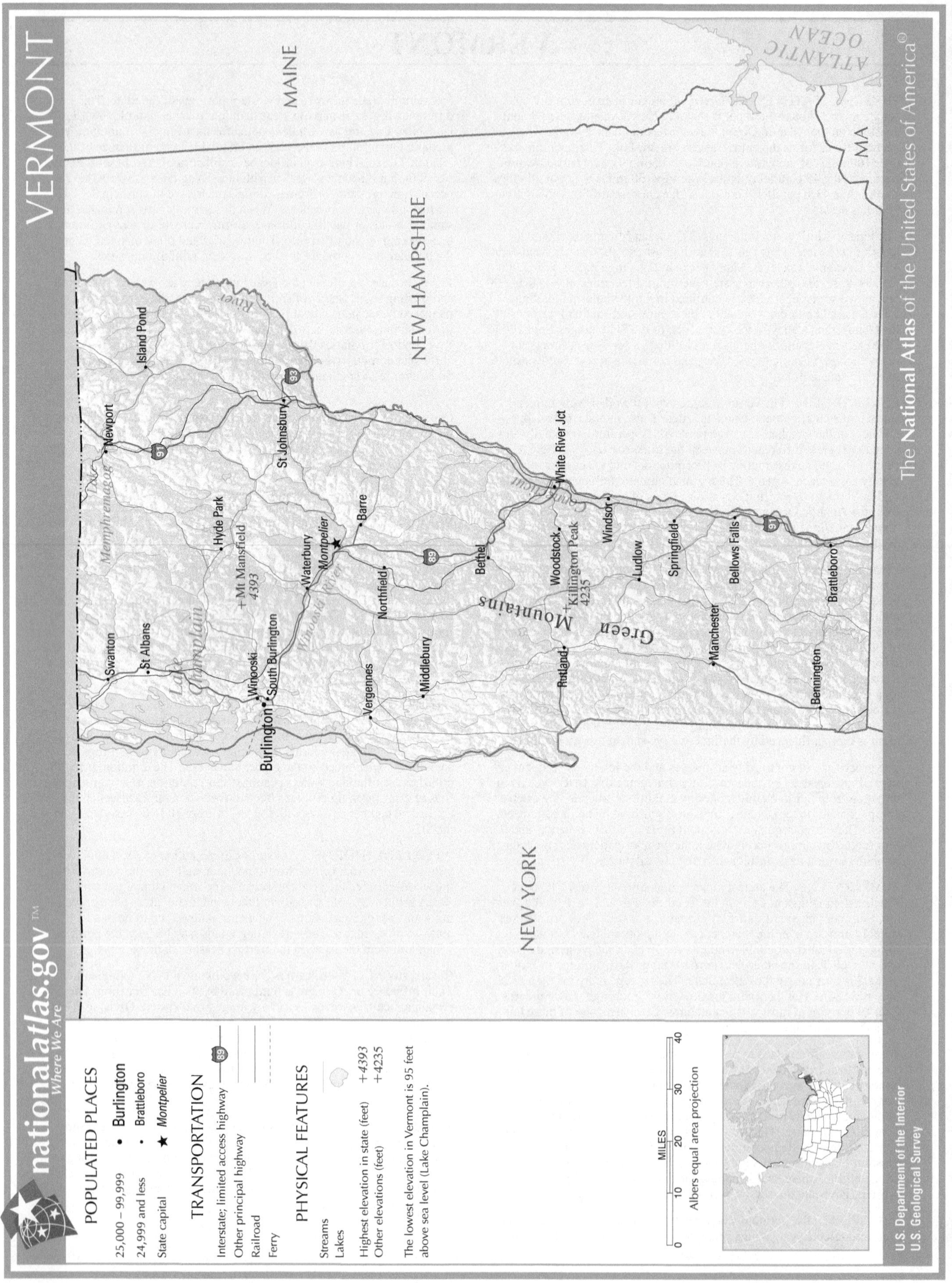
VERMONT
nationalatlas.gov™
Where We Are
POPULATED PLACES
25,000 – 99,999 • Burlington
24,999 and less • Brattleboro
State capital ★ Montpelier
TRANSPORTATION
Interstate; limited access highway 89
Other principal highway
Railroad
Ferry
PHYSICAL FEATURES
Streams
Lakes
Highest elevation in state (feet) +4393
Other elevations (feet) +4235
The lowest elevation in Vermont is 95 feet above sea level (Lake Champlain).
MILES
0 10 20 30 40
Albers equal area projection
U.S. Department of the Interior
U.S. Geological Survey
The National Atlas of the United States of America®
MAINE
NEW HAMPSHIRE
NEW YORK
MA
ATLANTIC OCEAN
Island Pond
Newport
St Johnsbury
Lake Memphremagog
Hyde Park
Mt Mansfield 4393
Swanton
St Albans
Lake Champlain
Winooski
South Burlington
Burlington
Waterbury
Montpelier
Barre
Winooski River
Northfield
Vergennes
Middlebury
Bethel
White River Jct
Connecticut River
Woodstock
Killington Peak 4235
Green Mountains
Rutland
Windsor
Ludlow
Springfield
Manchester
Bellows Falls
Brattleboro
Bennington
91
93
89

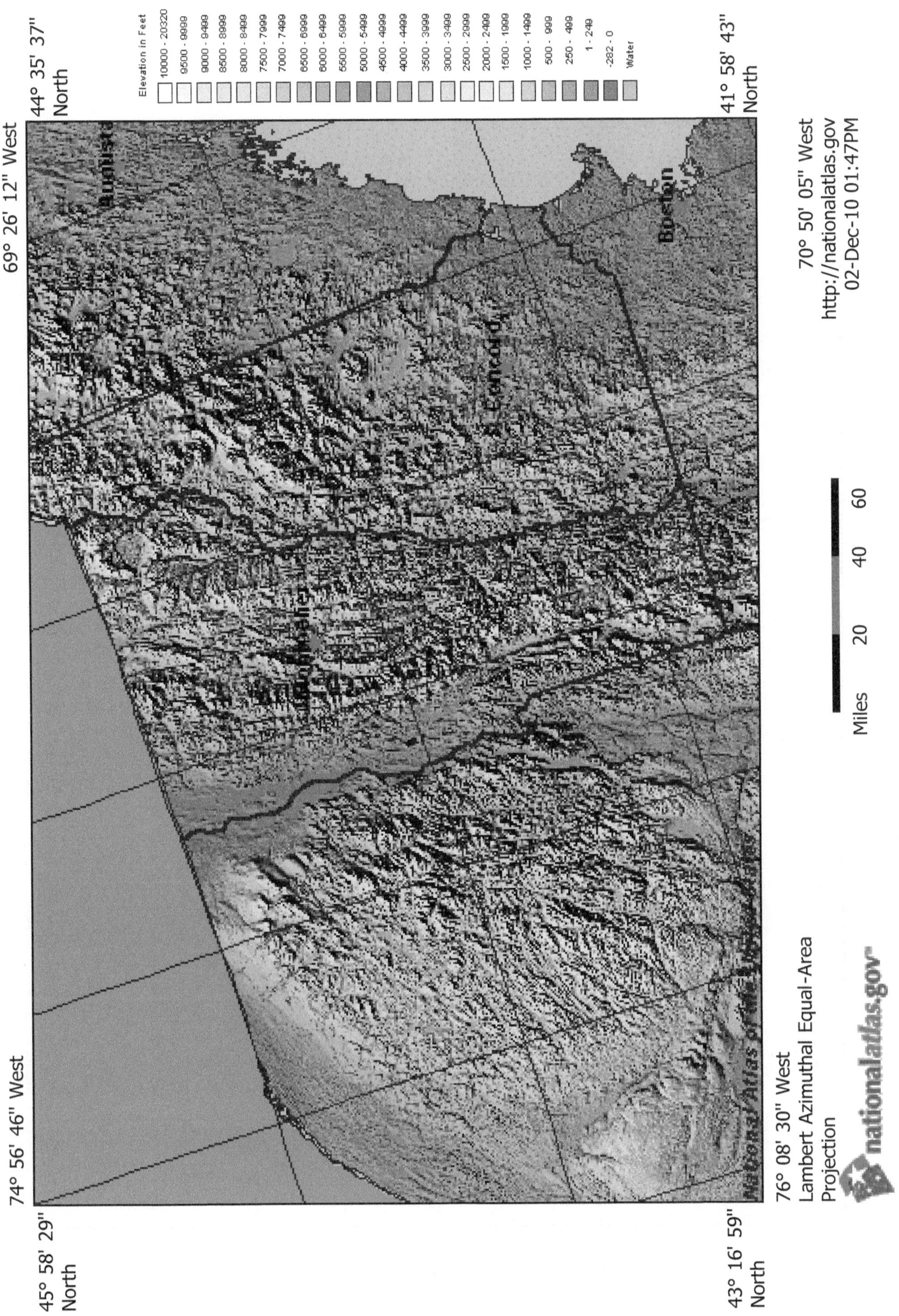
69° 26' 12" West
44° 35' 37" North
74° 56' 46" West
45° 58' 29" North
76° 08' 30" West
43° 16' 59" North
70° 50' 05" West
41° 58' 43" North
Elevation in Feet
10000 - 20320
9500 - 9999
9000 - 9499
8500 - 8999
8000 - 8499
7500 - 7999
7000 - 7499
6500 - 6999
6000 - 6499
5500 - 5999
5000 - 5499
4500 - 4999
4000 - 4499
3500 - 3999
3000 - 3499
2500 - 2999
2000 - 2499
1500 - 1999
1000 - 1499
500 - 999
250 - 499
1 - 249
-282 - 0
Water
Augusta
Concord
Boston
Miles
20
40
60
Lambert Azimuthal Equal-Area Projection
http://nationalatlas.gov
02-Dec-10 01:47PM
nationalatlas.gov

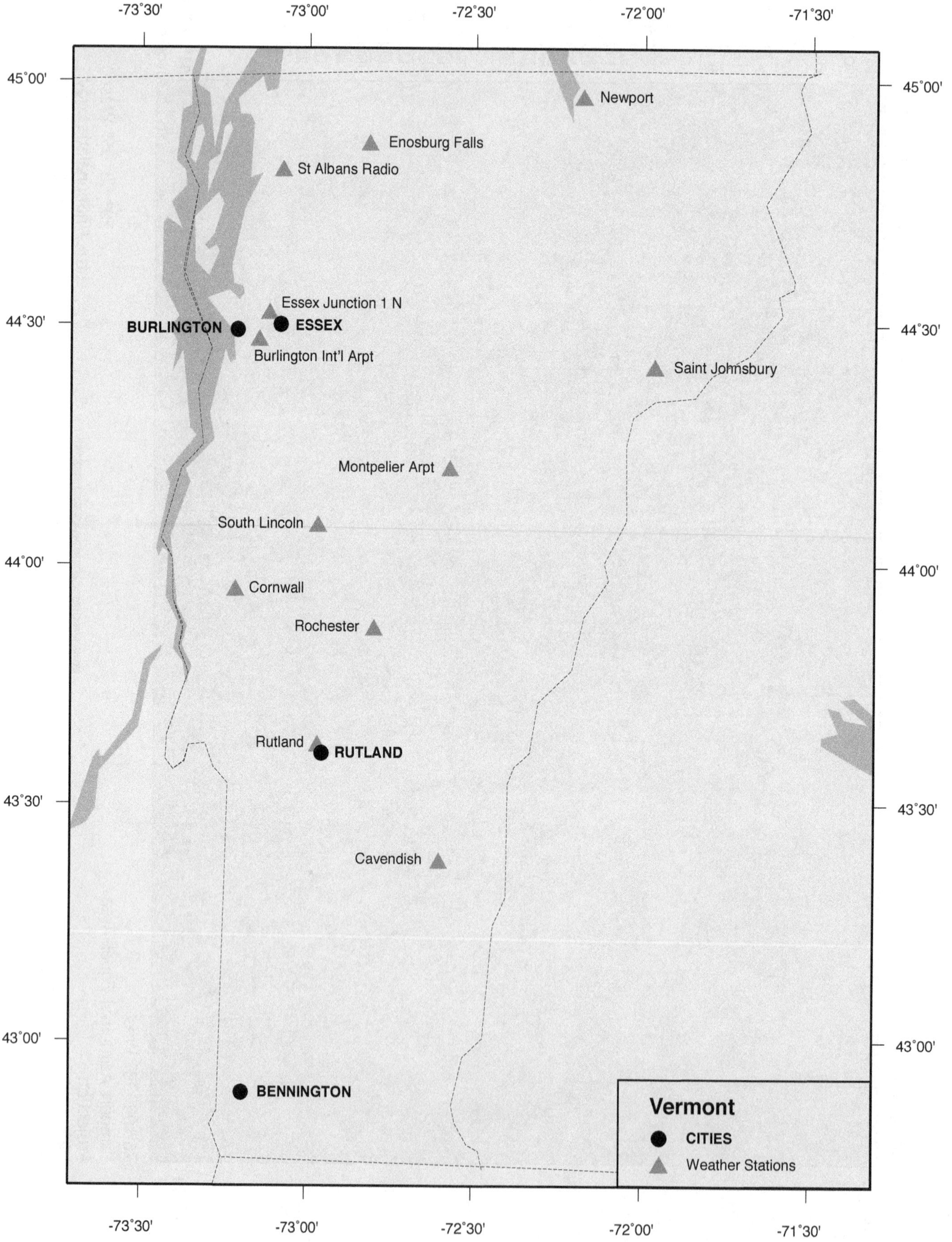
-73°30'
-73°00'
-72°30'
-72°00'
-71°30'
45°00'
44°30'
44°00'
43°30'
43°00'
Newport
Enosburg Falls
St Albans Radio
Essex Junction 1 N
BURLINGTON
ESSEX
Burlington Int'l Arpt
Saint Johnsbury
Montpelier Arpt
South Lincoln
Cornwall
Rochester
Rutland
RUTLAND
Cavendish
BENNINGTON
Vermont
CITIES
Weather Stations

Vermont Weather Stations by County

County	Station Name
Addison	Cornwall
	South Lincoln
Caledonia	Saint Johnsbury
Chittenden	Burlington Int'l Arpt
	Essex Junction 1 N
Franklin	Enosburg Falls
	St Albans Radio
Orleans	Newport
Rutland	Rutland
Washington	Montpelier Arpt
Windsor	Cavendish
	Rochester

See User Guide for station inclusion criteria.

Vermont Weather Stations by City

City	Station Name	Miles
Barre	Montpelier Arpt	3.1
	South Lincoln	24.3
Bennington	Grafton, NY	15.3
Brattleboro	Keene, NH	14.9
Burlington	Peru 2 WSW, NY	17.9
	Burlington Int'l Arpt	3.7
	Essex Junction 1 N	5.6
	St Albans Radio	23.9
Colchester	Peru 2 WSW, NY	18.1
	Burlington Int'l Arpt	5.4
	Essex Junction 1 N	4.4
	St Albans Radio	20.2
Essex	Peru 2 WSW, NY	23.9
	Burlington Int'l Arpt	3.8
	Essex Junction 1 N	1.7
	St Albans Radio	21.8
Essex Junction	Peru 2 WSW, NY	23.1
	Burlington Int'l Arpt	2.7
	Essex Junction 1 N	1.7
	St Albans Radio	22.5
Hartford	Grafton, NH	21.2
	Hanover, NH	4.3
	Cavendish	23.0
Middlebury	Cornwall	5.0
	Rochester	19.8
	South Lincoln	10.6
Milton	Chazy, NY	22.7
	Peru 2 WSW, NY	21.9
	Burlington Int'l Arpt	11.6
	Enosburg Falls	22.3
	Essex Junction 1 N	8.1
	St Albans Radio	12.8
Rutland	Whitehall, NY	21.7
	Cavendish	24.4
	Rochester	19.8
	Rutland	0.7
South Burlington	Peru 2 WSW, NY	20.6
	Burlington Int'l Arpt	1.8
	Essex Junction 1 N	5.4
Springfield	Mount Sunapee, NH	20.5
	Cavendish	8.1
Williston	Peru 2 WSW, NY	24.9
	Burlington Int'l Arpt	3.3
	Essex Junction 1 N	5.1

Note: Miles is the distance between the geographic center of the city and the weather station.

See User Guide for station inclusion criteria.

Vermont Weather Stations by Elevation

Feet	Station Name
1,370	South Lincoln
1,125	Montpelier Arpt
830	Rochester
799	Cavendish
770	Newport
700	Saint Johnsbury
620	Rutland
490	Cornwall
459	St Albans Radio
419	Enosburg Falls
339	Essex Junction 1 N
330	Burlington Int'l Arpt

Burlington Int'l Airport

Burlington is located on the eastern shore of Lake Champlain at the widest part of the lake. About 35 miles to the west lie the highest peaks of the Adirondacks, while the foothills of the Green Mountains begin 10 miles to the east and southeast.

Its northerly latitude assures the variety and vigor of a true New England climate, while thanks to the modifying influence of the lake, the many rapid and marked weather changes are tempered in severity. Due to its location in the path of the St. Lawrence Valley storm track and the lake effects, the city is one of the cloudiest in the United States.

Lake Champlain exercises a tempering influence on the local temperature. During the winter months and prior to the lake freezing, temperatures along the lake shore are often five to 10 degrees warmer than at the airport three and a half miles inland. At the airport the average occurrence of the last freeze in spring is around May 10th and that of the first in fall is early October, giving a growing season of 145 days. On average, there are few days a year with maxima of 90 degrees or higher. This moderate summer heat gives way to a cooler, but none the less pleasant fall period, usually extending well into October. High pressure systems moving down rapidly from central Canada or Hudson Bay produce the coldest temperatures during the winter months, but extended periods of very cold weather are rare.

Precipitation, although generally plentiful and well distributed throughout the year, is less in the Champlain Valley than in other areas of Vermont due to the shielding effect of the mountain barriers to the east and west. The heaviest rainfall usually occurs during summer thunderstorms, but excessively heavy rainfall is quite uncommon. Droughts are infrequent.

Because of the trend of the Champlain Valley between the Adirondack and Green Mountain ranges, most winds have a northerly or southerly component. The prevailing direction most of the year is from the south. Winds of damaging force are very uncommon.

Smoke pollution is nearly non-existent since there is no concentration of heavy industry here, however, haze has been on the increase over the years due to the large increase in industry to the north and south. During the spring and fall months, fog occasionally forms along the Winooski River to the north and east and may drift over the airport with favorable winds. In spite of the high percentage of cloudiness, periods of low aircraft ceilings and visibilities are usually of short duration, allowing this area to have one of the highest percentages of flying weather in New England.

Burlington Int'l Airport *Chittenden County* Elevation: 330 ft. Latitude: 44° 28' N Longitude: 73° 09' W

	JAN	FEB	MAR	APR	MAY	JUN	JUL	AUG	SEP	OCT	NOV	DEC	YEAR
Mean Maximum Temp. (°F)	27.3	30.4	39.9	54.6	67.2	76.3	80.8	79.0	70.3	57.1	45.3	33.1	55.1
Mean Temp. (°F)	18.8	21.3	30.8	44.7	56.4	65.8	70.6	68.8	60.4	48.2	38.0	25.6	45.8
Mean Minimum Temp. (°F)	10.2	12.2	21.7	34.8	45.4	55.2	60.3	58.5	50.5	39.2	30.7	18.1	36.4
Extreme Maximum Temp. (°F)	66	62	84	90	92	100	100	99	98	82	74	67	100
Extreme Minimum Temp. (°F)	-29	-27	-18	10	27	33	40	39	28	20	3	-26	-29
Days Maximum Temp. ≥ 90°F	0	0	0	0	0	2	3	2	0	0	0	0	7
Days Maximum Temp. ≤ 32°F	20	16	8	0	0	0	0	0	0	0	3	14	61
Days Minimum Temp. ≤ 32°F	29	26	26	13	1	0	0	0	0	8	18	27	148
Days Minimum Temp. ≤ 0°F	8	6	2	0	0	0	0	0	0	0	0	3	19
Heating Degree Days (base 65°F)	1,428	1,230	1,053	604	278	69	13	29	170	517	802	1,215	7,408
Cooling Degree Days (base 65°F)	0	0	0	3	18	101	193	154	40	2	0	0	511
Mean Precipitation (in.)	1.99	1.71	2.20	2.80	3.45	3.55	4.28	3.92	3.65	3.48	3.12	2.30	36.45
Maximum Precipitation (in.)*	4.7	5.4	3.6	6.5	6.3	7.7	6.1	11.5	6.3	6.2	6.8	5.9	50.2
Minimum Precipitation (in.)*	0.4	0.2	0.4	0.9	0.3	0.8	1.2	0.7	0.9	0.5	0.6	0.6	26.2
Extreme Maximum Daily Precip. (in.)	2.11	1.94	1.27	1.36	1.99	2.32	2.69	3.62	3.11	1.96	2.46	1.74	3.62
Days With ≥ 0.1" Precipitation	5	4	6	7	8	8	8	8	7	7	7	6	81
Days With ≥ 0.5" Precipitation	1	1	1	2	2	2	3	3	2	2	2	1	22
Days With ≥ 1.0" Precipitation	0	0	0	0	1	1	1	1	1	1	0	0	6
Mean Snowfall (in.)	19.9	16.3	15.8	4.5	trace	trace	trace	trace	trace	0.3	5.5	18.8	81.1
Maximum Snowfall (in.)*	42	34	40	21	4	0	0	0	trace	5	19	57	130
Maximum 24-hr. Snowfall (in.)*	15	17	16	13	4	0	0	0	trace	5	10	17	17
Maximum Snow Depth (in.)	22	30	31	16	trace	trace	trace	trace	trace	3	9	24	31
Days With ≥ 1.0" Snow Depth	24	24	16	2	0	0	0	0	0	0	4	18	88
Thunderstorm Days*	< 1	0	< 1	1	2	5	6	5	2	1	< 1	< 1	22
Foggy Days*	8	7	10	10	10	10	9	12	12	11	11	10	120
Predominant Sky Cover*	OVR	OVR	OVR	OVR	OVR	OVR	OVR	OVR	OVR	OVR	OVR	OVR	OVR
Mean Relative Humidity 7am (%)*	73	74	75	74	73	76	78	83	85	82	78	76	77
Mean Relative Humidity 4pm (%)*	65	61	58	52	51	54	53	56	60	61	67	69	59
Mean Dewpoint (°F)*	9	11	20	31	43	54	58	58	51	39	29	16	35
Prevailing Wind Direction*	S	S	S	S	S	S	S	S	S	S	S	S	S
Prevailing Wind Speed (mph)*	13	12	12	13	12	10	10	10	12	12	12	13	12
Maximum Wind Gust (mph)*	51	54	56	52	71	52	60	59	52	51	62	52	71

Note: (*) Period of record is 1948-1995

The period of record for National Weather Service station data is 1980 – 2009 except where noted. See User Guide for detailed explanation of data.

Cavendish *Windsor County* Elevation: 799 ft. Latitude: 43° 23' N Longitude: 72° 36' W

	JAN	FEB	MAR	APR	MAY	JUN	JUL	AUG	SEP	OCT	NOV	DEC	YEAR
Mean Maximum Temp. (°F)	28.9	33.0	41.2	54.7	67.4	76.1	80.8	79.3	71.0	58.3	45.6	33.6	55.8
Mean Temp. (°F)	17.7	20.5	29.6	42.5	54.3	63.4	68.0	66.4	58.1	45.9	36.0	23.9	43.9
Mean Minimum Temp. (°F)	6.5	7.9	18.1	30.2	41.0	50.6	55.2	53.5	45.1	33.4	26.4	14.2	31.8
Extreme Maximum Temp. (°F)	64	60	80	91	91	97	97	97	94	85	73	71	97
Extreme Minimum Temp. (°F)	-36	-29	-19	6	23	29	38	32	23	16	-1	-25	-36
Days Maximum Temp. ≥ 90°F	0	0	0	0	0	2	3	2	0	0	0	0	7
Days Maximum Temp. ≤ 32°F	19	13	5	0	0	0	0	0	0	0	2	13	52
Days Minimum Temp. ≤ 32°F	31	28	29	19	6	0	0	0	2	16	23	30	184
Days Minimum Temp. ≤ 0°F	11	9	3	0	0	0	0	0	0	0	0	5	28
Heating Degree Days (base 65°F)	1,459	1,252	1,089	671	338	108	31	53	222	585	862	1,266	7,936
Cooling Degree Days (base 65°F)	0	0	0	1	11	66	131	104	22	1	0	0	336
Mean Precipitation (in.)	3.35	2.79	3.82	3.95	4.19	4.31	3.87	4.00	3.92	4.36	4.12	3.62	46.30
Extreme Maximum Daily Precip. (in.)	2.05	1.67	2.50	3.10	3.01	3.51	3.50	4.19	5.34	3.52	1.97	1.84	5.34
Days With ≥ 0.1" Precipitation	6	6	7	7	8	8	8	7	7	7	7	7	85
Days With ≥ 0.5" Precipitation	2	2	3	3	3	3	3	3	3	3	3	3	34
Days With ≥ 1.0" Precipitation	1	1	1	1	1	1	1	1	1	1	1	1	12
Mean Snowfall (in.)	21.8	17.5	16.8	4.3	0.1	0.0	0.0	0.0	trace	0.5	5.1	17.7	83.8
Maximum Snow Depth (in.)	41	39	39	34	trace	0	0	0	trace	4	11	24	41
Days With ≥ 1.0" Snow Depth	28	28	29	7	0	0	0	0	0	0	5	25	122

Cornwall *Addison County* Elevation: 490 ft. Latitude: 43° 57' N Longitude: 73° 13' W

	JAN	FEB	MAR	APR	MAY	JUN	JUL	AUG	SEP	OCT	NOV	DEC	YEAR
Mean Maximum Temp. (°F)	27.9	31.2	41.0	55.4	67.8	76.0	80.6	78.8	70.9	57.7	46.0	33.0	55.5
Mean Temp. (°F)	19.0	21.4	31.3	44.7	56.4	65.0	69.7	67.9	60.0	47.9	37.9	24.9	45.5
Mean Minimum Temp. (°F)	10.0	11.5	21.5	34.0	44.8	53.9	58.9	57.0	49.1	38.0	29.7	16.7	35.4
Extreme Maximum Temp. (°F)	64	62	80	91	90	97	97	96	96	80	75	66	97
Extreme Minimum Temp. (°F)	-30	-24	-20	3	23	33	40	32	22	16	4	-23	-30
Days Maximum Temp. ≥ 90°F	0	0	0	0	0	1	2	1	0	0	0	0	4
Days Maximum Temp. ≤ 32°F	20	15	7	0	0	0	0	0	0	0	2	14	58
Days Minimum Temp. ≤ 32°F	29	26	26	14	2	0	0	0	1	9	19	29	155
Days Minimum Temp. ≤ 0°F	8	6	2	0	0	0	0	0	0	0	0	3	19
Heating Degree Days (base 65°F)	1,421	1,229	1,039	604	279	80	16	39	181	525	806	1,236	7,455
Cooling Degree Days (base 65°F)	0	0	0	3	18	86	170	136	37	1	0	0	451
Mean Precipitation (in.)	1.98	2.02	2.27	2.92	3.46	3.85	3.67	4.02	3.39	3.70	3.09	2.72	37.09
Extreme Maximum Daily Precip. (in.)	2.27	2.08	1.54	1.71	2.33	3.24	2.40	4.70	3.98	2.20	2.41	1.56	4.70
Days With ≥ 0.1" Precipitation	4	4	6	6	7	8	8	7	6	7	6	5	74
Days With ≥ 0.5" Precipitation	1	1	2	2	2	2	2	3	2	2	2	2	23
Days With ≥ 1.0" Precipitation	0	0	0	0	1	1	1	1	1	1	1	0	7
Mean Snowfall (in.)	13.7	13.2	10.0	2.4	trace	0.0	0.0	0.0	0.0	0.3	2.4	15.0	57.0
Maximum Snow Depth (in.)	25	28	25	15	0	0	0	0	0	5	7	24	28
Days With ≥ 1.0" Snow Depth	13	13	7	2	0	0	0	0	0	0	2	13	50

Enosburg Falls *Franklin County* Elevation: 419 ft. Latitude: 44° 52' N Longitude: 72° 49' W

	JAN	FEB	MAR	APR	MAY	JUN	JUL	AUG	SEP	OCT	NOV	DEC	YEAR
Mean Maximum Temp. (°F)	28.1	31.9	41.6	56.4	68.4	76.3	80.2	78.5	70.7	58.6	45.9	33.3	55.8
Mean Temp. (°F)	17.2	20.1	30.3	44.5	55.7	64.4	68.8	67.0	59.4	47.9	37.2	24.0	44.7
Mean Minimum Temp. (°F)	6.1	8.3	18.9	32.5	42.9	52.5	57.3	55.5	48.1	37.3	28.4	14.6	33.5
Extreme Maximum Temp. (°F)	67	62	82	89	89	94	94	95	92	81	74	66	95
Extreme Minimum Temp. (°F)	-41	-38	-28	5	22	27	34	34	22	18	-9	-37	-41
Days Maximum Temp. ≥ 90°F	0	0	0	0	0	1	1	1	0	0	0	0	3
Days Maximum Temp. ≤ 32°F	20	15	6	0	0	0	0	0	0	0	3	14	58
Days Minimum Temp. ≤ 32°F	30	27	26	16	4	0	0	0	1	10	19	28	161
Days Minimum Temp. ≤ 0°F	12	9	3	0	0	0	0	0	0	0	0	6	30
Heating Degree Days (base 65°F)	1,479	1,263	1,070	611	297	92	24	49	192	523	828	1,265	7,693
Cooling Degree Days (base 65°F)	0	0	0	2	15	80	148	119	32	2	0	0	398
Mean Precipitation (in.)	2.22	1.97	2.46	3.11	3.85	4.09	4.59	4.66	3.89	4.05	3.85	2.89	41.63
Extreme Maximum Daily Precip. (in.)	2.02	1.50	1.45	1.75	2.29	3.25	3.36	2.88	3.68	1.95	2.70	2.01	3.68
Days With ≥ 0.1" Precipitation	7	5	7	9	10	9	10	9	7	9	9	8	99
Days With ≥ 0.5" Precipitation	1	1	1	2	2	3	3	3	3	3	2	2	26
Days With ≥ 1.0" Precipitation	0	0	0	0	1	1	1	1	1	1	1	0	7
Mean Snowfall (in.)	19.2	17.3	14.3	3.9	trace	0.0	0.0	0.0	trace	0.5	6.1	20.6	81.9
Maximum Snow Depth (in.)	na	na	na	18	trace	0	na	0	trace	na	na	na	na
Days With ≥ 1.0" Snow Depth	na	na	18	2	0	0	0	0	0	0	na	na	na

Essex Junction 1 N *Chittenden County* Elevation: 339 ft. Latitude: 44° 31' N Longitude: 73° 07' W

	JAN	FEB	MAR	APR	MAY	JUN	JUL	AUG	SEP	OCT	NOV	DEC	YEAR
Mean Maximum Temp. (°F)	28.0	30.4	39.9	54.7	67.1	76.4	80.3	78.8	70.6	57.3	45.6	33.1	55.2
Mean Temp. (°F)	17.6	18.8	29.4	44.0	55.7	65.2	69.5	67.9	59.8	47.5	37.1	24.1	44.7
Mean Minimum Temp. (°F)	7.1	7.2	18.7	33.2	44.2	54.0	58.6	57.0	48.9	37.7	28.6	15.0	34.2
Extreme Maximum Temp. (°F)	66	60	80	91	91	98	100	98	97	82	74	64	100
Extreme Minimum Temp. (°F)	-31	-35	-22	2	25	30	39	36	27	19	-3	-26	-35
Days Maximum Temp. ≥ 90°F	0	0	0	0	0	2	3	2	0	0	0	0	7
Days Maximum Temp. ≤ 32°F	19	15	8	0	0	0	0	0	0	0	3	13	58
Days Minimum Temp. ≤ 32°F	30	27	27	15	3	0	0	0	1	9	20	29	161
Days Minimum Temp. ≤ 0°F	11	10	3	0	0	0	0	0	0	0	0	4	28
Heating Degree Days (base 65°F)	1,464	1,299	1,098	627	300	81	22	42	183	538	829	1,254	7,737
Cooling Degree Days (base 65°F)	0	0	0	3	18	98	168	140	35	2	0	0	464
Mean Precipitation (in.)	2.48	1.93	2.68	3.02	3.51	4.08	4.69	4.46	4.01	4.04	3.36	2.70	40.96
Extreme Maximum Daily Precip. (in.)	1.70	1.81	1.57	1.61	2.11	2.39	2.12	3.12	3.19	1.99	2.40	1.92	3.19
Days With ≥ 0.1" Precipitation	6	5	7	7	8	9	9	8	8	8	7	7	89
Days With ≥ 0.5" Precipitation	1	1	1	2	2	3	3	3	3	2	2	1	24
Days With ≥ 1.0" Precipitation	0	0	0	0	0	1	1	1	1	1	1	0	6
Mean Snowfall (in.)	20.6	17.6	15.6	4.3	trace	trace	0.0	0.0	trace	0.4	6.2	18.5	83.2
Maximum Snow Depth (in.)	21	29	31	23	trace	trace	0	0	trace	3	10	22	31
Days With ≥ 1.0" Snow Depth	26	26	20	3	0	0	0	0	0	0	5	20	100

The period of record for all cooperative weather station data is 1980 – 2009. See User Guide for detailed explanation of data.

Montpelier Arpt *Washington County* Elevation: 1,125 ft. Latitude: 44° 12' N Longitude: 72° 34' W

	JAN	FEB	MAR	APR	MAY	JUN	JUL	AUG	SEP	OCT	NOV	DEC	YEAR
Mean Maximum Temp. (°F)	25.5	29.0	38.2	52.4	64.9	73.6	78.1	76.1	68.1	55.2	43.3	30.5	52.9
Mean Temp. (°F)	16.5	19.1	28.7	42.3	53.6	62.5	67.2	65.2	57.2	45.5	35.4	22.3	43.0
Mean Minimum Temp. (°F)	7.3	9.2	19.1	32.2	42.2	51.3	56.3	54.3	46.4	35.7	27.4	14.0	32.9
Extreme Maximum Temp. (°F)	65	61	74	90	90	95	95	93	92	80	72	67	95
Extreme Minimum Temp. (°F)	-34	-28	-17	7	24	32	38	35	23	16	-4	-27	-34
Days Maximum Temp. ≥ 90°F	0	0	0	0	0	1	1	1	0	0	0	0	3
Days Maximum Temp. ≤ 32°F	22	18	9	1	0	0	0	0	0	0	5	18	73
Days Minimum Temp. ≤ 32°F	30	27	28	17	4	0	0	0	1	11	21	29	168
Days Minimum Temp. ≤ 0°F	10	7	2	0	0	0	0	0	0	0	0	5	24
Heating Degree Days (base 65°F)	1,499	1,292	1,118	676	355	123	37	73	244	599	882	1,318	8,216
Cooling Degree Days (base 65°F)	0	0	0	1	9	54	113	87	18	1	0	0	283
Mean Precipitation (in.)	2.22	1.98	2.28	2.71	3.41	3.51	3.92	3.94	3.20	3.49	3.14	2.70	36.50
Extreme Maximum Daily Precip. (in.)	1.99	1.76	2.14	1.25	3.90	2.43	2.19	3.78	3.37	2.52	2.07	2.62	3.90
Days With ≥ 0.1" Precipitation	5	5	6	7	8	7	7	7	6	7	7	6	78
Days With ≥ 0.5" Precipitation	1	1	1	2	2	2	3	3	2	2	2	1	22
Days With ≥ 1.0" Precipitation	0	0	0	0	1	1	1	1	1	1	0	0	6
Mean Snowfall (in.)	na	na	na	na	na	na	na	na	na	na	na	na	na
Maximum Snow Depth (in.)	na	na	na	na	na	na	na	na	na	na	na	na	na
Days With ≥ 1.0" Snow Depth	na	na	na	na	na	na	na	na	na	na	na	na	na

Newport *Orleans County* Elevation: 770 ft. Latitude: 44° 56' N Longitude: 72° 12' W

	JAN	FEB	MAR	APR	MAY	JUN	JUL	AUG	SEP	OCT	NOV	DEC	YEAR
Mean Maximum Temp. (°F)	25.5	30.4	39.5	53.9	67.1	75.2	79.2	77.5	69.2	56.2	42.9	30.6	53.9
Mean Temp. (°F)	15.5	19.0	28.4	42.6	54.8	63.7	68.0	66.2	58.1	46.5	35.0	21.9	43.3
Mean Minimum Temp. (°F)	5.4	7.5	17.3	31.2	42.5	52.2	56.7	54.8	47.0	36.6	27.1	13.2	32.6
Extreme Maximum Temp. (°F)	64	62	83	87	91	95	95	95	96	82	73	66	96
Extreme Minimum Temp. (°F)	-37	-38	-22	5	23	28	36	36	23	17	-5	-28	-38
Days Maximum Temp. ≥ 90°F	0	0	0	0	0	1	1	1	0	0	0	0	3
Days Maximum Temp. ≤ 32°F	21	16	8	0	0	0	0	0	0	0	4	16	65
Days Minimum Temp. ≤ 32°F	30	27	28	18	4	0	0	0	1	10	22	29	169
Days Minimum Temp. ≤ 0°F	12	10	3	0	0	0	0	0	0	0	0	6	31
Heating Degree Days (base 65°F)	1,531	1,297	1,127	667	321	100	29	54	222	569	893	1,329	8,139
Cooling Degree Days (base 65°F)	0	0	0	1	12	69	128	97	22	1	0	0	330
Mean Precipitation (in.)	2.65	2.21	2.78	2.79	3.64	3.79	4.31	4.47	3.39	3.76	3.50	3.21	40.50
Extreme Maximum Daily Precip. (in.)	2.08	2.33	1.52	1.48	2.00	1.77	1.70	3.51	3.00	2.26	2.61	2.06	3.51
Days With ≥ 0.1" Precipitation	7	6	7	8	9	9	9	9	7	8	8	8	95
Days With ≥ 0.5" Precipitation	1	1	1	2	2	2	3	3	2	3	2	2	24
Days With ≥ 1.0" Precipitation	0	0	0	0	0	1	1	1	1	1	0	0	5
Mean Snowfall (in.)	21.8	17.6	18.4	5.0	0.1	0.0	0.0	0.0	trace	1.0	7.1	23.1	94.1
Maximum Snow Depth (in.)	30	34	40	31	trace	0	0	0	trace	4	17	30	40
Days With ≥ 1.0" Snow Depth	30	28	27	6	0	0	0	0	0	0	7	24	122

Rochester *Windsor County* Elevation: 830 ft. Latitude: 43° 52' N Longitude: 72° 48' W

	JAN	FEB	MAR	APR	MAY	JUN	JUL	AUG	SEP	OCT	NOV	DEC	YEAR
Mean Maximum Temp. (°F)	28.7	32.6	40.3	54.2	66.8	74.6	78.9	77.7	70.5	58.2	46.0	33.6	55.2
Mean Temp. (°F)	17.8	20.2	28.7	42.1	53.3	62.0	66.5	65.5	58.0	46.4	36.3	23.9	43.4
Mean Minimum Temp. (°F)	6.9	7.8	16.9	30.0	39.8	49.3	54.0	53.2	45.4	34.5	26.7	14.2	31.6
Extreme Maximum Temp. (°F)	64	64	81	91	89	95	95	94	95	82	75	68	95
Extreme Minimum Temp. (°F)	-32	-28	-21	1	24	30	36	34	23	15	-1	-30	-32
Days Maximum Temp. ≥ 90°F	0	0	0	0	0	1	1	1	0	0	0	0	3
Days Maximum Temp. ≤ 32°F	19	13	7	0	0	0	0	0	0	0	2	14	55
Days Minimum Temp. ≤ 32°F	30	28	28	20	7	0	0	0	1	14	21	29	178
Days Minimum Temp. ≤ 0°F	11	9	3	0	0	0	0	0	0	0	0	5	28
Heating Degree Days (base 65°F)	1,458	1,260	1,121	680	362	130	43	65	224	572	853	1,267	8,035
Cooling Degree Days (base 65°F)	0	0	0	1	7	46	97	86	21	1	0	0	259
Mean Precipitation (in.)	3.27	2.79	3.40	3.86	4.34	4.92	4.61	4.49	4.27	4.52	3.81	3.75	48.03
Extreme Maximum Daily Precip. (in.)	2.06	2.48	2.32	3.43	3.53	3.42	3.70	3.30	5.33	2.58	2.23	3.05	5.33
Days With ≥ 0.1" Precipitation	6	6	7	8	9	9	9	8	7	8	7	7	91
Days With ≥ 0.5" Precipitation	2	2	2	3	3	3	3	3	3	3	3	3	33
Days With ≥ 1.0" Precipitation	1	1	1	1	1	1	1	1	1	1	1	1	12
Mean Snowfall (in.)	18.8	17.0	15.1	3.2	trace	0.0	0.0	0.0	0.0	0.3	4.1	18.1	76.6
Maximum Snow Depth (in.)	34	33	38	22	trace	0	0	0	0	3	12	30	38
Days With ≥ 1.0" Snow Depth	26	25	20	3	0	0	0	0	0	0	4	21	99

Rutland *Rutland County* Elevation: 620 ft. Latitude: 43° 37' N Longitude: 72° 58' W

	JAN	FEB	MAR	APR	MAY	JUN	JUL	AUG	SEP	OCT	NOV	DEC	YEAR
Mean Maximum Temp. (°F)	30.7	34.1	43.3	57.4	69.2	77.5	81.2	79.2	71.0	59.2	47.3	35.2	57.1
Mean Temp. (°F)	20.8	23.5	32.4	45.5	56.4	65.2	69.3	67.7	59.6	48.3	38.3	26.3	46.1
Mean Minimum Temp. (°F)	10.9	12.9	21.4	33.5	43.5	52.9	57.4	56.2	48.2	37.3	29.2	17.3	35.1
Extreme Maximum Temp. (°F)	67	67	86	92	92	95	96	95	92	83	79	69	96
Extreme Minimum Temp. (°F)	-36	-26	-19	5	26	32	39	36	24	17	3	-23	-36
Days Maximum Temp. ≥ 90°F	0	0	0	0	0	2	2	1	0	0	0	0	5
Days Maximum Temp. ≤ 32°F	17	12	5	0	0	0	0	0	0	0	2	12	48
Days Minimum Temp. ≤ 32°F	30	27	27	15	3	0	0	0	1	10	20	29	162
Days Minimum Temp. ≤ 0°F	7	5	2	0	0	0	0	0	0	0	0	3	17
Heating Degree Days (base 65°F)	1,364	1,166	1,004	580	276	72	18	36	182	513	795	1,194	7,200
Cooling Degree Days (base 65°F)	0	0	0	2	15	85	159	126	29	1	0	0	417
Mean Precipitation (in.)	2.47	2.13	2.71	2.85	3.67	4.00	4.76	4.14	3.86	3.56	3.24	2.86	40.25
Extreme Maximum Daily Precip. (in.)	2.51	2.23	2.10	1.85	2.12	3.55	2.66	3.06	3.77	2.82	1.82	3.65	3.77
Days With ≥ 0.1" Precipitation	6	5	6	7	8	8	8	8	6	7	8	7	84
Days With ≥ 0.5" Precipitation	2	1	2	2	2	3	4	3	2	2	2	2	27
Days With ≥ 1.0" Precipitation	0	0	0	0	1	1	1	1	1	1	0	0	6
Mean Snowfall (in.)	17.2	13.9	12.8	3.2	trace	0.0	0.0	0.0	trace	0.5	4.6	16.5	68.7
Maximum Snow Depth (in.)	32	***27***	28	21	trace	0	0	0	trace	***2***	***10***	***19***	***32***
Days With ≥ 1.0" Snow Depth	23	***22***	14	2	0	0	0	0	0	0	4	19	***84***

The period of record for all cooperative weather station data is 1980 – 2009. See User Guide for detailed explanation of data.

Saint Johnsbury *Caledonia County* Elevation: 700 ft. Latitude: 44° 25' N Longitude: 72° 01' W

	JAN	FEB	MAR	APR	MAY	JUN	JUL	AUG	SEP	OCT	NOV	DEC	YEAR
Mean Maximum Temp. (°F)	28.0	32.7	42.1	57.1	69.6	77.7	81.2	79.4	71.2	58.4	44.7	32.2	56.2
Mean Temp. (°F)	17.7	21.1	30.8	44.6	56.3	65.2	69.3	67.7	59.7	47.7	36.6	23.5	45.0
Mean Minimum Temp. (°F)	7.5	9.5	19.5	32.1	42.9	52.7	57.4	55.9	48.2	37.0	28.4	14.9	33.8
Extreme Maximum Temp. (°F)	63	62	84	92	91	98	98	94	92	84	73	67	98
Extreme Minimum Temp. (°F)	-32	-31	-24	7	21	30	37	34	25	17	-6	-31	-32
Days Maximum Temp. ≥ 90°F	0	0	0	0	0	2	2	1	0	0	0	0	5
Days Maximum Temp. ≤ 32°F	20	14	5	0	0	0	0	0	0	0	3	16	58
Days Minimum Temp. ≤ 32°F	30	27	27	16	4	0	0	0	1	11	20	29	165
Days Minimum Temp. ≤ 0°F	11	8	3	0	0	0	0	0	0	0	0	5	27
Heating Degree Days (base 65°F)	1,459	1,234	1,052	606	279	74	18	36	182	530	846	1,279	7,595
Cooling Degree Days (base 65°F)	0	0	0	2	16	88	159	126	30	1	0	0	422
Mean Precipitation (in.)	2.51	2.15	2.51	2.79	3.35	3.96	4.11	4.14	3.42	3.74	3.40	3.06	39.14
Extreme Maximum Daily Precip. (in.)	1.82	1.51	1.84	2.10	2.04	3.37	3.06	4.33	4.53	2.55	2.17	1.87	4.53
Days With ≥ 0.1" Precipitation	6	6	6	7	8	8	9	7	7	7	7	7	85
Days With ≥ 0.5" Precipitation	1	1	1	2	2	3	3	3	2	2	2	2	24
Days With ≥ 1.0" Precipitation	0	0	0	0	1	0	1	1	1	1	0	0	5
Mean Snowfall (in.)	21.4	17.6	15.5	4.7	0.0	0.0	0.0	0.0	trace	0.5	5.7	22.8	88.2
Maximum Snow Depth (in.)	25	34	35	25	trace	0	0	0	trace	1	12	23	35
Days With ≥ 1.0" Snow Depth	28	27	23	3	0	0	0	0	0	0	6	24	111

South Lincoln *Addison County* Elevation: 1,370 ft. Latitude: 44° 05' N Longitude: 72° 58' W

	JAN	FEB	MAR	APR	MAY	JUN	JUL	AUG	SEP	OCT	NOV	DEC	YEAR
Mean Maximum Temp. (°F)	25.7	28.8	37.2	50.8	63.6	72.0	76.0	74.4	66.7	54.4	43.5	31.3	52.0
Mean Temp. (°F)	15.5	17.8	26.7	40.3	52.1	60.8	65.1	63.5	55.6	44.2	34.9	22.1	41.5
Mean Minimum Temp. (°F)	5.2	6.7	16.1	29.7	40.7	49.6	54.1	52.6	44.4	34.0	26.1	12.9	31.0
Extreme Maximum Temp. (°F)	64	63	76	89	88	92	94	91	90	78	73	62	94
Extreme Minimum Temp. (°F)	-35	-29	-20	2	23	26	34	29	20	12	-4	-28	-35
Days Maximum Temp. ≥ 90°F	0	0	0	0	0	0	0	0	0	0	0	0	0
Days Maximum Temp. ≤ 32°F	21	18	11	1	0	0	0	0	0	0	5	16	72
Days Minimum Temp. ≤ 32°F	29	27	28	19	6	0	0	0	3	14	22	28	176
Days Minimum Temp. ≤ 0°F	12	10	4	0	0	0	0	0	0	0	0	6	32
Heating Degree Days (base 65°F)	1,531	1,330	1,183	735	399	158	70	100	289	636	897	1,323	8,651
Cooling Degree Days (base 65°F)	0	0	0	1	7	39	78	62	13	0	0	0	200
Mean Precipitation (in.)	2.84	2.22	3.07	3.77	4.31	4.65	4.74	5.28	4.16	4.79	4.06	3.33	47.22
Extreme Maximum Daily Precip. (in.)	1.75	2.12	1.85	3.40	1.96	3.65	***2.84***	***3.19***	3.97	2.94	***2.23***	***2.15***	***3.97***
Days With ≥ 0.1" Precipitation	7	6	8	8	10	9	9	8	8	9	8	8	98
Days With ≥ 0.5" Precipitation	1	1	2	2	3	3	3	3	3	3	2	2	28
Days With ≥ 1.0" Precipitation	0	0	1	1	1	1	1	1	1	1	1	1	10
Mean Snowfall (in.)	27.5	22.9	22.3	9.5	0.5	0.0	0.0	trace	0.0	2.3	11.6	28.2	124.8
Maximum Snow Depth (in.)	46	36	44	42	4	trace	0	trace	0	11	24	24	46
Days With ≥ 1.0" Snow Depth	28	26	24	7	0	0	0	0	0	1	9	23	118

St Albans Radio *Franklin County* Elevation: 459 ft. Latitude: 44° 49' N Longitude: 73° 05' W

	JAN	FEB	MAR	APR	MAY	JUN	JUL	AUG	SEP	OCT	NOV	DEC	YEAR
Mean Maximum Temp. (°F)	25.9	28.6	37.5	53.2	65.6	74.6	78.4	76.7	68.2	55.4	43.3	31.4	53.2
Mean Temp. (°F)	17.3	19.9	28.9	43.7	55.6	65.2	69.3	67.4	59.1	47.3	36.5	23.9	44.5
Mean Minimum Temp. (°F)	8.7	11.2	20.3	34.2	45.6	55.7	60.2	58.0	49.9	39.1	29.7	16.3	35.7
Extreme Maximum Temp. (°F)	64	63	78	88	88	96	94	96	90	79	73	64	96
Extreme Minimum Temp. (°F)	-31	-29	-17	6	25	31	38	36	23	19	-2	-25	-31
Days Maximum Temp. ≥ 90°F	0	0	0	0	0	1	1	0	0	0	0	0	2
Days Maximum Temp. ≤ 32°F	21	18	10	1	0	0	0	0	0	0	5	15	70
Days Minimum Temp. ≤ 32°F	29	26	27	13	1	0	0	0	1	8	18	28	151
Days Minimum Temp. ≤ 0°F	9	6	2	0	0	0	0	0	0	0	0	5	22
Heating Degree Days (base 65°F)	1,472	1,267	1,112	632	302	82	22	44	202	544	847	1,268	7,794
Cooling Degree Days (base 65°F)	0	0	0	1	17	95	163	126	31	2	0	0	435
Mean Precipitation (in.)	2.12	1.93	2.52	2.99	3.18	3.43	3.73	3.95	3.62	3.50	3.35	2.51	36.83
Extreme Maximum Daily Precip. (in.)	1.86	1.42	1.98	1.41	***3.11***	3.45	2.30	3.01	2.80	2.05	1.82	2.07	***3.45***
Days With ≥ 0.1" Precipitation	5	5	7	8	7	7	8	7	7	8	8	7	84
Days With ≥ 0.5" Precipitation	1	1	1	2	2	2	2	2	2	2	2	1	20
Days With ≥ 1.0" Precipitation	0	0	0	0	0	1	1	1	1	1	1	0	6
Mean Snowfall (in.)	17.5	16.6	15.4	5.3	0.1	0.0	0.0	0.0	trace	0.7	6.3	18.2	80.1
Maximum Snow Depth (in.)	30	31	37	18	1	0	0	0	trace	3	10	23	37
Days With ≥ 1.0" Snow Depth	22	23	17	2	0	0	0	0	0	0	5	18	87

The period of record for all cooperative weather station data is 1980 – 2009. See User Guide for detailed explanation of data.

Vermont Weather Station Rankings

Annual Extreme Maximum Temperature

Rank	Station Name	°F	Rank	Station Name	°F
	Highest			**Lowest**	
1	Burlington Int'l Arpt	100	1	South Lincoln	94
1	Essex Junction 1 N	*100*	2	Montpelier Arpt	95
3	Saint Johnsbury	98	2	Enosburg Falls	95
4	Cavendish	97	2	Rochester	95
4	Cornwall	97	5	Newport	96
6	Newport	96	5	Rutland	96
6	Rutland	96	5	St Albans Radio	96
6	St Albans Radio	96	8	Cavendish	97
9	Montpelier Arpt	95	8	Cornwall	97
9	Enosburg Falls	95	10	Saint Johnsbury	98
9	Rochester	95	11	Burlington Int'l Arpt	100
12	South Lincoln	94	11	Essex Junction 1 N	*100*

Annual Mean Maximum Temperature

Rank	Station Name	°F	Rank	Station Name	°F
	Highest			**Lowest**	
1	Rutland	57.1	1	South Lincoln	52.0
2	Saint Johnsbury	56.2	2	Montpelier Arpt	52.9
3	Cavendish	55.8	3	St Albans Radio	53.2
3	Enosburg Falls	55.8	4	Newport	53.9
5	Cornwall	*55.5*	5	Burlington Int'l Arpt	55.1
6	Essex Junction 1 N	*55.2*	6	Essex Junction 1 N	*55.2*
6	Rochester	55.2	6	Rochester	55.2
8	Burlington Int'l Arpt	55.1	8	Cornwall	*55.5*
9	Newport	53.9	9	Cavendish	55.8
10	St Albans Radio	53.2	9	Enosburg Falls	55.8
11	Montpelier Arpt	52.9	11	Saint Johnsbury	56.2
12	South Lincoln	52.0	12	Rutland	57.1

Rankings include 25 highest/lowest stations. If state has less than 25 stations, all stations are included. The period of record is 1980–2009. See User Guide for detailed explanation of data.

Annual Mean Temperature

Highest			Lowest		
Rank	**Station Name**	**°F**	**Rank**	**Station Name**	**°F**
1	Rutland	46.1	1	South Lincoln	41.5
2	Burlington Int'l Arpt	45.8	2	Montpelier Arpt	43.0
3	Cornwall	***45.5***	3	Newport	43.3
4	Saint Johnsbury	45.0	4	Rochester	43.4
5	Enosburg Falls	44.7	5	Cavendish	43.9
5	Essex Junction 1 N	***44.7***	6	St Albans Radio	44.5
7	St Albans Radio	44.5	7	Enosburg Falls	44.7
8	Cavendish	43.9	7	Essex Junction 1 N	***44.7***
9	Rochester	43.4	9	Saint Johnsbury	45.0
10	Newport	43.3	10	Cornwall	***45.5***
11	Montpelier Arpt	43.0	11	Burlington Int'l Arpt	45.8
12	South Lincoln	41.5	12	Rutland	46.1

Annual Mean Minimum Temperature

Highest			Lowest		
Rank	**Station Name**	**°F**	**Rank**	**Station Name**	**°F**
1	Burlington Int'l Arpt	36.4	1	South Lincoln	31.0
2	St Albans Radio	35.7	2	Rochester	31.6
3	Cornwall	***35.4***	3	Cavendish	31.9
4	Rutland	35.1	4	Newport	32.6
5	Essex Junction 1 N	***34.2***	5	Montpelier Arpt	33.0
6	Saint Johnsbury	33.8	6	Enosburg Falls	33.5
7	Enosburg Falls	33.5	7	Saint Johnsbury	33.8
8	Montpelier Arpt	33.0	8	Essex Junction 1 N	***34.2***
9	Newport	32.6	9	Rutland	35.1
10	Cavendish	31.9	10	Cornwall	***35.4***
11	Rochester	31.6	11	St Albans Radio	35.7
12	South Lincoln	31.0	12	Burlington Int'l Arpt	36.4

Rankings include 25 highest/lowest stations. If state has less than 25 stations, all stations are included. The period of record is 1980–2009. See User Guide for detailed explanation of data.

Annual Extreme Minimum Temperature

Highest Rank	Station Name	°F	Lowest Rank	Station Name	°F
1	Burlington Int'l Arpt	-29	1	Enosburg Falls	-41
2	Cornwall	-30	2	Newport	-38
3	St Albans Radio	-31	3	Cavendish	-36
4	Rochester	-32	3	Rutland	-36
4	Saint Johnsbury	-32	5	Essex Junction 1 N	***-35***
6	Montpelier Arpt	-34	5	South Lincoln	-35
7	Essex Junction 1 N	***-35***	7	Montpelier Arpt	-34
7	South Lincoln	-35	8	Rochester	-32
9	Cavendish	-36	8	Saint Johnsbury	-32
9	Rutland	-36	10	St Albans Radio	-31
11	Newport	-38	11	Cornwall	-30
12	Enosburg Falls	-41	12	Burlington Int'l Arpt	-29

July Mean Maximum Temperature

Highest Rank	Station Name	°F	Lowest Rank	Station Name	°F
1	Rutland	81.2	1	South Lincoln	76.0
1	Saint Johnsbury	81.2	2	Montpelier Arpt	78.1
3	Burlington Int'l Arpt	80.8	3	St Albans Radio	78.4
3	Cavendish	80.8	4	Rochester	79.0
5	Cornwall	80.6	5	Newport	79.2
6	Essex Junction 1 N	***80.3***	6	Enosburg Falls	80.2
7	Enosburg Falls	80.2	7	Essex Junction 1 N	***80.3***
8	Newport	79.2	8	Cornwall	80.6
9	Rochester	79.0	9	Burlington Int'l Arpt	80.8
10	St Albans Radio	78.4	9	Cavendish	80.8
11	Montpelier Arpt	78.1	11	Rutland	81.2
12	South Lincoln	76.0	11	Saint Johnsbury	81.2

 Rankings include 25 highest/lowest stations. If state has less than 25 stations, all stations are included. The period of record is 1980–2009. See User Guide for detailed explanation of data.

January Mean Minimum Temperature

Highest			Lowest		
Rank	Station Name	°F	Rank	Station Name	°F
1	Rutland	10.9	1	South Lincoln	5.2
2	Burlington Int'l Arpt	10.2	2	Newport	5.4
3	Cornwall	10.0	3	Enosburg Falls	6.1
4	St Albans Radio	8.7	4	Cavendish	6.5
5	Saint Johnsbury	7.5	5	Rochester	6.9
6	Montpelier Arpt	7.3	6	Essex Junction 1 N	*7.1*
7	Essex Junction 1 N	*7.1*	7	Montpelier Arpt	7.3
8	Rochester	6.9	8	Saint Johnsbury	7.5
9	Cavendish	6.5	9	St Albans Radio	8.7
10	Enosburg Falls	6.1	10	Cornwall	10.0
11	Newport	5.4	11	Burlington Int'l Arpt	10.2
12	South Lincoln	5.2	12	Rutland	10.9

Number of Days Annually Maximum Temperature ≥ 90°F

Highest			Lowest		
Rank	Station Name	Days	Rank	Station Name	Days
1	Burlington Int'l Arpt	7	1	South Lincoln	0
1	Cavendish	7	2	St Albans Radio	2
1	Essex Junction 1 N	*7*	3	Montpelier Arpt	3
4	Rutland	5	3	Enosburg Falls	3
4	Saint Johnsbury	5	3	Newport	3
6	Cornwall	4	3	Rochester	3
7	Montpelier Arpt	3	7	Cornwall	4
7	Enosburg Falls	3	8	Rutland	5
7	Newport	3	8	Saint Johnsbury	5
7	Rochester	3	10	Burlington Int'l Arpt	7
11	St Albans Radio	2	10	Cavendish	7
12	South Lincoln	0	10	Essex Junction 1 N	*7*

Number of Days Annually Maximum Temperature ≤ 32°F

Highest

Rank	Station Name	Days
1	Montpelier Arpt	73
2	South Lincoln	72
3	St Albans Radio	70
4	Newport	65
5	Burlington Int'l Arpt	61
6	Cornwall	58
6	Enosburg Falls	58
6	Essex Junction 1 N	***58***
6	Saint Johnsbury	58
10	Rochester	55
11	Cavendish	52
12	Rutland	48

Lowest

Rank	Station Name	Days
1	Rutland	48
2	Cavendish	52
3	Rochester	55
4	Cornwall	58
4	Enosburg Falls	58
4	Essex Junction 1 N	***58***
4	Saint Johnsbury	58
8	Burlington Int'l Arpt	61
9	Newport	65
10	St Albans Radio	70
11	South Lincoln	72
12	Montpelier Arpt	73

Number of Days Annually Minimum Temperature ≤ 32°F

Highest

Rank	Station Name	Days
1	Cavendish	184
2	Rochester	178
3	South Lincoln	176
4	Newport	169
5	Montpelier Arpt	168
6	Saint Johnsbury	165
7	Rutland	162
8	Enosburg Falls	161
8	Essex Junction 1 N	***161***
10	Cornwall	155
11	St Albans Radio	151
12	Burlington Int'l Arpt	148

Lowest

Rank	Station Name	Days
1	Burlington Int'l Arpt	148
2	St Albans Radio	151
3	Cornwall	155
4	Enosburg Falls	161
4	Essex Junction 1 N	***161***
6	Rutland	162
7	Saint Johnsbury	165
8	Montpelier Arpt	168
9	Newport	169
10	South Lincoln	176
11	Rochester	178
12	Cavendish	184

 Rankings include 25 highest/lowest stations. If state has less than 25 stations, all stations are included. The period of record is 1980–2009. See User Guide for detailed explanation of data.

Number of Days Annually Minimum Temperature ≤ 0°F

Highest			Lowest		
Rank	**Station Name**	**Days**	**Rank**	**Station Name**	**Days**
1	South Lincoln	32	1	Rutland	17
2	Newport	31	2	Burlington Int'l Arpt	19
3	Enosburg Falls	30	2	Cornwall	19
4	Cavendish	28	4	St Albans Radio	22
4	Essex Junction 1 N	***28***	5	Montpelier Arpt	24
4	Rochester	28	6	Saint Johnsbury	27
7	Saint Johnsbury	27	7	Cavendish	28
8	Montpelier Arpt	24	7	Essex Junction 1 N	***28***
9	St Albans Radio	22	7	Rochester	28
10	Burlington Int'l Arpt	19	10	Enosburg Falls	30
10	Cornwall	19	11	Newport	31
12	Rutland	17	12	South Lincoln	32

Number of Annual Heating Degree Days

Highest			Lowest		
Rank	**Station Name**	**Num.**	**Rank**	**Station Name**	**Num.**
1	South Lincoln	8,651	1	Rutland	7,200
2	Montpelier Arpt	8,216	2	Burlington Int'l Arpt	7,408
3	Newport	8,139	3	Cornwall	***7,455***
4	Rochester	8,035	4	Saint Johnsbury	7,595
5	Cavendish	7,936	5	Enosburg Falls	7,693
6	St Albans Radio	7,794	6	Essex Junction 1 N	***7,737***
7	Essex Junction 1 N	***7,737***	7	St Albans Radio	7,794
8	Enosburg Falls	7,693	8	Cavendish	7,936
9	Saint Johnsbury	7,595	9	Rochester	8,035
10	Cornwall	***7,455***	10	Newport	8,139
11	Burlington Int'l Arpt	7,408	11	Montpelier Arpt	8,216
12	Rutland	7,200	12	South Lincoln	8,651

Number of Annual Cooling Degree Days

Highest			Lowest		
Rank	Station Name	Num.	Rank	Station Name	Num.
1	Burlington Int'l Arpt	511	1	South Lincoln	200
2	Essex Junction 1 N	***464***	2	Rochester	259
3	Cornwall	***451***	3	Montpelier Arpt	283
4	St Albans Radio	435	4	Newport	330
5	Saint Johnsbury	422	5	Cavendish	336
6	Rutland	417	6	Enosburg Falls	398
7	Enosburg Falls	398	7	Rutland	417
8	Cavendish	336	8	Saint Johnsbury	422
9	Newport	330	9	St Albans Radio	435
10	Montpelier Arpt	283	10	Cornwall	***451***
11	Rochester	259	11	Essex Junction 1 N	***464***
12	South Lincoln	200	12	Burlington Int'l Arpt	511

Annual Precipitation

Highest			Lowest		
Rank	Station Name	Inches	Rank	Station Name	Inches
1	Rochester	48.03	1	Burlington Int'l Arpt	36.45
2	South Lincoln	47.22	2	Montpelier Arpt	36.50
3	Cavendish	46.30	3	St Albans Radio	36.83
4	Enosburg Falls	41.63	4	Cornwall	***37.09***
5	Essex Junction 1 N	***40.96***	5	Saint Johnsbury	39.14
6	Newport	40.50	6	Rutland	40.25
7	Rutland	40.25	7	Newport	40.50
8	Saint Johnsbury	39.14	8	Essex Junction 1 N	***40.96***
9	Cornwall	***37.09***	9	Enosburg Falls	41.63
10	St Albans Radio	36.83	10	Cavendish	46.30
11	Montpelier Arpt	36.50	11	South Lincoln	47.22
12	Burlington Int'l Arpt	36.45	12	Rochester	48.03

Rankings include 25 highest/lowest stations. If state has less than 25 stations, all stations are included. The period of record is 1980–2009. See User Guide for detailed explanation of data.

Annual Extreme Maximum Daily Precipitation

Highest Rank	Station Name	Inches	Lowest Rank	Station Name	Inches
1	Cavendish	5.34	1	Essex Junction 1 N	***3.19***
2	Rochester	5.33	2	St Albans Radio	***3.45***
3	Cornwall	***4.70***	3	Newport	3.51
4	Saint Johnsbury	4.53	4	Burlington Int'l Arpt	3.62
5	South Lincoln	***3.97***	5	Enosburg Falls	3.68
6	Montpelier Arpt	3.90	6	Rutland	3.77
7	Rutland	3.77	7	Montpelier Arpt	3.90
8	Enosburg Falls	3.68	8	South Lincoln	***3.97***
9	Burlington Int'l Arpt	3.62	9	Saint Johnsbury	4.53
10	Newport	3.51	10	Cornwall	***4.70***
11	St Albans Radio	***3.45***	11	Rochester	5.33
12	Essex Junction 1 N	***3.19***	12	Cavendish	5.34

Number of Days Annually With ≥ 0.1 Inches of Precipitation

Highest Rank	Station Name	Days	Lowest Rank	Station Name	Days
1	Enosburg Falls	99	1	Cornwall	***74***
2	South Lincoln	98	2	Montpelier Arpt	78
3	Newport	95	3	Burlington Int'l Arpt	81
4	Rochester	91	4	Rutland	84
5	Essex Junction 1 N	***89***	4	St Albans Radio	84
6	Cavendish	85	6	Cavendish	85
6	Saint Johnsbury	85	6	Saint Johnsbury	85
8	Rutland	84	8	Essex Junction 1 N	***89***
8	St Albans Radio	84	9	Rochester	91
10	Burlington Int'l Arpt	81	10	Newport	95
11	Montpelier Arpt	78	11	South Lincoln	98
12	Cornwall	***74***	12	Enosburg Falls	99

Rankings include 25 highest/lowest stations. If state has less than 25 stations, all stations are included. The period of record is 1980–2009. See User Guide for detailed explanation of data.

Number of Days Annually With ≥ 0.5 Inches of Precipitation

Highest Rank	Station Name	Days	Lowest Rank	Station Name	Days
1	Cavendish	34	1	St Albans Radio	20
2	Rochester	33	2	Montpelier Arpt	22
3	South Lincoln	28	2	Burlington Int'l Arpt	22
4	Rutland	27	4	Cornwall	23
5	Enosburg Falls	26	5	Essex Junction 1 N	*24*
6	Essex Junction 1 N	*24*	5	Newport	24
6	Newport	24	5	Saint Johnsbury	24
6	Saint Johnsbury	24	8	Enosburg Falls	26
9	Cornwall	23	9	Rutland	27
10	Montpelier Arpt	22	10	South Lincoln	28
10	Burlington Int'l Arpt	22	11	Rochester	33
12	St Albans Radio	20	12	Cavendish	34

Number of Days Annually With ≥ 1.0 Inches of Precipitation

Highest Rank	Station Name	Days	Lowest Rank	Station Name	Days
1	Cavendish	12	1	Newport	5
1	Rochester	12	1	Saint Johnsbury	5
3	South Lincoln	10	3	Montpelier Arpt	6
4	Cornwall	7	3	Burlington Int'l Arpt	6
4	Enosburg Falls	7	3	Essex Junction 1 N	*6*
6	Montpelier Arpt	6	3	Rutland	6
6	Burlington Int'l Arpt	6	3	St Albans Radio	6
6	Essex Junction 1 N	*6*	8	Cornwall	7
6	Rutland	6	8	Enosburg Falls	7
6	St Albans Radio	6	10	South Lincoln	10
11	Newport	5	11	Cavendish	12
11	Saint Johnsbury	5	11	Rochester	12

Rankings include 25 highest/lowest stations. If state has less than 25 stations, all stations are included. The period of record is 1980–2009. See User Guide for detailed explanation of data.

Annual Snowfall

Highest Rank	Highest Station Name	Highest Inches	Lowest Rank	Lowest Station Name	Lowest Inches
1	South Lincoln	124.8	1	Cornwall	57.0
2	Newport	94.1	2	Rutland	68.7
3	Saint Johnsbury	88.2	3	Rochester	76.6
4	Cavendish	83.8	4	St Albans Radio	80.1
5	Essex Junction 1 N	***83.2***	5	Burlington Int'l Arpt	81.1
6	Enosburg Falls	81.9	6	Enosburg Falls	81.9
7	Burlington Int'l Arpt	81.1	7	Essex Junction 1 N	***83.2***
8	St Albans Radio	80.1	8	Cavendish	83.8
9	Rochester	76.6	9	Saint Johnsbury	88.2
10	Rutland	68.7	10	Newport	94.1
11	Cornwall	57.0	11	South Lincoln	124.8

Annual Maximum Snow Depth

Highest Rank	Highest Station Name	Highest Inches	Lowest Rank	Lowest Station Name	Lowest Inches
1	South Lincoln	46	1	Cornwall	***28***
2	Cavendish	41	2	Burlington Int'l Arpt	31
3	Newport	40	2	Essex Junction 1 N	***31***
4	Rochester	38	4	Rutland	***32***
5	St Albans Radio	37	5	Saint Johnsbury	35
6	Saint Johnsbury	35	6	St Albans Radio	37
7	Rutland	***32***	7	Rochester	38
8	Burlington Int'l Arpt	31	8	Newport	40
8	Essex Junction 1 N	***31***	9	Cavendish	41
10	Cornwall	***28***	10	South Lincoln	46

Rankings include 25 highest/lowest stations. If state has less than 25 stations, all stations are included. The period of record is 1980–2009. See User Guide for detailed explanation of data.

Number of Days Annually With ≥ 1.0 Inch Snow Depth

Highest

Rank	Station Name	Days
1	Cavendish	122
1	Newport	122
3	South Lincoln	118
4	Saint Johnsbury	111
5	Essex Junction 1 N	***100***
6	Rochester	99
7	Burlington Int'l Arpt	88
8	St Albans Radio	87
9	Rutland	***84***
10	Cornwall	***50***

Lowest

Rank	Station Name	Days
1	Cornwall	***50***
2	Rutland	***84***
3	St Albans Radio	87
4	Burlington Int'l Arpt	88
5	Rochester	99
6	Essex Junction 1 N	***100***
7	Saint Johnsbury	111
8	South Lincoln	118
9	Cavendish	122
9	Newport	122

 Rankings include 25 highest/lowest stations. If state has less than 25 stations, all stations are included. The period of record is 1980–2009. See User Guide for detailed explanation of data.

Significant Storm Events in Vermont: 2000 – 2009

Location or County	Date	Type	Mag.	Deaths	Injuries	Property Damage ($mil.)	Crop Damage ($mil.)
Windsor County	01/07/00	Light Snow	na	1	2	0.0	0.0
Washington	12/17/00	Flood	na	0	0	1.0	0.0
Essex County	02/05/01	Winter Storm	na	1	0	0.0	0.0
Windsor	07/04/02	Lightning	na	1	0	0.0	0.0
Western Chittenden County	02/22/03	Winter Weather/Mix	na	1	0	0.0	0.0
Lamoille County	03/21/04	Winter Weather/Mix	na	1	0	0.0	0.0
Grand Isle County	06/26/04	Strong Wind	46 mph	1	0	0.0	0.0
Franklin	07/12/04	Lightning	na	1	1	0.0	0.0
Addison	08/28/04	Flash Flood	na	0	0	1.7	0.0
Rutland County	04/16/07	High Wind	79 mph	0	0	1.0	0.0
Washington	07/11/07	Flash Flood	na	0	0	1.5	0.0

Note: Deaths, injuries, and damages are date and location specific.

VIRGINIA

PHYSICAL FEATURES. Virginia is located on the east coast of the North American continent between latitudes 36.5° and 39.5° N. The State is triangular in shape with the longest north-south distance of about 200 miles and the longest east-west distance more than 400 miles. There are 40,815 square miles of area within the State of which 1,200 square miles are inland waters.

The State is composed of three natural topographic regions, namely: the Tidewater or coastal plains area, the Piedmont plateau or middle Virginia; and the western mountain region. Tidewater Virginia extends westward from the Atlantic Coast and west shore of the Chesapeake Bay to the "Fall Line." The "Fall Line" extends from Great Falls in the north, southward through Richmond to Emporia. It is divided into necks, or peninsulas, by four principal rivers and by numerous estuaries that open into the Chesapeake Bay. The principal rivers include the Potomac, Rappahannock, York, and the James. The Piedmont region is more than 200 miles wide in southern Virginia, but the Virginia section becomes quite narrow in the north. This region from east to west becomes more rolling and hilly with a few isolated mountains and ridges appearing a few miles east of the Blue Ridge. Elevations in general range from about 300 feet above sea level in the east to about 1,000 feet in the west. The James, the largest river crossing this region, divides it into two parts.

West of the Piedmont, the Blue Ridge Mountains traverse the State from southwest to northeast. They range from narrow ridges in the north to a high, wide plateau southwest from Roanoke. Elevations range generally from 1,500 to 3,500 feet. Mt. Rogers, in western Grayson County, towers to 5,719 feet, the highest point in the State. A great valley west of the Blue Ridge extends from Tennessee through Scott and Washington Counties in the south, northeastward to the northern-most point of the State. This great valley of Virginia is well drained. The north is drained by the north and south forks of the Shenandoah River, thence into the Potomac; the central portion by the Cow Pasture and Jackson Rivers flowing southeastward into the James; and the southwestern half of the valley is drained by the Roanoke River, the New River, and three forks of the Holston River.

GENERAL CLIMATE. The climate of Virginia is determined by its proximity to the Atlantic Ocean, latitude, and topography. The State is in the zone of prevailing westerly movement of the earth's atmosphere, in or near the mean path of winter storm tracks, and in the mean path of tropical, moist air from the southwest Atlantic and Gulf of Mexico much of the summer and early fall seasons. The mountains provide the usual elevation effects on temperatures, which are distinctly lower in this section, and there are wide variations over short distances as elevations change. Summers in the mountains are comparatively cool, and winters are more severe. In addition, these mountains produce various steering, blocking, and modifying effects on storms and general air movements in their vicinity. Temperature variations within the State due to latitude alone are very small. The longitudinal variations, however, show a sharper contrast, from the mountain extremes in the west toward an ocean influence in the east. The prevalence of winds with a westerly component prevents the extension of ocean influences very far westward from the coast.

Virginia lies in the zone of prevailing westerlies where the general motion is from west to east. Southerly and northerly winds are about equally frequent, reflecting the progression of weather systems over the State. The Appalachian mountains, however, act to deflect these winds to some extent with northeasterly and southwesterly directions occurring frequently. During the cold season a more intense circulation is present with frequent storms and outbreaks of cold polar air. Northerly winds are most common during this season. The storm track is well north of the State during the warm season and southerly winds with light speeds prevail.

Summers in Virginia are usually warm and humid, and several hot and humid periods usually occur each year. Principal sources of moisture are the Gulf of Mexico and the Atlantic Ocean. Relative humidity varies inversely with temperature — high in the morning and low in the afternoon. Tidewater locations have a much higher frequency of humidity and uncomfortable temperatures.

PRECIPITATION. The annual precipitation ranges from about 35 to 50 inches. The heaviest amounts occur in the extreme southwest, the southeast, and the south-central areas. Minimum amounts are found in the sheltered valleys west of the Blue Ridge Mountains. Precipitation is well distributed throughout the year without distinct wet and dry periods. Maximum rainfall occurs in the summer months and minimum in the fall months. Precipitation during the cold season is associated with migratory low-pressure storms. The amounts are quite evenly distributed during this season in comparison to the warm season when showers and thundershowers account for most of the rainfall. Excessive rainfall usually occurs in the fall season with the passage of hurricanes. Snow is common in winter. Average seasonal amounts range from less than 10 inches in Tidewater Virginia to around 20 inches west of the Blue Ridge, and up to 30 inches on the mountains. Occasionally, a major snowstorm will occur with snow depths greater than 10 inches.

The greater portion of the State lies in the Atlantic drainage. The extreme southwestern portion drains to the Ohio Basin. Floods occur in all months of the year. The greatest frequency occurs in late winter and early spring; snowmelt occasionally is a factor. July is the month of least flooding. A second period of high water shows up in late summer and fall in the Piedmont and Tidewater sections associated mainly with tropical storms. Intense convectional storms in summer occasionally cause local flash floods.

Virginia is also subject to drought periods. Drought may be defined broadly as a prolonged and abnormal moisture deficiency. Some portions of Virginia sustain real damage from drought on the average of one year out of three. Equitable distribution of ample precipitation has seldom, if ever, occurred over all of Virginia for an entire season. Almost every year some sections undergo periods of insufficient rainfall.

STORMS. Thunderstorms occur on the average of 32 to 50 days each year, the greater number occurring in the mountains of extreme southwestern Virginia, decreasing in number toward the northeastern part of the State. About 85 percent of the annual total occur during the period May to September. Only a small percentage of these can be classed as severe, however. Thunderstorms exact a sizable annual toll of damage when accompanied by severe lightning, wind, or hail. Tornadoes are local storms of short duration and usually small dimensions, formed of winds rotating at high speeds. Approximately four tornadoes are reported in Virginia each year. These tornadoes occur mainly east of the Blue Ridge, but a few have been observed in the mountains.

A hurricane is a tropical storm with winds of at least 74 m.p.h., which blow in a large spiral around a relatively calm center. Virginia has been affected by hurricanes since the early settlement days, but most have decreased in intensity before entering the State. Even though a hurricane may not enter the State, it can be much more destructive by passing closely offshore and maintaining its intense circulation. High tides along with waves and currents, and flooding from the torrential rains, cause damage. About 80 percent of the hurricanes occur during August, September, and October. An average of about two hurricanes each year come close enough to affect Virginia, but less than one enters the State.

Middle latitude storms sometimes develop south of Virginia and move northward along the Virginia coast. These storms, although usually weaker than hurricanes, produce similar type of damage. This type of storm, often referred to as a "Northeaster," generally occurs from late fall through the spring months. They often account for considerable damage from high tides, strong east or northeast winds, and heavy rain, mainly in Tidewater Virginia.

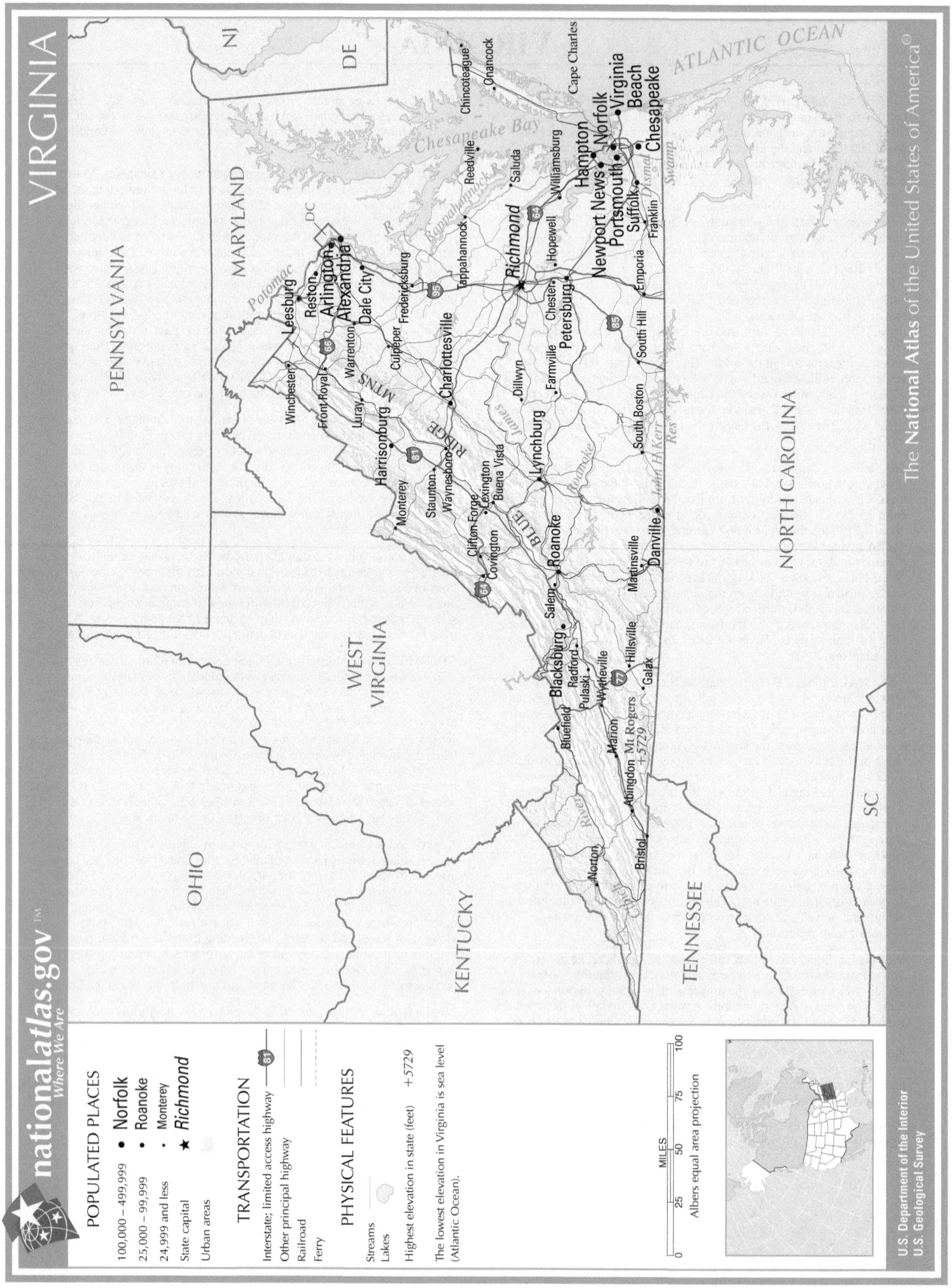
VIRGINIA
nationalatlas.gov™
Where We Are
POPULATED PLACES
100,000 – 499,999 • Norfolk
25,000 – 99,999 • Roanoke
24,999 and less · Monterey
State capital ★ Richmond
Urban areas
TRANSPORTATION
Interstate; limited access highway
Other principal highway
Railroad
Ferry
PHYSICAL FEATURES
Streams
Lakes
Highest elevation in state (feet) +5729
The lowest elevation in Virginia is sea level (Atlantic Ocean).
MILES
0 25 50 75 100
Albers equal area projection
U.S. Department of the Interior
U.S. Geological Survey
The National Atlas of the United States of America®
PENNSYLVANIA
MARYLAND
NJ
DE
DC
OHIO
WEST VIRGINIA
KENTUCKY
TENNESSEE
NORTH CAROLINA
SC
ATLANTIC OCEAN
Chesapeake Bay
Potomac R
Rappahannock R
James R
Roanoke R
Clinch River
John H Kerr Res
Dismal Swamp
BLUE RIDGE MTNS
Winchester
Front Royal
Leesburg
Reston
Arlington
Alexandria
Dale City
Warrenton
Luray
Culpeper
Fredericksburg
Harrisonburg
Charlottesville
Staunton
Waynesboro
Monterey
Lexington
Buena Vista
Clifton Forge
Covington
Lynchburg
Roanoke
Salem
Blacksburg
Radford
Pulaski
Wytheville
Bluefield
Marion
Mt Rogers +5729
Abingdon
Bristol
Norton
Hillsville
Galax
Martinsville
Danville
South Boston
South Hill
Emporia
Dillwyn
Farmville
Petersburg
Chester
Hopewell
Richmond
Tappahannock
Reedville
Saluda
Williamsburg
Hampton
Newport News
Norfolk
Portsmouth
Virginia Beach
Chesapeake
Suffolk
Franklin
Cape Charles
Onancock
Chincoteague
66
95
64
81
85
77

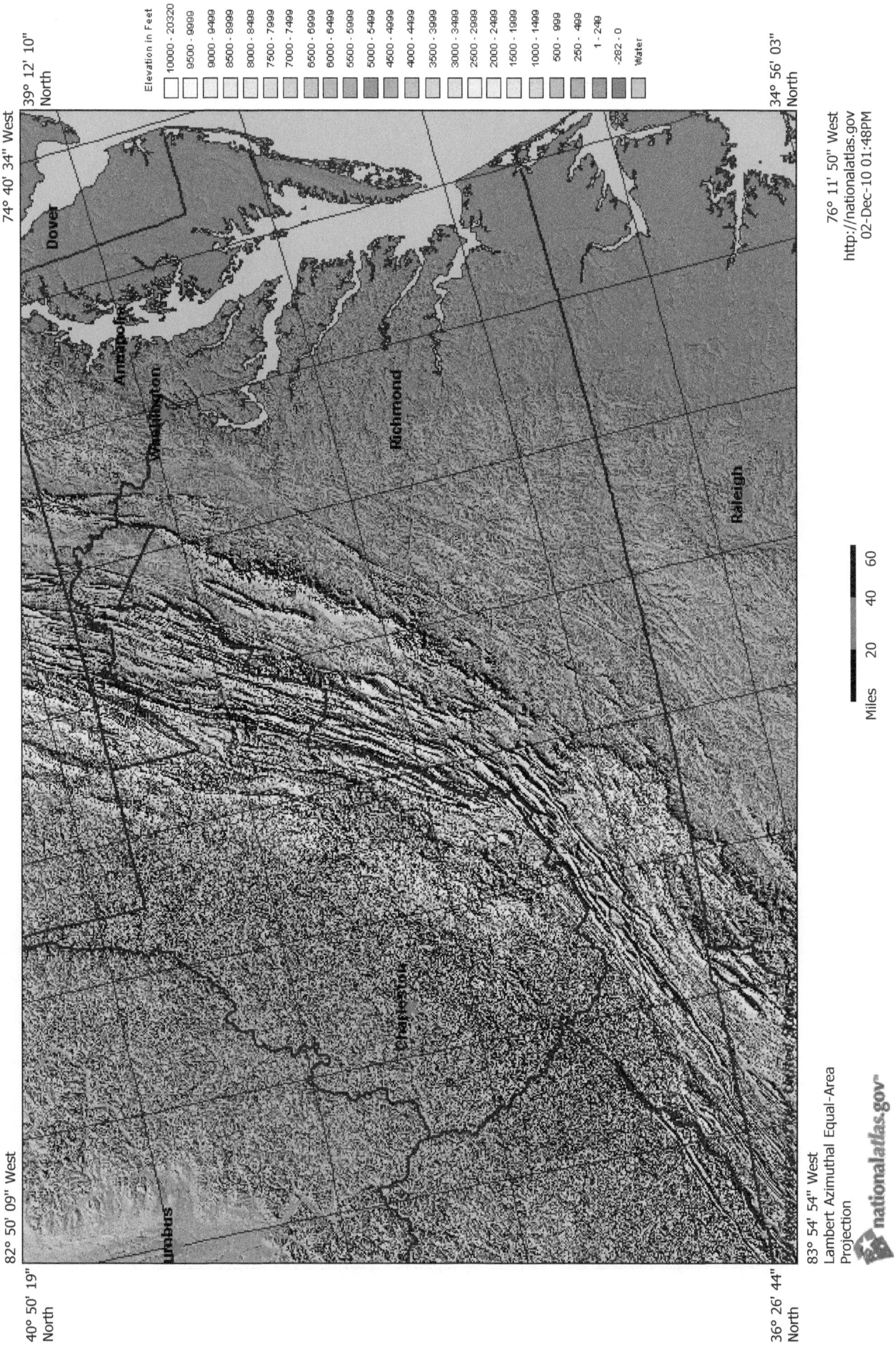
Elevation in Feet
10000 - 20320
9500 - 9999
9000 - 9499
8500 - 8999
8000 - 8499
7500 - 7999
7000 - 7499
6500 - 6999
6000 - 6499
5500 - 5999
5000 - 5499
4500 - 4999
4000 - 4499
3500 - 3999
3000 - 3499
2500 - 2999
2000 - 2499
1500 - 1999
1000 - 1499
500 - 999
250 - 499
1 - 249
-282 - 0
Water
39° 12' 10" North
74° 40' 34" West
34° 56' 03" North
76° 11' 50" West
http://nationalatlas.gov
02-Dec-10 01:48PM
40° 50' 19" North
82° 50' 09" West
36° 26' 44" North
83° 54' 54" West
Lambert Azimuthal Equal-Area Projection
Dover
Annapolis
Washington
Richmond
Raleigh
Charleston
Miles
20
40
60
nationalatlas.gov

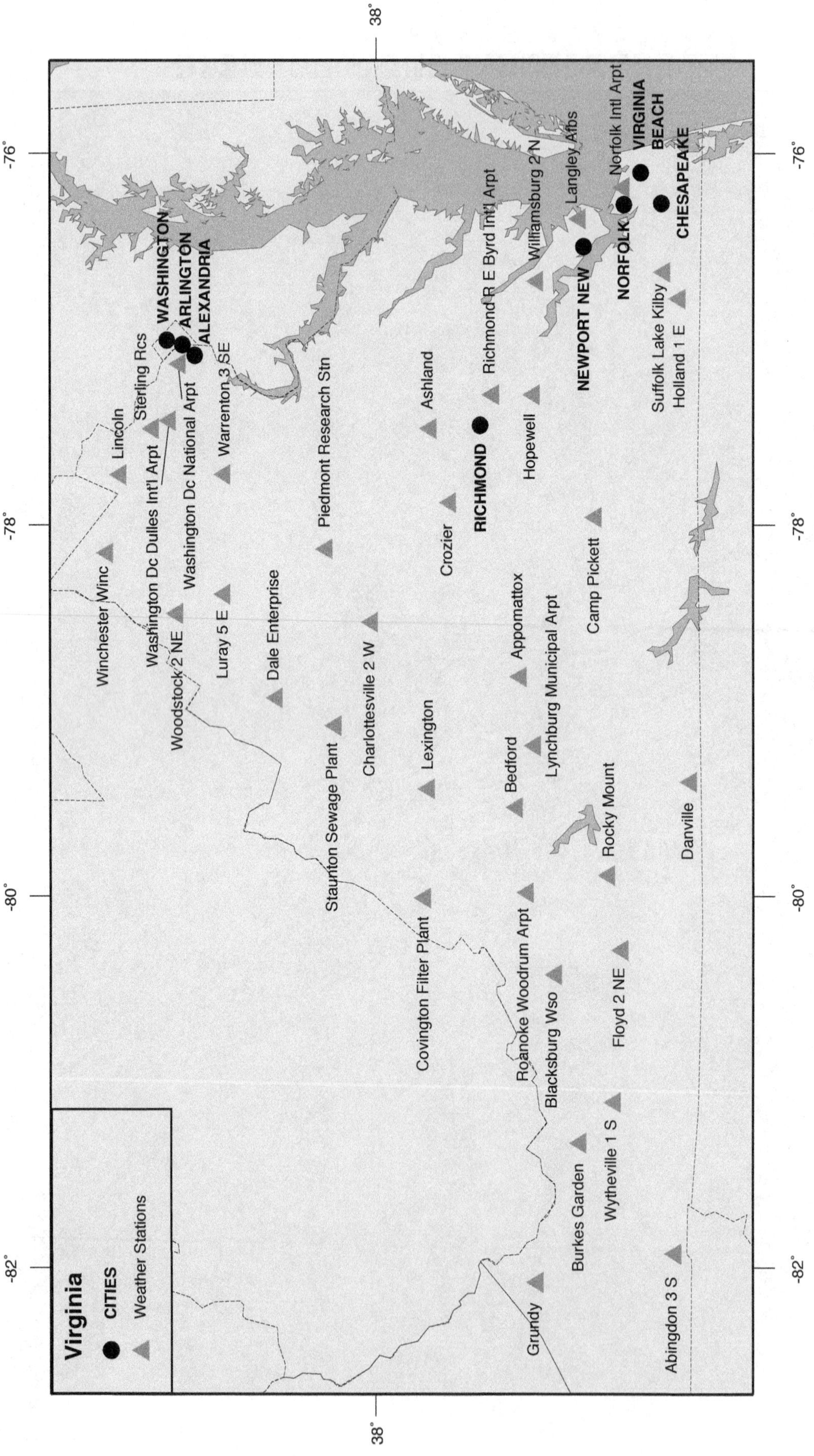
Virginia
CITIES
Weather Stations
38°
-76°
-78°
-80°
-82°
WASHINGTON
ARLINGTON
ALEXANDRIA
RICHMOND
NEWPORT NEW
NORFOLK
VIRGINIA BEACH
CHESAPEAKE
Lincoln
Sterling Rcs
Washington Dc Dulles Int'l Arpt
Washington Dc National Arpt
Warrenton 3 SE
Winchester Winc
Woodstock 2 NE
Luray 5 E
Dale Enterprise
Piedmont Research Stn
Staunton Sewage Plant
Charlottesville 2 W
Ashland
Crozier
Lexington
Richmond R E Byrd Int'l Arpt
Hopewell
Appomattox
Bedford
Lynchburg Municipal Arpt
Williamsburg 2 N
Langley Afbs
Norfolk Intl Arpt
Suffolk Lake Kilby
Holland 1 E
Camp Pickett
Rocky Mount
Danville
Covington Filter Plant
Roanoke Woodrum Arpt
Blacksburg Wso
Floyd 2 NE
Burkes Garden
Wytheville 1 S
Grundy
Abingdon 3 S

Virginia Weather Stations by County

County	Station Name
Albemarle	Charlottesville 2 W
Alleghany	Covington Filter Plant
Appomattox	Appomattox
Arlington	Washington DC National Arpt
Augusta	Staunton Sewage Plant
Bedford	Bedford
Buchanan	Grundy
Campbell	Lynchburg Municipal Arpt
Fauquier	Warrenton 3 SE
Floyd	Floyd 2 NE
Franklin	Rocky Mount
Frederick	Winchester Winc
Goochland	Crozier
Hampton (city)	Langley AFB
Hanover	Ashland
Henrico	Richmond R E Byrd Int'l Arpt
Loudoun	Lincoln Sterling RCS Washington DC Dulles Int'l Arpt
Montgomery	Blacksburg Wso
Norfolk	Norfolk Intl Arpt
Nottoway	Camp Pickett
Orange	Piedmont Research Stn
Page	Luray 5 E
Pittsylvania	Danville
Prince George	Hopewell
Roanoke	Roanoke Woodrum Arpt
Rockbridge	Lexington
Rockingham	Dale Enterprise
Shenandoah	Woodstock 2 NE
Suffolk (city)	Holland 1 E Suffolk Lake Kilby
Tazewell	Burkes Garden
Washington	Abingdon 3 S
Wythe	Wytheville 1 S
York	Williamsburg 2 N

See User Guide for station inclusion criteria.

Virginia Weather Stations by City

City	Station Name	Miles
Alexandria	Beltsville, MD	18.5
	Dalecarlia Reservoir, MD	7.9
	Glenn Dale Bell Stn, MD	18.7
	Laurel 3 W, MD	21.9
	Rockville 1 NE, MD	19.3
	Upper Marlboro 3 NNW, MD	17.0
	Sterling RCS	23.8
	Washington Dulles Int'l Arpt	20.7
	Washington National Arpt	4.5
Annandale	Beltsville, MD	22.4
	Dalecarlia Reservoir, MD	8.6
	Glenn Dale Bell Stn, MD	24.0
	Laurel 3 W, MD	24.9
	Rockville 1 NE, MD	19.4
	Upper Marlboro 3 NNW, MD	23.1
	Sterling RCS	17.9
	Washington Dulles Int'l Arpt	14.6
	Washington National Arpt	9.8
Arlington	Beltsville, MD	16.1
	Dalecarlia Reservoir, MD	4.2
	Glenn Dale Bell Stn, MD	17.4
	Laurel 3 W, MD	19.0
	Rockville 1 NE, MD	15.6
	Upper Marlboro 3 NNW, MD	17.1
	Sterling RCS	21.8
	Washington Dulles Int'l Arpt	19.2
	Washington National Arpt	3.7
Blacksburg	Blacksburg Wso	2.4
	Floyd 2 NE	21.6
	Union 3 SSE, WV	22.9
Burke	Dalecarlia Reservoir, MD	13.5
	Rockville 1 NE, MD	23.9
	Sterling RCS	17.9
	Washington Dulles Int'l Arpt	14.1
	Washington National Arpt	14.2
Cave Spring	Blacksburg Wso	21.7
	Roanoke Woodrum Arpt	6.5
	Rocky Mount	17.9
Centreville	Dalecarlia Reservoir, MD	18.7
	Lincoln	25.0
	Sterling RCS	10.1
	Warrenton 3 SE	20.5
	Washington Dulles Int'l Arpt	6.4
	Washington National Arpt	22.1
Chantilly	Dalecarlia Reservoir, MD	15.9
	Rockville 1 NE, MD	22.4
	Lincoln	24.5
	Sterling RCS	8.6
	Warrenton 3 SE	23.7
	Washington Dulles Int'l Arpt	4.7
	Washington National Arpt	19.9
Charlottesville	Charlottesville 2 W	1.3
	Piedmont Research Stn	24.0
Chesapeake	Langley AFB	22.8
	Norfolk Intl Arpt	10.8

City	Station Name	Miles
Chesapeake *(cont.)*	Suffolk Lake Kilby	17.7
Dale City	Dalecarlia Reservoir, MD	23.3
	Sterling RCS	24.4
	Warrenton 3 SE	22.9
	Washington Dulles Int'l Arpt	20.6
	Washington National Arpt	22.6
Danville	Reidsville 2 NW, NC	21.6
	Danville	1.5
Franconia	Beltsville, MD	23.4
	Dalecarlia Reservoir, MD	11.8
	Glenn Dale Bell Stn, MD	23.4
	Rockville 1 NE, MD	23.3
	Upper Marlboro 3 NNW, MD	20.9
	Sterling RCS	23.5
	Washington Dulles Int'l Arpt	19.9
	Washington National Arpt	9.4
Hampton	Langley AFB	2.8
	Norfolk Intl Arpt	13.5
Harrisonburg	Dale Enterprise	3.5
	Staunton Sewage Plant	22.3
Jefferson	Beltsville, MD	20.1
	Dalecarlia Reservoir, MD	6.1
	Glenn Dale Bell Stn, MD	22.1
	Laurel 3 W, MD	22.4
	Rockville 1 NE, MD	16.8
	Upper Marlboro 3 NNW, MD	21.9
	Sterling RCS	17.7
	Washington Dulles Int'l Arpt	14.7
	Washington National Arpt	8.4
Lake Ridge	Dalecarlia Reservoir, MD	19.9
	Sterling RCS	22.5
	Warrenton 3 SE	24.7
	Washington Dulles Int'l Arpt	18.6
	Washington National Arpt	19.3
Leesburg	Rockville 1 NE, MD	24.6
	Lincoln	8.6
	Sterling RCS	9.6
	Washington Dulles Int'l Arpt	13.5
Lynchburg	Appomattox	19.6
	Bedford	18.5
	Lynchburg Municipal Arpt	4.7
Manassas	Dalecarlia Reservoir, MD	23.0
	Sterling RCS	16.0
	Warrenton 3 SE	16.4
	Washington Dulles Int'l Arpt	12.6
McLean	Beltsville, MD	17.3
	Dalecarlia Reservoir, MD	3.2
	Glenn Dale Bell Stn, MD	20.3
	Laurel 3 W, MD	18.9
	Rockville 1 NE, MD	12.5
	Upper Marlboro 3 NNW, MD	21.5
	Sterling RCS	17.0
	Washington Dulles Int'l Arpt	14.8

See User Guide for station inclusion criteria.

City	Station Name	Miles
McLean *(cont.)*	Washington National Arpt	8.8
Mechanicsville	Ashland	11.6
	Hopewell	22.2
	Richmond R E Byrd Int'l Arpt	7.3
Mount Vernon	Beltsville, MD	24.3
	Dalecarlia Reservoir, MD	14.2
	Glenn Dale Bell Stn, MD	23.4
	Upper Marlboro 3 NNW, MD	19.9
	Washington Dulles Int'l Arpt	23.2
	Washington National Arpt	10.4
Newport News	Langley AFB	8.1
	Norfolk Intl Arpt	20.9
	Williamsburg 2 N	18.5
Norfolk	Langley AFB	13.8
	Norfolk Intl Arpt	3.3
	Suffolk Lake Kilby	22.0
Oakton	Beltsville, MD	24.4
	Dalecarlia Reservoir, MD	10.1
	Rockville 1 NE, MD	18.3
	Sterling RCS	12.4
	Washington Dulles Int'l Arpt	9.2
	Washington National Arpt	14.0
Petersburg	Hopewell	8.2
	Richmond R E Byrd Int'l Arpt	21.6
Portsmouth	Langley AFB	17.3
	Norfolk Intl Arpt	9.7
	Suffolk Lake Kilby	15.3
Reston	Dalecarlia Reservoir, MD	12.5
	Rockville 1 NE, MD	16.7
	Lincoln	23.4
	Sterling RCS	7.6
	Washington Dulles Int'l Arpt	5.7
	Washington National Arpt	17.9
Richmond	Ashland	14.8
	Crozier	24.5
	Hopewell	18.7
	Richmond R E Byrd Int'l Arpt	8.3
Roanoke	Bedford	24.9
	Blacksburg Wso	24.7
	Roanoke Woodrum Arpt	2.7
	Rocky Mount	20.6
Salem	Blacksburg Wso	19.8
	Roanoke Woodrum Arpt	5.3
	Rocky Mount	22.6
Springfield	Beltsville, MD	23.4
	Dalecarlia Reservoir, MD	10.7
	Glenn Dale Bell Stn, MD	24.0
	Rockville 1 NE, MD	22.1
	Upper Marlboro 3 NNW, MD	22.1
	Sterling RCS	21.3
	Washington Dulles Int'l Arpt	17.7
	Washington National Arpt	9.7

City	Station Name	Miles
Suffolk	Holland 1 E	12.3
	Norfolk Intl Arpt	22.5
	Suffolk Lake Kilby	2.8
Tuckahoe	Ashland	11.8
	Crozier	17.1
	Richmond R E Byrd Int'l Arpt	15.7
Virginia Beach	Langley AFB	22.7
	Norfolk Intl Arpt	7.7
West Springfield	Dalecarlia Reservoir, MD	12.0
	Rockville 1 NE, MD	22.9
	Upper Marlboro 3 NNW, MD	24.9
	Sterling RCS	19.2
	Washington Dulles Int'l Arpt	15.5
	Washington National Arpt	12.1
Winchester	Lincoln	24.4
	Winchester Winc	1.1
	Woodstock 2 NE	24.9
	Martinsburg E. WV Reg Arpt, WV	18.4
Woodbridge	Dalecarlia Reservoir, MD	21.6
	Washington Dulles Int'l Arpt	22.4
	Washington National Arpt	19.8

Note: Miles is the distance between the geographic center of the city and the weather station.

Virginia Weather Stations by Elevation

Feet	Station Name
3,299	Burkes Garden
2,625	Floyd 2 NE
2,450	Wytheville 1 S
2,009	Blacksburg Wso
1,919	Abingdon 3 S
1,640	Staunton Sewage Plant
1,399	Dale Enterprise
1,314	Rocky Mount
1,299	Luray 5 E
1,229	Covington Filter Plant
1,169	Grundy
1,148	Roanoke Woodrum Arpt
1,060	Lexington
975	Bedford
939	Lynchburg Municipal Arpt
910	Appomattox
870	Charlottesville 2 W
720	Winchester Winc
660	Woodstock 2 NE
520	Piedmont Research Stn
500	Lincoln
500	Warrenton 3 SE
410	Danville
350	Crozier
330	Camp Pickett
290	Washington DC Dulles Int'l Arpt
279	Sterling RCS
220	Ashland
164	Richmond R E Byrd Int'l Arpt
80	Holland 1 E
69	Williamsburg 2 N
40	Hopewell
23	Norfolk Intl Arpt
21	Suffolk Lake Kilby
9	Langley AFB
9	Washington DC National Arpt

See User Guide for station inclusion criteria.

Lynchburg Municipal Airport

Lynchburg is situated in the valley of the James River, and on the eastern edge of the Blue Ridge Mountains. The terrain is definitely hilly, with sheltered valleys which are visited by early autumn and late spring frosts. The climate is usually a pleasant one, being neither too hot in the summer, nor too cold in the winter. Rainfall is fairly evenly distributed throughout the year, but there is a distinct summertime rainfall, occasioned by afternoon thunderstorms.

Spring makes itself felt in March, when the mean monthly temperature increases about seven degrees over the February temperature. Autumn rapidly comes in October, which shows about a 10 degree drop below the September mean. The approaching autumn season brings periods of two to three days of cloudy, cool weather, with high humidity and light rain or drizzle. In midwinter, however, after the passage of a cold front, dry invigorating air, with clear skies, is the rule in Lynchburg. There are occasional snow showers, but the mountains to the immediate west act as a barrier and shelter the area from many storms and high winds.

The mountains also act as a barrier to extremely cold weather. Temperatures have fallen below zero only on a few days, and 100 degree heat is almost as rare, although this mark has been exceeded in the months of May through September.

Great variation in temperature is quite frequently noted during clear, still nights in the winter months. On some such nights, differences of as much as 10-15 degrees occur between the low valleys and the higher terrain.

Based on the 1951-1980 period, the average first occurrence of 32 degrees Fahrenheit in the fall is October 23 and the average last occurrence in the spring is April 13.

Lynchburg Municipal Airport *Campbell County* Elevation: 939 ft. Latitude: 37° 20' N Longitude: 79° 12' W

	JAN	FEB	MAR	APR	MAY	JUN	JUL	AUG	SEP	OCT	NOV	DEC	YEAR
Mean Maximum Temp. (°F)	45.4	49.3	57.7	68.0	75.5	83.0	86.5	85.4	78.4	68.4	58.5	48.2	67.0
Mean Temp. (°F)	36.0	39.0	46.5	56.1	64.0	72.2	76.0	74.9	67.9	56.9	47.5	38.6	56.3
Mean Minimum Temp. (°F)	26.5	28.8	35.3	44.1	52.4	61.3	65.5	64.4	57.3	45.3	36.5	29.0	45.5
Extreme Maximum Temp. (°F)	80	79	87	94	92	97	101	102	97	92	81	79	102
Extreme Minimum Temp. (°F)	-10	-10	5	20	31	40	49	46	35	23	15	-4	-10
Days Maximum Temp. ≥ 90°F	0	0	0	0	0	5	10	8	2	0	0	0	25
Days Maximum Temp. ≤ 32°F	4	2	0	0	0	0	0	0	0	0	0	2	8
Days Minimum Temp. ≤ 32°F	23	20	12	3	0	0	0	0	0	3	11	21	93
Days Minimum Temp. ≤ 0°F	0	0	0	0	0	0	0	0	0	0	0	0	0
Heating Degree Days (base 65°F)	893	727	570	281	103	10	1	1	45	266	518	812	4,227
Cooling Degree Days (base 65°F)	0	0	3	21	78	233	350	317	137	21	1	0	1,161
Mean Precipitation (in.)	3.13	2.88	3.57	3.35	3.67	3.53	4.38	3.08	3.71	3.10	3.44	3.18	41.02
Maximum Precipitation (in.)*	8.0	5.7	9.2	7.9	9.1	10.0	10.3	11.4	9.9	11.4	8.8	7.1	59.7
Minimum Precipitation (in.)*	0.5	0.3	0.7	0.3	1.4	0.5	1.1	0.7	trace	0.4	0.9	0.3	26.6
Extreme Maximum Daily Precip. (in.)	2.03	2.20	2.14	3.01	2.21	3.47	3.61	5.29	6.05	3.86	2.81	2.14	6.05
Days With ≥ 0.1" Precipitation	6	6	7	6	8	6	7	6	5	4	6	6	73
Days With ≥ 0.5" Precipitation	2	2	3	2	2	2	3	2	2	2	3	2	27
Days With ≥ 1.0" Precipitation	1	1	1	1	1	1	1	1	1	1	1	1	12
Mean Snowfall (in.)	***5.2***	***5.3***	***2.6***	***0.2***	***trace***	***trace***	***0.0***	***0.0***	***trace***	***trace***	***0.3***	***2.7***	***16.3***
Maximum Snowfall (in.)*	32	19	25	5	0	0	0	0	0	2	12	18	56
Maximum 24-hr. Snowfall (in.)*	12	13	13	3	0	0	0	0	0	2	6	10	13
Maximum Snow Depth (in.)	***21***	***15***	***13***	***trace***	***trace***	***trace***	***0***	***0***	***trace***	***trace***	***1***	***10***	***21***
Days With ≥ 1.0" Snow Depth	***4***	***3***	***1***	***0***	***0***	***0***	***0***	***0***	***0***	***0***	***0***	***3***	***11***
Thunderstorm Days*	< 1	< 1	2	4	7	8	10	7	3	1	1	< 1	43
Foggy Days*	13	13	13	11	16	13	16	19	16	13	12	12	167
Predominant Sky Cover*	OVR	OVR	OVR	OVR	OVR	SCT	OVR	SCT	OVR	CLR	OVR	OVR	OVR
Mean Relative Humidity 7am (%)*	72	72	73	72	80	83	86	88	88	85	78	74	79
Mean Relative Humidity 4pm (%)*	51	49	46	43	51	54	56	57	56	51	50	53	52
Mean Dewpoint (°F)*	22	24	31	39	52	61	65	65	58	46	35	26	44
Prevailing Wind Direction*	SW	SW	SW	SW	SW	SW	SW	SW	NE	NE	SW	SW	SW
Prevailing Wind Speed (mph)*	8	9	10	10	9	8	8	7	9	10	8	8	9
Maximum Wind Gust (mph)*	56	58	56	58	59	74	64	75	41	51	64	47	75

Note: (*) Period of record is 1948-1995

Norfolk Int'l Airport

The city of Norfolk, Virginia, is located near the coast and the southern border of the state. It is almost surrounded by water, with the Chesapeake Bay immediately to the north, Hampton Roads to the west, and the Atlantic Ocean only 18 miles to the east. It is traversed by numerous rivers and waterways and its average elevation above sea level is 13 feet. There are no nearby hilly areas and the land is low and level throughout the city. The climate is generally marine. The geographic location of the city with respect to the principal storm tracks, is especially favorable, being south of the average path of storms originating in the higher latitudes and north of the usual tracks of hurricanes and other tropical storms.

The winters are usually mild, while the autumn and spring seasons usually are delightful. Summers, though warm and long, frequently are tempered by cool periods, often associated with northeasterly winds off the Atlantic. Temperatures of 100 degrees or higher occur infrequently. Extreme cold waves seldom penetrate the area and temperatures of zero or below are almost nonexistent. Winters pass, on occasion, without a measurable amount of snowfall. Most of the snowfall in Norfolk is light and generally melts within 24 hours.

Based on the 1951-1980 period, the average first occurrence of 32 degrees Fahrenheit in the fall is November 17 and the average last occurrence in the spring is March 23.

Norfolk Int'l Airport *Norfolk County* Elevation: 23 ft. Latitude: 36° 54' N Longitude: 76° 12' W

	JAN	FEB	MAR	APR	MAY	JUN	JUL	AUG	SEP	OCT	NOV	DEC	YEAR
Mean Maximum Temp. (°F)	48.9	51.5	58.7	68.1	76.0	84.0	88.0	85.9	80.0	70.7	61.8	53.0	68.9
Mean Temp. (°F)	40.9	43.0	49.6	58.5	67.0	75.5	80.0	78.3	72.7	62.3	53.1	44.7	60.5
Mean Minimum Temp. (°F)	32.8	34.4	40.4	48.8	57.9	67.0	71.9	70.7	65.3	53.9	44.4	36.4	52.0
Extreme Maximum Temp. (°F)	80	82	88	94	100	101	103	104	99	94	85	80	104
Extreme Minimum Temp. (°F)	-3	9	18	28	39	50	57	49	47	34	23	7	-3
Days Maximum Temp. ≥ 90°F	0	0	0	0	2	7	14	9	2	0	0	0	34
Days Maximum Temp. ≤ 32°F	2	1	0	0	0	0	0	0	0	0	0	1	4
Days Minimum Temp. ≤ 32°F	15	12	5	0	0	0	0	0	0	0	3	11	46
Days Minimum Temp. ≤ 0°F	0	0	0	0	0	0	0	0	0	0	0	0	0
Heating Degree Days (base 65°F)	742	618	479	227	63	3	0	0	7	137	358	624	3,258
Cooling Degree Days (base 65°F)	1	1	9	39	131	326	472	420	245	61	9	2	1,716
Mean Precipitation (in.)	3.43	3.08	3.63	3.48	3.43	4.18	5.01	5.46	4.40	3.47	3.20	3.25	46.02
Maximum Precipitation (in.)*	9.9	6.2	10.4	7.3	10.1	9.7	14.4	14.3	13.8	10.1	7.0	6.1	65.0
Minimum Precipitation (in.)*	1.0	0.8	0.8	0.4	0.6	0.4	0.4	0.7	0.3	0.6	0.5	0.7	26.5
Extreme Maximum Daily Precip. (in.)	2.87	4.75	3.78	5.86	3.41	4.39	3.55	4.32	8.92	6.23	4.90	2.77	8.92
Days With ≥ 0.1" Precipitation	7	6	7	7	7	6	7	7	6	5	6	6	77
Days With ≥ 0.5" Precipitation	2	2	2	2	3	3	3	4	2	2	2	2	29
Days With ≥ 1.0" Precipitation	1	1	1	1	1	1	2	2	1	1	1	1	14
Mean Snowfall (in.)	2.7	2.8	***0.8***	***trace***	***trace***	***trace***	***0.0***	***trace***	***0.0***	***0.0***	***trace***	0.5	***6.8***
Maximum Snowfall (in.)*	14	24	14	1	0	0	0	0	0	0	1	15	42
Maximum 24-hr. Snowfall (in.)*	9	14	8	1	0	0	0	0	0	0	1	10	14
Maximum Snow Depth (in.)	na	na	na	na	na	na	na	na	na	na	na	na	na
Days With ≥ 1.0" Snow Depth	na	na	na	na	na	na	na	na	na	na	na	na	na
Thunderstorm Days*	< 1	1	2	3	5	6	9	7	3	1	1	< 1	38
Foggy Days*	13	12	12	11	13	12	12	15	14	14	13	12	153
Predominant Sky Cover*	OVR	OVR	OVR	OVR	OVR	OVR	SCT	SCT	OVR	OVR	OVR	OVR	OVR
Mean Relative Humidity 7am (%)*	74	74	74	73	77	79	81	84	83	82	79	75	78
Mean Relative Humidity 4pm (%)*	59	56	53	50	56	57	60	63	62	60	58	59	58
Mean Dewpoint (°F)*	30	30	36	44	55	63	69	68	63	52	42	33	49
Prevailing Wind Direction*	N	N	N	SW	SW	SW	SW	SW	NE	NE	SW	SW	SW
Prevailing Wind Speed (mph)*	13	14	14	13	12	12	10	9	13	13	10	12	12
Maximum Wind Gust (mph)*	69	59	66	62	66	69	63	63	67	75	55	53	75

Note: (*) Period of record is 1948-1995

Richmond R.E. Byrd Int'l Airport

Richmond is located in east-central Virginia at the head of navigation on the James River and along a line separating the Coastal Plains (Tidewater Virginia) from the Piedmont. The Blue Ridge Mountains lie about 90 miles to the west and the Chesapeake Bay 60 miles to the east. Elevations range from a few feet above sea level along the river to a little over 300 feet in parts of the western section of the city.

The climate might be classified as modified continental. Summers are warm and humid and winters generally mild. The mountains to the west act as a partial barrier to outbreaks of cold, continental air in winter. The cold winter air is delayed long enough to be modified, then further warmed as it subsides in its approach to Richmond. The open waters of the Chesapeake Bay and Atlantic Ocean contribute to the humid summers and mild winters. The coldest weather normally occurs in late December and January, when low temperatures usually average in the upper 20s, and the high temperatures in the upper 40s. Temperatures seldom lower to zero, but there have been several occurrences of below zero temperatures. Summertime high temperatures above 100 degrees are not uncommon, but do not occur every year.

Precipitation is rather uniformly distributed throughout the year. However, dry periods lasting several weeks do occur, especially in autumn when long periods of pleasant, mild weather are most common. There is considerable variability in total monthly amounts from year to year. Snow usually remains on the ground only one or two days at a time. Ice storms (freezing rain or glaze) are not uncommon, but they are seldom severe.

The James River reaches tidewater at Richmond where flooding may occur in every month of the year, most frequently in March and least in July. Hurricanes and tropical storms have been responsible for most of the flooding during the summer and early fall months. Hurricanes passing near Richmond have produced record rainfalls. In 1955, three hurricanes brought record rainfall to Richmond within a six-week period. The most noteworthy of these were Hurricanes Connie and Diane that brought heavy rains five days apart.

Damaging storms occur mainly from snow and freezing rain in winter and from hurricanes, tornadoes, and severe thunderstorms in other seasons. Damage may be from wind, flooding, or rain, or from any combination of these.

Based on the 1951-1980 period, the average first occurrence of 32 degrees Fahrenheit in the fall is October 26 and the average last occurrence in the spring is April 10.

Richmond R.E. Byrd Int'l Airport *Henrico County* Elevation: 164 ft. Latitude: 37° 31' N Longitude: 77° 19' W

	JAN	FEB	MAR	APR	MAY	JUN	JUL	AUG	SEP	OCT	NOV	DEC	YEAR
Mean Maximum Temp. (°F)	47.2	51.1	59.5	69.9	77.6	85.6	89.3	87.4	80.9	70.6	61.0	50.7	69.2
Mean Temp. (°F)	37.9	40.8	48.3	58.1	66.3	75.0	79.1	77.5	70.6	59.4	50.2	41.1	58.7
Mean Minimum Temp. (°F)	28.5	30.5	37.1	46.2	54.9	64.2	68.9	67.4	60.2	48.2	39.3	31.5	48.1
Extreme Maximum Temp. (°F)	81	82	91	96	98	101	102	104	100	95	86	81	104
Extreme Minimum Temp. (°F)	-6	-2	10	23	32	44	52	47	37	27	17	3	-6
Days Maximum Temp. ≥ 90°F	0	0	0	1	2	9	16	11	4	0	0	0	43
Days Maximum Temp. ≤ 32°F	3	1	0	0	0	0	0	0	0	0	0	2	6
Days Minimum Temp. ≤ 32°F	21	18	10	1	0	0	0	0	0	1	8	18	77
Days Minimum Temp. ≤ 0°F	0	0	0	0	0	0	0	0	0	0	0	0	0
Heating Degree Days (base 65°F)	834	677	517	236	72	5	0	1	25	206	442	734	3,749
Cooling Degree Days (base 65°F)	0	0	7	35	119	310	444	394	199	40	4	1	1,553
Mean Precipitation (in.)	3.12	2.69	4.02	3.35	3.85	3.92	4.64	4.60	3.99	3.14	3.26	3.16	43.74
Maximum Precipitation (in.)*	10.1	6.0	8.6	7.3	8.9	9.3	16.1	14.1	11.0	9.4	7.6	7.1	61.3
Minimum Precipitation (in.)*	0.6	0.3	0.9	0.5	0.4	0.4	0.5	0.6	0.3	0.3	0.2	0.4	26.8
Extreme Maximum Daily Precip. (in.)	1.89	2.56	3.14	3.35	3.05	2.98	3.70	6.68	4.53	2.94	3.51	2.62	6.68
Days With ≥ 0.1" Precipitation	6	6	7	7	7	6	7	6	5	5	5	6	73
Days With ≥ 0.5" Precipitation	2	2	3	2	3	3	3	3	3	2	2	2	30
Days With ≥ 1.0" Precipitation	1	1	1	1	1	1	1	1	1	1	1	1	12
Mean Snowfall (in.)	4.3	3.4	***1.2***	0.1	trace	0.0	trace	0.0	trace	0.0	0.2	1.8	***11.0***
Maximum Snowfall (in.)*	26	21	20	3	0	0	0	0	0	trace	9	13	47
Maximum 24-hr. Snowfall (in.)*	13	13	11	2	0	0	0	0	0	trace	7	8	13
Maximum Snow Depth (in.)	na	na	na	na	na	na	na	na	na	na	na	na	na
Days With ≥ 1.0" Snow Depth	na	na	na	na	na	na	na	na	na	na	na	na	na
Thunderstorm Days*	< 1	< 1	2	3	6	8	10	8	3	1	1	< 1	42
Foggy Days*	11	9	10	9	13	12	14	16	15	14	11	10	144
Predominant Sky Cover*	OVR	OVR	OVR	OVR	OVR	OVR	OVR	OVR	OVR	CLR	OVR	OVR	OVR
Mean Relative Humidity 7am (%)*	80	79	78	76	81	82	85	89	90	89	84	80	83
Mean Relative Humidity 4pm (%)*	55	50	46	43	51	53	56	58	57	53	51	55	52
Mean Dewpoint (°F)*	26	27	34	42	54	63	68	67	61	49	38	30	47
Prevailing Wind Direction*	N	N	SSW	SSW	S	S	SSW	S	N	N	S	SSW	S
Prevailing Wind Speed (mph)*	8	9	10	10	8	7	8	7	8	8	8	8	8
Maximum Wind Gust (mph)*	104	60	67	64	79	67	93	128	51	104	54	54	128

Note: (*) Period of record is 1948-1995

Roanoke Woodrum Airport

The climate of Roanoke is relatively mild. Roanoke is nestled among mountains which interrupt the Great Valley, extending from northernmost Virginia southwestward into east Tennessee. This location, at a point where the valley is pinched between the Blue Ridges and the Alleghenies, offers a natural barrier to the winter cold as it moves southward. It is also far enough inland that hurricanes lose much of their destructive force before reaching Roanoke. Finally, the rough terrain is an inhospitable breeding ground for tornadic activity. The elevation in the vicinity usually produces cool summer nights that make a light cover comfortable for sleeping. Although past records show extremes over 100 degrees and below zero, many years pass without either extreme being threatened.

Roanoke is located near the headwaters of the Roanoke River, which flows in a general southeasterly direction. Numerous creeks and small streams from nearby mountainous areas empty into the Roanoke River. The usual low water stage is one to 1.5 feet, and flood stage is 10 feet. Some low-lying streets in Roanoke and nearby Salem have to be blocked off during seven to eight foot stages, but damage is minor until the river overflows its banks. The highest stage on record exceeds 19 feet. Damage has been widespread on occasion and has amounted to several million dollars in the city of Roanoke alone.

The growing season averages 190 days. The average date of the last freezing temperature in spring is mid-April and the average date of the first freezing date in the fall is late October.

Rainfall is well apportioned throughout the year. Droughts are so infrequent that quoting actual records would be difficult. Snow usually falls each winter, ranging from only a trace to more than 60 inches.

Roanoke Woodrum Airport *Roanoke County* Elevation: 1,148 ft. Latitude: 37° 19' N Longitude: 79° 58' W

	JAN	FEB	MAR	APR	MAY	JUN	JUL	AUG	SEP	OCT	NOV	DEC	YEAR
Mean Maximum Temp. (°F)	45.8	49.5	57.8	67.9	75.7	83.2	87.0	85.9	78.5	68.7	58.5	48.2	67.2
Mean Temp. (°F)	36.8	39.6	47.2	56.6	64.5	72.6	76.6	75.5	68.1	57.5	48.1	39.3	56.9
Mean Minimum Temp. (°F)	27.7	29.7	36.5	45.2	53.2	62.0	66.3	65.0	57.7	46.3	37.7	30.3	46.5
Extreme Maximum Temp. (°F)	79	80	87	92	93	98	100	105	97	92	82	80	105
Extreme Minimum Temp. (°F)	-11	-1	9	20	32	41	47	42	34	24	13	-4	-11
Days Maximum Temp. ≥ 90°F	0	0	0	0	1	6	11	9	2	0	0	0	29
Days Maximum Temp. ≤ 32°F	4	2	0	0	0	0	0	0	0	0	0	2	8
Days Minimum Temp. ≤ 32°F	22	18	11	2	0	0	0	0	0	2	9	19	83
Days Minimum Temp. ≤ 0°F	0	0	0	0	0	0	0	0	0	0	0	0	0
Heating Degree Days (base 65°F)	869	711	552	271	97	9	0	1	44	248	501	790	4,093
Cooling Degree Days (base 65°F)	0	0	5	25	87	244	369	333	144	24	1	0	1,232
Mean Precipitation (in.)	2.90	2.84	3.51	3.51	3.97	3.85	4.02	3.49	3.71	2.91	3.34	2.89	40.94
Maximum Precipitation (in.)*	7.3	7.2	7.9	11.3	8.4	10.3	10.1	9.5	11.1	9.9	12.4	7.1	58.9
Minimum Precipitation (in.)*	0.3	0.1	0.4	0.5	1.3	0.6	0.4	0.7	0.1	trace	0.4	0.2	25.7
Extreme Maximum Daily Precip. (in.)	2.14	2.44	2.96	3.82	2.62	4.08	2.36	3.83	6.56	2.66	6.61	2.61	6.61
Days With ≥ 0.1" Precipitation	6	6	7	6	8	7	7	6	5	5	5	6	74
Days With ≥ 0.5" Precipitation	2	2	2	2	3	3	3	2	2	2	2	2	27
Days With ≥ 1.0" Precipitation	1	1	1	1	1	1	1	1	1	1	1	0	11
Mean Snowfall (in.)	***5.8***	***5.9***	***2.6***	***0.5***	***trace***	***trace***	***0.0***	***0.0***	***trace***	***trace***	***0.5***	***3.2***	***18.5***
Maximum Snowfall (in.)*	41	28	30	7	trace	0	0	0	0	1	14	23	73
Maximum 24-hr. Snowfall (in.)*	14	15	14	4	trace	0	0	0	0	1	8	15	15
Maximum Snow Depth (in.)	***23***	***18***	***16***	***3***	***trace***	***trace***	***0***	***0***	***trace***	***trace***	***3***	***14***	***23***
Days With ≥ 1.0" Snow Depth	***4***	***3***	***1***	***0***	***0***	***0***	***0***	***0***	***0***	***0***	***0***	***3***	***11***
Thunderstorm Days*	< 1	< 1	1	3	6	7	8	6	3	1	< 1	< 1	35
Foggy Days*	10	9	10	7	11	10	12	14	13	10	9	9	124
Predominant Sky Cover*	OVR	OVR	OVR	OVR	OVR	OVR	SCT	SCT	OVR	CLR	OVR	OVR	OVR
Mean Relative Humidity 7am (%)*	70	70	70	71	79	81	83	86	88	83	75	72	77
Mean Relative Humidity 4pm (%)*	51	48	45	44	51	53	54	54	54	49	50	52	51
Mean Dewpoint (°F)*	23	24	30	39	51	60	64	64	57	45	34	26	43
Prevailing Wind Direction*	WNW	WNW	NW	NW	SE	W	W	SE	SE	NW	NW	NW	WNW
Prevailing Wind Speed (mph)*	15	15	14	14	9	8	8	7	7	10	13	13	12
Maximum Wind Gust (mph)*	60	60	66	77	59	74	81	62	54	59	55	61	81

Note: (*) Period of record is 1948-1995

The period of record for National Weather Service station data is 1980 – 2009 except where noted. See User Guide for detailed explanation of data.

Washington Dulles Int'l Arpt.

Dulles International Airport is located in the Virginia Piedmont about 23 miles east of the Blue Ridge Mountains and 12 miles east of the Bull Run and Catoctin Mountains. The Blue Ridge rises to about 2,500 feet above sea level and the Bull Run Mountains to about 1,500 feet at their nearest points. Field elevation is 313 feet. The terrain near the airport is mostly low rolling hills about one-fourth wooded. Ponds located on and near the airport, along with poor air drainage contribute to the formation of local ground fog. Easterly winds cause an upslope effect from the Atlantic Ocean, 140 miles east, and from the Chesapeake Bay, about 55 miles east. Westerly winds create a slight foehn effect.

Its location in the middle latitudes, where the general atmospheric flow is from west to east, favors a continental climate with four well defined seasons. Summers are warm and at times humid, Winters are mild. Generally pleasant weather prevails in spring and autumn. The coldest period, when temperatures average 21 degrees, occurs in late January. The warmest period, averaging 88 degrees, occurs in the last half of July.

Precipitation is rather evenly distributed through the year. Annual precipitation has ranged from about 25 inches to more than 55 inches. Rainfalls of over 10 inches in a 24-hour period have been recorded during the passage of tropical storms. The seasonal snowfall is nearly 24 inches, but varies greatly from season to season. Snowfalls of four inches or more occur only twice each winter on average. Accumulations of over 20 inches from a single storm are extremely rare.

Storm damage results mainly from heavy snows and freezing rains in winter and from hurricanes and severe thunderstorms during the other seasons. Damage may result from wind, flooding or rain.

Prevailing winds are from the south except during the winter months when they are from the northwest. The windiest period is late winter and early spring. Winds are generally less during the night and early morning hours and increase to a high in the afternoon. Winds may reach 50 to 60 miles per hour or even higher during severe summer thunderstorms, hurricanes, and winter storms.

The growing season averages 169 days. The average date for the last freeze in spring is late April and the average date for the first freeze in the fall is mid October.

Washington Dulles Int'l Arpt. *Loudoun County* Elevation: 290 ft. Latitude: 38° 56' N Longitude: 77° 27' W

	JAN	FEB	MAR	APR	MAY	JUN	JUL	AUG	SEP	OCT	NOV	DEC	YEAR
Mean Maximum Temp. (°F)	42.2	46.2	55.0	66.3	74.8	83.3	87.6	86.4	79.1	67.8	57.0	45.9	66.0
Mean Temp. (°F)	33.0	36.0	43.8	54.1	62.9	71.9	76.5	75.2	67.6	55.7	46.1	36.5	55.0
Mean Minimum Temp. (°F)	23.8	25.8	32.5	41.9	51.0	60.5	65.3	64.0	56.2	43.5	35.1	27.1	43.9
Extreme Maximum Temp. (°F)	74	79	89	93	95	99	104	104	99	94	84	79	104
Extreme Minimum Temp. (°F)	-18	-10	-1	19	30	39	41	38	32	21	9	-4	-18
Days Maximum Temp. ≥ 90°F	0	0	0	0	1	6	12	10	3	0	0	0	32
Days Maximum Temp. ≤ 32°F	6	3	1	0	0	0	0	0	0	0	0	3	13
Days Minimum Temp. ≤ 32°F	25	21	16	4	0	0	0	0	0	4	13	23	106
Days Minimum Temp. ≤ 0°F	1	0	0	0	0	0	0	0	0	0	0	0	1
Heating Degree Days (base 65°F)	983	812	654	335	128	14	1	2	53	302	562	877	4,723
Cooling Degree Days (base 65°F)	0	0	3	15	71	228	363	327	139	20	1	0	1,167
Mean Precipitation (in.)	2.71	2.59	3.42	3.54	4.50	4.00	3.67	3.43	3.81	3.26	3.44	2.93	41.30
Maximum Precipitation (in.)*	6.6	5.8	7.6	7.3	10.3	8.6	7.2	10.7	11.3	9.2	7.8	6.7	55.4
Minimum Precipitation (in.)*	0.4	0.2	1.0	0.3	0.8	0.5	0.9	0.8	0.6	trace	0.2	0.4	28.9
Extreme Maximum Daily Precip. (in.)	1.79	2.17	2.21	2.90	3.73	5.94	3.50	4.68	5.11	3.50	2.59	2.26	5.94
Days With ≥ 0.1" Precipitation	6	5	7	7	8	7	6	6	6	5	6	6	75
Days With ≥ 0.5" Precipitation	2	2	2	2	3	3	2	2	3	2	2	2	27
Days With ≥ 1.0" Precipitation	1	1	1	1	1	1	1	1	1	1	1	0	11
Mean Snowfall (in.)	7.4	6.2	3.2	0.4	trace	trace	trace	trace	0.0	0.0	0.5	3.4	21.1
Maximum Snowfall (in.)*	29	28	16	4	trace	0	0	0	0	1	11	24	55
Maximum 24-hr. Snowfall (in.)*	11	23	14	3	trace	0	0	0	0	1	11	11	23
Maximum Snow Depth (in.)	24	22	13	1	trace	trace	trace	trace	0	0	4	18	24
Days With ≥ 1.0" Snow Depth	6	5	2	0	0	0	0	0	0	0	0	3	16
Thunderstorm Days*	< 1	< 1	1	2	4	6	6	5	2	1	1	< 1	28
Foggy Days*	13	10	12	10	14	16	19	20	18	14	12	12	170
Predominant Sky Cover*	OVR	OVR	OVR	OVR	OVR	OVR	OVR	OVR	OVR	OVR	OVR	OVR	OVR
Mean Relative Humidity 7am (%)*	77	77	78	77	82	84	86	89	89	88	82	78	82
Mean Relative Humidity 4pm (%)*	57	52	49	46	53	54	54	55	55	52	54	57	53
Mean Dewpoint (°F)*	21	22	30	39	52	61	65	64	58	45	35	26	43
Prevailing Wind Direction*	NW	NW	NW	NW	S	S	S	S	S	S	NW	NW	NW
Prevailing Wind Speed (mph)*	13	13	13	13	8	7	7	7	7	7	12	13	10
Maximum Wind Gust (mph)*	62	53	61	68	59	78	78	68	54	52	56	62	78

Note: (*) Period of record is 1962-1995

Washington National Airport

Washington lies at the western edge of the mid Atlantic Coastal Plain, about 50 miles east of the Blue Ridge Mountains and 35 miles west of Chesapeake Bay, adjacent to the Potomac and Anacostia Rivers. Elevations range from a few feet above sea level to about 400 feet in parts of the northwest section of the city.

Observations have been kept continuously since November 1870. Since June 1941 the official observations have been taken at Washington National Airport.

National Airport is located at the center of the urban heat island. As a result, low temperatures are the highest for the area. Differences between the airport and suburban locations are often 10 to 15 degrees. There is less variation in the high temperatures.

Summers are warm and humid and winters are cold, but not severe. Periods of pleasant weather often occur in the spring and fall. The summertime temperature is in the upper 80s and the winter is in the upper 20s. Precipitation is rather uniformly distributed throughout the year.

Thunderstorms can occur at any time but are most frequent during the late spring and summer. The storms are most often accompanied by downpours and gusty winds, but are not usually severe.

Tornadoes, which infrequently occur, have resulted in significant damage. Severe hailstorms have occurred in the spring.

Tropical storms can bring heavy rain, high winds and flooding, but extensive damage from wind and tidal flooding is rare. Wind gusts of nearly 100 mph and rainfall over seven inches have occurred during the passage of tropical storms and hurricanes.

Major flooding of the Potomac River can result from heavy rains over the basin, occasionally augmented by snowmelt, and above normal tides associated with hurricanes or severe storms along the coast. Flooding may also occur after a cold winter when the Potomac may be blocked with ice.

Although a snowfall of 10 inches or more in 24 hours is unusual, several notable falls of more than 25 inches have occurred. Normal snowfall during the winter season is 18 inches.

The average date of the last freezing temperature in the spring is April 1 and the average date for the first freezing temperature in the fall is November 10.

Washington National Airport *Arlington County* Elevation: 9 ft. Latitude: 38° 52' N Longitude: 77° 02' W

	JAN	FEB	MAR	APR	MAY	JUN	JUL	AUG	SEP	OCT	NOV	DEC	YEAR
Mean Maximum Temp. (°F)	43.6	47.4	55.9	66.7	75.5	84.2	88.5	86.8	79.7	68.4	57.9	47.2	66.8
Mean Temp. (°F)	36.2	39.1	46.7	56.9	66.1	75.1	79.8	78.3	71.2	59.6	49.6	40.0	58.2
Mean Minimum Temp. (°F)	28.8	30.9	37.5	47.1	56.6	66.1	71.1	69.8	62.6	50.7	41.2	32.7	49.6
Extreme Maximum Temp. (°F)	77	78	89	95	99	101	104	105	101	94	83	79	105
Extreme Minimum Temp. (°F)	-5	5	14	24	38	49	54	49	44	32	21	3	-5
Days Maximum Temp. ≥ 90°F	0	0	0	0	2	7	14	10	3	0	0	0	36
Days Maximum Temp. ≤ 32°F	5	2	0	0	0	0	0	0	0	0	0	2	9
Days Minimum Temp. ≤ 32°F	20	17	8	1	0	0	0	0	0	0	4	15	65
Days Minimum Temp. ≤ 0°F	0	0	0	0	0	0	0	0	0	0	0	0	0
Heating Degree Days (base 65°F)	886	725	563	260	72	4	0	1	20	199	457	770	3,957
Cooling Degree Days (base 65°F)	0	0	4	24	113	316	467	421	212	38	2	0	1,597
Mean Precipitation (in.)	2.85	2.52	3.53	3.12	4.00	3.77	3.68	2.88	3.58	3.37	3.18	3.01	39.49
Maximum Precipitation (in.)*	7.1	5.7	8.4	6.9	10.7	11.5	12.9	14.3	12.4	8.6	6.7	6.5	57.5
Minimum Precipitation (in.)*	0.3	0.4	0.7	trace	0.8	0.9	0.9	0.5	0.2	trace	0.3	0.2	26.9
Extreme Maximum Daily Precip. (in.)	1.84	2.27	2.29	2.41	2.63	5.19	2.18	2.43	3.67	3.67	2.57	2.36	5.19
Days With ≥ 0.1" Precipitation	6	5	7	7	7	6	6	5	5	5	5	6	70
Days With ≥ 0.5" Precipitation	2	2	2	2	3	3	3	2	2	2	2	2	27
Days With ≥ 1.0" Precipitation	1	0	1	1	1	1	1	1	1	1	1	1	11
Mean Snowfall (in.)	5.6	4.8	1.5	trace	trace	trace	trace	trace	0.0	0.0	0.5	2.3	14.7
Maximum Snowfall (in.)*	21	31	17	1	0	0	0	0	0	trace	12	16	44
Maximum 24-hr. Snowfall (in.)*	12	16	7	1	0	0	0	0	0	trace	12	11	16
Maximum Snow Depth (in.)	20	17	8	trace	trace	trace	trace	trace	0	0	12	16	20
Days With ≥ 1.0" Snow Depth	5	4	1	0	0	0	0	0	0	0	0	2	12
Thunderstorm Days*	< 1	< 1	1	3	5	6	7	5	2	1	1	< 1	31
Foggy Days*	11	10	10	9	12	10	10	11	12	13	11	11	130
Predominant Sky Cover*	OVR	OVR	OVR	OVR	OVR	OVR	OVR	OVR	OVR	OVR	OVR	OVR	OVR
Mean Relative Humidity 7am (%)*	71	70	70	70	75	76	77	81	82	81	76	72	75
Mean Relative Humidity 4pm (%)*	55	50	47	46	51	52	53	54	55	53	53	55	52
Mean Dewpoint (°F)*	23	24	31	40	52	61	66	65	59	48	37	27	45
Prevailing Wind Direction*	NW	NW	NW	S	S	S	S	S	S	S	S	NW	S
Prevailing Wind Speed (mph)*	14	14	14	9	9	9	9	9	9	9	9	14	10
Maximum Wind Gust (mph)*	71	69	73	66	64	66	83	67	64	70	66	67	83

Note: (*) Period of record is 1945-1995

The period of record for National Weather Service station data is 1980 – 2009 except where noted. See User Guide for detailed explanation of data.

Abingdon 3 S *Washington County* Elevation: 1,919 ft. Latitude: 36° 40' N Longitude: 81° 58' W

	JAN	FEB	MAR	APR	MAY	JUN	JUL	AUG	SEP	OCT	NOV	DEC	YEAR
Mean Maximum Temp. (°F)	44.5	49.0	57.9	66.9	74.8	82.0	84.6	84.2	78.5	68.6	58.0	47.4	66.4
Mean Temp. (°F)	34.2	37.6	45.1	53.5	61.8	69.7	72.9	72.1	65.7	54.9	45.6	36.7	54.2
Mean Minimum Temp. (°F)	23.7	26.2	32.4	40.1	48.7	57.4	61.1	60.0	52.9	41.3	33.2	26.0	41.9
Extreme Maximum Temp. (°F)	72	78	85	91	91	96	99	100	97	86	82	78	100
Extreme Minimum Temp. (°F)	-21	-17	-6	12	28	35	42	37	28	18	9	-12	-21
Days Maximum Temp. ≥ 90°F	0	0	0	0	0	2	5	4	1	0	0	0	12
Days Maximum Temp. ≤ 32°F	4	3	1	0	0	0	0	0	0	0	0	3	11
Days Minimum Temp. ≤ 32°F	25	22	16	7	1	0	0	0	0	6	15	23	115
Days Minimum Temp. ≤ 0°F	1	0	0	0	0	0	0	0	0	0	0	0	1
Heating Degree Days (base 65°F)	949	768	609	345	139	18	2	3	68	315	574	871	4,661
Cooling Degree Days (base 65°F)	0	0	1	8	46	165	255	229	95	10	0	0	809
Mean Precipitation (in.)	3.85	3.61	4.11	3.89	4.64	3.91	4.93	3.55	3.28	2.45	3.23	3.75	45.20
Extreme Maximum Daily Precip. (in.)	2.17	2.57	2.75	2.50	2.10	2.13	3.55	2.15	2.20	2.60	2.54	2.68	3.55
Days With ≥ 0.1" Precipitation	8	8	9	9	10	8	9	8	6	6	7	8	96
Days With ≥ 0.5" Precipitation	3	2	3	3	3	3	4	3	2	2	2	2	32
Days With ≥ 1.0" Precipitation	1	1	1	1	1	1	1	1	1	0	1	1	11
Mean Snowfall (in.)	5.6	3.8	1.7	0.2	0.0	0.0	0.0	0.0	0.0	trace	0.1	2.2	13.6
Maximum Snow Depth (in.)	18	16	14	16	0	0	0	0	0	1	2	8	18
Days With ≥ 1.0" Snow Depth	5	3	1	0	0	0	0	0	0	0	0	3	12

Appomattox *Appomattox County* Elevation: 910 ft. Latitude: 37° 21' N Longitude: 78° 50' W

	JAN	FEB	MAR	APR	MAY	JUN	JUL	AUG	SEP	OCT	NOV	DEC	YEAR
Mean Maximum Temp. (°F)	45.9	50.0	58.3	68.2	75.9	83.6	87.1	85.7	79.2	69.1	59.2	49.1	67.6
Mean Temp. (°F)	35.4	38.7	46.0	55.4	63.5	72.2	76.0	74.9	68.0	56.5	47.5	38.6	56.1
Mean Minimum Temp. (°F)	24.9	27.4	33.7	42.6	51.1	60.6	64.9	63.9	56.8	43.9	35.9	28.1	44.5
Extreme Maximum Temp. (°F)	78	80	89	93	93	97	100	103	98	93	82	79	103
Extreme Minimum Temp. (°F)	-14	-7	2	23	27	39	45	44	35	24	11	-8	-14
Days Maximum Temp. ≥ 90°F	0	0	0	1	0	6	11	8	2	0	0	0	28
Days Maximum Temp. ≤ 32°F	3	1	0	0	0	0	0	0	0	0	0	2	6
Days Minimum Temp. ≤ 32°F	24	20	13	3	0	0	0	0	0	3	11	21	95
Days Minimum Temp. ≤ 0°F	0	0	0	0	0	0	0	0	0	0	0	0	0
Heating Degree Days (base 65°F)	911	738	591	299	112	12	1	2	42	275	518	812	4,313
Cooling Degree Days (base 65°F)	0	0	4	19	72	234	349	314	138	19	1	0	1,150
Mean Precipitation (in.)	3.08	2.80	3.94	3.62	4.30	3.22	4.56	3.80	4.39	3.56	3.89	3.16	44.32
Extreme Maximum Daily Precip. (in.)	2.20	1.85	3.45	3.26	***2.65***	4.36	3.25	3.95	8.35	3.90	4.20	2.51	***8.35***
Days With ≥ 0.1" Precipitation	5	5	6	6	7	6	7	6	5	5	6	5	69
Days With ≥ 0.5" Precipitation	2	2	3	2	3	2	3	2	2	2	3	2	28
Days With ≥ 1.0" Precipitation	1	1	1	1	1	1	1	1	1	1	1	1	12
Mean Snowfall (in.)	4.7	3.7	0.9	trace	0.0	0.0	0.0	0.0	0.0	0.0	0.1	2.0	11.4
Maximum Snow Depth (in.)	***30***	***16***	***9***	***0***	***0***	***0***	***0***	***0***	***0***	***0***	1	***10***	***30***
Days With ≥ 1.0" Snow Depth	***1***	1	0	0	0	0	0	0	0	0	0	0	***2***

Ashland *Hanover County* Elevation: 220 ft. Latitude: 37° 45' N Longitude: 77° 29' W

	JAN	FEB	MAR	APR	MAY	JUN	JUL	AUG	SEP	OCT	NOV	DEC	YEAR
Mean Maximum Temp. (°F)	46.2	50.6	59.4	70.0	76.2	83.4	86.8	85.5	79.1	68.7	59.4	49.2	67.9
Mean Temp. (°F)	36.3	39.6	47.2	57.1	64.7	72.9	76.8	75.5	68.7	57.5	48.3	39.3	57.0
Mean Minimum Temp. (°F)	26.4	28.6	35.1	44.2	53.2	62.3	66.6	65.4	58.3	46.3	37.2	29.3	46.1
Extreme Maximum Temp. (°F)	80	82	90	95	95	100	100	103	102	92	82	80	103
Extreme Minimum Temp. (°F)	-9	-11	6	18	33	42	48	43	34	26	13	-1	-11
Days Maximum Temp. ≥ 90°F	0	0	0	1	1	5	11	8	2	0	0	0	28
Days Maximum Temp. ≤ 32°F	3	1	0	0	0	0	0	0	0	0	0	2	6
Days Minimum Temp. ≤ 32°F	23	19	14	3	0	0	0	0	0	2	11	21	93
Days Minimum Temp. ≤ 0°F	0	0	0	0	0	0	0	0	0	0	0	0	0
Heating Degree Days (base 65°F)	882	711	549	258	93	8	0	2	38	253	497	791	4,082
Cooling Degree Days (base 65°F)	0	0	6	28	92	251	372	333	156	28	2	1	1,269
Mean Precipitation (in.)	3.31	2.91	3.94	3.42	4.15	3.46	4.59	3.52	3.63	3.26	3.62	3.48	43.29
Extreme Maximum Daily Precip. (in.)	3.17	2.72	2.41	3.04	3.52	4.41	5.44	4.86	4.96	2.93	3.15	2.26	5.44
Days With ≥ 0.1" Precipitation	7	6	7	7	7	6	7	5	5	5	6	6	74
Days With ≥ 0.5" Precipitation	2	2	3	3	3	2	3	2	2	2	2	3	29
Days With ≥ 1.0" Precipitation	1	1	1	1	1	1	1	1	1	1	1	1	12
Mean Snowfall (in.)	6.4	4.7	1.8	0.1	trace	0.0	0.0	0.0	0.0	trace	0.5	3.0	16.5
Maximum Snow Depth (in.)	19	11	12	1	trace	0	0	0	0	trace	6	10	19
Days With ≥ 1.0" Snow Depth	5	3	1	0	0	0	0	0	0	0	0	2	11

Bedford *Bedford County* Elevation: 975 ft. Latitude: 37° 21' N Longitude: 79° 31' W

	JAN	FEB	MAR	APR	MAY	JUN	JUL	AUG	SEP	OCT	NOV	DEC	YEAR
Mean Maximum Temp. (°F)	45.9	***50.0***	***58.2***	***68.7***	***74.9***	***81.9***	85.5	83.9	***77.5***	***67.8***	***58.9***	***48.4***	***66.8***
Mean Temp. (°F)	36.7	***39.5***	***46.6***	***56.5***	***63.8***	***71.7***	***75.7***	74.1	***67.5***	***57.1***	***48.1***	***39.1***	***56.4***
Mean Minimum Temp. (°F)	27.4	***29.0***	***35.1***	***44.3***	***52.7***	***61.4***	***65.9***	64.2	***57.4***	***46.3***	***37.1***	***29.8***	***45.9***
Extreme Maximum Temp. (°F)	81	***79***	87	***94***	***94***	***96***	99	100	***97***	***86***	***82***	***81***	***100***
Extreme Minimum Temp. (°F)	-10	***-1***	7	***22***	***33***	***40***	***45***	42	***34***	***22***	***14***	***-6***	***-10***
Days Maximum Temp. ≥ 90°F	0	***0***	0	***1***	***0***	***3***	***8***	6	***1***	***0***	***0***	***0***	***19***
Days Maximum Temp. ≤ 32°F	3	***1***	0	***0***	***0***	***0***	***0***	0	***0***	***0***	***0***	***2***	***6***
Days Minimum Temp. ≤ 32°F	22	***19***	12	***2***	***0***	***0***	***0***	0	***0***	***2***	***10***	***19***	***86***
Days Minimum Temp. ≤ 0°F	0	***0***	0	***0***	***0***	***0***	***0***	0	***0***	***0***	***0***	***0***	***0***
Heating Degree Days (base 65°F)	871	***714***	***566***	***274***	***101***	***11***	***1***	3	***48***	***255***	***503***	***796***	***4,143***
Cooling Degree Days (base 65°F)	0	***0***	***4***	***25***	***71***	***219***	***341***	291	***128***	***16***	***1***	***0***	***1,096***
Mean Precipitation (in.)	3.20	***2.80***	***3.69***	***3.93***	***4.36***	***4.28***	4.55	3.58	***3.92***	***3.44***	***3.37***	***3.00***	***44.12***
Extreme Maximum Daily Precip. (in.)	2.30	na	***2.36***	***4.60***	***4.50***	***3.77***	***3.25***	***3.99***	***5.85***	***6.77***	***3.90***	***2.40***	na
Days With ≥ 0.1" Precipitation	6	***5***	***7***	***6***	***8***	***7***	7	6	***6***	***5***	***6***	***5***	***74***
Days With ≥ 0.5" Precipitation	2	***2***	***3***	***2***	***3***	***3***	3	2	***2***	***2***	***2***	***2***	***28***
Days With ≥ 1.0" Precipitation	1	***1***	***1***	***1***	***1***	***1***	1	1	***1***	***1***	***1***	***1***	***12***
Mean Snowfall (in.)	5.3	***4.6***	***1.9***	***trace***	***0.0***	***0.0***	0.0	0.0	***0.0***	***0.0***	***0.4***	***2.2***	***14.4***
Maximum Snow Depth (in.)	***10***	na	***15***	***1***	***0***	***0***	***0***	***0***	***0***	na	na	na	na
Days With ≥ 1.0" Snow Depth	***1***	na	***0***	***0***	***0***	***0***	0	0	***0***	***0***	***0***	***0***	na

Blacksburg Wso *Montgomery County* Elevation: 2,009 ft. Latitude: 37° 12' N Longitude: 80° 24' W

	JAN	FEB	MAR	APR	MAY	JUN	JUL	AUG	SEP	OCT	NOV	DEC	YEAR
Mean Maximum Temp. (°F)	41.8	45.7	53.5	63.5	71.9	79.3	82.7	81.9	75.7	65.7	55.5	44.5	63.5
Mean Temp. (°F)	31.6	34.9	41.8	51.3	59.7	67.9	71.5	70.4	63.7	52.7	43.5	34.3	52.0
Mean Minimum Temp. (°F)	21.4	24.1	30.1	39.0	47.4	56.4	60.3	58.9	51.5	39.7	31.5	24.1	40.4
Extreme Maximum Temp. (°F)	69	73	85	86	89	94	97	99	94	87	82	75	99
Extreme Minimum Temp. (°F)	-18	-5	3	14	26	35	42	36	22	18	9	-10	-18
Days Maximum Temp. ≥ 90°F	0	0	0	0	0	1	3	3	1	0	0	0	8
Days Maximum Temp. ≤ 32°F	6	4	1	0	0	0	0	0	0	0	0	5	16
Days Minimum Temp. ≤ 32°F	27	24	19	7	1	0	0	0	0	8	17	26	129
Days Minimum Temp. ≤ 0°F	1	0	0	0	0	0	0	0	0	0	0	1	2
Heating Degree Days (base 65°F)	1,030	846	713	410	186	32	5	9	99	379	638	945	5,292
Cooling Degree Days (base 65°F)	0	0	0	4	28	125	213	185	64	6	0	0	625
Mean Precipitation (in.)	2.97	2.76	3.76	3.65	4.31	3.84	4.41	3.47	3.02	2.81	2.93	2.89	40.82
Extreme Maximum Daily Precip. (in.)	2.26	2.32	2.95	3.42	2.08	4.07	3.33	3.44	3.52	2.63	2.55	2.69	4.07
Days With ≥ 0.1" Precipitation	6	6	8	8	9	7	9	6	5	5	6	6	81
Days With ≥ 0.5" Precipitation	2	2	3	2	3	3	3	2	2	2	2	2	28
Days With ≥ 1.0" Precipitation	1	0	1	1	1	1	1	1	1	1	0	0	9
Mean Snowfall (in.)	7.6	6.7	3.9	0.7	trace	0.0	0.0	0.0	0.0	trace	0.5	4.6	24.0
Maximum Snow Depth (in.)	27	15	18	5	trace	0	0	0	0	trace	2	14	27
Days With ≥ 1.0" Snow Depth	6	6	2	0	0	0	0	0	0	0	0	5	19

Burkes Garden *Tazewell County* Elevation: 3,299 ft. Latitude: 37° 05' N Longitude: 81° 20' W

	JAN	FEB	MAR	APR	MAY	JUN	JUL	AUG	SEP	OCT	NOV	DEC	YEAR
Mean Maximum Temp. (°F)	39.2	42.2	50.8	60.2	68.4	75.4	78.6	77.8	71.9	62.1	52.0	42.1	60.1
Mean Temp. (°F)	29.8	32.5	39.9	48.5	56.5	64.3	67.7	66.5	60.0	49.4	40.8	32.5	49.0
Mean Minimum Temp. (°F)	20.5	22.8	29.0	36.7	44.7	53.2	56.8	55.2	48.1	36.7	29.5	22.8	38.0
Extreme Maximum Temp. (°F)	66	70	78	81	83	89	93	94	90	83	77	70	94
Extreme Minimum Temp. (°F)	-26	-22	-2	3	19	29	34	31	21	11	2	-22	-26
Days Maximum Temp. ≥ 90°F	0	0	0	0	0	0	0	0	0	0	0	0	0
Days Maximum Temp. ≤ 32°F	9	6	3	0	0	0	0	0	0	0	2	7	27
Days Minimum Temp. ≤ 32°F	26	24	20	11	3	0	0	0	1	12	19	25	141
Days Minimum Temp. ≤ 0°F	2	1	0	0	0	0	0	0	0	0	0	1	4
Heating Degree Days (base 65°F)	1,084	912	772	491	265	69	24	32	164	478	720	1,000	6,011
Cooling Degree Days (base 65°F)	0	0	0	1	9	54	115	87	22	1	0	0	289
Mean Precipitation (in.)	3.83	3.38	4.13	3.67	4.69	4.15	4.69	4.05	3.35	2.91	3.14	3.70	45.69
Extreme Maximum Daily Precip. (in.)	4.56	2.61	2.70	1.80	2.25	2.27	3.78	2.98	2.75	2.45	3.90	2.10	4.56
Days With ≥ 0.1" Precipitation	8	7	9	8	10	9	9	8	7	6	7	8	96
Days With ≥ 0.5" Precipitation	2	2	3	3	3	3	3	3	2	2	2	2	30
Days With ≥ 1.0" Precipitation	1	1	1	1	1	1	1	1	1	1	1	1	12
Mean Snowfall (in.)	15.1	12.8	8.6	2.8	0.1	0.0	0.0	0.0	0.0	0.2	2.2	10.1	51.9
Maximum Snow Depth (in.)	21	14	18	17	trace	0	0	0	0	3	6	13	21
Days With ≥ 1.0" Snow Depth	13	11	5	1	0	0	0	0	0	0	2	9	41

Camp Pickett *Nottoway County* Elevation: 330 ft. Latitude: 37° 02' N Longitude: 77° 58' W

	JAN	FEB	MAR	APR	MAY	JUN	JUL	AUG	SEP	OCT	NOV	DEC	YEAR
Mean Maximum Temp. (°F)	47.5	51.4	59.1	69.3	76.8	84.4	88.1	86.7	80.3	70.1	61.0	50.7	68.8
Mean Temp. (°F)	36.1	39.0	46.2	55.8	64.2	72.7	77.0	75.5	68.6	57.1	48.1	39.2	56.6
Mean Minimum Temp. (°F)	24.7	26.6	33.2	42.2	51.5	61.0	65.9	64.3	56.8	44.0	35.2	27.6	44.4
Extreme Maximum Temp. (°F)	81	82	89	95	95	99	102	103	101	92	84	80	103
Extreme Minimum Temp. (°F)	-12	-3	6	11	32	37	41	41	35	22	13	-1	-12
Days Maximum Temp. ≥ 90°F	0	0	0	1	1	7	13	10	3	0	0	0	35
Days Maximum Temp. ≤ 32°F	3	1	0	0	0	0	0	0	0	0	0	2	6
Days Minimum Temp. ≤ 32°F	24	22	16	5	0	0	0	0	0	4	14	23	108
Days Minimum Temp. ≤ 0°F	1	0	0	0	0	0	0	0	0	0	0	0	1
Heating Degree Days (base 65°F)	888	729	581	294	104	11	0	2	40	263	501	794	4,207
Cooling Degree Days (base 65°F)	0	0	5	24	86	250	378	334	154	25	2	1	1,259
Mean Precipitation (in.)	3.67	3.11	4.27	3.80	4.14	3.95	4.38	4.38	3.94	3.66	3.49	3.40	46.19
Extreme Maximum Daily Precip. (in.)	2.80	3.78	2.90	4.60	5.66	3.00	3.31	4.96	5.91	4.10	4.57	3.00	5.91
Days With ≥ 0.1" Precipitation	7	6	7	7	7	7	7	6	5	5	6	6	76
Days With ≥ 0.5" Precipitation	3	2	4	3	3	3	3	3	3	3	3	2	35
Days With ≥ 1.0" Precipitation	1	1	1	1	1	1	1	1	1	1	1	1	12
Mean Snowfall (in.)	2.8	2.5	0.7	0.1	0.0	0.0	0.0	0.0	0.0	0.0	0.1	0.8	7.0
Maximum Snow Depth (in.)	12	14	13	1	0	0	0	0	0	0	3	5	14
Days With ≥ 1.0" Snow Depth	2	2	0	0	0	0	0	0	0	0	0	1	5

Charlottesville 2 W *Albemarle County* Elevation: 870 ft. Latitude: 38° 02' N Longitude: 78° 31' W

	JAN	FEB	MAR	APR	MAY	JUN	JUL	AUG	SEP	OCT	NOV	DEC	YEAR
Mean Maximum Temp. (°F)	45.2	49.2	57.4	68.5	75.7	83.9	87.4	86.0	79.2	68.9	59.0	47.8	67.4
Mean Temp. (°F)	36.1	39.3	46.6	56.9	64.9	73.2	76.9	75.4	68.7	58.2	49.0	39.0	57.0
Mean Minimum Temp. (°F)	26.9	29.4	35.7	45.3	53.9	62.4	66.3	64.7	58.1	47.5	39.0	30.0	46.6
Extreme Maximum Temp. (°F)	81	81	92	96	96	100	102	105	98	94	84	83	105
Extreme Minimum Temp. (°F)	-10	1	10	22	35	44	49	44	38	27	15	-3	-10
Days Maximum Temp. ≥ 90°F	0	0	0	1	1	7	11	9	3	0	0	0	32
Days Maximum Temp. ≤ 32°F	4	2	0	0	0	0	0	0	0	0	0	2	8
Days Minimum Temp. ≤ 32°F	23	19	12	2	0	0	0	0	0	0	8	19	83
Days Minimum Temp. ≤ 0°F	0	0	0	0	0	0	0	0	0	0	0	0	0
Heating Degree Days (base 65°F)	888	719	571	269	94	10	1	2	37	233	476	801	4,101
Cooling Degree Days (base 65°F)	0	0	7	34	96	261	375	331	155	30	3	1	1,293
Mean Precipitation (in.)	3.07	3.10	3.91	3.40	4.55	4.14	5.42	3.98	4.77	3.77	3.99	3.17	47.27
Extreme Maximum Daily Precip. (in.)	3.31	3.09	3.00	2.82	4.75	4.22	5.02	4.99	9.20	3.52	4.69	2.21	9.20
Days With ≥ 0.1" Precipitation	6	6	6	6	8	7	8	6	6	5	6	6	76
Days With ≥ 0.5" Precipitation	2	2	3	2	3	3	3	3	3	2	3	2	31
Days With ≥ 1.0" Precipitation	1	1	1	1	1	1	2	1	2	1	1	1	14
Mean Snowfall (in.)	4.6	5.5	2.5	0.1	0.0	0.0	0.0	0.0	0.0	0.0	0.5	4.3	17.5
Maximum Snow Depth (in.)	24	16	13	1	0	0	0	0	0	0	*4*	19	***24***
Days With ≥ 1.0" Snow Depth	4	4	1	0	0	0	0	0	0	0	0	2	11

The period of record for all cooperative weather station data is 1980 – 2009. See User Guide for detailed explanation of data.

Covington Filter Plant *Alleghany County* Elevation: 1,229 ft. Latitude: 37° 48' N Longitude: 80° 00' W

	JAN	FEB	MAR	APR	MAY	JUN	JUL	AUG	SEP	OCT	NOV	DEC	YEAR
Mean Maximum Temp. (°F)	46.0	50.3	59.0	70.2	78.2	84.8	88.0	87.0	80.4	70.9	59.9	48.7	68.6
Mean Temp. (°F)	35.1	38.1	45.4	55.2	63.3	71.0	74.7	73.8	66.9	56.4	46.5	37.6	55.3
Mean Minimum Temp. (°F)	24.0	26.0	31.8	40.1	48.4	57.2	61.3	60.4	53.4	41.9	33.0	26.5	42.0
Extreme Maximum Temp. (°F)	80	79	87	93	99	100	102	102	97	92	85	80	102
Extreme Minimum Temp. (°F)	-19	-5	1	15	27	36	41	39	28	20	11	-10	-19
Days Maximum Temp. ≥ 90°F	0	0	0	1	2	7	14	11	4	0	0	0	39
Days Maximum Temp. ≤ 32°F	3	1	0	0	0	0	0	0	0	0	0	2	6
Days Minimum Temp. ≤ 32°F	25	22	17	6	1	0	0	0	0	6	16	23	116
Days Minimum Temp. ≤ 0°F	1	0	0	0	0	0	0	0	0	0	0	0	1
Heating Degree Days (base 65°F)	921	753	601	303	114	13	1	2	53	275	549	843	4,428
Cooling Degree Days (base 65°F)	0	0	1	15	69	200	307	280	118	16	1	0	1,007
Mean Precipitation (in.)	2.47	2.27	3.23	3.29	4.09	3.32	3.89	3.20	3.26	2.49	3.32	2.54	37.37
Extreme Maximum Daily Precip. (in.)	2.65	2.04	1.85	2.18	3.88	3.50	2.34	3.45	3.22	2.55	8.00	1.70	8.00
Days With ≥ 0.1" Precipitation	6	5	7	7	9	7	8	6	5	5	6	6	77
Days With ≥ 0.5" Precipitation	1	1	2	2	3	2	3	2	2	2	2	2	24
Days With ≥ 1.0" Precipitation	0	0	1	1	1	1	1	1	1	1	1	0	9
Mean Snowfall (in.)	1.6	***0.9***	0.4	0.2	0.0	0.0	0.0	0.0	0.0	trace	0.1	2.1	***5.3***
Maximum Snow Depth (in.)	7	10	10	trace	0	0	0	0	0	0	1	*17*	*17*
Days With ≥ 1.0" Snow Depth	1	1	0	0	0	0	0	0	0	0	0	1	3

Crozier *Goochland County* Elevation: 350 ft. Latitude: 37° 40' N Longitude: 77° 53' W

	JAN	FEB	MAR	APR	MAY	JUN	JUL	AUG	SEP	OCT	NOV	DEC	YEAR
Mean Maximum Temp. (°F)	46.8	50.7	58.9	69.5	76.9	84.7	88.8	87.7	81.0	70.7	60.9	50.3	68.9
Mean Temp. (°F)	35.9	38.7	45.9	55.9	64.0	72.6	77.0	75.7	68.8	57.3	48.0	39.0	56.6
Mean Minimum Temp. (°F)	24.8	26.6	32.9	42.4	50.9	60.5	65.2	63.8	56.5	43.9	35.1	27.6	44.2
Extreme Maximum Temp. (°F)	83	81	89	97	96	101	103	105	101	97	85	83	105
Extreme Minimum Temp. (°F)	-8	-9	1	19	32	41	49	45	34	24	16	0	-9
Days Maximum Temp. ≥ 90°F	0	0	0	1	2	8	15	12	4	0	0	0	42
Days Maximum Temp. ≤ 32°F	4	2	0	0	0	0	0	0	0	0	0	1	7
Days Minimum Temp. ≤ 32°F	24	22	15	4	0	0	0	0	0	3	14	23	105
Days Minimum Temp. ≤ 0°F	0	0	0	0	0	0	0	0	0	0	0	0	0
Heating Degree Days (base 65°F)	897	738	589	290	109	10	0	2	40	258	505	801	4,239
Cooling Degree Days (base 65°F)	0	0	5	25	84	245	379	343	161	27	2	1	1,272
Mean Precipitation (in.)	3.23	2.65	3.73	3.42	4.21	3.46	3.90	3.94	3.40	3.16	3.64	3.31	42.05
Extreme Maximum Daily Precip. (in.)	2.77	1.61	2.49	3.93	2.42	2.33	3.29	6.51	4.37	3.37	4.26	2.38	6.51
Days With ≥ 0.1" Precipitation	6	5	7	6	7	6	7	5	5	5	6	6	71
Days With ≥ 0.5" Precipitation	2	2	3	2	3	2	3	3	2	2	2	2	28
Days With ≥ 1.0" Precipitation	1	0	1	1	1	1	1	1	1	1	1	1	11
Mean Snowfall (in.)	3.7	3.7	1.3	0.1	0.0	0.0	0.0	0.0	0.0	0.0	0.3	2.1	11.2
Maximum Snow Depth (in.)	19	15	11	2	0	0	0	0	0	0	4	16	19
Days With ≥ 1.0" Snow Depth	4	3	0	0	0	0	0	0	0	0	0	2	9

Dale Enterprise *Rockingham County* Elevation: 1,399 ft. Latitude: 38° 27' N Longitude: 78° 56' W

	JAN	FEB	MAR	APR	MAY	JUN	JUL	AUG	SEP	OCT	NOV	DEC	YEAR
Mean Maximum Temp. (°F)	42.4	46.0	54.3	65.2	73.7	82.3	85.8	84.5	77.4	66.6	55.8	45.1	64.9
Mean Temp. (°F)	32.4	35.2	42.4	52.4	61.2	70.1	73.9	72.5	65.4	54.2	44.7	35.2	53.3
Mean Minimum Temp. (°F)	22.2	24.4	30.5	39.5	48.6	57.9	62.0	60.4	53.3	41.7	33.5	25.2	41.6
Extreme Maximum Temp. (°F)	78	78	85	89	96	98	105	102	98	90	80	78	105
Extreme Minimum Temp. (°F)	-13	-13	2	14	27	39	44	39	30	20	13	-11	-13
Days Maximum Temp. ≥ 90°F	0	0	0	0	0	4	9	7	2	0	0	0	22
Days Maximum Temp. ≤ 32°F	6	3	1	0	0	0	0	0	0	0	0	4	14
Days Minimum Temp. ≤ 32°F	26	23	19	7	1	0	0	0	0	5	14	24	119
Days Minimum Temp. ≤ 0°F	1	0	0	0	0	0	0	0	0	0	0	1	2
Heating Degree Days (base 65°F)	1,005	836	694	380	160	21	2	5	77	340	602	917	5,039
Cooling Degree Days (base 65°F)	0	0	1	8	49	182	284	245	95	12	0	0	876
Mean Precipitation (in.)	2.28	2.16	2.89	3.12	3.71	3.35	4.06	3.52	3.52	2.49	2.87	2.47	36.44
Extreme Maximum Daily Precip. (in.)	2.05	1.91	2.32	2.28	2.10	2.20	2.06	4.21	5.95	3.25	1.87	1.58	5.95
Days With ≥ 0.1" Precipitation	5	5	6	7	8	7	8	6	5	4	6	5	72
Days With ≥ 0.5" Precipitation	1	1	2	2	2	2	3	2	2	2	2	2	23
Days With ≥ 1.0" Precipitation	0	0	1	0	1	1	1	1	1	1	1	0	8
Mean Snowfall (in.)	6.2	6.7	3.6	0.6	0.0	0.0	0.0	0.0	0.0	0.0	1.1	4.7	22.9
Maximum Snow Depth (in.)	30	21	18	6	0	0	0	0	0	0	4	16	30
Days With ≥ 1.0" Snow Depth	5	6	2	0	0	0	0	0	0	0	0	5	18

Danville *Pittsylvania County* Elevation: 410 ft. Latitude: 36° 35' N Longitude: 79° 23' W

	JAN	FEB	MAR	APR	MAY	JUN	JUL	AUG	SEP	OCT	NOV	DEC	YEAR
Mean Maximum Temp. (°F)	48.1	52.3	60.6	71.1	78.9	86.4	89.8	88.6	81.7	71.1	61.3	51.1	70.1
Mean Temp. (°F)	37.7	40.9	48.1	57.7	66.3	74.9	79.1	77.7	70.5	58.8	49.1	40.5	58.4
Mean Minimum Temp. (°F)	27.3	29.5	35.5	44.3	53.7	63.4	68.2	66.7	59.3	46.4	36.8	29.9	46.7
Extreme Maximum Temp. (°F)	80	81	91	95	97	102	105	105	101	94	84	81	105
Extreme Minimum Temp. (°F)	-5	4	11	25	33	45	51	47	38	28	17	2	-5
Days Maximum Temp. ≥ 90°F	0	0	0	1	3	11	18	15	4	0	0	0	52
Days Maximum Temp. ≤ 32°F	2	1	0	0	0	0	0	0	0	0	0	1	4
Days Minimum Temp. ≤ 32°F	22	19	12	2	0	0	0	0	0	1	12	20	88
Days Minimum Temp. ≤ 0°F	0	0	0	0	0	0	0	0	0	0	0	0	0
Heating Degree Days (base 65°F)	840	675	522	243	71	5	0	1	25	218	473	753	3,826
Cooling Degree Days (base 65°F)	0	0	5	32	118	310	442	400	196	32	2	0	1,537
Mean Precipitation (in.)	3.56	3.12	4.13	3.79	3.99	3.71	4.56	3.46	3.84	3.63	3.35	3.12	44.26
Extreme Maximum Daily Precip. (in.)	3.17	2.98	3.15	4.26	3.70	4.33	2.89	4.62	4.76	4.23	3.65	2.10	4.76
Days With ≥ 0.1" Precipitation	6	6	7	7	7	6	7	6	5	5	6	6	74
Days With ≥ 0.5" Precipitation	3	2	3	3	3	3	3	2	2	2	2	2	30
Days With ≥ 1.0" Precipitation	1	1	1	1	1	1	1	1	1	1	1	1	12
Mean Snowfall (in.)	2.1	1.3	0.6	0.1	0.0	0.0	0.0	0.0	0.0	0.0	0.0	0.7	4.8
Maximum Snow Depth (in.)	8	13	10	1	0	0	0	0	0	0	0	8	13
Days With ≥ 1.0" Snow Depth	2	1	0	0	0	0	0	0	0	0	0	1	4

The period of record for all cooperative weather station data is 1980 – 2009. See User Guide for detailed explanation of data.

Floyd 2 NE *Floyd County* Elevation: 2,625 ft. Latitude: 36° 56' N Longitude: 80° 18' W

	JAN	FEB	MAR	APR	MAY	JUN	JUL	AUG	SEP	OCT	NOV	DEC	YEAR
Mean Maximum Temp. (°F)	43.0	46.9	54.4	64.6	71.9	78.2	81.9	80.7	74.4	65.7	55.5	45.1	63.5
Mean Temp. (°F)	32.8	35.6	42.2	51.2	59.0	66.4	70.6	68.9	62.4	52.5	43.3	34.6	51.6
Mean Minimum Temp. (°F)	22.5	24.4	29.9	37.7	46.0	54.6	59.2	57.2	50.3	39.3	31.0	24.1	39.7
Extreme Maximum Temp. (°F)	76	73	83	85	90	91	95	97	92	84	78	74	97
Extreme Minimum Temp. (°F)	-19	-15	-7	0	22	***31***	***37***	***32***	24	***17***	***6***	***-11***	***-19***
Days Maximum Temp. ≥ 90°F	0	0	0	0	0	0	2	1	0	0	0	0	3
Days Maximum Temp. ≤ 32°F	5	3	1	0	0	0	0	0	0	0	0	4	13
Days Minimum Temp. ≤ 32°F	26	23	19	10	3	0	0	0	1	9	18	25	134
Days Minimum Temp. ≤ 0°F	1	0	0	0	0	0	0	0	0	0	0	1	2
Heating Degree Days (base 65°F)	991	823	700	411	199	44	8	17	119	383	645	936	5,276
Cooling Degree Days (base 65°F)	0	0	0	2	19	93	188	146	46	3	0	0	497
Mean Precipitation (in.)	2.74	2.54	3.78	3.55	3.78	4.00	3.41	3.17	3.53	2.98	3.53	2.41	39.42
Extreme Maximum Daily Precip. (in.)	***3.50***	3.00	3.20	3.43	2.93	***2.67***	3.79	***5.16***	3.50	***3.75***	***5.87***	***2.60***	***5.87***
Days With ≥ 0.1" Precipitation	5	4	6	6	8	7	7	6	5	4	5	5	68
Days With ≥ 0.5" Precipitation	2	2	2	2	3	3	2	2	2	2	3	2	27
Days With ≥ 1.0" Precipitation	0	1	1	1	1	1	1	1	1	1	1	0	10
Mean Snowfall (in.)	6.2	5.8	2.7	1.0	0.0	0.0	0.0	0.0	0.0	0.0	0.4	3.8	19.9
Maximum Snow Depth (in.)	***5***	na	***8***	***trace***	***0***	***0***	***0***	***0***	***0***	***0***	***trace***	na	na
Days With ≥ 1.0" Snow Depth	***1***	na	***0***	0	0	0	0	0	0	***0***	0	***1***	na

Grundy *Buchanan County* Elevation: 1,169 ft. Latitude: 37° 17' N Longitude: 82° 05' W

	JAN	FEB	MAR	APR	MAY	JUN	JUL	AUG	SEP	OCT	NOV	DEC	YEAR
Mean Maximum Temp. (°F)	45.8	50.1	59.1	69.2	76.5	83.2	86.3	85.5	80.0	70.5	60.2	48.6	67.9
Mean Temp. (°F)	34.9	38.1	45.5	54.5	62.9	70.9	74.6	73.9	67.5	56.4	46.6	37.5	55.3
Mean Minimum Temp. (°F)	23.9	26.2	31.8	39.7	49.3	58.5	62.8	62.3	54.9	42.3	32.9	26.4	42.6
Extreme Maximum Temp. (°F)	78	83	88	92	95	99	101	99	102	90	85	80	102
Extreme Minimum Temp. (°F)	-14	-12	-3	21	30	40	40	45	34	20	12	-11	-14
Days Maximum Temp. ≥ 90°F	0	0	0	0	1	5	10	8	3	0	0	0	27
Days Maximum Temp. ≤ 32°F	4	3	1	0	0	0	0	0	0	0	0	2	10
Days Minimum Temp. ≤ 32°F	25	21	17	7	0	0	0	0	0	5	16	23	114
Days Minimum Temp. ≤ 0°F	1	0	0	0	0	0	0	0	0	0	0	0	1
Heating Degree Days (base 65°F)	926	753	599	322	123	12	1	2	47	277	546	844	4,452
Cooling Degree Days (base 65°F)	0	0	1	13	64	195	305	285	128	18	1	0	1,010
Mean Precipitation (in.)	3.17	3.02	3.49	4.10	4.76	4.31	5.35	3.86	3.22	2.81	2.89	3.13	44.11
Extreme Maximum Daily Precip. (in.)	2.50	3.18	1.86	2.22	2.65	2.43	***2.42***	2.68	2.09	2.26	2.86	2.49	***3.18***
Days With ≥ 0.1" Precipitation	7	7	8	8	10	8	9	7	6	6	7	7	90
Days With ≥ 0.5" Precipitation	2	2	2	3	3	3	4	3	2	2	2	2	30
Days With ≥ 1.0" Precipitation	1	0	1	1	1	1	1	1	1	1	0	0	9
Mean Snowfall (in.)	6.2	3.8	2.7	1.0	0.0	0.0	0.0	0.0	0.0	trace	0.3	3.1	17.1
Maximum Snow Depth (in.)	10	8	16	20	0	0	0	0	0	trace	1	8	20
Days With ≥ 1.0" Snow Depth	5	3	2	0	0	0	0	0	0	0	0	3	13

Holland 1 E *Suffolk (city) County* Elevation: 80 ft. Latitude: 36° 41' N Longitude: 76° 46' W

	JAN	FEB	MAR	APR	MAY	JUN	JUL	AUG	SEP	OCT	NOV	DEC	YEAR
Mean Maximum Temp. (°F)	49.6	53.1	60.5	70.2	78.0	85.7	89.1	87.8	81.8	72.4	63.4	53.5	70.4
Mean Temp. (°F)	39.0	41.9	48.6	57.6	66.1	74.3	78.2	76.6	70.4	59.8	51.2	42.3	58.8
Mean Minimum Temp. (°F)	28.4	30.6	36.6	45.0	54.1	62.9	67.2	65.4	59.0	47.2	39.0	31.2	47.2
Extreme Maximum Temp. (°F)	80	81	88	94	97	100	104	104	99	95	84	81	104
Extreme Minimum Temp. (°F)	-5	-5	13	21	31	42	49	45	37	25	19	4	-5
Days Maximum Temp. ≥ 90°F	0	0	0	1	2	9	16	12	3	0	0	0	43
Days Maximum Temp. ≤ 32°F	2	1	0	0	0	0	0	0	0	0	0	1	4
Days Minimum Temp. ≤ 32°F	21	18	11	3	0	0	0	0	0	2	10	19	84
Days Minimum Temp. ≤ 0°F	0	0	0	0	0	0	0	0	0	0	0	0	0
Heating Degree Days (base 65°F)	799	649	508	248	75	7	0	1	23	197	414	696	3,617
Cooling Degree Days (base 65°F)	0	1	6	33	116	294	415	367	193	43	6	1	1,475
Mean Precipitation (in.)	3.86	3.13	3.98	3.51	3.80	3.69	5.26	5.17	5.02	3.70	3.39	3.44	47.95
Extreme Maximum Daily Precip. (in.)	2.80	1.82	2.50	2.71	2.25	4.20	3.95	4.22	8.60	6.42	3.99	2.29	8.60
Days With ≥ 0.1" Precipitation	8	6	7	6	7	6	8	7	6	5	6	7	79
Days With ≥ 0.5" Precipitation	3	2	3	2	3	2	4	3	2	2	2	3	31
Days With ≥ 1.0" Precipitation	1	1	1	1	1	1	2	2	1	1	1	1	14
Mean Snowfall (in.)	2.1	1.7	0.5	trace	0.0	0.0	0.0	0.0	0.0	0.0	trace	0.9	5.2
Maximum Snow Depth (in.)	8	12	13	trace	0	0	0	0	0	0	1	2	13
Days With ≥ 1.0" Snow Depth	1	1	0	0	0	0	0	0	0	0	0	0	2

Hopewell *Prince George County* Elevation: 40 ft. Latitude: 37° 18' N Longitude: 77° 18' W

	JAN	FEB	MAR	APR	MAY	JUN	JUL	AUG	SEP	OCT	NOV	DEC	YEAR
Mean Maximum Temp. (°F)	51.0	54.9	63.2	73.4	80.4	87.7	91.2	89.6	83.4	73.9	64.2	54.2	72.2
Mean Temp. (°F)	40.8	43.8	51.1	60.6	68.4	76.5	80.2	78.7	72.4	61.8	52.7	43.8	60.9
Mean Minimum Temp. (°F)	30.6	32.6	39.1	47.7	56.3	65.2	69.2	67.9	61.4	49.7	41.2	33.4	49.5
Extreme Maximum Temp. (°F)	81	82	91	96	99	101	105	104	103	93	88	85	105
Extreme Minimum Temp. (°F)	-11	4	12	23	35	40	47	46	38	24	16	3	-11
Days Maximum Temp. ≥ 90°F	0	0	0	1	3	13	20	16	6	1	0	0	60
Days Maximum Temp. ≤ 32°F	1	0	0	0	0	0	0	0	0	0	0	1	2
Days Minimum Temp. ≤ 32°F	19	15	9	1	0	0	0	0	0	1	7	15	67
Days Minimum Temp. ≤ 0°F	0	0	0	0	0	0	0	0	0	0	0	0	0
Heating Degree Days (base 65°F)	744	593	435	180	44	2	0	0	15	152	372	652	3,189
Cooling Degree Days (base 65°F)	1	1	12	55	156	353	479	433	245	61	9	2	1,807
Mean Precipitation (in.)	3.56	2.87	4.04	3.87	3.77	3.32	4.62	4.90	4.44	3.39	3.54	3.30	45.62
Extreme Maximum Daily Precip. (in.)	2.70	2.14	2.75	3.49	2.85	2.62	3.91	6.62	7.61	6.65	2.80	2.40	7.61
Days With ≥ 0.1" Precipitation	7	6	7	6	6	6	8	6	5	5	5	6	73
Days With ≥ 0.5" Precipitation	2	2	3	3	3	2	3	3	3	2	3	3	32
Days With ≥ 1.0" Precipitation	1	1	1	1	1	1	1	1	1	1	1	1	12
Mean Snowfall (in.)	2.6	1.4	0.5	0.0	0.0	0.0	0.0	0.0	0.0	0.0	0.1	trace	4.6
Maximum Snow Depth (in.)	***5***	***trace***	***trace***	0	0	0	0	0	0	***0***	0	***3***	***5***
Days With ≥ 1.0" Snow Depth	***0***	0	0	0	0	0	0	0	0	0	0	0	***0***

The period of record for all cooperative weather station data is 1980 – 2009. See User Guide for detailed explanation of data.

Langley AFB *Hampton (city) County* Elevation: 9 ft. Latitude: 37° 05' N Longitude: 76° 21' W

	JAN	FEB	MAR	APR	MAY	JUN	JUL	AUG	SEP	OCT	NOV	DEC	YEAR
Mean Maximum Temp. (°F)	47.8	50.5	57.8	67.4	75.1	83.0	87.5	85.4	79.1	69.7	60.7	52.0	68.0
Mean Temp. (°F)	40.0	42.3	49.0	58.1	66.4	74.9	79.7	78.0	71.8	61.3	52.1	43.9	59.8
Mean Minimum Temp. (°F)	32.1	33.9	40.2	48.8	57.7	66.8	71.9	70.5	64.4	52.9	43.4	35.8	51.5
Extreme Maximum Temp. (°F)	79	81	87	94	96	100	101	105	99	91	85	79	105
Extreme Minimum Temp. (°F)	-3	7	17	28	39	46	54	54	45	34	22	8	-3
Days Maximum Temp. ≥ 90°F	0	0	0	0	1	6	12	8	2	0	0	0	29
Days Maximum Temp. ≤ 32°F	2	1	0	0	0	0	0	0	0	0	0	1	4
Days Minimum Temp. ≤ 32°F	16	13	6	1	0	0	0	0	0	0	3	12	51
Days Minimum Temp. ≤ 0°F	0	0	0	0	0	0	0	0	0	0	0	0	0
Heating Degree Days (base 65°F)	769	637	496	235	68	5	0	0	13	160	388	648	3,419
Cooling Degree Days (base 65°F)	0	1	8	35	118	310	463	410	222	53	6	1	1,627
Mean Precipitation (in.)	3.67	3.39	4.36	3.33	3.52	3.42	4.34	4.40	4.22	3.26	3.36	3.33	44.60
Extreme Maximum Daily Precip. (in.)	2.46	4.51	3.51	2.97	2.27	3.98	3.51	3.69	7.15	4.51	2.46	2.69	7.15
Days With ≥ 0.1" Precipitation	6	6	7	7	6	5	7	6	5	5	6	6	72
Days With ≥ 0.5" Precipitation	3	2	3	3	3	2	3	3	2	2	3	2	30
Days With ≥ 1.0" Precipitation	1	1	1	1	1	1	1	1	1	1	1	1	12
Mean Snowfall (in.)	2.9	2.3	0.9	0.3	0.0	0.0	0.0	0.0	0.0	0.0	0.1	0.5	7.0
Maximum Snow Depth (in.)	11	13	19	trace	trace	0	0	0	0	0	trace	1	19
Days With ≥ 1.0" Snow Depth	2	1	0	0	0	0	0	0	0	0	0	0	3

Lexington *Rockbridge County* Elevation: 1,060 ft. Latitude: 37° 47' N Longitude: 79° 26' W

	JAN	FEB	MAR	APR	MAY	JUN	JUL	AUG	SEP	OCT	NOV	DEC	YEAR
Mean Maximum Temp. (°F)	46.3	50.2	58.7	69.3	76.7	83.8	86.9	86.3	79.1	69.3	59.0	48.6	67.9
Mean Temp. (°F)	35.1	37.8	45.2	54.9	63.1	71.4	75.1	74.5	67.1	56.0	46.2	37.4	55.3
Mean Minimum Temp. (°F)	23.9	25.5	31.6	40.5	49.5	58.9	63.3	62.5	55.0	42.8	33.4	26.2	42.7
Extreme Maximum Temp. (°F)	84	80	86	95	97	99	101	103	100	94	87	79	103
Extreme Minimum Temp. (°F)	-12	-15	0	14	30	35	45	42	32	22	13	-9	-15
Days Maximum Temp. ≥ 90°F	0	0	0	1	1	5	10	9	3	0	0	0	29
Days Maximum Temp. ≤ 32°F	3	1	0	0	0	0	0	0	0	0	0	1	5
Days Minimum Temp. ≤ 32°F	25	22	18	6	1	0	0	0	0	5	15	24	116
Days Minimum Temp. ≤ 0°F	1	0	0	0	0	0	0	0	0	0	0	0	1
Heating Degree Days (base 65°F)	919	761	609	310	115	10	1	1	54	287	557	848	4,472
Cooling Degree Days (base 65°F)	0	0	2	14	65	209	320	302	123	16	0	0	1,051
Mean Precipitation (in.)	2.68	2.63	3.35	3.49	3.95	4.23	3.94	3.24	3.40	2.88	3.41	2.98	40.18
Extreme Maximum Daily Precip. (in.)	2.11	2.47	2.28	3.80	1.95	5.18	2.55	3.15	3.96	4.52	3.49	2.02	5.18
Days With ≥ 0.1" Precipitation	5	5	6	7	8	7	7	5	5	4	6	5	70
Days With ≥ 0.5" Precipitation	2	1	2	2	3	3	2	2	2	2	3	2	26
Days With ≥ 1.0" Precipitation	1	1	1	1	1	1	1	1	1	1	1	1	12
Mean Snowfall (in.)	3.9	4.0	1.4	0.1	0.0	0.0	0.0	0.0	0.0	0.0	0.3	2.9	12.6
Maximum Snow Depth (in.)	16	13	6	1	0	0	0	0	0	0	3	14	16
Days With ≥ 1.0" Snow Depth	3	3	1	0	0	0	0	0	0	0	0	3	10

Lincoln *Loudoun County* Elevation: 500 ft. Latitude: 39° 08' N Longitude: 77° 43' W

	JAN	FEB	MAR	APR	MAY	JUN	JUL	AUG	SEP	OCT	NOV	DEC	YEAR
Mean Maximum Temp. (°F)	43.6	47.1	55.5	66.9	75.4	83.6	87.8	86.5	79.4	68.5	57.9	46.5	66.6
Mean Temp. (°F)	33.7	36.3	43.6	54.2	62.9	71.7	76.0	74.5	67.2	56.0	46.5	36.5	54.9
Mean Minimum Temp. (°F)	23.7	25.4	31.7	41.5	50.4	59.8	64.2	62.5	54.9	43.3	35.0	26.5	43.2
Extreme Maximum Temp. (°F)	76	81	88	94	96	98	105	102	100	94	83	79	105
Extreme Minimum Temp. (°F)	-10	-8	7	20	30	39	46	41	35	23	12	-3	-10
Days Maximum Temp. ≥ 90°F	0	0	0	0	1	6	13	9	3	0	0	0	32
Days Maximum Temp. ≤ 32°F	5	2	0	0	0	0	0	0	0	0	0	3	10
Days Minimum Temp. ≤ 32°F	26	22	18	5	0	0	0	0	0	4	13	24	112
Days Minimum Temp. ≤ 0°F	0	0	0	0	0	0	0	0	0	0	0	0	0
Heating Degree Days (base 65°F)	964	806	660	331	126	16	0	2	54	290	550	877	4,676
Cooling Degree Days (base 65°F)	0	0	3	15	68	224	349	304	126	17	1	0	1,107
Mean Precipitation (in.)	2.63	2.37	3.22	3.69	4.48	3.99	3.68	3.40	4.27	3.12	3.59	2.97	41.41
Extreme Maximum Daily Precip. (in.)	1.70	2.27	2.45	3.34	3.92	3.23	3.63	5.11	4.67	3.07	3.39	4.27	5.11
Days With ≥ 0.1" Precipitation	5	5	5	6	7	6	6	5	5	4	5	5	64
Days With ≥ 0.5" Precipitation	2	1	2	3	3	3	2	2	3	2	3	2	28
Days With ≥ 1.0" Precipitation	0	1	1	1	1	1	1	1	1	1	1	1	11
Mean Snowfall (in.)	5.9	5.7	3.7	0.2	0.0	0.0	0.0	0.0	0.0	0.0	0.3	3.1	18.9
Maximum Snow Depth (in.)	30	22	16	trace	0	0	0	0	0	0	4	16	30
Days With ≥ 1.0" Snow Depth	7	7	2	0	0	0	0	0	0	0	0	3	19

Luray 5 E *Page County* Elevation: 1,299 ft. Latitude: 38° 40' N Longitude: 78° 22' W

	JAN	FEB	MAR	APR	MAY	JUN	JUL	AUG	SEP	OCT	NOV	DEC	YEAR
Mean Maximum Temp. (°F)	43.5	48.3	55.8	67.7	75.1	82.8	86.1	84.8	78.8	69.0	58.8	47.6	66.5
Mean Temp. (°F)	32.2	36.1	43.0	53.5	61.6	69.6	73.4	72.1	65.6	55.2	46.1	36.4	53.7
Mean Minimum Temp. (°F)	20.8	23.9	30.2	39.4	48.0	56.4	60.6	59.4	52.3	41.4	33.3	25.2	40.9
Extreme Maximum Temp. (°F)	76	79	90	93	97	99	105	100	96	91	85	79	105
Extreme Minimum Temp. (°F)	-10	-14	-2	15	28	38	39	37	30	20	7	-7	-14
Days Maximum Temp. ≥ 90°F	0	0	0	0	1	5	10	7	2	0	0	0	25
Days Maximum Temp. ≤ 32°F	6	3	1	0	0	0	0	0	0	0	0	3	13
Days Minimum Temp. ≤ 32°F	27	23	18	7	1	0	0	0	0	6	15	23	120
Days Minimum Temp. ≤ 0°F	1	0	0	0	0	0	0	0	0	0	0	0	1
Heating Degree Days (base 65°F)	1,012	813	677	351	150	25	4	8	72	314	563	879	4,868
Cooling Degree Days (base 65°F)	0	0	3	13	52	171	269	235	97	17	1	0	858
Mean Precipitation (in.)	2.59	2.54	3.48	3.51	3.92	4.06	3.96	3.35	4.54	2.90	3.72	2.64	41.21
Extreme Maximum Daily Precip. (in.)	2.64	2.10	3.32	4.50	2.20	2.12	2.50	3.15	9.42	3.80	3.60	2.22	9.42
Days With ≥ 0.1" Precipitation	5	5	6	7	7	7	7	6	5	5	6	5	71
Days With ≥ 0.5" Precipitation	1	1	2	2	3	3	2	2	2	2	2	2	24
Days With ≥ 1.0" Precipitation	1	1	1	1	1	1	1	1	1	1	1	0	11
Mean Snowfall (in.)	5.3	5.9	4.4	0.4	0.0	0.0	0.0	0.0	0.0	trace	0.7	2.7	19.4
Maximum Snow Depth (in.)	18	26	38	2	0	0	0	0	0	trace	3	7	38
Days With ≥ 1.0" Snow Depth	3	3	1	0	0	0	0	0	0	0	0	1	8

The period of record for all cooperative weather station data is 1980 – 2009. See User Guide for detailed explanation of data.

Piedmont Research Stn *Orange County* Elevation: 520 ft. Latitude: 38° 13' N Longitude: 78° 07' W

	JAN	FEB	MAR	APR	MAY	JUN	JUL	AUG	SEP	OCT	NOV	DEC	YEAR
Mean Maximum Temp. (°F)	44.0	47.5	55.5	66.3	74.3	82.7	86.2	84.8	78.4	67.9	57.9	47.1	66.1
Mean Temp. (°F)	34.4	37.4	44.7	55.1	63.7	72.4	76.3	74.9	68.0	56.6	47.4	37.7	55.7
Mean Minimum Temp. (°F)	24.7	27.2	33.9	43.8	52.9	62.1	66.4	64.9	57.6	45.3	36.9	28.2	45.3
Extreme Maximum Temp. (°F)	81	79	88	93	95	98	101	102	99	92	83	79	102
Extreme Minimum Temp. (°F)	-6	-11	6	18	32	44	47	44	36	25	14	-4	-11
Days Maximum Temp. ≥ 90°F	0	0	0	0	1	5	10	7	2	0	0	0	25
Days Maximum Temp. ≤ 32°F	5	2	1	0	0	0	0	0	0	0	0	3	11
Days Minimum Temp. ≤ 32°F	25	22	14	2	0	0	0	0	0	1	10	22	96
Days Minimum Temp. ≤ 0°F	0	0	0	0	0	0	0	0	0	0	0	0	0
Heating Degree Days (base 65°F)	943	776	625	312	113	12	1	2	43	274	523	840	4,464
Cooling Degree Days (base 65°F)	0	0	4	21	79	241	358	316	141	21	1	0	1,182
Mean Precipitation (in.)	2.77	2.68	3.49	3.43	4.16	4.11	4.88	3.22	3.96	3.37	3.83	3.05	42.95
Extreme Maximum Daily Precip. (in.)	2.83	1.92	2.75	2.24	4.69	5.67	4.65	3.87	4.95	4.57	5.47	2.83	5.67
Days With ≥ 0.1" Precipitation	5	5	6	7	8	7	8	6	6	5	6	6	75
Days With ≥ 0.5" Precipitation	2	2	2	2	2	3	3	4	2	2	2	3	2	29
Days With ≥ 1.0" Precipitation	1	1	1	1	1	1	1	1	1	1	1	1	12
Mean Snowfall (in.)	5.9	5.5	2.2	0.2	0.0	0.0	0.0	0.0	0.0	trace	0.6	3.8	18.2
Maximum Snow Depth (in.)	22	18	10	2	0	0	0	0	0	trace	4	19	22
Days With ≥ 1.0" Snow Depth	5	4	1	0	0	0	0	0	0	0	0	3	13

Rocky Mount *Franklin County* Elevation: 1,314 ft. Latitude: 36° 59' N Longitude: 79° 54' W

	JAN	FEB	MAR	APR	MAY	JUN	JUL	AUG	SEP	OCT	NOV	DEC	YEAR
Mean Maximum Temp. (°F)	45.7	49.8	57.5	67.8	75.6	83.0	86.3	85.4	78.1	68.7	59.1	48.6	67.1
Mean Temp. (°F)	35.8	38.6	45.6	55.0	63.1	71.6	75.5	74.2	66.9	56.3	47.1	38.5	55.7
Mean Minimum Temp. (°F)	25.9	27.5	33.6	42.1	50.5	60.2	64.5	62.9	55.6	43.9	35.1	28.4	44.2
Extreme Maximum Temp. (°F)	82	79	86	92	93	97	102	101	98	91	82	78	102
Extreme Minimum Temp. (°F)	-11	-2	8	20	28	39	48	40	31	24	14	-4	-11
Days Maximum Temp. ≥ 90°F	0	0	0	0	0	5	9	8	2	0	0	0	24
Days Maximum Temp. ≤ 32°F	3	2	0	0	0	0	0	0	0	0	0	2	7
Days Minimum Temp. ≤ 32°F	23	21	15	4	0	0	0	0	0	4	13	21	101
Days Minimum Temp. ≤ 0°F	0	0	0	0	0	0	0	0	0	0	0	0	0
Heating Degree Days (base 65°F)	897	739	598	311	120	12	1	2	52	281	531	815	4,359
Cooling Degree Days (base 65°F)	0	0	2	18	67	217	332	293	116	17	1	0	1,063
Mean Precipitation (in.)	3.35	2.96	4.18	4.02	3.92	4.18	5.10	4.06	4.40	3.13	3.58	3.25	46.13
Extreme Maximum Daily Precip. (in.)	3.37	2.70	2.53	4.17	2.11	3.61	4.56	4.10	7.45	4.06	2.35	2.41	7.45
Days With ≥ 0.1" Precipitation	6	6	7	7	8	7	8	6	6	5	6	5	77
Days With ≥ 0.5" Precipitation	2	2	3	2	3	3	3	2	2	2	3	2	29
Days With ≥ 1.0" Precipitation	1	1	1	1	1	1	1	1	1	1	1	1	12
Mean Snowfall (in.)	5.4	4.6	2.2	0.3	0.0	0.0	0.0	0.0	0.0	trace	0.2	2.9	15.6
Maximum Snow Depth (in.)	24	18	12	2	0	0	0	0	0	trace	2	13	24
Days With ≥ 1.0" Snow Depth	3	3	1	0	0	0	0	0	0	0	0	2	9

Staunton Sewage Plant *Augusta County* Elevation: 1,640 ft. Latitude: 38° 10' N Longitude: 79° 05' W

	JAN	FEB	MAR	APR	MAY	JUN	JUL	AUG	SEP	OCT	NOV	DEC	YEAR
Mean Maximum Temp. (°F)	42.4	46.0	53.6	64.1	72.5	80.5	84.0	83.3	76.3	66.1	56.0	45.6	64.2
Mean Temp. (°F)	32.2	35.1	42.2	52.1	60.7	69.0	72.9	71.9	64.5	53.2	44.7	35.5	52.8
Mean Minimum Temp. (°F)	21.9	24.1	30.7	40.0	48.9	57.5	61.7	60.4	52.7	40.3	33.3	25.3	41.4
Extreme Maximum Temp. (°F)	77	78	83	89	92	96	100	102	93	88	81	76	102
Extreme Minimum Temp. (°F)	-16	-6	-10	12	27	35	41	37	22	18	10	-13	-16
Days Maximum Temp. ≥ 90°F	0	0	0	0	0	2	5	5	1	0	0	0	13
Days Maximum Temp. ≤ 32°F	6	3	1	0	0	0	0	0	0	0	0	4	14
Days Minimum Temp. ≤ 32°F	26	23	19	7	1	0	0	0	0	7	14	24	121
Days Minimum Temp. ≤ 0°F	1	0	0	0	0	0	0	0	0	0	0	1	2
Heating Degree Days (base 65°F)	1,010	840	702	391	169	30	3	8	89	367	603	908	5,120
Cooling Degree Days (base 65°F)	0	0	1	9	44	156	254	228	81	9	0	0	782
Mean Precipitation (in.)	2.60	2.51	3.41	3.32	3.75	3.62	3.98	3.66	4.15	2.75	3.10	2.66	39.51
Extreme Maximum Daily Precip. (in.)	1.82	3.50	2.15	2.72	1.70	3.57	5.40	2.96	5.50	3.40	3.27	1.90	5.50
Days With ≥ 0.1" Precipitation	6	5	6	6	8	6	7	7	6	4	6	5	72
Days With ≥ 0.5" Precipitation	2	2	2	2	3	3	3	3	2	2	2	2	28
Days With ≥ 1.0" Precipitation	0	1	1	1	1	1	1	1	1	1	1	1	11
Mean Snowfall (in.)	4.9	6.9	3.6	0.3	trace	0.0	0.0	0.0	0.0	0.0	0.6	4.6	20.9
Maximum Snow Depth (in.)	19	20	18	1	trace	0	0	0	0	0	6	24	24
Days With ≥ 1.0" Snow Depth	4	5	2	0	0	0	0	0	0	0	0	4	15

Sterling RCS *Loudoun County* Elevation: 279 ft. Latitude: 38° 59' N Longitude: 77° 29' W

	JAN	FEB	MAR	APR	MAY	JUN	JUL	AUG	SEP	OCT	NOV	DEC	YEAR
Mean Maximum Temp. (°F)	42.2	45.6	54.0	65.7	74.3	82.7	87.1	85.9	78.9	67.8	57.0	45.8	65.6
Mean Temp. (°F)	32.0	34.5	42.1	52.8	61.8	70.6	75.1	73.7	66.4	54.6	44.9	35.3	53.6
Mean Minimum Temp. (°F)	21.8	23.4	30.2	39.8	49.2	58.4	63.0	61.5	53.8	41.4	32.7	24.7	41.6
Extreme Maximum Temp. (°F)	75	80	90	95	95	97	103	104	99	92	83	81	104
Extreme Minimum Temp. (°F)	-19	-12	-2	17	28	36	39	36	30	19	8	-5	-19
Days Maximum Temp. ≥ 90°F	0	0	0	0	1	5	11	9	3	0	0	0	29
Days Maximum Temp. ≤ 32°F	6	3	1	0	0	0	0	0	0	0	0	3	13
Days Minimum Temp. ≤ 32°F	27	23	19	7	1	0	0	0	0	7	16	25	125
Days Minimum Temp. ≤ 0°F	1	0	0	0	0	0	0	0	0	0	0	0	1
Heating Degree Days (base 65°F)	1,015	856	706	373	152	23	1	5	68	331	597	916	5,043
Cooling Degree Days (base 65°F)	0	0	3	13	58	197	320	282	116	16	1	0	1,006
Mean Precipitation (in.)	2.86	2.65	3.68	3.68	4.59	3.97	3.66	3.42	3.93	3.48	3.64	3.02	42.58
Extreme Maximum Daily Precip. (in.)	2.05	2.26	2.63	2.76	4.09	4.67	3.87	5.79	6.64	4.72	4.61	2.12	6.64
Days With ≥ 0.1" Precipitation	6	6	7	7	7	7	7	5	5	5	6	6	74
Days With ≥ 0.5" Precipitation	2	2	3	2	3	2	2	2	2	2	3	2	27
Days With ≥ 1.0" Precipitation	1	0	1	1	1	1	1	1	1	1	1	1	11
Mean Snowfall (in.)	7.0	6.3	3.0	0.2	trace	0.0	0.0	0.0	0.0	0.0	0.3	2.8	19.6
Maximum Snow Depth (in.)	20	23	12	2	trace	0	0	0	0	0	4	19	23
Days With ≥ 1.0" Snow Depth	6	6	2	0	0	0	0	0	0	0	0	3	17

The period of record for all cooperative weather station data is 1980 – 2009. See User Guide for detailed explanation of data.

Suffolk Lake Kilby *Suffolk (city) County* Elevation: 21 ft. Latitude: 36° 44' N Longitude: 76° 36' W

	JAN	FEB	MAR	APR	MAY	JUN	JUL	AUG	SEP	OCT	NOV	DEC	YEAR
Mean Maximum Temp. (°F)	49.2	52.7	60.4	69.5	77.0	84.5	88.3	86.2	80.4	71.1	62.0	52.8	69.5
Mean Temp. (°F)	40.0	42.8	49.7	58.6	66.7	74.6	78.9	77.1	71.2	60.9	51.8	43.4	59.6
Mean Minimum Temp. (°F)	30.8	32.8	38.9	47.6	56.3	64.9	69.5	67.9	62.0	50.9	41.6	33.9	49.7
Extreme Maximum Temp. (°F)	79	81	88	94	98	98	101	103	98	93	83	80	103
Extreme Minimum Temp. (°F)	-5	4	14	26	37	46	54	48	41	30	21	4	-5
Days Maximum Temp. ≥ 90°F	0	0	0	0	1	6	13	9	2	0	0	0	31
Days Maximum Temp. ≤ 32°F	2	1	0	0	0	0	0	0	0	0	0	1	4
Days Minimum Temp. ≤ 32°F	18	15	8	1	0	0	0	0	0	0	5	15	62
Days Minimum Temp. ≤ 0°F	0	0	0	0	0	0	0	0	0	0	0	0	0
Heating Degree Days (base 65°F)	769	623	475	221	62	4	0	1	15	167	394	665	3,396
Cooling Degree Days (base 65°F)	1	1	6	34	120	300	438	383	208	48	6	1	1,546
Mean Precipitation (in.)	3.61	3.22	4.00	3.57	3.81	4.31	5.11	5.85	4.98	3.67	3.59	3.48	49.20
Extreme Maximum Daily Precip. (in.)	2.60	4.18	3.08	4.32	2.44	5.10	3.61	6.25	9.19	6.65	7.73	2.20	9.19
Days With ≥ 0.1" Precipitation	7	6	7	7	7	7	8	7	6	5	6	6	79
Days With ≥ 0.5" Precipitation	2	2	3	2	3	3	3	4	3	2	3	3	33
Days With ≥ 1.0" Precipitation	1	1	1	1	1	1	2	2	1	1	1	1	14
Mean Snowfall (in.)	2.4	2.2	0.7	0.0	0.0	0.0	0.0	0.0	0.0	0.0	0.1	0.7	6.1
Maximum Snow Depth (in.)	12	17	16	0	0	0	0	0	0	0	2	10	17
Days With ≥ 1.0" Snow Depth	1	1	0	0	0	0	0	0	0	0	0	0	2

Warrenton 3 SE *Fauquier County* Elevation: 500 ft. Latitude: 38° 41' N Longitude: 77° 46' W

	JAN	FEB	MAR	APR	MAY	JUN	JUL	AUG	SEP	OCT	NOV	DEC	YEAR
Mean Maximum Temp. (°F)	***43.1***	47.0	54.5	65.8	73.8	82.1	86.0	84.6	***78.5***	68.1	***57.1***	***45.9***	***65.5***
Mean Temp. (°F)	***33.6***	36.7	43.6	54.1	62.5	71.1	75.5	***73.8***	***67.1***	56.0	***46.6***	***36.5***	***54.8***
Mean Minimum Temp. (°F)	***23.8***	26.4	32.7	42.5	51.1	60.1	64.8	***63.2***	***55.6***	43.9	***36.0***	***27.1***	***43.9***
Extreme Maximum Temp. (°F)	75	80	90	93	94	99	102	104	***101***	94	84	***79***	***104***
Extreme Minimum Temp. (°F)	-10	-7	7	19	30	40	48	***44***	***27***	16	11	***-2***	***-10***
Days Maximum Temp. ≥ 90°F	0	0	0	0	1	4	9	7	***3***	0	0	***0***	***24***
Days Maximum Temp. ≤ 32°F	5	3	1	0	0	0	0	0	***0***	0	0	***3***	***12***
Days Minimum Temp. ≤ 32°F	***25***	***21***	15	3	0	0	0	***0***	***0***	2	10	***23***	***99***
Days Minimum Temp. ≤ 0°F	0	0	0	0	0	0	0	***0***	***0***	0	0	***0***	***0***
Heating Degree Days (base 65°F)	***968***	795	661	334	134	16	1	***3***	***56***	290	***546***	***877***	***4,681***
Cooling Degree Days (base 65°F)	***0***	0	4	15	63	206	331	***284***	***125***	19	***1***	***0***	***1,048***
Mean Precipitation (in.)	2.83	2.59	3.51	3.48	4.25	3.58	3.86	3.43	***3.90***	3.16	3.52	***3.19***	***41.30***
Extreme Maximum Daily Precip. (in.)	***1.61***	***2.11***	2.95	2.60	3.80	3.16	2.87	***4.20***	***2.72***	***3.95***	4.38	***2.40***	***4.38***
Days With ≥ 0.1" Precipitation	6	5	6	7	7	6	7	6	***6***	4	6	***6***	***72***
Days With ≥ 0.5" Precipitation	2	2	2	2	3	2	3	2	***3***	2	2	***2***	***27***
Days With ≥ 1.0" Precipitation	1	0	1	1	1	1	1	1	***1***	1	1	***1***	***11***
Mean Snowfall (in.)	6.4	***4.4***	2.8	0.2	0.0	0.0	0.0	0.0	***0.0***	0.0	0.5	***3.8***	***18.1***
Maximum Snow Depth (in.)	26	20	13	3	0	0	0	0	***0***	***0***	8	***19***	***26***
Days With ≥ 1.0" Snow Depth	7	6	2	0	0	0	0	0	***0***	***0***	0	***4***	***19***

Williamsburg 2 N *York County* Elevation: 69 ft. Latitude: 37° 18' N Longitude: 76° 42' W

	JAN	FEB	MAR	APR	MAY	JUN	JUL	AUG	SEP	OCT	NOV	DEC	YEAR
Mean Maximum Temp. (°F)	49.2	52.7	60.8	71.0	78.1	85.4	89.0	87.2	81.2	71.5	62.5	52.6	70.1
Mean Temp. (°F)	39.1	41.7	48.8	58.3	66.4	74.4	78.5	76.9	70.8	60.2	51.3	42.4	59.1
Mean Minimum Temp. (°F)	28.9	30.7	36.8	45.5	54.6	63.4	67.9	66.7	60.4	48.8	40.0	32.1	48.0
Extreme Maximum Temp. (°F)	81	83	90	94	98	100	103	104	100	93	85	82	104
Extreme Minimum Temp. (°F)	-7	1	12	22	34	41	52	46	38	26	18	0	-7
Days Maximum Temp. ≥ 90°F	0	0	0	0	2	8	15	11	3	0	0	0	39
Days Maximum Temp. ≤ 32°F	2	1	0	0	0	0	0	0	0	0	0	1	4
Days Minimum Temp. ≤ 32°F	21	17	11	2	0	0	0	0	0	1	7	18	77
Days Minimum Temp. ≤ 0°F	0	0	0	0	0	0	0	0	0	0	0	0	0
Heating Degree Days (base 65°F)	798	652	503	230	68	4	0	0	18	183	411	695	3,562
Cooling Degree Days (base 65°F)	1	1	8	35	117	293	425	378	199	40	5	1	1,503
Mean Precipitation (in.)	3.73	3.20	4.33	3.75	4.00	3.30	5.40	5.26	4.50	3.54	3.33	3.48	47.82
Extreme Maximum Daily Precip. (in.)	2.40	3.19	2.54	2.52	3.14	2.11	4.64	11.33	14.28	6.18	3.49	2.78	14.28
Days With ≥ 0.1" Precipitation	7	6	7	7	7	6	9	7	5	5	6	6	78
Days With ≥ 0.5" Precipitation	3	2	3	3	3	2	3	4	2	2	3	3	33
Days With ≥ 1.0" Precipitation	1	1	1	1	1	1	1	2	1	1	1	1	13
Mean Snowfall (in.)	2.1	2.1	0.6	0.1	0.0	0.0	0.0	0.0	0.0	0.0	0.3	0.4	5.6
Maximum Snow Depth (in.)	14	11	12	2	0	0	0	0	0	0	trace	4	14
Days With ≥ 1.0" Snow Depth	2	1	0	0	0	0	0	0	0	0	0	1	4

Winchester Winc *Frederick County* Elevation: 720 ft. Latitude: 39° 11' N Longitude: 78° 09' W

	JAN	FEB	MAR	APR	MAY	JUN	JUL	AUG	SEP	OCT	NOV	DEC	YEAR
Mean Maximum Temp. (°F)	40.8	44.4	***52.5***	***63.8***	72.4	81.4	85.4	83.8	76.5	65.5	54.9	43.8	***63.8***
Mean Temp. (°F)	32.3	35.0	***42.4***	***53.1***	61.9	71.0	75.2	73.6	66.0	54.7	45.4	35.4	***53.8***
Mean Minimum Temp. (°F)	23.7	25.6	***32.3***	***42.3***	51.3	60.6	65.0	63.2	55.4	43.9	35.8	27.0	***43.8***
Extreme Maximum Temp. (°F)	72	79	***88***	***92***	96	98	105	102	97	92	81	78	***105***
Extreme Minimum Temp. (°F)	-12	-3	***7***	***22***	32	40	49	39	35	24	14	-18	***-18***
Days Maximum Temp. ≥ 90°F	0	0	***0***	***0***	1	4	8	6	1	0	0	0	***20***
Days Maximum Temp. ≤ 32°F	7	4	***1***	***0***	0	0	0	0	0	0	0	4	***16***
Days Minimum Temp. ≤ 32°F	25	22	***17***	***3***	0	0	0	0	0	2	11	23	***103***
Days Minimum Temp. ≤ 0°F	1	0	***0***	***0***	0	0	0	0	0	0	0	0	***1***
Heating Degree Days (base 65°F)	1,008	841	***695***	***366***	149	19	1	5	70	327	583	910	***4,974***
Cooling Degree Days (base 65°F)	0	0	***3***	***15***	60	207	323	277	106	15	1	0	***1,007***
Mean Precipitation (in.)	2.50	2.18	***3.33***	***3.38***	4.00	3.60	3.48	3.03	3.79	2.93	3.35	2.77	***38.34***
Extreme Maximum Daily Precip. (in.)	1.39	2.00	***3.91***	***4.15***	2.77	3.48	2.21	3.90	3.73	3.23	3.00	***2.11***	***4.15***
Days With ≥ 0.1" Precipitation	6	5	***6***	***7***	8	7	7	6	6	5	5	5	***73***
Days With ≥ 0.5" Precipitation	2	1	***2***	***2***	3	2	3	2	2	2	3	2	***26***
Days With ≥ 1.0" Precipitation	1	0	***1***	***1***	1	1	1	1	1	1	1	0	***10***
Mean Snowfall (in.)	7.2	7.1	***3.4***	***trace***	0.0	0.0	0.0	0.0	0.0	0.0	0.5	4.3	***22.5***
Maximum Snow Depth (in.)	30	26	***12***	***1***	0	0	0	0	0	***0***	4	17	***30***
Days With ≥ 1.0" Snow Depth	7	7	***2***	***0***	0	0	0	0	0	0	0	5	***21***

The period of record for all cooperative weather station data is 1980 – 2009. See User Guide for detailed explanation of data.

Woodstock 2 NE *Shenandoah County* Elevation: 660 ft. Latitude: 38° 54' N Longitude: 78° 28' W

	JAN	FEB	MAR	APR	MAY	JUN	JUL	AUG	SEP	OCT	NOV	DEC	YEAR
Mean Maximum Temp. (°F)	43.7	47.3	55.8	66.6	75.1	83.3	87.1	86.1	79.7	69.1	58.0	46.7	66.5
Mean Temp. (°F)	32.9	35.7	43.1	53.0	62.0	70.6	74.6	73.3	66.4	55.1	45.6	36.0	54.0
Mean Minimum Temp. (°F)	22.0	24.0	30.3	39.4	48.8	57.8	62.1	60.5	52.9	41.1	33.1	25.2	41.4
Extreme Maximum Temp. (°F)	74	80	89	92	96	99	105	105	99	93	86	80	105
Extreme Minimum Temp. (°F)	-17	-13	-1	16	26	37	41	33	30	19	6	-10	-17
Days Maximum Temp. ≥ 90°F	0	0	0	0	1	6	11	9	3	0	0	0	30
Days Maximum Temp. ≤ 32°F	5	3	1	0	0	0	0	0	0	0	0	3	12
Days Minimum Temp. ≤ 32°F	27	24	19	7	1	0	0	0	0	6	15	25	124
Days Minimum Temp. ≤ 0°F	1	0	0	0	0	0	0	0	0	0	0	0	1
Heating Degree Days (base 65°F)	988	822	674	362	144	18	1	4	64	314	577	894	4,862
Cooling Degree Days (base 65°F)	0	0	2	10	58	192	306	269	111	14	0	0	962
Mean Precipitation (in.)	2.58	2.52	3.08	2.98	4.07	3.84	3.78	3.17	3.78	2.65	2.90	2.36	37.71
Extreme Maximum Daily Precip. (in.)	1.73	2.35	3.55	2.73	2.07	2.45	3.50	3.33	5.21	3.20	3.50	2.48	5.21
Days With ≥ 0.1" Precipitation	6	5	6	7	8	8	8	6	6	5	5	5	75
Days With ≥ 0.5" Precipitation	2	2	2	2	3	3	3	2	2	2	2	2	27
Days With ≥ 1.0" Precipitation	1	1	1	0	1	1	1	1	1	1	1	0	10
Mean Snowfall (in.)	7.0	7.0	3.6	0.1	0.0	0.0	0.0	0.0	0.0	trace	0.7	4.2	22.6
Maximum Snow Depth (in.)	27	32	22	2	0	0	0	0	0	trace	4	19	32
Days With ≥ 1.0" Snow Depth	4	2	1	0	0	0	0	0	0	0	0	3	10

Wytheville 1 S *Wythe County* Elevation: 2,450 ft. Latitude: 36° 56' N Longitude: 81° 06' W

	JAN	FEB	MAR	APR	MAY	JUN	JUL	AUG	SEP	OCT	NOV	DEC	YEAR
Mean Maximum Temp. (°F)	42.9	46.8	55.3	64.9	73.0	79.8	83.3	82.8	76.6	67.1	56.6	45.6	64.6
Mean Temp. (°F)	32.6	35.5	42.5	51.3	59.5	67.4	71.2	70.3	63.6	53.0	43.7	35.2	52.2
Mean Minimum Temp. (°F)	22.2	24.2	29.6	37.6	46.0	54.9	59.1	57.8	50.7	38.8	30.8	24.6	39.7
Extreme Maximum Temp. (°F)	72	75	83	87	89	93	98	97	95	87	79	76	98
Extreme Minimum Temp. (°F)	-20	-9	1	12	24	34	39	36	25	14	7	-13	-20
Days Maximum Temp. ≥ 90°F	0	0	0	0	0	1	3	3	0	0	0	0	7
Days Maximum Temp. ≤ 32°F	5	3	1	0	0	0	0	0	0	0	0	3	12
Days Minimum Temp. ≤ 32°F	27	24	20	9	3	0	0	0	1	9	18	24	135
Days Minimum Temp. ≤ 0°F	1	0	0	0	0	0	0	0	0	0	0	1	2
Heating Degree Days (base 65°F)	999	827	690	408	188	33	6	9	98	369	633	919	5,179
Cooling Degree Days (base 65°F)	0	0	0	3	25	110	206	182	63	5	0	0	594
Mean Precipitation (in.)	2.84	2.76	3.25	3.30	4.09	3.57	3.97	3.25	3.19	2.72	2.77	2.62	38.33
Extreme Maximum Daily Precip. (in.)	2.23	2.24	3.74	2.01	2.67	3.36	3.40	3.45	3.95	3.50	2.10	1.78	3.95
Days With ≥ 0.1" Precipitation	6	6	7	7	8	7	7	6	6	5	6	6	77
Days With ≥ 0.5" Precipitation	2	2	2	2	3	2	3	2	2	2	2	2	26
Days With ≥ 1.0" Precipitation	1	0	0	1	1	1	1	1	1	1	0	1	9
Mean Snowfall (in.)	6.6	4.9	2.7	0.9	0.0	0.0	0.0	0.0	0.0	trace	0.3	3.8	19.2
Maximum Snow Depth (in.)	22	13	18	10	0	0	0	0	0	1	2	13	22
Days With ≥ 1.0" Snow Depth	6	5	1	0	0	0	0	0	0	0	0	4	16

The period of record for all cooperative weather station data is 1980 – 2009. See User Guide for detailed explanation of data.

Virginia Weather Station Rankings

Annual Extreme Maximum Temperature

Highest Rank	Station Name	°F	Lowest Rank	Station Name	°F
1	Charlottesville 2 W	105	1	Burkes Garden	94
1	Crozier	105	2	Floyd 2 NE	97
1	Dale Enterprise	105	3	Wytheville 1 S	98
1	Danville	105	4	Blacksburg Wso	99
1	Hopewell	105	5	Abingdon 3 S	100
1	Langley AFB	*105*	5	Bedford	*100*
1	Lincoln	105	7	Covington Filter Plant	102
1	Luray 5 E	*105*	7	Grundy	102
1	Roanoke Woodrum Arpt	105	7	Lynchburg Municipal Arpt	102
1	Washington DC National Arpt	105	7	Piedmont Research Stn	102
1	Winchester Winc	*105*	7	Rocky Mount	102
1	Woodstock 2 NE	105	7	Staunton Sewage Plant	102
13	Holland 1 E	104	13	Appomattox	103
13	Norfolk Intl Arpt	104	13	Ashland	103
13	Richmond R E Byrd Int'l Arpt	104	13	Camp Pickett	103
13	Sterling RCS	104	13	Lexington	103
13	Warrenton 3 SE	*104*	13	Suffolk Lake Kilby	103
13	Washington DC Dulles Int'l Arpt	104	18	Holland 1 E	104
13	Williamsburg 2 N	104	18	Norfolk Intl Arpt	104
20	Appomattox	103	18	Richmond R E Byrd Int'l Arpt	104
20	Ashland	103	18	Sterling RCS	104
20	Camp Pickett	103	18	Warrenton 3 SE	*104*
20	Lexington	103	18	Washington DC Dulles Int'l Arpt	104
20	Suffolk Lake Kilby	103	18	Williamsburg 2 N	104
25	Covington Filter Plant	102	25	Charlottesville 2 W	105

Annual Mean Maximum Temperature

Highest Rank	Station Name	°F	Lowest Rank	Station Name	°F
1	Hopewell	72.3	1	Burkes Garden	60.1
2	Holland 1 E	70.4	2	Blacksburg Wso	63.5
3	Danville	70.1	2	Floyd 2 NE	63.5
3	Williamsburg 2 N	70.1	4	Winchester Winc	*63.8*
5	Suffolk Lake Kilby	69.5	5	Staunton Sewage Plant	64.2
6	Richmond R E Byrd Int'l Arpt	69.2	6	Wytheville 1 S	64.6
7	Crozier	68.9	7	Dale Enterprise	64.9
7	Norfolk Intl Arpt	68.9	8	Warrenton 3 SE	*65.5*
9	Camp Pickett	68.8	9	Sterling RCS	65.6
10	Covington Filter Plant	68.6	10	Washington DC Dulles Int'l Arpt	66.0
11	Langley AFB	*68.0*	11	Piedmont Research Stn	66.1
12	Ashland	67.9	12	Abingdon 3 S	66.4
12	Grundy	67.9	13	Luray 5 E	*66.5*
12	Lexington	67.9	13	Woodstock 2 NE	66.5
15	Appomattox	67.6	15	Lincoln	66.6
16	Charlottesville 2 W	67.4	16	Bedford	*66.8*
17	Roanoke Woodrum Arpt	67.2	16	Washington DC National Arpt	66.8
18	Rocky Mount	67.1	18	Lynchburg Municipal Arpt	67.0
19	Lynchburg Municipal Arpt	67.0	19	Rocky Mount	67.1
20	Bedford	*66.8*	20	Roanoke Woodrum Arpt	67.2
20	Washington DC National Arpt	66.8	21	Charlottesville 2 W	67.4
22	Lincoln	66.6	22	Appomattox	67.6
23	Luray 5 E	*66.5*	23	Ashland	67.9
23	Woodstock 2 NE	66.5	23	Grundy	67.9
25	Abingdon 3 S	66.4	23	Lexington	67.9

Rankings include 25 highest/lowest stations. If state has less than 25 stations, all stations are included. The period of record is 1980–2009. See User Guide for detailed explanation of data.

Annual Mean Temperature

Highest Rank	Station Name	°F	Lowest Rank	Station Name	°F
1	Hopewell	60.9	1	Burkes Garden	49.1
2	Norfolk Intl Arpt	60.5	2	Floyd 2 NE	51.6
3	Langley AFB	***59.8***	3	Blacksburg Wso	52.0
4	Suffolk Lake Kilby	59.6	4	Wytheville 1 S	52.2
5	Williamsburg 2 N	59.1	5	Staunton Sewage Plant	52.8
6	Holland 1 E	58.8	6	Dale Enterprise	53.3
7	Richmond R E Byrd Int'l Arpt	58.7	7	Sterling RCS	53.6
8	Danville	58.4	8	Luray 5 E	***53.7***
9	Washington DC National Arpt	58.2	9	Winchester Winc	***53.8***
10	Ashland	57.0	10	Woodstock 2 NE	54.0
10	Charlottesville 2 W	57.0	11	Abingdon 3 S	54.2
12	Roanoke Woodrum Arpt	56.9	12	Warrenton 3 SE	***54.8***
13	Camp Pickett	56.6	13	Lincoln	54.9
13	Crozier	56.6	14	Washington DC Dulles Int'l Arpt	55.0
15	Bedford	***56.4***	15	Covington Filter Plant	55.3
16	Lynchburg Municipal Arpt	56.3	15	Grundy	55.3
17	Appomattox	56.1	15	Lexington	55.3
18	Piedmont Research Stn	55.7	18	Piedmont Research Stn	55.7
18	Rocky Mount	55.7	18	Rocky Mount	55.7
20	Covington Filter Plant	55.3	20	Appomattox	56.1
20	Grundy	55.3	21	Lynchburg Municipal Arpt	56.3
20	Lexington	55.3	22	Bedford	***56.4***
23	Washington DC Dulles Int'l Arpt	55.0	23	Camp Pickett	56.6
24	Lincoln	54.9	23	Crozier	56.6
25	Warrenton 3 SE	***54.8***	25	Roanoke Woodrum Arpt	56.9

Annual Mean Minimum Temperature

Highest Rank	Station Name	°F	Lowest Rank	Station Name	°F
1	Norfolk Intl Arpt	52.0	1	Burkes Garden	38.0
2	Langley AFB	***51.5***	2	Floyd 2 NE	39.7
3	Suffolk Lake Kilby	49.7	2	Wytheville 1 S	39.7
4	Washington DC National Arpt	49.6	4	Blacksburg Wso	40.4
5	Hopewell	49.5	5	Luray 5 E	***40.9***
6	Richmond R E Byrd Int'l Arpt	48.1	6	Staunton Sewage Plant	41.4
7	Williamsburg 2 N	48.0	6	Woodstock 2 NE	41.4
8	Holland 1 E	47.2	8	Dale Enterprise	41.6
9	Danville	46.8	8	Sterling RCS	41.6
10	Charlottesville 2 W	46.6	10	Abingdon 3 S	41.9
11	Roanoke Woodrum Arpt	46.5	11	Covington Filter Plant	42.0
12	Ashland	46.1	12	Grundy	42.6
13	Bedford	***45.9***	13	Lexington	42.8
14	Lynchburg Municipal Arpt	45.5	14	Lincoln	43.2
15	Piedmont Research Stn	45.3	15	Winchester Winc	***43.8***
16	Appomattox	44.5	16	Warrenton 3 SE	***43.9***
17	Camp Pickett	44.4	16	Washington DC Dulles Int'l Arpt	43.9
18	Crozier	44.2	18	Crozier	44.2
18	Rocky Mount	44.2	18	Rocky Mount	44.2
20	Warrenton 3 SE	***43.9***	20	Camp Pickett	44.4
20	Washington DC Dulles Int'l Arpt	43.9	21	Appomattox	44.5
22	Winchester Winc	***43.8***	22	Piedmont Research Stn	45.3
23	Lincoln	43.2	23	Lynchburg Municipal Arpt	45.5
24	Lexington	42.8	24	Bedford	***45.9***
25	Grundy	42.6	25	Ashland	46.1

 Rankings include 25 highest/lowest stations. If state has less than 25 stations, all stations are included. The period of record is 1980–2009. See User Guide for detailed explanation of data.

Annual Extreme Minimum Temperature

Highest Rank	Highest Station Name	Highest °F	Lowest Rank	Lowest Station Name	Lowest °F
1	Langley AFB	*-3*	1	Burkes Garden	-26
1	Norfolk Intl Arpt	-3	2	Abingdon 3 S	-21
3	Danville	-5	3	Wytheville 1 S	-20
3	Holland 1 E	-5	4	Covington Filter Plant	-19
3	Suffolk Lake Kilby	-5	4	Floyd 2 NE	*-19*
3	Washington DC National Arpt	-5	4	Sterling RCS	-19
7	Richmond R E Byrd Int'l Arpt	-6	7	Blacksburg Wso	-18
8	Williamsburg 2 N	-7	7	Washington DC Dulles Int'l Arpt	-18
9	Crozier	-9	7	Winchester Winc	*-18*
10	Bedford	*-10*	10	Woodstock 2 NE	-17
10	Charlottesville 2 W	-10	11	Staunton Sewage Plant	-16
10	Lincoln	-10	12	Lexington	-15
10	Lynchburg Municipal Arpt	-10	13	Appomattox	-14
10	Warrenton 3 SE	*-10*	13	Grundy	-14
15	Ashland	-11	13	Luray 5 E	*-14*
15	Hopewell	-11	16	Dale Enterprise	-13
15	Piedmont Research Stn	-11	17	Camp Pickett	-12
15	Roanoke Woodrum Arpt	-11	18	Ashland	-11
15	Rocky Mount	-11	18	Hopewell	-11
20	Camp Pickett	-12	18	Piedmont Research Stn	-11
21	Dale Enterprise	-13	18	Roanoke Woodrum Arpt	-11
22	Appomattox	-14	18	Rocky Mount	-11
22	Grundy	-14	23	Bedford	*-10*
22	Luray 5 E	*-14*	23	Charlottesville 2 W	-10
25	Lexington	-15	23	Lincoln	-10

July Mean Maximum Temperature

Highest Rank	Highest Station Name	Highest °F	Lowest Rank	Lowest Station Name	Lowest °F
1	Hopewell	91.2	1	Burkes Garden	78.6
2	Danville	89.8	2	Floyd 2 NE	81.9
3	Richmond R E Byrd Int'l Arpt	89.3	3	Blacksburg Wso	82.7
4	Holland 1 E	89.1	4	Wytheville 1 S	83.3
5	Williamsburg 2 N	89.0	5	Staunton Sewage Plant	84.0
6	Crozier	88.8	6	Abingdon 3 S	84.6
7	Washington DC National Arpt	88.5	7	Winchester Winc	85.4
8	Suffolk Lake Kilby	88.3	8	Bedford	85.5
9	Camp Pickett	88.1	9	Dale Enterprise	85.8
10	Covington Filter Plant	88.0	10	Warrenton 3 SE	86.0
10	Norfolk Intl Arpt	88.0	11	Luray 5 E	86.1
12	Lincoln	87.8	12	Piedmont Research Stn	86.2
13	Washington DC Dulles Int'l Arpt	87.6	13	Grundy	86.3
14	Langley AFB	*87.5*	13	Rocky Mount	86.3
15	Charlottesville 2 W	87.4	15	Lynchburg Municipal Arpt	86.5
16	Appomattox	87.1	16	Ashland	86.9
16	Sterling RCS	87.1	16	Lexington	86.9
16	Woodstock 2 NE	87.1	18	Roanoke Woodrum Arpt	87.0
19	Roanoke Woodrum Arpt	87.0	19	Appomattox	87.1
20	Ashland	86.9	19	Sterling RCS	87.1
20	Lexington	86.9	19	Woodstock 2 NE	87.1
22	Lynchburg Municipal Arpt	86.5	22	Charlottesville 2 W	87.4
23	Grundy	86.3	23	Langley AFB	*87.5*
23	Rocky Mount	86.3	24	Washington DC Dulles Int'l Arpt	87.6
25	Piedmont Research Stn	86.2	25	Lincoln	87.8

Rankings include 25 highest/lowest stations. If state has less than 25 stations, all stations are included. The period of record is 1980–2009. See User Guide for detailed explanation of data.

January Mean Minimum Temperature

Highest Rank	Station Name	°F	Lowest Rank	Station Name	°F
1	Norfolk Intl Arpt	32.8	1	Burkes Garden	20.5
2	Langley AFB	*32.1*	2	Luray 5 E	20.8
3	Suffolk Lake Kilby	30.8	3	Blacksburg Wso	21.4
4	Hopewell	30.6	4	Sterling RCS	21.8
5	Williamsburg 2 N	28.9	5	Staunton Sewage Plant	21.9
6	Washington DC National Arpt	28.8	6	Woodstock 2 NE	22.0
7	Richmond R E Byrd Int'l Arpt	28.5	7	Dale Enterprise	22.2
8	Holland 1 E	28.4	7	Wytheville 1 S	22.2
9	Roanoke Woodrum Arpt	27.7	9	Floyd 2 NE	22.5
10	Bedford	27.4	10	Abingdon 3 S	23.7
11	Danville	27.3	10	Lincoln	23.7
12	Charlottesville 2 W	27.0	10	Winchester Winc	23.7
13	Lynchburg Municipal Arpt	26.5	13	Warrenton 3 SE	*23.8*
14	Ashland	26.4	13	Washington DC Dulles Int'l Arpt	23.8
15	Rocky Mount	25.9	15	Grundy	23.9
16	Appomattox	24.9	15	Lexington	23.9
17	Crozier	24.8	17	Covington Filter Plant	24.0
18	Camp Pickett	24.7	18	Camp Pickett	24.7
18	Piedmont Research Stn	24.7	18	Piedmont Research Stn	24.7
20	Covington Filter Plant	24.0	20	Crozier	24.8
21	Grundy	23.9	21	Appomattox	24.9
21	Lexington	23.9	22	Rocky Mount	25.9
23	Warrenton 3 SE	*23.8*	23	Ashland	26.4
23	Washington DC Dulles Int'l Arpt	23.8	24	Lynchburg Municipal Arpt	26.5
25	Abingdon 3 S	23.7	25	Charlottesville 2 W	27.0

Number of Days Annually Maximum Temperature ≥ 90°F

Highest Rank	Station Name	Days	Lowest Rank	Station Name	Days
1	Hopewell	60	1	Burkes Garden	0
2	Danville	52	2	Floyd 2 NE	3
3	Holland 1 E	43	3	Wytheville 1 S	7
3	Richmond R E Byrd Int'l Arpt	43	4	Blacksburg Wso	8
5	Crozier	42	5	Abingdon 3 S	12
6	Covington Filter Plant	39	6	Staunton Sewage Plant	13
6	Williamsburg 2 N	39	7	Bedford	*19*
8	Washington DC National Arpt	36	8	Winchester Winc	*20*
9	Camp Pickett	35	9	Dale Enterprise	22
10	Norfolk Intl Arpt	34	10	Rocky Mount	24
11	Charlottesville 2 W	32	10	Warrenton 3 SE	*24*
11	Lincoln	32	12	Luray 5 E	*25*
11	Washington DC Dulles Int'l Arpt	32	12	Lynchburg Municipal Arpt	25
14	Suffolk Lake Kilby	31	12	Piedmont Research Stn	25
15	Woodstock 2 NE	30	15	Grundy	27
16	Langley AFB	*29*	16	Appomattox	28
16	Lexington	29	16	Ashland	28
16	Roanoke Woodrum Arpt	29	18	Langley AFB	*29*
16	Sterling RCS	29	18	Lexington	29
20	Appomattox	28	18	Roanoke Woodrum Arpt	29
20	Ashland	28	18	Sterling RCS	29
22	Grundy	27	22	Woodstock 2 NE	30
23	Luray 5 E	*25*	23	Suffolk Lake Kilby	31
23	Lynchburg Municipal Arpt	25	24	Charlottesville 2 W	32
23	Piedmont Research Stn	25	24	Lincoln	32

 Rankings include 25 highest/lowest stations. If state has less than 25 stations, all stations are included. The period of record is 1980–2009. See User Guide for detailed explanation of data.

Number of Days Annually Maximum Temperature ≤ 32°F

Highest			Lowest		
Rank	Station Name	Days	Rank	Station Name	Days
1	Burkes Garden	27	1	Hopewell	2
2	Blacksburg Wso	16	2	Danville	4
2	Winchester Winc	***16***	2	Holland 1 E	4
4	Dale Enterprise	14	2	Langley AFB	***4***
4	Staunton Sewage Plant	14	2	Norfolk Intl Arpt	4
6	Floyd 2 NE	13	2	Suffolk Lake Kilby	4
6	Luray 5 E	***13***	2	Williamsburg 2 N	4
6	Sterling RCS	13	8	Lexington	5
6	Washington DC Dulles Int'l Arpt	13	9	Appomattox	6
10	Warrenton 3 SE	***12***	9	Ashland	6
10	Woodstock 2 NE	12	9	Bedford	***6***
10	Wytheville 1 S	12	9	Camp Pickett	6
13	Abingdon 3 S	11	9	Covington Filter Plant	6
13	Piedmont Research Stn	11	9	Richmond R E Byrd Int'l Arpt	6
15	Grundy	10	15	Crozier	7
15	Lincoln	10	15	Rocky Mount	7
17	Washington DC National Arpt	9	17	Charlottesville 2 W	8
18	Charlottesville 2 W	8	17	Lynchburg Municipal Arpt	8
18	Lynchburg Municipal Arpt	8	17	Roanoke Woodrum Arpt	8
18	Roanoke Woodrum Arpt	8	20	Washington DC National Arpt	9
21	Crozier	7	21	Grundy	10
21	Rocky Mount	7	21	Lincoln	10
23	Appomattox	6	23	Abingdon 3 S	11
23	Ashland	6	23	Piedmont Research Stn	11
23	Bedford	***6***	25	Warrenton 3 SE	***12***

Number of Days Annually Minimum Temperature ≤ 32°F

Highest			Lowest		
Rank	Station Name	Days	Rank	Station Name	Days
1	Burkes Garden	141	1	Norfolk Intl Arpt	46
2	Wytheville 1 S	135	2	Langley AFB	***51***
3	Floyd 2 NE	134	3	Suffolk Lake Kilby	62
4	Blacksburg Wso	129	4	Washington DC National Arpt	65
5	Sterling RCS	125	5	Hopewell	67
6	Woodstock 2 NE	124	6	Richmond R E Byrd Int'l Arpt	77
7	Staunton Sewage Plant	121	6	Williamsburg 2 N	77
8	Luray 5 E	***120***	8	Charlottesville 2 W	83
9	Dale Enterprise	119	8	Roanoke Woodrum Arpt	83
10	Covington Filter Plant	116	10	Holland 1 E	84
10	Lexington	116	11	Bedford	***86***
12	Abingdon 3 S	115	12	Danville	88
13	Grundy	114	13	Ashland	93
14	Lincoln	112	13	Lynchburg Municipal Arpt	93
15	Camp Pickett	108	15	Appomattox	95
16	Washington DC Dulles Int'l Arpt	106	16	Piedmont Research Stn	96
17	Crozier	105	17	Warrenton 3 SE	***99***
18	Winchester Winc	***103***	18	Rocky Mount	101
19	Rocky Mount	101	19	Winchester Winc	***103***
20	Warrenton 3 SE	***99***	20	Crozier	105
21	Piedmont Research Stn	96	21	Washington DC Dulles Int'l Arpt	106
22	Appomattox	95	22	Camp Pickett	108
23	Ashland	93	23	Lincoln	112
23	Lynchburg Municipal Arpt	93	24	Grundy	114
25	Danville	88	25	Abingdon 3 S	115

Rankings include 25 highest/lowest stations. If state has less than 25 stations, all stations are included. The period of record is 1980–2009. See User Guide for detailed explanation of data.

Number of Days Annually Minimum Temperature ≤ 0°F

Highest Rank	Highest Station Name	Highest Days	Lowest Rank	Lowest Station Name	Lowest Days
1	Burkes Garden	4	1	Appomattox	0
2	Blacksburg Wso	2	1	Ashland	0
2	Dale Enterprise	2	1	Bedford	*0*
2	Floyd 2 NE	2	1	Charlottesville 2 W	0
2	Staunton Sewage Plant	2	1	Crozier	0
2	Wytheville 1 S	2	1	Danville	0
7	Abingdon 3 S	1	1	Holland 1 E	0
7	Camp Pickett	1	1	Hopewell	0
7	Covington Filter Plant	1	1	Langley AFB	*0*
7	Grundy	1	1	Lincoln	0
7	Lexington	1	1	Lynchburg Municipal Arpt	0
7	Luray 5 E	*1*	1	Norfolk Intl Arpt	0
7	Sterling RCS	1	1	Piedmont Research Stn	0
7	Washington DC Dulles Int'l Arpt	1	1	Richmond R E Byrd Int'l Arpt	0
7	Winchester Winc	*1*	1	Roanoke Woodrum Arpt	0
7	Woodstock 2 NE	1	1	Rocky Mount	0
17	Appomattox	0	1	Suffolk Lake Kilby	0
17	Ashland	0	1	Warrenton 3 SE	*0*
17	Bedford	*0*	1	Washington DC National Arpt	0
17	Charlottesville 2 W	0	1	Williamsburg 2 N	0
17	Crozier	0	21	Abingdon 3 S	1
17	Danville	0	21	Camp Pickett	1
17	Holland 1 E	0	21	Covington Filter Plant	1
17	Hopewell	0	21	Grundy	1
17	Langley AFB	*0*	21	Lexington	1

Number of Annual Heating Degree Days

Highest Rank	Highest Station Name	Highest Num.	Lowest Rank	Lowest Station Name	Lowest Num.
1	Burkes Garden	6,011	1	Hopewell	3,189
2	Blacksburg Wso	5,292	2	Norfolk Intl Arpt	3,258
3	Floyd 2 NE	5,276	3	Suffolk Lake Kilby	3,396
4	Wytheville 1 S	5,179	4	Langley AFB	*3,419*
5	Staunton Sewage Plant	5,120	5	Williamsburg 2 N	3,562
6	Sterling RCS	5,043	6	Holland 1 E	3,617
7	Dale Enterprise	5,039	7	Richmond R E Byrd Int'l Arpt	3,749
8	Winchester Winc	*4,974*	8	Danville	3,826
9	Luray 5 E	*4,868*	9	Washington DC National Arpt	3,957
10	Woodstock 2 NE	4,862	10	Ashland	4,082
11	Washington DC Dulles Int'l Arpt	4,723	11	Roanoke Woodrum Arpt	4,093
12	Warrenton 3 SE	*4,681*	12	Charlottesville 2 W	4,101
13	Lincoln	4,676	13	Bedford	*4,143*
14	Abingdon 3 S	4,661	14	Camp Pickett	4,207
15	Lexington	4,472	15	Lynchburg Municipal Arpt	4,227
16	Piedmont Research Stn	4,464	16	Crozier	4,239
17	Grundy	4,452	17	Appomattox	4,313
18	Covington Filter Plant	4,428	18	Rocky Mount	4,359
19	Rocky Mount	4,359	19	Covington Filter Plant	4,428
20	Appomattox	4,313	20	Grundy	4,452
21	Crozier	4,239	21	Piedmont Research Stn	4,464
22	Lynchburg Municipal Arpt	4,227	22	Lexington	4,472
23	Camp Pickett	4,207	23	Abingdon 3 S	4,661
24	Bedford	*4,143*	24	Lincoln	4,676
25	Charlottesville 2 W	4,101	25	Warrenton 3 SE	*4,681*

 Rankings include 25 highest/lowest stations. If state has less than 25 stations, all stations are included. The period of record is 1980–2009. See User Guide for detailed explanation of data.

Number of Annual Cooling Degree Days

Rank	Station Name (Highest)	Num.	Rank	Station Name (Lowest)	Num.
1	Hopewell	1,807	1	Burkes Garden	289
2	Norfolk Intl Arpt	1,716	2	Floyd 2 NE	497
3	Langley AFB	***1,627***	3	Wytheville 1 S	594
4	Washington DC National Arpt	1,597	4	Blacksburg Wso	625
5	Richmond R E Byrd Int'l Arpt	1,553	5	Staunton Sewage Plant	782
6	Suffolk Lake Kilby	1,546	6	Abingdon 3 S	809
7	Danville	1,537	7	Luray 5 E	***858***
8	Williamsburg 2 N	1,503	8	Dale Enterprise	876
9	Holland 1 E	1,475	9	Woodstock 2 NE	962
10	Charlottesville 2 W	1,293	10	Sterling RCS	1,006
11	Crozier	1,272	11	Covington Filter Plant	1,007
12	Ashland	1,269	11	Winchester Winc	***1,007***
13	Camp Pickett	1,259	13	Grundy	1,010
14	Roanoke Woodrum Arpt	1,232	14	Warrenton 3 SE	***1,048***
15	Piedmont Research Stn	1,182	15	Lexington	1,051
16	Washington DC Dulles Int'l Arpt	1,167	16	Rocky Mount	1,063
17	Lynchburg Municipal Arpt	1,161	17	Bedford	***1,096***
18	Appomattox	1,150	18	Lincoln	1,107
19	Lincoln	1,107	19	Appomattox	1,150
20	Bedford	***1,096***	20	Lynchburg Municipal Arpt	1,161
21	Rocky Mount	1,063	21	Washington DC Dulles Int'l Arpt	1,167
22	Lexington	1,051	22	Piedmont Research Stn	1,182
23	Warrenton 3 SE	***1,048***	23	Roanoke Woodrum Arpt	1,232
24	Grundy	1,010	24	Camp Pickett	1,259
25	Covington Filter Plant	1,007	25	Ashland	1,269

Annual Precipitation

Rank	Station Name (Highest)	Inches	Rank	Station Name (Lowest)	Inches
1	Suffolk Lake Kilby	49.20	1	Dale Enterprise	36.44
2	Holland 1 E	47.95	2	Covington Filter Plant	37.37
3	Williamsburg 2 N	47.82	3	Woodstock 2 NE	37.71
4	Charlottesville 2 W	47.27	4	Wytheville 1 S	38.33
5	Camp Pickett	46.19	5	Winchester Winc	***38.34***
6	Rocky Mount	46.13	6	Floyd 2 NE	39.42
7	Norfolk Intl Arpt	46.02	7	Washington DC National Arpt	39.49
8	Burkes Garden	45.69	8	Staunton Sewage Plant	39.51
9	Hopewell	45.62	9	Lexington	40.18
10	Abingdon 3 S	45.20	10	Blacksburg Wso	40.82
11	Langley AFB	***44.60***	11	Roanoke Woodrum Arpt	40.94
12	Appomattox	44.32	12	Lynchburg Municipal Arpt	41.02
13	Danville	44.26	13	Luray 5 E	41.21
14	Bedford	***44.12***	14	Warrenton 3 SE	***41.30***
15	Grundy	44.11	14	Washington DC Dulles Int'l Arpt	41.30
16	Richmond R E Byrd Int'l Arpt	43.74	16	Lincoln	41.41
17	Ashland	43.29	17	Crozier	42.05
18	Piedmont Research Stn	42.95	18	Sterling RCS	42.58
19	Sterling RCS	42.58	19	Piedmont Research Stn	42.95
20	Crozier	42.05	20	Ashland	43.29
21	Lincoln	41.41	21	Richmond R E Byrd Int'l Arpt	43.74
22	Warrenton 3 SE	***41.30***	22	Grundy	44.11
22	Washington DC Dulles Int'l Arpt	41.30	23	Bedford	***44.12***
24	Luray 5 E	41.21	24	Danville	44.26
25	Lynchburg Municipal Arpt	41.02	25	Appomattox	44.32

Rankings include 25 highest/lowest stations. If state has less than 25 stations, all stations are included. The period of record is 1980–2009. See User Guide for detailed explanation of data.

Annual Extreme Maximum Daily Precipitation

Highest

Rank	Station Name	Inches
1	Williamsburg 2 N	14.28
2	Luray 5 E	***9.42***
3	Charlottesville 2 W	9.20
4	Suffolk Lake Kilby	9.19
5	Norfolk Intl Arpt	8.92
6	Holland 1 E	8.60
7	Appomattox	***8.35***
8	Covington Filter Plant	8.00
9	Hopewell	7.61
10	Rocky Mount	7.45
11	Langley AFB	***7.15***
12	Richmond R E Byrd Int'l Arpt	6.68
13	Sterling RCS	6.64
14	Roanoke Woodrum Arpt	6.61
15	Crozier	6.51
16	Lynchburg Municipal Arpt	6.05
17	Dale Enterprise	5.95
18	Washington DC Dulles Int'l Arpt	5.94
19	Camp Pickett	5.91
20	Floyd 2 NE	***5.87***
21	Piedmont Research Stn	5.67
22	Staunton Sewage Plant	5.50
23	Ashland	5.44
24	Woodstock 2 NE	5.21
25	Washington DC National Arpt	5.19

Lowest

Rank	Station Name	Inches
1	Grundy	***3.18***
2	Abingdon 3 S	3.55
3	Wytheville 1 S	3.95
4	Blacksburg Wso	4.07
5	Winchester Winc	***4.15***
6	Warrenton 3 SE	***4.38***
7	Burkes Garden	4.56
8	Danville	4.76
9	Lincoln	***5.11***
10	Lexington	5.18
11	Washington DC National Arpt	5.19
12	Woodstock 2 NE	5.21
13	Ashland	5.44
14	Staunton Sewage Plant	5.50
15	Piedmont Research Stn	5.67
16	Floyd 2 NE	***5.87***
17	Camp Pickett	5.91
18	Washington DC Dulles Int'l Arpt	5.94
19	Dale Enterprise	5.95
20	Lynchburg Municipal Arpt	6.05
21	Crozier	6.51
22	Roanoke Woodrum Arpt	6.61
23	Sterling RCS	6.64
24	Richmond R E Byrd Int'l Arpt	6.68
25	Langley AFB	***7.15***

Number of Days Annually With ≥ 0.1 Inches of Precipitation

Highest

Rank	Station Name	Days
1	Abingdon 3 S	96
1	Burkes Garden	96
3	Grundy	90
4	Blacksburg Wso	81
5	Holland 1 E	79
5	Suffolk Lake Kilby	79
7	Williamsburg 2 N	78
8	Covington Filter Plant	77
8	Norfolk Intl Arpt	77
8	Rocky Mount	77
8	Wytheville 1 S	77
12	Camp Pickett	76
12	Charlottesville 2 W	76
14	Piedmont Research Stn	75
14	Washington DC Dulles Int'l Arpt	75
14	Woodstock 2 NE	75
17	Ashland	74
17	Bedford	***74***
17	Danville	74
17	Roanoke Woodrum Arpt	74
17	Sterling RCS	74
22	Hopewell	73
22	Lynchburg Municipal Arpt	73
22	Richmond R E Byrd Int'l Arpt	73
22	Winchester Winc	***73***

Lowest

Rank	Station Name	Days
1	Lincoln	64
2	Floyd 2 NE	68
3	Appomattox	69
4	Lexington	70
4	Washington DC National Arpt	70
6	Crozier	71
6	Luray 5 E	71
8	Dale Enterprise	72
8	Langley AFB	***72***
8	Staunton Sewage Plant	72
8	Warrenton 3 SE	***72***
12	Hopewell	73
12	Lynchburg Municipal Arpt	73
12	Richmond R E Byrd Int'l Arpt	73
12	Winchester Winc	***73***
16	Ashland	74
16	Bedford	***74***
16	Danville	74
16	Roanoke Woodrum Arpt	74
16	Sterling RCS	74
21	Piedmont Research Stn	75
21	Washington DC Dulles Int'l Arpt	75
21	Woodstock 2 NE	75
24	Camp Pickett	76
24	Charlottesville 2 W	76

Rankings include 25 highest/lowest stations. If state has less than 25 stations, all stations are included. The period of record is 1980–2009. See User Guide for detailed explanation of data.

Number of Days Annually With ≥ 0.5 Inches of Precipitation

Highest Rank	Station Name	Days	Lowest Rank	Station Name	Days
1	Camp Pickett	35	1	Dale Enterprise	23
2	Suffolk Lake Kilby	33	2	Covington Filter Plant	24
2	Williamsburg 2 N	33	2	Luray 5 E	24
4	Abingdon 3 S	32	4	Lexington	26
4	Hopewell	32	4	Winchester Winc	***26***
6	Charlottesville 2 W	31	4	Wytheville 1 S	26
6	Holland 1 E	31	7	Floyd 2 NE	27
8	Burkes Garden	30	7	Lynchburg Municipal Arpt	27
8	Danville	30	7	Roanoke Woodrum Arpt	27
8	Grundy	30	7	Sterling RCS	27
8	Langley AFB	***30***	7	Warrenton 3 SE	***27***
8	Richmond R E Byrd Int'l Arpt	30	7	Washington DC Dulles Int'l Arpt	27
13	Ashland	29	7	Washington DC National Arpt	27
13	Norfolk Intl Arpt	29	7	Woodstock 2 NE	27
13	Piedmont Research Stn	29	15	Appomattox	28
13	Rocky Mount	29	15	Bedford	***28***
17	Appomattox	28	15	Blacksburg Wso	28
17	Bedford	***28***	15	Crozier	28
17	Blacksburg Wso	28	15	Lincoln	28
17	Crozier	28	15	Staunton Sewage Plant	28
17	Lincoln	28	21	Ashland	29
17	Staunton Sewage Plant	28	21	Norfolk Intl Arpt	29
23	Floyd 2 NE	27	21	Piedmont Research Stn	29
23	Lynchburg Municipal Arpt	27	21	Rocky Mount	29
23	Roanoke Woodrum Arpt	27	25	Burkes Garden	30

Number of Days Annually With ≥ 1.0 Inches of Precipitation

Highest Rank	Station Name	Days	Lowest Rank	Station Name	Days
1	Charlottesville 2 W	14	1	Dale Enterprise	8
1	Holland 1 E	14	2	Blacksburg Wso	9
1	Norfolk Intl Arpt	14	2	Covington Filter Plant	9
1	Suffolk Lake Kilby	14	2	Grundy	9
5	Williamsburg 2 N	13	2	Wytheville 1 S	9
6	Appomattox	12	6	Floyd 2 NE	10
6	Ashland	12	6	Winchester Winc	***10***
6	Bedford	***12***	6	Woodstock 2 NE	10
6	Burkes Garden	12	9	Abingdon 3 S	11
6	Camp Pickett	12	9	Crozier	11
6	Danville	12	9	Lincoln	11
6	Hopewell	12	9	Luray 5 E	11
6	Langley AFB	***12***	9	Roanoke Woodrum Arpt	11
6	Lexington	12	9	Staunton Sewage Plant	11
6	Lynchburg Municipal Arpt	12	9	Sterling RCS	11
6	Piedmont Research Stn	12	9	Warrenton 3 SE	***11***
6	Richmond R E Byrd Int'l Arpt	12	9	Washington DC Dulles Int'l Arpt	11
6	Rocky Mount	12	9	Washington DC National Arpt	11
19	Abingdon 3 S	11	19	Appomattox	12
19	Crozier	11	19	Ashland	12
19	Lincoln	11	19	Bedford	***12***
19	Luray 5 E	11	19	Burkes Garden	12
19	Roanoke Woodrum Arpt	11	19	Camp Pickett	12
19	Staunton Sewage Plant	11	19	Danville	12
19	Sterling RCS	11	19	Hopewell	12

Rankings include 25 highest/lowest stations. If state has less than 25 stations, all stations are included. The period of record is 1980–2009. See User Guide for detailed explanation of data.

Annual Snowfall

Highest

Rank	Station Name	Inches
1	Burkes Garden	51.9
2	Blacksburg Wso	24.0
3	Dale Enterprise	22.9
4	Woodstock 2 NE	22.6
5	Winchester Winc	***22.5***
6	Washington DC Dulles Int'l Arpt	21.1
7	Staunton Sewage Plant	20.9
8	Floyd 2 NE	19.9
9	Sterling RCS	19.6
10	Luray 5 E	19.4
11	Wytheville 1 S	19.2
12	Lincoln	18.9
13	Roanoke Woodrum Arpt	***18.5***
14	Piedmont Research Stn	18.2
15	Warrenton 3 SE	***18.1***
16	Charlottesville 2 W	17.5
17	Grundy	17.1
18	Ashland	16.5
19	Lynchburg Municipal Arpt	***16.3***
20	Rocky Mount	15.6
21	Washington DC National Arpt	14.7
22	Bedford	***14.4***
23	Abingdon 3 S	13.6
24	Lexington	12.6
25	Appomattox	11.4

Lowest

Rank	Station Name	Inches
1	Hopewell	4.6
2	Danville	4.8
3	Holland 1 E	5.2
4	Covington Filter Plant	***5.3***
5	Williamsburg 2 N	5.6
6	Suffolk Lake Kilby	6.1
7	Norfolk Intl Arpt	***6.8***
8	Camp Pickett	7.0
8	Langley AFB	***7.0***
10	Richmond R E Byrd Int'l Arpt	***11.0***
11	Crozier	11.2
12	Appomattox	11.4
13	Lexington	12.6
14	Abingdon 3 S	13.6
15	Bedford	***14.4***
16	Washington DC National Arpt	14.7
17	Rocky Mount	15.6
18	Lynchburg Municipal Arpt	***16.3***
19	Ashland	16.5
20	Grundy	17.1
21	Charlottesville 2 W	17.5
22	Warrenton 3 SE	***18.1***
23	Piedmont Research Stn	18.2
24	Roanoke Woodrum Arpt	***18.5***
25	Lincoln	18.9

Annual Maximum Snow Depth

Highest

Rank	Station Name	Inches
1	Luray 5 E	38
2	Woodstock 2 NE	32
3	Appomattox	***30***
3	Dale Enterprise	30
3	Lincoln	30
3	Winchester Winc	***30***
7	Blacksburg Wso	27
8	Warrenton 3 SE	***26***
9	Charlottesville 2 W	***24***
9	Rocky Mount	24
9	Staunton Sewage Plant	24
9	Washington DC Dulles Int'l Arpt	24
13	Roanoke Woodrum Arpt	***23***
13	Sterling RCS	23
15	Piedmont Research Stn	22
15	Wytheville 1 S	22
17	Burkes Garden	21
17	Lynchburg Municipal Arpt	***21***
19	Grundy	20
19	Washington DC National Arpt	20
21	Ashland	19
21	Crozier	19
21	Langley AFB	***19***
24	Abingdon 3 S	18
25	Covington Filter Plant	***17***

Lowest

Rank	Station Name	Inches
1	Hopewell	***5***
2	Danville	13
2	Holland 1 E	13
4	Camp Pickett	14
4	Williamsburg 2 N	14
6	Lexington	16
7	Covington Filter Plant	***17***
7	Suffolk Lake Kilby	17
9	Abingdon 3 S	18
10	Ashland	19
10	Crozier	19
10	Langley AFB	***19***
13	Grundy	20
13	Washington DC National Arpt	20
15	Burkes Garden	21
15	Lynchburg Municipal Arpt	***21***
17	Piedmont Research Stn	22
17	Wytheville 1 S	22
19	Roanoke Woodrum Arpt	***23***
19	Sterling RCS	23
21	Charlottesville 2 W	***24***
21	Rocky Mount	24
21	Staunton Sewage Plant	24
21	Washington DC Dulles Int'l Arpt	24
25	Warrenton 3 SE	***26***

Rankings include 25 highest/lowest stations. If state has less than 25 stations, all stations are included. The period of record is 1980–2009. See User Guide for detailed explanation of data.

Number of Days Annually With ≥ 1.0 Inch Snow Depth

Highest Rank	Station Name	Days	Lowest Rank	Station Name	Days
1	Burkes Garden	41	1	Hopewell	***0***
2	Winchester Winc	***21***	2	Appomattox	***2***
3	Blacksburg Wso	19	2	Holland 1 E	2
3	Lincoln	19	2	Suffolk Lake Kilby	2
3	Warrenton 3 SE	***19***	5	Covington Filter Plant	3
6	Dale Enterprise	18	5	Langley AFB	***3***
7	Sterling RCS	17	7	Danville	4
8	Washington DC Dulles Int'l Arpt	16	7	Williamsburg 2 N	4
8	Wytheville 1 S	16	9	Camp Pickett	5
10	Staunton Sewage Plant	15	10	Luray 5 E	8
11	Grundy	13	11	Crozier	9
11	Piedmont Research Stn	13	11	Rocky Mount	9
13	Abingdon 3 S	12	13	Lexington	10
13	Washington DC National Arpt	12	13	Woodstock 2 NE	10
15	Ashland	11	15	Ashland	11
15	Charlottesville 2 W	11	15	Charlottesville 2 W	11
15	Lynchburg Municipal Arpt	***11***	15	Lynchburg Municipal Arpt	***11***
15	Roanoke Woodrum Arpt	***11***	15	Roanoke Woodrum Arpt	***11***
19	Lexington	10	19	Abingdon 3 S	12
19	Woodstock 2 NE	10	19	Washington DC National Arpt	12
21	Crozier	9	21	Grundy	13
21	Rocky Mount	9	21	Piedmont Research Stn	13
23	Luray 5 E	8	23	Staunton Sewage Plant	15
24	Camp Pickett	5	24	Washington DC Dulles Int'l Arpt	16
25	Danville	4	24	Wytheville 1 S	16

Rankings include 25 highest/lowest stations. If state has less than 25 stations, all stations are included. The period of record is 1980–2009. See User Guide for detailed explanation of data.

Significant Storm Events in Virginia: 2000 – 2009

Location or County	Date	Type	Mag.	Deaths	Injuries	Property Damage ($mil.)	Crop Damage ($mil.)
Tazewell	07/08/01	Flash Flood	na	0	0	15.0	0.0
Campbell	04/28/02	Tornado	F2	0	11	3.0	0.0
Buchanan	05/02/02	Flash Flood	na	2	0	25.0	0.0
Northern and Northwest Virginia	02/14/03	Winter Storm	na	1	0	8.8	0.0
Eastern Virginia	09/18/03	Hurricane Isabel	na	2	0	506.0	10.9
Arlington, Fairfax, King George, Prince William, and Stafford Counties	09/18/03	Tropical Storm	na	0	29	55.1	0.1
Central and South Central Virginia	09/18/03	Tropical Storm	na	3	0	45.0	7.1
Northern Virginia	09/18/03	High Wind	58 mph	0	70	16.8	11.9
Interior Southeast Virginia	09/18/03	Hurricane Isabel	na	2	0	6.0	3.7
Northern Virginia	09/18/03	Flood	na	0	0	4.8	0.0
Tazewell County	11/19/03	Flood	na	0	0	6.1	0.0
Richmond	08/30/04	Flash Flood	na	3	0	20.0	0.0
Henry	09/17/04	Tornado	F2	0	4	53.8	0.0
Fairfax	06/25/06	Flash Flood	na	0	0	11.0	0.0
Fairfax	07/02/06	Thunderstorm Wind	69 mph	0	2	5.0	0.0
Eastern and Southeast Virginia	09/01/06	High Wind	60 mph	2	0	36.2	0.0
Northumberland County, Northern Neck, and Eastern Shore	09/01/06	Coastal Flood	na	0	0	28.6	0.0
Gloucester, Mathews, Middlesex, and York Counties	09/01/06	Coastal Flood	na	0	0	18.5	0.0
Franklin	10/07/06	Flash Flood	na	0	0	4.0	0.7
Suffolk	04/28/08	Tornado	F3	0	200	30.0	0.0
Colonial Heights	04/28/08	Tornado	F1	0	21	2.0	0.0
Stafford	05/08/08	Tornado	F2	0	0	10.0	0.0

Note: Deaths, injuries, and damages are date and location specific.

WASHINGTON

PHYSICAL FEATURES. Washington's western boundary is formed by the Pacific Ocean. There are two ranges of mountains parallel to the coast. The Cascade Mountains, 90 to 125 miles inland and 4,000 to 10,000 feet in elevation, are a topographic and climatic barrier separating the State into eastern and western Washington. The higher, wider and more rugged sections are in the northern part of the State. Some of the highest isolated volcanic peaks are Mt. Rainier (14,408 ft.), Mt. Adams (12,307 ft.), and Mt. Baker (10,730 ft.). These and other high peaks are snowcapped throughout the year. The only break in the Cascade Range is the narrow Columbia River gorge.

GENERAL CLIMATE. The location of the State of Washington on the windward coast in mid-latitudes is such that the climatic elements combine to produce a predominantly marine-type climate west of the Cascade Mountains, while east of the Cascades, the climate possesses both continental and marine characteristics. Considering its northerly latitude, 46 to 49°, Washington's climate is mild. There are several climatic controls which have a definite influence on the climate: (a) terrain; (b) Pacific Ocean; and (c) semi-permanent high and low pressure regions located over the north Pacific Ocean. The effect of these various controls combine to produce entirely different conditions within short distances.

The seasonal change in the temperature of the ocean is less than the seasonal change in the temperature of the land, thus the ocean is warmer in winter and cooler in summer than the adjoining land surfaces. The average temperature of the water along the coast and in the Strait of Juan de Fuca ranges from 45°F. in January to 53°F. in July; however, during the summer, some of the shallow bays and protected coves are five to 10 degrees warmer.

The first orographic lifting and major release of moisture occurs along the western slope of the Coastal Range. The second area of heavy orographic precipitation is along the windward slopes of the Cascade Range. Warming and drying of air as it descends along the lee (eastern) slopes of the Cascade Range results in near desert conditions in the lowest section of the Columbia Basin. Another orographic lifting of the air occurs as it flows eastward from the lowest elevations of the Inland Basin toward the Rocky Mountains. This lifting of air results in a gradual increase in precipitation from the lowest section of the basin to the higher elevations along the eastern border of the State.

The location and intensity of the semi-permanent high and low pressure areas over the north Pacific Ocean have a definite influence on the climate. Air circulates in a clockwise direction around the semi-permanent high pressure cell and in a counter-clockwise direction around the semi-permanent low pressure cell. During the spring and summer, the low pressure cell becomes weak and moves north of the Aleutian Islands. At the same time, the high pressure area spreads over most of the north Pacific Ocean. A circulation of air around the high pressure center brings a prevailing westerly and northwesterly flow of comparatively dry, cool and stable air into the Pacific Northwest. As the air moves inland, it becomes warmer and drier which results in a dry season beginning in the late spring and reaching a peak in midsummer.

In the fall and winter, the Aleutian low pressure center intensifies and moves southward reaching a maximum intensity in midwinter. At the same time, the high pressure area becomes weaker and moves southward. A circulation of air around these two pressure centers over the ocean brings a prevailing southwesterly and westerly flow of air into the Pacific Northwest. This air from over the ocean is moist and near the temperature of the water. Condensation occurs as the air moves inland over the cooler land and rises along the windward slopes of the mountains. This results in a wet season beginning in October, reaching a peak in winter, then gradually decreasing in the spring.

WESTERN WASHINGTON. West of the Cascade mountains, summers are cool and comparatively dry and winters are mild, wet and cloudy. The average number of clear or only partly cloudy days each month varies from four to eight in winter, eight to 15 in spring and fall, and 15 to 20 in summer. The percent of possible sunshine received each month ranges from approximately 25 percent in winter to 60 percent in summer. In the interior valleys, measurable rainfall is recorded on 150 days each year, and on 190 days in the mountains and along the coast. Thunderstorms over the lower elevations occur on four to eight days each year and over the mountains on seven to 15 days. Damaging hail storms rarely, if ever, occur in most localities of western Washington. During July and August, the driest months, it is not unusual for 2 to 4 weeks to pass with only a few showers; however, in December and January, the wettest months, precipitation is frequently recorded on 20 to 25 days or more each month. The range in annual precipitation is from approximately 20 inches in an area northeast of the Olympic Mountains to 150 inches along the southwestern slopes of these mountains. Snowfall is light in the lower elevations and heavy in the mountains.

During the wet season, rainfall is usually of light to moderate intensity and continuous over a period of time rather than heavy downpours for brief periods. The heavier intensities occur along the windward slopes of the mountains. During the latter half of the summer and early fall, the lower valleys are sometimes filled with fog or low clouds until noon, while at the same time, the higher elevations are sunny. The strongest winds are generally from the south or southwest and occur during the late fall and winter. In the interior valleys, wind velocities can be expected to reach 40 to 50 m.p.h. each winter. The daily variation in relative humidity in January is from approximately 87 percent at 4 a.m. to 78 percent at 4 p.m., and in July, from 85 percent at 4 a.m. to 47 percent at 4 p.m. During periods of easterly winds, the relative humidity occasionally drops to 25 percent or lower. The highest summer and lowest winter temperatures are usually recorded during periods of easterly winds.

The Olympic Mountains, located on the northern section of the Olympic Peninsula, tower to nearly 8,000 feet. This area receives the full force of storms moving inland from over the ocean, thus heavy precipitation and winds of gale force occur frequently during the winter season. The "rainforest" area along the southwestern and western slopes of the Olympic Mountains receives the heaviest precipitation in the continental United States. A belt on the northeastern slope of the Olympic Mountains in the "rain shadow" of the Olympic Mountains is the driest area in western Washington. This area frequently receives drizzle or light rain while other localities are experiencing light to moderate rainfall, and has slightly more sunshine and slightly less cloudiness than other localities in Puget Sound..

EASTERN WASHINGTON. This section of the State is part of the large inland basin between the Cascade and Rocky Mountains. In an easterly and northerly direction, the Rocky Mountains shield the inland basin from the winter season's cold air masses traveling southward across Canada. In a westerly direction, the Cascade range forms a barrier to the easterly movement of moist and comparatively mild air in winter and cool air in summer. Some of the air from each of these source regions reaches this section of the State and produces a climate which has some of the characteristics of both continental and marine types. Most of the air masses and weather systems crossing eastern Washington are traveling under the influence of the prevailing westerly winds. Infrequently, dry continental air masses enter the inland basin from the north or east. In the summer season, this air from over the continent results in low relative humidity and high temperatures while in winter, clear cold weather prevails. Extremes in both summer and winter temperatures generally occur when the inland basin is under the influence of air from over the continent.

East of the Cascades, summers are warmer, winters are colder, and precipitation is less than in western Washington. The average number of clear or only partly cloudy days each month varies from five to 10 in winter, 12 to 18 in spring and fall, and 20 to 28 in summer. The percent of possible sunshine received each month is from 20 to 30 percent in winter, 50 to 60 percent in spring and fall, and 80 to 85 percent in summer. The number of hours of sunshine possible on a clear day ranges from approximately 8 in December to 16 in June. In the driest areas, rainfall is recorded on 70 days each year .

Annual precipitation ranges from seven to nine inches near the confluence of the Snake and Columbia Rivers, 15 to 30 inches along the eastern border, and 75 to 90 inches near the summit of the Cascade Mountains. During July and August, it is not unusual for four to eight weeks to pass with only a few scattered showers. Thunderstorms can be expected on one to three days each month from April through September. Most thunderstorms in the warmest months occur as isolated cells covering only a few square miles. A few damaging hail storms are reported each summer.

During the coldest months, a loss of heat by radiation at night and moist air crossing the Cascades and mixing with the colder air in the inland basin results in cloudiness, fog, and occasional freezing drizzle. A "chinook" wind which produces a rapid rise in temperature occurs a few times each winter. During most of the year, the prevailing direction of the wind is from the southwest or west. The frequency of northeasterly winds is greatest in the fall and winter.

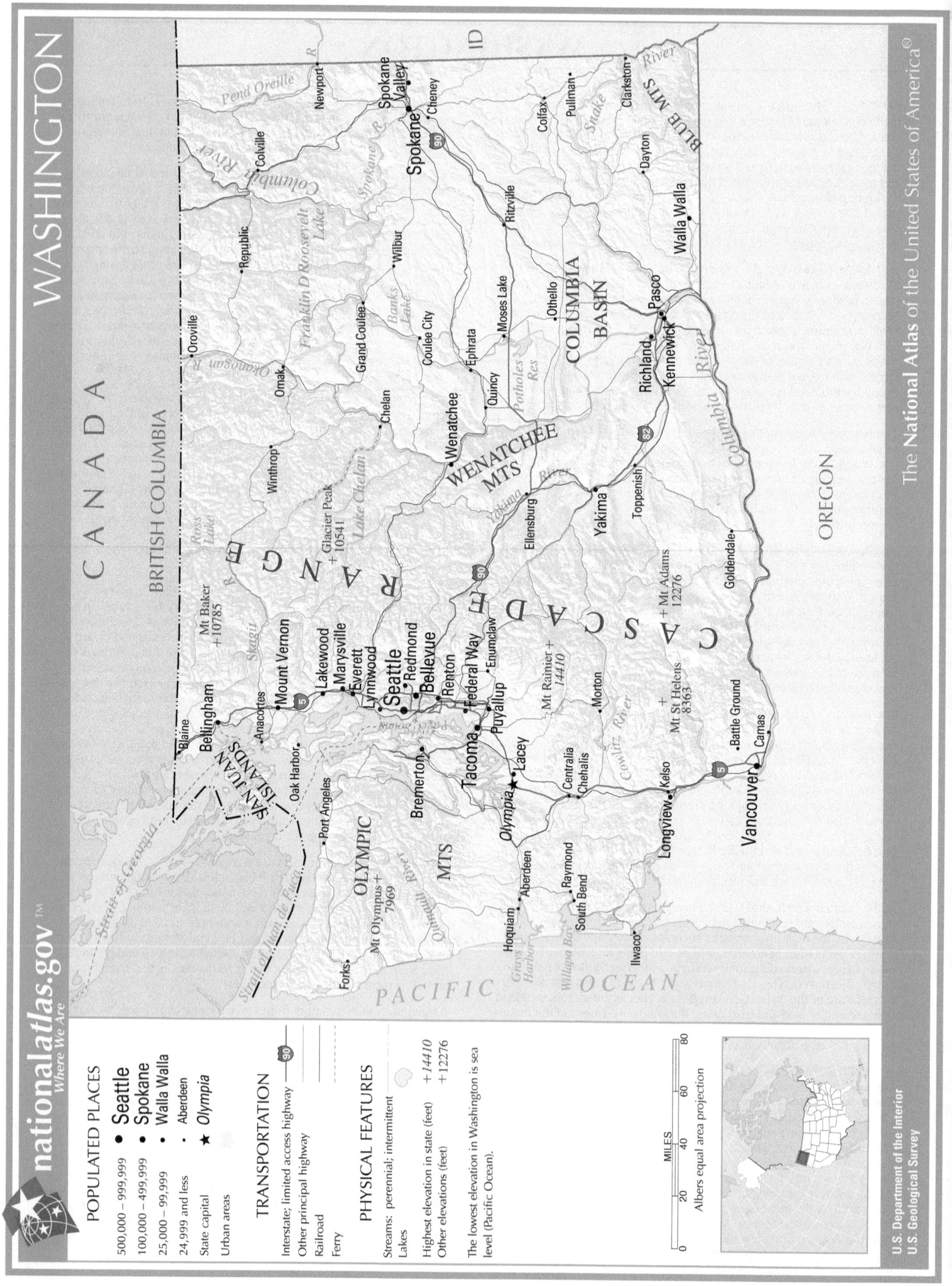
WASHINGTON
nationalatlas.gov™
Where We Are
POPULATED PLACES
500,000 – 999,999 Seattle
100,000 – 499,999 Spokane
25,000 – 99,999 Walla Walla
24,999 and less Aberdeen
State capital Olympia
Urban areas
TRANSPORTATION
Interstate; limited access highway
Other principal highway
Railroad
Ferry
PHYSICAL FEATURES
Streams: perennial; intermittent
Lakes
Highest elevation in state (feet) +14410
Other elevations (feet) +12276
The lowest elevation in Washington is sea level (Pacific Ocean).
MILES
0 20 40 60 80
Albers equal area projection
U.S. Department of the Interior
U.S. Geological Survey
The National Atlas of the United States of America®
CANADA
BRITISH COLUMBIA
ID
OREGON
PACIFIC OCEAN
CASCADE RANGE
OLYMPIC MTS
WENATCHEE MTS
BLUE MTS
COLUMBIA BASIN
SAN JUAN ISLANDS
Strait of Georgia
Strait of Juan de Fuca
Seattle
Spokane
Spokane Valley
Tacoma
Vancouver
Bellevue
Everett
Olympia
Yakima
Bellingham
Kennewick
Richland
Pasco
Walla Walla
Wenatchee
Mt Rainier +14410
Mt Adams +12276
Mt Baker +10785
Glacier Peak +10541
Mt St Helens 8363
Mt Olympus +7969

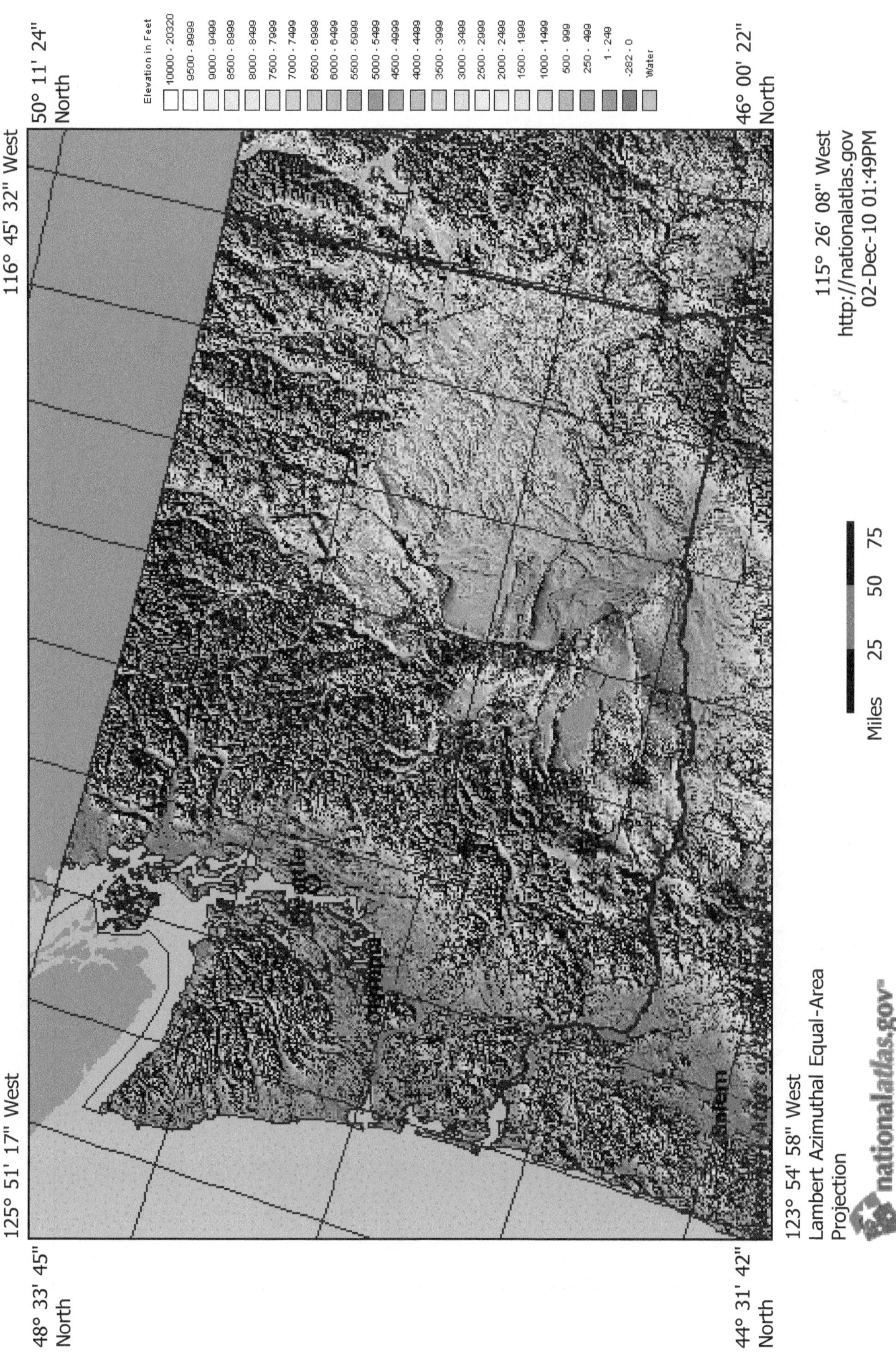
50° 11' 24" North
116° 45' 32" West
46° 00' 22" North
115° 26' 08" West
http://nationalatlas.gov
02-Dec-10 01:49PM
48° 33' 45" North
125° 51' 17" West
44° 31' 42" North
123° 54' 58" West
Lambert Azimuthal Equal-Area Projection
nationalatlas.gov
Miles
25
50
75
Elevation in Feet
10000 - 20320
9500 - 9999
9000 - 9499
8500 - 8999
8000 - 8499
7500 - 7999
7000 - 7499
6500 - 6999
6000 - 6499
5500 - 5999
5000 - 5499
4500 - 4999
4000 - 4499
3500 - 3999
3000 - 3499
2500 - 2999
2000 - 2499
1500 - 1999
1000 - 1499
500 - 999
250 - 499
1 - 249
-282 - 0
Water

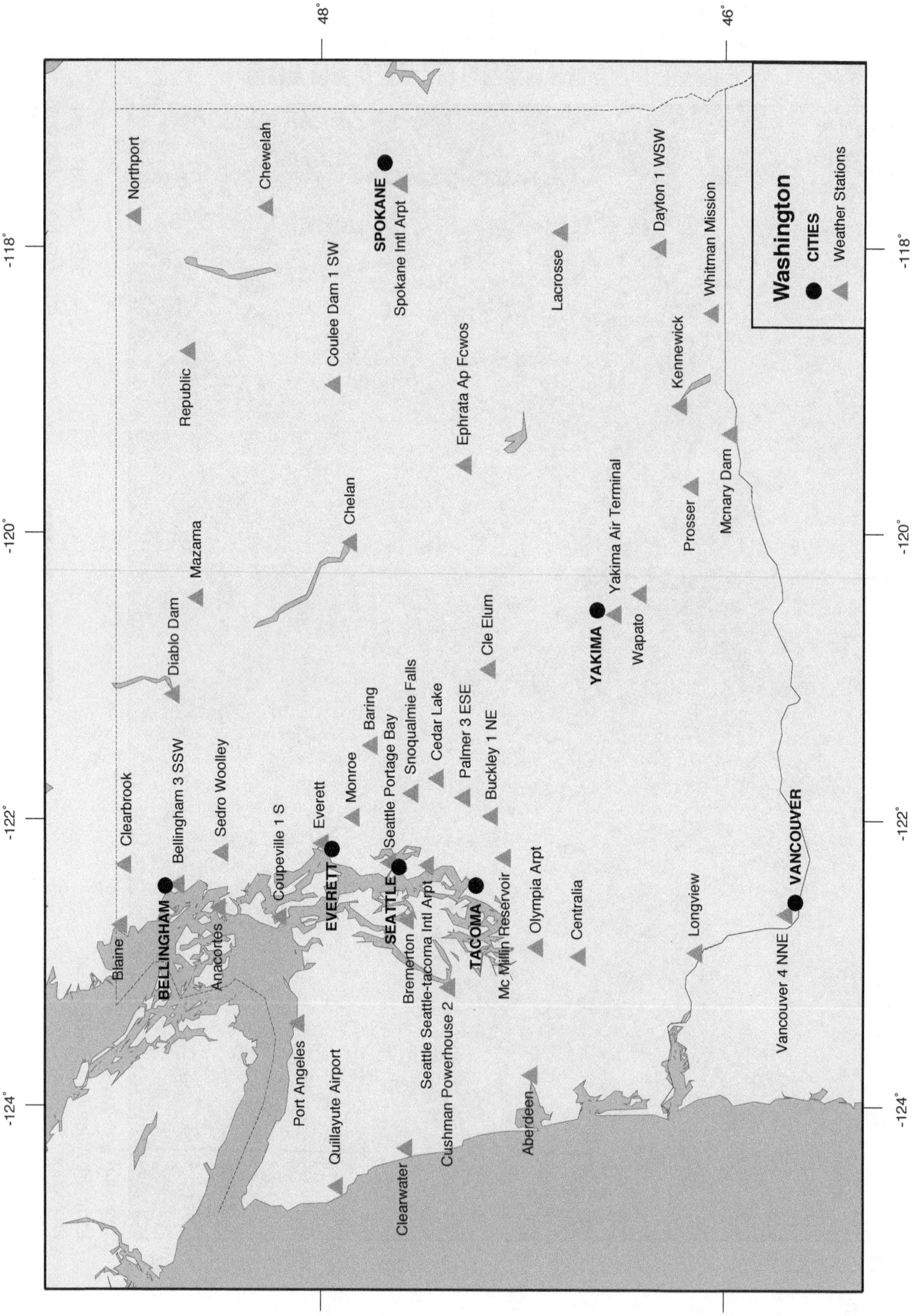
Washington
CITIES
Weather Stations
48°
46°
-118°
-120°
-122°
-124°
Northport
Chewelah
SPOKANE
Spokane Intl Arpt
Coulee Dam 1 SW
Republic
Lacrosse
Dayton 1 WSW
Whitman Mission
Kennewick
Ephrata Ap Fcwos
Mcnary Dam
Prosser
Chelan
Mazama
Yakima Air Terminal
YAKIMA
Wapato
Diablo Dam
Cle Elum
Baring
Snoqualmie Falls
Cedar Lake
Palmer 3 ESE
Buckley 1 NE
Monroe
Seattle Portage Bay
Everett
Clearbrook
Bellingham 3 SSW
Sedro Woolley
Coupeville 1 S
EVERETT
SEATTLE
TACOMA
BELLINGHAM
Blaine
Anacortes
Bremerton
Seattle Seattle-tacoma Intl Arpt
Mc Millin Reservoir
Olympia Arpt
Centralia
Longview
VANCOUVER
Vancouver 4 NNE
Port Angeles
Quillayute Airport
Seattle Cushman Powerhouse 2
Aberdeen
Clearwater

Washington Weather Stations by County

County	Station Name
Benton	Kennewick McNary Dam Prosser
Chelan	Chelan
Clallam	Port Angeles Quillayute Airport
Clark	Vancouver 4 NNE
Columbia	Dayton 1 WSW
Cowlitz	Longview
Ferry	Republic
Grant	Coulee Dam 1 SW Ephrata Arpt FCWOS
Grays Harbor	Aberdeen
Island	Coupeville 1 S
Jefferson	Clearwater
King	Baring Cedar Lake Palmer 3 ESE Seattle Portage Bay Seattle-Tacoma Intl Arpt Snoqualmie Falls
Kitsap	Bremerton
Kittitas	Cle Elum
Lewis	Centralia
Mason	Cushman Powerhouse 2
Okanogan	Mazama
Pierce	Buckley 1 NE McMillin Reservoir
Skagit	Anacortes Sedro Woolley
Snohomish	Everett Monroe
Spokane	Spokane Intl Arpt
Stevens	Chewelah Northport
Thurston	Olympia Arpt
Walla Walla	Whitman Mission
Whatcom	Bellingham 3 SSW Blaine Clearbrook

County	Station Name
Whatcom *(cont.)*	Diablo Dam
Whitman	Lacrosse
Yakima	Wapato Yakima Air Terminal

See User Guide for station inclusion criteria.

Washington Weather Stations by City

City	Station Name	Miles
Auburn	Buckley 1 NE	13.5
	Cedar Lake	23.9
	McMillin Reservoir	11.7
	Palmer 3 ESE	17.0
	Seattle Portage Bay	24.7
	Seattle-Tacoma Intl Arpt	12.6
	Snoqualmie Falls	24.8
Bellevue	Bremerton	24.8
	Cedar Lake	23.3
	Monroe	19.1
	Seattle Portage Bay	7.7
	Seattle-Tacoma Intl Arpt	11.9
	Snoqualmie Falls	15.3
Bellingham	Anacortes	17.5
	Bellingham 3 SSW	3.2
	Blaine	21.3
	Clearbrook	16.1
	Sedro Woolley	20.5
Bothell	Everett	14.5
	Monroe	11.6
	Seattle Portage Bay	9.6
	Seattle-Tacoma Intl Arpt	21.9
	Snoqualmie Falls	23.3
Bremerton	Bremerton	1.8
	Seattle Portage Bay	17.0
	Seattle-Tacoma Intl Arpt	17.3
Burien	Bremerton	17.2
	McMillin Reservoir	23.6
	Seattle Portage Bay	12.6
	Seattle-Tacoma Intl Arpt	1.3
	Snoqualmie Falls	24.4
Cascade-Fairwood	Buckley 1 NE	20.8
	Cedar Lake	20.2
	McMillin Reservoir	22.2
	Palmer 3 ESE	17.9
	Seattle Portage Bay	15.4
	Seattle-Tacoma Intl Arpt	7.3
	Snoqualmie Falls	17.0
East Hill-Meridian	Buckley 1 NE	18.9
	Cedar Lake	21.0
	McMillin Reservoir	19.5
	Palmer 3 ESE	17.3
	Seattle Portage Bay	17.4
	Seattle-Tacoma Intl Arpt	7.4
	Snoqualmie Falls	18.9
Edmonds	Bremerton	22.7
	Everett	14.4
	Monroe	17.4
	Seattle Portage Bay	11.2
	Seattle-Tacoma Intl Arpt	23.6
Everett	Everett	3.0
	Monroe	12.8
	Seattle Portage Bay	20.9
Federal Way	Bremerton	23.6

City	Station Name	Miles
Federal Way *(cont.)*	Buckley 1 NE	19.0
	McMillin Reservoir	13.1
	Palmer 3 ESE	23.0
	Seattle Portage Bay	23.2
	Seattle-Tacoma Intl Arpt	10.5
Kennewick	Kennewick	3.2
	McNary Dam	18.6
Kent	Buckley 1 NE	17.7
	Cedar Lake	22.7
	McMillin Reservoir	17.0
	Palmer 3 ESE	17.9
	Seattle Portage Bay	19.3
	Seattle-Tacoma Intl Arpt	7.8
	Snoqualmie Falls	21.5
Kirkland	Bremerton	24.4
	Everett	20.3
	Monroe	14.8
	Seattle Portage Bay	5.7
	Seattle-Tacoma Intl Arpt	16.4
	Snoqualmie Falls	19.3
Lacey	Centralia	22.2
	Olympia Arpt	5.8
Lakewood	Buckley 1 NE	24.9
	McMillin Reservoir	12.5
	Olympia Arpt	22.1
	Seattle-Tacoma Intl Arpt	23.2
Longview	Clatskanie, OR	11.9
	St Helens Rfd, OR	20.3
	Longview	2.1
Lynnwood	Everett	12.1
	Monroe	15.0
	Seattle Portage Bay	12.4
Marysville	Everett	5.7
	Monroe	16.7
Mount Vernon	Anacortes	15.2
	Bellingham 3 SSW	22.2
	Coupeville 1 S	23.5
	Sedro Woolley	6.4
North Creek	Everett	11.2
	Monroe	10.0
	Seattle Portage Bay	12.8
Olympia	Centralia	22.6
	Olympia Arpt	5.2
Paine Field-Lake Stickney	Everett	7.3
	Monroe	12.7
	Seattle Portage Bay	16.6
Pasco	Kennewick	1.7
	McNary Dam	22.0
Puyallup	Buckley 1 NE	13.5
	McMillin Reservoir	3.3

See User Guide for station inclusion criteria.

City	Station Name	Miles
Puyallup *(cont.)*	Palmer 3 ESE	22.1
	Seattle-Tacoma Intl Arpt	19.9
Redmond	Everett	21.7
	Monroe	13.9
	Seattle Portage Bay	8.4
	Seattle-Tacoma Intl Arpt	16.8
	Snoqualmie Falls	15.8
Renton	Bremerton	23.7
	Buckley 1 NE	23.8
	Cedar Lake	21.8
	McMillin Reservoir	24.7
	Palmer 3 ESE	20.4
	Seattle Portage Bay	12.4
	Seattle-Tacoma Intl Arpt	6.2
	Snoqualmie Falls	17.1
Richland	Kennewick	9.6
	McNary Dam	22.6
	Prosser	23.0
Sammamish	Cedar Lake	19.5
	Monroe	16.8
	Palmer 3 ESE	23.1
	Seattle Portage Bay	12.5
	Seattle-Tacoma Intl Arpt	16.3
	Snoqualmie Falls	10.4
Seattle	Bremerton	16.9
	Monroe	22.3
	Seattle Portage Bay	2.1
	Seattle-Tacoma Intl Arpt	11.2
	Snoqualmie Falls	23.9
Seattle Hill-Silver Firs	Everett	7.0
	Monroe	9.1
	Seattle Portage Bay	17.0
Shoreline	Bremerton	20.8
	Everett	17.1
	Monroe	17.7
	Seattle Portage Bay	7.7
	Seattle-Tacoma Intl Arpt	20.2
South Hill	Buckley 1 NE	14.0
	McMillin Reservoir	1.3
	Palmer 3 ESE	24.0
	Seattle-Tacoma Intl Arpt	23.8
Spokane	Spokane Intl Arpt	7.1
Tacoma	Bremerton	25.0
	Buckley 1 NE	22.2
	McMillin Reservoir	11.7
	Seattle-Tacoma Intl Arpt	17.2
University Place	McMillin Reservoir	14.1
	Olympia Arpt	24.2
	Seattle-Tacoma Intl Arpt	20.2
Vancouver	Beaverton 2 SSW, OR	17.1
	Headworks Ptld Wtr Bur, OR	24.3
	Oregon City, OR	19.5
	Portland Intl Arpt, OR	2.9

City	Station Name	Miles
Vancouver *(cont.)*	St Helens Rfd, OR	19.9
	Vancouver 4 NNE	4.9
Walla Walla	Dayton 1 WSW	23.5
	Whitman Mission	5.8
Yakima	Wapato	12.5
	Yakima Air Terminal	2.3

Note: Miles is the distance between the geographic center of the city and the weather station.

Washington Weather Stations by Elevation

Feet	Station Name
2,609	Republic
2,355	Spokane Intl Arpt
2,169	Mazama
1,919	Cle Elum
1,700	Coulee Dam 1 SW
1,669	Chewelah
1,560	Cedar Lake
1,557	Dayton 1 WSW
1,450	Lacrosse
1,350	Northport
1,258	Ephrata Arpt FCWOS
1,120	Chelan
1,063	Yakima Air Terminal
919	Palmer 3 ESE
891	Diablo Dam
840	Wapato
830	Prosser
771	Baring
685	Buckley 1 NE
631	Whitman Mission
579	McMillin Reservoir
439	Snoqualmie Falls
399	Seattle-Tacoma Intl Arpt
390	Kennewick
360	McNary Dam
209	Vancouver 4 NNE
206	Olympia Arpt
185	Centralia
179	Quillayute Airport
120	Monroe
109	Bremerton
89	Port Angeles
80	Clearwater
63	Clearbrook
60	Blaine
60	Everett
60	Sedro Woolley
49	Coupeville 1 S
21	Cushman Powerhouse 2
20	Anacortes
19	Seattle Portage Bay
15	Bellingham 3 SSW
12	Longview
9	Aberdeen

See User Guide for station inclusion criteria.

Olympia Airport

The climate of Olympia and vicinity is characterized by warm, generally dry summers and wet, mild winters.

Fall rains usually begin about mid-October, borne inland to the Cascade Mountains by frequent maritime disturbances originating in the Pacific Ocean. These rains continue with few interruptions through spring. Daytime temperatures will be in the 40s and low 50s, with nighttime temperatures in the 30s. The progression of the wet and mild Pacific disturbances is usually broken once or twice each winter by the formation of large anticyclones, which originate in Alaska and northwestern Canada, and move southward over the state of Washington. These southerly migrations of polar-continental air from the interior will normally lower daytime temperatures to about freezing and nighttime temperatures to 10 - 20 degrees. Often the onset of the cold weather is accompanied by a little snow, but during these cold snaps the air is dry and skies are clear.

During the spring months, the track of the Pacific storms moves gradually farther north, and the semi-permanent Pacific anticyclone also moves northward. The effects of the maritime disturbances lessen, and the periods of improving weather between storms lengthen. During the spring and early fall, clearing skies at night will usually be followed by fog or low stratus clouds in the early morning, which normally dissipate by noon.

Daily high temperatures average 70 to 80 degrees during July, August, and September. The temperature will equal or exceed 90 degrees about 6 days each summer, but as the warm weather is usually accompanied by lowering humidity, it is seldom uncomfortably hot. Rainfall is near one inch per month during July and August and about two inches per month during the transitional period of May, June, and September. About two-thirds of the days are sunny in July, August, and September, and about half are sunny during May and June.

Olympia and vicinity are quite well protected by the Coast Range from the strong south and southwest winds accompanying many of the Pacific storms during the fall and winter. Winds which reach hurricane force along the coast, only 45 miles away, will reach only 50 or 55 mph in gusts in this vicinity. The prevailing wind in Olympia is southerly during most of the year, but during the fair weather in the summers the wind is gentle and from the north to east.

The length of the growing season in the vicinity of Olympia varies with distance from the waterfront and elevation above sea level. The average length of the growing season is 166 days.

Olympia Airport *Thurston County* Elevation: 206 ft. Latitude: 46° 58' N Longitude: 122° 54' W

	JAN	FEB	MAR	APR	MAY	JUN	JUL	AUG	SEP	OCT	NOV	DEC	YEAR
Mean Maximum Temp. (°F)	45.9	49.4	54.2	59.4	65.8	70.9	77.1	77.9	72.3	60.7	50.7	44.6	60.7
Mean Temp. (°F)	39.2	40.8	44.3	48.2	54.1	58.9	63.7	63.9	58.8	50.3	43.4	38.4	50.3
Mean Minimum Temp. (°F)	32.6	32.1	34.4	37.0	42.5	46.9	50.2	49.9	45.3	39.8	36.0	32.1	39.9
Extreme Maximum Temp. (°F)	64	73	79	87	96	98	104	104	98	90	73	63	104
Extreme Minimum Temp. (°F)	0	2	9	23	26	33	38	37	26	14	0	-7	-7
Days Maximum Temp. ≥ 90°F	0	0	0	0	0	1	2	2	0	0	0	0	5
Days Maximum Temp. ≤ 32°F	0	0	0	0	0	0	0	0	0	0	0	1	1
Days Minimum Temp. ≤ 32°F	14	15	13	7	1	0	0	0	0	5	10	15	80
Days Minimum Temp. ≤ 0°F	0	0	0	0	0	0	0	0	0	0	0	0	0
Heating Degree Days (base 65°F)	792	678	635	497	333	188	78	68	187	450	643	819	5,368
Cooling Degree Days (base 65°F)	0	0	0	0	3	13	45	42	7	0	0	0	110
Mean Precipitation (in.)	7.73	5.32	5.25	3.57	2.22	1.73	0.63	0.93	1.59	4.45	8.75	7.45	49.62
Maximum Precipitation (in.)*	19.8	13.2	10.1	7.8	5.8	3.7	3.0	5.4	7.6	10.1	15.5	14.3	66.7
Minimum Precipitation (in.)*	0.3	0.2	0.5	0.4	0.2	0	trace	trace	trace	0.4	1.4	2.5	29.9
Extreme Maximum Daily Precip. (in.)	4.82	2.75	2.18	3.11	1.01	1.60	1.34	1.24	1.54	4.12	4.31	3.19	4.82
Days With ≥ 0.1" Precipitation	14	11	13	10	7	5	2	2	4	9	15	13	105
Days With ≥ 0.5" Precipitation	5	3	3	2	1	1	0	1	1	3	6	5	31
Days With ≥ 1.0" Precipitation	2	1	1	0	0	0	0	0	0	1	2	2	9
Mean Snowfall (in.)	na	na	na	na	na	na	na	na	na	na	na	na	na
Maximum Snowfall (in.)*	59	27	21	2	trace	trace	0	0	0	trace	15	21	60
Maximum 24-hr. Snowfall (in.)*	14	11	9	2	trace	trace	0	0	0	trace	10	10	14
Maximum Snow Depth (in.)	na	na	na	na	na	na	na	na	na	na	na	na	na
Days With ≥ 1.0" Snow Depth	na	na	na	na	na	na	na	na	na	na	na	na	na
Thunderstorm Days*	< 1	< 1	< 1	1	1	< 1	1	1	1	< 1	< 1	< 1	5
Foggy Days*	25	21	20	16	11	9	10	15	21	26	25	26	225
Predominant Sky Cover*	OVR	OVR	OVR	OVR	OVR	OVR	CLR	OVR	OVR	OVR	OVR	OVR	OVR
Mean Relative Humidity 7am (%)*	91	91	91	88	83	82	83	87	92	94	92	92	89
Mean Relative Humidity 4pm (%)*	80	71	61	55	52	53	49	50	54	68	79	84	63
Mean Dewpoint (°F)*	34	36	36	39	44	49	52	52	50	45	39	36	43
Prevailing Wind Direction*	SSW	SSW	SSW	SSW	SSW	SSW	SSW	SSW	SSW	SSW	SSW	SSW	SSW
Prevailing Wind Speed (mph)*	10	10	10	9	9	8	8	8	8	9	10	10	9
Maximum Wind Gust (mph)*	58	53	51	43	44	38	32	39	38	45	64	56	64

Note: (*) Period of record is 1948-1995

The period of record for National Weather Service station data is 1980 – 2009 except where noted. See User Guide for detailed explanation of data.

Quillayute Airport

Quillayute Airport, located on the coastal plain between the Pacific Ocean and the Olympic Mountains, is three miles inland from the coast, and 10 miles west of the city of Forks. The terrain is slightly rolling with a gradual increase in elevation from sea level to 180 feet at the station, to 350 feet in the vicinity of Forks. Foothills of the Olympic Mountains begin near the eastern edge of Forks.

In the late fall and winter, storm systems crossing the Pacific follow a more southerly path striking the coast at frequent intervals. The wet season begins in September or October. From October through January, rain may be expected on about 26 days per month, from February through March, on 20 days, from April to June, on 15 days, and from July to September, on 10 days. As the weather systems move inland, rainfall is usually of moderate intensity and continuous, rather than heavy downpours for brief periods. Gale force winds are not unusual. Most of the winter precipitation over the coastal plains falls as rain, however, snow can be expected each year.

Annual precipitation increases from approximately 90 inches near the coast, to amounts in excess of 120 inches over the coastal plains, to 200 inches or more on the wettest slopes of the Olympic Mountains.

During the rainy season, temperatures show little diurnal or day-to-day change. Maximums are in the 40s and minimums in the mid-30s. A few brief outbreaks of cold air from the interior of Canada can be expected each winter. Clear, dry, cold weather generally prevails during periods of easterly winds.

The dry season begins in May with the driest period between mid-July and mid-August. The total rainfall for July is less than .5 inch in one summer out of ten. It also exceeds five inches in one summer out of ten. During the warmest months, afternoon temperatures are in the upper 60s and lower 70s, reaching the upper 70s and the lower 80s on a few days. Occasionally, hot, dry air from the east of the Cascade Mountains reaches this area and temperatures are in the mid- or upper-90s for one to three days.

In summer and early fall, fog or low clouds form over the ocean and frequently move inland at night, but generally disappear by midday. In winter, under the influence of a surface high pressure system, centered off the coast, fog, low clouds, and drizzle are a daily occurence as long as this type of pressure continues.

Quillayute Airport *Clallam County* Elevation: 179 ft. Latitude: 47° 56' N Longitude: 124° 34' W

	JAN	FEB	MAR	APR	MAY	JUN	JUL	AUG	SEP	OCT	NOV	DEC	YEAR
Mean Maximum Temp. (°F)	47.3	49.6	51.8	55.4	60.1	63.7	67.9	69.0	66.8	58.7	51.0	46.5	57.3
Mean Temp. (°F)	41.4	42.2	44.1	46.9	51.5	55.5	59.2	59.6	56.7	50.2	44.5	40.5	49.4
Mean Minimum Temp. (°F)	35.4	34.8	36.4	38.2	42.8	47.2	50.4	50.3	46.5	41.6	37.9	34.4	41.3
Extreme Maximum Temp. (°F)	65	73	72	83	92	96	97	99	97	83	66	63	99
Extreme Minimum Temp. (°F)	9	11	19	23	30	34	38	37	30	23	18	10	9
Days Maximum Temp. ≥ 90°F	0	0	0	0	0	0	0	0	0	0	0	0	0
Days Maximum Temp. ≤ 32°F	0	0	0	0	0	0	0	0	0	0	0	1	1
Days Minimum Temp. ≤ 32°F	11	11	8	5	0	0	0	0	0	3	7	13	58
Days Minimum Temp. ≤ 0°F	0	0	0	0	0	0	0	0	0	0	0	0	0
Heating Degree Days (base 65°F)	724	637	641	537	414	284	182	166	246	453	609	752	5,645
Cooling Degree Days (base 65°F)	0	0	0	0	1	5	8	7	3	0	0	0	24
Mean Precipitation (in.)	14.51	10.54	10.85	7.77	4.94	3.41	2.12	2.41	3.78	10.22	15.85	12.96	99.36
Maximum Precipitation (in.)*	24.0	20.6	21.9	13.9	12.4	8.5	11.0	15.1	10.9	27.2	29.1	27.8	132.
Minimum Precipitation (in.)*	1.2	0.9	1.8	2.9	1.0	0.4	0.4	0.3	0.1	1.4	4.4	3.6	60.2
Extreme Maximum Daily Precip. (in.)	4.54	5.07	3.67	2.63	3.36	2.74	5.35	4.29	3.48	5.21	6.03	5.63	6.03
Days With ≥ 0.1" Precipitation	19	15	17	14	10	7	4	4	6	13	19	18	146
Days With ≥ 0.5" Precipitation	10	7	8	6	3	2	1	1	3	7	11	9	68
Days With ≥ 1.0" Precipitation	5	3	3	2	1	1	0	1	1	3	5	4	29
Mean Snowfall (in.)	na	na	na	na	na	na	na	na	na	na	na	na	na
Maximum Snowfall (in.)*	40	16	10	3	trace	0	0	0	trace	trace	16	12	58
Maximum 24-hr. Snowfall (in.)*	8	7	8	2	trace	0	0	0	trace	trace	8	7	8
Maximum Snow Depth (in.)	na	na	na	na	na	na	na	na	na	na	na	na	na
Days With ≥ 1.0" Snow Depth	na	na	na	na	na	na	na	na	na	na	na	na	na
Thunderstorm Days*	1	< 1	< 1	< 1	< 1	< 1	1	< 1	1	1	2	1	7
Foggy Days*	21	19	20	17	17	18	19	20	20	22	21	22	236
Predominant Sky Cover*	OVR	OVR	OVR	OVR	OVR	OVR	OVR	OVR	OVR	OVR	OVR	OVR	OVR
Mean Relative Humidity 7am (%)*	92	91	92	92	90	90	91	94	94	94	93	92	92
Mean Relative Humidity 4pm (%)*	83	77	72	68	66	67	65	67	67	75	84	87	73
Mean Dewpoint (°F)*	37	38	39	40	45	49	52	53	50	46	41	38	44
Prevailing Wind Direction*	NE	ENE	S	S	S	WNW	NW	S	S	S	ENE	ENE	S
Prevailing Wind Speed (mph)*	8	6	9	8	8	8	8	7	7	8	6	6	7
Maximum Wind Gust (mph)*	55	58	49	40	41	44	32	48	36	53	54	58	58

Note: (*) Period of record is 1966-1995

The period of record for National Weather Service station data is 1980 – 2009 except where noted. See User Guide for detailed explanation of data.

Seattle Portage Bay

Seattle is located on a hill between the salt waters of Puget Sound to the west and the fresh waters of Lake Washington to the east. The lake shore roughly parallels the shore of Puget Sound at distances varying from about two and a half to six miles. Hills rise abruptly from both shorelines and reach elevations of more than 300 feet in the central area to more than 500 feet in the northern and the southwestern sections. The north-south orientation of the city is matched on the east by the Cascade Mountains and the Olympic Mountains to the west and northwest.

The climate of Seattle is mild and moist, the result of the prevailing westerly winds off the Pacific Ocean approximately 90 miles to the west, and the Cascade Mountains which tend to shield the city from the cold continental air from the east. Winters are comparatively warm and summers cool because of the steady influx of marine air.

An average year will have less than three days during the summer with a high temperature of 90 degrees or more with the maximum temperature rarely reaching 100 degrees. Nighttime temperatures during the warmest months seldom remain above 65 degrees. Daily highs during the winter fail to rise above 32 degrees on an average of about two days per year, while the number of days with minimum temperatures of 32 degrees or less averages only 15 days per year.

The city lies within the lee side dry area caused by the Olympic Mountains. As a result, the normal precipitation of less than 36 inches is relatively light when compared to the 50 inches or more that falls on the nearby Cascade foothills. The western slopes of these hills and mountains lift the moist marine air, causing very heavy precipitation on the seaward slopes and significantly less at the summits. The winter wet season, usually from October to March, is the result of the air flowing around the Aleutian low pressure system, but, in the summer the Eastern Pacific high pressure system moves north and forces the moist marine air to the north of Washington and brings relatively dry and cool air to the state. The warmest temperatures of the summer usually occur when the Pacific high extends into southwest Canada creating a hot and dry flow of continental air across the Cascade Mountains into the Puget Sound area. Less than 20 percent of the annual rainfall occurs during the summer dry season, April through September.

The average winter snowfall is about nine inches but the snow seldom remains on the ground for more than two days at a time. Fog is a frequent occurrence during the late fall and winter months.

Seattle Portage Bay *King County* Elevation: 19 ft. Latitude: 47° 39' N Longitude: 122° 18' W

	JAN	FEB	MAR	APR	MAY	JUN	JUL	AUG	SEP	OCT	NOV	DEC	YEAR
Mean Maximum Temp. (°F)	na	na	na	na	na	na	na	na	na	na	na	na	na
Mean Temp. (°F)	na	na	na	na	na	na	na	na	na	na	na	na	na
Mean Minimum Temp. (°F)	na	na	na	na	na	na	na	na	na	na	na	na	na
Extreme Maximum Temp. (°F)	na	na	na	na	na	na	na	na	na	na	na	na	na
Extreme Minimum Temp. (°F)	na	na	na	na	na	na	na	na	na	na	na	na	na
Days Maximum Temp. ≥ 90°F	na	na	na	na	na	na	na	na	na	na	na	na	na
Days Maximum Temp. ≤ 32°F	na	na	na	na	na	na	na	na	na	na	na	na	na
Days Minimum Temp. ≤ 32°F	na	na	na	na	na	na	na	na	na	na	na	na	na
Days Minimum Temp. ≤ 0°F	na	na	na	na	na	na	na	na	na	na	na	na	na
Heating Degree Days (base 65°F)	na	na	na	na	na	na	na	na	na	na	na	na	na
Cooling Degree Days (base 65°F)	na	na	na	na	na	na	na	na	na	na	na	na	na
Mean Precipitation (in.)	na	na	na	na	na	na	na	na	na	na	na	na	na
Maximum Precipitation (in.)*	10.9	8.1	7.2	5.3	4.7	3.7	2.2	5.5	5.6	8.0	11.2	15.3	48.1
Minimum Precipitation (in.)*	0.6	0.3	0.4	0.2	0.3	trace	0	trace	trace	0.2	0.5	1.0	19.5
Extreme Maximum Daily Precip. (in.)	na	na	na	na	na	na	na	na	na	na	na	na	na
Days With ≥ 0.1" Precipitation	na	na	na	na	na	na	na	na	na	na	na	na	na
Days With ≥ 0.5" Precipitation	na	na	na	na	na	na	na	na	na	na	na	na	na
Days With ≥ 1.0" Precipitation	na	na	na	na	na	na	na	na	na	na	na	na	na
Mean Snowfall (in.)	na	na	na	na	na	na	na	na	na	na	na	na	na
Maximum Snowfall (in.)*	31	35	9	2	0	0	0	0	0	trace	10	14	64
Maximum 24-hr. Snowfall (in.)*	12	22	6	2	0	0	0	0	0	trace	6	10	22
Maximum Snow Depth (in.)	na	na	na	na	na	na	na	na	na	na	na	na	na
Days With ≥ 1.0" Snow Depth	na	na	na	na	na	na	na	na	na	na	na	na	na
Thunderstorm Days*	< 1	< 1	< 1	< 1	< 1	< 1	< 1	1	< 1	< 1	< 1	< 1	1
Foggy Days*	3	2	1	1	1	1	1	3	4	3	3	3	26
Predominant Sky Cover*	na	na	na	na	na	na	na	na	na	na	na	na	na
Mean Relative Humidity 7am (%)*	na	na	na	na	na	na	na	na	na	na	na	na	na
Mean Relative Humidity 4pm (%)*	na	na	na	na	na	na	na	na	na	na	na	na	na
Mean Dewpoint (°F)*	na	na	na	na	na	na	na	na	na	na	na	na	na
Prevailing Wind Direction*	na	na	na	na	na	na	na	na	na	na	na	na	na
Prevailing Wind Speed (mph)*	na	na	na	na	na	na	na	na	na	na	na	na	na
Maximum Wind Gust (mph)*	44	48	49	43	40	35	41	43	39	43	47	51	51

Note: (*) Period of record is 1900-1992

Seattle-Tacoma Int'l Airport

The Seattle-Tacoma International Airport is located 6 miles south of the Seattle city limits and 14 miles north of Tacoma. It is situated on a low ridge lying between Puget Sound on the west and the Green River valley on the east with terrain sloping moderately to the shores of Puget Sound some two miles to the west. The Olympic Mountains, rising sharply from Puget Sound, are about 50 miles to the northwest. Rather steep bluffs border the Green River Valley about 2.5 miles to the east and the foothills of the Cascade Range begin 10 to 15 miles to the east of the airport.

The mild climate of the Pacific Coast is modified by the Cascade Mountains and, to a lesser extent, by the Olympic Mountains. The climate is characterized by mild temperatures, a pronounced though not sharply defined rainy season, and considerable cloudiness, particularly during the winter months. The Cascades are very effective in shielding the Seattle-Tacoma area from the cold, dry continental air during the winter and the hot, dry continental air during the summer months. Southwesterly circulation keeps the average winter daytime temperatures in the 40s and the nighttime readings in the 30s. During the summer, daytime temperatures are usually in the 70s with nighttime lows in the 50s. Extremes of temperatures, both in the winter and summer, are usually of short duration. The dry season is centered around July and early August with July being the driest month of the year. The rainy season extends from October to March with December normally the wettest month, however, precipitation is rather evenly distributed through the winter and early spring months with more than 75 percent of the yearly precipitation falling during the winter wet season.

The occurrence of snow in the Seattle-Tacoma area is extremely variable and usually melts before accumulating measurable depths. There are winters on record with only a trace of snow, but at the other extreme, over 21 inches has fallen in a 24-hour period.

The highest winds recorded in the Seattle-Tacoma area were associated with strong storms crossing the state from the southwest. Prevailing winds are from the southwest but occasional severe winter storms will produce strong northerly winds. Winds during the summer months are relatively light with occasional land-sea breeze effects creating afternoon northerly winds of eight to 15 miles an hour. Fog or low clouds that form over the southern Puget Sound area in the late summer, fall, and early winter months, often dominate the weather conditions during the late night and early morning hours.

Based on the 1951-1980 period, the average first occurrence of 32 degrees Fahrenheit in the fall is November 11 and the average last occurrence in the spring is March 24.

Seattle-Tacoma Int'l Airport *King County* Elevation: 399 ft. Latitude: 47° 28' N Longitude: 122° 19' W

	JAN	FEB	MAR	APR	MAY	JUN	JUL	AUG	SEP	OCT	NOV	DEC	YEAR
Mean Maximum Temp. (°F)	46.5	49.4	53.2	58.2	64.3	69.5	75.4	75.8	70.2	59.4	50.6	45.3	59.8
Mean Temp. (°F)	41.5	43.2	46.3	50.2	55.8	60.7	65.5	65.8	61.1	52.6	45.4	40.5	52.4
Mean Minimum Temp. (°F)	36.4	36.8	39.3	42.2	47.3	51.9	55.6	55.8	52.0	45.8	40.1	35.7	44.9
Extreme Maximum Temp. (°F)	64	68	78	83	92	96	103	99	98	89	71	64	103
Extreme Minimum Temp. (°F)	14	7	20	32	35	42	47	46	39	30	10	9	7
Days Maximum Temp. ≥ 90°F	0	0	0	0	0	1	1	1	0	0	0	0	3
Days Maximum Temp. ≤ 32°F	1	0	0	0	0	0	0	0	0	0	0	1	2
Days Minimum Temp. ≤ 32°F	8	7	2	0	0	0	0	0	0	0	3	9	29
Days Minimum Temp. ≤ 0°F	0	0	0	0	0	0	0	0	0	0	0	0	0
Heating Degree Days (base 65°F)	723	611	573	436	284	145	49	36	130	377	582	753	4,699
Cooling Degree Days (base 65°F)	0	0	0	0	6	23	71	68	19	0	0	0	187
Mean Precipitation (in.)	5.49	3.55	3.66	2.70	1.87	1.54	0.70	0.88	1.34	3.35	6.64	5.31	37.03
Maximum Precipitation (in.)*	12.9	9.1	8.4	6.5	4.8	3.8	2.4	4.6	5.9	7.8	10.7	11.8	55.1
Minimum Precipitation (in.)*	0.6	0.3	0.6	0.3	0.1	0.1	trace	trace	trace	0.3	0.7	1.4	23.7
Extreme Maximum Daily Precip. (in.)	2.98	3.06	1.86	2.64	1.06	1.54	0.85	1.41	1.19	5.02	3.29	3.77	5.02
Days With ≥ 0.1" Precipitation	12	9	11	7	6	4	2	2	4	8	13	12	90
Days With ≥ 0.5" Precipitation	4	2	1	1	1	1	0	1	1	2	4	3	21
Days With ≥ 1.0" Precipitation	1	0	0	0	0	0	0	0	0	0	1	1	3
Mean Snowfall (in.)	na	na	na	na	na	na	na	na	na	na	na	na	na
Maximum Snowfall (in.)*	57	13	18	2	trace	0	0	0	0	2	18	22	61
Maximum 24-hr. Snowfall (in.)*	20	7	6	1	trace	0	0	0	0	2	8	9	20
Maximum Snow Depth (in.)	na	na	na	na	na	na	na	na	na	na	na	na	na
Days With ≥ 1.0" Snow Depth	na	na	na	na	na	na	na	na	na	na	na	na	na
Thunderstorm Days*	< 1	< 1	1	1	1	1	1	1	1	< 1	1	< 1	8
Foggy Days*	18	15	13	10	8	8	8	11	16	19	19	19	164
Predominant Sky Cover*	OVR	OVR	OVR	OVR	OVR	OVR	CLR	OVR	OVR	OVR	OVR	OVR	OVR
Mean Relative Humidity 7am (%)*	83	83	84	83	80	79	79	83	88	88	86	85	83
Mean Relative Humidity 4pm (%)*	75	69	63	57	54	53	49	51	56	68	76	79	62
Mean Dewpoint (°F)*	33	35	36	39	44	48	52	53	50	45	39	35	43
Prevailing Wind Direction*	S	S	SSW	SSW	SSW	SSW	SW	SSW	N	S	S	S	SSW
Prevailing Wind Speed (mph)*	12	10	13	12	10	9	9	9	9	10	12	12	10
Maximum Wind Gust (mph)*	64	60	53	44	46	33	29	38	39	45	67	60	67

Note: (*) Period of record is 1948-1995

The period of record for National Weather Service station data is 1980 – 2009 except where noted. See User Guide for detailed explanation of data.

Spokane Int'l Airport

Spokane lies on the eastern edge of the broad Columbia Basin area of Washington which is bounded by the Cascade Range on the west and the Rocky Mountains on the east. The elevations in eastern Washington vary from less than 400 feet above sea level near Pasco where the Columbia River flows out of Washington to over 5,000 feet in the mountain areas of the extreme eastern edge of the State. Spokane is located on the upper plateau area where the long gradual slope from the Columbia River meets the sharp rise of the Rocky Mountain Ranges.

Much of the urban area of Spokane lies along both sides of the Spokane River at an elevation of approximately 2,000 feet, but the residential areas have spread to the crests of the plateaus on either side of the river with elevations up to 2,500 feet above sea level. Spokane International Airport is situated on the plateau area 6 miles west-southwest and some 400 feet higher than the downtown business district.

The climate of Spokane combines some of the characteristics of damp coastal type weather and arid interior conditions. Most of the air masses which reach Spokane are brought in by the prevailing westerly and southwesterly circulations. Annual precipitation totals in the Spokane area are generally less than 20 inches. The lifting action of the air masses as they move up the east slope of the Columbia Basin frequently produces the cooling and condensation necessary for formation of clouds and precipitation.

Infrequently, the Spokane area comes under the influence of dry continental air masses from the north or east. On occasions when these air masses penetrate into eastern Washington the result is high temperatures and very low humidity in the summer and sub-zero temperatures in the winter.

In general, Spokane weather has the characteristics of a mild, arid climate during the summer months and a cold, coastal type in the winter. Approximately 70 percent of the total annual precipitation falls between the first of October and the end of March and about half of that falls as snow. The growing season usually extends over nearly six months from mid-April to mid-October. Winter weather includes many cloudy or foggy days and below freezing temperatures with occasional snowfall of several inches in depth. Sub-zero temperatures and traffic-stopping snowfalls are infrequent.

Based on the 1951-1980 period, the average first occurrence of 32 degrees Fahrenheit in the fall is October 6 and the average last occurrence in the spring is May 4.

Spokane Int'l Airport *Spokane County* Elevation: 2,355 ft. Latitude: 47° 37' N Longitude: 117° 32' W

	JAN	FEB	MAR	APR	MAY	JUN	JUL	AUG	SEP	OCT	NOV	DEC	YEAR
Mean Maximum Temp. (°F)	34.1	39.5	48.8	57.5	66.6	73.8	83.4	82.9	73.1	58.1	41.8	32.5	57.7
Mean Temp. (°F)	28.7	32.5	39.7	46.7	54.8	61.6	69.4	68.8	59.7	47.1	35.4	27.1	47.6
Mean Minimum Temp. (°F)	23.2	25.4	30.6	35.9	43.0	49.4	55.3	54.6	46.3	36.1	28.9	21.7	37.5
Extreme Maximum Temp. (°F)	56	63	70	86	96	101	103	103	98	86	67	56	103
Extreme Minimum Temp. (°F)	-22	-24	-7	21	24	33	37	37	22	7	-21	-18	-24
Days Maximum Temp. ≥ 90°F	0	0	0	0	0	1	8	8	1	0	0	0	18
Days Maximum Temp. ≤ 32°F	12	5	1	0	0	0	0	0	0	0	4	14	36
Days Minimum Temp. ≤ 32°F	26	23	20	9	2	0	0	0	1	9	19	28	137
Days Minimum Temp. ≤ 0°F	1	1	0	0	0	0	0	0	0	0	0	1	3
Heating Degree Days (base 65°F)	1,120	912	776	542	323	143	35	34	185	548	882	1,168	6,668
Cooling Degree Days (base 65°F)	0	0	0	0	14	48	178	159	34	1	0	0	434
Mean Precipitation (in.)	1.80	1.35	1.60	1.27	1.62	1.20	0.64	0.61	0.67	1.15	2.25	2.31	16.47
Maximum Precipitation (in.)*	5.0	3.9	3.8	3.1	5.7	3.1	2.3	1.8	2.0	4.0	5.1	5.1	26.1
Minimum Precipitation (in.)*	0.4	0.3	0.3	0.1	0.2	0.2	trace	trace	trace	trace	0.2	0.6	11.2
Extreme Maximum Daily Precip. (in.)	1.02	0.66	0.96	1.23	2.19	0.89	1.06	1.06	1.05	0.98	1.24	1.39	2.19
Days With ≥ 0.1" Precipitation	6	5	6	4	4	4	2	2	2	3	7	7	52
Days With ≥ 0.5" Precipitation	0	0	0	0	1	0	0	0	0	1	1	1	4
Days With ≥ 1.0" Precipitation	0	0	0	0	0	0	0	0	0	0	0	0	0
Mean Snowfall (in.)	12.6	7.0	3.5	1.0	0.1	trace	0.0	0.0	trace	0.2	6.2	13.7	44.3
Maximum Snowfall (in.)*	57	29	15	7	4	trace	0	0	0	6	25	42	99
Maximum 24-hr. Snowfall (in.)*	13	11	5	4	4	trace	0	0	0	6	9	11	13
Maximum Snow Depth (in.)	27	23	10	4	trace	trace	0	0	trace	trace	12	23	27
Days With ≥ 1.0" Snow Depth	17	10	3	0	0	0	0	0	0	0	5	16	51
Thunderstorm Days*	< 1	< 1	< 1	1	2	3	2	2	1	< 1	< 1	0	11
Foggy Days*	19	14	9	4	3	2	1	1	2	8	17	21	101
Predominant Sky Cover*	OVR	OVR	OVR	OVR	OVR	OVR	CLR	CLR	CLR	OVR	OVR	OVR	OVR
Mean Relative Humidity 7am (%)*	86	85	81	73	68	64	56	59	69	81	88	88	75
Mean Relative Humidity 4pm (%)*	79	69	55	43	40	37	27	28	34	50	75	83	52
Mean Dewpoint (°F)*	22	26	28	32	38	43	44	43	40	35	30	24	34
Prevailing Wind Direction*	NE	NE	SW	SW	SW	SW	SW	SW	SW	NE	NE	NE	SW
Prevailing Wind Speed (mph)*	7	8	14	14	12	12	10	10	12	7	7	7	10
Maximum Wind Gust (mph)*	67	55	64	62	53	49	51	54	47	62	58	55	67

Note: (*) Period of record is 1948-1995

Yakima Air Terminal

Yakima is located in a small east-west valley in the upper (northwestern) part of the Yakima Valley. Local topography is complex with a number of minor valleys and ridges giving a local relief of as much as 1,000 feet. This complex topography results in marked variations in air drainage, winds, and low temperatures within short distances.

The climate of the Yakima Valley is relatively mild and dry. It has characteristics of both maritime and continental climates, modified by the Cascade and the Rocky Mountains, respectively. Summers are dry and rather hot, and winters cool with only light snowfall. The maritime influence is strongest in winter when the prevailing westerlies are the strongest and most steady. The Selkirk and Rocky Mountains in British Columbia and Idaho shield the area from most of the very cold air masses that sweep down from Canada into the Great Plains and eastern United States. Sometimes a strong polar high pressure area over western Canada will occur at the same time that a low pressure area covers the southwestern United States. On these occasions, the cold arctic air will pour through the passes and down the river valleys of British Columbia, bringing very cold temperatures to Yakima. However, over one-half of the winters remain above zero.

The modifying influence of the Pacific Ocean is much less in summer. Afternoons are hot, but the dry air results in a rapid temperature fall after sunset, and nights are pleasantly cool with summertime low temperatures, usually in the 50s. Spells of four to 11 days of 100 degrees or more have occurred.

Temperatures below 32 degrees are infrequent during the period from mid-May through September. Temperatures below 40 degrees during July and August have occurred in about half of the years.

Precipitation follows a West Coast marine climate with the typical late fall and early winter high. However, since Yakima lies in the rain shadow of the Cascades, total amounts are small. The three months, November to January, total nearly half of the annual fall.

Irrigation is necessary for nearly all crops. Ample water supplies are available from the snowmelt in the Cascade Mountains which is collected in storage reservoirs for summer use.

Snowfall in the Yakima area is light, averaging 20 to 25 inches.

Summers are sunny, with about 85 percent of the possible sunshine. Winters are generally cloudy, with only a third of the possible sunshine.

Winds are mostly light, averaging about seven mph for the year, being somewhat stronger in late spring and weaker in winter. Speeds of 30 to 35 mph are reached at least once in about half the months and speeds over 40 mph occur in about one out of five months. The most common wind direction in downtown Yakima is northwest, while at the airport the wind is from the west in winter and the west-northwest in summer.

Yakima Air Terminal *Yakima County* Elevation: 1,063 ft. Latitude: 46° 34' N Longitude: 120° 33' W

	JAN	FEB	MAR	APR	MAY	JUN	JUL	AUG	SEP	OCT	NOV	DEC	YEAR
Mean Maximum Temp. (°F)	38.4	45.9	56.3	64.0	72.5	79.5	87.8	86.7	78.1	64.0	48.1	35.9	63.1
Mean Temp. (°F)	30.8	36.0	43.4	49.5	57.5	64.1	70.7	69.4	61.0	49.2	37.7	28.8	49.8
Mean Minimum Temp. (°F)	23.2	26.1	30.5	34.9	42.5	48.6	53.6	52.0	43.9	34.3	27.3	21.6	36.5
Extreme Maximum Temp. (°F)	64	68	78	89	102	105	109	104	100	88	73	67	109
Extreme Minimum Temp. (°F)	-17	-17	10	18	25	30	36	36	24	4	-13	-16	-17
Days Maximum Temp. ≥ 90°F	0	0	0	0	2	4	14	12	2	0	0	0	34
Days Maximum Temp. ≤ 32°F	8	2	0	0	0	0	0	0	0	0	2	11	23
Days Minimum Temp. ≤ 32°F	27	23	20	12	3	0	0	0	1	13	23	28	150
Days Minimum Temp. ≤ 0°F	1	0	0	0	0	0	0	0	0	0	0	1	2
Heating Degree Days (base 65°F)	1,052	813	663	460	248	92	21	22	148	484	813	1,117	5,933
Cooling Degree Days (base 65°F)	0	0	0	1	23	71	206	166	34	0	0	0	501
Mean Precipitation (in.)	1.11	0.79	0.62	0.56	0.56	0.62	0.21	0.27	0.34	0.52	1.05	1.54	8.19
Maximum Precipitation (in.)*	3.7	2.5	2.6	1.8	2.8	2.5	0.7	2.1	2.1	2.2	2.8	4.2	13.9
Minimum Precipitation (in.)*	0.1	trace	trace	trace	trace	trace	trace	0	0	0	trace	0.1	4.2
Extreme Maximum Daily Precip. (in.)	0.64	0.79	0.73	0.80	0.70	1.48	0.47	1.64	1.36	1.01	1.70	1.38	1.70
Days With ≥ 0.1" Precipitation	4	3	2	2	2	2	1	1	1	2	3	5	28
Days With ≥ 0.5" Precipitation	0	0	0	0	0	0	0	0	0	0	0	0	0
Days With ≥ 1.0" Precipitation	0	0	0	0	0	0	0	0	0	0	0	0	0
Mean Snowfall (in.)	6.2	2.8	0.8	trace	trace	0.0	0.0	0.0	0.0	0.1	3.3	9.5	22.7
Maximum Snowfall (in.)*	27	17	11	trace	trace	0	0	0	0	3	21	38	53
Maximum 24-hr. Snowfall (in.)*	14	8	7	trace	trace	0	0	0	0	2	11	14	14
Maximum Snow Depth (in.)	21	11	6	trace	trace	0	*0*	0	*0*	2	16	27	*27*
Days With ≥ 1.0" Snow Depth	15	5	0	0	0	0	*0*	0	*0*	0	2	14	*36*
Thunderstorm Days*	0	< 1	< 1	< 1	1	2	1	1	1	< 1	0	0	6
Foggy Days*	15	8	3	< 1	< 1	< 1	< 1	< 1	< 1	2	11	17	56
Predominant Sky Cover*	OVR	OVR	OVR	OVR	OVR	CLR	CLR	CLR	CLR	OVR	OVR	OVR	OVR
Mean Relative Humidity 7am (%)*	84	83	77	64	56	54	54	61	72	81	85	85	71
Mean Relative Humidity 4pm (%)*	72	59	41	33	30	30	26	28	32	43	63	75	44
Mean Dewpoint (°F)*	22	27	28	31	37	43	46	47	43	36	30	25	34
Prevailing Wind Direction*	W	W	W	W	W	NW	W	W	WNW	WNW	W	W	W
Prevailing Wind Speed (mph)*	6	7	8	8	8	10	8	7	8	8	7	6	8
Maximum Wind Gust (mph)*	66	59	61	56	69	69	59	44	55	54	59	61	69

Note: (*) Period of record is 1948-1995

The period of record for National Weather Service station data is 1980 – 2009 except where noted. See User Guide for detailed explanation of data.

Aberdeen *Grays Harbor County* Elevation: 9 ft. Latitude: 46° 58' N Longitude: 123° 49' W

	JAN	FEB	MAR	APR	MAY	JUN	JUL	AUG	SEP	OCT	NOV	DEC	YEAR
Mean Maximum Temp. (°F)	47.6	50.3	53.6	56.9	61.3	64.8	68.5	69.3	68.5	60.9	52.1	46.6	58.4
Mean Temp. (°F)	42.2	43.4	46.1	49.0	53.7	57.8	61.1	61.6	59.4	52.7	45.9	41.2	51.2
Mean Minimum Temp. (°F)	36.7	36.3	38.5	41.0	46.1	50.7	53.8	53.8	50.3	44.4	39.6	35.9	43.9
Extreme Maximum Temp. (°F)	61	73	79	85	92	98	98	105	100	86	69	62	105
Extreme Minimum Temp. (°F)	15	12	23	29	31	37	43	43	36	28	14	10	10
Days Maximum Temp. ≥ 90°F	0	0	0	0	0	0	0	0	0	0	0	0	0
Days Maximum Temp. ≤ 32°F	0	0	0	0	0	0	0	0	0	0	0	1	1
Days Minimum Temp. ≤ 32°F	8	8	4	1	0	0	0	0	0	0	4	10	35
Days Minimum Temp. ≤ 0°F	0	0	0	0	0	0	0	0	0	0	0	0	0
Heating Degree Days (base 65°F)	701	604	580	473	347	218	129	114	173	375	568	729	5,011
Cooling Degree Days (base 65°F)	0	0	0	0	5	8	16	15	12	1	0	0	57
Mean Precipitation (in.)	13.25	9.55	8.94	6.16	3.52	2.55	1.24	1.51	2.52	7.42	14.37	12.50	83.53
Extreme Maximum Daily Precip. (in.)	4.82	4.60	4.59	3.80	1.70	2.97	1.72	2.33	2.58	4.87	7.03	5.21	7.03
Days With ≥ 0.1" Precipitation	17	14	16	13	9	7	3	3	6	11	18	17	134
Days With ≥ 0.5" Precipitation	9	6	6	4	2	1	1	1	2	5	10	8	55
Days With ≥ 1.0" Precipitation	4	3	2	1	0	0	0	0	0	2	4	4	20
Mean Snowfall (in.)	0.4	0.2	0.1	0.0	0.0	0.0	0.0	0.0	0.0	0.0	0.1	trace	0.8
Maximum Snow Depth (in.)	6	6	1	0	0	0	0	0	0	0	4	4	6
Days With ≥ 1.0" Snow Depth	1	0	0	0	0	0	0	0	0	0	0	0	1

Anacortes *Skagit County* Elevation: 20 ft. Latitude: 48° 31' N Longitude: 122° 37' W

	JAN	FEB	MAR	APR	MAY	JUN	JUL	AUG	SEP	OCT	NOV	DEC	YEAR
Mean Maximum Temp. (°F)	46.6	49.4	53.2	58.0	63.3	68.1	72.7	73.0	67.8	59.2	51.0	45.9	59.0
Mean Temp. (°F)	41.3	42.8	46.3	50.3	55.4	59.7	63.2	63.4	59.3	52.1	45.5	40.7	51.7
Mean Minimum Temp. (°F)	36.0	36.2	39.3	42.7	47.4	51.2	53.7	53.7	50.6	45.0	39.9	35.5	44.3
Extreme Maximum Temp. (°F)	62	69	79	79	86	88	101	88	85	77	66	62	101
Extreme Minimum Temp. (°F)	11	9	21	31	35	41	45	42	36	27	10	8	8
Days Maximum Temp. ≥ 90°F	0	0	0	0	0	0	0	0	0	0	0	0	0
Days Maximum Temp. ≤ 32°F	1	0	0	0	0	0	0	0	0	0	0	1	2
Days Minimum Temp. ≤ 32°F	9	8	3	0	0	0	0	0	0	0	4	9	33
Days Minimum Temp. ≤ 0°F	0	0	0	0	0	0	0	0	0	0	0	0	0
Heating Degree Days (base 65°F)	727	620	572	433	294	162	74	65	170	392	579	746	4,834
Cooling Degree Days (base 65°F)	0	0	0	0	1	9	26	21	4	0	0	0	61
Mean Precipitation (in.)	3.64	2.32	2.40	1.91	1.85	1.50	0.84	1.06	1.47	2.71	4.68	3.34	27.72
Extreme Maximum Daily Precip. (in.)	1.65	1.20	1.09	1.04	1.49	***0.95***	0.98	1.60	1.59	1.80	2.25	1.53	***2.25***
Days With ≥ 0.1" Precipitation	10	7	8	7	5	4	3	2	4	7	12	10	79
Days With ≥ 0.5" Precipitation	2	1	1	1	1	1	0	1	1	1	2	2	14
Days With ≥ 1.0" Precipitation	0	0	0	0	0	0	0	0	0	0	1	0	1
Mean Snowfall (in.)	1.3	0.4	0.2	0.0	0.0	0.0	0.0	0.0	0.0	0.0	0.7	1.0	3.6
Maximum Snow Depth (in.)	***0***	0	1	0	0	0	0	0	0	0	14	***14***	***14***
Days With ≥ 1.0" Snow Depth	***0***	0	0	0	0	0	0	0	0	0	0	***0***	***0***

Baring *King County* Elevation: 771 ft. Latitude: 47° 46' N Longitude: 121° 29' W

	JAN	FEB	MAR	APR	MAY	JUN	JUL	AUG	SEP	OCT	NOV	DEC	YEAR
Mean Maximum Temp. (°F)	41.5	46.5	51.8	58.6	64.8	69.2	75.4	75.5	69.7	58.3	46.2	39.9	58.1
Mean Temp. (°F)	36.6	39.3	43.2	48.5	54.4	58.8	63.8	63.9	58.7	50.0	41.0	35.7	49.5
Mean Minimum Temp. (°F)	31.7	32.0	34.5	38.4	43.9	48.5	52.2	52.2	47.7	41.6	35.8	31.3	40.8
Extreme Maximum Temp. (°F)	62	73	80	91	100	95	101	98	98	86	67	60	101
Extreme Minimum Temp. (°F)	3	6	16	28	31	34	40	39	32	23	8	1	1
Days Maximum Temp. ≥ 90°F	0	0	0	0	0	1	1	1	0	0	0	0	3
Days Maximum Temp. ≤ 32°F	2	1	0	0	0	0	0	0	0	0	1	3	7
Days Minimum Temp. ≤ 32°F	17	15	11	4	0	0	0	0	0	2	8	18	75
Days Minimum Temp. ≤ 0°F	0	0	0	0	0	0	0	0	0	0	0	0	0
Heating Degree Days (base 65°F)	873	721	669	488	328	194	82	75	190	458	713	904	5,695
Cooling Degree Days (base 65°F)	0	0	0	0	6	16	53	48	10	0	0	0	133
Mean Precipitation (in.)	15.73	10.31	10.22	7.85	5.33	4.04	2.04	2.03	4.73	10.66	18.97	14.05	105.96
Extreme Maximum Daily Precip. (in.)	6.42	6.37	na	4.44	2.28	2.90	2.34	1.98	na	5.85	8.87	7.54	na
Days With ≥ 0.1" Precipitation	17	13	13	14	11	9	5	4	6	13	18	16	139
Days With ≥ 0.5" Precipitation	10	7	7	6	4	3	1	1	3	8	12	9	71
Days With ≥ 1.0" Precipitation	5	3	3	2	1	1	0	1	1	4	6	5	32
Mean Snowfall (in.)	17.5	7.7	4.1	0.8	trace	0.0	0.0	trace	0.0	trace	4.5	15.7	50.3
Maximum Snow Depth (in.)	36	29	13	1	trace	0	0	trace	0	trace	18	41	41
Days With ≥ 1.0" Snow Depth	16	10	4	0	0	0	0	0	0	0	3	12	45

Bellingham 3 SSW *Whatcom County* Elevation: 15 ft. Latitude: 48° 43' N Longitude: 122° 31' W

	JAN	FEB	MAR	APR	MAY	JUN	JUL	AUG	SEP	OCT	NOV	DEC	YEAR
Mean Maximum Temp. (°F)	47.0	49.4	53.1	58.4	63.8	68.7	73.4	73.3	67.6	58.9	51.1	46.1	59.2
Mean Temp. (°F)	41.4	42.5	46.1	50.5	55.6	60.1	64.0	64.0	59.0	52.1	45.4	40.7	51.8
Mean Minimum Temp. (°F)	35.7	35.6	39.0	42.5	47.4	51.5	54.5	54.6	50.4	45.2	39.7	35.2	44.3
Extreme Maximum Temp. (°F)	65	66	78	76	83	84	92	91	84	75	68	65	92
Extreme Minimum Temp. (°F)	9	5	17	28	30	37	43	44	37	23	11	6	5
Days Maximum Temp. ≥ 90°F	0	0	0	0	0	0	0	0	0	0	0	0	0
Days Maximum Temp. ≤ 32°F	1	0	0	0	0	0	0	0	0	0	1	1	3
Days Minimum Temp. ≤ 32°F	10	9	4	1	0	0	0	0	0	1	5	10	40
Days Minimum Temp. ≤ 0°F	0	0	0	0	0	0	0	0	0	0	0	0	0
Heating Degree Days (base 65°F)	725	629	580	429	285	148	58	53	176	394	580	748	4,805
Cooling Degree Days (base 65°F)	0	0	0	0	1	8	33	28	3	0	0	0	73
Mean Precipitation (in.)	4.45	2.67	3.14	2.60	2.39	1.73	1.06	1.34	1.49	3.66	6.04	4.04	34.61
Extreme Maximum Daily Precip. (in.)	1.91	1.46	1.80	1.52	1.40	1.23	1.51	1.87	1.91	2.75	2.73	1.35	2.75
Days With ≥ 0.1" Precipitation	12	8	10	7	6	5	3	3	4	9	13	12	92
Days With ≥ 0.5" Precipitation	3	1	1	1	1	1	0	1	1	2	4	2	18
Days With ≥ 1.0" Precipitation	1	0	0	0	0	0	0	0	0	0	1	0	2
Mean Snowfall (in.)	0.7	0.3	0.6	0.0	0.0	0.0	0.0	0.0	0.0	0.1	0.9	1.7	4.3
Maximum Snow Depth (in.)	10	4	6	0	0	0	0	0	0	3	12	38	38
Days With ≥ 1.0" Snow Depth	1	0	0	0	0	0	0	0	0	0	1	1	3

The period of record for all cooperative weather station data is 1980 – 2009. See User Guide for detailed explanation of data.

Blaine *Whatcom County* Elevation: 60 ft. Latitude: 49° 00' N Longitude: 122° 45' W

	JAN	FEB	MAR	APR	MAY	JUN	JUL	AUG	SEP	OCT	NOV	DEC	YEAR
Mean Maximum Temp. (°F)	43.7	47.0	51.4	57.0	63.0	68.1	71.8	71.5	66.1	56.6	48.6	42.7	57.3
Mean Temp. (°F)	38.4	40.4	44.0	48.6	54.3	59.2	62.5	62.2	57.3	49.5	43.1	37.6	49.7
Mean Minimum Temp. (°F)	33.0	33.7	36.5	40.2	45.5	50.3	53.2	52.9	48.4	42.3	37.6	32.4	42.2
Extreme Maximum Temp. (°F)	61	68	66	73	84	85	86	86	83	78	64	62	86
Extreme Minimum Temp. (°F)	1	5	19	26	30	38	41	39	32	19	6	3	1
Days Maximum Temp. ≥ 90°F	0	0	0	0	0	0	0	0	0	0	0	0	0
Days Maximum Temp. ≤ 32°F	2	0	0	0	0	0	0	0	0	0	1	2	5
Days Minimum Temp. ≤ 32°F	14	12	8	3	0	0	0	0	0	2	7	15	61
Days Minimum Temp. ≤ 0°F	0	0	0	0	0	0	0	0	0	0	0	0	0
Heating Degree Days (base 65°F)	818	690	646	485	325	170	85	91	226	474	649	843	5,502
Cooling Degree Days (base 65°F)	0	0	0	0	1	4	15	11	1	0	0	0	32
Mean Precipitation (in.)	5.60	3.73	3.68	2.92	2.61	2.19	1.38	1.31	1.75	3.76	6.53	5.24	40.70
Extreme Maximum Daily Precip. (in.)	2.25	2.04	1.83	1.61	1.50	1.60	1.40	2.75	2.20	1.83	2.15	2.40	2.75
Days With ≥ 0.1" Precipitation	13	10	11	9	7	5	4	3	4	9	15	13	103
Days With ≥ 0.5" Precipitation	4	2	2	1	1	1	1	1	1	2	4	3	23
Days With ≥ 1.0" Precipitation	1	0	0	0	0	0	0	0	0	1	1	1	4
Mean Snowfall (in.)	4.2	1.9	0.6	0.0	0.0	0.0	0.0	0.0	0.0	0.1	0.6	4.1	11.5
Maximum Snow Depth (in.)	16	8	4	0	0	0	0	0	0	2	6	21	21
Days With ≥ 1.0" Snow Depth	3	1	0	0	0	0	0	0	0	0	1	2	7

Bremerton *Kitsap County* Elevation: 109 ft. Latitude: 47° 34' N Longitude: 122° 41' W

	JAN	FEB	MAR	APR	MAY	JUN	JUL	AUG	SEP	OCT	NOV	DEC	YEAR
Mean Maximum Temp. (°F)	46.0	49.3	54.3	59.2	65.2	70.1	75.4	76.2	71.3	60.4	50.5	44.9	60.2
Mean Temp. (°F)	40.5	42.1	46.1	50.1	55.8	60.4	64.9	65.4	60.8	52.3	44.6	39.7	51.9
Mean Minimum Temp. (°F)	35.0	34.9	37.9	41.0	46.3	50.8	54.3	54.5	50.4	44.2	38.6	34.4	43.5
Extreme Maximum Temp. (°F)	62	71	***80***	83	***92***	***95***	***99***	101	97	***86***	***70***	***68***	***101***
Extreme Minimum Temp. (°F)	14	12	***19***	29	***31***	***38***	***44***	39	35	***27***	***13***	***7***	***7***
Days Maximum Temp. ≥ 90°F	0	0	0	0	0	1	1	1	0	0	0	0	3
Days Maximum Temp. ≤ 32°F	1	0	0	0	0	0	0	0	0	0	0	1	2
Days Minimum Temp. ≤ 32°F	11	10	5	1	0	0	0	0	0	0	5	12	44
Days Minimum Temp. ≤ 0°F	0	0	0	0	0	0	0	0	0	0	0	0	0
Heating Degree Days (base 65°F)	751	640	579	441	285	152	56	45	136	386	606	779	4,856
Cooling Degree Days (base 65°F)	0	0	0	0	6	22	60	63	18	0	0	0	169
Mean Precipitation (in.)	8.32	6.05	5.54	3.46	2.22	1.75	0.91	1.04	1.46	4.78	9.70	8.95	54.18
Extreme Maximum Daily Precip. (in.)	***4.30***	***3.09***	***2.90***	2.51	***1.64***	***1.96***	***1.50***	1.83	1.65	***3.98***	***4.21***	***7.50***	***7.50***
Days With ≥ 0.1" Precipitation	13	10	12	8	7	5	3	2	4	9	14	12	99
Days With ≥ 0.5" Precipitation	6	4	4	2	1	1	0	1	1	3	7	6	36
Days With ≥ 1.0" Precipitation	2	2	1	0	0	0	0	0	0	1	3	3	12
Mean Snowfall (in.)	***0.7***	1.1	0.3	0.0	trace	0.0	0.0	0.0	0.0	0.0	0.9	1.5	***4.5***
Maximum Snow Depth (in.)	7	***5***	***2***	0	***trace***	***0***	***0***	0	0	***0***	***11***	***9***	***11***
Days With ≥ 1.0" Snow Depth	***1***	0	***0***	0	0	0	0	0	0	0	1	1	***3***

Buckley 1 NE *Pierce County* Elevation: 685 ft. Latitude: 47° 10' N Longitude: 122° 00' W

	JAN	FEB	MAR	APR	MAY	JUN	JUL	AUG	SEP	OCT	NOV	DEC	YEAR
Mean Maximum Temp. (°F)	46.8	49.8	54.0	59.1	65.2	70.3	76.4	77.3	71.8	60.5	51.0	45.2	60.6
Mean Temp. (°F)	40.4	42.0	45.2	49.2	54.7	59.4	64.1	64.3	59.5	51.2	44.3	39.1	51.1
Mean Minimum Temp. (°F)	34.0	34.1	36.3	39.2	44.1	48.5	51.7	51.4	47.2	41.8	37.6	32.9	41.6
Extreme Maximum Temp. (°F)	66	72	78	83	95	95	102	103	97	89	70	63	103
Extreme Minimum Temp. (°F)	10	7	13	28	32	37	40	38	29	22	5	0	0
Days Maximum Temp. ≥ 90°F	0	0	0	0	0	1	2	1	0	0	0	0	4
Days Maximum Temp. ≤ 32°F	1	0	0	0	0	0	0	0	0	0	0	1	2
Days Minimum Temp. ≤ 32°F	12	11	8	3	0	0	0	0	0	2	6	14	56
Days Minimum Temp. ≤ 0°F	0	0	0	0	0	0	0	0	0	0	0	0	0
Heating Degree Days (base 65°F)	754	644	607	468	318	180	75	62	170	422	613	797	5,110
Cooling Degree Days (base 65°F)	0	0	0	0	4	20	54	49	12	1	0	0	140
Mean Precipitation (in.)	5.95	4.36	4.93	4.13	3.52	2.83	1.38	1.45	2.04	4.29	7.64	5.34	47.86
Extreme Maximum Daily Precip. (in.)	2.70	3.79	2.20	2.92	1.60	1.60	1.17	1.24	1.73	2.82	5.12	2.00	5.12
Days With ≥ 0.1" Precipitation	13	11	13	12	10	7	3	4	6	10	15	13	117
Days With ≥ 0.5" Precipitation	4	2	3	2	2	2	1	1	1	3	5	3	29
Days With ≥ 1.0" Precipitation	1	1	0	0	0	0	0	0	0	1	2	1	6
Mean Snowfall (in.)	1.7	1.5	0.6	0.1	0.0	0.0	0.0	0.0	0.0	0.0	1.2	2.3	7.4
Maximum Snow Depth (in.)	12	7	trace	trace	0	0	0	0	0	0	11	3	12
Days With ≥ 1.0" Snow Depth	0	0	0	0	0	0	0	0	0	0	0	0	0

Cedar Lake *King County* Elevation: 1,560 ft. Latitude: 47° 25' N Longitude: 121° 44' W

	JAN	FEB	MAR	APR	MAY	JUN	JUL	AUG	SEP	OCT	NOV	DEC	YEAR
Mean Maximum Temp. (°F)	40.7	43.9	47.9	53.1	59.9	64.9	71.6	72.1	65.8	56.1	45.4	39.5	55.1
Mean Temp. (°F)	36.0	37.8	40.7	44.7	50.7	55.5	60.9	61.5	56.1	48.3	40.3	35.1	47.3
Mean Minimum Temp. (°F)	31.3	31.7	33.4	36.2	41.5	46.1	50.2	50.8	46.4	40.4	35.2	30.7	39.5
Extreme Maximum Temp. (°F)	58	67	76	85	96	92	96	98	101	89	68	58	101
Extreme Minimum Temp. (°F)	6	3	14	26	30	34	40	40	33	22	7	2	2
Days Maximum Temp. ≥ 90°F	0	0	0	0	0	0	1	1	0	0	0	0	2
Days Maximum Temp. ≤ 32°F	4	1	0	0	0	0	0	0	0	0	1	3	9
Days Minimum Temp. ≤ 32°F	18	15	14	8	1	0	0	0	0	2	10	19	87
Days Minimum Temp. ≤ 0°F	0	0	0	0	0	0	0	0	0	0	0	0	0
Heating Degree Days (base 65°F)	892	761	747	603	438	287	152	132	267	512	734	919	6,444
Cooling Degree Days (base 65°F)	0	0	0	0	3	10	32	29	8	1	0	0	83
Mean Precipitation (in.)	12.78	8.71	10.08	8.28	6.51	5.50	2.62	2.54	4.52	8.48	15.42	11.11	96.55
Extreme Maximum Daily Precip. (in.)	5.32	3.59	2.78	3.89	2.25	3.51	2.30	2.08	2.90	5.91	7.33	3.14	7.33
Days With ≥ 0.1" Precipitation	16	13	16	15	12	10	5	4	8	12	19	16	146
Days With ≥ 0.5" Precipitation	9	6	7	7	5	4	2	2	3	6	11	8	70
Days With ≥ 1.0" Precipitation	4	2	3	2	2	1	1	1	1	2	5	4	28
Mean Snowfall (in.)	11.4	7.4	7.8	2.8	0.2	0.0	0.0	0.0	0.0	trace	3.4	11.4	44.4
Maximum Snow Depth (in.)	30	24	20	13	4	0	0	0	0	10	20	23	30
Days With ≥ 1.0" Snow Depth	13	9	7	2	0	0	0	0	0	0	3	12	46

The period of record for all cooperative weather station data is 1980 – 2009. See User Guide for detailed explanation of data.

Centralia *Lewis County* Elevation: 185 ft. Latitude: 46° 43' N Longitude: 122° 57' W

	JAN	FEB	MAR	APR	MAY	JUN	JUL	AUG	SEP	OCT	NOV	DEC	YEAR
Mean Maximum Temp. (°F)	47.3	50.9	55.9	61.6	67.7	72.7	78.6	79.4	74.0	62.5	51.8	45.9	62.4
Mean Temp. (°F)	41.5	43.3	47.0	51.2	56.9	61.7	66.4	66.7	61.7	53.2	45.6	40.5	53.0
Mean Minimum Temp. (°F)	35.7	35.7	38.0	40.8	46.1	50.6	54.1	53.9	49.4	43.9	39.4	35.1	43.5
Extreme Maximum Temp. (°F)	64	73	81	89	98	98	107	103	100	92	73	65	107
Extreme Minimum Temp. (°F)	5	0	19	27	30	37	41	41	33	20	7	2	0
Days Maximum Temp. ≥ 90°F	0	0	0	0	0	1	3	3	1	0	0	0	8
Days Maximum Temp. ≤ 32°F	0	0	0	0	0	0	0	0	0	0	0	1	1
Days Minimum Temp. ≤ 32°F	10	9	7	3	0	0	0	0	0	1	5	10	45
Days Minimum Temp. ≤ 0°F	0	0	0	0	0	0	0	0	0	0	0	0	0
Heating Degree Days (base 65°F)	722	606	553	406	253	122	37	30	118	359	574	753	4,533
Cooling Degree Days (base 65°F)	0	0	0	1	10	29	87	89	25	1	0	0	242
Mean Precipitation (in.)	6.73	5.03	4.84	3.52	2.43	1.90	0.61	0.93	1.51	4.18	7.96	7.04	46.68
Extreme Maximum Daily Precip. (in.)	4.13	3.34	1.90	2.71	1.04	1.16	1.63	1.63	1.17	3.13	3.96	2.80	4.13
Days With ≥ 0.1" Precipitation	14	12	13	10	7	5	2	2	4	9	15	14	107
Days With ≥ 0.5" Precipitation	4	3	3	2	1	1	0	0	1	2	6	5	28
Days With ≥ 1.0" Precipitation	1	1	0	0	0	0	0	0	0	1	2	1	6
Mean Snowfall (in.)	0.5	0.6	0.1	trace	0.0	0.0	0.0	0.0	0.0	0.0	0.1	0.3	1.6
Maximum Snow Depth (in.)	11	8	trace	0	0	0	0	0	0	0	4	10	11
Days With ≥ 1.0" Snow Depth	0	0	0	0	0	0	0	0	0	0	0	0	0

Chelan *Chelan County* Elevation: 1,120 ft. Latitude: 47° 50' N Longitude: 120° 02' W

	JAN	FEB	MAR	APR	MAY	JUN	JUL	AUG	SEP	OCT	NOV	DEC	YEAR
Mean Maximum Temp. (°F)	33.3	40.2	51.4	61.4	70.2	76.9	84.7	85.1	75.7	61.2	44.3	33.2	59.8
Mean Temp. (°F)	28.6	33.5	42.5	51.0	59.3	66.1	72.9	72.6	63.5	51.1	38.3	29.0	50.7
Mean Minimum Temp. (°F)	23.9	26.8	33.5	40.4	48.3	55.3	60.9	60.1	51.3	40.9	32.1	24.8	41.5
Extreme Maximum Temp. (°F)	62	61	72	86	98	98	106	105	97	88	72	58	106
Extreme Minimum Temp. (°F)	-5	-2	11	26	32	33	37	43	26	13	-3	-8	-8
Days Maximum Temp. ≥ 90°F	0	0	0	0	0	3	9	9	1	0	0	0	22
Days Maximum Temp. ≤ 32°F	13	4	0	0	0	0	0	0	0	0	2	13	32
Days Minimum Temp. ≤ 32°F	28	22	12	2	0	0	0	0	0	2	14	26	106
Days Minimum Temp. ≤ 0°F	0	0	0	0	0	0	0	0	0	0	0	0	0
Heating Degree Days (base 65°F)	1,122	884	692	413	196	60	11	7	98	425	795	1,108	5,811
Cooling Degree Days (base 65°F)	0	0	0	0	25	100	261	251	60	0	0	0	697
Mean Precipitation (in.)	1.65	1.21	0.89	0.61	0.97	0.84	0.35	0.30	0.32	0.69	1.60	1.86	11.29
Extreme Maximum Daily Precip. (in.)	1.40	1.07	0.73	1.10	1.80	1.88	1.23	0.88	0.83	0.76	1.30	1.50	1.88
Days With ≥ 0.1" Precipitation	5	4	3	2	3	2	1	1	1	2	5	6	35
Days With ≥ 0.5" Precipitation	1	0	0	0	0	0	0	0	0	0	1	1	3
Days With ≥ 1.0" Precipitation	0	0	0	0	0	0	0	0	0	0	0	0	0
Mean Snowfall (in.)	8.1	3.6	0.7	trace	0.0	0.0	0.0	0.0	0.0	trace	2.1	9.8	24.3
Maximum Snow Depth (in.)	na	17	na	trace	0	0	0	0	0	trace	3	na	na
Days With ≥ 1.0" Snow Depth	na	3	0	0	0	0	0	0	0	0	1	na	na

Chewelah *Stevens County* Elevation: 1,669 ft. Latitude: 48° 17' N Longitude: 117° 43' W

	JAN	FEB	MAR	APR	MAY	JUN	JUL	AUG	SEP	OCT	NOV	DEC	YEAR
Mean Maximum Temp. (°F)	34.9	41.7	52.3	62.1	71.1	77.9	87.1	87.3	77.4	61.2	43.0	33.5	60.8
Mean Temp. (°F)	27.5	32.0	40.1	47.7	55.8	62.1	68.5	67.6	58.5	46.3	35.0	26.6	47.3
Mean Minimum Temp. (°F)	20.1	22.1	28.0	33.3	40.4	46.3	49.8	47.9	39.5	31.3	27.0	19.8	33.8
Extreme Maximum Temp. (°F)	53	62	75	91	100	106	107	105	104	92	66	58	107
Extreme Minimum Temp. (°F)	-25	-20	-5	19	23	31	33	33	20	5	-19	-23	-25
Days Maximum Temp. ≥ 90°F	0	0	0	0	1	3	14	13	4	0	0	0	35
Days Maximum Temp. ≤ 32°F	10	3	0	0	0	0	0	0	0	0	2	11	26
Days Minimum Temp. ≤ 32°F	28	25	24	15	4	0	0	0	4	18	21	28	167
Days Minimum Temp. ≤ 0°F	2	1	0	0	0	0	0	0	0	0	0	2	5
Heating Degree Days (base 65°F)	1,156	925	764	512	292	126	36	41	208	573	894	1,186	6,713
Cooling Degree Days (base 65°F)	0	0	0	0	13	46	151	128	19	0	0	0	357
Mean Precipitation (in.)	2.41	1.77	1.94	1.61	1.97	1.88	1.15	0.75	0.83	1.26	2.48	2.89	20.94
Extreme Maximum Daily Precip. (in.)	4.25	1.50	1.22	1.30	2.35	1.60	1.23	1.44	0.88	1.00	1.37	2.02	4.25
Days With ≥ 0.1" Precipitation	7	5	6	5	6	5	3	2	2	4	7	7	59
Days With ≥ 0.5" Precipitation	1	1	1	1	1	1	1	0	0	0	1	2	10
Days With ≥ 1.0" Precipitation	0	0	0	0	0	0	0	0	0	0	0	0	0
Mean Snowfall (in.)	11.8	4.9	1.4	0.2	0.0	0.0	0.0	0.0	0.0	trace	4.1	13.0	35.4
Maximum Snow Depth (in.)	36	24	16	3	0	0	0	0	0	trace	15	27	36
Days With ≥ 1.0" Snow Depth	21	12	3	0	0	0	0	0	0	0	3	15	54

Cle Elum *Kittitas County* Elevation: 1,919 ft. Latitude: 47° 11' N Longitude: 120° 57' W

	JAN	FEB	MAR	APR	MAY	JUN	JUL	AUG	SEP	OCT	NOV	DEC	YEAR
Mean Maximum Temp. (°F)	36.2	41.3	50.2	57.7	65.7	72.0	79.9	80.4	73.2	59.1	43.2	34.0	57.7
Mean Temp. (°F)	29.8	32.6	39.9	45.8	53.2	59.7	66.3	66.0	57.9	46.8	36.2	28.1	46.9
Mean Minimum Temp. (°F)	23.5	23.9	29.5	33.9	40.6	47.4	52.6	51.5	42.6	34.4	29.1	22.2	35.9
Extreme Maximum Temp. (°F)	57	63	74	85	99	100	103	101	97	86	64	52	103
Extreme Minimum Temp. (°F)	-24	-20	8	18	22	32	34	30	21	10	-14	-23	-24
Days Maximum Temp. ≥ 90°F	0	0	0	0	1	1	6	6	1	0	0	0	15
Days Maximum Temp. ≤ 32°F	8	4	0	0	0	0	0	0	0	0	2	12	26
Days Minimum Temp. ≤ 32°F	27	24	21	13	3	0	0	0	4	13	20	28	153
Days Minimum Temp. ≤ 0°F	1	1	0	0	0	0	0	0	0	0	0	1	3
Heating Degree Days (base 65°F)	1,083	907	773	568	366	180	59	60	221	559	859	1,136	6,771
Cooling Degree Days (base 65°F)	0	0	0	0	6	28	106	99	15	0	0	0	254
Mean Precipitation (in.)	3.33	2.32	1.87	1.25	1.06	1.08	0.51	0.48	0.89	2.13	4.05	na	na
Extreme Maximum Daily Precip. (in.)	2.21	2.30	0.97	0.95	0.82	1.34	1.20	1.85	0.74	2.05	3.45	2.05	3.45
Days With ≥ 0.1" Precipitation	8	7	6	4	4	3	2	1	3	6	10	8	62
Days With ≥ 0.5" Precipitation	2	1	1	0	0	0	0	0	1	1	2	2	10
Days With ≥ 1.0" Precipitation	0	0	0	0	0	0	0	0	0	0	1	0	1
Mean Snowfall (in.)	23.8	12.8	6.6	0.6	0.1	trace	0.0	0.0	0.0	0.5	12.7	28.2	85.3
Maximum Snow Depth (in.)	43	31	16	3	trace	trace	0	0	0	3	22	85	85
Days With ≥ 1.0" Snow Depth	25	18	4	0	0	0	0	0	0	0	6	22	75

The period of record for all cooperative weather station data is 1980 – 2009. See User Guide for detailed explanation of data.

Clearbrook *Whatcom County* Elevation: 63 ft. Latitude: 48° 58' N Longitude: 122° 20' W

	JAN	FEB	MAR	APR	MAY	JUN	JUL	AUG	SEP	OCT	NOV	DEC	YEAR
Mean Maximum Temp. (°F)	43.5	47.8	53.3	59.8	65.9	70.5	75.7	76.4	71.1	59.6	48.9	42.4	59.6
Mean Temp. (°F)	38.2	40.8	45.0	49.9	55.6	60.2	63.7	63.7	58.8	50.8	43.0	37.4	50.6
Mean Minimum Temp. (°F)	32.9	33.8	36.6	39.9	45.2	49.9	51.8	50.9	46.5	42.0	37.1	32.3	41.6
Extreme Maximum Temp. (°F)	65	64	76	85	98	93	98	95	95	81	67	65	98
Extreme Minimum Temp. (°F)	6	2	19	27	30	37	39	37	29	19	0	5	0
Days Maximum Temp. ≥ 90°F	0	0	0	0	0	0	1	1	0	0	0	0	2
Days Maximum Temp. ≤ 32°F	3	1	0	0	0	0	0	0	0	0	1	3	8
Days Minimum Temp. ≤ 32°F	14	11	7	3	0	0	0	0	0	4	7	14	60
Days Minimum Temp. ≤ 0°F	0	0	0	0	0	0	0	0	0	0	0	0	0
Heating Degree Days (base 65°F)	824	677	614	447	289	150	68	66	183	433	654	848	5,253
Cooling Degree Days (base 65°F)	0	0	0	0	4	13	36	31	5	0	0	0	89
Mean Precipitation (in.)	5.75	3.65	4.23	3.56	3.26	2.68	1.70	1.63	2.36	4.84	6.82	5.08	45.56
Extreme Maximum Daily Precip. (in.)	2.30	3.09	2.06	1.79	1.68	2.47	1.92	1.96	2.51	2.35	2.81	2.29	3.09
Days With ≥ 0.1" Precipitation	12	9	11	10	8	7	4	4	5	10	14	12	106
Days With ≥ 0.5" Precipitation	4	2	2	2	2	2	1	1	2	3	4	3	28
Days With ≥ 1.0" Precipitation	1	0	0	1	0	0	0	0	0	1	1	1	5
Mean Snowfall (in.)	3.9	1.7	0.6	trace	0.0	0.0	0.0	0.0	0.0	trace	1.3	3.2	10.7
Maximum Snow Depth (in.)	7	4	1	0	0	0	0	0	0	trace	10	*14*	*14*
Days With ≥ 1.0" Snow Depth	1	0	0	0	0	0	0	0	0	0	0	1	2

Clearwater *Jefferson County* Elevation: 80 ft. Latitude: 47° 35' N Longitude: 124° 18' W

	JAN	FEB	MAR	APR	MAY	JUN	JUL	AUG	SEP	OCT	NOV	DEC	YEAR
Mean Maximum Temp. (°F)	46.4	50.1	53.7	58.4	63.1	66.6	70.8	71.8	69.4	60.0	50.7	44.8	58.8
Mean Temp. (°F)	40.8	42.1	45.0	48.3	52.8	56.7	60.3	60.6	57.5	50.9	44.3	39.4	49.9
Mean Minimum Temp. (°F)	35.2	34.0	36.3	38.1	42.5	46.7	49.6	49.3	45.6	41.9	37.9	34.0	40.9
Extreme Maximum Temp. (°F)	63	76	76	85	96	92	95	98	93	84	68	59	98
Extreme Minimum Temp. (°F)	13	7	21	25	28	32	37	36	29	22	11	4	4
Days Maximum Temp. ≥ 90°F	0	0	0	0	0	0	1	0	0	0	0	0	1
Days Maximum Temp. ≤ 32°F	0	0	0	0	0	0	0	0	0	0	0	1	1
Days Minimum Temp. ≤ 32°F	13	13	10	6	1	0	0	0	0	4	8	14	69
Days Minimum Temp. ≤ 0°F	0	0	0	0	0	0	0	0	0	0	0	0	0
Heating Degree Days (base 65°F)	744	642	612	495	372	246	150	138	220	429	614	786	5,448
Cooling Degree Days (base 65°F)	0	0	0	0	1	3	11	8	2	0	0	0	25
Mean Precipitation (in.)	16.26	11.66	12.29	8.51	5.41	3.62	2.36	2.68	4.41	10.63	17.09	14.11	109.03
Extreme Maximum Daily Precip. (in.)	5.71	7.94	5.53	4.40	2.42	2.29	2.65	3.08	4.59	4.25	4.96	4.17	7.94
Days With ≥ 0.1" Precipitation	18	14	17	14	10	8	4	4	6	13	19	17	144
Days With ≥ 0.5" Precipitation	11	8	9	6	4	3	1	2	3	7	12	10	76
Days With ≥ 1.0" Precipitation	6	4	4	2	1	1	1	1	1	4	6	5	36
Mean Snowfall (in.)	trace	0.0	0.0	0.0	0.0	0.0	0.0	0.0	0.0	0.0	0.0	0.4	0.4
Maximum Snow Depth (in.)	0	0	0	0	0	0	0	0	0	0	0	trace	trace
Days With ≥ 1.0" Snow Depth	0	0	0	0	0	0	0	0	0	0	0	0	0

Coulee Dam 1 SW *Grant County* Elevation: 1,700 ft. Latitude: 47° 57' N Longitude: 119° 00' W

	JAN	FEB	MAR	APR	MAY	JUN	JUL	AUG	SEP	OCT	NOV	DEC	YEAR
Mean Maximum Temp. (°F)	33.4	40.3	51.5	61.9	71.0	78.8	87.6	87.1	77.1	61.3	43.7	32.7	60.5
Mean Temp. (°F)	28.2	33.1	41.8	50.1	58.4	65.7	73.2	72.6	63.6	50.8	37.6	28.1	50.3
Mean Minimum Temp. (°F)	23.1	25.9	31.9	38.3	45.8	52.5	58.8	58.1	50.1	40.1	31.6	23.4	40.0
Extreme Maximum Temp. (°F)	61	61	73	85	100	102	107	104	103	84	69	58	107
Extreme Minimum Temp. (°F)	-13	-10	5	21	21	36	40	41	32	7	-10	-13	-13
Days Maximum Temp. ≥ 90°F	0	0	0	0	1	4	14	12	2	0	0	0	33
Days Maximum Temp. ≤ 32°F	13	4	0	0	0	0	0	0	0	0	2	14	33
Days Minimum Temp. ≤ 32°F	27	22	16	6	0	0	0	0	0	4	15	27	117
Days Minimum Temp. ≤ 0°F	1	0	0	0	0	0	0	0	0	0	0	1	2
Heating Degree Days (base 65°F)	1,133	894	713	441	224	72	12	8	106	437	814	1,138	5,992
Cooling Degree Days (base 65°F)	0	0	0	1	25	98	274	251	71	2	0	0	722
Mean Precipitation (in.)	1.07	0.95	0.97	0.87	1.20	0.99	0.61	0.30	0.46	0.65	1.26	1.42	10.75
Extreme Maximum Daily Precip. (in.)	0.70	0.90	0.95	0.81	0.97	2.31	1.20	0.77	1.35	1.36	0.75	0.95	2.31
Days With ≥ 0.1" Precipitation	4	3	3	3	3	3	1	1	1	2	5	5	34
Days With ≥ 0.5" Precipitation	0	0	0	0	1	0	0	0	0	0	0	0	1
Days With ≥ 1.0" Precipitation	0	0	0	0	0	0	0	0	0	0	0	0	0
Mean Snowfall (in.)	*3.2*	1.2	0.1	trace	0.0	0.0	0.0	0.0	0.0	0.0	0.8	*3.8*	*9.1*
Maximum Snow Depth (in.)	*23*	*10*	7	trace	0	*0*	*0*	0	0	0	*7*	*19*	*23*
Days With ≥ 1.0" Snow Depth	*7*	3	1	0	0	0	0	0	0	0	0	*6*	*17*

Coupeville 1 S *Island County* Elevation: 49 ft. Latitude: 48° 12' N Longitude: 122° 42' W

	JAN	FEB	MAR	APR	MAY	JUN	JUL	AUG	SEP	OCT	NOV	DEC	YEAR
Mean Maximum Temp. (°F)	46.2	48.9	53.0	58.0	63.2	67.1	71.6	72.5	67.5	58.4	50.2	45.0	58.5
Mean Temp. (°F)	41.2	42.3	45.6	49.5	54.5	58.2	61.8	62.1	57.7	50.9	44.6	40.1	50.7
Mean Minimum Temp. (°F)	36.1	35.6	38.2	41.0	45.8	49.2	51.9	51.6	47.9	43.4	39.1	35.2	42.9
Extreme Maximum Temp. (°F)	61	69	78	81	85	88	94	90	86	79	67	61	94
Extreme Minimum Temp. (°F)	8	5	14	29	33	40	43	38	34	26	6	6	5
Days Maximum Temp. ≥ 90°F	0	0	0	0	0	0	0	0	0	0	0	0	0
Days Maximum Temp. ≤ 32°F	1	0	0	0	0	0	0	0	0	0	0	1	2
Days Minimum Temp. ≤ 32°F	9	9	5	1	0	0	0	0	0	1	5	10	40
Days Minimum Temp. ≤ 0°F	0	0	0	0	0	0	0	0	0	0	0	0	0
Heating Degree Days (base 65°F)	731	636	594	458	318	201	109	92	211	431	604	764	5,149
Cooling Degree Days (base 65°F)	0	0	0	0	1	4	15	10	1	0	0	0	31
Mean Precipitation (in.)	2.43	1.69	1.90	1.60	1.76	1.34	0.82	0.73	1.21	1.95	3.17	2.44	21.04
Extreme Maximum Daily Precip. (in.)	1.24	0.82	0.91	0.87	1.43	1.19	1.30	1.12	2.25	1.63	1.78	1.96	2.25
Days With ≥ 0.1" Precipitation	8	6	6	5	5	4	3	2	4	6	9	8	66
Days With ≥ 0.5" Precipitation	1	0	0	1	1	0	0	0	0	1	1	1	6
Days With ≥ 1.0" Precipitation	0	0	0	0	0	0	0	0	0	0	0	0	0
Mean Snowfall (in.)	1.7	0.7	0.4	0.0	0.0	0.0	0.0	0.0	0.0	trace	1.0	1.4	5.2
Maximum Snow Depth (in.)	7	3	4	0	0	0	*0*	*0*	0	trace	16	8	*16*
Days With ≥ 1.0" Snow Depth	0	0	0	0	0	0	0	0	0	0	0	0	0

The period of record for all cooperative weather station data is 1980 – 2009. See User Guide for detailed explanation of data.

Cushman Powerhouse 2 *Mason County* Elevation: 21 ft. Latitude: 47° 22' N Longitude: 123° 10' W

	JAN	FEB	MAR	APR	MAY	JUN	JUL	AUG	SEP	OCT	NOV	DEC	YEAR
Mean Maximum Temp. (°F)	45.4	48.6	53.6	59.0	65.9	70.4	76.0	76.4	70.5	59.5	49.8	43.9	59.9
Mean Temp. (°F)	40.2	41.7	45.3	49.4	55.5	59.9	64.5	64.6	59.7	51.5	44.2	39.1	51.3
Mean Minimum Temp. (°F)	34.9	34.7	36.9	39.7	45.0	49.4	52.9	52.8	48.9	43.3	38.4	34.3	42.6
Extreme Maximum Temp. (°F)	63	71	75	83	92	94	96	97	91	82	68	66	97
Extreme Minimum Temp. (°F)	11	14	21	28	31	37	43	39	34	26	13	11	11
Days Maximum Temp. ≥ 90°F	0	0	0	0	0	0	2	0	0	0	0	0	2
Days Maximum Temp. ≤ 32°F	0	0	0	0	0	0	0	0	0	0	0	1	1
Days Minimum Temp. ≤ 32°F	12	11	6	2	0	0	0	0	0	1	5	13	50
Days Minimum Temp. ≤ 0°F	0	0	0	0	0	0	0	0	0	0	0	0	0
Heating Degree Days (base 65°F)	763	653	604	462	292	162	60	53	160	413	618	795	5,035
Cooling Degree Days (base 65°F)	0	0	0	0	4	17	52	48	8	0	0	0	129
Mean Precipitation (in.)	14.39	10.29	9.23	5.80	3.14	2.06	1.09	1.31	2.28	7.91	16.36	15.34	89.20
Extreme Maximum Daily Precip. (in.)	5.73	4.95	7.23	3.72	2.93	3.48	2.24	2.54	4.02	8.30	6.87	7.00	8.30
Days With ≥ 0.1" Precipitation	15	13	14	10	6	5	2	3	4	10	16	15	113
Days With ≥ 0.5" Precipitation	9	7	6	4	2	1	1	1	1	5	10	9	56
Days With ≥ 1.0" Precipitation	5	4	3	1	1	0	0	0	1	3	6	5	29
Mean Snowfall (in.)	1.5	1.8	0.3	0.0	0.0	0.0	0.0	0.0	0.0	0.0	0.2	2.2	6.0
Maximum Snow Depth (in.)	8	18	6	0	0	0	0	0	0	0	5	6	18
Days With ≥ 1.0" Snow Depth	1	0	0	0	0	0	0	0	0	0	0	1	2

Dayton 1 WSW *Columbia County* Elevation: 1,557 ft. Latitude: 46° 19' N Longitude: 118° 00' W

	JAN	FEB	MAR	APR	MAY	JUN	JUL	AUG	SEP	OCT	NOV	DEC	YEAR
Mean Maximum Temp. (°F)	41.1	46.0	54.5	61.2	69.1	77.1	86.8	86.6	77.3	64.0	49.0	39.9	62.7
Mean Temp. (°F)	34.1	37.4	44.5	49.7	56.9	63.9	71.1	70.7	62.3	51.2	40.6	33.1	51.3
Mean Minimum Temp. (°F)	27.1	28.8	34.5	38.1	44.7	50.6	55.4	54.8	47.4	38.2	32.2	26.3	39.8
Extreme Maximum Temp. (°F)	65	74	79	90	101	105	107	110	102	90	77	68	110
Extreme Minimum Temp. (°F)	-13	-17	5	12	21	31	39	38	26	12	-10	-21	-21
Days Maximum Temp. ≥ 90°F	0	0	0	0	1	4	13	12	4	0	0	0	34
Days Maximum Temp. ≤ 32°F	7	3	0	0	0	0	0	0	0	0	2	7	19
Days Minimum Temp. ≤ 32°F	22	19	11	5	1	0	0	0	1	6	15	24	104
Days Minimum Temp. ≤ 0°F	1	0	0	0	0	0	0	0	0	0	0	1	2
Heating Degree Days (base 65°F)	950	773	628	454	268	103	21	22	131	425	725	981	5,481
Cooling Degree Days (base 65°F)	0	0	0	2	24	77	217	207	58	2	0	0	587
Mean Precipitation (in.)	2.33	1.77	2.17	1.69	1.74	1.21	0.47	0.56	0.79	1.59	2.62	2.22	19.16
Extreme Maximum Daily Precip. (in.)	1.46	1.33	1.95	1.30	1.92	1.09	0.49	1.10	1.00	1.10	2.18	1.25	2.18
Days With ≥ 0.1" Precipitation	7	5	6	5	5	4	2	2	2	4	8	7	57
Days With ≥ 0.5" Precipitation	1	1	1	1	1	0	0	0	0	1	1	1	8
Days With ≥ 1.0" Precipitation	0	0	0	0	0	0	0	0	0	0	0	0	0
Mean Snowfall (in.)	6.1	2.7	1.3	0.1	0.0	0.0	0.0	0.0	0.0	0.1	0.8	6.3	17.4
Maximum Snow Depth (in.)	18	8	5	1	0	0	0	0	0	*1*	2	*22*	*22*
Days With ≥ 1.0" Snow Depth	6	3	1	0	0	0	0	0	0	0	1	5	16

Diablo Dam *Whatcom County* Elevation: 891 ft. Latitude: 48° 43' N Longitude: 121° 09' W

	JAN	FEB	MAR	APR	MAY	JUN	JUL	AUG	SEP	OCT	NOV	DEC	YEAR
Mean Maximum Temp. (°F)	38.9	43.3	49.7	57.5	64.9	70.1	77.0	77.9	70.9	57.6	44.5	38.0	57.5
Mean Temp. (°F)	34.2	36.7	41.5	47.5	54.3	59.6	64.9	65.6	59.5	49.3	39.5	33.9	48.9
Mean Minimum Temp. (°F)	29.5	30.1	33.4	37.5	43.7	49.0	52.9	53.2	47.9	41.0	34.6	29.7	40.2
Extreme Maximum Temp. (°F)	58	63	75	90	103	101	104	105	101	87	61	59	105
Extreme Minimum Temp. (°F)	0	1	11	25	29	38	39	43	34	18	6	-2	-2
Days Maximum Temp. ≥ 90°F	0	0	0	0	1	2	4	4	1	0	0	0	12
Days Maximum Temp. ≤ 32°F	4	1	0	0	0	0	0	0	0	0	1	3	9
Days Minimum Temp. ≤ 32°F	20	18	12	4	0	0	0	0	0	2	10	21	87
Days Minimum Temp. ≤ 0°F	0	0	0	0	0	0	0	0	0	0	0	0	0
Heating Degree Days (base 65°F)	948	792	720	518	332	183	75	63	181	481	757	958	6,008
Cooling Degree Days (base 65°F)	0	0	0	0	9	27	80	87	21	0	0	0	224
Mean Precipitation (in.)	12.13	7.50	7.25	4.81	3.08	2.47	1.63	1.67	2.91	8.21	15.10	11.29	78.05
Extreme Maximum Daily Precip. (in.)	4.65	6.10	4.03	3.95	2.06	1.47	2.45	2.21	2.78	7.23	7.32	4.58	7.32
Days With ≥ 0.1" Precipitation	15	11	13	11	8	7	4	4	6	12	17	15	123
Days With ≥ 0.5" Precipitation	8	5	4	3	2	1	1	1	2	5	10	8	50
Days With ≥ 1.0" Precipitation	4	2	2	1	0	0	0	0	1	3	5	4	22
Mean Snowfall (in.)	16.3	9.5	4.0	0.2	0.0	0.0	0.0	0.0	0.0	trace	3.1	15.8	48.9
Maximum Snow Depth (in.)	43	32	15	2	0	0	0	0	0	1	15	36	43
Days With ≥ 1.0" Snow Depth	14	10	3	0	0	0	0	0	0	0	2	11	40

Ephrata Arpt FCWOS *Grant County* Elevation: 1,258 ft. Latitude: 47° 18' N Longitude: 119° 31' W

	JAN	FEB	MAR	APR	MAY	JUN	JUL	AUG	SEP	OCT	NOV	DEC	YEAR
Mean Maximum Temp. (°F)	35.3	42.6	54.2	63.6	73.0	80.3	88.7	87.6	78.3	62.9	45.7	34.2	62.2
Mean Temp. (°F)	29.1	34.6	43.6	51.3	60.2	67.5	74.8	73.6	64.5	51.2	38.0	28.3	51.4
Mean Minimum Temp. (°F)	22.9	26.5	32.9	38.9	47.4	54.6	60.9	59.5	50.6	39.4	30.1	22.4	40.5
Extreme Maximum Temp. (°F)	59	64	75	90	101	104	108	106	106	86	72	60	108
Extreme Minimum Temp. (°F)	-16	-19	5	21	28	38	40	37	28	8	-15	-21	-21
Days Maximum Temp. ≥ 90°F	0	0	0	0	2	5	15	13	3	0	0	0	38
Days Maximum Temp. ≤ 32°F	11	4	0	0	0	0	0	0	0	0	2	12	29
Days Minimum Temp. ≤ 32°F	27	22	15	6	1	0	0	0	0	5	19	28	123
Days Minimum Temp. ≤ 0°F	1	1	0	0	0	0	0	0	0	0	0	1	3
Heating Degree Days (base 65°F)	1,106	854	657	407	185	49	7	6	93	425	804	1,130	5,723
Cooling Degree Days (base 65°F)	0	0	0	2	44	129	319	279	85	3	0	0	861
Mean Precipitation (in.)	0.88	0.80	0.67	0.48	0.63	0.57	0.39	0.19	0.35	0.49	1.03	1.20	7.68
Extreme Maximum Daily Precip. (in.)	0.59	0.90	0.85	0.58	0.80	0.95	1.74	0.93	0.63	0.92	0.82	0.76	1.74
Days With ≥ 0.1" Precipitation	4	3	2	2	2	2	1	1	1	2	3	4	27
Days With ≥ 0.5" Precipitation	0	0	0	0	0	0	0	0	0	0	0	0	0
Days With ≥ 1.0" Precipitation	0	0	0	0	0	0	0	0	0	0	0	0	0
Mean Snowfall (in.)	*5.3*	*3.3*	*0.7*	*0.1*	*0.0*	na	*0.0*	*0.0*	na	na	na	na	na
Maximum Snow Depth (in.)	*27*	*14*	*6*	*trace*	*0*	na	*0*	*0*	*0*	na	na	na	na
Days With ≥ 1.0" Snow Depth	*16*	*9*	*1*	*0*	*0*	na	*0*	*0*	*0*	na	na	na	na

Everett *Snohomish County* Elevation: 60 ft. Latitude: 47° 59' N Longitude: 122° 11' W

	JAN	FEB	MAR	APR	MAY	JUN	JUL	AUG	SEP	OCT	NOV	DEC	YEAR
Mean Maximum Temp. (°F)	46.9	49.8	53.9	58.9	64.2	68.9	73.4	74.6	69.1	60.1	51.5	45.4	59.7
Mean Temp. (°F)	40.7	42.1	45.7	50.0	55.4	60.2	64.0	64.5	59.0	51.4	44.5	39.5	51.4
Mean Minimum Temp. (°F)	34.5	34.4	37.5	41.1	46.6	51.4	54.5	54.3	48.9	42.7	37.5	33.6	43.1
Extreme Maximum Temp. (°F)	67	74	82	85	93	93	91	92	89	83	74	66	93
Extreme Minimum Temp. (°F)	9	6	18	28	34	40	44	40	31	25	0	6	0
Days Maximum Temp. ≥ 90°F	0	0	0	0	0	0	0	0	0	0	0	0	0
Days Maximum Temp. ≤ 32°F	0	0	0	0	0	0	0	0	0	0	0	1	1
Days Minimum Temp. ≤ 32°F	11	11	6	1	0	0	0	0	0	2	7	13	51
Days Minimum Temp. ≤ 0°F	0	0	0	0	0	0	0	0	0	0	0	0	0
Heating Degree Days (base 65°F)	746	640	591	443	292	150	66	54	179	414	606	784	4,965
Cooling Degree Days (base 65°F)	0	0	0	0	2	12	42	45	5	0	0	0	106
Mean Precipitation (in.)	4.43	3.09	3.61	3.00	2.55	2.37	1.18	1.14	1.77	3.52	5.53	5.01	37.20
Extreme Maximum Daily Precip. (in.)	2.33	1.64	1.76	1.23	1.11	1.72	1.16	1.51	1.63	1.95	***3.62***	2.52	***3.62***
Days With ≥ 0.1" Precipitation	11	9	11	8	7	6	3	3	5	9	11	11	94
Days With ≥ 0.5" Precipitation	3	1	2	2	1	1	1	1	1	2	3	3	21
Days With ≥ 1.0" Precipitation	0	0	0	0	0	0	0	0	0	0	1	1	2
Mean Snowfall (in.)	0.2	0.4	0.0	0.1	0.0	0.0	0.0	0.0	0.0	0.0	0.2	0.1	1.0
Maximum Snow Depth (in.)	0	0	0	0	0	0	0	0	0	0	0	10	10
Days With ≥ 1.0" Snow Depth	0	0	0	0	0	0	0	0	0	0	0	0	0

Kennewick *Benton County* Elevation: 390 ft. Latitude: 46° 13' N Longitude: 119° 06' W

	JAN	FEB	MAR	APR	MAY	JUN	JUL	AUG	SEP	OCT	NOV	DEC	YEAR
Mean Maximum Temp. (°F)	41.5	48.0	58.5	66.7	74.9	82.0	90.5	89.5	80.2	65.9	50.9	40.2	65.7
Mean Temp. (°F)	35.1	39.2	47.3	54.4	62.1	68.9	76.0	74.9	66.0	53.7	43.1	34.4	54.6
Mean Minimum Temp. (°F)	28.7	30.3	36.1	42.0	49.2	55.8	61.4	60.4	51.9	41.5	35.3	28.5	43.4
Extreme Maximum Temp. (°F)	69	74	80	91	104	107	109	110	100	89	79	69	110
Extreme Minimum Temp. (°F)	-11	-11	13	25	30	40	45	45	30	18	-8	-7	-11
Days Maximum Temp. ≥ 90°F	0	0	0	0	3	6	18	16	4	0	0	0	47
Days Maximum Temp. ≤ 32°F	6	2	0	0	0	0	0	0	0	0	1	7	16
Days Minimum Temp. ≤ 32°F	20	17	8	1	0	0	0	0	0	3	10	20	79
Days Minimum Temp. ≤ 0°F	0	0	0	0	0	0	0	0	0	0	0	0	0
Heating Degree Days (base 65°F)	921	724	541	314	137	28	2	2	59	345	650	942	4,665
Cooling Degree Days (base 65°F)	0	0	0	3	54	153	350	317	96	3	0	0	976
Mean Precipitation (in.)	1.09	0.80	0.74	0.56	0.65	0.47	0.21	0.19	0.30	0.61	0.96	1.14	7.72
Extreme Maximum Daily Precip. (in.)	0.92	0.57	0.62	0.70	1.18	0.61	0.85	0.55	0.81	1.21	1.33	0.85	1.33
Days With ≥ 0.1" Precipitation	4	3	3	2	2	2	1	1	1	2	3	4	28
Days With ≥ 0.5" Precipitation	0	0	0	0	0	0	0	0	0	0	0	0	0
Days With ≥ 1.0" Precipitation	0	0	0	0	0	0	0	0	0	0	0	0	0
Mean Snowfall (in.)	***1.3***	0.1	0.0	0.0	0.0	0.0	0.0	0.0	0.0	0.0	0.1	***0.6***	***2.1***
Maximum Snow Depth (in.)	na	***1***	***1***	***0***	***0***	***0***	***0***	***0***	***0***	***0***	***trace***	na	na
Days With ≥ 1.0" Snow Depth	na	0	0	0	0	0	0	0	0	0	0	***1***	na

Lacrosse *Whitman County* Elevation: 1,450 ft. Latitude: 46° 49' N Longitude: 117° 53' W

	JAN	FEB	MAR	APR	MAY	JUN	JUL	AUG	SEP	OCT	NOV	DEC	YEAR
Mean Maximum Temp. (°F)	38.7	45.4	54.1	62.8	71.6	79.7	89.4	88.4	78.3	63.6	47.6	36.8	63.0
Mean Temp. (°F)	31.9	36.2	42.7	49.3	56.5	63.5	70.6	69.8	60.7	49.1	38.9	30.4	50.0
Mean Minimum Temp. (°F)	25.0	27.1	31.3	35.7	41.4	47.3	52.0	51.3	43.2	34.6	30.1	23.8	36.9
Extreme Maximum Temp. (°F)	61	70	77	94	100	104	108	109	103	92	76	62	109
Extreme Minimum Temp. (°F)	-30	-24	0	17	21	26	31	28	19	3	-17	-23	-30
Days Maximum Temp. ≥ 90°F	0	0	0	0	1	4	16	14	4	0	0	0	39
Days Maximum Temp. ≤ 32°F	7	2	0	0	0	0	0	0	0	0	2	9	20
Days Minimum Temp. ≤ 32°F	24	21	17	10	4	0	0	0	2	11	17	26	132
Days Minimum Temp. ≤ 0°F	1	1	0	0	0	0	0	0	0	0	0	1	3
Heating Degree Days (base 65°F)	1,019	806	683	466	272	100	19	21	159	486	776	1,067	5,874
Cooling Degree Days (base 65°F)	0	0	0	1	16	61	200	178	37	1	0	0	494
Mean Precipitation (in.)	1.89	1.41	1.64	1.32	1.25	0.92	0.36	0.38	0.55	1.03	1.97	2.22	14.94
Extreme Maximum Daily Precip. (in.)	0.95	0.85	0.74	1.47	1.43	0.76	0.52	0.51	0.75	1.35	1.43	0.81	1.47
Days With ≥ 0.1" Precipitation	6	5	5	4	4	3	1	1	2	3	7	7	48
Days With ≥ 0.5" Precipitation	1	0	0	1	1	0	0	0	0	0	1	1	5
Days With ≥ 1.0" Precipitation	0	0	0	0	0	0	0	0	0	0	0	0	0
Mean Snowfall (in.)	5.8	2.4	0.9	0.1	trace	0.0	0.0	0.0	0.0	trace	1.4	6.3	16.9
Maximum Snow Depth (in.)	15	9	4	trace	trace	0	0	0	0	trace	7	16	16
Days With ≥ 1.0" Snow Depth	8	3	0	0	0	0	0	0	0	0	1	8	20

Longview *Cowlitz County* Elevation: 12 ft. Latitude: 46° 09' N Longitude: 122° 55' W

	JAN	FEB	MAR	APR	MAY	JUN	JUL	AUG	SEP	OCT	NOV	DEC	YEAR
Mean Maximum Temp. (°F)	46.8	51.1	56.2	61.2	67.5	71.8	77.9	78.7	74.2	63.2	52.2	45.5	62.2
Mean Temp. (°F)	40.9	43.1	47.1	50.8	56.4	60.7	65.7	65.9	61.9	53.7	45.7	40.1	52.7
Mean Minimum Temp. (°F)	34.9	35.0	37.9	40.3	45.2	49.6	53.4	53.0	49.4	44.2	39.3	34.6	43.1
Extreme Maximum Temp. (°F)	62	72	80	90	99	99	105	108	100	90	72	62	108
Extreme Minimum Temp. (°F)	9	5	23	28	31	37	41	41	35	24	12	5	5
Days Maximum Temp. ≥ 90°F	0	0	0	0	0	1	3	2	1	0	0	0	7
Days Maximum Temp. ≤ 32°F	0	0	0	0	0	0	0	0	0	0	0	1	1
Days Minimum Temp. ≤ 32°F	11	10	5	2	0	0	0	0	0	1	5	11	45
Days Minimum Temp. ≤ 0°F	0	0	0	0	0	0	0	0	0	0	0	0	0
Heating Degree Days (base 65°F)	741	613	548	420	270	147	48	40	118	344	570	766	4,625
Cooling Degree Days (base 65°F)	0	0	0	1	10	24	77	74	30	1	0	0	217
Mean Precipitation (in.)	6.63	5.01	4.74	3.76	2.88	2.17	0.86	1.17	1.89	3.86	7.76	6.84	47.57
Extreme Maximum Daily Precip. (in.)	3.45	3.78	2.01	2.42	1.31	1.18	1.15	1.97	1.39	2.32	4.04	2.83	4.04
Days With ≥ 0.1" Precipitation	14	12	14	11	8	6	3	3	5	9	15	14	114
Days With ≥ 0.5" Precipitation	4	3	2	2	1	1	0	1	1	2	5	5	27
Days With ≥ 1.0" Precipitation	1	1	0	0	0	0	0	0	0	0	1	1	4
Mean Snowfall (in.)	0.8	0.5	trace	0.0	0.0	0.0	0.0	0.0	0.0	0.0	0.1	0.3	1.7
Maximum Snow Depth (in.)	18	3	trace	0	0	0	0	0	0	0	2	4	18
Days With ≥ 1.0" Snow Depth	1	1	0	0	0	0	0	0	0	0	0	1	3

The period of record for all cooperative weather station data is 1980 – 2009. See User Guide for detailed explanation of data.

Mazama *Okanogan County* Elevation: 2,169 ft. Latitude: 48° 37' N Longitude: 120° 27' W

	JAN	FEB	MAR	APR	MAY	JUN	JUL	AUG	SEP	OCT	NOV	DEC	YEAR
Mean Maximum Temp. (°F)	29.7	36.5	46.9	58.4	67.2	74.2	82.5	82.8	73.5	56.6	37.7	27.2	56.1
Mean Temp. (°F)	22.9	27.8	36.5	45.3	53.6	60.7	67.3	67.3	58.3	44.7	31.4	21.0	44.7
Mean Minimum Temp. (°F)	16.1	19.1	26.0	32.1	39.9	47.1	52.2	51.7	43.1	32.7	25.0	14.7	33.3
Extreme Maximum Temp. (°F)	58	55	74	84	97	98	103	102	101	84	65	46	103
Extreme Minimum Temp. (°F)	-27	-17	-5	12	25	31	28	32	22	8	-14	-30	-30
Days Maximum Temp. ≥ 90°F	0	0	0	0	0	2	8	7	1	0	0	0	18
Days Maximum Temp. ≤ 32°F	19	7	1	0	0	0	0	0	0	0	6	23	56
Days Minimum Temp. ≤ 32°F	31	28	27	17	5	0	0	0	2	16	25	31	182
Days Minimum Temp. ≤ 0°F	3	2	0	0	0	0	0	0	0	0	1	5	11
Heating Degree Days (base 65°F)	1,297	1,043	877	586	353	154	46	45	216	623	1,001	1,358	7,599
Cooling Degree Days (base 65°F)	0	0	0	0	6	30	125	122	22	0	0	0	305
Mean Precipitation (in.)	3.70	2.28	1.72	1.07	1.06	1.11	0.82	0.57	0.69	1.78	3.64	3.75	22.19
Extreme Maximum Daily Precip. (in.)	3.07	2.14	1.14	1.58	1.23	1.52	1.14	0.88	0.77	3.23	2.74	2.95	3.23
Days With ≥ 0.1" Precipitation	9	6	5	3	3	3	2	2	2	4	8	9	56
Days With ≥ 0.5" Precipitation	2	1	1	0	0	1	0	0	0	1	2	2	10
Days With ≥ 1.0" Precipitation	1	0	0	0	0	0	0	0	0	0	1	1	3
Mean Snowfall (in.)	33.6	17.4	7.2	0.3	trace	0.0	0.0	0.0	0.0	2.1	16.4	37.2	114.2
Maximum Snow Depth (in.)	62	61	60	31	trace	0	0	0	0	14	24	62	62
Days With ≥ 1.0" Snow Depth	31	28	27	6	0	0	0	0	0	1	14	30	137

McMillin Reservoir *Pierce County* Elevation: 579 ft. Latitude: 47° 08' N Longitude: 122° 16' W

	JAN	FEB	MAR	APR	MAY	JUN	JUL	AUG	SEP	OCT	NOV	DEC	YEAR
Mean Maximum Temp. (°F)	45.6	48.3	52.8	57.7	63.9	69.0	75.1	75.8	69.8	59.3	50.2	44.4	59.3
Mean Temp. (°F)	39.3	40.7	44.4	48.3	54.0	58.9	63.6	63.9	58.6	50.3	43.4	38.3	50.3
Mean Minimum Temp. (°F)	32.9	33.0	35.9	38.8	44.2	48.7	52.0	51.9	47.3	41.3	36.6	32.2	41.2
Extreme Maximum Temp. (°F)	66	67	79	83	92	95	102	100	95	86	72	66	102
Extreme Minimum Temp. (°F)	5	4	13	25	30	36	40	37	30	23	2	-1	-1
Days Maximum Temp. ≥ 90°F	0	0	0	0	0	0	1	1	0	0	0	0	2
Days Maximum Temp. ≤ 32°F	1	0	0	0	0	0	0	0	0	0	0	1	2
Days Minimum Temp. ≤ 32°F	14	13	9	3	0	0	0	0	0	3	8	15	65
Days Minimum Temp. ≤ 0°F	0	0	0	0	0	0	0	0	0	0	0	0	0
Heating Degree Days (base 65°F)	790	680	632	495	337	192	84	71	194	448	641	822	5,386
Cooling Degree Days (base 65°F)	0	0	0	0	3	15	47	43	8	0	0	0	116
Mean Precipitation (in.)	5.82	4.24	4.50	3.56	2.65	2.29	1.02	0.98	1.55	3.68	7.04	5.74	43.07
Extreme Maximum Daily Precip. (in.)	2.50	2.72	2.15	2.60	1.19	1.84	1.30	1.95	1.24	3.07	3.59	2.09	3.59
Days With ≥ 0.1" Precipitation	13	10	13	10	8	6	3	3	5	9	15	13	108
Days With ≥ 0.5" Precipitation	4	3	2	1	1	1	1	0	1	2	5	4	25
Days With ≥ 1.0" Precipitation	1	1	0	0	0	0	0	0	0	0	1	1	4
Mean Snowfall (in.)	1.0	1.1	0.8	0.1	0.0	0.0	0.0	0.0	0.0	0.0	1.1	1.6	5.7
Maximum Snow Depth (in.)	14	7	11	trace	0	0	0	0	0	0	9	7	14
Days With ≥ 1.0" Snow Depth	2	1	0	0	0	0	0	0	0	0	1	2	6

McNary Dam *Benton County* Elevation: 360 ft. Latitude: 45° 57' N Longitude: 119° 18' W

	JAN	FEB	MAR	APR	MAY	JUN	JUL	AUG	SEP	OCT	NOV	DEC	YEAR
Mean Maximum Temp. (°F)	40.8	46.4	56.5	64.4	72.6	79.5	88.4	87.4	78.1	65.0	50.2	40.4	64.1
Mean Temp. (°F)	35.2	38.6	46.4	53.1	60.5	67.1	74.7	74.0	65.5	54.2	43.1	35.2	54.0
Mean Minimum Temp. (°F)	29.7	30.7	36.2	41.6	48.3	54.5	60.8	60.5	52.8	43.3	36.0	30.0	43.7
Extreme Maximum Temp. (°F)	67	70	78	88	104	104	108	106	99	87	75	68	108
Extreme Minimum Temp. (°F)	-4	-7	12	29	34	40	48	47	34	20	1	-9	-9
Days Maximum Temp. ≥ 90°F	0	0	0	0	1	4	15	12	2	0	0	0	34
Days Maximum Temp. ≤ 32°F	5	2	0	0	0	0	0	0	0	0	1	6	14
Days Minimum Temp. ≤ 32°F	18	15	6	1	0	0	0	0	0	2	8	19	69
Days Minimum Temp. ≤ 0°F	0	0	0	0	0	0	0	0	0	0	0	0	0
Heating Degree Days (base 65°F)	918	742	571	350	166	42	3	2	63	330	650	916	4,753
Cooling Degree Days (base 65°F)	0	0	0	1	34	112	309	289	85	3	0	0	833
Mean Precipitation (in.)	1.05	0.79	0.76	0.59	0.70	0.54	0.19	0.25	0.34	0.60	1.12	1.06	7.99
Extreme Maximum Daily Precip. (in.)	0.60	0.70	0.50	1.13	1.01	0.65	0.62	0.62	0.83	1.00	1.68	0.55	1.68
Days With ≥ 0.1" Precipitation	4	3	3	2	3	2	1	1	1	2	4	4	30
Days With ≥ 0.5" Precipitation	0	0	0	0	0	0	0	0	0	0	0	0	0
Days With ≥ 1.0" Precipitation	0	0	0	0	0	0	0	0	0	0	0	0	0
Mean Snowfall (in.)	***0.4***	***0.5***	trace	0.0	0.0	0.0	0.0	0.0	0.0	0.0	trace	***0.2***	***1.1***
Maximum Snow Depth (in.)	***12***	na	***5***	***0***	***0***	***0***	***0***	***0***	***0***	***0***	***trace***	na	na
Days With ≥ 1.0" Snow Depth	***1***	***0***	0	0	0	0	0	0	0	0	0	***0***	***1***

Monroe *Snohomish County* Elevation: 120 ft. Latitude: 47° 51' N Longitude: 121° 59' W

	JAN	FEB	MAR	APR	MAY	JUN	JUL	AUG	SEP	OCT	NOV	DEC	YEAR
Mean Maximum Temp. (°F)	46.3	50.1	54.6	59.9	65.9	***70.5***	76.2	77.0	71.0	60.2	50.2	44.1	***60.5***
Mean Temp. (°F)	40.1	42.2	46.0	50.3	56.0	***60.4***	64.8	65.2	60.0	51.4	44.0	38.6	***51.6***
Mean Minimum Temp. (°F)	34.0	34.1	37.3	40.6	46.1	***50.3***	53.4	53.4	48.9	42.5	37.8	33.0	***42.6***
Extreme Maximum Temp. (°F)	67	75	79	84	91	94	102	97	94	88	77	62	102
Extreme Minimum Temp. (°F)	6	1	12	26	31	38	43	41	32	0	1	1	0
Days Maximum Temp. ≥ 90°F	0	0	0	0	0	0	1	1	0	0	0	0	2
Days Maximum Temp. ≤ 32°F	1	0	0	0	0	0	0	0	0	0	0	1	2
Days Minimum Temp. ≤ 32°F	12	11	7	2	0	0	0	0	0	2	7	14	55
Days Minimum Temp. ≤ 0°F	0	0	0	0	0	0	0	0	0	0	0	0	0
Heating Degree Days (base 65°F)	764	639	582	435	276	***145***	53	42	154	415	623	812	***4,940***
Cooling Degree Days (base 65°F)	0	0	0	0	3	***15***	52	56	11	0	0	0	***137***
Mean Precipitation (in.)	6.10	4.06	4.84	3.75	3.23	2.61	1.33	1.42	2.49	4.55	7.62	6.44	48.44
Extreme Maximum Daily Precip. (in.)	3.92	2.55	1.75	1.89	1.58	2.55	1.26	1.94	2.03	3.12	2.40	3.94	3.94
Days With ≥ 0.1" Precipitation	14	11	13	10	9	7	3	4	6	10	15	14	116
Days With ≥ 0.5" Precipitation	4	2	3	2	2	1	1	1	2	3	6	4	31
Days With ≥ 1.0" Precipitation	1	0	0	0	0	0	0	0	0	1	2	1	5
Mean Snowfall (in.)	0.7	0.7	0.3	trace	0.0	0.0	0.0	0.0	0.0	0.0	0.6	1.9	4.2
Maximum Snow Depth (in.)	6	5	4	trace	0	0	0	0	0	0	8	22	22
Days With ≥ 1.0" Snow Depth	1	1	0	0	0	0	0	0	0	0	1	1	4

The period of record for all cooperative weather station data is 1980 – 2009. See User Guide for detailed explanation of data.

Northport *Stevens County* Elevation: 1,350 ft. Latitude: 48° 55' N Longitude: 117° 47' W

	JAN	FEB	MAR	APR	MAY	JUN	JUL	AUG	SEP	OCT	NOV	DEC	YEAR
Mean Maximum Temp. (°F)	33.5	40.2	52.0	63.0	72.3	78.7	86.8	87.0	76.4	58.6	41.9	32.8	60.3
Mean Temp. (°F)	28.0	32.1	40.6	48.7	57.0	63.3	69.4	68.9	59.9	46.8	35.5	27.6	48.1
Mean Minimum Temp. (°F)	22.5	24.1	29.1	34.5	41.6	47.8	51.7	50.7	43.3	35.0	29.1	22.4	36.0
Extreme Maximum Temp. (°F)	54	60	76	90	102	101	105	104	100	81	64	58	105
Extreme Minimum Temp. (°F)	-18	-11	-3	17	20	26	30	35	24	9	-11	-17	-18
Days Maximum Temp. ≥ 90°F	0	0	0	0	2	4	13	13	2	0	0	0	34
Days Maximum Temp. ≤ 32°F	11	4	0	0	0	0	0	0	0	0	2	13	30
Days Minimum Temp. ≤ 32°F	28	24	22	12	3	0	0	0	2	12	19	28	150
Days Minimum Temp. ≤ 0°F	1	0	0	0	0	0	0	0	0	0	0	1	2
Heating Degree Days (base 65°F)	1,139	923	750	480	256	95	21	24	172	557	879	1,152	6,448
Cooling Degree Days (base 65°F)	0	0	0	0	14	50	164	151	25	0	0	0	404
Mean Precipitation (in.)	2.04	1.35	1.65	1.62	2.23	2.39	1.38	1.06	1.14	1.29	2.12	2.45	20.72
Extreme Maximum Daily Precip. (in.)	1.90	0.88	1.41	0.97	2.10	2.49	1.76	1.48	1.23	1.05	1.28	1.10	2.49
Days With ≥ 0.1" Precipitation	7	5	6	5	6	6	4	3	3	5	7	8	65
Days With ≥ 0.5" Precipitation	1	0	0	0	1	1	1	0	1	0	1	1	7
Days With ≥ 1.0" Precipitation	0	0	0	0	0	0	0	0	0	0	0	0	0
Mean Snowfall (in.)	14.2	6.2	1.4	0.1	0.0	0.0	0.0	0.0	0.0	trace	5.9	18.2	46.0
Maximum Snow Depth (in.)	28	25	17	1	0	0	0	0	0	trace	15	31	31
Days With ≥ 1.0" Snow Depth	27	20	6	0	0	0	0	0	0	0	5	23	81

Palmer 3 ESE *King County* Elevation: 919 ft. Latitude: 47° 18' N Longitude: 121° 51' W

	JAN	FEB	MAR	APR	MAY	JUN	JUL	AUG	SEP	OCT	NOV	DEC	YEAR
Mean Maximum Temp. (°F)	44.0	47.3	51.4	56.7	62.7	67.5	73.8	74.4	69.1	58.9	48.4	42.8	58.1
Mean Temp. (°F)	38.6	40.4	43.5	47.4	53.0	57.6	62.5	63.1	58.6	50.5	42.6	37.5	49.6
Mean Minimum Temp. (°F)	33.1	33.4	35.5	38.0	43.2	47.6	51.5	51.8	48.0	42.0	36.7	32.2	41.1
Extreme Maximum Temp. (°F)	61	68	75	85	100	95	98	99	97	90	68	62	100
Extreme Minimum Temp. (°F)	8	-3	15	28	31	35	39	42	32	23	9	4	-3
Days Maximum Temp. ≥ 90°F	0	0	0	0	0	0	1	1	0	0	0	0	2
Days Maximum Temp. ≤ 32°F	1	1	0	0	0	0	0	0	0	0	1	2	5
Days Minimum Temp. ≤ 32°F	13	12	8	3	0	0	0	0	0	1	6	15	58
Days Minimum Temp. ≤ 0°F	0	0	0	0	0	0	0	0	0	0	0	0	0
Heating Degree Days (base 65°F)	812	690	661	522	372	233	111	94	199	444	665	845	5,648
Cooling Degree Days (base 65°F)	0	0	0	0	6	16	41	42	13	1	0	0	119
Mean Precipitation (in.)	10.99	7.96	9.11	7.35	6.16	5.29	2.58	2.61	3.98	7.08	12.61	9.67	85.39
Extreme Maximum Daily Precip. (in.)	5.30	3.88	3.20	3.15	2.00	2.34	2.07	2.30	3.25	5.87	8.10	2.87	8.10
Days With ≥ 0.1" Precipitation	16	13	17	15	12	10	5	5	8	12	18	16	147
Days With ≥ 0.5" Precipitation	8	6	7	5	4	4	2	2	3	5	9	7	62
Days With ≥ 1.0" Precipitation	3	2	2	1	2	1	1	1	1	2	4	3	23
Mean Snowfall (in.)	5.8	4.1	2.1	0.4	0.0	0.0	0.0	0.0	0.0	trace	1.3	4.4	18.1
Maximum Snow Depth (in.)	26	18	14	1	0	0	0	0	0	1	21	19	26
Days With ≥ 1.0" Snow Depth	5	3	1	0	0	0	0	0	0	0	1	4	14

Port Angeles *Clallam County* Elevation: 89 ft. Latitude: 48° 07' N Longitude: 123° 26' W

	JAN	FEB	MAR	APR	MAY	JUN	JUL	AUG	SEP	OCT	NOV	DEC	YEAR
Mean Maximum Temp. (°F)	46.1	47.7	50.9	55.5	60.6	64.7	68.4	68.8	65.5	57.0	49.6	45.5	56.7
Mean Temp. (°F)	40.9	41.8	44.4	48.3	53.4	57.4	60.6	60.7	57.4	50.5	44.2	40.5	50.0
Mean Minimum Temp. (°F)	35.7	35.9	37.9	41.1	46.1	50.0	52.8	52.5	49.3	43.8	38.7	35.4	43.3
Extreme Maximum Temp. (°F)	65	62	68	82	86	90	91	94	84	73	65	63	94
Extreme Minimum Temp. (°F)	10	10	20	26	30	36	40	40	35	29	6	12	6
Days Maximum Temp. ≥ 90°F	0	0	0	0	0	0	0	0	0	0	0	0	0
Days Maximum Temp. ≤ 32°F	0	0	0	0	0	0	0	0	0	0	0	1	1
Days Minimum Temp. ≤ 32°F	9	7	4	1	0	0	0	0	0	1	4	9	35
Days Minimum Temp. ≤ 0°F	0	0	0	0	0	0	0	0	0	0	0	0	0
Heating Degree Days (base 65°F)	739	649	631	493	355	228	144	138	224	444	618	753	5,416
Cooling Degree Days (base 65°F)	0	0	0	0	0	1	7	14	10	3	0	0	35
Mean Precipitation (in.)	3.88	2.44	2.21	1.43	1.08	0.93	0.56	0.65	0.94	2.66	4.57	4.22	25.57
Extreme Maximum Daily Precip. (in.)	3.64	1.57	1.50	1.58	1.22	0.87	1.10	1.22	1.20	2.38	2.47	2.01	3.64
Days With ≥ 0.1" Precipitation	9	6	6	4	3	3	2	2	2	7	10	9	63
Days With ≥ 0.5" Precipitation	2	1	1	1	0	0	0	0	0	2	3	3	13
Days With ≥ 1.0" Precipitation	1	0	0	0	0	0	0	0	0	0	1	1	3
Mean Snowfall (in.)	0.2	0.0	0.0	0.0	0.0	0.0	0.0	0.0	0.0	0.0	0.0	0.2	0.4
Maximum Snow Depth (in.)	***0***	0	0	0	***0***	***0***	***0***	***0***	***0***	***0***	6	***11***	***11***
Days With ≥ 1.0" Snow Depth	***0***	0	0	0	0	0	0	0	0	0	0	0	***0***

Prosser *Benton County* Elevation: 830 ft. Latitude: 46° 12' N Longitude: 119° 45' W

	JAN	FEB	MAR	APR	MAY	JUN	JUL	AUG	SEP	OCT	NOV	DEC	YEAR
Mean Maximum Temp. (°F)	39.9	***46.3***	***57.5***	***65.3***	73.7	80.4	***89.1***	88.5	***78.4***	65.4	49.5	38.2	***64.4***
Mean Temp. (°F)	33.0	***37.3***	***46.0***	***52.2***	60.0	66.3	***73.1***	72.0	***63.1***	52.1	40.5	31.7	***52.3***
Mean Minimum Temp. (°F)	26.1	***28.3***	***34.5***	***39.0***	46.3	52.1	***56.9***	55.5	***47.8***	38.9	31.5	25.2	***40.2***
Extreme Maximum Temp. (°F)	66	***69***	***78***	***88***	100	104	***111***	106	***99***	***85***	76	***66***	***111***
Extreme Minimum Temp. (°F)	-8	***-3***	***13***	***24***	27	35	***40***	36	***21***	***14***	-7	***-14***	***-14***
Days Maximum Temp. ≥ 90°F	0	***0***	***0***	***0***	2	5	***16***	15	***3***	0	0	0	***41***
Days Maximum Temp. ≤ 32°F	7	***3***	***0***	***0***	0	0	***0***	0	***0***	0	1	9	***20***
Days Minimum Temp. ≤ 32°F	24	***20***	***12***	***5***	0	0	***0***	0	***1***	6	17	25	***110***
Days Minimum Temp. ≤ 0°F	0	***0***	***0***	***0***	0	0	***0***	0	***0***	0	0	0	***0***
Heating Degree Days (base 65°F)	983	***776***	***580***	***380***	186	63	***12***	11	***112***	394	729	1,024	***5,250***
Cooling Degree Days (base 65°F)	0	***0***	***0***	***2***	40	108	***269***	235	***62***	2	0	0	***718***
Mean Precipitation (in.)	1.08	***0.80***	***0.73***	***0.63***	0.65	0.65	***0.18***	0.26	***0.44***	0.65	0.98	1.28	***8.33***
Extreme Maximum Daily Precip. (in.)	***0.71***	***0.55***	***0.61***	na	0.75	0.86	***0.43***	***0.78***	***0.98***	***1.09***	0.60	***0.70***	na
Days With ≥ 0.1" Precipitation	4	***3***	***2***	***2***	2	2	***1***	1	***1***	2	3	4	***27***
Days With ≥ 0.5" Precipitation	0	***0***	***0***	***0***	0	0	***0***	0	***0***	0	0	0	***0***
Days With ≥ 1.0" Precipitation	0	***0***	***0***	***0***	0	0	***0***	0	***0***	0	0	0	***0***
Mean Snowfall (in.)	***0.9***	***0.2***	***trace***	***0.0***	0.0	0.0	***0.0***	0.0	***0.0***	0.0	0.3	***1.6***	***3.0***
Maximum Snow Depth (in.)	***12***	na	na	na	***0***	***0***	na	***0***	na	na	***0***	na	na
Days With ≥ 1.0" Snow Depth	***2***	***0***	***0***	***0***	0	0	***0***	0	***0***	0	0	***3***	***5***

The period of record for all cooperative weather station data is 1980 – 2009. See User Guide for detailed explanation of data.

Republic *Ferry County* Elevation: 2,609 ft. Latitude: 48° 39' N Longitude: 118° 44' W

	JAN	FEB	MAR	APR	MAY	JUN	JUL	AUG	SEP	OCT	NOV	DEC	YEAR
Mean Maximum Temp. (°F)	30.4	37.9	48.0	57.9	66.5	72.9	81.6	81.7	72.2	56.4	38.5	28.4	56.0
Mean Temp. (°F)	24.1	28.9	37.0	44.4	52.3	58.4	64.7	64.1	55.6	43.6	31.7	22.5	43.9
Mean Minimum Temp. (°F)	17.7	19.9	25.9	30.8	38.0	43.8	47.7	46.5	38.9	30.7	24.9	16.5	31.8
Extreme Maximum Temp. (°F)	49	58	72	86	96	100	103	102	97	86	62	53	103
Extreme Minimum Temp. (°F)	-25	-18	-6	14	20	26	32	31	19	1	-20	-27	-27
Days Maximum Temp. ≥ 90°F	0	0	0	0	0	1	6	6	1	0	0	0	14
Days Maximum Temp. ≤ 32°F	16	6	1	0	0	0	0	0	0	0	6	21	50
Days Minimum Temp. ≤ 32°F	30	26	26	19	7	0	0	0	5	18	24	30	185
Days Minimum Temp. ≤ 0°F	3	2	0	0	0	0	0	0	0	0	1	3	9
Heating Degree Days (base 65°F)	1,262	1,014	861	611	391	206	75	84	282	658	992	1,312	7,748
Cooling Degree Days (base 65°F)	0	0	0	0	3	14	72	64	6	0	0	0	159
Mean Precipitation (in.)	1.45	1.18	1.32	1.26	2.03	1.90	1.28	0.80	0.84	0.95	1.71	2.06	16.78
Extreme Maximum Daily Precip. (in.)	0.88	0.87	1.91	0.90	1.68	1.62	1.44	2.50	1.13	0.90	0.82	1.42	2.50
Days With ≥ 0.1" Precipitation	5	4	4	4	6	5	3	2	3	3	6	7	52
Days With ≥ 0.5" Precipitation	0	0	0	0	1	1	1	0	0	0	0	1	4
Days With ≥ 1.0" Precipitation	0	0	0	0	0	0	0	0	0	0	0	0	0
Mean Snowfall (in.)	11.8	5.0	2.5	0.4	trace	0.0	0.0	0.0	0.0	0.4	6.4	16.7	43.2
Maximum Snow Depth (in.)	26	26	24	2	0	0	0	0	0	3	14	30	30
Days With ≥ 1.0" Snow Depth	29	24	8	0	0	0	0	0	0	0	7	25	93

Sedro Woolley *Skagit County* Elevation: 60 ft. Latitude: 48° 30' N Longitude: 122° 14' W

	JAN	FEB	MAR	APR	MAY	JUN	JUL	AUG	SEP	OCT	NOV	DEC	YEAR
Mean Maximum Temp. (°F)	46.4	49.5	53.8	58.9	64.6	69.1	74.1	75.2	69.5	60.2	50.8	45.1	59.8
Mean Temp. (°F)	40.5	42.2	46.1	50.2	55.5	59.8	63.4	63.9	59.0	51.5	44.7	39.5	51.3
Mean Minimum Temp. (°F)	34.4	34.8	38.2	41.5	46.3	50.5	52.6	52.6	48.4	42.7	38.6	33.8	42.9
Extreme Maximum Temp. (°F)	66	74	80	82	92	89	98	90	89	86	70	67	98
Extreme Minimum Temp. (°F)	10	8	20	27	30	39	42	42	36	26	9	8	8
Days Maximum Temp. ≥ 90°F	0	0	0	0	0	0	0	0	0	0	0	0	0
Days Maximum Temp. ≤ 32°F	1	0	0	0	0	0	0	0	0	0	1	1	3
Days Minimum Temp. ≤ 32°F	12	10	4	1	0	0	0	0	0	2	6	12	47
Days Minimum Temp. ≤ 0°F	0	0	0	0	0	0	0	0	0	0	0	0	0
Heating Degree Days (base 65°F)	754	638	580	436	292	161	77	60	179	412	602	784	4,975
Cooling Degree Days (base 65°F)	0	0	0	0	3	12	34	34	5	0	0	0	88
Mean Precipitation (in.)	5.71	3.74	4.38	3.80	3.09	2.81	1.52	1.64	2.61	4.65	7.40	5.04	46.39
Extreme Maximum Daily Precip. (in.)	2.64	2.54	1.41	2.25	1.61	2.50	1.42	2.72	1.80	2.61	2.80	1.87	2.80
Days With ≥ 0.1" Precipitation	13	10	12	10	8	6	4	3	5	9	15	13	108
Days With ≥ 0.5" Precipitation	3	2	2	2	2	2	1	1	2	3	5	4	29
Days With ≥ 1.0" Precipitation	1	0	0	0	0	0	0	0	0	1	2	0	4
Mean Snowfall (in.)	1.0	0.7	0.6	0.0	0.0	0.0	0.0	0.0	0.0	0.1	1.0	2.9	6.3
Maximum Snow Depth (in.)	10	8	4	0	0	0	0	0	0	0	18	19	19
Days With ≥ 1.0" Snow Depth	2	0	0	0	0	0	0	0	0	0	1	1	4

Snoqualmie Falls *King County* Elevation: 439 ft. Latitude: 47° 33' N Longitude: 121° 50' W

	JAN	FEB	MAR	APR	MAY	JUN	JUL	AUG	SEP	OCT	NOV	DEC	YEAR
Mean Maximum Temp. (°F)	46.6	49.5	53.7	58.4	63.8	68.6	74.6	76.0	70.2	60.0	50.6	45.0	59.7
Mean Temp. (°F)	40.4	41.8	45.0	48.8	54.2	58.9	63.6	64.1	58.6	50.7	44.0	39.3	50.8
Mean Minimum Temp. (°F)	34.2	34.1	36.3	39.2	44.5	49.2	52.4	52.1	46.9	41.4	37.4	33.6	41.8
Extreme Maximum Temp. (°F)	67	74	79	86	97	99	100	96	98	95	74	67	100
Extreme Minimum Temp. (°F)	0	1	17	28	31	38	40	40	30	24	5	3	0
Days Maximum Temp. ≥ 90°F	0	0	0	0	0	0	1	1	0	0	0	0	2
Days Maximum Temp. ≤ 32°F	1	0	0	0	0	0	0	0	0	0	1	1	3
Days Minimum Temp. ≤ 32°F	12	12	8	3	0	0	0	0	0	3	7	13	58
Days Minimum Temp. ≤ 0°F	0	0	0	0	0	0	0	0	0	0	0	0	0
Heating Degree Days (base 65°F)	755	649	613	480	333	193	84	70	195	437	624	789	5,222
Cooling Degree Days (base 65°F)	0	0	0	0	4	16	46	47	8	1	0	0	122
Mean Precipitation (in.)	8.70	5.48	6.25	4.71	3.83	3.01	1.46	1.31	2.76	5.41	10.21	8.34	61.47
Extreme Maximum Daily Precip. (in.)	3.38	2.16	2.33	2.03	1.28	1.83	1.09	1.39	1.73	2.20	4.64	3.22	4.64
Days With ≥ 0.1" Precipitation	14	11	14	12	10	8	4	3	6	11	16	14	123
Days With ≥ 0.5" Precipitation	6	4	4	3	3	2	1	1	2	4	7	6	43
Days With ≥ 1.0" Precipitation	2	1	1	1	1	0	0	0	0	1	3	2	11
Mean Snowfall (in.)	2.1	1.2	0.7	trace	0.0	0.0	0.0	0.0	0.0	0.0	1.1	2.7	7.8
Maximum Snow Depth (in.)	11	8	12	trace	0	0	***0***	0	0	***0***	1	***12***	***12***
Days With ≥ 1.0" Snow Depth	1	1	0	0	0	0	0	0	0	0	0	1	3

Vancouver 4 NNE *Clark County* Elevation: 209 ft. Latitude: 45° 41' N Longitude: 122° 39' W

	JAN	FEB	MAR	APR	MAY	JUN	JUL	AUG	SEP	OCT	NOV	DEC	YEAR
Mean Maximum Temp. (°F)	46.5	50.7	55.5	60.4	66.7	72.0	78.3	79.3	74.6	63.5	52.4	45.4	62.1
Mean Temp. (°F)	39.5	41.8	46.2	50.1	56.0	61.0	65.9	65.9	61.0	52.4	44.9	38.8	52.0
Mean Minimum Temp. (°F)	32.5	32.9	36.8	39.9	45.2	49.9	53.5	52.5	47.4	41.3	37.3	32.1	41.8
Extreme Maximum Temp. (°F)	64	69	77	87	99	103	106	103	103	90	70	64	106
Extreme Minimum Temp. (°F)	5	5	19	23	28	35	37	36	30	19	8	1	1
Days Maximum Temp. ≥ 90°F	0	0	0	0	0	1	3	3	1	0	0	0	8
Days Maximum Temp. ≤ 32°F	1	0	0	0	0	0	0	0	0	0	0	1	2
Days Minimum Temp. ≤ 32°F	15	14	8	3	0	0	0	0	0	3	8	15	66
Days Minimum Temp. ≤ 0°F	0	0	0	0	0	0	0	0	0	0	0	0	0
Heating Degree Days (base 65°F)	783	649	577	440	284	145	52	50	140	385	597	804	4,906
Cooling Degree Days (base 65°F)	0	0	0	0	11	31	88	87	26	1	0	0	244
Mean Precipitation (in.)	5.89	4.32	4.20	3.20	2.56	1.80	0.67	0.74	1.53	3.29	6.45	6.38	41.03
Extreme Maximum Daily Precip. (in.)	2.25	2.90	2.09	1.46	1.07	2.03	1.23	1.17	2.04	3.42	3.32	3.15	3.42
Days With ≥ 0.1" Precipitation	13	11	12	10	7	5	2	2	4	8	14	14	102
Days With ≥ 0.5" Precipitation	4	2	2	1	1	1	0	0	1	2	4	4	22
Days With ≥ 1.0" Precipitation	1	1	0	0	0	0	0	0	0	0	1	1	4
Mean Snowfall (in.)	2.1	0.9	0.2	0.0	0.0	0.0	0.0	0.0	0.0	0.0	trace	0.8	4.0
Maximum Snow Depth (in.)	8	4	trace	0	0	0	0	0	0	0	1	3	8
Days With ≥ 1.0" Snow Depth	1	1	0	0	0	0	0	0	0	0	0	0	2

The period of record for all cooperative weather station data is 1980 – 2009. See User Guide for detailed explanation of data.

Wapato *Yakima County* Elevation: 840 ft. Latitude: 46° 26' N Longitude: 120° 25' W

	JAN	FEB	MAR	APR	MAY	JUN	JUL	AUG	SEP	OCT	NOV	DEC	YEAR
Mean Maximum Temp. (°F)	39.2	47.3	58.0	65.6	74.4	81.0	89.3	88.5	80.1	66.3	49.7	36.9	64.7
Mean Temp. (°F)	31.7	37.2	45.8	52.3	60.4	67.0	74.0	72.6	64.1	51.6	39.6	29.6	52.2
Mean Minimum Temp. (°F)	24.2	27.1	33.5	39.0	46.5	53.0	58.6	56.6	48.0	36.8	29.4	22.3	39.6
Extreme Maximum Temp. (°F)	63	70	78	89	102	104	110	105	99	89	73	64	110
Extreme Minimum Temp. (°F)	-14	-19	6	23	28	33	40	35	29	12	-9	-18	-19
Days Maximum Temp. ≥ 90°F	0	0	0	0	2	5	16	14	4	0	0	0	41
Days Maximum Temp. ≤ 32°F	8	2	0	0	0	0	0	0	0	0	1	11	22
Days Minimum Temp. ≤ 32°F	27	22	14	6	1	0	0	0	0	9	20	28	127
Days Minimum Temp. ≤ 0°F	0	0	0	0	0	0	0	0	0	0	0	1	1
Heating Degree Days (base 65°F)	1,025	780	590	377	183	58	10	9	95	411	756	1,089	5,383
Cooling Degree Days (base 65°F)	0	0	0	4	49	125	295	251	75	2	0	0	801
Mean Precipitation (in.)	1.11	0.68	0.64	0.56	0.68	0.64	0.27	0.28	0.36	0.58	1.10	1.40	8.30
Extreme Maximum Daily Precip. (in.)	1.25	0.61	0.82	0.70	0.99	0.90	1.47	1.05	0.65	1.01	2.30	1.00	2.30
Days With ≥ 0.1" Precipitation	4	2	2	2	2	2	1	1	1	2	3	4	26
Days With ≥ 0.5" Precipitation	0	0	0	0	0	0	0	0	0	0	0	0	0
Days With ≥ 1.0" Precipitation	0	0	0	0	0	0	0	0	0	0	0	0	0
Mean Snowfall (in.)	4.5	2.0	0.4	trace	0.0	0.0	0.0	0.0	0.0	0.1	1.8	5.1	13.9
Maximum Snow Depth (in.)	15	8	7	trace	0	0	0	0	0	3	11	20	20
Days With ≥ 1.0" Snow Depth	10	4	1	0	0	0	0	0	0	0	1	10	26

Whitman Mission *Walla Walla County* Elevation: 631 ft. Latitude: 46° 03' N Longitude: 118° 27' W

	JAN	FEB	MAR	APR	MAY	JUN	JUL	AUG	SEP	OCT	NOV	DEC	YEAR
Mean Maximum Temp. (°F)	41.4	47.1	57.0	64.8	72.4	80.0	89.6	88.9	79.7	65.5	50.2	39.9	64.7
Mean Temp. (°F)	34.3	37.7	45.2	51.2	58.2	64.8	71.4	70.1	61.4	50.1	41.0	33.1	51.6
Mean Minimum Temp. (°F)	27.3	28.3	33.3	37.6	44.0	49.6	53.2	51.1	43.1	34.8	31.7	26.2	38.3
Extreme Maximum Temp. (°F)	68	76	82	88	98	104	110	110	103	89	82	70	110
Extreme Minimum Temp. (°F)	-22	-21	4	21	27	32	37	33	18	8	-13	-21	-22
Days Maximum Temp. ≥ 90°F	0	0	0	0	1	5	17	15	4	0	0	0	42
Days Maximum Temp. ≤ 32°F	7	3	0	0	0	0	0	0	0	0	2	9	21
Days Minimum Temp. ≤ 32°F	23	20	15	7	2	0	0	0	2	13	16	24	122
Days Minimum Temp. ≤ 0°F	0	1	0	0	0	0	0	0	0	0	0	1	2
Heating Degree Days (base 65°F)	943	764	606	408	226	78	15	20	139	455	713	981	5,348
Cooling Degree Days (base 65°F)	0	0	0	1	24	80	220	183	39	0	0	0	547
Mean Precipitation (in.)	1.62	1.38	1.58	1.43	1.45	1.06	0.39	0.43	0.61	1.17	1.81	1.66	14.59
Extreme Maximum Daily Precip. (in.)	1.04	0.85	1.05	1.40	1.52	1.09	0.66	1.30	0.82	1.50	1.90	1.00	1.90
Days With ≥ 0.1" Precipitation	5	5	5	4	4	3	1	1	2	3	6	5	44
Days With ≥ 0.5" Precipitation	0	0	0	1	1	0	0	0	0	0	1	0	3
Days With ≥ 1.0" Precipitation	0	0	0	0	0	0	0	0	0	0	0	0	0
Mean Snowfall (in.)	3.3	1.7	0.2	0.0	0.0	0.0	0.0	0.0	0.0	0.0	0.1	3.7	9.0
Maximum Snow Depth (in.)	11	12	8	0	0	0	0	0	0	1	trace	15	15
Days With ≥ 1.0" Snow Depth	5	2	0	0	0	0	0	0	0	0	0	4	11

The period of record for all cooperative weather station data is 1980 – 2009. See User Guide for detailed explanation of data.

Washington Weather Station Rankings

Annual Extreme Maximum Temperature

Highest			Lowest		
Rank	Station Name	°F	Rank	Station Name	°F
1	Prosser	***111***	1	Blaine	86
2	Dayton 1 WSW	110	2	Bellingham 3 SSW	***92***
2	Kennewick	110	3	Everett	93
2	Wapato	110	4	Coupeville 1 S	94
2	Whitman Mission	110	4	Port Angeles	94
6	Lacrosse	109	6	Cushman Powerhouse 2	97
6	Yakima Air Terminal	109	7	Clearbrook	98
8	Ephrata Arpt FCWOS	108	7	Clearwater	98
8	Longview	108	7	Sedro Woolley	98
8	McNary Dam	108	10	Quillayute Airport	99
11	Centralia	107	11	Palmer 3 ESE	100
11	Chewelah	107	11	Snoqualmie Falls	100
11	Coulee Dam 1 SW	107	13	Anacortes	101
14	Chelan	106	13	Baring	101
14	Vancouver 4 NNE	106	13	Bremerton	***101***
16	Aberdeen	105	13	Cedar Lake	101
16	Diablo Dam	105	17	McMillin Reservoir	102
16	Northport	105	17	Monroe	102
19	Olympia Arpt	104	19	Buckley 1 NE	103
20	Buckley 1 NE	103	19	Cle Elum	***103***
20	Cle Elum	***103***	19	Mazama	103
20	Mazama	103	19	Republic	103
20	Republic	103	19	Seattle-Tacoma Intl Arpt	103
20	Seattle-Tacoma Intl Arpt	103	19	Spokane Intl Arpt	103
20	Spokane Intl Arpt	103	25	Olympia Arpt	104

Annual Mean Maximum Temperature

Highest			Lowest		
Rank	Station Name	°F	Rank	Station Name	°F
1	Kennewick	65.7	1	Cedar Lake	55.1
2	Wapato	64.7	2	Republic	56.0
2	Whitman Mission	64.7	3	Mazama	56.1
4	Prosser	***64.4***	4	Port Angeles	56.7
5	McNary Dam	64.1	5	Blaine	57.3
6	Yakima Air Terminal	63.1	5	Quillayute Airport	57.3
7	Lacrosse	63.0	7	Diablo Dam	57.5
8	Dayton 1 WSW	62.7	8	Cle Elum	***57.7***
9	Centralia	62.4	8	Spokane Intl Arpt	57.7
10	Ephrata Arpt FCWOS	62.2	10	Baring	58.1
10	Longview	62.2	10	Palmer 3 ESE	58.1
12	Vancouver 4 NNE	62.1	12	Aberdeen	58.4
13	Chewelah	60.8	13	Coupeville 1 S	58.5
14	Olympia Arpt	60.7	14	Clearwater	58.8
15	Buckley 1 NE	60.6	15	Anacortes	59.0
16	Coulee Dam 1 SW	60.5	16	Bellingham 3 SSW	***59.2***
16	Monroe	***60.5***	17	McMillin Reservoir	59.3
18	Northport	60.3	18	Clearbrook	59.6
19	Bremerton	60.2	19	Everett	59.7
20	Cushman Powerhouse 2	59.9	20	Chelan	59.8
21	Chelan	59.8	20	Seattle-Tacoma Intl Arpt	59.8
21	Seattle-Tacoma Intl Arpt	59.8	20	Sedro Woolley	59.8
21	Sedro Woolley	59.8	20	Snoqualmie Falls	59.8
21	Snoqualmie Falls	59.8	24	Cushman Powerhouse 2	59.9
25	Everett	59.7	25	Bremerton	60.2

Rankings include 25 highest/lowest stations. If state has less than 25 stations, all stations are included. The period of record is 1980–2009. See User Guide for detailed explanation of data.

Annual Mean Temperature

Highest Rank	Station Name	°F	Lowest Rank	Station Name	°F
1	Kennewick	54.6	1	Republic	43.9
2	McNary Dam	54.0	2	Mazama	44.7
3	Centralia	53.0	3	Cle Elum	***46.9***
4	Longview	52.7	4	Cedar Lake	47.3
5	Seattle-Tacoma Intl Arpt	52.4	4	Chewelah	47.3
6	Prosser	***52.3***	6	Spokane Intl Arpt	47.6
7	Wapato	52.2	7	Northport	48.1
8	Vancouver 4 NNE	52.0	8	Diablo Dam	48.9
9	Bremerton	51.9	9	Quillayute Airport	49.4
10	Bellingham 3 SSW	***51.8***	10	Baring	49.5
11	Anacortes	51.7	11	Palmer 3 ESE	49.6
12	Monroe	***51.6***	12	Blaine	49.8
12	Whitman Mission	51.6	12	Yakima Air Terminal	49.8
14	Ephrata Arpt FCWOS	51.4	14	Clearwater	49.9
14	Everett	51.4	15	Lacrosse	50.0
14	Sedro Woolley	51.4	15	Port Angeles	50.0
17	Cushman Powerhouse 2	51.3	17	Coulee Dam 1 SW	50.3
17	Dayton 1 WSW	51.3	17	McMillin Reservoir	50.3
19	Aberdeen	51.2	17	Olympia Arpt	50.3
20	Buckley 1 NE	51.1	20	Clearbrook	50.6
21	Snoqualmie Falls	50.8	21	Chelan	50.7
22	Chelan	50.7	21	Coupeville 1 S	50.7
22	Coupeville 1 S	50.7	23	Snoqualmie Falls	50.8
24	Clearbrook	50.6	24	Buckley 1 NE	51.1
25	Coulee Dam 1 SW	50.3	25	Aberdeen	51.2

Annual Mean Minimum Temperature

Highest Rank	Station Name	°F	Lowest Rank	Station Name	°F
1	Seattle-Tacoma Intl Arpt	44.9	1	Republic	31.8
2	Anacortes	44.3	2	Mazama	33.3
2	Bellingham 3 SSW	***44.3***	3	Chewelah	33.8
4	Aberdeen	43.9	4	Cle Elum	***35.9***
5	McNary Dam	43.7	5	Northport	36.0
6	Centralia	43.6	6	Yakima Air Terminal	36.5
7	Bremerton	43.5	7	Lacrosse	36.9
8	Kennewick	43.4	8	Spokane Intl Arpt	37.5
9	Port Angeles	43.3	9	Whitman Mission	38.4
10	Everett	43.1	10	Cedar Lake	39.5
10	Longview	43.1	11	Wapato	39.6
12	Coupeville 1 S	42.9	12	Dayton 1 WSW	39.9
12	Sedro Woolley	42.9	12	Olympia Arpt	39.9
14	Cushman Powerhouse 2	42.6	14	Coulee Dam 1 SW	40.0
14	Monroe	***42.6***	15	Diablo Dam	40.2
16	Blaine	42.2	15	Prosser	***40.2***
17	Snoqualmie Falls	41.8	17	Ephrata Arpt FCWOS	40.5
17	Vancouver 4 NNE	41.8	18	Baring	40.8
19	Buckley 1 NE	41.6	19	Clearwater	40.9
19	Clearbrook	41.6	20	Palmer 3 ESE	41.1
21	Chelan	41.5	21	McMillin Reservoir	41.2
22	Quillayute Airport	41.3	22	Quillayute Airport	41.3
23	McMillin Reservoir	41.2	23	Chelan	41.5
24	Palmer 3 ESE	41.1	24	Buckley 1 NE	41.6
25	Clearwater	40.9	24	Clearbrook	41.6

Rankings include 25 highest/lowest stations. If state has less than 25 stations, all stations are included. The period of record is 1980–2009. See User Guide for detailed explanation of data.

Annual Extreme Minimum Temperature

Highest

Rank	Station Name	°F
1	Cushman Powerhouse 2	11
2	Aberdeen	10
3	Quillayute Airport	9
4	Anacortes	8
4	Sedro Woolley	8
6	Bremerton	*7*
6	Seattle-Tacoma Intl Arpt	7
8	Port Angeles	6
9	Bellingham 3 SSW	***5***
9	Coupeville 1 S	5
9	Longview	5
12	Clearwater	4
13	Cedar Lake	2
14	Baring	1
14	Blaine	1
14	Vancouver 4 NNE	1
17	Buckley 1 NE	0
17	Centralia	0
17	Clearbrook	0
17	Everett	0
17	Monroe	0
17	Snoqualmie Falls	0
23	McMillin Reservoir	-1
24	Diablo Dam	-2
25	Palmer 3 ESE	-3

Lowest

Rank	Station Name	°F
1	Lacrosse	-30
1	Mazama	-30
3	Republic	-27
4	Chewelah	-25
5	Cle Elum	***-24***
5	Spokane Intl Arpt	-24
7	Whitman Mission	-22
8	Dayton 1 WSW	-21
8	Ephrata Arpt FCWOS	-21
10	Wapato	-19
11	Northport	-18
12	Yakima Air Terminal	-17
13	Prosser	***-14***
14	Coulee Dam 1 SW	-13
15	Kennewick	-11
16	McNary Dam	-9
17	Chelan	-8
18	Olympia Arpt	-7
19	Palmer 3 ESE	-3
20	Diablo Dam	-2
21	McMillin Reservoir	-1
22	Buckley 1 NE	0
22	Centralia	0
22	Clearbrook	0
22	Everett	0

July Mean Maximum Temperature

Highest

Rank	Station Name	°F
1	Kennewick	90.5
2	Whitman Mission	89.6
3	Lacrosse	89.4
4	Wapato	89.3
5	Prosser	***89.1***
6	Ephrata Arpt FCWOS	88.7
7	McNary Dam	88.4
8	Yakima Air Terminal	87.8
9	Coulee Dam 1 SW	87.6
10	Chewelah	87.1
11	Dayton 1 WSW	86.8
11	Northport	86.8
13	Chelan	84.7
14	Spokane Intl Arpt	83.4
15	Mazama	82.5
16	Republic	81.6
17	Cle Elum	***79.9***
18	Centralia	78.6
19	Vancouver 4 NNE	78.3
20	Longview	77.9
21	Olympia Arpt	77.2
22	Diablo Dam	77.0
23	Buckley 1 NE	76.4
24	Monroe	76.2
25	Cushman Powerhouse 2	76.0

Lowest

Rank	Station Name	°F
1	Quillayute Airport	67.9
2	Port Angeles	68.4
3	Aberdeen	68.5
4	Clearwater	70.9
5	Cedar Lake	71.6
5	Coupeville 1 S	71.6
7	Blaine	71.8
8	Anacortes	72.7
9	Bellingham 3 SSW	***73.4***
9	Everett	73.4
11	Palmer 3 ESE	73.8
12	Sedro Woolley	74.1
13	Snoqualmie Falls	74.6
14	McMillin Reservoir	75.1
15	Baring	75.4
15	Bremerton	75.4
15	Seattle-Tacoma Intl Arpt	75.4
18	Clearbrook	75.7
19	Cushman Powerhouse 2	76.0
20	Monroe	76.2
21	Buckley 1 NE	76.4
22	Diablo Dam	77.0
23	Olympia Arpt	77.2
24	Longview	77.9
25	Vancouver 4 NNE	78.3

January Mean Minimum Temperature

Highest Rank	Station Name	°F	Lowest Rank	Station Name	°F
1	Aberdeen	36.7	1	Mazama	16.1
2	Seattle-Tacoma Intl Arpt	36.4	2	Republic	17.7
3	Coupeville 1 S	36.1	3	Chewelah	20.2
4	Anacortes	36.0	4	Northport	22.5
5	Bellingham 3 SSW	***35.7***	5	Ephrata Arpt FCWOS	22.9
5	Centralia	35.7	6	Coulee Dam 1 SW	23.1
5	Port Angeles	35.7	7	Spokane Intl Arpt	23.2
8	Quillayute Airport	35.4	7	Yakima Air Terminal	23.2
9	Clearwater	35.2	9	Cle Elum	***23.5***
10	Bremerton	35.0	10	Chelan	23.9
11	Cushman Powerhouse 2	34.9	11	Wapato	24.2
11	Longview	34.9	12	Lacrosse	25.0
13	Everett	34.5	13	Prosser	26.1
14	Sedro Woolley	34.4	14	Dayton 1 WSW	27.1
15	Snoqualmie Falls	34.2	15	Whitman Mission	27.3
16	Buckley 1 NE	34.0	16	Kennewick	28.7
16	Monroe	34.0	17	Diablo Dam	29.5
18	Palmer 3 ESE	33.1	18	McNary Dam	29.7
19	Blaine	33.0	19	Cedar Lake	31.3
20	Clearbrook	32.9	20	Baring	31.7
20	McMillin Reservoir	32.9	21	Vancouver 4 NNE	32.5
22	Olympia Arpt	32.6	22	Olympia Arpt	32.6
23	Vancouver 4 NNE	32.5	23	Clearbrook	32.9
24	Baring	31.7	23	McMillin Reservoir	32.9
25	Cedar Lake	31.3	25	Blaine	33.0

Number of Days Annually Maximum Temperature ≥ 90°F

Highest Rank	Station Name	Days	Lowest Rank	Station Name	Days
1	Kennewick	47	1	Aberdeen	0
2	Whitman Mission	42	1	Anacortes	0
3	Prosser	***41***	1	Bellingham 3 SSW	***0***
3	Wapato	41	1	Blaine	0
5	Lacrosse	39	1	Coupeville 1 S	0
6	Ephrata Arpt FCWOS	38	1	Everett	0
7	Chewelah	35	1	Port Angeles	0
8	Dayton 1 WSW	34	1	Quillayute Airport	0
8	McNary Dam	34	1	Sedro Woolley	0
8	Northport	34	10	Clearwater	1
8	Yakima Air Terminal	34	11	Cedar Lake	2
12	Coulee Dam 1 SW	33	11	Clearbrook	2
13	Chelan	22	11	Cushman Powerhouse 2	2
14	Mazama	18	11	McMillin Reservoir	2
14	Spokane Intl Arpt	18	11	Monroe	2
16	Cle Elum	***15***	11	Palmer 3 ESE	2
17	Republic	14	11	Snoqualmie Falls	2
18	Diablo Dam	12	18	Baring	3
19	Centralia	8	18	Bremerton	3
19	Vancouver 4 NNE	8	18	Seattle-Tacoma Intl Arpt	3
21	Longview	7	21	Buckley 1 NE	4
22	Olympia Arpt	5	22	Olympia Arpt	5
23	Buckley 1 NE	4	23	Longview	7
24	Baring	3	24	Centralia	8
24	Bremerton	3	24	Vancouver 4 NNE	8

 Rankings include 25 highest/lowest stations. If state has less than 25 stations, all stations are included. The period of record is 1980–2009. See User Guide for detailed explanation of data.

Number of Days Annually Maximum Temperature ≤ 32°F

Highest			Lowest		
Rank	Station Name	Days	Rank	Station Name	Days
1	Mazama	56	1	Aberdeen	1
2	Republic	50	1	Centralia	1
3	Spokane Intl Arpt	36	1	Clearwater	1
4	Coulee Dam 1 SW	33	1	Cushman Powerhouse 2	1
5	Chelan	32	1	Everett	1
6	Northport	30	1	Longview	1
7	Ephrata Arpt FCWOS	29	1	Olympia Arpt	1
8	Chewelah	26	1	Port Angeles	1
8	Cle Elum	***26***	1	Quillayute Airport	1
10	Yakima Air Terminal	23	10	Anacortes	2
11	Wapato	22	10	Bremerton	2
12	Whitman Mission	21	10	Buckley 1 NE	2
13	Lacrosse	20	10	Coupeville 1 S	2
13	Prosser	***20***	10	McMillin Reservoir	2
15	Dayton 1 WSW	19	10	Monroe	2
16	Kennewick	16	10	Seattle-Tacoma Intl Arpt	2
17	McNary Dam	14	10	Vancouver 4 NNE	2
18	Cedar Lake	9	18	Bellingham 3 SSW	***3***
18	Diablo Dam	9	18	Sedro Woolley	3
20	Clearbrook	8	18	Snoqualmie Falls	3
21	Baring	7	21	Blaine	5
22	Blaine	5	21	Palmer 3 ESE	5
22	Palmer 3 ESE	5	23	Baring	7
24	Bellingham 3 SSW	***3***	24	Clearbrook	8
24	Sedro Woolley	3	25	Cedar Lake	9

Number of Days Annually Minimum Temperature ≤ 32°F

Highest			Lowest		
Rank	Station Name	Days	Rank	Station Name	Days
1	Republic	185	1	Seattle-Tacoma Intl Arpt	29
2	Mazama	182	2	Anacortes	33
3	Chewelah	167	3	Aberdeen	35
4	Cle Elum	***153***	3	Port Angeles	35
5	Northport	150	5	Bellingham 3 SSW	***40***
5	Yakima Air Terminal	150	5	Coupeville 1 S	40
7	Spokane Intl Arpt	137	7	Bremerton	44
8	Lacrosse	132	8	Centralia	45
9	Wapato	127	8	Longview	45
10	Ephrata Arpt FCWOS	123	10	Sedro Woolley	47
11	Whitman Mission	122	11	Cushman Powerhouse 2	50
12	Coulee Dam 1 SW	117	12	Everett	51
13	Prosser	***110***	13	Monroe	55
14	Chelan	106	14	Buckley 1 NE	56
15	Dayton 1 WSW	104	15	Palmer 3 ESE	58
16	Cedar Lake	87	15	Quillayute Airport	58
16	Diablo Dam	87	15	Snoqualmie Falls	58
18	Olympia Arpt	80	18	Clearbrook	60
19	Kennewick	79	19	Blaine	61
20	Baring	75	20	McMillin Reservoir	65
21	Clearwater	69	21	Vancouver 4 NNE	66
21	McNary Dam	69	22	Clearwater	69
23	Vancouver 4 NNE	66	22	McNary Dam	69
24	McMillin Reservoir	65	24	Baring	75
25	Blaine	61	25	Kennewick	79

Rankings include 25 highest/lowest stations. If state has less than 25 stations, all stations are included. The period of record is 1980–2009. See User Guide for detailed explanation of data.

Number of Days Annually Minimum Temperature ≤ 0°F

Highest

Rank	Station Name	Days
1	Mazama	11
2	Republic	9
3	Chewelah	5
4	Cle Elum	*3*
4	Ephrata Arpt FCWOS	3
4	Lacrosse	3
4	Spokane Intl Arpt	3
8	Coulee Dam 1 SW	2
8	Dayton 1 WSW	2
8	Northport	2
8	Whitman Mission	2
8	Yakima Air Terminal	2
13	Wapato	1
14	Aberdeen	0
14	Anacortes	0
14	Baring	0
14	Bellingham 3 SSW	*0*
14	Blaine	0
14	Bremerton	0
14	Buckley 1 NE	0
14	Cedar Lake	0
14	Centralia	0
14	Chelan	0
14	Clearbrook	0
14	Clearwater	0

Lowest

Rank	Station Name	Days
1	Aberdeen	0
1	Anacortes	0
1	Baring	0
1	Bellingham 3 SSW	*0*
1	Blaine	0
1	Bremerton	0
1	Buckley 1 NE	0
1	Cedar Lake	0
1	Centralia	0
1	Chelan	0
1	Clearbrook	0
1	Clearwater	0
1	Coupeville 1 S	0
1	Cushman Powerhouse 2	0
1	Diablo Dam	0
1	Everett	0
1	Kennewick	0
1	Longview	0
1	McMillin Reservoir	0
1	McNary Dam	0
1	Monroe	0
1	Olympia Arpt	0
1	Palmer 3 ESE	0
1	Port Angeles	0
1	Prosser	*0*

Number of Annual Heating Degree Days

Highest

Rank	Station Name	Num.
1	Republic	7,748
2	Mazama	7,599
3	Cle Elum	*6,771*
4	Chewelah	6,713
5	Spokane Intl Arpt	6,668
6	Northport	6,448
7	Cedar Lake	6,444
8	Diablo Dam	6,008
9	Coulee Dam 1 SW	5,992
10	Yakima Air Terminal	5,933
11	Lacrosse	5,874
12	Chelan	5,811
13	Ephrata Arpt FCWOS	5,723
14	Baring	5,695
15	Palmer 3 ESE	5,648
16	Quillayute Airport	5,645
17	Blaine	5,502
18	Dayton 1 WSW	5,481
19	Clearwater	5,448
20	Port Angeles	5,416
21	McMillin Reservoir	5,386
22	Wapato	5,383
23	Olympia Arpt	5,368
24	Whitman Mission	5,348
25	Clearbrook	5,253

Lowest

Rank	Station Name	Num.
1	Centralia	4,533
2	Longview	4,625
3	Kennewick	4,665
4	Seattle-Tacoma Intl Arpt	4,699
5	McNary Dam	4,753
6	Bellingham 3 SSW	*4,805*
7	Anacortes	4,834
8	Bremerton	4,856
9	Vancouver 4 NNE	4,906
10	Monroe	*4,940*
11	Everett	4,965
12	Sedro Woolley	4,975
13	Aberdeen	5,011
14	Cushman Powerhouse 2	5,035
15	Buckley 1 NE	5,110
16	Coupeville 1 S	5,149
17	Snoqualmie Falls	5,222
18	Prosser	*5,250*
19	Clearbrook	5,253
20	Whitman Mission	5,348
21	Olympia Arpt	5,368
22	Wapato	5,383
23	McMillin Reservoir	5,386
24	Port Angeles	5,416
25	Clearwater	5,448

Rankings include 25 highest/lowest stations. If state has less than 25 stations, all stations are included. The period of record is 1980–2009. See User Guide for detailed explanation of data.

Number of Annual Cooling Degree Days

Highest Rank	Highest Station Name	Highest Num.	Lowest Rank	Lowest Station Name	Lowest Num.
1	Kennewick	976	1	Quillayute Airport	24
2	Ephrata Arpt FCWOS	861	2	Clearwater	25
3	McNary Dam	833	3	Coupeville 1 S	31
4	Wapato	801	4	Blaine	32
5	Coulee Dam 1 SW	722	5	Port Angeles	35
6	Prosser	***718***	6	Aberdeen	57
7	Chelan	697	7	Anacortes	61
8	Dayton 1 WSW	587	8	Bellingham 3 SSW	***73***
9	Whitman Mission	547	9	Cedar Lake	83
10	Yakima Air Terminal	501	10	Sedro Woolley	88
11	Lacrosse	494	11	Clearbrook	89
12	Spokane Intl Arpt	434	12	Everett	106
13	Northport	404	13	Olympia Arpt	110
14	Chewelah	357	14	McMillin Reservoir	116
15	Mazama	305	15	Palmer 3 ESE	119
16	Cle Elum	***254***	16	Snoqualmie Falls	122
17	Vancouver 4 NNE	244	17	Cushman Powerhouse 2	129
18	Centralia	242	18	Baring	133
19	Diablo Dam	224	19	Monroe	***137***
20	Longview	217	20	Buckley 1 NE	140
21	Seattle-Tacoma Intl Arpt	187	21	Republic	159
22	Bremerton	169	22	Bremerton	169
23	Republic	159	23	Seattle-Tacoma Intl Arpt	187
24	Buckley 1 NE	140	24	Longview	217
25	Monroe	***137***	25	Diablo Dam	224

Annual Precipitation

Highest Rank	Highest Station Name	Highest Inches	Lowest Rank	Lowest Station Name	Lowest Inches
1	Clearwater	109.03	1	Ephrata Arpt FCWOS	7.68
2	Baring	105.96	2	Kennewick	7.72
3	Quillayute Airport	99.36	3	McNary Dam	7.99
4	Cedar Lake	96.55	4	Yakima Air Terminal	8.19
5	Cushman Powerhouse 2	89.20	5	Wapato	8.30
6	Palmer 3 ESE	85.39	6	Prosser	***8.33***
7	Aberdeen	83.53	7	Coulee Dam 1 SW	10.75
8	Diablo Dam	78.05	8	Chelan	11.29
9	Snoqualmie Falls	61.47	9	Whitman Mission	14.59
10	Bremerton	54.18	10	Lacrosse	14.94
11	Olympia Arpt	49.62	11	Spokane Intl Arpt	16.47
12	Monroe	48.44	12	Republic	16.78
13	Buckley 1 NE	47.86	13	Dayton 1 WSW	19.16
14	Longview	47.57	14	Northport	20.72
15	Centralia	46.68	15	Chewelah	20.94
16	Sedro Woolley	46.39	16	Coupeville 1 S	21.04
17	Clearbrook	45.56	17	Mazama	22.19
18	McMillin Reservoir	43.07	18	Port Angeles	25.57
19	Vancouver 4 NNE	41.03	19	Anacortes	27.72
20	Blaine	40.70	20	Bellingham 3 SSW	***34.61***
21	Everett	37.20	21	Seattle-Tacoma Intl Arpt	37.03
22	Seattle-Tacoma Intl Arpt	37.03	22	Everett	37.20
23	Bellingham 3 SSW	***34.61***	23	Blaine	40.70
24	Anacortes	27.72	24	Vancouver 4 NNE	41.03
25	Port Angeles	25.57	25	McMillin Reservoir	43.07

Rankings include 25 highest/lowest stations. If state has less than 25 stations, all stations are included. The period of record is 1980–2009. See User Guide for detailed explanation of data.

Annual Extreme Maximum Daily Precipitation

Highest			Lowest		
Rank	Station Name	Inches	Rank	Station Name	Inches
1	Cushman Powerhouse 2	8.30	1	Kennewick	1.33
2	Palmer 3 ESE	8.10	2	Lacrosse	1.47
3	Clearwater	7.94	3	McNary Dam	1.68
4	Bremerton	***7.50***	4	Yakima Air Terminal	1.70
5	Cedar Lake	7.33	5	Ephrata Arpt FCWOS	1.74
6	Diablo Dam	7.32	6	Chelan	1.88
7	Aberdeen	7.03	7	Whitman Mission	1.90
8	Quillayute Airport	6.03	8	Dayton 1 WSW	2.18
9	Buckley 1 NE	5.12	9	Spokane Intl Arpt	2.19
10	Seattle-Tacoma Intl Arpt	5.02	10	Anacortes	***2.25***
11	Olympia Arpt	4.82	10	Coupeville 1 S	2.25
12	Snoqualmie Falls	4.64	12	Wapato	2.30
13	Chewelah	4.25	13	Coulee Dam 1 SW	2.31
14	Centralia	4.13	14	Northport	2.49
15	Longview	4.04	15	Republic	2.50
16	Monroe	3.94	16	Bellingham 3 SSW	***2.75***
17	Port Angeles	3.64	16	Blaine	2.75
18	Everett	***3.62***	18	Sedro Woolley	2.80
19	McMillin Reservoir	3.59	19	Clearbrook	3.09
20	Cle Elum	***3.45***	20	Mazama	3.23
21	Vancouver 4 NNE	3.42	21	Vancouver 4 NNE	3.42
22	Mazama	3.23	22	Cle Elum	***3.45***
23	Clearbrook	3.09	23	McMillin Reservoir	3.59
24	Sedro Woolley	2.80	24	Everett	***3.62***
25	Bellingham 3 SSW	***2.75***	25	Port Angeles	3.64

Number of Days Annually With ≥ 0.1 Inches of Precipitation

Highest			Lowest		
Rank	Station Name	Days	Rank	Station Name	Days
1	Palmer 3 ESE	147	1	Wapato	26
2	Cedar Lake	146	2	Ephrata Arpt FCWOS	27
2	Quillayute Airport	146	2	Prosser	***27***
4	Clearwater	144	4	Kennewick	28
5	Baring	139	4	Yakima Air Terminal	28
6	Aberdeen	134	6	McNary Dam	30
7	Diablo Dam	123	7	Coulee Dam 1 SW	34
7	Snoqualmie Falls	123	8	Chelan	35
9	Buckley 1 NE	117	9	Whitman Mission	44
10	Monroe	116	10	Lacrosse	48
11	Longview	114	11	Republic	52
12	Cushman Powerhouse 2	113	11	Spokane Intl Arpt	52
13	McMillin Reservoir	108	13	Mazama	56
13	Sedro Woolley	108	14	Dayton 1 WSW	57
15	Centralia	107	15	Chewelah	59
16	Clearbrook	106	16	Cle Elum	***62***
17	Olympia Arpt	105	17	Port Angeles	63
18	Blaine	103	18	Northport	65
19	Vancouver 4 NNE	102	19	Coupeville 1 S	66
20	Bremerton	99	20	Anacortes	79
21	Everett	94	21	Seattle-Tacoma Intl Arpt	90
22	Bellingham 3 SSW	***92***	22	Bellingham 3 SSW	***92***
23	Seattle-Tacoma Intl Arpt	90	23	Everett	94
24	Anacortes	79	24	Bremerton	99
25	Coupeville 1 S	66	25	Vancouver 4 NNE	102

 Rankings include 25 highest/lowest stations. If state has less than 25 stations, all stations are included. The period of record is 1980–2009. See User Guide for detailed explanation of data.

Number of Days Annually With ≥ 0.5 Inches of Precipitation

Highest Rank	Station Name	Days	Lowest Rank	Station Name	Days
1	Clearwater	76	1	Ephrata Arpt FCWOS	0
2	Baring	71	1	Kennewick	0
3	Cedar Lake	70	1	McNary Dam	0
4	Quillayute Airport	68	1	Prosser	*0*
5	Palmer 3 ESE	62	1	Wapato	0
6	Cushman Powerhouse 2	56	1	Yakima Air Terminal	0
7	Aberdeen	55	7	Coulee Dam 1 SW	1
8	Diablo Dam	50	8	Chelan	3
9	Snoqualmie Falls	43	8	Whitman Mission	3
10	Bremerton	36	10	Republic	4
11	Monroe	31	10	Spokane Intl Arpt	4
11	Olympia Arpt	31	12	Lacrosse	5
13	Buckley 1 NE	29	13	Coupeville 1 S	6
13	Sedro Woolley	29	14	Northport	7
15	Centralia	28	15	Dayton 1 WSW	8
15	Clearbrook	28	16	Chewelah	10
17	Longview	27	16	Cle Elum	*10*
18	McMillin Reservoir	25	16	Mazama	10
19	Blaine	23	19	Port Angeles	13
20	Vancouver 4 NNE	22	20	Anacortes	14
21	Everett	21	21	Bellingham 3 SSW	*18*
21	Seattle-Tacoma Intl Arpt	21	22	Everett	21
23	Bellingham 3 SSW	*18*	22	Seattle-Tacoma Intl Arpt	21
24	Anacortes	14	24	Vancouver 4 NNE	22
25	Port Angeles	13	25	Blaine	23

Number of Days Annually With ≥ 1.0 Inches of Precipitation

Highest Rank	Station Name	Days	Lowest Rank	Station Name	Days
1	Clearwater	36	1	Chelan	0
2	Baring	32	1	Chewelah	0
3	Cushman Powerhouse 2	29	1	Coulee Dam 1 SW	0
3	Quillayute Airport	29	1	Coupeville 1 S	0
5	Cedar Lake	28	1	Dayton 1 WSW	0
6	Palmer 3 ESE	23	1	Ephrata Arpt FCWOS	0
7	Diablo Dam	22	1	Kennewick	0
8	Aberdeen	20	1	Lacrosse	0
9	Bremerton	12	1	McNary Dam	0
10	Snoqualmie Falls	11	1	Northport	0
11	Olympia Arpt	9	1	Prosser	*0*
12	Buckley 1 NE	6	1	Republic	0
12	Centralia	6	1	Spokane Intl Arpt	0
14	Clearbrook	5	1	Wapato	0
14	Monroe	5	1	Whitman Mission	0
16	Blaine	4	1	Yakima Air Terminal	0
16	Longview	4	17	Anacortes	1
16	McMillin Reservoir	4	17	Cle Elum	*1*
16	Sedro Woolley	4	19	Bellingham 3 SSW	*2*
16	Vancouver 4 NNE	4	19	Everett	2
21	Mazama	3	21	Mazama	3
21	Port Angeles	3	21	Port Angeles	3
21	Seattle-Tacoma Intl Arpt	3	21	Seattle-Tacoma Intl Arpt	3
24	Bellingham 3 SSW	*2*	24	Blaine	4
24	Everett	2	24	Longview	4

Annual Snowfall

Highest			Lowest		
Rank	Station Name	Inches	Rank	Station Name	Inches
1	Mazama	114.2	1	Clearwater	0.4
2	Cle Elum	***85.3***	1	Port Angeles	0.4
3	Baring	50.3	3	Aberdeen	0.8
4	Diablo Dam	48.9	4	Everett	1.0
5	Northport	46.0	5	McNary Dam	***1.1***
6	Cedar Lake	44.4	6	Centralia	1.6
7	Spokane Intl Arpt	44.3	7	Longview	1.7
8	Republic	43.2	8	Kennewick	***2.1***
9	Chewelah	35.4	9	Prosser	***3.0***
10	Chelan	24.3	10	Anacortes	3.6
11	Yakima Air Terminal	22.7	11	Vancouver 4 NNE	4.0
12	Palmer 3 ESE	18.1	12	Monroe	4.2
13	Dayton 1 WSW	17.4	13	Bellingham 3 SSW	***4.3***
14	Lacrosse	16.9	14	Bremerton	***4.5***
15	Wapato	13.9	15	Coupeville 1 S	5.2
16	Blaine	11.5	16	McMillin Reservoir	5.7
17	Clearbrook	10.7	17	Cushman Powerhouse 2	6.0
18	Coulee Dam 1 SW	***9.1***	18	Sedro Woolley	6.3
19	Whitman Mission	9.0	19	Buckley 1 NE	7.4
20	Snoqualmie Falls	7.8	20	Snoqualmie Falls	7.8
21	Buckley 1 NE	7.4	21	Whitman Mission	9.0
22	Sedro Woolley	6.3	22	Coulee Dam 1 SW	***9.1***
23	Cushman Powerhouse 2	6.0	23	Clearbrook	10.7
24	McMillin Reservoir	5.7	24	Blaine	11.5
25	Coupeville 1 S	5.2	25	Wapato	13.9

Annual Maximum Snow Depth

Highest			Lowest		
Rank	Station Name	Inches	Rank	Station Name	Inches
1	Cle Elum	***85***	1	Clearwater	Trace
2	Mazama	62	2	Aberdeen	6
3	Diablo Dam	43	3	Vancouver 4 NNE	8
4	Baring	41	4	Everett	10
5	Bellingham 3 SSW	***38***	5	Bremerton	***11***
6	Chewelah	36	5	Centralia	11
7	Northport	31	5	Port Angeles	***11***
8	Cedar Lake	30	8	Buckley 1 NE	12
8	Republic	30	8	Snoqualmie Falls	***12***
10	Spokane Intl Arpt	27	10	Anacortes	***14***
10	Yakima Air Terminal	***27***	10	Clearbrook	***14***
12	Palmer 3 ESE	26	10	McMillin Reservoir	14
13	Coulee Dam 1 SW	***23***	13	Whitman Mission	15
14	Dayton 1 WSW	***22***	14	Coupeville 1 S	***16***
14	Monroe	22	14	Lacrosse	16
16	Blaine	21	16	Cushman Powerhouse 2	18
17	Wapato	20	16	Longview	18
18	Sedro Woolley	19	18	Sedro Woolley	19
19	Cushman Powerhouse 2	18	19	Wapato	20
19	Longview	18	20	Blaine	21
21	Coupeville 1 S	***16***	21	Dayton 1 WSW	***22***
21	Lacrosse	16	21	Monroe	22
23	Whitman Mission	15	23	Coulee Dam 1 SW	***23***
24	Anacortes	***14***	24	Palmer 3 ESE	26
24	Clearbrook	***14***	25	Spokane Intl Arpt	27

Rankings include 25 highest/lowest stations. If state has less than 25 stations, all stations are included. The period of record is 1980–2009. See User Guide for detailed explanation of data.

Number of Days Annually With ≥ 1.0 Inch Snow Depth

Highest Rank	Highest Station Name	Highest Days	Lowest Rank	Lowest Station Name	Lowest Days
1	Mazama	137	1	Anacortes	***0***
2	Republic	93	1	Buckley 1 NE	0
3	Northport	81	1	Centralia	0
4	Cle Elum	***75***	1	Clearwater	0
5	Chewelah	54	1	Coupeville 1 S	0
6	Spokane Intl Arpt	51	1	Everett	0
7	Cedar Lake	46	1	Port Angeles	***0***
8	Baring	45	8	Aberdeen	1
9	Diablo Dam	40	8	McNary Dam	***1***
10	Yakima Air Terminal	***36***	10	Clearbrook	2
11	Wapato	26	10	Cushman Powerhouse 2	2
12	Lacrosse	20	10	Vancouver 4 NNE	2
13	Coulee Dam 1 SW	***17***	13	Bellingham 3 SSW	***3***
14	Dayton 1 WSW	16	13	Bremerton	***3***
15	Palmer 3 ESE	14	13	Longview	3
16	Whitman Mission	11	13	Snoqualmie Falls	3
17	Blaine	7	17	Monroe	4
18	McMillin Reservoir	6	17	Sedro Woolley	4
19	Prosser	***5***	19	Prosser	***5***
20	Monroe	4	20	McMillin Reservoir	6
20	Sedro Woolley	4	21	Blaine	7
22	Bellingham 3 SSW	***3***	22	Whitman Mission	11
22	Bremerton	***3***	23	Palmer 3 ESE	14
22	Longview	3	24	Dayton 1 WSW	16
22	Snoqualmie Falls	3	25	Coulee Dam 1 SW	***17***

Rankings include 25 highest/lowest stations. If state has less than 25 stations, all stations are included. The period of record is 1980–2009. See User Guide for detailed explanation of data.

Significant Storm Events in Washington: 2000 – 2009

Location or County	Date	Type	Mag.	Deaths	Injuries	Property Damage ($mil.)	Crop Damage ($mil.)
Jefferson, Kitsap, Mason, Snohomish, Skagit, Whatcom, and Clallam Counties	10/20/03	Flood	na	0	0	9.5	0.0
Seattle Metropolitan Area and Central Cascade Foothills	12/04/03	High Wind	79 mph	0	3	15.0	0.0
Seattle Metropolitan and Tacoma Areas, and Northern Cascade Mountains and Foothills	03/10/05	Drought	na	0	0	12.0	0.0
Pierce	11/04/06	Heavy Rain	na	0	0	36.0	0.0
King	11/04/06	Flood	na	0	0	11.1	0.0
Lewis	11/04/06	Flood	na	2	0	8.8	0.0
Tacoma Area	12/14/06	High Wind	58 mph	2	2	11.0	0.0
Chelan and Western Grant Counties	01/07/07	High Wind	74 mph	0	0	10.0	0.0
Lewis	12/02/07	Flood	na	1	0	50.0	0.0
Kitsap	12/02/07	Heavy Rain	na	0	0	30.0	0.0
Central Coast	12/02/07	High Wind	81 mph	1	10	20.0	0.0
Thurston	12/03/07	Heavy Rain	na	0	0	14.0	0.0
King	12/03/07	Heavy Rain	na	0	0	12.0	0.0
Pacific	12/03/07	Flood	na	0	0	10.0	0.0
Snohomish	12/03/07	Heavy Rain	na	0	0	10.0	0.0
Eastern Washington and Spokane Area	01/04/09	Heavy Snow	na	0	0	10.0	0.0
King	01/07/09	Flood	na	0	0	14.0	0.0
Kittitas	01/07/09	Flood	na	0	0	10.0	0.0
Pierce	01/07/09	Flood	na	0	0	8.8	0.0
East Slopes, Central Cascade Mountains	10/10/09	Landslide	na	0	0	25.0	0.0

Note: Deaths, injuries, and damages are date and location specific.

WEST VIRGINIA

PHYSICAL FEATURES. West Virginia has an area of over 24,000 square miles. From southwest to northeast, the State is about 200 miles in length; width averages a little over one-half the length. There are two projections: the Northeastern Panhandle juts eastward between Maryland and Virginia; and the Northern Panhandle, a narrow strip stretching northward along the Ohio River between Ohio and Pennsylvania. The easternmost extremity of the State is about 150 miles from the Atlantic Ocean and the southwestern corner adjacent to Kentucky is nearly 400 miles away from the ocean. As a result, West Virginia lies beyond the immediate climatic effect of the Atlantic, and its climate is much more continental than maritime type. The most important aspect of this type of climate is the marked temperature contrast between summer and winter.

The physical configuration of the State accentuates its interior location. Excluding the Northeastern Panhandle, the State lies in the Allegheny Plateau. The eastern third of the plateau is part of the Appalachian Mountain chain and contains the highest land in the State. Peak elevations in this area range from about 2,500 feet to 4,860 feet (above sea level) at Spruce Knob, the highest point in West Virginia. The central and western thirds of the plateau slope generally westward to the Ohio River which lies at about 550 to 650 feet above sea level.

The Northeastern Panhandle is marked by long ridges and valleys, oriented southwest-northeast, intersected by the winding courses of the Potomac River and its tributaries. The main stream of the Potomac with its North Branch forms the northern border of this part of the State. Summit elevations exceed 4,000 feet (above sea level), but the land in general slopes eastward away from the main ridgeline to the west and finally reaches the lowest elevation in the State of 274 feet at Harpers Ferry. This section lies in the Atlantic Ocean drainage and is drained by the Potomac River. The remainder of the State drains into the Ohio River.

GENERAL CLIMATE. Physical features considerably modify the effects of the major climatic controls. The State's latitudinal position (from about 37° 15' N. latitude in the south to 40° in the north) places it in the zone of prevailing westerly winds, which are frequently interrupted by northward and southward surges of relatively warm and cold air, respectively. These atmospheric movements are accompanied by the passage of high and low-pressure areas; the latter are the large-dimension storms, known as extratropical cyclones, which are most common in the United States in the colder half-year. West Virginia lies near the average path of the extratropical cyclones that move in a general easterly direction across the United States. In the warmer half-year, the State is affected by the showers and thunderstorms that occur in the broad current of air that tends to sweep northeastward from the Gulf of Mexico.

The State has a moderately severe winter climate, accentuated and prolonged in the mountains, with frequent alternations of fair and stormy weather. Summer is marked by hot and showery weather; the heat is less pronounced in the mountains, which are more subject to thunderstorms and have fewer clear days the year-round. There are marked variations in temperature, precipitation, and the other weather elements, due to the rugged topography occurring not only between the mountains and plateau areas but also between different parts of the same county.

TEMPERATURE. Locations in the mountainous belt, regardless of their latitude, tend to have lower temperatures than those in the rest of the State. Average winter minimum temperatures range from the low 20s in the mountains of the Central and Northeastern Divisions and in the Northern Panhandle, to near 30°F. in the extreme southern and southwestern corners of the State. Average winter maximum readings are in the middle and upper 40s, except in the mountains and in the Northern Panhandle where they are close to 40°F. In summer, maximum temperatures average over 85°F. everywhere except in the mountains, where they are 5 to 10°F. cooler; average minimum temperatures during this season range from the middle 50s in the mountains to the middle 60s elsewhere. Spring and autumn mean temperatures average in the 50s, with similar geographical variations. The average date of the last freezing temperature in spring ranges from mid-April in the southwest to mid-May in the mountains; the average first occurrence of 32°F. in the fall similarly varies from late October to late September.

Despite the coolness of the mountains, they can on occasion be as hot as any other part of West Virginia. Temperatures near or over 100°F. have been recorded at all weather stations in the State. On the other hand, very low temperatures (below -30°F.) have been observed only in the mountains and in the North Central Division. These are extremes, and do not represent usual winter conditions. Cold waves, with near or subzero temperatures, occur on average three times a winter, but as a rule do not last more than two or three days.

Fog conditions over the State are complicated as to their causes and distribution. The valley fogs are usually of the radiation type, and occur characteristically when a high-pressure area is centered over or near the State. This situation is most common in late summer and fall. Low cloudiness and fog in the mountains are generally orographic in nature, the result of moist winds moving upslope, so that there is usually a great difference in cloud and fog conditions on opposite sides of a ridge.

PRECIPITATION. The precipitation pattern can be directly related to the rain and snow-producing atmospheric currents generally move across West Virginia on an eastward course. As they approach the mountains, these air currents are subject to orographic lifting, which acts to trigger potential precipitation or to intensify the rain or snow that may already be falling. As a result, average annual precipitation increases from the Ohio eastward to the Appalachians. On the other side of the mountains, there is the well-marked "rain shadow" where the air currents descend the leeward slopes and precipitation is correspondingly reduced, to increase only when more favorable topographic influences are encountered farther eastward and where the influence of the ocean and coastal storms is more pronounced.

Mean annual snowfall exhibits the same features, but to a more remarkable degree. The mountain belt receives over 60 inches of snow a year, on the average. Amounts over 20 inches have been experienced everywhere in of the State except west of longitude 81° 30' W. which usually receives about 15 inches. It is very unusual for a relatively small and compact area the size of West Virginia to exhibit such great differences in snowfall. Furthermore, the heavy snowfall at elevations under 5,000 feet (above sea level) is unusual in the East, for an area located south of 40° N. latitude. The snow, as a general rule, does not remain on the ground for extended periods over most of the State. Except in the higher portions of the plateau and in the mountains themselves. Snowstorms are usually followed by thawing periods and there is no large-scale melting in the spring of a seasonally accumulated snowpack.

SUNSHINE AND CLOUDINESS. West Virginia lies in a cloudy belt. Percentage of possible sunshine is only about 40 in winter, increasing to somewhat over 60 percent in early autumn. Cloudiness is most pronounced over the mountains. The average annual number of clear days ranges from about 80 in the mountains to about 120 in the western portion. In addition to cloudiness, the hours of sunshine are reduced by fog, particularly in the river valleys.

WINDS AND STORMS. The prevailing winds blow from westerly directions. There is a tendency outside of the mountain belt for southerly or southwesterly winds during summer and fall. Thunderstorms occur on an average of 40 to 50 days per year, being more frequent in the mountains and during June and July. Violent local winds accompanying thunderstorms are experienced every year in some part of the State, but tornadoes are rare. Destructive hailstorms occur on an average of about three per year. Though hurricanes have damaged the State, principally as a result of heavy rains, it is uncommon for this type of storm to strike West Virginia with full force. The remnants of the hurricanes which have affected the State have been more noted for their accompanying heavy rainfalls than for any high winds produced. Much more frequent and costly is the damage from intense large-area storms — that is, from exceptionally strong specimens of the ordinary lows that affect the State quite frequently during the colder half of the year. Such storms produce high winds and heavy rain or snow.

Warm-season thunderstorms, mostly those of June and July, often yield intense local rainfall and cause flash flooding in the narrow valleys that cut through the plateau and mountain districts. This kind of severe local flood is likely to occur in some part of the State every year. In contrast to flash flooding on the smaller streams, flooding in the larger streams is almost exclusively a cold season phenomenon. The ideal setup for the cold season floods is soil well saturated from previous rains, a good snow cover, and a more-or-less stationary front lying northeast-southwest across the State. Along this front separating two contrasting air masses, a succession of "waves" may move northeastward, resulting in copious warm rains for a period of at least several days and a rapid melting of the snow cover.

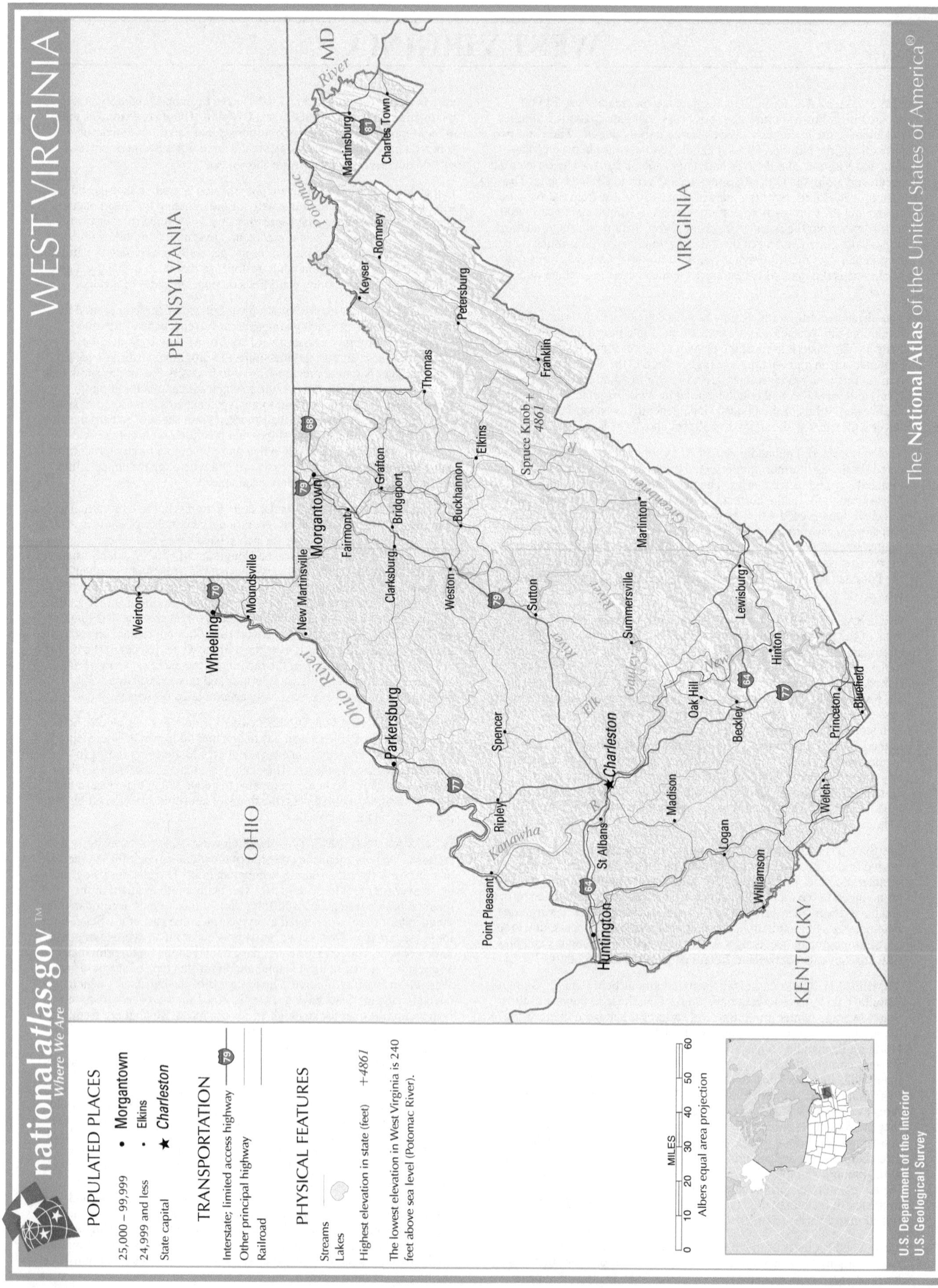
WEST VIRGINIA
nationalatlas.gov™
Where We Are
POPULATED PLACES
25,000 – 99,999 • Morgantown
24,999 and less • Elkins
State capital ★ Charleston
TRANSPORTATION
Interstate; limited access highway 79
Other principal highway
Railroad
PHYSICAL FEATURES
Streams
Lakes
Highest elevation in state (feet) +4861
The lowest elevation in West Virginia is 240 feet above sea level (Potomac River).
MILES
0 10 20 30 40 50 60
Albers equal area projection
U.S. Department of the Interior
U.S. Geological Survey
The National Atlas of the United States of America®
PENNSYLVANIA
MD
VIRGINIA
OHIO
KENTUCKY
Weirton
Wheeling
Moundsville
New Martinsville
Morgantown
Fairmont
Grafton
Bridgeport
Clarksburg
Weston
Buckhannon
Elkins
Thomas
Keyser
Romney
Petersburg
Franklin
Martinsburg
Charles Town
Spruce Knob + 4861
Marlinton
Lewisburg
Sutton
Summersville
Parkersburg
Spencer
Ripley
Point Pleasant
Charleston
St Albans
Huntington
Madison
Logan
Williamson
Oak Hill
Beckley
Hinton
Princeton
Bluefield
Welch
Ohio River
Potomac River
Kanawha R
Elk River
Gauley River
New R
Greenbrier R
70
79
68
81
77
64

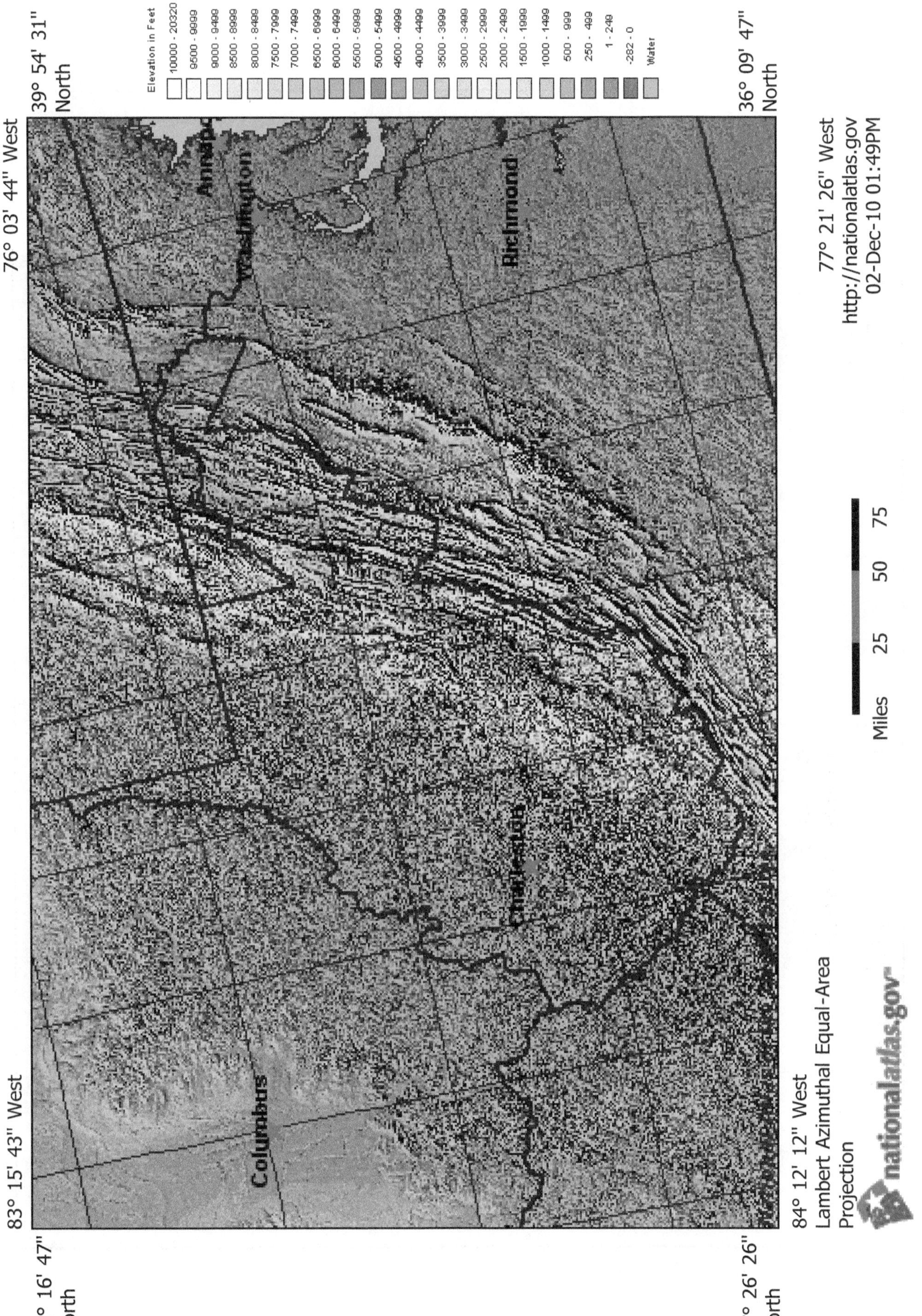

39° 54' 31" North
76° 03' 44" West
36° 09' 47" North
77° 21' 26" West
http://nationalatlas.gov
02-Dec-10 01:49PM
41° 16' 47" North
83° 15' 43" West
37° 26' 26" North
84° 12' 12" West
Lambert Azimuthal Equal-Area Projection
nationalatlas.gov
Miles 25 50 75
Elevation in Feet
10000 - 20320
9500 - 9999
9000 - 9499
8500 - 8999
8000 - 8499
7500 - 7999
7000 - 7499
6500 - 6999
6000 - 6499
5500 - 5999
5000 - 5499
4500 - 4999
4000 - 4499
3500 - 3999
3000 - 3499
2500 - 2999
2000 - 2499
1500 - 1999
1000 - 1499
500 - 999
250 - 499
1 - 249
-282 - 0
Water
Washington
Richmond
Charleston
Columbus

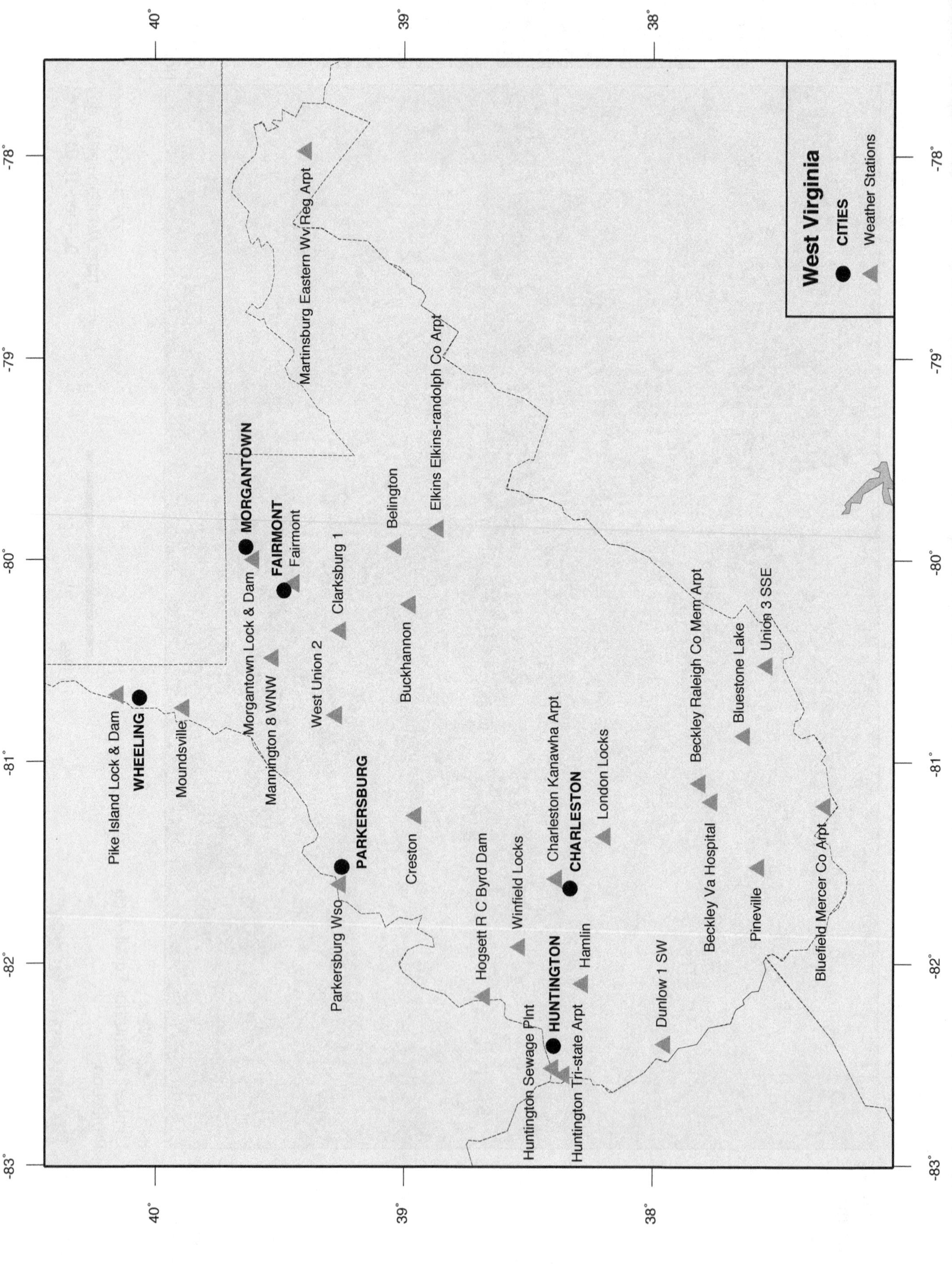
West Virginia
CITIES
Weather Stations
MORGANTOWN
FAIRMONT
WHEELING
PARKERSBURG
CHARLESTON
HUNTINGTON
Martinsburg Eastern Wv Reg Arpt
Elkins Elkins-randolph Co Arpt
Belington
Fairmont
Clarksburg 1
Morgantown Lock & Dam
Mannington 8 WNW
West Union 2
Buckhannon
Pike Island Lock & Dam
Moundsville
Parkersburg Wso
Creston
Hogsett R C Byrd Dam
Winfield Locks
Charleston Kanawha Arpt
London Locks
Hamlin
Huntington Sewage Plnt
Huntington Tri-state Arpt
Dunlow 1 SW
Beckley Raleigh Co Mem Arpt
Beckley Va Hospital
Bluestone Lake
Union 3 SSE
Pineville
Bluefield Mercer Co Arpt
40°
39°
38°
-78°
-79°
-80°
-81°
-82°
-83°

West Virginia Weather Stations by County

County	Station Name
Barbour	Belington
Berkeley	Martinsburg Eastern WV Reg Arpt
Doddridge	West Union 2
Harrison	Clarksburg 1
Kanawha	Charleston Kanawha Arpt London Locks
Lincoln	Hamlin
Marion	Fairmont Mannington 8 WNW
Marshall	Moundsville
Mason	Hogsett R C Byrd Dam
Mercer	Bluefield Mercer Co Arpt
Monongalia	Morgantown Lock & Dam
Monroe	Union 3 SSE
Ohio	Pike Island Lock and Dam
Putnam	Winfield Locks
Raleigh	Beckley Raleigh Co Mem Arpt Beckley Va Hospital
Randolph	Elkins Elkins-Randolph Co Arpt
Summers	Bluestone Lake
Upshur	Buckhannon
Wayne	Dunlow 1 SW Huntington Sewage Plant Huntington Tri-State Arpt
Wirt	Creston
Wood	Parkersburg WSO
Wyoming	Pineville

West Virginia Weather Stations by City

City	Station Name	Miles
Beckley	Beckley Va Hospital	1.3
	Beckley Raleigh Co Mem Arpt	4.0
	Bluestone Lake	19.5
	Pineville	24.1
Bluefield	Burkes Garden, VA	13.7
	Wytheville 1 S, VA	23.5
	Bluefield Mercer Co Arpt	2.8
Bridgeport	Belington	24.9
	Buckhannon	21.4
	Clarksburg 1	5.3
	Fairmont	13.8
	Mannington 8 WNW	21.2
Charleston	Charleston Kanawha Arpt	3.7
	London Locks	17.8
	Winfield Locks	19.8
Clarksburg	Buckhannon	21.7
	Clarksburg 1	1.0
	Fairmont	17.1
	Mannington 8 WNW	19.3
	West Union 2	22.5
Cross Lanes	Charleston Kanawha Arpt	10.9
	Hamlin	20.4
	Winfield Locks	10.4
Dunbar	Charleston Kanawha Arpt	8.5
	Hamlin	20.4
	London Locks	23.2
	Winfield Locks	15.1
Fairmont	Clarksburg 1	18.3
	Fairmont	1.2
	Mannington 8 WNW	19.2
	Morgantown Lock & Dam	13.5
Huntington	Ashland, KY	10.2
	Hamlin	20.2
	Hogsett R C Byrd Dam	23.1
	Huntington Tri-State Arpt	6.6
	Huntington Sewage Plant	4.5
Martinsburg	Winchester Winc, VA	21.5
	Martinsburg Eastern WV Reg Arpt	4.2
Morgantown	Chalk Hill 2 ENE, PA	24.6
	Uniontown 1 NE, PA	23.2
	Fairmont	15.1
	Morgantown Lock & Dam	1.5
Moundsville	Barnesville, OH	22.3
	Hannibal Lock & Dam, OH	19.0
	Moundsville	1.7
	Pike Island Lock and Dam	15.8
Parkersburg	Marietta Wwtp, OH	11.9
	Parkersburg WSO	1.4
South Charleston	Charleston Kanawha Arpt	7.2
	Hamlin	21.7
	London Locks	21.5

City	Station Name	Miles
S. Charleston *(cont.)*	Winfield Locks	16.7
St. Albans	Charleston Kanawha Arpt	12.7
	Hamlin	16.6
	Winfield Locks	11.9
Teays Valley	Charleston Kanawha Arpt	19.9
	Hamlin	14.3
	Hogsett R C Byrd Dam	20.9
	Winfield Locks	6.0
Vienna	Marietta Wwtp, OH	8.5
	Parkersburg WSO	4.3
Weirton	Cadiz, OH	24.7
	Steubenville, OH	3.8
	Montgomery Lock & Dam, PA	19.3
	Pittsburgh Intl Arpt, PA	18.7
	Pike Island Lock and Dam	19.2
Wheeling	Barnesville, OH	24.8
	Cadiz, OH	21.0
	Steubenville, OH	21.9
	Moundsville	12.1
	Pike Island Lock and Dam	5.5

Note: Miles is the distance between the geographic center of the city and the weather station.

See User Guide for station inclusion criteria.

West Virginia Weather Stations by Elevation

Feet	Station Name
2,891	Bluefield Mercer Co Arpt
2,503	Beckley Raleigh Co Mem Arpt
2,330	Beckley Va Hospital
2,109	Union 3 SSE
1,948	Elkins Elkins-Randolph Co Arpt
1,708	Belington
1,455	Buckhannon
1,390	Bluestone Lake
1,299	Fairmont
1,279	Pineville
1,200	Dunlow 1 SW
1,100	Mannington 8 WNW
1,016	Charleston Kanawha Arpt
990	Clarksburg 1
830	Huntington Tri-State Arpt
825	Morgantown Lock & Dam
790	West Union 2
649	Creston
642	Hamlin
640	Pike Island Lock and Dam
620	London Locks
620	Moundsville
615	Parkersburg WSO
570	Winfield Locks
569	Hogsett R C Byrd Dam
537	Martinsburg Eastern WV Reg Arpt
520	Huntington Sewage Plant

See User Guide for station inclusion criteria.

Beckley Memorial Airport

The city of Beckley is located in the Appalachian Mountains about 30 miles northwest of the high ridges through eastern West Virginia. The Raleigh County Memorial Airport is on a plateau about 2.5 miles east of the city. Beckley is almost surrounded by distant peaks. The entire area is on a broad plateau composed of rough, hilly ground and lush valleys. The generalized 2,000-foot contour line is about 25 miles to the northwest and runs from southwest to northeast. The generalized 3,000-foot contour is about 10 miles to the southeast and follows the general configuration of the Appalachians.

Due to the configuration the weather often remains clear over Beckley even though the low stratus clouds to the east may obscure the ridges and be solid to the east of these ridges. To a lesser degree, this location is largely responsible for the formation of heavy fogs at the Beckley Airport.

Beckley has a climate characterized by sharp temperature contrasts, both seasonal and day to day. The months of May through September are moderately cold, with April and October months of fairly rapid transition. Cold waves occur on an average of two or three times during the winter, but severe cold spells are seldom of more than two or three days duration. Below-zero temperatures, as well as temperatures in the 70s have been recorded during winter months. A low of -13 degrees may be expected once every 10 years and -16 degrees once every 25 years. Summer highs near 90 degrees have occurred, contrasting with lows in the 30s during the same months. Highs seldom reach above the mid-80s. Cool nights are common throughout the summer, with lowest temperatures usually ranging from the 50s to the low 60s.

Ample precipitation is well distributed throughout the year. July has the highest monthly average while October has the lowest average. Summer rainfall occurs mostly during thunderstorms or showery precipitation, while the heaviest winter precipitation usually is associated with storms originating to the southwest and moving northeastward over the Ohio Valley. The formation of storms in the eastern Gulf of Mexico which move up the east coast will sometimes bring heavy snow to the Beckley area. Snowfall occurs chiefly from November through March and occasionally in October and April. The average seasonal snowfall is greater than snowfall at stations to the west at lower elevations, and considerably less than the totals for stations at higher elevations to the east and northeast.

Beckley Memorial Airport *Raleigh County* Elevation: 2,503 ft. Latitude: 37° 48' N Longitude: 81° 07' W

	JAN	FEB	MAR	APR	MAY	JUN	JUL	AUG	SEP	OCT	NOV	DEC	YEAR
Mean Maximum Temp. (°F)	39.6	43.2	51.8	62.7	70.1	76.9	79.8	79.1	72.8	63.2	52.9	42.7	61.2
Mean Temp. (°F)	31.3	34.4	42.0	52.0	59.7	67.2	70.6	69.7	63.1	53.1	43.8	34.6	51.8
Mean Minimum Temp. (°F)	22.9	25.6	32.2	41.3	49.3	57.5	61.4	60.2	53.5	42.9	34.7	26.4	42.3
Extreme Maximum Temp. (°F)	73	72	81	85	89	89	94	96	92	86	79	73	96
Extreme Minimum Temp. (°F)	-22	-16	-5	11	27	38	41	36	30	18	8	-18	-22
Days Maximum Temp. ≥ 90°F	0	0	0	0	0	0	1	1	0	0	0	0	2
Days Maximum Temp. ≤ 32°F	10	6	2	0	0	0	0	0	0	0	1	7	26
Days Minimum Temp. ≤ 32°F	25	21	17	6	1	0	0	0	0	5	14	23	112
Days Minimum Temp. ≤ 0°F	1	0	0	0	0	0	0	0	0	0	0	1	2
Heating Degree Days (base 65°F)	1,039	858	706	393	189	37	8	12	109	369	630	937	5,287
Cooling Degree Days (base 65°F)	0	0	1	9	32	111	189	164	61	6	1	0	574
Mean Precipitation (in.)	2.82	2.74	3.49	3.45	4.48	3.94	5.06	3.56	2.99	2.56	2.89	2.96	40.94
Maximum Precipitation (in.)*	6.4	6.0	9.2	7.6	7.1	7.0	9.6	5.9	8.3	5.9	6.3	6.4	57.1
Minimum Precipitation (in.)*	0.5	0.5	1.7	0.3	1.0	1.5	1.6	1.7	0.5	0.1	1.0	0.6	32.6
Extreme Maximum Daily Precip. (in.)	2.10	2.11	1.91	2.19	2.06	2.47	3.48	3.06	3.25	3.13	2.50	1.77	3.48
Days With ≥ 0.1" Precipitation	7	7	8	8	9	8	9	7	6	6	6	7	88
Days With ≥ 0.5" Precipitation	2	1	2	2	3	3	3	2	2	1	2	2	25
Days With ≥ 1.0" Precipitation	0	0	0	0	1	1	1	1	1	0	0	0	5
Mean Snowfall (in.)	***17.1***	***15.3***	***8.7***	***2.9***	***0.1***	***trace***	***0.0***	***0.0***	***0.0***	***0.4***	***2.7***	***11.4***	***58.6***
Maximum Snowfall (in.)*	36	31	13	19	1	0	0	0	trace	7	13	27	94
Maximum 24-hr. Snowfall (in.)*	12	9	7	13	1	0	0	0	trace	7	6	14	14
Maximum Snow Depth (in.)	***24***	***19***	***30***	***15***	***trace***	***trace***	***0***	***0***	***0***	***2***	***5***	***21***	***30***
Days With ≥ 1.0" Snow Depth	***11***	***10***	***4***	***1***	***0***	***0***	***0***	***0***	***0***	***0***	***2***	***8***	***36***
Thunderstorm Days*	< 1	1	2	4	6	8	10	7	3	1	< 1	< 1	42
Foggy Days*	14	12	14	12	16	19	23	24	21	14	13	13	195
Predominant Sky Cover*	OVR	OVR	OVR	OVR	OVR	OVR	OVR	OVR	OVR	OVR	OVR	OVR	OVR
Mean Relative Humidity 7am (%)*	80	79	77	74	81	86	89	91	91	86	79	79	83
Mean Relative Humidity 4pm (%)*	65	61	54	48	54	59	61	62	62	55	58	65	59
Mean Dewpoint (°F)*	22	23	30	37	48	57	62	61	55	42	33	26	41
Prevailing Wind Direction*	WNW	WNW	WNW	WNW	SSE	WSW	WSW	SE	SE	SE	SSE	WNW	SSE
Prevailing Wind Speed (mph)*	13	13	13	13	10	9	8	9	9	12	12	12	12
Maximum Wind Gust (mph)*	61	62	70	60	58	55	61	46	48	49	60	56	70

Note: (*) Period of record is 1963-1995

Charleston Kanawha Airport

Charleston lies at the junction of the Kanawha and Elk Rivers in the western foothills of the Appalachian Mountains. The hilltops are around 1,100 feet above sea level, about 500 feet higher than the valleys. The Kanawha Airport is just over two miles northeast of the center-city area, on an artificial plateau constructed from several hilltops.

Weather records are maintained at the Kanawha Airport by National Weather Service personnel. This site tends to be slightly cooler than the river valleys during the afternoons. Conversely, the valleys can become cooler than the hilltops during clear, calm nights. The weather at Charleston is highly changeable, especially from mid-autumn through the spring.

Winters can vary greatly from one season to the next. Snow does not favor any given winter month, heavy snowstorms are infrequent, and most snowfalls are in the four inch or less category. Snow and ice usually do not persist on valley roads, but can linger longer on nearby hills and outlying rural roads.

Afternoon temperatures in the 40s and morning readings in the 20s are common during the winter. Yet, every winter typically has two or three extended cold spells when temperatures stay below freezing for a few consecutive days. Northwesterly winds are associated with the cold weather. Air reaching Charleston from the northwest can cause cloudiness and flurries, even when there is no nearby organized storm system. Winter conditions are much more severe over the higher mountains less than 50 miles to the northeast through the southeast. Temperatures warm rapidly in the spring and are accompanied by low daytime humidities.

Summer and early autumn have more day-to-day consistency in the weather. Sunshine is more abundant than in winter. Summer precipitation falls mostly in brief, but sometimes heavy, showers. Flash flooding can occur along small streams, but flooding is rare on the dam-controlled Kanawha and Elk Rivers.

Afternoon summer temperatures are mostly in the 80s. Readings above 95 degrees are rare. However, during a hot spell, haze and humidity can add to the unpleasantness and indoor air conditioning is recommended. Cooler and less humid air often penetrates the area from the north to end a hot spell.

Early morning fog is common from late June into October. By the end of October, the first 32 degree temperature has usually arrived.

Ample precipitation is well distributed throughout the year. July is quite often the wettest month of the year, while October averages the least rain. Droughts severe enough to limit water use are scarce. Any dry spells during the spring or autumn can cause conditions favorable for brush fires in outlying areas.

Charleston Kanawha Airport *Kanawha County* Elevation: 1,016 ft. Latitude: 38° 23' N Longitude: 81° 35' W

	JAN	FEB	MAR	APR	MAY	JUN	JUL	AUG	SEP	OCT	NOV	DEC	YEAR
Mean Maximum Temp. (°F)	43.3	47.4	56.7	68.0	75.3	82.7	85.8	84.9	78.4	68.1	57.4	46.6	66.2
Mean Temp. (°F)	34.6	37.7	45.7	55.9	63.6	71.7	75.5	74.4	67.5	56.5	46.9	37.7	55.6
Mean Minimum Temp. (°F)	25.8	28.0	34.7	43.8	51.9	60.7	65.1	63.9	56.4	44.8	36.4	28.8	45.0
Extreme Maximum Temp. (°F)	78	79	89	94	93	98	104	104	96	93	85	80	104
Extreme Minimum Temp. (°F)	-16	-12	0	19	29	40	47	42	34	23	13	-12	-16
Days Maximum Temp. ≥ 90°F	0	0	0	0	1	4	8	7	2	0	0	0	22
Days Maximum Temp. ≤ 32°F	6	4	1	0	0	0	0	0	0	0	0	4	15
Days Minimum Temp. ≤ 32°F	23	20	14	4	0	0	0	0	0	3	12	20	96
Days Minimum Temp. ≤ 0°F	1	0	0	0	0	0	0	0	0	0	0	0	1
Heating Degree Days (base 65°F)	937	765	597	293	115	12	0	2	52	280	538	840	4,431
Cooling Degree Days (base 65°F)	0	0	6	28	80	219	331	301	133	22	2	1	1,123
Mean Precipitation (in.)	3.01	3.16	3.95	3.31	4.62	4.24	4.96	3.97	3.29	2.67	3.67	3.24	44.09
Maximum Precipitation (in.)*	9.1	6.9	7.7	6.5	6.8	7.5	13.5	10.4	7.6	6.5	8.4	8.0	60.6
Minimum Precipitation (in.)*	1.1	0.5	1.3	0.5	0.8	0.7	2.0	0.7	0.6	0.1	0.6	0.4	30.3
Extreme Maximum Daily Precip. (in.)	1.66	2.68	2.76	1.66	2.26	2.73	3.44	2.65	4.15	1.55	3.61	1.72	4.15
Days With ≥ 0.1" Precipitation	8	8	9	8	9	8	8	7	6	6	7	8	92
Days With ≥ 0.5" Precipitation	2	2	3	2	3	3	3	3	2	2	3	2	30
Days With ≥ 1.0" Precipitation	0	0	1	0	1	1	1	1	1	0	1	0	7
Mean Snowfall (in.)	***11.0***	***9.2***	***6.3***	***1.5***	***trace***	***trace***	***trace***	***trace***	***trace***	na	na	***6.0***	na
Maximum Snowfall (in.)*	40	22	20	21	1	0	0	0	0	3	26	22	68
Maximum 24-hr. Snowfall (in.)*	16	10	17	11	1	0	0	0	0	3	13	11	17
Maximum Snow Depth (in.)	***19***	***13***	***18***	***17***	***trace***	***trace***	***trace***	***trace***	***trace***	na	na	***11***	na
Days With ≥ 1.0" Snow Depth	***9***	***7***	***3***	***0***	***0***	***0***	***0***	***0***	***0***	na	na	***5***	na
Thunderstorm Days*	1	1	2	4	7	8	10	7	3	1	1	< 1	45
Foggy Days*	15	13	13	13	22	25	28	29	26	23	16	15	238
Predominant Sky Cover*	OVR	OVR	OVR	OVR	OVR	OVR	OVR	OVR	OVR	OVR	OVR	OVR	OVR
Mean Relative Humidity 7am (%)*	77	77	75	75	83	87	90	92	91	88	80	78	83
Mean Relative Humidity 4pm (%)*	60	55	49	44	50	53	56	57	55	51	54	60	54
Mean Dewpoint (°F)*	24	25	31	39	51	60	65	64	58	46	35	28	44
Prevailing Wind Direction*	WSW	WSW	WSW	WSW	SW	SW	SW	SW	NE	SW	SW	WSW	SW
Prevailing Wind Speed (mph)*	10	10	12	10	8	8	8	7	6	8	9	10	9
Maximum Wind Gust (mph)*	76	68	60	66	58	49	67	64	44	46	49	62	76

Note: (*) Period of record is 1949-1995

Elkins-Randolph Co. Airport

Elkins, West Virginia, is located near the principal storm tracks and is therefore subjected to frequent weather changes throughout the year. While changes may be rigorous, they bring relief from summer heat waves and winter cold waves. The airport and city are located near the middle of a valley with a narrow floor and ridges at or near 3,000 feet. The ridges are oriented north northeast to south southwest, three to four miles to the east and west. The valley is located on the general northwest slope of the Appalachian Mountains which crest about 20 miles to the southeast at about 4,500 feet, with some higher peaks.

The seasonal climates vary greatly from year to year. When the Atlantic High extends westward, warm weather with high humidities occur in both summer and winter. Conversely, if the Atlantic High is displaced eastward and the circulation is principally from the northwest, weather is colder than normal.

Summers are characterized by warm, humid, showery weather, but the heat is moderated by elevation and orographically induced cloudiness. A daily high temperature of 90 or above may occasionally be expected during the summer months. Winters are moderately severe with rapid changes. Snowfall may be frequent, and at times, heavy. However, it seldom remains on the ground for extended periods. Snows often fall upon warm ground thereby causing preliminary melting, then freezing, resulting in slippery road conditions. Glaze formation upon the ground or upon wires and trees is rare. Cold spells alternate frequently with thaws, and snow is subject to frequent complete melting during the winter. Severe cold spells occur occasionally but they seldom last more than two or three days. A daily low of zero degrees or below can be expected several times annually.

Significant climatic characteristics are associated with air currents rising and descending over the mountains. During the winter when low clouds and snow flurries sometimes persist for 24 hours or more. Easterly and southerly winds, tend to diminish existing low cloud layers and keep ceilings higher than otherwise anticipated. Night time fog is common during the summer and the autumn but it usually dissipates rapidly after sunrise.

Tornadoes are rare in this area, and severe thunderstorms are very infrequent. However, occasionally intense local rainfall from warm-season thunderstorms causes flash flooding in the narrow valleys of the area. Due to the remote location of the city with respect to concentrated industry, the air is usually relatively unpolluted. The average last occurrence in the spring of temperatures as low as 32 is early to mid-May, and the first occurrence in the autumn is early October. The length of the growing season averages about 148 days.

Elkins-Randolph Co. Airport *Randolph County* Elevation: 1,948 ft. Latitude: 38° 53' N Longitude: 79° 51' W

	JAN	FEB	MAR	APR	MAY	JUN	JUL	AUG	SEP	OCT	NOV	DEC	YEAR
Mean Maximum Temp. (°F)	39.5	43.2	52.0	62.9	70.9	78.1	81.3	80.5	74.2	64.3	53.5	43.1	62.0
Mean Temp. (°F)	29.2	32.0	39.5	49.3	57.8	65.8	69.8	68.9	62.1	50.9	41.6	32.6	50.0
Mean Minimum Temp. (°F)	18.8	20.6	27.1	35.7	44.6	53.5	58.2	57.3	50.0	37.5	29.6	22.1	37.9
Extreme Maximum Temp. (°F)	76	75	83	89	93	92	99	94	93	87	82	74	99
Extreme Minimum Temp. (°F)	-24	-22	-14	3	21	33	32	38	29	15	3	-24	-24
Days Maximum Temp. ≥ 90°F	0	0	0	0	0	0	1	2	0	0	0	0	3
Days Maximum Temp. ≤ 32°F	10	6	2	0	0	0	0	0	0	0	1	7	26
Days Minimum Temp. ≤ 32°F	26	24	22	12	3	0	0	0	1	11	19	26	144
Days Minimum Temp. ≤ 0°F	3	2	0	0	0	0	0	0	0	0	0	1	6
Heating Degree Days (base 65°F)	1,104	928	783	465	236	57	12	18	125	433	696	997	5,854
Cooling Degree Days (base 65°F)	0	0	0	2	19	87	167	146	45	4	0	0	470
Mean Precipitation (in.)	3.23	3.08	4.05	3.92	5.08	4.44	5.42	4.02	3.63	2.83	3.40	3.26	46.36
Maximum Precipitation (in.)*	6.1	6.5	8.8	6.9	7.7	8.3	8.3	10.4	7.5	6.3	11.1	6.7	58.7
Minimum Precipitation (in.)*	1.0	0.8	1.4	1.0	1.4	1.7	1.3	1.1	0.3	0.3	1.2	0.9	34.1
Extreme Maximum Daily Precip. (in.)	1.76	2.48	2.11	2.07	3.35	2.31	2.73	2.68	2.78	3.29	5.02	1.92	5.02
Days With ≥ 0.1" Precipitation	9	8	10	10	10	9	9	8	7	6	8	9	103
Days With ≥ 0.5" Precipitation	1	2	2	2	3	3	4	3	2	2	2	2	28
Days With ≥ 1.0" Precipitation	0	0	1	1	1	1	1	1	1	0	1	0	8
Mean Snowfall (in.)	***24.6***	***17.7***	***13.0***	***5.6***	***trace***	***trace***	na	na	na	na	na	***15.6***	na
Maximum Snowfall (in.)*	54	32	34	25	1	0	0	0	0	4	38	37	125
Maximum 24-hr. Snowfall (in.)*	16	13	17	9	1	0	0	0	0	3	12	18	18
Maximum Snow Depth (in.)	***19***	***13***	***18***	***10***	***trace***	***trace***	na	***0***	na	na	na	***16***	na
Days With ≥ 1.0" Snow Depth	***14***	***11***	***6***	***1***	***0***	***0***	na	***0***	na	na	na	***9***	na
Thunderstorm Days*	< 1	1	2	4	7	8	9	6	3	1	1	< 1	42
Foggy Days*	14	13	15	15	21	24	27	29	27	23	16	16	240
Predominant Sky Cover*	OVR	OVR	OVR	OVR	OVR	OVR	OVR	OVR	OVR	OVR	OVR	OVR	OVR
Mean Relative Humidity 7am (%)*	81	81	82	83	87	92	94	96	95	90	83	82	87
Mean Relative Humidity 4pm (%)*	64	60	55	50	54	58	61	62	61	54	58	64	58
Mean Dewpoint (°F)*	22	23	29	37	48	57	62	61	54	42	32	25	42
Prevailing Wind Direction*	WNW	WNW	WNW	WNW	NW	NW	NW	NW	NW	NW	WNW	WNW	WNW
Prevailing Wind Speed (mph)*	12	12	12	12	9	8	7	7	7	8	10	12	9
Maximum Wind Gust (mph)*	59	49	63	69	60	69	52	46	44	46	59	54	69

Note: (*) Period of record is 1948-1995

Huntington Tri-State Airport

The Tri-State Airport is near the confluence of the Ohio and Big Sandy Rivers, located on a man-made plateau constructed by cutting the tops off several hills and filling intervening valleys. The elevation of the ground at the National Weather Service Office is 260 feet higher than at the Federal Building in downtown Huntington.

The temperature record for the valley locations is not compatible with that for the airport, which is generally cooler throughout the year. The summer season is moderately warm and humid, with the valley locations considerably warmer and more humid than the Tri-State Airport site. The winter months are moderately cold, with an occasional severe cold wave lasting a few days. The four seasons are nearly equal in length and autumn is the most pleasant, with warm days and cool nights.

The heaviest rainfall occurs in July and August, mostly in thunderstorms, and flash floods are common in the area. The winter rainfall occurs mostly prior to and with a frontal passage and frequently lasts from two to four days, causing frequent general flooding on all streams.

Snow seldom remains on the ground more than two days in the valleys. However, at higher elevations surrounding the airport, roads are frequently blocked for several days during the winter months.

Huntington Tri-State Airport *Wayne County* Elevation: 830 ft. Latitude: 38° 23' N Longitude: 82° 33' W

	JAN	FEB	MAR	APR	MAY	JUN	JUL	AUG	SEP	OCT	NOV	DEC	YEAR
Mean Maximum Temp. (°F)	42.3	46.5	56.3	67.6	75.3	82.8	86.1	85.4	78.7	67.9	56.6	45.7	65.9
Mean Temp. (°F)	34.1	37.4	45.9	56.1	64.1	72.2	75.9	75.0	67.8	56.6	46.9	37.4	55.8
Mean Minimum Temp. (°F)	25.8	28.1	35.4	44.6	52.8	61.5	65.7	64.5	56.8	45.2	37.0	29.0	45.5
Extreme Maximum Temp. (°F)	78	77	86	92	93	100	102	103	97	93	83	80	103
Extreme Minimum Temp. (°F)	-21	-9	-2	20	30	41	47	43	31	23	13	-13	-21
Days Maximum Temp. ≥ 90°F	0	0	0	0	1	4	9	8	2	0	0	0	24
Days Maximum Temp. ≤ 32°F	7	4	1	0	0	0	0	0	0	0	0	4	16
Days Minimum Temp. ≤ 32°F	23	19	13	3	0	0	0	0	0	3	11	20	92
Days Minimum Temp. ≤ 0°F	1	0	0	0	0	0	0	0	0	0	0	0	1
Heating Degree Days (base 65°F)	952	775	592	288	108	10	0	2	51	277	540	850	4,445
Cooling Degree Days (base 65°F)	0	0	7	29	86	231	345	318	142	23	3	1	1,185
Mean Precipitation (in.)	2.95	3.03	3.98	3.47	4.55	3.77	4.62	3.85	2.77	2.78	3.37	3.31	42.45
Maximum Precipitation (in.)*	6.4	8.7	8.6	6.6	9.3	7.6	8.6	6.9	6.3	5.7	7.4	8.7	60.0
Minimum Precipitation (in.)*	0.6	0.5	1.1	0.7	0.9	0.4	1.4	0.7	0.3	trace	0.7	0.3	30.0
Extreme Maximum Daily Precip. (in.)	1.49	2.83	3.26	1.76	3.73	2.36	2.95	3.25	3.89	2.71	2.56	2.21	3.89
Days With ≥ 0.1" Precipitation	7	7	8	8	8	8	8	6	5	6	6	7	84
Days With ≥ 0.5" Precipitation	2	2	3	2	3	3	3	3	2	2	2	2	29
Days With ≥ 1.0" Precipitation	1	1	1	1	1	1	1	1	1	1	1	1	12
Mean Snowfall (in.)	***6.6***	***7.0***	***4.1***	***1.0***	***trace***	***trace***	***0.0***	***trace***	na	***0.1***	***0.7***	***3.2***	na
Maximum Snowfall (in.)*	30	24	24	14	trace	0	0	0	0	2	5	13	51
Maximum 24-hr. Snowfall (in.)*	10	10	21	7	trace	0	0	0	0	2	4	7	21
Maximum Snow Depth (in.)	***14***	***13***	***22***	***14***	***trace***	***trace***	***0***	***trace***	na	***1***	***2***	***5***	na
Days With ≥ 1.0" Snow Depth	***7***	***6***	***2***	***0***	***0***	***0***	***0***	***0***	na	***0***	***0***	***3***	na
Thunderstorm Days*	< 1	1	3	4	6	7	9	7	3	1	1	< 1	42
Foggy Days*	12	11	12	11	18	20	24	26	23	16	13	12	198
Predominant Sky Cover*	OVR	OVR	OVR	OVR	OVR	OVR	OVR	OVR	OVR	OVR	OVR	OVR	OVR
Mean Relative Humidity 7am (%)*	78	77	76	76	85	88	90	92	92	87	80	79	83
Mean Relative Humidity 4pm (%)*	61	56	50	45	51	55	57	57	57	51	56	62	55
Mean Dewpoint (°F)*	23	24	32	40	52	61	66	65	58	45	35	28	44
Prevailing Wind Direction*	W	WSW	WSW	WSW	SW	SW	SW	SW	SW	ESE	SW	SW	SW
Prevailing Wind Speed (mph)*	10	9	10	10	7	7	7	7	7	5	8	8	8
Maximum Wind Gust (mph)*	60	53	54	56	55	56	56	49	46	39	55	62	62

Note: (*) Period of record is 1961-1995

Beckley Va Hospital *Raleigh County* Elevation: 2,330 ft. Latitude: 37° 46' N Longitude: 81° 12' W

	JAN	FEB	MAR	APR	MAY	JUN	JUL	AUG	SEP	OCT	NOV	DEC	YEAR
Mean Maximum Temp. (°F)	39.8	43.5	52.1	63.2	70.6	76.1	78.5	78.1	72.0	62.8	53.2	42.8	61.1
Mean Temp. (°F)	30.3	33.1	40.5	50.4	58.3	65.5	68.6	67.9	61.4	51.2	42.0	33.3	50.2
Mean Minimum Temp. (°F)	20.7	22.6	28.8	37.5	46.0	54.8	58.6	57.6	50.7	39.6	30.8	23.8	39.3
Extreme Maximum Temp. (°F)	71	73	82	88	88	89	93	96	90	83	79	75	96
Extreme Minimum Temp. (°F)	-23	-22	-10	9	24	34	38	35	27	18	6	-22	-23
Days Maximum Temp. ≥ 90°F	0	0	0	0	0	0	0	1	0	0	0	0	1
Days Maximum Temp. ≤ 32°F	10	6	2	0	0	0	0	0	0	0	1	7	26
Days Minimum Temp. ≤ 32°F	26	24	21	10	2	0	0	0	1	8	18	25	135
Days Minimum Temp. ≤ 0°F	2	1	0	0	0	0	0	0	0	0	0	1	4
Heating Degree Days (base 65°F)	1,070	897	753	436	217	51	17	21	137	423	682	975	5,679
Cooling Degree Days (base 65°F)	0	0	0	4	16	73	134	117	34	3	0	0	381
Mean Precipitation (in.)	2.66	2.47	3.21	3.54	4.47	3.30	5.30	3.53	2.89	2.41	2.87	2.95	39.60
Extreme Maximum Daily Precip. (in.)	1.97	1.60	1.90	2.24	3.02	2.00	5.31	3.80	3.11	2.86	2.17	1.95	5.31
Days With ≥ 0.1" Precipitation	7	7	8	8	9	8	9	7	5	5	7	8	88
Days With ≥ 0.5" Precipitation	2	1	2	2	3	2	4	2	2	1	2	2	25
Days With ≥ 1.0" Precipitation	0	0	0	1	1	1	1	1	1	0	1	0	7
Mean Snowfall (in.)	10.3	7.8	4.9	0.8	0.0	0.0	0.0	0.0	0.0	trace	1.6	7.2	32.6
Maximum Snow Depth (in.)	28	20	26	17	0	0	0	0	0	4	4	***17***	***28***
Days With ≥ 1.0" Snow Depth	11	8	3	1	0	0	0	0	0	0	1	8	32

Belington *Barbour County* Elevation: 1,708 ft. Latitude: 39° 02' N Longitude: 79° 56' W

	JAN	FEB	MAR	APR	MAY	JUN	JUL	AUG	SEP	OCT	NOV	DEC	YEAR
Mean Maximum Temp. (°F)	39.3	42.6	51.1	62.9	71.1	78.6	81.7	80.7	74.7	64.1	53.6	42.8	61.9
Mean Temp. (°F)	29.1	31.5	38.9	***49.2***	57.8	66.5	70.3	69.1	62.4	51.1	41.8	32.7	***50.0***
Mean Minimum Temp. (°F)	18.8	20.3	26.7	***35.5***	44.5	54.3	58.7	57.4	50.1	38.0	30.1	22.6	***38.1***
Extreme Maximum Temp. (°F)	71	75	86	88	91	94	99	94	92	86	83	76	99
Extreme Minimum Temp. (°F)	-25	-21	-10	12	19	34	36	38	30	19	6	-19	-25
Days Maximum Temp. ≥ 90°F	0	0	0	0	0	0	1	1	0	0	0	0	2
Days Maximum Temp. ≤ 32°F	9	6	2	0	0	0	0	0	0	0	1	7	25
Days Minimum Temp. ≤ 32°F	25	24	22	12	3	0	0	0	0	9	18	25	138
Days Minimum Temp. ≤ 0°F	3	2	0	0	0	0	0	0	0	0	0	1	6
Heating Degree Days (base 65°F)	1,105	943	802	***472***	240	53	11	20	122	430	689	979	***5,866***
Cooling Degree Days (base 65°F)	0	0	0	***4***	25	104	180	152	52	4	0	0	***521***
Mean Precipitation (in.)	3.38	3.28	4.36	4.36	5.40	5.10	5.27	3.81	4.00	2.99	3.72	3.78	49.45
Extreme Maximum Daily Precip. (in.)	1.28	2.67	1.84	na	***3.80***	2.99	3.84	2.48	***2.86***	1.52	***3.70***	***1.95***	na
Days With ≥ 0.1" Precipitation	10	8	10	9	10	9	9	7	7	7	8	10	104
Days With ≥ 0.5" Precipitation	2	1	3	3	4	4	4	3	3	2	3	2	34
Days With ≥ 1.0" Precipitation	0	0	1	0	1	1	1	1	1	0	1	0	7
Mean Snowfall (in.)	***14.1***	10.3	7.8	1.2	0.0	0.0	0.0	0.0	0.0	0.2	2.0	***9.0***	***44.6***
Maximum Snow Depth (in.)	***21***	***16***	***10***	***13***	***0***	***0***	0	0	***0***	***3***	***3***	***16***	***21***
Days With ≥ 1.0" Snow Depth	***13***	9	4	1	0	0	0	0	0	0	2	8	***37***

Bluefield Mercer Co Arpt *Mercer County* Elevation: 2,891 ft. Latitude: 37° 18' N Longitude: 81° 13' W

	JAN	FEB	MAR	APR	MAY	JUN	JUL	AUG	SEP	OCT	NOV	DEC	YEAR
Mean Maximum Temp. (°F)	41.0	44.6	53.1	63.5	70.7	77.0	80.0	79.4	73.2	64.1	54.1	44.2	62.1
Mean Temp. (°F)	33.0	35.9	43.8	53.6	61.2	68.2	71.5	70.8	64.4	54.9	45.6	36.3	53.3
Mean Minimum Temp. (°F)	25.0	27.5	34.5	43.7	51.6	59.4	63.0	62.1	55.6	45.7	37.0	28.4	44.4
Extreme Maximum Temp. (°F)	72	72	83	86	89	91	96	95	93	88	81	74	96
Extreme Minimum Temp. (°F)	-21	-9	-2	15	28	39	45	39	30	24	8	-13	-21
Days Maximum Temp. ≥ 90°F	0	0	0	0	0	0	1	1	0	0	0	0	2
Days Maximum Temp. ≤ 32°F	8	5	2	0	0	0	0	0	0	0	1	6	22
Days Minimum Temp. ≤ 32°F	24	19	14	5	0	0	0	0	0	3	11	21	97
Days Minimum Temp. ≤ 0°F	1	0	0	0	0	0	0	0	0	0	0	0	1
Heating Degree Days (base 65°F)	984	817	652	352	158	29	5	8	87	319	578	882	4,871
Cooling Degree Days (base 65°F)	0	0	3	17	46	132	214	194	77	13	1	0	697
Mean Precipitation (in.)	2.93	2.68	3.48	3.40	4.26	4.02	4.36	3.23	3.09	2.49	2.61	2.82	39.37
Extreme Maximum Daily Precip. (in.)	1.76	2.66	2.28	1.76	2.52	3.61	3.26	2.14	3.03	3.18	2.05	1.53	3.61
Days With ≥ 0.1" Precipitation	7	7	8	8	9	8	8	7	5	5	6	7	85
Days With ≥ 0.5" Precipitation	2	1	2	2	3	3	3	2	2	2	2	2	26
Days With ≥ 1.0" Precipitation	0	0	1	0	1	1	1	1	1	0	0	0	6
Mean Snowfall (in.)	na	na	na	na	na	na	na	na	na	na	na	na	na
Maximum Snow Depth (in.)	na	na	na	na	na	na	na	na	na	na	na	na	na
Days With ≥ 1.0" Snow Depth	na	na	na	na	na	na	na	na	na	na	na	na	na

Bluestone Lake *Summers County* Elevation: 1,390 ft. Latitude: 37° 38' N Longitude: 80° 53' W

	JAN	FEB	MAR	APR	MAY	JUN	JUL	AUG	SEP	OCT	NOV	DEC	YEAR
Mean Maximum Temp. (°F)	41.4	45.8	54.7	66.1	74.0	81.0	84.5	83.3	77.0	66.9	55.6	43.9	64.5
Mean Temp. (°F)	32.6	35.8	43.1	53.2	61.6	69.8	74.0	72.9	66.3	55.2	44.9	35.3	53.7
Mean Minimum Temp. (°F)	23.6	25.8	31.5	40.3	49.1	58.5	63.4	62.4	55.6	43.5	34.2	26.6	42.9
Extreme Maximum Temp. (°F)	77	78	85	90	90	95	98	99	96	86	80	77	99
Extreme Minimum Temp. (°F)	-17	-13	0	20	26	39	45	41	31	24	13	-9	-17
Days Maximum Temp. ≥ 90°F	0	0	0	0	0	2	5	4	1	0	0	0	12
Days Maximum Temp. ≤ 32°F	6	3	1	0	0	0	0	0	0	0	0	4	14
Days Minimum Temp. ≤ 32°F	25	22	18	5	1	0	0	0	0	3	14	23	111
Days Minimum Temp. ≤ 0°F	1	0	0	0	0	0	0	0	0	0	0	0	1
Heating Degree Days (base 65°F)	999	819	673	356	146	20	2	3	62	308	596	915	4,899
Cooling Degree Days (base 65°F)	0	0	0	9	48	169	287	254	107	11	0	0	885
Mean Precipitation (in.)	2.88	2.60	3.45	3.53	4.00	3.39	4.60	3.39	2.88	2.59	2.63	2.81	38.75
Extreme Maximum Daily Precip. (in.)	2.71	1.90	2.12	2.11	2.02	2.76	2.79	2.44	2.25	2.37	1.90	2.00	2.79
Days With ≥ 0.1" Precipitation	7	6	7	7	9	8	8	7	6	5	6	7	83
Days With ≥ 0.5" Precipitation	2	2	3	2	3	2	3	2	2	2	2	2	27
Days With ≥ 1.0" Precipitation	0	0	1	1	1	1	1	1	1	1	0	0	8
Mean Snowfall (in.)	7.4	5.2	2.8	0.4	trace	0.0	0.0	0.0	0.0	trace	0.5	4.0	20.3
Maximum Snow Depth (in.)	23	14	19	7	trace	0	0	0	0	1	3	19	23
Days With ≥ 1.0" Snow Depth	7	5	2	0	0	0	0	0	0	0	0	4	18

The period of record for all cooperative weather station data is 1980 – 2009. See User Guide for detailed explanation of data.

Buckhannon *Upshur County* Elevation: 1,455 ft. Latitude: 38° 59' N Longitude: 80° 13' W

	JAN	FEB	MAR	APR	MAY	JUN	JUL	AUG	SEP	OCT	NOV	DEC	YEAR
Mean Maximum Temp. (°F)	39.9	44.0	53.0	64.9	73.5	80.5	83.2	82.9	77.1	66.1	54.6	44.4	63.7
Mean Temp. (°F)	29.9	33.0	40.7	51.1	60.0	68.1	71.8	70.9	64.2	52.8	43.1	34.6	51.7
Mean Minimum Temp. (°F)	19.9	21.8	28.4	37.3	46.4	55.8	60.4	58.7	51.2	39.5	31.5	24.8	39.6
Extreme Maximum Temp. (°F)	71	77	84	93	92	95	96	96	96	90	81	76	96
Extreme Minimum Temp. (°F)	-30	-20	-13	12	24	36	41	37	28	20	7	-13	-30
Days Maximum Temp. ≥ 90°F	0	0	0	0	0	1	3	4	1	0	0	0	9
Days Maximum Temp. ≤ 32°F	10	6	2	0	0	0	0	0	0	0	1	6	25
Days Minimum Temp. ≤ 32°F	26	23	21	10	2	0	0	0	0	8	17	24	131
Days Minimum Temp. ≤ 0°F	3	2	0	0	0	0	0	0	0	0	0	1	6
Heating Degree Days (base 65°F)	1,080	900	746	416	184	33	4	9	91	376	651	936	5,426
Cooling Degree Days (base 65°F)	0	0	0	6	35	134	222	198	74	6	0	0	675
Mean Precipitation (in.)	3.40	3.02	4.31	3.93	5.05	5.07	5.13	4.23	3.48	3.33	3.69	3.82	48.46
Extreme Maximum Daily Precip. (in.)	1.36	3.43	1.88	1.96	2.10	4.95	3.63	2.49	2.77	2.46	3.26	2.05	4.95
Days With ≥ 0.1" Precipitation	9	7	9	9	10	9	9	8	7	7	8	9	101
Days With ≥ 0.5" Precipitation	2	2	3	2	3	3	4	3	3	2	2	2	31
Days With ≥ 1.0" Precipitation	0	0	1	1	1	1	1	1	1	1	1	1	10
Mean Snowfall (in.)	14.9	10.5	7.1	0.8	trace	0.0	0.0	0.0	0.0	0.1	2.2	8.0	43.6
Maximum Snow Depth (in.)	18	15	24	3	0	0	0	0	0	1	7	13	24
Days With ≥ 1.0" Snow Depth	15	10	4	0	0	0	0	0	0	0	1	7	37

Clarksburg 1 *Harrison County* Elevation: 990 ft. Latitude: 39° 16' N Longitude: 80° 21' W

	JAN	FEB	MAR	APR	MAY	JUN	JUL	AUG	SEP	OCT	NOV	DEC	YEAR
Mean Maximum Temp. (°F)	39.5	43.1	52.3	64.7	73.5	81.7	84.4	83.2	76.5	65.1	54.1	42.8	63.4
Mean Temp. (°F)	30.5	33.1	40.8	51.7	60.8	69.6	73.3	72.2	65.1	53.1	43.4	34.2	52.3
Mean Minimum Temp. (°F)	21.5	23.0	29.3	38.7	47.9	57.5	62.2	61.2	53.6	41.0	32.7	25.5	41.2
Extreme Maximum Temp. (°F)	73	77	84	93	92	97	97	98	94	87	80	74	98
Extreme Minimum Temp. (°F)	-24	-11	-6	18	30	38	47	40	35	21	12	-11	-24
Days Maximum Temp. ≥ 90°F	0	0	0	0	0	3	5	4	1	0	0	0	13
Days Maximum Temp. ≤ 32°F	9	6	2	0	0	0	0	0	0	0	1	6	24
Days Minimum Temp. ≤ 32°F	26	23	20	8	1	0	0	0	0	6	16	23	123
Days Minimum Temp. ≤ 0°F	1	1	0	0	0	0	0	0	0	0	0	0	2
Heating Degree Days (base 65°F)	1,063	896	743	401	171	24	2	6	81	371	642	949	5,349
Cooling Degree Days (base 65°F)	0	0	1	9	46	170	267	237	90	9	0	0	829
Mean Precipitation (in.)	3.32	3.15	4.22	3.66	4.78	4.39	4.80	3.88	3.17	3.07	3.91	3.41	45.76
Extreme Maximum Daily Precip. (in.)	1.55	2.80	2.50	1.67	2.88	3.00	2.47	3.11	2.43	1.83	5.00	2.17	5.00
Days With ≥ 0.1" Precipitation	8	8	9	9	10	9	8	7	6	7	8	8	97
Days With ≥ 0.5" Precipitation	2	2	3	2	3	3	4	3	2	2	3	2	31
Days With ≥ 1.0" Precipitation	1	0	1	1	1	1	1	1	1	1	1	1	11
Mean Snowfall (in.)	9.3	6.3	3.5	0.3	0.0	0.0	0.0	0.0	0.0	trace	0.7	4.3	24.4
Maximum Snow Depth (in.)	18	21	18	5	0	0	0	0	0	0	4	13	21
Days With ≥ 1.0" Snow Depth	11	7	3	0	0	0	0	0	0	0	1	5	27

Creston *Wirt County* Elevation: 649 ft. Latitude: 38° 57' N Longitude: 81° 16' W

	JAN	FEB	MAR	APR	MAY	JUN	JUL	AUG	SEP	OCT	NOV	DEC	YEAR
Mean Maximum Temp. (°F)	41.5	46.4	55.7	67.5	76.2	83.5	86.8	85.6	79.4	68.7	56.9	45.5	66.1
Mean Temp. (°F)	30.8	34.7	42.0	52.3	61.9	70.1	74.5	73.1	66.0	54.3	44.0	34.9	53.2
Mean Minimum Temp. (°F)	20.1	22.8	28.2	37.2	47.6	56.6	62.0	60.5	52.6	39.9	31.0	24.2	40.2
Extreme Maximum Temp. (°F)	76	80	90	95	96	103	106	105	98	90	85	80	106
Extreme Minimum Temp. (°F)	-30	-20	-6	15	25	38	42	41	29	18	8	-19	-30
Days Maximum Temp. ≥ 90°F	0	0	0	0	2	6	10	8	2	0	0	0	28
Days Maximum Temp. ≤ 32°F	7	4	1	0	0	0	0	0	0	0	0	5	17
Days Minimum Temp. ≤ 32°F	26	23	21	10	1	0	0	0	0	8	18	24	131
Days Minimum Temp. ≤ 0°F	2	1	0	0	0	0	0	0	0	0	0	1	4
Heating Degree Days (base 65°F)	1,053	852	708	384	149	23	2	5	76	338	624	928	5,142
Cooling Degree Days (base 65°F)	0	0	1	11	59	183	301	263	113	14	1	0	946
Mean Precipitation (in.)	3.16	3.40	4.25	3.40	4.79	4.24	4.80	3.93	3.44	3.03	3.75	3.21	45.40
Extreme Maximum Daily Precip. (in.)	2.38	3.24	2.42	2.08	2.36	2.98	3.26	3.55	2.64	2.20	2.64	1.63	3.55
Days With ≥ 0.1" Precipitation	8	7	9	8	9	8	8	7	5	6	8	8	91
Days With ≥ 0.5" Precipitation	2	2	3	2	4	3	4	3	2	2	3	2	32
Days With ≥ 1.0" Precipitation	1	1	1	1	1	1	1	1	1	1	1	0	11
Mean Snowfall (in.)	7.3	3.8	2.9	0.4	0.0	0.0	0.0	0.0	0.0	0.0	0.4	na	na
Maximum Snow Depth (in.)	18	13	15	8	0	0	0	0	0	0	2	5	18
Days With ≥ 1.0" Snow Depth	8	4	1	0	0	0	0	0	0	0	0	3	16

Dunlow 1 SW *Wayne County* Elevation: 1,200 ft. Latitude: 37° 57' N Longitude: 82° 24' W

	JAN	FEB	MAR	APR	MAY	JUN	JUL	AUG	SEP	OCT	NOV	DEC	YEAR
Mean Maximum Temp. (°F)	41.9	45.6	54.9	66.1	73.1	80.2	83.4	82.5	76.3	65.7	55.6	44.5	64.2
Mean Temp. (°F)	33.1	36.1	44.0	54.5	62.0	69.8	73.3	72.3	65.4	54.5	45.6	35.7	53.8
Mean Minimum Temp. (°F)	24.2	26.6	32.9	42.8	50.8	59.4	63.2	62.0	54.5	43.2	35.5	26.8	43.5
Extreme Maximum Temp. (°F)	73	77	87	90	90	94	100	100	94	87	83	78	100
Extreme Minimum Temp. (°F)	-20	-9	2	11	26	40	43	33	27	20	1	-15	-20
Days Maximum Temp. ≥ 90°F	0	0	0	0	0	1	4	4	1	0	0	0	10
Days Maximum Temp. ≤ 32°F	7	4	1	0	0	0	0	0	0	0	1	6	19
Days Minimum Temp. ≤ 32°F	24	20	16	5	1	0	0	0	0	5	12	21	104
Days Minimum Temp. ≤ 0°F	1	0	0	0	0	0	0	0	0	0	0	1	2
Heating Degree Days (base 65°F)	983	811	649	335	148	23	2	7	80	334	572	904	4,848
Cooling Degree Days (base 65°F)	0	0	4	26	62	174	268	239	99	15	1	1	889
Mean Precipitation (in.)	3.16	3.26	3.81	3.93	4.71	4.27	4.63	3.56	3.45	3.15	3.67	3.49	45.09
Extreme Maximum Daily Precip. (in.)	2.08	1.90	2.12	2.15	2.70	2.80	2.64	2.25	2.98	1.95	2.95	2.52	2.98
Days With ≥ 0.1" Precipitation	7	7	9	9	9	8	8	6	6	6	7	8	90
Days With ≥ 0.5" Precipitation	2	2	3	3	3	3	4	3	2	2	2	2	31
Days With ≥ 1.0" Precipitation	0	1	1	1	1	1	1	1	1	1	1	0	10
Mean Snowfall (in.)	6.3	3.6	2.7	0.7	0.0	0.0	0.0	0.0	0.0	trace	0.5	3.2	17.0
Maximum Snow Depth (in.)	20	13	18	2	0	0	0	0	0	trace	5	11	20
Days With ≥ 1.0" Snow Depth	5	4	1	0	0	0	0	0	0	0	0	4	14

The period of record for all cooperative weather station data is 1980 – 2009. See User Guide for detailed explanation of data.

Fairmont *Marion County* Elevation: 1,299 ft. Latitude: 39° 28' N Longitude: 80° 08' W

	JAN	FEB	MAR	APR	MAY	JUN	JUL	AUG	SEP	OCT	NOV	DEC	YEAR
Mean Maximum Temp. (°F)	38.7	42.4	51.9	64.1	72.4	79.9	83.3	82.3	75.9	64.5	53.4	42.1	62.6
Mean Temp. (°F)	30.2	33.0	41.1	52.0	60.6	68.4	72.4	71.4	64.6	53.2	43.8	33.9	52.0
Mean Minimum Temp. (°F)	21.7	23.5	30.2	39.9	48.6	57.0	61.5	60.4	53.2	41.8	34.1	25.6	41.5
Extreme Maximum Temp. (°F)	73	77	84	91	91	94	100	98	95	89	82	74	100
Extreme Minimum Temp. (°F)	-21	-8	-1	16	25	35	42	36	29	20	11	-16	-21
Days Maximum Temp. ≥ 90°F	0	0	0	0	0	1	4	3	1	0	0	0	9
Days Maximum Temp. ≤ 32°F	10	7	2	0	0	0	0	0	0	0	1	7	27
Days Minimum Temp. ≤ 32°F	26	23	19	7	1	0	0	0	0	5	14	24	119
Days Minimum Temp. ≤ 0°F	1	1	0	0	0	0	0	0	0	0	0	1	3
Heating Degree Days (base 65°F)	1,071	899	736	395	176	33	3	8	89	370	631	957	5,368
Cooling Degree Days (base 65°F)	0	0	2	12	45	143	240	212	82	10	1	0	747
Mean Precipitation (in.)	3.39	2.95	4.03	3.67	4.98	4.45	4.97	3.89	3.46	3.04	3.74	3.28	45.85
Extreme Maximum Daily Precip. (in.)	1.55	3.19	1.98	1.77	2.98	2.05	3.68	3.49	2.77	2.04	3.66	2.00	3.68
Days With ≥ 0.1" Precipitation	8	7	8	8	10	8	8	7	7	7	7	8	93
Days With ≥ 0.5" Precipitation	2	2	3	2	3	3	4	3	2	2	3	2	31
Days With ≥ 1.0" Precipitation	1	0	1	0	1	1	1	1	1	1	1	0	9
Mean Snowfall (in.)	11.3	7.5	5.3	0.9	0.0	0.0	0.0	0.0	0.0	0.2	1.7	5.8	32.7
Maximum Snow Depth (in.)	17	20	20	13	0	0	0	0	0	5	8	10	20
Days With ≥ 1.0" Snow Depth	11	8	4	0	0	0	0	0	0	0	1	6	30

Hamlin *Lincoln County* Elevation: 642 ft. Latitude: 38° 17' N Longitude: 82° 06' W

	JAN	FEB	MAR	APR	MAY	JUN	JUL	AUG	SEP	OCT	NOV	DEC	YEAR
Mean Maximum Temp. (°F)	43.9	47.9	57.2	68.5	76.9	84.1	87.4	86.9	80.9	70.1	58.9	47.5	67.5
Mean Temp. (°F)	32.9	35.8	43.6	53.7	62.8	70.9	75.1	74.1	67.1	55.1	45.3	36.2	54.4
Mean Minimum Temp. (°F)	21.5	23.6	30.0	38.9	48.6	57.7	62.6	61.2	53.2	39.9	31.3	24.6	41.1
Extreme Maximum Temp. (°F)	78	82	89	94	95	100	103	105	101	98	88	82	105
Extreme Minimum Temp. (°F)	-28	-19	-8	15	27	38	40	40	31	18	8	-17	-28
Days Maximum Temp. ≥ 90°F	0	0	0	0	2	6	12	11	4	0	0	0	35
Days Maximum Temp. ≤ 32°F	6	4	1	0	0	0	0	0	0	0	0	4	15
Days Minimum Temp. ≤ 32°F	26	23	19	8	1	0	0	0	0	8	17	24	126
Days Minimum Temp. ≤ 0°F	1	1	0	0	0	0	0	0	0	0	0	1	3
Heating Degree Days (base 65°F)	989	820	657	348	132	18	1	3	61	315	587	886	4,817
Cooling Degree Days (base 65°F)	0	0	2	16	70	203	320	294	131	16	0	0	1,052
Mean Precipitation (in.)	2.95	3.15	3.94	3.56	4.77	4.02	5.06	3.85	3.15	3.13	3.56	3.49	44.63
Extreme Maximum Daily Precip. (in.)	1.90	2.40	2.52	1.82	3.38	2.76	3.30	2.82	2.20	2.33	3.56	2.28	3.56
Days With ≥ 0.1" Precipitation	7	7	8	9	9	8	8	7	6	6	7	8	90
Days With ≥ 0.5" Precipitation	2	2	3	2	3	3	4	3	2	2	2	2	30
Days With ≥ 1.0" Precipitation	0	1	1	0	1	1	1	1	1	1	1	1	10
Mean Snowfall (in.)	6.7	5.3	2.7	0.8	trace	0.0	0.0	0.0	trace	trace	0.4	3.0	18.9
Maximum Snow Depth (in.)	17	13	16	13	trace	0	0	0	trace	trace	3	6	17
Days With ≥ 1.0" Snow Depth	6	4	1	0	0	0	0	0	0	0	0	3	14

Hogsett R C Byrd Dam *Mason County* Elevation: 569 ft. Latitude: 38° 41' N Longitude: 82° 11' W

	JAN	FEB	MAR	APR	MAY	JUN	JUL	AUG	SEP	OCT	NOV	DEC	YEAR
Mean Maximum Temp. (°F)	41.8	45.4	54.8	66.7	74.9	82.9	86.6	85.8	79.2	68.2	56.7	45.2	65.7
Mean Temp. (°F)	32.1	34.9	42.9	53.8	62.4	71.0	75.1	74.2	67.3	55.8	45.4	35.7	54.2
Mean Minimum Temp. (°F)	22.4	24.4	31.0	40.8	49.8	59.2	63.6	62.5	55.3	43.3	34.1	26.2	42.7
Extreme Maximum Temp. (°F)	75	77	88	91	93	100	102	102	97	91	82	78	102
Extreme Minimum Temp. (°F)	-24	-12	-6	15	29	36	45	41	34	23	11	-15	-24
Days Maximum Temp. ≥ 90°F	0	0	0	0	1	5	10	8	2	0	0	0	26
Days Maximum Temp. ≤ 32°F	7	4	1	0	0	0	0	0	0	0	0	4	16
Days Minimum Temp. ≤ 32°F	26	23	19	5	0	0	0	0	0	3	14	23	113
Days Minimum Temp. ≤ 0°F	1	0	0	0	0	0	0	0	0	0	0	0	1
Heating Degree Days (base 65°F)	1,012	845	679	344	138	15	1	2	53	296	582	900	4,867
Cooling Degree Days (base 65°F)	0	0	2	15	63	203	321	295	128	17	1	0	1,045
Mean Precipitation (in.)	2.97	2.93	3.82	3.40	4.15	3.56	4.12	3.37	3.06	2.73	3.12	3.22	40.45
Extreme Maximum Daily Precip. (in.)	2.38	2.57	3.90	3.20	2.12	2.40	4.70	3.11	4.78	4.36	2.04	2.58	4.78
Days With ≥ 0.1" Precipitation	7	6	8	8	8	7	7	6	5	6	6	7	81
Days With ≥ 0.5" Precipitation	2	2	3	2	3	3	3	2	2	2	2	2	28
Days With ≥ 1.0" Precipitation	0	1	1	0	1	1	1	1	1	1	1	0	9
Mean Snowfall (in.)	***3.0***	***1.8***	***1.7***	trace	0.0	0.0	0.0	0.0	0.0	0.0	trace	***1.8***	***8.3***
Maximum Snow Depth (in.)	11	10	20	7	0	0	0	0	0	0	trace	3	20
Days With ≥ 1.0" Snow Depth	6	3	1	0	0	0	0	0	0	0	0	1	11

Huntington Sewage Plant *Wayne County* Elevation: 520 ft. Latitude: 38° 25' N Longitude: 82° 31' W

	JAN	FEB	MAR	APR	MAY	JUN	JUL	AUG	SEP	OCT	NOV	DEC	YEAR
Mean Maximum Temp. (°F)	43.7	47.9	57.7	69.4	76.7	84.6	***87.8***	87.2	81.0	70.4	***58.2***	47.8	***67.7***
Mean Temp. (°F)	34.5	37.6	46.0	56.3	64.7	***73.4***	***76.8***	76.3	69.0	57.9	***47.1***	38.8	***56.5***
Mean Minimum Temp. (°F)	25.2	27.1	34.3	43.1	52.5	***62.3***	***66.0***	65.2	57.0	45.4	***35.8***	29.8	***45.3***
Extreme Maximum Temp. (°F)	78	80	88	104	95	***98***	102	***103***	***99***	***93***	***88***	***80***	***104***
Extreme Minimum Temp. (°F)	-19	-9	-2	22	32	***42***	***47***	***44***	***35***	***25***	***10***	***4***	***-19***
Days Maximum Temp. ≥ 90°F	0	0	0	1	1	7	12	11	3	0	0	0	35
Days Maximum Temp. ≤ 32°F	6	3	1	0	0	0	0	0	0	0	0	3	13
Days Minimum Temp. ≤ 32°F	22	20	14	3	0	0	0	0	0	2	11	19	91
Days Minimum Temp. ≤ 0°F	1	0	0	0	0	0	0	0	0	0	0	0	1
Heating Degree Days (base 65°F)	940	769	586	283	100	***8***	***0***	1	40	238	***533***	807	***4,305***
Cooling Degree Days (base 65°F)	0	0	4	28	97	***268***	***373***	358	167	26	***2***	1	***1,324***
Mean Precipitation (in.)	3.23	2.72	3.80	3.50	4.47	3.86	4.67	3.85	2.90	2.82	3.14	3.37	42.33
Extreme Maximum Daily Precip. (in.)	***1.86***	2.25	***3.10***	***1.64***	***2.01***	***2.43***	***3.30***	***2.94***	***3.00***	na	na	***2.00***	na
Days With ≥ 0.1" Precipitation	6	6	8	8	8	7	7	7	5	5	***6***	7	***80***
Days With ≥ 0.5" Precipitation	2	2	2	2	3	2	3	2	2	2	2	2	26
Days With ≥ 1.0" Precipitation	1	1	1	1	1	1	1	1	1	1	1	1	12
Mean Snowfall (in.)	***4.8***	3.4	1.1	trace	0.0	0.0	0.0	0.0	0.0	trace	trace	***1.5***	***10.8***
Maximum Snow Depth (in.)	***13***	***11***	***10***	***trace***	***0***	***0***	***0***	***0***	***0***	***0***	***trace***	na	na
Days With ≥ 1.0" Snow Depth	***4***	2	0	0	0	0	0	0	0	0	0	***1***	7

The period of record for all cooperative weather station data is 1980 – 2009. See User Guide for detailed explanation of data.

London Locks *Kanawha County* Elevation: 620 ft. Latitude: 38° 12' N Longitude: 81° 22' W

	JAN	FEB	MAR	APR	MAY	JUN	JUL	AUG	SEP	OCT	NOV	DEC	YEAR
Mean Maximum Temp. (°F)	43.4	47.2	56.2	67.5	75.0	82.6	85.6	84.8	78.7	67.9	57.5	46.7	66.1
Mean Temp. (°F)	34.6	37.5	45.1	55.1	63.3	71.9	75.7	75.0	68.6	57.3	47.1	38.0	55.8
Mean Minimum Temp. (°F)	25.8	27.7	33.8	42.8	51.7	61.0	65.7	65.1	58.5	46.6	36.7	29.3	45.4
Extreme Maximum Temp. (°F)	75	79	88	92	95	96	98	101	96	91	84	76	101
Extreme Minimum Temp. (°F)	-16	-7	-1	22	28	45	48	45	38	25	17	-7	-16
Days Maximum Temp. ≥ 90°F	0	0	0	0	1	4	7	7	2	0	0	0	21
Days Maximum Temp. ≤ 32°F	5	3	1	0	0	0	0	0	0	0	0	3	12
Days Minimum Temp. ≤ 32°F	23	19	15	3	0	0	0	0	0	1	11	20	92
Days Minimum Temp. ≤ 0°F	1	0	0	0	0	0	0	0	0	0	0	0	1
Heating Degree Days (base 65°F)	935	771	613	307	116	10	0	1	38	257	531	830	4,409
Cooling Degree Days (base 65°F)	0	0	2	18	70	226	339	317	153	24	1	0	1,150
Mean Precipitation (in.)	2.97	2.79	3.62	3.76	4.72	4.24	5.09	3.84	3.23	2.54	3.37	3.19	43.36
Extreme Maximum Daily Precip. (in.)	1.55	1.63	1.95	1.95	2.50	3.36	2.52	2.45	3.10	2.15	2.95	2.11	3.36
Days With ≥ 0.1" Precipitation	8	7	8	9	9	8	8	7	6	6	7	8	91
Days With ≥ 0.5" Precipitation	2	2	2	3	3	3	4	3	2	2	2	2	30
Days With ≥ 1.0" Precipitation	0	0	1	1	1	1	2	1	1	0	1	0	9
Mean Snowfall (in.)	na	na	***0.4***	0.0	0.0	0.0	0.0	0.0	0.0	0.0	0.0	na	na
Maximum Snow Depth (in.)	na	na	na	***1***	***0***	***0***	***0***	***0***	***0***	***0***	***2***	na	na
Days With ≥ 1.0" Snow Depth	na	***2***	1	0	0	0	0	0	0	0	0	***1***	na

Mannington 8 WNW *Marion County* Elevation: 1,100 ft. Latitude: 39° 32' N Longitude: 80° 30' W

	JAN	FEB	MAR	APR	MAY	JUN	JUL	AUG	SEP	OCT	NOV	DEC	YEAR
Mean Maximum Temp. (°F)	39.3	43.2	53.0	65.6	74.1	81.5	84.8	84.2	77.7	66.5	54.3	42.5	63.9
Mean Temp. (°F)	28.3	31.3	39.0	50.0	59.0	67.2	71.5	70.5	63.2	51.6	41.5	32.0	50.4
Mean Minimum Temp. (°F)	17.2	19.1	25.0	34.3	43.8	52.9	58.1	56.8	48.6	36.6	28.7	21.6	36.9
Extreme Maximum Temp. (°F)	75	80	88	93	94	97	103	100	96	88	82	75	103
Extreme Minimum Temp. (°F)	-34	-21	-13	12	25	25	36	34	27	14	2	-24	-34
Days Maximum Temp. ≥ 90°F	0	0	0	0	1	3	6	6	1	0	0	0	17
Days Maximum Temp. ≤ 32°F	9	5	1	0	0	0	0	0	0	0	1	7	23
Days Minimum Temp. ≤ 32°F	28	25	24	13	4	0	0	0	1	12	20	26	153
Days Minimum Temp. ≤ 0°F	4	2	1	0	0	0	0	0	0	0	0	1	8
Heating Degree Days (base 65°F)	1,132	946	802	450	212	46	7	15	110	414	698	1,015	5,847
Cooling Degree Days (base 65°F)	0	0	0	6	32	120	215	193	62	5	0	0	633
Mean Precipitation (in.)	3.71	3.40	4.39	3.81	4.90	4.44	5.37	4.12	3.71	3.26	4.04	3.87	49.02
Extreme Maximum Daily Precip. (in.)	1.54	3.10	2.16	1.88	2.13	2.69	3.00	3.07	3.57	2.04	4.29	2.18	4.29
Days With ≥ 0.1" Precipitation	9	8	9	9	10	9	8	7	7	7	9	9	101
Days With ≥ 0.5" Precipitation	2	2	3	2	3	3	4	3	2	2	3	2	31
Days With ≥ 1.0" Precipitation	1	0	1	0	1	1	1	1	1	1	1	1	10
Mean Snowfall (in.)	***15.0***	***9.8***	6.8	0.5	0.0	0.0	0.0	0.0	0.0	0.2	2.0	***8.4***	***42.7***
Maximum Snow Depth (in.)	27	29	28	12	0	0	0	0	0	2	5	***7***	***29***
Days With ≥ 1.0" Snow Depth	13	11	4	1	0	0	0	0	0	0	1	9	39

Martinsburg Eastern WV Reg Arpt *Berkeley County* Elevation: 537 ft. Latitude: 39° 24' N Longitude: 77° 59' W

	JAN	FEB	MAR	APR	MAY	JUN	JUL	AUG	SEP	OCT	NOV	DEC	YEAR
Mean Maximum Temp. (°F)	40.4	44.3	53.4	64.9	73.8	82.7	86.7	84.9	77.6	66.2	55.2	43.9	64.5
Mean Temp. (°F)	31.8	34.8	42.8	53.4	62.2	71.2	75.7	73.9	66.3	54.7	45.0	35.2	53.9
Mean Minimum Temp. (°F)	23.1	25.3	32.2	41.8	50.5	59.7	64.7	62.9	55.0	43.2	34.9	26.4	43.3
Extreme Maximum Temp. (°F)	75	83	88	93	96	100	107	103	100	89	82	78	107
Extreme Minimum Temp. (°F)	-18	-5	-3	19	30	39	49	40	32	22	13	-12	-18
Days Maximum Temp. ≥ 90°F	0	0	0	0	1	6	10	8	2	0	0	0	27
Days Maximum Temp. ≤ 32°F	7	4	1	0	0	0	0	0	0	0	0	4	16
Days Minimum Temp. ≤ 32°F	25	22	16	4	0	0	0	0	0	4	12	23	106
Days Minimum Temp. ≤ 0°F	1	0	0	0	0	0	0	0	0	0	0	0	1
Heating Degree Days (base 65°F)	1,022	847	683	354	143	16	1	4	66	326	593	918	4,973
Cooling Degree Days (base 65°F)	0	0	3	11	62	209	340	287	114	14	0	0	1,040
Mean Precipitation (in.)	2.38	2.27	3.50	3.36	4.04	3.75	3.80	3.09	3.42	3.06	3.16	2.66	38.49
Extreme Maximum Daily Precip. (in.)	1.47	2.91	2.31	3.42	2.56	3.15	3.07	2.69	3.19	3.50	3.33	2.12	3.50
Days With ≥ 0.1" Precipitation	6	5	7	6	8	7	7	6	6	5	6	6	75
Days With ≥ 0.5" Precipitation	1	1	2	2	3	3	2	2	2	2	2	2	24
Days With ≥ 1.0" Precipitation	0	0	1	1	1	1	1	1	1	1	1	0	9
Mean Snowfall (in.)	na	na	***4.7***	***0.4***	***trace***	na	na	***0.0***	***trace***	***trace***	***1.1***	na	na
Maximum Snow Depth (in.)	na	na	na	***3***	***trace***	na	na	na	na	na	na	na	na
Days With ≥ 1.0" Snow Depth	na	na	***3***	***0***	***0***	na	na	***0***	***0***	***0***	***1***	na	na

Morgantown Lock & Dam *Monongalia County* Elevation: 825 ft. Latitude: 39° 37' N Longitude: 79° 58' W

	JAN	FEB	MAR	APR	MAY	JUN	JUL	AUG	SEP	OCT	NOV	DEC	YEAR
Mean Maximum Temp. (°F)	39.6	43.5	53.0	64.8	72.5	80.1	83.6	82.6	76.4	65.6	54.5	43.3	63.3
Mean Temp. (°F)	31.1	34.0	42.1	52.5	60.9	69.2	73.3	72.2	65.7	54.5	44.5	34.9	52.9
Mean Minimum Temp. (°F)	22.5	24.4	31.1	40.2	49.2	58.2	62.9	61.8	54.9	43.5	34.5	26.4	42.5
Extreme Maximum Temp. (°F)	73	77	83	90	90	95	98	100	99	96	81	78	100
Extreme Minimum Temp. (°F)	-21	-8	-3	19	27	37	42	36	34	20	12	-15	-21
Days Maximum Temp. ≥ 90°F	0	0	0	0	0	1	4	3	1	0	0	0	9
Days Maximum Temp. ≤ 32°F	8	5	1	0	0	0	0	0	0	0	0	6	20
Days Minimum Temp. ≤ 32°F	25	22	18	7	1	0	0	0	0	3	13	23	112
Days Minimum Temp. ≤ 0°F	1	1	0	0	0	0	0	0	0	0	0	0	2
Heating Degree Days (base 65°F)	1,044	871	706	376	160	25	2	5	70	328	608	927	5,122
Cooling Degree Days (base 65°F)	0	0	1	8	41	157	265	236	97	11	0	0	816
Mean Precipitation (in.)	3.06	2.90	3.79	3.72	4.55	4.10	4.42	3.58	3.05	2.78	3.56	3.23	42.74
Extreme Maximum Daily Precip. (in.)	1.41	3.00	2.01	1.75	2.90	2.08	3.75	2.68	2.55	1.63	3.56	1.67	3.75
Days With ≥ 0.1" Precipitation	8	7	8	9	9	8	8	7	6	6	7	7	90
Days With ≥ 0.5" Precipitation	2	1	3	2	3	3	3	2	2	2	2	2	27
Days With ≥ 1.0" Precipitation	0	0	1	1	1	1	1	1	1	0	1	0	8
Mean Snowfall (in.)	na	na	***0.4***	trace	0.0	0.0	0.0	0.0	0.0	0.0	0.1	na	na
Maximum Snow Depth (in.)	20	***5***	13	trace	0	0	0	0	0	0	2	***6***	***20***
Days With ≥ 1.0" Snow Depth	6	***2***	1	0	0	0	0	0	0	0	0	***4***	***13***

The period of record for all cooperative weather station data is 1980 – 2009. See User Guide for detailed explanation of data.

Moundsville *Marshall County* Elevation: 620 ft. Latitude: 39° 54' N Longitude: 80° 45' W

	JAN	FEB	MAR	APR	MAY	JUN	JUL	AUG	SEP	OCT	NOV	DEC	YEAR
Mean Maximum Temp. (°F)	***38.8***	42.5	51.5	64.8	73.8	82.0	85.5	84.3	77.8	66.1	54.1	43.0	***63.7***
Mean Temp. (°F)	***30.1***	32.7	40.7	52.3	61.6	70.3	74.3	73.1	66.1	54.2	44.1	34.7	***52.9***
Mean Minimum Temp. (°F)	***21.3***	22.9	29.8	39.8	49.3	58.6	63.0	61.9	54.4	42.4	34.0	26.4	***42.0***
Extreme Maximum Temp. (°F)	74	78	***84***	***92***	92	98	***99***	99	96	90	82	78	***99***
Extreme Minimum Temp. (°F)	-20	-5	-3	***19***	28	38	***45***	40	31	23	12	-11	***-20***
Days Maximum Temp. ≥ 90°F	0	0	0	0	0	4	7	6	1	0	0	0	18
Days Maximum Temp. ≤ 32°F	9	6	2	0	0	0	0	0	0	0	0	5	22
Days Minimum Temp. ≤ 32°F	25	23	19	6	1	0	0	0	0	4	14	22	114
Days Minimum Temp. ≤ 0°F	2	1	0	0	0	0	0	0	0	0	0	0	3
Heating Degree Days (base 65°F)	***1,076***	907	748	384	154	22	1	5	70	340	622	932	***5,261***
Cooling Degree Days (base 65°F)	***0***	0	1	10	55	188	296	263	110	13	0	0	***936***
Mean Precipitation (in.)	3.09	2.32	3.52	3.58	4.46	4.50	4.18	3.86	3.32	2.79	3.69	3.13	42.44
Extreme Maximum Daily Precip. (in.)	***1.95***	1.55	1.66	***1.71***	2.16	2.04	***3.40***	2.54	7.11	1.46	3.77	1.34	***7.11***
Days With ≥ 0.1" Precipitation	***7***	6	8	9	9	8	8	6	6	6	8	8	***89***
Days With ≥ 0.5" Precipitation	***2***	1	2	2	4	3	3	3	2	2	2	2	***28***
Days With ≥ 1.0" Precipitation	1	0	1	1	1	1	1	1	1	0	1	0	9
Mean Snowfall (in.)	***6.1***	***4.4***	***2.7***	trace	0.0	0.0	0.0	0.0	0.0	trace	0.1	***2.1***	***15.4***
Maximum Snow Depth (in.)	***28***	***16***	***21***	***1***	***0***	***0***	***0***	***0***	***0***	***1***	***3***	na	na
Days With ≥ 1.0" Snow Depth	***8***	***5***	***1***	0	0	0	0	0	0	0	0	***2***	***16***

Parkersburg WSO *Wood County* Elevation: 615 ft. Latitude: 39° 16' N Longitude: 81° 34' W

	JAN	FEB	MAR	APR	MAY	JUN	JUL	AUG	SEP	OCT	NOV	DEC	YEAR
Mean Maximum Temp. (°F)	40.1	44.0	53.7	66.0	75.1	83.3	86.6	86.0	79.2	67.1	55.4	43.8	65.0
Mean Temp. (°F)	31.6	34.5	42.6	53.7	62.9	71.7	75.6	74.6	67.3	55.2	45.2	35.4	54.2
Mean Minimum Temp. (°F)	23.1	24.9	31.4	41.3	50.7	60.1	64.5	63.2	55.4	43.3	34.9	26.9	43.3
Extreme Maximum Temp. (°F)	76	78	85	94	96	102	105	103	98	94	82	78	105
Extreme Minimum Temp. (°F)	-26	-5	2	17	29	38	45	42	34	20	10	-10	-26
Days Maximum Temp. ≥ 90°F	0	0	0	0	1	6	10	10	3	0	0	0	30
Days Maximum Temp. ≤ 32°F	8	5	1	0	0	0	0	0	0	0	0	5	19
Days Minimum Temp. ≤ 32°F	25	22	18	5	0	0	0	0	0	4	13	22	109
Days Minimum Temp. ≤ 0°F	1	0	0	0	0	0	0	0	0	0	0	0	1
Heating Degree Days (base 65°F)	1,026	857	689	350	132	15	1	3	58	317	589	911	4,948
Cooling Degree Days (base 65°F)	0	0	2	18	74	223	336	308	134	20	1	0	1,116
Mean Precipitation (in.)	2.85	2.67	3.87	3.43	4.38	4.07	4.85	3.64	3.08	2.72	3.17	3.07	41.80
Extreme Maximum Daily Precip. (in.)	1.63	2.91	3.64	2.00	2.23	4.16	4.20	2.83	3.75	1.73	2.03	2.75	4.20
Days With ≥ 0.1" Precipitation	7	6	8	8	9	7	8	7	5	6	7	7	85
Days With ≥ 0.5" Precipitation	2	2	3	2	3	3	3	3	2	2	2	2	29
Days With ≥ 1.0" Precipitation	0	0	1	1	1	1	1	1	1	1	0	0	8
Mean Snowfall (in.)	4.6	2.7	1.5	0.7	0.0	0.0	0.0	0.0	0.0	trace	0.2	***1.4***	***11.1***
Maximum Snow Depth (in.)	23	14	17	0	0	0	0	0	0	0	2	***4***	***23***
Days With ≥ 1.0" Snow Depth	4	3	1	0	0	0	0	0	0	0	0	1	9

Pike Island Lock and Dam *Ohio County* Elevation: 640 ft. Latitude: 40° 09' N Longitude: 80° 42' W

	JAN	FEB	MAR	APR	MAY	JUN	JUL	AUG	SEP	OCT	NOV	DEC	YEAR
Mean Maximum Temp. (°F)	37.6	40.6	49.6	61.8	71.1	79.6	83.0	82.2	75.6	64.3	52.7	41.1	61.6
Mean Temp. (°F)	30.4	32.5	40.1	51.1	60.5	69.5	73.6	72.8	66.1	54.6	44.3	34.1	52.4
Mean Minimum Temp. (°F)	23.1	24.3	30.5	40.2	49.9	59.3	64.1	63.4	56.5	44.9	35.9	27.1	43.3
Extreme Maximum Temp. (°F)	71	73	82	89	91	95	100	98	93	87	78	74	100
Extreme Minimum Temp. (°F)	-17	-4	3	19	31	42	45	43	37	25	13	-8	-17
Days Maximum Temp. ≥ 90°F	0	0	0	0	0	1	4	3	1	0	0	0	9
Days Maximum Temp. ≤ 32°F	10	7	2	0	0	0	0	0	0	0	1	7	27
Days Minimum Temp. ≤ 32°F	25	22	19	5	0	0	0	0	0	1	11	22	105
Days Minimum Temp. ≤ 0°F	1	0	0	0	0	0	0	0	0	0	0	0	1
Heating Degree Days (base 65°F)	1,067	913	767	418	175	26	2	4	64	328	615	951	5,330
Cooling Degree Days (base 65°F)	0	0	0	7	42	168	275	253	104	13	1	0	863
Mean Precipitation (in.)	2.89	2.27	3.29	3.12	4.08	3.82	3.90	3.75	3.17	2.52	3.25	2.86	38.92
Extreme Maximum Daily Precip. (in.)	2.00	1.87	1.57	1.26	2.41	2.27	3.40	3.21	6.86	1.55	3.15	1.95	6.86
Days With ≥ 0.1" Precipitation	7	6	8	8	9	8	7	6	6	6	7	7	85
Days With ≥ 0.5" Precipitation	2	1	2	2	3	3	3	3	2	2	2	2	27
Days With ≥ 1.0" Precipitation	0	0	1	0	1	1	1	1	1	0	1	0	7
Mean Snowfall (in.)	6.2	4.3	2.9	0.7	0.0	0.0	0.0	0.0	0.0	trace	0.4	2.6	17.1
Maximum Snow Depth (in.)	12	20	6	5	0	0	0	0	0	trace	1	6	20
Days With ≥ 1.0" Snow Depth	9	6	2	0	0	0	0	0	0	0	0	5	22

Pineville *Wyoming County* Elevation: 1,279 ft. Latitude: 37° 34' N Longitude: 81° 32' W

	JAN	FEB	MAR	APR	MAY	JUN	JUL	AUG	SEP	OCT	NOV	DEC	YEAR
Mean Maximum Temp. (°F)	41.7	46.2	55.6	66.8	74.8	81.8	84.6	84.1	77.8	67.1	56.0	44.5	65.1
Mean Temp. (°F)	32.5	35.8	43.4	53.3	62.0	70.2	74.0	73.3	66.5	54.9	44.6	35.4	53.8
Mean Minimum Temp. (°F)	23.2	25.4	31.2	39.7	49.1	58.6	63.3	62.5	55.2	42.5	33.1	26.2	42.5
Extreme Maximum Temp. (°F)	74	77	86	91	92	96	98	100	97	89	82	80	100
Extreme Minimum Temp. (°F)	-17	-16	-6	19	26	38	42	43	33	23	11	-13	-17
Days Maximum Temp. ≥ 90°F	0	0	0	0	0	2	5	5	1	0	0	0	13
Days Maximum Temp. ≤ 32°F	6	4	1	0	0	0	0	0	0	0	0	4	15
Days Minimum Temp. ≤ 32°F	25	22	18	7	1	0	0	0	0	5	15	23	116
Days Minimum Temp. ≤ 0°F	1	0	0	0	0	0	0	0	0	0	0	0	1
Heating Degree Days (base 65°F)	1,001	819	663	355	139	16	1	3	57	319	606	911	4,890
Cooling Degree Days (base 65°F)	0	0	1	10	53	180	287	267	109	11	0	0	918
Mean Precipitation (in.)	3.58	3.23	3.83	3.97	4.98	4.03	5.41	3.78	3.26	2.88	3.24	3.47	45.66
Extreme Maximum Daily Precip. (in.)	2.75	2.32	1.46	2.22	3.95	3.62	4.75	2.48	2.46	2.34	2.60	2.05	4.75
Days With ≥ 0.1" Precipitation	8	7	9	8	9	8	9	7	6	6	7	8	92
Days With ≥ 0.5" Precipitation	2	2	3	3	3	3	4	3	2	2	2	2	31
Days With ≥ 1.0" Precipitation	1	0	1	1	1	1	2	1	1	0	1	0	10
Mean Snowfall (in.)	7.3	4.5	2.9	0.8	trace	0.0	0.0	0.0	0.0	trace	0.4	3.4	19.3
Maximum Snow Depth (in.)	18	12	21	18	trace	0	0	0	0	trace	2	14	21
Days With ≥ 1.0" Snow Depth	7	4	2	0	0	0	0	0	0	0	0	3	16

The period of record for all cooperative weather station data is 1980 – 2009. See User Guide for detailed explanation of data.

Union 3 SSE *Monroe County* Elevation: 2,109 ft. Latitude: 37° 33' N Longitude: 80° 32' W

	JAN	FEB	MAR	APR	MAY	JUN	JUL	AUG	SEP	OCT	NOV	DEC	YEAR
Mean Maximum Temp. (°F)	41.9	45.4	54.2	64.6	72.8	79.6	83.3	82.1	75.7	66.1	55.4	44.4	63.8
Mean Temp. (°F)	31.9	34.5	41.9	51.3	59.5	67.4	71.5	70.1	63.0	52.4	43.2	34.1	51.7
Mean Minimum Temp. (°F)	21.7	23.6	29.4	38.0	46.2	55.1	59.6	57.9	50.3	38.6	30.9	23.8	39.6
Extreme Maximum Temp. (°F)	76	77	83	88	90	92	96	96	92	85	82	74	96
Extreme Minimum Temp. (°F)	-23	-26	-11	11	21	32	36	35	24	13	7	-22	-26
Days Maximum Temp. ≥ 90°F	0	0	0	0	0	1	2	2	0	0	0	0	5
Days Maximum Temp. ≤ 32°F	7	4	1	0	0	0	0	0	0	0	0	5	17
Days Minimum Temp. ≤ 32°F	26	23	19	9	2	0	0	0	1	9	17	24	130
Days Minimum Temp. ≤ 0°F	1	0	0	0	0	0	0	0	0	0	0	1	2
Heating Degree Days (base 65°F)	1,021	854	711	409	191	36	6	11	110	389	647	950	5,335
Cooling Degree Days (base 65°F)	0	0	1	5	27	115	213	175	58	5	0	0	599
Mean Precipitation (in.)	2.46	2.23	3.11	3.38	4.14	3.45	3.83	3.34	3.18	2.31	2.68	2.47	36.58
Extreme Maximum Daily Precip. (in.)	2.21	1.76	1.77	2.56	2.34	2.36	2.12	2.95	2.53	2.14	3.05	1.90	3.05
Days With ≥ 0.1" Precipitation	6	6	7	8	9	7	8	7	6	5	6	6	81
Days With ≥ 0.5" Precipitation	2	1	2	2	3	2	3	2	2	1	2	1	23
Days With ≥ 1.0" Precipitation	0	0	1	0	1	1	1	1	1	0	1	0	7
Mean Snowfall (in.)	6.8	5.6	4.5	0.7	trace	0.0	0.0	0.0	0.0	0.1	0.8	4.9	23.4
Maximum Snow Depth (in.)	21	11	16	10	trace	0	0	0	0	2	4	13	21
Days With ≥ 1.0" Snow Depth	8	6	3	0	0	0	0	0	0	0	1	5	23

West Union 2 *Doddridge County* Elevation: 790 ft. Latitude: 39° 17' N Longitude: 80° 46' W

	JAN	FEB	MAR	APR	MAY	JUN	JUL	AUG	SEP	OCT	NOV	DEC	YEAR
Mean Maximum Temp. (°F)	40.3	43.8	52.8	65.1	73.2	80.8	83.8	83.5	77.3	66.3	55.2	43.9	63.8
Mean Temp. (°F)	30.0	32.5	40.3	51.0	59.9	68.5	72.1	71.6	64.7	52.8	42.7	33.8	51.7
Mean Minimum Temp. (°F)	19.6	21.1	27.8	36.9	46.4	56.0	60.4	59.7	52.0	39.1	30.2	23.7	39.4
Extreme Maximum Temp. (°F)	74	78	86	90	92	97	103	101	96	91	82	78	103
Extreme Minimum Temp. (°F)	-33	-17	-7	16	25	35	38	40	28	19	9	-18	-33
Days Maximum Temp. ≥ 90°F	0	0	0	0	0	2	4	5	1	0	0	0	12
Days Maximum Temp. ≤ 32°F	9	5	2	0	0	0	0	0	0	0	0	6	22
Days Minimum Temp. ≤ 32°F	27	24	22	10	1	0	0	0	0	8	19	25	136
Days Minimum Temp. ≤ 0°F	3	2	0	0	0	0	0	0	0	0	0	1	6
Heating Degree Days (base 65°F)	1,079	914	758	419	191	33	6	7	87	380	661	959	5,494
Cooling Degree Days (base 65°F)	0	0	0	6	38	143	233	221	85	8	0	0	734
Mean Precipitation (in.)	3.37	3.15	4.37	3.67	5.17	4.31	5.42	3.72	3.41	3.22	3.45	3.55	46.81
Extreme Maximum Daily Precip. (in.)	1.50	2.75	1.97	2.27	2.30	2.98	3.40	3.83	3.16	2.40	2.37	2.38	3.83
Days With ≥ 0.1" Precipitation	8	7	9	9	10	8	9	7	6	7	7	8	95
Days With ≥ 0.5" Precipitation	2	2	3	2	4	3	4	2	2	2	2	2	30
Days With ≥ 1.0" Precipitation	1	0	1	1	1	1	2	1	1	1	1	1	12
Mean Snowfall (in.)	9.1	***4.9***	***3.2***	0.1	0.0	0.0	0.0	0.0	0.0	trace	0.4	3.2	***20.9***
Maximum Snow Depth (in.)	24	15	18	1	0	0	0	0	0	trace	2	7	24
Days With ≥ 1.0" Snow Depth	10	8	3	0	0	0	0	0	0	0	1	5	27

Winfield Locks *Putnam County* Elevation: 570 ft. Latitude: 38° 32' N Longitude: 81° 55' W

	JAN	FEB	MAR	APR	MAY	JUN	JUL	AUG	SEP	OCT	NOV	DEC	YEAR
Mean Maximum Temp. (°F)	42.7	46.3	55.3	67.3	74.9	82.9	86.3	85.9	79.3	68.7	57.6	46.3	66.1
Mean Temp. (°F)	33.5	36.2	43.7	54.1	62.7	71.4	75.5	74.9	67.9	56.6	46.5	37.1	55.0
Mean Minimum Temp. (°F)	24.2	26.1	32.1	41.1	50.4	59.8	64.7	63.9	56.5	44.5	35.4	27.9	43.9
Extreme Maximum Temp. (°F)	77	79	86	93	96	102	101	103	98	96	87	80	103
Extreme Minimum Temp. (°F)	-18	-7	1	21	32	40	48	43	35	27	13	-11	-18
Days Maximum Temp. ≥ 90°F	0	0	0	0	1	5	9	8	2	0	0	0	25
Days Maximum Temp. ≤ 32°F	6	3	1	0	0	0	0	0	0	0	0	4	14
Days Minimum Temp. ≤ 32°F	25	21	17	4	0	0	0	0	0	2	12	21	102
Days Minimum Temp. ≤ 0°F	1	0	0	0	0	0	0	0	0	0	0	0	1
Heating Degree Days (base 65°F)	970	809	655	336	132	15	1	2	46	276	548	857	4,647
Cooling Degree Days (base 65°F)	0	0	2	16	67	212	332	316	140	23	2	0	1,110
Mean Precipitation (in.)	2.51	2.64	3.59	3.17	3.91	3.56	4.59	4.20	3.09	2.70	3.26	2.87	40.09
Extreme Maximum Daily Precip. (in.)	1.59	1.87	2.20	1.79	2.01	2.90	3.05	3.92	2.69	3.34	4.00	2.00	4.00
Days With ≥ 0.1" Precipitation	6	6	8	8	8	7	8	7	5	6	6	7	82
Days With ≥ 0.5" Precipitation	2	2	2	2	3	3	4	3	2	2	2	2	29
Days With ≥ 1.0" Precipitation	0	0	1	0	1	1	1	1	1	1	1	0	8
Mean Snowfall (in.)	4.2	2.8	2.3	0.9	0.0	0.0	0.0	0.0	0.0	trace	trace	1.5	11.7
Maximum Snow Depth (in.)	19	10	27	trace	0	0	0	0	0	trace	trace	3	27
Days With ≥ 1.0" Snow Depth	4	3	1	0	0	0	0	0	0	0	0	1	9

The period of record for all cooperative weather station data is 1980 – 2009. See User Guide for detailed explanation of data.

West Virginia Weather Station Rankings

Annual Extreme Maximum Temperature

Highest Rank	Station Name	°F	Lowest Rank	Station Name	°F
1	Martinsburg Eastern WV Reg Arpt	107	1	Beckley Raleigh Co Mem Arpt	96
2	Creston	***106***	1	Beckley Va Hospital	96
3	Hamlin	105	1	Bluefield Mercer Co Arpt	96
3	Parkersburg WSO	105	1	Buckhannon	96
5	Charleston Kanawha Arpt	104	1	Union 3 SSE	96
5	Huntington Sewage Plant	***104***	6	Clarksburg 1	98
7	Huntington Tri-State Arpt	103	7	Belington	99
7	Mannington 8 WNW	103	7	Bluestone Lake	99
7	West Union 2	103	7	Elkins Elkins-Randolph Co Arpt	99
7	Winfield Locks	103	7	Moundsville	***99***
11	Hogsett R C Byrd Dam	102	11	Dunlow 1 SW	100
12	London Locks	101	11	Fairmont	100
13	Dunlow 1 SW	100	11	Morgantown Lock & Dam	100
13	Fairmont	100	11	Pike Island Lock and Dam	100
13	Morgantown Lock & Dam	100	11	Pineville	100
13	Pike Island Lock and Dam	100	16	London Locks	101
13	Pineville	100	17	Hogsett R C Byrd Dam	102
18	Belington	99	18	Huntington Tri-State Arpt	103
18	Bluestone Lake	99	18	Mannington 8 WNW	103
18	Elkins Elkins-Randolph Co Arpt	99	18	West Union 2	103
18	Moundsville	***99***	18	Winfield Locks	103
22	Clarksburg 1	98	22	Charleston Kanawha Arpt	104
23	Beckley Raleigh Co Mem Arpt	96	22	Huntington Sewage Plant	***104***
23	Beckley Va Hospital	96	24	Hamlin	105
23	Bluefield Mercer Co Arpt	96	24	Parkersburg WSO	105

Annual Mean Maximum Temperature

Highest Rank	Station Name	°F	Lowest Rank	Station Name	°F
1	Huntington Sewage Plant	***67.7***	1	Beckley Va Hospital	61.1
2	Hamlin	67.5	2	Beckley Raleigh Co Mem Arpt	61.2
3	Charleston Kanawha Arpt	66.2	3	Pike Island Lock and Dam	61.6
4	Creston	***66.1***	4	Belington	61.9
4	London Locks	66.1	5	Elkins Elkins-Randolph Co Arpt	62.0
4	Winfield Locks	66.1	6	Bluefield Mercer Co Arpt	62.1
7	Huntington Tri-State Arpt	65.9	7	Fairmont	62.6
8	Hogsett R C Byrd Dam	65.7	8	Morgantown Lock & Dam	63.3
9	Pineville	65.1	9	Clarksburg 1	63.4
10	Parkersburg WSO	65.0	10	Buckhannon	63.7
11	Bluestone Lake	64.5	10	Moundsville	***63.7***
11	Martinsburg Eastern WV Reg Arpt	64.5	12	Union 3 SSE	63.8
13	Dunlow 1 SW	64.2	12	West Union 2	63.8
14	Mannington 8 WNW	63.9	14	Mannington 8 WNW	63.9
15	Union 3 SSE	63.8	15	Dunlow 1 SW	64.2
15	West Union 2	63.8	16	Bluestone Lake	64.5
17	Buckhannon	63.7	16	Martinsburg Eastern WV Reg Arpt	64.5
17	Moundsville	***63.7***	18	Parkersburg WSO	65.0
19	Clarksburg 1	63.4	19	Pineville	65.1
20	Morgantown Lock & Dam	63.3	20	Hogsett R C Byrd Dam	65.7
21	Fairmont	62.6	21	Huntington Tri-State Arpt	65.9
22	Bluefield Mercer Co Arpt	62.1	22	Creston	***66.1***
23	Elkins Elkins-Randolph Co Arpt	62.0	22	London Locks	66.1
24	Belington	61.9	22	Winfield Locks	66.1
25	Pike Island Lock and Dam	61.6	25	Charleston Kanawha Arpt	66.2

 Rankings include 25 highest/lowest stations. If state has less than 25 stations, all stations are included. The period of record is 1980–2009. See User Guide for detailed explanation of data.

Annual Mean Temperature

Highest			Lowest		
Rank	Station Name	°F	Rank	Station Name	°F
1	Huntington Sewage Plant	***56.5***	1	Belington	***50.0***
2	Huntington Tri-State Arpt	55.8	1	Elkins Elkins-Randolph Co Arpt	50.0
2	London Locks	55.8	3	Beckley Va Hospital	50.2
4	Charleston Kanawha Arpt	55.6	4	Mannington 8 WNW	50.4
5	Winfield Locks	55.0	5	Buckhannon	51.7
6	Hamlin	54.4	5	Union 3 SSE	51.7
7	Hogsett R C Byrd Dam	54.2	5	West Union 2	51.7
7	Parkersburg WSO	54.2	8	Beckley Raleigh Co Mem Arpt	51.8
9	Dunlow 1 SW	53.9	9	Fairmont	52.0
9	Martinsburg Eastern WV Reg Arpt	53.9	10	Clarksburg 1	52.3
11	Pineville	53.8	11	Pike Island Lock and Dam	52.5
12	Bluestone Lake	53.7	12	Morgantown Lock & Dam	52.9
13	Bluefield Mercer Co Arpt	53.3	12	Moundsville	***52.9***
14	Creston	***53.2***	14	Creston	***53.2***
15	Morgantown Lock & Dam	52.9	15	Bluefield Mercer Co Arpt	53.3
15	Moundsville	***52.9***	16	Bluestone Lake	53.7
17	Pike Island Lock and Dam	52.5	17	Pineville	53.8
18	Clarksburg 1	52.3	18	Dunlow 1 SW	53.9
19	Fairmont	52.0	18	Martinsburg Eastern WV Reg Arpt	53.9
20	Beckley Raleigh Co Mem Arpt	51.8	20	Hogsett R C Byrd Dam	54.2
21	Buckhannon	51.7	20	Parkersburg WSO	54.2
21	Union 3 SSE	51.7	22	Hamlin	54.4
21	West Union 2	51.7	23	Winfield Locks	55.0
24	Mannington 8 WNW	50.4	24	Charleston Kanawha Arpt	55.6
25	Beckley Va Hospital	50.2	25	Huntington Tri-State Arpt	55.8

Annual Mean Minimum Temperature

Highest			Lowest		
Rank	Station Name	°F	Rank	Station Name	°F
1	Huntington Tri-State Arpt	45.5	1	Mannington 8 WNW	36.9
2	London Locks	45.4	2	Elkins Elkins-Randolph Co Arpt	37.9
3	Huntington Sewage Plant	***45.3***	3	Belington	***38.1***
4	Charleston Kanawha Arpt	45.0	4	Beckley Va Hospital	39.3
5	Bluefield Mercer Co Arpt	44.4	5	West Union 2	39.4
6	Winfield Locks	43.9	6	Buckhannon	39.6
7	Dunlow 1 SW	43.5	6	Union 3 SSE	39.6
8	Martinsburg Eastern WV Reg Arpt	43.3	8	Creston	***40.2***
8	Parkersburg WSO	43.3	9	Hamlin	41.1
8	Pike Island Lock and Dam	43.3	10	Clarksburg 1	41.2
11	Bluestone Lake	42.9	11	Fairmont	41.5
12	Hogsett R C Byrd Dam	42.7	12	Moundsville	***42.0***
13	Morgantown Lock & Dam	42.5	13	Beckley Raleigh Co Mem Arpt	42.3
13	Pineville	42.5	14	Morgantown Lock & Dam	42.5
15	Beckley Raleigh Co Mem Arpt	42.3	14	Pineville	42.5
16	Moundsville	***42.0***	16	Hogsett R C Byrd Dam	42.7
17	Fairmont	41.5	17	Bluestone Lake	42.9
18	Clarksburg 1	41.2	18	Martinsburg Eastern WV Reg Arpt	43.3
19	Hamlin	41.1	18	Parkersburg WSO	43.3
20	Creston	***40.2***	18	Pike Island Lock and Dam	43.3
21	Buckhannon	39.6	21	Dunlow 1 SW	43.5
21	Union 3 SSE	39.6	22	Winfield Locks	43.9
23	West Union 2	39.4	23	Bluefield Mercer Co Arpt	44.4
24	Beckley Va Hospital	39.3	24	Charleston Kanawha Arpt	45.0
25	Belington	***38.1***	25	Huntington Sewage Plant	***45.3***

Annual Extreme Minimum Temperature

Highest Rank	Station Name	°F	Lowest Rank	Station Name	°F
1	Charleston Kanawha Arpt	-16	1	Mannington 8 WNW	-34
1	London Locks	-16	2	West Union 2	-33
3	Bluestone Lake	-17	3	Buckhannon	-30
3	Pike Island Lock and Dam	-17	3	Creston	*-30*
3	Pineville	-17	5	Hamlin	-28
6	Martinsburg Eastern WV Reg Arpt	-18	6	Parkersburg WSO	-26
6	Winfield Locks	-18	6	Union 3 SSE	-26
8	Huntington Sewage Plant	*-19*	8	Belington	-25
9	Dunlow 1 SW	-20	9	Clarksburg 1	-24
9	Moundsville	*-20*	9	Elkins Elkins-Randolph Co Arpt	-24
11	Bluefield Mercer Co Arpt	-21	9	Hogsett R C Byrd Dam	-24
11	Fairmont	-21	12	Beckley Va Hospital	-23
11	Huntington Tri-State Arpt	-21	13	Beckley Raleigh Co Mem Arpt	-22
11	Morgantown Lock & Dam	-21	14	Bluefield Mercer Co Arpt	-21
15	Beckley Raleigh Co Mem Arpt	-22	14	Fairmont	-21
16	Beckley Va Hospital	-23	14	Huntington Tri-State Arpt	-21
17	Clarksburg 1	-24	14	Morgantown Lock & Dam	-21
17	Elkins Elkins-Randolph Co Arpt	-24	18	Dunlow 1 SW	-20
17	Hogsett R C Byrd Dam	-24	18	Moundsville	*-20*
20	Belington	-25	20	Huntington Sewage Plant	*-19*
21	Parkersburg WSO	-26	21	Martinsburg Eastern WV Reg Arpt	-18
21	Union 3 SSE	-26	21	Winfield Locks	-18
23	Hamlin	-28	23	Bluestone Lake	-17
24	Buckhannon	-30	23	Pike Island Lock and Dam	-17
24	Creston	*-30*	23	Pineville	-17

July Mean Maximum Temperature

Highest Rank	Station Name	°F	Lowest Rank	Station Name	°F
1	Huntington Sewage Plant	*87.9*	1	Beckley Va Hospital	78.5
2	Hamlin	87.4	2	Beckley Raleigh Co Mem Arpt	79.8
3	Creston	*86.9*	3	Bluefield Mercer Co Arpt	80.0
4	Martinsburg Eastern WV Reg Arpt	86.7	4	Elkins Elkins-Randolph Co Arpt	81.3
5	Hogsett R C Byrd Dam	86.6	5	Belington	81.7
5	Parkersburg WSO	86.6	6	Pike Island Lock and Dam	83.0
7	Winfield Locks	86.3	7	Buckhannon	83.2
8	Huntington Tri-State Arpt	86.1	8	Fairmont	83.3
9	Charleston Kanawha Arpt	85.8	8	Union 3 SSE	83.3
10	London Locks	85.6	10	Dunlow 1 SW	83.4
11	Moundsville	85.5	11	Morgantown Lock & Dam	83.6
12	Mannington 8 WNW	84.8	12	West Union 2	83.8
13	Pineville	84.6	13	Clarksburg 1	84.4
14	Bluestone Lake	84.5	14	Bluestone Lake	84.5
15	Clarksburg 1	84.4	15	Pineville	84.6
16	West Union 2	83.8	16	Mannington 8 WNW	84.8
17	Morgantown Lock & Dam	83.6	17	Moundsville	85.5
18	Dunlow 1 SW	83.4	18	London Locks	85.6
19	Fairmont	83.3	19	Charleston Kanawha Arpt	85.8
19	Union 3 SSE	83.3	20	Huntington Tri-State Arpt	86.1
21	Buckhannon	83.2	21	Winfield Locks	86.3
22	Pike Island Lock and Dam	83.0	22	Hogsett R C Byrd Dam	86.6
23	Belington	81.7	22	Parkersburg WSO	86.6
24	Elkins Elkins-Randolph Co Arpt	81.3	24	Martinsburg Eastern WV Reg Arpt	86.7
25	Bluefield Mercer Co Arpt	80.0	25	Creston	*86.9*

 Rankings include 25 highest/lowest stations. If state has less than 25 stations, all stations are included. The period of record is 1980–2009. See User Guide for detailed explanation of data.

January Mean Minimum Temperature

Highest			Lowest		
Rank	**Station Name**	**°F**	**Rank**	**Station Name**	**°F**
1	Charleston Kanawha Arpt	25.8	1	Mannington 8 WNW	17.2
1	Huntington Tri-State Arpt	25.8	2	Belington	18.8
1	London Locks	25.8	2	Elkins Elkins-Randolph Co Arpt	18.8
4	Huntington Sewage Plant	25.2	4	West Union 2	19.6
5	Bluefield Mercer Co Arpt	25.0	5	Buckhannon	19.9
6	Dunlow 1 SW	24.2	6	Creston	***20.1***
6	Winfield Locks	24.2	7	Beckley Va Hospital	20.7
8	Bluestone Lake	23.6	8	Moundsville	***21.3***
9	Pineville	23.2	9	Clarksburg 1	21.5
10	Martinsburg Eastern WV Reg Arpt	23.1	9	Hamlin	21.5
10	Parkersburg WSO	23.1	11	Fairmont	21.7
10	Pike Island Lock and Dam	23.1	11	Union 3 SSE	21.7
13	Beckley Raleigh Co Mem Arpt	22.9	13	Hogsett R C Byrd Dam	22.4
14	Morgantown Lock & Dam	22.5	14	Morgantown Lock & Dam	22.5
15	Hogsett R C Byrd Dam	22.4	15	Beckley Raleigh Co Mem Arpt	22.9
16	Fairmont	21.7	16	Martinsburg Eastern WV Reg Arpt	23.1
16	Union 3 SSE	21.7	16	Parkersburg WSO	23.1
18	Clarksburg 1	21.5	16	Pike Island Lock and Dam	23.1
18	Hamlin	21.5	19	Pineville	23.2
20	Moundsville	***21.3***	20	Bluestone Lake	23.6
21	Beckley Va Hospital	20.7	21	Dunlow 1 SW	24.2
22	Creston	***20.1***	21	Winfield Locks	24.2
23	Buckhannon	19.9	23	Bluefield Mercer Co Arpt	25.0
24	West Union 2	19.6	24	Huntington Sewage Plant	25.2
25	Belington	18.8	25	Charleston Kanawha Arpt	25.8

Number of Days Annually Maximum Temperature ≥ 90°F

Highest			Lowest		
Rank	**Station Name**	**Days**	**Rank**	**Station Name**	**Days**
1	Hamlin	35	1	Beckley Va Hospital	1
1	Huntington Sewage Plant	35	2	Beckley Raleigh Co Mem Arpt	2
3	Parkersburg WSO	30	2	Belington	2
4	Creston	***28***	2	Bluefield Mercer Co Arpt	2
5	Martinsburg Eastern WV Reg Arpt	27	5	Elkins Elkins-Randolph Co Arpt	3
6	Hogsett R C Byrd Dam	26	6	Union 3 SSE	5
7	Winfield Locks	25	7	Buckhannon	9
8	Huntington Tri-State Arpt	24	7	Fairmont	9
9	Charleston Kanawha Arpt	22	7	Morgantown Lock & Dam	9
10	London Locks	21	7	Pike Island Lock and Dam	9
11	Moundsville	18	11	Dunlow 1 SW	10
12	Mannington 8 WNW	17	12	Bluestone Lake	12
13	Clarksburg 1	13	12	West Union 2	12
13	Pineville	13	14	Clarksburg 1	13
15	Bluestone Lake	12	14	Pineville	13
15	West Union 2	12	16	Mannington 8 WNW	17
17	Dunlow 1 SW	10	17	Moundsville	18
18	Buckhannon	9	18	London Locks	21
18	Fairmont	9	19	Charleston Kanawha Arpt	22
18	Morgantown Lock & Dam	9	20	Huntington Tri-State Arpt	24
18	Pike Island Lock and Dam	9	21	Winfield Locks	25
22	Union 3 SSE	5	22	Hogsett R C Byrd Dam	26
23	Elkins Elkins-Randolph Co Arpt	3	23	Martinsburg Eastern WV Reg Arpt	27
24	Beckley Raleigh Co Mem Arpt	2	24	Creston	***28***
24	Belington	2	25	Parkersburg WSO	30

Number of Days Annually Maximum Temperature ≤ 32°F

Highest Rank	Station Name	Days	Lowest Rank	Station Name	Days
1	Fairmont	27	1	London Locks	12
1	Pike Island Lock and Dam	27	2	Huntington Sewage Plant	13
3	Beckley Raleigh Co Mem Arpt	26	3	Bluestone Lake	14
3	Beckley Va Hospital	26	3	Winfield Locks	14
3	Elkins Elkins-Randolph Co Arpt	26	5	Charleston Kanawha Arpt	15
6	Belington	25	5	Hamlin	15
6	Buckhannon	25	5	Pineville	15
8	Clarksburg 1	24	8	Hogsett R C Byrd Dam	16
9	Mannington 8 WNW	23	8	Huntington Tri-State Arpt	16
10	Bluefield Mercer Co Arpt	22	8	Martinsburg Eastern WV Reg Arpt	16
10	Moundsville	22	11	Creston	*17*
10	West Union 2	22	11	Union 3 SSE	17
13	Morgantown Lock & Dam	20	13	Dunlow 1 SW	19
14	Dunlow 1 SW	19	13	Parkersburg WSO	19
14	Parkersburg WSO	19	15	Morgantown Lock & Dam	20
16	Creston	*17*	16	Bluefield Mercer Co Arpt	22
16	Union 3 SSE	17	16	Moundsville	22
18	Hogsett R C Byrd Dam	16	16	West Union 2	22
18	Huntington Tri-State Arpt	16	19	Mannington 8 WNW	23
18	Martinsburg Eastern WV Reg Arpt	16	20	Clarksburg 1	24
21	Charleston Kanawha Arpt	15	21	Belington	25
21	Hamlin	15	21	Buckhannon	25
21	Pineville	15	23	Beckley Raleigh Co Mem Arpt	26
24	Bluestone Lake	14	23	Beckley Va Hospital	26
24	Winfield Locks	14	23	Elkins Elkins-Randolph Co Arpt	26

Number of Days Annually Minimum Temperature ≤ 32°F

Highest Rank	Station Name	Days	Lowest Rank	Station Name	Days
1	Mannington 8 WNW	153	1	Huntington Sewage Plant	91
2	Elkins Elkins-Randolph Co Arpt	144	2	Huntington Tri-State Arpt	92
3	Belington	138	2	London Locks	92
4	West Union 2	136	4	Charleston Kanawha Arpt	96
5	Beckley Va Hospital	135	5	Bluefield Mercer Co Arpt	97
6	Buckhannon	131	6	Winfield Locks	102
6	Creston	*131*	7	Dunlow 1 SW	104
8	Union 3 SSE	130	8	Pike Island Lock and Dam	105
9	Hamlin	126	9	Martinsburg Eastern WV Reg Arpt	106
10	Clarksburg 1	123	10	Parkersburg WSO	109
11	Fairmont	119	11	Bluestone Lake	111
12	Pineville	116	12	Beckley Raleigh Co Mem Arpt	112
13	Moundsville	114	12	Morgantown Lock & Dam	112
14	Hogsett R C Byrd Dam	113	14	Hogsett R C Byrd Dam	113
15	Beckley Raleigh Co Mem Arpt	112	15	Moundsville	114
15	Morgantown Lock & Dam	112	16	Pineville	116
17	Bluestone Lake	111	17	Fairmont	119
18	Parkersburg WSO	109	18	Clarksburg 1	123
19	Martinsburg Eastern WV Reg Arpt	106	19	Hamlin	126
20	Pike Island Lock and Dam	105	20	Union 3 SSE	130
21	Dunlow 1 SW	104	21	Buckhannon	131
22	Winfield Locks	102	21	Creston	*131*
23	Bluefield Mercer Co Arpt	97	23	Beckley Va Hospital	135
24	Charleston Kanawha Arpt	96	24	West Union 2	136
25	Huntington Tri-State Arpt	92	25	Belington	138

Rankings include 25 highest/lowest stations. If state has less than 25 stations, all stations are included. The period of record is 1980–2009. See User Guide for detailed explanation of data.

Number of Days Annually Minimum Temperature ≤ 0°F

Highest			Lowest		
Rank	Station Name	Days	Rank	Station Name	Days
1	Mannington 8 WNW	8	1	Bluefield Mercer Co Arpt	1
2	Belington	6	1	Bluestone Lake	1
2	Buckhannon	6	1	Charleston Kanawha Arpt	1
2	Elkins Elkins-Randolph Co Arpt	6	1	Hogsett R C Byrd Dam	1
2	West Union 2	6	1	Huntington Sewage Plant	1
6	Beckley Va Hospital	4	1	Huntington Tri-State Arpt	1
6	Creston	***4***	1	London Locks	1
8	Fairmont	3	1	Martinsburg Eastern WV Reg Arpt	1
8	Hamlin	3	1	Parkersburg WSO	1
8	Moundsville	3	1	Pike Island Lock and Dam	1
11	Beckley Raleigh Co Mem Arpt	2	1	Pineville	1
11	Clarksburg 1	2	1	Winfield Locks	1
11	Dunlow 1 SW	2	13	Beckley Raleigh Co Mem Arpt	2
11	Morgantown Lock & Dam	2	13	Clarksburg 1	2
11	Union 3 SSE	2	13	Dunlow 1 SW	2
16	Bluefield Mercer Co Arpt	1	13	Morgantown Lock & Dam	2
16	Bluestone Lake	1	13	Union 3 SSE	2
16	Charleston Kanawha Arpt	1	18	Fairmont	3
16	Hogsett R C Byrd Dam	1	18	Hamlin	3
16	Huntington Sewage Plant	1	18	Moundsville	3
16	Huntington Tri-State Arpt	1	21	Beckley Va Hospital	4
16	London Locks	1	21	Creston	***4***
16	Martinsburg Eastern WV Reg Arpt	1	23	Belington	6
16	Parkersburg WSO	1	23	Buckhannon	6
16	Pike Island Lock and Dam	1	23	Elkins Elkins-Randolph Co Arpt	6

Number of Annual Heating Degree Days

Highest			Lowest		
Rank	Station Name	Num.	Rank	Station Name	Num.
1	Belington	***5,866***	1	Huntington Sewage Plant	***4,305***
2	Elkins Elkins-Randolph Co Arpt	5,854	2	London Locks	4,409
3	Mannington 8 WNW	5,847	3	Charleston Kanawha Arpt	4,431
4	Beckley Va Hospital	5,679	4	Huntington Tri-State Arpt	4,445
5	West Union 2	5,494	5	Winfield Locks	4,647
6	Buckhannon	5,426	6	Hamlin	4,817
7	Fairmont	5,368	7	Dunlow 1 SW	4,848
8	Clarksburg 1	5,349	8	Hogsett R C Byrd Dam	4,867
9	Union 3 SSE	5,335	9	Bluefield Mercer Co Arpt	4,871
10	Pike Island Lock and Dam	5,330	10	Pineville	4,890
11	Beckley Raleigh Co Mem Arpt	5,287	11	Bluestone Lake	4,899
12	Moundsville	***5,261***	12	Parkersburg WSO	4,948
13	Creston	***5,142***	13	Martinsburg Eastern WV Reg Arpt	4,973
14	Morgantown Lock & Dam	5,122	14	Morgantown Lock & Dam	5,122
15	Martinsburg Eastern WV Reg Arpt	4,973	15	Creston	***5,142***
16	Parkersburg WSO	4,948	16	Moundsville	***5,261***
17	Bluestone Lake	4,899	17	Beckley Raleigh Co Mem Arpt	5,287
18	Pineville	4,890	18	Pike Island Lock and Dam	5,330
19	Bluefield Mercer Co Arpt	4,871	19	Union 3 SSE	5,335
20	Hogsett R C Byrd Dam	4,867	20	Clarksburg 1	5,349
21	Dunlow 1 SW	4,848	21	Fairmont	5,368
22	Hamlin	4,817	22	Buckhannon	5,426
23	Winfield Locks	4,647	23	West Union 2	5,494
24	Huntington Tri-State Arpt	4,445	24	Beckley Va Hospital	5,679
25	Charleston Kanawha Arpt	4,431	25	Mannington 8 WNW	5,847

Rankings include 25 highest/lowest stations. If state has less than 25 stations, all stations are included. The period of record is 1980–2009. See User Guide for detailed explanation of data.

Number of Annual Cooling Degree Days

Highest			Lowest		
Rank	Station Name	Num.	Rank	Station Name	Num.
1	Huntington Sewage Plant	***1,324***	1	Beckley Va Hospital	381
2	Huntington Tri-State Arpt	1,185	2	Elkins Elkins-Randolph Co Arpt	470
3	London Locks	1,150	3	Belington	***521***
4	Charleston Kanawha Arpt	1,123	4	Beckley Raleigh Co Mem Arpt	574
5	Parkersburg WSO	1,116	5	Union 3 SSE	599
6	Winfield Locks	1,110	6	Mannington 8 WNW	633
7	Hamlin	1,052	7	Buckhannon	675
8	Hogsett R C Byrd Dam	1,045	8	Bluefield Mercer Co Arpt	697
9	Martinsburg Eastern WV Reg Arpt	1,040	9	West Union 2	734
10	Creston	***946***	10	Fairmont	747
11	Moundsville	***936***	11	Morgantown Lock & Dam	816
12	Pineville	918	12	Clarksburg 1	829
13	Dunlow 1 SW	889	13	Pike Island Lock and Dam	863
14	Bluestone Lake	885	14	Bluestone Lake	885
15	Pike Island Lock and Dam	863	15	Dunlow 1 SW	889
16	Clarksburg 1	829	16	Pineville	918
17	Morgantown Lock & Dam	816	17	Moundsville	***936***
18	Fairmont	747	18	Creston	***946***
19	West Union 2	734	19	Martinsburg Eastern WV Reg Arpt	1,040
20	Bluefield Mercer Co Arpt	697	20	Hogsett R C Byrd Dam	1,045
21	Buckhannon	675	21	Hamlin	1,052
22	Mannington 8 WNW	633	22	Winfield Locks	1,110
23	Union 3 SSE	599	23	Parkersburg WSO	1,116
24	Beckley Raleigh Co Mem Arpt	574	24	Charleston Kanawha Arpt	1,123
25	Belington	***521***	25	London Locks	1,150

Annual Precipitation

Highest			Lowest		
Rank	Station Name	Inches	Rank	Station Name	Inches
1	Belington	49.45	1	Union 3 SSE	36.58
2	Mannington 8 WNW	49.02	2	Martinsburg Eastern WV Reg Arpt	38.49
3	Buckhannon	48.46	3	Bluestone Lake	38.75
4	West Union 2	46.81	4	Pike Island Lock and Dam	38.92
5	Elkins Elkins-Randolph Co Arpt	46.36	5	Bluefield Mercer Co Arpt	39.37
6	Fairmont	45.85	6	Beckley Va Hospital	39.60
7	Clarksburg 1	45.76	7	Winfield Locks	40.09
8	Pineville	45.66	8	Hogsett R C Byrd Dam	40.45
9	Creston	***45.40***	9	Beckley Raleigh Co Mem Arpt	40.94
10	Dunlow 1 SW	45.09	10	Parkersburg WSO	41.80
11	Hamlin	44.63	11	Huntington Sewage Plant	42.33
12	Charleston Kanawha Arpt	44.09	12	Moundsville	42.44
13	London Locks	43.36	13	Huntington Tri-State Arpt	42.45
14	Morgantown Lock & Dam	42.74	14	Morgantown Lock & Dam	42.74
15	Huntington Tri-State Arpt	42.45	15	London Locks	43.36
16	Moundsville	42.44	16	Charleston Kanawha Arpt	44.09
17	Huntington Sewage Plant	42.33	17	Hamlin	44.63
18	Parkersburg WSO	41.80	18	Dunlow 1 SW	45.09
19	Beckley Raleigh Co Mem Arpt	40.94	19	Creston	***45.40***
20	Hogsett R C Byrd Dam	40.45	20	Pineville	45.66
21	Winfield Locks	40.09	21	Clarksburg 1	45.76
22	Beckley Va Hospital	39.60	22	Fairmont	45.85
23	Bluefield Mercer Co Arpt	39.37	23	Elkins Elkins-Randolph Co Arpt	46.36
24	Pike Island Lock and Dam	38.92	24	West Union 2	46.81
25	Bluestone Lake	38.75	25	Buckhannon	48.46

 Rankings include 25 highest/lowest stations. If state has less than 25 stations, all stations are included. The period of record is 1980–2009. See User Guide for detailed explanation of data.

Annual Extreme Maximum Daily Precipitation

Highest			Lowest		
Rank	Station Name	Inches	Rank	Station Name	Inches
1	Moundsville	***7.11***	1	Bluestone Lake	2.79
2	Pike Island Lock and Dam	6.86	2	Dunlow 1 SW	***2.98***
3	Beckley Va Hospital	5.31	3	Union 3 SSE	3.05
4	Elkins Elkins-Randolph Co Arpt	5.02	4	London Locks	3.36
5	Clarksburg 1	5.00	5	Beckley Raleigh Co Mem Arpt	3.48
6	Buckhannon	4.95	6	Martinsburg Eastern WV Reg Arpt	3.50
7	Hogsett R C Byrd Dam	4.78	7	Creston	***3.55***
8	Pineville	4.75	8	Hamlin	3.56
9	Mannington 8 WNW	4.29	9	Bluefield Mercer Co Arpt	3.61
10	Parkersburg WSO	4.20	10	Fairmont	3.68
11	Charleston Kanawha Arpt	4.15	11	Morgantown Lock & Dam	3.75
12	Winfield Locks	4.00	12	West Union 2	3.83
13	Huntington Tri-State Arpt	3.89	13	Huntington Tri-State Arpt	3.89
14	West Union 2	3.83	14	Winfield Locks	4.00
15	Morgantown Lock & Dam	3.75	15	Charleston Kanawha Arpt	4.15
16	Fairmont	3.68	16	Parkersburg WSO	4.20
17	Bluefield Mercer Co Arpt	3.61	17	Mannington 8 WNW	4.29
18	Hamlin	3.56	18	Pineville	4.75
19	Creston	***3.55***	19	Hogsett R C Byrd Dam	4.78
20	Martinsburg Eastern WV Reg Arpt	3.50	20	Buckhannon	4.95
21	Beckley Raleigh Co Mem Arpt	3.48	21	Clarksburg 1	5.00
22	London Locks	3.36	22	Elkins Elkins-Randolph Co Arpt	5.02
23	Union 3 SSE	3.05	23	Beckley Va Hospital	5.31
24	Dunlow 1 SW	***2.98***	24	Pike Island Lock and Dam	6.86
25	Bluestone Lake	2.79	25	Moundsville	***7.11***

Number of Days Annually With ≥ 0.1 Inches of Precipitation

Highest			Lowest		
Rank	Station Name	Days	Rank	Station Name	Days
1	Belington	104	1	Martinsburg Eastern WV Reg Arpt	75
2	Elkins Elkins-Randolph Co Arpt	103	2	Huntington Sewage Plant	***80***
3	Buckhannon	101	3	Hogsett R C Byrd Dam	81
3	Mannington 8 WNW	101	3	Union 3 SSE	81
5	Clarksburg 1	97	5	Winfield Locks	82
6	West Union 2	95	6	Bluestone Lake	83
7	Fairmont	93	7	Huntington Tri-State Arpt	84
8	Charleston Kanawha Arpt	92	8	Bluefield Mercer Co Arpt	85
8	Pineville	92	8	Parkersburg WSO	85
10	Creston	***91***	8	Pike Island Lock and Dam	85
10	London Locks	91	11	Beckley Raleigh Co Mem Arpt	88
12	Dunlow 1 SW	90	11	Beckley Va Hospital	88
12	Hamlin	90	13	Moundsville	***89***
12	Morgantown Lock & Dam	90	14	Dunlow 1 SW	90
15	Moundsville	***89***	14	Hamlin	90
16	Beckley Raleigh Co Mem Arpt	88	14	Morgantown Lock & Dam	90
16	Beckley Va Hospital	88	17	Creston	***91***
18	Bluefield Mercer Co Arpt	85	17	London Locks	91
18	Parkersburg WSO	85	19	Charleston Kanawha Arpt	92
18	Pike Island Lock and Dam	85	19	Pineville	92
21	Huntington Tri-State Arpt	84	21	Fairmont	93
22	Bluestone Lake	83	22	West Union 2	95
23	Winfield Locks	82	23	Clarksburg 1	97
24	Hogsett R C Byrd Dam	81	24	Buckhannon	101
24	Union 3 SSE	81	24	Mannington 8 WNW	101

Rankings include 25 highest/lowest stations. If state has less than 25 stations, all stations are included. The period of record is 1980–2009. See User Guide for detailed explanation of data.

Number of Days Annually With ≥ 0.5 Inches of Precipitation

Highest			Lowest		
Rank	Station Name	Days	Rank	Station Name	Days
1	Belington	34	1	Union 3 SSE	23
2	Creston	*32*	2	Martinsburg Eastern WV Reg Arpt	24
3	Buckhannon	31	3	Beckley Raleigh Co Mem Arpt	25
3	Clarksburg 1	31	3	Beckley Va Hospital	25
3	Dunlow 1 SW	31	5	Bluefield Mercer Co Arpt	26
3	Fairmont	31	5	Huntington Sewage Plant	26
3	Mannington 8 WNW	31	7	Bluestone Lake	27
3	Pineville	31	7	Morgantown Lock & Dam	27
9	Charleston Kanawha Arpt	30	7	Pike Island Lock and Dam	27
9	Hamlin	30	10	Elkins Elkins-Randolph Co Arpt	28
9	London Locks	30	10	Hogsett R C Byrd Dam	28
9	West Union 2	30	10	Moundsville	*28*
13	Huntington Tri-State Arpt	29	13	Huntington Tri-State Arpt	29
13	Parkersburg WSO	29	13	Parkersburg WSO	29
13	Winfield Locks	29	13	Winfield Locks	29
16	Elkins Elkins-Randolph Co Arpt	28	16	Charleston Kanawha Arpt	30
16	Hogsett R C Byrd Dam	28	16	Hamlin	30
16	Moundsville	*28*	16	London Locks	30
19	Bluestone Lake	27	16	West Union 2	30
19	Morgantown Lock & Dam	27	20	Buckhannon	31
19	Pike Island Lock and Dam	27	20	Clarksburg 1	31
22	Bluefield Mercer Co Arpt	26	20	Dunlow 1 SW	31
22	Huntington Sewage Plant	26	20	Fairmont	31
24	Beckley Raleigh Co Mem Arpt	25	20	Mannington 8 WNW	31
24	Beckley Va Hospital	25	20	Pineville	31

Number of Days Annually With ≥ 1.0 Inches of Precipitation

Highest			Lowest		
Rank	Station Name	Days	Rank	Station Name	Days
1	Huntington Sewage Plant	12	1	Beckley Raleigh Co Mem Arpt	5
1	Huntington Tri-State Arpt	12	2	Bluefield Mercer Co Arpt	6
1	West Union 2	12	3	Beckley Va Hospital	7
4	Clarksburg 1	11	3	Belington	7
4	Creston	*11*	3	Charleston Kanawha Arpt	7
6	Buckhannon	10	3	Pike Island Lock and Dam	7
6	Dunlow 1 SW	10	3	Union 3 SSE	7
6	Hamlin	10	8	Bluestone Lake	8
6	Mannington 8 WNW	10	8	Elkins Elkins-Randolph Co Arpt	8
6	Pineville	10	8	Morgantown Lock & Dam	8
11	Fairmont	9	8	Parkersburg WSO	8
11	Hogsett R C Byrd Dam	9	8	Winfield Locks	8
11	London Locks	9	13	Fairmont	9
11	Martinsburg Eastern WV Reg Arpt	9	13	Hogsett R C Byrd Dam	9
11	Moundsville	9	13	London Locks	9
16	Bluestone Lake	8	13	Martinsburg Eastern WV Reg Arpt	9
16	Elkins Elkins-Randolph Co Arpt	8	13	Moundsville	9
16	Morgantown Lock & Dam	8	18	Buckhannon	10
16	Parkersburg WSO	8	18	Dunlow 1 SW	10
16	Winfield Locks	8	18	Hamlin	10
21	Beckley Va Hospital	7	18	Mannington 8 WNW	10
21	Belington	7	18	Pineville	10
21	Charleston Kanawha Arpt	7	23	Clarksburg 1	11
21	Pike Island Lock and Dam	7	23	Creston	*11*
21	Union 3 SSE	7	25	Huntington Sewage Plant	12

Rankings include 25 highest/lowest stations. If state has less than 25 stations, all stations are included. The period of record is 1980–2009. See User Guide for detailed explanation of data.

Annual Snowfall

Highest			Lowest		
Rank	Station Name	Inches	Rank	Station Name	Inches
1	Beckley Raleigh Co Mem Arpt	***58.6***	1	Hogsett R C Byrd Dam	***8.3***
2	Belington	***44.6***	2	Huntington Sewage Plant	***10.8***
3	Buckhannon	43.6	3	Parkersburg WSO	***11.1***
4	Mannington 8 WNW	***42.7***	4	Winfield Locks	11.7
5	Fairmont	32.7	5	Moundsville	***15.4***
6	Beckley Va Hospital	32.6	6	Dunlow 1 SW	17.0
7	Clarksburg 1	24.4	7	Pike Island Lock and Dam	17.1
8	Union 3 SSE	23.4	8	Hamlin	18.9
9	West Union 2	***20.9***	9	Pineville	19.3
10	Bluestone Lake	20.3	10	Bluestone Lake	20.3
11	Pineville	19.3	11	West Union 2	***20.9***
12	Hamlin	18.9	12	Union 3 SSE	23.4
13	Pike Island Lock and Dam	17.1	13	Clarksburg 1	24.4
14	Dunlow 1 SW	17.0	14	Beckley Va Hospital	32.6
15	Moundsville	***15.4***	15	Fairmont	32.7
16	Winfield Locks	11.7	16	Mannington 8 WNW	***42.7***
17	Parkersburg WSO	***11.1***	17	Buckhannon	43.6
18	Huntington Sewage Plant	***10.8***	18	Belington	***44.6***
19	Hogsett R C Byrd Dam	***8.3***	19	Beckley Raleigh Co Mem Arpt	***58.6***

Annual Maximum Snow Depth

Highest			Lowest		
Rank	Station Name	Inches	Rank	Station Name	Inches
1	Beckley Raleigh Co Mem Arpt	***30***	1	Hamlin	17
2	Mannington 8 WNW	***29***	2	Creston	***18***
3	Beckley Va Hospital	***28***	3	Dunlow 1 SW	***20***
4	Winfield Locks	27	3	Fairmont	20
5	Buckhannon	24	3	Hogsett R C Byrd Dam	20
5	West Union 2	24	3	Morgantown Lock & Dam	***20***
7	Bluestone Lake	23	3	Pike Island Lock and Dam	20
7	Parkersburg WSO	***23***	8	Belington	***21***
9	Belington	***21***	8	Clarksburg 1	21
9	Clarksburg 1	21	8	Pineville	21
9	Pineville	21	8	Union 3 SSE	21
9	Union 3 SSE	21	12	Bluestone Lake	23
13	Dunlow 1 SW	***20***	12	Parkersburg WSO	***23***
13	Fairmont	20	14	Buckhannon	24
13	Hogsett R C Byrd Dam	20	14	West Union 2	24
13	Morgantown Lock & Dam	***20***	16	Winfield Locks	27
13	Pike Island Lock and Dam	20	17	Beckley Va Hospital	***28***
18	Creston	***18***	18	Mannington 8 WNW	***29***
19	Hamlin	17	19	Beckley Raleigh Co Mem Arpt	***30***

Number of Days Annually With ≥ 1.0 Inch Snow Depth

Highest

Rank	Station Name	Days
1	Mannington 8 WNW	39
2	Belington	*37*
2	Buckhannon	37
4	Beckley Raleigh Co Mem Arpt	*36*
5	Beckley Va Hospital	32
6	Fairmont	30
7	Clarksburg 1	27
7	West Union 2	27
9	Union 3 SSE	23
10	Pike Island Lock and Dam	22
11	Bluestone Lake	18
12	Creston	*16*
12	Moundsville	*16*
12	Pineville	16
15	Dunlow 1 SW	*14*
15	Hamlin	14
17	Morgantown Lock & Dam	*13*
18	Hogsett R C Byrd Dam	11
19	Parkersburg WSO	9
19	Winfield Locks	9
21	Huntington Sewage Plant	*7*

Lowest

Rank	Station Name	Days
1	Huntington Sewage Plant	*7*
2	Parkersburg WSO	9
2	Winfield Locks	9
4	Hogsett R C Byrd Dam	11
5	Morgantown Lock & Dam	*13*
6	Dunlow 1 SW	*14*
6	Hamlin	14
8	Creston	*16*
8	Moundsville	*16*
8	Pineville	16
11	Bluestone Lake	18
12	Pike Island Lock and Dam	22
13	Union 3 SSE	23
14	Clarksburg 1	27
14	West Union 2	27
16	Fairmont	30
17	Beckley Va Hospital	32
18	Beckley Raleigh Co Mem Arpt	*36*
19	Belington	*37*
19	Buckhannon	37
21	Mannington 8 WNW	39

 Rankings include 25 highest/lowest stations. If state has less than 25 stations, all stations are included. The period of record is 1980–2009. See User Guide for detailed explanation of data.

Significant Storm Events in West Virginia: 2000 – 2009

Location or County	Date	Type	Mag.	Deaths	Injuries	Property Damage ($mil.)	Crop Damage ($mil.)
Wyoming	07/08/01	Flash Flood	na	1	0	60.0	0.0
Mcdowell	07/08/01	Flash Flood	na	0	0	50.0	0.0
Fayette	07/08/01	Flash Flood	na	0	0	47.0	0.0
Raleigh	07/08/01	Flash Flood	na	0	0	40.0	0.0
Mcdowell	05/02/02	Flash Flood	na	2	0	85.0	0.0
Eastern Panhandle	02/14/03	Winter Storm	na	0	1	7.6	0.0
Western West Virginia	02/15/03	Flood	na	2	0	8.6	0.0
Northwest and Northcentral West Virginia	02/16/03	Ice Storm	na	0	0	9.5	0.0
Kanawha	06/16/03	Flash Flood	na	0	0	7.0	0.0
West and Central West Virginia	11/12/03	Flood	na	1	0	13.5	0.0
Western West Virginia	11/19/03	Flood	na	2	0	12.0	0.0
Mingo	05/30/04	Flash Flood	na	0	0	9.0	0.0
Logan	05/30/04	Flash Flood	na	0	0	7.0	0.0
Ohio Co.	09/17/04	Flood	na	0	0	40.0	0.0
Hancock Co.	09/17/04	Flood	na	0	0	36.0	0.0
Brooke County	09/17/04	Flood	na	0	0	20.0	0.0
Northwest West Virginia	09/17/04	Flood	na	1	0	9.5	0.0
Wetzel County	09/18/04	Flood	na	0	0	7.0	0.0
Mingo	05/09/09	Flood	na	0	0	24.0	0.0
Wyoming	05/09/09	Flood	na	0	0	10.0	0.0

Note: Deaths, injuries, and damages are date and location specific.

WISCONSIN

PHYSICAL FEATURES. Wisconsin lies in the upper Midwest between Lake Superior, Upper Michigan, Lake Michigan, and the Mississippi and St. Croix Rivers. Its greatest length is 320 miles, greatest width 295 miles, and total area 56,066 square miles. Glaciation has largely determined the topography and soils of the State. The various glaciations created a rolling terrain with nearly 9,000 lakes and several areas of marshes and swamps. Elevations range from about 600 feet above sea level along the Lake Superior and Lake Michigan shores and in the Mississippi flood plain in southwestern Wisconsin, to nearly 1,950 feet above sea level at Rib and Strawberry Hills.

The Northern Highlands, a plateau extending across northern Wisconsin, is an area of about 15,000 square miles with elevations from 1,000 to 1,800 feet above sea level. This area is the location of many lakes and the origin of most of the major streams in the State. The slope down to the narrow Lake Superior plain is quite steep. A comparatively flat, crescent shaped lowland lies immediately south of the Northern Highlands, embodying nearly one-fourth of Wisconsin. The eastern ridges and lowlands lie to the southeast of the central plains. The western uplands of southwestern Wisconsin west of the ridges and lowlands and south of the central plains contains approximately one-fourth of the State. This area is the roughest section of the State, rising 200 to 350 feet above the central plains and 100 to 200 feet above the Eastern Ridges and Lowlands. The Mississippi River bluffs rise 230 to 650 feet.

GENERAL CLIMATE. The Wisconsin climate is typically continental with some modification by Lakes Michigan and Superior. The winters are cold and snowy, and the summers are warm. About two-thirds of the annual precipitation falls during the growing season (freeze-free period). The rapid succession of storms moving from west to east and southwest to northeast account for the stimulating climate.

TEMPERATURE. The average annual temperature varies from 39°F. to 49.5°F. During more than one-half of the winters temperatures fall to -40°F. or lower, and almost every winter -30°F. or colder is reported from northern Wisconsin. Summer temperatures above 90°F. or higher average two to four days in northern counties to about 14 days in southern districts. During marked cool outbreaks in the summer months, the central lowlands occasionally report freezing temperatures. The freeze-free season averages around 80 days per year in the upper northeast and north-central lowlands, to about 180 days in the Milwaukee area. The pronounced moderating effect of Lake Michigan is well illustrated by the fact that the growing season of 140 to 150 days along the east-central coastal area is of the same duration as in the southwestern Wisconsin valleys. The short growing season in the central portion of the State is attributed to a number of factors, among them being an inward cold air drainage and the low heat capacities of the peat and sandy soils. The average date of last spring freeze ranges from early May along the Lake Michigan coastal area and southern counties to early June in the northernmost counties. The first autumn freezes occur in late August and early September in northern and central lowlands to mid-October along the Lake Michigan coast line. However, July freeze is not unusual in the north and central Wisconsin lowlands.

PRECIPITATION. The mean annual precipitation totals 30 to 34 inches over most of the Western Uplands and Northern Highlands, diminishing to about 28 inches along most of the Wisconsin coastal area bordering Lake Michigan and 28 to 30 inches over most of the Wisconsin Central Plain and Lake Superior Coastal area. The higher average annual precipitation coincides generally with the highest elevations, particularly to the windward slopes of the Western Uplands and Northern Highlands. Thunderstorms average about 30 per year in northern Wisconsin to about 40 per year in southern counties, occurring mostly in the summer. Occasional hail, wind, and lightning damage are reported.

The average seasonal snowfall varies from about 30 inches to well over 100 inches along the steep western slope of the Gogebic Range. The heavy snowfall along the Gogebic Range is a result of the prevailing cold northerly winter winds blowing across the relatively warm Lake Superior. Relatively greater average snowfall is recorded over the Western Uplands and Eastern Ridges than in adjacent lowland areas. The mean dates of the first snowfall of consequence, an inch or more, varies from early November in northern localities to around December 1 in southern Wisconsin counties. Average annual duration of snowcover ranges from 85 days in southern-most Wisconsin to more than 140 days along Lake Superior.

The drainage of Wisconsin is into Lake Superior, Lake Michigan, and the Mississippi River. The Mississippi and St. Croix Rivers form most of the western boundary. About one-half of the northwestern portion of the State is drained through the Chippewa River, while the remainder of this region drains directly into the Mississippi or the St. Croix and into Lake Superior. The Wisconsin River has its source at a small lake nearly 1,600 feet above mean sea level on the Upper Michigan boundary and drains most of central Wisconsin. Most of the Wisconsin River tributaries also spring from the many lakes in the north. Except for the Rock River, a Mississippi River tributary which flows through northern Illinois, eastern Wisconsin drains into Lake Michigan, a large part through Green Bay.

Most of the streams and lakes in Wisconsin are ice-covered from late November to late March. Snow covers the ground in practically all the winter months, except in the extreme southern areas. Flooding is most frequent, and most serious, during April due to the melting of snow associated with spring rains. During this period, flood conditions are often aggravated by ice jams which back up the flood waters. Excessive rains of the thunderstorm type sometimes produce tributary flooding or flash flooding along the smaller streams and creeks. Major flooding occurs on the Mississippi River, on the average, about three years in 10.

Tornadoes occur in Wisconsin. Most of the very destructive tornadoes occur in the northwestern quarter of the State. Wisconsin tornado frequency is highest in June and July, followed in order by April, May, and September.

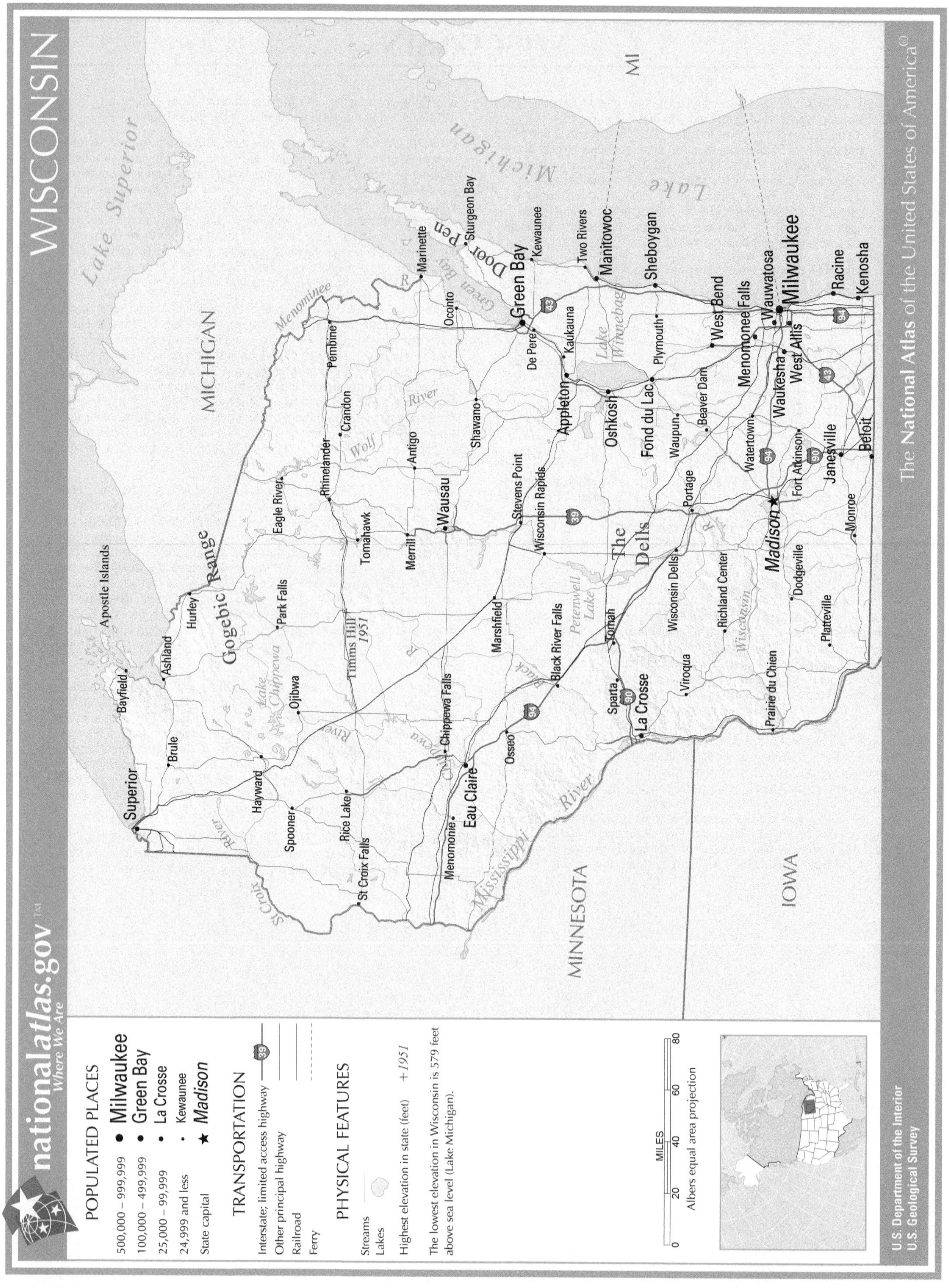
WISCONSIN
nationalatlas.gov™
Where We Are
POPULATED PLACES
500,000 – 999,999 Milwaukee
100,000 – 499,999 Green Bay
25,000 – 99,999 La Crosse
24,999 and less Kewaunee
State capital Madison
TRANSPORTATION
Interstate; limited access highway
Other principal highway
Railroad
Ferry
PHYSICAL FEATURES
Streams
Lakes
Highest elevation in state (feet) +1951
The lowest elevation in Wisconsin is 579 feet above sea level (Lake Michigan).
MILES
0 20 40 60 80
Albers equal area projection
U.S. Department of the Interior
U.S. Geological Survey
The National Atlas of the United States of America®
Lake Superior
Lake Michigan
MICHIGAN
MI
MINNESOTA
IOWA
Apostle Islands
Gogebic Range
Door Pen
Green Bay
Lake Winnebago
Lake Chippewa
Petenwell Lake
Timms Hill 1951
The Dells
Mississippi River
St Croix River
Chippewa River
Wisconsin River
Wolf River
Black R
Menominee
Superior
Brule
Bayfield
Ashland
Hurley
Hayward
Spooner
Rice Lake
St Croix Falls
Ojibwa
Park Falls
Eagle River
Rhinelander
Tomahawk
Merrill
Wausau
Antigo
Crandon
Pembine
Marinette
Oconto
Shawano
Sturgeon Bay
Kewaunee
Green Bay
De Pere
Kaukauna
Appleton
Oshkosh
Fond du Lac
Two Rivers
Manitowoc
Sheboygan
Plymouth
West Bend
Menomonee Falls
Wauwatosa
Milwaukee
West Allis
Waukesha
Racine
Kenosha
Beaver Dam
Waupun
Watertown
Fort Atkinson
Janesville
Beloit
Monroe
Madison
Portage
Wisconsin Dells
Stevens Point
Wisconsin Rapids
Marshfield
Tomah
Black River Falls
Sparta
La Crosse
Viroqua
Richland Center
Dodgeville
Platteville
Prairie du Chien
Chippewa Falls
Eau Claire
Menomonie
Osseo
39
43
94
90

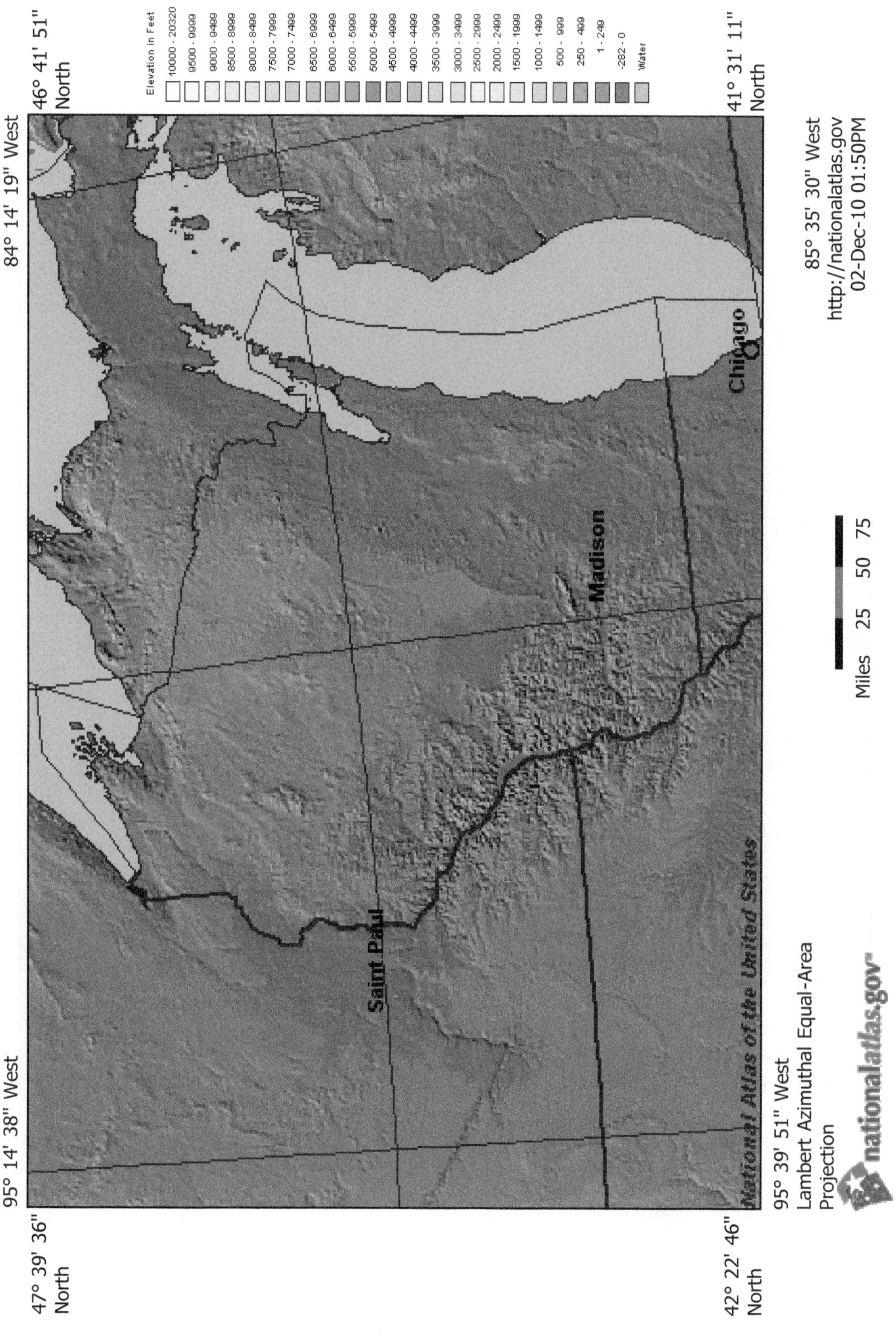
Elevation in Feet
10000 - 20320
9500 - 9999
9000 - 9499
8500 - 8999
8000 - 8499
7500 - 7999
7000 - 7499
6500 - 6999
6000 - 6499
5500 - 5999
5000 - 5499
4500 - 4999
4000 - 4499
3500 - 3999
3000 - 3499
2500 - 2999
2000 - 2499
1500 - 1999
1000 - 1499
500 - 999
250 - 499
1 - 249
-282 - 0
Water
46° 41' 51" North
84° 14' 19" West
41° 31' 11" North
85° 35' 30" West
http://nationalatlas.gov
02-Dec-10 01:50PM
Chicago
Madison
Saint Paul
Miles 25 50 75
National Atlas of the United States
95° 14' 38" West
47° 39' 36" North
42° 22' 46" North
95° 39' 51" West
Lambert Azimuthal Equal-Area
Projection
nationalatlas.gov

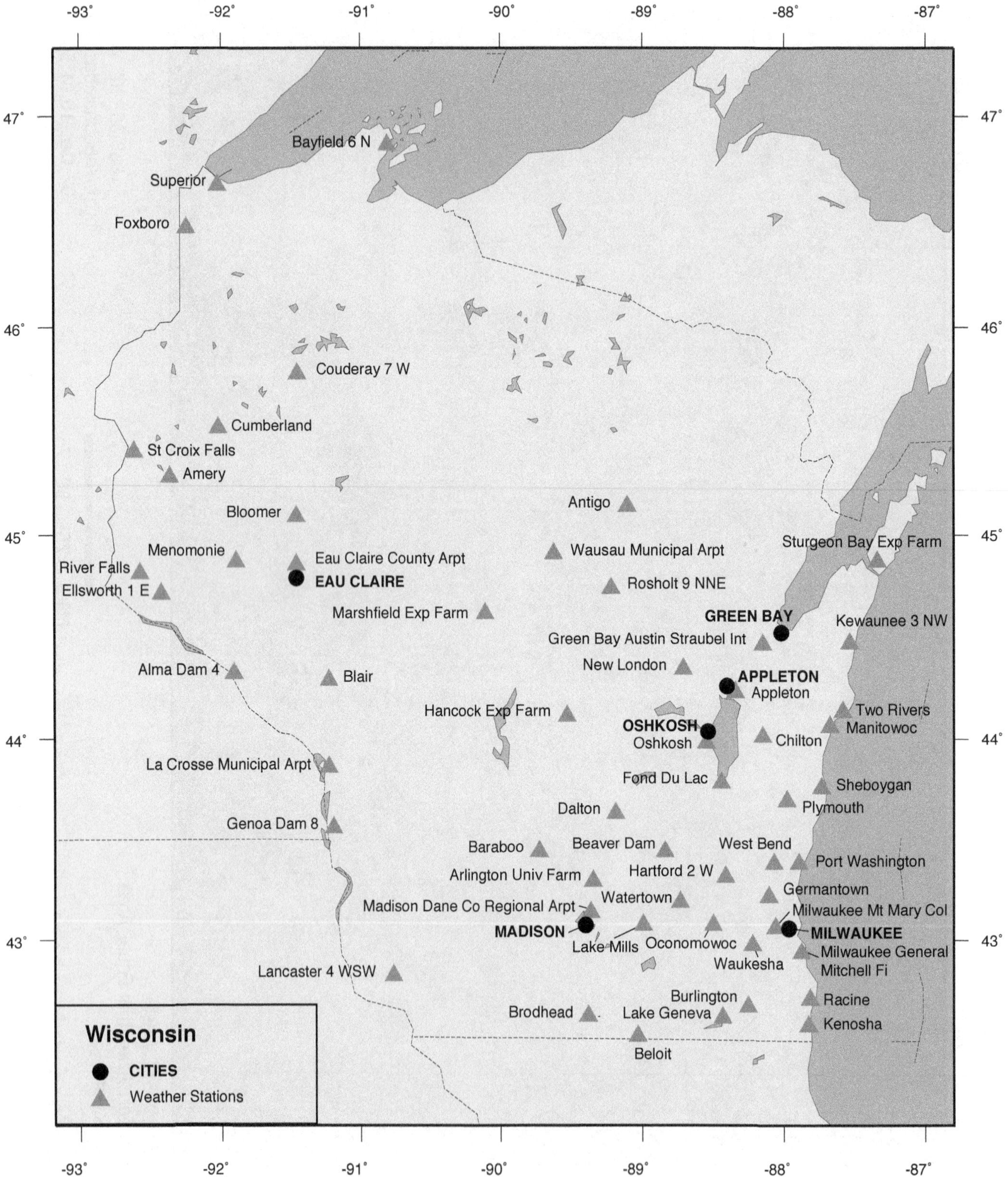
-93°
-92°
-91°
-90°
-89°
-88°
-87°
47°
46°
45°
44°
43°
Bayfield 6 N
Superior
Foxboro
Couderay 7 W
Cumberland
St Croix Falls
Amery
Bloomer
Antigo
Menomonie
Eau Claire County Arpt
Wausau Municipal Arpt
Sturgeon Bay Exp Farm
River Falls
EAU CLAIRE
Ellsworth 1 E
Rosholt 9 NNE
Marshfield Exp Farm
GREEN BAY
Kewaunee 3 NW
Green Bay Austin Straubel Int
New London
Alma Dam 4
Blair
APPLETON
Appleton
Hancock Exp Farm
Two Rivers
Manitowoc
OSHKOSH
Oshkosh
Chilton
La Crosse Municipal Arpt
Fond Du Lac
Sheboygan
Dalton
Plymouth
Genoa Dam 8
Baraboo
Beaver Dam
West Bend
Port Washington
Arlington Univ Farm
Hartford 2 W
Germantown
Watertown
Madison Dane Co Regional Arpt
Milwaukee Mt Mary Col
MADISON
MILWAUKEE
Lake Mills
Oconomowoc
Milwaukee General Mitchell Fi
Waukesha
Lancaster 4 WSW
Burlington
Racine
Brodhead
Lake Geneva
Kenosha
Beloit
Wisconsin
CITIES
Weather Stations

Wisconsin Weather Stations by County

County	Station Name
Barron	Cumberland
Bayfield	Bayfield 6 N
Brown	Green Bay Austin Straubel Intl
Buffalo	Alma Dam 4
Calumet	Chilton
Chippewa	Bloomer Eau Claire County Arpt
Columbia	Arlington Univ Farm
Dane	Madison Dane Co Regional Arpt
Dodge	Beaver Dam
Door	Sturgeon Bay Exp Farm
Douglas	Foxboro Superior
Dunn	Menomonie
Fond Du Lac	Fond Du Lac
Grant	Lancaster 4 WSW
Green	Brodhead
Green Lake	Dalton
Jefferson	Lake Mills Watertown
Kenosha	Kenosha
Kewaunee	Kewaunee 3 NW
La Crosse	La Crosse Municipal Arpt
Langlade	Antigo
Manitowoc	Manitowoc Two Rivers
Marathon	Rosholt 9 NNE Wausau Municipal Arpt
Milwaukee	Milwaukee General Mitchell Field Milwaukee Mt Mary Col
Outagamie	Appleton New London
Ozaukee	Port Washington
Pierce	Ellsworth 1 E River Falls
Polk	Amery St Croix Falls

County	Station Name
Racine	Burlington Racine
Rock	Beloit
Sauk	Baraboo
Sawyer	Couderay 7 W
Sheboygan	Plymouth Sheboygan
Trempealeau	Blair
Vernon	Genoa Dam 8
Walworth	Lake Geneva
Washington	Germantown Hartford 2 W West Bend
Waukesha	Oconomowoc Waukesha
Waushara	Hancock Exp Farm
Winnebago	Oshkosh
Wood	Marshfield Exp Farm

See User Guide for station inclusion criteria.

Wisconsin Weather Stations by City

City	Station Name	Miles
Appleton	Appleton	1.9
	Chilton	20.2
	Green Bay Austin Straubel Intl	20.0
	New London	16.8
	Oshkosh	18.7
Beloit	Rockford Greater Rockford Arpt, IL	22.2
	Beloit	1.1
	Brodhead	19.1
Brookfield	Germantown	10.6
	Hartford 2 W	23.9
	Milwaukee Mt Mary Col	4.5
	Milwaukee General Mitchell Field	13.6
	Oconomowoc	19.3
	Waukesha	6.5
	West Bend	21.1
Eau Claire	Bloomer	19.9
	Eau Claire County Arpt	3.8
	Menomonie	22.1
Fond du Lac	Chilton	23.0
	Fond Du Lac	1.8
	Oshkosh	17.6
	Plymouth	23.8
Franklin	Burlington	21.3
	Germantown	22.6
	Kenosha	25.0
	Milwaukee Mt Mary Col	11.6
	Milwaukee General Mitchell Field	6.3
	Racine	17.8
	Waukesha	14.1
Green Bay	Green Bay Austin Straubel Intl	6.2
	Kewaunee 3 NW	23.8
Greenfield	Germantown	18.6
	Milwaukee Mt Mary Col	7.5
	Milwaukee General Mitchell Field	4.9
	Racine	21.1
	Waukesha	12.6
Janesville	Beloit	12.9
	Brodhead	19.4
Kenosha	Antioch, IL	15.4
	Burlington	21.0
	Kenosha	1.9
	Racine	8.7
La Crosse	Caledonia, MN	18.0
	Genoa Dam 8	16.6
	La Crosse Municipal Arpt	4.2
Madison	Arlington Univ Farm	15.8
	Lake Mills	24.6
	Madison Dane Co Regional Arpt	4.9
Manitowoc	Chilton	24.1
	Manitowoc	1.0
	Sheboygan	24.1
	Two Rivers	5.9

City	Station Name	Miles
Menomonee Falls	Germantown	4.3
	Hartford 2 W	19.7
	Milwaukee Mt Mary Col	7.3
	Milwaukee General Mitchell Field	17.7
	Oconomowoc	20.0
	Port Washington	20.0
	Waukesha	11.4
	West Bend	14.7
Milwaukee	Germantown	13.7
	Milwaukee Mt Mary Col	3.9
	Milwaukee General Mitchell Field	7.9
	Port Washington	23.1
	Waukesha	14.2
	West Bend	22.4
Mount Pleasant	Antioch, IL	20.9
	Burlington	20.7
	Kenosha	10.4
	Milwaukee General Mitchell Field	16.4
	Racine	3.6
New Berlin	Burlington	23.9
	Germantown	16.4
	Milwaukee Mt Mary Col	7.0
	Milwaukee General Mitchell Field	10.6
	Oconomowoc	21.6
	Waukesha	7.0
Oak Creek	Burlington	23.9
	Kenosha	22.5
	Milwaukee Mt Mary Col	14.1
	Milwaukee General Mitchell Field	4.5
	Racine	14.2
	Waukesha	19.0
Oshkosh	Appleton	18.1
	Chilton	20.0
	Fond Du Lac	16.3
	New London	23.9
	Oshkosh	0.5
Racine	Antioch, IL	23.0
	Burlington	23.1
	Kenosha	11.0
	Milwaukee General Mitchell Field	16.2
	Racine	2.2
Sheboygan	Manitowoc	23.2
	Plymouth	12.1
	Sheboygan	0.4
Sun Prairie	Arlington Univ Farm	9.9
	Lake Mills	17.3
	Madison Dane Co Regional Arpt	7.1
	Watertown	25.0
Superior	Cloquet, MN	21.1
	Duluth Intl Arpt, MN	10.5
	Foxboro	18.1
	Superior	3.5
Waukesha	Burlington	24.8

See User Guide for station inclusion criteria.

City	Station Name	Miles
Waukesha *(cont.)*	Germantown	15.6
	Hartford 2 W	24.1
	Milwaukee Mt Mary Col	11.1
	Milwaukee General Mitchell Field	17.6
	Oconomowoc	14.6
	Waukesha	0.6
Wausau	Rosholt 9 NNE	23.9
	Wausau Municipal Arpt	3.2
Wauwatosa	Germantown	11.9
	Milwaukee Mt Mary Col	0.8
	Milwaukee General Mitchell Field	9.7
	Oconomowoc	24.2
	Port Washington	23.8
	Waukesha	11.0
	West Bend	21.5
West Allis	Germantown	15.3
	Milwaukee Mt Mary Col	4.2
	Milwaukee General Mitchell Field	7.2
	Racine	24.4
	Waukesha	10.8
West Bend	Germantown	14.7
	Hartford 2 W	13.1
	Plymouth	24.1
	Port Washington	16.3
	West Bend	6.5

Note: Miles is the distance between the geographic center of the city and the weather station.

Wisconsin Weather Stations by Elevation

Feet	Station Name
1,521	Antigo
1,299	Couderay 7 W
1,250	Marshfield Exp Farm
1,240	Cumberland
1,200	Wausau Municipal Arpt
1,160	Rosholt 9 NNE
1,080	Arlington Univ Farm
1,076	Hancock Exp Farm
1,069	Amery
1,040	Lancaster 4 WSW
1,029	Ellsworth 1 E
979	Bloomer
979	Hartford 2 W
939	West Bend
932	Foxboro
915	River Falls
890	Eau Claire County Arpt
879	Lake Geneva
859	Blair
859	Dalton
857	Madison Dane Co Regional Arpt
855	Oconomowoc
852	Lake Mills
850	Germantown
839	Beaver Dam
839	Chilton
833	Plymouth
830	Waukesha
825	Watertown
823	Baraboo
819	Bayfield 6 N
805	New London
790	Brodhead
779	Beloit
779	Menomonie
770	St Croix Falls
759	Fond Du Lac
750	Burlington
750	Appleton
750	Oshkosh
726	Milwaukee Mt Mary Col
702	Kewaunee 3 NW
687	Green Bay Austin Straubel Intl
671	Milwaukee General Mitchell Field
669	Alma Dam 4
660	Manitowoc
655	Sturgeon Bay Exp Farm
650	La Crosse Municipal Arpt
647	Sheboygan
639	Genoa Dam 8
629	Superior
600	Kenosha
600	Port Washington
599	Two Rivers
595	Racine

See User Guide for station inclusion criteria.

Green Bay Int'l Airport

The Green Bay climate is modified by surrounding topography. The modification is caused by the Bay of Green Bay, Lakes Michigan, and Superior, and to a lesser extent, the slightly higher surrounding terrain terminating in the Fox River Valley. The city of Green Bay is located at the mouth of the Fox River, one of the largest rivers flowing northward in the United States. It empties into the south end of the Bay.

The modified continental climate of Green Bay is shown by the few occurrences of 90 degree temperatures in the summer season and the few occurrences of sub-zero temperatures in the winter season. The narrow temperature range stems from the lake effects and the limited hours of sunshine caused by cloudiness.

Precipitation normally falls in the five-month period May through September. Three-fifths of the annual total is in the growing season, most often falling during thunderstorms. During the winter months, snowfall is less than in nearby communities where the ground is slightly higher.

The comparatively low range in temperature along with the greater portion of the precipitation falling during the growing season is conducive to the development of the dairy industry. Cherry and apple orchards are important crops in nearby lake communities. The growing of potatoes and canning vegetables are predominant inland. Paper products are the major manufacturing industry.

High winds, excessive precipitation, and electrical storms cause occasional damage. Snowstorms are the principal winter hazard. While the winters are long in Green Bay, the extremes are never as severe as the northern latitude location would indicate.

Based on the 1951-1980 period, the average first occurrence of 32 degrees Fahrenheit in the fall is October 2 and the average last occurrence in the spring is May 12.

Green Bay Int'l Airport *Brown County* Elevation: 687 ft. Latitude: 44° 29' N Longitude: 88° 08' W

	JAN	FEB	MAR	APR	MAY	JUN	JUL	AUG	SEP	OCT	NOV	DEC	YEAR
Mean Maximum Temp. (°F)	25.4	29.1	39.8	54.8	67.0	76.4	80.8	78.5	70.9	57.3	43.1	29.6	54.4
Mean Temp. (°F)	17.5	21.0	31.3	44.6	55.8	65.5	69.9	68.0	60.0	47.7	35.4	22.3	44.9
Mean Minimum Temp. (°F)	9.6	12.9	22.8	34.4	44.6	54.6	58.9	57.5	49.1	38.1	27.6	15.0	35.4
Extreme Maximum Temp. (°F)	53	61	78	89	90	98	103	99	92	87	74	64	103
Extreme Minimum Temp. (°F)	-28	-28	-13	11	26	36	43	39	28	16	-3	-27	-28
Days Maximum Temp. ≥ 90°F	0	0	0	0	0	2	3	1	0	0	0	0	6
Days Maximum Temp. ≤ 32°F	22	17	7	0	0	0	0	0	0	0	4	17	67
Days Minimum Temp. ≤ 32°F	30	27	26	13	2	0	0	0	1	9	22	29	159
Days Minimum Temp. ≤ 0°F	9	5	1	0	0	0	0	0	0	0	0	5	20
Heating Degree Days (base 65°F)	1,467	1,238	1,038	609	298	79	17	32	183	531	883	1,318	7,693
Cooling Degree Days (base 65°F)	0	0	0	3	21	101	175	131	40	3	0	0	474
Mean Precipitation (in.)	1.17	1.08	1.88	2.60	2.92	3.79	3.24	3.46	3.01	2.43	2.12	1.49	29.19
Maximum Precipitation (in.)*	2.6	3.6	4.7	5.9	8.2	10.3	7.0	9.0	7.8	5.0	5.3	3.1	38.4
Minimum Precipitation (in.)*	0.1	trace	0.3	0.5	0.1	0.3	0.8	0.9	0.3	trace	0.2	0.1	17.8
Extreme Maximum Daily Precip. (in.)	0.94	1.53	1.25	1.86	2.05	4.90	4.12	2.57	2.72	2.06	2.23	1.24	4.90
Days With ≥ 0.1" Precipitation	4	3	5	6	7	7	6	7	6	6	5	4	66
Days With ≥ 0.5" Precipitation	0	0	1	2	2	3	2	2	2	1	1	1	17
Days With ≥ 1.0" Precipitation	0	0	0	0	0	1	1	1	1	0	0	0	4
Mean Snowfall (in.)	13.5	9.5	8.6	2.9	0.2	trace	trace	trace	trace	0.2	4.1	12.9	51.9
Maximum Snowfall (in.)*	30	21	24	12	4	0	0	0	trace	2	17	27	92
Maximum 24-hr. Snowfall (in.)*	9	9	13	10	4	0	0	0	trace	1	10	14	14
Maximum Snow Depth (in.)	21	18	17	5	2	trace	trace	trace	trace	1	10	19	21
Days With ≥ 1.0" Snow Depth	25	23	13	2	0	0	0	0	0	0	3	18	84
Thunderstorm Days*	< 1	< 1	1	2	4	6	7	6	4	2	1	< 1	33
Foggy Days*	9	10	11	10	9	9	11	14	12	11	12	11	129
Predominant Sky Cover*	OVR	OVR	OVR	OVR	OVR	OVR	OVR	OVR	OVR	OVR	OVR	OVR	OVR
Mean Relative Humidity 6am (%)*	78	79	81	79	79	82	86	90	89	85	82	81	83
Mean Relative Humidity 3pm (%)*	68	65	63	54	52	55	55	58	59	59	67	71	60
Mean Dewpoint (°F)*	9	12	22	32	43	54	60	59	51	40	27	15	35
Prevailing Wind Direction*	W	W	NE	NE	NE	SW	SW	SW	SSW	SW	W	W	SW
Prevailing Wind Speed (mph)*	12	10	12	13	12	10	9	9	10	12	12	10	10
Maximum Wind Gust (mph)*	69	55	58	68	81	70	60	54	48	46	54	53	81

Note: (*) Period of record is 1949-1995

La Crosse Municipal Airport

The city of La Crosse is situated on the east bank of the Mississippi River at the confluence of the Mississippi, Black, and La Crosse Rivers. The official records are taken at the La Crosse Municipal Airport which is six and a half miles north of the main Post Office, on the north end of French Island. This island is about six miles long from north to south and two to four miles wide with the Mississippi River to the west and the old channel of the Black River to the east. A sandy plain exists on each side of the river extending between the Wisconsin and Minnesota bluffs which rise 450 to 500 feet above the valley floor. The distance from bluff to bluff averages about five miles.

The prevailing winds in the area are from the northwest from January through April and southerly during the remainder of the year. The situation of the city and airport in a natural bowl between the hills results in somewhat colder temperatures at night due to the settling of cooler air. Valley fogs often persist to mid-forenoon. Steepsided hills with narrow valleys are characteristic of most of the surrounding area.

The flow of the Mississippi River is regulated by dams built for the purpose of navigation, but the reservoirs have limited storage capacity. La Crosse is in the area of Pool No. eight with a mean sea level elevation of 631 feet. When the river reaches an elevation of 639 feet, with open gate operation, there is considerable flooding of land near the river and some industrial sections of the city.

The invigorating continental-type climate results in wide and frequent variations in temperature. General storms moving eastward or northeastward into the area bring warmer weather and supply most of our moisture. These are usually followed by cooler air from Canada. The winters are cold and humid. The summers are warm with moderate humidities, while periods of hot and humid weather occur occasionally, usually lasting from a few days to a week at a time.

Sixty percent of the precipitation falls during the main growing season, extending from May through September. Most of the summer rainfall occurs during scattered thunderstorms. Some damage from heavy rains, high winds, and hail occurs each year, but tornadoes are infrequent and cover very small areas. Snow is frequent and is the predominant form of precipitation in winter. Heavy snow sometimes falls with larger amounts over the ridges.

Based on the 1951-1980 period, the average first occurrence of 32 degrees Fahrenheit in the fall is October 13 and the average last occurrence in the spring is April 29.

La Crosse Municipal Airport *La Crosse County* Elevation: 650 ft. Latitude: 43° 52' N Longitude: 91° 15' W

	JAN	FEB	MAR	APR	MAY	JUN	JUL	AUG	SEP	OCT	NOV	DEC	YEAR
Mean Maximum Temp. (°F)	26.3	31.5	43.7	59.4	71.1	80.4	84.7	81.8	73.5	59.8	44.3	30.0	57.2
Mean Temp. (°F)	17.7	22.6	34.2	48.6	60.0	69.5	74.0	71.5	63.0	50.0	36.3	22.4	47.5
Mean Minimum Temp. (°F)	9.0	13.6	24.7	37.8	48.8	58.4	63.2	61.2	52.5	40.1	28.4	14.8	37.7
Extreme Maximum Temp. (°F)	57	64	83	93	95	102	108	105	95	91	75	67	108
Extreme Minimum Temp. (°F)	-33	-35	-9	7	26	39	46	40	29	14	-3	-30	-35
Days Maximum Temp. ≥ 90°F	0	0	0	0	1	4	7	4	1	0	0	0	17
Days Maximum Temp. ≤ 32°F	20	14	5	0	0	0	0	0	0	0	4	17	60
Days Minimum Temp. ≤ 32°F	30	26	24	9	0	0	0	0	0	6	20	29	144
Days Minimum Temp. ≤ 0°F	9	6	1	0	0	0	0	0	0	0	0	5	21
Heating Degree Days (base 65°F)	1,461	1,193	947	494	195	34	4	13	133	467	853	1,313	7,107
Cooling Degree Days (base 65°F)	0	0	1	9	47	175	289	221	80	8	0	0	830
Mean Precipitation (in.)	1.13	1.06	2.04	3.32	3.49	4.16	4.14	4.43	3.61	2.21	1.95	1.30	32.84
Maximum Precipitation (in.)*	2.9	2.6	3.8	7.3	8.8	10.8	9.3	9.8	10.5	5.1	6.2	2.9	44.1
Minimum Precipitation (in.)*	0.1	0	0.3	0.6	0.9	1.3	0.2	0.5	0.4	trace	trace	0.3	16.6
Extreme Maximum Daily Precip. (in.)	0.98	1.29	1.58	2.17	2.87	3.82	5.24	4.05	3.35	2.28	2.80	1.42	5.24
Days With ≥ 0.1" Precipitation	4	3	5	7	7	7	7	7	6	5	4	4	66
Days With ≥ 0.5" Precipitation	0	1	1	2	2	3	3	3	2	1	1	0	19
Days With ≥ 1.0" Precipitation	0	0	0	1	1	1	1	1	1	0	0	0	6
Mean Snowfall (in.)	11.6	8.2	7.5	1.9	trace	trace	trace	trace	trace	0.2	4.1	10.3	43.8
Maximum Snowfall (in.)*	30	31	34	17	1	0	0	0	trace	2	30	30	91
Maximum 24-hr. Snowfall (in.)*	10	10	13	10	1	0	0	0	trace	2	13	14	14
Maximum Snow Depth (in.)	27	23	19	5	trace	trace	trace	trace	trace	1	15	17	27
Days With ≥ 1.0" Snow Depth	23	21	10	1	0	0	0	0	0	0	3	19	77
Thunderstorm Days*	< 1	< 1	1	3	5	8	8	7	5	2	1	< 1	40
Foggy Days*	11	11	12	9	8	8	10	14	13	10	12	13	131
Predominant Sky Cover*	OVR	OVR	OVR	OVR	OVR	OVR	OVR	OVR	OVR	OVR	OVR	OVR	OVR
Mean Relative Humidity 6am (%)*	78	79	81	79	79	84	88	90	90	83	82	81	83
Mean Relative Humidity 3pm (%)*	64	61	57	49	49	52	54	55	56	53	63	68	57
Mean Dewpoint (°F)*	8	13	22	34	46	57	62	61	52	40	27	15	37
Prevailing Wind Direction*	NW	NW	NW	NW	S	S	S	S	S	S	S	S	S
Prevailing Wind Speed (mph)*	12	12	13	14	12	10	10	9	10	12	10	10	12
Maximum Wind Gust (mph)*	na	na	na	na	na	na	na	na	na	na	na	na	na

Note: (*) Period of record is 1948-1995

Madison Regional Airport

Madison is set on a narrow isthmus of land between Lakes Mendota and Monona. Lake Mendota (15 square miles) lies northwest of Lake Monona (five square miles) and the lakes are only two-thirds of a mile apart at one point. Drainage at Madison is southeast through two other lakes into the Rock River, which flows south into Illinois, and then west to the Mississippi. The westward flowing Wisconsin River is only 20 miles northwest of Madison. Madison lakes are normally frozen from mid-December to early April.

Madison has the typical continental climate of interior North America with a large annual temperature range and with frequent short period temperature changes. The range of extreme temperatures is from about 110 to -40 degrees. Winter temperatures (December-February) average near 20 degrees and the summer average (June-August) is in the upper 60s. Daily temperatures average below 32 degrees about 120 days and above 40 degrees for about 210 days of the year.

Madison lies in the path of the frequent cyclones and anticyclones which move eastward over this area during fall, winter and spring. In summer, the cyclones have diminished intensity and tend to pass farther north. The most frequent air masses are of polar origin. Occasional outbreaks of arctic air affect this area during the winter months. Although northward moving tropical air masses contribute considerable cloudiness and precipitation, the true Gulf air mass does not reach this area in winter, and only occasionally at other seasons. Summers are pleasant, with only occasional periods of extreme heat or high humidity.

There are no dry and wet seasons, but about 60 percent of the annual precipitation falls in the five months of May through September. Cold season precipitation is lighter, but lasts longer. Soil moisture is usually adequate in the first part of the growing season. During July, August, and September, the crops depend on current rainfall, which is mostly from thunderstorms and tends to be erratic and variable. Average occurrence of thunderstorms is just under 7 days per month during this period.

March and November are the windiest months. Tornadoes are infrequent. Dane County has about one tornado in every three to five years.

The ground is covered with one inch or more of snow about 60 percent of the time from about December 10 to near February 25 in an average winter. The soil is usually frozen from the first of December through most of March with an average frost penetration of 25 to 30 inches. The growing season averages 175 days.

Farming is diversified with the main emphasis on dairying. Field crops are mainly corn, oats, clover, and alfalfa, but barley, wheat, rye, and tobacco are also raised. Canning factories pack peas, sweet corn, and lima beans. Fruits are mainly apples, strawberries, and raspberries.

Madison Regional Airport *Dane County* Elevation: 857 ft. Latitude: 43° 08' N Longitude: 89° 21' W

	JAN	FEB	MAR	APR	MAY	JUN	JUL	AUG	SEP	OCT	NOV	DEC	YEAR
Mean Maximum Temp. (°F)	27.2	31.7	43.5	57.8	69.2	78.7	82.4	80.0	72.5	59.3	44.8	31.1	56.5
Mean Temp. (°F)	19.1	23.2	34.0	46.7	57.5	67.3	71.5	69.4	61.3	49.0	36.4	23.5	46.6
Mean Minimum Temp. (°F)	11.0	14.7	24.4	35.5	45.8	55.8	60.7	58.6	50.0	38.5	28.0	15.9	36.6
Extreme Maximum Temp. (°F)	56	64	82	94	92	101	101	102	93	87	74	64	102
Extreme Minimum Temp. (°F)	-27	-29	-8	0	24	35	42	38	26	13	-2	-25	-29
Days Maximum Temp. ≥ 90°F	0	0	0	0	0	2	4	2	0	0	0	0	8
Days Maximum Temp. ≤ 32°F	20	14	5	0	0	0	0	0	0	0	4	16	59
Days Minimum Temp. ≤ 32°F	30	27	24	11	2	0	0	0	1	9	20	29	153
Days Minimum Temp. ≤ 0°F	8	5	1	0	0	0	0	0	0	0	0	4	18
Heating Degree Days (base 65°F)	1,416	1,175	956	548	254	56	9	24	162	496	851	1,280	7,227
Cooling Degree Days (base 65°F)	0	0	0	5	29	130	219	166	56	5	0	0	610
Mean Precipitation (in.)	1.24	1.43	2.19	3.36	3.49	4.37	4.00	4.45	3.30	2.36	2.39	1.74	34.32
Maximum Precipitation (in.)*	2.4	2.8	5.0	7.1	6.3	9.9	10.9	9.5	9.2	5.6	5.1	4.1	43.3
Minimum Precipitation (in.)*	0.1	0.1	0.3	1.1	0.6	0.8	1.5	0.7	0.1	0.1	0.1	0.3	21.1
Extreme Maximum Daily Precip. (in.)	1.07	1.56	2.78	1.94	3.66	4.51	3.75	3.40	3.67	2.78	1.96	2.19	4.51
Days With ≥ 0.1" Precipitation	4	4	5	7	7	7	7	7	6	5	5	5	69
Days With ≥ 0.5" Precipitation	1	1	1	2	2	2	3	3	2	1	1	1	20
Days With ≥ 1.0" Precipitation	0	0	0	1	1	1	1	1	1	0	1	0	7
Mean Snowfall (in.)	12.8	10.2	6.9	2.8	0.2	trace	trace	trace	trace	0.5	3.7	13.1	50.2
Maximum Snowfall (in.)*	28	37	25	17	3	0	0	0	trace	3	18	33	83
Maximum 24-hr. Snowfall (in.)*	13	12	12	13	3	0	0	0	trace	3	8	17	17
Maximum Snow Depth (in.)	23	20	16	8	4	trace	trace	trace	trace	1	9	17	23
Days With ≥ 1.0" Snow Depth	23	21	9	1	0	0	0	0	0	0	3	18	75
Thunderstorm Days*	< 1	< 1	2	4	5	7	8	7	5	2	1	< 1	41
Foggy Days*	13	11	13	11	11	10	11	14	14	12	13	14	147
Predominant Sky Cover*	OVR	OVR	OVR	OVR	OVR	OVR	OVR	OVR	OVR	OVR	OVR	OVR	OVR
Mean Relative Humidity 6am (%)*	78	80	81	80	79	81	85	89	90	85	83	82	83
Mean Relative Humidity 3pm (%)*	67	63	59	51	49	51	53	55	56	54	64	69	57
Mean Dewpoint (°F)*	10	14	23	34	45	55	61	60	51	40	28	17	37
Prevailing Wind Direction*	WNW	WNW	NW	S	S	S	S	S	S	S	S	WNW	S
Prevailing Wind Speed (mph)*	12	12	13	12	10	9	9	9	10	10	10	12	10
Maximum Wind Gust (mph)*	58	62	67	63	64	83	83	64	64	62	55	58	83

Note: (*) Period of record is 1948-1995

Milwaukee Gen. Mitchell Field

Milwaukee possesses a continental climate characterized by a wide range of temperatures between summer and winter. Precipitation is moderate and occurs mostly in the spring, less in the autumn, and very little in the wintertime. Rainfall is well distributed for agricultural purposes, although spring planting is sometimes delayed by wet ground and cold weather.

Milwaukee is in a region of frequently changeable weather and its climate is influenced by general easterly-moving storms which traverse the nations midsection. The most severe winter storms, which produce in excess of 10 inches of snow, develop in the southern Great Plains and move northeast across Illinois and Indiana.

Occasionally during the cold season, frigid air masses from Canada push southeast across the Great Lakes region. These arctic air masses account for the coldest winter temperatures. If northwesterly wind circulation persists, repeated incursions of arctic air will result in a period of bitterly cold weather lasting several days.

Summer temperatures, which reach into the 90s but rarely exceed 100 degrees, occur with brisk southwest winds that carry hot air from the plains and lower Mississippi River Valley across the city. A combination of high temperatures and humidity occasionally develops, usually building up over a period of several days when persistent southerly winds transport moisture from the Gulf of Mexico into the area.

The Gulf is a major source of moisture for Milwaukee in all seasons. Cold-season precipitation (rain, snow, or a mixture) is usually of relatively long duration and low intensity, and occasionally persists for two days or more, whereas in the warm season, relatively short-duration and high-intensity showery rainfall, usually lasting a few hours or less, predominates.

The Great Lakes significantly influence the local climate. Temperature extremes are modified by Lake Michigan and, to a lesser extent, the other Great Lakes. In late autumn and winter, air masses that are initially very cold often reach the city only after being tempered by passage over one or more of the lakes. Similarly, air masses that approach from the northeast in the spring and summer are cooler because of movement over the Great Lakes.

Lake-induced snows usually occur a few times each winter, but snow accumulation is rarely heavy.

Milwaukee Gen. Mitchell Field *Milwaukee County* Elevation: 671 ft. Latitude: 42° 57' N Longitude: 87° 54' W

	JAN	FEB	MAR	APR	MAY	JUN	JUL	AUG	SEP	OCT	NOV	DEC	YEAR
Mean Maximum Temp. (°F)	29.4	32.9	42.7	54.3	65.4	75.7	80.5	78.7	71.8	59.4	46.3	33.4	55.9
Mean Temp. (°F)	22.6	26.1	35.1	45.8	56.0	66.4	72.0	70.9	63.3	51.3	39.2	26.9	48.0
Mean Minimum Temp. (°F)	15.7	19.1	27.5	37.3	46.6	57.0	63.4	63.0	54.8	43.1	32.1	20.3	40.0
Extreme Maximum Temp. (°F)	63	68	82	91	93	101	103	103	96	87	75	68	103
Extreme Minimum Temp. (°F)	-26	-26	-6	12	29	37	47	44	32	18	5	-20	-26
Days Maximum Temp. ≥ 90°F	0	0	0	0	0	2	4	2	1	0	0	0	9
Days Maximum Temp. ≤ 32°F	18	13	5	0	0	0	0	0	0	0	2	13	51
Days Minimum Temp. ≤ 32°F	29	25	22	7	0	0	0	0	0	3	15	27	128
Days Minimum Temp. ≤ 0°F	4	2	0	0	0	0	0	0	0	0	0	2	8
Heating Degree Days (base 65°F)	1,309	1,095	919	574	301	80	10	13	118	426	768	1,176	6,789
Cooling Degree Days (base 65°F)	0	0	1	6	29	128	233	202	73	7	0	0	679
Mean Precipitation (in.)	1.79	1.68	2.26	3.58	3.35	3.83	3.42	4.09	3.21	2.65	2.70	2.10	34.66
Maximum Precipitation (in.)*	4.0	3.9	6.9	7.3	7.6	8.3	7.7	9.0	9.4	7.0	7.1	5.4	42.2
Minimum Precipitation (in.)*	0.3	0	0.3	1.3	0.5	0.7	1.0	0.5	trace	0.1	0.6	0.3	19.1
Extreme Maximum Daily Precip. (in.)	1.54	1.29	1.28	2.06	2.15	4.93	4.42	6.81	2.96	2.33	2.22	2.24	6.81
Days With ≥ 0.1" Precipitation	5	4	5	7	7	6	6	7	6	6	6	5	70
Days With ≥ 0.5" Precipitation	1	1	2	3	2	3	2	3	2	2	2	1	24
Days With ≥ 1.0" Precipitation	0	0	0	1	1	1	1	1	1	0	1	0	7
Mean Snowfall (in.)	14.8	10.9	7.6	2.1	0.1	trace	trace	trace	trace	0.3	2.5	11.7	50.0
Maximum Snowfall (in.)*	34	42	27	16	3	0	0	0	0	6	16	28	88
Maximum 24-hr. Snowfall (in.)*	14	17	11	12	3	0	0	0	0	4	10	13	17
Maximum Snow Depth (in.)	32	23	14	9	2	trace	trace	trace	trace	6	10	32	32
Days With ≥ 1.0" Snow Depth	21	17	7	1	0	0	0	0	0	0	1	12	59
Thunderstorm Days*	< 1	< 1	2	4	4	6	7	6	4	2	1	< 1	36
Foggy Days*	11	11	12	11	11	10	10	13	12	11	12	13	137
Predominant Sky Cover*	OVR	OVR	OVR	OVR	OVR	OVR	OVR	OVR	OVR	OVR	OVR	OVR	OVR
Mean Relative Humidity 6am (%)*	76	77	79	78	77	79	82	86	85	82	80	79	80
Mean Relative Humidity 3pm (%)*	68	66	64	58	57	58	59	62	61	60	66	69	62
Mean Dewpoint (°F)*	13	16	24	34	44	55	61	61	53	41	30	19	38
Prevailing Wind Direction*	WNW	WNW	WNW	NNE	NNE	NNE	SW	SW	SSW	SSW	WNW	WNW	WNW
Prevailing Wind Speed (mph)*	13	13	13	14	14	12	10	10	12	12	13	13	13
Maximum Wind Gust (mph)*	66	67	77	67	74	76	81	64	62	53	56	61	81

Note: (*) Period of record is 1948-1995

The period of record for National Weather Service station data is 1980 – 2009 except where noted. See User Guide for detailed explanation of data.

Alma Dam 4 *Buffalo County* Elevation: 669 ft. Latitude: 44° 20' N Longitude: 91° 56' W

	JAN	FEB	MAR	APR	MAY	JUN	JUL	AUG	SEP	OCT	NOV	DEC	YEAR
Mean Maximum Temp. (°F)	25.6	30.6	42.0	58.4	69.9	78.6	82.5	80.2	72.1	58.9	43.0	29.0	55.9
Mean Temp. (°F)	17.7	22.5	33.7	48.3	59.7	68.7	73.1	71.0	62.9	50.2	35.8	21.9	47.1
Mean Minimum Temp. (°F)	9.7	14.3	25.3	38.1	49.5	58.7	63.6	61.7	53.7	41.4	28.6	14.8	38.3
Extreme Maximum Temp. (°F)	55	62	80	89	92	96	100	101	90	91	73	64	101
Extreme Minimum Temp. (°F)	-38	-35	-8	7	24	36	49	42	25	18	-4	-32	-38
Days Maximum Temp. ≥ 90°F	0	0	0	0	0	2	3	2	0	0	0	0	7
Days Maximum Temp. ≤ 32°F	21	15	6	0	0	0	0	0	0	0	5	18	65
Days Minimum Temp. ≤ 32°F	30	26	23	8	0	0	0	0	0	5	20	29	141
Days Minimum Temp. ≤ 0°F	8	5	1	0	0	0	0	0	0	0	0	5	19
Heating Degree Days (base 65°F)	1,461	1,196	964	503	197	39	3	13	130	460	869	1,329	7,164
Cooling Degree Days (base 65°F)	0	0	0	6	40	155	260	205	75	7	0	0	748
Mean Precipitation (in.)	0.87	0.77	1.70	3.28	4.24	4.66	4.66	5.12	4.11	2.46	2.08	0.97	34.92
Extreme Maximum Daily Precip. (in.)	0.73	1.32	1.56	2.20	2.70	3.73	5.91	2.88	3.59	1.79	1.88	1.41	5.91
Days With ≥ 0.1" Precipitation	3	3	4	7	8	8	7	8	7	6	4	3	68
Days With ≥ 0.5" Precipitation	0	0	1	2	3	3	3	4	3	2	1	0	22
Days With ≥ 1.0" Precipitation	0	0	0	1	1	1	1	2	1	0	0	0	7
Mean Snowfall (in.)	9.1	6.6	7.0	1.2	trace	0.0	0.0	0.0	0.0	trace	3.2	8.7	35.8
Maximum Snow Depth (in.)	24	24	21	6	trace	0	0	0	0	1	15	23	24
Days With ≥ 1.0" Snow Depth	26	23	13	1	0	0	0	0	0	0	3	19	85

Amery *Polk County* Elevation: 1,069 ft. Latitude: 45° 18' N Longitude: 92° 22' W

	JAN	FEB	MAR	APR	MAY	JUN	JUL	AUG	SEP	OCT	NOV	DEC	YEAR
Mean Maximum Temp. (°F)	21.3	26.8	38.3	54.7	67.3	76.1	80.6	78.3	69.6	55.7	39.4	25.3	52.8
Mean Temp. (°F)	11.9	17.1	29.0	44.0	56.1	65.3	69.9	67.7	58.8	45.8	31.5	17.2	42.9
Mean Minimum Temp. (°F)	2.5	7.4	19.6	33.2	44.9	54.5	59.2	57.0	48.0	35.7	23.5	9.0	32.9
Extreme Maximum Temp. (°F)	54	57	80	90	94	98	101	101	92	86	73	61	101
Extreme Minimum Temp. (°F)	-35	-38	-16	3	20	34	41	34	23	12	-13	-43	-43
Days Maximum Temp. ≥ 90°F	0	0	0	0	0	1	2	2	0	0	0	0	5
Days Maximum Temp. ≤ 32°F	25	18	9	1	0	0	0	0	0	0	9	22	84
Days Minimum Temp. ≤ 32°F	30	28	27	14	2	0	0	0	1	12	25	31	170
Days Minimum Temp. ≤ 0°F	14	9	3	0	0	0	0	0	0	0	1	9	36
Heating Degree Days (base 65°F)	1,641	1,349	1,111	627	290	81	19	41	219	590	998	1,478	8,444
Cooling Degree Days (base 65°F)	0	0	0	3	21	97	178	132	39	3	0	0	473
Mean Precipitation (in.)	0.92	0.83	1.68	2.72	3.44	4.50	3.91	4.20	3.71	2.84	1.81	1.19	31.75
Extreme Maximum Daily Precip. (in.)	1.71	0.97	1.25	2.31	2.13	3.02	3.72	3.44	4.08	2.65	2.20	1.51	4.08
Days With ≥ 0.1" Precipitation	3	3	4	6	7	8	7	7	6	6	4	4	65
Days With ≥ 0.5" Precipitation	0	0	1	2	2	3	3	3	2	2	1	0	19
Days With ≥ 1.0" Precipitation	0	0	0	1	1	1	1	1	1	1	0	0	7
Mean Snowfall (in.)	9.5	7.4	9.6	2.4	0.0	0.0	0.0	0.0	0.0	0.7	6.7	9.4	45.7
Maximum Snow Depth (in.)	29	26	22	12	0	0	0	0	0	4	18	20	29
Days With ≥ 1.0" Snow Depth	29	26	19	2	0	0	0	0	0	0	7	23	106

Antigo *Langlade County* Elevation: 1,521 ft. Latitude: 45° 09' N Longitude: 89° 07' W

	JAN	FEB	MAR	APR	MAY	JUN	JUL	AUG	SEP	OCT	NOV	DEC	YEAR
Mean Maximum Temp. (°F)	21.4	26.0	36.1	52.7	65.1	73.8	***78.6***	76.4	67.9	54.1	38.8	24.5	***51.3***
Mean Temp. (°F)	12.0	15.6	26.1	42.0	53.4	***62.5***	***67.0***	65.1	56.8	44.1	30.9	16.0	***40.9***
Mean Minimum Temp. (°F)	2.4	5.1	16.2	31.2	41.6	***51.1***	***55.3***	53.8	45.6	34.1	23.0	7.4	***30.6***
Extreme Maximum Temp. (°F)	48	56	73	87	***89***	***93***	***96***	95	91	83	71	***59***	***96***
Extreme Minimum Temp. (°F)	-39	-38	-23	-1	***20***	***30***	***37***	33	22	14	-10	***-35***	***-39***
Days Maximum Temp. ≥ 90°F	0	0	0	0	0	0	1	1	0	0	0	0	2
Days Maximum Temp. ≤ 32°F	26	20	11	1	0	0	0	0	0	0	9	23	90
Days Minimum Temp. ≤ 32°F	31	28	28	17	5	0	0	0	2	15	25	30	181
Days Minimum Temp. ≤ 0°F	14	11	4	0	0	0	0	0	0	0	1	10	40
Heating Degree Days (base 65°F)	1,641	1,393	1,197	686	365	***127***	***45***	73	264	642	1,015	1,515	***8,963***
Cooling Degree Days (base 65°F)	0	0	0	2	12	***59***	***112***	83	24	2	0	0	***294***
Mean Precipitation (in.)	0.79	0.73	1.28	2.46	3.15	3.82	3.39	3.73	3.60	2.99	1.75	1.04	28.73
Extreme Maximum Daily Precip. (in.)	0.76	0.80	***1.31***	1.98	***2.02***	3.16	***3.54***	2.57	2.64	4.34	1.72	***0.90***	***4.34***
Days With ≥ 0.1" Precipitation	2	2	4	6	7	8	6	7	7	6	5	4	64
Days With ≥ 0.5" Precipitation	0	0	1	1	2	3	2	3	2	2	1	0	17
Days With ≥ 1.0" Precipitation	0	0	0	0	0	1	1	1	1	1	0	0	5
Mean Snowfall (in.)	11.3	8.5	8.5	3.6	0.3	0.0	0.0	0.0	trace	1.1	6.4	13.3	53.0
Maximum Snow Depth (in.)	23	28	20	13	2	0	0	0	trace	***5***	***13***	***25***	***28***
Days With ≥ 1.0" Snow Depth	28	27	23	4	0	0	0	0	0	1	7	25	115

Appleton *Outagamie County* Elevation: 750 ft. Latitude: 44° 15' N Longitude: 88° 22' W

	JAN	FEB	MAR	APR	MAY	JUN	JUL	AUG	SEP	OCT	NOV	DEC	YEAR
Mean Maximum Temp. (°F)	25.5	29.4	40.4	55.4	68.1	77.3	81.8	79.1	71.3	57.1	43.0	29.0	54.8
Mean Temp. (°F)	17.9	21.2	31.5	45.2	57.1	66.8	71.7	69.5	61.4	48.1	35.4	21.8	45.6
Mean Minimum Temp. (°F)	10.2	13.0	22.5	35.0	46.2	56.3	61.5	59.8	51.4	38.9	27.8	14.6	36.4
Extreme Maximum Temp. (°F)	52	59	81	89	94	101	102	103	92	87	75	61	103
Extreme Minimum Temp. (°F)	-29	-29	-9	9	25	35	43	40	25	15	0	-23	-29
Days Maximum Temp. ≥ 90°F	0	0	0	0	0	2	4	2	0	0	0	0	8
Days Maximum Temp. ≤ 32°F	22	17	7	1	0	0	0	0	0	0	5	18	70
Days Minimum Temp. ≤ 32°F	30	27	26	12	2	0	0	0	0	8	21	30	156
Days Minimum Temp. ≤ 0°F	8	5	1	0	0	0	0	0	0	0	0	5	19
Heating Degree Days (base 65°F)	1,455	1,232	1,034	591	270	66	10	24	159	522	880	1,333	7,576
Cooling Degree Days (base 65°F)	0	0	0	4	33	127	224	169	57	4	0	0	618
Mean Precipitation (in.)	1.21	1.04	1.83	2.88	3.14	3.90	3.27	3.84	3.05	2.43	2.08	1.47	30.14
Extreme Maximum Daily Precip. (in.)	1.23	1.73	1.85	2.30	2.29	4.18	3.84	3.26	2.67	1.54	1.82	1.64	4.18
Days With ≥ 0.1" Precipitation	4	3	5	7	7	7	6	7	6	6	5	4	67
Days With ≥ 0.5" Precipitation	0	0	1	2	2	2	2	3	2	1	1	1	17
Days With ≥ 1.0" Precipitation	0	0	0	1	0	1	1	1	1	0	0	0	5
Mean Snowfall (in.)	11.6	8.5	7.3	2.4	0.2	0.0	0.0	0.0	trace	0.2	3.0	11.5	44.7
Maximum Snow Depth (in.)	22	22	20	3	2	0	0	0	trace	1	8	20	22
Days With ≥ 1.0" Snow Depth	24	22	11	1	0	0	0	0	0	0	3	18	79

The period of record for all cooperative weather station data is 1980 – 2009. See User Guide for detailed explanation of data.

Arlington Univ Farm *Columbia County* Elevation: 1,080 ft. Latitude: 43° 18' N Longitude: 89° 21' W

	JAN	FEB	MAR	APR	MAY	JUN	JUL	AUG	SEP	OCT	NOV	DEC	YEAR
Mean Maximum Temp. (°F)	26.6	31.1	42.4	57.7	69.6	78.7	82.3	80.3	73.1	59.9	44.1	30.4	56.3
Mean Temp. (°F)	18.1	22.4	33.1	46.5	57.6	66.9	71.0	69.1	61.3	49.0	35.7	22.3	46.1
Mean Minimum Temp. (°F)	9.6	13.7	23.7	35.1	45.5	55.1	59.6	57.8	49.6	38.0	27.1	14.3	35.8
Extreme Maximum Temp. (°F)	55	61	81	90	91	100	100	102	93	88	75	63	102
Extreme Minimum Temp. (°F)	-36	-30	-9	7	19	34	41	34	25	14	-5	-26	-36
Days Maximum Temp. ≥ 90°F	0	0	0	0	0	2	4	3	1	0	0	0	10
Days Maximum Temp. ≤ 32°F	21	15	6	0	0	0	0	0	0	0	4	17	63
Days Minimum Temp. ≤ 32°F	31	27	26	12	2	0	0	0	1	9	22	30	160
Days Minimum Temp. ≤ 0°F	9	6	1	0	0	0	0	0	0	0	0	5	21
Heating Degree Days (base 65°F)	1,447	1,199	983	555	250	55	13	26	161	495	873	1,317	7,374
Cooling Degree Days (base 65°F)	0	0	0	5	26	120	205	159	57	5	0	0	577
Mean Precipitation (in.)	1.10	1.17	1.85	3.29	3.60	4.64	3.92	4.19	3.78	2.52	2.35	1.45	33.86
Extreme Maximum Daily Precip. (in.)	0.93	1.60	1.42	2.10	2.96	3.90	5.10	3.10	3.26	2.44	2.25	1.88	5.10
Days With ≥ 0.1" Precipitation	4	4	5	7	8	7	7	7	7	6	6	5	73
Days With ≥ 0.5" Precipitation	1	1	1	2	2	3	3	3	2	2	1	1	22
Days With ≥ 1.0" Precipitation	0	0	0	1	1	1	1	1	1	0	0	0	6
Mean Snowfall (in.)	9.8	7.8	5.3	1.7	0.1	0.0	0.0	0.0	0.0	0.3	3.4	10.1	38.5
Maximum Snow Depth (in.)	27	25	18	6	trace	0	0	0	0	2	12	25	27
Days With ≥ 1.0" Snow Depth	24	22	10	1	0	0	0	0	0	0	4	18	79

Baraboo *Sauk County* Elevation: 823 ft. Latitude: 43° 27' N Longitude: 89° 44' W

	JAN	FEB	MAR	APR	MAY	JUN	JUL	AUG	SEP	OCT	NOV	DEC	YEAR
Mean Maximum Temp. (°F)	27.9	32.6	43.6	57.8	69.4	78.8	82.8	80.5	72.8	59.7	45.1	31.6	56.9
Mean Temp. (°F)	17.4	21.7	32.4	45.3	56.7	66.2	70.4	67.9	59.6	47.2	34.9	21.9	45.1
Mean Minimum Temp. (°F)	6.8	10.7	21.1	32.7	44.0	53.6	57.9	55.2	46.4	34.8	24.7	12.1	33.3
Extreme Maximum Temp. (°F)	57	63	84	92	92	102	102	102	96	87	76	64	102
Extreme Minimum Temp. (°F)	-36	-41	-18	-2	22	31	38	34	22	10	-12	-35	-41
Days Maximum Temp. ≥ 90°F	0	0	0	0	0	3	5	3	1	0	0	0	12
Days Maximum Temp. ≤ 32°F	20	13	5	0	0	0	0	0	0	0	4	15	57
Days Minimum Temp. ≤ 32°F	31	27	27	16	3	0	0	0	2	14	24	30	174
Days Minimum Temp. ≤ 0°F	11	7	2	0	0	0	0	0	0	0	0	7	27
Heating Degree Days (base 65°F)	1,471	1,219	1,004	590	276	68	18	40	199	550	896	1,331	7,662
Cooling Degree Days (base 65°F)	0	0	0	6	26	112	192	137	45	5	0	0	523
Mean Precipitation (in.)	1.11	1.12	1.97	3.54	3.77	5.07	4.25	4.83	3.66	2.60	2.29	1.36	35.57
Extreme Maximum Daily Precip. (in.)	0.90	1.17	3.80	3.05	2.75	5.31	7.78	5.09	3.02	2.96	2.10	1.57	7.78
Days With ≥ 0.1" Precipitation	4	3	4	7	8	7	7	7	7	6	5	4	69
Days With ≥ 0.5" Precipitation	1	1	1	2	3	3	3	3	2	2	1	1	23
Days With ≥ 1.0" Precipitation	0	0	0	1	1	2	1	1	1	0	0	0	7
Mean Snowfall (in.)	10.5	8.4	6.4	2.1	trace	0.0	0.0	0.0	0.0	0.4	3.4	10.8	42.0
Maximum Snow Depth (in.)	20	20	16	6	trace	0	0	0	0	3	12	18	20
Days With ≥ 1.0" Snow Depth	23	22	10	2	0	0	0	0	0	0	4	17	78

Bayfield 6 N *Bayfield County* Elevation: 819 ft. Latitude: 46° 53' N Longitude: 90° 49' W

	JAN	FEB	MAR	APR	MAY	JUN	JUL	AUG	SEP	OCT	NOV	DEC	YEAR
Mean Maximum Temp. (°F)	22.8	28.1	37.0	50.5	63.5	71.6	76.8	75.6	66.7	54.0	39.1	27.1	51.1
Mean Temp. (°F)	14.5	18.8	27.6	40.4	51.7	60.2	66.2	65.7	57.2	45.2	32.1	19.9	41.6
Mean Minimum Temp. (°F)	6.1	9.5	18.2	30.3	39.9	48.8	55.6	55.7	47.6	36.2	25.1	12.7	32.1
Extreme Maximum Temp. (°F)	53	61	78	88	91	96	101	96	93	85	74	61	101
Extreme Minimum Temp. (°F)	-29	-34	-17	2	17	22	37	37	28	15	-3	-24	-34
Days Maximum Temp. ≥ 90°F	0	0	0	0	0	0	1	1	0	0	0	0	2
Days Maximum Temp. ≤ 32°F	25	18	10	1	0	0	0	0	0	0	8	21	83
Days Minimum Temp. ≤ 32°F	31	28	28	19	5	0	0	0	1	10	25	30	177
Days Minimum Temp. ≤ 0°F	11	8	3	0	0	0	0	0	0	0	0	5	27
Heating Degree Days (base 65°F)	1,561	1,302	1,152	733	415	175	59	63	247	609	980	1,391	8,687
Cooling Degree Days (base 65°F)	0	0	0	1	10	38	103	90	20	1	0	0	263
Mean Precipitation (in.)	1.75	1.03	1.80	2.75	3.33	3.60	3.85	3.62	3.94	2.91	2.71	1.67	32.96
Extreme Maximum Daily Precip. (in.)	1.26	1.08	1.64	2.80	2.35	3.37	4.40	2.11	3.01	1.95	2.81	1.70	4.40
Days With ≥ 0.1" Precipitation	5	3	4	6	7	8	7	7	7	7	5	5	71
Days With ≥ 0.5" Precipitation	0	0	1	1	2	2	3	3	3	2	2	0	19
Days With ≥ 1.0" Precipitation	0	0	0	1	1	1	1	1	1	0	1	0	7
Mean Snowfall (in.)	26.7	13.2	14.5	5.5	0.6	0.0	0.0	0.0	trace	0.7	13.7	26.3	101.2
Maximum Snow Depth (in.)	33	34	32	21	12	0	0	0	trace	5	22	28	34
Days With ≥ 1.0" Snow Depth	31	28	28	8	0	0	0	0	0	0	10	27	132

Beaver Dam *Dodge County* Elevation: 839 ft. Latitude: 43° 27' N Longitude: 88° 51' W

	JAN	FEB	MAR	APR	MAY	JUN	JUL	AUG	SEP	OCT	NOV	DEC	YEAR
Mean Maximum Temp. (°F)	27.0	31.5	42.8	57.5	69.2	78.8	82.2	80.2	73.2	59.9	44.9	30.8	56.5
Mean Temp. (°F)	19.0	23.0	33.7	46.9	58.0	67.6	71.5	69.7	62.1	49.6	36.8	23.3	46.7
Mean Minimum Temp. (°F)	11.0	14.4	24.6	36.3	46.7	56.4	60.7	59.1	50.9	39.1	28.6	15.8	37.0
Extreme Maximum Temp. (°F)	55	61	80	90	90	98	98	100	93	86	73	65	100
Extreme Minimum Temp. (°F)	-31	-29	-9	9	27	36	43	40	28	14	0	-24	-31
Days Maximum Temp. ≥ 90°F	0	0	0	0	0	2	3	2	1	0	0	0	8
Days Maximum Temp. ≤ 32°F	21	15	6	0	0	0	0	0	0	0	4	16	62
Days Minimum Temp. ≤ 32°F	30	27	25	10	1	0	0	0	0	7	20	29	149
Days Minimum Temp. ≤ 0°F	8	5	1	0	0	0	0	0	0	0	0	4	18
Heating Degree Days (base 65°F)	1,421	1,183	965	542	243	47	8	18	142	478	841	1,285	7,173
Cooling Degree Days (base 65°F)	0	0	0	5	30	131	215	168	59	5	0	0	613
Mean Precipitation (in.)	1.32	1.32	2.05	3.25	3.49	4.56	4.26	3.81	3.66	2.64	2.38	1.66	34.40
Extreme Maximum Daily Precip. (in.)	1.35	1.64	3.46	2.47	2.96	4.01	3.95	3.14	4.41	3.00	3.85	1.60	4.41
Days With ≥ 0.1" Precipitation	4	4	5	7	7	7	7	7	6	6	5	5	70
Days With ≥ 0.5" Precipitation	1	1	1	2	2	3	3	3	2	2	2	1	23
Days With ≥ 1.0" Precipitation	0	0	0	1	1	1	1	1	1	0	0	0	6
Mean Snowfall (in.)	9.8	8.3	5.6	1.3	0.1	0.0	0.0	0.0	0.0	0.2	1.8	10.6	37.7
Maximum Snow Depth (in.)	25	26	21	6	0	0	0	0	0	3	8	24	26
Days With ≥ 1.0" Snow Depth	21	18	8	1	0	0	0	0	0	0	2	16	66

The period of record for all cooperative weather station data is 1980 – 2009. See User Guide for detailed explanation of data.

Beloit *Rock County* Elevation: 779 ft. Latitude: 42° 30' N Longitude: 89° 02' W

	JAN	FEB	MAR	APR	MAY	JUN	JUL	AUG	SEP	OCT	NOV	DEC	YEAR
Mean Maximum Temp. (°F)	28.4	32.7	44.3	58.5	69.8	79.5	83.1	81.1	74.2	61.3	46.6	32.2	57.6
Mean Temp. (°F)	20.7	24.7	35.3	48.1	58.9	68.6	72.6	70.9	63.2	50.9	38.4	24.9	48.1
Mean Minimum Temp. (°F)	13.0	16.6	26.1	37.6	47.9	57.7	62.2	60.6	52.2	40.5	30.2	17.6	38.5
Extreme Maximum Temp. (°F)	61	69	84	92	93	101	102	102	96	88	75	66	102
Extreme Minimum Temp. (°F)	-26	-25	-9	7	25	34	43	43	30	17	2	-23	-26
Days Maximum Temp. ≥ 90°F	0	0	0	0	0	3	5	4	1	0	0	0	13
Days Maximum Temp. ≤ 32°F	19	13	5	0	0	0	0	0	0	0	3	14	54
Days Minimum Temp. ≤ 32°F	30	26	24	8	1	0	0	0	0	6	18	28	141
Days Minimum Temp. ≤ 0°F	5	4	0	0	0	0	0	0	0	0	0	4	13
Heating Degree Days (base 65°F)	1,367	1,134	915	509	223	42	6	14	124	437	790	1,235	6,796
Cooling Degree Days (base 65°F)	0	0	0	8	41	156	249	202	77	8	0	0	741
Mean Precipitation (in.)	1.44	1.45	2.12	3.54	3.79	4.67	3.69	4.40	3.70	2.71	2.72	1.98	36.21
Extreme Maximum Daily Precip. (in.)	1.50	2.30	2.70	2.21	2.63	5.77	3.21	5.00	3.30	1.90	2.73	1.64	5.77
Days With ≥ 0.1" Precipitation	4	4	4	7	8	7	6	6	5	5	5	5	66
Days With ≥ 0.5" Precipitation	1	1	1	3	3	3	3	3	3	2	2	1	26
Days With ≥ 1.0" Precipitation	0	0	0	1	1	1	1	1	1	1	1	0	8
Mean Snowfall (in.)	9.5	7.2	3.2	0.8	trace	0.0	0.0	0.0	0.0	trace	1.3	9.9	31.9
Maximum Snow Depth (in.)	19	16	8	5	trace	0	0	0	0	trace	5	20	20
Days With ≥ 1.0" Snow Depth	20	16	5	0	0	0	0	0	0	0	1	14	56

Blair *Trempealeau County* Elevation: 859 ft. Latitude: 44° 18' N Longitude: 91° 14' W

	JAN	FEB	MAR	APR	MAY	JUN	JUL	AUG	SEP	OCT	NOV	DEC	YEAR
Mean Maximum Temp. (°F)	25.2	30.5	41.9	57.4	68.9	78.1	82.4	80.0	71.6	59.0	42.6	28.9	55.6
Mean Temp. (°F)	14.3	19.1	30.9	45.0	56.3	65.8	70.2	67.9	59.0	46.5	32.8	18.8	43.9
Mean Minimum Temp. (°F)	3.3	7.6	19.9	32.5	43.6	53.5	58.0	55.8	46.4	34.0	23.0	8.7	32.2
Extreme Maximum Temp. (°F)	56	61	83	91	90	100	105	101	93	88	75	64	105
Extreme Minimum Temp. (°F)	-40	-45	-17	-4	22	31	38	33	24	9	-11	-39	-45
Days Maximum Temp. ≥ 90°F	0	0	0	0	0	2	4	2	0	0	0	0	8
Days Maximum Temp. ≤ 32°F	22	15	6	0	0	0	0	0	0	0	5	18	66
Days Minimum Temp. ≤ 32°F	31	28	27	16	3	0	0	0	2	15	25	30	177
Days Minimum Temp. ≤ 0°F	13	9	3	0	0	0	0	0	0	0	1	9	35
Heating Degree Days (base 65°F)	1,567	1,293	1,050	599	286	76	17	37	213	568	958	1,425	8,089
Cooling Degree Days (base 65°F)	0	0	0	4	23	107	185	135	41	2	0	0	497
Mean Precipitation (in.)	0.91	1.02	1.80	3.21	4.06	4.40	4.16	4.70	4.39	2.44	2.05	1.09	34.23
Extreme Maximum Daily Precip. (in.)	0.89	2.22	1.53	2.82	2.75	3.74	3.36	5.31	5.69	4.50	2.02	1.29	5.69
Days With ≥ 0.1" Precipitation	3	3	5	7	7	7	7	7	7	5	4	3	65
Days With ≥ 0.5" Precipitation	0	0	1	2	3	3	3	3	2	1	1	0	19
Days With ≥ 1.0" Precipitation	0	0	0	1	1	1	1	1	1	1	0	0	7
Mean Snowfall (in.)	9.6	7.2	8.1	1.8	trace	0.0	0.0	0.0	0.0	0.2	3.7	9.2	39.8
Maximum Snow Depth (in.)	20	19	23	10	trace	0	0	0	0	3	11	19	23
Days With ≥ 1.0" Snow Depth	27	26	18	2	0	0	0	0	0	0	5	23	101

Bloomer *Chippewa County* Elevation: 979 ft. Latitude: 45° 06' N Longitude: 91° 29' W

	JAN	FEB	MAR	APR	MAY	JUN	JUL	AUG	SEP	OCT	NOV	DEC	YEAR
Mean Maximum Temp. (°F)	22.8	28.2	39.9	57.0	69.3	78.2	82.6	80.0	71.3	57.2	40.9	26.4	54.5
Mean Temp. (°F)	13.5	18.3	30.0	45.4	57.2	66.4	70.9	68.6	59.7	46.5	32.6	18.1	43.9
Mean Minimum Temp. (°F)	4.1	8.3	20.1	33.8	45.1	54.7	59.2	57.1	48.1	35.8	24.3	9.7	33.4
Extreme Maximum Temp. (°F)	51	57	81	90	94	99	103	104	94	86	73	62	104
Extreme Minimum Temp. (°F)	-37	-36	-16	4	22	34	42	35	25	14	-15	-35	-37
Days Maximum Temp. ≥ 90°F	0	0	0	0	0	2	5	2	0	0	0	0	9
Days Maximum Temp. ≤ 32°F	24	17	8	1	0	0	0	0	0	0	6	21	77
Days Minimum Temp. ≤ 32°F	31	27	26	14	3	0	0	0	1	12	24	30	168
Days Minimum Temp. ≤ 0°F	13	9	3	0	0	0	0	0	0	0	1	8	34
Heating Degree Days (base 65°F)	1,593	1,316	1,077	586	264	66	15	32	197	567	964	1,449	8,126
Cooling Degree Days (base 65°F)	0	0	0	5	29	116	205	150	45	2	0	0	552
Mean Precipitation (in.)	0.89	0.78	1.63	2.85	3.54	4.25	3.81	4.62	3.71	2.58	1.93	1.03	31.62
Extreme Maximum Daily Precip. (in.)	1.50	1.35	1.65	2.04	3.82	3.92	3.30	5.05	3.31	2.32	2.62	1.00	5.05
Days With ≥ 0.1" Precipitation	3	3	4	6	7	8	7	7	6	6	4	3	64
Days With ≥ 0.5" Precipitation	0	0	1	2	2	3	3	3	2	2	1	0	19
Days With ≥ 1.0" Precipitation	0	0	0	1	1	1	1	1	1	1	0	0	7
Mean Snowfall (in.)	10.9	7.5	8.3	1.7	trace	0.0	0.0	0.0	trace	0.6	5.1	10.2	44.3
Maximum Snow Depth (in.)	26	24	18	4	trace	0	0	0	trace	5	10	20	26
Days With ≥ 1.0" Snow Depth	26	27	17	1	0	0	0	0	0	0	6	21	98

Brodhead *Green County* Elevation: 790 ft. Latitude: 42° 37' N Longitude: 89° 23' W

	JAN	FEB	MAR	APR	MAY	JUN	JUL	AUG	SEP	OCT	NOV	DEC	YEAR
Mean Maximum Temp. (°F)	28.0	32.4	44.2	58.6	70.0	79.7	83.1	81.0	73.9	60.9	46.1	31.5	57.4
Mean Temp. (°F)	18.7	22.9	34.0	46.9	58.1	67.8	71.6	69.5	61.3	48.9	36.5	22.9	46.6
Mean Minimum Temp. (°F)	9.4	13.0	23.8	35.2	46.1	55.9	60.1	58.0	48.6	36.9	26.9	14.2	35.7
Extreme Maximum Temp. (°F)	59	69	83	91	94	101	101	102	96	89	76	67	102
Extreme Minimum Temp. (°F)	-30	-34	-13	7	26	35	42	38	25	14	-4	-26	-34
Days Maximum Temp. ≥ 90°F	0	0	0	0	0	3	5	3	1	0	0	0	12
Days Maximum Temp. ≤ 32°F	19	13	5	0	0	0	0	0	0	0	3	15	55
Days Minimum Temp. ≤ 32°F	30	27	26	12	1	0	0	0	1	11	22	29	159
Days Minimum Temp. ≤ 0°F	8	6	1	0	0	0	0	0	0	0	0	6	21
Heating Degree Days (base 65°F)	1,429	1,185	954	543	242	47	9	23	160	498	848	1,299	7,237
Cooling Degree Days (base 65°F)	0	0	0	6	34	138	221	170	54	6	0	0	629
Mean Precipitation (in.)	1.43	1.66	2.12	3.59	3.77	4.82	3.79	4.44	3.55	2.94	2.40	1.96	36.47
Extreme Maximum Daily Precip. (in.)	1.40	1.80	2.58	2.88	2.64	4.00	6.62	3.83	3.41	2.82	2.71	1.58	6.62
Days With ≥ 0.1" Precipitation	4	4	5	7	8	7	6	7	5	6	5	5	69
Days With ≥ 0.5" Precipitation	1	1	1	2	3	3	2	3	2	2	2	1	23
Days With ≥ 1.0" Precipitation	0	0	0	1	1	2	1	1	1	1	0	0	8
Mean Snowfall (in.)	10.6	7.6	4.6	0.7	0.1	0.0	0.0	0.0	0.0	0.1	1.4	10.5	35.6
Maximum Snow Depth (in.)	na	na	na	na	*trace*	*0*	*0*	*0*	*0*	na	na	na	na
Days With ≥ 1.0" Snow Depth	na	na	*5*	0	0	0	0	0	0	0	0	na	na

The period of record for all cooperative weather station data is 1980 – 2009. See User Guide for detailed explanation of data.

Burlington *Racine County* Elevation: 750 ft. Latitude: 42° 39' N Longitude: 88° 15' W

	JAN	FEB	MAR	APR	MAY	JUN	JUL	AUG	SEP	OCT	NOV	DEC	YEAR
Mean Maximum Temp. (°F)	27.8	32.1	42.6	56.3	67.6	77.5	81.3	79.7	72.7	59.7	45.8	32.2	56.3
Mean Temp. (°F)	19.7	23.6	33.4	45.7	56.3	66.2	70.5	69.1	61.2	49.0	37.3	24.6	46.4
Mean Minimum Temp. (°F)	11.6	15.1	24.1	35.1	44.9	54.9	59.7	58.5	49.7	38.2	28.6	16.9	36.4
Extreme Maximum Temp. (°F)	60	66	78	90	94	102	105	102	100	87	74	67	105
Extreme Minimum Temp. (°F)	-27	-27	-9	3	23	33	42	40	26	18	0	-18	-27
Days Maximum Temp. ≥ 90°F	0	0	0	0	0	2	4	2	1	0	0	0	9
Days Maximum Temp. ≤ 32°F	20	14	6	0	0	0	0	0	0	0	3	15	58
Days Minimum Temp. ≤ 32°F	30	26	25	12	2	0	0	0	0	9	20	29	153
Days Minimum Temp. ≤ 0°F	7	4	0	0	0	0	0	0	0	0	0	4	15
Heating Degree Days (base 65°F)	1,398	1,161	974	579	291	74	17	26	158	495	826	1,247	7,246
Cooling Degree Days (base 65°F)	0	0	0	6	27	118	196	161	52	5	0	0	565
Mean Precipitation (in.)	1.67	1.51	1.96	3.46	3.52	3.82	3.44	3.99	3.28	2.53	2.62	2.03	33.83
Extreme Maximum Daily Precip. (in.)	1.54	1.75	1.91	1.95	2.88	3.20	3.22	3.50	2.76	2.40	1.98	2.21	3.50
Days With ≥ 0.1" Precipitation	4	4	5	7	7	7	5	6	6	6	6	5	68
Days With ≥ 0.5" Precipitation	1	1	1	2	2	2	2	3	2	1	2	1	20
Days With ≥ 1.0" Precipitation	0	0	0	1	1	1	1	1	1	0	0	0	6
Mean Snowfall (in.)	11.7	7.6	4.5	1.1	trace	0.0	0.0	0.0	0.0	trace	1.3	9.6	35.8
Maximum Snow Depth (in.)	***25***	na	na	***5***	***trace***	***0***	***0***	***0***	***0***	***trace***	***5***	na	na
Days With ≥ 1.0" Snow Depth	***16***	na	***4***	0	0	0	0	0	0	0	1	***10***	na

Chilton *Calumet County* Elevation: 839 ft. Latitude: 44° 02' N Longitude: 88° 09' W

	JAN	FEB	MAR	APR	MAY	JUN	JUL	AUG	SEP	OCT	NOV	DEC	YEAR
Mean Maximum Temp. (°F)	25.8	29.8	40.5	55.8	67.9	77.7	81.6	79.6	72.1	58.4	43.8	30.0	55.3
Mean Temp. (°F)	18.0	21.5	31.6	45.2	56.3	66.6	70.7	69.2	61.3	48.7	35.9	22.8	45.6
Mean Minimum Temp. (°F)	10.1	13.3	22.8	34.5	44.9	55.2	59.7	58.6	50.3	38.9	28.1	15.5	36.0
Extreme Maximum Temp. (°F)	52	63	79	89	92	99	103	100	93	87	74	65	103
Extreme Minimum Temp. (°F)	-30	-28	-10	8	24	35	37	41	26	17	1	-21	-30
Days Maximum Temp. ≥ 90°F	0	0	0	0	0	2	3	2	0	0	0	0	7
Days Maximum Temp. ≤ 32°F	22	16	7	0	0	0	0	0	0	0	4	17	66
Days Minimum Temp. ≤ 32°F	30	27	26	13	2	0	0	0	0	7	21	29	155
Days Minimum Temp. ≤ 0°F	8	5	1	0	0	0	0	0	0	0	0	4	18
Heating Degree Days (base 65°F)	1,453	1,223	1,029	592	288	65	15	25	159	503	864	1,303	7,519
Cooling Degree Days (base 65°F)	0	0	0	4	27	121	199	161	54	5	0	0	571
Mean Precipitation (in.)	1.33	1.15	1.76	2.64	3.16	3.96	3.43	3.63	3.62	2.56	2.21	1.59	31.04
Extreme Maximum Daily Precip. (in.)	1.05	0.78	3.00	1.85	2.37	4.42	3.82	2.41	5.31	2.26	1.57	1.55	5.31
Days With ≥ 0.1" Precipitation	4	3	5	6	6	7	7	7	7	6	5	4	67
Days With ≥ 0.5" Precipitation	1	1	1	2	2	2	2	2	2	1	1	1	18
Days With ≥ 1.0" Precipitation	0	0	0	0	1	1	1	1	1	0	0	0	5
Mean Snowfall (in.)	11.9	8.1	6.6	2.3	0.3	0.0	0.0	0.0	0.0	0.3	3.6	9.8	42.9
Maximum Snow Depth (in.)	23	18	12	4	5	0	0	0	0	3	7	18	23
Days With ≥ 1.0" Snow Depth	24	21	11	1	0	0	0	0	0	0	4	18	79

Couderay 7 W *Sawyer County* Elevation: 1,299 ft. Latitude: 45° 48' N Longitude: 91° 28' W

	JAN	FEB	MAR	APR	MAY	JUN	JUL	AUG	SEP	OCT	NOV	DEC	YEAR
Mean Maximum Temp. (°F)	21.9	27.3	38.7	53.1	67.8	75.9	80.9	78.2	69.2	55.9	39.7	26.5	52.9
Mean Temp. (°F)	11.8	16.2	28.0	41.5	54.3	63.1	68.9	66.4	57.0	44.5	30.6	17.1	41.6
Mean Minimum Temp. (°F)	1.2	4.7	17.4	29.8	40.3	50.2	56.8	54.5	44.6	33.1	21.6	7.6	30.1
Extreme Maximum Temp. (°F)	54	59	75	86	92	98	102	100	91	85	72	59	102
Extreme Minimum Temp. (°F)	-50	-55	-26	-5	15	22	30	30	17	3	-27	-52	-55
Days Maximum Temp. ≥ 90°F	0	0	0	0	0	1	3	2	0	0	0	0	6
Days Maximum Temp. ≤ 32°F	25	18	8	1	0	0	0	0	0	0	8	22	82
Days Minimum Temp. ≤ 32°F	30	27	27	20	8	2	0	0	4	16	26	30	190
Days Minimum Temp. ≤ 0°F	15	11	5	0	0	0	0	0	0	0	1	10	42
Heating Degree Days (base 65°F)	1,650	1,376	1,133	702	347	130	36	67	264	630	1,025	1,479	8,839
Cooling Degree Days (base 65°F)	0	0	0	2	20	79	165	118	30	1	0	0	415
Mean Precipitation (in.)	1.12	1.29	2.16	2.97	3.69	4.44	4.60	4.55	4.49	3.72	2.07	1.33	36.43
Extreme Maximum Daily Precip. (in.)	1.30	1.47	2.60	2.50	2.60	2.20	4.15	3.65	3.00	5.00	2.45	1.60	5.00
Days With ≥ 0.1" Precipitation	4	4	5	7	7	9	8	8	8	7	5	4	76
Days With ≥ 0.5" Precipitation	0	1	1	2	3	4	3	3	3	2	1	1	24
Days With ≥ 1.0" Precipitation	0	0	0	1	1	1	1	1	1	1	0	0	7
Mean Snowfall (in.)	na	***9.6***	***8.5***	***3.0***	0.1	0.0	0.0	0.0	0.0	1.1	***3.4***	na	na
Maximum Snow Depth (in.)	44	39	***38***	35	7	0	0	0	0	5	27	***36***	***44***
Days With ≥ 1.0" Snow Depth	26	24	***20***	3	0	0	0	0	0	0	7	***23***	***103***

Cumberland *Barron County* Elevation: 1,240 ft. Latitude: 45° 32' N Longitude: 92° 01' W

	JAN	FEB	MAR	APR	MAY	JUN	JUL	AUG	SEP	OCT	NOV	DEC	YEAR
Mean Maximum Temp. (°F)	22.0	27.3	38.8	55.5	68.4	77.0	81.3	78.9	69.9	55.8	39.3	25.0	53.3
Mean Temp. (°F)	12.3	16.9	28.3	44.2	56.8	66.0	70.6	68.3	59.2	46.0	31.4	16.9	43.1
Mean Minimum Temp. (°F)	2.5	6.5	17.8	32.8	45.1	54.9	59.9	57.7	48.4	36.1	23.4	8.7	32.8
Extreme Maximum Temp. (°F)	52	57	80	92	96	97	103	101	92	85	71	60	103
Extreme Minimum Temp. (°F)	-35	-38	-22	2	18	36	42	37	24	11	-16	-39	-39
Days Maximum Temp. ≥ 90°F	0	0	0	0	0	2	3	2	0	0	0	0	7
Days Maximum Temp. ≤ 32°F	25	18	8	1	0	0	0	0	0	0	8	22	82
Days Minimum Temp. ≤ 32°F	31	27	28	14	1	0	0	0	1	11	25	31	169
Days Minimum Temp. ≤ 0°F	14	9	4	0	0	0	0	0	0	0	1	9	37
Heating Degree Days (base 65°F)	1,628	1,355	1,129	621	272	65	14	30	205	584	1,002	1,486	8,391
Cooling Degree Days (base 65°F)	0	0	0	3	23	101	195	139	36	2	0	0	499
Mean Precipitation (in.)	1.02	0.96	1.66	2.77	3.50	4.45	4.22	4.35	4.09	3.20	1.95	1.14	33.31
Extreme Maximum Daily Precip. (in.)	1.54	1.84	1.78	1.94	2.95	3.80	4.34	3.48	2.86	5.75	2.14	1.56	5.75
Days With ≥ 0.1" Precipitation	3	3	4	6	7	7	7	7	6	7	5	4	66
Days With ≥ 0.5" Precipitation	0	0	1	2	3	3	3	3	3	2	1	0	21
Days With ≥ 1.0" Precipitation	0	0	0	0	1	1	1	1	1	1	0	0	6
Mean Snowfall (in.)	10.9	9.6	10.1	4.0	trace	0.0	0.0	0.0	trace	0.9	7.7	11.6	54.8
Maximum Snow Depth (in.)	***36***	***29***	***31***	***12***	***trace***	***0***	***0***	***0***	***trace***	***6***	***20***	***37***	***37***
Days With ≥ 1.0" Snow Depth	***21***	***18***	***15***	2	0	0	0	0	0	0	4	***16***	***76***

The period of record for all cooperative weather station data is 1980 – 2009. See User Guide for detailed explanation of data.

Dalton *Green Lake County* Elevation: 859 ft. Latitude: 43° 39' N Longitude: 89° 12' W

	JAN	FEB	MAR	APR	MAY	JUN	JUL	AUG	SEP	OCT	NOV	DEC	YEAR
Mean Maximum Temp. (°F)	28.3	33.0	44.0	59.1	70.8	80.0	83.7	81.7	73.3	60.2	44.5	32.2	57.6
Mean Temp. (°F)	19.4	23.6	33.8	47.0	58.3	67.5	71.6	69.9	61.4	49.2	35.7	24.0	46.8
Mean Minimum Temp. (°F)	10.4	14.2	23.5	34.9	45.8	54.9	59.4	58.0	49.5	38.3	26.9	15.8	36.0
Extreme Maximum Temp. (°F)	57	63	83	91	92	102	103	103	94	86	76	64	103
Extreme Minimum Temp. (°F)	-29	-34	-14	4	22	33	40	33	24	11	-6	-28	-34
Days Maximum Temp. ≥ 90°F	0	0	0	0	0	3	5	3	1	0	0	0	12
Days Maximum Temp. ≤ 32°F	20	13	5	0	0	0	0	0	0	0	3	15	56
Days Minimum Temp. ≤ 32°F	31	26	25	13	3	0	0	0	1	9	21	29	158
Days Minimum Temp. ≤ 0°F	8	5	1	0	0	0	0	0	0	0	0	5	19
Heating Degree Days (base 65°F)	1,408	1,164	961	538	235	51	9	21	162	486	871	1,264	7,170
Cooling Degree Days (base 65°F)	0	0	0	6	33	132	220	178	61	6	0	0	636
Mean Precipitation (in.)	1.35	1.15	1.77	2.97	3.78	4.45	4.26	3.83	4.06	2.53	2.64	1.36	34.15
Extreme Maximum Daily Precip. (in.)	3.30	1.74	2.64	2.63	4.69	2.81	4.68	2.95	4.18	3.48	2.36	1.15	4.69
Days With ≥ 0.1" Precipitation	4	3	4	7	7	8	7	7	6	6	6	4	69
Days With ≥ 0.5" Precipitation	0	1	1	2	2	3	3	3	3	1	1	1	21
Days With ≥ 1.0" Precipitation	0	0	0	0	1	1	1	1	1	0	1	0	6
Mean Snowfall (in.)	11.5	7.2	7.4	2.7	0.2	0.0	0.0	0.0	trace	0.6	4.2	9.3	43.1
Maximum Snow Depth (in.)	23	18	15	5	trace	0	0	0	trace	4	12	19	23
Days With ≥ 1.0" Snow Depth	21	20	8	1	0	0	0	0	0	0	3	14	67

Eau Claire County Arpt *Chippewa County* Elevation: 890 ft. Latitude: 44° 52' N Longitude: 91° 29' W

	JAN	FEB	MAR	APR	MAY	JUN	JUL	AUG	SEP	OCT	NOV	DEC	YEAR
Mean Maximum Temp. (°F)	23.5	29.3	40.5	57.1	70.2	78.6	82.8	80.1	70.7	57.4	40.6	26.9	54.8
Mean Temp. (°F)	14.5	19.8	30.8	45.5	58.0	67.0	71.7	69.4	59.8	46.9	32.3	18.7	44.5
Mean Minimum Temp. (°F)	5.4	10.3	21.1	33.9	45.7	55.4	60.6	58.6	48.8	36.4	23.9	10.4	34.2
Extreme Maximum Temp. (°F)	54	63	84	91	93	100	104	104	96	89	76	64	104
Extreme Minimum Temp. (°F)	-33	-35	-11	6	22	35	44	39	28	13	-12	-32	-35
Days Maximum Temp. ≥ 90°F	0	0	0	0	1	3	5	2	1	0	0	0	12
Days Maximum Temp. ≤ 32°F	23	15	8	1	0	0	0	0	0	0	7	20	74
Days Minimum Temp. ≤ 32°F	30	27	27	14	2	0	0	0	1	11	25	30	167
Days Minimum Temp. ≤ 0°F	11	8	2	0	0	0	0	0	0	0	1	8	30
Heating Degree Days (base 65°F)	1,561	1,272	1,052	585	245	61	10	24	200	555	975	1,430	7,970
Cooling Degree Days (base 65°F)	0	0	0	6	35	129	227	168	49	2	0	0	616
Mean Precipitation (in.)	1.02	0.85	1.77	2.75	3.54	4.39	3.94	4.98	3.89	2.27	1.92	0.96	32.28
Extreme Maximum Daily Precip. (in.)	0.70	0.93	2.08	1.93	2.02	2.74	2.38	4.12	5.98	2.05	3.24	0.99	5.98
Days With ≥ 0.1" Precipitation	3	2	4	6	7	8	8	7	7	5	4	3	64
Days With ≥ 0.5" Precipitation	0	0	1	2	2	3	3	3	2	1	1	0	18
Days With ≥ 1.0" Precipitation	0	0	0	0	1	1	1	1	1	0	0	0	5
Mean Snowfall (in.)	na	na	na	na	na	na	na	na	na	na	na	na	na
Maximum Snow Depth (in.)	na	na	na	na	na	na	na	na	na	na	na	na	na
Days With ≥ 1.0" Snow Depth	na	na	na	na	na	na	na	na	na	na	na	na	na

Ellsworth 1 E *Pierce County* Elevation: 1,029 ft. Latitude: 44° 44' N Longitude: 92° 28' W

	JAN	FEB	MAR	APR	MAY	JUN	JUL	AUG	SEP	OCT	NOV	DEC	YEAR
Mean Maximum Temp. (°F)	23.9	29.6	41.5	58.0	69.2	78.0	81.9	79.1	72.1	59.0	41.7	27.4	55.1
Mean Temp. (°F)	14.4	19.7	31.4	45.9	57.4	66.4	70.6	67.9	60.3	47.8	33.0	18.9	44.5
Mean Minimum Temp. (°F)	4.9	9.7	21.2	33.7	45.4	54.8	59.2	56.6	48.5	36.5	24.2	10.2	33.7
Extreme Maximum Temp. (°F)	53	59	80	87	93	98	105	97	91	89	77	63	105
Extreme Minimum Temp. (°F)	-37	-37	-15	3	21	33	38	35	22	12	-13	-40	-40
Days Maximum Temp. ≥ 90°F	0	0	0	0	0	2	3	1	0	0	0	0	6
Days Maximum Temp. ≤ 32°F	23	16	6	0	0	0	0	0	0	0	6	20	71
Days Minimum Temp. ≤ 32°F	31	28	27	14	2	0	0	0	1	12	24	30	169
Days Minimum Temp. ≤ 0°F	12	8	2	0	0	0	0	0	0	0	1	8	31
Heating Degree Days (base 65°F)	1,562	1,274	1,036	571	255	63	13	34	181	532	954	1,425	7,900
Cooling Degree Days (base 65°F)	0	0	0	4	25	112	193	130	49	5	0	0	518
Mean Precipitation (in.)	0.97	0.77	2.01	3.07	3.94	4.31	4.32	5.11	4.16	2.66	2.24	1.16	34.72
Extreme Maximum Daily Precip. (in.)	1.50	0.95	2.17	2.75	2.35	2.74	4.53	3.91	7.10	2.20	2.10	1.31	7.10
Days With ≥ 0.1" Precipitation	3	2	5	6	8	8	7	7	6	6	5	4	67
Days With ≥ 0.5" Precipitation	0	0	1	2	3	2	3	3	3	2	1	0	20
Days With ≥ 1.0" Precipitation	0	0	0	1	1	1	1	2	1	1	0	0	8
Mean Snowfall (in.)	10.6	6.8	9.8	1.9	trace	0.0	0.0	0.0	0.0	0.3	5.5	9.8	44.7
Maximum Snow Depth (in.)	na	na	na	na	na	na	na	na	na	na	na	na	na
Days With ≥ 1.0" Snow Depth	na	na	na	0	0	0	0	0	0	0	1	na	na

Fond Du Lac *Fond Du Lac County* Elevation: 759 ft. Latitude: 43° 48' N Longitude: 88° 27' W

	JAN	FEB	MAR	APR	MAY	JUN	JUL	AUG	SEP	OCT	NOV	DEC	YEAR
Mean Maximum Temp. (°F)	25.8	30.1	40.8	55.1	67.4	76.8	80.8	78.3	71.0	57.7	43.5	30.4	54.8
Mean Temp. (°F)	18.4	22.3	32.5	45.9	57.4	67.0	71.4	69.5	61.7	49.1	36.2	23.4	46.2
Mean Minimum Temp. (°F)	11.0	14.3	24.0	36.7	47.3	57.2	61.9	60.6	52.4	40.4	28.9	16.3	37.6
Extreme Maximum Temp. (°F)	53	64	81	90	92	100	103	102	94	85	74	65	103
Extreme Minimum Temp. (°F)	-28	-29	-10	9	28	35	46	41	30	18	0	-24	-29
Days Maximum Temp. ≥ 90°F	0	0	0	0	0	2	3	2	0	0	0	0	7
Days Maximum Temp. ≤ 32°F	21	16	7	0	0	0	0	0	0	0	4	16	64
Days Minimum Temp. ≤ 32°F	30	27	25	9	1	0	0	0	0	5	20	29	146
Days Minimum Temp. ≤ 0°F	7	5	1	0	0	0	0	0	0	0	0	4	17
Heating Degree Days (base 65°F)	1,437	1,199	1,000	572	263	62	9	20	150	491	856	1,283	7,342
Cooling Degree Days (base 65°F)	0	0	0	6	33	128	215	167	59	5	0	0	613
Mean Precipitation (in.)	1.16	1.08	1.66	2.61	3.17	3.76	3.44	3.72	3.47	2.49	2.02	1.26	29.84
Extreme Maximum Daily Precip. (in.)	2.83	1.30	2.38	2.38	3.81	4.07	3.34	4.45	6.83	3.70	1.82	1.68	6.83
Days With ≥ 0.1" Precipitation	3	3	4	6	7	6	7	7	6	6	5	4	64
Days With ≥ 0.5" Precipitation	1	1	1	1	2	2	2	2	2	2	1	1	18
Days With ≥ 1.0" Precipitation	0	0	0	0	1	1	1	1	1	0	0	0	5
Mean Snowfall (in.)	10.1	8.0	6.4	1.6	0.1	0.0	0.0	0.0	0.0	0.2	2.8	8.9	38.1
Maximum Snow Depth (in.)	19	17	10	6	1	0	0	0	0	1	10	15	19
Days With ≥ 1.0" Snow Depth	23	20	9	1	0	0	0	0	0	0	3	16	72

The period of record for all cooperative weather station data is 1980 – 2009. See User Guide for detailed explanation of data.

Foxboro *Douglas County* Elevation: 932 ft. Latitude: 46° 29' N Longitude: 92° 17' W

	JAN	FEB	MAR	APR	MAY	JUN	JUL	AUG	SEP	OCT	NOV	DEC	YEAR
Mean Maximum Temp. (°F)	22.5	27.9	38.1	52.8	65.8	***74.2***	79.3	77.5	68.9	55.4	38.4	25.4	***52.2***
Mean Temp. (°F)	11.3	16.1	26.9	40.3	51.2	***59.9***	66.1	65.0	57.0	44.2	29.4	15.6	***40.3***
Mean Minimum Temp. (°F)	0.1	4.5	15.7	27.7	36.6	***45.5***	52.9	52.6	45.0	33.0	20.4	5.7	***28.3***
Extreme Maximum Temp. (°F)	54	59	79	89	92	98	104	99	92	88	73	57	104
Extreme Minimum Temp. (°F)	-42	-42	-35	-4	17	21	32	29	21	-1	-24	-43	-43
Days Maximum Temp. ≥ 90°F	0	0	0	0	0	1	3	1	0	0	0	0	5
Days Maximum Temp. ≤ 32°F	24	18	9	1	0	0	0	0	0	0	9	21	82
Days Minimum Temp. ≤ 32°F	30	26	28	21	9	1	0	0	3	15	26	30	189
Days Minimum Temp. ≤ 0°F	16	11	4	0	0	0	0	0	0	0	2	11	44
Heating Degree Days (base 65°F)	1,662	1,373	1,175	738	427	***184***	58	74	259	639	1,061	1,528	***9,178***
Cooling Degree Days (base 65°F)	0	0	0	0	6	***35***	101	82	24	2	0	0	***250***
Mean Precipitation (in.)	0.82	0.72	1.34	2.58	3.03	3.87	4.30	3.75	4.00	2.74	1.89	1.01	30.05
Extreme Maximum Daily Precip. (in.)	1.15	0.95	1.10	***2.21***	2.56	2.25	3.30	3.86	4.75	2.65	2.57	1.15	***4.75***
Days With ≥ 0.1" Precipitation	3	2	4	5	6	6	6	6	6	5	4	3	56
Days With ≥ 0.5" Precipitation	0	0	0	2	2	2	3	2	3	2	1	0	17
Days With ≥ 1.0" Precipitation	0	0	0	0	1	1	1	1	1	1	0	0	6
Mean Snowfall (in.)	na	na	na	na	na	***0.0***	***0.0***	***0.0***	***trace***	na	na	na	na
Maximum Snow Depth (in.)	na	na	na	na	na	na	na	na	na	na	na	na	na
Days With ≥ 1.0" Snow Depth	na	na	na	na	na	***0***	***0***	***0***	***0***	na	na	na	na

Genoa Dam 8 *Vernon County* Elevation: 639 ft. Latitude: 43° 34' N Longitude: 91° 14' W

	JAN	FEB	MAR	APR	MAY	JUN	JUL	AUG	SEP	OCT	NOV	DEC	YEAR
Mean Maximum Temp. (°F)	27.0	31.7	43.3	59.0	70.3	79.2	83.0	80.8	72.9	59.9	44.3	30.3	56.8
Mean Temp. (°F)	18.9	23.4	34.7	48.9	60.0	69.2	73.4	71.5	63.3	50.8	36.9	23.2	47.8
Mean Minimum Temp. (°F)	10.8	15.1	26.0	38.7	49.6	59.2	63.8	62.1	53.6	41.7	29.4	15.9	38.8
Extreme Maximum Temp. (°F)	55	63	81	93	92	101	109	100	93	90	75	65	109
Extreme Minimum Temp. (°F)	-34	-38	-9	6	26	40	47	42	28	15	-3	-26	-38
Days Maximum Temp. ≥ 90°F	0	0	0	0	0	2	4	3	0	0	0	0	9
Days Maximum Temp. ≤ 32°F	20	14	5	0	0	0	0	0	0	0	4	17	60
Days Minimum Temp. ≤ 32°F	30	26	23	8	0	0	0	0	0	5	19	29	140
Days Minimum Temp. ≤ 0°F	8	5	1	0	0	0	0	0	0	0	0	4	18
Heating Degree Days (base 65°F)	1,422	1,169	934	486	190	31	3	9	122	439	838	1,291	6,934
Cooling Degree Days (base 65°F)	0	0	0	8	42	165	271	217	77	7	0	0	787
Mean Precipitation (in.)	1.09	0.97	1.84	3.51	3.93	4.37	4.44	5.18	3.66	2.35	2.14	1.21	34.69
Extreme Maximum Daily Precip. (in.)	0.83	1.52	1.70	2.81	3.96	4.90	3.35	7.10	2.92	1.46	2.27	1.27	7.10
Days With ≥ 0.1" Precipitation	3	3	5	7	8	7	7	7	6	5	5	3	66
Days With ≥ 0.5" Precipitation	0	0	1	2	3	3	3	3	3	2	1	1	22
Days With ≥ 1.0" Precipitation	0	0	0	1	1	1	1	1	1	0	0	0	6
Mean Snowfall (in.)	8.1	5.5	3.9	0.5	0.0	0.0	0.0	0.0	0.0	trace	2.7	7.9	28.6
Maximum Snow Depth (in.)	30	30	23	5	0	0	0	0	0	trace	14	23	30
Days With ≥ 1.0" Snow Depth	21	19	8	0	0	0	0	0	0	0	3	18	69

Germantown *Washington County* Elevation: 850 ft. Latitude: 43° 13' N Longitude: 88° 07' W

	JAN	FEB	MAR	APR	MAY	JUN	JUL	AUG	SEP	OCT	NOV	DEC	YEAR
Mean Maximum Temp. (°F)	27.0	31.0	41.2	54.7	66.2	76.3	80.6	78.8	71.6	58.6	45.0	31.4	55.2
Mean Temp. (°F)	18.9	22.6	32.3	44.7	55.2	64.8	69.6	68.0	60.4	48.2	36.4	23.6	45.4
Mean Minimum Temp. (°F)	10.6	14.0	23.4	34.6	44.2	53.4	58.6	57.3	49.1	37.6	27.8	15.7	35.5
Extreme Maximum Temp. (°F)	56	64	83	89	90	99	102	102	95	87	74	67	102
Extreme Minimum Temp. (°F)	-40	-28	-10	9	22	27	38	36	22	14	-3	-25	-40
Days Maximum Temp. ≥ 90°F	0	0	0	0	0	2	3	2	0	0	0	0	7
Days Maximum Temp. ≤ 32°F	20	15	7	1	0	0	0	0	0	0	4	16	63
Days Minimum Temp. ≤ 32°F	30	27	26	13	3	0	0	0	1	10	21	29	160
Days Minimum Temp. ≤ 0°F	8	5	1	0	0	0	0	0	0	0	0	4	18
Heating Degree Days (base 65°F)	1,425	1,193	1,006	607	320	92	26	38	179	520	851	1,279	7,536
Cooling Degree Days (base 65°F)	0	0	0	5	24	95	175	140	46	5	0	0	490
Mean Precipitation (in.)	1.49	1.38	1.93	3.56	3.62	4.01	3.89	4.30	3.60	2.64	2.51	1.72	34.65
Extreme Maximum Daily Precip. (in.)	1.58	1.56	2.18	2.63	3.55	5.25	3.91	3.78	4.07	1.86	2.70	1.17	5.25
Days With ≥ 0.1" Precipitation	4	4	5	6	7	7	6	7	7	6	5	5	69
Days With ≥ 0.5" Precipitation	1	1	1	2	2	3	2	3	3	2	2	1	23
Days With ≥ 1.0" Precipitation	0	0	0	1	1	1	1	1	1	0	0	0	6
Mean Snowfall (in.)	13.4	9.6	5.7	1.5	0.3	0.0	0.0	0.0	0.0	0.1	2.3	11.2	44.1
Maximum Snow Depth (in.)	30	33	16	6	6	0	0	0	0	trace	10	27	33
Days With ≥ 1.0" Snow Depth	18	15	7	1	0	0	0	0	0	0	2	14	57

Hancock Exp Farm *Waushara County* Elevation: 1,076 ft. Latitude: 44° 07' N Longitude: 89° 32' W

	JAN	FEB	MAR	APR	MAY	JUN	JUL	AUG	SEP	OCT	NOV	DEC	YEAR
Mean Maximum Temp. (°F)	25.7	30.8	41.7	57.8	69.5	78.2	81.7	79.4	71.8	58.5	43.1	29.1	55.6
Mean Temp. (°F)	16.7	21.2	31.7	46.1	57.5	66.8	70.6	68.8	60.9	48.3	34.8	20.9	45.4
Mean Minimum Temp. (°F)	7.7	11.5	21.7	34.3	45.5	55.4	59.4	58.0	50.0	38.1	26.5	12.6	35.1
Extreme Maximum Temp. (°F)	54	63	84	90	90	100	105	102	93	84	74	62	105
Extreme Minimum Temp. (°F)	-34	-37	-17	-1	22	33	39	33	23	9	-10	-32	-37
Days Maximum Temp. ≥ 90°F	0	0	0	0	0	2	4	2	0	0	0	0	8
Days Maximum Temp. ≤ 32°F	22	16	6	0	0	0	0	0	0	0	5	19	68
Days Minimum Temp. ≤ 32°F	30	27	26	13	2	0	0	0	1	9	22	30	160
Days Minimum Temp. ≤ 0°F	10	7	2	0	0	0	0	0	0	0	0	7	26
Heating Degree Days (base 65°F)	1,491	1,234	1,025	566	256	61	15	28	171	515	899	1,362	7,623
Cooling Degree Days (base 65°F)	0	0	0	5	31	122	195	152	55	5	0	0	565
Mean Precipitation (in.)	1.00	1.00	1.73	3.04	3.84	4.48	4.10	4.10	3.40	2.50	2.10	1.13	32.42
Extreme Maximum Daily Precip. (in.)	1.02	1.46	2.20	2.29	3.37	9.43	5.75	3.62	2.97	2.13	1.87	1.10	9.43
Days With ≥ 0.1" Precipitation	3	3	5	6	8	8	7	7	7	6	5	3	68
Days With ≥ 0.5" Precipitation	0	0	1	2	3	3	3	3	2	2	1	0	20
Days With ≥ 1.0" Precipitation	0	0	0	1	1	1	1	1	1	0	0	0	6
Mean Snowfall (in.)	12.7	10.0	10.6	3.2	0.1	0.0	0.0	0.0	trace	0.5	4.8	12.5	54.4
Maximum Snow Depth (in.)	28	29	28	6	trace	0	0	0	trace	4	9	27	29
Days With ≥ 1.0" Snow Depth	25	25	15	2	0	0	0	0	0	0	4	22	93

The period of record for all cooperative weather station data is 1980 – 2009. See User Guide for detailed explanation of data.

Hartford 2 W *Washington County* Elevation: 979 ft. Latitude: 43° 20' N Longitude: 88° 25' W

	JAN	FEB	MAR	APR	MAY	JUN	JUL	AUG	SEP	OCT	NOV	DEC	YEAR
Mean Maximum Temp. (°F)	26.9	31.0	41.7	55.9	67.6	77.5	81.3	79.3	72.0	58.8	44.5	30.8	55.6
Mean Temp. (°F)	18.1	22.0	32.5	45.3	56.2	65.8	69.9	68.1	60.3	48.1	36.0	22.7	45.4
Mean Minimum Temp. (°F)	9.2	12.9	23.2	34.6	44.8	54.0	58.4	56.9	48.6	37.4	27.5	14.5	35.2
Extreme Maximum Temp. (°F)	55	63	81	88	94	100	105	101	96	89	75	65	105
Extreme Minimum Temp. (°F)	-35	-29	-15	1	24	31	40	36	24	17	-4	-29	-35
Days Maximum Temp. ≥ 90°F	0	0	0	0	0	2	4	2	1	0	0	0	9
Days Maximum Temp. ≤ 32°F	20	15	6	1	0	0	0	0	0	0	4	16	62
Days Minimum Temp. ≤ 32°F	30	27	25	12	2	0	0	0	1	9	21	29	156
Days Minimum Temp. ≤ 0°F	9	6	1	0	0	0	0	0	0	0	0	5	21
Heating Degree Days (base 65°F)	1,449	1,210	1,000	590	291	77	20	36	181	521	864	1,306	7,545
Cooling Degree Days (base 65°F)	0	0	0	5	25	107	180	140	46	4	0	0	507
Mean Precipitation (in.)	1.34	1.16	1.68	3.01	3.31	4.05	3.99	3.92	3.51	2.70	2.25	1.60	32.52
Extreme Maximum Daily Precip. (in.)	1.16	1.80	2.10	2.25	2.73	4.95	3.95	3.96	5.20	2.27	2.67	1.30	5.20
Days With ≥ 0.1" Precipitation	4	3	5	6	7	7	6	7	6	6	5	5	67
Days With ≥ 0.5" Precipitation	1	0	1	2	2	2	3	3	3	2	1	1	21
Days With ≥ 1.0" Precipitation	0	0	0	1	1	1	1	1	1	1	0	0	7
Mean Snowfall (in.)	10.2	7.0	5.4	1.4	0.4	0.0	0.0	0.0	0.0	0.1	1.7	8.7	34.9
Maximum Snow Depth (in.)	21	19	15	7	6	0	0	0	0	trace	10	25	25
Days With ≥ 1.0" Snow Depth	21	19	8	1	0	0	0	0	0	0	2	15	66

Kenosha *Kenosha County* Elevation: 600 ft. Latitude: 42° 34' N Longitude: 87° 49' W

	JAN	FEB	MAR	APR	MAY	JUN	JUL	AUG	SEP	OCT	NOV	DEC	YEAR
Mean Maximum Temp. (°F)	30.3	33.5	42.3	52.4	62.5	73.1	79.0	78.0	71.1	59.4	47.1	34.4	55.3
Mean Temp. (°F)	22.9	26.3	34.8	44.6	54.2	64.5	71.0	70.3	62.8	51.2	39.6	27.3	47.5
Mean Minimum Temp. (°F)	15.5	18.9	27.2	36.7	45.8	55.9	62.9	62.5	54.5	42.9	32.0	20.0	39.6
Extreme Maximum Temp. (°F)	65	69	83	90	89	101	104	100	96	88	75	70	104
Extreme Minimum Temp. (°F)	-31	-23	-7	10	27	38	41	42	30	20	5	-29	-31
Days Maximum Temp. ≥ 90°F	0	0	0	0	0	1	3	2	0	0	0	0	6
Days Maximum Temp. ≤ 32°F	17	12	5	0	0	0	0	0	0	0	2	11	47
Days Minimum Temp. ≤ 32°F	28	26	22	8	0	0	0	0	0	3	15	26	128
Days Minimum Temp. ≤ 0°F	5	2	0	0	0	0	0	0	0	0	0	2	9
Heating Degree Days (base 65°F)	1,298	1,089	930	608	344	99	12	14	119	426	755	1,163	6,857
Cooling Degree Days (base 65°F)	0	0	0	2	16	92	204	184	61	5	0	0	564
Mean Precipitation (in.)	1.75	1.47	2.46	3.72	3.83	3.57	3.57	4.13	3.53	2.92	2.80	2.21	35.96
Extreme Maximum Daily Precip. (in.)	1.47	1.61	2.17	2.39	2.86	4.06	3.12	4.88	3.06	2.81	2.05	2.74	4.88
Days With ≥ 0.1" Precipitation	5	3	5	7	7	6	6	6	6	6	6	5	68
Days With ≥ 0.5" Precipitation	1	1	2	3	3	2	3	3	2	2	2	1	25
Days With ≥ 1.0" Precipitation	0	0	0	1	1	1	1	1	1	1	1	0	8
Mean Snowfall (in.)	12.4	8.7	5.4	0.8	trace	0.0	0.0	0.0	0.0	0.1	1.1	8.3	36.8
Maximum Snow Depth (in.)	19	26	12	6	trace	0	0	0	0	1	4	16	26
Days With ≥ 1.0" Snow Depth	18	12	5	0	0	0	0	0	0	0	1	8	44

Kewaunee 3 NW *Kewaunee County* Elevation: 702 ft. Latitude: 44° 29' N Longitude: 87° 32' W

	JAN	FEB	MAR	APR	MAY	JUN	JUL	AUG	SEP	OCT	NOV	DEC	YEAR
Mean Maximum Temp. (°F)	27.1	30.2	38.7	50.4	61.4	71.6	77.3	76.2	68.8	55.8	43.4	31.0	52.6
Mean Temp. (°F)	20.1	22.9	31.2	42.4	52.2	62.2	68.2	67.7	60.0	47.9	36.4	24.2	44.6
Mean Minimum Temp. (°F)	13.0	15.5	23.7	34.4	43.0	52.8	59.1	59.1	51.2	39.9	29.4	17.4	36.5
Extreme Maximum Temp. (°F)	53	56	75	85	91	95	100	98	90	83	73	66	100
Extreme Minimum Temp. (°F)	-29	-20	-9	10	27	31	41	40	28	20	3	-20	-29
Days Maximum Temp. ≥ 90°F	0	0	0	0	0	1	2	1	0	0	0	0	4
Days Maximum Temp. ≤ 32°F	20	15	7	0	0	0	0	0	0	0	2	15	59
Days Minimum Temp. ≤ 32°F	29	26	24	10	1	0	0	0	0	5	16	27	138
Days Minimum Temp. ≤ 0°F	6	4	1	0	0	0	0	0	0	0	0	3	14
Heating Degree Days (base 65°F)	1,384	1,182	1,041	673	395	129	30	31	173	525	850	1,261	7,674
Cooling Degree Days (base 65°F)	0	0	0	0	6	53	136	121	29	1	0	0	346
Mean Precipitation (in.)	1.36	1.07	1.50	2.71	2.92	3.29	3.30	3.50	3.33	2.66	2.50	1.53	29.67
Extreme Maximum Daily Precip. (in.)	1.20	1.23	1.72	2.20	1.54	3.75	2.25	4.40	3.78	2.41	2.00	0.94	4.40
Days With ≥ 0.1" Precipitation	4	3	5	6	6	6	6	6	6	6	5	5	64
Days With ≥ 0.5" Precipitation	1	0	1	2	2	2	2	2	2	2	2	1	19
Days With ≥ 1.0" Precipitation	0	0	0	0	1	1	1	1	1	1	0	0	6
Mean Snowfall (in.)	12.3	9.9	6.3	1.8	0.1	0.0	0.0	0.0	0.0	trace	1.8	9.9	42.1
Maximum Snow Depth (in.)	24	26	17	4	0	0	0	0	0	trace	3	30	30
Days With ≥ 1.0" Snow Depth	21	22	11	1	0	0	0	0	0	0	2	12	69

Lake Geneva *Walworth County* Elevation: 879 ft. Latitude: 42° 36' N Longitude: 88° 26' W

	JAN	FEB	MAR	APR	MAY	JUN	JUL	AUG	SEP	OCT	NOV	DEC	YEAR
Mean Maximum Temp. (°F)	29.6	34.8	45.1	59.0	71.2	81.3	85.6	83.1	75.0	61.8	46.5	33.5	58.9
Mean Temp. (°F)	21.9	26.6	35.8	48.2	59.5	69.4	74.4	72.2	63.9	51.6	38.5	26.3	49.0
Mean Minimum Temp. (°F)	14.2	18.3	26.4	37.4	47.7	57.6	63.1	61.3	52.7	41.4	30.4	19.1	39.1
Extreme Maximum Temp. (°F)	58	67	81	90	94	104	104	106	98	87	74	67	106
Extreme Minimum Temp. (°F)	-27	-25	-7	9	27	37	43	40	28	17	2	-23	-27
Days Maximum Temp. ≥ 90°F	0	0	0	0	1	5	9	5	1	0	0	0	21
Days Maximum Temp. ≤ 32°F	19	11	4	0	0	0	0	0	0	0	2	13	49
Days Minimum Temp. ≤ 32°F	29	25	23	9	1	0	0	0	0	5	18	28	138
Days Minimum Temp. ≤ 0°F	5	3	0	0	0	0	0	0	0	0	0	3	11
Heating Degree Days (base 65°F)	1,331	1,081	900	505	211	39	4	10	116	417	791	1,193	6,598
Cooling Degree Days (base 65°F)	0	0	0	7	46	179	301	240	89	7	0	0	869
Mean Precipitation (in.)	1.86	1.63	2.17	3.55	3.68	3.94	3.57	3.60	3.93	2.87	2.84	2.19	35.83
Extreme Maximum Daily Precip. (in.)	1.15	2.15	1.56	2.08	2.99	2.91	3.65	3.00	3.38	2.70	1.80	2.65	3.65
Days With ≥ 0.1" Precipitation	5	4	6	7	7	7	7	6	6	5	6	5	71
Days With ≥ 0.5" Precipitation	1	1	1	3	3	2	2	3	2	2	2	1	23
Days With ≥ 1.0" Precipitation	0	0	0	1	1	1	1	1	1	1	0	0	7
Mean Snowfall (in.)	13.0	8.3	5.9	2.0	0.1	0.0	0.0	0.0	0.0	0.2	2.8	11.3	43.6
Maximum Snow Depth (in.)	25	20	11	8	trace	0	0	0	0	1	5	21	25
Days With ≥ 1.0" Snow Depth	22	17	6	1	0	0	0	0	0	0	3	14	63

The period of record for all cooperative weather station data is 1980 – 2009. See User Guide for detailed explanation of data.

Lake Mills *Jefferson County* Elevation: 852 ft. Latitude: 43° 05' N Longitude: 88° 55' W

	JAN	FEB	MAR	APR	MAY	JUN	JUL	AUG	SEP	OCT	NOV	DEC	YEAR
Mean Maximum Temp. (°F)	28.0	32.5	43.4	58.7	71.1	80.3	84.1	81.3	74.1	60.8	***45.9***	31.4	***57.6***
Mean Temp. (°F)	19.8	23.8	34.1	47.8	59.3	68.6	73.0	70.7	62.8	50.4	***37.7***	23.9	***47.6***
Mean Minimum Temp. (°F)	11.5	15.0	24.6	36.8	47.4	56.8	61.8	60.0	51.4	39.9	***29.6***	16.4	***37.6***
Extreme Maximum Temp. (°F)	55	64	81	89	92	103	102	104	95	88	74	66	104
Extreme Minimum Temp. (°F)	-29	-20	-8	8	26	37	45	41	30	15	0	-24	-29
Days Maximum Temp. ≥ 90°F	0	0	0	0	0	3	6	3	1	0	0	0	13
Days Maximum Temp. ≤ 32°F	19	13	5	0	0	0	0	0	0	0	2	15	54
Days Minimum Temp. ≤ 32°F	29	26	24	9	1	0	0	0	0	6	19	28	142
Days Minimum Temp. ≤ 0°F	7	5	0	0	0	0	0	0	0	0	0	4	16
Heating Degree Days (base 65°F)	1,396	1,159	952	516	210	40	4	14	129	452	***810***	1,266	***6,948***
Cooling Degree Days (base 65°F)	0	0	0	6	40	153	258	201	68	7	***0***	0	***733***
Mean Precipitation (in.)	1.22	1.30	1.92	3.25	3.62	4.46	4.02	4.78	3.78	2.68	2.35	1.70	35.08
Extreme Maximum Daily Precip. (in.)	1.30	1.66	2.41	3.10	3.20	2.90	2.76	5.59	3.59	2.31	3.00	1.62	5.59
Days With ≥ 0.1" Precipitation	3	4	4	6	7	7	6	6	6	6	5	4	64
Days With ≥ 0.5" Precipitation	1	1	1	2	2	3	3	3	2	2	2	1	23
Days With ≥ 1.0" Precipitation	0	0	0	1	1	1	1	1	1	0	0	0	6
Mean Snowfall (in.)	9.8	8.9	5.2	1.6	0.1	0.0	0.0	0.0	0.0	0.1	2.1	10.7	38.5
Maximum Snow Depth (in.)	21	17	12	13	trace	0	0	0	0	trace	5	22	22
Days With ≥ 1.0" Snow Depth	20	18	8	1	0	0	0	0	0	0	1	15	63

Lancaster 4 WSW *Grant County* Elevation: 1,040 ft. Latitude: 42° 50' N Longitude: 90° 47' W

	JAN	FEB	MAR	APR	MAY	JUN	JUL	AUG	SEP	OCT	NOV	DEC	YEAR
Mean Maximum Temp. (°F)	25.4	30.5	42.4	57.1	68.1	77.3	81.1	79.2	71.5	58.7	43.6	29.4	55.4
Mean Temp. (°F)	17.2	22.1	33.5	46.8	57.7	67.1	71.1	69.3	61.2	48.7	35.5	21.7	46.0
Mean Minimum Temp. (°F)	9.0	13.7	24.6	36.5	47.3	56.9	61.1	59.3	50.9	38.6	27.3	13.9	36.6
Extreme Maximum Temp. (°F)	57	64	79	95	91	100	100	103	93	87	74	62	103
Extreme Minimum Temp. (°F)	-28	-31	-12	6	25	37	44	40	27	15	-5	-27	-31
Days Maximum Temp. ≥ 90°F	0	0	0	0	0	1	3	2	0	0	0	0	6
Days Maximum Temp. ≤ 32°F	22	16	6	0	0	0	0	0	0	0	5	18	67
Days Minimum Temp. ≤ 32°F	31	27	25	10	1	0	0	0	0	9	22	30	155
Days Minimum Temp. ≤ 0°F	9	6	1	0	0	0	0	0	0	0	0	6	22
Heating Degree Days (base 65°F)	1,475	1,208	970	544	245	52	11	23	162	504	879	1,337	7,410
Cooling Degree Days (base 65°F)	0	0	0	5	26	122	208	163	56	5	0	0	585
Mean Precipitation (in.)	0.87	1.06	1.96	3.54	4.08	5.14	4.04	4.31	3.13	2.60	2.44	1.39	34.56
Extreme Maximum Daily Precip. (in.)	0.94	1.30	3.60	4.56	2.80	4.60	3.17	4.05	2.20	2.16	4.01	1.79	4.60
Days With ≥ 0.1" Precipitation	3	3	5	7	8	7	7	7	6	5	5	4	67
Days With ≥ 0.5" Precipitation	0	1	1	2	3	3	3	3	2	2	2	1	23
Days With ≥ 1.0" Precipitation	0	0	0	1	1	1	1	1	1	1	1	0	8
Mean Snowfall (in.)	10.3	7.4	5.8	1.9	0.2	0.0	0.0	0.0	0.0	0.3	3.1	10.3	39.3
Maximum Snow Depth (in.)	28	18	16	7	3	0	0	0	0	6	9	18	28
Days With ≥ 1.0" Snow Depth	22	18	10	1	0	0	0	0	0	0	3	17	71

Manitowoc *Manitowoc County* Elevation: 660 ft. Latitude: 44° 05' N Longitude: 87° 41' W

	JAN	FEB	MAR	APR	MAY	JUN	JUL	AUG	SEP	OCT	NOV	DEC	YEAR
Mean Maximum Temp. (°F)	27.6	30.7	39.8	53.1	64.3	74.4	79.2	77.6	70.0	56.9	44.1	31.5	54.1
Mean Temp. (°F)	20.3	23.4	32.2	44.1	54.5	64.4	69.9	68.9	61.4	49.1	37.2	24.7	45.8
Mean Minimum Temp. (°F)	12.9	16.1	24.5	35.0	44.5	54.3	60.6	60.1	52.7	41.2	30.2	17.8	37.5
Extreme Maximum Temp. (°F)	54	57	79	90	89	97	101	96	97	88	76	64	101
Extreme Minimum Temp. (°F)	-26	-27	-9	4	26	35	37	41	29	20	3	-21	-27
Days Maximum Temp. ≥ 90°F	0	0	0	0	0	1	2	1	0	0	0	0	4
Days Maximum Temp. ≤ 32°F	19	15	6	0	0	0	0	0	0	0	3	15	58
Days Minimum Temp. ≤ 32°F	30	26	25	11	1	0	0	0	0	4	18	28	143
Days Minimum Temp. ≤ 0°F	6	3	1	0	0	0	0	0	0	0	0	3	13
Heating Degree Days (base 65°F)	1,380	1,170	1,010	622	330	93	16	23	147	488	829	1,244	7,352
Cooling Degree Days (base 65°F)	0	0	0	1	12	81	175	150	45	3	0	0	467
Mean Precipitation (in.)	1.44	1.27	1.53	3.00	3.01	3.41	3.43	3.59	3.06	2.60	2.35	1.65	30.34
Extreme Maximum Daily Precip. (in.)	1.75	1.40	2.95	2.27	2.08	4.27	4.20	2.60	3.40	2.00	2.10	1.35	4.27
Days With ≥ 0.1" Precipitation	4	4	4	7	6	6	6	7	6	6	5	4	65
Days With ≥ 0.5" Precipitation	1	1	1	2	2	2	2	3	2	2	1	1	20
Days With ≥ 1.0" Precipitation	0	0	0	1	1	1	1	1	1	0	0	0	6
Mean Snowfall (in.)	***5.6***	***6.9***	na	0.8	trace	0.0	0.0	0.0	0.0	trace	1.3	***6.5***	na
Maximum Snow Depth (in.)	***30***	na	***12***	***4***	***0***	***0***	***0***	***0***	***0***	***trace***	***2***	na	na
Days With ≥ 1.0" Snow Depth	***10***	***9***	4	0	0	0	0	0	0	0	0	na	na

Marshfield Exp Farm *Wood County* Elevation: 1,250 ft. Latitude: 44° 38' N Longitude: 90° 08' W

	JAN	FEB	MAR	APR	MAY	JUN	JUL	AUG	SEP	OCT	NOV	DEC	YEAR
Mean Maximum Temp. (°F)	24.4	29.3	40.3	56.7	68.6	77.5	81.6	79.4	71.1	57.9	41.9	27.7	54.7
Mean Temp. (°F)	15.4	19.8	30.5	45.1	56.5	65.7	70.0	68.2	59.7	47.2	33.6	19.6	44.3
Mean Minimum Temp. (°F)	6.3	10.3	20.7	33.4	44.4	53.9	58.2	56.8	48.2	36.5	25.2	11.4	33.8
Extreme Maximum Temp. (°F)	55	58	80	91	91	97	104	102	97	84	74	63	104
Extreme Minimum Temp. (°F)	-33	-33	-15	5	22	33	41	35	26	14	-7	-27	-33
Days Maximum Temp. ≥ 90°F	0	0	0	0	0	2	3	2	0	0	0	0	7
Days Maximum Temp. ≤ 32°F	23	17	7	1	0	0	0	0	0	0	5	20	73
Days Minimum Temp. ≤ 32°F	31	27	27	14	2	0	0	0	1	11	24	30	167
Days Minimum Temp. ≤ 0°F	11	7	2	0	0	0	0	0	0	0	0	7	27
Heating Degree Days (base 65°F)	1,533	1,272	1,062	594	278	71	15	31	193	548	937	1,403	7,937
Cooling Degree Days (base 65°F)	0	0	0	2	23	100	175	137	41	3	0	0	481
Mean Precipitation (in.)	0.93	0.85	1.74	2.82	3.67	4.27	3.66	4.46	3.87	2.61	2.12	1.23	32.23
Extreme Maximum Daily Precip. (in.)	1.12	1.07	2.30	2.18	2.35	3.52	3.02	4.02	2.95	2.29	1.90	1.60	4.02
Days With ≥ 0.1" Precipitation	3	3	4	6	7	8	7	7	7	6	5	4	67
Days With ≥ 0.5" Precipitation	0	0	1	2	2	3	2	3	2	2	1	0	18
Days With ≥ 1.0" Precipitation	0	0	0	1	1	1	1	1	1	0	0	0	6
Mean Snowfall (in.)	11.3	9.2	9.9	3.1	trace	0.0	0.0	0.0	0.0	0.9	5.1	12.2	51.7
Maximum Snow Depth (in.)	17	22	19	5	trace	0	0	0	0	4	11	20	22
Days With ≥ 1.0" Snow Depth	19	18	13	1	0	0	0	0	0	0	3	18	72

The period of record for all cooperative weather station data is 1980 – 2009. See User Guide for detailed explanation of data.

Menomonie *Dunn County* Elevation: 779 ft. Latitude: 44° 53' N Longitude: 91° 56' W

	JAN	FEB	MAR	APR	MAY	JUN	JUL	AUG	SEP	OCT	NOV	DEC	YEAR
Mean Maximum Temp. (°F)	25.8	31.2	42.8	59.6	70.6	78.9	83.0	80.8	72.7	59.7	43.4	29.1	56.5
Mean Temp. (°F)	16.4	21.3	32.3	47.0	58.1	67.0	71.5	69.4	61.1	48.7	34.7	20.8	45.7
Mean Minimum Temp. (°F)	6.9	11.3	21.8	34.5	45.6	55.0	60.0	58.0	49.5	37.6	25.9	12.4	34.9
Extreme Maximum Temp. (°F)	55	60	82	90	93	98	99	100	95	90	76	64	100
Extreme Minimum Temp. (°F)	-38	-40	-15	5	22	30	41	37	28	12	-13	-36	-40
Days Maximum Temp. ≥ 90°F	0	0	0	0	0	2	5	2	1	0	0	0	10
Days Maximum Temp. ≤ 32°F	21	15	5	0	0	0	0	0	0	0	5	18	64
Days Minimum Temp. ≤ 32°F	30	27	26	13	2	0	0	0	1	10	23	30	162
Days Minimum Temp. ≤ 0°F	10	7	2	0	0	0	0	0	0	0	1	7	27
Heating Degree Days (base 65°F)	1,502	1,231	1,006	537	237	56	10	24	167	504	904	1,364	7,542
Cooling Degree Days (base 65°F)	0	0	0	6	31	122	219	169	58	5	0	0	610
Mean Precipitation (in.)	0.81	0.79	1.76	2.66	3.65	4.54	3.84	4.01	3.78	2.42	1.82	1.00	31.08
Extreme Maximum Daily Precip. (in.)	1.03	1.23	1.86	2.32	2.91	2.50	3.34	2.88	4.39	2.58	3.41	1.04	4.39
Days With ≥ 0.1" Precipitation	3	2	4	6	8	8	7	7	6	6	4	3	64
Days With ≥ 0.5" Precipitation	0	0	1	2	3	3	2	3	3	1	1	0	19
Days With ≥ 1.0" Precipitation	0	0	0	1	1	1	1	1	1	1	0	0	7
Mean Snowfall (in.)	10.7	7.5	8.8	1.2	trace	0.0	0.0	trace	0.0	0.2	4.0	9.2	41.6
Maximum Snow Depth (in.)	27	29	19	5	trace	0	0	trace	0	trace	13	29	29
Days With ≥ 1.0" Snow Depth	25	22	14	1	0	0	0	0	0	0	4	18	84

Milwaukee Mt Mary Col *Milwaukee County* Elevation: 726 ft. Latitude: 43° 04' N Longitude: 88° 02' W

	JAN	FEB	MAR	APR	MAY	JUN	JUL	AUG	SEP	OCT	NOV	DEC	YEAR
Mean Maximum Temp. (°F)	30.0	34.4	45.0	58.0	69.3	80.0	84.4	82.1	74.8	61.0	47.2	34.1	58.3
Mean Temp. (°F)	22.6	26.6	36.1	47.9	58.5	68.9	73.9	72.3	64.4	51.6	39.4	27.0	49.1
Mean Minimum Temp. (°F)	15.2	18.7	27.1	37.7	47.7	57.7	63.4	62.3	54.0	42.2	31.6	19.8	39.8
Extreme Maximum Temp. (°F)	59	67	85	91	95	104	108	108	98	90	76	68	108
Extreme Minimum Temp. (°F)	-26	-25	-5	12	27	34	47	43	31	19	4	-22	-26
Days Maximum Temp. ≥ 90°F	0	0	0	0	1	4	8	5	1	0	0	0	19
Days Maximum Temp. ≤ 32°F	17	12	4	0	0	0	0	0	0	0	2	12	47
Days Minimum Temp. ≤ 32°F	29	25	22	8	1	0	0	0	0	4	16	27	132
Days Minimum Temp. ≤ 0°F	5	2	0	0	0	0	0	0	0	0	0	2	9
Heating Degree Days (base 65°F)	1,307	1,080	892	515	238	44	5	9	102	417	761	1,171	6,541
Cooling Degree Days (base 65°F)	0	0	1	8	44	167	287	241	92	8	0	0	848
Mean Precipitation (in.)	1.40	1.28	1.61	3.33	3.21	3.74	3.38	3.82	3.28	2.42	2.33	1.66	31.46
Extreme Maximum Daily Precip. (in.)	1.35	1.60	1.29	2.25	2.42	5.55	2.45	3.80	2.94	2.35	2.46	1.51	5.55
Days With ≥ 0.1" Precipitation	4	4	4	6	7	6	6	6	6	5	5	5	64
Days With ≥ 0.5" Precipitation	1	1	1	2	2	2	2	3	2	2	1	1	20
Days With ≥ 1.0" Precipitation	0	0	0	1	1	1	1	1	1	0	0	0	6
Mean Snowfall (in.)	11.2	9.0	5.3	1.5	0.1	0.0	0.0	0.0	0.0	0.1	1.9	8.9	38.0
Maximum Snow Depth (in.)	21	20	16	7	2	0	0	0	0	2	11	19	21
Days With ≥ 1.0" Snow Depth	19	14	5	1	0	0	0	0	0	0	1	11	51

New London *Outagamie County* Elevation: 805 ft. Latitude: 44° 21' N Longitude: 88° 43' W

	JAN	FEB	MAR	APR	MAY	JUN	JUL	AUG	SEP	OCT	NOV	DEC	YEAR
Mean Maximum Temp. (°F)	25.7	30.2	40.8	56.3	68.1	77.4	81.3	79.1	71.7	58.0	43.3	29.6	55.1
Mean Temp. (°F)	16.8	20.7	30.9	45.0	***56.6***	65.8	69.8	67.9	59.8	47.3	34.7	21.2	***44.7***
Mean Minimum Temp. (°F)	7.8	11.2	20.9	33.7	***44.7***	54.2	58.3	56.7	47.8	36.5	26.0	12.9	***34.2***
Extreme Maximum Temp. (°F)	53	60	81	92	90	99	105	99	92	86	74	63	105
Extreme Minimum Temp. (°F)	-33	-32	-13	8	25	35	42	35	22	11	-3	-27	-33
Days Maximum Temp. ≥ 90°F	0	0	0	0	0	2	3	2	0	0	0	0	7
Days Maximum Temp. ≤ 32°F	22	16	7	0	0	0	0	0	0	0	4	17	66
Days Minimum Temp. ≤ 32°F	30	27	26	14	2	0	0	0	1	11	23	30	164
Days Minimum Temp. ≤ 0°F	10	7	2	0	0	0	0	0	0	0	0	6	25
Heating Degree Days (base 65°F)	1,488	1,246	1,051	596	***282***	73	19	37	192	546	903	1,350	***7,783***
Cooling Degree Days (base 65°F)	0	0	0	4	***27***	105	176	134	41	4	0	0	***491***
Mean Precipitation (in.)	***1.19***	0.98	1.78	2.70	3.44	4.07	3.89	4.04	3.01	2.61	1.92	1.49	***31.12***
Extreme Maximum Daily Precip. (in.)	***1.67***	***1.20***	***2.12***	***1.95***	***1.81***	***2.48***	***4.30***	***2.89***	***2.14***	***1.70***	***2.20***	***1.65***	***4.30***
Days With ≥ 0.1" Precipitation	3	2	4	6	7	7	7	7	6	6	4	***4***	***63***
Days With ≥ 0.5" Precipitation	1	1	1	2	2	3	3	3	2	2	1	1	22
Days With ≥ 1.0" Precipitation	0	0	0	0	1	1	1	1	1	0	0	0	5
Mean Snowfall (in.)	10.3	7.6	7.6	***1.6***	trace	0.0	0.0	0.0	0.0	0.1	3.2	***9.4***	***39.8***
Maximum Snow Depth (in.)	na	na	***23***	***4***	***0***	***0***	***0***	***0***	***0***	***2***	***8***	na	na
Days With ≥ 1.0" Snow Depth	na	na	***7***	1	0	0	0	0	0	0	1	***9***	na

Oconomowoc *Waukesha County* Elevation: 855 ft. Latitude: 43° 06' N Longitude: 88° 30' W

	JAN	FEB	MAR	APR	MAY	JUN	JUL	AUG	SEP	OCT	NOV	DEC	YEAR
Mean Maximum Temp. (°F)	27.7	31.9	43.0	56.9	68.2	78.1	81.9	80.0	72.7	59.7	45.3	32.0	56.5
Mean Temp. (°F)	19.2	23.2	33.8	46.7	57.4	67.2	71.5	69.9	61.8	49.4	36.9	24.1	46.8
Mean Minimum Temp. (°F)	10.6	14.4	24.6	36.5	46.8	56.2	61.0	59.6	50.8	39.0	28.5	16.2	37.0
Extreme Maximum Temp. (°F)	59	64	81	88	91	100	100	101	95	87	74	67	101
Extreme Minimum Temp. (°F)	-29	-29	-13	4	26	35	43	40	27	14	-2	-22	-29
Days Maximum Temp. ≥ 90°F	0	0	0	0	0	2	4	2	1	0	0	0	9
Days Maximum Temp. ≤ 32°F	20	14	6	0	0	0	0	0	0	0	4	15	59
Days Minimum Temp. ≤ 32°F	30	27	24	10	1	0	0	0	1	8	20	29	150
Days Minimum Temp. ≤ 0°F	8	5	1	0	0	0	0	0	0	0	0	4	18
Heating Degree Days (base 65°F)	1,414	1,177	960	548	260	57	10	20	151	483	835	1,260	7,175
Cooling Degree Days (base 65°F)	0	0	0	7	32	128	218	177	61	6	0	0	629
Mean Precipitation (in.)	1.41	1.47	2.03	3.45	3.66	4.13	3.93	4.46	3.71	2.83	2.36	1.84	35.28
Extreme Maximum Daily Precip. (in.)	1.21	1.41	2.53	2.37	2.69	3.56	3.38	5.38	3.91	2.82	2.38	1.40	5.38
Days With ≥ 0.1" Precipitation	4	4	5	7	8	7	6	7	6	6	5	5	70
Days With ≥ 0.5" Precipitation	1	1	1	2	2	3	3	3	3	2	2	1	24
Days With ≥ 1.0" Precipitation	0	0	0	1	1	1	1	1	1	1	0	0	7
Mean Snowfall (in.)	10.6	8.3	5.5	1.6	0.3	0.0	0.0	0.0	trace	0.1	2.2	11.0	39.6
Maximum Snow Depth (in.)	14	16	13	6	4	0	0	0	trace	1	6	14	16
Days With ≥ 1.0" Snow Depth	22	18	7	1	0	0	0	0	0	0	2	16	66

The period of record for all cooperative weather station data is 1980 – 2009. See User Guide for detailed explanation of data.

Oshkosh *Winnebago County* Elevation: 750 ft. Latitude: 44° 01' N Longitude: 88° 33' W

	JAN	FEB	MAR	APR	MAY	JUN	JUL	AUG	SEP	OCT	NOV	DEC	YEAR
Mean Maximum Temp. (°F)	26.1	30.2	40.6	55.1	67.5	77.3	81.6	79.3	71.7	58.2	43.9	30.2	55.1
Mean Temp. (°F)	17.9	21.7	31.8	45.6	57.5	67.4	71.9	69.8	61.7	49.0	36.1	22.7	46.1
Mean Minimum Temp. (°F)	9.8	13.2	22.9	35.9	47.5	57.6	61.9	60.2	51.6	39.8	28.3	15.1	37.0
Extreme Maximum Temp. (°F)	54	62	80	91	91	98	101	100	93	87	74	65	101
Extreme Minimum Temp. (°F)	-29	-30	-8	10	27	37	46	41	28	19	0	-27	-30
Days Maximum Temp. ≥ 90°F	0	0	0	0	0	2	3	2	1	0	0	0	8
Days Maximum Temp. ≤ 32°F	21	16	7	0	0	0	0	0	0	0	4	17	65
Days Minimum Temp. ≤ 32°F	30	27	25	10	1	0	0	0	0	6	20	29	148
Days Minimum Temp. ≤ 0°F	8	6	1	0	0	0	0	0	0	0	0	5	20
Heating Degree Days (base 65°F)	1,453	1,217	1,023	581	256	57	8	21	154	495	859	1,306	7,430
Cooling Degree Days (base 65°F)	0	0	0	5	31	136	228	176	61	6	0	0	643
Mean Precipitation (in.)	1.22	1.08	1.81	2.81	3.16	4.10	3.57	3.89	3.35	2.43	2.42	1.53	31.37
Extreme Maximum Daily Precip. (in.)	1.15	1.82	2.48	2.28	2.80	5.16	3.23	3.83	4.58	2.36	2.30	1.78	5.16
Days With ≥ 0.1" Precipitation	4	3	4	6	7	7	7	7	6	6	5	4	66
Days With ≥ 0.5" Precipitation	0	0	1	2	2	3	2	3	2	2	1	1	19
Days With ≥ 1.0" Precipitation	0	0	0	1	1	1	1	1	1	0	1	0	7
Mean Snowfall (in.)	10.2	6.5	6.4	1.1	0.0	0.0	0.0	0.0	0.0	0.1	2.5	9.3	36.1
Maximum Snow Depth (in.)	*15*	na	*17*	*3*	*0*	*0*	*0*	*0*	*0*	*trace*	*7*	na	na
Days With ≥ 1.0" Snow Depth	*13*	na	*6*	0	0	0	0	0	0	0	1	na	na

Plymouth *Sheboygan County* Elevation: 833 ft. Latitude: 43° 44' N Longitude: 87° 58' W

	JAN	FEB	MAR	APR	MAY	JUN	JUL	AUG	SEP	OCT	NOV	DEC	YEAR
Mean Maximum Temp. (°F)	27.2	31.0	41.2	55.3	66.6	76.7	81.3	79.1	71.6	58.3	44.3	31.3	55.3
Mean Temp. (°F)	19.7	23.0	32.7	45.3	55.9	65.9	70.9	69.2	61.4	48.9	36.7	24.2	46.2
Mean Minimum Temp. (°F)	12.2	15.0	24.2	35.3	45.1	55.0	60.4	59.3	51.1	39.5	29.0	17.0	36.9
Extreme Maximum Temp. (°F)	53	64	80	89	91	101	102	101	92	87	74	67	102
Extreme Minimum Temp. (°F)	-29	-27	-9	11	25	33	43	39	27	15	1	-20	-29
Days Maximum Temp. ≥ 90°F	0	0	0	0	0	2	4	2	0	0	0	0	8
Days Maximum Temp. ≤ 32°F	20	15	7	1	0	0	0	0	0	0	4	16	63
Days Minimum Temp. ≤ 32°F	30	27	25	11	2	0	0	0	0	6	20	29	150
Days Minimum Temp. ≤ 0°F	6	4	1	0	0	0	0	0	0	0	0	4	15
Heating Degree Days (base 65°F)	1,398	1,179	994	589	300	78	17	26	155	495	843	1,259	7,333
Cooling Degree Days (base 65°F)	0	0	0	4	25	111	207	164	53	4	0	0	568
Mean Precipitation (in.)	1.44	1.33	1.95	3.37	3.96	4.11	3.63	4.26	3.65	2.92	2.84	1.81	35.27
Extreme Maximum Daily Precip. (in.)	1.38	1.10	3.16	2.05	4.94	4.15	3.74	5.21	6.12	2.49	3.97	1.75	6.12
Days With ≥ 0.1" Precipitation	4	3	5	7	7	7	7	7	6	7	6	5	71
Days With ≥ 0.5" Precipitation	1	1	1	2	3	3	2	3	2	2	2	1	23
Days With ≥ 1.0" Precipitation	0	0	0	1	1	1	1	1	1	0	1	0	7
Mean Snowfall (in.)	13.8	10.4	8.7	2.9	0.2	0.0	0.0	0.0	0.0	0.1	3.7	12.2	52.0
Maximum Snow Depth (in.)	*27*	na	*20*	*7*	*3*	*0*	*0*	*0*	*0*	*trace*	*11*	na	na
Days With ≥ 1.0" Snow Depth	*16*	na	*7*	1	0	0	0	0	0	0	2	*9*	na

Port Washington *Ozaukee County* Elevation: 600 ft. Latitude: 43° 23' N Longitude: 87° 52' W

	JAN	FEB	MAR	APR	MAY	JUN	JUL	AUG	SEP	OCT	NOV	DEC	YEAR
Mean Maximum Temp. (°F)	29.5	32.8	41.3	51.7	61.4	72.0	78.0	77.4	70.2	58.1	45.7	33.2	54.3
Mean Temp. (°F)	21.9	25.1	33.6	43.8	53.1	63.2	69.5	69.2	61.6	49.7	38.2	25.9	46.2
Mean Minimum Temp. (°F)	14.2	17.2	25.8	35.7	44.7	54.3	61.0	61.0	53.1	41.3	30.7	18.6	38.1
Extreme Maximum Temp. (°F)	56	61	82	92	90	102	106	103	94	87	75	68	106
Extreme Minimum Temp. (°F)	-25	-29	-3	11	25	29	45	42	28	16	0	-20	-29
Days Maximum Temp. ≥ 90°F	0	0	0	0	0	1	3	2	0	0	0	0	6
Days Maximum Temp. ≤ 32°F	18	12	5	0	0	0	0	0	0	0	3	13	51
Days Minimum Temp. ≤ 32°F	29	25	23	9	0	0	0	0	0	4	17	27	134
Days Minimum Temp. ≤ 0°F	5	3	0	0	0	0	0	0	0	0	0	3	11
Heating Degree Days (base 65°F)	1,332	1,126	967	629	372	114	20	20	142	469	797	1,205	7,193
Cooling Degree Days (base 65°F)	0	0	0	1	9	68	166	157	48	2	0	0	451
Mean Precipitation (in.)	1.58	1.32	1.85	3.35	3.38	3.86	3.84	4.12	3.46	2.42	2.25	1.82	33.25
Extreme Maximum Daily Precip. (in.)	1.34	1.60	1.75	2.50	2.95	9.87	4.15	2.80	3.50	1.85	2.59	2.50	9.87
Days With ≥ 0.1" Precipitation	4	3	5	6	7	6	6	7	6	5	5	4	64
Days With ≥ 0.5" Precipitation	1	1	1	2	2	2	3	3	2	1	1	1	20
Days With ≥ 1.0" Precipitation	0	0	0	1	1	1	1	1	1	1	0	0	7
Mean Snowfall (in.)	11.0	8.2	5.5	0.9	trace	0.0	0.0	0.0	0.0	0.1	1.0	8.8	35.5
Maximum Snow Depth (in.)	25	17	12	9	trace	0	0	0	0	2	7	33	33
Days With ≥ 1.0" Snow Depth	21	16	7	1	0	0	0	0	0	0	1	11	57

Racine *Racine County* Elevation: 595 ft. Latitude: 42° 42' N Longitude: 87° 47' W

	JAN	FEB	MAR	APR	MAY	JUN	JUL	AUG	SEP	OCT	NOV	DEC	YEAR
Mean Maximum Temp. (°F)	29.6	32.6	41.1	51.4	61.4	72.1	78.0	77.3	70.2	58.4	46.2	33.7	54.3
Mean Temp. (°F)	22.4	25.8	34.5	44.6	54.1	64.3	71.0	70.7	63.1	51.0	39.5	27.0	47.3
Mean Minimum Temp. (°F)	15.2	19.0	27.9	37.7	46.6	56.5	64.0	64.1	56.0	43.6	32.8	20.3	40.3
Extreme Maximum Temp. (°F)	64	63	83	91	90	100	104	100	95	89	74	66	104
Extreme Minimum Temp. (°F)	-31	-24	-7	12	29	39	49	45	34	21	6	-23	-31
Days Maximum Temp. ≥ 90°F	0	0	0	0	0	1	3	2	0	0	0	0	6
Days Maximum Temp. ≤ 32°F	18	13	6	0	0	0	0	0	0	0	2	12	51
Days Minimum Temp. ≤ 32°F	29	25	21	6	0	0	0	0	0	2	13	26	122
Days Minimum Temp. ≤ 0°F	5	2	0	0	0	0	0	0	0	0	0	3	10
Heating Degree Days (base 65°F)	1,313	1,102	940	609	345	96	11	11	114	432	759	1,171	6,903
Cooling Degree Days (base 65°F)	0	0	0	2	12	81	203	195	65	4	0	0	562
Mean Precipitation (in.)	1.65	1.65	2.26	3.78	3.89	3.74	3.27	4.19	3.77	2.79	2.97	2.15	36.11
Extreme Maximum Daily Precip. (in.)	1.63	1.57	1.78	3.06	3.69	2.86	3.99	4.10	3.97	3.15	2.27	1.90	4.10
Days With ≥ 0.1" Precipitation	5	4	5	7	7	7	6	6	6	6	6	5	70
Days With ≥ 0.5" Precipitation	1	1	1	3	3	2	2	3	3	2	2	1	24
Days With ≥ 1.0" Precipitation	0	0	0	1	1	1	1	1	1	1	1	0	8
Mean Snowfall (in.)	14.7	10.2	5.4	1.4	0.1	0.0	0.0	0.0	0.0	0.1	1.5	9.3	42.7
Maximum Snow Depth (in.)	29	23	14	4	1	0	0	0	0	trace	6	*25*	*29*
Days With ≥ 1.0" Snow Depth	17	14	6	0	0	0	0	0	0	0	1	9	47

The period of record for all cooperative weather station data is 1980 – 2009. See User Guide for detailed explanation of data.

River Falls *Pierce County* Elevation: 915 ft. Latitude: 44° 51' N Longitude: 92° 37' W

	JAN	FEB	MAR	APR	MAY	JUN	JUL	AUG	SEP	OCT	NOV	DEC	YEAR
Mean Maximum Temp. (°F)	23.8	28.8	40.8	57.8	69.4	78.3	82.5	79.9	71.7	58.1	41.2	27.1	54.9
Mean Temp. (°F)	14.6	19.4	30.8	45.8	57.4	66.7	71.1	68.9	60.5	47.7	33.0	18.9	44.6
Mean Minimum Temp. (°F)	5.4	9.8	20.8	33.9	45.3	55.1	59.7	57.8	49.3	37.2	24.6	10.7	34.1
Extreme Maximum Temp. (°F)	53	57	81	92	94	99	102	101	93	90	77	66	102
Extreme Minimum Temp. (°F)	-32	-35	-15	5	19	33	39	34	27	13	-15	-36	-36
Days Maximum Temp. ≥ 90°F	0	0	0	0	0	2	4	2	0	0	0	0	8
Days Maximum Temp. ≤ 32°F	23	16	7	0	0	0	0	0	0	0	7	20	73
Days Minimum Temp. ≤ 32°F	31	26	25	14	3	0	0	0	1	11	24	30	165
Days Minimum Temp. ≤ 0°F	12	8	2	0	0	0	0	0	0	0	1	8	31
Heating Degree Days (base 65°F)	1,559	1,282	1,054	573	261	64	13	27	181	533	955	1,423	7,925
Cooling Degree Days (base 65°F)	0	0	0	5	31	122	210	154	54	5	0	0	581
Mean Precipitation (in.)	0.84	0.71	1.49	2.62	3.59	4.31	4.27	4.76	3.57	2.76	1.51	0.87	31.30
Extreme Maximum Daily Precip. (in.)	1.53	0.77	*2.13*	1.83	2.30	5.02	3.24	5.52	2.39	3.84	1.72	1.53	*5.52*
Days With ≥ 0.1" Precipitation	3	2	3	6	8	8	6	7	6	6	4	3	62
Days With ≥ 0.5" Precipitation	0	0	1	2	2	3	3	3	3	1	1	0	19
Days With ≥ 1.0" Precipitation	0	0	0	0	1	1	1	2	1	1	0	0	7
Mean Snowfall (in.)	9.1	7.7	9.3	2.3	trace	trace	0.0	0.0	trace	0.4	6.4	8.6	43.8
Maximum Snow Depth (in.)	27	26	22	14	trace	trace	0	0	0	4	18	22	27
Days With ≥ 1.0" Snow Depth	19	17	10	1	0	0	0	0	0	0	5	16	68

Rosholt 9 NNE *Marathon County* Elevation: 1,160 ft. Latitude: 44° 45' N Longitude: 89° 15' W

	JAN	FEB	MAR	APR	MAY	JUN	JUL	AUG	SEP	OCT	NOV	DEC	YEAR
Mean Maximum Temp. (°F)	23.7	28.4	39.0	55.0	67.1	75.9	79.9	78.0	70.0	56.2	41.1	27.1	53.4
Mean Temp. (°F)	14.0	18.2	28.4	43.1	54.6	63.7	67.6	66.1	57.7	45.2	32.2	18.5	42.4
Mean Minimum Temp. (°F)	4.2	8.0	17.7	31.2	42.1	51.5	55.3	54.2	45.4	34.2	23.3	9.8	31.4
Extreme Maximum Temp. (°F)	53	59	78	89	89	95	103	98	91	83	73	60	103
Extreme Minimum Temp. (°F)	-41	-38	-30	2	15	26	35	31	19	10	-10	-35	-41
Days Maximum Temp. ≥ 90°F	0	0	0	0	0	1	2	1	0	0	0	0	4
Days Maximum Temp. ≤ 32°F	24	18	8	1	0	0	0	0	0	0	6	21	78
Days Minimum Temp. ≤ 32°F	31	28	28	18	4	0	0	0	2	14	25	30	180
Days Minimum Temp. ≤ 0°F	12	9	4	0	0	0	0	0	0	0	1	8	34
Heating Degree Days (base 65°F)	1,577	1,316	1,129	653	330	104	36	56	238	610	977	1,434	8,460
Cooling Degree Days (base 65°F)	0	0	0	2	16	72	123	98	27	2	0	0	340
Mean Precipitation (in.)	1.04	0.88	1.51	2.92	3.69	3.99	3.53	4.45	3.68	2.98	2.14	1.35	32.16
Extreme Maximum Daily Precip. (in.)	0.92	1.65	1.40	2.15	2.50	2.62	2.07	6.65	2.86	2.20	2.00	1.66	6.65
Days With ≥ 0.1" Precipitation	3	3	4	6	7	7	7	7	7	6	5	4	66
Days With ≥ 0.5" Precipitation	0	0	1	2	3	3	3	3	2	2	1	1	21
Days With ≥ 1.0" Precipitation	0	0	0	0	1	1	1	1	1	1	0	0	6
Mean Snowfall (in.)	11.0	9.8	8.6	2.8	0.2	0.0	0.0	0.0	0.0	0.5	6.0	12.7	51.6
Maximum Snow Depth (in.)	37	38	27	16	3	0	0	0	0	4	12	23	38
Days With ≥ 1.0" Snow Depth	28	27	21	3	0	0	0	0	0	0	6	25	110

Sheboygan *Sheboygan County* Elevation: 647 ft. Latitude: 43° 45' N Longitude: 87° 43' W

	JAN	FEB	MAR	APR	MAY	JUN	JUL	AUG	SEP	OCT	NOV	DEC	YEAR
Mean Maximum Temp. (°F)	30.6	33.6	42.1	53.3	64.1	75.2	81.1	79.9	72.1	59.4	46.0	34.1	56.0
Mean Temp. (°F)	22.9	25.9	34.2	44.7	54.6	65.2	71.5	70.9	63.1	50.8	38.8	27.1	47.5
Mean Minimum Temp. (°F)	15.2	18.1	26.3	36.1	45.2	55.1	61.9	62.0	54.2	42.2	31.6	20.0	39.0
Extreme Maximum Temp. (°F)	58	63	82	92	92	101	108	100	96	88	76	65	108
Extreme Minimum Temp. (°F)	-26	-25	-6	14	29	36	47	43	33	21	4	-21	-26
Days Maximum Temp. ≥ 90°F	0	0	0	0	0	2	4	3	1	0	0	0	10
Days Maximum Temp. ≤ 32°F	17	12	4	0	0	0	0	0	0	0	2	11	46
Days Minimum Temp. ≤ 32°F	29	25	23	8	0	0	0	0	0	3	15	27	130
Days Minimum Temp. ≤ 0°F	5	2	0	0	0	0	0	0	0	0	0	3	10
Heating Degree Days (base 65°F)	1,298	1,099	947	604	327	81	8	9	116	437	778	1,168	6,872
Cooling Degree Days (base 65°F)	0	0	0	2	14	93	219	201	67	4	0	0	600
Mean Precipitation (in.)	1.74	1.50	1.88	3.09	3.28	3.62	3.18	3.88	3.32	2.73	2.62	1.75	32.59
Extreme Maximum Daily Precip. (in.)	1.01	1.59	2.60	2.12	4.21	4.07	4.41	10.84	5.19	2.04	3.67	1.61	10.84
Days With ≥ 0.1" Precipitation	5	4	5	6	7	7	6	6	7	6	6	5	70
Days With ≥ 0.5" Precipitation	1	1	1	2	2	2	2	2	2	2	2	1	20
Days With ≥ 1.0" Precipitation	0	0	0	1	1	1	1	1	1	0	0	0	6
Mean Snowfall (in.)	13.7	11.1	6.7	1.8	trace	0.0	0.0	0.0	0.0	0.1	2.0	8.8	44.2
Maximum Snow Depth (in.)	25	28	16	4	trace	0	0	0	0	trace	11	36	36
Days With ≥ 1.0" Snow Depth	18	16	7	1	0	0	0	0	0	0	1	11	54

St Croix Falls *Polk County* Elevation: 770 ft. Latitude: 45° 25' N Longitude: 92° 39' W

	JAN	FEB	MAR	APR	MAY	JUN	JUL	AUG	SEP	OCT	NOV	DEC	YEAR
Mean Maximum Temp. (°F)	24.2	29.5	41.5	57.9	70.3	79.2	83.6	81.0	72.3	58.6	41.6	27.6	55.6
Mean Temp. (°F)	12.8	17.8	30.0	45.3	57.4	66.8	71.4	69.4	60.6	47.4	32.5	17.8	44.1
Mean Minimum Temp. (°F)	1.4	6.0	18.5	32.5	44.4	54.5	59.2	57.7	48.9	36.2	23.2	8.0	32.5
Extreme Maximum Temp. (°F)	57	63	83	93	96	99	105	102	94	90	76	66	105
Extreme Minimum Temp. (°F)	-42	-43	-24	-1	16	30	38	34	25	11	-17	-39	-43
Days Maximum Temp. ≥ 90°F	0	0	0	0	1	3	6	3	1	0	0	0	14
Days Maximum Temp. ≤ 32°F	22	16	6	0	0	0	0	0	0	0	6	20	70
Days Minimum Temp. ≤ 32°F	31	27	27	15	3	0	0	0	1	12	25	31	172
Days Minimum Temp. ≤ 0°F	15	10	4	0	0	0	0	0	0	0	1	10	40
Heating Degree Days (base 65°F)	1,613	1,331	1,077	589	262	61	11	24	179	544	970	1,458	8,119
Cooling Degree Days (base 65°F)	0	0	0	4	33	123	218	168	54	4	0	0	604
Mean Precipitation (in.)	0.67	0.62	1.29	2.60	3.54	4.03	3.95	4.07	3.75	2.80	1.39	0.76	29.47
Extreme Maximum Daily Precip. (in.)	1.07	0.88	1.00	2.09	2.37	3.00	4.70	4.16	3.75	3.70	1.82	1.00	4.70
Days With ≥ 0.1" Precipitation	2	2	4	6	7	7	7	6	6	6	4	3	60
Days With ≥ 0.5" Precipitation	0	0	1	2	3	3	3	3	2	2	1	0	20
Days With ≥ 1.0" Precipitation	0	0	0	0	1	1	1	1	1	1	0	0	6
Mean Snowfall (in.)	8.4	6.1	7.0	1.5	0.0	0.0	0.0	0.0	0.0	0.4	6.3	8.0	37.7
Maximum Snow Depth (in.)	39	38	24	10	trace	0	0	0	0	4	31	30	39
Days With ≥ 1.0" Snow Depth	28	25	17	1	0	0	0	0	0	0	6	22	99

The period of record for all cooperative weather station data is 1980 – 2009. See User Guide for detailed explanation of data.

Sturgeon Bay Exp Farm *Door County* Elevation: 655 ft. Latitude: 44° 52' N Longitude: 87° 20' W

	JAN	FEB	MAR	APR	MAY	JUN	JUL	AUG	SEP	OCT	NOV	DEC	YEAR
Mean Maximum Temp. (°F)	26.1	29.3	38.6	52.1	64.0	74.0	78.9	77.5	69.7	56.2	43.0	30.6	53.3
Mean Temp. (°F)	18.6	21.4	30.5	42.8	53.5	63.5	68.9	68.1	60.4	48.0	36.4	24.2	44.7
Mean Minimum Temp. (°F)	11.1	13.4	22.4	33.5	43.0	53.1	58.8	58.6	51.1	39.8	29.7	17.8	36.0
Extreme Maximum Temp. (°F)	52	54	76	85	90	96	99	98	92	83	74	60	99
Extreme Minimum Temp. (°F)	-29	-28	-8	5	26	32	40	40	27	20	5	-19	-29
Days Maximum Temp. ≥ 90°F	0	0	0	0	0	1	1	1	0	0	0	0	3
Days Maximum Temp. ≤ 32°F	22	17	8	1	0	0	0	0	0	0	3	16	67
Days Minimum Temp. ≤ 32°F	30	27	26	13	2	0	0	0	0	5	19	29	151
Days Minimum Temp. ≤ 0°F	7	5	1	0	0	0	0	0	0	0	0	3	16
Heating Degree Days (base 65°F)	1,432	1,228	1,062	658	357	104	23	31	169	520	853	1,257	7,694
Cooling Degree Days (base 65°F)	0	0	0	0	9	66	151	133	38	1	0	0	398
Mean Precipitation (in.)	1.72	1.24	1.93	2.79	3.10	3.53	3.37	3.48	3.21	3.08	2.48	1.81	31.74
Extreme Maximum Daily Precip. (in.)	1.32	1.06	1.60	1.98	1.76	2.80	3.96	3.79	2.10	2.80	1.95	1.33	3.96
Days With ≥ 0.1" Precipitation	5	4	5	7	7	7	7	7	7	7	6	5	74
Days With ≥ 0.5" Precipitation	1	0	1	2	2	2	2	2	2	2	1	1	18
Days With ≥ 1.0" Precipitation	0	0	0	1	1	1	1	1	1	1	0	0	7
Mean Snowfall (in.)	14.8	10.6	8.0	2.3	0.1	0.0	0.0	0.0	trace	0.1	2.7	13.2	51.8
Maximum Snow Depth (in.)	42	41	27	7	1	0	0	0	trace	1	6	29	42
Days With ≥ 1.0" Snow Depth	24	26	18	2	0	0	0	0	0	0	3	17	90

Superior *Douglas County* Elevation: 629 ft. Latitude: 46° 42' N Longitude: 92° 01' W

	JAN	FEB	MAR	APR	MAY	JUN	JUL	AUG	SEP	OCT	NOV	DEC	YEAR
Mean Maximum Temp. (°F)	22.7	26.7	35.4	47.9	58.8	68.9	76.7	74.5	66.6	53.2	38.9	26.0	49.7
Mean Temp. (°F)	13.8	17.9	27.6	39.6	49.6	58.9	67.0	65.9	57.8	45.4	31.9	18.3	41.1
Mean Minimum Temp. (°F)	4.9	9.0	19.9	31.3	40.5	48.9	57.2	57.2	49.0	37.3	24.9	10.6	32.6
Extreme Maximum Temp. (°F)	53	59	72	85	94	98	101	99	94	89	70	57	101
Extreme Minimum Temp. (°F)	-33	-37	-19	0	22	21	41	36	24	14	-11	-32	-37
Days Maximum Temp. ≥ 90°F	0	0	0	0	0	1	2	1	0	0	0	0	4
Days Maximum Temp. ≤ 32°F	25	19	12	1	0	0	0	0	0	0	7	21	85
Days Minimum Temp. ≤ 32°F	31	27	28	16	3	0	0	0	1	8	23	30	167
Days Minimum Temp. ≤ 0°F	12	8	2	0	0	0	0	0	0	0	1	8	31
Heating Degree Days (base 65°F)	1,582	1,325	1,151	755	474	204	54	61	229	603	985	1,443	8,866
Cooling Degree Days (base 65°F)	0	0	0	0	4	28	123	95	22	1	0	0	273
Mean Precipitation (in.)	0.88	0.76	1.46	2.48	3.05	3.87	4.03	3.67	4.18	2.94	1.90	1.07	30.29
Extreme Maximum Daily Precip. (in.)	0.80	0.85	1.64	2.82	1.80	2.83	4.07	3.68	4.00	3.98	1.87	1.41	4.07
Days With ≥ 0.1" Precipitation	3	2	4	5	7	8	7	6	7	6	4	3	62
Days With ≥ 0.5" Precipitation	0	0	1	2	2	3	3	2	3	2	1	0	19
Days With ≥ 1.0" Precipitation	0	0	0	0	1	1	1	1	1	1	0	0	6
Mean Snowfall (in.)	13.3	9.2	9.1	2.3	0.1	0.0	0.0	0.0	0.0	0.3	6.9	11.9	53.1
Maximum Snow Depth (in.)	50	50	41	23	1	0	0	0	0	3	40	36	50
Days With ≥ 1.0" Snow Depth	27	24	20	3	0	0	0	0	0	0	7	20	101

Two Rivers *Manitowoc County* Elevation: 599 ft. Latitude: 44° 08' N Longitude: 87° 34' W

	JAN	FEB	MAR	APR	MAY	JUN	JUL	AUG	SEP	OCT	NOV	DEC	YEAR
Mean Maximum Temp. (°F)	27.2	29.9	38.3	49.4	59.3	68.9	74.8	75.1	66.9	54.7	43.0	31.3	51.6
Mean Temp. (°F)	20.1	22.8	31.4	42.2	51.5	60.9	67.1	67.6	59.7	47.9	36.7	24.7	44.4
Mean Minimum Temp. (°F)	13.0	15.7	24.4	35.0	43.6	52.8	59.3	60.2	52.3	40.9	30.3	18.0	37.1
Extreme Maximum Temp. (°F)	53	57	77	82	89	95	96	97	89	80	73	62	97
Extreme Minimum Temp. (°F)	-25	-26	-7	12	24	36	44	42	29	20	3	-21	-26
Days Maximum Temp. ≥ 90°F	0	0	0	0	0	0	1	0	0	0	0	0	1
Days Maximum Temp. ≤ 32°F	20	16	7	0	0	0	0	0	0	0	3	15	61
Days Minimum Temp. ≤ 32°F	30	27	24	10	1	0	0	0	0	4	18	28	142
Days Minimum Temp. ≤ 0°F	6	4	1	0	0	0	0	0	0	0	0	3	14
Heating Degree Days (base 65°F)	1,385	1,186	1,037	678	415	149	29	25	178	525	843	1,244	7,694
Cooling Degree Days (base 65°F)	0	0	0	0	2	32	101	113	24	0	0	0	272
Mean Precipitation (in.)	1.52	1.37	2.00	2.88	3.11	3.33	3.10	3.44	3.17	2.47	2.32	1.69	30.40
Extreme Maximum Daily Precip. (in.)	1.37	1.10	3.16	1.85	1.80	3.90	3.31	4.37	4.72	1.74	1.75	1.38	4.72
Days With ≥ 0.1" Precipitation	4	4	5	7	7	7	6	6	6	6	6	5	69
Days With ≥ 0.5" Precipitation	1	1	1	2	2	2	2	2	2	2	1	1	19
Days With ≥ 1.0" Precipitation	0	0	0	1	1	1	1	1	1	0	0	0	6
Mean Snowfall (in.)	11.2	7.9	***5.3***	0.9	0.0	0.0	0.0	0.0	0.0	0.1	1.8	***9.3***	***36.5***
Maximum Snow Depth (in.)	41	40	18	6	0	0	0	0	0	2	***9***	39	***41***
Days With ≥ 1.0" Snow Depth	23	23	12	1	0	0	0	0	0	0	2	14	75

Watertown *Jefferson County* Elevation: 825 ft. Latitude: 43° 11' N Longitude: 88° 44' W

	JAN	FEB	MAR	APR	MAY	JUN	JUL	AUG	SEP	OCT	NOV	DEC	YEAR
Mean Maximum Temp. (°F)	27.0	31.2	42.5	56.9	68.7	78.6	82.3	80.3	72.9	59.7	45.1	31.2	56.4
Mean Temp. (°F)	18.6	22.6	33.5	46.6	57.7	67.7	71.8	69.8	61.8	49.4	37.0	23.4	46.7
Mean Minimum Temp. (°F)	10.2	13.9	24.5	36.2	46.8	56.7	61.2	59.3	50.7	39.1	28.7	15.7	36.9
Extreme Maximum Temp. (°F)	57	64	81	91	94	101	101	102	95	87	74	66	102
Extreme Minimum Temp. (°F)	-31	-27	-9	10	25	35	47	41	26	16	1	-27	-31
Days Maximum Temp. ≥ 90°F	0	0	0	0	0	3	4	3	1	0	0	0	11
Days Maximum Temp. ≤ 32°F	20	15	6	0	0	0	0	0	0	0	4	16	61
Days Minimum Temp. ≤ 32°F	30	27	24	10	1	0	0	0	0	8	20	29	149
Days Minimum Temp. ≤ 0°F	8	6	1	0	0	0	0	0	0	0	0	4	19
Heating Degree Days (base 65°F)	1,433	1,193	971	552	251	50	8	21	149	482	835	1,281	7,226
Cooling Degree Days (base 65°F)	0	0	0	6	33	138	225	178	61	6	0	0	647
Mean Precipitation (in.)	1.27	1.33	1.85	3.18	3.55	4.92	4.51	4.38	3.88	2.85	2.41	1.77	35.90
Extreme Maximum Daily Precip. (in.)	1.20	1.37	2.36	2.83	3.51	3.98	6.65	2.49	5.10	3.11	2.82	3.00	6.65
Days With ≥ 0.1" Precipitation	4	4	5	7	7	7	7	7	6	6	5	5	70
Days With ≥ 0.5" Precipitation	0	1	1	2	3	3	3	3	2	2	1	1	22
Days With ≥ 1.0" Precipitation	0	0	0	1	1	2	1	1	1	0	0	0	7
Mean Snowfall (in.)	10.2	8.2	4.4	1.2	0.2	0.0	0.0	0.0	trace	0.1	1.9	9.3	35.5
Maximum Snow Depth (in.)	17	14	11	9	3	0	0	0	0	1	8	16	17
Days With ≥ 1.0" Snow Depth	18	16	6	1	0	0	0	0	0	0	2	12	55

The period of record for all cooperative weather station data is 1980 – 2009. See User Guide for detailed explanation of data.

Waukesha *Waukesha County* Elevation: 830 ft. Latitude: 43° 01' N Longitude: 88° 14' W

	JAN	FEB	MAR	APR	MAY	JUN	JUL	AUG	SEP	OCT	NOV	DEC	YEAR
Mean Maximum Temp. (°F)	27.9	32.9	43.3	56.7	68.2	78.2	82.6	80.5	73.3	60.1	45.6	32.5	56.8
Mean Temp. (°F)	20.2	25.0	34.4	46.8	57.6	67.3	72.2	70.6	62.7	50.4	37.7	25.2	47.5
Mean Minimum Temp. (°F)	12.4	17.0	25.5	36.8	46.9	56.5	61.8	60.6	52.0	40.6	29.8	17.8	38.1
Extreme Maximum Temp. (°F)	58	66	82	91	91	100	109	98	96	87	74	68	109
Extreme Minimum Temp. (°F)	-27	-28	-9	7	26	34	42	40	30	19	2	-23	-28
Days Maximum Temp. ≥ 90°F	0	0	0	0	0	3	5	3	1	0	0	0	12
Days Maximum Temp. ≤ 32°F	20	13	5	0	0	0	0	0	0	0	3	15	56
Days Minimum Temp. ≤ 32°F	30	26	24	9	1	0	0	0	0	5	18	28	141
Days Minimum Temp. ≤ 0°F	6	3	0	0	0	0	0	0	0	0	0	3	12
Heating Degree Days (base 65°F)	1,384	1,125	942	549	255	59	9	16	133	454	812	1,227	6,965
Cooling Degree Days (base 65°F)	0	0	0	6	31	137	240	196	69	7	0	0	686
Mean Precipitation (in.)	1.39	1.42	1.76	3.51	3.52	4.23	3.74	4.73	3.44	2.70	2.45	1.85	34.74
Extreme Maximum Daily Precip. (in.)	1.45	1.60	1.68	2.30	2.71	3.93	4.61	5.02	3.22	1.77	2.42	1.65	5.02
Days With ≥ 0.1" Precipitation	4	4	4	7	7	7	6	7	6	6	5	5	68
Days With ≥ 0.5" Precipitation	1	1	1	2	3	3	2	3	2	2	2	1	23
Days With ≥ 1.0" Precipitation	0	0	0	1	1	1	1	2	1	0	0	0	7
Mean Snowfall (in.)	12.2	8.2	5.6	2.0	trace	0.0	0.0	0.0	0.0	0.1	1.9	10.0	40.0
Maximum Snow Depth (in.)	22	16	12	9	trace	0	0	0	0	2	10	20	22
Days With ≥ 1.0" Snow Depth	21	18	6	1	0	0	0	0	0	0	2	14	62

Wausau Municipal Arpt *Marathon County* Elevation: 1,200 ft. Latitude: 44° 55' N Longitude: 89° 38' W

	JAN	FEB	MAR	APR	MAY	JUN	JUL	AUG	SEP	OCT	NOV	DEC	YEAR
Mean Maximum Temp. (°F)	23.6	28.4	39.4	55.1	67.5	76.4	80.7	78.0	69.1	55.7	40.2	27.1	53.4
Mean Temp. (°F)	15.2	19.5	30.2	44.6	56.3	65.5	70.1	67.9	59.0	46.5	32.8	19.6	43.9
Mean Minimum Temp. (°F)	6.8	10.5	20.9	34.0	45.0	54.6	59.5	57.8	48.9	37.3	25.5	12.2	34.4
Extreme Maximum Temp. (°F)	51	59	79	88	94	97	102	99	90	84	73	61	102
Extreme Minimum Temp. (°F)	-32	-33	-15	4	23	35	40	39	27	16	-6	-26	-33
Days Maximum Temp. ≥ 90°F	0	0	0	0	0	2	3	1	0	0	0	0	6
Days Maximum Temp. ≤ 32°F	24	18	8	1	0	0	0	0	0	0	7	21	79
Days Minimum Temp. ≤ 32°F	30	27	27	13	2	0	0	0	1	10	24	30	164
Days Minimum Temp. ≤ 0°F	10	7	2	0	0	0	0	0	0	0	0	7	26
Heating Degree Days (base 65°F)	1,538	1,282	1,073	610	286	77	17	35	209	568	958	1,401	8,054
Cooling Degree Days (base 65°F)	0	0	0	4	23	99	182	132	37	2	0	0	479
Mean Precipitation (in.)	1.06	0.92	1.77	2.75	3.53	4.47	3.71	4.28	3.95	2.85	2.00	1.31	32.60
Extreme Maximum Daily Precip. (in.)	1.48	1.28	1.42	1.92	3.05	4.46	2.71	2.81	3.42	1.83	2.04	1.47	4.46
Days With ≥ 0.1" Precipitation	3	3	5	7	7	7	7	7	7	6	5	4	68
Days With ≥ 0.5" Precipitation	0	0	1	2	2	3	2	3	2	2	1	0	18
Days With ≥ 1.0" Precipitation	0	0	0	0	1	1	1	1	1	0	0	0	5
Mean Snowfall (in.)	13.1	9.6	10.3	4.3	0.1	trace	0.0	trace	trace	1.3	7.0	13.6	59.3
Maximum Snow Depth (in.)	26	150	25	14	trace	trace	0	trace	trace	7	12	19	150
Days With ≥ 1.0" Snow Depth	30	27	19	2	0	0	0	0	0	0	6	26	110

West Bend *Washington County* Elevation: 939 ft. Latitude: 43° 22' N Longitude: 88° 05' W

	JAN	FEB	MAR	APR	MAY	JUN	JUL	AUG	SEP	OCT	NOV	DEC	YEAR
Mean Maximum Temp. (°F)	27.6	32.2	41.9	55.3	67.5	77.5	81.5	79.2	71.5	59.1	44.5	32.1	55.8
Mean Temp. (°F)	19.9	24.2	33.1	45.2	55.8	65.5	70.3	68.7	60.5	48.9	36.5	24.7	46.1
Mean Minimum Temp. (°F)	12.1	16.2	24.2	35.0	44.1	53.4	58.9	58.1	49.5	38.7	28.5	17.3	36.3
Extreme Maximum Temp. (°F)	54	65	82	88	91	100	103	105	95	85	74	64	105
Extreme Minimum Temp. (°F)	-30	-25	-11	2	21	33	37	38	25	14	-3	-24	-30
Days Maximum Temp. ≥ 90°F	0	0	0	0	0	2	4	2	0	0	0	0	8
Days Maximum Temp. ≤ 32°F	20	14	6	0	0	0	0	0	0	0	3	14	57
Days Minimum Temp. ≤ 32°F	30	27	26	12	2	0	0	0	1	8	20	29	155
Days Minimum Temp. ≤ 0°F	7	4	1	0	0	0	0	0	0	0	0	3	15
Heating Degree Days (base 65°F)	1,392	1,147	984	594	303	81	16	30	174	494	849	1,241	7,305
Cooling Degree Days (base 65°F)	0	0	0	6	25	102	186	151	45	3	0	0	518
Mean Precipitation (in.)	1.44	1.20	1.67	3.14	3.15	3.71	4.03	4.00	3.69	2.60	2.64	1.53	32.80
Extreme Maximum Daily Precip. (in.)	1.05	1.46	2.55	1.93	3.44	3.39	4.50	2.58	2.75	1.57	2.26	1.54	4.50
Days With ≥ 0.1" Precipitation	5	3	5	7	7	7	7	7	6	7	6	5	72
Days With ≥ 0.5" Precipitation	1	1	1	2	2	3	3	3	3	2	2	1	24
Days With ≥ 1.0" Precipitation	0	0	0	1	1	1	1	1	1	0	0	0	6
Mean Snowfall (in.)	14.5	8.0	6.8	3.0	0.1	0.0	0.0	0.0	0.0	0.2	2.9	9.8	45.3
Maximum Snow Depth (in.)	20	19	15	7	trace	0	0	0	0	trace	7	19	20
Days With ≥ 1.0" Snow Depth	24	21	11	1	0	0	0	0	0	0	3	15	75

Wisconsin Weather Station Rankings

Annual Extreme Maximum Temperature

Highest			Lowest		
Rank	**Station Name**	**°F**	**Rank**	**Station Name**	**°F**
1	Genoa Dam 8	109	1	Antigo	***96***
1	Waukesha	***109***	2	Two Rivers	97
3	La Crosse Municipal Arpt	108	3	Sturgeon Bay Exp Farm	99
3	Milwaukee Mt Mary Col	108	4	Beaver Dam	100
3	Sheboygan	108	4	Kewaunee 3 NW	100
6	Lake Geneva	***106***	4	Menomonie	100
6	Port Washington	106	7	Alma Dam 4	101
8	Blair	105	7	Amery	101
8	Burlington	105	7	Bayfield 6 N	***101***
8	Ellsworth 1 E	***105***	7	Manitowoc	101
8	Hancock Exp Farm	105	7	Oconomowoc	101
8	Hartford 2 W	105	7	Oshkosh	101
8	New London	105	7	Superior	101
8	St Croix Falls	105	14	Arlington Univ Farm	102
8	West Bend	***105***	14	Baraboo	102
16	Bloomer	104	14	Beloit	102
16	Eau Claire County Arpt	***104***	14	Brodhead	102
16	Foxboro	104	14	Couderay 7 W	102
16	Kenosha	104	14	Germantown	102
16	Lake Mills	104	14	Madison Dane Co Regional Arpt	102
16	Marshfield Exp Farm	104	14	Plymouth	102
16	Racine	104	14	River Falls	102
23	Appleton	103	14	Watertown	102
23	Chilton	103	14	Wausau Municipal Arpt	102
23	Cumberland	103	25	Appleton	103

Annual Mean Maximum Temperature

Highest			Lowest		
Rank	**Station Name**	**°F**	**Rank**	**Station Name**	**°F**
1	Lake Geneva	***58.9***	1	Superior	49.7
2	Milwaukee Mt Mary Col	58.3	2	Bayfield 6 N	***51.1***
3	Beloit	57.6	3	Antigo	***51.3***
3	Dalton	***57.6***	4	Two Rivers	51.6
3	Lake Mills	***57.6***	5	Foxboro	***52.2***
6	Brodhead	57.4	6	Kewaunee 3 NW	***52.6***
7	La Crosse Municipal Arpt	57.2	7	Amery	52.8
8	Baraboo	56.9	8	Couderay 7 W	52.9
9	Genoa Dam 8	56.8	9	Cumberland	53.3
9	Waukesha	***56.8***	9	Sturgeon Bay Exp Farm	53.3
11	Beaver Dam	56.5	11	Rosholt 9 NNE	53.4
11	Madison Dane Co Regional Arpt	56.5	11	Wausau Municipal Arpt	53.4
11	Menomonie	56.5	13	Manitowoc	54.1
11	Oconomowoc	56.5	14	Port Washington	54.3
15	Arlington Univ Farm	56.4	14	Racine	54.3
15	Watertown	56.4	16	Green Bay Austin Straubel Intl	54.4
17	Burlington	56.3	17	Bloomer	54.5
18	Sheboygan	56.0	18	Marshfield Exp Farm	54.7
19	Alma Dam 4	55.9	19	Appleton	54.8
19	Milwaukee General Mitchell Field	55.9	19	Eau Claire County Arpt	***54.8***
21	West Bend	***55.8***	19	Fond Du Lac	54.8
22	Blair	55.6	22	River Falls	55.0
22	Hancock Exp Farm	55.6	23	Ellsworth 1 E	***55.1***
22	Hartford 2 W	55.6	23	New London	55.1
22	St Croix Falls	55.6	23	Oshkosh	55.1

 Rankings include 25 highest/lowest stations. If state has less than 25 stations, all stations are included. The period of record is 1980–2009. See User Guide for detailed explanation of data.

Annual Mean Temperature

Highest			Lowest		
Rank	Station Name	°F	Rank	Station Name	°F
1	Milwaukee Mt Mary Col	49.1	1	Foxboro	***40.3***
2	Lake Geneva	***49.0***	2	Antigo	***41.0***
3	Beloit	48.1	3	Superior	41.2
4	Milwaukee General Mitchell Field	48.0	4	Bayfield 6 N	***41.6***
5	Genoa Dam 8	47.9	4	Couderay 7 W	41.6
6	Lake Mills	***47.6***	6	Rosholt 9 NNE	42.4
7	Kenosha	47.5	7	Amery	42.9
7	La Crosse Municipal Arpt	47.5	8	Cumberland	43.1
7	Sheboygan	47.5	9	Blair	43.9
7	Waukesha	***47.5***	9	Bloomer	43.9
11	Racine	47.3	9	Wausau Municipal Arpt	43.9
12	Alma Dam 4	47.1	12	St Croix Falls	44.1
13	Beaver Dam	46.8	13	Marshfield Exp Farm	44.3
13	Dalton	***46.8***	14	Two Rivers	44.4
13	Oconomowoc	46.8	15	Eau Claire County Arpt	***44.5***
16	Watertown	46.7	15	Ellsworth 1 E	***44.5***
17	Brodhead	46.6	17	Kewaunee 3 NW	***44.6***
17	Madison Dane Co Regional Arpt	46.6	17	River Falls	44.6
19	Burlington	46.4	19	New London	***44.7***
20	Fond Du Lac	46.2	19	Sturgeon Bay Exp Farm	44.7
20	Plymouth	46.2	21	Green Bay Austin Straubel Intl	44.9
20	Port Washington	46.2	22	Baraboo	45.1
23	Arlington Univ Farm	46.1	23	Germantown	45.4
23	Oshkosh	46.1	23	Hancock Exp Farm	45.4
23	West Bend	***46.1***	23	Hartford 2 W	45.4

Annual Mean Minimum Temperature

Highest			Lowest		
Rank	Station Name	°F	Rank	Station Name	°F
1	Racine	40.3	1	Foxboro	***28.3***
2	Milwaukee General Mitchell Field	40.0	2	Couderay 7 W	30.1
3	Milwaukee Mt Mary Col	39.8	3	Antigo	***30.6***
4	Kenosha	39.6	4	Rosholt 9 NNE	31.4
5	Lake Geneva	***39.1***	5	Bayfield 6 N	***32.1***
6	Sheboygan	39.0	6	Blair	32.2
7	Genoa Dam 8	38.8	7	St Croix Falls	32.6
8	Beloit	38.5	7	Superior	32.6
9	Alma Dam 4	38.3	9	Cumberland	32.8
10	Waukesha	***38.2***	10	Amery	32.9
11	Port Washington	38.1	11	Baraboo	33.3
12	La Crosse Municipal Arpt	37.7	12	Bloomer	33.4
13	Fond Du Lac	37.6	13	Ellsworth 1 E	***33.7***
13	Lake Mills	***37.6***	14	Marshfield Exp Farm	33.8
15	Manitowoc	37.5	15	River Falls	34.1
16	Two Rivers	37.1	16	Eau Claire County Arpt	***34.2***
17	Beaver Dam	37.0	16	New London	***34.2***
17	Oconomowoc	37.0	18	Wausau Municipal Arpt	34.4
17	Oshkosh	37.0	19	Menomonie	34.9
20	Plymouth	36.9	20	Hancock Exp Farm	35.1
20	Watertown	36.9	21	Hartford 2 W	35.2
22	Lancaster 4 WSW	36.6	22	Green Bay Austin Straubel Intl	35.4
22	Madison Dane Co Regional Arpt	36.6	23	Germantown	35.5
24	Kewaunee 3 NW	***36.5***	24	Brodhead	35.7
25	Appleton	36.4	25	Arlington Univ Farm	35.8

Annual Extreme Minimum Temperature

Highest Rank	Highest Station Name	Highest °F	Lowest Rank	Lowest Station Name	Lowest °F
1	Beloit	-26	1	Couderay 7 W	-55
1	Milwaukee General Mitchell Field	-26	2	Blair	-45
1	Milwaukee Mt Mary Col	-26	3	Amery	-43
1	Sheboygan	-26	3	Foxboro	-43
1	Two Rivers	-26	3	St Croix Falls	-43
6	Burlington	-27	6	Baraboo	-41
6	Lake Geneva	***-27***	6	Rosholt 9 NNE	-41
6	Manitowoc	-27	8	Ellsworth 1 E	***-40***
9	Green Bay Austin Straubel Intl	-28	8	Germantown	-40
9	Waukesha	***-28***	8	Menomonie	-40
11	Appleton	-29	11	Antigo	***-39***
11	Fond Du Lac	-29	11	Cumberland	-39
11	Kewaunee 3 NW	-29	13	Alma Dam 4	-38
11	Lake Mills	-29	13	Genoa Dam 8	-38
11	Madison Dane Co Regional Arpt	-29	15	Bloomer	-37
11	Oconomowoc	-29	15	Hancock Exp Farm	-37
11	Plymouth	-29	15	Superior	-37
11	Port Washington	-29	18	Arlington Univ Farm	-36
11	Sturgeon Bay Exp Farm	-29	18	River Falls	-36
20	Chilton	-30	20	Eau Claire County Arpt	***-35***
20	Oshkosh	-30	20	Hartford 2 W	-35
20	West Bend	***-30***	20	La Crosse Municipal Arpt	-35
23	Beaver Dam	-31	23	Bayfield 6 N	***-34***
23	Kenosha	-31	23	Brodhead	-34
23	Lancaster 4 WSW	-31	23	Dalton	-34

July Mean Maximum Temperature

Highest Rank	Highest Station Name	Highest °F	Lowest Rank	Lowest Station Name	Lowest °F
1	Lake Geneva	***85.6***	1	Two Rivers	74.8
2	La Crosse Municipal Arpt	84.7	2	Superior	76.7
3	Milwaukee Mt Mary Col	84.4	3	Bayfield 6 N	***76.8***
4	Lake Mills	84.1	4	Kewaunee 3 NW	77.3
5	Dalton	83.7	5	Port Washington	78.0
6	St Croix Falls	83.6	5	Racine	78.0
7	Beloit	83.1	7	Antigo	***78.6***
7	Brodhead	83.1	8	Sturgeon Bay Exp Farm	78.9
9	Genoa Dam 8	83.0	9	Kenosha	79.0
9	Menomonie	83.0	10	Manitowoc	79.2
11	Baraboo	82.8	11	Foxboro	79.3
11	Eau Claire County Arpt	***82.8***	12	Rosholt 9 NNE	79.9
13	Bloomer	82.6	13	Milwaukee General Mitchell Field	80.5
13	Waukesha	82.6	14	Amery	80.6
15	Alma Dam 4	82.5	14	Germantown	80.6
15	River Falls	82.5	16	Wausau Municipal Arpt	80.7
17	Blair	82.4	17	Fond Du Lac	80.8
17	Madison Dane Co Regional Arpt	82.4	17	Green Bay Austin Straubel Intl	80.8
19	Arlington Univ Farm	82.3	19	Couderay 7 W	80.9
19	Watertown	82.3	20	Lancaster 4 WSW	81.1
21	Beaver Dam	82.2	20	Sheboygan	81.1
22	Ellsworth 1 E	81.9	22	Burlington	81.3
22	Oconomowoc	81.9	22	Cumberland	81.3
24	Appleton	81.8	22	Hartford 2 W	81.3
25	Hancock Exp Farm	81.7	22	New London	81.3

Rankings include 25 highest/lowest stations. If state has less than 25 stations, all stations are included. The period of record is 1980–2009. See User Guide for detailed explanation of data.

January Mean Minimum Temperature

Highest Rank	Station Name	°F	Lowest Rank	Station Name	°F
1	Milwaukee General Mitchell Field	15.7	1	Foxboro	0.1
2	Kenosha	15.5	2	Couderay 7 W	1.2
3	Milwaukee Mt Mary Col	15.2	3	St Croix Falls	1.4
3	Racine	15.2	4	Amery	2.5
3	Sheboygan	15.2	4	Antigo	2.5
6	Lake Geneva	*14.2*	4	Cumberland	2.5
6	Port Washington	14.2	7	Blair	3.3
8	Beloit	13.0	8	Bloomer	4.1
8	Kewaunee 3 NW	13.0	9	Rosholt 9 NNE	4.2
8	Two Rivers	13.0	10	Ellsworth 1 E	4.9
11	Manitowoc	12.9	10	Superior	4.9
12	Waukesha	*12.4*	12	Eau Claire County Arpt	*5.4*
13	Plymouth	12.2	12	River Falls	5.4
14	West Bend	*12.1*	14	Bayfield 6 N	6.1
15	Burlington	11.6	15	Marshfield Exp Farm	6.3
16	Lake Mills	11.5	16	Baraboo	6.8
17	Sturgeon Bay Exp Farm	11.1	16	Wausau Municipal Arpt	6.8
18	Beaver Dam	11.0	18	Menomonie	6.9
18	Fond Du Lac	11.0	19	Hancock Exp Farm	7.7
18	Madison Dane Co Regional Arpt	11.0	20	New London	7.8
21	Genoa Dam 8	10.8	21	La Crosse Municipal Arpt	9.0
22	Germantown	10.6	21	Lancaster 4 WSW	9.0
22	Oconomowoc	10.6	23	Hartford 2 W	9.2
24	Dalton	10.5	24	Brodhead	9.4
25	Appleton	10.2	25	Arlington Univ Farm	9.6

Number of Days Annually Maximum Temperature ≥ 90°F

Highest Rank	Station Name	Days	Lowest Rank	Station Name	Days
1	Lake Geneva	*21*	1	Two Rivers	1
2	Milwaukee Mt Mary Col	19	2	Antigo	2
3	La Crosse Municipal Arpt	17	2	Bayfield 6 N	*2*
4	St Croix Falls	14	4	Sturgeon Bay Exp Farm	3
5	Beloit	13	5	Kewaunee 3 NW	4
5	Lake Mills	13	5	Manitowoc	4
7	Baraboo	12	5	Rosholt 9 NNE	4
7	Brodhead	12	5	Superior	4
7	Dalton	12	9	Amery	5
7	Eau Claire County Arpt	*12*	9	Foxboro	5
7	Waukesha	*12*	11	Couderay 7 W	6
12	Watertown	11	11	Ellsworth 1 E	*6*
13	Arlington Univ Farm	10	11	Green Bay Austin Straubel Intl	6
13	Menomonie	10	11	Kenosha	6
13	Sheboygan	10	11	Lancaster 4 WSW	6
16	Bloomer	9	11	Port Washington	6
16	Burlington	9	11	Racine	6
16	Genoa Dam 8	9	11	Wausau Municipal Arpt	6
16	Hartford 2 W	9	19	Alma Dam 4	7
16	Milwaukee General Mitchell Field	9	19	Chilton	7
16	Oconomowoc	9	19	Cumberland	7
22	Appleton	8	19	Fond Du Lac	7
22	Beaver Dam	8	19	Germantown	7
22	Blair	8	19	Marshfield Exp Farm	7
22	Hancock Exp Farm	8	19	New London	7

Number of Days Annually Maximum Temperature ≤ 32°F

Highest Rank	Station Name	Days	Lowest Rank	Station Name	Days
1	Antigo	90	1	Sheboygan	46
2	Superior	85	2	Kenosha	47
3	Amery	84	2	Milwaukee Mt Mary Col	47
4	Bayfield 6 N	***83***	4	Lake Geneva	***49***
5	Couderay 7 W	82	5	Milwaukee General Mitchell Field	51
5	Cumberland	82	5	Port Washington	51
5	Foxboro	82	5	Racine	51
8	Wausau Municipal Arpt	79	8	Beloit	54
9	Rosholt 9 NNE	78	8	Lake Mills	54
10	Bloomer	77	10	Brodhead	55
11	Eau Claire County Arpt	***74***	11	Dalton	56
12	Marshfield Exp Farm	73	11	Waukesha	***56***
12	River Falls	73	13	Baraboo	57
14	Ellsworth 1 E	***71***	13	West Bend	***57***
15	Appleton	70	15	Burlington	58
15	St Croix Falls	70	15	Manitowoc	58
17	Hancock Exp Farm	68	17	Kewaunee 3 NW	59
18	Green Bay Austin Straubel Intl	67	17	Madison Dane Co Regional Arpt	59
18	Lancaster 4 WSW	67	17	Oconomowoc	59
18	Sturgeon Bay Exp Farm	67	20	Genoa Dam 8	60
21	Blair	66	20	La Crosse Municipal Arpt	60
21	Chilton	66	22	Two Rivers	61
21	New London	66	22	Watertown	61
24	Alma Dam 4	65	24	Beaver Dam	62
24	Oshkosh	65	24	Hartford 2 W	62

Number of Days Annually Minimum Temperature ≤ 32°F

Highest Rank	Station Name	Days	Lowest Rank	Station Name	Days
1	Couderay 7 W	190	1	Racine	122
2	Foxboro	189	2	Kenosha	128
3	Antigo	181	2	Milwaukee General Mitchell Field	128
4	Rosholt 9 NNE	180	4	Sheboygan	130
5	Bayfield 6 N	***177***	5	Milwaukee Mt Mary Col	132
5	Blair	177	6	Port Washington	134
7	Baraboo	174	7	Kewaunee 3 NW	138
8	St Croix Falls	172	7	Lake Geneva	***138***
9	Amery	170	9	Genoa Dam 8	140
10	Cumberland	169	10	Alma Dam 4	141
10	Ellsworth 1 E	***169***	10	Beloit	141
12	Bloomer	168	10	Waukesha	***141***
13	Eau Claire County Arpt	***167***	13	Lake Mills	142
13	Marshfield Exp Farm	167	13	Two Rivers	142
13	Superior	167	15	Manitowoc	143
16	River Falls	165	16	La Crosse Municipal Arpt	144
17	New London	164	17	Fond Du Lac	146
17	Wausau Municipal Arpt	164	18	Oshkosh	148
19	Menomonie	162	19	Beaver Dam	149
20	Arlington Univ Farm	160	19	Watertown	149
20	Germantown	160	21	Oconomowoc	150
20	Hancock Exp Farm	160	21	Plymouth	150
23	Brodhead	159	23	Sturgeon Bay Exp Farm	151
23	Green Bay Austin Straubel Intl	159	24	Burlington	153
25	Dalton	158	24	Madison Dane Co Regional Arpt	153

 Rankings include 25 highest/lowest stations. If state has less than 25 stations, all stations are included. The period of record is 1980–2009. See User Guide for detailed explanation of data.

Number of Days Annually Minimum Temperature ≤ 0°F

Highest			Lowest		
Rank	**Station Name**	**Days**	**Rank**	**Station Name**	**Days**
1	Foxboro	44	1	Milwaukee General Mitchell Field	8
2	Couderay 7 W	42	2	Kenosha	9
3	Antigo	40	2	Milwaukee Mt Mary Col	9
3	St Croix Falls	40	4	Racine	10
5	Cumberland	37	4	Sheboygan	10
6	Amery	36	6	Lake Geneva	***11***
7	Blair	35	6	Port Washington	11
8	Bloomer	34	8	Waukesha	***12***
8	Rosholt 9 NNE	34	9	Beloit	13
10	Ellsworth 1 E	***31***	9	Manitowoc	13
10	River Falls	31	11	Kewaunee 3 NW	14
10	Superior	31	11	Two Rivers	14
13	Eau Claire County Arpt	***30***	13	Burlington	15
14	Baraboo	27	13	Plymouth	15
14	Bayfield 6 N	***27***	13	West Bend	***15***
14	Marshfield Exp Farm	27	16	Lake Mills	16
14	Menomonie	27	16	Sturgeon Bay Exp Farm	16
18	Hancock Exp Farm	26	18	Fond Du Lac	17
18	Wausau Municipal Arpt	26	19	Beaver Dam	18
20	New London	25	19	Chilton	18
21	Lancaster 4 WSW	22	19	Genoa Dam 8	18
22	Arlington Univ Farm	21	19	Germantown	18
22	Brodhead	21	19	Madison Dane Co Regional Arpt	18
22	Hartford 2 W	21	19	Oconomowoc	18
22	La Crosse Municipal Arpt	21	25	Alma Dam 4	19

Number of Annual Heating Degree Days

Highest			Lowest		
Rank	**Station Name**	**Num.**	**Rank**	**Station Name**	**Num.**
1	Foxboro	***9,178***	1	Milwaukee Mt Mary Col	6,541
2	Antigo	***8,963***	2	Lake Geneva	***6,598***
3	Superior	8,866	3	Milwaukee General Mitchell Field	6,789
4	Couderay 7 W	8,839	4	Beloit	6,796
5	Bayfield 6 N	***8,687***	5	Kenosha	6,857
6	Rosholt 9 NNE	8,460	6	Sheboygan	6,872
7	Amery	8,444	7	Racine	6,903
8	Cumberland	8,391	8	Genoa Dam 8	6,934
9	Bloomer	8,126	9	Lake Mills	***6,948***
10	St Croix Falls	8,119	10	Waukesha	***6,965***
11	Blair	8,089	11	La Crosse Municipal Arpt	7,107
12	Wausau Municipal Arpt	8,054	12	Alma Dam 4	7,164
13	Eau Claire County Arpt	***7,970***	13	Dalton	***7,170***
14	Marshfield Exp Farm	7,937	14	Beaver Dam	7,173
15	River Falls	7,925	15	Oconomowoc	7,175
16	Ellsworth 1 E	***7,900***	16	Port Washington	7,193
17	New London	***7,783***	17	Watertown	7,226
18	Sturgeon Bay Exp Farm	7,694	18	Madison Dane Co Regional Arpt	7,227
18	Two Rivers	7,694	19	Brodhead	7,237
20	Green Bay Austin Straubel Intl	7,693	20	Burlington	7,246
21	Kewaunee 3 NW	***7,674***	21	West Bend	***7,305***
22	Baraboo	7,662	22	Plymouth	7,333
23	Hancock Exp Farm	7,623	23	Fond Du Lac	7,342
24	Appleton	7,576	24	Manitowoc	7,352
25	Hartford 2 W	7,545	25	Arlington Univ Farm	7,374

Number of Annual Cooling Degree Days

Highest			Lowest		
Rank	Station Name	Num.	Rank	Station Name	Num.
1	Lake Geneva	***869***	1	Foxboro	***250***
2	Milwaukee Mt Mary Col	848	2	Bayfield 6 N	***263***
3	La Crosse Municipal Arpt	830	3	Two Rivers	272
4	Genoa Dam 8	787	4	Superior	273
5	Alma Dam 4	748	5	Antigo	***294***
6	Beloit	741	6	Rosholt 9 NNE	340
7	Lake Mills	***733***	7	Kewaunee 3 NW	***346***
8	Waukesha	***686***	8	Sturgeon Bay Exp Farm	398
9	Milwaukee General Mitchell Field	679	9	Couderay 7 W	415
10	Watertown	647	10	Port Washington	451
11	Oshkosh	643	11	Manitowoc	467
12	Dalton	***636***	12	Amery	473
13	Brodhead	629	13	Green Bay Austin Straubel Intl	474
13	Oconomowoc	629	14	Wausau Municipal Arpt	479
15	Appleton	618	15	Marshfield Exp Farm	481
16	Eau Claire County Arpt	***616***	16	Germantown	490
17	Beaver Dam	613	17	New London	***491***
17	Fond Du Lac	613	18	Blair	497
19	Madison Dane Co Regional Arpt	610	19	Cumberland	499
19	Menomonie	610	20	Hartford 2 W	507
21	St Croix Falls	604	21	Ellsworth 1 E	***518***
22	Sheboygan	600	21	West Bend	***518***
23	Lancaster 4 WSW	585	23	Baraboo	523
24	River Falls	581	24	Bloomer	552
25	Arlington Univ Farm	577	25	Racine	562

Annual Precipitation

Highest			Lowest		
Rank	Station Name	Inches	Rank	Station Name	Inches
1	Brodhead	36.47	1	Antigo	28.73
2	Couderay 7 W	36.43	2	Green Bay Austin Straubel Intl	29.19
3	Beloit	36.21	3	St Croix Falls	29.47
4	Racine	36.11	4	Kewaunee 3 NW	29.67
5	Kenosha	35.96	5	Fond Du Lac	29.84
6	Watertown	35.90	6	Foxboro	30.05
7	Lake Geneva	***35.83***	7	Appleton	30.14
8	Baraboo	35.57	8	Superior	30.29
9	Oconomowoc	35.28	9	Manitowoc	30.34
10	Plymouth	35.27	10	Two Rivers	30.40
11	Lake Mills	35.08	11	Chilton	31.04
12	Alma Dam 4	34.92	12	Menomonie	31.08
13	Waukesha	***34.74***	13	New London	***31.12***
14	Ellsworth 1 E	***34.72***	14	River Falls	31.30
15	Genoa Dam 8	34.69	15	Oshkosh	31.37
16	Milwaukee General Mitchell Field	34.66	16	Milwaukee Mt Mary Col	31.46
17	Germantown	34.65	17	Bloomer	31.62
18	Lancaster 4 WSW	34.56	18	Sturgeon Bay Exp Farm	31.74
19	Beaver Dam	34.40	19	Amery	31.75
20	Madison Dane Co Regional Arpt	34.32	20	Rosholt 9 NNE	32.16
21	Blair	34.23	21	Marshfield Exp Farm	32.23
22	Dalton	34.15	22	Eau Claire County Arpt	***32.28***
23	Arlington Univ Farm	33.86	23	Hancock Exp Farm	32.42
24	Burlington	33.83	24	Hartford 2 W	32.52
25	Cumberland	33.31	25	Sheboygan	32.59

Rankings include 25 highest/lowest stations. If state has less than 25 stations, all stations are included. The period of record is 1980–2009. See User Guide for detailed explanation of data.

Annual Extreme Maximum Daily Precipitation

Highest			Lowest		
Rank	**Station Name**	**Inches**	**Rank**	**Station Name**	**Inches**
1	Sheboygan	10.84	1	Burlington	3.50
2	Port Washington	9.87	2	Lake Geneva	***3.65***
3	Hancock Exp Farm	9.43	3	Sturgeon Bay Exp Farm	3.96
4	Baraboo	7.78	4	Marshfield Exp Farm	4.02
5	Ellsworth 1 E	***7.10***	5	Superior	4.07
5	Genoa Dam 8	7.10	6	Amery	4.08
7	Fond Du Lac	6.83	7	Racine	4.10
8	Milwaukee General Mitchell Field	6.81	8	Appleton	4.18
9	Rosholt 9 NNE	6.65	9	Manitowoc	4.27
9	Watertown	6.65	10	New London	***4.30***
11	Brodhead	6.62	11	Antigo	***4.34***
12	Plymouth	6.12	12	Menomonie	4.39
13	Eau Claire County Arpt	***5.98***	13	Bayfield 6 N	***4.40***
14	Alma Dam 4	5.91	13	Kewaunee 3 NW	4.40
15	Beloit	5.77	15	Beaver Dam	4.41
16	Cumberland	5.75	16	Wausau Municipal Arpt	4.46
17	Blair	5.69	17	West Bend	***4.50***
18	Lake Mills	5.59	18	Madison Dane Co Regional Arpt	4.51
19	Milwaukee Mt Mary Col	5.55	19	Lancaster 4 WSW	4.60
20	River Falls	***5.52***	20	Dalton	4.69
21	Oconomowoc	5.38	21	St Croix Falls	4.70
22	Chilton	5.31	22	Two Rivers	4.72
23	Germantown	5.25	23	Foxboro	***4.75***
24	La Crosse Municipal Arpt	5.24	24	Kenosha	4.88
25	Hartford 2 W	5.20	25	Green Bay Austin Straubel Intl	4.90

Number of Days Annually With ≥ 0.1 Inches of Precipitation

Highest			Lowest		
Rank	**Station Name**	**Days**	**Rank**	**Station Name**	**Days**
1	Couderay 7 W	76	1	Foxboro	56
2	Sturgeon Bay Exp Farm	74	2	St Croix Falls	60
3	Arlington Univ Farm	73	3	River Falls	62
4	West Bend	***72***	3	Superior	62
5	Bayfield 6 N	***71***	5	New London	***63***
5	Lake Geneva	***71***	6	Antigo	64
5	Plymouth	71	6	Bloomer	64
8	Beaver Dam	70	6	Eau Claire County Arpt	***64***
8	Milwaukee General Mitchell Field	70	6	Fond Du Lac	64
8	Oconomowoc	70	6	Kewaunee 3 NW	64
8	Racine	70	6	Lake Mills	64
8	Sheboygan	70	6	Menomonie	64
8	Watertown	70	6	Milwaukee Mt Mary Col	64
14	Baraboo	69	6	Port Washington	64
14	Brodhead	69	15	Amery	65
14	Dalton	69	15	Blair	65
14	Germantown	69	15	Manitowoc	65
14	Madison Dane Co Regional Arpt	69	18	Beloit	66
14	Two Rivers	69	18	Cumberland	66
20	Alma Dam 4	68	18	Genoa Dam 8	66
20	Burlington	68	18	Green Bay Austin Straubel Intl	66
20	Hancock Exp Farm	68	18	La Crosse Municipal Arpt	66
20	Kenosha	68	18	Oshkosh	66
20	Waukesha	***68***	18	Rosholt 9 NNE	66
20	Wausau Municipal Arpt	68	25	Appleton	67

Rankings include 25 highest/lowest stations. If state has less than 25 stations, all stations are included. The period of record is 1980–2009. See User Guide for detailed explanation of data.

Number of Days Annually With ≥ 0.5 Inches of Precipitation

Highest			Lowest		
Rank	Station Name	Days	Rank	Station Name	Days
1	Beloit	26	1	Antigo	17
2	Kenosha	25	1	Appleton	17
3	Couderay 7 W	24	1	Foxboro	17
3	Milwaukee General Mitchell Field	24	1	Green Bay Austin Straubel Intl	17
3	Oconomowoc	24	5	Chilton	18
3	Racine	24	5	Eau Claire County Arpt	*18*
3	West Bend	*24*	5	Fond Du Lac	18
8	Baraboo	23	5	Marshfield Exp Farm	18
8	Beaver Dam	23	5	Sturgeon Bay Exp Farm	18
8	Brodhead	23	5	Wausau Municipal Arpt	18
8	Germantown	23	11	Amery	19
8	Lake Geneva	*23*	11	Bayfield 6 N	*19*
8	Lake Mills	23	11	Blair	19
8	Lancaster 4 WSW	23	11	Bloomer	19
8	Plymouth	23	11	Kewaunee 3 NW	19
8	Waukesha	*23*	11	La Crosse Municipal Arpt	19
17	Alma Dam 4	22	11	Menomonie	19
17	Arlington Univ Farm	22	11	Oshkosh	19
17	Genoa Dam 8	22	11	River Falls	19
17	New London	22	11	Superior	19
17	Watertown	22	11	Two Rivers	19
22	Cumberland	21	22	Burlington	20
22	Dalton	21	22	Ellsworth 1 E	*20*
22	Hartford 2 W	21	22	Hancock Exp Farm	20
22	Rosholt 9 NNE	21	22	Madison Dane Co Regional Arpt	20

Number of Days Annually With ≥ 1.0 Inches of Precipitation

Highest			Lowest		
Rank	Station Name	Days	Rank	Station Name	Days
1	Beloit	8	1	Green Bay Austin Straubel Intl	4
1	Brodhead	8	2	Antigo	5
1	Ellsworth 1 E	*8*	2	Appleton	5
1	Kenosha	8	2	Chilton	5
1	Lancaster 4 WSW	8	2	Eau Claire County Arpt	*5*
1	Racine	8	2	Fond Du Lac	5
7	Alma Dam 4	7	2	New London	5
7	Amery	7	2	Wausau Municipal Arpt	5
7	Baraboo	7	9	Arlington Univ Farm	6
7	Bayfield 6 N	*7*	9	Beaver Dam	6
7	Blair	7	9	Burlington	6
7	Bloomer	7	9	Cumberland	6
7	Couderay 7 W	7	9	Dalton	6
7	Hartford 2 W	7	9	Foxboro	6
7	Lake Geneva	*7*	9	Genoa Dam 8	6
7	Madison Dane Co Regional Arpt	7	9	Germantown	6
7	Menomonie	7	9	Hancock Exp Farm	6
7	Milwaukee General Mitchell Field	7	9	Kewaunee 3 NW	6
7	Oconomowoc	7	9	La Crosse Municipal Arpt	6
7	Oshkosh	7	9	Lake Mills	6
7	Plymouth	7	9	Manitowoc	6
7	Port Washington	7	9	Marshfield Exp Farm	6
7	River Falls	7	9	Milwaukee Mt Mary Col	6
7	Sturgeon Bay Exp Farm	7	9	Rosholt 9 NNE	6
7	Watertown	7	9	Sheboygan	6

Rankings include 25 highest/lowest stations. If state has less than 25 stations, all stations are included. The period of record is 1980–2009. See User Guide for detailed explanation of data.

Annual Snowfall

Highest			Lowest		
Rank	Station Name	Inches	Rank	Station Name	Inches
1	Bayfield 6 N	***101.2***	1	Genoa Dam 8	28.6
2	Wausau Municipal Arpt	59.3	2	Beloit	31.9
3	Cumberland	54.8	3	Hartford 2 W	34.9
4	Hancock Exp Farm	54.4	4	Port Washington	35.5
5	Superior	53.1	4	Watertown	35.5
6	Antigo	53.0	6	Brodhead	35.6
7	Plymouth	52.0	7	Alma Dam 4	35.8
8	Green Bay Austin Straubel Intl	51.9	7	Burlington	35.8
9	Sturgeon Bay Exp Farm	51.8	9	Oshkosh	36.1
10	Marshfield Exp Farm	51.7	10	Two Rivers	***36.5***
11	Rosholt 9 NNE	51.6	11	Kenosha	36.8
12	Madison Dane Co Regional Arpt	50.2	12	Beaver Dam	37.7
13	Milwaukee General Mitchell Field	50.0	12	St Croix Falls	37.7
14	Amery	45.7	14	Milwaukee Mt Mary Col	38.0
15	West Bend	***45.3***	15	Fond Du Lac	38.1
16	Appleton	44.7	16	Arlington Univ Farm	38.5
16	Ellsworth 1 E	***44.7***	16	Lake Mills	38.5
18	Bloomer	44.3	18	Lancaster 4 WSW	39.3
19	Sheboygan	44.2	19	Oconomowoc	39.6
20	Germantown	44.1	20	Blair	39.8
21	La Crosse Municipal Arpt	43.8	20	New London	***39.8***
21	River Falls	43.8	22	Waukesha	***40.0***
23	Lake Geneva	***43.6***	23	Menomonie	41.6
24	Dalton	***43.1***	24	Baraboo	42.0
25	Chilton	42.9	25	Kewaunee 3 NW	42.1

Annual Maximum Snow Depth

Highest			Lowest		
Rank	Station Name	Inches	Rank	Station Name	Inches
1	Wausau Municipal Arpt	150	1	Oconomowoc	16
2	Superior	50	2	Watertown	17
3	Couderay 7 W	***44***	3	Fond Du Lac	19
4	Sturgeon Bay Exp Farm	42	4	Baraboo	20
5	Two Rivers	***41***	4	Beloit	20
6	St Croix Falls	39	4	West Bend	***20***
7	Rosholt 9 NNE	38	7	Green Bay Austin Straubel Intl	21
8	Cumberland	***37***	7	Milwaukee Mt Mary Col	21
9	Sheboygan	36	9	Appleton	22
10	Bayfield 6 N	***34***	9	Lake Mills	22
11	Germantown	33	9	Marshfield Exp Farm	22
11	Port Washington	33	9	Waukesha	***22***
13	Milwaukee General Mitchell Field	32	13	Blair	23
14	Genoa Dam 8	30	13	Chilton	23
14	Kewaunee 3 NW	***30***	13	Dalton	***23***
16	Amery	29	13	Madison Dane Co Regional Arpt	23
16	Hancock Exp Farm	29	17	Alma Dam 4	24
16	Menomonie	29	18	Hartford 2 W	25
16	Racine	***29***	18	Lake Geneva	***25***
20	Antigo	***28***	20	Beaver Dam	26
20	Lancaster 4 WSW	28	20	Bloomer	26
22	Arlington Univ Farm	27	20	Kenosha	26
22	La Crosse Municipal Arpt	27	23	Arlington Univ Farm	27
22	River Falls	27	23	La Crosse Municipal Arpt	27
25	Beaver Dam	26	23	River Falls	27

Rankings include 25 highest/lowest stations. If state has less than 25 stations, all stations are included. The period of record is 1980–2009. See User Guide for detailed explanation of data.

Number of Days Annually With ≥ 1.0 Inch Snow Depth

Highest			Lowest		
Rank	Station Name	Days	Rank	Station Name	Days
1	Bayfield 6 N	***132***	1	Kenosha	44
2	Antigo	115	2	Racine	47
3	Rosholt 9 NNE	110	3	Milwaukee Mt Mary Col	51
3	Wausau Municipal Arpt	110	4	Sheboygan	54
5	Amery	106	5	Watertown	55
6	Couderay 7 W	***103***	6	Beloit	56
7	Blair	101	7	Germantown	57
7	Superior	101	7	Port Washington	57
9	St Croix Falls	99	9	Milwaukee General Mitchell Field	59
10	Bloomer	98	10	Waukesha	***62***
11	Hancock Exp Farm	93	11	Lake Geneva	***63***
12	Sturgeon Bay Exp Farm	90	11	Lake Mills	63
13	Alma Dam 4	85	13	Beaver Dam	66
14	Green Bay Austin Straubel Intl	84	13	Hartford 2 W	66
14	Menomonie	84	13	Oconomowoc	66
16	Appleton	79	16	Dalton	***67***
16	Arlington Univ Farm	79	17	River Falls	68
16	Chilton	79	18	Genoa Dam 8	69
19	Baraboo	78	18	Kewaunee 3 NW	***69***
20	La Crosse Municipal Arpt	77	20	Lancaster 4 WSW	71
21	Cumberland	***76***	21	Fond Du Lac	72
22	Madison Dane Co Regional Arpt	75	21	Marshfield Exp Farm	72
22	Two Rivers	75	23	Madison Dane Co Regional Arpt	75
22	West Bend	***75***	23	Two Rivers	75
25	Fond Du Lac	72	23	West Bend	***75***

Rankings include 25 highest/lowest stations. If state has less than 25 stations, all stations are included. The period of record is 1980–2009. See User Guide for detailed explanation of data.

Significant Storm Events in Wisconsin: 2000 – 2009

Location or County	Date	Type	Mag.	Deaths	Injuries	Property Damage ($mil.)	Crop Damage ($mil.)
Milwaukee	03/08/00	Tornado	F1	0	16	4.5	0.0
Manitowoc	05/12/00	Hail	2.50 in.	0	30	46.0	4.0
Calumet	05/12/00	Hail	2.00 in.	0	0	32.2	0.0
Waushara	05/12/00	Hail	2.75 in.	0	0	26.0	0.0
Pierce	05/01/01	Hail	2.75 in.	0	0	20.0	0.0
Burnett	06/18/01	Tornado	F3	2	16	10.0	0.0
Rusk	09/02/02	Tornado	F3	0	27	25.0	0.0
Ozaukee and Sheboygan Counties	10/11/02	Fog	na	11	0	0.0	0.0
South-central and Southeast Wisconsin	06/01/04	Flood	na	0	0	35.5	216.0
Dane	08/18/05	Tornado	F3	1	23	34.3	0.7
Barron	09/21/05	Hail	3.00 in.	0	0	30.0	0.0
Columbia	06/25/06	Hail	1.00 in.	0	0	500.0	1.7
Kenosha	08/24/06	Lightning	na	0	0	14.0	0.0
Wood	06/07/07	Hail	5.50 in.	0	0	45.0	0.0
St. Croix	08/13/07	Thunderstorm Wind	90 mph	0	0	35.0	10.0
Vernon	08/18/07	Flash Flood	na	0	0	28.2	0.5
Crawford	08/18/07	Flash Flood	na	0	0	20.0	0.4
Kenosha	01/07/08	Tornado	F3	0	15	13.7	0.0
Jefferson	06/08/08	Flash Flood	na	0	0	102.2	35.0
Milwaukee	06/08/08	Flash Flood	na	0	0	77.9	0.0
Waukesha	06/08/08	Flash Flood	na	0	0	62.9	1.0
Columbia	06/08/08	Flash Flood	na	0	0	15.6	40.0
Sauk	06/09/08	Flash Flood	na	0	0	22.4	15.0
Winnebago	06/12/08	Flash Flood	na	0	0	18.6	5.0

Note: Deaths, injuries, and damages are date and location specific.

WYOMING

PHYSICAL FEATURES AND GENERAL CLIMATE. Wyoming is a name of Delaware Indian origin and is variously interpreted as "large plains" or "end of the plains." Thus, the name describes the State's outstanding topographic feature. There are, of course, several mountain ranges, but the mountains themselves cover less area than the high plains. The topography and variations in elevation make it difficult to divide the State into homogeneous, climatological areas.

The mean elevation is about 6,700 feet above sea level. Even excluding the mountain ranges, the average elevation over the southern portion is well over 6,000 feet, while much of the northern portion is some 2,500 feet lower. The lowest point, 3,125 feet, is near the northeast corner where the Belle Fourche River crosses the State line to South Dakota. The highest point is Gannett Peak at 13,785 feet, which is part of the Wind River Range in the west-central portion. Since the mountain ranges lie in a general north to south direction, they are perpendicular to the prevailing westerlies. Therefore, the mountain ranges provide effective barriers which force the air currents moving in from the Pacific Ocean to drop much of their moisture. It naturally follows that the mountain ranges and the western slopes receive the greatest amount of precipitation. Outside of the mountains, the State is considered semiarid.

The Continental Divide splits the State from near the northwest corner to a point along the southern border about midway. This leaves most of the drainage areas to the east. Precipitation drains into three great river systems: the Columbia; the Colorado; and the Missouri. The Snake with its tributaries in the northwest portion flows to the Columbia; the Green River draining most of the Southwest portion joins the Colorado; the Yellowstone, Wind River, Big Horn, Tongue, and Powder drainage areas cover most of the north portion and flow northward into Montana, entering the Missouri there; the Belle Fourche, Cheyenne, and Niobrara covering the east-central portion flow eastward; and the Platte (mostly North Platte), draining all of the southeast, flows eastward over Nebraska. There is a relatively small area along the southwest border that is drained by the Bear going to the Great Salt Lake. In the south-central portion west of Rawlins, there is an area called the Great Divide Basin which extends from near Rawlins to nearly 100 miles westward and about 50 miles in a north to south direction. Part of this is often referred to as the Red Desert. There is no drainage from the Great Divide Basin. Precipitation here, which averages only seven to 10 inches annually, follows usually dry creekbeds to ponds or small lakes, also often dry.

Rapid runoff from heavy thunderstorm rains causes flash flooding on the headwater streams of the State, and when the time of these storms coincides with the melting of the snowpack, the flooding is intensified.

PRECIPITATION. Like the other states in the western part of the country, precipitation varies considerably from one location to another. The period of maximum precipitation occurs in the spring and early summer for most of the State. It is greater over the mountain ranges and usually at the higher elevations, although elevation alone is not the only influence. Mountain ranges block the flow of moisture laden air from the east as well as from the west. During the summer months showers are quite frequent but light and often amount to only a few hundredths of an inch. Occasionally there will be some very heavy rain associated with thunderstorms covering a few square miles. There are usually several local storms each year with one to two inches of rain in a 24-hour period. On rarer occasions 24-hour amounts range from three to five inches.

SNOWFALL. Snow falls frequently from November through May. Generally snowfall at lower elevations is light to moderate. About five times a year on the average, weather stations at the lower elevations will have snowfall exceeding five inches. Wind will frequently accompany or follow a snowstorm and pile the snow into drifts several feet deep, often causing blizzard or near blizzard conditions in parts of the State for a few hours; however, it is uncommon for a severe blizzard to last long.

The total annual amount of snow varies considerably over the State as does the rainfall. At the lower elevations of the east portion, the range is mostly from 60 to 70 inches annually. Over the drier southwest portion, amounts vary from 45 to 55 inches at most places. Snow is very light in the Big Horn Basin with annual averages from 15 to 20 inches over the lower portion to 30 to 40 inches on the sides of the Basin where elevations range from 5,000 to 6,000 feet. The mountains receive a great deal more and over the higher ranges annual amounts are well over 200 inches.

TEMPERATURES. Because of the elevation, Wyoming has a relatively cool climate. Above the 6,000-foot level the temperature rarely exceeds 100°F. The warmest parts of the State are the lower portion of the Big Horn Basin, the lower elevations of the central and northeast portions, and along the east border. With increasing elevation, average values drop rapidly. A few places in the mountains, at about 9,000-feet level, show an average high in July close to 70°F. Summer nights are almost invariably cool, even though daytime readings may be quite high at times. For most places outside of the mountains, the mean low temperature in July is in the range from 50 to 60°F. The mountains and high valleys are much cooler, with average lows in the middle of the summer in the 30s and low 40s with occasional drops below freezing.

In the wintertime it is characteristic to have rapid and frequent changes between mild and cold spells. Usually there are less than 10 cold waves during a winter, and frequently less than half that number for most of the State. The majority of cold waves move southward on the east side of the Divide, with only an occasional cold wave for the west side. Sometimes only the northeast portion will be affected by the cold air as it slides on to the east over the plains. Many of the cold waves are not accompanied by enough snow to cause severe conditions. Numerous valleys provide ideal pockets for the collection of cold air drainage at night. Protecting mountain ranges prevent the wind from stirring the air, and the colder heavier air continues to deepen in valleys, often sending readings well below zero. It is common to have temperatures in the valleys considerably lower than on the nearby mountain sides. Except for the occasional cold waves and an infrequent blizzard, the winters are not severe. Even January, the coldest month, has occasional mild periods when maximum readings will reach the 50s and 60s.

Early freezes in the fall and late in the spring are characteristic of the Wyoming climate. This has the effect of seemingly long winters and short growing seasons.

SUNSHINE. For most of the State, sunshine ranges from approximately 60 percent of the possible amount during the winter to about 75 percent during the summer. Mountain areas receive less, and in the wintertime the estimated amount over the northwestern mountains is about 45 percent. Although the average amount of sunshine is less in winter, the low point on the annual variations is not during the coldest month (January or February). One low period of sunshine comes in November or December, and another in April or May. These periods of low sunshine correspond fairly closely to the periods of greatest temperature changes, i.e., in the late fall when average temperatures are dropping rapidly and in the spring when the average is climbing rapidly. To be sure, sunshine will not be much higher during the coldest months, but cold air masses are apt to be more stable at that time, and frontal activity is followed by a slightly longer period of sunshine. In the summertime when sunshine is greatest—not only in time but also intensity—it is characteristic for the forenoons to be mostly clear. Cumulus clouds develop nearly every day and frequently blot out the sun for a portion of the afternoons. Because of the altitude—providing less atmosphere for the sun's rays to penetrate—and because of the very small amount of fog, haze, and smoke, the intensity of sunshine is unusually high.

OTHER CLIMATIC ELEMENTS. Hailstorms are the most destructive type of local storm for this State. Tornadoes occur over Wyoming, but they are small and have a short duration. Many of them touch the ground for only a few minutes before receding into the clouds. The season for these local storms extends from April through September. June has the greatest number on the average, with May next.

Wind is an important factor of the Wyoming climate. This is largely due to the high elevation and the enormous stretches of rolling plains. Most of Wyoming is quite windy, and during the colder months from November through March there are frequent periods when the wind reaches 30 to 40 m.p.h., with occasional gusts much higher. Prevailing directions in the different localities vary from west-southwest through west to northwest. In many localities winds are so strong and constant from those directions that trees show a definite lean toward the east or southeast.

The average relative humidity is quite low and, while this has a distinct advantage in providing comfortable summer weather, it is related to the rather low amount of moisture. During the warmer part of the summer days, the average drops to about 25 to 30 percent. Late at night when the temperature is lowest the humidity will generally be up to 65 to 75 percent. Low relative humidity, high percentage of sunshine, and rather high average winds add their influence in causing a large amount of evaporation.

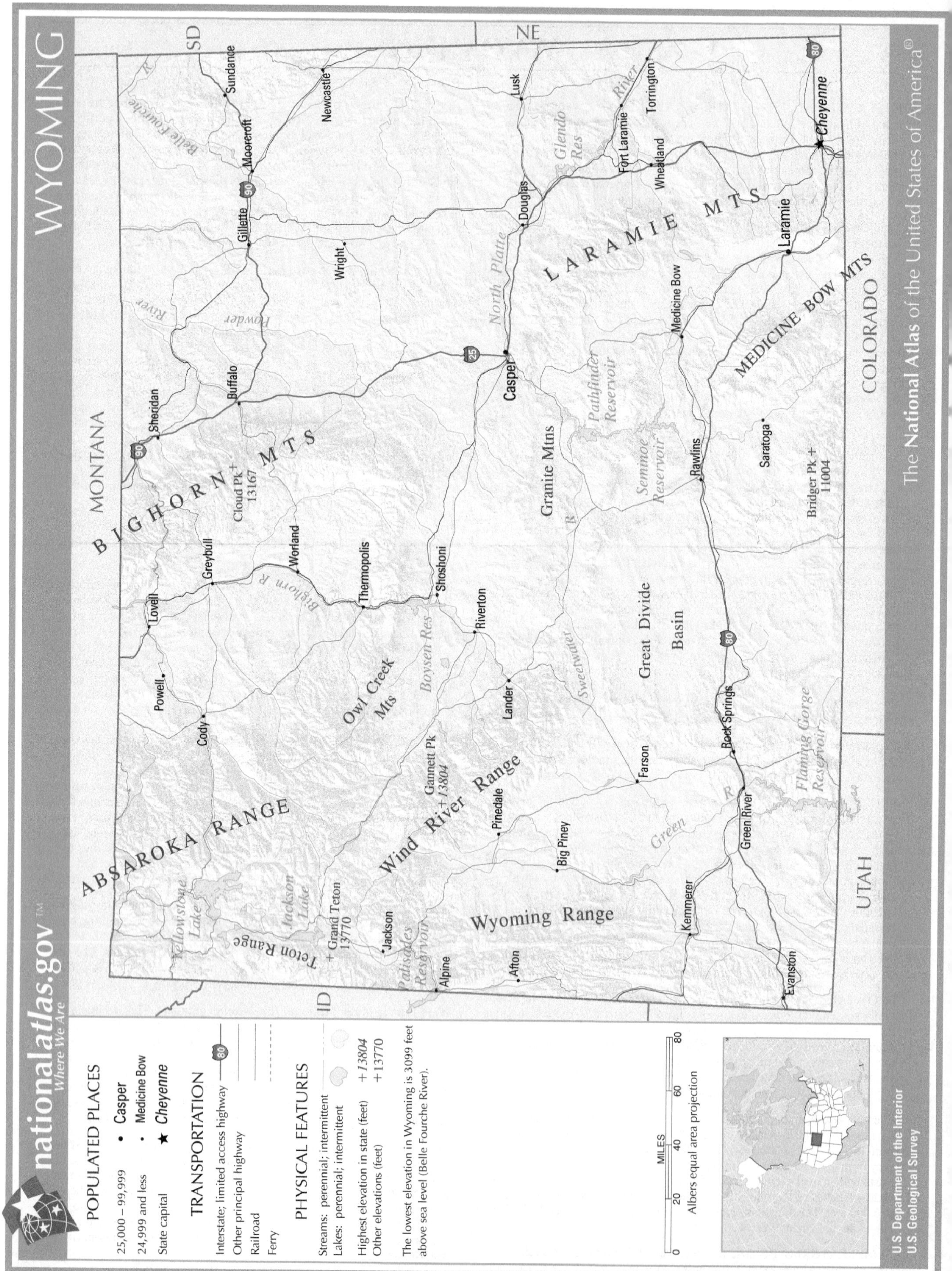
WYOMING
nationalatlas.gov™
Where We Are
POPULATED PLACES
25,000 – 99,999
• Casper
24,999 and less
• Medicine Bow
State capital
★ Cheyenne
TRANSPORTATION
Interstate; limited access highway
80
Other principal highway
Railroad
Ferry
PHYSICAL FEATURES
Streams: perennial; intermittent
Lakes: perennial; intermittent
Highest elevation in state (feet)
+13804
Other elevations (feet)
+13770
The lowest elevation in Wyoming is 3099 feet above sea level (Belle Fourche River).
MILES
0
20
40
60
80
Albers equal area projection
U.S. Department of the Interior
U.S. Geological Survey
The National Atlas of the United States of America®
MONTANA
SD
NE
COLORADO
UTAH
ID
BIGHORN MTS
LARAMIE MTS
MEDICINE BOW MTS
ABSAROKA RANGE
Wind River Range
Wyoming Range
Teton Range
Owl Creek Mts
Granite Mtns
Great Divide Basin
Cloud Pk + 13167
Gannett Pk + 13804
+ Grand Teton 13770
Bridger Pk + 11004
Yellowstone Lake
Jackson Lake
Palisades Reservoir
Boysen Res
Pathfinder Reservoir
Seminoe Reservoir
Glendo Res
Flaming Gorge Reservoir
Belle Fourche
Powder River
North Platte
Bighorn R
Sweetwater
Green
Green R
Sheridan
Buffalo
Gillette
Moorcroft
Sundance
Newcastle
Wright
Lusk
Douglas
Casper
Fort Laramie
Torrington
Wheatland
Cheyenne
Laramie
Medicine Bow
Saratoga
Rawlins
Rock Springs
Green River
Farson
Lander
Riverton
Shoshoni
Thermopolis
Worland
Greybull
Lovell
Powell
Cody
Pinedale
Big Piney
Kemmerer
Evanston
Afton
Alpine
Jackson
90
25
80

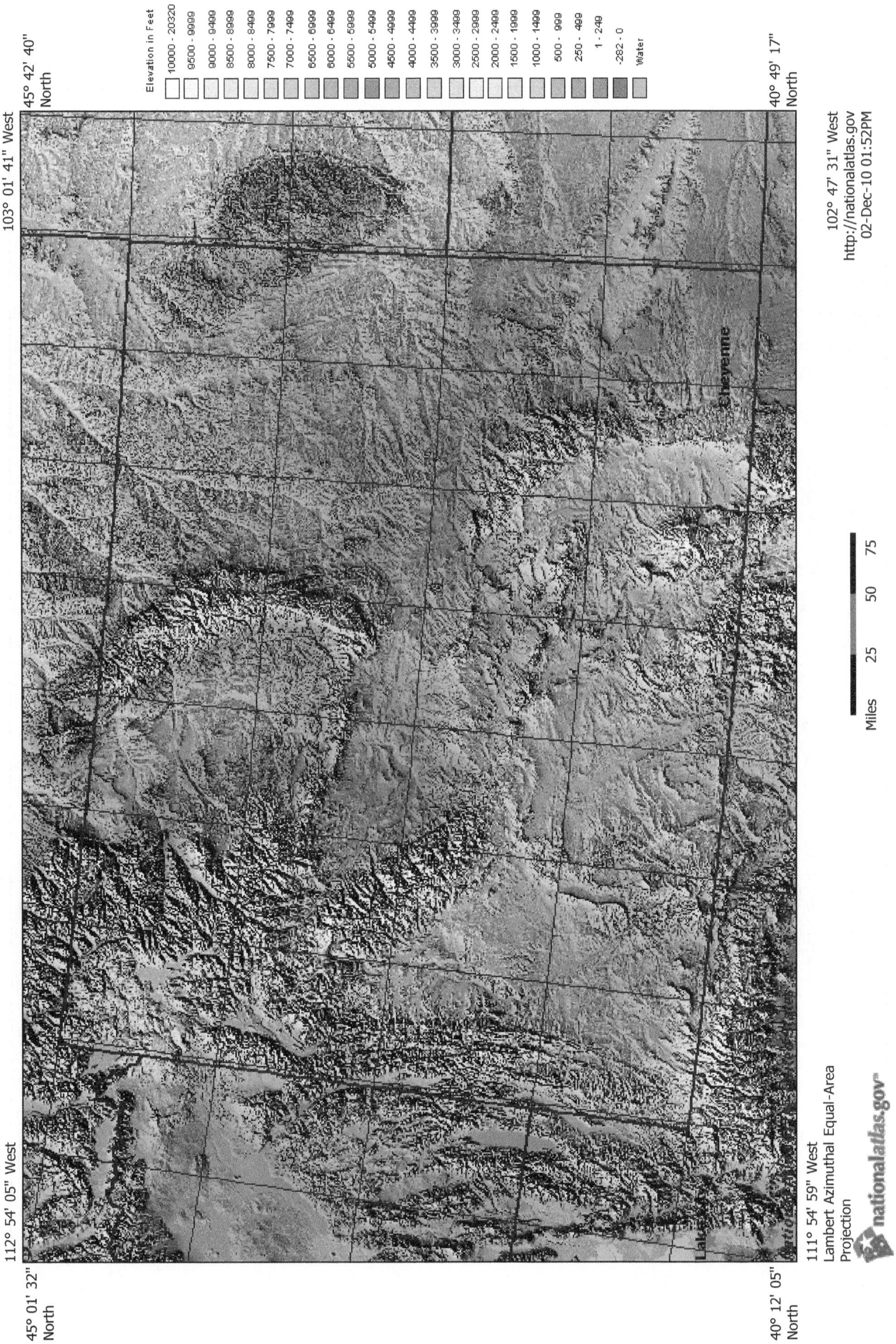
Elevation in Feet
10000 - 20320
9500 - 9999
9000 - 9499
8500 - 8999
8000 - 8499
7500 - 7999
7000 - 7499
6500 - 6999
6000 - 6499
5500 - 5999
5000 - 5499
4500 - 4999
4000 - 4499
3500 - 3999
3000 - 3499
2500 - 2999
2000 - 2499
1500 - 1999
1000 - 1499
500 - 999
250 - 499
1 - 249
-282 - 0
Water
103° 01' 41" West
45° 42' 40" North
40° 49' 17" North
102° 47' 31" West
http://nationalatlas.gov
02-Dec-10 01:52PM
Cheyenne
Miles
25
50
75
112° 54' 05" West
45° 01' 32" North
111° 54' 59" West
Lambert Azimuthal Equal-Area Projection
nationalatlas.gov
40° 12' 05" North

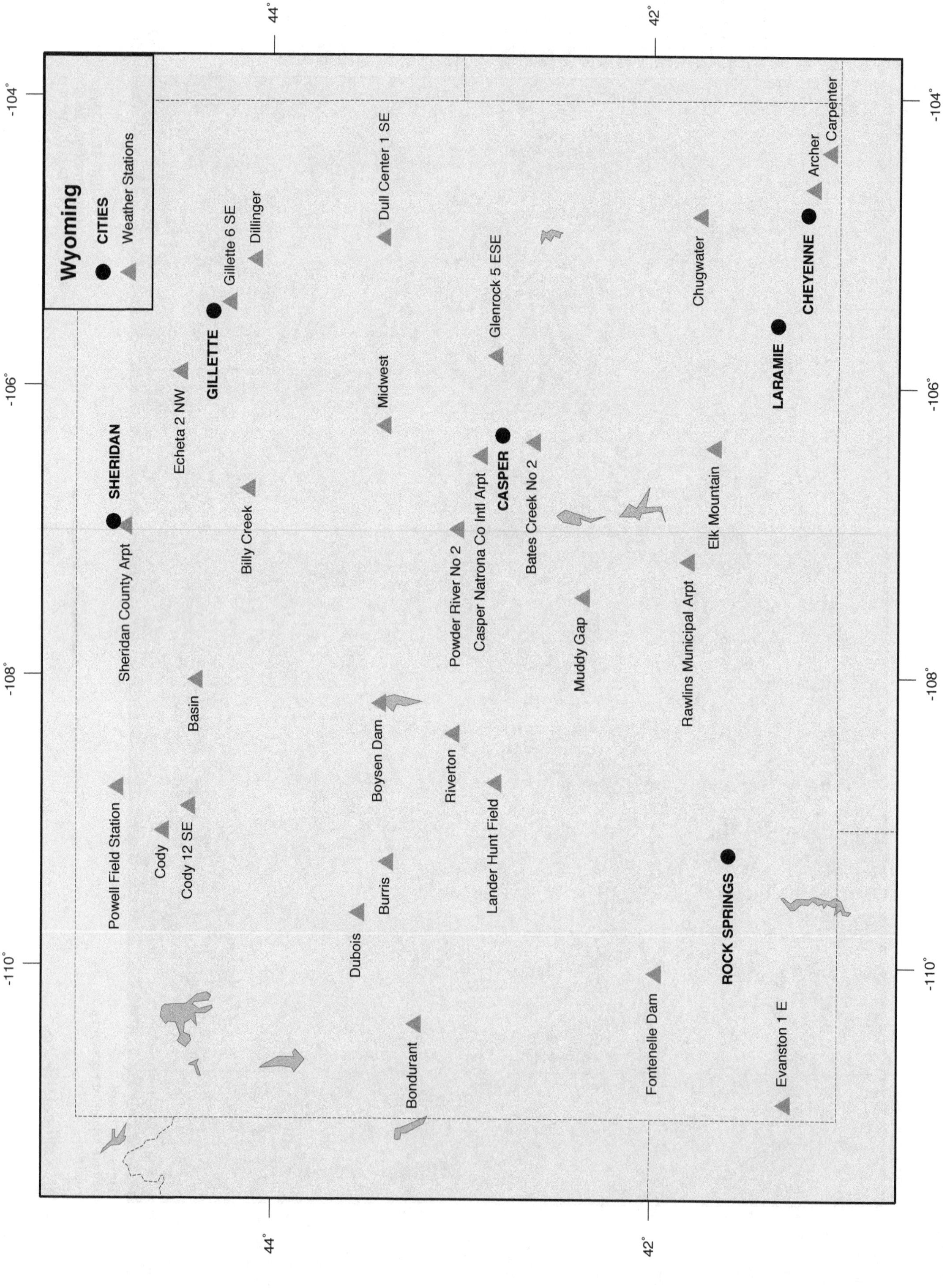
Wyoming
CITIES
Weather Stations
-104°
-106°
-108°
-110°
44°
42°
SHERIDAN
GILLETTE
CASPER
LARAMIE
CHEYENNE
ROCK SPRINGS
Sheridan County Arpt
Echeta 2 NW
Gillette 6 SE
Dillinger
Dull Center 1 SE
Billy Creek
Midwest
Glenrock 5 ESE
Powder River No 2
Casper Natrona Co Intl Arpt
Bates Creek No 2
Muddy Gap
Rawlins Municipal Arpt
Elk Mountain
Chugwater
Archer
Carpenter
Powell Field Station
Cody
Cody 12 SE
Basin
Boysen Dam
Riverton
Lander Hunt Field
Burris
Dubois
Bondurant
Fontenelle Dam
Evanston 1 E

Wyoming Weather Stations by County

County	Station Name
Big Horn	Basin
Campbell	Dillinger
	Echeta 2 NW
	Gillette 6 SE
Carbon	Elk Mountain
	Muddy Gap
	Rawlins Municipal Arpt
Converse	Dull Center 1 SE
	Glenrock 5 ESE
Fremont	Boysen Dam
	Burris
	Dubois
	Lander Hunt Field
	Riverton
Johnson	Billy Creek
Laramie	Archer
	Carpenter
Lincoln	Fontenelle Dam
Natrona	Bates Creek No 2
	Casper Natrona Co Intl Arpt
	Midwest
	Powder River No 2
Park	Cody
	Cody 12 SE
	Powell Field Station
Platte	Chugwater
Sheridan	Sheridan County Arpt
Sublette	Bondurant
Uinta	Evanston 1 E

See User Guide for station inclusion criteria.

Wyoming Weather Stations by City

City	Station Name	Miles
Casper	Bates Creek No 2	14.1
	Casper Natrona Co Intl Arpt	8.5
Cheyenne	Archer	7.7
	Carpenter	23.4
Cody	Cody	1.9
	Cody 12 SE	10.7
	Powell Field Station	22.9
Douglas	Glenrock 5 ESE	21.0
Evanston	Woodruff, UT	21.2
	Evanston 1 E	0.8
Gillette	Dillinger	23.3
	Echeta 2 NW	23.6
	Gillette 6 SE	5.2
Jackson	Driggs, ID	24.9
	Bondurant	23.7
Lander	Lander Hunt Field	1.1
	Riverton	22.5
Ranchettes	Archer	8.0
	Carpenter	24.3
Rawlins	Rawlins Municipal Arpt	1.9
Riverton	Lander Hunt Field	22.7
	Riverton	0.5
Sheridan	Sheridan County Arpt	2.1

Note: Miles is the distance between the geographic center of the city and the weather station.

See User Guide for station inclusion criteria.

Wyoming Weather Stations by Elevation

Feet	Station Name
7,265	Elk Mountain
6,959	Dubois
6,825	Evanston 1 E
6,735	Rawlins Municipal Arpt
6,535	Bondurant
6,479	Fontenelle Dam
6,245	Muddy Gap
6,120	Burris
6,009	Archer
6,009	Bates Creek No 2
5,700	Powder River No 2
5,557	Lander Hunt Field
5,390	Carpenter
5,337	Casper Natrona Co Intl Arpt
5,304	Chugwater
5,248	Cody 12 SE
4,990	Cody
4,975	Billy Creek
4,955	Riverton
4,948	Glenrock 5 ESE
4,859	Midwest
4,810	Boysen Dam
4,640	Gillette 6 SE
4,415	Dull Center 1 SE
4,370	Powell Field Station
4,310	Dillinger
4,000	Echeta 2 NW
3,963	Sheridan County Arpt
3,836	Basin

See User Guide for station inclusion criteria.

Casper Int'l Airport

Casper is located in the central portion of Wyoming in the North Platte River Valley at an elevation of about 5,300 feet. The country immediately surrounding Casper is mostly rolling and hilly with considerable flat prairie land in each direction except toward the south where Casper Mountain rises some 3,500 feet above the valley floor. The prairie land is used mainly for grazing.

The National Weather Service Office is located at Natrona County International Airport, some eight miles west-northwest of the Casper Post Office and about 200 feet higher in elevation.

The climate of Casper is semi-arid. Most of the air masses reaching this area move in from the Pacific and the mountains to the west are effective moisture barriers. About 70 percent of the annual precipitation occurs during the growing season of late spring and summer, mostly in thunderstorms. Monthly snowfall amounts are unusually uniform from November through February, and a bit heavier in March and April. Snow has occurred as early in the season as September and as late as early June.

Casper experiences large diurnal and annual temperature ranges. This is due to the advent of both warm and cold air masses and the relatively high elevation which permits rapid incoming and outgoing radiation. The mean daily temperature averages about 71 degrees in summer and 22 degrees in winter. Temperatures during winter months average a few degrees higher and summer temperatures average several degrees cooler than locations in the Missouri Valley to the east.

Windy days are quite frequent during winter and spring months. Usually the stronger winds are from the southwest and this tends to raise the temperature because the air is moving downslope.

Based on the 1951-1980 period, the average first occurrence of 32 degrees Fahrenheit in the fall is September 22 and the average last occurrence in the spring is May 22.

Casper Int'l Airport *Natrona County* Elevation: 5,337 ft. Latitude: 42° 54' N Longitude: 106° 28' W

	JAN	FEB	MAR	APR	MAY	JUN	JUL	AUG	SEP	OCT	NOV	DEC	YEAR
Mean Maximum Temp. (°F)	35.3	38.3	48.1	57.3	67.7	79.4	88.6	86.7	74.6	59.7	45.2	34.9	59.7
Mean Temp. (°F)	25.0	27.5	35.5	43.4	52.9	62.9	71.2	69.5	58.5	45.7	33.9	24.6	45.9
Mean Minimum Temp. (°F)	14.6	16.7	22.9	29.3	38.0	46.4	53.8	52.2	42.3	31.7	22.6	14.4	32.1
Extreme Maximum Temp. (°F)	59	68	75	84	95	102	104	101	97	87	72	63	104
Extreme Minimum Temp. (°F)	-32	-32	-15	-6	17	31	34	34	16	1	-21	-41	-41
Days Maximum Temp. ≥ 90°F	0	0	0	0	0	6	16	13	2	0	0	0	37
Days Maximum Temp. ≤ 32°F	11	8	4	1	0	0	0	0	0	1	6	12	43
Days Minimum Temp. ≤ 32°F	29	26	27	20	7	0	0	0	3	16	24	29	181
Days Minimum Temp. ≤ 0°F	5	3	1	0	0	0	0	0	0	0	2	5	16
Heating Degree Days (base 65°F)	1,234	1,054	906	643	373	118	11	23	220	592	926	1,244	7,344
Cooling Degree Days (base 65°F)	0	0	0	0	5	63	210	168	30	0	0	0	476
Mean Precipitation (in.)	0.51	0.57	0.81	1.26	2.03	1.53	1.40	0.86	1.08	1.11	0.75	0.58	12.49
Maximum Precipitation (in.)*	1.4	1.4	2.4	3.9	6.5	4.1	3.0	2.7	3.4	4.2	2.7	3.7	20.5
Minimum Precipitation (in.)*	trace	0.1	0.3	0.1	0.3	trace	0.1	trace	0.1	trace	trace	trace	6.6
Extreme Maximum Daily Precip. (in.)	0.53	0.59	0.88	0.90	2.22	2.15	1.78	2.21	2.01	2.06	0.99	1.26	2.22
Days With ≥ 0.1" Precipitation	2	2	3	4	5	4	3	2	3	3	3	2	36
Days With ≥ 0.5" Precipitation	0	0	0	0	1	1	1	0	1	0	0	0	4
Days With ≥ 1.0" Precipitation	0	0	0	0	0	0	0	0	0	0	0	0	0
Mean Snowfall (in.)	9.8	10.2	11.0	11.3	3.4	0.1	trace	trace	1.8	7.6	10.3	11.2	76.7
Maximum Snowfall (in.)*	39	24	36	56	25	3	0	0	12	22	37	63	138
Maximum 24-hr. Snowfall (in.)*	10	10	15	17	13	3	0	0	7	13	12	24	24
Maximum Snow Depth (in.)	na	na	na	na	na	na	na	na	na	na	na	na	na
Days With ≥ 1.0" Snow Depth	na	na	na	na	na	na	na	na	na	na	na	na	na
Thunderstorm Days*	0	< 1	< 1	1	6	8	9	7	3	< 1	< 1	0	34
Foggy Days*	3	3	4	4	4	2	1	1	2	3	3	3	33
Predominant Sky Cover*	OVR	OVR	OVR	OVR	OVR	CLR	CLR	CLR	CLR	CLR	OVR	OVR	OVR
Mean Relative Humidity 6am (%)*	67	71	74	74	74	68	63	63	65	66	69	68	68
Mean Relative Humidity 3pm (%)*	54	52	45	38	36	29	23	22	28	34	48	54	38
Mean Dewpoint (°F)*	13	16	20	25	34	40	43	41	33	27	20	15	27
Prevailing Wind Direction*	SW	SW	SW	SW	SW	WSW	WSW	SW	SW	SW	SW	SW	SW
Prevailing Wind Speed (mph)*	20	18	17	15	15	14	12	13	15	16	18	20	16
Maximum Wind Gust (mph)*	67	67	64	69	64	64	67	67	63	62	60	67	69

Note: (*) Period of record is 1949-1995

The period of record for National Weather Service station data is 1980 – 2009 except where noted. See User Guide for detailed explanation of data.

Lander Hunt Field

Lander, located in the central Wyoming valley of the Popo Agie River, lies at the foot and east of the Wind River Range. Situated on a flat-topped mesa, the airport station is one and a half miles south-southeast and approximately 200 feet above the town.

The terrain to the north, east and south varies from rolling to broken with some grass covered hills two to five miles distant, rising approximately 400 feet above the station elevation. To the west and southwest the foothills of the Wind River Range begin about three miles from the station, sloping upward to over 12,000 feet above sea level along the Continental Divide, 20 miles distant.

Because Lander is in a pocket, winds from all directions except northeast are downslope and produce a Chinook effect, most noticable in winds from westerly quadrants. The airport, on its mesa, receives more wind than the town of Lander. Because of light winds, steep temperature inversions are the rule during winter nights and early mornings. Temperatures in the valley will be as much as 15 degrees lower than at the airport on calm, clear nights when there is a snow cover. However, when the wind is calm and the humidities low, the chilling effect is much less than is usual in extreme cold. For several days each winter, temperatures are 20 to 30 degrees lower than in the surrounding areas where higher wind speeds occur. The sheltered location, however, offers protection from most severe storms that sweep down from Canada.

Lander does not have a true spring season, and snow has been recorded in June.

Usually on 15 to 20 days a year the temperature reaches or exceeds 90 degrees. Even the warmest days are not oppressive, the humidity being low, and the nights being cool. The normal daily range of summer temperature is near 30 degrees.

Mountains block moisture from the Pacific, creating a semi-arid climate. The heaviest and most persistent precipitation comes when the wind in the lower levels is from easterly quadrants, through a combination of low pressure to the south, usually over Colorado, and high pressure to the north over Montana or the western Dakotas. More than a third of the annual precipitation occurs in April and May, with another but lesser peak in September and October. Summer moisture comes from occasional showers but is very erratic and spotty. Since about one-third of the annual snowfall comes in March and April, when the temperature is comparatively high, the snow soon melts.

Hardier plants and vegetables do well in this area. The average first occurrence of 32 degrees Fahrenheit in the fall is September 24 and the average last occurrence in the spring is May 22.

Lander Hunt Field *Fremont County* Elevation: 5,557 ft. Latitude: 42° 49' N Longitude: 108° 44' W

	JAN	FEB	MAR	APR	MAY	JUN	JUL	AUG	SEP	OCT	NOV	DEC	YEAR
Mean Maximum Temp. (°F)	33.2	37.1	47.7	57.0	67.1	78.0	87.3	85.2	73.2	58.8	43.1	32.3	58.3
Mean Temp. (°F)	21.9	25.8	35.9	44.4	53.9	63.5	71.7	70.0	59.1	45.9	31.7	21.3	45.4
Mean Minimum Temp. (°F)	10.5	14.4	24.0	31.8	40.8	48.9	56.2	54.7	44.9	33.0	20.2	10.3	32.5
Extreme Maximum Temp. (°F)	62	65	74	82	93	99	101	100	94	84	70	64	101
Extreme Minimum Temp. (°F)	-27	-25	-9	6	21	32	39	37	17	-3	-18	-37	-37
Days Maximum Temp. ≥ 90°F	0	0	0	0	0	3	14	9	1	0	0	0	27
Days Maximum Temp. ≤ 32°F	14	9	3	1	0	0	0	0	0	1	7	15	50
Days Minimum Temp. ≤ 32°F	31	28	27	16	4	0	0	0	2	14	27	31	180
Days Minimum Temp. ≤ 0°F	6	4	1	0	0	0	0	0	0	0	2	6	19
Heating Degree Days (base 65°F)	1,330	1,102	895	610	342	113	12	18	204	584	993	1,347	7,550
Cooling Degree Days (base 65°F)	0	0	0	0	7	75	228	180	33	0	0	0	523
Mean Precipitation (in.)	0.43	0.57	1.15	1.85	2.16	1.21	0.77	0.61	1.05	1.33	0.85	0.56	12.54
Maximum Precipitation (in.)*	1.3	2.2	3.3	5.5	6.0	5.3	2.5	2.3	4.7	4.9	3.4	1.6	21.9
Minimum Precipitation (in.)*	trace	trace	0.3	0.2	0.1	trace	0	trace	trace	trace	trace	trace	6.4
Extreme Maximum Daily Precip. (in.)	0.46	0.82	1.02	1.87	1.91	1.73	1.02	2.20	1.72	1.56	0.99	0.86	2.20
Days With ≥ 0.1" Precipitation	2	2	3	5	4	3	2	2	3	3	2	2	33
Days With ≥ 0.5" Precipitation	0	0	1	1	2	1	0	0	1	1	1	0	8
Days With ≥ 1.0" Precipitation	0	0	0	0	0	0	0	0	0	0	0	0	0
Mean Snowfall (in.)	8.3	10.2	16.2	16.7	4.8	0.1	trace	trace	2.7	10.1	13.3	9.9	92.3
Maximum Snowfall (in.)*	27	44	52	66	34	18	0	0	33	40	49	28	200
Maximum 24-hr. Snowfall (in.)*	14	20	16	22	16	16	0	0	14	19	23	16	23
Maximum Snow Depth (in.)	na	na	na	na	na	na	na	na	na	na	na	na	na
Days With ≥ 1.0" Snow Depth	na	na	na	na	na	na	na	na	na	na	na	na	na
Thunderstorm Days*	0	0	< 1	1	5	7	10	7	3	< 1	< 1	0	33
Foggy Days*	2	2	1	2	1	< 1	< 1	< 1	1	1	2	2	14
Predominant Sky Cover*	OVR	OVR	OVR	OVR	OVR	SCT	CLR	CLR	CLR	CLR	OVR	CLR	CLR
Mean Relative Humidity 6am (%)*	69	69	67	65	66	60	55	55	59	64	69	69	64
Mean Relative Humidity 3pm (%)*	57	51	42	36	36	30	26	25	31	36	49	54	39
Mean Dewpoint (°F)*	8	13	18	24	33	39	42	40	34	27	17	10	26
Prevailing Wind Direction*	SW	SW	SW	SW	WSW	SW	WSW	WSW	SW	SW	WSW	SE	SW
Prevailing Wind Speed (mph)*	9	9	9	10	9	10	9	9	9	9	9	7	9
Maximum Wind Gust (mph)*	86	69	63	63	69	63	66	67	67	53	68	75	86

Note: (*) Period of record is 1948-1995

Sheridan County Airport

Sheridan is located east of the Rocky Mountains at an elevation of a little less than 4,000 feet. To the northwest, east, and southeast are rolling hills, but to the southwest and west the Bighorn Mountains rise abruptly, oriented generally northwest-southeast. The foothills are only about 15 miles from Sheridan, and within 30 miles to the southwest the average elevation is near 10,000 feet, with Cloud Peak rising to 13,175 feet.

During the winter months, a few days after the outbreak of cold arctic air from Canada, the winds generally shift to the west or southwest and increase in velocity. These downslope winds produce a pronounced warming or Chinook. At other times, a gentle downslope flow will persist for several days and result in a prolonged period of mild weather. The Chinook is very effective in moderating the weather of the winter season, which otherwise would be more severe. On the other hand, winds from the east or northeast blowing toward the mountains are upslope and usually cause cooling, persistent low clouds, and often heavy precipitation. The upslope precipitation occurs at times all through the year, but most frequently during the winter and spring. In the summer, the mountains act as a breeding ground for thunderstorms that frequently move away from the mountains toward the northeast and give afternoon or evening showers to Sheridan.

Based on the 1951-1980 period, the average first occurrence of 32 degrees Fahrenheit in the fall is September 20 and the average last occurrence in the spring is May 20.

The climate of Sheridan can be described generally as semi-arid with long cold winters and short hot summers. However, during all of the winter months, more than 50 percent of the possible sunshine is received, while the hot days in the summer are marked by very low humidity and nights are cool. During July, the warmest month, even though temperatures of 90 degrees or above occur frequently, the nights are cool. January is usually the coldest month.

The yearly precipitation pattern for Sheridan is heavy in the spring and early summer. The three winter months constitute the period with the least moisture. Amounts of snowfall are quite generous during the winter, but the water content of the snow is usually low. This dry snow is ordinarily not injurious to livestock and does not result in serious inconvenience or discomfort to the public. During the spring months of March and April, however, precipitation often begins as rain, gradually turning to rain and snow mixed or to heavy wet snow. These snowstorms are frequently accompanied by strong winds and drifting. As a result, these two months are considered to have the most disagreeable weather of the year and are most likely to cause livestock loss. March has more snow than any other month.

Sheridan County Airport *Sheridan County* Elevation: 3,963 ft. Latitude: 44° 46' N Longitude: 106° 58' W

	JAN	FEB	MAR	APR	MAY	JUN	JUL	AUG	SEP	OCT	NOV	DEC	YEAR
Mean Maximum Temp. (°F)	36.1	39.2	48.1	57.8	67.2	77.0	87.4	86.4	74.4	60.1	46.5	35.7	59.7
Mean Temp. (°F)	24.1	27.1	35.5	44.4	53.3	62.2	70.7	69.4	58.5	45.9	33.5	23.7	45.7
Mean Minimum Temp. (°F)	12.0	15.1	22.7	30.8	39.3	47.3	53.9	52.4	42.6	31.6	20.5	11.5	31.6
Extreme Maximum Temp. (°F)	69	76	80	86	94	105	107	106	103	92	81	72	107
Extreme Minimum Temp. (°F)	-35	-32	-14	0	16	29	37	32	6	-9	-20	-37	-37
Days Maximum Temp. ≥ 90°F	0	0	0	0	0	3	13	13	3	0	0	0	32
Days Maximum Temp. ≤ 32°F	11	8	4	1	0	0	0	0	0	1	5	11	41
Days Minimum Temp. ≤ 32°F	30	27	27	17	5	0	0	0	3	16	27	30	182
Days Minimum Temp. ≤ 0°F	6	4	1	0	0	0	0	0	0	0	2	6	19
Heating Degree Days (base 65°F)	1,262	1,064	909	613	363	132	19	29	223	588	938	1,276	7,416
Cooling Degree Days (base 65°F)	0	0	0	1	5	54	202	174	35	1	0	0	472
Mean Precipitation (in.)	0.60	0.56	1.00	1.55	2.32	2.06	1.13	0.72	1.47	1.36	0.73	0.58	14.08
Maximum Precipitation (in.)*	1.9	2.7	3.0	4.8	6.8	6.1	3.8	3.0	3.1	3.4	2.4	2.4	23.8
Minimum Precipitation (in.)*	0.1	0	0.1	0.2	0.3	0.3	0.1	trace	0.1	trace	0.1	0.1	8.2
Extreme Maximum Daily Precip. (in.)	1.31	0.76	0.70	1.17	2.45	1.90	1.40	0.92	2.02	1.20	0.80	0.68	2.45
Days With ≥ 0.1" Precipitation	2	2	4	5	5	5	3	2	4	4	2	2	40
Days With ≥ 0.5" Precipitation	0	0	0	1	1	1	1	0	1	1	0	0	6
Days With ≥ 1.0" Precipitation	0	0	0	0	0	0	0	0	0	0	0	0	0
Mean Snowfall (in.)	***10.5***	***9.5***	na	na	***1.5***	na	na	na	na	na	na	na	na
Maximum Snowfall (in.)*	33	35	37	40	13	4	0	0	21	18	26	44	158
Maximum 24-hr. Snowfall (in.)*	12	10	10	23	7	3	0	0	13	13	10	12	23
Maximum Snow Depth (in.)	***12***	***13***	***10***	***21***	***9***	na	na	na	na	na	na	na	na
Days With ≥ 1.0" Snow Depth	***22***	***18***	***10***	***3***	***1***	na	na	na	na	na	na	na	na
Thunderstorm Days*	0	< 1	< 1	1	4	9	9	7	3	< 1	< 1	0	33
Foggy Days*	2	3	3	3	2	1	< 1	< 1	1	2	2	2	21
Predominant Sky Cover*	OVR	OVR	OVR	OVR	OVR	BRK	SCT	SCT	CLR	OVR	OVR	OVR	OVR
Mean Relative Humidity 5am (%)*	71	73	75	74	77	78	72	68	71	71	73	71	73
Mean Relative Humidity 5pm (%)*	64	61	52	45	46	45	34	30	37	46	62	66	49
Mean Dewpoint (°F)*	11	16	21	28	38	46	48	45	38	30	21	14	30
Prevailing Wind Direction*	NW	NW	NW	NW	NW	NW	NW	NW	NW	NW	NW	NW	NW
Prevailing Wind Speed (mph)*	13	13	15	15	14	13	12	12	13	13	13	13	13
Maximum Wind Gust (mph)*	71	69	68	69	66	58	64	60	67	64	73	69	73

Note: (*) Period of record is 1948-1995

The period of record for National Weather Service station data is 1980 – 2009 except where noted. See User Guide for detailed explanation of data.

Archer *Laramie County* Elevation: 6,009 ft. Latitude: 41° 09' N Longitude: 104° 39' W

	JAN	FEB	MAR	APR	MAY	JUN	JUL	AUG	SEP	OCT	NOV	DEC	YEAR
Mean Maximum Temp. (°F)	40.7	42.5	48.8	56.9	66.3	76.7	85.3	83.8	74.8	61.7	47.9	40.9	60.5
Mean Temp. (°F)	27.5	29.1	35.2	42.5	51.8	61.3	68.7	67.2	58.1	46.1	34.2	27.6	45.8
Mean Minimum Temp. (°F)	14.3	15.7	21.6	28.0	37.3	45.8	52.1	50.5	41.5	30.5	20.6	14.2	31.0
Extreme Maximum Temp. (°F)	69	70	76	82	95	101	102	102	97	86	78	69	102
Extreme Minimum Temp. (°F)	-22	-28	-13	-2	16	29	37	31	8	-4	-16	-30	-30
Days Maximum Temp. ≥ 90°F	0	0	0	0	0	3	10	7	2	0	0	0	22
Days Maximum Temp. ≤ 32°F	7	6	4	1	0	0	0	0	0	1	4	8	31
Days Minimum Temp. ≤ 32°F	30	27	28	21	8	1	0	0	4	18	27	30	194
Days Minimum Temp. ≤ 0°F	4	3	1	0	0	0	0	0	0	0	1	4	13
Heating Degree Days (base 65°F)	1,155	1,009	915	669	405	151	29	36	226	577	917	1,152	7,241
Cooling Degree Days (base 65°F)	0	0	0	0	3	45	150	110	27	0	0	0	335
Mean Precipitation (in.)	0.39	0.50	1.08	1.56	2.67	2.82	2.11	2.02	1.68	0.99	0.66	0.38	16.86
Extreme Maximum Daily Precip. (in.)	0.61	1.53	1.85	1.77	1.98	3.29	1.73	1.87	1.34	1.11	0.78	0.47	3.29
Days With ≥ 0.1" Precipitation	1	2	3	4	6	6	5	5	4	3	2	1	42
Days With ≥ 0.5" Precipitation	0	0	1	1	2	2	1	1	1	0	0	0	9
Days With ≥ 1.0" Precipitation	0	0	0	0	0	0	0	0	0	0	0	0	0
Mean Snowfall (in.)	6.3	6.7	9.8	7.8	1.2	0.0	0.0	0.0	1.1	3.8	7.6	6.8	51.1
Maximum Snow Depth (in.)	23	15	19	15	7	0	0	0	6	16	15	13	23
Days With ≥ 1.0" Snow Depth	11	11	8	4	1	0	0	0	0	2	9	13	59

Basin *Big Horn County* Elevation: 3,836 ft. Latitude: 44° 23' N Longitude: 108° 02' W

	JAN	FEB	MAR	APR	MAY	JUN	JUL	AUG	SEP	OCT	NOV	DEC	YEAR
Mean Maximum Temp. (°F)	30.3	38.2	51.4	62.1	71.8	81.7	90.3	88.8	76.3	61.3	44.7	32.0	60.7
Mean Temp. (°F)	17.1	24.6	37.2	47.3	57.1	66.2	73.3	71.2	59.5	46.2	31.8	19.5	45.9
Mean Minimum Temp. (°F)	4.0	11.0	23.0	32.4	42.4	50.7	56.2	53.4	42.8	31.0	18.8	7.0	31.0
Extreme Maximum Temp. (°F)	59	73	81	89	98	110	107	115	99	88	77	67	115
Extreme Minimum Temp. (°F)	-38	-41	-14	-2	18	30	40	34	16	-1	-19	-41	-41
Days Maximum Temp. ≥ 90°F	0	0	0	0	1	7	18	16	3	0	0	0	45
Days Maximum Temp. ≤ 32°F	15	8	2	0	0	0	0	0	0	1	5	14	45
Days Minimum Temp. ≤ 32°F	31	28	27	15	3	0	0	0	2	18	28	31	183
Days Minimum Temp. ≤ 0°F	11	5	1	0	0	0	0	0	0	0	2	8	27
Heating Degree Days (base 65°F)	1,478	1,135	855	527	262	74	10	17	197	577	991	1,405	7,528
Cooling Degree Days (base 65°F)	0	0	0	1	24	117	274	215	39	0	0	0	670
Mean Precipitation (in.)	0.23	0.17	0.37	0.72	1.29	1.08	0.50	0.33	0.77	0.66	0.28	0.31	6.71
Extreme Maximum Daily Precip. (in.)	0.50	0.31	0.95	0.79	2.00	1.15	0.95	1.00	1.40	1.20	0.70	0.90	2.00
Days With ≥ 0.1" Precipitation	1	1	1	2	4	4	2	1	2	2	1	1	22
Days With ≥ 0.5" Precipitation	0	0	0	0	1	0	0	0	0	0	0	0	1
Days With ≥ 1.0" Precipitation	0	0	0	0	0	0	0	0	0	0	0	0	0
Mean Snowfall (in.)	3.4	2.7	2.8	1.0	0.1	trace	0.0	0.0	1.0	1.1	2.1	4.1	18.3
Maximum Snow Depth (in.)	8	8	7	4	trace	trace	0	0	12	6	12	13	13
Days With ≥ 1.0" Snow Depth	18	11	8	3	0	0	0	0	0	0	4	11	47

Bates Creek No 2 *Natrona County* Elevation: 6,009 ft. Latitude: 42° 38' N Longitude: 106° 23' W

	JAN	FEB	MAR	APR	MAY	JUN	JUL	AUG	SEP	OCT	NOV	DEC	YEAR
Mean Maximum Temp. (°F)	35.0	37.0	45.8	54.7	64.7	75.6	83.6	82.3	71.2	58.1	44.1	35.0	57.2
Mean Temp. (°F)	23.8	25.8	34.2	42.2	51.8	61.4	68.9	67.6	57.3	45.2	33.0	24.1	44.6
Mean Minimum Temp. (°F)	12.5	14.6	22.5	29.8	38.8	47.2	54.2	53.0	43.3	32.2	21.8	13.1	31.9
Extreme Maximum Temp. (°F)	60	62	72	78	88	96	98	96	90	80	70	63	98
Extreme Minimum Temp. (°F)	-22	-36	-11	-1	17	30	38	35	14	1	-16	-38	-38
Days Maximum Temp. ≥ 90°F	0	0	0	0	0	2	5	2	0	0	0	0	9
Days Maximum Temp. ≤ 32°F	11	8	4	1	0	0	0	0	0	1	5	12	42
Days Minimum Temp. ≤ 32°F	30	28	28	19	6	0	0	0	3	16	25	30	185
Days Minimum Temp. ≤ 0°F	4	3	1	0	0	0	0	0	0	0	1	4	13
Heating Degree Days (base 65°F)	1,271	1,102	949	676	406	149	25	34	249	607	955	1,262	7,685
Cooling Degree Days (base 65°F)	0	0	0	0	3	48	153	123	22	0	0	0	349
Mean Precipitation (in.)	0.61	0.70	0.96	1.32	2.22	1.42	1.06	0.84	1.02	1.37	0.74	0.61	12.87
Extreme Maximum Daily Precip. (in.)	0.66	0.82	1.41	1.17	3.01	1.55	1.42	0.96	1.15	2.35	0.68	0.90	3.01
Days With ≥ 0.1" Precipitation	2	2	3	4	6	4	3	3	3	3	3	2	38
Days With ≥ 0.5" Precipitation	0	0	0	1	1	1	0	0	0	1	0	0	4
Days With ≥ 1.0" Precipitation	0	0	0	0	0	0	0	0	0	0	0	0	0
Mean Snowfall (in.)	10.6	11.6	13.1	10.6	2.1	0.1	0.0	0.0	0.6	6.5	8.0	11.0	74.2
Maximum Snow Depth (in.)	16	24	19	18	14	2	0	0	5	17	10	23	24
Days With ≥ 1.0" Snow Depth	25	22	10	3	1	0	0	0	0	2	8	20	91

Billy Creek *Johnson County* Elevation: 4,975 ft. Latitude: 44° 08' N Longitude: 106° 43' W

	JAN	FEB	MAR	APR	MAY	JUN	JUL	AUG	SEP	OCT	NOV	DEC	YEAR
Mean Maximum Temp. (°F)	38.1	39.7	47.2	55.7	64.9	75.0	84.8	83.6	72.2	58.9	46.4	37.8	58.7
Mean Temp. (°F)	24.6	27.1	34.6	42.7	51.7	61.0	69.2	67.6	56.9	44.7	33.2	24.5	44.8
Mean Minimum Temp. (°F)	11.0	14.5	21.9	29.6	38.6	46.9	53.5	51.4	41.7	30.4	19.9	11.0	30.9
Extreme Maximum Temp. (°F)	66	71	78	85	91	100	104	102	98	87	81	72	104
Extreme Minimum Temp. (°F)	-32	-41	-17	-1	15	30	35	31	11	-12	-26	-39	-41
Days Maximum Temp. ≥ 90°F	0	0	0	0	0	3	10	9	2	0	0	0	24
Days Maximum Temp. ≤ 32°F	9	7	4	1	0	0	0	0	0	1	5	10	37
Days Minimum Temp. ≤ 32°F	30	27	27	19	7	1	0	0	4	18	26	30	189
Days Minimum Temp. ≤ 0°F	6	4	1	0	0	0	0	0	0	0	2	5	18
Heating Degree Days (base 65°F)	1,247	1,065	937	663	410	167	37	53	268	623	948	1,251	7,669
Cooling Degree Days (base 65°F)	0	0	0	0	6	52	174	139	32	0	0	0	403
Mean Precipitation (in.)	0.29	0.35	0.61	1.32	2.31	2.15	1.59	0.90	1.22	1.00	0.46	0.28	12.48
Extreme Maximum Daily Precip. (in.)	0.62	0.78	0.81	1.64	2.77	3.50	1.68	1.24	0.99	1.38	0.68	0.35	3.50
Days With ≥ 0.1" Precipitation	1	1	2	4	6	6	4	3	4	3	1	1	36
Days With ≥ 0.5" Precipitation	0	0	0	1	1	1	1	0	1	0	0	0	5
Days With ≥ 1.0" Precipitation	0	0	0	0	0	0	0	0	0	0	0	0	0
Mean Snowfall (in.)	5.0	6.0	6.7	6.3	0.9	trace	0.0	0.0	0.8	3.0	5.0	4.8	38.5
Maximum Snow Depth (in.)	10	10	10	22	4	trace	0	0	3	8	11	11	22
Days With ≥ 1.0" Snow Depth	14	12	7	2	0	0	0	0	0	1	6	11	53

The period of record for all cooperative weather station data is 1980 – 2009. See User Guide for detailed explanation of data.

Bondurant *Sublette County* Elevation: 6,535 ft. Latitude: 43° 14' N Longitude: 110° 26' W

	JAN	FEB	MAR	APR	MAY	JUN	JUL	AUG	SEP	OCT	NOV	DEC	YEAR
Mean Maximum Temp. (°F)	23.3	28.2	38.2	48.9	60.7	70.0	78.6	78.2	68.4	54.3	36.6	23.1	50.7
Mean Temp. (°F)	9.2	12.6	23.0	34.1	44.5	51.0	57.3	55.9	47.5	36.5	22.7	9.5	33.7
Mean Minimum Temp. (°F)	-4.9	-3.2	7.5	19.3	28.3	31.9	35.7	33.7	26.5	18.7	8.9	-3.8	16.6
Extreme Maximum Temp. (°F)	46	50	65	76	85	89	95	93	87	79	66	49	95
Extreme Minimum Temp. (°F)	-47	-52	-35	-18	9	14	18	13	3	-14	-35	-49	-52
Days Maximum Temp. ≥ 90°F	0	0	0	0	0	0	1	0	0	0	0	0	1
Days Maximum Temp. ≤ 32°F	24	18	6	1	0	0	0	0	0	1	10	25	85
Days Minimum Temp. ≤ 32°F	29	28	30	27	23	17	10	14	23	28	29	30	288
Days Minimum Temp. ≤ 0°F	19	16	9	1	0	0	0	0	0	0	8	18	71
Heating Degree Days (base 65°F)	1,725	1,479	1,294	919	628	416	236	275	518	876	1,262	1,715	11,343
Cooling Degree Days (base 65°F)	0	0	0	0	0	0	2	1	0	0	0	0	3
Mean Precipitation (in.)	2.08	1.67	1.41	1.04	1.76	1.62	1.30	1.20	1.42	1.30	1.89	2.10	18.79
Extreme Maximum Daily Precip. (in.)	1.32	1.00	0.98	1.35	0.94	1.32	1.11	1.58	1.38	1.09	1.10	1.40	1.58
Days With ≥ 0.1" Precipitation	6	5	4	3	5	4	4	4	4	4	5	6	54
Days With ≥ 0.5" Precipitation	1	1	1	0	1	1	0	0	0	1	1	1	8
Days With ≥ 1.0" Precipitation	0	0	0	0	0	0	0	0	0	0	0	0	0
Mean Snowfall (in.)	28.2	21.3	14.4	4.2	1.4	0.4	0.0	0.0	0.4	3.8	18.7	30.4	123.2
Maximum Snow Depth (in.)	52	63	56	47	14	4	0	0	1	12	32	47	63
Days With ≥ 1.0" Snow Depth	30	28	29	18	1	0	0	0	0	2	17	29	154

Boysen Dam *Fremont County* Elevation: 4,810 ft. Latitude: 43° 24' N Longitude: 108° 10' W

	JAN	FEB	MAR	APR	MAY	JUN	JUL	AUG	SEP	OCT	NOV	DEC	YEAR
Mean Maximum Temp. (°F)	31.2	37.4	50.0	60.0	70.4	81.1	90.3	88.2	75.7	60.9	44.0	29.8	59.9
Mean Temp. (°F)	19.0	24.5	37.1	47.0	57.0	66.8	75.2	73.3	61.5	48.1	33.3	19.5	46.9
Mean Minimum Temp. (°F)	6.7	11.6	24.2	33.9	43.6	52.5	60.1	58.3	47.4	35.3	22.6	9.2	33.8
Extreme Maximum Temp. (°F)	62	65	76	88	94	103	105	102	99	88	71	65	105
Extreme Minimum Temp. (°F)	-29	-30	-10	6	20	31	42	42	22	8	-15	-33	-33
Days Maximum Temp. ≥ 90°F	0	0	0	0	0	6	19	16	2	0	0	0	43
Days Maximum Temp. ≤ 32°F	15	8	2	0	0	0	0	0	0	0	5	16	46
Days Minimum Temp. ≤ 32°F	29	27	25	12	2	0	0	0	1	9	25	29	159
Days Minimum Temp. ≤ 0°F	9	5	1	0	0	0	0	0	0	0	1	6	22
Heating Degree Days (base 65°F)	1,421	1,138	856	534	262	71	5	7	155	517	944	1,405	7,315
Cooling Degree Days (base 65°F)	0	0	0	1	21	132	328	271	58	1	0	0	812
Mean Precipitation (in.)	0.23	0.28	0.60	0.95	1.79	1.20	0.85	0.49	0.93	0.78	0.38	0.31	8.79
Extreme Maximum Daily Precip. (in.)	0.32	0.41	0.85	1.30	2.00	1.29	1.95	1.10	1.32	1.30	0.47	1.25	2.00
Days With ≥ 0.1" Precipitation	1	1	2	3	4	3	2	2	3	2	1	1	25
Days With ≥ 0.5" Precipitation	0	0	0	0	1	1	0	0	0	0	0	0	2
Days With ≥ 1.0" Precipitation	0	0	0	0	0	0	0	0	0	0	0	0	0
Mean Snowfall (in.)	na	na	3.8	1.2	0.1	0.0	0.0	0.0	0.0	0.3	1.4	na	na
Maximum Snow Depth (in.)	na	na	na	na	1	2	0	0	trace	14	na	na	na
Days With ≥ 1.0" Snow Depth	na	na	2	1	0	0	0	0	0	0	2	na	na

Burris *Fremont County* Elevation: 6,120 ft. Latitude: 43° 22' N Longitude: 109° 17' W

	JAN	FEB	MAR	APR	MAY	JUN	JUL	AUG	SEP	OCT	NOV	DEC	YEAR
Mean Maximum Temp. (°F)	37.8	40.5	48.1	56.4	65.0	73.8	81.6	79.9	69.7	58.5	44.8	36.4	57.7
Mean Temp. (°F)	24.7	26.7	34.1	41.9	50.6	58.4	65.2	63.3	54.1	44.0	32.2	23.8	43.3
Mean Minimum Temp. (°F)	11.6	12.8	20.0	27.4	36.1	43.0	48.8	46.7	38.4	29.5	19.5	11.1	28.7
Extreme Maximum Temp. (°F)	62	66	73	84	89	95	95	94	88	81	72	64	95
Extreme Minimum Temp. (°F)	-38	-32	-19	-1	13	26	31	32	11	-6	-18	-45	-45
Days Maximum Temp. ≥ 90°F	0	0	0	0	0	1	3	1	0	0	0	0	5
Days Maximum Temp. ≤ 32°F	9	6	2	0	0	0	0	0	0	1	5	10	33
Days Minimum Temp. ≤ 32°F	30	27	29	22	10	1	0	0	6	19	27	29	200
Days Minimum Temp. ≤ 0°F	6	4	1	0	0	0	0	0	0	0	2	6	19
Heating Degree Days (base 65°F)	1,241	1,078	952	686	441	207	57	82	324	645	977	1,270	7,960
Cooling Degree Days (base 65°F)	0	0	0	0	1	17	71	37	4	0	0	0	130
Mean Precipitation (in.)	0.17	0.27	0.49	0.98	1.69	1.27	0.95	0.62	0.95	0.71	0.31	0.18	8.59
Extreme Maximum Daily Precip. (in.)	0.30	0.68	0.68	1.43	2.05	1.25	1.67	0.60	1.50	0.93	0.66	0.45	2.05
Days With ≥ 0.1" Precipitation	1	1	2	3	5	4	3	3	3	2	1	1	29
Days With ≥ 0.5" Precipitation	0	0	0	0	1	1	0	0	1	0	0	0	3
Days With ≥ 1.0" Precipitation	0	0	0	0	0	0	0	0	0	0	0	0	0
Mean Snowfall (in.)	3.3	4.0	5.7	6.5	1.3	0.2	0.0	0.0	1.3	2.9	3.8	3.5	32.5
Maximum Snow Depth (in.)	8	14	15	15	11	4	0	0	6	16	8	7	16
Days With ≥ 1.0" Snow Depth	4	5	4	2	0	0	0	0	0	1	4	5	25

Carpenter *Laramie County* Elevation: 5,390 ft. Latitude: 41° 03' N Longitude: 104° 22' W

	JAN	FEB	MAR	APR	MAY	JUN	JUL	AUG	SEP	OCT	NOV	DEC	YEAR
Mean Maximum Temp. (°F)	41.7	43.6	50.9	60.1	69.8	80.0	87.0	84.7	76.0	63.4	48.8	41.1	62.2
Mean Temp. (°F)	28.6	30.1	37.0	45.1	54.7	64.1	70.9	68.9	60.0	48.1	35.5	28.0	47.6
Mean Minimum Temp. (°F)	15.4	16.7	23.0	30.2	39.7	48.2	54.7	53.2	44.0	32.9	22.2	14.9	32.9
Extreme Maximum Temp. (°F)	70	70	78	88	93	101	103	100	96	87	76	70	103
Extreme Minimum Temp. (°F)	-29	-28	-9	-1	18	31	40	36	15	-6	-14	-31	-31
Days Maximum Temp. ≥ 90°F	0	0	0	0	0	5	12	8	2	0	0	0	27
Days Maximum Temp. ≤ 32°F	7	5	3	1	0	0	0	0	0	0	4	7	27
Days Minimum Temp. ≤ 32°F	30	27	27	17	5	0	0	0	2	14	26	29	177
Days Minimum Temp. ≤ 0°F	3	3	1	0	0	0	0	0	0	0	1	4	12
Heating Degree Days (base 65°F)	1,123	980	862	588	319	93	10	21	178	516	877	1,140	6,707
Cooling Degree Days (base 65°F)	0	0	0	0	8	73	200	150	35	0	0	0	466
Mean Precipitation (in.)	0.30	0.27	0.86	1.30	2.28	2.35	2.52	1.69	1.43	0.80	0.47	0.26	14.53
Extreme Maximum Daily Precip. (in.)	0.61	0.44	1.20	1.45	1.72	2.15	5.50	1.95	2.05	1.00	0.80	0.74	5.50
Days With ≥ 0.1" Precipitation	1	1	2	4	6	6	5	4	4	2	2	1	38
Days With ≥ 0.5" Precipitation	0	0	0	1	1	1	2	1	1	0	0	0	7
Days With ≥ 1.0" Precipitation	0	0	0	0	0	0	0	0	0	0	0	0	0
Mean Snowfall (in.)	5.1	4.8	8.3	3.9	0.6	trace	trace	0.0	0.5	2.5	4.7	4.9	35.3
Maximum Snow Depth (in.)	17	10	12	7	3	trace	trace	0	4	8	19	23	23
Days With ≥ 1.0" Snow Depth	6	7	4	1	0	0	0	0	0	1	4	6	29

The period of record for all cooperative weather station data is 1980 – 2009. See User Guide for detailed explanation of data.

Chugwater *Platte County* Elevation: 5,304 ft. Latitude: 41° 45' N Longitude: 104° 49' W

	JAN	FEB	MAR	APR	MAY	JUN	JUL	AUG	SEP	OCT	NOV	DEC	YEAR
Mean Maximum Temp. (°F)	40.4	42.1	49.4	58.3	67.7	78.4	86.6	84.6	75.0	62.0	48.6	39.8	61.1
Mean Temp. (°F)	28.9	30.0	36.4	43.9	53.2	62.7	70.0	68.2	58.4	46.5	36.1	28.2	46.9
Mean Minimum Temp. (°F)	17.4	17.9	23.2	29.5	38.7	47.0	53.3	51.8	41.7	30.8	23.6	16.6	32.6
Extreme Maximum Temp. (°F)	69	70	76	84	94	101	102	99	98	86	77	69	102
Extreme Minimum Temp. (°F)	-28	-28	-16	1	14	27	35	34	10	-5	-22	-35	-35
Days Maximum Temp. ≥ 90°F	0	0	0	0	0	4	12	8	1	0	0	0	25
Days Maximum Temp. ≤ 32°F	8	6	3	1	0	0	0	0	0	1	4	8	31
Days Minimum Temp. ≤ 32°F	28	25	26	19	6	0	0	0	4	18	24	28	178
Days Minimum Temp. ≤ 0°F	3	3	1	0	0	0	0	0	0	0	1	4	12
Heating Degree Days (base 65°F)	1,112	983	881	626	364	119	20	27	218	568	860	1,135	6,913
Cooling Degree Days (base 65°F)	0	0	0	0	5	57	180	135	27	0	0	0	404
Mean Precipitation (in.)	0.50	0.58	1.09	1.63	2.92	2.08	1.72	1.66	1.36	1.16	0.66	0.65	16.01
Extreme Maximum Daily Precip. (in.)	0.53	0.59	2.62	1.32	3.30	2.00	1.80	1.93	1.95	1.95	1.63	1.81	3.30
Days With ≥ 0.1" Precipitation	2	2	3	4	7	5	4	4	4	3	2	2	42
Days With ≥ 0.5" Precipitation	0	0	0	1	2	1	1	1	1	1	0	0	8
Days With ≥ 1.0" Precipitation	0	0	0	0	1	0	0	0	0	0	0	0	1
Mean Snowfall (in.)	9.2	9.3	11.9	9.1	2.3	0.0	0.0	0.0	1.3	5.0	9.8	11.1	69.0
Maximum Snow Depth (in.)	22	21	22	13	16	0	0	0	5	20	24	24	24
Days With ≥ 1.0" Snow Depth	13	11	9	4	0	0	0	0	0	2	9	14	62

Cody *Park County* Elevation: 4,990 ft. Latitude: 44° 33' N Longitude: 109° 04' W

	JAN	FEB	MAR	APR	MAY	JUN	JUL	AUG	SEP	OCT	NOV	DEC	YEAR
Mean Maximum Temp. (°F)	37.6	40.5	49.1	57.5	66.3	75.5	84.0	82.4	72.2	59.4	45.8	36.8	58.9
Mean Temp. (°F)	26.9	29.4	37.4	45.3	53.8	62.3	70.0	68.4	58.8	47.2	35.5	26.6	46.8
Mean Minimum Temp. (°F)	16.1	18.2	25.6	33.0	41.2	49.1	55.9	54.3	45.4	35.1	25.1	16.3	34.6
Extreme Maximum Temp. (°F)	63	66	74	83	89	99	100	100	96	84	74	65	100
Extreme Minimum Temp. (°F)	-26	-37	-15	4	20	31	39	35	14	-4	-17	-34	-37
Days Maximum Temp. ≥ 90°F	0	0	0	0	0	2	8	4	1	0	0	0	15
Days Maximum Temp. ≤ 32°F	9	6	2	1	0	0	0	0	0	1	4	10	33
Days Minimum Temp. ≤ 32°F	28	25	24	14	4	0	0	0	2	12	22	28	159
Days Minimum Temp. ≤ 0°F	4	3	1	0	0	0	0	0	0	0	1	4	13
Heating Degree Days (base 65°F)	1,176	1,002	849	586	351	130	22	31	216	545	878	1,185	6,971
Cooling Degree Days (base 65°F)	0	0	0	0	9	57	182	143	36	2	0	0	429
Mean Precipitation (in.)	0.35	0.33	0.59	1.09	1.83	1.68	1.15	0.89	1.12	0.87	0.47	0.29	10.66
Extreme Maximum Daily Precip. (in.)	1.15	0.83	0.61	1.95	1.98	2.40	0.90	0.68	1.21	0.90	0.83	0.76	2.40
Days With ≥ 0.1" Precipitation	1	1	2	3	6	5	3	3	4	3	2	1	34
Days With ≥ 0.5" Precipitation	0	0	0	0	1	1	1	0	0	0	0	0	3
Days With ≥ 1.0" Precipitation	0	0	0	0	0	0	0	0	0	0	0	0	0
Mean Snowfall (in.)	7.8	6.8	7.3	***5.4***	0.6	trace	0.0	0.0	0.2	4.3	6.0	7.3	***45.7***
Maximum Snow Depth (in.)	***18***	***14***	***10***	***12***	6	0	0	0	3	***8***	***8***	***14***	***18***
Days With ≥ 1.0" Snow Depth	***9***	***4***	***3***	***1***	0	0	0	0	0	1	***4***	7	***29***

Cody 12 SE *Park County* Elevation: 5,248 ft. Latitude: 44° 25' N Longitude: 108° 54' W

	JAN	FEB	MAR	APR	MAY	JUN	JUL	AUG	SEP	OCT	NOV	DEC	YEAR
Mean Maximum Temp. (°F)	38.3	40.3	48.4	56.5	65.4	75.6	84.6	83.8	71.9	57.7	45.9	37.7	58.9
Mean Temp. (°F)	25.0	27.6	35.7	43.3	52.1	61.1	68.9	67.5	56.3	43.8	33.0	24.5	44.9
Mean Minimum Temp. (°F)	11.7	14.6	23.0	30.1	38.6	46.6	53.2	51.2	40.7	29.9	20.1	11.3	30.9
Extreme Maximum Temp. (°F)	65	68	77	84	89	101	102	100	97	88	73	69	102
Extreme Minimum Temp. (°F)	-29	-40	-18	0	13	31	36	31	7	-8	-23	-41	-41
Days Maximum Temp. ≥ 90°F	0	0	0	0	0	2	10	7	1	0	0	0	20
Days Maximum Temp. ≤ 32°F	8	6	3	1	0	0	0	0	0	1	4	9	32
Days Minimum Temp. ≤ 32°F	29	27	27	19	7	0	0	0	4	18	26	30	187
Days Minimum Temp. ≤ 0°F	6	4	1	0	0	0	0	0	0	0	2	6	19
Heating Degree Days (base 65°F)	1,234	1,049	900	644	399	162	32	44	275	650	953	1,248	7,590
Cooling Degree Days (base 65°F)	0	0	0	0	6	50	161	129	22	1	0	0	369
Mean Precipitation (in.)	***0.21***	0.21	0.54	0.90	1.91	1.68	1.02	0.77	0.91	0.66	0.32	0.20	***9.33***
Extreme Maximum Daily Precip. (in.)	***0.40***	***0.52***	***1.00***	***1.03***	1.80	2.54	***1.70***	1.18	***1.27***	***0.73***	0.54	***0.35***	***2.54***
Days With ≥ 0.1" Precipitation	***1***	1	2	3	5	5	3	3	3	2	1	1	***30***
Days With ≥ 0.5" Precipitation	***0***	0	0	0	1	1	0	0	1	0	0	0	***3***
Days With ≥ 1.0" Precipitation	***0***	0	0	0	0	0	0	0	0	0	0	0	***0***
Mean Snowfall (in.)	***1.5***	na	***1.0***	***0.8***	0.2	0.0	0.0	0.0	0.1	0.4	0.8	na	na
Maximum Snow Depth (in.)	na	na	na	***2***	***trace***	0	***0***	***0***	***1***	na	***3***	na	na
Days With ≥ 1.0" Snow Depth	na	na	***1***	***0***	0	0	0	0	0	***1***	***0***	***1***	na

Dillinger *Campbell County* Elevation: 4,310 ft. Latitude: 44° 06' N Longitude: 105° 07' W

	JAN	FEB	MAR	APR	MAY	JUN	JUL	AUG	SEP	OCT	NOV	DEC	YEAR
Mean Maximum Temp. (°F)	35.3	38.3	46.8	57.3	67.2	78.1	88.0	86.5	74.7	59.5	45.3	35.0	59.3
Mean Temp. (°F)	22.9	25.9	34.1	43.4	53.2	63.1	71.1	69.8	58.5	45.0	32.2	22.4	45.1
Mean Minimum Temp. (°F)	10.5	13.5	21.3	29.4	39.2	47.9	54.4	52.9	42.3	30.6	19.2	9.8	30.9
Extreme Maximum Temp. (°F)	66	70	78	87	93	103	108	104	101	90	77	70	108
Extreme Minimum Temp. (°F)	-34	-38	-25	-4	15	30	36	30	12	-16	-24	-45	-45
Days Maximum Temp. ≥ 90°F	0	0	0	0	0	5	14	13	3	0	0	0	35
Days Maximum Temp. ≤ 32°F	11	8	4	1	0	0	0	0	0	1	5	12	42
Days Minimum Temp. ≤ 32°F	30	28	28	19	6	0	0	0	4	17	27	30	189
Days Minimum Temp. ≤ 0°F	7	5	2	0	0	0	0	0	0	0	2	6	22
Heating Degree Days (base 65°F)	1,299	1,099	952	643	364	125	18	27	228	613	977	1,314	7,659
Cooling Degree Days (base 65°F)	0	0	0	0	5	72	216	183	39	0	0	0	515
Mean Precipitation (in.)	0.35	0.50	0.95	1.74	2.52	2.20	1.66	1.21	1.11	1.24	0.58	0.53	14.59
Extreme Maximum Daily Precip. (in.)	0.36	1.30	1.05	1.81	2.22	1.41	1.93	1.34	1.57	1.72	0.96	0.57	2.22
Days With ≥ 0.1" Precipitation	1	2	3	5	6	6	4	3	3	3	2	2	40
Days With ≥ 0.5" Precipitation	0	0	0	1	1	1	1	1	1	1	0	0	7
Days With ≥ 1.0" Precipitation	0	0	0	0	0	0	0	0	0	0	0	0	0
Mean Snowfall (in.)	5.3	6.0	7.4	5.2	0.8	0.1	0.0	0.0	0.1	1.4	5.4	7.2	38.9
Maximum Snow Depth (in.)	11	***16***	***16***	***24***	4	2	0	0	0	***4***	9	14	***24***
Days With ≥ 1.0" Snow Depth	***7***	***5***	***4***	1	0	0	0	0	0	0	4	11	***32***

Dubois *Fremont County* Elevation: 6,959 ft. Latitude: 43° 32' N Longitude: 109° 38' W

	JAN	FEB	MAR	APR	MAY	JUN	JUL	AUG	SEP	OCT	NOV	DEC	YEAR
Mean Maximum Temp. (°F)	34.6	***36.8***	***43.5***	***50.6***	60.7	70.3	79.2	77.8	67.1	55.2	41.6	33.6	***54.2***
Mean Temp. (°F)	23.9	***24.7***	***31.4***	***37.6***	46.7	54.9	***61.7***	59.9	51.2	41.2	30.5	23.2	***40.6***
Mean Minimum Temp. (°F)	13.3	***12.6***	***19.2***	***24.6***	32.6	39.4	***44.1***	41.9	35.2	27.1	19.3	12.8	***26.8***
Extreme Maximum Temp. (°F)	59	***66***	***73***	***79***	***85***	92	97	***92***	86	80	70	56	***97***
Extreme Minimum Temp. (°F)	-35	***-34***	***-17***	***-2***	***10***	20	27	***27***	8	2	-24	-42	***-42***
Days Maximum Temp. ≥ 90°F	0	***0***	***0***	0	0	0	1	1	0	0	0	0	***2***
Days Maximum Temp. ≤ 32°F	12	***8***	***4***	1	0	0	0	0	0	1	6	12	***44***
Days Minimum Temp. ≤ 32°F	30	***28***	***28***	25	15	3	0	1	10	24	26	29	***219***
Days Minimum Temp. ≤ 0°F	4	***5***	***2***	0	0	0	0	0	0	0	2	5	***18***
Heating Degree Days (base 65°F)	1,266	***1,127***	***1,035***	***815***	562	303	***121***	162	409	731	1,029	1,290	***8,850***
Cooling Degree Days (base 65°F)	0	***0***	***0***	***0***	0	5	***25***	9	0	0	0	0	***39***
Mean Precipitation (in.)	0.27	***0.33***	***0.41***	1.12	1.51	1.23	1.15	0.84	1.26	0.65	0.51	0.30	***9.58***
Extreme Maximum Daily Precip. (in.)	0.28	***0.85***	***0.35***	***1.52***	***1.87***	1.10	***1.39***	***0.63***	***1.61***	***0.64***	***0.56***	***0.50***	***1.87***
Days With ≥ 0.1" Precipitation	1	***1***	***2***	3	4	4	4	3	4	2	2	1	***31***
Days With ≥ 0.5" Precipitation	0	***0***	***0***	0	1	0	0	0	1	0	0	0	***2***
Days With ≥ 1.0" Precipitation	0	***0***	***0***	0	0	0	0	0	0	0	0	0	***0***
Mean Snowfall (in.)	3.9	***5.2***	***5.7***	8.2	3.4	0.5	0.0	0.0	2.4	3.6	5.6	5.3	***43.8***
Maximum Snow Depth (in.)	***6***	na	na	na	***5***	***3***	***0***	***0***	***14***	***7***	***7***	***8***	na
Days With ≥ 1.0" Snow Depth	***5***	***5***	***3***	***3***	1	0	0	0	1	1	***5***	***6***	***30***

Dull Center 1 SE *Converse County* Elevation: 4,415 ft. Latitude: 43° 25' N Longitude: 104° 58' W

	JAN	FEB	MAR	APR	MAY	JUN	JUL	AUG	SEP	OCT	NOV	DEC	YEAR
Mean Maximum Temp. (°F)	37.3	40.4	49.6	59.3	69.4	80.0	90.0	88.4	76.7	61.8	46.7	36.3	61.3
Mean Temp. (°F)	25.6	28.2	36.4	45.3	55.1	64.7	73.1	71.5	60.5	47.2	34.7	24.8	47.3
Mean Minimum Temp. (°F)	13.7	15.9	23.1	31.2	40.8	49.4	56.1	54.5	44.2	32.6	22.6	13.4	33.1
Extreme Maximum Temp. (°F)	68	71	80	87	94	106	107	103	99	87	78	67	107
Extreme Minimum Temp. (°F)	-28	-37	-18	1	17	30	41	37	14	-8	-21	-42	-42
Days Maximum Temp. ≥ 90°F	0	0	0	0	0	5	17	16	4	0	0	0	42
Days Maximum Temp. ≤ 32°F	9	7	3	1	0	0	0	0	0	1	5	11	37
Days Minimum Temp. ≤ 32°F	29	26	26	17	5	0	0	0	2	14	25	29	173
Days Minimum Temp. ≤ 0°F	5	4	1	0	0	0	0	0	0	0	1	5	16
Heating Degree Days (base 65°F)	1,216	1,034	880	585	310	92	9	14	178	544	903	1,239	7,004
Cooling Degree Days (base 65°F)	0	0	0	1	12	90	265	222	50	0	0	0	640
Mean Precipitation (in.)	0.21	0.49	0.90	1.58	2.20	2.03	1.55	1.29	1.10	0.99	0.52	0.35	13.21
Extreme Maximum Daily Precip. (in.)	0.25	1.02	1.58	2.22	1.62	3.24	2.22	1.53	1.28	1.73	0.85	0.58	3.24
Days With ≥ 0.1" Precipitation	1	2	2	4	5	5	4	3	3	3	2	1	35
Days With ≥ 0.5" Precipitation	0	0	0	1	1	1	1	1	1	1	0	0	7
Days With ≥ 1.0" Precipitation	0	0	0	0	0	0	0	0	0	0	0	0	0
Mean Snowfall (in.)	4.9	6.7	9.8	7.5	1.0	0.0	0.0	0.0	0.6	3.4	6.3	6.8	47.0
Maximum Snow Depth (in.)	14	9	14	18	2	0	0	0	6	13	14	19	19
Days With ≥ 1.0" Snow Depth	13	10	8	2	0	0	0	0	0	1	6	14	54

Echeta 2 NW *Campbell County* Elevation: 4,000 ft. Latitude: 44° 29' N Longitude: 105° 54' W

	JAN	FEB	MAR	APR	MAY	JUN	JUL	AUG	SEP	OCT	NOV	DEC	YEAR
Mean Maximum Temp. (°F)	***36.8***	***40.2***	***49.7***	60.0	68.7	***80.6***	***89.5***	***87.5***	***75.5***	61.6	45.2	35.9	***60.9***
Mean Temp. (°F)	***23.9***	***27.2***	***36.0***	45.0	53.9	***64.6***	***72.1***	***70.2***	***58.7***	46.3	32.3	23.3	***46.1***
Mean Minimum Temp. (°F)	***10.9***	***14.1***	***22.3***	30.0	39.1	***48.4***	***54.8***	***52.9***	***41.8***	31.0	19.4	10.5	***31.3***
Extreme Maximum Temp. (°F)	67	***70***	81	88	96	***106***	***111***	***105***	***99***	***90***	78	66	***111***
Extreme Minimum Temp. (°F)	-42	***-42***	-21	0	13	***29***	***34***	***30***	***10***	***-19***	-20	-54	***-54***
Days Maximum Temp. ≥ 90°F	0	***0***	0	0	0	***6***	***16***	***13***	***3***	0	0	0	***38***
Days Maximum Temp. ≤ 32°F	***10***	7	3	1	0	0	0	***0***	***0***	1	5	10	***37***
Days Minimum Temp. ≤ 32°F	30	***27***	26	18	6	***0***	0	***0***	***4***	17	26	29	***183***
Days Minimum Temp. ≤ 0°F	***7***	***5***	1	0	0	0	0	***0***	***0***	0	2	6	***21***
Heating Degree Days (base 65°F)	***1,270***	***1,061***	***893***	593	346	***100***	***16***	***27***	***224***	574	974	1,288	***7,366***
Cooling Degree Days (base 65°F)	***0***	***0***	***0***	1	9	***94***	***245***	***195***	***40***	1	0	0	***585***
Mean Precipitation (in.)	***0.41***	***0.64***	1.07	2.11	2.58	2.35	1.45	***1.10***	***1.49***	1.44	0.79	0.53	***15.96***
Extreme Maximum Daily Precip. (in.)	***0.47***	na	***1.25***	***2.55***	***2.02***	***2.02***	***1.45***	***2.35***	***1.98***	***1.75***	***1.12***	***0.75***	na
Days With ≥ 0.1" Precipitation	***2***	***2***	3	6	7	***6***	4	***2***	***4***	4	3	2	***45***
Days With ≥ 0.5" Precipitation	***0***	***0***	0	1	2	***1***	1	***1***	***1***	1	0	0	***8***
Days With ≥ 1.0" Precipitation	***0***	***0***	0	0	1	***0***	0	***0***	***0***	0	0	0	***1***
Mean Snowfall (in.)	***7.1***	***7.4***	10.9	7.7	1.5	0.0	0.0	***0.0***	***0.9***	***2.5***	***6.7***	8.7	***53.4***
Maximum Snow Depth (in.)	na	na	na	***19***	***9***	***0***	***0***	na	***1***	na	na	na	na
Days With ≥ 1.0" Snow Depth	na	na	***6***	***2***	0	***0***	0	***0***	***0***	***1***	***5***	***11***	na

Elk Mountain *Carbon County* Elevation: 7,265 ft. Latitude: 41° 41' N Longitude: 106° 25' W

	JAN	FEB	MAR	APR	MAY	JUN	JUL	AUG	SEP	OCT	NOV	DEC	YEAR
Mean Maximum Temp. (°F)	33.7	35.0	42.1	50.6	61.2	72.8	80.4	78.0	68.6	55.6	41.9	33.7	54.5
Mean Temp. (°F)	24.1	25.1	31.8	38.7	48.1	57.5	64.2	62.3	53.7	42.9	31.7	24.0	42.0
Mean Minimum Temp. (°F)	14.5	15.1	21.4	26.8	34.9	42.2	48.1	46.5	38.6	30.2	21.5	14.2	29.5
Extreme Maximum Temp. (°F)	55	56	75	75	85	92	94	93	89	79	68	58	94
Extreme Minimum Temp. (°F)	-25	-30	-17	-5	14	26	34	29	6	-5	-17	-35	-35
Days Maximum Temp. ≥ 90°F	0	0	0	0	0	0	2	0	0	0	0	0	2
Days Maximum Temp. ≤ 32°F	13	9	5	2	0	0	0	0	0	1	6	13	49
Days Minimum Temp. ≤ 32°F	30	27	27	22	10	1	0	0	6	17	25	29	194
Days Minimum Temp. ≤ 0°F	3	3	1	0	0	0	0	0	0	0	1	3	11
Heating Degree Days (base 65°F)	1,260	1,123	1,023	782	517	228	69	104	336	677	993	1,265	8,377
Cooling Degree Days (base 65°F)	0	0	0	0	0	10	52	26	3	0	0	0	91
Mean Precipitation (in.)	0.67	0.73	1.19	1.27	1.77	0.93	0.83	0.89	1.09	0.99	0.93	0.78	12.07
Extreme Maximum Daily Precip. (in.)	2.10	0.83	1.55	1.72	2.40	3.25	1.93	1.83	1.21	1.27	1.51	1.60	3.25
Days With ≥ 0.1" Precipitation	2	2	3	3	4	2	2	2	3	3	2	2	30
Days With ≥ 0.5" Precipitation	0	0	1	1	1	0	0	0	1	1	0	0	5
Days With ≥ 1.0" Precipitation	0	0	0	0	0	0	0	0	0	0	0	0	0
Mean Snowfall (in.)	8.2	9.5	13.0	9.8	3.3	trace	0.0	0.0	0.8	6.5	8.6	10.2	69.9
Maximum Snow Depth (in.)	28	21	16	16	20	1	0	0	9	20	17	24	28
Days With ≥ 1.0" Snow Depth	18	19	12	6	1	0	0	0	1	3	10	15	85

The period of record for all cooperative weather station data is 1980 – 2009. See User Guide for detailed explanation of data.

Evanston 1 E *Uinta County* Elevation: 6,825 ft. Latitude: 41° 16' N Longitude: 110° 57' W

	JAN	FEB	MAR	APR	MAY	JUN	JUL	AUG	SEP	OCT	NOV	DEC	YEAR
Mean Maximum Temp. (°F)	32.2	34.7	43.8	54.6	63.3	73.7	81.8	80.2	70.7	58.5	42.4	33.0	55.7
Mean Temp. (°F)	21.6	23.5	32.2	41.3	48.8	57.2	64.3	63.1	54.3	43.8	30.8	22.0	41.9
Mean Minimum Temp. (°F)	10.9	12.3	20.5	27.7	34.1	40.5	46.8	46.0	37.9	28.9	19.2	10.9	28.0
Extreme Maximum Temp. (°F)	57	60	75	77	85	94	99	92	88	80	69	59	99
Extreme Minimum Temp. (°F)	-20	-30	-8	0	15	22	31	25	14	2	-17	-31	-31
Days Maximum Temp. ≥ 90°F	0	0	0	0	0	0	2	0	0	0	0	0	2
Days Maximum Temp. ≤ 32°F	16	11	3	0	0	0	0	0	0	0	7	14	51
Days Minimum Temp. ≤ 32°F	30	28	29	23	12	3	0	0	6	21	28	30	210
Days Minimum Temp. ≤ 0°F	6	5	1	0	0	0	0	0	0	0	2	5	19
Heating Degree Days (base 65°F)	1,340	1,165	1,010	704	494	235	61	78	316	652	1,020	1,328	8,403
Cooling Degree Days (base 65°F)	0	0	0	0	0	7	47	26	2	0	0	0	82
Mean Precipitation (in.)	0.79	0.65	0.76	1.00	1.71	1.07	0.78	0.94	1.23	1.05	0.97	0.66	11.61
Extreme Maximum Daily Precip. (in.)	1.28	0.90	0.86	1.50	2.00	1.18	1.22	1.31	1.24	1.42	0.86	0.71	2.00
Days With ≥ 0.1" Precipitation	3	2	2	3	5	3	2	3	3	3	3	2	34
Days With ≥ 0.5" Precipitation	0	0	0	0	1	0	0	0	1	0	0	0	2
Days With ≥ 1.0" Precipitation	0	0	0	0	0	0	0	0	0	0	0	0	0
Mean Snowfall (in.)	11.3	7.1	4.3	1.7	1.1	0.2	trace	0.0	0.2	1.3	8.3	9.3	44.8
Maximum Snow Depth (in.)	28	27	24	8	5	5	trace	0	4	8	14	19	28
Days With ≥ 1.0" Snow Depth	25	23	11	1	0	0	0	0	0	1	9	21	91

Fontenelle Dam *Lincoln County* Elevation: 6,479 ft. Latitude: 41° 59' N Longitude: 110° 04' W

	JAN	FEB	MAR	APR	MAY	JUN	JUL	AUG	SEP	OCT	NOV	DEC	YEAR
Mean Maximum Temp. (°F)	25.1	29.1	39.8	50.6	60.9	71.3	81.2	79.5	68.0	54.6	37.8	25.8	52.0
Mean Temp. (°F)	11.2	15.0	26.6	35.8	45.6	54.6	62.9	60.8	50.2	38.0	23.8	12.1	36.4
Mean Minimum Temp. (°F)	-2.8	0.8	13.3	21.0	30.3	37.9	44.6	42.1	32.4	21.3	9.8	-1.7	20.7
Extreme Maximum Temp. (°F)	52	56	66	79	83	94	100	94	86	78	66	57	100
Extreme Minimum Temp. (°F)	-43	-46	-33	-1	6	14	21	17	4	-6	-28	-45	-46
Days Maximum Temp. ≥ 90°F	0	0	0	0	0	1	3	1	0	0	0	0	5
Days Maximum Temp. ≤ 32°F	23	16	7	1	0	0	0	0	0	1	10	22	80
Days Minimum Temp. ≤ 32°F	31	28	31	29	18	6	1	2	14	29	29	31	249
Days Minimum Temp. ≤ 0°F	18	13	3	0	0	0	0	0	0	0	6	18	58
Heating Degree Days (base 65°F)	1,663	1,409	1,184	868	594	312	105	141	437	831	1,228	1,635	10,407
Cooling Degree Days (base 65°F)	0	0	0	0	0	7	46	18	1	0	0	0	72
Mean Precipitation (in.)	0.30	0.30	0.44	0.79	1.28	0.75	0.65	0.71	0.95	0.64	0.43	0.24	7.48
Extreme Maximum Daily Precip. (in.)	0.40	0.57	0.56	1.20	1.42	1.08	0.79	1.04	1.82	1.02	0.51	0.53	1.82
Days With ≥ 0.1" Precipitation	1	1	2	3	4	2	2	3	3	2	2	1	26
Days With ≥ 0.5" Precipitation	0	0	0	0	1	0	0	0	0	0	0	0	1
Days With ≥ 1.0" Precipitation	0	0	0	0	0	0	0	0	0	0	0	0	0
Mean Snowfall (in.)	4.6	na	3.4	2.1	0.5	0.0	0.0	0.0	0.0	1.2	na	na	na
Maximum Snow Depth (in.)	na	na	na	5	2	0	0	0	1	9	na	na	na
Days With ≥ 1.0" Snow Depth	na	na	na	1	0	0	0	0	0	1	na	na	na

Gillette 6 SE *Campbell County* Elevation: 4,640 ft. Latitude: 44° 14' N Longitude: 105° 26' W

	JAN	FEB	MAR	APR	MAY	JUN	JUL	AUG	SEP	OCT	NOV	DEC	YEAR
Mean Maximum Temp. (°F)	34.3	37.5	46.3	55.9	65.6	76.3	85.5	84.4	72.5	58.1	44.1	34.1	57.9
Mean Temp. (°F)	24.0	27.0	34.7	43.5	52.9	62.8	70.7	69.6	58.5	45.6	33.1	24.0	45.5
Mean Minimum Temp. (°F)	13.5	16.4	23.1	31.1	40.3	49.2	55.9	54.8	44.5	33.1	22.2	13.8	33.2
Extreme Maximum Temp. (°F)	67	70	80	88	92	101	107	101	98	85	75	66	107
Extreme Minimum Temp. (°F)	-31	-35	-16	-5	14	32	37	35	18	-9	-23	-37	-37
Days Maximum Temp. ≥ 90°F	0	0	0	0	0	3	11	8	2	0	0	0	24
Days Maximum Temp. ≤ 32°F	11	9	5	1	0	0	0	0	0	1	6	12	45
Days Minimum Temp. ≤ 32°F	30	27	26	18	5	0	0	0	2	14	25	30	177
Days Minimum Temp. ≤ 0°F	6	4	2	0	0	0	0	0	0	0	1	5	18
Heating Degree Days (base 65°F)	1,265	1,068	932	638	375	130	21	30	226	595	950	1,265	7,495
Cooling Degree Days (base 65°F)	0	0	0	1	8	69	206	179	39	0	0	0	502
Mean Precipitation (in.)	0.49	0.60	1.12	1.81	2.86	2.39	1.75	1.33	1.46	1.47	0.61	0.63	16.52
Extreme Maximum Daily Precip. (in.)	0.67	1.31	1.55	2.43	2.63	2.38	2.25	2.60	2.05	2.16	0.55	0.80	2.63
Days With ≥ 0.1" Precipitation	2	2	4	5	7	6	4	3	4	4	2	2	45
Days With ≥ 0.5" Precipitation	0	0	0	1	2	1	1	1	1	1	0	0	8
Days With ≥ 1.0" Precipitation	0	0	0	0	1	0	0	0	0	0	0	0	1
Mean Snowfall (in.)	7.5	7.6	11.1	9.5	1.5	0.1	0.0	0.0	0.7	4.5	6.8	9.4	58.7
Maximum Snow Depth (in.)	11	14	15	21	5	trace	1	0	2	8	8	19	21
Days With ≥ 1.0" Snow Depth	17	12	10	3	1	0	0	0	0	2	8	16	69

Glenrock 5 ESE *Converse County* Elevation: 4,948 ft. Latitude: 42° 50' N Longitude: 105° 47' W

	JAN	FEB	MAR	APR	MAY	JUN	JUL	AUG	SEP	OCT	NOV	DEC	YEAR
Mean Maximum Temp. (°F)	38.0	40.6	48.8	59.0	68.9	80.7	88.7	86.4	75.4	61.0	45.9	37.5	60.9
Mean Temp. (°F)	27.7	29.9	37.1	45.6	55.0	65.4	72.5	70.5	59.8	47.2	35.2	27.6	47.8
Mean Minimum Temp. (°F)	17.4	19.1	25.4	32.2	41.1	49.9	56.2	54.4	44.4	33.4	24.4	17.7	34.6
Extreme Maximum Temp. (°F)	69	68	80	86	92	104	107	102	98	88	74	66	107
Extreme Minimum Temp. (°F)	-28	-26	-11	4	15	32	39	35	17	-9	-20	-40	-40
Days Maximum Temp. ≥ 90°F	0	0	0	0	0	6	14	10	2	0	0	0	32
Days Maximum Temp. ≤ 32°F	9	6	3	1	0	0	0	0	0	0	5	10	34
Days Minimum Temp. ≤ 32°F	27	23	23	15	4	0	0	0	2	13	22	26	155
Days Minimum Temp. ≤ 0°F	4	3	1	0	0	0	0	0	0	0	1	4	13
Heating Degree Days (base 65°F)	1,149	987	858	576	311	81	8	14	192	546	888	1,152	6,762
Cooling Degree Days (base 65°F)	0	0	0	1	8	97	246	189	40	1	0	0	582
Mean Precipitation (in.)	0.27	0.44	0.79	1.24	1.97	1.40	0.90	0.69	1.04	1.00	0.63	0.33	10.70
Extreme Maximum Daily Precip. (in.)	0.56	1.10	1.48	1.30	2.15	na	1.10	0.87	1.38	1.15	1.10	0.55	na
Days With ≥ 0.1" Precipitation	1	1	2	3	5	3	2	2	3	3	2	1	28
Days With ≥ 0.5" Precipitation	0	0	0	1	1	1	0	0	1	1	0	0	5
Days With ≥ 1.0" Precipitation	0	0	0	0	0	0	0	0	0	0	0	0	0
Mean Snowfall (in.)	2.7	na	na	na	trace	trace	0.0	0.0	trace	0.8	na	na	na
Maximum Snow Depth (in.)	na	na	na	na	na	0	0	0	trace	na	na	na	na
Days With ≥ 1.0" Snow Depth	na	na	na	0	0	0	0	0	0	0	na	na	na

The period of record for all cooperative weather station data is 1980 – 2009. See User Guide for detailed explanation of data.

Midwest *Natrona County* Elevation: 4,859 ft. Latitude: 43° 25' N Longitude: 106° 17' W

	JAN	FEB	MAR	APR	MAY	JUN	JUL	AUG	SEP	OCT	NOV	DEC	YEAR
Mean Maximum Temp. (°F)	36.8	39.5	49.5	***58.5***	***68.6***	***80.3***	***89.2***	***87.4***	***76.2***	62.0	45.6	35.7	***60.8***
Mean Temp. (°F)	25.1	27.5	36.5	***44.4***	***54.3***	***64.2***	***71.8***	***69.7***	***59.0***	46.9	33.3	24.4	***46.4***
Mean Minimum Temp. (°F)	13.3	15.4	23.5	***30.3***	***39.9***	***48.1***	***54.4***	***52.0***	***41.8***	31.8	21.2	13.0	***32.1***
Extreme Maximum Temp. (°F)	64	70	74	***86***	***92***	***103***	***105***	***101***	***98***	87	74	65	***105***
Extreme Minimum Temp. (°F)	-28	-31	-16	***0***	***18***	***31***	***38***	***34***	***18***	-3	-29	-40	***-40***
Days Maximum Temp. ≥ 90°F	0	0	0	***0***	***0***	***6***	***17***	***13***	3	0	0	0	***39***
Days Maximum Temp. ≤ 32°F	10	7	3	***1***	***0***	***0***	***0***	***0***	0	1	5	11	***38***
Days Minimum Temp. ≤ 32°F	30	27	26	***18***	***5***	***0***	***0***	***0***	3	16	25	28	***178***
Days Minimum Temp. ≤ 0°F	5	4	1	***0***	***0***	***0***	***0***	***0***	0	0	1	5	***16***
Heating Degree Days (base 65°F)	1,231	1,055	875	***611***	***335***	***101***	***12***	***24***	***210***	554	944	1,253	***7,205***
Cooling Degree Days (base 65°F)	0	0	0	***1***	***10***	***84***	***231***	***177***	***36***	0	0	0	***539***
Mean Precipitation (in.)	0.27	0.49	1.01	***1.23***	***2.48***	***1.67***	***1.25***	***0.63***	***0.90***	1.15	0.52	0.46	***12.06***
Extreme Maximum Daily Precip. (in.)	0.42	1.06	1.14	***1.35***	***2.10***	***2.01***	***1.43***	na	***1.80***	***1.43***	0.75	0.61	na
Days With ≥ 0.1" Precipitation	1	1	3	***4***	***5***	***4***	***3***	***2***	***2***	3	2	2	***32***
Days With ≥ 0.5" Precipitation	0	0	0	***1***	***2***	***1***	***1***	***0***	***1***	1	0	0	***7***
Days With ≥ 1.0" Precipitation	0	0	0	***0***	***1***	***0***	***0***	***0***	***0***	0	0	0	***1***
Mean Snowfall (in.)	6.4	7.6	9.9	***6.0***	***1.1***	***0.0***	***0.0***	***0.0***	0.3	4.3	6.4	7.5	***49.5***
Maximum Snow Depth (in.)	9	11	20	***17***	***5***	***0***	***0***	***0***	7	10	25	9	***25***
Days With ≥ 1.0" Snow Depth	11	9	6	***3***	***0***	***0***	***0***	***0***	0	2	5	12	***48***

Muddy Gap *Carbon County* Elevation: 6,245 ft. Latitude: 42° 22' N Longitude: 107° 27' W

	JAN	FEB	MAR	APR	MAY	JUN	JUL	AUG	SEP	OCT	NOV	DEC	YEAR
Mean Maximum Temp. (°F)	***32.8***	***35.6***	***46.3***	57.0	66.8	***77.7***	***86.7***	84.7	73.4	59.4	***41.7***	32.4	***57.9***
Mean Temp. (°F)	***24.1***	***26.0***	***34.8***	***43.5***	52.6	***62.3***	***70.4***	68.8	58.6	46.3	***32.0***	23.6	***45.2***
Mean Minimum Temp. (°F)	***15.3***	***16.2***	***23.2***	***29.9***	38.4	***46.7***	***54.2***	52.9	43.6	33.1	***22.3***	14.8	***32.6***
Extreme Maximum Temp. (°F)	53	60	73	79	89	97	99	102	92	82	68	58	102
Extreme Minimum Temp. (°F)	-26	-28	-15	-6	14	29	36	31	12	2	-17	-40	-40
Days Maximum Temp. ≥ 90°F	0	0	0	0	0	3	9	5	0	0	0	0	17
Days Maximum Temp. ≤ 32°F	13	9	3	1	0	0	0	0	0	1	7	14	48
Days Minimum Temp. ≤ 32°F	28	25	25	***17***	***6***	1	0	0	3	13	22	28	***168***
Days Minimum Temp. ≤ 0°F	3	3	1	0	0	0	0	0	0	0	1	3	11
Heating Degree Days (base 65°F)	***1,262***	***1,095***	***931***	***640***	381	***130***	***15***	20	211	574	***982***	1,276	***7,517***
Cooling Degree Days (base 65°F)	***0***	***0***	***0***	***0***	4	***54***	***191***	149	25	0	***0***	0	***423***
Mean Precipitation (in.)	***0.34***	0.41	1.01	1.27	1.85	1.04	***0.73***	0.52	1.01	0.89	***0.79***	0.36	***10.22***
Extreme Maximum Daily Precip. (in.)	***0.97***	***0.53***	***2.05***	***1.18***	***2.70***	***1.18***	***0.98***	***0.75***	***1.70***	***1.40***	***1.31***	0.58	***2.70***
Days With ≥ 0.1" Precipitation	***1***	1	2	4	5	2	2	2	3	2	***2***	1	***27***
Days With ≥ 0.5" Precipitation	***0***	0	1	1	1	1	0	0	1	1	***0***	0	***6***
Days With ≥ 1.0" Precipitation	***0***	0	0	0	0	0	0	0	0	0	***0***	0	***0***
Mean Snowfall (in.)	na	***6.2***	***9.8***	***8.2***	1.4	0.1	0.0	0.0	0.5	3.2	***8.8***	5.6	na
Maximum Snow Depth (in.)	na	na	na	na	***7***	***0***	***0***	***0***	***12***	***16***	na	na	na
Days With ≥ 1.0" Snow Depth	na	***4***	***3***	2	0	0	0	0	0	1	na	***2***	na

Powder River No 2 *Natrona County* Elevation: 5,700 ft. Latitude: 43° 02' N Longitude: 106° 59' W

	JAN	FEB	MAR	APR	MAY	JUN	JUL	AUG	SEP	OCT	NOV	DEC	YEAR
Mean Maximum Temp. (°F)	***35.1***	38.1	48.1	57.5	***66.9***	***78.4***	***88.8***	***86.6***	***74.8***	***59.3***	***44.2***	***35.0***	***59.4***
Mean Temp. (°F)	***23.0***	25.9	35.0	43.3	***52.1***	***61.3***	***70.5***	***68.4***	***58.1***	***44.5***	***31.5***	***22.5***	***44.7***
Mean Minimum Temp. (°F)	***10.5***	13.4	22.0	29.0	***37.3***	***44.5***	***52.2***	***50.1***	***41.0***	***29.7***	***18.8***	***9.9***	***29.9***
Extreme Maximum Temp. (°F)	60	65	74	***82***	***91***	***101***	109	***104***	95	***86***	***73***	***60***	***109***
Extreme Minimum Temp. (°F)	-28	-33	-18	5	***15***	***29***	34	32	10	-5	-30	-45	***-45***
Days Maximum Temp. ≥ 90°F	0	0	0	0	***0***	***4***	15	11	1	0	***0***	0	***31***
Days Maximum Temp. ≤ 32°F	11	7	3	1	***0***	***0***	0	0	0	1	***6***	11	***40***
Days Minimum Temp. ≤ 32°F	29	26	26	20	***7***	***0***	0	0	4	18	25	28	***183***
Days Minimum Temp. ≤ 0°F	6	4	1	0	***0***	***0***	0	0	0	0	2	6	***19***
Heating Degree Days (base 65°F)	***1,297***	1,098	922	646	***396***	***145***	***18***	***33***	***226***	***627***	***999***	***1,311***	7,718
Cooling Degree Days (base 65°F)	***0***	0	0	0	0	***3***	***43***	***196***	***143***	***25***	***0***	***0***	***410***
Mean Precipitation (in.)	***0.30***	0.37	***0.71***	0.82	***2.13***	***1.35***	0.94	0.67	0.91	***0.89***	***0.52***	***0.32***	***9.93***
Extreme Maximum Daily Precip. (in.)	***0.85***	0.80	***1.45***	***1.25***	***1.93***	na	***1.22***	***1.20***	***1.45***	na	***1.10***	***0.50***	na
Days With ≥ 0.1" Precipitation	***1***	1	***2***	2	***4***	***3***	2	2	2	***2***	2	***1***	***24***
Days With ≥ 0.5" Precipitation	***0***	0	***0***	0	***1***	***1***	1	0	1	***1***	0	***0***	***5***
Days With ≥ 1.0" Precipitation	***0***	0	***0***	0	***1***	***0***	0	0	0	***0***	0	***0***	***1***
Mean Snowfall (in.)	***4.9***	***6.2***	***8.4***	***5.5***	***1.3***	***trace***	0.0	0.0	1.2	***5.7***	***5.5***	na	na
Maximum Snow Depth (in.)	***16***	13	***25***	***13***	***11***	na	***0***	***0***	7	na	***18***	na	na
Days With ≥ 1.0" Snow Depth	***10***	9	***5***	***2***	***0***	***0***	0	0	0	***2***	7	***8***	***43***

Powell Field Station *Park County* Elevation: 4,370 ft. Latitude: 44° 47' N Longitude: 108° 46' W

	JAN	FEB	MAR	APR	MAY	JUN	JUL	AUG	SEP	OCT	NOV	DEC	YEAR
Mean Maximum Temp. (°F)	32.6	38.2	48.7	58.4	67.7	76.7	85.4	84.7	72.5	58.7	44.3	32.8	58.4
Mean Temp. (°F)	20.2	25.3	35.0	44.4	54.4	62.4	69.5	67.8	56.8	44.2	31.7	20.7	44.4
Mean Minimum Temp. (°F)	7.8	12.3	21.3	30.3	41.0	48.2	53.6	50.8	41.1	29.7	19.0	8.5	30.3
Extreme Maximum Temp. (°F)	58	69	77	85	93	99	104	102	95	87	75	66	104
Extreme Minimum Temp. (°F)	-27	-33	-15	4	19	32	32	33	16	-5	-18	-34	-34
Days Maximum Temp. ≥ 90°F	0	0	0	0	0	3	11	9	1	0	0	0	24
Days Maximum Temp. ≤ 32°F	14	7	3	1	0	0	0	0	0	1	5	14	45
Days Minimum Temp. ≤ 32°F	31	28	28	18	4	0	0	0	4	19	28	31	191
Days Minimum Temp. ≤ 0°F	7	4	1	0	0	0	0	0	0	0	1	6	19
Heating Degree Days (base 65°F)	1,382	1,116	922	613	333	131	29	36	263	637	993	1,368	7,823
Cooling Degree Days (base 65°F)	0	0	0	0	12	61	176	130	25	0	0	0	404
Mean Precipitation (in.)	***0.20***	0.12	***0.31***	0.56	1.38	1.39	0.91	0.46	0.69	0.60	0.18	0.15	***6.95***
Extreme Maximum Daily Precip. (in.)	0.50	***0.28***	***0.61***	***0.82***	1.75	2.08	***1.10***	0.40	0.97	***1.26***	0.32	***0.46***	***2.08***
Days With ≥ 0.1" Precipitation	1	0	1	2	4	4	3	2	2	2	1	0	22
Days With ≥ 0.5" Precipitation	0	0	0	0	1	1	0	0	0	0	0	0	2
Days With ≥ 1.0" Precipitation	0	0	0	0	0	0	0	0	0	0	0	0	0
Mean Snowfall (in.)	na	***0.8***	***2.7***	***0.5***	***0.4***	***0.0***	***0.0***	***0.0***	***0.1***	***1.0***	na	***2.7***	na
Maximum Snow Depth (in.)	na	na	na	na	***1***	***0***	***0***	***0***	***5***	na	na	na	na
Days With ≥ 1.0" Snow Depth	na	***1***	***1***	***0***	***0***	***0***	***0***	***0***	***0***	***1***	***1***	na	na

The period of record for all cooperative weather station data is 1980 – 2009. See User Guide for detailed explanation of data.

Rawlins Municipal Arpt *Carbon County* Elevation: 6,735 ft. Latitude: 41° 48' N Longitude: 107° 12' W

	JAN	FEB	MAR	APR	MAY	JUN	JUL	AUG	SEP	OCT	NOV	DEC	YEAR
Mean Maximum Temp. (°F)	*31.6*	*34.8*	*44.0*	*53.9*	*64.3*	*76.2*	*83.9*	*82.1*	*71.0*	*57.0*	*41.7*	*32.0*	*56.0*
Mean Temp. (°F)	*22.4*	*25.3*	*33.3*	*41.1*	*50.5*	*60.7*	*67.8*	*66.3*	*56.4*	*44.5*	*31.8*	*22.9*	*43.6*
Mean Minimum Temp. (°F)	*13.2*	*15.7*	*22.6*	*28.2*	*36.7*	*45.1*	*51.7*	*50.5*	*41.8*	*32.0*	*21.9*	*13.8*	*31.1*
Extreme Maximum Temp. (°F)	*56*	*57*	*68*	*77*	*84*	*94*	*97*	*98*	*95*	*81*	*70*	*56*	*98*
Extreme Minimum Temp. (°F)	*-32*	*-36*	*-23*	*-5*	*13*	*26*	*32*	*31*	*8*	*1*	*-23*	*-35*	*-36*
Days Maximum Temp. ≥ 90°F	*0*	*0*	*0*	*0*	*0*	*1*	*6*	*2*	*0*	*0*	*0*	*0*	*9*
Days Maximum Temp. ≤ 32°F	*16*	*10*	*4*	*1*	*0*	*0*	*0*	*0*	*0*	*1*	*7*	*15*	*54*
Days Minimum Temp. ≤ 32°F	*30*	*27*	*27*	*21*	*8*	*1*	*0*	*0*	*4*	*16*	*25*	*29*	*188*
Days Minimum Temp. ≤ 0°F	*4*	*3*	*1*	*0*	*0*	*0*	*0*	*0*	*0*	*0*	*1*	*5*	*14*
Heating Degree Days (base 65°F)	*1,314*	*1,118*	*974*	*712*	*443*	*153*	*25*	*34*	*261*	*628*	*989*	*1,298*	*7,949*
Cooling Degree Days (base 65°F)	*0*	*0*	*0*	*0*	*0*	*29*	*120*	*81*	*11*	*0*	*0*	*0*	*241*
Mean Precipitation (in.)	*0.47*	*0.48*	*0.73*	*0.95*	*1.52*	*0.94*	*0.85*	*0.78*	*0.91*	*0.86*	*0.58*	*0.41*	*9.48*
Extreme Maximum Daily Precip. (in.)	*0.71*	*0.60*	*0.62*	*1.15*	*1.66*	*0.91*	*1.42*	*0.81*	*0.84*	*1.44*	*0.53*	*0.57*	*1.66*
Days With ≥ 0.1" Precipitation	*1*	*1*	*3*	*3*	*4*	*3*	*2*	*2*	*3*	*3*	*2*	*1*	*28*
Days With ≥ 0.5" Precipitation	*0*	*0*	*0*	*0*	*1*	*1*	*0*	*0*	*0*	*0*	*0*	*0*	*2*
Days With ≥ 1.0" Precipitation	*0*	*0*	*0*	*0*	*0*	*0*	*0*	*0*	*0*	*0*	*0*	*0*	*0*
Mean Snowfall (in.)	na	na	na	na	na	na	na	na	na	na	na	na	na
Maximum Snow Depth (in.)	na	na	na	na	na	na	na	na	na	na	na	na	na
Days With ≥ 1.0" Snow Depth	na	na	na	na	na	na	na	na	na	na	na	na	na

Riverton *Fremont County* Elevation: 4,955 ft. Latitude: 43° 02' N Longitude: 108° 23' W

	JAN	FEB	MAR	APR	MAY	JUN	JUL	AUG	SEP	OCT	NOV	DEC	YEAR
Mean Maximum Temp. (°F)	30.7	37.6	50.0	60.1	69.9	80.1	89.1	87.5	75.4	60.9	43.9	30.0	59.6
Mean Temp. (°F)	16.4	22.6	35.2	44.8	54.6	63.6	71.1	68.9	57.9	44.7	29.6	16.5	43.8
Mean Minimum Temp. (°F)	2.0	7.5	20.4	29.5	39.2	46.9	53.0	50.4	40.4	28.5	15.3	2.9	28.0
Extreme Maximum Temp. (°F)	60	70	78	87	96	101	104	103	98	90	73	65	104
Extreme Minimum Temp. (°F)	-45	-34	-19	5	20	28	30	31	13	-2	-28	-46	-46
Days Maximum Temp. ≥ 90°F	0	0	0	0	0	6	17	14	2	0	0	0	39
Days Maximum Temp. ≤ 32°F	16	9	3	0	0	0	0	0	0	0	6	17	51
Days Minimum Temp. ≤ 32°F	30	28	29	20	5	0	0	0	4	22	29	30	197
Days Minimum Temp. ≤ 0°F	13	8	1	0	0	0	0	0	0	0	4	12	38
Heating Degree Days (base 65°F)	1,502	1,194	917	599	325	110	16	21	230	623	1,055	1,498	8,090
Cooling Degree Days (base 65°F)	0	0	0	0	9	73	211	151	24	0	0	0	468
Mean Precipitation (in.)	0.28	0.33	0.53	0.93	1.53	1.21	0.79	0.47	0.80	0.86	0.42	0.35	8.50
Extreme Maximum Daily Precip. (in.)	0.85	0.57	1.08	1.00	1.46	2.20	1.33	0.97	1.50	1.32	1.20	2.05	2.20
Days With ≥ 0.1" Precipitation	1	1	2	3	4	3	2	1	2	2	1	1	23
Days With ≥ 0.5" Precipitation	0	0	0	0	1	1	0	0	0	1	0	0	3
Days With ≥ 1.0" Precipitation	0	0	0	0	0	0	0	0	0	0	0	0	0
Mean Snowfall (in.)	5.0	5.8	5.7	4.6	0.7	trace	0.0	trace	0.7	3.7	4.5	5.0	35.7
Maximum Snow Depth (in.)	***16***	***14***	***15***	***8***	12	trace	0	0	2	***10***	*7*	na	na
Days With ≥ 1.0" Snow Depth	***16***	***11***	5	2	0	0	0	0	0	1	5	***14***	***54***

Wyoming Weather Station Rankings

Annual Extreme Maximum Temperature

Highest

Rank	Station Name	°F
1	Basin	115
2	Echeta 2 NW	***111***
3	Powder River No 2	***109***
4	Dillinger	108
5	Dull Center 1 SE	107
5	Gillette 6 SE	107
5	Glenrock 5 ESE	***107***
5	Sheridan County Arpt	107
9	Boysen Dam	105
9	Midwest	***105***
11	Billy Creek	104
11	Casper Natrona Co Intl Arpt	104
11	Powell Field Station	104
11	Riverton	104
15	Carpenter	***103***
16	Archer	***102***
16	Chugwater	102
16	Cody 12 SE	102
16	Muddy Gap	102
20	Lander Hunt Field	101
21	Cody	100
21	Fontenelle Dam	100
23	Evanston 1 E	99
24	Bates Creek No 2	98
24	Rawlins Municipal Arpt	***98***

Lowest

Rank	Station Name	°F
1	Elk Mountain	94
2	Bondurant	95
2	Burris	95
4	Dubois	***97***
5	Bates Creek No 2	98
5	Rawlins Municipal Arpt	***98***
7	Evanston 1 E	99
8	Cody	100
8	Fontenelle Dam	100
10	Lander Hunt Field	101
11	Archer	***102***
11	Chugwater	102
11	Cody 12 SE	102
11	Muddy Gap	102
15	Carpenter	***103***
16	Billy Creek	104
16	Casper Natrona Co Intl Arpt	104
16	Powell Field Station	104
16	Riverton	104
20	Boysen Dam	105
20	Midwest	***105***
22	Dull Center 1 SE	107
22	Gillette 6 SE	107
22	Glenrock 5 ESE	***107***
22	Sheridan County Arpt	107

Annual Mean Maximum Temperature

Highest

Rank	Station Name	°F
1	Carpenter	***62.2***
2	Dull Center 1 SE	61.3
3	Chugwater	61.1
4	Echeta 2 NW	***60.9***
4	Glenrock 5 ESE	***60.9***
6	Midwest	***60.8***
7	Basin	60.7
8	Archer	***60.5***
9	Boysen Dam	59.9
10	Casper Natrona Co Intl Arpt	59.7
10	Sheridan County Arpt	59.7
12	Riverton	59.6
13	Powder River No 2	***59.4***
14	Dillinger	59.3
15	Cody	58.9
15	Cody 12 SE	58.9
17	Billy Creek	58.7
18	Powell Field Station	58.4
19	Lander Hunt Field	58.3
20	Gillette 6 SE	57.9
20	Muddy Gap	***57.9***
22	Burris	57.7
23	Bates Creek No 2	57.3
24	Rawlins Municipal Arpt	***56.0***
25	Evanston 1 E	***55.7***

Lowest

Rank	Station Name	°F
1	Bondurant	***50.7***
2	Fontenelle Dam	52.0
3	Dubois	***54.2***
4	Elk Mountain	54.5
5	Evanston 1 E	***55.7***
6	Rawlins Municipal Arpt	***56.0***
7	Bates Creek No 2	57.3
8	Burris	57.7
9	Gillette 6 SE	57.9
9	Muddy Gap	***57.9***
11	Lander Hunt Field	58.3
12	Powell Field Station	58.4
13	Billy Creek	58.7
14	Cody	58.9
14	Cody 12 SE	58.9
16	Dillinger	59.3
17	Powder River No 2	***59.4***
18	Riverton	59.6
19	Casper Natrona Co Intl Arpt	59.7
19	Sheridan County Arpt	59.7
21	Boysen Dam	59.9
22	Archer	***60.5***
23	Basin	60.7
24	Midwest	***60.8***
25	Echeta 2 NW	***60.9***

 Rankings include 25 highest/lowest stations. If state has less than 25 stations, all stations are included. The period of record is 1980–2009. See User Guide for detailed explanation of data.

Annual Mean Temperature

Highest			Lowest		
Rank	Station Name	°F	Rank	Station Name	°F
1	Glenrock 5 ESE	***47.8***	1	Bondurant	***33.7***
2	Carpenter	***47.6***	2	Fontenelle Dam	36.4
3	Dull Center 1 SE	47.3	3	Dubois	***40.6***
4	Boysen Dam	46.9	4	Evanston 1 E	***41.9***
4	Chugwater	46.9	5	Elk Mountain	42.0
6	Cody	46.8	6	Burris	43.3
7	Midwest	***46.4***	7	Rawlins Municipal Arpt	***43.6***
8	Echeta 2 NW	***46.1***	8	Riverton	43.8
9	Basin	45.9	9	Powell Field Station	44.4
9	Casper Natrona Co Intl Arpt	45.9	10	Bates Creek No 2	44.6
11	Archer	***45.8***	11	Powder River No 2	***44.7***
12	Sheridan County Arpt	45.7	12	Billy Creek	44.8
13	Gillette 6 SE	45.5	13	Cody 12 SE	44.9
14	Lander Hunt Field	45.4	14	Dillinger	45.1
15	Muddy Gap	***45.2***	15	Muddy Gap	***45.2***
16	Dillinger	45.1	16	Lander Hunt Field	45.4
17	Cody 12 SE	44.9	17	Gillette 6 SE	45.5
18	Billy Creek	44.8	18	Sheridan County Arpt	45.7
19	Powder River No 2	***44.7***	19	Archer	***45.8***
20	Bates Creek No 2	44.6	20	Basin	45.9
21	Powell Field Station	44.4	20	Casper Natrona Co Intl Arpt	45.9
22	Riverton	43.8	22	Echeta 2 NW	***46.1***
23	Rawlins Municipal Arpt	***43.6***	23	Midwest	***46.4***
24	Burris	43.3	24	Cody	46.8
25	Elk Mountain	42.0	25	Boysen Dam	46.9

Annual Mean Minimum Temperature

Highest			Lowest		
Rank	Station Name	°F	Rank	Station Name	°F
1	Cody	34.6	1	Bondurant	16.6
1	Glenrock 5 ESE	***34.6***	2	Fontenelle Dam	20.7
3	Boysen Dam	33.8	3	Dubois	***26.8***
4	Gillette 6 SE	33.2	4	Evanston 1 E	28.0
5	Dull Center 1 SE	33.1	4	Riverton	28.0
6	Carpenter	***32.9***	6	Burris	28.8
7	Chugwater	32.6	7	Elk Mountain	29.5
7	Muddy Gap	***32.6***	8	Powder River No 2	***29.9***
9	Lander Hunt Field	32.5	9	Powell Field Station	30.3
10	Casper Natrona Co Intl Arpt	32.1	10	Billy Creek	30.9
10	Midwest	***32.1***	10	Cody 12 SE	30.9
12	Bates Creek No 2	31.9	10	Dillinger	30.9
13	Sheridan County Arpt	31.6	13	Archer	***31.0***
14	Echeta 2 NW	***31.3***	13	Basin	31.0
15	Rawlins Municipal Arpt	***31.1***	15	Rawlins Municipal Arpt	***31.1***
16	Archer	***31.0***	16	Echeta 2 NW	***31.3***
16	Basin	31.0	17	Sheridan County Arpt	31.6
18	Billy Creek	30.9	18	Bates Creek No 2	31.9
18	Cody 12 SE	30.9	19	Casper Natrona Co Intl Arpt	32.1
18	Dillinger	30.9	19	Midwest	***32.1***
21	Powell Field Station	30.3	21	Lander Hunt Field	32.5
22	Powder River No 2	***29.9***	22	Chugwater	32.6
23	Elk Mountain	29.5	22	Muddy Gap	***32.6***
24	Burris	28.8	24	Carpenter	***32.9***
25	Evanston 1 E	28.0	25	Dull Center 1 SE	33.1

Rankings include 25 highest/lowest stations. If state has less than 25 stations, all stations are included. The period of record is 1980–2009. See User Guide for detailed explanation of data.

Annual Extreme Minimum Temperature

Rank	Highest: Station Name	°F	Rank	Lowest: Station Name	°F
1	Archer	***-30***	1	Echeta 2 NW	***-54***
2	Carpenter	***-31***	2	Bondurant	-52
2	Evanston 1 E	***-31***	3	Fontenelle Dam	-46
4	Boysen Dam	-33	3	Riverton	-46
5	Powell Field Station	-34	5	Burris	-45
6	Chugwater	-35	5	Dillinger	-45
6	Elk Mountain	-35	5	Powder River No 2	***-45***
8	Rawlins Municipal Arpt	***-36***	8	Dubois	***-42***
9	Cody	-37	8	Dull Center 1 SE	-42
9	Gillette 6 SE	-37	10	Basin	-41
9	Lander Hunt Field	-37	10	Billy Creek	-41
9	Sheridan County Arpt	-37	10	Casper Natrona Co Intl Arpt	-41
13	Bates Creek No 2	-38	10	Cody 12 SE	-41
14	Glenrock 5 ESE	***-40***	14	Glenrock 5 ESE	***-40***
14	Midwest	***-40***	14	Midwest	***-40***
14	Muddy Gap	-40	14	Muddy Gap	-40
17	Basin	-41	17	Bates Creek No 2	-38
17	Billy Creek	-41	18	Cody	-37
17	Casper Natrona Co Intl Arpt	-41	18	Gillette 6 SE	-37
17	Cody 12 SE	-41	18	Lander Hunt Field	-37
21	Dubois	***-42***	18	Sheridan County Arpt	-37
21	Dull Center 1 SE	-42	22	Rawlins Municipal Arpt	***-36***
23	Burris	-45	23	Chugwater	-35
23	Dillinger	-45	23	Elk Mountain	-35
23	Powder River No 2	***-45***	25	Powell Field Station	-34

July Mean Maximum Temperature

Rank	Highest: Station Name	°F	Rank	Lowest: Station Name	°F
1	Basin	90.3	1	Bondurant	78.6
1	Boysen Dam	90.3	2	Dubois	79.2
3	Dull Center 1 SE	90.0	3	Elk Mountain	80.4
4	Echeta 2 NW	***89.5***	4	Fontenelle Dam	81.2
5	Midwest	***89.2***	5	Burris	81.6
6	Riverton	89.1	6	Evanston 1 E	81.8
7	Powder River No 2	***88.8***	7	Bates Creek No 2	83.6
8	Glenrock 5 ESE	***88.7***	8	Rawlins Municipal Arpt	***83.9***
9	Casper Natrona Co Intl Arpt	88.6	9	Cody	84.0
10	Dillinger	88.0	10	Cody 12 SE	84.6
11	Sheridan County Arpt	87.4	11	Billy Creek	84.8
12	Lander Hunt Field	87.3	12	Archer	***85.3***
13	Carpenter	***87.0***	13	Powell Field Station	85.4
14	Muddy Gap	***86.7***	14	Gillette 6 SE	85.5
15	Chugwater	86.6	15	Chugwater	86.6
16	Gillette 6 SE	85.5	16	Muddy Gap	***86.7***
17	Powell Field Station	85.4	17	Carpenter	***87.0***
18	Archer	***85.3***	18	Lander Hunt Field	87.3
19	Billy Creek	84.8	19	Sheridan County Arpt	87.4
20	Cody 12 SE	84.6	20	Dillinger	88.0
21	Cody	84.0	21	Casper Natrona Co Intl Arpt	88.6
22	Rawlins Municipal Arpt	***83.9***	22	Glenrock 5 ESE	***88.7***
23	Bates Creek No 2	83.6	23	Powder River No 2	***88.8***
24	Evanston 1 E	81.8	24	Riverton	89.1
25	Burris	81.6	25	Midwest	***89.2***

 Rankings include 25 highest/lowest stations. If state has less than 25 stations, all stations are included. The period of record is 1980–2009. See User Guide for detailed explanation of data.

January Mean Minimum Temperature

Highest			Lowest		
Rank	Station Name	°F	Rank	Station Name	°F
1	Chugwater	17.4	1	Bondurant	-4.9
1	Glenrock 5 ESE	17.4	2	Fontenelle Dam	-2.8
3	Cody	16.1	3	Riverton	2.0
4	Carpenter	15.4	4	Basin	4.0
5	Muddy Gap	***15.3***	5	Boysen Dam	6.7
6	Casper Natrona Co Intl Arpt	14.6	6	Powell Field Station	7.8
7	Elk Mountain	14.5	7	Dillinger	10.5
8	Archer	14.3	7	Lander Hunt Field	10.5
9	Dull Center 1 SE	13.8	7	Powder River No 2	***10.5***
10	Gillette 6 SE	13.5	10	Echeta 2 NW	***10.9***
11	Dubois	13.3	10	Evanston 1 E	10.9
11	Midwest	13.3	12	Billy Creek	11.0
13	Rawlins Municipal Arpt	***13.2***	13	Burris	11.6
14	Bates Creek No 2	12.5	14	Cody 12 SE	11.7
15	Sheridan County Arpt	12.0	15	Sheridan County Arpt	12.0
16	Cody 12 SE	11.7	16	Bates Creek No 2	12.5
17	Burris	11.6	17	Rawlins Municipal Arpt	***13.2***
18	Billy Creek	11.0	18	Dubois	13.3
19	Echeta 2 NW	***10.9***	18	Midwest	13.3
19	Evanston 1 E	10.9	20	Gillette 6 SE	13.5
21	Dillinger	10.5	21	Dull Center 1 SE	13.8
21	Lander Hunt Field	10.5	22	Archer	14.3
21	Powder River No 2	***10.5***	23	Elk Mountain	14.5
24	Powell Field Station	7.8	24	Casper Natrona Co Intl Arpt	14.6
25	Boysen Dam	6.7	25	Muddy Gap	***15.3***

Number of Days Annually Maximum Temperature ≥ 90°F

Highest			Lowest		
Rank	Station Name	Days	Rank	Station Name	Days
1	Basin	45	1	Bondurant	1
2	Boysen Dam	43	2	Dubois	***2***
3	Dull Center 1 SE	42	2	Elk Mountain	2
4	Midwest	***39***	2	Evanston 1 E	2
4	Riverton	39	5	Burris	5
6	Echeta 2 NW	***38***	5	Fontenelle Dam	5
7	Casper Natrona Co Intl Arpt	37	7	Bates Creek No 2	9
8	Dillinger	35	7	Rawlins Municipal Arpt	***9***
9	Glenrock 5 ESE	***32***	9	Cody	15
9	Sheridan County Arpt	32	10	Muddy Gap	17
11	Powder River No 2	***31***	11	Cody 12 SE	20
12	Carpenter	***27***	12	Archer	***22***
12	Lander Hunt Field	27	13	Billy Creek	24
14	Chugwater	25	13	Gillette 6 SE	24
15	Billy Creek	24	13	Powell Field Station	24
15	Gillette 6 SE	24	16	Chugwater	25
15	Powell Field Station	24	17	Carpenter	***27***
18	Archer	***22***	17	Lander Hunt Field	27
19	Cody 12 SE	20	19	Powder River No 2	***31***
20	Muddy Gap	17	20	Glenrock 5 ESE	***32***
21	Cody	15	20	Sheridan County Arpt	32
22	Bates Creek No 2	9	22	Dillinger	35
22	Rawlins Municipal Arpt	***9***	23	Casper Natrona Co Intl Arpt	37
24	Burris	5	24	Echeta 2 NW	***38***
24	Fontenelle Dam	5	25	Midwest	***39***

Rankings include 25 highest/lowest stations. If state has less than 25 stations, all stations are included. The period of record is 1980–2009. See User Guide for detailed explanation of data.

Number of Days Annually Maximum Temperature ≤ 32°F

Highest			Lowest		
Rank	Station Name	Days	Rank	Station Name	Days
1	Bondurant	85	1	Carpenter	***27***
2	Fontenelle Dam	80	2	Archer	***31***
3	Rawlins Municipal Arpt	***54***	2	Chugwater	31
4	Evanston 1 E	51	4	Cody 12 SE	32
4	Riverton	51	5	Burris	33
6	Lander Hunt Field	50	5	Cody	33
7	Elk Mountain	49	7	Glenrock 5 ESE	***34***
8	Muddy Gap	48	8	Billy Creek	37
9	Boysen Dam	46	8	Dull Center 1 SE	37
10	Basin	45	8	Echeta 2 NW	***37***
10	Gillette 6 SE	45	11	Midwest	***38***
10	Powell Field Station	45	12	Powder River No 2	***40***
13	Dubois	***44***	13	Sheridan County Arpt	41
14	Casper Natrona Co Intl Arpt	43	14	Bates Creek No 2	42
15	Bates Creek No 2	42	14	Dillinger	42
15	Dillinger	42	16	Casper Natrona Co Intl Arpt	43
17	Sheridan County Arpt	41	17	Dubois	***44***
18	Powder River No 2	***40***	18	Basin	45
19	Midwest	***38***	18	Gillette 6 SE	45
20	Billy Creek	37	18	Powell Field Station	45
20	Dull Center 1 SE	37	21	Boysen Dam	46
20	Echeta 2 NW	***37***	22	Muddy Gap	48
23	Glenrock 5 ESE	***34***	23	Elk Mountain	49
24	Burris	33	24	Lander Hunt Field	50
24	Cody	33	25	Evanston 1 E	51

Number of Days Annually Minimum Temperature ≤ 32°F

Highest			Lowest		
Rank	Station Name	Days	Rank	Station Name	Days
1	Bondurant	288	1	Glenrock 5 ESE	***155***
2	Fontenelle Dam	249	2	Boysen Dam	159
3	Dubois	***219***	2	Cody	159
4	Evanston 1 E	***210***	4	Muddy Gap	***168***
5	Burris	200	5	Dull Center 1 SE	173
6	Riverton	197	6	Carpenter	***177***
7	Archer	***194***	6	Gillette 6 SE	177
7	Elk Mountain	194	8	Chugwater	178
9	Powell Field Station	191	8	Midwest	***178***
10	Billy Creek	189	10	Lander Hunt Field	180
10	Dillinger	189	11	Casper Natrona Co Intl Arpt	181
12	Rawlins Municipal Arpt	***188***	12	Sheridan County Arpt	182
13	Cody 12 SE	187	13	Basin	183
14	Bates Creek No 2	185	13	Echeta 2 NW	***183***
15	Basin	183	13	Powder River No 2	***183***
15	Echeta 2 NW	***183***	16	Bates Creek No 2	185
15	Powder River No 2	***183***	17	Cody 12 SE	187
18	Sheridan County Arpt	182	18	Rawlins Municipal Arpt	***188***
19	Casper Natrona Co Intl Arpt	181	19	Billy Creek	189
20	Lander Hunt Field	180	19	Dillinger	189
21	Chugwater	178	21	Powell Field Station	191
21	Midwest	***178***	22	Archer	***194***
23	Carpenter	***177***	22	Elk Mountain	194
23	Gillette 6 SE	177	24	Riverton	197
25	Dull Center 1 SE	173	25	Burris	200

 Rankings include 25 highest/lowest stations. If state has less than 25 stations, all stations are included. The period of record is 1980–2009. See User Guide for detailed explanation of data.

Number of Days Annually Minimum Temperature ≤ 0°F

Highest			Lowest		
Rank	Station Name	Days	Rank	Station Name	Days
1	Bondurant	71	1	Elk Mountain	11
2	Fontenelle Dam	58	1	Muddy Gap	11
3	Riverton	38	3	Carpenter	*12*
4	Basin	27	3	Chugwater	12
5	Boysen Dam	22	5	Archer	*13*
5	Dillinger	22	5	Bates Creek No 2	13
7	Echeta 2 NW	*21*	5	Cody	13
8	Burris	19	5	Glenrock 5 ESE	*13*
8	Cody 12 SE	19	9	Rawlins Municipal Arpt	*14*
8	Evanston 1 E	19	10	Casper Natrona Co Intl Arpt	16
8	Lander Hunt Field	19	10	Dull Center 1 SE	16
8	Powder River No 2	*19*	10	Midwest	*16*
8	Powell Field Station	19	13	Billy Creek	18
8	Sheridan County Arpt	19	13	Dubois	*18*
15	Billy Creek	18	13	Gillette 6 SE	18
15	Dubois	*18*	16	Burris	19
15	Gillette 6 SE	18	16	Cody 12 SE	19
18	Casper Natrona Co Intl Arpt	16	16	Evanston 1 E	19
18	Dull Center 1 SE	16	16	Lander Hunt Field	19
18	Midwest	*16*	16	Powder River No 2	*19*
21	Rawlins Municipal Arpt	*14*	16	Powell Field Station	19
22	Archer	*13*	16	Sheridan County Arpt	19
22	Bates Creek No 2	13	23	Echeta 2 NW	*21*
22	Cody	13	24	Boysen Dam	22
22	Glenrock 5 ESE	*13*	24	Dillinger	22

Number of Annual Heating Degree Days

Highest			Lowest		
Rank	Station Name	Num.	Rank	Station Name	Num.
1	Bondurant	*11,343*	1	Carpenter	*6,707*
2	Fontenelle Dam	10,407	2	Glenrock 5 ESE	*6,762*
3	Dubois	*8,850*	3	Chugwater	6,913
4	Evanston 1 E	*8,403*	4	Cody	6,971
5	Elk Mountain	8,377	5	Dull Center 1 SE	7,004
6	Riverton	8,090	6	Midwest	*7,205*
7	Burris	7,960	7	Archer	*7,241*
8	Rawlins Municipal Arpt	*7,949*	8	Boysen Dam	*7,315*
9	Powell Field Station	7,823	9	Casper Natrona Co Intl Arpt	7,344
10	Powder River No 2	*7,718*	10	Echeta 2 NW	*7,366*
11	Bates Creek No 2	7,685	11	Sheridan County Arpt	7,416
12	Billy Creek	7,669	12	Gillette 6 SE	7,495
13	Dillinger	7,659	13	Muddy Gap	*7,517*
14	Cody 12 SE	7,590	14	Basin	7,528
15	Lander Hunt Field	7,550	15	Lander Hunt Field	7,550
16	Basin	7,528	16	Cody 12 SE	7,590
17	Muddy Gap	*7,517*	17	Dillinger	7,659
18	Gillette 6 SE	7,495	18	Billy Creek	7,669
19	Sheridan County Arpt	7,416	19	Bates Creek No 2	7,685
20	Echeta 2 NW	*7,366*	20	Powder River No 2	*7,718*
21	Casper Natrona Co Intl Arpt	7,344	21	Powell Field Station	7,823
22	Boysen Dam	*7,315*	22	Rawlins Municipal Arpt	*7,949*
23	Archer	*7,241*	23	Burris	7,960
24	Midwest	*7,205*	24	Riverton	8,090
25	Dull Center 1 SE	7,004	25	Elk Mountain	8,377

Number of Annual Cooling Degree Days

Highest			Lowest		
Rank	Station Name	Num.	Rank	Station Name	Num.
1	Boysen Dam	***812***	1	Bondurant	3
2	Basin	670	2	Dubois	***39***
3	Dull Center 1 SE	640	3	Fontenelle Dam	72
4	Echeta 2 NW	***585***	4	Evanston 1 E	***82***
5	Glenrock 5 ESE	***582***	5	Elk Mountain	91
6	Midwest	***539***	6	Burris	130
7	Lander Hunt Field	523	7	Rawlins Municipal Arpt	***241***
8	Dillinger	515	8	Archer	***335***
9	Gillette 6 SE	502	9	Bates Creek No 2	349
10	Casper Natrona Co Intl Arpt	476	10	Cody 12 SE	369
11	Sheridan County Arpt	472	11	Billy Creek	403
12	Riverton	468	12	Chugwater	404
13	Carpenter	***466***	12	Powell Field Station	404
14	Cody	429	14	Powder River No 2	***410***
15	Muddy Gap	***423***	15	Muddy Gap	***423***
16	Powder River No 2	***410***	16	Cody	429
17	Chugwater	404	17	Carpenter	***466***
17	Powell Field Station	404	18	Riverton	468
19	Billy Creek	403	19	Sheridan County Arpt	472
20	Cody 12 SE	369	20	Casper Natrona Co Intl Arpt	476
21	Bates Creek No 2	349	21	Gillette 6 SE	502
22	Archer	***335***	22	Dillinger	515
23	Rawlins Municipal Arpt	***241***	23	Lander Hunt Field	523
24	Burris	130	24	Midwest	***539***
25	Elk Mountain	91	25	Glenrock 5 ESE	***582***

Annual Precipitation

Highest			Lowest		
Rank	Station Name	Inches	Rank	Station Name	Inches
1	Bondurant	18.79	1	Basin	6.71
2	Archer	***16.86***	2	Powell Field Station	***6.95***
3	Gillette 6 SE	16.52	3	Fontenelle Dam	7.48
4	Chugwater	16.01	4	Riverton	8.50
5	Echeta 2 NW	***15.96***	5	Burris	8.59
6	Dillinger	14.59	6	Boysen Dam	8.79
7	Carpenter	***14.53***	7	Cody 12 SE	***9.33***
8	Sheridan County Arpt	14.08	8	Rawlins Municipal Arpt	***9.48***
9	Dull Center 1 SE	13.21	9	Dubois	***9.58***
10	Bates Creek No 2	12.87	10	Powder River No 2	***9.93***
11	Lander Hunt Field	12.54	11	Muddy Gap	***10.22***
12	Casper Natrona Co Intl Arpt	12.49	12	Cody	10.66
13	Billy Creek	12.48	13	Glenrock 5 ESE	***10.70***
14	Elk Mountain	12.07	14	Evanston 1 E	11.61
15	Midwest	***12.06***	15	Midwest	***12.06***
16	Evanston 1 E	11.61	16	Elk Mountain	12.07
17	Glenrock 5 ESE	***10.70***	17	Billy Creek	12.48
18	Cody	10.66	18	Casper Natrona Co Intl Arpt	12.49
19	Muddy Gap	***10.22***	19	Lander Hunt Field	12.54
20	Powder River No 2	***9.93***	20	Bates Creek No 2	12.87
21	Dubois	***9.58***	21	Dull Center 1 SE	13.21
22	Rawlins Municipal Arpt	***9.48***	22	Sheridan County Arpt	14.08
23	Cody 12 SE	***9.33***	23	Carpenter	***14.53***
24	Boysen Dam	8.79	24	Dillinger	14.59
25	Burris	8.59	25	Echeta 2 NW	***15.96***

Rankings include 25 highest/lowest stations. If state has less than 25 stations, all stations are included. The period of record is 1980–2009. See User Guide for detailed explanation of data.

Annual Extreme Maximum Daily Precipitation

Highest

Rank	Station Name	Inches
1	Carpenter	***5.50***
2	Billy Creek	3.50
3	Chugwater	3.30
4	Archer	***3.29***
5	Elk Mountain	3.25
6	Dull Center 1 SE	3.24
7	Bates Creek No 2	3.01
8	Muddy Gap	***2.70***
9	Gillette 6 SE	2.63
10	Cody 12 SE	***2.54***
11	Sheridan County Arpt	2.45
12	Cody	2.40
13	Casper Natrona Co Intl Arpt	2.22
13	Dillinger	2.22
15	Lander Hunt Field	2.20
15	Riverton	2.20
17	Powell Field Station	***2.08***
18	Burris	2.05
19	Basin	2.00
19	Boysen Dam	***2.00***
19	Evanston 1 E	2.00
22	Dubois	***1.87***
23	Fontenelle Dam	1.82
24	Rawlins Municipal Arpt	***1.66***
25	Bondurant	***1.58***

Lowest

Rank	Station Name	Inches
1	Bondurant	***1.58***
2	Rawlins Municipal Arpt	***1.66***
3	Fontenelle Dam	1.82
4	Dubois	***1.87***
5	Basin	2.00
5	Boysen Dam	***2.00***
5	Evanston 1 E	2.00
8	Burris	2.05
9	Powell Field Station	***2.08***
10	Lander Hunt Field	2.20
10	Riverton	2.20
12	Casper Natrona Co Intl Arpt	2.22
12	Dillinger	2.22
14	Cody	2.40
15	Sheridan County Arpt	2.45
16	Cody 12 SE	***2.54***
17	Gillette 6 SE	2.63
18	Muddy Gap	***2.70***
19	Bates Creek No 2	3.01
20	Dull Center 1 SE	3.24
21	Elk Mountain	3.25
22	Archer	***3.29***
23	Chugwater	3.30
24	Billy Creek	3.50
25	Carpenter	***5.50***

Number of Days Annually With ≥ 0.1 Inches of Precipitation

Highest

Rank	Station Name	Days
1	Bondurant	54
2	Echeta 2 NW	***45***
2	Gillette 6 SE	45
4	Archer	***42***
4	Chugwater	42
6	Dillinger	40
6	Sheridan County Arpt	40
8	Bates Creek No 2	38
8	Carpenter	***38***
10	Billy Creek	36
10	Casper Natrona Co Intl Arpt	36
12	Dull Center 1 SE	35
13	Cody	34
13	Evanston 1 E	34
15	Lander Hunt Field	33
16	Midwest	***32***
17	Dubois	***31***
18	Cody 12 SE	***30***
18	Elk Mountain	30
20	Burris	29
21	Glenrock 5 ESE	***28***
21	Rawlins Municipal Arpt	***28***
23	Muddy Gap	***27***
24	Fontenelle Dam	26
25	Boysen Dam	25

Lowest

Rank	Station Name	Days
1	Basin	22
1	Powell Field Station	22
3	Riverton	23
4	Powder River No 2	***24***
5	Boysen Dam	25
6	Fontenelle Dam	26
7	Muddy Gap	***27***
8	Glenrock 5 ESE	***28***
8	Rawlins Municipal Arpt	***28***
10	Burris	29
11	Cody 12 SE	***30***
11	Elk Mountain	30
13	Dubois	***31***
14	Midwest	***32***
15	Lander Hunt Field	33
16	Cody	34
16	Evanston 1 E	34
18	Dull Center 1 SE	35
19	Billy Creek	36
19	Casper Natrona Co Intl Arpt	36
21	Bates Creek No 2	38
21	Carpenter	***38***
23	Dillinger	40
23	Sheridan County Arpt	40
25	Archer	***42***

Rankings include 25 highest/lowest stations. If state has less than 25 stations, all stations are included. The period of record is 1980–2009. See User Guide for detailed explanation of data.

Number of Days Annually With ≥ 0.5 Inches of Precipitation

Highest			Lowest		
Rank	Station Name	Days	Rank	Station Name	Days
1	Archer	*9*	1	Basin	1
2	Bondurant	8	1	Fontenelle Dam	1
2	Chugwater	8	3	Boysen Dam	2
2	Echeta 2 NW	*8*	3	Dubois	*2*
2	Gillette 6 SE	8	3	Evanston 1 E	2
2	Lander Hunt Field	8	3	Powell Field Station	2
7	Carpenter	*7*	3	Rawlins Municipal Arpt	*2*
7	Dillinger	7	8	Burris	3
7	Dull Center 1 SE	7	8	Cody	3
7	Midwest	*7*	8	Cody 12 SE	*3*
11	Muddy Gap	*6*	8	Riverton	3
11	Sheridan County Arpt	6	12	Bates Creek No 2	4
13	Billy Creek	5	12	Casper Natrona Co Intl Arpt	4
13	Elk Mountain	5	14	Billy Creek	5
13	Glenrock 5 ESE	*5*	14	Elk Mountain	5
13	Powder River No 2	*5*	14	Glenrock 5 ESE	*5*
17	Bates Creek No 2	4	14	Powder River No 2	*5*
17	Casper Natrona Co Intl Arpt	4	18	Muddy Gap	*6*
19	Burris	3	18	Sheridan County Arpt	6
19	Cody	3	20	Carpenter	*7*
19	Cody 12 SE	*3*	20	Dillinger	7
19	Riverton	3	20	Dull Center 1 SE	7
23	Boysen Dam	2	20	Midwest	*7*
23	Dubois	*2*	24	Bondurant	8
23	Evanston 1 E	2	24	Chugwater	8

Number of Days Annually With ≥ 1.0 Inches of Precipitation

Highest			Lowest		
Rank	Station Name	Days	Rank	Station Name	Days
1	Chugwater	1	1	Archer	*0*
1	Echeta 2 NW	*1*	1	Basin	0
1	Gillette 6 SE	1	1	Bates Creek No 2	0
1	Midwest	*1*	1	Billy Creek	0
1	Powder River No 2	*1*	1	Bondurant	0
6	Archer	*0*	1	Boysen Dam	0
6	Basin	0	1	Burris	0
6	Bates Creek No 2	0	1	Carpenter	*0*
6	Billy Creek	0	1	Casper Natrona Co Intl Arpt	0
6	Bondurant	0	1	Cody	0
6	Boysen Dam	0	1	Cody 12 SE	*0*
6	Burris	0	1	Dillinger	0
6	Carpenter	*0*	1	Dubois	*0*
6	Casper Natrona Co Intl Arpt	0	1	Dull Center 1 SE	0
6	Cody	0	1	Elk Mountain	0
6	Cody 12 SE	*0*	1	Evanston 1 E	0
6	Dillinger	0	1	Fontenelle Dam	0
6	Dubois	*0*	1	Glenrock 5 ESE	*0*
6	Dull Center 1 SE	0	1	Lander Hunt Field	0
6	Elk Mountain	0	1	Muddy Gap	*0*
6	Evanston 1 E	0	1	Powell Field Station	0
6	Fontenelle Dam	0	1	Rawlins Municipal Arpt	*0*
6	Glenrock 5 ESE	*0*	1	Riverton	0
6	Lander Hunt Field	0	1	Sheridan County Arpt	0
6	Muddy Gap	*0*	25	Chugwater	1

 Rankings include 25 highest/lowest stations. If state has less than 25 stations, all stations are included. The period of record is 1980–2009. See User Guide for detailed explanation of data.

Annual Snowfall

Highest			Lowest		
Rank	Station Name	Inches	Rank	Station Name	Inches
1	Bondurant	123.2	1	Basin	18.3
2	Lander Hunt Field	92.3	2	Burris	***32.5***
3	Casper Natrona Co Intl Arpt	76.7	3	Carpenter	***35.3***
4	Bates Creek No 2	74.2	4	Riverton	35.7
5	Elk Mountain	69.9	5	Billy Creek	38.5
6	Chugwater	69.0	6	Dillinger	38.9
7	Gillette 6 SE	58.7	7	Dubois	***43.8***
8	Echeta 2 NW	***53.4***	8	Evanston 1 E	***44.8***
9	Archer	***51.1***	9	Cody	***45.7***
10	Midwest	***49.5***	10	Dull Center 1 SE	47.0
11	Dull Center 1 SE	47.0	11	Midwest	***49.5***
12	Cody	***45.7***	12	Archer	***51.1***
13	Evanston 1 E	***44.8***	13	Echeta 2 NW	***53.4***
14	Dubois	***43.8***	14	Gillette 6 SE	58.7
15	Dillinger	38.9	15	Chugwater	69.0
16	Billy Creek	38.5	16	Elk Mountain	69.9
17	Riverton	35.7	17	Bates Creek No 2	74.2
18	Carpenter	***35.3***	18	Casper Natrona Co Intl Arpt	76.7
19	Burris	***32.5***	19	Lander Hunt Field	92.3
20	Basin	18.3	20	Bondurant	123.2

Annual Maximum Snow Depth

Highest			Lowest		
Rank	Station Name	Inches	Rank	Station Name	Inches
1	Bondurant	63	1	Basin	13
2	Elk Mountain	28	2	Burris	***16***
2	Evanston 1 E	***28***	3	Cody	***18***
4	Midwest	***25***	4	Dull Center 1 SE	19
5	Bates Creek No 2	24	5	Gillette 6 SE	21
5	Chugwater	24	6	Billy Creek	22
5	Dillinger	***24***	7	Archer	***23***
8	Archer	***23***	7	Carpenter	***23***
8	Carpenter	***23***	9	Bates Creek No 2	24
10	Billy Creek	22	9	Chugwater	24
11	Gillette 6 SE	21	9	Dillinger	***24***
12	Dull Center 1 SE	19	12	Midwest	***25***
13	Cody	***18***	13	Elk Mountain	28
14	Burris	***16***	13	Evanston 1 E	***28***
15	Basin	13	15	Bondurant	63

Number of Days Annually With ≥ 1.0 Inch Snow Depth

Highest			Lowest		
Rank	**Station Name**	**Days**	**Rank**	**Station Name**	**Days**
1	Bondurant	154	1	Burris	***25***
2	Bates Creek No 2	91	2	Carpenter	***29***
2	Evanston 1 E	***91***	2	Cody	***29***
4	Elk Mountain	85	4	Dubois	***30***
5	Gillette 6 SE	69	5	Dillinger	***32***
6	Chugwater	62	6	Powder River No 2	***43***
7	Archer	***59***	7	Basin	47
8	Dull Center 1 SE	54	8	Midwest	***48***
8	Riverton	***54***	9	Billy Creek	53
10	Billy Creek	53	10	Dull Center 1 SE	54
11	Midwest	***48***	10	Riverton	***54***
12	Basin	47	12	Archer	***59***
13	Powder River No 2	***43***	13	Chugwater	62
14	Dillinger	***32***	14	Gillette 6 SE	69
15	Dubois	***30***	15	Elk Mountain	85
16	Carpenter	***29***	16	Bates Creek No 2	91
16	Cody	***29***	16	Evanston 1 E	***91***
18	Burris	***25***	18	Bondurant	154

Rankings include 25 highest/lowest stations. If state has less than 25 stations, all stations are included. The period of record is 1980–2009. See User Guide for detailed explanation of data.

Significant Storm Events in Wyoming: 2000 – 2009

Location or County	Date	Type	Mag.	Deaths	Injuries	Property Damage ($mil.)	Crop Damage ($mil.)
Hot Springs	08/07/00	Wild/Forest Fire	na	1	1	0.0	0.0
Southeast Big Horn County	12/01/00	Avalanche	na	1	0	0.0	0.0
Southeast Big Horn County	12/09/00	Avalanche	na	1	0	0.0	0.0
Southeast Big Horn County	12/25/00	Avalanche	na	1	0	0.0	0.0
Southeast Big Horn County	02/06/01	Avalanche	na	1	0	0.0	0.0
Laramie	08/26/02	Hail	2.75 in.	0	0	30.0	0.0
Campbell	06/21/03	Hail	2.75 in.	0	0	17.0	0.0
Fremont Couny-Wind River Basin	09/18/04	Wildfire	na	0	9	1.0	0.0
Campbell	08/12/05	Tornado	F2	2	13	5.0	0.0
Fremont County-East Wind River Mountains	12/27/05	Avalanche	na	1	0	0.0	0.0
Fremont County-Lander Foothills	04/10/06	Wildfire	na	0	0	1.0	0.0
Natrona County-Casper Mountain	08/12/06	Wildfire	na	0	0	1.2	0.0
Teton County-Darby Canyon	03/10/07	Avalanche	na	1	1	0.0	0.0
Sweetwater	08/17/07	Flash Flood	na	0	0	0.2	0.0
Albany County-Snowy Range	01/02/08	Avalanche	na	1	0	0.0	0.0
Lincoln County-Cottonwood Lake	01/12/08	Avalanche	na	3	0	0.0	0.0
Natrona	06/18/08	Dust Devil	na	1	0	0.0	0.0
Teton County-Teton Village	12/27/08	Avalanche	na	1	0	0.0	0.0
Northern Wyoming-Absaroka Mountains	01/02/09	Avalanche	na	1	0	0.0	0.0
Natrona	07/03/09	Flash Flood	na	0	1	5.0	0.0

Note: Deaths, injuries, and damages are date and location specific.

Weather Station Rankings: United States

Highest Annual Extreme Maximum Temperature

Rank	Station Name	°F
1	Death Valley, CA	129
2	Bullhead City, AZ	126
3	Fountain Hills, AZ	125
3	Laveen 3 SSE, AZ	125
3	Needles Airport, CA	125
6	Alamo Dam, AZ	124
6	Maricopa 4 N, AZ	124
6	Willow Beach, AZ	124
6	Yuma Citrus Station, AZ	***124***
6	Yuma Proving Ground, AZ	124
11	Parker Reservoir, CA	123
12	Blythe, CA	122
12	Borrego Desert Park, CA	122
12	Gila Bend, AZ	122
12	Phoenix Sky Harbor Intl Arpt, AZ	122
16	Beaver Dam, AZ	120
16	Casa Grande, AZ	***120***
16	Castle Hot Springs, AZ	120
16	Yucca 1 NNE, AZ	120
20	Florence, AZ	119
20	Hayfield Pumping Plant, CA	119
20	Kofa Mine, AZ	119
20	Lees Ferry, AZ	***119***
24	Ash Mountain, CA	118
24	Organ Pipe Cactus N M, AZ	118
24	Redlands, CA	118
27	Amargosa Farms Garey, NV	117
27	Boquillas Ranger Stn, TX	***117***
27	Castolon, TX	117
27	Childress Municipal Arpt, TX	117
27	Childs, AZ	***117***
27	Cottonwood 2 E, SD	117
27	Desert Natl Wl Range, NV	117
27	Grandfalls 3 SSE, TX	***117***
27	Haiwee, CA	117
27	Las Vegas-McCarran Intl Arpt, NV	117
27	Pierre Municipal Arpt, SD	117
27	St George, UT	117
27	Tucson Intl Arpt, AZ	117
27	Wichita Falls Municipal Arpt, TX	117
41	Arches Np Hqs, UT	116
41	Canoga Park Pierce College, CA	***116***
41	Cascabel, AZ	116
41	Cedar Butte 1 NE, SD	116
41	Chattanooga 3 NE, OK	116
41	Clifton, AZ	***116***
41	Columbus, TX	116
41	Encinal, TX	***116***
41	Falcon Dam, TX	116
41	Gail, TX	116
41	Midland Regional Air Terminal, TX	116
41	Newman, CA	***116***
41	Penwell, TX	116
41	Ponca City Municipal Arpt, OK	116
41	Rio Grande City 1 SE, TX	116
41	Riverside Fire Sta 3, CA	116
41	Victorville Pump Plant, CA	116
58	Altus Irig Res Station, OK	115
58	Barstow Fire Station, CA	115
58	Basin, WY	115
58	Bridgeport, TX	***115***
58	Brownlee Dam, ID	115
58	Buffalo, OK	115
58	Candelaria, TX	115
58	Coalinga, CA	115
58	Cordes, AZ	115
58	Covelo, CA	115
58	Crystal City, TX	115
58	Dell City 5 SSW, TX	115
58	Elsinore, CA	115
58	Falfurrias, TX	115
58	Frederick, OK	115
58	Henrietta, TX	***115***
58	Hot Springs 1 NNE, AR	115
58	Morrilton, AR	***115***
58	Mountain Home, ID	115
58	Stockton Metropolitan Arpt, CA	115
58	Tatum, NM	115
58	Tucson 17 NW, AZ	***115***
58	Tucson NWSO, AZ	115
58	Waurika, OK	115
82	Amistad Dam, TX	114
82	Anson, TX	***114***
82	Anvil Ranch, AZ	114
82	Bakersfield, TX	114
82	Big Spring, TX	***114***
82	Bitter Lakes Wl Refuge, NM	114
82	Carlsbad, NM	114
82	Conchas Dam, NM	114
82	Dupree 15 SSE, SD	114
82	El Paso Intl Arpt, TX	114
82	Fairfield, CA	114
82	Faulkton 1 NW, SD	114
82	Friant Government Camp, CA	114
82	Healdton, OK	114
82	Hobbs, NM	***114***
82	Independence, CA	114
82	Laredo 2, TX	114
82	Lubbock Regional Arpt, TX	114
82	Medford Jackson County Arpt, OR	114

Rankings include 100 highest and 100 lowest stations in each category. The period of record is 1980–2009. See User Guide for detailed explanation of data.

Lowest Annual Extreme Maximum Temperature

Rank	Station Name	°F
1	St Paul Island Arpt, AK	66
2	Mount Washington, NH	72
3	Cold Bay Arpt, AK	76
4	Haleakala R S 338, HI	78
5	Barrow W Post-W Rogers Arpt, AK	79
6	Cannery Creek, AK	80
7	Dutch Harbor, AK	***81***
7	Homer Arpt, AK	81
9	Glacier Bay, AK	***82***
9	Homer 8 NW, AK	82
9	Kodiak State USCG Base, AK	82
12	Cabin Creek, CO	83
12	Kula Hospital 267, HI	83
12	Kuparuk, AK	***83***
12	Port San Juan, AK	83
16	Anchorage Intl Arpt, AK	84
16	Glen Alps, AK	84
16	Iliamna Arpt, AK	84
16	Intricate Bay, AK	***84***
16	Kenai Municipal Arpt, AK	84
16	Sitka Japonski Arpt, AK	84
22	Juneau Int'l Arpt, AK	85
22	King Salmon Arpt, AK	85
22	Kotzebue Ralph Wein Memorial, AK	85
22	Nome Municipal Arpt, AK	85
22	Puntilla, AK	85
22	Sutton 2 E, AK	85
28	Alta, UT	86
28	Anderson Lake, AK	***86***
28	Blaine, WA	86
28	Chulitna River Lodge, AK	***86***
28	Elfin Cove, AK	86
33	Bethel Airport, AK	87
33	Cantwell 2 E, AK	***87***
33	Eureka, CA	87
33	Kitoi Bay, AK	87
33	Nabesna, AK	87
33	Seward, AK	***87***
39	Alyeska, AK	88
39	Antero Reservoir, CO	88
39	Little Port Walter, AK	88
39	Yakutat State Arpt, AK	88
43	Cordova, AK	89
43	Gulkana Intermediate Field, AK	89
43	Hayes River, AK	***89***
43	McGrath Arpt, AK	89
43	Northway Airport, AK	89
43	Skwentna, AK	89
43	Talkeetna State Arpt, AK	89
43	Whites Crossing, AK	89
51	Big Delta Allen AAF, AK	90
51	Blowhard Mtn Radar, UT	***90***
51	Cooke City 2 W, MT	90
51	Cooper Landing 6 W, AK	90
51	Gascon, NM	90
51	Kanalohuluhulu 1075, HI	90
51	Lihue Arpt, HI	90
58	Bodie, CA	91
58	Indian Lake 2 SW, NY	91
58	Tanana Ralph M Calhoun Mem Arpt, AK	91
61	Aspen 1 SW, CO	92
61	Bellingham 3 SSW, WA	***92***
61	Bright Angel R S, AZ	92
61	Center 4 SSW, CO	92
61	Eielson Field, AK	92
61	Electric Lake U P & L, UT	***92***
61	Hohnholz Ranch, CO	***92***
61	Morrisville 5 SW, NY	***92***
61	Norfolk 2 SW, CT	92
70	Alpine, AZ	93
70	Annette Island Arpt, AK	93
70	Bailey, CO	93
70	Bettles Field, AK	93
70	Chama, NM	93
70	Crescent City 3 NNW, CA	93
70	Driggs, ID	93
70	Everett, WA	93
70	Hawaii Volcanos Np Hq 54, HI	93
70	Healy 2 NW, AK	***93***
70	Hilo International Arpt, HI	93
70	Molokai Airport, HI	93
70	Tully Heiberg Forest, NY	***93***
83	Big Bear Lake, CA	94
83	Boonville 2 SSW, NY	94
83	Brassua Dam, ME	94
83	Burkes Garden, VA	94
83	Chalk Hill 2 ENE, PA	94
83	Cochetopa Creek, CO	94
83	College Observatory, AK	94
83	Coupeville 1 S, WA	94
83	Elk Mountain, WY	94
83	Fairbanks Intl Arpt, AK	94
83	Fort Bragg 5 N, CA	94
83	Grafton, NY	***94***
83	Grand Marais, MN	94
83	Middle Dam, ME	94
83	Opihihale 2 24.1, HI	94
83	Port Angeles, WA	94
83	South Lincoln, VT	94
100	Allagash, ME	***95***

Rankings include 100 highest and 100 lowest stations in each category. The period of record is 1980–2009. See User Guide for detailed explanation of data.

Highest Annual Mean Maximum Temperature

Rank	Station Name	°F	Rank	Station Name	°F
1	Death Valley, CA	91.3	48	Saint Leo, FL	83.9
2	Gila Bend, AZ	89.8	52	Arcadia, FL	83.8
3	Bullhead City, AZ	89.1	53	Alice, TX	***83.7***
4	Blythe, CA	***88.3***	53	Brownsville Intl Arpt, TX	83.7
5	Boquillas Ranger Stn, TX	***88.1***	53	Castle Hot Springs, AZ	83.7
6	Yuma Proving Ground, AZ	88.0	53	Tucson Intl Arpt, AZ	83.7
7	Borrego Desert Park, CA	87.9	57	Charlotte 5 NNW, TX	83.6
8	Castolon, TX	87.7	57	Fort Lauderdale, FL	83.6
8	Maricopa 4 N, AZ	87.7	57	Tucson NWSO, AZ	83.6
10	Casa Grande, AZ	***87.4***	60	Avon Park 2 W, FL	83.3
11	Laveen 3 SSE, AZ	87.2	60	Plant City, FL	83.3
12	Alamo Dam, AZ	87.1	62	Kissimmee 2, FL	83.2
12	Needles Airport, CA	87.1	62	West Palm Beach Intl Arpt, FL	83.2
12	Oasis Ranger Station, FL	87.1	64	Fort Pierce, FL	83.1
15	Willow Beach, AZ	***87.0***	64	Stuart 1 S, FL	***83.1***
16	Phoenix Sky Harbor Intl Arpt, AZ	86.8	66	Anvil Ranch, AZ	83.0
17	Organ Pipe Cactus N M, AZ	86.7	67	Key West Intl Arpt, FL	82.9
18	Parker Reservoir, CA	86.6	68	Orlando Intl Arpt, FL	82.8
19	Falcon Dam, TX	86.5	69	Cascabel, AZ	82.7
19	Fountain Hills, AZ	86.5	70	Parrish, FL	82.5
21	Rio Grande City 1 SE, TX	86.4	70	Tarpon Springs Sewage Plant, FL	82.5
22	Florence, AZ	85.9	70	Weeki Wachee, FL	82.5
22	Laredo 2, TX	85.9	73	Clermont 7 S, FL	82.4
22	McAllen Miller Intl Arpt, TX	***85.9***	73	Langtry, TX	82.4
25	Myakka River State Park, FL	85.5	73	Vero Beach Municipal Arpt, FL	***82.4***
26	Candelaria, TX	85.4	76	High Springs, FL	82.2
26	McCook, TX	85.4	77	Cuero, TX	82.1
28	Hayfield Pumping Plant, CA	85.1	77	Robstown, TX	82.1
28	Raymondville, TX	85.1	77	Sanford Experiment Stn, FL	82.1
30	Immokalee 3 NNW, FL	***85.0***	80	Beaver Dam, AZ	***82.0***
30	Naples, FL	85.0	80	Brooksville Chin Hill, FL	***82.0***
30	South Phoenix, AZ	85.0	80	Tampa Intl Arpt, FL	82.0
33	Archbold Bio Station, FL	84.9	83	Floresville, TX	81.9
33	Weslaco 2 E, TX	84.9	83	Molokai Airport, HI	81.9
35	Encinal, TX	***84.8***	83	Yucca 1 NNE, AZ	81.9
35	Honolulu Intl Arpt, HI	84.8	86	Amistad Dam, TX	81.8
35	Ke-Ahole Point 68.13, HI	***84.8***	87	Del Rio Intl Arpt, TX	81.7
35	McAllen, TX	***84.8***	87	Melbourne Regional Arpt, FL	81.7
39	Punta Gorda 4 ESE, FL	84.7	89	Corpus Christi Intl Arpt, TX	81.6
40	Fort Myers Page Field, FL	84.6	90	Amargosa Farms Garey, NV	81.5
40	Kofa Mine, AZ	84.6	90	Childs, AZ	***81.5***
42	Falfurrias, TX	84.3	90	Columbus, TX	81.5
42	Kahului Arpt, HI	84.3	93	Deland 1 SSE, FL	81.4
44	Flamingo Ranger Stn, FL	84.2	93	Grandfalls 3 SSE, TX	***81.4***
44	Tucson 17 NW, AZ	***84.2***	93	Hilo International Arpt, HI	81.4
46	Mountain Lake, FL	84.1	93	Perry, FL	81.4
47	Miami Intl Arpt, FL	84.0	97	Canoga Park Pierce College, CA	***81.3***
48	Carrizo Springs, TX	83.9	97	Titusville, FL	81.3
48	Crystal City, TX	83.9	99	Lihue Arpt, HI	81.2
48	Harlingen, TX	83.9	100	St Petersburg, FL	81.1

Rankings include 100 highest and 100 lowest stations in each category. The period of record is 1980–2009. See User Guide for detailed explanation of data.

Lowest Annual Mean Maximum Temperature

Rank	Station Name	°F	Rank	Station Name	°F
1	Barrow W Post-W Rogers Arpt, AK	17.0	51	Cordova, AK	47.2
2	Kuparuk, AK	*18.3*	52	Cooke City 2 W, MT	*47.3*
3	Kotzebue Ralph Wein Memorial, AK	28.7	53	Glacier Bay, AK	*47.6*
4	Bettles Field, AK	32.6	54	Electric Lake U P & L, UT	*47.7*
5	Mount Washington, NH	34.1	55	Alta, UT	47.9
5	Northway Airport, AK	34.1	56	Juneau Int'l Arpt, AK	48.0
7	Nabesna, AK	34.2	57	Warroad, MN	48.2
7	Nome Municipal Arpt, AK	34.2	58	Grand Marais, MN	48.4
9	Tanana Ralph M Calhoun Mem Arpt, AK	35.4	59	Cabin Creek, CO	48.6
10	Eagle, AK	36.6	59	Duluth Intl Arpt, MN	48.6
11	McGrath Arpt, AK	36.8	59	International Falls Int'l Arpt, MN	48.6
11	Tok, AK	*36.8*	62	Cavalier 7 NW, ND	48.7
13	Eielson Field, AK	37.0	63	Hancock Houghton Co Arpt, MI	48.9
14	Cantwell 2 E, AK	*37.4*	63	Pembina, ND	48.9
14	North Pole, AK	37.4	65	Gunflint Lake 10 NW, MN	*49.0*
16	Bethel Airport, AK	37.6	66	Eustis, ME	*49.1*
17	Fairbanks Intl Arpt, AK	37.8	66	Red Lake Indian Agency, MN	*49.1*
18	Big Delta Allen AAF, AK	37.9	68	Caribou Municipal Arpt, ME	49.2
19	College Observatory, AK	38.2	68	Edmore 1 NW, ND	49.2
19	Gulkana Intermediate Field, AK	38.2	70	Hibbing Chisholm-Hibbing Arpt, MN	49.3
19	Puntilla, AK	38.2	70	Whitefish Point, MI	49.3
22	St Paul Island Arpt, AK	39.5	72	Allagash, ME	*49.4*
23	Healy 2 NW, AK	*39.7*	73	Brassua Dam, ME	49.6
24	Glen Alps, AK	40.2	73	Little Port Walter, AK	49.6
25	Chulitna River Lodge, AK	*40.8*	73	Tower 3 S, MN	49.6
26	Iliamna Arpt, AK	42.3	76	Bottineau, ND	49.7
27	Hayes River, AK	*42.6*	76	Hebgen Dam, MT	49.7
28	Homer 8 NW, AK	42.9	76	Marquette County Arpt, MI	49.7
28	Whites Crossing, AK	42.9	76	Superior, WI	49.7
30	Kenai Municipal Arpt, AK	43.2	80	Manistique, MI	49.8
31	King Salmon Arpt, AK	43.4	81	Ironwood, MI	49.9
32	Anchorage Intl Arpt, AK	43.6	81	Sitka Japonski Arpt, AK	49.9
32	Cold Bay Arpt, AK	43.6	83	Two Harbors, MN	50.0
34	Skwentna, AK	*43.9*	84	Sault Ste Marie Sanderson Field, MI	50.1
35	Blowhard Mtn Radar, UT	*44.1*	85	Devils Lake Kdlr, ND	50.2
36	Talkeetna State Arpt, AK	44.3	86	Munising, MI	50.3
37	Anderson Lake, AK	*44.6*	87	Stanley 3 NNW, ND	50.4
38	Cannery Creek, AK	44.8	88	Cass Lake, MN	50.5
39	Alyeska, AK	44.9	88	Middle Dam, ME	50.5
40	Intricate Bay, AK	*45.2*	90	Bergland Dam, MI	50.6
41	Homer Arpt, AK	45.3	91	Argyle 4 E, MN	50.7
42	Sutton 2 E, AK	45.8	91	Bondurant, WY	*50.7*
43	Seward, AK	*45.9*	91	Carrington, ND	*50.7*
44	Cooper Landing 6 W, AK	*46.1*	91	Crookston NW Exp Stn, MN	50.7
44	Dutch Harbor, AK	*46.1*	91	Hansboro 4 NNE, ND	50.7
46	Port San Juan, AK	*46.6*	96	Stambaugh 2 SSE, MI	50.8
47	Kitoi Bay, AK	46.7	97	Agassiz Refuge, MN	50.9
48	Kodiak State USCG Base, AK	46.9	98	Indian Lake 2 SW, NY	51.0
48	Yakutat State Arpt, AK	46.9	99	Bayfield 6 N, WI	*51.1*
50	Elfin Cove, AK	*47.0*	99	Boonville 2 SSW, NY	51.1

Rankings include 100 highest and 100 lowest stations in each category. The period of record is 1980–2009. See User Guide for detailed explanation of data.

Highest Annual Mean Temperature

Rank	Station Name	°F
1	Key West Intl Arpt, FL	78.1
2	Honolulu Intl Arpt, HI	77.8
3	Ke-Ahole Point 68.13, HI	***77.5***
4	Miami Intl Arpt, FL	77.0
5	Death Valley, CA	76.7
6	Oasis Ranger Station, FL	76.3
7	Fort Lauderdale, FL	76.1
8	Kahului Arpt, HI	76.0
9	Lihue Arpt, HI	75.8
10	Kii-Kahuku 911, HI	***75.6***
10	McAllen Miller Intl Arpt, TX	***75.6***
10	West Palm Beach Intl Arpt, FL	75.6
13	Flamingo Ranger Stn, FL	75.4
14	Fort Myers Page Field, FL	75.1
15	Naples, FL	75.0
15	Phoenix Sky Harbor Intl Arpt, AZ	75.0
17	Stuart 1 S, FL	***74.9***
18	Brownsville Intl Arpt, TX	74.6
18	Bullhead City, AZ	74.6
18	McAllen, TX	***74.6***
18	Molokai Airport, HI	74.6
18	Yuma Proving Ground, AZ	74.6
23	Falcon Dam, TX	74.5
23	Needles Airport, CA	74.5
23	Parker Reservoir, CA	74.5
23	Weslaco 2 E, TX	74.5
27	Laredo 2, TX	74.3
27	Punta Gorda 4 ESE, FL	74.3
27	Rio Grande City 1 SE, TX	74.3
30	Gila Bend, AZ	74.2
31	Hilo International Arpt, HI	74.1
31	McCook, TX	74.1
31	Port Isabel, TX	74.1
34	Harlingen, TX	74.0
34	St Petersburg, FL	74.0
36	Immokalee 3 NNW, FL	***73.9***
37	Raymondville, TX	73.8
38	Kofa Mine, AZ	73.5
38	Myakka River State Park, FL	73.5
40	Fort Pierce, FL	73.4
40	Vero Beach Municipal Arpt, FL	***73.4***
42	Borrego Desert Park, CA	73.2
42	Tampa Intl Arpt, FL	73.2
44	Willow Beach, AZ	***73.1***
45	Tarpon Springs Sewage Plant, FL	73.0
46	Mountain Lake, FL	72.9
46	Saint Leo, FL	72.9
48	Orlando Intl Arpt, FL	72.8
49	Blythe, CA	***72.7***
49	Crystal City, TX	72.7
51	Alice, TX	***72.6***
51	Falfurrias, TX	72.6
51	Kissimmee 2, FL	72.6
51	Laveen 3 SSE, AZ	72.6
55	Melbourne Regional Arpt, FL	72.5
55	Plant City, FL	72.5
57	Avon Park 2 W, FL	72.4
58	Arcadia, FL	72.3
58	Parrish, FL	72.3
58	Robstown, TX	72.3
61	Corpus Christi Intl Arpt, TX	72.2
61	Port Mansfield, TX	***72.2***
63	Fountain Hills, AZ	72.1
64	Archbold Bio Station, FL	72.0
64	Clermont 7 S, FL	72.0
64	Encinal, TX	***72.0***
64	Titusville, FL	72.0
68	Sanford Experiment Stn, FL	71.9
69	Castolon, TX	71.8
70	Brooksville Chin Hill, FL	***71.5***
71	Carrizo Springs, TX	71.4
72	Casa Grande, AZ	***71.3***
72	Charlotte 5 NNW, TX	71.3
72	Tucson NWSO, AZ	71.3
75	Crescent City, FL	***71.1***
75	Florence, AZ	***71.1***
77	Alamo Dam, AZ	71.0
77	Daytona Beach Regional Arpt, FL	71.0
77	Organ Pipe Cactus N M, AZ	71.0
80	Aransas Wildlife Refuge, TX	70.9
80	Weeki Wachee, FL	70.9
82	Maricopa 4 N, AZ	70.8
83	New Orleans Audubon, LA	70.6
84	Del Rio Intl Arpt, TX	70.5
84	Deland 1 SSE, FL	70.5
84	Victoria Regional Arpt, TX	70.5
87	Boquillas Ranger Stn, TX	***70.4***
87	Federal Point, FL	70.4
87	South Phoenix, AZ	70.4
90	Tucson 17 NW, AZ	***70.3***
91	Bay City Waterworks, TX	70.2
91	Castle Hot Springs, AZ	70.2
91	Houston William P Hobby Arpt, TX	70.2
91	St Augustine WFOY, FL	70.2
95	Amistad Dam, TX	70.1
95	Cuero, TX	70.1
95	Hayfield Pumping Plant, CA	70.1
98	Opihihale 2 24.1, HI	69.9
98	Thompsons 3 WSW, TX	69.9
100	Langtry, TX	69.8

Rankings include 100 highest and 100 lowest stations in each category. The period of record is 1980–2009. See User Guide for detailed explanation of data.

Lowest Annual Mean Temperature

Rank	Station Name	°F
1	Barrow W Post-W Rogers Arpt, AK	11.5
2	Kuparuk, AK	***11.7***
3	Kotzebue Ralph Wein Memorial, AK	22.8
4	Bettles Field, AK	23.3
4	Northway Airport, AK	23.3
6	Tok, AK	***24.6***
7	Nabesna, AK	24.7
8	Eagle, AK	25.3
9	Tanana Ralph M Calhoun Mem Arpt, AK	25.6
10	North Pole, AK	26.2
11	Cantwell 2 E, AK	***26.7***
12	McGrath Arpt, AK	27.2
13	Nome Municipal Arpt, AK	27.4
14	Mount Washington, NH	27.5
15	Eielson Field, AK	27.6
16	Fairbanks Intl Arpt, AK	27.9
17	Gulkana Intermediate Field, AK	28.1
18	Puntilla, AK	28.2
19	College Observatory, AK	28.4
20	Big Delta Allen AAF, AK	29.3
21	Healy 2 NW, AK	***30.0***
22	Bethel Airport, AK	30.7
23	Whites Crossing, AK	32.5
24	Chulitna River Lodge, AK	***32.8***
25	Hayes River, AK	***33.4***
26	Bondurant, WY	***33.7***
26	Skwentna, AK	***33.7***
28	Glen Alps, AK	33.8
29	Cooke City 2 W, MT	***34.1***
30	Electric Lake U P & L, UT	***34.3***
31	King Salmon Arpt, AK	35.1
32	Talkeetna State Arpt, AK	35.2
33	Kenai Municipal Arpt, AK	35.3
34	Stanley, ID	35.4
35	St Paul Island Arpt, AK	35.5
36	Iliamna Arpt, AK	35.9
36	Sutton 2 E, AK	35.9
38	Antero Reservoir, CO	36.0
38	Cooper Landing 6 W, AK	***36.0***
40	Tower 3 S, MN	36.1
41	Blowhard Mtn Radar, UT	***36.4***
41	Cabin Creek, CO	36.4
41	Dixie, ID	***36.4***
41	Fontenelle Dam, WY	36.4
45	Allagash, ME	***36.5***
46	Intricate Bay, AK	***36.6***
47	Anderson Lake, AK	***36.7***
47	Homer 8 NW, AK	36.7
49	Anchorage Intl Arpt, AK	37.0
49	Hebgen Dam, MT	37.0
51	Alyeska, AK	37.7
51	Gunflint Lake 10 NW, MN	***37.7***
51	Pembina, ND	37.7
54	International Falls Int'l Arpt, MN	37.8
54	Island Park, ID	***37.8***
56	Warroad, MN	37.9
57	Cavalier 7 NW, ND	38.1
57	Edmore 1 NW, ND	38.1
57	Hibbing Chisholm-Hibbing Arpt, MN	38.1
60	Bodie, CA	38.3
61	Cannery Creek, AK	38.4
62	Alta, UT	38.5
62	Bottineau, ND	38.5
62	Eustis, ME	***38.5***
65	Hansboro 4 NNE, ND	38.7
65	Stambaugh 2 SSE, MI	38.7
65	Stanley 3 NNW, ND	38.7
68	Homer Arpt, AK	38.8
68	Upham 3 N, ND	38.8
70	Cold Bay Arpt, AK	38.9
70	Hohnholz Ranch, CO	***38.9***
72	Red Lake Indian Agency, MN	***39.0***
72	Wildhorse Reservoir, NV	***39.0***
74	Argyle 4 E, MN	39.1
74	Brassua Dam, ME	39.1
74	Champion Van Riper Prk, MI	39.1
74	Cochetopa Creek, CO	39.1
78	Bergland Dam, MI	39.2
79	Cass Lake, MN	39.3
80	Duluth Intl Arpt, MN	39.5
80	Westby, MT	***39.5***
82	Caribou Municipal Arpt, ME	39.6
82	Opheim 10 N, MT	39.6
82	Woodruff, UT	39.6
85	Cordova, AK	39.7
86	Middle Dam, ME	39.8
87	Butte Bert Mooney Arpt, MT	39.9
87	Grand Marais, MN	39.9
87	Ironwood, MI	39.9
90	Kenmare 1 WSW, ND	40.0
91	Agassiz Refuge, MN	40.1
91	Crookston NW Exp Stn, MN	40.1
91	Marquette County Arpt, MI	40.1
94	Carrington, ND	***40.2***
95	Bridgewater, ME	40.3
95	Cascade 1 NW, ID	40.3
95	Chilly Barton Flat, ID	40.3
95	Foxboro, WI	***40.3***
95	Yakutat State Arpt, AK	40.3
100	Devils Lake Kdlr, ND	40.4

Rankings include 100 highest and 100 lowest stations in each category. The period of record is 1980–2009. See User Guide for detailed explanation of data.

Highest Annual Mean Minimum Temperature

Rank	Station Name	°F
1	Key West Intl Arpt, FL	73.2
2	Honolulu Intl Arpt, HI	70.8
3	Lihue Arpt, HI	70.4
4	Kii-Kahuku 911, HI	***70.2***
5	Ke-Ahole Point 68.13, HI	***70.1***
6	Miami Intl Arpt, FL	69.8
7	Fort Lauderdale, FL	68.6
8	West Palm Beach Intl Arpt, FL	67.8
9	Kahului Arpt, HI	67.6
10	Molokai Airport, HI	67.3
11	Port Isabel, TX	67.2
12	St Petersburg, FL	66.9
13	Hilo International Arpt, HI	66.8
14	Stuart 1 S, FL	***66.7***
15	Flamingo Ranger Stn, FL	66.5
16	Port Mansfield, TX	65.6
17	Fort Myers Page Field, FL	65.5
18	Brownsville Intl Arpt, TX	65.4
18	Oasis Ranger Station, FL	65.4
20	McAllen Miller Intl Arpt, TX	***65.2***
21	Naples, FL	64.9
22	Tampa Intl Arpt, FL	64.4
23	Vero Beach Municipal Arpt, FL	***64.3***
24	McAllen, TX	***64.2***
25	Weslaco 2 E, TX	64.1
26	Harlingen, TX	63.9
27	Fort Pierce, FL	63.7
27	Punta Gorda 4 ESE, FL	63.7
29	Tarpon Springs Sewage Plant, FL	63.5
30	Dauphin Island #2, AL	63.3
30	Melbourne Regional Arpt, FL	63.3
30	Phoenix Sky Harbor Intl Arpt, AZ	63.3
33	Aransas Wildlife Refuge, TX	63.2
34	McCook, TX	62.8
34	Orlando Intl Arpt, FL	62.8
36	Corpus Christi Intl Arpt, TX	62.7
36	Immokalee 3 NNW, FL	***62.7***
38	Raymondville, TX	62.6
38	Titusville, FL	62.6
40	Falcon Dam, TX	62.5
40	Laredo 2, TX	62.5
42	Kofa Mine, AZ	62.4
42	Parker Reservoir, CA	62.4
42	Robstown, TX	62.4
45	Rio Grande City 1 SE, TX	62.1
46	Death Valley, CA	62.0
46	Jacksonville Beach, FL	62.0
46	Kissimmee 2, FL	62.0
46	Parrish, FL	62.0
50	Needles Airport, CA	61.9
50	New Orleans Audubon, LA	61.9
50	Saint Leo, FL	61.9
53	Mountain Lake, FL	61.7
53	Plant City, FL	61.7
55	Alice, TX	***61.5***
55	Clermont 7 S, FL	61.5
55	Daytona Beach Regional Arpt, FL	61.5
55	Sanford Experiment Stn, FL	61.5
59	Avon Park 2 W, FL	61.4
59	Crystal City, TX	61.4
59	Houston William P Hobby Arpt, TX	61.4
59	Myakka River State Park, FL	61.4
63	Crescent City, FL	***61.3***
63	Hackberry 8 SSW, LA	***61.3***
65	Yuma Proving Ground, AZ	61.2
66	Bay City Waterworks, TX	61.1
67	St Augustine WFOY, FL	61.0
68	Brooksville Chin Hill, FL	***60.9***
68	Falfurrias, TX	60.9
68	Opihihale 2 24.1, HI	60.9
71	Arcadia, FL	60.8
72	Federal Point, FL	60.7
73	Fernandina Beach, FL	60.5
74	Charleston City, SC	60.4
75	Baytown, TX	60.3
75	New Orleans Intl Arpt, LA	60.3
75	Victoria Regional Arpt, TX	60.3
78	Biloxi, MS	***60.2***
79	Galliano, LA	60.1
80	Bullhead City, AZ	60.0
80	St Bernard, LA	***60.0***
82	Angleton 2 W, TX	59.9
82	Port Arthur Jefferson County, TX	59.9
84	Houma, LA	59.7
84	Sugar Land, TX	***59.7***
84	Thompsons 3 WSW, TX	59.7
87	Deland 1 SSE, FL	59.6
88	Apalachicola Municipal Arpt, FL	59.4
89	Houston Bush Intercontinental, TX	59.3
89	Weeki Wachee, FL	59.3
91	Anahuac, TX	59.2
91	Del Rio Intl Arpt, TX	59.2
91	Gulfport Naval Center, MS	59.2
91	Pensacola Regional Arpt, FL	59.2
95	Archbold Bio Station, FL	59.1
95	Encinal, TX	***59.1***
95	Franklin 3 NW, LA	59.1
98	Lake Charles Municipal Arpt, LA	59.0
98	Willow Beach, AZ	***59.0***
100	Austin Municipal Arpt, TX	58.9

Rankings include 100 highest and 100 lowest stations in each category. The period of record is 1980–2009. See User Guide for detailed explanation of data.

Lowest Annual Mean Minimum Temperature

Rank	Station Name	°F	Rank	Station Name	°F
1	Kuparuk, AK	***5.0***	51	Chilly Barton Flat, ID	25.6
2	Barrow W Post-W Rogers Arpt, AK	6.0	52	Cooper Landing 6 W, AK	***25.8***
3	Northway Airport, AK	12.4	52	Flagstaff 4 SW, AZ	***25.8***
3	Tok, AK	***12.4***	52	Reese River O'Toole, NV	25.8
5	Eagle, AK	14.0	55	Butte Bert Mooney Arpt, MT	25.9
6	Bettles Field, AK	14.1	56	Sutton 2 E, AK	26.0
7	North Pole, AK	15.0	57	Opheim 10 N, MT	26.1
8	Nabesna, AK	15.1	58	Angle, UT	26.2
9	Cantwell 2 E, AK	***15.8***	58	Austin 3 S, OR	26.2
9	Tanana Ralph M Calhoun Mem Arpt, AK	15.8	58	Cascade 1 NW, ID	26.2
11	Bondurant, WY	16.6	58	Talkeetna State Arpt, AK	26.2
12	Kotzebue Ralph Wein Memorial, AK	16.9	62	McGaffey 5 SE, NM	26.3
13	McGrath Arpt, AK	17.7	62	Upham 3 N, ND	26.3
14	Fairbanks Intl Arpt, AK	18.0	64	Gunflint Lake 10 NW, MN	***26.4***
14	Gulkana Intermediate Field, AK	18.0	65	Champion Van Riper Prk, MI	26.5
16	Eielson Field, AK	18.2	65	Fort Valley, AZ	26.5
16	Puntilla, AK	18.2	65	Pembina, ND	26.5
18	Stanley, ID	18.4	65	Stambaugh 2 SSE, MI	26.5
19	Antero Reservoir, CO	18.6	69	Cheesman, CO	26.6
20	College Observatory, AK	18.7	69	Hansboro 4 NNE, ND	26.6
21	Bodie, CA	19.5	71	Dubois, WY	***26.8***
22	Healy 2 NW, AK	***20.3***	72	Edmore 1 NW, ND	26.9
23	Big Delta Allen AAF, AK	20.5	72	International Falls Int'l Arpt, MN	26.9
24	Nome Municipal Arpt, AK	20.6	72	King Salmon Arpt, AK	26.9
25	Fontenelle Dam, WY	20.7	72	Stanley 3 NNW, ND	26.9
26	Mount Washington, NH	20.8	76	Hibbing Chisholm-Hibbing Arpt, MN	27.0
27	Cooke City 2 W, MT	***20.9***	77	Bottineau, ND	27.2
28	Electric Lake U P & L, UT	***21.0***	77	Driggs, ID	27.2
29	Cochetopa Creek, CO	21.3	77	Gibbs Ranch, NV	27.2
30	Dixie, ID	***21.6***	77	Glen Alps, AK	27.2
31	Wildhorse Reservoir, NV	***22.0***	77	Westby, MT	***27.2***
32	Whites Crossing, AK	22.2	82	Argyle 4 E, MN	27.4
33	Tower 3 S, MN	22.6	82	Kenai Municipal Arpt, AK	27.4
34	Hohnholz Ranch, CO	***22.7***	82	Millegan 14 SE, MT	***27.4***
35	Island Park, ID	***23.3***	85	Cavalier 7 NW, ND	27.5
36	Skwentna, AK	***23.4***	85	Warroad, MN	27.5
37	Allagash, ME	***23.5***	87	Divide, MT	27.6
38	Bethel Airport, AK	23.8	88	Aspen 1 SW, CO	27.8
38	Woodruff, UT	23.8	88	Bergland Dam, MI	27.8
40	Alamosa Bergman Field, CO	23.9	90	Denton 1 NNE, MT	27.9
41	Hayes River, AK	***24.1***	90	Eustis, ME	***27.9***
42	Hebgen Dam, MT	24.2	90	Evergreen, CO	27.9
43	Cabin Creek, CO	24.3	90	Intricate Bay, AK	***27.9***
44	Cimarron, CO	24.6	94	Cass Lake, MN	28.0
44	Spring Valley State Park, NV	***24.6***	94	Donner Memorial St Pk, CA	28.0
46	Boca, CA	24.7	94	Evanston 1 E, WY	28.0
47	Chulitna River Lodge, AK	***24.8***	94	Riverton, WY	28.0
48	Bailey, CO	24.9	98	Blackleaf, MT	***28.1***
49	Center 4 SSW, CO	25.1	98	Dickinson Exp Stn, ND	28.1
50	Chama, NM	25.4	100	Alpine, AZ	28.3

Rankings include 100 highest and 100 lowest stations in each category. The period of record is 1980–2009. See User Guide for detailed explanation of data.

Highest Annual Extreme Minimum Temperature

Rank	Station Name	°F
1	Ke-Ahole Point 68.13, HI	56
2	Hilo International Arpt, HI	54
3	Honolulu Intl Arpt, HI	53
3	Lihue Arpt, HI	53
5	Kahului Arpt, HI	50
6	Opihihale 2 24.1, HI	49
7	Molokai Airport, HI	46
8	Kii-Kahuku 911, HI	43
9	Key West Intl Arpt, FL	41
10	Kula Hospital 267, HI	37
11	Santa Monica Pier, CA	***35***
12	San Diego Lindbergh Field, CA	34
13	Los Angeles Civic Center, CA	33
13	Los Angeles Intl Arpt, CA	33
15	Culver City, CA	32
16	Hawaii Volcanos Np Hq 54, HI	31
17	Miami Intl Arpt, FL	30
18	Fort Lauderdale, FL	29
18	Haleakala R S 338, HI	29
18	Kanalohuluhulu 1075, HI	29
21	Long Beach Daugherty Fld, CA	28
21	West Palm Beach Intl Arpt, FL	28
23	Fort Myers Page Field, FL	27
23	Laguna Beach, CA	***27***
23	San Francisco Int'l Arpt, CA	27
26	Kofa Mine, AZ	26
26	Naples, FL	26
26	Oasis Ranger Station, FL	26
26	Phoenix Sky Harbor Intl Arpt, AZ	26
26	San Francisco Oceanside, CA	***26***
31	Escondido No 2, CA	***25***
31	Parker Reservoir, CA	25
31	Tucson NWSO, AZ	25
31	Yuma Citrus Station, AZ	***25***
35	Berkeley, CA	***24***
35	Flamingo Ranger Stn, FL	24
35	St Petersburg, FL	24
35	Yuma Proving Ground, AZ	24
39	Borrego Desert Park, CA	23
39	Bullhead City, AZ	23
39	Castle Hot Springs, AZ	23
39	Fountain Hills, AZ	23
39	Punta Gorda 4 ESE, FL	23
39	San Francisco, CA	23
39	Stuart 1 S, FL	23
46	Burbank Valley Pump Plant, CA	22
46	Morro Bay Fire Dept, CA	22
46	Riverside Fire Sta 3, CA	22
46	Salinas No 2, CA	22
46	Santa Barbara, CA	***22***
51	Melbourne Regional Arpt, FL	21
51	Santa Maria Public Arpt, CA	21
51	South Phoenix, AZ	21
51	Vero Beach Municipal Arpt, FL	***21***
51	Visalia, CA	21
51	Willow Beach, AZ	21
57	Antioch Pump Plant #3, CA	20
57	Balch Power House, CA	20
57	Immokalee 3 NNW, FL	***20***
57	Laveen 3 SSE, AZ	20
61	Alamo Dam, AZ	19
61	Bakersfield Meadows Field, CA	19
61	Crescent City 3 NNW, CA	19
61	Elsinore, CA	***19***
61	Fort Pierce, FL	19
61	Kissimmee 2, FL	19
61	Modesto, CA	19
61	Organ Pipe Cactus N M, AZ	19
61	Orlando Intl Arpt, FL	19
61	Redlands, CA	19
61	Sanford Experiment Stn, FL	19
61	Tampa Intl Arpt, FL	19
61	Tarpon Springs Sewage Plant, FL	19
61	Titusville, FL	19
61	Tucson 17 NW, AZ	***19***
61	Tucson Intl Arpt, AZ	19
61	Woodland 1 WNW, CA	19
78	Arcadia, FL	18
78	Avon Park 2 W, FL	18
78	Camp Pardee, CA	18
78	Canoga Park Pierce College, CA	***18***
78	Colusa 2 SSW, CA	18
78	Florence, AZ	18
78	Fresno Air Terminal, CA	18
78	Fort Bragg 5 N, CA	18
78	Hayfield Pumping Plant, CA	18
78	Livermore, CA	18
78	McAllen, TX	***18***
78	McAllen Miller Intl Arpt, TX	***18***
78	Myakka River State Park, FL	18
78	Parrish, FL	18
78	Petaluma Fire Station 2, CA	18
78	Sacramento Executive Arpt, CA	18
78	Saint Leo, FL	18
78	Yucca 1 NNE, AZ	18
96	Ash Mountain, CA	17
96	Casa Grande, AZ	***17***
96	Clermont 7 S, FL	17
96	Fairfield, CA	17
96	Gilroy, CA	17

Rankings include 100 highest and 100 lowest stations in each category. The period of record is 1980–2009. See User Guide for detailed explanation of data.

Lowest Annual Extreme Minimum Temperature

Rank	Station Name	°F
1	Tanana Ralph M Calhoun Mem Arpt, AK	-76
2	McGrath Arpt, AK	-75
3	Bettles Field, AK	-69
4	Eagle, AK	-68
4	Tok, AK	***-68***
6	Northway Airport, AK	-65
7	North Pole, AK	-63
8	Eielson Field, AK	-60
8	Tower 3 S, MN	-60
10	Big Delta Allen AAF, AK	-59
11	Fairbanks Intl Arpt, AK	-58
11	Kuparuk, AK	***-58***
13	Barrow W Post-W Rogers Arpt, AK	-55
13	College Observatory, AK	-55
13	Couderay 7 W, WI	-55
16	Brainerd, MN	-54
16	Echeta 2 NW, WY	***-54***
16	Island Park, ID	***-54***
16	Nome Municipal Arpt, AK	-54
16	Stanley, ID	-54
21	Gulkana Intermediate Field, AK	-53
21	Skwentna, AK	-53
23	Bondurant, WY	-52
23	Busby, MT	-52
23	Butte Bert Mooney Arpt, MT	-52
23	Chester, MT	-52
23	Healy 2 NW, AK	***-52***
28	Antero Reservoir, CO	-51
28	Ridgeway 1 S, MT	-51
30	Big Sandy, MT	-50
30	Chinook, MT	-50
30	Denton 1 NNE, MT	-50
30	Havre City-County Arpt, MT	-50
30	Hibbing Chisholm-Hibbing Arpt, MN	-50
30	Intricate Bay, AK	***-50***
30	Puntilla, AK	-50
30	Velva, ND	-50
30	Whites Crossing, AK	-50
30	Williston Sloulin Intl Arpt, ND	-50
40	Cantwell 2 E, AK	***-49***
40	Content 3 SSE, MT	-49
40	Dixie, ID	***-49***
40	Kotzebue Ralph Wein Memorial, AK	-49
44	Argyle 4 E, MN	-48
44	Bethel Airport, AK	-48
44	Cass Lake, MN	-48
44	Culbertson, MT	-48
44	Electric Lake U P & L, UT	***-48***
44	King Salmon Arpt, AK	-48
44	Moorhead 9 NE, MT	-48
44	Nabesna, AK	-48
44	Upham 3 N, ND	-48
53	Allagash, ME	***-47***
53	Almont, ND	***-47***
53	Blackleaf, MT	***-47***
53	Hardin, MT	-47
53	Huntley Experiment Stn, MT	-47
53	Opheim 10 N, MT	-47
53	Stanley 3 NNW, ND	-47
60	Agassiz Refuge, MN	-46
60	Bozeman Gallatin Fld, MT	-46
60	Edmore 1 NW, ND	-46
60	Fontenelle Dam, WY	-46
60	Medicine Lake 3 SE, MT	-46
60	Riverton, WY	-46
60	Talkeetna State Arpt, AK	-46
60	Warroad, MN	-46
60	Woodruff, UT	-46
60	Wyola 1 SW, MT	***-46***
70	Aberdeen Regional Arpt, SD	-45
70	Blair, WI	-45
70	Burris, WY	-45
70	Cascade 5 S, MT	-45
70	Columbia 8 N, SD	-45
70	Crookston NW Exp Stn, MN	-45
70	Detroit Lakes 1 NNE, MN	***-45***
70	Dillinger, WY	-45
70	Gouverneur 3 NW, NY	-45
70	Hansboro 4 NNE, ND	-45
70	International Falls Int'l Arpt, MN	-45
70	Kenai Municipal Arpt, AK	-45
70	Mount Washington, NH	-45
70	Powder River No 2, WY	***-45***
70	Stambaugh 2 SSE, MI	-45
70	Stephenson 8 WNW, MI	***-45***
86	Belle Fourche, SD	***-44***
86	Bismarck Municipal Arpt, ND	-44
86	Brandenberg, MT	-44
86	Castlewood, SD	-44
86	Chazy, NY	-44
86	Cut Bank Muni Arpt, MT	-44
86	Drake 9 NE, ND	-44
86	Fort Assinniboine, MT	-44
86	Gunflint Lake 10 NW, MN	***-44***
86	Hayden, CO	-44
86	Millegan 14 SE, MT	***-44***
86	Red Lake Indian Agency, MN	***-44***
86	Valley City 3 NNW, ND	-44
99	Ada, MN	-43
99	Amery, WI	-43

Rankings include 100 highest and 100 lowest stations in each category. The period of record is 1980–2009. See User Guide for detailed explanation of data.

Highest July Mean Maximum Temperature

Rank	Station Name	°F	Rank	Station Name	°F
1	Death Valley, CA	116.4	51	Carrizo Springs, TX	98.6
2	Bullhead City, AZ	112.2	51	Fresno Air Terminal, CA	98.6
3	Willow Beach, AZ	110.5	53	Grandfalls 3 SSE, TX	98.4
4	Needles Airport, CA	109.3	53	Victorville Pump Plant, CA	98.4
5	Gila Bend, AZ	109.0	55	Langtry, TX	98.3
6	Blythe, CA	***108.7***	56	Chattanooga 3 NE, OK	98.1
7	Alamo Dam, AZ	108.3	56	El Mirage, CA	98.1
8	Parker Reservoir, CA	107.7	58	Porterville, CA	***98.0***
9	Maricopa 4 N, AZ	107.6	59	Bishop Arpt, CA	97.9
10	Borrego Desert Park, CA	107.5	60	Bakersfield Meadows Field, CA	97.8
11	Yuma Proving Ground, AZ	106.9	60	Elsinore, CA	***97.8***
12	Laveen 3 SSE, AZ	106.5	60	McCook, TX	97.8
13	Beaver Dam, AZ	***106.3***	60	Searchlight, NV	97.8
14	Casa Grande, AZ	106.2	64	Beatty 8 N, NV	97.7
14	Phoenix Sky Harbor Intl Arpt, AZ	106.2	65	Amistad Dam, TX	97.6
16	Fountain Hills, AZ	106.1	65	Tejon Rancho, CA	97.6
17	Hayfield Pumping Plant, CA	104.8	67	Altus Irig Res Station, OK	97.5
18	Las Vegas-McCarran Intl Arpt, NV	104.2	67	Buffalo, OK	97.5
19	Florence, AZ	104.1	69	McAllen Miller Intl Arpt, TX	97.4
20	Amargosa Farms Garey, NV	103.9	69	Wichita Falls Municipal Arpt, TX	97.4
20	Kofa Mine, AZ	103.9	71	Crystal City, TX	97.3
20	Yucca 1 NNE, AZ	103.9	71	Falfurrias, TX	97.3
23	Lees Ferry, AZ	***103.8***	73	Bowie, AZ	97.1
24	Organ Pipe Cactus N M, AZ	103.5	73	Dell City 5 SSW, TX	97.1
25	Boquillas Ranger Stn, TX	***103.0***	73	White Sands Natl Mon, NM	97.1
26	St George, UT	***102.7***	76	Raymondville, TX	97.0
27	South Phoenix, AZ	102.4	76	Waco Madison Cooper Arpt, TX	97.0
28	Castle Hot Springs, AZ	102.3	78	Bernardo, NM	96.9
28	Castolon, TX	102.3	78	Del Rio Intl Arpt, TX	96.9
28	Desert Natl Wl Range, NV	102.3	80	Charlotte 5 NNW, TX	96.8
31	Childs, AZ	***102.2***	80	Haiwee, CA	96.8
32	Barstow Fire Station, CA	102.1	80	Newman, CA	96.8
33	Tucson 17 NW, AZ	101.3	80	Walters, OK	96.8
34	Pahrump, NV	100.8	84	Bridgeport, TX	96.7
35	Laredo 2, TX	100.4	84	Waurika, OK	96.7
35	Tucson Intl Arpt, AZ	100.4	84	Whitney Dam, TX	96.7
37	Falcon Dam, TX	100.3	87	Clinton, OK	96.6
38	Coalinga, CA	100.2	87	Frederick, OK	96.6
38	Tucson NWSO, AZ	100.2	87	Henrietta, TX	***96.6***
40	Candelaria, TX	99.9	87	Pilot Point, TX	***96.6***
41	Friant Government Camp, CA	99.7	91	Caballo Dam, NM	96.4
41	Pahranagat W L Refuge, NV	***99.7***	92	Alice, TX	96.3
43	Independence, CA	99.6	92	Floresville, TX	96.3
44	Clifton, AZ	99.5	92	La Tuna 1 S, TX	96.3
45	Cascabel, AZ	99.4	92	McAllen, TX	96.3
45	Rio Grande City 1 SE, TX	99.4	96	Cordes, AZ	96.2
47	Arches Np Hqs, UT	99.2	96	Ferris, TX	96.2
48	Encinal, TX	***98.9***	96	Fort Hancock 5 SSE, TX	96.2
49	Anvil Ranch, AZ	98.8	96	Lovelock Derby Field, NV	***96.2***
50	Ash Mountain, CA	98.7	100	Bitter Lakes Wl Refuge, NM	96.1

Rankings include 100 highest and 100 lowest stations in each category. The period of record is 1980–2009. See User Guide for detailed explanation of data.

Lowest July Mean Maximum Temperature

Rank	Station Name	°F	Rank	Station Name	°F
1	Barrow W Post-W Rogers Arpt, AK	46.7	51	San Francisco, CA	68.2
2	St Paul Island Arpt, AK	50.9	51	Sutton 2 E, AK	68.2
3	Mount Washington, NH	54.0	53	Cooper Landing 6 W, AK	68.3
4	Cold Bay Arpt, AK	55.5	54	Port Angeles, WA	68.4
5	Kuparuk, AK	55.8	55	Aberdeen, WA	68.5
6	Dutch Harbor, AK	56.9	56	Gulkana Intermediate Field, AK	68.7
7	Elfin Cove, AK	58.1	57	Whites Crossing, AK	68.9
8	Nome Municipal Arpt, AK	58.2	58	Cabin Creek, CO	69.3
9	Glen Alps, AK	58.8	58	McGrath Arpt, AK	69.3
10	Kotzebue Ralph Wein Memorial, AK	59.7	60	Healy 2 NW, AK	***69.5***
11	Yakutat State Arpt, AK	60.2	61	Cloverdale, OR	69.8
12	Homer 8 NW, AK	60.3	61	Santa Monica Pier, CA	69.8
13	Sitka Japonski Arpt, AK	60.4	63	Big Delta Allen AAF, AK	69.9
14	Kodiak State USCG Base, AK	60.6	63	Kanalohuluhulu 1075, HI	69.9
15	Homer Arpt, AK	61.2	65	Bettles Field, AK	70.0
15	Kitoi Bay, AK	61.2	65	Northway Airport, AK	70.0
17	Cordova, AK	61.6	67	Skwentna, AK	70.2
17	Seward, AK	61.6	68	Grand Marais, MN	70.8
19	Cannery Creek, AK	62.1	69	Clearwater, WA	70.9
20	Port San Juan, AK	62.2	70	Cedar Lake, WA	71.6
21	Kenai Municipal Arpt, AK	62.6	70	Coupeville 1 S, WA	71.6
22	Little Port Walter, AK	62.7	70	Eielson Field, AK	71.6
23	San Francisco Oceanside, CA	62.9	70	Salinas No 2, CA	71.6
24	Iliamna Arpt, AK	63.0	74	Tanana Ralph M Calhoun Mem Arpt, AK	71.7
25	Bethel Airport, AK	63.6	75	Blaine, WA	71.8
25	Glacier Bay, AK	***63.6***	76	Alta, UT	72.0
27	Eureka, CA	63.9	77	San Francisco Int'l Arpt, CA	72.1
28	Juneau Int'l Arpt, AK	64.0	78	Hawaii Volcanos Np Hq 54, HI	72.3
28	King Salmon Arpt, AK	64.0	79	Whitefish Point, MI	72.4
30	Annette Island Arpt, AK	64.1	80	College Observatory, AK	72.5
31	Puntilla, AK	64.7	81	Berkeley, CA	72.6
32	Blowhard Mtn Radar, UT	***64.8***	82	Anacortes, WA	72.7
33	Alyeska, AK	65.1	82	Fairbanks Intl Arpt, AK	72.7
34	Nabesna, AK	65.3	84	North Pole, AK	72.8
35	Anchorage Intl Arpt, AK	65.4	85	Eagle, AK	72.9
36	Haleakala R S 338, HI	65.6	86	Electric Lake U P & L, UT	73.3
37	Crescent City 3 NNW, CA	65.7	86	Manistique, MI	73.3
38	Morro Bay Fire Dept, CA	65.8	88	Bellingham 3 SSW, WA	***73.4***
39	Cantwell 2 E, AK	***66.0***	88	Everett, WA	73.4
40	Anderson Lake, AK	66.1	88	Tok, AK	73.4
40	Chulitna River Lodge, AK	***66.1***	91	Santa Maria Public Arpt, CA	73.7
42	Intricate Bay, AK	66.2	92	Palmer 3 ESE, WA	73.8
43	Fort Bragg 5 N, CA	66.4	93	Eastport, ME	73.9
44	Seaside, OR	66.9	94	Cooke City 2 W, MT	74.1
45	Port Orford 2, OR	67.3	94	Sedro Woolley, WA	74.1
46	Bandon 2 NNE, OR	67.5	96	Indian Lake 2 SW, NY	74.2
47	Astoria Clatsop County Arpt, OR	67.6	97	Kula Hospital 267, HI	74.3
48	Hayes River, AK	67.8	98	Clatskanie, OR	74.4
49	Quillayute Airport, WA	67.9	99	Eustis, ME	***74.5***
50	Talkeetna State Arpt, AK	68.1	100	Snoqualmie Falls, WA	74.6

Rankings include 100 highest and 100 lowest stations in each category. The period of record is 1980–2009. See User Guide for detailed explanation of data.

Highest January Mean Minimum Temperature

Rank	Station Name	°F	Rank	Station Name	°F
1	Ke-Ahole Point 68.13, HI	***66.5***	51	Sanford Experiment Stn, FL	47.9
2	Honolulu Intl Arpt, HI	66.1	52	Avon Park 2 W, FL	47.8
3	Kii-Kahuku 911, HI	65.8	53	Arcadia, FL	47.7
4	Lihue Arpt, HI	65.5	53	Culver City, CA	47.7
5	Key West Intl Arpt, FL	64.5	55	Kofa Mine, AZ	47.6
6	Hilo International Arpt, HI	63.7	56	Corpus Christi Intl Arpt, TX	47.4
7	Kahului Arpt, HI	63.6	56	Daytona Beach Regional Arpt, FL	47.4
8	Molokai Airport, HI	63.1	58	Federal Point, FL	46.8
9	Miami Intl Arpt, FL	59.9	59	Archbold Bio Station, FL	46.7
10	Fort Lauderdale, FL	58.7	59	Falcon Dam, TX	46.7
11	Opihihale 2 24.1, HI	57.5	61	Aransas Wildlife Refuge, TX	46.4
12	West Palm Beach Intl Arpt, FL	57.0	61	Long Beach Daugherty Fld, CA	46.4
13	Flamingo Ranger Stn, FL	56.1	61	Robstown, TX	46.4
13	Stuart 1 S, FL	***56.1***	64	San Francisco, CA	46.3
15	Oasis Ranger Station, FL	54.7	64	St Augustine WFOY, FL	46.3
16	St Petersburg, FL	54.1	66	Jacksonville Beach, FL	46.2
17	Naples, FL	53.8	67	Kanalohuluhulu 1075, HI	46.1
18	Fort Myers Page Field, FL	53.7	68	Chula Vista, CA	46.0
19	Port Isabel, TX	53.2	68	New Orleans Audubon, LA	46.0
20	Vero Beach Municipal Arpt, FL	***52.4***	70	Crescent City, FL	45.9
21	Kula Hospital 267, HI	52.3	70	Rio Grande City 1 SE, TX	45.9
22	Punta Gorda 4 ESE, FL	51.8	72	Santa Barbara, CA	45.8
23	Brownsville Intl Arpt, TX	51.7	73	Dauphin Island #2, AL	45.7
24	Fort Pierce, FL	51.5	74	Alice, TX	***45.6***
24	Immokalee 3 NNW, FL	***51.5***	74	Phoenix Sky Harbor Intl Arpt, AZ	45.6
26	Tampa Intl Arpt, FL	51.1	76	Laredo 2, TX	45.5
27	Santa Monica Pier, CA	50.8	77	Deland 1 SSE, FL	45.1
28	McAllen Miller Intl Arpt, TX	***50.6***	77	Houston William P Hobby Arpt, TX	45.1
29	Melbourne Regional Arpt, FL	50.4	79	Bay City Waterworks, TX	45.0
29	Tarpon Springs Sewage Plant, FL	50.4	79	San Francisco Oceanside, CA	***45.0***
31	Port Mansfield, TX	49.9	81	Falfurrias, TX	44.8
32	Harlingen, TX	49.8	82	Weeki Wachee, FL	44.7
32	Los Angeles Civic Center, CA	49.8	83	Borrego Desert Park, CA	44.5
34	San Diego Lindbergh Field, CA	49.7	83	Yuma Proving Ground, AZ	44.5
35	Parrish, FL	49.6	85	Fernandina Beach, FL	44.2
35	Weslaco 2 E, TX	49.6	86	Angleton 2 W, TX	44.1
37	Hawaii Volcanos Np Hq 54, HI	49.5	86	Crystal City, TX	44.1
38	Orlando Intl Arpt, FL	49.4	86	New Orleans Intl Arpt, LA	44.1
39	McAllen, TX	49.3	89	Galliano, LA	44.0
39	Saint Leo, FL	49.3	89	Victoria Regional Arpt, TX	44.0
41	Myakka River State Park, FL	49.2	91	Bullhead City, AZ	43.9
42	Mountain Lake, FL	49.0	91	Hackberry 8 SSW, LA	43.9
42	Plant City, FL	49.0	91	San Francisco Int'l Arpt, CA	43.9
44	Kissimmee 2, FL	48.9	91	Thompsons 3 WSW, TX	43.9
44	Los Angeles Intl Arpt, CA	48.9	95	Parker Reservoir, CA	43.8
46	Titusville, FL	48.8	96	Berkeley, CA	***43.7***
47	Clermont 7 S, FL	48.4	96	Needles Airport, CA	43.7
48	Brooksville Chin Hill, FL	48.1	96	Port Arthur Jefferson County, TX	43.7
48	McCook, TX	48.1	99	Biloxi, MS	***43.5***
48	Raymondville, TX	48.1	99	Laguna Beach, CA	***43.5***

Rankings include 100 highest and 100 lowest stations in each category. The period of record is 1980–2009. See User Guide for detailed explanation of data.

Lowest January Mean Minimum Temperature

Rank	Station Name	°F	Rank	Station Name	°F
1	Northway Airport, AK	-23.7	49	Whites Crossing, AK	-1.5
2	Kuparuk, AK	*-23.6*	52	Stanley 3 NNW, ND	-1.1
3	Tok, AK	-20.7	53	Georgetown 1 E, MN	-1.0
4	Barrow W Post-W Rogers Arpt, AK	-19.4	53	Velva, ND	-1.0
5	North Pole, AK	-18.5	55	Detroit Lakes 1 NNE, MN	-0.9
6	Eagle, AK	-18.0	56	Stanley, ID	-0.8
7	Bettles Field, AK	-17.7	57	Carrington, ND	*-0.7*
8	Tanana Ralph M Calhoun Mem Arpt, AK	-16.6	57	Devils Lake Kdlr, ND	-0.7
9	Fairbanks Intl Arpt, AK	-16.0	59	Hinckley, MN	*-0.6*
10	McGrath Arpt, AK	-15.5	60	Forman 5 SSE, ND	-0.5
11	Eielson Field, AK	-15.3	60	Grand Forks Univ Nws, ND	-0.5
12	Nabesna, AK	-12.1	62	Brassua Dam, ME	-0.4
13	College Observatory, AK	-11.3	62	Fergus Falls, MN	-0.4
14	Gulkana Intermediate Field, AK	-10.6	64	Center 4 SSW, CO	-0.3
15	Kotzebue Ralph Wein Memorial, AK	-9.5	64	Stambaugh 2 SSE, MI	-0.3
16	Tower 3 S, MN	-9.1	66	Kenmare 1 WSW, ND	-0.2
17	Cantwell 2 E, AK	*-8.8*	67	Fargo Hector Field, ND	0.0
18	Allagash, ME	*-8.3*	67	Rothsay, MN	0.0
19	Big Delta Allen AAF, AK	-7.9	69	Foxboro, WI	0.1
20	Pembina, ND	-6.9	70	Bridgewater, ME	0.3
21	Warroad, MN	-6.7	71	Columbia 8 N, SD	0.4
22	International Falls Int'l Arpt, MN	-5.8	72	Caribou Municipal Arpt, ME	0.5
23	Upham 3 N, ND	-5.6	73	Bethel Airport, AK	0.6
24	Healy 2 NW, AK	*-5.5*	73	Williston Sloulin Intl Arpt, ND	0.6
25	Argyle 4 E, MN	-5.4	75	Opheim 10 N, MT	0.7
25	Edmore 1 NW, ND	-5.4	76	Crosby, ND	0.9
27	Cass Lake, MN	-5.3	77	Skwentna, AK	1.0
28	Cavalier 7 NW, ND	-5.1	78	Medicine Lake 3 SE, MT	1.1
28	Gunflint Lake 10 NW, MN	-5.1	78	Middle Dam, ME	1.1
30	Bondurant, WY	-4.9	80	Couderay 7 W, WI	1.2
31	Hansboro 4 NNE, ND	-4.8	81	Culbertson, MT	1.3
32	Bottineau, ND	-4.6	82	Electric Lake U P & L, UT	1.4
33	Antero Reservoir, CO	-4.2	82	Jamestown Municipal Arpt, ND	1.4
34	Red Lake Indian Agency, MN	-3.9	82	St Croix Falls, WI	1.4
35	Agassiz Refuge, MN	-3.5	85	Champion Van Riper Prk, MI	1.5
35	Crookston NW Exp Stn, MN	-3.5	85	Corinna, ME	1.5
37	Cochetopa Creek, CO	-3.4	85	Duluth Intl Arpt, MN	1.5
38	Mount Washington, NH	-3.3	85	Eustis, ME	*1.5*
39	Hibbing Chisholm-Hibbing Arpt, MN	-3.2	89	Cloquet, MN	1.6
40	Puntilla, AK	-3.0	89	North Stratford, NH	*1.6*
41	Brainerd, MN	-2.8	91	Butte, ND	1.8
41	Fontenelle Dam, WY	-2.8	91	Center 4 SE, ND	1.8
41	Nome Municipal Arpt, AK	-2.8	91	St Cloud Municipal Arpt, MN	1.8
41	Valley City 3 NNW, ND	-2.8	94	Ashley, ND	1.9
45	Westby, MT	-2.4	94	Bergland Dam, MI	1.9
46	Colgate, ND	-2.1	94	Castlewood, SD	1.9
47	Ada, MN	-1.9	97	Riverton, WY	2.0
48	Grand Rapids Forestry Lab, MN	-1.8	97	Wildhorse Reservoir, NV	2.0
49	Alamosa Bergman Field, CO	-1.5	97	Wilton, ND	2.0
49	Drake 9 NE, ND	-1.5	100	Bismarck Municipal Arpt, ND	2.1

Rankings include 100 highest and 100 lowest stations in each category. The period of record is 1980–2009. See User Guide for detailed explanation of data.

Highest Number of Days Annually Maximum Temperature ≥ 90°F

Rank	Station Name	Days
1	Death Valley, CA	194
2	Boquillas Ranger Stn, TX	***192***
3	Gila Bend, AZ	190
4	Castolon, TX	186
5	Bullhead City, AZ	180
6	Maricopa 4 N, AZ	179
6	Rio Grande City 1 SE, TX	179
8	Falcon Dam, TX	178
9	Yuma Proving Ground, AZ	177
10	Casa Grande, AZ	176
10	Laveen 3 SSE, AZ	176
12	Borrego Desert Park, CA	175
12	Laredo 2, TX	175
14	Alamo Dam, AZ	173
15	Blythe, CA	172
15	Fountain Hills, AZ	172
15	Parker Reservoir, CA	172
15	Phoenix Sky Harbor Intl Arpt, AZ	172
19	McAllen Miller Intl Arpt, TX	***171***
20	Needles Airport, CA	170
20	Organ Pipe Cactus N M, AZ	170
22	Florence, AZ	168
23	Willow Beach, AZ	167
24	Candelaria, TX	165
25	South Phoenix, AZ	164
26	McCook, TX	163
27	Encinal, TX	***161***
28	Oasis Ranger Station, FL	158
29	Hayfield Pumping Plant, CA	157
29	Tucson 17 NW, AZ	***157***
31	Kofa Mine, AZ	156
32	McAllen, TX	***155***
32	Raymondville, TX	155
32	Yuma Citrus Station, AZ	***155***
35	Tucson NWSO, AZ	153
36	Tucson Intl Arpt, AZ	152
37	Carrizo Springs, TX	150
37	Weslaco 2 E, TX	150
39	Castle Hot Springs, AZ	149
39	Crystal City, TX	149
41	Langtry, TX	146
42	Beaver Dam, AZ	145
43	Alice, TX	144
43	Cascabel, AZ	144
43	Charlotte 5 NNW, TX	144
43	Falfurrias, TX	144
43	Myakka River State Park, FL	144
48	Yucca 1 NNE, AZ	143
49	Anvil Ranch, AZ	142
49	Harlingen, TX	142
51	Childs, AZ	***140***
52	Amargosa Farms Garey, NV	139
52	Amistad Dam, TX	139
54	Archbold Bio Station, FL	136
55	Las Vegas-McCarran Intl Arpt, NV	134
56	Brownsville Intl Arpt, TX	133
57	Barstow Fire Station, CA	132
57	Del Rio Intl Arpt, TX	132
59	Clifton, AZ	***130***
59	Floresville, TX	130
61	Cuero, TX	129
62	Saint Leo, FL	128
63	Columbus, TX	127
64	Coalinga, CA	126
64	Naples, FL	126
64	Robstown, TX	126
67	St George, UT	125
68	Desert Natl Wl Range, NV	124
68	Punta Gorda 4 ESE, FL	124
70	Immokalee 3 NNW, FL	***123***
70	Lees Ferry, AZ	***123***
70	Pahrump, NV	123
73	Bakersfield, TX	122
73	Fort Hancock 5 SSE, TX	122
75	Dell City 5 SSW, TX	121
76	Fort Myers Page Field, FL	120
76	Mountain Lake, FL	120
78	Porterville, CA	***119***
79	Bowie, AZ	118
79	San Antonio Intl Arpt, TX	118
81	Friant Government Camp, CA	117
81	San Marcos, TX	117
83	Austin Municipal Arpt, TX	116
83	Balmorhea, TX	116
85	Brenham, TX	115
86	Arcadia, FL	114
86	Corpus Christi Intl Arpt, TX	114
86	New Braunfels, TX	114
86	Penwell, TX	114
86	Victoria Regional Arpt, TX	114
91	Carlsbad Cavern City Air Term, NM	113
91	Somerville Dam, TX	113
91	Waco Madison Cooper Arpt, TX	113
94	Ballinger 2 NW, TX	112
94	Brownwood, TX	112
94	Jal, NM	112
94	La Tuna 1 S, TX	112
94	Nogales 6 N, AZ	112
94	Victorville Pump Plant, CA	112
94	White Sands Natl Mon, NM	112

Rankings include 100 highest and 100 lowest stations in each category. The period of record is 1980–2009. See User Guide for detailed explanation of data.

Lowest Number of Days Annually Maximum Temperature ≥ 90°F

Rank	Station Name	Days
1	Aberdeen, WA	0
1	Alpine, AZ	0
1	Alta, UT	0
1	Anacortes, WA	0
1	Antero Reservoir, CO	0
1	Aspen 1 SW, CO	0
1	Astoria Clatsop County Arpt, OR	0
1	Bandon 2 NNE, OR	0
1	Barrow W Post-W Rogers Arpt, AK*	0
1	Bellingham 3 SSW, WA	*0*
1	Benton 5 SW, NH	0
1	Blaine, WA	0
1	Blowhard Mtn Radar, UT	*0*
1	Bodie, CA	0
1	Boonville 2 SSW, NY	0
1	Brassua Dam, ME	0
1	Burkes Garden, VA	0
1	Cabin Creek, CO	0
1	Chalk Hill 2 ENE, PA	0
1	Chatham WSMO, MA	0
1	Cloverdale, OR	0
1	Cold Bay Arpt, AK*	0
1	Cooke City 2 W, MT	0
1	Coupeville 1 S, WA	0
1	Crescent City 3 NNW, CA	0
1	Cross Village, MI	0
1	Eastport, ME	*0*
1	Electric Lake U P & L, UT	*0*
1	Eureka, CA	0
1	Eustis, ME	*0*
1	Everett, WA	0
1	Fort Bragg 5 N, CA	0
1	Gascon, NM	0
1	Grafton, NY	*0*
1	Grand Marais, MN	0
1	Haleakala R S 338, HI	0
1	Hawaii Volcanos Np Hq 54, HI	0
1	Hilo International Arpt, HI	0
1	Indian Lake 2 SW, NY	0
1	Kanalohuluhulu 1075, HI	0
1	Kula Hospital 267, HI	0
1	Lihue Arpt, HI	0
1	Manistique, MI	0
1	Middle Dam, ME	0
1	Morrisville 5 SW, NY	*0*
1	Morro Bay Fire Dept, CA	0
1	Mount Washington, NH	0
1	Opihihale 2 24.1, HI	0
1	Pleasant Mount 1 W, PA	0
1	Port Angeles, WA	0
1	Port Orford 2, OR	0
1	Quillayute Airport, WA	0
1	San Francisco Oceanside, CA	0
1	Santa Monica Pier, CA	*0*
1	Seaside, OR	0
1	Sedro Woolley, WA	0
1	South Lincoln, VT	0
1	St Paul Island Arpt, AK*	0
1	Tully Heiberg Forest, NY	*0*
1	Wales, NY	*0*
1	Whitefish Point, MI	0
62	Allegany State Park, NY	1
62	Bailey, CO	1
62	Beckley Va Hospital, WV	1
62	Big Bear Lake, CA	1
62	Bondurant, WY	1
62	Bradford 4 SW Res 5, PA	1
62	Bright Angel R S, AZ	1
62	Center 4 SSW, CO	1
62	Chama, NM	1
62	Clearwater, WA	1
62	Conklingville Dam, NY	1
62	Edgartown, MA	1
62	Frankfort 2 NE, MI	1
62	Fort Lewis, CO	1
62	Hebgen Dam, MT	1
62	Hohnholz Ranch, CO	*1*
62	Newcastle, ME	1
62	Norfolk 2 SW, CT	1
62	Sault Ste Marie Sanderson Field, MI	1
62	Stambaugh 2 SSE, MI	1
62	Two Harbors, MN	1
62	Two Rivers, WI	1
84	Allagash, ME	*2*
84	Antigo, WI	2
84	Bayfield 6 N, WI	*2*
84	Beckley Raleigh Co Mem Arpt, WV	2
84	Belington, WV	2
84	Bergland Dam, MI	2
84	Binghamton Edwin A Link Field, NY	2
84	Bluefield Mercer Co Arpt, WV	2
84	Bridgewater, ME	2
84	Canton 4 SE, NY	2
84	Caribou Municipal Arpt, ME	2
84	Cedar Lake, WA	2
84	Champion Van Riper Prk, MI	2
84	Chula Vista, CA	2
84	Clearbrook, WA	2
84	Cochetopa Creek, CO	2
84	Cushman Powerhouse 2, WA	2

Note: (*) Figures for Alaska stations are based on a maximum temperature of 70°F

Rankings include 100 highest and 100 lowest stations in each category. The period of record is 1980–2009. See User Guide for detailed explanation of data.

Highest Number of Days Annually Maximum Temperature ≤ 32°F

Rank	Station Name	Days
1	Barrow W Post-W Rogers Arpt, AK	247
2	Kuparuk, AK	***236***
3	Kotzebue Ralph Wein Memorial, AK	196
4	Bettles Field, AK	180
5	Tanana Ralph M Calhoun Mem Arpt, AK	169
6	Northway Airport, AK	167
7	Nome Municipal Arpt, AK	166
8	Mount Washington, NH	164
9	Nabesna, AK	163
10	Tok, AK	***161***
11	Eagle, AK	156
11	Fairbanks Intl Arpt, AK	156
13	McGrath Arpt, AK	153
13	North Pole, AK	153
15	College Observatory, AK	152
16	Eielson Field, AK	150
17	Cantwell 2 E, AK	***148***
18	Big Delta Allen AAF, AK	147
19	Puntilla, AK	***143***
20	Gulkana Intermediate Field, AK	141
21	Bethel Airport, AK	134
22	Chulitna River Lodge, AK	***124***
23	Whites Crossing, AK	119
24	Healy 2 NW, AK	***118***
25	Hayes River, AK	***116***
26	Pembina, ND	109
27	Cavalier 7 NW, ND	108
28	Anchorage Intl Arpt, AK	107
28	Warroad, MN	107
30	Edmore 1 NW, ND	106
30	International Falls Int'l Arpt, MN	106
30	Skwentna, AK	106
33	Bottineau, ND	105
34	Talkeetna State Arpt, AK	104
35	Argyle 4 E, MN	103
35	Crookston NW Exp Stn, MN	103
35	Glen Alps, AK	103
38	Duluth Intl Arpt, MN	102
39	Hibbing Chisholm-Hibbing Arpt, MN	101
39	Red Lake Indian Agency, MN	***101***
41	Gunflint Lake 10 NW, MN	***100***
41	Tower 3 S, MN	100
43	Agassiz Refuge, MN	99
44	Devils Lake Kdlr, ND	98
44	Sutton 2 E, AK	98
46	Grand Forks Univ Nws, ND	97
46	Hancock Houghton Co Arpt, MI	97
46	Hansboro 4 NNE, ND	97
46	Kenai Municipal Arpt, AK	97
50	Cooke City 2 W, MT	96
50	Ironwood, MI	96
50	Marquette County Arpt, MI	96
50	Stanley 3 NNW, ND	96
50	Upham 3 N, ND	96
55	Carrington, ND	***95***
55	Cass Lake, MN	95
55	Electric Lake U P & L, UT	***95***
58	Colgate, ND	94
58	Hebgen Dam, MT	94
60	Allagash, ME	***93***
60	Bergland Dam, MI	93
60	Caribou Municipal Arpt, ME	93
60	Fargo Hector Field, ND	93
60	Fergus Falls, MN	93
65	Ada, MN	92
65	Alexandria Chandler Field, MN	92
65	Anderson Lake, AK	***92***
65	Rothsay, MN	92
65	Stambaugh 2 SSE, MI	92
70	Blowhard Mtn Radar, UT	***91***
70	Eustis, ME	***91***
70	Grand Rapids Forestry Lab, MN	91
73	Antigo, WI	90
73	Detroit Lakes 1 NNE, MN	***90***
73	Drake 9 NE, ND	90
73	Georgetown 1 E, MN	90
73	Valley City 3 NNW, ND	90
78	Brainerd, MN	89
78	Jamestown Municipal Arpt, ND	89
80	Minot FAA Arpt, ND	88
80	Westby, MT	88
82	Kenmare 1 WSW, ND	87
82	Presque Isle, ME	87
82	Wilton, ND	87
85	Alta, UT	86
85	Brassua Dam, ME	86
85	Cloquet, MN	86
85	Crosby, ND	86
85	Sault Ste Marie Sanderson Field, MI	86
90	Bondurant, WY	85
90	Forman 5 SSE, ND	85
90	Superior, WI	85
93	Amery, WI	84
93	Cambridge State Hosp, MN	***84***
93	Iliamna Arpt, AK	84
93	King Salmon Arpt, AK	84
93	Velva, ND	84
98	Artichoke Lake, MN	83
98	Bayfield 6 N, WI	***83***
98	Champion Van Riper Prk, MI	83

Rankings include 100 highest and 100 lowest stations in each category. The period of record is 1980–2009. See User Guide for detailed explanation of data.

Lowest Number of Days Annually Maximum Temperature ≤ 32°F

Rank	Station Name	Days
1	Aiken 4 NE, SC	0
1	Alamo Dam, AZ	0
1	Alamogordo, NM	0
1	Albany 3 SE, GA	0
1	Alexander City, AL	0
1	Alexandria, LA	0
1	Alice, TX	0
1	Allendale 2 NW, SC	*0*
1	Alma Bacon County Arpt, GA	0
1	Alpine, TX	*0*
1	Amargosa Farms Garey, NV	0
1	Amistad Dam, TX	0
1	Amite, LA	0
1	Anahuac, TX	0
1	Andalusia 3 W, AL	0
1	Anderson, SC	0
1	Andrews, SC	0
1	Angleton 2 W, TX	0
1	Angwin Pac Union Col, CA	0
1	Antioch Pump Plant #3, CA	0
1	Anvil Ranch, AZ	0
1	Apalachicola Municipal Arpt, FL	0
1	Appling 2 NW, GA	0
1	Aransas Wildlife Refuge, TX	0
1	Arcadia, FL	0
1	Archbold Bio Station, FL	0
1	Ash Mountain, CA	0
1	Ashland, OR	0
1	Auberry 2 NW, CA	0
1	Auburn, CA	0
1	Augusta Bush Field, GA	0
1	Austin Municipal Arpt, TX	0
1	Avon Park 2 W, FL	0
1	Bakersfield Meadows Field, CA	0
1	Balch Power House, CA	0
1	Bandon 2 NNE, OR	0
1	Barstow Fire Station, CA	0
1	Baton Rouge Ryan Arpt, LA	0
1	Bay City Waterworks, TX	0
1	Bay Minette 3 NNW, AL	0
1	Bay St Louis Nasa, MS	0
1	Bayboro 3 E, NC	*0*
1	Baytown, TX	0
1	Beatty 8 N, NV	*0*
1	Beaufort 7 SW, SC	*0*
1	Beaumont Research Ctr, TX	0
1	Beaver Dam, AZ	0
1	Ben Lomond No 4, CA	0
1	Berkeley, CA	*0*
1	Bernardo, NM	0
1	Bessemer 3 WSW, AL	0
1	Biloxi, MS	*0*
1	Bishop Arpt, CA	0
1	Blanco, TX	0
1	Blythe, CA	0
1	Boerne, TX	0
1	Bogalusa, LA	0
1	Boquillas Ranger Stn, TX	*0*
1	Borrego Desert Park, CA	0
1	Bowie, AZ	0
1	Boyce 3 WNW, LA	0
1	Brenham, TX	0
1	Brookhaven City, MS	0
1	Brooklet 1 W, GA	0
1	Brooksville Chin Hill, FL	0
1	Brownsville Intl Arpt, TX	0
1	Brunswick, GA	0
1	Bullhead City, AZ	0
1	Bunkie, LA	0
1	Burbank Valley Pump Plant, CA	0
1	Caballo Dam, NM	0
1	Cachuma Lake, CA	0
1	Calistoga, CA	0
1	Cameron, TX	0
1	Camilla 3 SE, GA	0
1	Camp Pardee, CA	0
1	Camp Wood, TX	0
1	Candelaria, TX	0
1	Canelo 1 NW, AZ	*0*
1	Canoga Park Pierce College, CA	*0*
1	Carrizo Springs, TX	0
1	Carville 2 SW, LA	0
1	Casa Grande, AZ	0
1	Cascabel, AZ	0
1	Castle Hot Springs, AZ	0
1	Castolon, TX	0
1	Centreville WSMO, AL	0
1	Charleston City, SC	0
1	Charleston Intl Arpt, SC	0
1	Charlotte 5 NNW, TX	0
1	Childs, AZ	*0*
1	Chipley 3 E, FL	0
1	Chula Vista, CA	0
1	Clark Hill 1 W, SC	0
1	Clayton, AL	*0*
1	Clermont 7 S, FL	0
1	Cleveland, TX	0
1	Clifton, AZ	*0*
1	Cloverdale, OR	0
1	Coalinga, CA	0

Rankings include 100 highest and 100 lowest stations in each category. The period of record is 1980–2009. See User Guide for detailed explanation of data.

Highest Number of Days Annually Minimum Temperature ≤ 32°F

Rank	Station Name	Days
1	Barrow W Post-W Rogers Arpt, AK	312
2	Bodie, CA	303
3	Kuparuk, AK	***290***
4	Bondurant, WY	288
5	Stanley, ID	282
6	Dixie, ID	***271***
7	Boca, CA	270
8	Antero Reservoir, CO	265
9	Cooke City 2 W, MT	264
10	Wildhorse Reservoir, NV	***263***
11	Cantwell 2 E, AK	***262***
12	Tok, AK	***259***
13	Hohnholz Ranch, CO	***256***
14	Electric Lake U P & L, UT	***255***
15	Puntilla, AK	***254***
16	Nabesna, AK	252
17	Cochetopa Creek, CO	250
17	Fort Valley, AZ	250
19	Eagle, AK	249
19	Fontenelle Dam, WY	249
21	Austin 3 S, OR	245
21	Flagstaff 4 SW, AZ	***245***
23	Northway Airport, AK	244
24	Island Park, ID	***243***
24	North Pole, AK	243
26	Cabin Creek, CO	242
27	Kotzebue Ralph Wein Memorial, AK	241
28	Reese River O'Toole, NV	240
29	Bailey, CO	239
29	Bettles Field, AK	239
29	Gulkana Intermediate Field, AK	239
29	Mount Washington, NH	239
33	Woodruff, UT	238
34	Spring Valley State Park, NV	237
35	Cascade 1 NW, ID	235
35	Tanana Ralph M Calhoun Mem Arpt, AK	235
37	Chama, NM	234
38	Cimarron, CO	233
38	Nome Municipal Arpt, AK	233
40	Donner Memorial St Pk, CA	231
41	College Observatory, AK	229
42	Alamosa Bergman Field, CO	228
42	Hayes River, AK	***228***
44	McGrath Arpt, AK	227
44	Sutton 2 E, AK	227
46	Angle, UT	226
46	McGaffey 5 SE, NM	226
46	Tower 3 S, MN	226
49	Cheesman, CO	224
50	Chilly Barton Flat, ID	222
50	Fairbanks Intl Arpt, AK	222
50	Hebgen Dam, MT	222
53	Alpine, AZ	221
53	Butte Bert Mooney Arpt, MT	221
53	Whites Crossing, AK	221
56	Brothers, OR	220
57	Dubois, WY	***219***
57	Evergreen, CO	219
59	Bethel Airport, AK	218
59	Glen Alps, AK	218
61	Allagash, ME	***217***
61	Eielson Field, AK	217
63	Ely Yelland Field, NV	216
63	Idaho City, ID	216
65	Center 4 SSW, CO	215
66	Big Delta Allen AAF, AK	214
66	Powell, ID	214
68	Chiloquin 7 NW, OR	213
68	Gibbs Ranch, NV	***213***
68	Millegan 14 SE, MT	***213***
68	Talkeetna State Arpt, AK	213
72	Chulitna River Lodge, AK	***212***
72	Skwentna, AK	212
74	Alta, UT	211
74	Aspen 1 SW, CO	211
74	Stambaugh 2 SSE, MI	211
77	Driggs, ID	210
77	Evanston 1 E, WY	***210***
77	Healy 2 NW, AK	***210***
77	Opheim 10 N, MT	210
81	Drummond, MT	208
81	Middle Fork Lodge, ID	208
83	Agate 3 E, NE	207
83	Montello 1 SE, NV	207
85	Boulder, MT	206
85	Cooper Landing 6 W, AK	206
85	Enterprise 20 NNE, OR	***206***
85	Idaho Falls 16 SE, ID	206
89	Burns Municipal Arpt, OR	205
89	Champion Van Riper Prk, MI	205
89	Divide, MT	205
92	Coalville, UT	204
92	Fort Lewis, CO	204
92	Stanley 3 NNW, ND	204
92	Upham 3 N, ND	204
96	Blowhard Mtn Radar, UT	***203***
96	Denton 1 NNE, MT	203
96	Dickinson Exp Stn, ND	203
96	Huntsville Monastery, UT	203
100	Alturas, CA	202

Rankings include 100 highest and 100 lowest stations in each category. The period of record is 1980–2009. See User Guide for detailed explanation of data.

Lowest Number of Days Annually Minimum Temperature ≤ 32°F

Rank	Station Name	Days
1	Berkeley, CA	*0*
1	Chula Vista, CA	0
1	Culver City, CA	0
1	Flamingo Ranger Stn, FL	0
1	Fort Lauderdale, FL	0
1	Fort Myers Page Field, FL	0
1	Haleakala R S 338, HI	0
1	Hawaii Volcanos Np Hq 54, HI	0
1	Hilo International Arpt, HI	0
1	Honolulu Intl Arpt, HI	0
1	Kahului Arpt, HI	0
1	Kanalohuluhulu 1075, HI	0
1	Ke-Ahole Point 68.13, HI	0
1	Key West Intl Arpt, FL	0
1	Kii-Kahuku 911, HI	0
1	Kofa Mine, AZ	0
1	Kula Hospital 267, HI	0
1	Lihue Arpt, HI	0
1	Long Beach Daugherty Fld, CA	0
1	Los Angeles Civic Center, CA	0
1	Los Angeles Intl Arpt, CA	0
1	Miami Intl Arpt, FL	0
1	Molokai Airport, HI	0
1	Naples, FL	0
1	Oasis Ranger Station, FL	0
1	Opihihale 2 24.1, HI	0
1	Phoenix Sky Harbor Intl Arpt, AZ	0
1	Port Isabel, TX	0
1	San Diego Lindbergh Field, CA	0
1	San Francisco, CA	0
1	San Francisco Int'l Arpt, CA	0
1	San Francisco Oceanside, CA	0
1	Santa Barbara, CA	*0*
1	Santa Monica Pier, CA	*0*
1	St Petersburg, FL	0
1	Stuart 1 S, FL	0
1	West Palm Beach Intl Arpt, FL	0
38	McAllen Miller Intl Arpt, TX	*1*
38	Orlando Intl Arpt, FL	1
38	Parker Reservoir, CA	1
38	Punta Gorda 4 ESE, FL	1
38	Tampa Intl Arpt, FL	1
38	Vero Beach Municipal Arpt, FL	*1*
38	Weslaco 2 E, TX	1
45	Borrego Desert Park, CA	2
45	Brownsville Intl Arpt, TX	2
45	Bullhead City, AZ	2
45	Fort Pierce, FL	2
45	Harlingen, TX	2
45	Immokalee 3 NNW, FL	*2*
45	Laguna Beach, CA	2
45	McAllen, TX	*2*
45	Needles Airport, CA	2
45	Tarpon Springs Sewage Plant, FL	2
45	Titusville, FL	2
45	Yuma Proving Ground, AZ	2
57	Burbank Valley Pump Plant, CA	3
57	Escondido No 2, CA	*3*
57	Falcon Dam, TX	3
57	McCook, TX	3
57	Melbourne Regional Arpt, FL	3
57	Parrish, FL	3
57	Port Mansfield, TX	3
57	Saint Leo, FL	3
65	Avon Park 2 W, FL	4
65	Clermont 7 S, FL	4
65	Dauphin Island #2, AL	4
65	Daytona Beach Regional Arpt, FL	4
65	Federal Point, FL	4
65	Jacksonville Beach, FL	4
65	Kissimmee 2, FL	4
65	Morro Bay Fire Dept, CA	4
65	Mountain Lake, FL	4
65	Myakka River State Park, FL	4
65	New Orleans Audubon, LA	4
65	Plant City, FL	4
65	Raymondville, TX	4
65	Redlands, CA	4
65	Riverside Fire Sta 3, CA	4
65	Sanford Experiment Stn, FL	4
65	Willow Beach, AZ	4
65	Yuma Citrus Station, AZ	*4*
83	Alice, TX	5
83	Arcadia, FL	5
83	Brooksville Chin Hill, FL	5
83	Castle Hot Springs, AZ	5
83	Corpus Christi Intl Arpt, TX	5
83	Crescent City, FL	5
83	Robstown, TX	5
83	Tucson NWSO, AZ	5
91	Aransas Wildlife Refuge, TX	6
91	Charleston City, SC	6
91	Eureka, CA	6
91	Fernandina Beach, FL	6
91	Hackberry 8 SSW, LA	*6*
91	Houston William P Hobby Arpt, TX	6
91	Salinas No 2, CA	6
91	St Augustine WFOY, FL	6
99	Bay City Waterworks, TX	7
99	Fountain Hills, AZ	7

Rankings include 100 highest and 100 lowest stations in each category. The period of record is 1980–2009. See User Guide for detailed explanation of data.

Highest Number of Days Annually Minimum Temperature ≤ 0°F

Rank	Station Name	Days
1	Kuparuk, AK	***167***
2	Barrow W Post-W Rogers Arpt, AK	162
3	Northway Airport, AK	133
4	Tok, AK	***127***
5	Bettles Field, AK	125
6	North Pole, AK	119
7	Eagle, AK	116
8	Fairbanks Intl Arpt, AK	113
9	Tanana Ralph M Calhoun Mem Arpt, AK	112
10	Eielson Field, AK	108
10	Kotzebue Ralph Wein Memorial, AK	108
12	McGrath Arpt, AK	106
13	Nabesna, AK	103
14	Cantwell 2 E, AK	***100***
15	Gulkana Intermediate Field, AK	98
16	College Observatory, AK	97
17	Healy 2 NW, AK	***87***
18	Big Delta Allen AAF, AK	83
19	Puntilla, AK	82
20	Nome Municipal Arpt, AK	72
21	Allagash, ME	***71***
21	Bondurant, WY	71
23	Tower 3 S, MN	69
24	Whites Crossing, AK	66
25	Antero Reservoir, CO	65
26	Pembina, ND	63
27	Bethel Airport, AK	62
27	Warroad, MN	62
29	Gunflint Lake 10 NW, MN	***60***
29	International Falls Int'l Arpt, MN	60
29	Mount Washington, NH	60
29	Stanley, ID	60
33	Cavalier 7 NW, ND	58
33	Edmore 1 NW, ND	58
33	Fontenelle Dam, WY	58
36	Argyle 4 E, MN	57
36	Bottineau, ND	57
36	Cass Lake, MN	57
36	Hansboro 4 NNE, ND	57
36	Upham 3 N, ND	57
41	Cochetopa Creek, CO	56
42	Red Lake Indian Agency, MN	***54***
43	Skwentna, AK	53
44	Agassiz Refuge, MN	52
44	Crookston NW Exp Stn, MN	52
44	Hibbing Chisholm-Hibbing Arpt, MN	52
47	Grand Rapids Forestry Lab, MN	50
47	Stanley 3 NNW, ND	50
49	Drake 9 NE, ND	49
49	Stambaugh 2 SSE, MI	49
49	Valley City 3 NNW, ND	49
52	Ada, MN	48
52	Brainerd, MN	48
52	Brassua Dam, ME	48
52	Colgate, ND	48
52	Electric Lake U P & L, UT	***48***
52	Westby, MT	48
58	Carrington, ND	***47***
58	Devils Lake Kdlr, ND	***47***
58	Velva, ND	47
61	Alamosa Bergman Field, CO	46
61	Detroit Lakes 1 NNE, MN	***46***
61	Georgetown 1 E, MN	46
61	Kenmare 1 WSW, ND	46
61	Talkeetna State Arpt, AK	46
66	Bergland Dam, MI	45
66	Champion Van Riper Prk, MI	45
66	Grand Forks Univ Nws, ND	45
66	Opheim 10 N, MT	45
70	Eustis, ME	***44***
70	Fergus Falls, MN	44
70	Forman 5 SSE, ND	44
70	Foxboro, WI	44
70	Hayes River, AK	***44***
70	Middle Dam, ME	44
70	Rothsay, MN	44
77	Cooke City 2 W, MT	43
77	Crosby, ND	43
77	Fargo Hector Field, ND	43
77	Wildhorse Reservoir, NV	***43***
81	Bridgewater, ME	42
81	Caribou Municipal Arpt, ME	42
81	Cloquet, MN	42
81	Couderay 7 W, WI	42
81	Duluth Intl Arpt, MN	42
81	Hinckley, MN	42
81	King Salmon Arpt, AK	42
81	North Stratford, NH	***42***
81	Williston Sloulin Intl Arpt, ND	42
90	Columbia 8 N, SD	41
91	Antigo, WI	40
91	Center 4 SE, ND	40
91	Dickinson Exp Stn, ND	40
91	Hebgen Dam, MT	40
91	Island Park, ID	***40***
91	Jamestown Municipal Arpt, ND	40
91	Medicine Lake 3 SE, MT	40
91	St Croix Falls, WI	40
91	Woodruff, UT	40
100	Alexandria Chandler Field, MN	39

Rankings include 100 highest and 100 lowest stations in each category. The period of record is 1980–2009. See User Guide for detailed explanation of data.

Lowest Number of Days Annually Minimum Temperature ≤ 0°F

Rank	Station Name	Days
1	Aberdeen, MS	0
1	Aberdeen, WA	0
1	Aberdeen Phillips Field, MD	0
1	Abilene Municipal Arpt, TX	0
1	Ada, OK	0
1	Aiken 4 NE, SC	0
1	Alamo Dam, AZ	0
1	Alamogordo, NM	0
1	Albany, TX	*0*
1	Albany 3 SE, GA	0
1	Albemarle, NC	0
1	Albuquerque Intl Arpt, NM	0
1	Alcalde, NM	0
1	Alexander City, AL	0
1	Alexandria, LA	0
1	Alice, TX	0
1	Alicia, AR	0
1	Allendale 2 NW, SC	*0*
1	Alma Bacon County Arpt, GA	0
1	Alpine, TX	*0*
1	Altus Irig Res Station, OK	0
1	Alum Fork, AR	0
1	Amargosa Farms Garey, NV	0
1	Amistad Dam, TX	0
1	Amite, LA	0
1	Anacortes, WA	0
1	Anadarko 3 E, OK	0
1	Anahuac, TX	0
1	Andalusia 3 W, AL	0
1	Anderson, SC	0
1	Andrews, SC	0
1	Angleton 2 W, TX	0
1	Angwin Pac Union Col, CA	0
1	Annapolis Police Brks, MD	*0*
1	Annette Island Arpt, AK	0
1	Anniston Calhoun Co Arpt, AL	0
1	Anson, TX	*0*
1	Antioch Pump Plant #3, CA	0
1	Antlers, OK	0
1	Anvil Ranch, AZ	0
1	Apalachicola Municipal Arpt, FL	0
1	Appling 2 NW, GA	0
1	Appomattox, VA	0
1	Aransas Wildlife Refuge, TX	0
1	Arcadia, FL	0
1	Archbold Bio Station, FL	0
1	Arches Np Hqs, UT	0
1	Arcola, NC	0
1	Ardmore, OK	0
1	Arkadelphia 2 N, AR	0
1	Arkansas Post, AR	0
1	Arlington, OR	0
1	Artesia 6 S, NM	0
1	Ash Mountain, CA	0
1	Asheboro 2 W, NC	0
1	Asheville, NC	0
1	Asheville Regional Arpt, NC	0
1	Ashland, LA	0
1	Ashland, OR	0
1	Ashland, VA	0
1	Assateague Island, MD	*0*
1	Astoria Clatsop County Arpt, OR	0
1	Athens, TN	0
1	Athens, TX	0
1	Athens Municipal Arpt, GA	0
1	Atlanta Hartsfield Intl Arpt, GA	0
1	Atlantic City State Marina, NJ	0
1	Auberry 2 NW, CA	0
1	Auburn, CA	0
1	Augusta Bush Field, GA	0
1	Aurora 6 N, NC	0
1	Austin Municipal Arpt, TX	0
1	Avon Park 2 W, FL	0
1	Bakersfield, TX	0
1	Bakersfield Meadows Field, CA	0
1	Balch Power House, CA	0
1	Ballinger 2 NW, TX	0
1	Balmorhea, TX	0
1	Baltimore Blt-Washngtn Int'l, MD	0
1	Bandon 2 NNE, OR	0
1	Bankhead Lock and Dam, AL	0
1	Bardwell Dam, TX	0
1	Baring, WA	0
1	Barstow Fire Station, CA	0
1	Bastrop, LA	0
1	Batesville 2 SW, MS	0
1	Batesville Livestock, AR	0
1	Baton Rouge Ryan Arpt, LA	0
1	Bay City Waterworks, TX	0
1	Bay Minette 3 NNW, AL	0
1	Bay St Louis Nasa, MS	0
1	Bayboro 3 E, NC	*0*
1	Baytown, TX	0
1	Beatty 8 N, NV	*0*
1	Beaufort 7 SW, SC	*0*
1	Beaumont Research Ctr, TX	0
1	Beaver Dam, AZ	0
1	Beaverton 2 SSW, OR	*0*
1	Bedford, VA	*0*
1	Beedeville 4 NE, AR	0

Rankings include 100 highest and 100 lowest stations in each category. The period of record is 1980–2009. See User Guide for detailed explanation of data.

Highest Number of Annual Heating Degree Days

Rank	Station Name	Num.	Rank	Station Name	Num.
1	Barrow W Post-W Rogers Arpt, AK	19,472	51	Anchorage Intl Arpt, AK	10,142
2	Kuparuk, AK	***19,413***	52	Warroad, MN	10,101
3	Kotzebue Ralph Wein Memorial, AK	15,334	53	Gunflint Lake 10 NW, MN	***10,078***
4	Bettles Field, AK	15,170	54	International Falls Int'l Arpt, MN	10,055
5	Northway Airport, AK	15,160	55	Edmore 1 NW, ND	10,031
6	Tok, AK	***14,696***	56	Cavalier 7 NW, ND	10,000
7	Nabesna, AK	14,639	57	Bottineau, ND	9,911
8	Eagle, AK	14,434	58	Hibbing Chisholm-Hibbing Arpt, MN	9,887
9	Tanana Ralph M Calhoun Mem Arpt, AK	14,335	59	Island Park, ID	***9,874***
10	North Pole, AK	14,108	60	Alyeska, AK	9,857
11	Cantwell 2 E, AK	***13,926***	61	Hansboro 4 NNE, ND	9,816
12	McGrath Arpt, AK	13,728	62	Upham 3 N, ND	9,796
13	Nome Municipal Arpt, AK	13,629	63	Stanley 3 NNW, ND	9,774
14	Eielson Field, AK	13,619	64	Argyle 4 E, MN	9,712
15	Mount Washington, NH	13,608	65	Red Lake Indian Agency, MN	***9,704***
16	Fairbanks Intl Arpt, AK	13,508	66	Eustis, ME	***9,683***
17	Gulkana Intermediate Field, AK	13,389	67	Stambaugh 2 SSE, MI	9,673
18	Puntilla, AK	***13,355***	68	Bodie, CA	9,658
19	College Observatory, AK	13,318	69	Cass Lake, MN	9,617
20	Big Delta Allen AAF, AK	12,995	70	Cannery Creek, AK	9,608
21	Healy 2 NW, AK	***12,724***	71	Alta, UT	9,582
22	Bethel Airport, AK	12,449	72	Westby, MT	***9,533***
23	Whites Crossing, AK	11,767	73	Champion Van Riper Prk, MI	9,527
24	Chulitna River Lodge, AK	***11,676***	74	Bergland Dam, MI	9,505
25	Hayes River, AK	***11,452***	75	Brassua Dam, ME	9,495
26	Bondurant, WY	***11,343***	76	Homer Arpt, AK	9,471
27	Skwentna, AK	***11,341***	77	Cold Bay Arpt, AK	9,451
28	Glen Alps, AK	11,313	78	Wildhorse Reservoir, NV	***9,442***
29	Cooke City 2 W, MT	***11,182***	79	Duluth Intl Arpt, MN	9,426
30	Electric Lake U P & L, UT	***11,086***	80	Opheim 10 N, MT	9,425
31	King Salmon Arpt, AK	10,811	81	Hohnholz Ranch, CO	***9,424***
32	Talkeetna State Arpt, AK	10,785	82	Crookston NW Exp Stn, MN	9,414
33	Kenai Municipal Arpt, AK	10,732	83	Agassiz Refuge, MN	9,383
34	Stanley, ID	10,731	84	Cochetopa Creek, CO	9,373
35	St Paul Island Arpt, AK	10,681	85	Kenmare 1 WSW, ND	9,371
36	Tower 3 S, MN	10,592	86	Caribou Municipal Arpt, ME	9,352
37	Iliamna Arpt, AK	10,543	87	Carrington, ND	***9,349***
38	Cooper Landing 6 W, AK	***10,516***	88	Ironwood, MI	9,319
39	Sutton 2 E, AK	10,515	89	Devils Lake Kdlr, ND	9,295
40	Antero Reservoir, CO	10,471	90	Valley City 3 NNW, ND	9,284
41	Allagash, ME	***10,423***	91	Middle Dam, ME	9,261
42	Fontenelle Dam, WY	10,407	92	Marquette County Arpt, MI	9,233
43	Blowhard Mtn Radar, UT	***10,354***	93	Woodruff, UT	9,217
44	Dixie, ID	***10,351***	94	Drake 9 NE, ND	9,215
45	Cabin Creek, CO	10,330	95	Colgate, ND	***9,180***
46	Intricate Bay, AK	***10,289***	96	Foxboro, WI	***9,178***
47	Homer 8 NW, AK	10,249	97	Grand Rapids Forestry Lab, MN	9,173
48	Anderson Lake, AK	***10,216***	98	Grand Marais, MN	9,157
49	Pembina, ND	10,158	99	Cordova, AK	9,154
50	Hebgen Dam, MT	10,151	100	Butte Bert Mooney Arpt, MT	9,141

Rankings include 100 highest and 100 lowest stations in each category. The period of record is 1980–2009. See User Guide for detailed explanation of data.

Lowest Number of Annual Heating Degree Days

Rank	Station Name	Num.	Rank	Station Name	Num.
1	Hilo International Arpt, HI	0	51	Rio Grande City 1 SE, TX	821
1	Honolulu Intl Arpt, HI	0	52	Deland 1 SSE, FL	839
1	Kahului Arpt, HI	0	53	Crescent City, FL	***842***
1	Kii-Kahuku 911, HI	***0***	54	Yuma Proving Ground, AZ	844
1	Lihue Arpt, HI	0	55	Weeki Wachee, FL	849
6	Molokai Airport, HI	***2***	56	Los Angeles Civic Center, CA	850
7	Opihihale 2 24.1, HI	13	57	Corpus Christi Intl Arpt, TX	878
8	Key West Intl Arpt, FL	61	58	St Augustine WFOY, FL	894
9	Miami Intl Arpt, FL	127	59	Federal Point, FL	895
10	Fort Lauderdale, FL	149	59	Phoenix Sky Harbor Intl Arpt, AZ	895
11	Oasis Ranger Station, FL	170	61	Laredo 2, TX	906
12	Flamingo Ranger Stn, FL	171	62	Alice, TX	***910***
13	West Palm Beach Intl Arpt, FL	217	63	Borrego Desert Park, CA	913
14	Stuart 1 S, FL	***236***	64	Robstown, TX	929
15	Naples, FL	251	65	Kofa Mine, AZ	947
16	Fort Myers Page Field, FL	273	66	Gila Bend, AZ	968
17	Punta Gorda 4 ESE, FL	327	67	Falfurrias, TX	971
18	Immokalee 3 NNW, FL	***333***	68	Crystal City, TX	977
19	St Petersburg, FL	401	69	Aransas Wildlife Refuge, TX	1,020
20	Vero Beach Municipal Arpt, FL	***404***	70	Bullhead City, AZ	1,023
21	Fort Pierce, FL	406	71	Jacksonville Beach, FL	1,035
22	Myakka River State Park, FL	417	72	Usher Tower, FL	1,041
23	Mountain Lake, FL	508	73	San Diego Lindbergh Field, CA	1,047
24	Melbourne Regional Arpt, FL	516	74	Parker Reservoir, CA	1,049
25	Tampa Intl Arpt, FL	529	75	Needles Airport, CA	1,077
26	Kissimmee 2, FL	531	76	Encinal, TX	***1,112***
27	Arcadia, FL	536	77	Charlotte 5 NNW, TX	1,118
28	Tarpon Springs Sewage Plant, FL	537	78	New Orleans Audubon, LA	1,120
29	Port Isabel, TX	539	79	Death Valley, CA	1,133
29	Saint Leo, FL	539	80	Gainesville Regional Arpt, FL	***1,143***
31	Orlando Intl Arpt, FL	543	81	Blythe, CA	***1,151***
32	Brownsville Intl Arpt, TX	547	82	Bay City Waterworks, TX	1,152
33	Plant City, FL	550	82	Long Beach Daugherty Fld, CA	1,152
34	Parrish, FL	563	84	High Springs, FL	1,161
35	Archbold Bio Station, FL	573	85	Organ Pipe Cactus N M, AZ	1,163
36	Avon Park 2 W, FL	580	86	Culver City, CA	***1,175***
37	McAllen Miller Intl Arpt, TX	***584***	87	Victoria Regional Arpt, TX	1,184
38	Weslaco 2 E, TX	619	88	Laveen 3 SSE, AZ	1,186
39	Clermont 7 S, FL	620	89	Tucson NWSO, AZ	1,192
40	Titusville, FL	630	90	Houston William P Hobby Arpt, TX	1,210
41	Brooksville Chin Hill, FL	***659***	91	Perry, FL	1,217
42	Harlingen, TX	673	92	Los Angeles Intl Arpt, CA	1,219
42	McAllen, TX	***673***	93	Chula Vista, CA	***1,235***
44	Sanford Experiment Stn, FL	676	94	Fountain Hills, AZ	1,238
45	Raymondville, TX	736	95	Hawaii Volcanos Np Hq 54, HI	1,242
46	McCook, TX	757	96	Angleton 2 W, TX	1,243
47	Daytona Beach Regional Arpt, FL	767	97	Carrizo Springs, TX	1,245
48	Kula Hospital 267, HI	778	98	Fernandina Beach, FL	1,252
49	Port Mansfield, TX	***785***	99	Apalachicola Municipal Arpt, FL	1,255
50	Falcon Dam, TX	796	99	Cuero, TX	1,255

Rankings include 100 highest and 100 lowest stations in each category. The period of record is 1980–2009. See User Guide for detailed explanation of data.

Highest Number of Annual Cooling Degree Days

Rank	Station Name	Num.	Rank	Station Name	Num.
1	Death Valley, CA	5,512	51	Immokalee 3 NNW, FL	***3,674***
2	Key West Intl Arpt, FL	4,925	52	Boquillas Ranger Stn, TX	***3,641***
3	Honolulu Intl Arpt, HI	4,778	53	Florence, AZ	***3,633***
4	Phoenix Sky Harbor Intl Arpt, AZ	4,665	54	Tampa Intl Arpt, FL	3,625
5	Needles Airport, CA	4,663	55	Myakka River State Park, FL	3,611
6	Ke-Ahole Point 68.13, HI	***4,645***	56	Molokai Airport, HI	3,607
7	Parker Reservoir, CA	4,637	57	Corpus Christi Intl Arpt, TX	3,593
8	Bullhead City, AZ	4,629	58	Tucson NWSO, AZ	3,586
9	Miami Intl Arpt, FL	4,586	59	Fort Pierce, FL	3,577
10	McAllen Miller Intl Arpt, TX	***4,549***	60	Vero Beach Municipal Arpt, FL	***3,558***
11	Yuma Proving Ground, AZ	4,460	61	Tarpon Springs Sewage Plant, FL	3,557
12	Gila Bend, AZ	4,448	62	Saint Leo, FL	3,530
13	Oasis Ranger Station, FL	4,396	63	Port Mansfield, TX	***3,521***
14	Laredo 2, TX	4,389	64	Charlotte 5 NNW, TX	3,513
15	Falcon Dam, TX	4,378	65	Mountain Lake, FL	3,499
16	Willow Beach, AZ	***4,332***	66	Orlando Intl Arpt, FL	3,498
17	Rio Grande City 1 SE, TX	4,318	67	Langtry, TX	3,494
18	Fort Lauderdale, FL	4,292	68	Del Rio Intl Arpt, TX	3,443
19	McAllen, TX	***4,264***	69	Organ Pipe Cactus N M, AZ	3,438
20	McCook, TX	4,193	70	Tucson 17 NW, AZ	***3,428***
20	Weslaco 2 E, TX	4,193	71	Las Vegas-McCarran Intl Arpt, NV	3,425
22	Kofa Mine, AZ	4,172	72	Hilo International Arpt, HI	3,417
23	West Palm Beach Intl Arpt, FL	4,164	73	Kissimmee 2, FL	3,408
24	Brownsville Intl Arpt, TX	4,131	74	Plant City, FL	3,396
25	Kahului Arpt, HI	4,099	75	Hayfield Pumping Plant, CA	3,391
26	Blythe, CA	***4,091***	76	South Phoenix, AZ	3,380
27	Laveen 3 SSE, AZ	4,071	77	Avon Park 2 W, FL	3,379
28	Raymondville, TX	4,058	78	Amistad Dam, TX	3,367
29	Fort Myers Page Field, FL	4,054	79	Melbourne Regional Arpt, FL	3,366
30	Flamingo Ranger Stn, FL	4,051	80	Parrish, FL	3,319
31	Harlingen, TX	4,042	81	Castle Hot Springs, AZ	3,318
32	Lihue Arpt, HI	4,036	82	Victoria Regional Arpt, TX	3,303
33	Borrego Desert Park, CA	4,029	83	Arcadia, FL	3,297
34	Naples, FL	3,994	84	Titusville, FL	3,283
35	Port Isabel, TX	3,969	85	Sanford Experiment Stn, FL	3,276
36	Stuart 1 S, FL	***3,956***	86	Aransas Wildlife Refuge, TX	3,270
37	Fountain Hills, AZ	3,949	86	Clermont 7 S, FL	3,270
38	Kii-Kahuku 911, HI	***3,947***	88	Tucson Intl Arpt, AZ	3,257
39	Castolon, TX	3,933	89	New Orleans Audubon, LA	3,255
40	Crystal City, TX	3,875	90	Yucca 1 NNE, AZ	3,248
41	Falfurrias, TX	3,844	91	Archbold Bio Station, FL	3,237
42	Alamo Dam, AZ	3,835	92	Floresville, TX	3,228
43	Punta Gorda 4 ESE, FL	3,805	93	San Antonio Intl Arpt, TX	3,222
44	Alice, TX	***3,800***	94	Cuero, TX	3,216
45	St Petersburg, FL	3,781	95	Houston William P Hobby Arpt, TX	3,198
46	Encinal, TX	***3,759***	96	Austin Municipal Arpt, TX	3,187
47	Maricopa 4 N, AZ	3,741	97	Thompsons 3 WSW, TX	3,178
48	Casa Grande, AZ	***3,736***	98	Crescent City, FL	***3,175***
49	Carrizo Springs, TX	3,688	99	Sugar Land, TX	***3,160***
50	Robstown, TX	3,675	100	Bay City Waterworks, TX	3,140

Rankings include 100 highest and 100 lowest stations in each category. The period of record is 1980–2009. See User Guide for detailed explanation of data.

Lowest Number of Annual Cooling Degree Days

Rank	Station Name	Num.
1	Barrow W Post-W Rogers Arpt, AK	0
1	Cabin Creek, CO	0
1	Cold Bay Arpt, AK	0
1	Glacier Bay, AK	*0*
1	Homer 8 NW, AK	0
1	Homer Arpt, AK	0
1	Kenai Municipal Arpt, AK	0
1	Kuparuk, AK	*0*
1	Little Port Walter, AK	0
1	Mount Washington, NH	0
1	Puntilla, AK	*0*
1	St Paul Island Arpt, AK	0
1	Yakutat State Arpt, AK	0
14	Antero Reservoir, CO	1
14	Bodie, CA	1
14	Cannery Creek, AK	1
14	Cordova, AK	1
14	Dutch Harbor, AK	*1*
14	Elfin Cove, AK	*1*
14	Glen Alps, AK	1
14	Intricate Bay, AK	*1*
14	Kitoi Bay, AK	1
14	Port San Juan, AK	*1*
14	Sitka Japonski Arpt, AK	1
14	Sutton 2 E, AK	1
26	Alyeska, AK	2
26	Cantwell 2 E, AK	*2*
26	Haleakala R S 338, HI	2
26	Iliamna Arpt, AK	2
26	King Salmon Arpt, AK	2
26	Nabesna, AK	2
32	Bondurant, WY	3
32	Cooke City 2 W, MT	*3*
32	Electric Lake U P & L, UT	*3*
32	Eureka, CA	3
32	Kodiak State USCG Base, AK	3
32	Nome Municipal Arpt, AK	3
38	Anchorage Intl Arpt, AK	4
38	Anderson Lake, AK	*4*
38	Bethel Airport, AK	4
38	Cooper Landing 6 W, AK	4
38	Juneau Int'l Arpt, AK	4
43	Bandon 2 NNE, OR	5
44	Gulkana Intermediate Field, AK	6
45	Fort Bragg 5 N, CA	7
45	Kotzebue Ralph Wein Memorial, AK	7
47	Blowhard Mtn Radar, UT	*8*
47	Chulitna River Lodge, AK	*8*
47	Crescent City 3 NNW, CA	8
47	Seward, AK	*8*
51	Hayes River, AK	*9*
52	Gascon, NM	10
52	Port Orford 2, OR	10
52	Skwentna, AK	*10*
55	Dixie, ID	*11*
55	Whites Crossing, AK	11
57	Stanley, ID	12
58	Alpine, AZ	13
58	Hohnholz Ranch, CO	*13*
60	Northway Airport, AK	14
61	Talkeetna State Arpt, AK	15
62	Bailey, CO	17
63	Annette Island Arpt, AK	19
64	Seaside, OR	21
64	Tok, AK	*21*
66	Alta, UT	22
67	Astoria Clatsop County Arpt, OR	23
67	Kanalohuluhulu 1075, HI	23
67	McGrath Arpt, AK	23
70	Quillayute Airport, WA	24
71	Clearwater, WA	25
71	Cloverdale, OR	25
73	Healy 2 NW, AK	*27*
73	San Francisco Oceanside, CA	*27*
75	Hebgen Dam, MT	29
76	Cochetopa Creek, CO	30
77	Center 4 SSW, CO	31
77	Coupeville 1 S, WA	31
79	Blaine, WA	32
80	Big Delta Allen AAF, AK	33
80	North Pole, AK	33
82	Chama, NM	35
82	Eagle, AK	35
82	Port Angeles, WA	35
82	Tanana Ralph M Calhoun Mem Arpt, AK	35
86	Aspen 1 SW, CO	38
86	Boca, CA	38
88	Dubois, WY	*39*
88	Island Park, ID	*39*
90	Bettles Field, AK	40
91	Bright Angel R S, AZ	*45*
92	Donner Memorial St Pk, CA	48
92	Fort Valley, AZ	48
94	Eielson Field, AK	50
95	McGaffey 5 SE, NM	51
96	Morro Bay Fire Dept, CA	52
97	Wildhorse Reservoir, NV	*54*
98	Woodruff, UT	55
99	Flagstaff 4 SW, AZ	*56*
100	Aberdeen, WA	57

Highest Annual Precipitation

Rank	Station Name	Inches	Rank	Station Name	Inches
1	Little Port Walter, AK	236.26	51	Franklin 3 NW, LA	64.45
2	Yakutat State Arpt, AK	156.10	52	Galliano, LA	64.34
3	Port San Juan, AK	130.88	53	De Funiak Springs, FL	***64.21***
4	Hilo International Arpt, HI	127.30	54	Dunsmuir Treatment Plant, CA	63.71
5	Cannery Creek, AK	120.88	55	Wiggins, MS	***63.49***
6	Clearwater, WA	109.03	56	Houma, LA	63.45
7	Hawaii Volcanos Np Hq 54, HI	106.93	57	Slidell, LA	63.44
8	Baring, WA	105.96	58	Amite, LA	63.42
9	Elfin Cove, AK	103.14	59	St Bernard, LA	***62.93***
10	Annette Island Arpt, AK	101.90	60	New Orleans Audubon, LA	62.90
11	Quillayute Airport, WA	99.36	61	Juneau Int'l Arpt, AK	62.82
12	Cedar Lake, WA	96.55	62	Bay St Louis Nasa, MS	62.76
13	Mount Washington, NH	96.20	63	New Orleans Intl Arpt, LA	62.55
14	Cordova, AK	91.37	64	Hattiesburg 5 SW, MS	62.44
15	Detroit Dam, OR	90.44	65	West Palm Beach Intl Arpt, FL	62.37
16	Cushman Powerhouse 2, WA	89.20	66	Dutch Harbor, AK	***62.31***
17	Sitka Japonski Arpt, AK	88.01	67	Bogalusa, LA	62.25
18	Palmer 3 ESE, WA	85.39	68	Panama City 5 NE, FL	62.17
19	Aberdeen, WA	83.53	69	Kanalohuluhulu 1075, HI	***62.07***
20	Cloverdale, OR	78.84	69	Tryon, NC	62.07
21	Kodiak State USCG Base, AK	78.45	71	Liberty, TX	61.82
22	Diablo Dam, WA	78.05	72	Stuart 1 S, FL	61.76
23	Headworks Ptld Wtr Bur, OR	77.92	73	Grand Coteau, LA	61.73
24	Bonneville Dam, OR	76.89	74	Dauphin Island #2, AL	61.65
25	Seward, AK	75.48	75	Miami Intl Arpt, FL	61.61
26	Belknap Springs 8 N, OR	74.01	76	Snoqualmie Falls, WA	61.47
27	Seaside, OR	73.73	77	Wewahitchka, FL	61.42
28	Port Orford 2, OR	71.94	78	Idleyld Park 4 NE, OR	61.32
29	Thibodaux 3 ESE, LA	71.40	79	Bunkie, LA	61.31
30	Alyeska, AK	70.68	80	Baton Rouge Ryan Arpt, LA	61.26
31	Glacier Bay, AK	***70.06***	81	Lafayette Regional Arpt, LA	61.21
32	Bay Minette 3 NNW, AL	69.43	82	Alexandria, LA	61.07
33	Saucier Exp Forest, MS	69.25	83	New Iberia, LA	61.04
34	Clayton 1 SSW, GA	68.83	84	Crowley 2 NE, LA	61.00
35	Kitoi Bay, AK	68.65	85	Port Arthur Jefferson County, TX	60.92
36	Fairhope 2 NE, AL	68.07	86	Jasper, AL	60.88
37	De Sabla, CA	67.87	87	Bienville 3 NE, LA	60.53
38	Coden, AL	***67.81***	88	Sam Rayburn Dam, TX	60.52
39	Crescent City 3 NNW, CA	67.76	89	Bridgeport 5 NW, AL	60.46
40	Corvallis Water Bureau, OR	66.77	90	Brookhaven City, MS	60.44
41	Astoria Clatsop County Arpt, OR	66.66	91	Andalusia 3 W, AL	60.19
42	Mobile Regional Arpt, AL	66.39	92	Jackson, AL	60.04
43	Fort Lauderdale, FL	65.80	93	Fulton 3 W, MS	60.03
44	Gulfport Naval Center, MS	65.69	94	Bankhead Lock and Dam, AL	60.01
45	Waveland, MS	***65.67***	94	Baytown, TX	60.01
46	Pascagoula 3 NE, MS	65.22	96	Chipley 3 E, FL	59.92
47	Biloxi, MS	***65.08***	97	Lawrenceburg Filter Plant, TN	59.89
48	Reserve, LA	64.94	98	Hackberry 8 SSW, LA	59.79
49	Pensacola Regional Arpt, FL	64.71	99	Jena 4 WSW, LA	***59.77***
50	De Ridder, LA	64.51	100	Lsu Ben Hur Farm, LA	59.74

Rankings include 100 highest and 100 lowest stations in each category. The period of record is 1980–2009. See User Guide for detailed explanation of data.

Lowest Annual Precipitation

Rank	Station Name	Inches
1	Death Valley, CA	2.21
2	Yuma Proving Ground, AZ	3.62
3	Blythe, CA	3.67
4	Yuma Citrus Station, AZ	***3.80***
5	Kuparuk, AK	***3.98***
6	Las Vegas-McCarran Intl Arpt, NV	4.17
7	Barrow W Post-W Rogers Arpt, AK	4.45
8	Amargosa Farms Garey, NV	4.55
9	Monument Valley, AZ	***4.63***
10	Hayfield Pumping Plant, CA	4.71
11	Needles Airport, CA	4.73
12	Desert Natl Wl Range, NV	4.86
13	Fallon Experiment Stn, NV	5.00
14	Barstow Fire Station, CA	5.02
15	Bishop Arpt, CA	5.05
16	Dyer, NV	5.06
16	Pahrump, NV	5.06
18	Tonopah Airport, NV	5.17
19	Lovelock Derby Field, NV	***5.24***
20	Independence, CA	5.39
21	Bullhead City, AZ	5.62
22	Willow Beach, AZ	5.69
23	El Mirage, CA	5.72
24	Beatty 8 N, NV	***5.92***
25	Lovelock, NV	6.08
26	Victorville Pump Plant, CA	6.16
27	Bakersfield Meadows Field, CA	6.27
28	Borrego Desert Park, CA	6.31
29	Pahranagat W L Refuge, NV	6.34
30	Parker Reservoir, CA	6.45
31	Callao, UT	6.56
32	Kofa Mine, AZ	6.69
33	Basin, WY	6.71
34	Eskdale, UT	6.78
35	Lees Ferry, AZ	***6.81***
36	Grand View 2 W, ID	6.86
37	Gila Bend, AZ	6.89
38	Powell Field Station, WY	***6.95***
39	Winslow Municipal Arpt, AZ	7.05
40	Center 4 SSW, CO	7.06
41	Haiwee, CA	7.19
42	Alamosa Bergman Field, CO	7.27
43	Reno Cannon Intl Arpt, NV	7.37
44	Bruneau, ID	7.43
45	Howe, ID	7.44
46	Beaver Dam, AZ	7.45
47	Fontenelle Dam, WY	7.48
48	Reese River O'Toole, NV	7.57
49	Ephrata Arpt FCWOS, WA	7.68
50	Kennewick, WA	7.72
51	Gerlach, NV	***7.78***
51	Yucca 1 NNE, AZ	7.78
53	Maricopa 4 N, AZ	7.83
54	Phoenix Sky Harbor Intl Arpt, AZ	7.92
55	Searchlight, NV	7.96
56	McNary Dam, WA	7.99
57	Chilly Barton Flat, ID	8.00
58	Teec Nos Pos, AZ	8.03
59	Lages, NV	***8.09***
59	Winnemucca Municipal Arpt, NV	8.09
61	Brothers, OR	8.11
62	Montello 1 SE, NV	***8.12***
63	Coalinga, CA	8.13
64	Imlay, NV	8.17
65	Castle Dale, UT	8.19
65	Wupatki N M, AZ	8.19
65	Yakima Air Terminal, WA	8.19
68	Wapato, WA	8.30
69	Prosser, WA	***8.33***
70	St George, UT	8.40
71	Kings River Valley, NV	8.46
72	Laveen 3 SSE, AZ	8.48
73	Riverton, WY	8.50
73	South Phoenix, AZ	8.50
75	Rome 2 NW, OR	8.51
76	Blue Eagle Ranch Hanks, NV	8.57
77	Alamo Dam, AZ	8.58
78	Burris, WY	8.59
79	Holbrook, AZ	8.64
80	Arches Np Hqs, UT	8.65
80	Dugway, UT	8.65
82	Bernardo, NM	8.73
83	Boysen Dam, WY	8.79
84	Casa Grande, AZ	***8.89***
85	Angle, UT	***8.93***
86	Battle Mountain, NV	8.99
87	Arlington, OR	9.07
88	Aberdeen Exp Station, ID	9.19
88	Black Rock, UT	9.19
88	Tok, AK	***9.19***
91	La Tuna 1 S, TX	9.20
92	Fort Hancock 5 SSE, TX	9.25
93	Grand Junction 6 ESE, CO	9.26
94	Beowawe, NV	9.27
95	Canyonlands The Neck, UT	9.30
96	Cody 12 SE, WY	***9.33***
97	Chaco Canyon Natl Mon, NM	9.38
98	Denio, NV	9.41
99	Grand Junction Walker Field, CO	9.43
100	Albuquerque Intl Arpt, NM	9.44

Rankings include 100 highest and 100 lowest stations in each category. The period of record is 1980–2009. See User Guide for detailed explanation of data.

Highest Annual Extreme Maximum Daily Precipitation

Rank	Station Name	Inches	Rank	Station Name	Inches
1	Dauphin Island #2, AL	23.99	51	Castana Experiment Farm, IA	12.02
2	Key West Intl Arpt, FL	22.75	52	Kanalohuluhulu 1075, HI	11.97
3	Bay City Waterworks, TX	20.85	53	Melbourne Regional Arpt, FL	11.85
4	Haleakala R S 338, HI	18.50	54	Ruston La Tech, LA	11.84
4	Liberty, TX	18.50	55	Port Arthur Jefferson County, TX	11.80
6	New Braunfels, TX	***18.35***	56	Portland Intl Jetport, ME	11.74
7	Southport 5 N, NC	***18.30***	57	Marcus Hook, PA	***11.68***
8	Andalusia 3 W, AL	17.88	58	Walters, OK	***11.64***
9	Aurora, IL	16.91	59	Monroe NLU, LA	11.50
10	Louisville 1 E, GA	16.42	60	Cape Girardeau Municipal Arpt, MO	11.49
11	Hilo International Arpt, HI	16.17	61	Ben Lomond No 4, CA	11.47
12	Stuart 1 S, FL	***16.05***	62	Conway, SC	11.35
13	San Marcos, TX	15.78	63	Biloxi, MS	***11.30***
14	Baytown, TX	15.74	64	St Augustine WFOY, FL	11.28
15	Lake Charles Municipal Arpt, LA	15.67	65	San Antonio Intl Arpt, TX	11.26
16	Bay Minette 3 NNW, AL	15.58	66	Clayton, AL	***11.20***
17	Greenville, AL	15.36	67	Chestertown, MD	11.06
18	Bay St Louis Nasa, MS	***15.32***	68	Henderson, TX	11.05
19	Somerville Dam, TX	15.25	69	Pageland, SC	11.00
20	Beaumont Research Ctr, TX	15.21	70	Yorktown Heights 1 W, NY	10.95
21	Thibodaux 3 ESE, LA	15.16	71	New Orleans Audubon, LA	10.94
22	Seward, AK	***15.05***	72	Ashland, LA	10.88
23	Fairhope 2 NE, AL	14.52	73	Sheboygan, WI	10.84
24	Williamsburg 2 N, VA	14.28	74	Greenville, NC	10.75
25	Saucier Exp Forest, MS	14.05	75	Aransas Wildlife Refuge, TX	10.73
26	Sam Rayburn Dam, TX	14.00	76	Hattiesburg 5 SW, MS	10.68
27	De Ridder, LA	13.60	77	Apalachicola Municipal Arpt, FL	***10.67***
27	Joliet Brandon Rd Dam, IL	13.60	78	Punta Gorda 4 ESE, FL	10.65
29	Little Port Walter, AK	13.55	79	Houma, LA	10.60
30	Slidell, LA	13.42	79	Sugar Land, TX	***10.60***
31	Wilmington New Hanover County, NC	13.38	81	De Funiak Springs, FL	***10.55***
32	Anahuac, TX	13.20	82	Experiment, GA	***10.50***
33	Atlantic 1 NE, IA	13.18	83	Shreveport Regional Arpt, LA	10.44
34	Cleveland, TX	13.17	84	Geary, OK	***10.41***
35	Bunkie, LA	13.15	85	Brenham, TX	10.38
36	Hawaii Volcanos Np Hq 54, HI	13.06	85	Lafayette Regional Arpt, LA	10.38
37	Hot Springs 1 NNE, AR	12.97	87	Houston Bush Intercontinental, TX	10.34
38	Jena 4 WSW, LA	***12.96***	88	Wichita Mid-Continent Arpt, KS	10.31
39	Minden, LA	12.87	89	Yakutat State Arpt, AK	10.22
40	Longwood, NC	12.85	90	Sanford Experiment Stn, FL	***10.17***
41	West Pelzer 2 W, SC	***12.81***	91	Clinton 2 NE, NC	10.05
42	Panama City 5 NE, FL	12.80	92	Bankhead Lock and Dam, AL	10.03
43	Clayton 1 SSW, GA	12.75	93	Alexandria, LA	10.02
44	Jacksonville Beach, FL	12.56	93	Loris 1 S, SC	***10.02***
44	Miami Intl Arpt, FL	12.56	95	Black Mountain 2 W, NC	10.00
46	Fort Scott, KS	12.50	95	Grand Coteau, LA	10.00
47	Angleton 2 W, TX	12.36	95	High Springs, FL	10.00
48	Coden, AL	***12.15***	98	Port Washington, WI	9.87
49	Fort Pierce, FL	12.11	98	Victoria Regional Arpt, TX	9.87
50	Perry, FL	12.10	100	Corpus Christi Intl Arpt, TX	9.85

Rankings include 100 highest and 100 lowest stations in each category. The period of record is 1980–2009. See User Guide for detailed explanation of data.

Lowest Annual Extreme Maximum Daily Precipitation

Rank	Station Name	Inches
1	Kuparuk, AK	***1.02***
2	Burns Municipal Arpt, OR	1.07
3	Chilly Barton Flat, ID	1.15
3	Montello 1 SE, NV	***1.15***
5	Imlay, NV	***1.17***
5	Lovelock Derby Field, NV	***1.17***
7	Reese River O'Toole, NV	1.18
8	Grand Junction 6 ESE, CO	1.20
9	Winnemucca Municipal Arpt, NV	1.21
10	Barrow W Post-W Rogers Arpt, AK	1.28
10	Elko Municipal Arpt, NV	1.28
10	Oakley, ID	1.28
13	Tonopah Airport, NV	1.30
14	Grand Junction Walker Field, CO	1.31
15	Kotzebue Ralph Wein Memorial, AK	1.32
16	Kennewick, WA	1.33
17	Lovelock, NV	1.35
18	Cochetopa Creek, CO	1.36
18	Las Vegas-McCarran Intl Arpt, NV	1.36
20	Buhl No 2, ID	1.38
21	Blue Eagle Ranch Hanks, NV	***1.39***
22	Bakersfield Meadows Field, CA	1.42
22	Salmon, ID	1.42
24	Rexburg Ricks College, ID	***1.43***
25	Altamont, UT	1.44
26	Canyonlands The Neck, UT	1.45
26	Ephraim Sorensens Fld, UT	1.45
26	Pocatello Municipal Arpt, ID	1.45
29	Battle Mountain, NV	***1.46***
29	Dugway, UT	1.46
31	Butte Bert Mooney Arpt, MT	1.47
31	Death Valley, CA	1.47
31	Lacrosse, WA	1.47
34	Alamosa Bergman Field, CO	1.49
35	Dubois Experiment Stn, ID	1.51
35	Gulkana Intermediate Field, AK	1.51
37	Drummond, MT	1.52
37	Lund, NV	***1.52***
39	Denio, NV	1.55
39	Echo Dam, UT	1.55
39	Fallon Experiment Stn, NV	1.55
39	Payette, ID	***1.55***
43	Barstow Fire Station, CA	1.57
43	Fruita 1 W, CO	***1.57***
45	Bondurant, WY	***1.58***
46	King Salmon Arpt, AK	1.59
46	Porterville, CA	***1.59***
46	Reynolds, ID	1.59
49	Grand View 2 W, ID	***1.60***
50	Dinosaur Natl Monumnt, CO	1.61
50	Winslow Municipal Arpt, AZ	1.61
52	Arches Np Hqs, UT	1.62
53	Divide, MT	***1.63***
54	Angle, UT	***1.64***
55	Tulelake, CA	1.65
56	Fort Hall 1 NNE, ID	***1.66***
56	Rawlins Municipal Arpt, WY	***1.66***
58	Bruneau, ID	1.67
59	Beowawe, NV	1.68
59	McNary Dam, WA	1.68
59	Mountain Home, ID	***1.68***
59	Wupatki N M, AZ	1.68
63	Brownlee Dam, ID	1.70
63	Darby, MT	1.70
63	Eureka Ranger Stn, MT	1.70
63	Parma Experiment Stn, ID	1.70
63	Yakima Air Terminal, WA	1.70
68	Heber, UT	1.71
68	Lages, NV	***1.71***
70	Burley Municipal Arpt, ID	1.72
70	Nome Municipal Arpt, AK	1.72
70	Stevensville, MT	1.72
73	Bethel Airport, AK	1.73
73	Grace, ID	1.73
73	Idaho Falls 2 ESE, ID	1.73
73	McGrath Arpt, AK	1.73
73	Pahranagat W L Refuge, NV	***1.73***
78	Ephrata Arpt FCWOS, WA	1.74
78	Woodruff, UT	1.74
80	Aberdeen Exp Station, ID	1.75
80	Beaver Dam, AZ	***1.75***
80	Cimarron, CO	1.75
80	Corrales, NM	***1.75***
80	Emmett 2 E, ID	1.75
80	Wildhorse Reservoir, NV	***1.75***
86	Wanship Dam, UT	1.76
87	Boise Air Terminal, ID	1.77
87	College Observatory, AK	1.77
89	Electric Lake U P & L, UT	***1.80***
89	Johnson Pass, UT	1.80
89	Lewiston Nez Perce County Arpt, ID	1.80
92	Fontenelle Dam, WY	1.82
93	Anaconda, MT	1.83
93	Libby Dam Base, MT	***1.83***
95	Hayden, CO	1.84
96	Amargosa Farms Garey, NV	1.85
96	Boulder, MT	1.85
96	Eureka, NV	***1.85***
96	Malad City, ID	***1.85***
96	Uravan, CO	1.85

Rankings include 100 highest and 100 lowest stations in each category. The period of record is 1980–2009. See User Guide for detailed explanation of data.

Highest Number of Days Annually With ≥ 0.1 Inches of Precipitation

Rank	Station Name	Days
1	Little Port Walter, AK	208
2	Hilo International Arpt, HI	190
3	Yakutat State Arpt, AK	188
4	Elfin Cove, AK	180
5	Annette Island Arpt, AK	169
6	Sitka Japonski Arpt, AK	168
7	Port San Juan, AK	166
8	Cannery Creek, AK	165
9	Hawaii Volcanos Np Hq 54, HI	160
10	Mount Washington, NH	155
11	Cordova, AK	151
12	Palmer 3 ESE, WA	147
13	Cedar Lake, WA	146
13	Juneau Int'l Arpt, AK	146
13	Quillayute Airport, WA	146
16	Clearwater, WA	144
16	Kitoi Bay, AK	144
18	Baring, WA	139
19	Headworks Ptld Wtr Bur, OR	137
20	Glacier Bay, AK	***136***
21	Aberdeen, WA	134
21	Cloverdale, OR	134
21	Detroit Dam, OR	134
24	Kodiak State USCG Base, AK	131
25	Alyeska, AK	127
25	Astoria Clatsop County Arpt, OR	127
27	Bonneville Dam, OR	126
28	Dutch Harbor, AK	***125***
29	Diablo Dam, WA	123
29	Snoqualmie Falls, WA	123
31	Seaside, OR	119
32	Estacada 2 SE, OR	118
33	Buckley 1 NE, WA	117
34	Boonville 2 SSW, NY	116
34	Monroe, WA	116
36	Derry 4 SW, PA	115
36	Seward, AK	115
38	Belknap Springs 8 N, OR	114
38	Clatskanie, OR	114
38	Longview, WA	114
41	Cold Bay Arpt, AK	113
41	Cushman Powerhouse 2, WA	113
43	Chalk Hill 2 ENE, PA	112
44	Port Orford 2, OR	110
45	Corvallis Water Bureau, OR	109
45	Idleyld Park 4 NE, OR	109
47	Chardon, OH	108
47	McMillin Reservoir, WA	108
47	Sedro Woolley, WA	108
50	Centralia, WA	107
50	Lookout Point Dam, OR	107
52	Bandon 2 NNE, OR	106
52	Bradford 4 SW Res 5, PA	106
52	Clearbrook, WA	106
55	Olympia Arpt, WA	105
56	Belington, WV	104
56	Oakland 1 SE, MD	104
58	Allegany State Park, NY	103
58	Blaine, WA	103
58	Elkins Elkins-Randolph Co Arpt, WV	103
58	Morrisville 5 SW, NY	103
58	Tully Heiberg Forest, NY	***103***
58	Wales, NY	***103***
64	Vancouver 4 NNE, WA	102
65	Buckhannon, WV	101
65	Mannington 8 WNW, WV	101
67	Cottage Grove 1 S, OR	100
67	Gatlinburg 2 SW, TN	100
67	Munising, MI	***100***
67	N Willamette Exp Stn, OR	***100***
71	Bremerton, WA	99
71	Enosburg Falls, VT	99
73	South Lincoln, VT	98
73	Westfield 2 SSE, NY	***98***
75	Clarion 3 SW, PA	97
75	Clarksburg 1, WV	97
75	Dannemora, NY	97
75	Erie Intl Arpt, PA	97
75	Utica Oneida County Arpt, NY	***97***
80	Abingdon 3 S, VA	96
80	Bergland Dam, MI	96
80	Burkes Garden, VA	96
80	Grafton, NY	***96***
80	Uniontown 1 NE, PA	96
85	Beaverton 2 SSW, OR	95
85	Buffalo Greater Buffalo Int'l, NY	95
85	Cottage Grove Dam, OR	95
85	Hiram, OH	95
85	Newport, VT	95
85	West Union 2, WV	95
91	Alta, UT	94
91	Baxter, KY	94
91	Corvallis State Univ, OR	94
91	Delhi 2 SE, NY	94
91	Dorset, OH	94
91	Everett, WA	94
91	Lowville, NY	94
98	Fairmont, WV	93
98	Powell, ID	93
100	Allardt, TN	92

Rankings include 100 highest and 100 lowest stations in each category. The period of record is 1980–2009. See User Guide for detailed explanation of data.

Lowest Number of Days Annually With ≥ 0.1 Inches of Precipitation

Rank	Station Name	Days
1	Death Valley, CA	5
2	Blythe, CA	8
2	Yuma Citrus Station, AZ	*8*
2	Yuma Proving Ground, AZ	8
5	Hayfield Pumping Plant, CA	10
6	Barrow W Post-W Rogers Arpt, AK	11
6	Independence, CA	11
6	Kuparuk, AK	*11*
6	Las Vegas-McCarran Intl Arpt, NV	11
10	Bishop Arpt, CA	12
10	Monument Valley, AZ	*12*
10	Needles Airport, CA	12
13	Bullhead City, AZ	13
13	Dyer, NV	13
13	Parker Reservoir, CA	13
16	Amargosa Farms Garey, NV	14
16	Desert Natl Wl Range, NV	14
16	Kofa Mine, AZ	14
16	Pahrump, NV	14
16	Victorville Pump Plant, CA	14
21	Borrego Desert Park, CA	15
21	Fallon Experiment Stn, NV	15
21	Pahranagat W L Refuge, NV	15
21	Willow Beach, AZ	15
25	Barstow Fire Station, CA	16
25	Beatty 8 N, NV	*16*
25	El Mirage, CA	16
25	Ke-Ahole Point 68.13, HI	16
25	Phoenix Sky Harbor Intl Arpt, AZ	16
30	Gila Bend, AZ	17
30	Haiwee, CA	17
30	Lovelock Derby Field, NV	*17*
30	Maricopa 4 N, AZ	17
30	Searchlight, NV	17
30	Tonopah Airport, NV	17
36	Alamo Dam, AZ	18
36	Culver City, CA	*18*
36	Lees Ferry, AZ	*18*
36	Riverside Fire Sta 3, CA	18
36	Yucca 1 NNE, AZ	18
41	Bakersfield Meadows Field, CA	19
41	Casa Grande, AZ	19
41	Chula Vista, CA	19
41	Coalinga, CA	19
41	Elsinore, CA	19
41	Howe, ID	19
41	Laveen 3 SSE, AZ	19
41	Santa Monica Pier, CA	*19*
49	Callao, UT	20
49	Eskdale, UT	20
49	La Tuna 1 S, TX	20
49	Long Beach Daugherty Fld, CA	20
49	Mitchell Caverns, CA	20
49	Organ Pipe Cactus N M, AZ	20
49	San Diego Lindbergh Field, CA	20
49	South Phoenix, AZ	20
57	Lovelock, NV	21
57	Reno Cannon Intl Arpt, NV	21
59	Basin, WY	22
59	Florence, AZ	22
59	Grand View 2 W, ID	22
59	Los Angeles Intl Arpt, CA	22
59	Penwell, TX	22
59	Powell Field Station, WY	22
59	Winslow Municipal Arpt, AZ	22
66	Beaver Dam, AZ	*23*
66	Bernardo, NM	23
66	Boquillas Ranger Stn, TX	*23*
66	Canoga Park Pierce College, CA	*23*
66	Castolon, TX	23
66	Center 4 SSW, CO	23
66	Dell City 5 SSW, TX	23
66	Holbrook, AZ	23
66	Jal, NM	23
66	Laguna Beach, CA	23
66	Los Angeles Civic Center, CA	23
66	Riverton, WY	23
66	Santa Barbara, CA	*23*
66	Teec Nos Pos, AZ	23
80	Alamosa Bergman Field, CO	24
80	Burbank Valley Pump Plant, CA	24
80	Chilly Barton Flat, ID	24
80	Cooper Landing 6 W, AK	*24*
80	Encinal, TX	*24*
80	Fairmont, CA	24
80	Fort Hancock 5 SSE, TX	24
80	Gerlach, NV	*24*
80	Kings River Valley, NV	24
80	Lages, NV	*24*
80	Ojai, CA	24
80	Powder River No 2, WY	*24*
80	Redlands, CA	24
80	Sunnyside, NV	24
80	Tejon Rancho, CA	24
80	Tok, AK	*24*
80	Wupatki N M, AZ	24
97	Boysen Dam, WY	25
97	Carlsbad, NM	25
97	Columbus, NM	25
97	El Paso Intl Arpt, TX	25

Rankings include 100 highest and 100 lowest stations in each category. The period of record is 1980–2009. See User Guide for detailed explanation of data.

Highest Number of Days Annually With ≥ 0.5 Inches of Precipitation

Rank	Station Name	Days
1	Little Port Walter, AK	129
2	Yakutat State Arpt, AK	97
3	Port San Juan, AK	85
4	Cannery Creek, AK	79
5	Clearwater, WA	76
6	Annette Island Arpt, AK	73
7	Baring, WA	71
8	Cedar Lake, WA	70
8	Hilo International Arpt, HI	70
10	Elfin Cove, AK	69
11	Quillayute Airport, WA	68
12	Detroit Dam, OR	66
13	Mount Washington, NH	65
14	Cloverdale, OR	62
14	Palmer 3 ESE, WA	62
14	Sitka Japonski Arpt, AK	62
17	Cordova, AK	60
18	Headworks Ptld Wtr Bur, OR	58
19	Cushman Powerhouse 2, WA	56
19	Kodiak State USCG Base, AK	56
21	Aberdeen, WA	55
22	Bonneville Dam, OR	53
23	Hawaii Volcanos Np Hq 54, HI	51
23	Port Orford 2, OR	51
25	Diablo Dam, WA	50
26	Seaside, OR	49
27	Belknap Springs 8 N, OR	48
27	Kitoi Bay, AK	48
29	Seward, AK	47
30	Corvallis Water Bureau, OR	46
31	Astoria Clatsop County Arpt, OR	45
32	Alyeska, AK	44
32	Clayton 1 SSW, GA	44
32	Idleyld Park 4 NE, OR	44
32	Jasper, AL	44
36	Bankhead Lock and Dam, AL	43
36	Franklin 3 NW, LA	43
36	Snoqualmie Falls, WA	43
39	Amite, LA	42
39	Bridgeport 5 NW, AL	42
39	Chipley 3 E, FL	42
39	De Funiak Springs, FL	*42*
39	Thibodaux 3 ESE, LA	42
44	Bay Minette 3 NNW, AL	41
44	Booneville, MS	41
44	Dunsmuir Treatment Plant, CA	41
44	Hattiesburg 5 SW, MS	41
44	Lafayette Regional Arpt, LA	41
44	Mobile Regional Arpt, AL	41
50	Alum Fork, AR	40
50	Bessemer 3 WSW, AL	40
50	Brookhaven City, MS	40
50	Centreville WSMO, AL	40
50	Coden, AL	*40*
50	D Lo 2 SW, MS	40
50	De Sabla, CA	40
50	Fort Lauderdale, FL	40
50	Fulton 3 W, MS	40
50	Galliano, LA	40
50	Grand Coteau, LA	40
50	Pensacola Regional Arpt, FL	40
50	Reserve, LA	40
50	Russellville No 2, AL	40
50	Saucier Exp Forest, MS	40
50	Tuscaloosa Municipal Arpt, AL	40
66	Alexander City, AL	39
66	Alexandria, LA	39
66	Athens, TN	39
66	Bandon 2 NNE, OR	39
66	Bogalusa, LA	39
66	Crescent City 3 NNW, CA	39
66	Deland 1 SSE, FL	39
66	Demopolis Lock and Dam, AL	39
66	Estacada 2 SE, OR	39
66	Fairhope 2 NE, AL	39
66	Fayette, AL	*39*
66	Forest 3 S, MS	39
66	Gatlinburg 2 SW, TN	39
66	Geneva No 2, AL	39
66	Gulfport Naval Center, MS	39
66	Iuka 5s, MS	39
66	Lafayette 5 SW, GA	39
66	Lawrenceburg Filter Plant, TN	39
66	Louisville, MS	39
66	Pinson, AL	39
66	Sam Rayburn Dam, TX	39
66	Talladega, AL	39
66	Usher Tower, FL	39
66	West Palm Beach Intl Arpt, FL	39
66	Wewahitchka, FL	39
91	Baton Rouge Ryan Arpt, LA	38
91	Bay St Louis Nasa, MS	38
91	Bienville 3 NE, LA	38
91	Biloxi, MS	*38*
91	Birmingham Municipal Arpt, AL	38
91	Boyce 3 WNW, LA	38
91	Bunkie, LA	38
91	Carville 2 SW, LA	38
91	Cleveland Filter Plant, TN	38
91	Crossett 2 SSE, AR	38

Rankings include 100 highest and 100 lowest stations in each category. The period of record is 1980–2009. See User Guide for detailed explanation of data.

Lowest Number of Days Annually With ≥ 0.5 Inches of Precipitation

Rank	Station Name	Days
1	Barrow W Post-W Rogers Arpt, AK	0
1	Blythe, CA	0
1	Brothers, OR	0
1	Bruneau, ID	0
1	Buhl No 2, ID	0
1	Burns Municipal Arpt, OR	0
1	Callao, UT	0
1	Center 4 SSW, CO	0
1	Death Valley, CA	0
1	Denio, NV	0
1	Desert Natl Wl Range, NV	0
1	Dyer, NV	0
1	Ephrata Arpt FCWOS, WA	0
1	Eskdale, UT	0
1	Fallon Experiment Stn, NV	0
1	Grand Junction 6 ESE, CO	0
1	Grand View 2 W, ID	0
1	Howe, ID	0
1	Imlay, NV	0
1	Kennewick, WA	0
1	Kings River Valley, NV	0
1	Kuparuk, AK	*0*
1	Lages, NV	*0*
1	Lovelock, NV	0
1	Lovelock Derby Field, NV	*0*
1	McNary Dam, WA	0
1	Montello 1 SE, NV	0
1	Monument Valley, AZ	*0*
1	Needles Airport, CA	0
1	Pahranagat W L Refuge, NV	0
1	Parma Experiment Stn, ID	0
1	Pendleton Municipal Arpt, OR	0
1	Prosser, WA	*0*
1	Reese River O'Toole, NV	0
1	Salmon, ID	0
1	Tonopah Airport, NV	0
1	Wapato, WA	0
1	Winnemucca Municipal Arpt, NV	0
1	Yakima Air Terminal, WA	0
1	Yuma Citrus Station, AZ	*0*
1	Yuma Proving Ground, AZ	0
42	Aberdeen Exp Station, ID	1
42	Alamosa Bergman Field, CO	1
42	Amargosa Farms Garey, NV	1
42	American Falls 3 NW, ID	1
42	Arches Np Hqs, UT	1
42	Arlington, OR	1
42	Bakersfield Meadows Field, CA	1
42	Basin, WY	1
42	Battle Mountain, NV	1
42	Beatty 8 N, NV	*1*
42	Beaver Dam, AZ	1
42	Beowawe, NV	1
42	Black Rock, UT	1
42	Burley Municipal Arpt, ID	1
42	Canyon De Chelly, AZ	1
42	Castle Dale, UT	1
42	Chaco Canyon Natl Mon, NM	1
42	Chilly Barton Flat, ID	1
42	Coulee Dam 1 SW, WA	1
42	Drewsey, OR	1
42	Dugway, UT	1
42	Elko Municipal Arpt, NV	1
42	Ely Yelland Field, NV	1
42	Fontenelle Dam, WY	1
42	Fruita 1 W, CO	1
42	Gerlach, NV	*1*
42	Gibbs Ranch, NV	1
42	Grand Junction Walker Field, CO	1
42	Hayfield Pumping Plant, CA	1
42	Kotzebue Ralph Wein Memorial, AK	1
42	Las Vegas-McCarran Intl Arpt, NV	1
42	Lewiston Nez Perce County Arpt, ID	1
42	Milford Airport, UT	*1*
42	Pahrump, NV	1
42	Paisley, OR	1
42	Payette, ID	1
42	Reynolds, ID	1
42	Rome 2 NW, OR	1
42	Tulelake, CA	1
42	Willow Beach, AZ	1
82	Abiquiu Dam, NM	2
82	Altamont, UT	2
82	Barnes Station, OR	2
82	Barstow Fire Station, CA	2
82	Bishop Arpt, CA	2
82	Blue Eagle Ranch Hanks, NV	2
82	Boise Air Terminal, ID	2
82	Boysen Dam, WY	2
82	Condon, OR	2
82	Dubois, WY	*2*
82	Dubois Experiment Stn, ID	2
82	Eagle, AK	2
82	El Mirage, CA	2
82	Evanston 1 E, WY	2
82	Fairbanks Intl Arpt, AK	2
82	Fort Hall 1 NNE, ID	2
82	Gulkana Intermediate Field, AK	2
82	Independence, CA	2
82	Malad City, ID	2

Rankings include 100 highest and 100 lowest stations in each category. The period of record is 1980–2009. See User Guide for detailed explanation of data.

Highest Number of Days Annually With ≥ 1.0 Inches of Precipitation

Rank	Station Name	Days
1	Little Port Walter, AK	82
2	Yakutat State Arpt, AK	52
3	Port San Juan, AK	43
4	Cannery Creek, AK	37
5	Clearwater, WA	36
6	Baring, WA	32
7	Hilo International Arpt, HI	30
8	Annette Island Arpt, AK	29
8	Cushman Powerhouse 2, WA	29
8	Quillayute Airport, WA	29
11	Cedar Lake, WA	28
12	Mount Washington, NH	26
13	Cordova, AK	25
13	Detroit Dam, OR	25
13	Elfin Cove, AK	25
16	De Sabla, CA	24
17	Amite, LA	23
17	Clayton 1 SSW, GA	23
17	Coden, AL	***23***
17	Fairhope 2 NE, AL	23
17	Franklin 3 NW, LA	23
17	Palmer 3 ESE, WA	23
17	Saucier Exp Forest, MS	23
17	Slidell, LA	23
17	St Bernard, LA	***23***
17	Thibodaux 3 ESE, LA	23
27	Bankhead Lock and Dam, AL	22
27	Bay Minette 3 NNW, AL	22
27	De Ridder, LA	22
27	Diablo Dam, WA	22
27	Gulfport Naval Center, MS	22
27	Mobile Regional Arpt, AL	22
27	Reserve, LA	22
27	Waveland, MS	***22***
35	Baton Rouge Ryan Arpt, LA	21
35	Bienville 3 NE, LA	21
35	Bonneville Dam, OR	21
35	Brookhaven City, MS	21
35	Bunkie, LA	21
35	Dunsmuir Treatment Plant, CA	21
35	Fulton 3 W, MS	21
35	Hawaii Volcanos Np Hq 54, HI	21
35	Houma, LA	21
35	Jackson, AL	21
35	Jena 4 WSW, LA	***21***
35	New Orleans Intl Arpt, LA	21
35	Pascagoula 3 NE, MS	21
35	Port Orford 2, OR	21
35	Tryon, NC	21
50	Aberdeen, WA	20
50	Alexandria, LA	20
50	Arkadelphia 2 N, AR	20
50	Bastrop, LA	20
50	Belzoni, MS	***20***
50	Biloxi, MS	***20***
50	Bogalusa, LA	20
50	Bridgeport 5 NW, AL	20
50	Calaveras Big Trees, CA	20
50	Canton, MS	***20***
50	Cloverdale, OR	20
50	Crossett 2 SSE, AR	20
50	D Lo 2 SW, MS	20
50	De Funiak Springs, FL	***20***
50	Deland 1 SSE, FL	20
50	Eudora, AR	20
50	Eupora 2 E, MS	20
50	Forest 3 S, MS	20
50	Fort Lauderdale, FL	20
50	Fort Myers Page Field, FL	20
50	Grand Coteau, LA	20
50	Hattiesburg 5 SW, MS	20
50	Jasper, AL	20
50	Lawrenceburg Filter Plant, TN	20
50	Louisville, MS	20
50	Myakka River State Park, FL	20
50	Pensacola Regional Arpt, FL	20
50	Ruston La Tech, LA	20
50	Seward, AK	20
50	Sheridan, AR	20
50	Sitka Japonski Arpt, AK	20
50	Tallulah, LA	20
82	Alexander City, AL	19
82	Alum Fork, AR	19
82	Alyeska, AK	19
82	Beaumont Research Ctr, TX	19
82	Bessemer 3 WSW, AL	19
82	Boyce 3 WNW, LA	19
82	Calhoun City 2 NW, MS	19
82	Carville 2 SW, LA	19
82	Chipley 3 E, FL	19
82	Corvallis Water Bureau, OR	19
82	Dalton, GA	***19***
82	Dauphin Island #2, AL	19
82	Dequeen, AR	19
82	Geneva No 2, AL	19
82	Greenville, AL	19
82	Kodiak State USCG Base, AK	19
82	Lake Providence, LA	19
82	Lsu Ben Hur Farm, LA	19
82	Meridian Key Field, MS	19

Rankings include 100 highest and 100 lowest stations in each category. The period of record is 1980–2009. See User Guide for detailed explanation of data.

Lowest Number of Days Annually With ≥ 1.0 Inches of Precipitation

Rank	Station Name	Days
1	Aberdeen Exp Station, ID	0
1	Abiquiu Dam, NM	0
1	Alamo Dam, AZ	0
1	Alamogordo, NM	0
1	Alamosa Bergman Field, CO	0
1	Albuquerque Intl Arpt, NM	0
1	Alcalde, NM	0
1	Alder 17 S, MT	0
1	Alpine, UT	*0*
1	Altamont, UT	0
1	Altenbern, CO	0
1	Alturas, CA	0
1	Amargosa Farms Garey, NV	0
1	American Falls 3 NW, ID	0
1	Anaconda, MT	0
1	Anchorage Intl Arpt, AK	0
1	Anderson Lake, AK	*0*
1	Angle, UT	*0*
1	Antelope 1 NW, OR	0
1	Antero Reservoir, CO	0
1	Anvil Ranch, AZ	0
1	Archer, WY	*0*
1	Arches Np Hqs, UT	0
1	Arlington, OR	0
1	Artesia 6 S, NM	0
1	Arthur 4 NW, NV	0
1	Ashton, ID	0
1	Aspen 1 SW, CO	0
1	Augustine 2 E, NM	0
1	Austin, NV	*0*
1	Austin 3 S, OR	0
1	Bakersfield Meadows Field, CA	0
1	Barnes Station, OR	0
1	Barrow W Post-W Rogers Arpt, AK	0
1	Barstow Fire Station, CA	0
1	Basin, WY	0
1	Bates Creek No 2, WY	0
1	Battle Mountain, NV	0
1	Bayview Model Basin, ID	0
1	Beatty 8 N, NV	*0*
1	Beaver Dam, AZ	0
1	Bend, OR	0
1	Beowawe, NV	0
1	Bernardo, NM	0
1	Betatakin, AZ	0
1	Bethel Airport, AK	0
1	Bettles Field, AK	0
1	Biddle 8 SW, MT	0
1	Big Delta Allen AAF, AK	0
1	Bigfork 13 S, MT	0
1	Billings Logan Int'l Arpt, MT	0
1	Billings Water Plant, MT	0
1	Billy Creek, WY	0
1	Bingham 2 NE, NM	0
1	Bishop Arpt, CA	0
1	Black Rock, UT	0
1	Blue Eagle Ranch Hanks, NV	0
1	Blythe, CA	0
1	Bodie, CA	0
1	Boise 7 N, ID	0
1	Boise Air Terminal, ID	0
1	Bondurant, WY	0
1	Bonners Ferry, ID	0
1	Boquillas Ranger Stn, TX	*0*
1	Borrego Desert Park, CA	0
1	Boulder, CO	0
1	Boulder, MT	0
1	Boulder, UT	0
1	Bowie, AZ	0
1	Boysen Dam, WY	0
1	Bozeman Gallatin Fld, MT	0
1	Bozeman Montana St Univ, MT	0
1	Brandenberg, MT	0
1	Bredette, MT	0
1	Bridger 1 S, MT	*0*
1	Brigham City Waste Plt, UT	0
1	Brockway 3 WSW, MT	0
1	Brothers, OR	0
1	Brownlee Dam, ID	0
1	Bruneau, ID	0
1	Buhl No 2, ID	0
1	Bullhead City, AZ	0
1	Burley Municipal Arpt, ID	0
1	Burns Municipal Arpt, OR	0
1	Burris, WY	0
1	Busby, MT	0
1	Butte Bert Mooney Arpt, MT	0
1	Byers 5 ENE, CO	0
1	Caballo Dam, NM	0
1	Cabin Creek, CO	0
1	Callao, UT	0
1	Candelaria, TX	0
1	Canon City, CO	*0*
1	Cantwell 2 E, AK	*0*
1	Canyon De Chelly, AZ	0
1	Canyonlands The Neck, UT	0
1	Carlyle 12 NW, MT	0
1	Carpenter, WY	*0*
1	Carter 14 W, MT	0
1	Casper Natrona Co Intl Arpt, WY	0

Rankings include 100 highest and 100 lowest stations in each category. The period of record is 1980–2009. See User Guide for detailed explanation of data.

Highest Annual Snowfall

Rank	Station Name	Inches
1	Alta, UT	527.2
2	Mount Washington, NH	278.4
3	Blowhard Mtn Radar, UT	***248.1***
4	Island Park, ID	***222.0***
5	Alyeska, AK	212.6
6	Hayes River, AK	***207.6***
7	Marquette County Arpt, MI	203.0
8	Boonville 2 SSW, NY	197.5
9	Chulitna River Lodge, AK	196.0
10	Cooke City 2 W, MT	***192.1***
11	Ironwood, MI	187.2
12	Donner Memorial St Pk, CA	185.4
13	Dixie, ID	***182.2***
14	Hebgen Dam, MT	180.2
15	Bergland Dam, MI	177.8
16	Aspen 1 SW, CO	176.9
17	Glen Alps, AK	167.9
18	Munising, MI	***151.7***
19	Yakutat State Arpt, AK	150.2
20	Cannery Creek, AK	142.3
21	Lindbergh Lake, MT	133.3
22	Bright Angel R S, AZ	133.2
23	Grand Marais 2 E, MI	***132.9***
24	Cabin Creek, CO	132.1
25	Gascon, NM	131.7
26	Millegan 14 SE, MT	***128.7***
27	Powell, ID	***126.1***
28	South Lincoln, VT	124.8
29	Syracuse Hancock Int'l Arpt, NY	124.5
30	Cantwell 2 E, AK	***124.3***
31	Morrisville 5 SW, NY	124.1
32	Eustis, ME	***123.8***
33	Bondurant, WY	123.2
34	Whitefish Point, MI	122.6
35	Skwentna, AK	121.7
36	Lowville, NY	121.4
36	West Glacier, MT	121.4
38	Tully Heiberg Forest, NY	***115.8***
39	Wildhorse Reservoir, NV	***115.6***
40	Marquette, MI	115.3
41	Hayden, CO	114.8
42	Champion Van Riper Prk, MI	***114.6***
43	Mazama, WA	114.2
44	Boyne Falls, MI	114.1
45	Caribou Municipal Arpt, ME	112.9
46	Calaveras Big Trees, CA	112.7
47	Wales, NY	***110.8***
48	Elfin Cove, AK	110.1
49	Homer 8 NW, AK	108.3
50	Port San Juan, AK	107.6
51	Hohnholz Ranch, CO	***106.6***
52	Canyon Dam, CA	106.0
53	Frankfort 2 NE, MI	104.9
54	Chama, NM	103.2
55	Chardon, OH	102.8
55	Little Port Walter, AK	102.8
57	Brassua Dam, ME	102.7
58	Bayfield 6 N, WI	***101.2***
59	Erie Intl Arpt, PA	99.6
60	Rochester Intl Arpt, NY	99.4
61	Oakland 1 SE, MD	98.0
62	McGrath Arpt, AK	97.3
63	Puntilla, AK	***95.7***
64	Muskegon County Arpt, MI	***95.1***
65	Allagash, ME	***94.9***
66	Newport, VT	94.1
67	Buffalo Greater Buffalo Int'l, NY	94.0
68	Boca, CA	92.9
68	Dover-Foxcroft, ME	92.9
70	Bozeman Montana St Univ, MT	92.8
70	Cheboygan, MI	92.8
72	Dutch Harbor, AK	***92.4***
73	Lander Hunt Field, WY	92.3
74	Bettles Field, AK	91.7
75	Presque Isle, ME	88.3
76	Saint Johnsbury, VT	88.2
77	Boulder, CO	87.7
77	Chalk Hill 2 ENE, PA	87.7
77	Juneau Int'l Arpt, AK	87.7
80	Alfred, NY	87.6
81	Bridgewater, ME	86.8
82	Allegan 5 NE, MI	***86.6***
83	Bailey, CO	86.1
84	Fort Lewis, CO	85.8
85	Benton Harbor Ross Field, MI	85.7
85	Millinocket, ME	***85.7***
87	Duluth Intl Arpt, MN	85.5
88	Cle Elum, WA	***85.3***
89	Cascade 1 NW, ID	85.2
90	Gouverneur 3 NW, NY	84.6
91	Westfield 2 SSE, NY	***84.5***
92	North Stratford, NH	***84.3***
93	Cavendish, VT	83.8
94	Essex Junction 1 N, VT	***83.2***
94	Grafton, NY	***83.2***
96	Winchester, ID	82.9
97	Binghamton Edwin A Link Field, NY	82.8
98	Vanceboro 2, ME	82.7
99	Evergreen, CO	82.6
100	Ashton, ID	82.1

Rankings include 100 highest and 100 lowest stations in each category. The period of record is 1980–2009. See User Guide for detailed explanation of data.

Lowest Annual Snowfall

Rank	Station Name	Inches
1	Arcadia, FL	0.0
1	Archbold Bio Station, FL	0.0
1	Avon Park 2 W, FL	0.0
1	Balch Power House, CA	0.0
1	Bay City Waterworks, TX	0.0
1	Baytown, TX	0.0
1	Berkeley, CA	***0.0***
1	Blythe, CA	0.0
1	Brooksville Chin Hill, FL	0.0
1	Brunswick, GA	0.0
1	Bullhead City, AZ	0.0
1	Burbank Valley Pump Plant, CA	0.0
1	Cachuma Lake, CA	0.0
1	Camilla 3 SE, GA	0.0
1	Camp Pardee, CA	0.0
1	Carrizo Springs, TX	0.0
1	Chipley 3 E, FL	0.0
1	Clermont 7 S, FL	0.0
1	Cordele, GA	0.0
1	Dauphin Island #2, AL	0.0
1	Death Valley, CA	0.0
1	Deland 1 SSE, FL	0.0
1	Escondido No 2, CA	***0.0***
1	Falcon Dam, TX	0.0
1	Falfurrias, TX	0.0
1	Federal Point, FL	0.0
1	Flamingo Ranger Stn, FL	0.0
1	Friant Government Camp, CA	0.0
1	Fort Lauderdale, FL	0.0
1	Fort Pierce, FL	0.0
1	Gila Bend, AZ	0.0
1	Gilroy, CA	0.0
1	Haleakala R S 338, HI	0.0
1	Hawaii Volcanos Np Hq 54, HI	0.0
1	High Springs, FL	0.0
1	Hollister 2, CA	0.0
1	Immokalee 3 NNW, FL	***0.0***
1	Jackson, AL	0.0
1	Kanalohuluhulu 1075, HI	0.0
1	Ke-Ahole Point 68.13, HI	0.0
1	Kii-Kahuku 911, HI	0.0
1	Kissimmee 2, FL	0.0
1	Kula Hospital 267, HI	0.0
1	Laguna Beach, CA	0.0
1	Lake City 2 E, FL	0.0
1	Laveen 3 SSE, AZ	0.0
1	Lihue Arpt, HI	0.0
1	Maricopa 4 N, AZ	0.0
1	Melbourne Regional Arpt, FL	0.0
1	Molokai Airport, HI	***0.0***
1	Mountain Lake, FL	0.0
1	Naples, FL	0.0
1	Newman, CA	0.0
1	Oasis Ranger Station, FL	0.0
1	Ojai, CA	0.0
1	Opihihale 2 24.1, HI	0.0
1	Panama City 5 NE, FL	0.0
1	Parker Reservoir, CA	0.0
1	Parrish, FL	0.0
1	Perry, FL	0.0
1	Plant City, FL	0.0
1	Porterville, CA	***0.0***
1	Punta Gorda 4 ESE, FL	0.0
1	Redlands, CA	0.0
1	Riverside Fire Sta 3, CA	0.0
1	Saint Leo, FL	0.0
1	Salinas No 2, CA	0.0
1	San Francisco Oceanside, CA	***0.0***
1	Sanford Experiment Stn, FL	0.0
1	Santa Barbara, CA	0.0
1	Santa Monica Pier, CA	0.0
1	South Phoenix, AZ	0.0
1	St Petersburg, FL	0.0
1	Stockton Fire Stn #4, CA	0.0
1	Stuart 1 S, FL	0.0
1	Tarpon Springs Sewage Plant, FL	0.0
1	Titusville, FL	0.0
1	Weeki Wachee, FL	0.0
1	Weslaco 2 E, TX	0.0
1	Wewahitchka, FL	0.0
1	Willow Beach, AZ	0.0
1	Woodside Fire Stn 1, CA	0.0
1	Yuma Citrus Station, AZ	***0.0***
1	Yuma Proving Ground, AZ	0.0
85	Albany 3 SE, GA	Trace
85	Anahuac, TX	Trace
85	Angleton 2 W, TX	Trace
85	Antioch Pump Plant #3, CA	Trace
85	Anvil Ranch, AZ	Trace
85	Apalachicola Municipal Arpt, FL	Trace
85	Bay St Louis Nasa, MS	Trace
85	Beaumont Research Ctr, TX	Trace
85	Beaver Dam, AZ	***Trace***
85	Belzoni, MS	***Trace***
85	Boquillas Ranger Stn, TX	***Trace***
85	Borrego Desert Park, CA	Trace
85	Boyce 3 WNW, LA	Trace
85	Brownsville Intl Arpt, TX	***Trace***
85	Bunkie, LA	Trace
85	Calistoga, CA	Trace

Rankings include 100 highest and 100 lowest stations in each category. The period of record is 1980–2009. See User Guide for detailed explanation of data.

Highest Annual Maximum Snow Depth

Rank	Station Name	Inches
1	Alta, UT	***150***
1	Wausau Municipal Arpt, WI	150
3	Blowhard Mtn Radar, UT	***148***
4	Barrow W Post-W Rogers Arpt, AK	140
5	Hayes River, AK	***117***
6	Canyon Dam, CA	115
7	Chulitna River Lodge, AK	112
8	Puntilla, AK	***103***
9	Donner Memorial St Pk, CA	94
10	Cannery Creek, AK	92
11	Alyeska, AK	89
11	Bright Angel R S, AZ	89
11	Island Park, ID	***89***
11	Nome Municipal Arpt, AK	89
15	Skwentna, AK	88
16	Sutton 2 E, AK	86
17	Cle Elum, WA	***85***
17	Dixie, ID	***85***
19	Benton Harbor Ross Field, MI	80
19	Cantwell 2 E, AK	***80***
19	Glacier Bay, AK	***80***
22	Bodie, CA	78
22	Little Port Walter, AK	78
24	Homer 8 NW, AK	77
25	Whites Crossing, AK	76
26	Yakutat State Arpt, AK	75
27	Cooke City 2 W, MT	72
28	Boca, CA	70
29	Belknap Springs 8 N, OR	69
29	Port San Juan, AK	69
31	Fergus Falls, MN	***68***
31	McGrath Arpt, AK	68
33	Lindbergh Lake, MT	65
33	Tower 3 S, MN	***65***
35	Powell, ID	***64***
36	Bondurant, WY	63
36	Bonneville Dam, OR	63
36	Marquette County Arpt, MI	63
36	Wildhorse Reservoir, NV	***63***
40	Elfin Cove, AK	62
40	Kotzebue Ralph Wein Memorial, AK	62
40	Mazama, WA	62
43	Berlin, NH	61
43	Kalispell Arpt, MT	***61***
43	Manistique, MI	***61***
46	Aspen 1 SW, CO	***60***
46	Champion Van Riper Prk, MI	60
46	Cooper Landing 6 W, AK	***60***
46	Dover-Foxcroft, ME	60
46	Tully Heiberg Forest, NY	***60***
46	West Glacier, MT	60
52	Bettles Field, AK	59
52	Saint Maries 1 W, ID	59
54	Boonville 2 SSW, NY	57
55	Chama, NM	56
55	Hebgen Dam, MT	56
57	Bonners Ferry, ID	***55***
58	Ashton, ID	54
58	Fairbanks Intl Arpt, AK	54
60	Alpena Wastewater Pl, MI	53
60	Bridgton 3 NW, ME	***53***
60	Eureka, SD	***53***
63	Allagash, ME	***52***
63	College Observatory, AK	52
63	Grand Marais, MN	52
63	Laurelton Center, PA	***52***
63	McClusky, ND	52
68	Eustis, ME	***51***
68	Morrisville 5 SW, NY	51
68	Pleasant Mount 1 W, PA	51
68	Priest River Exp Stn, ID	51
72	Bridgewater, ME	50
72	Cascade 1 NW, ID	50
72	Chazy, NY	***50***
72	Francis E Walter Dam, PA	50
72	Millegan 14 SE, MT	***50***
72	Superior, WI	50
78	Bergland Dam, MI	49
78	Columbia 8 N, SD	49
78	East Hiram, ME	49
78	Fort Lewis, CO	49
78	Mankato, MN	***49***
83	Frankfort 2 NE, MI	48
83	Fort Meade, SD	48
83	Huntsville Monastery, UT	48
86	Arthur 4 NW, NV	***47***
86	Caribou Municipal Arpt, ME	47
86	Chardon, OH	47
86	Ironwood, MI	47
90	Brockton, MA	***46***
90	Cold Bay Arpt, AK	46
90	Farmington 3 NW, MN	***46***
90	Idaho City, ID	46
90	South Lincoln, VT	46
90	Two Harbors, MN	46
96	Acadia National Park, ME	45
96	Bailey, CO	45
96	Chiloquin 7 NW, OR	45
96	Concord Municipal Arpt, NH	45
96	Conklingville Dam, NY	45

Rankings include 100 highest and 100 lowest stations in each category. The period of record is 1980–2009. See User Guide for detailed explanation of data.

Lowest Annual Maximum Snow Depth

Rank	Station Name	Inches
1	Alice, TX	*0*
1	Arcadia, FL	0
1	Archbold Bio Station, FL	0
1	Avon Park 2 W, FL	0
1	Baytown, TX	0
1	Berkeley, CA	*0*
1	Blythe, CA	0
1	Brooksville Chin Hill, FL	0
1	Brunswick, GA	0
1	Bullhead City, AZ	0
1	Burbank Valley Pump Plant, CA	0
1	Burnet, TX	0
1	Cachuma Lake, CA	0
1	Camilla 3 SE, GA	0
1	Camp Pardee, CA	0
1	Chipley 3 E, FL	0
1	Cordele, GA	0
1	Crescent City 3 NNW, CA	0
1	Culver City, CA	*0*
1	Dauphin Island #2, AL	0
1	Death Valley, CA	0
1	Deland 1 SSE, FL	0
1	Dell City 5 SSW, TX	0
1	Demopolis Lock and Dam, AL	0
1	Enterprise 5 NNW, AL	*0*
1	Escondido No 2, CA	*0*
1	Fairfield, CA	0
1	Falcon Dam, TX	0
1	Falfurrias, TX	0
1	Federal Point, FL	0
1	Flamingo Ranger Stn, FL	0
1	Fountain Hills, AZ	0
1	Friant Government Camp, CA	0
1	Fort Lauderdale, FL	0
1	Fort Pierce, FL	0
1	Gila Bend, AZ	0
1	Gilroy, CA	0
1	Gulfport Naval Center, MS	0
1	Haleakala R S 338, HI	0
1	Hawaii Volcanos Np Hq 54, HI	0
1	High Springs, FL	0
1	Hollister 2, CA	0
1	Immokalee 3 NNW, FL	*0*
1	Jackson, AL	0
1	Jacksonville Beach, FL	0
1	Kanalohuluhulu 1075, HI	0
1	Ke-Ahole Point 68.13, HI	0
1	Kii-Kahuku 911, HI	0
1	King City, CA	0
1	Kissimmee 2, FL	0
1	Kula Hospital 267, HI	0
1	Laguna Beach, CA	*0*
1	Lake City 2 E, FL	0
1	Laveen 3 SSE, AZ	0
1	Lihue Arpt, HI	0
1	Maricopa 4 N, AZ	0
1	McGregor, TX	0
1	Melbourne Regional Arpt, FL	0
1	Molokai Airport, HI	*0*
1	Mountain Lake, FL	0
1	Naples, FL	0
1	Newman, CA	0
1	Oasis Ranger Station, FL	0
1	Ojai, CA	0
1	Opihihale 2 24.1, HI	0
1	Panama City 5 NE, FL	0
1	Parker Reservoir, CA	0
1	Parrish, FL	0
1	Pascagoula 3 NE, MS	0
1	Perry, FL	0
1	Plant City, FL	0
1	Punta Gorda 4 ESE, FL	0
1	Redlands, CA	0
1	Riverside Fire Sta 3, CA	0
1	Saint Leo, FL	0
1	Salinas No 2, CA	0
1	San Francisco Oceanside, CA	*0*
1	Sanford Experiment Stn, FL	0
1	Santa Barbara, CA	0
1	Santa Monica Pier, CA	*0*
1	Searchlight, NV	0
1	South Phoenix, AZ	0
1	St Petersburg, FL	0
1	Stockton Fire Stn #4, CA	0
1	Stuart 1 S, FL	0
1	Tarpon Springs Sewage Plant, FL	0
1	Tejon Rancho, CA	0
1	Titusville, FL	0
1	U of GA Plant Sci Farm, GA	0
1	Victorville Pump Plant, CA	0
1	Warrenton, GA	0
1	Weeki Wachee, FL	0
1	Weslaco 2 E, TX	0
1	Wewahitchka, FL	0
1	Willow Beach, AZ	*0*
1	Woodside Fire Stn 1, CA	*0*
1	Yucca 1 NNE, AZ	0
1	Yuma Citrus Station, AZ	*0*
1	Yuma Proving Ground, AZ	0
100	Albany 3 SE, GA	Trace

Rankings include 100 highest and 100 lowest stations in each category. The period of record is 1980–2009. See User Guide for detailed explanation of data.

Highest Number of Days Annually With ≥ 1.0 Inch Snow Depth

Rank	Station Name	Days
1	Kuparuk, AK	***243***
2	Barrow W Post-W Rogers Arpt, AK	242
3	Bettles Field, AK	216
4	Kotzebue Ralph Wein Memorial, AK	214
5	Blowhard Mtn Radar, UT	***213***
6	Cantwell 2 E, AK	***209***
7	Alta, UT	***206***
7	Chulitna River Lodge, AK	206
9	Hayes River, AK	***204***
10	Eagle, AK	198
10	McGrath Arpt, AK	198
12	Puntilla, AK	***196***
12	Tok, AK	196
14	College Observatory, AK	195
15	Nabesna, AK	193
15	North Pole, AK	193
17	Fairbanks Intl Arpt, AK	192
18	Cannery Creek, AK	190
19	Cooke City 2 W, MT	189
20	Skwentna, AK	187
21	Mount Washington, NH	186
21	Nome Municipal Arpt, AK	186
23	Healy 2 NW, AK	***181***
24	Eielson Field, AK	***178***
25	Alyeska, AK	177
26	Dixie, ID	***174***
27	Homer 8 NW, AK	171
28	Aspen 1 SW, CO	165
29	Sutton 2 E, AK	160
30	Hebgen Dam, MT	158
31	Island Park, ID	***156***
31	Lindbergh Lake, MT	156
33	Bethel Airport, AK	155
34	Bailey, CO	154
34	Bondurant, WY	154
34	Eustis, ME	***154***
37	Whites Crossing, AK	153
38	Marquette County Arpt, MI	152
39	Bergland Dam, MI	151
40	Anchorage Intl Arpt, AK	148
41	Allagash, ME	***146***
41	West Glacier, MT	146
43	Ironwood, MI	145
44	Whitefish Point, MI	139
45	Duluth Intl Arpt, MN	137
45	Mazama, WA	137
47	Cloquet, MN	136
48	Anderson Lake, AK	***135***
48	Bright Angel R S, AZ	135
48	Caribou Municipal Arpt, ME	135
51	Boonville 2 SSW, NY	134
51	Donner Memorial St Pk, CA	134
53	Agassiz Refuge, MN	133
53	International Falls Int'l Arpt, MN	133
55	Bayfield 6 N, WI	***132***
56	Champion Van Riper Prk, MI	131
56	Grand Marais 2 E, MI	***131***
58	Ashton, ID	130
58	Marquette, MI	130
58	Stambaugh 2 SSE, MI	130
61	Dover-Foxcroft, ME	129
61	Hohnholz Ranch, CO	***129***
63	Bodie, CA	128
64	Cavalier 7 NW, ND	127
64	Upham 3 N, ND	127
66	Bridgewater, ME	126
67	Cascade 1 NW, ID	125
68	Millegan 14 SE, MT	***124***
68	Powell, ID	***124***
68	Tully Heiberg Forest, NY	***124***
71	Cavendish, VT	122
71	Glacier Bay, AK	***122***
71	Newport, VT	122
74	Bottineau, ND	120
74	Hayden, CO	120
76	Stanley 3 NNW, ND	119
77	Bridgton 3 NW, ME	***118***
77	South Lincoln, VT	118
79	Grand Marais, MN	117
79	Idaho City, ID	117
79	Yakutat State Arpt, AK	117
82	Bozeman Montana St Univ, MT	116
82	Drake 9 NE, ND	116
82	Dubois Experiment Stn, ID	116
82	East Hiram, ME	116
82	North Stratford, NH	***116***
82	Wildhorse Reservoir, NV	***116***
88	Antigo, WI	115
88	Brainerd, MN	115
88	Morrisville 5 SW, NY	115
91	Iron Mtn-Kingsford WWTP, MI	114
92	Port San Juan, AK	113
93	Berlin, NH	112
93	Edmore 1 NW, ND	112
93	Intricate Bay, AK	***112***
93	Priest River Exp Stn, ID	112
97	Corinna, ME	111
97	Saint Johnsbury, VT	111
99	Cross Village, MI	110
99	Rosholt 9 NNE, WI	110

Rankings include 100 highest and 100 lowest stations in each category. The period of record is 1980–2009. See User Guide for detailed explanation of data.

Lowest Number of Days Annually With ≥ 1.0 Inch Snow Depth

Rank	Station Name	Days
1	Aberdeen, MS	0
1	Ada, OK	0
1	Aiken 4 NE, SC	0
1	Alamo Dam, AZ	0
1	Alamogordo, NM	*0*
1	Albany, TX	*0*
1	Albany 3 SE, GA	0
1	Albemarle, NC	*0*
1	Alexander City, AL	0
1	Alexandria, LA	0
1	Alice, TX	0
1	Alicia, AR	*0*
1	Allendale 2 NW, SC	*0*
1	Alpine, TX	*0*
1	Amargosa Farms Garey, NV	*0*
1	Amistad Dam, TX	0
1	Amite, LA	0
1	Anacortes, WA	*0*
1	Anahuac, TX	0
1	Andalusia 3 W, AL	0
1	Anderson, SC	0
1	Andrews, SC	0
1	Angleton 2 W, TX	0
1	Angwin Pac Union Col, CA	0
1	Antioch Pump Plant #3, CA	0
1	Antlers, OK	*0*
1	Anvil Ranch, AZ	0
1	Apalachicola Municipal Arpt, FL	0
1	Appling 2 NW, GA	0
1	Aransas Wildlife Refuge, TX	0
1	Arcadia, FL	0
1	Archbold Bio Station, FL	0
1	Arkadelphia 2 N, AR	0
1	Ash Mountain, CA	0
1	Ashland, LA	0
1	Ashland, OR	0
1	Athens, TX	0
1	Auberry 2 NW, CA	0
1	Auburn, CA	0
1	Augusta Bush Field, GA	*0*
1	Aurora 6 N, NC	0
1	Austin Municipal Arpt, TX	*0*
1	Avon Park 2 W, FL	0
1	Bakersfield, TX	0
1	Ballinger 2 NW, TX	0
1	Balmorhea, TX	*0*
1	Bandon 2 NNE, OR	0
1	Bankhead Lock and Dam, AL	0
1	Bardwell Dam, TX	0
1	Barstow Fire Station, CA	0
1	Bastrop, LA	0
1	Batesville 2 SW, MS	0
1	Bay City Waterworks, TX	0
1	Bay Minette 3 NNW, AL	0
1	Bay St Louis Nasa, MS	0
1	Bayboro 3 E, NC	*0*
1	Baytown, TX	0
1	Beaumont Research Ctr, TX	0
1	Beaver Dam, AZ	*0*
1	Beaverton 2 SSW, OR	*0*
1	Beedeville 4 NE, AR	*0*
1	Belhaven 5 SE, NC	0
1	Belle Mina 2 N, AL	0
1	Belzoni, MS	*0*
1	Ben Lomond No 4, CA	0
1	Benbrook Dam, TX	0
1	Benton, AR	*0*
1	Berkeley, CA	*0*
1	Bessemer 3 WSW, AL	0
1	Bienville 3 NE, LA	0
1	Big Spring, TX	*0*
1	Biloxi, MS	*0*
1	Birmingham Municipal Arpt, AL	0
1	Bishopville 8 NNW, SC	0
1	Blairsville Exp Sta, GA	0
1	Blakely Mountain Dam, AR	0
1	Blanco, TX	0
1	Blythe, CA	*0*
1	Boerne, TX	0
1	Bogalusa, LA	0
1	Boquillas Ranger Stn, TX	*0*
1	Borrego Desert Park, CA	0
1	Bowie, AZ	*0*
1	Boyce 3 WNW, LA	0
1	Brady, TX	0
1	Brenham, TX	0
1	Bridgeport, TX	0
1	Bridgeport 5 NW, AL	0
1	Brookhaven City, MS	0
1	Brooklet 1 W, GA	0
1	Brooksville Chin Hill, FL	0
1	Brownsville Intl Arpt, TX	*0*
1	Brownwood, TX	0
1	Bruneau, ID	*0*
1	Brunswick, GA	0
1	Buckley 1 NE, WA	0
1	Bullhead City, AZ	0
1	Bunkie, LA	0
1	Burbank Valley Pump Plant, CA	0
1	Burlington Fire Stn #5, NC	0

Rankings include 100 highest and 100 lowest stations in each category. The period of record is 1980–2009. See User Guide for detailed explanation of data.

Five-Year Averages:
1950 - 2009

Annual Mean Maximum Temperature

Five-Year Averages: 1950 - 2009

State	Weather Station	1950-1954	1955-1959	1960-1964	1965-1969	1970-1974	1975-1979	1980-1984	1985-1989	1990-1994	1995-1999	2000-2004	2005-2009
Alabama	Birmingham-Shuttlesworth Int'l Airport	74.9	73.7	73.5	72.1	73.0	72.2	73.4	73.4	74.2	74.1	73.4	na
Alaska	Anchorage Int'l Airport	na	42.1	42.4	na	40.5	44.2	43.4	43.7	43.5	43.2	45.0	43.0
Arizona	Phoenix Sky Harbor Int'l Airport	85.9	84.1	84.6	84.7	85.7	86.0	86.2	87.6	86.4	85.9	87.2	87.3
Arkansas	Little Rock National Airport	73.5	72.2	72.8	72.0	72.7	71.7	72.0	72.8	73.0	73.7	72.4	73.7
California	Los Angeles Int'l Airport	69.2	72.3	69.4	69.8	69.8	70.8	71.0	70.4	71.0	70.5	69.4	70.0
California	San Francisco Int'l Airport	64.1	66.3	64.8	64.6	64.6	65.0	65.7	66.4	66.2	65.5	65.6	65.4
Colorado	Denver Stapleton Int'l Airport	64.8	63.8	64.1	64.1	64.4	64.3	63.5	64.4	65.1	na	65.5	na
Connecticut	Bridgeport-Sikorsky Memorial Airport	60.7	59.8	58.8	59.0	60.0	59.2	59.4	59.6	60.9	60.2	59.7	60.5
Delaware	Wilmington-New Castle Airport	64.5	63.3	62.7	62.8	64.3	62.8	63.8	63.8	65.1	63.9	63.4	64.5
Florida	Jacksonville Int'l Airport	80.2	79.5	78.9	78.7	79.6	78.3	79.0	79.5	80.1	79.1	78.9	79.3
Florida	Miami Int'l Airport	83.5	82.9	82.5	82.1	82.6	81.9	83.1	84.2	84.6	84.0	83.9	84.4
Georgia	Atlanta Hartsfield Int'l Airport	72.7	71.9	70.1	69.8	71.4	70.9	71.6	72.4	73.1	72.3	71.6	72.3
Hawaii	Honolulu Int'l Airport	na	82.0	83.4	na	84.0	84.3	84.6	85.5	85.0	84.9	84.5	na
Idaho	Boise Air Terminal	62.7	62.0	62.7	63.6	63.1	62.4	61.5	63.0	63.9	64.1	64.3	64.2
Illinois	Chicago O'Hare Int'l Airport	na	na	58.2	58.2	58.6	58.5	58.2	59.0	59.1	59.0	59.0	59.1
Indiana	Indianapolis Int'l Airport	63.0	61.8	61.3	61.9	62.4	61.5	61.9	62.5	63.0	62.6	62.5	62.9
Iowa	Des Moines Int'l Airport	59.6	59.9	58.5	58.6	59.3	59.6	60.0	60.8	59.9	59.3	60.6	60.6
Kansas	Wichita Mid-Continent Airport	na	67.5	67.2	67.4	66.8	67.6	67.2	67.8	na	67.6	68.4	68.6
Kentucky	Lexington Bluegrass Airport	66.5	65.1	64.4	63.9	64.9	63.8	64.4	65.2	65.5	64.9	64.9	65.6
Louisiana	New Orleans Int'l Airport	78.6	77.5	77.2	76.9	78.2	77.2	77.7	77.5	78.3	78.4	78.2	78.7
Maine	Portland Int'l Jetport	56.2	55.2	55.0	54.8	54.5	54.5	55.3	55.4	55.9	55.8	55.4	55.8
Maryland	Baltimore/Washington Int'l Airport	65.7	64.5	64.7	64.7	65.0	65.3	64.7	65.2	66.3	66.0	65.0	65.8
Massachusetts	Boston Logan Int'l Airport	60.1	58.9	58.5	57.6	58.9	59.7	59.2	58.5	60.0	59.2	58.8	59.0
Michigan	Detroit Metro Airport	na	na	58.0	57.9	58.1	58.0	57.8	58.5	59.3	59.0	58.8	59.2
Minnesota	Minneapolis-Saint Paul Int'l Airport	53.7	54.9	54.2	53.2	53.4	54.3	54.4	55.4	54.6	55.0	55.3	55.7
Mississippi	Jackson Int'l Airport	na	na	na	75.4	76.7	75.1	76.1	76.3	76.4	76.0	75.7	76.7
Missouri	St Louis-Lambert Int'l Airport	66.8	65.7	64.7	64.8	65.6	64.5	65.0	66.1	66.5	65.7	66.3	66.6
Montana	Billings Logan Int'l Airport	58.2	58.2	59.3	57.4	57.1	57.0	59.7	59.5	59.8	58.6	59.5	60.0
Nebraska	Omaha Eppley Airfield	61.5	61.8	61.3	61.8	62.0	62.2	59.8	na	61.8	na	62.5	62.1
Nevada	Las Vegas-McCarran Int'l Airport	na	na	79.3	79.2	78.9	80.4	79.0	80.6	79.8	79.9	80.4	80.7
New Hampshire	Concord Municipal Airport	58.3	na	57.6	56.7	56.4	56.9	57.3	57.2	58.2	58.1	57.8	57.8
New Jersey	Newark Int'l Airport	63.2	62.5	62.3	61.9	63.1	62.0	63.0	63.5	65.1	63.6	63.1	63.8
New Mexico	Albuquerque Int'l Airport	71.5	70.2	69.4	69.7	70.0	70.5	71.0	69.8	70.5	70.3	70.3	70.1
New York	Buffalo Niagara Int'l Airport	57.3	56.8	55.8	55.4	55.6	55.2	55.9	56.6	57.2	56.5	56.1	57.0
New York	New York LaGuardia Airport	62.9	61.9	60.9	60.7	60.9	60.6	61.1	62.0	63.5	62.9	62.3	63.3
North Carolina	Charlotte Douglas Int'l Airport	72.3	72.3	70.6	69.6	70.1	70.1	69.8	71.2	72.4	71.4	70.9	71.8
North Dakota	Fargo Hector Int'l Airport	50.5	51.8	52.9	50.1	50.5	50.5	51.6	52.7	52.8	51.7	52.4	52.4
Ohio	Columbus Intl Airport	63.3	63.1	61.5	60.7	61.4	60.4	61.0	62.2	63.2	62.8	62.1	63.0
Oklahoma	Oklahoma City-Will Rogers World Arpt	72.1	70.1	70.8	71.1	70.7	71.0	71.1	70.5	na	71.8	71.3	73.2
Oregon	Portland Int'l Airport	61.3	61.2	61.1	62.8	63.0	62.0	62.6	63.2	63.9	63.0	63.2	62.9
Pennsylvania	Philadelphia Int'l Airport	64.8	63.4	62.4	62.6	63.7	63.5	63.0	64.3	65.8	64.6	64.4	64.8
Rhode Island	Providence TF Green Airport	na	59.0	58.8	58.9	59.7	59.2	60.2	59.9	61.3	60.8	60.1	60.8
South Carolina	Columbia Metro Airport	76.6	75.5	74.9	74.1	76.1	75.0	74.2	75.7	76.4	75.3	74.9	75.4
South Dakota	Sioux Falls Foss Field	56.0	57.6	57.1	56.1	56.3	56.0	56.9	57.8	56.9	56.0	57.4	57.2
Tennessee	Memphis Int'l Airport	73.0	71.6	70.9	70.8	71.3	71.5	71.8	72.2	72.7	72.2	72.1	73.3
Texas	Dallas-Fort Worth Int'l Airport	na	76.1	76.3	75.7	76.1	75.9	76.0	76.1	76.3	77.0	76.1	78.5
Texas	El Paso Int'l Airport	78.2	77.1	77.1	76.9	77.6	77.7	78.1	77.3	78.6	78.2	77.9	78.4
Texas	Houston Intercontinental Airport	na	na	na	na	78.8	78.1	79.0	79.1	79.5	80.3	79.3	80.5
Utah	Salt Lake City Int'l Airport	63.7	64.2	63.6	64.0	63.5	64.2	63.1	63.9	64.1	64.8	64.0	64.0
Vermont	Burlington Int'l Airport	55.1	53.9	53.5	52.5	53.0	53.7	54.5	54.5	55.4	55.8	55.0	55.6
Virginia	Norfolk Int'l Airport	69.1	68.6	67.3	66.7	68.5	68.7	68.0	68.8	70.4	68.5	68.6	69.0
Virginia	Washington-Reagan National Airport	66.6	65.6	65.5	66.5	67.1	67.1	67.0	66.3	67.5	67.0	66.2	67.0
Washington	Seattle-Tacoma Int'l Airport	57.9	58.1	58.6	59.9	58.7	60.0	59.0	60.1	60.8	59.9	59.4	59.7
West Virginia	Charleston Int'l Airport	67.2	66.0	64.9	64.9	65.7	64.6	65.8	66.2	67.2	65.5	65.7	66.8
Wisconsin	Milwaukee-Mitchell Int'l Airport	55.4	55.4	54.7	54.4	53.9	54.1	54.4	55.8	56.8	56.0	56.0	56.1
Wyoming	Casper/Natrona County Int'l Airport	58.8	58.4	58.3	58.4	57.4	57.9	59.1	59.2	60.4	59.3	59.9	60.0

Note: na indicates that data is not available for one or more years in the five-year period.

Annual Mean Temperature

Five-Year Averages: 1950 - 2009

State	Weather Station	1950-1954	1955-1959	1960-1964	1965-1969	1970-1974	1975-1979	1980-1984	1985-1989	1990-1994	1995-1999	2000-2004	2005-2009
Alabama	Birmingham-Shuttlesworth Int'l Airport	63.3	62.9	62.5	61.0	62.1	61.6	62.1	62.2	63.0	63.2	63.0	na
Alaska	Anchorage Int'l Airport	na	34.3	35.2	na	33.9	37.5	36.8	37.1	36.5	36.4	38.4	36.5
Arizona	Phoenix Sky Harbor Int'l Airport	71.0	70.9	70.1	70.2	71.9	72.9	74.3	75.6	74.8	74.2	75.6	75.8
Arkansas	Little Rock National Airport	62.9	62.5	61.5	61.1	62.0	61.3	61.9	62.0	62.7	63.2	62.3	63.3
California	Los Angeles Int'l Airport	61.3	64.0	61.9	62.8	62.6	63.3	63.8	63.0	63.7	63.5	62.7	63.2
California	San Francisco Int'l Airport	55.8	57.6	56.6	56.5	56.6	56.8	57.6	58.0	58.3	58.1	58.4	57.9
Colorado	Denver Stapleton Int'l Airport	51.0	50.6	49.7	49.7	49.8	50.4	50.7	50.8	51.3	na	51.3	na
Connecticut	Bridgeport-Sikorsky Memorial Airport	52.4	51.6	50.7	51.3	52.3	51.9	51.5	51.6	52.8	52.5	52.2	52.9
Delaware	Wilmington-New Castle Airport	54.6	54.0	53.1	53.4	55.2	53.6	54.1	54.5	55.6	54.7	54.4	55.3
Florida	Jacksonville Int'l Airport	69.9	69.6	68.9	68.8	68.8	67.4	68.0	68.6	69.6	68.6	68.3	68.6
Florida	Miami Int'l Airport	75.7	75.4	75.4	75.2	76.3	75.8	75.9	76.5	77.7	77.1	77.1	77.5
Georgia	Atlanta Hartsfield Int'l Airport	62.5	62.4	60.3	59.8	61.4	60.6	61.8	62.7	63.6	62.7	62.4	62.9
Hawaii	Honolulu Int'l Airport	na	75.7	76.8	na	77.0	77.0	77.3	77.8	77.8	77.9	78.2	na
Idaho	Boise Air Terminal	50.9	50.5	50.9	51.8	51.8	50.5	50.0	50.5	51.4	52.8	53.2	53.0
Illinois	Chicago O'Hare Int'l Airport	na	na	48.3	48.7	49.9	49.1	48.5	49.3	49.9	50.1	50.0	50.3
Indiana	Indianapolis Int'l Airport	52.7	52.2	51.3	52.1	52.7	51.7	52.3	52.6	53.4	53.2	53.3	53.9
Iowa	Des Moines Int'l Airport	49.5	49.9	48.9	48.7	49.9	49.8	50.5	50.5	50.3	50.1	51.0	51.2
Kansas	Wichita Mid-Continent Airport	na	56.5	56.5	56.1	55.6	55.8	56.3	56.6	na	56.8	57.3	57.5
Kentucky	Lexington Bluegrass Airport	56.0	55.3	54.5	54.3	55.2	54.2	54.9	55.4	56.0	55.3	55.5	55.9
Louisiana	New Orleans Int'l Airport	69.2	69.1	67.4	67.2	68.5	67.9	68.4	68.3	68.9	69.7	69.7	70.3
Maine	Portland Int'l Jetport	45.8	44.9	44.3	44.9	45.4	44.8	45.9	45.8	46.5	46.5	46.2	46.8
Maryland	Baltimore/Washington Int'l Airport	55.8	55.0	54.1	54.5	55.6	55.6	54.9	55.4	56.3	55.8	55.2	56.0
Massachusetts	Boston Logan Int'l Airport	52.2	51.3	50.7	50.4	51.3	52.0	51.6	50.8	52.1	51.8	51.4	51.7
Michigan	Detroit Metro Airport	na	na	48.0	48.4	48.8	48.1	48.3	49.4	50.5	50.3	50.3	50.6
Minnesota	Minneapolis-Saint Paul Int'l Airport	44.6	45.6	44.1	43.7	44.1	44.7	45.3	45.8	45.5	45.8	46.7	47.1
Mississippi	Jackson Int'l Airport	na	na	na	63.4	65.4	63.8	64.6	64.6	65.1	65.0	64.7	65.5
Missouri	St Louis-Lambert Int'l Airport	56.6	56.2	54.7	54.8	55.3	54.4	55.9	56.7	57.7	56.7	57.2	57.4
Montana	Billings Logan Int'l Airport	46.7	46.9	47.9	46.4	46.0	45.8	48.3	47.9	48.3	47.5	48.3	48.5
Nebraska	Omaha Eppley Airfield	51.0	51.4	50.9	50.8	51.0	50.9	49.4	na	50.9	na	51.8	51.5
Nevada	Las Vegas-McCarran Int'l Airport	na	na	65.9	66.0	66.0	67.1	67.0	67.8	67.8	68.4	69.5	70.2
New Hampshire	Concord Municipal Airport	46.6	na	45.7	44.8	44.7	44.7	45.6	45.5	46.3	46.8	46.3	46.5
New Jersey	Newark Int'l Airport	54.4	54.0	53.8	53.7	55.2	54.0	54.7	55.1	56.4	55.3	55.0	55.5
New Mexico	Albuquerque Int'l Airport	58.1	57.4	56.1	56.0	55.8	56.1	56.9	56.6	57.3	57.7	58.3	58.0
New York	Buffalo Niagara Int'l Airport	48.8	48.4	47.0	47.2	47.7	47.3	47.8	48.3	48.8	48.5	48.3	49.0
New York	New York LaGuardia Airport	55.5	54.8	54.0	54.0	54.2	53.8	54.4	54.9	56.2	56.1	55.6	56.6
North Carolina	Charlotte Douglas Int'l Airport	61.2	61.2	59.8	59.1	59.8	59.8	59.6	61.1	62.5	61.1	60.1	60.7
North Dakota	Fargo Hector Int'l Airport	40.2	41.3	41.8	39.3	40.2	40.3	41.6	42.1	42.4	41.7	42.2	42.4
Ohio	Columbus Intl Airport	52.8	52.7	51.1	51.0	52.0	50.9	51.5	52.3	53.4	53.4	53.1	53.9
Oklahoma	Oklahoma City-Will Rogers World Arpt	60.7	59.3	59.8	60.0	59.6	59.5	60.1	60.2	na	60.8	60.4	61.8
Oregon	Portland Int'l Airport	52.4	52.5	52.3	53.5	53.8	53.2	54.2	54.0	54.7	54.7	54.6	54.2
Pennsylvania	Philadelphia Int'l Airport	55.7	54.6	52.7	53.4	55.2	54.5	54.2	54.9	56.8	56.0	55.9	56.4
Rhode Island	Providence TF Green Airport	na	50.1	49.8	49.7	50.7	50.2	51.1	50.7	51.9	51.8	51.4	52.1
South Carolina	Columbia Metro Airport	64.2	63.8	62.9	62.1	64.2	62.8	62.2	63.6	64.5	63.9	63.9	64.2
South Dakota	Sioux Falls Foss Field	44.8	46.0	45.9	44.4	45.0	44.9	46.2	46.3	46.3	45.5	46.4	46.6
Tennessee	Memphis Int'l Airport	62.4	61.7	60.9	61.0	61.9	62.2	62.8	62.6	63.1	62.9	62.9	63.8
Texas	Dallas-Fort Worth Int'l Airport	na	65.6	65.4	65.1	65.6	64.9	65.3	65.4	66.1	66.6	66.2	68.0
Texas	El Paso Int'l Airport	64.8	64.4	63.7	63.4	63.1	62.9	63.9	62.6	64.9	65.0	65.2	65.7
Texas	Houston Intercontinental Airport	na	na	na	na	68.2	66.9	68.8	68.9	69.5	69.7	69.6	70.4
Utah	Salt Lake City Int'l Airport	51.7	51.5	50.8	51.3	51.7	52.2	52.5	52.6	52.7	53.5	53.2	52.9
Vermont	Burlington Int'l Airport	45.8	44.6	43.1	42.9	43.7	44.6	45.4	45.0	45.7	46.5	45.7	46.4
Virginia	Norfolk Int'l Airport	60.2	59.9	58.6	58.1	60.2	59.8	59.4	60.1	61.5	60.4	60.6	60.9
Virginia	Washington-Reagan National Airport	57.7	57.2	56.4	56.9	58.1	58.4	58.5	57.6	58.6	58.3	57.8	58.5
Washington	Seattle-Tacoma Int'l Airport	49.9	50.6	51.1	52.5	51.5	52.5	51.9	52.2	53.0	52.7	52.2	52.3
West Virginia	Charleston Int'l Airport	56.2	55.3	54.3	54.0	55.3	54.2	55.0	55.6	56.6	55.1	55.4	56.2
Wisconsin	Milwaukee-Mitchell Int'l Airport	47.0	46.6	45.7	45.9	45.9	46.0	46.3	47.5	48.9	48.2	48.2	48.5
Wyoming	Casper/Natrona County Int'l Airport	44.9	45.6	45.5	44.9	44.4	44.6	45.6	45.6	46.9	45.7	45.9	45.6

Note: na indicates that data is not available for one or more years in the five-year period.

Annual Mean Minimum Temperature

Five-Year Averages: 1950 - 2009

State	Weather Station	1950-1954	1955-1959	1960-1964	1965-1969	1970-1974	1975-1979	1980-1984	1985-1989	1990-1994	1995-1999	2000-2004	2005-2009
Alabama	Birmingham-Shuttlesworth Int'l Airport	51.7	52.0	51.4	49.7	51.2	51.0	50.7	50.8	51.8	52.2	52.6	na
Alaska	Anchorage Int'l Airport	na	26.5	28.0	na	27.2	30.8	30.2	30.4	29.5	29.5	31.8	30.1
Arizona	Phoenix Sky Harbor Int'l Airport	56.0	57.7	55.6	55.6	58.0	59.8	62.4	63.4	63.1	62.4	64.0	64.2
Arkansas	Little Rock National Airport	52.3	52.7	50.1	50.2	51.2	50.8	51.7	51.3	52.4	52.8	52.2	52.9
California	Los Angeles Int'l Airport	53.4	55.8	54.3	55.7	55.5	55.8	56.7	55.6	56.4	56.4	55.9	56.4
California	San Francisco Int'l Airport	47.3	48.8	48.2	48.3	48.5	48.5	49.4	49.7	50.3	50.7	51.1	50.4
Colorado	Denver Stapleton Int'l Airport	37.2	37.4	35.3	35.2	35.2	36.5	37.7	37.2	37.6	na	37.0	na
Connecticut	Bridgeport-Sikorsky Memorial Airport	44.1	43.4	42.6	43.5	44.5	44.6	43.5	43.5	44.7	44.9	44.7	45.2
Delaware	Wilmington-New Castle Airport	44.6	44.6	43.4	44.0	46.1	44.2	44.4	45.2	46.1	45.5	45.4	46.1
Florida	Jacksonville Int'l Airport	59.5	59.6	58.8	58.9	58.0	56.5	56.9	57.7	59.0	58.1	57.5	57.7
Florida	Miami Int'l Airport	67.9	67.8	68.2	68.2	70.0	69.6	68.6	68.8	70.7	70.2	70.2	70.5
Georgia	Atlanta Hartsfield Int'l Airport	52.5	52.8	50.4	49.8	51.4	50.3	51.9	53.0	54.1	53.1	53.0	53.5
Hawaii	Honolulu Int'l Airport	na	69.3	70.2	na	70.0	69.6	70.0	70.0	70.6	70.9	71.9	na
Idaho	Boise Air Terminal	39.0	38.9	39.1	39.9	40.6	38.6	38.5	37.9	38.9	41.4	42.0	41.8
Illinois	Chicago O'Hare Int'l Airport	na	na	38.3	39.1	41.1	39.6	38.7	39.5	40.6	41.1	40.9	41.5
Indiana	Indianapolis Int'l Airport	42.4	42.5	41.2	42.2	43.0	41.8	42.6	42.7	43.9	43.8	44.1	44.8
Iowa	Des Moines Int'l Airport	39.4	39.8	39.2	38.8	40.5	39.9	40.9	40.1	40.6	40.9	41.3	41.7
Kansas	Wichita Mid-Continent Airport	na	45.5	45.7	44.8	44.5	44.0	45.3	45.4	na	46.0	46.2	46.3
Kentucky	Lexington Bluegrass Airport	45.5	45.4	44.5	44.6	45.5	44.5	45.5	45.5	46.4	45.6	46.1	46.3
Louisiana	New Orleans Int'l Airport	59.8	60.6	57.5	57.4	58.8	58.5	59.1	59.2	59.5	60.9	61.2	61.8
Maine	Portland Int'l Jetport	35.3	34.5	34.1	35.0	36.2	35.0	36.3	36.2	37.1	37.3	37.1	37.7
Maryland	Baltimore/Washington Int'l Airport	45.9	45.5	43.5	44.3	46.1	45.8	45.1	45.6	46.2	45.5	45.3	46.0
Massachusetts	Boston Logan Int'l Airport	44.3	43.5	42.8	43.2	43.7	44.2	43.9	43.1	44.2	44.4	44.0	44.4
Michigan	Detroit Metro Airport	na	na	37.9	38.8	39.5	38.2	38.7	40.3	41.6	41.6	41.8	41.9
Minnesota	Minneapolis-Saint Paul Int'l Airport	35.4	36.3	33.9	34.1	34.9	35.0	36.2	36.1	36.3	36.5	38.1	38.5
Mississippi	Jackson Int'l Airport	na	na	na	51.4	54.0	52.5	53.0	52.9	53.7	53.9	53.7	54.1
Missouri	St Louis-Lambert Int'l Airport	46.5	46.7	44.6	44.7	45.0	44.3	46.8	47.3	48.9	47.7	48.0	48.1
Montana	Billings Logan Int'l Airport	35.1	35.4	36.4	35.3	34.9	34.4	37.0	36.4	36.7	36.3	37.0	37.1
Nebraska	Omaha Eppley Airfield	40.5	41.0	40.5	39.7	39.9	39.6	38.9	na	39.9	na	41.0	40.8
Nevada	Las Vegas-McCarran Int'l Airport	na	na	52.5	52.9	53.0	53.7	54.9	54.9	55.8	56.9	58.5	59.5
New Hampshire	Concord Municipal Airport	34.8	na	33.7	32.8	33.0	32.4	33.8	33.9	34.4	35.5	34.8	35.1
New Jersey	Newark Int'l Airport	45.7	45.5	45.4	45.5	47.4	46.0	46.4	46.6	47.7	47.0	46.8	47.1
New Mexico	Albuquerque Int'l Airport	44.7	44.5	42.8	42.2	41.6	41.7	42.7	43.4	43.9	45.1	46.2	45.8
New York	Buffalo Niagara Int'l Airport	40.2	40.0	38.2	39.0	39.7	39.3	39.7	40.0	40.4	40.4	40.4	41.0
New York	New York LaGuardia Airport	48.1	47.6	47.0	47.4	47.4	47.1	47.7	47.8	48.8	49.4	48.8	49.8
North Carolina	Charlotte Douglas Int'l Airport	50.0	50.1	48.9	48.6	49.4	49.5	49.4	50.8	52.5	50.7	49.2	49.5
North Dakota	Fargo Hector Int'l Airport	29.9	30.9	30.6	28.4	29.9	30.0	31.6	31.5	32.0	31.7	31.9	32.4
Ohio	Columbus Intl Airport	42.2	42.4	40.7	41.2	42.6	41.4	41.9	42.3	43.5	43.9	44.1	44.7
Oklahoma	Oklahoma City-Will Rogers World Arpt	49.3	48.5	48.8	48.8	48.4	48.0	48.9	49.8	na	49.7	49.4	50.4
Oregon	Portland Int'l Airport	43.5	43.7	43.3	44.0	44.4	44.3	45.6	44.8	45.5	46.4	46.0	45.6
Pennsylvania	Philadelphia Int'l Airport	46.5	45.7	43.0	44.2	46.6	45.4	45.3	45.5	47.8	47.3	47.5	47.8
Rhode Island	Providence TF Green Airport	na	41.2	40.7	40.5	41.6	41.2	42.0	41.4	42.5	42.9	42.5	43.3
South Carolina	Columbia Metro Airport	51.8	52.1	50.9	50.1	52.2	50.6	50.0	51.4	52.6	52.4	52.7	52.9
South Dakota	Sioux Falls Foss Field	33.5	34.3	34.5	32.7	33.7	33.8	35.5	34.8	35.6	34.9	35.3	36.0
Tennessee	Memphis Int'l Airport	51.7	51.8	50.9	51.2	52.5	52.9	53.7	53.0	53.6	53.6	53.7	54.3
Texas	Dallas-Fort Worth Int'l Airport	na	55.1	54.4	54.5	54.9	53.9	54.6	54.6	55.8	56.3	56.2	57.4
Texas	El Paso Int'l Airport	51.4	51.6	50.3	50.0	48.6	48.2	49.8	47.9	51.2	51.6	52.5	52.8
Texas	Houston Intercontinental Airport	na	na	na	na	57.5	55.7	58.5	58.6	59.5	59.0	59.8	60.3
Utah	Salt Lake City Int'l Airport	39.8	38.8	37.9	38.7	39.7	40.2	41.8	41.2	41.2	42.1	42.4	41.8
Vermont	Burlington Int'l Airport	36.5	35.2	32.6	33.3	34.5	35.5	36.2	35.4	36.0	37.2	36.4	37.2
Virginia	Norfolk Int'l Airport	51.3	51.3	49.8	49.5	51.7	50.7	50.7	51.4	52.6	52.2	52.5	52.6
Virginia	Washington-Reagan National Airport	48.7	48.6	47.3	47.3	49.0	49.7	49.9	48.9	49.6	49.6	49.4	50.1
Washington	Seattle-Tacoma Int'l Airport	41.7	43.1	43.5	45.0	44.4	44.9	44.7	44.4	45.2	45.3	44.9	44.9
West Virginia	Charleston Int'l Airport	45.1	44.6	43.6	43.1	44.8	43.7	44.1	45.0	45.9	44.5	45.0	45.5
Wisconsin	Milwaukee-Mitchell Int'l Airport	38.6	37.8	36.6	37.2	37.9	37.8	38.1	39.3	41.0	40.5	40.3	40.8
Wyoming	Casper/Natrona County Int'l Airport	33.0	32.8	32.7	31.4	31.3	31.3	32.0	31.9	33.4	32.0	31.7	31.3

Note: na indicates that data is not available for one or more years in the five-year period.

Annual Extreme Maximum Temperature

Five-Year Averages: 1950 - 2009

State	Weather Station	1950-1954	1955-1959	1960-1964	1965-1969	1970-1974	1975-1979	1980-1984	1985-1989	1990-1994	1995-1999	2000-2004	2005-2009
Alabama	Birmingham-Shuttlesworth Int'l Airport	106	100	102	102	101	105	106	101	103	103	103	105
Alaska	Anchorage Int'l Airport	na	81	80	na	80	82	76	82	80	80	84	79
Arizona	Phoenix Sky Harbor Int'l Airport	118	118	114	115	116	117	116	118	122	121	117	118
Arkansas	Little Rock National Airport	107	104	108	105	105	104	109	112	106	107	109	106
California	Los Angeles Int'l Airport	101	108	110	101	102	105	104	106	98	97	101	96
California	San Francisco Int'l Airport	94	97	106	98	103	100	100	105	100	95	105	97
Colorado	Denver Stapleton Int'l Airport	102	99	100	100	103	99	100	103	104	na	102	na
Connecticut	Bridgeport-Sikorsky Memorial Airport	99	103	97	100	97	96	97	95	98	100	100	97
Delaware	Wilmington-New Castle Airport	102	102	98	102	100	97	100	100	100	100	99	97
Florida	Jacksonville Int'l Airport	103	100	99	100	99	100	103	102	100	103	103	98
Florida	Miami Int'l Airport	98	97	95	96	96	94	98	98	98	98	95	98
Georgia	Atlanta Hartsfield Int'l Airport	103	99	98	98	98	98	105	102	102	102	101	104
Hawaii	Honolulu Int'l Airport	na	92	91	na	92	93	94	94	95	94	96	93
Idaho	Boise Air Terminal	105	106	111	107	105	108	106	108	109	108	110	107
Illinois	Chicago O'Hare Int'l Airport	na	na	99	97	97	98	102	104	101	104	96	102
Indiana	Indianapolis Int'l Airport	104	96	97	99	99	96	100	103	97	99	96	96
Iowa	Des Moines Int'l Airport	103	105	100	100	104	103	108	104	97	101	101	100
Kansas	Wichita Mid-Continent Airport	na	107	110	106	107	109	112	110	na	108	109	109
Kentucky	Lexington Bluegrass Airport	103	96	98	98	97	94	103	103	99	103	99	102
Louisiana	New Orleans Int'l Airport	100	97	97	98	98	97	102	100	100	100	101	101
Maine	Portland Int'l Jetport	96	97	94	96	96	103	95	97	98	97	95	95
Maryland	Baltimore/Washington Int'l Airport	102	102	100	102	99	100	105	104	102	102	100	102
Massachusetts	Boston Logan Int'l Airport	100	100	98	98	99	102	99	99	99	100	101	98
Michigan	Detroit Metro Airport	na	na	97	98	99	102	96	104	99	100	99	97
Minnesota	Minneapolis-Saint Paul Int'l Airport	98	100	99	99	101	100	100	105	100	101	99	101
Mississippi	Jackson Int'l Airport	na	na	na	103	102	99	106	105	103	104	107	106
Missouri	St Louis-Lambert Int'l Airport	115	100	105	106	103	101	107	103	102	103	104	105
Montana	Billings Logan Int'l Airport	103	104	105	103	102	104	105	104	103	105	108	106
Nebraska	Omaha Eppley Airfield	108	107	107	99	110	103	107	na	106	na	104	105
Nevada	Las Vegas-McCarran Int'l Airport	na	na	113	114	116	116	114	116	115	116	115	117
New Hampshire	Concord Municipal Airport	99	na	99	102	96	101	98	96	98	101	99	98
New Jersey	Newark Int'l Airport	105	101	100	105	100	102	101	101	105	104	105	102
New Mexico	Albuquerque Int'l Airport	102	104	103	102	105	105	105	103	107	103	104	100
New York	Buffalo Niagara Int'l Airport	98	95	94	94	90	92	93	97	95	97	93	95
New York	New York LaGuardia Airport	102	101	97	107	97	99	99	99	101	103	104	102
North Carolina	Charlotte Douglas Int'l Airport	104	102	100	99	98	100	103	103	100	100	99	104
North Dakota	Fargo Hector Int'l Airport	99	102	100	100	99	106	102	106	96	100	98	102
Ohio	Columbus Intl Airport	104	100	98	97	95	96	101	101	99	100	96	97
Oklahoma	Oklahoma City-Will Rogers World Arpt	107	107	106	108	107	106	110	109	na	110	108	107
Oregon	Portland Int'l Airport	99	102	104	107	104	105	107	105	103	101	103	106
Pennsylvania	Philadelphia Int'l Airport	102	101	100	104	99	100	99	102	101	103	101	98
Rhode Island	Providence TF Green Airport	na	97	97	96	95	104	100	97	102	na	100	100
South Carolina	Columbia Metro Airport	107	104	102	106	104	105	107	106	106	104	104	107
South Dakota	Sioux Falls Foss Field	102	103	101	106	108	106	102	110	104	107	101	100
Tennessee	Memphis Int'l Airport	106	103	101	103	100	100	108	104	101	102	107	106
Texas	Dallas-Fort Worth Int'l Airport	na	107	108	104	106	108	113	107	106	110	111	107
Texas	El Paso Int'l Airport	107	107	109	106	108	112	110	108	114	108	106	107
Texas	Houston Intercontinental Airport	na	na	na	na	100	102	107	102	104	105	109	104
Utah	Salt Lake City Int'l Airport	102	102	107	102	104	104	101	104	106	106	107	105
Vermont	Burlington Int'l Airport	99	97	97	98	94	99	96	97	97	100	99	96
Virginia	Norfolk Int'l Airport	103	99	101	99	97	102	104	100	103	101	98	102
Virginia	Washington-Reagan National Airport	103	101	100	101	98	100	103	104	101	105	100	102
Washington	Seattle-Tacoma Int'l Airport	96	97	99	98	95	98	99	98	100	97	96	103
West Virginia	Charleston Int'l Airport	102	97	96	97	99	96	99	104	100	98	96	104
Wisconsin	Milwaukee-Mitchell Int'l Airport	99	101	98	97	99	99	99	103	100	103	98	98
Wyoming	Casper/Natrona County Int'l Airport	104	100	96	99	101	102	101	102	102	103	101	104

Note: na indicates that data is not available for one or more years in the five-year period.

Annual Extreme Minimum Temperature

Five-Year Averages: 1950 - 2009

State	Weather Station	1950-1954	1955-1959	1960-1964	1965-1969	1970-1974	1975-1979	1980-1984	1985-1989	1990-1994	1995-1999	2000-2004	2005-2009
Alabama	Birmingham-Shuttlesworth Int'l Airport	5	3	-2	-4	5	3	-1	-6	2	4	7	12
Alaska	Anchorage Int'l Airport	na	-27	-30	-21	-28	-34	-23	-30	-24	-28	-18	-24
Arizona	Phoenix Sky Harbor Int'l Airport	17	26	20	21	19	26	34	28	26	32	32	29
Arkansas	Little Rock National Airport	-5	9	-4	2	6	4	0	-2	11	5	10	13
California	Los Angeles Int'l Airport	33	36	30	32	35	33	35	33	35	37	36	35
California	San Francisco Int'l Airport	28	30	29	29	24	29	31	31	27	31	35	32
Colorado	Denver Stapleton Int'l Airport	-25	-13	-25	-13	-18	-11	-21	-24	-25	na	-8	na
Connecticut	Bridgeport-Sikorsky Memorial Airport	-1	-5	-5	-3	4	0	-7	-2	-2	2	-2	2
Delaware	Wilmington-New Castle Airport	2	-4	-4	1	-2	-6	-14	-14	-5	0	4	1
Florida	Jacksonville Int'l Airport	23	17	12	20	19	19	11	7	24	19	19	20
Florida	Miami Int'l Airport	36	35	34	34	35	31	32	30	41	37	36	38
Georgia	Atlanta Hartsfield Int'l Airport	3	5	-3	-3	2	1	-5	-8	6	6	8	12
Hawaii	Honolulu Int'l Airport	na	55	54	52	53	53	53	54	54	53	57	57
Idaho	Boise Air Terminal	-17	-9	-12	2	-23	-14	-18	-15	-25	-2	1	-6
Illinois	Chicago O'Hare Int'l Airport	na	na	-19	-20	-17	-17	-26	-27	-21	-19	-9	-18
Indiana	Indianapolis Int'l Airport	-19	-13	-18	-12	-20	-20	-21	-23	-27	-12	-11	-12
Iowa	Des Moines Int'l Airport	-15	-20	-22	-23	-24	-19	-22	-22	-18	-26	-12	-19
Kansas	Wichita Mid-Continent Airport	na	-10	-12	-5	-9	-11	-21	-16	na	-7	0	-1
Kentucky	Lexington Bluegrass Airport	-15	-6	-21	-10	-11	-12	-17	-19	-20	-10	-7	-3
Louisiana	New Orleans Int'l Airport	19	25	14	18	17	19	14	11	26	16	25	28
Maine	Portland Int'l Jetport	-21	-20	-22	-22	-26	-20	-20	-13	-18	-13	-17	-16
Maryland	Baltimore/Washington Int'l Airport	5	-4	-7	-1	2	-3	-7	-6	-5	-1	5	2
Massachusetts	Boston Logan Int'l Airport	-1	-12	-4	-4	-3	-4	-7	-4	-4	0	-7	-2
Michigan	Detroit Metro Airport	na	na	-13	-8	-14	-18	-21	-15	-20	-10	-7	-15
Minnesota	Minneapolis-Saint Paul Int'l Airport	-29	-21	-32	-31	-34	-32	-29	-25	-27	-32	-24	-22
Mississippi	Jackson Int'l Airport	na	na	na	7	9	6	3	2	14	10	13	19
Missouri	St Louis-Lambert Int'l Airport	-7	-5	-11	-8	-10	-14	-15	-18	-8	-12	0	0
Montana	Billings Logan Int'l Airport	-27	-28	-26	-25	-27	-23	-32	-28	-26	-30	-17	-19
Nebraska	Omaha Eppley Airfield	-18	-15	-17	-17	-22	-21	-23	na	-13	na	-12	-16
Nevada	Las Vegas-McCarran Int'l Airport	na	na	8	15	12	17	19	16	11	20	23	23
New Hampshire	Concord Municipal Airport	-22	na	-27	-23	-29	-30	-33	-23	-28	-18	-20	-24
New Jersey	Newark Int'l Airport	5	0	-2	1	2	-2	-7	-8	-2	3	0	3
New Mexico	Albuquerque Int'l Airport	-5	3	-7	1	-17	-7	8	0	-7	3	10	5
New York	Buffalo Niagara Int'l Airport	-5	-12	-20	-11	-8	-18	-16	-10	-10	-10	-7	-6
New York	New York LaGuardia Airport	6	0	-2	1	6	-1	-1	-3	-3	4	2	5
North Carolina	Charlotte Douglas Int'l Airport	11	5	2	4	4	5	2	-5	6	7	8	9
North Dakota	Fargo Hector Int'l Airport	-36	-27	-34	-35	-33	-35	-31	-33	-33	-39	-36	-31
Ohio	Columbus Intl Airport	-14	-8	-15	-11	-12	-19	-16	-19	-22	-3	-6	-11
Oklahoma	Oklahoma City-Will Rogers World Arpt	-1	-4	-3	1	-1	-3	-3	-8	na	-3	6	6
Oregon	Portland Int'l Airport	-3	6	6	8	8	13	12	9	12	11	18	12
Pennsylvania	Philadelphia Int'l Airport	5	5	-5	4	1	-4	-7	-6	-5	3	4	3
Rhode Island	Providence TF Green Airport	na	-9	-6	-5	-5	-13	-12	-5	-3	-2	-6	-2
South Carolina	Columbia Metro Airport	12	4	6	7	5	9	4	-1	13	14	13	13
South Dakota	Sioux Falls Foss Field	-26	-26	-31	-30	-36	-28	-26	-29	-29	-29	-19	-26
Tennessee	Memphis Int'l Airport	-11	6	-13	2	6	8	0	-4	9	4	10	12
Texas	Dallas-Fort Worth Int'l Airport	na	7	4	9	8	9	5	-1	10	8	14	15
Texas	El Paso Int'l Airport	5	8	-8	9	3	1	10	6	15	6	13	13
Texas	Houston Intercontinental Airport	na	na	na	na	19	17	11	7	19	19	22	26
Utah	Salt Lake City Int'l Airport	-4	-14	-18	-3	-15	-8	-6	-14	-11	-12	-5	-2
Vermont	Burlington Int'l Airport	-22	-30	-26	-27	-25	-30	-27	-22	-29	-23	-20	-21
Virginia	Norfolk Int'l Airport	17	11	12	8	8	5	7	-3	5	11	15	15
Virginia	Washington-Reagan National Airport	11	5	3	7	3	2	-5	-4	-4	5	8	8
Washington	Seattle-Tacoma Int'l Airport	0	6	10	6	12	13	9	7	12	15	20	14
West Virginia	Charleston Int'l Airport	-2	-5	-12	-6	-7	-10	-13	-15	-16	-12	-2	-2
Wisconsin	Milwaukee-Mitchell Int'l Airport	-24	-17	-24	-23	-22	-18	-26	-25	-21	-26	-10	-12
Wyoming	Casper/Natrona County Int'l Airport	-26	-25	-31	-28	-40	-34	-39	-29	-41	-27	-30	-32

Note: na indicates that data is not available for one or more years in the five-year period.

Number of Days Annually Maximum Temperature ≥ 90°F

Five-Year Averages: 1950 - 2009

State	Weather Station	1950-1954	1955-1959	1960-1964	1965-1969	1970-1974	1975-1979	1980-1984	1985-1989	1990-1994	1995-1999	2000-2004	2005-2009
Alabama	Birmingham-Shuttlesworth Int'l Airport	na	66	68	37	42	48	62	57	61	72	46	66
Alaska	Anchorage Int'l Airport	na	na	na	na	na	na	na	na	na	na	na	na
Arizona	Phoenix Sky Harbor Int'l Airport	na	154	161	163	169	168	162	182	174	166	176	173
Arkansas	Little Rock National Airport	na	70	81	65	69	68	74	77	70	84	60	78
California	Los Angeles Int'l Airport	na	6	4	3	4	6	5	4	3	5	1	5
California	San Francisco Int'l Airport	na	3	3	1	4	4	6	4	1	3	6	4
Colorado	Denver Stapleton Int'l Airport	na	33	43	24	35	34	31	37	35	na	48	na
Connecticut	Bridgeport-Sikorsky Memorial Airport	na	11	3	6	6	3	6	6	10	7	5	6
Delaware	Wilmington-New Castle Airport	na	21	14	16	18	14	25	22	23	23	12	19
Florida	Jacksonville Int'l Airport	na	94	83	68	71	69	82	88	94	70	69	77
Florida	Miami Int'l Airport	na	43	49	40	26	23	71	93	89	87	74	97
Georgia	Atlanta Hartsfield Int'l Airport	na	43	24	19	21	30	48	50	48	46	29	41
Hawaii	Honolulu Int'l Airport	na	1	3	46	17	18	33	63	44	48	24	23
Idaho	Boise Air Terminal	na	44	46	46	50	41	39	50	51	47	54	61
Illinois	Chicago O'Hare Int'l Airport	na	na	16	11	13	17	20	22	15	19	12	14
Indiana	Indianapolis Int'l Airport	na	16	15	19	13	13	24	20	16	20	11	16
Iowa	Des Moines Int'l Airport	na	32	16	17	25	27	31	27	14	19	19	20
Kansas	Wichita Mid-Continent Airport	na	66	61	51	63	68	71	61	na	57	62	58
Kentucky	Lexington Bluegrass Airport	na	24	18	16	10	14	21	28	19	26	15	27
Louisiana	New Orleans Int'l Airport	na	65	66	54	66	73	75	67	84	80	73	88
Maine	Portland Int'l Jetport	na	5	3	4	4	4	4	5	5	4	4	4
Maryland	Baltimore/Washington Int'l Airport	na	31	29	36	26	27	30	32	33	34	21	32
Massachusetts	Boston Logan Int'l Airport	na	15	10	8	12	14	17	10	17	13	11	10
Michigan	Detroit Metro Airport	na	na	12	9	10	15	11	15	13	13	9	11
Minnesota	Minneapolis-Saint Paul Int'l Airport	na	20	15	12	16	18	14	18	6	10	13	16
Mississippi	Jackson Int'l Airport	na	na	na	73	84	73	87	91	85	85	69	89
Missouri	St Louis-Lambert Int'l Airport	na	48	36	33	41	43	44	45	43	41	37	45
Montana	Billings Logan Int'l Airport	na	31	31	26	30	26	36	29	27	25	36	34
Nebraska	Omaha Eppley Airfield	na	40	32	25	41	44	33	na	25	na	34	32
Nevada	Las Vegas-McCarran Int'l Airport	na	na	136	130	130	137	125	138	139	128	142	136
New Hampshire	Concord Municipal Airport	na	na	11	8	10	18	9	9	11	12	12	11
New Jersey	Newark Int'l Airport	na	27	22	21	23	18	24	29	35	22	22	25
New Mexico	Albuquerque Int'l Airport	75	71	67	57	63	67	77	50	64	52	65	57
New York	Buffalo Niagara Int'l Airport	na	9	4	2	0	3	1	5	3	2	2	4
New York	New York LaGuardia Airport	na	19	12	14	14	9	16	16	20	17	17	20
North Carolina	Charlotte Douglas Int'l Airport	na	64	46	31	26	36	35	51	51	44	29	45
North Dakota	Fargo Hector Int'l Airport	na	17	18	11	13	15	15	19	8	11	10	13
Ohio	Columbus Intl Airport	na	30	20	13	9	13	12	20	19	22	11	21
Oklahoma	Oklahoma City-Will Rogers World Arpt	na	70	70	65	70	70	75	63	na	71	67	79
Oregon	Portland Int'l Airport	na	7	7	10	18	9	10	16	15	13	11	16
Pennsylvania	Philadelphia Int'l Airport	na	25	14	19	20	21	22	29	33	28	22	24
Rhode Island	Providence TF Green Airport	na	9	5	6	7	7	17	9	10	11	8	10
South Carolina	Columbia Metro Airport	na	83	83	61	71	64	69	86	85	76	64	74
South Dakota	Sioux Falls Foss Field	na	32	24	20	26	28	24	25	15	15	18	13
Tennessee	Memphis Int'l Airport	na	62	60	53	54	66	70	73	67	69	61	80
Texas	Dallas-Fort Worth Int'l Airport	na	106	102	84	87	107	102	96	96	102	93	115
Texas	El Paso Int'l Airport	na	102	113	94	101	113	114	97	112	114	120	102
Texas	Houston Intercontinental Airport	na	na	na	na	82	93	102	100	105	111	103	116
Utah	Salt Lake City Int'l Airport	na	62	64	56	61	55	48	55	54	56	66	64
Vermont	Burlington Int'l Airport	na	6	4	4	4	9	4	7	7	8	7	5
Virginia	Norfolk Int'l Airport	na	41	29	23	22	34	32	43	42	32	28	31
Virginia	Washington-Reagan National Airport	na	33	32	42	33	35	41	38	42	40	22	35
Washington	Seattle-Tacoma Int'l Airport	na	3	3	2	3	2	1	4	4	3	2	4
West Virginia	Charleston Int'l Airport	na	22	17	19	14	14	25	29	24	16	10	28
Wisconsin	Milwaukee-Mitchell Int'l Airport	na	14	9	7	10	6	7	14	12	8	8	6
Wyoming	Casper/Natrona County Int'l Airport	na	27	23	25	25	24	38	34	32	32	40	40

Note: na indicates that data is not available for one or more years in the five-year period.

Number of Days Annually Maximum Temperature ≤ 32°F

Five-Year Averages: 1950 - 2009

State	Weather Station	1950-1954	1955-1959	1960-1964	1965-1969	1970-1974	1975-1979	1980-1984	1985-1989	1990-1994	1995-1999	2000-2004	2005-2009
Alabama	Birmingham-Shuttlesworth Int'l Airport	na	1	2	1	3	4	2	3	0	2	1	0
Alaska	Anchorage Int'l Airport	na	118	119	113	126	100	101	100	107	117	96	116
Arizona	Phoenix Sky Harbor Int'l Airport	na	0	0	0	0	0	0	0	0	0	0	0
Arkansas	Little Rock National Airport	na	3	6	4	6	9	7	6	2	4	3	1
California	Los Angeles Int'l Airport	na	0	0	0	0	0	0	0	0	0	0	0
California	San Francisco Int'l Airport	na	0	0	0	0	0	0	0	0	0	0	0
Colorado	Denver Stapleton Int'l Airport	na	22	27	18	21	20	23	26	17	na	18	na
Connecticut	Bridgeport-Sikorsky Memorial Airport	na	22	27	23	22	31	22	23	18	17	24	17
Delaware	Wilmington-New Castle Airport	na	17	21	18	14	25	18	18	11	15	17	13
Florida	Jacksonville Int'l Airport	na	0	0	0	0	0	0	0	0	0	0	0
Florida	Miami Int'l Airport	na	0	0	0	0	0	0	0	0	0	0	0
Georgia	Atlanta Hartsfield Int'l Airport	na	2	3	1	2	3	2	2	1	2	1	1
Hawaii	Honolulu Int'l Airport	na	0	0	0	0	0	0	0	0	0	0	0
Idaho	Boise Air Terminal	na	22	26	14	15	24	23	34	23	11	15	18
Illinois	Chicago O'Hare Int'l Airport	na	na	58	46	40	54	52	47	38	43	47	44
Indiana	Indianapolis Int'l Airport	na	31	41	35	29	42	33	34	21	30	29	27
Iowa	Des Moines Int'l Airport	na	56	63	58	51	62	48	45	42	51	45	44
Kansas	Wichita Mid-Continent Airport	na	21	24	20	21	29	24	22	na	18	17	16
Kentucky	Lexington Bluegrass Airport	na	19	25	22	19	30	21	22	13	19	20	18
Louisiana	New Orleans Int'l Airport	na	0	1	0	0	0	0	0	0	0	0	0
Maine	Portland Int'l Jetport	na	42	49	46	50	52	46	46	40	38	43	46
Maryland	Baltimore/Washington Int'l Airport	na	14	19	15	11	17	16	16	9	11	11	11
Massachusetts	Boston Logan Int'l Airport	na	27	32	27	26	29	31	26	24	20	26	25
Michigan	Detroit Metro Airport	na	na	53	44	45	56	51	46	35	40	44	45
Minnesota	Minneapolis-Saint Paul Int'l Airport	na	82	80	83	82	88	77	72	65	74	71	74
Mississippi	Jackson Int'l Airport	na	na	na	0	0	3	2	3	0	1	1	0
Missouri	St Louis-Lambert Int'l Airport	na	23	31	27	25	39	26	24	15	23	20	17
Montana	Billings Logan Int'l Airport	42	43	41	50	44	58	38	41	35	40	39	36
Nebraska	Omaha Eppley Airfield	na	43	50	44	39	51	49	na	38	na	38	40
Nevada	Las Vegas-McCarran Int'l Airport	na	na	0	0	0	0	0	0	0	0	0	0
New Hampshire	Concord Municipal Airport	na	na	44	48	53	60	47	50	44	40	45	49
New Jersey	Newark Int'l Airport	na	18	22	18	18	28	20	21	10	13	18	15
New Mexico	Albuquerque Int'l Airport	3	3	7	5	6	6	1	6	3	2	1	2
New York	Buffalo Niagara Int'l Airport	na	51	63	58	53	61	56	50	39	49	53	52
New York	New York LaGuardia Airport	na	19	24	21	20	30	23	22	13	12	18	13
North Carolina	Charlotte Douglas Int'l Airport	na	1	3	2	4	2	3	2	1	1	1	1
North Dakota	Fargo Hector Int'l Airport	na	100	92	104	104	112	96	93	84	100	94	91
Ohio	Columbus Intl Airport	na	28	42	36	32	48	34	32	18	26	33	28
Oklahoma	Oklahoma City-Will Rogers World Arpt	na	10	13	8	10	15	9	11	na	8	8	7
Oregon	Portland Int'l Airport	na	5	3	3	4	3	4	2	2	3	1	3
Pennsylvania	Philadelphia Int'l Airport	na	16	22	20	15	26	22	18	9	14	16	13
Rhode Island	Providence TF Green Airport	na	25	29	27	28	34	27	25	20	17	22	21
South Carolina	Columbia Metro Airport	na	0	1	1	1	0	1	1	0	0	0	0
South Dakota	Sioux Falls Foss Field	na	68	69	71	71	83	68	61	62	71	66	63
Tennessee	Memphis Int'l Airport	na	5	8	6	6	10	5	9	3	5	4	2
Texas	Dallas-Fort Worth Int'l Airport	na	1	4	1	2	5	4	4	1	4	2	1
Texas	El Paso Int'l Airport	na	0	1	0	1	0	0	1	0	0	0	0
Texas	Houston Intercontinental Airport	na	na	na	na	0	0	1	1	0	0	0	0
Utah	Salt Lake City Int'l Airport	na	17	32	24	23	19	21	29	22	12	27	25
Vermont	Burlington Int'l Airport	na	70	75	80	73	73	65	69	52	61	64	63
Virginia	Norfolk Int'l Airport	na	5	8	5	4	5	6	4	2	2	3	2
Virginia	Washington-Reagan National Airport	na	10	15	8	7	9	10	13	5	9	9	7
Washington	Seattle-Tacoma Int'l Airport	na	2	2	3	4	1	2	2	2	2	1	3
West Virginia	Charleston Int'l Airport	na	16	22	22	16	25	18	17	9	16	18	14
Wisconsin	Milwaukee-Mitchell Int'l Airport	na	58	71	59	62	71	60	55	41	50	51	54
Wyoming	Casper/Natrona County Int'l Airport	na	48	46	46	48	54	41	50	37	42	43	43

Note: na indicates that data is not available for one or more years in the five-year period.

Number of Days Annually Minimum Temperature ≤ 32°F

Five-Year Averages: 1950 - 2009

State	Weather Station	1950-1954	1955-1959	1960-1964	1965-1969	1970-1974	1975-1979	1980-1984	1985-1989	1990-1994	1995-1999	2000-2004	2005-2009
Alabama	Birmingham-Shuttlesworth Int'l Airport	na	55	54	71	51	59	59	61	48	51	50	43
Alaska	Anchorage Int'l Airport	na	208	200	187	198	179	198	193	194	196	185	191
Arizona	Phoenix Sky Harbor Int'l Airport	na	6	16	15	9	4	0	3	0	0	0	0
Arkansas	Little Rock National Airport	na	48	70	67	53	65	56	57	43	44	55	52
California	Los Angeles Int'l Airport	na	0	0	0	0	0	0	0	0	0	0	0
California	San Francisco Int'l Airport	na	1	3	4	3	2	0	1	1	1	0	0
Colorado	Denver Stapleton Int'l Airport	na	155	158	168	165	149	152	148	149	na	156	na
Connecticut	Bridgeport-Sikorsky Memorial Airport	na	105	107	108	99	93	99	105	93	94	95	95
Delaware	Wilmington-New Castle Airport	na	104	111	106	90	101	97	98	90	92	98	90
Florida	Jacksonville Int'l Airport	na	13	14	9	15	28	21	22	9	13	20	14
Florida	Miami Int'l Airport	na	0	0	0	0	0	0	0	0	0	0	0
Georgia	Atlanta Hartsfield Int'l Airport	na	38	57	66	53	63	47	44	28	38	42	39
Hawaii	Honolulu Int'l Airport	na	0	0	0	0	0	0	0	0	0	0	0
Idaho	Boise Air Terminal	na	134	128	124	106	121	118	129	129	104	111	112
Illinois	Chicago O'Hare Int'l Airport	na	na	143	134	117	131	139	132	127	123	122	122
Indiana	Indianapolis Int'l Airport	na	124	126	118	117	120	115	114	105	106	104	105
Iowa	Des Moines Int'l Airport	na	144	143	140	129	136	129	138	134	131	129	125
Kansas	Wichita Mid-Continent Airport	na	114	114	110	118	116	107	107	na	100	104	104
Kentucky	Lexington Bluegrass Airport	na	100	103	99	91	99	96	95	83	91	91	91
Louisiana	New Orleans Int'l Airport	na	7	20	20	15	18	12	13	6	7	6	2
Maine	Portland Int'l Jetport	na	159	169	158	150	159	149	150	146	144	147	145
Maryland	Baltimore/Washington Int'l Airport	na	99	109	107	88	93	95	94	93	93	102	92
Massachusetts	Boston Logan Int'l Airport	na	95	106	99	100	93	97	105	90	89	95	93
Michigan	Detroit Metro Airport	na	na	142	138	133	142	136	131	121	122	118	121
Minnesota	Minneapolis-Saint Paul Int'l Airport	na	153	166	159	157	153	151	156	161	153	145	147
Mississippi	Jackson Int'l Airport	na	na	na	56	38	58	51	51	39	40	45	40
Missouri	St Louis-Lambert Int'l Airport	na	96	109	106	104	108	97	92	75	87	87	88
Montana	Billings Logan Int'l Airport	156	155	143	150	159	153	141	142	141	141	148	142
Nebraska	Omaha Eppley Airfield	na	139	137	138	138	138	149	na	141	na	135	138
Nevada	Las Vegas-McCarran Int'l Airport	na	na	44	39	40	29	17	28	24	10	10	9
New Hampshire	Concord Municipal Airport	na	na	172	175	178	180	168	174	166	166	165	166
New Jersey	Newark Int'l Airport	na	91	92	92	77	88	83	87	74	79	82	84
New Mexico	Albuquerque Int'l Airport	99	103	118	116	123	128	124	105	109	89	89	89
New York	Buffalo Niagara Int'l Airport	na	135	143	133	134	134	128	126	124	128	123	124
New York	New York LaGuardia Airport	na	76	78	79	70	76	70	77	62	57	68	61
North Carolina	Charlotte Douglas Int'l Airport	na	59	74	79	66	67	68	59	35	52	70	65
North Dakota	Fargo Hector Int'l Airport	na	179	176	187	181	176	181	177	180	176	175	169
Ohio	Columbus Intl Airport	na	119	129	124	113	123	116	113	105	105	104	99
Oklahoma	Oklahoma City-Will Rogers World Arpt	na	83	87	81	77	86	76	70	na	67	74	69
Oregon	Portland Int'l Airport	na	48	49	38	38	49	31	45	38	23	28	38
Pennsylvania	Philadelphia Int'l Airport	na	89	111	105	87	94	96	95	76	77	83	81
Rhode Island	Providence TF Green Airport	na	120	122	125	121	119	110	119	108	109	111	110
South Carolina	Columbia Metro Airport	na	55	60	69	55	62	64	61	44	48	54	48
South Dakota	Sioux Falls Foss Field	na	167	166	174	168	167	162	166	167	172	162	162
Tennessee	Memphis Int'l Airport	na	58	69	66	51	59	48	53	40	40	48	45
Texas	Dallas-Fort Worth Int'l Airport	na	39	52	42	34	44	39	43	23	29	36	27
Texas	El Paso Int'l Airport	na	50	64	61	62	68	57	76	49	46	47	39
Texas	Houston Intercontinental Airport	na	na	na	na	21	31	15	17	9	14	12	7
Utah	Salt Lake City Int'l Airport	na	139	140	138	120	120	110	116	116	110	117	120
Vermont	Burlington Int'l Airport	na	155	176	168	161	152	146	152	148	147	151	144
Virginia	Norfolk Int'l Airport	na	52	68	66	40	62	55	56	38	37	45	43
Virginia	Washington-Reagan National Airport	na	72	81	85	65	68	61	72	61	61	67	64
Washington	Seattle-Tacoma Int'l Airport	na	43	39	25	28	34	26	35	30	22	23	33
West Virginia	Charleston Int'l Airport	na	98	104	111	97	104	103	97	86	101	97	94
Wisconsin	Milwaukee-Mitchell Int'l Airport	na	146	151	148	140	139	137	134	120	126	127	123
Wyoming	Casper/Natrona County Int'l Airport	na	177	172	189	186	183	178	178	170	181	187	185

Note: na indicates that data is not available for one or more years in the five-year period.

Number of Days Annually Minimum Temperature ≤ 0°F

Five-Year Averages: 1950 - 2009

State	Weather Station	1950-1954	1955-1959	1960-1964	1965-1969	1970-1974	1975-1979	1980-1984	1985-1989	1990-1994	1995-1999	2000-2004	2005-2009
Alabama	Birmingham-Shuttlesworth Int'l Airport	na	0	0	0	0	0	0	0	0	0	0	0
Alaska	Anchorage Int'l Airport	na	47	33	43	44	24	21	17	28	27	12	23
Arizona	Phoenix Sky Harbor Int'l Airport	na	0	0	0	0	0	0	0	0	0	0	0
Arkansas	Little Rock National Airport	na	0	0	0	0	0	0	0	0	0	0	0
California	Los Angeles Int'l Airport	na	0	0	0	0	0	0	0	0	0	0	0
California	San Francisco Int'l Airport	na	0	0	0	0	0	0	0	0	0	0	0
Colorado	Denver Stapleton Int'l Airport	na	5	14	8	11	7	7	10	5	na	3	na
Connecticut	Bridgeport-Sikorsky Memorial Airport	na	0	1	0	0	0	2	0	1	0	1	0
Delaware	Wilmington-New Castle Airport	na	0	1	0	0	1	3	1	0	0	0	0
Florida	Jacksonville Int'l Airport	na	0	0	0	0	0	0	0	0	0	0	0
Florida	Miami Int'l Airport	na	0	0	0	0	0	0	0	0	0	0	0
Georgia	Atlanta Hartsfield Int'l Airport	na	0	0	0	0	0	1	0	0	0	0	0
Hawaii	Honolulu Int'l Airport	na	0	0	0	0	0	0	0	0	0	0	0
Idaho	Boise Air Terminal	na	2	2	0	3	5	5	9	3	0	0	1
Illinois	Chicago O'Hare Int'l Airport	na	na	18	10	10	16	13	13	7	5	5	7
Indiana	Indianapolis Int'l Airport	na	4	12	5	6	13	9	7	3	3	3	2
Iowa	Des Moines Int'l Airport	na	13	21	13	15	22	15	17	10	12	8	11
Kansas	Wichita Mid-Continent Airport	na	1	3	1	4	5	6	4	na	1	0	0
Kentucky	Lexington Bluegrass Airport	na	2	4	3	3	4	4	4	1	1	0	0
Louisiana	New Orleans Int'l Airport	na	0	0	0	0	0	0	0	0	0	0	0
Maine	Portland Int'l Jetport	na	13	19	15	12	16	13	9	9	5	8	5
Maryland	Baltimore/Washington Int'l Airport	na	0	1	0	0	1	1	1	0	0	0	0
Massachusetts	Boston Logan Int'l Airport	na	1	1	1	0	1	2	0	0	0	1	0
Michigan	Detroit Metro Airport	na	na	8	4	6	11	9	7	3	2	2	3
Minnesota	Minneapolis-Saint Paul Int'l Airport	na	28	34	36	32	40	29	30	24	25	19	21
Mississippi	Jackson Int'l Airport	na	na	na	0	0	0	0	0	0	0	0	0
Missouri	St Louis-Lambert Int'l Airport	na	2	5	2	2	6	5	2	1	3	0	0
Montana	Billings Logan Int'l Airport	na	17	18	17	17	26	17	18	15	15	10	13
Nebraska	Omaha Eppley Airfield	na	11	18	10	16	21	18	na	9	na	7	10
Nevada	Las Vegas-McCarran Int'l Airport	na	na	0	0	0	0	0	0	0	0	0	0
New Hampshire	Concord Municipal Airport	na	na	21	22	23	31	23	18	16	9	15	12
New Jersey	Newark Int'l Airport	na	0	0	0	0	2	1	0	1	0	0	0
New Mexico	Albuquerque Int'l Airport	0	0	1	0	1	0	0	0	1	0	0	0
New York	Buffalo Niagara Int'l Airport	na	2	5	4	4	6	6	3	2	2	3	2
New York	New York LaGuardia Airport	na	0	0	0	0	0	0	0	1	0	0	0
North Carolina	Charlotte Douglas Int'l Airport	na	0	0	0	0	0	0	0	0	0	0	0
North Dakota	Fargo Hector Int'l Airport	na	52	54	58	52	59	46	48	39	45	41	43
Ohio	Columbus Intl Airport	na	4	7	4	3	9	5	4	2	2	1	2
Oklahoma	Oklahoma City-Will Rogers World Arpt	na	0	1	0	0	1	2	1	na	0	0	0
Oregon	Portland Int'l Airport	na	0	0	0	0	0	0	0	0	0	0	0
Pennsylvania	Philadelphia Int'l Airport	na	0	1	0	0	2	1	0	0	0	0	0
Rhode Island	Providence TF Green Airport	na	2	3	3	3	4	3	1	0	0	1	0
South Carolina	Columbia Metro Airport	na	0	0	0	0	0	0	0	0	0	0	0
South Dakota	Sioux Falls Foss Field	na	31	33	37	31	40	27	29	23	26	22	25
Tennessee	Memphis Int'l Airport	na	0	1	0	0	0	0	0	0	0	0	0
Texas	Dallas-Fort Worth Int'l Airport	na	0	0	0	0	0	0	0	0	0	0	0
Texas	El Paso Int'l Airport	na	0	0	0	0	0	0	0	0	0	0	0
Texas	Houston Intercontinental Airport	na	na	na	na	0	0	0	0	0	0	0	0
Utah	Salt Lake City Int'l Airport	na	2	5	0	5	1	1	2	3	1	0	0
Vermont	Burlington Int'l Airport	na	24	29	27	29	26	22	24	21	14	17	16
Virginia	Norfolk Int'l Airport	na	0	0	0	0	0	0	0	0	0	0	0
Virginia	Washington-Reagan National Airport	na	0	0	0	0	0	0	0	0	0	0	0
Washington	Seattle-Tacoma Int'l Airport	na	0	0	0	0	0	0	0	0	0	0	0
West Virginia	Charleston Int'l Airport	na	1	4	0	1	2	3	2	1	0	0	0
Wisconsin	Milwaukee-Mitchell Int'l Airport	na	14	17	13	16	16	14	12	6	7	4	6
Wyoming	Casper/Natrona County Int'l Airport	na	17	18	18	16	25	18	20	13	17	12	14

Note: na indicates that data is not available for one or more years in the five-year period.

Number of Annual Heating Degree Days

Five-Year Averages: 1950 - 2009

State	Weather Station	1950-1954	1955-1959	1960-1964	1965-1969	1970-1974	1975-1979	1980-1984	1985-1989	1990-1994	1995-1999	2000-2004	2005-2009
Alabama	Birmingham-Shuttlesworth Int'l Airport	na	2730	2881	3042	2733	2979	2933	2850	2565	2635	2653	na
Alaska	Anchorage Int'l Airport	na	11104	10793	10646	11276	9929	10198	10077	10289	10361	9635	10281
Arizona	Phoenix Sky Harbor Int'l Airport	na	1327	1564	1499	1328	1152	872	895	924	936	896	843
Arkansas	Little Rock National Airport	na	3004	3310	3208	3016	3263	3221	3086	2843	2846	3004	2789
California	Los Angeles Int'l Airport	na	1153	1589	1365	1422	1257	1166	1214	1123	1215	1330	1275
California	San Francisco Int'l Airport	na	2780	3121	3113	3127	3044	2801	2582	2536	2594	2540	2659
Colorado	Denver Stapleton Int'l Airport	na	5887	6162	6045	6077	5901	5920	5826	5608	na	5747	na
Connecticut	Bridgeport-Sikorsky Memorial Airport	na	5586	5748	5690	5369	5436	5592	5549	5220	5264	5387	5195
Delaware	Wilmington-New Castle Airport	na	5031	5222	5170	4662	5108	5020	4905	4534	4763	4841	4623
Florida	Jacksonville Int'l Airport	na	1230	1347	1331	1184	1567	1432	1371	1117	1271	1376	1270
Florida	Miami Int'l Airport	na	208	208	186	151	203	190	186	51	131	122	85
Georgia	Atlanta Hartsfield Int'l Airport	na	2766	3235	3239	2831	3112	2988	2715	2433	2642	2674	2624
Hawaii	Honolulu Int'l Airport	na	na	na	na	na	na	na	0	0	0	0	na
Idaho	Boise Air Terminal	na	5978	5880	5529	5579	5869	5997	6016	5691	5251	5292	5392
Illinois	Chicago O'Hare Int'l Airport	na	na	6764	6539	6270	6602	6750	6501	6206	6231	6164	6165
Indiana	Indianapolis Int'l Airport	na	5592	5844	5610	5405	5813	5649	5510	5140	5295	5211	5131
Iowa	Des Moines Int'l Airport	na	6517	6762	6710	6459	6604	6369	6298	6190	6341	6050	6052
Kansas	Wichita Mid-Continent Airport	na	4739	4748	4659	4897	4918	4936	4613	na	4526	4453	4357
Kentucky	Lexington Bluegrass Airport	na	4713	4923	4881	4542	4981	4797	4700	4372	4616	4533	4478
Louisiana	New Orleans Int'l Airport	na	1319	1659	1619	1359	1632	1466	1421	1269	1225	1308	1129
Maine	Portland Int'l Jetport	na	7549	7687	7529	7407	7591	7252	7246	7033	6983	7102	6925
Maryland	Baltimore/Washington Int'l Airport	na	4758	4992	4941	4521	4586	4792	4684	4370	4511	4644	4469
Massachusetts	Boston Logan Int'l Airport	na	5723	5810	5897	5660	5446	5685	5769	5412	5467	5608	5522
Michigan	Detroit Metro Airport	na	na	6712	6589	6482	6753	6674	6365	5968	6091	6044	6004
Minnesota	Minneapolis-Saint Paul Int'l Airport	na	7766	8173	8253	8199	8078	7808	7709	7606	7615	7365	7310
Mississippi	Jackson Int'l Airport	na	na	na	2568	2152	2558	2474	2365	2180	2259	2322	2164
Missouri	St Louis-Lambert Int'l Airport	na	4711	5085	4969	4824	5223	4870	4613	4237	4509	4395	4390
Montana	Billings Logan Int'l Airport	na	7112	6831	7231	7422	7445	6715	6745	6552	6862	6729	6623
Nebraska	Omaha Eppley Airfield	na	6114	6227	6139	6169	6306	6699	na	6063	na	5910	6045
Nevada	Las Vegas-McCarran Int'l Airport	na	na	2590	2456	2622	2299	2211	2163	2210	1937	2005	1801
New Hampshire	Concord Municipal Airport	na	na	7370	7644	7706	7793	7421	7418	7171	7005	7201	7117
New Jersey	Newark Int'l Airport	na	5056	5070	5155	4710	5031	4917	4824	4439	4639	4746	4638
New Mexico	Albuquerque Int'l Airport	na	4165	4490	4399	4514	4439	4300	4138	4099	3919	3908	3903
New York	Buffalo Niagara Int'l Airport	na	6585	6940	6921	6722	6898	6738	6565	6376	6485	6510	6369
New York	New York LaGuardia Airport	na	4849	4984	5030	4905	4993	4902	4740	4421	4398	4585	4355
North Carolina	Charlotte Douglas Int'l Airport	na	3122	3467	3531	3293	3346	3457	3169	2718	3032	3233	3125
North Dakota	Fargo Hector Int'l Airport	na	9102	8985	9697	9430	9494	9003	8861	8625	8963	8775	8687
Ohio	Columbus Intl Airport	na	5435	5840	5822	5459	5938	5703	5508	5127	5214	5214	5069
Oklahoma	Oklahoma City-Will Rogers World Arpt	na	3870	3792	3601	3721	3820	3762	3595	na	3429	3523	3218
Oregon	Portland Int'l Airport	na	4730	4803	4465	4441	4568	4227	4340	4117	4115	4154	4325
Pennsylvania	Philadelphia Int'l Airport	na	4879	5314	5198	4732	4917	5025	4820	4278	4482	4528	4424
Rhode Island	Providence TF Green Airport	na	5978	6013	6114	5866	5952	5745	5797	5431	5444	5622	5445
South Carolina	Columbia Metro Airport	na	2552	2774	2827	2334	2664	2878	2633	2297	2485	2520	2400
South Dakota	Sioux Falls Foss Field	na	7734	7690	8053	7942	8048	7571	7535	7438	7727	7440	7351
Tennessee	Memphis Int'l Airport	na	3181	3432	3309	3064	3125	3075	3054	2796	2874	2902	2762
Texas	Dallas-Fort Worth Int'l Airport	na	2497	2572	2364	2269	2601	2518	2427	2172	2184	2244	1943
Texas	El Paso Int'l Airport	na	2456	2722	2630	2589	2729	2585	2724	2362	2337	2418	2164
Texas	Houston Intercontinental Airport	na	na	na	na	1476	1811	1543	1523	1318	1331	1386	1212
Utah	Salt Lake City Int'l Airport	na	5814	6146	5818	5801	5591	5551	5595	5538	5230	5512	5621
Vermont	Burlington Int'l Airport	na	7839	8245	8310	8115	7843	7565	7657	7426	7161	7435	7205
Virginia	Norfolk Int'l Airport	na	3409	3718	3801	3189	3441	3558	3416	2990	3224	3214	3153
Virginia	Washington-Reagan National Airport	na	4226	4446	4303	3932	3932	3942	4187	3826	3911	3987	3877
Washington	Seattle-Tacoma Int'l Airport	na	5266	5136	4679	5008	4669	4823	4750	4492	4599	4767	4749
West Virginia	Charleston Int'l Airport	na	4574	4827	4872	4446	4861	4670	4523	4158	4533	4422	4283
Wisconsin	Milwaukee-Mitchell Int'l Airport	na	7230	7466	7368	7398	7393	7295	6961	6482	6716	6664	6616
Wyoming	Casper/Natrona County Int'l Airport	na	7470	7478	7588	7834	7757	7478	7440	6961	7371	7384	7427

Note: na indicates that data is not available for one or more years in the five-year period.

Number of Annual Cooling Degree Days

Five-Year Averages: 1950 - 2009

State	Weather Station	1950-1954	1955-1959	1960-1964	1965-1969	1970-1974	1975-1979	1980-1984	1985-1989	1990-1994	1995-1999	2000-2004	2005-2009
Alabama	Birmingham-Shuttlesworth Int'l Airport	na	na	na	na	na	na	1970	1918	1948	2083	2042	na
Alaska	Anchorage Int'l Airport	na	na	na	na	na	na	1	2	4	2	8	3
Arizona	Phoenix Sky Harbor Int'l Airport	na	na	na	na	na	na	4380	4853	4599	4390	4887	4883
Arkansas	Little Rock National Airport	na	na	na	na	na	na	2197	2127	2110	2312	2127	2291
California	Los Angeles Int'l Airport	na	na	na	na	na	na	833	579	753	742	577	710
California	San Francisco Int'l Airport	na	na	na	na	na	na	175	129	170	167	204	162
Colorado	Denver Stapleton Int'l Airport	na	na	na	na	na	na	786	767	737	na	846	na
Connecticut	Bridgeport-Sikorsky Memorial Airport	na	na	na	na	na	na	772	767	888	827	837	885
Delaware	Wilmington-New Castle Airport	na	na	na	na	na	na	1150	1197	1225	1127	1080	1209
Florida	Jacksonville Int'l Airport	na	na	na	na	na	na	2620	2789	2888	2701	2662	2676
Florida	Miami Int'l Airport	na	na	na	na	na	na	4271	4472	4775	4651	4621	4731
Georgia	Atlanta Hartsfield Int'l Airport	na	na	na	na	na	na	1913	1994	2039	1919	1821	1974
Hawaii	Honolulu Int'l Airport	na	na	na	na	na	na	4597	4773	4775	4808	4908	na
Idaho	Boise Air Terminal	na	na	na	na	na	na	637	823	847	895	1079	1143
Illinois	Chicago O'Hare Int'l Airport	na	na	na	na	na	na	822	877	801	896	802	925
Indiana	Indianapolis Int'l Airport	na	na	na	na	na	na	1106	1112	1038	1100	1064	1193
Iowa	Des Moines Int'l Airport	na	na	na	na	na	na	1185	1121	945	1008	1055	1135
Kansas	Wichita Mid-Continent Airport	na	na	na	na	na	na	1859	1677	na	1648	1769	1719
Kentucky	Lexington Bluegrass Airport	na	na	na	na	na	na	1235	1290	1194	1189	1171	1286
Louisiana	New Orleans Int'l Airport	na	na	na	na	na	na	2828	2745	2797	3049	3128	3166
Maine	Portland Int'l Jetport	na	na	na	na	na	na	372	362	409	363	359	389
Maryland	Baltimore/Washington Int'l Airport	na	na	na	na	na	na	1221	1306	1314	1262	1166	1287
Massachusetts	Boston Logan Int'l Airport	na	na	na	na	na	na	900	707	829	775	752	797
Michigan	Detroit Metro Airport	na	na	na	na	na	na	676	796	788	841	783	869
Minnesota	Minneapolis-Saint Paul Int'l Airport	na	na	na	na	na	na	736	820	601	724	814	912
Mississippi	Jackson Int'l Airport	na	na	na	na	na	na	2436	2332	2302	2351	2332	2437
Missouri	St Louis-Lambert Int'l Airport	na	na	na	na	na	na	1667	1716	1691	1599	1643	1724
Montana	Billings Logan Int'l Airport	na	na	na	na	na	na	728	646	557	577	744	722
Nebraska	Omaha Eppley Airfield	na	na	na	na	na	na	1096	na	1031	na	1194	1220
Nevada	Las Vegas-McCarran Int'l Airport	na	na	na	na	na	na	3041	3289	3359	3302	3770	3786
New Hampshire	Concord Municipal Airport	na	na	na	na	na	na	437	433	481	479	481	479
New Jersey	Newark Int'l Airport	na	na	na	na	na	na	1261	1315	1437	1222	1199	1280
New Mexico	Albuquerque Int'l Airport	na	na	na	na	na	na	1447	1191	1379	1380	1558	1451
New York	Buffalo Niagara Int'l Airport	na	na	na	na	na	na	573	594	595	563	526	641
New York	New York LaGuardia Airport	na	na	na	na	na	na	1138	1184	1311	1280	1259	1402
North Carolina	Charlotte Douglas Int'l Airport	na	na	na	na	na	na	1601	1838	1921	1708	1541	1669
North Dakota	Fargo Hector Int'l Airport	na	na	na	na	na	na	553	630	497	576	549	559
Ohio	Columbus Intl Airport	na	na	na	na	na	na	890	985	1009	1084	991	1120
Oklahoma	Oklahoma City-Will Rogers World Arpt	na	na	na	na	na	na	2071	1951	na	1993	1940	2161
Oregon	Portland Int'l Airport	na	na	na	na	na	na	357	423	468	468	458	495
Pennsylvania	Philadelphia Int'l Airport	na	na	na	na	na	na	1178	1258	1411	1303	1324	1388
Rhode Island	Providence TF Green Airport	na	na	na	na	na	na	786	689	772	763	741	843
South Carolina	Columbia Metro Airport	na	na	na	na	na	na	1942	2220	2233	2179	2206	2215
South Dakota	Sioux Falls Foss Field	na	na	na	na	na	na	811	836	719	710	753	763
Tennessee	Memphis Int'l Airport	na	na	na	na	na	na	2382	2285	2218	2224	2264	2453
Texas	Dallas-Fort Worth Int'l Airport	na	na	na	na	na	na	2745	2673	2668	2886	2778	3137
Texas	El Paso Int'l Airport	na	na	na	na	na	na	2306	1972	2446	2423	2603	2509
Texas	Houston Intercontinental Airport	na	na	na	na	na	na	3038	3055	3067	3129	3163	3296
Utah	Salt Lake City Int'l Airport	na	na	na	na	na	na	1089	1194	1159	1137	1336	1334
Vermont	Burlington Int'l Airport	na	na	na	na	na	na	493	484	509	532	502	539
Virginia	Norfolk Int'l Airport	na	na	na	na	na	na	1608	1746	1820	1655	1711	1756
Virginia	Washington-Reagan National Airport	na	na	na	na	na	na	1669	1603	1597	1589	1477	1638
Washington	Seattle-Tacoma Int'l Airport	na	na	na	na	na	na	124	198	221	186	177	225
West Virginia	Charleston Int'l Airport	na	na	na	na	na	na	1126	1218	1198	1012	1009	1180
Wisconsin	Milwaukee-Mitchell Int'l Airport	na	na	na	na	na	na	568	712	734	704	644	708
Wyoming	Casper/Natrona County Int'l Airport	na	na	na	na	na	na	504	481	475	426	513	462

Note: na indicates that data is not available for one or more years in the five-year period.

Annual Precipitation (in.)

Five-Year Averages: 1950 - 2009

State	Weather Station	1950-1954	1955-1959	1960-1964	1965-1969	1970-1974	1975-1979	1980-1984	1985-1989	1990-1994	1995-1999	2000-2004	2005-2009
Alabama	Birmingham-Shuttlesworth Int'l Airport	50.72	50.70	55.64	55.47	56.83	56.39	54.96	46.96	51.20	57.91	61.66	52.28
Alaska	Anchorage Int'l Airport	na	15.89	16.48	13.62	13.35	15.79	17.08	18.25	16.13	15.53	16.38	16.44
Arizona	Phoenix Sky Harbor Int'l Airport	6.91	7.35	5.02	8.09	7.27	7.54	10.08	7.22	10.49	7.13	6.44	6.06
Arkansas	Little Rock National Airport	46.78	54.88	42.27	49.41	53.81	53.02	50.88	51.31	53.20	43.56	46.29	53.54
California	Los Angeles Int'l Airport	10.84	11.20	10.17	13.08	10.63	13.68	16.80	8.94	12.33	17.08	11.78	10.26
California	San Francisco Int'l Airport	18.63	21.37	18.89	22.11	19.88	18.06	25.83	14.78	17.96	24.95	21.05	18.09
Colorado	Denver Stapleton Int'l Airport	13.71	17.36	12.95	17.92	15.71	14.25	15.48	15.77	15.70	na	14.28	na
Connecticut	Bridgeport-Sikorsky Memorial Airport	43.02	39.16	32.30	37.93	51.89	44.99	43.27	38.66	42.12	41.59	43.00	46.92
Delaware	Wilmington-New Castle Airport	42.71	42.83	37.17	36.24	45.07	45.60	41.34	40.03	42.63	40.91	46.18	44.80
Florida	Jacksonville Int'l Airport	51.18	50.64	52.24	55.68	57.31	49.09	47.61	51.60	58.27	53.44	51.51	52.96
Florida	Miami Int'l Airport	52.91	62.11	52.10	72.32	52.16	52.07	58.61	51.96	64.65	68.40	64.31	61.75
Georgia	Atlanta Hartsfield Int'l Airport	43.17	44.56	53.60	49.34	48.90	50.94	50.41	49.15	56.31	46.81	45.67	49.54
Hawaii	Honolulu Int'l Airport	na	26.49	19.59	32.02	21.47	18.32	19.47	19.77	15.65	16.64	16.02	16.67
Idaho	Boise Air Terminal	11.78	12.20	11.97	10.03	11.64	12.40	15.26	11.13	10.20	12.90	9.85	10.88
Illinois	Chicago O'Hare Int'l Airport	na	na	28.36	34.50	37.96	34.64	41.18	35.19	36.53	34.07	35.31	39.05
Indiana	Indianapolis Int'l Airport	41.48	41.20	38.07	37.87	38.87	41.21	38.53	41.74	42.91	40.89	44.69	45.83
Iowa	Des Moines Int'l Airport	30.17	26.50	32.36	27.68	35.77	32.41	36.83	31.86	40.26	32.73	29.95	38.27
Kansas	Wichita Mid-Continent Airport	na	27.78	34.20	28.43	29.75	28.00	28.05	31.05	na	36.03	32.02	39.08
Kentucky	Lexington Bluegrass Airport	45.76	46.12	43.73	41.38	52.17	49.70	38.62	40.26	46.87	48.90	49.24	46.30
Louisiana	New Orleans Int'l Airport	53.37	59.33	55.60	53.21	64.77	67.56	66.12	61.29	69.99	57.49	63.30	57.08
Maine	Portland Int'l Jetport	48.09	36.82	40.30	41.68	45.51	49.08	46.75	40.88	46.49	46.52	39.50	58.78
Maryland	Baltimore/Washington Int'l Airport	43.39	40.14	40.80	36.18	44.94	46.43	38.01	39.14	39.36	42.38	44.88	45.58
Massachusetts	Boston Logan Int'l Airport	48.07	50.17	41.36	39.48	42.72	41.68	42.72	40.71	44.66	41.91	41.27	46.78
Michigan	Detroit Metro Airport	na	na	28.39	34.39	29.84	31.46	33.80	34.41	34.26	30.99	34.42	33.66
Minnesota	Minneapolis-Saint Paul Int'l Airport	26.31	23.76	24.31	29.37	24.65	29.59	31.20	28.57	32.27	30.02	30.64	28.48
Mississippi	Jackson Int'l Airport	na	na	na	46.36	55.13	64.26	61.69	48.25	54.02	53.55	59.36	50.93
Missouri	St Louis-Lambert Int'l Airport	29.56	35.73	33.69	35.64	36.07	34.84	44.90	37.29	40.32	38.88	40.39	41.43
Montana	Billings Logan Int'l Airport	12.00	16.01	14.17	15.23	16.29	16.48	14.80	13.04	14.57	14.46	10.34	13.90
Nebraska	Omaha Eppley Airfield	28.66	29.35	32.51	32.39	29.79	28.85	28.84	na	33.54	na	27.78	31.18
Nevada	Las Vegas-McCarran Int'l Airport	na	na	2.81	4.31	4.18	5.74	4.89	3.00	5.06	4.24	4.71	3.22
New Hampshire	Concord Municipal Airport	42.83	na	33.25	34.92	37.21	37.32	39.60	35.89	35.66	39.27	38.59	52.37
New Jersey	Newark Int'l Airport	44.81	40.63	38.73	37.36	44.01	49.05	47.74	45.26	44.53	45.26	44.56	49.11
New Mexico	Albuquerque Int'l Airport	5.44	8.28	7.45	9.08	9.03	8.50	8.74	10.03	10.82	9.17	7.85	9.95
New York	Buffalo Niagara Int'l Airport	36.98	39.52	32.74	35.47	36.48	43.62	38.57	41.51	43.21	38.41	39.20	42.04
New York	New York LaGuardia Airport	47.88	43.72	38.94	36.53	43.96	46.58	43.59	43.09	42.68	43.23	45.38	49.93
North Carolina	Charlotte Douglas Int'l Airport	38.42	42.83	43.40	39.52	44.37	49.44	40.79	39.93	44.19	42.61	41.62	41.06
North Dakota	Fargo Hector Int'l Airport	17.92	19.73	19.34	19.02	21.00	20.97	18.59	18.30	20.69	23.93	24.84	25.92
Ohio	Columbus Intl Airport	36.22	36.73	32.27	38.57	40.89	38.66	37.28	36.17	39.00	38.85	43.65	40.94
Oklahoma	Oklahoma City-Will Rogers World Arpt	26.84	35.55	31.34	28.01	33.92	30.84	34.45	41.34	na	35.09	32.33	36.26
Oregon	Portland Int'l Airport	41.30	37.00	36.74	36.47	40.77	33.85	40.89	29.85	32.26	47.10	31.42	33.75
Pennsylvania	Philadelphia Int'l Airport	42.04	39.50	37.93	38.60	44.09	46.71	43.07	39.22	37.90	40.12	42.43	45.06
Rhode Island	Providence TF Green Airport	47.05	43.82	43.56	39.31	47.56	50.24	47.60	44.32	44.95	43.89	44.82	53.42
South Carolina	Columbia Metro Airport	42.37	44.55	51.17	47.77	58.37	51.49	44.67	46.33	49.40	42.47	41.87	43.95
South Dakota	Sioux Falls Foss Field	25.13	22.84	24.92	23.91	24.53	24.89	24.31	22.25	27.61	24.73	26.62	27.66
Tennessee	Memphis Int'l Airport	50.45	56.22	47.70	44.88	56.37	56.02	55.64	49.97	51.90	60.45	56.75	48.49
Texas	Dallas-Fort Worth Int'l Airport	na	32.79	30.34	35.48	36.96	29.74	34.49	31.08	43.59	34.26	38.18	33.34
Texas	El Paso Int'l Airport	6.41	9.12	7.08	7.34	8.77	8.07	11.04	9.93	10.34	8.20	6.99	11.80
Texas	Houston Intercontinental Airport	na	na	na	na	51.26	48.88	47.86	42.07	51.00	46.10	57.87	52.91
Utah	Salt Lake City Int'l Airport	14.16	13.79	14.19	16.23	17.85	14.93	20.52	13.80	14.95	17.68	14.49	14.78
Vermont	Burlington Int'l Airport	33.22	35.30	30.24	31.41	36.81	35.14	38.26	32.68	34.64	37.42	34.77	40.84
Virginia	Norfolk Int'l Airport	42.48	49.02	48.71	39.17	44.52	47.86	44.60	42.26	44.85	47.47	49.16	47.71
Virginia	Washington-Reagan National Airport	43.22	38.09	36.17	36.24	41.71	42.31	37.08	37.43	37.18	40.16	41.34	43.70
Washington	Seattle-Tacoma Int'l Airport	41.98	41.45	39.54	38.25	40.37	34.04	37.65	32.23	35.31	44.53	34.08	38.38
West Virginia	Charleston Int'l Airport	45.45	42.66	40.95	37.28	44.31	46.50	42.03	42.73	43.51	45.30	48.21	42.74
Wisconsin	Milwaukee-Mitchell Int'l Airport	32.12	27.80	28.53	31.21	32.12	33.76	36.18	35.87	35.67	32.13	32.62	35.43
Wyoming	Casper/Natrona County Int'l Airport	10.22	11.51	10.02	11.63	13.01	12.81	14.46	12.18	12.84	13.05	9.50	12.85

Note: na indicates that data is not available for one or more years in the five-year period.

Annual Extreme Maximum Daily Precipitation (in.)

Five-Year Averages: 1950 - 2009

State	Weather Station	1950-1954	1955-1959	1960-1964	1965-1969	1970-1974	1975-1979	1980-1984	1985-1989	1990-1994	1995-1999	2000-2004	2005-2009
Alabama	Birmingham-Shuttlesworth Int'l Airport	5.89	3.85	5.46	4.55	6.91	4.61	4.41	5.47	2.80	6.94	9.75	4.01
Alaska	Anchorage Int'l Airport	na	2.00	1.62	1.21	1.09	1.23	1.32	2.71	1.30	2.76	1.57	1.32
Arizona	Phoenix Sky Harbor Int'l Airport	na	1.52	1.50	1.73	2.43	1.24	1.98	2.32	1.66	1.59	1.53	1.40
Arkansas	Little Rock National Airport	3.98	7.68	3.97	6.79	7.58	8.10	5.11	6.23	4.08	3.02	3.11	5.05
California	Los Angeles Int'l Airport	3.28	4.56	3.91	5.60	2.25	2.27	2.63	2.66	3.23	3.50	4.53	1.98
California	San Francisco Int'l Airport	1.81	2.99	2.62	4.07	2.39	2.21	5.59	1.83	2.34	3.16	2.60	2.64
Colorado	Denver Stapleton Int'l Airport	2.06	2.34	1.80	3.25	3.27	1.71	2.68	1.76	1.98	na	3.81	na
Connecticut	Bridgeport-Sikorsky Memorial Airport	3.69	4.76	4.46	3.69	6.18	4.30	4.79	3.45	4.66	5.28	3.99	5.30
Delaware	Wilmington-New Castle Airport	5.18	3.23	4.65	4.43	4.15	3.89	2.76	6.63	2.72	8.29	5.72	4.36
Florida	Jacksonville Int'l Airport	6.78	6.47	4.15	7.82	7.35	5.40	4.80	6.40	7.83	6.14	6.07	6.80
Florida	Miami Int'l Airport	7.88	7.02	6.41	5.67	4.22	11.51	7.25	3.90	8.59	6.81	12.56	4.63
Georgia	Atlanta Hartsfield Int'l Airport	na	5.30	3.73	4.34	4.64	4.44	3.65	4.90	4.32	6.68	4.93	5.14
Hawaii	Honolulu Int'l Airport	na	15.32	6.40	6.40	4.75	7.47	3.71	7.89	2.85	4.51	5.43	3.81
Idaho	Boise Air Terminal	1.13	1.91	1.09	1.27	0.84	1.73	1.60	0.79	1.77	0.97	0.90	0.91
Illinois	Chicago O'Hare Int'l Airport	na	na	2.88	4.25	2.55	3.48	4.47	6.49	3.14	3.44	4.45	6.64
Indiana	Indianapolis Int'l Airport	3.27	3.88	3.80	4.00	2.29	4.46	2.41	5.09	4.15	3.51	7.20	3.81
Iowa	Des Moines Int'l Airport	2.76	3.10	4.42	2.18	3.80	6.18	3.18	3.45	4.23	3.23	3.55	4.15
Kansas	Wichita Mid-Continent Airport	na	4.14	3.74	4.65	3.18	2.72	2.82	3.76	na	5.79	2.78	10.31
Kentucky	Lexington Bluegrass Airport	3.08	2.57	3.89	3.56	3.11	4.30	3.03	3.38	4.99	5.56	3.36	4.76
Louisiana	New Orleans Int'l Airport	6.18	9.85	5.37	4.49	5.39	8.52	6.41	4.33	6.47	5.64	7.67	6.07
Maine	Portland Int'l Jetport	7.49	3.05	7.49	4.03	5.21	3.59	3.48	3.32	7.75	11.74	3.36	5.03
Maryland	Baltimore/Washington Int'l Airport	5.85	4.91	3.42	3.82	4.04	4.39	3.26	5.00	2.62	5.02	4.45	4.37
Massachusetts	Boston Logan Int'l Airport	5.63	7.06	3.00	3.51	3.15	2.52	4.12	3.58	4.21	6.11	4.29	3.84
Michigan	Detroit Metro Airport	na	na	3.21	3.19	2.81	3.08	2.61	2.23	2.73	4.34	3.71	2.97
Minnesota	Minneapolis-Saint Paul Int'l Airport	2.44	3.00	2.16	2.39	2.39	7.28	2.91	9.15	2.59	3.71	2.95	4.61
Mississippi	Jackson Int'l Airport	na	na	na	4.10	4.87	6.35	4.95	3.95	4.72	6.49	7.38	4.07
Missouri	St Louis-Lambert Int'l Airport	4.16	3.95	2.60	2.78	2.87	4.79	3.37	3.15	2.96	5.59	3.31	4.58
Montana	Billings Logan Int'l Airport	2.83	2.44	1.88	2.19	1.67	2.53	2.11	1.50	2.06	2.91	2.27	1.62
Nebraska	Omaha Eppley Airfield	2.82	3.27	3.31	6.24	3.53	2.35	3.07	na	4.07	na	3.05	3.37
Nevada	Las Vegas-McCarran Int'l Airport	na	na	1.07	1.09	1.01	1.56	1.36	0.83	1.29	1.29	1.13	0.94
New Hampshire	Concord Municipal Airport	3.56	na	4.12	2.16	3.71	2.18	2.43	2.25	3.84	3.53	2.42	5.12
New Jersey	Newark Int'l Airport	3.64	3.44	3.15	4.71	5.93	6.73	3.29	3.15	2.97	6.22	3.10	6.18
New Mexico	Albuquerque Int'l Airport	1.61	1.92	1.64	1.74	1.08	0.93	1.75	1.39	1.45	1.45	1.92	1.47
New York	Buffalo Niagara Int'l Airport	2.28	2.55	3.88	3.41	2.33	4.89	2.42	5.01	2.78	1.89	3.24	3.55
New York	New York LaGuardia Airport	3.32	6.40	3.63	3.12	4.73	4.20	3.73	4.00	2.74	4.63	3.85	6.69
North Carolina	Charlotte Douglas Int'l Airport	3.40	3.59	3.45	3.26	3.47	4.51	2.37	3.26	4.21	6.88	4.14	5.36
North Dakota	Fargo Hector Int'l Airport	3.93	3.37	2.69	2.85	2.95	4.02	3.10	1.92	4.42	3.03	4.64	3.33
Ohio	Columbus Intl Airport	2.88	4.79	3.40	2.25	2.28	2.66	2.55	2.85	5.13	3.17	3.06	2.51
Oklahoma	Oklahoma City-Will Rogers World Arpt	4.52	4.52	3.37	3.11	7.53	3.21	5.60	5.38	na	3.79	3.90	6.28
Oregon	Portland Int'l Airport	2.43	1.99	2.31	2.23	2.42	1.84	2.08	2.33	2.44	2.69	2.05	2.53
Pennsylvania	Philadelphia Int'l Airport	3.46	3.29	4.60	4.69	4.77	3.99	4.40	4.38	3.45	6.63	4.68	5.53
Rhode Island	Providence TF Green Airport	na	3.28	5.39	3.73	4.23	6.31	5.15	3.37	3.06	3.57	2.66	4.38
South Carolina	Columbia Metro Airport	4.23	5.79	4.20	5.06	5.40	3.95	2.95	3.81	4.84	5.17	4.47	3.77
South Dakota	Sioux Falls Foss Field	2.91	4.26	1.78	4.02	4.54	4.59	3.99	2.40	3.35	2.68	4.22	3.27
Tennessee	Memphis Int'l Airport	3.42	3.69	3.54	3.48	4.08	5.42	4.04	5.65	3.84	4.48	5.88	3.48
Texas	Dallas-Fort Worth Int'l Airport	na	4.85	3.00	4.71	3.30	4.05	3.63	3.38	4.22	3.81	4.39	3.90
Texas	El Paso Int'l Airport	na	2.00	1.77	1.65	2.26	1.69	2.20	1.46	1.64	1.15	1.37	2.84
Texas	Houston Intercontinental Airport	na	na	na	na	7.47	8.16	9.25	10.34	4.56	4.81	8.13	7.73
Utah	Salt Lake City Int'l Airport	1.62	1.46	2.28	1.38	2.19	1.62	2.27	1.57	1.53	1.48	1.40	1.10
Vermont	Burlington Int'l Airport	2.58	3.59	2.48	2.04	2.60	2.36	3.11	2.69	2.46	3.62	2.21	2.42
Virginia	Norfolk Int'l Airport	3.46	6.48	7.41	4.72	3.81	4.31	4.13	2.86	5.86	6.23	4.39	8.92
Virginia	Washington-Reagan National Airport	3.74	5.44	4.83	4.35	6.11	4.76	2.31	3.17	2.29	3.67	2.46	5.19
Washington	Seattle-Tacoma Int'l Airport	2.98	3.41	1.64	2.26	2.70	1.76	2.72	2.98	2.95	3.06	5.02	3.77
West Virginia	Charleston Int'l Airport	2.38	4.13	5.60	2.76	2.34	2.91	2.60	2.07	2.47	3.44	4.15	3.10
Wisconsin	Milwaukee-Mitchell Int'l Airport	3.04	2.72	2.79	2.34	2.78	3.01	2.37	6.81	2.45	4.23	4.42	4.93
Wyoming	Casper/Natrona County Int'l Airport	2.07	0.98	1.90	1.22	1.82	1.96	2.14	2.15	1.74	2.06	2.22	2.21

Note: na indicates that data is not available for one or more years in the five-year period.

Number of Days Annually With ≥ 0.1 Inches of Precipitation

Five-Year Averages: 1950 - 2009

State	Weather Station	1950-1954	1955-1959	1960-1964	1965-1969	1970-1974	1975-1979	1980-1984	1985-1989	1990-1994	1995-1999	2000-2004	2005-2009
Alabama	Birmingham-Shuttlesworth Int'l Airport	na	79	78	80	91	79	79	75	81	84	83	77
Alaska	Anchorage Int'l Airport	na	42	52	45	44	49	50	54	47	42	51	50
Arizona	Phoenix Sky Harbor Int'l Airport	na	16	15	20	15	18	25	15	22	16	17	15
Arkansas	Little Rock National Airport	na	68	66	70	76	75	68	70	76	70	72	68
California	Los Angeles Int'l Airport	na	22	14	19	18	26	30	18	21	24	20	21
California	San Francisco Int'l Airport	na	38	34	39	38	34	44	28	35	48	38	41
Colorado	Denver Stapleton Int'l Airport	na	41	31	43	38	35	41	43	42	na	33	na
Connecticut	Bridgeport-Sikorsky Memorial Airport	na	76	64	67	78	79	76	70	79	76	72	82
Delaware	Wilmington-New Castle Airport	na	76	69	63	73	80	70	70	73	71	77	72
Florida	Jacksonville Int'l Airport	na	74	74	74	80	78	70	77	81	78	76	71
Florida	Miami Int'l Airport	na	86	75	95	84	82	83	81	89	93	84	83
Georgia	Atlanta Hartsfield Int'l Airport	na	77	76	79	80	78	77	74	80	77	73	73
Hawaii	Honolulu Int'l Airport	na	29	35	42	37	28	30	32	26	29	23	28
Idaho	Boise Air Terminal	na	37	38	36	39	41	50	38	37	43	35	33
Illinois	Chicago O'Hare Int'l Airport	na	na	59	69	77	67	79	68	70	64	64	73
Indiana	Indianapolis Int'l Airport	na	78	70	72	79	77	78	74	79	74	75	80
Iowa	Des Moines Int'l Airport	na	52	60	56	65	57	72	57	72	61	56	70
Kansas	Wichita Mid-Continent Airport	na	48	49	50	52	49	52	51	na	54	51	54
Kentucky	Lexington Bluegrass Airport	na	82	75	79	90	90	80	76	85	80	85	83
Louisiana	New Orleans Int'l Airport	na	79	76	75	85	84	76	78	82	73	76	75
Maine	Portland Int'l Jetport	na	75	70	74	81	83	76	78	77	81	74	87
Maryland	Baltimore/Washington Int'l Airport	na	70	68	63	78	77	70	68	74	73	78	73
Massachusetts	Boston Logan Int'l Airport	na	83	71	73	82	78	74	75	76	73	75	83
Michigan	Detroit Metro Airport	na	na	65	66	70	75	73	75	74	68	75	74
Minnesota	Minneapolis-Saint Paul Int'l Airport	na	50	55	61	na	61	65	60	65	63	59	56
Mississippi	Jackson Int'l Airport	na	na	na	71	80	80	71	73	78	73	78	70
Missouri	St Louis-Lambert Int'l Airport	na	66	65	68	67	67	72	63	70	69	67	74
Montana	Billings Logan Int'l Airport	na	46	36	42	43	43	43	36	37	40	34	35
Nebraska	Omaha Eppley Airfield	na	48	58	53	57	56	57	na	63	na	51	55
Nevada	Las Vegas-McCarran Int'l Airport	na	na	9	12	13	11	12	7	14	11	13	9
New Hampshire	Concord Municipal Airport	na	na	68	72	78	77	74	75	74	81	78	86
New Jersey	Newark Int'l Airport	na	77	76	70	75	85	70	75	81	73	74	79
New Mexico	Albuquerque Int'l Airport	na	21	23	26	24	27	27	27	30	26	22	26
New York	Buffalo Niagara Int'l Airport	na	90	81	81	94	96	89	91	95	91	99	95
New York	New York LaGuardia Airport	na	81	72	68	76	81	70	73	79	73	75	76
North Carolina	Charlotte Douglas Int'l Airport	na	73	73	71	81	82	69	68	72	72	73	66
North Dakota	Fargo Hector Int'l Airport	na	43	40	46	43	49	42	40	45	45	56	53
Ohio	Columbus Intl Airport	na	76	73	77	91	82	79	78	80	74	83	82
Oklahoma	Oklahoma City-Will Rogers World Arpt	na	50	52	50	50	48	52	56	na	49	56	49
Oregon	Portland Int'l Airport	na	96	98	90	95	95	97	76	79	110	88	91
Pennsylvania	Philadelphia Int'l Airport	na	74	69	65	72	79	72	68	72	72	74	73
Rhode Island	Providence TF Green Airport	na	79	69	69	77	80	80	76	78	78	76	83
South Carolina	Columbia Metro Airport	na	73	73	72	82	76	68	70	78	68	67	67
South Dakota	Sioux Falls Foss Field	na	40	54	51	50	47	47	47	53	54	50	56
Tennessee	Memphis Int'l Airport	na	80	71	67	81	77	75	71	76	73	79	66
Texas	Dallas-Fort Worth Int'l Airport	na	49	45	54	53	48	49	50	66	51	57	48
Texas	El Paso Int'l Airport	na	23	17	18	22	20	24	28	28	23	19	24
Texas	Houston Intercontinental Airport	na	na	na	na	68	68	63	59	69	65	67	65
Utah	Salt Lake City Int'l Airport	na	38	37	46	49	43	58	40	44	50	43	45
Vermont	Burlington Int'l Airport	na	80	77	77	84	87	85	76	77	79	74	90
Virginia	Norfolk Int'l Airport	na	76	75	71	76	73	76	78	74	76	78	70
Virginia	Washington-Reagan National Airport	na	70	66	68	76	73	70	65	70	69	76	67
Washington	Seattle-Tacoma Int'l Airport	na	104	97	94	101	85	96	81	89	101	85	89
West Virginia	Charleston Int'l Airport	na	86	90	80	98	98	95	89	93	91	91	89
Wisconsin	Milwaukee-Mitchell Int'l Airport	na	59	57	66	69	65	73	69	74	65	64	74
Wyoming	Casper/Natrona County Int'l Airport	na	37	28	38	35	33	41	35	39	37	26	35

Note: na indicates that data is not available for one or more years in the five-year period.

Number of Days Annually With ≥ 0.5 Inches of Precipitation

Five-Year Averages: 1950 - 2009

State	Weather Station	1950-1954	1955-1959	1960-1964	1965-1969	1970-1974	1975-1979	1980-1984	1985-1989	1990-1994	1995-1999	2000-2004	2005-2009
Alabama	Birmingham-Shuttlesworth Int'l Airport	na	36	35	35	40	36	37	32	37	41	39	37
Alaska	Anchorage Int'l Airport	na	5	6	3	4	5	6	6	6	6	5	5
Arizona	Phoenix Sky Harbor Int'l Airport	na	3	1	3	3	3	6	1	7	2	2	4
Arkansas	Little Rock National Airport	na	33	26	29	36	35	32	34	37	33	35	34
California	Los Angeles Int'l Airport	na	6	8	7	6	8	10	6	8	12	9	6
California	San Francisco Int'l Airport	na	14	11	18	15	12	18	10	12	15	14	10
Colorado	Denver Stapleton Int'l Airport	na	9	5	8	6	7	9	6	6	na	5	na
Connecticut	Bridgeport-Sikorsky Memorial Airport	na	23	20	24	33	31	30	26	27	25	31	30
Delaware	Wilmington-New Castle Airport	na	31	24	25	31	31	30	29	31	28	31	30
Florida	Jacksonville Int'l Airport	na	35	34	32	35	34	32	31	35	35	33	33
Florida	Miami Int'l Airport	na	36	31	42	32	34	35	32	36	43	39	40
Georgia	Atlanta Hartsfield Int'l Airport	na	32	39	37	34	35	33	33	40	32	28	34
Hawaii	Honolulu Int'l Airport	na	9	11	19	11	7	7	10	8	7	7	8
Idaho	Boise Air Terminal	na	3	4	2	2	2	3	3	1	3	0	2
Illinois	Chicago O'Hare Int'l Airport	na	na	15	25	25	21	24	21	21	24	21	23
Indiana	Indianapolis Int'l Airport	na	27	26	26	29	27	24	29	27	28	29	33
Iowa	Des Moines Int'l Airport	na	16	21	18	23	20	26	21	25	22	18	24
Kansas	Wichita Mid-Continent Airport	na	18	23	17	21	20	17	18	na	25	22	24
Kentucky	Lexington Bluegrass Airport	na	30	27	28	39	32	26	27	31	32	34	30
Louisiana	New Orleans Int'l Airport	na	38	37	37	42	45	40	39	42	36	38	33
Maine	Portland Int'l Jetport	na	28	25	25	30	32	31	26	30	29	26	36
Maryland	Baltimore/Washington Int'l Airport	na	25	30	23	31	31	28	28	26	29	30	34
Massachusetts	Boston Logan Int'l Airport	na	36	27	25	30	28	29	26	32	24	27	31
Michigan	Detroit Metro Airport	na	na	16	22	18	20	20	20	21	19	21	22
Minnesota	Minneapolis-Saint Paul Int'l Airport	na	12	15	19	na	15	19	15	20	17	19	17
Mississippi	Jackson Int'l Airport	na	na	na	30	35	40	37	33	35	35	41	33
Missouri	St Louis-Lambert Int'l Airport	na	25	22	23	25	21	30	25	30	28	26	26
Montana	Billings Logan Int'l Airport	na	5	6	7	7	6	6	6	7	5	2	6
Nebraska	Omaha Eppley Airfield	na	18	22	20	18	18	17	na	21	na	19	18
Nevada	Las Vegas-McCarran Int'l Airport	na	na	1	1	1	2	2	1	1	3	1	1
New Hampshire	Concord Municipal Airport	na	na	20	24	24	25	28	23	23	26	26	34
New Jersey	Newark Int'l Airport	na	27	26	24	30	33	36	30	30	32	30	33
New Mexico	Albuquerque Int'l Airport	na	3	2	2	3	2	2	5	4	4	2	5
New York	Buffalo Niagara Int'l Airport	na	25	18	21	20	29	23	25	27	24	22	24
New York	New York LaGuardia Airport	na	27	26	25	28	30	30	29	27	30	32	33
North Carolina	Charlotte Douglas Int'l Airport	na	30	28	29	30	33	29	27	31	29	28	29
North Dakota	Fargo Hector Int'l Airport	na	12	11	11	11	10	9	8	11	14	13	15
Ohio	Columbus Intl Airport	na	25	19	27	25	26	24	21	26	27	27	28
Oklahoma	Oklahoma City-Will Rogers World Arpt	na	24	22	22	24	18	22	28	na	25	21	21
Oregon	Portland Int'l Airport	na	20	17	19	25	16	23	18	18	28	14	20
Pennsylvania	Philadelphia Int'l Airport	na	27	27	22	28	33	28	25	26	30	27	30
Rhode Island	Providence TF Green Airport	na	30	31	26	32	31	32	29	31	29	33	32
South Carolina	Columbia Metro Airport	na	28	32	29	37	33	34	31	33	29	28	28
South Dakota	Sioux Falls Foss Field	na	12	16	13	15	16	14	14	19	15	14	16
Tennessee	Memphis Int'l Airport	na	40	33	29	38	38	36	33	36	42	36	33
Texas	Dallas-Fort Worth Int'l Airport	na	20	20	24	24	19	25	21	30	22	26	23
Texas	El Paso Int'l Airport	na	3	2	4	3	3	6	4	5	4	3	5
Texas	Houston Intercontinental Airport	na	na	na	na	31	29	28	27	32	29	33	31
Utah	Salt Lake City Int'l Airport	na	5	5	8	9	6	6	6	5	8	6	5
Vermont	Burlington Int'l Airport	na	19	18	19	22	21	24	17	21	22	20	25
Virginia	Norfolk Int'l Airport	na	29	29	26	30	32	30	31	27	32	34	29
Virginia	Washington-Reagan National Airport	na	26	24	22	25	27	29	26	26	28	31	31
Washington	Seattle-Tacoma Int'l Airport	na	22	26	21	24	21	21	17	19	28	18	20
West Virginia	Charleston Int'l Airport	na	27	24	23	29	30	27	29	31	31	28	30
Wisconsin	Milwaukee-Mitchell Int'l Airport	na	15	17	20	21	22	25	23	23	19	21	23
Wyoming	Casper/Natrona County Int'l Airport	na	3	3	2	4	4	5	4	5	5	1	4

Note: na indicates that data is not available for one or more years in the five-year period.

Number of Days Annually With ≥ 1.0 Inches of Precipitation

Five-Year Averages: 1950 - 2009

State	Weather Station	1950-1954	1955-1959	1960-1964	1965-1969	1970-1974	1975-1979	1980-1984	1985-1989	1990-1994	1995-1999	2000-2004	2005-2009
Alabama	Birmingham-Shuttlesworth Int'l Airport	na	13	18	18	18	19	17	15	15	16	20	16
Alaska	Anchorage Int'l Airport	na	1	1	0	0	0	0	1	0	1	1	0
Arizona	Phoenix Sky Harbor Int'l Airport	na	1	0	0	0	0	1	0	0	0	0	0
Arkansas	Little Rock National Airport	na	16	13	14	15	16	17	14	15	14	13	15
California	Los Angeles Int'l Airport	na	1	1	2	3	4	3	1	3	5	1	2
California	San Francisco Int'l Airport	na	5	5	4	4	5	6	1	2	5	6	3
Colorado	Denver Stapleton Int'l Airport	na	2	1	3	1	1	1	2	1	na	3	na
Connecticut	Bridgeport-Sikorsky Memorial Airport	na	6	5	10	18	13	11	7	9	10	10	10
Delaware	Wilmington-New Castle Airport	na	9	9	7	11	13	10	10	11	13	11	11
Florida	Jacksonville Int'l Airport	na	16	13	17	16	12	14	13	19	18	15	17
Florida	Miami Int'l Airport	na	20	15	23	14	12	17	16	18	20	21	19
Georgia	Atlanta Hartsfield Int'l Airport	na	15	19	14	12	16	17	16	16	12	14	15
Hawaii	Honolulu Int'l Airport	na	6	5	8	5	4	4	3	3	1	3	4
Idaho	Boise Air Terminal	na	0	0	0	0	0	0	0	0	0	0	0
Illinois	Chicago O'Hare Int'l Airport	na	na	6	3	7	7	10	6	9	7	9	8
Indiana	Indianapolis Int'l Airport	na	9	9	9	6	11	8	10	12	9	10	11
Iowa	Des Moines Int'l Airport	na	6	8	6	7	9	7	7	11	8	6	10
Kansas	Wichita Mid-Continent Airport	na	5	10	6	8	8	6	7	na	10	10	13
Kentucky	Lexington Bluegrass Airport	na	10	13	10	13	12	8	11	12	11	13	11
Louisiana	New Orleans Int'l Airport	na	19	17	17	20	20	22	19	22	19	18	15
Maine	Portland Int'l Jetport	na	4	11	10	13	14	13	11	11	10	10	16
Maryland	Baltimore/Washington Int'l Airport	na	8	10	9	12	13	9	8	11	11	12	14
Massachusetts	Boston Logan Int'l Airport	na	13	10	10	11	13	10	9	10	9	9	13
Michigan	Detroit Metro Airport	na	na	4	7	3	3	5	7	5	4	6	4
Minnesota	Minneapolis-Saint Paul Int'l Airport	5	4	3	5	4	4	8	3	5	4	6	6
Mississippi	Jackson Int'l Airport	na	na	na	12	20	19	18	15	18	17	18	16
Missouri	St Louis-Lambert Int'l Airport	na	8	6	7	9	6	12	10	9	7	12	12
Montana	Billings Logan Int'l Airport	na	1	1	1	0	1	1	0	2	0	0	0
Nebraska	Omaha Eppley Airfield	na	8	7	6	6	11	6	na	7	na	7	10
Nevada	Las Vegas-McCarran Int'l Airport	na	na	0	0	0	0	0	0	0	0	0	0
New Hampshire	Concord Municipal Airport	na	na	5	7	9	10	10	8	8	7	10	14
New Jersey	Newark Int'l Airport	na	10	9	8	11	13	13	17	10	12	13	13
New Mexico	Albuquerque Int'l Airport	0	0	0	0	0	0	0	0	0	0	0	0
New York	Buffalo Niagara Int'l Airport	4	4	2	5	3	8	7	7	8	7	4	6
New York	New York LaGuardia Airport	11	10	10	10	10	13	12	11	10	11	11	14
North Carolina	Charlotte Douglas Int'l Airport	10	10	12	8	13	14	13	11	10	11	10	13
North Dakota	Fargo Hector Int'l Airport	na	3	4	1	5	3	2	4	4	5	5	4
Ohio	Columbus Intl Airport	na	3	6	9	7	6	6	5	6	9	10	9
Oklahoma	Oklahoma City-Will Rogers World Arpt	na	11	9	6	10	9	11	15	na	12	8	10
Oregon	Portland Int'l Airport	na	3	6	4	4	2	4	2	3	5	2	3
Pennsylvania	Philadelphia Int'l Airport	na	7	10	10	10	12	12	11	8	8	12	11
Rhode Island	Providence TF Green Airport	na	11	14	10	12	15	11	11	9	11	13	14
South Carolina	Columbia Metro Airport	na	12	15	14	17	18	14	12	16	12	13	13
South Dakota	Sioux Falls Foss Field	na	5	6	6	7	5	5	4	5	4	7	6
Tennessee	Memphis Int'l Airport	na	17	13	17	18	18	20	14	18	20	17	17
Texas	Dallas-Fort Worth Int'l Airport	na	8	7	10	12	7	13	8	13	10	10	10
Texas	El Paso Int'l Airport	na	0	1	0	1	1	1	0	1	0	0	2
Texas	Houston Intercontinental Airport	na	na	na	na	15	14	14	13	17	16	16	15
Utah	Salt Lake City Int'l Airport	na	1	0	0	1	0	0	0	0	0	0	0
Vermont	Burlington Int'l Airport	na	4	4	1	4	2	4	5	5	7	6	7
Virginia	Norfolk Int'l Airport	na	14	12	9	12	10	12	10	10	11	12	15
Virginia	Washington-Reagan National Airport	na	7	9	8	10	13	9	9	9	8	10	14
Washington	Seattle-Tacoma Int'l Airport	na	4	7	4	6	4	4	4	3	7	3	5
West Virginia	Charleston Int'l Airport	na	7	9	7	8	12	6	9	10	9	11	6
Wisconsin	Milwaukee-Mitchell Int'l Airport	na	4	5	6	6	8	8	9	6	5	6	8
Wyoming	Casper/Natrona County Int'l Airport	0	0	0	0	2	1	1	0	0	0	0	1

Note: na indicates that data is not available for one or more years in the five-year period.

Annual Snowfall (in.)

Five-Year Averages: 1950 - 2009

State	Weather Station	1950-1954	1955-1959	1960-1964	1965-1969	1970-1974	1975-1979	1980-1984	1985-1989	1990-1994	1995-1999	2000-2004	2005-2009
Alabama	Birmingham-Shuttlesworth Int'l Airport	0.4	1.3	3.1	0.8	0.7	0.7	2.3	1.9	3.5	na	na	0.4
Alaska	Anchorage Int'l Airport	na	93.5	70.0	68.4	62.4	75.2	57.6	62.7	87.9	na	na	82.3
Arizona	Phoenix Sky Harbor Int'l Airport	trace	trace	trace	trace	trace	trace	0.0	trace	0.1	na	na	na
Arkansas	Little Rock National Airport	2.6	3.1	10.3	7.9	4.3	6.9	4.4	6.8	0.2	na	na	na
California	Los Angeles Int'l Airport	trace	trace	trace	0.0	trace	trace	0.0	0.0	trace	na	na	na
California	San Francisco Int'l Airport	trace	trace	0.3	trace	trace	trace	trace	trace	trace	na	na	na
Colorado	Denver Stapleton Int'l Airport	64.9	71.3	60.9	52.9	72.0	58.0	60.8	60.0	66.0	na	45.1	na
Connecticut	Bridgeport-Sikorsky Memorial Airport	16.9	26.2	32.4	36.4	22.5	28.7	17.1	na	28.5	na	na	35.2
Delaware	Wilmington-New Castle Airport	13.0	22.2	29.5	25.1	11.0	27.2	17.9	22.0	13.0	na	na	21.4
Florida	Jacksonville Int'l Airport	trace	0.3	trace	0.0	trace	trace	trace	0.3	trace	trace	na	na
Florida	Miami Int'l Airport	trace	0.0	0.0	0.0	0.0	0.0	0.0	0.0	0.0	trace	na	na
Georgia	Atlanta Hartsfield Int'l Airport	1.2	1.1	2.7	2.5	0.7	1.4	4.7	2.7	2.9	na	na	1.3
Hawaii	Honolulu Int'l Airport	na	0.0	0.0	0.0	0.0	0.0	0.0	0.0	0.0	na	na	na
Idaho	Boise Air Terminal	na	na	na	na	20.4	20.8	21.4	18.6	19.1	16.1	17.9	19.8
Illinois	Chicago O'Hare Int'l Airport	na	na	37.8	43.2	33.7	44.1	42.6	34.1	33.2	na	31.2	45.8
Indiana	Indianapolis Int'l Airport	20.4	20.2	28.1	28.2	23.5	34.2	30.9	21.1	20.4	na	27.1	24.5
Iowa	Des Moines Int'l Airport	28.9	32.4	42.5	25.1	37.5	38.7	44.8	24.9	29.6	na	na	42.3
Kansas	Wichita Mid-Continent Airport	na	15.6	19.2	10.8	19.6	17.2	19.8	18.8	na	15.1	14.2	14.7
Kentucky	Lexington Bluegrass Airport	16.1	10.9	24.1	23.0	14.7	23.0	12.9	14.9	13.7	na	na	10.1
Louisiana	New Orleans Int'l Airport	na	0.4	0.5	trace	0.1	trace	trace	0.2	trace	na	na	na
Maine	Portland Int'l Jetport	63.4	83.2	84.7	82.7	79.1	74.2	56.3	55.5	na	na	58.5	78.7
Maryland	Baltimore/Washington Int'l Airport	11.2	18.3	37.3	29.0	11.6	22.4	18.9	21.0	11.7	na	22.8	17.3
Massachusetts	Boston Logan Int'l Airport	31.0	42.7	49.4	50.7	38.8	48.4	34.8	32.4	50.3	na	41.5	53.0
Michigan	Detroit Metro Airport	na	na	32.5	35.7	46.4	44.5	43.2	47.3	41.6	na	37.9	52.6
Minnesota	Minneapolis-Saint Paul Int'l Airport	58.0	32.5	43.0	60.2	na	56.7	70.3	54.4	52.2	na	na	43.4
Mississippi	Jackson Int'l Airport	na	na	na	1.8	0.1	1.4	1.3	0.6	0.3	1.1	na	na
Missouri	St Louis-Lambert Int'l Airport	11.3	14.5	25.5	15.8	17.0	35.4	23.1	18.9	17.4	na	16.3	16.3
Montana	Billings Logan Int'l Airport	56.8	76.3	56.0	52.2	60.4	69.8	63.4	56.7	48.9	59.6	49.4	56.4
Nebraska	Omaha Eppley Airfield	25.8	27.7	39.0	30.3	31.9	29.6	25.5	na	28.4	na	na	28.6
Nevada	Las Vegas-McCarran Int'l Airport	na	na	0.9	0.4	2.8	2.1	trace	0.2	0.3	na	na	na
New Hampshire	Concord Municipal Airport	50.7	na	64.5	67.2	70.2	74.8	60.0	56.5	61.2	na	na	79.0
New Jersey	Newark Int'l Airport	12.9	32.7	39.9	30.0	16.5	33.3	25.4	21.5	27.3	na	na	30.3
New Mexico	Albuquerque Int'l Airport	7.1	13.2	7.8	8.0	15.4	12.2	10.6	13.2	10.4	8.9	na	9.2
New York	Buffalo Niagara Int'l Airport	76.8	107.3	94.9	82.3	98.7	123.2	81.4	88.6	83.1	na	115.2	96.3
New York	New York LaGuardia Airport	15.4	28.4	30.9	26.4	15.2	24.6	23.2	19.9	27.6	na	31.6	27.8
North Carolina	Charlotte Douglas Int'l Airport	1.6	3.4	8.6	10.7	7.8	5.2	9.2	5.3	1.0	2.1	8.0	1.5
North Dakota	Fargo Hector Int'l Airport	40.5	20.3	30.9	35.5	40.0	47.9	37.1	47.4	50.7	na	45.3	53.5
Ohio	Columbus Intl Airport	24.5	26.0	34.5	29.8	28.1	31.8	27.5	27.3	22.9	na	29.0	27.9
Oklahoma	Oklahoma City-Will Rogers World Arpt	8.0	7.7	10.5	10.7	8.5	8.8	7.7	13.2	na	na	7.9	7.5
Oregon	Portland Int'l Airport	na	na	na	na	4.4	3.3	4.3	4.5	5.7	na	na	na
Pennsylvania	Philadelphia Int'l Airport	12.4	19.1	30.2	28.5	13.0	30.3	22.9	18.9	14.8	na	23.1	23.3
Rhode Island	Providence TF Green Airport	na	35.1	45.7	45.0	28.7	39.4	29.8	30.7	36.7	na	na	41.3
South Carolina	Columbia Metro Airport	trace	2.7	1.1	1.8	4.5	1.2	2.5	1.9	0.9	0.3	na	0.2
South Dakota	Sioux Falls Foss Field	51.8	38.5	42.8	41.1	27.3	42.3	43.6	38.8	43.1	na	41.9	43.7
Tennessee	Memphis Int'l Airport	2.6	3.2	9.3	9.3	3.5	5.9	4.2	7.0	1.1	na	na	na
Texas	Dallas-Fort Worth Int'l Airport	na	1.6	5.7	2.1	1.3	7.1	0.9	2.8	0.3	na	na	na
Texas	El Paso Int'l Airport	3.4	5.3	5.6	5.3	5.0	4.3	11.9	9.7	3.5	na	na	na
Texas	Houston Intercontinental Airport	na	na	na	na	1.0	0.1	0.3	0.7	trace	trace	trace	0.5
Utah	Salt Lake City Int'l Airport	55.9	59.3	59.9	71.1	76.3	67.9	66.0	45.2	60.0	61.6	54.3	na
Vermont	Burlington Int'l Airport	71.1	80.5	65.3	93.9	101.4	84.3	71.6	68.2	81.2	82.6	90.6	92.1
Virginia	Norfolk Int'l Airport	2.7	8.0	10.5	10.7	7.6	7.0	11.4	8.7	3.3	na	na	0.9
Virginia	Washington-Reagan National Airport	10.1	15.4	27.1	23.9	10.5	17.4	16.7	20.0	8.4	na	15.9	12.9
Washington	Seattle-Tacoma Int'l Airport	na	na	na	na	13.8	3.9	4.9	8.4	6.0	na	na	na
West Virginia	Charleston Int'l Airport	na	22.4	na	33.9	30.4	47.0	31.7	38.9	32.1	na	na	25.6
Wisconsin	Milwaukee-Mitchell Int'l Airport	52.5	40.2	50.7	46.6	52.4	60.3	48.7	46.3	51.3	na	41.8	65.6
Wyoming	Casper/Natrona County Int'l Airport	73.1	77.3	56.2	71.0	87.5	95.6	104.3	79.3	69.0	na	62.7	70.0

Note: na indicates that data is not available for one or more years in the five-year period.

Annual Maximum Snow Depth (in.)

Five-Year Averages: 1950 - 2009

State	Weather Station	1950-1954	1955-1959	1960-1964	1965-1969	1970-1974	1975-1979	1980-1984	1985-1989	1990-1994	1995-1999	2000-2004	2005-2009
Alabama	Birmingham-Shuttlesworth Int'l Airport	na	2	8	1	1	1	1	5	13	na	na	trace
Alaska	Anchorage Int'l Airport	na	47	32	31	22	29	21	25	34	na	na	24
Arizona	Phoenix Sky Harbor Int'l Airport	na	0	trace	0	0	0	0	trace	trace	na	na	na
Arkansas	Little Rock National Airport	na	4	8	7	4	5	5	13	1	na	na	na
California	Los Angeles Int'l Airport	trace	0	trace	0	0	0	0	0	trace	na	na	na
California	San Francisco Int'l Airport	na	0	1	0	0	0	trace	trace	trace	na	na	na
Colorado	Denver Stapleton Int'l Airport	13	16	12	11	13	17	24	17	13	na	22	na
Connecticut	Bridgeport-Sikorsky Memorial Airport	5	na	19	18	14	17	13	13	20	na	na	10
Delaware	Wilmington-New Castle Airport	na	na	13	13	6	20	14	14	9	na	na	13
Florida	Jacksonville Int'l Airport	na	0	trace	0	0	0	0	1	trace	trace	na	na
Florida	Miami Int'l Airport	na	0	0	0	0	0	0	0	0	trace	na	na
Georgia	Atlanta Hartsfield Int'l Airport	na	1	3	2	1	4	3	2	5	1	na	1
Hawaii	Honolulu Int'l Airport	na	0	0	0	0	0	0	0	0	na	na	na
Idaho	Boise Air Terminal	na	na	na	na	7	6	13	13	10	10	5	7
Illinois	Chicago O'Hare Int'l Airport	na	na	11	27	12	28	10	15	15	na	na	12
Indiana	Indianapolis Int'l Airport	6	5	9	13	13	20	13	8	9	na	9	12
Iowa	Des Moines Int'l Airport	13	9	18	10	14	17	13	15	10	na	16	16
Kansas	Wichita Mid-Continent Airport	na	7	17	7	13	9	11	11	na	8	10	7
Kentucky	Lexington Bluegrass Airport	8	5	12	10	7	14	7	9	10	na	na	4
Louisiana	New Orleans Int'l Airport	na	2	3	0	1	0	0	1	trace	na	na	na
Maine	Portland Int'l Jetport	27	28	20	33	54	31	24	30	34	na	30	28
Maryland	Baltimore/Washington Int'l Airport	6	16	13	17	5	22	23	17	9	na	18	18
Massachusetts	Boston Logan Int'l Airport	11	na	19	17	9	29	18	14	19	na	na	na
Michigan	Detroit Metro Airport	na	na	8	11	19	15	18	12	12	na	12	14
Minnesota	Minneapolis-Saint Paul Int'l Airport	na	12	27	30	na	24	38	18	23	na	na	14
Mississippi	Jackson Int'l Airport	na	na	na	2	trace	3	6	1	2	1	na	na
Missouri	St Louis-Lambert Int'l Airport	10	11	11	8	12	17	20	11	11	na	7	10
Montana	Billings Logan Int'l Airport	12	35	17	14	18	24	12	14	12	11	8	10
Nebraska	Omaha Eppley Airfield	13	11	27	18	11	13	17	na	9	na	26	14
Nevada	Las Vegas-McCarran Int'l Airport	na	na	3	2	8	6	trace	trace	trace	na	na	na
New Hampshire	Concord Municipal Airport	na	na	27	37	26	21	23	23	24	22	na	na
New Jersey	Newark Int'l Airport	na	18	25	14	6	19	19	14	18	na	na	14
New Mexico	Albuquerque Int'l Airport	3	11	4	4	8	5	4	9	5	4	na	10
New York	Buffalo Niagara Int'l Airport	na	27	na	34	23	42	22	26	16	30	44	22
New York	New York LaGuardia Airport	na	13	26	16	6	14	22	10	19	na	20	16
North Carolina	Charlotte Douglas Int'l Airport	na	4	8	12	6	9	9	12	2	2	13	4
North Dakota	Fargo Hector Int'l Airport	18	8	14	17	14	24	29	30	24	na	na	na
Ohio	Columbus Intl Airport	13	6	10	10	10	17	9	11	9	na	13	18
Oklahoma	Oklahoma City-Will Rogers World Arpt	na	5	6	6	6	7	6	12	na	na	7	14
Oregon	Portland Int'l Airport	na	na	na	na	5	5	10	2	6	na	na	na
Pennsylvania	Philadelphia Int'l Airport	9	12	12	12	6	20	22	10	12	na	23	21
Rhode Island	Providence TF Green Airport	na	na	30	15	10	27	13	11	15	na	na	20
South Carolina	Columbia Metro Airport	na	8	2	3	14	5	4	4	1	1	na	trace
South Dakota	Sioux Falls Foss Field	24	19	31	34	12	18	18	17	12	18	22	19
Tennessee	Memphis Int'l Airport	na	5	14	12	3	2	4	8	2	na	na	na
Texas	Dallas-Fort Worth Int'l Airport	na	4	8	3	2	8	2	3	trace	na	na	na
Texas	El Paso Int'l Airport	na	7	7	7	5	6	9	14	2	na	na	na
Texas	Houston Intercontinental Airport	na	na	na	na	1	trace	trace	trace	trace	trace	trace	trace
Utah	Salt Lake City Int'l Airport	11	10	11	11	14	12	13	13	25	17	14	na
Vermont	Burlington Int'l Airport	14	33	21	33	32	29	19	21	31	22	26	30
Virginia	Norfolk Int'l Airport	na	11	5	9	8	5	14	9	3	na	na	na
Virginia	Washington-Reagan National Airport	6	14	13	16	8	22	17	18	5	na	16	16
Washington	Seattle-Tacoma Int'l Airport	na	na	na	na	11	3	8	8	7	na	na	na
West Virginia	Charleston Int'l Airport	na	5	9	12	11	23	9	17	18	na	na	11
Wisconsin	Milwaukee-Mitchell Int'l Airport	22	18	24	16	21	33	19	23	21	na	32	15
Wyoming	Casper/Natrona County Int'l Airport	12	9	11	8	20	14	21	12	12	na	na	na

Note: na indicates that data is not available for one or more years in the five-year period.

Number of Days Annually With ≥ 1.0 Inch Snow Depth

Five-Year Averages: 1950 - 2009

State	Weather Station	1950-1954	1955-1959	1960-1964	1965-1969	1970-1974	1975-1979	1980-1984	1985-1989	1990-1994	1995-1999	2000-2004	2005-2009
Alabama	Birmingham-Shuttlesworth Int'l Airport	na	na	na	1	0	1	1	0	1	na	na	0
Alaska	Anchorage Int'l Airport	na	na	na	162	164	156	136	132	156	na	na	162
Arizona	Phoenix Sky Harbor Int'l Airport	na	na	na	0	0	0	0	0	0	na	na	na
Arkansas	Little Rock National Airport	na	na	na	3	2	6	1	3	0	na	na	na
California	Los Angeles Int'l Airport	na	na	na	0	0	0	0	0	0	na	na	na
California	San Francisco Int'l Airport	na	na	na	0	0	0	0	0	0	na	na	na
Colorado	Denver Stapleton Int'l Airport	na	na	na	39	55	41	59	59	52	na	38	na
Connecticut	Bridgeport-Sikorsky Memorial Airport	na	na	na	32	28	32	23	22	22	na	na	34
Delaware	Wilmington-New Castle Airport	na	na	na	20	11	26	17	20	11	na	na	14
Florida	Jacksonville Int'l Airport	na	na	na	0	0	0	0	0	0	0	na	na
Florida	Miami Int'l Airport	na	na	na	0	0	0	0	0	0	0	na	na
Georgia	Atlanta Hartsfield Int'l Airport	na	na	na	2	0	1	na	1	0	1	na	0
Hawaii	Honolulu Int'l Airport	na	na	na	0	0	0	0	0	0	na	na	na
Idaho	Boise Air Terminal	na	na	na	18	16	30	38	39	24	8	13	16
Illinois	Chicago O'Hare Int'l Airport	na	na	na	44	39	61	48	44	39	na	na	52
Indiana	Indianapolis Int'l Airport	na	na	na	24	24	43	33	27	17	na	31	24
Iowa	Des Moines Int'l Airport	na	na	na	50	56	65	54	47	48	na	48	57
Kansas	Wichita Mid-Continent Airport	na	na	na	13	17	26	19	20	na	11	14	12
Kentucky	Lexington Bluegrass Airport	na	na	na	20	11	30	13	14	8	na	na	8
Louisiana	New Orleans Int'l Airport	na	na	na	0	0	0	0	0	0	na	na	na
Maine	Portland Int'l Jetport	na	na	na	97	85	85	75	78	61	na	68	81
Maryland	Baltimore/Washington Int'l Airport	na	na	na	17	7	17	15	17	8	na	20	13
Massachusetts	Boston Logan Int'l Airport	na	na	na	42	38	45	30	31	35	na	na	na
Michigan	Detroit Metro Airport	na	na	na	51	50	65	47	48	41	na	49	52
Minnesota	Minneapolis-Saint Paul Int'l Airport	na	na	na	96	106	107	96	96	94	na	na	82
Mississippi	Jackson Int'l Airport	na	na	na	0	0	1	0	1	0	0	na	na
Missouri	St Louis-Lambert Int'l Airport	na	na	na	14	16	43	25	20	15	na	20	15
Montana	Billings Logan Int'l Airport	na	na	na	66	63	88	60	67	54	52	56	47
Nebraska	Omaha Eppley Airfield	na	na	na	45	50	55	50	na	41	na	34	43
Nevada	Las Vegas-McCarran Int'l Airport	na	na	na	0	1	0	0	0	0	na	na	na
New Hampshire	Concord Municipal Airport	na	na	na	102	106	99	76	84	71	73	na	na
New Jersey	Newark Int'l Airport	na	na	na	30	na	30	20	22	19	na	na	22
New Mexico	Albuquerque Int'l Airport	na	na	na	6	8	11	4	4	7	2	na	4
New York	Buffalo Niagara Int'l Airport	na	na	na	77	79	86	76	62	67	67	85	76
New York	New York LaGuardia Airport	na	na	na	23	14	27	16	17	22	na	24	20
North Carolina	Charlotte Douglas Int'l Airport	na	na	na	5	4	2	4	5	0	1	4	0
North Dakota	Fargo Hector Int'l Airport	na	na	na	113	na	116	81	109	93	na	na	na
Ohio	Columbus Intl Airport	na	na	na	24	21	42	30	27	21	na	25	25
Oklahoma	Oklahoma City-Will Rogers World Arpt	na	na	na	6	6	12	6	12	na	na	9	7
Oregon	Portland Int'l Airport	na	na	na	na	3	2	2	1	2	na	na	na
Pennsylvania	Philadelphia Int'l Airport	na	na	na	20	9	na	17	20	9	na	23	15
Rhode Island	Providence TF Green Airport	na	na	na	42	35	36	30	33	29	na	na	28
South Carolina	Columbia Metro Airport	na	na	na	2	2	1	0	1	0	0	na	0
South Dakota	Sioux Falls Foss Field	na	na	na	73	82	na	75	71	71	73	62	74
Tennessee	Memphis Int'l Airport	na	na	na	5	2	5	2	5	1	na	na	na
Texas	Dallas-Fort Worth Int'l Airport	na	na	na	1	1	5	0	2	0	na	na	na
Texas	El Paso Int'l Airport	na	na	na	2	2	1	4	4	1	na	na	na
Texas	Houston Intercontinental Airport	na	na	na	na	0	0	0	0	0	0	0	0
Utah	Salt Lake City Int'l Airport	na	na	na	52	57	42	51	59	59	40	48	na
Vermont	Burlington Int'l Airport	na	na	na	99	na	98	87	88	84	88	96	87
Virginia	Norfolk Int'l Airport	na	na	na	7	3	4	5	4	1	na	na	na
Virginia	Washington-Reagan National Airport	na	na	na	16	5	14	12	17	8	na	14	8
Washington	Seattle-Tacoma Int'l Airport	na	na	na	10	7	2	2	6	3	na	na	na
West Virginia	Charleston Int'l Airport	na	na	na	24	19	38	31	32	15	na	na	14
Wisconsin	Milwaukee-Mitchell Int'l Airport	na	na	na	52	71	85	68	60	52	na	49	75
Wyoming	Casper/Natrona County Int'l Airport	na	na	na	62	na	76	65	74	59	na	na	na

Note: na indicates that data is not available for one or more years in the five-year period.

All-Time Weather Records

All-Time Record Minimum Temperature by State

State	Location	Value	Date	Station ID	Status*
Alabama	New Market	-27 °F	30-Jan-66	015867	E
Alaska	Prospect Creek Camp	-80 °F	23-Jan-71	507778	E
Arizona	Hawley Lake	-40 °F	7-Jan-71	023926	E
Arkansas	Brook Farm Pond	-29 °F	13-Feb-05	032930	E
California	Boca	-45 °F	20-Jan-37	040931	E
Colorado	Maybell	-61 °F	1-Feb-85	055446	E
Connecticut	Falls Village	-32 °F	16-Feb-43	062658	E1
	Coventry	-32 °F	22-Jan-61	061689	E1
Delaware	Millsboro	-17 °F	January 17, 1893	076020	E
Florida	Tallahassee	-2 °F	February 13, 1899	088754	E
Georgia	CCC Fire Camp F-16	-17 °F	27-Jan-40		EA
Hawaii	Mauna Kea Observatory	12 °F	17-May-79	516183	E
Idaho	Island Park Dam	-60 °F	18-Jan-43	104598	E
Illinois	Congerville	-36 °F	5-Jan-99	111836	E
Indiana	New Whiteland	-36 °F	19-Jan-94	126304	E
Iowa	Washta	-47 °F	12-Jan-12	138693	E1
	Elkader	-47 °F	3-Feb-96	132603	E1
Kansas	Lebanon	-40 °F	13-Feb-05	144598	E
Kentucky	Shelbyville	-37 °F	19-Jan-94	157324	E
Louisiana	Minden	-16 °F	February 13, 1899	166244	E
Maine	Big Black River	-50 °F	16-Jan-09	USGS BBRM1	NS
Maryland	Oakland	-40 °F	13-Jan-12	186620	E
Massachusetts	Taunton	-35 °F	5-Jan-04	198367	E1
	Coldbrook	-35 °F	15-Feb-43	191589	E1
	Chester	-35 °F	12-Jan-81	191430	E1
Michigan	Vanderbilt	-51 °F	9-Feb-34	208417	E
Minnesota	Tower	-60 °F	2-Feb-96	218311	E
Mississippi	Corinth	-19 °F	30-Jan-66	221962	E
Missouri	Warsaw	-40 °F	13-Feb-05	238733	E
Montana	Rogers Pass	-70 °F	20-Jan-54	247156	E
Nebraska	Bridgeport	-47 °F	February 12, 1899	251145	E1
	Oshkosh	-47 °F	22-Dec-89	256385	E1
Nevada	San Jacinto	-50 °F	8-Jan-37	267284	E
New Hampshire	Mount Washington	-46 °F	8-Jan-68	275639	N
New Jersey	River Vale	-34 °F	5-Jan-04	287620	E
New Mexico	Gavilan	-50 °F	1-Feb-51	293505	E
New York	Old Forge	-52 °F	18-Feb-79	306184	E1
North Carolina	Mount Mitchell	-34 °F	21-Jan-85	315923	E
North Dakota	Parshall	-60 °F	15-Feb-36	326867	E
Ohio	Milligan	-39 °F	February 10, 1899	335310	E
Oklahoma	Vinita	-27 °F	13-Feb-05	349203	N1
	Watts	-27 °F	18-Jan-30	349382	N1
	Guthrie	-27 °F	4-Jan-47	343821	N1
Oregon	Ukiah	-54 °F	9-Feb-33	358726	E1
	Seneca	-54 °F	10-Feb-33	357675	E1
Pennsylvania	Smethport	-42 °F	5-Jan-04	368190	E
Rhode Island	Wood River Junction	-28 °F	11-Jan-42	379327	NA
South Carolina	Caesar's Head	-19 °F	21-Jan-85	381256	E
South Dakota	McIntosh	-58 °F	17-Feb-36	395381	E
Tennessee	Mountain City	-32 °F	30-Dec-17	406287	E
Texas	Seminole	-23 °F	8-Feb-33	418201	E
Utah	Strawberry Tunnel (East)	-50 °F	5-Jan-13	422319	NA
Vermont	Bloomfield	-50 °F	30-Dec-33	430690	E
Virginia	Mountain Lake Biological Stn	-30 °F	21-Jan-85	445828	E
Washington	Mazama	-48 °F	30-Dec-68	455133	E2
	Winthrop	-48 °F	30-Dec-68	459376	E2
West Virginia	Lewisburg	-37 °F	30-Dec-17	465224	E
Wisconsin	Couderay	-55 °F	February 2 & 4, 1996	471847	E1
Wyoming	Riverside Ranger Stn	-66 °F	9-Feb-33		EA

These values have been evaluated by the NOAA National Climatic Data Center and/or by the State Climate Extremes Committee and determined to be valid. The data may come from sources other than official NOAA-supervised weather stations, but are archived, officially recognized observations.

** Record Status*

Locations without associated station IDs are not archived in NCDC's digital data collection. They may be derived from historical documents (official or otherwise) in NCDC archives or may be archived elsewhere. Please contact NCDC at ncdc.info@noaa.gov for more information.

E *Value is unchanged from previous extremes tables last updated by NCDC between 1998 and 2006. Value exceeds all other valid values.*

N *Value is changed from extremes tables last updated by NCDC between 1998 and 2006. Value exceeds all other valid values.*

1 *Value ties values from earlier dates.*

2 *Value set at multiple stations on the same date.*

3 *Value set at multiple locations on the same date and ties values from earlier dates.*

S *Value has been officially reviewed by a State Climate Extremes Committee.*

A *Additional information is available. Official value may be exceeded by a widely accepted unofficial value that is not supported by a direct, calibrated observation (e.g., estimates, uncalibrated instruments, anecdotal reports). Please refer to the state extremes page footnotes.*

All-Time Record Maximum Temperature by State

State	Location	Value	Date	Station ID	Status*
Alabama	Centerville	112 °F	6-Sep-25	011520	E
Alaska	Fort Yukon	100 °F	27-Jun-15	503175	E
Arizona	Lake Havasu City	128 °F	29-Jun-94	024761	E
Arkansas	Ozark	120 °F	10-Aug-36	035508	E
California	Greenland Ranch	134 °F	10-Jul-13	043603	E
Colorado	Sedgwick	114 °F	11-Jul-54	057513	N1A
	Las Animas	114 °F	1-Jul-33	054834	N1A
Connecticut	Torrington	106 °F	23-Aug-16	068438	E1
	Danbury	106 °F	15-Jul-95	061762	E1
Delaware	Millsboro	110 °F	21-Jul-30	076020	E
Florida	Monticello	109 °F	29-Jun-31	085879	E
Georgia	Louisville	112 °F	24-Jul-52	095314	E1
	Greenville 2 NNW	112 °F	20-Aug-83	093915	E1
Hawaii	Pahala	100 °F	27-Apr-31	517421	E
Idaho	Orofino	118 °F	28-Jul-34	106681	E
Illinois	East St. Louis	117 °F	14-Jul-54	112614	E
Indiana	Collegeville	116 °F	14-Jul-36	121719	E
Iowa	Keokuk No. 2	118 °F	20-Jul-34	134372	EA
Kansas	Fredonia	121 °F	18-Jul-36	142894	E1
	Alton	121 °F	24-Jul-36	140201	E1
Kentucky	Greensburg	114 °F	28-Jul-30	153430	E
Louisiana	Plain Dealing 4W	114 °F	10-Aug-36	167344	E
Maine	North Bridgton	105 °F	July 4 & 10, 1911	175875	E1
Maryland	Boettcherville	109 °F	July 3, 1898	180960	E3
	Keedysville	109 °F	6-Aug-18	184780	E3
	Cumberland	109 °F	August 6 & 7, 1918	182280	E3
	Cumberland	109 °F	10-Jul-36	182280	E3
	Frederick	109 °F	10-Jul-36	183348	E3
Massachusetts	New Bedford	107 °F	2-Aug-75	195246	E2
	Chester	107 °F	2-Aug-75	191430	E2
Michigan	Mio	112 °F	13-Jul-36	205531	E2
	Stanwood	112 °F	13-Jul-36	207834	E2
Minnesota	Beardsley	115 °F	29-Jul-17	210541	N1A
Mississippi	Holly Springs 2N	115 °F	29-Jul-30	224168	E
Missouri	Union	118 °F	14-Jul-54	238515	E3
	Warsaw	118 °F	14-Jul-54	238733	E3
Montana	Glendive	117 °F	July 20, 1893	243581	E1
	Medicine Lake	117 °F	5-Jul-37	245572	E1
Nebraska	Geneva	118 °F	15-Jul-34	253175	E1
	Hartington	118 °F	17-Jul-36	253630	E1
	Minden	118 °F	24-Jul-36	255565	E1
Nevada	Laughlin	125 °F	29-Jun-94	264480	E
New Hampshire	Nashua	106 °F	4-Jul-11	275712	E
New Jersey	Runyon	110 °F	10-Jul-36	287825	E
New Mexico	Waste Isolation Pilot Plant	122 °F	27-Jun-94	299569	E
New York	Troy	108 °F	22-Jul-26	308597	E
North Carolina	Fayetteville	110 °F	21-Aug-83	093740	E
North Dakota	Steele	121 °F	6-Jul-36	328366	E
Ohio	Gallipolis	113 °F	21-Jul-34	333029	E
Oklahoma	Alva	120 °F	18-Jul-36	340193	E1A
	Altus	120 °F	19-Jul-36	340179	E1A
	Poteau	120 °F	10-Aug-36	347246	E1A
	Altus	120 °F	12-Aug-36	340179	E1A
	Tipton	120 °F	27-Jun-94	348879	E1A
Oregon	Prineville	119 °F	July 29, 1898	356883	E1
	Pendleton	119 °F	August 10, 1898	356541	E1
Pennsylvania	Phoenixville	111 °F	July 9 & 10, 1936	366927	E1
Rhode Island	Providence	104 °F	2-Aug-75	376698	E
South Carolina	Blackville	111 °F	4-Sep-25	380764	E1
	Calhoun Falls	111 °F	8-Sep-25	381277	E1
	Camden	111 °F	28-Jun-54	381310	E1

Continued on next page.

State	Location	Value	Date	Station ID	Status*
South Dakota	Gann Valley	120 °F	5-Jul-36	393217	N1
	Fort Pierre	120 °F	15-Jul-06	393076	N1
Tennessee	Perryville	113 °F	29-Jul-30	407099	E1
	Perryville	113 °F	9-Aug-30	407099	E1
Texas	Seymour	120 °F	12-Aug-36	418221	E1
	Monahans	120 °F	28-Jun-94	415999	E1
Utah	St. George	117 °F	5-Jul-85	427516	EA
Vermont	Vernon	107 °F	7-Jul-12	438600	N
Virginia	Columbia	110 °F	July 5 & 7, 1900	441929	E1
	Balcony Falls	110 °F	15-Jul-54	440411	E1
Washington	Wahluke	118 °F	24-Jul-28	458903	E1
	Ice Harbor Dam	118 °F	5-Aug-61	453883	E1
West Virginia	Moorefield	112 °F	4-Aug-30	466163	E1
	Martinsburg	112 °F	10-Jul-36	465707	E1
Wisconsin	Wisconsin Dells	114 °F	13-Jul-36	479319	E
Wyoming	Basin	115 °F	8-Aug-83	480540	N1
	Diversion Dam	115 °F	15-Jul-88	482595	N1

These values have been evaluated by the NOAA National Climatic Data Center and/or by the State Climate Extremes Committee and determined to be valid. The data may come from sources other than official NOAA-supervised weather stations, but are archived, officially recognized observations.

** Record Status*

Locations without associated station IDs are not archived in NCDC's digital data collection. They may be derived from historical documents (official or otherwise) in NCDC archives or may be archived elsewhere. Please contact NCDC at ncdc.info@noaa.gov for more information.

E *Value is unchanged from previous extremes tables last updated by NCDC between 1998 and 2006. Value exceeds all other valid values.*

N *Value is changed from extremes tables last updated by NCDC between 1998 and 2006. Value exceeds all other valid values.*

1 *Value ties values from earlier dates.*

2 *Value set at multiple stations on the same date.*

3 *Value set at multiple locations on the same date and ties values from earlier dates.*

S *Value has been officially reviewed by a State Climate Extremes Committee.*

A *Additional information is available. Official value may be exceeded by a widely accepted unofficial value that is not supported by a direct, calibrated observation (e.g., estimates, uncalibrated instruments, anecdotal reports). Please refer to the state extremes page footnotes.*

All-Time Record 24-hr Precipitation by State

State	Location	Value	Date	Station ID	Status*
Alabama	Dauphin Island Sea Lab	32.52 in.	July 19-20, 1997	012172	EA
Alaska	Angoon	15.20 in.	12-Oct-82	500310	E
Arizona	Workman Creek	11.40 in.	September 4-5, 1970	029534	E
Arkansas	Big Fork	14.06 in.	3-Dec-82	030664	E
California	Hoegees Camp	25.83 in.	January 22-23, 1943	044017	EA
Colorado	Holly	11.08 in.	17-Jun-65	054076	EA
Connecticut	Burlington	12.77 in.	19-Aug-55	060973	E
Delaware	Dover	8.50 in.	13-Jul-75	072730	E
Florida	Key West	23.28 in.	November 11-12, 1980	084570	NA
Georgia	Americus	21.10 in.	6-Jul-94	090253	E
Hawaii	Kilauea Sugar Co. (Kauai)	38.00 in.	January 24-25, 1956	514561	EA
Idaho	Rattlesnake Creek	7.17 in.	23-Nov-09	107545	E
Illinois	Aurora	16.91 in.	18-Jul-96	110338	E
Indiana	Princeton	10.50 in.	6-Aug-05	127125	E
Iowa	Atlantic 1Nebraska	13.18 in.	14-Jun-98	130364	NA
Kansas	Woodruff 3WSW	13.53 in.	22-Jun-67	149028	N
Kentucky	Dunmor	10.40 in.	28-Jun-60	152366	E
Louisiana	Hackberry	22.00 in.	August 28-29, 1962	163979	E
Maine	Portland	13.32 in.	October 20-21, 1996	176905	E
Maryland	Jewell	14.75 in.	July 26-27, 1897		E
Massachusetts	Westfield	18.15 in.	August 18-19, 1955	199191	E
Michigan	Bloomingdale	9.78 in.	Aug 31 -Sept 1, 1914	200864	E
Minnesota	Hokah 1S	15.10 in.	19-Aug-07	213808	NS
Mississippi	Columbus	15.68 in.	9-Jul-68	221870	E
Missouri	Edgerton	18.18 in.	20-Jul-65	232474	E
Montana	Circle (Springbrook)	11.50 in.	20-Jun-21	247796	E
Nebraska	York	13.15 in.	July 8-9, 1950	259510	E
Nevada	Mount Charleston	7.78 in.	20-Oct-04	265400	N
New Hampshire	Mount Washington	11.07 in.	October 20-21, 1996	275639	N
New Jersey	Tuckerton	14.81 in.	August 19-20, 1939	288899	E
New Mexico	Lake Maloya	11.28 in.	May 18-19, 1955	294742	E
New York	NYC Central Park	11.15 in.	October 8-9, 1903	305801	EA
North Carolina	Altapass	22.22 in.	July 15-16, 1916	310160	E
North Dakota	Litchville	8.10 in.	29-Jun-75	325230	E
Ohio	Lockington Dam	10.75 in.	August 7-8, 1995		EA
Oklahoma	Enid	15.68 in.	11-Oct-73	342912	E
Oregon	Nehalem 9 Nebraska	11.77 in.	6-Nov-06	355971	N
Pennsylvania	York 3SSW Pump Stn	13.50 in.	22-Jun-72	369933	NA
Rhode Island	Westerly	12.13 in.	September 16-17, 1932	378911	E
South Carolina	Myrtle Beach	14.80 in.	16-Sep-99	386153	NA
South Dakota	Groton	8.74 in.	6-May-07	393456	NSA
Tennessee	Milan	13.60 in.	13-Sep-82	406012	N
Texas	Alvin	42.00 in.	July 25-26, 1979		EA
Utah	Deer Creek Dam	5.08 in.	1-Feb-63	422057	NA
Vermont	Mount Mansfield	9.92 in.	17-Sep-99	435416	N
Virginia	Williamsburg 2N	14.28 in.	16-Sep-99	449151	NA
Washington	Mt. Mitchell #2	14.26 in.	November 23-24, 1986	455668	E
West Virginia	Brushy Run	12.02 in.	18-Jun-49	461204	NA
Wisconsin	Mellen	11.72 in.	24-Jun-46	475286	E
Wyoming	Cheyenne	6.06 in.	1-Aug-85	481675	E

These values have been evaluated by the NOAA National Climatic Data Center and/or by the State Climate Extremes Committee and determined to be valid. The data may come from sources other than official NOAA-supervised weather stations, but are archived, officially recognized observations.

** Record Status*

Locations without associated station IDs are not archived in NCDC's digital data collection. They may be derived from historical documents (official or otherwise) in NCDC archives or may be archived elsewhere. Please contact NCDC at ncdc.info@noaa.gov for more information.

***E** Value is unchanged from previous extremes tables last updated by NCDC between 1998 and 2006. Value exceeds all other valid values.*

***N** Value is changed from extremes tables last updated by NCDC between 1998 and 2006. Value exceeds all other valid values.*

***1** Value ties values from earlier dates.*

***2** Value set at multiple stations on the same date.*

***3** Value set at multiple locations on the same date and ties values from earlier dates.*

***S** Value has been officially reviewed by a State Climate Extremes Committee.*

***A** Additional information is available. Official value may be exceeded by a widely accepted unofficial value that is not supported by a direct, calibrated observation (e.g., estimates, uncalibrated instruments, anecdotal reports). Please refer to the state extremes page footnotes.*

All-Time Record 24-hr Snow Fall by State

State	Location	Value	Date	Station ID	Status*
Alabama	Walunt Grove	20.0 in.	13-Mar-93	018648	N
Alaska	Mile 47 Camp	78.0 in.	9-Feb-63	505878	N
Arizona	Heber Ranger Stn	38.0 in.	14-Dec-67	023961	N1
	Alpine	38.0 in.	25-Feb-87	020170	N1
Arkansas	Corning	25.0 in.	22-Jan-18	031632	N
California	Echo Summit Sierra at Tahoe	67.0 in.	5-Jan-82	042671	N
Colorado	Silver Lake	75.8 in.	April 14-15, 1921	057648	E
Connecticut	Falls Village	30.0 in.	10-Feb-69	062658	N1
Delaware	Dover	25.0 in.	19-Feb-79	072730	E
Florida	Milton Exp. Stn.	4.0 in.	6-Mar-54	085793	E
Georgia	Cedartown 3	19.3 in.	3-Mar-42	091732	E
Hawaii	Haleakali (Maui)	6.5 in.	2-Feb-36	510992	N
Idaho	Anderson Dam	31.0 in.	18-Dec-67	100282	N
Illinois	Astoria	36.0 in.	28-Feb-00	110291	N
Indiana	Salem	33.0 in.	23-Dec-04	127755	N
Iowa	Lenox	24.0 in.	20-Apr-18	134746	N
Kansas	Pratt	30.0 in.	28-Mar-09	146549	NSA
Kentucky	Simers	26.0 in.	3-Mar-42	157396	N
Louisiana	Colfax	13.0 in.	13-Feb-60	161941	NA
Maine	Orono	40.0 in.	30-Dec-62	176430	N
Maryland	Clear Spring 1E	31.0 in.	29-Mar-42	181890	E
Massachusetts	Natick	29.0 in.	1-Apr-97	195175	E
Michigan	Herman	32.0 in.	2-Dec-85	203744	N
Minnesota	Wolf Ridge ELC	36.0 in.	7-Jan-94	219134	E
Mississippi	Mt. Pleasant	18.0 in.	23-Dec-63	226084	N2
	Tunica 2	18.0 in.	23-Dec-63	228998	N2
Missouri	Cape Girardeau	24.0 in.	25-Feb-79	003935	N3
	Jackson	24.0 in.	25-Feb-79	231289	N3
Montana	Shonkin 7S	48.0 in.	29-May-82	247540	E1
	Millegan 14SE	48.0 in.	27-Dec-03	245712	E1
Nebraska	Dalton	27.0 in.	21-Dec-06	252145	N
Nevada	Dagget Pass	36.0 in.	21-Dec-96	262119	N
New Hampshire	Mount Washington	49.3 in.	25-Feb-69	275639	N
New Jersey	Charlotteburg Reservoir	32.0 in.	14-Dec-15	287833	N
New Mexico	Kelly Ranch	41.0 in.	3-Feb-64	294461	N
New York	Watertown	49.0 in.	Nov 14-15, 1900	309000	EA
North Carolina	Mount Mitchell	36.0 in.	13-Mar-93	315923	N
North Dakota	Minot Airport	27.0 in.	27-Apr-84	024013	N
Ohio	Warren 3S	30.0 in.	20-Apr-01	338769	N
Oklahoma	Woodward	26.0 in.	28-Mar-09	349760	NSA
	Freedom	26.0 in.	28-Mar-09	343358	NSA
Oregon	Hood River ES	47.0 in.	9-Jan-80	354003	N
Pennsylvania	Morgantown	38.0 in.	20-Mar-58	365956	E
Rhode Island	Woonsocket	30.0 in.	7-Feb-78	379423	E
South Carolina	Rimini 2SSW	24.0 in.	Feb 9-10, 1973	387313	N
South Dakota	Lead	52.0 in.	14-Mar-73	394834	N
Tennessee	Mt. Leconte	30.0 in.	14-Mar-93	406328	N
Texas	Follett	25.0 in.	28-Mar-09	413225	NSA
Utah	Alta	38.0 in.	2-Dec-82	420072	NA
Vermont	Jay Peak	42.0 in.	5-Feb-95	434189	N
Virginia	Luray 5E	33.5 in.	3-Mar-94	445096	E
Washington	Crystal Mountain Ski Resort	65.0 in.	24-Feb-94	NWAC	NA
West Virginia	Flat Top	35.0 in.	Jan 27-28, 1998	463072	NA
Wisconsin	Neillsville	26.0 in.	Dec 26-27, 1904	475808	E
Wyoming	Hunter Station	49.0 in.	21-Mar-24	484770	N

These values have been evaluated by the NOAA National Climatic Data Center and/or by the State Climate Extremes Committee and determined to be valid. The data may come from sources other than official NOAA-supervised weather stations, but are archived, officially recognized observations.

** Record Status*

Locations without associated station IDs are not archived in NCDC's digital data collection. They may be derived from historical documents (official or otherwise) in NCDC archives or may be archived elsewhere. Please contact NCDC at ncdc.info@noaa.gov for more information.

E *Value is unchanged from previous extremes tables last updated by NCDC between 1998 and 2006. Value exceeds all other valid values.*

N *Value is changed from extremes tables last updated by NCDC between 1998 and 2006. Value exceeds all other valid values.*

1 *Value ties values from earlier dates.*

2 *Value set at multiple stations on the same date.*

3 *Value set at multiple locations on the same date and ties values from earlier dates.*

S *Value has been officially reviewed by a State Climate Extremes Committee.*

A *Additional information is available. Official value may be exceeded by a widely accepted unofficial value that is not supported by a direct, calibrated observation (e.g., estimates, uncalibrated instruments, anecdotal reports). Please refer to the state extremes page footnotes.*

All-Time Record Snow Depth by State

State	Location	Value	Date	Station ID	Status*
Alabama	Reform	22 in.	24-Jan-40	016847	N
Alaska	Valdez Municipal Airport	192 in.	Mar 7 & Apr 11, 2008	509685	N1
Arizona	Hawley Lake	91 in.	21-Dec-67	023926	N
Arkansas	Calico Rock 2WSW	26 in.	22-Jan-18	031132	N
California	Tamarack	451 in.	11-Mar-11	048781	E
Colorado	Wolf Creek Pass 1E	251 in.	31-Mar-79	059181	N
Connecticut	Norfolk 2SW	55 in.	5-Feb-61	065445	E
Delaware	Bridgeville	25 in.	19-Feb-79	071330	N1
	Wilmington Apt	25 in.	18-Feb-03	079595	N1
Florida	Milton Exp. Stn	4 in.	6-Mar-54	085793	N
Georgia	Chatsworth 2	18 in.	13-Mar-93	091863	N
Hawaii	Haleakali (Maui)	5 in.	6-Apr-38	510992	N
Idaho	Mullan Pass VOR/DMaine	182 in.	Feb 20 & 22, 1954	024154	N1
Illinois	Astoria	41 in.	28-Feb-00	110291	N1
	Gebhard Woods St.Pk.	41 in.	31-Jan-79	113369	N1
Indiana	Hammond	47 in.	28-Jan-18	123650	N
Iowa	Lake Park	52 in.	Feb 28 & Mar 1, 1969	134561	E1
Kansas	Syracuse	40 in.	31-Dec-18	148038	N
Kentucky	La Grange	31 in.	20-Jan-78	154595	E
Louisiana	Rayne	24 in.	February 15, 1895	167678	N
Maine	Farmington	84 in.	28-Feb-69	172765	E
Maryland	Frostburg 2	54 in.	15-Mar-93	183415	E
Massachusetts	Great Barrington Airport	62 in.	13-Jan-96	193208	E
Michigan	Eagle Harbor	117 in.	January 27-31, 1948	202332	N1
Minnesota	Meadowlands 1NNW	88 in.	February 15-21, 1969	215298	E1
Mississippi	Mount Pleasant	18 in.	23-Dec-63	226084	N
Missouri	Union	36 in.	March 19 & 20, 1960	238515	E1
Montana	Summit	147 in.	18-Feb-75	247978	E
Nebraska	Fremont	44 in.	16-Feb-36	253050	N
Nevada	Spooners Station	271 in.	March 12 & 13, 1911	267710	N1
New Hampshire	Pinkham Notch	164 in.	27-Feb-69	276818	N
New Jersey	Canistear Reservoir	52 in.	5-Feb-61	281327	E
New Mexico	Lee's Ranch	96 in.	15-Mar-41	294903	N
New York	Whiteface Mountain	119 in.	20-Apr-43	309383	N
North Carolina	Mount Mitchell	50 in.	March 3-6, 1942	315921	N1
	Mount Mitchell	50 in.	14-Mar-93	315923	N1
North Dakota	Berlin	65 in.	March 11 & 12, 1897	320720	N1
Ohio	Chardon	47 in.	14-Nov-96	331458	N
Oklahoma	Buffalo 2SSW	36 in.	22-Feb-71	331243	N
Oregon	Crater Lake NP HQ	252 in.	3-Apr-83	351946	N
Pennsylvania	Gouldsboro	60 in.	March 22 & 23, 1958	363394	N1
Rhode Island	North Foster 1E	42 in.	7-Feb-78	375270	E
South Carolina	Ceasars Head	29 in.	18-Feb-69	381256	N
South Dakota	Lead	73 in.	1-Mar-98	394834	E
Tennessee	Mount Leconte	63 in.	March 14 & 15, 1993	406328	N1
Texas	Vega 2NW	33 in.	7-Feb-56	419330	N
Utah	Alta	179 in.	April 5 & 7, 1958	420072	N1A
Vermont	Mount Mansfield	149 in.	2-Apr-69	435416	N
Virginia	Big Meadows	47 in.	7-Jan-96	440720	E
Washington	Rainier Paradise RS	367 in.	March 9 & 10, 1956	456898	N1
West Virginia	Snowshoe	62 in.	8-Mar-78	468308	N
Wisconsin	Flambeau Reservoir	83 in.	6-Apr-33	472814	N
Wyoming	Grassy Lake Dam	128 in.	4-Feb-43	484050	N

These values have been evaluated by the NOAA National Climatic Data Center and/or by the State Climate Extremes Committee and determined to be valid. The data may come from sources other than official NOAA-supervised weather stations, but are archived, officially recognized observations.

**Record Status*

Locations without associated station IDs are not archived in NCDC's digital data collection. They may be derived from historical documents (official or otherwise) in NCDC archives or may be archived elsewhere. Please contact NCDC at ncdc.info@noaa.gov for more information.

E *Value is unchanged from previous extremes tables last updated by NCDC between 1998 and 2006. Value exceeds all other valid values.*

N *Value is changed from extremes tables last updated by NCDC between 1998 and 2006. Value exceeds all other valid values.*

1 *Value ties values from earlier dates.*

2 *Value set at multiple stations on the same date.*

3 *Value set at multiple locations on the same date and ties values from earlier dates.*

S *Value has been officially reviewed by a State Climate Extremes Committee.*

A *Additional information is available. Official value may be exceeded by a widely accepted unofficial value that is not supported by a direct, calibrated observation (e.g., estimates, uncalibrated instruments, anecdotal reports). Please refer to the state extremes page footnotes.*

Storm Events: United States

100 Storm Events with the Greatest Number of Fatalities: 2000-2009

Rank	Location or County	Date	Type	Mag.	Deaths	Injuries	Property Damage ($mil.)	Crop Damage ($mil.)
1	Chambers, Harris, Houston, and Montgomery Counties, TX	09/21/05	Excessive Heat	na	49	0	0.0	0.0
2	Interior Central California, CA	07/16/06	Excessive Heat	na	46	18	0.1	492.4
3	Southeast New York, NY	08/01/06	Excessive Heat	na	42	0	0.0	0.0
4	Greater Phoenix Area, AZ	07/12/05	Excessive Heat	na	30	0	0.0	0.0
5	Cook County, IL	08/01/06	Excessive Heat	na	24	0	0.0	0.0
5	Southeast Pennsylvania, PA	08/01/06	Excessive Heat	na	24	40	0.0	0.0
7	Galveston Island, TX	06/05/01	Tropical Storm	na	22	0	5,150.0	0.0
7	Southeast Pennsylvania, PA	08/06/01	Excessive Heat	na	22	0	0.0	0.0
9	Northwest and Central Maryland, MD	07/02/02	Excessive Heat	na	21	0	0.0	0.0
10	Vanderburgh County, IN	11/06/05	Tornado	F3	20	200	15.0	0.0
11	Southeast Texas, TX	07/06/00	Excessive Heat	na	19	0	0.0	0.0
12	Dyer County, TN	04/02/06	Tornado	F3	16	70	20.0	0.0
12	Southern California, CA	07/21/06	Excessive Heat	na	16	27	0.0	0.0
14	Southeast Pennsylvania, PA	07/01/02	Excessive Heat	na	15	0	0.0	0.0
14	Mississippi Gulf Coast, MS	08/29/05	Hurricane Katrina	na	15	104	5,880.0	1,510.0
16	Cook County, IL	08/06/01	Excessive Heat	na	14	0	0.0	0.0
16	San Diego County, CA	10/25/03	Wildfire	na	14	90	1,040.0	6.5
16	San Bernardino County Mountain, CA	12/25/03	Landslide	na	14	10	5.0	0.0
16	Newton County, MO	05/10/08	Tornado	F4	14	200	35.0	0.0
20	Lake County, FL	02/02/07	Tornado	F3	13	9	46.0	0.0
20	Macon County, TN	02/05/08	Tornado	F3	13	44	14.1	1.0
22	Cook County, IL	07/01/02	Excessive Heat	na	12	0	0.0	0.0
22	Southern Arizona, AZ	05/20/05	Excessive Heat	na	12	0	0.0	0.0
22	Carson and Gray County, TX	03/12/06	Wildfire	na	12	8	49.9	45.4
25	Mitchell County, GA	02/13/00	Tornado	F3	11	175	20.0	2.0
25	Tuscaloosa County, AL	12/16/00	Tornado	F4	11	144	12.5	0.0
25	Cook County, IL	07/15/02	Excessive Heat	na	11	0	0.0	0.0
25	Ozaukee and Sheboygan Counties, WI	10/11/02	Fog	na	11	0	0.0	0.0
25	Madison County, TN	05/04/03	Tornado	F4	11	66	30.0	0.0
25	Kiowa County, KS	05/04/07	Tornado	F5	11	63	250.0	0.0
25	Texas Gulf Coast near Galveston, TX	09/12/08	Storm Surge/Tide	na	11	0	4,000.0	0.0
32	Cook County, IL	07/21/01	Excessive Heat	na	10	0	0.0	0.0
32	Los Angeles, Southern Santa Barbara, and Ventura Counties, CA	01/10/05	Landslide	na	10	0	0.0	0.0
32	Statewide, OK	07/16/06	Heat	na	10	100	0.0	0.0
32	Cook County, IL	02/01/07	Extreme Cold/Wind Chill	na	10	0	0.0	0.0
36	Bay Area, CA	06/14/00	Excessive Heat	na	9	102	0.0	0.0
36	Southeast Pennsylvania, PA	08/01/02	Excessive Heat	na	9	0	0.0	0.0
36	Tohono Oodham Nation, Cochise and Santa Cruz Counties, AZ	07/02/05	Excessive Heat	na	9	0	0.0	0.0
36	Cook County, IL	07/15/06	Excessive Heat	na	9	0	0.0	0.0
36	Coffee County, AL	03/01/07	Tornado	F4	9	50	250.0	0.0
36	Butler County, IA	05/25/08	Tornado	F5	9	50	75.0	0.0
42	North Texas, TX	07/01/00	Excessive Heat	na	8	0	0.0	0.0
42	Western and Central Oklahoma, OK	07/04/01	Excessive Heat	na	8	0	0.0	0.0
42	Southeast Pennsylvania, PA	08/11/02	Excessive Heat	na	8	0	0.0	0.0
42	La Salle County, IL	04/20/04	Tornado	F3	8	7	0.0	0.0
42	Statewide, OK	08/01/06	Heat	na	8	0	0.0	0.0
42	Columbus County, NC	11/16/06	Tornado	F3	8	20	0.5	0.0
42	Lake County, FL	02/02/07	Tornado	F3	8	10	52.0	0.0
42	San Diego County Valleys, CA	10/21/07	Wildfire	na	8	61	75.0	0.0
42	Carter County, OK	02/10/09	Tornado	F4	8	0	3.0	0.0
51	Chester and Philadelphia Counties, PA	05/06/00	Excessive Heat	na	7	0	0.0	0.0
51	Cook County, IL	06/21/02	Excessive Heat	na	7	0	0.0	0.0
51	Northwest and Central Maryland, MD	08/01/02	Excessive Heat	na	7	0	0.0	0.0
51	Walker County, AL	11/10/02	Tornado	F3	7	40	2.5	0.0
51	Morgan County, TN	11/10/02	Tornado	F3	7	28	0.9	0.0

Rank	Location or County	Date	Type	Mag.	Deaths	Injuries	Property Damage ($mil.)	Crop Damage ($mil.)
51	Southwest and West Central Florida, FL	08/13/04	Hurricane Charley	na	7	780	5,420.0	285.0
51	Extreme Western Florida Panhandle, FL	09/13/04	Hurricane Ivan	na	7	0	4,000.0	25.0
51	Southeast Pennsylvania, PA	07/25/05	Excessive Heat	na	7	0	0.0	0.0
51	Kauai County, HI	03/13/06	Flash Flood	na	7	0	0.0	0.0
51	Sumner County, TN	04/07/06	Tornado	F3	7	121	69.0	0.0
51	Cook County, IL	12/02/06	Extreme Cold/Wind Chill	na	7	5	0.0	0.0
51	Maverick County, TX	04/24/07	Tornado	F3	7	0	80.0	0.0
51	Sumner County, TN	02/05/08	Tornado	F3	7	14	10.0	0.0
51	Carroll and Shelby Counties, TN	06/17/09	Heat	na	7	0	0.0	0.0
65	Grady County, GA	02/14/00	Tornado	F3	6	15	3.5	3.0
65	Pontotoc County, MS	02/24/01	Tornado	F3	6	43	28.0	0.0
65	Cook County, IL	07/29/01	Excessive Heat	na	6	0	0.0	0.0
65	Central Maryland, MD	06/25/02	Excessive Heat	na	6	0	0.0	0.0
65	Walton County, FL	06/08/03	Rip Current	na	6	0	0.0	0.0
65	Chase County, KS	08/30/03	Flash Flood	na	6	0	0.2	0.0
65	Centre and Clinton Counties, PA	01/06/04	Winter Weather/Mix	na	6	12	1.5	0.0
65	Northwestern Florida, FL	09/15/04	Hurricane Ivan	na	6	16	90.4	0.0
65	Bucks, Chester, Delaware, Montgomery, and Philadelphia Counties, PA	07/18/05	Excessive Heat	na	6	0	0.0	0.0
65	Southeast Florida, FL	08/25/05	Hurricane Katrina	na	6	0	100.0	423.0
65	Gibson County, TN	04/02/06	Tornado	F3	6	42	25.0	0.0
65	Northwest and Central Maryland, MD	08/01/06	Heat	na	6	5	0.0	0.0
65	Baker County, GA	03/01/07	Tornado	F2	6	3	1.2	0.0
65	Ottawa County, OK	05/10/08	Tornado	F4	6	150	15.0	0.0
79	Northern Arizona, AZ	03/20/00	Winter Storm	na	5	0	0.0	0.0
79	Caddo Parish, LA	07/14/00	Excessive Heat	na	5	0	0.0	0.0
79	North Texas, TX	08/01/00	Excessive Heat	na	5	0	0.0	0.0
79	Philadelphia County, PA	08/07/00	Excessive Heat	na	5	0	0.0	0.0
79	North Texas, TX	09/01/00	Excessive Heat	na	5	0	0.0	0.0
79	Southeast Texas, TX	09/01/00	Excessive Heat	na	5	0	0.0	0.0
79	Central and Eastern Missouri, MO	07/07/01	Excessive Heat	na	5	61	0.0	0.0
79	Southern Minnesota, MN	08/04/01	Excessive Heat	na	5	0	0.0	0.0
79	Carlton and Southern St. Louis Counties, MN	08/07/01	Excessive Heat	na	5	0	0.0	0.0
79	Jackson County, MO	07/06/02	Excessive Heat	na	5	0	0.0	0.0
79	Lawrence County, MO	05/04/03	Tornado	F3	5	33	27.5	0.0
79	Broome County, NY	06/13/03	Flash Flood	na	5	0	0.1	0.0
79	Stanly County, NC	06/16/03	Flash Flood	na	5	0	0.0	0.0
79	Southeast Pennsylvania, PA	08/02/05	Excessive Heat	na	5	0	0.0	0.0
79	South Florida, FL	10/24/05	Hurricane Wilma	na	5	0	10,000.0	0.0
79	Texas Panhandle Region, TX	12/17/05	Winter Weather/Mix	na	5	15	0.1	0.0
79	Little Colorado River Valley, White Mountains, and Mogollon Rim, AZ	01/25/06	Ice Storm	na	5	0	0.0	0.0
79	Frederick County, MD	06/27/06	Flash Flood	na	5	1	0.5	0.0
79	Central, South Central, and Southeast Kansas, KS	07/16/06	Heat	na	5	0	0.0	0.0
79	Winona County, MN	08/18/07	Flash Flood	na	5	0	0.3	0.1
79	Cook County, IL	01/22/08	Extreme Cold/Wind Chill	na	5	0	0.0	0.0
79	Pope County, AR	02/05/08	Tornado	F3	5	15	11.5	0.0
79	Cook County, IL	12/21/08	Cold/Wind Chill	na	5	0	0.0	0.0
79	Harris County, TX	04/18/09	Flash Flood	na	5	0	3.5	0.0

Note: Deaths, injuries, and damages are date and location specific.

100 Storm Events with the Greatest Number of Injuries: 2000-2009

Rank	Location or County	Date	Type	Mag.	Deaths	Injuries	Property Damage ($mil.)	Crop Damage ($mil.)
1	Southwest and West Central Florida, FL	08/13/04	Hurricane Charley	na	7	780	5,420.0	285.0
2	St. Charles and St. Louis Metro Area, MO	08/04/07	Excessive Heat	na	2	519	0.0	0.0
3	St. Louis City, MO	07/13/06	Excessive Heat	na	4	437	0.0	0.0
4	Franklin, Jefferson, St. Charles, and St. Louis Counties, MO	07/14/06	Excessive Heat	na	3	306	0.0	0.0
5	Southeast Lower Michigan, MI	08/06/01	Excessive Heat	na	1	200	0.0	0.0
5	Mitchell County, GA	03/20/03	Tornado	F3	4	200	6.0	0.0
5	Western Shore Counties of Chesapeake Bay, MD	09/18/03	Tropical Storm	na	1	200	530.4	0.1
5	Vanderburgh County, IN	11/06/05	Tornado	F3	20	200	15.0	0.0
5	Suffolk County, VA	04/28/08	Tornado	F3	0	200	30.0	0.0
5	Newton County, MO	05/10/08	Tornado	F4	14	200	35.0	0.0
11	Mitchell County, GA	02/13/00	Tornado	F3	11	175	20.0	2.0
12	Ottawa County, OK	05/10/08	Tornado	F4	6	150	15.0	0.0
13	Tuscaloosa County, AL	12/16/00	Tornado	F4	11	144	12.5	0.0
14	Potter County, TX	12/22/07	Winter Weather	na	1	137	1.2	0.0
15	Pemiscot County, MO	04/02/06	Tornado	F3	2	130	60.0	0.0
16	Eastern Central Missouri, MO	08/28/00	Excessive Heat	na	1	125	0.0	0.0
17	Charles County, MD	04/28/02	Tornado	F4	1	122	114.0	0.0
18	Sumner County, TN	04/07/06	Tornado	F3	7	121	69.0	0.0
19	Mississippi Gulf Coast, MS	08/29/05	Hurricane Katrina	na	15	104	5,880.0	1,510.0
20	St. Louis County and St. Louis City, MO	07/02/00	Excessive Heat	na	4	103	0.0	0.0
21	Bay Area, CA	06/14/00	Excessive Heat	na	9	102	0.0	0.0
22	Greene County, OH	09/20/00	Tornado	F4	1	100	15.0	0.0
22	Statewide, OK	07/16/06	Heat	na	10	100	0.0	0.0
24	Marion County, IN	09/20/02	Tornado	F2	0	97	40.0	0.0
25	Eastern Central Missouri, MO	07/03/03	Excessive Heat	na	3	93	0.0	0.0
25	Southeastern Missouri, MO	07/21/05	Excessive Heat	na	2	93	0.0	0.0
27	Allegheny County, PA	09/17/04	Flood	na	1	92	26.0	0.0
28	San Diego County, CA	10/25/03	Wildfire	na	14	90	1,040.0	6.5
29	Oklahoma County, OK	05/08/03	Tornado	F4	0	89	160.0	0.0
30	Tarrant County, TX	03/28/00	Tornado	F3	2	80	0.0	0.0
31	Weld County, CO	05/22/08	Tornado	F3	1	78	147.0	0.0
32	Van Buren County, AR	02/05/08	Tornado	F4	3	77	22.7	0.0
33	Eastern Central Missouri, MO	07/21/01	Excessive Heat	na	3	71	0.0	0.0
34	Northern Virginia, VA	09/18/03	High Wind	58 mph	0	70	16.8	11.9
34	Dyer County, TN	04/02/06	Tornado	F3	16	70	20.0	0.0
36	Madison County, TN	05/04/03	Tornado	F4	11	66	30.0	0.0
37	Central and Eastern Missouri, MO	07/20/05	Excessive Heat	na	4	65	0.0	0.0
38	Kiowa County, KS	05/04/07	Tornado	F5	11	63	250.0	0.0
39	Central and Eastern Missouri, MO	07/07/01	Excessive Heat	na	5	61	0.0	0.0
39	San Diego County Valleys, CA	10/21/07	Wildfire	na	8	61	75.0	0.0
41	Eastern Central Missouri, MO	08/01/02	Excessive Heat	na	1	59	0.0	0.0
42	Rutherford County, TN	04/10/09	Tornado	F4	2	58	100.0	0.0
43	Prince George's County, MD	09/24/01	Tornado	F3	2	55	100.0	0.0
43	Lowndes County, MS	11/10/02	Tornado	F3	0	55	60.0	0.0
45	Allegheny County, PA	05/31/02	Thunderstorm Wind	105 mph	1	54	10.0	0.0
45	Eastern Central Missouri, MO	08/15/03	Excessive Heat	na	2	54	0.0	0.0
47	Madison County, TN	02/05/08	Tornado	F4	0	51	100.0	0.0
48	Travis County, TX	11/15/01	Flash Flood	na	2	50	0.5	0.0
48	Northern Utah, UT	03/07/02	Winter Storm	na	2	50	0.2	0.0
48	Coffee County, AL	03/01/07	Tornado	F4	9	50	250.0	0.0
48	Autauga County, AL	02/17/08	Tornado	F3	0	50	10.0	0.0
48	Butler County, IA	05/25/08	Tornado	F5	9	50	75.0	0.0
53	Benton County, MO	07/05/04	Thunderstorm Wind	81 mph	1	48	0.3	0.0
53	Monona County, IA	06/11/08	Tornado	F3	4	48	0.0	0.0
55	Greene County, AR	04/02/06	Tornado	F3	0	47	25.0	0.0

Rank	Location or County	Date	Type	Mag.	Deaths	Injuries	Property Damage ($mil.)	Crop Damage ($mil.)
56	Pittsburg and Tulsa Counties, OK	08/01/08	Excessive Heat	na	2	46	0.0	0.0
57	Cleveland County, OK	05/08/03	Tornado	F3	0	45	210.0	0.0
57	St. Louis City, and Jefferson, St. Charles, and St. Louis Counties, MO	07/09/04	Excessive Heat	na	1	45	0.0	0.0
59	Macon County, TN	02/05/08	Tornado	F3	13	44	14.1	1.0
60	Pontotoc County, MS	02/24/01	Tornado	F3	6	43	28.0	0.0
61	Wayne County, IL	04/21/02	Tornado	F3	1	42	4.0	0.0
61	Gibson County, TN	04/02/06	Tornado	F3	6	42	25.0	0.0
61	Volusia County, FL	02/02/07	Tornado	F3	0	42	52.0	0.0
61	Volusia County, FL	02/02/07	Tornado	F3	0	42	52.0	0.0
65	Central and Southern San Joaquin County Valley, CA	02/05/02	Fog	na	3	40	0.4	0.0
65	Walker County, AL	11/10/02	Tornado	F3	7	40	2.5	0.0
65	Houston County, TX	09/14/04	Lightning	na	1	40	0.0	0.0
65	Hopkins County, KY	11/15/05	Tornado	F4	0	40	31.0	0.0
65	Southeast Pennsylvania, PA	08/01/06	Excessive Heat	na	24	40	0.0	0.0
70	Horry County, SC	07/06/01	Tornado	F2	0	39	8.0	0.0
71	St. Louis City and Boone, Lincoln, St. Charles, and St. Louis Counties, MO	09/01/00	Excessive Heat	na	1	38	0.0	0.0
71	San Diego County, CA	08/01/02	Wild/Forest Fire	na	0	38	10.0	0.0
73	Cedar County, MO	05/04/03	Tornado	F3	3	37	40.0	3.0
74	Terrebonne Parish, LA	03/15/00	Tornado	F2	0	36	10.0	0.0
74	Bolivar County, MS	11/24/01	Tornado	F4	0	36	6.0	0.0
76	San Bernardino, CA	10/21/03	Wildfire	na	0	35	50.0	0.0
76	Baxter County, AR	02/05/08	Tornado	F2	1	35	15.7	0.0
78	Lawrence County, MO	05/04/03	Tornado	F3	5	33	27.5	0.0
78	Curry County, NM	03/23/07	Tornado	F2	2	33	16.5	0.0
80	Tazewell County, IL	05/10/03	Tornado	F3	0	32	10.0	0.0
81	Rutherford County, TN	04/28/02	Tornado	F3	0	31	2.3	0.0
81	Daviess County, IN	11/15/05	Tornado	F3	0	31	11.6	0.0
83	Manitowoc County, WI	05/12/00	Hail	2.50 in.	0	30	46.0	4.0
83	Prentiss County, MS	02/24/01	Tornado	F3	0	30	2.0	0.0
83	Bexar County, TX	03/19/02	Tornado	F2	0	30	2.0	0.0
83	Wyandotte County, KS	05/04/03	Tornado	F4	2	30	15.5	0.0
83	Lancaster County, NE	05/22/04	Tornado	F4	1	30	100.0	0.0
83	Warrick County, IN	11/06/05	Tornado	F3	4	30	65.0	0.0
83	Johnson County, IA	04/13/06	Tornado	F2	0	30	12.0	0.0
83	Le Sueur County, MN	08/24/06	Tornado	F3	1	30	20.0	4.0
83	Houston County, MN	08/18/07	Flash Flood	na	0	30	27.0	0.7
83	Fulton County, GA	03/14/08	Tornado	F2	1	30	25.0	0.0
83	Polk County, AR	04/09/09	Tornado	F3	3	30	130.0	0.0
83	Santa Barbara County, CA	05/05/09	Wildfire	na	0	30	17.0	0.0
95	Arlington, Fairfax, King George, Prince William, and Stafford Counties, VA	09/18/03	Tropical Storm	na	0	29	55.1	0.1
95	Pender County, NC	08/13/04	Tornado	F2	3	29	1.3	0.0
97	Barton County, KS	04/21/01	Tornado	F4	1	28	43.0	0.0
97	Morgan County, IN	09/20/02	Tornado	F3	0	28	15.0	0.0
97	Morgan County, TN	11/10/02	Tornado	F3	7	28	0.9	0.0
97	Palm Beach, FL	08/07/03	Tornado	F1	0	28	80.0	0.0
97	Desha County, AR	02/24/07	Tornado	F3	0	28	45.0	0.0

Note: Deaths, injuries, and damages are date and location specific.

100 Storm Events with the Greatest Property Damage: 2000-2009

Rank	Location or County	Date	Type	Mag.	Deaths	Injuries	Property Damage ($mil.)	Crop Damage ($mil.)
1	Southeast Louisiana, LA	08/28/05	Hurricane Katrina	na	0	0	16,930.0	0.0
2	South Florida, FL	10/24/05	Hurricane Wilma	na	5	0	10,000.0	0.0
3	Mississippi Coast, MS	08/28/05	Hurricane Katrina	na	0	0	7,350.0	0.0
4	Mississippi Gulf Coast, MS	08/29/05	Hurricane Katrina	na	15	104	5,880.0	1,510.0
5	Southwest and West Central Florida, FL	08/13/04	Hurricane Charley	na	7	780	5,420.0	285.0
6	Galveston Island, TX	06/05/01	Tropical Storm	na	22	0	5,150.0	0.0
7	Brevard, Indian River, Martin, St. Lucie, and Volusia Co., FL	09/04/04	Hurricane Frances	na	0	0	4,830.0	93.2
8	Extreme Western Florida Panhandle, FL	09/13/04	Hurricane Ivan	na	7	0	4,000.0	25.0
8	Southwest Louisiana, LA	09/23/05	Hurricane Rita	na	1	0	4,000.0	0.0
8	Texas Gulf Coast near Galveston, TX	09/12/08	Storm Surge/Tide	na	11	0	4,000.0	0.0
11	Southwest Alabama, AL	09/13/04	Hurricane Ivan	na	0	0	2,500.0	25.0
12	Southeast Texas, TX	09/23/05	Hurricane Rita	na	1	0	2,090.0	0.0
13	Extreme Northwest Florida, FL	07/09/05	Hurricane Dennis	na	0	0	1,500.0	0.3
14	Osceola, Orange, Seminole, and Volusia Cos., FL	08/13/04	High Wind	105 mph	4	0	1,300.0	0.0
15	San Diego County, CA	10/25/03	Wildfire	na	14	90	1,040.0	6.5
16	Jefferson County, AL	05/07/03	Flash Flood	na	0	0	1,000.0	0.0
16	Southwest Alabama, AL	08/27/05	Hurricane Katrina	na	0	0	1,000.0	0.0
16	Harris and Matagorda Co., TX	09/12/08	Hurricane Ike	na	0	0	1,000.0	0.0
19	Hardee, Highlands, and Polk Counties, FL	08/13/04	High Wind	108 mph	1	12	929.0	175.0
20	Knox, Stark, and Trumbull Counties, OH	03/07/08	Winter Storm	na	0	0	750.0	0.0
20	Linn County, IA	06/01/08	Flood	na	0	0	750.0	0.0
20	Jackson County, OK	06/05/08	Thunderstorm Wind	87 mph	0	0	750.0	0.0
23	Highlands and Polk Counties, FL	09/25/04	High Wind	70 mph	0	0	702.0	0.0
24	East Carroll Parish, LA	05/10/09	Thunderstorm Wind	81 mph	0	0	700.0	0.2
25	San Bernardino County, CA	10/25/03	Wildfire	na	4	5	696.4	0.0
26	Statewide, IA	08/01/03	Drought	na	0	0	645.1	0.0
27	Southeast Florida, FL	09/04/04	Hurricane Frances	na	0	0	621.0	90.0
28	Tehama County, CA	09/29/00	Wild/Forest Fire	na	0	0	547.0	0.0
29	Western Shore Counties of Chesapeake Bay, MD	09/18/03	Tropical Storm	na	1	200	530.4	0.1
30	Eastern Virginia, VA	09/18/03	Hurricane Isabel	na	2	0	506.0	10.9
31	Columbia County, WI	06/25/06	Hail	1.00 in.	0	0	500.0	1.7
31	Acadia Parish, LA	10/26/06	Flood	na	0	0	500.0	0.0
31	Greater Lake Tahoe Area, CA	06/24/07	Wildfire	na	0	3	500.0	0.0
31	Southeast Texas, TX	09/12/08	Hurricane Ike	na	0	0	500.0	0.0
31	Jefferson and Orange County, TX	09/12/08	Storm Surge/Tide	na	0	0	500.0	0.0
36	Broward and Miami-Dade Co., FL	10/03/00	Flood	na	0	0	450.0	500.0
37	Eastern North Carolina, NC	09/17/03	Hurricane Isabel	na	0	0	435.6	14.2
38	Southeast Louisiana, LA	09/23/05	Storm Surge	na	0	0	432.0	0.0
39	St Louis County, MO	04/10/01	Hail	2.50 in.	0	0	400.0	0.0
40	Brevard, Indian River, Martin, St. Lucie, and Volusia Co., FL	09/25/04	Hurricane Jeanne	na	0	0	379.9	8.7
41	Southwest and Central Louisiana, LA	10/03/02	Hurricane Lili	na	0	3	368.0	168.0
42	Southwest Arkansas, AR	12/12/00	Ice Storm	na	0	0	360.0	0.0
43	Jefferson County, CO	07/20/09	Hail	1.25 in.	0	0	350.0	0.0
44	Glades, Hendry, Palm Beach, Broward, and Miami-Dade Co., FL	09/25/04	Hurricane Jeanne	na	0	0	323.0	30.0
45	Lake County, OH	07/28/06	Flash Flood	na	1	0	320.0	0.0
46	St Louis County, MO	04/10/01	Hail	1.50 in.	0	0	300.0	0.0
46	Douglas County, NE	04/10/01	Hail	1.75 in.	0	1	300.0	0.0
46	Northwestern Oklahoma, OK	01/30/02	Ice Storm	na	0	0	300.0	0.0
46	West and Central Utah, UT	01/10/05	Flood	na	1	6	300.0	0.0
50	San Bernardino County, CA	11/01/03	Wildfire	na	2	7	278.6	0.0
51	Southeast Mississippi, MS	08/27/05	Hurricane Katrina	na	0	0	250.0	0.0
51	Delaware County, NY	06/27/06	Flash Flood	na	2	0	250.0	0.0
51	Coffee County, AL	03/01/07	Tornado	F4	9	50	250.0	0.0
51	Kiowa County, KS	05/04/07	Tornado	F5	11	63	250.0	0.0
55	Johnson County, IA	06/01/08	Flood	na	0	0	230.0	0.0

Rank	Location or County	Date	Type	Mag.	Deaths	Injuries	Property Damage ($mil.)	Crop Damage ($mil.)
56	Cleveland County, OK	05/08/03	Tornado	F3	0	45	210.0	0.0
57	Central and South Central Minnesota, MN	04/01/01	Flood	na	3	1	200.0	0.0
57	Douglas County, NE	04/30/01	Hail	1.75 in.	0	0	200.0	0.0
57	Roseau County, MN	06/10/02	Flood	na	0	0	200.0	0.0
57	Broome County, NY	06/27/06	Flash Flood	na	0	0	200.0	0.0
61	El Paso County, TX	08/01/06	Flash Flood	na	0	0	180.0	0.0
62	Central Florida, FL	09/05/04	Tropical Storm	na	1	0	179.4	0.0
63	Williamson County, IL	05/08/09	Thunderstorm Wind	100 mph	0	1	175.0	0.0
64	Sussex County, NJ	08/12/00	Flood	na	0	0	166.5	0.0
65	Southwest Arkansas, AR	12/24/00	Ice Storm	na	0	0	165.0	0.0
66	Midland County, TX	04/11/09	Hail	2.00 in.	0	1	161.2	0.0
67	Southeast Lower Michigan, MI	04/03/03	Ice Storm	na	1	2	161.1	0.0
68	Arapahoe County, CO	06/07/09	Hail	3.00 in.	0	0	161.0	0.0
69	Oklahoma County, OK	05/08/03	Tornado	F4	0	89	160.0	0.0
69	Travis County, TX	03/25/09	Hail	3.00 in.	0	0	160.0	0.0
71	Extreme Southeast Texas, TX	09/23/05	Hurricane Rita	na	3	3	159.5	0.0
72	San Diego County Valleys, CA	10/22/07	Wildfire	na	0	5	151.1	15.0
73	Maricopa County, AZ	07/25/06	Thunderstorm Wind	92 mph	0	1	150.0	0.0
73	Blaine, Canadian, Kay, Logan, Major, and Payne Counties, OK	12/09/07	Ice Storm	na	0	0	150.0	0.0
73	Bartholomew County, IN	06/05/08	Flood	na	0	0	150.0	150.0
73	St. Mary Parish, LA	09/01/08	Hurricane Gustav	na	0	0	150.0	30.0
73	Orange County Coastal Areas, San Bernardino and Riverside Counties, CA	11/15/08	Wildfire	na	0	0	150.0	0.0
78	South Central Louisiana Coast, LA	10/02/02	Hurricane Lili	na	0	0	149.5	0.0
79	Weld County, CO	05/22/08	Tornado	F3	1	78	147.0	0.0
80	Denver County, CO	06/09/04	Hail	0.75 in.	0	0	146.5	0.0
81	Burnet County, TX	06/26/07	Flash Flood	na	2	0	137.0	0.0
82	West Central Florida, FL	09/25/04	Tropical Storm	na	0	0	134.8	0.0
83	Hennepin County, MN	09/21/05	Thunderstorm Wind	81 mph	1	0	130.0	0.0
83	Polk County, AR	04/09/09	Tornado	F3	3	30	130.0	0.0
85	Franklin and Logan Counties, OH	09/14/08	High Wind	75 mph	0	0	128.7	0.0
86	Hardee, Highlands, Polk, and Sumter Cos., FL	09/05/04	High Wind	69 mph	0	0	127.2	0.0
87	Northern Ohio, OH	01/05/05	Ice Storm	na	0	0	124.9	0.0
88	Northeast Texas, TX	12/12/00	Ice Storm	na	0	0	123.0	0.0
89	Bexar County, TX	05/06/01	Hail	4.00 in.	0	0	120.0	30.0
89	Columbia County, AR	10/11/01	Flash Flood	na	0	0	120.0	0.0
89	Southwest Alabama, AL	07/09/05	Hurricane Dennis	na	0	0	120.0	0.1
89	Bowie County, TX	03/31/08	Hail	2.75 in.	0	0	120.0	0.0
93	Napa County, CA	12/31/05	Flood	na	0	0	115.0	32.5
94	Charles County, MD	04/28/02	Tornado	F4	1	122	114.0	0.0
95	Morton County, ND	06/09/01	Hail	2.75 in.	0	0	113.0	0.0
95	Burleigh County, ND	06/09/01	Hail	1.75 in.	0	0	113.0	0.0
97	Sumter County, GA	03/01/07	Tornado	F3	2	8	110.0	0.0
98	Southeast Louisiana, LA	09/25/02	Tropical Storm	na	0	0	108.6	0.0
99	Marin County, CA	12/31/05	Flood	na	0	0	108.0	0.0
99	Marin County, CA	01/01/06	Flood	na	0	0	108.0	0.0

Note: Deaths, injuries, and damages are date and location specific.

Deadliest Hurricanes: 2000-2009

Rank	Location or County	Date	Type	Mag.	Deaths	Injuries	Property Damage ($mil.)	Crop Damage ($mil.)
1	Galveston Island, TX	06/05/01	Tropical Storm Allison	na	22	0	5,150.0	0.0
2	Mississippi Gulf Coast, MS	08/29/05	Hurricane Katrina	na	15	104	5,880.0	1,510.0
3	Texas Gulf Coast near Galveston, TX	09/12/08	Hurricane Ike (Storm Surge)	na	11	0	4,000.0	0.0
4	Southwest and West Central Florida, FL	08/13/04	Hurricane Charley	na	7	780	5,420.0	285.0
4	Extreme Western Florida Panhandle, FL	09/13/04	Hurricane Ivan	na	7	0	4,000.0	25.0
6	Southeast Florida Coast, FL	08/25/05	Hurricane Katrina	na	6	0	100.0	423.0
7	South Florida, FL	10/24/05	Hurricane Wilma	na	5	0	10,000.0	0.0
8	Central Florida Coast, FL	09/04/04	Hurricane Frances	na	4	0	0.0	0.0
9	Central and South Central Virginia, VA	09/18/03	Tropical Storm Isabel	na	3	0	45.0	7.1
9	Southeast Texas/Southwest Louisiana, TX	09/23/05	Hurricane Rita	na	3	3	159.5	0.0
11	Eastern Virginia, VA	09/18/03	Hurricane Isabel	na	2	0	506.0	10.9
11	Volusia Co., FL	08/13/04	Hurricane Charley	na	2	0	52.0	0.0

Note: Deaths, injuries, and damages are date and location specific.

Hurricanes Causing the Greatest Amount of Property Damage: 2000-2009

Rank	Location or County	Date	Type	Mag.	Deaths	Injuries	Property Damage ($mil.)	Crop Damage ($mil.)
1	Southeast Louisiana, LA	08/28/05	Hurricane Katrina	na	0	0	16,930.0	0.0
2	South Florida, FL	10/24/05	Hurricane Wilma	na	5	0	10,000.0	0.0
3	Mississippi Coast, MS	08/28/05	Hurricane Katrina	na	0	0	7,350.0	0.0
4	Mississippi Gulf Coast, MS	08/29/05	Hurricane Katrina	na	15	104	5,880.0	1,510.0
5	Southwest and West Central Florida, FL	08/13/04	Hurricane Charley	na	7	780	5,420.0	285.0
6	Galveston Island, TX	06/05/01	Tropical Storm Allison	na	22	0	5,150.0	0.0
7	Brevard, Indian River, Martin, St. Lucie, and Volusia Co., FL	09/04/04	Hurricane Frances	na	0	0	4,830.0	93.2
8	Extreme Western Florida Panhandle, FL	09/13/04	Hurricane Ivan	na	7	0	4,000.0	25.0
8	Southwest Louisiana, LA	09/23/05	Hurricane Rita	na	1	0	4,000.0	0.0
10	Southwest Alabama, AL	09/13/04	Hurricane Ivan	na	0	0	2,500.0	25.0
11	Southeast Texas, TX	09/23/05	Hurricane Rita	na	1	0	2,090.0	0.0
12	Extreme Northwest Florida, FL	07/09/05	Hurricane Dennis	na	0	0	1,500.0	0.3
13	Southwest Alabama, AL	08/27/05	Hurricane Katrina	na	0	0	1,000.0	0.0
13	Harris and Matagorda Co., TX	09/12/08	Hurricane Ike	na	0	0	1,000.0	0.0
15	Southeast Florida, FL	09/04/04	Hurricane Frances	na	0	0	621.0	90.0
16	Western Shore Counties of Chesapeake Bay, MD	09/18/03	Tropical Storm Isabel	na	1	200	530.4	0.1
17	Eastern Virginia, VA	09/18/03	Hurricane Isabel	na	2	0	506.0	10.9
18	Southeast Texas, TX	09/12/08	Hurricane Ike	na	0	0	500.0	0.0
19	Eastern North Carolina, NC	09/17/03	Hurricane Isabel	na	0	0	435.6	14.2
20	Brevard, Indian River, Martin, St. Lucie, and Volusia Co., FL	09/25/04	Hurricane Jeanne	na	0	0	379.9	8.7
21	Southwest and Central Louisiana, LA	10/03/02	Hurricane Lili	na	0	3	368.0	168.0
22	Glades, Hendry, Palm Beach, Broward, and Miami-Dade Co., FL	09/25/04	Hurricane Jeanne	na	0	0	323.0	30.0
23	Southeast Mississippi, MS	08/27/05	Hurricane Katrina	na	0	0	250.0	0.0
24	Central Florida, FL	09/05/04	Tropical Storm Frances	na	1	0	179.4	0.0
25	Extreme Southeast Texas, TX	09/23/05	Hurricane Rita	na	3	3	159.5	0.0
26	St. Mary Parish, LA	09/01/08	Hurricane Gustav	na	0	0	150.0	30.0
27	South Central Louisiana Coast, LA	10/02/02	Hurricane Lili	na	0	0	149.5	0.0
28	West Central Florida, FL	09/25/04	Tropical Storm Jeanne	na	0	0	134.8	0.0
29	District of Columbia, DC	09/18/03	Tropical Storm Isabel	na	0	0	125.0	0.0
30	Southwest Alabama, AL	07/09/05	Hurricane Dennis	na	0	0	120.0	0.1
31	Southeast Louisiana, LA	09/25/02	Tropical Storm Isidore	na	0	0	108.6	0.0
32	Lee Co., FL	10/24/05	Hurricane Wilma	na	0	0	101.0	0.0
33	Southeast Florida, FL	08/25/05	Hurricane Katrina	na	6	0	100.0	423.0
33	Northwest Florida, FL	08/27/05	Tropical Storm Katrina	na	0	0	100.0	0.0
33	Iberia and Upper St. Martin Parish, LA	09/01/08	Hurricane Gustav	na	0	0	100.0	30.0
33	Calcasieu, Cameron, and Lafayette Parish, LA	09/01/08	Hurricane Gustav	na	1	0	100.0	5.0
33	Acadia and St. Landry Parish, LA	09/01/08	Hurricane Gustav	na	0	0	100.0	25.0
33	Jefferson and Newton Co., TX	09/12/08	Hurricane Ike	na	0	0	100.0	0.0

Note: Deaths, injuries, and damages are date and location specific.

Deadliest Tornados: 2000-2009

Rank	Location or County	Date	Type	Mag.	Deaths	Injuries	Property Damage ($mil.)	Crop Damage ($mil.)
1	Vanderburgh County, IN	11/06/05	Tornado	F3	20	200	15.0	0.0
2	Dyer County, TN	04/02/06	Tornado	F3	16	70	20.0	0.0
3	Newton County, MO	05/10/08	Tornado	F4	14	200	35.0	0.0
4	Lake County, FL	02/02/07	Tornado	F3	13	9	46.0	0.0
4	Macon County, TN	02/05/08	Tornado	F3	13	44	14.1	1.0
6	Tuscaloosa County, AL	12/16/00	Tornado	F4	11	144	12.5	0.0
6	Mitchell County, GA	02/13/00	Tornado	F3	11	175	20.0	2.0
6	Madison County, TN	05/04/03	Tornado	F4	11	66	30.0	0.0
6	Kiowa County, KS	05/04/07	Tornado	F5	11	63	250.0	0.0
10	Coffee County, AL	03/01/07	Tornado	F4	9	50	250.0	0.0
10	Butler County, IA	05/25/08	Tornado	F5	9	50	75.0	0.0
12	La Salle County, IL	04/20/04	Tornado	F3	8	7	0.0	0.0
12	Columbus County, NC	11/16/06	Tornado	F3	8	20	0.5	0.0
12	Lake County, FL	02/02/07	Tornado	F3	8	10	52.0	0.0
12	Carter County, OK	02/10/09	Tornado	F4	8	0	3.0	0.0
16	Walker County, AL	11/10/02	Tornado	F3	7	40	2.5	0.0
16	Morgan County, TN	11/10/02	Tornado	F3	7	28	0.9	0.0
16	Sumner County, TN	04/07/06	Tornado	F3	7	121	69.0	0.0
16	Maverick County, TX	04/24/07	Tornado	F3	7	0	80.0	0.0
16	Sumner County, TN	02/05/08	Tornado	F3	7	14	10.0	0.0
21	Grady County, GA	02/14/00	Tornado	F3	6	15	3.5	3.0
21	Pontotoc County, MS	02/24/01	Tornado	F3	6	43	28.0	0.0
21	Gibson County, TN	04/02/06	Tornado	F3	6	42	25.0	0.0
21	Baker County, GA	03/01/07	Tornado	F2	6	3	1.2	0.0
21	Ottawa County, OK	05/10/08	Tornado	F4	6	150	15.0	0.0
26	Lawrence County, MO	05/04/03	Tornado	F3	5	33	27.5	0.0
26	Pope County, AR	02/05/08	Tornado	F3	5	15	11.5	0.0
28	Cumberland County, TN	11/10/02	Tornado	F3	4	18	0.5	0.0
28	Mitchell County, GA	03/20/03	Tornado	F3	4	200	6.0	0.0
28	Camden County, MO	05/04/03	Tornado	F3	4	27	5.0	1.0
28	Calhoun County, FL	09/15/04	Tornado	F2	4	5	2.5	0.0
28	Warrick County, IN	11/06/05	Tornado	F3	4	30	65.0	0.0
28	Randolph County, MO	03/12/06	Tornado	F3	4	26	5.0	0.0
28	Lawrence County, AL	02/06/08	Tornado	F4	4	23	0.0	0.0
28	Monona County, IA	06/11/08	Tornado	F3	4	48	0.0	0.0
28	Allen County, KY	02/06/08	Tornado	F3	4	11	1.2	0.0
37	Ashley County, AR	11/24/01	Tornado	F3	3	11	2.0	0.0
37	Walker County, AL	11/10/02	Tornado	F3	3	20	2.5	0.0
37	Crawford County, KS	05/04/03	Tornado	F4	3	20	7.2	1.0
37	Cherokee County, KS	05/04/03	Tornado	F3	3	19	2.7	1.0
37	Cedar County, MO	05/04/03	Tornado	F3	3	37	40.0	3.0
37	De Kalb County, MO	05/29/04	Tornado	F4	3	6	0.3	0.0
37	Pemiscot County, MO	10/18/04	Tornado	F2	3	7	0.3	0.0
37	Pender County, NC	08/13/04	Tornado	F2	3	29	1.3	0.0
37	Van Buren County, AR	02/05/08	Tornado	F4	3	77	22.7	0.0
37	Van Buren County, AR	05/02/08	Tornado	F3	3	6	10.0	0.0
37	Muhlenberg County, KY	02/05/08	Tornado	F3	3	24	21.3	0.0
37	Shelby County, TN	02/05/08	Tornado	F2	3	13	100.0	0.0
37	Hardin County, TN	02/05/08	Tornado	F4	3	5	17.6	0.0
37	Polk County, AR	04/09/09	Tornado	F3	3	30	130.0	0.0

Note: Deaths, injuries, and damages are date and location specific.

Tornados Causing the Greatest Amount of Property Damage: 2000-2009

Rank	Location or County	Date	Type	Mag.	Deaths	Injuries	Property Damage ($mil.)	Crop Damage ($mil.)
1	Coffee County, AL	03/01/07	Tornado	F4	9	50	250.0	0.0
1	Kiowa County, KS	05/04/07	Tornado	F5	11	63	250.0	0.0
3	Cleveland County, OK	05/08/03	Tornado	F3	0	45	210.0	0.0
4	Oklahoma County, OK	05/08/03	Tornado	F4	0	89	160.0	0.0
5	Weld County, CO	05/22/08	Tornado	F3	1	78	147.0	0.0
6	Polk County, AR	04/09/09	Tornado	F3	3	30	130.0	0.0
7	Charles County, MD	04/28/02	Tornado	F4	1	122	114.0	0.0
8	Sumter County, GA	03/01/07	Tornado	F3	2	8	110.0	0.0
9	Prince George's County, MD	09/24/01	Tornado	F3	2	55	100.0	0.0
9	Washita County, OK	10/09/01	Tornado	F3	0	9	100.0	0.0
9	Lancaster County, NE	05/22/04	Tornado	F4	1	30	100.0	0.0
9	Shelby County, TN	02/05/08	Tornado	F2	3	13	100.0	0.0
9	Madison County, TN	02/05/08	Tornado	F4	0	51	100.0	0.0
9	Rutherford County, TN	04/10/09	Tornado	F4	2	58	100.0	0.0
15	Palm Beach County, FL	08/07/03	Tornado	F1	0	28	80.0	0.0
15	Maverick County, TX	04/24/07	Tornado	F3	7	0	80.0	0.0
17	Nueces County, TX	10/24/02	Tornado	F2	1	20	75.0	0.0
17	Arkansas County, AR	05/10/08	Tornado	F3	0	9	75.0	0.0
17	Butler County, IA	05/25/08	Tornado	F5	9	50	75.0	0.0
20	Labette County, KS	04/19/00	Tornado	F3	0	27	71.0	0.0
21	Henry County, GA	07/06/05	Tornado	F2	0	0	70.0	0.0
22	Sumner County, TN	04/07/06	Tornado	F3	7	121	69.0	0.0
23	Warrick County, IN	11/06/05	Tornado	F3	4	30	65.0	0.0
24	Daviess County, KY	01/03/00	Tornado	F3	0	18	64.0	0.0
25	Sumter County, FL	02/02/07	Tornado	F3	0	15	62.0	0.0
26	Lowndes County, MS	11/10/02	Tornado	F3	0	55	60.0	0.0
26	Clay County, MO	05/04/03	Tornado	F2	0	0	60.0	0.0
26	Pemiscot County, MO	04/02/06	Tornado	F3	2	130	60.0	0.0
29	Henry County, VA	09/17/04	Tornado	F2	0	4	53.8	0.0
30	Lake County, FL	02/02/07	Tornado	F3	8	10	52.0	0.0
30	Volusia County, FL	02/02/07	Tornado	F3	0	42	52.0	0.0
30	Volusia County, FL	02/02/07	Tornado	F3	0	42	52.0	0.0
33	Grayson County, KY	05/23/00	Tornado	F3	0	16	50.0	0.0
33	Rankin County, MS	04/24/03	Tornado	F3	0	6	50.0	0.0
33	Dyer County, TN	05/04/03	Tornado	F2	0	10	50.0	0.0
33	Volusia County, FL	12/25/06	Tornado	F0	0	6	50.0	0.0
33	Christian County, MO	03/12/06	Tornado	F3	0	3	50.0	0.0
33	Franklin County, OH	10/11/06	Tornado	F2	0	0	50.0	0.0
33	Grand Forks County, ND	08/26/07	Tornado	F4	1	18	50.0	2.0
33	Pulaski County, AR	04/03/08	Tornado	F1	0	1	50.0	0.0
33	Caddo County, OK	05/13/09	Tornado	F2	0	0	50.0	0.0
42	Lake County, FL	02/02/07	Tornado	F3	13	9	46.0	0.0
42	Cherokee County, GA	05/20/08	Tornado	F1	0	4	46.0	0.0
44	Mckean County, PA	07/21/03	Tornado	F1	0	0	45.7	0.0
45	Stark County, OH	04/28/02	Tornado	F2	0	2	45.5	0.0
46	Desha County, AR	02/24/07	Tornado	F3	0	28	45.0	0.0
47	Barton County, KS	04/21/01	Tornado	F4	1	28	43.0	0.0
48	Marion County, IN	09/20/02	Tornado	F2	0	97	40.0	0.0
48	Cedar County, MO	05/04/03	Tornado	F3	3	37	40.0	3.0
48	Eaton County, MI	08/24/07	Tornado	F3	0	5	40.0	0.0

Note: Deaths, injuries, and damages are date and location specific.

Deadliest Floods: 2000-2009

Rank	Location or County	Date	Type	Mag.	Deaths	Injuries	Property Damage ($mil.)	Crop Damage ($mil.)
1	Monroe County, MI	02/10/01	Flood	na	3	0	0.0	0.0
1	Central Minnesota, MN	04/01/01	Flood	na	3	1	200.0	0.0
1	Kuskokwim Valley, AK	05/07/02	Flood	na	3	0	1.0	0.0
1	South Central Indiana, IN	01/04/04	Flood	na	3	0	0.0	0.0
1	Haywood County, NC	09/16/04	Flood	na	3	0	15.0	0.0
6	Ohio River at Portsmouth, OH	02/20/00	Flood	na	2	2	0.0	0.0
6	Howard County, TX	03/22/00	Flood	na	2	1	0.0	0.0
6	Southern and Central Missouri, MO	05/07/02	Flood	na	2	0	14.2	0.2
6	West Branch of the Delaware River at Delhi, NY	10/29/03	Flood	na	2	1	0.0	0.0
6	Central Tennessee, TN	02/15/03	Flood	na	2	0	0.0	0.0
6	Central Virginia, VA	02/22/03	Flood	na	2	1	3.0	0.0
6	Buchanan and Dickenson Counties, VA	11/19/03	Flood	na	2	0	0.5	0.0
6	Western West Virginia, WV	02/15/03	Flood	na	2	0	8.6	0.0
6	Western West Virginia, WV	11/19/03	Flood	na	2	0	12.0	0.0
6	Boyd, Carter, and Greenup Counties, KY	03/05/04	Flood	na	2	0	0.0	0.0
6	Buncombe County, NC	09/16/04	Flood	na	2	0	40.0	0.0
6	Central Pennsylvania, PA	09/17/04	Flood	na	2	0	50.0	0.0
6	North Central and Northeast Connecticut, CT	10/15/05	Flood	na	2	0	6.0	0.0
6	Central and Southern New Hampshire, NH	10/08/05	Flood	na	2	0	5.7	0.2
6	Bell, Comanche, Falls, and Mills Counties, TX	08/10/05	Flood	na	2	0	0.0	0.0
6	Essex County, MA	05/13/06	Flood	na	2	0	7.0	0.0
6	Monroe County, PA	06/27/06	Flood	na	2	0	16.0	0.0
6	Lewis County, WA	11/04/06	Flood	na	2	0	8.8	0.0
6	York County, ME	04/16/07	Flood	na	2	0	25.0	0.0
6	Somervell County, TX	05/29/07	Flood	na	2	0	0.0	0.0
6	Yell County, AR	04/11/08	Flood	na	2	0	0.0	0.0
6	Jefferson County, IL	03/18/08	Flood	na	2	0	0.0	0.0
6	Fulton County, IN	01/08/08	Flood	na	2	1	0.1	0.0
6	Tunica County, MS	04/01/08	Flood	na	2	0	0.2	0.0
6	Labette County, KS	04/27/09	Flood	na	2	0	0.5	0.0
6	Hutchinson County, TX	09/02/09	Flood	na	2	0	0.0	0.0

Note: Deaths, injuries, and damages are date and location specific.

Floods Causing the Greatest Amount of Property Damage: 2000-2009

Rank	Location or County	Date	Type	Mag.	Deaths	Injuries	Property Damage ($mil.)	Crop Damage ($mil.)
1	Linn County, IA	06/01/08	Flood	na	0	0	750.0	0.0
2	Acadia Parish, LA	10/26/06	Flood	na	0	0	500.0	0.0
3	Broward and Miami-Dade Counties, FL	10/03/00	Flood	na	0	0	450.0	500.0
4	West and Central Utah, UT	01/10/05	Flood	na	1	6	300.0	0.0
5	Johnson County, IA	06/01/08	Flood	na	0	0	230.0	0.0
6	Central and South Central Minnesota, MN	04/01/01	Flood	na	3	1	200.0	0.0
6	Roseau County, MN	06/10/02	Flood	na	0	0	200.0	0.0
8	Sussex County, NJ	08/12/00	Flood	na	0	0	166.5	0.0
9	Bartholomew County, IN	06/05/08	Flood	na	0	0	150.0	150.0
10	Napa County, CA	12/31/05	Flood	na	0	0	115.0	32.5
11	Marin County, CA	12/31/05	Flood	na	0	0	108.0	0.0
11	Marin County, CA	01/01/06	Flood	na	0	0	108.0	0.0
13	Sonoma County, CA	12/31/05	Flood	na	0	0	104.0	3.0
13	Sonoma County, CA	01/01/06	Flood	na	0	0	104.0	3.0
15	Southeast Michigan, MI	05/23/04	Flood	na	0	0	100.0	0.0
15	Jefferson Davis Parish, LA	10/26/06	Flood	na	0	0	100.0	0.0
17	Morgan County, IN	06/04/08	Flood	na	0	0	80.0	100.0
18	Volusia County, FL	05/19/09	Flood	na	0	0	68.6	0.0
19	St Lucie County, FL	08/19/08	Flood	na	0	0	67.0	20.0
20	Klamath and Russian River Basins, CA	12/29/05	Flood	na	0	0	60.8	8.0
21	Benson, Nelson, and Ramsey Counties, ND	08/01/01	Flood	na	0	0	50.0	0.0
21	Central Pennsylvania, PA	09/17/04	Flood	na	2	0	50.0	0.0
21	Chenango County, NY	06/27/06	Flood	na	0	0	50.0	0.0
21	Broome County, NY	06/27/06	Flood	na	0	0	50.0	0.0
21	Lewis County, WA	12/02/07	Flood	na	1	0	50.0	0.0
21	Vigo County, IN	06/01/08	Flood	na	0	0	50.0	50.0
21	Owen County, IN	06/04/08	Flood	na	0	0	50.0	60.0
28	Somerset County, NJ	04/15/07	Flood	na	0	0	48.0	0.0
29	Clay County, IN	06/04/08	Flood	na	0	0	45.0	45.0
30	Brown County, TX	07/06/02	Flood	na	0	0	42.0	0.0
31	Central Indiana, IN	07/05/03	Flood	na	0	0	41.6	12.0
32	Buncombe County, NC	09/07/04	Flood	na	0	0	40.0	1.0
32	Buncombe County, NC	09/16/04	Flood	na	2	0	40.0	0.0
32	Ohio County, WV	09/17/04	Flood	na	0	0	40.0	0.0
32	Monroe County, PA	04/02/05	Flood	na	0	0	40.0	0.0
32	Northhampton County, PA	04/02/05	Flood	na	0	0	40.0	0.0
32	Bucks County, PA	04/03/05	Flood	na	0	0	40.0	0.0
38	Hancock County, WV	09/17/04	Flood	na	0	0	36.0	0.0
38	Columbia County, OR	12/03/07	Flood	na	0	0	36.0	0.0
40	South Central and Southeast Wisconsin, WI	06/01/04	Flood	na	0	0	35.5	216.0
41	Montgomery County, PA	06/16/01	Flood	na	1	0	33.5	0.0
42	Eastern Kentucky, KY	05/31/04	Flood	na	0	0	33.0	0.0
43	Trumbull County, OH	07/21/03	Flood	na	0	0	32.0	0.0
44	Hunterdon County, NJ	04/02/05	Flood	na	0	0	30.0	0.0
44	Hood River County, OR	11/07/06	Flood	na	0	0	30.0	0.0
44	Bucks County, PA	06/28/06	Flood	na	0	0	30.0	0.0
44	Jackson County, IN	06/05/08	Flood	na	0	0	30.0	30.0
48	Warren County, NJ	09/18/04	Flood	na	0	0	28.0	0.0
49	Cumberland River, KY	03/17/02	Flood	na	0	0	26.5	0.0
49	Nern P.W. Snd, AK	10/09/06	Flood	na	0	0	26.5	0.0
49	Tillamook County, OR	12/02/07	Flood	na	0	0	26.5	0.0
52	Allegheny County, PA	09/17/04	Flood	na	1	92	26.0	0.0
52	Morris County, NJ	04/15/07	Flood	na	0	0	26.0	0.0
54	Southeast Ohio, OH	09/17/04	Flood	na	0	0	25.5	0.0

Note: Deaths, injuries, and damages are date and location specific.

Deadliest Flash Floods: 2000-2009

Rank	Location or County	Date	Type	Mag.	Deaths	Injuries	Property Damage ($mil.)	Crop Damage ($mil.)
1	Kauai County, HI	03/13/06	Flash Flood	na	7	0	0.0	0.0
2	Chase County, KS	08/30/03	Flash Flood	na	6	0	0.2	0.0
3	Broome County, NY	06/13/03	Flash Flood	na	5	0	0.1	0.0
3	Stanly County, NC	06/16/03	Flash Flood	na	5	0	0.0	0.0
3	Frederick County, MD	06/27/06	Flash Flood	na	5	1	0.5	0.0
3	Winona County, MN	08/18/07	Flash Flood	na	5	0	0.3	0.1
3	Harris County, TX	04/18/09	Flash Flood	na	5	0	3.5	0.0
8	Bexar County, TX	07/01/02	Flash Flood	na	4	0	0.0	0.0
8	Baltimore City, MD	11/19/03	Flash Flood	na	4	0	0.0	0.0
8	Tutuila County, AS	05/19/03	Flash Flood	na	4	6	50.0	1.0
8	Lewis County, KY	05/27/04	Flash Flood	na	4	0	0.0	0.0
8	Delaware County, NY	06/19/07	Flash Flood	na	4	0	30.0	0.0
8	Bell County, TX	05/24/07	Flash Flood	na	4	0	0.1	0.0
14	Crawford County, IL	08/07/00	Flash Flood	na	3	0	1.0	0.0
14	Kanawha County, WV	02/18/00	Flash Flood	na	3	0	0.5	0.0
14	Coconino County, AZ	08/11/01	Flash Flood	na	3	0	0.0	0.0
14	Hamilton County, OH	07/17/01	Flash Flood	na	3	0	3.5	0.0
14	San Bernardino County, CA	08/26/03	Flash Flood	na	3	0	0.0	0.0
14	Summit County, OH	07/21/03	Flash Flood	na	3	0	100.0	0.0
14	Cannon County, TN	05/05/03	Flash Flood	na	3	0	0.0	0.0
14	Tarrant County, TX	04/30/04	Flash Flood	na	3	0	0.0	0.0
14	Richmond County, VA	08/30/04	Flash Flood	na	3	0	20.0	0.0
14	Perry County, IN	05/25/06	Flash Flood	na	3	0	0.0	0.0
14	Luzerne County, PA	06/27/06	Flash Flood	na	3	0	100.0	0.0
14	Caddo County, OK	08/18/07	Flash Flood	na	3	0	0.0	0.0
14	Cooke County, TX	06/18/07	Flash Flood	na	3	0	28.0	0.0
14	Harris County, TX	08/16/07	Flash Flood	na	3	0	0.7	0.0
14	Pima County, AZ	08/03/08	Flash Flood	na	3	0	0.0	0.0
14	St Louis County, MO	09/14/08	Flash Flood	na	3	0	0.0	0.0
14	Mckinley County, NM	07/11/08	Flash Flood	na	3	0	0.0	0.0

Note: Deaths, injuries, and damages are date and location specific.

Flash Floods Causing the Greatest Amount of Property Damage: 2000-2009

Rank	Location or County	Date	Type	Mag.	Deaths	Injuries	Property Damage ($mil.)	Crop Damage ($mil.)
1	Jefferson County, AL	05/07/03	Flash Flood	na	0	0	1,000.0	0.0
2	Lake County, OH	07/28/06	Flash Flood	na	1	0	320.0	0.0
3	Delaware County, NY	06/27/06	Flash Flood	na	2	0	250.0	0.0
4	Broome County, NY	06/27/06	Flash Flood	na	0	0	200.0	0.0
5	El Paso County, TX	08/01/06	Flash Flood	na	0	0	180.0	0.0
6	Burnet County, TX	06/26/07	Flash Flood	na	2	0	137.0	0.0
7	Columbia County, AR	10/11/01	Flash Flood	na	0	0	120.0	0.0
8	Jefferson County, WI	06/08/08	Flash Flood	na	0	0	102.2	35.0
9	Franklin County, MO	05/07/00	Flash Flood	na	2	0	100.0	0.0
9	Cass County, ND	06/19/00	Flash Flood	na	0	0	100.0	0.0
9	Summit County, OH	07/21/03	Flash Flood	na	3	0	100.0	0.0
9	Luzerne County, PA	09/18/04	Flash Flood	na	0	0	100.0	0.0
9	Tioga County, NY	06/27/06	Flash Flood	na	0	0	100.0	0.0
9	Sullivan County, NY	06/27/06	Flash Flood	na	1	0	100.0	0.0
9	Susquehanna County, PA	06/27/06	Flash Flood	na	1	0	100.0	0.0
9	Luzerne County, PA	06/27/06	Flash Flood	na	3	0	100.0	0.0
9	Hancock County, OH	08/21/07	Flash Flood	na	0	0	100.0	5.0
9	Bartholomew County, IN	06/07/08	Flash Flood	na	0	0	100.0	0.0
19	Johnson County, IN	06/07/08	Flash Flood	na	0	0	90.0	90.0
20	Mcdowell County, WV	05/02/02	Flash Flood	na	2	0	85.0	0.0
21	Montgomery County, KS	07/01/07	Flash Flood	na	1	0	81.1	0.0
22	Honolulu County, HI	10/30/04	Flash Flood	na	0	0	80.0	0.0
23	Milwaukee County, WI	06/08/08	Flash Flood	na	0	0	77.9	0.0
24	Hawaii County, HI	11/01/00	Flash Flood	na	0	0	70.0	0.0
24	Richland County, OH	08/21/07	Flash Flood	na	0	0	70.0	5.0
24	Brevard County, FL	08/20/08	Flash Flood	na	0	0	70.0	0.0
27	Waukesha County, WI	06/08/08	Flash Flood	na	0	0	62.9	1.0
28	Crawford County, OH	08/21/07	Flash Flood	na	0	0	62.0	3.0
29	Wyoming County, WV	07/08/01	Flash Flood	na	1	0	60.0	0.0
29	Wyoming County, PA	06/27/06	Flash Flood	na	0	0	60.0	0.0
31	Stark County, OH	07/27/03	Flash Flood	na	0	0	52.0	0.0
32	Mcdowell County, WV	07/08/01	Flash Flood	na	0	0	50.0	0.0
32	Madison County, MS	04/06/03	Flash Flood	na	0	0	50.0	0.0
32	Scott County, MS	04/06/03	Flash Flood	na	1	0	50.0	0.0
32	Lauderdale County, MS	04/07/03	Flash Flood	na	0	0	50.0	0.0
32	Tutuila County, AS	05/19/03	Flash Flood	na	4	6	50.0	1.0
32	Burlington County, NJ	07/12/04	Flash Flood	na	0	0	50.0	0.0
32	Otsego County, NY	06/27/06	Flash Flood	na	0	0	50.0	0.0
32	Chenango County, NY	06/27/06	Flash Flood	na	1	0	50.0	0.0
32	Oneida County, NY	06/27/06	Flash Flood	na	0	0	50.0	0.0
32	Wayne County, PA	06/27/06	Flash Flood	na	1	0	50.0	0.0
32	Lackawanna County, PA	06/27/06	Flash Flood	na	0	0	50.0	0.0
43	Fayette County, WV	07/08/01	Flash Flood	na	0	0	47.0	0.0
44	Cattaraugus County, NY	08/09/09	Flash Flood	na	1	1	45.0	0.0
44	Jefferson County, KY	08/04/09	Flash Flood	na	0	0	45.0	0.0
46	Lucas County, OH	06/21/06	Flash Flood	na	0	0	42.0	0.0
47	Raleigh County, WV	07/08/01	Flash Flood	na	0	0	40.0	0.0
48	Fillmore County, MN	08/18/07	Flash Flood	na	0	0	38.0	0.3
49	Cook County, IL	08/02/01	Flash Flood	na	0	0	37.0	0.0
50	Cuyahoga County, OH	06/22/06	Flash Flood	na	0	0	35.0	0.0
50	Olmsted County, MN	08/18/07	Flash Flood	na	0	0	35.0	0.0
50	Cook County, IL	09/13/08	Flash Flood	na	1	0	35.0	0.0
53	Ottawa County, MI	06/19/09	Flash Flood	na	0	0	34.0	0.0

Note: Deaths, injuries, and damages are date and location specific.

Hail Storms Causing the Greatest Amount of Property Damage: 2000-2009

Rank	Location or County	Date	Type	Mag.	Deaths	Injuries	Property Damage ($mil.)	Crop Damage ($mil.)
1	Columbia County, WI	06/25/06	Hail	1.00 in.	0	0	500.0	1.7
2	St Louis County, MO	04/10/01	Hail	2.50 in.	0	0	400.0	0.0
3	Jefferson County, CO	07/20/09	Hail	1.25 in.	0	0	350.0	0.0
4	St Louis County, MO	04/10/01	Hail	1.50 in.	0	0	300.0	0.0
4	Douglas County, NE	04/10/01	Hail	1.75 in.	0	1	300.0	0.0
6	Douglas County, NE	04/30/01	Hail	1.75 in.	0	0	200.0	0.0
7	Midland County, TX	04/11/09	Hail	2.00 in.	0	1	161.2	0.0
8	Arapahoe County, CO	06/07/09	Hail	3.00 in.	0	0	161.0	0.0
9	Travis County, TX	03/25/09	Hail	3.00 in.	0	0	160.0	0.0
10	Denver County, CO	06/09/04	Hail	0.75 in.	0	0	146.5	0.0
11	Bexar County, TX	05/06/01	Hail	4.00 in.	0	0	120.0	30.0
11	Bowie County, TX	03/31/08	Hail	2.75 in.	0	0	120.0	0.0
13	Burleigh County, ND	06/09/01	Hail	1.75 in.	0	0	113.0	0.0
13	Morton County, ND	06/09/01	Hail	2.75 in.	0	0	113.0	0.0
15	Summit County, OH	06/08/07	Hail	4.25 in.	0	0	105.0	0.0
16	St Charles County, MO	04/10/01	Hail	2.00 in.	0	0	100.0	0.0
16	St Louis County, MO	04/10/01	Hail	2.75 in.	0	0	100.0	0.0
16	Travis County, TX	03/25/05	Hail	2.00 in.	0	0	100.0	0.0
16	Franklin County, OH	10/04/06	Hail	2.00 in.	0	0	100.0	0.0
16	Licking County, OH	10/04/06	Hail	1.75 in.	0	1	100.0	0.0
16	Hays County, TX	04/20/06	Hail	4.25 in.	0	1	100.0	0.0
16	El Paso County, TX	09/16/09	Hail	1.75 in.	0	10	100.0	0.0
23	Burleigh County, ND	07/21/05	Hail	2.50 in.	0	0	93.0	0.0
24	Pueblo County, CO	07/29/09	Hail	1.75 in.	0	7	90.0	20.0
25	Miller County, AR	03/31/08	Hail	4.00 in.	0	0	85.0	0.0
26	Franklin County, OH	04/20/03	Hail	1.75 in.	0	0	80.0	0.0
27	Montgomery County, OH	04/09/01	Hail	1.75 in.	0	0	70.0	0.0
27	Sedgwick County, KS	04/24/06	Hail	3.00 in.	0	0	70.0	0.0
29	Jefferson Parrish, LA	01/23/00	Hail	1.00 in.	0	0	65.0	0.0
29	Delaware County, OH	04/20/03	Hail	1.50 in.	0	0	65.0	0.0
29	Tulsa County, OK	04/05/05	Hail	3.00 in.	0	0	65.0	0.0
32	Pulaski County, AR	06/30/09	Hail	2.75 in.	0	0	60.0	1.0
33	St Charles County, MO	04/10/01	Hail	1.00 in.	0	0	50.0	0.0
33	St Charles County, MO	04/10/01	Hail	1.50 in.	0	0	50.0	0.0
33	St Louis County, MO	04/10/01	Hail	1.75 in.	0	0	50.0	0.0
33	Scotts Bluff County, NE	07/04/01	Hail	3.00 in.	0	12	50.0	0.0
33	Buffalo County, NE	06/12/02	Hail	5.00 in.	0	15	50.0	2.0
33	Washington County, AR	07/13/03	Hail	2.75 in.	0	0	50.0	0.0
33	Cameron County, TX	04/08/03	Hail	2.75 in.	0	5	50.0	0.0
33	Rice County, MN	08/24/06	Hail	2.75 in.	0	0	50.0	2.3
41	Adams County, CO	06/20/01	Hail	2.50 in.	0	5	49.0	0.0
42	Manitowoc County, WI	05/12/00	Hail	2.50 in.	0	30	46.0	4.0
43	Wood County, WI	06/07/07	Hail	5.50 in.	0	0	45.0	0.0
44	Socorro County, NM	10/05/04	Hail	3.00 in.	0	0	40.0	0.0
44	Adams County, NE	05/11/05	Hail	2.75 in.	0	0	40.0	2.5
44	Cleveland County, OK	11/05/08	Hail	1.75 in.	0	0	40.0	0.0
47	Tarrant County, TX	03/30/09	Hail	2.75 in.	0	0	35.0	0.0
48	Calumet County, WI	05/12/00	Hail	2.00 in.	0	0	32.2	0.0
49	Florence County, SC	05/25/00	Hail	4.50 in.	0	2	30.0	0.0
49	Laurel County, KY	05/01/02	Hail	4.50 in.	0	0	30.0	2.0
49	Laramie County, WY	08/26/02	Hail	2.75 in.	0	0	30.0	0.0
49	Barron County, WI	09/21/05	Hail	3.00 in.	0	0	30.0	0.0
49	Cass County, ND	09/21/07	Hail	3.50 in.	0	0	30.0	0.0
49	Stark County, OH	07/26/08	Hail	2.50 in.	0	0	30.0	0.0
55	Waushara County, WI	05/12/00	Hail	2.75 in.	0	0	26.0	0.0

Note: Deaths, injuries, and damages are date and location specific.

Appendices

National Climate Centers

National Oceanic and Atmospheric Administration
1401 Constitution Avenue, NW
Room 5128
Washington, DC 20230
Tel: 202-482-6090
Fax: 202-482-3154
http://www.noaa.gov
Dr. Jane Lubchenco, Administrator

National Climatic Data Center
Federal Building
151 Patton Avenue
Asheville NC 28801-5001
Tel: 828-271-4800
Fax: 828-271-4876
http://www.ncdc.noaa.gov
Thomas R Karl, Director

Climate Prediction Center
World Weather Building
5200 Auth Road
Camp Springs, MD 20746
Tel: 301-763-8000
http://www.cpc.ncep.noaa.gov
R W Higgins, PhD, Director

Office of Oceanic and Atmospheric Research
Silver Spring Metro Center
Building 3, Room 11458
1315 East-West Highway
Silver Spring, MD 20910
Tel: 301-713-2458
http://www.oar.noaa.gov

National Weather Service Headquarters
1325 East-West Highway
Silver Spring, MD 20910
http://www.nws.noaa.gov

National Huricane Center
11691 S.W. 17th Street
Miami, Florida 33165-2149
Tel: 305-229-4470
http://www.nhc.noaa.gov

Storm Prediction Center
120 David L Boren Blvd
Norman, Oklahoma 73072
Tel: 405-579-0771
http://www.spc.noaa.gov
Russell Schneider, Director

Aviation Weather Center
7220 NW 101st Terrace, Room 118
Kansas City, Missouri 64153-2371
Tel: 816-584-7200
http://www.aviationweather.gov

Regional Climate Centers

High Plains

Dr. Martha Shulski, Director
High Plains Regional Climate Center
727 Hardin Hall, 3310 Holdrege St
School of Natural Resources,University of Nebraska
Lincoln, NE 68583-0997
Tel: 402-472-6709
Fax: 402-472-8736
E-mail: info@hprcc.unl.edu
http://www.hprcc.unl.edu

Midwest

Steve Hilberg, Director
Midwestern Regional Climate Center
Illinois State Water Survey
2204 Griffith Drive
Champaign, IL 61820
Tel: 217-244-8226
Fax: 217-244-0220
E-mail: mrcc@isws.illinois.edu
http://mrcc.isws.illinois.edu

Northeast

Arthur DeGaetano, Director
Northeast Regional Climate Center
1123 Bradfield Hall
Cornell University
Ithaca, NY 14853-1901
Tel: 607-255-1751
Fax: 607-255-2106
E-mail: nrcc@cornell.edu
http://www.nrcc.cornell.edu

Southeast

Dr. Charles E. Konrad II, Director
Southeast Regional Climate Center
University of North Carolina at Chapel Hill
Saunders Hall Campus Box 3220
Chapel Hill, NC 27599-3220
Tel: 919-843-9721
Fax: 919-843-9060
E-mail: sercc@climate.ncsu.edu
http://www.sercc.com

South

Dr. Kevin Robbins, Director
Southern Regional Climate Center
Louisiana State University
E328 Howe-Russell Complex
Baton Rouge, LA 70803
Tel: 225-388-5021
Fax: 225-388-2912
E-mail: krobbins@srcc.lsu.edu
http://www.srcc.lsu.edu

West

Dr. Tim Brown, Director
Western Regional Climate Center
2215 Raggio Parkway
Reno, NV 89512
Tel: 775-674-7010
Fax: 775-674-7016
E-mail: wrcc@dri.edu
http://www.wrcc.dri.edu

State Climate Centers

Alabama

Dr. John Christy, State Climatologist
National Space Science and Technology Center
Room 4082
320 Sparkman Drive
Huntsville, Alabama 35805
Tel: 256-961-7771
http://nsstc.uah.edu/oasc

Alaska

Dr. Gerd Wendler, Director
Alaska Climate Research Center
University of Alaska Fairbanks
903 Koyukuk Drive
PO Box 757320
Fairbanks, AK 99775-7320
Tel: 907-474-7885
Fax: 907-474-7290
E-mail: webmaster@climate.gi.alaska.edu
http://climate.gi.alaska.edu

Arizona

Dr Nancy Selover, State Climatologist
State Climate Office
Arizona State University
PO Box 871508
Tempe, AZ 85287-1508
Tel: 480-965-0580
Fax: 480-965-1473
E-mail: selover@asu.edu
http://azclimate.asu.edu

Arkansas

No state climate center at this time.

California

Michael Anderson
Acting State Climatologist
CA Dept of Water Resources
Division of Flood Management
3310 El Camino Avenue
Suite 200
Sacramento CA 95821
Tel: 916-574-2830
Fax: 916-574-2767
E-mail: manderso@water.ca.gov
http://www.climate.water.ca.gov/

Colorado

Nolan Doesken, State Climatologist
Colorado Climate Center
Dept of Atmospheric Science
Colorado State University
1371 General Delivery
Fort Collins CO 80523-1371
Tel: 970-491-8545
Fax: 970-491-3314
E-mail: nolan@atmos.colostate.edu
http://ccc.atmos.colostate.edu

Connecticut

Dr. X Harrison Yang, State Climatologist
Natural Resources Management and Engineering
University of Connecticut
1376 Storrs Rd
Storrs CT 06269
Tel: 860-486-0135
Fax: 860-486-5408
E-mail: cscc@canr.uconn.edu
http://www.canr.uconn.edu

Delaware

Dr. Daniel J. Leathers
Center for Climatic Research
210 Newark Hall
Department of Geography
University of Delaware
Newark DE 19716
Tel: 302-831-2294
Fax: 302-831-6654
E-mail: leathers@udel.edu
http://www.udel.edu/leathers/stclim.html

Florida

David Zierden, State Climatologist
Florida Climate Center
Florida State University
Center for Ocean-Atmospheric Prediction Studies
2035 E Paul Dirac Dr, 223 RM Johnson Bldg
Tallahassee, FL 32306-2840
Tel: 850-644-3417
Fax: 850-644-5092
E-mail: climate@coaps.fsu.edu
http://www.coaps.fsu.edu/climate_center

Georgia

David Stooksbury, PhD, State Climatologist
Bioligical & Agricultural Engineering Dept.
Driftmier Engineering Center
University of Georgia
Athens GA 30602
Tel: 706-583-0156
Fax: 706-542-8806
E-mail: stooks@engr.uga.edu
http://climate.engr.uga.edu

Hawaii

Pao-Shin Chu, Ph.D., Associate Professor
Department of Meteorology
University of Hawaii at Manoa
2525 Correa Road, HIG 318
Honolulu HI 96822
Tel: 808-956-2573
Fax: 808-956-2877
E-mail: hclimate@hawaii.edu
http://lumahai.soest.hawaii.edu

Idaho

Dr. Russell Qualls, State Coordinator
Dept of Bio & Ag Eng
University of Idaho
PO Box 440904
Moscow ID 83844-0904
Tel: 208-885-6184
E-mail: rqualls@uidaho.edu
http://snow.cals.uidaho.edu

Illinois

Dr. Jim Angel, State Climatologist
Illinois State Water Survey
Institute of Natural Resource Sustainability
University of Illinois
2204 Griffith Drive
Champaign IL 61820-7463
Tel: 217-333-0729
Fax: 217-244-0220
E-mail: jimangel@illinois.edu
http://www.isws.illiois.edu

Indiana

Dr. Dev Niyogi
LILY 2-420
915 W State Street
Purdue University
West Lafayette IN 47907-2054
Tel: 765-418-9575
Fax: 765-496-2926
E-mail: climate@purdue.org
http://iclimate.org

Iowa

Harry Hillaker, Bureau Chief
Iowa Dept. of Agriculture
502 E 9th St
Des Moines, IA 50319
Tel: 515-281-5321
E-mail: climatology@iowaagriculture.gov
http://www.iowaagriculture.gov

Kansas

Mary Knapp, Dept of Communications
Weather Data Library
211 Umberger Hall
Kansas State University
Manhattan KS 66506-3402
Tel: 785-532-7019
Fax: 785-532-6487
E-mail: mknapp@oznet.ksu.edu
http://www.ksre.ksu.edu/wdl

Kentucky

Stuart Foster, Director, State Climatologist
Kentucky Climate Center
Dept of Geography & Geology
Western Kentucky University
1906 College Heights Blve
Bowling Green KY 42101-1066
Tel: 270-745-5983
http://kyclim.wku.edu

Louisiana

Barry Keim, State Climatologist
Department of Geography & Anthropology
Louisiana State University
Baton Rouge LA 70803-4105
Tel: 504-388-6870
Fax: 504-388-2912
E-mail: losc@lsu.edu
http://www.losc.lsu.edu

Maine

Dr. George L Jacobson, State Climatologist
Climate Change Institute
University of Maine
Orno, ME 04469-5790
Tel: 207-581-2991
http://climatechange.umaine.edu/

Maryland

Dr. Kenneth E. Pickering
Maryland State Climatologist Office
Office of Atomospheric and Oceanic Science
University of Maryland
College Park, MD 20742
Tel: 301-405-7223
Fax: 301-314-9482
E-mail: climate@atmos.umd.edu
http://www.aosc.umd.edu/~climate

Massachusetts

Dr. David Taylor
Mass Dept. of Conservation and Recreation
Office of Water Resources
610 Mulpus Road
Lunenburg, MA 01462-1825
Tel: 978-582-1148
E-mail: climat@wx.com
http://www.mass.gov/dcr/watersupply/rainfall/

Michigan

Mr. Geoffrey Anderson
Michigan State Climatologist's Office
Department of Geography
417 Natural Sciences Bldg.
Michigan State University
East Lansing MI 48824-1115
Tel: 517-355-0231
Fax: 517-432-1076
http://climate.geo.msu.edu

Minnesota

Jim Zandlo
Minnesota State Climatology Office
University of Minnesota
439 Borlaug Hall, University of Minnesota
1991 Upper Buford Circl
St. Paul MN 55108-6028
Tel: 651-296-4214
E-mail: climate@umn.edu
http://www.climate.unm.edu/doc/about_us.htm

Mississippi

Dr. Charles L. Wax
Office of the Mississippi State Climatologist
P.O. Box 5448
Mississippi State, MS 39762-5448
Tel: 662-325-3915
http://geosciences.msstate.edu/prospective.htm

Missouri

Dr. Patrick Guinan
Missouri State Climatologist
School of Natural Resources
102 Anheuser-Busch Natural Resources Building
Columbia, MO 65211
Tel: 573-882-5908
Fax: 573-884-5133
E-mail: GuinanP@missouri.edu
http://www.climate.missouri.edu

Montana

No state climate center at this time.

Nebraska

Allen Dutcher
Nebraska State Climate Office
724 Hardin Hall
Lincoln NE 68583-0987
Tel: 402-472-5206
Fax: 402-472-2946
E-mail: adutcher1@unl.edu
http://www.snr.unl.edu/neclimateoffice/index.asp

Nevada

Dr. Jeffrey Underwood
Nevada State Climate Office
University of Nevada, Reno
Mackay Science Building
Room 315
Reno, NV 89557-0118
Tel: 775-784-1723
Fax: 775-784-1058
E-mail: climate@unr.edu
http://www.climate.unr.edu/contact/

New Hampshire

Mary Stampone
New Hampshire State Climate office
102 Huddleston Hall
73 Main Street
Durham NH 03824
Tel: 603-862-3136
Fax: 603-862-4362
E-mail: mary.stampone@unh.edu
http://www.unh.edu/stateclimatologist/

New Jersey

Dr. David A. Robinson
Office of the New Jersey State Climatologist
Rutgers University
54 Joyce Kilmer Avenue
Lucy Stone Hall B224
Piscataway NJ 08854-8054
Tel: 732-445-4741
Fax: 732-445-0006
E-mail: drobins@rci.rutgers.edu
http://climate.rutgers.edu/stateclim

New Mexico

Dr. David Dubois
New Mexico State Climatologist
Dept. of Plant and Environmental Science
New Mexico State University

Las Cruces, NM 88003-8003
Tel: 575-646-2974
Fax: 575-646-6041
E-mail: dwdubois@nmsu.edu
http://weather.nmsu.edu

New York

Mr. Mark Wysocki
New York State Climate Office
Department of Earth and Atmospheric Sciences
1114 Bradfield Hall
Cornell University
Ithaca NY 14853
Tel: 607-255-3034
Fax: 607-255-2106
E-mail: nysc@cornell.edu
http://nysc.eas.cornell.edu

North Carolina

Dr. Sethu Raman
State Climate Office of North Carolina
Campus Box 7236
NC State University
Raleigh NC 27695-7236
Tel: 919-515-1440
Fax: 919-515-1446
E-mail: sethu_raman@ncsu.edu
http://www.nc-climate.ncsu.edu

North Dakota

Dr. Adnan Akyuz
State Climatology Office of North Dakota
Walster Hall 231
NDSU Dept. 7680
P.O. Box 6050
Fargo, ND 58108-6050
Tel: 701-231-6577
Fax: 701-231-7861
E-mail: adnan.akyuz@ndsu.edu
http://www.ndsu.edu/ndsco/

Ohio

Dr. Jeffrey C. Rogers
The State Climatology Office for Ohio
Department of Geography
Ohio State University
103 Bricker Hall
Columbus OH 43210-1361
Tel: 614-292-0148
E-mail: jcrogers@magnus.acs.ohio-state.edu
http://www.geography.ohio-state.edu
faculty/rogers/statclim.html

Oklahoma

Dr. Renee McPherson
Oklahoma Climatological Survey
120 David L. Boren Blvd.
Suite 2900
Norman OK 73072-7305
Tel: 405-325-2541
Fax: 405-325-2550
E-mail: ocs@ou.edu
http://climate.ok.gov

Oregon

Mr. Phil Mote
Oregon Climate Service
Strand Agricultural Hall 326
Oregon State University
Corvallis OR 97331-2209
Tel: 541-737-8927
Fax: 541-737-5710
E-mail: oregon@coas.oregonstate.edu
http://www.ocs.coas.oregonstate.edu

Pennsylvania

Mr. Paul Knight
Pennsylvania State Climatologist
Department of Meteorology
503 Walker Building
University Park, PA 16802
Tel: 814-865-8732
Fax: 814-865-3663
E-mail: psc@mail.meteo.psu.edu
http://climate.met.psu.edu/www_prod

Puerto Rico

Dr. Amos Winter
Dept of Marine Sciences
College of Arts and Sciences
University of Puerto Rico
Mayaguez, PR 00681-9013
Tel: 787-265-5416

Rhode Island

No state climate center at this time.

South Carolina

Hope Mizzell
South Carolina State Climatology Office
1000 Assembly Street
Columbia SC 29201
Tel: 803-734-9568
Fax: 803-765-9080
E-mail: mizzellh@dnr.sc.gov
http://www.dnr.sc.gov/climate/sco

South Dakota

Dr. Dennis Todey
South Dakota Office of Climate and Weather
SAE 213 Box 2120
South Dakota State University
Brookings, SD 57007
Tel: 605-688-5678
Fax: 605-688-6764
E-mail: dennis.todey@sdstate.edu
http://climate.sdstate.edu

Tennessee

No state climate center at this time.

Texas

John Nielsen-Gammon
Texas State Climatologist
Department of Atmospheric Sciences
Texas A&M University
3150 TAMUS
College Station TX 77843-3150
Tel: 979-845-5044
Fax: 979-862-4466
E-mail: osc@ariel.met.tamu.edu
http://www.atmo.tamu.edu/osc

Utah

Mr. Robert Gillies
Utah State Climatologist
Utah Climate Center
Utah State University
4825 Old Main Hill
Logan UT 84322-4825
Tel: 435-797-2664
Fax: 435-797-2117
E-mail: djensen@cc.usu.edu
http://climate.usu.edu

Vermont

Dr. Lesley-Ann Dupigny-Giroux
Vermont State Climate Center
University of Vermont
Department of Geography
200 Old Mill Building
94 University Place
Burlington VT 05405-0114
Tel: 802-656-3060
Fax: 802-656-3042
E-mail: State.Climatologist@uvm.edu
http://www.uvm.edu

Virginia

Dr. Patrick J. Michaels
University of Virginia Climatology Office
Department of Environmental Sciences
291 McCormick Road
PO Box 400123
Charlottesville VA 22904-4123
Tel: 434-924-0548
E-mail: climate@virginia.edu
http://www.climate.virginia.edu

Washington

Nick Bond
Washington State Climatologist
University of Washington
3737 Brooklyn Avenue NE
Box 355672
Seattle WA 98195
Tel: 206-543-3145
Fax: 206-543-0308
E-mail: climate@atmos.washington.edu
http://www.climate.washington.edu

Wisconsin

John Young
Wisconsin State Climatology Office
University of Wisconsin
1225 West Dayton Street
Madison WI 53706-1612
Tel: 608-263-2374
Fax: 608-263-7679
E-mail: stclim@aos.wisc.edu
http://www.aos.wisc.edu

Wyoming

Steve Gray
Wyoming State Climatologist
Water Resource Data Center
Dept. 3943
1000 East University Avenue
Laramie WY 82071-3943
Tel: 307-766-6659
Fax: 307-766-3785
E-mail: pochop@uwyo.edu
http://www.wrds@uwyo.edu

Glossary of Terms

Ablation The process of being removed. Snow ablation usually refers to removal by melting

Absolute Humidity The density of water vapor. It is the mass of the water vapor divided by the volume that it occupies.

Accretion Growth of precipitation particles by collision of ice crystals with supercooled liquid droplets which freeze on impact

Accessory Clouds Clouds that are dependent on a larger cloud system for development and continuance. Accessory clouds associated with the thunderstorm include roll, shelf, mammatus, and wall clouds.

Acid Rain Cloud or rain droplets containing pollutants, such as oxides of sulfur and nitrogen, to make them acidic (e.g. pH 5.6).

Additive data A group of coded remarks in a weather observation that includes pressure tendency, amount of precipitation, and maximum/minimum temperature during specified periods of time.

Adiabatic changes in temperature caused by the expansion (cooling) or compression (warming) of a body of air as it rises or descends in the atmosphere.

Adiabatic Process The change of temperature of air without transferring heat. In an adiabatic process compression results in warming, and expansion results in cooling.

Advection The horizontal transport of air, moisture or other atmospheric properties. Commonly used with temperatures, i.e., "warm air advection".

Advection Fog a type of fog that results from the advection of moist air over a cold surface and the cooling of the air to its dew point that follows; this type of fog is most common in coastal regions.

Advisory Advisories are issued for weather situations that cause significant inconveniences but do not meet warning criteria and, if caution is not exercised, could lead to life-threatening situations. Advisories are issued for significant events that are occurring, are imminent, or have a very high probability of occurrence.

Aerosol Particles of matter, solid or liquid, larger than a molecule but small enough to remain suspended in the atmosphere (up to 100ï¿½1/2 m diameter). Natural origins include salt particles from sea spray and clay particles as a result of weathering of rocks. Aerosols can also originate as a result of man's activities and in this case are often considered pollutants.

Aerovane Aerovanes are commonly used at many weather stations and airports to measure both wind direction and speed. They are similar to wind vanes and cup anemometers except have three-bladed propellers attached to the end of the vane.

AFOS the Automation of Field Operations and Services; AFOS is the computer system that links National Weather Service offices and other computer networks, such as the NOAA Weather Wire, to transmit weather information.

AGL above ground level.

Air the mixture of gases that make-up the earth's atmosphere.Air Mass A large body of air that has similar horizontal temperature and moisture characteristics.

Air-mass Thunderstorm Generally, a thunderstorm not associated with a front or other type of synoptic-scale forcing mechanism. Air mass thunderstorms typically are associated with warm, humid air in the summer months; they develop during the afternoon in response to insolation, and dissipate rather quickly after sunset.

Air Parcel An imaginary small body of air that is used to explain the behavior of air. A parcel is large enough to contain a very great number of molecules, but small enough so that the properties assigned to it are approximately uniform throughout. Air Pollution The existence in the air of substances in concentrations that are determined unacceptable. Contaminants in the air we breathe come mainly from manufacturing industries, electric power plants, automobiles, buses, and trucks.

Air Pressure (atmospheric pressure) air pressure is the force exerted on a surface by the weight of the air above it. The internationally recognized unit for measuring this pressure is the kilopascal.

Airstream A significant body of air flowing in the same general circulation.

Albedo The percentage of light reflected by an object. Snow covered areas have a high albedo (0.9 or 90%) due to their white color.

Alberta Clipper A small, fast-moving low-pressure system that forms in western Canada and travels southeastward into the United States. These storms, which generally bring little precipitation, generally precede an Arctic air mass.

Altimeter An active instrument (see active system) used to measure the altitude of an object above a fixed level.

Altimeter setting That pressure value to which an aircraft altimeter scale is set so that it will indicate the altitude above mean sea-level of an aircraft on the ground at the location for which the value was determined.

Altitude Height expressed as the distance above a reference point, which is normally sea level or ground level.

Altocumulus Mid-altitude clouds with a cumuliform shape. Altostratus Mid-altitude clouds with a flat sheet-like shape. Anabatic wind flowing up an incline, such as up a hillside; upslope wind.

Anafront A front at which the warm is ascending the frontal surface up to high altitudes.

Anemometer An instrument that measures wind speed.

Aneroid barometer An instrument built around a metal structure that bends with changing air pressure. These changes are recorded on a pointer that moves back and forth across a printed scale.

Angular Momentum the energy of motion of a spinning body or mass of air or water.

Angular Velocity the rate at which a spinning body rotates.

Anomaly The deviation of (usually) temperature or precipitation in a given region over a specified period from the normal value for the same region.

Anticyclone A large body of air in which the atmospheric pressure is higher than the pressure in the surrounding air. The winds blow clockwise around an anticyclone in in the Northern Hemisphere. Anticyclonic describes the movement of air around a high pressure, and rotation about the local vertical opposite the earth's rotation. This is clockwise in the Northern Hemisphere.

Anvil Cloud The flat, spreading top of a Cb (cumulonimbus), often shaped like an anvil. Thunderstorm anvils may spread hundreds of miles downwind from the thunderstorm itself, and sometimes may spread upwind (see back-sheared anvil).

Anvil Crawler A lightning discharge occurring within the anvil of a thunderstorm, characterized by one or more channels that appear to crawl along the underside of the anvil. They typically appear during the weakening or dissipating stage of the parent thunderstorm, or during an active MCS.

Anvil Dome A large overshooting top or penetrating top.

Anvil Rollover A circular or semicircular lip of clouds along the underside of the upwind part of a back-sheared anvil, indicating rapid expansion of the anvil. See cumuliform anvil, knuckles, mushroom.

Anvil Zits Frequent (often continuous or nearly continuous), localized lightning discharges occurring from within a thunderstorm anvil.

Arctic Air a mass of very cold, dry air that usually originates over the Arctic Ocean north of Canada and Alaska.

Arctic High a very cold high pressure that originates over the Arctic Ocean.

Arcus A low, horizontal cloud formation associated with the leading edge of thunderstorm outflow (i.e., the gust front). Roll clouds and shelf clouds both are types of arcus clouds.

Aridity A general term used to describe areas suffering from lack of rain or drought. More specifically, a condition in which evaporation exceeds precipitation.

ASOS Automated Surface Observing System. This system observes sky conditions, temperature and dewpoint, wind direction and speed, and barometric pressure, and precipitation.

Atmosphere The mass of air surrounding the earth and bound to it more or less permanently by the earth's gravitational attraction.

Atmospheric Pressure (also called air pressure or barometric pressure) The pressure asserted by the mass of the column of air directly above any specific point.

Atmospheric Stability An indication of how easily a parcel of air is lifted. If the air is very stable it is difficult to make the parcel rise. If the air is very unstable the parcel may rise on its own once started.

Aurora Borealis Also known as the northern lights. The luminous, radiant emission from the upper atmosphere over middle and high latitudes, and centered around the earth's magnetic poles. These silent fireworks are often seen on clear winter nights in a variety of shapes and colors.

Automated Weather Station An unmanned station with various sensors that measure weather elements such as temperature/wind/pressure and transmit these readings for use by meteorologists.

VHRR Advanced Very High Resolution Radiometer. Main sensor on U.S. polar orbiting satellites.

Avalanche a large mass of rapidly moving snow down a steep mountain slope.AVN Aviation Model generated every 12 hours by NCEP. AWIPS Advanced Weather Information Processing System. New NWS computer system integrating graphics, satellite and radar imagery. The successor to AFOS.

Back Door Cold Front A front that moves east to west in direction rather than the normal west to east movement. For instance, one that enters Southern New England from the Gulf of Maine.

Back-building Thunderstorm A thunderstorm in which new development takes place on the upwind side (usually the west or southwest side), such that the storm seems to remain stationary or propagate in a backward direction.

Back-sheared Anvil A thunderstorm anvil which spreads upwind, against the flow aloft. A back-sheared anvil often implies a very strong updraft and a high severe weather potential.

Backing Wind Wind which shifts in a counterclockwise direction with time at a given location (e.g. from southerly to southeasterly), or change direction in a counterclockwise sense with height (e.g. westerly at the surface but becoming more southerly aloft). Backing winds with height are indicative of cold air advection (CAA). The opposite of veering winds.

Ball lightning A relatively rarely seen form of lightning, generally consisting of an orange or reddish ball of the order of a few cm to 30 cm in diameter and of moderate luminosity, which may move up to 1 m/s horizontally with a lifetime of a second or two. Barber Pole A thunderstorm updraft with a visual appearance including cloud striations that are curved in a manner similar to the stripes of a barber pole. The structure typically is most pronounced on the leading edge of the updraft, while drier air from the rear flank downdraft often erodes the clouds on the trailing side of the updraft.

Baroclinic Zone A region in which a temperature gradient exists on a constant pressure surface. Baroclinic zones are favored areas for strengthening and weakening systems.

Barogram The graphic record of pressure produced by a barograph.

Barograph An instrument that provides a continuous record of atmospheric pressure.

Barometer An instrument for measuring atmospheric pressure.

Barometric pressure The actual pressure value indicated by a pressure sensor.

Barometric Tendency The amount and direction of change in barometer readings over a three-hour period.

Barotropic System A weather system in which temperature and pressure surfaces are coincident, i.e., temperature is uniform (no temperature gradient) on a constant pressure surface. Barotropic systems are characterized by a lack of wind shear, and thus are generally unfavorable areas for severe thunderstorm development.

Bear's Cage A region of storm-scale rotation, in a thunderstorm, which is wrapped in heavy precipitation. This area often coincides with a radar hook echo and/or mesocyclone, especially one associated with an HP storm. The term reflects the danger involved in observing such an area visually, which must be done at close range in low visibility.

Beaufort Scale A scale that indicates the wind speed using the effect wind has on certain familiar objects.

Beaver('s) Tail A particular type of inflow band with a relatively broad, flat appearance suggestive of a beaver's tail. It is attached to a supercell's general updraft and is oriented roughly parallel to the pseudo-warm front, i.e., usually east to west or southeast to northwest.

Black Ice thin, new ice that forms on fresh water or dew covered surfaces; it is common on roadways during the fall and early winter and appears "black" because of its transparency.

Blizzard Includes winter storm conditions of sustained winds or frequent gusts of 35 mph or more that cause major blowing and drifting of snow, reducing visibility to less than one-quarter mile for 3 or more hours. Extremely cold temperatures often are associated with dangerous blizzard conditions.

Blizzard warning Issued when blizzard condition are expected or are occurring.Blocking High A high pressure area (anticyclone), often aloft, that remains nearly stationary or moves slowly compared to west-to-east motion. It blocks the movement eastward movement of low pressure areas (cyclones) at its latitude..

Blowing Dust dust that is raised by the wind to moderate heights above the ground to a degree that horizontal visibility decreases to less than seven miles. Visibilities of 1/8 mile or less over a widespread area are criteria for a Blowing Dust Advisory.

Blowing Sand Sand particles picked up from the surface of the earth by the wind to moderate heights above the ground, reducing the reported horizontal visibility to less than 7 statute miles.

Blowing Snow Wind driven snow that reduces visibility to six miles or less causing significant drifting. Blowing snow may be snow that is falling and/or loose snow on the ground picked up by the wind.

Blowing spray Water droplets torn by the wind from a body of water, generally from the crests of waves, and carried up into the air in such quantities that they reduce the reported horizontal visibility to less than 7 statute miles.

Blustery Descriptive term for gusty winds that accompany cold weather.

Bomb Cyclone An extratropical area of low pressure in which the central pressure drops at least 24 millibars in 24 hours.

Boundary Layer In general, a layer of air adjacent to a bounding surface. Specifically, the term most often refers to the planetary boundary layer, which is the layer within which the effects of friction are significant. For the earth, this layer is considered to be roughly the lowest one or two kilometers of the atmosphere.

Bow echo A radar echo which is linear but bent outward in a bow shape. Damaging straight-line winds often occur near the "crest" or center of a bow echo. Areas of circulation also can develop at either end of a bow echo, which sometimes can lead to tornado formation—especially in the left (usually northern) end, where the circulation exhibits cyclonic rotation.

Box (or Watch Box) A severe thunderstorm or tornado watch.

Breezy Wind in the range of 15 mph to 25 mph with mild or warm temperatures.

Brisk Wind in the range of 15 to 25 mph when the temperature is cold.

Broken Clouds Clouds which cover between 5/8ths and 7/8ths of the sky.

Buoyancy That property of an object that enables it to float on the surface of a liquid, or as in the case with air parcels, to ascend and remain freely suspended in the atmosphere.

Bubble High A mesoscale area of high pressure, typically associated with cooler air from the rainy downdraft area of a thunderstorm or a complex of thunderstorms. A gust front or outflow boundary separates a bubble high from the surrounding air.

Bulk Richardson Number (or BRN) A non-dimensional number relating vertical stability and vertical shear (generally, stability divided by shear). High values indicate unstable and/or weakly-sheared environments; low values indicate weak instability and/or strong vertical shear. Generally, values in the range of around 50 to 100 suggest environmental conditions favorable for supercell development.

Bust An inaccurate forecast, usually a situation in which significant weather is expected, but does not occur.

BWER Bounded Weak Echo Region. (Also known as a vault.) Radar signature within a thunderstorm characterized by a local minimum in radar reflectivity at low levels which extends upward into, and is surrounded by, higher reflectivities aloft. This feature is associated with a strong updraft and is almost always found in the inflow region of a thunderstorm. It cannot be seen visually.

CAA Cold Air Advection

Calm the absence of apparent motion in the air.

Cap (or Capping Inversion) A layer of relatively warm air aloft (usually several thousand feet above the ground) which suppresses or delays the development of thunderstorms. Air parcels rising into this layer become cooler than the surrounding air, which inhibits their ability to rise further. As such, the cap often prevents or delays thunderstorm development even in the presence of extreme instability.

CAPE Convective Available Potential Energy. A measure of the amount of energy available for convection. CAPE is directly related to the maximum potential vertical speed within an updraft; thus, higher values indicate greater potential for severe weather. Observed values in thunderstorm environments often may exceed 1,000 joules per kilogram (j/kg), and in extreme cases may exceed 5,000 j/kg. However, as with other indices or indicators, there are no threshold values above which severe weather becomes imminent.

Cb Cumulonimbus cloud

Ceiling The height of the lowest layer of broken or overcast clouds.

Ceilometer A device used to evaluate the height of clouds or the vertical visibility into a surface-based obscuration.

Cell Convection in the form of a single updraft, downdraft, or updraft/downdraft couplet, typically seen as a vertical dome or tower as in a cumulus or towering cumulus cloud. A typical thunderstorm consists of several cells

Celsius a temperature scale in which zero is the freezing point of water and one hundred is the boiling point.

Chance A 30, 40 or 50 percent chance of occurrence of measurable precipitation.

Chinook Wind A strong downslope wind that causes the air to warm rapidly as a result of compressive heating; called a foehn wind in Europe.

Circulation The pattern of the movement of air. General circulation is the flow of air of large, semi-permanent weather systems, while secondary circulation is the flow of air of more temporary weather systems.

Cirriform High altitude ice clouds with a very thin wispy appearance.

Cirrocumulus Cirrus clouds with vertical development. Cirrostratus Cirrus clouds with a flat sheetlike appearance. Cirrus High clouds, usually above 18,000 feet, composed of ice crystals and appearing in the form of white, delicate filaments or white or mostly white patches or narrow bands. Clear Sky condition of less than 1/10 cloud coverage.

Clear Slot A local region of clearing skies or reduced cloud cover, indicating an intrusion of drier air; often seen as a bright area with higher cloud bases on the west or southwest side of a wall cloud.

Climate The prevalent long term weather conditions in a particular area. Climatic elements include precipitation, temperature, humidity, sunshine and wind velocity and phenomena such as fog, frost, and hail storms. Climate cannot be considered a satisfactory indicator of actual conditions since it is based upon a vast number of elements taken as an average.

Climate change This strictly refers to all forms of climatic inconsistency. But it is often used in a more restricted sense to imply a significant change. Within the media, climate change has been used synonymously with global warming. Scientists, however, use the term in a wider sense to include past climate changes also.

Climate Normals Averages of temperatures, precipitation, snowfall, etc. made over standard 30 year periods. These normals span across 3 decades and are rederived every 10 years.Climatology the scientific study of climate.

Closed Low A low pressure area with a distinct center of cyclonic circulation which can be completely encircled by one or more isobars or height contour lines. The term usually is used to distinguish a low pressure area aloft from a low-pressure trough. Closed lows aloft typically are partially or completely detached from the main westerly current, and thus move relatively slowly.

Cloud A visible cluster of tiny water and/or ice particles in the atmosphere.

Cloud Base For a given cloud or cloud layer, it is the lowest level in the atmosphere where cloud particles are visible.

Cloud Condensation Nuclei small particles in the air on which water vapor condenses and forms cloud droplets.

Cloud Streets Rows of cumulus or cumulus-type clouds aligned parallel to the low-level flow. Cloud streets sometimes can be seen from the ground, but are seen best on satellite photographs.

Cloud Tags Ragged, detached cloud fragments; fractus or scud.

Cloudburst A sudden, intense rainfall that is normally of short duration.

Cloudy the state of the sky when 7/10ths or more of the sky is covered by clouds.

Coastal Flood Warning Issued when there is widespread coastal flooding expected within 12 hours, more than just typical overwash.

Coastal Flooding The inundation of land areas along the coast caused by sea water above normal tidal actions. This is often caused by prolonged strong onshore flow of wind and/or high astronomical tides.

Coastal Forecast A forecast of wind, wave and weather conditions between the coastline and 25 miles offshore.

Coastal Waters include the area from a line approximating the mean high water along the mainland or island as far out as 25 miles including the bays, harbors and sounds.

Cold Advection (CAA) Transport of cold air into a region by horizontal winds.

Cold Air Damming Cold air damming occurs when a cold dome of high pressure settles over northeastern New England. The clockwise circulation around the high pressure center brings northeasterly winds to the mid Atlantic region. The northeasterly winds bank cold air against the eastern slopes of the Appalachian Mountains. Warmer air from the west or southwest is lifted above the cold air as it moves instead of warming the surface.

Cold-air Funnel A funnel cloud or (rarely) a small, relatively weak tornado that can develop from a small shower or thunderstorm when the air aloft is unusually cold (hence the name). They are much less violent than other types of tornadoes.

Cold Front A narrow transition zone separating advancing colder air from retreating warmer air. The air behind a cold front is cooler and typically drier than the air it is replacing.

Cold Low a low pressure system with cold air mass from near the surface to all vertical levels (also called a cold core low).

Cold Pool A region of relatively cold air, represented on a weather map analysis as a relative minimum in temperature surrounded by closed isotherms. Cold pools aloft represent regions of relatively low stability, while surface-based cold pools are regions of relatively stable air.

Collar Cloud Frequently used as a synonym for wall cloud, although it actually is a generally circular ring of cloud surrounding the upper portion of a wall cloud.

Comma Cloud A synoptic scale cloud pattern with a characteristic comma-like shape, often seen on satellite photographs associated with large and intense low-pressure systems.

Condensation The process by which water vapor becomes a liquid; the opposite of evaporation, which is the conversion of liquid to vapor.

Condensation Nuclei Small particles in the air around which water vapor condenses.

Conduction The transfer of heat by molecular action between bodies that are in contact.

Confluence A pattern of wind flow in which air flows inward toward an axis oriented parallel to the general direction of flow. It is the opposite of difluence. Confluence is not the same as convergence. Winds often accelerate as they enter a confluent zone, resulting in speed divergence which offsets the (apparent) converging effect of the confluent flow.

Congestus (or Cumulus Congestus) A large cumulus cloud with great vertical development, usually with a cauliflower-like appearance, but lacking the characteristic anvil shaped top of a Cb.

Continental Air Mass A dry air mass originating over a large land area.

Contrail A cloud-like stream formed in cold, clear air behind the engines of an airplane.

Convection The transfer of heat within a the air by its movement. The term is used specifically to describe vertical transport of heat and moisture, especially by updrafts and downdrafts in an unstable atmosphere.

Convective Outlook A forecast containing the area(s) of expected thunderstorm occurrence and expected severity over the contiguous United States, issued several times daily by the SPC.

Convective Temperature The approximate temperature that the air near the ground must warm to in order for surface-based convection to develop, based on analysis of a sounding.

Convergence An atmospheric condition that exists when the winds cause a horizontal net inflow of air into a specified region. Divergence is the opposite, where winds cause a horizontal net outflow of air from a specified region.

Coordinated Universal Time (UTC) The time in the zero degree meridian time zone.

Combined Seas The combined height of swell and wind waves.

Cooling Degree Day A form of degree day used to estimate the required energy for cooling. one cooling degree day occurs for each degree the daily mean temperature is above 65 degrees Fahrenheit.

Coriolis Force An apparent force caused by the rotation of the Earth. In the Northern Hemisphere winds are deflected to the right, and in the Southern Hemisphere to the left. In synoptic scale weather systems (hurricanes and large mid-latitude storms), the Coriolis force causes the air to rotate around a low pressure center in a cyclonic direction. The air flowing around a hurricane spins counter-clockwise in the northern hemisphere

Corona a disk of light surrounding the sun or moon; this is a result of the diffraction of light by small water droplets.CRS Console Replacement System. This consists of a computer system and computer voice that is used to automate NOAA Weather Radio.

Cumulonimbus Cloud A vertically developed cloud, often capped by an anvil shaped cloud. Also called a thunderstorm cloud, it is frequently accompanied by heavy showers, lightning, thunder, and sometimes hail or gusty winds. Cumulus Cloud A cloud in the shape of individual detached domes, with a flat base and a bulging upper portion resembling cauliflower.

Cumulus Congestus A large cumulus cloud with great vertical development, usually with a cauliflower-like appearance, but lacking the characteristic anvil shaped top of a Cb.Cut Off Low An upper level low pressure system that is no longer in the normal west to east upper air flow. Usually a cut-off low will lie to the South of the established upper air flow.

Cyclogenesis Development or intensification of a low-pressure center

Cyclone An area of low pressure around which winds blow counterclockwise in the Northern Hemisphere. Also the term used for a hurricane in the Indian Ocean and in the Western Pacific Ocean.

Cyclonic Circulation (or Cyclonic Rotation) Circulation (or rotation) which is in the same sense as the Earth's rotation, i.e., counterclockwise (in the Northern Hemisphere) as would be seen from above.

Dart Leader In lightning, the leader which, after the first stroke, initiates each succeeding stroke of a composite flash of lightning.

Debris Cloud A rotating "cloud" of dust or debris, near or on the ground, often appearing beneath a condensation funnel and surrounding the base of a tornado.

Decouple The tendency for the surface wind to become much lighter than wind above it at night when the surface temperature cools.

Degree Day a measure of the departure of the daily mean temperature from the normal daily temperature; heating and cooling Degree Days are the departure of the daily mean temperature from sixty-five degrees Fahrenheit.

Dendrite hexagonal ice crystals with complex and often fernlike branches.

Dense Fog a fog in which the visibility is less than one-quarter mile.

Dense Fog Advisory Issued when fog is expected to reduce visibility to 1/4 mile or less over a widespread are for at least 3 hours.

Density Of Air The mass of air divided by its volume. The air's density depends on its temperature, its pressure and how much water vapor is in the air.

Density Altitude The pressure altitude corrected for temperature deviations from the standard atmosphere. It is used by pilots when setting aircraft performance.Depression a region of low atmospheric pressure that is usually accompanied by low clouds and precipitation.

Depth Hoar Large (one to several millimeters in diameter), cohesionless, coarse, faceted snow crystals which result from the presence of strong temperature gradients within the snowpack

Derechoe A widespread and usually fast-moving windstorm associated with convection. Derechoes include any family of downburst clusters produced by an extratropical MCS, and can produce damaging straight-line winds over areas hundreds of miles long and more than 100 miles across.

Dew Moisture from water vapor in the air that has condensed on objects near the ground, whose temperatures have fallen below the dewpoint temperature. Dew Point The temperature to which the air must be cooled for water vapor to condense and form fog or clouds.

Diamond Dust A fall of non-branched (snow crystals are branched) ice crystals in the form of needles, columns, or plates. (same as ice crystals)

Differential Motion Cloud motion that appears to differ relative to other nearby cloud elements, e.g. clouds moving from left to right relative to other clouds in the foreground or background. Cloud rotation is one example of differential motion, but not all differential motion indicates rotation. For example, horizontal wind shear along a gust front may result in differential cloud motion without the presence of rotation.

Difluence (or Diffluence) A pattern of wind flow in which air moves outward (in a "fan-out" pattern) away from a central axis that is oriented parallel to the general direction of the flow. It is the opposite of confluence.

Dirty ridge Most of the time, upper-level ridges bring fairly clear weather as the storms are steered around the ridge. Sometimes, however, strong storms undercut the ridge and create precipitation. Ridges that experience this undercutting by storms are known as dirty ridges because of the unusual precipitation.

Disturbance a disruption of the atmosphere that usually refers to a low pressure area, cool air and inclement weather.

Diurnal Daily; related to actions which are completed in the course of a calendar day, and which typically recur every calendar day (e.g., diurnal temperature rises during the day, and falls at night).

Divergence The expansion or spreading out of a vector field; usually said of horizontal winds. It is the opposite of convergence.

Doldrums the regions on either side of the equator where air pressure is low and winds are light.

Doppler Radar A type of weather radar that determines whether atmospheric motion is toward or away from the radar. It determines the intensity of rainfall and uses the Doppler effect to measure the velocity of droplets in the atmosphere.

Downburst A strong downdraft resulting in an outward burst of damaging winds on or near the ground. Downburst winds can produce damage similar to a strong tornado.

Downdraft A column of generally cool air that rapidly sinks to the ground, usually accompanied by precipitation as in a shower or thunderstorm. .

Downslope wind Air that descends an elevated plain and consequently warms and dries. Occurs when prevailing wind direction is from the same direction as the elevated terrain and often produces fair weather conditions.

Downstream In the same direction as a stream or other flow, or toward the direction in which the flow is moving.

Drifting snow Uneven distribution of snowfall caused by strong surface winds. Drifting snow does not reduce visibility.

Dry Adiabat A line of constant potential temperature on a thermodynamic chart.

Dry Line A boundary separating moist and dry air masses, and an important factor in severe weather frequency in the Great Plains.

Dry-line Bulge A bulge in the dry line, representing the area where dry air is advancing most strongly at lower levels

Drizzle Small, slowly falling water droplets, with diameters between .2 and .5 millimeters.

Drought Abnormally dry weather in a region over an extended period sufficient to cause a serious hydrological (water cycle) imbalance in the affected area. This can cause such problems as crop damage and water-supply shortage.

Dry Punch A surge of drier air; normally a synoptic-scale or mesoscale process. A dry punch at the surface results in a dry line bulge.

Dry Slot A zone of dry (and relatively cloud-free) air which wraps east or northeastward into the southern and eastern parts of a synoptic scale or mesoscale low pressure system. A dry slot generally is seen best on satellite photographs.

Dryline A boundary which separates warm, dry air from warm, moist air. The differences in the two air masses may be significant. The dry line is usually a boundary of instability along which thunderstorms form.

Dust Devil A small, rapidly rotating wind that is made visible by the dust, dirt or debris it picks up. Also called a whirlwind. Dust devils usually develop during hot, sunny days over dry and dusty or sandy areas.

Dust Storm An area where high surface winds have picked up loose dust, reducing visibility to less than one-half mile.

Dust Plume A non-rotating "cloud" of dust raised by straight-line winds. Often seen in a microburst or behind a gust front.

Dust Whirl A rotating column of air rendered visible by dust.

Dynamics Generally, any forces that produce motion or affect change. In operational meteorology, dynamics usually refer specifically to those forces that produce vertical motion in the atmosphere.

Easterly Wave A wavelike disturbance in the tropical easterly winds that usually moves from east to west. Such waves can grow into tropical depressions.

ECMF European Center for Meteorology Forecast model.

Eddy A small volume of air that behaves differently from the predominant flow of the layer in which it exists, seemingly having a life of its own. An example of such would be a tornado, which has its own distinct rotation, but is different than the large-scale flow of air surrounding the thunderstorm in which the tornado is born. El Nii¿1/2o A major warming of the equatorial waters in the eastern Pacific Ocean. El Nii¿1/2o events usually occur every 3 to 7 years, and are related to shifts in global weather patterns. (Spanish for the "Christ Child", named this because it often begins around Christmas.)

Enhanced greenhouse effect The natural greenhouse effect has been enhanced by man's emissions of greenhouse gases. Increased concentrations of carbon dioxide, methane and nitrous oxide trap more infra-red radiation, so heating up the atmosphere.

Enhanced Wording An option used by the SPC in tornado and severe thunderstorm watches when the potential for strong/violent tornadoes, or unusually widespread damaging straight-line winds, is high.

Entrance Region The region upstream from a wind speed maximum in a jet stream (jet max), in which air is approaching (entering) the region of maximum winds, and therefore is accelerating. This acceleration results in a vertical circulation that creates divergence in the upper-level winds in the right half of the entrance region (as would be viewed looking along the direction of flow). This divergence results in upward motion of air in the right rear quadrant (or right entrance region) of the jet max. Severe weather potential sometimes increases in this area as a result.

ENSO El Nino-Southern Oscillation.

Equilibrium Level (or EL) On a sounding, the level above the level of free convection (LFC) at which the temperature of a rising air parcel again equals the temperature of the environment.

ETA "Eta" (from Greek) model generated every 12 hours by NCEP

Evaporation the process of a liquid changing into a vapor or gas.

Excessive Heat Warning Issued within 12 hours of the onset of the following conditions: heat index of at least 105 degrees Fahrenheit for more than 3 hours per day for 2 consecutive days or heat index more than 115 degrees Fahrenheit for any period of time.

Excessive Heat Watch Issued for the potential of the following conditions within 12 to 36 hours: heat index of at least 105 degrees Fahrenheit for more than 3 hours per day for 2 consecutive days or heat index more than 115 degrees Fahrenheit for any period of time.

Exit Region The region downstream from a wind speed maximum in a jet stream (jet max), in which air is moving away from the region of maximum winds, and therefore is decelerating. This deceleration results in divergence in the upper-level winds in the left half of the exit region (as would be viewed looking along the direction of flow). This divergence results in upward motion of air in the left front quadrant (or left exit region) of the jet max. Severe weather potential sometimes increases in this area as a result.

Extended Outlook a basic forecast of general weather conditions three to five days in the future.

Extratropical cyclone A storm that forms outside the tropics, sometimes as a tropical storm or hurricane changes. See table below for differences between extratropical and tropical cyclones. Eye The low pressure center of a tropical cyclone. Winds are normally calm and sometimes the sky clears. Eye wall The ring of thunderstorms that surrounds a storm's eye. The heaviest rain, strongest winds and worst turbulence are normally in the eye wall.

Fahrenheit the standard scale used to measure temperature in the United States; in which the freezing point of water is thirty-two degrees and the boiling point is two hundred and twelve degrees.

Fair describes weather in which there is less than 4/10ths of opaque cloud cover, no precipitation, and there is no extreme visibility, wind or temperature conditions.

Fall Wind a strong, cold, downslope wind.

Feeder Bands Lines or bands of low-level clouds that move (feed) into the updraft region of a thunderstorm, usually from the east through south (i.e., parallel to the inflow). This term also is used in tropical meteorology to describe spiral-shaped bands of convection surrounding, and moving toward, the center of a tropical cyclone. Fetch The area in which ocean waves are generated by the wind. Also refers to the length of the fetch area, measured in the direction of the wind.

Few A cloud layer that covers between 1/8th and 2/8ths of the sky.

Flanking Line A line of cumulus connected to and extending outward from the most active portion of a parent cumulonimbus, usually found on the southwest side of the storm. The cloud line has roughly a stair step appearance with the taller clouds adjacent to the parent cumulonimbus. It is most frequently associated with strong or severe thunderstorms.

Flash Flood A flood that occurs within a few hours (usually less than six) of heavy or excessive rainfall, dam or levee failure or water released from an ice jam.

Flash Flood Warning Issued to inform the public, emergency management, and other cooperating agencies that flash flooding is in progress, imminent, or highly likely.

Flash Flood Watch Issued to indicate current or developing hydrologic conditions that are favorable for flash flooding in and close to the watch area, but the occurrence is neither certain or imminent.

Flood a condition that occurs when water overflows the natural or artificial confines of a stream or river; the water also may accumulate by drainage over low-lying areas.

Flood Crest The highest stage or flow occurring in a flood.

Flood Warning Issued when there is expected inundation of a normally dry area near a stream, other water course; or unusually severe ponding of water.

Flood Stage The stage at which water overflowing the banks of a river, stream or body of water begins to cause damage.Flurries Light snow falling for short durations. No accumulation or just a light dusting is all that is expected.

Foehn A warm dry wind on the lee side of a mountain range. The heating and drying are due to adiabatic compression as the wind descend downslope.

Fog Water that has condensed close to ground level, producing a cloud of very small droplets that reduces visibility to less than one km (three thousand and three hundred feet).

Fogbow A rainbow that has a white band that appears in fog, and is fringed with red on the outside and blue on the inside.

Forecast A forecast provides a description of the most significant weather conditions expected during the current and following days. The exact content depends upon the intended user, such as the Public or Marine forecast audiences.

Fractus Ragged, detached cloud fragments

Freeze Occurs when the surface air temperature is expected to be 32 degrees Fahrenheit or below over a widespread area for a significant period of time.

Freeze Warning Issued during the growing season when surface temperatures are expected to drop below freezing over a large area for an extended period of time, regardless if frost develops or not.

Freezing The change in a substance from a liquid to a solid state.

Freezing Drizzle Drizzle that falls in liquid form and then freezes upon impact with the ground or an item with a temperature of 32 degrees Fahrenheit or less, possibly producing a thin coating of ice. Even in small amounts, freezing drizzle may cause traveling problems.

Freezing fog A suspension of numerous minute ice crystals in the air, or water droplets at temperatures below 0 Celsius, based at the Earth's surface, which reduces horizontal visibility; also called ice fog.

Freezing Level The altitude in the atmosphere where the temperature drops to 32F.

Freezing Nuclei Particles suspended in the air around which ice crystals form.

Freezing Rain Rain that freezes on objects such as trees, cars and roads, forming a coating or glaze of ice. Temperatures at higher levels are warm enough for rain to form, but surface temperatures are below 32 degrees Fahrenheit, causing the rain to freeze on impact.

Freshet the annual spring rise of streams in cold climates as a result of snow melt; freshet also refers to a flood caused by rain or melting snow.

Frog Storm the first bad weather in spring after a warm period.

Front The boundary or transition zone between two different air masses. The basic frontal types are cold fronts, warm fronts and occluded fronts.

Frost The formation of thin ice crystals on the ground or other surfaces. Frost develops when the temperature of the exposed surface falls below 32 degrees Fahrenheit and water vapor is deposited as a solid.

Frost Advisory Issued during the growing season when widespread frost formation is expected over an extensive area. Surface temperatures are usually in the mid 30s Fahrenheit.

Frost Point When the temperature to which air must be cooled to in order to be saturated is below freezing.

Frozen Dew When liquid dew changes into tiny beads of ice. The change occurs after dew formation and then the temperature falls below freezing.

Fujita Scale System developed by Dr. Theodore Fujita to classify tornadoes based on wind damage. Scale is from F0 for weakest to F5 for strongest tornadoes.

Fujiwhara effect The Fujiwhara effect describes the rotation of two storms around each other.

Funnel Cloud A rotating, cone-shaped column of air extending downward from the base of a thunderstorm but not touching the ground. When it reaches the ground it is called a tornado.

Gale Sustained wind speeds from 34 to 47 knots (39 to 54 mph).

Gale Warning A marine weather warning for gale force winds from a non tropical system.

Geostationary Satellite A satellite positioned over the equator that rotates at the same rate as the earth, remaining over the same spot.

Glaciation The transformation of cloud particles from water droplets to ice crystals. Thus, a cumulonimbus cloud is said to have a "glaciated" upper portion.

Glaze a layer or coating of ice that is generally smooth and clear, and forms on exposed objects by the freezing of liquid raindrops.

Global Warming A theory that increased concentrations of greenhouse gases are causing an elevation in the Earth's surface temperature.

GOES Geostationary Operational Environmental Satellite

GOES-8 One of the Geostationary Operational Environmental Satellites. They are owned and run by the National Oceanic and Atmospheric Administration (NOAA), while NASA designs and launches them.

Gradient The time rate or spatial rate of change of an atmospheric property.

Graupel Small pellets of ice created when supercooled water droplets coat, or rime, a snowflake. The pellets are cloudy or white, not clear like sleet, and often are mistaken for hail.

Gravity Wave A wave disturbance in which buoyancy acts as the restoring force on parcels displaced from hydrostatic equilibrium. Waves on the ocean are examples of gravity waves.

Greenhouse Effect The warming of the atmosphere by the trapping of longwave radiation (heat) being radiated to space. The gases most responsible for this effect are water vapor and carbon dioxide.

Ground Fog Shallow fog (less than twenty feet deep) produced over the land by the cooling of the lower atmosphere as it comes in contact with the ground. Also known as radiation fog.

Growing Degree Day A form of degree day to estimate the approximate dates when a crop will be ready to harvest. one growing degree day occurs when the daily mean temperature is one degree above the minimum temperature required for the growth of that specific crop.

Growing Season The period of time between the last killing frost of spring and the first killing frost of autumn.

Gust A brief sudden increase in wind speed. Generally the duration is less than 20 seconds and the fluctuation greater than 10 mph. Gust Front The leading edge of the downdraft from a thunderstorm. A gust front may precede the thunderstorm by several minutes and have winds that can easily exceed 80 mph.

Gustnado (or Gustinado) Gust front tornado. A small tornado, usually weak and short-lived, that occurs along the gust front of a thunderstorm. Often it is visible only as a debris cloud or dust whirl near the ground. .

Hail Precipitation in the form of balls or irregular lumps of ice produced by liquid precipitation, freezing and being coated by layers of ice as it is lifted and cooled in strong updrafts of thunderstorms..

Halo A ring or arc that encircles the sun or moon. Halos are caused by the refraction of light through the ice crystals in cirrus clouds.

Hard Freeze freeze where vegetation is killed and the ground surface is frozen solid.

Harmattan a hot, dry, and dusty northeasterly or easterly wind that occurs in West Africa north of the equator and is caused by the outflow of air from subtropical high pressure areas.

Haze Fine dust or salt particles in the air that reduce visibility.

Heat Advisory Issued within 12 hours of the onset of the following conditions: heat index of at least 105 degrees but less than 115 degrees for less than 3 hours per day. Nighttime lows remain above 80 degrees for 2 consecutive days.

Heat Balance The equilibrium existing between the radiation received and emitted by a planetary system.Heat Index An index that combines air temperature and humidity to give an apparent temperature (how hot it feels).

Heat Island A dome of elevated temperatures over an urban area caused by the heat absorbed by structures and pavement.

Heat Lightning Lightning that can be seen, but is too far away for the thunder to be heard.

Heating Degree Day A form of degree day used to estimate the required energy for heating. One heating degree day occurs for each degree the daily mean temperature is below 65 degrees Fahrenheit.

Heavy snow Depending on the region of the USA, this generally means that four or more inches of snow has accumulated in 12 hours, or six or more inches of snow in 24 hours.

Heavy Snow Warning Older terminology replaced by winter storm warning for heavy snow. Issued when 7 or more inches of snow or sleet is expected in the next 24 hours. A warning is used for winter weather conditions posing a threat to life and property.

Heavy Surf the result of large waves breaking on or near the shore resulting from swells or produced by a distant storm.

Helicity A property of a moving fluid which represents the potential for helical flow (i.e. flow which follows the pattern of a corkscrew) to evolve. Helicity is proportional to the strength of the flow, the amount of vertical wind shear, and the amount of turning in the flow (i.e. vorticity).

High An area of high pressure, usually accompanied by anticyclonic and outward wind flow. Also known as an anticyclone.

High Risk (of severe thunderstorms) Severe weather is expected to affect more than 10 percent of the area.

High Wind Warning Issued when sustained winds from 40 to 73 mph are expected for at least 1 hour; or any wind gusts are expected to reach 58 mph or more.

High Wind Watch Issued when conditions are favorable for the development of high winds over all of or part of the forecast area but the occurrence is still uncertain. The criteria of a high wind watch are listed under the high wind warning and should include the area affected, the reason for the watch and the potential impact of the winds.

Hodograph A plot representing the vertical distribution of horizontal winds, using polar coordinates. A hodograph is obtained by plotting the end points of the wind vectors at various altitudes, and connecting these points in order of increasing height.

Hook Echo A radar pattern sometimes observed in the southwest quadrant of a tornadic thunderstorm. Appearing like a fishhook turned in toward the east, the hook echo is precipitation aloft around the periphery of a rotating column of air 2-10 miles in diameter.

Horse Latitudes Subtropical regions where anticyclones produce settled weather.

Hot Spot Typically large areas of pavement, these "hot spots" are heated much quicker by the sun than surrounding grasses and forests. As a result, air rises upwards from the relatively hot surface of the pavement, reaches its condensation level, condenses, and forms a cloud above the "hot spot".

Humidity The amount of water vapor in the atmosphere.

Hurricane A severe tropical cyclone with sustained winds over 74 mph (64 knots). Normally applied to such storms in the Atlantic Basin and the Pacific Ocean east of the International Date Line.

Hurricane Warning Warning issued when sustained winds of 74 mph (64 knots) or more are expected within 24 hours. This implies a dangerous storm surge.Hydrology The study of the waters of the earth with relation to the effects of precipitation and evaporation upon the water in streams, rivers, lakes, and its effect on land surfaces.

Hydrologic Cycle The composite picture of the interchange of water substance between the earth, the atmosphere and the seas which includes the change of state and vertical and horizontal transport.

Hydrosphere The totality of water encompassing the Earth, comprising all the bodies of water, ice, and water vapor in the atmosphere.

Hygrometer An instrument used to measure humidity.

Ice age Periods in the history of the earth characterized by a growth of the ice caps towards the equator and a general lowering of global surface temperatures, especially in temperate mid-latitudes. The most recent ice age ended about 10,000 years ago. Ice advances in this period are known to have altered the whole pattern of global atmospheric circulation.

Ice Crystals A barely visible crystalline form of ice that has the shape of needles, columns or plates. Ice crystals are so small that they seem to be suspended in air. Ice crystals occur at very low temperatures (around zero degrees F and colder) in a stable atmosphere.

Ice Fog A suspension of numerous minute ice crystals in the air, or water droplets at temperatures below 0 Celsius, based at the Earth's surface, which reduces horizontal visibility. Usually occurs at -20F and below.

Ice Jam An accumulation of broken river ice caught in a narrow channel that frequently produces local floods during a spring break-up.

Ice pellets Precipitation of transparent or translucent pellets of ice, which are round or irregular, rarely conical, and which have a diameter of 0.2 inch (5 mm), or less. There are two main types. Hard grains of ice consisting of frozen raindrops and pellets of snow encased in a thin layer of ice.

Ice Storm Liquid rain falling and freezing on contact with cold objects creating ice build-ups of 1/4th inch or more that can cause severe damage.

Ice storm warning Older terminology replaced by winter storm warning for severe icing. Issued when 1/2 inch or more of accretion of freezing rain is expected. This may lead to dangerous walking or driving conditions and the pulling down of power lines and trees. A warning is used for winter weather conditions posing a threat to life and property.

Indefinite ceiling The ceiling classification applied when the reported ceiling value represents the vertical visibility upward into surface-based obscuration.

Inflow Bands (or Feeder Bands) Bands of low clouds, arranged parallel to the low-level winds and moving into or toward a thunderstorm.

Inflow Jets Local jets of air near the ground flowing inward toward the base of a tornado.

Inflow Notch A radar signature characterized by an indentation in the reflectivity pattern on the inflow side of the storm. The indentation often is V-shaped, but this term should not be confused with V-notch. Supercell thunderstorms often exhibit inflow notches, usually in the right quadrant of a classic supercell, but sometimes in the eastern part of an HP storm or in the rear part of a storm (rear inflow notch).

Inflow Stinger A beaver tail cloud with a stinger-like shape.

Infra-Red Radiation Electromagnetic radiation of lower frequencies and longer wavelengths than visible light (greater than 0.7 microns (ï¿1/2 m)). Solar ultra-violet radiation is absorbed by the Earth's surface and re-emitted as infra-red radiation.

Indian Summer An unseasonably warm period near the middle of autumn, usually following a substantial period of cool weather.

Insolation Incoming solar radiation. Solar heating; sunshine.

Instability A state of the atmosphere in which convection takes place spontaneously, leading to cloud formation and precipitation.

Intertropical Convergence Zone (ITCZ) The region where the northeasterly and southeasterly trade winds converge, forming an often continuous band of clouds or thunderstorms near the equator.

Inversion An increase in temperature with height. The reverse of the normal cooling with height in the atmosphere. Temperature inversions trap atmospheric pollutants in the lower troposphere, resulting in higher concentrations of pollutants at ground levels than would usually be experienced.

Ionosphere Also known as the thermosphere. A layer in the atmosphere above the mesosphere extending from about 80km above the Earth's surface. It can be considered a distinct layer due to a rise in air temperature with increasing height. Atmospheric densities here are very low.

Iridescence Brilliant patches of green or pink sometimes seen near the edges of high or medium-level clouds.

Isentropic Lift Lifting of air that is traveling along an upward-sloping isentropic surface. Situations involving isentropic lift often are characterized by widespread stratiform clouds and precipitation.

Isentropic Surface A two-dimensional surface containing points of equal potential temperature.

Isobar A line of equal barometric pressure on a weather map.

Isodrosotherm A line of equal dew point temperature.

Isohyet A line of equal precipitation amounts.

Isopleth General term for a line of equal value of some quantity. Isobars, isotherms, etc. all are examples of isopleths.

Isotach A line of equal wind speed.

Isotherm A line of equal temperature on a weather map.

January Thaw A period of mild weather popularly supposed to recur each year in late January.

Jet streak A local wind speed maximum within a jet stream.

Jet Stream Strong winds concentrated within a narrow band in the upper atmosphere. It normally refers to horizontal, high-altitude winds. The jet stream often "steers" surface features such as front and low pressure systems.

Katabatic Wind blowing down an incline, such as down a hillside; downslope wind.

Katafront A front (usually a cold front) at which the warm air descents the frontal surface.

Kelvin Temperature Scale A temperature scale in which 0 degrees is the point at which all molecular motion ceases (absolute zero).

Killing Frost Frost severe enough to end the growing season. This usually occurs at temperatures below 28F.

Kilopascal The internationally recognized unit for measuring atmospheric pressure. It is equal to 10 millibars.

Knot A measure of speed. It is one nautical mile per hour (1.15 mph). A nautical mile is one minute of one degree of latitude.

Knuckles Lumpy protrusions on the edges, and sometimes the underside, of a thunderstorm anvil. They usually appear on the upwind side of a back-sheared anvil, and indicate rapid expansion of the anvil due to the presence of a very strong updraft. They are not mammatus clouds.

Lake effect The effect of a lake (usually a large one) in modifying the weather near the shore and down wind. It is often refers to the enhanced rain or snow that falls downwind from the lake. This effect can also result in enhanced snowfall along the east coast of New England in winter.

Laminar Smooth, non-turbulent. Often used to describe cloud formations which appear to be shaped by a smooth flow of air traveling in parallel layers or sheets.

La Nina A cooling of the equatorial waters in the Pacific Ocean.

Land Breeze A wind that blows from the land towards a body of water. Also known as an offshore breeze. It occurs when the land is cooler than the water.

Landspout A tornado that does not arise from organized storm-scale rotation and therefore is not associated with a wall cloud (visually) or a mesocyclone (on radar). Landspouts typically are observed beneath Cbs or towering cumulus clouds (often as no more than a dust whirl), and essentially are the land-based equivalents of waterspouts.

Lapse Rate The change in temperature with altitude in the atmosphere.

Latent Heat The heat energy that must be absorbed when a substance changes from solid to liquid and liquid to gas, and which is released when a gas condenses and a liquid solidifies.

Layer An array of clouds and/or obscurations whose bases are at approximately the same level.

Left Front Quadrant (or Left Exit Region) The area downstream from and to the left of an upper-level jet max (as would be viewed looking along the direction of flow). Upward motion and severe thunderstorm potential sometimes are increased in this area relative to the wind speed maximum.

Left Mover A thunderstorm which moves to the left relative to the steering winds, and to other nearby thunderstorms; often the northern part of a splitting storm.

Leeward Situated away from the wind; downwind—opposite of windward

Lenticular Clouds A cloud that generally has the form of a smooth lens. They usually appear in formation as the result of orographic origin. Viewed from the ground, the clouds appear stationary as the air rushes through them.

Lifted Index (or LI) A common measure of atmospheric instability. Its value is obtained by computing the temperature that air near the ground would have if it were lifted to some higher level (around 18,000 feet, usually) and comparing that temperature to the actual temperature at that level. Negative values indicate instability—the more negative, the more unstable the air is, and if thunderstorms develop they are more likely to be stronger.

Lifting The forcing of air in a vertical direction by an upslope in terrain or by the movement of a denser air mass.

Lifting Condensation Level The level in the atmosphere where a lifted air parcel reaches its saturation point, and as a result, the water vapor within condenses into water droplets.

Lightning Any form of visible electrical discharges produced by thunderstorms.

Likely In probability of precipitation statements, the equivalent of a 60 or 70 percent chance.

Loaded Gun (Sounding) A sounding characterized by extreme instability but containing a cap, such that explosive thunderstorm development can be expected if the cap can be weakened or the air below it heated sufficiently to overcome it.

Longwave Trough A trough in the prevailing westerly flow aloft which is characterized by large length and (usually) long duration. Generally, there are no more than about five longwave troughs around the Northern Hemisphere at any given time. Their position and intensity govern general weather patterns (e.g., hot/cold, wet/dry) over periods of days, weeks, or months.

Low An area of low pressure, usually accompanied by cyclonic and inward wind flow. Also known as a cyclone.

Low-level Jet A region of relatively strong winds in the lower part of the atmosphere.

Macroburst Large downburst with a 2.5 mile or greater outflow diameter and damaging winds lasting 5 to 20 minutes.

Mamma Clouds Also called mammatus, these clouds appear as hanging, rounded protuberances or pouches on the under-surface of a cloud. With thunderstorms, mammatus are seen on the underside of the anvil. These clouds do not produce tornadoes, funnels, hail, or any other type of severe weather, although they often accompany severe thunderstorms.

Maritime Air Mass An air mass that forms over water. It is usually humid, and may be cold or warm.

Maximum Temperature The highest temperature during a specified time period.

Mean Sea Level (MSL) The average height of the sea surface, based upon hourly observation of the tide height on the open coast or in adjacent waters that have free access to the sea.

Mean Temperature The average of a series of temperatures taken over a period of time, such as a day or a month.

Medium Range In forecasting, (generally) three to seven days in advance.

Mercury Barometer An instrument that measures barometric pressure by measuring the level of mercury in a column.

Meridional flow A type of atmospheric circulation pattern in which the north and south component of motion is unusually pronounced. Opposite of zonal flow.

Mesocyclone A storm-scale region of rotation, typically around 2-6 miles in diameter and often found in the right rear flank of a supercell (or often on the eastern, or front, flank of an HP storm). The circulation of a mesocyclone covers an area much larger than the tornado that may develop within it.

Mesohigh A mesoscale high pressure area, usually associated with MCSs or their remnants.

Mesolow (or Sub-synoptic Low) A mesoscale low-pressure center. Severe weather potential often increases in the area near and just ahead of a mesolow.

Mesonet A regional network of observing stations (usually surface stations) designed to diagnose mesoscale weather features and their associated processes.

Mesoscale Size scale referring to weather systems smaller than synoptic-scale systems but larger than single storm clouds. Horizontal dimensions generally range from around 50 miles to several hundred miles. Squall lines are an example of mesoscale weather systems.

Mesoscale Convective Complex (MCC) A large mesoscale convective system, generally round or oval-shaped, which normally reaches peak intensity at night. The formal definition includes specific minimum criteria for size, duration, and eccentricity (i.e., "roundness"), based on the cloud shield as seen on infrared satellite photographs:

Mesoscale Convective System (MCS) A complex of thunderstorms which becomes organized on a scale larger than the individual thunderstorms, and normally persists for several hours or more. MCSs may be round or linear in shape, and include systems such as tropical cyclones, squall lines, and MCCs (among others). MCS often is used to describe a cluster of thunderstorms that does not satisfy the size, shape, or duration criteria of an MCC.

Mesosphere A layer of the atmosphere separated by the ionosphere above and the stratosphere below extending from about 50km-80km above the Earth's surface. The air temperature in mesosphere decreases with height.

META The mesoscale ETA model. A mathematical model of the atmosphere run on a computer that makes forecasts out to 30 hours.

Metamorphism Changes in the structure and texture of snow grains which results from variations in temperature, migration of liquid water and water vapor, and pressure within the snow cover

METAR A weather observation near ground level. It may include date and time, wind, visibility, weather and obstructions to vision, sky condition, temperature and dew point, sea level pressure, precipitation amount and other data used for aircraft operations.

Meteorologist A person who studies meteorology. Some examples include research meteorologist, climatologist, operational meteorologist, TV meteorologist.

Meteorology The study of the physics, chemistry, and dynamics of the atmosphere and the direct effects of the atmosphere upon the Earth's surface, the oceans, and life in general.

Microburst A strong localized downdraft from a thunderstorm with peak gusts lasting 2 to 5 minutes.

Microclimate A local climate that differs from the main climate around it.

Mid-Latitudes The areas in the northern and southern hemispheres between the tropics and the Arctic and Antarctic circles.

Millibar A metric unit of atmospheric pressure. 1 mb = 100 Pa (pascal). Normal surface pressure is approximately 1013 millibars.

Minimum Temperature The lowest temperature during a specified time period.

Mist Consists of microscopic water droplets suspended in the air which produce a thin grayish veil over the landscape. It reduces visibility to a lesser extent than fog.

Mixing Air movements (usually vertical) that make the properties of the air with a parcel homogeneous. It may result in a lapse rate approaching the moist or dry adiabatic rate.

Model A mathematical representation of a process, system, or object developed to understand its behavior or to make predictions. The representation always involves certain simplifications and assumptions.

Moderate Risk (of severe thunderstorms) Severe thunderstorms are expected to affect between 5 and 10 percent of the area.

Moisture Advection Transport of moisture by horizontal winds.

Moisture Convergence A measure of the degree to which moist air is converging into a given area, taking into account the effect of converging winds and moisture advection. Areas of persistent moisture convergence are favored regions for thunderstorm development, if other factors (e.g., instability) are favorable.

Monsoon A persistent seasonal wind, often responsible for seasonal precipitation regime. It is most commonly used to describe meteorological changes in southern and eastern Asia.

Mountain Breeze System of winds that blow downhill during the night.

Morning Glory An elongated cloud band, visually similar to a roll cloud, usually appearing in the morning hours, when the atmosphere is relatively stable. Morning glories result from perturbations related to gravitational waves in a stable boundary layer.

MOS Model Output Statistics.

MRF Medium Range Forecast model generated every 12 hours by NCEP.

MSL Mean sea level.

MSLP Mean sea level pressure.

Muggy Colloquially descriptive of warm and especially humid weather.

Multicell Cluster Thunderstorm A thunderstorm consisting of two or more cells, of which most or all are often visible at a given time as distinct domes or towers in various stages of development.

Multivortex Tornado A tornado in which two or more condensation funnels or debris clouds are present at the same time, often rotating about a common center or about each other. Multiple-vortex tornadoes can be especially damaging.

Mushroom A thunderstorm with a well-defined anvil rollover, and thus having a visual appearance resembling a mushroom.

NCDC: National Climatic Data Center. Located in Asheville, North Carolina, the agency that archives climatic and forecast data from the National Weather Service. NCEP: National Centers for Environmental Prediction. Central computer and communications facility of the National Weather Service; located in Washington, DC.

Negative Tilt Trough An upper level system which is tilted to the west with increasing latitude (i.e., with an axis from southeast to northwest). A negative-tilt trough often is a sign of a developing or intensifying system. NEXRAD: NEXt Generation RADar. A NWS network of about 140 Doppler radars operating nationwide. NGM: Nested Grid Model generated every 12 hours by NCEP.NHC: National Hurricane Center. The office of the National Weather Service in Miami that is responsible for tracking and forecasting tropical cyclones.

NOAA National Oceanic and Atmospheric Administration. A branch of the U.S. Department of Commerce, NOAA is the parent organization of the National Weather Service.

NOAA WEATHER WIRE (NWWS) A computer dissemination network that sends National Weather Service products to the media and public.

NOAA WEATHER RADIO (NWR) Continuous, 24 hour a day VHF broadcasts of weather observations and forecasts directly from National Weather Service offices. A special tone allows certain receivers to alarm when watches or warnings are issued.

Nocturnal Related to nighttime, or occurring at night.

Nor'easter A low-pressure disturbance forming along the South Atlantic coast and moving northeast along the Middle Atlantic and New England coasts to the Atlantic Provinces of Canada. It usually causes strong northeast winds with rain or snow. Also called a Northeaster or Coastal Storm.

Normal The long-term average value of a meteorological element for a certain area. For example, "temperatures are normal for this time of year" Usually averaged over 30 years.

Northern Lights Also known as the aurora borealis. The luminous, radiant emission from the upper atmosphere over middle and high latitudes, and centered around the earth's magnetic poles. These silent fireworks are often seen on clear winter nights in a variety of shapes and colors.

Nowcast A short-term weather forecast, generally out to six hours or less.

NSSL The National Severe Storms Laboratory.

Nucleus a particle of any nature upon which molecules of water or ice accumulate.

Numerical Forecasting Forecasting the weather through digital computations carried out by supercomputers.

NWP Numerical Weather Prediction.

NWS National Weather Service.

Obscuration Any phenomenon in the atmosphere, other than precipitation, that reduces the horizontal visibility in the atmosphere.

Occluded Front A complex frontal system that occurs when a cold front overtakes a warm front. Also known as an occlusion.

Offshore Breeze A wind that blows from the land towards a body of water. Also known as a land breeze. Offshore Forecast A marine weather forecast for the waters between 60 and 250 miles off the coast.

Omega A term used to describe vertical motion in the atmosphere. The "omega equation" used in numerical weather models is composed of two terms, the "differential vorticity advection" term and the "thickness advection" term. Put more simply, omega is determined by the amount of spin (or large scale rotation) and warm (or cold) advection present in the atmosphere. On a weather forecast chart, high values of omega (or a strong omega field) relate to upward vertical motion in the atmosphere. If this upward vertical motion is strong enough and in a sufficiently moist airmass, precipitation results.

Onshore Breeze A wind that blows from a body of water towards the land. Also known as a seabreeze.

Orographic Related to, or caused by, physical geography (such as mountains or sloping terrain).

Orographic Lift The lifting of air as it passes over terrain features such hills or mountains. This can create orographic clouds and/or precipitation.

Orphan Anvil An anvil from a dissipated thunderstorm, below which no other clouds remain.

Outflow Air that flows outward from a thunderstorm.

Outflow Boundary A storm-scale or mesoscale boundary separating thunderstorm-cooled air (outflow) from the surrounding air; similar in effect to a cold front, with passage marked by a wind shift and usually a drop in temperature.

Outflow Winds Winds that blow down fjords and inlets from the land to the sea.

Overcast Sky condition when greater than 9/10 of the sky is covered by clouds.

Overrunning A condition that exists when a relatively warm air mass moves up and over a colder and denser air mass on the surface. The result is usually low clouds, fog and steady, light precipitation.

Overshooting Top (or Penetrating Top) A dome-like protrusion above a thunderstorm anvil, representing a very strong updraft and hence a higher potential for severe weather with that storm.

Ozone A form of oxygen in which the molecule is made of 3 atoms instead of the usual two. Ozone is usually found in the stratosphere, and responsible for filtering out much of the sun's ultraviolet radiation. It is also a primary component of smog.

Ozone Hole A thinning of the ozone layer over Antarctica, which occurs each spring.

Partly Cloudy Sky condition when between 3/10 and 7/10 of the sky is covered. Used more frequently at night.

Partly Sunny Similar to partly cloudy. Used to emphasize daytime sunshine.

Patches Used with fog to denote random occurrence over relatively small areas.

Pendant Echo Radar signature generally similar to a hook echo, except that the hook shape is not as well defined.

Permafrost A soil layer below the surface of tundra regions that remains frozen permanently.

Polar Air A mass of very cold, very dry air that forms in polar regions.

Polar front The semi-permanent, semi-continuous front that encircles the northern hemisphere separating air masses of tropical and polar origin.

Polar Stratospheric Clouds (PSCs) High altitude clouds that form in the stratosphere above Antarctica during the Southern Hemisphere winter. Their presence seems to initiate the ozone loss experienced during the ensuing Southern Hemisphere spring.

Polar vortex A circumpolar wind circulation which isolates the Antarctic continent during the cold Southern Hemisphere winter, heightening ozone depletion.

Pollutant Strictly too much of any substance in the wrong place or at the wrong time is a pollutant. More specifically, atmospheric pollution may be defined as the presence of substances in the atmosphere, resulting from man-made activities or from natural processes, causing adverse effects to man and the environment.

Polycrystal A snowflake composed of many individual ice crystals.

POP Probability of Precipitation. Probability forecasts are subjective estimates of the chances of encountering measurable precipitation at some time during the forecast period.

Popcorn Convection Clouds, showers and thundershowers that form on a scattered basis with little or no apparent organization, usually during the afternoon in response to diurnal heating.

Positive Area The area on a sounding representing the layer in which a lifted parcel would be warmer than the environment; thus, the area between the environmental temperature profile and the path of the lifted parcel.

Positive-tilt Trough An upper level system which is tilted to the east with increasing latitude (i.e., from southwest to northeast). A positive-tilt trough often is a sign of a weakening weather system, and generally is less likely to result in severe weather than a negative-tilt trough if all other factors are equal.

Potential Temperature The temperature a parcel of dry air would have if brought adiabatically (i.e., without transfer of heat or mass) to a standard pressure level of 1000 mb.

Precipitation Liquid or solid water that falls from the atmosphere and reaches the ground.

Precipitation Shaft A visible column of rain and/or hail falling from a cloud base. When viewed against a light background, heavy precipitation appears very dark gray, sometimes with a turquoise tinge. This turquoise tinge has been commonly attributed to hail, but its actual cause is unknown.

Pressure The force exerted by the interaction of the atmosphere and gravity. Also known as atmospheric pressure.

Pressure Change The net difference between pressure readings at the beginning and ending of a specified interval of time.

Pressure Falling Rapidly A decrease in station pressure at a rate of 0.06 inch of mercury or more per hour which totals 0.02 inch or more.

Pressure Gradient The rate of decrease of pressure with distance at a fixed level.

Pressure Gradient Force Force acting on air that causes it to move from areas of higher pressure to areas of lower pressure.

Pressure Rising Rapidly An increase in station pressure at a rate of 0.06 inch of mercury or more per hour which totals 0.02 inch or more.

Pressure Tendency The character and amount of atmospheric pressure change during a specified period of time, usually the 3-hour period preceding an observation.

Pressure Unsteady A pressure that fluctuates by 0.03 inch of mercury or more from the mean pressure during the period of measurement.

Prevailing Westerlies Winds in the middle latitudes (approximately 30 degrees to 60 degrees) that generally blow from west to east.

Prevailing Wind The direction from which the wind blows most frequently in any location.

Profiler An instrument designed to measure horizontal winds directly above its location, and thus measure the vertical wind profile. Profilers operate on the same principles as Doppler radar.

Psychrometer An instrument used for measuring the water vapor content of the atmosphere. It consists of two thermometers, one of which is an ordinary glass thermometer, while the other has its bulb covered with a jacket of clean muslin which is saturated with distilled water prior to use.

Pulse Storm A thunderstorm within which a brief period (pulse) of strong updraft occurs, during and immediately after which the storm produces a short episode of severe weather. These storms generally are not tornado producers, but often produce large hail and/or damaging winds. See overshooting top, cyclic storm.

PVA Positive Vorticity Advection. Advection of higher values of vorticity into an area, which often is associated with upward motion (lifting) of the air. PVA typically is found in advance of disturbances aloft (i.e., shortwaves), and is a property which often enhances the potential precipitation.

QPF Quantitative Precipitation Forecast

Quality Of Snow The amount of ice in a snow sample expressed as a percent of the weight of the sample.

Radar An instrument used to detect precipitation by measuring the strength of the electromagnetic signal reflected back. (RADAR= Radio Detection and Ranging)

Radiation Energy emitted in the form of electromagnetic waves. Radiation has differing characteristics depending upon the wavelength. Radiation from the Sun has a short wavelength (ultra-violet) while energy re-radiated from the Earth's surface and the atmosphere has a long wavelength (infra-red).

Radiation Fog Fog produced over the land by the cooling of the lower atmosphere as it comes in contact with the ground. Also known as ground fog.

Radiational Cooling Cooling process of the Earth's surface and adjacent air, which occurs when infrared (heat) energy radiates from the surface of the Earth upward through the atmosphere into space. Air near the surface transfers its thermal energy to the nearby ground through conduction, so that radiative cooling lowers the temperature of both the surface and the lowest part of the atmosphere.

Radiosonde An instrument attached to a weather balloon that transmits pressure, humidity, temperature and winds as it ascends to the upper atmosphere.

Rain Liquid water droplets that fall from the atmosphere, having diameters greater than drizzle (0.5 mm).

Rain Foot A horizontal bulging near the surface in a precipitation shaft, forming a foot-shaped prominence. It is a visual indication of a wet microburst.

Rain-Free Base A horizontal, dark cumulonimbus base that has no visible precipitation beneath it. This structure usually marks the location of the thunderstorm updraft. Tornadoes most commonly develop (1) from wall clouds that are attached to the rain-free base, or (2) from the rain-free base itself. This is particularly true when the rain-free base is observed to the south or southwest of the precipitation shaft.

Rain Gauge An instrument used to measure rainfall amounts.

Rain Shadow The region on the lee side of a mountain or mountain range where the precipitation is noticeably less than on the windward side.

Rainbow Optical phenomena when light is refracted and reflected by moisture in the air into concentric arcs of color. Raindrops act like prisms, breaking the light into the colors of a rainbow, with red on the outer, and blue on the inner edge.

Rankine Temperature Scale A temperature scale with the degree of the Fahrenheit temperature scale and the zero point of the Kelvin temperature scale.

Rawinsonde A balloon that is tracked by radar to measure wind speeds and wind directions in the atmosphere.

Reflectivity Radar term referring to the ability of a radar target to return energy; used to estimate precipitation intensity and rainfall rates.

Refraction The bending of light as it passes through areas of different density, such as from air through ice crystals.

Relative Humidity The amount of water vapor in the air, compared to the amount the air could hold if it was totally saturated. (Expressed as a percentage).

Retrogression (or Retrograde Motion) Movement of a weather system in a direction opposite to that of the basic flow in which it is embedded, usually referring to a closed low or a longwave trough which moves westward.

Return Flow South winds on the back (west) side of an eastward-moving surface high pressure system. Return flow over the central and eastern United States typically results in a return of moist air from the Gulf of Mexico (or the Atlantic Ocean).

RFC River Forecast Center. The Northeast River Forecast Center is located in Taunton, MA..

Ridge An elongated area of high pressure in the atmosphere. Opposite of a trough.

Right Entrance Region (or Right Rear Quadrant) The area upstream from and to the right of an upper-level jet max (as would be viewed looking along the direction of flow). Upward motion and severe thunderstorm potential sometimes are increased in this area relative to the wind speed maximum.

Right Mover A thunderstorm that moves appreciably to the right relative to the main steering winds and to other nearby thunderstorms. Right movers typically are associated with a high potential for severe weather. (Supercells often are right movers.)

Rime Tiny balls of ice that form when tiny drops of water (usually not precipitation) freeze on contact with the surface.

River Flood Warning Issued when main stem rivers (such as the Merrimack, Charles, Connecticut, etc) are expected to reach a level above flood stage.

Roll Cloud A relatively rare, low-level horizontal, tube-shaped accessory cloud completely detached from the cumulonimbus base. When present, it is located along the gust front and most frequently observed on the leading edge of a line of thunderstorms. The roll cloud will appear to be slowly "rolling" about its horizontal axis. Roll clouds are not and do not produce tornadoes.

Rope (or Rope Funnel) A narrow, often contorted condensation funnel usually associated with the decaying stage of a tornado.

Rope Cloud In satellite meteorology, a narrow, rope-like band of clouds sometimes seen on satellite images along a front or other boundary.

Rope Stage The dissipating stage of a tornado, characterized by thinning and shrinking of the condensation funnel into a rope (or rope funnel). Damage still is possible during this stage.

Rossby Waves Long waves that form in air or water that flows almost parallel to the equator, which results form the effect of the earth's rotation.

Rotor Cloud A turbulent cloud formation found in the lee of some large mountain barriers. The air in the cloud rotates around an axis parallel to the mountain range.

RUC Rapid Update Cycle, a numerical model run at NCEP that focuses on short-term (up to 12 h) forecasts and small-scale (mesoscale) weather features. Forecasts are prepared every 3 hours for the contiguous United States.

Runway Visual Range (RVR) An instrumentally-derived value, based on standard calibrations, that represents the horizontal distance a pilot may see down the runway from the approach end.Saffir-Simpson Hurricane Damage Potential Scale A scale that measures hurricane intensity, developed by Herbert Saffir and Robert Simpson.

St. Elmo's Fire A luminous, and often audible, electric discharge that is intermediate in nature between a spark discharge and a point discharge (with its diffuse, quiescent, and non-luminous character). It occurs from objects, especially pointed ones, when the electric field strength near their surfaces attains a value near 100,000 volts per m. Aircraft flying through active electrical storms often develop corona discharge streamers from antennas and propellers, and even from the entire fuselage and wing structure. It is seen also, during stormy weather, emanating from the yards and masts of ships at sea.

Sandstorm Particles of sand carried aloft by a strong wind. The sand particles are mostly confined to the lowest ten feet, and rarely rise more than fifty feet above the ground.

Santa Ana Winds Relatively warm, dry winds that blow into Southern California coastal areas from an anticyclone located over the high deserts of California or Nevada. The warmth and dryness are due to compressional heating.

Satellite Photo A photograph of the earth taken by weather satellites that shows areas of cloud.

Saturation A condition of the atmosphere in which a certain volume of air holds the maximum water vapor it can hold at a specific temperature.

Saturation Vapor Pressure (water) The maximum amount of water vapor necessary to keep moist air in equilibrium with a surface of pure water. This is the maximum water vapor the air can hold for any given combination of temperature and pressure

Scattered A cloud layer that covers between 3/8ths and 1/2 of the sky.

Scud Clouds Small, ragged, low cloud fragments that are unattached to a larger cloud base and often seen with and behind cold fronts and thunderstorm gust fronts. Such clouds generally are associated with cool moist air, such as thunderstorm outflow.

Secondary Cold Front A front that follows a primary cold front and ushers in even colder air.

Sea Breeze A wind that blows from a sea or ocean towards a land mass. Also known as an onshore breeze. It occurs when the land is warmer than the water.

Sea-level Pressure The pressure value obtained by the theoretical reduction or increase of barometric pressure to sea-level.

Sensible Heat The excess radiative energy that has passed from the Earth's surface to the atmosphere through advection, conduction, and convection processes.

Severe Thunderstorm A strong thunderstorm with wind gusts in excess of 58 mph (50 knots) and/or hail with a diameter of 3/4" or more. A thunderstorm with winds greater than 39 mph and/or hail greater than ï¿½1/2 inch is defined as approaching severe.

Severe Thunderstorm Warning Issued when thunderstorms are expected to have wind gusts to 58 mph or above or hail 3/4 inch or more in diameter.

Severe Thunderstorm Watch Issued when conditions are favorable for the development of severe thunderstorms in and close to a defined area.

Shallow fog Fog in which the visibility at 6 feet above ground level is 5/8ths of a mile or more.

Shear (Wind Shear) Variation in wind speed and/or direction over a short distance. Shear usually refers to vertical wind shear, i.e., the change in wind with height, but the term also is used in Doppler radar to describe changes in radial velocity over short horizontal distances.

Shelf Cloud A low-level horizontal accessory cloud that appears to be wedge-shaped as it approaches. It is usually attached to the thunderstorm base and forms along the gust front. The leading edge of the shelf is often smooth and at times layered or terraced. It is most often seen along the leading edge of an approaching line of thunderstorms, accompanied by gusty straight winds as it passes overhead and followed by precipitation. The underside is concave upward, turbulent, boiling, or wind-torn. Tornadoes rarely occur with the shelf cloud.

Short-Fuse Warning A warning issued by the NWS for a local weather hazard of relatively short duration. Short-fuse warnings include tornado warnings, severe thunderstorm warnings, and flash flood warnings. Tornado and severe thunderstorm warnings typically are issued for periods of an hour or less, flash flood warnings typically for three hours or less.

Shortwave (Shortwave Trough) A disturbance in the mid or upper part of the atmosphere which induces upward motion ahead of it. If other conditions are favorable, the upward motion can contribute to thunderstorm development ahead of a shortwave.

Shortwave Radiation The radiation received from the sun and emitted in the spectral wavelengths less than 4 microns. It is also called 'solar radiation'.

Shower Precipitation that is intermittent, both in time, space or intensity.

Sky Condition The state of the sky in terms of such parameters as sky cover, layers and associated heights, ceiling, and cloud types.

Sky Cover The amount of the sky which is covered by clouds or obscurations in contact with the surface.

Sleet Rain drops that freeze into ice pellets before reaching the ground. Sleet usually bounces when hitting a surface and does not stick to objects. Forms when snow enters a warm layer of air above the surface and melts and then enters a deep layer of sub freezing air near the surface and refreezes.

Slight Risk (of severe thunderstorms) Severe thunderstorms are expected to affect between 2 and 5 percent of the area. A slight risk generally implies that severe weather events are expected to be isolated.

Sling Psychrometer A psychrometer in which the wet and dry bulb thermometers are mounted upon a frame connected to a handle. The psychrometer may be whirled by hand in order to provided the necessary ventilation.

Slight Chance In probability of precipitation statements, usually equivalent to a 20 percent chance.

Small Craft Advisory A marine advisory for winds 25 to 33 knots (29 to 38 mph) or seas of 5 feet or more, that may cause hazardous conditions for operators of small vessels.

Smog Pollution formed by the interaction of pollutants and sunlight (photochemical smog), usually restricting visibility, and occasionally hazardous to health.

Smoke A suspension in the air of small particles produced by combustion. A transition to haze may occur when smoke particles have traveled great distances (25 to 100 statute miles or more) and when the larger particles have settled out and the remaining particles have become widely scattered through the atmosphere.

Snow Frozen precipitation composed of ice particles in complex hexagonal patterns. Snow forms in cold clouds by the direct transfer of water vapor to ice. Snow Advisory Older terminology replaced by winter weather advisory. An advisory issued when 4, 5, or 6 inches of snow or sleet is expected in 24 hours. It is expected to create hazardous or restricted travel conditions, but not as severe as expected with a winter storm.

Snow Depth The vertical height of frozen precipitation on the ground. For this purpose, frozen precipitation includes ice pellets, glaze, hail, any combination of these, and sheet ice formed directly or indirectly from precipitation.Snow Flurries Light snow showers, usually of an intermittent nature and short duration with no measurable accumulation.

Snow Grains Precipitation of very small, white, opaque grains of ice.

Snow Pellets Precipitation of white, opaque grains of ice. The grains are round or sometimes conical. Diameters range from about 0.08 to 0.2 inch (2 to 5 mm).

Snow Shower Snow falling at varying intensities for brief periods of time. Some accumulation is possible.

Snow Squalls Intense, but of limited duration, periods of moderate to heavy snowfall, accompanied by strong, gusty surface winds and possible lightning.

Snowburst Very intense shower of snow, often of short duration, that greatly restricts visibility and produces periods of rapid snow accumulation.

Snowfall The depth of new snow that has accumulated since the previous day or since the previous observation.

Snowflake White ice crystals that have combined in a complex branched hexagonal form.

Solar Energy The energy produced by the sun.

Sounder A special kind of radiometer that measures changes in atmospheric temperature with height, as well as the content of various chemical species in the atmosphere at various levels. The High Resolution Infrared Radiation Sounder (HIRS), found on NOAA polar-orbiting satellites, is a passive instrument. See passive system.

Sounding A plot of the vertical profile of temperature and dew point (and often winds) above a fixed location (example). Soundings are used extensively in weather forecasting, e.g., to determine instability, locate temperature inversions etc.

Southern Oscillation A periodic reversal of the pressure pattern across the tropical Pacific Ocean during El Nino events.

Special Marine Warning Issued for brief or sudden occurrence of sustained wind or frequent gusts of 34 knots or more. This is usually associated with severe thunderstorms or waterspouts.

SPC Storm Prediction Center. Located in Norman, OK. This office is responsible for monitoring and forecasting severe convective weather in the continental U.S. This includes the issuance of Tornado and Severe Thunderstorm Watches.

Speed Shear The component of wind shear which is due to a change in wind speed with height, e.g., southwesterly winds of 20 mph at 10,000 feet increasing to 50 mph at 20,000 feet. Speed shear is an important factor in severe weather development, especially in the middle and upper levels of the atmosphere.

Spin-up A small-scale vortex initiation, such as what may be seen when a gustnado, landspout, or suction vortex forms.

Spray An ensemble of water droplets torn by the wind from an extensive body of water, generally from the crests of waves, and carried up into the air in such quantities that it reduces the horizontal visibility.

Squall A strong wind characterized by a sudden onset in which the wind speed increases at least 16 knots and is sustained at 22 knots or more for at least one minute.

Squall Line Any non-frontal line or narrow band of active thunderstorms. The term is usually used to describe solid or broken lines of strong or severe thunderstorms.

Stability An indication of how easily a parcel of air is lifted. If the air is very stable it is difficult to make the parcel rise. If the air is very unstable the parcel may rise on its own once started.

Stable Air Air with little or no tendency to rise, that is usually accompanied by clear dry weather.

Standard Atmosphere A hypothetical vertical distribution of the atmospheric temperature, pressure, and density, which by international agreement is considered to be representative of the atmosphere for pressure-altimeter calibrations and other purposes (29.92INS or 1013hPa).

Standing Lenticular Cloud A, more or less, isolated cloud with sharp outlines that is generally in the form of a smooth lens or almond. These clouds often form on the lee side of and generally parallel to mountain ranges. Depending on their height above the surface, they may be reported as stratocumulus standing lenticular cloud (SCSL); altocumulus standing lenticular cloud (ACSL); or cirrocumulus standing lenticular cloud (CCSL).

Statement Provides the public with information concerning the status of existing warnings.

Station Identifier A group of four alphabetic characters used to identify a location that makes weather observations.

Station Pressure The pressure that is read from a barometer but is not adjusted to sea level.

Stationary Front The boundary between cool and warm air masses in that are not moving.

Stationary wave Wave (flow pattern with periodicity in time and/or space) that is fixed relative to Earth.

Steam fog Fog that is formed when water vapor is added to air which is much colder than the vapor's source. This is most common when very cold air drifts across relatively warm water.

Steering Winds (Steering Currents) A prevailing synoptic scale flow which governs the movement of smaller features embedded within it.

Storm In marine usage, winds 48 knots (55 mph) or greater. Storm Surge A rise of the sea level alone the shore that builds up as a storm (usually a hurricane) moves over water. It is a result of the winds of the storm and low atmospheric pressures.

Storm Track the path that a low pressure area follows.

Storm Warning A marine wind warning for sustained winds greater of 48 knots (55 mph) or more from a non-tropical system.

Storm-relative Measured relative to a moving thunderstorm, usually referring to winds, wind shear, or helicity.

Storm-scale Referring to weather systems with sizes on the order of individual thunderstorms. See synoptic scale, mesoscale.

Straight Line Winds Thunderstorm winds most often found with the gust front. They originate from downdrafts and can cause damage which occurs in a "straight line", as opposed to tornadic wind damage which has circular characteristics.

Stratiform Having extensive horizontal development, as opposed to the more vertical development characteristic of convection. Stratiform clouds cover large areas but show relatively little vertical development.

Stratocumulus Low-level clouds, existing in a relatively flat layer but having individual elements. Elements often are arranged in rows, bands, or waves.

Stratosphere- The layer of atmosphere above the troposphere and below the mesosphere (between 10 km and 50 km) generally characterized by an increase in temperature with height.

Stratus A flat, low, generally gray cloud layer with a fairly uniform base. Stratus may appear in the form of ragged patches, but otherwise does not exhibit individual cloud elements as do cumulus and stratocumulus clouds.

Striations Grooves or channels in cloud formations, arranged parallel to the flow of air and therefore depicting the airflow relative to the parent cloud.

Sublimation The change from ice directly to water vapor or from water vapor to ice with out going through the liquid water phase.

Subsidence Downward moving (sinking) air over a broad area that is associated with warming air and little cloud formation.

Subtropical Jet The branch of the jet stream that is found in the lower latitudes.

Subtropical storm A low pressure system that develops in subtropical waters (north of 20 north degrees latitude) and initially has non-tropical features (see table below for a list of tropical features) but does have some element of a tropical cyclone's cloud structure (located close to the center rather than away from the center of circulation).

Suction Vortex (sometimes Suction Spot) A small but very intense vortex within a tornado circulation. Several suction vortices typically are present in a multiple-vortex tornado. Much of the extreme damage associated with violent tornadoes (F4 and F5 on the Fujita scale) is attributed to suction vortices.

Supercell Thunderstorm A severe thunderstorm whose updrafts and downdrafts are in near balance allowing the storm to maintain itself for several hours. Supercells often produce large hail and tornadoes.

Supercooled Water Water that stays in liquid form if undisturbed even though it has been cooled to a temperature below its normal freezing point.

Supersaturation The condition which occurs in the atmosphere when the relative humidity is greater than 100 percent.

Surface Hoar The deposition (sublimation) of ice crystals on a surface which occurs when the temperature of the surface is colder than the air above and colder than the frost point of that air.

Surface Pressure The pressure that is read from a barometer but is not adjusted to sea level.

Sustained Winds The wind speed obtained by averaging the observed values over a one minute period.

SWEAT Index Severe Weather ThrEAT index. A stability index developed by the Air Force which incorporates instability, wind shear, and wind speeds.

Synoptic Chart Chart showing meteorological conditions over a region at a given time; weather map.

Synoptic Scale (Large Scale) Size scale referring generally to weather systems with horizontal dimensions of several hundred miles or more. Most high and low pressure areas seen on weather maps are synoptic-scale systems. Compare with mesoscale.

TAF A weather forecast for aircraft operations at an airport.

Tail Cloud A low tail-shaped cloud extending outward from the northern quadrant of a wall cloud. Motions in the tail cloud are toward the wall cloud with rapid updraft at the junction of tail and wall cloud. This horizontal cloud is not a funnel or tornado.

Tail-end Charlie The thunderstorm at the southernmost end of a squall line or other line or band of thunderstorms.

Teleconnection A strong statistical relationship between weather in different parts of the globe. For example, there appears to be a teleconnection between the tropics and North America during El Niï¿1/2o.

Temperate Zone The area of the globe between the tropics and the polar regions.

Temperature a measure of the warmth or coldness of an object or substance with reference to a standard value.

Terrestrial Radiation The total infrared radiation emitted by the Earth.

Thermal A small rising parcel of warm air produced when the earth's surface is unevenly heated.

Thermodynamics In general, the relationships between heat and other properties (such as temperature, pressure, density, etc.) In forecast discussions, thermodynamics usually refers to the distribution of temperature and moisture (both vertical and horizontal) as related to the diagnosis of atmospheric instability.

Thermometer An instrument for measuring temperature.

Theta-e (or Equivalent Potential Temperature) The temperature a parcel of air would have if a) it was lifted until it became saturated, b) all water vapor was condensed out, and c) it was returned adiabatically (i.e., without transfer of heat or mass) to a pressure of 1000 millibars.

Theta-e Ridge An axis of relatively high values of theta-e. Severe weather and excessive rainfall often occur near or just upstream from a theta-e ridge.

Thunder The sound caused by a lightning stroke as it heats the air and causes it to rapidly expand.

Thunderstorm A storm with lightning and thunder, produced by a cumulonimbus cloud, usually producing gusty winds, heavy rain and sometimes hail.

Tilted Storm or Tilted Updraft A thunderstorm or cloud tower which is not purely vertical but instead exhibits a slanted or tilted character. It is a sign of vertical wind shear, a favorable condition for severe storm development.

Topography Generally, the lay-out of the major natural and man-made physical features of the earth's surface. Bridges, highways, trees, rivers and fields are all components that make up this topography.

Tornadic Activity The occurrence or disappearance of tornadoes, funnel clouds, or waterspouts.

Tornado A violent rotating column of air, in contact with the ground, pendant from a cumulonimbus cloud. A tornado does not require the visible presence of a funnel cloud. It has a typical width of tens to hundreds of meters and a lifespan of minutes to hours.

Tornado Alley The area of the United States in which tornadoes are most frequent. It encompasses the great lowland areas of the Mississippi, the Ohio, and lower Missouri River Valleys. Although no state is entirely free of tornadoes, they are most frequent in the Plains area between the Rocky Mountains and Appalachians

Tornado Family A series of tornadoes produced by a single supercell, resulting in damage path segments along the same general line.

Tornado Warning Issued when there is likelihood of a tornado within the given area based on radar or actual sighting. It is usually accompanied by conditions indicated for Severe Thunderstorm Warning.

Total-Totals Index A stability index and severe weather forecast tool, equal to the temperature at 850 mb plus the dew point at 850 mb, minus twice the temperature at 500 mb.

Towering Cumulus A large cumulus cloud with great vertical development, usually with a cauliflower-like appearance, but lacking the characteristic anvil shaped top of a Cb. (Often shortened to "towering cu," and abbreviated TCU.)

Trade Winds Persistent tropical winds that blow from the subtropical high pressure centers towards the equatorial low. They blow northeasterly in the Northern Hemisphere.

Transverse Bands Bands of clouds oriented perpendicular to the flow in which they are embedded. They often are seen best on satellite photographs. When observed at high levels (i.e., in cirrus formations), they may indicate severe or extreme turbulence.

Transverse Rolls Elongated low-level clouds, arranged in parallel bands and aligned parallel to the low-level winds but perpendicular to the mid-level flow.

Triple Point The intersection point between two boundaries (dry line, outflow boundary, cold front, warm front etc.), often a focus for thunderstorm development.

Tropical Air An air mass that has warm temperatures and high humidities and develops over tropical or sub-tropical areas.

Tropical Depression Tropical mass of thunderstorms with a cyclonic wind circulation and winds near the surface between 23 mph and 39 mph.Tropical Disturbance An organized mass of thunderstorms in the tropics than lasts for more than 24 hours, has a slight cyclonic circulation, and winds less than 23 mph. Tropical Storm An organized low pressure system in the tropics with wind speeds between 38 and 74 mph.

Tropical Storm Warning A warning issued when sustained winds of 39 to 73 mph (34 to 63 knots) are expected within 24 hours.

Tropical wave A kink or bend in the normally straight flow of surface air in the tropics which forms a low pressure trough, or pressure boundary, and showers and thunderstorms. Can develop into a tropical cyclone.

Tropics The area of the globe from latitudes 23.5 degrees north to 23.5 degrees south.

Tropopause The boundary between troposphere and the stratosphere. It is usually characterized by an abrupt change in temperature with height from positive (decreasing temperature with height) to neutral or negative (temperature constant or increasing with height).

Troposphere The layer of the atmosphere from the earth's surface up to the tropopause, characterized by decreasing temperature with height. It's the layer of the atmosphere where most of the weather occurs.

Trough An elongated area of relatively low atmospheric pressure surface or aloft. Usually not associated with a closed circulation, and thus used to distinguish from a closed low. The opposite of ridge.

Turbulence Disrupted flow in the atmosphere that produces gusts and eddies. At times this can be violent and can cause the up and down movement of a plane.

Turkey Tower A narrow, individual cloud tower that develops and falls apart rapidly.

TVS Tornadic Vortex Signature. Doppler radar signature in the radial velocity field indicating intense, concentrated rotation—more so than a mesocyclone.

Twister A colloquial term for a tornado.

Typhoon A hurricane that forms in the Western Pacific Ocean.

UKMET United Kingdom forecast model.

Ultraviolet radiation The energy range just beyond the violet end of the visible spectrum. Although ultraviolet radiation constitutes only about 5 percent of the total energy emitted from the sun, it is the major energy source for the stratosphere and mesosphere, playing a dominant role in both energy balance and chemical composition.

Unstable Air Air that rises easily and can form clouds and rain.

Updraft A small-scale current of rising air. This is often associated with cumulus and cumulonimbus clouds.

Upper Level System A general term for any large-scale or mesoscale disturbance capable of producing upward motion (lift) in the middle or upper parts of the atmosphere.

Upslope Flow Air that flows toward higher terrain, and hence is forced to rise. The added lift often results in widespread low cloudiness and stratiform precipitation if the air is stable, or an increased chance of thunderstorm development if the air is unstable.

Upstream Toward the source of the flow, or located in the area from which the flow is coming.

UTC Coordinated Universal Time. The time in the zero degree meridian time zone.

UVI Ultraviolet Index

UVV Upward Vertical Velocity.

Valley Breeze System of winds that blow uphill during the day.

Vapor Pressure The pressure exerted by water vapor molecules in a given volume of air

Variable Ceiling A ceiling of less than 3,000 feet which rapidly increases or decreases in height by established criteria during the period of observation.

Veering Wind Wind which changes in a clockwise direction with time at a given location (e.g., from southerly to westerly), or which change direction in a clockwise sense with height (e.g., southeasterly at the surface turning to southwesterly aloft). Veering winds with height are indicative of warm air advection (WAA).

Vertical Shear The rate of change of wind speed or direction, with a given change in height.

Vertically-stacked System A low-pressure system, usually a closed low or cutoff low, which is not tilted with height, i.e., located similarly at all levels of the atmosphere.

Vicinity A proximity qualifier used to indicate weather phenomena observed between 5 and 10 statute miles of the usual point of observation but not at the station.

VIL Vertically-Integrated Liquid water. A property computed by RADAP II and WSR-88D units that takes into account the three-dimensional reflectivity of an echo. The maximum VIL of a storm is useful in determining its potential severity, especially in terms of maximum hail size.

Visibility The greatest horizontal distance an observer can see and identify a prominent object.

Virtual temperature The temperature a parcel of air would have if the moisture in it were removed and its specific heat was added to the parcel.

Virga Precipitation falling from the base of a cloud and evaporating before it reaches the ground.

Volcanic Ash Fine particles of rock powder that originate from a volcano and that may remain suspended in the atmosphere for long periods.

Vort Max (Short for vorticity maximum), a center, or maximum, in the vorticity field of an airmass.

Vorticity A measure of the local rotation in a fluid flow. In weather analysis and forecasting, it usually refers to the vertical component of rotation (i.e., rotation about a vertical axis) and is used most often in reference to synoptic scale or mesoscale weather systems. By convention, positive values indicate cyclonic rotation.

Vortex An atmospheric feature that tends to rotate. It has vorticity and usually has closed streamlines.

WAA Warm Air Advection

Walker cell A zonal circulation of the atmosphere confined to equatorial regions and driven principally by the oceanic temperature gradient. In the Pacific, air flows westward from the colder, eastern area to the warm, western ocean, where it acquires warmth and moisture and subsequently rises. A return flow aloft and subsidence over the eastern ocean complete the cell.

Wall Cloud A local and often abrupt lowering of a rain-free cumulonimbus base into a low-hanging accessory cloud, from 1 to 4 miles in diameter. The wall cloud is usually situated in the southwest portion of the storm below an intense updraft marked by the main cumulonimbus cloud and associated with a very strong or severe thunderstorm. When seen from several miles away, many wall clouds exhibit rapid upward motion and rotation in the same sense as a tornado, except with considerably lower speed. A rotating wall cloud usually develops before tornadoes or funnel clouds by a time which can range from a few minutes up to possibly an hour.

Warm Advection Transport of warm air into an area by horizontal winds. Low-level warm advection sometimes is referred to (erroneously) as overrunning.

Warm Front A narrow transitions zone separating advancing warmer air from retreating cooler air. The air behind a warm front is warmer and typically more humid than the air it is replacing. Warning Forecast issued when a particular weather or flood hazard is "imminent" or already occurring (e.g., tornado warning, flash flood warning). A warning is used for conditions posing a threat to life or property.

Warning Stage The level of a river or stream which may cause minor flooding, and at which concerned interests should take action. Watch Forecast issued well in advance to alert the public of the possibility of a particular weather related hazard (e.g. tornado watch, flash flood watch). The occurrence, location and timing may still be uncertain.

Watch Box (or Box) A severe thunderstorm or tornado watch.

Water a transparent, odorless, tasteless liquid; composed of hydrogen and oxygen.

Water Equivalent The liquid content of solid precipitation that has accumulated on the ground (snow depth). The accumulation may consist of snow, ice formed by freezing precipitation, freezing liquid precipitation, or ice formed by the refreezing of melted snow.

Water Vapor Water substance in a gaseous state that comprises one of the most important of all the constituents of the atmosphere.Waterspout A rapidly rotating column of air extending from a cumulonimbus cloud with a circulation that reaches the surface of the water, (i.e. a tornado over water).

Wave In meteorology any pattern identifiable on a weather map that has a cyclic pattern, or, a small cyclonic circulation in the early stages of development that moves along a cold front.

Wave Crest The highest point in a wave.

Wave Trough The lowest point in a wave.

Wavelength Physical distance of one period (wave repeat).

Weather State of the atmosphere with respect to heat or cold, wetness or dryness, calm or storm, clearness or cloudiness. Also, weather is the meteorological day-to-day variations of the atmosphere and their effects on life and human activity. It includes temperature, pressure, humidity, clouds, wind, precipitation and fog.

Weather Balloon Large balloon filled with helium or hydrogen that carries a radiosonde (weather instrument) aloft to measure temperature pressure and humidity as the balloon rises through the air. It is attached to a small parachute so that when the balloon inevitably breaks, the radiosonde doesn't hurtle back to earth dangerously quickly.

Weather Synopsis a description of weather patterns affecting a large area.

Wedge (or Wedge Tornado) A large tornado with a condensation funnel that is at least as wide (horizontally) at the ground as it is tall (vertically) from the ground to cloud base.

WFO Weather Forecast Office.

Whiteout A condition caused by falling and/or blowing snow that reduces visibility to nothing or zero miles; typically only a few feet. Whiteouts can occur rapidly often blinding motorists and creating chain-reaction crashes involving multiple vehicles. Whiteouts are most frequent during blizzards.

Wind Air in motion relative to the surface of the earth.

Wind Advisory Issued for sustained winds 31 to 39 mph for at least 1 hour or any gusts 46 to 57 mph. However, winds of this magnitude occurring over an area that frequently experiences such winds would not require the issuance a wind advisory.

Wind Aloft The wind speeds and wind directions at various levels in the atmosphere above the area of surface.

Wind Chill The additional cooling effect resulting from wind blowing on bare skin. The wind chill is based on the rate of heat loss from exposed skin caused by the combined effects of wind and cold. The (equivalent) wind chill temperature is the temperature the body "feels" for a certain combination of wind and air temperature

Wind Chill Factor The apparent temperature which describes the cooling effect on exposed skin by the combination of temperature and wind, expressed as the loss of body heat. Increased wind speed will accelerate the loss of body heat. The formula to calculate wind chill is: WC=.0817(3.71 V^.5 + 5.81 - .25 v)(T-91.4)+91.4 where V=wind speed in MPH and T=temperature F.

Wind Chill Advisory Issued when the wind chill index is expected to be between -25F and -39F for at least 3 hours. This is using the wind chill of the sustained wind, not gusts.

Wind Chill Warning Issued when life-threatening wind chills of -40F or colder are expected for at least 3 hours. This is using the wind chill of the sustained wind, not gusts.

Wind Direction The direction from which the wind is blowing.

Wind Shear Variation in wind speed and/or direction over a short distance. Shear usually refers to vertical wind shear, i.e., the change in wind with height, but the term also is used in Doppler radar to describe changes in radial velocity over short horizontal distances.

Wind Speed The rate at which air is moving horizontally past a given point. It may be a 2-minute average speed (reported as wind speed) or an instantaneous speed (reported as a peak wind speed, or gust).Wind Vane An instrument that determines the direction from which a wind is blowing.

Wind Wave A wave that is caused by the action of wind on the surface of water.

Windward Upwind, or the direction from which the wind is blowing; the opposite of leeward.

Winter Storm A heavy snow event. A snow accumulation of more than 6 inches in 12 hrs or more than 12 inches in 24 hrs.

Winter Storm Watch A significant winter storm may affect your area, but its occurrence, location and timing are still uncertain. A winter storm watch is issued to provide 12 to 36 hours notice of the possibility of severe winter weather. A watch will often be issued when neither the path of a developing winter storm nor the consequences of the weather event are as yet well defined. Ideally, the winter storm watch will eventually be upgraded to a warning when the nature and location of the developing weather event becomes more apparent. A winter storm watch is intended to provide enough lead time so those who need to set plans in motion can do so.

Winter Storm Warning Issued when 7 or more inches of snow or sleet is expected in the next 24 hours, or 1/2 inch or more of accretion of freezing rain is expected. A warning is used for winter weather conditions posing a threat to life and property.

Winter Weather Advisory Issued when 4, 5, or 6 inches of snow or sleet is expected in 24 hours; or any accretion of freezing rain or freezing drizzle is expected on road surfaces; or when blowing or drifting snow is expected to occasionally reduce visibility to 1/4 mile or less.

Wiresonde an atmospheric sounding instrument that is used to obtain temperature and humidity information between ground level and height of a few thousand feet; this instrument is supported by a captive balloon while traveling from the ground level.

World Meteorological Organization (WMO) A specialized UN agency responsible for the establishment of meteorological stations and networks, and the monitoring of meteorological observations.

Wrapping Gust Front A gust front which wraps around a mesocyclone, cutting off the inflow of warm moist air to the mesocyclone circulation and resulting in an occluded mesocyclone.

WSR-88D Weather Surveillance Radar – 1988 Doppler; NEXRAD unit.

Yellow Wind a strong, cold, dry west wind of eastern Asia that blows across the plains during winter and carries a yellow dust from the desert.

Youg a hot wind during unsettled summer weather in the Mediterranean.

Young Ice newly formed flat, sea or lake ice generally between two and eight inches thick.

Zigzag Lightning ordinary lightning of a cloud-to-ground discharge that appears to have a single lightning channel.

Zodiac the position of the sun throughout a year as it appears to move through successive star groups or constellations.Zonal Flow (Zonal Wind) Large-scale atmospheric flow in which the east-west component (i.e., latitudinal) is dominant.

Zone Of Maximum Precipitation The belt of elevation at which the annual precipitation is greatest in a mountain region.

Zulu time Same as UTC, Universal Coordinated Time. Is is called Zulu because Z is often appended to the time to distinguish it from local time.

Source: NOAA, National Weather Service

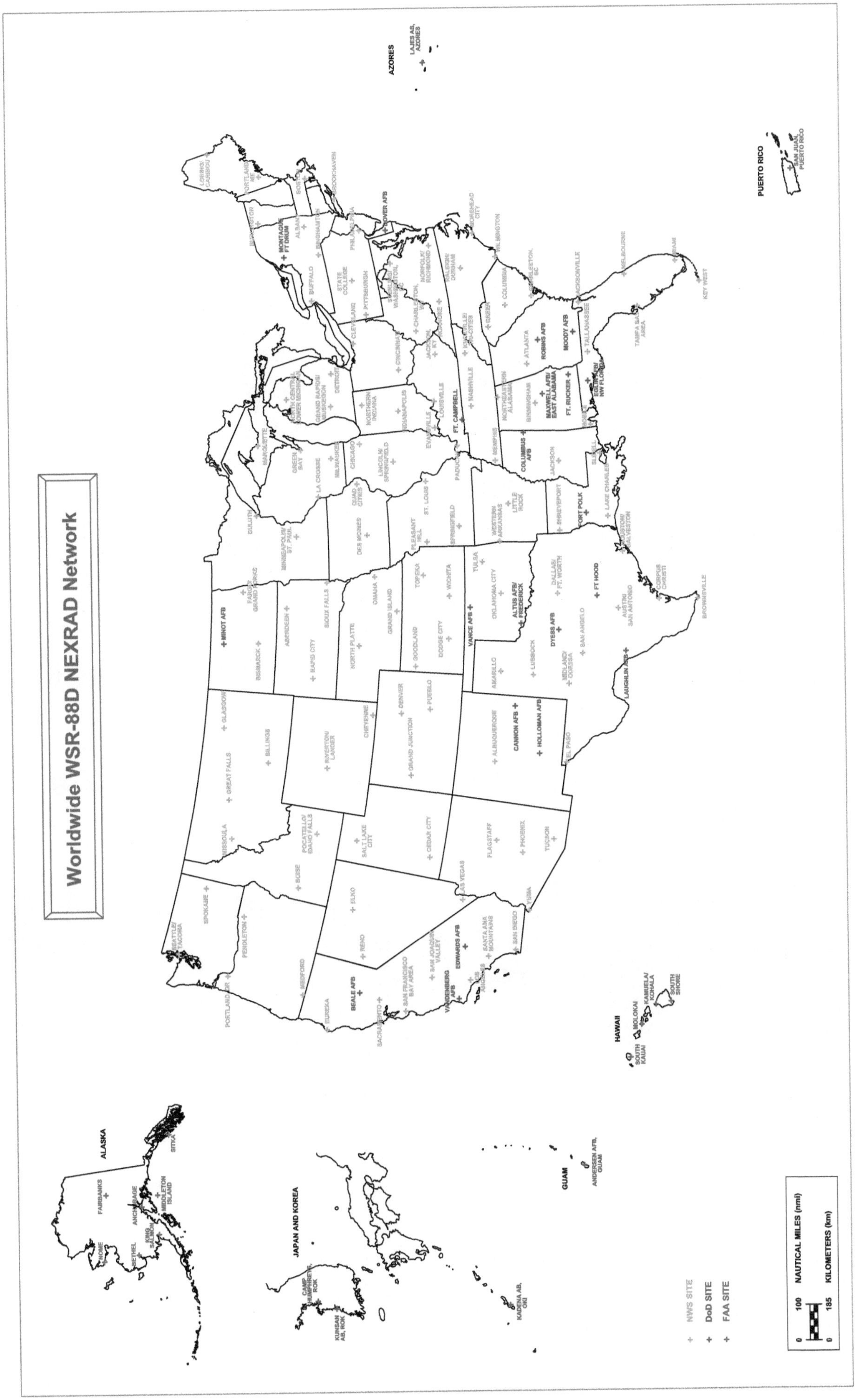
Worldwide WSR-88D NEXRAD Network
ALASKA
JAPAN AND KOREA
GUAM
HAWAII
PUERTO RICO
AZORES
NWS SITE
DoD SITE
FAA SITE
NAUTICAL MILES (nmi)
KILOMETERS (km)

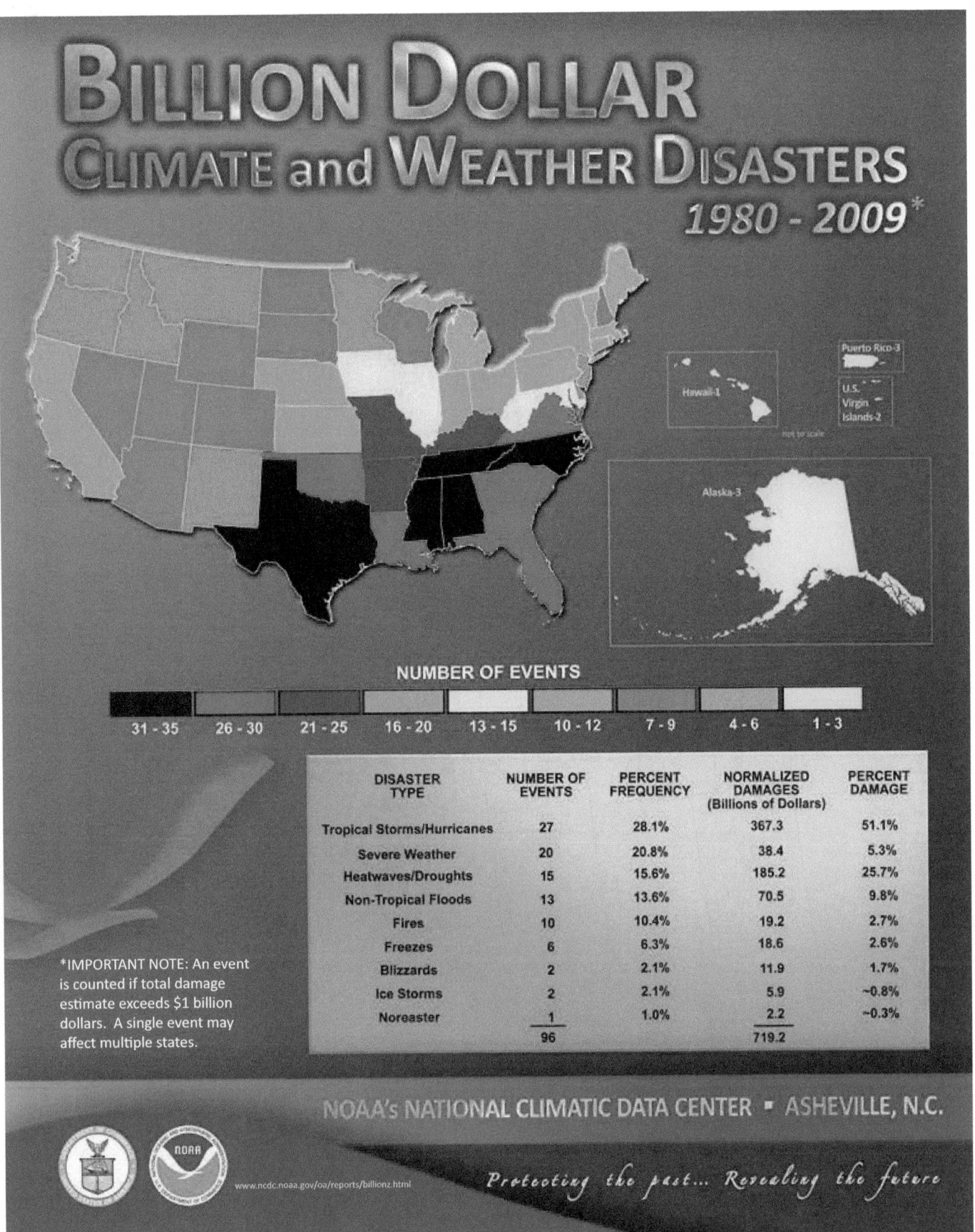

BILLION DOLLAR CLIMATE and WEATHER DISASTERS 1980 - 2009*

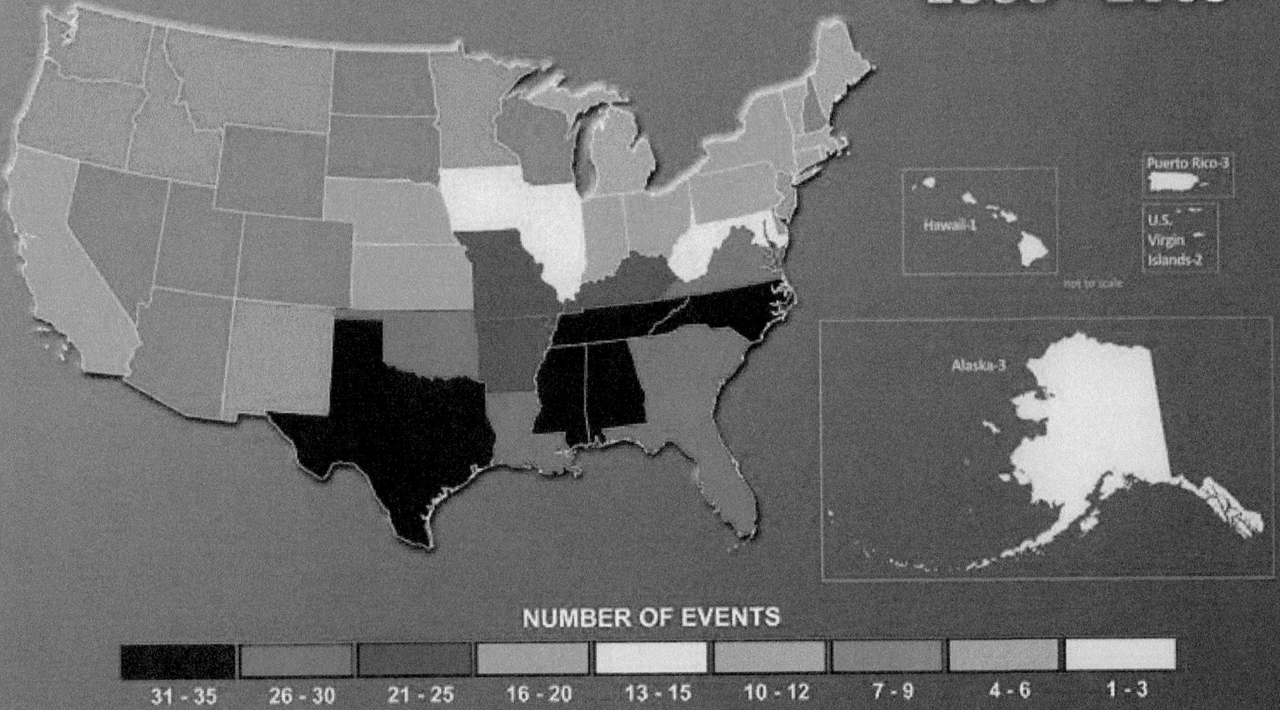

DISASTER TYPE	NUMBER OF EVENTS	PERCENT FREQUENCY	NORMALIZED DAMAGES (Billions of Dollars)	PERCENT DAMAGE
Tropical Storms/Hurricanes	27	28.1%	367.3	51.1%
Severe Weather	20	20.8%	38.4	5.3%
Heatwaves/Droughts	15	15.6%	185.2	25.7%
Non-Tropical Floods	13	13.6%	70.5	9.8%
Fires	10	10.4%	19.2	2.7%
Freezes	6	6.3%	18.6	2.6%
Blizzards	2	2.1%	11.9	1.7%
Ice Storms	2	2.1%	5.9	~0.8%
Noreaster	1	1.0%	2.2	~0.3%
	96		719.2	

*IMPORTANT NOTE: An event is counted if total damage estimate exceeds $1 billion dollars. A single event may affect multiple states.

NOAA's NATIONAL CLIMATIC DATA CENTER ▪ ASHEVILLE, N.C.

www.ncdc.noaa.gov/oa/reports/billionz.html

Protecting the past... Revealing the future

Billion Dollar Weather Disasters 1980 - 2009

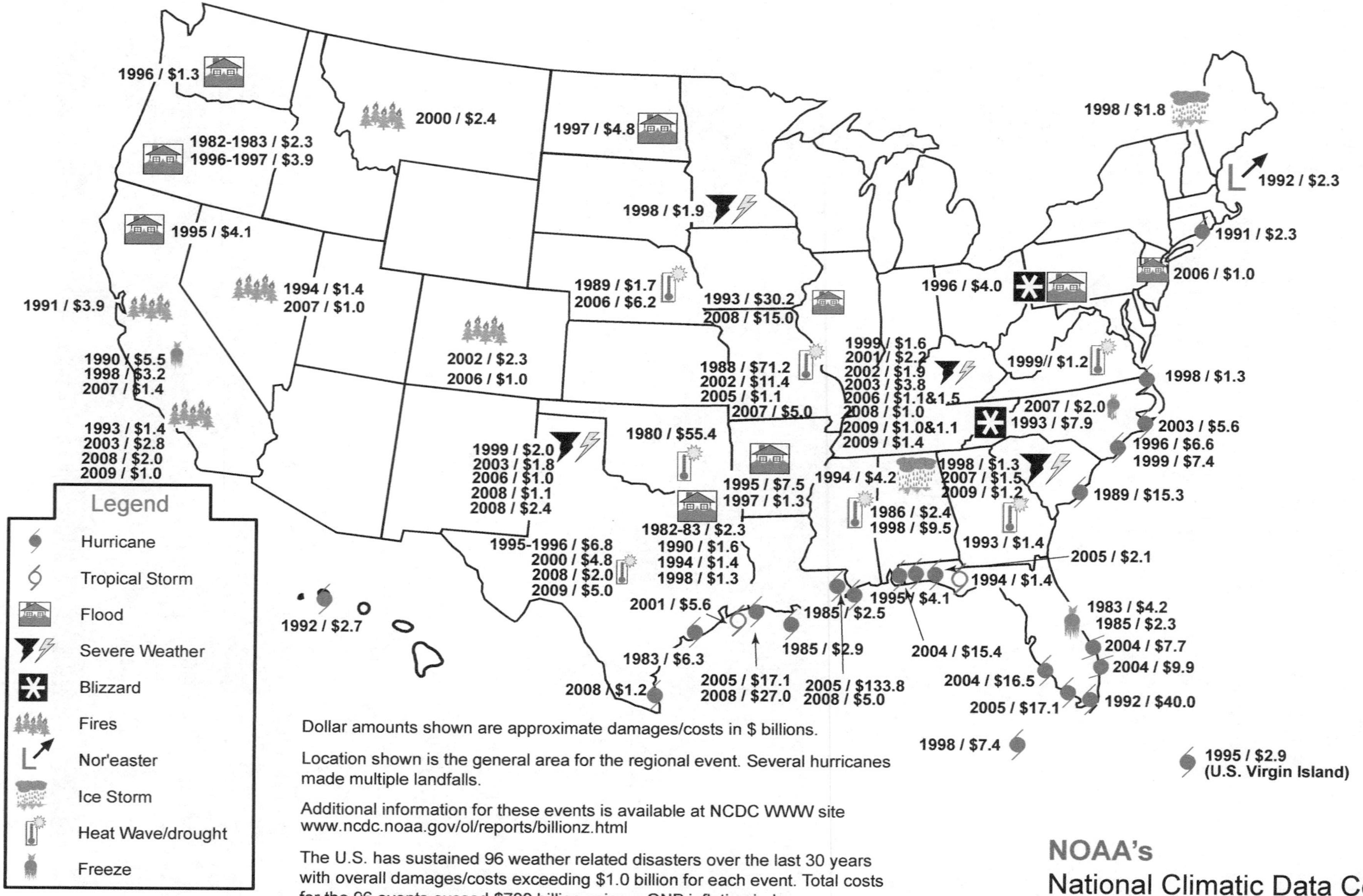

Dollar amounts shown are approximate damages/costs in $ billions.

Location shown is the general area for the regional event. Several hurricanes made multiple landfalls.

Additional information for these events is available at NCDC WWW site
www.ncdc.noaa.gov/ol/reports/billionz.html

The U.S. has sustained 96 weather related disasters over the last 30 years with overall damages/costs exceeding $1.0 billion for each event. Total costs for the 96 events exceed $700 billion using a GNP inflation index.

NOAA's
National Climatic Data Center

1980-2009 Billion Dollar U.S. Weather Disasters

(Damage Amounts in Billions of Dollars and Costs Normalized to 2007 Dollars Using GNP Inflation / Wealth Index)

1980	Drought / Heat Wave e $55.4 ~10,000 Deaths				
1983	Hurricane Alicia $6.3 21 Deaths	Florida Freeze ~ $4.2 No Deaths	Gulf Storms / Flooding ~ $2.3 ~ 50 Deaths	W Storms / Flooding ~ $2.3 ~ 45 Deaths	
1985	Florida Freeze ~ $2.3 No Deaths	Hurricane Elena $2.5 4 Deaths	Hurricane Juan $2.9 63 Deaths		
1986	Drought / Heat Wave $2.4 ~100 Deaths				
1988	Drought / Heat Wave e $71.2 ~7,500 Deaths				
1989	Hurricane Hugo > $15.3 86 Deaths	N Plains Drought > $1.7 No Deaths			
1990	S Plains Flooding > $1.6 13 Deaths	California Freeze > $5.5 No Deaths			
1991	Hurricane Bob $2.3 18 Deaths	Oakland CA Firestorm ~ $3.9 25 Deaths			
1992	Hurricane Andrew ~ $40.0 61 Deaths	Hurricane Iniki ~ $2.7 7 Deaths	Nor'easter $2.3 19 Deaths		
1993	E Storm / Blizzard $7.9 ~ 270 Deaths	SE Drought / Heat Wave ~ $1.4 > 16 Deaths	Midwest Flooding ~ $30.2 48 Deaths	CA Wildfires ~ $1.4 4 Deaths	
1994	SE Ice Storm ~ $4.2 9 Deaths	Tropical Storm Alberto ~ $1.4 32 Deaths	Texas Flooding ~ $1.4 19 Deaths	W Fire Season ~ $1.4 No Deaths	
1995	CA Flooding > $4.1 27 Deaths	SE / SW Severe Wx $7.5 32 Deaths	Hurricane Marilyn e $2.9 13 Deaths	Hurricane Opal > $4.1 27 Deaths	
1996	Blizzard / Flooding ~ $4.0 187 Deaths	Pacific NW Flooding ~ $1.3 9 Deaths	S Plains Drought ~ $6.8 No Deaths	Hurricane Fran > $6.6 37 Deaths	
1997	Midwest Flood / Tornadoes e $1.3 67 Deaths	N Plains Flooding ~ $4.8 11 Deaths	W Coast Flooding ~ $3.9 36 Deaths		
1998	New England Ice Storm > $1.8 16 Deaths	SE Severe Wx > $1.3 132 Deaths	MN Severe Storms / Hail > $1.9 1 Death	S Drought / Heat Wave $9.5 > 200 Deaths	Hurricane Bonnie ~ $1.3 3 Deaths
	Hurricane Georges e $7.4 16 Deaths	Texas Flooding ~ $1.3 31 Deaths	California Freeze $3.2 No Deaths		
1999	AR - TN Tornadoes ~ $1.6 17 Deaths	OK - KS Tornadoes > $2.0 55 Deaths	E Drought / Heat Wave > $1.2 e 502 Deaths	Hurricane Floyd e > $7.4 77 Deaths	
2000	Drought / Heat Wave e > $4.8 ~ 140 Deaths	Western Fires > $2.4 No Deaths			
2001	Tropical Storm Allison e ~ $5.6 > 43 Deaths	Midwest / OH Valley Hail / Tornadoes > $2.2 > 3 Deaths			
2002	30-State Drought e > $11.4 No Deaths	Western Fires > $2.3 ~21 Deaths	Severe Wx / Tornadoes > $1.9 7 Deaths		
2003	Severe Wx / Hail > $1.8 3 Deaths	Severe Wx / Tornadoes > $3.8 51 Deaths	Hurricane Isabel ~ $5.6 55 Deaths	S California Wildfires > $2.8 22 Deaths	
2004	Hurricane Charley e ~ $16.5 35 Deaths	Hurricane Frances e ~ $9.9 48 Deaths	Hurricane Ivan e > $15.4 57 Deaths	Hurricane Jeanne e > $7.7 28 Deaths	
2005	Hurricane Dennis e > $2.2 > 15 Deaths	Hurricane Katrina e ~ $133.8 > 1833 Deaths	Hurricane Rita e ~ $17.1 119 Deaths	Midwest Drought e > $1.1 No Deaths	Hurricne Wilma e ~ $17.1 35 Deaths
2006	Numerous Wildfires > $1.0 28 Deaths	Widespread Drought e > $6.2 * Deaths	Severe Storms Tornadoes e > $1.0 10 Deaths	Northeast Flooding > $1.0 20 Deaths	MW / SE Tornadoes > $1.5 10 Deaths
	MW / Ohio Valley Tornadoes ~ $1.1 27 Deaths				
2007	Great Plains East Drought > $5.0 * Deaths	Western Wildfires > $1.0 12 Deaths	Spring Freeze > $2.0 No Deaths	East / South Severe Weather > $1.5 9 Deaths	California Freeze > $1.4 1 Deaths
2008	Southeast / Midwest Tornadoes > $1.0 57 Deaths	MW / Ohio Valley Svr Wx / Tornadoes > $2.4 13 Deaths	MW / Mid-Atl. Svr Wx / Tornadoes > $1.1 18 Deaths	Midwest Flooding e > $15.0 24 Deaths	U.S. Wild Fires > $2.0 16 Deaths
	Hurricane Dolly > $1.2 3 Deaths	Hurricane Gustav > $5.0 53 Deaths	Hurricane Ike > $27.0 > 112 Deaths	Widespread Drought > $2.0 No Deaths	
2009	Southeast / Ohio Valley Severe Weather > $1.4 10 Deaths	Midwest / Southeast Tornadoes > $1.0 No Deaths	South / Southeast Tornadoes & Severe Weather > $1.2 6 Deaths	Midwest, South, East Severe Weather > $1.1 No Deaths	Western Wild Fires > $1.0 10 Deaths
	Southwest / G. Plains Drought e > $5.0 No Deaths				

e = estimated > = greater than/at least ~ = approximately/about * = undetermined

< 5	5-20	20-30	30-40	> 40

Amounts in Billions of Dollars

Source: NOAA's National Climatic Data Center Asheville, NC 28801-5001 www.ncdc.noaa.gov/oa/reports/billionz.html

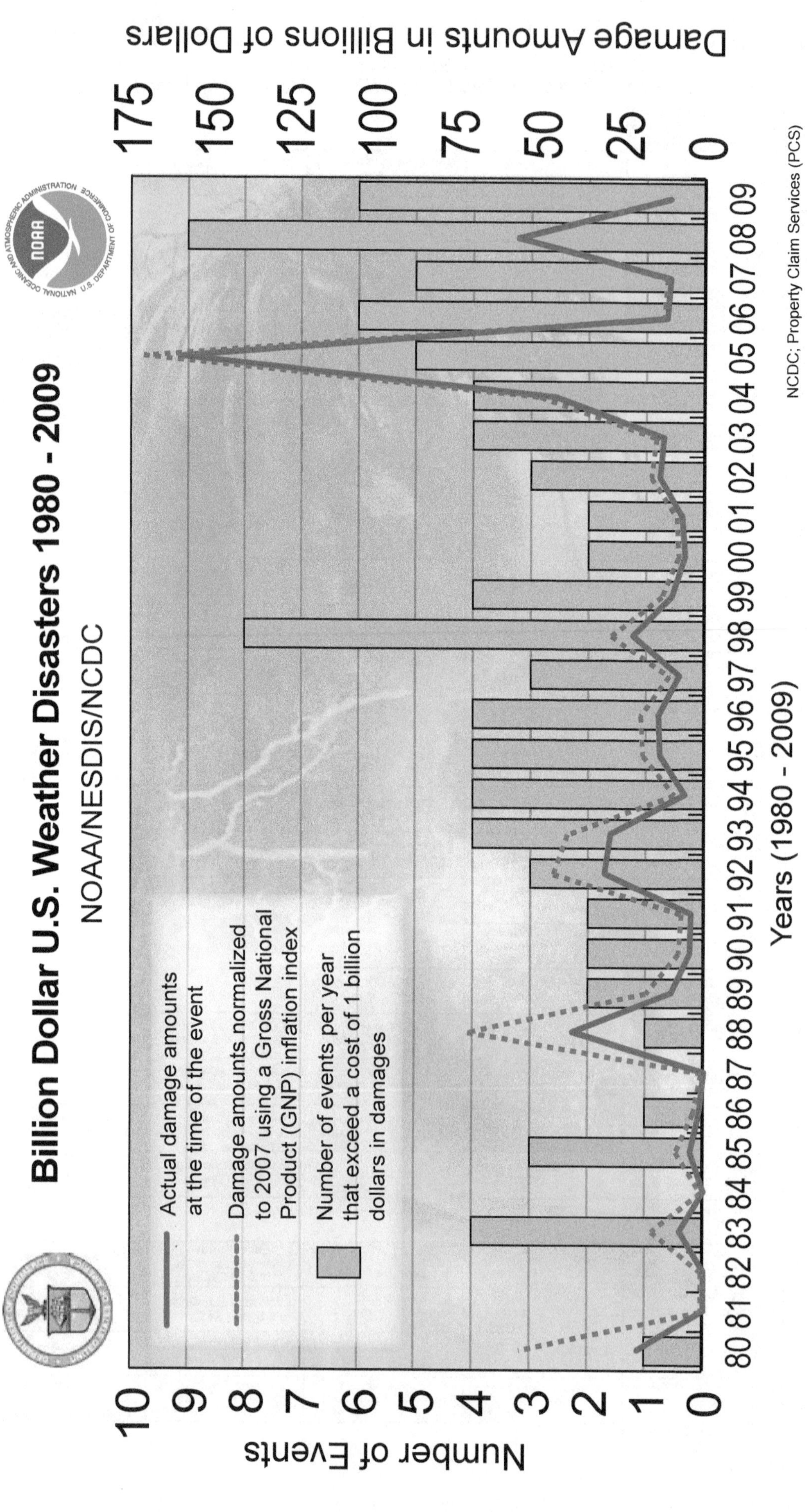
Billion Dollar U.S. Weather Disasters 1980 - 2009
NOAA/NESDIS/NCDC
Actual damage amounts at the time of the event
Damage amounts normalized to 2007 using a Gross National Product (GNP) inflation index
Number of events per year that exceed a cost of 1 billion dollars in damages
Number of Events
0 1 2 3 4 5 6 7 8 9 10
Damage Amounts in Billions of Dollars
0 25 50 75 100 125 150 175
80 81 82 83 84 85 86 87 88 89 90 91 92 93 94 95 96 97 98 99 00 01 02 03 04 05 06 07 08 09
Years (1980 - 2009)
NCDC; Property Claim Services (PCS)

Billion Dollar U.S. Weather Disasters, 1980 - 2009
National Climatic Data Center Asheville, NC 01/01/2010

http://www.ncdc.noaa.gov/oa/reports/billionz.html

The U.S. has sustained 96 weather-related disasters over the past 30 years in which overall damages/costs reached or exceeded $1 billion. The total normalized losses for the 96 events exceed $700 billion. Events are listed below beginning with the most recent. Two damage figures are given for events prior to 2007–the first figure represents actual dollar costs at the time of the event and is not adjusted for inflation. The value in parenthesis is the costs normalized to 2007 dollars using a GNP inflation index.

2009 **Southwest/Great Plains Drought** Entire year, 2009. Drought conditions occurred during much of the year across parts of the Southwest, Great Plains, and southern Texas causing agricultural losses in numerous states (TX, OK, KS, CA, NM, AZ). The largest agriculture losses occurred in TX and CA. Estimate of over $5.0 billion in damages/costs.

Western Wildfires Summer-Fall 2009. Residual and sustained drought conditions across western and south-central states resulted in thousands of wildfires. Most affected states include CA, AZ, NM, TX, OK, and UT. National acreage burned exceeding 5.9 million. Over 200 homes and structures destroyed in the California "Station" fire alone. Over $1.0 billion in damages/costs (including annual fire suppression costs); 10 deaths.

Midwest, South and Eastern Severe Weather June 2009. Sustained outbreak of thunderstorms and high winds from a strong derecho event over the central, southern, and eastern states (TX, OK, MO, NE, KS, AR, AL, MS, TN, NC, SC, KY, PA). Over $1.1 billion in damages/costs; no deaths reported.

South/Southeast Tornadoes and Severe Weather April 2009. Outbreak of tornadoes, hail and severe thunderstorms over the south and southeastern states (AL, AR, GA, KY, MO, SC, TN) with 85 confirmed tornadoes. Over $1.2 billion in damages/costs; 6 deaths.

Midwest/Southeast Tornadoes March 2009. Outbreak of tornadoes over central and southern states (NE, KS, OK, IA, TX, LA, MS, AL, GA, TN, KY) with 56 tornadoes confirmed. Over $1.0 billion in damages/costs with majority of damage in TX; no deaths reported.

Southeast/Ohio Valley Severe Weather February 2009. Complex of severe thunderstorms and high winds across the region (TN, KY, OK, OH, VA, WV, PA). Over $1.4 billion in damages/costs with majority of damage in OK and OH; 10 deaths.

2008 **Widespread Drought** Entire year, 2008. Severe drought and heat caused agricultural losses in areas of the south and west. Record low lake levels also occurred in areas of the southeast. Includes states of CA, TX, NC, SC, GA, and TN. Estimate of over $2.0 billion in damages/costs.

Hurricane Ike September 2008. Category 2 hurricane makes landfall in Texas causing considerable storm surge in coastal TX and significant wind and flooding damage in TX, LA, AR, TN, IL, IN, KY, MO, OH, MI and PA. Severe gasoline shortages occurred in the southeast US due to damaged oil platforms, storage tanks, pipelines and off-line refineries. Estimate of over $27.0 billion in damages/costs; 112 deaths; dozens of people missing.

Hurricane Gustav September 2008. Category 2 hurricane makes landfall in Louisiana causing significant wind, storm surge, and flooding damage in AL, AR, LA, and MS. Estimate of at least $5.0 billion in damages/costs; 53 deaths.

Hurricane Dolly July 2008. Category 2 hurricane makes landfall in southern Texas causing considerable wind and flooding damage in TX and NM. Over $1.2 billion in damages/costs; 3 deaths.

US Wildfires Summer-Fall 2008. Drought conditions across numerous western, central and southeastern states (AK, AZ, CA, NM, ID, UT, MT, NV, OR, WA, CO, TX, OK, NC, FL) resulted in thousands of wildfires; national acreage burned exceeding 5.2 million acres (mainly in the west) and over 1,000 homes and structures destroyed in California fires alone. Over $2.0 billion in damages/costs; 16 deaths.

Midwest Flood June 2008. Heavy rain and flooding caused significant agricultural loss and property damage in IA, IL, IN, MO, MN, NE, and WI with IA being hardest hit with widespread rainfall totals ranging from 4 to over 16 inches. Estimate of over $15 billion in damages/costs; 24 deaths.

Midwest/Mid-Atlantic Severe Weather/Tornadoes June 2008. An outbreak of tornadoes and thunderstorms over the Midwest/Mid-Atlantic states (IA, IL, IN, KS, NE, MI, MN, MO, OK, WI, MD, VA, WV). Over $1.1 billion in damages/costs; 18 deaths.

Midwest/Ohio Valley Severe Weather/Tornadoes May 2008. Outbreak of tornadoes over the Midwest/Ohio Valley regions (IL, IN, IA, KS, MN, NE, OK, WY, CO) with 235 tornadoes confirmed. Over $2.4 billion in damages/costs; 13 deaths.

Southeast/Midwest Tornadoes February 2008. Series of tornadoes and severe thunderstorms across the Southeast and Midwest states (AL, AR, IN, KY, MS, OH, TN, TX) with 87 tornadoes confirmed. Over $1.0 billion in damages/costs; 57 deaths.

2007 **Great Plains and Eastern Drought** Entire year 2007. Severe drought with periods of extreme heat over most of the southeast and portions of the Great Plains, Ohio Valley, and Great Lakes area, resulting in major reductions in crop yields, along with very low stream-flows and lake levels. Includes states of ND, SD, NE, KS, OK, TX, MN, WI, IA, MO, AR, LA, MS, AL, GA, NC, SC, FL, TN, VA, WV, KY, IN, IL, OH, MI, PA, NY. Preliminary estimate of well over $5.0 billion in damage/costs; some deaths reported due to heat but not beyond typical annual averages.

Western Wildfires Summer-Fall 2007. Continued drought conditions and high winds over much of the western US (AK, AZ, CA, ID, UT, MT, NV, OR, WA) resulting in numerous wildfires; with national acreage burned exceeding 8.9 million acres (mainly in the west) and over 3,000 homes and structures destroyed in southern California alone. Well over $1.0 billion in damages/costs; at least 12 deaths.

Spring Freeze April 2007. Widespread severe freeze over much of the east and midwest (AL, AR, GA, IL, IN, IA, KS, KY, MS, MO, NE, NC, OH, OK, SC, TN, VA, WV), causing significant losses in fruit crops, field crops (especially wheat), and the ornamental industry. Temperatures in the teens/20's accompanied by rather high winds nullified typical crop-protection systems. Over $2.0 billion in damage/costs; no deaths reported.

East/South Severe Weather April 2007. Flooding, hail, tornadoes, and severe thunderstorms across numerous states (CT, DE, GA, LA, ME, MD, MA, MS, NH, NJ, NY, NC, PA, RI, SC, TX, VT, VA) in mid-April, including 3 "killer" tornadoes. Over $1.5 billion in damages/costs; 9 deaths.

California Freeze January 2007. Widespread agricultural freeze – for nearly two weeks in January, overnight temperatures over a good portion of California dipped into the 20's, destroying numerous agricultural crops; with citrus, berry, and vegetable crops most affected. $1.4 billion estimated in damage/costs; 1 fatality reported.

2006 **Widespread Drought** Spring-Summer 2006. Rather severe drought affected crops especially during the spring-summer, centered over the Great Plains region with other areas affected across portions of the south and far west – including states of ND, SD, NE, KS, OK, TX, MN, IA, MO, AR, LA, MS, AL, GA, FL, MT, WY, CO, NM, CA. Estimate of over $6.0 (6.2) billion in damages/costs; some heat-related deaths but not beyond typical annual averages.

Northeast Flooding June 2006. Severe flooding over portions of the northeast due to several weeks of heavy rainfall, affecting the states of NY, PA, DE, MD, NJ, and VA. Over $1.0 billion in damage/costs; at least 20 deaths reported.

Midwest/Southeast Tornadoes April 2006. Severe weather and numerous tornadoes affecting the states of OK, KS, MO, NE, KY, OH, TN, IN, MS, GA, and AL on April 6-8 with 3 "killer" tornadoes in TN. Over $1.5 billion in damages/costs; 10 deaths.

Midwest/Ohio Valley Tornadoes April 2006. Significant outbreak of tornadoes and severe weather affecting the states of IL, IN, IA, AR, MO, KY, and TN on April 2nd with 5 "killer" tornadoes. Approximately $1.1 billion in damages/costs; 27 deaths.

Severe Storms and Tornadoes March 2006. Outbreak of tornadoes over portions of the midwest and south during a week-long period—affecting the states of AL, AR, KY, MS, TN, TX, IN, KS, MO, and OK. Over $1.0 billion in damage/costs; at least 10 deaths.

Numerous Wildfires Entire year 2006. Numerous wildfires mainly over the western half of the country due to dry weather and high winds, burning nearly 10 million acres (new record for period since 1960), with the most affected states being AK, AZ, CA, CO, FL, ID, MT, NM, NV, OK, OR, TX, WA, WY. Well over $1.0 billion in overall damages/costs; at least 28 fatalities, including 20 firefighters.

2005 **Hurricane Wilma** October 2005. Category 3 hurricane hits SW Florida resulting in strong damaging winds and major flooding across southeastern Florida. Prior to landfall, Wilma as a Category 5 recorded the lowest pressure (882 mb) ever recorded in the Atlantic basin. Estimate of approximately $16.0 (17.1) billion in damages/costs; estimated 35 deaths.

Hurricane Rita September 2005. Category 3 hurricane hits Texas-Louisiana border coastal region, creating significant storm surge and wind damage along the coast, and some inland flooding in the FL panhandle, AL, MS, LA, AR, and TX. Prior to landfall, Rita reached the third lowest pressure (897 mb) ever recorded in the Atlantic basin. Estimate of approximately $16.0 (17.1) billion in damage/costs; 119 deaths reported—most being indirect (many related to evacuations).

Hurricane Katrina August 2005. Category 3 hurricane initially impacts the U.S. as a Category 1 near Miami, FL, then as a strong Category 3 along the eastern LA-western MS coastlines, resulting in severe storm surge damage (maximum surge probably exceeded 25 feet) along the LA-MS-AL coasts, wind damage, and the failure of parts of the levee system in New Orleans. Inland effects included high winds and some flooding in the states of AL, MS, FL, TN, KY, IN, OH, and GA. Estimate of approximately $125 (133.8) billion in damage/costs, making this the most expensive natural disaster in U.S. history; approximately 1833 deaths—the highest U.S. total since the 1928 major hurricane in southern Florida.

Hurricane Dennis July 2005. Category 3 hurricane makes landfall in western Florida panhandle resulting in storm surge and wind damage along the FL-AL coasts, along with scattered wind and flood damage in GA, MS, and TN. Estimate of over $2.0 (2.1) billion in damage/costs; at least 15 deaths.

Midwest Drought Spring-Summer 2005. Rather severe localized drought causes significant crop losses (especially for corn and soybeans) in the states of AR, IL, IN, MO, OH, and WI. Estimate of over $1.0 (1.1) billion in damage/costs; no reported deaths.

2004 Hurricane Jeanne September 2004. Category 3 hurricane makes landfall in east-central Florida, causing considerable wind, storm surge, and flooding damage in FL, with some flood damage also in the states of GA, SC, NC, VA, MD, DE, NJ, PA, and NY. Puerto Rico also affected. Estimate of over $7.0 (7.7) billion in damage/costs; at least 28 deaths.

Hurricane Ivan September 2004. Category 3 hurricane makes landfall on Gulf coast of Alabama, with significant wind, storm surge, and flooding damage in coastal AL and FL panhandle, along with wind/flood damage in the states of GA, MS, LA, SC, NC, VA, WV, MD, TN, KY, OH, DE, NJ, PA, and NY. Estimate of over $14.0 (15.4) billion in damage/costs; at least 57 deaths.

Hurricane Frances September 2004. Category 2 hurricane makes landfall in east-central Florida, causing significant wind, storm surge, and flooding damage in FL, along with considerable flood damage in the states of GA, SC, NC, and NY due to 5-15 inch rains. Estimate of over $9.0 (9.9) billion in damage/costs; at least 48 deaths.

Hurricane Charley August 2004. Category 4 hurricane makes landfall in southwest Florida, resulting in major wind and some storm surge damage in FL, along with some damage in the states of SC and NC. Estimate of over $15.0 (16.5) billion in damage/costs; at least 35 deaths.

2003 Southern California Wildfires Late October-early November 2003. Dry weather, high winds, and resulting wildfires in Southern California. More than 743,000 acres of brush and timber burned, over 3,700 homes destroyed; over $2.5 (2.8) billion in damage/costs; 22 deaths.

Hurricane Isabel September 2003. Category 2 hurricane makes landfall in eastern North Carolina, causing considerable storm surge damage along the coasts of NC, VA, and MD, with wind damage and some flooding due to 4-12 inch rains in NC, VA, MD, DE, WV, NJ, NY, and PA; approximately $5.0 (5.6) billion in damage/costs; 55 deaths.

Severe Storms and Tornadoes Early May 2003. Numerous tornadoes over the midwest, MS valley, OH/TN valleys, and portions of the southeast, with a modern record one-week total of approximately 400 tornadoes reported; over $3.4 (3.8) billion in damage/costs; 51 deaths.

Storms and Hail Early April 2003. Severe storms and large hail over the southern plains and lower MS valley, with Texas hardest hit, and much of the monetary losses due to hail; over $1.6 (1.8) billion in damage/costs; 3 deaths.

2002 Widespread Drought Spring through Fall 2002. Moderate to extreme drought over large portions of 30 states, including the western states, the Great Plains, and much of the eastern U.S.; estimate of over $10.0 (11.4) billion in damage/costs; no deaths reported.

Western Fire Season Spring through Fall 2002. Major fires over 11 western states from the Rockies to the west coast, due to drought and periodic high winds, with over 7.1 million acres burned; over $2.0 (2.3) billion in damage/costs; 21 deaths.

Central/Eastern Severe Weather/Tornadoes Late April - Early May 2002. Numerous tornadoes over the Central and Eastern states (NC, GA, VA, TX, AR, MO, MS, TN, IL, IN, KY, PA, MD, NY, OH, WV, KS). Over $1.7 (1.9) billion in damages/costs; 7 deaths.

2001 Tropical Storm Allison June 2001. The persistent remnants of Tropical Storm Allison produce rainfall amounts of 30-40 inches in portions of coastal Texas and Louisiana, causing severe flooding especially in the Houston area, then moves slowly northeastward; fatalities and significant damage reported in TX, LA, MS, FL, VA, and PA; estimate of approximately $5.0 (5.6) billion in damage/costs; at least 43 deaths.

Midwest and Ohio Valley Hail and Tornadoes April 2001. Storms, tornadoes, and hail in the states of TX, OK, KS, NE, IA, MO, IL, IN, WI, MI, OH, KY, WV, and PA, over a 6-day period; over $1.9 (2.2) billion in damage/costs, with the most significant losses due to hail; at least 3 deaths.

2000 Drought/Heat Wave Spring-Summer 2000. Severe drought and persistent heat over south-central and southeastern states causing significant losses to agriculture and related industries; estimate of over $4.0 (4.8) billion in damage/costs; estimated 140 deaths nationwide.

Western Fire Season Spring-Summer 2000. Severe fire season in western states due to drought and frequent winds, with nearly 7 million acres burned; estimate of over $2.0 (2.4) billion in damage/costs (includes fire suppression); no deaths reported.

1999 Hurricane Floyd September 1999. Large, category 2 hurricane makes landfall in eastern NC, causing 10-20 inch rains in 2 days, with severe flooding in NC and some flooding in SC, VA, MD, PA, NY, NJ, DE, RI, CT, MA, NH, and VT; estimate of at least $6.0 (7.4) billion in damage/costs; 77 deaths.

Eastern Drought/Heat Wave Summer 1999. Very dry summer and high temperatures, mainly in eastern U.S., with extensive agricultural losses; over $1.0 (1.2) billion in damage/costs; estimated 502 deaths.

Oklahoma-Kansas Tornadoes May 1999. Outbreak of F4-F5 tornadoes hit the states of Oklahoma and Kansas, along with Texas and Tennessee, Oklahoma City area hardest hit; over $1.6 (2.0) billion in damage/costs; 55 deaths.

Arkansas-Tennessee Tornadoes January 1999. Two outbreaks of tornadoes in 6-day period strike Arkansas and Tennessee; approximately $1.3 (1.6) billion in damage/costs; 17 deaths.

1998 California Freeze December 1998. A severe freeze damaged fruit and vegetable crops in the Central and Southern San Joaquin Valley. Extended intervals of sub 27 degree F temperatures occurred over an 8-day period. $2.5 (3.2) billion estimated damages/costs.

Texas Flooding October-November 1998. Severe flooding in southeast Texas from 2 heavy rain events, with 10-20 inch rainfall totals; approximately $1.0 (1.3) billion in damage/costs; 31 deaths.

Hurricane Georges September 1998. Category 2 hurricane strikes Puerto Rico, Florida Keys, and Gulf coasts of Louisiana, Mississippi, Alabama, and Florida panhandle, 15-30 inch 2-day rain totals in parts of AL/FL; estimated $5.9 (7.4) billion in damage/costs; 16 deaths.

Hurricane Bonnie August 1998. Category 3 hurricane strikes eastern North Carolina and Virginia, extensive agricultural damage due to winds and flooding, with 10-inch rains in 2 days in some locations; approximately $1.0 (1.3) billion in damage/costs; 3 deaths.

Southern Drought/Heat Wave Summer 1998. Severe drought and heat wave from Texas/Oklahoma eastward to the Carolinas; $6.0-$9.0 (7.6-11.3) billion in damage/costs to agriculture and ranching; at least 200 deaths.

Minnesota Severe Storms/Hail May 1998. Very damaging severe thunderstorms with large hail over wide areas of Minnesota; over $1.5 (1.9) billion in damage/costs; 1 death.

Southeast Severe Weather Winter-Spring 1998. Tornadoes and flooding related to El Nino in southeastern states; over $1.0 (1.3) billion in damage/costs; at least 132 deaths.

Northeast Ice Storm January 1998. Intense ice storm hits Maine, New Hampshire, Vermont, and New York, with extensive forestry losses; over $1.4 (1.8) billion in damage/costs; 16 deaths.

1997 Northern Plains Flooding April-May 1997. Severe flooding in Dakotas and Minnesota due to heavy spring snowmelt; approximately $3.7 (4.8) billion in damage/costs; 11 deaths.

MS and OH Valleys Flooding & Tornadoes March 1997. Tornadoes and severe flooding hit the states of AR, MO, MS, TN, IL, IN, KY, OH, and WV, with over 10 inches of rain in 24 hours in Louisville; estimated $1.0 (1.3) billion in damage/costs; 67 deaths.

West Coast Flooding December 1996-January 1997. Torrential rains (10-40 inches in 2 weeks) and snowmelt produce severe flooding over portions of CA, WA, OR, ID, NV, and MT; approximately $3.0 (3.9) billion in damage/costs; 36 deaths.

1996 Hurricane Fran September 1996. Category 3 hurricane strikes North Carolina and Virginia, over 10-inch 24-hour rains in some locations and extensive agricultural and other losses; over $5.0 (6.6) billion in damage/costs; 37 deaths.

Southern Plains Severe Drought Fall 1995 through Summer 1996. Severe drought in agricultural regions of southern plains--Texas and Oklahoma most severely affected; approximately $5.0 (6.8) billion in damage/costs; no deaths.

Pacific Northwest Severe Flooding February 1996. Very heavy, persistent rains (10-30 inches) and melting snow over OR, WA, ID, and western MT; approximately $1.0 (1.3) billion in damage/costs; 9 deaths.

Blizzard of '96 Followed by Flooding January 1996. Very heavy snowstorm (1-4 feet) over Appalachians, Mid-Atlantic, and Northeast; followed by severe flooding in parts of same area due to rain & snowmelt; approximately $3.0 (4.0) billion in damage/costs; 187 deaths.

1995 Hurricane Opal October 1995. Category 3 hurricane strikes Florida panhandle, Alabama, western Georgia, eastern Tennessee, and the western Carolinas, causing storm surge, wind, and flooding damage; over $3.0 (4.1) billion in damage/costs; 27 deaths.

Hurricane Marilyn September 1995. Category 2 hurricane devastates U.S. Virgin Islands; estimated $2.1 (2.9) billion in damage/costs; 13 deaths

Texas/Oklahoma/Louisiana/Mississippi Severe Weather and Flooding May 1995. Torrential rains, hail, and tornadoes across Texas - Oklahoma and southeast Louisiana - southern Mississippi, with Dallas and New Orleans areas (10-25 inch rains in 5 days) hardest hit; $5.0-$6.0 (6.8-8.2) billion in damage/costs; 32 deaths.

California Flooding January-March 1995. Frequent winter storms cause 20-70 inch rainfall and periodic flooding across much of California; over $3.0 (4.1) billion in damage/costs; 27 deaths.

1994 Western Fire Season Summer-Fall 1994. Severe fire season in western states due to dry weather; approximately $1.0 (1.4) billion in damage/costs; death toll undetermined.

Texas Flooding October 1994. Torrential rain (10-25 inches in 5 days) and thunderstorms cause flooding across much of southeast Texas; approximately $1.0 (1.4) billion in damage/costs; 19 deaths.

Tropical Storm Alberto July 1994. Remnants of slow-moving Alberto bring torrential 10-25 inch rains in 3 days, widespread flooding and agricultural damage in parts of Georgia, Alabama, and panhandle of Florida; approximately $1.0 (1.4) billion in damage/costs; 32 deaths.

Southeast Ice Storm February 1994. Intense ice storm with extensive damage in portions of TX, OK, AR, LA, MS, AL, TN, GA, SC, NC, and VA; approximately $3.0 (4.2) billion in damage/costs; 9 deaths.

1993 California Wildfires Fall 1993. Dry weather, high winds and wildfires in Southern California; approximately $1.0 (1.4) billion in damage/costs; 4 deaths.

Midwest Flooding Summer 1993. Severe, widespread flooding in central U.S. due to persistent heavy rains and thunderstorms; approximately $21.0 (30.2) billion in damage/costs; 48 deaths.

Drought/Heat Wave Summer 1993. Southeastern U.S.; about $1.0 (1.4) billion damage/costs to agriculture; at least 16 deaths.

Storm/Blizzard March 1993. "Storm of the Century" hits entire eastern seaboard with tornadoes (FL), high winds, and heavy snows (2-4 feet); $5.0-$6.0 (7.2-8.6) billion damage/costs; approximately 270 deaths.

1992 **Nor'easter of 1992** December 1992. Slow-moving storm batters northeast U.S. coast, New England hardest hit; $1.0-$2.0 (1.5-3.0) billion in damage/costs; 19 deaths.

Hurricane Iniki September 1992. Category 4 hurricane hits Hawaiian island of Kauai; about $1.8 (2.7) billion in damage/costs; 7 deaths.

Hurricane Andrew August 1992. Category 4 hurricane hits Florida and Louisiana, high winds damage or destroy over 125,000 homes; approximately $27.0 (40.0) billion in damage/costs; 61 deaths.

1991 **Oakland Firestorm** October 1991. Oakland, California firestorm due to low humidities and high winds; approximately $2.5 (3.9) billion in damage/costs; 25 deaths.

Hurricane Bob August 1991. Category 2 hurricane--Mainly coastal North Carolina, Long Island, and New England; $1.5 (2.3) billion in damage/costs; 18 deaths.

1990 **California Freeze** December 1990. Severe freeze in the Central and Southern San Joaquin Valley caused the loss of citrus, avocado trees, and other crops in many areas. Several days of subfreezing temperatures occurred, with some valley locations in the teens. $3.4 (5.5) billion in direct and indirect economic losses, including damage to public buildings, utilities, crops, and residences.

Texas/Oklahoma/Louisiana/Arkansas Flooding May 1990. Torrential rains cause flooding along the Trinity, Red, and Arkansas Rivers in TX, OK, LA, and AR; over $1.0 (1.6) billion in damage/costs; 13 deaths.

1989 **Hurricane Hugo** September 1989. Category 4 hurricane devastates South and North Carolina with ~ 20 foot storm surge and severe wind damage after hitting Puerto Rico and the U.S. Virgin Islands; over $9.0 (15.3) billion in damage/costs (about $7.1 (12.1) billion in Carolinas); 86 deaths (57--U.S. mainland, 29--U.S. Islands).

Northern Plains Drought Summer 1989. Severe summer drought over much of the northern plains with significant losses to agriculture; at least $1.0 (1.7) billion in damage/costs; no deaths reported.

1988 **Drought/Heat Wave** Summer 1988. 1988 drought in central and eastern U.S. with very severe losses to agriculture and related industries; estimated $40.0 (71.2) billion in damage/costs; estimated 5,000 to 10,000 deaths (includes heat stress-related).

1986 **Southeast Drought/Heat Wave** Summer 1986. Severe summer drought in parts of the southeastern U.S. with severe losses to agriculture; $1.0-$1.5 (1.9-2.8) billion in damage/costs; estimated 100 deaths.

1985 **Hurricane Juan** October-November 1985. Category 1 hurricane--Louisiana and Southeast U.S.--severe flooding; $1.5 (2.9) billion in damage/costs; 63 deaths.

Hurricane Elena August-September 1985. Category 3 hurricane--Florida to Louisiana; $1.3 (2.5) billion in damage/costs; 4 deaths.

Florida Freeze January 1985. Severe freeze central/northern Florida; about $1.2 (2.3) billion in damage to citrus industry; no deaths.

1983 **Florida Freeze** December 1983. Severe freeze central/northern Florida; about $2.0 (4.2) billion in damage to citrus industry; no deaths.

Hurricane Alicia August 1983. Category 3 hurricane--Texas; $3.0 (6.3) billion in damage/costs; 21 deaths.

Western Storms and Flooding 1982 - Early 1983. Storms and flooding related to El Nino, especially in the states of WA, OR, CA, AZ, NV, ID, UT, and MT; approximately $1.1 (2.3) billion in damage/costs; at least 45 deaths.

Gulf States Storms and Flooding 1982 - Early 1983. Storms and flooding related to El Nino, especially in the states of TX, AR, LA, MS, AL, GA, and FL; approximately $1.1 (2.3) billion in damage/costs; at least 50 deaths.

1980 **Drought/Heat Wave** June-September 1980. Central and eastern U.S.; estimated $20.0 (55.4) billion in damage/costs to agriculture and related industries; estimated 10,000 deaths (includes heat stress-related).

These statistics were taken from a wide variety of sources and represent, to the best of our ability, the estimated total costs of these events---that is, the costs in terms of dollars and lives that would not have been incurred had the event not taken place. Insured and uninsured losses are included in damage estimates, and direct plus indirect deaths (i.e., related to the event, would not have occurred otherwise) are included in fatality totals. Economic costs are included for wide-scale, long-lasting events such as drought.

Estimates are periodically updated as more data/information become available. Sources include Storm Data (NCDC publication), the National Weather Service, the Federal Emergency Management Agency, other U.S. government agencies, individual state emergency management agencies, state and regional climate centers, and insurance industry estimates including Property Claim Services and Munich Re. The WWW version of this report (http://www.ncdc.noaa.gov/oa/reports/billionz.html -- accessible via NCDC homepage) includes links to detailed technical reports on many of these events.

Authors: Neal Lott, Tom Ross, Adam Smith, Tamara Houston, Karsten Shein.

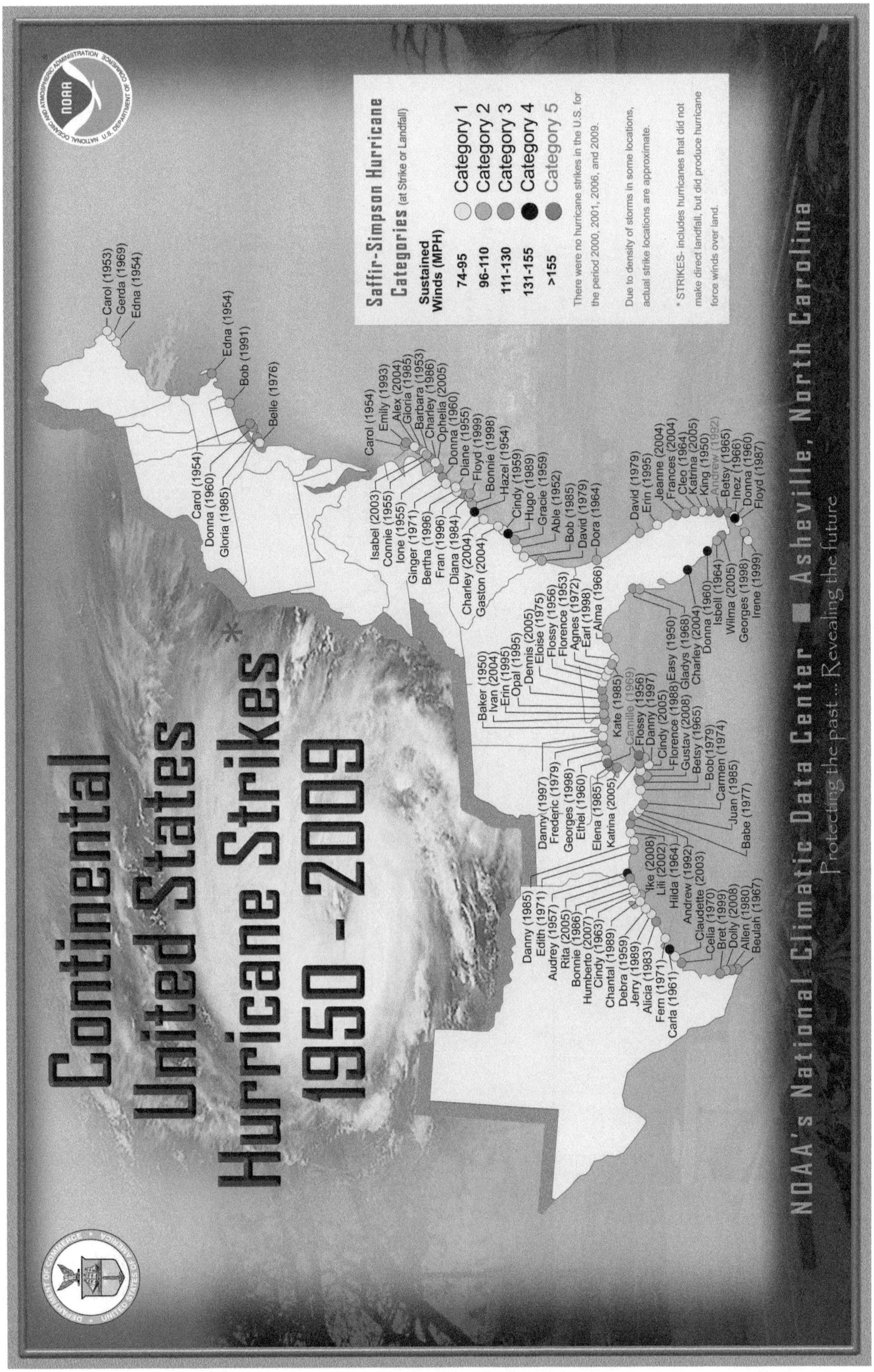

Continental United States Hurricane Strikes 1950 - 2009
Saffir-Simpson Hurricane Categories (at Strike or Landfall)
Sustained Winds (MPH)
74-95 Category 1
96-110 Category 2
111-130 Category 3
131-155 Category 4
>155 Category 5
There were no hurricane strikes in the U.S. for the period 2000, 2001, 2006, and 2009.
Due to density of storms in some locations, actual strike locations are approximate.
* STRIKES- includes hurricanes that did not make direct landfall, but did produce hurricane force winds over land.
Carol (1953) Gerda (1969) Edna (1954)
Edna (1954) Bob (1991) Belle (1976)
Carol (1954) Donna (1960) Gloria (1985)
Carol (1954) Emily (1993) Alex (2004) Gloria (1985) Barbara (1953) Charley (1986) Ophelia (2005) Donna (1960) Diane (1955) Floyd (1999) Bonnie (1998) Hazel (1954) Cindy (1959) Hugo (1989) Gracie (1959) Able (1952) Bob (1985) David (1979) Dora (1964)
Isabel (2003) Connie (1955) Ione (1955) Ginger (1971) Bertha (1996) Fran (1996) Diana (1984) Charley (2004) Gaston (2004)
David (1979) Erin (1995) Jeanne (2004) Frances (2004) Cleo (1964) Katrina (2005) King (1950) Andrew (1992) Betsy (1965) Inez (1966) Donna (1960) Floyd (1987)
Baker (1950) Ivan (2004) Erin (1995) Opal (1995) Dennis (2005) Eloise (1975) Flossy (1956) Florence (1953) Agnes (1972) Earl (1998) Alma (1966)
Easy (1950) Gladys (1968) Charley (2004) Donna (1960) Isbell (1964) Wilma (2005) Georges (1998) Irene (1999)
Kate (1985) Camille (1969) Flossy (1956) Danny (1997) Cindy (2005) Florence (1988) Gustav (2008) Betsy (1965) Bob (1979) Carmen (1974) Juan (1985) Babe (1977)
Danny (1997) Frederic (1979) Georges (1998) Ethel (1960) Elena (1985) Katrina (2005)
Danny (1985) Edith (1971) Audrey (1957) Rita (2005) Bonnie (1986) Humberto (2007) Cindy (1963) Chantal (1989) Debra (1959) Jerry (1989) Alicia (1983) Fern (1971) Carla (1961)
Ike (2008) Lili (2002) Hilda (1964) Andrew (1992) Claudette (2003) Celia (1970) Bret (1999) Dolly (2008) Allen (1980) Beulah (1967)
NOAA's National Climatic Data Center ■ Asheville, North Carolina
Protecting the past... Revealing the future

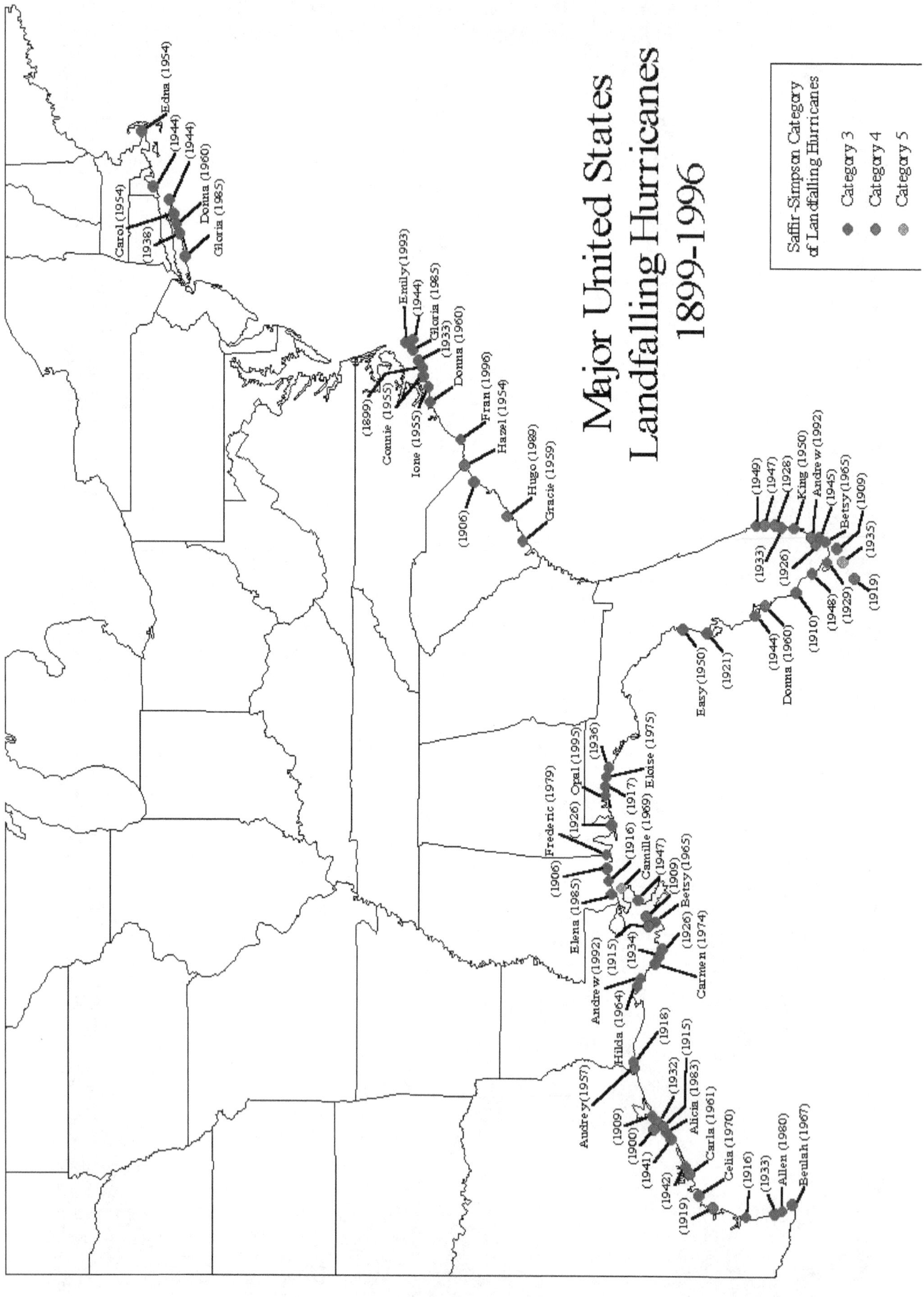
Major United States
Landfalling Hurricanes
1899-1996
Saffir-Simpson Category
of Landfalling Hurricanes
Category 3
Category 4
Category 5
Edna (1954)
(1944)
(1944)
(1960)
Carol (1954)
Donna (1960)
(1938)
Gloria (1985)
Emily (1993)
(1944)
Gloria (1985)
(1933)
Donna (1960)
(1899)
Connie (1955)
Ione (1955)
Fran (1996)
Hazel (1954)
Hugo (1989)
(1906)
Gracie (1959)
(1949)
(1947)
(1928)
King (1950)
Andrew (1992)
(1945)
Betsy (1965)
(1909)
(1935)
(1933)
(1926)
(1919)
(1929)
(1948)
(1910)
Donna (1960)
(1944)
Easy (1950)
(1921)
(1936)
Opal (1995)
Frederic (1979)
Eloise (1975)
(1917)
(1926)
(1916)
Camille (1969)
(1906)
(1947)
Elena (1985)
(1909)
Betsy (1965)
(1915)
(1934)
(1926)
Andrew (1992)
Carmen (1974)
Hilda (1964)
(1918)
(1915)
Audrey (1957)
(1932)
(1909)
Alicia (1983)
(1900)
Carla (1961)
(1941)
(1942)
Celia (1970)
(1919)
(1916)
(1933)
Allen (1980)
Beulah (1967)

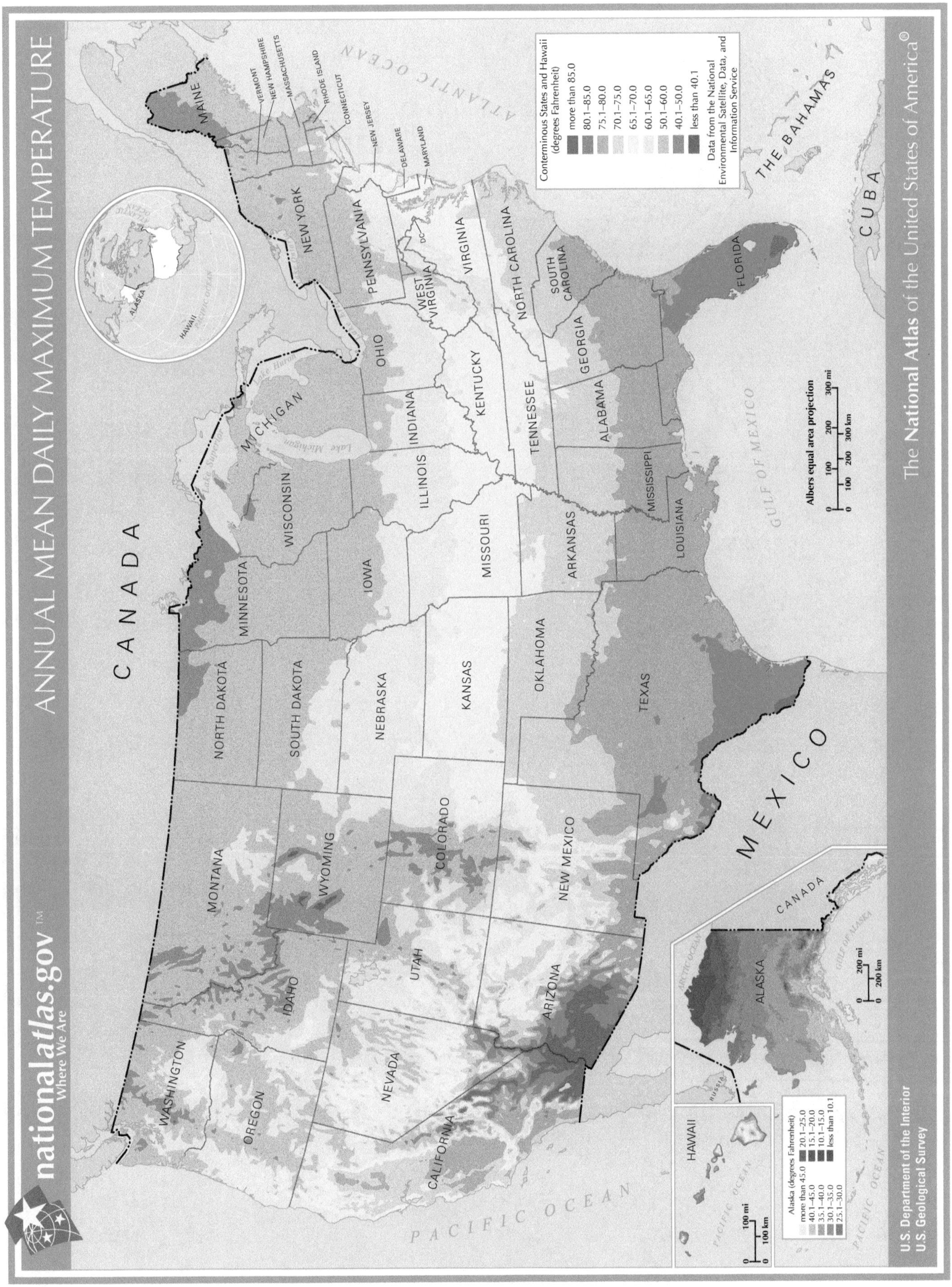
ANNUAL MEAN DAILY MAXIMUM TEMPERATURE
nationalatlas.gov™
Where We Are
Conterminous States and Hawaii (degrees Fahrenheit)
more than 85.0
80.1–85.0
75.1–80.0
70.1–75.0
65.1–70.0
60.1–65.0
50.1–60.0
40.1–50.0
less than 40.1
Data from the National Environmental Satellite, Data, and Information Service
Alaska (degrees Fahrenheit)
more than 45.0
40.1–45.0
35.1–40.0
30.1–35.0
25.1–30.0
20.1–25.0
15.1–20.0
10.1–15.0
less than 10.1
Albers equal area projection
CANADA
MEXICO
PACIFIC OCEAN
ATLANTIC OCEAN
GULF OF MEXICO
THE BAHAMAS
CUBA
WASHINGTON
OREGON
CALIFORNIA
NEVADA
IDAHO
MONTANA
WYOMING
UTAH
ARIZONA
COLORADO
NEW MEXICO
NORTH DAKOTA
SOUTH DAKOTA
NEBRASKA
KANSAS
OKLAHOMA
TEXAS
MINNESOTA
IOWA
MISSOURI
ARKANSAS
LOUISIANA
WISCONSIN
ILLINOIS
MICHIGAN
INDIANA
OHIO
KENTUCKY
TENNESSEE
MISSISSIPPI
ALABAMA
GEORGIA
FLORIDA
SOUTH CAROLINA
NORTH CAROLINA
VIRGINIA
WEST VIRGINIA
DC
MARYLAND
DELAWARE
NEW JERSEY
PENNSYLVANIA
NEW YORK
CONNECTICUT
RHODE ISLAND
MASSACHUSETTS
NEW HAMPSHIRE
VERMONT
MAINE
ALASKA
HAWAII
The National Atlas of the United States of America®
U.S. Department of the Interior
U.S. Geological Survey

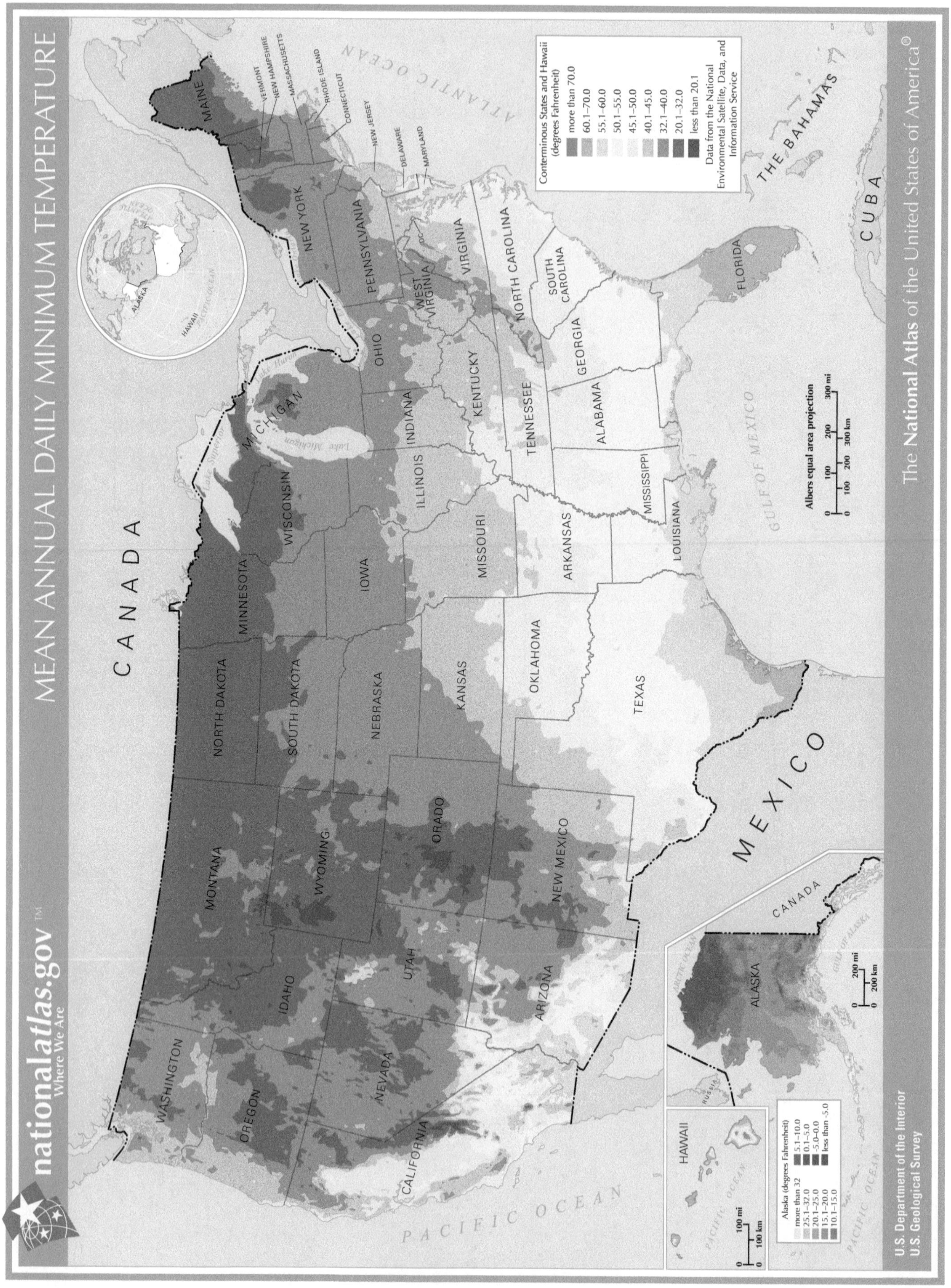
MEAN ANNUAL DAILY MINIMUM TEMPERATURE
nationalatlas.gov™
Where We Are
Conterminous States and Hawaii (degrees Fahrenheit)
more than 70.0
60.1–70.0
55.1–60.0
50.1–55.0
45.1–50.0
40.1–45.0
32.1–40.0
20.1–32.0
less than 20.1
Data from the National Environmental Satellite, Data, and Information Service
Alaska (degrees Fahrenheit)
more than 32
25.1–32.0
20.1–25.0
15.1–20.0
10.1–15.0
5.1–10.0
0.1–5.0
-5.0–0.0
less than -5.0
Albers equal area projection
CANADA
MEXICO
PACIFIC OCEAN
ATLANTIC OCEAN
GULF OF MEXICO
THE BAHAMAS
CUBA
HAWAII
ALASKA
The National Atlas of the United States of America®
U.S. Department of the Interior
U.S. Geological Survey

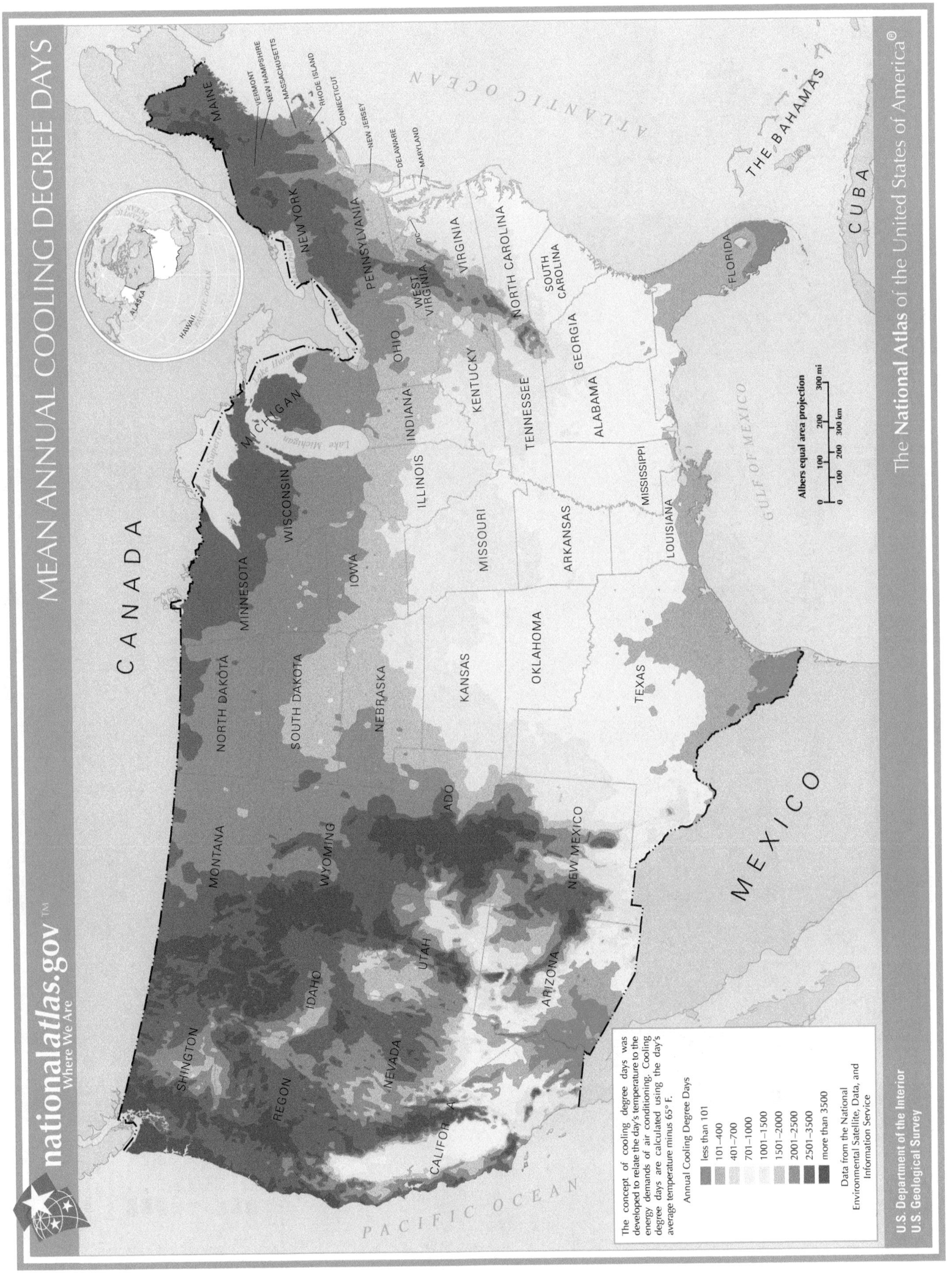
MEAN ANNUAL COOLING DEGREE DAYS
nationalatlas.gov™
Where We Are
The concept of cooling degree days was developed to relate the day's temperature to the energy demands of air conditioning. Cooling degree days are calculated using the day's average temperature minus 65° F.
Annual Cooling Degree Days
less than 101
101–400
401–700
701–1000
1001–1500
1501–2000
2001–2500
2501–3500
more than 3500
Data from the National Environmental Satellite, Data, and Information Service
Albers equal area projection
0 100 200 300 mi
0 100 200 300 km
U.S. Department of the Interior
U.S. Geological Survey
The National Atlas of the United States of America®
CANADA
MEXICO
PACIFIC OCEAN
ATLANTIC OCEAN
GULF OF MEXICO
THE BAHAMAS
CUBA
ALASKA
HAWAII
MAINE
VERMONT
NEW HAMPSHIRE
MASSACHUSETTS
RHODE ISLAND
CONNECTICUT
NEW JERSEY
DELAWARE
MARYLAND
DC
NEW YORK
PENNSYLVANIA
WEST VIRGINIA
VIRGINIA
NORTH CAROLINA
SOUTH CAROLINA
GEORGIA
FLORIDA
OHIO
MICHIGAN
Lake Huron
Lake Michigan
Lake Superior
INDIANA
KENTUCKY
TENNESSEE
ALABAMA
MISSISSIPPI
ILLINOIS
WISCONSIN
MINNESOTA
IOWA
MISSOURI
ARKANSAS
LOUISIANA
NORTH DAKOTA
SOUTH DAKOTA
NEBRASKA
KANSAS
OKLAHOMA
TEXAS
MONTANA
WYOMING
ADO
NEW MEXICO
SHINGTON
IDAHO
UTAH
ARIZONA
REGON
NEVADA
CALIFOR A

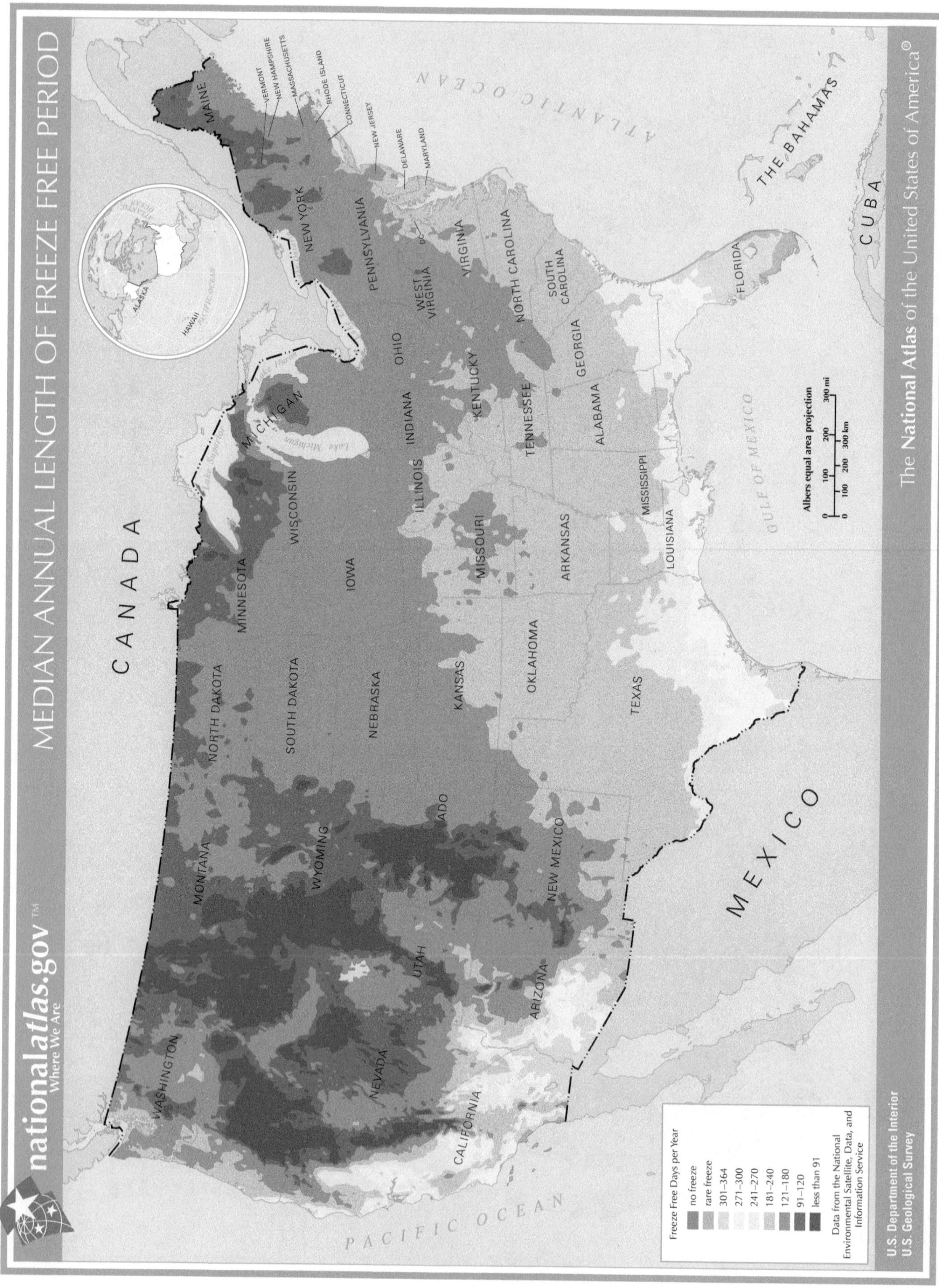
MEDIAN ANNUAL LENGTH OF FREEZE FREE PERIOD
nationalatlas.gov™
Where We Are
CANADA
MEXICO
PACIFIC OCEAN
ATLANTIC OCEAN
GULF OF MEXICO
THE BAHAMAS
CUBA
ALASKA
HAWAII
WASHINGTON
MONTANA
NORTH DAKOTA
MINNESOTA
WISCONSIN
MICHIGAN
SOUTH DAKOTA
WYOMING
NEBRASKA
IOWA
ILLINOIS
INDIANA
OHIO
PENNSYLVANIA
NEW YORK
MAINE
VERMONT
NEW HAMPSHIRE
MASSACHUSETTS
RHODE ISLAND
CONNECTICUT
NEW JERSEY
DELAWARE
MARYLAND
DC
WEST VIRGINIA
VIRGINIA
NORTH CAROLINA
SOUTH CAROLINA
GEORGIA
FLORIDA
ALABAMA
MISSISSIPPI
TENNESSEE
KENTUCKY
MISSOURI
ARKANSAS
LOUISIANA
KANSAS
OKLAHOMA
TEXAS
NEW MEXICO
ARIZONA
UTAH
NEVADA
CALIFORNIA
Lake Superior
Lake Michigan
Lake Huron
Freeze Free Days per Year
no freeze
rare freeze
301–364
271–300
241–270
181–240
121–180
91–120
less than 91
Data from the National Environmental Satellite, Data, and Information Service
Albers equal area projection
0 100 200 300 mi
0 100 200 300 km
U.S. Department of the Interior
U.S. Geological Survey
The National Atlas of the United States of America®

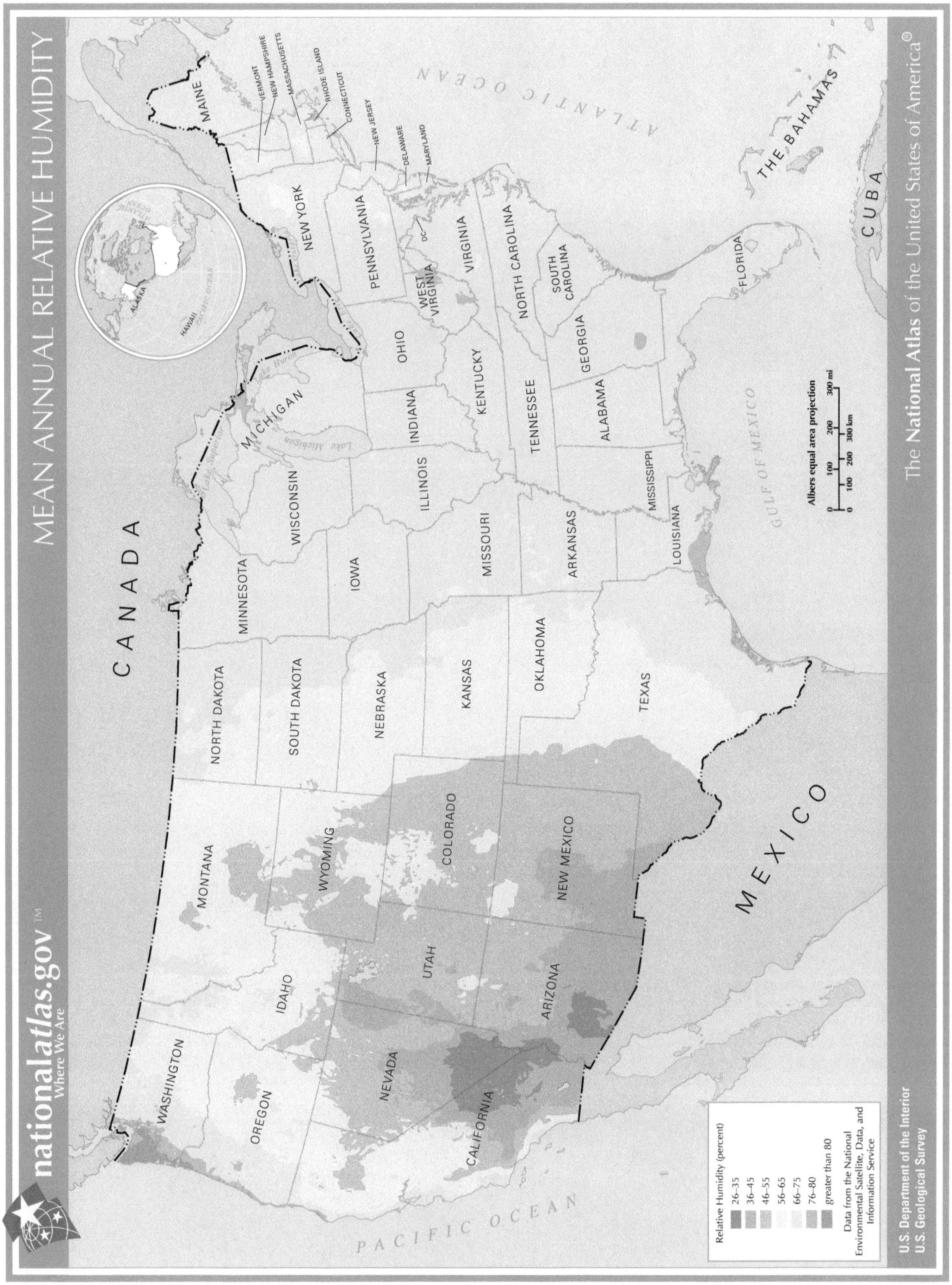
MEAN ANNUAL RELATIVE HUMIDITY
nationalatlas.gov™
Where We Are
The National Atlas of the United States of America®
U.S. Department of the Interior
U.S. Geological Survey
Relative Humidity (percent)
26–35
36–45
46–55
56–65
66–75
76–80
greater than 80
Data from the National Environmental Satellite, Data, and Information Service
Albers equal area projection
0 100 200 300 mi
0 100 200 300 km
CANADA
MEXICO
PACIFIC OCEAN
ATLANTIC OCEAN
GULF OF MEXICO
THE BAHAMAS
CUBA
WASHINGTON
OREGON
CALIFORNIA
NEVADA
IDAHO
MONTANA
WYOMING
UTAH
ARIZONA
COLORADO
NEW MEXICO
NORTH DAKOTA
SOUTH DAKOTA
NEBRASKA
KANSAS
OKLAHOMA
TEXAS
MINNESOTA
IOWA
MISSOURI
ARKANSAS
LOUISIANA
WISCONSIN
ILLINOIS
MICHIGAN
INDIANA
OHIO
KENTUCKY
TENNESSEE
MISSISSIPPI
ALABAMA
GEORGIA
FLORIDA
SOUTH CAROLINA
NORTH CAROLINA
VIRGINIA
WEST VIRGINIA
DC
MARYLAND
DELAWARE
NEW JERSEY
PENNSYLVANIA
NEW YORK
CONNECTICUT
RHODE ISLAND
MASSACHUSETTS
NEW HAMPSHIRE
VERMONT
MAINE
Lake Superior
Lake Michigan
Lake Huron
ALASKA
HAWAII

Grey House Publishing

Grey House Publishing
2010 Title List

Visit **www.greyhouse.com** for Product Information, Table of Contents and Sample Pages

eneral Reference

erican Environmental Leaders: From Colonial Times to the Present
African Biographical Dictionary
cyclopedia of African-American Writing
cyclopedia of American Industries
cyclopedia of Emerging Industries
cyclopedia of Global Industries
cyclopedia of Gun Control & Gun Rights
cyclopedia of Invasions & Conquests
cyclopedia of Prisoners of War & Internment
cyclopedia of Religion & Law in America
cyclopedia of Rural America
cyclopedia of the United States Cabinet, 1789-2010
cyclopedia of Warrior Peoples & Fighting Groups
vironmental Resource Handbook
m Suffrage to the Senate: America's Political Women
bal Terror & Political Risk Assessment
torical Dictionary of War Journalism
man Rights in the United States
tions of the World
itical Corruption in America
eakers of the House of Representatives, 1789-2009
e Environmental Debate: A Documentary History
e Evolution Wars: A Guide to the Debates
e Religious Right: A Reference Handbook
e Value of a Dollar: 1860-2009
e Value of a Dollar: Colonial Era
iversity & College Museums, Galleries & Related Facilities
eather America
orld Cultural Leaders of the 20th & 21st Centuries
orking Americans 1880-1999 Vol. I: The Working Class
orking Americans 1880-1999 Vol. II: The Middle Class
orking Americans 1880-1999 Vol. III: The Upper Class
orking Americans 1880-1999 Vol. IV: Their Children
orking Americans 1880-2003 Vol. V: At War
orking Americans 1880-2005 Vol. VI: Women at Work
orking Americans 1880-2006 Vol. VII: Social Movements
orking Americans 1880-2007 Vol. VIII: Immigrants
orking Americans 1770-1869 Vol. IX: Revol. War to the Civil War
orking Americans 1880-2009 Vol. X: Sports & Recreation
orking Americans 1880-2010 Vol. XI: Entrepreneurs & Inventors

owker's Books In Print® Titles

oks In Print®
oks In Print® Supplement
erican Book Publishing Record® Annual
erican Book Publishing Record® Monthly
oks Out Loud™
wker's Complete Video Directory™
ildren's Books In Print®
Hi Textbooks & Serials In Print®
thcoming Books®
ge Print Books & Serials™
v Books & Serials In Print™
dical & Health Care Books In Print™
blishers, Distributors & Wholesalers of the US™
oject Guide to Books In Print®
oject Guide to Children's Books In Print®

Business Information

Directory of Business Information Resources
Directory of Mail Order Catalogs
Directory of Venture Capital & Private Equity Firms
Food & Beverage Market Place
Grey House Homeland Security Directory
Grey House Performing Arts Directory
Hudson's Washington News Media Contacts Directory
New York State Directory
Sports Market Place Directory
The Rauch Guides – Industry Market Research Reports

Statistics & Demographics

America's Top-Rated Cities
America's Top-Rated Small Towns & Cities
America's Top-Rated Smaller Cities
Comparative Guide to American Suburbs
Comparative Guide to Health in America
Profiles of... Series – State Handbooks

Health Information

Comparative Guide to American Hospitals
Comparative Guide to Health in America
Complete Directory for Pediatric Disorders
Complete Directory for People with Chronic Illness
Complete Directory for People with Disabilities
Complete Mental Health Directory
Directory of Health Care Group Purchasing Organizations
Directory of Hospital Personnel
HMO/PPO Directory
Medical Device Register
Older Americans Information Directory

Education Information

Charter School Movement
Comparative Guide to American Elementary & Secondary Schools
Complete Learning Disabilities Directory
Educators Resource Directory
Special Education

TheStreet.com Ratings Guides

TheStreet.com Ratings Consumer Box Set
TheStreet.com Ratings Guide to Bank Fees & Service Charges
TheStreet.com Ratings Guide to Banks & Thrifts
TheStreet.com Ratings Guide to Bond & Money Market Mutual Funds
TheStreet.com Ratings Guide to Common Stocks
TheStreet.com Ratings Guide to Credit Unions
TheStreet.com Ratings Guide to Exchange-Traded Funds
TheStreet.com Ratings Guide to Health Insurers
TheStreet.com Ratings Guide to Life & Annuity Insurers
TheStreet.com Ratings Guide to Property & Casualty Insurers
TheStreet.com Ratings Guide to Stock Mutual Funds
TheStreet.com Ratings Ultimate Guided Tour of Stock Investing

Canadian General Reference

Associations Canada
Canadian Almanac & Directory
Canadian Environmental Resource Guide
Canadian Parliamentary Guide
Financial Services Canada
History of Canada
Libraries Canada

ey House Publishing
19 Route 22, PO Box 56, Amenia NY 12501-0056 | (800) 562-2139 | www.greyhouse.com | books@greyhouse.com